THE AUTHORITY SINCE 1868

THE WORLD ALMANAC
AND BOOK OF FACTS
1992

WORLD ALMANAC
AN IMPRINT OF PHAROS BOOKS • A SCRIPPS HOWARD COMPANY
NEW YORK

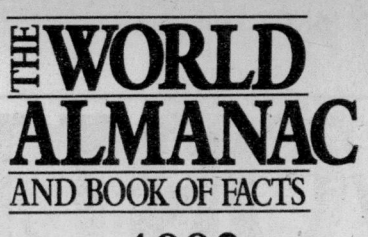

THE WORLD ALMANAC AND BOOK OF FACTS
1992

Editor: Mark S. Hoffman
Associate Editor: June Foley   **Senior Assistant Editor:** Thomas McGuire
Chronology & Special Features: Donald Young   **Index:** Aris Georgiadis
Editorial Assistant: Michael Northrop

Pharos Books
Senior Vice President & Publisher: David Hendin
Vice President & Associate Publisher: Phyllis Henrici
Publicity Manager: Anina Crossfield   **Sales Manager:** Patricia Hughes
Director of Manufacturing: Randy Lang

The editors acknowledge with thanks the many letters of helpful comment and criticism from readers of THE WORLD ALMANAC, and invite further suggestions and observations. Because of the volume of mail directed to the editorial offices, it is not possible to reply to each letter writer. However, every communication is read by the editors and all comments and suggestions receive careful attention. Inquiries regarding contents should be sent to: Editor, The World Almanac, 200 Park Avenue, New York, NY 10166.

THE WORLD ALMANAC is published annually in November.

THE WORLD ALMANAC does not decide wagers.

The first edition of THE WORLD ALMANAC, a 120-page volume with 12 pages of advertising, was published by the New York World in 1868, 124 years ago. Annual publication was suspended in 1876. Joseph Pulitzer, publisher of the New York World, revived THE WORLD ALMANAC in 1886 with the goal of making it a "compendium of universal knowledge." It has been published annually since then. In 1931, it was acquired by the Scripps Howard Newspapers; until 1951, it bore the imprint of the New York World-Telegram and thereafter, until 1967, that of the New York World-Telegram and Sun. It is now published in paper and clothbound editions by Pharos Books, a Scripps Howard company.

THE WORLD ALMANAC & BOOK OF FACTS 1992
Copyright© Pharos Books 1991
Library of Congress Catalog Card Number 4-3781
International Standard Serial Number (ISSN) 0084-1382
Pharos Books (softcover) ISBN 0-88687-642-7
Pharos Books (hardcover) ISBN 0-88687-643-5
Microform Edition since 1868: University Microfilms Intl.
Printed in the United States of America
The softcover and hardcover editions distributed to the trade in the United States
by St. Martin's Press.

WORLD ALMANAC
An Imprint of Pharos Books
A Scripps Howard Company
200 Park Avenue, New York, NY 10166

1992 HIGHLIGHTS

GENERAL INDEX

Addenda, Late News, Changes

Attorney General (p. 379)

Pres. Bush, Oct. 16, nominated Deputy Attorney General William P. Barr to be the next Attorney General.

Cambodia (p. 745)

Cambodia's warring factions signed a peace treaty, Oct. 23, aimed at ending the war, mass murder, foreign occupation, starvation, and exile that has devastated the country over the past 21 years.

Chronology

A man smashed a truck into a restaurant in Killeen, Tex., Oct. 16, and shot 22 people dead and wounded at least 22 others with a semiautomatic pistol. He then shot himself. The 23 deaths made the attack the worst mass murder in the U.S.

Dominican Republic (p. 755)

The address of the embassy is 1715 22nd St., NW, Washington, DC 20008.

Dow Jones Industrial Average (p. 143)

The Dow Jones industrial average reached an all-time high of 3,077.15 on Oct. 18.

Earthquakes (p. 546)

An earthquake, measuring between 6.1 and 7.1 on the Richter scale, hit the Uttar Kashi region of India on Oct. 20; death toll estimates reached as high as 670 people.

European Community (p. 828)

The 12-nation EC and the 7-member European Free Trade Assn. agreed to form a new common market, to be known as the European Economic Area, thus forming the world's largest trading bloc.

Fires (p. 544)

At least 22 people were killed as a fire swept through the Oakland and Berkeley Hills area of California, Oct. 20.

Flags (pp. F1-F3)

Due to deadline constraints, the flags for Estonia, Latvia, Lithuania, Marshall Islands, and Micronesia are not included.

Mayors (p. 603)

Willie Herenton was the first black to be elected mayor of Memphis, Tenn., Oct. 4.

Nations (pp. 765; 766; 773; 795; 804; 819)

Haiti: Pres. Jean-Bertrand Aristide was ousted in a coup, Sept. 30.

Hungary: Prime Minister Petre Roman resigned, Sept. 26.

Japan: Kiichi Miyazawa was chosen to replace Toshiki Kaifu as Prime Minister, Oct. 27.

Romania: Theodor Stolojan was named Prime Minister, Oct. 16.

Sweden: Prime Minister Carl Bildt headed a coalition of 4 conservative parties that ousted the Social Democrats, Sept. 15.

Zaire: Etienne Tshisekedi was named Prime Minister, Oct. 1.

Nobel Prizes (pp. 320-322)

(Each 1991 Nobel Prize included a cash award of about $985,000 to $1 million)

Physiology or Medicine: Edwin Neher, and Bert Sakmann, both German, were awarded the prize for discoveries in basic cell function that have shed light on the causes of several diseases, including diabetes and cystic fibrosis, and that are preparing the way for "tailor-made" drugs.

Literature: Nadine Gordimer, a South African, became the first woman to win the Nobel Prize for literature in 25 years. Gordimer's short stories and novels depict the contradictions and conflicts of a racist society.

Peace: Daw Aung San Suu Kyi, leader of the opposition to the military government in Myanmar (formerly Burma) was awarded the prize. Daughter of U Aung San, the assassinated founder of modern Burma, she has been under house arrest in the capital since July 1989.

Memorial Prize in Economic Sciences: The award went to Ronald H. Coase, a British-born economist retired from the Univ. of Chicago Law School, for his work on the role of institutions in the economy.

Physics: Pierre-Gilles de Gennes, a professor at the College de France in Paris, won the prize, for his discoveries about the ordering of molecules in substances ranging from the "super glue" used in aircraft constructions to a form of liquid helium.

Chemistry: The award was presented to Richard R. Ernst, who is Swiss, for his refinements in nuclear magnetic resonance spectroscopy, an important new technique of chemical analysis.

Obituaries (p. 957)

Ford, Tennessee Ernie, 72; country & western singer, "16 Tons;" Virginia, Oct. 17.

Roddenberry, Gene, 70; creator of Star Trek; Santa Monica, Cal., Oct. 24.

Patents (p. 199)

The National Institutes of Health applied for a patent that would cover rights to 340 pieces of genetic code, most of which have yet to be deciphered.

Standard Time, International (p. 297)

Soviet officials corrected an error dating from the Stalin era, when the USSR did not return to winter time after six months of daylight saving time. To correct the mistake, officials decided to leave clocks alone last spring and "fall back" one hour at the end of September 1991. Moscow time is now two hours ahead of Greenwich Mean Time, instead of three.

Heroes of Young America: The Twelfth Annual Poll

General H. Norman Schwarzkopf, commander of the U.S. Central Command in the Persian Gulf, who led U.S. and allied troops to victory over Iraq in 1991, was named the "Top Hero" of Young America in *The World Almanac's* twelfth annual poll of high school students. The students in grades 8 through 12 were asked to select those individuals in public life they admired most. The schools chosen to participate represented a geographic cross-section of the United States. In addition to choosing a top hero/heroine, the teenagers were asked to make selections in 8 other categories as well as answering 5 general questions on current events and entertainment.

The Top Hero/Heroine

A graduate of West Point, the 56-year old Gen. Schwarzkopf, who retired from the military in September 1991, was a four-star Army general. His leadership in Operation Desert Storm along with his engaging personality as a public speaker made him a hero not only to America's young, but to the vast majority of Americans. Schwarzkopf served two tours of combat duty during the Vietnam War and was the deputy commander of the U.S. invasion of Grenada in 1983. When asked about his duties as a soldier and about the costs of war, Schwarzkopf told *U.S. News & World Report:* "Yes, I am antiwar. A professional soldier understands that war means killing people, war means maiming people, war means families left without fathers and mothers . . . All you have to do is hold your first soldier who is dying in your arms, and have that terribly futile feeling that I can't do anything about it . . . Then you understand the horror of war. Any soldier worth his salt should be antiwar. And still there are things worth fighting for."

The second place finisher and "Top Heroine" was actress Julia Roberts, star of *Pretty Woman.* The third place winner was Pres. George Bush, whose popularity soared during the Persian Gulf war. In fourth place was former top hero Michael Jordan. Barbara Bush placed fifth, the highest finish ever for any first lady. Pop singer Mariah Carey was the sixth-place winner and actor/director Kevin Costner of *Dances with Wolves* finished seventh. TV talk show host Oprah Winfrey placed eighth, followed by pop star Madonna. Last year's top heroine Paula Abdul was tied with Supreme Court Justice Sandra Day O'Connor for tenth place.

Most Influential Person/Public Issues

When asked to name "the person most directly influential in your life, other than your parents," the students split their votes evenly between **teachers** and **friends.**

According to the poll, the "most important public issue facing teenagers" is **drug abuse,** which ranked highest in last year's poll. Receiving almost as many votes as substance abuse was **AIDS.** Other issues receiving substantial mention included the **environment,** the **quality of education,** and **prejudice/racism.**

Songs, TV Shows, and Movies

The students chose "More Than Words" by Extreme and "I Wanna Sex You Up" by Color Me Badd as their favorite songs of 1991. Their favorite television show for the year was "Beverly Hills 90210" followed by "In Living Color" and "Fresh Prince of Bel Aire." There was a tie between *Ghost* and *New Jack City* as favorite movie, with *Silence of the Lambs* and *Dances with Wolves* also receiving many votes.

Listed below are the top male and female vote-getters in each category. The winner is listed first.

Top Hero

Gen. H. Norman Schwarzkopf, commander, Operation Desert Storm
Julia Roberts, actress

Politicians and Newsmakers
H. Norman Schwarzkopf, Army general
Sandra Day O'Connor, Supreme Court Justice

Music and Dance
Mariah Carey, pop singer
LL Cool J, rap singer

Artists, Writers, Filmmakers
Steven King, writer
Alice Walker, writer

Comedy
Eddie Murphy, actor/comedian
Kirstie Alley, actress

News and Sports Media
Barbara Walters, TV journalist
Tom Brokaw, TV journalist

Television Performers/Non-Comedy
Oprah Winfrey, talk show host
Richard Dean Anderson, actor

Sports
Michael Jordan, basketball player
Jennifer Capriati, tennis player

Movie Performers/Non-Comedy
Kevin Costner, actor
Whoopi Goldberg, actress

The Heroes of Young America: 1980-1991

1980	Burt Reynolds	1984	Michael Jackson	1988	Eddie Murphy
1981	Burt Reynolds	1985	Eddie Murphy	1989	Michael Jordan
1982	Alan Alda	1986	Bill Cosby	1990	Paula Abdul
1983	Sylvester Stallone	1987	Tom Cruise	1991	H. Norman Schwarzkopf

The World Almanac

and Book of Facts for 1992
The Top 10 News Stories

Just as the republics of the U.S.S.R. were about to sign a new union agreement, a coup took place, but was quickly rebuffed leading to the demise of the communist party and the reorganization of the Soviet Union. At the same time, Europe saw the end of the Warsaw Pact and dramatic changes in NATO.

Encountering little resistance, and utilizing the latest military technology, the U.S.-led coalition defeated Iraqi forces in the Persian Gulf War, thereby liberating Kuwait, but leaving Saddam Hussein in power.

Savings and Loan failures, recession, unemployment, health care costs, budget deficits, the BCCI scandal, and scaled-down defense budgets were some of the issues contributing to the uncertain state of the U.S. economy.

Seizing the opportunity to gain their independence in the wake of the turmoil in the Soviet Union, the Baltic states of Estonia, Latvia, and Lithuania became independent nations and were admitted to the U.N. along with North and South Korea, Micronesia, and the Marshall Islands.

Incidents of racially motivated violence surged as Americans struggled with such race-related issues as police brutality, job opportunities, and multiculturalism in U.S. schools.

Experience as a jurist, his views on abortion and equal opportunity in the work place, and charges of sexual harassment marked the hearings to confirm Clarence Thomas as Justice Thurgood Marshall's replacement on the Supreme Court. Thomas was confirmed by the Senate, 52-48.

Joint agreements between the U.S. and the Soviet Union on nuclear and conventional weapons disarmament, including START, were seen as a direct result of the end of the Cold War.

After the Persian Gulf War, progress in arranging peace talks between Israel and its neighbors was seen for the first time in many years.

Keeping his promise to end institutionalized apartheid, Pres. De Klerk made progress toward racial equality in South Africa.

Entering the 21st century, the World Health Organization estimated, 30 million adults and 10 million children worldwide will be infected with the AIDS virus.

After the Failure of a Coup, Soviet Union is Reorganized and Communist Rule Ends

The attempted coup d'etat in the Soviet Union in August 1991 stunned the world, yet it did not really come as a surprise. The conditions were ripe for an extralegal putsch by hard-line Communists and other conservative forces. Food shops in the cities were often empty while vegetables rotted in the fields because of an ineffective system of harvest. Veteran bureaucrats chafed at the loss of their power and perquisites as the political system evolved fitfully toward a democracy. Military commanders were still embarrassed by the withdrawal from Afghanistan, and were angered by the collapse of Communist rule in Eastern Europe and cuts in the defense budget. Many of the Union's 15 republics added to the instability with incessant demands for sovereignty or greater autonomy.

The overthrow of Pres. Mikhail Gorbachev was frequently predicted, and conservatives did not conceal their intense desire to slow the move toward reform of the Soviet system. In October 1990, conservatives had helped block a 500-day plan aimed at establishing a market economy. Foreign Minister Eduard Shevardnadze, a close adviser to Gorbachev, resigned in December 1990, warning that a dictatorship was coming. In June 1991, Prime Minister Valentin Pavlov led an unsuccessful effort in Parliament to strip Gorbachev of some of his power. The U.S. Central Intelligence Agency had predicted a coup.

On Aug. 16, Aleksandr Yakovlev, a leading reformer, resigned from the Communist Party and said a coup was being readied. The catalyzing event was the planned signing, on Aug. 20, of a new Union Treaty that would have shifted some authority from the central government to participating republics. Inexplicably, Gorbachev chose the previous weekend for a vacation in the Crimea.

The coup leaders made their move on Aug. 18. And yet, from the beginning, the coup faltered, and fell apart on the morning of Aug. 21. A general took over

from Yazov at a meeting and ordered the troops and tanks out of Moscow. Troops deployed elsewhere were ordered to stand down.

Having lost its military muscle, the Emergency Committee disintegrated. Some were arrested, though one, Pugo, committed suicide. Kryuchkov flew to the Crimea to negotiate with Gorbachev, returned to Moscow with him, and was arrested.

On arriving in Moscow on the night of Aug. 22, Gorbachev still seemed shaken by his 3 days of captivity. It quickly became apparent that he would have to share the decision-making process with Yeltsin. Widely blamed for the collapsing economy and seen by other reformers as far too cautious in supporting change, Gorbachev again held back, at first defending the Communist Party against the actions of a few. In the housecleaning that followed, Yeltsin imposed his will, occasionally forcing out Gorbachev's men and putting his own friends in office. Gorbachev's loss of stature was illustrated by Shevardnadze's speculation that the president himself might have orchestrated the coup.

But Gorbachev, at first seen as only a figurehead after the coup attempt, recovered his power as Yeltsin seemed to overplay his hand. Yeltsin shut down newspapers that had supported the Communist line. He negotiated economic agreements with neighboring republics as if Russia and they were sovereign states. He warned that borders must be redrawn if other republics contained large Russian populations. The very size and post-coup emerging power of the Russian Republic worried Russia's neighbors.

In this climate, Gorbachev's hand was strengthened again. His great influence with world leaders would prove critical in the weeks ahead, especially after Pres. Bush announced more cutbacks in nuclear arms. Also, Gorbachev shifted to a bolder posture, resigning as general secretary of the Communist Party, Aug. 24, and ending party influence in the military and the government.

During the transition that followed the failure of the coup, superficial change came easily. Statues of Communist heroes were toppled, Leningrad became St. Petersburg again, and the country was now called the Union of Sovereign States. Structural reforms would require more time. Although the Union Treaty was abandoned, the Soviet Parliament in early September approved new government bodies that empowered the republics—now fewer in number after the Baltic republics were granted full independence. It remained to be seen whether any government could tackle effectively the massive economic agenda, which would probably include an end to price controls and state monopolies, the creation of a banking system, and the privatization of agriculture and industry.

The failure of the coup and the subsequent overthrow of the Communist Party appeared to break the tense deadlock that had existed since Gorbachev began to introduce reform in 1985. But by October, the democratic leaders were squabbling among themselves, ethnic unrest was reported again, and the amount of grain stored for the winter stood at its lowest level in a half-century.

The August coup had failed because society had changed in the Gorbachev years. The young people who stood in the streets in defiance of the tanks wanted to preserve not just the abstract concept of democracy but, as well, the freer, more spontaneous lifestyle that they had come to believe was their right.

Don Young, Special Features Editor

Chronology of Events

Hard-line Communists and conservative bureaucrats seized power briefly in the Soviet Union in August. But their attempted coup d'etat failed in the face of popular opposition, refusal of some military and security units to obey their orders, and international protests. Public resistance was led by Russian Pres. Boris Yeltsin. The president of the Soviet Union, Mikhail Gorbachev, was restored to office, but his authority was diminished and he was forced to share power with Yeltsin. The 3 Baltic republics quickly won their independence, other republics sought the same objective, and Gorbachev and the Soviet parliament put an end to 74 years of Communist Party rule.

Gorbachev, with members of his family and several aides, was vacationing at his residence in the Crimea on Aug. 18, when he and they were detained by representatives of the coup leaders. On the morning of Aug. 19, Tass, the national news agency, announced that Gorbachev was ill and that Vice Pres. Gennadi Yanayev and 7 other officials, the State Committee for the State of Emergency, as they called themselves, had assumed leadership of the country.

The committee banned opposition political activity, and hundreds of tanks moved into Moscow.

In addition to Yanayev, the most prominent members of the emergency committee were Premier Valentin Pavlov, Defense Minister Dmitri Yazov, Interior Minister Boris Pugo, and KGB Chairman Vladimir Kryuchkov. Several had been vocal critics of reform of the Soviet system, but Gorbachev had placed his trust in them.

The committee issued a statement on the morning of Aug. 19. It said the country had become ungovernable, and that "Our prime concern is the solution of the food and housing problems." The committee promised to restore law and order while supporting democratic processes. Six of the committee members appeared at a press conference, Aug. 19. Yanayev, who identified himself as acting president, said Gorbachev was "very tired," but expressed the hope that he would someday resume his office.

Troops surrounded the Russian parliament building in Moscow, but a number of tanks deserted to the side of Yeltsin, who was organizing opposition from the building with the support of members of his government. In a dramatic gesture, he stood atop a tank whose crew joined him, called for a general strike and demanded the restoration of Gorbachev. A large crowd cheered him. Citizens barricaded streets around the parliament building with cars and buses. Meanwhile, military rule in support of the coup was imposed in the Baltic states.

Pres. George Bush's initial response to the coup was restrained, but by the evening of Aug. 19, he said the U.S. would not accept the legitimacy of the new government and he called for Gorbachev's return. Some other Western leaders were quicker to speak out more forcefully against the coup, while the leaders of Libya and Iraq welcomed it.

Yeltsin, speaking by phone, Aug. 20, with Bush and British Prime Minister John Major, received their backing. Leaders of some other Soviet republics, including those in Kazakhstan and the Ukraine, denounced the coup. Yeltsin, Former Foreign Minister Eduard Shevardnadze, and other supporters of democracy appeared before a crowd of 150,000 at the parliament building. In Leningrad (once again St. Petersburg), 200,000 rallied against the coup, and in Kishinev, the capital of the republic of Moldavia, 400,000 turned out.

It was reported, Aug. 20, that Pavlov had fallen ill and had resigned as premier and as a member of the emergency committee.

By the night of Aug. 20-21, the Russian parliament building was defended by hundreds of paratroopers and thousands of citizens who opposed the coup. As armored vehicles supporting the coup approached the building, the defenders fought back with Molotov cocktails. Three defenders were killed, 2 crushed under tanks. But the advancing tanks stopped, then fell back.

The foreign ministers of the European Community, Aug. 20, froze more than $1 billion in credits for food purchase and technical aid that had been promised the Soviet Union. Pres. Bush swore in Robert Strauss, the new ambassador to the Soviet Union, who left immediately for Moscow to assess the situation.

Abruptly, the coup collapsed on Aug. 21. Tanks and troops pulled out of Moscow and the Baltic region and returned to their bases. Some coup leaders flew to the Crimea in an attempt to meet with Gorbachev. The Presidium of the Supreme Soviet voided the decrees of the emergency committee. Bush and other Western leaders acclaimed the outcome, and attributed it to the commitment of the Soviet people to democratic values.

Early on Aug. 22, Gorbachev arrived back in Moscow by plane. Later that day, he held a press conference, saying he had erred in placing trust in those who later betrayed him. He said that when representatives of the coup leaders first confronted him in the Crimea, he refused to resign and predicted that their country would reject the coup. Gorbachev said that on his return he had fired all those who had participated in the rebellion. He paid tribute to the resistance by the population and noted the leading role played by Yeltsin.

One of the coup leaders, Pugo, committed suicide, **Aug. 22**, by shooting himself. Other members of the emergency committee were arrested.

Aug. 22 was a day of public celebration. In Moscow, the crowd painted graffiti on the KGB building and removed a statue of the founder of the KGB. Throughout the country other statues of Communist leaders, including Lenin, were toppled in the following days.

Aug. 23 was a day of confusion in the government, as men appointed temporarily to office the day before were in turn removed. Yeltsin rejected men named by Gorbachev to head the KGB and the defense ministry, and forced him to choose others. Gorbachev dismissed Aleksandr Bessmertnykh, the foreign minister, who claimed to have been ill during the coup.

Gorbachev and Yeltsin appeared together before the Russian parliament, **Aug. 23**, and Yeltsin insisted that Gorbachev read notes taken at a meeting of government ministers during the coup, which revealed that almost all of them had gone along with the coup. Yeltsin, asserting more power, suspended publication of *Pravda* and 5 other Communist papers, **Aug. 23.**

The 74-year reign of the Communist Party, dating from 1917, effectively ended **Aug. 24**. Gorbachev resigned as general secretary of the party; issued decrees that disbanded the Central Committee, including the party's ruling Politburo; placed all party property under control of the Soviet parliament; and banned party activities in the police, military, KGB, government agencies, and state-owned enterprises. Thus, the coup, which had been orchestrated by prominent Communists, had become the party's last hurrah. Gorbachev, **Aug. 24**, also removed the rest of the cabinet, and made the Russian premier, Ivan Silayev, head of a committee to deal with the economy.

In Moscow, **Aug. 24**, 100,000 joined a funeral procession to honor the 3 men who had died resisting tanks in front of parliament. Nationwide, it appeared that fewer than a dozen people had lost their lives during the 3-day crisis. It was reported, **Aug. 24**, that Marshal Sergei Akhromeyev, national security adviser to Gorbachev, had hanged himself.

Anatoly Lukyanov, Speaker of the Soviet parliament, resigned, **Aug. 26**, but he denied charges that he had been the chief ideologist of the coup.

During the next days, Gorbachev and other leaders concentrated on seeing what could be salvaged of the Soviet Union, and what form it would take. By the end of August, 10 of the 15 republics—Lithuania, Georgia, Estonia, Latvia, Ukraine, Byelorussia, Moldavia, Azerbaijan, Uzbekistan, and Kirghizia—had voted for independence. Gorbachev, backed by Yeltsin, made a special effort to keep the Ukraine, the "bread basket" of the nation, from leaving the fold. Some of the newly "independent" republics seemed willing to consider a form of confederation.

On **Aug. 28**, the Russian prosecutor's office charged 13 former officials, including the surviving members of the State Committee for the State of Emergency, with high treason.

The Soviet parliament, **Aug. 29**, suspended all activities of the Communist Party pending an investigation of its part in the coup.

The new leaders of the KGB and the defense ministry declared, **Aug. 30**, that they would seek to reform their organizations.

On **Sept. 2**, Bush announced formal U.S. diplomatic recognition for Estonia, Latvia, and Lithuania.

Speaking to the Soviet parliament, **Sept. 2**, Gorbachev proposed creation of a transitional political structure called a State Council, that would consist of Pres. Gorbachev and the heads of all republics choosing to stay in the Soviet Union. The plan, which also included an Interrepublic Economic Committee and a Supreme Soviet, was approved by Congress, **Sept. 5**. It would remain in place pending a rewrite of the Soviet constitution and the drafting of a new union treaty.

Lukyanov, **Sept. 5**, was added to the list of those charged with treason.

As one of its first acts the new State Council, **Sept. 6**, recognized the independence of Estonia, Latvia, and Lithuania.

Gorbachev said, **Sept. 11**, that the USSR would soon begin to negotiate with Cuba over the withdrawal of Soviet military forces.

The Persian Gulf War: An Analysis

By Anthony H. Cordesman (Copyright, 1991 ©, by Anthony H. Cordesman)

On August 1, 1990, Iraq shattered world peace by invading Kuwait—a nation that had been its ally and supporter throughout the eight years of the Iran-Iraq War. While Iraq initially claimed that it invaded Kuwait because of its oil policies, and then in support of a non-existent Kuwaiti rebel government, it became obvious in a matter of days that its true goal was outright annexation.

The Origins of the Gulf War

The strategic importance of the war that followed is illustrated by the motives that drove Iraq's dictator, Saddam Hussein, to launch his invasion. While Iraq claimed it was reasserting control over a territory stolen from it by colonial powers, these claims had no historical validity: first, Iraq was an artificial creation of Britain, created following the break-up of the Turkish Empire at the end of World War I; second, even Turkey had only the most tenuous historical claim to Kuwait, which had only existed as a small settlement on the coast of the Gulf; and third, modern Kuwait had been created within its present boundaries when British intervention protected it from Saudi conquest during the 1920s.

Iraq's claims that Kuwait was violating its oil quota, and was stealing oil from Iraq's Rumalia oil field, were equally false. Iraq itself had consistently refused to accept any OPEC oil quota, and Kuwait had agreed to reduce its oil exports before Iraq invaded. Part of the Rumalia oil field was on Kuwaiti territory, and Kuwait was taking only limited oil from the field. Further, Kuwait had provided Iraq with billions of dollars worth of oil during the Iraq-Iran War, and had sold the oil produced from Rumalia to benefit Iraq.

The real reasons for the conflict were Saddam Hussein's ambitions. Instead of moving towards peaceful reconstruction after the cease fire in the Iran-Iraq War in August 1988, he continued to build-up his military machine—although it had already received more than $60 billion worth of arms during 1980-1988, and had cost Iraq as much as one-third of its gross domestic product. He spent at least an additional $4 billion on acquiring missiles and biological, chemical, and nuclear weapons. The end result was an Iraqi foreign debt of some $80-$100 billion, and a situation where Iraq could not fund its military machine, pay its debts, and provide a minimum level of civil development and recovery from the Iran-Iraq War.

Invading Kuwait offered Saddam Hussein a potential source of capital—since Kuwait's "Fund for the Future" alone was worth well in excess of $100 billion. It offered a vast new source of oil production and oil reserves, and it offered something Iraq lacked—a deep water port on the Gulf far enough away from Iran to be defendable. At the same time, it allowed Iraq to position its forces near Saudi Arabia's main oil fields and facilities, and gave it the political and military potential to dominate the oil rich Southern Gulf states. Annexing Kuwait gave Saddam Hussein the opportunity to nearly double his oil reserves from 100 billion to 198 billion barrels (a total of nearly 25% of the world's total reserves), and gain dominant influence over nations with another 28% of the world's total reserves.

The Importance of the U.S. and U.N. Reaction

In launching his invasion, Saddam Hussein fatally miscalculated the reaction of his neighbors, the United States, and the other nations of the world. Initially, he failed to intimidate Saudi Arabia. Although he rapidly moved Iraqi divisions to the Saudi border, and seemed ready to invade Saudi Arabia if it suppported Kuwait's government in exile, Saudi Arabia firmly resisted Iraqi pressure and rapidly gained the support of other Gulf states like Bahrain, Oman, Qatar, and the United Arab Emirates.

Additionally, he totally miscalculated the reaction of the U.S. and the rest of the world. Saddam Hussein apparently expected that the U.S. would protest his seizure of Kuwait, but not take the large scale military action necessary to secure Saudi Arabia and actually liberate Kuwait. These expectations seem to have been based on an exaggerated view of Iraq's military capabilities, after its "victory" in the Iran-Iraq War, and his feeling that a U.S. that had withdrawn from Vietnam and Lebanon was too weak and indecisive to act. At the same time, he seems to have counted on the Soviet Union to give him at least tacit support in avoiding a war, and on the Arab world to protect him from outside intervention.

In fact, the U.S. reacted quickly and decisively. It froze Iraqi assets within hours after the invasion. It joined with the Soviet Union to condemn Iraq's actions, proposed an economic boycott and blockade of Iraq, and dispatched a mission to Saudi Arabia to discuss military cooperation. The U.S. strengthened its naval forces in the area days after the invasion. On August 7, 1990, it announced it would send land, air, and naval forces to Saudi Arabia.

The rest of the world proved equally firm. While the Soviet Union did occasionally temporize and seek to head off a conflict, it never gave Iraq any tangible support for its position. The USSR put consistent pressure on Iraq to leave Kuwait, and all of the major states in the Arab world—including Egypt and Syria—strongly opposed Iraq and many sent military forces to defend Saudi Arabia and liberate Kuwait. Only Jordan, Libya, the PLO, and Yemen gave Iraq support. Iran steadily hardened its position against Iraq, and Europe and the developing world united against it from the start.

Equally important, this international unity in opposing aggression allowed the United Nations to take unprecedented action. It reacted immediately to condemn Iraq. On August 2, 1990, the Security Council voted 14 to 0 to demand Iraq's immediate and unconditional withdrawal from Kuwait. It supported the U.S. in creating a naval and then air blockade, and an embargo on Iraqi imports and exports. The Security Council opposed Iraq's efforts to use foreign hostages to prevent political and military pressure, showing a unity that eventually helped force Saddam to release all the foreign hostages he had taken after the U.N. first enforced its blockade.

During the months that followed, the U.N. voted for eleven more resolutions that put steadily growing pressure on Iraq. This culminated on November 29, 1990 with a resolution that established a deadline that authorized the nations allied with Kuwait "to use all necessary means" if Iraq did not withdraw from Kuwait by January 15, 1991.

As a result, Iraq came under steadily escalating pressure from early August to the end of the United Nations' deadline. It suffered from the economic costs of the blockade, ceased to be able to export oil, and lost all significant sources of arms imports. It could not draw on most of Kuwait's assets, and was forced into a massive military effort to defend the Saudi-Kuwaiti border and Iraq's border with Saudi Arabia. By some estimates, Iraq deployed some 545,000 men (12 heavy and 31 light divisions) in the Kuwaiti theater of operations by January 15th.

During this same period, the U.S. steadily built up from a few token air units to a land-sea-air force of 527,000 men and women. By mid January, 1991, this force included over 110 naval vessels, 2,000 tanks, 2,200 armored personnel carriers, 1,800 fixed-wing aircraft, and 1,700 helicopters. In addition to U.S. forces, the 28-nation Coalition included about 118,000 Saudi troops, 43,000 British troops with 170 tanks and 72 combat aircraft, 40,000 Egyptian troops with two armored divisions of 250 tanks, 16,000 French troops with tanks and combat aircraft, and 20,000 Syrian troops with two divisions, and troops and aircraft from Canada, Oman, Qatar, and the United Arab Emirates.

The end result was that the Gulf War began with the largest set of opposing military forces since the Korean War. While it is difficult to make reliable comparisons of the force ratios involved, U.S. reports after the war indicate that the total Coalition had well in excess of 600,000 ground troops to Iraq's 545,000; 3,360 tanks to 4,230; 3,633 artillery weapons to 3,110; 4,050 other armored vehicles to 2,870; 1,959 helicopters to 160, and some 2,700 aircraft to 770.

The Course of the Gulf War

The fighting began on January 17, 1991, when U.S.-led air units launched a devastating series of air attacks against Iraq's command and control facilities, communications systems, air bases, and land based air defenses. These attacks involved the first use of sea launched cruise missiles and stealth aircraft, which flew 31% of the attacks during the first day, and attacked even heavily defended targets like downtown Baghdad with complete immunity. Within days, the Coalition air forces shattered Iraq's air warfare capabilities, and left Iraq with no way to strike at allied forces except to launch its Scud missiles.

Iraq began these Scud strikes with attacks on Israel and Saudi Arabia on the second day of the war, and persisted until the war ended in a ceasefire. Although the Iraqis launched 40 Scud variants against Israel, and 46 against Saudi Arabia, they never succeeded in doing major military damage. Equally important, they did not provoke Israel into retaliating, in part because the U.S. rushed Patriot air defense missiles to both Israel and Saudi Arabia. The Arab members of the Coalition remained united throughout the war. The only major impact of the Scuds was to force the Coalition air forces into a massive hide and seek game to try to kill Iraqi Scud units. While the attacks on the Iraqi Scuds did divert sorties from other targets, they also broadened the damage to Iraqi targets outside the Kuwaiti theater of operations.

The only strategic damage Iraq was able to inflict on Kuwait and the Coalition during the war was to set some 600 Kuwaiti oil wells on fire—fires that may take until 1993 to fully extinguish. These fires, however, did nothing to affect allied air operations or slow the pace of the war. If anything, the oil fires and continued atrocities against the Kuwaiti people, gave even more impetus to the military efforts to liberate Kuwait.

By the third day of the war, the Coalition air strikes against Iraq's main air defenses and air units were so successful that their targets expanded to include more Iraqi strategic targets like electric power plants, key headquarters, civil and army communications, and Iraq's plants and facilities for the production of biological, chemical, and nuclear warfare.

Although Iraq had begun the war with 770 combat aircraft, 25 main operating bases, 30 dispersal bases, and a massive network of surface-to-air missiles, the Coalition's advantage in air command and control, training, technology, and weapons gave it decisive air superiority. Iraq was unable to win a single air-to-air engagement, while losing 35 aircraft in air-to-air combat. By the 6th day of the air war, Iraq found itself virtually unable to use its air force or air defenses, and Iraqi aircraft began to flee to Iran—hoping that Iran would return the aircraft and pilots after the war. Iraq halted any significant effort to use its aircraft in combat after the 14th day of the air war, and Iraq's remaining air defenses proved vulnerable to electronic warfare and anti-radiation missiles throughout the conflict.

On the eighth day of the air war, the Coalition air forces were able to shift from the mission of gaining air superiority over Iraq and Kuwait, disrupting Iraqi command and control, and destroying Iraq's weapons of mass destruction to a primary focus on destroying the Iraqi field army in the Kuwaiti Theater of Operations. This phase lasted for the next 26 days. It involved massive strikes by unguided and precision weapons on land forces like the Republican Guards, key supply and communications facilities in the border area, artillery units, other tank forces, and Iraq's defensive barriers.

By the time the ground war began at 0400 hours on February 24, 1991, Iraqi ground forces had been hit by well in excess of 40,000 attack sorties. By the time the air-land phase ended on February 28th, the coalition had dropped a total of 88,500 tons of ordnance, 6,520 tons of which were precision guided weapons, and had killed a total of 216 aircraft, destroyed nearly 600 aircraft shelters, and damaged 375 others. Coalition air forces had also destroyed 54 bridges, or made them inoperable.

The land phase of battle was equally decisive. It pitted the "air-land battle" concept that the U.S. had developed to meet the Warsaw Pact's most modern forces in Europe against an Iraqi force which was equipped with modern weapons, but had trained and organized to fight a relatively static trench war against Iran, who lacked significant air power.

Iraq's only "success" in the land war occurred well before Coalition forces drove into Kuwait and Iraq. It was a brief incursion into the Saudi border town of Khafji on January 29. This attack was rapidly repulsed by Saudi, Qatari, and U.S. Marine forces, and did more to reveal Iraq's weaknesses in organization and equipment than serve the Iraqi cause. It did nothing to halt many of the Coalition land forces from making a massive shift from positions along the coast and to the south of Kuwait to areas west of Kuwait—shifts that later allowed them to drive deep into Iraq without the

Iraqis having any conclusive warning that they had moved.

This shift began on January 17, and soon positioned the U.S. Marine Expeditionary Force—and Saudi, Syrian, and Egyptian forces—to drive north from the center of Kuwait's southern border towards Kuwait City. At the same time, French and U.S. forces in the VIIth Corps drove far to the West, where they could launch an attack to cut off southern Iraq from Baghdad and drive around Kuwait to move against Basra from the West. British and U.S. Army forces in the XVIIIth Corps drove to areas on the Saudi-Iraqi border just west of Kuwait. The allied commander, General Norman Schwarzkopf, was able to position two full armored corps along the Iraqi border to the west of Kuwait, without the Iraqis detecting these movements, in what he later called his "hail Mary play."

The Iraqi forces proved to have been heavily demoralized even before the land attack by the preceding air bombardment, the breakdown of resupply, a lack of leadership, and poor organization of their defenses. The Coalition then compounded this situation by massive surprise land attacks, rapidly moving 24 hour-a-day armored and heliborne maneuvers, precisely targeted artillery fire, deceptions like the threat of an amphibious landing, effective use of air and attack helicopter support, and use of advanced land warfare technologies. These technologies ranged from thermal tank sights that could spot Iraqi targets long before they could see Coalition armor, to hand-held satellite navigation devices that allowed Coalition forces to precisely locate themselves in the desert.

The devastating impact of the 1000 hour air battle, and 100 hour air-land battle that followed, is indicated by the fact that Coalition forces succeeded in reaching every objective and achieved a rate of advance so fast that many allied forces did not stop at their original objectives.

The scale of the Iraqi defeat is also evident from U.S. estimates indicating that Coalition forces had destroyed nearly 4,000 Iraqi tanks, over 1,000 other armored vehicles, and nearly 3,000 artillery weapons. These estimates compare with Coalition combat losses of 4 tanks, 9 other armored vehicles, and 1 artillery weapon. Further, although Coalition air forces had flown some 109,876 sorties by the end of the war, the Coalition lost only 38 aircraft—the lowest loss rate of any air combat in history and less than the normal accident rate per sortie in combat training. The difference in manpower losses, the most important cost of any war, is harder to quantify. U.S. intelligence has issued rough estimates that 100,000 Iraqi soldiers died in combat. Allies killed, minus casualties to friendly fire, totalled less than 200.

The Political and Military Consequences of the Conflict

It may take a decade before the full implications of the Coalition victory in the Gulf War can be fully understood. Within the immediate region of the Gulf, it was a war that shattered the Iraqi military machine and Saddam Hussein's regional ambitions, aligned the conservative southern Gulf states with the West, and helped shift Iran towards a more moderate position. From a broader Arab perspective, it deeply divided the Arab world. Arab fought against Arab. At the same time, the Palestinian and Jordanian alignment with Iraq, and de facto cooperation between Israel and Kuwait and Saudi Arabia, shattered the illusion of Arab unity against Israel. This both created new opportunities for a U.S. peace initiative, and new causes of tension within the region.

From an Israeli perspective, it critically weakened the strongest military power in the Arab world, while demonstrating Israel's vulnerability to missile attacks and its potential vulnerability to weapons of mass destruction.

From an American perspective, the U.S. emerged as the leader of a 28-nation coalition, backed by the United Nations. It also emerged as a military power that took 43 days to inflict one of the most decisive and shattering military defeats in military history. Nearly two decades after the U.S. withdrawal from Vietnam, and almost a decade after U.S. withdrawal from Lebanon, the reputation of U.S. military forces was decisively restored.

From an international perspective, this demonstration of U.S. military power came at a time when the Soviet Union was already in a deep political and economic crisis, and was drifting towards dissolution. The bipolar world that existed from 1945 to 1990 was already eroding, and one of the most dramatic indications of this was that the Soviet Union found itself with little choice other than to cooperate with the U.S. against a state that it had sold over $22 billion worth of arms in the preceding decade.

The end result was the liberation of Kuwait, the destruction of Iraq's ability to invade or use military pressure against its neighbors, the virtual elimination of most of Iraq's capability to build and use weapons of mass destruction, and the Iraqi agreement to cease-fire terms that promised to steadily weaken its military capabilities for years to come.

More broadly, however, the war did not destroy Saddam Hussein's control over Iraq. It did not bring a stable peace to the Gulf, and it did not create more liberal or democratic regimes. While President Bush talked during the conflict of a new world order, and the United Nations played its most active role in dealing with a major conflict since the Korean War, few elements of such a new world order emerged.

The Arab portion of the Coalition that defeated Iraq did not hold together for more than a few months, or produce any decisive momentum towards a lasting peace in the Gulf or between the Arab states and Israel. Major new uncertainties arose outside the region because of the breakup of the Soviet Union, and new conflicts in the developing world. Rather than marking the end of history, the Gulf War has already emerged as a critical and unstable factor in a new period of change.

Anthony H. Cordesman is an Adjunct Professor of National Security Studies at Georgetown University, National Security Assistant to Senator John McCain of Arizona, and a consultant to ABC. He is the author of Lessons of Modern War *(Westview, 1990) and* Weapons of Mass Destruction in the Middle East *(Brassey's 1991).*

Columbus: A Man for that Season

by Daniel J. Boorstin (Copyright 1991©, by Daniel J. Boorstin)

"It was wonderful," Mark Twain shrewdly observed, "to find America, but it would have been more wonderful to miss it." Europe in Columbus's time was turbulent with rivals for world-trade, and the glittering prize was commerce with "the Indies"—the fabled Orient. Columbus's own career was an allegory of converging and competing nations, languages, and cultures which eventually would be embodied in American civilization. He demonstrated brilliantly on the sea the bold experimental spirit that the Renaissance of his age was revealing in science and the arts.

Born in 1451 in Genoa (just one year before Leonardo da Vinci and long before there was an Italy), Columbus first spoke Genoese, then only a dialect and not a written language. He had little formal schooling and could not read or write Italian. When he was only 25, while serving on a Flemish vessel coming northward through the Straits of Gibraltar, his ship was attacked by a French armada. Using one of his sinking ship's long oars as a life raft, he luckily reached the shore of Portugal near Lagos, where Prince Henry the Navigator had directed bold ventures down the west coast of Africa. With his brother Bartholomew, he set up shop in Lisbon selling mariner's charts. As he became acquainted with the books of geography, he began to wonder whether it might not be possible to reach Asia by sailing westward.

This was not such an outrageous notion at the time, for geographers and mariners had no doubt that the earth was a sphere. But they disagreed wildly on its dimensions, and on the extent of the Western ocean and on how far Asia extended eastward. Columbus's optimistic imagination pieced together Biblical lore and the conclusions of geographers ancient and modern to conclude that a voyage westward to the Orient and back to Europe was quite feasible. But he failed to persuade the King of Portugal. It was unfortunate for Columbus that Dias, carrying a Portuguese flag, returned triumphantly up the Tagus River in 1488 with his three caravels (Columbus and his brother Bartholomew were on the dock!) from a voyage which had finally proved that there was an open sea-passage to India around the Cape of Good Hope. Why should King John gamble on Columbus's westward scheme now that the Portuguese had a clear path the other way?

Meanwhile, when his brother Bartholomew failed to sell the idea to King Henry VIII of England or King Charles VIII of France, Columbus redoubled his efforts to enlist the Spanish sovereigns. Queen Isabella was persuaded by her treasurer Santangel that Columbus's "Enterprise of the Indies" would cost no more than a week's royal entertainment. Inspired by the desire to outdo her Portuguese neighbor and by fear that Columbus's bargain venture might be taken up by others, she suddenly decided to take the small gamble herself—and even without having to pawn her jewels. Her messenger caught Columbus just as he was about to leave for a last-ditch effort to enlist the King of France.

The rest of the story is familiar enough. But Columbus's achievement in reaching across the ocean to America was more than a triumph of imagination and salesmanship. It was a work of extraordinary skill at sea achieved with the benefits of wide-ranging experience. By the age of forty-one when Columbus received Isabella's go-ahead message, he had sailed the waters bounding Europe—from the Eastern Mediterranean to the outer Azores, and from the Arctic circle to nearly the equator. He probably knew the sea winds and currents, crucial for his venture, as well as any other sea captain of his time. A practical man, he added to this knowledge his personal magnetism and the stick-to-itiveness essential to all great adventures. To cajole his crew and discourage mutiny he was not above using guile when his men feared they were going beyond the point of no return and were terrified by the green gulfweed blanket of the Sargasso Sea. He even falsified his daily log to make it seem that they had not gone as far as they really had.

In an age obsessed by the role of information and the media in shaping history, it is especially worth our noting that what made Columbus's venture into a historic discovery was his ability to get the word out. *Feedback* was what distinguished this voyage from others before. Some five centuries earlier, the Vikings in their "Vinland" voyages had actually reached America. But they had not *discovered* America for Europeans because there was practically no feedback from their voyages. Columbus's feat was not only to get there and back, but also to get the news out. A pioneer of feedback, he made his "Enterprise of the Indies" a discovery voyage that opened the floodgates of knowledge and stirred world-wide ventures of exploration. Columbus had discovered the best westward passage for sailing ships from Europe, by going southward to the Canaries to avoid the strong westerly winds of the North Atlantic. Then he made another, insufficiently celebrated, discovery—the best eastward passage. This he accomplished by going above the "horse latitudes" where he could be carried home by the strong westerly winds of the North Atlantic. Modern racing yachtsmen still follow Columbus's course.

By a fortunate coincidence, less than a half-century before Columbus, Gutenberg had opened for Europe the paths of information. Now, as never before, it was possible speedily to spread the word of momentous discoveries. The "letter" written in Spanish that Columbus sent as a report to Santangel, the crown official who had persuaded Queen Isabella, was printed in Barcelona about April 1, 1493, six months after he had sighted an American island, and only a month after his return to Spain. Then it was translated into Latin (still the language of the learned in Western Europe) dated April 29, and again printed in Rome in May as an eight-page pamphlet entitled *De Insulis Inventis* (On Islands Discovered). Frequently reprinted, by the standards of its day it was a best seller. Columbus had not only succeeded in this risky American voyage. He had put his brand name on it and transformed personal experience into widespread knowledge. So, too, he had dramatized the opening of a new epoch in the Western World's way of informing itself. Seafaring secrets, once closely guarded by European sovereigns, had become news. Once sent out, that information could never be recaptured.

There are elements of both comedy and tragedy in the end of Columbus's career. He never realized what he had done. From his third voyage to America, he was sent back to Spain in chains and in fear of the gallows for his alleged corruption and maladministration of an American island colony. He never was reinstated in his honors, and died in poverty and humiliation. Ironically, too, Columbus died believing he had reached Asia. A bitter relic of his Catholic orthodoxy and his hope that his voyage would spread the faith was his firm belief that the Caribbean lands he coasted were the Terrestrial Paradise.

The skill, technology and good fortune that brought to Europeans the word of "islands" they had never imagined, also carried a larger message for future centuries. Columbus had only begun to reveal to the peoples of Europe (though never to himself) the infinite dimensions of their ignorance. On the five-hundredth anniversary of Columbus's landfall, as we venture into the unknowns of outer space, the meanings of the encounters of worlds old and new are still unfolding.

Daniel J. Boorstin, historian and the Librarian of Congress Emeritus, is the author of The Discoverers.

Voyages of Columbus

Christopher Columbus, the most famous explorer, was born Cristoforo Colombo in or near Genoa, Italy probably in 1451, but made his discoveries sailing for the Spanish rulers Ferdinand and Isabella. Dates of his voyages, places he discovered, and other information follow:

1492—First voyage. Left Palos, Spain, Aug. 3 with 88 men (est.). His fleet consisted of 3 vessels—the *Nina,* the *Pinta,* and the *Santa Maria.* Discovered San Salvador, (Guanahani or Watling Is., Bahamas) Oct. 12. Also Cuba, Hispaniola (Haiti-Dominican Republic); built Fort La Navidad on latter.

1493—Second voyage, first part, Sept. 25, with 17 ships, 1,500 men. Dominica (Lesser Antilles) Nov. 3; Guadeloupe, Montserrat, Antigua, San Martin, Santa Cruz, Puerto Rico, Virgin Islands. Settled Isabela on Hispaniola. **Second part** (Columbus having remained in Western Hemisphere), Jamaica, Isle of Pines, La Mona Is.

1498—Third voyage. Left Spain, May 30, 1498, 6 ships. Discovered Trinidad. Saw South American continent, Aug. 1, 1498, but called it Isla Sancta (Holy Island). Entered Gulf of Paria and landed, first time on continental soil. At mouth of Orinoco, Aug. 14, he decided this was the mainland.

1502—Fourth voyage, 4 caravels, 150 men. St. Lucia, Guanaja off Honduras; Cape Gracias a Dios, Honduras; San Juan River, Costa Rica; Almirante, Portobelo, and Laguna de Chiriqui, Panama.

U.S. Population by Age, Sex and Households, 1990

Source: Bureau of the Census, U.S. Dept. of Commerce; 1990 Census

Total population	248,709,873	**Households by Type**	
Sex		Total households.	91,947,410
Male	121,239,418	Family households (families)	64,517,947
Female	127,470,455	Married-couple families	50,708,322
Age		Percent of total households	55.1
Under 5 years	18,354,443	Other family, male householder	3,143,582
5 to 17 years	45,249,989	Other family, female householder	10,666,043
18 to 20 years	11,726,868	Nonfamily households	27,429,463
21 to 24 years	15,010,898	Percent of total households	29.8
25 to 44 years	80,754,835	Householder living alone	22,580,420
45 to 54 years	25,223,086	Householder 65 years and over	8,824,845
55 to 59 years	10,531,756	Persons living in households	242,012,129
60 to 64 years	10,616,167	Persons per household	2.63
65 to 74 years	18,106,558		
75 to 84 years	10,055,108		
85 years and over	3,080,165		
Median age	32.9		
Under 18 years	63,604,432	**Group Quarters**	
Percent of total population	25.6	Persons living in group quarters	6,697,744
65 years and over	31,241,831	Institutionalized persons	3,334,018
Percent of total population	12.6	Other persons in group quarters	3,363,726

Residence of the Population, 1990

Source: Economic Research Service, U.S. Department of Agriculture; and Bureau of the Census, U.S. Dept. of Commerce, 1990.

(Numbers in thousands)

Residence	Total	Metropolitan	Nonmetropolitan	Residence	Total	Metropolitan	Nonmetropolitan
Total	246,081[1]	191,023	55,057	Total	100.0	77.6	22.4
Urban	179,117	160,174	18,943	Urban	100.0	89.4	10.6
Rural	66,964	30,849	36,115	Rural	100.0	46.1	53.9
Rural nonfarm	62,373	29,636	32,737	Rural nonfarm	100.0	47.5	52.5
Rural farm	4,591	1,213	3,378	Rural farm	100.0	26.4	73.6

Percent distribution
(1) Refers only to civilian noninstitutionalized population.

Projections of Total Population by Race: 1992 to 2025

Source: Bureau of the Census, U.S. Dept. of Commerce

Year	Total Population (1,000)				By Race (middle series)					
	Lowest series	Middle series	Highest series	Zero migration	Number (1,000)			Percent distribution		
					White	Black	Other races	White	Black	Other races
1992	251,592	254,521	257,235	250,781	213,301	31,988	9,232	83.8	12.6	3.6
1993	252,906	256,466	259,888	252,083	214,542	32,398	9,527	83.7	12.6	3.7
1994	254,121	258,338	262,526	253,308	215,714	32,801	9,823	83.5	12.7	3.8
1995	255,239	260,138	265,151	254,459	216,820	33,199	10,119	83.3	12.8	3.9
2000	259,576	268,266	278,228	259,304	221,514	35,129	11,624	82.6	13.1	4.3
2005	262,363	275,604	291,710	263,189	225,424	37,003	13,177	81.8	13.4	4.8
2010	264,193	282,575	305,882	266,528	228,978	38,833	14,764	81.0	13.7	5.2
2015	265,072	288,997	320,494	269,131	232,081	40,564	16,352	80.3	14.0	5.7
2020	264,536	294,364	335,022	270,493	234,330	42,128	17,906	79.6	14.3	6.1
2025	262,218	298,252	348,985	270,234	235,369	43,473	19,410	78.9	14.6	6.5

For the series shown, the following assumptions were made about fertility (ultimate lifetime births per woman), mortality (ultimate life expectancy in 2080), and immigration (ultimate yearly net immigration). Lowest series: 1.5 births per woman, 77.9 years, and 300,000 net immigration. Middle series: 1.8 births per woman, 81.2 years, and 500,000 net immigration. Highest series: 2.2 births per woman, 88.0 years, and 800,000 net immigration. Zero migration series: 1.8 births per woman and 81.2 years.

1990 Census Count of the Homeless

The Bureau of the Census released results of its Shelter and Street Night (S-Night) operations conducted across the U.S. during the night of March 20-21, 1990, in an effort to include persons in the 1990 census who might not have been counted using standard procedures. Census officials said that the S-Night results and other 1990 census data that will be released in the future will *not* be considered as a count of the U.S. "homeless" population.

The operation found a total of 178,828 persons in emergency shelters for the homeless, and 49,793 persons visible at pre-identified street locations. New York City had the highest count, with 23,383 persons found in emergency shelters and 10,447 persons found in street locations. Other cities which had among the highest counts included Los Angeles, San Francisco, Washington, DC, and Chicago.

The Census Bureau's figures were disputed by almost all of the cities involved in the count. In addition to the cities' claims that the count was substantially below their own estimates, advocates for the homeless found the totals to be useless, especially when compared to previous estimates of 1 million to 3 million for the entire homeless population. In 1987, the Urban Inst., a nonprofit research organization, made an estimate of 500,000 to 600,000 homeless in America.

CHRONOLOGY OF THE YEAR'S EVENTS

Reported Month by Month in 3 Categories: National, International, and General
Nov. 1, 1990 to Oct. 15, 1991

NOVEMBER

National

Economic Indicators Decline — Twice during November, the Commerce Dept. reported a decline in the leading economic indicators. On Nov. 2, the department said that its index had fallen 0.8 percent in September. The Labor Dept. reported, Nov. 2, that unemployment had held steady at 5.7 percent in October, but also that the number of payroll jobs had declined by 68,000 in October. The Dow Jones industrial average, which had closed at nearly 3,000 in July, fell to 2440.84 on Nov. 7. Thereafter, it began to rise again. The Labor Dept. said, Nov. 9, that producer prices for finished goods had risen by 1.1 percent in October. The department reported, Nov. 16, that consumer prices had risen by 0.6 percent in October. The Commerce Dept. said, Nov. 16, that the U.S. merchandise trade deficit had declined to $9.41 billion in September. The department reported, Nov. 28, that the gross national product had grown at an annual rate of 1.7 percent in the third quarter. Alan Greenspan, chairman of the Federal Reserve Board, said, Nov. 28, that the U.S. economy had entered a "meaningful downturn" but was unsure if a recession would result. The Commerce Dept. reported, Nov. 30, that the economic indicators had fallen 1.2 percent in October. The index had now declined for 4 consecutive months. A decline for 3 straight months was traditionally seen as an indicator of a recession.

Democrats Gain in Congressional Elections — The Democratic Party made small gains in both the Senate and the House of Representatives in elections held on Nov. 6. In the Senate, only one seat changed parties. In Minnesota, Paul Wellstone (D), a college professor, defeated the incumbent Republican, Sen. Rudy Boschwitz. Wellstone ran as a populist opposed to "special interests." In a near upset, Sen. Bill Bradley (D, N.J.) barely squeaked through in a state where the tax policies of a Democratic governor had proved unpopular. Jesse Helms (R, N.C.), the Senate's most outspoken conservative, turned back a strong challenge by Harvey Gantt, a black. The Democrats emerged with a 56-44 margin in the Senate. In the House, the Democrats picked up 8 seats for a 267-167 margin over the Republicans. One independent, Bernard Sanders, a socialist and former mayor of Burlington, was elected in Vermont. About 96 percent of the incumbents seeking re-election were successful; only 15 lost. Among prominent leaders of the House, only Newt Gingrich (R, Ga.) had a close call. In gubernatorial elections, 14 statehouses changed parties, with the Democrats holding a 28-19 margin, compared with 29-21 before the election. Independents won in Alaska and Connecticut, and a runoff would be required in Arizona. The Democrats captured the governorships of Florida and Texas, but the Republicans held on to California. Gov. Mario Cuomo (D, N.Y.) was reelected easily. The results failed to show an anticipated backlash against incumbents. In several states, initiatives supported by environmentalists were defeated.

Inquiry Involving 5 Senators Begins — On Nov. 15, the Senate Ethics Committee began hearings in a case involving conduct by 5 members of the Senate. The senators who were the subject of the inquiry were informally referred to in the press as the "Keating 5." On Nov. 15, the committee special counsel, Robert Bennett, recounted the relationship between the senators and Charles Keating, who had been chairman of the Lincoln Savings and Loan Association in California. The collapse of the S&L in 1989 had cost the government $2 billion. Bennett said that 2 senators, Alan Cranston (D, Cal.) and Dennis DeConcini (D, Ariz.) had been "by far the most active" in the allegedly improper activity. He said that Donald Riegle (D, Mich.) had played a greater role than he later recalled, and that John Glenn (D, Ohio) and John McCain (R, Ariz.) had not played any meaningful role. Bennett described a meeting on April 2, 1987 between 4 of the senators (Riegle excepted) and Edwin Gray, then chairman of the Federal Home Loan Bank Board. He said the senators pressured Gray to ease regulations that restricted investments by thrifts into high-risk investments. According to Bennett, the 5 senators met with banking regulators on April 7, 1987, and the regulators revealed that the Lincoln S&L was the subject of a criminal investigation. Bennett asserted, however, that Cranston and DeConcini had continued to do favors for Keating. He said that efforts by the senators in behalf of Keating coincided with large political contributions by Keating. Addressing the committee, Nov. 16, Cranston said he had done no favors for Keating in exchange for political contributions. McCain, Glenn, and Riegle on Nov. 16, and DeConcini on Nov. 19, also said that they had done nothing wrong. Gray testified, Nov. 26 and 27, that the senators had subjected him to "years of private threats and public vilification" in an effort to get the board to lift regulations against high-risk investments by Keating.

International

Thatcher Resigns as Prime Minister — Margaret Thatcher, the "Iron Lady" of British politics, resigned as prime minister, and was succeeded by John Major, one of her political allies in the Conservative Party. Thatcher, in office for 11½ years, had survived criticism from fellow Conservatives in the past, but by the beginning of November her grip on the party had begun to fall apart. On Nov. 1, Sir Geoffrey Howe, deputy prime minister and leader of the House of Commons, resigned. Reflecting the views of others in the party, he protested the prime minister's opposition to closer economic and monetary integration of Europe. Speaking in Commons, Nov. 13, Howe questioned Thatcher's view that Britain would lose its "national identity" in an integrated Europe, and he warned that Britain was in danger of being "shut out" of Europe. The party split came at a time when Conservatives were being blamed for high inflation and for imposing an unpopular tax to fund local government. On Nov. 14, former Defense Secretary Michael Hesseltine announced that he would challenge Thatcher for the party leadership. The Conservative members of Commons held their first ballot in the leadership contest, Nov. 20. Thatcher led Hesseltine, 204-152, but fell 4 votes short of the 15 percent majority required on the first ballot. Thatcher, who was in Paris, said she would remain in the contest. But on Nov. 22, she informed her cabinet that she would resign. During 11½ years in power, Thatcher had been a strong advocate of a free-market economy, had disposed of many state-owned enterprises, and had restrained the power of labor unions. In foreign affairs, she had been a staunch ally of the United States and had led the nation to victory over Argentina in the Falklands war. After Thatcher announced her resignation, Foreign Secretary

Douglas Hurd and Chancellor of the Exchequer John Major joined the contest to succeed her. In the ballot taken Nov. 27, Major received 185 votes, Hesseltine 131, and Hurd 56. Hesseltine and Hurd then withdrew and Major was declared elected. Major, 47, had enjoyed a rapid rise in British politics. He had quit school at 16, worked for a bank, entered Conservative politics, and was elected to Parliament in 1979. He had held a number of government posts, including foreign secretary. Major named his cabinet, Nov. 28, and on Nov. 29, he told Parliament he would give priority to dealing with the European Community and with the unpopular local government tax.

JDL Leader Assassinated — Rabbi Meir Kahane, a militant and controversial political leader, was assassinated in New York City, Nov. 5. Kahane, who had been born in Brooklyn, had founded the Jewish Defense League, which advocated aggressive self-defense by Jews. A strong supporter of Soviet Jews, Kahane had moved to Israel in 1971 and was elected to the Knesset in 1984, where he advocated expulsion of Arabs from Israel and the occupied territories. Kahane was shot dead in a mid-Manhattan hotel after making a speech. The gunman also wounded a bystander and a policeman before being shot and wounded himself. He was identified as El Sayyid A. Nosair, a Moslem and U.S. citizen who had been born in Egypt. Nosair was indicted, Nov. 20, for 2d-degree murder and on other charges.

Woman Elected President of Ireland — For the first time ever, a woman was elected president of Ireland. In the voting that occurred on Nov. 7, the leader was Brian Lenihan of the dominant Fianna Fail political faction. Mary Robinson, the candidate of the Labour Party and the Workers Party, placed second. Neither had a majority and when, according to Irish law, the votes of the 3d-place finisher were distributed according to the 2d-choice preferences of those voters, Robinson received a majority and was declared elected, Nov. 9. Robinson's views were quite liberal; she opposed the legal prohibition on divorce and the constitutional ban on abortion. As president, however, she would have only limited powers.

Indian Prime Minister Resigns — Prime Minister Vishwanath Pratap Singh resigned, Nov. 7, after he lost a vote of confidence, 346-142, in parliament. His opposition to construction of a Hindu temple on the site of a mosque and his plan to provide more government jobs for low-caste Hindus had antagonized influential leaders in Indian politics. Pres. Ramaswamy Venkataraman picked Chandra Shekhar, a Socialist, as prime minister, Nov. 9, and the latter was sworn in, Nov. 10.

USSR Debates New Union Treaty — Soviet Pres. Mikhail Gorbachev submitted a proposal for a restructuring of the relationship between the national government and the 15 republics. The Nov. 7 celebration of the Bolshevik Revolution was marked as well in the Soviet Union by anti-Communist rallies. In Moscow, on Nov. 7, a gunman fired 2 shots near the reviewing stand where Gorbachev and other dignitaries were watching the parade. No one was injured and the gunman was arrested. In a speech to the Supreme Soviet (national legislature), Nov. 16, Gorbachev said unnamed officials were seeking to discredit him. On Nov. 17, the Supreme Soviet approved a plan he had put forward earlier that day for an emergency reorganization of the executive branch. The plan would put the executive branch directly under presidential control, but allow the 15 republics more decision-making powers. The office of premier would be abolished and the council of the heads of the republics, chaired by Gor-

bachev, would be elevated to the key role in the government. At a press conference, Nov. 23, Gorbachev gave more details of the union treaty, which would replace a treaty adopted in 1922. The USSR would be renamed the Union of Sovereign Soviet Republics, with the word Socialist dropped from the title. In a powerful executive branch, the president and vice president would be elected directly by the people. The office of premier would be retained, and republics could determine their form of government and economic system. The 3 Baltic republics and Georgia had already said they would not sign the treaty and would seek independence. Boris Yeltsin, president of the Russian Federation and a leading reformer, called, Nov. 21, for a national referendum on the proposal. Defense Minister Dmitri Yazov, Nov. 27, sanctioned the use of force to combat a "breakdown" of order.

Paris Summit Marks End of Cold War — A formal conclusion to the era of Cold War between East and West was formally celebrated at a summit conference in Paris. On his way to the summit, Pres. George Bush visited Czechoslovakia, addressing 100,000 in Wenceslas Square in Prague on Nov. 17, before speaking again to the Federal Assembly. Bush met with German Chancellor Helmut Kohl in Berlin, Nov. 18. Soviet Pres. Mikhail Gorbachev met with Pope John Paul II in the Vatican, Nov. 18, and then signed a Soviet-Italian friendship treaty with Italian Premier Giulio Andreotti. The Conference on Security and Cooperation in Europe opened in Paris, Nov. 19, with the United States, Canada, and all the nations of Europe represented (except Albania, which sent observers). On Nov. 19, Bush and Gorbachev, as well as other leaders of NATO and the Warsaw Pact, signed the Treaty on Conventional Armed Forces in Europe, which limited each military force in the region to 20,000 main battle tanks, 30,000 other armored combat vehicles, 20,000 pieces of artillery, and 6,800 combat aircraft. On Nov. 21, the last day of the summit, the leaders signed the Charter of Paris for a New Europe, which declared an end to "the era of confrontation and division in Europe" and pledged a "new era of democracy, peace and unity."

Bulgarian Premier Resigns — A general strike led by the opposition brought about the resignation of Premier Andrei Lukanov of Bulgaria. Lukanov's government had survived a no-confidence vote in parliament on Nov. 23. His cabinet was composed entirely of members of the Socialist (formerly Communist) Party. An anti-socialist labor federation launched its strike, Nov. 26. It spread throughout the country, and on Nov. 29, Lukanov resigned, saying he had been unable to create a consensus behind solutions for Bulgaria's economic difficulties. On Dec. 7, parliament elected a political independent, Dimitar Popov, to the office of premier.

Polish Premier Quits After Rebuff at Polls — The first round of voting for a president of Poland proved inconclusive on Nov. 25. Lech Walesa, leader of the Solidarity movement, led with 40 percent. Stanislaw Tyminski, a newcomer to Polish politics, placed 2d with 23 percent. Tyminski had emigrated to Canada in 1969 and owned a computer-systems company there and a cable TV company in Peru. He had returned to Poland to seek the presidency as an outsider challenging establishment figures. Premier Tadeusz Mazowiecki finished 3d in the field of 6 candidates with 18 percent. On Nov. 26, he announced his resignation, but said he and his cabinet would remain in office until a new premier was appointed by the next president. Mazowiecki had imposed a tough economic reform program on Poland. Walesa and Tyminski would face a runoff election to determine the next president.

General

Nations Plan Effort on Global Warming — At the Second World Climate Conference in Geneva on **Nov. 7,** more than 130 countries reached an agreement to begin drafting a convention on global warming. The signatories agreed to seek "feasible national programs or strategies" to limit emissions of carbon dioxide and other greenhouse gases. Many delegates criticized the United States and the Soviet Union for successfully leading opposition to establishing firm targets for reducing carbon dioxide.

"Junk-Bond" Expert Sentenced — In New York District Court on **Nov. 21,** Judge Kimba Wood sentenced Michael Milken, a former employee of Drexel Burnham Lambert Inc., to 10 years in prison for securities fraud. Milken had helped facilitate the corporate takeover boom of the 1980s through the promotion of high-risk, high-yield securities known as "junk bonds." He pleaded guilty in April 1990 to fraud—6 felony counts—and agreed to pay fines and make restitution totaling $600 million. In imposing a sentence that was longer than some had predicted, Judge Wood dismissed assertions by Milken's lawyers that the crimes were little more than technicalities. She said a prison term was necessary to deter others in the financial industry from engaging in similar practices.

Players Fined for Harassing Reporter — A professional football team and 3 of its players were fined in connection with the harassment of a woman reporter. The incident that led to the fines had occurred in September and had been widely deplored by advocates of equal rights for women. In a report issued for the National Football League by Philip Heymann, a Harvard law professor, the incident reportedly began while Lisa Olson, a reporter for the *Boston Herald,* was interviewing Maurice Hurst, a player for the New England Patriots, in the team's locker room in Foxboro, Mass. According to the report, Zeke Mowatt stood naked a few feet from Olson, and he and 2 other players made inappropriate remarks or gestures. The report said Olson had been "degraded and humiliated." On **Nov. 27,** National Football League Commissioner Paul Tagliabue levied fines totaling $72,500 against the team and the 3 players.

Disasters — At least 112 people were killed, **Nov. 14,** when a typhoon with 150-mile-an-hour winds struck the central Philippines.

DECEMBER

National

Jobless Rate at 3-Year High — The Labor Dept., **Dec. 7,** put the unemployment rate at 5.9 percent in November, up from 5.7 percent in October. The November percentage was the highest in 3 years. Furthermore, the number of payroll jobs lost in October and November (including an upward revision for the October total) was put at 445,000, the greatest for any 2 consecutive months since the 1982 recession. On **Dec. 7,** the Federal Reserve Board cut the federal funds rate, the overnight-loan rate between banks, from 7.5 to 7.25 percent. The Labor Dept. reported, **Dec. 14,** that producer prices for finished goods rose 0.5 percent in November. The department said, **Dec. 18,** that consumer prices had risen 0.3 percent in November. With statistical evidence mounting that the U.S. had entered a recession in the fourth quarter, the Federal Reserve Board, **Dec. 18,** cut its rate for loans to its member institutions from 7 to 6.5 percent. This cut, an effort to stimulate the economy, was the first in the discount rate since 1986. The Commerce Dept., **Dec. 18,** put the merchandise trade deficit in October at $11.61 billion,

the highest level since February 1988. The department said, **Dec. 28,** that the leading economic indicators had declined 1.2 percent in November. The index had now dropped for 5 consecutive months, with a decline of 3 straight months generally regarded as indicating a recession. On Wall Street, the Dow Jones industrial average closed for the year, **Dec. 31,** at 2633.66, down 119.54 points, or 4.3 percent, for 1990.

Keating Hearings Continue — The Senate Ethics Committee continued its hearings into the relationship between 5 senators and Charles Keating, former chairman of the failed Lincoln Savings and Loan Association in California. M. Danny Wall, a former chairman of the Federal Home Bank Board, testified, **Dec. 4,** that Sen. Alan Cranston (D, Cal.) had made a large number of phone calls to his office concerning Lincoln and that he would have been very disturbed about the calls had he known that Keating was a large contributor to Cranston's senatorial campaign. William Black, a federal bank regulator, testified, **Dec. 5,** that a decision by the board to limit high-risk investments by Lincoln had been reversed after a call from an aide to Cranston. James Grogan, a former lobbyist for Keating, testified, **Dec. 14** and **15,** that Keating had not expected to exchange money for favors from the senators, but he acknowledged that his contributions had gotten their attention.

Minority Scholarships Debated — Michael Williams, assistant secretary of Education for civil rights, disclosed, **Dec. 11,** that his department regarded college scholarships set aside exclusively for minorities as discriminatory and therefore in violation of federal civil rights law. The department announced, **Dec. 12,** that it would prohibit institutions receiving federal funds from awarding scholarships on the basis of race. Grants given on the basis of financial need would not be affected. In a development unrelated to the new policy, Education Secretary Lauro Cavazos resigned, **Dec. 12.** News reports said that Pres. George Bush had felt that Cavazos, the first Hispanic-American Cabinet member, had not been active enough in developing a national education agenda. On **Dec. 17,** Bush nominated Lamar Alexander, a former governor of Tennessee, to succeed Cavazos. Meanwhile, criticism of the department's new policy on scholarships had been widespread. On **Dec. 18,** Williams announced a partial reversal, saying that the department would allow colleges receiving federal money to give scholarships to minority students if the money came from private donors or from U.S. programs established to aid minority students. Williams said he had been "politically naive" in announcing the previous policy.

Population Put at 249.6 Million — The Census Bureau released its final figures, **Dec. 26,** and reported that the 1990 U.S. population was 249,632,692, or 10.2 percent more than the total for 1980. The "final" figure was 3.8 percent greater than the preliminary figure released in August, and might be revised further if an undercount could be shown. The West, up 22 percent, led the nation in growth between 1980 and 1990. The South was up 13.5 percent, the Northeast 3.4 percent, and the Midwest 1.3 percent. California would gain 7 seats in the U.S. House of Representatives, while Florida would pick up 4 and Texas 3. Among states losing Congressional seats, New York led the list with 3.

International

President of Chad Overthrown — A 3-week offensive by rebel forces in Chad ended in success, **Dec. 1,** when Pres. Hissene Habré fled into exile in Cameroon. Rebel leader Idris Deby, a French-trained professional soldier, entered the capital, Ndjamena, **Dec. 2,** and proclaimed himself interim president, **Dec. 4**. Deby had mounted his offensive from the Sudan, where he had fled in 1989 after being implicated in a coup against Habré.

USSR Offered Food, Other Help — The Soviet Union, facing the possibility of a famine, received pledges of assistance from the U.S. and other countries in November and December. On **Dec. 1**, food rationing was initiated in Leningrad and 3 other Soviet cities. Soviet Foreign Minister Eduard Shevardnadze, **Dec. 10**, appealed to the U.S. for food. On **Dec. 12**, joining Germany, Australia, Saudi Arabia and other countries, Pres. George Bush announced that the U.S. would provide help—in the form of loan guarantees to allow the Soviets to buy U.S. food. He also promised emergency shipments of food and medical supplies. In acting, Bush waived a legal requirement barring normal trade with countries not having market economies or unrestricted emigration. Bush also announced that he and Soviet Pres. Mikhail Gorbachev would hold a summit meeting in Moscow in February.

Kohl's Party Wins All-German Election — The Christian Democratic Union, the party of Chancellor Helmut Kohl, finished first, **Dec. 2**, in the first general election to the Bundestag in reunified Germany. Kohl's party and its allies would retain their majority in the Bundestag, the lower house of parliament. The principal opposition party, the Social Democratic Party, had its poorest showing since 1957. In the area that was formerly East Germany, the Party of Democratic Socialism, the successor to the Communist Party, polled 10 percent of the vote and captured 17 seats in the Bundestag. In his campaign, Kohl had stressed his role in bringing about the reunification of Germany. On **Dec. 20**, members of the new Bundestag met in the old Reichstag in Berlin.

Argentine Revolt Thwarted — Several hundred army troops staged a rebellion in Argentina, **Dec. 3**, and were able to seize the army headquarters in Buenos Aires as well as a barracks. Forces loyal to Pres. Carlos Saúl Menem moved swiftly to quash the revolt, recapturing the 2 sites and bombing advancing tanks. The unsuccessful attempt resulted in 21 deaths. U.S. Pres. George Bush, in a trip through South America that also included visits to Brazil, Uruguay, Chile, and Venezuela, addressed the Argentine legislature, **Dec. 5**, and proclaimed that the "day of the dictator" had ended in Latin America.

Walesa Elected President of Poland — Lech Walesa won a runoff election for the presidency of Poland in December. On **Dec. 7**, Premier Tadeusz Mazowiecki, who had been eliminated from contention in the first round, urged members of the Solidarity union movement, which Walesa headed, to close ranks behind Walesa. In the voting on **Dec. 9**, Walesa defeated Polish-Canadian businessman Stanislaw Tyminski, getting 74 percent of the vote. Walesa resigned as chairman of Solidarity, **Dec. 12**. Tyminski returned to Canada, **Dec. 12**, after posting a bond of $100,000 relating to a government charge that he had slandered Mazowiecki during the campaign. Poland's outgoing president, Wojciech Jaruzelski, apologized, **Dec. 12**, for "each harm, pain and injustice" suffered by Poles during his 9 years in office. Walesa was sworn in as president, **Dec. 22**. On **Dec. 29**, he named Jan Krzysztof Bielecki, an economist, as premier.

U.N. Rebukes Israel on Territories — Prime Minister Yitzhak Shamir of Israel met with Pres. George Bush, **Dec. 11**, at the White House. Bush have assurances that the U.S. would not tie Iraq's withdrawal from Kuwait to any proposal to resolve the Palestinian question. This helped improve U.S.-Israeli relations, but then, on **Dec. 20**, the U.S. joined in a unanimous vote for a U.N. Security Council resolution that called the occupied West Bank and Gaza Strip "occupied territories" and deplored Israel's treatment of Arab civilians there. Under the resolution, the U.N. Secretary General would monitor the safety of Palestinians in the territories. The resolution also opposed Israel's plan to resume deporting Arabs from the territories. Shamir and other Israeli leaders denounced the resolution.

Soviet Foreign Minister Resigns — Eduard Shevardnadze, a close adviser to Soviet Pres. Mikhail Gorbachev for many years, resigned as foreign minister. On **Dec. 19**, Premier Nikolai Ryzhkov, addressing the Congress of People's Deputies, said perestroika (restructuring) had failed and that he assumed personal responsibility for the failure for the economy. On **Dec. 20**, Shevardnadze astonished the deputies by announcing during a speech that he would step down. He said he was tired of defending his policies against conservative Communist critics. Although he predicted that democracy and freedom were the way of the future, he said that dictatorship was on the horizon, but he added, "No one knows what this dictatorship will be like." Gorbachev, apparently taken by surprise, deplored the resignation as "unforgivable" at a time of crisis in the Soviet Union, and he denied the country was on the brink of any kind of dictatorship. Gorbachev warned, **Dec. 22**, that "necessary measures" would be taken in Moldavia unless that republic met demands he had made. In response, the Moldavian parliament, **Dec. 30**, said it would review a law that made the Moldavian language official in the republic and also agreed not to form a special defense force in Moldavia.

General

Comatose Woman Allowed to Die — A long legal dispute over whether a patient had a "right to die" came to an end in December. Mary Beth Cruzan had suffered permanent brain damage in a car accident in Missouri in 1983. Hospitalized in a "persistent vegetative state," she had been fed since then through a tube into her stomach. In June 1990, the U.S. Supreme Court had rejected an appeal from her parents to remove the tube and allow her to die. But a probate court judge in Jasper County, Mo. ruled, **Dec. 14**, that they had a right to remove the tube because 3 of Nancy's co-workers had testified in November that she had once said that she would never want to live under such circumstances. Two hours after the court ruling, the tube was removed. Twelve days later, on **Dec. 26**, she died.

Two Convicted of Killing Environmentalist — A rancher and his son were found guilty, **Dec. 15**, in the murder of Chico Mendes, a defender of the Amazon rain forest in Brazil. Mendes, a leader of the rubber tappers, men who collected latex from forest trees, had resisted the burning and cutting of the forest by ranchers. Mendes had gained international recognition as an environmental champion for his efforts to save the world's largest tropical forest. In 1988 he had been shot to death.

Decline in Use of Drugs Reported — The National Institute on Drug Abuse released a survey, **Dec. 19**, showing a decline in the use of drugs by Americans since 1988. Pres. George Bush called the findings "very encouraging news." The report said that an estimated 27 million Americans had used some illegal drug during the past year. According to the results, those who used cocaine at least once a month declined in number by 45 percent, to about 1.6 million. The number using marijuana once a month or more often declined by 12 percent to about 10.2 million. The number of persons who smoked cigarettes or consumed alcohol had also declined.

JANUARY

National

Inflation, Unemployment Rose in 1990 — Data released in January showed that inflation and unemployment rose in 1990. On **Jan. 2**, most big U.S. banks lowered their prime lending rate, the interest charged on loans to preferred customers, from 10 percent to 9.5 percent. The Labor Dept. reported, **Jan. 4**, that in December 1990 unemployment had reached a 3-year high of 6.1 percent. In the second half of 1990, more than 1 million payroll jobs had been lost. The department said, **Jan. 11**, that prices paid producers for finished goods had declined 0.6 percent in December but that the index for the entire year was up 5.6 percent. The department reported, **Jan. 16**, that consumer prices had risen 6.1 percent in 1990, the highest annual rate since 1981. The increase in December had been 0.3 percent. The Commerce Dept. reported, **Jan. 17**, that housing construction dropped in 1990 to its lowest level in 8 years. On **Jan. 17**, following the outbreak of the war in the Persian Gulf region, oil prices plunged $10.56 a barrel on the New York Mercantile Exchange. Also on **Jan. 17**, the Dow Jones Industrial Average rose 114.60, the second-highest one-day point gain ever. Alan Greenspan, chairman of the Federal Reserve Board, reported to Congress, **Jan. 22** and **23**, that the nation's money supply was growing too slowly and that the board might cut interest rates again. The Commerce Dept. reported, **Jan. 25**, that the gross national product declined at a 2.1 percent annual rate in the 4th quarter of 1990; for all of 1990, the growth rate was 0.9 percent, the lowest since the 2.5 percent decline in 1982. The department said, **Jan. 30**, that the leading economic indicators had edged upward 0.1 percent in December, ending a string of 6 monthly declines.

Regulators Take Over Bank — On **Jan. 4**, the Bank of New England Corp. announced that it had lost $450 million in the 4th quarter of 1990. On **Jan. 5**, worried investors withdrew $1 billion. Federal regulators then intervened, **Jan. 6**, taking control of the bank and declaring 3 subsidiaries insolvent. The Federal Deposit Insurance Corporation said it would insure deposits in full—not just those up to $100,000. The cost of the bailout was put at $2.3 billion.

Stealth Attack-Plane Canceled — Defense Secretary Dick Cheney announced, **Jan. 7**, that he was canceling the Navy's A-12 Stealth attack-plane project. The A-12 Avenger was being developed by McDonnell Douglas Corp. and General Dynamics Corp. The Navy had planned to pay $52 billion for 620 of the planes. Cheney said the companies had not been able to "design, develop, fabricate, assemble, and test the A-12 aircraft within the contract schedule." He said it was not in the national interest to bail the companies out. The companies denied they had defaulted on the contract. The Pentagon had never previously canceled such an expensive program.

Republican Chairman Appointed — Agriculture Secretary Clayton Yeutter, **Jan. 7**, was named by the White House to become chairman of the Republican National Committee. The committee leadership had been confused since early 1990, when Chairman Lee Atwater had fallen ill. William Bennett had first accepted, and then declined, the position late in 1990. Yeutter, a former president of the Chicago mercantile exchange, had served as U.S. trade representative under Pres. Ronald Reagan.

International

Coup Thwarted in Haiti — Rebels in Haiti sought to prevent Jean-Bertrand Aristide from taking office as president. He had been elected in December 1990, and was scheduled to succeed Pres. Ertha Pascal-Trouillot in February. On **Jan. 6**, Roger Lafontant, a former leader of the Tonton Macoutes, the private militia of the 2 Duvalier presidents, and armed supporters seized the presidential palace. Pascal-Trouillot announced her resignation. But loyalist troops attacked the palace, **Jan. 7**, rescued her, and captured Lafontant and his supporters. In the next 3 days, at least 70 people were killed in violent riots triggered by the coup.

2 PLO Leaders Killed — On **Jan. 4**, the U.N. Security Council had voted unanimously to condemn Israel for its treatment of Palestinians in territories occupied by Israel. In the previous week, at least 10 Arabs had been killed and hundreds had been injured in violent clashes with Israelis. On **Jan. 5**, the U.S. State Department expressed concern over Israel's use of lethal force against demonstrators. In Tunis, **Jan. 14**, 2 Palestine Liberation Organization leaders and a 3rd man were shot dead. In a **Jan. 15** statement, Al Fatah, the mainline faction of the PLO, blamed a dissident group for the assassinations. On **Jan. 17**, after war broke out in the Persian Gulf region, Israel began enforcing a sweeping curfew on Palestinians from the West Bank and the Gaza Strip. They were restricted to their homes except for a few hours every few days, when they could buy food. On **Jan. 29**, PLO guerrillas sympathetic to Iraq attacked Israeli settlements from southern Lebanon. From **Jan. 29** to **31**, Israeli forces struck at a Palestinian refugee camp and other targets.

Baltic Crackdown Turns Violent — Lithuanians and Latvians were killed as Soviet troops moved forcefully against the 2 Baltic republics. The Soviet defense ministry said, **Jan. 7**, that it would send thousands of troops to 7 republics to seize draft dodgers and enforce conscription. Pres. Vytautas Landsbergis of Lithuania said the Kremlin was "looking for bloodshed," **Jan. 7**, and on **Jan. 8**, the Latvian parliament condemned the troop move as an "invasion" of the Baltic republics. Pres. Mikhail Gorbachev told Lithuania, **Jan. 10**, that it must accept Soviet central authority. In Lithuania on **Jan. 10**, supporters of the Moscow government went on strike. Hundreds of unarmed supporters of independence surrounded communications facilities in Vilnius, the Lithuanian capital, **Jan. 13**. Soviet paratroopers fired on the people, some of whom were crushed by tanks. Fifteen people were killed and 140 were injured. Boris Yeltsin, president of the Russian Federation, and the 3 Baltic republics signed a mutual-security agreement, **Jan. 13**, binding all the signatories to defend any that were attacked by the Kremlin. Yeltsin denounced the killings in Lithuania, and on **Jan. 14**, called on Russian troops to refuse to shoot civilians. Gorbachev, **Jan. 14**, said he had not given the order to attack the demonstrators. The Supreme Soviet, **Jan. 14**, confirmed Finance Minister Valentin Pavlov as the new premier (his predecessor, Nikolai Ryzhkov, had fallen ill), and on **Jan. 15**, confirmed Aleksandr Bessmertnykh as the new foreign minister. In Vilnius, **Jan. 16**, as many as 500,000 people attended a funeral for 9 of those killed 3 days earlier. In Moscow, **Jan. 20**, 100,000 to 300,000 people demonstrated against the crackdown in the Baltics. Just hours later, in Riga, the capital of Latvia, Soviet para-military troops stormed a government building; 4 Latvians were killed.

General

3 AIDS Cases Traced to Dentist — Louis Sullivan, secretary of Health, **Jan. 3**, removed acquired immune deficiency syndrome from the list of diseases that would automatically bar an infected person from entering the United States. Leprosy, syphilis, gonorrhea, and 3 other diseases were also dropped from the list. The Centers for Disease Control said, **Jan. 17**, that a total of 3 patients of a Florida dentist, David Acer, now deceased, had apparently become infected with the AIDS virus as a result of contact with him. The CDC could not say exactly how the patients had been infected. The American Medical Association and the American Dental Association, **Jan. 17**, appealed to doctors and dentists to warn patients, or give up surgery if they had the virus. The CDC said, **Jan. 24**, that 161,073 persons had contracted AIDS in the United States, and that 100,777 of these had died.

Pan Am Bankrupt, Eastern Closes — Pan American World Airways filed for bankruptcy, **Jan. 8**. This occurred a month after Continental Airlines Holdings Inc. had done the same. Pan Am said it hoped to get needed cash from the sale of overseas routes. Eastern Airlines stopped flying, **Jan. 18**, and gave up a 2-year effort to escape bankruptcy. An increase in jet fuel prices during the Persian Gulf crisis had been the final blow for Eastern.

Superpower Summit Postponed — Sec. of State James Baker and Soviet Foreign Minister Aleksandr Bessmertnykh announced in Washington, **Jan. 28**, that a summit scheduled for February in Moscow between Pres. George Bush and Pres. Mikhail Gorbachev had been postponed indefinitely. The official explanation was that Bush needed to stay in Washington while the Persian Gulf war was continuing. Problems with the strategic-arms reduction treaty, which was to be signed in Moscow, were also cited. Unidentified sources in the White House said the postponement was also related to the Soviet crackdown in the Baltics.

FEBRUARY

National

Jobless Rate Continues to Rise — The Labor Dept. reported, **Feb. 1**, that the unemployment rate continued to edge upward in January, to 6.2 percent. Some 232,000 payroll jobs were lost during January. In a report issued **Feb. 12**, the president's Council of Economic Advisers predicted that the recession would end soon. The report called on the Federal Reserve Board to increase the money supply. The report attributed the recession to the jump in oil prices after Iraq invaded Kuwait, a credit crunch, and a decline in consumer confidence. The Commerce Dept. said, **Feb. 15**, that the merchandise trade deficit stood at $101 billion in 1990, the lowest amount since 1983. Producer prices fell 0.1 percent in January, the Labor Dept. reported, **Feb 15**. The department said, **Feb. 20**, that consumer prices had risen 0.4 percent in January.

Bush Budget Has Big Deficit — Pres. George Bush submitted a $1.446 trillion budget to Congress, **Feb. 4**, for the 1992 fiscal year. With revenues projected at $1.165 trillion, the deficit was forecast at $280.9 billion, the 2nd-highest ever. The figures reflected neither the full cost of the Persian Gulf War nor of the savings and loan industry bailout. Bush again backed a capital gains tax. Wealthy taxpayers would be subject to an increase in Medicare taxes, and wealthy farmers would lose crop support payments.

President Presents Energy Plan — Pres. George Bush announced a comprehensive national energy plan, **Feb. 20**. Its objectives, he said, were to increase domestic production and encourage conservation, while ensuring continued economic growth. Bush proposed to open the Arctic National Wildlife Refuge and

some other areas in Alaska to oil exploration, and to explore the outer continental shelf off California and in the Gulf of Mexico. The plan also stressed nuclear power, increased spending on transportation technology, and efficiency standards for electric lights. Congressional critics said the plan did not focus enough on conservation or the use of renewable fuels.

Arizona Elects Governor — Arizona voters, **Feb. 26**, elected J. Fife Symington 3rd, a Phoenix real estate developer, as their next governor. Symington, a Republican, defeated Terry Goddard, a Democrat, by 52 to 48 percent in a runoff election. In November, neither candidate had obtained the required majority of all votes cast.

Keating Committee Finds Misconduct — On **Feb. 27**, the Senate Ethics Committee reported on its investigation of the so-called Keating Five. It found "substantial credible evidence" of misconduct by Sen. Alan Cranston (D, Cal.). The senators said Cranston or his staff members had on at least four occasions contacted regulators on Keating's behalf in close juxtaposition to receiving or soliciting money from Keating. Cranston could face disciplinary action by the Senate. The Committee issued only mild reprimands to four other senators.

International

Pres. De Klerk Targets Apartheid Laws — In an address to parliament, **Feb. 1**, Pres. F.W. De Klerk of South Africa said he would seek repeal of laws on which the apartheid system was based. He cited laws that reserved 87 percent of the nation's land for the white minority, segregated residential areas, and separated South Africans into four races. He also proposed a "multiparty conference" to consider a new constitution. Nelson Mandela, deputy president of the African National Congress, welcomed the proposals, **Feb. 2**, and the U.S. and British governments expressed their approval.

Israel Eases Palestinian Curfew — The Israeli cabinet, **Feb. 3**, approved admitting the Moledet (Homeland) Party to the government's ruling coalition. The party advocated expelling all Palestinians from the occupied territories. Israeli authorities, **Feb. 5**, began easing the curfew imposed on Palestinians in January, and some soon began to return to their work in Israel. Their absence had been a setback to the Israeli economy. From **Feb. 5 to 7**, Israeli planes and commandos attacked bases of the Palestine Liberation Organization.

Lithuanians Vote to Secede — Lithuanians voted, **Feb. 9**, on whether to secede from the Soviet Union. Pres. Mikhail Gorbachev, **Feb. 5**, issued a decree calling the plebiscite illegal. In the nonbinding vote, 90.4 percent of the voters supported independence.

Albania Gets New Government — Pro-democracy demonstrations in Albania led to the appointment of a new government. On **Feb. 6**, students at Enver Hoxha Univ. went on strike. They called for political and economic reforms and the ouster of some leading government officials. At a military academy on **Feb. 22**, a policeman and three civilians were killed during an exchange of gunfire. On **Feb. 22**, Pres. Ramiz Alia, who had supported modest reform, removed Premier Adil Carcani, who had held office since 1982, and named Fatos Nano, an economist and reformer, to succeed him.

IRA Fires at Prime Minister — Three mortar shells were fired from a van toward 10 Downing Street, the residence in London of British Prime Minister John Major, on **Feb. 7**. Major was meeting with senior cabinet members at the residence, but no one was injured.

The Provisional Irish Republican Army claimed responsibility. The IRA also claimed responsibility for a bomb that exploded in the Victoria Station rail terminal in London, **Feb. 18**, which killed a man and injured 40 people.

Warsaw Pact Alliance Fading — Soviet Pres. Mikhail Gorbachev notified the Warsaw Pact countries, **Feb. 11**, that the military side of the alliance would disband on **Apr. 1**. Hungary, Czechoslovakia, and Bulgaria had already indicated they would withdraw from the alliance if it did not disband.

Yeltsin Asks Gorbachev to Resign — Soviet Pres. Mikhail Gorbachev said, **Feb. 13**, that the nation was not yet ready to give up central economic controls. Soviet Premier Valentin Pavlov, **Feb. 18**, submitted to parliament a plan for raising prices on most goods and services by an average of 60 percent. Wages and pensions would be increased to cover most of the added costs. Boris Yeltsin, president of the Russian Federation, **Feb. 19**, called on Gorbachev to resign. He criticized the president for wanting to hold on to the old system, for not wanting to grant independence to republics desiring it, and for leading the country to dictatorship under the name of "presidential rule."

Yugoslavia Closer to Disintegration — The apparent breakup of the nation of Yugoslavia continued, as the parliament of Slovenia, **Feb. 20**, approved amendments to its constitution invalidating federal laws in that republic. The parliament also declared that the process of disunion had begun. The parliament of Croatia passed legislation, **Feb. 21**, asserting a veto power over all federal laws applying to that republic.

General

Collision at Airport Kills 34 — The collision of two planes, **Feb. 1**, on a runway at Los Angeles International Airport killed 34 persons and injured 24. A USAir jet that was landing struck a SkyWest plane that was taxiing for takeoff. According to federal investigators, **Feb. 3**, an air traffic controller may have given both planes clearance to be on the same runway at the same time.

Disasters — At least 1,200 persons were killed, **Feb. 1**, by an earthquake that struck Afghanistan and Pakistan. More than 122 people were killed, **Feb. 15**, in Phang Nga province, Thailand, after a trailer-truck carrying dynamite overturned; the dynamite then exploded, killing some of those who had gathered at the scene.

MARCH

National

Unemployment at 4-Year High — Statistics released in March continued to show the impact of the recession. The Commerce Dept. reported, **Mar. 1**, that the leading economic indicators had declined 0.4 percent in January. With revisions in previous data, this was the 6th straight monthly decline. The Labor Dept. reported, **Mar. 8**, that the unemployment rate in February was 6.5 percent, the highest in 4 years. The number of payroll jobs declined by 184,000 in February. The department reported, **Mar. 15**, that producer prices for finished goods declined 0.6 percent in February. It reported, **Mar. 19**, that consumer prices edged upward 0.2 percent in February. Despite near-record exports, the merchandise trade deficit stood at $7 billion in January, the Commerce Dept. said, **Mar. 20**. The leading economic indicators reversed themselves in February, according to the Commerce Dept., **Mar. 29**. For that

month, the index rose 1.1 percent, ending the 6-month decline.

Governor Switches Parties — Gov. Charles (Buddy) Roemer 3rd of Louisiana announced, **Mar. 11**, that he was switching from the Democratic to the Republican party. He called the GOP "most open to new ideas, new thinking, new people." As a Congressman in the 1980s, Roemer had supported the policies of Pres. Ronald Reagan, a Republican. Roemer faced a tough re-election campaign later in 1991.

$78 Billion for S&L Bailout Approved — Congress approved a $78 billion package to help bail out insolvent savings and loan associations. The Senate acted, **Mar. 19**, the House, **Mar. 21**. A previous outlay of $50 billion had nearly been exhausted. The new funding included $30 billion to cover losses at 225 institutions, and $48 billion for capital that would help facilitate their sale.

Reagan Supports Handgun Bill — Former Pres. Ronald Reagan, **Mar. 28**, endorsed a bill before Congress that would require a 7-day waiting period on the purchase of handguns. During this time, law enforcement personnel could check the background of the purchasers. Reagan gave his endorsement during a speech at George Washington University in Washington, D.C., that marked the 10th anniversary of the attempt on his life. The legislation was known as the Brady bill. James Brady, the president's press secretary, had been seriously wounded in the assassination attempt, and his wife, Sarah, had strongly advocated the legislation. In supporting the bill, Reagan broke with the views of the National Rifle Association.

International

Soviet People Vote to Preserve Union — During another turbulent month in the Soviet Union, the people voted to keep their federal union. On **Mar. 1**, nearly 200,000 coal miners went on strike in the Ukraine, Kazakhstan, and Russia, demanding higher pay. The strike spread and soon included a demand by the miners that Pres. Mikhail Gorbachev resign. In nonbinding plebiscites, **Mar. 3**, voters in Estonia and Latvia backed independence from the Soviet Union. The final draft of the union treaty, published **Mar. 9**, proposed to transform the nation into a "democratic state, formed as a result of a voluntary union of equal republics," from which any republic could secede. Boris Yeltsin, president of Russia, **Mar. 9**, urged democratic forces to "declare war on the leadership ... which has led us into a quagmire." Hundreds of thousands of Yeltsin's supporters demonstrated in Moscow and other cities, **Mar. 10**. Mayor Gavril Popov of Moscow urged citizens not to support the treaty. With only 9 of 15 republics officially participating, the treaty was approved, **Mar. 17**, with 77 percent of some 105 million voters reportedly saying yes. In an apparent boost for Yeltsin, Russian voters approved direct election of their president. Gorbachev, **Mar. 25**, banned demonstrations for 3 weeks in Moscow, but on **Mar. 28**, more than 100,000 Yeltsin supporters turned out anyway.

Iraq Suppresses Internal Revolts — In the wake of its defeat in the Persian Gulf war, Iraq faced serious internal revolts by Kurds and Shiite Moslems, which it was able to put down. The U.N. Security Council, **Mar. 2**, approved terms governing the end of hostilities between Iraq and the allied forces. Iraq was requested to rescind its annexation of Kuwait, release all prisoners of war, return Kuwaiti property, and end all military action. Iraq, **Mar. 3**, agreed to "fulfill its obligations." Allied and Iraqi commanders met, **Mar. 3**, to arrange a cease-fire. Gen. Norman Schwarzkopf said that allied forces, which controlled about 20 percent of Iraq, would pull back on the signing of a cease-fire. On Mar. 4 and 5, Iraq released 45 allied prisoners of war, and said it held no more. But the Red Cross said that at least 7,000 Kuwaitis were unaccounted for. The allies held up to 175,000 Iraqi prisoners. Baghdad radio reported, Mar. 5, that the annexation of Kuwait had been voided. Israel said, Mar. 5, that Scud missiles had killed 2 of its citizens and injured 239. Meanwhile, Shiite Moslems in southern Iraq had rebelled against government control, and fighting in Basra, a major city, was reported, Mar. 5. Pres. George Bush, addressing Congress, Mar. 6, said that the allies, in prevailing in the Persian Gulf, had passed the first test under the new world order. Defense Secretary Dick Cheney said, Mar. 7, that the 540,000 U.S. troops could be brought home by mid-summer. Troops began leaving Saudi Arabia, Mar. 7, and began arriving in the U.S., Mar. 8. All 21 former U.S. POWs arrived at Andrews Air Force Base in Maryland, Mar. 10. As anti-government insurgencies spread inside Iraq, Bush said, Mar. 13, that he was concerned about the use of helicopters to attack the rebels, which he called a violation of the cease-fire. Schwarzkopf, Mar. 15, warned Iraq against using fixed-wing aircraft in the fighting. Pres. Saddam Hussein said, Mar. 16, that the Shiite revolt had been crushed. U.N. officials said, Mar. 20, that more than 30,000 Iraqis had fled into Iran to escape the fighting. Enforcing Schwarzkopf's warning, a U.S. fighter, Mar. 20, shot down an Iraqi warplane in northern Iraq. A U.N. investigatory team reported, Mar. 21, that allied bombs had "wrought near-apocalyptic results upon the infrastructure of what had been . . . a rather highly urbanized and mechanized society." The United Nations, Mar. 22, effectively ended its food embargo against Iraq. A U.S. fighter downed another Iraqi warplane, Mar. 22. Gen. Colin Powell, chairman of the Joint Chiefs of Staff, said, Mar. 22, that a U.S. military presence would be maintained in southern Iraq for some months until a U.N. security arrangement was in place. Bush said, Mar. 27, that he would adopt a "wait and see" attitude toward the internal revolts and that he thought the Hussein regime would fall without U.S. intervention. Iran denied, Mar. 27, that it was aiding the Iraqi rebels, including the Kurds, who were reported gaining ground in the north. Schwarzkopf, in a taped interview aired Mar. 27, said he had wanted to "continue the march" to wipe out the Iraqi army, but Cheney said, Mar. 27, that the general had not urged a continuation of the war. A Shiite leader said, Mar. 28, that the Shiites were still conducting guerrilla warfare against government forces. The government recaptured Kirkuk from the Kurds, Mar. 30, and hundreds of thousands of Kurds were reported fleeing into the mountains.

Kuwait Faces War's Aftermath — The withdrawal of Iraqi forces did not immediately restore stable conditions in Kuwait. Kuwaiti oil officials said, Mar. 5, that Iraq had sabotaged Kuwait's oil refineries, eliminated all above-ground oil storage facilities, and destroyed about half of the centers where oil, gas, and water were separated. Sec. of State James Baker, meeting with Kuwaiti officials, Mar. 9, obtained a promise that the emirate would move toward democracy. The emir returned, Mar. 14, but was criticized for having delayed his return from exile for so long. The government announced, Mar. 17, that parliamentary elections would be held in 6 months to a year. The premier resigned, Mar. 20, partly as a result of complaints that the government was too slow to restore basic services, including electricity and drinkable water. Middle East Watch, a U.S.-based human rights organization, said, Mar. 21, that Kuwaiti soldiers and vigilantes had tor-

tured or beaten at least 400 people, most of them Palestinians, and that at least 30 of these had died. Meanwhile, oil wells set afire by Iraqis continued to burn. Temperatures fell under the clouds of noxious fumes, which were bringing illness to many Kuwaitis.

Yugoslav Leader Quits, Returns — Unrest returned to Yugoslavia as anti-communists in the republic of Serbia took to the streets to demand the removal of Serbian Pres. Slobodan Milosevic, a Marxist. Clashes with security forces left 2 people dead, Mar. 9. One of every 6 workers in the republic was unemployed. The federal collective presidency, consisting of the presidents of the republics, voted, Mar. 15, not to declare a national state of emergency, which would have allowed a military intervention, whereupon Borisav Jovic, the nominal national head of state, and a supporter of Milosevic, resigned. Two others resigned from the collective presidency, Mar. 16, and Milosevic said, Mar. 16, that Serbia would no longer recognize the legitimacy of the federal government. Jovic returned to his office, Mar. 20.

Baker Visits Israel — During his first trip to Israel as secretary of state, James Baker met, Mar. 12, with Israeli Prime Minister Yitzhak Shamir. Baker sought Israeli concessions, including giving up all or part of the occupied territories as part of a peace settlement. He also met separately with Palestinian leaders, Mar. 12. Israel did not immediately reject Baker's proposals.

Albanian Voters Back Communists — In the first multiparty national election since World War II, held on Mar. 31, Albanian voters chose to stick with the ruling Workers' (Communist) Party. In voting for seats in the People's Assembly, the Workers' Party won about two thirds of the popular vote and a large majority in the parliament. The opposition Democratic Party did well in urban areas, but rural areas backed the Communists.

General

Beating of Suspect Stirs Outcry — Police in Los Angeles stopped a driver, Rodney Glenn King, Mar. 3, made him lie on the pavement, and then beat him. From his window, George Holliday recorded the incident on videotape. The 2-minute tape, showing King being kicked and beaten with nightsticks by several policeman, was shown on television, both locally and nationally, and prompted loud protests from civil rights groups. No charges were filed against King, a black man, but he remained hospitalized with skull fractures, a broken leg, an injured eye, and other injuries. Attorney General Richard Thornburgh said, Mar. 14, that the U.S. Justice Dept. would review other recent complaints about police brutality. On Mar. 15, 4 white police officers were indicted on charges that included assault with a deadly weapon and inflicting bodily injury. Los Angeles Police Chief Daryl Gates resisted demands that he resign. The city's Police Commission suspended Gates, Apr. 4, but the Los Angeles City Council, Apr. 5, overruled the suspension.

Cholera Takes Heavy Toll in Peru — Cholera, a highly contagious disease, struck Peru early in 1991 and by March a serious epidemic was occurring. Cholera is caused by bacteria in feces-contaminated food and water. No similar epidemic had been reported in the Western Hemisphere since early in the 19th century. The first case was reported in January, and by Mar. 5, 259 victims had died. On Mar. 8, the number of cases in Peru stood at 55,000.

Exxon Signs Oil Spill Plea Bargain — The Exxon Corp. signed a plea bargain, Mar. 13, with the U.S. government and the state of Alaska relating to charges growing out of the oil spill in Alaskan waters in 1989 from the *Exxon Valdez.* Exxon agreed to pay a criminal fine of $100 million and to pay $900 million in civil damages to repair damage to the Alaskan coast. Exxon agreed to plead guilty to one count of killing migratory birds, and its subsidiary, Exxon Shipping Co., accepted a charge of negligent discharge of pollutants and the killing of wildlife. Exxon would continue to clean up the coastline, on which it had already spent $2.2 billion.

Disasters — More than 160 Somali refugees, fleeing from their war-torn country, drowned, **Mar. 1,** when an overcrowded dhow ran aground several hundred yards from shore off Kenya ... A transport plane crashed at a Saudi air force base, **Mar. 21,** killing 92 soldiers from Senegal serving in a multinational force in the Persian Gulf; 6 Saudi crewmembers also died in the disaster, which occurred in skies blackened by smoke from burning oil wells in Kuwait.

APRIL

National

Daley Re-Elected Chicago Mayor — Mayor Richard M. Daley of Chicago was re-elected **Apr. 2,** in a landslide vote. Daley, a Democrat, the son of former Mayor Richard J. Daley, had first won the office when he was chosen in a special election to fill the unexpired term of the late Harold Washington. His latest victory, with 71 percent of the vote, came at a time of relative calm in Chicago politics.

Unemployment at 6.8 Percent — The Labor Dept. reported, **Apr. 5,** that the unemployment rate in March stood at 6.8 percent, a jump of 0.3 percentage points. The unemployment rate had not been higher since late 1986. Also, the number of payroll jobs declined by 205,000 in March. The department said, **Apr. 11,** that producer prices for finished goods had declined 0.3 percent in March, and on **Apr. 12,** it said consumer prices had fallen 0.1 percent in March—for the first time since April 1986. Ignoring the recession, the stock markets remained strong, and on **Apr. 17,** the Dow Jones industrial average finished above 3000 for the first time, closing at 3004.46. The Commerce Dept. reported, **Apr. 18,** that the merchandise trade deficit stood at $5.33 billion in February, its lowest level in 8 years. The department said, **Apr. 26,** that the U.S. gross national product had declined by 2.8 percent, at an annual rate, in the first quarter. To stimulate economic growth, the Federal Reserve Board—for the 2nd time in 1991—cut the rate for loans to member institutions, from 6 percent to 5.5 percent, on **Apr. 30.**

Appeals Court Nominee Rejected — U.S. District Judge Kenneth Ryskamp's nomination to serve on the U.S. 11th Circuit Court of Appeals was rejected, **Apr. 11,** by the Senate Judiciary Committee. Opponents of the nomination contended that some of his public comments and a club membership indicated he was insensitive toward minorities. The committee voted, 8-6, not to approve the nomination and then, by a 7-7 vote, failed also to agree to send his nomination to the full Senate with no recommendation. Ryskamp's was the first judicial nomination made by Pres. George Bush that failed to win approval.

Legislation Ends Rail Strike — Railroad unions representing 235,000 employees went on strike, **Apr. 17.** The principal issue related to the number of workers needed to run a freight train and the number of miles an employee had to travel to earn a day's pay. The railroads argued that only an engineer and a conductor were needed to operate a train safely. Legislation adopted by Congress, **Apr. 17,** provided for a 3-member panel, to be appointed by the president, that

would have 65 days to resolve the dispute. If there was no settlement within that time, the recommendations of an emergency board already appointed by Pres. George Bush would take effect. The strike ended after Bush signed the legislation, **Apr. 18.**

House, Senate Adopt Budget — The House, **Apr. 17,** rejected, 335-89, a budget submitted in January by Pres. George Bush for the 1992 fiscal year. It then approved a $1.46 trillion budget by a 261-163 vote. Many difficult budget issues had been worked out in bipartisan budget talks held in October 1990. The House plan, providing for no tax increases and no cuts in federal benefit programs, projected a deficit of $289.6 billion. On **Apr. 25,** the Senate approved its budget plan by a voice vote. It provided for $1.448 trillion in spending and projected a deficit of $286 billion. A conference committee would reconcile differences between the 2 plans.

Tsongas Enters Presidential Race — Paul Tsongas, a former U.S. Senator from Massachusetts, announced his candidacy for the Democratic presidential nomination on **Apr. 30.** He was the first major candidate to enter the 1992 presidential race. Suffering from lymphoma, Tsongas had retired from the Senate in 1985, but said he had recovered from the illness. In making his announcement, he stressed economic issues. His support of commercial nuclear power and a cut in the capital-gains tax promised to set him apart from more liberal candidates for the Democratic nomination.

International

U.S., Allies Assist Iraqi Refugees — Refugees from Iraq, mostly Kurds, began to receive international help. On **Apr. 1,** a coalition of Kurdish insurgent groups appealed to the U.S. and other Western nations to help the Kurds, whose insurgency was being beaten down by Iraqi government forces. On **Apr. 2,** France and Turkey asked the United Nations to intervene on behalf of insurgents in Iraq. The U.S. State Dept. reiterated, **Apr. 2,** its hands-off policy toward the insurrections by Kurds and Shiites in Iran. Pres. George Bush, **Apr. 3,** said that the coalition that had won the Persian Gulf war "did not go there to settle all the internal affairs of Iraq." The U.N. Security Council, **Apr. 3,** approved a resolution establishing a permanent cease-fire in the Gulf war that would require Iraq to destroy all its chemical, biological, and nuclear weapons; destroy all but its short-term missiles; and renounce international terrorism. The U.N. Security Council, **Apr. 5,** condemned Iraq's suppression of Kurds and other dissidents. The Iraqi government, **Apr. 5,** offered amnesty to Kurds who had joined the rebellion, but Kurdish leaders said they didn't trust the offer. As the refugee tide into Iran and Turkey grew to 1 million, Bush, **Apr. 5,** ordered an airlift of food and supplies to the refugees. Iraq, **Apr. 6,** formally accepted the cease-fire terms, but called them unfair and vindictive. Sec. of State James Baker visited a refugee camp on the Iraq-Turkey border, **Apr. 8,** heard pleas for help, and promised an international relief effort. The U.N. Security Council, **Apr. 9,** authorized a 1,440-member peacekeeping force to patrol the Iraq-Kuwait border. The U.S. said, **Apr. 10,** that it had warned Iraq not to initiate any military action in northeastern Iraq, the region where fleeing Kurds were concentrated. Conditions worsened in the refugee camps, with diarrhea, dehydration, and exposure taking a death toll of up to 1,000 persons a day along the Iraq-Turkey border. Bush announced, **Apr. 16,** that U.S., British, and French military personnel would build and run refugee camps in northern Iraq. It was estimated that up to 10,000 U.S. troops would be brought into Iraq to run the camps, each of which would accommodate up to 100,000 Kurds. On **Apr. 17,** U.S. Army Special Forces units arrived in Iraq and began to select sites for the camps. Iraq and the United Nations agreed, **Apr. 18,** to allow the United Nations to set up centers in northern and southern Iraq to aid the refugees. Iraq would participate in these efforts. U.S. forces, **Apr. 21,** began to construct refugee camps. U.N. observers entered northern Iraq, **Apr. 24.** Kurdish leaders, meeting with government officials in Baghdad, **Apr. 24,** said that Pres. Saddam Hussein had agreed to guarantee the Kurds a safe return to their homes. Iraqi forces, **Apr. 26,** withdrew from the town of Zakho, where their presence had discouraged the refugees from returning to the vicinity. The United Nations estimated, **Apr. 26,** that refugees were dying at the rate of 4,000 per day. Given assurances for their safety by the U.S. commander, **Apr. 29,** Kurds began returning to the Zakho area. Relief officials estimated, **Apr. 30,** that refugees were returning to Iraq at the rate of 25,000 per day.

Kuwait's Premier Promises Elections — Advocates of democracy in Kuwait demanded, **Apr. 1,** that the emir of Kuwait, Sheik Jabir al-Ahmad Al Sabah, schedule an election. The emir, **Apr. 7,** promised elections in 1991, "God willing." He said the government would study expanding the franchise; only males descended from families that had lived in Kuwait before 1920 were eligible to vote, barely 2 percent of the population. Amnesty International reported, **Apr. 19,** that hundreds of persons suspected of collaborating with the Iraqis had been beaten, tortured, or killed by Kuwaiti soldiers and vigilantes. The new cabinet, announced **Apr. 20,** was dominated by members of the ruling Sabah family, as before. Meeting with the emir in Kuwait, **Apr. 22,** Sec. of State James Baker said that the U.S. wanted to see Kuwait take meaningful steps toward democratization and protection of human rights.

Gorbachev Survives New Challenge — Soviet Pres. Mikhail Gorbachev turned back an attempt within the Communist leadership to curb his power. In Minsk, in the capital of Byelorussia, thousands of workers went on strike, **Apr. 4,** protesting price increases and demanding higher wages and Gorbachev's removal. On **Apr. 9,** following a unanimous vote of its parliament, the republic of Georgia became the 5th republic to declare independence from the Soviet Union. Gorbachev warned, **Apr. 9,** that the economy was "coming apart" and that "institutions of power are paralyzed." He demanded that all republics continue to pay into the central budget and produce goods for the Union. The Supreme Soviet, **Apr. 23,** approved legislation supporting Gorbachev's proposals. The program included a ban on strikes and demonstrations during work hours, the privatizing of one-third of small business firms by the end of 1991, the freeing of most prices from government controls by October, and nullification of republic laws in conflict with national laws. Gorbachev and leaders of 9 republics reached an agreement, **Apr. 23.** Republics were granted the right to secede under certain circumstances and were promised a larger role in national decision-making. The republics pledged to honor economic agreements with the central government and to enforce law and order. At a plenary meeting of the Central Committee of the Communist Party, **Apr. 24,** Gorbachev persuaded delegates to reject motions that would have required him to give a self-critical account of his leadership and that would have barred him from being both president and general secretary of the party. On **Apr. 25,** following new attacks on his leadership, Gorbachev offered to resign, but the delegates then passed a motion rejecting the offer.

Israel Considers Regional Peace Talks — During a trip to the Middle East, Sec. of State James Baker met, **Apr. 9** and **10,** with Israeli officials and with a delegation of Palestinians from occupied territories. Israel indicated a willingness to attend a regional peace conference sponsored by the U.S. and the Soviet Union. Ariel Sharon, the Israeli Housing Minister, said, **Apr. 10,** that he would continue to promote Jewish settlement of the occupied territories. On **Apr. 16,** as Israeli settlers arrived at one settlement, representatives of Gush Emunim, an Israeli religious group, said that the resettlement was "a message to Baker." A second settlement was launched, **Apr. 23,** and on **Apr. 24,** Baker criticized the settlement policy. On, **Apr. 26,** Israel reaffirmed its opposition to a role in a peace conference for either the United Nations or the Palestine Liberation Organization .

Gorbachev Visits Japan — During the first visit ever by a Soviet president to Japan, Mikhail Gorbachev met with Premier Toshiki Kaifu in Tokyo, **Apr. 17-19.** Addressing the Japanese Diet, **Apr. 17,** Gorbachev noted that the Soviet Union was reducing its military presence in the Pacific, and he appealed to the Japanese to invest in the Soviet economy. Gorbachev and Kaifu were unable to resolve a dispute over the Kurile Islands, which the Soviet Union had seized from Japan at the end of World War II. In South Korea, **Apr. 20,** Gorbachev and Pres. Roh Tae Woo agreed to a tenfold increase in Soviet-Korean trade, and the 2 presidents urged North Korea to allow international agencies to inspect its nuclear facilities.

General

Kennedy Nephew Accused of Rape — William Kennedy Smith, 30, a nephew of Sen. Edward Kennedy (D, Mass.), was under investigation after a woman claimed that he had raped her. The alleged attack occurred early on **Mar. 30,** at the Kennedy family estate in Palm Beach, Fla. Police identified Smith, **Apr. 4,** as the suspect in the incident. The woman filing the complaint and another woman had met Smith, his uncle, and his cousin Patrick Kennedy at a bar that night and had then gone to the estate. Smith, a medical student, denied, **Apr. 11,** that he had raped the woman. Several news organizations, including NBC News (**Apr. 16**) and *The New York Times* (**Apr. 17**) revealed the name of the alleged victim. Women's rights organizations protested the publication of the name, noting that women in rape cases are often unfairly stigmatized.

Senator, Ex-Senator Die in Plane Crashes — A helicopter and a chartered plane collided over a suburb of Philadelphia, **Apr. 4,** killing all 5 aboard the 2 craft, including Sen. John Heinz (R, Pa.). Also, 2 children were killed by falling wreckage. Heinz, a member of the Senate since 1977, had previously served in the House. He was heir to the H. J. Heinz food company fortune. On **Apr. 5,** former U.S. Senator John Tower (R, Tex.) was among 23 people killed when a commercial plane crashed in Brunswick, Ga. During 4 terms in the Senate (1961-85), Tower had served as chairman of the Armed Services Committee. Although he was a leading authority on national defense, the Senate in 1989 rejected Tower's nomination to be Sec. of Defense, primarily because of allegations of drinking and womanizing. An astronaut, Navy Captain Manley Lanier Carter, was among those killed in the Georgia crash.

Exxon Oil Spill Agreement Rejected — A plea bargain reached in March between Exxon Corp. and the U.S. Justice Dept., related to the *Exxon Valdez* oil spill in Alaska in 1989, was rejected by a judge in April. On

Apr. 9, the National Oceanic and Atmospheric Administration issued a summary of 58 studies showing that the spill had caused more ecological damage than previously thought. Seabird deaths alone were now put as high as 580,000. Some damage to the natural ecology was now thought to be permanent. U.S. District Judge H. Russel Holland, in Anchorage, **Apr. 24,** rejected the plea bargain, saying that the $100 million in fines Exxon agreed to pay in settlement of criminal charges did not "adequately punish" the company and would not "achieve deterrence."

Cyclone Kills 125,000 in Bangladesh — A cyclone struck the coastal areas and islands of Bangladesh, **Apr. 30,** and claimed at least 125,000 lives. Millions were homeless. The cyclone took a heavy toll among fishermen in 2,000 boats. Aside from devastating the fishing industry, the cyclone wiped out rice fields on which many people relied for a living.

Disasters — An auto ferry crashed into an oil tanker in thick fog outside Livorno harbor, on Italy's northwest coast, **Apr. 10,** causing the death of about 140 people ... An earthquake that struck Costa Rica and Panama, **Apr. 22,** killed about 95 people ... An earthquake in the mountains of the Soviet republic of Georgia, **Apr. 29,** killed more than 100 people and left tens of thousands homeless.

MAY

National

Economic Indicators Up Again — The Commerce Dept. reported, **May 1,** that the leading economic indicators had risen again in March, by 0.5 percent, the second straight monthly increase after 6 consecutive declines. The Labor Dept. said, **May 3,** that the unemployment rate had edged downward, from 6.8 percent to 6.6 percent, in April. Payroll jobs declined again in April, by 124,000, but this was just about one half of the previous decline. The department reported, **May 10,** that producer prices for finished goods had risen 0.2 percent in April, the first increase in wholesale prices in 6 months. It reported, **May 14,** that consumer prices had risen 0.2 percent in April. The Commerce Dept. said, **May 17,** that the merchandise trade deficit had fallen to $4.05 billion in March, the smallest deficit since 1983. On **May 31,** the department reported that the leading economic indicators had continued to rise in April, by 0.6 percent. On Wall Street, the Dow Jones industrial average ended the month, **May 31,** at an all-time high of 3,027.50.

President Has Thyroid Disorder — Pres. George Bush experienced fatigue and shortness of breath while jogging at Camp David, **May 4.** After a doctor detected an irregular heart beat, Bush entered Bethesda Naval Hospital in Maryland. Although no damage to the heart had occurred, doctors treated the irregular beat with digoxin and then procainamide. By **May 6,** Bush had responded well enough to leave the hospital and resume his regular schedule. Doctors said, **May 7,** that the cause of Bush's condition—afrial fibrillation—was a mild hyperthyroid condition. They said, **May 9,** that the condition resulted from Graves' Disease, in which the immune system attacked the thyroid. Bush's wife, Barbara, had been diagnosed with the same disease in 1989. George Bush took medicine to slow production of the thyroxine hormone and to prevent formation of blood clots.

House Approves Handgun Bill — The House, **May 8,** voted, 239-186, in favor of the Brady Handgun Violence Prevention Act, which provided for a 7-day waiting period for purchases of handguns, while police could check out any criminal record by prospective buyers. It rejected an amendment providing for computerized background checks of would-be buyers. Opponents saw this approach as too expensive and too slow to implement. The National Rifle Association had lobbied against the Brady bill.

Director of CIA to Retire — Pres. George Bush announced, **May 8,** that William Webster would retire as director of central intelligence. Pres. Ronald Reagan had appointed Webster to head the Central Intelligence Agency in 1987. Webster, who had once been a federal appeals court judge, said he would resume his legal career. On **May 14,** Bush nominated Robert Gates to succeed Webster. Gates had also been nominated to head the CIA in 1987, when William Casey retired, but he withdrew his name from consideration when senators brought up his name in connection with the Iran-contra affair. In 1991, Gates was serving as deputy national security adviser.

International

Tensions Build Within Yugoslavia — A shootout between Croatians and Serbs in Borovo Selo, in Yugoslavia's republic of Croatia, **May 2,** resulted in the deaths of 12 policemen and 3 civilians. Serbs inside Croatia were seeking to join Serbia, a republic to the south. Col. Gen. Veljko Kadijevic, the country's Defense secretary, said, **May 6,** that "Yugoslavia has entered a state of civil war." The military went on combat alert, **May 6,** and on **May 7,** the military began to call up reserves. On **May 15,** Stipe Mesic of Croatia, vice chairman of the collective presidency, was scheduled to become chairman, or titular head of state. An opponent of Serbian nationalism, Mesic would have become Yugoslavia's first non-Communist leader since World War II. But Borisav Jovic of Serbia, who held the chairmanship, blocked Mesic from getting a majority vote. In a referendum held **May 19,** voters in Croatia overwhelmingly endorsed having a sovereign state within a loose Yugoslav confederation. Mesic, **May 20,** unilaterally declared himself to be the head of state, but the administrative chief of the presidency's secretariat rejected this claim. Croatia, **May 29,** declared itself to be independent.

U.N. Security Guards Enter Iraq — Lightly armed security guards representing the United Nations entered Iraq in May to protect returning refugees. On **May 5,** U.S. forces began to move south from Turkey into Iraq to create a safe zone in the area of Dahok and to encourage the return of Kurdish refugees. From **May 7 to 9,** U.S. troops of the 3rd Armored Division withdrew from positions along the Iraq-Kuwait border into Kuwait, marking the end of the U.S. occupation of southern Iraq. On **May 13,** officials from the U.N. Office of the High Commissioner for Refugees replaced U.S. military personnel as administrators of a Kurdish refugee camp near Zakho. The U.S. State Dept. said, **May 14,** that about 250,000 Kurdish refugees had already left the mountains in Turkey or on the border and returned to Iraq. Iraq agreed on **May 18,** to let 400 to 500 U.N. guards protect refugees at centers inside Iraq. The guards would occupy both Kurdish and Shiite refugee centers. Ten U.N. guards began to patrol Dahok on **May 19.** Iraq and allied military commanders agreed, **May 22,** that allied troops and relief workers could occupy Dahok, and all Iraqi soldiers and secret police were withdrawn by **May 24.** By **May 26,** about 50,000 people had returned to Dahok.

Hopes Up for Mideast Peace Conference — The Saudi foreign minister announced, **May 11,** that members of the Gulf Cooperation Council—Bahrain, Kuwait, Oman, Qatar, Saudi Arabia, and United Arab Emirates—were ready to take part in an Israeli-Arab peace conference. Sec. of State James Baker agreed, **May 16**, to an Israeli proposal for Israel to participate in a peace conference that included a joint Jordanian-Palestinian delegation. Appearing before a panel of the House Appropriations Committee on **May 22**, Baker said that the accelerated pace of Israeli settlements in the occupied territories had been the biggest obstacle to arranging a peace conference. Addressing graduates at the U.S. Air Force Academy on **May 29**, Pres. George Bush presented several proposals aimed at banning weapons of mass destruction in the Middle East. He called on the major suppliers of arms to the region to exercise restraint. He also called for a freeze on surface-to-surface ballistic missiles in the Middle East, a ban on elements used in nuclear weapons, a commitment by regional countries to stand by a ban on biological weapons, and a promise by the same countries to ban chemical weapons.

Winnie Mandela Convicted in Kidnappings — Winnie Mandela, wife of Nelson Mandela, leader of the African National Congress, was convicted in a criminal trial in Johannesburg, South Africa, **May 13**. The trial grew out of the abduction and subsequent beating of 4 black youths by black supporters of Winnie Mandela in 1988. One boy died as a result of a beating. Mandela was found guilty of 4 counts of kidnapping and acting as accessory to assault. Judge Michael Stegmann, in rendering a verdict and sentencing Mandela, said he did not believe her claim that she did not know of the beatings until after they occurred. He called her "a calm, composed, unblushing and unprincipled liar." The judge, **May 14**, sentenced her to 6 years in prison. Her attorney immediately filed an appeal.

Queen Elizabeth Speaks to Congress — Queen Elizabeth II, accompanied by Prince Philip, began a 2-week visit to the United States, **May 14**. In an address to Congress, **May 16**, the first ever by a British monarch, she praised the U.S. for its leading role in the Persian Gulf war. In Tampa, Fla., **May 20**, she presented an honorary knighthood to Gen. H. Norman Schwarzkopf, commander of U.S. forces in the gulf. On **May 22**, the Queen began a visit to Texas.

Woman Named Premier of France — French Premier Michel Rocard resigned, **May 15**. He had headed a minority Socialist government since 1988, and had had problems in getting support in the National Assembly for his legislative programs. Pres. François Mitterrand, **May 15**, named Edith Cresson as premier. A Socialist and longtime supporter of Mitterrand, Cresson had headed several ministries under Rocard before leaving the government in 1990. She was France's first woman premier.

Ethiopian Capital Falls to Rebels — The president of Ethiopia, Lt. Col. Mengistu Haile Mariam, resigned, **May 21**, and left the country, as rebel forces closed in on the capital of Addis Ababa. Mengistu, who had led the effort to overthrow Emperor Haile Selassie in 1974, had later brought Marxism to Ethiopia and had been propped up by Soviet aid until the USSR began cutting back on military and economic assistance in recent years. When Mengistu left, Lt. Gen. Tesfaye Gebre-Kidan was named acting president. An official said, **May 21**, that his government would negotiate with the rebels. On **May 24** and **25**, Israel airlifted 14,000 Ethiopian Jews to Israel. On **May 27**, U.S. mediators persuaded the government and the rebels, who consisted of 3 separate groups, to sign a cease-fire that would spare the capital from chaos and allow the rebels to enter the city. The rebels occupied Addis Ababa, **May 28**, and promised to set up a democratic government.

Rajiv Gandhi Is Assassinated — Rajiv Gandhi, former prime minister and leader of India's Congress (I) Party, was assassinated, **May 21**. He had become prime minister in 1984 after his mother, Indira Gandhi, had been shot to death by her own bodyguards. His grandfather, Jawaharlal Nehru, had also served as prime minister. Rajiv Gandhi had lost the prime minister's office in 1989 after voters concluded that his government was incompetent and corrupt. At the time of his death, Gandhi was attempting a political comeback, in an election compaign for seats in the lower house of Parliament. He had made a campaign stop in Sriperumbudur, southwest of Madras. Police later determined that a bomb had been concealed by a woman who approached Gandhi. The explosion of the bomb killed 16 other persons, including the assassin. On **May 23**, Gandhi's widow declined to assume the leadership of the party. Gandhi was cremated, **May 24**, on the banks of the Jumma River in a traditional Hindu funeral ceremony. On **May 29**, the Congress (I) Party named P.V. Narasimha Rao, a former foreign minister, as provisional leader of the party.

NATO Alliance to Be Restructured — The North Atlantic Treaty Organization, formed in 1949 to check Communist expansion in Europe, reached a major turning point in May. With the end of the Cold War, 5 members, including the United States, were planning to cut the size of their military units. On **May 28**, NATO Defense ministers agreed to a restructuring that would create 8 NATO corps of up to 70,000 troops each. One of these would be an all-German force assigned to eastern Germany to balance remaining Soviet forces in the region. Under the new plan, U.S. troop strength would be cut by up to 50 percent within 5 or 6 years.

Angola, Rebels Sign Peace Accord — The government of Angola and a rebel faction that had fought it for 16 years signed a peace agreement, **May 31**. A cease-fire then went into effect. The pact was signed by Pres. José Eduardo dos Santos and Jonas Savimbi, head of the National Union for Total Independence of Angola (Unita). The Soviet Union, which had supported the government, and the United States, which had supported Unita, had pressed the parties to reach an agreement. Under the settlement, both sides would work for a single armed force, democracy, and a market economy.

General

Exxon, Governor Reject Settlement — A civil settlement between the Exxon Corp. and the state of Alaska relating to the oil spill in Prince William Sound in 1989 collapsed in May. In April, a criminal penalty in the case to which Exxon had agreed had been rejected by a federal judge as too lenient. On **May 2**, the Alaska House of Representatives rejected, 26-14, the $1 billion civil agreement, the opponents contending that it did not adequately penalize Exxon or provide enough money to clean up the sound. On **May 3**, both Exxon and Gov. Walter Hickel withdrew from the settlement.

Pope Warns Capitalist Nations — Pope John Paul II released a 25,000-word encyclical, **May 2**, in which he admonished capitalist nations not to allow the collapse of communism to blind them to the necessity of surmounting injustices in their own economic systems. The pope called the free market "the most efficient instrument for utilizing resources and effectively responding to needs," but he added, "there are many human needs which find no place on the market," and noted that many people lack the purchasing power to utilize the market. In the encyclical, "Centesimus Annus," the pope said that communism had collapsed because of the opposition of workers, its inefficiency, and the spiritual void of its atheism. The pope urged the world to find an alternative to war for resolving disputes, and cited with approval the largely peaceful revolutions in eastern Europe.

Kennedy's Nephew Charged in Rape Case — After an investigation that lasted nearly 6 weeks, William Kennedy Smith, a nephew of Sen. Edward Kennedy (D, Mass.) was charged, **May 9,** in Palm Beach, Fla. with a felony count of sexual battery and a misdemeanor count of battery. Sexual battery was Florida's legal term for rape. Allegations had been leveled against Smith by a woman who had visited the Kennedy family estate in Palm Beach in March. Smith surrendered to Palm Beach police, **May 11,** and was released after posting bond. He called the woman's claims "an outrageous lie." On **May 31,** Smith entered a plea of not guilty.

Disasters — A chartered plane from Austria exploded in midair, **May 26,** soon after taking off from Bangkok. All 223 persons aboard were killed. The cause of the disaster, which claimed the 12th highest death toll in aviation history, was not immediately determined.

JUNE

National

House Approves Civil Rights Bill — On **June 5,** the U.S. House of Representatives approved, 273-158, a civil rights bill that sought to reverse decisions handed down by the U.S. Supreme Court in 1989. Under the bill, individuals would have an easier time suing and collecting damages in job-discrimination cases. The legislation would also permit women, religious minorities, and the disabled to win compensatory and punitive damages if they were subject to job discrimination. Pres. George Bush opposed the bill, saying it would establish quotas in hiring and promotion.

Students Do Poorly in Math Test — The U.S. Dept. of Education, **June 6,** released results of a mathematics test in which 125,000 students across the nation had taken part. The majority of those tested did not do as well as had been expected for the grades they were in. State-by-state breakdowns were issued only for 8th grade students. Those living in the Northwest and Upper Midwest did the best, and figures tended to suggest that students who watched a lot of television did less well.

Unemployment Rate Up to 6.9 Percent — The Labor Dept. reported, **June 7,** that the nation's unemployment rate jumped in May to 6.9 percent from 6.6 percent. On the other hand, after declining for 11 months, the number of payroll jobs in the economy rose by 59,000 in May. The department said, **June 13,** that producer prices had risen by 0.6 percent in May, and it reported, **June 14,** that consumer prices had risen 0.3 percent at the same time. The Commerce Dept. said, **June 19,** that the merchandise trade deficit had remained relatively narrow in April, at $4.78 billion. The department said, **June 28,** that the leading economic indicators had advanced 0.8 percent in May, the 4th straight rise.

Plan Offered to Help Children — The National Commission on Children, **June 24,** set forth proposals aimed at improving the lives of American children. The commission recommended that each family receive $1,000 tax credit per child, and that all children and pregnant women be covered by national health insurance. Other proposals were to increase funding for Head Start in order to cover all eligible children and to step up enforcement of efforts to collect child-support payments. Sen. John D. (Jay) Rockefeller (D, W.Va.) headed the bipartisan commission.

Justice Thurgood Marshall Retires — Thurgood Marshall, the only black ever to serve on the U.S. Supreme Court, announced, **June 27,** that he would retire when a successor was approved. Marshall, a pioneering civil rights lawyer, had argued the case (Brown v. Board of Education) before the Supreme Court in 1954 that had ended the "separate but equal" school systems in the U.S. Pres. Lyndon Johnson had nominated him to the high court in 1967. Marshall, who was 82, had become increasingly frustrated by the conservative trend on the court in recent years. In one dissent he had written, "Power, not reason, is the new currency of this Court's decision-making."

International

U.S., USSR Agree on Conventional Forces — At a meeting in Lisbon on **June 1,** Sec. of State James Baker and Soviet Foreign Minister Aleksandr Bessmertnykh reached an agreement on a Conventional Forces in Europe treaty. Although the accord had been signed in 1990, a dispute had subsequently arisen over the Soviet Union's reclassification of 3 infantry divisions as naval coastal-defense forces, a category not limited by the treaty. Details of the agreement were not announced. Baker told reporters that he hoped Pres. George Bush and Pres. Mikhail Gorbachev would meet later in June or in July to sign a treaty reducing strategic nuclear weapons.

Kuwait Elections Scheduled for 1992 — The Emir of Kuwait announced, **June 2,** that parliamentary elections had been set for October 1992. At a demonstration in Kuwait City, **June 4,** about 1,000 opponents of the government protested the long delay before the election. Sec. of State James Baker told a Senate committee, **June 12,** that the Kuwait regime "doesn't follow our standards and it's not a full-fledged democracy." During mid-June, 21 defendants in Kuwait were sentenced to death for collaborating with Iraqi forces during the occupation. Six were sentenced, **June 15,** for having worked on a newspaper published by Iraq in Kuwait. On **June 26,** all of these death sentences were commuted to life terms in prison.

Albania's Communist Government Falls — On **June 4,** two months after winning a free election, the Communist government of Albania resigned. Strikers, demanding wage increases and better working conditions for women and representing about half of the work force, had dealt a severe blow to the government. The opposition Albanian Democratic Party agreed to support an interim government, and, on **June 5,** Pres. Ramiz Alia named Ylli Bufi, a Communist, to head such a government. The parliament, **June 12,** approved a 24-member cabinet that included 12 opposition members. Bufi warned that Albania was facing "catastrophic" economic problems. The Albanian Workers' (Communist) Party officially changed its name to the Albanian Socialist Party on **June 12.** During a European trip, Sec. of State James Baker visited Tirana, the capital of Albania, **June 22.** He received an immensely enthusiastic welcome from at least 200,000 people. Baker said to the throng, "Welcome to the assembly of free peoples building a Europe whole and free."

Gorbachev Seeks International Aid — On **June 4,** Pres. George Bush named Robert Strauss as ambassador to the Soviet Union. Strauss, a prominent Democrat, was influential in the worlds of politics and finance. Pres. Mikhail Gorbachev, speaking in Oslo, Norway, **June 5,** at a ceremony honoring him as recipient of the 1990 Nobel Peace Prize, said the failure of other nations to help the Soviet economy would have a negative impact on world peace. He said economic aid from abroad was critical to the success of perestroika.

On **June 11,** Bush approved loan guarantees of up to $1.5 billion to allow the Soviet Union to buy U.S. grain. He said a team of experts would be sent to the Soviet Union to help in a restructuring of the food distribution system.

Croatia, Slovenia Declare Independence — On **June 6,** with Croatia and Slovenia preparing to secede, the presidents of the 6 republics of Yugoslavia agreed to consider a plan to turn the country into a loose confederation. In separate actions taken on **June 25,** the parliaments of Croatia and Slovenia declared that their republics were independent and sovereign, but they did not actually secede. Clashes began, **June 27,** between Yugoslav troops and Slovenian militias, and it was reported that 100 persons were killed or wounded. Yugoslav army units, **June 28,** took control of several border posts from Slovenian authorities. Croatia and Slovenia agreed, **June 29,** to suspend their declarations of independence, and Yugoslav officials agreed to pull back federal troops and let a Croatian assume the country's presidency. Sporadic fighting continued, and the Yugoslav army said, **June 30,** that it would take "decisive military action" unless Slovenia agreed to an unconditional cease-fire.

Yeltsin Elected President of Russia — Boris Yeltsin, with about 60 percent of the vote, was elected president of Russia, **June 12.** Running as an independent, he became the first leader of Russia ever to be chosen in a popular vote. Yeltsin had been serving as chairman of the Russian parliament. He had pressed for democratic and economic reforms at a faster pace than Soviet Pres. Mikhail Gorbachev had allowed. Former Soviet Prime Minister Nikolai Ryzhkov, a conservative Communist, ran a distant second to Yeltsin. The mayors of Moscow and Leningrad, both allies of Yeltsin, were easily re-elected. In a nonbinding referendum, residents of Leningrad voted to change the name of the city back to St. Petersburg, its name before World War I.

India Gets New Prime Minister — The Congress (I) Party, led until his assassination in May by Rajiv Gandhi, won a plurality in the Indian elections that were concluded on **June 15.** Violence related to the election climaxed that day when terrorists fired on 2 passenger trains in the state of Punjab, killing at least 76 people. In the voting, the Congress (I) Party picked up seats but remained short of an absolute majority. On **June 20,** Pres. Ramaswamy Venkataraman named P. V. Narasimha Rao, president of the Congress (I) Party, as prime minister. Rao was sworn in, **June 21,** as prime minister.

Apartheid Law Repealed — On **June 17,** the Parliament of South Africa repealed a law that was a key to maintaining the apartheid system of racial separation. The law, the Population Registration Act of 1950, had required that every citizen be registered as a white, black, Asian, or colored (mixed race). Opposition to repeal in the House of Assembly came from the Conservative Party, which supported apartheid. Repeal meant that South Africa had met 4 of the 5 conditions set by the U.S. Congress for suspension of economic sanctions. The release of political prisoners was still an issue, but the Bush administration said, **June 17,** that sanctions would be lifted by the end of the summer.

Soviet Troops Leave 2 Countries — The last Soviet troops and their dependents left Hungary by train, **June 19.** A similar exit was completed in Czechoslovakia, **June 21.** The departures were in compliance with agreements made in 1990. At one time, there had been about 50,000 Soviet troops in Hungary and about 73,500 in Czechoslovakia. The 2 former Soviet satellites. as well as Poland, were demanding monetary compensation from the Soviet Union for environmental damage at the former Soviet bases.

Drug Kingpin Surrenders in Colombia — Pablo Escobar Gaviria, believed to be the leader of the Medellín cocaine cartel, surrendered to authorities in Columbia, **June 19.** An assembly rewriting Colombia's constitution had just voted to forbid the extradition of Colombian nationals. Escobar had been indicted in the U.S. for drug trafficking and murder. Escobar's drug gangs were believed to be responsible for hundreds of murders. Escobar was taken to a prison built especially for him near his hometown of Envigado, and near Medellín. The facility was more like a well-appointed home than a prison. U.S. officials said they doubted that Escobar's imprisonment would have much effect on the flow of cocaine out of Colombia.

Berlin to Become German Capital — On **June 20,** the German parliament's lower body, the Bundestag, voted, 337-320, to move the capital of the newly united nation from Bonn to Berlin. The moving of government operations was expected to take place over a decade.

Allied Force to Protect Kurds — In order to protect Iraqi Kurds after allied troops pulled out of the safe zone in northern Iraq, the U.S. and its European allies agreed, **June 21,** to station a military task force in southern Turkey, near the Iraq border. It was agreed, **June 25,** that about 5,000 U.S., British, French, and Dutch troops would remain in Turkey, backed up by U.S. attack and fighter aircraft based at Incirlik, Turkey. On **June 28,** when U.N. inspectors sought to investigate machinery that the U.S. said was being used to make nuclear weapons, Iraqi soldiers east of Baghdad fired over the heads of the inspectors, and thwarted the inquiry. Pres. George Bush said, **June 28,** "We can't allow this," and the U.N. Security Council, **June 28,** ordered Iraq to hand over the equipment.

General

Shuttle Trip Focuses on Medical Problems — During a mission that took place from **June 5** to **14,** the crew of the space shuttle *Columbia* studied the biological effects of space travel. It was known that weightlessness caused faster heatbeats, atrophy of muscles, loss of calcium, and movement of bodily fluids. The shuttle carried the Space Lab module, a pressurized cylinder containing medical instruments. Also aboard were 29 rats, which would be dissected later, and 2,478 jellyfish, which had organs similar to those in the human ear, and whose adaptation to weightlessness would be studied. Astronauts would donate samples of blood, urine, and saliva for analysis.

Volcano Erupts in Philippines — Major eruptions at Pinatubo, a volcanic mountain 55 miles northwest of Manila, in the Philippines, occurred on **June 12** and **13.** On **June 10,** when it became apparent that a major eruption would soon occur, U.S. military personnel began to evacuate Clark Air Force Base, which was about 10 miles east of the mountain. Some 16,000 persons transferred to Subic Bay Naval Base. Lava poured down the mountainside, and white ash covered nearby towns. More than 20,000 Filipinos were also evacuated from the area. On **June 17,** the Philippines Red Cross put the death toll from the volcano at 76. Civil defense officials said in the Philippines, **July 14,** that more than 40 tribespeople who had hidden in caves to escape the erupting Pinatubo volcano had been buried alive; the overall death toll in the eruption, which occurred **June 9,** was put at up to 435.

Pres. Taylor's Remains Exhumed — An attempt was made to solve an historical mystery involving Zachary Taylor, the 12th president of the U.S. Taylor had died suddenly in office on July 9, 1850, and his death was attributed to acute gastrointestinal illness. This occurred during a tense moment in the controversy over slavery, and some historians speculated that Taylor might have been poisoned with arsenic. An historical novelist, Clara Rising, asked that Taylor's body be exhumed, and this was done at a cemetary in Louisville, Ky., **June 17.** Never before had a president's body been exhumed. The State Chief Medical Examiner and the coroner's office conducted tests, and reported, **June 26,** that no trace of arsenic had been found.

Disasters — A passenger train crashed into a standing freight train in southern Pakistan, **June 8,** causing death to more than 100 persons and injury to about 250 ... Torrential rains in Antofagasta, Chile, **June 18,** created mudslides that killed at least 61 persons and injured about 750 ... About 120 persons, most of whom were illegal immigrants who had been expelled from Malaysia, were feared drowned, **June 26,** after 2 ships collided about 150 miles southwest of Kuala Lumpur.

JULY

National

Bush Nominates Thomas for Supreme Court — On July 1, Pres. George Bush nominated Judge Clarence Thomas of the U.S. Court of Appeals for the District of Columbia Circuit Court to serve on the U.S. Supreme Court. If approved by the Senate, Thomas, a black, would succeed Thurgood Marshall, the first black ever to serve on the high court, who had announced his retirement. From humble beginnings in Pinpoint, Ga., Thomas had obtained a law degree from Yale. A political conservative, he had served as head of the Equal Employment Opportunities Commission during the Reagan administration. In a Feb. 20, 1987 letter to the editor of the *Wall Street Journal*, Thomas advocated "black self-help" while calling racial quotas "race-conscious legal devices that only further deepen the original problem." The National Organization for Women opposed the nomination, **July 5,** because of his perceived or presumed views on women's rights and his opposition to workplace preferences for minorities and women. The National Education Association, **July 5,** expressed its "grave concern" over Thomas's positions. On **July 31,** both the National Association for the Advancement of Colored People and the AFL-CIO declared their opposition.

G.N.P. Expansion Signals Economic Upturn — Growth in the gross national product was reported in July, suggesting that the recession might be ending. However, the Labor Dept. reported, **July 5,** that unemployment in June had edged upward by 0.1 percentage point to 7.0 percent. The department said, **July 12,** that producer prices for finished goods had fallen 0.3 percent in June. In a report that could impact the economy, White House Budget Director Richard Darman said, **July 15,** that the 1992 federal budget deficit would be $348.3 billion, $67.4 billion more than the previous estimate. The Labor Dept. said, **July 17,** that consumer prices had risen 0.2 percent in June. On **July 18,** the Commerce Dept. put the merchandise trade deficit in May at $4.57 billion, little changed from the previous month's revised estimate of $4.51 billion. The department reported, **July 26,** that the G.N.P., the broadest measure of the economy, had risen 0.4 percent at an annual rate during the second quarter of 1991. Prior to this report, the G.N.P. had slumped by a cumulative total of 1.1 percent, and Michael Boskin,

the President's chief economic adviser, said that "the recession appears to have ended."

Ex-CIA Official Admits Lying to Congress — The seemingly dormant Iran-contra investigation came back to life, **July 9,** when a former official of the Central Intelligence Agency pleaded guilty to deceiving Congress. Alan D. Fiers, Jr., who made the admission, had been head of the CIA's Central American Task Force from 1984 to 1986. In the fall of 1986, Fiers had told the House and Senate committees that he didn't know details about the sale of arms to Iran and the transfer of proceeds to the contras in Nicaragua. But according to a statement from the prosecution, Fiers acknowledged that he had learned about these operations from Col. Oliver North, a central figure in the scheme. Based on the prosecution statement, it appeared that other CIA officials from that time might face legal problems. On July 16, the Senate Intelligence Committee postponed until September hearings on the nomination of Robert Gates to be head of the CIA. Gates had been deputy director in 1986.

Federal Reserve Board Chairman Reappointed — Pres. George Bush announced, **July 10,** that he would renominate Alan Greenspan to a second 4-year term as chairman of the Federal Reserve Board. The Senate would need to confirm. During his first term, Greenspan had followed a tight-money policy in order to restrain inflationary pressures. Although largely successful in this regard, he had also been criticized for not stimulating growth to head off a recession.

34 Military Bases to Be Closed — A long controversy over the closing of U.S. domestic military installations was resolved when Pres. George Bush, **July 10,** approved the recommendations of the Defense Base Closure and Realignment Commission. The commission had proposed that 34 bases be closed and that 48 others be realigned. It estimated that shutting down the 34 installations would save $2.3 billion per year through 1997, although it would also cost $4.1 billion just to close them down. The end of the cold war and the federal budget crunch had precipitated the move to shut down bases. However, members of Congress whose districts were affected had in many cases vehemently opposed the closings, arguing economic hardship. Hence, it had been agreed in advance that, to avoid a legislative donnybrook, Congress would have to accept or reject the recommendations without amendment. Rejection could come only in a joint resolution of both houses. On July 30, the issue was settled when the House voted, 364-60, to accept the recommendations. Installations to be closed included Fort Ord Army Base in California, the Philadelphia Naval Shipyard and the Philadelphia Naval Station.

House Democrats Elect Bonior — The Democrats in the U.S. House elected a successor to Rep. William Gray (Pa.), the majority whip, who announced, **June 20,** that he would resign from the House in September. Gray, the highest ranking black in Congress, was to become president of the United Negro College Fund. On July 11, David Bonior (Mich.) was chosen as Gray's replacement. The whip's responsibility was to line up votes during legislative battles. House Majority Leader Richard Gephardt (Mo.), announced, **July 17,** that he would not seek the Democratic presidential nomination in 1992.

Changes in 1990 Census Count Rejected — Commerce Secretary Mosbacher announced, **July 15,** that there would be no adjustment in the figures for the 1990 census that had been previously reported. Based on a survey whose results were announced in April, Census Bureau officials had put the undercount at 5.3 million people. The General Accounting Office had estimated that the census had missed at least 9.7 million people. Mosbacher agreed that an undercount had occurred and that a disproportionate number of those who had been missed were members of minorities. But he was reluctant, he said, "to abandon a 200-year tradition of how we actually count people."

Senators Give Themselves A Raise — The U.S. Senate voted, July 17, 53-45, to raise the pay of senators to $125,100. This matched the salary received by members of the U.S. House and, like the House in 1989, the Senate voted to eliminate speaking fees.

International

3-month Truce Accepted in Yugoslavia— July began in Yugoslavia with a tense cease-fire in effect. On July 1, the federal army began calling up reservists. Slovenia demanded, July 1, that trapped federal forces give up their weapons and equipment before withdrawing to their bases. The cease-fire broke down, July 2, in Slovenia, and combat resumed. But on July 7, a 3-member team of foreign ministers from Luxembourg, Portugal, and the Netherlands succeeded in mediating a truce between Slovenia and the federal government. The truce, approved by Slovenia's parliament, July 10, provided for a 3-month cooling-off period. During this time, Slovenia and Croatia would suspend their pursuit of independence and federal troops would return to their bases. On July 18, the federal collective presidency ordered federal troops to pull out of Slovenia. On July 22, 14 to 20 people were killed in Croatia in fighting between Croats and Serbs. The president of Croatia, Franjo Tudjman, walked out of talks on the form of the future government.

Soviet Party Congress to Weigh New Course—The Central Committee of the Communist Party of the Soviet Union agreed to schedule a party congress for late 1991 that could lead to a new path for Soviet communism. The Supreme Soviet, the standing national legislature, July 1, passed a law to allow the sale of state-owned enterprises. This action, which was unprecedented, would favor Soviet citizens over foreigners as purchasers. On July 1, former Foreign Minister Eduard Shevardnadze and 8 other leading Soviet citizens founded the Democratic Reform Movement, an open challenge to Communist hardliners. Aleksandr Yakovlev, an aide to Soviet Pres. Mikhail Gorbachev, was another founder. Gorbachev called the formation of the movement a "positive step," and Yakovlev said in a newspaper article, July 2, that the Communist Party was "incapable of listening to the voice of reason." Shevardnadze resigned from the party, July 3. On July 24, Gorbachev announced that he had reached agreement with 9 of 15 Soviet republics on a draft treaty that would decentralize the system of power-sharing in the Soviet Union. He said that, except for the formula for taxation, all major differences between the central government and the republics had been settled. In a speech to the Central Committee, July 25, Gorbachev proposed a sweeping overhaul in party ideology. He proposed that the party support private ownership of property, a free-market economy, reject totalitarian methods, and favor individual freedoms over the collective good. Nor, he said, should party members be required to embrace atheism. The Central Committee, already upset by a decree by Russian Pres. Boris Yeltsin banning party cells from factories and state offices, agreed, July 26, to the convening of a party congress in November to deal with Gorbachev's new program.

Warsaw Pact Enters History Books—The Warsaw Pact ceased to exist, July 1. Its military structure had been disbanded in March. The remaining Political Consultative Committee was abolished at a summit of leaders of member nations in Prague. The leaders voided the 1955 Treaty of Friendship, Cooperation and Mutual Assistance, which had created the pact.

Bank Target of International Investigation—The Bank of Commerce and Credit International, which had offices in 69 countries, became the subject of a number of investigations. The bank was controlled by Sheik Zayed bin Sultan Al Nahayan, the ruler of Abu Dhabi in the United Arab Emirates. In the U.S., units of BCCI had pleaded guilty to money-laundering schemes. On July 5, regulators in 7 countries, including the U.S., acted to shut down the bank. Gov. Robin Leigh-Pemberton of the Bank of England cited evidence of "fraudulent conduct on a world-wide scale." Leigh-Pemberton said, July 23, that top executives of the bank were implicated in wrongdoing. Throughout the month, a number of unsubstantiated press reports linked prominent figures with shady doings involving the bank. The U.S. Federal Reserve Board said, July 29, that it would seek a $200 million penalty against the bank for violating U.S. banking laws. In New York City, July 29, a state grand jury indicted the bank and 2 former top executives on charges that included fraud, theft, and money-laundering.

Bush Lifts South African Sanctions—Pres. George Bush, July 10, lifted economic sanctions imposed on South Africa by Congress in 1986. The U.S. State Department told Bush, July 5, that the release of political prisoners by South Africa, the last of the requirements imposed by Congress, had been met. On July 9, the International Olympic Committee lifted its 21-year boycott of South Africa, noting the dismantling of the apartheid system and the racial integration of South African sports. Bush ended bans on loans and investments in South Africa, and opened the door to the imports of South African uranium, steel, sugar, textiles, gold coins, and other products. Commercial air service between the 2 countries could now be established.

Iraq Admits Uranium Research—In a report to the United Nations on July 8, Iraq acknowledged that it had been conducting research aimed at producing enriched uranium, a component of nuclear weapons. Iraq, however, denied that the equipment and material revealed for the first time was part of a weapons program. Within the next weak, the U.S., Britain, and France indicated they would use force if Iraq did not destroy its nuclear-weapons technology in compliance with a U.N. resolution. The U.S. Defense Department said, July 12, that the U.S. would join with 7 allies in deploying a ground force in Turkey to protect the Kurds. By July 15, the allies had completed withdrawal from a "safe zone" in northern Iraq established to aid Kurdish refugees. U.N. inspectors said, July 17 and 18, that allied bombing during the war had destroyed Iraq's facilities for enriching uranium. Fighting flared anew between Iraqi government troops and Kurdish guerillas, and on July 19, U.N. officials estimated that 500 people had been killed or wounded. U.N. inspectors reported to the Security Council, July 30, that Iraq had buried equipment in order to conceal its nuclear program. The inspectors said buildings at testing sites had been torn down. It was also reported that Iraq had more than 4 times as many chemical weapons as it had previously admitted having.

Bush, Gorbachev Agree to Reduce Nuclear Arsenals—The signing of a treaty to reduce nuclear-weapons stockpiles highlighted an historic month in international summitry. Secy. of State James Baker and Soviet Foreign Minister Aleksandr Bessmertnykh met in Washington, July 11-14, to work out details on a strategic-arms reduction treaty (START), the subject of negotiations since 1982. The treaty would be the first ever to reduce, not just limit, long-range nuclear arms. The scene shifted to London, July 15, and the opening of the so-called Group of 7 summit involving the leaders of the world's major industrial democracies. In a communique issued July 16, the G-7 presidents and prime ministers said they would continue sanctions against Iraq until Iraq complied fully with all U.N. resolutions, and they warned Iraq of "severe measures" unless the government dismantled its nuclear, chemical, and biological weapons programs. The communique also backed the U.S. peace plan in the Middle East and hailed the dismantling of apartheid in South Africa. Pres. Mikhail Gorbachev arrived in London, July 16; never before had a Soviet leader been invited to attend the G-7 summit. In an address to the other leaders, July 17, Gorbachev gave his vision for economic and political reform in the Soviet Union. The G-7 leaders, whose communique had also endorsed reform in the Soviet Union, approved a package of assistance to the USSR that included "special association" with the International Monetary Fund and the World Bank, technical assistance on energy production and food distribution, and help in expanding Soviet international trade. Meanwhile, Baker and Bessmertnykh met in London and brought the START talks to a successful conclusion with an agreement on the throw weights of missiles. Bush and Gorbachev said, July 17, they would sign the treaty later in July in Moscow. Bush arrived in the Soviet capital, July 29. On July 30, Bush praised Gorbachev for "instituting reforms that changed the world," and said he would ask Congress to grant preferred tariff terms, "most-favored-nation status," to the Soviet Union. The 2 leaders signed the nuclear-weapons treaty, July 31. The treaty, which must be approved by the U.S. Congress and the Soviet Parliament, would reduce strategic (long-range) offensive arms by 30 percent over 7 years. At a press conference, the 2 presidents said it would not be practical to scrap all nuclear weapons in their arsenals because of similar weapons held by other countries.

Mideast Nations OK Terms for Peace Conference— Secy. of State James Baker visited the Middle East and received commitments for a peace conference between Israel and its Arab neighbors. Egypt and Saudi Arabia had previously agreed to the U.S. proposal. Baker announced, July 18, that Syria had agreed to come to a conference. Lebanon's foreign minister announced his country's participation July 20. Jordan's King Hussein met with Baker, July 21, and then said that Jordan would be "among the first to attend" a conference. Israeli Prime Minister Yitzhak Shamir said, July 24, that the Palestine Liberation Organization could have no role in a peace conference, and that Israel would not negotiate with Palestinians from East Jerusalem because that might imply that the status of the city was negotiable. Yasir Arafat, chairman of the PLO, rejected, July 24, any participation with those restrictions.

Israeli Police Blamed in Shootings—Judge Ezra Kama, who headed an Israeli judicial inquiry into the violent episode on Jerusalem's Temple Mount in Oct. 1990, made his report on July 18, At least 17 Arabs had been killed in the incident, and a government commission had said that Palestinians had provoked the clash with Israeli border police. But Kama put the responsibility on the police, whom he said had fired indiscriminately into the crowd and had used live ammunition "without reasonable need."

Bush Travels to Greece, Turkey—Pres. George Bush visited Greece and Turkey, where he offered military aid and assistance in helping to resolve the controversy between the nations over Cyprus. He said in Athens, July 19, that the U.S. could serve as a catalyst for a settlement over Cyprus, but that the countries

directly affected would have to resolve the dispute. In Turkey, July 19-21, Bush thanked that country for its support during the Persian Gulf war.

General

Report Criticizes L.A. Police—The Los Angeles Police Department was criticized, July 9, in a report released by an independent commission. The commission, appointed by Mayor Tom Bradley and Police Chief Daryl Gates, was headed by Warren Christopher, a former deputy secretary of state. The inquiry was triggered by the beating of a black motorist by several L.A. policemen. The report said that police were isolated from the communities that they were to serve, and that "officers are encouraged to command and confront, not to communicate." The commission studied more than 2,000 alleged instances of the use of excessive force by police. It recommended that Gates retire after a successor was found, and it called for a "major overhaul" of the police disciplinary system. Gates announced, July 22, that he would retire in April 1992 if a replacement had been found.

Total Eclipse of Sun—A total eclipse of the sun by the moon, July 11, provided a spectacular sky show for thousands of people in Hawaii, Mexico, Central America, and Brazil. In some areas, the sun was covered for nearly 7 minutes, almost the maximum possible length for any eclipse. Viewing was especially dramatic for astronomers at the summit of Mauna Kea volcano on the island of Hawaii, where powerful telescopes in large observatories were focused on the event. High altitude dust from the eruption in June of Mt. Pinatubo in the Philippines, as well as clouds in some places, diminished the view. During totality, viewers could see glowing streaks of gas rising up to 100,000 miles above the solar surface.

Pan Am and Delta Reach Agreement—On July 11, Pan American World Airways agreed to sell many of its remaining assets to Delta Air Lines. For $260 million, Pan Am would part with its Boston-New York-Washington shuttle, its European routes, and 45 jets. A Pan Am representative called it the beginning of an orderly liquidation of the airline. For many years, Pan Am had been the U.S.'s only international commercial air carrier. But Pan Am had filed for bankruptcy in Jan. 1991, brought down by airline deregulation, declining international travel, and soaring fuel costs.

Dangerous Pesticide Spilled Into River—Seven cars of a freight train slipped off a track, July 14, while the train was crossing a bridge over the Sacramento River near Dunsmuir, Calif. The tanker car ruptured and spilled metam sodium, a farm pesticide used to kill weeds and insects, into the river. Some 200 people were hospitalized after inhaling the fumes or suffering skin irritation. As the pesticide was carried downstream, vegetation along the banks withered, and at least 100,000 rainbow trout were killed. The pesticide entered Lake Shasta, the state's largest reservoir, July 17.

Major Banks Announce Merger Plans—On July 15, Chemical Banking Corp. and Manufacturers Hanover Corp. announced a merger agreement that, if approved, would create the 2nd largest bank in the U.S., after Citicorp. The merger partners, both based in New York, would have combined assets of $135.46 billion. On July 22, 2 other major banks, NCNB Corp. and C&S/Sovran Corp., announced a plan to merge. The banks were based in Charlotte, N.C. and in Norfolk, Va., and Atlanta, respectively. The new institution, NationsBank, would be the 3rd in size in the U.S.

Man Charged in Serial Killings—On July 22, police in Milwaukee arrested Jeffrey Dahmer, 31, after finding human skulls, heads, and other body parts in his apartment. The police filed an affidavit, **July 24**, which said that Dahmer had admitted killing 11 men; he had lured the victims to his apartment, drugged them, strangled them, and often dismembered the bodies. On **July 25**, Dahmer was charged with 4 counts of intentional homicide. In May, 3 police officers had returned a 14-year-old boy, who had been found on the street naked and bleeding, to Dahmer's custody when the latter persuaded them that the youth was his boyfriend. The officers were suspended, **July 26**.

Disasters—A Chinese newspaper reported, **July 9**, that flooding in eastern and central China had killed 847 people through the end of June . . . All 261 persons aboard died, **July 11**, when a jetliner carrying Nigerian Moslems home from a visit to holy sites in Saudi Arabia crashed at an airport in Jidda, Saudi Arabia, while attempting an emergency landing. The pilot had reported a fire in the landing gear just after takeoff from Jidda . . . The collapse of a dam, **July 28**, in northeastern Romania caused a flood that killed at least 66 people and forced 10,000 out of their homes.

AUGUST

National

Surge in Jobless Rate Ends — The Labor Dept. reported, **Aug. 2**, that the unemployment rate backed off in July from a 5-year high, declining from 7.0 percent to 6.8 percent. However, the number of payroll jobs declined in July by 51,000. On **Aug. 6**, the Federal Reserve reduced the federal funds interest rate, the overnight loan-rate between banks, from 5.75 percent to 5.5 percent, its lowest level in a decade. The move was seen as an effort to stimulate the economy. The Labor Dept. reported, **Aug. 9**, that producer prices had fallen 0.2 percent in July, and reported, **Aug. 14**, that consumer prices had risen 0.2 percent at the same time. The Commerce Dept., **Aug. 16**, put the merchandise trade deficit in June at $4.02 billion, its lowest level in 8 years. Correcting an earlier estimate, the Commerce Dept. said, **Aug. 28**, that the gross national product had shrunk 0.1 percent at an annual rate during the 2nd quarter. The department said, **Aug. 30**, that the leading economic indicators had risen 1.2 percent in July, the biggest monthly jump in 3 years.

"October Surprise" Rumors to Be Investigated — Democratic leaders in the Congress—Sen. George Mitchell (Me.) and House Speaker Thomas S. Foley (Wash.)—announced, **Aug. 5**, that committees would investigate allegations that members of Ronald Reagan's 1980 campaign team had sought to delay release of U.S. hostages held by Iran until after the election. Reagan was challenging the reelection bid by Pres. Jimmy Carter. According to some rumors, Reagan strategists had gotten involved in a deal with Iran for fear that Carter would spring an "October Surprise," gaining the hostages' release shortly before the election. Sen. Terry Sanford (D, N.C.) and Rep. Lee Hamilton (D, Ind.) would head the investigatory committees.

Protests on Abortion Bring Legal Showdown — A prolonged confrontation at an abortion clinic in Wichita, Kan., resulted in the intervention of the U.S. Justice Dept. Demonstrations, by members of the antiabortion group Operation Rescue, had begun in mid-July. U.S. District Judge Patrick Kelly issued a temporary restraining order barring protestors from blocking access to the clinic, and ordered U.S. marshals to help protect visitors to the clinic. By early August, nearly 2,000 arrests had been made. On **August 6**, the U.S. Justice Dept. filed a brief in U.S. Circuit Court contending that the Federal courts had no jurisdiction in the dispute. Rather, the Department said, such matters as trespass were for local jurisdictions. On **Aug. 16**, Pres. George Bush called Operation Rescue's tactics excessive, and refused to meet with leaders of the organization. Meanwhile, foes of abortion were still being arrested by the hundreds.

Two More Democrats Decline to Challenge Bush — Two U.S. senators announced they would not seek the Democratic presidential nomination in 1992, joining a growing list of Democrats who had decided not to challenge Pres. George Bush. Sen. John D. Rockefeller, 4th (W. Va.) took his name out of consideration, **Aug. 7**. On **Aug. 9**, Attorney Gen. Richard Thornburgh announced his resignation, effective **Aug. 15**, to seek the U.S. Senate seat from Pennsylvania. On **Aug. 21**, Sen. Albert Gore, Jr. (Tenn.), who had run for president in 1988, said he would not try again in 1992.

Securities Firm Admits Violations — Salomon Brothers, a division of Salomon, Inc., revealed, **Aug. 9**, that its bidding in U.S. Treasury auctions had been marred by "irregularities and rule violations." In an **Aug. 14** statement, the firm said that 3 top officials had known about one such violation in April but had not reported it. Salomon had submitted bids in the names of clients without informing them. Resignations of Chairman John Gutfreund and Pres. Thomas Strauss were accepted at a board meeting on **Aug. 16**. The new interim chairman, Warren Buffett, promised an internal investigation. The Treasury Dept., **Aug. 18**, limited Salomon's role in future auctions to purchasing securities for its own account, not for clients.

Supreme Court Nominee Called Qualified — An American Bar Association committee announced, **Aug. 27**, that it had found Judge Clarence Thomas "qualified" to serve on the U.S. Supreme Court. Pres. George Bush had submitted Thomas's name for the court in July. No one on the 15-member committee gave Thomas the highest rating of "Well qualified." Two found him to be "not qualified."

International

Israel Agrees to Peace Talks — Prime Minister Yitzhak Shamir of Israel announced, **Aug. 1**, that his country would participate in Middle East peace talks, but only if the Palestine Liberation Organization were excluded, as well as any Palestinian delegates from East Jerusalem. Palestinian leaders told Secy. of State James Baker, **Aug. 2**, in Jerusalem, that they rejected these conditions. On **Aug. 4**, the Israeli cabinet approved Shamir's announcement.

Bush Visits Ukraine — After his historic summit conference with Pres. Mikhail Gorbachev in Moscow, Pres. George Bush visited the Ukraine, **Aug. 1**. He conferred with Ukrainian Pres. Leonid Kravchuk. In addressing the Ukrainian parliament, Bush promised U.S. support to republics "who pursue freedom, democracy, and economic liberty," but he did not give the strong encouragement for Ukrainian independence that some had hoped to hear.

Another Truce in Croatia Fails — Yugoslavia's federal collective presidency, **Aug. 6**, approved a ceasefire between Croat forces and Serb guerrillas living in the republic. The truce took effect **Aug. 7**. But the ceasefire broke down, and on **Aug. 25**, Yugoslav federal forces shelled and bombed Croat positions.

Italy Returns Albanian Refugees — For the 3rd time in 1991, Albanian refugees in large numbers fled to Italy. About 18,000 arrived, **Aug. 8**, in southern Italy after seizing ships in the Albanian port of Durres. Most of the refugees were unemployed. Offering clothing and $40 per person, Italian authorities induced most to return to Albania. Some refused and clashed with Italian riot police, **Aug. 9-12.** Many were held under guard in a soccer stadium. The last of the refugees were deported, **Aug. 17.**

British, U.S. Hostages Freed — John McCarthy, a British journalist kidnapped in 1986, was freed, **Aug. 8,** by Islamic Jihad, a Shiite Moslem faction, in Lebanon. McCarthy gave a letter from Islamic Jihad to U.N. Secretary General Javier Pérez de Cuéllar, **Aug. 11,** implying that all its hostages would be freed if Palestinians and Lebanese held elsewhere were released. Israel held about 400 prisoners. Edward Tracy, a U.S. native held hostage since 1986, was released, **Aug. 11,** by the Revolutionary Justice Organization, another Shiite group in Lebanon.

Clark Clifford Resigns as Head of Bank — The international scandal involving the Bank of Credit and Commerce International led to the resignation of Clark Clifford as chairman of First American Bankshares, Inc. Robert Altman, the president of the latter bank, also resigned, **Aug. 13.** Neither had been charged with any wrongdoing. Clifford had served as secretary of defense and as an adviser to several Democratic presidents. Both Clifford and Altman claimed that they had not known that BCCI had obtained a controlling interest, illegally, in First American, which was the largest bank in Washington, D.C.

U.N. Allows Iraq Oil Sale for Food, Medicine — The U.N. Security Council voted, 13-1, **Aug. 15,** to let Iraq sell up to $1.6 billion worth of oil to obtain money for food and medicine. This represented an exception to sanctions imposed on Iraq after the Gulf war. The United Nations would administer proceeds from the sale in an escrow account, and would supervise distribution of the food and medicine. The Security Council also stipulated, **Aug. 15,** that 30 percent of Iraq's future revenue from oil would go to a fund to compensate relatives of victims who died as a result of Iraq's invasion of Kuwait.

General

571 Escape Sinking Cruise Ship — A major disaster was averted when all 571 passengers and crew on a cruise ship escaped before the vessel went down. The *Oceanos,* operated by a Greek shipping company, was off the coast of South Africa, **Aug. 3,** when it began taking on water. South African Air Force helicopters airlifted 200 people to safety, and the rest were picked up from lifeboats or the sea. The ship sank into the Indian Ocean, **Aug. 4.** The captain, Yiannis Avranas, said a piston had burst in the engine room and torn a hole in the hull. Some passengers complained that the captain and crew had abandoned the ship without supervising rescue operations.

Two More Big Banks Merge — BankAmerica Corp. and Security Pacific Corp. announced, **Aug. 12,** that they would merge. The agreement, if regulators approved, would involve a $4.47 billion stock swap. As measured by assets, the merged bank would be the second largest in the U.S.

Arsonist Found Guilty in Deaths of 87 — Julio Gonzalez, a Cuban immigrant, was found guilty, **Aug. 19,** of felony murder, murder with depraved indifference to human life, arson, and assault in the deaths of 87 people in a fire in New York City in 1990. The fire had occurred at the Happy Land social club in the Bronx. Prosecutors had charged that Gonzalez had started the fire after an argument with his ex-girl friend at the club.

Disasters — A bus crash in Zimbabwe, near Troutbeck, **Aug. 3,** caused the death of 87 people, including 80 schoolchildren. ... An Indian Airlines jetliner crashed in Imphal, India, **Aug. 16,** shortly before a scheduled landing, killing all 69 aboard.

SEPTEMBER

National

Charges Against Oliver North Dropped — The Iran-Contra story continued to unfold, nearly 5 years after the broad outlines of the scandal first became public knowledge. On **Sept. 6,** Clair George, former director of operations at the Central Intelligence Agency, was indicted on charges that he had lied to members of Congress and to a grand jury. The indictment was based primarily on testimony by Alan Fiers, another former CIA official, who had pleaded guilty to lying to Congress. In 1989, Oliver North had been convicted of obstructing a congressional investigation, destroying documents, and accepting an illegal gratuity. In 1990, a federal appeals court had overturned one conviction and sent the others back to the federal district court, instructing it to determine whether the testimony of any witness had been influenced by immunized testimony North had given to Congress. On **Sept. 11,** former National Security Adviser Robert McFarlane told District Judge Gerhard Gesell that his testimony had been influenced by North's immunized testimony. Lawrence Walsh, the special prosecutor in the Iran-Contra case, then stated that it appeared unlikely that a successful prosecution could be achieved, and on **Sept. 16,** Gesell declared that the case against North was "terminated," with all charges dropped.

Committee Split on Thomas Nomination to Supreme Court — The Senate Judiciary Committee was unable to reach a consensus on the nomination of Judge Clarence Thomas to serve on the U.S. Supreme Court. Thomas testified at the committee's confirmation hearings on **Sept. 10-13** and **16.** A number of senators sought to ascertain his views on whether a woman had a constitutional right to an abortion, but Thomas declined to respond. He would not comment on the Roe v. Wade case, which legalized abortions, saying that to do so would compromise his judicial impartiality. He appeared to back off from conservative positions that he had stated publicly while serving in the Reagan administration. Many witnesses appeared before the committee, both for and against the nomination. Dean Guido Calabresi of the Yale Law School said, **Sept. 17,** that he supported Thomas, whom he described as an independent-minded person who had shown he might grow intellectually once on the court. Prof. Charles Lawrence of Stanford Law School, a black, noted that Justice Thurgood Marshall, whom Thomas would replace, had been an advocate of the least powerful members of society, but he said that Thomas had chosen to serve "those who are most powerful in this society, and has served them well." In its vote on Thomas's nomination, taken **Sept. 27,** the committee divided equally, 7-7. Six Republicans and one Democrat supported the nomination, and 7 Democrats opposed it. The committee then voted to send the nomination to the full Senate without any recommendation.

Interest Rates Lowered Again — Key interest rates were lowered in September, with evidence the economy was not gaining momentum. The Labor Dept. reported, **Sept. 6,** that the unemployment rate remained unchanged in August at 6.8 percent. Payroll jobs edged upward by 34,000. The department reported, **Sept. 12,** that producer prices had risen 0.2 percent in August, and it reported, **Sept. 13,** that consumer prices had risen in August by the same amount. The Federal Reserve Board, **Sept. 13,** reduced its rate for loans to member institutions from 5.5 percent to 5 percent, its lowest level in 18 years. The Fed also reduced the federal-funds rate, the rate on overnight loans between banks, from 5.5 percent to 5.25 percent. The Commerce Dept. said, Sept. 19, that the U.S. foreign trade deficit had risen sharply in July to $5.9 billion.

3 Democrats Enter Presidential Race — Three Democrats announced that they would seek the presidency in 1992. Gov. L. Douglas Wilder of Virginia declared his candidacy, Sept. 13. Wilder, the first black to serve as a governor of any state since the Reconstruction era, described himself as a long shot. Depicting himself as a challenger to the Washington establishment, he promised to cut "tens of billions" of dollars from the federal budget. Sen. Tom Harkin (Iowa) announced his candidacy, Sept. 15. A Navy pilot during the Vietnam war, he had served in the House for 10 years before entering the Senate in 1985. A strong advocate of liberal policies, Harkin appeared ready to paint Pres. George Bush as an elitist out of touch with common people. Sen. Bob Kerrey announced, Sept. 30, that he would seek the Democratic nomination. While serving in the Navy in Vietnam, he had lost part of a leg in combat and had been awarded the Medal of Honor. A restauranteur, Kerrey was elected governor of Nebraska in 1982, and entered the Senate in 1989. He complained of a federal government that was cynical, short-sighted, and neglectful, and that had let the nation drift.

Hearings Open on Nominee to Head CIA — Robert Gates, nominated by Pres. George Bush to serve as director of the Central Intelligence Agency, began his testimony, Sept. 16, before the Senate Intelligence Committee, which was considering the nomination. Gates had been chosen for the same position by Pres. Ronald Reagan in 1987, but his nomination had failed in the face of concern about his possible early knowledge about the Iran-Contra affair. Gates, who was the CIA's deputy director in 1986, at a time when Iran-Contra was unfolding, said in his new testimony that he should have been more skeptical of what he had been told, and should have asked more questions. He said he had had only fragmentary information about Iran-Contra before it became public. Sen. Howard Metzenbaum (D, Ohio) noted, Sept. 16, that Gates had said 33 times, in response to written questions, that he could not recall events related to the affair. Sen. Bill Bradley (D, N.J.) accused Gates, Sept. 17, of altering intelligence analyses to fit Reagan administration policies. On Sept. 19, Alan Fiers, who had headed the CIA's Latin American operations and who had just pleaded guilty to lying to Congress, testified that Gates had received earlier and more frequent warnings about Iran-Contra than he had acknowledged.

International

Civil War Continues in Yugoslavia — A plan approved by the European Community to end the civil war in Yugoslavia was accepted, Sept. 2, by the Yugoslav federal presidency, but on the same day federal forces had renewed an offensive against Croatia. Peace talks sponsored by the European Community opened, Sept. 7, in the Netherlands. In a referendum on Sept. 8, voters in another republic, Macedonia, declared their independence from Yugoslavia. The EC-sponsored talks led to another agreement, signed Sept. 17, which provided for an end to hostilities in Croatia and a withdrawal of all forces. But all sides ignored the Sept. 18 cease-fire deadline.

Gen. Noriega's Drug Trial Opens — Gen. Manuel Antonio Noriega, the former leader of Panama who was ousted and captured by U.S. invading forces

nearly 2 years earlier, went on trial in Miami, Sept. 5, accused of laundering money and helping Colombian drug traffickers transport drugs. Seven of his 15 co-defendants had made plea-bargain agreements with the U.S. government and were to testify against Noriega. Opening its case, Sept. 16, the prosecution said it would show that Noriega had sought to make Panama a cocaine trafficking and manufacturing center.

U.S., Israel at Odds on Loan Guarantees — Ten billion dollars in loan guarantees became the center of a dispute between the U.S. and Israel. Under a loan-guarantee agreement, the U.S. would give assurance that Israel would repay loans from commercial banks, allowing Israel to obtain more favorable terms. Israel wanted the guarantees in order to deal with its incoming flood of emigrants from the Soviet Union. But on Sept. 6, Pres. George Bush asked Congress to postpone consideration of the Israeli request, saying that disputes over the loans could upset plans for a Middle East peace conference, which the U.S. supported. The Bush administration wanted the Israelis to stop building settlements in the occupied territories. Secy. of State James Baker met, Sept. 16 and 17, with Israeli Prime Minister Yitzhak Shamir, but they were unable to reach an agreement that would permit a quick U.S. approval of the guarantees.

Israel Frees 51 Palestinians — On Sept. 11, Israel freed 51 Lebanese and Palestinian guerrillas and returned the bodies of 9 others. In return, the Shiite group Hizballah (Party of God) confirmed that 2 Israeli soldiers captured in 1986 were dead. The body of a 3rd soldier was returned to Israel, Sept. 12.

Peace Plan Signed in South Africa — The South African government and 2 major black organizations, the African National Congress and Inkatha, signed an agreement, Sept. 14, aimed at ending black factional fighting that had resulted in thousands of deaths. Twenty smaller groups also signed the accord. The signatories agreed not to resort to violence or inflammatory language and to observe a code of conduct for political parties and security forces. Under the agreement, special courts would deal with political violence.

Philippine Senate Opposes U.S. Base — The Philippine Senate, Sept. 16, rejected a treaty that would have extended the U.S. lease on Subic Bay Naval Station. Critics of the base saw it as a vestige of U.S. colonialism and as a potential site of nuclear weapons. Pres. Corazon Aquino had said that she would seek a public referendum on the issue, but on Sept. 19, Aquino, who favored the base, said she would seek a vote by the public only if there was a widespread demand for one.

Saudi Fined as Front Man for BCCI — A Saudi businessman, Ghaith Pharaon, was being fined $37 million, the U.S. Federal Reserve Board announced, Sept. 17. The Fed said he had purchased Independence Bank in Encino, Calif., in 1985, for about $23 million, saying he was buying it for himself with his own money. But the Fed said the bank had been purchased, illegally, by the Bank of Credit and Commerce International, linked to corrupt activities in many countries.

7 Countries Admitted to United Nations — The U.N. General Assembly convened in New York on Sept. 17, and the delegates voted to admit 7 new countries. They were the newly independent Baltic countries—Estonia, Latvia, and Lithuania—and North Korea, South Korea, the Marshall Islands, and Micronesia. The admission of the 2 Koreas reflected another gradual lessening of Cold War tensions. Total U.N. membership now stood at 166.

Iraq Detains U.N. Inspectors — Iraq backed down after a tense confrontation with a U.N. inspection team. After Pres. Saddam Hussein refused to allow helicopter inspections of his military installations, Pres. George Bush, **Sept. 18,** authorized U.S. warplanes to fly into Iraq to protect U.N. inspectors. On **Sept. 23,** 44 U.N. inspectors were detained in Baghdad after they found secret Iraqi plans for building nuclear weapons and sought to remove them. The U.N. Security Council said, **Sept. 24,** that Iraq had agreed to allow helicopters to enter Iraq without challenge. Meanwhile, the inspectors, after being freed, were detained again as they made copies of the secret documents. After spending 4 nights in a bus and several cars, surrounded by Iraqi guards, the inspectors were freed again, **Sept. 28,** and allowed to take the documentation with them.

Salvadoran Accord Brings Hope for Peace — Pres. Alfredo Cristiani of El Salvador and 5 commanders of guerrilla forces reached an agreement, **Sept. 25,** that was seen as a prelude to a cease-fire in the country's long civil war. U.N. Secretary Gen. Javier Pérez de Cuéllar had set up the negotiations that led to the so-called New York Agreement. The accord dealt with the integration of rebel forces into Salvadoran life. Under the agreement, rebels would be able to join a civilian-controlled police force and could keep land that they have occupied. On **Sept. 28,** a Salvadoran colonel, Guillermo Alfredo Benavides Moreno, was found responsible by a jury in San Salvador for the slayings in 1989 of 6 Jesuit priests, a cook, and her daughter. The jury determined that he had sent the patrol that had killed the victims.

Prime Minister of Romania Resigns — Thousands of Romanian miners poured into Bucharest, **Sept. 25,** to demand pay increases and better working conditions. Demonstrators stormed the Parliament building, and security forces responded with tear gas. Within 2 days, the protests had resulted in 3 deaths and injuries to 137 people. On **Sept. 27,** Prime Minister Petre Roman announced his resignation.

U.S. to Give Up Some Nuclear Weapons — Pres. George Bush announced, **Sept. 27,** that the U.S. would eliminate tactical nuclear weapons on land and at sea in Asia and Europe. He also called a halt to 24-hour alerts for U.S. long-range bombers, and asked for more negotiations with the Soviet Union to reduce stockpiles of long-range missiles. Explaining his decision, Bush said that a Soviet invasion of Western Europe was "no longer a realistic threat." Pres. Mikhail Gorbachev, **Sept. 28,** hailed Bush's announcement as "a new major breakthrough" and a "great event." A spokesman said Gorbachev was prepared to reciprocate.

President of Haiti Overthrown — The first freely elected president of Haiti, Jean-Bertrand Aristide, was ousted in a military coup, **Sept. 30.** At least 26 were killed and 200 wounded in the brief fighting between the military and supporters of the president. Aristide, a Roman Catholic priest who was popular among Haiti's poor, flew into exile in Venezuela.

General

25 Die in Fire at Plant — A fire at a chicken-processing plant in Hamlet, N.C., **Sept. 3,** killed 25 people and injured 55. The deaths were attributed to smoke inhalation. Several doors to the plant, operated by Imperial Food Products, were locked or blocked, allegedly to prevent thefts by employees. John Brooks, the state Labor Secretary, said, **Sept. 4,** that his office had not inspected the plant during its 11 years of operation because of a lack of manpower.

Cheerleader's Mother Guilty in Murder Plot — Wanda Webb Holloway of Channelview, Tex., was found guilty, **Sept. 3,** of trying to hire a man to kill the mother of another student at her daughter's school. Holloway's daughter and the daughter of the intended murder victim were rivals for a place on the school's cheerleading squad. Prosecutors alleged that Holloway hoped to upset the victim's daughter so that she would be less competitive in trying for a place on the cheerleading squad. Holloway, **Sept. 4,** was sentenced to 15 years in prison.

Access to Dead Sea Scrolls Opened — The monopoly by a few scholars over the Dead Sea Scrolls appeared to be ending. The scrolls, some 800 manuscripts in Hebrew and Aramaic, were found in caves east of Jerusalem between 1947 and 1956. They contained Biblical manuscripts and a wealth of information on Judaism and the origins of Christianity. Photographs of many of the manuscripts had never been made public, with a few editors controlling access. But the *New York Times* reported, **Sept. 22,** that the Huntington Library in San Marino, Calif., had decided to open its collection of some 3,000 film negatives of the scrolls. Some of the controlling editors reportedly called the photos stolen property. Dr. William Moffett, the Huntington Library director, said that only authors retain property rights to unpublished material, and that the manuscripts were in the public domain.

8 to Spend 2 Years in "Biosphere" — Four men and 4 women entered a huge airtight greenhouse, **Sept. 26,** with the intention of remaining inside for 2 years. They and their sponsors called the 3.15-acre glass and steel structure Biosphere 2, with the earth itself being described as Biosphere 1. In addition to a farm and the living quarters for its human occupants, the structure contained 5 ecosystems—a rain forest, ocean, marsh, desert, and savanna—populated with 3,800 plant and animal species. The purpose of the $150 million experiment was to see if all the species could live in ecological harmony without any food from the outside.

Disasters — More than 100 people were killed **Sept. 5-6,** when a passenger train and a train carrying timber collided near Dolisie, in the Congo.

OCTOBER

National

Nominee to Head CIA Rebuts Critics — The qualifications of Robert Gates to head the Central Intelligence Agency were hotly debated before the Senate Intelligence Committee. On **Oct. 1** and **2,** a number of former CIA analysts testified for and against his nomination. Critics said he had slanted intelligence reports to conform with the anticommunist views of the Reagan administration, and with his own belief in a pervasive worldwide Soviet military threat. Harold Ford, an analyst for 30 years, said Gates's "pressures" on analysts "clearly constitute a skewing of intelligence." He said Gates often "ignored or scorned" the views of others. Melvin Goodman, another former analyst, said Gates imposed his views on others without supporting evidence. Jennifer Glaudemans, a former Soviet analyst for the CIA, said Gates had "politicized intelligence analysis and is responsible for an overall degradation of the analytical process." But other witnesses denied that Gates had approached the analysis process in that way, and on **Oct. 3,** the nominee himself mounted a vigorous counterattack before the committee. Gates said, "I never distorted intelligence to support policy or to please a policy-maker," and he presented a case-by-case rebuttal of 20 allegations. He denied that his pessimistic view of the Soviet Union had caused the CIA to miss the major shifts in policy under Gorbachev. He added, "The CIA is not a place for the faint-hearted," and said that some analysts may have resented his demand that they put aside "flabby, complacent thinking" in preparing their reports.

Rubber Checks, Unpaid Bills Embarrass House — A bank that served members of the U.S. House was closed in October after embarrassing revelations. The bank operated at the Capitol with only House members for depositors. After the General Accounting Office revealed that in a recent 12-month period 8,331 checks had been written against insufficient funds, the House leadership, **Sept. 26,** said that the bank would no longer be allowed to cover such checks, as had been the practice. Funds of other depositors had been used to cover shortages. A number of House members apologized publicly for having written some of the bad checks. House Speaker Tom Foley (D, Wash.) said, **Oct. 3,** that the bank would be closed at the end of 1991 and that the House Ethics Committee would investigate. It was also reported, **Oct. 3,** that members of the House owed about $300,000 in unpaid bills that they and their guests had run up at the House restaurant. Foley also expressed concern about the practice of having the House sergeant-at-arms office fix parking tickets for House members. On **Oct. 8,** the Speaker said that the sergeant-at-arms would no longer intervene with the District of Columbia government with regard to such tickets.

Arkansas Governor Seeks Presidency — Gov. Bill Clinton of Arkansas announced his candidacy for the 1992 Democratic presidential nomination, **Oct. 3.** Clinton, who was 45, was 32 when first elected governor and was now in his 6th term. He criticized the domestic policies of the Reagan and Bush administrations, and said he would restore the American dream for "the forgotten middle class." On **Oct. 5,** former Sen. Eugene McCarthy (Minn.) launched his 5th campaign for the presidency.

Jobless Rate Down Slightly — The Labor Dept. reported, **Oct. 4,** that the unemployment rate declined in September from 6.8 to 6.7 percent. Across the nation, payroll jobs rose in number by 24,000. The department said, **Oct. 11,** that producer prices edged upward by 0.1 percent in September. Citicorp, the nation's largest banking company, announced, **Oct. 15,** that it had lost $885 million in the 3rd quarter. The bank had been battered by bad loans. John Reed, its chairman, said "there is little prospect for immediate improvement" in the economy. The company eliminated its dividend. The Dow Jones industrial average closed, **Oct. 18,** at 3,077.15, an all-time high.

International

U.S. to Leave Philippines — A majority of the Philippines Senate, **Oct. 2,** signed a draft resolution authorizing Pres. Corazon Aquino to negotiate for the withdrawal of U.S. forces from the Subic Bay Naval Station by 1994. Aquino said she would not seek a national referendum on the issue. The 3-year period for the withdrawal would give Filipinos, who relied on the presence of the base for income, time to find other jobs.

Accord Bars Exploitation of Antarctica — On **Oct. 4,** 24 countries signed an agreement that would bar exploration for minerals and oil in Antarctica for 50 years. The accord, a protocol to the 1959 treaty that had barred nuclear and military activity in Antarctica, also contained regulations for protecting wildlife, waste disposal, and marine pollution. Signatories included the United States, the Soviet Union, France, Britain, China, Germany, and Canada.

Kaifu to Step Down as Japanese Premier — Prime Minister Toshiki Kaifu dropped his effort, **Oct. 4,** to win a second term. A member of the Liberal Democratic Party, which had governed Japan without interruption for 36 years, Kaifu had become prime minister in 1989. At that time, the party needed a prime minister who would project a clean image in the wake of bribery and sex scandals. Thereafter, he supported legislation to cleanse Japan of the influence of wealthy political contributors. This antagonized leaders of his party, who served notice that they would not support him for another term. On **Oct. 11,** the largest faction of the party endorsed Kiichi Miyazawa, one of the designers of Japan's postwar economic recovery, to succeed Kaifu. This seemed to assure that Miyazawa would be the next prime minister, although, ironically, he had been implicated in the same bribery scandal that had brought Kaifu to power.

Gorbachev Announces Nuclear-Weapons Cutbacks — Pres. Mikhail Gorbachev, **Oct. 5,** made a dramatic response to Pres. George Bush's September initiative on nuclear-weapons reductions. Gorbachev said the Soviet Union would reduce its number of strategic warheads within 7 years to 5,000, which would be 1,000 fewer than the number agreed to in the new strategic-arms treaty with the U.S. He said the Soviet armed forces would be cut from about 3.7 million to 3 million, and that nuclear testing would be halted for one year. Strategic bombers would no longer be on ready-alert status—matching the step Bush had taken. Gorbachev also promised to destroy all nuclear warheads for short-range missiles and nuclear mines. Also, the Soviet president said his country would store or destroy nuclear warheads from anti-aircraft rockets and all tactical nuclear weapons on ships, submarines, and land-based naval aircraft.

Nuclear-Weapons Center Found in Iraq — In a report to the U.N. Security Council that became known on **Oct. 7,** U.N. inspectors said that they had found a document indicating that Iraq's nuclear-weapons program was based about 40 miles south of Baghdad. The report said that at this site Pres. Saddam Hussein planned "to design and produce a nuclear device." Meanwhile, in northern Iraq, clashes between government troops and Kurdish guerrillas intensified, and on **Oct. 8,** the Kurds put the casualty toll at more than 400 over a 4-day period. The guerrillas killed at least 60 captured soldiers.

General

Stratospheric Ozone Level at New Low — The National Aeronautics and Space Administration reported, **Oct. 9,** that a satellite above Antarctica had found that the ozone level in the stratosphere had fallen to the lowest level on record. The depletion of ozone had first been reported in 1986. Some authorities believe that a decline in the ozone level will lead to an increased frequency of skin cancer and cataracts, because more ultraviolet radiation will penetrate the atmosphere. Chloroflurocarbons used in refrigerants, solvents, and other products were considered to be the culprits in ozone depletion.

Disasters — A military transport plane crashed shortly after takeoff, **Oct. 5,** in Jakarta, Indonesia, killing all 132 aboard and one person on the ground. The plane was carrying airmen who had participated in an Armed Forces Day ceremony.

Amid Controversy, Clarence Thomas Becomes Associate Justice of the Supreme Court

The Senate approved the nomination of Clarence Thomas to serve as an associate justice of the U.S. Supreme Court, but only after investigating an allegation of sexual harassment that had been leveled against him. Thomas, a U.S. circuit court judge, had been nominated for the Supreme Court in July by Pres. George Bush. An African-American, Thomas succeeded Thurgood Marshall, the first black ever to serve on the high court.

The Senate Judiciary Committee had conducted hearings on the Thomas nomination in September, and, after dividing, 7-7, failed to make any recommendation to the full Senate. Informal surveys indicated that the Senate was likely to approve the nomination, although a number of senators said that the 43-year-old Thomas was not qualified by experience and that he had been unduly evasive on abortion and other matters likely to be considered by the court.

On Oct. 6, National Public Radio and Newsday, a New York newspaper, reported that Anita Hill, a professor of law at the University of Oklahoma, had submitted an affidavit to the Judiciary Committee. In it, she stated that between 1981 and 1983, when she worked for Thomas, he had frequently asked her out and that, when she declined, he described in detail pornographic films that he had seen. She had been his assistant at the Department of Education and later worked for him when he headed the Equal Employment Opportunity Commission.

Hill, who was 35 and black, held a news conference, Oct. 7, in Norman, Okla. She said that she had also been interviewed by the FBI, and that she had hoped to keep her communications confidential. It became apparent that a senator or a member of his staff had leaked her statements to the press.

The Senate had been scheduled to vote on the Thomas nomination on Oct. 8, but that day became one of tumult on Capitol Hill. Feminist organizations complained that the members of the Judiciary Committee had all known about the allegations but had not treated them seriously. Seven women, all Democratic members of the House, marched on the Senate to demand that the Thomas vote be delayed. Thomas issued a statement saying, "I totally and unequivocally deny Anita Hill's allegations." As support for Thomas appeared to erode, the Democratic and Republican leadership agreed to postpone the confirmation vote for one week. Hearings were scheduled by the Judiciary Committee.

Pres. Bush met with Thomas, Oct. 9, and reiterated his strong support for, and confidence in, his nominee. Meanwhile, the allegations triggered a national discussion of the problem of sexual harassment in the workplace. Polls showed that large numbers of women, and some men, had experienced harassment of this nature, but that most of them had been unwilling to come forward with complaints, even though federal law forbade such harassment.

With an immense audience watching on television across the nation, Thomas and Hill appeared before the Judiciary Committee, Oct. 11. Hill's explicit account and Thomas's angry rebuttal left most who heard them stunned and incredulous. Hill said she had not volunteered to raise the issue, but had done so only because Senate aides had asked her if she was aware of any harassment.

Hill testified, "He talked about pornographic materials depicting individuals with large penises or large breasts involved in various sex acts," and added, "On several occasions Thomas told me graphically of his own sexual prowess." She described, in detail, other things that she claimed he had said. Hill, who was accompanied by 3 lawyers, her parents, and other members of her family, said she had not made the allegations before because "I was aware that he could affect my future career and did not wish to burn all my bridges." She said she had been hospitalized in 1983 for acute stomach pain, which she attributed to stress caused by Thomas.

Hill said that when she left the EEOC in 1983, Thomas told her that "if I ever told anyone about his behavior toward me it could ruin his career."

Hardly controlling his anger, Thomas denied that the conversations recounted by Hill had ever taken place, and said that the charges were "drowning my life, my career and my integrity." He added, "You have robbed me of something that can never be restored." He called the hearings "a national disgrace. From my standpoint as a black American it is a high-tech lynching for uppity blacks who in any way deign to think for themselves, to do for themselves." He also said, "No job is worth what I've been through—no job. No horror in my life has been so debilitating."

Thomas said his relationship with Hill had always been "both cordial and professional. At no time did I become aware ... that she felt I had said or done anything to change the cordial nature of our relationship."

Testifying, Oct. 12, Thomas complained that Hill's testimony had reinforced stereotypes about the "sexual prowess of black men ... about the sex organs of black men."

Several Republicans on the committee sought to discredit Hill's testimony, Oct. 12. Sen. Orrin Hatch (Utah) suggested that she could have found details of the alleged conversations in a novel and in a court case on sexual harassment. Sen. Arlen Spector (Pa.) accused her of perjury on one aspect of her testimony. Hatch hinted that Hill might be in collusion with liberal groups who had hired "slick lawyers" to discredit Thomas.

On Oct. 13, at a rare Sunday session, 3 friends of Professor Hill and a professional colleague of hers appeared before the committee, and all testified that during the 1980s she had confided in them that she had been harassed by a supervisor. According to their testimony, she had not gone into the details that the committee had heard, and she had not always identified Thomas. Hill's witnesses included a judge, a lawyer, and a law professor.

Two panels of witnesses consisting of former members of Thomas's staff—13 women in all—testified. They said they had never known Thomas to have conducted himself in the way Hill had described. One suggested Hill had an unrequited sexual interest in Thomas. Another, Diane Holt, who had been Thomas's secretary, said that phone logs kept after Hill left the EEOC showed that she had phoned Thomas on a number of occasions over a period of years and left friendly messages for Thomas, and that she had talked with him on some occasions.

Charles Kothe, former dean of the Oral Roberts University Law Center, also testified. Hill had taught at Oral Roberts before joining the Oklahoma faculty. Kothe said that he had seen Thomas and Hill together at a function at Oral Roberts, and that they had been quite friendly. Republican senators cited this meeting, plus the phone calls, as evidence that Hill had not been repelled, as one might expect, by Thomas's alleged treatment of her.

On Oct. 13, Hill voluntarily took a polygraph test. It was administered by Paul Minor, who had trained FBI agents in the use of such tests. Minor said the test showed that Hill was telling the truth about Thomas. Senator Hatch noted that such a test would not be admissable in a court of law. It was suggested that someone suffering from a "delusional disorder" could pass the polygraph test if they really believed they were telling the truth.

On Oct. 14, Hill said, "I have been deeply hurt and offended by the nature of the attacks on my character."

The vote on Thomas's confirmation was scheduled for 6 p.m., Oct. 15, and the debate in the Senate continued all that day. Sen. John Danforth (R, Mo.), for whom Thomas had once worked and who had been his most ardent supporter in the Senate, said, "Clarence Thomas is going to surprise a lot of people ... He is going to be the people's justice." Sen. George Mitchell (D, Me.), the majority leader, said that Bush had nominated Thomas because Thomas opposed abortion, and

that the chance for abortion rights was lost when Thomas was nominated.

Many senators debated whether Hill's assertions were credible. Some, unable to resolve the matter, said that Thomas should be given the benefit of the doubt. Others contended that it would not be wise to seat a justice on the court if there were a cloud over his head.

Phone calls and telegrams from constituents, apparently running to the hundreds of thousands, flooded the capital. Senators worried about the sensibilities of both black and women voters, but it was clear that both blacks and women were divided in their opinions. Overall, public opinion surveys showed majority support for the confirmation of Thomas.

The final vote was 52-48 in favor of confirmation, with 41 Republicans and 11 Democrats, mostly southerners, in the majority. Two Republicans and 46 Democrats voted against Thomas.

In a statement issued at his home, Judge Thomas said, "This is more a time for healing, not a time for anger or animus or animosity."

U.S. and Allied Forces Defeat Iraq and Liberate Kuwait

The United States and its allies defeated Iraq in January and February 1991 and liberated Kuwait, which Iraq had overrun in August 1990. After Iraq's invasion, for nearly 6 months, diplomats of many nations had sought in vain to persuade Pres. Saddam Hussein to pull his occupying forces out of the oil-rich sheikhdom. Finally, in January, the allies launched an attack on Iraq from the air that sharply reduced Hussein's offensive and defensive military capacity. In a ground war in February that lasted just 100 hours, the U.S.-led attackers killed or captured many thousands of Iraqi soldiers and sent the rest into retreat before Pres. George Bush ordered a cease-fire.

The Iraqis left Kuwait looted and devastated, its skies blackened by smoke from oil-well fires that the invaders had ignited. In the aftermath of defeat, Iraq itself was torn by a civil war between supporters and opponents of Saddam Hussein.

In August, September, and October 1990, in the first 3 months after Iraq attacked Kuwait, the U.S. built up a large defensive force in Saudi Arabia to discourage Hussein from further aggression that might give him control of the world's oil supply. But by November, the Bush administration was shifting to a new strategy. After Sec. of State James Baker met with King Fahd in Saudi Arabia, Nov. 5, the 2 nations announced that in the event of war, the Saudis would have prime responsibility for defense of the kingdom, but the allies could launch offensive action against Iraq from Saudi territory subject to joint authorization by Bush and Fahd.

Baker met in Moscow, Nov. 8, with Soviet Pres. Mikhail Gorbachev and Foreign Minister Eduard Shevardnadze. The latter said after the meeting that the use of force "could not be ruled out." Bush, Nov. 8, ordered a near doubling of U.S. forces in the Persian Gulf region to as many as 430,000, with the additional buildup to be completed by early 1991. Bush said this was to insure that the coalition forces had "an adequate offensive military option."

On Nov. 13, Baker said justification for the U.S. mobilization came down to "one word ... jobs." He said that control of oil by Hussein could bring on a worldwide economic recession. On Nov. 14, with criticism of the expanding U.S. buildup beginning to grow in the U.S., Bush promised Congressional leaders that he would consult with Congress before using force in the Gulf.

Iraq had been holding foreign hostages, using some of them as human shields at military installations the Allies might attack by air. On Nov. 18, Iraq offered to release all the hostages beginning at the end of the year providing there was no outbreak of war. On Nov. 19, Iraq said it would add 250,000 troops to the 430,000 it had already deployed in Kuwait and southern Iraq.

On Nov. 22, Pres. and Mrs. Bush visited 4 military sites in the region to help the troops celebrate Thanksgiving. During his visits, Bush cited another justification for war—noting that Hussein was coming closer to creating a nuclear weapons arsenal. Bush met in Cairo, Nov. 23, with Pres. Hosni Mubarak of Egypt, a strong supporter of the allied effort, and met in Geneva, Nov. 23 with Pres. Hafez al-Assad of Syria, who was a longtime adversary of Hussein in the Arab world.

On Nov. 29, the U.N. Security Council authorized the use of force if Iraq did not pull out of Kuwait by Jan. 15, 1991. In adopting resolution 678 by a 12-2 vote, with 1 abstention, the Council granted such authority to individual nations for only the 2d time, the first being at the beginning of the Korean War in 1950. Iraq's U.N. ambassador, Abdul Amir al-Anbari, argued that the Council approved an "integrated and comprehensive" Mideast peace plan that would include the plight of the Palestinians.

Following Congressional hearings in which leading Americans questioned the rush toward war, Bush said, Nov. 30, that he was ready to send Baker to Baghdad, the capital of Iraq, in a final effort to reach a peaceful settlement, but he reiterated that a total Iraqi withdrawal from Kuwait would be required.

Hussein said, Dec. 6, he would free all foreign hostages being held in Iraq and Kuwait. Hostages known to be in the 2 countries included about 900 Americans, 1,200 Britons, and 200 Japanese. Some were being used as human shields, but Hussein said this was no longer necessary because Iraq had built up its defenses. Iraq's National Assembly, Dec. 7, approved the release of the hostages, most of whom were flown to their homelands within the next week. The U.S. State Department said, Dec. 11, that more than 500 Americans had chosen to stay in the 2 countries because they had dual citizenship with Iraq or Kuwait or were long-time residents.

Lt. Gen. Calvin Waller, deputy U.S. commander in the Gulf, said, Dec. 19, that his ground troops would not be ready to take the offensive by **Jan. 15**, the date the U.N. had given Hussein as a deadline for leaving Kuwait. He said reinforcements ordered to the Gulf in November would not be combat-ready until as late as mid-February. Hussein said, **Dec. 21**, that Iraq would not pull out of Kuwait by the deadline.

On **Dec. 22**, 21 U.S. sailors drowned when an Israeli ferry taking them from shore leave to the *U.S.S. Saratoga* capsized. The U.S. command ordered the troops to observe Christmas discreetly, **Dec. 25**, in deference to their Saudi hosts. The Pentagon said, **Dec. 31**, that a total of 52 U.S. servicemen had died in the Gulf region, mostly in accidents.

On **Jan. 3**, Bush proposed talks between Baker and Iraqi Foreign Minister Tariq Aziz as a "last attempt to go the extra mile for peace," but Bush added that there would be "no negotiations, no compromises." On **Jan. 4**, Iraq agreed to set up a meeting. On **Jan. 8**, Bush asked Congress to authorize use of "all necessary means" to expel Iraq from Kuwait.

Baker and Aziz met for 6½ hours in Geneva on **Jan. 9**, but failed to resolve the crisis. Baker said Iraq had shown no flexibility, and Aziz complained that Baker had repeatedly threatened him, and said Iraq would vigorously defend itself. He also said Israel would be attacked if war broke out. Baker had told Aziz that linking settlement of the Israeli-Palestinian question to Iraq's aggression was not acceptable. Bush complained that Iraq's position constituted "a total stiff arm, a total rebuff."

On **Jan. 10**, the Israeli defense ministry warned citizens of Israel to prepare for an attack from Iraq. Bush, **Jan. 10**, urged Israel, in a call to Prime Minister Yitzhak Shamir, to stay out of the war.

Congress, **Jan. 10**, began debate over whether to authorize Bush to use force against Iraq. In a letter made public, **Jan. 10**, Central Intelligence Agency Director William Webster said economic sanctions alone could not oust Iraq from Kuwait for 6 to 12 months. Many in Congress, however, continued to urge that sanctions be given more time to work. Supporters of Bush's policy argued that the U.S. must show its resolve and give the president a free hand to use force if needed. On **Jan. 12**, the Senate, 52-47, and the House, 250-183, authorized Bush to use military power to expel Iraq from Kuwait.

U.N. Secretary General Javier Pérez de Cuéllar met with Hussein in Baghdad, **Jan. 13**, but failed to persuade him to pull out of Kuwait. The British Parliament, **Jan. 15**, and the French National Assembly, **Jan. 16**, authorized the use of force against Iraq.

The war began on **Jan. 17**, the second day after the deadline set by the United Nations for Iraqi withdrawal from Kuwait. On the evening of **Jan. 16** in the U.S., within a few hours after planes reached their targets in Iraq, Bush spoke on television, saying he had no choice but force. He said Allied planes had struck at Iraq's nuclear bomb potential, chemical weapons facilities, and artillery and tanks. He saw victory in war as leading to a "new world order" based on the rule of law.

At the onset of hostilities, the 28-nation allied force reportedly had about 690,000 troops in the region. Of these, 425,000 were Americans. Iraq's army was put at about 1 million men. The Allies had more aircraft and helicopters, Iraq more tanks and artillery pieces. High-tech U.S. arms included F-117-A Stealth fighters, ship-launched Tomahawk cruise missiles, and the Patriot radar-guided antimissile missile.

In the first 14 hours of what the Allies called Operation Desert Storm, more than 1,000 sorties, or individual missions, were launched against Iraq. Baghdad was pounded with cruise missiles and bombs, with the defense ministry, presidential palace, telecommunications, and the airport targeted. Iraq infantry and armor near Kuwait were also pounded. Defense Secretary Dick Cheney and Gen. Colin Powell, chairman of the Joint Chiefs of Staff, said, **Jan. 17**, that Iraqi antiaircraft fire had been heavy but that the Iraqi air force had made little response. Allied casualties were reported to be light.

On **Jan. 17**, Israel declared a state of emergency. On that day, Iraq fired 8 Scud missiles at Israel, causing light damage and few casualties in Tel Aviv, and 1 at Saudi Arabia. These Soviet-made missiles were notoriously inaccurate. A Patriot knocked down the one aimed at Saudi Arabia.

Iraq, **Jan. 20**, broadcast a videotape of 7 captured Allied pilots, including 3 Americans, 2 Britons, and one each from Italy and Kuwait. The U.S. pilots appeared dazed and bruised. Several pilots made statements condemning the attacks on Iraq.

Gen. H. Norman Schwarzkopf, the U.S. commander in the region, said, **Jan. 20**, that the Allies had not yet achieved air superiority because Iraqi missiles were still being fired and Iraq still had airplanes it could utilize. He said the Allies were attacking the elite Iraqi Republican Guard units in southern Iraq.

Deputy Sec. of State Lawrence Eagleburger met, **Jan. 21**, with Israeli leaders in Jerusalem and said they had agreed not to retaliate against Iraq without consulting the United States first. Iraq said, **Jan. 21**, that it would disperse Allied prisoners—now growing in number—to strategic sites to discourage air attacks.

Of 22 Scuds fired at Saudi Arabia by **Jan. 23**, 18 had been downed by Patriots. None had caused damage.

Powell said, **Jan. 23**, that air superiority had been achieved, that Iraq's 2 operating nuclear plants were "finished," and that chemical and biological warfare facilities had been badly damaged. By **Jan. 24**, Allied combat missions totaled 8,000, with Allied military casualties—dead and missing—put at 30.

Oil began flowing into the Persian Gulf, **Jan. 23**, and on **Jan. 25**, the U.S. blamed the spill on Iraq, calling it an act of "environmental terrorism." The spill threatened the operation of Allied naval vessels, some of which utilized sea water for cooling, and environmentalists said the oil was a disaster for sea life.

Scuds fired, **Jan. 25**, killed one person each in Israel and Saudi Arabia.

On **Jan. 26**, the Pentagon said that two dozen Iraqi aircraft had flown to Iran. Many more soon joined them, and Iran, which had declared its neutrality, said they would be impounded until the war ended.

In an attempt to stop the flow of oil into the gulf, the U.S., **Jan. 27**, bombed installations that controlled the flow of oil from storage facilities.

Baker and Aleksandr Bessmertnykh, the new Soviet foreign minister, issued a statement in Washington, **Jan. 29**, which held out the possibility of a cease-fire if Iraq left Kuwait.

In his State of the Union speech, **Jan. 29**, Bush emphasized that the liberation of Kuwait was the purpose of the war, not to bring about "the destruction of Iraq, its culture, or its people."

Iraqi troops, supported by tanks and artillery rockets, seized the town of Khafji, in Saudi Arabia, **Jan. 29**. Troops from the U.S., Saudi Arabia, and Qatar retaliated, and 11 U.S. Marines were reported killed, **Jan. 30**. The town was retaken by **Jan. 31**, with 500 Iraqis taken prisoner and 200 killed or wounded.

By month's end, the oil slick in the gulf was 60 miles long and 20 miles wide, the largest slick ever reported.

It was reported, **Feb. 3,** that 7 Marines killed, **Jan. 30,** had been struck by a missile from a U.S. aircraft.

On **Feb. 6,** King Hussein of Jordan appeared to drop his stance of neutrality. He asserted that nations allied against Iraq were attempting to put all Arabs "under direct foreign hegemony."

Pérez de Cuéllar said, **Feb. 7,** that there had apparently been thousands of Iraqi civilian casualties.

Cheney and Powell arrived in Saudi Arabia, **Feb. 8,** to review the military situation. They met with Saudi officials and Allied commanders on **Feb. 9.** Allied officials reported, **Feb. 11,** that 39 Iraqi planes had been shot down and that 142 had now flown to Iran.

On **Feb. 13,** two U.S. bombs destroyed a building in Baghdad where civilians had sought shelter. Iraq claimed hundreds of civilians had been killed. U.S. officials said the building was being used for military communications.

The U.S. command said, **Feb. 14,** that the allies had destroyed 1,300 of 4,280 Iraqi tanks, 800 of 1,870 armored personnel carriers, and 1,100 of 3,110 artillery pieces.

On **Feb. 15,** for the first time since the war began, Iraq offered to pull out of Kuwait. But the offer was tied to agreements that sanctions would be lifted and the issue of reparations dropped. Under Iraq's proposal, its debts to Allied nations would be forgiven, and Israel would have to withdraw from its occupied territories. Bush rejected the offer as a "cruel hoax" and called on the Iraqi military and citizenry to "take matters into their own hands" and force Hussein from power.

Schwarzkopf said, **Feb. 19,** that the Iraqi forces were "on the verge of collapse." Lt. Gen. Thomas Kelly, chief of operations for the Joint Chiefs of Staff, said, **Feb. 19,** that "we are ready now" to attack on the ground. On **Feb. 21,** the estimate of Iraqi tanks destroyed was put at 2,100.

On **Feb. 22,** while Aziz was in Moscow, the Soviet Union announced that Iraq had agreed to pull out of Kuwait in a fixed time frame. With the total withdrawal, all U.N. resolutions would cease to be in effect. Bush announced, **Feb. 22,** that unless Iraq began its withdrawal by noon, **Feb. 23** (Eastern Standard

Time), Iraq would face a ground offensive.

Bush, **Feb. 22,** also denounced Iraq for setting fire to Kuwaiti oil installations. Hundreds were aflame and black smoke covered up to half of Kuwait and parts of neighboring countries.

On the evening of **Feb. 23,** Bush announced that his deadline had passed and his demands had not been met. He said that the ground offensive had already been launched.

Some 200,000 Allied troops participated in the ground offensive, which began at about dawn on **Feb. 24,** in the Persian Gulf region. The attacks spread across a 300-mile area west from the gulf. U.S. Marines and Army airborne and armored units were joined by units from France, Great Britain, Saudi Arabia, and other Arab countries. Some Allied forces struck directly into Kuwait, but others crossed from Saudi Arabia into Iraq far to the west, beyond the Iraqi defensive lines. U.S. and British armored units moved first north, then northeast, and out-flanked elite Iraqi Republican Guard forces dug in north of Kuwait.

U.S. Marines and Arab forces striking directly into Kuwait achieved a quick breakthrough, and were joined in Kuwait by Allied armored forces entering from the west.

Fragments of an Iraqi Scud missile struck a makeshift barracks in Dhahran, Saudi Arabia, **Feb. 25,** killing 28 U.S. soldiers, including 3 women, and wounding at least 89 others.

Iraqi troops began to pull out of Kuwait City, **Feb. 25.** On **Feb. 26,** Kuwaiti resistance leaders claimed control of the city, and U.S. pilots reported that roads leading north were jammed with retreating Iraqis. U.S. airborne units reached the Euphrates River, **Feb. 26,** cutting off some escape routes. The first U.S. military convoy entered Kuwait City, **Feb. 27.**

In a letter received at the United Nations, **Feb. 27,** Aziz formally accepted U.N. resolutions requiring that Iraq annul its annexation of Kuwait and pay reparations. Iraq's ambassador said all 12 U.N. resolutions would be accepted.

Schwarzkopf said, **Feb. 27,** that the Iraqi army had collapsed because of poor leadership, and he ridiculed Hussein's leadership abilities. He denied that the U.S. intended to take over Iraq, and he called the low level of U.S. casualties "miraculous," but added that it would never be miraculous for the families of those killed in the war.

On **Feb. 27** and **28,** 800 U.S. tanks clashed with 300 Iraqi tanks north of Kuwait. It was reported that Iraq lost 200 tanks, the U.S. none.

On **Feb. 27,** Bush announced a suspension of Allied military operations, declaring, "Kuwait is liberated." He went on, "Iraq's army is defeated. Our military objectives are met." He said offensive operations would cease at midnight (EST), 100 hours after they began. He said a permanent cease-fire would require that Iraqi commanders meet with their Allied counterparts and that Iraq free all prisoners of war and other detainees. Iraq announced a cease-fire, **Feb. 28.**

Estimates of Iraqis killed and wounded ran as high as 100,000, and the Allies held up to 175,000 prisoners. It was reported that 29 Iraqi divisions were destroyed or battered, and that Iraq had lost all but 500 of its 4,200 tanks. Some Iraqi prisoners said the month-long pounding from the air had weakened the capacity and resolve to resist the ground attack.

A British white paper on defense reported, **July 9,** that allied combat deaths in the war had been as follows: United States 147, Saudi Arabia 33, Britain 24, Egypt 10, United Arab Emirates 6, France 2, and Kuwait 1, for a total of 223. *Facts on File* reported that a Defense Department spokesman said, **July 17,** that the U.S. had suffered 148 combat deaths and 120 noncombat deaths during the war, plus 13 deaths since the cease-fire of Feb. 28. U.S. personnel wounded in combat totaled 458. Eleven U.S. women had been killed in combat and 4 in noncombat situations, according to the spokesman.

The Defense Dept. said, **Aug. 13,** that 35 of 148 U.S. combat deaths in the war had been the result of Americans firing on other Americans. As well, 72 of 467 Americans wounded in combat had been injured because of so-called friendly fire.

(See Cordesman article and Chronology for additional coverage.)

Notable Decisions of the U.S. Supreme Court, 1990-91

(For further information, see *Supreme Court, Chronology,* and *Addenda.*)

The Supreme Court began its 1990-91 term on Oct. 1. The Court issued 112 signed decisions, the lowest number since 1970. Of those decisions, 34.8% were unanimous, and 19% were decided by 5-4 votes; the newest justice, David H. Souter, cast the fifth vote for the conservative majority in 13 cases. Five decisions overturned court precedents. Among the most notable actions, the Court:

Declined to hear, thus let stand, a ruling allowing a homosexual former sergeant to re-enlist in the Army. The sergeant had re-enlisted three times in a 14-year career, before the Army cited stricter regulations against homosexuality and forced him to retire. In 1989 a U.S. Court of Appeals ruled that invocation of the stricter policy was unjust, due to the individual's several enlistments and "exceptionally outstanding" military record. (Nov. 5)

Declined to hear, thus let stand, a prohibition of begging in the New York City subway system, despite the contention that panhandling was a form of free speech protected by the Constitution. (Nov. 26)

Ruled, 6-2, to further curb police interrogation of criminal suspects by disallowing questioning, once the suspect asked to speak with a lawyer, unless the lawyer was present. The ruling broadened the court's 1966 landmark ruling, Miranda vs. Arizona, which had been extended in a 1981 ruling, Edwards vs. Arizona. (Dec. 3)

Ruled, 6-2, that a taxpayer who sincerely believed that federal income tax laws did not apply to him or her could not be convicted of tax evasion, since tax laws required "willful" conduct. Also ruled that a person's belief that a tax was unconstitutional did not protect him from criminal liability for refusal to pay taxes. The court's rulings affected only criminal provisions of the tax laws, not civil actions, more commonly used by the IRS. (Jan. 8)

Ruled, unanimously, that convicted prisoners called to testify as witnesses in federal court must be paid the same $30-per-day fee as other federal witnesses. This ruling overturned a federal appeals court ruling that had upheld a federal policy against paying witness fees to prisoners. (Jan. 8)

Ruled, 5-3, that court orders for busing to end school desegregation could end if school districts had done everything "practicable" to eliminate the "vestiges of past discrimination." (Jan. 15)

Declined to hear, thus let stand, a case on the issue of "victim impact" statements during the sentencing phase of capital cases. The high court had ruled in 1987 that testimony by family and friends of a murder victim was too inflammatory for jurors to hear during the sentencing phase. (Jan. 22)

Declined to hear, thus let stand, a N.J. Supreme Court ruling that the Tiger Inn, an all-male eating club at Princeton Univ., had practiced illegal sex discrimination. Under the state supreme court ruling, the Tiger Inn would have to admit women when it accepted new members; 2 other all-male Princeton clubs had agreed to admit women before the case reached the U.S. Supreme Court. (Jan. 22)

Ruled, 7-2, that illegal immigrants could sue the Immigration and Naturalization Service over the administration of the 1986 immigration law. This ruling allowed illegal immigrants to initiate class-action lawsuits against the federal government, which had contended that federal courts lacked jurisdiction in these cases. (Feb. 20)

Ruled, 6-3, that employers could not bar women from jobs where they might be exposed to materials hazardous to developing fetuses. The 9 judges unanimously agreed that a "fetal protection" policy constituted overt discrimination against women. (Mar. 20)

Declined to hear, thus let stand, a case challenging the Federal Aviation Administration's "age 60 rule," which prohibited pilots 60 or older from flying commercial planes that seated more than 30 passengers. (Mar. 25)

Ruled, 5-4, that the use of coerced confession in a criminal trial did not automatically void a conviction. This changed the precedent set in 1967 that a coerced confession could never be considered a "harmless error." (Mar. 26)

Ruled, 6-3, that a federal law prohibiting employment discrimination did not apply to the operations of U.S. companies outside the country. (Mar. 26)

Ruled, 9-0, that the white pages of a telephone directory, listing names, addresses, and phone numbers, were not protected under federal copyright law. The case was considered to have wide-ranging implications for publishers of fact-based directories and databases. (Mar. 27)

Ruled, 7-2, that criminal defendants could object to a prosecutor's race-based peremptory challenges of potential jurors, regardless of the race of the defendant or the potential juror. (Apr. 1)

Declined to hear, thus let stand, a life sentence imposed for a crime committed by a 13-year-old boy. (Apr. 15)

Ruled, 6-3, to apply a more restrictive standard regarding challenges filed by state prisoners to the constitutionality of their convictions. (April 16)

Ruled, 7-2, that states could apply a sales tax to one form of communication—in this case, cable TV services; and not to another—here, newspapers or magazines. (Apr. 16)

Ruled, unanimously, that passengers on international flights could not sue airlines for purely emotional or mental injuries suffered in accidents or near collisions. (April 17)

Ruled, unanimously, to uphold the authority of the National Labor Relations Board to define bargaining units for contract negotiations in an entire industry. The case concerned a 1989 NLRB decision to break with its case-by-case policy for determining bargaining units. (Apr. 23)

Ruled, 7-2, that evidence discarded by a fleeing suspect was not protected by the Fourth Amendment's guarantee against illegal search and seizure. (April 23)

Ruled, 6-3, to prohibit a prisoner from filing certain kinds of petitions without paying the court's $300 filing fee. The high court also changed its rules to deter "frivolous" appeals from indigent petitioners. (Apr. 29)

Ruled, 5-4, that suspects arrested without warrants could be held in custody for up to 48 hours while waiting for a judge to determine whether the arrest was proper. The Court had previously ruled that when an arrest was made without a warrant, a "prompt" hearing to determine probable cause was required. (May 13)

Ruled, 7-2, that states, in certain cases, could limit an accused rapist's ability to present evidence about his prior sexual relationship with the alleged victim. (May 20)

Ruled, unanimously, that a spouse could not use federal bankruptcy law to circumvent a lien placed on the couple's home as part of a divorce settlement. (May 23)

Ruled, 5-3, to uphold federal regulations that prohibited federally funded family planning clinics from providing any information about abortion. The clinics would be required to direct all pregnant women to prenatal-care facilities; advisement of an abortion option would be allowed only if continuing the pregnancy was a threat to the woman's life. (May 23)

Ruled, 6-3, that prosecutors needed to demonstrate that an elected official had used "force, violence or fear" in soliciting campaign donations in order to prove that the official had engaged in extortion. (May 23)

Ruled, 7-2, that a suspect who gave police permission to search his car for narcotics also gave implicit permission to search closed containers in the car's passenger compartment. (May 23)

Declined to hear, thus let stand, a 1990 ruling by the U.S. Court of Appeals for the District of Columbia that had suspended the felony convictions of former National Security Council staff member Oliver L. North. North had been convicted in 1989 for his role in the Iran-Contra arms scandal. (May 28)

Ruled, 6-3, that a prosecutor's removal of potential jurors fluent in Spanish from a case involving an Hispanic defendant did not necessarily violate the Constitution. The high court held that a prosecutor could dismiss potential jurors fluent in both Spanish and English based on their answers to questions about their willingness to abide by the court's official translation of testimony given in Spanish. (May 28)

Ruled, 6-3, that police, without a court warrant, could search bags, suitcases, or other containers in the trunk of a car, overturning a precedent set in 1979 that required warrants for luggage searches. (May 30)

Ruled, 8-1, that public employee unions could not charge nonmembers for activities not directly related to collective-bargaining efforts. (May 30)

Ruled, 6-3, that potential jurors in civil cases could not be excluded on the basis of race, thus expanding the ban since 1986 on race-based juror exclusions from criminal cases. (June 3)

Ruled, 5-4, that if a criminal case had received substantial pretrial publicity, the judge need not question jurors specifically about what they had heard or read about the crime; a promise of impartiality from potential jurors was sufficient to protect a defendant's Sixth Amendment right to a fair trial. (June 3)

Ruled, 5-3, that federal judges had broad power to fine people who abused the court system. The Court upheld a $997,000 fine against a Louisiana businessman who had withheld information from a federal judge and filed fraudulent legal actions to avoid fulfilling a contract. The fine was calculated to cover legal costs for the opposing party, previously not allowed in cases of legal system abuse. (June 6)

Ruled, 6-3, that a criminal suspect represented by an attorney in a criminal case could, under certain circumstances, be questioned by police about a second, separate crime without the attorney present. The decision limited the rights for suspects guaranteed by the Supreme Court in the landmark 1966 Miranda v. Arizona decision. (June 13)

Ruled, 5-3, that to challenge the constitutionality of prison conditions, such as unsanitary bathrooms and dining areas, inmates must prove the conditions were the result of deliberate indifference by prison officials. (June 17)

Ruled, 6-3, that police in quest of drug traffickers could board buses and, with permission, search passengers' luggage, without violating the Fourth Amendment guarantee against illegal search and seizure. (June 20)

Ruled, 6-3, that the federal Voting Rights Act applied to judicial elections. The Voting Rights Act, passed in 1965 and amended in 1982, made it illegal for states and localities to maintain voting practices or district boundaries that effectively discriminated against voters on the basis of race. (June 20)

Ruled, 7-2, that altered quotes attributed to a public figure could be considered libelous, but only if the alterations materially changed the meaning of what the person had actually said. According to the Supreme Court's First Amendment doctrine established in the landmark 1964 case, New York Times v. Sullivan, a public figure could prove libel by showing that an article that injured his reputation was not only incorrect but was published with "actual malice" and "reckless disregard for the truth." (June 20)

Ruled, 5-4, that states and cities could ban totally nude dancing in order to protect morality and order. (June 21)

Ruled, 6-3, to tighten restrictions on the rights of state prisoners to appeal their cases in federal courts, overturning a landmark 1963 decision. (June 24)

Clarence Thomas Becomes 106th Justice

Clarence Thomas became the nation's 106th Supreme Court Justice, Oct. 23, 1991, at a last-minute, private swearing-in ceremony at the U.S. Supreme Court building.

There was no public announcement of the event until after it had taken place. Chief Justice William H. Rehnquist administered the judicial oath, with three witnesses in attendance: Mr. Thomas's wife; Sen. John C. Danforth; and Robb M. Jones, the Chief Justice's administrative assistant.

The court's public information officer said the swearing-in had been arranged at the request of Justice Thomas, who wanted to start work immediately and to have his staff on the Supreme Court payroll.

The judicial oath is contained in the Judiciary Act of 1789, and is required by law of all Federal judges. By this oath, judges pledge to "administer justice without respect to persons, and do equal right to the poor and to the rich."

How Cases Come to the Supreme Court

Cases come to the Supreme Court in 3 ways: (1) There are 2 kinds of cases in the court's original jurisdiction—i.e., heard without prior consideration in any other court—and these are relatively few: those in which a state is a party; and those affecting foreign ministers or ambassadors; (2) The Supreme Court receives appeals from the lower federal courts, including district courts, courts of appeals, and a few specialized tribunals such as the U.S. Court of Claims. The Supreme Court has a statutory obligation to hear certain types of appeals, but most cases come up for review on the writ of certiorari, a discretionary writ that the court can grant or refuse as it chooses. The writ is granted on the affirmative vote of 4 justices; (3) The Supreme Court reviews appeals from state supreme courts that present a substantial "federal question," usually where a constitutional right has been denied in the state courts. Article VI makes the federal Constitution, laws, and treaties "the supreme Law of the Land," binding on state judges, and the Supreme Court review enforces this.

In both civil and criminal law, the Supreme Court is the final court of appeal.

Major Actions of the 102nd Congress, 1991

(As of Oct. 15. For further information, see *Congress, Chronology,* and *Addenda.*)

The 102nd Congress convened Jan. 3, 1991.

Legislation Passed by Congress and Signed or Vetoed by Pres. Bush

Covert Action Rules. Congress approved legislation, July 31, creating a new set of rules for U.S. covert action. In Nov. 1990, Pres. Bush had vetoed similar legislation within the fiscal 1991 intelligence budget authorization. The House, July 30, passed the bill, 419-4; the Senate carried it by voice vote, July 31. The bill defined covert action as that taken by the U.S. government "to influence political, economic, or military conditions abroad, where it is intended that the role of the U.S. government will not be apparent or acknowledged publicly." It required the pres. to report all covert activities to Congress and to authorize all activities in advance with a written presidential finding, including a determination that the covert action was necessary "to support identifiable foreign policy objectives." The pres. would also be required to notify Congress when any third country or private citizen was to be involved in carrying out or financing any covert action. Pres. Bush signed the bill **Aug. 15.**

D.C. Appropriations. Congress cleared a $4.6 billion fiscal 1992 appropriations bill for the District of Columbia, by a 239-180 vote in the House, Aug. 1, and a voice vote in the Senate, Aug. 2. Pres. Bush vetoed the bill, **Aug. 17,** contending that it would have permitted the city to fund abortions—although they would have been funded with locally generated revenues rather than federal dollars.

Legislative Appropriations. The fiscal 1992 legislative branch appropriations bill was passed by voice votes in the House, July 31, and the Senate, Aug. 2. Pres. Bush signed the bill, **Aug. 14.** At $2.3 billion, it funded the operations of Congress as well as branch agencies such as the Library of Congress and General Accounting Office. It also included a pay raise of $23,200, and a ban on honoria for senators; an expansion of the limits on gifts that members of Congress and their employees could accept from non-relatives; and the elimination of most rules requiring public disclosure of gifts.

Energy and Water Appropriations. Congress gave final passage to a $21.8 billion fiscal 1992 energy and water appropriations bill, on a 392-32 vote in the House, July 31, and a voice vote in the Senate, Aug. 2. The bill was signed by Pres. Bush, **Aug. 17.** Included was $11.97 billion in defense-related atomic programs and $9.9 billion in domestic spending, $484 million of the latter for a superconducting supercollider, an advanced atom smasher under construction in Texas. Also included was $3.68 billion for the cleanup of nuclear-weapons production sites. One provision narrowed the definition of wetlands, opening up for development some lands that had been federally protected.

Benefits for Long-Term Unemployed. Pres. Bush signed a bill, **Aug. 17,** providing expanded benefits to the long-term unemployed. However, he refused to declare a fiscal emergency, required to release the up to $5.8 billion to pay for the additional benefits. Congress had passed the bill Aug. 2. Under the 1990 budget agreement between Congress and the White House, new spending that was not balanced by cuts elsewhere in the budget, or by increased revenues, was permitted only in cases of "dire emergency." The pres., by not declaring an emergency, formally supported the extension of jobless benefits but prevented the spending.

Benefits Vetoed. Pres. Bush vetoed, **Oct. 11,** a similar bill that included a declaration of emergency. The second measure would have provided $6.5 billion for 20 weeks of additional benefits in states where the total unemployment rate over the previous six months averaged 8 percent or more, 13 weeks in states where the rate was 7 percent or more, and 7 weeks in all others. The pres. objected to the three levels as a "complex, cumbersome system." He also objected to using a state's total unemployment as a standard, rather than the rate of unemployment among insured workers—about half those employed—used by current law and Republican bills. The Senate failed by 2 votes to override the veto, Oct. 16.

Iraq Resolution. The U.S. Senate voted, 97-2, on **Aug. 2,** in favor of a resolution supporting the use of "all necessary means," including military force, to rid Iraq of weapons of mass destruction.

Historical Anniversaries

1892—100 Years Ago

U.S. president Benjamin Harrison failed to win re-election, as Grover Cleveland, president the term before Harrison's, was returned to office. The People's, or Populist, Party attempted to replace the Democrats as the country's 2d party by forming an alliance of farmers of the West and South with industrial workers of the East. They received more than a million votes, 22 percent of the total, advocating an 8-hour workday, graduated income tax, secret ballot, popular election of U.S. senators, and public ownership of railroads, telegraph, and telephone.

An economic depression began in the U.S.

Ellis Island, in the Upper Bay of New York Harbor, became the nation's chief immigration station, after the Castle Garden station established in 1855 had received almost 7.7 million immigrants.

The Geary Chinese Exclusion Act was passed by Congress, extending for 10 more years laws requiring Chinese laborers to register, and deporting those not specifically allowed to stay in the U.S.

Science and Technology: Nikola Tesla, an American immigrant born in Croatia, developed the first motor that could effectively utilize alternating currents of power. The first successful gas-powered auto was made in the U.S., when brothers Charles and Franklin Duryea completed a gas-powered car with a 4-cycle water-cooled engine, testing it indoors for fear of ridicule. The first motorcar with pneumatic tires was produced by Frenchmen Rene Panhard and E.C. Levassor. An improved carburetor that mixed vaporized fuel with air to create combustible gas was invented by Gottlieb Daimler of Germany. Chicago's first elevated railway began the "Loop" that would circle the city's downtown area. Telephone service began between New York and Chicago. Other inventions: the escalator, book matches, the tin-plated steel bottle cap, the Ferris Wheel; and Liederkrantz cheese, a milder Limburger. Also, Player's Navy Cut cigarettes were manufactured, cigarettes were produced in the first push-up cardboard packs, and Fig Newtons were introduced.

Labor and Industry: General Electric Company was created, through the merger of 2 rival companies; Coca-Cola Company was founded; the first Hawaiian pineapple cannery opened. Strikes took place in several states, including one of the most bitter industrial disputes in U.S. labor history, involving steelworkers at a Carnegie mill in Homestead, Pa. Protesting wage cuts and demanding union recognition, the workers went on strike, and the company called in 300 Pinkerton guards to suppress them. In the armed battle that followed, several guards and strikers were killed or wounded. The National Guard was called in, and remained for 3 months, until the strike was broken and most workers returned to their 12-hour shifts. It would be 40 years before there would be an important union of steelworkers.

Religion: The First Church of Christ, Scientist, was established in Boston, Mass. by Mary Baker Eddy. The Protestant Episcopal Cathedral of St. John the Divine, planned as the largest church in America, began construction on a 3-block site in upper Manhattan, New York City. As of 1992, it would not yet be completed.

Medicine: *A Manual of Bacteriology*, by Lt. Col. George Miller Sternberg, the first comprehensive work on the subject, was written. The American School of Osteopathy was founded at Kirksville, Mo. The Ladies Home Journal refused to carry patent medicine ads.

Sports: The first title prizefight with padded gloves and Marquis of Queensbury rules, including 3-minute rounds, was held in New Orleans. "Gentleman Jim" Corbett knocked out "The Great John L" Sullivan in the 21st round, to take the championship.

Crime: Lisbeth Bordon, age 32, was accused of murdering her father and stepmother with blows from an ax in their Fall River, Mass. home. Her acquittal did not stop the spread of a jingle in which she "gave her father 40 whacks" and when she was done "gave her mother forty-one."

Books: Fiction: *The Adventures of Sherlock Holmes* by Arthur Conan Doyle, the first Sherlock Holmes story widely read in America. Poetry: *Barrack-Room Ballads*, including "Gunga Din," "If," and "The Road to Mandalay" by Rudyard Kipling.

Journalism: Jimmy Swinnerton's cartoons of bears and tigers, forerunners of the comic strip, appeared in the *San Francisco Examiner*.

Painting: "The Spirit of the Dead Watching" and "Aha ce feii" (Why, you are jealous) by Paul Gauguin; "At the Moulin Rouge" by Henri de Toulouse-Lautrec; "Woman Sweeping" by Jean Vuillard.

Theater: "Lady Windemere's Fan" by Oscar Wilde; "Charley's Aunt" by Brandon Thomas. **Ballet:** "The Nutcracker Suite" by Petr Illich Tchaikovsky. **Opera:** "Pagliacci" by Ruggiero Leoncavallo. **Music:** "Te Deum" by Anton Dvorak. **Popular Songs:** "Daisy Bell (A Bicycle Built for Two)" by Harry Dacre; "The Bowery" by Percy Gaunt, lyrics by Charles H. Hoyt; "After the Ball is Over" by Charles K. Harris.

1792—200 Years Ago

Austria and Prussia formed an alliance against France, and France declared war on Austria. In Paris, a mob stormed the Tuileries Palace, and an insurrectionary commune replaced the legally elected one. Under the commune's pressure, the Assembly suspended Louis XVI and ordered elections for a new body, the National Convention. Mass arrests of royalist sympathizers were followed by the September massacres in which mobs stormed jails and killed hundreds of prisoners. The Convention held its first meeting Sept. 21, and immediately abolished the monarchy, established the First Republic, and proceeded to try the king for treason. Louis XVI would be convicted and executed in Jan. 1793.

The first great feminist document, *The Vindication of the Rights of Women*, was published in London. Its author, Mary Wollstonecraft, would marry the English political philosopher William Godwin, and die giving birth to a daughter; that daughter, also named Mary, would marry the poet Percy Bysshe Shelley and write, in 1818 at age 19, the novel *Frankenstein*.

George Washington was reelected U.S. president; John Adams reelected vice president.

The cornerstone of the U.S. Capitol was laid in Washington, D.C.

The U.S. Mint was founded by Congress and began producing decimal coins of gold, silver, and copper in Philadelphia.

The New York Stock Exchange was organized at the Merchant's Coffee House in Manhattan.

Kentucky, formerly part of Virginia, was admitted to the Union as the 15th state.

General Anthony Wayne was appointed commander of military forces in Ohio county, after the defeat of Gen. Arthur St. Clair by Native Americans the previous year. Increasing Native American hostility in the Northwest Territory brought passage of the Militia Act, which permitted states to raise armed forces of all able-bodied, free, white males, age 18-45.

Duncan Fife (later Phyfe), a Scottish-American cabinetmaker, set up a New York shop for producing furniture, mostly chairs, tables, sofas and sideboards of mahogany.

The first volume of *Modern Chivalry*, a satire of frontier life by Hugh Henry Brackenridge, was published.

The song "Oh! Dear, What Can the Matter Be?" was published in London.

The first U.S. cracker bakery opened in Newburyport, Mass.

1692—300 Years Ago

The Massacre of the Macdonald clan by the Campbells at Glencoe, Scotland began years of highland feuding.

Salem, the Mass. colony, was swept by accusations of witchcraft. Several hundred men and women were arrested, many imprisoned, dozens brought to trial. Twenty people were executed and at least one died in jail, all of whom swore their innocence. Samuel Sewall, one of the 9 judges, would publicly disclaim his decisions 5 years later; another judge would become better known as an ancestor of Nathaniel Hawthorne, author of *The Scarlet Letter*, written in 1850 but set in 17th-century Puritan Salem.

Aesop's Fables were published in London, translated by Sir Roger L'Estrange from the stories of the Greek slave in the 6th century, B.C., and some traced to earlier tales.

1592—400 Years Ago

Galileo Galilei, a 28-year-old professor of mathematics, left the Univ. of Pisa, Italy, after controversy about his finding that contrary to Aristotle, objects of different weights fall to the ground with equal velocity and uniform acceleration. Galileo joined the Univ. of Padua, where in 1609 he would construct the first astronomical telescope, with which he would confirm the Copernican theory that the earth moved, with other planets, around the sun—a turning point in scientific and philosophic thought.

"Two Gentlemen of Verona," "Titus Andronicus" and "King Richard III," the first dramatic works of the 28-year-old actor and playwright William Shakespeare, were produced in London.

Tintoretto (Jacopo Robusti) painted "The Last Supper."

Heineken Beer began in a Dutch brewery called De Hooiberg—The Haystack.

1492—500 Years Ago

Christopher Columbus set off from Palos, Spain on Fri., Aug. 3 with 52 men aboard his flagship *Santa Maria*, 18 aboard the *Pinta*, commanded by Martín Alonso Pinzón, and 18 on the *Niña*, commanded by Vicente Yáñez Pinzón. Land was sighted Oct. 12, and that day Columbus stepped onto a small island in the Bahamas and took possession for Spain, believing he had discovered the "Indies." He also explored the northeastern coast of Cuba and the northeastern coast of Hispaniola before the *Santa Maria* was wrecked, on Christmas Eve. Leaving some men to found the first colony, Columbus returned to Spain, where he would be named "admiral of the ocean sea." (For more information, see *Index* under Columbus.)

1492—While Columbus Sailed

Castille's Isabella and Aragon's Ferdinand, determined to unify the Iberian peninsula and halt the advance of the Ottoman Turks, conquered Granada. That same year they decreed that Spanish Jews be given three months in which to convert to Catholicism or be expelled from the country. This order was ruthlessly executed by the inquisitor-general, Tomas de Torquemada.

Leonardo da Vinci (1452-1519), Italian artist and scientist, and towering example of the Renaissance man, the universal genius, designed a flying machine resembling a bird's wing after studying the flights of birds.

Lorenzo de'Medici, Lorenzo the Magnificent, died. An astute politician, patron of the arts, literature, and learning; a scholar and a poet, he had conducted the affairs of the Florentine state without an official title.

Pope Innocent VIII died, and Roderigo Borgia became Pope Alexander VI.

Charles VIII (1470-98), king of France under the regency of his sister Anne de Beaujeau, invaded Italy, beginning the Italian Wars, but also bringing the Italian Renaissance to France.

Henry VII (1457-1509) of England invaded France, following French support of a Flemish-born imposter, Perkin Warbeck, as claimant to the English throne.

Martin Behaim, a German traveler and cosmographer, constructed the first terrestrial globe for his native city of Nuremberg. Influenced by the ancient geographer Ptolemy, it also attempts to include some contemporary knowledge of geography, but shows no details of lands beyond the Atlantic.

Reports of Native Americans smoking, snuffing, and chewing tobacco came back from the New World. Native Americans of the Caribbean area rolled tobacco into cigars and also smoked it in a *tobago*, a pipe—the derivation of the word tobacco.

New World foods were discovered, including maize, sweet potatoes, plaintain, peppers, pineapples, turtle meat, and allspice.

UNITED STATES POPULATION
The Changing Face of the United States

by
Barbara Everitt Bryant
Director
Bureau of the Census, U.S. Dept. of Commerce

From the first U.S. census in 1790 to last year's 200th anniversary, the decennial census has changed. For instance:

The first census was taken by 17 U.S. Marshals and a support staff of less than 600 people. The 1990 census questionnaire was mailed to nearly 100 million housing units. It took a staff of over 315,000 civil servants to follow up on those who did not respond and process the data.

The first census was taken for the purposes of determining taxation and representation in the U.S. Congress. Last year's census was conducted for the purposes of representation and the allocation of federal funds. Additionally, state and local governments, nonprofit organizations, and private sector businesses will use the data generated by the 1990 census.

In 1790, the census asked questions about free white males 16 years and older, free white males under 16, free white females, slaves, and other persons. American Indians were specifically excluded. The 1990 census asked about all persons and the relationships of people living in households.

The 1790 census cost $300,000 in 1990 dollars. The 1990 census cost $2.6 billion. This works out to about $1,040 per person counted.

The first census found 3.9 million people. The 1990 census found 248.7 million people.

However, some things have stayed the same between the 1790 and 1990 census. One thing that has not changed is disappointment with the outcome of the census. George Washington was disappointed with the 1790 census because he believed there were over 4 million Americans. Another thing that has stayed the same from 1790 until today is the fundamental reason that Americans have kept the census around for 200 years—we need to know who we are, what we do for a living, where and how we live, and something about the quality of our lives.

Who We Are

If you gave America a face in 1990, it would have shown the first sign of wrinkles, it would have been full of color, and it would have been a married female. Census Bureau facts show that:

Age: The nation's median age is 32.9 years. This is up from 30 years in 1980.

Nearly 26% of Americans are under 18 years of age (63.6 million). Over 12% of Americans are 65 years and older (31.2 million).

Sex: 51% of the American population is female. There are 6.2 million more women than men in America.

Households: The nation has about 91.9 million households. 70% of these are family households; down from 73% in 1980.

55% of U.S. households are maintained by married couples. However this is down from 1980 when 60% of U.S. households were married couples.

Only 26% of households with children under 18 included a married couple. This is down from 31% in 1980. The number of single parent households has increased by 2.8 million since 1980.

Persons living alone accounted for 25% of households in 1990.

Minorities: Asian-Pacific Islanders are the fastest growing minority group. In 1990 they accounted for 2.9% of the population. This is up from 1.5% of the population in 1980. 7.3 million people identified themselves as Asian-Pacific Islanders in 1990.

The nation's Hispanic population growth exceeded that of Asian-Pacific Islanders in total numbers but not in percent. Hispanics grew from 6.4% in 1980 to 9% of the population in 1990; or 22.4 million people.

The percentage of Black Americans increased from 11.7% in 1980 to 12.1% in 1990; or 30 million people.

The American Indian/Eskimo/Aleut populations grew from 0.6% of the population in 1980 to 0.8% of the population in 1990; or 2 million people.

Approximately 25% of the U.S. population growth comes from **immigration.** The rest of the population growth comes from births.

Work Force

Less than 2% of Americans live on farms. This is a decrease in the farm population of over 2% a year between 1980 and 1990.

6.1% of Americans were unemployed between May, 1990 and May, 1991.

The number of women-owned businesses (sole proprietorship, partnership, or subchapter S companies) jumped 55% in the late 1980's. The number of firms owned by Asian-Pacific Islanders grew 89%; Hispanic-owned firms grew 81%, American Indian/Eskimo/Aleut-owned firms grew 58%; and Black-owned firms grew 38%.

Personal and business services grew 13 times faster than the population in the late 1980's.

The Federal government funds one-third of all industrial research and development.

Most state and local government employees are in education-related activities; two-fifths of the 4.3 million state employees and over one-half of the 10.4 million local government workers.

Two-thirds of the work force were covered by a pension of some sort. Social Security covered 92% of civilian wage and salary workers. 95% of government employees were covered by pensions whereas only 29% of agricultural and personal service workers were covered by employer-sponsored pensions.

87% of Americans had **health insurance.** Those most likely to have health insurance were the elderly, the employed, and those with at least a high-school diploma.

Retail sales in 1990 exceeded $1.8 trillion. This accounted for about one-third of the U.S. gross national product.

About one-third of retail sales are durable goods such as automobiles and furniture.

Where and How We Live

When we paint this part of the American portrait, we find that a majority (55.6%) live in the South and West. Because of the shifting of the American popula-

72

tion between 1980 and 1990, 19 seats in the House of Representatives changed. Eight states gained seats (California +7, Florida +4, Texas +3, and Arizona, Georgia, North Carolina, Virginia, and Washington +1 each) and thirteen states lost seats (New York -3; Illinois, Michigan, Ohio, and Pennsylvania -2 each; and Iowa, Kansas, Kentucky, Louisiana, Massachusetts, Montana, New Jersey, and West Virginia -1 each).

The five most populous states are California (29.8 million), New York (18 million), Texas (17 million), Florida (12.9 million) and Pennsylvania (11.9 million). California's population is now larger than the total population of Canada.

The five least populated states are Delaware (666,000), North Dakota (639,000), Vermont (563,000), Alaska (550,000), and Wyoming (454,000).

Most Americans live in metropolitan areas. 50.2% of the U.S. population live in one of the 39 metropolitan areas that has a population of at least 1 million. In total, 77.5% of the U.S. population live in metropolitan areas.

The five largest metropolitan areas are New York/New Jersey/Long Island/Connecticut (18.1 million), Los Angeles/Anaheim/Riverside (14.5 million), Chicago/Gary/Lake Counties (8.1 million), San Francisco/Oakland/San Jose (6.3 million), and Philadelphia/Wilmington/Trenton (5.9 million).

The Los Angeles/Anaheim/Riverside metropolitan area experienced 26% growth compared to 3% growth in the New York/New Jersey/Long Island/Connecticut metropolitan area.

In 1992, the new combined Washington D.C./Baltimore metropolitan area should become the fourth largest metropolitan area with San Francisco/Oakland/San Jose moving to fifth place.

In the San Francisco/Oakland/San Jose metropolitan area, San Jose is now larger than San Francisco.

The five largest cities are New York (7.3 million), Los Angeles (3.5 million), Chicago (2.8 million), Houston (1.6 million), and Philadelphia (1.6 million).

The five largest counties are Los Angeles, CA (8.9 million), Cook, IL (5.1 million), Harris, TX (2.8 million), San Diego, CA (2.5 million), and Orange, CA (2.4 million).

The West grew by 22.3% during the 1980's and the South grew by 13.4%. The population of the total U.S. grew 9.8% during the 1980's. Despite the dramatic growth figures in the West and South, the 1980's had the second lowest growth rate in census history. Only the 7.3% rate during the Depression decade of the 1930's was lower.

The average number of people living in a U.S. household in 1990 was 2.63. This is a reduction from 1980 when it was 2.75 people per household. In 1790, there were 5.79 people living in the average U.S. household.

The median value of an owner-occupied, single-family home is $79,100. This is a 68% increase from the 1980 median value of $47,200. Even when adjusted for inflation, median value of owner-occupied homes increased 5% in the past decade; from $75,000 to $79,100.

The median rent is $374 a month. This is an 89% increase from 1980 when the median rent was $198. When adjusted for inflation the increase was 19%; from $314 to $374.

The vacancy rate in housing is just over 10%; up from 9% in 1980. Vacancies include seasonal housing units that were unoccupied on April 1, 1990.

Fewer people own houses in 1990 (64.2%) than in 1980 (66%).

There was a 16% growth in housing units between 1980 and 1990. Most of this growth occurred in the South and West.

Property taxes increased between 8% and 9% during the 1980's.

Quality of Life

Education: More Americans are high school graduates than at any time in U.S. history; over 78%. About 23% of Americans have obtained a degree beyond high school. There is a direct correlation between education and income. The average monthly earnings without a high school diploma are $452; high school diploma, $921; bachelor's degree, $1,829; doctorate, $3,637; professional degree, $4,003.

We spend an annual average of $2,635 per student in our public schools and universities.

Assets: Home ownership accounts for over 40% of Americans net worth. Interest-earning assets account for 25%. About 44% of our country's net worth is concentrated in 25% of our households.

Computers: Although only about 15% of Americans own their own computer, this is nearly double the early 1980's. 46% of children and nearly 30% of adults use a computer at school, home, or work.

Child care: Employed women spend about 7% of their family income on child care for their preschoolers. Most of this care takes place in a home environment such as with relatives or neighbors (66%). About 25% of child care comes from organized facilities such as nursery schools and day care centers.

Assistance: About 4% of the American population age 15 and older needs assistance with everyday activities. This increases to 45% of persons 85 and over who need assistance. Most of the assistance is provided by female relatives.

Federal Aid: The Federal government dispensed over $1 trillion in fiscal year 1990 to the states. California received $116 billion of these funds. On a per capita basis, Virginia received the most with spending of over $4,500 per person. Federal funds were divided up in this manner:

$498 billion in payments to individuals such as Social Security;

$146 billion in salaries to military and civilian employees;

$189 billion in contracts;

$134 billion in grants for such things as Medicaid, Aid to Families with Dependent Children, and highway construction; and

$36 billion in research grants and agricultural subsidies.

Lotteries: 32 states operate lotteries. During fiscal year 1990, these lotteries produced $8.5 billion in net revenue. During this same time, state general expenditures amounted to $506.7 billion.

State expenditures for highways was up 3.7% in 1990 to $44.3 billion. Expenditures for hospitals rose 5.7% to 22.4 billion in 1990.

Through information such as this, the American public is able to see the value of the decennial census, the economic and agricultural censuses that are taken every five years, and the on-going monthly, quarterly, and annual surveys. Although the picture that the 1990 census and periodic surveys paint may discomfort some Americans, it is essential for our continued national health that we fully understand that our country is changing. Census information gives us the picture of how the United States is changing.

U.S. Population by Official

(Members of the Armed Forces overseas or

State	1790[1]	1800[1]	1810[1]	1820	1830	1840	1850	1860	1870	1880	1890
Ala. . .	....	1	9	127,901	309,527	590,756	771,623	964,201	996,992	1,262,505	1,513,401
Alas. .	....	....	....	....	....	....	....	....	....	33,426	32,052
Ariz. .	....	....	....	....	....	....	....	....	9,658	40,440	88,243
Ark. . .	....	....	1	14,273	30,388	97,574	209,897	435,450	484,471	802,525	1,128,211
Cal. . .	....	....	....	....	....	....	92,597	379,994	560,247	864,694	1,213,398
Col. . .	....	....	....	....	....	....	....	34,277	39,864	194,327	413,249
Conn. .	238	251	262	275,248	297,675	309,978	370,792	460,147	537,454	622,700	746,258
Del. . .	59	64	73	72,749	76,748	78,085	91,532	112,216	125,015	146,608	168,493
D.C. . .	....	....	8	16	23,336	30,261	33,745	51,687	75,080	131,700	177,624	230,392
Fla. . .	....	....	....	....	34,730	54,477	87,445	140,424	187,748	269,493	391,422
Ga. . .	83	163	252	340,989	516,823	691,392	906,185	1,057,286	1,184,109	1,542,180	1,837,353
Ha. . .	....	....	....	....	....	....	....	....	....	....	....
Ida. . .	....	....	....	....	....	....	....	....	14,999	32,610	88,548
Ill. . .	....	....	12	55,211	157,445	476,183	851,470	1,711,951	2,539,891	3,077,871	3,826,352
Ind. . .	....	6	25	147,178	343,031	685,866	988,416	1,350,428	1,680,637	1,978,301	2,192,404
Ia. . .	....	....	....	....	....	43,112	192,214	674,913	1,194,020	1,624,615	1,912,297
Kan. .	....	....	....	....	....	....	....	107,206	364,399	996,096	1,428,108
Ky.. . .	74	221	407	564,317	687,917	779,828	982,405	1,155,684	1,321,011	1,648,690	1,858,635
La.. . .	....	....	77	153,407	215,739	352,411	517,762	708,002	726,915	939,946	1,118,588
Me. . .	97	152	229	298,335	399,455	501,793	583,169	628,279	626,915	648,936	661,086
Md. . .	320	342	381	407,350	447,040	470,019	583,034	687,049	780,894	934,943	1,042,390
Mass. .	379	423	472	523,287	610,408	737,699	994,514	1,231,066	1,457,351	1,783,085	2,238,947
Mich. .	....	....	5	8,896	31,639	212,267	397,654	749,113	1,184,059	1,636,937	2,093,890
Minn. .	....	....	....	....	....	....	6,077	172,023	439,706	780,773	1,310,283
Miss. .	....	8	31	75,448	136,621	375,651	606,526	791,305	827,922	1,131,597	1,289,600
Mo. . .	....	....	20	66,586	140,455	383,702	682,044	1,182,012	1,721,295	2,168,380	2,679,185
Mon.. .	....	....	....	....	....	....	....	....	20,595	39,159	142,924
Neb.. .	....	....	....	....	....	....	....	28,841	122,993	452,402	1,062,656
Nev.. .	....	....	....	....	....	....	....	6,857	42,491	62,266	47,355
N.H.. .	142	184	214	244,161	269,328	284,574	317,976	326,073	318,300	346,991	376,530
N.J.. .	184	211	246	277,575	320,823	373,306	489,555	672,035	906,096	1,131,116	1,444,933
N.M.. .	....	....	....	....	....	....	61,547	93,516	91,874	119,565	160,282
N.Y.. .	340	589	959	1,372,812	1,918,608	2,428,921	3,097,394	3,880,735	4,382,759	5,082,871	6,003,174
N.C.. .	394	478	556	638,829	737,987	753,419	869,039	992,622	1,071,361	1,399,750	1,617,949
N.D.. .	....	....	....	....	....	....	....	....	*2,405	36,909	190,983
Oh. . .	....	45	231	581,434	937,903	1,519,467	1,980,329	2,339,511	2,665,260	3,198,062	3,672,329
Okla. .	....	....	....	....	....	....	....	....	....	....	258,657
Ore. . .	....	....	....	....	....	....	12,093	52,465	90,923	174,768	317,704
Pa. . .	434	602	810	1,049,458	1,348,233	1,724,033	2,311,786	2,906,215	3,521,951	4,282,891	5,258,113
R.I. . .	69	69	77	83,059	97,199	108,830	147,545	174,620	217,353	276,531	345,506
S.C.. .	249	346	415	502,741	581,185	594,398	668,507	703,708	705,606	995,577	1,151,149
S.D.. .	....	....	....	....	....	....	....	4,837[2]	11,776[2]	98,268	348,600
Tenn..	36	106	262	422,823	681,904	829,210	1,002,717	1,109,801	1,258,520	1,542,359	1,767,518
Tex.. .	....	....	....	....	....	....	212,592	604,215	818,579	1,591,749	2,235,527
Ut. . .	....	....	....	....	....	....	11,380	40,273	86,786	143,963	210,779
Vt. . .	85	154	218	235,981	280,652	291,948	314,120	315,098	330,551	332,286	332,422
Va. . .	692	808	878	938,261	1,044,054	1,025,227	1,119,348	1,219,630	1,225,163	1,512,565	1,655,980
Wash..	....	....	....	....	....	....	1,201	11,594	23,955	75,116	357,232
W. Va..	56	79	105	136,808	176,924	224,537	302,313	376,688	442,014	618,457	762,794
Wis. . .	....	....	....	....	....	30,945	305,391	775,881	1,054,670	1,315,497	1,693,330
Wy. . .	....	....	....	....	....	....	....	....	9,118	20,789	62,555
U.S.. . .	3,929	5,308	7,240	9,638,453	12,860,702	17,063,353[3]	23,191,876	31,443,321[3]	38,558,371	50,189,209	62,979,766

Note: Where possible, population shown is that of 1990 area of state.
(1) Totals for 1790, 1800, and 1810 are in thousands. (2) 1860 figure is for Dakota Territory; 1870 figures are for parts of Dakota Territory. (3) U.S. total includes persons (5,318 in 1830 and 6,100 in 1840) on public ships in the service of the United States not credited to any region, division, or state.

Congressional Apportionment

	1990	1980		1990	1980		1990	1980		1990	1980		1990	1980
Ala.. .	7	7	Ida.. .	2	2	Minn..	8	8	N. D..	1	1	Vt.. . .	1	1
Alas..	1	1	Ill.. . .	20	22	Miss..	5	5	Oh.. .	19	21	Va.. .	11	10
Ariz..	6	5	Ind.. .	10	10	Mo.. .	9	9	Okla..	6	6	Wash..	9	8
Ark.. .	4	4	Ia.. . .	5	6	Mon..	1	2	Ore.. .	5	5	W. Va..	3	4
Cal.. .	52	45	Kan..	4	5	Neb..	3	3	Pa.. .	21	23	Wis.. .	9	9
Col.. .	6	6	Ky.. .	6	7	Nev..	2	2	R. I.. .	2	2	Wy.. .	1	1
Conn..	6	6	La.. .	7	8	N. H..	2	2	S. C..	6	6			
Del.. .	1	1	Me.. .	2	2	N. J..	13	14	S. D..	1	1	Totals.	435	435
Fla.. .	23	19	Md.. .	8	8	N. M..	3	3	Tenn..	9	9			
Ga.. .	11	10	Mass..	10	11	N. Y.. .	31	34	Tex...	30	27			
Ha.. .	2	2	Mich..	16	18	N. C.. .	12	11	Ut.. . .	3	3			

The primary reason the Constitution provided for a census of the population every 10 years was to give a basis for apportionment of representatives among the states. This apportionment largely determines the number of electoral votes allotted to each state.

The number of representatives of each state in Congress is determined by the state's population, but each state is entitled to one representative regardless of population. A Congressional apportionment has been made after each decennial census except that of 1920.

Under provisions of a law that became effective Nov. 15, 1941, apportionment of representatives is made by the method of equal proportions. In the application of this method, the apportionment is made so that the average population per representative has the least possible variation between one state and any other. The first House of Representatives, in 1789, had 65 members, as provided by the Constitution. As the population grew, the number of representatives was increased, but the total membership has been fixed at 435 since the apportionment based on the 1910 census.

Census from 1790 to 1990

other U.S. nationals overseas are not included.)

1900	1910	1920	1930	1940	1950	1960	1970	1980	1990
1,828,697	2,138,093	2,348,174	2,646,248	2,832,961	3,061,743	3,266,740	3,444,354	3,894,025	4,040,587
63,592	64,356	55,036	59,278	72,524	128,643	226,167	302,583	401,851	550,043
122,931	204,354	334,162	435,573	499,261	749,587	1,302,161	1,775,399	2,716,546	3,665,228
1,311,564	1,574,449	1,752,204	1,854,482	1,949,387	1,909,511	1,786,272	1,923,322	2,286,357	2,350,725
1,485,053	2,377,549	3,426,861	5,677,251	6,907,387	10,586,223	15,717,204	19,971,069	23,667,764	29,760,021
539,700	799,024	939,629	1,035,791	1,123,296	1,325,089	1,753,947	2,209,596	2,889,735	3,294,394
908,420	1,114,756	1,380,631	1,606,903	1,709,242	2,007,280	2,535,234	3,032,217	3,107,564	3,287,116
184,735	202,322	223,003	238,380	266,505	318,085	446,292	548,104	594,338	666,168
278,718	331,069	437,571	486,869	663,091	802,178	763,956	756,668	638,432	606,900
528,542	752,619	968,470	1,468,211	1,897,414	2,771,305	4,951,560	6,791,418	[2]9,746,961	12,937,926
2,216,331	2,609,121	2,895,832	2,908,506	3,123,723	3,444,578	3,943,116	4,587,930	5,462,982	6,478,216
154,001	191,874	255,881	368,300	422,770	499,794	632,772	769,913	964,691	1,108,229
161,772	325,594	431,866	445,032	524,873	588,637	667,191	713,015	944,127	1,006,749
4,821,550	5,638,591	6,485,280	7,630,654	7,897,241	8,712,176	10,081,158	11,110,285	11,427,409	11,430,602
2,516,462	2,700,876	2,930,390	3,238,503	3,427,796	3,934,224	4,662,498	5,195,392	5,490,214	5,544,159
2,231,853	2,224,771	2,404,021	2,470,939	2,538,268	2,621,073	2,757,537	2,825,368	2,913,808	2,776,755
1,470,495	1,690,949	1,769,257	1,880,999	1,801,028	1,905,299	2,178,611	2,249,071	2,364,236	2,477,574
2,147,174	2,289,905	2,416,630	2,614,589	2,845,627	2,944,806	3,038,156	3,220,711	3,660,324	3,685,296
1,381,625	1,656,388	1,798,509	2,101,593	2,363,880	2,683,516	3,257,022	3,644,637	4,206,116	4,219,973
694,466	742,371	768,014	797,423	847,226	913,774	969,265	993,722	1,125,043	1,227,928
1,188,044	1,295,346	1,449,661	1,631,526	1,821,244	2,343,001	3,100,689	3,923,897	4,216,933	4,781,468
2,805,346	3,366,416	3,852,356	4,249,614	4,316,721	4,690,514	5,148,578	5,689,170	5,737,093	6,016,425
2,420,982	2,810,173	3,668,412	4,842,325	5,256,106	6,371,766	7,823,194	8,881,826	9,262,044	9,295,297
1,751,394	2,075,708	2,387,125	2,563,953	2,792,300	2,982,483	3,413,864	3,806,103	4,075,970	4,375,099
1,551,270	1,797,114	1,790,618	2,009,821	2,183,796	2,178,914	2,178,141	2,216,994	2,520,770	2,573,216
3,106,665	3,293,335	3,404,055	3,629,367	3,784,664	3,954,653	4,319,813	4,677,623	4,916,766	5,117,073
243,329	376,053	548,889	537,606	559,456	591,024	674,767	694,409	786,690	799,065
1,066,300	1,192,214	1,296,372	1,377,963	1,315,834	1,325,510	1,411,330	1,485,333	1,569,825	1,578,385
42,335	81,875	77,407	91,058	110,247	160,083	285,278	488,738	800,508	1,201,833
411,588	430,572	443,083	465,293	491,524	533,242	606,921	737,681	920,610	1,109,252
1,883,669	2,537,167	3,155,900	4,041,334	4,160,165	4,835,329	6,066,782	7,171,112	7,365,011	7,730,188
195,310	327,301	360,350	423,317	531,818	681,187	951,023	1,017,055	1,303,302	1,515,069
7,268,894	9,113,614	10,385,227	12,588,066	13,479,142	14,830,192	16,782,304	18,241,391	17,558,165	17,990,455
1,893,810	2,206,287	2,559,123	3,170,276	3,571,623	4,061,929	4,556,155	5,084,411	5,880,095	6,628,637
319,146	577,056	646,872	680,845	641,935	619,636	632,446	617,792	652,717	638,800
4,157,545	4,767,121	5,759,394	6,646,697	6,907,612	7,946,627	9,706,397	10,657,423	10,797,603	10,847,115
790,391	1,657,155	2,028,283	2,396,040	2,336,434	2,233,351	2,328,284	2,559,463	3,025,487	3,145,585
413,536	672,765	783,389	953,786	1,089,684	1,521,341	1,768,687	2,091,533	2,633,156	2,842,321
6,302,115	7,665,111	8,720,017	9,631,350	9,900,180	10,498,012	11,319,366	11,800,766	11,864,720	11,881,643
428,556	542,610	604,397	687,497	713,346	791,896	859,488	949,723	947,154	1,003,464
1,340,316	1,515,400	1,683,724	1,738,765	1,899,804	2,117,027	2,382,594	2,590,713	3,120,729	3,486,703
401,570	583,888	636,547	692,849	642,961	652,740	680,514	666,257	690,768	696,004
2,020,616	2,184,789	2,337,885	2,616,556	2,915,841	3,291,718	3,567,089	3,926,018	4,591,023	4,877,185
3,048,710	3,896,542	4,663,228	5,824,715	6,414,824	7,711,194	9,579,677	11,198,655	14,225,513	16,986,510
276,749	373,351	449,396	507,847	550,310	688,862	890,627	1,059,273	1,461,037	1,722,850
343,641	355,956	352,428	359,611	359,231	377,747	389,881	444,732	511,456	562,758
1,854,184	2,061,612	2,309,187	2,421,851	2,677,773	3,318,680	3,966,949	4,651,448	5,346,797	6,187,358
518,103	1,141,990	1,356,621	1,563,396	1,736,191	2,378,963	2,853,214	3,413,244	4,132,353	4,866,692
958,800	1,221,119	1,463,701	1,729,205	1,901,974	2,005,552	1,860,421	1,744,237	1,950,186	1,793,477
2,069,042	2,333,860	2,632,067	2,939,006	3,137,587	3,434,575	3,951,777	4,417,821	4,705,642	4,891,769
92,531	145,965	194,402	225,565	250,742	290,529	330,066	332,416	469,557	453,588
76,212,168	92,228,496	106,021,537	123,202,624	132,164,569	151,325,798	179,323,175	203,302,031	226,542,203	248,709,873

U.S. Center of Population, 1790-1990

Center of Population is that point which may be considered as center of population gravity of the U.S. or that point upon which the U.S. would balance if it were a rigid plane without weight and the population distributed thereon with each individual being assumed to have equal weight and to exert an influence on a central point proportional to his distance from that point. The 1990 center is 818.6 miles from the 1790 center of population, and 39.5 miles southwest of the 1980 center.

Year	N. Lat.			W.Long.			Approximate location
	°	'	"	°	'	"	
1790	39	16	30	76	11	12	23 miles east of Baltimore, Md.
1800	39	16	6	76	56	30	18 miles west of Baltimore, Md.
1810	39	11	30	77	37	12	40 miles northwest by west of Washington, D.C. (in Va.)
1820	39	5	42	78	33	0	16 miles east of Moorefield, W. Va.[1]
1830	38	57	54	79	16	54	19 miles west-southwest of Moorefield, W. Va.[1]
1840	39	2	0	80	18	0	16 miles south of Clarksburg, W. Va.[1]
1850	38	59	0	81	19	0	23 miles southeast of Parkersburg, W. Va.[1]
1860	39	0	24	82	48	48	20 miles south by east of Chillicothe, Oh.
1870	39	12	0	83	35	42	48 miles east by north of Cincinnati, Oh.
1880	39	4	8	84	39	40	8 miles west by south of Cincinnati, Oh. (in Ky.)
1890	39	11	56	85	32	53	20 miles east of Columbus, Ind.
1900	39	9	36	85	48	54	6 miles southeast of Columbus, Ind.
1910	39	10	12	86	32	20	In the city of Bloomington, Ind.
1920	39	10	21	86	43	15	8 miles south-southeast of Spencer, Owen County, Ind.
1930	39	3	45	87	8	6	3 miles northeast of Linton, Greene County, Ind.
1940	38	56	54	87	22	35	2 miles southeast by east of Carlisle, Haddon township, Sullivan Co., Ind.
1950 (inc. Alaska & Hawaii)	38	48	15	88	22	8	3 miles northeast of Louisville, Clay County, Ill.
1960	38	35	58	89	12	35	6 1/2 miles northwest of Centralia, Clinton Co., Ill.
1970	38	27	47	89	42	22	5 miles east southeast of Mascoutah, St. Clair County, Ill.
1980	38	8	13	90	34	26	1/4 mile west of De Soto, Jefferson Co., Mo.
1990	37	52	20	91	12	55	9.7 miles northwest of Steelville, Mo.

(1) West Virginia was set off from Virginia Dec. 31, 1862, and admitted as a state June 20, 1863.

Percent Distribution of the Population by Age

Source: U.S. Bureau of the Census

U.S. Population Abroad, by Selected Country: 1989

Source: U.S. Dept. of State

(In thousands. As of May 1. Data compiled as part of noncombatant personnel evacuation requirements report)

Country	Total[1]	Resident U.S. citizen	U.S. tourists	Country	Total[1]	Resident U.S. citizen	U.S. tourists
Total[2]	4,244.4	2,241.7	1,164.5	Japan	94.6	34.9	8.6
Australia	84.2	67.0	13.9	Jerusalem	35.3	30.0	5.1
Belgium	19.5	12.8	4.5	Mexico	690.2	425.4	262.0
Brazil	53.8	41.5	11.6	Netherlands	32.5	22.5	3.9
Canada	650.7	259.7	388.9	Panama	27.1	7.5	0.3
Colombia	23.5	20.8	2.1	Philippines	197.6	120.6	3.4
Costa Rica	27.7	23.7	3.6	Portugal	32.1	20.8	8.6
Dominican Republic	65.7	48.8	15.6	Saudi Arabia	25.1	20.1	1.2
Egypt	26.2	17.8	2.7	South Korea	54.9	11.7	15.5
France	134.3	44.6	88.5	Spain	106.1	61.4	26.0
Greece	67.5	54.0	9.6	Switzerland	36.5	24.1	11.4
Hong Kong	25.0	17.3	6.6	Turkey	23.0	11.2	2.8
Ireland	36.5	31.8	4.4	United Kingdom	256.9	170.1	42.5
Israel	93.7	77.2	15.9	Venezuela	24.0	20.3	3.3
Italy	157.7	83.4	49.4	West Germany	627.8	152.3	12.3

(1) Includes Dept. of Defense noncombatant employees, other U.S. government employees, and dependents of U.S. military and civilian employees, not shown separately. (2) Includes other countries not shown separately.

Estimated Population of American Colonies: 1630-1780

Source: U.S. Bureau of the Census (thousands)

Colony	1780	1770	1750	1740	1720	1700	1690	1670	1650	1630
Total	2,780.4	2,148.1	1,170.8	905.6	466.2	250.9	210.4	111.9	50.4	4.6
Maine (counties)[1]	49.1	31.3	...	...	...	...	...	...	1.0	0.4
New Hampshire[2]	87.8	62.4	27.5	23.3	9.4	5.0	4.2	1.8	1.3	0.5
Vermont[3]	47.6	10.0	...	...	...	...	...	...	...	...
Plymouth and Massachusetts[1,2,4]	268.6	235.3	188.0	151.6	91.0	55.9	56.9	35.3	15.6	0.9
Rhode Island[2]	52.9	58.2	33.2	25.3	11.7	5.9	4.2	2.2	0.8	...
Connecticut[2]	206.7	183.9	111.3	89.6	58.8	26.0	21.6	12.6	4.1	...
New York[2]	210.5	162.9	76.7	63.7	36.9	19.1	13.9	5.8	4.1	0.4
New Jersey[2]	139.6	117.4	71.4	51.4	29.8	14.0	8.0	1.0	...	...
Pennsylvania[2]	327.3	240.1	119.7	85.6	31.0	18.0	11.4	...	...	...
Delaware[2]	45.4	35.5	28.7	19.9	5.4	2.5	1.5	0.7	0.2	...
Maryland[2]	245.5	202.6	141.1	116.1	66.1	29.6	24.0	13.2	4.5	...
Virginia[2]	538.0	447.0	231.0	180.4	87.8	58.6	53.0	35.3	18.7	2.5
North Carolina[2]	270.1	197.2	73.0	51.8	21.3	10.7	7.6	3.8	...	...
South Carolina[2]	180.0	124.2	64.0	45.0	17.0	5.7	3.9	0.2	...	...
Georgia[2]	56.1	23.4	5.2	2.0	...	...	...	...	...	...
Kentucky[5]	45.0	15.7	...	...	...	...	...	...	...	...
Tennessee[6]	10.0	1.0	...	...	...	...	...	...	...	...

(1) For 1660-1750, Maine counties included with Massachusetts. Maine was a part of Massachusetts until it became a separate state in 1820. (2) One of the original 13 states. (3) Admitted to statehood in 1791. (4) Plymouth became a part of the Province of Massachusetts in 1691. (5) Admitted to statehood in 1792. (6) Admitted to statehood in 1796.

Race and Hispanic Origin for the United States: 1990 and 1980

Source: Bureau of the Census, U.S. Dept. of Commerce

	1990 Census		1980 Census		Percent change 1980-1990
	Number	Percent	Number	Percent	
Race					
All persons	248,709,873	100.0	226,545,805	100.0	9.8
White	199,686,070	80.3	188,371,622	83.1	6.0
Black.	29,986,060	12.1	26,495,025	11.7	13.2
American Indian, Eskimo, or Aleut	1,959,234	0.8	1,420,400	0.6	37.9
American Indian	1,878,285	0.8	1,364,033	0.6	37.7
Eskimo	57,152	0.0	42,162	0.0	35.6
Aleut	23,797	0.0	14,205	0.0	67.5
Asian or Pacific Islander	7,273,662	2.9	3,500,439[1]	1.5	107.8
Chinese	1,645,472	0.7	806,040	0.4	104.1
Filipino	1,406,770	0.6	774,652	0.3	81.6
Japanese	847,562	0.3	700,974	0.3	20.9
Asian Indian	815,447	0.3	361,531	0.2	125.6
Korean.	798,849	0.3	354,593	0.2	125.3
Vietnamese	614,547	0.2	261,729	0.1	134.8
Hawaiian	211,014	0.1	166,814	0.1	26.5
Samoan	62,964	0.0	41,948	0.0	50.1
Guamanian	49,345	0.0	32,158	0.0	53.4
Other Asian or Pacific Islander	821,692	0.3	NA	NA	NA
Other race	9,804,847	3.9	6,758,319	3.0	45.1
Hispanic Origin					
Hispanic origin[2]	22,354,059	9.0	14,608,673	6.4	53.0
Mexican	13,495,938	5.4	8,740,439	3.9	54.4
Puerto Rican	2,727,754	1.1	2,013,945	0.9	35.4
Cuban	1,043,932	0.4	803,226	0.4	30.0
Other Hispanic.	5,086,435	2.0	3,051,063	1.3	66.7
Not of Hispanic origin	226,355,814	91.0	211,937,132	93.6	6.8

(NA) Not Available from 1980 100-percent tabulations. (1) The 1980 numbers for Asians or Pacific Islanders shown in this table are not entirely comparable with 1990 counts. The 1980 count of 3,500,439 Asians or Pacific Islanders based on 100-percent tabulations includes only the nine specific Asian or Pacific Islander groups listed separately in the 1980 race item. The 1980 total Asian or Pacific Islander population of 3,726,440 from sample tabulations is comparable to the 1990 count; these figures include groups not listed separately in the race item on the 1980 census form. (2) Persons of Hispanic origin may be of any race.ig Def. of Race & Hispanic Origin

Definitions of Race and Hispanic Origin Groups

Source: Bureau of the Census, U.S. Dept. of Commerce

Race

The concept of race as used by the Census Bureau reflects self-identification; it does not denote any clear-cut scientific definition of biological stock. The data for race represent self-classification by people according to the race with which they most closely identify.

Persons identified their race by classifying themselves in one of the categories listed, i.e., White, Black, American Indian, Eskimo, Aleut, Chinese, Filipino, Japanese, Korean, Vietnamese, Hawaiian, Samoan, Guamanian, Other race. In cases where persons did not identify with any of the given race categories they were directed to identify as "Other API" ("API" means Asian or Pacific Islander) or "Other race" and write in the name of their race in the space provided. Thus, data for the Asian or Pacific Islander groups not listed on the census questionnaire but contained in the tables— Cambodian, Hmong, Laotian, Thai, Bangladeshi, Burmese, Indonesian, Malayan, Okinawan, Pakistani, Sri Lankan, Tongan, Tahitian, Northern Mariana Islander, Palauan, and Fijian—were tabulated from write-in responses.

The "Other race" category includes persons not included in the race categories described above. Persons reporting in the "Other race" category and providing write-in entries such as a Spanish/Hispanic origin group (i.e., Mexican, Cuban, Puerto Rican) are included here.

Spanish/Hispanic origin

Persons of Spanish/Hispanic origin or descent are those who classify themselves in one of the specific Hispanic origin categories listed on the census questionnaire—for example, Mexican, Puerto Rican, or Cuban—as well as those who indicated that they were of other Spanish/Hispanic origin. Persons reporting "Other Spanish/Hispanic" are those whose origins are from other Spanish-speaking countries of the Caribbean, Central or South America, or from Spain, or persons identifying themselves generally as Spanish, Spanish-American, Hispano, Hispanic, Latino, etc.

Spanish origin and race are distinct; thus, persons of Spanish/Hispanic origin may be of any race.

The Census

On April 1, 1990, the Bureau of the Census began to take the 21st decennial census of the United States. The Census Bureau took the first census in 1790, when it counted 3.9 million people, and has conducted a census every 10 years over the past 200 years, as mandated by the U.S. Constitution, Article 1, Section 2. The primary purpose of the census was, and is, to provide population counts needed to apportion seats in the U.S. House of Representatives, and to subsequently determine state legislative district boundaries. In addition, the findings of the 1990 census are critical to many other national, state, and local programs, which: determine compliances with the Voting Rights Act and amendments; allocate funds from federal grant programs; identify areas needing bilingual education; assess the need for equal employment opportunity programs; allocate funds and analyze programs for American Indians and Alaska Natives; identify areas needing energy assistance; develop programs to reduce unemployment; identify areas needing programs to stimulate economic growth; establish fair lending practices; assess the need for developing or expanding low-income housing programs; and identify areas requiring child assistance programs. For state and local government programs, the census results will help: develop social services programs, including programs for the elderly and handicapped; assess transportation systems and improve commuting patterns; identify areas for low-cost housing programs; establish occupational and vocational education programs; plan school district boundaries and school construction programs; and assess the need for state housing bonds for below-market interest rates on mortgages.

U.S. Places of 5,000 or More Population—With ZIP and Area Codes

Source: Bureau of the Census; U.S. Commerce Dept., 1990 Census

This listing presents the official 1990 Census counts. They show the official urban population of the United States. "Urban population" is defined as all persons living in (a) places of 5,000 inhabitants or more, incorporated as cities, villages, boroughs (except Alaska), and towns (except in New England, New York, New Jersey, Pennsylvania and Wisconsin), but excluding those persons living in the rural portions of extended cities; (b) unincorporated places of 5,000 inhabitants or more; and (c) other territory, incorporated or unincorporated, included in urbanized areas.

The non-urban portion of an extended city contains one or more areas, each at least 5 square miles in extent and with a population density of less than 100 persons per square mile. The area or areas constitute at least 25 percent of the legal city's land area of a total of 25 square miles or more.

In New England, New York, New Jersey, Pennsylvania, and Wisconsin, minor civil divisions called "towns" often include rural areas and one or more urban areas. Only the urban areas of these "towns" are included here, except in the case of New England where entire town populations, which may include some rural population, are shown; these towns are indicated by italics. Boroughs in Alaska may contain one or more urban areas which are included here. Population in Hawaii is counted by county subdivisions.

(u) means place is unincorporated.

The ZIP Code of each place appears before the name of that place, if it is obtainable. Telephone Area Code appears in parentheses after the name of the state or, if a state has more than one number, after the name of the place.

CAUTION—Where an asterisk (*) appears before the ZIP Code, ask your local postmaster for the correct ZIP Code for a specific address within the place listed.

Note: Due to deadline constraints, zip and area codes for places that reached 5,000 population in 1990 are not included.

Alabama (205)

ZIP code	Place	1990	1980
35007	Alabaster	14,732	7,079
35950	Albertville	14,507	12,039
35010	Alexander City	14,917	13,807
36420	Andalusia	9,269	10,415
36201	Anniston	26,623	29,135
35016	Arab	6,321	6,053
35611	Athens	16,901	14,558
36502	Atmore	8,046	8,789
35954	Attalla	6,859	7,737
36830	Auburn	33,830	28,471
36507	Bay Minette	7,168	7,455
35020	Bessemer	33,497	31,729
*35203	Birmingham	265,968	284,413
35957	Boaz	6,928	7,151
36426	Brewton	5,885	6,680
35215	Center Point(u)	22,658	23,317
36611	Chickasaw	6,649	7,402
35045	Clanton	7,669	5,832
35055	Cullman	13,367	13,084
	Daleville	5,117	4,250
	Daphne	11,290	3,406
35601	Decatur	48,761	42,002
36732	Demopolis	7,512	7,678
36301	Dothan	53,589	48,750
36330	Enterprise	20,123	18,033
36027	Eufaula	13,220	12,097
35064	Fairfield	12,200	13,242
36532	Fairhope	8,485	7,286
35630	Florence	36,426	37,029
35214	Forestdale(u)	10,395	10,814
35967	Fort Payne	11,838	11,485
36360	Fort Rucker(u)	7,593	8,932
35068	Fultondale	6,400	6,217
*35901	Gadsden	42,523	47,565
35071	Gardendale	9,251	8,005
36037	Greenville	7,492	7,807
35976	Guntersville	7,038	7,041
	Hamilton	5,787	5,093
35640	Hartselle	10,795	8,858
35209	Homewood	22,922	21,412
35226	Hoover	39,788	18,996
35020	Hueytown	15,280	13,452
*35804	Huntsville	159,789	142,513
35210	Irondale	9,454	6,510
36545	Jackson	5,819	6,073
36265	Jacksonville	10,283	9,735
35501	Jasper	13,553	11,894
36863	Lanett	8,985	8,922
35094	Leeds	9,946	8,638
	Madison	14,904	4,057
35228	Midfield	5,559	6,182
	Millbrook	6,050	3,101
*36601	Mobile	196,278	200,452
36460	Monroeville	6,993	5,674
*36104	Montgomery	187,106	177,857
35223	Mountain Brook	19,810	19,718
35660	Muscle Shoals	9,611	8,911
35476	Northport	17,366	14,291
36801	Opelika	22,122	21,896
36467	Opp	6,985	7,204
36203	Oxford	9,362	8,939
36360	Ozark	12,922	13,188
35124	Pelham	9,765	6,759

ZIP code	Place	1990	1980
35125	Pell City	8,118	6,616
36867	Phenix City	25,312	26,928
36272	Piedmont	5,288	5,544
	Pinson-Clay-Chalkville	10,987	....
35127	Pleasant Grove	8,458	7,102
36067	Prattville	19,587	18,647
36610	Prichard	34,311	39,541
35901	Rainbow City	7,673	6,299
36274	Roanoke	6,362	5,809
35653	Russellville	7,812	8,195
36201	Saks(u)	11,138	11,118
36571	Saraland	11,751	9,833
	Satsuma	5,194	3,822
35768	Scottsboro	13,786	14,758
36701	Selma	23,755	26,684
35660	Sheffield	10,380	11,903
35901	Southside	5,580	5,141
35150	Sylacauga	12,520	12,708
35160	Talladega	18,175	19,128
	Tallassee	5,112	4,763
35217	Tarrant City	8,046	8,148
36582	Theodore(u)	6,509	6,392
36619	Tillman's Corner(u)	17,988	15,941
36081	Troy	13,051	13,124
	Trussville	8,266	3,507
35401	Tuscaloosa	77,759	75,211
35674	Tuscumbia	8,413	9,137
36083	Tuskegee	12,257	13,327
	Valley	8,173	8,946
35216	Vestavia Hills	19,749	15,722

Alaska (907)

ZIP code	Place	1990	1980
*99502	Anchorage	226,338	174,431
	College	11,249	4,043
99702	Eielson AFB(u)	5,251	5,232
*99701	Fairbanks	30,843	22,645
99801	Juneau	26,751	19,528
99611	Kenai	6,327	4,324
99901	Ketchikan	8,263	7,198
	Kodiak	6,365	4,756
99835	Sitka	8,588	7,803

Arizona (602)

ZIP code	Place	1990	1980
85220	Apache Junction	18,100	9,935
85323	Avondale	16,169	8,168
85603	Bisbee	6,288	7,154
	Buckeye	5,038	3,434
86430	Bullhead City	21,951	10,719
	Camp Verde	6,243	3,824
85222	Casa Grande	19,082	14,971
*85224	Chandler	90,533	29,673
	Chinle	5,059	2,815
85228	Coolidge	6,927	6,851
	Cottonwood	5,918	4,550
	Cottonwood-Verde Village	7,037	....
85607	Douglas	12,822	13,058
	El Mirage	5,001	4,307
85231	Eloy	7,211	6,240

ZIP code	Place	1990	1980
*86001	Flagstaff	45,857	34,743
.....	Florence	7,510	3,391
.....	Flowing Wells	14,013	....
.....	Fortuna Foothills	7,737	....
.....	Fountain Hills	10,030	2,771
85234	Gilbert	29,188	5,717
*85301	Glendale	148,134	97,172
85501	Globe	6,062	6,886
.....	Goodyear	6,258	2,747
85614	Green Valley(u)	13,231	7,999
.....	Guadalupe	5,458	4,506
86401	Kingman	12,722	9,257
86403	Lake Havasu City	24,363	15,909
*85201	Mesa	288,091	152,404
.....	Mohave Valley	6,962	....
.....	New Kingman-Butler	11,627	....
85621	Nogales	19,489	15,683
.....	Oro Valley	6,670	1,489
86040	Page(u)	6,598	4,907
85253	Paradise Valley	11,671	11,085
.....	Payson	8,377	5,068
85345	Peoria	50,618	12,171
*85026	Phoenix	983,403	789,704
86301	Prescott	26,455	19,865
.....	Prescott Valley	8,858	2,284
85546	Safford	7,359	7,010
*85251	Scottsdale	130,069	88,622
.....	Sedona	7,720	5,319
.....	Show Low	5,019	4,298
85635	Sierra Vista	32,983	24,937
.....	Sierra Vista Southeast	9,237	....
.....	Somerton	5,282	3,969
85713	South Tucson	5,093	6,554
*85351	Sun City(u)	38,126	40,505
.....	Sun City West	15,997	3,772
.....	Sun Lakes	6,578	....
.....	Suprise	7,122	3,723
*85282	Tempe	141,865	106,919
86045	Tuba City(u)	7,323	5,045
*85726	Tucson	405,390	330,537
86047	Winslow	8,190	7,921
*85364	Yuma	54,923	42,481

Arkansas (501)

ZIP code	Place	1990	1980
71923	Arkadelphia	10,014	10,005
.....	Ashdown	5,150	4,218
.....	Bella Vista	9,083	2,589
72501	Batesville	9,187	8,447
72015	Benton	18,177	17,717
72712	Bentonville	11,257	8,756
72315	Blytheville	22,906	23,844
.....	Bryant	5,269	2,682
.....	Cabot	8,319	4,806
71701	Camden	14,380	15,356
72830	Clarksville	5,833	5,237
72032	Conway	26,481	20,375
71635	Crossett	6,282	6,706
71639	Dumas	5,520	6,091
71730	El Dorado	23,146	25,270
72701	Fayetteville	42,099	36,608
72335	Forrest City	13,364	13,803
72901	Fort Smith	72,798	71,626
72601	Harrison	9,922	9,567
.....	Heber Springs	5,628	4,589
72342	Helena	7,491	9,598
71801	Hope	9,643	10,290
71901	Hot Springs	32,462	35,781
.....	Hot Springs Village	6,361	2,083
72076	Jacksonville	29,101	27,589
72401	Jonesboro	46,535	31,530
*72201	Little Rock	175,795	159,151
71753	Magnolia	11,151	11,909
72104	Malvern	9,256	10,163
72360	Marianna	5,910	6,220
.....	Maumelle	6,714	1,368
71953	Mena	5,475	5,154
71655	Monticello	8,116	8,259
72110	Morrilton	6,551	7,355
72653	Mountain Home	9,027	8,066
72112	Newport	7,459	8,339
*72114	North Little Rock	61,741	64,388
72370	Osceola	8,930	8,881
72450	Paragould	18,540	15,248
71601	Pine Bluff	57,140	56,636
72455	Pocahontas	6,151	5,995
72756	Rogers	24,692	17,429
72801	Russellville	21,260	14,518
72143	Searcy	15,180	13,612
72116	Sherwood	18,893	10,423
72761	Siloam Springs	8,151	7,940
72764	Springdale	29,941	23,458
72160	Stuttgart	10,420	10,941
75502	Texarkana	22,631	21,459
72472	Trumann	6,304	6,395
72956	Van Buren	14,979	12,020
71671	Warren	6,455	7,646
72390	West Helena	9,695	11,367

ZIP code	Place	1990	1980
72301	West Memphis	28,259	28,138
72396	Wynne	8,817	7,927

California

ZIP code	Place		1990	1980
94501	Adelanto		8,517	2,164
.....	Agoura Hills		20,390	11,399
.....	Alameda		76,459	63,852
94507	Alamo(u)	(415)	12,277	8,505
94706	Albany	(415)	16,327	15,130
*91802	Alhambra	(818)	82,106	64,767
.....	Aliso		7,612	....
90249	Alondra Park(u)	(310)	12,215	12,096
92001	Alpine(u)	(619)	9,695	5,368
91001	Altadena(u)	(818)	42,658	40,510
.....	Alta Sierra		5,709	2,168
94590	American Canyon(u)	(707)	7,706	5,712
*92803	Anaheim	(714)	266,406	219,494
96007	Anderson	(916)	8,299	7,381
94509	Antioch	(415)	62,195	42,683
92307	Apple Valley(u)	(619)	46,079	16,748
95003	Aptos(u)	(408)	9,061	7,039
91006	Arcadia	(818)	48,290	45,993
95521	Arcata	(707)	15,197	12,849
95825	Arden-Arcade(u)	(916)	92,040	87,570
93420	Arroyo Grande	(805)	14,378	11,290
90701	Artesia	(310)	15,464	14,301
93203	Arvin	(805)	9,286	6,863
94577	Ashland(u)	(415)	16,590	13,893
93422	Atascadero	(805)	23,138	16,232
94025	Atherton	(415)	7,163	7,797
95301	Atwater	(209)	22,282	17,530
95603	Auburn	(916)	10,592	7,540
92505	August(u)	(714)	6,376	5,445
.....	Avenal		9,770	4,137
91746	Avocado Heights(u)	(818)	14,232	11,721
91702	Azusa	(818)	41,333	29,380
*93302	Bakersfield	(805)	174,820	105,611
91706	Baldwin Park	(818)	69,330	50,554
92220	Banning	(714)	20,570	14,020
92311	Barstow	(619)	21,472	17,690
93402	Baywood-Los Osos(u)	(805)	14,377	10,933
95903	Beale AFB East(u)	(916)	6,912	6,329
92223	Beaumont	(714)	9,685	6,818
90201	Bell	(213)	34,365	25,450
90706	Bellflower	(213)	61,815	53,441
90201	Bell Gardens	(213)	42,355	34,117
94002	Belmont	(415)	24,127	24,505
94510	Benicia	(707)	24,437	15,376
95005	Ben Lomond(u)	(408)	7,884	7,238
*94704	Berkeley	(415)	102,724	103,328
*90213	Beverly Hills	(310)	31,971	32,646
92314	Big Bear(u)	(714)	5,351	4,896
.....	Blackhawk		6,199	....
92316	Bloomington(u)	(714)	15,116	12,781
92225	Blythe	(619)	8,428	6,805
.....	Bonadella Ranchos-Madera Ranchos		5,705	3,272
92002	Bonita(u)	(619)	12,542	6,257
.....	Bostonia		13,670	....
95006	Boulder Creek(u)	(408)	6,725	5,662
.....	Boyes Hot Springs		5,973	4,177
92227	Brawley	(619)	18,923	14,946
92621	Brea	(714)	32,873	27,913
.....	Brentwood		7,563	4,434
*90620	Buena Park	(714)	68,784	64,165
*91505	Burbank	(818)	93,643	84,625
94010	Burlingame	(415)	26,801	26,173
92231	Calexico	(619)	18,633	14,412
.....	California City		5,955	2,743
93010	Camarillo	(805)	52,303	37,797
.....	Cambria		5,382	3,061
95682	Cameron Park(u)	(916)	11,897	5,607
95008	Campbell	(408)	36,048	26,843
.....	Camp Pendleton North		10,373	2,065
92055	Camp Pendleton South(u)	(714)	11,299	7,952
.....	Canyon Lake		7,938	2,039
95010	Capitola	(408)	10,171	9,095
*92008	Carlsbad	(619)	63,126	35,490
95608	Carmichael(u)	(916)	48,702	43,108
93013	Carpinteria	(805)	13,747	10,835
90744	Carson	(310)	83,995	81,221
92077	Casa de Oro-Mt. Helix(u)	(619)	30,727	19,651
94546	Castro Valley(u)	(415)	48,619	44,011
.....	Castroville		5,272	4,396
.....	Cathedral City		30,085	11,096
95307	Ceres	(209)	26,314	13,281
90701	Cerritos	(310)	53,240	53,020
91724	Charter Oak(u)	(818)	8,858	6,840
94541	Cherryland(u)	(415)	11,088	9,425
92223	Cherry Valley(u)	(714)	5,945	5,012
95926	Chico	(916)	40,079	26,716
91710	Chino	(714)	59,682	40,165
.....	Chino Hills		27,608	....
93610	Chowchilla	(209)	5,930	5,122
*92010	Chula Vista	(619)	135,163	83,927
95610	Citrus(u)	(916)	9,481	12,450
95610	Citrus Heights(u)	(916)	107,439	85,911

ZIP code	Place	Area	1990	1980
91711	Claremont	(714)	32,503	31,028
.....	Clayton		7,317	4,325
.....	Clearlake		11,804	8,343
93612	Clovis	(209)	50,323	33,021
92236	Coachella	(619)	16,896	9,129
93210	Coalinga	(209)	8,212	6,593
92324	Colton	(714)	40,213	21,310
90022	Commerce	(310)	12,135	10,509
*90220	Compton	(310)	90,454	81,350
*94520	Concord	(415)	111,348	103,763
93212	Corcoran	(209)	13,364	6,454
.....	Corning		5,870	4,745
91720	Corona	(714)	76,095	37,791
92118	Coronado	(619)	26,540	18,790
94925	Corte Madera	(415)	8,272	8,074
*92626	Costa Mesa	(714)	96,357	82,562
.....	Cotati		5,714	3,346
.....	Country Club(u)	(209)	9,325	9,585
*91722	Covina	(818)	43,207	32,746
92325	Crestline(u)	(714)	8,594	6,715
90201	Cudahy	(310)	22,817	18,275
*90230	Culver City	(310)	38,793	38,139
95014	Cupertino	(408)	40,263	34,297
90630	Cypress	(714)	42,655	40,738
*94017	Daly City	(415)	92,311	78,519
92629	Dana Point	(714)	31,896	21,271
*94526	Danville	(415)	31,306	26,143
95616	Davis	(916)	46,209	36,640
90250	Del Aire(u)	(310)	8,040	8,487
93215	Delano	(805)	22,762	16,491
.....	Del Monte Forest		5,069	....
92240	Desert Hot Springs	(619)	11,668	5,941
91765	Diamond Bar(u)	(714)	53,672	30,736
93618	Dinuba	(209)	12,743	9,907
.....	Discovery Bay		5,351	1,326
95620	Dixon	(916)	10,401	7,541
*90241	Downey	(310)	91,444	82,602
91010	Duarte	(818)	20,688	16,766
94568	Dublin	(415)	23,229	13,496
.....	Earlimart		5,881	4,578
90220	East Compton(u)	(310)	7,967	6,435
.....	East Foothills		14,898	....
92343	East Hemet(u)	(714)	17,611	14,712
90638	East La Mirada(u)	(310)	9,367	9,468
90022	East Los Angeles(u)	(310)	126,379	110,017
94303	East Palo Alto	(415)	23,451	18,106
.....	East Pasadena		5,910	....
93257	East Porterville(u)	(209)	5,790	5,218
.....	East San Gabriel		12,736	....
93523	Edwards AFB(u)	(805)	7,423	8,554
*92020	El Cajon	(619)	88,693	73,892
92243	El Centro	(619)	31,384	23,996
94530	El Cerrito	(415)	22,869	22,731
.....	El Dorado Hills		6,395	....
95624	Elk Grove(u)	(916)	17,483	10,959
*91734	El Monte	(818)	106,209	79,494
93446	El Paso de Robles	(310)	18,583	9,163
93030	El Rio(u)	(805)	6,419	5,674
90245	El Segundo	(310)	15,223	13,752
94803	El Sobrante(u)	(415)	9,852	10,535
92630	El Toro(u)	(714)	62,685	38,153
92709	El Toro Station(u)	(714)	6,869	7,632
.....	Emeryville		5,740	3,714
92024	Encinitas	(619)	55,386	36,550
*92025	Escondido	(619)	108,635	64,355
95501	Eureka	(707)	27,025	24,153
93221	Exeter	(209)	7,276	5,606
94930	Fairfax	(415)	6,931	7,391
94533	Fairfield	(707)	77,211	58,099
95628	Fair Oaks(u)	(916)	26,867	22,602
.....	Fairview		6,049	....
92028	Fallbrook(u)	(619)	22,095	14,041
93223	Farmersville	(209)	6,235	5,544
.....	Felton		5,350	4,564
93015	Fillmore	(805)	11,992	9,602
90001	Florence-Graham(u)	(310)	57,147	48,662
95828	Florin(u)	(916)	24,330	16,523
95630	Folsom	(916)	29,802	11,003
*92335	Fontana	(714)	87,535	36,804
95841	Foothill Farms(u)	(916)	17,135	13,700
95437	Fort Bragg	(707)	6,078	5,019
95540	Fortuna	(707)	8,788	7,591
94404	Foster City	(415)	28,176	23,287
92708	Fountain Valley	(714)	53,691	55,080
95019	Freedom(u)	(408)	8,361	6,416
*94536	Fremont	(415)	173,339	131,945
*93706	Fresno	(209)	354,202	217,491
*92631	Fullerton	(714)	114,144	102,246
95632	Galt	(209)	8,889	5,514
90247	Gardena	(310)	49,847	45,165
95205	Garden Acres(u)	(213)	8,547	7,361
*92640	Garden Grove	(714)	143,050	123,307
92392	George AFB(u)	(619)	5,085	7,061
95020	Gilroy	(408)	31,487	21,641
92509	Glen Avon(u)	(714)	12,663	8,444
*91209	Glendale	(818)	180,038	139,060
91740	Glendora	(818)	47,828	38,500
.....	Golden Hills		5,423	....
92324	Grand Terrace	(714)	10,946	8,498
95945	Grass Valley	(916)	9,048	6,697
93308	Greenacres(u)	(805)	7,379	5,381
.....	Greenfield		7,464	4,181
93433	Grover City	(805)	11,656	8,827
.....	Guadalupe		5,479	3,629
91745	Hacienda Heights	(818)	52,354	49,422
94019	Half Moon Bay	(415)	8,886	7,282
93230	Hanford	(209)	30,897	20,958
90716	Hawaiian Gardens	(310)	13,639	10,548
90250	Hawthorne	(310)	71,349	56,437
*94544	Hayward	(415)	111,498	93,585
95448	Healdsburg	(707)	9,469	7,217
92343	Hemet	(714)	36,094	22,531
94547	Hercules	(415)	16,829	5,963
90254	Hermosa Beach	(310)	18,219	18,070
92345	Hesperia	(619)	50,418	20,612
92346	Highland	(714)	34,439	21,720
94010	Hillsborough	(415)	10,667	10,372
95023	Hollister	(408)	19,212	11,488
91720	Home Gardens(u)	(714)	7,780	5,783
*92647	Huntington Beach	(714)	181,519	170,505
90255	Huntington Park	(310)	56,065	45,932
92032	Imperial Beach	(619)	26,512	22,689
92201	Indio	(619)	36,793	21,611
*90306	Inglewood	(310)	109,602	94,162
.....	Interlake		6,404	....
.....	Ione		6,516	2,207
*92711	Irvine	(714)	110,330	62,134
.....	Isla Vista		20,395	....
.....	Kentfield		6,030	....
.....	Kerman		5,448	4,002
93930	King City	(408)	7,634	5,495
93631	Kingsburg	(209)	7,205	5,115
91011	La Canada-Flintridge	(818)	19,378	20,153
91214	La Crescenta-Montrose(u)	(818)	16,968	16,531
90045	Ladera Heights(u)	(310)	6,316	6,647
94549	Lafayette	(415)	23,501	20,837
.....	Laguna		9,828	....
*92651	Laguna Beach	(714)	23,170	17,858
92653	Laguna Hills(u)	(714)	46,731	33,600
92677	Laguna Niguel(u)	(714)	44,400	12,237
90631	La Habra	(714)	51,266	45,232
.....	La Habra Heights		6,226	4,786
92352	Lake Arrowhead(u)	(714)	6,539	6,272
92330	Lake Elsinore	(714)	18,285	5,982
.....	Lakeland Village		5,159	2,796
.....	Lake Los Angeles		7,977	....
.....	Lakeside(u)		39,412	23,921
92041	La Mesa	(619)	52,931	50,308
90638	La Mirada	(310)	40,452	40,986
93241	Lamont(u)	(805)	11,517	9,616
93534	Lancaster	(805)	97,291	48,027
90624	La Palma	(310)	15,392	15,399
91747	La Puente	(818)	36,955	30,882
.....	La Quinta		11,215	4,027
*90714	Lakewood	(310)	73,557	74,511
.....	La Riviera(u)	(916)	10,986	10,906
.....	Larkfield-Wikiup		6,779	....
94939	Larkspur	(415)	11,070	11,064
.....	Lathrop		6,841	4,112
91750	La Verne	(714)	30,897	23,508
90260	Lawndale	(310)	27,331	23,460
92045	Lemon Grove	(619)	23,984	20,780
93245	Lemoore	(209)	13,622	8,832
90304	Lennox(u)	(310)	22,757	18,445
93207	Lincoln Village(u)	(916)	7,248	4,132
95901	Linda(u)	(916)	13,033	10,225
93247	Lindsay	(209)	8,338	6,936
95062	Live Oak(u) (Santa Cruz)	(916)	15,212	11,482
94550	Livermore	(415)	56,741	48,349
95534	Livingston	(209)	7,317	5,326
*95240	Lodi	(209)	51,874	35,221
92354	Loma Linda	(714)	17,400	10,694
90717	Lomita	(310)	19,382	18,807
93436	Lompoc	(805)	37,649	26,267
*90801	Long Beach	(310)	429,433	361,498
.....	Loomis		5,705	3,663
90720	Los Alamitos	(714)	11,676	11,529
94022	Los Altos	(415)	26,303	25,769
94022	Los Altos Hills	(415)	7,514	7,421
*90052	Los Angeles	(213)	3,485,398	2,968,528
93635	Los Banos	(209)	14,519	10,341
95030	Los Gatos	(408)	27,357	26,906
.....	Los Serranos		7,099	....
94903	Lucas Valley-Marinwood(u)	(415)	5,982	6,409
90262	Lynwood	(310)	61,945	48,289
93250	Mc Farland	(805)	7,005	5,151
95521	McKinleyville(u)	(707)	10,749	7,772
93637	Madera	(209)	29,281	21,732
.....	Madera Acres		5,245	2,173
.....	Magalia		8,987	....
90266	Manhattan Beach	(310)	32,063	31,542
95336	Manteca	(209)	40,773	24,925
.....	March AFB		5,523	3,607
93933	Marina	(408)	26,436	20,647
90292	Marina Del Rey(u)	(310)	7,431	8,065
94553	Martinez	(415)	31,808	22,582
95901	Marysville	(916)	12,324	9,898
90270	Maywood	(213)	27,850	21,810

ZIP code	Place		1990	1980
93640	Mendota	(209)	6,821	5,038
94025	Menlo Park	(415)	28,040	26,438
.....	Mentone		5,675	....
*95340	Merced	(209)	56,216	36,423
94030	Millbrae	(415)	20,412	20,058
94941	Mill Valley	(415)	13,038	12,967
95035	Milpitas	(408)	50,686	37,820
91752	Mira Loma(u)	(714)	15,786	8,707
.....	Mira Monte		7,744	....
92675	Mission Viejo	(714)	72,820	48,503
*95350	Modesto	(209)	164,730	106,963
91016	Monrovia	(818)	35,761	30,531
91763	Montclair	(714)	28,434	22,628
90640	Montebello	(213)	59,564	52,929
93940	Monterey	(408)	31,954	27,558
91754	Monterey Park	(818)	60,738	54,338
.....	Moorpark		25,494	7,798
94556	Moraga	(415)	15,852	15,014
.....	Moreno Valley		118,779	28,139
95037	Morgan Hill	(408)	23,928	17,060
93442	Morro Bay	(805)	9,664	9,064
*94042	Mountain View	(415)	67,460	58,655
92405	Muscoy(u)	(714)	7,541	6,188
94558	Napa	(707)	61,842	50,879
92050	National City	(619)	54,249	48,772
.....	Needles		5,191	4,120
94560	Newark	(415)	37,861	32,126
*92660	Newport Beach	(714)	66,643	62,556
93444	Nipomo(u)	(805)	7,109	5,247
91760	Norco	(714)	23,302	19,732
95603	North Auburn(u)	(916)	10,301	7,619
94025	North Fair Oaks(u)	(415)	13,912	10,308
95660	North Highlands(u)	(916)	42,105	37,825
90650	Norwalk	(310)	94,279	84,901
94947	Novato	(415)	47,585	43,916
95361	Oakdale	(209)	11,961	8,474
*94615	Oakland	(415)	372,242	339,337
.....	Oakley		18,374	2,816
.....	Oceano		6,169	4,478
*92054	Oceanside	(619)	128,398	76,698
93308	Oildale(u)	(805)	26,553	23,382
93023	Ojai	(805)	7,613	6,816
95961	Olivehurst(u)	(916)	9,738	8,929
*91761	Ontario	(714)	133,179	88,820
95060	Opal Cliffs(u)	(408)	5,940	5,041
*92667	Orange	(714)	110,658	91,450
.....	Orange Cove		5,604	4,026
95662	Orangevale(u)	(916)	26,266	20,585
94563	Orinda	(415)	16,642	17,030
.....	Orland		5,052	4,031
.....	Orosi		5,486	4,076
95965	Oroville	(916)	11,960	8,683
.....	Oroville East		8,462	....
93030	Oxnard	(805)	142,216	108,195
94044	Pacifica	(415)	37,670	36,866
93950	Pacific Grove	(408)	16,117	15,755
.....	Palermo		5,260	2,572
93550	Palmdale	(805)	68,842	12,277
92260	Palm Desert	(619)	23,252	11,801
.....	Palm Desert Country		5,626	....
92262	Palm Springs	(619)	40,181	32,359
*94302	Palo Alto	(415)	55,900	55,225
90274	Palos Verdes Estates	(310)	13,512	14,376
95969	Paradise	(916)	25,408	22,571
90723	Paramount	(310)	47,669	36,407
95823	Parkway-Sacramento So.(u)	(916)	31,903	26,815
.....	Parlier		7,938	2,902
*91109	Pasadena	(818)	131,591	118,072
.....	Patterson		8,626	3,908
.....	Pedley		8,869	....
92370	Perris	(714)	21,460	6,827
94952	Petaluma	(707)	43,184	33,834
90660	Pico Rivera	(213)	59,177	53,387
94611	Piedmont	(415)	10,602	10,498
94564	Pinole	(415)	17,460	14,253
93449	Pismo Beach	(805)	7,669	5,364
94565	Pittsburg	(415)	47,564	33,465
92670	Placentia	(714)	41,259	35,041
95667	Placerville	(916)	8,355	6,739
94523	Pleasant Hill	(415)	31,585	25,547
94566	Pleasanton	(415)	50,553	35,160
*91766	Pomona	(714)	131,723	92,742
93257	Porterville	(209)	29,563	19,707
93041	Port Hueneme	(805)	20,319	17,803
92064	Poway	(619)	43,516	33,439
.....	Prunedale		7,393	....
93534	Quartz Hill(u)	(213)	9,626	7,421
92065	Ramona(u)	(619)	13,040	8,173
95670	Rancho Cordova(u)	(916)	48,731	42,881
91730	Rancho Cucamonga	(714)	101,409	55,250
92270	Rancho Mirage	(619)	9,778	6,281
90274	Rancho Palos Verdes	(310)	41,659	36,577
.....	Rancho San Diego		6,977	....
.....	Rancho Santa Margarita		11,390	....
96080	Red Bluff	(916)	12,363	9,490
96001	Redding	(916)	66,462	42,103
92373	Redlands	(714)	60,394	43,619
*90277	Redondo Beach	(310)	60,167	57,102
*94064	Redwood City	(415)	66,072	54,951

ZIP code	Place		1990	1980
93654	Reedley	(209)	15,791	11,071
92376	Rialto	(714)	72,388	37,862
*94802	Richmond	(415)	87,425	74,676
93555	Ridgecrest	(619)	27,725	15,929
95003	Rio Del Mar(u)	(408)	8,919	7,067
95673	Rio Linda(u)	(916)	9,481	7,359
.....	Ripon		7,455	3,509
95367	Riverbank	(209)	8,547	5,695
*92502	Riverside	(714)	226,505	170,591
95677	Rocklin	(916)	19,033	7,344
94572	Rodeo(u)	(415)	7,589	8,286
94928	Rohnert Park	(707)	36,326	22,965
90274	Rolling Hills Estates	(310)	7,789	7,701
.....	Rosamond		7,430	2,869
95401	Roseland(u)	(707)	8,779	7,915
91770	Rosemead	(818)	51,638	42,604
95826	Rosemont(u)	(916)	22,851	18,888
95678	Roseville	(916)	44,685	24,347
90720	Rossmoor(u)	(714)	9,893	10,457
91745	Rowland Heights(u)	(818)	42,647	28,252
92509	Rubidoux(u)	(714)	24,367	16,763
*95813	Sacramento	(916)	369,365	275,741
93901	Salinas	(408)	108,777	80,479
94960	San Anselmo	(415)	11,743	12,067
*92403	San Bernardino	(714)	164,164	118,794
94066	San Bruno	(415)	38,961	35,417
93001	San Buenaventura (Ventura)	(805)	92,575	73,774
94070	San Carlos	(415)	26,167	24,710
92672	San Clemente	(714)	41,100	27,325
*92109	San Diego	(619)	1,110,549	875,538
.....	San Diego County Estates		6,874	....
91773	San Dimas	(714)	32,397	24,014
*91340	San Fernando	(818)	22,580	17,731
*94101	San Francisco	(415)	723,959	678,974
91776	San Gabriel	(818)	37,120	30,072
93657	Sanger	(209)	16,839	12,542
92383	San Jacinto	(714)	16,210	7,098
*95101	San Jose	(408)	782,248	629,400
92675	San Juan Capistrano	(714)	26,183	18,959
*94577	San Leandro	(415)	68,223	63,952
94580	San Lorenzo(u)	(415)	19,987	20,545
93401	San Luis Obispo	(805)	41,958	34,252
92069	San Marcos	(619)	38,974	17,479
91108	San Marino	(818)	12,959	13,307
*94402	San Mateo	(415)	85,486	77,640
94806	San Pablo	(415)	25,158	19,750
*94901	San Rafael	(415)	48,404	44,700
94583	San Ramon	(415)	35,303	20,511
*92711	Santa Ana	(714)	293,742	204,023
*93102	Santa Barbara	(805)	85,571	74,414
*95050	Santa Clara	(408)	93,613	87,700
.....	Santa Clarita		110,642	66,730
95060	Santa Cruz	(408)	49,040	41,483
90670	Santa Fe Springs	(310)	15,520	14,520
93454	Santa Maria	(805)	61,284	39,685
*90406	Santa Monica	(310)	86,905	88,314
93060	Santa Paula	(805)	25,062	20,658
*95402	Santa Rosa	(707)	113,313	82,658
92071	Santee	(619)	52,902	40,298
95070	Saratoga	(408)	28,061	29,261
94965	Sausalito	(415)	7,152	7,338
95066	Scotts Valley	(408)	8,615	6,891
90740	Seal Beach	(310)	25,098	25,975
93955	Seaside	(408)	38,901	36,567
95472	Sebastopol	(707)	7,004	5,595
93662	Selma	(209)	14,757	10,942
93263	Shafter	(805)	8,409	7,010
91024	Sierra Madre	(818)	10,762	10,837
90806	Signal Hill	(310)	8,371	5,734
*93065	Simi Valley	(805)	100,217	77,500
92075	Solana Beach	(619)	12,962	12,250
93960	Soledad	(408)	7,146	5,928
95476	Sonoma	(707)	8,121	6,054
95073	Soquel(u)	(408)	9,188	6,212
91733	South El Monte	(213)	20,850	16,623
90280	South Gate	(213)	86,284	66,784
95705	South Lake Tahoe	(916)	21,586	20,681
95965	South Oroville(u)	(916)	7,463	7,246
91030	South Pasadena	(818)	23,936	22,681
94080	South San Francisco	(415)	54,312	49,393
91770	South San Gabriel(u)	(213)	7,700	5,421
91744	South San Jose Hills(u)	(818)	17,814	16,049
90605	South Whittier(u)	(310)	49,514	43,815
95991	South Yuba(u)	(916)	8,816	7,530
*92077	Spring Valley(u)	(619)	55,331	40,191
94305	Stanford(u)	(415)	18,097	11,045
90680	Stanton	(714)	30,491	23,723
*95204	Stockton	(209)	210,943	148,283
94585	Suisun City	(707)	22,686	11,087
92381	Sun City(u)	(714)	14,930	8,460
*94086	Sunnyvale	(408)	117,229	106,618
96130	Susanville	(916)	7,279	6,520
93268	Taft	(805)	5,902	5,316
94941	Tamalpais-Homestead Valley(u)	(415)	9,601	8,511
.....	Tehachapi		5,791	4,126
.....	Temecula		27,099	4,289
91780	Temple City	(818)	31,100	28,972
.....	Thermalito		5,646	4,961

ZIP code	Place	1990	1980
*91360	Thousand Oaks....... (805)	104,352	77,072
94920	Tiburon............ (415)	7,532	6,685
*90510	Torrance.......... (310)	133,107	129,881
95396	Tracy............. (209)	33,558	18,428
93274	Tulare............ (209)	33,249	22,530
95380	Turlock........... (209)	42,198	26,287
92680	Tustin............ (714)	50,689	32,248
92705	Tustin-Foothills(u)... (714)	24,358	26,174
92277	Twentynine Palms(u)..... (619)	11,821	8,802
92278	Twentynine Palms Base... (619)	10,606	7,079
.....	Twin Lakes...........	5,379	4,502
95482	Ukiah............. (707)	14,599	12,035
94587	Union City........ (415)	53,762	39,406
91786	Upland............ (714)	63,374	47,647
*95688	Vacaville.......... (707)	71,479	43,367
91744	Valinda(u)......... (818)	18,735	18,700
*94590	Vallejo........... (707)	109,199	80,303
92343	Valle Vista(u)....... (714)	8,751	5,474
93437	Vandenberg AFB(u).... (805)	9,846	5,839
93436	Vandenberg Village(u)... (805)	5,971	5,839
92392	Victorville......... (619)	40,674	14,220
90043	View Park-Windsor Hills(u). (310)	11,769	12,101
92667	Villa Park.......... (714)	6,299	7,137
.....	Vincent............	13,713	....
93277	Visalia............ (209)	75,636	49,729
92083	Vista............. (619)	71,872	35,834
*91789	Walnut............ (714)	29,105	12,478
*94596	Walnut Creek....... (415)	60,569	54,033
90255	Walnut Park(u)...... (213)	14,722	11,811
93280	Wasco............ (805)	12,412	9,613
95076	Watsonville........ (408)	31,099	23,662
90044	West Athens(u)...... (310)	8,859	8,531
90502	West Carson(u)...... (310)	20,143	17,997
90247	West Compton(u)..... (310)	5,451	5,907
*91793	West Covina........ (818)	96,086	80,292
90069	West Hollywood...... (213)	36,118	35,754
.....	Westlake Village	7,455	6,130
92683	Westminster........ (714)	78,118	71,133
90047	Westmont(u)........ (310)	31,044	27,916
94565	West Pittsburg(u)..... (415)	17,453	8,773
91746	West Puente Valley(u)... (818)	20,254	20,445
95591	West Sacramento..... (916)	28,898	24,482
*90606	West Whittier-Los Nietos(u). (310)	24,164	21,001
*90605	Whittier.......... (310)	77,671	68,558
.....	Wildomar...........	10,411	....
.....	Willits............	5,027	4,008
90222	Willowbrook(u)...... (213)	32,772	30,845
.....	Willows...........	5,988	4,777
.....	Windsor...........	13,371	....
.....	Winton............	7,559	4,995
.....	Woodcrest..........	7,796	....
93286	Woodlake.......... (209)	5,678	4,343
95695	Woodland.......... (916)	39,802	30,235
94062	Woodside.......... (415)	5,035	5,291
92686	Yorba Linda........ (714)	52,422	28,254
96097	Yreka City......... (916)	6,948	5,916
95991	Yuba City.......... (916)	27,437	18,736
92399	Yucaipa(u)......... (714)	32,824	27,654
92284	Yucca Valley(u)...... (619)	13,701	8,294

Colorado

ZIP code	Place	1990	1980
80840	Air Force Academy..... (719)	9,062	8,655
81101	Alamosa........... (719)	7,579	6,830
80401	Applewood(u)....... (303)	11,069	12,040
*80001	Arvada........... (303)	89,235	84,576
.....	Aspen............	5,049	3,678
*80010	Aurora........... (303)	222,103	158,588
.....	Black Forest........	8,143	3,372
*80302	Boulder........... (303)	83,312	76,685
80601	Brighton.......... (303)	14,203	12,773
80020	Broomfield......... (303)	24,638	20,730
81212	Canon City......... (719)	12,687	13,037
.....	Castle Rock........	8,708	3,921
.....	Castlewood(u)....... (303)	24,392	16,413
80110	Cherry Hills Village... (303)	5,245	5,127
81220	Cimarron Hills....... (303)	11,160	6,597
81520	Clifton........... (303)	12,671	5,223
*80901	Colorado Springs..... (719)	281,140	215,105
80120	Columbine......... (303)	23,969	23,523
80022	Commerce City...... (303)	16,466	16,234
81321	Cortez........... (303)	7,284	7,095
81625	Craig............ (303)	8,091	8,133
*80817	Denver........... (303)	467,610	492,686
80022	Derby(u).......... (303)	6,043	8,578
81301	Durango.......... (303)	12,430	11,649
*80110	Englewood......... (303)	29,387	30,021
80620	Evans............ (303)	5,877	5,063
80439	Evergreen......... (303)	7,582	6,376
80221	Federal Heights...... (303)	9,342	7,838
80913	Fort Carson(u)...... (303)	11,309	13,219
*80521	Fort Collins........ (303)	87,758	65,092
.....	Fort Lupton........	5,159	4,251
80701	Fort Morgan........ (303)	9,068	8,768
80817	Fountain.......... (719)	9,984	8,324
.....	Fruitvale..........	5,222	....
.....	Gateway...........	7,510	....

ZIP code	Place	1990	1980
.....	Glenwood Springs	6,561	4,637
80401	Golden............ (303)	13,116	12,237
81501	Grand Junction...... (303)	29,034	27,956
*80631	Greeley........... (303)	60,536	53,006
80110	Greenwood Village.... (303)	7,589	5,729
80501	Gunbarrel......... (303)	9,388	5,172
.....	Highlands Ranch	10,181	....
.....	Ken Caryl.......... (303)	24,391	10,661
80026	Lafayette.......... (303)	14,548	8,985
81050	La Junta.......... (719)	7,637	8,338
80215	Lakewood......... (303)	126,481	113,808
81052	Lamar............ (719)	8,343	7,713
*80120	Littleton.......... (303)	33,685	28,631
80501	Longmont......... (303)	51,555	42,942
80027	Louisville......... (303)	12,361	5,593
*80537	Loveland.......... (303)	37,352	30,215
81401	Montrose......... (303)	8,854	8,722
80233	Northglenn........ (303)	27,195	29,847
.....	Orchard Mesa........	5,977	4,876
.....	Parker............	5,450	290
*81003	Pueblo........... (719)	98,640	101,686
.....	Redlands..........	9,355	....
80911	Security-Widefield(u)... (719)	23,822	18,768
80221	Sherrelwood(u)....... (303)	16,636	17,629
80122	Southglenn........ (303)	43,087	37,787
80477	Steamboat Springs... (303)	6,695	5,098
80751	Sterling.......... (303)	10,362	11,385
80906	Stratmoor......... (719)	5,854	5,519
80229	Thornton......... (303)	55,031	42,054
81082	Trinidad.......... (719)	8,580	9,663
80229	Welby(u).......... (303)	10,218	9,668
*80030	Westminster....... (303)	74,625	50,211
80221	Westminster East(u)... (303)	5,197	6,002
80033	Wheat Ridge....... (303)	29,419	30,293
.....	Windsor...........	5,062	4,277

Connecticut (203)

See Note on Page 78

ZIP code	Place	1990	1980
06401	Ansonia	18,403	19,039
06001	Avon	13,937	11,201
.....	Beacon Falls	5,083	....
06037	Berlin	16,787	15,121
06801	Bethel	17,541	8,835
06002	Bloomfield	19,483	18,608
06405	Branford	27,603	5,688
*06602	Bridgeport	141,686	142,546
06010	Bristol	57,370	55,487
06804	Brookfield	14,113	12,872
06234	Brooklyn	6,681	5,691
06013	Burlington	7,026	5,660
06019	Canton	8,268	7,635
.....	Central Manchester	30,934	....
06410	Cheshire	12,199	5,759
06413	Clinton	12,767	11,195
06415	Colchester	10,980	7,761
06340	Conning Towers-Nautilus Park(u).	10,013	9,665
06238	Coventry	10,063	8,895
06416	Cromwell	12,286	10,265
06810	Danbury	65,585	60,470
06820	Darien	18,130	18,892
06418	Derby	12,199	12,199
06422	Durham	5,732	5,143
06423	East Haddam	6,676	5,621
06424	East Hampton	10,428	8,572
06108	East Hartford	50,452	52,563
06512	East Haven	26,144	25,028
06333	East Lyme	13,870	11,399
06016	East Windsor	10,081	8,925
06425	Easton	6,303	5,962
06029	Ellington	11,197	9,711
06082	Enfield	45,532	42,695
06426	Essex	5,904	5,078
06430	Fairfield	53,418	54,849
06032	Farmington	20,608	16,407
06033	Glastonbury Center.....	27,901	7,082
06035	Granby	9,369	7,956
06830	Greenwich	58,441	59,578
06351	Griswold	10,384	8,967
06340	Groton	45,144	9,837
06437	Guilford	19,848	17,375
06333	Haddam	6,769	6,383
06514	Hamden	52,434	51,071
*06101	Hartford	139,739	136,392
.....	Harwinton	5,228	....
06082	Hazardville(u)	5,179	5,436
06037	Kensington(u)	8,306	7,502
06239	Killingly	15,889	14,519
06339	Ledyard	14,913	13,735
06759	Litchfield	8,365	7,365
06443	Madison	14,031	9,768
06040	Manchester	21,103	51,618
06250	Mansfield	20,634	19,994
.....	Marlborough	5,535	....
06450	Meriden	59,479	57,118
06762	Middlebury	6,145	5,995

ZIP code	Place	1990	1980
06457	Middletown	42,762	39,040
06460	Milford	49,938	48,168
06468	Monroe	16,896	14,010
06353	Montville	16,673	16,455
06770	Naugatuck	30,625	26,456
*06050	New Britain	75,491	73,840
06840	New Canaan	17,864	17,931
06810	New Fairfield	12,911	11,260
.....	New Hartford	5,769	.....
*06510	New Haven	130,474	126,089
06111	Newington	29,208	28,841
06320	New London	28,540	28,842
06776	New Milford	23,629	5,775
06470	Newtown	20,779	19,107
06471	North Branford	12,996	11,554
06473	North Haven	22,249	22,080
06856	Norwalk	78,331	77,767
06360	Norwich	37,391	38,074
06779	Oakville(u)	8,741	8,737
06371	Old Lyme	6,535	6,159
06475	Old Saybrook	9,552	9,287
06477	Orange	12,830	13,237
.....	Oxford	8,685	.....
02891	Pawcatuck(u)	5,289	5,216
06374	Plainfield	14,363	17,392
06062	Plainville	16,401	16,733
06782	Plymouth	11,832	10,732
06480	Portland	8,418	5,645
.....	Preston	5,006	.....
06712	Prospect	7,775	6,807
06260	Putnam	6,835	6,855
.....	Putnam	9,031	8,580
06875	Redding	7,927	7,272
06877	Ridgefield Center(u)	6,363	6,066
.....	Ridgefield	20,919	20,120
06067	Rocky Hill	16,554	14,559
06483	Seymour	14,288	13,434
06484	Shelton	35,418	31,314
06082	Sherwood Manor(u)	6,357	6,303
06070	Simsbury	22,023	5,577
.....	Somers	9,108	.....
06488	Southbury	15,818	14,156
06489	Southington	38,518	36,879
06074	South Windsor	22,090	17,198
06082	Southwood Acres(u)	8,963	9,779
06075	Stafford	11,091	9,268
*06904	Stamford	108,056	102,466
06378	Stonington	16,919	6,220
06268	Storrs(u)	12,198	11,394
06497	Stratford	49,389	49,389
06078	Suffield	11,427	9,294
06786	Terryville(u)	5,426	5,234
06787	Thomaston	6,947	6,272
06277	Thompson	8,668	8,141
.....	Thompsonville	8,458	.....
06084	Tolland	11,001	9,694
06790	Torrington	33,687	30,987
06611	Trumbull	32,016	32,000
06066	Vernon	29,841	27,974
06492	Wallingford	40,822	17,827
*06701	Waterbury	108,961	103,266
06385	Waterford	17,930	17,843
06795	Watertown	20,456	19,489
06107	West Hartford	60,110	61,301
06516	West Haven	54,021	53,184
06498	Westbrook	5,414	5,216
06883	Weston	8,648	8,284
06880	Westport	24,410	24,407
06109	Wethersfield	25,651	25,651
06226	Willimantic	14,746	14,652
.....	Willington	5,979	.....
06897	Wilton	15,989	15,351
06094	Winchester	11,524	10,841
06280	Windham	22,039	21,062
06095	Windsor	27,817	25,204
06096	Windsor Locks	12,358	12,190
06098	Winsted	8,254	8,092
06716	Wolcott	13,700	13,008
06525	Woodbridge	7,924	7,761
06798	Woodbury	8,131	6,942
06281	Woodstock	6,008	5,117

Delaware (302)

ZIP code	Place	1990	1980
19713	Brookside(u)	15,307	15,255
19703	Claymont(u)	9,800	10,022
19901	Dover	27,630	23,507
19802	Edgemoor(u)	5,853	7,397
19805	Elsmere	5,935	6,493
19963	Milford	6,040	5,366
*19711	Newark	25,098	25,247
.....	Pike Creek	10,163	.....
19973	Seaford	5,689	5,256
.....	Smyrna	5,231	4,750
19804	Stanton(u)	5,028	5,495
19803	Talleyville(u)	6,346	6,880

ZIP code	Place	1990	1980
*19899	Wilmington	71,529	70,195
19720	Wilmington Manor	8,568	9,233

District of Columbia (202)

ZIP code	Place	1990	1980
*20013	Washington	606,900	638,432

Florida

ZIP code	Place	1990	1980
*32701	Altamonte Springs ...... (407)	34,879	21,105
.....	Andover	6,251	.....
.....	Apollo Beach	6,025	4,014
32703	Apopka (407)	13,512	6,019
33821	Arcadia (813)	6,488	6,002
32233	Atlantic Beach (904)	11,636	7,847
33823	Auburndale (813)	8,858	6,501
.....	Aventura(u) (305)	14,914	9,698
33825	Avon Park (813)	8,042	8,026
32807	Azalea Park(u) (407)	8,926	8,301
33830	Bartow (813)	14,716	14,780
.....	Bay Hill	5,346	.....
.....	Bayonet Point(u) (813)	21,860	16,455
33505	Bayshore Gardens(u) (813)	17,062	14,945
33589	Beacon Square(u) (813)	6,265	6,513
.....	Bee Ridge	6,406	3,313
32073	Bellair-Meadowbrook Terrace(u) (904)	15,606	12,144
33430	Belle Glade (407)	16,177	16,535
.....	Belle Isle	5,272	2,848
32506	Belleview(u) (904)	19,386	15,439
32665	Beverly Hills(u) (904)	6,163	5,024
.....	Bloomingdale	13,912	.....
.....	Boca Del Mar	17,754	.....
*33487	Boca Raton (407)	61,492	49,447
33959	Bonita Springs(u) (813)	13,600	5,435
*33435	Boynton Beach (407)	46,194	35,624
*34206	Bradenton (813)	43,779	30,228
33511	Brandon(u) (813)	57,985	41,826
32525	Brent(u) (904)	21,624	21,872
33317	Broadview Park(u) (305)	6,109	6,022
33313	Broadview-Pompano Park(u) (305)	5,230	5,256
*34601	Brooksville (904)	7,440	5,582
33311	Browardale(u) (305)	6,257	7,571
33142	Brownsville(u) (305)	15,607	18,058
.....	Buena Ventura Lakes	14,148	.....
32401	Callaway (904)	12,253	7,154
32920	Cape Canaveral (407)	8,014	5,733
33904	Cape Coral (813)	74,991	32,103
33055	Carol City(u) (305)	53,331	47,349
.....	Carrollwood	7,195	.....
.....	Carrollwood Village	15,051	.....
32707	Casselberry (407)	18,911	15,037
33401	Century Village(u) (305)	8,363	10,619
*34615	Clearwater City (813)	93,784	85,170
32711	Clermont (904)	6,910	5,461
33440	Clewiston (813)	6,085	5,219
32922	Cocoa (407)	17,722	16,096
32931	Cocoa Beach (407)	12,123	10,926
32922	Cocoa West(u) (407)	6,160	6,432
33066	Coconut Creek (305)	27,485	6,288
33064	Collier Manor-Cresthaven(u) (305)	7,322	7,045
33801	Combee Settlement(u) (813)	5,463	5,400
32809	Conway(u) (407)	13,159	24,027
33314	Cooper City (305)	20,791	10,140
33134	Coral Gables (305)	40,091	43,241
33065	Coral Springs (305)	79,443	37,349
.....	Coral Terrace(u) (305)	23,255	22,702
32536	Crestview (904)	9,886	7,617
33803	Crystal Lake(u) (813)	5,300	6,827
33157	Cutler(u) (305)	16,201	15,593
33157	Cutler Ridge(u) (305)	21,268	20,886
33880	Cypress Gardens(u) (813)	9,188	8,043
.....	Cypress Lake(u) (813)	10,491	8,721
.....	Dade City	5,633	4,923
33004	Dania (305)	13,024	11,796
33314	Davie (305)	47,217	20,515
*32015	Daytona Beach (904)	61,921	54,176
.....	De Bary	7,176	4,980
33441	Deerfield Beach (305)	46,325	39,193
32433	DeFuniak Springs (904)	5,120	5,563
32720	De Land (904)	16,491	15,354
*33444	Delray Beach (407)	47,181	34,329
33617	Del Rio(u) (813)	8,248	7,409
32725	Deltona(u) (407)	50,828	15,710
.....	Destin (904)	8,080	3,913
.....	Doctor Phillips	7,963	.....
*34698	Dunedin (813)	34,012	30,203
33610	East Lake-Orient Park (u) (813)	6,171	5,612
33940	East Naples(u) (813)	22,951	12,127
32032	Edgewater (904)	15,337	6,726
32542	Eglin AFB(u) (904)	8,347	7,574
33614	Egypt Lake(u) (813)	14,580	11,932
34680	Elfers(u) (813)	12,356	11,396
*34223	Englewood(u) (813)	15,025	10,229
32504	Ensley(u) (904)	16,362	14,422
32726	Eustis (904)	12,967	9,453

ZIP code	Place	1990	1980
32804	Fairview Shores(u) . . . . . (305)	13,192	10,174
32034	Fernandina Beach . . . . . (904)	8,765	7,224
32730	Fern Park(u) . . . . (407)	8,294	8,890
32504	Ferry Pass(u) . . . . (904)	26,301	16,910
33030	Florida City . . . . (305)	5,806	6,174
.....	Florida Ridge	12,218	4,988
32751	Forest City(u) . . . . (407)	10,638	6,819
.....	Forest Island Park.	5,988	.....
*33319	Fort Lauderdale. . . . . . (305)	149,377	153,279
*33901	Fort Myers. . . . . (813)	45,206	36,638
33931	Fort Myers Beach(u). . . . (813)	9,284	5,753
.....	Fort Myers Shores	5,460	4,426
*34950	Fort Pierce. . . . . (407)	36,830	33,802
33452	Fort Pierce NW(u) . . . . . (407)	5,833	5,929
.....	Fort Pierce South	5,320	3,324
32548	Fort Walton Beach . . . . (904)	21,471	20,829
.....	Fruit Cove	5,904	3,906
.....	Fruitville	9,808	3,070
*32601	Gainesville. . . . . (904)	84,770	81,371
33801	Gibsonia(u) . . . . (813)	5,168	5,011
.....	Gibsonton	7,706	.....
32960	Gifford(u) . . . . (305)	6,278	6,240
.....	Gladeview(u). . . . . (305)	15,637	18,919
33143	Glenvar Heights(u). . . . . (305)	14,823	13,216
.....	Golden Gate.	14,148	4,327
33055	Golden Glades(u). . . . . (305)	25,474	23,154
32733	Goldenrod(u). . . . . (407)	12,362	13,681
32560	Gonzalez(u) . . . . (904)	7,669	6,084
33170	Goulds(u) . . . . (305)	7,284	7,078
.....	Greater Northdale.	16,318	.....
33463	Greenacres City. . . . . . (407)	18,683	8,870
32561	Gulf Breeze. . . . . (904)	5,530	5,478
33581	Gulf Gate Estates(u) . . . (813)	11,622	9,248
33707	Gulfport. . . . . (813)	11,727	11,180
33844	Haines City. . . . . (813)	11,683	10,799
33009	Hallandale. . . . . (305)	30,996	36,460
.....	Hammocks.	10,897	.....
.....	Hamptons at Boca Raton	11,686	.....
*33010	Hialeah. . . . . (305)	188,004	145,254
.....	Hialeah Gardens	7,713	2,700
.....	Highpoint.	13,818	.....
33455	Hobe Sound(u) . . . . . . (407)	11,507	6,822
34690	Holiday(u). . . . . (813)	19,360	18,392
32017	Holly Hill. . . . . (904)	11,141	9,953
*33022	Hollywood. . . . . (305)	121,697	121,323
33030	Homestead . . . . (305)	26,866	20,668
33030	Homestead AFB. . . . . . (305)	5,153	7,594
.....	Homosassa Springs	6,271	1,426
34667	Hudson(u) . . . . (813)	7,344	5,789
33934	Immokalee(u). . . . . . . (813)	14,120	11,038
32937	Indian Harbour Beach . . (407)	6,933	5,967
.....	Inverness.	5,797	4,095
33880	Inwood(u) . . . . (813)	6,824	6,668
.....	Iona	9,565	.....
33162	Ives Estates(u) . . . . . . (305)	13,531	12,623
32250	Jacksonville Beach. . . . . (904)	17,839	15,462
*32201	Jacksonville. . . . . (904)	635,230	540,920
.....	Jan Phyl Village.	5,308	2,785
33568	Jasmine Estates(u) . . . . (813)	17,136	11,995
*34957	Jensen Beach(u). . . . . . (407)	9,884	6,639
33458	Jupiter. . . . . (407)	24,986	9,868
.....	Kendale Lakes(u). . . . . (305)	48,524	32,769
33156	Kendall(u). . . . . (305)	87,271	73,758
.....	Kendall Lakes West . . .	6,038	.....
33149	Key Biscayne(u). . . . . . (305)	8,854	6,313
33037	Key Largo(u) . . . . (305)	11,336	7,447
33040	Key West . . . . (305)	24,832	24,382
.....	Kings Point(u) . . . . . . (305)	12,422	8,724
32741	Kissimmee. . . . . (407)	30,050	15,487
.....	Lady Lake	8,071	1,193
32055	Lake City. . . . . (904)	10,005	9,257
*33802	Lakeland. . . . . (813)	70,576	47,406
33801	Lakeland Highlands(u). . . (813)	9,972	10,426
.....	Lake Lorraine(u) . . . . . (904)	6,779	5,427
33054	Lake Lucerne(u) . . . . . . (305)	9,478	9,762
33612	Lake Magdalene(u). . . . (813)	15,973	13,331
.....	Lake Mary	5,929	2,853
33403	Lake Park . . . . (407)	6,704	6,909
.....	Lakes by the Bay	5,615	.....
.....	Lakeside(u). . . . . (904)	29,137	10,534
33853	Lake Wales. . . . . (813)	9,670	8,466
.....	Lakewood Park	7,211	3,411
33460	Lake Worth. . . . . (407)	28,564	27,048
.....	Land O' Lakes.	7,892	4,515
33460	Lantana. . . . . (407)	8,392	8,048
*34640	Largo. . . . . (813)	65,674	57,958
33313	Lauderdale Lakes. . . . . (305)	27,341	25,426
33313	Lauderhill. . . . . (305)	49,708	37,271
34272	Laurel(u). . . . . (813)	8,245	6,368
33717	Lealman(u). . . . . (813)	21,748	19,873
32748	Leesburg. . . . . (904)	14,903	13,191
*33936	Lehigh Acres(u) . . . . . . (813)	13,611	9,604
33033	Leisure City(u) . . . . . . (305)	19,379	17,905
33064	Lighthouse Point. . . . . . (305)	10,378	11,488
.....	Lindgren Acres(u). . . . . (305)	22,290	11,986
32060	Live Oak. . . . . (904)	6,332	6,732
32810	Lockhart(u). . . . . (407)	11,636	10,569
34228	Longboat Key . . . . (813)	5,937	4,843
*32750	Longwood . . . . (407)	13,316	10,029

ZIP code	Place	1990	1980
33549	Lutz(u). . . . . (813)	10,552	5,555
32444	Lynn Haven. . . . . (904)	9,298	6,239
.....	McGregor	6,504	.....
32751	Maitland. . . . . (407)	9,110	8,763
33550	Mango(u). . . . . (813)	8,700	6,493
33050	Marathon(u). . . . . (305)	8,857	7,568
.....	Marco	9,493	4,679
33063	Margate . . . . (305)	42,985	35,900
32446	Marianna . . . . (904)	6,292	7,006
*32901	Melbourne. . . . . (407)	59,646	46,536
33314	Melrose Park(u). . . . . . (904)	6,477	5,662
33561	Memphis(u). . . . . (813)	6,760	5,501
32952	Merritt Island(u). . . . . . (407)	32,886	30,708
*33152	Miami. . . . . (305)	358,548	346,681
33139	Miami Beach. . . . . (305)	92,639	96,298
33023	Miami Gardens —Utopia-Carver(u) . . . . . (305)	7,448	9025
33014	Miami Lakes(u) . . . . . . (305)	12,750	9,809
33153	Miami Shores . . . . (305)	10,084	9,244
33166	Miami Springs. . . . . . . (305)	13,268	12,350
.....	Micco	8,757	.....
.....	Middleburg	6,223	3,585
32570	Milton. . . . . (904)	7,216	7,206
32754	Mims(u). . . . . (407)	9,412	7,583
33023	Miramar . . . . (305)	40,663	32,813
32757	Mount Dora. . . . . (904)	7,196	5,883
32506	Myrtle Grove(u) . . . . . . (904)	17,402	14,238
*33962	Naples. . . . . (813)	19,505	17,581
33940	Naples Park(u) . . . . . . (813)	8,002	5,438
33032	Naranja-Princeton(u). . . . (305)	5,790	10,381
32233	Neptune Beach. . . . . . (904)	6,816	5,248
*34652	New Port Richey. . . . . . (813)	14,044	11,196
33552	New Port Richey East(u). . (813)	9,683	6,147
32069	New Smyrna Beach . . . . (904)	16,543	13,557
32578	Niceville. . . . . (904)	10,507	8,543
33169	Norland(u) . . . . (305)	22,109	19,471
33308	North Andrews Gardens(u) . (305)	9,002	8,967
.....	North Bay Village	5,383	4,920
33903	North Fort Myers(u). . . . (813)	30,027	22,808
33068	North Lauderdale. . . . . (305)	26,506	18,479
33161	North Miami . . . . (305)	49,998	42,566
33160	North Miami Beach. . . . (305)	35,359	36,553
33940	North Naples(u). . . . . . (813)	13,422	7,950
33408	North Palm Beach. . . . . (407)	11,343	11,344
33596	North Port . . . . (813)	11,973	6,205
.....	North Sarasota	6,702	4,997
33860	Oak Ridge(u) . . . . (813)	15,388	15,477
.....	Oakland Party	26,326	22,944
32670	Ocala. . . . . (904)	42,045	37,170
32548	Ocean City(u). . . . . . . (904)	5,422	5,582
32761	Ocoee. . . . . (407)	12,778	7,803
33163	Ojus(u). . . . . (305)	15,519	17,344
.....	Oldsmar	8,361	2,608
33165	Olympia Heights(u) . . . . (305)	37,792	33,112
33054	Opa-Locka. . . . . (305)	15,283	14,460
33054	Opa-Locka North(u). . . . (305)	6,568	5,721
.....	Orange City	5,347	2,795
32073	Orange Park. . . . . (904)	9,488	8,766
*32801	Orlando. . . . . (407)	164,693	128,291
32811	Orlovista(u). . . . . (407)	5,990	6,474
32074	Ormond Beach. . . . . . . (904)	29,721	21,438
32074	Ormond By-The-Sea(u) . . (904)	8,157	7,665
32765	Oviedo. . . . . (407)	11,114	3,074
.....	Page Park-Pine Manor . .	5,116	5,006
32570	Pace(u). . . . . (904)	6,277	5,006
33476	Pahokee. . . . . (407)	6,822	6,346
32077	Palatka. . . . . (904)	10,201	10,175
32905	Palm Bay. . . . . (407)	62,632	18,560
33480	Palm Beach. . . . . (407)	9,814	9,729
33403	Palm Beach Gardens. . . . (407)	22,965	14,407
.....	Palm Coast	14,287	2,837
34221	Palmetto. . . . . (813)	9,268	8,637
33157	Palmetto Estates(u). . . . (305)	12,293	11,116
*34683	Palm Harbor(u) . . . . . . (813)	50,256	5,215
33619	Palm River-Clair Mel(u). . (813)	13,691	14,447
33460	Palm Springs. . . . . (407)	9,763	8,166
33012	Palm Springs North(u) . . (407)	5,300	5,838
.....	Palm Valley	9,960	.....
32401	Panama City. . . . . (904)	34,378	33,346
33023	Pembroke Pines. . . . . . (305)	65,452	35,776
*32502	Pensacola. . . . . (904)	58,165	57,619
33157	Perrine(u). . . . . (305)	15,576	16,129
32347	Perry. . . . . (904)	7,151	8,254
32809	Pine Castle(u). . . . . . . (407)	8,276	9,992
32808	Pine Hills(u). . . . . (407)	35,322	35,771
.....	Pine Island Ridge	5,244	.....
*34665	Pinellas Park. . . . . (813)	43,426	32,811
33168	Pinewood(u). . . . . (305)	15,518	16,252
33317	Plantation. . . . . (305)	66,692	48,653
33566	Plant City. . . . . (813)	22,754	17,064
33067	Pompano Beach. . . . . . (305)	72,411	52,618
33064	Pompano Beach Highlands(u)	17,915	16,154
33950	Port Charlotte(u). . . . . . (813)	41,535	25,770
32019	Port Orange. . . . . (904)	35,317	18,756
.....	Port John.	8,933	1,837
34952	Port St. Lucie . . . . (407)	55,866	14,690
.....	Port Salerno.	7,786	4,511
.....	Princeton.	7,073	.....
*33950	Punta Goda. . . . . (813)	10,747	6,797

ZIP code	Place		1990	1980
32351	Quincy	(904)	7,444	8,591
33156	Richmond Heights(u)	(305)	8,583	8,577
33312	Riverland(u)	(305)	5,376	5,919
.....	Riverview	.....	6,478	....
33404	Riviera Beach	(407)	27,639	26,489
32955	Rockledge	(407)	16,023	11,877
.....	Royal Palm Beach	.....	14,589	3,423
33570	Ruskin(u)	(813)	6,046	5,117
34695	Safety Harbor	(813)	15,124	6,461
32084	St. Augustine	(904)	11,692	11,985
34769	St. Cloud	(407)	12,453	7,840
*33702	St. Petersburg	(813)	238,629	238,647
33706	St. Petersburg Beach	(813)	9,200	9,354
.....	San Carlos Park	.....	11,785	3,590
33432	Sandalfoot Cove(u)	(305)	14,214	5,299
32771	Sanford	(407)	32,387	23,176
.....	Sanibel	.....	5,468	3,363
*34604	Sarasota	(813)	50,961	48,868
33577	Sarasota Springs(u)	(813)	16,088	13,860
32937	Satellite Beach	(407)	9,889	9,163
.....	Scott Lake(u)	(305)	14,588	14,154
.....	Sebastian	.....	10,205	2,831
*33870	Sebring	(813)	8,900	8,736
.....	Seffner	.....	5,371	....
.....	Seminole	.....	9,251	4,856
33578	Siesta Key(u)	(813)	7,772	7,010
.....	Silver Springs Shores	.....	6,421	3,983
32809	Sky Lake(u)	(407)	6,202	6,692
32703	South Apopka(u)	(407)	6,360	5,687
33505	South Bradenton(u)	(813)	20,398	14,297
32021	South Daytona	(904)	12,482	11,252
33579	Southgate(u)	(813)	7,324	7,322
.....	South Gate Ridge	.....	5,924	4,259
33143	South Miami	(305)	10,404	10,895
33157	South Miami Heights(u)	(305)	30,030	23,559
.....	South Pasadena	.....	5,644	4,188
32937	South Patrick Shores(u)	(407)	10,249	9,816
.....	South Sarasota	.....	5,298	4,267
33595	South Venice(u)	(813)	11,951	8,075
32401	Springfield	(904)	8,715	7,220
34606	Spring Hill(u)	(904)	31,117	6,468
32091	Starke	(904)	5,226	5,306
*34994	Stuart	(407)	11,936	9,467
33573	Sun City Center(u)	(813)	8,326	5,605
33160	Sunny Isles(u)	(305)	11,772	12,564
33304	Sunrise	(305)	64,407	39,681
33139	Sunset(u)	(305)	15,810	13,531
33144	Sweetwater	(305)	13,909	8,067
*32303	Tallahassee	(904)	124,773	81,548
33313	Tamarac	(305)	44,822	29,376
33144	Tamiami(u)	(305)	33,845	17,607
*33625	Tampa	(813)	280,015	271,577
*34689	Tarpon Springs	(813)	17,906	13,251
.....	Tavares	.....	7,383	4,398
33617	Temple Terrace	(813)	16,444	11,097
32780	Titusville	(407)	39,394	31,910
32505	Town 'n' Country(u)	(904)	60,946	37,834
33707	Treasure Island	(813)	7,266	6,316
32807	Union Park(u)	(407)	6,890	19,175
33620	University (Hillsborough)(u)	(813)	23,750	24,514
.....	Upper Grand Lagoon	.....	7,855	3,314
*34285	Venice	(813)	16,922	12,153
33595	Venice Gardens(u)	(813)	7,701	6,568
32960	Vero Beach	(407)	17,350	16,176
32960	Vero Beach South(u)	(407)	16,973	12,636
.....	Villages of Oriole	.....	5,698	8,724
33901	Villas(u)	(813)	9,898	8,724
32507	Warrington(u)	(904)	16,040	15,792
33314	Washington Park(u)	(305)	6,930	7,240
32703	Wekiva Springs(u)	(407)	23,026	13,386
.....	Wellington	.....	20,670	4,622
33155	Westchester(u)	(305)	29,883	29,272
.....	Westgate-Belvedere Homes	.....	6,880	....
33138	West Little River(u)	(305)	33,575	32,492
32901	West Melbourne	(407)	8,399	5,078
33144	West Miami	(305)	5,727	6,076
*33404	West Palm Beach	(407)	67,643	63,305
.....	West Park	.....	10,347	....
32505	West Pensacola(u)	(904)	22,107	24,371
33168	Westview(u)	(305)	9,668	9,102
33165	Westwood Lakes(u)	(305)	11,522	11,478
.....	Whiskey Creek	.....	5,061	....
33305	Wilton Manors(u)	(305)	11,804	12,742
33803	Winston(u)	(813)	9,118	9,315
*32787	Winter Garden	(407)	9,745	6,789
33880	Winter Haven	(813)	24,725	21,119
*32789	Winter Park	(407)	22,242	22,339
32708	Winter Springs	(407)	22,151	10,475
32548	Wright(u)	(904)	18,945	13,011
.....	Yulee	.....	6,915	....
33599	Zephyrhills	(813)	8,220	5,742

Georgia

ZIP code	Place		1990	1980
31620	Adel	(912)	5,093	5,592
*31701	Albany	(912)	78,122	74,425
.....	Alpharetta	.....	13,002	3,128
31709	Americus	(912)	16,512	16,120
*30601	Athens	(404)	45,734	42,549
*30304	Atlanta	(404)	394,017	425,022
*30901	Augusta	(404)	44,639	47,532
31717	Bainbridge	(912)	10,712	10,553
30032	Belvedere Park(u)	(404)	18,089	17,766
31723	Blakely	(912)	5,595	5,880
31520	Brunswick	(912)	16,433	17,605
30518	Buford	(404)	8,771	6,578
31728	Cairo	(912)	9,035	8,777
30701	Calhoun	(404)	7,135	5,563
31730	Camilla	(912)	5,008	5,414
30032	Candler-McAfee(u)	(404)	29,491	27,306
30117	Carrollton	(404)	16,029	14,078
30120	Cartersville	(404)	12,035	9,247
30125	Cedartown	(404)	7,978	8,619
30341	Chamblee	(404)	7,137.	7,668
.....	Clarkston	.....	5,385	4,539
30337	College Park	(404)	20,457	24,632
*31902	Columbus	(404)	178,681	169,441
30027	Conley(u)	(404)	5,528	6,033
30207	Conyers	(404)	7,380	6,567
31015	Cordele	(912)	10,321	11,184
.....	Country Club Estates	.....	7,500	....
30209	Covington	(404)	10,026	10,586
30720	Dalton	(404)	21,761	20,581
31742	Dawson	(912)	5,295	5,699
*30030	Decatur	(404)	17,336	18,404
31520	Dock Junction(u)	(912)	7,094	6,189
30340	Doraville	(404)	7,626	7,414
31533	Douglas	(912)	10,464	10,980
30134	Douglasville	(404)	11,635	7,641
30333	Druid Hills(u)	(404)	12,174	12,700
31021	Dublin	(912)	16,312	16,083
.....	Duluth	.....	9,029	2,956
30338	Dunwoody(u)	(404)	26,302	17,768
31023	Eastman	(912)	5,513	5,330
30344	East Point	(404)	34,402	37,486
30635	Elberton	(404)	5,682	5,686
.....	Evans	.....	13,713	....
30060	Fair Oaks(u)	(404)	6,996	8,486
30535	Fairview(u)	(404)	6,444	6,558
.....	Fayetteville	.....	5,827	2,715
31750	Fitzgerald	(912)	8,612	10,187
30050	Forest Park	(404)	16,925	18,782
31905	Fort Benning South(u)	(404)	14,617	15,074
30905	Fort Gordon(u)	(404)	9,140	14,069
30741	Fort Oglethorpe	(404)	5,880	5,443
31313	Fort Stewart(u)	(912)	13,774	15,031
31030	Fort Valley	(912)	8,198	9,000
.....	Gaines School	.....	11,354	....
30501	Gainesville	(404)	17,885	15,280
31408	Garden City	(912)	7,410	6,895
.....	Georgetown	.....	5,554	2,785
30316	Gresham Park(u)	(404)	9,000	6,232
30223	Griffin	(404)	21,347	20,728
30354	Hapeville	(404)	5,483	6,166
31313	Hinesville	(404)	21,603	11,309
31545	Jesup	(912)	8,958	9,418
30144	Kennesaw	(404)	8,936	5,095
30728	La Fayette	(404)	6,313	6,517
30240	La Grange	(404)	25,597	24,204
.....	Lakeview	.....	5,237	5,403
30245	Lawrenceville	(404)	16,848	8,928
.....	Lilburn	.....	9,301	3,765
30057	Lithia Springs(u)	(404)	11,403	9,145
30059	Mableton(u)	(404)	25,725	25,111
*31201	Macon	(912)	106,612	116,896
30060	Marietta	(404)	44,129	30,821
30907	Martinez(u)	(404)	33,731	16,472
31061	Milledgeville	(912)	17,727	12,176
30655	Monroe	(404)	9,759	8,854
.....	Morrow	.....	5,168	3,791
31768	Moultrie	(912)	14,865	15,105
30075	Mountain Park(u)	(404)	11,025	9,425
30263	Newnan	(404)	12,497	11,449
.....	Norcross	.....	5,947	3,363
30319	North Atlanta(u)	(404)	27,812	30,521
30033	North Decatur(u)	(404)	13,936	11,830
30033	North Druid Hills(u)	(404)	14,170	12,438
30032	Panthersville(u)	(404)	9,874	11,366
30269	Peachtree City	(404)	19,027	6,429
31069	Perry	(912)	9,452	9,453
.....	Powder Springs	.....	6,893	3,381
31643	Quitman	(912)	5,292	5,188
.....	Reden	.....	24,376	....
*30274	Riverdale	(404)	9,359	7,121
30161	Rome	(404)	30,326	28,915
30075	Roswell	(404)	47,923	23,337
.....	St. Marys	.....	8,187	3,596
31522	St. Simons(u)	(912)	12,026	6,566
31082	Sandersville	(912)	6,290	6,137
30328	Sandy Springs(u)	(404)	67,842	46,877
*31401	Savannah	(912)	137,560	141,654
30079	Scottdale(u)	(404)	8,636	8,770
30080	Smyrna	(404)	30,981	20,312
30278	Snellville	(404)	12,084	8,514
30901	South Augusta(u)	(404)	55,998	51,072
30458	Statesboro	(912)	15,854	14,866

ZIP code	Place	1990	1980
.....	Stone Mountain	6,494	4,867
.....	Summerville	5,025	4,878
30401	Swainsboro . . . . (912)	7,361	7,602
31791	Sylvester . . . . (912)	5,702	5,860
30286	Thomaston . . . . (404)	9,127	9,682
31792	Thomasville . . . . (912)	17,457	18,463
30824	Thomson . . . . (404)	6,862	7,001
31794	Tifton . . . . (912)	14,215	13,749
30577	Toccoa . . . . (404)	8,266	8,869
30084	Tucker(u) . . . . (404)	25,781	25,399
.....	Union City	8,375	4,780
31601	Valdosta . . . . (912)	39,806	37,596
30474	Vidalia . . . . (912)	11,078	10,393
.....	Villa Rica	6,542	3,420
.....	Vinings	7,417	....
31093	Warner Robins . . . . . . (912)	43,726	39,893
31501	Waycross . . . . (912)	16,410	19,371
30830	Waynesboro . . . . (404)	5,701	5,760
30901	West Augusta(u) . . . . . . (404)	27,637	24,242
31410	Wilmington Island(u) . . . (912)	11,230	7,546
30680	Winder . . . . (404)	7,373	6,705

Hawaii (808)

See Note on Page 78

ZIP code	Place	1990	1980
96706	Aiea	8,906	32,879
.....	Aliamanu	8,835	....
96706	Ewa	14,315	14,369
.....	Halawa	13,408	....
.....	Heeia	5,010	5,432
.....	Hickman	6,553	4,425
96720	Hilo	37,808	35,269
*96815	Honolulu	365,272	365,048
96732	Kahului	16,889	12,978
.....	Kailua	9,126	4,751
.....	Kailua	36,818	35,812
.....	Kaneohe	35,448	29,919
.....	Kaneohe Station	11,662	....
.....	Kapaa	8,149	4,467
96753	Kihei	11,107	5,644
96761	Lahaina	9,073	6,095
.....	Laie	5,577	4,643
.....	Lihue	5,536	4,000
.....	Maili	6,059	5,026
.....	Makaha	7,990	6,582
.....	Makailo	9,828	7,691
96768	Makawao-Paia	5,405	2,900
.....	Mililani Town	29,359	21,365
.....	Nanakuli	9,575	8,185
.....	Pearl City	30,993	42,575
.....	Pukalani	5,879	3,950
.....	Schofield Barracks	19,597	....
.....	Village Park	7,407	18,851
96786	Wahiawa	17,386	16,911
96792	Waianae	8,758	7,941
96793	Wailuku	10,688	10,260
.....	Waimalu	29,967	....
.....	Waimea	5,972	1,179
.....	Waipahu	31,435	29,139
.....	Waipio	11,812	....
.....	Waipio Acre	5,304	4,091

Idaho (208)

ZIP code	Place	1990	1980
.....	Ammon	5,002	4,669
83221	Blackfoot	9,646	10,065
*83708	Boise City	125,738	102,249
83318	Burley	8,702	8,761
83605	Caldwell	18,400	17,699
83201	Chubbuck	7,791	7,052
83814	Coeur D'Alene	24,563	19,913
.....	Garden City	6,369	4,571
*83401	Idaho Falls	43,929	39,739
83338	Jerome	6,529	6,891
83501	Lewiston	28,082	27,986
83642	Meridian	9,596	6,658
83843	Moscow	18,519	16,513
83647	Mountain Home	7,913	7,540
83648	Mountain Home AFB(u) . .	5,936	6,403
*83651	Nampa	28,365	25,112
83661	Payette	5,592	5,448
*83201	Pocatello	46,080	46,340
83854	Post Falls	7,349	5,738
83440	Rexburg	14,302	11,559
83350	Rupert	5,455	5,476
.....	Sandpoint	5,203	4,460
83301	Twin Falls	27,591	26,209

Illinois

ZIP code	Place	1990	1980
60101	Addison . . . . (708)	32,058	29,826
60102	Algonquin . . . . (708)	11,663	5,834
60658	Alsip . . . . (708)	18,227	17,134

ZIP code	Place	1990	1980
62002	Alton . . . . (618)	32,905	34,171
.....	Antioch	6,105	4,419
*60004	Arlington Heights . . . . (708)	75,460	66,116
*60507	Aurora . . . . (708)	99,581	81,293
60010	Barrington . . . . (708)	9,504	9,029
60103	Bartlett . . . . (708)	19,373	13,254
61607	Bartonville . . . . (309)	5,643	6,137
60510	Batavia . . . . (708)	17,076	12,574
.....	Beach Park	9,513	8,468
62618	Beardstown . . . . (217)	5,270	6,338
*62220	Belleville . . . . (618)	42,785	41,580
60104	Bellwood . . . . (708)	20,241	19,811
61008	Belvidere . . . . (815)	15,958	15,176
60106	Bensenville . . . . (708)	17,767	16,106
62812	Benton . . . . (618)	7,216	7,778
60162	Berkeley . . . . (708)	5,137	5,467
60402	Berwyn . . . . (708)	45,426	46,849
62010	Bethalto . . . . (618)	9,507	8,630
60108	Bloomingdale . . . . (708)	16,614	12,659
61701	Bloomington . . . . (309)	51,972	44,189
60406	Blue Island . . . . (708)	21,203	21,855
60439	Bolingbrook . . . . (708)	40,843	37,261
60538	Boulder Hill(u) . . . . . . (708)	8,894	9,333
60914	Bourbonnais . . . . (815)	13,934	13,280
60915	Bradley . . . . (815)	10,792	11,015
60455	Bridgeview . . . . (708)	14,402	14,155
60153	Broadview . . . . (708)	8,713	8,618
60513	Brookfield . . . . (708)	18,876	19,395
60090	Buffalo Grove . . . . . . (708)	36,427	22,230
60459	Burbank . . . . (708)	27,600	28,462
.....	Burr Ridge	7,669	3,838
62206	Cahokia . . . . (618)	17,550	18,904
60409	Calumet City . . . . (708)	37,840	39,697
60643	Calumet Park . . . . (708)	8,418	8,788
61520	Canton . . . . (309)	13,922	14,626
62901	Carbondale . . . . (618)	27,033	26,414
62626	Carlinville . . . . (217)	5,416	5,439
62821	Carmi . . . . (618)	5,564	6,107
60187	Carol Stream . . . . (708)	31,716	15,472
60110	Carpentersville . . . . . . (708)	23,049	23,272
60013	Cary . . . . (708)	10,043	6,640
62801	Centralia . . . . (618)	14,274	15,126
62206	Centreville . . . . (618)	7,489	9,747
61820	Champaign . . . . (217)	63,502	58,267
61920	Charleston . . . . (217)	20,398	19,355
62629	Chatham . . . . (217)	6,074	5,597
62233	Chester . . . . (618)	8,194	8,401
*60607	Chicago . . . . (312)	2,783,726	3,005,072
60411	Chicago Heights . . . . . (708)	33,072	37,026
60415	Chicago Ridge . . . . . . (708)	13,643	13,473
61523	Chillicothe . . . . (309)	5,959	6,176
60650	Cicero . . . . (708)	67,436	61,232
60514	Clarendon Hills . . . . . . (708)	6,994	6,870
61727	Clinton . . . . (217)	7,437	8,014
62234	Collinsville . . . . (618)	22,446	19,475
.....	Columbia	5,524	4,269
60477	Country Club Hills . . . . (708)	15,431	14,676
60525	Countryside . . . . (708)	5,716	6,242
60435	Crest Hill . . . . (815)	10,643	9,252
60445	Crestwood . . . . (708)	10,823	10,852
60417	Crete . . . . (708)	6,773	5,417
61611	Creve Coeur . . . . (309)	5,938	6,851
60014	Crystal Lake . . . . (815)	24,512	18,590
61832	Danville . . . . (217)	33,828	38,985
60559	Darien . . . . (708)	18,341	14,956
*62521	Decatur . . . . (217)	83,885	93,939
60015	Deerfield . . . . (708)	17,327	17,432
60115	De Kalb . . . . (815)	34,925	33,157
*60016	Des Plaines . . . . (708)	53,223	53,568
61021	Dixon . . . . (815)	15,144	15,710
60419	Dolton . . . . (708)	23,930	24,766
60515	Downers Grove . . . . . . (708)	46,858	42,259
62832	Du Quoin . . . . (618)	6,697	6,594
62024	East Alton . . . . (618)	7,063	7,096
61244	East Moline . . . . (309)	20,147	20,907
61611	East Peoria . . . . (309)	21,378	22,385
*62201	East St. Louis . . . . (618)	40,944	55,200
62025	Edwardsville . . . . (618)	14,579	12,480
62401	Effingham . . . . (217)	11,851	11,270
60120	Elgin . . . . (708)	77,010	63,668
60007	Elk Grove Village . . . . . (708)	33,429	28,679
60126	Elmhurst . . . . (708)	42,029	44,276
60635	Elmwood Park . . . . . . (708)	23,206	24,016
*60204	Evanston . . . . (708)	73,233	73,706
60642	Evergreen Park . . . . . . (708)	20,874	22,260
62837	Fairfield . . . . (618)	5,439	5,944
62208	Fairview Heights . . . . . (618)	14,351	12,111
62839	Flora . . . . (618)	5,054	5,379
60422	Flossmoor . . . . (708)	8,651	8,423
60130	Forest Park . . . . (708)	14,918	15,177
60020	Fox Lake . . . . (708)	7,478	6,831
.....	Frankfort	7,180	4,357
.....	Frankfort Square	6,227	....
60131	Franklin Park . . . . (708)	18,485	17,507
61032	Freeport . . . . (815)	25,840	26,266
60030	Gages . . . . (708)	8,349	3,814
61401	Galesburg . . . . (309)	33,530	35,305
61254	Geneseo . . . . (309)	5,990	6,373
60134	Geneva . . . . (708)	12,617	9,881

ZIP code	Place		1990	1980
62034	Glen Carbon	(618)	7,731	5,197
60022	Glencoe	(708)	8,499	9,200
60137	Glendale Heights	(618)	27,973	23,251
60137	Glen Ellyn	(708)	24,944	23,691
60025	Glenview	(708)	37,093	32,060
60425	Glenwood	(708)	9,289	10,538
.....	Godfrey	...	5,436	
.....	Goodings Grove	...	14,054	
62040	Granite City	(618)	32,862	36,815
60030	Grayslake	(708)	7,388	5,260
60031	Gurnee	(708)	13,701	7,179
60103	Hanover Park	(708)	32,895	28,719
62946	Harrisburg	(618)	9,289	10,410
60033	Harvard	(815)	5,975	5,126
60426	Harvey	(708)	29,771	35,810
60656	Harwood Heights	(708)	7,680	8,228
60429	Hazel Crest	(708)	13,334	13,973
62948	Herrin	(618)	10,857	10,708
60457	Hickory Hills	(708)	13,021	13,778
62249	Highland	(618)	7,525	7,122
60035	Highland Park	(708)	30,575	30,599
60040	Highwood	(708)	5,331	5,455
60162	Hillside	(708)	7,672	8,279
60521	Hinsdale	(708)	16,029	16,726
60172	Hoffman Estates	(708)	46,561	37,272
60430	Homewood	(708)	19,278	19,724
60942	Hoopeston	(217)	5,871	6,411
.....	Inverness	...	6,503	4,046
60143	Itasca	(708)	6,947	7,129
62650	Jacksonville	(217)	19,324	20,284
62052	Jerseyville	(618)	7,382	7,506
*60431	Joliet	(815)	76,836	77,956
60458	Justice	(708)	11,137	10,552
60901	Kankakee	(815)	27,575	29,633
61443	Kewanee	(309)	12,969	14,508
60525	La Grange	(708)	15,362	15,693
60525	La Grange Park	(708)	12,861	13,359
.....	Lake Bluff	...	5,513	4,434
60045	Lake Forest	(708)	17,836	15,245
60102	Lake in the Hills	(708)	5,866	5,651
60047	Lake Zurich	(708)	14,947	8,225
60438	Lansing	(708)	28,086	29,039
61301	La Salle	(815)	9,717	10,347
60439	Lemont	(708)	7,348	5,640
60048	Libertyville	(708)	19,174	16,520
62656	Lincoln	(217)	15,418	16,327
60645	Lincolnwood	(708)	11,365	11,921
60046	Lindenhurst	(708)	8,038	6,220
60532	Lisle	(708)	19,512	13,638
62056	Litchfield	(217)	6,883	7,204
60441	Lockport	(815)	9,401	9,192
60148	Lombard	(708)	39,408	36,879
61111	Loves Park	(815)	15,462	13,192
.....	Lynwood	...	6,535	4,195
60534	Lyons	(708)	9,828	9,925
60050	McHenry	(815)	16,177	10,737
.....	Machesney Park	...	19,033	19,514
61455	Macomb	(309)	19,952	19,863
62959	Marion	(618)	14,545	14,031
60426	Markham	(708)	13,136	15,172
.....	Mascoutah	...	5,511	4,962
60443	Matteson	(708)	11,378	10,223
61938	Mattoon	(217)	18,441	19,293
60153	Maywood	(708)	27,139	27,998
*60160	Melrose Park	(708)	20,859	20,735
61342	Mendota	(815)	7,018	7,134
62960	Metropolis	(618)	6,734	7,171
60445	Midlothian	(708)	14,372	14,274
61264	Milan	(309)	5,831	6,371
.....	Mokena	...	6,128	4,578
61265	Moline	(309)	43,202	46,407
61462	Monmouth	(309)	9,489	10,706
60450	Morris	(815)	10,270	8,833
61550	Morton	(309)	13,799	14,178
60053	Morton Grove	(708)	22,408	23,747
62863	Mount Carmel	(618)	8,287	8,908
60056	Mount Prospect	(708)	53,170	52,634
62864	Mount Vernon	(618)	16,988	17,193
60060	Mundelein	(708)	21,215	17,053
62966	Murphysboro	(618)	9,176	9,866
60540	Naperville	(708)	85,351	42,601
60451	New Lenox	(815)	9,627	5,792
60648	Niles	(708)	28,284	30,363
61761	Normal	(309)	40,023	35,672
60656	Norridge	(708)	14,459	16,483
60542	North Aurora	(708)	5,940	5,205
60062	Northbrook	(708)	32,308	30,778
60064	North Chicago	(708)	34,978	38,774
60164	Northlake	(708)	12,505	12,166
60546	North Riverside	(708)	6,005	6,764
60521	Oak Brook	(708)	9,178	6,676
60452	Oak Forest	(708)	26,203	25,040
*60454	Oak Lawn	(708)	56,182	60,590
*60301	Oak Park	(708)	53,648	54,887
62269	O'Fallon	(618)	16,073	12,173
62450	Olney	(618)	8,664	9,026
.....	Orland Hills	...	5,510	2,784
60462	Orland Park	(708)	35,720	23,045
61350	Ottawa	(815)	17,451	18,166

ZIP code	Place		1990	1980
60067	Palatine	(708)	39,253	32,176
60463	Palos Heights	(708)	11,478	11,096
60465	Palos Hills	(708)	17,803	16,654
62557	Pana	(217)	5,796	6,040
61944	Paris	(217)	8,987	9,885
60466	Park Forest	(708)	24,656	26,222
60068	Park Ridge	(708)	36,175	38,704
61554	Pekin	(309)	32,254	33,967
*61601	Peoria	(309)	113,504	124,160
61614	Peoria Heights	(309)	6,930	7,453
61354	Peru	(815)	9,302	10,886
.....	Plano	...	5,104	4,875
61764	Pontiac	(815)	11,428	11,227
61356	Princeton	(815)	7,197	7,342
60070	Prospect Heights	(708)	15,239	11,823
62301	Quincy	(217)	39,681	42,554
61866	Rantoul	(217)	17,212	20,161
60471	Richton Park	(708)	10,523	9,403
60627	Riverdale	(708)	13,671	13,233
60305	River Forest	(708)	11,669	12,392
60171	River Grove	(708)	9,961	10,368
60546	Riverside	(708)	8,774	9,236
60472	Robbins	(708)	7,498	8,853
62454	Robinson	(618)	6,740	7,285
61068	Rochelle	(815)	8,769	8,982
61071	Rock Falls	(815)	9,654	10,633
*61125	Rockford	(815)	139,426	139,712
61201	Rock Island	(309)	40,552	46,821
60008	Rolling Meadows	(708)	22,591	20,167
60441	Romeoville	(815)	14,074	15,519
60172	Roselle	(708)	20,819	17,034
60073	Round Lake Beach	(708)	16,434	12,921
60174	St. Charles	(708)	22,501	17,492
62881	Salem	(618)	7,470	7,813
60548	Sandwich	(815)	5,567	5,356
60411	Sauk Village	(708)	9,926	10,906
60172	Schaumburg	(708)	68,586	53,355
60176	Schiller Park	(708)	11,189	11,458
62225	Scott AFB(u)	(618)	7,245	8,648
.....	Shorewood	...	6,264	4,714
61282	Silvis	(309)	6,926	7,130
60076	Skokie	(708)	59,432	60,278
60177	South Elgin	(708)	7,474	5,970
*60473	South Holland	(708)	22,105	24,977
*62703	Springfield	(217)	105,227	100,054
61362	Spring Valley	(815)	5,246	5,822
60475	Steger	(708)	8,584	9,269
61081	Sterling	(815)	15,132	16,281
60402	Stickney	(708)	5,678	5,893
60103	Streamwood	(708)	30,987	23,456
61364	Streator	(815)	14,121	14,795
60501	Summit	(708)	9,971	10,110
62221	Swansea	(618)	8,201	5,529
60178	Sycamore	(815)	9,708	9,219
62568	Taylorville	(217)	11,133	11,386
60477	Tinley Park	(708)	37,121	26,178
.....	Troy	...	6,046	3,772
.....	University Park	...	6,204	6,245
61801	Urbana	(217)	36,344	35,978
62471	Vandalia	(618)	6,114	5,338
60061	Vernon Hills	(708)	15,319	9,827
60181	Villa Park	(708)	22,253	23,155
60555	Warrenville	(708)	11,333	7,519
61571	Washington	(309)	10,099	10,364
62204	Washington Park	(618)	7,431	8,223
.....	Waterloo	...	5,072	4,646
60970	Watseka	(815)	5,424	5,543
60084	Wauconda	(708)	6,294	5,688
60085	Waukegan	(708)	69,392	67,653
60153	Westchester	(708)	17,301	17,730
60185	West Chicago	(708)	14,796	12,550
60558	Western Springs	(708)	11,984	12,876
62896	West Frankfort	(618)	8,526	9,437
60559	Westmont	(708)	21,228	17,353
61604	West Peoria(u)	(309)	5,314	5,219
60187	Wheaton	(708)	51,464	43,043
60090	Wheeling	(708)	29,911	23,266
.....	Willowbrook	...	8,598	4,953
60091	Wilmette	(708)	26,690	28,221
.....	Winfield	...	7,096	4,422
60093	Winnetka	(708)	12,174	12,772
60096	Winthrop Harbor	(708)	6,240	5,427
60097	Wonder Lake(u)	(815)	6,664	5,917
60191	Wood Dale	(708)	12,425	11,251
60515	Woodridge	(708)	26,256	21,763
62095	Wood River	(618)	11,490	12,446
60098	Woodstock	(815)	14,353	11,725
60482	Worth	(708)	11,208	11,592
60099	Zion	(708)	19,775	17,865

Indiana

ZIP code	Place		1990	1980
46001	Alexandria	(317)	5,709	6,028
46011	Anderson	(317)	59,459	64,695
46703	Angola	(219)	5,824	5,486
46706	Auburn	(219)	9,379	8,122
47421	Bedford	(812)	13,817	14,410

ZIP code	Place		1990	1980
46107	Beech Grove	(317)	13,383	13,196
47401	Bloomington	(812)	60,633	52,663
46714	Bluffton	(219)	9,020	8,705
47601	Boonville	(812)	6,724	6,300
47834	Brazil	(812)	7,640	7,852
46112	Brownsburg	(317)	7,628	6,242
46032	Carmel	(317)	25,380	18,272
46303	Cedar Lake	(219)	8,885	8,754
47111	Charlestown	(812)	5,889	5,596
46304	Chesterton	(219)	9,124	8,531
47130	Clarksville	(812)	19,833	15,164
47842	Clinton	(317)	5,040	5,267
46725	Columbia City	(219)	5,706	5,091
47201	Columbus	(812)	31,802	30,614
47331	Connersville	(317)	15,550	17,023
47933	Crawfordsville	(317)	13,584	13,325
46307	Crown Point	(219)	17,728	16,455
46733	Decatur	(219)	8,644	8,649
46514	Dunlap(u)	(219)	5,705	5,397
46311	Dyer	(219)	10,923	9,555
46312	East Chicago	(219)	33,892	39,786
46514	Elkhart	(219)	43,627	41,305
46036	Elwood	(317)	9,494	10,867
*47708	Evansville	(812)	126,272	130,496
	Fishers		7,508	2,008
*46802	Fort Wayne	(219)	173,072	172,391
46041	Frankfort	(317)	14,754	15,168
46131	Franklin	(317)	12,907	11,563
	Garrett		5,349	4,751
*46401	Gary	(219)	116,646	151,968
46933	Gas City	(317)	6,296	6,370
46526	Goshen	(219)	23,797	19,665
	Granger		20,241	.....
46135	Greencastle	(317)	8,984	8,403
46140	Greenfield	(317)	11,657	11,288
47240	Greensburg	(812)	9,286	9,254
46142	Greenwood	(317)	26,265	19,327
46319	Griffith	(219)	17,916	17,026
*46320	Hammond	(219)	84,236	93,714
47348	Hartford City	(317)	6,960	7,622
46322	Highland	(219)	23,696	25,935
46342	Hobart	(219)	21,822	22,987
47542	Huntingburg	(812)	5,242	5,376
46750	Huntington	(219)	16,389	16,202
*46206	Indianapolis	(317)	731,327	700,807
47546	Jasper	(812)	10,030	9,097
47130	Jeffersonville	(812)	21,841	21,220
46755	Kendallville	(219)	7,773	7,299
46901	Kokomo	(317)	44,962	47,808
*47901	Lafayette	(317)	43,764	43,011
	Lakes of the Four Seasons		6,556	.....
46405	Lake Station	(219)	13,899	15,087
46350	La Porte	(219)	21,507	21,796
46226	Lawrence	(317)	26,763	25,591
46052	Lebanon	(317)	12,059	11,456
47441	Linton	(812)	5,814	6,315
46947	Logansport	(219)	16,812	17,731
46356	Lowell	(219)	6,430	5,827
47250	Madison	(812)	12,006	12,472
46952	Marion	(317)	32,618	35,874
46151	Martinsville	(317)	11,677	11,311
46410	Merrillville	(219)	27,257	27,677
46360	Michigan City	(219)	33,822	36,850
46544	Mishawaka	(219)	42,608	40,201
47960	Monticello	(219)	5,237	5,162
46158	Mooresville	(317)	5,541	5,349
47620	Mount Vernon	(812)	7,217	7,656
*47302	Muncie	(317)	71,035	77,216
46321	Munster	(219)	19,949	20,671
	Nappanee		5,510	4,694
47150	New Albany	(812)	36,322	37,103
47362	New Castle	(317)	17,753	20,056
46774	New Haven	(219)	9,320	6,714
46060	Noblesville	(317)	17,655	12,253
46962	North Manchester	(219)	6,383	5,998
47265	North Vernon	(812)	5,311	5,768
47130	Oak Park(u)	(812)	5,630	5,871
46970	Peru	(317)	12,843	13,764
46168	Plainfield	(317)	10,433	9,191
46563	Plymouth	(219)	8,303	7,693
46368	Portage	(219)	29,060	27,409
47371	Portland	(219)	6,483	7,074
47670	Princeton	(812)	8,127	8,976
	Rensselaer		5,045	4,944
47374	Richmond	(317)	38,705	41,349
46975	Rochester	(317)	5,969	5,050
46173	Rushville	(317)	5,533	6,113
47167	Salem	(812)	5,619	5,290
46375	Schererville	(219)	19,926	13,209
47170	Scottsburg	(812)	5,334	5,068
	Sellersburg		5,745	3,211
47274	Seymour	(812)	15,576	15,050
46176	Shelbyville	(317)	15,336	14,989
*46624	South Bend	(219)	105,511	109,727
46383	South Haven(u)	(219)	6,112	6,679
46224	Speedway	(317)	13,092	12,641
47586	Tell City	(812)	8,088	8,704
*47808	Terre Haute	(812)	57,483	61,125
46383	Valparaiso	(219)	24,414	22,247
47591	Vincennes	(812)	19,859	20,857
46992	Wabash	(219)	12,127	12,985
46580	Warsaw	(219)	10,968	10,647
47501	Washington	(812)	10,838	11,325
47906	West Lafayette	(317)	25,907	21,247
	Westville		5,255	2,887
46394	Whiting	(219)	5,155	5,630
47394	Winchester	(317)	5,095	5,659
.....	Zionsville		5,281	3,948

Iowa

ZIP code	Place		1990	1980
50511	Algona	(515)	6,015	6,289
50009	Altoona	(515)	7,191	5,764
50010	Ames	(515)	47,198	45,775
	Anamosa		5,100	4,958
50021	Ankeny	(515)	18,482	15,429
50022	Atlantic	(712)	7,432	7,789
52722	Bettendorf	(319)	28,132	27,381
50036	Boone	(515)	12,392	12,602
52601	Burlington	(319)	27,208	29,529
51401	Carroll	(712)	9,579	9,705
50613	Cedar Falls	(319)	34,298	36,322
*52401	Cedar Rapids	(319)	108,751	110,243
52544	Centerville	(515)	5,936	6,558
50616	Charles City	(515)	7,878	8,778
51012	Cherokee	(712)	6,026	7,004
51632	Clarinda	(712)	5,104	5,458
50428	Clear Lake City	(515)	8,183	7,458
52732	Clinton	(319)	29,201	32,828
50053	Clive	(515)	7,462	6,064
52240	Coralville	(319)	10,347	7,687
51501	Council Bluffs	(712)	54,315	56,449
50801	Creston	(515)	7,911	8,429
*52802	Davenport	(319)	95,333	103,264
52101	Decorah	(319)	8,063	7,991
51442	Denison	(712)	6,604	6,675
*50318	Des Moines	(515)	193,187	191,003
52001	Dubuque	(319)	57,546	62,374
51334	Estherville	(712)	6,720	7,518
52556	Fairfield	(515)	9,768	9,428
50501	Fort Dodge	(515)	25,894	29,423
52627	Fort Madison	(319)	11,618	13,520
50112	Grinnell	(515)	8,902	8,868
51537	Harlan	(712)	5,148	5,357
50644	Independence	(319)	5,972	6,392
50125	Indianola	(515)	11,340	10,843
52240	Iowa City	(319)	59,738	50,508
50126	Iowa Falls	(515)	5,424	6,174
52632	Keokuk	(515)	12,451	13,536
50138	Knoxville	(515)	8,232	8,143
51031	Le Mars	(712)	8,454	8,276
	Manchester		5,137	4,942
52060	Maquoketa	(319)	6,111	6,313
52302	Marion	(319)	20,403	19,474
50158	Marshalltown	(515)	25,178	26,938
50401	Mason City	(515)	29,040	30,144
52641	Mount Pleasant	(319)	8,027	7,322
52761	Muscatine	(319)	22,881	23,467
50201	Nevada	(515)	6,009	5,912
50208	Newton	(515)	14,789	15,292
	Norwalk		5,726	2,676
50662	Oelwein	(319)	6,493	7,564
52577	Oskaloosa	(515)	10,632	10,989
52501	Ottumwa	(515)	24,488	27,381
50219	Pella	(515)	9,270	8,349
50220	Perry	(515)	6,652	7,053
51566	Red Oak	(712)	6,264	6,810
51601	Shenandoah	(712)	5,572	6,274
	Sioux Center		5,074	4,588
*51101	Sioux City	(712)	80,505	82,003
51301	Spencer	(712)	11,066	11,726
50588	Storm Lake	(712)	8,769	8,814
50322	Urbandale	(515)	23,500	17,869
52349	Vinton	(319)	5,103	5,040
52353	Washington	(319)	7,074	6,584
*50701	Waterloo	(319)	66,467	75,985
50677	Waverly	(319)	8,539	8,444
50595	Webster City	(515)	7,894	8,572
50265	West Des Moines	(515)	31,702	21,894
50311	Windsor Heights	(515)	5,190	5,474

Kansas

ZIP code	Place		1990	1980
67410	Abilene	(913)	6,242	6,572
67005	Arkansas City	(316)	12,762	13,201
66002	Atchison	(913)	10,656	11,407
67010	Augusta	(316)	7,876	6,968
66012	Bonner Springs	(913)	6,413	6,266
67337	Coffeyville	(316)	12,917	15,185
67701	Colby	(913)	5,396	5,544
66901	Concordia	(913)	6,167	6,847
67037	Derby	(316)	14,699	9,786
67801	Dodge City	(316)	21,129	18,001
67042	El Dorado	(316)	11,504	11,551

ZIP code	Place		1990	1980
66801	Emporia	(316)	25,512	25,287
66442	Fort Riley North(u)	(913)	12,848	16,086
66701	Fort Scott	(316)	8,362	8,893
67846	Garden City	(316)	24,097	18,256
67530	Great Bend	(316)	15,427	16,608
67601	Hays	(913)	17,767	16,301
67060	Haysville	(316)	8,364	8,006
67501	Hutchinson	(316)	39,308	40,284
67301	Independence	(316)	9,942	10,598
66749	Iola	(316)	6,351	6,938
66441	Junction City	(913)	20,604	19,305
*66110	Kansas City	(913)	149,767	161,148
66043	Lansing	(913)	7,120	5,307
66044	Lawrence	(913)	65,608	52,738
66048	Leavenworth	(913)	38,495	33,656
66206	Leawood	(913)	19,693	13,360
66215	Lenexa	(913)	34,034	18,639
67901	Liberal	(316)	16,573	14,911
67460	McPherson	(316)	12,422	11,753
66502	Manhattan	(913)	37,712	32,644
66203	Merriam	(913)	11,821	10,794
66222	Mission	(913)	9,504	8,643
67114	Newton	(316)	16,700	16,332
66061	Olathe	(913)	63,352	37,258
66067	Ottawa	(913)	10,667	11,016
66204	Overland Park	(913)	111,790	81,784
.....	Park City	.....	5,050	4,056
67357	Parsons	(316)	11,924	12,898
66762	Pittsburg	(316)	17,775	18,770
66208	Prairie Village	(913)	23,186	24,657
67124	Pratt	(316)	6,887	6,885
66203	Roeland Park	(913)	7,706	7,962
67401	Salina	(913)	42,303	41,843
*66203	Shawnee	(913)	37,993	29,653
*66603	Topeka	(913)	119,883	118,690
.....	Ulysses	.....	5,474	4,653
67152	Wellington	(316)	8,411	8,212
*67202	Wichita	(316)	304,011	279,838
67156	Winfield	(316)	11,931	10,736

Kentucky

ZIP code	Place		1990	1980
41101	Alexandria	.....	5,592	4,735
41101	Ashland	(606)	23,622	27,064
40004	Bardstown	(502)	6,801	6,155
41073	Bellevue	(606)	6,997	7,678
40403	Berea	(606)	9,126	8,226
42101	Bowling Green	(502)	40,641	40,450
40218	Buechel(u)	(502)	7,081	6,912
.....	Burlington	.....	6,070	.....
42718	Campbellsville	(502)	9,577	8,715
40701	Corbin	(606)	7,419	8,075
*41011	Covington	(606)	43,264	49,585
41031	Cynthiana	(606)	6,497	5,881
40422	Danville	(606)	12,420	12,942
41074	Dayton	(606)	6,576	6,979
.....	Douglass Hills	.....	5,549	4,384
41017	Edgewood	(606)	8,143	7,243
42701	Elizabethtown	(502)	18,167	15,380
41018	Elsmere	(606)	6,847	7,203
41018	Erlanger	(606)	15,979	14,466
40118	Fairdale(u)	(502)	6,563	7,315
40291	Fern Creek(u)	(502)	16,406	16,866
41139	Flatwoods	(606)	7,799	8,354
41042	Florence	(606)	18,624	15,586
42223	Fort Campbell North(u)	(502)	18,861	17,211
40121	Fort Knox(u)	(502)	21,495	31,055
41017	Fort Mitchell	(606)	7,438	7,294
41075	Fort Thomas	(606)	16,032	16,012
.....	Fort Wright	.....	6,570	4,481
40601	Frankfort	(502)	25,968	25,973
42134	Franklin	(502)	7,607	7,738
40324	Georgetown	(502)	11,414	10,972
42141	Glasgow	(502)	12,351	12,958
40330	Harrodsburg	(606)	7,335	7,265
41701	Hazard	(606)	5,416	5,371
42420	Henderson	(502)	25,945	24,834
40228	Highview(u)	(502)	14,814	13,286
40229	Hillview	(502)	6,119	5,196
42240	Hopkinsville	(502)	29,809	27,318
41051	Independence	(606)	10,444	7,998
40299	Jeffersontown	(502)	23,221	15,795
40342	Lawrenceburg	(502)	5,911	5,167
40033	Lebanon	(502)	5,695	6,590
*40511	Lexington-Fayette	(606)	225,366	204,165
.....	London	.....	5,757	4,002
*40201	Louisville	(502)	269,063	298,694
.....	Lyndon	.....	8,037	1,553
42431	Madisonville	(502)	16,200	16,979
42066	Mayfield	(502)	9,935	10,705
41056	Maysville	(606)	7,169	7,983
40965	Middlesborough	(606)	11,328	12,251
.....	Middletown	.....	5,016	4,262
42633	Monticello	(606)	5,357	5,677
40351	Morehead	(606)	8,357	7,789
40353	Mount Sterling	(606)	5,362	5,820
.....	Mount Washington	.....	5,226	3,997

ZIP code	Place		1990	1980
42071	Murray	(502)	14,439	14,248
40218	Newburg(u)	(502)	21,647	24,612
*41071	Newport	(606)	18,871	21,587
40356	Nicholasville	(606)	13,603	10,400
40219	Okolona(u)	(502)	18,902	20,039
42301	Owensboro	(502)	53,549	54,450
42001	Paducah	(502)	27,256	29,315
40361	Paris	(606)	8,730	7,935
.....	Pikeville	.....	6,324	4,756
40258	Pleasure Ridge Park(u)	(502)	25,131	27,332
42445	Princeton	(502)	6,940	7,073
40160	Radcliff	(502)	19,772	14,656
40475	Richmond	(606)	21,155	21,705
42276	Russellville	(502)	7,454	7,520
.....	St. Dennis	.....	10,326	.....
40207	St. Matthews	(502)	15,800	13,519
40065	Shelbyville	(502)	6,238	5,329
40216	Shively	(502)	15,535	16,645
42501	Somerset	(606)	10,733	10,649
.....	Taylor Mill	.....	5,530	4,509
40272	Valley Station(u)	(502)	22,840	24,474
40383	Versailles	(606)	7,269	6,427
.....	Villa Hills	.....	7,739	4,384
41101	Westwood(u)	(606)	5,300	5,973
40769	Williamsburg	(606)	5,493	5,560
40391	Winchester	(606)	15,799	15,216

Louisiana

ZIP code	Place		1990	1980
70510	Abbeville	(318)	11,187	12,391
71301	Alexandria	(318)	49,188	51,648
70032	Arabi(u)	(504)	8,787	10,248
70094	Avondale(u)	(504)	5,813	6,699
70714	Baker	(504)	13,233	12,865
71220	Bastrop	(318)	13,916	15,527
*70821	Baton Rouge	(504)	219,531	220,394
70360	Bayou Cane(u)	(504)	15,876	15,723
70037	Belle Chasse(u)	(504)	8,512	5,412
70427	Bogalusa	(504)	14,280	16,976
71010	Bossier City	(318)	52,721	50,817
70517	Breaux Bridge	(318)	6,515	5,922
.....	Bridge	.....	8,327	.....
.....	Brownfields	.....	5,229	.....
71291	Brownsville-Bawcomville(u)	(318)	7,397	7,252
71322	Bunkie	(318)	5,044	5,364
.....	Carencro	.....	5,429	3,712
70043	Chalmette(u)	(504)	31,860	33,847
71291	Claiborne(u)	(318)	8,300	6,278
70433	Covington	(504)	7,691	7,892
70526	Crowley	(318)	13,983	16,036
70345	Cut Off(u)	(504)	5,325	5,049
70726	Denham Springs	(504)	8,381	8,563
70634	De Ridder	(318)	9,868	10,337
.....	Destrehan	.....	8,031	2,382
70346	Donaldsonville	(504)	7,949	7,901
70072	Estelle(u)	(504)	14,091	12,724
70535	Eunice	(318)	11,162	12,479
.....	Fort Polk South	.....	10,911	12,498
70538	Franklin	(318)	9,004	9,584
.....	Gardere	.....	7,209	.....
70737	Gonzales	(504)	7,003	7,287
.....	Grambling	.....	5,484	4,226
70053	Gretna	(504)	17,208	20,615
70401	Hammond	(504)	15,871	15,226
70123	Harahan	(504)	9,927	11,384
70058	Harvey(u)	(504)	21,222	22,709
70360	Houma	(504)	30,495	32,602
70544	Jeanerette	(318)	6,205	6,511
70121	Jefferson(u)	(504)	14,521	15,550
70546	Jennings	(318)	11,305	12,401
70062	Kenner	(504)	72,033	66,382
70445	Lacombe(u)	(504)	6,523	5,146
70501	Lafayette	(318)	94,440	80,584
70601	Lake Charles	(318)	70,580	75,226
71254	Lake Providence	(318)	5,380	6,361
70068	Laplace(u)	(504)	24,194	16,112
70373	Larose(u)	(504)	5,772	5,234
71446	Leesville	(318)	7,638	9,054
70448	Mandeville	(504)	7,083	6,076
71052	Mansfield	(318)	5,389	6,485
71351	Marksville	(318)	5,526	5,113
70072	Marrero(u)	(504)	36,671	36,548
.....	Meraux	.....	8,849	.....
.....	Merrydale	.....	10,395	.....
*70004	Metairie(u)	(504)	149,428	164,160
71055	Minden	(318)	13,661	15,064
71201	Monroe	(318)	54,909	57,597
70380	Morgan City	(504)	14,531	16,114
70601	Moss Bluff(u)	(318)	8,039	7,004
71457	Natchitoches	(318)	16,609	16,664
70560	New Iberia	(318)	31,828	32,766
*70013	New Orleans	(504)	496,938	557,927
.....	New Roads	.....	5,303	3,924
71463	Oakdale	(318)	6,832	7,155
.....	Oak Hills Place	.....	5,479	.....
70570	Opelousas	(318)	18,151	18,903
71360	Pineville	(318)	12,251	12,034

ZIP code	Place		1990	1980
70764	Plaquemine	(504)	7,186	7,521
70454	Ponchatoula	(504)	5,425	5,469
70767	Port Allen	(504)	6,277	6,114
70601	Prien(u)	(318)	6,448	6,224
70394	Raceland(u)	(504)	5,564	6,302
70578	Rayne	(318)	8,502	9,066
.....	Red Chute		5,431	....
70084	Reserve(u)	(504)	14,800	17,146
70123	River Ridge(u)	(504)	14,806	....
71270	Ruston	(318)	20,027	20,585
70582	St. Martinville	(318)	7,137	7,965
.....	St. Rose		6,259	....
.....	Shenandoah		13,429	....
*71102	Shreveport	(318)	198,525	206,989
70458	Slidell	(504)	24,124	26,718
71075	Springhill	(318)	5,668	6,516
70663	Sulphur	(318)	20,125	19,709
71282	Tallulah	(318)	8,526	11,341
70056	Terrytown(u)	(504)	23,787	23,548
70301	Thibodaux	(504)	14,035	15,810
70053	Timberlane(u)	(504)	12,614	11,579
.....	Village St. George		6,242	....
70586	Ville Platte	(318)	9,037	9,201
70092	Violet(u)	(504)	8,574	11,678
70094	Waggaman(u)	(504)	9,405	9,004
70669	Westlake	(318)	5,007	5,246
71291	West Monroe	(318)	14,096	14,993
70094	Westwego	(504)	11,218	12,663
71483	Winnfield	(318)	6,138	7,311
71295	Winnsboro	(318)	5,755	5,921
70791	Zachary	(504)	9,036	7,297

Maine (207)

See Note on Page 78

ZIP code	Place	1990	1980
04210	Auburn	24,309	23,128
04330	Augusta	21,325	21,819
04401	Bangor	33,181	31,643
04530	Bath	9,799	10,246
04915	Belfast	6,355	6,243
.....	Berwick	5,995	....
04005	Biddeford	20,710	19,638
04412	Brewer	9,021	9,017
04011	Brunswick Center(u)	14,683	10,990
04011	Brunswick	20,906	17,366
04093	Buxton	6,494	5,775
.....	Camden	5,060	....
04107	Cape Elizabeth	8,854	7,838
04736	Caribou	9,415	9,916
04021	Cumberland	5,836	5,284
04605	Ellsworth	5,975	5,179
04937	Fairfield	6,718	6,113
04105	Falmouth	7,610	6,853
04938	Farmington	7,436	6,730
04032	Freeport	6,905	5,863
04345	Gardiner	6,746	6,485
04038	Gorham	11,856	10,101
04444	Hampden	5,974	5,250
.....	Harpswell	5,012	....
04730	Houlton Center(u)	5,627	5,730
04730	Houlton	6,613	6,766
04239	Jay	5,080	5,080
04043	Kennebunk	8,004	6,621
03904	Kittery Center(u)	5,151	5,465
03904	Kittery	9,372	9,314
04240	Lewiston	39,757	40,481
04750	Limestone	9,922	8,719
04457	Lincoln	5,587	5,066
04250	Lisbon	9,457	8,769
04750	Loring(u)	5,494	6,572
04462	Millinocket Center(u)	6,922	7,567
04462	Millinocket	7,567	7,742
04963	Oakland	5,595	5,162
04064	Old Orchard Beach Ctr.(u)	7,789	6,023
04064	Old Orchard Beach	7,789	6,291
04468	Old Town	8,317	8,422
04473	Orono Center(u)	9,789	9,891
04473	Orono	10,573	10,578
*04101	Portland	64,358	61,572
04769	Presque Isle	10,550	11,172
04841	Rockland	7,972	7,919
04276	Rumford Compact(u)	5,419	6,256
04276	Rumford	7,078	8,240
04072	Saco	15,181	12,921
04073	Sanford Center(u)	10,296	10,268
04073	Sanford	20,463	18,020
04074	Scarborough	12,518	11,347
04976	Skowhegan Center(u)	6,990	6,517
04976	Skowhegan	8,725	8,098
.....	South Berwick	5,877	....
04106	South Portland	23,163	22,712
04084	Standish	7,678	5,946
04086	Topsham	8,746	6,147
04901	Waterville	17,173	17,779
04090	Wells	7,778	8,211
04092	Westbrook	16,121	14,976

ZIP code	Place	1990	1980
04082	Windham	13,020	11,282
04901	Winslow Center(u)	5,436	5,903
04901	Winslow	7,997	8,057
04364	Winthrop	5,986	5,889
04096	Yarmouth	7,862	6,585
03909	York	9,818	8,465

Maryland (301)

ZIP code	Place	1990	1980
21001	Aberdeen	13,087	11,533
21005	Aberdeen Proving Ground(u)	5,267	5,722
20783	Adelphi(u)	13,524	12,530
20331	Andrews AFB(u)	10,228	10,064
*21401	Annapolis	33,187	31,740
21227	Arbutus(u)	19,750	20,163
21012	Arnold(u)	20,251	12,285
20906	Aspen Hill(u)	45,494	47,455
.....	Ballenger Creek	5,546	2,659
*21233	Baltimore	736,014	786,741
21014	Bel Air	8,860	7,814
21050	Bel Air North(u)	14,880	5,043
21014	Bel Air South(u)	26,421	8,461
20705	Beltsville(u)	14,476	12,760
*20815	Bethesda(u)	62,936	62,736
20710	Bladensburg	8,064	7,691
*20715	Bowie	37,589	33,695
.....	Bowleys Quarters	5,595	....
21225	Brooklyn Park(u)	10,987	11,508
.....	Burtonsville	5,853	2,046
20818	Cabin John-Brookmont(u)	5,341	5,135
20619	California(u)	7,626	5,770
.....	Calverton	12,046	....
21613	Cambridge	11,514	11,703
20748	Camp Springs(u)	16,392	16,118
21401	Cape St. Clair(u)	7,878	6,022
21234	Carney(u)	25,578	21,488
21228	Catonsville(u)	35,233	33,208
.....	Chesapeake Ranch Estates	5,423	....
20785	Cheverly	6,023	5,751
20815	Chevy Chase(u)	8,559	12,232
20783	Chillum(u)	31,309	32,775
20735	Clinton(u)	19,987	16,438
20904	Cloverly(u)	7,904	5,153
21030	Cockeysville(u)	18,668	17,013
20904	Colesville(u)	18,819	14,359
20740	College Park	21,927	23,614
*21044	Columbia(u)	75,883	52,518
20743	Coral Hills(u)	11,032	11,602
21114	Crofton(u)	12,781	12,009
21502	Cumberland	23,706	25,933
.....	Damascus	9,817	4,129
20747	District Heights	6,704	6,799
21222	Dundalk(u)	65,800	71,293
21601	Easton	9,372	7,536
20737	East Riverdale(u)	14,187	14,117
21219	Edgemere(u)	9,226	9,078
21040	Edgewood	23,903	19,455
.....	Eldersburg	9,720	4,959
.....	Elkridge	12,953	....
21921	Elkton	9,073	6,468
21043	Ellicott City(u)	41,396	21,784
21221	Essex(u)	40,872	39,614
20904	Fairland(u)	19,828	5,154
21047	Fallston(u)	5,730	5,572
21061	Ferndale(u)	16,355	14,314
20747	Forestville(u)	16,731	16,401
20755	Fort Meade(u)	12,509	14,083
.....	Fort Washington	24,032	....
21701	Frederick	40,148	28,086
.....	Friendly(u)	9,028	8,848
21532	Frostburg	8,075	7,715
*20877	Gaithersburg	39,542	26,424
.....	Garrison	5,045	....
20874	Germantown(u)	41,145	9,721
.....	Glenarden	5,025	4,993
21061	Glen Burnie(u)	37,305	37,263
20769	Glenn Dale(u)	9,689	5,106
.....	Greater Upper Marlboro	11,528	....
20770	Greenbelt	21,096	17,332
21122	Green Haven(u)	14,416	6,577
.....	Green Valley	9,424	4,934
21740	Hagerstown	35,445	34,132
21740	Halfway(u)	8,873	8,659
21078	Havre De Grace	8,952	8,763
20903	Hillandale(u)	10,318	9,686
20748	Hillcrest Heights	17,136	17,021
*20780	Hyattsville	13,864	12,709
.....	Jessup	6,537	4,288
21085	Joppatowne(u)	11,084	11,348
20785	Kentland(u)	7,967	8,596
20772	Kettering(u)	9,901	6,972
21122	Lake Shore(u)	13,269	10,181
20785	Landover(u)	5,052	5,374
20787	Langley Park(u)	17,474	14,038
20706	Lanham-Seabrook(u)	16,792	15,814
21227	Lansdowne-Baltimore Highlands(u)	15,509	16,759
.....	La Plata	5,841	2,484

ZIP code	Place	1990	1980
20772	Largo(u)	9,475	5,557
*20707	Laurel	19,438	12,103
20653	Lexington Pk.(u)	9,943	10,361
21090	Linthicum(u)	7,547	7,457
21207	Lochearn(u)	25,240	26,908
21037	Londontowne(u)	6,992	6,052
.....	Long Meadow	5,594	1,203
21093	Lutherville-Timonium(u)	16,442	17,854
20748	Marlow Heights(u)	5,885	5,824
.....	Marlton	5,523	.....
20707	Maryland City(u)	6,813	6,949
.....	Mays Chapel(u)	10,132	5,213
21220	Middle River(u)	24,616	26,756
.....	Milford Mill(u)	22,547	20,354
.....	Mitchellville	12,593	.....
20879	Montgomery Village(u)	32,315	18,725
20822	Mount Rainier	7,954	7,361
21402	Naval Academy(u)	5,420	5,367
20784	New Carrollton	12,002	12,632
20815	North Bethesda(u)	29,656	22,671
20895	North Kensington(u)	8,607	9,039
20707	North Laurel(u)	15,008	6,093
.....	North Potomac	18,456	.....
.....	Ocean City	5,146	4,946
21113	Odenton(u)	12,833	13,270
20832	Olney(u)	23,019	13,026
21206	Overlea(u)	12,137	12,965
21117	Owings Mills(u)	9,474	9,526
20745	Oxon Hill(u)	35,794	36,267
20785	Palmer Park(u)	7,019	7,986
21234	Parkville	31,617	35,159
.....	Parole	10,054	3,377
21122	Pasadena(u)	10,012	7,439
21126	Perry Hall(u)	22,723	13,455
21208	Pikesville(u)	24,815	22,555
20854	Potomac(u)	45,634	40,402
2:227	Pumphrey(u).	5,483	5,666
21133	Randallstown(u)	26,277	25,927
.....	Redland(u)	16,145	10,759
21136	Reisterstown(u)	19,314	19,385
.....	Riverdale	5,185	4,761
21122	Riviera Beach(u)	11,376	8,812
*20850	Rockville	44,835	43,811
.....	Rosaryville	8,976	.....
21237	Rosedale(u)	18,703	19,956
.....	Rossmoor	6,182	8,646
21221	Rossville(u)	9,492	8,646
20601	St. Charles(u)	28,717	13,921
21801	Salisbury	20,592	16,429
.....	Savage-Guilford	9,669	2,928
20743	Seat Pleasant	5,359	5,217
21144	Severn(u)	24,499	20,147
21146	Severna Park	25,879	21,253
*20907	Silver Spring(u)	76,046	72,893
21061	South Gate(u)	27,564	24,185
20895	South Kensington(u)	8,777	9,344
20707	South Laurel(u)	18,591	18,034
20912	Suitland-Silver Hills(u)	35,111	32,164
20748	Takoma Park	16,700	16,231
21204	Temple Hills(u)	6,865	6,630
20601	Towson(u)	49,445	51,083
20743	Waldorf(u)	15,058	9,782
20743	Walker Mill(u)	10,920	10,651
21157	Westminster	13,068	8,808
20902	Wheaton Glenmont(u)	53,720	48,598
.....	White Marsh	8,183	.....
20903	White Oak(u)	18,671	13,700
21207	Woodlawn	32,907	.....
21207	Woodlawn(u)	5,329	5,306

Massachusetts

See Note on Page 78

ZIP code	Place	Area	1990	1980
02351	Abington	(617)	13,817	13,887
01720	Acton	(508)	17,872	17,544
02743	Acushnet	(508)	9,554	8,704
01220	Adams Center(u)	(413)	6,356	6,857
.....	Adams	(413)	9,445	10,381
01001	Agawam	(413)	27,323	26,271
01913	Amesbury Center(u)	(508)	12,109	12,236
.....	Amesbury	(508)	14,997	13,971
01002	Amherst Center	(413)	17,824	17,773
.....	Amherst	(413)	35,228	33,229
.....	Andover		8,242	8,445
01810	Andover	(508)	29,151	26,370
02174	Arlington	(617)	44,630	44,630
01721	Ashland	(508)	12,066	9,165
01331	Athol Center(u)	(617)	8,732	8,708
.....	Athol	(508)	11,451	10,634
02703	Attleboro	(508)	38,383	34,196
01501	Auburn	(508)	15,005	14,845
*01432	Ayer	(508)	6,871	6,993
02630	Barnstable	(508)	40,949	30,898
01730	Bedford	(617)	12,996	13,067
01007	Belchertown	(413)	10,579	8,339
02019	Bellingham	(508)	14,877	14,300
02178	Belmont	(617)	24,720	24,720
01915	Beverly	(508)	38,195	37,655
01821	Billerica	(508)	37,609	36,727
01504	Blackstone	(508)	8,023	6,570
*02109	Boston	(617)	574,283	562,994
02532	Bourne	(508)	16,064	13,874
01921	Boxford	(508)	6,266	5,374
02184	Braintree	(617)	33,836	36,337
02631	Brewster	(508)	8,440	5,226
02324	Bridgewater	(508)	21,249	7,242
*02403	Brockton	(508)	92,788	95,172
02146	Brookline	(617)	54,718	55,062
01803	Burlington	(617)	23,302	23,486
*02138	Cambridge	(617)	95,802	95,322
02021	Canton	(617)	18,530	18,182
02330	Carver	(508)	10,590	6,988
.....	Centerville		9,190	3,640
01507	Charlton	(508)	9,576	6,719
02633	Chatham	(508)	6,579	6,071
01824	Chelmsford	(508)	32,383	32,388
02150	Chelsea	(617)	28,710	25,431
*01021	Chicopee	(413)	56,632	55,112
01510	Clinton	(508)	13,222	7,943
01778	Cochituate(u)	(617)	6,046	6,126
02025	Cohasset	(617)	7,075	7,174
01742	Concord	(508)	17,076	16,293
01226	Dalton	(413)	7,155	6,797
01923	Danvers	(508)	24,174	24,174
02714	Dartmouth	(508)	27,244	23,966
02026	Dedham	(617)	23,782	25,298
.....	Deerfield		5,018	.....
02638	Dennis	(508)	13,864	12,360
02715	Dighton	(508)	5,631	5,352
.....	Douglas		5,438	.....
01826	Dracut	(508)	25,594	21,249
01570	Dudley	(508)	9,540	8,717
02332	Duxbury	(617)	13,895	11,807
02333	East Bridgewater	(508)	11,104	9,945
02536	East Falmouth(u)	(617)	5,577	5,181
01027	Easthampton	(413)	15,537	15,580
01028	East Longmeadow	(413)	13,367	12,905
02334	Easton	(508)	19,807	16,623
02149	Everett	(617)	35,701	37,195
02719	Fairhaven	(508)	16,132	15,759
*02722	Fall River	(617)	92,703	92,574
.....	Falmouth	(508)	27,960	41,194
01420	Fitchburg	(508)	41,194	39,580
01433	Fort Devens(u)	(617)	8,973	9,546
02035	Foxborough	(508)	14,637	5,706
01701	Framingham	(508)	64,994	65,113
02038	Franklin Center(u)	(508)	9,965	9,296
.....	Franklin	(508)	22,095	18,217
02702	Freetown	(508)	8,522	7,058
01440	Gardner	(508)	20,125	17,900
01833	Georgetown	(508)	6,384	5,687
01930	Gloucester	(508)	28,716	27,768
01519	Grafton	(508)	13,035	11,238
01033	Granby	(413)	5,565	5,380
01230	Great Barrington	(413)	7,725	7,405
01301	Greenfield Center(u)	(508)	14,016	14,198
.....	Greenfield	(413)	18,666	18,436
01450	Groton	(508)	7,511	6,154
01834	Groveland	(508)	5,214	5,040
02338	Halifax	(617)	6,526	5,513
01936	Hamilton	(508)	7,280	6,960
02339	Hanover	(617)	11,912	11,358
02341	Hanson	(617)	9,028	8,508
01451	Harvard	(508)	12,329	12,170
02645	Harwich	(508)	10,275	8,971
01830	Haverhill	(508)	51,418	46,865
02043	Hingham	(617)	19,821	5,454
02343	Holbrook	(617)	11,041	11,041
01520	Holden	(508)	14,628	13,336
01746	Holliston	(508)	12,926	12,622
01040	Holyoke	(413)	43,704	44,678
.....	Hopedale		5,666	.....
01748	Hopkinton	(508)	9,191	7,114
01749	Hudson Center(u).	(508)	14,267	14,156
01749	Hudson	(508)	17,233	14,267
02045	Hull	(617)	10,466	10,466
02601	Hyannis(u)	(617)	14,120	9,118
.....	Ipswich	(508)	11,873	11,158
02364	Kingston	(617)	9,045	7,362
02346	Lakeville	(508)	7,785	5,931
01523	Lancaster	(508)	6,661	6,334
*01842	Lawrence	(508)	70,207	63,175
01238	Lee	(413)	5,849	6,247
01524	Leicester	(508)	10,191	9,446
01240	Lenox	(413)	5,069	6,523
01453	Leominster	(508)	38,145	34,508
02173	Lexington	(617)	28,974	29,479
01773	Lincoln	(617)	7,666	7,098
01460	Littleton	(508)	7,051	6,970
01106	Longmeadow	(413)	15,467	15,467
*01853	Lowell	(508)	103,439	92,418
01056	Ludlow	(413)	18,820	18,150
01462	Lunenburg	(508)	9,117	8,405
*01901	Lynn	(617)	81,245	78,471
01940	Lynnfield	(617)	11,274	11,267

ZIP code	Place	1990	1980
02148	Malden (617)	53,884	53,386
01944	Manchester (508)	5,286	5,424
02048	Mansfield (508)	16,568	7,170
01945	Marblehead (617)	19,971	19,971
01752	Marlborough (508)	31,813	30,617
02050	Marshfield (617)	21,531	20,916
.....	Marstons Mills	8,017	....
.....	Mashpee	7,884	....
02739	Mattapoisett (508)	5,850	5,597
01754	Maynard (508)	10,325	10,325
02052	Medfield (508)	10,531	5,985
02155	Medford (617)	57,407	58,076
02053	Medway (508)	9,931	8,447
02176	Melrose (617)	28,150	30,055
01844	Methuen (508)	39,990	36,701
02346	Middleborough Center(u) (508)	6,837	7,012
.....	Middleborough (508)	17,867	16,404
01757	Milford Center(u) (508)	23,339	21,730
.....	Milford (508)	25,355	23,390
01527	Millbury (508)	12,228	11,808
02054	Millis (508)	7,613	6,908
02186	Milton (617)	25,725	25,860
01057	Monson (413)	7,776	7,315
01351	Montague (413)	8,316	8,011
02554	Nantucket (508)	6,012	5,087
01760	Natick (508)	30,510	29,461
02192	Needham (617)	27,557	27,901
*02741	New Bedford (508)	99,922	98,478
.....	Newbury	5,623	....
01950	Newburyport (508)	16,317	15,900
02158	Newton (617)	82,585	83,622
02056	Norfolk (508)	9,270	6,363
01247	North Adams (413)	16,797	18,063
01002	North Amherst(u) (413)	6,239	5,616
01060	Northampton (413)	29,289	29,286
01845	North Andover (508)	22,792	20,129
*02760	North Attleborough (508)	25,038	16,178
01532	Northborough (508)	11,929	5,761
01534	Northbridge (508)	13,371	12,246
01864	North Reading (508)	12,002	11,455
02766	Norton (508)	14,265	12,690
02061	Norwell (617)	9,279	9,182
02062	Norwood (617)	28,700	29,711
01364	Orange (508)	7,312	6,844
02653	Orleans (508)	5,838	5,306
01540	Oxford Center(u) (508)	5,969	6,369
.....	Oxford (508)	12,588	11,680
01069	Palmer (413)	12,054	11,389
01960	Peabody (508)	47,039	45,976
02359	Pembroke (617)	14,544	13,487
01463	Pepperell (508)	10,098	8,061
01866	Pinehurst(u) (617)	6,614	6,588
01201	Pittsfield (413)	48,622	51,974
02762	Plainville (508)	6,871	5,857
*02360	Plymouth Center(u) (508)	7,258	7,232
.....	Plymouth (508)	45,608	35,913
02169	Quincy (617)	84,985	84,743
02368	Randolph (617)	30,093	28,218
02767	Raynham (508)	9,867	9,085
01867	Reading (617)	22,539	22,678
02769	Rehoboth (508)	8,656	7,570
02151	Revere (617)	42,786	42,423
02370	Rockland (617)	16,123	15,695
01966	Rockport (508)	7,482	5,448
01970	Salem (508)	38,091	38,276
01950	Salisbury (508)	6,882	5,973
02563	Sandwich (508)	15,489	8,727
01906	Saugus (617)	25,549	25,549
02066	Scituate (617)	16,786	5,180
02771	Seekonk (508)	13,046	12,269
02067	Sharon (617)	15,517	5,893
01464	Shirley (508)	6,118	5,124
01545	Shrewsbury (508)	24,146	22,674
02725	Somerset (508)	17,655	18,813
02143	Somerville (617)	76,210	77,372
.....	South Amherst	5,053	4,861
01772	Southborough (508)	6,628	6,193
01550	Southbridge Center(u) (508)	12,882	14,261
.....	Southbridge (508)	17,816	13,631
01075	South Hadley (413)	16,685	16,399
01077	Southwick (413)	7,667	7,382
02664	South Yarmouth(u) (617)	10,358	7,525
01562	Spencer Center (617)	6,306	6,350
.....	Spencer (508)	11,645	10,774
*01101	Springfield (413)	156,983	152,319
01564	Sterling (508)	6,481	5,440
02180	Stoneham (617)	22,203	21,424
02072	Stoughton (617)	26,777	26,710
01775	Stow (508)	5,328	5,144
01566	Sturbridge (508)	7,775	5,976
01776	Sudbury (508)	14,358	14,027
01527	Sutton (508)	6,824	5,855
01907	Swampscott (617)	13,650	13,837
02777	Swansea (508)	15,411	15,461
02780	Taunton (508)	49,832	45,001
01468	Templeton (508)	6,438	6,070
01876	Tewksbury (508)	27,266	24,635
01983	Topsfield (508)	5,754	5,709
01469	Townsend (508)	8,496	7,201
01879	Tyngsborough (508)	8,642	5,683
01569	Uxbridge (508)	10,415	8,374
01880	Wakefield (617)	24,825	24,895
02081	Walpole (508)	20,212	5,495
02154	Waltham (617)	57,878	58,200
01082	Ware Center(u) (413)	6,533	6,806
.....	Ware (413)	9,808	8,953
.....	Wareham (508)	19,232	18,457
02172	Watertown (617)	33,284	34,384
01778	Wayland (508)	11,874	12,170
01570	Webster Center(u) (508)	11,849	11,175
.....	Webster (508)	16,196	14,480
02181	Wellesley (617)	26,615	27,209
01581	Westborough (508)	14,133	13,619
01583	West Boylston (508)	6,611	6,204
02379	West Bridgewater (508)	6,389	6,359
01742	West Concord(u) (617)	5,761	5,331
01085	Westfield (413)	38,372	36,465
01886	Westford (508)	16,392	13,434
01473	Westminster (508)	6,191	5,139
02193	Weston (617)	10,200	11,169
02790	Westport (508)	13,852	13,763
01089	West Springfield (413)	27,537	27,042
02090	Westwood (617)	12,557	13,212
.....	West Yarmouth	5,409	3,852
02188	Weymouth (617)	54,063	55,601
01588	Whitinsville(u) (508)	5,639	5,379
02382	Whitman (617)	13,240	13,534
01095	Wilbraham (413)	12,635	12,053
01267	Williamstown (413)	8,220	8,741
01887	Wilmington (508)	17,654	17,471
01475	Winchendon (508)	8,805	7,019
01890	Winchester (617)	20,267	20,701
02152	Winthrop (617)	18,127	19,294
01801	Woburn (617)	35,943	36,626
*01613	Worcester (508)	169,759	161,799
02093	Wrentham (508)	9,006	7,580
02675	Yarmouth (508)	21,174	18,449

Michigan

ZIP code	Place	1990	1980
49221	Adrian (517)	22,097	21,276
49224	Albion (517)	10,066	11,059
.....	Allendale	6,950	....
48101	Allen Park (313)	31,092	34,196
48801	Alma (517)	9,034	9,652
49707	Alpena (517)	11,354	12,214
*48106	Ann Arbor (313)	109,592	107,969
.....	Auburn Hills	17,076	15,388
49016	Battle Creek (616)	53,540	35,724
48706	Bay City (517)	38,936	41,593
48505	Beecher(u) (313)	14,465	17,178
48809	Belding (616)	5,969	5,634
49022	Benton Harbor (616)	12,818	14,707
49022	Benton Heights(u) (616)	5,465	6,787
48072	Berkley (313)	16,960	18,637
48009	Beverly Hills (313)	10,610	11,598
49307	Big Rapids (616)	12,603	14,361
*48012	Birmingham (313)	19,997	21,689
48013	Bloomfield(u) (313)	42,137	42,876
.....	Bridgeport	8,569	....
.....	Brighton	5,686	4,268
.....	Buena Vista	8,196	....
*48502	Burton (313)	27,617	29,976
49601	Cadillac (616)	10,104	10,199
.....	Canton	57,047	....
48724	Carrollton(u) (517)	6,521	7,482
48015	Center Line (313)	9,026	9,293
48813	Charlotte (517)	8,083	8,251
48017	Clawson (313)	13,874	15,103
48043	Clinton(u) (313)	85,866	72,400
49036	Coldwater (517)	9,607	9,461
49321	Comstock Park(u) (616)	6,530	5,506
49508	Cutlerville(u) (616)	11,228	8,256
48423	Davison (313)	5,693	6,087
*48120	Dearborn (313)	89,286	90,660
48127	Dearborn Heights (313)	60,838	67,706
*48233	Detroit (313)	1,027,974	1,203,368
49047	Dowagiac (616)	6,409	6,307
48021	East Detroit (313)	35,283	38,280
49506	East Grand Rapids (616)	10,807	10,914
48823	East Lansing (517)	50,677	51,392
49001	Eastwood(u) (517)	6,340	7,186
48229	Ecorse (313)	12,180	14,447
49829	Escanaba (906)	13,659	14,355
49022	Fair Plain(u) (616)	8,051	8,289
48024	Farmington (313)	10,132	11,022
48024	Farmington Hills (313)	74,652	58,056
48430	Fenton (313)	8,444	8,098
48220	Ferndale (313)	25,084	26,227
48134	Flat Rock (313)	7,290	6,853
*48502	Flint (313)	140,761	159,611
48433	Flushing (313)	8,542	8,624
.....	Forest Hills	16,690	....
48026	Fraser (313)	13,899	14,560
48135	Garden City (313)	31,846	35,640
48439	Grand Blanc (313)	7,760	6,848

ZIP code	Place		1990	1980
49417	Grand Haven	(616)	11,951	11,763
48837	Grand Ledge	(517)	7,579	6,920
*49501	Grand Rapids	(616)	189,126	181,843
49418	Grandville	(616)	15,624	12,412
48838	Greenville	(616)	8,101	8,019
48138	Grosse Ile(u).	(313)	9,781	9,320
48236	Grosse Pointe.	(313)	5,681	5,901
48236	Grosse Pointe Farms.	(313)	10,092	10,551
48236	Grosse Pointe Park.	(313)	12,857	13,562
48236	Grosse Pointe Woods	(313)	17,715	18,886
48212	Hamtramck.	(313)	18,372	21,300
48225	Harper Woods.	(313)	14,903	16,361
48625	Harrison(u).	(517)	24,685	23,649
48840	Haslett(u).	(517)	10,230	7,025
49058	Hastings.	(616)	6,549	6,418
48030	Hazel Park.	(313)	20,051	20,914
48203	Highland Park.	(313)	20,121	27,909
49242	Hillsdale.	(517)	8,170	7,432
49423	Holland.	(616)	30,745	26,281
.....	Holly		5,595	4,874
48842	Holt(u)	(517)	11,744	10,097
49931	Houghton	(906)	7,498	7,512
48843	Howell.	(517)	8,184	6,976
.....	Hudsonville		6,170	4,844
48070	Huntington Woods	(313)	6,419	6,937
48141	Inkster.	(313)	30,772	35,190
48846	Ionia.	(616)	5,935	5,920
49801	Iron Mountain	(906)	8,525	8,341
49938	Ironwood.	(906)	6,849	7,741
49849	Ishpeming.	(906)	7,200	7,538
*49201	Jackson.	(517)	37,446	39,739
49428	Jenison(u).	(616)	17,882	16,230
*49001	Kalamazoo	(616)	80,277	79,722
49508	Kentwood.	(616)	37,826	30,438
49801	Kingsford.	(906)	5,480	5,290
49843	K.I. Sawyer(u).	(906)	6,577	7,345
48144	Lambertville(u).	(313)	7,860	6,341
*48924	Lansing.	(517)	127,321	130,414
48446	Lapeer.	(313)	7,759	6,198
48146	Lincoln Park.	(313)	41,832	45,105
*48150	Livonia.	(313)	100,850	104,814
49431	Ludington.	(616)	8,507	8,937
48071	Madison Heights.	(313)	32,196	35,375
49660	Manistee.	(616)	6,734	7,665
49855	Marquette.	(906)	21,977	23,288
49068	Marshall.	(616)	6,891	7,201
48040	Marysville.	(313)	8,515	7,345
48854	Mason.	(517)	6,768	6,019
48122	Melvindale.	(313)	11,216	12,322
49858	Menominee.	(906)	9,398	10,099
48640	Midland.	(517)	38,053	37,269
48042	Milford.	(313)	5,511	5,041
48161	Monroe.	(313)	22,902	23,531
48043	Mount Clemens.	(313)	18,405	18,991
48858	Mount Pleasant.	(517)	23,285	23,746
*49440	Muskegon.	(616)	40,283	40,823
49444	Muskegon Heights.	(616)	13,176	14,611
48047	New Baltimore.	(313)	5,798	5,439
49120	Niles.	(616)	12,458	13,115
.....	Northview(u).		13,712	11,662
48167	Northville.	(313)	6,226	5,698
49441	Norton Shores.	(616)	21,755	22,025
48050	Novi.	(313)	32,998	22,525
48237	Oak Park.	(313)	30,462	31,537
48864	Okemos(u).	(517)	20,216	8,882
48867	Owosso.	(517)	16,322	16,455
49770	Petoskey.	(616)	6,056	6,097
48170	Plymouth.	(313)	9,560	9,986
.....	Plymouth Township.		23,646	
*48053	Pontiac.	(313)	71,166	76,715
49081	Portage.	(616)	41,042	38,157
48060	Port Huron.	(313)	33,694	33,981
48239	Redford(u).	(313)	54,387	58,441
48218	River Rouge.	(313)	11,314	12,912
48192	Riverview.	(313)	13,894	14,569
48063	Rochester.	(313)	7,130	7,203
.....	Rochester Hills		61,766	40,704
48174	Romulus.	(313)	22,897	24,857
48066	Roseville.	(313)	51,412	54,311
*48068	Royal Oak.	(313)	65,410	70,893
*48605	Saginaw.	(517)	69,512	77,508
.....	Saginaw Township North.		23,018	
.....	Saginaw Township South		13,987	
.....	St. Clair.		5,116	4,780
*48083	St. Clair Shores.	(313)	68,107	76,210
48879	St. Johns.	(517)	7,284	7,376
49085	St. Joseph.	(616)	9,214	9,622
48176	Saline.	(313)	6,660	6,483
49783	Sault Ste. Marie.	(906)	14,689	14,448
.....	Shelby.		48,655	
.....	Shields.		6,634	
*48075	Southfield.	(313)	75,728	75,568
48198	Southgate.	(313)	30,771	32,058
49090	South Haven.	(616)	5,563	5,943
48178	South Lyon.	(313)	5,857	5,214
.....	South Monroe.		5,266	4,232
49015	Springfield.	(616)	5,582	5,917
*48078	Sterling Heights.	(313)	117,810	108,999
49091	Sturgis.	(616)	10,130	9,468

ZIP code	Place		1990	1980
48180	Taylor.	(313)	70,811	77,568
49286	Tecumseh.	(517)	7,462	7,320
.....	Temperance.		6,542	
49093	Three Rivers.	(616)	7,413	7,015
49684	Traverse City.	(616)	15,155	15,516
48183	Trenton.	(313)	20,586	22,762
48084	Troy.	(313)	72,884	67,102
48087	Utica.	(313)	5,081	5,282
49504	Walker.	(616)	17,279	15,088
.....	Walled Lake.		6,278	4,748
*48089	Warren.	(313)	144,864	161,134
48095	Waterford(u).	(313)	66,692	64,250
.....	Waverly.		15,614	
48184	Wayne.	(313)	19,899	21,159
48033	West Bloomfield(u).	(313)	54,843	41,962
48185	Westland.	(313)	84,724	84,603
49007	Westwood(u).	(616)	8,957	8,519
48096	Wixom.	(313)	8,550	6,705
48183	Woodhaven.	(313)	11,631	10,902
48753	Wurtsmith(u).	(517)	5,080	5,166
*48192	Wyandotte.	(313)	30,938	34,006
49509	Wyoming.	(616)	63,891	59,616
48197	Ypsilanti.	(313)	24,846	24,031
.....	Zeeland		5,417	4,764

Minnesota

ZIP code	Place		1990	1980
56007	Albert Lea.	(507)	18,310	19,200
56308	Alexandria.	(612)	7,838	7,608
55303	Andover.	(612)	15,216	9,387
55303	Anoka.	(612)	17,192	15,634
55124	Apple Valley.	(612)	34,598	21,818
55112	Arden Hills.	(612)	9,199	8,012
55912	Austin.	(507)	21,907	23,020
56601	Bemidji.	(218)	11,245	10,949
55433	Blaine.	(612)	38,975	28,558
55420	Bloomington.	(612)	86,335	81,831
56401	Brainerd.	(218)	12,353	11,489
55429	Brooklyn Center.	(612)	28,887	31,230
55429	Brooklyn Park.	(612)	56,381	43,332
.....	Buffalo		6,856	4,560
55337	Burnsville.	(612)	51,288	35,674
.....	Cambridge.		5,094	3,287
55316	Champlin.	(612)	16,849	9,006
55317	Chanhassen.	(612)	11,732	6,359
55318	Chaska.	(612)	11,339	8,346
55719	Chisholm.	(218)	5,290	5,930
55720	Cloquet.	(218)	10,885	11,142
55421	Columbia Heights.	(612)	18,910	20,029
55433	Coon Rapids.	(612)	52,978	35,826
.....	Corcoran.		5,199	4,252
55016	Cottage Grove	(612)	22,935	18,994
56716	Crookston.	(218)	8,119	8,628
55428	Crystal.	(612)	23,788	25,543
56501	Detroit Lakes.	(218)	6,635	7,106
55806	Duluth.	(218)	85,493	92,811
55121	Eagan.	(612)	47,409	20,700
55005	East Bethel.	(612)	8,050	6,626
56721	East Grand Forks.	(218)	8,658	8,537
*55343	Eden Prairie.	(612)	39,311	16,263
55435	Edina.	(612)	46,070	46,073
55330	Elk River.	(612)	11,143	6,785
56031	Fairmont.	(507)	11,265	11,506
55113	Falcon Heights.	(507)	5,380	5,291
55021	Faribault.	(507)	17,085	16,241
.....	Farmington.		5,940	4,370
56537	Fergus Falls.	(218)	12,362	12,519
.....	Forest Lake.		5,833	4,596
55432	Fridley.	(612)	28,335	30,228
55416	Golden Valley.	(612)	20,971	22,775
55744	Grand Rapids.	(218)	7,976	7,934
*55303	Ham Lake.	(612)	8,924	7,832
55033	Hastings.	(612)	15,445	12,827
55811	Hermantown.	(218)	6,761	6,759
55746	Hibbing.	(218)	18,046	21,193
55343	Hopkins.	(612)	16,534	15,336
55350	Hutchinson.	(612)	11,523	9,244
56649	International Falls.	(218)	8,325	5,611
55075	Inver Grove Heights.	(612)	22,477	17,171
55042	Lake Elmo.	(612)	5,903	5,296
55044	Lakeville.	(612)	24,854	14,790
.....	Lino Lakes.		8,807	4,966
55355	Litchfield.	(612)	6,041	5,904
55110	Little Canada.	(612)	8,971	7,102
56345	Little Falls.	(612)	7,232	7,250
.....	Mahtomedi.		5,569	3,851
56001	Mankato.	(507)	31,477	28,646
55369	Maple Grove.	(612)	38,736	20,525
55109	Maplewood.	(612)	30,954	26,990
56258	Marshall.	(507)	12,023	11,161
55118	Mendota Heights.	(612)	9,431	7,288
*55401	Minneapolis.	(612)	368,383	370,951
55343	Minnetonka.	(612)	48,370	38,683
56265	Montevideo.	(612)	5,499	5,845
56560	Moorhead.	(218)	32,295	29,998
56267	Morris.	(612)	5,613	5,367
55364	Mound.	(612)	9,634	9,280

ZIP code	Place	1990	1980
55112	Mounds View .... (612)	12,541	12,593
55112	New Brighton .... (612)	22,207	23,269
54428	New Hope .... (612)	21,853	23,087
56073	New Ulm .... (507)	13,132	13,755
55057	Northfield .... (507)	14,684	12,562
56001	North Mankato .... (507)	10,164	9,145
55109	North St. Paul .... (612)	12,376	11,921
55119	Oakdale .... (612)	18,374	12,123
55323	Orono .... (612)	7,285	6,845
55060	Owatonna .... (507)	19,386	18,632
55427	Plymouth .... (612)	50,889	31,615
55372	Prior Lake .... (612)	11,482	7,284
55303	Ramsey .... (612)	12,408	10,093
55066	Red Wing .... (612)	15,134	13,736
55423	Richfield .... (612)	35,710	37,851
55422	Robbinsdale .... (612)	14,396	14,422
55901	Rochester .... (507)	70,745	57,906
55068	Rosemount .... (612)	8,622	5,083
55113	Roseville .... (612)	33,485	35,820
55418	St. Anthony .... (612)	7,727	7,981
56301	St. Cloud .... (612)	48,812	42,566
55426	St. Louis Park .... (612)	43,787	42,931
*55101	St. Paul .... (612)	272,235	270,230
56082	St. Peter .... (507)	9,421	9,056
.....	Sartell	5,393	3,427
56379	Sauk Rapids .... (612)	7,825	5,793
.....	Savage	9,906	3,954
55379	Shakopee .... (612)	11,739	9,941
55126	Shoreview .... (612)	24,587	17,300
.....	Shorewood	5,917	4,646
55075	South St. Paul .... (612)	20,197	21,235
55432	Spring Lake Park ..... (612)	6,532	6,477
55082	Stillwater .... (612)	13,882	12,290
56701	Thief River Falls ..... (218)	8,010	9,105
55110	Vadnais Heights ...... (612)	11,041	5,111
55792	Virginia .... (218)	9,410	11,056
.....	Waite Park	5,020	3,496
56093	Waseca .... (507)	8,385	8,219
55118	West St. Paul .... (612)	19,248	18,527
55110	White Bear Lake ...... (612)	24,704	22,538
56201	Willmar .... (612)	17,531	15,895
55987	Winona .... (507)	25,399	25,075
55119	Woodbury .... (612)	20,075	10,297
56187	Worthington .... (507)	9,977	10,243

Mississippi (601)

ZIP code	Place	1990	1980
39730	Aberdeen	6,837	7,184
38821	Amory	7,093	7,307
38606	Batesville	6,403	5,162
39520	Bay St. Louis	8,063	7,850
*39530	Biloxi	46,319	49,311
38829	Booneville	7,955	6,199
39042	Brandon	11,077	9,626
39601	Brookhaven	10,243	10,800
39046	Canton	10,062	11,116
38614	Clarksdale	19,717	21,137
38732	Cleveland	15,384	14,524
39056	Clinton	21,847	14,660
39429	Columbia	6,815	7,733
39701	Columbus	23,799	27,503
38834	Corinth	11,820	13,178
.....	Crystal Springs	5,643	4,902
39532	D'Iberville(u)	6,566	6,236
39074	Forest	5,060	5,229
39553	Gautier(u)	10,088	10,392
38701	Greenville	45,226	40,613
38930	Greenwood	18,906	20,115
38901	Grenada	10,864	11,508
.....	Gulf Hills	5,004	4,512
39501	Gulfport	40,775	39,676
39401	Hattiesburg	41,882	40,829
38635	Holly Springs	7,261	7,285
.....	Horn Lake	9,069	4,326
38751	Indianola	11,809	8,050
*39205	Jackson	196,637	202,895
39090	Kosciusko	6,986	7,415
39440	Laurel	18,827	21,897
38756	Leland	6,366	6,667
39560	Long Beach	15,804	14,199
39339	Louisville	7,169	7,323
39648	McComb	11,591	12,331
.....	Madison	7,471	2,241
39301	Meridian	41,036	46,577
39563	Moss Point	17,837	18,998
39120	Natchez	19,460	22,209
38652	New Albany	6,775	7,072
39564	Ocean Springs	14,658	14,504
39567	Orange Grove(u)	15,676	13,476
38655	Oxford	9,984	9,882
39567	Pascagoula	25,899	29,318
39571	Pass Christian	5,557	5,014
39208	Pearl	19,588	18,602
39465	Petal	7,883	8,476
39350	Philadelphia	6,758	6,434
39466	Picayune	10,633	10,361
39157	Ridgeland	11,714	5,461

ZIP code	Place	1990	1980
.....	Ripley	5,371	4,271
.....	St. Martin	6,349	....
38671	Southaven(u)	17,949	16,441
39759	Starkville	18,458	16,139
38801	Tupelo	30,685	23,905
39180	Vicksburg	20,908	25,434
.....	Waveland	5,369	4,186
39367	Waynesboro	5,143	5,349
.....	West Hattiesburg	5,450	....
39773	West Point	8,489	8,811
38967	Winona	5,705	6,177
39194	Yazoo City	12,427	12,092

Missouri

ZIP code	Place	1990	1980
63123	Affton(u) .... (314)	21,106	23,181
63010	Arnold .... (314)	18,828	19,141
65605	Aurora .... (417)	6,459	6,437
63011	Ballwin .... (314)	21,816	12,656
63137	Bellefontaine Neighbors . (314)	10,922	12,082
64012	Belton .... (816)	18,150	12,708
63134	Berkeley .... (314)	12,450	15,922
63031	Black Jack .... (314)	6,128	5,293
64015	Blue Springs .... (816)	40,153	25,936
65613	Bolivar .... (417)	6,845	5,919
65233	Boonville .... (816)	7,095	6,959
63114	Breckenridge Hills .... (816)	5,404	5,666
63144	Brentwood .... (314)	8,150	8,209
63044	Bridgeton .... (314)	17,779	18,445
63701	Cape Girardeau ...... (314)	34,438	34,361
64836	Carthage .... (417)	10,747	11,104
63830	Caruthersville .... (314)	7,389	7,958
63834	Charleston .... (314)	5,085	5,230
.....	Chesterfield	37,991	28,384
64601	Chillicothe .... (816)	8,804	9,089
63105	Clayton .... (314)	13,874	14,306
64735	Clinton .... (816)	8,703	8,366
65201	Columbia .... (314)	69,101	62,061
63128	Concord(u) .... (314)	19,859	20,896
63126	Crestwood .... (314)	11,234	12,815
63141	Creve Coeur .... (314)	12,304	11,743
63136	Dellwood .... (314)	5,245	6,200
63020	De Soto .... (314)	5,993	5,993
63131	Des Peres .... (314)	8,395	7,953
63841	Dexter .... (314)	7,559	7,043
63011	Ellisville .... (314)	7,545	6,233
64024	Excelsior Springs ..... (816)	10,354	10,424
63640	Farmington .... (314)	11,598	8,270
63135	Ferguson .... (314)	22,286	24,549
63028	Festus .... (314)	8,105	7,574
*63033	Florissant .... (314)	51,206	55,721
65473	Fort Leonard Wood(u) .. (314)	15,863	21,262
65251	Fulton .... (314)	10,033	11,046
64118	Gladstone .... (816)	26,243	24,990
.....	Glasgow Village	5,199	....
63122	Glendale .... (314)	5,945	6,035
64030	Grandview .... (816)	24,967	24,561
63401	Hannibal .... (314)	18,004	18,811
64701	Harrisonville .... (816)	7,683	6,372
*63042	Hazelwood .... (314)	15,324	13,098
*64051	Independence .... (816)	112,301	111,797
63755	Jackson .... (314)	9,256	7,827
65101	Jefferson City .... (314)	35,481	33,619
63136	Jennings .... (314)	15,905	16,934
64801	Joplin .... (417)	40,961	39,126
*64108	Kansas City .... (816)	435,146	448,028
63857	Kennett .... (314)	10,941	10,145
63501	Kirksville .... (816)	17,152	17,167
63122	Kirkwood .... (314)	27,291	27,739
63124	Ladue .... (314)	8,847	9,369
.....	Lake St. Louis	7,400	3,843
65536	Lebanon .... (417)	9,983	9,507
64063	Lee's Summit .... (816)	46,418	28,741
63125	Lemay(u) .... (314)	18,005	35,424
64068	Liberty .... (816)	20,459	16,251
63552	Macon .... (816)	5,571	5,680
63863	Malden .... (314)	5,123	6,096
63011	Manchester .... (314)	6,542	6,351
63143	Maplewood .... (314)	9,962	10,960
65340	Marshall .... (816)	12,711	12,781
63043	Maryland Heights(u) .... (314)	25,407	26,413
64468	Maryville .... (816)	10,663	9,558
.....	Mehlville	27,557	....
65265	Mexico .... (314)	11,290	12,276
65270	Moberly .... (816)	12,839	13,418
65708	Monett .... (417)	6,529	6,148
64850	Murphy(u) .... (314)	9,342	8,121
64850	Neosho .... (417)	9,254	9,493
64772	Nevada .... (417)	8,597	9,044
63121	Northwoods .... (314)	5,106	5,831
.....	Oakville	31,750	....
63366	O'Fallon .... (314)	18,698	8,677
63132	Olivette .... (314)	7,573	7,952
63114	Overland .... (314)	17,987	19,620
63775	Perryville .... (314)	6,933	7,343
63120	Pine Lawn .... (314)	5,092	6,570
63901	Poplar Bluff .... (314)	16,996	17,139

ZIP code	Place	1990	1980
.....	Raymore	5,592	3,154
64133	Raytown (816)	30,601	31,831
.....	Republic	6,292	4,485
64085	Richmond (816)	5,738	5,499
63117	Richmond Heights (314)	10,448	11,516
63124	Rock Hill (314)	5,217	5,702
65401	Rolla (314)	14,090	13,303
63074	St. Ann (314)	14,489	15,523
63301	St. Charles (314)	54,555	37,379
63114	St. John (314)	7,466	7,854
*64501	St. Joseph (816)	71,852	76,691
*63155	St. Louis (314)	396,685	452,801
63376	St. Peters (314)	45,779	15,700
63126	Sappington(u) (314)	10,917	11,388
65301	Sedalia (816)	19,800	20,927
63119	Shrewsbury (314)	6,416	5,077
63801	Sikeston (314)	17,641	17,431
63138	Spanish Lake(u) (314)	20,322	20,632
*65801	Springfield (417)	140,494	133,116
63080	Sullivan (314)	5,661	5,461
.....	Town and Country	9,519	3,187
64683	Trenton (816)	6,129	6,811
63084	Union (314)	5,909	5,506
63130	University City (314)	40,087	42,690
64093	Warrensburg (816)	15,244	13,807
63090	Washington (314)	10,704	9,251
64870	Webb City (417)	7,449	7,309
63119	Webster Groves (314)	22,987	23,097
.....	Wentzville	5,088	3,193
65775	West Plains (417)	8,913	7,741

Montana (406)

ZIP code	Place	1990	1980
59711	Anaconda-Deer Lodge County	10,278	12,518
*59101	Billings	81,151	66,818
59715	Bozeman	22,660	21,645
59701	Butte-Silver Bow	33,336	37,205
*59401	Great Falls	55,097	56,894
59501	Havre	10,201	10,891
59601	Helena	24,569	23,938
.....	Helena Valley West Central	6,327	.....
59901	Kalispell	11,917	10,689
59044	Laurel	5,686	5,481
59457	Lewistown	6,051	7,104
59047	Livingston	6,701	6,994
59402	Malmstrom AFB(u)	5,938	6,675
59301	Miles City	8,461	9,602
*59801	Missoula	42,918	33,351
59801	Orchard Homes(u)	10,317	10,837
59270	Sidney	5,217	5,726

Nebraska

ZIP code	Place	1990	1980
69301	Alliance (308)	9,765	9,920
68310	Beatrice (402)	12,354	12,891
68005	Bellevue (402)	30,982	21,813
68008	Blair (402)	6,860	6,418
69337	Chadron (308)	5,588	5,933
.....	Chalco	7,337	.....
68601	Columbus (402)	19,480	17,328
68025	Fremont (402)	23,680	23,979
69341	Gering (308)	7,946	7,760
68801	Grand Island (308)	39,386	33,180
68901	Hastings (402)	22,837	23,045
68949	Holdrege (308)	5,671	5,624
68847	Kearney (402)	24,396	21,158
68128	La Vista (402)	9,840	9,588
68850	Lexington (308)	6,601	7,040
*68501	Lincoln (402)	191,972	171,932
69001	McCook (308)	8,112	8,404
68410	Nebraska City (402)	6,547	7,127
68701	Norfolk (402)	21,476	19,449
69101	North Platte (308)	22,605	24,509
68113	Offutt AFB West(u) (402)	10,883	8,787
69153	Ogallala (308)	5,095	5,638
*68108	Omaha (402)	335,795	313,939
68046	Papillion (402)	10,372	6,399
68048	Plattsmouth (402)	6,412	6,295
68127	Ralston (402)	6,236	5,143
69361	Scottsbluff (308)	13,711	14,156
68434	Seward (402)	5,634	5,713
69162	Sidney (308)	5,959	6,010
68776	South Sioux City (402)	9,677	9,339
68787	Wayne (402)	5,142	5,240
68467	York (402)	7,884	7,723

Nevada (702)

ZIP code	Place	1990	1980
89005	Boulder City	12,567	9,590
*89701	Carson City	40,443	32,022
89112	East Las Vegas(u)	11,087	6,449
89801	Elko	14,736	8,758
.....	Enterprise	6,412	.....
.....	Fallon	6,438	4,262

ZIP code	Place	1990	1980
.....	Fernley	5,164	.....
.....	Gardnerville Ranchos	7,455	3,542
89015	Henderson	64,942	24,363
89450	Incline Village-Crystal Bay(u)	7,119	6,225
*89114	Las Vegas	258,295	164,674
89110	Nellis AFB(u)	8,377	7,476
*89030	North Las Vegas	47,707	42,739
.....	Pahrump	7,424	84,818
89109	Paradise(u)	124,682	84,818
*89501	Reno	133,850	100,756
*89431	Sparks	53,367	40,780
.....	Spring Creek	5,866	4,155
.....	Spring Valley	51,726	.....
89110	Sunrise Manor(u)	95,362	44,155
89431	Sun Valley(u)	11,391	8,822
89101	Winchester(u)	23,365	19,728
.....	Winnemucca	6,134	4,140

New Hampshire (603)

See Note on Page 78

ZIP code	Place	1990	1980
.....	Amherst	9,068	.....
.....	Atkinson	5,188	.....
.....	Barrington	6,164	.....
03102	Bedford	12,563	9,481
.....	Belmont	5,796	.....
03570	Berlin	11,824	13,084
.....	Bow	5,500	.....
03743	Claremont	13,902	14,557
03301	Concord	36,006	30,400
03818	Conway	7,940	7,158
03038	Derry Compact(u)	20,446	12,248
.....	Derry	29,603	18,875
03820	Dover	25,042	22,377
03824	Durham Compact(u)	9,236	8,448
.....	Durham	11,818	10,652
.....	Epping	5,162	.....
03833	Exeter Compact(u)	9,556	8,947
.....	Exeter	12,481	11,024
.....	Farmington	5,739	.....
03235	Franklin	8,304	7,901
.....	Gilford	5,867	.....
03045	Goffstown	14,621	11,315
.....	Hampstead	6,732	.....
03842	Hampton Compact(u)	7,989	6,779
.....	Hampton	12,278	10,493
03755	Hanover Compact(u)	6,538	6,861
.....	Hanover	9,212	9,119
.....	Hollis	5,705	.....
03106	Hooksett	8,767	7,303
03051	Hudson	19,530	7,626
.....	Jaffrey	5,361	.....
03431	Keene	22,430	21,449
.....	Kingston	5,591	.....
03246	Laconia	15,743	15,575
03766	Lebanon	12,183	11,134
.....	Litchfield	5,516	.....
03561	Littleton	5,827	5,558
03053	Londonderry	19,781	10,114
*03101	Manchester	99,567	90,936
03054	Merrimack	22,156	15,406
03055	Milford	11,795	8,015
*03060	Nashua	79,662	67,865
.....	Newmarket	7,157	.....
03773	Newport	6,110	6,229
03076	Pelham	9,408	8,090
.....	Pembroke	6,561	.....
.....	Peterborough	5,239	.....
03865	Plaistow	7,316	5,609
.....	Plymouth	5,811	.....
03801	Portsmouth	25,925	26,254
03077	Raymond	8,713	5,453
03867	Rochester	26,630	21,560
03079	Salem	25,746	24,124
03874	Seabrook	6,503	5,917
03878	Somersworth	11,249	10,350
.....	Suncook	5,214	4,698
.....	Swanzey	6,236	.....
.....	Weare	6,193	.....
03087	Windham	9,000	5,664

New Jersey

ZIP code	Place	1990	1980
08201	Absecon (609)	7,298	6,859
07401	Allendale (201)	5,900	5,901
07712	Asbury Park (908)	16,799	17,015
*08401	Atlantic City (609)	37,986	40,199
08106	Audubon (609)	9,205	9,533
.....	Avenel	15,504	.....
08007	Barrington (609)	6,774	7,418
07002	Bayonne (201)	61,444	65,047
08722	Beachwood (201)	9,324	7,687
07109	Belleville (201)	34,213	35,367
08031	Bellmawr (609)	12,603	13,721
07719	Belmar (908)	5,877	6,771

ZIP code	Place		1990	1980
07621	Bergenfield	(201)	24,458	25,568
07922	Berkeley Hts. Twp.	(201)	11,980	12,549
08009	Berlin	(609)	5,672	5,786
07924	Bernardsville	(908)	6,597	6,715
08012	Blackwood(u)	(609)	5,120	5,219
07003	Bloomfield	(201)	45,061	47,792
07003	Bloomingdale	(201)	7,530	7,867
07603	Bogota	(201)	7,824	8,344
07005	Boonton	(201)	8,343	8,620
08805	Bound Brook	(908)	9,487	9,710
08723	Brick Twp	(201)	66,473	53,629
08302	Bridgeton	(609)	18,942	18,795
08203	Brigantine	(609)	11,354	8,318
08015	Browns Mills(u)	(609)	11,429	10,568
07828	Budd Lake	(201)	7,272	6,523
08016	Burlington	(609)	9,835	10,246
07405	Butler	(201)	7,392	7,616
07006	Caldwell	(201)	7,549	7,624
*08101	Camden	(609)	87,492	84,910
07072	Carlstadt	(201)	5,510	6,166
08069	Carney's Point	(609)	7,686	7,574
07008	Carteret	(908)	19,025	20,598
07009	Cedar Grove Twp.	(201)	12,053	12,600
07928	Chatham	(201)	8,007	8,537
*08002	Cherry Hill Twp.	(609)	69,319	68,785
08077	Cinnaminson Twp.	(609)	14,583	16,072
07066	Clark Twp.	(201)	14,629	16,699
08312	Clayton	(609)	6,155	6,013
08021	Clementon	(609)	5,601	5,764
07010	Cliffside Park	(201)	20,393	21,464
*07015	Clifton	(201)	71,742	74,388
07624	Closter	(201)	8,094	8,164
08108	Collingswood	(609)	15,289	15,838
	Colonia		18,238	
07016	Cranford Twp.	(908)	22,624	24,573
07626	Cresskill	(201)	7,558	7,609
	Crestwood Village	(201)	8,030	7,965
07801	Dover	(201)	15,115	14,681
07628	Dumont	(201)	17,187	18,334
08812	Dunellen	(908)	6,528	6,593
08816	East Brunswick Twp.	(201)	43,548	37,711
07936	East Hanover	(201)	9,926	9,319
*07019	East Orange	(201)	73,552	77,878
07073	East Rutherford	(201)	7,902	7,849
07724	Eatontown	(908)	13,800	12,703
	Edgewater Borough		5,001	4,628
08010	Edgewater Park	(609)	8,388	9,273
08817	Edison Twp.	(201)	88,680	70,193
*07201	Elizabeth	(908)	110,002	106,201
07407	Elmwood Park	(201)	17,623	18,377
07630	Emerson	(201)	6,930	7,793
*07631	Englewood	(201)	24,850	23,701
07632	Englewood Cliffs	(201)	5,634	5,698
08618	Ewing Twp.	(609)	34,185	34,842
07006	Fairfield	(201)	7,615	7,987
07701	Fair Haven	(201)	5,270	5,679
07410	Fair Lawn	(201)	30,548	32,229
07022	Fairview	(201)	10,733	10,519
07023	Fanwood	(908)	7,115	7,767
08518	Florence-Roebling(u)	(609)	8,564	7,677
07932	Florham Park	(201)	8,521	9,359
	Ford		14,392	
08640	Fort Dix(u)	(609)	10,205	14,297
07024	Fort Lee	(201)	31,997	32,449
07417	Franklin Lakes	(201)	9,873	8,769
07728	Freehold	(908)	10,742	10,020
07026	Garfield	(201)	26,727	26,803
08753	Gilford Park	(201)	8,668	6,528
08028	Glassboro	(609)	15,614	14,574
08029	Glendora	(609)	5,201	5,632
07028	Glen Ridge	(201)	7,076	7,855
07452	Glen Rock	(201)	10,883	11,497
08030	Gloucester City	(609)	12,649	13,121
07093	Guttenberg	(201)	8,268	7,340
*07602	Hackensack	(201)	37,049	36,039
07840	Hackettstown	(908)	8,120	8,850
08033	Haddonfield	(609)	11,628	12,337
08035	Haddon Heights	(609)	7,860	8,361
07508	Haledon	(201)	6,951	6,607
08037	Hammonton	(609)	12,208	12,298
07981	Hanover Twp.	(201)	11,538	11,846
07029	Harrison	(201)	13,425	12,242
07604	Hasbrouck Heights	(201)	11,488	12,166
07506	Hawthorne	(201)	17,084	18,200
08904	Highland Park	(201)	13,279	13,396
	Hightstown		5,126	4,581
07642	Hillsdale	(201)	9,750	10,495
07205	Hillside Twp.	(201)	21,044	21,440
07030	Hoboken	(201)	33,397	42,460
08753	Holiday City-Berkeley	(201)	14,293	9,019
	Holiday City South		5,452	
07843	Hopatcong	(201)	15,586	15,531
07111	Irvington	(201)	59,774	61,473
	Iselin		16,141	
	Jamesburg		5,294	4,114
*07303	Jersey City	(201)	228,537	223,532
07734	Keansburg	(908)	11,069	10,613
07032	Kearny	(201)	34,874	35,735
08824	Kendall Park(u)	(201)	7,127	7,419

ZIP code	Place		1990	1980
07033	Kenilworth	(201)	7,574	8,221
07735	Keyport	(908)	7,586	7,413
07405	Kinnelon	(201)	8,470	7,770
07871	Lake Mohawk(u)	(201)	8,930	8,498
08701	Lakewood(u)	(908)	26,095	22,863
08879	Laurence Harbor(u)	(201)	6,361	6,737
......	Lawrenceville		6,446	.....
......	Leisure Village			
	West-Pine Lake Park		10,139	.....
07605	Leonia	(201)	8,365	8,027
07035	Lincoln Park	(201)	10,978	8,806
	Lincroft		6,193	.....
07036	Linden	(908)	36,701	37,836
08021	Lindenwold	(609)	18,734	18,196
08221	Linwood	(609)	6,866	6,144
07424	Little Falls Twp.	(201)	11,294	11,496
07643	Little Ferry	(201)	9,989	9,399
07739	Little Silver	(201)	5,721	5,548
07039	Livingston Twp.	(201)	26,609	28,040
07644	Lodi	(201)	22,355	23,956
07740	Long Branch	(908)	28,658	29,819
07071	Lyndhurst Twp.	(201)	18,262	20,326
08641	McGuire AFB(u)	(609)	7,580	7,853
07940	Madison	(201)	15,850	15,357
08859	Madison Park	(201)	7,490	7,447
08736	Manasquan	(908)	5,369	5,354
08835	Manville	(201)	10,567	11,278
08052	Maple Shade Twp.	(609)	19,211	20,525
07040	Maplewood Twp.	(201)	21,756	22,950
08402	Margate City	(609)	8,431	9,179
08053	Marlton(u)	(609)	10,228	9,411
07747	Matawan	(908)	9,270	8,837
07607	Maywood	(201)	9,473	9,895
08619	Mercerville-Hamilton Sq.(u)	(609)	26,873	25,446
08840	Metuchen	(908)	12,804	13,762
08846	Middlesex	(201)	13,055	13,480
07432	Midland Park	(201)	7,047	7,381
07041	Milburn Twp.	(201)	18,630	19,543
08850	Milltown	(201)	6,968	7,136
08332	Millville	(609)	25,992	24,815
*07042	Montclair	(201)	37,729	38,321
07645	Montvale	(201)	6,946	7,318
08057	Moorestown-Lenola(u)	(609)	13,242	13,695
07950	Morris Plains	(201)	5,219	5,305
07960	Morristown	(201)	16,189	16,614
07092	Mountainside	(201)	6,657	7,118
08060	Mount Holly Twp.	(609)	10,639	10,818
	Mystic Island		7,400	4,929
*07102	Newark	(201)	275,221	329,248
08901	New Brunswick	(908)	41,711	41,442
07646	New Milford	(201)	15,990	16,876
07974	New Providence	(201)	11,439	12,426
07860	Newton	(201)	7,521	7,748
07032	North Arlington	(201)	13,790	16,587
07047	North Bergen Twp.	(201)	48,414	47,019
08902	North Brunswick Twp.	(201)	31,287	22,220
07006	North Caldwell	(201)	6,706	5,832
08225	Northfield	(609)	7,305	7,795
07508	North Haledon	(201)	7,987	8,177
07060	North Plainfield	(201)	18,820	19,108
	North Wildwood		5,017	4,714
07110	Nutley	(201)	27,099	28,998
07436	Oakland	(201)	11,997	13,443
	Ocean Acres		5,587	4,850
08226	Ocean City	(609)	15,512	13,949
07757	Oceanport	(201)	6,146	5,888
08857	Old Bridge	(201)	22,151	21,815
07649	Oradell	(201)	8,024	8,658
*07050	Orange	(201)	29,925	31,136
07650	Palisades Park	(201)	14,536	13,732
08065	Palmyra	(609)	7,056	7,085
07652	Paramus	(201)	25,067	26,474
07656	Park Ridge	(201)	8,102	8,515
07054	Parsippany-Troy Hills	(201)	48,478	49,868
*07055	Passaic	(201)	58,041	52,463
*07510	Paterson	(201)	140,891	137,970
08066	Paulsboro	(609)	6,577	6,944
08110	Pennsauken Twp.	(609)	34,733	33,775
08069	Penns Grove	(609)	5,228	5,760
08070	Pennsville Center(u)	(609)	12,218	12,467
07440	Pequannock Twp.	(201)	12,844	13,776
*08861	Perth Amboy	(908)	41,967	38,951
08865	Phillipsburg	(908)	15,757	16,647
08021	Pine Hill	(201)	9,854	8,684
08071	Pitman	(609)	9,365	9,7447
*07061	Plainfield	(908)	46,567	45,555
08232	Pleasantville	(609)	16,027	13,435
08742	Point Pleasant	(908)	18,177	17,747
08742	Point Pleasant Beach	(908)	5,112	5,415
07442	Pompton Lakes	(201)	10,539	10,660
08540	Princeton	(609)	12,016	12,035
07508	Prospect Park	(201)	5,053	5,142
07065	Rahway	(908)	25,325	26,723
08057	Ramblewood(u)	(609)	6,181	6,475
07446	Ramsey	(201)	13,228	12,899
08869	Raritan	(201)	5,798	6,128
07701	Red Bank	(908)	10,636	12,031
07657	Ridgefield	(201)	9,996	10,294
07660	Ridgefield Park	(201)	12,454	12,738

ZIP code	Place		1990	1980
*07451	Ridgewood	(201)	24,152	25,208
07456	Ringwood	(201)	12,623	12,625
07661	River Edge	(201)	10,603	11,111
08075	Riverside Twp.	(609)	7,974	7,941
07675	River Vale	(201)	9,410	9,489
07726	Robertsville	(201)	9,841	8,461
07662	Rochelle Park Twp.	(201)	5,587	5,603
07866	Rockaway	(201)	6,243	6,852
07203	Roselle	(908)	20,314	20,641
07204	Roselle Park	(201)	12,805	13,377
07760	Rumson	(201)	6,701	7,623
08078	Runnemede	(609)	9,042	9,461
*07070	Rutherford	(201)	17,790	19,068
07662	Saddle Brook Twp.	(201)	13,296	14,084
08079	Salem	(609)	6,883	6,959
08872	Sayreville	(201)	34,986	29,969
07076	Scotch Plains Twp.	(201)	21,160	20,774
07094	Secaucus	(201)	14,061	13,719
08753	Silverton	(201)	9,175	7,236
08083	Somerdale	(609)	5,440	5,900
08873	Somerset	(201)	22,070	21,731
08244	Somers Point	(609)	11,216	10,330
08876	Somerville	(908)	11,632	11,973
08879	South Amboy	(908)	7,863	8,322
07079	South Orange Vill. Twp.	(201)	16,390	15,864
07080	South Plainfield	(908)	20,489	20,521
08882	South River	(908)	13,692	14,361
08884	Spotswood	(201)	7,983	7,840
07081	Springfield Twp.	(201)	13,420	13,955
07762	Spring Lake Heights	(908)	5,341	5,424
08084	Stratford	(609)	7,614	8,005
07747	Strathmore(u)	(201)	7,060	
07876	Succasunna-Kenvil	(201)	11,781	10,931
07901	Summit	(908)	19,757	21,071
07666	Teaneck Twp.	(201)	37,825	39,007
07670	Tenafly	(201)	13,326	13,552
07724	Tinton Falls	(201)	12,361	7,740
*08753	Toms River(u)	(908)	7,524	7,465
07512	Totowa	(201)	10,177	11,448
*08608	Trenton	(609)	88,675	92,124
08520	Twin Rivers	(609)	7,715	7,742
07083	Union Twp.	(201)	50,024	50,184
07735	Union Beach	(201)	6,156	6,354
07087	Union City	(201)	58,012	55,593
07458	Upper Saddle River.	(201)	7,198	7,958
08406	Ventnor City.	(609)	11,005	11,704
07044	Verona	(201)	13,597	14,166
08251	Villas	(609)	8,136	5,909
08360	Vineland	(609)	54,780	53,753
07463	Waldwick	(201)	9,757	10,802
07057	Wallington	(201)	10,828	10,741
07465	Wanaque	(201)	9,711	10,025
07882	Washington	(908)	6,474	6,429
07675	Washington Twp. (Bergen).	(908)	9,245	9,550
07060	Watchung	(201)	5,110	5,290
07470	Wayne Twp.	(201)	47,025	46,474
07087	Weehawken Twp.	(201)	12,385	13,168
07006	West Caldwell	(201)	10,422	11,407
*07091	Westfield	(908)	28,870	30,447
07728	West Freehold	(201)	11,166	9,929
07764	West Long Branch	(201)	7,690	7,380
07480	West Milford Twp.	(201)	25,430	22,750
07093	West New York	(201)	38,125	39,194
07052	West Orange	(201)	39,103	39,510
07424	West Paterson	(201)	10,982	11,293
07675	Westwood	(201)	10,446	10,714
07885	Wharton	(201)	5,405	5,485
08610	White Horse	(609)	9,397	10,098
07886	White Meadow Lake(u).	(201)	8,002	8,429
08094	Williamstown	(609)	10,891	5,768
08046	Willingboro Twp.	(609)	36,291	39,912
07095	Woodbridge Twp.	(908)	17,434	90,074
08096	Woodbury	(609)	10,904	10,353
07675	Woodcliff Lake	(201)	5,303	5,644
07075	Wood-Ridge	(201)	7,506	7,929
07481	Wyckoff Twp.	(201)	15,372	15,500
08620	Yardville-Groveville.	(609)	9,248	9,414
.....	Yorketown	(201)	6,313	5,330

New Mexico (505)

ZIP code	Place		1990	1980
88310	Alamogordo		27,596	24,024
*87101	Albuquerque		384,736	332,920
.....	Anthony		5,160	
88210	Artesia		10,610	10,385
87410	Aztec		5,479	5,512
87002	Belen		6,547	5,617
.....	Bernalillo		5,960	2,988
.....	Bloomfield		5,214	4,881
88220	Carlsbad		24,952	25,496
88101	Clovis		30,954	31,194
.....	Corrales		5,453	2,791
88030	Deming		10,970	9,964
87532	Espanola		8,389	6,803
87401	Farmington		33,997	31,222
87301	Gallup		19,154	18,167
87020	Grants		8,626	11,439

ZIP code	Place		1990	1980
88240	Hobbs		29,115	29,153
88330	Holloman AFB(u)		5,891	7,245
*88001	Las Cruces		62,126	45,086
87701	Las Vegas		14,753	14,322
87544	Los Alamos(u)		11,455	11,039
.....	Los Lunas		6,013	3,525
88260	Lovington		9,322	9,727
87107	North Valley(u)		12,507	5,096
87114	Paradise Hills		5,513	5,096
88130	Portales		10,690	9,940
87740	Raton		7,372	8,225
87124	Rio Rancho Estates.		32,505	9,985
88201	Roswell		44,654	39,676
87115	Sandia(u).		6,742	5,288
*87501	Santa Fe		55,859	49,160
87420	Shiprock		7,687	7,237
88061	Silver City		10,683	9,887
87801	Socorro		8,159	7,173
87105	South Valley(u)		35,701	38,916
.....	Sunland		8,179	4,313
87901	Truth or Consequences		6,221	5,219
88401	Tucumcari		6,831	6,765
87544	White Rock		6,192	6,560
87327	Zuni Pueblo		5,857	5,551

New York

ZIP code	Place		1990	1980
.....	Airmont		7,835	.....
*12207	Albany	(518)	101,082	101,727
11507	Albertson(u)	(516)	5,166	5,561
.....	Albion		5,863	4,897
11701	Amityville	(516)	9,286	9,076
12010	Amsterdam	(518)	20,714	21,872
12603	Arlington(u)	(914)	11,948	11,305
13021	Auburn	(315)	31,258	32,548
*11702	Babylon	(516)	12,249	12,388
11510	Baldwin(u)	(516)	22,719	31,630
.....	Baldwin Harbor		7,899	.....
13027	Baldwinsville	(315)	6,591	6,446
14020	Batavia	(716)	16,310	16,703
14810	Bath	(607)	5,801	6,042
11705	Bayport(u)	(516)	7,702	9,282
11706	Bay Shore(u)	(516)	21,279	10,784
11709	Bayville	(516)	7,193	7,034
.....	Baywood		7,351	.....
12508	Beacon	(914)	13,243	12,937
11710	Bellmore(u)	(516)	16,438	18,106
11714	Bethpage(u)	(516)	15,761	16,840
*13902	Binghamton	(607)	53,008	55,860
11716	Bohemia(u)	(516)	9,556	9,308
11717	Brentwood(u)	(516)	45,218	44,321
10510	Briarcliff Manor	(914)	7,070	7,115
14610	Brighton (u)	(716)	34,455	35,776
14420	Brockport	(716)	8,749	9,776
10708	Bronxville	(914)	6,028	6,267
*14240	Buffalo	(716)	328,123	357,870
14424	Canandaigua	(716)	10,725	10,419
13617	Canton	(315)	6,379	7,055
11514	Carle Place(u)	(516)	5,107	5,470
11516	Cedarhurst	(516)	5,716	6,162
11720	Centereach(u)	(516)	26,720	30,136
11934	Center Moriches(u)	(516)	5,987	5,703
11721	Centerport(u)	(516)	5,333	6,576
11722	Central Islip(u)	(516)	26,028	19,734
14225	Cheektowaga(u)	(716)	84,387	92,145
.....	Chestnut Ridge		7,517	8,217
12043	Cobleskill	(518)	5,268	5,272
12047	Cohoes	(518)	16,825	18,144
12205	Colonie	(518)	8,019	8,869
11725	Commack(u)	(516)	36,124	34,719
10920	Congers(u)	(914)	8,003	7,123
11726	Copiague(u)	(516)	20,769	20,132
11727	Coram(u)	(516)	30,111	24,752
14830	Corning	(607)	11,938	12,953
13045	Cortland	(607)	19,801	20,138
10520	Croton-on-Hudson	(914)	7,018	6,889
.....	Dansville		5,002	4,979
11729	Deer Park(u)	(516)	28,840	30,394
12054	Delmar(u)	(518)	8,360	8,423
14043	Depew	(716)	17,673	19,819
13214	DeWitt(u)	(315)	8,244	9,024
11746	Dix Hills(u)	(516)	25,849	26,693
10522	Dobbs Ferry	(914)	9,940	10,053
14048	Dunkirk	(716)	13,989	15,310
14052	East Aurora	(716)	6,647	6,803
10709	Eastchester(u)	(914)	18,537	20,305
12302	East Glenville(u)	(518)	6,518	6,537
11576	East Hills.	(516)	6,746	7,160
11730	East Islip(u)	(516)	14,325	13,852
11758	East Massapequa(u)	(516)	19,550	13,987
11554	East Meadow(u)	(516)	36,909	39,317
11731	East Northport(u)	(516)	20,411	20,187
11772	East Patchogue(u)	(516)	20,195	18,139
14445	East Rochester	(716)	6,932	7,596
11518	East Rockaway	(516)	10,152	10,917
.....	East Shoreham		5,461	.....
*14901	Elmira	(607)	33,724	35,327

ZIP code	Place		1990	1980
11003	Elmont(u)	(516)	28,612	27,592
11731	Elwood(u)	(516)	10,916	11,847
13760	Endicott	(607)	13,531	14,457
13760	Endwell(u)	(607)	12,602	13,745
13219	Fairmount(u)	(315)	12,266	13,415
14450	Fairport	(716)	5,943	5,970
11735	Farmingdale	(516)	8,022	7,946
11738	Farmingville(u)	(516)	14,842	13,398
*11001	Floral Park	(516)	15,947	16,805
.....	Fort Drum		11,578	....
11768	Fort Salonga(u)	(516)	9,176	9,550
11010	Franklin Square(u)	(516)	28,205	29,051
14063	Fredonia	(716)	10,436	11,126
11520	Freeport	(516)	39,894	38,272
13069	Fulton	(315)	12,929	13,312
11530	Garden City	(516)	21,686	22,927
11040	Garden City Park(u)	(516)	7,437	7,712
14624	Gates-North Gates(u)	(716)	14,995	15,244
14454	Geneseo	(716)	7,187	6,746
14456	Geneva	(315)	14,143	15,133
11542	Glen Cove	(516)	24,149	24,618
12801	Glens Falls	(518)	15,023	15,897
12801	Glens Falls North(u)	(518)	7,976	6,956
12078	Gloversville	(518)	16,656	17,836
.....	Goshen		5,255	4,874
*11022	Great Neck	(516)	8,745	9,168
11020	Great Neck Plaza	(516)	5,897	5,604
14616	Greece(u)	(716)	15,632	16,177
11740	Greenlawn(u)	(516)	13,208	13,869
12083	Greenville(u)	(518)	9,528	8,706
14075	Hamburg	(716)	10,442	10,582
11946	Hampton Bays(u)	(516)	7,893	7,256
10528	Harrison	(914)	23,308	23,046
10530	Hartsdale(u)	(914)	9,587	10,216
10706	Hastings-on-Hudson	(914)	8,000	8,573
11787	Hauppauge(u)	(516)	19,750	20,960
10927	Haverstraw	(914)	9,438	8,800
*11551	Hempstead	(516)	49,453	40,404
13350	Herkimer	(315)	7,945	8,383
11557	Hewlett(u)	(516)	6,620	6,986
*11802	Hicksville(u)	(516)	40,174	43,245
10977	Hillcrest(u)	(914)	6,447	5,733
.....	Hilton		5,216	4,151
11741	Holbrook(u)	(516)	25,273	24,382
11742	Holtsville(u)	(516)	14,972	13,515
14843	Hornell	(607)	9,877	10,234
14845	Horseheads	(607)	6,802	7,348
12534	Hudson	(518)	8,034	7,986
12839	Hudson Falls	(518)	7,651	7,419
11743	Huntington(u)	(516)	18,243	21,727
11746	Huntington Station(u)	(516)	28,247	28,769
13357	Ilion	(315)	8,888	9,450
11696	Inwood(u)	(516)	7,767	8,228
14617	Irondequoit(u)	(716)	52,322	57,648
10533	Irvington	(914)	6,348	5,774
11751	Islip(u)	(516)	18,924	13,438
11752	Islip Terrace(u)	(516)	5,530	5,588
14850	Ithaca	(607)	29,541	28,732
14701	Jamestown	(716)	34,681	35,775
10535	Jefferson Valley-Yorktown(u)	(914)	14,118	13,380
11753	Jericho(u)	(516)	13,141	12,739
13790	Johnson City	(607)	16,890	17,126
12095	Johnstown	(518)	9,058	9,360
14217	Kenmore	(716)	17,180	18,474
11754	Kings Park(u)	(516)	17,773	16,131
12401	Kingston	(914)	23,095	24,481
.....	Kiryas Joel		7,437	2,088
14218	Lackawanna	(716)	20,585	22,701
10512	Lake Carmel(u)	(914)	8,489	7,295
11755	Lake Grove	(516)	9,612	9,692
11779	Lake Ronkonkoma(u)	(516)	18,997	38,336
11552	Lakeview(u)	(516)	5,476	5,276
14086	Lancaster	(716)	11,940	13,056
10538	Larchmont	(914)	6,181	6,308
12110	Latham(u)	(518)	10,131	11,182
11559	Lawrence	(516)	6,513	6,175
11756	Levittown(u)	(516)	53,286	57,045
11757	Lindenhurst	(516)	26,879	26,919
13365	Little Falls	(315)	5,829	6,156
14094	Lockport	(716)	24,426	24,844
11561	Long Beach	(516)	33,510	34,073
12211	Loudonville(u)	(518)	10,822	11,480
11563	Lynbrook	(516)	19,208	20,424
10541	Mahopac(u)	(914)	7,755	7,681
12953	Malone	(518)	6,777	7,668
11565	Malverne	(516)	9,054	9,262
10543	Mamaroneck	(914)	17,325	17,616
11030	Manhasset(u)	(516)	7,718	8,485
11050	Manorhaven(u)	(516)	5,672	5,384
.....	Manorville		6,198	....
11758	Massapequa(u)	(516)	22,018	24,454
11762	Massapequa Park	(516)	18,044	19,779
13662	Massena	(315)	11,719	12,851
11950	Mastic(u)	(516)	13,778	10,413
11951	Mastic Beach(u)	(516)	10,293	8,318
13211	Mattydale(u)	(315)	6,418	7,511
12118	Mechanicville	(518)	5,249	5,500
11763	Medford(u)	(516)	21,274	20,418
14103	Medina	(716)	6,686	6,392

ZIP code	Place		1990	1980
11746	Melville(u)	(516)	12,586	8,139
11566	Merrick(u)	(516)	23,042	24,478
11953	Middle Island(u)	(516)	7,848	5,703
10940	Middletown	(914)	24,160	21,454
11764	Miller Place(u)	(516)	9,315	7,877
11501	Mineola	(516)	18,994	20,757
10950	Monroe	(914)	6,672	5,996
10952	Monsey(u)	(914)	13,986	12,380
12701	Monticello	(914)	6,597	6,306
.....	Mount Ivy.		6,013	....
10549	Mount Kisco	(914)	9,108	8,025
11766	Mount Sinai(u)	(516)	8,023	6,591
*10551	Mount Vernon	(914)	67,153	66,713
12590	Myers Corner(u)	(914)	5,599	5,180
10954	Nanuet(u)	(914)	14,065	12,578
11767	Nesconset(u)	(516)	10,712	10,706
14513	Newark	(315)	9,849	10,017
12550	Newburgh	(914)	26,454	23,438
11590	New Cassel(u)	(516)	10,257	9,635
10956	New City(u)	(914)	33,673	35,859
11040	New Hyde Park(u).	(516)	9,728	9,801
.....	New Paltz		5,463	4,938
10801	New Rochelle	(914)	67,265	70,794
*12550	New Windsor Center(u)	(914)	8,898	7,812
*10001	New York	(212)	7,322,564	7,071,639
*14302	Niagara Falls	(716)	61,840	71,384
11701	North Amityville(u)	(516)	13,849	13,140
11703	North Babylon(u)	(516)	18,081	19,019
11706	North Bay Shore(u)	(516)	12,799	35,020
11710	North Bellmore(u)	(516)	19,707	20,630
11713	North Bellport(u)	(516)	8,182	7,432
11757	North Lindenhurst(u)	(516)	10,563	11,511
11758	North Massapequa(u)	(516)	19,365	21,385
11566	North Merrick(u)	(516)	12,113	12,848
11040	North New Hyde Park(u).	(516)	14,359	15,114
11772	North Patchogue(u)	(516)	7,374	7,126
11768	Northport	(516)	7,572	7,651
13212	North Syracuse	(315)	7,363	7,970
10591	North Tarrytown	(914)	8,152	7,994
14120	North Tonawanda	(716)	34,989	35,760
11580	North Valley Stream(u)	(516)	14,574	14,530
11793	North Wantagh(u)	(516)	12,276	12,677
13815	Norwich	(607)	7,613	8,082
10960	Nyack	(914)	6,558	6,428
11769	Oakdale(u)	(516)	7,875	8,090
11572	Oceanside(u)	(516)	32,423	33,639
13669	Ogdensburg	(315)	13,521	12,375
11804	Old Bethpage(u)	(516)	5,610	6,215
14760	Olean	(716)	16,946	18,207
13421	Oneida	(315)	10,850	10,810
13820	Oneonta	(607)	13,954	14,933
12550	Orange Lake(u)	(914)	5,196	5,120
10562	Ossining	(914)	22,582	20,196
13126	Oswego	(315)	19,195	19,793
11771	Oyster Bay(u)	(516)	6,687	6,497
11772	Patchogue	(516)	11,060	11,291
10965	Pearl River(u)	(914)	15,314	15,893
10566	Peekskill	(914)	19,536	18,236
10803	Pelham	(914)	6,413	6,848
10803	Pelham Manor	(914)	5,443	6,130
14527	Penn Yan	(315)	5,248	5,242
11714	Plainedge(u)	(516)	8,739	9,629
11803	Plainview(u)	(516)	26,207	28,037
12901	Plattsburgh	(518)	21,255	21,057
12903	Plattsburgh AFB(u)	(518)	5,483	5,905
10570	Pleasantville	(914)	6,592	6,749
10573	Port Chester	(914)	24,728	23,565
11777	Port Jefferson	(516)	7,455	6,731
11776	Port Jefferson Station(u)	(516)	7,232	17,009
12771	Port Jervis	(914)	9,060	8,699
11050	Port Washington(u)	(516)	15,387	14,521
13676	Potsdam	(315)	10,251	10,635
*12601	Poughkeepsie	(914)	28,844	29,757
12144	Rensselaer	(518)	8,255	9,047
11961	Ridge(u)	(516)	11,734	8,977
11901	Riverhead(u)	(516)	8,814	6,339
*14603	Rochester	(716)	231,636	241,741
*11570	Rockville Centre	(516)	24,727	25,412
11778	Rocky Point(u)	(516)	8,596	7,012
12205	Roessleville(u)	(518)	10,753	11,685
13440	Rome	(315)	44,350	43,826
11779	Ronkonkoma	(516)	20,391	....
11575	Roosevelt(u)	(516)	15,030	14,109
11577	Roslyn Heights(u)	(516)	6,405	6,546
12303	Rotterdam(u)	(518)	21,228	22,933
10580	Rye	(914)	14,936	15,083
.....	Rye Brook		7,765	7,996
11780	St. James(u)	(516)	12,703	12,122
14779	Salamanca	(716)	6,566	6,890
.....	Salisbury		12,226	....
12983	Saranac Lake	(518)	5,377	5,578
12866	Saratoga Springs	(518)	25,001	23,906
11782	Sayville(u)	(516)	16,550	12,013
10583	Scarsdale	(914)	16,987	17,650
*12301	Schenectady	(518)	65,566	67,972
10940	Scotchtown(u)	(914)	8,765	7,352
12302	Scotia	(518)	7,359	7,280
11579	Sea Cliff	(516)	5,054	5,364
11783	Seaford(u)	(516)	15,597	16,117

ZIP code	Place	1990	1980
.....	Searingtown	5,020	.....
11784	Selden(u) (516)	20,608	17,259
13148	Seneca Falls (315)	7,370	7,466
11733	Setauket-East Setauket(u) (516)	13,634	10,176
11967	Shirley(u) (516)	22,936	18,072
11787	Smithtown(u) (516)	25,638	30,906
13209	Solvay (315)	6,717	7,140
11789	South Beach(u) (516)	9,102	8,071
11735	South Farmingdale(u) (516)	15,377	16,439
14850	South Hill(u) (607)	5,423	.....
11746	South Huntington(u) (516)	9,624	14,854
.....	South Lockport	7,112	3,366
.....	Southold	5,192	4,770
14904	Southport(u) (607)	7,753	8,329
11581	South Valley Stream(u) (516)	5,328	5,462
10977	Spring Valley (914)	21,802	20,537
11790	Stony Brook(u) (516)	13,726	16,155
11980	Stony Point(u) (914)	10,587	8,686
10901	Suffern (914)	11,055	10,794
11791	Syosset(u) (516)	18,967	9,818
*13201	Syracuse (315)	163,860	170,105
10983	Tappan(u) (914)	6,867	8,267
10591	Tarrytown (914)	10,739	10,648
.....	Terryville	10,275	.....
.....	Thiells	5,204	.....
10594	Thornwood(u) (914)	7,025	7,197
14150	Tonawanda (716)	17,284	18,693
.....	Tonawanda	65,284	72,795
*12180	Troy (518)	54,269	56,638
10707	Tuckahoe (914)	6,302	6,076
11553	Uniondale(u) (516)	20,328	20,016
*13503	Utica (315)	68,637	75,632
10989	Valley Cottage(u) (914)	9,007	8,214
*11580	Valley Stream (516)	33,946	35,769
.....	Wading River	5,317	.....
12586	Walden (914)	5,836	5,659
11793	Wantagh(u) (516)	18,567	19,817
.....	Warwick	5,984	4,320
13165	Waterloo (315)	5,116	5,303
13601	Watertown (315)	29,429	27,861
12189	Watervliet (518)	11,061	11,354
14580	Webster (716)	5,464	5,499
14895	Wellsville (716)	5,241	5,769
11704	West Babylon(u) (516)	42,410	41,699
11590	Westbury (516)	13,060	13,871
14905	West Elmira(u) (607)	5,218	5,485
12801	West Glens Falls(u) (518)	5,964	5,331
10993	West Haverstraw (914)	9,183	9,181
11552	West Hempstead(u) (516)	17,689	18,536
11743	West Hills(u) (516)	5,849	6,071
11795	West Islip(u) (516)	28,419	29,533
12203	Westmere(u) (518)	6,750	6,881
10996	West Point(u) (914)	8,024	8,105
14224	West Seneca(u) (716)	47,866	51,210
13219	Westvale(u) (315)	5,952	6,169
.....	Wheatley Heights	5,027	.....
10602	White Plains (914)	48,718	46,999
14221	Williamsville (716)	5,583	6,017
11596	Williston Park (516)	7,516	8,216
11797	Woodbury(u) (516)	8,008	7,043
11598	Woodmere(u) (516)	15,578	17,205
11798	Wyandach(u) (516)	8,950	13,215
*10701	Yonkers (914)	188,082	195,351
10598	Yorktown Heights(u) (914)	7,690	7,696

North Carolina

ZIP code	Place	1990	1980
28001	Albemarle (704)	14,939	15,110
27263	Archdale (919)	6,913	5,326
27203	Asheboro (919)	16,362	15,252
*28801	Asheville (704)	61,607	54,022
.....	Belmont	8,434	4,607
.....	Black Mountain	5,418	4,083
28607	Boone (704)	12,915	10,191
28712	Brevard (704)	5,388	5,323
27215	Burlington (919)	39,498	37,266
28542	Camp Le Jeune(u) (919)	36,716	30,764
27510	Carrboro (919)	11,553	7,336
27511	Cary (919)	43,858	21,763
27514	Chapel Hill (919)	38,719	32,421
*28202	Charlotte (704)	395,934	315,474
27012	Clemmons(u) (919)	6,020	4,842
28328	Clinton (919)	8,204	7,552
28025	Concord (704)	27,347	16,942
.....	Conover	5,465	4,245
28334	Dunn (919)	8,336	8,962
*27701	Durham (919)	136,611	101,149
27288	Eden (919)	15,238	15,672
27932	Edenton (919)	5,268	5,357
27909	Elizabeth City (919)	14,292	14,004
*28302	Fayetteville (919)	75,695	59,507
28043	Forest City (704)	7,475	7,688
28307	Fort Bragg(u) (919)	34,744	37,834
27529	Garner (919)	14,967	10,073
28052	Gastonia (704)	54,732	47,218
27530	Goldsboro (919)	40,709	31,871
27253	Graham (919)	10,426	8,674

ZIP code	Place	1990	1980
*27420	Greensboro (919)	183,521	155,642
27834	Greenville (919)	44,972	35,740
.....	Half Moon	6,306	3,592
.....	Hamlet	6,196	4,720
28532	Havelock (919)	20,268	17,718
27536	Henderson (919)	15,655	13,522
28739	Hendersonville (704)	7,284	6,862
28601	Hickory (704)	28,301	20,757
*27260	High Point (919)	69,496	63,479
26348	Hope Mills (919)	8,184	5,412
28540	Jacksonville (919)	30,013	18,237
28081	Kannapolis(u) (704)	29,696	30,303
27284	Kernersville (919)	10,836	5,875
28086	Kings Mountain (704)	8,763	9,080
28501	Kinston (919)	25,295	25,234
28352	Laurinburg (919)	11,643	11,480
28645	Lenoir (704)	14,192	13,748
27292	Lexington (704)	16,581	15,711
.....	Lincolnton	6,847	4,879
28358	Lumberton (919)	18,601	18,241
.....	Masonboro	7,010	3,881
.....	Matthews	13,651	1,648
28212	Mint Hill (704)	11,567	7,915
28110	Monroe (704)	16,127	12,639
28115	Mooresville (704)	9,317	8,575
.....	Morehead	6,046	4,359
28655	Morganton (704)	15,085	13,763
27030	Mount Airy (919)	7,156	6,862
.....	Mount Holly	7,710	4,530
28560	New Bern (919)	17,363	14,557
27604	New Hope (Wake)(u) (919)	5,694	6,745
28540	New River Station(u)	9,732	5,401
28658	Newton (704)	9,304	7,624
27565	Oxford (919)	7,913	7,709
.....	Pinehurst	5,103	1,746
.....	Piney Green-White Oak(u) (919)	8,999	6,058
*27611	Raleigh (919)	207,951	150,255
27320	Reidsville (919)	12,183	12,492
27870	Roanoke Rapids (919)	15,722	14,702
28379	Rockingham (919)	9,399	8,300
27801	Rocky Mount (919)	48,997	41,526
27573	Roxboro (919)	7,332	7,532
28601	St. Stephens(u) (704)	8,734	10,797
28144	Salisbury (704)	23,087	22,677
27330	Sanford (919)	14,475	14,773
.....	Seagate	5,444	3,422
28150	Shelby (704)	14,669	15,310
.....	Smith Creek	7,461	.....
27577	Smithfield (919)	7,540	7,288
28387	Southern Pines (919)	9,129	8,620
.....	South Gastonia	5,487	4,767
28390	Spring Lake (919)	7,524	6,273
28677	Statesville (919)	17,567	18,622
27886	Tarboro (919)	11,037	8,741
27360	Thomasville (919)	15,915	14,144
27370	Trinity(u) (919)	5,469	6,887
.....	Wake Forest	5,769	3,780
27889	Washington (919)	9,075	8,418
28786	Waynesville (704)	6,758	6,765
28472	Whiteville (919)	5,078	5,565
27892	Williamston (919)	5,503	6,159
28401	Wilmington (919)	55,530	44,000
27893	Wilson (919)	36,930	34,424
*27102	Winston-Salem (919)	143,485	131,885

North Dakota (701)

ZIP code	Place	1990	1980
58501	Bismarck	49,256	44,485
58301	Devils Lake	7,782	7,442
58601	Dickinson	16,097	15,924
58102	Fargo	74,111	61,383
58201	Grand Forks	49,425	43,765
58201	Grand Forks AFB(u)	9,343	3,390
58401	Jamestown	15,571	16,280
58554	Mandan	15,177	15,513
58701	Minot	34,544	32,843
58701	Minot AFB(u)	9,095	9,880
58072	Valley City	7,163	7,774
58075	Wahpeton	8,751	9,064
58078	West Fargo	12,287	10,099
58801	Williston	13,131	13,336

Ohio

ZIP code	Place	1990	1980
45810	Ada (419)	5,413	5,669
*44309	Akron (216)	223,019	237,177
44601	Alliance (216)	23,376	24,315
44001	Amherst (216)	10,332	10,638
44805	Ashland (419)	20,079	20,326
44004	Ashtabula (216)	21,633	23,449
45701	Athens (614)	21,265	19,743
44202	Aurora (216)	9,192	8,177
44515	Austintown(u) (216)	32,371	33,636
44011	Avon (216)	7,337	7,241

ZIP code	Place		1990	1980	ZIP code	Place		1990	1980
44012	Avon Lake	(216)	15,066	13,222	44839	Huron	(419)	7,030	7,123
44203	Barberton	(216)	27,623	29,751	44131	Independence	(216)	6,500	6,607
44140	Bay Village	(216)	17,000	17,846	45638	Ironton	(614)	12,751	14,290
44122	Beachwood	(216)	10,677	9,983	45640	Jackson	(614)	6,144	6,675
45385	Beavercreek	(513)	33,626	31,589	44240	Kent	(216)	28,835	26,164
44146	Bedford	(216)	14,822	15,056	43326	Kenton	(419)	8,356	8,605
44146	Bedford Heights	(216)	12,131	13,214	45236	Kenwood(u)	(513)	7,469	9,928
43906	Bellaire	(614)	6,028	8,241	45429	Kettering	(513)	60,569	61,186
45305	Bellbrook	(513)	6,511	5,174	44094	Kirtland	(216)	5,681	5,969
43311	Bellefontaine	(513)	12,142	11,888	44107	Lakewood	(216)	59,718	61,963
44811	Bellevue	(419)	8,146	8,187	43130	Lancaster	(614)	34,507	34,953
45714	Belpre	(614)	6,796	7,193	.....	Landen	.....	9,263	2,870
44017	Berea	(216)	19,051	19,567	45036	Lebanon	(513)	10,453	9,636
43209	Bexley	(614)	13,088	13,405	*45802	Lima	(419)	45,549	47,827
43004	Blacklick Estates(u)	(614)	10,080	11,223	43228	Lincoln Village(u)	(614)	9,958	10,548
45242	Blue Ash	(513)	11,860	9,510	43138	Logan	(614)	6,725	6,557
44512	Boardman(u)	(216)	38,596	39,161	43140	London	(614)	7,807	6,958
43402	Bowling Green	(419)	28,176	25,728	*44052	Lorain	(216)	71,245	75,416
44141	Brecksville	(216)	11,818	10,132	44641	Louisville	(216)	8,087	7,996
45211	Bridgetown North	(513)	11,748	11,460	45140	Loveland	(513)	9,990	9,106
44141	Broadview Heights	(216)	12,219	10,920	44124	Lyndhurst	(216)	15,982	18,092
44144	Brooklyn	(216)	11,706	12,342	44056	Macedonia	(216)	7,509	6,571
44142	Brook Park	(216)	22,865	26,195	.....	Mack South	.....	5,767	....
44212	Brunswick	(216)	28,230	28,104	45243	Madeira	(513)	9,141	9,341
43506	Bryan	(419)	8,348	7,879	*44901	Mansfield	(419)	50,627	53,927
44820	Bucyrus	(419)	13,496	13,433	44137	Maple Heights	(216)	27,089	29,735
43725	Cambridge	(614)	11,748	13,573	45750	Marietta	(614)	15,026	16,467
44405	Campbell	(216)	10,038	11,619	43302	Marion	(614)	34,075	37,040
44406	Canfield	(216)	5,409	5,535	43935	Martins Ferry	(614)	7,990	9,331
*44711	Canton	(216)	84,161	93,077	43040	Marysville	(513)	9,656	7,414
45822	Celina	(419)	9,650	9,137	45040	Mason	(513)	11,452	8,692
45459	Centerville	(513)	21,082	18,886	44646	Massillon	(216)	31,007	30,557
45211	Cheviot	(513)	9,616	9,888	43537	Maumee	(419)	15,561	15,747
45601	Chillicothe	(614)	21,923	23,420	44124	Mayfield Heights	(216)	19,847	21,550
*45234	Cincinnati	(513)	364,040	385,409	44256	Medina	(216)	19,231	15,268
43113	Circleville	(614)	11,666	11,700	44060	Mentor	(216)	47,358	42,065
*44101	Cleveland	(216)	505,616	573,822	44060	Mentor-on-the-Lake	(216)	8,271	7,919
44118	Cleveland Heights	(216)	54,052	56,438	45342	Miamisburg	(513)	17,834	15,304
43410	Clyde	(419)	5,776	5,489	44130	Middleburg Heights	(216)	14,702	16,218
*43235	Columbus	(614)	632,910	565,021	45042	Middletown	(513)	46,022	43,719
44030	Conneaut	(216)	13,241	13,835	45150	Milford	(513)	5,660	5,679
44410	Cortland	(216)	5,666	5,011	45242	Montgomery	(513)	9,753	10,084
43812	Coshocton	(614)	12,193	13,405	45439	Moraine	(513)	5,989	5,325
45238	Covedale(u)	(513)	6,669	5,830	45231	Mount Healthy	(513)	7,580	7,562
*44222	Cuyahoga Falls	(216)	48,950	50,526	43050	Mount Vernon	(614)	14,550	14,323
*45401	Dayton	(513)	182,044	193,536	.....	Munroe Falls	.....	5,359	4,731
45236	Deer Park	(513)	6,181	6,745	43545	Napoleon	(419)	8,884	8,614
43512	Defiance	(419)	16,768	16,810	43055	Newark	(614)	44,389	41,200
43015	Delaware	(614)	20,030	18,780	45344	New Carlisle	(513)	6,049	6,498
45833	Delphos	(419)	7,093	7,314	43764	New Lexington	(614)	5,117	5,179
.....	Dent	.....	6,416	....	44663	New Philadelphia	(216)	15,698	16,883
44622	Dover	(216)	11,329	11,782	44446	Niles	(216)	21,128	23,088
.....	Drexel	.....	5,143	....	45239	Northbrook(u)	(513)	11,471	8,357
.....	Dry Run	.....	5,389	....	44720	North Canton	(216)	14,748	14,228
.....	Dublin	.....	16,366	3,855	45239	North College Hill	(513)	11,002	11,114
44112	East Cleveland	(216)	33,096	36,957	.....	Northgate	.....	7,864	....
44094	Eastlake	(216)	21,161	22,104	44057	North Madison(u)	(216)	8,699	8,741
43920	East Liverpool	(216)	13,654	16,687	44070	North Olmsted	(216)	34,204	36,486
44413	East Palestine	(216)	5,168	5,306	45502	Northridge(u)	(513)	5,939	5,559
45320	Eaton	(513)	7,396	6,839	45414	Northridge(u) (Montgomery)	(513)	9,448	9,720
.....	Edgewood	.....	5,189	3,099	44039	North Ridgeville	(216)	21,564	21,522
*44035	Elyria	(216)	56,746	57,538	44133	North Royalton	(216)	23,197	17,671
45322	Englewood	(513)	11,432	11,329	.....	Northview(u)	(513)	10,337	9,973
44117	Euclid	(216)	54,875	59,999	43619	Northwood	(419)	5,506	5,495
45324	Fairborn	(513)	31,300	29,702	44203	Norton	(216)	11,477	12,242
45014	Fairfield	(513)	39,729	30,777	44857	Norwalk	(419)	14,731	14,358
44313	Fairlawn	(216)	5,779	6,100	45212	Norwood	(513)	23,674	26,342
44126	Fairview Park	(216)	18,028	19,311	45873	Oakwood	(513)	8,957	9,372
45840	Findlay	(419)	35,703	35,594	44074	Oberlin	(216)	8,191	8,660
.....	Finneytown	.....	13,096	....	44138	Olmsted Falls	(216)	6,741	5,868
45405	Forest Park	(513)	18,609	18,566	43616	Oregon	(419)	18,334	18,675
.....	Forestville	.....	9,185	....	44667	Orrville	(216)	7,712	7,511
45426	Fort McKinley(u)	(513)	9,740	10,161	45431	Overlook-Page Manor(u)	(513)	13,242	14,825
44830	Fostoria	(419)	14,983	15,743	45056	Oxford	(513)	18,937	17,655
45005	Franklin	(513)	11,026	10,711	44077	Painesville	(216)	15,699	16,391
43420	Fremont	(419)	17,648	17,834	44129	Parma	(216)	87,876	92,548
43230	Gahanna	(614)	27,791	18,001	44130	Parma Heights	(216)	21,448	23,112
44833	Galion	(419)	11,859	12,391	44124	Pepper Pike	(216)	6,185	6,177
44125	Garfield Heights	(216)	31,739	34,938	44646	Perry Heights(u)	(216)	9,055	9,206
44041	Geneva	(216)	6,597	6,655	43551	Perrysburg	(419)	12,551	10,215
44420	Girard	(216)	11,304	12,517	.....	Pickerington	.....	5,668	3,917
43212	Grandview Heights	(614)	7,010	7,420	45356	Piqua	(513)	20,612	20,480
45123	Greenfield	(513)	5,172	5,150	44319	Portage Lakes(u)	(216)	13,373	11,310
45331	Greenville	(513)	12,863	12,999	43452	Port Clinton	(419)	7,106	7,223
45239	Groesbeck(u)	(513)	6,684	9,594	45662	Portsmouth	(614)	22,676	25,943
43123	Grove City	(614)	19,661	16,816	44266	Ravenna	(216)	12,069	11,987
*45012	Hamilton	(513)	61,368	63,189	45215	Reading	(513)	12,038	12,843
45030	Harrison	(513)	7,518	5,855	43068	Reynoldsburg	(614)	25,748	20,661
43055	Heath	(614)	7,231	6,969	44143	Richmond Heights	(213)	9,611	10,095
44124	Highland Heights	(216)	6,249	5,739	44270	Rittman	(216)	6,147	6,063
43026	Hilliard	(614)	11,796	8,131	44116	Rocky River	(216)	20,410	21,084
45133	Hillsboro	(513)	6,235	6,356	43460	Rossford	(419)	5,861	5,978
44484	Howland(u)	(216)	6,732	7,441	45217	St. Bernard	(513)	5,344	5,396
44425	Hubbard	(216)	8,248	9,245	43950	St. Clairsville	(614)	5,162	5,452
45424	Huber Heights(u)	(513)	38,696	35,480	45885	St. Marys	(419)	8,441	8,414
43081	Huber Ridge(u)	(614)	5,255	5,835	44460	Salem	(216)	12,233	12,869
.....	Hudson	.....	5,159	4,615	44870	Sandusky	(419)	29,764	31,360

ZIP code	Place		1990	1980
44870	Sandusky South(u)	(419)	6,336	6,548
44131	Seven Hills	(216)	12,339	13,650
44120	Shaker Heights	(216)	30,831	32,487
45241	Sharonville	(513)	13,153	10,108
44054	Sheffield Lake	(216)	9,825	10,484
44875	Shelby	(419)	9,564	9,703
	Shiloh		11,607	11,735
45365	Sidney	(513)	18,710	17,657
45236	Silverton	(513)	5,859	6,172
44139	Solon	(216)	18,548	14,341
44121	South Euclid	(216)	23,866	25,713
	Springboro		6,590	4,962
45246	Springdale	(216)	10,621	10,111
*45501	Springfield	(513)	70,487	72,563
43952	Steubenville	(614)	22,125	26,400
44224	Stow	(216)	27,702	25,303
44240	Streetsboro	(216)	9,932	9,055
44136	Strongsville	(216)	35,308	28,577
44471	Struthers	(216)	12,284	13,624
43560	Sylvania	(419)	17,301	15,527
44278	Tallmadge	(216)	14,870	15,269
45243	The Village of Indian Hill	(513)	5,383	5,521
44883	Tiffin	(419)	18,604	19,549
45371	Tipp City	(513)	6,027	5,595
*43601	Toledo	(419)	332,943	354,635
43964	Toronto	(614)	6,127	6,934
45067	Trenton	(513)	6,189	6,401
45426	Trotwood	(513)	8,816	7,802
45373	Troy	(513)	19,478	19,086
44087	Twinsburg	(216)	9,606	7,632
44683	Uhrichsville	(614)	5,604	6,130
45322	Union	(513)	5,501	5,219
44118	University Heights	(216)	14,790	15,401
43221	Upper Arlington	(614)	34,128	35,648
43351	Upper Sandusky	(419)	5,906	5,967
43078	Urbana	(513)	11,353	10,762
45377	Vandalia	(513)	13,882	13,161
45891	Van Wert	(419)	10,891	11,035
44089	Vermilion	(216)	11,127	11,012
44281	Wadsworth	(216)	15,718	15,166
45895	Wapakoneta	(419)	9,214	8,402
*44481	Warren	(216)	50,793	56,629
44122	Warrensville Heights	(216)	15,745	16,565
43160	Washington C.H.	(614)	12,983	12,682
43567	Wauseon	(419)	6,322	6,173
45692	Wellston	(614)	6,049	6,016
45449	West Carrollton	(513)	14,403	13,148
43081	Westerville	(614)	30,269	23,414
44145	Westlake	(216)	27,018	19,483
	Wheelersburg		5,113	4,796
43213	Whitehall	(614)	20,572	21,299
45239	White Oak(u)	(513)	12,430	9,563
44092	Wickliffe	(216)	14,558	16,790
44890	Willard	(419)	6,210	5,720
44094	Willoughby	(216)	20,510	19,329
44094	Willoughby Hills	(216)	8,427	8,612
44094	Willowick	(216)	15,269	17,834
45177	Wilmington	(513)	11,199	10,431
45459	Woodbourne-Hyde Park(u)	(513)	7,837	8,826
44691	Wooster	(216)	22,191	19,289
43085	Worthington	(614)	14,869	14,666
	Wright-Patterson AFB		8,579	....
45215	Wyoming	(513)	8,128	8,282
45385	Xenia	(513)	24,664	24,653
*44501	Youngstown	(216)	95,732	115,511
43701	Zanesville	(614)	26,778	28,655

Oklahoma

ZIP code	Place		1990	1980
74820	Ada	(405)	15,820	15,902
73521	Altus	(405)	21,910	23,101
73717	Alva	(405)	5,495	6,416
73005	Anadarko	(405)	6,586	6,378
73401	Ardmore	(405)	23,079	23,689
74003	Bartlesville	(918)	34,256	34,568
73008	Bethany	(405)	20,075	22,038
74008	Bixby	(918)	9,502	6,969
74631	Blackwell	(405)	7,538	8,400
74012	Broken Arrow	(918)	58,043	35,761
73018	Chickasha	(405)	14,988	15,828
73020	Choctaw	(405)	8,545	7,520
74017	Claremore	(918)	13,280	12,085
73601	Clinton	(405)	9,298	8,796
	Coweta		6,159	4,554
74023	Cushing	(918)	7,218	7,720
73115	Del City	(405)	23,928	28,523
73533	Duncan	(405)	21,732	22,517
74701	Durant	(405)	12,823	11,972
73034	Edmond	(405)	52,315	34,637
73644	Elk City	(405)	10,428	9,579
73036	El Reno	(405)	15,414	15,486
73701	Enid	(405)	45,309	50,363
73503	Fort Sill(u)	(405)	12,107	15,924
73542	Frederick	(405)	5,221	6,153
	Glenpool		6,688	2,706
73044	Guthrie	(405)	10,518	10,312
73942	Guymon	(405)	7,803	8,492
74437	Henryetta	(918)	5,872	6,432
74743	Hugo	(405)	5,978	7,172
74745	Idabel	(405)	6,957	7,622
74037	Jenks	(918)	7,493	5,876
73501	Lawton	(405)	80,561	80,054
74501	McAlester	(918)	16,370	17,255
74354	Miami	(918)	13,142	14,237
73110	Midwest City	(405)	52,267	49,559
74868	Moore	(405)	40,318	35,063
74401	Muskogee	(918)	37,708	40,011
73064	Mustang	(405)	10,434	7,496
73069	Norman	(405)	80,071	68,020
*73125	Oklahoma City	(405)	444,719	404,014
74447	Okmulgee	(918)	13,441	16,263
74055	Owasso	(918)	11,151	6,149
73075	Pauls Valley	(405)	6,150	5,664
74601	Ponca City	(405)	26,359	26,238
74953	Poteau	(918)	7,210	7,089
74361	Pryor Creek	(918)	8,327	8,483
74955	Sallisaw	(918)	7,122	6,403
74063	Sand Springs	(918)	15,346	13,121
74066	Sapulpa	(918)	18,074	15,853
74868	Seminole	(405)	7,071	8,590
74801	Shawnee	(405)	26,017	26,506
74074	Stillwater	(405)	36,676	38,268
74464	Tahlequah	(918)	10,398	9,708
74873	Tecumseh	(405)	5,570	5,123
73120	The Village	(405)	10,353	11,114
*74101	Tulsa	(918)	367,302	360,919
74301	Vinita	(918)	5,804	6,740
74467	Wagoner	(918)	6,894	6,191
73132	Warr Acres	(405)	9,288	9,940
73096	Weatherford	(405)	10,124	9,640
73801	Woodward	(405)	12,340	13,781
73099	Yukon	(405)	20,935	17,112

Oregon (503)

ZIP code	Place	1990	1980
97321	Albany	29,462	26,511
97005	Aloha(u)	34,284	28,353
97601	Altamont(u)	18,591	19,805
97520	Ashland	16,234	14,943
97103	Astoria	10,069	9,998
97814	Baker	9,140	9,471
97005	Beaverton	53,310	31,962
97701	Bend	20,469	17,263
97013	Canby	8,983	7,659
97225	Cedar Hills(u)	9,294	9,619
	Cedar Mill	9,697	22,118
97502	Central Point	7,509	6,357
	City of the Dalles	11,060	10,820
97420	Coos Bay	15,076	14,424
	Cornelius	6,148	4,462
97330	Corvallis	44,757	40,960
97424	Cottage Grove	7,402	7,148
97338	Dallas	9,422	8,530
*97401	Eugene	112,669	105,664
	Florence	5,162	4,411
97116	Forest Grove	13,559	11,499
97301	Four Corners(u)	12,156	11,331
97223	Garden Home-Whitford(u)	6,652	6,926
97027	Gladstone	10,152	9,500
97526	Grants Pass	17,488	15,032
97030	Gresham	68,235	33,005
97303	Hayesville(u)	14,318	9,213
97230	Hazelwood(u)	11,480	25,541
97838	Hermiston	10,040	9,408
97123	Hillsboro	37,520	27,664
	Jennings Lodge	6,530	....
97303	Keizer(u)	21,884	19,785
97601	Klamath Falls	17,737	16,661
97850	La Grande	11,766	11,354
97034	Lake Oswego	30,576	22,527
97355	Lebanon	10,950	10,413
97367	Lincoln City	5,892	5,469
97128	McMinnville	17,894	14,080
97501	Medford	46,951	39,746
97862	Milton-Freewater	5,533	5,086
97222	Milwaukie	18,692	17,931
97361	Monmouth	6,288	5,594
97132	Newberg	13,086	10,394
97365	Newport	8,437	7,519
97459	North Bend	9,614	9,779
	North Springfield(u)	5,451	6,140
97268	Oak Grove(u)	12,576	11,640
	Oak Hills	6,450	....
	Oatfield	15,348	....
97914	Ontario	9,392	8,814
97045	Oregon City	14,698	14,673
97801	Pendleton	15,126	14,521
*97208	Portland	437,319	368,148
97236	Powellhurst(u)	28,756	20,132
97754	Prineville	5,355	5,276
97225	Raleigh Hills(u)	6,066	6,517

ZIP code	Place	1990	1980
97756	Redmond	7,163	6,452
97404	River Road(u)	9,443	10,370
.....	Rockcreek	8,282	.....
97470	Roseburg	17,032	16,644
.....	Roseburg North	6,831	.....
97051	St. Helens	7,535	7,064
*97301	Salem	107,786	89,091
97401	Santa Clara(u)	12,834	14,288
97138	Seaside	5,359	5,193
97381	Silverton	5,635	5,168
97477	Springfield	44,683	41,621
.....	Stayton	5,011	4,396
.....	Sutherlin	5,020	4,560
97386	Sweet Home	6,850	6,921
97223	Tigard	29,344	14,799
97060	Troutdale	7,852	5,908
97062	Tualatin	15,013	7,483
.....	West Haven-Sylvan	6,009	.....
97068	West Linn	16,367	11,358
97225	West Slope(u)	7,959	5,364
97501	White City(u)	5,891	5,445
.....	Wilsonville	7,106	2,920
97071	Woodburn	13,404	11,196

Pennsylvania

ZIP code	Place	1990	1980
15001	Aliquippa (412)	13,374	17,094
*18101	Allentown (215)	105,090	103,758
*16603	Altoona (814)	51,881	57,078
19002	Ambler (215)	6,609	6,628
15003	Ambridge (412)	8,133	9,575
18403	Archbald (717)	6,291	6,295
19003	Ardmore(u) (215)	12,646	.....
15068	Arnold (412)	6,113	6,853
.....	Audubon	6,113	6,853
15202	Avalon (412)	5,784	6,240
15005	Baden (412)	5,074	5,318
15234	Baldwin (412)	21,923	24,714
18013	Bangor (215)	5,383	5,006
15009	Beaver (412)	5,028	5,441
15010	Beaver Falls (412)	10,687	12,525
16823	Bellefonte (814)	6,358	6,300
15202	Bellevue (412)	9,126	10,128
16603	Berwick (717)	10,976	11,850
15102	Bethel Park (412)	33,823	34,755
*18016	Bethlehem (215)	71,428	70,419
18447	Blakely (717)	7,222	7,438
17815	Bloomsburg (717)	12,439	11,717
19422	Blue Bell	6,091	.....
.....	Boothwyn	5,069	.....
16701	Bradford (814)	9,625	11,211
15227	Brentwood (412)	10,823	11,859
15017	Bridgeville (412)	5,445	6,154
19007	Bristol (215)	10,405	10,867
19015	Brookhaven (215)	8,567	7,912
.....	Broomall	10,930	.....
16001	Butler (412)	15,714	17,026
15419	California (412)	5,748	5,703
17011	Camp Hill (717)	7,831	8,422
15317	Canonsburg (412)	9,200	10,459
18407	Carbondale (717)	10,664	11,255
17013	Carlisle (717)	18,419	18,314
15106	Carnegie (412)	9,278	10,099
15108	Carnot-Moon(u) (412)	10,187	11,102
15234	Castle Shannon (412)	9,135	10,164
18032	Catasauqua (215)	6,662	6,711
17201	Chambersburg (717)	16,647	16,174
15022	Charleroi (412)	5,014	5,717
*19013	Chester (215)	41,856	45,794
19013	Chester Twp(u) (215)	5,399	5,687
15025	Clairton (412)	9,656	12,188
16214	Clarion (814)	6,457	6,198
18411	Clarks Summit (717)	5,433	5,272
16830	Clearfield (814)	6,633	7,580
19018	Clifton Heights (215)	7,111	7,320
19320	Coatesville (215)	11,038	10,698
19023	Collingdale (215)	9,175	9,539
.....	Colonial Park	13,777	.....
17512	Columbia (717)	10,701	10,466
15425	Connellsville (412)	9,229	10,319
19428	Conshohocken (215)	8,064	8,591
15108	Coraopolis (412)	6,747	7,308
16407	Corry (814)	7,216	7,149
15205	Crafton (412)	7,188	7,623
.....	Croydon	9,967	.....
17821	Danville (717)	5,165	5,239
19023	Darby (215)	11,140	11,513
19036	Darby Twp(u) (215)	10,955	12,264
19333	Devon-Berwyn(u) (215)	5,019	5,246
18519	Dickson City (717)	6,276	6,699
15033	Donora (412)	5,928	7,524
15216	Dormont (412)	9,772	11,275
19335	Downingtown (215)	7,749	7,650
18901	Doylestown (215)	8,575	8,717
.....	Drexel Hill	29,744	.....
15801	Du Bois (814)	8,286	9,290

ZIP code	Place	1990	1980
18512	Dunmore (717)	15,403	16,781
15110	Duquesne (412)	8,525	10,094
19401	East Norriton(u) (215)	13,324	12,711
18042	Easton (215)	26,276	26,027
18301	East Stroudsburg (717)	8,781	8,039
.....	East York	8,487	.....
15005	Economy (412)	9,519	9,538
16412	Edinboro (814)	7,736	6,324
18704	Edwardsville (717)	5,399	5,729
17022	Elizabethtown (717)	9,952	8,233
16117	Ellwood City (412)	8,894	9,998
18049	Emmaus (215)	11,157	11,001
.....	Enola	5,961	.....
17522	Ephrata (717)	12,133	11,095
*16501	Erie (814)	108,718	119,123
18643	Exeter (717)	5,691	5,493
.....	Fairless Hills	9,026	.....
16121	Farrell (412)	6,841	8,645
.....	Feasterville-Trevose	6,696	.....
.....	Fernway	9,072	3,843
19032	Folcroft (215)	7,506	8,231
15221	Forest Hills (412)	8,173	8,198
18704	Forty Fort (717)	5,049	5,590
15238	Fox Chapel (814)	5,319	5,049
16323	Franklin (814)	7,329	8,146
15143	Franklin Park (412)	10,109	6,135
18052	Fullerton(u) (215)	13,127	8,055
17325	Gettysburg (717)	7,025	7,194
15045	Glassport (412)	5,582	6,242
19036	Glenolden (215)	7,260	7,633
.....	Glenside	8,704	.....
15601	Greensburg (412)	16,318	17,558
16125	Greenville (412)	6,734	7,730
16127	Grove City (412)	8,240	8,162
.....	Hampton Township	15,568	.....
17331	Hanover (717)	14,399	14,890
.....	Harleysville	7,405	3,673
*17105	Harrisburg (717)	52,376	53,264
.....	Harrison Township	11,763	.....
19040	Hatboro (215)	7,382	7,579
18201	Hazleton (717)	24,730	27,318
18055	Hellertown (215)	5,662	6,025
.....	Hermitage	15,300	16,365
17033	Hershey(u)	11,860	13,249
16648	Hollidaysburg (814)	5,624	5,892
16001	Homeacre-Lyndora(u) (412)	7,511	8,333
19044	Horsham(u) (215)	15,051	9,900
16652	Huntingdon (814)	6,843	7,042
15701	Indiana (412)	15,174	16,051
15644	Jeannette (412)	11,221	13,106
15344	Jefferson (412)	9,533	8,643
18229	Jim Thorpe (717)	5,048	5,263
*15901	Johnstown (814)	28,134	35,496
15108	Kennedy Twp(u) (412)	7,152	7,159
.....	Kennett Square	5,218	4,715
.....	King of Prussia	18,406	.....
18704	Kingston (717)	14,507	15,681
16201	Kittanning (412)	5,120	5,432
.....	Kulpsville	5,183	.....
*17604	Lancaster (717)	55,551	54,725
19446	Lansdale (215)	16,362	16,526
19050	Lansdowne (215)	11,712	11,891
15650	Latrobe (412)	9,265	10,799
.....	Leacock-Leola-Bareville	5,685	.....
17042	Lebanon (717)	24,800	25,711
18235	Lehighton (215)	5,914	5,826
.....	Levittown	55,362	.....
17837	Lewisburg (717)	5,785	5,407
17044	Lewistown (717)	9,341	9,830
.....	Linglestown	5,862	.....
.....	Lionville-Marchwood	6,468	.....
17543	Lititz (717)	8,280	7,590
17745	Lock Haven (717)	9,230	9,617
.....	Lower Allen	6,329	.....
15068	Lower Burrell (412)	12,251	13,200
15237	McCandless Twp(u) (412)	28,781	26,250
*15134	McKeesport (412)	26,016	31,012
15136	McKees Rocks (412)	7,691	8,742
17948	Mahanoy City (717)	5,209	6,167
17545	Manheim (717)	5,011	5,015
.....	Maple	5,881	.....
16335	Meadville (814)	14,318	15,544
17055	Mechanicsburg (717)	9,452	9,487
*19063	Media (215)	5,957	6,119
17057	Middletown (Dauphin) (717)	9,254	10,122
18017	Middletown (Northampton)(u) (215)	6,866	5,801
17551	Millersville (717)	8,099	7,668
17847	Milton (717)	6,746	6,730
15061	Monaca (412)	6,739	7,661
15062	Monessen (412)	9,901	11,928
.....	Montgomeryville	9,114	.....
18507	Moosic (717)	5,339	6,068
19067	Morrisville (215)	9,765	9,845
17851	Mount Carmel (717)	7,196	8,190
17552	Mount Joy (717)	6,398	5,680
15228	Mount Lebanon(u) (412)	33,362	34,414
15120	Munhall (412)	13,158	14,535

ZIP code	Place	1990	1980
15146	Municipality of Monroeville. . (412)	29,169	30,977
15668	Municipality of Murrysville. . (412)	17,240	16,036
18634	Nanticoke. . . . . (717)	12,267	13,044
18064	Nazareth. . . . . (215)	5,713	5,443
.....	Nether Providence Twp(u). . (215)	13,229	12,730
15066	New Brighton. . . . . (412)	6,854	7,364
*16101	New Castle. . . . . (412)	28,334	33,621
17070	New Cumberland. . . . . . . (717)	7,665	8,051
15068	New Kensington. . . . . . . (412)	15,894	17,660
*19401	Norristown. . . . . (215)	30,749	34,684
18067	Northampton. . . . . (215)	8,717	8,240
15104	North Braddock. . . . . . . (412)	7,036	8,711
15137	North Versailles(u). . . . . . (412)	12,302	13,294
16421	Northwest Harbor-Creek(u). . (814)	6,662	7,485
19074	Norwood. . . . . (215)	6,162	6,647
15139	Oakmont. . . . . (412)	6,961	7,039
.....	O'Hara.	9,096	
16301	Oil City. . . . . (814)	11,949	13,881
18518	Old Forge. . . . . (717)	8,834	9,304
18447	Olyphant. . . . . (717)	5,222	5,204
.....	Oreland.	5,695	
18071	Palmerton. . . . . (215)	5,394	5,455
17078	Palmyra. . . . . (717)	6,910	7,228
19301	Paoli(u). . . . . (215)	5,603	5,277
.....	Park Forest Village	6,703	
17331	Parkville(u). . . . . (717)	6,014	5,009
15235	Penn Hills(u). . . . . (412)	51,430	57,632
.....	Penn Wynne	5,807	
18944	Perkasie . . . . (215)	7,787	5,241
*19104	Philadelphia. . . . . (215)	1,585,577	1,688,210
19460	Phoenixville . . . . (215)	15,066	14,165
15219	Pittsburgh . . . . (412)	369,879	423,959
*18640	Pittston. . . . . (717)	9,389	9,9303
15236	Pleasant Hills. . . . . (412)	8,884	9,604
15239	Plum . . . . (412)	25,609	25,309
18651	Plymouth. . . . . (717)	7,134	7,605
.....	Plymouth Meeting.	6,241	
19464	Pottstown . . . . (215)	21,831	22,729
17901	Pottsville. . . . . (717)	16,603	18,195
.....	Progress	9,654	
19076	Prospect Park. . . . . (215)	6,764	6,593
15767	Punxsutawney. . . . . (814)	6,782	7,479
18951	Quakertown. . . . . (215)	8,982	8,867
19087	Radnor Twp(u). . . . . (215)	28,705	27,676
*19603	Reading . . . . (215)	78,380	78,686
17356	Red Lion. . . . . (717)	6,130	5,824
18954	Richboro(u) . . . . (215)	5,332	5,141
19078	Ridley Park . . . . (215)	7,592	7,889
.....	Robinson	10,830	
15237	Ross Twp(u). . . . . (412)	33,482	35,102
15857	St. Marys . . . . (814)	5,511	6,417
.....	Sanatoga.	5,534	3,723
18840	Sayre. . . . . (717)	5,791	6,951
17972	Schuylkill Haven . . . . . . (717)	5,610	5,977
15683	Scottdale. . . . . (412)	5,184	5,833
15106	Scott Twp(u). . . . . (412)	17,118	20,413
*18503	Scranton . . . . (717)	81,805	88,117
17870	Selinsgrove . . . . (717)	5,384	5,227
15116	Shaler Twp(u). . . . . (412)	30,533	33,694
17872	Shamokin . . . . (717)	9,184	10,357
16146	Sharon . . . . (412)	17,493	19,057
19079	Sharon Hill. . . . . (215)	5,771	6,221
17976	Shenandoah. . . . . (717)	6,221	7,589
19607	Shillington . . . . (215)	5,062	5,601
17404	Shiloh(u). . . . . (717)	8,245	5,315
17257	Shippensburg . . . . (717)	5,331	5,261
15501	Somerset . . . . (814)	6,454	6,474
18964	Souderton . . . . (215)	5,957	6,657
.....	South Park.	14,292	
17701	South Williamsport . . . . . (717)	6,496	6,581
19064	Springfield(u) . . . . (215)	24,160	25,326
16801	State College. . . . . (814)	38,923	36,130
17113	Steelton . . . . (717)	5,152	6,484
15136	Stowe Twp(u). . . . . (412)	7,681	9,202
18360	Stroudsburg . . . . (717)	5,312	5,148
16323	Sugar Creek. . . . . (814)	5,532	5,954
17801	Sunbury . . . . (717)	11,591	12,292
19081	Swarthmore . . . . (215)	6,157	5,950
15218	Swissvale . . . . (412)	10,637	11,345
18704	Swoyersville. . . . . (717)	5,630	5,795
18252	Tamaqua. . . . . (717)	7,943	8,843
15084	Tarentum . . . . (412)	5,674	6,419
18517	Taylor . . . . (717)	6,941	7,246
16354	Titusville . . . . (814)	6,434	6,884
19401	Trooper(u). . . . . (215)	5,137	7,370
15145	Turtle Creek. . . . . (412)	6,556	6,959
16686	Tyrone . . . . (814)	5,743	6,346
15401	Uniontown. . . . . (412)	12,034	14,510
19063	Upper Providence Twp(u) . . (215)	9,727	9,477
15241	Upper St. Clair(u). . . . . . (412)	19,692	19,023
15690	Vandergrift. . . . . (412)	5,904	6,823
.....	Village Green-Green Ridge . . .	9,026	
16365	Warren. . . . . (814)	11,122	12,146
15301	Washington . . . . (412)	15,864	18,363
17268	Waynesboro. . . . . (717)	9,578	9,726
.....	Weigelstown(u). . . . . (717)	8,665	5,213
*19380	West Chester. . . . . (215)	18,041	17,435

ZIP code	Place	1990	1980
19380	West Goshen(u). . . . . . . (215)	8,948	7,998
15122	West Mifflin . . . . (412)	23,644	26,322
15905	Westmont. . . . . (814)	5,789	6,113
19401	West Norriton(u) . . . . (215)	15,209	14,034
18643	West Pittston . . . . (717)	5,590	5,980
15229	West View. . . . . (412)	7,734	7,648
18052	Whitehall. . . . . (215)	14,451	15,143
15131	White Oak . . . . (717)	8,761	9,480
*18701	Wilkes-Barre. . . . . (717)	47,523	51,551
15221	Wilkinsburg . . . . (412)	21,080	23,669
15145	Wilkins Twp(u). . . . . (412)	7,487	8,472
17701	Williamsport . . . . (717)	31,933	33,401
.....	Willow Grove	16,325	
.....	Willow Street	5,817	
15025	Wilson . . . . (412)	7,830	7,564
.....	Woodlyn	10,151	
.....	Wyndmoor	5,682	
19610	Wyomissing . . . . (215)	7,332	6,551
19050	Yeadon . . . . (215)	11,980	11,727
*17405	York . . . . (717)	42,192	44,619

Rhode Island (401)

See Note on Page 78

ZIP code	Place	1990	1980
02806	Barrington	15,849	16,174
02809	Bristol.	21,625	20,128
02830	Burrillville.	16,230	13,164
02863	Central Falls	17,637	16,995
02816	Coventry	31,083	27,065
02910	Cranston	76,060	71,992
02864	Cumberland	29,038	27,069
02864	Cumberland Hill(u)	6,379	5,421
02818	East Greenwich	11,865	10,211
02914	East Providence	50,380	50,980
02814	Glocester	9,227	7,550
02828	Greenville(u).	8,303	7,576
02833	Hopkinton	6,873	6,406
02919	Johnston.	26,542	24,907
02881	Kingston(u).	6,504	5,479
02865	Lincoln	18,045	16,949
02840	Middletown.	19,460	17,216
02882	Narragansett	14,985	12,088
02840	Newport	28,227	29,259
02843	Newport East(u).	11,080	11,030
02852	North Kingstown.	23,786	21,938
02908	North Providence	32,090	29,188
02876	North Smithfield	10,497	9,972
.....	Pascoag	5,011	3,807
*02800	Pawtucket.	72,644	71,204
02871	Portsmouth	16,857	14,257
*02904	Providence.	160,728	156,804
02857	Scituate	9,796	8,405
02917	Smithfield	19,163	16,886
02879	South Kingstown	24,631	20,414
02878	Tiverton	14,312	7,259
02864	Valley Falls(u)	11,175	10,892
*02880	Wakefield-Peacedale(u) . . .	7,134	6,474
02885	Warren	11,385	10,640
*02887	Warwick	85,427	87,123
02891	Westerly	21,605	18,580
02891	Westerly Center(u)	16,477	14,093
02893	West Warwick	29,268	27,026
02895	Woonsocket	43,877	45,914

South Carolina (803)

ZIP code	Place	1990	1980
29620	Abbeville	5,778	5,833
29801	Aiken	19,872	14,978
29621	Anderson.	26,184	27,546
29812	Barnwell	5,255	5,572
29902	Beaufort	9,576	8,634
29841	Belvedere(u).	6,133	6,859
29512	Bennettsville	9,345	8,774
29611	Berea(u)	13,535	13,164
.....	Brookdale(u).	5,339	6,123
.....	Burton	6,917	3,619
29020	Camden	6,696	7,462
29033	Cayce	11,163	11,701
*29401	Charleston.	80,414	69,779
29520	Cheraw	5,505	5,654
29706	Chester.	7,158	6,820
29631	Clemson	11,096	8,118
29325	Clinton	7,987	8,596
*29201	Columbia.	98,052	101,229
29526	Conway	9,819	10,240
29532	Darlington	7,311	7,989
29204	Dentsville(u)	11,839	13,579
29536	Dillon	6,829	7,060
29640	Easley	15,195	14,264
29501	Florence	29,813	29,842
29206	Forest Acres.	7,197	6,062
29340	Gaffney	13,145	13,453
29605	Gantt(u)	13,891	13,719
.....	Garden City	6,305	

ZIP code	Place	1990	1980
29440	Georgetown	9,517	10,144
29445	Goose Creek	24,692	17,811
*29602	Greenville	58,282	58,242
29646	Greenwood	20,807	21,613
29651	Greer	10,322	10,525
29410	Hanahan	13,176	13,224
29550	Hartsville	8,372	7,631
29928	Hilton Head Island(u)	23,694	11,239
29621	Homeland Park(u)	6,569	6,720
	Irmo	11,280	3,957
29456	Ladson(u)	13,540	13,246
29560	Lake City	7,153	6,731
29720	Lancaster	8,914	9,703
29360	Laurens	9,694	10,587
29571	Marion	7,658	7,700
29662	Mauldin	11,587	8,143
	Moncks Corner	5,607	4,179
29464	Mount Pleasant	30,108	14,464
29574	Mullins	5,910	6,068
29577	Myrtle Beach	24,848	18,446
29108	Newberry	10,542	9,866
29841	North	15,351	13,593
29406	North Charleston	70,218	62,479
	North Myrtle Beach	8,636	3,960
29565	Oak Grove(u)	7,173	7,092
29115	Orangeburg	13,739	14,933
	Parker	11,072	
29905	Parris Island(u)	7,172	7,752
	Red Bank	5,950	
	Red Hill	6,112	
29730	Rock Hill	41,643	35,327
29210	St. Andrews	25,692	20,245
29609	Sans Souci(u)	7,612	8,393
29678	Seneca	7,726	7,436
	Seven Oaks(u)	15,722	16,604
29681	Simpsonville	11,708	9,037
	Socastee	10,426	1,082
*29301	Spartanburg	43,467	43,826
29483	Summerville	22,519	6,492
29150	Sumter	41,943	24,921
29687	Taylors(u)	19,619	15,201
29379	Union	9,836	10,523
29607	Wade-Hampton(u)	20,014	20,180
29488	Walterboro	5,492	6,209
29611	Welcome(u)	6,560	6,922
29169	West Columbia	10,588	10,409
29206	Woodfield(u)	8,862	9,588
29745	York	6,709	6,412

South Dakota (605)

ZIP code	Place	1990	1980
57401	Aberdeen	24,927	25,851
57006	Brookings	16,270	14,951
	Ellsworth AFB	7,017	4,766
57350	Huron	12,448	13,000
57042	Madison	6,257	6,210
57301	Mitchell	13,798	13,916
57501	Pierre	12,906	11,973
57701	Rapid City	54,523	46,492
	Rapid Valley	5,968	3,265
*57101	Sioux Falls	100,814	81,343
	Spearfish	6,966	5,251
57785	Sturgis	5,330	5,184
57069	Vermillion	10,034	10,136
57201	Watertown	17,592	15,649
57078	Yankton	12,703	12,011

Tennessee

ZIP code	Place		1990	1980
37701	Alcoa	(615)	6,400	6,870
37303	Athens	(615)	12,054	12,080
38134	Bartlett	(901)	26,989	17,170
37660	Bloomingdale(u)	(615)	10,953	12,088
38008	Bolivar	(901)	5,969	6,597
37027	Brentwood	(615)	16,392	9,431
37620	Bristol	(615)	23,421	23,986
38012	Brownsville	(901)	10,019	9,307
*37401	Chattanooga	(615)	152,466	169,514
37040	Clarksville	(615)	75,494	54,777
37311	Cleveland	(615)	30,354	26,415
37716	Clinton	(615)	8,972	5,245
	Collegedale		5,048	4,607
38017	Collierville	(901)	14,427	7,839
37663	Colonial Heights(u)	(615)	6,716	6,744
38401	Columbia	(615)	28,583	26,571
38501	Cookeville	(615)	21,744	20,535
38019	Covington	(901)	7,487	6,065
38555	Crossville	(615)	6,930	6,394
37321	Dayton	(615)	5,671	5,233
37055	Dickson	(615)	8,791	7,040
38024	Dyersburg	(901)	16,317	15,856
37801	Eagleton Village(u)	(615)	5,169	5,331
	East Brainerd		11,594	
37412	East Ridge	(615)	21,101	21,236
37643	Elizabethton	(615)	11,931	12,431
	Erwin		5,015	4,739
	Farragut		12,793	5,992
37334	Fayetteville	(615)	6,921	7,559
37064	Franklin	(615)	20,098	12,407
37066	Gallatin	(615)	18,794	17,191
38138	Germantown	(901)	32,893	21,467
37072	Goodlettsville	(615)	11,219	8,327
37743	Greeneville	(615)	13,532	14,097
	Green Hill		6,763	
37918	Halls(u)	(615)	6,450	10,363
37748	Harriman	(615)	7,119	8,303
37341	Harrison(u)	(615)	7,191	6,206
37075	Hendersonville	(615)	32,188	26,561
38343	Humboldt	(901)	9,651	10,209
38301	Jackson	(901)	48,949	49,258
37760	Jefferson City	(615)	5,494	5,612
37601	Johnson City	(615)	49,381	39,753
*37662	Kingsport	(615)	36,365	32,027
*37901	Knoxville	(615)	165,121	175,045
37766	La Follette	(615)	7,192	8,198
37086	LaVergne	(615)	7,499	5,495
38464	Lawrenceburg	(615)	10,412	10,184
37087	Lebanon	(615)	15,208	11,872
37771	Lenoir City	(615)	6,147	5,180
37091	Lewisburg	(615)	9,879	8,760
38351	Lexington	(901)	5,810	5,934
38201	McKenzie	(901)	5,168	5,405
37110	McMinnville	(615)	11,194	10,683
37355	Manchester	(615)	7,709	7,250
38237	Martin	(901)	8,600	8,898
37701	Maryville	(615)	19,208	17,480
*38101	Memphis	(901)	610,337	646,174
37343	Middle Valley(u)	(615)	12,255	11,420
38358	Milan	(901)	7,512	8,083
38053	Millington	(901)	17,866	20,236
37814	Morristown	(615)	21,385	19,570
	Mount Juliet		5,389	2,879
37130	Murfreesboro	(615)	44,922	32,845
*37202	Nashville-Davidson	(615)	488,374	455,651
37821	Newport	(615)	7,123	7,580
37830	Oak Ridge	(615)	27,310	27,662
38242	Paris	(901)	9,332	10,728
	Portland		5,165	4,030
37849	Powell(u)	(615)	7,534	7,220
38478	Pulaski	(615)	7,895	7,184
37415	Red Bank White Oak	(615)	12,322	13,129
38063	Ripley	(901)	6,188	6,366
37854	Rockwood	(615)	5,348	5,687
38372	Savannah	(901)	6,547	6,992
	Sevierville		7,178	4,556
	Seymour		7,026	
	Shelbyville		14,049	13,530
37377	Signal Mountain	(615)	7,034	5,818
37167	Smyrna	(615)	13,647	8,839
37379	Soddy-Daisy	(615)	8,240	8,388
	South Cleveland		5,372	4,360
37172	Springfield	(615)	11,227	10,814
	Sweetwater		5,066	4,725
37388	Tullahoma	(615)	16,761	15,800
38261	Union City	(901)	10,513	10,436
37398	Winchester	(615)	6,305	5,821

Texas

ZIP code	Place		1990	1980
*79604	Abilene	(915)	106,654	98,315
75001	Addison	(214)	8,783	5,553
78516	Alamo	(512)	8,210	5,831
78209	Alamo Heights	(512)	6,502	6,252
77039	Aldine(u)	(713)	11,133	12,623
78332	Alice	(512)	19,788	20,961
75002	Allen	(214)	18,309	8,314
79830	Alpine	(915)	5,637	5,465
77511	Alvin	(713)	19,220	16,515
*79105	Amarillo	(806)	157,615	149,230
	Anderson Mill		9,468	
79714	Andrews	(915)	10,678	11,061
77515	Angleton	(409)	17,140	13,929
78336	Aransas Pass	(512)	7,180	7,173
*76010	Arlington	(817)	261,721	160,113
75751	Athens	(214)	10,967	10,197
75551	Atlanta	(214)	6,118	6,272
*78710	Austin	(512)	465,622	345,890
76020	Azle	(817)	8,868	5,822
75149	Balch Springs	(214)	17,406	13,746
77414	Bay City	(409)	18,170	17,837
77520	Baytown	(713)	63,850	56,923
*77704	Beaumont	(409)	114,323	118,102
76021	Bedford	(817)	43,762	20,821
78102	Beeville	(512)	13,547	14,574
77401	Bellaire	(713)	13,842	14,950
76704	Bellmead	(817)	8,336	7,569
76513	Belton	(817)	12,476	10,660
76126	Benbrook	(817)	19,564	13,579
79720	Big Spring	(915)	23,093	24,804
75418	Bonham	(214)	6,686	7,338

ZIP code	Place		1990	1980
79007	Borger	(806)	15,675	15,837
76825	Brady	(915)	5,946	5,969
76024	Breckenridge	(817)	5,665	6,921
77833	Brenham	(409)	11,952	10,966
77611	Bridge City	(409)	8,034	7,667
79316	Brownfield	(806)	9,560	10,387
78520	Brownsville	(512)	98,962	84,997
76801	Brownwood	(915)	18,387	19,396
.....	Brushy Creek	.....	5,833	
77801	Bryan	(409)	55,002	44,337
76354	Burkburnett	(817)	10,145	10,668
76028	Burleson	(817)	16,113	11,734
76520	Cameron	(817)	5,580	5,721
79015	Canyon	(806)	11,365	10,724
.....	Canyon Lake		9,975	
78834	Carrizo Springs	(512)	5,745	6,886
75006	Carrollton	(214)	82,169	40,595
75633	Carthage	(214)	6,496	6,447
75104	Cedar Hill	(214)	19,976	6,849
.....	Cedar Park		5,161	3,474
77530	Channelview(u)	(713)	25,564	17,471
79201	Childress	(817)	5,055	5,817
76031	Cleburne	(817)	22,205	19,218
77327	Cleveland	(713)	7,124	5,977
77015	Clover Leaf(u)	(713)	18,230	17,317
77531	Clute	(409)	8,910	9,577
76834	Coleman	(915)	5,410	5,960
77840	College Station	(409)	52,456	37,272
76034	Colleyville	(817)	12,724	6,700
75428	Commerce	(214)	6,825	8,136
77301	Conroe	(409)	27,610	18,034
78109	Converse	(512)	8,887	5,150
.....	Coppell		16,881	3,826
76522	Copperas Cove	(817)	24,079	19,469
*78408	Corpus Christi	(512)	257,453	232,134
75110	Corsicana	(214)	22,911	21,712
75835	Crockett	(713)	7,024	7,405
76036	Crowley	(817)	6,974	5,852
78839	Crystal City	(512)	8,263	8,334
77954	Cuero	(512)	6,700	7,124
79022	Dalhart	(806)	6,246	6,854
*75260	Dallas	(214)	1,006,877	904,599
.....	Dayton		5,151	4,908
77536	Deer Park	(713)	27,652	22,648
78840	Del Rio	(512)	30,705	30,034
75020	Denison	(214)	21,505	23,884
76201	Denton	(817)	66,270	48,063
.....	Denver City		5,145	4,704
75115	De Soto	(214)	30,544	15,538
77539	Dickinson	(713)	9,497	7,505
78537	Donna	(512)	12,652	9,952
79029	Dumas	(806)	12,871	12,194
75116	Duncanville	(214)	35,748	27,781
.....	Eagle Mountain		5,847	
78852	Eagle Pass	(512)	20,651	21,407
78539	Edinburg	(512)	29,885	24,075
77957	Edna	(512)	5,343	5,650
77437	El Campo	(619)	10,511	10,462
*79910	El Paso	(915)	515,342	425,259
78543	Elsa	(512)	5,242	5,061
75119	Ennis	(214)	13,883	12,110
76039	Euless	(817)	38,149	24,002
76140	Everman	(817)	5,672	5,387
.....	Fabens		5,599	4,285
78355	Falfurrias	(512)	5,788	6,103
75234	Farmers Branch	(214)	24,250	24,863
.....	First Colony		18,327	
.....	Floresville		5,247	4,381
.....	Flower Mound		15,527	4,402
76119	Forest Hill	(817)	11,482	11,684
79906	Fort Bliss(u)	(915)	13,915	12,687
76544	Fort Hood(u)	(817)	35,580	31,250
79735	Fort Stockton	(915)	8,524	8,688
*76101	Fort Worth	(817)	447,619	385,164
78624	Fredericksburg	(512)	6,934	6,412
77541	Freeport	(409)	11,389	13,444
77546	Friendswood	(713)	22,814	10,719
.....	Frisco		6,141	3,499
76240	Gainesville	(817)	14,256	14,081
77547	Galena Park	(713)	10,033	9,879
77550	Galveston	(409)	59,070	61,902
*75040	Garland	(214)	180,650	138,857
76528	Gatesville	(817)	11,492	6,078
78626	Georgetown	(512)	14,842	9,468
75647	Gladewater	(214)	6,027	6,548
78629	Gonzales	(512)	6,527	7,152
76046	Graham	(817)	8,986	9,170
*75050	Grand Prairie	(214)	99,616	71,462
76051	Grapevine	(817)	29,202	11,801
75401	Greenville	(214)	23,071	22,161
77619	Groves	(409)	16,513	17,090
76117	Haltom City	(817)	32,856	29,014
76541	Harker Heights	(817)	12,841	7,345
78550	Harlingen	(512)	48,735	43,543
77859	Hearne	(713)	5,132	5,418
75652	Henderson	(214)	11,139	11,473
79045	Hereford	(806)	14,745	15,853

ZIP code	Place		1990	1980
76643	Hewitt	(817)	8,983	5,247
75205	Highland Park	(214)	8,739	8,909
77562	Highlands	(713)	6,632	6,467
.....	Highland Village		7,027	3,246
76645	Hillsboro	(817)	7,072	7,397
77563	Hitchcock	(713)	5,868	6,103
78861	Hondo	(512)	6,018	6,057
*77013	Houston	(713)	1,630,553	1,595,138
77338	Humble	(713)	12,060	6,729
77340	Huntsville	(409)	27,925	23,936
76053	Hurst	(817)	33,574	31,420
78362	Ingleside	(512)	5,696	5,436
76367	Iowa Park	(817)	6,072	6,184
*75061	Irving	(214)	155,037	109,943
77029	Jacinto City	(713)	9,343	8,953
75766	Jacksonville	(214)	12,765	12,264
75951	Jasper	(409)	6,959	6,959
.....	Jollyville		15,206	
77450	Katy	(713)	8,005	5,660
.....	Kaufman		5,238	4,658
.....	Keller		13,683	4,156
79745	Kermit	(915)	6,875	8,015
78028	Kerrville	(512)	17,384	15,276
75662	Kilgore	(214)	11,066	11,331
76541	Killeen	(817)	63,535	46,296
78363	Kingsville	(512)	25,276	28,808
.....	Kingwood	(713)	37,397	16,261
78219	Kirby	(713)	8,326	6,435
78236	Lackland AFB(u)	(512)	9,352	14,459
77566	Lake Jackson	(409)	22,776	19,102
77568	La Marque	(409)	14,120	15,372
79631	Lamesa	(806)	10,809	11,790
76550	Lampasas	(512)	6,382	6,165
75146	Lancaster	(214)	22,117	14,807
77571	La Porte	(713)	27,910	14,062
78040	Laredo	(512)	122,899	91,449
77573	League City	(713)	30,159	16,578
78238	Leon Valley	(512)	9,581	9,088
79336	Levelland	(806)	13,986	13,809
75067	Lewisville	(214)	46,521	24,273
77575	Liberty	(713)	7,733	7,945
79339	Littlefield	(806)	6,489	7,409
78233	Live Oak	(512)	10,023	8,183
.....	Livingston		5,019	4,928
78644	Lockhart	(512)	9,205	7,953
75601	Longview	(214)	70,311	62,762
*79408	Lubbock	(806)	186,206	174,361
75901	Lufkin	(409)	30,206	28,562
.....	Lumberton		6,640	2,480
78501	McAllen	(512)	84,021	66,281
75069	McKinney	(214)	21,283	16,256
76063	Mansfield	(817)	15,607	8,102
76661	Marlin	(817)	6,386	7,099
75670	Marshall	(214)	23,682	24,921
76368	Mathis	(512)	5,423	5,667
78570	Mercedes	(512)	12,694	11,851
75149	Mesquite	(214)	101,484	67,053
76667	Mexia	(817)	6,933	7,094
79701	Midland	(915)	89,443	70,525
.....	Midlothian		5,141	3,219
76067	Mineral Wells	(817)	14,870	14,468
78572	Mission	(512)	28,653	22,653
.....	Mission Bend		24,945	
77459	Missouri City	(713)	36,176	24,423
79756	Monahans	(915)	8,101	8,397
75455	Mount Pleasant	(214)	12,291	11,003
75961	Nacogdoches	(409)	30,872	27,149
77868	Navasota	(409)	6,296	5,971
77627	Nederland	(409)	16,192	16,855
.....	New Boston		5,057	4,628
78130	New Braunfels	(512)	27,334	22,402
76118	North Richland Hills	(817)	45,895	30,592
*79760	Odessa	(915)	89,699	90,027
77630	Orange	(409)	19,381	23,628
75801	Palestine	(214)	18,042	15,948
79065	Pampa	(806)	19,959	21,396
75460	Paris	(214)	24,699	25,498
*77501	Pasadena	(713)	119,363	112,560
77581	Pearland	(713)	18,697	13,248
78061	Pearsall	(512)	6,924	7,383
.....	Pecan Grove		9,502	
79772	Pecos	(915)	12,069	12,855
79070	Perryton	(806)	7,607	7,991
78577	Pharr	(512)	32,921	21,381
79072	Plainview	(806)	21,700	22,187
*75075	Plano	(214)	128,713	72,331
78064	Pleasanton	(512)	7,678	6,346
77640	Port Arthur	(409)	58,724	61,251
78374	Portland	(512)	12,224	12,023
77979	Port Lavaca	(512)	10,886	10,911
77651	Port Neches	(409)	12,974	13,944
78580	Raymondville	(512)	8,880	9,493
.....	Rendon		7,658	
*75080	Richardson	(214)	74,840	72,496
76118	Richland Hills	(817)	7,978	7,977
77469	Richmond	(713)	9,801	9,692
78582	Rio Grande City(u)	(512)	9,891	8,930

ZIP code	Place		1990	1980
77019	River Oaks	(817)	6,580	6,890
76701	Robinson	(817)	7,111	6,074
78380	Robstown	(512)	12,849	12,100
76567	Rockdale	(512)	5,235	5,611
75087	Rockwall	(214)	10,486	5,939
.....	Roma		8,059	3,384
77471	Rosenberg	(713)	20,183	17,840
78664	Round Rock	(512)	30,923	12,740
75088	Rowlett	(214)	23,260	7,522
.....	Sachse		5,346	1,640
76179	Saginaw	(817)	8,551	5,736
76901	San Angelo	(915)	84,474	73,240
*78284	San Antonio	(512)	935,933	785,940
78586	San Benito	(512)	20,125	17,988
78589	San Juan	(512)	10,815	7,608
78666	San Marcos	(512)	28,743	23,420
77550	Santa Fe	(713)	8,429	6,172
78154	Schertz	(512)	10,555	7,262
.....	Seabrook		6,685	4,670
75159	Seagoville	(214)	8,969	7,304
78155	Seguin	(512)	18,853	17,854
79360	Seminole	(915)	6,342	6,080
75090	Sherman	(214)	31,601	30,413
77656	Silsbee	(409)	6,368	7,684
78387	Sinton	(512)	5,549	6,044
79364	Slaton	(806)	6,078	6,804
79549	Snyder	(915)	12,195	12,705
.....	Socorro		22,995	12,341
77587	South Houston	(713)	14,207	13,293
.....	Southlake		7,065	2,808
.....	Spring		33,111	....
.....	Stafford		8,397	4,755
76401	Stephenville	(817)	13,502	11,881
77478	Sugar Land	(713)	24,529	8,826
75482	Sulphur Springs	(214)	14,062	12,804
79556	Sweetwater	(915)	11,967	12,242
76574	Taylor	(512)	11,472	10,619
76501	Temple	(817)	46,109	42,354
75160	Terrell	(214)	12,490	13,269
75501	Texarkana	(214)	31,656	31,271
77590	Texas City	(409)	40,822	41,201
75056	The Colony	(214)	22,113	11,586
77380	The Woodlands	(713)	29,205	8,443
.....	Tomball		6,370	3,996
.....	Town West		6,166	....
75701	Tyler	(214)	75,450	70,508
78148	Universal City	(512)	13,057	10,720
76308	University Park	(214)	22,259	22,254
78801	Uvalde	(512)	14,729	14,178
76384	Vernon	(817)	12,001	12,695
77901	Victoria	(512)	55,076	50,695
77662	Vidor	(409)	10,935	11,834
*76701	Waco	(817)	103,590	101,261
76148	Watauga	(817)	20,009	10,284
75165	Waxahachie	(214)	18,168	14,624
76086	Weatherford	(817)	14,804	12,049
.....	Wells Branch		7,094	....
78596	Weslaco	(512)	21,877	19,331
.....	West Odessa		16,568	....
77005	West University Place	(713)	12,920	12,010
77488	Wharton	(409)	9,011	9,033
.....	White Oak		5,136	4,415
76108	White Settlement	(817)	15,472	13,508
*76307	Wichita Falls	(817)	96,259	94,201
78239	Windcrest	(512)	5,331	5,332
76710	Woodway	(817)	8,695	7,091
.....	Wylie		8,716	3,152
77995	Yoakum	(512)	5,611	6,148
.....	Zapata		7,119	3,831

Utah (801)

ZIP code	Place	1990	1980
84003	American Fork	15,696	12,564
*84010	Bountiful	36,659	32,877
84302	Brigham City	15,644	15,596
.....	Canyon Rim	10,527	....
84720	Cedar City	13,443	10,972
84014	Centerville	11,500	8,069
84015	Clearfield	21,435	17,982
84015	Clinton	7,945	5,777
84121	Cottonwood(u)	28,766	22,665
.....	Cottonwood West	17,476	....
84020	Draper	7,257	5,521
84109	East Millcreek(u)	21,184	24,150
.....	Farmington	9,028	4,691
.....	Highland	5,002	2,435
84117	Holladay-Cottonwood(u)	14,095	22,189
84037	Kaysville	13,961	9,811
84118	Kearns(u)	28,374	21,353
*84041	Layton	41,784	22,862
84043	Lehi	6,475	6,848
.....	Little Cottonwood Creek Valley	5,042	....
84321	Logan	32,762	26,844
84044	Magna(u)	17,829	13,138
84047	Midvale	11,886	10,146
.....	Millcreek	32,230	....

ZIP code	Place	1990	1980
84117	Mount Olympus(u)	7,413	6,068
84107	Murray	31,282	25,750
84404	North Ogden	11,668	9,309
84054	North Salt Lake	6,474	5,548
*84401	Ogden	63,909	64,407
.....	Oquirrh	7,593	....
*84057	Orem	67,561	52,399
84651	Payson	9,510	8,246
84062	Pleasant Grove	13,476	10,833
84501	Price	8,712	9,086
*84601	Provo	86,835	74,111
84701	Richfield	5,593	5,482
.....	Riverdale	6,419	6,031
84065	Riverton	11,261	7,032
84067	Roy	24,603	19,694
84770	St. George	28,502	11,350
*84101	Salt Lake City	159,936	163,034
*84070	Sandy City	75,058	52,210
.....	Smithfield	5,566	4,993
84065	South Jordan	12,220	7,492
84403	South Ogden	12,105	11,366
84115	South Salt Lake	10,129	10,413
84660	Spanish Fork	11,272	9,825
84663	Springville	13,950	12,101
84015	Sunset	5,128	5,733
84107	Taylorsville(u)	52,351	17,448
84074	Tooele	13,887	14,335
84047	Union-East Midvale(u)	13,684	9,665
84078	Vernal	6,644	6,600
84403	Washington Terrace	8,189	8,212
*84084	West Jordan	42,892	27,325
*84119	West Valley City	86,976	72,509
84070	White City(u)	6,506	7,180
.....	Woods Cross	5,384	4,263

Vermont (802)

See Note on Page 78

ZIP code	Place	1990	1980
05641	Barre	9,482	9,824
.....	Barre	7,411	6,509
05201	Bennington	16,451	15,815
.....	Bennington(u)	9,532	9,349
05301	Brattleboro Center(u)	8,612	8,596
.....	Brattleboro	12,241	11,886
05401	Burlington	39,127	37,712
05446	Colchester	14,731	12,629
05451	Essex	16,498	14,392
05452	Essex Junction	8,396	7,033
05753	Middlebury	8,034	6,007
05602	Montpelier	8,247	8,241
05701	Rutland	18,230	18,436
05478	St. Albans	7,339	7,308
05819	St. Johnsbury	7,608	6,424
05401	South Burlington	12,809	10,679
.....	Springfield	9,579	10,190
05404	Winooski	6,649	6,318

Virginia

ZIP code	Place		1990	1980
.....	Abingdon		7,003	4,318
*22313	Alexandria	(703)	111,183	103,217
22003	Annandale(u)	(703)	50,975	49,524
.....	Aquia Harbour		6,308	2,870
*22210	Arlington(u)	(703)	170,936	152,599
.....	Ashland		5,864	4,640
22041	Bailey's Crossroads(u)	(703)	19,507	12,564
24523	Bedford	(703)	6,073	5,991
22307	Belle Haven(u)	(703)	6,427	6,520
23234	Bellwood(u)	(804)	6,178	6,439
23234	Bensley(u)	(804)	5,093	5,299
24060	Blacksburg	(703)	34,590	30,638
24605	Bluefield	(703)	5,363	5,946
23235	Bon Air(u)	(804)	16,413	16,224
24201	Bristol	(703)	18,426	19,042
24416	Buena Vista	(703)	6,406	6,717
.....	Bull Run		5,525	....
22015	Burke(u)	(703)	57,734	33,835
24018	Cave Spring(u)	(703)	24,053	21,682
22020	Centreville(u)	(703)	26,585	7,473
22021	Chantilly(u)	(703)	29,337	12,259
*22906	Charlottesville	(804)	40,341	39,916
*23320	Chesapeake	(804)	151,976	114,486
23831	Chester(u)	(804)	14,986	11,728
24073	Christiansburg	(703)	15,004	10,345
24078	Collinsville(u)	(703)	7,280	7,517
23834	Colonial Heights	(804)	16,064	16,509
.....	Commonwealth		5,538	3,505
.....	Countryside		8,349	....
24426	Covington	(703)	6,991	9,063
22701	Culpeper	(703)	8,581	6,621
22191	Dale City(u)	(703)	47,170	33,127
24541	Danville	(804)	53,056	45,642
23228	Dumbarton(u)	(804)	8,526	8,149
22027	Dunn Loring(u)	(703)	6,509	6,077

ZIP code	Place		1990	1980
23222	East Highland Park(u)	(804)	11,850	11,797
......	Emporia		5,306	4,840
......	Ettrick		5,290	4,890
22030	Fairfax	(703)	19,622	19,390
*22046	Falls Church	(703)	9,578	9,515
23901	Farmville	(804)	6,046	6,067
......	Forest		5,624	....
22060	Fort Belvoir(u)	(703)	8,590	7,726
22308	Fort Hunt(u)	(703)	12,989	14,294
23801	Fort Lee(u)	(804)	6,895	9,784
22310	Franconia(u)	(703)	19,882	8,476
23851	Franklin	(804)	7,864	7,308
22401	Fredericksburg	(703)	19,027	15,322
22630	Front Royal	(703)	11,880	11,126
24333	Galax	(703)	6,670	6,524
23060	Glen Allen(u)	(804)	9,010	6,202
23062	Gloucester Point(u)	(804)	8,509	5,841
......	Great Falls		6,945	2,419
*22306	Groveton(u)	(703)	19,997	18,860
*23660	Hampton	(804)	133,793	122,617
22801	Harrisonburg	(703)	30,707	19,671
*22070	Herndon	(703)	16,139	11,449
23075	Highland Springs(u)	(804)	13,823	12,146
24019	Hollins(u)	(703)	13,305	12,295
23860	Hopewell	(804)	23,101	23,397
22303	Huntington(u)	(703)	7,489	5,813
22306	Hybla Valley(u)	(703)	15,491	15,533
22043	Idylwood(u)	(703)	14,710	11,982
22042	Jefferson(u)	(804)	25,782	24,342
22041	Lake Barcroft(u)	(703)	8,686	8,725
22191	Lake Ridge(u)	(703)	23,862	11,072
23228	Lakeside(u)	(804)	12,081	12,289
23060	Laurel(u)	(804)	13,011	10,569
22075	Leesburg	(703)	16,202	8,357
22450	Lexington	(703)	6,959	7,292
22312	Lincolnia(u)	(703)	13,041	10,350
22079	Lorton(u)	(703)	15,385	5,813
......	Montclair		11,399	....
23231	Montrose(u)	(804)	6,405	5,349
22121	Mount Vernon(u)	(703)	27,485	24,058
22122	Newington(u)	(703)	17,965	8,313
*23607	Newport News	(804)	170,045	144,903
*23501	Norfolk	(804)	261,229	266,979
22151	North Springfield(u)	(703)	8,996	9,538
22124	Oakton(u)	(703)	24,610	19,150
23803	Petersburg	(804)	38,386	41,055
22043	Pimmit Hills(u)	(703)	6,019	6,658
23662	Poquoson	(804)	11,005	8,726
*23705	Portsmouth	(804)	103,907	104,577
24301	Pulaski	(703)	9,985	10,1069
22134	Quantico Station(u)	(703)	7,425	7,121
24141	Radford	(703)	15,940	13,225
22090	Reston(u)	(703)	48,556	36,407
*23232	Richmond	(804)	203,056	219,214
*24001	Roanoke	(703)	96,397	100,220
22310	Rose Hill(u)	(703)	12,675	11,926
24153	Salem	(703)	23,756	23,958
22044	Seven Corners(u)	(703)	72,80	6,058
24592	South Boston	(804)	6,997	7,093
*22150	Springfield	(703)	23,706	21,435
22401	Staunton	(703)	24,461	21,857
22170	Sterling Park(u)	(703)	20,512	16,080
......	Stuarts Draft		5,087	1,776
......	Sudley		7,321	4,674
23434	Suffolk	(804)	52,141	47,621
22170	Sugarland Run(u)	(703)	9,357	6,258
24502	Timberlake(u)	(804)	10,314	9,697
23229	Tuckahoe(u)	(804)	42,629	39,868
22101	Tysons Corner(u)	(703)	13,124	10,065
......	University Heights		6,900	6,736
22180	Vienna	(703)	14,852	15,469
24179	Vinton	(703)	7,665	8,027
*23458	Virginia Beach	(804)	393,069	262,199
22980	Waynesboro	(703)	18,549	15,329
22110	West Gate(u)	(703)	6,565	7,119
22152	West Springfield(u)	(703)	28,126	25,012
23185	Williamsburg	(804)	11,530	9,870
22601	Winchester	(703)	21,947	20,217
24592	Wolf Trap(u)	(804)	13,133	9,875
22191	Woodbridge(u)	(703)	26,401	24,004
24382	Wytheville	(703)	8,038	7,135
......	Yorkshire		5,699	4,940

Washington

ZIP code	Place		1990	1980
98520	Aberdeen	(206)	16,565	18,739
98036	Alderwood Manor(u)	(206)	22,945	16,524
98221	Anacortes	(206)	11,451	9,013
......	Artondale		7,141	....
98002	Auburn	(206)	33,102	26,417
*98009	Bellevue	(206)	86,874	73,903
98225	Bellingham	(206)	52,179	45,794
98390	Bonney Lake	(206)	7,494	5,328
98011	Bothell	(206)	12,345	7,943
98310	Bremerton	(206)	38,142	36,208
......	Brier		5,633	2,915
98178	Bryn Mawr-Skyway(u)	(206)	12,514	11,754
98166	Burien(u)	(206)	25,089	23,189
98607	Camas	(206)	6,442	5,681
98055	Cascade-Fairwood(u)	(206)	30,107	16,939
......	Cascade Park East		6,996	....
......	Cascade Park West		6,656	....
98531	Centralia	(206)	12,101	11,555
98532	Chehalis	(206)	6,527	6,100
99004	Cheney	(509)	7,723	7,630
99403	Clarkston	(509)	6,753	6,903
99324	College Place	(509)	6,308	5,771
......	Country Homes		5,126	....
......	Covington-Sawyer-Wilderness		24,321	....
98198	Des Moines	(206)	17,283	7,378
99213	Dishman(u)	(509)	9,671	10,169
......	East Hill-Meridian(u)		42,696	....
......	East Port Orchard		5,409	4,631
......	East Renton Highlands(u)	(206)	13,218	12,033
98801	East Wenatchee Bench(u)	(509)	12,539	11,410
......	Edgewood-North Hill		9,120	....
98020	Edmonds	(206)	30,744	27,679
......	Elk Plain		12,197	....
98926	Ellensburg	(509)	12,361	11,752
......	Ellsworth North		5,796	....
98022	Enumclaw	(206)	7,227	5,427
98823	Ephrata	(509)	5,349	5,359
99210	Esperance(u)	(509)	11,236	11,120
*98201	Everett	(206)	69,961	54,413
......	Evergreen		11,249	....
98055	Fairwood(u)	(206)	5,807	5,337
......	Federal Way		67,554	....
......	Ferndale		5,398	3,855
98466	Fircrest	(206)	5,258	5,477
......	Five Corners		6,776	....
98433	Fort Lewis(u)	(206)	22,224	23,761
98930	Grandview	(509)	7,169	5,615
......	Harbour Pointe		9,107	....
98660	Hazel Dell North(u)	(206)	6,924	15,386
......	Hazel Dell South		5,796	....
98550	Hoquiam	(206)	8,972	9,719
98011	Inglewood-Finn Hill(u)	(206)	29,132	12,467
98027	Issaquah	(206)	7,786	5,536
98626	Kelso	(206)	11,820	11,129
98028	Kenmore(u)	(206)	8,917	7,281
99336	Kennewick	(509)	42,155	34,397
98031	Kent	(206)	37,960	22,961
98033	Kingsgate(u)	(206)	14,259	12,652
98033	Kirkland	(206)	40,052	18,785
98503	Lacey	(206)	19,279	13,940
98155	Lake Forest North(u)	(206)	8,002	7,995
......	Lakeland North(u)	(206)	14,402	11,451
......	Lakeland South(u)	(206)	9,027	5,225
......	Lake Serene-North Lynnwood		14,290	54,533
......	Lake Shore		6,268	....
......	Lakewood(u)		58,412	....
98632	Longview	(206)	31,499	31,052
......	Lynden		5,709	4,022
98036	Lynnwood	(206)	28,695	22,641
......	Martha Lake(u)	(206)	10,155	7,022
98270	Marysville	(206)	10,328	5,080
98040	Mercer Island	(206)	20,816	21,522
......	Midland		5,587	....
......	Mill Creek		7,172	1,803
......	Minnehaha		9,661	....
98837	Moses Lake	(509)	11,235	10,629
98043	Mountlake Terrace	(206)	19,320	16,534
98273	Mount Vernon	(206)	17,647	13,009
......	Mukilteo		7,007	1,426
98006	Newport Hills(u)	(206)	14,736	12,245
......	Normandy Park		6,709	4,268
98155	North City-Ridgecrest(u)	(206)	13,832	13,551
......	North Creek-Canyon Park		23,236	13,551
......	North Hill(u)	(206)	5,706	10,170
98270	North Marysville(u)	(206)	18,711	15,159
98277	Oak Harbor	(206)	17,176	12,271
*98501	Olympia	(206)	33,840	27,447
99214	Opportunity(u)	(509)	22,326	21,241
98662	Orchards North(u)	(206)	6,479	8,828
......	Orchards South		12,956	....
......	Otis Orchards-East Farms		5,811	4,597
......	Paine Field-Lake Stickney		18,670	....
98444	Parkland(u)	(206)	20,882	23,355
......	Parkwood		6,853	4,599
99301	Pasco	(509)	20,337	18,428
......	Pine Lake		13,940	....
98362	Port Angeles	(206)	17,710	17,311
98368	Port Townsend	(206)	7,001	6,067

ZIP code	Place	1990	1980
.....	Prairie Ridge............	8,278	....
99163	Pullman............ (509)	23,478	23,579
98371	Puyallup............ (206)	23,875	18,251
98052	Redmond............ (206)	35,800	23,318
98055	Renton............ (206)	41,688	31,031
99352	Richland............ (509)	32,315	33,578
98160	Richmond Beach-Innis Arden (206)	7,242	6,700
98113	Richmond Highlands(u)... (206)	26,037	24,463
98188	Riverton-Boulevard Park(u) . (206)	15,337	14,182
.....	Sahalee............	13,951	....
.....	Salmon Creek............	11,989	....
.....	Sea-Tac............	22,694	....
*98109	Seattle............ (206)	516,259	493,846
98284	Sedro Woolley............ (206)	6,031	6,110
.....	Selah............	5,113	4,500
98584	Shelton............ (206)	7,241	7,629
98155	Sheridan Beach(u)...... (206)	6,518	6,873
.....	Silverdale............	7,660	....
98201	Silver Lake-Fircrest(u)....	24,474	10,299
98290	Snohomish............ (206)	6,499	5,294
.....	South Hill............	12,963	....
98387	Spanaway(u)............ (206)	15,001	8,868
*99210	Spokane............ (509)	177,196	171,300
.....	Steilacoom............	5,728	4,886
.....	Summit............	6,312	....
.....	Sumner............	6,281	4,936
98944	Sunnyside............ (509)	11,238	9,225
98402	Tacoma............ (206)	176,664	158,501
98501	Tanglewilde-Thompson Place(u)	6,061	5,910
98948	Toppenish............ (509)	7,419	6,517
.....	Tukwila............	11,874	3,578
98502	Tumwater............ (206)	9,976	6,705
98406	University Place(u)...... (206)	27,701	20,381
*98660	Vancouver............ (206)	46,380	42,834
.....	Vancouver Mall............	6,938	....
99037	Veradale(u)............ (509)	7,836	7,256
99362	Walla Walla............ (509)	26,478	25,618
.....	Waller............	6,415	....
98801	Wenatchee............ (509)	21,756	17,257
.....	West Lake Sammamish......	6,087	....
.....	West Lake Stevens......	12,453	....
99301	West Pasco(u)............ (509)	7,312	6,210
.....	West Valley............	6,594	....
98166	White Center-Shorewood(u). (206)	20,531	19,362
.....	Woodinville............	23,654	....
.....	Woodmont Beach............	7,493	....
*98901	Yakima............ (509)	54,827	49,826

West Virginia (304)

ZIP code	Place	1990	1980
25801	Beckley............	18,296	20,492
24701	Bluefield............	12,756	16,060
26330	Bridgeport............	6,739	6,604
26201	Buckhannon............	5,909	6,820
*25301	Charleston............	57,287	63,968
26301	Clarksburg............	18,059	22,371
.....	Cross Lanes............	10,878	....
25064	Dunbar............	8,697	9,285
26241	Elkins............	7,420	8,536
26554	Fairmont............	20,210	23,863
26354	Grafton............	5,524	6,845
*25701	Huntington............	54,844	63,684
26726	Keyser............	5,870	6,569
25401	Martinsburg............	14,073	13,063
26505	Morgantown............	25,879	27,605
26041	Moundsville............	10,753	12,419
26155	New Martinsville......	6,705	7,109
25143	Nitro............	6,851	8,074
25901	Oak Hill............	6,812	7,120
26101	Parkersburg............	33,862	39,946
.....	Pea Ridge............	6,535	....
24740	Princeton............	7,043	7,538
25177	St. Albans............	11,194	12,402
25303	South Charleston......	13,645	15,968
.....	Teays Valley............	8,436	....
26105	Vienna............	10,862	11,618
26062	Weirton............	22,124	25,371
26003	Wheeling............	34,882	43,070

Wisconsin

ZIP code	Place	1990	1980
54301	Allouez(u)............ (414)	14,431	14,882
.....	Altoona............	5,889	4,393
54409	Antigo............ (715)	8,276	8,653
53411	Appleton............ (414)	65,695	58,913
54806	Ashland............ (715)	8,695	9,115
54304	Ashwaubenon............ (414)	16,376	14,486
53913	Baraboo............ (608)	9,203	8,081
53916	Beaver Dam............ (414)	14,196	14,149
.....	Bellevue Town............	7,541	....
53511	Beloit............ (608)	35,573	35,207
54923	Berlin............ (414)	5,371	5,478
53005	Brookfield............ (414)	35,184	34,035
53209	Brown Deer............ (414)	12,236	12,921

ZIP code	Place	1990	1980
53105	Burlington............ (414)	8,855	8,385
53012	Cedarburg............ (414)	9,895	9,005
54729	Chippewa Falls...... (715)	12,727	12,270
53110	Cudahy............ (414)	18,659	19,547
.....	Delafield............	5,347	4,083
53115	Delavan............ (414)	6,073	5,684
54115	De Pere............ (414)	16,569	14,892
54701	Eau Claire............ (715)	56,856	51,509
.....	Elkhorn............	5,337	4,605
53122	Elm Grove............ (414)	6,261	6,735
.....	Fitchburg............	15,648	11,965
54935	Fond Du Lac............ (414)	37,757	35,863
53538	Fort Atkinson............ (414)	10,227	9,785
53217	Fox Point............ (414)	7,238	7,649
53132	Franklin............ (414)	21,855	16,871
53022	Germantown............ (414)	13,658	10,729
53209	Glendale............ (414)	14,088	13,882
53024	Grafton............ (414)	9,340	8,381
*54305	Green Bay............ (414)	96,466	87,899
53129	Greendale............ (414)	15,128	16,928
53220	Greenfield............ (414)	33,403	31,353
53130	Hales Corners............ (414)	7,623	7,110
53027	Hartford............ (414)	8,188	7,159
53029	Hartland............ (414)	6,906	5,559
54303	Howard............ (414)	9,874	8,240
54016	Hudson............ (715)	6,378	5,434
53545	Janesville............ (608)	52,133	51,071
53549	Jefferson............ (414)	6,078	5,647
54130	Kaukauna............ (414)	11,982	11,310
53140	Kenosha............ (414)	80,352	77,685
54136	Kimberly............ (414)	5,406	5,881
54601	La Crosse............ (608)	51,003	48,347
53147	Lake Geneva............ (414)	5,979	5,612
54140	Little Chute............ (414)	9,207	7,907
.....	McFarland............	5,232	3,783
*53701	Madison............ (608)	191,262	170,616
54220	Manitowoc............ (414)	32,520	32,547
54143	Marinette............ (715)	11,843	11,965
54449	Marshfield............ (715)	19,291	18,290
54952	Menasha............ (414)	14,711	14,728
53051	Menomonee Falls...... (414)	26,840	27,845
54751	Menomonie............ (715)	13,547	12,769
53092	Mequon............ (414)	18,885	16,193
54452	Merrill............ (715)	9,860	9,578
53562	Middleton............ (608)	13,289	11,851
*53203	Milwaukee............ (414)	628,088	636,297
53716	Monona............ (608)	8,637	8,809
53566	Monroe............ (608)	10,241	10,027
53150	Muskego............ (414)	16,813	15,277
54956	Neenah............ (414)	23,219	22,432
53151	New Berlin............ (414)	33,592	30,529
54961	New London............ (414)	6,658	6,210
.....	New Richmond............	5,106	4,306
53154	Oak Creek............ (414)	19,513	16,932
53066	Oconomowoc............ (414)	10,993	9,909
54650	Onalaska............ (608)	11,284	9,249
54901	Oshkosh............ (414)	55,006	49,620
53818	Platteville............ (608)	9,708	9,580
.....	Pleasant Prairie......	11,961	12,176
54467	Plover............ (715)	8,176	5,310
53073	Plymouth............ (414)	6,769	6,027
53901	Portage............ (608)	8,640	7,896
53074	Port Washington...... (414)	9,338	8,612
53821	Prairie du Chien...... (608)	5,659	5,859
*53401	Racine............ (414)	84,298	85,725
53959	Reedsburg............ (608)	5,834	5,038
54501	Rhinelander............ (715)	7,427	7,873
54868	Rice Lake............ (715)	7,998	7,691
.....	Richland Center......	5,018	4,997
54971	Ripon............ (414)	7,241	7,111
54022	River Falls............ (715)	10,610	9,019
53207	St. Francis............ (414)	9,245	10,095
54166	Shawano............ (715)	7,598	7,013
53081	Sheboygan............ (414)	49,676	48,085
53085	Sheboygan Falls...... (414)	5,823	5,253
53211	Shorewood............ (414)	14,116	14,327
53172	South Milwaukee...... (414)	20,958	21,069
54656	Sparta............ (608)	7,788	6,934
54481	Stevens Point...... (715)	23,006	22,970
53589	Stoughton............ (608)	8,786	7,589
54235	Sturgeon Bay............ (414)	9,176	8,847
53590	Sun Prairie............ (608)	15,333	12,931
54880	Superior............ (715)	27,134	29,571
.....	Sussex............	5,039	3,482
54660	Tomah............ (608)	7,570	7,204
54241	Two Rivers............ (414)	13,030	13,354
.....	Verona............	5,374	3,336
53094	Watertown............ (414)	19,142	18,113
53186	Waukesha............ (414)	56,958	50,365
.....	Waunakee............	5,897	3,866
53963	Waupun............ (414)	8,207	8,132
54401	Wausau............ (715)	37,060	32,426
53213	Wauwatosa............ (414)	49,366	51,308
53214	West Allis............ (414)	63,221	63,982
53095	West Bend............ (414)	23,916	21,484
54476	Weston(u)............ (715)	9,714	8,775
53217	Whitefish Bay............ (414)	14,272	14,930

ZIP code	Place		1990	1980
53190	Whitewater	(414)	12,636	11,520
54494	Wisconsin Rapids	(715)	18,245	17,995

Wyoming (307)

ZIP code	Place	1990	1980
*82601	Casper	46,742	51,016
*82001	Cheyenne	50,008	47,283
82414	Cody	7,897	6,599
82633	Douglas	5,076	6,030
82930	Evanston	10,903	6,265

ZIP code	Place	1990	1980
82716	Gillette	17,635	12,134
82935	Green River	12,711	12,807
82520	Lander	7,023	7,867
82070	Laramie	26,687	24,410
82435	Powell	5,292	5,310
82301	Rawlins	9,380	11,547
82501	Riverton	9,202	9,562
82901	Rock Springs	19,050	19,458
82801	Sheridan	13,900	15,146
82240	Torrington	5,651	5,441
82401	Worland	5,742	6,391

Census and Areas of Counties and States

Source: Bureau of the Census, U.S. Dept. of Commerce
With names of county seats or court houses

Population figures listed below are final counts in the 1990 census, conducted on Apr. 1, 1990.

Alabama

(67 counties, 50,767 sq. mi. land; pop., 4,040,587)

County	Pop.	County Seat or court house	Land area sq. mi.
Autauga	34,222	Prattville	597
Baldwin	98,280	Bay Minette	1,589
Barbour	25,417	Clayton	884
Bibb	16,576	Centreville	625
Blount	39,248	Oneonta	643
Bullock	11,042	Union Springs	625
Butler	21,892	Greenville	779
Calhoun	116,034	Anniston	611
Chambers	36,876	Lafayette	596
Cherokee	19,543	Centre	553
Chilton	32,458	Clanton	695
Choctaw	16,018	Butler	909
Clarke	27,240	Grove Hill	1,230
Clay	13,252	Ashland	605
Cleburne	12,730	Heflin	561
Coffee	40,240	Elba	680
Colbert	51,666	Tuscumbia	589
Conecuh	14,054	Evergreen	854
Coosa	11,063	Rockford	657
Covington	36,478	Andalusia	1,038
Crenshaw	13,635	Luverne	611
Cullman	67,613	Cullman	738
Dale	49,633	Ozark	561
Dallas	48,130	Selma	975
De Kalb	54,651	Fort Payne	778
Elmore	49,210	Wetumpka	622
Escambia	35,518	Brewton	951
Etowah	99,840	Gadsden	542
Fayette	17,962	Fayette	630
Franklin	27,814	Russellville	643
Geneva	23,647	Geneva	578
Greene	10,153	Eutaw	631
Hale	15,498	Greensboro	661
Henry	15,374	Abbeville	557
Houston	81,331	Dothan	577
Jackson	47,796	Scottsboro	1,070
Jefferson	651,525	Birmingham	1,119
Lamar	15,715	Vernon	605
Lauderdale	79,661	Florence	661
Lawrence	31,513	Moulton	693
Lee	87,146	Opelika	609
Limestone	46,005	Athens	559
Lowndes	12,658	Hayneville	714
Macon	24,928	Tuskegee	614
Madison	238,912	Huntsville	806
Marengo	23,084	Linden	982
Marion	29,830	Hamilton	743
Marshall	70,832	Guntersville	567
Mobile	378,643	Mobile	1,238
Monroe	23,968	Monroeville	1,019
Montgomery	209,085	Montgomery	793
Morgan	100,043	Decatur	575
Perry	12,759	Marion	718
Pickens	20,699	Carrollton	890
Pike	27,595	Troy	672
Randolph	19,881	Wedowee	584
Russell	46,860	Phenix City	634
St. Clair	50,009	Ashville & Pell City	646
Shelby	99,358	Columbiana	800
Sumter	16,174	Livingston	907
Talladega	74,107	Talladega	753
Tallapoosa	38,826	Dadeville	701
Tuscaloosa	150,522	Tuscaloosa	1,336
Walker	67,670	Jasper	804
Washington	16,694	Chatom	1,081
Wilcox	13,568	Camden	883
Winston	22,053	Double Springs	613

Alaska

(25 divisions, 570,833 sq. mi. land; pop., 550,043)

Census area	Pop.	Land area sq. mi.
Aleutian Islands	2,464	10,890
Aleutians West Census Area	9,478	531
Anchorage Borough	226,338	1,732

Census division	Pop.	Land area sq. mi.
Bethel	13,656	36,104
Bristol Bay Borough	1,410	531
Dillingham	4,012	46,042
Fairbanks North Star Borough	77,720	7,404
Haines Borough	2,117	2,374
Juneau Borough	26,751	2,626
Kenai Peninsula Borough	40,802	16,056
Ketchikan Gateway Borough	13,828	1,242
Kodiak Island Borough	13,309	4,796
Lake and Peninsula Borough	1,668	.....
Matanuska-Susitna Borough	39,683	24,502
Nome	8,288	23,871
North Slope Borough	5,979	90,955
Northwest Arctic Borough	6,113	.....
Prince of Wales-Outer Ketchikan	6,278	7,660
Sitka Borough	8,588	2,938
Skagway-Yakutat-Angoon	4,385	13,239
Southeast Fairbanks	5,913	24,169
Valdez-Cordova	9,952	39,229
Wade Hampton	5,791	17,816
Wrangell-Petersburg	7,042	6,167
Yukon-Koyukuk	8,478	159,099

Arizona

(15 counties, 113,508 sq. mi. land; pop. 3,665,228)

County	Pop.	County seat or court house	Land area sq. mi.
Apache	61,591	Saint Johns	11,211
Cochise	97,624	Bisbee	6,218
Coconino	96,591	Flagstaff	18,608
Gila	40,216	Globe	4,752
Graham	26,554	Safford	4,630
Greenlee	8,008	Clifton	1,837
La Paz	13,844	Parker	4,430
Maricopa	2,122,101	Phoenix	9,127
Mohave	93,497	Kingman	13,285
Navajo	77,658	Holbrook	9,955
Pima	666,880	Tucson	9,187
Pinal	116,379	Florence	5,343
Santa Cruz	29,676	Nogales	1,238
Yavapai	107,714	Prescott	8,123
Yuma	106,895	Yuma	5,564

Arkansas

(75 counties, 52,078 sq. mi. land; pop. 2,350,725)

County	Pop.	County Seat or court house	Land area sq. mi.
Arkansas	21,653	DeWitt & Stuttgart	1,006
Ashley	24,319	Hamburg	934
Baxter	31,186	Mountain Home	546
Benton	97,499	Bentonville	843
Boone	28,297	Harrison	584
Bradley	11,793	Warren	654
Calhoun	5,826	Hampton	628
Carroll	18,654	Berryville and Eureka Sp.	634
Chicot	15,713	Lake Village	649
Clark	21,437	Arkadelphia	867
Clay	18,107	Corning; Piggott	641
Cleburne	19,411	Heber Springs	551
Cleveland	7,781	Rison	599
Columbia	25,691	Magnolia	767
Conway	19,151	Morrilton	558
Craighead	68,956	Jonesboro and Lake City	713
Crawford	42,493	Van Buren	594
Crittenden	49,939	Marion	599
Cross	19,225	Wynne	622
Dallas	9,614	Fordyce	668
Desha	16,798	Arkansas City	746
Drew	17,369	Monticello	831
Faulkner	60,006	Conway	645
Franklin	14,897	Charleston and Ozark	609
Fulton	10,037	Salem	616
Garland	73,397	Hot Spgs. Nat'l Pk.	657
Grant	13,948	Sheridan	633
Greene	31,804	Paragould	579
Hempstead	21,621	Hope	725
Hot Spring	26,115	Malvern	615
Howard	13,569	Nashville	574
Independence	31,192	Batesville	763
Izard	11,364	Melbourne	581
Jackson	18,944	Newport	633
Jefferson	85,487	Pine Bluff	882
Johnson	18,221	Clarksville	676
Lafayette	9,643	Lewisville	518
Lawrence	17,457	Walnut Ridge	589
Lee	13,053	Marianna	602
Lincoln	13,690	Star City	562
Little River	13,966	Ashdown	516
Logan	20,557	Booneville & Paris	717
Lonoke	39,268	Lonoke	783
Madison	11,618	Huntsville	837
Marion	12,001	Yellville	587
Miller	38,467	Texarkana	619
Mississippi	57,525	Blytheville and Osceola	896
Monroe	11,333	Clarendon	609
Montgomery	7,841	Mount Ida	774
Nevada	10,101	Prescott	620
Newton	7,666	Jasper	823
Ouachita	30,574	Camden	737
Perry	7,969	Perryville	550
Phillips	28,838	Helena	685
Pike	10,086	Murfreesboro	598
Poinsett	24,664	Harrisburg	762
Polk	17,347	Mena	860
Pope	45,883	Russellville	820
Prairie	9,518	Des Arc and De Valls Bluff	656
Pulaski	349,660	Little Rock	767
Randolph	16,558	Pocahontas	656
St. Francis	28,497	Forrest City	638
Saline	64,183	Benton	725
Scott	10,205	Waldron	896
Searcy	7,841	Marshall	668
Sebastian	99,590	Fort Smith; Greenwood	535
Sevier	13,637	De Queen	560
Sharp	14,109	Ash Flat	606
Stone	9,775	Mountain View	606
Union	46,719	El Dorado	1,053
Van Buren	14,008	Clinton	709
Washington	113,409	Fayetteville	951
White	54,676	Searcy	1,040
Woodruff	9,520	Augusta	592
Yell	17,759	Danville and Dardanelle	930

California

(58 counties, 156,299 sq. mi. land; pop. 29,760,021)

County	Pop.	County Seat or court house	Land area sq. mi.
Alameda	1,279,182	Oakland	736
Alpine	1,113	Markleeville	738
Amador	30,039	Jackson	589
Butte	182,120	Oroville	1,646
Calaveras	31,998	San Andreas	1,021
Colusa	16,275	Colusa	1,152
Contra Costa	803,732	Martinez	730
Del Norte	23,460	Crescent City	1,007
El Dorado	125,995	Placerville	1,715
Fresno	667,490	Fresno	5,978
Glenn	24,798	Willows	1,319
Humboldt	119,118	Eureka	3,579
Imperial	109,303	El Centro	4,173
Inyo	18,281	Independence	10,223
Kern	543,477	Bakersfield	8,130
Kings	101,469	Hanford	1,392
Lake	50,631	Lakeport	1,262
Lassen	27,598	Susanville	4,553
Los Angeles	8,863,164	Los Angeles	4,070
Madera	88,090	Madera	2,145
Marin	230,096	San Rafael	523
Mariposa	14,302	Mariposa	1,456
Mendocino	80,345	Ukiah	3,512
Merced	178,403	Merced	1,944
Modoc	9,678	Alturas	4,064
Mono	9,956	Bridgeport	3,018
Monterey	355,660	Salinas	3,303
Napa	110,765	Napa	744
Nevada	78,510	Nevada City	960
Orange	2,410,556	Santa Ana	798
Placer	172,796	Auburn	1,416
Plumas	19,739	Quincy	2,573
Riverside	1,170,413	Riverside	7,214
Sacramento	1,041,219	Sacramento	971
San Benito	36,697	Hollister	1,388
San Bernardino	1,418,380	San Bernardino	20,064
San Diego	2,498,016	San Diego	4,212
San Francisco	723,959	San Francisco	46
San Joaquin	480,628	Stockton	1,415
San Luis Obispo	217,162	San Luis Obispo	3,308
San Mateo	649,623	Redwood City	447
Santa Barbara	369,608	Santa Barbara	2,748
Santa Clara	1,497,577	San Jose	1,293
Santa Cruz	229,734	Santa Cruz	446
Shasta	147,036	Redding	3,786
Sierra	3,318	Downieville	959
Siskiyou	43,531	Yreka	6,281
Solano	340,421	Fairfield	834
Sonoma	388,222	Santa Rosa	1,604
Stanislaus	370,522	Modesto	1,506
Sutter	64,415	Yuba City	602
Tehama	49,625	Red Bluff	2,953
Trinity	13,063	Weaverville	3,190
Tulare	311,921	Visalia	4,808
Tuolumne	48,456	Sonora	2,234
Ventura	669,016	Ventura	1,862
Yolo	141,092	Woodland	1,014
Yuba	58,228	Marysville	640

Colorado

(63 counties, 103,595 sq. mi. land; pop. 3,294,394)

County	Pop.	County Seat or court house	Land area sq. mi.
Adams	265,038	Brighton	1,235
Alamosa	13,617	Alamosa	719
Arapahoe	391,511	Littleton	800
Archuleta	5,345	Pagosa Springs	1,353
Baca	4,556	Springfield	2,554
Bent	5,048	Las Animas	1,517
Boulder	225,339	Boulder	742
Chaffee	12,684	Salida	1,008
Cheyenne	2,397	Cheyenne Wells	1,783
Clear Creek	7,619	Georgetown	396
Conejos	7,453	Conejos	1,284
Costilla	3,190	San Luis	1,227
Crowley	3,946	Ordway	790
Custer	1,926	Westcliffe	740
Delta	20,980	Delta	1,141
Denver	467,610	Denver	111
Dolores	1,504	Dove Creek	1,064
Douglas	60,391	Castle Rock	841
Eagle	21,928	Eagle	1,690
Elbert	9,646	Kiowa	1,851
El Paso	397,014	Colorado Springs	2,129
Fremont	32,273	Canon City	1,538
Garfield	29,974	Glenwood Springs	2,952
Gilpin	3,070	Central City	149
Grand	7,966	Hot Sulphur Springs	1,854
Gunnison	10,273	Gunnison	3,238
Hinsdale	467	Lake City	1,115
Huerfano	6,009	Walsenburg	1,584
Jackson	1,605	Walden	1,614
Jefferson	438,430	Golden	768
Kiowa	1,688	Eads	1,758
Kit Carson	7,140	Burlington	2,160
Lake	6,007	Leadville	379
La Plata	32,284	Durango	1,692
Larimer	186,136	Fort Collins	2,604
Las Animas	13,765	Trinidad	4,771
Lincoln	4,529	Hugo	2,586
Logan	17,567	Sterling	1,818
Mesa	93,145	Grand Junction	3,309
Mineral	558	Creede	877
Moffat	11,357	Craig	4,732
Montezuma	18,672	Cortez	2,038
Montrose	24,423	Montrose	2,240

County	Pop.	County Seat or court house	Land area sq. mi.
Morgan	21,939	Fort Morgan	1,276
Otero	20,185	LaJunta	1,247
Ouray	2,295	Ouray	542
Park	7,174	Fairplay	2,192
Phillips	4,189	Holyoke	688
Pitkin	12,661	Aspen	968
Prowers	13,347	Lamar	1,629
Pueblo	123,051	Pueblo	2,377
Rio Blanco	5,972	Meeker	3,222
Rio Grande	10,770	Del Norte	913
Routt	14,088	Steamboat Springs	2,367
Saguache	4,619	Saguache	3,167
San Juan	745	Silverton	388
San Miguel	3,653	Telluride	1,287
Sedgwick	2,690	Julesburg	540
Summit	12,881	Breckenridge	607
Teller	12,468	Cripple Creek	559
Washington	4,812	Akron	2,520
Weld	131,821	Greeley	3,990
Yuma	8,954	Wray	2,365

Connecticut

(8 counties, 4,872 sq. mi. land; pop. 3,287,116)

County	Pop.	County Seat or court house	Land area sq. mi.
Fairfield	827,645	Bridgeport	632
Hartford	851,783	Hartford	739
Litchfield	174,092	Litchfield	921
Middlesex	143,196	Middletown	373
New Haven	804,219	New Haven	610
New London	254,957	Norwich	669
Tolland	128,699	Rockville	412
Windham	102,525	Putnam	515

Delaware

(3 counties, 1,932 sq. mi. land; pop. 666,168)

County	Pop.	County Seat or court house	Land area sq. mi.
Kent	110,993	Dover	595
New Castle	441,946	Wilmington	396
Sussex	113,229	Georgetown	942

District of Columbia

(63 sq. mi. land; pop. 606,900)

Florida

(67 counties, 54,153 sq. mi. land; pop. 12,937,926)

County	Pop.	County Seat or court house	Land area sq. mi.
Alachua	181,596	Gainesville	901
Baker	18,486	Macclenny	585
Bay	126,994	Panama City	758
Bradford	22,515	Starke	293
Brevard	398,978	Titusville	995
Broward	1,255,488	Fort Lauderdale	1,211
Calhoun	11,011	Blountstown	568
Charlotte	110,975	Punta Gorda	690
Citrus	93,515	Inverness	629
Clay	105,986	Green Cove Spgs.	592
Collier	152,099	Naples	1,994
Columbia	42,613	Lake City	796
Dade	1,937,094	Miami	1,955
De Soto	23,865	Arcadia	636
Dixie	10,585	Cross City	701
Duval	672,971	Jacksonville	776
Escambia	262,798	Pensacola	660
Flagler	28,701	Bunnell	491
Franklin	8,967	Apalachicola	545
Gadsden	41,105	Quincy	518
Gilchrist	9,667	Trenton	354
Glades	7,591	Moore Haven	763
Gulf	11,504	Port St. Joe	559
Hamilton	10,930	Jasper	517
Hardee	19,499	Wauchula	637
Hendry	25,773	La Belle	1,163
Hernando	101,115	Brooksville	477
Highlands	68,432	Sebring	1,029
Hillsborough	834,054	Tampa	1,053
Holmes	15,778	Bonifay	488
Indian River	90,208	Vero Beach	497
Jackson	41,375	Marianna	942
Jefferson	11,296	Monticello	609
Lafayette	5,578	Mayo	545
Lake	152,104	Tavares	954
Lee	335,113	Fort Myers	803
Leon	192,493	Tallahassee	676
Levy	25,923	Bronson	1,100
Liberty	5,569	Bristol	837
Madison	16,569	Madison	710
Manatee	211,707	Bradenton	747
Marion	194,833	Ocala	1,610
Martin	100,900	Stuart	555
Monroe	78,024	Key West	1,034
Nassau	43,941	Fernandina Beach	649
Okaloosa	143,776	Crestview	936
Okeechobee	29,627	Okeechobee	770
Orange	677,491	Orlando	910
Osceola	107,728	Kissimmee	1,350
Palm Beach	863,518	West Palm Beach	1,993
Pasco	281,131	Dade City	738
Pinellas	851,659	Clearwater	280
Polk	405,382	Bartow	1,823
Putnam	65,070	Palatka	733
St. Johns	83,829	Saint Augustine	617
St. Lucie	150,171	Fort Pierce	581
Santa Rosa	81,608	Milton	1,024
Sarasota	277,776	Sarasota	573
Seminole	287,529	Sanford	298
Sumter	31,577	Bushnell	561
Suwannee	26,780	Live Oak	690
Taylor	17,111	Perry	1,058
Union	10,252	Lake Butler	246
Volusia	370,712	De Land	1,113
Wakulla	14,202	Crawfordville	601
Walton	27,760	De Funiak Springs	1,066
Washington	16,919	Chipley	590

Georgia

(159 counties, 58,056 sq. mi. land; pop. 6,478,216)

County	Pop.	County Seat or court house	Land area sq. mi.
Appling	15,744	Baxley	510
Atkinson	6,213	Pearson	344
Bacon	9,566	Alma	286
Baker	3,615	Newton	347
Baldwin	39,530	Milledgeville	257
Banks	10,308	Horner	234
Bartow	29,721	Winder	163
Bartow	55,911	Cartersville	456
Ben Hill	16,245	Fitzgerald	254
Berrien	14,153	Nashville	456
Bibb	149,967	Macon	253
Bleckley	10,430	Cochran	219
Brantley	11,077	Nahunta	445
Brooks	15,398	Quitman	491
Bryan	15,438	Pembroke	441
Bulloch	43,125	Statesboro	678
Burke	20,579	Waynesboro	833
Butts	15,326	Jackson	187
Calhoun	5,013	Morgan	284
Camden	30,167	Woodbine	649
Candler	7,744	Metter	248
Carroll	71,422	Carrollton	501
Catoosa	42,464	Ringgold	162
Charlton	8,496	Folkston	780
Chatham	216,935	Savannah	443
Chattahoochee	16,934	Cusseta	250
Chattooga	22,242	Summerville	313
Cherokee	90,204	Canton	424
Clarke	87,594	Athens	122
Clay	3,364	Fort Gaines	196
Clayton	182,052	Jonesboro	148
Clinch	6,160	Homerville	821
Cobb	447,745	Marietta	343
Coffee	29,592	Douglas	602
Colquitt	36,645	Moultrie	557
Columbia	66,031	Appling	290
Cook	13,456	Adel	233
Coweta	53,853	Newnan	444
Crawford	8,991	Knoxville	328
Crisp	20,011	Cordele	275
Dade	13,147	Trenton	176
Dawson	9,429	Dawsonville	210
Decatur	25,511	Bainbridge	586
De Kalb	545,837	Decatur	270
Dodge	17,607	Eastman	504
Dooly	9,901	Vienna	397
Dougherty	96,311	Albany	330
Douglas	71,120	Douglasville	203
Early	11,854	Blakely	516
Echols	2,334	Statenville	421
Effingham	25,687	Springfield	482
Elbert	18,949	Elberton	367
Emanuel	20,546	Swainsboro	688
Evans	8,724	Claxton	186
Fannin	15,992	Blue Ridge	384
Fayette	62,415	Fayetteville	199
Floyd	81,251	Rome	519
Forsyth	44,083	Cumming	226
Franklin	16,650	Carnesville	264
Fulton	648,951	Atlanta	534
Gilmer	13,368	Ellijay	427
Glascock	2,357	Gibson	144

County	Pop.	County Seat or court house	Land area sq. mi.
Glynn	62,496	Brunswick	412
Gordon	35,072	Calhoun	355
Grady	20,279	Cairo	459
Greene	11,793	Greensboro	389
Gwinnett	352,910	Lawrenceville	435
Habersham	27,621	Clarkesville	278
Hall	95,428	Gainesville	379
Hancock	8,908	Sparta	470
Haralson	21,966	Buchanan	283
Harris	17,788	Hamilton	464
Hart	19,712	Hartwell	230
Heard	8,628	Franklin	292
Henry	58,741	McDonough	321
Houston	89,208	Perry	380
Irwin	8,649	Ocilla	362
Jackson	30,005	Jefferson	342
Jasper	8,453	Monticello	371
Jeff Davis	12,032	Hazlehurst	335
Jefferson	17,408	Louisville	529
Jenkins	8,247	Millen	353
Johnson	8,329	Wrightsville	306
Jones	20,739	Gray	394
Lamar	13,038	Barnesville	186
Lanier	5,531	Lakeland	194
Laurens	39,988	Dublin	816
Lee	16,250	Leesburg	358
Liberty	52,745	Hinesville	517
Lincoln	7,442	Lincolnton	196
Long	6,202	Ludowici	402
Lowndes	75,981	Valdosta	507
Lumpkin	14,573	Dahlonega	287
McDuffie	20,119	Thomson	256
McIntosh	8,634	Darien	425
Macon	13,114	Oglethorpe	404
Madison	21,050	Danielsville	285
Marion	5,590	Buena Vista	366
Meriwether	22,411	Greenville	506
Miller	6,280	Colquitt	284
Mitchell	20,275	Camilla	512
Monroe	17,113	Forsyth	397
Montgomery	7,163	Mount Vernon	244
Morgan	12,883	Madison	349
Murray	26,147	Chatsworth	345
Muscogee	179,278	Columbus	218
Newton	41,808	Covington	277
Oconee	17,618	Watkinsville	186
Oglethorpe	9,763	Lexington	442
Paulding	41,611	Dallas	312
Peach	21,189	Fort Valley	152
Pickens	14,432	Jasper	232
Pierce	13,328	Blackshear	344
Pike	10,224	Zebulon	219
Polk	33,815	Cedartown	311
Pulaski	8,108	Hawkinsville	249
Putnam	14,137	Eatonton	344
Quitman	2,209	Georgetown	146
Rabun	11,648	Clayton	370
Randolph	8,023	Cuthbert	431
Richmond	189,719	Augusta	326
Rockdale	54,091	Conyers	132
Schley	3,588	Ellaville	169
Screven	13,842	Sylvania	655
Seminole	9,010	Donalsonville	225
Spalding	54,457	Griffin	199
Stephens	23,257	Toccoa	177
Stewart	5,654	Lumpkin	452
Sumter	30,228	Americus	489
Talbot	6,524	Talbotton	395
Taliaferro	1,915	Crawfordville	196
Tattnall	17,722	Reidsville	484
Taylor	7,642	Butler	382
Telfair	11,000	McRae	444
Terrell	10,653	Dawson	337
Thomas	38,986	Thomasville	551
Tift	34,998	Tifton	268
Toombs	24,072	Lyons	371
Towns	6,754	Hiawassee	165
Treutlen	5,994	Soperton	202
Troup	55,536	La Grange	414
Turner	8,703	Ashburn	289
Twiggs	9,806	Jeffersonville	362
Union	11,993	Blairsville	320
Upson	26,300	Thomaston	326
Walker	58,340	La Fayette	446
Walton	38,586	Monroe	330
Ware	35,471	Waycross	907
Warren	6,078	Warrenton	286
Washington	19,112	Sandersville	684
Wayne	22,356	Jesup	647
Webster	2,263	Preston	210
Wheeler	4,903	Alamo	299
White	13,006	Cleveland	242
Whitfield	72,462	Dalton	291
Wilcox	7,008	Abbeville	382
Wilkes	10,597	Washington	470
Wilkinson	10,228	Irwinton	451
Worth	19,745	Sylvester	575

Hawaii

(5 counties, 6,645 sq. mi. land; pop. 1,108,229)

County	Pop.	County Seat or court house	Land area sq. mi.
Hawaii	120,317	Hilo	4,034
Honolulu	836,231	Honolulu	596
Kalawao	130		
Kauai	51,177	Lihue	620
Maui*	100,374	Wailuku	1,175

Idaho

(44 counties, 82,412 sq. mi. land; pop. 1,006,749)

County	Pop.	County Seat or court house	Land area sq. mi.
Ada	205,775	Boise	1,052
Adams	3,254	Council	1,362
Bannock	66,026	Pocatello	1,112
Bear Lake	6,084	Paris	990
Benewah	7,937	Saint Maries	784
Bingham	37,583	Blackfoot	2,096
Blaine	13,552	Hailey	2,634
Boise	3,509	Idaho City	1,901
Bonner	26,622	Sandpoint	1,726
Bonneville	72,207	Idaho Falls	1,840
Boundary	8,332	Bonners Ferry	1,268
Butte	2,918	Arco	2,236
Camas	727	Fairfield	1,071
Canyon	90,076	Caldwell	584
Caribou	6,963	Soda Springs	1,763
Cassia	19,532	Burley	2,560
Clark	762	Dubois	1,763
Clearwater	8,505	Orofino	2,236
Custer	4,133	Challis	4,927
Elmore	21,205	Mountain Home	3,071
Franklin	9,232	Preston	664
Fremont	10,937	Saint Anthony	1,852
Gem	11,844	Emmett	558
Gooding	11,633	Gooding	728
Idaho	13,783	Grangeville	8,497
Jefferson	16,543	Rigby	1,093
Jerome	15,138	Jerome	601
Kootenai	69,795	Coeur d'Alene	1,240
Latah	30,617	Moscow	1,077
Lemhi	6,899	Salmon	4,564
Lewis	3,516	Nezperce	478
Lincoln	3,308	Shoshone	1,205
Madison	23,674	Rexberg	468
Minidoka	19,361	Rupert	757
Nez Perce	33,754	Lewiston	845
Oneida	3,492	Malad City	1,200
Owyhee	8,392	Murphy	7,643
Payette	16,434	Payette	405
Power	7,086	American Falls	1,403
Shoshone	13,931	Wallace	2,641
Teton	3,439	Driggs	448
Twin Falls	53,580	Twin Falls	1,944
Valley	6,109	Cascade	3,670
Washington	8,550	Weiser	1,454

Illinois

(102 counties, 55,645 sq. mi. land; pop. 11,430,602)

County	Pop.	County Seat or court house	Land area sq. mi.
Adams	66,090	Quincy	852
Alexander	10,626	Cairo	236
Bond	14,991	Greenville	377
Boone	30,806	Belvidere	282
Brown	5,836	Mount Sterling	306
Bureau	35,688	Princeton	869
Calhoun	5,322	Hardin	250
Carroll	16,905	Mount Carroll	444
Cass	13,437	Virginia	374
Champaign	173,025	Urbana	998
Christian	34,418	Taylorville	710
Clark	15,921	Marshall	506
Clay	14,460	Louisville	469
Clinton	33,944	Carlyle	472
Coles	51,644	Charleston	509
Cook	5,105,067	Chicago	958
Crawford	19,464	Robinson	446
Cumberland	10,670	Toledo	346
De Kalb	77,932	Sycamore	634
De Witt	16,516	Clinton	397
Douglas	19,464	Tuscola	417
Du Page	781,666	Wheaton	337
Edgar	19,595	Paris	623
Edwards	7,440	Albion	223
Effingham	31,704	Effingham	478
Fayette	20,893	Vandalia	709
Ford	14,275	Paxton	486

Illinois (continued)

County	Pop.	County Seat or court house	Land area sq. mi.
Franklin	40,319	Benton	414
Fulton	38,080	Lewiston	871
Gallatin	6,909	Shawneetown	325
Greene	15,317	Carrollton	543
Grundy	32,337	Morris	423
Hamilton	8,499	McLeansboro	436
Hancock	21,373	Carthage	796
Hardin	5,189	Elizabethtown	181
Henderson	8,096	Oquawka	373
Henry	51,159	Cambridge	824
Iroquois	30,787	Watseka	1,118
Jackson	61,067	Murphysboro	590
Jasper	10,609	Newton	496
Jefferson	37,020	Mount Vernon	570
Jersey	20,539	Jerseyville	373
Jo Daviess	21,821	Galena	603
Johnson	11,347	Vienna	346
Kane	317,471	Geneva	524
Kankakee	96,255	Kankakee	679
Kendall	39,413	Yorkville	322
Knox	56,393	Galesburg	720
Lake	516,418	Waukegan	454
La Salle	106,913	Ottawa	1,139
Lawrence	15,972	Lawrenceville	374
Lee	34,392	Dixon	725
Livingston	39,301	Pontiac	1,046
Logan	30,798	Lincoln	619
McDonough	35,244	Macomb	590
McHenry	183,241	Woodstock	606
McLean	129,180	Bloomington	1,185
Macon	117,206	Decatur	581
Macoupin	47,679	Carlinville	865
Madison	249,238	Edwardsville	728
Marion	41,561	Salem	573
Marshall	12,846	Lacon	388
Mason	16,269	Havana	536
Massac	14,752	Metropolis	241
Menard	11,164	Petersburg	315
Mercer	17,290	Aledo	559
Monroe	22,422	Waterloo	388
Montgomery	30,728	Hillsboro	705
Morgan	36,397	Jacksonville	568
Moultrie	13,930	Sullivan	325
Ogle	45,957	Oregon	759
Peoria	182,827	Peoria	621
Perry	21,412	Pinckneyville	443
Piatt	15,548	Monticello	439
Pike	17,577	Pittsfield	830
Pope	4,373	Golconda	374
Pulaski	7,523	Mound City	203
Putnam	5,730	Hennepin	160
Randolph	34,583	Chester	583
Richland	16,545	Olney	360
Rock Island	148,723	Rock Island	423
St. Clair	262,852	Belleville	672
Saline	26,551	Harrisburg	385
Sangamon	178,386	Springfield	866
Schuyler	7,498	Rushville	436
Scott	5,644	Winchester	251
Shelby	22,261	Shelbyville	747
Stark	6,534	Toulon	288
Stephenson	48,052	Freeport	564
Tazewell	123,692	Pekin	650
Union	17,619	Jonesboro	414
Vermilion	88,257	Danville	900
Wabash	13,111	Mt. Carmel	224
Warren	19,181	Monmouth	543
Washington	14,965	Nashville	563
Wayne	17,241	Fairfield	715
White	16,522	Carmi	497
Whiteside	60,186	Morrison	682
Will	357,313	Joliet	844
Williamson	57,733	Marion	427
Winnebago	252,913	Rockford	516
Woodford	32,653	Eureka	527

Indiana

(92 counties, 35,932 sq. mi. land; pop. 5,544,159)

County	Pop.	County Seat or court house	Land area sq. mi.
Adams	31,095	Decatur	340
Allen	300,836	Fort Wayne	659
Bartholomew	63,657	Columbus	409
Benton	9,441	Fowler	407
Blackford	14,067	Hartford City	166
Boone	38,147	Lebanon	423
Brown	14,080	Nashville	312
Carroll	18,809	Delphi	372
Cass	38,413	Logansport	414
Clark	87,777	Jeffersonville	376
Clay	24,705	Brazil	360
Clinton	30,974	Frankfort	405
Crawford	9,914	English	307
Daviess	27,533	Washington	432
Dearborn	38,835	Lawrenceburg	307
Decatur	23,645	Greensburg	373
DeKalb	35,324	Auburn	364
Delaware	119,659	Muncie	392
Dubois	36,616	Jasper	429
Elkhart	156,198	Goshen	466
Fayette	26,015	Connersville	215
Floyd	64,404	New Albany	150
Fountain	17,808	Covington	398
Franklin	19,580	Brookville	385
Fulton	18,840	Rochester	369
Gibson	31,913	Princeton	490
Grant	74,169	Marion	415
Greene	30,410	Bloomfield	546
Hamilton	108,936	Noblesville	398
Hancock	45,527	Greenfield	307
Harrison	29,890	Corydon	486
Hendricks	75,717	Danville	409
Henry	48,139	New Castle	394
Howard	80,827	Kokomo	293
Huntington	35,427	Huntington	366
Jackson	37,730	Brownstown	513
Jasper	24,960	Rensselaer	561
Jay	21,512	Portland	384
Jefferson	29,797	Madison	363
Jennings	23,661	Vernon	378
Johnson	88,109	Franklin	321
Knox	39,884	Vincennes	520
Kosciusko	65,294	Warsaw	540
Lagrange	29,477	Lagrange	380
Lake	475,594	Crown Point	501
La Porte	107,066	La Porte	600
Lawrence	42,836	Bedford	452
Madison	130,669	Anderson	453
Marion	797,159	Indianapolis	396
Marshall	42,182	Plymouth	444
Martin	10,369	Shoals	339
Miami	36,897	Peru	369
Monroe	108,978	Bloomington	385
Montgomery	34,436	Crawfordsville	505
Morgan	55,920	Martinsville	409
Newton	13,551	Kentland	401
Noble	37,877	Albion	413
Ohio	5,315	Rising Sun	87
Orange	18,409	Paoli	408
Owen	17,281	Spencer	386
Parke	15,410	Rockville	444
Perry	19,107	Cannelton	382
Pike	12,509	Petersburg	341
Porter	128,932	Valparaiso	418
Posey	25,968	Mount Vernon	409
Pulaski	12,643	Winamac	435
Putnam	30,315	Greencastle	482
Randolph	27,148	Winchester	454
Ripley	24,616	Versailles	447
Rush	18,129	Rushville	408
St. Joseph	247,052	South Bend	459
Scott	20,991	Scottsburg	191
Shelby	40,307	Shelbyville	413
Spencer	19,490	Rockport	400
Starke	22,747	Knox	309
Steuben	27,446	Angola	308
Sullivan	18,993	Sullivan	452
Switzerland	7,738	Vevay	223
Tippecanoe	130,598	Lafayette	502
Tipton	16,119	Tipton	260
Union	6,976	Liberty	162
Vanderburgh	165,058	Evansville	236
Vermillion	16,773	Newport	260
Vigo	106,107	Terre Haute	405
Wabash	35,069	Wabash	398
Warren	8,176	Williamsport	366
Warrick	44,920	Boonville	391
Washington	23,717	Salem	516
Wayne	71,951	Richmond	404
Wells	25,948	Bluffton	370
White	23,265	Monticello	506
Whitley	27,651	Columbia City	336

Iowa

(99 counties; 55,965 sq. mi. land; pop. 2,776,755)

County	Pop.	County Seat or court house	Land area sq. mi.
Adair	8,409	Greenfield	570
Adams	4,866	Corning	425
Allamakee	13,855	Waukon	633
Appanoose	13,743	Centerville	498
Audubon	7,334	Audubon	444
Benton	22,429	Vinton	718
Black Hawk	123,798	Waterloo	573
Boone	25,186	Boone	573
Bremer	22,813	Waverly	439
Buchanan	20,844	Independence	572
Buena Vista	19,965	Storm Lake	575
Butler	15,731	Allison	582
Calhoun	11,508	Rockwell City	571

County	Pop.	County Seat or court house	Land area sq. mi.	County	Pop.	County Seat or court house	Land area sq. mi.
Carroll	21,423	Carroll	570	Barton	29,382	Great Bend	895
Cass	15,128	Atlantic	565	Bourbon	14,966	Fort Scott	638
Cedar	17,381	Tipton	582	Brown	11,128	Hiawatha	572
Cerro Gordo	46,733	Mason City	569	Butler	50,580	El Dorado	1,443
Cherokee	14,098	Cherokee	577	Chase	3,021	Cottonwood Falls	777
Chickasaw	13,295	New Hampton	505	Chautauqua	4,407	Sedan	644
Clarke	8,287	Osceola	431	Cherokee	21,374	Columbus	590
Clay	17,585	Spencer	569	Cheyenne	3,243	Saint Francis	1,021
Clayton	19,054	Elkader	779	Clark	2,418	Ashland	975
Clinton	51,040	Clinton	695	Clay	9,158	Clay Center	632
Crawford	16,775	Denison	714	Cloud	11,023	Concordia	718
Dallas	29,755	Adel	591	Coffey	8,404	Burlington	615
Davis	8,312	Bloomfield	504	Comanche	2,313	Coldwater	789
Decatur	8,338	Leon	535	Cowley	36,915	Winfield	1,128
Delaware	18,035	Manchester	578	Crawford	35,568	Girard	595
Des Moines	42,614	Burlington	414	Decatur	4,021	Oberlin	894
Dickinson	14,909	Spirit Lake	381	Dickinson	18,958	Abilene	852
Dubuque	86,403	Dubuque	607	Doniphan	8,134	Troy	388
Emmet	11,569	Estherville	394	Douglas	81,798	Lawrence	461
Fayette	21,843	West Union	731	Edwards	3,787	Kinsley	620
Floyd	17,058	Charles City	501	Elk	3,327	Howard	650
Franklin	11,364	Hampton	583	Ellis	26,004	Hays	900
Fremont	8,226	Sidney	515	Ellsworth	6,586	Ellsworth	717
Greene	10,045	Jefferson	571	Finney	33,070	Garden City	1,302
Grundy	12,029	Grundy Center	501	Ford	27,463	Dodge City	1,099
Guthrie	10,935	Guthrie Center	590	Franklin	21,994	Ottawa	577
Hamilton	16,071	Webster City	576	Geary	30,453	Junction City	377
Hancock	12,638	Garner	571	Gove	3,231	Gove	1,072
Hardin	19,094	Eldora	569	Graham	3,543	Hill City	898
Harrison	14,730	Logan	697	Grant	7,159	Ulysses	575
Henry	19,226	Mount Pleasant	436	Gray	5,396	Cimarron	868
Howard	9,809	Cresco	473	Greeley	1,774	Tribune	778
Humboldt	10,756	Dakota City	436	Greenwood	7,847	Eureka	1,135
Ida	8,365	Ida Grove	432	Hamilton	2,388	Syracuse	998
Iowa	14,630	Marengo	587	Harper	7,124	Anthony	802
Jackson	19,950	Maquoketa	638	Harvey	31,028	Newton	540
Jasper	34,795	Newton	731	Haskell	3,886	Sublette	578
Jefferson	16,310	Fairfield	440	Hodgeman	2,177	Jetmore	860
Johnson	96,119	Iowa City	614	Jackson	11,525	Holton	658
Jones	19,444	Anamosa	576	Jefferson	15,905	Oskaloosa	535
Keokuk	11,624	Sigourney	580	Jewell	4,251	Mankato	910
Kossuth	18,591	Algona	974	Johnson	355,054	Olathe	478
Lee	38,687	Fort Madison and Keokuk	522	Kearny	4,027	Lakin	868
Linn	168,767	Cedar Rapids	724	Kingman	8,292	Kingman	865
Louisa	11,592	Wapello	402	Kiowa	3,660	Greensburg	723
Lucas	9,070	Chariton	432	Labette	23,693	Oswego	653
Lyon	11,952	Rock Rapids	588	Lane	2,375	Dighton	717
Madison	12,483	Winterset	563	Leavenworth	64,371	Leavenworth	463
Mahaska	21,522	Oskaloosa	571	Lincoln	3,653	Lincoln	720
Marion	30,001	Knoxville	560	Linn	8,254	Mound City	601
Marshall	38,276	Marshalltown	573	Logan	3,081	Oakley	1,073
Mills	13,202	Glenwood	439	Lyon	34,732	Emporia	844
Mitchell	10,928	Osage	470	McPherson	27,268	McPherson	900
Monona	10,034	Onawa	697	Marion	12,888	Marion	944
Monroe	8,114	Albia	434	Marshall	11,705	Marysville	878
Montgomery	12,076	Red Oak	424	Meade	4,247	Meade	979
Muscatine	39,907	Muscatine	442	Miami	23,466	Paola	590
O'Brien	15,444	Primghar	574	Mitchell	7,203	Beloit	717
Osceola	7,267	Sibley	399	Montgomery	38,816	Independence	646
Page	16,870	Clarinda	535	Morris	6,198	Council Grove	693
Palo Alto	10,669	Emmetsburg	562	Morton	3,480	Elkhart	731
Plymouth	23,388	Le Mars	864	Nemaha	10,446	Seneca	719
Pocahontas	9,525	Pocahontas	577	Neosho	17,035	Erie	576
Polk	327,140	Des Moines	582	Ness	4,033	Ness City	1,074
Pottawattamie	82,628	Council Bluffs	953	Norton	5,947	Norton	873
Poweshiek	19,033	Montezuma	585	Osage	15,248	Lyndon	695
Ringgold	5,420	Mount Ayr	535	Osborne	4,867	Osborne	882
Sac	12,324	Sac City	576	Ottawa	5,634	Minneapolis	721
Scott	150,979	Davenport	459	Pawnee	7,555	Larned	755
Shelby	13,230	Harlan	591	Phillips	6,590	Phillipsburg	887
Sioux	29,903	Orange City	769	Pottawatomie	16,128	Westmoreland	828
Story	74,252	Nevada	574	Pratt	9,702	Pratt	735
Tama	17,419	Toledo	721	Rawlins	3,404	Atwood	1,069
Taylor	7,114	Bedford	537	Reno	62,389	Hutchinson	1,259
Union	12,750	Creston	426	Republic	6,482	Belleville	719
Van Buren	7,676	Keosauqua	484	Rice	10,610	Lyons	728
Wapello	35,687	Ottumwa	434	Riley	67,139	Manhattan	593
Warren	36,033	Indianola	573	Rooks	6,039	Stockton	888
Washington	19,612	Washington	570	Rush	3,842	LaCrosse	718
Wayne	7,067	Corydon	526	Russell	7,835	Russell	869
Webster	40,342	Fort Dodge	718	Saline	49,301	Salina	721
Winnebago	12,122	Forest City	401	Scott	5,289	Scott City	718
Winneshiek	20,847	Decorah	690	Sedgwick	403,662	Wichita	1,007
Woodbury	98,276	Sioux City	873	Seward	18,743	Liberal	640
Worth	7,991	Northwood	401	Shawnee	160,976	Topeka	549
Wright	14,269	Clarion	579	Sheridan	3,043	Hoxie	896
				Sherman	6,926	Goodland	1,057
				Smith	5,078	Smith Center	897
				Stafford	5,365	Saint John	788
				Stanton	2,333	Johnson	681
				Stevens	5,048	Hugoton	727
				Sumner	25,841	Wellington	1,183
				Thomas	8,258	Colby	1,075

Kansas

(105 counties, 81,778 sq. mi. land; pop. 2,477,574)

County	Pop.	County Seat or court house	Land area sq. mi.	County	Pop.	County Seat or court house	Land area sq. mi.
Allen	14,638	Iola	505	Trego	3,694	Wakeeney	890
Anderson	7,803	Garnett	584	Wabaunsee	6,603	Alma	797
Atchison	16,932	Atchison	431	Wallace	1,821	Sharon Springs	914
Barber	5,874	Medicine Lodge	1,136	Washington	7,073	Washington	898

County	Pop.	County Seat or court house	Land area sq. mi.
Wichita	2,758	Leoti	719
Wilson	10,289	Fredonia	575
Woodson	4,116	Yates Center	498
Wyandotte	161,993	Kansas City	149

Kentucky

(120 counties, 39,669 sq. mi. land; pop. 3,685,296)

County	Pop.	County Seat or court house	Land area sq. mi.
Adair	15,360	Columbia	407
Allen	14,628	Scottsville	338
Anderson	14,571	Lawrenceburg	204
Ballard	7,902	Wickliffe	254
Barren	34,001	Glasgow	482
Bath	9,692	Owingsville	277
Bell	31,506	Pineville	361
Boone	57,589	Burlington	246
Bourbon	19,236	Paris	292
Boyd	51,150	Catlettsburg	160
Boyle	25,641	Danville	182
Bracken	7,766	Brooksville	203
Breathitt	15,703	Jackson	495
Breckinridge	16,312	Hardinsburg	565
Bullitt	47,567	Shepherdsville	300
Butler	11,245	Morgantown	431
Caldwell	13,232	Princeton	347
Calloway	30,735	Murray	386
Campbell	83,866	Alexandria	152
Carlisle	5,238	Bardwell	191
Carroll	9,292	Carrollton	130
Carter	24,340	Grayson	407
Casey	14,211	Liberty	445
Christian	68,941	Hopkinsville	722
Clark	29,496	Winchester	255
Clay	21,746	Manchester	471
Clinton	9,135	Albany	196
Crittenden	9,196	Marion	360
Cumberland	6,784	Burkesville	304
Daviess	87,189	Owensboro	463
Edmonson	10,357	Brownsville	302
Elliott	6,455	Sandy Hook	234
Estill	14,614	Irvine	256
Fayette	225,366	Lexington	285
Fleming	12,292	Flemingsburg	351
Floyd	43,586	Prestonsburg	393
Franklin	43,781	Frankfort	212
Fulton	8,271	Hickman	211
Gallatin	5,393	Warsaw	99
Garrard	11,579	Lancaster	232
Grant	15,737	Williamstown	259
Graves	33,550	Mayfield	557
Grayson	21,050	Leitchfield	493
Green	10,371	Greensburg	289
Greenup	36,742	Greenup	347
Hancock	7,864	Hawesville	189
Hardin	89,240	Elizabethtown	629
Harlan	36,574	Harlan	468
Harrison	16,248	Cynthiana	310
Hart	14,890	Munfordville	412
Henderson	43,044	Henderson	438
Henry	12,823	New Castle	291
Hickman	5,566	Clinton	245
Hopkins	46,126	Madisonville	552
Jackson	11,955	McKee	346
Jefferson	664,937	Louisville	386
Jessamine	30,508	Nicholasville	174
Johnson	23,248	Paintsville	264
Kenton	142,031	Independence	163
Knott	17,906	Hindman	352
Knox	29,676	Barbourville	388
Larue	11,679	Hodgenville	263
Laurel	43,438	London	434
Lawrence	13,998	Louisa	420
Lee	7,422	Beattyville	211
Leslie	13,642	Hyden	402
Letcher	27,000	Whitesburg	339
Lewis	13,029	Vanceburg	484
Lincoln	20,045	Stanford	337
Livingston	9,062	Smithland	312
Logan	24,416	Russellville	556
Lyon	6,624	Eddyville	209
McCracken	62,879	Paducah	251
McCreary	15,603	Whitley City	427
McLean	9,628	Calhoun	256
Madison	57,508	Richmond	443
Magoffin	13,077	Salyersville	310
Marion	16,499	Lebanon	347
Marshall	27,205	Benton	304
Martin	12,526	Inez	230
Mason	16,666	Maysville	241
Meade	24,170	Brandenburg	306
Menifee	5,092	Frenchburg	203
Mercer	19,148	Harrodsburg	250
Metcalfe	8,963	Edmonton	291
Monroe	11,401	Tompkinsville	331
Montgomery	19,561	Mount Sterling	199
Morgan	11,648	West Liberty	382
Muhlenberg	31,318	Greenville	478
Nelson	29,710	Bardstown	424
Nicholas	6,725	Carlisle	197
Ohio	21,105	Hartford	596
Oldham	33,263	La Grange	190
Owen	9,035	Owenton	354
Owsley	5,036	Booneville	198
Pendleton	12,036	Falmouth	281
Perry	30,283	Hazard	341
Pike	72,583	Pikeville	785
Powell	11,686	Stanton	180
Pulaski	49,489	Somerset	660
Robertson	2,124	Mount Olivet	100
Rockcastle	14,803	Mount Vernon	318
Rowan	20,353	Morehead	282
Russell	14,716	Jamestown	250
Scott	23,867	Georgetown	286
Shelby	24,824	Shelbyville	385
Simpson	15,145	Franklin	236
Spencer	6,801	Taylorsville	192
Taylor	21,146	Campbellsville	270
Todd	10,940	Elkton	377
Trigg	10,361	Cadiz	421
Trimble	6,090	Bedford	148
Union	16,557	Morganfield	341
Warren	76,673	Bowling Green	548
Washington	10,441	Springfield	301
Wayne	17,468	Monticello	446
Webster	13,955	Dixon	336
Whitley	33,326	Williamsburg	443
Wolfe	6,503	Campton	223
Woodford	19,955	Versailles	192

Louisiana

(64 parishes, 44,521 sq. mi. land; pop. 4,219,973)

County	Pop.	County Seat or court house	Land area sq. mi.
Acadia	55,882	Crowley	657
Allen	21,226	Oberlin	765
Ascension	58,214	Donaldsonville	296
Assumption	22,753	Napoleonville	342
Avoyelles	39,159	Marksville	846
Beauregard	30,083	De Ridder	1,163
Bienville	15,979	Arcadia	816
Bossier	86,088	Benton	845
Caddo	248,253	Shreveport	894
Calcasieu	168,134	Lake Charles	1,082
Caldwell	9,810	Columbia	541
Cameron	9,260	Cameron	1,417
Catahoula	11,065	Harrisonburg	732
Claiborne	17,405	Homer	765
Concordia	20,828	Vidalia	717
De Soto	25,346	Mansfield	880
East Baton Rouge	380,105	Baton Rouge	458
East Carroll	9,709	Lake Providence	426
East Feliciana	19,211	Clinton	455
Evangeline	33,274	Ville Platte	667
Franklin	22,387	Winnsboro	635
Grant	17,526	Colfax	653
Iberia	68,297	New Iberia	589
Iberville	31,049	Plaquemine	638
Jackson	15,705	Jonesboro	579
Jefferson	448,306	Gretna	348
Jefferson Davis	30,722	Jennings	655
Lafayette	164,762	Lafayette	270
Lafourche	85,860	Thibodaux	1,141
La Salle	13,662	Jena	638
Lincoln	41,745	Ruston	472
Livingston	70,526	Livingston	661
Madison	12,463	Tallulah	631
Morehouse	31,938	Bastrop	807
Natchitoches	36,689	Natchitoches	1,264
Orleans	496,938	New Orleans	199
Ouachita	142,191	Monroe	627
Plaquemines	25,575	Pointe a la Hache	1,035
Pointe Coupee	22,540	New Roads	566
Rapides	131,556	Alexandria	1,341
Red River	9,387	Coushatta	394
Richland	20,629	Rayville	563
Sabine	22,646	Many	855
St. Bernard	66,631	Chalmette	486
St. Charles	42,437	Hahnville	286
St. Helena	9,874	Greensburg	409
St. James	20,879	Convent	248
St. John The Baptist	39,996	Edgard	213
St. Landry	80,331	Opelousas	936
St. Martin	43,978	Saint Martinville	749
St. Mary	58,086	Franklin	613
St. Tammany	144,508	Covington	873
Tangipahoa	85,709	Amite	783
Tensas	7,103	Saint Joseph	623
Terrebonne	96,982	Houma	1,367

County	Pop.	County Seat or court house	Land area sq. mi.
Union	20,690	Farmerville	884
Vermilion	50,055	Abbeville	1,205
Vernon	61,961	Leesville	1,332
Washington	43,185	Franklinton	676
Webster	41,989	Minden	602
West Baton Rouge	19,419	Port Allen	194
West Carroll	12,093	Oak Grove	360
West Feliciana	12,915	Saint Francisville	406
Winn	16,269	Winnfield	953

Maine

(16 counties, 30,995 sq. mi. land; pop. 1,227,928)

County	Pop.	County Seat or court house	Land area sq. mi.
Androscoggin	105,259	Auburn	477
Aroostook	86,936	Houlton	6,721
Cumberland	243,135	Portland	876
Franklin	29,008	Farmington	1,699
Hancock	46,948	Ellsworth	1,537
Kennebec	115,904	Augusta	876
Knox	36,310	Rockland	370
Lincoln	30,357	Wiscasset	458
Oxford	52,602	South Paris	2,053
Penobscot	146,601	Bangor	3,430
Piscataquis	18,653	Dover-Foxcroft	3,986
Sagadahoc	33,535	Bath	257
Somerset	49,767	Skowhegan	3,930
Waldo	33,018	Belfast	730
Washington	35,308	Machias	2,586
York	164,587	Alfred	1,008

Maryland

(23 cos., 1 ind. city, 9,837 sq. mi. land; pop. 4,781,468)

County	Pop.	County Seat or court house	Land area sq. mi.
Allegany	74,946	Cumberland	421
Anne Arundel	427,239	Annapolis	418
Baltimore	692,134	Towson	598
Calvert	51,372	Prince Frederick	213
Caroline	27,035	Denton	321
Carroll	123,372	Westminster	452
Cecil	71,347	Elkton	360
Charles	101,154	La Plata	452
Dorchester	30,236	Cambridge	593
Frederick	150,208	Frederick	663
Garrett	28,138	Oakland	657
Harford	182,132	Bel Air	448
Howard	187,328	Ellicott City	251
Kent	17,842	Chestertown	278
Montgomery	757,027	Rockville	495
Prince Georges	729,268	Upper Marlboro	487
Queen Annes	33,953	Centreville	372
St. Mary's	75,974	Leonardtown	373
Somerset	23,440	Princess Anne	338
Talbot	30,549	Easton	259
Washington	121,393	Hagerstown	455
Wicomico	74,339	Salisbury	379
Worcester	35,028	Snow Hill	475
Independent City			
Baltimore	736,014	.....	80

Massachusetts

(14 counties; 7,824 sq. mi. land; pop. 6,016,425)

County	Pop.	County Seat or court house	Land area sq. mi.
Barnstable	186,605	Barnstable	400
Berkshire	139,352	Pittsfield	929
Bristol	506,325	Taunton	557
Dukes	11,639	Edgartown	102
Essex	670,080	Salem	495
Franklin	70,092	Greenfield	702
Hampden	456,310	Springfield	618
Hampshire	146,568	Northampton	528
Middlesex	1,398,468	Cambridge	822
Nantucket	6,012	Nantucket	47
Norfolk	616,087	Dedham	400
Plymouth	435,276	Plymouth	655
Suffolk	663,906	Boston	57
Worcester	709,705	Worcester	1,513

Michigan

(83 counties; 56,954 sq. mi. land; pop. 9,295,297)

County	Pop.	County Seat or court house	Land area sq. mi.
Alcona	10,145	Harrisville	679
Alger	8,972	Munising	912
Allegan	90,509	Allegan	832
Alpena	30,605	Alpena	567
Antrim	18,185	Bellaire	480
Arenac	14,931	Standish	367
Baraga	7,954	L'Anse	901
Barry	50,057	Hastings	560
Bay	111,723	Bay City	447
Benzie	12,200	Beulah	322
Berrien	161,378	Saint Joseph	576
Branch	41,502	Coldwater	508
Calhoun	135,982	Marshall	712
Cass	49,477	Cassopolis	496
Charlevoix	21,468	Charlevoix	421
Cheboygan	21,398	Cheboygan	720
Chippewa	34,604	Sault Sainte Marie	1,590
Clare	24,952	Harrison	570
Clinton	57,883	Saint Johns	573
Crawford	12,260	Grayling	559
Delta	37,780	Escanaba	1,173
Dickinson	26,831	Iron Mountain	770
Eaton	92,879	Charlotte	579
Emmet	25,040	Petoskey	468
Genesee	430,459	Flint	642
Gladwin	21,896	Gladwin	505
Gogebic	18,052	Bessemer	1,105
Grand Traverse	64,273	Traverse City	466
Gratiot	38,982	Ithaca	570
Hillsdale	43,431	Hillsdale	603
Houghton	35,446	Houghton	1,014
Huron	34,951	Bad Axe	830
Ingham	281,912	Mason	560
Ionia	57,024	Ionia	577
Iosco	30,209	Tawas City	546
Iron	13,175	Crystal Falls	1,163
Isabella	54,624	Mount Pleasant	577
Jackson	149,756	Jackson	705
Kalamazoo	223,411	Kalamazoo	562
Kalkaska	13,497	Kalkaska	563
Kent	500,631	Grand Rapids	862
Keweenaw	1,701	Eagle River	543
Lake	8,583	Baldwin	568
Lapeer	74,768	Lapeer	658
Leelanau	16,527	Leland	341
Lenawee	91,476	Adrian	753
Livingston	115,645	Howell	574
Luce	5,763	Newberry	904
Mackinac	10,674	Saint Ignace	1,025
Macomb	717,400	Mount Clemens	482
Manistee	21,265	Manistee	543
Marquette	70,887	Marquette	1,821
Mason	25,537	Ludington	494
Mecosta	37,308	Big Rapids	560
Menominee	24,920	Menominee	1,045
Midland	75,651	Midland	525
Missaukee	12,147	Lake City	565
Monroe	133,600	Monroe	557
Montcalm	53,059	Stanton	713
Montmorency	8,936	Atlanta	550
Muskegon	158,983	Muskegon	507
Newaygo	38,202	White Cloud	847
Oakland	1,083,592	Pontiac	875
Oceana	22,454	Hart	541
Ogemaw	18,681	West Branch	570
Ontonagon	8,854	Ontonagon	1,311
Osceola	20,146	Reed City	569
Oscoda	7,842	Mio	568
Otsego	17,957	Gaylord	516
Ottawa	187,768	Grand Haven	567
Presque Isle	13,743	Rogers City	656
Roscommon	19,776	Roscommon	528
Saginaw	211,946	Saginaw	815
St. Clair	145,607	Port Huron	734
St. Joseph	58,913	Centreville	503
Sanilac	39,928	Sandusky	964
Schoolcraft	8,302	Manistique	1,173
Shiawassee	69,770	Corunna	540
Tuscola	55,498	Caro	812
Van Buren	70,060	Paw Paw	611
Washtenaw	282,937	Ann Arbor	710
Wayne	2,111,687	Detroit	615
Wexford	26,360	Cadillac	566

Minnesota

(87 counties; 79,548 sq. mi. land; pop., 4,375,099)

County	Pop.	County Seat or court house	Land area sq. mi.
Aitkin	12,425	Aitkin	1,834
Anoka	243,641	Anoka	430
Becker	27,881	Detroit Lakes	1,312
Beltrami	34,384	Bemidji	2,507
Benton	30,185	Foley	408
Big Stone	6,285	Ortonville	497
Blue Earth	54,044	Mankato	749
Brown	26,984	New Ulm	610
Carlton	29,259	Carlton	864
Carver	47,915	Chaska	351
Cass	21,791	Walker	2,033

County	Pop.	County Seat or court house	Land area sq. mi.	County	Pop.	County Seat or court house	Land area sq. mi.
Chippewa	13,228	Montevideo	584	Copiah	27,592	Hazlehurst	779
Chisago	30,521	Center City	417	Covington	16,527	Collins	416
Clay	50,422	Moorhead	1,049	De Soto	67,910	Hernando	483
Clearwater	8,309	Bagley	999	Forrest	68,314	Hattiesburg	469
Cook	3,868	Grand Marais	1,412	Franklin	8,377	Meadville	566
Cottonwood	12,694	Windom	640	George	16,673	Lucedale	483
Crow Wing	44,249	Brainerd	1,008	Greene	10,220	Leakesville	718
Dakota	275,227	Hastings	574	Grenada	21,555	Grenada	421
Dodge	15,731	Mantorville	439	Hancock	31,760	Bay Saint Louis	478
Douglas	28,674	Alexandria	643	Harrison	165,365	Gulfport	581
Faribault	16,937	Blue Earth	714	Hinds	254,441	Jackson & Raymond	875
Fillmore	20,777	Preston	862	Holmes	21,604	Lexington	759
Freeborn	33,060	Albert Lea	705	Humphreys	12,134	Belzoni	430
Goodhue	40,690	Red Wing	763	Issaquena	1,909	Mayersville	406
Grant	6,246	Elbow Lake	547	Itawamba	20,017	Fulton	540
Hennepin	1,032,431	Minneapolis	541	Jackson	115,243	Pascagoula	731
Houston	18,497	Caledonia	564	Jasper	17,114	Bat Springs & Paulding	678
Hubbard	14,939	Park Rapids	936	Jefferson	8,653	Fayette	523
Isanti	25,921	Cambridge	440	Jefferson Davis	14,051	Prentiss	409
Itasca	40,863	Grand Rapids	2,661	Jones	62,031	Ellisville & Laurel	696
Jackson	11,677	Jackson	699	Kemper	10,356	De Kalb	766
Kanabec	12,802	Mora	527	Lafayette	31,826	Oxford	669
Kandiyohi	38,761	Willmar	784	Lamar	30,424	Purvis	499
Kittson	5,767	Hallock	1,104	Lauderdale	75,555	Meridian	705
Koochiching	16,299	International Falls	3,108	Lawrence	12,458	Monticello	435
Lac qui Parle	8,924	Madison	772	Leake	18,436	Carthage	584
Lake	10,415	Two Harbors	2,053	Lee	65,581	Tupelo	451
Lake of the Woods	4,076	Baudette	1,296	Leflore	37,341	Greenwood	605
Le Sueur	23,239	Le Center	446	Lincoln	30,278	Brookhaven	587
Lincoln	6,890	Ivanhoe	538	Lowndes	59,308	Columbus	517
Lyon	24,789	Marshall	714	Madison	53,794	Canton	718
McLeod	32,030	Glencoe	489	Marion	25,544	Columbia	548
Mahnomen	5,044	Mahnomen	559	Marshall	30,361	Holly Springs	709
Marshall	10,993	Warren	1,760	Monroe	36,582	Aberdeen	772
Martin	22,914	Fairmont	706	Montgomery	12,388	Winona	408
Meeker	20,846	Litchfield	624	Neshoba	24,800	Philadelphia	572
Mille Lacs	18,670	Milaca	578	Newton	20,291	Decatur	580
Morrison	29,604	Little Falls	1,124	Noxubee	12,604	Macon	698
Mower	37,385	Austin	711	Oktibbeha	38,375	Starkville	459
Murray	9,660	Slayton	702	Panola	29,996	Batesville & Sardis	694
Nicollet	28,076	Saint Peter	440	Pearl River	38,714	Poplarville	818
Nobles	20,098	Worthington	714	Perry	10,865	New Augusta	651
Norman	7,975	Ada	877	Pike	36,882	Magnolia	410
Olmsted	106,470	Rochester	655	Pontotoc	22,237	Pontotoc	499
Otter Tail	50,714	Fergus Falls	1,973	Prentiss	23,278	Booneville	418
Pennington	13,306	Thief River Falls	618	Quitman	10,490	Marks	406
Pine	21,264	Pine City	1,421	Rankin	87,161	Brandon	782
Pipestone	10,491	Pipestone	466	Scott	24,137	Forest	610
Polk	32,498	Crookston	1,982	Sharkey	7,066	Rolling Fork	435
Pope	10,745	Glenwood	668	Simpson	23,953	Mendenhall	591
Ramsey	485,765	Saint Paul	154	Smith	14,798	Raleigh	635
Red Lake	4,525	Red Lake Falls	433	Stone	10,750	Wiggins	446
Redwood	17,254	Redwood Falls	882	Sunflower	32,867	Indianola	706
Renville	17,673	Olivia	984	Tallahatchie	15,210	Charleston & Sumner	651
Rice	49,183	Faribault	501	Tate	21,432	Senatobia	406
Rock	9,806	Luverne	483	Tippah	19,523	Ripley	458
Roseau	15,026	Roseau	1,677	Tishomingo	17,683	Iuka	434
St. Louis	198,213	Duluth	6,125	Tunica	8,164	Tunica	460
Scott	57,846	Shakopee	357	Union	22,085	New Albany	416
Sherburne	41,945	Elk River	435	Walthall	14,352	Tylertown	404
Sibley	14,366	Gaylord	593	Warren	47,880	Vicksburg	596
Stearns	118,791	Saint Cloud	1,338	Washington	67,935	Greenville	733
Steele	30,729	Owatonna	431	Wayne	19,517	Waynesboro	813
Stevens	10,634	Morris	560	Webster	10,222	Walthall	424
Swift	10,724	Benson	743	Wilkinson	9,678	Woodville	678
Todd	23,363	Long Prairie	941	Winston	19,433	Louisville	610
Traverse	4,463	Wheaton	575	Yalobusha	12,033	Coffeeville & Water Valley	478
Wabasha	19,744	Wabasha	537	Yazoo	25,506	Yazoo City	933
Wadena	13,154	Wadena	538				
Waseca	18,079	Waseca	422				
Washington	145,896	Stillwater	390				
Watonwan	11,682	Saint James	435				
Wilkin	7,516	Breckenridge	751				
Winona	47,828	Winona	630				
Wright	68,710	Buffalo	672				
Yellow Medicine	11,684	Granite Falls	758				

Mississippi

(82 counties, 47,233 sq. mi. land; pop. 2,573,216)

Missouri

(114 cos., 1 ind. city, 68,945 sq. mi. land; pop. 5,117,073)

County	Pop.	County Seat or court house	Land area sq. mi.
Adams	35,356	Natchez	456
Alcorn	31,722	Corinth	401
Amite	13,328	Liberty	732
Attala	18,481	Kosciusko	737
Benton	8,046	Ashland	407
Bolivar	41,875	Cleveland & Rosedale	892
Calhoun	14,908	Pittsboro	573
Carroll	9,237	Carrollton & Vaiden	634
Chickasaw	18,085	Houston & Okolona	503
Choctaw	9,071	Ackerman	420
Claiborne	11,370	Port Gibson	494
Clarke	17,313	Quitman	692
Clay	21,120	West Point	415
Coahoma	31,665	Clarksdale	559

County	Pop.	County Seat or court house	Land area sq. mi.
Adair	24,577	Kirksville	567
Andrew	14,632	Savannah	435
Atchison	7,457	Rockport	542
Audrain	23,599	Mexico	697
Barry	27,547	Cassville	773
Barton	11,312	Lamar	596
Bates	15,025	Butler	849
Benton	13,859	Warsaw	729
Bollinger	10,619	Marble Hill	621
Boone	112,379	Columbia	687
Buchanan	83,083	Saint Joseph	409
Butler	38,765	Poplar Buff	698
Caldwell	8,380	Kingston	430
Callaway	32,809	Fulton	842
Camden	27,495	Camdenton	641
Cape Girardeau	61,633	Jackson	577
Carroll	10,748	Carrollton	695
Carter	5,515	Van Buren	509
Cass	63,808	Harrisonville	701
Cedar	12,093	Stockton	470
Chariton	9,202	Keytesville	758
Christian	32,644	Ozark	564

County	Pop.	County Seat or court house	Land area sq. mi.
Clark	7,547	Kahoka	507
Clay	153,411	Liberty	403
Clinton	16,595	Plattsburg	423
Cole	63,579	Jefferson City	392
Cooper	14,835	Boonville	567
Crawford	19,173	Steelville	744
Dade	7,449	Greenfield	491
Dallas	12,646	Buffalo	543
Daviess	7,865	Gallatin	568
De Kalb	9,967	Maysville	425
Dent	13,702	Salem	755
Douglas	11,876	Ava	814
Dunklin	33,112	Kennett	547
Franklin	80,603	Union	922
Gasconade	14,006	Hermann	521
Gentry	6,848	Albany	493
Greene	207,949	Springfield	677
Grundy	10,536	Trenton	437
Harrison	8,469	Bethany	725
Henry	20,044	Clinton	729
Hickory	7,335	Hermitage	379
Holt	6,034	Oregon	457
Howard	9,631	Fayette	465
Howell	31,447	West Plains	928
Iron	10,726	Ironton	552
Jackson	633,232	Independence	611
Jasper	90,465	Carthage	641
Jefferson	171,380	Hillsboro	661
Johnson	42,514	Warrensburg	834
Knox	4,482	Edina	507
Laclede	27,158	Lebanon	768
Lafayette	31,107	Lexington	632
Lawrence	30,236	Mount Vernon	613
Lewis	10,233	Monticello	509
Lincoln	28,892	Troy	627
Linn	13,885	Linneus	620
Livingston	14,592	Chillicothe	537
McDonald	16,938	Pineville	540
Macon	15,345	Macon	797
Madison	11,127	Fredericktown	497
Maries	7,976	Vienna	528
Marion	27,682	Palmyra	438
Mercer	3,723	Princeton	454
Miller	20,700	Tuscumbia	593
Mississippi	14,442	Charleston	410
Moniteau	12,298	California	417
Monroe	9,104	Paris	670
Montgomery	11,355	Montgomery City	540
Morgan	15,574	Versailles	594
New Madrid	20,928	New Madrid	658
Newton	44,445	Neosho	627
Nodaway	21,709	Maryville	875
Oregon	9,470	Alton	792
Osage	12,018	Linn	606
Ozark	8,598	Gainesville	731
Pemiscot	21,921	Caruthersville	517
Perry	16,648	Perryville	473
Pettis	35,437	Sedalia	686
Phelps	35,248	Rolla	674
Pike	15,969	Bowling Green	673
Platte	57,867	Platte City	421
Polk	21,826	Bolivar	636
Pulaski	41,307	Waynesville	550
Putnam	5,079	Unionville	520
Ralls	8,476	New London	482
Randolph	24,370	Huntsville	477
Ray	21,971	Richmond	568
Reynolds	6,661	Centerville	809
Ripley	12,303	Doniphan	631
St. Charles	212,907	St. Charles	558
St. Clair	8,457	Osceola	699
St. Francois	48,904	Farmington	451
St. Louis	993,529	Clayton	506
Ste. Genevieve	16,037	Ste. Genevieve	504
Saline	23,523	Marshall	755
Schuyler	4,236	Lancaster	309
Scotland	4,822	Memphis	438
Scott	39,376	Benton	423
Shannon	7,613	Eminence	1,004
Shelby	6,942	Shelbyville	501
Stoddard	28,895	Bloomfield	815
Stone	19,078	Galena	451
Sullivan	6,326	Milan	651
Taney	25,561	Forsyth	608
Texas	21,476	Houston	1,180
Vernon	19,041	Nevada	837
Warren	19,534	Warrenton	429
Washington	20,380	Potosi	762
Wayne	11,543	Greenville	762
Webster	23,753	Marshfield	594
Worth	2,440	Grant City	266
Wright	16,758	Hartville	682

Independent City

St. Louis	396,685	.....	61

Montana

(56 counties, 145,388 sq. mi. land; pop., 799,065)

County	Pop.	County Seat or court house	Land area sq. mi.
Beaverhead	8,424	Dillon	5,529
Big Horn	11,337	Hardin	4,983
Blaine	6,728	Chinook	4,257
Broadwater	3,318	Townsend	1,189
Carbon	8,080	Red Lodge	2,056
Carter	1,503	Ekalaka	3,342
Cascade	77,691	Great Falls	2,699
Chouteau	5,452	Fort Benton	3,987
Custer	11,697	Miles City	3,776
Daniels	2,266	Scobey	1,427
Dawson	9,505	Glendive	2,374
Deer Lodge	10,278	Anaconda	740
Fallon	3,103	Baker	1,623
Fergus	12,083	Lewistown	4,340
Flathead	59,218	Kalispell	5,112
Gallatin	50,463	Bozeman	2,510
Garfield	1,589	Jordan	4,491
Glacier	12,121	Cut Bank	2,994
Golden Valley	912	Ryegete	1,172
Granite	2,548	Philipsburg	1,729
Hill	17,654	Havre	2,897
Jefferson	7,939	Boulder	1,657
Judith Basin	2,282	Stanford	1,871
Lake	21,041	Polson	1,445
Lewis & Clark	47,495	Helena	3,461
Liberty	2,295	Chester	1,426
Lincoln	17,481	Libby	3,616
McCone	2,276	Circle	2,626
Madison	5,989	Virginia City	3,520
Meagher	1,819	White Sulphur Springs	2,392
Mineral	3,315	Superior	1,216
Missoula	78,666	Missoula	2,582
Musselshell	4,106	Roundup	1,871
Park	14,562	Livingston	1,665
Petroleum	519	Winnett	1,652
Phillips	5,163	Malta	5,130
Pondera	6,433	Conrad	1,632
Powder River	2,090	Broadus	3,288
Powell	6,620	Deer Lodge	2,329
Prairie	1,383	Terry	1,732
Ravalli	25,010	Hamilton	2,384
Richland	10,716	Sidney	2,081
Roosevelt	10,999	Wolf Point	2,357
Rosebud	10,505	Forsyth	5,019
Sanders	8,669	Thompson Falls	2,749
Sheridan	4,732	Plentywood	1,681
Silver Bow	33,941	Butte	718
Stillwater	6,536	Columbus	1,793
Sweet Grass	3,154	Big Timber	1,903
Teton	6,271	Choteau	2,275
Toole	5,046	Shelby	1,931
Treasure	874	Hysham	975
Valley	8,239	Glasgow	4,936
Wheatland	2,246	Harlowton	1,419
Wibaux	1,191	Wibaux	888
Yellowstone	113,419	Billings	2,624

Nebraska

(93 counties, 76,644 sq. mi. land; pop., 1,578,385)

County	Pop.	County Seat or court house	Land area sq. mi.
Adams	29,625	Hastings	564
Antelope	7,965	Neligh	859
Arthur	462	Arthur	711
Banner	852	Harrisburg	747
Blaine	675	Brewster	714
Boone	6,667	Albion	687
Box Butte	13,130	Alliance	1,077
Boyd	2,835	Butte	532
Brown	3,657	Ainsworth	1,214
Buffalo	37,447	Kearney	945
Burt	7,868	Tekamah	486
Butler	8,601	David City	584
Cass	21,318	Plattsmouth	557
Cedar	10,131	Hartington	740
Chase	4,381	Imperial	894
Cherry	6,307	Valentine	5,961
Cheyenne	9,494	Sidney	1,196
Clay	7,123	Clay Center	574
Colfax	9,139	Schuyler	410
Cuming	10,117	West Point	575
Custer	12,270	Broken Bow	2,571
Dakota	16,742	Dakota City	258
Dawes	9,021	Chadron	1,397
Dawson	19,940	Lexington	982
Deuel	2,237	Chappell	437
Dixon	6,143	Ponca	474
Dodge	34,500	Fremont	534
Douglas	416,444	Omaha	333
Dundy	2,582	Benkelman	920

County	Pop.	County Seat or court house	Land area sq. mi.
Fillmore	7,103	Geneva	576
Franklin	3,938	Franklin	576
Frontier	3,101	Stockville	976
Furnas	5,553	Beaver City	721
Gage	22,794	Beatrice	858
Garden	2,460	Oshkosh	1,680
Garfield	2,141	Burwell	570
Gosper	1,928	Elwood	461
Grant	769	Hyannis	775
Greeley	3,006	Greeley	570
Hall	48,925	Grand Island	537
Hamilton	8,862	Aurora	543
Harlan	3,810	Alma	555
Hayes	1,222	Hayes Center	713
Hitchcock	3,750	Trenton	709
Holt	12,599	O'Neill	2,406
Hooker	793	Mullen	721
Howard	6,055	Saint Paul	564
Jefferson	8,759	Fairbury	575
Johnson	4,673	Tecumseh	377
Kearney	6,629	Minden	519
Keith	8,584	Ogallala	1,039
Keya Paha	1,029	Springview	769
Kimball	4,108	Kimball	952
Knox	9,534	Center	1,105
Lancaster	213,641	Lincoln	839
Lincoln	32,508	North Platte	2,525
Logan	878	Stapleton	571
Loup	683	Taylor	574
McPherson	546	Tryon	859
Madison	32,655	Madison	575
Merrick	8,042	Central City	478
Morrill	5,423	Bridgeport	1,405
Nance	4,275	Fullerton	439
Nemaha	7,980	Auburn	409
Nuckolls	5,786	Nelson	576
Otoe	14,252	Nebraska City	615
Pawnee	3,317	Pawnee City	433
Perkins	3,367	Grant	885
Phelps	9,715	Holdrege	540
Pierce	7,827	Pierce	575
Platte	29,820	Columbus	669
Polk	5,675	Osceola	437
Red Willow	11,705	McCook	718
Richardson	9,937	Falls City	553
Rock	2,019	Bassett	1,003
Saline	12,715	Wilber	575
Sarpy	102,583	Papillion	238
Saunders	18,285	Wahoo	753
Scotts Bluff	36,025	Gering	725
Seward	15,450	Seward	575
Sheridan	6,750	Rushville	2,453
Sherman	3,718	Loup City	564
Sioux	1,549	Harrison	2,070
Stanton	6,244	Stanton	431
Thayer	6,635	Hebron	575
Thomas	851	Thedford	713
Thurston	6,936	Pender	391
Valley	5,169	Ord	567
Washington	16,607	Blair	386
Wayne	9,364	Wayne	443
Webster	4,279	Red Cloud	575
Wheeler	948	Bartlett	575
York	14,428	York	576

Nevada

(16 cos., 1 ind. city, 109,894 sq. mi. land; pop., 1,201,833)

County	Pop.	County Seat or court house	Land area sq. mi.
Churchill	17,938	Fallon	4,990
Clark	741,459	Las Vegas	7,881
Douglas	27,637	Minden	708
Elko	33,530	Elko	17,135
Esmeralda	1,344	Goldfield	3,587
Eureka	1,547	Eureka	4,175
Humboldt	12,844	Winnemucca	9,698
Lander	6,266	Austin	5,515
Lincoln	3,775	Pioche	10,635
Lyon	20,001	Yerington	2,007
Mineral	6,475	Hawthorne	3,744
Nye	17,781	Tonopah	18,155
Pershing	4,336	Lovelock	6,036
Storey	2,526	Virginia City	264
Washoe	254,667	Reno	6,317
White Pine	9,264	Ely	8,902
Independent City			
Carson City	40,443	Carson City	146

New Hampshire

(10 counties, 8,993 sq. mi. land; pop., 1,109,252)

County	Pop.	County Seat or court house	Land area sq. mi.
Belknap	49,216	Laconia	404
Carroll	35,410	Ossipee	933
Cheshire	70,121	Keene	711
Coos	34,828	Lancaster	1,804
Grafton	74,929	Woodsville	1,719
Hillsborough	336,073	Nashua	876
Merrimack	120,005	Concord	936
Rockingham	245,845	Exeter	699
Strafford	104,233	Dover	370
Sullivan	38,592	Newport	540

New Jersey

(21 counties, 7,468 sq. mi. land; pop., 7,730,188)

County	Pop.	County Seat or court house	Land area sq. mi.
Atlantic	224,327	Mays Landing	568
Bergen	825,380	Hackensack	237
Burlington	395,066	Mount Holly	808
Camden	502,824	Camden	223
Cape May	95,089	Cape May Court House	263
Cumberland	138,053	Bridgeton	498
Essex	778,206	Newark	127
Gloucester	230,082	Woodbury	327
Hudson	553,099	Jersey City	46
Hunterdon	107,776	Flemington	426
Mercer	325,824	Trenton	227
Middlesex	671,780	New Brunswick	316
Monmouth	553,124	Freehold	472
Morris	421,353	Morristown	470
Ocean	433,203	Toms River	641
Passaic	453,060	Paterson	187
Salem	65,294	Salem	338
Somerset	240,279	Somerville	305
Sussex	130,943	Newton	526
Union	493,819	Elizabeth	103
Warren	91,607	Belvidere	359

New Mexico

(33 counties, 121,335 sq. mi. land; pop., 1,515,069)

County	Pop.	County Seat or court house	Land area sq. mi.
Bernalillo	480,577	Albuquerque	1,169
Catron	2,563	Reserve	6,929
Chaves	57,849	Roswell	6,066
Cibola	23,794	Grants	4,468
Colfax	12,925	Raton	3,762
Curry	42,207	Clovis	1,408
De Baca	2,252	Fort Sumner	2,323
Dona Ana	135,510	Las Cruces	3,819
Eddy	48,605	Carlsbad	4,184
Grant	27,676	Silver City	3,969
Guadalupe	4,156	Santa Rosa	3,032
Harding	987	Mosquero	2,122
Hidalgo	5,958	Lordsburg	3,445
Lea	55,765	Lovington	4,389
Lincoln	12,219	Carrizozo	4,832
Los Alamos	18,115	Los Alamos	109
Luna	18,110	Deming	2,965
McKinley	60,686	Gallup	5,442
Mora	4,264	Mora	1,930
Otero	51,928	Alamogordo	6,626
Quay	10,823	Tucumcari	2,874
Rio Arriba	34,365	Tierra Amarilla	5,856
Roosevelt	16,702	Portales	2,453
Sandoval	63,319	Bernalillo	3,707
San Juan	91,605	Aztec	5,521
San Miguel	25,743	Las Vegas	4,709
Santa Fe	98,928	Santa Fe	1,905
Sierra	9,912	Truth or Consequences	4,178
Socorro	14,764	Socorro	6,625
Taos	23,118	Taos	2,204
Torrance	10,285	Estancia	3,335
Union	4,124	Clayton	3,830
Valencia	45,235	Los Lunas	5,616

New York

(62 counties, 47,377 sq. mi. land; pop., 17,990,455)

County	Pop.	County Seat or court house	Land area sq. mi.
Albany	292,594	Albany	524
Allegany	50,470	Belmont	1,032
Bronx	1,203,789	Bronx	42
Broome	212,160	Binghamton	712
Cattaraugus	84,234	Little Valley	1,306
Cayuga	82,313	Auburn	695
Chautauqua	141,895	Mayville	1,064
Chemung	95,195	Elmira	411
Chenango	51,768	Norwich	897
Clinton	85,969	Plattsburgh	1,043
Columbia	62,982	Hudson	638

County	Pop.	County Seat or court house	Land area sq. mi.
Cortland	48,963	Cortland	500
Delaware	47,225	Delhi	1,440
Dutchess	259,462	Poughkeepsie	804
Erie	968,532	Buffalo	1,046
Essex	37,152	Elizabethtown	1,806
Franklin	46,540	Malone	1,642
Fulton	54,191	Johnstown	497
Genesee	60,060	Batavia	495
Greene	44,739	Catskill	648
Hamilton	5,279	Lake Pleasant	1,721
Herkimer	65,797	Herkimer	1,416
Jefferson	110,943	Watertown	1,273
Kings	2,300,664	Brooklyn	70
Lewis	26,796	Lowville	1,283
Livingston	62,372	Geneseo	633
Madison	69,120	Wampsville	656
Monroe	713,968	Rochester	663
Montgomery	51,981	Fonda	404
Nassau	1,287,348	Mineola	287
New York	1,487,536	New York	22
Niagara	220,756	Lockport	526
Oneida	250,836	Utica	1,219
Onondaga	466,973	Syracuse	784
Ontario	95,101	Canandaigua	644
Orange	307,647	Goshen	826
Orleans	41,846	Albion	391
Oswego	121,771	Oswego	954
Otsego	60,517	Cooperstown	1,004
Putnam	83,941	Carmel	231
Queens	1,951,598	Jamaica	109
Rensselaer	154,429	Troy	655
Richmond	378,977	Saint George	59
Rockland	265,475	New City	175
St. Lawrence	111,974	Canton	2,728
Saratoga	181,276	Ballston Spa	810
Schenectady	149,285	Schenectady	206
Schoharie	31,859	Schoharie	624
Schuyler	18,662	Watkins Glen	329
Seneca	33,683	Ovid & Waterloo	327
Steuben	99,088	Bath	1,396
Suffolk	1,321,864	Riverhead	911
Sullivan	69,277	Monticello	976
Tioga	52,337	Owego	519
Tompkins	94,097	Ithaca	477
Ulster	165,304	Kingston	1,131
Warren	59,209	Queensbury	882
Washington	59,330	Hudson Falls	836
Wayne	89,123	Lyons	605
Westchester	874,866	White Plains	438
Wyoming	42,507	Warsaw	595
Yates	22,810	Penn Yan	339

North Carolina

(100 counties, 48,843 sq. mi. land; pop., 6,628,637)

County	Pop.	County Seat or court house	Land area sq. mi.
Alamance	108,213	Graham	433
Alexander	27,544	Taylorsville	259
Alleghany	9,590	Sparta	235
Anson	23,474	Wadesboro	533
Ashe	22,209	Jefferson	426
Avery	14,867	Newland	247
Beaufort	42,283	Washington	826
Bertie	20,388	Windsor	701
Bladen	28,663	Elizabethtown	879
Brunswick	50,985	Southport	860
Buncombe	174,821	Asheville	659
Burke	75,744	Morganton	504
Cabarrus	98,935	Concord	364
Caldwell	70,709	Lenoir	471
Camden	5,904	Camden	240
Carteret	52,556	Beaufort	526
Caswell	20,693	Yanceyville	428
Catawba	118,412	Newton	396
Chatham	38,759	Pittsboro	708
Cherokee	20,170	Murphy	452
Chowan	13,506	Edenton	182
Clay	7,155	Hayesville	214
Cleveland	84,714	Shelby	468
Columbus	49,587	Whiteville	938
Craven	81,613	New Bern	701
Cumberland	274,566	Fayetteville	657
Currituck	13,736	Currituck	256
Dare	22,746	Manteo	391
Davidson	126,677	Lexington	548
Davie	27,859	Mocksville	267
Duplin	39,995	Kenansville	819
Durham	181,835	Durham	298
Edgecombe	56,558	Tarboro	506
Forsyth	265,878	Winston-Salem	412
Franklin	36,414	Louisburg	494
Gaston	175,093	Gastonia	357
Gates	9,305	Gatesville	338
Graham	7,196	Robbinsville	289
Granville	38,345	Oxford	534
Greene	15,384	Snow Hill	266
Guilford	347,420	Greensboro	651
Halifax	55,516	Halifax	724
Harnett	67,822	Lillington	601
Haywood	46,942	Waynesville	555
Henderson	69,285	Hendersonville	374
Hertford	22,523	Winton	356
Hoke	22,856	Raeford	391
Hyde	5,411	Swanquarter	624
Iredell	92,931	Statesville	574
Jackson	26,846	Sylva	491
Johnston	81,306	Smithfield	795
Jones	9,414	Trenton	470
Lee	41,374	Sanford	259
Lenoir	57,274	Kinston	402
Lincoln	50,319	Lincolnton	298
McDowell	35,681	Marion	437
Macon	23,499	Franklin	517
Madison	16,953	Marshall	451
Martin	25,078	Williamston	461
Mecklenburg	511,433	Charlotte	528
Mitchell	14,433	Bakersville	222
Montgomery	23,346	Troy	490
Moore	59,013	Carthage	701
Nash	76,677	Nashville	540
New Hanover	120,284	Wilmington	185
Northampton	20,798	Jackson	538
Onslow	149,838	Jacksonville	763
Orange	93,851	Hillsboro	400
Pamlico	11,372	Bayboro	341
Pasquotank	31,298	Elizabeth City	228
Pender	28,885	Burgaw	875
Perquimans	10,447	Hertford	246
Person	30,180	Roxboro	398
Pitt	107,924	Greenville	657
Polk	14,416	Columbus	238
Randolph	106,546	Asheboro	789
Richmond	44,518	Rockingham	477
Robeson	105,179	Lumberton	949
Rockingham	86,064	Wentworth	569
Rowan	110,605	Salisbury	519
Rutherford	56,918	Rutherfordton	568
Sampson	47,297	Clinton	947
Scotland	33,754	Laurinburg	319
Stanly	51,765	Albemarle	396
Stokes	37,223	Danbury	452
Surry	61,704	Dobson	539
Swain	11,268	Bryson City	526
Transylvania	25,520	Brevard	378
Tyrrell	3,856	Columbia	407
Union	84,211	Monroe	639
Vance	38,892	Henderson	249
Wake	423,380	Raleigh	854
Warren	17,265	Warrenton	427
Washington	13,997	Plymouth	332
Watauga	36,952	Boone	314
Wayne	104,666	Goldsboro	554
Wilkes	59,393	Wilkesboro	752
Wilson	66,061	Wilson	374
Yadkin	30,488	Yadkinville	336
Yancey	15,419	Burnsville	314

North Dakota

(53 counties, 69,300 sq. mi. land; pop., 638,800)

County	Pop.	County Seat or court house	Land area sq. mi.
Adams	3,174	Hettinger	988
Barnes	12,545	Valley City	1,498
Benson	7,198	Minnewaukan	1,412
Billings	1,108	Medora	1,152
Bottineau	8,011	Bottineau	1,668
Bowman	3,596	Bowman	1,162
Burke	3,002	Bowbells	1,118
Burleigh	60,131	Bismarck	1,618
Cass	102,874	Fargo	1,767
Cavalier	6,064	Langdon	1,507
Dickey	6,107	Ellendale	1,139
Divide	2,899	Crosby	1,288
Dunn	4,005	Manning	1,993
Eddy	2,951	New Rockford	634
Emmons	4,830	Linton	1,499
Foster	3,983	Carrington	640
Golden Valley	2,108	Beach	1,003
Grand Forks	70,683	Grand Forks	1,440
Grant	3,549	Carson	1,660
Griggs	3,303	Cooperstown	708
Hettinger	3,445	Mott	1,133
Kidder	3,332	Steele	1,362
La Moure	5,383	La Moure	1,150
Logan	2,847	Napoleon	1,000
McHenry	6,528	Towner	1,887
McIntosh	4,021	Ashley	984
McKenzie	6,383	Watford City	2,754
McLean	10,457	Washburn	2,065
Mercer	9,808	Stanton	1,044

County	Pop.	County Seat or court house	Land area sq. mi.
Morton	23,700	Mandan	1,921
Mountrail	7,021	Stanley	1,837
Nelson	4,410	Lakota	991
Oliver	2,381	Center	723
Pembina	9,238	Cavalier	1,120
Pierce	5,052	Rugby	1,037
Ramsey	12,681	Devils Lake	1,241
Ransom	5,921	Lisbon	862
Renville	3,160	Mohall	874
Richland	18,148	Wahpeton	1,436
Rolette	12,772	Rolla	914
Sargent	4,549	Forman	857
Sheridan	2,148	McClusky	989
Sioux	3,761	Fort Yates	1,099
Slope	907	Amidon	1,219
Stark	22,832	Dickinson	1,338
Steele	2,420	Finley	713
Stutsman	22,241	Jamestown	2,263
Towner	3,627	Cando	1,035
Traill	8,752	Hillsboro	861
Walsh	13,840	Grafton	1,290
Ward	57,921	Minot	2,041
Wells	5,864	Fessenden	1,288
Williams	21,129	Williston	2,074

County	Pop.	County Seat or court house	Land area sq. mi.
Portage	142,585	Ravenna	493
Preble	40,113	Eaton	426
Putnam	33,819	Ottawa	484
Richland	126,137	Mansfield	497
Ross	69,330	Chillicothe	692
Sandusky	61,963	Fremont	409
Scioto	80,327	Portsmouth	613
Seneca	59,733	Tiffin	553
Shelby	44,915	Sidney	409
Stark	367,585	Canton	574
Summit	514,990	Akron	412
Trumbull	227,813	Warren	612
Tuscarawas	84,090	New Philadelphia	570
Union	31,969	Marysville	437
Van Wert	30,464	Van Wert	410
Vinton	11,098	McArthur	414
Warren	113,909	Lebanon	403
Washington	62,254	Marietta	640
Wayne	101,461	Wooster	557
Williams	36,956	Bryan	422
Wood	113,269	Bowling Green	619
Wyandot	22,254	Upper Sandusky	406

Ohio

(88 counties, 41,004 sq. mi. land; pop., 10,847,115)

County	Pop.	County Seat	Land area sq. mi.
Adams	25,371	West Union	586
Allen	109,755	Lima	405
Ashland	47,507	Ashland	424
Ashtabula	99,821	Jefferson	703
Athens	59,549	Athens	508
Auglaize	44,585	Wapakoneta	398
Belmont	71,074	Saint Clairsville	537
Brown	34,966	Georgetown	493
Butler	291,479	Hamilton	470
Carroll	26,521	Carrollton	393
Champaign	36,019	Urbana	429
Clark	147,548	Springfield	398
Clermont	150,187	Batavia	456
Clinton	35,415	Wilmington	410
Columbiana	108,276	Lisbon	534
Coshocton	35,427	Coshocton	566
Crawford	47,870	Bucyrus	403
Cuyahoga	1,412,140	Cleveland	459
Darke	53,619	Greenville	600
Defiance	39,350	Defiance	414
Delaware	66,929	Delaware	443
Erie	76,779	Sandusky	264
Fairfield	103,461	Lancaster	506
Fayette	27,466	Washington C. H.	405
Franklin	961,437	Columbus	543
Fulton	38,498	Wauseon	407
Gallia	30,954	Gallipolis	471
Geauga	81,129	Chardon	408
Greene	136,731	Xenia	416
Guernsey	39,024	Cambridge	522
Hamilton	866,228	Cincinnati	412
Hancock	65,536	Findlay	532
Hardin	31,111	Kenton	471
Harrison	16,085	Cadiz	400
Henry	29,108	Napoleon	415
Highland	35,728	Hillsboro	553
Hocking	25,533	Logan	423
Holmes	32,849	Millersburg	424
Huron	56,240	Norwalk	494
Jackson	30,230	Jackson	420
Jefferson	80,298	Steubenville	410
Knox	47,473	Mount Vernon	529
Lake	215,499	Painesville	231
Lawrence	61,834	Ironton	457
Licking	128,300	Newark	686
Logan	42,310	Bellefontaine	458
Lorain	271,126	Elyria	495
Lucas	462,361	Toledo	341
Madison	37,068	London	467
Mahoning	264,806	Youngstown	417
Marion	64,274	Marion	403
Medina	122,354	Medina	422
Meigs	22,987	Pomeroy	432
Mercer	39,443	Celina	457
Miami	93,182	Troy	410
Monroe	15,497	Woodsfield	457
Montgomery	573,809	Dayton	458
Morgan	14,194	McConnelsville	420
Morrow	27,749	Mount Gilead	406
Muskingum	82,068	Zanesville	654
Noble	11,336	Caldwell	399
Ottawa	40,029	Port Clinton	253
Paulding	20,488	Paulding	419
Perry	31,557	New Lexington	412
Pickaway	48,255	Circleville	503
Pike	24,249	Waverly	443

Oklahoma

(77 counties, 68,655 sq. mi. land; pop., 3,145,585)

County	Pop.	County Seat	Land area sq. mi.
Adair	18,421	Stillwell	577
Alfalfa	6,416	Cherokee	864
Atoka	12,778	Atoka	980
Beaver	6,023	Beaver	1,808
Beckham	18,812	Sayre	904
Blaine	11,470	Watonga	920
Bryan	32,089	Durant	902
Caddo	29,550	Anadarko	1,286
Canadian	74,409	El Reno	901
Carter	42,919	Ardmore	828
Cherokee	34,049	Tahlequah	748
Choctaw	15,302	Hugo	762
Cimarron	3,301	Boise City	1,842
Cleveland	174,253	Norman	529
Coal	5,780	Coalgate	520
Comanche	111,486	Lawton	1,076
Cotton	6,651	Walters	656
Craig	14,104	Vinita	763
Creek	60,915	Sapulpa	930
Custer	26,897	Arapaho	981
Delaware	28,070	Jay	720
Dewey	5,551	Taloga	1,007
Ellis	4,497	Arnett	1,232
Garfield	56,735	Enid	1,060
Garvin	26,605	Pauls Valley	813
Grady	41,747	Chickasha	1,106
Grant	5,689	Medford	1,004
Greer	6,559	Mangum	638
Harmon	3,793	Hollis	537
Harper	4,063	Buffalo	1,039
Haskell	10,940	Stigler	570
Hughes	13,023	Holdenville	806
Jackson	28,764	Altus	817
Jefferson	7,010	Waurika	769
Johnston	10,032	Tishomingo	639
Kay	48,056	Newkirk	921
Kingfisher	13,212	Kingfisher	906
Kiowa	11,347	Hobart	1,019
Latimer	10,333	Wilburton	728
Le Flore	43,270	Poteau	1,585
Lincoln	29,216	Chandler	964
Logan	29,011	Guthrie	748
Love	8,157	Marietta	519
McClain	22,795	Purcell	582
McCurtain	33,433	Idabel	1,826
McIntosh	16,779	Eufaula	599
Major	8,055	Fairview	958
Marshall	10,829	Madill	372
Mayes	33,366	Pryor	644
Murray	12,042	Sulphur	420
Muskogee	68,078	Muskogee	815
Noble	11,045	Perry	736
Nowata	9,992	Nowata	540
Okfuskee	11,551	Okemah	628
Oklahoma	599,611	Oklahoma City	708
Okmulgee	36,490	Okmulgee	698
Osage	41,645	Pawhuska	2,265
Ottawa	30,561	Miami	465
Pawnee	15,575	Pawnee	551
Payne	61,507	Stillwater	691
Pittsburg	40,581	McAlester	1,251
Pontotoc	34,119	Ada	717
Pottawatomie	58,760	Shawnee	783
Pushmataha	10,997	Antlers	1,417
Roger Mills	4,147	Cheyenne	1,146
Rogers	55,170	Claremore	683
Seminole	25,412	Wewoka	639
Sequoyah	33,828	Sallisaw	678

County	Pop.	County Seat or court house	Land area sq. mi.
Stephens	42,299	Duncan	884
Texas	16,419	Guymon	2,040
Tillman	10,384	Frederick	904
Tulsa	503,341	Tulsa	572
Wagoner	47,883	Wagoner	559
Washington	48,066	Bartlesville	423
Washita	11,441	Cordell	1,006
Woods	9,103	Alva	1,291
Woodward	18,976	Woodward	1,242

Oregon

(36 counties, 96,184 sq. mi. land; pop., 2,842,321)

County	Pop.	County Seat or court house	Land area sq. mi.
Baker	15,317	Baker	3,072
Benton	70,811	Corvallis	679
Clackamas	278,850	Oregon City	1,870
Clatsop	33,301	Astoria	805
Columbia	37,557	Saint Helens	651
Coos	60,273	Coquille	1,606
Crook	14,111	Prineville	2,984
Curry	19,327	Gold Beach	1,609
Deschutes	74,958	Bend	3,025
Douglas	94,649	Roseburg	5,044
Gilliam	1,717	Condon	1,213
Grant	7,853	Canyon City	4,525
Harney	7,060	Burns	10,174
Hood River	16,903	Hood River	521
Jackson	146,389	Medford	2,787
Jefferson	13,676	Madras	1,789
Josephine	62,649	Grants Pass	1,640
Klamath	57,702	Klamath Falls	5,954
Lake	7,186	Lakeview	8,251
Lane	282,912	Eugene	4,562
Lincoln	38,889	Newport	980
Linn	91,227	Albany	2,296
Malheur	26,038	Vale	9,861
Marion	228,483	Salem	1,184
Morrow	7,625	Heppner	2,044
Multnomah	583,887	Portland	431
Polk	49,541	Dallas	741
Sherman	1,918	Moro	827
Tillamook	21,570	Tillamook	1,101
Umatilla	59,249	Pendleton	3,218
Union	23,598	La Grande	2,035
Wallowa	6,911	Enterprise	3,150
Wasco	21,683	The Dalles	2,384
Washington	311,554	Hillsboro	725
Wheeler	1,396	Fossil	1,713
Yamhill	65,551	McMinnville	715

Pennsylvania

(67 counties, 44,888 sq. mi. land; pop., 11,881,643)

County	Pop.	County Seat or court house	Land area sq. mi.
Adams	78,274	Gettysburg	521
Allegheny	1,336,449	Pittsburgh	727
Armstrong	73,478	Kittanning	646
Beaver	186,093	Beaver	436
Bedford	47,919	Bedford	1,017
Berks	336,523	Reading	861
Blair	130,542	Hollidaysburg	527
Bradford	60,967	Towanda	1,152
Bucks	541,174	Doylestown	610
Butler	152,013	Butler	789
Cambria	163,029	Ebensburg	691
Cameron	5,913	Emporium	398
Carbon	56,846	Jim Thorpe	384
Centre	123,786	Bellefonte	1,106
Chester	376,396	West Chester	758
Clarion	41,699	Clarion	607
Clearfield	78,097	Clearfield	1,149
Clinton	37,182	Lock Haven	891
Columbia	63,202	Bloomsburg	486
Crawford	86,169	Meadville	1,011
Cumberland	195,257	Carlisle	547
Dauphin	237,813	Harrisburg	528
Delaware	547,651	Media	184
Elk	34,878	Ridgeway	830
Erie	275,572	Erie	804
Fayette	145,351	Uniontown	794
Forest	4,802	Tionesta	428
Franklin	121,082	Chambersburg	774
Fulton	13,837	McConnellsburg	438
Greene	39,550	Waynesburg	577
Huntingdon	44,164	Huntingdon	877
Indiana	89,994	Indiana	829
Jefferson	46,083	Brookville	657
Juniata	20,625	Mifflintown	392
Lackawanna	219,039	Scranton	461
Lancaster	422,822	Lancaster	952
Lawrence	96,246	New Castle	363
Lebanon	113,744	Lebanon	363
Lehigh	291,130	Allentown	348
Luzerne	328,149	Wilkes-Barre	891
Lycoming	118,710	Williamsport	1,237
McKean	47,131	Smethport	979
Mercer	121,003	Mercer	672
Mifflin	46,197	Lewistown	413
Monroe	95,709	Stroudsburg	609
Montgomery	678,111	Norristown	486
Montour	17,735	Danville	131
Northampton	247,105	Easton	376
Northumberland	96,771	Sunbury	461
Perry	41,172	New Bloomfield	557
Philadelphia	1,585,577	Philadelphia	136
Pike	27,966	Milford	550
Potter	16,717	Coudersport	1,081
Schuylkill	152,585	Pottsville	782
Snyder	36,680	Middleburg	329
Somerset	78,218	Somerset	1,073
Sullivan	6,104	Laporte	451
Susquehanna	40,380	Montrose	826
Tioga	41,126	Wellsboro	1,131
Union	36,176	Lewisburg	317
Venango	59,381	Franklin	679
Warren	45,050	Warren	885
Washington	204,584	Washington	958
Wayne	39,944	Honesdale	731
Westmoreland	370,321	Greensburg	1,033
Wyoming	28,076	Tunkhannock	399
York	339,574	York	906

Rhode Island

(5 counties, 1,055 sq. mi. land; pop., 1,003,464)

County	Pop.	County Seat or court house	Land area sq. mi.
Bristol	48,859	Bristol	26
Kent	161,135	East Greenwich	172
Newport	87,194	Newport	107
Providence	596,270	Providence	416
Washington	110,006	West Kingston	333

South Carolina

(46 counties, 30,203 sq. mi. land; pop., 3,486,703)

County	Pop.	County Seat or court house	Land area sq. mi.
Abbeville	23,862	Abbeville	508
Aiken	120,940	Aiken	1,092
Allendale	11,722	Allendale	413
Anderson	145,196	Anderson	718
Bamberg	16,902	Bamberg	395
Barnwell	20,293	Barnwell	558
Beaufort	86,425	Beaufort	579
Berkeley	128,776	Moncks Corner	1,108
Calhoun	12,753	Saint Matthews	380
Charleston	295,039	Charleston	938
Cherokee	44,506	Gaffney	396
Chester	32,170	Chester	580
Chesterfield	38,577	Chesterfield	802
Clarendon	28,450	Manning	602
Colleton	34,377	Walterboro	1,052
Darlington	61,851	Darlington	563
Dillon	29,114	Dillon	406
Dorchester	83,060	Saint George	575
Edgefield	18,375	Edgefield	490
Fairfield	22,295	Winnsboro	685
Florence	114,344	Florence	804
Georgetown	46,302	Georgetown	822
Greenville	320,167	Greenville	795
Greenwood	59,567	Greenwood	451
Hampton	18,191	Hampton	561
Horry	144,053	Conway	1,143
Jasper	15,487	Ridgeland	655
Kershaw	43,599	Camden	723
Lancaster	54,516	Lancaster	552
Laurens	58,092	Laurens	712
Lee	18,437	Bishopville	411
Lexington	167,611	Lexington	707
McCormick	8,868	McCormick	350
Marion	33,899	Marion	493
Marlboro	29,361	Bennettsville	483
Newberry	33,172	Newberry	634
Oconee	57,494	Walhalla	629
Orangeburg	84,803	Orangeburg	1,111
Pickens	93,894	Pickens	499
Richland	285,720	Columbia	762
Saluda	16,357	Saluda	456
Spartanburg	226,800	Spartanburg	814
Sumter	102,637	Sumter	665
Union	30,337	Union	515
Williamsburg	36,815	Kingstree	934
York	131,497	York	685

South Dakota

(67 counties, 75,952 sq. mi. land; pop., 696,004)

County	Pop.	County Seat or court house	Land area sq. mi.
Aurora	3,135	Plankinton	707
Beadle	18,253	Huron	1,259
Bennett	3,206	Martin	1,182
Bon Homme	7,089	Tyndall	552
Brookings	25,207	Brookings	795
Brown	35,580	Aberdeen	1,722
Brule	5,485	Chamberlain	815
Buffalo	1,759	Gannvalley	475
Butte	7,914	Belle Fourche	2,251
Campbell	1,965	Mound City	732
Charles Mix	9,131	Lake Andes	1,090
Clark	4,403	Clark	953
Clay	13,186	Vermillion	409
Codington	22,698	Watertown	694
Corson	4,195	McIntosh	2,467
Custer	6,179	Custer	1,559
Davison	17,503	Mitchell	436
Day	6,978	Webster	1,022
Deuel	4,522	Clear Lake	631
Dewey	5,523	Timber Lake	2,310
Douglas	3,746	Armour	434
Edmunds	4,356	Ipswich	1,149
Fall River	7,353	Hot Springs	4,742
Faulk	2,744	Faulkton	1,004
Grant	8,372	Milbank	681
Gregory	5,359	Burke	1,013
Haakon	2,624	Philip	1,822
Hamlin	4,974	Hayti	512
Hand	4,272	Miller	1,437
Hanson	2,994	Alexandria	433
Harding	1,669	Buffalo	2,678
Hughes	14,817	Pierre	757
Hutchinson	8,262	Olivet	816
Hyde	1,696	Highmore	860
Jackson	2,811	Kadoka	1,872
Jerauld	2,425	Wessington Spgs.	530
Jones	1,324	Murdo	971
Kingsbury	5,925	De Smet	824
Lake	10,550	Madison	560
Lawrence	20,655	Deadwood	800
Lincoln	15,427	Canton	578
Lyman	3,638	Kennebec	1,679
McCook	5,688	Salem	576
McPherson	3,228	Leola	1,148
Marshall	4,844	Britton	848
Meade	21,878	Sturgis	3,481
Mellette	2,137	White River	1,311
Miner	3,272	Howard	570
Minnehaha	123,809	Sioux Falls	810
Moody	6,507	Flandreau	520
Pennington	81,343	Rapid City	2,783
Perkins	3,932	Bison	2,884
Potter	3,190	Gettysburg	869
Roberts	9,914	Sisseton	1,102
Sanborn	2,833	Woonsocket	569
Shannon	9,902	(Attached to Fall River)	2,094
Spink	7,981	Redfield	1,505
Stanley	2,453	Fort Pierre	1,431
Sully	1,589	Onida	972
Todd	8,352	(Attached to Tripp)	1,388
Tripp	6,924	Winner	1,618
Turner	8,576	Parker	617
Union	10,189	Elk Point	453
Walworth	6,087	Selby	707
Yankton	19,252	Yankton	518
Ziebach	2,220	Dupree	1,969

Tennessee

(95 counties, 41,155 sq. mi. land; pop., 4,877,185)

County	Pop.	County Seat or court house	Land area sq. mi.
Anderson	68,250	Clinton	339
Bedford	30,411	Shelbyville	475
Benton	14,524	Camden	392
Bledsoe	9,669	Pikeville	407
Blount	85,969	Maryville	558
Bradley	73,712	Cleveland	327
Campbell	35,079	Jacksboro	479
Cannon	10,467	Woodbury	266
Carroll	27,514	Huntingdon	600
Carter	51,505	Elizabethton	341
Cheatham	27,140	Ashland City	304
Chester	12,819	Henderson	289
Claiborne	26,137	Tazewell	432
Clay	7,238	Celina	227
Cocke	29,141	Newport	432
Coffee	40,339	Manchester	428
Crockett	13,378	Alamo	266
Cumberland	34,736	Crossville	682
Davidson	510,784	Nashville	501
Decatur	10,472	Decaturville	330
De Kalb	14,360	Smithville	291
Dickson	35,061	Charlotte	491
Dyer	34,854	Dyersburg	520
Fayette	25,559	Somerville	705
Fentress	14,669	Jamestown	498
Franklin	34,725	Winchester	543
Gibson	46,315	Trenton	602
Giles	25,741	Pulaski	610
Grainger	17,095	Rutledge	273
Greene	55,853	Greeneville	619
Grundy	13,362	Altamont	361
Hamblen	50,480	Morristown	156
Hamilton	285,536	Chattanooga	539
Hancock	6,739	Sneedville	223
Hardeman	23,377	Bolivar	670
Hardin	22,633	Savannah	578
Hawkins	44,565	Rogersville	486
Haywood	19,437	Brownsville	534
Henderson	21,844	Lexington	520
Henry	27,888	Paris	560
Hickman	16,754	Centerville	610
Houston	7,018	Erin	200
Humphreys	15,795	Waverly	528
Jackson	9,297	Gainesboro	308
Jefferson	33,016	Dandridge	265
Johnson	13,766	Mountain City	297
Knox	335,749	Knoxville	506
Lake	7,129	Tiptonville	169
Lauderdale	23,491	Ripley	474
Lawrence	35,303	Lawrenceburg	617
Lewis	9,247	Hohenwald	282
Lincoln	28,157	Fayetteville	571
Loudon	31,255	Loudon	235
McMinn	42,383	Athens	429
McNairy	22,422	Selmer	562
Macon	15,906	Lafayette	307
Madison	77,982	Jackson	558
Marion	24,860	Jasper	512
Marshall	21,539	Lewisburg	376
Maury	54,812	Columbia	616
Meigs	8,033	Decatur	189
Monroe	30,541	Madisonville	648
Montgomery	100,498	Clarksville	539
Moore	4,721	Lynchburg	129
Morgan	17,300	Wartburg	523
Obion	31,717	Union City	550
Overton	17,636	Livingston	433
Perry	6,612	Linden	412
Pickett	4,548	Byrdstown	159
Polk	13,643	Benton	438
Putnam	51,373	Cookeville	399
Rhea	24,344	Dayton	309
Roane	47,227	Kingston	357
Robertson	41,494	Springfield	476
Rutherford	118,570	Murfreesboro	606
Scott	18,358	Huntsville	528
Sequatchie	8,863	Dunlap	266
Sevier	51,043	Sevierville	590
Shelby	826,330	Memphis	772
Smith	14,143	Carthage	313
Stewart	9,479	Dover	454
Sullivan	143,596	Blountville	415
Sumner	103,281	Gallatin	529
Tipton	37,568	Covington	454
Trousdale	5,920	Hartsville	114
Unicoi	16,549	Erwin	186
Union	13,694	Maynardville	218
Van Buren	4,846	Spencer	273
Warren	32,992	McMinnville	431
Washington	92,315	Jonesboro	326
Wayne	13,935	Waynesboro	734
Weakley	31,972	Dresden	581
White	20,090	Sparta	373
Williamson	81,021	Franklin	584
Wilson	67,675	Lebanon	570

Texas

(254 counties, 262,017 sq. mi. land; pop., 16,986,510)

County	Pop.	County Seat or court house	Land area sq. mi.
Anderson	48,024	Palestine	1,077
Andrews	14,338	Andrews	1,501
Angelina	69,884	Lufkin	807
Aransas	17,892	Rockport	280
Archer	7,973	Archer City	907
Armstrong	2,021	Claude	909
Atascosa	30,533	Jourdanton	1,218
Austin	19,832	Bellville	656
Bailey	7,064	Muleshoe	826
Bandera	10,562	Bandera	793
Bastrop	38,263	Bastrop	895
Baylor	4,385	Seymour	862

County	Pop.	County Seat or court house	Land area sq. mi.	County	Pop.	County Seat or court house	Land area sq. mi.
Bee	25,135	Beeville	880	Hockley	24,199	Levelland	908
Bell	191,088	Belton	1,055	Hood	28,981	Granbury	425
Bexar	1,185,394	San Antonio	1,248	Hopkins	28,833	Sulphur Springs	789
Blanco	5,972	Johnson City	714	Houston	21,375	Crockett	1,234
Borden	799	Gail	900	Howard	32,343	Big Spring	901
Bosque	15,125	Meridian	989	Hudspeth	2,915	Sierra Blanca	4,567
Bowie	81,665	Boston	891	Hunt	64,343	Greenville	840
Brazoria	191,707	Angleton	1,407	Hutchinson	25,689	Stinnett	872
Brazos	121,862	Bryan	589	Irion	1,629	Mertzon	1,052
Brewster	8,681	Alpine	6,169	Jack	6,981	Jacksboro	920
Briscoe	1,971	Silverton	887	Jackson	13,039	Edna	844
Brooks	8,204	Falfurrias	942	Jasper	31,102	Jasper	921
Brown	34,371	Brownwood	936	Jeff Davis	1,946	Fort Davis	2,257
Burleson	13,625	Caldwell	669	Jefferson	239,397	Beaumont	937
Burnet	22,677	Burnet	994	Jim Hogg	5,109	Hebbronville	1,136
Caldwell	26,392	Lockhart	546	Jim Wells	37,679	Alice	867
Calhoun	19,053	Port Lavaca	540	Johnson	97,165	Cleburne	730
Callahan	11,859	Baird	899	Jones	16,490	Anson	931
Cameron	260,120	Brownsville	906	Karnes	12,455	Karnes City	753
Camp	9,904	Pittsburg	203	Kaufman	52,220	Kaufman	788
Carson	6,576	Panhandle	924	Kendall	14,589	Boerne	663
Cass	29,982	Linden	937	Kenedy	460	Sarita	1,389
Castro	9,070	Dimmitt	899	Kent	1,010	Jayton	878
Chambers	20,088	Anahuac	616	Kerr	36,304	Kerrville	1,107
Cherokee	41,049	Rusk	1,052	Kimble	4,122	Junction	1,250
Childress	5,953	Childress	707	King	354	Guthrie	914
Clay	10,024	Henrietta	1,086	Kinney	3,119	Brackettville	1,359
Cochran	4,377	Morton	775	Kleberg	30,274	Kingsville	853
Coke	3,424	Robert Lee	908	Knox	4,837	Benjamin	845
Coleman	9,710	Coleman	1,277	Lamar	43,949	Paris	919
Collin	264,036	McKinney	851	Lamb	15,072	Littlefield	1,013
Collingsworth	3,573	Wellington	909	Lampasas	13,521	Lampasas	714
Colorado	18,383	Columbus	965	La Salle	5,254	Cotulla	1,517
Comal	51,832	New Braunfels	555	Lavaca	18,690	Hallettsville	971
Comanche	13,381	Comanche	930	Lee	12,854	Giddings	631
Concho	3,044	Paint Rock	992	Leon	12,665	Centerville	1,079
Cooke	30,777	Gainesville	893	Liberty	52,726	Liberty	1,174
Coryell	64,213	Gatesville	1,057	Limestone	20,946	Groesbeck	930
Cottle	2,247	Paducah	895	Lipscomb	3,143	Lipscomb	933
Crane	4,652	Crane	782	Live Oak	9,556	George West	1,057
Crockett	4,078	Ozona	2,806	Llano	11,631	Llano	939
Crosby	7,304	Crosbyton	899	Loving	107	Mentone	670
Culberson	3,407	Van Horn	3,815	Lubbock	222,636	Lubbock	900
Dallam	5,461	Dalhart	1,505	Lynn	6,758	Tahoka	888
Dallas	1,852,810	Dallas	880	McCulloch	8,778	Brady	1,071
Dawson	14,349	Lamesa	903	McLennan	189,123	Waco	1,031
Deaf Smith	19,153	Hereford	1,497	McMullen	817	Tilden	1,163
Delta	4,857	Cooper	278	Madison	10,931	Madisonville	472
Denton	273,525	Denton	911	Marion	9,984	Jefferson	385
Dewitt	18,840	Cuero	910	Martin	4,956	Staton	914
Dickens	2,571	Dickens	907	Mason	3,423	Mason	934
Dimmit	10,433	Carrizo Springs	1,307	Matagorda	36,928	Bay City	1,127
Donley	3,696	Clarendon	929	Maverick	36,378	Eagle Pass	1,287
Duval	12,918	San Diego	1,795	Medina	27,312	Hondo	1,331
Eastland	18,488	Eastland	924	Menard	2,252	Menard	902
Ector	118,934	Odessa	903	Midland	106,611	Midland	902
Edwards	2,266	Rocksprings	2,121	Milam	22,946	Cameron	1,019
Ellis	85,167	Waxahachie	939	Mills	4,531	Goldthwaite	748
El Paso	591,610	El Paso	1,014	Mitchell	8,016	Colorado City	912
Erath	27,991	Stephenville	1,080	Montague	17,274	Montague	928
Falls	17,712	Marlin	770	Montgomery	182,201	Conroe	1,047
Fannin	24,804	Bonham	895	Moore	17,865	Dumas	905
Fayette	20,095	La Grange	950	Morris	13,200	Daingerfield	256
Fisher	4,842	Roby	897	Motley	1,532	Matador	959
Floyd	8,497	Floydada	992	Nacogdoches	54,753	Nacogdoches	939
Foard	1,794	Crowell	703	Navarro	39,926	Corsicana	1,068
Fort Bend	225,421	Richmond	876	Newton	13,569	Newton	935
Franklin	7,802	Mount Vernon	294	Nolan	16,594	Sweetwater	915
Freestone	15,818	Fairfield	888	Nueces	291,145	Corpus Christi	847
Frio	13,472	Pearsall	1,133	Ochiltree	9,128	Perryton	919
Gaines	14,123	Seminole	1,504	Oldham	2,278	Vega	1,485
Galveston	217,399	Galveston	399	Orange	80,509	Orange	362
Garza	5,143	Post	895	Palo Pinto	25,055	Palo Pinto	949
Gillespie	17,204	Fredericksburg	1,061	Panola	22,035	Carthage	812
Glasscock	1,447	Garden City	900	Parker	64,785	Weatherford	902
Goliad	5,980	Goliad	859	Parmer	9,863	Farwell	885
Gonzales	17,205	Gonzales	1,068	Pecos	14,675	Fort Stockton	4,777
Gray	23,967	Pampa	921	Polk	30,687	Livingston	1,061
Grayson	95,021	Sherman	934	Potter	97,874	Amarillo	902
Gregg	104,948	Longview	273	Presidio	6,637	Marfa	3,857
Grimes	18,828	Anderson	799	Rains	6,715	Emory	243
Guadalupe	64,873	Seguin	713	Randall	89,673	Canyon	917
Hale	34,671	Plainview	1,005	Reagan	4,514	Big Lake	1,173
Hall	3,905	Memphis	877	Real	2,412	Leakey	697
Hamilton	7,733	Hamilton	836	Red River	14,317	Clarksville	1,054
Hansford	5,848	Spearman	921	Reeves	15,852	Pecos	2,626
Hardeman	5,283	Quanah	688	Refugio	7,976	Refugio	771
Hardin	41,320	Kountze	898	Roberts	1,025	Miami	915
Harris	2,818,199	Houston	1,734	Robertson	15,511	Franklin	864
Harrison	57,483	Marshall	908	Rockwall	25,604	Rockwall	128
Hartley	3,634	Channing	1,462	Runnels	11,294	Ballinger	1,056
Haskell	6,820	Haskell	901	Rusk	43,735	Henderson	932
Hays	65,614	San Marcos	678	Sabine	9,586	Hemphill	486
Hemphill	3,720	Canadian	903	San Augustine	7,999	San Augustine	524
Henderson	58,543	Athens	888	San Jacinto	16,372	Coldspring	572
Hidalgo	383,545	Edinburg	1,569	San Patricio	58,749	Sinton	693
Hill	27,146	Hillsboro	968	San Saba	5,401	San Saba	1,136

County	Pop.	County Seat or court house	Land area sq. mi.
Schleicher	2,990	Eldorado	1,309
Scurry	18,634	Snyder	900
Shackelford	3,316	Albany	915
Shelby	22,034	Center	791
Sherman	2,858	Stratford	923
Smith	151,309	Tyler	932
Somervell	5,360	Glen Rose	188
Starr	40,518	Rio Grande City	1,226
Stephens	9,010	Breckenridge	894
Sterling	1,438	Sterling City	923
Stonewall	2,013	Aspermont	925
Sutton	4,135	Sonora	1,455
Swisher	8,133	Tulia	902
Tarrant	1,170,103	Fort Worth	868
Taylor	119,655	Abilene	917
Terrell	1,410	Sanderson	2,357
Terry	13,218	Brownfield	887
Throckmorton	1,880	Throckmorton	912
Titus	24,009	Mount Pleasant	412
Tom Green	98,458	San Angelo	1,515
Travis	576,407	Austin	989
Trinity	11,445	Groveton	692
Tyler	16,646	Woodville	922
Upshur	31,370	Gilmer	587
Upton	4,447	Rankin	1,243
Uvalde	23,340	Uvalde	1,564
Val Verde	38,721	Del Rio	3,150
Van Zandt	37,944	Canton	855
Victoria	74,361	Victoria	887
Walker	50,917	Huntsville	786
Waller	23,390	Hempstead	514
Ward	13,115	Monahans	836
Washington	26,154	Brenham	610
Webb	133,239	Laredo	3,362
Wharton	39,955	Wharton	1,086
Wheeler	5,879	Wheeler	904
Wichita	122,378	Wichita Falls	606
Wilbarger	15,121	Vernon	947
Willacy	17,705	Raymondville	589
Williamson	139,551	Georgetown	1,137
Wilson	22,650	Floresville	807
Winkler	8,626	Kermit	840
Wise	34,679	Decatur	902
Wood	29,380	Quitman	689
Yoakum	8,786	Plains	800
Young	18,126	Graham	919
Zapata	9,279	Zapata	999
Zavala	12,162	Crystal City	1,298

Utah

(29 counties, 82,073 sq. mi. land; pop. 1,722,850)

County	Pop.	County Seat or court house	Land area sq. mi.
Beaver	4,765	Beaver	2,586
Box Elder	36,485	Brigham City	5,614
Cache	70,183	Logan	1,171
Carbon	20,228	Price	1,479
Daggett	690	Manila	699
Davis	187,941	Farmington	299
Duchesne	12,645	Duchesne	3,233
Emery	10,332	Castle Dale	4,449
Garfield	3,980	Panguitch	5,148
Grand	6,620	Moab	3,689
Iron	20,789	Parowan	3,301
Juab	5,817	Nephi	3,396
Kane	5,169	Kanab	3,898
Millard	11,333	Fillmore	6,818
Morgan	5,528	Morgan	603
Piute	1,277	Junction	759
Rich	1,725	Randolph	1,034
Salt Lake	725,956	Salt Lake City	756
San Juan	12,621	Monticello	7,725
Sanpete	16,259	Manti	1,587
Sevier	15,431	Richfield	1,910
Summit	15,518	Coalville	1,871
Tooele	26,601	Tooele	6,919
Uintah	22,211	Vernal	4,479
Utah	263,590	Provo	2,018
Wasatch	10,089	Heber City	1,191
Washington	48,560	Saint George	2,422
Wayne	2,177	Loa	2,461
Weber	158,330	Ogden	566

Vermont

(14 counties, 9,273 sq. mi. land; pop. 562,758)

County	Pop.	County Seat or court house	Land area sq. mi.
Addison	32,953	Middlebury	773
Bennington	35,845	Bennington	677
Caledonia	27,846	Saint Johnsbury	651
Chittenden	131,761	Burlington	540
Essex	6,405	Guildhall	666
Franklin	39,980	Saint Albans	649
Grand Isle	5,318	North Hero	89
Lamoille	19,735	Hyde Park	461
Orange	26,149	Chelsea	690
Orleans	24,053	Newport	697
Rutland	62,142	Rutland	932
Washington	54,928	Montpelier	690
Windham	41,588	Newfane	787
Windsor	54,055	Woodstock	972

Virginia

(95 cos., 41 ind. cities, 39,704 sq. mi. land; pop. 6,187,358)

County	Pop.	County Seat or court house	Land area sq. mi.
Accomack	31,703	Accomac	476
Albemarle	68,040	Charlottesville	725
Alleghany	13,176	Covington	446
Amelia	8,787	Amelia, C.H.	357
Amherst	28,578	Amherst	479
Appomattox	12,298	Appomattox	336
Arlington	170,936	Arlington	26
Augusta	54,677	Staunton	969
Bath	4,799	Warm Springs	538
Bedford	45,656	Bedford	747
Bland	6,514	Bland	359
Botetourt	24,992	Fincastle	545
Brunswick	15,987	Lawrenceville	563
Buchanan	31,333	Grundy	504
Buckingham	12,873	Buckingham	583
Campbell	47,572	Rustburg	505
Caroline	19,217	Bowling Green	535
Carroll	26,594	Hillsville	478
Charles City	6,282	Charles City	181
Charlotte	11,688	Charlotte Courthouse	477
Chesterfield	209,274	Chesterfield	434
Clarke	12,101	Berryville	178
Craig	4,372	New Castle	330
Culpeper	27,791	Culpeper	382
Cumberland	7,825	Cumberland	300
Dickenson	17,620	Clintwood	331
Dinwiddie	20,960	Dinwiddie	507
Essex	8,689	Tappahannock	263
Fairfax	818,584	Fairfax	394
Fauquier	48,741	Warrenton	651
Floyd	12,005	Floyd	381
Fluvanna	12,429	Palmyra	290
Franklin	39,549	Rocky Mount	683
Frederick	45,723	Winchester	415
Giles	16,366	Pearisburg	362
Gloucester	30,131	Gloucester	225
Goochland	14,163	Goochland	281
Grayson	16,278	Independence	446
Greene	10,297	Stanardsville	157
Greensville	8,853	Emporia	300
Halifax	29,033	Halifax	816
Hanover	63,306	Hanover	467
Henrico	217,881	Richmond	238
Henry	56,942	Martinsville	382
Highland	2,635	Monterey	416
Isle of Wight	25,053	Isle of Wight	319
James City	34,859	Williamsburg	153
King and Queen	6,289	King and Queen	317
King George	13,527	King George	180
King William	10,913	King William	278
Lancaster	10,896	Lancaster	133
Lee	24,496	Jonesville	437
Loudoun	86,129	Leesburg	521
Louisa	20,325	Louisa	497
Lunenburg	11,419	Lunenburg	432
Madison	11,949	Madison	322
Mathews	8,348	Mathews	87
Mecklenburg	29,241	Boydton	616
Middlesex	8,653	Saluda	134
Montgomery	73,913	Christiansburg	390
Nelson	12,778	Lovingston	474
New Kent	10,445	New Kent	213
Northampton	13,061	Eastville	226
Northumberland	10,524	Heathsville	185
Nottoway	14,993	Nottoway	316
Orange	21,421	Orange	342
Page	21,690	Luray	313
Patrick	17,473	Stuart	481
Pittsylvania	55,655	Chatham	995
Powhatan	15,328	Powhatan	261
Prince Edward	17,320	Farmville	354
Prince George	27,394	Prince George	266
Prince William	215,686	Manassas	339
Pulaski	34,496	Pulaski	318
Rappahannock	6,622	Washington	267
Richmond	7,273	Warsaw	193
Roanoke	79,332	Salem	251
Rockbridge	18,350	Lexington	603
Rockingham	57,482	Harrisonburg	865
Russell	28,667	Lebanon	479
Scott	23,204	Gate City	535
Shenandoah	31,636	Woodstock	512

County	Pop.	County Seat or court house	Land area sq. mi.
Smyth	3? 370	Marion	452
Southampton	1?,550	Courtland	603
Spotsylvania	57,403	Spotsylvania	404
Stafford	61,236	Stafford	271
Surry	6,145	Surry	281
Sussex	10,248	Sussex	491
Tazewell	45,960	Tazewell	520
Warren	26,142	Front Royal	217
Washington	45,887	Abingdon	562
Westmoreland	15,480	Montross	227
Wise	39,573	Wise	405
Wythe	25,466	Wytheville	465
York	42,422	Yorktown	113
Independent cities			
Alexandria	111,183		15
Bedford	6,073		7
Bristol	18,426		12
Buena Vista	6,406		3
Charlottesville	40,341		10
Chesapeake	151,976		340
Clifton Forge	4,679		3
Colonial Heights	16,064		8
Covington	6,991		4
Danville	53,056		17
Emporia	5,306		2
Fairfax	19,622		6
Falls Church	9,578		2
Franklin	7,864		4
Fredericksburg	19,027		6
Galax	6,670		8
Hampton	133,793		51
Harrisonburg	30,707		6
Hopewell	23,101		10
Lexington	6,959		2
Lynchburg	66,049		50
Manassas	27,957		8
Manassas Park	6,734		2
Martinsville	16,162		11
Newport News	170,045		65
Norfolk	261,229		53
Norton	4,247		7
Petersburg	38,386		23
Poquoson	11,005		17
Portsmouth	103,907		30
Radford	15,940		7
Richmond	203,056		60
Roanoke	96,397		43
Salem	23,756		14
South Boston	6,997		6
Staunton	24,461		9
Suffolk	52,141		409
Virginia Beach	393,069		256
Waynesboro	18,549		8
Williamsburg	11,530		5
Winchester	21,947		9

Washington

(39 counties, 66,511 sq. mi. land; pop., 4,866,692)

County	Pop.	County Seat or court house	Land area sq. mi.
Adams	13,603	Ritzville	1,921
Asotin	17,605	Asotin	635
Benton	112,560	Prosser	1,715
Chelan	52,250	Wenatchee	2,916
Clallam	56,464	Port Angeles	1,753
Clark	238,053	Vancouver	627
Columbia	4,024	Dayton	865
Cowlitz	82,119	Kelso	1,140
Douglas	26,205	Waterville	1,817
Ferry	6,295	Republic	2,200
Franklin	37,473	Pasco	1,243
Garfield	2,248	Pomeroy	706
Grant	54,758	Ephrata	2,660
Grays Harbor	64,175	Montesano	1,918
Island	60,195	Coupeville	212
Jefferson	20,146	Port Townsend	1,805
King	1,507,319	Seattle	2,128
Kitsap	189,731	Port Orchard	393
Kittitas	26,725	Ellensburg	2,308
Klickitat	16,616	Goldendale	1,880
Lewis	59,358	Chehalis	2,409
Lincoln	8,864	Davenport	2,310
Mason	38,341	Shelton	961
Okanogan	33,350	Okanogan	5,281
Pacific	18,882	South Bend	908
Pend Oreille	8,915	Newport	1,400
Pierce	586,203	Tacoma	1,675
San Juan	10,035	Friday Harbor	179
Skagit	79,555	Mount Vernon	1,735
Skamania	8,289	Stevenson	1,672
Snohomish	465,642	Everett	2,098
Spokane	361,364	Spokane	1,762
Stevens	30,948	Colville	2,470
Thurston	161,238	Olympia	727
Wahkiakum	3,327	Cathlamet	261
Walla Walla	48,439	Walla Walla	1,261
Whatcom	127,780	Bellingham	2,125
Whitman	38,775	Colfax	2,151
Yakima	188,823	Yakima	4,287

West Virginia

(55 counties, 24,119 sq. mi. land; pop., 1,793,477)

County	Pop.	County Seat or court house	Land area sq. mi.
Barbour	15,699	Philippi	343
Berkeley	59,253	Martinsburg	321
Boone	25,870	Madison	503
Braxton	12,998	Sutton	513
Brooke	26,992	Wellsburg	90
Cabell	96,827	Huntington	282
Calhoun	7,885	Grantsville	280
Clay	9,983	Clay	346
Doddridge	6,994	West Union	321
Fayette	47,952	Fayetteville	667
Gilmer	7,669	Glenville	340
Grant	10,428	Petersburg	480
Greenbrier	34,693	Lewisburg	1,025
Hampshire	16,498	Romney	644
Hancock	35,233	New Cumberland	84
Hardy	10,977	Moorefield	585
Harrison	69,371	Clarksburg	417
Jackson	25,938	Ripley	464
Jefferson	35,926	Charles Town	209
Kanawha	207,619	Charleston	901
Lewis	17,223	Weston	389
Lincoln	21,382	Hamlin	439
Logan	43,032	Logan	456
McDowell	35,233	Welch	535
Marion	57,249	Fairmont	312
Marshall	37,356	Moundsville	305
Mason	25,178	Point Pleasant	433
Mercer	64,980	Princeton	420
Mineral	26,697	Keyser	329
Mingo	33,739	Williamson	424
Monongalia	75,509	Morgantown	363
Monroe	12,406	Union	473
Morgan	12,128	Berkeley Springs	230
Nicholas	26,775	Summersville	650
Ohio	50,871	Wheeling	106
Pendleton	8,054	Franklin	698
Pleasants	7,546	St. Marys	131
Pocahontas	9,008	Marlinton	942
Preston	29,037	Kingwood	651
Putnam	42,835	Winfield	346
Raleigh	76,819	Beckley	608
Randolph	27,803	Elkins	1,040
Ritchie	10,233	Harrisville	454
Roane	15,120	Spencer	484
Summers	14,204	Hinton	353
Taylor	15,144	Grafton	174
Tucker	7,728	Parsons	421
Tyler	9,796	Middlebourne	258
Upshur	22,867	Buckhannon	355
Wayne	41,636	Wayne	508
Webster	10,729	Webster Springs	556
Wetzel	19,258	New Martinsville	359
Wirt	5,192	Elizabeth	235
Wood	86,915	Parkersburg	367
Wyoming	28,990	Pineville	502

Wisconsin

(72 counties, 54,426 sq. mi. land; pop., 4,891,769)

County	Pop.	County Seat or court house	Land area sq. mi.
Adams	15,682	Friendship	648
Ashland	16,307	Ashland	1,048
Barron	40,750	Barron	865
Bayfield	14,008	Washburn	1,462
Brown	194,594	Green Bay	524
Buffalo	13,584	Alma	699
Burnett	13,084	Grantsburg	818
Calumet	34,291	Chilton	326
Chippewa	52,360	Chippewa Falls	1,017
Clark	31,647	Neillsville	1,218
Columbia	45,088	Portage	771
Crawford	15,940	Prairie du Chien	566
Dane	367,085	Madison	1,205
Dodge	76,559	Juneau	887
Door	25,690	Sturgeon Bay	492
Douglas	41,758	Superior	1,305
Dunn	35,909	Menomonie	853
Eau Claire	85,183	Eau Claire	638
Florence	4,590	Florence	486
Fond du Lac	90,083	Fond du Lac	725
Forest	8,776	Crandon	1,011
Grant	49,264	Lancaster	1,144
Green	30,339	Monroe	583
Green Lake	18,651	Green Lake	357

County	Pop.	County Seat or court house	Land area sq. mi.	County	Pop.	County Seat or court house	Land area sq. mi.
Iowa	20,150	Dodgeville	760	Walworth	75,000	Elkhorn	556
Iron	6,153	Hurley	751	Washburn	13,772	Shell Lake	815
Jackson	16,588	Black River Falls	998	Washington	95,328	West Bend	430
Jefferson	67,783	Jefferson	562	Waukesha	304,715	Waukesha	554
Juneau	21,650	Mauston	774	Waupaca	46,104	Waupaca	754
Kenosha	128,181	Kenosha	273	Waushara	19,385	Wautoma	628
Kewaunee	18,878	Kewaunee	343	Winnebago	140,320	Oshkosh	449
La Crosse	97,904	La Crosse	457	Wood	73,605	Wisconsin Rapids	801
Lafayette	16,076	Darlington	634				
Langlade	19,505	Antigo	873				
Lincoln	26,993	Merrill	886				
Manitowoc	80,421	Manitowoc	594				
Marathon	115,400	Wausau	1,559				
Marinette	40,548	Marinette	1,395				
Marquette	12,321	Montello	455				
Menominee	3,890	Keshena	359				
Milwaukee	959,275	Milwaukee	241				
Monroe	36,633	Sparta	904				
Oconto	30,226	Oconto	1,002				
Oneida	31,679	Rhinelander	1,130				
Outagamie	140,510	Appleton	642				
Ozaukee	72,831	Port Washington	235				
Pepin	7,107	Durand	231				
Pierce	32,765	Ellsworth	577				
Polk	34,773	Balsam Lake	919				
Portage	61,405	Stevens Point	810				
Price	15,600	Phillips	1,256				
Racine	175,034	Racine	335				
Richland	17,521	Richland Center	585				
Rock	139,510	Janesville	723				
Rusk	15,079	Ladysmith	913				
St. Croix	50,251	Hudson	723				
Sauk	46,975	Baraboo	838				
Sawyer	14,181	Hayward	1,255				
Shawano	37,157	Shawano	897				
Sheboygan	103,877	Sheboygan	515				
Taylor	18,901	Medford	975				
Trempealeau	25,263	Whitehall	736				
Vernon	25,617	Viroqua	808				
Vilas	17,707	Eagle River	867				

Wyoming

(23 counties, 96,989 sq. mi. land; pop., 453,588)

County	Pop.	County Seat or court house	Land area sq. mi.
Albany	30,797	Laramie	4,268
Big Horn	10,525	Basin	3,139
Campbell	29,370	Gillette	4,796
Carbon	16,659	Rawlins	7,877
Converse	11,128	Douglas	4,271
Crook	5,294	Sundance	2,855
Fremont	33,662	Lander	9,181
Goshen	12,373	Torrington	2,186
Hot Springs	4,809	Thermopolis	2,005
Johnson	6,145	Buffalo	4,166
Laramie	73,142	Cheyenne	2,684
Lincoln	12,625	Kemmerer	4,070
Natrona	61,226	Casper	5,347
Niobrara	2,499	Lusk	2,684
Park	23,178	Cody	6,936
Platte	8,145	Wheatland	2,023
Sheridan	23,562	Sheridan	2,532
Sublette	4,843	Pinedale	4,872
Sweetwater	38,823	Green River	10,352
Teton	11,172	Jackson	4,011
Uinta	18,705	Evanston	2,085
Washakie	8,388	Worland	2,243
Weston	6,518	Newcastle	2,402

Population of Outlying Areas

Source: Bureau of the Census U.S. Dept. of Commerce
Population figures are final counts from the census conducted on Apr. 1, 1990.

Puerto Rico

ZIP code	Municipios	Pop.	Land area sq. mile	ZIP code	Municipios	Pop.	Land area sq. mile	ZIP code	Municipios	Pop.	Land area sq. mile
00601	Adjuntas	19,451	67	00648	Fajardo	36,882	31	00719	Naranjito	27,914	28
00602	Aguada	35,911	31	00650	Florida	8,689	10	00720	Orocovis	21,158	64
00603	Aguadilla	59,335	37	00653	Guanica	19,984	37	00723	Patillas	19,633	47
00607	Aguas Buenas	25,424	30	00654	Guayama	41,588	65	00724	Penuelas	22,515	45
00609	Aibonito	24,971	31	00656	Guayanilla	21,581	42	00731	Ponce	187,749	117
00610	Anasco	25,234	40	00657	Guaynabo	92,886	27	00742	Quebradillas	21,425	23
00612	Arecibo	93,385	127	00658	Gurabo	28,737	28	00743	Rincon	12,213	14
00615	Arroyo	18,910	15	00659	Hatillo	32,703	42	00745	Rio Grande	45,648	62
00617	Barceloneta	20,947	24	00660	Hormigueros	15,212	11	00747	Sabana Grande	22,843	36
00618	Barranquitas	25,605	34	00661	Humacao	55,203	45	00751	Salinas	28,335	71
00619	Bayamon	220,262	45	00662	Isabela	39,147	56	00753	San German	34,962	54
00623	Cabo Rojo	38,521	72	00664	Jayuya	15,527	44	*00936	San Juan	437,745	47
00625	Caguas	133,447	59	00665	Juana Diaz	45,198	61	00754	San Lorenzo	35,163	53
00627	Camuy	28,917	47	00666	Juncos	30,612	27	00755	San Sebastian	38,799	71
00629	Canovanas	36,816	33	00667	Lajas	23,271	60	00757	Santa Isabel	19,318	35
00630	Carolina	177,806	48	00669	Lares	29,015	62	00758	Toa Alta	44,101	28
00632	Catano	34,587	6	00670	Las Marias	9,306	46	00759	Toa Baja	89,454	24
00633	Cayey	46,553	52	00671	Las Piedras	27,896	34	00760	Trujillo Alto	61,120	21
00635	Ceiba	17,145	27	00672	Loiza	29,307	21	00761	Utuado	34,980	115
00638	Ciales	18,084	67	00673	Luquillo	18,100	26	00762	Vega Alta	34,559	28
00639	Cidra	35,601	36	00701	Manati	38,692	46	00763	Vega Baja	55,997	48
00640	Coamo	33,837	78	00706	Marico	6,206	37	00765	Vieques	8,602	53
00642	Comerio	20,265	29	00707	Maunabo	12,347	21	00766	Villalba	23,559	37
00643	Corozal	33,095	43	00708	Mayaguez	100,371	77	00767	Yabucoa	36,483	55
00645	Culebra	1,542	13	00716	Moca	32,926	50	00768	Yauco	42,058	69
00646	Dorado	30,759	24	00717	Morovis	25,288	39	Total		3,522,037	3,459
				00718	Naguabo	22,620	52				

ZIP code	Area	Pop.	Land area sq. mile	ZIP code	Area	Pop.	Land area sq. mile	ZIP code	Area	Pop.	Land area sq. mile
	American Samoa			96912	Dededo	31,728	30	.....	Umatac	897	6
96799	American Samoa	46,773	77	96916	Inarajan	2,469	19	.....	Yigo	14,213	35
					Mangilao	10,483	10	96914	Yona	5,338	20
	Guam			96916	Merizo	1,742	6		Total	133,152	209
96910	Agana	1,139	1	.....	Mongmong-Toto-Maite	5,845	2				
	Agana Hts.	3,646	1		Piti	1,827	7		**Virgin Islands**		
96915	Agat	4,960	10	96915	Santa Rita	11,857	17	.....	St. Croix	50,139	80
	Asan	2,070	6		Sinajana	2,658	1	.....	St. John	3,504	20
96913	Barrigada	8,846	5		Talofofo	2,310	17	.....	St. Thomas	48,166	3
.....	Chalan-Pago-Ordot	4,451	6	96911	Tamuning	16,673	6	00801	Charlotte Amalie	12,331	
								00820	Christiansted	2,555	

ZIP code	Area	Pop.	Land area sq. mile	ZIP code	Area	Pop.	Land area sq. mile	ZIP code	Area	Pop.	Land area sq. mile
00840	Frederiksted.....	1,064			Palau........	15,122	192				
	Total	101,809	132		Ponape	NA	176		No. Mariana		
	Trust Territory of				Truk...........	NA	49		Islands.......	43,345	184
	Pacific Islands				Yap	NA	46				
	Kosrae	NA	42		Total	NA	533				
	Marshall Islands....	NA	70								

U.S. Area and Population: 1790 to 1990

Source: Bureau of the Census

	Area (square miles)			Population		
Census date	Gross	Land	Water	Number	Per sq. mile of land	Increase over preceding census Number	%
1990 (Apr. 1)..........	3,787,425	3,536,342	251,083[1]	248,709,873	70.3	22,164,068	9.8
1980 (Apr. 1)..........	3,618,770	3,539,289	79,481	226,542,203	64.0	23,240,172	11.4
1970 (Apr. 1)..........	3,618,770	3,536,855	81,915	203,302,031	57.5	23,978,856	13.4
1960 (Apr. 1)..........	3,618,770	3,540,911	77,859	179,323,175	50.6	27,997,377	18.5
1950 (Apr. 1)..........	3,618,770	3,552,206	66,564	151,325,798	42.6	19,161,229	14.5
1940 (Apr. 1)..........	3,618,770	3,554,608	64,162	132,164,569	37.2	8,961,945	7.3
1930 (Apr. 1)..........	3,618,770	3,551,608	67,162	123,202,624	34.7	17,181,087	16.2
1920 (Jan. 1)..........	3,618,770	3,546,931	71,839	106,021,537	29.9	13,793,041	15.0
1910 (Apr. 15).........	3,618,770	3,547,045	71,725	92,228,496	26.0	16,016,328	21.0
1900 (June 1).........	3,618,770	3,547,314	71,456	76,212,168	21.5	13,232,402	21.0
1890 (June 1).........	3,612,299	3,540,705	71,594	62,979,766	17.8	12,790,557	25.5
1880 (June 1).........	3,612,299	3,540,705	71,594	50,189,209	14.2	11,630,838	30.2
1870 (June 1).........	3,612,299	3,540,705	71,594	38,558,371	10.9	7,115,050	22.6
1860 (June 1).........	3,021,295	2,969,640	51,655	31,443,321	10.6	8,251,445	35.6
1850 (June 1).........	2,991,655	2,940,042	51,613	23,191,876	7.9	6,122,423	35.9
1840 (June 1).........	1,792,552	1,749,462	43,090	17,069,453	9.8	4,203,433	32.7
1830 (June 1).........	1,792,552	1,749,462	43,090	12,866,020	7.4	3,227,567	33.5
1820 (June 1).........	1,792,552	1,749,462	43,090	9,638,453	5.5	2,398,572	33.1
1810 (Aug. 6).........	1,722,685	1,681,828	40,857	7,239,881	4.3	1,931,398	36.4
1800 (Aug. 4)..........	891,364	864,746	26,618	5,308,483	6.1	1,379,269	35.1
1790 (Aug. 2)..........	891,364	864,746	26,618	3,929,214	4.5	—	—

(1) Comprises inland, coastal, Great Lakes, and territorial water. Data for prior years cover inland water only.
NOTE: Percent changes are computed on basis of change in population since preceding census date, and period covered therefore is not always exactly 10 years.
　　Population density figures given for various years represent the area within the boundaries of the United States which was under the jurisdiction on date in question, including in some cases considerable areas not organized or settled and not covered by the census. In 1870, for example, Alaska was not covered by the census.
　　Revised figure of 39,818,449 for the 1870 population includes adjustments for undernumeration in the Southern states. On the basis of the revised figure, the population increased by 8,375,128, or 26.6 percent between 1860 and 1870, and by 10,370,760, or 26.1 percent between 1870 and 1880.

Resident Population by Sex, Race, Residence, and Median Age: 1790 to 1990

Source: U.S. Bureau of the Census (thousands, except as indicated)

Date	Sex		Race				Residence		Median Age (years)		
	Male	Female	White	Black Number	Percent	Other	Urban	Rural	All races	White	Black
Conterminous U.S.[1]											
1790 (Aug. 2)...	NA	NA	3,172	757	19.3	NA	202	3,728	NA	NA	NA
1810 (Aug. 6)...	NA	NA	5,862	1,378	19.0	NA	525	6,714	NA	16.0	NA
1820 (Aug. 7)...	4,897	4,742	7,867	1,772	18.4	NA	693	8,945	16.7	16.5	17.2
1840 (June 1)...	8,689	8,381	14,196	2,874	16.8	NA	1,845	15,224	17.8	17.9	17.3
1860 (June 1)...	16,085	15,358	26,923	4,442	14.1	79	6,217	25,227	19.4	19.7	17.7
1870 (June 1)..	19,494	19,065	33,589	4,880	12.7	89	9,902	28,656	20.2	20.4	18.5
1880 (June 1)..	25,519	24,637	43,403	6,581	13.1	172	14,130	36,026	20.9	21.4	18.0
1890 (June 1)..	32,237	30,711	55,101	7,489	11.9	358	22,106	40,841	22.0	22.5	17.8
1900 (June 1)..	38,816	37,178	66,809	8,834	11.6	351	30,160	45,835	22.9	23.4	19.4
1920 (Jan. 1)...	53,900	51,810	94,821	10,463	9.9	427	54,158	51,553	25.3	25.6	22.3
1930 (Apr. 1)...	62,137	60,638	110,287	11,891	9.7	597	68,955	53,820	26.4	26.9	23.5
1940 (Apr. 1)...	66,062	65,608	118,215	12,866	9.8	589	74,424	57,246	29.0	29.5	25.3
United States											
1950 (Apr. 1)...	75,187	76,139	135,150	15,045	9.9	1,131	96,847	54,479	30.2	30.7	26.2
1960 (Apr. 1)...	88,331	90,992	158,832	18,872	10.5	1,620	125,269	54,054	29.5	30.3	23.5
1970 (Apr. 1)[2] ..	98,926	104,309	178,098	22,581	11.1	2,557	149,325	53,887	28.0	28.9	22.4
1980 (Apr. 1)[3] ..	110,053	116,493	194,713	26,683	11.8	5,150	167,051	59,495	30.0	30.9	24.9
1983 (July 1)...	113,119	120,365	199,849	28,056	12.0	6,379	NA	NA	30.8	31.7	25.9
1984 (July 1)...	115,022	121,455	201,290	28,457	12.0	6,730	NA	NA	31.1	32.0	26.3
1985 (July 1, est)	116,160	122,576	202,769	28,810	12.1	7,097	NA	NA	31.4	32.3	26.6
1990 (Apr. 1)...	121,239	127,470	199,686	29,986	12.1	9,805	NA	NA	32.9	NA	NA

(NA) Not available. (1) Excludes Alaska and Hawaii. (2) The revised 1970 resident population count is 203,302,031, which incorporates changes due to errors found after tabulations were completed. The race and sex data shown here reflect the official 1970 census count while the residence data come from the tabulated count. (3) The race data shown for April 1, 1980 have been modified.

Counties with 1990 Population over 1 Million

Source: U.S. Bureau of the Census, U.S. Dept. of Commerce, 1990 Census

County	April 1, 1990 census	April 1, 1980 census	Percent change 1980-90	County	April 1, 1990 census	April 1, 1980 census	Percent change 1980-90
Los Angeles, CA	8,863,164	7,477,238	18.5	San Bernardino, CA	1,418,380	895,016	58.5
Cook, IL	5,105,067	5,253,628	-2.8	Cuyahoga, OH	1,412,140	1,498,400	-5.8
Harris, TX	2,818,199	2,409,547	17.0	Middlesex, MA	1,398,468	1,367,034	2.3
San Diego, CA	2,498,016	1,861,846	34.2	Allegheny, PA	1,336,449	1,450,195	-7.8
Orange, CA	2,410,556	1,932,921	24.7	Suffolk, NY	1,321,864	1,284,231	2.9
Kings, NY	2,300,664	2,231,028	3.1	Nassau, NY	1,287,348	1,321,582	-2.6
Maricopa, AZ	2,122,101	1,509,175	40.6	Alameda, CA	1,279,182	1,105,379	15.7
Wayne, MI	2,111,687	2,337,843	-9.7	Broward, FL	1,255,488	1,018,257	23.3
Queens, NY	1,951,598	1,891,325	3.2	Bronx, NY	1,203,789	1,168,972	3.0
Dade, FL	1,937,094	1,625,509	19.2	Bexar, TX	1,185,394	988,971	19.9
Dallas, TX	1,852,810	1,556,419	19.0	Riverside, CA	1,170,413	663,199	76.5
Philadelphia, PA	1,585,577	1,688,210	-6.1	Tarrant, TX	1,170,103	860,880	35.9
King, WA	1,507,319	1,269,898	18.7	Oakland, MI	1,083,592	1,011,793	7.1
Santa Clara, CA	1,497,577	1,295,071	15.6	Sacramento, CA	1,041,219	783,381	32.9
New York, NY	1,487,536	1,428,285	4.1	Hennepin, MN	1,032,431	941,411	9.7

Los Angeles County, the nation's largest, also had the largest numeric increase, 1.4 million, followed by San Diego and Maricopa (Phoenix) each with over 600,000, and San Bernardino and Riverside each with more than 500,000. New York City encompasses 5 counties, 4 of which exceed a million population. The largest is Kings (Brooklyn), with 2.3 million, followed by Queens, New York (Manhattan), and the Bronx. For the first time since 1950, the population of all five counties increased.

Population by State: 1990

Source: U.S. Bureau of the Census, U.S. Dept. of Commerce, 1990 Census

State	1990 population	Percent change 1980-90	Minority population 1990	Minority percent change 1980-90	State	1990 population	Percent change 1980-90	Minority population 1990	Minority percent change 1980-90
U.S.	248,709,873	9.8%	60,581,577	30.9%	Colo.	3,294,394	14.0	635,449	27.2
Cal.	29,760,021	25.7	12,730,895	61.1	Conn.	3,287,116	5.8	532,932	43.2
N.Y.	17,990,455	2.5	5,530,266	25.9	Okla.	3,145,585	4.0	597,997	31.6
Tex.	16,986,510	19.4	6,694,830	37.2	Ore.	2,842,321	7.9	262,589	48.3
Fla.	12,937,926	32.7	3,462,600	52.3	Ia.	2,776,755	-4.7	112,915	24.8
Pa.	11,881,643	0.1	1,459,585	13.3	Miss.	2,573,216	2.1	949,018	3.5
Ill.	11,430,602	0.0	2,880,394	14.5	Kan.	2,477,574	4.8	287,050	27.5
Oh.	10,847,115	0.5	1,402,493	10.4	Ark.	2,350,725	2.8	417,643	2.7
Mich.	9,295,297	0.4	1,645,346	11.4	W.Va.	1,793,477	-8.0	74,581	-13.3
N.J.	7,730,188	5.0	2,011,222	30.7	Utah	1,722,850	17.9	151,596	37.1
N.C.	6,628,637	12.7	1,657,510	14.1	Neb.	1,578,385	0.5	118,290	25.2
Ga.	6,478,216	18.6	1,934,791	24.9	N.M.	1,515,069	16.3	750,905	21.7
Va.	6,187,358	15.7	1,485,708	27.3	Me.	1,227,928	9.2	24,571	30.7
Mass.	6,016,425	4.9	736,133	66.2	Nev.	1,201,833	50.1	255,476	90.5
Ind.	5,544,159	1.0	578,917	7.9	N.H.	1,109,252	20.5	29,768	97.1
Mo.	5,117,073	4.1	668,608	10.5	Ha.	1,108,229	14.9	760,585	14.4
Wis.	4,891,769	4.0	427,092	42.3	Id.	1,006,749	6.7	78,088	35.2
Tenn.	4,877,185	6.2	849,554	9.2	R.I.	1,003,464	5.9	107,355	71.8
Wash.	4,866,692	17.8	645,070	58.8	Mont.	799,065	1.6	65,187	24.7
Md.	4,781,468	13.4	1,455,359	32.2	S.D.	696,004	0.8	61,216	14.9
Minn.	4,375,099	7.3	273,833	71.7	Del.	666,168	12.1	138,076	24.2
La.	4,219,973	0.3	1,443,951	5.8	N.D.	638,800	-2.1	37,208	26.1
Ala.	4,040,587	3.8	1,080,420	4.1	D. of C.	606,900	-4.9	440,769	-7.0
Ky.	3,685,296	0.7	307,274	1.7	Vt.	562,758	10.0	10,574	39.4
Ariz.	3,665,228	34.8	1,039,043	50.2	Alas.	550,043	36.9	143,321	47.4
S.C.	3,486,703	11.7	1,096,647	10.8	Wyo.	453,588	-3.4	40,877	8.7

*Note: "Minority" includes blacks, Asians, other races, and Hispanics.

Density of Population by States

(Per square mile, land area only)

State	1920	1960	1980	1990	State	1920	1960	1980	1990	State	1920	1960	1980	1990
Ala.	45.8	64.2	76.6	79.6	La.	39.6	72.2	94.5	96.9	Oh.	141.4	236.6	263.3	264.9
Alas.*	0.1	0.4	0.7	1.0	Me.	25.7	31.3	36.3	39.8	Okla.	29.2	33.8	44.1	45.8
Ariz.	2.9	11.5	23.9	32.3	Md.	145.8	313.5	428.7	489.2	Ore.	8.2	18.4	27.4	29.6
Ark.	33.4	34.2	43.9	45.1	Mass.	479.2	657.3	733.3	767.6	Pa.	194.5	251.4	264.3	265.1
Cal.	22.0	100.4	151.4	190.8	Mich.	63.8	137.7	162.6	163.6	R.I.	566.4	819.3	897.8	960.3
Col.	9.1	16.9	27.9	31.8	Minn.	29.5	43.1	51.2	55.0	S.C.	55.2	78.7	103.4	115.8
Conn.	286.4	520.6	637.8	678.4	Miss.	38.6	46.0	53.4	54.9	S.D.	8.3	9.0	9.1	9.2
Del.	113.5	225.2	307.6	340.8	Mo.	49.5	62.6	71.3	74.3	Tenn.	56.1	86.2	111.6	118.3
D.C.	7,292.9	12,523.9	10,132.3	9,882.8	Mon.	3.8	4.6	5.4	5.5	Tex.	17.8	36.4	54.3	64.9
Fla.	17.7	91.5	180.0	239.6	Neb.	16.9	18.4	20.5	20.5	Ut.	5.5	10.8	17.8	21.0
Ga.	49.3	67.8	94.1	111.9	Nev.	.7	2.6	7.3	10.9	Vt.	38.6	42.0	55.2	60.8
Ha.*	39.9	98.5	150.1	172.5	N.H.	49.1	67.2	102.4	123.7	Va.	57.4	99.6	134.7	156.3
Ida.	5.2	8.1	11.5	12.2	N.J.	420.0	805.5	986.2	1,042.0	Wash.	20.3	42.8	62.1	73.1
Ill.	115.7	180.4	205.3	205.6	N.M.	2.9	7.8	10.7	12.5	W.Va.	60.9	77.2	80.8	74.5
Ind.	81.3	128.8	152.8	154.6	N.Y.	217.9	350.6	370.6	381.0	Wis.	47.6	72.6	86.5	90.1
Ia.	43.2	49.2	52.1	49.7	N.C.	52.5	93.2	120.4	136.1	Wy.	2.0	3.4	4.9	4.7
Kan.	21.6	26.6	28.9	30.3	N.D.	9.2	9.1	9.4	9.3					
Ky.	60.1	76.2	92.3	92.8						U.S.	*29.9	50.6	64.0	70.3

*For purposes of comparison, Alaska and Hawaii included in above tabulation for 1920, even though not states then.

The 50 Fastest-Growing Metropolitan Areas

Source: Bureau of the Census. U.S. Dept. of Commerce 1990 Census

	1990 population	Percent-change 1980-1990		1990 population	Percent-change 1980-1990		1990 population	Percent-change 1980-1990
1. Naples, FL . . .	152,099	76.9	18. Sarasota, FL . .	277,776	37.3	36. Olympia, WA . .	161,238	29.8
2. Riverside-San			19. Fort			37. Fresno, CA . . .	667,490	29.7
Bernardino, CA			Worth-Arlington,-			38. Santo		
. . . .	2,588,793	66.1	TX	1,332,053	36.9	Rosa-Petaluma,-		
3. Fort Pierce, FL .	251,071	66.1	20. McAllen-Edinburg			CA	388,222	29.6
4. Fort Myers-Cape			Mission, TX . .	383,545	35.4	39. Midland, TX . . .	106,611	29.0
Coral, FL . . .	335,113	63.3	21. Vallejo-Fairfield-Na-			40. Bremerton, WA .	189,731	28.9
5. Las Vegas, NV .	741,459	60.1	pa, CA	451,186	34.9	41. Colorado		
6. Ocala, FL	194,833	59.1	22. Bakersfield, CA .	543,477	34.8	Springs, CO . .	397,014	28.3
7. Orlando, FL . . .	1,072,748	53.3	23. Sacramento, CA	1,481,102	34.7	42. Tampa-St.		
8. West Palm			24. Laredo, TX . . .	133,239	34.2	Petersburg-Clear-		
Beach-Boca			25. San Diego, CA .	2,498,016	34.2	water, FL . .	2,067,959	28.2
Raton-Delray			26. Jacksonville, FL	149,838	32.9	43. Redding, CA . . .	147,036	27.2
Beach,FL . . .	863,518	49.7	27. Merced, CA . . .	178,403	32.6	44. Portsmouth-Dover-		
9. Melbourne-			28. Atlanta, GA . . .	2,833,511	32.5	-Rochester,		
Titusville-Palm			29. Reno, NV	254,667	31.5	NH[1]	350,078	27.0
Bay, FL . . .	398,978	46.2	30. Raleigh-Durham,			45. Visalia-Tulare-Port-		
10. Austin, TX	781,572	45.6	NC	735,480	31.2	erville, CA . .	311,921	26.9
11. Daytona Beach,			31. Fort Walton			46. Chico, CA	182,120	26.6
FL	370,712	43.3	Beach, FL . .	143,776	30.8	47. Oxnard-Ventura,		
12. Bradenton, FL .	211,707	42.6	32. Dallas, TX	2,553,362	30.4	CA	669,016	26.4
13. Las Cruces, NM	135,510	40.7	33. Bryan-College			48. Lakeland-Winter		
14. Phoenix, AZ . .	2,122,101	40.6	Station, TX . .	121,862	30.2	Haven, FL . .	405,382	26.0
15. Yuma, AZ	106,895	40.3	34. Panama City, FL	126,994	29.9	49. Santa Fe, NM . .	117,043	25.7
16. Modesto, CA . .	370,522	39.3	35. Anchorage, AK .	226.338	29.8	50. Jacksonville, FL	906,727	25.5
17. Stockton, CA . .	480,628	38.4						

(1) New England County Metropolitan Area (NECMA)

Metropolitan Statistical Areas: 1980–1990

Source: Bureau of the Census. U.S. Dept. of Commerce
(MSAs over 400,000 listed by 1990 population)

Metropolitan areas are defined for federal statistical use by the Office of Management and Budget, with technical assistance from the Census Bureau. Most individual metropolitan areas are designated as "metropolitan statistical areas" (MSAs). Metropolitan areas over one million may under specified circumstances be subdivided into component "primary metropolitan statistical areas"

(PMSAs), in which case the area as a whole is designated a "consolidated metropolitan statistical area" (CMSA). The 1980 and 1990 data refer to the areas as defined effective June 30, 1990. After detailed results of the census become available, OMB expects to issue revised definitions of all metropolitan areas by June 30, 1992.

MSA	1990 census	1980 census	Percent Change 1980 to 1990
New York-Northern New Jersey-Long Island, NY-NJ-CT CMSA	18,087,251	17,539,532	3.1
Los Angeles-Anaheim-Riverside, CA CMSA	14,531,529	11,497,549	26.4
Chicago-Gary-Lake County, IL-IN-WI CMSA	8,065,633	7,937,290	1.6
San Francisco-Oakland-San Jose, CA CMSA	6,253,311	5,367,900	16.5
Philadelphia-Wilmington-Trenton, PA-NJ-DE-MD CMSA	5,899,345	5,680,509	3.9
Detroit-Ann Arbor, MI CMSA.	4,665,236	4,752,764	−1.8
Boston-Lawrence-Salem, MA-NH CMSA	4,171,643	3,971,792	5.0
Washington, D.C.-MD-VA . .	3,923,574	3,250,921	20.7
Dallas-Fort Worth, TX CMSA	3,885,415	2,930,568	32.6
Houston-Galveston-Brazoria, TX CMSA	3,711,043	3,099,942	19.7
Miami-Fort Lauderdale, FL CMSA	3,192,582	2,643,766	20.8
Atlanta, GA.	2,833,511	2,138,136	32.5
Cleveland-Akron-Lorain, OH CMSA	2,759,823	2,834,062	−2.6
Seattle-Tacoma, WA CMSA.	2,559,164	2,093,285	22.3
San Diego, CA.	2,498,016	1,861,846	34.2
Minneapolis-St. Paul, MN-WI.	2,464,124	2,137,133	15.3
St. Louis, MO-IL.	2,444,099	2,376,968	2.8
Baltimore, MD	2,382,172	2,199,497	8.3
Pittsburgh-Beaver Valley, PA CMSA	2,242,798	2,423,311	−7.4
Phoenix, AZ	2,122,101	1,509,175	40.6
Tampa-St. Petersburg-Clearwater, FL	2,067,959	1,613,600	28.2
Denver-Boulder, CO CMSA .	1,848,319	1,618,461	14.2
Cincinnati-Hamilton, OH-KY-IN CMSA	1,744,124	1,660,257	5.1

MSA	1990 census	1980 census	Percent Change 1980 to 1990
Milwaukee-Racine, WI CMSA	1,607,183	1,570,152	2.4
Kansas City, MO-KS	1,566,280	1,433,464	9.3
Sacramento, CA.	1,481,102	1,099,814	34.7
Portland-Vancouver, OR-WA CMSA	1,477,895	1,297,977	13.9
Norfolk-Virginia Beach-Newport News, VA	1,396,107	1,160,311	20.3
Columbus, OH.	1,377,419	1,243,827	10.7
San Antonio, TX.	1,302,099	1,072,125	21.5
Indianapolis, IN	1,249,822	1,166,575	7.1
New Orleans, LA	1,238,816	1,256,668	−1.4
Buffalo-Niagara Falls, NY CMSA	1,189,288	1,242,826	−4.3
Charlotte-Gastonia-Rock Hill, NC-SC.	1,162,093	971,447	19.6
Providence-Pawtucket-Fall River, RI-MA CMSA	1,141,510	1,083,139	5.4
Hartford-New Britain-Middletown, CT CMSA	1,085,837	1,013,508	7.1
Orlando, FL	1,072,748	699,904	53.3
Salt Lake City-Ogden, UT . .	1,072,227	910,222	17.8
Rochester, NY	1,002,410	971,230	3.2
Nashville, TN.	985,026	850,505	15.8
Memphis, TN-AR-MS	981,747	913,472	7.5
Oklahoma City, OK	958,839	860,969	11.4
Louisville, KY-IN	952,662	956,426	−0.4
Dayton-Springfield, OH	951,270	942,083	1.0
Greensboro-Winston-Salem-High Point, NC	942,091	851,444	10.6
Birmingham, AL	907,810	883,993	2.7
Jacksonville, FL	906,727	722,252	25.5
Albany-Schenectady-Troy, NY	874,304	835,880	4.6
Richmond-Petersburg, VA . .	865,640	761,311	13.7
West Palm Beach-Boca Raton-Delray Beach, FL. . . .	863,518	576,758	49.7

MSA	Population 1990 census	Population 1980 census	Percent Change 1980 to 1990	MSA	Population 1990 census	Population 1980 census	Percent Change 1980 to 1990
Honolulu, HI	836,231	762,565	9.7	Springfield, MA	529,519	515,259	2.8
Austin, TX	781,572	536,688	45.6	Baton Rouge, LA	528,264	494,151	6.9
Las Vegas, NV.	741,459	463,087	60.1	Little Rock-North Little Rock,			
Raleigh-Durham, NC	735,480	560,774	31.2	AK	513,117	474,463	8.1
Scranton-Wilkes-Barre, PA. .	734,175	728,796	0.7	Charleston, SC	506,875	430,346	17.8
Tulsa, OK	708,954	657,173	7.9	Youngstown-Warren, OH. . .	492,619	531,350	−7.3
Grand Rapids, MI	688,399	601,680	14.4	Wichita, KS.	485,270	442,401	9.7
Allentown-Bethlehem-Easton,				Stockton, CA.	480,628	347,342	38.4
PA-NJ	686,688	635,481	8.1	Albuquerque, NM	480,577	420,261	14.4
Fresno, CA.	667,490	514,621	29.7	Mobile, AL	476,923	443,536	7.5
Tucson, AZ.	666,880	531,443	25.5	Columbia, SC	453,331	409,953	10.6
Syracuse, NY	659,864	642,971	2.6	Worcester, MA	436,905	402,918	8.4
Greenville-Spartanburg, SC .	640,861	570,210	12.4	Johnson City-Kingsport-Bris-			
Omaha, NE-IA	618,262	585,122	5.7	tol, TN-VA	436,047	433,638	0.6
Toledo, OH	614,128	616,864	−0.4	Chattanooga, TN-GA	433,210	426,443	1.6
Knoxville, TN.	604,816	565,970	6.9	Lansing-East Lansing, MI. . .	432,674	419,750	3.1
El Paso, TX	591,610	479,899	23.3	Flint, MI.	430,459	450,449	−4.4
Harrisburg-Lebanon-Carlisle,				Lancaster, PA	422,822	362,346	16.7
PA	587,986	556,242	5.7	York, PA	417,848	381,255	9.6
Bakersfield, CA	543,477	403,089	34.8	Lakeland-Winter Haven, FL .	405,382	321,652	26.0
New Haven-Meriden, CT . . .	530,180	500,462	5.9				

Final 1990 census figures show that the nation has 39 metropolitan areas of at least 1 million population, including 4 that have reached that size since 1980. **The 39 areas have 124.8 million people, or 50.2 percent of the U.S. population.** The 1950 census showed only 14 metropolitan areas of 1 million people, and their combined population of about 45 million amounted to less than 30 percent of the national total.

The census shows that the U.S. population living in all metropolitan areas totals 192,725,741, an increase of just over 20 million (11.6 percent) since 1980. The same areas grew 10.6 percent in the 1970s. The population living outside metropolitan areas totals 55,984,132, an increase of 2.1 million (3.9 percent). **The metropolitan population in 1990 constitutes 77.5 percent of the U.S. total** compared with 76.2 percent in 1980. Ninety percent of the nation's growth in the 1980s took place in metropolitan areas.

Fastest Growing Cities, 1980-1990

Source: Bureau of the Census, U.S. Dept. of Commerce, 1990 Census

Cities of more than 100,000 in 1990 that had the largest percentage increases in population from 1980.

	City	Suburb of . . .	1990	1980	Change
1.	Moreno Valley, Calif.	Riverside	118,779	28,309	319.6%
2.	Mesa, Ariz.	Phoenix	288,091	152,404	89.0
3.	Rancho Cucamonga, Calif.	Los Angeles	101,409	55,250	83.5
4.	Plano, Tex.	Dallas	128,713	72,331	77.9
5.	Irvine, Calif.	Los Angeles	110,330	62,134	77.6
6.	Escondido, Calif.	San Diego	108,635	64,355	68.8
7.	Oceanside, Calif.	Los Angeles	128,398	76,698	67.4
8.	Santa Clarita, Calif.	Los Angeles	110,642	66,730	65.8
9.	Bakersfield, Calif.		174,820	105,611	65.5
10.	Arlington, Tex.	Dallas	261,721	160,113	63.5
11.	Fresno, Calif.	—	354,202	217,491	62.9
12.	Chula Vista, Calif.	San Diego	135,163	83,927	61.0
13.	Las Vegas, Nev.	—	258,295	164,674	56.9
14.	Modesto, Calif.	—	164,730	106,963	54.0
15.	Tallahassee, Fla.	—	124,773	81,548	53.0
16.	Glendale, Ariz.	Phoenix	148,134	97,172	52.4
17.	Mesquite, Tex.	Dallas	101,484	67,053	51.3
18.	Ontario, Calif.	Los Angeles	133,179	88,820	49.9
19.	Virginia Beach, Va.	Norfolk	393,069	262,199	49.9
20.	Scottsdale, Ariz.	Phoenix	130,069	88,622	46.5
21.	Santa Ana, Calif.	Los Angeles	293,742	204,023	44.0
22.	Stockton, Calif.	—	210,943	148,283	42.3
23.	Pomona, Calif.	Los Angeles	131,723	92,742	42.0
24.	Irving, Tex.	Dallas	155,037	109,943	41.0
25.	Aurora, Colo.	Denver	222,103	158,588	40.1
26.	Raleigh, N.C.	—	207,951	150,255	38.4
27.	San Bernardino, Calif.	—	164,164	118,794	38.2
28.	Santa Rosa, Calif.	San Francisco	113,313	82,658	37.1
29.	Overland Park, Kan.	Kansas City	111,790	81,784	36.7
30.	Vallejo, Calif.	San Francisco	109,199	80,303	36.0
31.	Thousand Oaks, Calif.	Los Angeles	104,352	77,072	35.4
32.	Salinas, Calif.	—	108,777	80,479	35.2
33.	Durham, N.C.	—	136,611	101,149	35.1
34.	Austin, Tex.	—	465,622	345,890	34.6
35.	Laredo, Tex.	—	122,899	91,449	34.4
36.	Sacramento, Calif.	—	369,365	275,741	34.0
37.	El Monte, Calif.	Los Angeles	106,209	79,494	33.6
38.	Reno, Nev.	—	133,850	100,756	32.8
39.	Riverside, Calif.	—	226,505	170,591	32.8
40.	Chesapeake, Va.	Norfolk	151,967	114,486	32.7
41.	Tempe, Ariz.	Phoenix	141,865	106,919	32.7
42.	Oxnard, Calif.	Los Angeles	142,216	108,195	31.4
43.	Fremont, Calif.	San Jose/Oakland	173,339	131,945	31.4
44.	Colorado Springs, Colo.	—	281,140	215,105	30.7
45.	Garland, Tex.	Dallas	180,650	138,857	30.1

Population of U.S. Cities

Source: U.S. Bureau of the Census (100 most populated cities ranked by April, 1990 census)

Rank	City	1990	1980	1970	1960	1950	1900	1850
1	New York, NY	7,322,564	7,071,639	7,895,563	7,781,984	7,891,957	3,437,202	696,115
2	Los Angeles, Ca.	3,485,398	2,966,850	2,811,801	2,479,015	1,970,358	102,479	1,610
3	Chicago, Ill.	2,783,726	3,005,072	3,369,357	3,550,404	3,620,962	1,698,575	29,963
4	Houston, Tx	1,630,553	1,595,138	1,233,535	938,219	596,163	44,633	2,396
5	Philadelphia, Pa	1,585,577	1,688,210	1,949,996	2,002,512	2,071,605	1,293,697	121,376
6	San Diego, Ca.	1,110,549	875,538	697,471	573,224	334,387	17,700	...
7	Detroit, Mi	1,027,974	1,203,339	1,514,063	1,670,144	1,849,568	285,704	21,019
8	Dallas, Tx	1,006,877	904,078	844,401	679,684	434,462	42,638	...
9	Phoenix, Az	983,403	789,704	584,303	439,170	106,818	5,544	...
10	San Antonio, Tx	935,933	785,880	654,153	587,718	408,442	53,321	3,488
11	San Jose, Ca	782,248	629,442	459,913	204,196	95,280	21,500	...
12	Indianapolis, In	741,952	700,807	736,856	476,258	427,173	169,164	8,091
13	Baltimore, Md	736,014	786,775	905,787	939,024	949,708	508,957	169,054
14	San Francisco, Ca.	723,959	678,974	715,674	740,316	775,357	342,782	34,776
15	Jacksonville, Fl	672,971	540,920	504,265	201,030	204,517	28,429	1,045
16	Columbus, Oh.	632,910	564,871	540,025	471,316	375,901	125,560	17,882
17	Milwaukee, Wi	628,088	636,212	717,372	741,324	637,392	285,315	20,061
18	Memphis, Tn	610,337	646,356	623,988	497,524	396,000	102,320	8,841
19	Washington, DC	606,900	638,333	756,668	763,956	802,178	278,718	40,001
20	Boston, Ma.	574,283	562,994	641,071	697,197	801,444	560,892	136,881
21	Seattle, Wa	516,259	493,846	530,831	557,087	467,591	80,671	...
22	El Paso, Tx.	515,342	425,259	322,261	276,687	130,485	15,906	...
23	Nashville-Davidson, Tn	510,784	455,651	426,029	170,874	174,307	80,865	10,165
24	Cleveland, Oh	505,616	573,822	750,879	876,050	914,808	381,768	17,034
25	New Orleans, La	496,938	557,515	593,471	627,525	570,445	287,104	116,375
26	Denver, Co.	467,610	492,365	514,678	493,887	415,786	133,859	...
27	Austin, Tx.	465,622	345,496	253,539	186,545	132,459	22,258	629
28	Fort Worth, Tx	447,619	385,164	393,455	356,268	278,778	26,688	...
29	Oklahoma City, Ok	444,719	403,213	368,164	324,253	243,504	10,037	...
30	Portland, Or	437,319	366,383	379,967	372,676	373,628	90,426	...
31	Kansas City, Mo.	435,146	448,159	507,330	475,539	456,622	163,752	...
32	Long Beach, Ca.	429,433	361,334	358,879	344,168	250,767	2,252	...
33	Tucson, Az.	405,390	330,537	262,933	212,892	45,454	7,531	...
34	St. Louis, Mo.	396,685	453,085	622,236	750,026	856,796	575,238	77,860
35	Charlotte, NC	395,934	314,447	241,420	201,564	134,042	18,091	1,065
36	Atlanta, Ga.	394,017	425,022	495,039	487,455	331,314	89,872	2,572
37	Virginia Beach, Va.	393,069	262,199	172,106	8,091	5,390	...	...
38	Albuquerque, NM	384,736	331,767	244,501	201,189	96,815	6,238	...
39	Oakland, Ca.	372,242	339,337	361,561	367,548	384,575	66,960	...
40	Pittsburgh, Pa	369,879	423,938	520,089	604,332	676,806	321,616	46,601
41	Sacramento, Ca.	369,365	275,741	257,105	191,667	137,572	29,282	6,820
42	Minneapolis, Mn	368,383	370,951	434,400	482,872	521,718	202,718	...
43	Tulsa, Ok.	367,302	360,919	330,350	261,685	182,740	1,390	...
44	Honolulu, CDP, Hi.	365,272	762,874	630,528	294,194	248,034	39,306	...
45	Cincinnati, Oh.	364,040	385,457	453,514	502,550	503,998	325,902	115,435
46	Miami, Fla.	358,548	346,865	334,859	291,688	249,276	1,681	...
47	Fresno, Ca.	354,202	218,202	165,655	133,929	91,669	12,470	...
48	Omaha, Ne.	335,795	314,255	346,929	301,598	251,117	102,555	...
49	Toledo, Oh.	332,943	354,635	383,062	318,003	303,616	131,822	3,829
50	Buffalo, NY.	328,123	357,870	462,768	532,759	580,132	352,387	42,261
51	Wichita, Ks.	304,011	279,272	276,554	254,698	168,279	24,671	...
52	Santa Ana, Ca.	293,742	203,713	155,710	100,350	45,533	4,933	...
53	Mesa, Az.	288,091	152,453	63,049	33,772	16,790	722	...
54	Colorado Springs, Co.	281,140	215,150	135,517	70,194	45,472	21,085	...
55	Tampa, Fl	280,015	271,523	277,714	274,970	124,681	15,839	...
56	Newark, NJ	275,221	329,248	381,930	405,220	438,776	246,070	38,894
57	St. Paul, Mn	272,235	270,230	309,866	313,411	311,349	163,065	1,112
58	Louisville, Ky.	269,063	298,451	361,706	390,639	369,129	204,731	43,194
59	Anaheim, Ca.	266,406	219,311	166,408	104,184	14,556	1,456	...
60	Birmingham, Al	265,968	284,413	300,910	340,887	326,037	38,415	...
61	Arlington, Tx	261,721	160,113	90,229	44,775	7,692	1,079	...
62	Norfolk, Va.	261,229	266,979	307,951	304,869	213,513	46,624	14,326
63	Las Vegas, Nv	258,295	164,674	125,787	64,405	24,624	...	...
64	Corpus Christi, Tx.	257,453	231,999	204,525	167,690	108,287	4,703	...
65	St. Petersburg, Fl	238,629	238,647	216,159	181,298	96,738	1,575	...
66	Rochester, NY.	231,636	241,741	295,011	318,611	332,488	162,608	36,403
67	Jersey City, NJ	228,537	223,532	260,350	276,101	299,017	206,433	6,856
68	Riverside, Ca	226,505	170,876	140,089	84,332	46,764	7,973	...
69	Anchorage, Ak.	226,338	174,431	48,081	44,237	11,254	...	...
70	Lexington-Fayette, Ky.	225,366	204,165	108,137	62,810	55,534	26,369	8,159
71	Akron, Oh.	223,019	237,177	275,425	290,351	274,605	42,728	3,266
72	Aurora, Co.	222,103	158,588	74,974	48,548	11,421	202	...
73	Baton Rouge, La	219,531	346,029	165,921	152,419	125,629	11,269	3,905
74	Stockton, Ca.	210,943	149,779	109,963	86,321	70,853	17,506	...
75	Raleigh, NC	207,951	150,255	122,830	93,931	65,679	13,643	4,518
76	Richmond, Va	203,056	219,214	249,332	219,958	230,310	85,050	27,570
77	Shreveport, La.	198,525	205,820	182,064	164,372	127,206	16,013	1,728
78	Jackson, Ms.	196,637	202,895	153,968	144,422	98,271	7,816	1,861
79	Mobile, Al.	196,278	200,452	190,026	194,856	129,009	38,469	20,515
80	Des Moines, Ia.	193,187	191,003	201,404	208,982	177,965	62,139	...
81	Lincoln, Ne.	191,972	171,932	149,518	128,521	98,884	40,169	...
82	Madison, Wi	191,262	170,616	171,809	126,706	96,056	19,164	1,525
83	Grand Rapids, Mi	189,126	181,843	197,649	177,313	176,515	87,565	2,686
84	Yonkers, NY	188,082	195,351	204,297	190,634	152,798	47,931	...

Rank	City	1990	1980	1970	1960	1950	1900	1850
85	Hialeah, Fl	188,004	145,254	102,452	66,972	19,676	...	...
86	Montgomery, Al	187,106	177,857	133,386	134,393	106,525	30,346	8,728
87	Lubbock, Tx	186,206	173,979	149,101	126,691	71,747	...	...
88	Greensboro, NC	183,521	170,279	144,076	119,574	74,389	10,035	...
89	Dayton, Oh	182,044	203,371	243,023	262,332	243,872	85,333	10,977
90	Huntington Beach, Ca	181,519	170,505	115,960	11,492	5,237	...	...
91	Garland, Tx	180,650	138,857	81,437	38,501	10,571	819	...
92	Glendale, Ca.	180,038	139,060	133,000	119,000	96,000	...	...
93	Columbus, Ga	179,278	169,441	155,028	116,779	79,611	17,614	9,621
94	Spokane, Wa	177,196	171,300	170,516	181,608	161,721	36,848	...
95	Tacoma, Wa	176,664	158,501	154,407	147,979	143,673	37,714	...
96	Little Rock, Ar	175,795	158,461	132,483	107,813	102,213	38,307	2,167
97	Bakersfield, Cal	174,820	105,611	...	56,848	...	...	...
98	Fremont, Ca	173,339	131,945	100,869	43,790	...	...	...
99	Fort Wayne, In.	173,072	172,196	178,269	161,776	133,607	45,115	4,282
100	Newport News, Va	170,045	144,903	138,000	114,000	42,000	...	...

Cities with Largest Percentage Loss in Population, 1980-1990

Source: Bureau of the Census. U.S. Dept. of Commerce, 1990 Census

City	1990	1980	Change	City	1990	1980	Change
1. Gary, Ind.	116,646	151,968	−23.2%	16. Birmingham, Ala.	265,968	288,297	−7.7
2. Newark	275,221	329,248	−16.4	17. Richmond	203,056	219,214	−7.4
3. Detroit	1,027,974	1,203,369	−14.6	18. Chicago	2,783,726	3,005,072	−7.4
4. Pittsburgh	369,879	423,960	−12.8	19. Atlanta	394,017	425,022	−7.3
5. St. Louis	396,685	452,804	−12.4	20. Kansas City, Kan.	149,767	161,148	−7.1
6. Cleveland	505,616	573,822	−11.9	21. Baltimore	736,014	786,741	−6.4
7. Flint, Mich.	140,761	159,611	−11.8	22. Akron, Ohio	223,019	237,590	−6.1
8. New Orleans	496,938	557,927	−10.9	23. Toledo, Ohio	332,943	354,635	−6.1
9. Warren, Mich.	144,864	161,134	−10.1	24. Philadelphia	1,585,577	1,688,210	−6.1
10. Chattanooga, Tenn.	152,466	169,514	−10.1	25. Dayton, Ohio	182,044	193,549	−5.9
11. Louisville, Ky.	269,063	298,694	−9.9	26. Knoxville, Tenn.	165,121	175,045	−5.7
12. Peoria, Ill.	113,504	124,813	−9.1	27. Memphis	610,337	646,170	−5.5
13. Macon, Ga.	106,612	116,896	−8.8	28. Cincinnati	364,040	385,410	−5.5
14. Erie, Pa.	108,718	119,123	−8.7	29. Denver	467,610	492,694	−5.1
15. Buffalo	328,123	357,870	−8.3	30. District of Columbia	606,900	638,432	−4.9

The 50 Most Racially Diverse Counties in the U.S.

Source: Bureau of the Census. U.S. Dept. of Commerce

(Rank of counties where proportions of non-Hispanic whites, non-Hispanic blacks, Hispanics, and non-Hispanic other races are nearest to being equal; 1990 Census)

Fourteen of the 50 most diverse counties have populations of 1 million or more, and 33 are in metropolitan areas. Four of New York City's five boroughs, as well as the counties that contain San Francisco, Los Angeles, Chicago, Houston, San Diego, Miami, Dallas, Philadelphia, San Jose, San Bernardino, and Oakland are on the list.

Of the 60 counties with populations more than 99.5 percent non-Hispanic white in 1990, 12 are in Nebraska, 12 are in North Dakota, 7 are in Kentucky, and 6 are in South Dakota.

Rank/County	State	Rank/County	State	Rank/County	State
1. Queens	New York	18. Fresno	California	35. Socorro	New Mexico
2. San Francisco .	California	19. San Joaquin. . .	California	36. Aleutians West	Alaska
3. Los Angeles. . .	California	20. Santa Clara. . .	California	Census Area .	
4. Kings.	New York	21. San Mateo . . .	California	37. Passaic	New Jersey
5. Alameda.	California	22. Cook.	Illinois	38. Pinal	Arizona
6. New York	New York	23. Merced	California	39. Alexandria (city)	Virginia
7. Bronx	New York	24. Hoke.	North Carolina	40. Waller	Texas
8. Hudson	New Jersey	25. Chattahoochee .	Georgia	41. Caldwell.	Texas
9. Fort Bend	Texas	26. Kings.	California	42. San Diego	California
10. Cibola	New Mexico	27. Dallas	Texas	43. Liberty	Georgia
11. Harris	Texas	28. Suffolk.	Massachusetts	44. Prince George's	Maryland
12. Robeson.	North Carolina	29. Hendry.	Florida	45. Wharton	Texas
13. Solano	California	30. Matagorda. . . .	Texas	46. Philadelphia . . .	Pennsylvania
14. Essex	New Jersey	31. Graham	Arizona	47. Bell.	Texas
15. Dade	Florida	32. Denver.	Colorado	48. Otero	New Mexico
16. Sandoval	New Mexico	33. San Juan	New Mexico	49. Union.	New Jersey
17. Monterey	California	34. San Bernardino .	California	50. Coconino	Arizona

1990 Population of U.S. Counties, Under Age 18

Source: Bureau of the Census. U.S. Dept. of Commerce

(Counties with the **highest** share of residents under age 18, among counties of 10,000 or more; 1990 census)

The national average for counties' population under age 18 is 26 percent. Thirty-one percent of the nation's 64 million children are members of minorities, who, on average, have more children than do non-Hispanic whites. However, Utah, with only 8.8 percent minority population, has 11 of the 25 counties with the highest share of children. Sixty-nine percent of Utah residents belong to the Church of Jesus Christ of Latter Day Saints, and the birthrate for Mormon women was 2.5 births per woman in 1987, compared with 1.9 nationwide.

(continued)

Rank/County, State	Percent under 18	Rank/County, State	Percent under 18	Rank/County, State	Percent under 18
1. San Juan, Ut.	43.3	18. Rolette, N.D.	38.2	35. Washington, Ut.	36.2
2. Emery, Ut.	43.0	19. Lincoln, Wy.	38.1	36. Tooele, Ut.	36.2
3. Duchesne, Ut.	43.0	20. Sanpete, Ut.	38.0	37. Holmes, Oh.	35.8
4. Millard, Ut.	42.9	21. Maverick, Tex.	38.0	38. Humphreys, Miss.	35.8
5. Apache, Az.	41.7	22. Freemont, Ida.	37.9	39. Zavala, Tex.	35.7
6. Uintah, Ut.	41.4	23. Utah, Ut.	37.7	40. Campbell, Wy.	35.7
7. Box Elder, Ut.	40.6	24. Glacier, Mont.	37.1	41. Iron, Ut.	35.5
8. Jefferson, Id.	40.4	25. Webb, Tex.	36.7	42. Deaf Smith, Tex.	35.3
9. Davis, Ut.	40.2	26. Big Horn, Mont.	36.7	43. Matanuska-Susitna	35.3
10. Uinta, Wy.	39.8	27. Hidalgo, Tex.	36.6	Borough, Alas.	
11. Wasatch, Ut.	39.5	28. Cassia, Ida.	36.6	44. Cameron, Tex.	35.3
12. Starr, Tex.	39.4	29. Willacy, Tex.	36.6	45. Roosevelt, Mont.	35.2
13. Sevier, Ut.	39.3	30. Cache, Ut.	36.5	46. Bonneville, Ida.	35.2
14. Bethel Census Area,	39.0	31. Rosebud, Mont.	36.5	47. Lagrange, Ind.	35.1
Alas.		32. Gaines, Tex.	36.4	48. Minidoka, Ida.	35.1
15. McKinley, N.M.	38.8	33. San Juan, N.M.	36.4	49. Holmes, Miss.	35.0
16. Bingham, Ida.	38.6	34. Dimmit, Tex.	36.3	50. Frio, Tex.	34.8
17. Navajo, Az.	38.4				

(Counties with the **lowest** share of residents under age 18, among counties of 10,000 or more; 1990 Census)

Of the 25 counties with the **lowest** share of children, 3 are adult resort/vacation areas: Williamsburg, Llano, and Pitkin (Aspen); 8 of the counties are popular Florida retirement places, as is Watauga; 4 (New York, San Francisco, Alexandria, and Arlington) are urban areas that contain high concentrations of affluent single residents; and the other 9 are predominantly rural counties dominated by large colleges or universities.

Rank/County, State	Percent under 18	Rank/County, State	Percent under 18	Rank/County, State	Percent under 18
1. Williamsburg (city), Va.	9.2	19. Montgomery, Va.	17.9	36. District of Columbia,	19.3
2. Radford (city), Va.	12.7	20. Charlottesville (city), Va.	18.0	D.C.	
3. Arlington, Va.	15.1	21. Centre, Pa.	18.3	37. Suffolk, Mass.	19.3
4. Alexandria (city), Va.	15.4	22. McDonough, Ill.	18.4	38. Polk, N.C.	19.4
5. Charlotte, Fl.	15.6	23. Monroe, Ind.	18.4	39. Tompkins, N.Y.	19.4
6. Harrisonburg (city), Va.	15.6	24. Hernando, Fl.	18.4	40. Indian River, Fl.	19.4
7. Sarasota, Fl.	15.7	25. Fredericksburg (city),	18.6	41. Baxter, Ark.	19.4
8. San Francisco, Cal.	16.1	Va.		42. Calloway, Ky.	19.5
9. Llano, Tex.	16.4	26. Highlands, Fl.	18.7	43. Lee, Fl.	19.6
10. New York, N.Y.	16.6	27. Amador, Cal.	18.8	44. Palm Beach, Fl.	19.6
11. Pitkin, Col.	16.8	28. Orange, N.C.	18.9	45. Salem (city), Va.	19.7
12. Watauga, N.C.	17.1	29. Jackson, Ill.	19.0	46. Volusia, Fl.	19.7
13. Monroe, Fl.	17.4	30. Walker, Tex.	19.0	47. West Feliciana Parish,	19.7
14. Martin, Fl.	17.6	31. Flagler, Fl.	19.1	La.	
15. Citrus, Fl.	17.6	32. Marin, Cal.	19.1	48. Story, Ia.	19.8
16. Whitman, Wash.	17.8	33. Fairfax (city), Va.	19.2	49. Johnson, Ill.	19.8
17. Pinellas, Fl.	17.8	34. Manatee, Fl.	19.2	50. Macon, N.C.	19.8
18. Pasco, Fl.	17.9	35. Hampshire, Mass.	19.3		

Poverty and Income

Source: Bureau of the Census, U.S. Dept. of Commerce

According to a Census Bureau report based on interviews with 60,000 households in March 1991, there were 2.1 million more Americans living in poverty in 1990 than in the previous year. An estimated 33.6 million people were living in poverty in 1990, making the poverty rate 13.5 percent, up from 12.8 percent in 1989. The poverty rate is intended to reflect the percentage of Americans living below a threshold of minimal need, estimated at $13,359 for a family of four in 1990. In calculating the rate, the bureau counts only cash income and not benefits like subsidized housing, Medicaid, or food stamps.

The 13.5 percent poverty rate is higher than at any time in the 1970s, but is below the recent high of 15 percent in 1983.

The main increase in poverty occurred among white and Hispanic people, and took place in the Northeast. (The rate is not adjusted for regional variations in the cost of living.) The rate rose for both children and the elderly, and increased inside metropolitan areas. The poverty rate for whites rose to 10.7 percent, from 10 percent in 1989; for Hispanics, the percent increased

from 26.1 to 28.1 in 1990. The rate for blacks remained the highest for any group, at 31.9 percent. Regionally, the South had the highest poverty rate at 15.8 percent. The poverty rate for children was 20.6 percent in 1990, up from 19.6 percent in 1989. The rate for the elderly was 12.2 percent, a small increase from 1989, but was significantly lower than the 1967 rate of 29.5 percent. Married couples continued to have the nation's lowest poverty rate: 5.7 percent.

The report also said that the median household income fell 1.7 percent, to $29,943. The main decrease was among white men. In 1990, black married couple families had 84 percent of the income of married whites, an all-time high; women's earnings rose to 71 percent of those of men, also an all-time high. However, the gains were a result of declines in the earnings of white men, not in gains by other groups. Men's earnings fell 3.6 percent, to an average of $27,866 (the third consecutive year of decline). Women's earnings remained unchanged at $19,816. On a per capita basis, real income for all Americans declined for the first time in 8 years, by 2.9 percent, to $14,387.

Poverty by Family Status, Sex, and Race

Source: U.S. Bureau of the Census, Current Population Reports
By thousands

	1989 No.[1]	%[2]	1988 No.[1]	%[2]	1986 No.[1]	%[2]	1978 No.[1]	%[2]
Total poor	31,528	12.8	31,745	13.0	32,370	13.6	24,497	11.4
In families	24,066	11.5	24,048	11.6	24,754	12.0	19,062	10.0
Head	6,784	10.3	6,874	10.4	7,023	10.9	5,280	9.1
Related children	12,001	19.0	11,935	19.0	12,257	19.8	9,722	15.7
Other relatives	5,281	6.6	5,238	6.6	5,475	6.9	4,509	5.7
Unrelated individuals	6,760	19.2	7,070	20.6	6,846	21.6	5,435	22.1
In families with a female householder, no husband present	11,668	35.9	11,972	37.2	11,944	38.3	9,269	35.6
Head	3,504	32.2	3,642	33.4	3,613	34.6	2,654	31.4
Related children	6,808	51.1	6,955	52.9	6,943	54.4	5,687	50.6
Other relatives	1,356	16.3	1,375	16.9	1,388	17.5	928	14.6
Unrelated female individuals	4,221	22.2	4,225	23.1	4,311	25.1	3,611	26.0
All other	12,398	7.0	12,076	6.9	12,811	7.3	9,793	5.9
Head	3,280	5.9	3,232	5.9	3,410	6.3	2,626	5.3
Related children	5,193	10.4	4,980	10.0	5,313	10.8	4,035	7.9
Other relatives	3,925	5.5	3,863	5.4	4,087	5.8	3,131	4.8
Unrelated male individuals	2,539	15.7	2,844	17.7	2,536	17.5	1,824	17.1
Total white poor	20,785	10.0	20,715	10.1	22,183	11.0	16,259	8.7
In families	15,179	8.6	15,001	8.6	16,393	9.4	12,050	7.3
Head	4,409	7.8	4,471	7.9	4,811	8.6	3,523	6.9
Female	1,858	25.4	1,945	26.5	2,041	28.2	1,391	23.5
Related children	7,164	14.1	7,095	14.0	7,714	15.3	5,674	11.0
Other relatives	3,606	5.3	3,435	5.0	3,868	5.7	2,852	4.5
Unrelated individuals	5,063	16.9	5,314	16.9	5,198	19.2	4,209	19.8
Total black poor	9,302	30.7	9,356	31.3	8,983	31.1	7,625	30.6
In families	7,704	29.7	7,650	30.0	7,401	29.7	6,493	29.5
Head	2,077	27.8	2,089	28.2	1,987	28.0	1,622	27.5
Female	1,524	46.5	1,579	49.0	1,488	50.1	1,208	50.6
Related children	4,257	43.2	4,148	42.8	4,039	42.7	3,781	41.2
Other relatives	1,370	15.9	1,413	16.8	1,375	16.5	1,094	15.7
Unrelated individuals	1,471	35.2	1,509	36.8	1,431	38.5	1,132	38.6

(1) Beginning in 1979, total includes members of unrelated subfamilies not shown separately. For earlier years, unrelated subfamily members are included in the "in family" category. (2) Percent of total population in that general category who fell below poverty level. For example, of all black female heads of households in 1978, 50.6% were poor.

Poverty Level by Family Size 1988, 1989

	1988	1989		1988	1989
1 persons	$6,024	$6,310	3 persons	$9,435	$9,885
Under 65 years	6,155	6,451	4 persons	12,092	12,674
65 years and over	5,674	5,947	5 persons	14,304	14,990
2 persons	7,704	8,076	6 persons	16,146	16,921
Householder under 65 years	7,958	8,343	7 persons	18,232	19,162
Householder 65 years and over	7,157	7,501	8 persons	20,253	21,328
			9 persons or more	24,129	25,480

Income Distribution by Population Fifths

Families, 1989 Race	Top income of each fifth					Percent distribution of total income					
	Lowest	Second	Third	Fourth	Top 5%	Lowest fifth	Second fifth	Third fifth	Fourth fifth	Highest fifth	Top 5%
Total	$16,003	$28,000	$40,800	$59,550	$98,963	4.6	10.6	16.5	23.7	44.6	17.9
White	17,938	29,888	42,450	61,039	101,354	5.0	11.0	16.6	23.4	44.0	17.6
Black and other	(NA)	(NA)	(NA)	(NA)	(NA)	(NA)	(NA)	(NA)	(NA)	(NA)	(NA)
Black	7,868	15,500	26,054	41,956	69,545	3.4	8.8	15.4	25.2	47.3	17.1
Region											
Northeast	$18,744	$32,056	$46,825	$67,598	$112,000	4.6	10.7	16.6	23.7	44.4	17.7
Midwest	16,896	28,836	40,512	57,050	92,700	4.9	11.4	17.0	23.8	42.9	17.0
South	13,832	24,680	37,000	54,762	91,230	4.3	10.1	16.2	23.9	45.6	18.2
West	17,364	29,294	42,000	61,698	102,293	4.9	10.7	16.4	23.4	44.6	18.0

Persons Below Poverty Level, 1960-1989

Year	Number Below Poverty Level (mil.)				Percent Below Poverty Level				Average income cutoffs for non-farm family of 4[3] at poverty level
	All races[1]	White	Black	Hispanic origin[2]	All races[1]	White	Black	Spanish origin[2]	
1960	39.9	28.3	NA	NA	22.2	17.8	NA	NA	$3,022
1965	33.2	22.5	NA	NA	17.3	13.3	NA	NA	3,223
1970	25.4	17.5	7.5	NA	12.6	9.9	33.5	NA	3,968
1975	25.9	17.8	7.5	3.0	12.3	9.7	31.3	26.9	5,500
1980[4]	29.3	19.7	8.6	3.5	13.0	10.2	32.5	25.7	8,414
1986[4]	32.4	22.2	9.0	5.1	13.6	11.0	31.1	27.3	11,203
1988	31.7	20.7	9.4	5.4	13.0	10.1	31.3	26.7	12,092
1989	31.5	20.8	9.3	5.4	12.8	10.0	30.7	26.2	12,674

NA = Not Available. (1) Includes other races not shown separately. (2) Persons of Spanish origin may be of any race. (3) Beginning in 1981, income cutoffs for nonfarm families are applied to both farm and nonfarm families. (4) Data based on revised poverty definition.

Poverty Rate

The poverty rate is the proportion of the population whose income falls below the government's official poverty level, which is adjusted each year to take account of inflation.

The national poverty rate was higher in 1986 than in any year from 1969 through 1980. The rate reached a peak of 15.2 percent in 1983.

Aid to Families with Dependent Children

Source: Admin. and Human Services for Children and Families, Office of Family Assistance, U.S. Dept. of Health.

FY 1990 State	Total Assistance Payments[1]	Average Monthly Caseload	Average Monthly Recipients	Average Monthly Children	Average Payment per Family	Average Payment per Person
Alabama	$61,804,672	45,322	129,998	92,631	$113.64	$39.62
Alaska	59,463,336	7,664	20,234	13,191	646.57	244.90
Arizona	139,270,358	43,127	124,040	86,735	269.11	93.57
Arkansas	56,553,341	24,721	71,450	51,082	190.64	65.96
California	4,982,812,565	652,070	1,902,048	1,293,804	636.79	218.31
Colorado	136,318,903	35,363	102,157	68,768	321.24	111.20
Connecticut	296,652,382	43,548	120,086	81,324	567.67	205.86
Delaware	28,866,161	8,274	21,165	14,468	290.73	113.66
District of Col.	84,159,466	18,534	48,872	34,403	378.40	143.50
Florida	423,581,977	134,815	369,907	264,152	261.83	95.43
Georgia	321,443,905	101,849	293,366	205,991	263.01	91.31
Guam	5,047,329	1,172	4,106	2,946	358.88	102.44
Hawaii	98,922,949	14,336	43,917	29,293	575.03	187.71
Idaho	19,481,502	6,139	16,577	11,302	264.45	97.93
Illinois	856,675,407	208,410	635,839	435,516	342.54	112.28
Indiana	170,491,825	53,931	153,709	104,768	263.44	92.43
Iowa	152,443,355	34,698	98,040	63,607	366.12	129.58
Kansas	105,290,301	25,800	77,046	52,373	340.08	113.88
Kentucky	179,372,227	66,383	175,421	117,309	225.17	85.21
Louisiana	188,514,020	93,869	281,501	199,001	167.36	55.81
Maine	100,896,026	19,892	50,009	35,254	422.68	150.12
Maryland	295,757,470	66,918	185,507	124,413	368.31	132.86
Massachusetts	635,204,330	94,816	263,371	167,992	558.28	200.99
Michigan	1,216,485,727	218,137	655,101	426,871	464.73	154.75
Minnesota	351,554,572	56,845	170,575	110,283	515.37	171.75
Mississippi	86,184,982	60,023	178,588	128,690	119.66	40.22
Missouri	232,527,261	70,940	210,772	139,414	273.15	91.93
Montana	39,950,317	9,724	28,963	18,673	342.37	114.95
Nebraska	58,912,265	14,627	42,636	29,218	335.64	115.15
Nevada	27,180,914	8,147	22,594	15,879	278.03	100.25
New Hampshire	32,173,794	6,261	16,329	10,688	428.23	164.20
New Jersey	452,382,770	107,008	309,036	212,827	352.30	121.99
New Mexico	60,365,281	21,315	61,445	42,585	236.00	81.87
New York	2,277,981,698	344,610	981,153	657,765	550.86	193.48
North Carolina	246,538,960	86,464	223,442	151,806	237.61	91.95
North Dakota	24,324,772	5,565	15,534	10,334	364.25	130.49
Ohio	874,486,332	225,868	632,283	414,381	322.64	115.26
Oklahoma	130,189,614	38,810	111,867	76,924	279.54	96.98
Oregon	145,267,648	32,739	89,016	59,892	369.76	135.99
Pennsylvania	797,895,165	177,678	520,683	345,192	374.22	127.70
Puerto Rico	73,161,987	59,264	189,610	129,684	102.88	32.15
Rhode Island	99,333,977	16,657	46,150	30,358	496.96	179.37
South Carolina	95,726,167	38,893	110,931	79,619	205.11	71.91
South Dakota	21,768,921	6,698	18,991	13,340	270.84	95.52
Tennessee	167,069,875	76,483	211,185	143,897	182.03	65.93
Texas	416,551,175	208,897	611,281	427,701	166.17	56.79
Utah	64,104,689	15,522	45,134	30,548	344.16	118.36
Vermont	48,261,772	7,743	21,934	13,661	519.41	183.36
Virgin Islands	2,958,415	884	3,203	2,412	278.89	76.97
Virginia	177,368,980	56,154	150,858	103,972	263.22	97.98
Washington	439,258,601	81,312	228,191	147,587	450.18	160.41
West Virginia	110,564,238	36,888	111,084	68,498	249.77	82.94
Wisconsin	441,739,720	79,360	237,430	158,030	463.86	155.04
Wyoming	19,310,337	5,281	14,135	9,462	304.71	113.84
U.S. Total	**$18,630,604,733**	**3,976,448**	**11,464,500**	**7,760,510**	**$390.44**	**$135.42**

(1) Total assistance payments include AFDC-Basic, AFDC-Unemployed Parent, Title IV-A Payments under JOBS, Home repair, and payments to Indian tribes.

Supplemental Security Income (SSI) Program
Recipients and Payments, 1955-1990

Category		1955, Dec.	1965, Dec.	1970, Dec.	1975, Dec.[1]	1980, Dec.	1985, Dec.	1990, Dec.
Aged:	Recipients	2,538,000	2,087,000	2,082,000	2,307,105	1,807,776	1,504,469	1,454,041
	Total amt.	$127,003,000	$131,674,000	$161,642,000	$209,777,000	$221,303,000	$247,133,000	$309,225,000
	Avg. amt.	$50.05	$63.10	$77.65	$90.93	$128.20	$164.26	$212.66
Blind:	Recipients	104,000	85,100	81,000	74,489	78,401	82,220	83,686
	Total amt.	$5,803,000	$6,922,000	$8,446,000	$10,918,000	$16,381,000	$22,555,000	$28,581,000
	Avg. amt.	$55.55	$81.35	$104.35	$146.57	$213.23	$274.32	$341.52
Disabled:	Recipients	241,000	557,000	935,000	1,932,681	2,255,840	2,551,332	3,279,400
	Total amt.	$11,750,000	$37,035,000	$91,325,000	$272,800,000	$444,322,000	$665,774,000	$1,103,598,000
	Avg. amt.	$48.75	$66.50	$97.65	$141.15	$197.90	$260.95	$336.52

(1) In 1972, Congress replaced the categorical Federal-State programs of Old-Age Assistance, Aid to the Blind, and Aid to the Permanently and Totally Disabled with the Federal Supplemental Security Income (SSI) program effective Jan. 1974. The SSI program is administered by the Social Security Admin.

Immigration by Country of Last Residence 1820-1990

Source: U.S. Immigration and Naturalization Service

(thousands)

Country	Total 1820-1990	Total 1961-1970	Total 1971-1980	Total 1981-1990	1985	1988[10]	1989[11]	1990	Percent 1820-1990	Percent 1961-1970	Percent 1971-1980	Percent 1981-1990
All countries*	56,994	3,321.7	4,493.3	7,338.0	570.0	643.0	1,090.9	1,536.5	100.0	100.0	100.0	100.0
Europe	37,101	1,123.5	800.4	761.5	69.5	71.8	94.3	124.0	65.1	33.8	17.8	10.4
Austria[1]	4,343	20.6	9.5	18.9	1.9	2.5	2.8	3.8	7.8	.6	0.2	0.3
Hungary	211	5.4	6.6	5.9	0.6	0.7	0.7	1.0	0.4	.2	0.1	0.1
Belgium	146	9.2	5.3	6.6	0.8	0.7	0.7	0.8	0.3	.3	0.1	0.1
Czechoslovakia	371	3.3	6.0	5.4	0.7	0.7	0.5	0.6	0.7	.1	0.1	0.1
Denmark	37	9.2	4.4	2.8	0.5	0.6	0.6	0.7	0.1	.3	0.1	0.1
Finland	787	4.2	2.9	32.3	0.2	0.3	0.3	0.3	1.4	.1	0.1	0.4
France	7,083	45.2	25.1	92.1	3.5	3.6	4.1	4.3	12.4	1.4	0.6	1.3
Germany[1]	5,119	190.8	74.4	159.0	10.2	9.7	10.4	12.1	8.9	5.7	1.7	2.2
Great Britain[2]	704	214.5	137.4	38.5	15.6	14.7	17.0	19.0	1.2	6.5	3.1	0.5
Greece	4,723	86.0	92.4	31.9	3.5	4.7	4.6	3.9	8.3	2.6	2.1	0.4
Ireland	5,373	33.0	11.5	67.2	1.3	5.1	7.0	9.7	9.4	1.0	0.3	0.9
Italy	375	214.1	129.4	12.3	6.4	5.3	11.1	16.2	0.7	6.4	2.9	0.2
Netherlands	754	30.6	10.5	4.2	1.2	1.2	1.2	1.5	1.3	.9	0.2	0.1
Norway[9]	606	15.5	3.9	83.2	0.4	0.4	0.6	0.6	1.1	.5	0.1	1.1
Poland[1]	501	53.5	37.2	40.3	7.4	7.3	13.3	18.4	0.9	1.6	0.8	0.5
Portugal	285	76.1	101.7	20.5	3.8	3.3	3.9	4.0	0.5	2.3	2.3	0.3
Spain	1,246	44.7	39.1	11.1	2.3	2.0	2.2	2.7	2.2	1.3	0.9	0.2
Sweden[9]	359	17.1	6.5	8.0	1.2	1.2	1.2	1.4	0.6	.5	0.1	0.1
Switzerland	3,444	18.5	8.2	57.6	1.0	0.9	1.1	1.3	6.0	.6	0.2	0.8
USSR[1,3]	136	2.5	39.0	18.7	1.5	1.4	4.6	14.8	0.2	.1	0.9	0.3
Yugoslavia	294	20.4	30.5	37.3	1.5	2.0	2.5	2.8	0.5	.6	0.7	0.5
Other Europe	4,547	9.1	18.9	7.7	4.0	3.4	4.0	4.1	0.2	.2	0.2	0.2
Asia	6,019	427.6	1,588.2	2,738.1	255.2	254.7	296.4	321.9	10.6	12.9	35.2	37.3
China[4]	897[4]	34.8	124.3	298.9	33.1	34.3	39.3	22.7	1.6	1.0	2.8	4.1
Hong Kong	302[5]	75.0	113.5	98.2	10.8	11.8	15.2	14.4	0.5	2.3	2.5	1.3
India	456	27.2	164.1	250.7	24.5	25.3	28.6	28.8	0.8	.8	3.7	3.4
Iran	177[4]	10.3	45.1	116.0	12.3	9.8	13.0	14.9	0.3	.3	1.0	1.6
Israel	138[4]	29.6	37.7	44.2	4.3	4.4	5.5	5.9	0.2	.9	0.8	0.6
Japan	462[4]	40.0	49.8	47.0	4.6	5.1	5.4	6.4	0.8	1.2	1.1	0.6
Jordan	74	11.7	27.5	31.1	2.7	3.1	3.8	4.3	0.1	.4	0.6	0.4
Korea	642[4,5]	34.5	267.6	333.8	34.8	34.2	33.0	31.0	1.1	1.0	6.0	4.5
Lebanon	95[8]	15.2	41.3	33.2	2.5	3.5	3.8	4.0	0.2	.5	0.9	0.5
Philippines	1,026	98.4	355.0	548.7	53.1	61.0	66.1	71.3	1.8	3.0	7.9	7.5
Turkey	412	10.1	13.4	23.4	1.7	2.2	2.5	3.2	0.7	.3	0.3	0.3
Vietnam	459[6]	4.3	172.8	281.0	20.4	12.8	13.3	14.8	0.8	1.1	3.8	3.8
Other Asia	879	36.5	176.1	631.4	50.4	47.1	66.7	100.0	1.5	1.1	3.8	8.6
America	13,068	1,716.4	1,982.5	3,615.6	225.5	294.9	672.6	1,051.0	22.9	51.7	44.3	49.3
Argentina	131[7]	49.7	29.9	27.3	1.9	2.6	3.8	6.0	0.2	1.5	0.7	0.4
Brazil	98[7]	29.3	17.8	26.1	2.6	3.0	3.7	4.6	0.2	.9	0.4	0.4
Canada	4,296[7]	413.3	169.9	158.0	16.4	15.8	18.3	24.6	7.5	12.4	3.8	2.2
Colombia	296	72.0	77.3	122.9	11.8	10.2	14.9	23.8	0.5	2.2	1.7	1.7
Cuba	748[8]	208.5	264.9	144.6	17.1	16.6	9.5	9.4	1.3	6.3	5.9	2.0
Dominican Rep.	510[7]	93.3	148.1	252.0	23.9	27.2	26.7	42.1	0.9	2.8	3.3	3.4
Ecuador	155[7]	36.8	50.1	56.2	4.6	4.7	7.6	12.5	0.3	1.1	1.1	0.8
El Salvador	296[7]	15.0	34.4	213.5	10.1	12.0	57.6	79.6	0.5	.5	0.8	2.9
Guatemala	137[7]	15.9	25.9	89.0	4.4	5.8	19.2	32.9	0.2	.5	0.6	1.2
Haiti	235[8]	34.5	56.3	138.4	9.9	34.8	13.3	19.9	0.4	1.0	1.3	1.9
Honduras	91[7]	15.7	17.4	49.6	3.7	4.3	7.6	12.0	0.2	.5	0.4	0.7
Mexico	3,888[7]	453.9	640.3	1,655.7	61.3	95.2	405.6	680.2	6.8	13.7	14.3	22.6
Panama	94[7]	19.4	23.5	33.5	3.2	3.0	3.9	3.9	0.2	.6	0.5	0.5
Peru	121	19.1	29.2	63.5	4.1	5.8	10.0	15.4	0.2	.6	0.6	0.9
West Indies	1,209	133.9	271.8	336.8	28.5	32.3	38.0	41.0	2.1	4.0	6.1	4.9
Other America	798	106.1	125.7	263.7	22.0	21.5	32.7	58.0	1.4	3.1	2.8	3.6
Africa	334	29.0	80.8	176.8	15.2	17.1	22.5	32.8	0.6	.9	1.8	2.4
Australia and New Zealand	147	19.6	23.8	24.1	2.5	2.5	2.9	3.4	0.3	.6	0.5	0.3
Other Oceania	57	5.6	17.6	20.5	2.1	1.8	2.0	3.0	0.1	.1	0.4	0.3
Unknown or Not Reported	267	—	—	0.8	—	—	—	0.5	0.5	—	—	0.1

* Figures may not add to total due to rounding. (1) 1938-1945, Austria included with Germany; 1899-1919, Poland included with Austria-Hungary, Germany, and USSR. (2) Beginning 1952, includes data for United Kingdom not specified, formerly included with "Other Europe". (3) Europe and Asia. (4) Prior to 1951, included with "Other Asia". (5) Prior to 1951, Philippines included with "All other". (6) Prior to 1953, data for Vietnam not available. (7) Prior to 1951, included with "Other America". (8) Prior to 1951, included with "West Indies". (9) Norway and Sweden were combined from 1820-1868. (10) First full year with Immigration Reform and Control Act of 1986 in effect. (11) Data include 478,814 previously illegal aliens who were granted permanent resident status under section 245A of the Immigration Reform and Control Act of 1986. These aliens are not new residents of the United States.

ECONOMICS

U.S. Budget Receipts and Outlays—1987-1990

Source: Financial Management Service, U.S. Dept. of the Treasury
(Fiscal year ends Sept. 30)
(millions of dollars)

Classification	Fiscal 1987	Fiscal 1988	Fiscal 1989	Fiscal 1990
Net Receipts				
Individual income taxes	$392,557	$401,181	$445,690	$466,884
Corporation income taxes	83,926	94,195	103,291	93,507
Social insurance taxes and contributions:				
Federal old-age and survivors insurance	194,541	220,337	240,595	255,031
Federal disability insurance	18,861	21,154	23,071	26,625
Federal hospital insurance	55,992	59,859	65,396	68,556
Railroad retirement fund	3,634	3,743	3,798	3,679
Total employment taxes and contributions . .	273,028	305,093	332,859	353,891
Other insurance and retirement:				
Unemployment	25,575	24,584	22,011	21,635
Federal employees retirement	4,613	4,537	4,428	4,405
Non-federal employees	102	122	119	117
Total social insurance taxes and				
contributions	303,318	334,335	359,416	380,047
Excise taxes	32,457	35,540	34,386	35,345
Estate and gift taxes	7,493	7,594	8,745	11,500
Customs duties	15,085	15,411	16,334	16,607
Deposits of earnings-Federal Reserve Banks	16,817	17,163	19,604	24,319
All other miscellaneous receipts.	2,490	2,746	3,235	3,151
Net Budget Receipts	$854,143	$908,166	$990,701	$1,031,462
Net Outlays				
Legislative Branch.	$1,812	$1,852	$2,095	$2,233
The Judiciary.	1,178	1,337	1,492	1,641
Executive Office of the President:				
The White House Office.	25	26	27	30
Office of Management and Budget.	37	41	42	44
Total Executive Office	109	121	124	157
Funds appropriated to the President:				
International security assistance	6,820	4,273	1,012	8,352
Multinational assistance	1,306	1,498	1,492	1,695
Agency for International Development.	1,294	1,404	1,215	1,774
International Development Assistance.	2,673	2,980	2,780	3,528
Total funds appropriated to the President. . .	10,406	7,252	4,257	10,087
Agriculture Department:				
Food stamp program	12,405	13,145	13,725	15,923
Farmer's Home Admin.	3,748	7,277	7,608	6,713
Forest service	2,221	2,688	2,944	2,934
Total Agriculture Department.	49,593	44,003	48,316	46,012
Commerce Department				
Total Commerce Department.	2,156	2,279	2,571	3,734
Bureau of the Census	217	333	557	1,575
Defense Department:				
Military personnel	72,020	76,337	80,676	75,622
Operation and maintenance	76,178	84,475	87,001	88,340
Procurement	80,744	77,166	81,620	80,972
Research, development, test, evaluation	33,596	34,792	37,002	37,458
Military construction	5,853	5,874	5,275	5,080
Total Defense Department (military) **. . . . . . .**	273,938	281,935	294,881	289,755
Defense Department (civil)	20,659	22,047	23,450	24,975
Education Department	16,800	18,246	21,608	23,109
Energy Department	10,688	11,166	11,387	12,023
Health and Human Services Department:				
Food and Drug Administration	422	463	510	553
National Institutes of Health.	5,222	6,334	6,992	7,492
Public Health Service	9,886	11,408	12,250	14,007
Health Care Financing Adm.	130,472	144,654	163,028	184,893
Human Development Services	5,448	5,886	6,850	6,877
Total Health and Human Services Dept.	148,893	158,991	172,301	193,679
Social Security (Off Budget)	202,422	214,178	227,473	244,998
Housing and Urban Development Department. . . .	15,464	18,956	19,680	20,167
Interior Department	5,045	5,147	5,308	5,794
Justice Department:				
Federal Bureau of Investigation	1,216	1,384	1,528	1,473
Total Justice Department	4,333	5,426	6,232	6,739
Labor Department:				
Unemployment Trust Fund	20,527	18,598	18,730	20,250
Total Labor Department	23,453	21,870	22,657	25,316
State Department	2,788	3,421	3,722	3,979
Transportation Department:				
Federal Aviation Adm	4,895	5,192	5,740	6,391
Total Transportation Department	25,431	26,404	26,607	28,637
Treasury Department:				
Internal Revenue Service	7,513	9,363	11,049	12,053
Interest on the public debt.	195,390	214,145	240,863	264,853
Total Treasury Department	180,345	201,644	230,566	255,268
Veterans Affairs Department.	—	29,249	30,041	28,998
Environmental Protection Agency	4,903	4,872	4,906	5,106
General Services Administration.	74	−281	−462	−122

(continued)

Classification	Fiscal 1987	Fiscal 1988	Fiscal 1989	Fiscal 1990
Net Receipts				
National Aeronautics and Space Administration . . .	7,591	9,092	11,036	12,429
Office of Personnel Management	26,966	29,191	29,073	31,949
Small Business Administration.	−72	−54	85	692
Independent agencies:				
Action	159	153	163	169
Board for International Broadcasting.	156	194	199	208
Corporation for Public Broadcasting	200	214	228	229
District of Columbia	560	550	538	578
Equal Employment Opportunity Commission . .	158	176	182	181
Export-Import Bank of the United States	−2,300	−894	47	357
Federal Communications Commission.	79	52	49	79
Federal Deposit Insurance Corporation	−1,438	2,146	2,847	6,429
Federal Trade Commission	66	69	65	57
Interstate Commerce Comm..	—	43	44	43
Legal Services Corporation.	309	306	309	291
National Archives & Record Adm.	96	102	71	157
National Foundation on the Arts and Humanities	310	322	309	307
National Labor Relations Board	127	132	136	141
National Science Foundation	1,562	1,665	1,752	1,838
Nuclear Regulatory Commission.	393	232	189	221
Railroad Retirement Board	4,196	4,147	4,315	4,477
Securities and Exchange Commission.	108	126	140	129
Smithsonian Institution.	242	260	288	302
Tennessee Valley Authority.	1,091	1,089	348	−312
U.S. Information Agency	830	843	888	888
Total independent agencies	14,266	23,446	33,770	73,514
Undistributed offsetting receipts	−72,400	−78,474	−89,155	−99,025
Net Budget Outlays.	1,003,804	1,063,318	1,144,020	1,251,850
Less net receipts.	854,143	908,166	990,701	1,031,462
Deficit	$−149,661	$−155,151	$−153,319	$−220,388

U.S. Net Receipts and Outlays

Source: U.S. Dept. of the Treasury; annual statements for year ending June 30
(thousands of dollars)

Yearly average	Receipts	Outlays	Yearly average	Receipts	Outlays	Yearly average	Receipts	Outlays
1789-1800[1]	$5,717	$5,776	1866-1870.	$447,301	$377,642	1901-1905.	$559,481	$535,559
1801-1810[2].	13,056	9,086	1871-1875	336,830	287,460	1906-1910	628,507	639,178
1811-1820[2].	21,032	23,943	1876-1880	288,124	255,598	1911-1915	710,227	720,252
1821-1830[2].	21,928	16,162	1881-1885	366,961	257,691	1916-1920	3,483,652	8,065,333
1831-1840[2].	30,461	24,495	1886-1890	375,448	279,134	1921-1925	4,306,673	3,578,989
1841-1850[2].	28,545	34,097	1891-1895	352,891	363,599	1926-1930	4,069,138	3,182,807
1851-1860.	60,237	60,163	1896-1900	434,877	457,451	1931-1935	2,770,973	5,214,874
1861-1865	160,907	683,785						

(1) Average for period March 4, 1789, to Dec. 31, 1800. (2) Years ended Dec. 31, 1801 to 1842; average for 1841-1850 is for the period Jan. 1, 1841, to June 30, 1850.

Summary of Receipts, Outlays, and Surpluses or Deficits; 1934-1986

(Millions of dollars)

Source: Financial Management Service, U.S. Treasury Dept.

Year	Receipts	Total Outlays	Surplus or Deficit (−)	Year	Receipts	Total Outlays	Surplus or Deficit (−)
1934	2,955	6,541	−3,586	1961	94,388	97,723	−3,335
1935	3,609	6,412	−2,803	1962	99,676	106,821	−7,146
1936	3,923	8,228	−4,304	1963	106,560	111,316	−4,756
1937	5,387	7,580	−2,193	1964	112,613	118,528	−5,915
1938	6,751	6,840	−89	1965	116,817	118,228	−1,411
1939	6,295	9,141	−2,846	1966	130,835	134,532	−3,698
1940	6,548	9,468	−2,920	1967	148,822	157,464	−8,643
1941	8,712	13,653	−4,941	1968	152,973	178,134	−25,161
1942	14,634	35,137	−20,503	1969	186,882	183,640	3,242
1943	24,001	78,555	−54,554	1970	192,807	195,649	−2,842
1944	43,747	91,304	−47,557	1971	187,139	210,172	−23,033
1945	45,159	92,712	−47,553	1972	207,309	230,681	−23,373
1946	39,296	55,232	−15,936	1973	230,799	245,707	−14,908
1947	38,514	34,496	4,018	1974	263,224	269,359	−6,135
1948	41,560	29,764	11,796	1975	279,090	332,332	−53,242
1949	39,415	38,835	580	1976	298,060	371,779	−73,719
1950	39,443	42,562	−3,119	Transition quarter[1] . .	81,232	95,973	−14,741
1951	51,616	45,514	6,102	1977	355,559	409,203	−53,644
1952	66,167	67,686	−1,519	1978	399,561	458,729	−59,168
1953	69,608	76,101	−6,493	1979	463,302	503,464	−40,162
1954	69,701	70,855	−1,154	1980	517,112	590,920	−73,808
1955	65,451	68,444	−2,993	1981	599,272	678,209	−78,936
1956	74,587	70,640	3,947	1982	617,766	745,706	−127,940
1957	79,990	76,578	3,412	1983	600,562	808,327	−207,764
1958	79,636	82,405	−2,769	1984	666,457	851,781	−185,324
1959	79,249	92,098	−12,849	1985	734,057	946,316	−212,260
1960	92,492	92,191	301	1986	769,091	990,231	−221,140

(1) Effective fiscal year 1977, fiscal year is reckoned Oct. 1-Sept. 30; Transition Quarter covers July 1, 1976-Sept. 30, 1976.

The Federal Budget Process

Source: Executive Office of the President, Office of Management and Budget.

CBO = Congressional Budget Office; GRH = Gramm-Rudman-Hollings (*Balanced Budget and Emergency Deficit Control Act of 1985*); OMB = Office of Management and Budget.

Executive budget process	Timing	Congressional budget process
Agencies subject to executive branch review submit initial budget request materials.	Sept. 1	
Fiscal year begins. President's initial GRH sequester order takes effect (amounts are withheld from obligation pending issuance of final order).	Oct. 1	Fiscal year begins.
	Oct. 10	CBO issues revised GRH report to OMB and Congress.
OMB reports on changes in initial GRH estimates and determinations resulting from legislation enacted and regulations promulgated after its initial report to Congress. President issues final GRH sequester order, which is effective immediately, and transmits message to Congress within 15 days of final order. Agencies not subject to executive branch review submit budget request materials.	Oct. 15	
Legislative branch and the judiciary submit budget request materials.	Nov. 15 Nov.- Dec.	Comptroller General issues GRH compliance report.
President transmits the budget to Congress.	1st Mon. after Jan. 3	Congress receives the President's budget.
OMB sends allowance letters to agencies.	Jan.-Feb.	
	Feb. 15	CBO reports to the Budget Committees on the President's budget.
	Feb. 25	Committees submit views and estimates to Budget Committee in their own house.
OMB and the President conduct reviews to establish presidential policy to guide agencies in developing the next budget.	Apr.- June	
	Apr. 1	Senate Budget Committee reports concurrent resoluion on the budget.
	Apr. 15	Congress completes action on concurrent resolution.
	May 15	House may consider appropriations bills in the absence of a concurrent resolution on the budget.
	June 10	House Appropriations Committee reports last appropriations bill.
	June 15	Congress completes action on reconciliation legislation.
	June 30	House completes action on annual appropriations bills.
President transmits the mid-session review, updating the budget estimates.	July 15	Congress receives mid-session review of the budget.
OMB provides agencies with policy guidance for the upcoming budget.	July- Aug.	
Date of "snapshot" of projected deficits for the upcoming fiscal year for initial OMB and CBO GRH reports.	Aug. 15	
	Aug. 20	CBO issues its initial GRH report to OMB and Congress.
OMB issues its initial GRH report providing estimates and determinations to the President and Congress. President issues initial GRH sequester order and sends message to Congress within 15 days.	Aug. 25	

Public Debt of the U.S.

Source: Bureau of Public Debt, U.S. Dept. of the Treasury

Fiscal year	Debt (billions)	Per. cap. (dollars)	Interest paid (billions)	Pct. of federal outlays	Fiscal year	Debt (billions)	Per. cap. (dollars)	Interest paid (billions)	Pct. of federal outlays
1870	$2.4	$61.06	—	—	1976	$620.4	$2,852	$37.1	10.0
1880	2.0	41.60	—	—	1977	698.8	3,170	41.9	10.2
1890	1.1	17.80	—	—	1978	771.5	3,463	48.7	10.6
1900	1.2	16.60	—	—	1979	826.5	3,669	59.8	11.9
1910	1.1	12.41	—	—	1980	907.7	3,985	74.9	12.7
1920	24.2	228	—	—	1981	997.9	4,338	95.6	14.1
1930	16.1	131	—	—	1982	1,142.0	4,913	117.4	15.7
1940	43.0	325	$1.0	10.5	1983	1,377.2	5,870	128.8	15.9
1945	258.7	1,849	3.8	4.1	1984	1,572.3	6,640	153.8	18.1
1950	256.1	1,688	5.7	13.4	1985	1,823.1	7,598	178.9	18.9
1955	272.8	1,651	6.4	9.4	1986	2,125.3	8,774	190.2	19.2
1960	284.1	1,572	9.2	10.0	1987	2,350.3	9,615	195.4	19.5
1965	313.8	1,613	11.3	9.6	1988	2,602.3	10,534	214.1	20.1
1970	370.1	1,814	19.3	9.9	1989	2,857.4	11,545	240.9	21.0
1975	533.2	2,475	32.7	9.8	1990	3,233.3	13,000	264.8	21.1

Note: Through 1976 the fiscal year ended June 30. From 1977 on, fiscal year ends Sept. 30.

U.S. International Transactions

Source: Bureau of Economic Analysis, U.S. Dept. of Commerce

(millions of dollars)

	1960	1965	1970	1975	1980	1985	1989	1990
Exports of goods services and income[1]	$30,556	$42,722	$68,387	$157,936	$343,241	$366,049	$606,593	$652,936
Merchandise, adjusted, excluding military[2]	19,650	26,461	42,469	107,088	224,269	215,935	361,451	389,550
Transfers under U.S. military agency sales contracts	2,030	2,465	4,214	6,256	9,029	8,699	8,391	9,899
Travel	919	1,380	2,331	4,697	10,588	17,663	35,173	40,579
Passenger fares	175	271	544	1,039	2,591	4,323	10,374	12,251
Other transportation	1,607	2,175	3,125	5,840	11,618	14,674	20,709	22,407
Royalties and license fees[3]	837	1,534	2,331	4,300	7,085	5,995	11,934	15,291
Other private services	570	714	1,294	2,920	6,276	15,601	29,299	32,173
U.S. Government miscellaneous services	153	285	332	446	398	878	612	695
Income receipts on U.S. assets abroad:	4,616	7,437	11,748	25,351	71,388	82,282	128,651	130,091
Direct investment	3,621	5,506	8,169	16,595	37,146	28,295	53,997	54,444
Other private receipts	646	1,421	2,671	7,644	31,680	48,487	69,014	65,702
U.S. Government receipts	349	510	907	1,112	2,562	5,499	5,640	-9,945
Imports of goods, services and income	-23,670	-32,708	-59,901	-33,745	-333,774	-473,998	-697,407	-722,730
Merchandise, adjusted, excluding military[2]	-14,758	-21,510	-39,866	-98,185	-249,750	-338,083	-477,368	-497,665
Direct defense expenditures	-3,087	-2,952	-4,855	-4,795	-10,851	-12,795	-14,595	-17,119
Travel	-1,750	-2,438	-3,980	-6,417	-10,397	-25,155	-34,548	-38,671
Passenger fares	-513	-717	-1,215	-2,263	-3,607	-6,650	-8,387	-8,963
Other transportation	-1,402	-1,951	-2,843	-5,708	-11,790	-15,643	-20,699	-23,463
Royalties and license fees[3]	-74	-135	-244	-472	-724	-891	-2,158	-2,644
Other private services	-593	-461	-827	-1,551	-2,909	-5,840	-11,644	-13,819
U.S. Government miscellaneous services	-254	-457	-576	-789	-1,214	-1,735	-2,045	-2,240
Income payments on foreign assets in the U.S.								
Direct investment payments	-394	-657	-875	-2,234	-8,635	-6,079	-11,513	-1,782
Other private payments	-511	-942	-3,617	-5,788	-21,214	-37,064	-78,594	-78,494
U.S. Government payments	-332	-489	-1,024	-4,542	-12,684	-22,972	-35,856	-37,870
Unilateral transfers, net	-4,062	-4,583	-6,156	-7,075	-8,349	-15,473	-15,491	-22,329
U.S. Government grants	-3,367	-3,444	-4,449	-5,101	-5,486	-11,268	-11,071	-17,486
U.S. Government pensions and other transfers	-273	-463	-611	-1,068	-1,818	-2,138	-2,517	-2,947
Private remittances and other transfers	-423	-677	-1,096	-906	-1,044	-2,068	-1,903	-1,896
U.S. assets abroad, net (increase/ capital outflow (-))	-4,099	-5,716	-9,337	-39,703	-86,118	-27,721	-128,610	-57,706
U.S. official reserve assets, net	2,145	1,225	2,481	-849	-8,155	-3,858	25,293	-2,158
U.S. Government assets, other than official reserve assets, net	-1,100	-1,605	-1,589	-3,474	-5,162	-2,821	1,320	2,976
U.S. private assets, net	-5,144	-5,336	-10,229	-35,380	-72,802	-21,043	-104,637	-58,524
Foreign assets in U.S., net (increase/ capital inflow (+))	2,294	742	6,359	15,670	58,112	130,012	216,549	86,303
Statistical discrepancy (sum of above items with sign reversed)	-1,019	-457	-219	5,917	25,736	20,041	18,366	63,526
Memoranda:								
Balance on merchandise trade	4,892	4,951	2,603	8,903	-25,481	-122,148	-115,917	-108,115
Balance on investment income	3,379	5,350	6,233	12,707	28,856	16,166	2,688	11,945
Balance on services	-1,385	-287	-349	3,501	6,093	-877	22,415	36,378
Balance on goods, services, and income	6,886	10,014	8,486	25,191	9,467	-106,859	-90,814	-69,794
Balance on current account	2,824	5,431	2,331	18,116	1,119	-122,332	-106,305	-92,123

(1) Excludes transfers of goods and services under U.S. military grant programs. (2) Excludes exports of goods under U.S. military agency sales contracts identified in Census export documents, excludes imports of goods under direct defense expenditures identified in Census import documents, and reflects various other adjustments. (3) Redefined in 1982.

U.S. Direct Investment Abroad in Selected Countries

Source: Bureau of Economic Analysis, U.S. Dept. of Commerce

(millions of dollars)

	1988	1989	1990		1988	1989	1990
All countries	$335,893	370,091	421,494	Netherlands	16,145	18,133	22,779
Africa				Portugal	546	488	590
Egypt	1,637	1,744	1,451	Spain	4,966	6,096	7,480
Libya	315	252	246	United Kingdom	49,459	59,827	64,983
Nigeria	660	406	210	Other Europe			
S. Africa	1,252	843	889	Austria	669	588	767
Asia and Pacific (excl. Japan) . . .				Finland	408	476	542
Hong Kong	5,240	5,949	6,537	Norway	4,371	3,547	3,633
India	436	527	639	Sweden	1,119	1,129	1,526
Indonesia	2,921	3,770	3,827	Switzerland	18,734	19,209	23,733
Malaysia	1,135	1,174	1,425	Turkey	246	310	507
Philippines	1,513	1,657	1,655	Japan	18,009	18,488	20,994
Singapore	2,311	2,318	3,971	South America			
South Korea	1,501	1,855	2,096	Argentina	2,597	2,684	2,889
Taiwan	1,622	1,921	2,273	Brazil	12,609	14,522	15,416
Thailand	1,132	1,271	1,515	Chile	672	1,069	1,341
Australia	12,823	13,331	14,529	Colombia	2,248	1,977	2,043
Bermuda	19,022	17,717	18,972	Ecuador	431	393	389
Canada	62,656	65,548	68,431	Peru	976	939	600
European Communities	131,069	149,545	172,940	Venezuela	1,903	1,503	1,581
Belgium	7,501	7,941	9,462	Central America			
Denmark	1,161	1,234	1,633	Mexico	5,712	7,280	9,360
France	13,041	14,069	17,134	Panama	6,874	7,889	8,521
Germany[1]	21,832	24,550	27,715	Middle East			
Greece	195	265	300	Israel	700	756	818
Ireland	6,886	6,522	6,776	Saudi Arabia	1,782	1,955	2,523
Italy	9,496	10,294	12,971	United Arab Emirates	672	652	584
Luxembourg	841	1,127	1,119				

(1) Does not include E. Germany in 1988 and 1989.

National Income by Industry

Source: Bureau of Economic Analysis, U.S. Dept. of Commerce

(billions of dollars)

	1960	1965	1970	1975	1980	1989	1990
National income without capital consumption adjustment	$428.6	$583.6	$835.1	$1,315.0	$2,263.9	$4,228.5	$4,445.8
Domestic industries	425.1	577.8	827.8	1,297.4	2,216.3	4,190.9	4,404.1
Private industries	371.6	500.8	695.4	1,088.3	1,894.5	3,584.9	3,755.7
Agriculture, forestry, fisheries	17.8	21.0	25.9	46.5	61.4	101.0	103.4
Mining	5.6	6.1	8.4	21.2	43.8	36.4	42.2
Construction	22.5	32.3	47.4	69.9	126.6	225.1	255.1
Manufacturing	125.3	171.6	215.6	317.5	532.1	803.8	806.5
Durable goods	73.4	105.6	127.7	185.0	313.7	465.6	461.5
Nondurable goods	52.0	66.1	87.9	132.5	218.4	338.2	345.0
Transportation, public utilities	35.8	47.0	64.4	101.1	177.3	314.2	328.8
Transportation	18.5	23.7	31.5	48.0	85.8	136.6	144.0
Communication	8.2	11.5	17.6	26.8	48.1	87.4	92.8
Electric, gas, and sanitary services . .	9.1	11.7	86.8	90.2	43.4	90.2	92.0
Wholesale trade	25.0	32.5	47.5	83.0	143.3	247.4	261.7
Retail trade	41.3	55.1	79.9	123.1	189.4	360.1	377.1
Finance, insurance, and real estate	51.3	67.4	96.4	143.9	279.5	613.8	647.5
Services	46.9	67.9	109.8	182.1	341.0	883.0	963.4
Government, government enterprises . .	53.5	76.9	132.4	209.1	321.8	606.9	648.4
Rest of the world	3.5	5.8	7.3	17.5	47.6	37.6	41.7

National Income by Type of Income

Source: Bureau of Economic Analysis, U.S. Dept. of Commerce

(billions of dollars)

	1960	1965	1970	1975	1980	1989	1990
National income[1]	$424.9	$585.2	$832.6	$1,289.1	$2,203.5	$4,223.3	$4,418.4
Compensation of employees	296.7	399.8	618.3	948.7	1,638.2	3,079.0	3,244.2
Wages and salaries	272.8	363.7	551.5	814.7	1,372.0	2,573.2	2,705.3
Government	49.2	69.9	117.1	176.1	260.1	476.6	508.0
Other	223.7	293.8	434.3	638.6	1,111.8	2,096.6	2,197.2
Supplements to wages, salary	23.8	36.1	66.8	134.0	266.3	505.8	538.9
Employer contrib. for social ins . . .	12.6	18.3	34.3	68.0	127.9	263.9	280.8
Other labor income	11.2	17.8	32.5	65.9	138.4	241.9	258.1
Proprietors' income	52.1	65.1	80.2	125.4	180.7	379.3	402.5
Farm	11.6	13.0	14.7	25.4	20.5	48.6	49.9
Nonfarm	40.5	52.1	65.4	100.0	160.1	330.7	352.6
Rental income of persons	15.3	18.1	18.2	13.5	6.6	8.2	6.9
with capital consump. adjust.							
Corp. profits with inventory adjustment	49.8	76.2	69.5	123.9	194.0	286.1	293.3
Corp. profits before tax	49.9	77.4	76.0	134.8	237.1	307.7	304.7
Corp. profits tax liability	22.7	30.9	34.4	50.9	84.8	135.1	132.1
Corp. profits after tax	27.2	46.5	41.7	83.9	152.3	172.6	172.5
Dividends	12.9	19.1	22.5	29.6	54.7	123.5	133.9
Undistributed profits	14.3	27.4	19.2	54.3	97.6	49.1	38.7
Inventory valuation adjustment	-.2	-1.2	-6.6	-11.0	-43.1	-21.7	-11.4
Net interest	11.3	20.9	41.2	83.8	200.9	445.1	466.7

(1) *National income* is the aggregate of labor and property earnings which arises in the current production of goods and services. It is the sum of employee compensation, proprietors' income, rental income, corporate profits, and net interest. It measures the total factor costs of the goods and services produced by the economy. Income is measured before deduction of taxes on income.

Gross National Product, Net National Product, National Income, and Personal Income

Source: Bureau of Economic Analysis, U.S. Dept. of Commerce
(billions of dollars)

	1960	1970	1975	1980	1989	1990
Gross national product[1]	$515.3	$1,015.5	$1,598.4	$2,732.0	$5,200.8	$5,465.1
Less: Capital consumption allowances.	46.4	88.8	161.8	303.8	554.4	575.6
Equals: Net national product	468.9	926.6	1,436.6	2,428.1	4,646.4	4,889.5
Less: Indirect business tax and nontax liability .	45.3	94.0	140.0	213.3	414.0	440.3
Business transfer payments	2.0	4.1	7.4	12.1	32.4	35.0
Statistical discrepancy	−2.8	−1.1	2.5	4.9	−17.0	−1.7
Plus: Subsidies less current surplus of						
government enterprises	.4	2.9	2.4	5.7	6.3	2.5
Equals: National income	424.9	832.6	1,289.1	2,203.5	4,223.3	4,418.4
Less: Corporate profits with inventory						
valuation and capital consumption adjustment	49.5	74.7	117.6	177.2	311.6	298.3
Net interest	11.3	41.2	83.8	200.9	445.1	466.7
Contributions for social insurance	21.9	62.2	118.5	216.5	476.8	506.9
Wage accruals less disbursement	.0	.0	.1	.0	0	0
Plus: Government transfer payment to persons.	27.5	81.8	185.7	312.6	604.5	659.7
Personal interest income	24.9	69.3	122.5	271.9	643.2	680.4
Personal dividend income	12.9	22.2	28.7	52.9	114.4	123.8
Business transfer payments	2.0	4.1	7.4	12.1	32.4	35.0
Equals: Personal income	409.4	831.8	1,313.4	2,258.5	4,384.3	4,645.5

(1) Gross National Product is the market value of all goods and services that have been bought for final use during a year. The GNP is considered the most comprehensive measure of a nation's economic activity.

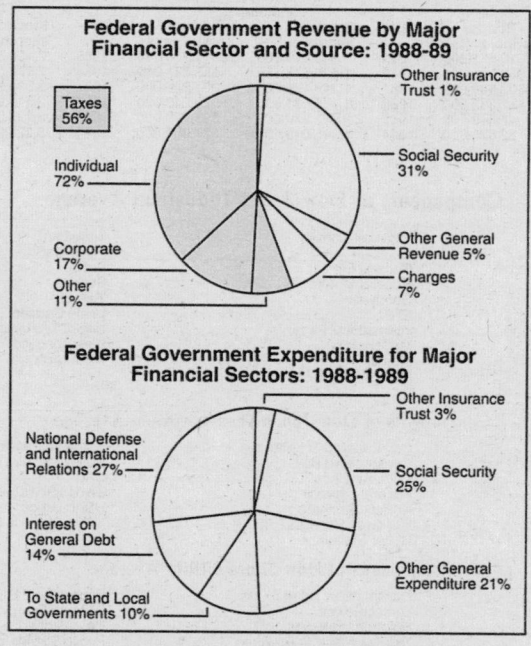

Federal Government Revenue by Major Financial Sector and Source: 1988-89

Taxes 56%

Individual 72%

Corporate 17%

Other 11%

Other Insurance Trust 1%

Social Security 31%

Other General Revenue 5%

Charges 7%

Federal Government Expenditure for Major Financial Sectors: 1988-1989

National Defense and International Relations 27%

Interest on General Debt 14%

To State and Local Governments 10%

Other Insurance Trust 3%

Social Security 25%

Other General Expenditure 21%

Dow Jones Industrial Average Since 1961

	High		Year		Low			High		Year		Low	
Dec.	13	734.91	1961	Jan.	3	610.25	Jan.	3	999.75	1977	Nov.	2	800.85
Jan.	3	726.01	1962	June	26	535.76	Sept.	8	907.74	1978	Feb.	28	742.12
Dec.	18	767.21	1963	Jan.	2	646.79	Oct.	5	897.61	1979	Nov.	7	796.67
Nov.	18	891.71	1964	Jan.	2	766.08	Nov.	20	1000.17	1980	Apr.	21	759.13
Dec.	31	969.26	1965	June	28	840.59	Apr.	27	1024.05	1981	Sept.	25	824.01
Feb.	9	995.15	1966	Oct.	7	744.32	Dec.	27	1070.55	1982	Aug.	12	776.92
Sept.	25	943.08	1967	Jan.	3	786.41	Nov.	29	1287.20	1983	Jan.	3	1027.04
Dec.	3	985.21	1968	Mar.	21	825.13	Jan.	6	1286.64	1984	July	24	1086.57
May	14	968.85	1969	Dec.	17	769.93	Dec.	16	1553.10	1985	Jan.	4	1184.96
Dec.	29	842.00	1970	May	6	631.16	Dec.	2	1955.57	1986	Jan.	22	1502.29
Apr.	28	950.82	1971	Nov.	23	797.97	Aug.	25	2722.42	1987	Oct.	19	1738.74
Dec.	11	1036.27	1972	Jan.	26	889.15	Oct.	21	2183.50	1988	Jan.	20	1879.14
Jan.	11	1051.70	1973	Dec.	5	788.31	Oct.	9	2791.41	1989	Jan.	3	2144.64
Mar.	13	891.66	1974	Dec.	6	577.60	July	16	2999.75	1990	Oct.	11	2365.10
July	15	881.81	1975	Jan.	2	632.04	Aug.	28	3055.23	1991*	Jan.	9	2470.30
Sept.	21	1014.79	1976	Jan.	2	858.71					*As	of	9/20/91

Stock Exchanges
N.Y. Stock Exchange Transactions

Year	Yearly volume Stock shares	Bonds par values	Year	Yearly volume Stock shares	Bonds par values
1900	138,981,000	$579,293,000	1975	4,693,427,000	$5,178,300,000
1905	260,569,000	1,026,254,000	1980	11,352,294,000	5,190,304,000
1910	163,705,000	634,863,000	1981	11,853,740,659	5,733,071,000
1915	172,497,000	961,700,000	1982	16,458,036,768	7,155,443,000
1920	227,636,000	3,868,422,000	1983	21,589,576,997	7,572,315,000
1925	459,717,623	3,427,042,210	1984	23,071,031,447	6,982,291,000
1929	1,124,800,410	2,996,398,000	1985	27,510,706,353	9,046,453,000
1930	810,632,546	2,720,301,800	1986	35,680,016,341	10,475,399,000
1935	381,635,752	3,339,458,000	1987	47,801,308,660	9,726,244,000
1940	207,599,749	1,669,438,000	1988	40,438,346,358	7,594,644,000
1950	524,799,621	1,112,425,170	1989	41,698,538,270	8,836,374,000
1960	766,693,818	1,346,419,750	1990	39,836,374,000	10,893,702,000
1970	2,937,359,448	4,494,864,600			

American Stock Exchange Transactions

Year	Yearly volume Stock shares	Bonds[1] princ. amts.	Year	Yearly volume Stock shares	Bonds[1] princ. amts.	Year	Yearly volume Stock shares	Bonds[1] princ. amts.
1929	476,140,375	$513,551,000	1970	843,116,260	$641,270,000	1985	2,100,860,000	$645,182,000
1930	222,270,065	863,541,000	1980	1,626,072,625	355,723,000	1986	2,978,540,000	810,264,000
1940	42,928,337	303,902,000	1981	1,343,400,220	301,226,000	1987	3,505,950,000	684,965,000
1945	143,309,392	167,333,000	1982	1,485,831,536	325,240,000	1988	2,515,210,000	604,950,000
1950	107,792,340	47,549,000	1983	2,081,270,000	395,190,000	1989	3,125,030,000	709,010,000
1960	286,039,982	32,670,000	1984	1,545,010,000	371,990,000	1990	3,328,918,000	767,108,000

(1) Corporate

Components of Dow Jones Industrial Average

Allied-Signal	Eastman Kodak	Morgan (J.P.)
Aluminum Co. of Amer.	Exxon	Philip Morris
American Express	General Electric	Procter & Gamble
AT&T	General Motors	Sears
Bethlehem Steel	Goodyear	Texaco
Boeing	IBM	Union Carbide
Caterpillar	International Paper	United Technologies
Chevron	McDonald's	Westinghouse
Coca-Cola	Merck	Woolworth
Disney (Walt)	Minn. Mining & Manuf.	
DuPont		

Components of Dow Jones Transportation Average

AMR Corp.	Consolidated Freightways	Santa Fe Pacific
Airborne Freight	Consolidated Rail	Southwest Air Lines
Alaska Air	Delta Air Lines	UAL
American President	Federal Express	Union Pacific
Burlington Northern	Norfolk Southern	USAir Group
CSX	Roadway Services	XTRA Corp
Carolina Freight	Ryder System	

Components of Dow Jones Utility Average

American Electric Power	Consolidated Natural Gas	Panhandle Eastern
Arkla	Detroit Edison	Peoples Energy
Centerior Energy	Houston Industries	Philadelphia Electric
Commonwealth Edison	Niagara Mohawk Power	Public Service Enterprises
Consolidated Edison	Pacific Gas & Electric	SCE

Stock Ownership Increased in the 1980s

One in 5 U.S. residents, a total of 51 million people, own stocks or invest in stock mutual funds. A telephone survey of 5,000 households conducted by the New York Stock Exchange in mid-1990 showed that 21.1 percent of the population owned stocks, up from 13.5 percent in 1980.

Nearly 30 million individuals owned stock listed on the New York Stock Exchange; some 26 million owned stocks via mutual funds, up 130 percent since 1985.

NASDAQ in 1990

NASDAQ, The National Association of Securities Dealers Automated Quotations reported turnover volume of 33.3 billion shares in 1990. The number of companies with shares traded in this market was over 5,000 at the start of 1991, making NASDAQ the third-largest market in the world, after the New York and Tokyo exchanges.

Most Active Common Stocks in 1990

New York Exchange	Volume (millions of shares)	American Exchange	Volume (millions of shares)	NASDAQ	Volume (millions of shares)
Philip Morris	524.55	Hillhaven	105.18	MCI	600.93
A.T.&T.	425.07	BAT	105.09	Telematics Intl.	517.75
Citicorp	421.43	Continental Air	101.62	Intel	471.25
I.B.M.	402.98	Enscor	90.03	Oracle Systems	408.62
General Electric	396.37	Echo Bay Mines	87.88	Apple Computer	396.30
Fannie Mae	323.53	Amdahl	77.69	Sun Microsystems	361.04
American Express	315.28	Fruit of the Loom	76.60	TIE/Comm.	349.99
Wal-Mart	303.15	Wang Labs	60.92	Microsoft	217.93
Exxon	294.81	Dow Chemical†	47.26	Seagate Tech.	213.12
General Motors	294.08	Western Digital	46.60	Novell	173.13
Boeing	274.96	Corroon & Black	41.44	Reuters Holdings	171.59
Waste Management	271.92	Jan Bell Marketing	38.36	McCaw Cellular	171.30
Bristol-Myers Squibb	254.81	Bolar Pharmaceutical	37.40	Lotus Development	157.71
Chase Manhattan	251.90	Diasonics	34.97	Liz Claiborne	154.78
Eastman Kodak	248.93	New York Times	33.65	Adobe Systems	145.09
Conner Peripherals	232.89	ALZA	31.79	Quantum	141.07
Pepsico	224.39	Hasbro	30.00	DSC Comm.	132.98
McDonald's	219.63			Nordstrom	131.44
† Contingent value rate					

Top Mutual Funds

Source: Lipper Analytical Services Inc.

Ten Years 12/31/80 To 12/31/90	Percent	Five-Years 12/31/85 To 12/31/90	Percent	1990 12/31/89 To 12/31/90	Percent
Fidelity Magellan	587.97	GT Global Japan	242.48	Fidelity Sel Bio Tech	44.38
Merrill Pacific; A	577.48	Financial Port: Health	224.08	Fidelity Pound Perform	36.53
Phoenix: Growth	420.37	GT Global Pacific	191.94	Shearson Curr: Pound	35.33
CGM Capital Development	412.23	Nomura Pacific Basin	181.49	Financial Port: Health	25.79
Sequoia Fund	411.88	Merrill Pacific; A	176.41	Fidelity Sel Health	24.28
Fidelity Destiny I	400.31	First Inv Global	162.29	Kemper Global Income	22.66
Quest for Value	399.28	Fidelity Destiny II	159.97	Equity Strategies	22.52
Japan Fund	397.10	Fidelity Sel Food	153.36	Shearson Curr: D-Mark	21.67
Oppenheimer Target	388.37	Oppenheimer Gld & Sp Min	150.79	Fidelity D-Mark Perform	21.30
Lindner Dividend	384.08	Japan Fund	148.71	Scudder Global: Intl Bond	21.08
FPA Paramount	381.45	Templeton: Foreign	148.06	Phoenix Multi: Cap Apprec	20.47
United: Income	379.06	Trustees Commingled: Intl	145.29	Intl Cash: Hard Currency	20.34
Washington Mutual Inv	375.01	Vanguard Spl: Health	140.89	Intl Cash: High Inc Currency	18.47
New England: Growth	373.79	Fidelity Overseas	136.86	Fidelity Sel Computer	18.40
Mutual: Qualified	363.86	Fidelity Sel Health	133.48	Franklin Prt: Tx-Ad Intl	18.39
Lindner Fund	362.87	Oppenheimer Global	133.29	Mass Finl Wrldwide Govt	17.90
Phoenix: Balanced	361.28	T Rowe Price Intl: Stock	131.55	Paine Wbr Inv: Mstr Global	17.73
SoGen International	354.26	GT Global International	131.28	Vanguard Spl: Health	16.79
Franklin Cust: Utilities	353.26	Europacific Growth	125.73	Van Eck: World Income	16.78
Investment Co of America	335.29	Fidelity Sel Telecomm	122.36	Dean Witter Wrldwd Inc	16.63
Twentieth Cent: Select	332.85	Putnam Health Science	121.46	Wasatch: Income	16.47
Janus Fund	331.39	Shearson Telecom: Inc	120.60	Putnam Global Govt Inc	16.33
IDS New Dimensions	330.93	GAM: International	120.01	Fidelity Sel Medical	16.24
Windsor Fund	330.57	AIM: Weingarten Equity	119.32	T Rowe Price Intl: Bond	16.02
New York Venture	328.52	Strong Opportunity	118.98	Merrill Ret Global Bd; A	15.59

Global Stock Markets

Source: Morgan Stanley Capital International Perspective (52 weeks as of Sept. 5, 1991)

(in Local Currencies)

Index	Sept. 5, 1991	52-week Range		Index	Sept. 5, 1991	52-week Range	
The World	406.3	420.5	332.2	The World	406.3	420.5	332.2
E.A.F.E.[1]	520.9	550.8	435.6	Japan	1005.2	1155.1	861.5
Australia	338.2	342.1	250.2	Netherlands	336.2	338.5	268.2
Austria	449.7	515.7	377.4	New Zealand	66.8	81.6	56.7
Belgium	392.4	416.9	327.6	Norway	803.4	967.3	659.4
Canada	392.1	401.6	338.3	Singapore/Malaysia	738.4	810.4	604.8
Denmark	839.0	859.2	630.8	Spain	224.4	237.8	169.9
Finland	65.7	81.8	55.5	Sweden	1229.6	1391.2	928.4
France	518.4	520.6	402.9	Switzerland	212.7	216.1	158.1
Germany	257.3	271.4	213.2	United Kingdom	797.5	801.8	585.4
Hong Kong	2924.0	2980.7	1995.5	United States	362.8	369.7	273.7
Italy	391.7	443.4	348.0				
(1) Europe, Australia, Far East Index.							

Leading U.S. Businesses in 1990

Source: FORTUNE Magazine; World Almanac Research

(millions of dollars of sales, unless otherwise noted)

Aerospace

Boeing	$27,595
United Technologies	21,783
McDonnell Douglas	16,351
Allied-Signal	12,396
General Dynamics	10,182
Lockheed	9,977
Textron	7,918
Martin Marietta	6,143
Northrop	5,503
Grumman	4,041

Apparel

Levi Strauss	$4,247
VF	2,624
Claiborne (Liz)	1,755
Fruit of the Loom	1,427
Hartmarx	1,310
Crystal Brands	876
Leslie Fay	859
Gitano Group	807
Kellwood	780
Phillips-Van Heusen	735

Beverages

Pepsico	$17,803
Anheuser-Busch	10,751
Coca-Cola	10,406
Coca-Cola Ent. (Bottler)	4,041
Seagram (J.E.)	3,412
Coors (Adolph)	1,868
Brown-Forman	1,024

Building Materials

PPG Industries	$6,118
Owens-Illinois	4,071
American Standard	3,647
Owens-Corning Fiber.	3,111
Corning	2,980
Armstrong World Ind.	2,536
USG	2,102
Lafarge	1,598
Holnam	1,075
Southdown	566

Chemicals

Du Pont (E.I.) De Nemours	$39,839
Dow Chemical	20,005
Monsanto	9,047
Union Carbide	7,621
Grace (W.R.)	6,775
Lyondell Petrochem.	6,508
Bayer USA	5,904
Hoechst Celanese	5,881
BASF	5,381
American Cyanamid	4,822

Computers (incl. office equip.)

IBM	$69,018
Hewlett-Packard	13,233
Digital Equipment	13,085
Unisys	10,111
NCR	6,395
Apple Computer	5,558
Compaq Computer	3,626
Pitney Bowes	3,267
Wang Laboratories	2,635
Sun Microsystems	2,481

Electronics

General Electric	$58,414
Westinghouse Electric	12,915
Rockwell International	12,443
Motorola	10,885
Raytheon	9,362
TRW	8,169
Emerson Electric	7,573
Whirlpool	6,647
Texas Instruments	6,567
Cooper Industries	6,222

Food

Philip Morris	$44,323
Conagra	15,518
Sara Lee	11,652
Archer Daniels	7,925
Borden	7,633
Ralston Purina	7,133
General Mills	6,487
Campbell Soup	6,223
Heinz (H.J.)	6,112
CPC International	5,800

Forest Products

International Paper	$12,960
Georgia-Pacific	12,665
Weyerhaeuser	9,024
Kimberly-Clark	6,448
Stone Container	5,770
James River	5,423
Scott Paper	5,391
Champion International	5,159
Mead	4,796
Boise Cascade	4,190

Furniture

Johnson Controls	$4,515
Interco	2,224
Leggett & Platt	1,089
Lear Seating	1,068
Miller (Herman)	869
Hon Industries	668
Sealy Holdings	642
Kimball International	620
La-Z-Boy Chair	595

Industrial and Farm Equip.

Tenneco	$14,893
Caterpillar	11,540
Deere	7,881
Black & Decker	4,877
Dresser Industries	4,528
Ingersoll-Rand	3,738
Cummins Engine	3,462
Baker Hughes	2,614
Parker Hannifin	2,512
Great Amer. Mgmt.	2,435

Life Insurance[1]

Prudential of America	$133,456
Metropolitan Life	103,228
Aetna Life	52,343
Equitable Life Assurance	50,302
Teachers Insurance & Annuity	49,894
New York Life	39,876
Connecticut General Life	37,407
John Hancock Mutual Life	33,750
Travelers	33,028
Northwestern Mutual Life	31,377

Metal Products

Kiewit (Peter) Sons'	$5,087
Gillette	4,394
Masco	3,235
Crown Cork & Seal	3,080
Illinois Tool Works	2,551
McDermott	2,327
Sequa	2,243
Tyco Laboratories	2,103
Stanley Works	1,977
Harsco	1,767

Metals

Aluminum Co. of Amer.	$10,865
LTV	6,138
Reynolds Metals	6,076
Bethlehem Steel	4,929
Inland Steel Ind.	3,870
Amax	3,811
Phelps Dodge	2,656
National Steel	2,508
Maxxam	2,361
Penn Central	2,154

Motor Vehicles and Parts

General Motors	$126,017
Ford Motor	98,275
Chrysler	30,868
Dana	5,225
Eaton	4,102
Navistar	3,854
Paccar	2,818
Arvin Industries	1,770
Echlin	1,607
Fleetwood Enterprises	1,563

Petroleum Refining

Exxon	$105,885
Mobil	58,770
Texaco	41,235
Chevron	39,262
Amoco	28,277
Shell Oil	24,423
USX	19,462
Atlantic Richfield	18,819
Phillips Petroleum	14,032
Sun	11,909

Pharmaceuticals

Johnson & Johnson	$11,232
Bristol-Myers Squibb	10,509
Merck	7,824
American Home Products	6,917
Pfizer	6,600
Abbott Laboratories	6,210
Lilly (Eli)	5,192
Warner-Lambert	4,769
Schering-Plough	3,323
Upjohn	3,033

Publishing & Printing

Times Mirror	$3,633
Donnelly (R.R.)	3,498
Gannett	3,446
Berkshire Hathaway	2,625
Tribune	2,353
Knight-Ridder	2,305
Reader's Digest	2,056
McGraw-Hill	1,939
New York Times	1,777
Dow Jones	1,728

Retail[2]

Sears Roebuck	$55,972
Wal-Mart Stores	32,602
K Mart	32,080
American Stores	22,156
Kroger	20,261
J.C. Penney	17,410
Safeway Stores	14,874
Dayton Hudson	14,739
Great Atlantic & Pacific Tea	11,164

Rubber and Plastics Products

Goodyear Tire	$11,453
Premark International	2,721
Rubbermaid	1,539
Raychem	1,136
Hanna (M.A.)	1,120
Cooper Tire & Rubber	897
Schulman	681
Standard Products	653
Carlisle	625
Bandag	596

Scientific and Photographic Equip.

Eastman Kodak	$19,075
Xerox	18,382
Minnesota Mining	13,021
Baxter International	8,148
Honeywell	6,985
EG&G	2,478
Becton Dickinson	2,013
Polaroid	2,006
Tektronix	1,412
Bausch & Lomb	1,386

Soaps, Cosmetics

Procter & Gamble	$24,376
Unilever U.S.	8,680
Colgate-Palmolive	5,740
Avon Products	3,509
Clorox	1,502
International Flavors	963
Alberto-Culver	796
Helene Curtis Ind.	736
Stanhome	676
NCH	628

Textiles

Wickes	$3,649
Burlington Holdings	2,290
Springs Industries	1,879
West Point-Pepperell	1,754
Shaw Industries	1,475
Amoskeag	1,276
DWG	1,239
JPS Textile Group	822

Cone Mills	684
Interface	623

Tobacco

RJR Nabisco Holdings	$13,879
American Brands	8,270
Universal	2,815
Lorillard	1,605
Standard Commercial	945
Dibrell Brothers	768
UST	755

Toys, Sporting Goods

Hasbro	$1,520
Mattel	1,471
Tonka	789

Transportation[3]

United Parcel Service	$13,629
AMR	11,804
UAL	11,160
Delta Air Lines	8,582
CSX	8,306
NWA	7,257
Union Pacific	7,059
Federal Express	7,026
USAir Group	6,563
Continental Airlines	6,284

Utilities[1]

GTE	$33,769

BellSouth	30,207
Bell Atlantic	27,999
US West	27,050
NYNEX	26,651
Southwestern Bell	22,196
Pacific Gas & Electric	21,958
American Information Tech.	21,715
Pacific Telesis Group	21,581
Southern	19,955

(1) Millions of dollars of assets as of Dec. 31, 1990; (2) Incl. revenue from nonretailing activities; (3) Incl. revenue from nontransportation activities.

U.S. Industrial Corporations with Largest Sales in 1990

Source: *FORTUNE Magazine*

Company (1989 rank)	Sales[1] (billions)	Income[1] (or loss) (millions)	Company (1989 rank)	Sales[1] (billions)	Income[1] (or loss) (millions)
General Motors (1)	$126.0	($1,985)	Tenneco (26)	14.9	$561
Exxon (3)	105.9	5,010	Phillips Petroleum (30)	14.0	779
Ford Motor (2)	98.3	860	RJR Nabisco (24)	13.9	(429)
IBM (4)	69.0	6,020	Hewlett-Packard (33)	13.2	739
Mobil (6)	58.8	1,929	Digital Equipment (27)	13.1	74
General Electric (5)	58.4	4,303	Minnesota Mining & Mfg. (32)	13.0	1,308
Philip Morris (7)	44.3	3,540	International Paper (35)	13.0	569
Texaco (10)	41.2	1,450	Westinghouse Electric (28)	12.9	268
Du Pont (9)	39.8	2,310	Georgia-Pacific (41)	12.7	365
Chevron (11)	39.3	2,157	Rockwell International (29)	12.4	624
Chrysler (8)	30.9	68	Allied-Signal (31)	12.4	462
Amoco (12)	28.3	1,913	Sun (46)	11.9	229
Boeing (15)	27.6	1,385	Sara Lee (34)	11.7	470
Shell Oil (13)	24.4	1,036	Caterpillar (38)	11.5	210
Procter & Gamble (14)	24.4	1,602	Goodyear Tire & Rubber (39)	11.5	(38)
Occidental Petroleum (16)	21.9	(1,695)	Johnson & Johnson (47)	11.2	1,143
United Technologies (17)	21.8	751	Motorola (48)	10.9	499
Dow Chemical (20)	20.0	1,384	Aluminum Co. of America (37)	10.9	295
USX (19)	19.5	818	Anheuser-Busch (49)	10.8	842
Eastman Kodak (18)	19.1	703	Unocal (40)	10.7	401
Atlantic Richfield (22)	18.8	2,011	Bristol-Myers Squibb (50)	10.5	1,748
Xerox (21)	18.4	243	Coca-Cola (51)	10.4	1,382
Pepsico (23)	17.8	1,077	General Dynamics (44)	10.2	(578)
McDonnell Douglas (25)	16.6	306	Unisys (43)	10.1	(436)
Conagra (36)	15.5	232	Lockheed (45)	10.0	335

(1) Fiscal year.

Leading Franchises in 1990

Source: *Entrepreneur* magazine

Fast food and service businesses dominated *Entrepreneur* magazine's list of the top franchises in the U.S. Rankings are based on a company's age, number of units, start-up costs and growth rate. It is estimated that franchising accounts for some $700 billion in retail revenue in the U.S. annually.

Company	Business	Minimum start-up	Company	Business	Minimum start-up
Subway	fast food	$32,400	Domino's Pizza	pizza	$76,500
McDonald's	fast food	610,000	Budget Rent A Car	car rentals	150,000
Jani-King	commercial cleaning	6,500	Dairy Queen	ice cream	375,000
Little Caesar's Pizza	pizza	117,000	Midas	auto repair	182,000
Hardee's	fast food	694,280	Burger King	fast food	333,600
Chem-Dry	cleaning services	3,800	H&R Block	income-tax services	5,000
Arby's	fast food	525,000	Coverall North America	commercial cleaning	350
Electronic Realty Associates	real estate services	1,110	Choice Hotels International	hotels, motels	76,000
Kentucky Fried Chicken	fast food	150,000	Nutri System	diet centers	60,000
Jazzercise	fitness centers	2,000	Century 21 Real Estate	real estate	15,000
Service Master	commercial cleaning	8,700	Big Boy Restaurants	restaurants	450,000
Intelligent Electronics	computer products, services	150,000	Mail Boxes Etc.	shipping services	35,000
			Re/Max International	real estate	2,800

Largest Corporate Mergers or Acquisitions in U.S.

(as of mid-1991)

Company	Acquirer	Dollars	Year
RJR Nabisco	Kohlberg Kravis Roberts	24.9 bln.	1988
Warner Communications	Time	13.9 bln.	1989
Gulf Oil	Chevron	13.3 bln.	1984
Kraft	Philip Morris	11.5 bln.	1988
Squibb	Bristol-Myers	11.5 bln.	1989
Getty Oil	Texaco	10.1 bln.	1984
Conoco	DuPont	8.0 bln.	1981
Standard Oil	British Petroleum	7.9 bln.*	1987
Federated Dept. Stores	Campeau	7.4 bln.	1988
NCR	AT&T	7.4 bln.	1991
MCA	Matsushita	6.5 bln.	1990
Marathon Oil	U.S. Steel	6.5 bln.	1981
Contel	GTE	6.2 bln.	1990
Beatrice	Kohlberg Kravis Roberts	6.2 bln.	1986
RCA	General Electric	6.2 bln.	1986
Superior Oil	Mobil Oil	5.7 bln.	1984
Pillsbury	Grand Metropolitan	5.7 bln.	1988
General Foods	Philip Morris	5.6 bln.	1986
Safeway Stores	Kohlberg Kravis Roberts	5.3 bln.	1986
Farmers Group	B.A.T. Industries	5.2 bln.	1988
Southern Pacific	Santa Fe Railroad	5.2 bln.	1983
Southland	J.T. Acquisition	5.1 bln.	1987
Hughes Aircraft	General Motors	5.0 bln.	1985
Nabisco	R.J. Reynolds	4.9 bln.	1985
Signal Cos.	Allied Corp.	4.9 bln.	1986
Sperry	Burroughs	4.8 bln.	1986
Connecticut General	INA	4.3 bln.	1981
Borg-Warner	AV Holdings	4.2 bln.	1987
Texasgulf	Elf Aquitaine	4.2 bln.	1981
Cities Service	Occidental Petroleum	4.0 bln.	1982
Bank America	Security Pacific	4.0 bln.	1991
Dome Petroleum	Amoco	3.8 bln.	1987
R.H. Macy	various investors	3.7 bln.	1986
American Hospital	Baxter Travenol	3.7 bln.	1986
Owens-Illinois	Kohlberg Kravis Roberts	3.6 bln.	1987
Belridge Oil	Shell Oil	3.6 bln.	1979
NWA	Checchi Group	3.6 bln.	1988
Allied Stores	Campeau	3.5 bln.	1986
Fort Howard Paper	Morgan Stanley Group	3.5 bln.	1988
ABC Broadcasting	Capital Cities Comm.	3.5 bln.	1985
Columbia Pictures	Sony	3.4 bln.	1989
Viacom	National Amusements	3.4 bln.	1987
McCaw Cellular	LIN Broadcasting	3.3 bln.	1989
Panhandle Eastern	Texas Eastern	3.2 bln.	1989
Chesebrough-Pond's	Unilever N.V.	3.1 bln.	1987
MidCon	Occidental Petroleum	3.0 bln.	1986
American Medical Intl.	IMA Holdings	3.0 bln.	1989
Texas Oil and Gas	USX Corp.	3.0 bln.	1986
Emhart	Black & Decker	2.8 bln.	1989
Carnation	Nestle	2.8 bln.	1984
Celanese	American Hoechst	2.7 bln.	1987
Esmark	Beatrice Foods	2.7 bln.	1984
G.D. Searle	Monsanto	2.7 bln.	1986
Continental Group	Kiewit-Murdock	2.7 bln.	1984
St. Joe Minerals	Fluor	2.6 bln.	1981
Electronic Data Systems	General Motors	2.6 bln.	1984
Firestone Tire	Bridgestone	2.6 bln.	1988
Macmillan	Maxwell Comm.	2.6 bln.	1988
Associated Dry Goods	May Dept. Stores	2.5 bln.	1986

*For the 45% of Standard Oil that British Petroleum did not already own.

Capital Gains Tax

Source: U.S. Chamber of Commerce

The following shows how the top effective tax rate on capital gains has changed since 1960.

Year	Effective rate (percent)	Year	Effective rate (percent)	Year	Effective rate (percent)	Year	Effective rate (percent)
1960	25.0	1970	32.2	1976	49.1	1987	28.0
1968	26.9	1971	34.4	1979	28.0	1988	33.0
1969	27.5	1972	45.5	1981	20.0	1991	28.0

Philanthropy in the U.S.

Source: American Association of Fund-Raising Counsel Trust for Philanthropy

(billions of dollars)

Sources of Contributors

	Corporations	Foundations	Bequests	Individuals	Total Amount
1970	$.80	$1.90	$2.13	$16.19	$21.02
1975	1.20	1.65	2.23	23.53	28.61
1980	2.36	2.81	2.86	40.71	48.74
1985	4.47	4.90	4.77	66.17	80.31
1988	4.80	6.15	6.57	86.35	103.87
1989	5.60	6.55	6.97	96.78	115.90
1990	5.90	7.08	7.79	101.90	122.57

Uses of Contributions

	Religion	Education	Health	Human service	Arts, culture & humanities	Public/ society benefit
1970	$9.34	$2.60	$3.44	$2.92	$.66	$.46
1975	12.81	2.83	3.61	2.94	1.56	.79
1980	22.23	4.96	5.34	4.91	3.15	1.46
1985	37.46	8.17	7.72	8.50	5.08	2.22
1988	48.09	10.23	9.58	10.49	6.79	3.21
1989	62.51	10.95	9.93	11.39	7.50	3.84
1990*	65.76	12.41	9.90	11.82	7.89	4.92

* In 1990, $2.29 billion went to Environment/Wildlife, $2.23 billion to International Affairs, and $5.34 billion were undesignated.

Personal Consumption Expenditures in the U.S.

Source: Bureau of Economic Analysis, U.S. Dept. of Commerce

(billions of dollars)

	1985	1986	1987	1988	1989	Average Annual % change 1980-1985	1985-1989
Personal consumption expenditures	$2,629.0	$2,797.4	$3,009.4	$3,238.2	$3,450.1	8.7	6.2
Food & Tobacco	503.8	533.7	566.4	599.6	636.9	6.4	5.3
Food purchased for off-premise consumption	322.7	339.1	353.7	372.6	395.4	5.9	4.5
Purchased meals and beverages	139.9	151.6	165.5	176.6	188.8	6.9	6.9
Tobacco products	32.2	33.6	35.6	36.9	41.7	9.1	5.9
Clothing, accessories, jewelry	193.3	207.5	222.3	240.0	257.8	7.4	6.7
Shoes	22.9	24.3	25.9	27.5	29.8	6.3	6.0
Clothing and accessories less shoes	133.4	142.4	152.5	163.4	174.7	7.7	6.2
Jewelry and watches	20.5	22.8	24.7	26.4	27.4	5.9	6.7
Personal care	38.8	41.4	44.4	48.5	52.3	7.4	7.0
Toilet articles, preparations	23.1	24.6	26.3	27.9	29.7	—	5.7
Barbershops, beauty parlors, baths, health clubs	15.7	16.8	18.2	20.4	22.6	—	8.8
Housing	403.0	434.2	468.9	502.3	533.9	9.0	6.5
Owner-occupied nonfarm dwellings space rent	272.7	293.7	316.9	339.2	361.7	8.9	6.5
Tenant-occupied nonfarm dwellings rent	103.8	114.3	123.6	132.9	141.2	10.9	7.2
Rental value of farm dwellings	10.9	9.7	10.3	10.4	10.3	-.2	-1.1
Household operation	334.1	347.5	363.3	386.1	404.9	7.5	4.2
Furniture, incl. bedding	28.0	30.4	31.8	32.9	33.6	6.0	3.3
Kitchen, other household appliances	23.7	25.5	26.7	28.4	29.4	—	4.8
China, glassware, tableware, utensils	13.0	14.3	15.3	16.5	18.0	—	7.7
Other durable house furnishings	28.2	30.6	33.5	37.0	39.2	—	7.8
Semidurable house furnishings	14.0	15.2	16.0	17.3	18.7	7.0	6.7
Cleaning, household supplies, paper products	26.4	27.8	29.1	30.8	32.8	5.6	4.8
Household utilities	124.2	122.4	125.8	132.6	139.3	8.2	2.4
Telephone, telegraph	40.4	42.7	44.1	47.2	48.7	7.8	4.1
Medical care	327.5	357.6	399.0	444.0	483.5	11.8	9.5
Drug preparations, sundries	26.1	30.2	32.3	34.3	36.4	8.4	5.9
Physicians	73.5	80.6	94.0	106.1	113.0	11.8	10.7
Dentists	21.5	22.8	25.0	27.1	29.0	9.4	7.0
Privately controlled hospitals and sanitariums	140.2	152.4	166.3	182.9	201.1	11.3	8.7
Health insurance	21.6	22.4	25.3	27.7	29.6	11.9	7.4
Personal business	169.9	192.5	215.4	227.1	243.1	11.9	8.6
Brokerage charges, investment counseling	14.8	19.7	20.5	17.6	19.2	—	5.9
Bank service charges, trust services, safe deposit box rental	11.7	13.0	14.6	15.6	17.5	—	9.9
Legal services	28.0	30.9	35.0	39.6	42.9	15.2	10.6
Funeral, burial expenses	6.3	6.6	7.0	7.5	7.9	7.4	5.1
Transportation	359.5	366.3	379.7	407.5	425.7	8.6	3.7
User-operated transportation	330.1	335.9	346.3	371.0	387.6	8.8	3.5
New autos	87.4	101.3	93.5	101.1	99.7	13.5	2.8
Used autos	35.1	33.6	38.5	40.9	41.6	18.7	3.7
Repair, greasing, washing, parking, storage, rental	49.1	52.0	55.9	63.2	69.6	8.7	8.4
Gasoline and oil	90.6	73.5	75.3	77.3	83.8	1.6	-1.5
Tolls	1.4	1.7	1.9	1.7	1.7	—	4.3
Insurance premiums less claims paid	9.9	12.6	15.4	16.7	17.0	—	14.3
Purchased local transportation	7.2	7.8	8.2	8.7	8.9	4.4	4.7
Transit systems	3.6	3.8	4.0	4.2	4.3	8.4	3.8
Taxicab	3.1	3.3	3.5	3.8	3.9	—	5.2
Railway (commutation)	.5	.6	.7	.7	.7	10.8	8.0
Purchased intercity transportation	22.2	22.6	25.5	27.7	29.2	6.9	6.3
Railway (excl. commutation)	.6	.7	.7	.8	.9	—	10.0
Bus	1.2	1.1	1.4	1.6	1.3	—	1.6
Airline	18.5	18.8	20.8	22.8	24.2	6.7	6.2
Recreation	185.7	201.2	223.2	245.1	264.4	10.1	8.5
Books, maps	8.1	8.6	9.5	10.5	11.4	—	8.1
Magazines, newspapers, sheet music	13.2	13.9	15.4	17.0	18.5	4.9	8.0
Nondurable toys and sport supplies	21.1	23.1	26.2	28.0	30.2	7.6	8.6
Wheel goods, durable toys, sports equipment, boats, pleasure aircraft	26.7	29.7	33.2	35.4	36.2	—	7.1
Radio and TV receivers, records, musical instruments	37.0	38.8	41.6	47.1	51.1	13.2	7.6
Flowers, seeds, potted plants	5.5	5.8	7.0	7.5	8.1	—	9.5
Admissions to specified spectator amusements	9.5	10.2	11.3	12.1	13.4	—	8.2
Motion picture theaters	3.6	3.9	4.2	4.4	5.0	—	7.8
Legitimate theater, opera	3.0	3.3	4.0	4.5	4.9	—	12.7
Spectator sports	2.9	2.9	3.0	3.2	3.5	—	4.1
Clubs, fraternal organizations	4.8	5.0	5.5	5.9	6.3	—	6.3
Commerical amusements	15.1	16.0	17.1	18.7	20.2	—	6.8
Private education, research	43.3	46.6	50.9	57.7	64.3	9.7	9.7
Higher education	15.7	16.9	17.7	19.3	20.9	—	6.6
Elementary and secondary schools	13.8	14.5	15.5	17.0	18.6	—	7.0
Religious and welfare activities	57.1	62.9	68.1	75.9	82.9	9.2	9.0

Consumer Price Index

The Consumer Price Index (CPI) is a measure of the average change in prices over time of basic consumer goods and services. From Jan. 1978, the Bureau of Labor Statistics began publishing CPI's for two population groups: (1) a CPI for All Urban Consumers (CPI-U) which covers about 80% of the total population; and (2) a CPI for Urban Wage Earners and Clerical Workers (CPI-W) which covers about 32% of the total population. The CPI-U includes, in addition to wage earners and clerical workers, groups such as professional, managerial, and technical workers, the self-employed, short-term workers, the unemployed, retirees and others not in the labor force.

The CPI is based on prices of food, clothing, shelter, fuels, transportation fares, charges for doctors' and dentists' services, drugs, and the other goods and services bought for day-to-day living. The index had been measuring price changes from a designated reference date—1967—which equaled 100.0.

Beginning with the release of data for January 1988, the standard reference base period for the Consumer Price Index is 1982-84. The rebasing is in keeping with the government's policy that index bases should be updated periodically. The 1982-84 period was chosen to coincide with the time period of the updated CPI's expenditure weights, which are based upon the Consumer Expenditure Surveys for 1982, 1983, and 1984. All of the CPI figures in the following tables have been changed to reflect the new reference base.

Consumer Price Indexes, 1991

Source: Bureau of Labor Statistics. U.S. Depart. of Labor

(1982-84=100)	CPI-U Unadjusted indexes June 1991	CPI-U Unadjusted percent change to June 1991 from— June 1990	CPI-U Unadjusted percent change to June 1991 from— May 1991	Seasonally adjusted percent change from— May to June	CPI-W Unadjusted indexes June 1991	CPI-W Unadjusted percent change to June 1991 from— June 1990	CPI-W Unadjusted percent change to June 1991 from— May 1991	Seasonally adjusted percent change from— May to June
Food, beverages.........	137.7	4.6	0.3	0.5	137.4	4.5	0.3	0.4
Housing..............	133.3	4.0	0.5	0.1	131.1	3.9	0.5	0.1
Apparel, upkeep.........	126.9	2.9	−1.9	−0.1	126.7	2.7	−1.7	0.2
Transportation..........	123.7	4.7	0.3	0.2	123.1	4.6	0.3	0.2
Medical care...........	176.2	8.8	0.6	0.6	175.6	8.5	0.6	0.6
Entertainment..........	138.1	4.7	0.2	0.2	136.7	4.4	0.2	0.2
Other goods, services.....	170.0	7.7	0.5	0.8	170.5	8.0	0.6	0.9
Services	145.8	5.0	0.6	0.2	144.1	4.9	0.5	0.2
Special Indexes								
All items less food........	135.7	4.9	0.2	0.1	133.4	4.7	0.2	0.2
Commodities less food	120.9	4.4	−0.3	0.1	120.5	4.4	−0.1	0.2
Nondurables	125.8	4.7	−0.2	−0.2	130.3	4.7	−0.1	−0.1
Energy	103.5	4.0	1.4	−1.0	103.3	4.1	1.3	−0.9
All items less energy	140.5	4.7	0.1	0.4	138.6	4.6	0.1	0.4

Consumer Price Indexes for Selected Items and Groups

Source: Bureau of Labor Statistics, U.S. Dept. of Labor

(all urban consumers = CPI-U)

(1982-84 = 100. Annual averages of monthly figures)

	1970	1975	1980	1985	1987	1988	1989	1990
All Items	38.8	53.8	82.4	107.6	113.6	118.3	124.0	130.7
Food and beverages.............	40.1	60.2	86.7	105.6	113.5	118.2	124.9	132.1
Food...................	39.2	59.8	86.8	105.6	113.5	118.2	125.1	132.4
Food at home	39.9	61.8	88.4	104.3	111.9	116.6	124.2	132.3
Cereals, bakery prods..	37.1	62.9	83.9	107.9	114.8	122.1	132.4	140.0
Meats, poultry, fish, eggs	44.6	67.0	92.0	100.1	110.5	114.3	121.3	130.0
Dairy prods..............	44.7	62.6	90.9	103.2	105.9	108.4	115.6	126.5
Fruits, vegetables.........	37.8	56.9	82.1	106.4	119.1	128.1	138.0	149.0
Sugar, sweets............	30.5	65.3	90.5	105.8	111.0	114.0	119.4	124.7
Fats, oils...............	39.2	73.5	89.3	106.9	108.1	113.1	121.2	126.3
Nonalcoholic beverages	27.1	41.3	91.4	104.3	107.5	107.5	111.3	113.5
Other prepared foods	39.6	58.9	83.6	106.4	113.8	118.0	125.5	131.2
Food away from home	37.5	54.5	83.4	108.3	117.0	121.8	127.4	133.4
Alcoholic beverages..........	52.1	65.9	86.4	106.4	114.1	118.6	123.5	129.3
Housing..................	36.4	50.7	81.1	107.7	114.2	118.5	123.0	128.5
Shelter	35.5	48.8	81.0	109.8	121.3	127.1	132.8	140.0
Rent	46.5	58.0	80.9	111.8	123.1	127.8	132.8	146.7
Maintenance, repairs.......	35.8	54.1	82.4	106.5	111.8	114.7	118.0	122.2
Fuel, other utilities	29.1	45.4	75.4	106.5	103.0	104.4	107.8	111.6
Electricity	31.8	50.0	75.8	106.9	110.0	111.5	114.7	117.4
Household furnishings & operation......	46.8	63.4	86.3	103.8	107.1	109.4	111.2	113.3
House furnishings...........	55.5	69.8	88.5	101.7	103.6	105.1	105.5	106.7
Apparel & upkeep..............	59.2	72.5	90.9	105.0	110.6	115.4	118.6	124.1
Apparel commodities	63.3	76.7	92.9	104.0	108.9	113.7	116.7	122.0
Men's & boys'...........	62.2	75.5	89.4	105.0	109.1	113.4	117.0	120.4
Women's & girls'..........	71.8	85.5	96.0	104.9	110.4	114.9	116.4	122.5
Footwear...............	56.8	69.6	91.8	102.3	105.1	109.9	114.4	117.4
Transportation................	37.5	50.1	83.1	106.4	105.4	108.7	114.1	120.5
Private..................	37.5	50.6	84.2	106.2	104.2	107.6	112.9	118.8
New cars..............	53.0	62.9	88.4	106.1	114.6	116.9	119.2	121.4
Used cars..............	31.2	43.8	62.3	113.7	113.1	118.0	120.4	117.6
Gasoline	27.9	45.1	97.5	98.6	80.1	80.8	88.5	101.0
Auto insurance..........	42.0	48.4	82.0	119.2	146.2	156.6	166.6	177.9
Public..................	35.2	43.5	69.0	110.5	121.1	123.3	129.5	142.6
Airline fares	28.3	38.0	68.0	112.5	122.8	124.2	131.6	148.4
Medical care................	34.0	47.5	74.9	113.5	130.1	138.6	149.3	162.8

(continued)

	1970	1975	1980	1985	1987	1988	1989	1990
Prescription drugs	47.4	51.2	72.5	120.1	140.8	152.0	165.2	181.7
Physicians' services	34.5	48.1	76.5	113.3	130.4	139.8	150.1	160.8
Dental services.	39.2	53.2	78.9	114.2	128.8	137.5	146.1	155.8
Hospital room	23.6	38.3	68.0	115.4	131.1	143.3	158.1	175.4
Entertainment	**47.5**	**62.0**	**83.6**	**107.9**	**115.3**	**120.3**	**126.5**	**132.4**
Other goods & services	**40.9**	**53.9**	**75.2**	**114.5**	**128.5**	**137.0**	**147.7**	**159.0**
Tobacco products	43.1	54.7	72.0	116.7	133.6	145.8	164.4	181.5
Personal care	43.5	57.9	81.9	106.3	115.1	119.4	125.0	130.4
Toilet goods	42.7	58.0	79.6	107.6	113.9	118.1	123.2	128.2
Personal care services	44.2	57.7	83.7	108.9	116.2	120.7	126.8	132.8
Personal, educational expenses	35.5	48.7	70.9	119.1	138.5	147.9	158.1	170.2

Consumer Price Indexes Annual Percent Change

Source: Bureau of Labor Statistics, U.S. Dept. of Labor

The Consumer Price Index (CPI-U) measures the average change in prices of goods and services purchased by all urban consumers.

	1978[1]	1979	1980	1981	1982	1983	1985	1986	1987	1988	1989	1990
All items.	7.6	11.3	13.5	10.3	6.2	3.2	3.6	1.9	3.6	4.1	4.8	5.4
Food	9.9	11.0	8.6	7.8	4.1	2.1	2.3	3.2	4.1	4.1	5.8	5.8
Shelter.	10.2	13.9	17.6	11.7	7.1	2.3	5.6	5.5	4.7	4.8	4.5	5.4
Rent, residential . . .	6.9	7.2	8.9	8.7	7.6	5.8	6.2	5.8	4.1	3.8	3.9	5.6
Fuel & other utilities . .	6.9	10.8	16.4	14.6	9.8	5.6	1.6	−2.3	−1.1	−1.4	3.3	3.5
Apparel and upkeep . .	3.6	4.3	7.1	4.8	2.6	2.5	2.8	0.9	4.4	4.3	2.8	4.6
Private transportation .	4.7	14.7	17.4	11.4	3.5	2.3	2.5	−4.7	−3.0	3.3	4.9	5.2
New cars	7.7	7.9	8.1	6.0	3.9	2.6	3.2	4.2	3.6	2.0	2.0	1.8
Gasoline.	4.2	35.5	38.9	11.3	−5.3	−3.3	.8	−21.9	−4.0	0.9	9.5	14.1
Public transportation . .	3.0	6.6	25.7	24.1	10.9	4.8	4.5	5.9	3.5	1.8	5.0	10.1
Medical care	8.4	9.2	11.0	10.7	11.6	8.8	6.3	7.5	6.6	6.5	7.7	9.0
Entertainment	5.3	6.7	9.0	7.8	6.5	4.3	3.9	3.4	3.3	4.3	5.2	4.7
Commodities	7.2	11.3	12.3	8.4	4.1	2.9	2.1	−0.9	3.2	3.5	4.7	5.2

(1) Change from 1977.

Consumer Price Index by Region and Selected Cities

Source: Bureau of Labor Statistics, U.S. Dept. of Labor

	CPI-U Indexes			Percent change to June 1991	CPI-W Indexes			Percent change to June 1991
Area (1982-84 = 100)	Apr. 1991	May 1991	June 1991	from— June 1990	Apr. 1991	May 1991	June 1991	from— June 1990
U.S. city average	135.2	135.6	136.0	4.7	133.3	133.8	134.1	4.5
Northeast urban	141.6	141.7	142.1	5.3	139.9	140.1	140.5	5.2
More than 1,200,000.	141.8	142.1	142.6	5.3	139.2	139.5	140.0	5.0
500,000 to 1,200,000	141.9	141.5	141.6	5.4	140.2	139.9	140.1	5.4
50,000 to 500,000	140.5	140.4	140.5	5.3	142.5	142.6	142.8	5.2
North Central urban.	131.5	132.3	132.6	4.5	129.2	130.1	130.4	4.5
More than 1,200,000.	132.6	133.8	134.2	4.4	129.4	130.5	131.0	4.3
360,000 to 1,200,000	130.4	130.9	131.5	4.7	128.0	128.4	129.1	4.9
50,000 to 360,000	132.5	132.8	132.5	4.7	131.0	131.3	131.0	4.6
Less than 50,000	127.0	127.8	127.9	4.6	126.6	127.5	127.6	4.6
South urban	132.1	132.5	132.8	4.3	131.0	131.5	131.8	4.3
More than 1,200,000.	132.7	133.4	133.6	4.5	131.2	132.1	-132.3	4.4
450,000 to 1,200,000	133.2	133.8	134.0	4.5	130.3	131.0	131.2	4.4
50,000 to 450,000	131.1	131.1	131.5	4.9	131.2	131.3	131.8	4.9
Less than 50,000	130.9	130.6	131.3	2.4	131.3	131.1	131.8	2.6
West urban	136.2	136.3	136.8	4.6	134.1	134.3	134.7	4.3
More than 1,250,000.	137.8	138.1	138.7	4.6	134.2	134.6	135.1	4.4
50,000 to 330,000	133.2	132.6	133.2	4.3	132.2	131.6	132.2	4.3
Selected areas								
Chicago, Ill.–Gary-Lake County, Ill., Ind., Wis.	136.1	136.8	137.3	4.3	132.1	132.7	133.1	4.1
L.A.–Anaheim, Riverside, Cal. .	140.7	140.8	140.8	4.3	136.3	136.5	136.4	4.0
New York, N.Y.–Northern N.J., Long Island, N.Y.	143.7	144.0	144.6	5.5	141.0	141.4	142.1	5.3
Philadelphia, Wilmington, Trenton, Pa., Del., N.J., M.D. . . .	140.8	141.3	141.8	5.0	140.8	141.2	141.8	4.6
San Francisco–Oakland, San Jose, Cal.	135.8	136.2	137.6	4.6	134.2	134.8	136.0	4.1
Baltimore, Md..	—	135.4	—	—	—	134.4	—	—
Boston, Lawrence, Salem, Mass., N.H.	—	143.5	—	—	—	143.4	—	—
Cleveland, Akron, Lorain Oh. . .	—	134.3	—	—	—	127.8	—	—
Miami, Ft. Lauderdale, Fla. . . .	—	132.0	—	—	—	130.2	—	—
St. Louis, E. St. Louis, Mo., Ill. .	—	131.3	—	—	—	130.6	—	—
Washington, D.C.–Md.–Va. . . .	—	140.9	—	—	—	139.6	—	—
Dallas–Fort Worth, Tex.	129.5	—	130.1	5.1	128.2	—	129.4	5.0
Detroit, Ann Arbor, Mich.. . . .	131.7	—	133.5	4.5	128.3	—	130.1	4.3
Houston, Galveston, Brazoria, Tex.	123.5	—	124.9	4.3	123.6	—	125.2	4.3
Pittsburgh, Beaver Valley, Pa. .	130.3	—	130.7	4.6	124.9	—	125.3	4.2

Percent Change in Consumer Prices in Selected Countries

Source: International Monetary Fund

Country	1970-1975, avg.	1975-1980, avg.	1980-1985, avg.	1986-1987, avg.	1987-1988, avg.	1988-1989, avg.	1989-1990, avg.
United States	6.7	8.9	5.5	3.7	4.0	4.8	5.4
Canada	7.3	8.7	7.4	4.4	4.0	5.0	4.8
France	8.8	10.5	9.6	3.3	2.7	3.5	3.4
Germany	6.1	4.1	3.9	0.2	1.3	2.8	2.7
Italy	11.3	16.3	13.7	4.7	5.1	6.3	6.5
Japan	11.5	6.5	2.7	0	0.7	2.3	3.1
Spain	12.1	18.6	12.2	5.3	4.8	6.8	6.7
Sweden	8.0	10.5	9.0	4.2	5.8	6.4	10.5
Switzerland	7.7	2.3	4.3	1.4	1.9	3.2	5.4
United Kingdom	13.0	14.4	7.2	4.1	4.9	7.8	9.5

Index of Leading Economic Indicators

Source: Bureau of Economic Analysis, U.S. Dept. of Commerce

The index of leading economic indicators, which is issued to project the economy's performance six months or a year ahead, was up 1.2 percent in July 1991, the largest monthly increase in 3 years. Analysts said that the increase suggests that the economy may be on the verge of a recovery from the recession.

The index is made up of eleven measurements of economic activity that tend to change direction long before the overall economy does. The volatility of the index, caused in part by the fact that many of the statistics covered do not reach the Commerce Department until weeks after the initial report, usually results in at least one revision after the initial reporting.

Leading Indicators: Component Analysis

Components	Contribution to change June to July 1991	Components	Contribution to change June to July 1991
Average work week of production workers in manufacturing	−0.70	adjusted for inflation	+0.31
Average weekly claims for state unemployment insurance[1]	+0.14	New building permits issued	+0.01
		Change in manufactureres unfilled orders, durable goods	+0.27
New orders for consumer goods and materials, adjusted for inflation	+0.39	Change in sensitive materials prices	+0.03
		Index of stock prices	+0.03
Vendor performance (companies receiving slower deliveries from suppliers)	+0.14	Money supply: M-2, adjusted for inflation	−0.17
Contracts and orders for plant and equipment,		Index of consumer expectations	−0.06
		Leading indicators index, percent change	**+1.20**

(1) Series is inverted in computing index; that is, a decrease in the series is considered upward movement.

Distribution of Total Personal Income

Source: Bureau of Economic Analysis; U.S. Dept. of Commerce

(billions of dollars)

Year	Personal income	Personal taxes	Disposable Personal income	Personal outlays	Personal Savings — Amount	As pct. of disposable income
1960	$ 402.3	$ 50.4	$ 352.0	$ 332.3	$ 19.7	5.6%
1965	540.7	64.9	475.8	442.1	33.7	7.1
1970	811.1	115.8	695.3	639.5	55.8	8.0
1975	1,265.0	168.9	1,096.1	1,001.8	94.3	8.6
1976	1,391.2	196.8	1,194.4	1,111.9	82.5	6.9
1977	1,540.4	226.4	1,314.0	1,236.0	78.0	5.9
1978	1,732.7	258.7	1,474.0	1,384.6	89.4	6.1
1979	1,951.2	301.0	1,650.2	1,553.5	96.7	5.9
1980	2,165.3	336.5	1,828.9	1,718.7	110.2	6.0
1981	2,429.5	387.7	2,041.7	1,904.3	137.4	6.7
1982	2,584.6	404.1	2,180.5	2,044.5	136.0	6.2
1983	2,838.6	410.5	2,428.1	2,297.4	130.6	5.4
1984	3,108.7	440.2	2,668.6	2,504.5	164.1	6.1
1985	3,325.3	486.6	2,838.7	2,713.3	125.4	4.4
1986	3,526.2	512.9	3,013.3	2,888.5	124.9	4.1
1987	3,776.6	571.7	3,205.9	3,104.1	101.8	3.2
1988	4,070.8	591.6	3,479.2	3,333.6	145.6	4.2
1989	4,384.3	658.8	3,725.5	3,553.7	171.8	4.6
1990	4,645.5	699.4	3,946.1	3,766.0	180.1	4.6

Notable Bankruptcy Filings

Year	Company	Year	Company	Year	Company
1970	Penn Central	1988	Financial Corp. of America	1990	Drexel Burnham Lambert
1982	Manville	1989	MCorp	1990	Allied/Federal
1983	Baldwin-United	1989	Southmark	1990	Ames Department Stores
1985	Wheeling-Pittsburgh Steel	1989	Lomas Financial	1990	Continental Airlines
1986	LTV Corp.	1989	American Continental	1990	Pan Am
1987	Texaco				

Percent Change in Federal Aid to State and Local Governments

Source: U.S. Office of Management and Budget

Type of aid, function, and major program	1970-1975	1975-1980	1980-1985	1985-1989
Grant-in-aid shared revenue	106%	83%	15%	16%
National defense	100	25	68	47
Natural resources & environment	492	120	-24	-8
Energy	72	1,060	6	-17
Agriculture	-33	40	325	-29
Transportation[2]	27	123	30	6
Commerce & housing credit	-50	50	-33	—
Community & regional development[2]	59	128	-19	-17
Education, employment, training, social services[2]	89	80	-18	25
Health[2]	128	78	55	49
Income security[2]	60	97	46	22
Veterans benefits & services	83	172	1	40
Administration of justice	1,626	-27	-82	277
General government[4]	106	36	31	1,048

Foreign Direct Investment in the U.S.

Source: Bureau of Economic Analysis; U.S. Dept. of Commerce

(billions of dollars)

Five countries accounted for over 75 percent of the $403.7 billion worth of foreign direct investment in the U.S. at the end of 1990.

	1970	1975	1980	1985	1988	1989	1990
All Countries	$13.2	$27.6	$83.0	$184.6	$328.8	$401.0	$403.7
Canada	3.1	5.3	12.1	17.1	27.3	32.0	27.7
Germany	0.680	1.4	7.5	14.8	23.8	28.0	27.8
Japan	0.229	0.591	4.7	19.3	53.3	70.0	108.1
Netherlands	2.1	5.3	19.1	37.0	48.9	60.0	83.5
Switzerland	1.5	2.1	5.0	10.5	15.8	—	64.3
United Kingdom	4.1	6.3	14.1	43.5	101.9	119.0	17.5

Consumer Credit Outstanding, 1970 to 1990

Source: Federal Reserve System

(billions of dollars)

Estimated amounts of credit outstanding as of end of year. Not seasonally adjusted.

Type of Credit	1970	1975	1980	1985	1986	1987	1988	1989	1990
Credit outstanding	133.8	207.5	355.4	601.8	659.8	693.2	743.6	794.7	808.9
Ratio to disposable personal income[1] (percent)	18.7	18.2	18.5	21.2	21.9	21.7	21.4	21.3	20.5
Installment	105.5	168.7	302.1	526.5	581.8	619.8	674.9	730.9	748.3
Automobile paper	36.3	57.2	111.9	210.3	247.5	265.8	284.3	290.7	284.8
Revolving	5.1	15.0	58.5	128.9	143.7	161.8	184.0	210.3	232.3
Mobile home paper	2.5	14.4	18.7	26.9	27.1	25.9	25.1	22.2	20.7
All other loans	61.6	85.3	112.9	160.4	163.6	166.3	181.3	207.6	210.5
Commercial banks	48.7	82.9	147.0	245.1	266.8	287.2	324.8	342.8	347.5
Finance companies	27.6	32.7	62.3	111.9	134.7	141.1	146.2	140.8	137.5
Credit unions	13.0	25.7	44.0	72.7	77.1	81.0	88.3	93.1	92.9
Retailers[2]	13.9	18.2	28.7	43.0	43.3	46.0	48.4	44.2	43.6
Other[3]	2.3	9.2	20.1	53.8	59.9	64.4	67.1	61.2	50.4
Noninstallment	28.3	38.8	53.3	75.3	78.0	73.5	68.8	63.8	60.6

(1) Based on fourth quarter seasonally adjusted disposable personal income at annual rates as published by the U.S. Bureau of Economic Analysis. (2) Excludes 30-day charge credit held by travel and entertainment companies. (3) Comprises savings institutions and gasoline companies.

Bankruptcy Petitions, 1905-1990

(Thousands)

Source: Administrative Office of the U.S. Courts. Annual Report of the Director

Year	Filed	Pending	Year	Filed	Pending	Year	Filed	Pending	Year	Filed	Pending
1905	17	28	1940	53	55	1975	254	202	1985	365	609
1910	18	28	1945	13	21	1980	278	346	1986	478	729
1915	28	44	1950	33	38	1981	360	362	1987	561	809
1920	14	30	1955	59	56	1982	368	461	1988	594	815
1925	46	60	1960	110	95	1983	375	537	1989	643	879
1930	63	61	1965	180	162	1984	344	578	1990	725	974
1935	69	65	1970	194	191						

For fiscal years ending in year shown. Covers all U.S. bankruptcy courts. Bankruptcy petitions "Filed" means the commencement of a proceeding through the presentation of a petition to the clerk of the bankruptcy court; "Pending" is a proceeding in which the administration has not been completed.

State Finances

Revenues, Expenditures, Debts, Taxes, and U.S. Aid

(fiscal year 1990)

Source: Census Bureau, U.S. Dept. of Commerce

State	Revenue (millions)	Expenditures (millions)	Debt (millions)	Per cap. debt	Per cap. taxes	Per cap. U.S. aid
Alabama.	$9,041	$8,108	$3,979	$984	$945	$509
Alaska.	5,500	4,688	5,536	10,064	2,811	1,131
Arizona	8,598	8,265	2,193	598	1,194	352
Arkansas	4,511	4,223	1,747	743	961	486
California	88,704	78,867	28,866	969	1,458	539
Colorado	7,527	6,510	2,422	735	931	413
Connecticut	9,591	9,886	10,988	3,342	1,602	533
Delaware	2,316	2,128	2,978	4,471	1,696	460
Florida.	23,868	21,723	9,950	769	1,027	309
Georgia	13,108	12,213	3,117	481	1,092	444
Hawaii	4,326	3,832	3,396	3,064	2,107	550
Idaho.	2,417	2,047	977	970	1,130	490
Illinois	24,313	22,072	15,262	1,335	1,127	392
Indiana.	11,456	10,414	4,140	746	1,100	406
Iowa	6,728	6,317	1,875	675	1,193	464
Kansas	5,136	4,705	306	123	1,077	386
Kentucky	8,593	7,772	5,295	1,437	1,156	486
Louisiana	10,096	9,420	12,770	3,026	968	568
Maine	3,246	3,044	2,125	1,730	1,271	563
Maryland	12,195	11,296	6,644	1,389	1,349	438
Massachusetts . . .	17,034	18,736	18,715	3,110	1,557	549
Michigan.	23,405	23,098	9,170	986	1,220	449
Minnesota.	13,162	11,355	3,764	860	1,558	519
Mississippi.	5,344	4,838	1,343	521	931	579
Missouri	9,343	8,326	5,250	1,025	965	352
Montana.	2,225	2,007	1,396	1,746	1,073	685
Nebraska	3,073	2,885	1,361	862	958	431
Nevada	3,266	2,929	1,573	1,308	1,317	304
New Hampshire . .	1,922	1,972	3,338	3,010	536	336
New Jersey	22,624	21,454	18,908	2,446	1,349	471
New Mexico.	4,731	4,172	1,830	1,208	1,329	514
New York	64,253	59,139	46,547	2,587	1,590	717
North Carolina . . .	14,485	13,493	3,071	463	1,186	399
North Dakota	1,810	1,755	872	1,364	1,059	693
Ohio	28,516	25,237	11,209	1,033	1,054	439
Oklahoma.	7,201	6,515	3,714	1,180	1,105	427
Oregon	7,001	6,352	6,558	2,307	980	576
Pennsylvania	27,223	24,531	10,926	919	1,112	443
Rhode Island	3,034	3,014	3,616	3,604	1,229	665
South Carolina . . .	8,750	7,910	3,894	1,116	1,128	495
South Dakota. . . .	1,494	1,344	1,787	2,568	718	647
Tennessee	9,110	8,403	2,618	536	870	508
Texas	30,975	26,027	7,864	462	866	382
Utah	4,302	3,857	1,790	1,039	1,026	560
Vermont.	1,592	1,565	1,259	2,236	1,182	699
Virginia.	13,607	12,632	6,083	983	1,066	340
Washington	14,999	13,567	5,686	1,168	1,525	461
West Virginia	4,435	4,212	2,471	1,378	1,243	525
Wisconsin	13,388	11,416	6,119	1,250	1,340	483
Wyoming	1,900	1,641	938	2,066	1,347	1,110
United States . . .	**$825,473**	**$571,909**	**$318,237**	**$1,282**	**$1,211**	**$477**

Federal Deposit Insurance Corporation (FDIC)

The primary purpose of the Federal Deposit Insurance Corporation (FDIC) is to insure deposits in all banks approved for insurance coverage benefits under the Federal Deposit Insurance Act. The major functions of the FDIC are to pay off depositors of insured banks closed without adequate provision having been made to pay depositors' claims, to act as receiver for all national banks placed in receivership and for state banks placed in receivership when appointed receiver by state authorities, and to prevent the continuance or development of unsafe and unsound banking practices. The FDIC's entire income consists of assessments on insured banks and income from investments; it receives no appropriations from Congress. It may borrow from the U.S. Treasury not to exceed $3 billion outstanding, but has made no such borrowings since it was organized in 1933. The FDIC surplus (Deposit Insurance Fund) as of Jan. 1, 1991 was $4.5 billion.

Federal Reserve System
(as of Aug. 1991)

The Federal Reserve System is the central bank for the United States. The system was established on December 23, 1913, originally to give the country an elastic currency, to provide facilities for discounting commercial paper, and to improve the supervision of banking. Since then, the System's responsibilities have been broadened. Over the years, stability and growth of the economy, a high level of employment, stability in the purchasing power of the dollar, and reasonable balance in transactions with foreign countries have come to be recognized as primary objectives of governmental economic policy.

The Federal Reserve System consists of the Board of Governors, the 12 District Reserve Banks and their branch offices, and the Federal Open Market Committee. Several advisory councils help the Board meet its varied responsibilities.

The hub of the System is the seven member Board of Governors in Washington. The members of the Board are appointed by the President and confirmed by the Senate, to serve 14-year terms. The President also appoints the Chairman and Vice-Chairman of the Board from among the board members for 4-year terms that may be renewed. Currently, the board members are: Alan Greenspan, Chairman; Edward W. Kelley, Jr.; David W. Mullins, Jr., Vice Chairman; Wayne D. Angell; John P. La Ware.

The Board is the policy-making body. In addition to its policy making responsibilities, it supervises the budget and operations of the Reserve Banks, approves the appointments of their presidents and appoints 3 of each District Bank's directors, including the chairman and vice chairman of each Reserve Bank's board.

The 12 Reserve Banks and their branch offices serve as the decentralized portion of the System, carrying out day-to-day operations such as circulating currency and coin, providing fiscal agency functions and payments mechanism services. The District Banks are located in Boston, New York, Philadelphia, Cleveland, Richmond, Atlanta, Chicago, St. Louis, Minneapolis, Kansas City, Dallas and San Francisco.

The System's principal function is monetary policy, which it controls using three tools: reserve requirements, the discount rate and open market operations. Uniform reserve requirements, set by the Board, are applied to the transaction accounts and nonpersonal time deposits of all depository institutions. Responsibility for setting the discount rate (the interest rate at which depository institutions can borrow money from the Reserve Banks) is shared by the Board of Governors and the Reserve Banks. Changes in the discount rate are recommended by the individual Boards of Directors of the Reserve Banks and are subject to approval by the Board of Governors. The most important tool of monetary policy is open market operations (the purchase and sale of government securities). Responsibility for influencing the cost and availability of money and credit through the purchase and sale of government securities lies with the Federal Open Market Committee (FOMC). This committee is composed of the 7 members of the Board of Governors, the president of the Federal Reserve Bank of New York, and 4 other Federal Reserve Bank presidents, who serve one-year terms on a rotating basis. The committee bases its decisions on current economic and financial developments and outlook, setting yearly growth objectives for key measures of money supply and credit. The decisions of the committee are carried out by the Domestic Trading Desk of the Federal Reserve Bank of New York.

The Federal Reserve Act prescribes a Federal Advisory Council, consisting of one member from each Federal Reserve District, elected annually by the Board of Directors of each of the 12 Federal Reserve Banks. They meet with the Federal Reserve Board four times a year to discuss business and financial conditions and to make advisory recommendations.

The Consumer Advisory Council is a statutory body, including both consumer and creditor representatives, which advises the Board of Governors on its implementation of consumer regulations and other consumer-related matters.

Following the passage of the Monetary Control Act of 1980, the Board of Governors established the Thrift Institutions Advisory Council to provide information and views on the special needs and problems of thrift institutions. The group is comprised of representatives of mutual savings banks, savings and loan associations, and credit unions.

Federal Reserve Board Discount Rate

The discount rate is the rate of interest set by the Federal Reserve that member banks are charged when borrowing money through the Federal Reserve System.

Effective Date	Rate	Effective Date	Rate	Effective Date	Rate	Effective Date	Rate
1980: Feb. 15	13	Nov. 2	13	Dec. 15	8½	Aug. 21	5½
May 30	12	Dec. 4	12	1984: April 9	9	1987: Sept. 4	6
June 13	11	1982: July 20	11½	Nov. 21	8½	1988: Aug. 9	6½
July 28	10	Aug. 2	11	Dec. 24	8	1989: Feb. 24	7
Sept. 26	11	Aug. 16	10½	1985: May 20	7½	1990: Dec. 18	6½
Nov. 17	12	Aug. 27	10	1986: March 7	7	1991: Feb. 1	6
Dec. 5	13	Oct. 12	9½	April 21	6½	1991: Apr. 30	5½
1981: May 5	14	Nov. 22	9	July 11	6	Sept. 13	5

Chapter 11

Chapter 11 refers to the provisions in the Federal Bankruptcy Act for court-supervised reorganization of debtor companies. A company files for Chapter 11 protection when it can no longer pay its creditors or when it expects future liabilities it cannot hope to pay, like product liability damage awards. In 1991, the U.S. Supreme Court ruled that the provision of Federal bankruptcy law that permits corporations to reorganize while continuing to operate was also available for use by individuals.

Process
1. Judge issues automatic stay
- Creditors cannot press suits for repayment.
- Debts are frozen.
- Company's day-to-day operations continue.
- Significant spending must have judge's approval.
- Secured creditors can ask court for hardship exemption from debt freeze.
2. Unsecured creditors form a committee
- Representatives are chosen to deal with the company.
- Creditors can ask the court to appoint an examiner to investigate possible fraud or mismanagement.
- Court can name a trustee to run the company.

3. The committee and company negotiate a reorganization plan.
- Parties negotiate a repayment plan for frozen debts. This step can take months or years.
4. Creditors approve the plan
- Must have assent of majority of creditors as well as creditors who are owed two-thirds of the debt.
5. Judge approves the plan

Reorganized Company Emerges
- It must meet the terms of the agreed repayment plan.
- It operates as a normal company.

The Savings and Loan Crisis

President Bush signed legislation March 23, 1991, giving the Resolution Trust Corporation, the government organization created in 1989 to handle the savings & loan industry bailout, $30 billion to cover losses at failed S&Ls. The legislation also provided $48 billion in working capital allowing the RTC to temporarily take over thrifts' bad assets so that the institutions would be easier to sell. There is no way to forecast how much the U.S. government will eventually pay to save the troubled industry. The following is the General Accounting Office estimate of the cost of the bailout as of June 1991. (*See Chronology for additional information.*)

Estimates of Major Costs through the Year 2029

$175 billion — **Extra interest costs if rates rise or recession strikes**

$133 billion — **Assumed cost of interest payments over the next 40 years**

$37 billion — **Administrative costs**

$155 billion — **The principal - what the bailout would cost if it could be paid for outright today**

$500 billion · $325 billion

All Banks in U.S.—Number, Deposits

Source: Federal Reserve System

Comprises all national banks in the United States and all state commercial banks, trust companies, mutual stock savings banks, private and industrial banks, and special types of institutions that are treated as banks by the federal bank supervisory agencies. Data as of June 30 prior to 1975.

Year	Number of banks					Total deposits (millions of dollars)					
	Total all banks	F.R.S. members		Nonmembers		Total all banks	F.R.S. members		Nonmembers		
		Total	Nat'l	State	Mutual savings	Other		Total	Nat'l	State	Mutual savings	Other
1925..	26,479	9,538	8,066	1,472	621	18,320	$51,641	$32,457	$19,912	$12,546	$7,089	$12,095
1930..	23,855	8,315	7,247	1,068	604	14,936	59,828	38,069	23,235	14,834	9,117	12,642
1935..	16,047	6,410	5,425	985	569	9,068	51,149	34,938	22,477	12,461	9,830	6,381
1940..	14,955	6,398	5,164	1,234	551	8,008	70,770	51,729	33,014	18,715	10,631	8,410
1945..	14,542	6,840	5,015	1,825	539	7,163	151,033	118,378	76,534	41,844	14,413	18,242
1950..	14,674	6,885	4,971	1,914	527	7,262	163,770	122,707	82,430	40,277	19,927	21,137
1955..	14,309	6,611	4,744	1,867	525	7,173	208,850	154,670	98,636	56,034	27,310	26,870
1960..	14,006	6,217	4,542	1,675	513	7,276	249,163	179,519	116,178	63,341	35,316	34,328
1965..	14,295	6,235	4,803	1,432	504	7,556	362,611	259,743	171,528	88,215	50,980	51,889
1970..	14,167	5,805	4,638	1,167	496	7,866	502,542	346,289	254,322	91,967	69,285	86,968
1975..	15,108	5,787	4,741	1,046	475	8,846	896,879	590,999	447,590	143,409	110,569	195,311
1980..	15,145	5,422	4,425	997	460	9,263	1,333,399	843,030	651,848	191,182	150,000	340,369
1985..	14,713	6,044	4,964	1,080	344	8,325	1,973,816	1,285,562	1,033,631	251,931	137,535	500,179
1987..	14,068	5,736	4,630	1,106	371	7,961	2,150,569	1,415,436	1,139,441	275,995	168,320	566,813
1988..	13,500	5,435	4,363	1,072	376	7,689	2,287,274	1,510,695	1,223,410	287,285	183,045	593,533
1989..	13,102	5,245	4,198	1,047	374	7483	2,412,396	1,606,884	1,307,977	298,907	188,592	616,920
1990..	12,736	5,034	4,013	1,021	361	7,341	2,522,473	1,679,699	1,374,099	305,570	183,522	659,282

Largest U.S. Commercial Banks

Source: American Banker; based on deposits Dec. 31, 1990.

(thousands)

Rank	Deposits	Rank	Deposits
Citibank NA, New York	$112,586,000	NCNB National Bank of Florida, Tampa	$9,856,891
Bank of America NT&SA, San Francisco . .	77,027,000	Citizens & Southern National Bank, Atlanta. .	9,665,732
Chase Manhattan Bank NA, New York	59,862,000	Seattle-First National Bank	9,563,041
Security Pacific National Bank, Los Angeles .	45,376,676	Bank of New England NA, Boston (a)	9,406,853
Wells Fargo Bank NA, San Francisco	42,716,399	Shawmut Bank, NA, Boston.	8,985,225
Manufacturers Hanover Trust Co., New York.	41,384,000	Valley National Bank, Phoenix	8,676,899
Morgan Guaranty Trust Co., New York . . . '	37,847,005	First Fidelity Bank, NA, Newark, N.J..	8,518,761
Bank of New York	33,468,870	Norwest Bank Minnesota NA, Minneapolis . .	8,372,123
Chemical Bank, New York	30,667,000	First Bank NA, Minneapolis	8,371,501
Bankers Trust Co., New York.	28,844,000	Comerica Bank-Detroit	8,175,956
NCNB Texas National Bank, Dallas	26,593,824	Midlantic National Bank, Newark, N.J.	8,132,110
First National Bank, Chicago	25,289,561	Mellon Bank (East) PSFS, NA, Philadelphia. .	8,111,122
First National Bank, Boston	20,079,100	Meridian Bank, Reading, Pa.`.	8,006,495
NBD Bank, NA, Detroit	16,864,551	Bank of Hawaii, Honolulu	7,967,360
Continental Bank NA, Chicago	16,455,000	Michigan National Bank, Farmington Hills . . .	7,717,635
Marine Midland Bank NA, Buffalo, N.Y.	16,356,546	Boatmen's National Bank, St. Louis	7,664,598
First Interstate Bank of California, Los Angeles	15,831,927	Crestar Bank, Richmond	7,612,797
Republic National Bank, New York.	15,750,448	State Street Bank & Trust Co., Boston	7,597,039
First Union National Bank of Florida, Jackson-ville	12,468,080	United States National Bank, Portland, Ore. .	7,575,817
		Banco Popular de Puerto Rico, San Juan . . .	7,434,524
National Westminster Bank USA, New York .	12,425,567	Ameritrust Co. NA, Cleveland	7,193,000
Bank One, Texas, NA, Dallas	12,283,510	Harris Trust & Savings Bank, Chicago.	6,881,758
First Union National Bank, Charlotte, N.C. . .	12,076,946	Connecticut Bank & Trust Co. NA, Hartford (a)	6,860,236
Union Bank, San Francisco	11,922,019	Huntington National Bank, Columbus, Oh. . .	6,837,531
Wachovia Bank & Trust Co., NA, Winston-Salem, N.C.	11,889,754	Manufacturers National Bank, Detroit	6,812,205
		Boston Safe Deposit & Trust Co..	6,785,766
Mellon Bank, NA, Pittsburgh	11,834,294	Texas Commerce Bank NA, Houston	6,781,939
Maryland National Bank, Baltimore	11,817,985	Fleet National Bank, Providence, R.I.	6,781,823
NCNB National Bank of North Carolina, Charlotte	11,802,446	Fidelity Bank, NA, Philadelphia	6,622,814
		Security Pacific Bank Washington, Seattle . .	6,512,827
Corestates Bank, NA, Philadelphia	11,796,851	First National Bank, Atlanta	6,479,114
Sovran Bank NA, Richmond	11,420,893	Provident National Bank, Philadelphia	6,314,140
Southeast Bank NA, Miami	11,167,261	National Westminster Bank NJ, Jersey City. .	6,165,963
Pittsburgh National Bank	10,910,127	AmSouth Bank NA, Birmingham, Ala.	6,143,236
Connecticut National Bank, Hartford.	9,890,645	First Interstate Bank of Arizona NA, Phoenix .	6,136,112

Largest Banks In The World

Source: American Banker; based on assets Dec. 31, 1990, or nearest fiscal year-end.
(thousands of U.S. dollars)

Bank, country	Assets	Bank, country	Assets
Dai-Ichi Kangyo Bank Ltd., Tokyo, Japan	$428,167,138	Union Bank of Switzerland, Zurich, Switzerland. .	$183,442,672
Sumitomo Bank Ltd., Osaka, Japan	409,160,814	Yasuda Trust & Banking Co. Ltd., Tokyo, Japan .	175,552,377
Mitsui Taiyo Kobe Bank, Ltd., Tokyo, Japan. . . .	408,754,426	Daiwa Bank, Ltd., Osaka, Japan	171,238,796
Sanwa Bank Ltd., Osaka, Japan	402,698,762	Citibank NA, New York, U.S.	155,394,000
Fuji Bank, Ltd., Tokyo, Japan	399,545,460	Swiss Bank Corp., Basle, Switzerland	151,260,091
Mitsubishi Bank Ltd., Tokyo, Japan.	391,528,117	HongKong and Shanghai Banking Corp., Hong Kong	148,488,419
Credit Agricole Mutuel, Paris, France	305,205,855	Commerzbank, Frankfurt, Germany	144,165,999
Banque Nationale de Paris, France	291,872,593	Toyo Trust & Banking Co. Ltd., Tokyo, Japan. . .	141,744,451
Industrial Bank of Japan, Ltd., Tokyo, Japan . . .	290,067,481	Bayerische Vereinsbank, Munich, Germany	137,747,100
Credit Lyonnais, Paris, France	287,330,254	Banca Nazionale del Lavoro, Rome, Italy	137,713,846
Deutsche Bank, AG, Frankfurt, Germany	266,286,359	Deutsche Genossenschaftsbank, Frankfurt, Germany	136,453,081
Barclays Bank Plc, London, U.K.	258,983,040		
Tokai Bank Ltd., Nagoya, Japan	249,751,219	Westdeutsche Landesbank Girozentrale, Duesseldorf, Germany	135,824,394
Norinchukin Bank, Tokyo, Japan	249,666,549	Istituto Bancario San Paolo di Torino, Turin, Italy .	133,486,857
Mitsubishi Trust & Banking Corp., Tokyo, Japan .	237,695,565	Nippon Credit Bank, Ltd., Tokyo, Japan	128,321,130
National Westminster Bank Plc, London, U.K. . .	232,512,000	Algemene Bank Nederland, Amsterdam, Netherlands	122,042,365
Bank of Tokyo, Ltd., Japan	223,184,577	Rabobank Nederland, Utrecht, Netherlands. . . .	119,728,479
Societe Generale, Paris, France	219,983,123	Credit Suisse, Zurich, Switzerland	117,345,984
Sumitomo Trust & Banking Co., Ltd., Osaka, Japan	218,916,042	Bayerische Hypotheken-und Wechsel-Bank, Munich, Germany	116,410,504
Mitsui Trust & Banking Co., Ltd., Tokyo, Japan . .	210,934,667		
Long-Term Credit Bank of Japan Ltd., Tokyo, Japan	200,678,534		
Dresdner Bank, Frankfurt, Germany	186,935,644		

Bank Failures

Source: Federal Deposit Insurance Corp

Year	Closed or Assisted	Year	Closed or Assisted	Year	Closed or Assisted	Year	Closed or Assisted
1934	61	1960	2	1971	6	1982	42
1935	32	1961	9	1972	3	1983	48
1936	72	1963	2	1973	6	1984	72
1937	84	1964	8	1975	14	1985	120
1938	81	1965	9	1976	17	1986	145
1939	72	1966	8	1978	7	1987	184
1940	48	1967	4	1979	10	1988	221
1955	5	1969	9	1980	10	1989	207
1959	3	1970	8	1981	10	1990	169

U.S. Currency and Coin

Source: Financial Management Service. U.S. Dept. of the Treasury (Mar. 31, 1991)

Amounts Outstanding and in Circulation

	Amounts outstanding	Less amounts held by: United States Treasury	Federal Reserve Banks[1]	Amounts in circulation
Currency				
Federal Reserve notes[1]	$311,041,235,308	$7,153,876	$43,650,650,908	$267,383,430,524
United States notes	322,539,056	33,448,039	213	289,090,804
Currency no longer issued.	265,201,084	217,746	17,697	264,965,641
Total	$311,628,975,448	$40,819,661	$43,650,668,818	$267,937,486,969
Coin[2]				
Dollars[3]	$2,024,703,898	$314,682,901	$96,332,849	$1,613,688,148
Fractional coin	17,961,858,000	275,466,852	562,645,172	17,123,745,976
Total	$19,986,561,898	$590,149,753	$658,978,021	$18,737,434,124
Total currency and coin.	$331,615,537,346	$630,969,414	$44,309,646,839	$286,674,921,093

Currency in Circulation by Denominations

Denomination	Total currency in circulation	Federal Reserve Notes[1]	U.S. Notes	Currency no longer issued
1 Dollar	$4,829,861,685	$4,678,919,795	$143,481	$150,798,409
2 Dollars	847,271,760	714,466,036	132,792,858	12,866
5 Dollars	5,903,633,895	5,756,184,845	111,619,305	35,829,745
10 Dollars	11,663,315,870	11,639,310,550	5,955	23,999,365
20 Dollars	65,905,027,584	65,884,889,100	3,390	20,135,094
50 Dollars	33,550,188,675	33,538,644,600	25	11,544,050
100 Dollars	144,913,269,400	144,846,639,600	44,525,700	22,104,100
500 Dollars	148,015,500	147,826,000	—	189,500
1,000 Dollars	171,666,998	171,459,998	—	207,000
5,000 Dollars	1,785,000	1,740,000	—	45,000
10,000 Dollars	3,450,000	3,350,000	—	100,000
Fractional parts	487	—	—	487
Partial notes[4]	115	—	90	25
Total currency	$267,937,486,969	$267,383,430,524	$289,090,804	$264,965,641

Comparative Totals of Money in Circulation — Selected Dates

Date	Dollars (in millions)	Per capita[5]	Date	Dollars (in millions)	Per capita[5]	Date	Dollars (in millions)	Per capita[5]
Mar. 31, 1991	286,675.0	1,138.62	June 30, 1975	81,196.4	380.08	June 30, 1940	7,847.5	59.40
Mar. 31, 1990	257,664.4	1,028.71	June 30, 1970	54,351.0	265.39	June 30, 1935	5,567.1	43.75
June 30, 1989	249,182.7	1,002.54	June 30, 1965	39,719.8	204.14	June 30, 1930	4,522.0	36.74
June 30, 1988	235,415.9	956.57	June 30, 1960	32,064.6	177.47	June 30, 1925	4,815.2	41.56
June 30, 1987	215,158.6	883.45	June 30, 1955	30,229.3	182.90	June 30, 1920	5,467.6	51.36
June 30, 1985	185,890.7	778.58	June 30, 1950	27,156.3	179.03	June 30, 1915	3,319.6	33.01
June 30, 1980	127,097.2	558.28	June 30, 1945	26,746.4	191.14	June 30, 1910	3,148.7	34.07

(1) Issued on and after July 1, 1929. (2) Excludes coin sold to collectors at premium prices. (3) Includes $481,781,898 in standard silver dollars. (4) Represents value of certain partial denominations not presented for redemption. (5) Based on Bureau of the Census estimates of population.

The requirement for a gold reserve against U.S. notes was repealed by Public Law 90-269 approved Mar. 18, 1968. Silver certificates issued on and after July 1, 1929 became redeemable from the general fund on June 24, 1968. The amount of security after those dates has been reduced accordingly.

Gold Reserves of Central Banks and Governments

Source: IMF. *International Financial Statistics*

(Million fine troy ounces)

Year end	All countries[1]	United States	Canada	Japan	Belgium	France	Germany	Italy	Netherlands	Switzerland	United Kingdom
1973	1.022.24	275.97	21.95	21.11	42.17	100.91	117.61	82.48	54.33	83.20	21.01
1974	1,020.24	275.97	21.95	21.11	42.17	100.93	117.61	82.48	54.33	83.20	21.03
1975	1,018.71	274.71.	21.95	21.11	42.17	100.93	117.61	82.48	54.33	83.20	21.03
1976	1,014.23	274.68	21.62	21.11	42.17	101.02	117.61	82.48	54.33	83.28	21.03
1977	1,029.19	277.55	22.01	21.62	42.45	101.67	118.30	82.91	54.63	83.28	22.23
1978	1,036.82	276.41	22.13	23.97	42.59	101.99	118.64	83.12	54.78	83.28	22.83
1979	944.44	264.60	22.18	24.23	34.21	81.92	95.25	66.71	43.97	83.28	18.25
1980	952.99	264.32	20.98	24.23	34.18	81.85	95.18	66.67	43.94	83.28	18.84
1981	953.72	264.11	20.46	24.23	34.18	81.85	95.18	66.67	43.94	83.28	19.03
1982	949.16	264.03	20.26	24.23	34.18	81.85	95.18	66.67	43.94	83.28	19.01
1983	947.84	263.39	20.17	24.23	34.18	81.85	95.18	66.67	43.94	83.28	19.03
1984	946.79	262.79	20.14	24.23	34.18	81.85	95.18	66.67	43.94	83.28	19.03
1985	949.39	262.65	20.11	24.23	34.18	81.85	95.18	66.67	43.94	83.28	19.01
1986	949.11	262.04	19.72	24.23	33.63	81.85	95.18	66.67	43.94	83.28	19.01
1987	944.49	262.38	18.52	24.23	33.67	81.85	95.18	66.67	43.94	83.28	19.00
1988	944.92	261.87	17.14	24.23	30.23	81.85	95.18	66.67	43.94	83.28	18.99
1989	938.95	261.93	16.10	24.23	30.23	81.85	95.18	66.67	43.94	83.28	18.94
1990	940.29	261.91	14.76	24.23	30.23	81.85	95.18	66.67	43.94	83.28	18.94

(1) Covers IMF members with reported gold holdings. For countries not listed above, see *International Financial Statistics*, a monthly publication of the International Monetary Fund.

United States Mint

Source: United States Mint, U.S. Dept. of the Treasury

The United States Mint was created by Act of Congress April 2, 1792, which established the U.S. national coinage system. Initially, operations were conducted at Philadelphia, then the nation's capital. Supervision of the Mint was a function of the secretary of state, but in 1799, it became an independent agency reporting directly to the president. The Mint was made a statutory bureau of the Treasury Department in 1873, with a director appointed by the president to oversee its operations through headquarters offices in the Treasury Department in Washington, D.C.

The Mint manufactures all U.S. coins and distributes them through the Federal Reserve banks and branches. The Mint also maintains physical custody of the treasury's monetary stocks of gold and silver, moving, storing and releasing from custody as authorized. There are 6 field facilities. Mints are located in Philadelphia and Denver; the San Francisco Mint and San Francisco Old Mint perform coinage operations and numismatic functions; two depositories, one at Fort Knox, Ky., for the storage of gold, and the other at West Point, N.Y., where gold and silver are stored and coinage is produced by congressional authorization. A museum is maintained at the San Francisco Old Mint.

The traditional 90% silver coinage was phased out and cupronickel clad coinage introduced when the Coinage Act of 1965 removed all silver from the dime and quarter and reduced the silver content of the half dollar to 40%. In 1970, legislative action removed the remaining silver from the half dollar and in providing for the resumption of dollar coinage, directed that both denominations produced for circulation also be cupronickel clad metal. Changes in the design, weight and size of the standard silver dollar were approved by Congress in 1978, and beginning in 1979, a smaller cupronickel dollar coin bearing the likeness of Susan B. Anthony and the Apollo II moon landing was released.

A change in the composition of the cent was effected in 1982, when the current copper-plated zinc cent was introduced to replace the traditional 95% copper cent.

The Mint manufactures and sells bronze medals of a national character, produces numismatic coins and coin sets. Special government-sponsored numismatic coinage includes congressionally authorized 90% silver half dollars produced in 1982 to mark the 250th anniversary of George Washington's birth, and 90% gold $10 coins dated 1984 and two 90% silver dollars dated 1983 and 1984, respectively, commemorating the 1984 Olympic games, and a 90% gold $5 coin, a 90% silver dollar coin and a cupronickel half dollar for the Statue of Liberty Centennial in 1986. The Mint issued a 1987 dated 90% gold $5 coin and a 1987 dated 90% silver dollar coin honoring the 200th Anniversary of the U.S. Constitution. Other Congressionally authorized commemoratives include the 1990 Eisenhower silver dollar and the 1991 Mt. Rushmore gold, silver and lead coin series. Congress has also directed the U.S. Mint to commence the production and sale of legal tender gold and silver bullion coins designated as "American Eagle Bullion Coins" by the mint. The coins in the series contain .9167 fine gold, and have a face value of $50 (1 oz.), $25 ($\frac{1}{2}$ oz.), $10 ($\frac{1}{4}$ oz.), and $5 ($\frac{1}{10}$ oz.). The American Eagle silver bullion coin has a face value of $1 and contains 1 troy ounce of .999 fine silver. Information concerning these and other Mint coin programs and coin availability, may be secured from the United States Mint, 10001 Aerospace Road, Lanham, MD 20706.

Domestic Coin Production

	Cents	Nickels	Dimes	Quarters	Halves	Total
1981	12,864,985,677	1,022,305,843	1,388,934,143	1,177,438,833	57,383,533	16,520,790,029
1982	16,725,504,368	666,081,544	1,062,188,584	980,973,788	23,959,102	19,458,707,386
1983	14,219,554,428	1,098,341,276	1,377,154,224	1,291,341,446	66,611,244	18,053,002,618
1984	13,720,317,906	1,264,444,146	1,561,472,976	1,223,028,064	52,291,158	17,821,554,250
1985	10,935,889,813	1,106,862,408	1,293,180,932	1,295,781,850	38,520,996	14,670,235,999
1986	8,934,262,191	898,702,633	1,155,976,667	1,055,497,993	28,473,778	12,072,913,262
1987	9,561,856,445	782,090,085	1,415,912,883	1,238,094,177	99,481,000	12,998,053,071
1988	11,346,550,443	1,435,131,652	1,992,935,488	1,158,862,687	25,626,096	15,959,106,366
1989	12,837,140,268	1,497,523,652	2,240,355,488	1,417,290,422	41,196,188	18,033,506,018
1990	12,031,422,711	1,415,222,474	1,956,105,597	1,560,357,858	43,614,192	17,006,722,832

Portraits on U.S. Treasury Bills, Bonds, Notes and Savings Bonds

Denomination	Savings bonds	Treas. bills	Treas. bonds	Treas. notes
50	Washington		Jefferson	
75	Adams			
100	Jefferson		Jackson	
200	Madison			
500	Hamilton		Washington	
1,000	Franklin	H. McCulloch	Lincoln	Lincoln
5,000	Revere	J.G. Carlisle	Monroe	Monroe
10,000	Wilson	J. Sherman.	Cleveland	Cleveland.
50,000		C. Glass.		
100,000		A Gallatin.	Grant.	Grant
1,000,000		O. Wolcott.	T. Roosevelt.	T. Roosevelt
100,000,000				Madison.
500,000,000				McKinley

Large Denominations of U.S. Currency Discontinued

The largest denomination of United States currency now being issued is the $100 bill. Issuance of currency in denominations larger than $100 was discontinued in 1969.

As large denomination bills reach the Federal Reserve Bank they are removed from circulation.

Because some of the discontinued currency is expected to be in the hands of holders for many years, the description of the various denominations below is continued:

Amt.	Portrait	Embellishment on back	Amt.	Portrait	Embellishment on back
$ 1	Washington	Great Seal of U.S.	$ 100	Franklin	Independence Hall
2	Jefferson	Signers of Declaration	500	McKinley	Ornate denominational marking
5	Lincoln	Lincoln Memorial	1,000	Cleveland	Ornate denominational marking
10	Hamilton	U.S. Treasury	5,000	Madison	Ornate denominational marking
20	Jackson	White House	10,000	Chase	Ornate denominational marking
50	Grant	U.S. Capitol	100,000*	Wilson	Ornate denominational marking

*For use only in transactions between Federal Reserve System and Treasury Department.

AGRICULTURE
U.S. Farms

Source: U.S. Department of Agriculture

The Department of Agriculture estimated the number of U.S. farms in June, 1989 at 2.17 million, a drop of 1.1 percent from June, 1988, when there were 2.19 million farms. The decline continued a slide that began in 1982, when there were 2.4 million farms. The size of the average U.S. farm increased in 1989 to 456 acres, from 453 acres in 1988. Overall, about 991 million U.S. acres were devoted to agriculture, as of June 1989.

State	Number of Farms	% Change	State	Number of Farms	% Change	State	Number of Farms	% Change
Alabama	47,000	−2.1	Louisiana	35,000	6.1	Ohio	87,000	2.4
Alaska	600	−3.2	Maine	7,300	0.0	Oklahoma	69,000	−1.4
Arizona	8,100	0.0	Maryland	15,600	−2.5	Oregon	37,000	1.4
Arkansas	49,000	0.0	Mass.	6,900	0.0	Pennsylvania	54,000	−1.8
California	84,000	0.0	Michigan	55,000	−1.8	Rhode Island	770	0.0
Colorado	27,300	0.0	Minnesota	90,000	−2.2	S. Carolina	25,500	−1.9
Connecticut	4,000	0.0	Mississippi	41,000	−2.4	S. Dakota	35,000	0.0
Delaware	3,000	0.0	Missouri	108,000	−1.8	Tennessee	91,000	0.0
Florida	41,000	0.0	Montana	24,700	0.4	Texas	186,000	−0.5
Georgia	48,000	−2.0	Nebraska	57,000	−1.7	Utah	13,000	−2.3
Hawaii	4,650	0.0	Nevada	2,500	−3.8	Vermont	7,100	0.0
Idaho	22,300	−0.9	New Hampshire	3,200	0.0	Virginia	47,000	−2.1
Illinois	86,000	−2.3	New Jersey	8,300	0.0	Washington	38,000	0.0
Indiana	71,000	−4.1	New Mexico	14,000	0.0	West Virginia	21,000	0.0
Iowa	105,000	−1.9	New York	39,000	−4.9	Wisconsin	81,000	−1.2
Kansas	69,000	0.0	N. Carolina	65,000	−4.4	Wyoming	8,900	0.0
Kentucky	96,000	−1.0	N. Dakota	33,500	0.0	Total	2,173,220	−1.1

Farm Income—Marketings and Government Payments

Source: Economic Research Service, U.S. Department of Agriculture

(1,000 dollars)

State	1989 Farm marketings Total	Crops	Livestock and products	1990 Farm marketings Total	Crops	Livestock and products	Government payments
AL	$2,670,904	$696,322	$1,974,582	$2,737,422	$654,909	$2,082,513	$82,226
AK	28,631	19,771	8,860	26,539	18,977	7,562	1,117
AZ	1,926,022	1,181,836	744,186	1,865,492	1,046,246	819,246	43,349
AR	4,156,869	1,496,114	2,660,755	4,259,205	1,552,776	2,706,429	312,696
CA	18,050,380	12,857,370	5,193,010	18,858,873	13,343,714	5,515,159	252,333
CO	3,969,206	1,320,629	2,648,577	4,213,419	1,184,074	3,029,345	236,723
CT	426,259	239,892	186,367	445,901	250,068	195,833	2,123
DE	661,640	159,032	502,608	643,661	183,829	459,832	3,213
FL	6,246,284	5,030,897	1,215,387	5,708,300	4,448,019	1,260,281	37,155
GA	3,907,761	1,626,283	2,281,478	3,842,186	1,574,081	2,268,105	130,593
HI	585,002	493,215	91,787	587,689	499,245	88,444	519
ID	2,745,336	1,661,606	1,083,730	2,934,519	1,780,841	1,153,678	133,431
IL	6,978,820	4,727,437	2,251,383	7,937,793	5,460,821	2,476,972	506,603
IN	4,281,440	2,455,574	1,825,866	4,930,668	2,871,067	2,059,601	244,170
IA	9,048,625	3,755,249	5,293,376	10,319,173	4,437,024	5,882,149	753,733
KS	6,548,317	2,132,274	4,416,043	6,994,864	2,098,649	4,896,215	834,746
KY	2,924,151	1,266,117	1,658,034	3,098,398	1,400,075	1,698,323	81,610
LA	1,707,682	1,093,656	614,026	1,921,224	1,284,157	637,067	154,631
ME	444,038	227,953	216,085	460,387	240,492	219,895	6,982
MD	1,336,215	477,149	859,066	1,345,165	516,701	828,464	17,386
MA	433,955	321,032	112,923	418,462	302,525	115,937	3,023
MI	2,922,761	1,611,462	1,311,299	3,183,356	1,785,034	1,398,322	168,831
MN	6,513,260	2,819,850	3,693,410	7,011,173	3,253,477	3,757,696	511,759
MS	2,275,837	981,002	1,294,835	2,432,964	1,111,288	1,321,676	185,969
MO	3,920,049	1,751,019	2,169,030	3,938,589	1,667,974	2,270,615	299,065
MT	1,553,782	624,526	929,256	1,605,731	742,052	863,679	299,599
NE	8,725,832	3,079,816	5,646,016	8,845,164	2,807,674	6,037,490	624,646
NV	243,589	101,556	142,033	333,435	115,085	218,350	5,347
NH	138,824	73,429	65,395	133,892	70,720	63,172	1,856
NJ	661,691	464,363	197,328	647,383	451,510	195,873	15,744
NM	1,458,917	484,706	974,211	1,528,793	482,814	1,045,979	63,840
NY	2,853,916	917,270	1,936,646	3,006,046	1,022,887	1,983,159	59,304
NC	4,592,584	2,082,348	2,510,236	4,866,512	2,213,714	2,652,798	73,255
ND	2,151,510	1,482,514	668,996	2,537,350	1,723,899	813,451	545,378
OH	3,786,524	2,088,064	1,698,460	4,171,818	2,335,424	1,836,394	197,006
OK	3,514,760	1,137,297	2,377,463	3,554,437	1,191,312	2,363,125	319,040
OR	2,284,656	1,546,451	738,205	2,311,783	1,557,088	754,695	89,137
PA	3,602,210	991,513	2,610,697	3,767,174	1,053,407	2,713,767	41,414
RI	78,317	65,461	12,856	70,793	58,269	12,524	191
SC	1,234,700	680,310	554,390	1,175,560	599,038	576,522	62,637
SD	2,982,194	950,887	2,031,307	3,348,717	1,036,068	2,312,649	332,851
TN	1,945,725	863,290	1,082,435	2,038,610	928,009	1,110,601	91,029
TX	10,923,494	4,062,624	6,860,870	11,980,527	4,268,378	7,712,149	974,702
UT	755,279	188,181	567,098	754,826	178,686	576,140	34,897
VT	429,318	50,247	379,071	446,722	48,951	397,771	5,793
VA	2,039,137	694,323	1,344,814	2,119,633	740,881	1,378,752	32,378
WA	3,689,120	2,456,532	1,232,588	3,815,779	2,420,139	1,395,640	205,425
WV	310,275	60,316	249,959	338,132	69,517	268,615	6,049
WI	5,399,559	1,049,982	4,349,577	5,706,149	1,124,923	4,581,226	181,243
WY	827,171	162,735	664,436	766,767	157,193	609,574	31,283
U.S.	$160,892,528	$76,761,482	$84,131,046	$169,987,155	$80,363,701	$89,623,454	$9,298,030

160

Farms—Number and Acreage by State, 1980, 1991

Source: Natl. Agricultural Statistics Service: U.S. Dept. of Agriculture

State	Farms (1,000) 1980	1991	Acreage (mil.) 1980	1991	Acreage per Farm 1980	1991	State	Farms (1,000) 1980	1991	Acreage (mil.) 1980	1991	Acreage per Farm 1980	1991
U.S.	2,437	2,105	1,039	983	426	467	Nebraska	65	56	48	47	734	841
Alabama	59	45	12	10	207	218	Nevada	3	3	9	9	3,100	3,560
Alaska	(z)	1	2	1	3,378	1,768	New Hampshire	3	3	1	(z)	160	166
Arizona	7	8	38	36	5,080	4,500	New Jersey	10	8	1	1	109	106
Arkansas	58	46	17	16	280	337	New Mexico	13	14	47	44	3,467	3,281
California	79	84	34	30	417	361	New York	48	38	9	8	200	218
Colorado	26	26	36	33	1,358	1,262	North Carolina	92	60	12	10	126	160
Connecticut	4	4	(z)	(z)	117	108	North Dakota	41	33	42	40	1,043	1,224
Delaware	4	3	1	1	186	197	Ohio	96	80	16	16	171	196
Florida	38	40	13	11	344	263	Oklahoma	72	70	35	33	481	471
Georgia	59	46	15	12	254	263	Oregon	34	37	18	18	517	481
Hawaii	4	5	2	2	458	372	Pennsylvania	61	53	9	8	145	153
Idaho	24	21	15	14	623	631	Rhode Island	1	1	(z)	(z)	87	94
Illinois	108	82	29	29	269	348	South Carolina	35	24	6	5	188	213
Indiana	88	65	17	16	193	246	South Dakota	39	35	45	44	1,169	1,263
Iowa	121	102	34	34	284	328	Tennessee	96	87	14	12	142	143
Kansas	75	69	48	48	644	694	Texas	192	185	138	131	715	708
Kentucky	103	91	15	14	143	155	Utah	13	13	12	11	919	850
Louisiana	37	30	10	9	273	293	Vermont	7	7	2	2	226	219
Maine	8	7	2	1	195	203	Virginia	59	45	10	9	169	196
Maryland	17	15	3	2	157	146	Washington	37	37	16	16	429	432
Massachusetts	6	7	1	1	116	99	West Virginia	20	20	4	4	191	185
Michigan	66	54	11	11	175	200	Wisconsin	94	79	19	18	200	222
Minnesota	104	88	30	30	291	341	Wyoming	9	9	35	35	3,846	3,867
Mississippi	56	38	15	13	265	337							
Missouri	121	107	31	30	261	284							
Montana	24	25	62	60	2,601	2,431							

(z) Less than 500 farms or 500,000 acres

Livestock on Farms in the U.S.

Source: Natl. Agricultural Statistics Service: U.S. Dept. of Agriculture (in thousands)

Year (On Jan. 1)	All cattle	Milk cows	All sheep	Hogs[3]	Year (On Jan. 1)	All cattle	Milk cows	All sheep	Hogs[3]
1890	60,014	15,000	44,518	48,130	1955	96,592	23,462	31,582	50,474
1900	59,739	16,544	48,105	51,055	1960	96,236	19,527	33,170	59,026
1910	58,993	19,450	50,239	48,072	1965	109,000	16,981[2]	25,127	56,106
1920	70,400	21,455	40,743	60,159	1970	112,369	12,091	20,423	57,046
1925	63,373	22,575	38,543	55,770	1975	132,028	11,220	14,515	54,693
1930	61,003	23,032	51,565	55,705	1980	111,242	10,758	12,699	67,318
1935	68,846	26,082	51,808	39,066	1985	109,582	10,777	10,716	54,073
1940	68,309	24,940	52,107	61,165	1989	98,065	10,212	10,858	55,469
1945	85,573	27,770	46,520	59,373	1990	98,162	10,149	11,363	53,821
1950	77,963	23,853	29,826	58,937	1991	99,436	10,159	11,200	54,462

(1) Total estimated value on farms as of Jan. 1, 1991, was (avg. value per head in parentheses): sheep & lambs $734,868,000 ($65.60); hogs & pigs $4,657,391 ($85.40). (2) New series, milk cows & heifers that have calved, from 1965. (3) As of Dec. 1 of preceding year.

U.S. Meat Production and Consumption

Source: Economic Research Service, U.S. Agriculture Department (million lbs.)

Year	Beef Production	Beef Consumption[1]	Veal Production	Veal Consumption[1]	Lamb and mutton Production	Lamb and mutton Consumption[1]	Pork (exclud. lard) Production	Pork (exclud. lard) Consumption[1]	All meats[3] Production	All meats[3] Consumption[1]	Lard Production	Lard Consumption[2]
1940	7,175	7,257	981	981	876	873	10,044	9,701	19,076	18,812	2,288	1,901
1950	9,534	9,529	1,230	1,206	597	596	10,714	10,390	22,075	21,721	2,631	1,891
1960	14,728	15,465	1,109	1,118	769	857	13,905	14,057	30,511	31,497	2,562	1,358
1970	21,685	23,391	588	610	551	663	14,699	14,871	37,523	39,535	1,913	939
1980	21,643	23,513	400	418	318	349	16,617	16,690	38,978	40,953	1,207	588
1985	23,728	25,472	515	533	359	386	14,807	15,733	39,409	42,125	927	425
1989	23,087[R]	24,330[R]	355	356	342	406	15,813	16,571[R]	39,592	41,664	(4)	(4)
1990	22,743	24,031	227	325	363	419	15,354	16,030	38,787	40,885	(4)	(4)

(1) Includes shipments. (2) Direct use. Excludes lard used in indirect food use such as table spreads and shortenings. (3) Meats may not add to total. (4) Discontinued series. R = Revised.

Selected Indexes of Farm Inputs: 1960 to 1988

Source: Economic Research Service, U.S. Dept. of Agriculture

(1977 = 100. Inputs based on physical quantities of resources used in production.)

Input	1960	1965	1970	1975	1980	1981	1982	1983	1985	1986	1987	1988[1]
Total	99	97	96	97	103	102	99	97	92	87	86	85
Farm labor	177	144	112	106	96	96	93	97	85	80	78	75
Farm real estate[2]	103	103	105	97	103	104	102	101	95	93	92	91
Mechanical power and machinery	83	80	85	96	101	98	92	88	80	75	72	71
Agricultural chemicals[3]	32	49	75	83	123	129	118	105	123	110	111	113
Feed, seed, and livestock purchases[4]	77	86	96	93	114	108	108	110	106	103	111	107
Taxes and interest	95	101	102	100	100	99	92	97	91	93	92	86

(1) Preliminary. (2) Includes service buildings, improvements. (3) Includes fertilizer, lime, and pesticides. (4) Nonfarm portion.

U.S. Egg Production

Source: Economic Research Service, U.S. Dept. of Agriculture

State	Eggs Produced[1] 1989	1990	Price Per Dozen 1989	1990	Value of Production 1989	1990
	(millions)		(Cents)		(1,000 Dollars)	
Ala.	2,183	2,206	83.9	92.4	$152,628	$169,862
Alas.	0.7	0.7	155.0	151.0	90	88
Ariz.	79	73	63.0	67.5	4,148	4,106
Ark.	3,352	3,620	85.0	86.4	237,433	260,640
Cal.	7,317	7,472	65.9	69.6	401,825	433,376
Col.	824	788	76.0	77.8	52,187	51,089
Conn.	934	1,023	107.0	106.0	83,282	90,365
Del.	146	170	111.0	117.0	13,505	16,575
Fla.	2,628	2,586	56.2	62.0	123,078	133,610
Ga.	4,211	4,302	81.0	80.6	284,243	288,951
Ha.	226.6	227.5	79.2	85.0	14,956	16,115
Ida.	217	187	84.1	79.1	15,208	12,326
Ill.	793	793	65.4	65.0	43,219	42,954
Ind.	5,529	5,445	61.0	62.7	281,058	284,501
Ia.	2,140	2,151	53.3	56.5	95,052	101,276
Kan.	387	404	54.3	54.5	17,512	18,348
Ky.	407	407	64.1	67.7	21,741	22,962
La.	299	273	109.0	115.0	27,159	26,163
Me.	1,140	1,069	102.0	101.0	96,900	89,974
Md.	966	954	72.1	76.3	58,041	60,659
Mass.	238	235	109.0	105.0	21,618	20,563
Mich.	1,454	1,404	56.4	58.1	68,338	67,977
Minn.	2,236	2,499	52.0	57.7	96,893	120,160
Miss.	1,289	1,434	83.4	87.8	89,586	104,921
Mo.	1,485	1,580	54.0	55.4	66,825	72,943
Mont.	180	172	75.0	68.0	11,250	9,747
Neb.	1,037	1,202	47.8	50.3	41,307	50,384
Nev.	2.3	2.2	56.0	53.9	107	99
N.H.	53	43	107.0	109.0	4,726	3,906
N.J.	437	442	74.0	85.0	26,948	31,308
N.M.	294	283	71.0	74.0	17,395	17,452
N.Y.	1,063	975	64.4	68.1	57,048	55,331
N.C.	3,312	2,986	80.3	82.8	221,628	206,034
N.D.	47	51	50.0	55.2	1,958	2,346
Oh.	4,367	4,667	50.4	59.1	183,414	229,850
Okla.	886	869	97.2	101.0	71,766	73,141
Ore.	678	652	75.6	76.8	42,714	41,728
Pa.	5,232	4,976	59.0	61.0	257,240	251,947
R.I.	46	42	104.0	102.0	3,987	3,570
S.C.	1,342	1,422	67.3	70.0	75,264	82,950
S.D.	373	435	47.0	48.0	14,609	17,400
Tenn.	389	277	66.5	70.2	21,557	16,204
Tex.	3,304	3,317	81.1	76.7	223,295	212,012
Ut.	460	456	65.0	64.0	24,917	24,320
Vt.	37	31	107.0	106.0	3,299	2,738
Va.	942	894	78.9	85.6	61,937	63,772
Wash.	1,299	1,287	73.1	74.1	79,131	79,472
W. Va.	121	136	102.0	104.0	10,285	11,787
Wis.	851	910	55.0	60.1	39,004	45,576
Wyo.	2.3	1.7	82.6	83.0	158	118
U.S.[2]	67,236	67,832	68.9	71.6	3,861,469	4,044,696

(1) Estimates cover the 12 month period Dec. 1, previous year through Nov. 30. (2) States may not add to U.S. total due to rounding.

Farm-Real Estate Debt Outstanding by Lender Groups[1]

Source: Economic Research Service, U.S. Dept. of Agriculture

Dec. 31	Total farm-real estate debt[2]	Amounts held by principal lender groups				
		Federal land banks[2]	Farmers Home Adminis-tration[3]	Life in-surance com-panies[4]	All commer-cial banks	Other[5]
	$1,000	$1,000	$1,000	$1,000	$1,000	$1,000
1955	9,048,676	1,480,000	413,000	2,272,000	1,275,000	3,609,000
1960	12,867,524	2,539,000	723,000	2,975,000	1,592,000	5,039,000
1965	21,220,912	4,240,000	1,497,000	4,802,000	2,607,000	8,070,000
1970	30,492,357	7,145,363	2,440,043	5,610,300	3,772,377	11,524,000
1975	49,852,888	16,029,468	3,368,747	6,726,000	6,296,286	17,432,000
1980	97,486,996	36,196,103	8,163,270	12,927,800	8,563,457	31,636,000
1982	111,312,036	47,821,589	9,169,874	12,801,546	8,391,800	33,127,000
1985	105,739,201	44,583,842	10,426,971	11,830,400	11,384,920	27,507,000
1986	95,879,799	37,757,626	10,348,597	10,940,200	12,710,650	24,123,000
1987	87,717,601	32,637,687	10,083,239	9,895,800	14,455,162	20,646,000
1988	82,952,518	30,326,707	9,606,796	9,581,700	15,416,700	18,020,000
1989	80,476,478	28,501,000	8,719,822	9,597,900	16,646,179	17,011,577
1990	80,806,457	28,795,000	8,092,986	10,186,300	17,227,171	16,505,000

(1) Includes opertator households. (2) Includes data for joint stock land banks and real estate loans by Agricultural Credit Assn. (3) Includes loans made directly by FmHA for farm ownership, soil and water loans to individuals, Indian tribe land acquisition, grazing associations, and half of economic emergency loans. Also includes loans for rural housing on farm tracts and labor housing. (4) American Council of Life Insurance. (5) Estimated by ERS, USDA. Includes CCC storage and drying facility loans.

Persons in Farm Occupations, 1820-1990

Source: Economic Research Service, U.S. Department of Agriculture; and Bureau of the Census, U.S. Department of Commerce, 1990.

(numbers in thousands)

Year	Total workers[1]	Farm occupations Number	Farm occupations % of total	Year	Total workers[1]	Farm occupations Number	Farm occupations % of total
1820	2,881	2,069	71.8	1950	59,230	6,858	11.6
1850	7,697	4,902	63.7	1960	67,990	4,132	6.1
1870	12,925	6,850	53.0	1970	79,802	2,881	3.6
1900	29,030	10,888	37.5	1980	104,058	2,818	2.7
1920	42,206	11,390	27.0	1985 (March)	106,214	2,949	2.8
1930	48,686	10,321	21.2	1990 (March)	117,491	2,864	2.4
1940	51,742	8,995	17.4				

(1) Total workers for 1985 to 1990 are employed workers 15 years and over; total workers for 1970 and 1980 are members of the experienced civilian labor force 16 years and over; total workers for 1900 to 1960 are members of the experienced civilian labor forced 14 years and over; and total workers for 1820 to 1890 are gainful workers 10 years and over.

Grain, Hay, Potato, Cotton, Soybean, Tobacco Production

Source: Economic Research Service, U.S. Agriculture Department

1990 State	Barley 1,000 bushels	Corn, grain 1,000 bushels	Cotton lint 1,000 bales	All Hay 1,000 tons	Oats 1,000 bushels	Potatoes 1,000 cwt.	Soybeans 1,000 bushels	Tobacco 1,000 pounds	All Wheat 1,000 bushels
Alabama	—	13,920	400	1,125	1,250	1,943	7,480	—	6,650
Alaska	—	—	—	—	—	—	—	—	—
Arizona	1,575	1,120	1,015	1,421	—	1,794	—	—	9,266
Arkansas	—	6,935	1,100	1,738	2,700	—	90,450	—	49,000
California	10,000	25,600	2,806	8,307	3,000	17,684	—	—	47,906
Colorado	12,000	128,650	—	3,805	2,250	24,136	—	—	86,950
Connecticut	—	(1)	—	198	—	—	—	3,007	—
Delaware	1,890	19,780	—	68	—	2,009	6,766	—	3,060
Florida	—	5,325	45	552	—	9,792	1,425	19,044	1,815
Georgia	—	37,400	410	1,140	2,240	—	9,800	103,845	20,650
Hawaii	—	—	—	—	—	—	—	—	—
Idaho	56,160	3,900	—	4,084	1,980	112,340	—	—	99,600
Illinois	—	1,320,800	—	3,348	11,560	837	354,900	—	91,200
Indiana	—	703,050	—	2,220	4,830	858	171,380	13,440	50,440
Iowa	—	1,562,400	—	7,095	40,800	160	323,900	—	3,375
Kansas	924	188,500	(1)	6,100	6,600	—	46,800	—	472,000
Kentucky	1,020	120,000	—	4,848	(1)	—	39,040	442,253	20,000
Louisiana	—	21,576	1,180	660	—	—	42,000	—	12,870
Maine	—	(1)	—	423	2,015	20,520	—	—	—
Maryland	4,284	53,100	—	678	986	324	17,820	9,443	9,880
Massachusetts	—	(1)	—	233	—	650	—	805	—
Michigan	2,580	238,050	—	5,335	13,050	12,115	43,320	—	41,250
Minnesota	50,400	762,600	—	6,560	48,180	16,110	179,400	—	138,620
Mississippi	—	11,200	1,851	1,035	—	—	39,900	—	15,600
Missouri	—	205,800	305	6,865	2,226	957	124,500	5,928	76,000
Montana	56,580	855	—	4,495	2,800	2,492	—	—	145,865
Nebraska	880	934,400	—	7,370	13,440	3,539	81,420	—	85,500
Nevada	675	—	—	1,359	—	2,345	—	—	980
New Hampshire	—	(1)	—	159	—	—	—	—	—
New Jersey	372	8,850	—	246	(1)	1,012	3,996	—	1,247
New Mexico	(1)	7,975	126	1,376	—	3,400	—	—	8,125
New York	—	60,760	—	4,377	8,235	7,890	—	—	7,105
North Carolina	1,590	72,760	271	1,011	2,440	3,380	32,400	639,639	22,550
North Dakota	129,850	36,800	—	3,745	30,600	16,675	12,870	—	385,220
Ohio	—	417,450	—	4,620	16,100	1,911	135,720	18,915	79,650
Oklahoma	697	10,032	380	3,926	2,280	—	4,410	—	201,600
Oregon	9,100	2,700	—	2,826	4,590	23,014	—	—	57,616
Pennsylvania	4,140	109,610	—	4,719	15,840	5,400	11,275	19,780	10,500
Rhode Island	—	(1)	—	18	—	294	—	—	—
South Carolina	676	14,400	145	456	1,824	—	13,875	109,905	14,440
South Dakota	24,500	234,000	—	6,300	53,200	1,980	53,760	—	128,004
Tennessee	—	43,860	490	3,255	—	—	33,750	112,218	17,640
Texas	608	130,500	5,085	8,000	9,225	3,072	5,000	—	130,200
Utah	8,505	2,660	—	2,123	816	1,643	—	—	7,170
Vermont	—	(1)	—	772	—	—	—	—	—
Virginia	5,280	36,500	7	2,600	(1)	1,980	16,800	110,269	12,220
Washington	22,620	14,000	—	3,056	2,640	67,980	—	—	150,080
West Virginia	—	5,250	—	1,142	342	—	—	2,720	552
Wisconsin	2,700	354,000	—	9,120	47,570	23,075	17,630	13,723	10,085
Wyoming	9,250	6,000	—	2,076	1,540	561	—	—	6,113
Total U.S.	418,856	7,933,068	15,617	146,985	357,149	393,872	1,921,787	1,624,934	2,738,594

(1) Estimates discontinued.

Production of Chief U.S. Crops

Source: National Agricultural Statistics Service: U.S. Dept. of Agriculture

Year	Corn for grain 1,000 bushels	Oats 1,000 bushels	Barley 1,000 bushels	Sorghum for grain 1,000 bushels	All Wheat 1,000 bushels	Rye 1,000 bushels	Flax-seed 1,000 bushels	Cotton lint 1,000 bales	Cotton seed 1,000 tons
1970..	4,152,243	915,236	416,091	683,179	1,351,558	36,840	29,416	10,192	4,068
1975..	5,828,961	638,960	379,162	754,354	2,126,927	15,924	15,553	8,302	3,218
1980..	6,639,396	458,792	361,135	579,343	2,380,934	15,958	7,728	11,122	4,470
1982..	8,235,101	592,630	515,935	835,083	2,764,967	19,533	10,278	11,963	4,744
1984..	7,672,130	473,661	598,034	866,241	2,594,777	32,407	7,022	12,982	5,149
1985..	8,875,453	518,490	590,213	1,120,271	2,424,115	20,373	8,293	13,432	5,279
1986..	8,225,764	384,996	608,532	938,869	2,090,570	19,067	11,538	9,731	3,801
1987..	7,131,300	373,713	521,499	730,809	2,107,685	19,526	7,444	14,760	5,769
1988..	4,928,681	217,600	289,994	576,686	1,812,201	14,689	1,615	15,412	6,062
1989..	7,525,493	373,587	404,203	615,420	2,036,618	13,647	1,215	12,196	4,677
1990..	7,933,068	357,149	418,856	571,483	2,738,594	10,098	3,812	15,617	5,967

Year	Tobacco 1,000 lbs.	All Hay 1,000 tons	Beans dry edible 1,000 cwt.	Peas dry edible 1,000 cwt.	Peanuts 1,000 lbs.	Soy-beans 1,000 bushels	Pota-toes 1,000 cwt.	Sweet pota-toes 1,000 cwt.
1970.....	1,906,453	126,969	17,399	3,315	2,983,121	1,127,100	325,716	13,164
1975.....	2,182,304	132,397	17,442	2,731	3,846,722	1,548,344	321,978	12,891
1980.....	1,786,225	130,740	26,729	3,285	2,302,762	1,797,543	303,905	10,953
1982.....	1,994,494	149,241	25,563	NA	3,440,255	2,190,297	355,131	14,833
1984.....	1,727,962	150,582	21,070	NA	4,405,945	1,860,863	362,612	12,902
1985.....	1,511,638	148,719	22,298	NA	4,122,787	2,099,056	407,109	14,573
1986.....	1,161,940	155,385	22,960	3,196	3,697,085	1,942,568	361,511	12,368
1987.....	1,188,868	147,319	26,031	3,385	3,616,010	1,938,087	385,774	11,611
1988.....	1,369,500	126,010	19,253	3,868	3,980,917	1,548,841	356,438	10,945
1989.....	1,367,188	145,512	23,729	3,883	3,989,995	1,923,666	370,444	11,358
1990.....	1,606,851	146,985	32,429	2,372	3,602,770	1,921,787	393,867	13,020

Year	Rice 1,000 cwt.	Sugar-cane 1,000 tons	Sugar beets 1,000 tons	Pecans 1,000 tons	Al-monds 1,000 tons	Wal-nuts 1,000 tons	Fil-berts 1,000 tons	Oranges* 1,000 boxes	Grape-fruit* 1,000 boxes
1970......	NA	23,996	26,378	NA	NA	111.8	9.3	185,770	53,910
1975......	NA	28,344	29,704	NA	NA	199.3	12.1	237,810	61,610
1980......	146,150	26,963	23,502	91.8	264.4	197.0	15.4	273,630	73,200
1982......	153,637	29,770	20,894	109.3	283.5	234.0	18.8	176,690	70,550
1984......	138,810	27,340	22,134	116.2	467.2	213.0	13.4	169,440	53,840
1985......	134,913	28,213	22,529	122.2	375.6	219.0	24.6	158,350	56,150
1986......	133,356	30,311	25,150	136.4	201.3	180.0	15.1	175,440	57,870
1987......	129,603	29,218	28,072	131.1	519.0	247.0	21.8	181,175	63,775
1988......	159,897	29,904	24,810	154.1	451.9	209.0	16.5	200,250	68,700
1989......	154,487	29,426	25,131	125.3	394.7	229.0	13.0	209,050	69,500
1990......	154,919	27,090	27,593	102.5	531.7	227.0	21.7	186,075	48,600

NA = Not available. *Crop year ending in year cited.

Harvested Acreage of Principal U.S. Crops

Source: National Agricultural Statistics Service: U.S. Dept. of Agriculture (thousands of acres)

State	1988	1989	1990P	State	1988	1989	1990P
Alabama	2,389	2,338	2,352	Nebraska	16,765	17,450	18,194
Arizona	784	830	802	Nevada	549	554	520
Arkansas	7,538	7,603	8,080	New Hampshire	99	93	91
California	5,107	4,900	4,719	New Jersey	368	380	364
Colorado	5,609	5,677	5,862	New Mexico	936	968	907
Connecticut.	124	128	129	New York	3,439	3,560	3,538
Delaware	504	537	496	North Carolina	4,104	4,526	4,371
Florida	1,115	1,128	1,074	North Dakota.	16,216	20,660	21,229
Georgia	3,754	4,205	3,788	Ohio	9,731	10,259	10,132
Hawaii.	86	81	76	Oklahoma	8,482	9,396	9,673
Idaho	4,018	4,333	4,271	Oregon	2,168	2,339	2,290
Illinois	21,581	22,977	22,809	Pennsylvania	4,199	4,198	4,094
Indiana	11,082	11,631	11,484	Rhode Island	11	10	10
Iowa.	23,092	24,097	23,276	South Carolina	2,022	2,283	2,049
Kansas	19,191	18,794	20,978	South Dakota.	13,508	15,210	15,552
Kentucky	4,968	5,487	5,505	Tennessee	4,548	4,570	4,477
Louisiana	4,308	4,093	4,367	Texas	16,527	16,697	18,546
Maine	346	364	361	Utah.	1,026	983	992
Maryland	1,493	1,602	1,552	Vermont.	453	442	441
Massachusetts	143	136	135	Virginia	2,708	2,768	2,726
Michigan	6,401	6,360	6,510	Washington	3,890	4,045	4,168
Minnesota	18,767	18,661	18,779	West Virginia	644	663	668
Mississippi	5,149	4,614	4,718	Wisconsin	8,430	8,615	8,550
Missouri.	12,684	13,249	12,685	Wyoming	1,674	1,628	1,735
Montana	7,118	9,475	8,926	**Total U.S. . . . .**	**289,846**	**305,597**	**309,051**

P = Preliminary. * States may not add due to rounding.

Average Prices Received by U.S. Farmers

Source: Natl. Agricultural Statistics Service, U.S. Dept. of Agriculture

The figures represent dollars per 100 lbs. for hogs, beef cattle, veal calves, sheep, lamb, and milk (wholesale), dollars per head for milk cows; cents per lb. for milk fat (in cream), chickens, broilers, turkeys, and wool; cents for eggs per dozen.

Weighted calendar year prices for livestock and livestock products other than wool. 1943 through 1963, wool prices are weighted on marketing year basis. The marketing year has been changed (1964) from a calendar year to a Dec.-Nov. basis for hogs, chickens, broilers and eggs.

Year	Hogs	Cattle (beef)	Calves (veal)	Sheep	Lambs	Cows (milk)	All milk (excl. brolers)	Chickens (excl. brolers)	Broilers	Turkeys	Eggs	Wool
1930	8.84	7.71	9.68	4.74	7.76	74	2.21	...	...	20.2	23.7	19.5
1940	5.39	7.56	8.83	3.95	8.10	61	1.82	13.0	17.3	15.2	18.0	28.4
1950	18.00	23.30	26.30	11.60	25.10	198	3.89	22.2	27.4	32.8	36.3	62.1
1960	15.30	20.40	22.90	5.61	17.90	223	4.21	12.2	16.9	25.4	36.1	42.0
1970	22.70	27.10	34.50	7.51	26.40	332	5.71	9.1	13.6	22.6	39.1	35.4
1975	46.10	32.20	27.20	11.30	42.10	412	8.75	9.9	26.3	34.8	54.5	44.8
1979	41.80	66.10	88.80	26.30	66.70	1,040	12.00	14.4	25.9	41.3	58.3	86.3
1980	38.00	62.40	76.80	21.30	63.60	1,190	13.05	11.0	27.7	41.3	56.3	88.1
1984	47.10	57.30	59.90	16.40	60.10	895	13.46	15.9	33.7	48.9	72.3	79.5
1985	44.00	53.70	62.10	23.90	67.70	860	12.76	14.8	30.1	49.1	57.1	63.3
1986	49.30	52.60	61.10	25.60	69.00	820	12.51	12.5	34.5	47.1	61.6	66.8
1987	51.20	61.10	78.50	29.50	77.60	920	12.54	11.0	28.7	34.8	54.9	91.7
1988	42.30	66.60	89.20	25.60	69.10	990	12.26	11.0	33.1	38.6	52.8	1.38
1989	42.50	69.50	90.80	24.40	66.10	1,030	13.56	14.9	36.6	40.9	68.9	1.24
1990	53.70	74.60	95.60	23.20	55.50	1,160	13.73	6.2	32.6	39.3	71.6	80.0

The figures represent cents per lb. for cotton, apples, and peanuts; dollars per bushel for oats, wheat, corn, barley, and soybeans; dollars per 100 lbs. for rice, sorghum, and potatoes; dollars per ton for cottonseed and baled hay.

Weighted crop year prices. Crop years are as follows: apples, June-May; wheat, oats, barley, hay and potatoes, July-June; cotton, rice, peanuts and cottonseed, August-July; soybeans, September-August; and corn and sorghum grain, October-September.

Year	Corn	Wheat	Upland cotton[1]	Oats	Barley	Rice	Soybeans	Sorghum	Peanuts	Cottonseed	Hay	Potatoes	Apples
1930	.598	.663	9.46	0.311	.420	1.74	1.34	1.02	5.01	22.00	11.00	1.47	...
1940	.618	.674	9.83	0.298	.393	1.80	.892	.873	3.72	21.70	9.78	.850	...
1950	1.52	2.00	39.90	0.788	1.19	5.09	2.47	1.88	10.9	86.60	21.10	1.50	...
1960	13.00	1.74	30.08	0.599	.840	4.55	2.13	1.49	10.0	42.50	21.70	2.00	2.72
1970	1.33	1.33	21.86	0.623	.973	5.17	2.85	2.04	12.8	56.40	26.10	2.21	6.52
1975	2.54	3.55	51.10	1.45	2.42	8.35	4.92	4.21	19.6	97.00	52.10	4.48	8.80
1979	2.52	3.78	62.3	1.36	2.29	10.50	6.28	4.18	20.6	121.00	59.50	3.43	15.40
1980	3.11	3.91	74.4	1.79	2.86	12.80	7.57	5.25	25.1	129.00	71.00	6.55	12.1
1984	2.63	3.39	58.7	1.67	2.29	8.04	5.84	4.15	27.9	99.50	72.70	5.69	15.5
1985	2.23	3.08	56.8	1.23	1.98	6.53	5.05	3.45	24.4	66.00	67.60	3.92	17.3
1986	1.50	2.42	51.5	1.21	1.61	3.75	4.78	2.45	29.2	80.00	59.80	5.03	19.1
1987	1.94	2.57	63.7	1.56	1.81	7.27	5.88	3.04	28.0	82.50	65.00	4.38	12.7
1988	2.54	3.72	55.6	2.61	2.80	6.83	7.42	4.05	27.9	118.00	85.20	6.02	17.4
1989	2.36	3.72	63.6	1.49	2.42	7.35	5.69	3.76	27.8	105.00	85.40	7.36	13.9
1990	2.30	2.61	66.4	1.14	2.14	6.50	5.75	3.75	34.1	121.00	83.20	6.15	20.9

(1) Beginning 1964, 480 lb. net weight bales.

Grain Storage Capacity at Principal Grain Centers in U.S.

Source: Chicago Board of Trade Market Information Department, Aug. 1991

(bushels)

Cities	Capacity	Cities	Capacity
Atlantic Coast...............	21,200,000	Fort Worth................	68,600,000
Great Lakes		Texas High Plains...........	79,500,000
Toledo......................	53,600,000	Enid.......................	79,700,000
Buffalo.....................	15,200,000	**Gulf Points**	
Chicago....................	52,400,000	South Mississippi..........	44,700,000
Milwaukee..................	6,600,000	North Texas Gulf...........	24,200,000
Duluth.....................	64,500,000	South Texas Gulf..........	15,300,000
River Points		**Plains**	
Minneapolis................	105,800,000	Wichita....................	37,400,000
Peoria.....................	3,300,000	Topeka....................	54,100,000
St. Louis...................	17,700,000	Salina.....................	49,500,000
Sioux City..................	3,700,000	Hutchinson................	42,000,000
Omaha-Council Bluffs.......	23,100,000	Hastings-Grand Island......	25,300,000
Atchison...................	15,200,000	Lincoln....................	33,700,000
St. Joseph.................	22,300,000	**Pacific N.W.**	
Kansas City, Mo............	95,200,000	Puget Sound (incl. Portland)........	35,100,000
Southwest		California interior	NA

Atlantic Coast — Albany, N.Y., Philadelphia, Pa., Baltimore, Md., Norfolk, Va. **Gulf Points** — New Orleans, Baton Rouge, Ama. Belle Chase, La., Mobile, Ala. **North Texas Gulf** — Houston, Galveston, Beaumont, Port Arthur, Texas. **South Texas Gulf** — Corpus Christi, Brownsville, Texas. **Pacific N.W.** — Seattle, Tacoma, Wash., Portland, Oreg., Columbia River. **Texas High Plains** — Amarillo, Lubbock, Hereford, Plainview, Texas. NA = Not available.

Government Payments by Programs and State[1]

Source: Economic Research Service, U.S. Dept. of Agriculture (thousands)

1990 State	Feed Grain	Wheat	Rice	Cotton	Wool Act	Conservation[2]	Miscellaneous[3]	Total
Alabama	$6,728	$6,655	0	$17,823	$19	$30,481	$20,520	$82,226
Alaska	27	0	0	0	0	975	115	1,117
Arizona	2,214	5,370	0	29,307	1,488	1,706	3,264	43,349
Arkansas	11,901	45,942	185,015	27,544	109	16,860	25,325	312,696
California	6,340	27,752	92,150	57,995	4,463	14,452	49,181	252,333
Colorado	37,355	83,713	0	0	3,690	88,699	23,266	236,723
Connecticut	465	0	0	0	12	446	1,200	2,123
Delaware	1,613	339	0	0	3	298	960	3,213
Florida	3,599	1,266	70	1,213	4	8,887	22,116	37,155
Georgia	22,174	22,781	0	14,603	12	32,726	38,297	130,593
Hawaii	0	0	0	0	9	510	0	519
Idaho	1,987	76,273	0	0	1,546	39,750	13,875	133,431
Illinois	367,119	43,381	0	0	346	56,892	38,865	506,603
Indiana	173,796	22,445	0	0	158	32,304	15,467	244,170
Iowa	507,923	928	0	0	1,206	171,218	72,458	753,733
Kansas	160,106	409,156	0	16	924	168,149	96,395	834,746
Kentucky	35,240	10,673	0	0	87	28,992	6,618	81,610
Louisiana	6,113	6,695	71,644	36,937	14	9,830	23,398	154,631
Maine	540	2	0	0	26	4,570	1,844	6,982
Maryland	7,873	2,123	0	0	43	2,514	4,833	17,386
Massachusetts	178	0	0	0	17	659	2,169	3,023
Michigan	84,258	25,576	0	0	618	16,996	41,383	168,831
Minnesota	221,961	109,121	0	0	756	105,459	74,462	511,759
Mississippi	6,092	14,162	36,611	65,325	8	37,860	25,911	185,969
Missouri	82,564	63,078	12,794	9,103	695	103,071	27,760	299,065
Montana	5,314	159,482	0	0	3,609	111,342	19,852	299,599
Nebraska	351,287	96,746	0	0	720	81,036	94,857	624,646
Nevada	37	627	0	0	437	1,012	3,234	5,347
New Hampshire	154	0	0	0	16	677	1,009	1,856
New Jersey	2,531	555	0	0	11	670	11,977	15,744
New Mexico	9,992	11,271	0	3,128	3,955	21,017	14,477	63,840
New York	24,122	5,383	0	0	160	8,204	21,435	59,304
North Carolina	29,562	9,984	0	4,393	38	11,918	17,360	73,255
North Dakota	22,887	330,490	0	0	890	121,070	70,041	545,378
Ohio	100,718	34,307	0	0	728	22,184	39,069	197,006
Oklahoma	11,096	219,124	158	9,896	2,251	55,596	20,919	319,040
Oregon	1,714	47,853	0	0	1,378	29,053	9,139	89,137
Pennsylvania	13,265	1,599	0	0	246	10,624	15,680	41,414
Rhode Island	0	0	0	0	2	171	18	191
South Carolina	14,514	11,873	0	6,881	1	19,307	10,061	62,637
South Dakota	83,199	98,811	0	0	3,185	83,753	63,903	332,851
Tennessee	16,096	12,441	65	16,047	27	26,966	19,387	91,029
Texas	146,910	141,235	66,373	140,469	53,669	180,542	245,504	974,702
Utah	695	5,914	0	0	2,852	11,380	14,056	34,897
Vermont	502	2	0	0	43	2,139	3,107	5,793
Virginia	11,338	5,307	0	77	363	8,003	7,290	32,378
Washington	4,082	131,118	0	0	310	56,716	13,199	205,425
West Virginia	1,530	118	0	0	192	2,306	1,903	6,049
Wisconsin	99,779	3,267	0	0	226	45,865	32,106	181,243
Wyoming	1,683	6,362	0	0	4,633	12,286	6,319	31,283
Total U.S.	$2,701,173	$2,311,300	$464,880	$440,757	$96,195	$1,898,141	$1,385,584	$9,298,030

(1) Includes both cash payments and payment-in-kind (PIK). (2) Includes amount paid under agriculture and conservation programs (Conservation Bonus, Conservation Reserve, Agriculture Conservation, Emergency Conservation, and Great Plains Program). (3) The programs included: Rural Clean Water, Clean Lakes, Animal Waste Management, Forest Incentive, Water Bank, Milk Indemnity, Dairy Termination, Emergency Feed, Extended Warehouse Storage, Extended Farm Storage, Milk Diversion, Disaster Program Crops, Disaster Program Non-Crops, Colorado River Salinity, Warehouse Storage Deduction, Livestock Emergency Assistance, Interest Penalty Payments, Disaster, and Loan Deficiency.

Federal Food Assistance Programs[1]

Source: Food and Nutrition Service, U.S. Agriculture Department (millions of dollars)

	1982	1983	1984	1985	1986	1987	1988	1989	1990	1991
Food Stamp Pgm.[2,6]	$10,145	$11,847	$11,579	$11,703	$11,638	$11,605	$12,317	$12,908	$15,510	$18,751
P.R. Nutrition Asst. Grant[3,11]	898	825	825	825	820	853	879	908	937	974
Natl. School Lunch Pgm.[4]	2,942	3,203	3,335	3,380	3,537	3,685	3,730	3,769	3,834	3,945
School Breakfast Pgm.	317	344	364	379	406	447	482	513	596	683
Special Supp. Food Pgm. for Women, Infants, Children[5]	949	1,126	1,388	1,489	1,583	1,680	1,798	1,911	2,123	2,347
Summer Food Service Pgm.[4]	87	93	96	112	115	129	133	146	164	179
Child and Adult Care Food Pgm.[4]	324	356	407	452	496	548	628	703	820	956
Special Milk Pgm.	18	17	16	16	16	15	19	18	19	21
Nutrition Prg. for the Elderly[4]	102	120	127	134	137	139	146	144	142	140
Needy Family Pgm.[4]	41	44	51	60	60	63	62	65	66	73
Commodity Supp. Food Pgm.[4,7]	28	42	48	48	48	56	62	73	84	96
Food Distribution to Charitable Inst.[4,8]	117	154	190	170	240	158	159	136	104	66
TEFAP (The Emerg. Food Asst. Pgm.)	180	998	1,075	1,026	895	895	645	276	257	289
Other Costs[9]	44	49	48	53	56	59	55	96	141	156
Total[10]	$16,192	$19,218	$19,549	$19,847	$20,048	$20,332	$21,114	$21,666	$24,794	$28,676

(continued)

(1) Data are for Fiscal (not Calendar) years. 1990 and prior years are updated per current reports; 1991 data represent the program level under current law in the 1991 budget. (2) Excludes Puerto Rico. (3) Grant was initiated in June 1982; prior data are Food Stamp costs. (4) Includes the value of commodities (entitlement, bonus and cash-in-lieu). (5) Includes program studies and Farmers Market Demo. Projects. (6) Includes SAE and other FS program costs; excludes transfers. (7) Includes Elderly Feeding Projects. (8) Includes Summer Camps. (9) Includes Child Nutrition State Admin. Expenses, CN Nutrition Studies & Education, and the costs of commodities distributed to Soup Kitchens/Food Banks. (10) Excludes food program administration (FPA) costs, Northern Marianas Nutrition Assistance Grant, and Disaster Relief. The Marianas Grant was $0.9 million in FY 1982, and $3.7 million for subsequent years. (11) 1990 includes $10 million tranferred to APHIS for tick eradication, a function previously included in Nutrition Assistance grants.

Age and Sex of the Farm and Nonfarm Population, 1990

Source: Economic Research Service, U.S. Department of Agriculture; and Bureau of the Census, U.S. Department of Commerce, 1990.

(Numbers in thousands)

Age	Both sexes	Farm Male	Female	Both sexes	Nonfarm Male	Female
All ages	4,591	2,383	2,208	241,490	116,979	124,511
Under 15 years	940	480	459	53,775	27,531	26,244
15 to 19	356	190	166	16,755	8,456	8,298
20 to 24	232	134	99	17,567	8,514	9,053
25 to 29	238	127	111	20,598	10,094	10,504
30 to 34	294	158	136	21,624	10,659	10,965
35 to 39	302	154	148	19,574	9,608	9,966
40 to 44	331	160	171	17,136	8,363	8,772
45 to 49	287	155	132	13,612	6,603	7,009
50 to 54	306	147	159	11,197	5,414	5,783
55 to 59	314	164	151	10,247	4,866	5,381
60 to 64	290	150	140	10,379	4,844	5,535
65 to 69	275	143	132	9,856	4,449	5,407
70 to 74	183	104	80	7,751	3,373	4,378
75 years and over	244	118	126	11,421	4,206	7,215
Median age (years)	38.9	38.3	39.5	32.8	31.8	33.7
Percent Distribution						
All ages	100.0	100.0	100.0	100.0	100.0	100.0
Under 15 years.	20.5	20.1	20.8	22.3	23.5	21.1
15 to 19	7.8	8.0	7.5	6.9	7.2	6.7
20 to 24	5.1	5.6	4.5	7.3	7.3	7.3
25 to 29	5.2	5.3	5.0	8.5	8.6	8.4
30 to 34	6.4	6.6	6.2	9.0	9.1	8.8
35 to 39	6.6	6.5	6.7	8.1	8.2	8.0
40 to 44	7.2	6.7	7.7	7.1	7.1	7.0
45 to 49	6.3	6.5	6.0	5.6	5.6	5.6
50 to 54	6.7	6.2	7.2	4.6	4.6	4.6
55 to 59	6.8	6.9	6.8	4.2	4.2	4.3
60 to 64	6.3	6.3	6.3	4.3	4.1	4.4
65 to 69	6.0	6.0	6.0	4.1	3.8	4.3
70 to 74	4.0	4.4	3.6	3.2	2.9	3.5
75 years and over	5.3	5.0	5.7	4.7	3.6	5.8

U.S. Farms, 1940-1991

Source: U.S. Dept. of Agriculture

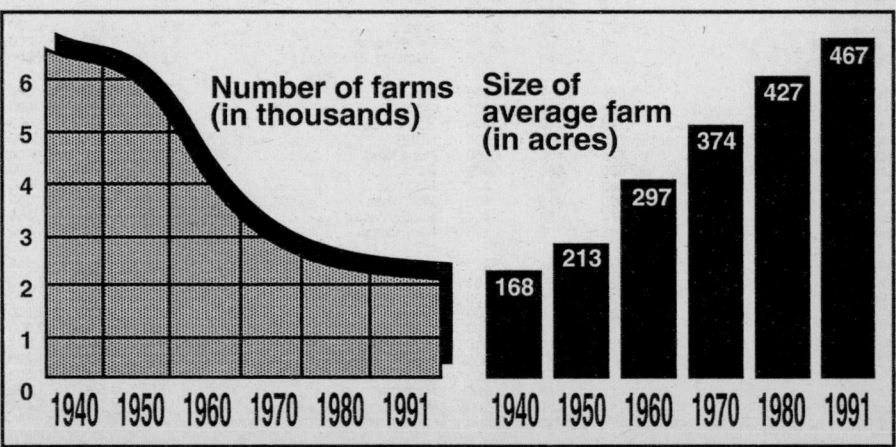

World Wheat, Rice and Corn Production, 1989

Source: U.N. Food and Agriculture Organization

(thousands of metric tons)

Country	Wheat	Rice	Corn
World, total	538,056	506,291	470,318
Afghanistan	1,925	490	750
Argentina	10,000	469	4,260
Australia	14,200	748	217
Austria	1,363	—	1,491
Bangladesh	834	26,600	3
Belgium-Lux.	1,478	—	62
Brazil	5,407	11,107	26,508
Bulgaria	5,402	50	2,421
Burma (Myanmar)	230	13,581	270
Canada	24,383	—	6,400
Chile	1,766	185	938
China	91,002	179,403	75,840
Colombia	81	1,884	1,052
Cuba	—	550	95
Czechoslovakia	6,356	—	1,000
Denmark	3,221	—	—
Ecuador	33	806	431
Egypt	3,148	2,680	3,748
Ethiopia	850	—	1,600
Finland	497	—	—
France	31,817	97	12,926
Germany (GDR)	3,477	—	—
Germany (FDR)	11,065	—	1,574
Greece	2,005	110	1,700
Hungary	6,559	45	6,949
India	53,995	107,500	7,800
Indonesia	—	43,566	6,324
Iran	5,800	1,200	40
Iraq	491	140	70
Ireland	498	—	—
Israel	201	—	20
Italy	7,408	1,130	6,251
Japan	985	12,934	1
Cambodia	—	2,100	115
Korea (DPR)	900	6,400	3,000
Korean Republic	2	8,200	118
Laos	—	1,220	47
Madagascar	—	2,290	220
Malaysia	—	1,697	34
Mexico	3,900	441	9,900
Nepal	830	2,870	900
Netherlands	1,047	—	5
New Zealand	135	—	139
Pakistan	14,419	4,796	1,120
Panama	—	180	100
Peru	159	1,091	1,010
Philippines	—	9,459	4,522
Poland	8,462	—	244
Portugal	605	153	674
Romania	6,000	175	11,800
South Africa	2,720	3	11,700
Soviet Union	90,500	2,525	17,000
Spain	5,465	341	3,224
Sri Lanka	—	1,949	36
Sweden	1,764	—	—
Switzerland	580	—	195
Syria	1,020	—	108
Thailand	—	21,300	4,456
Turkey	15,729	300	2,000
United Kingdom	13,900	—	—
United States	55,407	7,007	191,197
Uruguay	473	537	60
Venezuela	—	313	921
Vietnam	—	18,100	900
Yugoslavia	5,599	30	9,415

Note: Some figures are FAO estimates. Where production is small or nonexistent, — is indicated.

Wheat, Rice and Corn—Exports and Imports of 10 Leading Countries

Source: Economic Research Service, U.S. Dept. of Agriculture

(thousands of metric tons)

Leading Exporters	Exports[1] 1980	1989	1990P	Leading Importers	Imports[1] 1980	1989	1990P
Wheat				**Wheat**			
U.S.	41,204	33,557	29,257	USSR	16,000	14,600	14,500
Canada	16,262	17,413	20,500	China	13,789	13,000	9,500
France	13,423	18,200	17,250	Egypt	5,423	7,000	6,500
Australia	9,577	10,713	12,800	Japan	5,840	5,630	5,600
Argentina	3,845	6,060	5,300	Italy	3,028	5,100	5,000
United Kingdom	1,100	3,700	3,750	Algeria	2,294	4,300	4,600
Germany, Fed Rep[2]	1,502	4,200	3,000	Iran	1,896	5,200	4,500
Italy	1,620	2,700	2,550	Brazil	3,910	1,900	4,300
Saudi Arabia	0	1,700	2,000	South Korea	2,095	2,000	4,200
Denmark	180	1,040	1,800	Germany, Fed Rep 2/	1,317	2,000	2,000
Rice				**Rice**			
Thailand	3,049	3,927	4,200	Iran	583	850	1,000
U.S.	3,028	2,542	2,351	Brazil	0	405	600
Pakistan	1,163	749	1,200	Saudi Arabia	356	525	530
Vietnam	5	1,500	1,000	USSR	1,283	400	400
Italy	475	495	650	Hong Kong	362	400	400
China	580	300	550	Senegal	340	390	400
Australia	468	461	470	Malaysia	167	367	360
India	900	420	400	Philippines	0	575	350
Burma	674	186	400	South Africa	126	300	350
Spain	45	136	173	Ivory Coast	275	283	300
Corn				**Corn**			
United States	60,737	60,169	43,817	Japan	13,989	16,200	16,200
China	125	3,150	5,500	USSR	11,800	18,600	7,700
France	2,380	8,100	5,000	South Korea	2,355	6,100	5,000
Argentina	9,098	2,800	4,400	Taiwan	2,703	4,950	4,900
Thailand	2,142	1,179	1,200	Mexico	3,833	5,000	2,000
Belgium-Luxembourg	1,742	29	410	Netherlands	2,638	2,004	1,835
Spain	1	160	300	Spain	4,251	1,900	1,700
Greece	0	150	300	Egypt	984	1,350	1,500
Kenya	0	148	200	Malaysia	717	1,520	1,490
Germany, Fed Rep[2]	140	150	150	Algeria	206	1,250	1,400

(1) Marketing years; (2) Data for total Germany not yet available; p = preliminary

EMPLOYMENT

U.S. Labor Force, Employment and Unemployment

Source: Bureau of Labor Statistics, U.S. Dept. of Labor

In Feb. 1991 the unemployment rate rose to 6.5%, its highest point in nearly 4 years; the rate rose again to 6.8% in March, to 6.9% in May, and in July was 6.8%.

(numbers in thousands)

Employment status	Annual averages			1991			
	1988	1989	1990	Jan.	March	May	July
Civilian labor force	121,669	123,869	124,787	124,638	125,326	125,232	125,214
Employed	114,968	117,342	117,914	116,922	116,754	116,591	116,712
Unemployed	6,701	6,528	6,874	7,715	8,572	8,640	8,501
Unemployment rate	5.5	5.3	5.5	6.2	6.8	6.9	6.8

Selected Unemployment Indicators
(quarterly averages, seasonally adjusted)

Category Characteristic	1988			1989				1990				1991
	II	III	IV	I	II	III	IV	I	II	III	IV	I	II
Total (all civilian workers) . . .	5.5	5.5	5.3	5.2	5.3	5.3	5.3	5.2	5.3	5.6	5.9	6.6	6.8
Men, 20 years and over. . .	4.8	4.7	4.6	4.4	4.4	4.6	4.6	4.6	4.8	5.0	5.4	6.1	6.4
Women, 20 years and over .	4.9	4.9	4.7	4.6	4.8	4.7	4.8	4.7	4.6	4.9	5.1	5.5	5.7
Both sexes, 16 to 19 years .	15.1	15.5	14.5	15.0	15.0	15.0	15.2	14.5	14.8	16.0	16.4	18.0	18.8
White	4.7	4.8	4.6	4.4	4.5	4.5	4.5	4.6	4.6	4.8	5.1	5.8	6.0
Black and other	10.6	10.0	9.9	10.2	9.8	9.8	10.3	9.6	9.3	10.5	10.9	10.8	11.3
Black	12.0	11.4	11.3	11.5	11.3	11.3	11.8	10.8	10.4	11.6	12.0	12.1	12.9
Hispanic origin	8.8	7.9	7.8	7.3	8.0	8.6	8.1	7.5	7.6	8.1	8.7	9.7	9.3
Married men, spouse present	3.2	3.2	3.1	3.0	3.0	3.1	3.0	3.2	3.3	3.4	3.7	4.3	4.5
Married women, spouse present.	3.8	3.9	3.7	3.5	3.9	3.8	3.9	3.7	3.6	3.8	4.0	4.4	4.6
Women who maintain families	8.3	8.0	7.9	8.0	8.0	8.1	8.0	7.8	7.6	8.5	8.6	9.0	9.4
Full-time workers	5.1	5.1	5.0	4.9	4.9	5.0	5.0	4.9	5.0	5.2	5.7	6.3	6.5
Part-time workers	7.6	7.7	7.1	7.1	7.3	7.2	7.4	7.2	7.4	7.6	7.4	8.1	8.6
Unemployed 15 weeks and over[1]	1.3	1.3	1.2	1.1	1.1	1.1	1.1	1.1	1.1	1.3	1.3	1.6	1.9
Labor force time lost[2]	6.3	6.4	6.2	6.0	6.0	6.0	5.9	5.9	6.0	6.3	6.7	7.4	7.6
Industry													
Nonagricultural private wage and salary workers	5.5	5.5	5.4	5.3	5.3	5.4	5.4	5.5	5.5	5.7	6.1	6.8	7.2
Goods-producing industries.	6.4	6.5	6.4	6.1	6.0	6.3	6.3	6.6	6.5	6.8	7.8	8.8	9.3
Mining.	8.4	7.1	8.1	6.9	4.8	6.8	5.2	5.9	3.8	4.3	4.9	6.9	7.4
Construction	10.6	10.1	10.4	10.0	9.8	10.2	9.6	9.4	10.6	11.2	13.4	14.7	15.1
Manufacturing	5.2	5.4	5.1	5.0	5.0	5.2	5.4	5.8	5.4	5.7	6.3	7.1	7.7
Durable goods	4.8	5.1	4.9	4.7	4.6	4.8	5.3	5.6	5.3	5.8	8.5	7.7	8.1
Nondurable goods . . .	5.7	5.8	5.5	5.4	5.5	5.6	5.6	6.1	5.5	6.6	6.0	6.4	7.1
Service-producing industries	5.0	5.0	5.0	4.9	5.0	5.0	4.9	5.0	5.0	5.2	5.4	6.0	6.2
Transportation and public utilities	4.0	3.7	3.9	3.9	4.0	4.1	3.6	3.9	3.5	3.9	4.1	5.1	5.4
Wholesale and retail trade	6.1	6.2	6.0	5.9	5.8	6.0	6.2	6.1	6.2	6.3	6.7	7.4	7.5
Finance and service industries	4.5	4.4	4.4	4.4	4.5	4.4	4.3	4.4	4.5	4.6	4.7	5.2	5.5
Government workers.	2.9	2.9	2.6	2.7	2.8	2.8	2.7	2.4	2.5	2.8	2.8	3.3	3.1
Agricultural wage and salary workers.	10.6	11.2	9.5	9.2	10.0	8.6	10.6	9.6	9.6	9.6	10.2	12.4	11.1

(1) Unemployment as a percent of the civilian labor force. (2) Aggregate hours lost by the unemployed and persons on part time for economic reasons as a percent of potentially available labor force hours.

Employed Persons by Occupation, Sex, and Age

Source: Bureau of Labor Statistics, U.S. Dept. of Labor

(in thousands)

Occupation	Total 16 years and over		Men 16 years and over		Women 16 years and over	
	1989	1990	1989	1990	1989	1990
Total.	117,342	117,914	64,315	64,435	53,027	53,479
Managerial and professional specialty	30,398	30,657	16,652	16,619	13,746	14,038
Executive, administrative and managerial.	14,848	14,839	8,944	8,897	5,904	5,843
Technical, sales and administrative support	36,127	36,675	12,687	12,933	23,440	23,742
Technicians and related support	3,645	3,842	1,887	1,954	1,759	1,888
Sales occupations	14,065	14,191	7,124	7,208	6,841	6,983
Administrative support, including clerical.	18,416	18,041	3,676	3,771	14,741	14,870
Service occupations.	15,556	16,759	6,164	6,288	9,381	9,470
Private household	872	782	36	29	836	753
Protective service	1,960	1,988	1,854	1,897	305	291
Service, except private household and protective	12,724	12,989	4,474	4,582	8,250	8,427
Precision production, craft, and repair.	13,818	13,641	12,627	12,482	1,190	1,159
Mechanics and repairers	4,550	4,448	4,397	4,289	153	159
Construction trades	5,142	5,147	5,034	5,051	108	98
Other precision production, craft, and repair	4,126	4,046	3,196	3,142	929	904
Operators, fabricators, and laborers	18,022	17,775	13,327	13,249	4,695	4,528
Machine operators, assemblers, and inspectors	8,248	8,071	4,878	4,842	3,370	3,228
Transportation and material moving occupations	4,886	4,849	4,436	4,413	450	436
Handlers, equipment cleaners, helpers, and laborers	4,888	4,855	4,013	3,994	875	881

Selected Unemployment Insurance Data by State

Calendar year 1990, state programs only.

Source: Employment and Training Admin., U.S. Dept. of Labor

	Insured claimants[1]	Beneficiaries[2]	Exhaustions[3]	Initial claims[4]	Benefits paid[5]	Avg. weekly benefit for total unemployment	Employers subject to state law
AL.	195,920	168,817	28,052	418,752	$182,253,711	$115.57	80,289
AK	43,019	39,675	17,690	76,996	90,654,617	162.81	13,176
AR	128,217	91,356	20,963	238,650	139,803,534	133.33	49,066
AZ	117,209	82,922	22,214	188,861	147,099,909	135.04	79,109
CA	1,543,089	1,209,519	331,970	3,048,524	2,231,731,302	131.32	767,697
CO	96,051	71,021	25,019	137,803	143,450,484	167.98	89,419
CT	153,250	154,771	41,875	283,742	442,822,129	200.57	95,132
DC	30,791	24,443	10,881	39,729	89,100,799	212.67	20,865
DE	27,616	21,635	2,490	53,313	42,233,110	175.62	18,672
FL.	341,714	254,021	88,603	510,467	468,326,877	146.49	311,377
GA	326,391	250,477	51,654	489,064	318,089,229	142.96	142,831
HI	33,610	22,319	3,475	55,887	48,126,348	195.85	26,588
IA	100,543	82,251	16,556	157,733	145,564,599	160.91	61,956
ID	46,080	39,009	9,837	105,759	59,084,208	145.18	26,209
IL	248,174	352,228	111,202	770,881	945,853,769	170.28	246,675
IN	194,902	138,465	27,035	370,999	147,045,344	106.96	109,077
KS	81,395	66,791	19,843	157,107	151,959,998	171.00	58,573
KY	158,888	130,746	21,912	336,136	194,325,773	136.26	71,381
LA	113,858	85,268	23,303	228,666	126,456,051	102.36	80,449
MA	280,461	302,927	115,139	586,281	1,142,925,601	217.39	151,995
MD	173,365	118,893	26,265	249,867	267,209,760	170.04	112,823
ME	69,972	58,511	15,751	155,527	114,459,921	158.79	33,676
MI	665,733	466,000	125,639	1,206,869	1,165,835,850	203.94	178,726
MN	155,129	133,322	39,890	242,490	362,229,569	189.63	100,061
MO	235,673	178,495	48,074	496,625	294,517,734	134.74	126,548
MS	102,356	77,362	18,946	221,470	102,585,486	111.22	45,781
MT	29,546	23,656	7,363	51,170	38,131,827	136,89	23,867
NC	402,999	298,778	32,693	1,001,155	322,889,883	151.76	134,990
ND	16,128	14,323	5,467	30,687	23,484,559	136.08	17,766
NE	36,874	27,374	6,874	61,397	35,550,548	120.31	39,785
NH	61,490	49,012	4,238	77,780	59,513,824	128.42	32,921
NJ.	376,304	325,056	120,546	609,192	1,052,409,133	206.98	204,807
NM	33,953	27,370	8,991	59,470	54,040,507	126.22	33,767
NV	67,199	46,155	10,757	97,074	90,912,043	162.44	28,498
NY	679,137	615,228	216,735	1,217,861	1,872,818,171	180.59	441,361
OH	431,798	337,797	73,554	825,532	664,943,339	154.82	207,701
OK	69,577	60,563	17,009	165,148	106,400,863	150.08	64,901
OR	148,162	125,881	26,495	327,910	255,913,884	162.22	77,338
PA	574,045	472,039	108,398	1,184,449	1,224,809,204	188.53	233,679
PR	71,302	117,704	56,586	227,056	130,358,534	78.71	50,205
RI	72,120	61,479	19,762	137,226	171,106,705	193.59	27,806
SC	170,705	115,213	19,305	371,889	135,386,488	130.42	70,624
SD	9,164	7,240	854	18,686	9,201,104	119.62	18,888
TN	253,030	260,857	50,995	541,085	253,744,255	113.03	93,666
TX	461,121	345,506	139,823	739,991	783,579,070	161.98	318,352
UT	40,555	33,207	8,479	62,619	58,182,071	163.21	32,687
VA	214,112	168,503	21,755	443,483	189,132,686	146.05	128,895
VI	1,706	1,099	256	2,323	1,644,787	127.19	3,296
VT.	31,371	26,175	4,443	49,460	52,479,421	149.12	18,986
WA	228,952	187,998	43,972	482,386	425,683,131	168.78	134,944
WI	226,410	195,976	40,227	449,059	362,126,513	170.90	103,039
WV	60,494	53,615	10,926	92,217	98,913,549	146.14	35,098
WY	14,037	9,509	2,474	28,538	20,307,974	158.80	15,059
Total. . . .	10,445,697	8,628,557	2,323,255	20,183,041	$18,057,409,445	$153.43	5,693,077

(1) Claimants whose base-period earnings or whose employment, covered by the unemployment insurance program, was sufficient to make them eligible for unemployment insurance benefits as provided by state law. (2) First payments. (3) Final payments. Claimants who exhaust their benefit rights in one benefit year may be entitled to further benefits in the following benefit year. (4) Excludes intrastate transitional claims. (5) Adjusted for voided benefit checks and transfers under interstate combined wage plan.

Employment and Unemployment in the U.S.

Source: Bureau of Labor Statistics, U.S. Dept. of Labor

Civilian labor force, persons 16 years of age and over (in thousands)

Year*	Employed	Unemployed	Unemployment Rate	Year*	Employed	Unemployed	Unemployment Rate
1940[1]	47,520	8,120	14.6%	1983	100,834	10,717	9.6
1950	58,918	3,288	5.0	1984	105,005	8,539	7.5
1960	65,778	3,852	5.5	1985	107,150	8,312	7.2
1970	78,678	4,093	4.9	1986[2]	109,597	8,237	7.0
1975	85,846	7,929	8.5	1987	112,440	7,425	6.2
1978	96,048	6,202	6.1	1988	114,988	6,701	5.5
1980	99,303	7,637	7.1	1989	117,342	6,528	5.3
1981	100,397	8,273	7.6	1990	117,914	6,874	5.5
1982	99,526	10,678	9.7				

(1) Persons 14 years of age and over; (2) Not strictly comparable with prior years.
*Early unemployment rates: 1915, 9.7; 1916, 4.8; 1917, 4.8; 1918, 1.4; 1919, 2.3; 1920, 4.0; 1921, 11.9; 1922, 7.6; 1923, 3.2; 1924, 5.5; 1925, 4.0; 1926, 1.9; 1927, 4.1; 1928, 4.4; 1929, 3.2; 1930, 8.7; 1931, 15.9; 1932, 23.6; 1933, 24.9; 1934, 21.7; 1935, 20.1; 1936, 16.9; 1937, 14.3; 1938, 19.0; 1939, 17.2.

Employment and Training Services and Unemployment Insurance

Source: Employment and Training Administration, U.S. Dept. of Labor

Employment Service

The Federal-State Employment Service consists of the United States Employment Service and affiliated state employment services which make up the nation's public employment service system. During program year 1987, the public employment service listed 7.2 million job openings and placed more than 3.8 million people in jobs.

The employment service refers employable applicants to job openings that use their highest skills and helps the unemployed obtain services or training to make them employable. It also provides special attention to handicapped workers, migrants and seasonal farmworkers, workers who lose their jobs because of foreign trade competition, and other worker groups. Veterans receive priority services including referral to jobs and training. During program year 1987, 455,813 veterans were placed in jobs.

Job Training

The Job Training Partnership Act (JTPA), which became fully operational on October 1, 1983, provides job training and employment services for economically disadvantaged youth and adults, dislocated workers, and others who face significant employment barriers. The goal of the Act is to move as many jobless workers as possible into permanent, unsubsidized, self-sustaining employment.

Since its inception, JTPA has provided approximately four and a half million Americans with training and employment services. Its placement rate is 68 percent, making it one of the most successful job and training efforts ever undertaken.

Title I of the Act's five titles basically establishes an administrative structure for the delivery of job and training services. Generally, state governors receive bloc grants from the Labor Department, and the funds are then distributed to Service Delivery Areas — areas of 200,000 population or more where local elected officials work with Private Industry Councils to plan and conduct local training projects.

Title II is in two parts, with Title II-A spelling out the Act's provision of employment and training projects for the economically disadvantaged. In program year 1987 (July 1, 1987 to June 30, 1988), these projects served more than 1.3 million people.

Title II-A outlines a summer youth program offering basic and remedial education, institutional and on-the-job training, work experience, and supportive services. This program had nearly 640,000 participants in program year 1987.

Title III, Economic Dislocation and Worker Adjustment Assistance, provides for job and training help for dislocated workers — workers who lose jobs and are unlikely to return to their previous industries or occupations. This includes workers who lose their jobs because of plant closings or mass layoffs; long-term unemployed persons with limited local opportunities for jobs in their fields; farmers, ranchers, and other self-employed persons who become jobless due to general economic conditions or natural disasters; and, under certain circumstances, displaced homemakers. Such assistance benefitted nearly 183,000 workers in program year 1987.

Title IV authorizes programs to address the employment and training needs of specific groups facing significant barriers to productive employment, including Native Americans, migrant and seasonal farmworkers, and the disabled. In program year 1987, these programs served 33,000 Native Americans; 46,800 migrant and seasonal farmworkers; and 8,550 disabled persons.

In addition, Title IV includes the Job Corps, which each year enrolls approximately 100,000 young people between the ages of 16 and 21 in 107 residential job training centers throughout the United States; the National Commission for Employment Policy; and nationally administered programs for technical assistance, labor market information, research and evaluation, and pilots and demonstrations.

Title V contains miscellaneous provisions, including amendments to the Wagner-Peyser Act of 1933 — the legislation authorizing the federal-state Employment Service.

Trade Ajustment Assistance for Workers

The Trade Adjustment Assistance (TAA) is available to workers who lose their jobs or whose hours of work and wages are reduced as a result of increased imports. TAA includes a variety of benefits and reemployment services to help unemployed workers prepare for and obtain suitable employment. Workers may be eligible for training, job search, relocation and other reemployment services. Additionally, weekly trade readjustment allowances (TRA) may be payable to eligible workers following their exhaustion of unemployment insurance benefits. In fiscal year 1989, about 23,700 workers received $186 million in TRA payments; about 15,200 workers entered training; about 900 workers were involved in job search visits; and about 1,000 workers relocated in order to obtain long term jobs.

The TAA program is administered by the Employment and Training Administration's Office of Trade Adjustment Assistance. State employment security agencies serve as agents of the U.S., under an agreement with the Secretary of Labor, for administering the TAA benefit provisions in the Trade Act of 1974.

Unemployment Insurance

Unlike old-age and survivors insurance, entirely a federal program, the unemployment insurance program is a Federal-State system that provides insured wage earners with partial replacement of wages lost during involuntary unemployment. The program protects most workers. During calendar year 1990, an estimated 106.3 million workers in commerce, industry, agriculture, and government, including the armed forces, were covered under the Federal-State system. In addition, an estimated 296,000 railroad workers were insured against unemployment by the Railroad Retirement Board.

Each state, as well as the District of Columbia, Puerto Rico, and the Virgin Islands, has its own law and operates its own program. The amount and duration of the weekly benefits are determined by state laws, based on prior wages and length of employment. States are required to extend the duration of benefits when unemployment rises to and remains above specified state levels; costs of extended benefits are shared by the state and federal governments.

Under the Federal Unemployment Tax Act, as amended in 1985, the tax rate is 6.2% on the first $7,000 paid to each employee of employers with one or more employees in 20 weeks of the year or a quarterly payroll of $1,500. A credit of up to 5.4% is allowed for taxes paid under state unemployment insurance laws that meet certain criteria, leaving the federal share at 0.8% of taxable wages.

Social Security Requirement

The Social Security Act requires, as a condition of such grants, prompt payment of due benefits. The Federal Unemployment Tax Act provides safeguards for workers' right to benefits if they refuse jobs that fail to meet certain labor standards. Through the Unemployment Insurance Service of the Employment and Training Administration, the Secretary of Labor determines whether states qualify for grants and for tax offset credit from employers.

Benefits are financed solely by employer contributions, except in Alaska, Pennsylvania and New Jersey where employees also contribute. Benefits are paid through the states' public employment offices, at which unemployed workers must register for work and to which they must report regularly for referral to a possible job during the time when they are drawing weekly benefit payments. During the fiscal year 1989, $14.30 billion in benefits was paid under state unemployment insurance programs to 7 million beneficiaries. They received an average weekly payment of $152.08 for total unemployment for an average of 13.3 weeks.

Distribution of Wage and Salary Workers Paid Hourly Rates

Source: Bureau of Labor Statistics, U.S. Dept. of Labor

(Annual average, 2nd quarter 1990-1st quarter 1991; in thousands)

	Total paid hourly rates	$3.80* or less	$4.25 or less	$5.00 or less	$5.01 or more
Sex and Age					
Total, 16 years and over	62,112	3,189	8,058	15,588	46,524
16 to 24 years	14,716	1,642	4,227	7,478	7,238
20 to 24 years	9,220	603	1,641	3,414	5,805
25 years and over	47,396	1,547	3,831	8,110	39,287
25 to 54 years	40,994	1,247	3,098	6,618	34,376
25 to 34 years	18,237	646	1,611	3,308	14,929
35 to 44 years	14,092	381	934	2,073	12,019
45 to 54 years	8,666	220	553	1,237	7,428
55 years and over	6,402	300	733	1,492	4,910
55 to 64 years	5,026	175	448	939	4,087
65 years and over	1,375	125	285	552	823
Men, 16 years and over	31,355	1,050	2,929	6,102	25,253
16 to 24 years	7,689	659	1,853	3,522	4,167
20 to 24 years	4,892	217	672	1,565	3,327
25 years and over	23,666	391	1,077	2,580	21,086
Women, 16 years and over	30,757	2,139	5,129	9,486	21,271
16 to 24 years	7,027	983	2,374	3,956	3,071
20 to 24 years	4,328	386	969	1,849	2,478
25 years and over	23,730	1,156	2,755	5,529	18,200
Family Relationship					
Husbands	16,414	198	569	1,446	14,969
Wives	15,330	662	1,681	3,491	11,839
Women who maintain families	3,925	268	603	1,110	2,815
Men who maintain families	1,212	28	73	185	1,027
Race and Hispanic Origin					
White					
Total, 16 years and over	52,115	2,588	6,600	12,818	39,298
Men	26,393	834	2,365	4,955	21,439
Women	25,722	1,754	4,236	7,863	17,859
Black					
Total, 16 years and over	8,010	528	1,248	2,272	5,738
Men	3,965	184	474	934	3,031
Women	4,045	345	774	1,339	2,706
Hispanic origin					
Total, 16 years and over	5,834	270	867	1,914	3,920
Men	3,514	115	420	1,011	2,503
Women	2,320	156	448	903	1,417
Full- and Part-Time Status and Sex					
Full-time workers					
Total, 16 years and over	46,746	1,117	3,212	7,536	39,210
Men	26,654	394	1,232	3,274	23,381
Women	20,092	723	1,980	4,263	15,829
Part-time workers					
Total, 16 years and over	15,365	2,072	4,846	8,052	7,314
Men	4,701	656	1,697	2,829	1,872
Women	10,665	1,416	3,149	5,223	5,442

Note: Data exclude the incorporated self-employed; *$3.80 = minimum wage Apr. 1, 1990-Mar. 31, 1991.

Federal Minimum Hourly Wage Rates Since 1950

Source: U.S. Dept. of Labor.

(Employee estimates as of September 1984, except as indicated. The Fair Labor Standards Act of 1938 and subsequent amendments provide for minimum wage coverage applicable to specified nonsupervisory employment categories. Exempt from coverage are executives and administrators or professionals).

	Minimum Rates for Nonfarm Workers			Minimum rates for farm workers[4]		Minimum Rates for Nonfarm Workers			Minimum rates for farm workers[4]
Effective date	Laws prior to 1966[1]	Percent, avg earnings[2]	1966 and later[3]		Effective date	Laws prior to 1966[1]	Percent, avg earnings[2]	1966 and later[3]	
Jan. 25, 1950	$.75	54	(X)	(X)	Jan. 1, 1975	2.10	45	2.00	1.80
Mar. 1, 1956	1.00	52	(X)	(X)	Jan. 1, 1976	2.30	46	2.20	2.00
Sept. 3, 1961	1.15	50	(X)	(X)	Jan. 1, 1977	(5)	(5)	2.30	2.20
Sept. 3, 1963	1.25	51	(X)	(X)	Jan. 1, 1978	2.65	44	2.65	2.65
Feb. 1, 1967	1.40	50	$1.00	$1.00	Jan. 1, 1979	2.90	45	2.90	2.90
Feb. 1, 1968	1.60	54	1.15	1.15	Jan. 1, 1980	3.10	45	3.10	3.10
Feb. 1, 1969	(5)	(5)	1.30	1.30	Jan. 1, 1981	3.35	43	3.35	3.35
Feb. 1, 1970	(5)	(5)	1.45	(5)	Apr. 1, 1990	3.80[6]		3.80[6]	3.80[6]
Feb. 1, 1971	(5)	(5)	1.60	(5)	Apr. 1, 1991	4.25[6]		4.25[6]	4.25[6]
May 1, 1974	2.00	46	1.90	1.60					

(X) Not applicable. (1) Applies to workers covered prior to 1961 Amendments and, after Sept. 1965, to workers covered by 1961 Amendments. Rates set by 1961 Amendments were: Sept. 1961, $1.00; Sept. 1964, $1.15; and Sept. 1965, $1.25. (2) Percent of gross average hourly earnings of production workers in manufacturing. (3) Applies to workers newly covered by Amendments of 1966, 1974, and 1977, and Title IX of Education Amendments of 1972. (4) Included in coverage as of 1966, 1974, and 1977 Amendments. (5) No change in rate. (6) Training wage for workers age 16-19 in first six months of first job: 1990, $3.35; 1991, $3.62 and from Apr. 1, 1991, additional requirements re subsequent employment by a different employer for an additional 90 days. The training wage expires Mar. 31, 1993.

Average Weekly Earnings of Production Workers by Major Industry, 1966-1990

Source: Bureau of Labor Statistics, U.S. Dept. of Labor

(annual averages)

Year	Mining	Construction	Manufacturing	Transportation and public utilities	Wholesale trade
1966.	$130.24	$146.26	$112.19	$128.13	$111.11
1967.	135.89	154.95	114.49	130.82	116.06
1968.	142.71	164.49	122.51	138.85	122.31
1969.	154.80	181.54	129.51	147.74	129.85
1970.	164.40	195.45	133.33	155.93	137.26
1971.	172.14	211.67	142.44	168.82	144.18
1972.	189.14	221.19	154.71	187.86	151.69
1973.	201.40	235.89	166.46	203.31	160.34
1974.	219.14	249.25	176.80	217.48	170.33
1975.	249.31	266.08	190.79	233.44	183.05
1976.	273.90	283.73	209.32	256.71	194.66
1977.	301.20	295.65	228.90	278.90	209.13
1978.	332.88	318.69	249.27	302.80	228.14
1979.	365.07	342.99	269.34	325.58	247.93
1980.	397.06	367.78	288.62	351.25	267.96
1981.	438.75	399.26	318.00	382.18	291.06
1982.	459.88	426.82	330.26	402.48	309.85
1983.	479.40	442.97	354.08	420.81	329.18
1984.	503.58	458.51	374.03	438.13	342.27
1985.	519.93	464.46	386.37	450.30	351.74
1986.	525.81	466.75	396.01	458.64	358.11
1987.	531.70	480.44	406.31	471.58	365.76
1988.	541.44	495.73	418.81	475.69	380.24
1989.	569.75	512.41	430.09	490.53	394.82
1990.	603.73	526.40	441.86	504.14	411.10

Note: Production workers = production or nonsupervisory workers on private nonagriculture payrolls

Training Wage

Source: U.S. Dept. of Labor

Under the 1989 Amendments to the Fair Labor Standards Act (FLSA), the 1991 minimum wage changes will also affect the training wage, which increases to a minimum of $3.62 per hour on April 1, 1991. The training wage may be paid for up to a cumulative total of 90 days to employees under age 20, where all of the following conditions are met:

* An employer paying the training wage obtains proof of age and evidence from the employee of any previous employment during which the employee was paid the training wage;

* Before employment begins, the employer provides a written notice to each employee to be paid at the training wage describing the training wage provisions and statutory remedies available for violations (the text of the required notice is provided in Regulations, 29 CFR Part 517, which may be obtained from local offices of the Wage and Hour Division of the U.S. Dept. of Labor);

* An employer may not pay employees the training wage for more than 25 percent of the total hours worked by all employees at an establishment in any month; and,

* An employer cannot displace employees or reduce wages in order to hire employees at the training wage, and cannot hire an employee in a training wage position if the employer has laid off any employee from that or an essentially equivalent position in the previous 6 months.

* An employer must comply with all Federal, State, or local child labor laws.

An employee may continue to be paid at the training wage for a cumulative total of 90 additional days by a different employer, if in addition to the conditions above, that (subsequent) employer meets all of the following conditions:

* The employer provides on-the-job training which includes personal and job specific skills;

* The employer keeps on file, and provides employees with, a written training plan;

* The employer posts, in a prominent place, a notice of vacant or filled training wage positions. The employer must also furnish a copy of this position notice annually to the Dept. of Labor; and

* The employer did not employ the employee at the training wage during any portion of the first 90-day period.

The training wage, which expires March 31, 1993, does not apply to migrant or seasonal agricultural workers or to nonimmigrant agricultural workers performing temporary or seasonal work. Also, FLSA contains a number of exemptions from its minimum wage requirements, and the training wage provisions do not apply to any such employees.

Women in Unions

Source: Bureau of Labor Statistics, U.S. Dept. of Labor

	1983	1984	1985	1986	1987	1988
Number (thousands)	5,908	5,829	5,732	5,802	5,842	5,982
Union Women as % of Employed Women.	14.6	13.8	13.2	12.9	12.6	12.6
Union Women as % of Total Union Membership	33.3	33.6	33.7	34.2	34.5	35.2
Median Weekly Earnings of Union Women	$307	$326	$350	$368	$388	$403
Median Weekly Earnings of Union Men	$411	$444	$465	$482	$494	$506
Median Weekly Earnings of Non-union Women	$238	$251	$262	$274	$288	$300
Median Weekly Earnings of Non-union Men	$353	$362	$383	$394	$406	$416
Union Women's Median Weekly Earnings as % of Men's	74.4	73.4	72.3	76.3	78.5	79.6
Non-union Women's Median Weekly Earnings as % of Men's	67.4	69.3	68.4	69.5	70.9	72.1

Note: Data refer to members of a labor union or an employee association similar to a union.

Full-Time Employees Participating in Selected Employee Benefit Programs, 1989 and 1990

Source: Bureau of Labor Statistics, U.S. Dept. of Labor

(in percent)

Employee benefit program	Small private establishments, 1990		Full-time employees in medium and large private establishments, 1989	Employee benefit program	Small private establishments, 1990		Full-time employees in medium and large private establishments, 1989
	All full-time employees in small private establishments	Full-time employees in small independent private businesses			All full-time employees in small private establishments	Full-time employees in small independent private businesses	
Paid time off				Medical care . . .	69	66	92
Holidays.	83	80	97	Dental care	30	23	66
Vacations.	88	86	97	Life insurance . .	64	57	94
Personal leave . .	11	10	22				
Lunch period . . .	8	8	10	**Retirement**			
Rest period	48	46	71	All retirement[3] . .	42	35	81
Funeral leave. . .	47	38	84	Defined benefit			
Jury duty leave. .	54	47	90	pension.	20	12	63
Military leave . . .	21	15	53	Defined			
Sick leave.	48	41	68	contribution. . .	31	28	48
Maternity leave. .	2	2	3	Retirement[4] . . .	27	26	36
Paternity leave . .	(2)	(2)	1	Capital			
Unpaid time off				accumulation[5]	4	2	14
Maternity leave. .	17	14	37	**Other benefits**			
Paternity leave . .	8	7	18	Flexible benefits			
				plans	2	(2)	9
Insurance				Reimbursement			
Sickness and accident				accounts	8	5	23
insurance. . . .	26	23	43	Child care.	1	1	5
Long-term disability							
insurance. . . .	19	14	45				

(1) In 1989, survey coverage excluded executives and employees in constant travel status, such as airline pilots, as well as data for Alaska and Hawaii. Except for maternity and paternity leave and reimbursement accounts, benefits paid for entirely by the employee were excluded from the tabulations. (2) Less than 0.5 percent. (3) Includes defined benefit pension plans and defined contribution retirement plans. Some employees participated in both types of plans. (4) Includes money purchase pension, profit sharing, savings and thrift, stock bonus, employee stock ownership, and Simplified Employee Pension plans in which employer contributions must remain in the participant's account until retirement age, death, disability, separation from service, age 59-1/2, or hardship. (5) Includes plans in which participants may withdraw employer contributions from their accounts without regard to the conditions listed in (4).

Employer Cost for Employee Compensation as Percent of Total Compensation

Source: Bureau of Labor Statistics, U.S. Dept. of Labor

(March, 1990)

Industry, occupational category, employment size	Total compensation	Wage and salaries	Benefit costs					
			Total	Paid leave	Supplemental pay	Insurance	Retirement and savings	Legally required
				Percent of total compensation				
Goods-producing industries[1]	100.0	69.2	30.8	6.8	3.5	7.2	3.5	9.7
1-99 workers	100.0	72.2	27.8	4.6	2.9	5.4	3.1	11.7
100 workers or more	100.0	67.8	32.2	7.8	3.7	8.0	3.7	8.8
100-499 workers.	100.0	69.9	30.1	6.5	3.2	7.4	3.1	9.9
500 workers or more	100.0	66.4	33.6	8.6	4.1	8.3	4.1	8.1
Service-producing industries[2]. . . .	100.0	74.0	26.0	6.9	2.0	5.6	2.8	8.7
1-99 workers	100.0	75.4	24.6	6.0	2.1	5.2	2.4	8.9
100 workers or more	100.0	72.6	27.4	7.8	1.9	6.1	3.2	8.4
100-499 workers.	100.0	74.0	26.0	7.0	1.7	5.7	2.6	8.9
500 workers or more	100.0	71.5	28.5	8.4	2.0	6.4	3.6	8.0
White-collar workers	100.0	73.8	26.2	7.7	1.9	5.8	3.1	7.6
1-99 workers	100.0	75.6	24.4	6.6	2.1	5.3	2.6	7.8
100 workers or more	100.0	72.6	27.4	8.5	1.9	6.2	3.4	7.4
100-499 workers.	100.0	74.1	25.9	7.7	1.6	5.9	2.8	7.8
500 workers or more	100.0	71.6	28.4	9.0	2.0	6.4	3.8	7.1
Blue-collar workers	100.0	68.9	31.1	5.9	3.6	7.0	3.2	11.1
1-99 workers	100.0	71.9	28.1	4.6	2.8	5.6	2.9	12.1
100 workers or more	100.0	66.5	33.5	7.0	4.2	8.2	3.5	10.3
100-499 workers.	100.0	69.1	30.9	5.9	3.6	7.3	3.0	11.0
500 workers or more	100.0	64.4	35.6	7.9	4.8	8.9	4.0	9.6

(1) Includes mining, construction, and manufacturing; (2) Includes transportation, communication, and public utilities; wholesale and retail trade; finance, insurance, and real estate; and service industries.

Occupations with Projected Largest Job Growth, 1988-2000

Source: Bureau of Labor Statistics; U.S. Dept. of Labor, May, 1990

(Numbers in thousands)

Occupation	Employment 1988	Employment 2000	Numerical change	% change	Occupation	Employment 1988	Employment 2000	Numerical change	% change
Paralegals.	83	145	62	75.3	Human services workers.	118	171	53	44.9
Medical assistants .	149	253	104	70.0					
Radiologic technologists and technicians	132	218	87	66.0	Occupational therapy assistants and aides	8	13	4	44.7
Homemaker-home health aides . . .	327	537	207	63.3	Respiratory therapists.	56	79	23	41.3
Data processing equipment repairers.	71	115	44	61.2	Correction officers .	186	262	76	40.8
					Employment interviewers	81	113	33	40.5
Medical record technicians	47	75	28	59.9	Electrical and electronics engineers	439	615	176	40.1
Medical secretaries	207	327	120	58.0	Receptionists	833	1,164	331	39.8
Physical therapists .	68	107	39	57.0	Registered nurses .	1,577	2,190	613	38.9
Surgical technicians	35	55	20	56.4	Flight attendants . .	88	123	34	38.7
Operations research analysts.	55	85	30	55.4	Electromedical and biomedical equipment repairers . .	7	10	3	37.2
Securities and financial services sales workers.	200	309	109	54.8	Recreational therapists.	26	35	10	36.9
Travel agents	142	219	77	54.1					
Actuaries	16	24	8	53.6	Licensed practical nurses.	626	855	229	36.6
Computer systems analysts.	403	617	214	53.3	Guards.	795	1,050	256	32.2
Physical and corrective therapy assistants.	39	60	21	52.5	Nursing aides, orderlies, and attendants	1,184	1,562	378	31.9
Subway and streetcar operators. . .	8	13	4	52.0	Lawyers.	582	763	180	31.0
					Waiters and waitresses	1,786	2,338	551	30.9
EEG technologists .	6	10	3	50.4					
Occupational therapists.	33	48	16	48.8	Food service and lodging managers	560	721	161	28.8
					Child care workers .	670	856	186	27.8
Computer programmers.	519	769	250	48.1	Cooks, restaurant .	572	728	155	27.2

Earnings by Occupation and Sex

Source: Bureau of Labor Statistics, U.S. Dept. of Labor

(Median usual weekly earnings of full-time wage and salary workers; 2nd quarterly averages, not seasonally adjusted)

	Median weekly earnings			
	1990 Men	1990 Women	1991 Men	1991 Women
Managerial and professional specialty	717	507	741	519
Executive, administrative, and managerial	722	484	737	495
Professional specialty	712	525	744	548
Technical, sales, and administrative support.	494	329	498	351
Technicians and related support	561	426	564	442
Sales occupations	506	284	499	311
Administrative support, including clerical	438	332	456	349
Service occupations	317	231	320	243
Private household.	(1)	161	(1)	164
Protective service	454	369	494	436
Service, except private household and protective.	273	231	279	244
Precision production, craft, and repair	487	319	488	354
Mechanics and repairers.	477	476	472	541
Construction trades.	486	(1)	478	(1)
Other precision production, craft, and repair.	503	295	517	320
Operators, fabricators, and laborers.	379	262	391	275
Machine operators, assemblers, and inspectors	391	261	403	272
Transportation and material moving occupations	426	296	421	320
Handlers, equipment cleaners, helpers, and laborers.	308	249	316	269
Farming, forestry, and fishing	262	214	269	220

(1) Data not shown where base is less than 100,000.

Work Stoppages (Strikes) in the U.S.

Source: Bureau of Labor Statistics, U.S. Dept. of Labor

(involving 1,000 workers or more)

Year	Number stoppages[1]	Workers involved[1] (thousands)	Work days idle[1] (thousands)		Number stoppages[1]	Workers involved[1] (thousands)	Work days idle[1] (thousands)
1955	363	2,055	21,100	1977	298	1,212	21,258
1960	222	896	13,260	1978	219	1,006	23,774
1965	268	999	15,140	1979	235	1,021	20,409
1966	321	1,300	16,000	1980	187	795	20,844
1967	381	2,192	31,320	1981	145	729	16,908
1968	392	1,855	35,567	1982	96	656	9,061
1969	412	1,576	29,397	1983	81	909	17,461
1970	381	2,468	52,761	1984	62	376	8,499
1971	298	2,516	35,538	1985	54	324	7,079
1972	250	975	16,764	1986	69	533	11,861
1973	317	1,400	16,260	1987	46	174	4,481
1974	424	1,796	31,809	1988	40	118	4,364
1975	235	965	17,563	1989	51	452	16,996
1976	231	1,519	23,962	1990	44	201	6,580

(1) The number of stoppages and workers relate to stoppages that began in the year. Days of idleness include all stoppages in effect. Workers are counted more than once if they were involved in more than one stoppage during the year.

Changes in Mass Layoffs, 1989-1990

Source: Bureau of Labor Statistics. U.S. Dept. of Labor

Industry	Mass Layoff Events Number	Percent	Employees Laid Off Number	Percent	Initial Claimants for Unemployment Insurance Number	Percent
Total, all industries[1]	344	12.6	21,856	3.9	35,732	8.1
Agriculture	18	23.1	3,128	15.5	1,725	16.7
Manufacturing	281	20.4	27,100	10.3	50,737	21.9
Food and kindred products	5	2.0	3,001	5.9	5,915	16.1
Transportation equipment	57	41.0	1,167	2.4	10,481	26.4
Apparel and other textile products	32	21.1	467	1.9	3,930	16.0
Electronic and other electrical equipment	1	.6	-1,931	-6.2	409	1.4
Industrial machinery and equipment	31	27.7	2,121	8.8	6,228	27.5
Non manufacturing	45	3.5	-8,372	-3.0	-16,730	-8.5
Mining	2	3.5	-4,285	-33.9	912	13.1
Construction	-57	-13.5	-15,508	-23.9	-13,644	-24.9
Transportation and public utilities	-14	-8.2	-38,584	-56.8	-23,678	-51.8
Wholesale and retail trade	10	3.9	-1,024	-1.7	2,691	7.0
Finance, insurance, and real estate	22	75.9	9,015	173.7	5,759	178.4
Services	60	23.3	1,154	2.2	7,279	23.7
Government	22	26.8	40,860	214.8	3,951	24.0
Reason						
Bankruptcy	19	23.8	7,749	41.7	9,963	104.1
Business ownership change	-4	-4.9	-2,158	-11.3	-4,093	-27.5
Contract completion	-21	-9.5	-9,341	-18.9	-6,425	-17.2
Domestic relocation	47	70.1	7,310	65.3	5,664	64.5
Import competition	27	64.3	1,807	22.0	536	6.3
Seasonal work	-2	-.2	-8,082	-4.6	7,451	6.5
Slack work	300	46.8	43,321	44.0	61,218	67.2
Weather-related curtailment	16	23.5	402	3.5	-39	-.5
Other reasons	2	.5	9,433	7.9	-16,984	-17.4

(1) Data on layoffs in both years were reported by employers in 42 states and the District of Columbia. Those states *not* reporting were: California, Indiana, Maryland, Michigan, North Dakota, Ohio, Oregon, and Wyoming.

Occupational Injuries and Rates for Industries with 100,000 or More Injury Cases, 1989

Source: Bureau of Labor Statistics, U.S. Dept. of Labor

Industry	Total cases (in thousands)	Incidence rate[1]	Industry	Total cases (in thousands)	Incidence rate[1]
Motor vehicles and equipment manufacturing	161.4	18.9	Grocery stores	251.8	12.5
Nursing and personal care facilities	160.0	15.2	Hotels and motels	128.1	10.8
			Department stores	154.1	10.7
Trucking and courier services, except air	191.0	13.3	Eating and drinking places	351.9	8.4
			Hospitals	222.6	8.0
Groceries and related products —wholesale	104.2	13.1			

(1) Incident rates represent the number of injuries per 100 full-time workers.

Injuries and Illnesses in Industry

Source: Bureau of Labor Statistics, U.S. Dept. of Labor

(in thousands)

Industry division	Total cases[1] 1988	Total cases[1] 1989	Lost workday cases 1988	Lost workday cases 1989	Nonfatal cases without lost workdays 1988	Nonfatal cases without lost workdays 1989	Lost workdays 1988	Lost workdays 1989
Injuries and Illnesses[2]	**6,440.4**	**6,576.3**	**2,977.8**	**3,073.9**	**3,458.7**	**3,497.9**	**56,996.1**	**60,123.7**
Agriculture, forestry, and fishing[2]	101.9	102.3	52.7	53.3	49.0	48.8	952.1	946.4
Mining[3]	64.4	60.6	37.7	34.5	26.3	26.0	1,113.2	976.4
Construction	655.2	646.5	307.2	304.8	346.9	340.6	6,381.4	6,464.2
Manufacturing	2,463.9	2,465.5	1,079.6	1,093.7	1,383.6	1,371.1	20,264.8	21,311.3
Durable goods.	1,597.1	1,581.6	669.5	673.4	927.2	907.8	12,520.6	13,081.2
Nondurable goods	866.8	883.8	410.1	420.2	456.4	463.3	7,744.2	8,230.1
Transportation and public utilities	464.6	481.0	264.5	277.3	199.3	203.0	6,170.5	6,341.4
Wholesale and retail trade	1,533.4	1,603.3	683.4	719.2	849.4	883.3	11,914.2	12,767.4
Wholesale trade.	434.2	455.8	217.6	233.3	216.4	222.4	3,941.5	4,232.8
Retail trade	1,099.1	1,147.4	465.7	485.9	633.1	660.9	7,972.7	8,534.6
Finance, insurance, and real estate . . .	119.5	118.6	55.6	54.5	63.8	63.8	1,024.6	1,055.0
Services	1,037.6	1,098.5	497.1	536.6	540.3	561.4	9,175.2	10,261.6
Injuries	**6,199.6**	**6,292.5**	**2,880.4**	**2,955.5**	**3,315.6**	**3,333.0**	**54,339.7**	**56,704.9**
Agriculture, forestry, and fishing[3]	97.3	98.0	51.3	52.2	45.8	45.6	933.2	932.6
Mining.	62.5	58.6	37.1	33.9	25.0	24.6	1,100.3	958.4
Construction	648.3	638.8	304.4	301.2	343.0	336.6	6,338.4	6,386.0
Manufacturing	2,287.2	2,261.0	1,007.3	1,007.4	1,279.2	1,253.0	18,194.5	18,627.5
Durable goods.	1,479.5	1,453.5	625.0	623.7	854.0	829.5	11,203.5	11,509.6
Nondurable goods	807.8	807.5	382.3	383.7	425.2	423.5	6,991.0	7,117.9
Transportation and public utilities	455.6	472.6	261.3	273.9	193.6	198.1	6,103.2	6,266.6
Wholesale and retail trade	1,518.1	1,583.6	676.3	710.9	841.2	871.8	11,689.2	12,550.9
Wholesale trade.	427.8	447.0	214.7	230.3	212.8	216.6	3,882.5	4,161.4
Retail trade	1,090.3	1,136.5	461.6	480.6	628.4	655.2	7,806.6	8,389.5
Finance, insurance, and real estate . . .	116.3	115.0	54.0	52.6	62.3	62.1	970.4	988.3
Services	1,014.2	1,064.9	488.6	523.4	525.4	541.1	9,010.5	9,994.7
Illnesses	**240.8**	**283.7**	**97.4**	**118.4**	**143.1**	**164.9**	**2,656.4**	**3,418.8**
Agriculture, forestry, and fishing[3]	4.6	4.3	1.4	1.1	3.2	3.2	18.9	13.9
Mining.	1.9	2.0	.6	.6	1.3	1.4	12.8	18.0
Construction	6.9	7.7	2.8	3.6	4.0	3.9	43.0	78.2
Manufacturing	176.6	204.5	72.2	86.3	104.3	118.1	2,070.2	2,683.7
Durable goods.	117.7	128.1	44.4	49.8	73.2	78.3	1,317.1	1,571.6
Nondurable goods	59.0	76.3	27.8	36.5	31.1	39.8	753.1	1,112.2
Transportation and public utilities	9.0	8.4	3.2	3.4	5.7	4.9	67.4	74.8
Wholesale and retail trade	15.2	19.7	7.1	8.2	8.2	11.4	225.1	216.5
Wholesale trade.	6.5	8.8	3.0	3.0	3.5	5.8	59.0	71.4
Retail trade	8.8	10.9	4.1	5.2	4.7	5.6	166.1	145.1
Finance, insurance, and real estate . . .	3.1	3.7	1.6	2.0	1.5	1.7	54.2	66.7
Services	23.5	33.6	8.5	13.2	14.9	20.3	164.7	266.9

(1) Includes fatalities; (2) Excludes farms with fewer than 11 employees; (3) Excludes independent mining contractors. **Note:** Because of rounding, components may not add to totals.

Average Annual Pay, by State, 1989 and 1990

Source: Bureau of Labor Statistics, U.S. Dept. of Labor

State	Average annual pay 1989[1]	Average annual pay 1990[2]	% Change 1989-90[3]	State	Average annual pay 1989[1]	Average annual pay 1990[2]	% Change 1989-90[3]
United States	$22,563	$23,602	4.6	Missouri	$20,900	$21,716	3.9
Alabama	19,593	20,468	4.5	Montana	17,224	17,895	3.9
Alaska	29,704	29,946	0.8	Nebraska	17,690	18,577	5.0
Arizona	20,809	21,443	3.0	Nevada	21,333	22,358	4.8
Arkansas	17,418	18,204	4.5	New Hampshire	21,553	22,609	4.9
California	24,917	26,180	5.1	New Jersey	26,780	28,449	6.2
Colorado	21,940	22,908	4.4	New Mexico	18,667	19,347	3.6
Connecticut	27,500	28,995	5.4	New York	27,303	28,873	5.8
Delaware	23,268	24,423	5.0	North Carolina	19,321	20,220	4.7
District of Columbia	32,106	33,717	5.0	North Dakota	16,932	17,626	4.1
Florida	20,072	21,032	4.8	Ohio	21,986	22,843	3.9
Georgia	21,072	22,114	4.9	Oklahoma	19,533	20,288	3.9
Hawaii	21,624	23,167	7.1	Oregon	20,303	21,332	5.1
Idaho	18,146	18,991	4.7	Pennsylvania	22,313	23,457	5.1
Illinois	24,212	25,312	4.5	Rhode Island	21,128	22,388	6.0
Indiana	20,931	21,699	3.7	South Carolina	18,797	19,669	4.6
Iowa	18,420	19,224	4.4	South Dakota	15,810	16,430	3.9
Kansas	19,475	20,238	3.9	Tennessee	19,712	20,611	4.6
Kentucky	19,001	19,947	5.0	Texas	21,740	22,700	4.4
Louisiana	19,750	20,646	4.5	Utah	19,362	20,074	3.7
Maine	19,202	20,154	5.0	Vermont	19,497	20,532	5.3
Maryland	23,469	24,730	5.4	Virginia	21,882	22,750	4.0
Massachusetts	25,233	26,689	5.8	Washington	21,617	22,646	4.8
Michigan	24,767	25,376	2.5	West Virginia	19,788	20,715	4.7
Minnesota	22,155	23,126	4.4	Wisconsin	20,204	21,101	4.4
Mississippi	17,047	17,718	3.9	Wyoming	19,230	20,049	4.3

(1) Includes workers covered by Unemployment Insurance (UI) and Unemployment Compensation for Federal Employees (UCFE) programs. (2) Data are preliminary. (3) Percent changes were computed from unrounded average annual pay data and may differ from those computed using data rounded to the nearest dollar.

Civilian Employment of the Federal Government

Source: Workforce Analysis and Statistics Division, U.S. Office of Personnel Management
(Payroll in thousands of dollars, for May 1991)

Agency	All Areas Employment	All Areas Payroll	United States Employment	United States Payroll	Wash., D.C. MSA Employment	Wash., D.C. MSA Payroll	Overseas Employment	Overseas Payroll
Total, all agencies[1]	3,100,889*	9,366,150*	2,961,241*	8,999,900*	366,096*	1,228,987*	139,648*	366,250*
Legislative branch	38,387*	121,606*	38,329*	121,379*	36,043*	113,542*	58*	227*
Congress.	20,265	59,432	20,265	59,432	20,265	59,432	—	—
U.S. Senate	7,649	21,835	7,649	21,835	7,649	21,835	—	—
House of Rep Summary. . . .	12,598	37,549	12,598	37,549	12,598	37,549	—	—
Comm. on Scty & Coop in Eur	18	48	18	48	18	48	—	—
Architect of the Capitol	2,298	5,395	2,298	5,395	2,298	5,395	—	—
Botanic Garden	53	136	53	136	53	136	—	—
Committee on Agri Workers . . .	5*	11*	5*	11*	5*	11*	—*	—*
Comm Int Mig&Coop Econ Dev .	9*	33*	9*	33*	9*	33*	—*	—*
Congressional Budget Ofc	221	960	221	960	221	960	—	—
Copyright Royalty Tribunal. . . .	10	42	10	42	10	42	—	—
General Accounting Ofc	5,314	19,217	5,263	19,033	3,490	12,841	51	184
Government Printing Ofc.	4,908	20,714	4,908	20,714	4,420	19,139	—	—
John C Stennis Ctr Pub Dev . . .	6	16	6	16	—	—	—	—
Library of Congress.	4,747	13,743	4,740	13,700	4,727	13,667	7	43
Nat Comm on AIDS Syndrome .	8*	30*	8*	30*	7*	28*	—*	—*
Nat Comm Prev Infant Mort . . .	10*	20*	10*	20*	10*	20*	—*	—*
Ofc Technology Assessment . .	195	512	195	512	195	512	—	—
Physician Payment Rev Comm .	1*	1*	1*	1*	1*	1*	—*	—*
Prospty Paymt Assessmt Com .	5*	5*	5*	5*	5*	5*	—*	—*
U.S. Tax Court.	332	1,339	332	1,339	327	1,320	—	—
Judicial Branch	24,664	74,742	24,390	73,913	2,032	7,048	274	829
Supreme Court	350	940	350	940	350	940	—	—
U.S. Courts	24,247	73,578	23,973	72,749	1,615	5,884	274	829
U.S. Court of Vets Appeals . . .	67	224	67	224	67	224	—	—
Executive Branch	3,037,838*	9,169,802*	2,898,522*	8,804,608*	328,021*	1,108,397*	139,316*	365,194*
Exec Ofc of the President	1,767	6,590	1,758	6,543	1,758	6,543	9	47
White House Office	371	1,293	371	1,293	371	1,293	—	—
Ofc of Vice President	17	95	17	95	17	95	—	—
Ofc of Mgt & Budget	591	2,388	591	2,388	591	2,388	—	—
Office of Administration	229	625	229	625	229	625	—	—
Council Economic Advisors . .	32	128	32	128	32	128	—	—
Council on Environ Qual	23	92	23	92	23	92	—	—
Ofc of Policy Development . .	35	124	35	124	35	124	—	—
Exec Residence at WH	92	343	92	343	92	343	—	—
Natl Crit Materials Coun	2	2	2	2	2	2	—	—
National Security Council . . .	62	211	62	211	62	211	—	—
National Space Council	7	30	7	30	7	30	—	—
Ofc of Natl Drug Control. . . .	88	398	88	398	88	398	—	—
Ofc of Sci and Tech Policy . .	37	120	37	120	37	120	—	—
Ofc of U.S. Trade Rep	181	741	172	694	172	694	9	47
Executive Departments.	2,039,059	5,534,291	1,920,059	5,224,145	246,662	807,316	119,000	310,146
State.	25,534	88,841	9,415	31,381	8,483	27,811	16,119	57,460
Treasury.	175,150	412,170	174,066	408,443	23,056	74,537	1,084	3,727
Defense, Total	1,009,371	2,775,288	916,286	2,550,028	86,640	276,907	93,085	225,260
Dept of the Army.	352,164	864,574	309,141	775,046	26,913	58,652	43,023	89,528
Dept of the Navy.	325,742	961,400	302,248	924,771	36,614	133,250	23,494	36,629
Dept of the Air Force	224,390	640,904	211,370	590,032	6,497	19,618	13,020	50,872
Defense Log Agcy.	57,172	138,186	56,796	136,605	3,252	12,377	376	1,581
Other Defense Activities . .	49,903	170,224	36,731	123,574	13,364	53,010	13,172	46,650
Justice	87,265	278,920	85,750	273,748	20,645	66,436	1,515	5,172
Interior	77,808	190,723	77,388	189,572	9,295	29,054	420	1,151
Agriculture.	118,403	271,950	116,844	268,811	12,840	39,761	1,559	3,139
Commerce	40,092	106,472	39,253	103,160	19,638	61,930	839	3,312
Labor	18,123	58,925	18,089	58,780	6,648	22,597	34	145
Health and Human Services .	126,728	347,502	126,027	345,633	29,615	95,819	701	1,869
Housing & Urban Dev	13,745	40,149	13,622	39,795	3,444	12,277	123	354
Transportation	68,049	262,244	67,510	260,029	9,965	39,549	539	2,215
Energy.	18,712	65,396	18,705	65,357	6,753	26,043	7	39
Education	4,862	15,753	4,858	15,739	3,322	11,331	4	14
Veterans Affairs	255,217	619,958	252,246	613,669	6,318	23,264	2,971	6,289
Independent agencies	997,012*	3,628,921*	976,705*	3,573,920*	79,601*	294,538*	20,307*	55,001*
Environmtl Protect Agcy	17,856	54,779	17,837	54,723	5,903	20,228	19	56
Equal Employ Opp Comm	2,886	8,487	2,886	8,487	767	2,548	—	—
Federal Deposit Ins Corp.	21,138	67,712	21,124	67,665	2,992	11,846	14	47
Fed Emergency Mgmt Agcy . . .	3,597	10,406	3,510	10,240	1,555	5,171	87	166
General Svcs Admin.	20,715	56,263	20,620	55,986	6,937	21,878	95	277
Natl Archives & Recds, Admin. .	3,049	5,370	3,049	5,370	1,147	2,829	—	—
Natl Aero Space Admin	25,529	113,484	25,521	113,404	5,752	24,925	8	80
Nuclear Regulatory Comm. . . .	3,488	16,606	3,488	16,606	2,304	11,342	—	—
Office of Personnel Mgmt	6,588	14,685	6,568	14,651	2,854	7,656	20	34
Panama Canal Commission . . .	8,944	17,925	17	49	7	27	8,927	17,876
Small Business Admin	4,991	14,527	4,890	14,246	983	3,340	101	281
Smithsonian, Summary.	5,274	12,980	5,116	12,646	4,792	11,668	158	334
Tennessee Valley Auth.	24,801	86,023	24,801	86,023	9	36	—	—
U.S. Information Agency	8,301	26,501	4,158	16,774	3,915	15,379	4,143	9,727
U.S. Intnatl Dev Coop Agcy . . .	4,675	17,195	2,401	8,772	2,393	8,712	2,274	8,423
U.S. Postal Service	811,110	3,024,547	807,599	3,008,761	22,024	93,021	3,511	15,786

(1) Included in Total are other independent agencies with fewer than 2,500 employees.
*Preliminary or previous month's employment totals (or portions thereof) were used for current month.

Labor Union Directory

Source: Bureau of Labor Statistics, U.S. Dept. of Labor; World Almanac questionnaire

(*) Independent union; all others affiliated with AFL-CIO.

American Federation of Labor & Congress of Industrial Organizations (AFL-CIO), 815 16th St. NW, Washington, DC 20006; 14.5 mln. members.

Actors and Artistes of America, Associated (AAAA), 165 W. 46th St., New York, NY 10036; founded 1919; Theodore Bikel, Pres.; no individual members, 7 National Performing Arts Unions are affiliates; approx. 220,000 combined membership.

Actors' Equity Association, 165 W. 46th St., New York, NY 10036; founded 1913; Colleen Dewhurst, Pres.; 39,000 active members.

Air Line Pilots Association, 1625 Massachusetts Ave. NW, Washington, DC 20036. J. Randolph Babbitt, Pres.; 43,000 members.

Aluminum Brick & Glass Workers International Union (ABGWIU), 3362 Hollenberg Drive, Bridgeton, MO 63044; founded 1953; Ernie Labaff, Pres. (since 1985); 51,800 members, 390 locals.

Automobile, Aerospace & Agricultural Implement Workers of America, International Union, United (UAW), 8000 E. Jefferson Ave., Detroit, MI 48214; founded 1935; Owen Bieber, Pres. (since 1983); 1,000,000 members, 1,194 locals.

Bakery, Confectionery & Tobacco Workers International Union (BC&T), 10401 Connecticut Ave., Kensington, MD 20895; founded 1886; John DeConcini, Pres. (since 1978); 139,000 members, 139 locals.

Boilermakers, Iron Shipbuilders, Blacksmiths, Forgers and Helpers, International Brotherhood of (IBBISB/BF&H), 570 New Brotherhood Bldg., 753 State Ave., Kansas City, KS 66101; founded 1880; Charles W. Jones, Pres. (since 1983) 95,000 members, 375 locals.

Bricklayers and Allied Craftsmen, International Union of, 815 15th St. NW, Washington, DC 20005; John T. Joyce, Pres.; 106,000 members, 525 locals.

Carpenters and Joiners of America, United Brotherhood of, 101 Constitution Ave. NW, Washington, DC 20001; founded 1881; Sigurd Lucassen, Gen. Pres.; 595,000 members, 1,500 locals.

Chemical Workers Union, International (ICWU), 1655 West Market St., Akron, OH 44313; founded 1944; Frank D. Martino, Pres. (since 1975); 50,000 members, 350 locals.

Clothing and Textile Workers Union, Amalgamated (ACTWU), 15 Union Square, New York, NY 10003; founded 1976; union founded 1914; Jack Sheinkman, Pres. (since 1987); 272,669 members, 1,400 locals.

Communications Workers of America, 501 3rd St. NW, Washington, DC 20001-2797; Morton Bahr, Pres.; 700,000 members, 1,200 locals.

Distillery, Wine & Allied Workers International Union (DWU), 66 Grand Ave., Englewood, NJ 07631; founded 1940; George J. Orlando, Pres. (since 1984); 15,500 members, 57 locals.

***Education Association, National,** 1201 16th St. NW, Washington, DC 20036; Keith Geiger, Pres. (since 1989); 2,000,000 members, 12,000 affiliates.

Electrical Workers, International Brotherhood of (IBEW), 1125 15th St., NW, Washington, DC 20005; founded 1891; J.J. Barry, Int'l Pres.; 900,000 members, 1,400 locals.

Electronic, Electrical, Salaried, Machine and Furniture Workers, International Union of (IUE), 1126 16th St. NW, Washington, DC 20036; founded 1949; William H. Bywater, Pres. (since 1982); 160,000 members, 500 locals.

Farm Workers of America, United (UFW), P.O. Box 62, Keene, CA 93531; founded 1962; Cesar E. Chavez, Pres. (since 1962); 100,000 members.

***Federal Employees, National Federation of (NFFE),** 1016 16th St. NW, Washington, DC 20036; founded 1917; Sheila K. Velazco, Pres.; 60,000+ members, 487 locals.

Fire Fighters, International Association of, 1750 New York Ave. NW, Washington, DC 20006; Alfred K. Whitehead, Pres.; 172,401 members, 1,943 locals.

Firemen and Oilers, International Brotherhood of, 1100 Circle 75 Parkway, Suite 350, Atlanta, GA 30339; Jimmy L. Walker, Pres.; 30,000 members.

Food and Commercial Workers International Union, United, (UFCW) 1775 K St., NW, Washington, DC 20006; founded 1979 following merger; William H. Wynn, Int'l Pres. (since 1977); 1.3 million members, 600 locals.

Garment Workers of America, United (UGWA), 4207 Lebanon Rd., Hermitage, TN 37076; founded 1891; Dave Johnson, Gen. Pres.; 20,000 members, 120 locals.

Glass, Molders, Pottery, Plastics & Allied Workers Intl. Union (GMP), 608 E. Baltimore Pike, P.O. Box 607, Media, PA 19063; founded 1842; James E. Hatfield, Int'l Pres. (since 1977); 90,000 members, 435 locals.

Government Employees, American Federation of (AFGE) AFL-CIO, 80 F St., NW, Washington, DC 20001; founded 1932; John N. Sturdivant, Natl. Pres. (since 1988); 172,000 members, 1,300 locals.

Grain Millers, American Federation of (AFGM), 4949 Olson Memorial Hwy., Minneapolis, MN 55422; founded 1948; Larry R. Jackson, Gen. Pres.; 30,000 members, 210 locals.

Graphic Communications International Union (GCIU), 1900 L St., NW, Washington, DC 20036; founded 1983; James J. Norton, Pres. (since 1985); 182,706 members, 520 locals.

Hotel Employees and Restaurant Employees International Union, 1219-28th St., NW, Washington, DC 20007; Edward T. Henley, Gen. Pres.; 330,000 members, 190 locals.

Industrial Workers of America, International Union, Allied (AIW), 3520 W. Oklahoma Ave., Milwaukee, WI 53215; founded 1935; Dominick D'Ambrosio, Intl. Pres. (since 1975); 61,000 members, 330 locals.

Iron Workers, International Association of Bridge Structural and Ornamental, 1750 New York Ave. NW, Washington, DC 20006; Jake West, Gen. Pres.; 145,000 members, 300 locals.

Laborers' International Union of North America (LIUNA), 905 16th St. NW, Washington, DC 20006; founded 1903; Angelo Fosco, Gen. Pres. (since 1976); 450,000 members, 696 locals.

Ladies Garment Workers Union, International (ILGWU), 1710 Broadway, New York, NY 10019; founded 1900; Jay Mazur, Pres. (since 1986); 175,000 members, 340 locals.

Leather Goods, Plastic and Novelty Workers' Union, International, 265 W. 14th St., New York, NY 10011; Domenic DiPaolo, Gen. Pres.; 20,000 members, 85 locals.

Letter Carriers, National Association of (NALC), 100 Indiana Ave. NW, Washington, DC 20001; founded 1889; Vincent R. Sombrotto, Pres. (since 1978); 311,202 members, 3,466 locals.

***Locomotive Engineers, Brotherhood of (BLE),** The Standard Bldg., Cleveland, OH 44113; founded 1863; Larry McFather, Pres. (since 1987); 56,000 members, 650 divisions.

Longshoremen's Association, International, 17 Battery Pl., New York, NY 10004; John Bowers, Pres.; 76,579 members, 331 locals.

***Longshoremen's & Warehousemen's Union, International (ILWU),** 1188 Franklin St., San Francisco, CA 94109; founded 1937; James R. Herman, Pres. (since 1977); 55,000 members, 58 locals.

Machinists and Aerospace Workers, International Association of (IAM), 1300 Connecticut Ave. NW, Washington, DC 20036; founded 1888; George J. Kourpias , Int'l Pres.; 826,875 members, 1,700 locals.

Maintenance of Way Employes, Brotherhood of (BMWE), 12050 Woodward Ave., Detroit, MI 48203; founded 1887; Mac. A. Fleming, Pres. 75,000 members, 827 locals.

Marine & Shipbuilding Workers of America, Industrial Union of (IUMSWA), 5101 River Rd., #110, Bethesda, MD 20816; founded 1934; (merged with Machinists and Aerospace Workers, effective Dec. 1, 1990).

Marine Engineer Beneficial Assn./National Maritime Union (MEBA/NMU), 444 N. Capitol St. NW, Suite 800, Washington, D.C. 20001; C.E. DeFries, Pres.; 50,000 members.

***Mine Workers of America, United (UMWA),** 900 15th St. NW, Washington, DC 20005; founded 1890; Richard Trumka, Int'l Pres. (since 1982); 186,000 members, 800 locals.

Musicians of the United States and Canada, American Federation of (AF of M), 1501 Broadway, Suite 600, New York, NY 10036; founded 1896; Mark Tully Massagli, Pres.; 206,000 members, 480 locals.

Newspaper Guild, The (TNG), 8611 Second Ave., Silver Spring, MD 20910; founded 1933; Charles Dale, Pres. (since 1987); 33,000 members, 80 locals.

Novelty & Production Workers, Intl. Union of Allied, 1815 Franklin Ave., Valley Stream, NY 11581; Julius Isaacson, Pres. 30,000 members, 18 locals.

***Nurses Association, American,** 2420 Pershing Rd., Kansas City, MO 64108; Lucille A. Joel, Ed.D, R.N., F.A.A.N., Pres.; 53 constituent state assns.

(continued)

Office and Professional Employees International Union (OPEIU), 265 W. 14th St., New York, NY 10011; founded 1945 (AFL Charter); John Kelly, Int'l Pres. (since 1979); 135,000 members, 300 locals.

Oil, Chemical and Atomic Workers International Union (OCAW), PO Box 2812, Denver, CO 80201; Robert E. Wages, Pres.; 100,000 members, 400 locals.

Operating Engineers, International Union of (IUOE), 1125 17th St. NW, Washington, DC 20036; founded 1896; Frank Hanley, Gen. Pres.; 375,000 members, 200 locals.

Painters and Allied Trades, International Brotherhood of (IBPAT), 1750 New York Ave. NW, Washington, DC 20006; founded 1887; William A. Duval, Gen. Pres. (since 1984); 149,177 members, 626 locals.

Paperworkers International Union, United (UPIU), 3340 Perimeter Hill Dr., Nashville, TN 37202; founded 1884; Wayne E. Glenn, Pres. (since 1978); 230,000 members, 1,100 locals.

*Plant Guard Workers of America, International Union, United (UPGWA), 25510 Kelly Rd., Roseville, MI 48066; founded 1948; Gene McConville, Pres.; 28,000 members, 176 locals.

Plasterers' and Cement Mason's International Association of the United States & Canada; Operative, 1125 17th St. NW, Washington, DC 20036; Vincent J. Panepinto, Gen. Pres.; 65,000 members, 365 locals.

Plumbing and Pipe Fitting Industry of the United States and Canada, United Association of Journeymen and Apprentices of the, 901 Massachusetts Ave. NW, Washington, DC 20001; Marvin J. Boede, Pres.; 325,000 members.

*Police, Fraternal Order of, 2100 Gardiner Lane, Louisville, KY 40205; Dewey R. Stokes, Natl. Pres. and Charles R. Orms, Natl. Secy.; 225,000 members, 1,860 affiliates.

*Postal Supervisors, National Association of, 490 L'Enfant Plaza SW, Suite 3200, Washington, DC 20024-2120; Rubin Handelman, Pres.; 44,000 members, 443 locals.

Postal Workers Union, American (APWU), 1300 L St. NW, Washington, DC 20005; founded 1971; Moe Biller, Pres. (since 1980); 330,000 members, 2,000 locals.

Railway Carmen Division of Transportation Communications Int'l. Union (BRC Division/TCU), 4929 Main St., Kansas City, MO 64112; founded 1888; W.G. Fairchild, Gen. Pres. (since 1989); 50,000 members, 310 locals.

Retail, Wholesale and Department Store Union, 30 E. 29th St., New York, NY 10016; Lenore Miller, Pres.; 200,000 members, 250 locals.

Roofers, Waterproofers & Allied Workers, United Union of, 1125 17th St. NW, Washington, DC 20036; Earl J. Kruse, Pres.; 27,000 members, 138 locals.

Rubber, Cork, Linoleum and Plastic Workers of America, United (URW), 87 South High St., Akron, OH 44308; founded 1935; Kenneth L. Coss; Int'l Pres.; 100,000 members, 400 locals.

*Rural Letter Carriers' Association, National, 4th floor, 1630 Duke St., Alexandria, VA 22314; founded 1903; Vernon H. Meier, Pres. (since 1989); 80,000 members; 47 state organizations.

Seafarers International Union of North America (SIUNA), 5201 Auth Way, Camp Springs, MD 20746; founded 1938; Michael Sacco, Pres.; 85,000 members.

Service Employees International Union (SEIU), 1313 L St. NW, Washington, DC 20005; founded 1921; John J. Sweeney, Pres. (since 1980); 950,000 members, 300 locals.

Sheet Metal Workers' international Association (SMWIA), 1750 New York Ave. NW, Washington, DC 20006; founded 1888; Edward J. Carlough, Gen. Pres. (since 1970); 150,000 members, 245 locals.

State, County and Municipal Employees, American Federation of, 1625 L St. NW, Washington, DC 20036; Gerald McEntee, Pres.; 1,200,000 members, 2,991 locals.

Steelworkers of America, United (USWA), 5 Gateway Center, Pittsburgh, PA 15222; founded 1936; Lynn Williams, Int'l Pres. (since 1984); 750,000 members, 3,500 locals.

Teachers, American Federation of (AFT), 555 New Jersey Ave. NW, Washington, DC 20001; founded 1916; Albert Shanker, Pres. (since 1974); 750,000 members, 2,400 locals.

Teamsters, Chauffeurs, Warehousemen and Helpers of America, International Brotherhood of (IBT), 25 Louisiana Ave. NW, Washington, DC 20001; founded 1903; William J. McCarthy, Gen. Pres.; 1,600,000 members, 700 locals.

Television and Radio Artists, American Federation of, 260 Madison Ave., New York, NY 10016; founded 1937; Reed Farrell, Pres.; 67,000 members, 38 locals.

Textile Workers of America, United (UTWA), 2 Echelon Plaza, Laurel Rd., P.O. Box 749, Voorhees, NJ 08043-0749; founded 1901; Vernon Mustard, Intl. Pres. (since 1986); 26,000 members, 180 locals.

Theatrical Stage Employes and Moving Picture Machine Operators of the United States and Canada, International Alliance of, 1515 Broadway, New York, NY 10036; Alfred W. Di Tolla, Pres.; 61,471 members, 750 locals.

Transit Union, Amalgamated (ATU), 5025 Wisconsin Ave. NW, Washington, DC 20016; founded 1892; James La Sala, Intl. Pres. (since 1986); 165,000 members, 275 locals.

Transport Workers Union of America, 80 West End Ave., New York, NY 10023; founded 1934; George Leitz, Int'l Pres. (since 1985); 100,000 members, 94 locals.

Transportation Communications International Union (TCU), 3 Research Place, Rockville, MD 20850; Richard I. Kilroy, Int'l Pres. (since 1981); 160,000 members, 750 locals.

*Transportation Union, United (UTU), 14600 Detroit Ave., Cleveland, OH 44107; founded 1969; Fred A. Hardin, Pres. (since 1979); 100,000 members; 769 locals.

*Treasury Employees Union, National (NTEU), 901 E. St. N.W. Suite 600, Washington, DC 20004; founded 1938; Robert M. Tobias, Natl. Pres. (since 1983); 140,000 represented, 250 chapters.

*University Professors, American Association of (AAUP), 1012-14th St., Washington, DC 20005; founded 1915; Carol Simpson Stern, Pres.; 40,000 members, 600 chapters.

Upholstery Division - United Steelworkers of America, 25 N. 4th St., Philadelphia, PA 19106; founded 1882; Ernest F. Shock, dir.; approx. 18,000 members, 91 locals.

Utility Workers Union of America (UWUA), 815 16th St. NW, Washington, DC 20006; founded 1945; Marshall M. Hicks, Natl. Pres. (since 1980); 60,000 members, 220 locals.

International Woodworkers of America —U.S. (IWA—U.S.), 25 Cornell, Gladstone, OR 97027; founded 1987; Wilson (Bill) Hubbell, Natl. Pres.; 28,000 members, 100 locals.

U.S. Union Membership, 1930-1990

Source: Bureau of Labor Statistics, U.S. Dept. of Labor

Year	Labor[1] force (thousands)	Union[2] members (thousands)	Percent	Year	Labor[1] force (thousands)	Union[2] members (thousands)	Percent
1930	29,424	3,401	11.6	1980	90,564	19,843	21.9
1935	27,053	3,584	13.2	1983	88,290	17,717	20.1
1940	32,376	8,717	26.9	1984	92,194	17,340	18.8
1945	40,394	14,322	35.5	1985	94,521	16,996	18.0
1950	45,222	14,267	31.5	1986	96,903	16,975	17.5
1955	50,675	16,802	33.2	1987	99,303	16,913	17.0
1960	54,234	17,049	31.4	1988	101,407	17,002	16.8
1965	60,815	17,299	28.4	1989	103,480	16,960	16.4
1970	70,920	19,381	27.3	1990	103,905	16,740	16.1
1975	76,945	19,611	25.5				

(1) Does not include agricultural employment; from 1983 data do not include self-employed or unemployed persons. (2) From 1930 to 1980 data are the number of dues paying members of traditional trade unions with members counted regardless of employment status; from 1983 members include employee associations that engage in collective bargaining with employers.

TAXES

Federal Income Tax

Source: George W. Smith III, CPA, *Cut Your Own Taxes and Save*, Pharos Books.

During the past decade, Congress enacted some of the most dramatic changes to our tax law in over forty years. Its purpose was to create a more equitable income tax system for all taxpayers. Many of the provisions resulting from these massive changes will affect all taxpayers not only when completing their 1991 income tax return but also for years to come.

History of the United States Income Tax

The history of taxation in the United States centers primarily around the income tax and is consistent with the pattern of taxation in almost every highly developed country. Although the Massachusetts Bay Colony enacted an income tax in 1643, the first U.S. income tax was not created until the Civil War. However, this infant income tax had little vitality and it expired soon after the war.

In 1894, another income tax act was passed by Congress. Unfortunately for Congress, this new law was to be short lived. The Supreme Court held that the tax law was unconstitutional and invalidated the entire statute the following year.

By this time, income tax legislation had become a very important political issue. Congress did not give up and passed the Sixteenth Amendment to the United States Constitution. This amendment was passed by Congress on July 12, 1909 and laid the foundation for the basic framework of our modern income tax system. It was ratified by the required number of state legislatures early in 1913 and states broadly and explicitly:

"The Congress shall have the power to lay and collect taxes on incomes, from whatever source derived, without apportionment among the several States, and without regard to any census or enumeration."

Congress quickly expanded on this newly sanctioned source of revenue. Corporations as well as individuals became subject to the new income tax. Since then, various revenue acts have been passed. One of the most important of these acts was the Current Tax Payment Act of 1943. This act instituted for the first time the "pay-as-you go" system, which requires the regular withholding of tax from each employee's paycheck and the filing of estimated tax payments, remains the basic method for the collection of our income taxes today.

During the past few decades, Congress enacted several major tax acts. However, the Tax Reform Act of 1986 represents the most extensive overhaul of the tax code since 1954. This Act contains approximately 1,850 separate Code amendments. Because of the scope and magnitude of these amendments, Congress decided to redesignate the 1954 Code as the Internal Revenue Code of 1986. The complete phase out of consumer interest in 1991 resulted from this Act.

Tax Law Changes
and
Recent Developments

- For 1991, the highest marginal income tax rate for individuals, estates and trusts was raised to 31%. There are now three income tax rates: 15%, 28% and 31%.
- Starting in 1991, the maximum income tax rate for capital gains is 28%.
- Face-lifts, tummy tucks, liposuction and many other elective cosmetic surgeries are no longer a deductible medical expense starting in 1991.
- Interest earned on Series EE bonds issued in 1990 or later may be exempt from federal income tax if used to pay tuition and fees for a taxpayer, spouse or dependents to attend a college, university or qualified technical school during the year the bonds are redeemed. This exclusion is subject to an income phaseout if adjusted gross income exceeds $41,950 for a single taxpayer; $62,900 for taxpayers filing jointly. The full phase out occurs at $57,700 for a single taxpayer and $94,350 for taxpayers filing jointly.
- Parents may elect to include on their income tax return the unearned income of a dependent child under age 14 whose income is more than $550 but less than $5,000. The income must consist solely of interest, dividends or Alaska Permanent Fund dividends. This election is not available if estimated tax payments were made in the child's name. Form 8814, Parent's Election to Report Child's Interest and Dividends, is required to report this income.
- For individuals age 55 or over, the 3 out of 5 year home use rule for the sale of a principal residence has been expanded. Certain incapacitated individuals who reside in state licensed facilities may exclude from gross income up to $125,000 of gain resulting from the sale of their house if the house was used as their principal residence for at least one year out of the last 5 years. This is a once-in-a-lifetime exclusion.
- The 25% deduction of health insurance costs for self-employed individuals has been extended through 1991.
- For a taxpayer to be eligible for the child and dependent care credit, the dependent must be under age 13. The taxpayer must also report the name, address, and identification number of the child-care provider on their income tax return or the taxpayer will not be entitled to the credit.

- An individual may not claim an exemption for a dependent child for 1991 if the child qualifies as a full time student and is over age 23 at the end of the year unless the child's gross income is less than $2,150.
- Beginning in 1991 certain itemized deductions will be reduced by 3% of a taxpayer's adjusted gross income that is in excess of $100,000 ($50,000 for married taxpayers filing separate tax returns).
- A taxpayer must list the social security number of any dependent claimed on his income tax return who is at least 1 year old by the end of the tax year. The penalty for noncompliance can be $50 per omitted number.
- A business deduction is not allowed for the base rate on the first telephone line into a personal residence. This disallowance does not affect the deductibility of long distance calls or optional services such as call waiting, call forwarding, three-way calling or extra directory listings as long as they are business related.
- The medicare hospital insurance portion of the FICA tax has been increased in 1991 to 1.45% for the first $125,000 of wages and self-employment income.
- IRA investments are allowed for certain gold and silver coins issued by the U.S. Government. Investments also may include coins issued by a state government.
- Jury duty pay surrendered by an employee to an employer in return for his normal salary is deductible as an adjustment to income—not as an itemized deduction.
- The IRS no longer requires the filing of Form 4562, Depreciation and Amortization, for individuals claiming a deduction for depreciation on nonlisted property placed in service in a previous year. Non-listed property includes all property eligible for depreciation other than passenger automobiles, property used for entertainment or recreational purposes, cellular phones and computer or peripheral equipment.
- For 1991, the standard mileage rate for business use of an automobile has been increased to 27½ cents per mile. This rate applies to all business miles driven.
- The business use of a cellular phone must now be for the convenience of the employer and a condition of employ-

ment to be an allowable business deduction for an employee. All phone calls must be substantiated and business related.

• Self-employed persons are entitled to an income tax deduction up to one-half of the social security self-employment (SE) tax liability. The SE tax rate for 1991 is 15.3 percent.

1991 Individual Tax Rates

There are three rates for 1991 — 15%, 28%, and 31%. The dollar bracket amounts have been adjusted for inflation.

Single

Tax Rates	Bracket
15%	$0 to $20,350
28%	$20,351-49,300
31%	Over $49,300

Married Filing Jointly or Qualifying Widow(er)

Tax Rates	Bracket
15%	$0 to $34,000
28%	$34,001-82,150
31%	Over $82,150

Married Filing Separately

Tax Rate	Bracket
15%	$0 to $17,000
28%	$17,001 to 41,075
31%	Over $41,075

Head of Household

Tax Rate	Bracket
15%	$0 to $27,300
28%	$27,301 to 70,450
31%	Over $70,450

The maximum tax rate on net capital gains for an individual, estate or a trust is 28%.

The alternative minimum tax rate for a taxpayer other than a corporation has been raised to 24%.

Standard Deduction

The standard deduction is a flat amount that is subtracted from adjusted gross income for taxpayers who do not itemize their deductions. The amount of the basic standard deduction depends upon the taxpayer's filing status and is adjusted annually for inflation.

Taxpayers with itemized deductions such as medical expenses, charitable contributions, home mortgage interest, taxes, etc., totaling more than the standard deduction amount should not use the standard deduction. Instead, they should itemize their deductions.

1991 Basic Standard Deduction

Single	$3,450
Married filing jointly or Qualifying widow(er)	$5,700
Married filing separately	$2,850
Head of household	$5,000

An individual claimed as a dependent on another person's income tax return may only claim on their own return the larger of $550, or the amount of earned income up to the basic standard deduction which the taxpayer would nor-

mally be allowed. Earned income includes wages, salaries, commissions, tips, net profit from self-employment—any money received as compensation for personal services rendered. It also includes any part of a scholarship or fellowship grant that must be included in gross income.

Example: A dependent parent, age 60, had unearned income (interest and dividends) of $1,700 during 1991. She had no earned income. Her basic standard deduction would be $550. She would have taxable income of $1,150. A dependent cannot claim their own personal exemption.

Example: A dependent son had $10,000 of unearned income and $100 of earned income. He is entitled to a $550 standard deduction. He is limited to this amount because he is a dependent and his earned income is less than $550. The taxpayer would, therefore, have $9,550 in taxable income.

Example: A dependent daughter with $4,000 of earned income and $600 of unearned income would claim a maximum $3,400 standard deduction because her earned income of $4,000 is greater than the standard deduction. She would have taxable income of $1,200.

Additional Standard Deduction for Age and Blindness

Elderly or blind taxpayers may claim an additional standard deduction in addition to the basic standard deduction. Taxpayers who are age 65 or over or blind at the end of 1991 qualify for this additional standard deduction. Taxpayers who itemize deductions cannot claim the additional or basic standard deduction. Individuals who claim this deduction because of blindness must attach a doctor's statement to their income tax return The additional and basic standard deduction are adjusted each year for inflation.

1991 Additional Standard Deduction

Single or Head of household, age 65 or over or blind	$ 850
Single or Head of household, age 65 or over and blind	$1,700
Married filing jointly, or Qualifying widow(er), age 65 or over or blind (per person)	$ 650
Married filing jointly or Qualifying widow(er), age 65 or over and blind (per person)	$1,300
Married filing separately, age 65 or over or blind	$ 650

Married filing separately, age 65 or
over and blind $1,300

Example: A single, sixty-five year old individual would have a standard deduction of $4,250 computed as follows:

Basic standard deduction for a single person	$3,400
Additional standard deduction for age	850
Total	$4,250

Example: A seventy year old husband and a fifty-eight year old blind wife filing jointly would be entitled to a standard deduction totaling $7,000 computed as follows.

Basic standard deduction for married filing jointly	$5,700
Additional standard deduction for (husband's) age	650
Additional standard deduction for (wife's) blindness	650
Total	$7,000

Dependent and Personal Exemptions

The 1991 exemption amount is $2,150. This amount is adjusted each year for inflation.

For tax years 1991 through 1995, the deduction for exemptions is phased out for certain higher income taxpayers. The exemption amount is reduced by 2% for each $2,500 ($1,250 for married filing separately) or a fraction thereof by which adjusted gross income exceeds the threshold amount.

The threshold amount at which the phaseout of the tax benefit for the personal exemption begins is as follows:

Married filing jointly	$150,000
Qualifying widow(er)	$150,000
Head of household	$125,000
Single	$100,000
Married filing separately	$ 75,000

The exemption amount is fully phased out when adjusted gross income is more than $122,500 ($61,250 for married filing separately) over the threshold amount.

Adjustments to Income

Individual Retirement Accounts (IRAs)

Taxpayers who do not have a qualified retirement plan where they are employed may take an IRA deduction up to

the lesser of $2,000, or the amount of their earned income, regardless of their total income. Income earned from IRAs will remain tax-free until the taxpayer withdraws it.

Taxpayers may still make contributions to their IRAs even if they are covered by a qualified retirement plan by their employer. However, there are limits as to the amount that can be deducted on their income tax return. If either husband or wife has a qualified plan both spouses are subject to these limitations.

For 1991, married taxpayers filing jointly with adjusted gross income of $40,000 or less may take an IRA deduction whether or not they are active participants in a qualified retirement plan. Single taxpayers in qualified retirement plans may also deduct IRAs if their adjusted gross income is $25,000 or less. The IRA deduction phases out over the next

$10,000 of adjusted gross income if taxpayers are active participants in a qualified retirement plan. Consequently, married couples filing jointly with adjusted gross income over $50,000 or single filers with adjusted gross income over $35,000 may not deduct any contributions to their IRAs.

A qualified retirement plan generally includes: (1) a qualified pension, profit-sharing or stock bonus plan; (2) a qualified annuity plan; (3) a simplified employee pension plan; or (4) a plan established for its employees by the federal, state or other political subdivision or by an agency of these entities.

Itemized Deductions

- Itemized deductions are reduced for higher income taxpayers. Beginning in 1991 through 1995, total itemized deductions otherwise allowed are reduced by 3% of a taxpayer's adjusted gross income in excess of $100,000 ($50,000 for married taxpayers filing separately). This provision does not affect medical expenses, investment interest expense, casualty losses or wagering losses to the extent of wagering gains and cannot be more than 80% of allowable itemized deductions.
- Medical expenses are deductible, but only for the amount that exceeds 7.5 percent of adjusted gross income. Starting in 1991, many elective cosmetic surgeries including hair transplants and other similar procedures are no longer a deductible medical expense. Only cosmetic surgery for congenital abnormality, personal injury resulting from an accident or trauma or a disfiguring disease is allowed as a medical deduction.
- Consumer interest such as finance charges on personal credit cards and installment interest on personal automobile loans is no longer deductible.
- Investment interest for 1991 is now only deductible to the extent of net investment income.
- Mortgage interest on a taxpayer's first and second homes remains fully deductible. However, there are limitations.
- Home equity loans are deductible up to the first $100,000 in equity debt.
- In 1991, charitable contributions of tangible personal property which is related to the donee's tax-exempt purpose is not subject to the alternative minimum tax.
- State and local income taxes, real estate taxes, and personal property taxes remain fully deductible. Sales taxes are not deductible.

- Casualty and theft losses are deductible subject to the $100 limitation and the 10% of adjusted gross income rule.
- Miscellaneous deductions, such as union and professional dues, tax preparation fees, safe deposit box rental and employee business expenses are deductible, but only for the amount that exceeds 2 percent of adjusted gross income.

Moving Expenses

Taxpayers who change jobs during the year can usually deduct some of their moving expenses. These expenses include the cost of moving household goods, travel to the new home, househunting trips, temporary living quarters, and other related expenses. To qualify, the move must be job-related and it must meet several other requirements including a distance and time test. The expenses for moving household goods and traveling to a new home have some limitations. All other deductible moving expenses, such as househunting trips or temporary living quarters, are subject to a $3,000 ceiling. Meal expenses are only 80% deductible. Moving expenses are deductible only if the taxpayer itemizes deductions on Schedule A of Form 1040. Moves within the U.S. are reported on Form 3903, Moving Expenses.

Employee Business Expense

All employee business expenses including meals, travel, automobile, gifts and entertainment are allowed only as itemized miscellaneous deductions. Only 80% of the cost of customer meals and entertainment is deductible. These expenses are then subject to the 2% of adjusted gross income limitation for miscellaneous deductions.

Earned Income Credit, Young Child Credit, and Health Insurance Credit

Low income workers who have dependent children and maintain a household are eligible for a refundable earned income credit. The credit for 1991 is calculated on earned income such as wages and tips with a maximum credit of $1,192 for a taxpayer with one qualifying child and $1,235 for a taxpayer with two or more qualifying children. When income is more than $11,250, the credit begins to phase out until it is completely phased out at $21,245.

Starting in 1991, and in addition to the basic earned income credit, a supplemental young child care credit is also available to low income workers with a qualifying child who has not attained the age of one as of the close of the calendar year. The maximum credit is $357. If this supplemental credit is claimed, the dependent care credit may not be claimed.

Also new for 1991 is a supplemental credit for health insurance premium costs that cover one or more qualifying children. The maximum credit is $428. If medical expenses are itemized on Schedule A, or the 25% deduction for health insurance which self-employed individuals are entitled to is taken, these amounts must be reduced dollar for dollar by the amount of the allowable supplemental health insurance credit.

If an individual qualifies, the credits are refundable even if the taxpayer is not required to file an income tax return. However, a tax return must be filed in order to receive these credits. To assist individuals, the IRS publishes a table showing the earned income credit at various levels of income.

Taxing Children's Income

A child who may be claimed as a dependent by another taxpayer may not claim their own exemption on their tax return. Children under age 14 with at least one living parent may use up to $550 of their standard deduction against unearned income. Unearned income includes dividend and interest income. If the child's unearned income is more than $1,100, that income will be taxed at the child's tax rate, or the parent's rate, whichever is higher.

A parent has the option of including the child's unearned income on their tax return. However, if the unearned income is reported on the child's tax return, only the amount over $1,100 is subject to this treatment. Therefore, the child does

get the benefit of a lower tax rate on the first $1,100 of unearned income.

For example, assuming the child has $3,000 of interest income, the child's taxable income would be $2,450, allowing for the $550 standard deduction. Assuming that the parent's rate is 28%, the child's tax would be $616 ($84 from the tax table plus 28% of $1,900).

Who Must File

Whether a U.S. citizens or resident alien living in the United States must file an income tax return depends on the person's gross income, filing status, and age.

Generally, U.S. citizens or resident aliens will have to file an income tax return if their gross income for the year is at least as much as the amount shown in the following table.

Filing Status	1991 Gross Income
Single	
• Under 65	$5,550
• 65 or older	$6,400
Married filing jointly	
• Both spouses under 65	$10,000
• One spouse 65 or older	$10,650
• Both spouses 65 or older	$11,300
Married filing separately	$2,150
Head of household	
• Under 65	$7,150
• 65 or older	$8,000
Qualifying widow(er)	
• Under 65	$7,850
• 65 or older	$8,500

Example: John and Mary Smith intend to file a joint return for 1991. John's income is all from wages. Mary receives no income subject to tax. Neither John nor Mary is blind. John is 67 years old but Mary will not be 65 until next year. For 1991, their combined gross income subject to tax will be $11,200. They will have to file a tax return because their gross income will be at least $10,650.

If Mary were age 65, they would not have to file a 1991 tax return because their gross income would be less than $11,300 as shown in the table.

Some Exceptions to Filing Requirements. An individual must file a tax return if:

- Net earnings from self employment for the year are $400 or more.
- Advance earned income credit payments were received during the year from their employer.
- Qualifications for the earned income, young child or health insurance credit are met.
- An income tax refund is due.
- Gross income is less than the filing requirement amount but additional taxes are owed for:
- Social security tax on unreported tips;
- Alternative minimum tax;
- Recapture of investment credit;
- Tax attributable to qualified retirement plans (including IRAs), annuities, and modified endowment contracts.

When to File

U.S. individual income tax returns for 1991 are required to be filed with the Internal Revenue Service no later than Wednesday, April 15, 1992.

What if you can't file on time? Submitting Form 4868, Application for Automatic Extension of Time to File U.S. Individual Income Tax Return, gives you an automatic four-month extension of time until August 15 to file your tax return. However, this is not an extension of time to pay your taxes. You still have to pay the Internal Revenue Service any money owed by midnight April 15, 1992. Penalties and interest may be assessed for any income tax balance not paid. Form 4868 also provides space for you to estimate your tax obligation, if any.

Which Form to File

You may be able to use the short Form 1040EZ for 1991 if:
- You are single and do not claim any dependents.
- You are not 65 or older or blind.
- You have income only from wages, salaries, tips, taxable scholarships or fellowships, and not more than $400 of interest income.
- Your taxable income is less than $50,000.
- You do not itemize deductions or claim any adjustments to income or have tax credits.
- You did not make estimated tax payments.

You may be able to use Form 1040A for 1991 if:
- You have income from wages, salaries, tips, taxable scholarships or fellowships, interest, and dividends.
- You have income from Individual Retirement Account (IRA) distributions, pensions, annuities, unemployment compensation, and social security or railroad retirement benefits.
- Your taxable income is less than $50,000.
- You do not itemize deductions.
- You claim a deduction for qualified contributions to an IRA.
- You claim a credit for child and dependent care expenses, credit for the elderly or the disabled, the earned income credit, or the supplemental young child or health insurance credit.
- You have made estimated tax payments.
- You filed for an extension of time to file.

Forms 1040EZ and 1040A are easier to complete than the longer Form 1040. Even if you do meet the above tests, you will have to file Form 1040 for 1991 if any of the following situations apply.

You must use Form 1040 if:
- Your taxable income is $50,000 or more.
- You itemize deductions.
- You receive any nontaxable dividends or capital gain distributions.
- You have foreign accounts and/or foreign trusts.
- You have taxable refunds of state and local income taxes.
- You have business, farm or rental income.
- You have miscellaneous income not allowed on Form 1040EZ or 1040A such as alimony or lottery winnings.
- You have certain adjustments to income such as alimony paid.
- You can claim a foreign tax credit or certain other credits to which you are entitled.
- You have other taxes such as self-employment tax or the alternative minimum tax.
- You file any of these forms:

Form 2555, Foreign Earned Income.
Form 3903, Moving Expense.
Form 4972, Tax on Lump-Sum Distributions.
Form 5329, Return for Additional Taxes Attributable to Qualified Retirement Plans.
Form 8814, Parent's Election To Report Child's Interest and Dividends.

Electronic Filing

Electronic filing is a process of transmitting completed personal income tax returns to the Internal Revenue Service. Originating as a pilot program in 1986, over 7.5 million taxpayers filed electronically during 1991.

Electronic filing shortens the average time for processing returns to within 3 weeks. Refunds may also be deposited directly into your savings or checking account. Since electronic filing automates most of the manual steps needed to process standard paper returns, processing is faster, less expensive, and more accurate.

The electronic filing method can be used by many tax return preparers. These preparers are equipped to send tax re-

Declaration for Electronic Filing. This form is not a power of attorney and it does not authorize your tax preparer to receive information from the IRS about your account.

turn information over telephone lines to an Internal Revenue Service Center. The preparer will ask you to sign a declaration form, Form 8453, U.S. Individual Income Tax

Frequently Used Tax Forms

706
U.S. Estate (and Generation-Skipping Transfer) Tax Return
Used for the estate of a deceased United States resident or citizen.

709—A
U.S. Short Form Gift Tax Return
Used by married couples to report nontaxable gifts of more than $10,000 but less than $20,000.

1040
U.S. Individual Income Tax Return
Used by citizens and residents of the United States to report income tax.

1040-ES
Estimated Tax for individuals
Used to make estimated tax payments as a means for paying currently any income tax (including self-employment tax and the alternative minimum tax) due in excess of the tax withheld from wages, salaries, and other payments for personal services. It is not required unless the total tax exceeds withholding (if any) and applicable tax credits by $500 or more.

1040NR
U.S. Nonresident Alien Income Tax Return
Used by all nonresident alien individuals who file a U.S. tax return, whether or not engaged in a trade or business within the United States. Also used as required for filing nonresident alien fiduciary (estate and trust) returns.

1040X
Amended U.S. Individual Income Tax Return
Used to correct Form 1040, Form 1040A or 1040EZ that you have already filed.

1041
U.S. Fiduciary Income Tax Return
Used by a fiduciary for domestic estate or domestic trust.

1065
U.S. Partnership Return of Income
Used by partnerships as an information return.

1116
Computation of Foreign Tax Credit—Individual, Fiduciary, or Nonresident Alien Individual
Used to figure and support the foreign tax credit claimed for the amount of any income, war profits, and excess profits taxes paid or accrued during the tax year to any foreign country or U.S. possession.

1120
U.S. Corporation Income Tax Return
Used by a corporation to report income tax.

1120S
U.S. Income Tax Return for an S Corporation
Used by S corporations to report taxes under Subchapter S of the IRC and as an information return.

1139
Corporation Application for Tentative Refund

Used by corporations that have certain carrybacks and desire a quick refund of taxes.

1310
Statement of Person Claiming Refund Due a Deceased Taxpayer
Used by a claimant to secure payment of refund on behalf of a deceased taxpayer.

2106
Employee Business Expenses
For use by employee and outside salespersons to support deductions from income for travel, transportation, and expenses (except moving expenses).

2119
Sale of Your Home
For use by individuals who sold their principal residence. Also used by those individuals 55 or older who elect to exclude gain on the sale of their principal residence.

2120
Multiple Support Declaration
Used as a statement to disclaim as an income tax exemption an individual to whose support the taxpayer and others have contributed.

2441
Child and Dependent Care Expenses
Used to figure the credit for child and dependent care expenses.

2848
Power of Attorney and Declaration of Representative
Used as an authorization for one person to act for another in any tax matter (except alcohol and tobacco taxes and firearms activities).

3903
Moving Expenses
For optional use to support deductions from income for expenses of travel, transportation (including meals and lodging), and certain expenses of selling an old residence and buying a new residence for employees or self-employed individuals moving to a new job location in the U.S. or its possessions.

4562
Depreciation and Amortization
For use by: individuals, estates and trusts, partnerships, and corporations claiming depreciation, amortization, and section 179 expense deduction. Also used to provide required information for automobiles and all other "listed property."

4684
Casualties and Thefts
For use by all taxpayers for reporting gains and losses from casualties and thefts.

4868
Application for Automatic Extension of Time To File U.S. Individual Income

Tax Return
This extension form is not required to be filed as in prior years.

5329
Return for Additional Taxes Attributable to Qualified Retirement Plans (Including IRAs), Annuities, and Modified Endowment Contracts
Used to report tax on excess contributions, premature distributions, excess distributions and excess accumulations.

5500EZ
Annual Return of One-Participant (Owners and Their Spouses) Pension Benefit Plan
Used to report on a pension, profit-sharing, etc., plan covering an individual, partner or an individual and spouse or partners and spouses who wholly own a business.

6251
Alternative Minimum Tax—Individuals
Used by individuals to report tax preference items and to figure their alternative minimum tax liability.

7004
Application for Automatic Extension of Time To File Corporation Income Tax Return
Used by corporations and certain exempt organizations to request an automatic extension of 6 months to file their income tax returns.

8283
Noncash Charitable Contributions
Used by taxpayers to report contributions of property in which the total claimed fair market value of all property contributed exceeds $500.

8582
Passive Activity Loss Limitations
Used to determine limitations on passive activity losses.

8606
Nondeductible IRA Contributions, IRA Basis, and Nontaxable IRA Distributions
Used to report the nondeductible amount of IRA, contributions and distributions. It is also used to determine IRA basis.

8615
Computation of Tax for Children Under Age 14 Who Have Investment Income of More Than $1,000
Used to figure the tax on unearned income of more than $1,000 belonging to a child under age 14.

8815
Exclusion of interest from Series EE U.S. Savings Bonds issued after 1989.
Used to figure the amount of interest on post-1989 Series EE U.S. Savings Bonds that can be excluded from income when the bonds are cashed and qualified higher education expenses are paid.

Internal Revenue Service Audit

There are two important facts that should be remembered regarding the IRS audit program. First, fewer than one out of every hundred individual tax returns will be audited in 1992. Second, the IRS is good at selecting returns for audit that will yield additional income taxes.

Returns to be audited are chosen by one of the following six methods and also by random selection:
• The Discriminate Function System (DIF)
• Taxpayer Compliance Measurement Program (TCMP)
• Matching Information Documents

• Targeted Group Projects
• Discrepancies in Your Return
• Tips from Informants

If your return is audited and you feel you are not being treated fairly, or that proper attention is not being paid to your statements, you have a right to ask for a hearing at the IRS appellate level. If you are still dissatisfied, you can take your case to the United States Tax Court. If the total amount in question is less than $10,000, your case can be handled under the Small Tax Case procedures. If you are still dissatisfied, your next move would be the United States   Circuit Court of Appeals.

Your Rights As a Taxpayer

Congress responded to complaints that taxpayers were not being treated fairly by the IRS and passed a comprehensive law to force the IRS to explain, in easy to understand language, the actions it proposes to take against a taxpayer and to relax some of its audit and collection procedures. This law is called "The Taxpayer Bill of Rights."

Some of the features of this bill of rights are:
- Plain English statements
- Allowing recordings of audit conferences
- Not requiring taxpayers to attend the examination

- New audit location rules
- Guidelines for installment payment of taxes
- Acting on wrong IRS advice
- Hardship relief
- Specific basis of IRS decision
- Levies on property
- Suing the IRS for damages

You can obtain the IRS Publication 1, "Your Rights As a Taxpayer," free by calling 1-800-TAX-FORM.

Federal Tax Filing Dates, 1992

January 15

Individuals. File an estimated tax payment for 1991 if you did not pay your income tax for the year through withholding (or did not pay in enough tax that way). Use Form 1040-ES. This is the final installment date for 1991 estimated tax. However, you do not have to make this payment if you file your 1991 return (Form 1040) and pay any tax due by January 31, 1992.

Farmers and fishermen. Pay your estimated tax for 1991 using Form 1040-ES. You can then file your 1991 income tax return (Form 1040) by April 15. If you do not pay at this time, file your 1991 return by March 1.

January 31

All employers. Give your employees their Form W-2 for 1991. In addition, furnish Notice 797, *You May Be Eligible for a Refund on Your Federal Income Tax Return Because of the Earned Income Credit (EIC)*, to each employee you employed during 1991 who did not have any tax withheld during 1991.

Individuals. File your income tax return (Form 1040) for 1991 if you did not pay your last installment of estimated tax by January 15. Filing your return now prevents any penalty for late payment of the last installment.

February 15

Individuals. If you claimed exemption from income tax withholding last year on Form W-4, you must file a new Form W-4 by this date to continue your exemption for another year with your employer.

March 2

Farmers and fishermen. File your 1991 income tax return (Form 1040) to avoid an underpayment penalty if you owe estimated tax. However, you have until April 15 if you paid your 1991 estimated tax by January 15, 1992.

March 16

Corporations. File a 1991 calendar year income tax return (Form 1120 or 1120-A) and pay any tax due. If you want an automatic 6-month extension, file Form 7004 and deposit what you estimate you owe.

S Corporations. File a 1991 calendar year income tax return (Form 1120S) and pay any tax due. If you want an automatic 6-month extension, file Form 7004 and deposit what you estimate you owe.

Corporations. File Form 2553 to choose to be treated as an S corporation, beginning with calendar year 1992. If Form 2553 is filed late, S treatment will begin with calendar year 1993.

April 15

Individuals. File an income tax return for 1991 (Form 1040, 1040A, or 1040EZ) and pay any tax due. If you want an automatic 4-month extension, pay 90% of this year's liability or 100% of last year's tax and file 1040 or 1040A by August 15.

Individuals. If you are not paying your 1992 income tax through withholding (or will not pay in enough tax during the year that way), pay the first installment of your 1992 estimated tax by this date. Use Form 1040-ES.

Partnerships. File a 1991 calendar year return (Form 1065).

C and S Corporations. Deposit the 1st installment of your estimated income tax for 1992.

June 15

Individuals. Make a payment of your 1992 estimated tax by this date if you are not paying your income tax for the year through withholding (or will not pay in enough tax that way). Use Form 1040-ES. This is the 2nd installment date for estimated tax in 1992.

C and S Corporations. Deposit the 2nd installment of your estimated income tax for 1992.

August 17

Individuals. If you were given an automatic 4-month extension to file your income tax return for 1991, file Form 1040 and pay any tax, interest, and penalties due.

September 15

Individuals. Make a payment of your 1992 estimated tax by this date, if you are not paying your income tax for the year through withholding (or will not pay in enough tax that way). Use Form 1040-ES. This is the 3rd installment date for estimated tax in 1992.

Corporations. File a 1991 income tax return (Form 1120 or 1120A) and pay any tax due. This due date applies only if you were given an automatic 6-month extension from March 15.

S Corporations. File a 1991 income tax return (Form 1120S) and pay any tax due. This due date applies only if you were given an automatic 6-month extension from March 15.

C and S Corporations. Deposit the 3rd installment of your estimated income tax for 1992.

December 15

C and S Corporations. Deposit the 4th installment of your estimated income tax for 1992.

Free IRS Tax Services

IRS Information and Assistance

The Internal Revenue Service provides over 100 publications on various topics to help taxpayers understand the complex tax laws. Most of these publications are revised annually.

Most taxpayers should be able to meet the requirements of the tax laws by using information such as tax package instructions, publications, taxpayer education programs, films, and library programs.

Toll-free telephone numbers and walk-in assistance are available to answer questions on a taxpayer's account, IRS procedures, or technical inquiries on tax-related matters.
• **Telephone Service**
Toll-free telephone assistance is available in all 50 states, the District of Columbia, Puerto Rico, and the Virgin Islands. Through the toll-free system, taxpayers may obtain assistance on their questions.
During periods of peak demand for telephone assistance, it may be difficult to get through. Generally, early in the morning and later in the week are the best times to call the IRS.
Telephone service for deaf taxpayers. Toll-free telephone assistance for deaf taxpayers is available for those who have access to TV/Telephone-TTY equipment. The hours of operation for this service are 8:00 a.m. to 6:45 p.m. Eastern Standard Time for January thru April 15 and 8:00 a.m. to 4:30 p.m. for April 16 thru December. Residents in the U.S. including Alaska, Hawaii, Puerto Rico, and the Virgin Islands may call 1-800-429-4059.
• **Information for the Blind**
Braille materials are available at Regional Libraries for the Blind and Physically Handicapped in conjunction with the

Library of Congress. These materials include Publications 17 and 334, Forms 1040, 1040A, and 1040EZ, and Schedules A and B, and instructions.
• **Walk-In Service**
While the Internal Revenue Service will not prepare tax returns, assistors are available in most IRS offices throughout the country to help taxpayers prepare their own returns. Taxpayers will be expected to help themselves to the maximum extent possible. However, they will be provided assistance and, at the same time, provided the opportunity of learning how to research and prepare their own tax returns. An assistor will "walk-through" a return with a number of taxpayers in a group setting.
In many IRS offices a walk-in counter is available to help with inquiries that do not involve preparation of a return, such as receipt of an IRS notice or bill. Certain technical information or publications may also be obtained at most IRS offices.
Taxpayers who wish assistance with their tax returns should bring in their tax packages, Forms W-2 and 1099, and any other information (such as a copy of last year's return) which will enable the IRS to help.

Taxpayer Education Programs

The Internal Revenue Service has a number of programs designed to educate the public about our nation's voluntary compliance tax system and each citizen's share in it so that the system works as smoothly as possible. The more that citizens understand about their role in this tax system, the better they will be able to carry out their responsibilities with the minimum amount of confusion. Most of these taxpayer education programs offer opportunity for citizen involvement through service as a volunteer.
• **Understanding Taxes**
This is a tax education program that begins in the schools, where young people are taught about their tax rights and responsibilities under our voluntary compliance tax system. They also learn how to fill out basic tax returns. Since many of them already are working, often at their first job, this learning has immediate practical value. They also learn about the history of taxes and current issues in taxation, such as tax reform. All materials a teacher may need are available free of charge, including a series of video programs. These films were produced in cooperation with the states. Workshops are conducted during the year to help prepare teachers for course instruction.
• **Small Business Workshops**
These workshops help people start small businesses by providing them with the information they need to carry out their tax responsibilities, including tax withholding, making correct and timely tax deposits, and filing a business return.

Some sessions focus on the needs of the self-employed, minority entrepreneurs, and specialized business groups. Active or retired businesspersons often volunteer their services and provide invaluable information.
• **Volunteer Income Tax Assistance**
The Volunteer Income Tax Assistance program (VITA) provides free tax assistance to elderly, non-English-speaking, handicapped people, and also to members of the military. Generally, those who receive these services can't afford professional tax assistance. After completing the IRS training, volunteers provide free help at special locations.
• **Tax Counseling for the Elderly**
Tax Counseling for the Elderly (TCE) provides free tax assistance to people 60 or older, especially those who are disabled or have other special needs. Non-profit organizations under cooperative agreements with the IRS provide local assistance.
Both VITA and TCE sites are usually located in neighborhood centers, libraries, churches, and other places in the community.
• **Community Outreach Tax Assistance**
This is a year-round program of assistance to groups who need help understanding the tax laws, especially as they apply to members of their profession or group, such as teaching, business, or farming. Seminars are conducted at times and locations in the community that are convenient for members of the group.

Federal Death Taxes and the State "Pick-Up" Credit

Source: Advisory Commission on Intergovernmental Relations, 1991

Federal death taxes are made up of two components—gift taxes and estate taxes. Gift taxes are levied on the donor, *while the donor is alive*, on transfers above $10,000 ($20,000 for joint gifts), *per donee*, for a single year. Estate taxes are levied on the entire taxable estate (gross estate less administrative expenses, bequests to spouse, debts, charitable contributions, and funeral expenses) *after the death of the donor*. Gift taxes paid during the donor's lifetime are credited dollar for dollar against estate taxes due at time of death.

Although estate and gift tax rates begin at the first dollar of taxable estate, there is a unified credit of $192,800 against transfer tax liability. This is equivalent to a $600,000 exemption. In addition to the unified credit, a credit for state death taxes is also allowed; see the table below for maximum state death tax credit (Pick-Up").

Unified Transfer Tax Rates[1]			Maximum State Death Tax Credit		
Taxable Estate	Tax on Lower Amount	Rate on Excess	Adjusted Taxable Estate[2]	Federal Credit	Rate on Excess
$10,000 or less	$0	18%	$40,000-89,999	$0	0.8%
10,000-19,999	1,800	20	90,000-139,999	400	1.6
20,000-39,999	3,800	22	140,000-239,999	1,200	2.4
40,000-59,999	8,200	24	240,000-439,999	3,600	3.2
60,000-79,999	13,000	26	440,000-639,999	10,000	4.0
80,000-99,999	18,200	28	640,000-839,999	18,000	4.8
100,000-149,999	23,800	30	840,000-1,039,999	27,600	5.6
150,000-249,999	38,800	32	1,040,000-1,539,999	38,800	6.4
250,000-499,999	70,800	34	1,540,000-2,039,999	70,800	7.2
500,000-749,999	155,800	37	2,040,000-2,539,999	106,800	8.0

(continued)

Unified Transfer Tax Rates[1]				Maximum State Death Tax Credit		
Taxable Estate	Tax on Lower Amount	Rate on Excess		Adjusted Taxable Estate[2]	Federal Credit	Rate on Excess
$750,000-999,999	$248,300	39%		2,540,000-3,039,999	$146,800	8.8%
1,000,000-1,249,999	345,800	41		3,040,000-3,539,999	190,800	9.6
1,250,000-1,499,999	448,300	43		5,040,000-6,039,999	402,800	12.0
2,500,000-2,999,999	1,025,800	53		6,040,000-7,039,999	522,800	12.8
over 3,000,000[3]	1,290,800	55		7,040,000-8,039,999	650,800	13.6
				8,040,000-9,039,999	786,800	14.4
				9,040,000-10,039,999	930,800	15.2
				over 10,040,000	1,082,800	16.0

(1) For decedents dying from 1984 through 1992. (2) Taxable estate less $60,000. (3) On taxable estates between $10,000,000 and $21,040,000, an additional tax of 5% of the transfer above $10,000,000 is imposed.

State Government Individual Income Taxes

Source: Advisory Commission on Intergovernmental Relations

(As of October 1990. Only basic rates, brackets, and exemptions are shown. Local income tax rates, even those mandated by the state, are not included. Taxable income rates and brackets listed below apply to single taxpayers and married taxpayers filing "combined separate" returns in states where this is permitted.)

State	Tax Rates (range in percent)	Taxable Income Brackets Lowest: Amount Under	Highest: Amount Over	Personal Exemptions Single	Married-Joint Return	Dependents	Standard Deduction[a] Percent	Single	Married-Joint Return	Federal Income Tax Deductible[b]
AL-*	2.0-5.0%	$500	$3,000	$1,500	$3,000	$300	20%	$2,000	$4,000	yes
AK	No state income tax									
AZ[c]	3.8-7.0	10,000	150,000	2,000	4,000	2,000	NA	3,500	7,000	no
AR	1.0-7.0	3,000	25,000	20	40	20	10	1,000	1,000	no
CA[c]*	1.0-9.3	4,213	27,646	58[d]	116[d]	58[d]	NA	2,169	4,339	no
CO*	5 percent of modified federal taxable income									
CT*	Limited income tax									
DE-*	3.2-7.7	5,000	40,000					2,300	3,000	no
HI*	2.0-10.0	1,500	20,500	1,040	2,080	1,040	NA	1,500	1,900	no
ID	2.0-8.2	1,000	20,000	Same as federal						no
IL	3.0	Flat rate		1,000	2,000	1,000	NA	NA	NA	no
IN-[c]	3.4	Flat rate		1,000	2,000	1,000	NA	NA	NA	no
IA-[c]	0.4-9.98	1,038	46,710	20[d]	40[d]	15[d]	NA	1,260	3,100	yes
KS*	4.5-5.95	27,500	27,500	2,000	4,000	2,000	NA	3,000	5,000	yes
KY-*	2.0-6.0	3,000	8,000	20	40	20	NA	650	650	yes
LA	2.0-6.0	10,000	50,000	4,500	9,000	1,000	Combined with exemptions			yes
ME	2.0-8.5	4,050	16,200	2,050	4,100	2,050	NA	3,250	5,450	no
MD-*	2.0-5.0	1,000	3,000	1,200	2,400	1,200	15	2,000	4,000	no
MA*	5.0-10.0	Flat rate		2,200	4,400	1,000	NA	NA	NA	no
MI-*	4.6	Flat rate		2,100	4,200	2,100	NA	NA	NA	no
MN*	6.0-8.0	13,000	13,000	Same as federal						no
MS	3.0-5.0	5,000	10,000	6,000	9,500	1,500	15	2,300	3,400	no
MO-*	1.5-6.0	1,000	9,000	1,200	2,400	400	NA	Same as federal[e]		yes
MT[c]	2.0-11.0	1,600	55,000	1,260	2,520	1,260	20	2,360	4,720	yes
NE*	2.2-6.41	1,230	27,000	1,230	2,460	1,230	NA	Same as federal		
NV	No state income tax									
NH*	Limited income tax									
NJ*	2.0-3.5	20,000	50,000	1,000	2,000	1,000	NA	NA	NA	no
NM	1.8-8.5	5,200	64,000	2,000	4,000	2,000	NA	Same as federal		no
NY-*	4.0-7.875	5,500	13,000	0	0	1,000	NA	6,000	9,500	no
NC*	6.0-7.0	12,750	12,750	2,000	4,000	2,000	NA	3,000	5,000	no
ND*	2.67-12.0	3,000	50,000	Same as federal						yes
OH*	0.743-6.9	5,000	100,000	650	1,300	650	NA	NA	NA	no
OK*	0.5-7.0	1,000	10,000	1,000	2,000	1,000	15	2,000	2,000	no
OR*[c]	5.0-9.0	2,000	5,000	98	96	98	NA	1,800	3,000	yes
PA-*	2.1	Flat rate		NA	NA	NA	NA	NA	NA	no
RI	22.96 percent of federal income tax liability									no
SC[c]	2.75-7.0	2,030	10,150	Same as federal						no
SD	No state income tax									
TN*	Limited income tax									
TX	No state income tax									
UT*	2.55-7.2	750	3,750	75 percent of federal exemptions			Same as federal[e]			yes
VT*	28 percent of federal income tax liablity									no
VA	2.0-5.75	3,000	16,000	800	1,600	800	NA	3,000	5,000	no
WA	No state income tax									
WV*	3.0-6.5	10,000	60,000	2,000	4,000	2,000	NA	NA	NA	no
WI*	4.9-6.93	7,500	15,000	0	0	50[d]	NA	5,200	8,900	no
WY	No state income tax									

Notes: (NA) = not applicable. (+) = states in which one or more local governments levy a local income tax. (a) The lesser of (1) the percentage indicated, multiplied by adjusted gross income, or (2) the dollar value listed. In some states, when a standard deduction computed using a percentage of AGI is less than the fixed amount shown above, a minimum dollar deduction is allowed. Maryland and Utah have a minimum deduction as well. (b) A state provision that allows the taxpayer to deduct fully the federal income tax reduces the effective marginal tax rate for persons in the highest state and federal tax brackets by approximately 30% of the nominal tax rate—the deduction is of a lesser benefit to other taxpayers with lower federal and state top tax brackets. (c) Indexed by an inflation factor. (d) Tax credit per dependent. Taxpayers 65 or older receive a $25 credit.

(continued)

*State Notes:

Alabama: Social Security taxes are included in itemized deductions. Taxable income brackets for married filing joint over $6,000, taxed at highest rate.

Arkansas: Tax credit per dependent. Taxpayers 65 or older receive a $20 credit.

California: Taxpayers 65 and older receive additional $58 credit.

Colorado: Modifications for federal interest income, non-Colorado state and local interest income, and Colorado pension exclusion.

Connecticut: There is an income tax on interest, capital gains, and dividend income only. The rate of this tax ranges from 1% of interest and dividend income for taxpayers with an AGI of $54,000-$57,999 to 12% of such income of taxpayers with an AGI over $100,000. Capital gains are taxed at 7% after an exemption of $100 is applied.

Delaware: Lowest personal income tax rate (3.2%) applies to income in the $2,000-5,000 bracket. Taxable income under $2,000 is not subject to tax and is refered to as the "zero bracket" amount.

District of Columbia: Exemption will increase to $1,370 by 1991.

Hawaii: A refundable food/excise tax credit of at least $55 per exemption is granted; credit of $60 per exemption is granted for 1990; a refundable medical services excise tax credit of 4% of qualified medical expenses, subject to limitation, is granted.

Idaho: Idaho allows a refundable $15/exemption credit.

Illinois: Effective 1/1/90 an additional $1,000 exemption for persons 65 years of age or older. An additional $1,000 exemption for persons who are blind.

Indiana: Additional $1,000 exemption if taxpayer or spouse is over 65 or blind.

Iowa: Tax may not reduce after-tax income of taxpayer below $5,000 (single) or $7,500 (married filing joint, head-of-household, surviving spouse). Only limitation for the standard deduction is that the deduction otherwise allowable of $1,260 or $3,100 may not exceed the amount of income remaining after the federal tax deduction.

Kansas: A child care credit equal to 25% of the federal child care credit is allowed to taxpayers claiming the federal credit. These rates and brackets apply to single persons not deducting federal income tax. For individuals deducting the tax, rates range from 4.75% of the first $2,000 to 8.5% on income over $30,000.

Kentucky: Federal income tax paid only for years prior to 1990 is deductible in 1990; no deduction for 1991. Tax credit per dependent. Taxpayers 65 or older receive a $60 credit.

Maryland: All counties have a local income tax surcharge of at least 20% of the state tax liability; most counties have a surcharge of 50%. Single taxpayers have a minimum standard deduction of $1,500, and married taxpayers a minimum standard deduction of $3,000. Blind and elderly get an additional exemption of $1,000.

Massachusetts: 10% (flat rate) imposed on net capital gains, interest, and dividends of residents, and Massachusetts business income of nonresidents. All other net income taxed at 5%. No tax is imposed on a single person whose gross income is $8,000 or less ($12,000 married). Social Security taxes are deducted from taxable income up to $2,000 per taxpayer.

Michigan: Persons who can be claimed as a dependent on someone else's return get an exception of $1,000. If their AGI is $1,500 or less, they owe no tax.

Missouri: For taxpayers itemizing deductions, Social Security taxes are deductible.

Minnesota: Additional rate of 0.5% on certain income classes to reflect federal phaseout of personal exemptions and the 15% federal tax bracket. Total rate on brackets of higher income is 8.5%.

Montana: Taxable income brackets, personal exemption level, and standard deduction levels are indexed annually for inflation.

Nebraska: Taxable income brackets will vary by filing status.

New Hampshire: There is a 5% tax on interest and dividends in excess of $1,200 ($2,400 married). There is no filing requirement for an individual whose total interest and dividend income, after deducting all interest from U.S. obligations, New Hampshire and Vermont banks or credit unions; and dividends from New Hampshire non-holding company bonds is less than $1,200 ($2,400 for joint filers) for a taxable period.

New Jersey: No taxpayer is subject to tax if gross income is $3,000 or less ($1,500 married, filing separately).

New Mexico: Several rebates are available for lower income taxpayers. A minimum deduction exists but does not apply since it is lower than the federal standard deduction. The extra federal deduction for the aged and blind does not apply, although the state has its own provisions. An exception of $2,500 ($1,250 for married filing separate rate) is allowed for each "special needs" child adopted on or after 1/1/88.

New York: Rates are scheduled to be reduced further in 1991, when the top rate will be 7.7%.

North Carolina: Breaking point for higher marginal tax rate varies according to filing status. Taxable income brackets shown are for single taxpayers.

North Dakota: Information in table applies to the long form method. As an alternative, taxpayers may use the short form method where the tax is 14% of the adjusted federal income tax liability.

Ohio: Taxpayers take a $20 tax credit per exemption.

Oklahoma: These rates and brackets apply to single persons not deducting federal income tax. For individuals deducting the tax, rates range from 0.5% of the first $1,000 to 10% on income over $16,000 (single rate).

Oregon: Federal tax deduction limited to $3,000 ($1,500 if married filing separately).

Pennsylvania: There are eight classes of income: (1) comprehensive; (2) net profits; (3) interest; (4) dividends; (5) sale or exchange of property; (6) rents, royalties, patents, and copyrights; (7) income derived through estates or trusts; and (f) gambling and lottery winnings.

Tennessee: Interest and dividends taxed at 6%. Persons over 65 having total annual gross income derived from any and all sources of $9,000 or less are exempt. Blindness is a basis for total exemption.

Utah: One-half of federal tax liability is deductible.

Vermont: Refundable state earned income tax credit (28% of federal credit, maximum $267).

West Virginia: Eliminated standard deduction; all itemized deductions prohibited and replaced with larger personal exemptions.

Wisconsin: The standard deduction is gradually phased out as income increases; deduction is completely phased out at $50,830 of AGI for single filers and $55,000 of AGI for joint filers.

ENERGY

Major Energy Developments

Source: Energy Information Administration. *Annual Energy Review 1990*

The most dramatic energy-related event of 1990 was the Iraqi invasion of Kuwait on Aug. 2, which resulted in higher energy prices and heightened concern about the future availability of crude oil. Higher energy prices, combined with other factors such as mild weather early in the year and slow economic growth, restrained energy demand. U.S. total energy consumption in 1990 remained at the 1989 level of 81 quadrillion Btu. Domestic production of crude oil continued to suffer from the effects of years of low oil prices and from the expectation (before the Iraqi invasion of Kuwait) that prices would remain low. In 1990, production in the lower 48 states declined to 5.5 million barrels per day, and even Alaskan production declined for the second consecutive year. Production of other major forms of energy increased, with coal production exceeding 1 billion short tons for the first time, and natural gas production rising 2 percent to 18 trillion cubic feet.

U.S. net imports of all forms of energy combined decreased 2 percent in 1990 to 13.8 quadrillion Btu. Lower net imports of petroleum accounted for 0.2 quadrillion Btu, and a 0.1-quadrillion-Btu increase in natural gas net imports offset an equal increase in coal net exports. But higher crude oil prices contributed to an increase in the real value of energy net imports, which rose $6.5 billion to $41.6 billion, with crude oil and petroleum product net imports accounting for $6.4 billion of the increase. Petroleum continued to account for most of the energy trade, with petroleum net imports totalling 7.1 million barrels per day, down 0.1 million barrels per day. (See *Chronology* and *Index* for further information).

World Production of Crude Oil[1], 1960-1990

Source: Energy Information Administration. *Annual Energy Review. 1990* (in millions of barrels per day)

Year	Total[2] OPEC	Canada	China	Mexico	U.K.	U.S.	USSR	Other	Total World
1960	8.70	0.52	0.10	0.27	[3]	7.04	2.91	1.42	20.96
1965	14.34	0.81	0.23	0.32	[3]	7.80	4.79	2.01	30.30
1970	23.41	1.26	0.60	0.49	[3]	9.64	6.97	3.50	45.87
1971	25.33	1.35	0.78	0.49	[3]	9.46	7.44	3.64	48.48
1972	27.09	1.53	0.90	0.51	[3]	9.44	7.88	3.77	51.13
1973	30.99	1.80	1.09	0.47	[3]	9.21	8.33	3.80	55.68
1975	27.15	1.43	1.49	0.71	0.01	8.38	9.47	4.14	52.78
1977	31.30	1.32	1.87	0.98	0.77	8.25	10.49	4.62	59.59
1978	29.88	1.32	2.08	1.21	1.08	8.71	10.95	4.78	60.00
1979	31.00	1.50	2.12	1.46	1.57	8.55	11.19	5.09	62.48
1980	26.99	1.44	2.11	1.94	1.62	8.60	11.46	5.20	59.35
1981	22.84	1.29	2.01	2.31	1.81	8.57	11.55	5.39	55.78
1982	19.15	1.27	2.05	2.75	2.07	8.65	11.62	5.65	53.18
1983	17.89	1.36	2.12	2.69	2.29	8.69	11.68	6.25	52.97
1984	17.86	1.44	2.30	2.78	2.48	8.88	11.58	6.90	54.20
1985	16.63	1.47	2.51	2.75	2.53	8.97	11.25	7.54	53.65
1986	18.73	1.47	2.62	2.44	2.54	8.68	11.54	7.85	55.87
1987	18.85	1.54	2.69	2.55	2.41	8.35	11.69	8.24	56.31
1988	20.79	1.62	2.73	2.51	2.23	8.14	11.82	8.67	58.51
1989	22.66	1.56	2.76	2.51	1.79	7.61	11.42	9.31	59.61
1990	23.69	1.53	2.77	2.55	1.83	7.30	11.68	9.72	60.07

(1) Includes lease condensate, excludes natural gas plant liquids; (2) Current membership of the Organization of the Petroleum Exporting Countries consist of Algeria, Ecuador, Gabon, Indonesia, Iran, Iraq, Kuwait, Libya, Nigeria, Qatar, Saudi Arabia, United Arab Emirates, and Venezuela; production from the Neutral Zone between Kuwait and Saudi Arabia is included in "Total OPEC" production. (3) Less than 5,000 barrels per day.

Energy Consumption by Major Source, 1950-1990

Source: U.S. Dept. of Energy

(quadrillion Btu)

Petroleum

Natural Gas

Coal

Hydroelectric Power

Nuclear Electric Power

The Sources of Energy

Source: U.S. Dept. of Energy

Other (solar, wind, hydro etc.) 8.1%

Nuclear 6.9%

Coal 22.2%

Petroleum 40.3%

Natural Gas 22.5%

Petroleum Imports
As a percentage of all petroleum used.

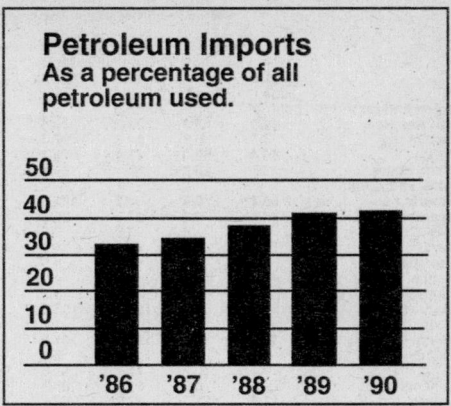

U.S. Net Imports[1] of Energy by Source

Source: Energy Information Administration, *Monthly Energy Review, March 1991*

(Quadrillion Btu)

Annual Total	Coal	Crude Oil[2]	Petroleum Products[3]	Natural Gas	Electricity[4]	Coal Coke	Total
1973	−1.422	6.883	6.097	0.981	0.148	−0.007	12.680
1975	−1.738	8.708	3.800	.904	.064	.014	11.752
1980	−2.391	10.586	2.912	.957	.217	−.035	12.247
1981	−2.918	8.854	2.522	.857	.347	−.016	9.646
1982	−2.768	6.917	2.128	.898	.306	−.022	7.460
1983	−2.013	6.731	2.351	.887	.372	−.016	8.311
1984	−2.119	6.918	2.970	.792	.409	−.011	8.959
1985	−2.389	6.381	2.570	.896	.423	−.013	7.868
1988	−2.446	10.698	3.308	1.221	.325	.040	13.146
1989	−2.566[R]	12.296[R]	3.029[R]	1.278[R]	.113[R]	.030	14.182[R]
1990	−2.704	12.429	2.671	1.410	.018	−.005	13.829

(1) Net imports equals imports minus exports. Minus sign indicates exports greater than imports. (2) Includes crude oil, lease condensate, and imports of crude oil for the Strategic Petroleum Reserve. (3) Includes petroleum products, unfinished oils, pentanes plus, and gasoline blending components. (4) Assumed to be hydroelectricity; estimated at the average input heat rate for fossil fuel steam-electric power plant generation. E = Estimate; R = Revised. **Notes:** Geographic coverage-50 States and District of Columbia. Totals may not equal sum of components due to independent rounding.

U.S Dependence on Petroleum Net Imports[1]

Source: Energy Information Administration, *Monthly Energy Review, March 1991*

Annual Average Rate	Net Imports[2]				Net Imports as % of U.S. Petroleum Products Supplied		
	From Arab OPEC[3]	From OPEC[4]	From All Countries	Petroleum Products Supplied	From Arab OPEC[3]	From OPEC[4]	From All Countries
	Thousand Barrels per Day				Percent		
1973	914	2,991	6,025	17,308	5.3	17.3	34.8
1975	1,382	3,599	5,846	16,322	8.5	22.0	35.8
1980	2,549	4,293	6,365	17,056	14.9	25.2	37.3
1981	1,844	3,315	5,401	16,058	11.5	20.6	33.6
1982	852	2,136	4,298	15,296	5.6	14.0	28.1
1983	630	1,843	4,312	15,231	4.1	12.1	28.3
1984	817	2,037	4,715	15,726	5.2	13.0	30.0
1985	470	1,821	4,286	15,726	3.0	11.6	27.3
1988	1,837	3,513	6,587	17,283	10.6	20.3	38.1
1989	2,128	4,124	7,202	17,325	12.3	23.8	41.6
1990	2,320	4,264	7,090	16,916	13.2	25.2	41.9

(1) Beginning in October 1977, Strategic Petroleum Reserves are included. (2) Net imports equals imports minus exports. Imports from members of the Organization of Petroleum Exporting Countries (OPEC) exclude indirect imports, which are petroleum products imported primarily from Caribbean and West European areas and refined from crude oil produced by OPEC. (3) The Arab members of OPEC are Algeria, Iraq, Kuwait, Libya, Qatar, Saudi Arabia, and the United Arab Emirates. Net imports from the Neutral Zone between Kuwait and Saudi Arabia are included in net imports from "Arab OPEC." (4) OPEC consists of Ecuador, Gabon, Indonesia, Iran, Nigeria, and Venezuela, as well as the Arab members. **Notes:** Geographic coverage is the 50 States and the District of Columbia. Annual averages may not equal average of quarters due to independent rounding.

World Crude Oil and Natural Gas Reserves, Jan. 1, 1990

Source: Energy Information Administration. *Annual Energy Review 1990*

Region and Country	Crude Oil (billion barrels) Oil and Gas Journal	World Oil	Natural Gas (trillion cubic feet) Oil and Gas Journal	World Oil	Region and Country	Crude Oil (billion barrels) Oil and Gas Journal	World Oil	Natural Gas (trillion cubic feet) Oil and Gas Journal	World Oil
North America....	89.0	85.3	334.8	336.8	Iran..........	92.9	62.5	500.0	600.0
Canada	6.1	6.8	94.3	97.0	Iraq..........	100.0	100.0	95.0	110.0
Mexico........	56.4	52.0	73.4	72.7	Kuwait[1]........	97.1	98.4	54.6	52.6
United States ..	26.5	26.5	167.1	167.1	Oman.........	4.3	4.3	9.3	9.9
Central and South					Qatar.........	4.5	2.6	163.1	162.0
America	68.7	70.9	160.3	162.6	Saudi Arabia[1]	257.6	262.5	187.3	188.4
Argentina	2.3	2.2	27.3	26.3	United Arab Emirates	98.1	55.7	200.8	193.4
Bolivia	0.2	0.2	5.5	5.7	Other.........	5.7	6.4	9.6	18.0
Brazil.........	2.8	2.8	3.8	4.1	Africa	58.8	60.8	266.6	221.6
Colombia.......	2.1	2.0	4.0	4.0	Algeria	9.2	9.2	114.0	114.2
Ecuador.......	1.5	1.4	4.0	4.0	Cameroon......	0.4	0.5	3.8	3.8
Trinidad and Tobago	0.5	0.6	10.0	8.7	Egypt.........	4.5	4.3	11.7	11.5
Venezuela	58.5	60.5	100.8	105.7	Libya	22.8	22.8	25.5	29.2
Other.........	0.8	1.3	4.9	4.1	Nigeria	16.0	16.7	87.4	47.4
Western Europe...	18.8	17.3	190.2	201.2	Tunisia	1.8	1.8	3.1	3.1
Denmark.......	0.8	0.5	4.4	3.0	Other.........	4.2	5.5	21.1	12.4
Italy..........	0.7	0.7	11.7	11.6	Far East and Oceania	46.5	46.8	283.3	345.7
Netherlands	0.2	0.2	61.1	60.9	Australia	1.7	2.8	16.5	73.5
Norway........	11.5	11.0	82.2	93.1	Brunei	1.4	1.2	11.4	12.2
United Kingdom....	4.3	3.8	20.8	19.8	China	24.0	21.5	35.3	33.0
West Germany ...	0.4	0.2	6.6	6.4	India	7.5	4.3	23.0	20.8
Other.........	0.9	0.8	3.3	6.4	Indonesia.......	8.2	12.0	87.0	85.7
Eastern Europe and					Maylaysia	2.9	3.7	51.9	53.6
U.S.S.R........	60.1	59.6	1,528.0	1,568.1	New Zealand	0.1	0.2	5.1	4.0
U.S.S.R........	58.4	57.9	1,500.0	1,550.0	Pakistan	0.1	0.3	18.0	22.9
Other[2]	1.7	1.7	28.0	18.1	Thailand	0.2	0.3	6.9	14.5
Middle East......	660.2	592.5	1,226.1	1,340.5	Other.........	0.3	0.6	28.3	25.4
Bahrain........	0.1	0.1	6.5	6.3	World Total......	1,002.2	933.2	3,989.4	4,176.6

(1) Includes one-half of the reserves in the Neutral Zone between Kuwait and Saudi Arabia. (2) Includes Albania, Bulgaria, Cuba, Czechoslovakia, East Germany, Hungary, Mongolia, North Korea, Poland, Romania, Yugoslavia, and Vietnam. **Note:** Sum of components may not equal total due to independent rounding.

U.S. Total Energy Production by Source, 1960-1990

Source: Energy Information Administration, *Annual Energy Review 1990* (quadrillion Btu, except as noted)

Year	Coal	Natural Gas[1]	Crude Oil[2]	Natural Gas Plant Liquids	Hydroelectric Power[3]	Nuclear Electric Power[4]	Geothermal[4]	Total	Percent Change[5]
1960	10.82	12.66	14.93	1.46	1.61	0.01	0	41.49	2.2
1965	13.06	15.78	16.52	1.88	2.06	0.04	(6)	49.34	3.4
1970	14.61	21.67	20.40	2.51	2.63	0.24	0.01	62.07	5.0
1975	14.99	19.64	17.73	2.37	3.15	1.90	0.07	59.86	−1.6
1980	18.60	19.91	18.25	2.25	2.90	2.74	0.11	64.76	1.5
1982	18.64	18.25	18.31	2.19	3.26	3.13	0.10	63.89	−0.8
1984	19.72	17.93	18.85	2.27	3.31	3.55	0.16	65.81	7.6
1985	19.33	16.92	18.99	2.24	2.94	4.15	0.20	64.78	−1.6
1986	19.51	16.47	18.38	2.15	3.03	4.47	0.22	64.25	−0.8
1987	20.14	17.05	17.67	2.22	2.59	4.91	0.23	64.82	0.9
1988	20.74	17.52[R]	17.28	2.26	2.31	5.66	0.22[R]	66.01[R]	1.8[R]
1989	21.35[R]	17.78[R]	16.12	2.16	2.77[R]	5.68[R]	0.20[R]	66.06[R]	0.6
1990	22.61	18.05	15.46	2.16	2.92	6.19	0.18	67.59	2.3

(1) Dry natural gas; (2) Includes lease condensate; (3) Electric utility and industrial generation of hydroelectric power; (4) Generated by electric utilities; (5) Percent change from previous year calculated from data prior to rounding; (6) Less than 0.005 quadrillion Btu; R = Revised.

U.S. Total Energy Consumption by Source, 1960-1990

Source: Energy Information Administration, *Annual Energy Review, 1990* (quadrillion Btu, except as noted)

Year	Coal	Natural Gas	Petroleum[1]	Hydroelectric Power[2]	Nuclear Electric Power[3]	Geothermal[3]	Total	Percent Change[4]
1960	9.84	12.39	19.92	1.66	0.01	(5)	43.80	3.9
1965	11.58	15.77	23.25	2.06	0.04	(5)	52.68	4.3
1970	12.26	21.79	29.52	2.65	0.24	0.01	66.43	3.5
1975	12.66	19.95	32.73	3.22	1.90	0.07	70.55	−2.8
1980	15.42	20.39	34.20	3.12	2.74	0.11	75.96	−3.7
1982	15.32	18.51	30.23	3.56	3.13	0.10	70.84	−4.3
1984	17.07	18.51	31.05	3.72	3.55	0.16	74.06	5.1
1985	17.48	17.85	30.92	3.36	4.15	0.20	73.96	−0.1
1986	17.26	16.71	32.20	3.40	4.47	0.22	74.26	0.4
1987	18.01	17.67	32.87	3.07	4.91	0.23	76.77	3.5[R]
1988	18.85	18.55	34.22[R]	2.64	5.66	0.22[R]	80.20	4.4[R]
1989	18.94[R]	19.38[R]	34.21	2.88[R]	5.68[R]	0.20[R]	81.35[R]	1.4[R]
1990	19.05	19.41	33.64	2.94	6.19	0.18	81.44	0.1

(1) Petroleum products supplied including natural gas plant liquids and crude oil burned as fuel; (2) Electric utility and industrial generation of hydroelectric power and net electricity imports; (3) Generated by electric utilities; (4) Percent change from previous year calculated from data prior to rounding; (5) Less than 0.005 quadrillion Btu; R = Revised.

U.S. Coal Production and Consumption, 1965-1990

Source: Energy Information Administration, *Annual Energy Review 1990* (million short tons)

	Production					Consumption				
Year	Bituminous Coal	Sub-bituminous Coal	Lignite	Anthracite	Total	Electric Utilities	Coke Plants	Other Industry & Misc.	Residential & Commercial	Total
1965	512.1	(1)	(1)	14.9	527.0	244.8	95.3	105.6	25.7	472.0
1970	578.5	16.4	8.0	9.7	612.7	320.2	96.5	90.2	16.1	523.2
1975	577.5	51.1	19.8	6.2	654.6	406.0	83.6	63.6	9.4	562.6
1976	588.4	64.8	25.5	6.2	684.9	448.4	84.7	61.8	8.9	603.8
1977	581.0	82.1	28.2	5.9	697.2	477.1	77.7	61.5	9.0	625.3
1978	534.0	96.8	34.4	5.0	670.2	481.2	71.4	63.1	9.5	625.2
1979	612.3	121.5	42.5	4.8	781.1	527.1	77.4	67.7	8.4	680.5
1980	628.8	147.7	47.2	6.1	829.7	569.3	66.7	60.3	6.5	702.7
1981	608.0	159.7	50.7	5.4	823.8	596.8	61.0	67.4	7.4	732.6
1982	620.2	160.9	52.4	4.6	838.1	593.7	40.9	64.1	8.2	706.9
1983	568.6	151.0	58.3	4.1	782.1	625.2	37.0	66.0	8.4	736.7
1984	649.5	179.2	63.1	4.2	895.9	664.4	44.0	73.7	9.1	791.3
1985	613.9	192.7	72.4	4.7	883.6	693.8	41.1	75.4	7.8	818.0
1986	620.1	189.6	76.4	4.3	890.3	685.1	36.0	75.6	7.7	804.3
1987	636.6	200.2	78.4	3.6	918.8	717.9	37.0	75.2	6.9	836.9
1988	638.1	223.5	85.1	3.6	950.3	758.4	41.9	76.3	7.1	883.7
1989	659.8R	231.2R	86.4R	3.3R	980.7R	766.9R	41.4R	76.1	6.2	890.6R
1990	697.9	245.2	89.6	3.1	1,035.9	771.5	38.8	75.9	6.3	892.5

(1) Included in bituminous; (p) = preliminary; (R) = revised.

Major U.S. Dams and Reservoirs

Source: Committee on Register of Dams, Corps of Engineers, U.S. Army, Aug. 1991

Highest Dams

Order	Dam Name	River	State	Type	Feet	Meters	Year Complete
1	Oroville	Feather	Cal.	E	754	230	1968
2	Hoover	Colorado	Nev.	A	725	221	1936
3	Dworshak	N Fork Clearwater	Id.	G	718	219	1973
4	Glen Canyon	Colorado	Ariz.	A	708	216	1966
5	New Bullards Bar	North Yuba	Cal.	A	636	194	1970
6	New Melones	Stanislaus	Cal.	R	626	191	1979
7	Swift	Lewis	Wash.	E	610	186	1958
8	Mossyrock	Cowlitz	Wash.	A	607	185	1968
9	Shasta	Sacramento	Cal.	G	600	183	1945
10	Hungry Horse	S Fork Flathead	Mon.	A	564	172	1953
11	Grand Coulee	Columbia	Wash.	G	551	168	1942
12	Ross	Skagit	Wash.	A	541	165	1949

E = Embankment, Earthfill; R = Embankment, Rockfill; G = Gravity; A = Arch.

Largest Embankment Dams

Order	Dam Name	River	State	Type	Cubic yards X 1000	Cubic Meters X 1000	Year Complete
1	Fort Peck	Missouri	Mon.	E	125,624	96,050	1937
2	Oahe	Missouri	S.D.	E	91,996	70,339	1958
3	Oroville	Feather	Cal.	E	77,997	59,635	1968
4	San Luis	San Luis Creek	Cal.	E	77,897	59,559	1967
5	Garrison	Missouri	N.D.	E	66,498	50,843	1953
6	Cochiti	Rio Grande	N.M.	E	65,693	50,228	1975
7	Earthquake Lake	Madison	Mon.	E-G	49,998	38,228	1959
8	Fort Randall	Missouri	S.D.	E	49,962	38,200	1952
9	Castaic	Castaic Creek	Cal.	E	43,998	33,640	1973
10	Ludington P/S	Lake Michigan	Mich.	E	37,699	28,824	1973
11	Kingsley	N. Platte	Neb.	E	31,999	24,466	1941
12	Warm Springs	Dry Creek	Cal.	E	29,977	22,920	1982

E = Embankment, Earthfill; R = Embankment, Rockfill; E-R = Embankment, Earth & Rockfill; G = Gravity; A = Arch.

Largest Man-Made Reservoirs

Order	Dam Name	Reservoir	Location	Acre-Feet	Cubic Meters x 1000	Year Completed
1	Hoover	Lake Mead	Nev.	28,253,000	34,850,000	1936
2	Glen Canyon	Lake Powell	Ariz.	26,997,000	33,300,000	1966
3	Garrison	Lake Sakakawea	N.D.	22,635,000	27,920,000	1953
4	Oahe	Lake Oahe	S.D.	22,238,000	27,430,000	1958
5	Fort Peck	Fort Peck Lake	Mon.	17,933,000	22,120,000	1937
6	Grand Coulee	F D Roosevelt Lake	Wash.	9,558,000	11,790,000	1942
7	Libby	Lake Koocanusa	Mon.	5,813,000	7,170,000	1973
8	Fort Randall	Lake Francis Case	S.D.	4,621,000	5,700,000	1952
9	Shasta	Lake Shasta	Cal.	4,548,000	5,610,000	1945
10	Toledo Bend	Toledo Bend Lake	La.	4,475,000	5,520,000	1968
11	Wolf Creek	Cumberland Lake	Ky.	3,997,000	4,930,000	1951
12	Flaming Gorge	Flaming Gorge Reservoir	Ut.	3,786,000	4,670,000	1964

1 acre foot = 1 acre of water, 1 foot deep

World's Largest Capacity Hydro Plants

Source: U.S. Committee on Large Dams, of the Intl. Commission on Large Dams, Aug. 1991

Rank order	Name	Country	Rated capacity now (MW)	Rated capacity planned (MW)	Rank order	Name	Country	Rated capacity now (MW)	Rated capacity planned (MW)
1	Turukhansk (Lower Tungu-ska)*	USSR		20,000	13=	Bratsk	USSR	4,500	4,500
2	Itaipu	Brazil/Paraguay	7,400	13,320	13=	Ust-Ilim	USSR	3,675	4,500
3	Grand Coulee	USA	9,070	10,830	15	Cabora Bassa	Mozambique	2,425	4,150
4	Guri (Raúl Leoni)	Venezuela	10,300	10,300	16	Boguchany	USSR		4,000
5	Tucuruí	Brazil	2,640	7,260	17=	Rogun*	USSR		3,600
6	Sayano Shu-shensk*	USSR	6,400	6,400	17=	Oak Creek	USA	3,600	3,600
7=	Corpus Posadas	Argentina/ Paraguay	4,700	6,000	19	Paulo Afonso I	Brazil	1,524	3,409
7=	Krasnoyarsk	USSR	6,000	6,000	20	Pati*	Argentina		3,300
9	La Grande 2	Canada	5,328	5,328	21=	Ilha Solteira	Brazil	3,200	3,200
10	Churchill Falls	Canada	5,225	5,225	21=	Brumley Gap*	USA	3,200	3,200
11	Xingo	Brazil	3,012	5,020	23	Chapetón*	Argentina		3,000
12	Tarbela	Pakistan	1,750	4,678	24	Gezhouba	China	2,715	2,715
					25	John Day	USA	2,160	2,700
					25	Nurek	USSR	900	2,700
					25=	Yacyreta*	Argentina/Paraguay		2,700

*Planned or under construction.

Major Dams of the World

Source: U.S. Committee on Large Dams, of the Intl. Commission of Large Dams, Aug. 1991

World's Highest Dams

Rank order	Name	Country	Height above lowest formation (m)	Rank order	Name	Country	Height above lowest formation (m)
1	Rogun*	USSR	335	11	Mica	Canada	242
2	Nurek	USSR	300	12	Mauvoisin	Switzerland	237
3	Grand Dixence	Switzerland	285	13	Chivor	Colombia	237
4	Inguri	USSR	272	14	El Cajón	Honduras	234
5	Chicoasén	Mexico	261	15	Chirkei	USSR	233
6	Tehri*	India	261	16	Oroville	USA	230
7	Kishau*	India	253	17	Bhakra	India	226
8=	Ertan	China	245	18	Hoover	USA	221
9=	Sayano-Shushensk*	USSR	245	19	Contra	Switzerland	220
10	Guavio*	Colombia	243	20	Mratinje	Yugoslavia	220

*Under construction.

World's Largest Volume Embankment Dams

Rank order	Name	Country	Volume cubic meters × 1000	Rank Order	Name	Country	Volume cubic meters × 1000
1	Tarbela	Pakistan	148,500	11	Gardiner	Canada	65,000
2	Fort Peck	USA	96,050	12	Afsluitdijk	Netherlands	63,400
3	Tucuruí	Brazil	85,200	13	Mangla	Pakistan	63,379
4	Atatürk*	Turkey	85,000	14	Oroville	USA	59,635
5	Yacireta*	Argentina	81,000	15	San Luis	USA	59,559
6	Rogun*	USSR	75,500	16	Nurek	USSR	58,000
7	Oahe	USA	70,339	17	Tanda	Pakistan	57,250
8	Guri	Venezuela	70,000	18	Garrison	USA	50,843
9	Parambikulam	India	69,165	19	Chochiti	USA	50,228
10	High Island West	Hong Kong	67,000	20	Oosterschelde	Netherlands	50,000

*Under construction.

World's Largest Capacity Manmade Reservoirs

Rank order	Name	Country	Capacity cubic meters × 1000	Rank Order	Name	Country	Capacity cubic meters × 1000
1	Owen Falls	Uganda	204,800	11	Cabora Bassa	Mozambique	63,000
2	Bratsk	USSR	169,000	12	La Grande 2	Canada	61,715
3	Aswan (High)	Egypt	162,000	13	La Grande 3	Canada	60,020
4	Kariba	Zimbabwe/Zambia	160,368	14	Ust-Ilim	USSR	59,300
5	Akosombo	Ghana	147,960	15	Boguchany*	USSR	58,200
6	Daniel Johnson	Canada	141,851	16	Kuibyshev	USSR	58,000
7	Guri	Venezuela	135,000	17	Serra de Mesa	Brazil	54,400
8	Krasnoyarsk	USSR	73,300	18	Caniapiscau Barrage KA 3	Canada	53,790
9	W A C Bennett (Portage Mt.)	Canada	70,309	19	Bukhtarma	USSR	49,800
10	Zeya	USSR	68,400	20	Atatürk	Turkey	48,700

*Under construction

Net Electricity Generation at Electric Utilities by Energy Source

Source: Energy Information Administration. *Annual Energy Review 1990* (billion kilowatthours)

	Coal	Petroleum	Natural Gas	Nuclear Electric Power	Hydro-electric Power	Geothermal and Other[1]	Total
1975	853	289	300	173	300	3	1,918
1980	1,162	246	346	251	276	6	2,286
1981	1,203	206	346	273	261	6	2,295
1982	1,192	147	305	283	309	5	2,241
1983	1,259	144	274	294	332	6	2,310
1984	1,342	120	297	328	321	9	2,416
1985	1,402	100	292	384	281	11	2,470
1986	1,386	137	249	414	291	12	2,487
1987	1,464	118	273	455	250	12	2,572
1988	1,541	149	253	527	223	12	2,704
1989	1,554R	158	267R	529	265R	11	2,784R
1990P	1,557	117	263	577	280	11	2,805

(1) Other = wood, waste, wind, photovoltaic, and solar thermal energy sources connected to electric utility distribution systems. P = Preliminary, R = Revised.

U.S. Passenger Car Efficiency, 1966-1989

Source: Energy Information Administration. *Annual Energy Review 1990*

	Mileage		Fuel Consumption		Fuel Rate	
Year	Thousand Miles per Car	Index 1973 = 100.0	Gallons per Car	Index 1973 = 100.0	Miles per Gallon	Index 1973 = 100.0
1966	9.92	96.7	703	91.2	14.1	106.0
1968	10.14	98.8	731	94.8	13.9	104.5
1970	10.27	100.0	760	98.6	13.5	101.5
1975	9.69	94.4	716	93.9	13.5	101.5
1977	9.88	96.3	716	93.9	13.8	103.8
1980	9.14	89.1	591	76.7	15.5	116.5
1981	9.19	89.6	576	74.7	15.9	119.6
1982	9.43	91.9	566	73.4	16.7	125.6
1983	9.48	92.4	553	71.7	17.1	128.6
1984	9.56	93.2	536	69.5	17.8	133.8
1985	9.56	93.2	525	68.1	18.2	136.8
1986	9.61	93.7	526	68.2	18.3	137.6
1987	9.88	96.3	514	66.7	19.2	144.4
1988	10.12	98.6R	509R	66.0R	19.9R	150.4R
1989	10.38	101.2	506	65.6	20.5	154.1

(P) =Preliminary

Household Energy Consumption and Expenditures by Application and Fuel Source, 1978-1987

Source: Energy Information Administration. *Annual Energy Review 1990*

Application/Fuel Source	Consumption (Quadrillion Btu)				Expenditures (Billion Dollars)			
	1978	1980	1984	1987	1978	1980	1984	1987
Space Heating								
Natural Gas	4.26	3.32	3.51	3.38	$11.49	$12.80	$20.66	$18.05
Electricity[1]	0.41	0.28	0.30	0.28	3.53	3.71	5.71	5.53
Distillate Fuel Oil and Kerosene	2.05	1.32	1.10	1.05	8.06	10.59	8.51	6.25
Liquefied Petrol. Gases .	0.23	0.25	0.21	0.22	1.05	1.90	2.00	1.85
Total	6.95	5.17	5.13	4.94	24.14	29.00	36.85	31.68
Air Conditioning[2]								
Electricity[1]	0.31	0.32	0.36	0.44	3.97	5.07	7.51	9.77
Water Heating								
Natural Gas	1.04	1.24	1.10	1.10	2.88	4.79	6.63	6.02
Electricity[1]	0.29	0.31	0.32	0.31	3.15	4.54	6.44	6.45
Distillate Fuel Oil and Kerosene	0.14	0.24	0.15	0.17	0.56	1.89	1.09	0.94
Liquefied Petrol. Gases .	0.06	0.07	0.06	0.06	0.36	0.59	0.58	0.50
Total	1.53	1.86	1.62	1.64	6.94	11.80	14.76	13.91
Appliances								
Natural Gas	0.28	0.38	0.35	0.34	0.93	1.71	2.31	2.02
Electricity[1]	1.46	1.55	1.53	1.72	19.24	26.82	34.95	39.83
Liquefied Petrol. Gases .	0.03	0.04	0.04	0.04	0.25	0.41	0.54	0.46
Total	1.77	1.97	1.92	2.10	20.42	28.94	37.81	42.33
Total[2]	10.56	9.32	9.04	9.13	55.47	74.81	97.00	97.75
Natural Gas[2]	5.58	4.94	4.98	4.83	15.30	19.30	29.80	26.15
Electricity[1]	2.47	2.46	2.48	2.76	29.89	40.14	54.50	61.58
Distillate Fuel Oil and Kerosene	2.19	1.55	1.26	1.22	8.62	12.48	9.60	7.21
Liquefied Petrol. Gases .	0.33	0.36	0.31	0.32	1.66	2.89	3.10	2.81

(1) Includes electricity generated for distribution from wood, waste, geothermal, wind, photovoltaic, and solar thermal electricity. (2) A small amount of natural gas used for air conditioning is included in "Total" and "Natural Gas" under "Total."
Note: Sum of components may not equal total due to independent rounding.

World Nuclear Power

Source: International Atomic Energy Agency, Dec. 31, 1990

Country	Reactors in Operation No. of Units	Reactors in Operation Total MW(e)[1]	Reactors under Construction No. of Units	Reactors under Construction Total MW(e)[1]	Nuclear Electricity Supplied, 1990 TW(e) .h[1]	Nuclear Electricity Supplied, 1990 % of Total	Total Operating Experience to December 31, 1990 Years	Total Operating Experience to December 31, 1990 Months
Argentina	2	935	1	692	6.6	19.8	24	7
Belgium	7	5,500	—	—	40.4	60.1	100	7
Brazil	1	626	1	1,245	2.1	1.0	8	9
Bulgaria	5	2,585	2	1,906	13.5	35.7	53	8
Canada	20	13,993	2	1,762	68.8	14.8	243	1
China[2]	—	—	3	2,148	—	—	—	—
Cuba	—	—	2	816	—	—	—	—
Czechoslovakia	8	3,264	6	3,336	23.0	28.4	60	1
Finland	4	2,310	—	—	18.1	35.0	47	4
France	56	55,778	6	8,305	297.7	74.5	598	8
Germany[3]	26	24,430	6	3,319	139.1	33.1	406	5
Hungary	4	1,645	—	—	12.9	51.4	22	2
India	7	1,374	7	1,540	5.1	2.2	86	1
Iran	—	—	2	2,392	—	—	—	—
Italy	—	—	—	—	—	—	81	0
Japan	41	30,917	10	9,012	186.4	27.1	472	8
Korea, South	9	7,220	2	1,900	50.2	49.1	54	1
Mexico	1	654	1	654	2.9	2.6	1	9
Netherlands	2	508	—	—	3.3	4.9	39	9
Pakistan	1	125	—	—	0.4	1.1E	19	3
Romania	—	—	5	3,125	—	—	—	—
S. Africa	2	1,842	—	—	8.4	5.6	12	3
Spain	9	7,067	—	—	51.9	35.9	101	7
Sweden	12	9,817	—	—	65.3	45.9	159	2
Switzerland	5	2,952	—	—	22.3	42.6	78	10
United Kingdom	37	11,506	1	1,188	58.6	19.7	888	10
United States	112	100,630	1	1,165	576.8	20.6	1,482	9
USSR	45	34,673	25	21,255	211.5	12.2	514	3
Yugoslavia	1	632	—	—	4.4	5.3	9	3
Total*	423[2]	325,873[2]	83[4]	65,760[4]	1,901.2	—	5,622	11

1 terawatt-hour (TW(e).h) = 10[6] megawatt-hour (MW(e).h). For an average power plant, 1 TW(e).h = 0.39 megatonnes of coal equivalent (input) and 0.23 megatonnes of oil equivalent (input). (2) Total includes data for Taiwan, China: 6 units, 4890 MW(e) in operation; 31.6 TW(e).h of nuclear electricity generation, or 35.2% of total electricity generated there; 56 yrs., 1 month of total operating experience. (3) Germany reported DE-4, AVR-Juelich as shut down in 1988. (4) Construction was cancelled for 3 reactors during 1990. E = Estimate.

U.S. Nuclear Power Plant Operations

Source: Energy Information Administration, *Monthly Energy Review*, March 1991

	Operable Reactors Number	Nuclear-Based Electricity Generation Million Net Kilowatthours	Nuclear Portion of Domestic Electricity Generation Percent		Operable Reactors Number	Nuclear-Based Electricity Generation Million Net Kilowatthours	Nuclear Portion of Domestic Electricity Generation Percent
1976	61	191,104	9.4	1984	86	327,634	13.6
1977	65	250,883	11.8	1985	95	383,691	15.5
1978	70	276,403	12.5	1986	100	414,038	16.6
1979	68	255,155	11.4	1987	107	455,270	17.7
1980	70	251,116	11.0	1988	108	526,973	19.5
1981	74	272,674	11.9	1989	110	529,355	19.0
1982	77	282,773	12.6	1990	111	576,784	20.6
1983	80	293,677	12.7				

Status of U.S. Nuclear Reactor Units

Source: Energy Information Administration, *Monthly Energy Review*, March 1991

	Licensed for Operation Operable	Licensed for Operation In Startup	Construction Permits Granted	Construction Permits Pending	On Order	Announced	Total	Total Design Capacity Million Net Kilowatts
			Number of Reactor Units					
1980	70	2	82	12	3	0	169	163
1981	74	0	75	11	3	0	163	157
1982	77	2	60	3	2	0	144	135
1983	80	3	53	0	2	0	138	129
1984	86	6	38	0	2	0	132	123
1985	95	3	30	0	2	0	130	121
1986	100	7	19	0	2	0	128	119
1987	107	4	14	0	2	0	127	119
1988	108	3	12	0	0	0	123	115
1989	110	1	10	0	0	0	121	113
1990	111	0	9	0	0	0	120	113

SCIENCE AND TECHNOLOGY

Scientific Achievements and Discoveries: 1991

Origins of Life on Earth

Antarctica was connected to the western coast of North America about half a billion years ago, according to Eldridge M. Moores of the Univ. of Calif. at Davis and Ian W.D. Dalziel of the Univ. of Texas at Austin. The geologists' theory is the first to suggest that the two land masses were once linked. Their theory holds that the Earth's land masses were once arranged so differently that North America looked like a slice of pizza between Antarctica and South America. The change in the Earth's appearance came during the Late Precambrian geological period (from a billion to half a billion years ago) before life emerged from the sea. The theory supports the idea that a continental mass was torn away from North America on a line that runs down through the middle of the Rocky Mountains today.

Tiny glass fragments from Haiti, presumably produced in the extreme heat of an asteroid or comet impact, are the clearest evidence yet that a massive object from outer space smashed into Earth 65 million years ago, at the time of the mass extinction of the dinosaurs and many other forms of life. Analysis of the glass fragments by a team of geologists led by Haraldur Sigurdsson of the Univ. of Rhode Island has provided evidence to raise doubts about the theory that widespread volcanic eruptions caused the ecological disaster at the time. The new theory states that the extraterrestrial impact very likely occurred in the area of the Gulf of Mexico or the Caribbean Sea. A crater on the Yucatan Peninsula, long since covered by sediment, may be the place where the object hit and scattered glassy debris at least as far as Haiti.

For the first time, scientists have firmly established that Neanderthals lived in Western Europe as recently as 36,000 years ago. This is several thousand years after the first modern humans are believed to have appeared there. The finding, by a group of French scientists, supports the view that anatomically modern people did not evolve from Neanderthals, but rather coexisted with and eventually supplanted them through superior intellect and culture. The finding also strengthens the notion that modern humans first appeared in one region, probably Africa, and then colonized the world. The conclusions are primarily based on a Neanderthal skeleton discovered at an archeological site near the village of St. Cesaire, north of Bordeaux, France.

Astronomical Findings

Astronomers at the Nuffield Radio Astronomy Laboratories at the Univ. of Manchester in England believe they have discovered a planet (defined as any large object that orbits a star) around a distant star. The discovery would be the first established detection of a planet beyond the solar system. The massive object appears to be orbiting the remnant of a star that collapsed in a violent explosion. Although the existence of other planetary systems is generally assumed, astronomers have yet to find conclusive evidence of their existence, and as a result, the British findings have been met with great doubt and caution.

An object more distant from Earth than any seen before, some 12 billion light-years away, was discovered by astronomers from Princeton University's Inst. for Advanced Study, and the Calif. Inst. of Technology. The faint object, a quasar that shines with a brightness comparable to that of hundreds of galaxies, was found by using the 200-inch telescope at Mt. Palomar, Calif. Because of the great distance its light had to cover before reaching Earth, astronomers are seeing the quasar as it was some 12 billion years ago, when the universe was very young. Quasars are found near the edge of the observable universe.

Based on findings from a German X-ray telescope orbiting Earth, theories on the origin of the universe have been brought into question. The telescope has detected strong evidence indicating the extensive clustering of quasars. The Big Bang theory holds that the universe began in an explosive instant with all matter and energy expanding in a smooth condition. The observation of clusters of quasars makes this theory difficult to prove. Another theory, the cold dark matter model, which proposes that cold invisible matter is a major attractive force, is also in dispute as a result of the latest findings.

The much maligned Hubble Space Telescope has revealed two extremely large and hot stars expelling large amounts of matter, which observers believe is a prelude to their impending destruction in catastrophic explosions. Hubble has also revealed an image of a luminous ring of matter surrounding a star that has already exploded. One of the stars is Melnick 42, which is 169,000 light-years away in the galaxy called the Large Magellanic Cloud. Melnick is 80 to 100 times more massive, 8 times hotter, and a million times brighter than the Sun. However, it is only 2 million years old, compared with the 4.6 billion-year-old solar system. Scientists predict that Melnick should explode as a supernova in the next million years or so, while the Sun is expected to continue shining for several billion years.

The Magellan space probe launched in May 1989, has completed its first survey of Venus. It has produced detailed images of the surface of Venus composed of huge lava flows, thousands of cracks and craters, and numerous features indicating the forces of volcanic activity. Magellan has also produced the first before and after pictures ever made of a huge landslide that is believed to have been caused by a "venus-quake."

Genetics

Geneticists have found that genes may behave differently depending on whether they are inherited from the father or the mother. This finding contradicts longstanding belief based on Gregor Mendel's conclusion that inheritable characteristics are passed down from parent to offspring and the results are the same no matter which parent contributes a gene. Geneticists now suspect that some common diseases, such as juvenile diabetes and congenital heart disease, may be "preferentially" passed on.

Two cancer patients, a 29-year-old woman and a 42-year-old man, who were not expected to live more than a few months, became the first people to receive gene therapy in an attempt to defeat otherwise incurable tumors. The patients, who were both suffering from metastatic melanoma, a lethal type of skin cancer, were infused with about 100 million white blood cells, which enfolded a genetically engineered copy of a gene that makes a potent anti-cancer enzyme. Six months after the first treatment, Steven A. Rosenberg of the National Cancer Inst. announced that both patients were still alive and that two other patients with advanced melanoma were added to the therapy program. Dr. Rosenberg said that it was too early to tell whether any of the patients were benefiting from their twice-weekly infusions, but that he remained "desperate and optimistic."

Researchers have identified the **gene behind Marfan syndrome**, a common disease of the body's connective tissue. Isolation of the gene will lead, it is hoped, to a simple test for detecting those who carry the trait for the disease. Marfan syndrome is thought to be the cause for **Abraham Lincoln's** towering frame and outsized hands and feet. A committee has received permission to examine samples of Lincoln's hair, bone chips, and blood, obtained at the time of the President's assassination, to determine if he suffered from the potentially fatal disease.

Among the latest findings on the **genetic basis of disease**, researchers have determined the general location of a gene that appears to cause a common form of diabetes, isolated a gene that initiates **colon cancer**, found that a tiny mutation in a particular gene causes **Alzheimer's disease** (which now afflicts 1 in 5 Americans who live to age 85); and discovered the gene apparently responsible for the most common type of inherited **mental retardation**.

Linda Buck and Richard Axel, of the Howard Hughes Medical Inst. at Columbia Univ., have discovered a huge **family of genes that are active exclusively in nose cells**, which help to explain the fundamental **mechanism of smell**. Each of the different genes seems designed to respond to a small group of different odors, and together the sensory genes can recognize all the 10,000 or so scents that mammals can smell.

Medicine

According to research findings of Simon LeVay, a neurobiologist at the Salk Inst. in La Jolla, Calif., the **brains of homosexual men are structurally different from those of heterosexual men** in a region thought to influence male sexual behavior. LeVay reported that in homosexual men, one segment of the **hypothalmus**, an important structure in the forebrain, is only a quarter to a half the size of the same region in heterosexual men. If the findings are confirmed, it would be the first time that **sexual preference could be explained at the biological level**. The findings are preliminary and involve only a small number of brain tissue samples. Other scientists reacted cautiously, stressing the importance of social environment, regardless of any biological link, in shaping and defining sexuality.

In Dec. 1990, the U.S. Food and Drug Admin. approved the **first substantially new contraceptive in 25 years**. The new method consists of a set of small soft tubes that are implanted under a woman's skin, where they release a hormone that can prevent conception for five years. **Norplant**, sold in the U.S. by Wyeth-Ayerst Laboratories, is thus far the **most effective contraceptive ever put on the market**, with a reported failure rate one-tenth to one-twentieth that of birth control pills, which fail 6 percent of the time. The implant is particularly valuable for women who want long-term protection, but do not wish to be sterilized. Fertility is restored by the next menstrual cycle after the implants are removed.

The results of a large study by the **United Network for Organ Sharing** show that 92 percent of those who receive a kidney from a cadaver live at least one year after the transplant. The study of all 12,735 transplants of five major organs performed in 1988 also showed that the one-year survival rate for those who received a pancreas was 89 percent; a heart, 83 percent; a liver, 76 percent; a lung, 48 percent; and a heart-lung combination, 57 percent.

A report, based on the examination of nearly 27,000 cases of birth defects, concludes that the **rate of common birth defects does not rise even as women who give birth approach their late 40's.** The report challenges the conventional belief that older women are at greater risk of having infants with birth defects. The analysis does not include cases of Down's syndrome, which are known to be more prevalent among older women, but does include such disorders as spina bifida, cleft palate, hair lip, heart defects, and limb deformities. Patricia A. Baird of the Univ. of British Columbia, the primary author of the report, said, "We can now reassure an older woman that if the amnio (fluid tested in the prenatal stage) is O.K., she should feel just as optimistic about the outcome of her pregnancy as a younger woman."

AIDS

Based on World Health Organization estimates, **40 million people are expected to be infected with HIV,** the virus that causes AIDS, by the year 2000. As of June 1991, there are an estimated 10 million infected adults; more than 366,000 cases have been reported in 162 countries. According to W.H.O. official James Chin, "Increasingly, **heterosexual transmission will become the predominant mode of HIV transmission throughout the world,**" and women will account for increasing numbers of cases. Heterosexual transmission is expected to account for up to 70 percent of the infections and homosexual transmission about 10 percent. Intravenous drug users will account for 10 percent. About **500,000 children now have AIDS,** due to transmission of the virus from their mothers in pregnancy. As of May 31, 1991, the Federal Centers for Disease Control in Atlanta said that **179,136 Americans have been afflicted with AIDS since 1981.** U.S. Department of Health and Human Services reported that AIDS killed 24,120 people in the U.S. in 1990, an increase of 13 percent from 1989.

Dissociative Disorder

An unusual and difficult to explain **sense of remoteness** is emerging as one of the most common feelings people have in life-threatening accidents, according to recent studies. Surprisingly, the same research suggests that bizarre experiences like the sense of being an automaton, **feelings of unreality** and amnesia are far more prevalent among otherwise normal people than psychiatrists had believed. If these experiences are severe and disruptive, such experiences may indicate that a person suffers from one of a group of psychiatric problems known as dissociative disorders. From 5 to 10 percent of the general population may suffer from such disorders, according to estimates from the first systematic study of their prevalence, conducted by Colin Ross, a psychiatrist at the Univ. of Manitoba. Based on a survey of 1,055 men and women in Canada, the study found that 29 percent said they occasionally felt as though they were **watching themselves in a movie.** While only 1 percent said it happened all of the time, 14 percent of the people said they sometimes looked in a mirror and **could not recognize themselves.** Many of the symptoms of dissociative disorder are familiar to most people from time to time, such as realizing that one has not heard part of a conversation. Marlene Steinberg, a psychiatrist at Yale Univ. medical school, said, "The symptoms are elusive because they involve a strange sense of absence of feeling or curious sense of reality."

Puberty and Evolution

The high numbers of girls in their early teens who become mothers, especially in American cities, are responding to a pattern in human evolution that induces people growing up in extremely stressful circumstances to **bear children early and often.** This controversial theory, drawing on sociobiology, posits that teenage mothers are implementing a reproductive strategy which, from an evolutionary viewpoint, is a wise decision.

Jay Belsky, a psychologist at Pennsylvania State Univ., who is the leading formulator of the new theory, believes that children who grow up in dangerous conditions are encouraged to increase the chances of having their genes survive into the next generation by choosing earlier sexual relations, earlier motherhood, and more children. One of the more noteworthy predictions of the theory is that girls who grow up in households where there is great emotional stress, and especially where the father is absent, will undergo **puberty at an earlier age** than other girls. "We propose that the time of puberty is regulated and influenced to some extent by these earlier experiences, rather than being a fixed biological given," said Dr. Belsky.

Patents

New methods to measure **a nation's technical strength, based on an analysis of influential patents,** show that while the United States ranks first in the world, Japan is quickly gaining. The technical strength is measured by an index based on the number of influential patents a nation holds. Through 1989, according to this index, the U.S. placed first, with Japan in second place and Germany a distant third. The other top-rated nations, in order, were: Great Britain; France; the Netherlands; Switzerland; Canada; Sweden; Italy; Taiwan; South Korea; U.S.S.R.; Belgium; and Panama. (Scores for Taiwan, South Korea and U.S.S.R. were estimated.) The competition between the U.S. and Japan is typified by Hitachi of Japan recently surpassing I.B.M. in overall technical strength and by Fuji Photo overtaking Eastman Kodak. The patent data is compiled by CHI Research Inc., of Haddon Heights, N.J., which tracks technical trends for the U.S. government. To create the index, the importance of a nation's patents and scientific papers are measured by analyzing how frequently they are cited, revealing the extent of high-quality work and providing an indication of industrial health and future prosperity. Scientific papers are important because inventors increasingly rely on them when developing their own ideas. **Citation analysis** (the method used to judge papers' value) has limitations, including the tendency of authors and inventors to cite their own work disproportionately and the tendency of certain papers or patents to become highly cited merely because they document a method or technique that becomes widely used. Additionally, some critics say cultural differences in the significance placed on patents can skew the results.

The **5 millionth U.S patent** has been given to researchers at the Univ. of Florida for a **genetically engineered microbe** that helps convert wastepaper and yard trash into ethanol fuel. The new bacteria can convert most sugars, making it possible to extract fuel from almost anything produced by plants (grass clippings, wheat stalks, cardboard, grocery bags, and newsprint). The new microbe was developed by Lonnie O. Ingram, a professor of microbiology at the Univ. of Florida; Tyrell Conway, a former post-doctoral student at the university; and Flavio Alterthum, a visiting professor who is now chairman of the microbiology department at the Univ. of Sao Paulo in Brazil.

Some of the more "interesting" U.S. patents awarded in 1991 include: a treatment to speed the healing of bone fractures using electromagnetic fields; a machine to **measure the fats, oils, and moisture in baked goods** as they come off the assembly line; a device to politely **deflect unwanted phone calls** with the push of a button—the person receiving the call can hang up and activate a recorded message that explains that he or she does not accept such calls (the device allows people to prepare alternate messages as well); a system that tells **golfers** on a driving range where their balls have landed; a **life-expectancy timepiece** to tell people how much time they have before they will die—people would set the starting point for the countdown by using actuarial tables to determine their life expectancy based on their age, health, and other life-style factors; a sheet of wire mesh that is designed to reinforce asphalt patchwork and **prevent** it from sinking and cracking and forming a **pothole**; a device that **measures a person's exposure to ultraviolet rays** and sounds an alarm when it is too great; a room **air-conditioner that blows air over ice,** which is quieter, more convenient, and, in some cases, cheaper to operate than those more modern units on the market today; a hand-held device to accurately **distinguish life and death,** designed to pick up faint electrical signals from the heart and brain that may be otherwise difficult to obtain in a person whose heartbeat and breathing may have stopped; a **magnetic hammer** intended to make it easier to bang in nails without striking one's fingers by allowing a person to position the nail without having to hold it by hand; an **orbital debris sweeper** to clear particles of fast-moving space waste from the paths of satellites and other spacecraft; software that allows **telephones to ring with different melodies,** depending on the source of a call; an **automobile cruise-control** system that automatically adjusts the car's speed to keep a safe distance from vehicles in front; a new **breathing tube** that makes it much safer to put patients on mechanical respirators (by 71-year-old Henry J. Heimlich, who pioneered the Heimlich maneuver, the technique for helping choking victims to breathe again); a battery-powered device that uses a small electrical jolt to **take the itch out of bug bites;** a device that combines the ancient Chinese practice of acupuncture with modern electronics to **bring relief from nausea** without the use of drugs; and a device that can **measure the presence of alcohol** within 15 seconds by analyzing vapor from the tears in an eye.

Inventors Hall of Fame

The National Inventors Hall of Fame selected Gertrude Belle Elion to be honored for her pioneering research at the Burroughs Wellcome Co. that led to the development of drugs to combat leukemia, septic shock and tissue rejection in patients undergoing kidney transplants. The 73-year-old Ms. Elion became the **first woman to be named to the Hall of Fame,** a nonprofit organization based in Akron, Ohio, established in 1973. Inductees are selected by a panel of scientists, patent attorneys, and other experts. As of March 1991, 94 inventors had been named to the hall.

Critical Technologies

In April 1991, the White House listed 22 areas of technological development that should be treated as "critical to the national prosperity and to national security." The 22 areas of technology are: surface transportation; environment; materials processing; electronic and photomic materials; ceramics; composites; high-performance metals and alloys; flexible computer integrated manufacturing; intelligent processing equipment; micro-and nano-fabrication; systems-management; software; microelectronics and optoelectronics; high-performance computing/networking; high-definition imaging and displays; sensors and signal processing; data storage; computer simulation; applied molecular biology; medical; aeronautics; and energy.

Inventions and Discoveries

Invention	Date	Inventor	Nation.
Adding machine	1642	Pascal	French
Adding machine	1885	Burroughs	U.S.
Aerosol spray	1926	Rotheim	Norwegian
Air brake	1868	Westinghouse	U.S.
Air conditioning	1911	Carrier	U.S.
Air pump	1654	Guericke	German
Airplane, automatic pilot	1912	Sperry	U.S.
Airplane, experimental	1896	Langley	U.S.
Airplane jet engine	1939	Ohain	German
Airplane with motor	1903	Wright bros.	U.S.
Airplane, hydro	1911	Curtiss	U.S.
Airship	1852	Giffard	French
Airship, rigid dirigible	1900	Zeppelin	German
Arc welder	1919	Thomson	U.S.
Autogyro	1920	de la Cierva	Spanish
Automobile, differential gear	1885	Benz	German
Automobile, electric	1892	Morrison	U.S.
Automobile, exp'mtl	1864	Marcus	Austrian
Automobile, gasoline	1889	Daimler	German
Automobile, gasoline	1892	Duryea	U.S.
Automobile magneto	1897	Bosch	German
Automobile muffler	...	Maxim, H.P.	U.S.
Automobile self-starter	1911	Kettering	U.S.
Babbitt metal	1839	Babbitt	U.S.
Bakelite	1907	Baekeland	Belg., U.S.
Balloon	1783	Montgolfier	French
Barometer	1643	Torricelli	Italian
Bicycle, modern	1885	Starley	English
Bifocal lens	1780	Franklin	U.S.
Block signals, railway	1867	Hall	U.S.
Bomb, depth	1916	Tait	U.S.
Bottle machine	1895	Owens	U.S.
Braille printing	1829	Braille	French
Burner, gas	1855	Bunsen	German
Calculating machine	1833	Babbage	English
Camera—see also Photography			
Camera, Kodak	1888	Eastman, Walker	U.S.
Camera, Polaroid Land	1948	Land	U.S.
Car coupler	1873	Janney	U.S.
Carburetor, gasoline	1893	Maybach	German
Card time recorder	1894	Cooper	U.S.
Carding machine	1797	Whittemore	U.S.
Carpet sweeper	1876	Bissell	U.S.
Cassette, audio	1963	Philips Co.	Dutch
Cassette, videotape	1969	Sony	Japanese
Cash register	1879	Ritty	U.S.
Cathode ray oscilloscope	1897	Braun	German
Cathode ray tube	1878	Crookes	English
CAT scan (computerized tomography)	1973	Hounsfield	English
Cellophane	1908	Brandenberger	Swiss
Celluloid	1870	Hyatt	U.S.
Cement, Portland	1824	Aspdin	English
Chronometer	1761	Harrison	English
Circuit breaker	1925	Hilliard	U.S.
Circuit, integrated	1959	Kilby, Noyce, Texas Instr	U.S
Clock, pendulum	1657	Huygens	Dutch
Coaxial cable system	1929	Affel, Espensched	U.S.
Coke oven	1893	Hoffman	Austrian
Compressed air rock drill	1871	Ingersoll	U.S.
Comptometer	1887	Felt	U.S.
Computer, automatic sequence	1944	Aiken et al.	U.S.
Computer, mini	1960	Digital Corp.	U.S.
Condenser microphone (telephone)	1916	Wente	U.S.
Contraceptive, oral	1954	Pincus, Rock	U.S.
Corn, hybrid	1917	Jones	U.S.
Cotton gin	1793	Whitney	U.S.
Cream separator	1878	DeLaval	Swedish
Cultivator, disc	1878	Mallon	U.S.
Cystoscope	1878	Nitze	German

Invention	Date	Inventor	Nation.
Electrocardiograph	1903	Einthoven	Dutch
Electroencephalograph	1929	Berger	German
Electromagnet	1824	Sturgeon	English
Electron spectrometer	1944	Deutsch, Elliott, Evans	U.S.
Electron tube multigrid	1913	Langmuir	U.S.
Electroplating	1805	Brugnatelli	Italian
Electrostatic generator	1929	Van de Graaff	U.S.
Elevator brake	1852	Otis	U.S.
Elevator, push button	1922	Larson	U.S.
Engine, automatic transmission	1910	Fottinger	German
Engine, coal-gas 4-cycle	1876	Otto	German
Engine, compression ignition	1883	Daimler	German
Engine, electric ignition	1883	Benz	German
Engine, gas, compound	1926	Eickemeyer	U.S.
Engine, gas, gasoline	1872	Brayton, Geo.	U.S.
Engine, gasoline	1889	Daimler	German
Engine, steam, piston	1705	Newcomen	English
Engine, steam, piston	1769	Watt	Scottish
Engraving, half-tone	1852	Talbot	U.S.
Fiberglass	1938	Owens-Corning	U.S.
Fiber optics	1955	Kapany	English
Filament, tungsten	1913	Coolidge	U.S.
Flanged rail	1831	Stevens	U.S.
Flatiron, electric	1882	Seely	U.S.
Food, frozen	1924	Birdseye	U.S.
Furnace (for steel)	1858	Siemens	German
Galvanometer	1820	Swieger	German
Gas discharge tube	1922	Hull	U.S.
Gas lighting	1792	Murdoch	Scottish
Gas mantle	1885	Welsbach	Austrian
Gasoline (lead ethyl)	1922	Midgley	U.S.
Gasoline, cracked	1913	Burton	U.S.
Gasoline, high octane	1930	Ipatieff	Russian
Geiger counter	1913	Geiger	German
Glass, laminated safety	1909	Benedictus	French
Glider	1853	Cayley	English
Gun, breechloader	1811	Thornton	U.S.
Gun, Browning	1897	Browning	U.S.
Gun, magazine	1875	Hotchkiss	U.S.
Gun, silencer	1908	Maxim, H.P.	U.S.
Guncotton	1847	Schoenbein	German
Gyrocompass	1911	Sperry	U.S.
Gyroscope	1852	Foucault	French
Harvester-thresher	1818	Lane	U.S.
Heart, artificial	1982	Jarvik	U.S.
Helicopter	1939	Sikorsky	U.S.
Hydrometer	1768	Baume	French
Ice-making machine	1851	Gorrie	U.S.
Iron lung	1928	Drinker, Shaw	U.S.
Kaleidoscope	1817	Brewster	Scottish
Kinetoscope	1889	Edison	U.S.
Lacquer, nitrocellulose	1921	Flaherty	U.S.
Lamp, arc	1847	Staite	English

(continued)

Invention	Date	Inventor	Nation.
Lamp, flourescent	1938	General Electric, Westinghouse	U.S.
Lamp, incandescent	1879	Edison	U.S.
Lamp, incand., frosted	1924	Pipkin	U.S.
Lamp, incand., gas	1913	Langmuir	U.S.
Lamp, Klieg	1911	Kliegl, A.&J.	U.S.
Lamp, mercury vapor	1912	Hewitt	U.S.
Lamp, miner's safety	1816	Davy	English
Lamp, neon	1909	Claude	French
Lathe, turret	1845	Fitch	U.S.
Launderette	1934	Cantrell	U.S.
Lens, achromatic	1758	Dollond	English
Lens, fused bifocal	1908	Borsch	U.S.
Leydenjar (condenser)	1745	von Kleist	German
Lightning rod	1752	Franklin	U.S.
Linoleum	1860	Walton	English
Linotype	1884	Mergenthaler	U.S.
Lock, cylinder	1851	Yale	U.S.
Locomotive, electric	1851	Vail	U.S.
Locomotive, exp'mtl	1802	Trevithick	English
Locomotive, exp'mtl	1812	Fenton et al.	English
Locomotive, exp'mtl	1813	Hedley	English
Locomotive, exp'mtl	1814	Stephenson	English
Locomotive practical	1829	Stephenson	English
Locomotive, 1st U.S.	1830	Cooper, P.	U.S.
Loom, power	1785	Cartwright	English
Loudspeaker, dynamic	1924	Rice, Kellogg	U.S.
Machine gun	1861	Gatling	U.S.
Machine gun, improved	1872	Hotchkiss	U.S.
Machine gun (Maxim)	1883	Maxim, H.S.U.S., Eng.	
Magnet, electro	1828	Henry	U.S.
Mantle, gas	1885	Welsbach	Austrian
Mason jar	1858	Mason, J.	U.S.
Match, friction	1827	John Walker	English
Mercerized textiles	1843	Mercer, J.	English
Meter, induction	1888	Shallenberg	U.S.
Metronome	1816	Malezel	German
Micrometer	1636	Gascoigne	English
Microphone	1877	Berliner	U.S.
Microscope, compound	1590	Janssen	Dutch
Microscope, electronic	1931	Knoll, Ruska	German
Microscope, field ion.	1951	Mueller	German
Monitor, warship	1861	Ericsson	U.S.
Monotype	1887	Lanston	U.S.
Motor, AC	1892	Tesla	U.S.
Motor, DC	1837	Davenport	U.S.
Motor, induction	1887	Tesla	U.S.
Motorcycle	1885	Daimler	German
Movie machine	1894	Jenkins	U.S.
Movie, panoramic	1952	Waller	U.S.
Movie, talking	1927	Warner Bros.	U.S.
Mower, lawn	1831	Budding, Ferrabee	English
Mowing machine	1822	Bailey	U.S.
Neoprene	1930	Carothers	U.S.
Nylon synthetic	1930	Carothers	U.S.
Nylon	1937	Du Pont lab.	U.S.
Oil cracking furnace	1891	Gavrilov	Russian
Oil filled power cable	1921	Emanueli	Italian
Oleomargarine	1869	Mege-Mouries	French
Ophthalmoscope	1851	Helmholtz	German
Paper machine	1809	Dickinson	U.S.
Parachute	1785	Blanchard	French
Pen, ballpoint	1838	Biro	Hungarian
Pen, fountain	1884	Waterman	U.S.
Pen, steel	1780	Harrison	English
Pendulum	1583	Galileo	Italian
Percussion cap	1807	Forsythe	Scottish
Phonograph	1877	Edison	U.S.
Photo, color	1892	Ives	U.S.
Photo film, celluloid	1893	Reichenbach	U.S.
Photo film, transparent	1884	Eastman, Goodwin	U.S.
Photoelectric cell	1895	Elster	German
Photographic paper	1835	Talbot	U.S.
Photography	1835	Talbot	English
Photography	1835	Daguerre	French
Photography	1816	Niepce	French
Photophone	1880	Bell	U.S.-Scot.
Phototelegraphy	1925	Bell Labs	U.S.
Piano	1709	Cristofori	Italian
Piano, player	1863	Fourneaux	French
Pin, safety	1849	Hunt	U.S.
Pistol (revolver)	1836	Colt	U.S.

Invention	Date	Inventor	Nation.
Plow, cast iron	1785	Ransome	English
Plow, disc	1896	Hardy	U.S.
Pneumatic hammer	1890	King	U.S.
Powder, smokeless	1884	Vieille	French
Printing press, rotary	1845	Hoe	U.S.
Printing press, web	1865	Bullock	U.S.
Propeller, screw	1804	Stevens	U.S.
Propeller, screw	1837	Ericsson	Swedish
Pulsars	1967	Bell	English
Punch card accounting	1889	Hollerith	U.S.
Quasars	1963	Schmidt	U.S.
Radar	1940	Watson-Watt	Scottish
Radio amplifier	1906	De Forest	U.S.
Radio beacon	1928	Donovan	U.S.
Radio crystal oscillator	1918	Nicolson	U.S.
Radio receiver, cascade tuning	1913	Alexanderson,	U.S.
Radio receiver, heterodyne	1913	Fessenden	U.S.
Radio transmitter triode modulation	1914	Alexanderson	U.S.
Radio tube-diode	1905	Fleming	English
Radio tube oscillator	1915	De Forest	U.S.
Radio tube triode	1906	De Forest	U.S.
Radio, signals	1895	Marconi	Italian
Radio, magnetic detector	1902	Marconi	Italian
Radio FM 2-path	1933	Armstrong	U.S.
Rayon	1883	Swan	English
Razor, electric	1917	Schick	U.S.
Razor, safety	1895	Gillette	U.S.
Reaper	1834	McCormick	U.S.
Record, cylinder	1887	Bell, Tainter	U.S.
Record, disc	1887	Berliner	U.S.
Record, long playing	1947	Goldmark	U.S.
Record, wax cylinder	1888	Edison	U.S.
Refrigerants, low-boiling fluorine compound	1930	Midgely and co-workers	U.S.
Refrigerator car	1868	David	U.S.
Resin, synthetic	1931	Hill	English
Richter scale	1935	Richter	U.S.
Rifle, repeating	1860	Spencer	U.S.
Rocket engine	1926	Goddard	U.S.
Rubber, vulcanized	1839	Goodyear	U.S.
Saw, band	1808	Newberry	English
Saw, circular	1777	Miller	English
Searchlight, arc	1915	Sperry	U.S.
Sewing machine	1846	Howe	U.S.
Shoe-sewing machine	1860	McKay	U.S.
Shrapnel shell	1784	Shrapnel	English
Shuttle, flying	1733	Kay	English
Sleeping-car	1865	Pullman	U.S.
Slide rule	1620	Oughtred	English
Soap, hardwater	1928	Bertsch	German
Spectroscope	1859	Kirchoff, Bunsen	German
Spectroscope (mass)	1918	Dempster	U.S.
Spinning jenny	1767	Hargreaves	English
Spinning mule	1779	Crompton	English
Steamboat, exp'mtl	1778	Jouffroy	French
Steamboat, exp'mtl	1785	Fitch	U.S.
Steamboat, exp'mtl	1787	Rumsey	U.S.
Steamboat, exp'mtl	1788	Miller	Scottish
Steamboat, exp'mtl	1803	Fulton	U.S.
Steamboat, exp'mtl	1804	Stevens	U.S.
Steamboat, practical	1802	Symington	Scottish
Steamboat, practical	1807	Fulton	U.S.
Steam car	1770	Cugnot	French
Steam turbine	1884	Parsons	English
Steel (converter)	1856	Bessemer	English
Steel alloy	1891	Harvey	U.S.
Steel alloy, high-speed	1901	Taylor, White	U.S.
Steel, electric	1900	Heroult	French
Steel, manganese	1884	Hadfield	English
Steel, stainless	1916	Brearley	English
Stereoscope	1838	Wheatstone	English
Stethoscope	1819	Laennec	French
Stethoscope, binaural	1840	Cammann	U.S.
Stock ticker	1870	Edison	U.S.
Storage battery, rechargeable	1859	Plante	French
Stove, electric	1896	Hadaway	U.S.
Submarine	1891	Holland	U.S.
Submarine, even keel	1894	Lake	U.S.

Invention	Date	Inventor	Nation.
Submarine, torpedo	1776	Bushnell	U.S.
Superconductivity (BCS theory	1957	Bardeen, Cooper, Schreiffer	U.S.
Tank, military	1914	Swinton	English
Tape recorder, magnetic	1899	Poulsen	Danish
Teflon	1938	Du Pont	U.S.
Telegraph, magnetic	1837	Morse	U.S.
Telegraph, quadruplex	1864	Edison	U.S.
Telegraph, railroad	1887	Woods	U.S.
Telegraph, wireless high frequency	1895	Marconi	Italian
Telephone	1876	Bell	U.S.-Scot.
Telephone amplifier	1912	De Forest	U.S.
Telephone, automatic	1891	Stowger	U.S.
Telephone, radio	1900	Poulsen, Fessenden	Danish
Telephone, radio	1906	De Forest	U.S.
Telephone, radio, l. d	1915	AT&T	U.S.
Telephone, recording	1898	Poulsen	Danish
Telephone, wireless	1899	Collins	U.S.
Telescope	1608	Lippershey	Neth.
Telescope	1609	Galileo	Italian
Telescope, astronomical	1611	Kepler	German
Teletype	1928	Morkrum, Kleinschmidt	U.S.
Television, iconoscope	1923	Zworykin	U.S.
Television, electronic	1927	Farnsworth	U.S.
Television, (mech. scanner)	1923	Baird	Scottish
Thermometer	1593	Galileo	Italian
Thermometer	1730	Reaumur	French
Thermometer, mercury	1714	Fahrenheit	German
Time recorder	1890	Bundy	U.S.
Time, self-regulator	1918	Bryce	U.S.
Tire, double-tube	1845	Thomson	Scottish
Tire, pneumatic	1888	Dunlop	Scottish
Toaster, automatic	1918	Strite	U.S.
Tool, pneumatic	1865	Law	English
Torpedo, marine	1804	Fulton	U.S.
Tractor, crawler	1904	Holt	U.S.
Transformer A.C.	1885	Stanley	U.S.
Transistor	1947	Shockley, Brattain, Bardeen	U.S.
Trolley car, electric	1884 -87	Van DePoele, Sprague	U.S.
Tungsten, ductile	1912	Coolidge	U.S.
Tupperware	1945	Tupper	U.S.
Turbine, gas	1849	Bourdin	French
Turbine, hydraulic	1849	Francis	U.S.
Turbine, steam	1884	Parsons	English
Type, movable	1447	Gutenberg	German
Typewriter	1867	Sholes, Soule, Glidden	U.S.
Vacuum cleaner, electric	1907	Spangler	U.S.
Velcro	1948	de Mestral	Swiss
Video game ("Pong")	1972	Buschnel	U.S.
Video home system (VHS)	1975	Matsushita, JVC	Japanese
Washer, electric	1901	Fisher	U.S.
Welding, atomic hydrogen	1924	Langmuir, Palmer	U.S.
Welding, electric	1877	Thomson	U.S.
Wind tunnel	1912	Eiffel	French
Wire, barbed	1874	Glidden	U.S.
Wire, barbed	1875	Haisn	U.S.
Wrench, double-acting	1913	Owen	U.S.
X-ray tube	1913	Coolidge	U.S.
Zipper	1891	Judson	U.S.

Discoveries and Innovations: Chemistry, Physics, Biology, Medicine

	Date	Discoverer	Nation.
Acetylene gas	1862	Berthelot	French
ACTH	1927	Evans, Long	U.S.
Adrenalin	1901	Takamine	Japanese
Aluminum, electrolytic process	1886	Hall	U.S.
Aluminum, isolated	1825	Oersted	Danish
Anesthesia, ether	1842	Long	U.S.
Anesthesia, local	1885	Koller	Austrian
Anesthesia, spinal	1898	Bier	German
Aniline dye	1856	Perkin	English
Anti-rabies	1885	Pasteur	French
Antiseptic surgery	1867	Lister	English
Antitoxin, diphtheria	1891	Von Behring	German
Argyrol	1897	Bayer	German
Arsphenamine	1910	Ehrlich	German
Aspirin	1889	Dresser	German
Atabrine	...	Mietzsch, et al.	German
Atomic numbers	1913	Moseley	English
Atomic theory	1803	Dalton	English
Atomic time clock	1947	Libby	U.S.
Atom-smashing theory	1919	Rutherford	English
Bacitracin	1945	Johnson, et al.	U.S.
Bacteria (described)	1676	Leeuwenhoek	Dutch
Barbital	1903	Fischer	German
Bleaching powder	1798	Tennant	English
Blood, circulation	1628	Harvey	English
Bordeaux mixture	1885	Millardet	French
Bromine from sea	1924	Edgar Kramer	U.S.
Calcium carbide	1888	Wilson	U.S.
Calculus	1670	Newton	English
Camphor synthetic	1896	Haller	French
Canning (food)	1804	Appert	French
Carbomycin	1952	Tanner	U.S.
Carbon oxides	1925	Fisher	German
Chloramphenicol	1947	Burkholder	U.S.
Chlorine	1774	Scheele	Swedish
Chloroform	1831	Guthrie, S.	U.S.
Chlortetracycline	1948	Duggen	U.S.
Classification of plants and animals	1735	Linnaeus	Swedish
Cocaine	1860	Niermann	German
Combustion explained	1777	Lavoisier	French
Conditioned reflex	1914	Pavlov	Russian
Cortisone	1936	Kendall	U.S.
Cortisone, synthesis	1946	Sarett	U.S.
Cosmic rays	1910	Gockel	Swiss
Cyanamide	1905	Frank, Caro	German
Cyclotron	1930	Lawrence	U.S.
DDT (not applied as insecticide until 1939)	1874	Zeidler	German
Deuterium	1932	Urey, Brickwedde, Murphy	U.S.
DNA (structure)	1951	Crick	English
		Watson	U.S.
		Wilkins	English
Electric resistance (law)	1827	Ohm	German
Electric waves	1888	Hertz	German
Electrolysis	1852	Faraday	English
Electromagnetism	1819	Oersted	Danish
Electron	1897	Thomson, J.	English
Electron diffraction	1936	Thomson, G.	English
		Davisson	U.S.
Electroshock treatment	1938	Cerletti, Bini	Italian
Erythromycin	1952	McGuire	U.S.
Evolution, natural selection	1858	Darwin	English
Falling bodies, law	1590	Galileo	Italian
Gases, law of combining volumes	1808	Gay-Lussac	French
Geometry, analytic	1619	Descartes	French
Gold (cyanide process for extraction)	1887	MacArthur, Forest	British
Gravitation, law	1687	Newton	English
Holograph	1948	Gabor	British
Human heart transplant	1967	Barnard	S. African
Indigo, synthesis of	1880	Baeyer	German
Induction, electric	1830	Henry	U.S.

	Date	Discoverer	Nation.
Insulin	1922	Banting, Best,	Canadian,
		Macleod	Scottish
Intelligence testing	1905	Binet, Simon	French
Isoniazid	1952	Hoffman-	
		La-Roche	U.S.
		Domagk	German
Isotopes, theory	1912	Soddy	English
Laser (light amplification by stimulated emission			
of radiation)	1958	Townes, Schaw-	
		low	U.S.
Light, velocity	1675	Roemer	Danish
Light, wave theory	1690	Huygens	Dutch
Lithography	1796	Senefelder	Bohemian
Lobotomy	1935	Egas Moniz	Portuguese
LSD-25	1943	Hoffman	Swiss
Mendelian laws	1866	Mendel	Austrian
Mercator projection			
(map)	1568	Mercator (Kremer)	Flemish
Methanol	1661	Boyle	Irish
Milk condensation	1853	Borden	U.S.
Molecular hypothesis	1811	Avogadro	Italian
Motion, laws of	1687	Newton	English
Neomycin	1949	Waksman,	
		Lechevalier	U.S.
Neutron	1932	Chadwick	English
Nitric acid	1648	Glauber	German
Nitric oxide	1772	Priestley	English
Nitroglycerin	1846	Sobrero	Italian
Oil cracking process	1891	Dewar	U.S.
Oxygen	1774	Priestley	English
Oxytetracycline	1950	Finlay, et al.	U.S.
Ozone	1840	Schonbein	German
Paper, sulfite process	1867	Tilghman	U.S.
Paper, wood pulp,			
sulfate process	1884	Dahl	German
Penicillin	1929	Fleming	Scottish
practical use	1941	Florey, Chain.	English
Periodic law and			
table of elements	1869	Mendeleyev	Russian
Planetary motion, laws	1609	Kepler	German
Plutonium fission	1940	Kennedy, Wahl,	
		Seaborg, Segre	U.S.
Polymyxin	1947	Ainsworth	English
Positron	1932	Anderson	U.S.
Proton	1919	Rutherford	N. Zealand
Psychoanalysis	1900	Freud	Austrian

	Date	Discoverer	Nation.
Quantum theory	1900	Planck	German
Quasars	1963	Matthews,	
		Sandage	U.S.
Quinine synthetic	1946	Woodward,	
		Doering	U.S.
Radioactivity	1896	Becquerel.	French
Radium	1898	Curie, Pierre	French
		Curie, Marie	Pol.-Fr.
Relativity theory	1905	Einstein	German
Reserpine	1949	Jal Vaikl	Indian
Schick test	1913	Schick	U.S.
Silicon	1823	Berzelius	Swedish
Streptomycin	1945	Waksman	U.S.
Sulfadiazine	1940	Roblin	U.S.
Sulfanilamide	1935	Bovet, Trefouel.	French
Sulfanilamide theory	1908	Gelmo	German
Sulfapyridine	1938	Ewins, Phelps	English
Sulfathiazole	...	Fosbinder, Walter	U.S.
Sulfuric acid	1831	Phillips	English
Sulfuric acid, lead	1746	Roebuck	English
Thiacetazone	1950	Belmisch,	
		Mietzsch,	
		Domagk	German
Tuberculin	1890	Koch	German
Uranium fission		Hahn, Meitner,	
(theory)	1939	Strassmann	German
		Bohr	Danish
		Fermi	Italian
		Einstein,	
		Pegram,	
		Wheeler.	U.S.
Uranium fission,		Fermi,	
atomic reactor	1942	Szilard	U.S.
Vaccine, measles	1954	Enders, Peebles	U.S.
Vaccine, polio	1953	Salk	U.S.
Vaccine, polio, oral	1955	Sabin	U.S.
Vaccine, rabies	1885	Pasteur	French
Vaccine, smallpox	1796	Jenner	English
Vaccine, typhus	1909	Nicolle.	French
Van Allen belts,			
radiation	1958	Van Allen	U.S.
Vitamin A	1913	McCollum, Davis.	U.S.
Vitamin B	1916	McCollum.	U.S.
Vitamin C	1912	Holst, Froelich	Norwegian
Vitamin D	1922	McCollum.	U.S.
Wassermann test	1906	Wassermann	German
Xerography	1938	Carlson	U.S.
X-ray	1895	Roentgen	German

Chemical Elements, Atomic Weights, Discoverers

Atomic weights, based on the exact number 12 as the assigned atomic mass of the principal isotope of carbon, carbon 12, are provided through the courtesy of the International Union of Pure and Applied Chemistry and Butterworth Scientific Publications.

For the radioactive elements, with the exception of uranium and thorium, the mass number of either the isotope of longest half-life (*) or the better known isotope (**) is given.

Chemical element	Symbol	Atomic number	Atomic weight	Year discov.	Discoverer
Actinium	Ac	89	227*	1899	Debierne
Aluminum	Al	13	26.9815	1825	Oersted
Americium	Am	95	243*	1944	Seaborg, et al.
Antimony	Sb	51	121.75	1450	Valentine
Argon	Ar	18	39.948	1894	Rayleigh, Ramsay
Arsenic	As	33	74.9216	13th c.	Albertus Magnus
Astatine	At	85	210*	1940	Corson, et al.
Barium	Ba	56	137.34	1808	Davy
Berkelium	Bk	97	249**	1949	Thompson, Ghiorso, Seaborg
Beryllium	Be	4	9.0122	1798	Vauquelin
Bismuth	Bi	83	208.980	15th c.	Valentine
Boron	B	5	10.811a	1808	Gay-Lussac, Thenard
Bromine	Br	35	79.904b	1826	Balard
Cadmium	Cd	48	112.40	1817	Stromeyer
Calcium	Ca	20	40.08	1808	Davy
Californium	Cf	98	251*	1950	Thompson, et al.
Carbon	C	6	12.01115a	B.C.	Unknown
Cerium	Ce	58	140.12	1803	Klaproth
Cesium	Cs	55	132.905	1860	Bunsen, Kirchhoff
Chlorine	Cl	17	35.453b	1774	Scheele
Chromium	Cr	24	51.996b	1797	Vauquelin
Cobalt	Co	27	58.9332	1735	Brandt
Copper	Cu	29	63.546b	B.C.	

Chemical element	Symbol	Atomic number	Atomic weight	Year discov.	Discoverer
Curium	Cm	96	247*	1944	Seaborg, James, Ghiorso
Dysprosium	Dy	66	162.50	1886	Boisbaudran
Einsteinium	Es	99	254*	1952	Ghiorso, et al.
Erbium	Er	68	167.26	1843	Mosander
Europium	Eu	63	151.96	1901	Demarcay
Fermium	Fm	100	257*	1953	Ghiorso, et al.
Fluorine	F	9	18.9984	1771	Scheele
Francium	Fr	87	223*	1939	Perey
Gadolinium	Gd	64	157.25	1886	Marignac
Gallium	Ga	31	69.72	1875	Boisbaudran
Germanium	Ge	32	72.59	1886	Winkler
Gold	Au	79	196.967	B.C.	unknown
Hafnium	Hf	72	178.49	1923	Coster, Hevesy
Hahnium	Ha	105	262*	1970	Ghiorso, et al.
Helium	He	2	4.0026	1868	Janssen, Lockyer
Holmium	Ho	67	164.930	1878	Soret, Delafontaine
Hydrogen	H	1	1.00797a	1766	Cavendish
Indium	In	49	114.82	1863	Reich, Richter
Iodine	I	53	126.9044	1811	Courtois
Iridium	Ir	77	192.2	1804	Tennant
Iron	Fe	26	55.847b	B.C.	unknown
Krypton	Kr	36	83.80	1898	Ramsay, Travers
Lanthanum	La	57	138.91	1839	Mosander
Lawrencium	Lr	103	262*	1961	Ghiorso, T. Sikkeland, A.E. Larsh, and R.M. Latimer
Lead	Pb	82	207.19	B.C.	unknown
Lithium	Li	3	6.939	1817	Arfvedson
Lutetium	Lu	71	174.97	1907	Welsbach, Urbain
Magnesium	Mg	12	24.312	1829	Bussy
Manganese	Mn	25	54.9380	1774	Gahn
Mendelevium	Md	101	258*	1955	Ghiorso, et al.
Mercury	Hg	80	200.59	B.C.	unknown
Molybdenum	Mo	42	95.94	1782	Hjelm
Neodymium	Nd	60	144.24	1885	Welsbach
Neon	Ne	10	20.183	1898	Ramsay, Travers
Neptunium	Np	93	237*	1940	McMillan, Abelson
Nickel	Ni	28	58.71	1751	Cronstedt
Niobium[1]	Nb	41	92.906	1801	Hatchett
Nitrogen	N	7	14.0067	1772	Rutherford
Nobelium	No	102	259*	1958	Ghiorso, et al.
Osmium	Os	76	190.2	1804	Tennant
Oxygen	O	8	15.9994a	1774	Priestley, Scheele
Palladium	Pd	46	106.4	1803	Wollaston
Phosphorus	P	15	30.9738	1669	Brand
Platinum	Pt	78	195.09	1735	Ulloa
Plutonium	Pu	94	242**	1940	Seaborg, et al.
Polonium	Po	84	210**	1898	P. and M. Curie
Potassium	K	19	39.102	1807	Davy
Praseodymium	Pr	59	140.907	1885	Welsbach
Promethium	Pm	61	147**	1945	Glendenin, Marinsky, Coryell
Protactinium	Pa	91	231*	1917	Hahn, Meitner
Radium	Ra	88	226*	1898	P. & M. Curie, Bemont
Radon	Rn	86	222*	1900	Dorn
Rhenium	Re	75	186.2	1925	Noddack, Tacke, Berg
Rhodium	Rh	45	102.905	1803	Wollaston
Rubidium	Rb	37	85.47	1861	Bunsen, Kirchhoff
Ruthenium	Ru	44	101.07	1845	Klaus
Rutherfordium	Rf	104	261*	1969	Ghiorso, et al.
Samarium	Sm	62	150.35	1879	Boisbaudran
Scandium	Sc	21	44.956	1879	Nilson
Selenium	Se	34	78.96	1817	Berzelius
Silicon	Si	14	28.086a	1823	Berzelius
Silver	Ag	47	107.868b	B.C.	unknown
Sodium	Na	11	22.9898	1807	Davy
Strontium	Sr	38	87.62	1790	Crawford
Sulfur	S	16	32.064a	B.C.	unknown
Tantalum	Ta	73	180.948	1802	Ekeberg
Technetium	Tc	43	99**	1937	Perrier and Segre
Tellurium	Te	52	127.60	1782	Von Reichenstein
Terbium	Tb	65	158.924	1843	Mosander
Thallium	Tl	81	204.37	1861	Crookes
Thorium	Th	90	232.038	1828	Berzelius
Thulium	Tm	69	168.934	1879	Cleve
Tin	Sn	50	118.69	B.C.	unknown
Titanium	Ti	22	47.90	1791	Gregor
Tungsten (Wolfram)	W	74	183.85	1783	d'Elhujar
Uranium	U	92	238.03	1789	Klaproth
Vanadium	V	23	50.942	1830	Sefstrom
Xenon	Xe	54	131.30	1898	Ramsay, Travers
Ytterbium	Yb	70	173.04	1878	Marignac
Yttrium	Y	39	88.905	1794	Gadolin
Zinc	Zn	30	65.37	B.C.	unknown
Zirconium	Zr	40	91.22	1789	Klaproth

(1) Formerly Columbium. (a) Atomic weights so designated are known to be variable because of natural variations in isotopic composition. The observed ranges are: hydrogen±0.0001; boron±0.003; carbon±0.005; oxygen±0.0001; silicon±0.001; sulfur±0.003. (b) Atomic weights so designated are believed to have the following experimental uncertainties: chlorine±0.001; chromium±0.001; iron±0.003; bromine±0.001; silver±0.001; copper±0.001.

METEOROLOGY

National Weather Service Watches and Warnings

Source: National Weather Service, NOAA, U.S. Dept. of Commerce; *Glossary of Meteorology*, American Meteorological Society

National Weather Service forecasters issue a Severe Thunderstorm or Tornado Watch for a specific area where threatening weather is most likely to occur during the valid time of the watch. A Severe Thunderstorm Watch is issued for a specific area where severe thunderstorms are most likely. A Tornado Watch is issued when severe thunderstorms that produce tornados are likely to occur in a specific area. A Watch alerts people to check for threatening weather, make plans for action, and listen for a Tornado Warning. A Tornado Warning means that a tornado has been sighted or indicated by radar, and that safety precautions should be taken at once. A Hurricane Watch means that an existing hurricane poses a threat to coastal and inland communities in the area specified by the Watch. A Hurricane Warning means hurricane force winds and/or dangerously high water and exceptionally high waves are expected in a specified coastal area within 24 hours.

Tornado—A violent rotating column of air in contact with the ground and pendant from a thundercloud, usually recognized as a funnel-shaped vortex accompanied by a loud roar. With rotating winds est. up to 300 mph., on a local scale, it is the most destructive storm. Tornado paths have varied in length from a few feet to nearly 300 miles (avg. 5 mi.); diameter from a few feet to over a mile (average 220 yards); average forward speed, 30 mph.

Cyclone—An atmospheric circulation of winds rotating counterclockwise in the northern hemisphere and clockwise in the southern hemisphere. Tornadoes, hurricanes, and the lows shown on weather maps are all examples of cyclones having various sizes and intensities. Cyclones are usually accompanied by precipitation or stormy weather.

Hurricane—A severe cyclone originating over tropical ocean waters and having winds 74 miles an hour or higher. (In the western Pacific, such storms are known as typhoons.) The area of strong winds takes the form of a circle or an oval, sometimes as much as 500 miles in diameter. In the lower latitudes hurricanes usually move toward the west or northwest at 10 to 15 mph. When the center approaches 25° to 30° North Latitude, direction of motion often changes to northeast, with increased forward speed.

Blizzard—A severe weather condition characterized by strong winds bearing a great amount of snow. The National Weather Service specifies a wind of 35 miles an hour or higher, and sufficient falling and/or blowing snow to reduce visibility to less than $1/4$ of a mile for a duration of three hours or longer.

Severe Thunderstorm—A thunderstorm with winds of 58 mph. or greater and/or hail three-fourths of an inch or larger in diameter.

Flood—The condition that occurs when water overflows the natural or artificial confines of a stream or other body of water, or accumulates by drainage over low-lying areas.

National Weather Service Marine Warnings and Advisories

Small Craft Advisory: A Small Craft Advisory alerts mariners to sustained (exceeding two hours) weather and/or sea conditions either present or forecast, potentially hazardous to small boats. Although there is no definition of a small craft, hazardous conditions generally include winds of 18 to 33 knots and/or dangerous wave conditions. It is the responsibility of the mariner, based on his experience, location and size or type of boat, to determine if the conditions are hazardous. When a mariner becomes aware of a Small Craft Advisory, he should immediately obtain the latest marine forecast to determine the reason for the Advisory.

Gale Warning indicates that winds within the range 34 to 63 knots, not directly associated with a tropical storm, are forecast for the area.

Tropical Storm Warning indicates that winds of 34 to 63 knots are forecast in a specified coastal area in 24 hours or less. Only issued for winds produced by tropical weather systems.

Storm Warning indicates that winds 48 knots and above, no matter how high the speed, not directly associated with a tropical storm, are forecast for the area.

Hurricane Warning indicates that winds 64 knots and above are forecast for the area. Only issued for winds produced by tropical weather systems.

Special Marine Warning: A warning for potentially hazardous weather conditions, usually of short duration (2 hours or less) and producing wind speeds of 34 knots or more, not adequately covered by existing marine warnings.

Primary sources of dissemination are commercial radio, TV, U.S. Coast Guard Radio stations, and NOAA VHF-FM broadcasts. These broadcasts on 162.40 to 162.55 MHz can usually be received 20-40 miles from the transmitting antenna site, depending on terrain and quality of the receiver used. Where transmitting antennas are on high ground, the range may be somewhat greater, reaching 60 miles or more.

Speed of Winds in the U.S.

Source: Natl. Climatic Data Center, NESDIS, NOAA, U.S. Department of Commerce
Miles per hour — average through 1990. High through 1990. Wind velocities in true values.

Station	Avg.	High	Station	Avg.	High	Station	Avg.	High
Albuquerque, N.M.	9.1	(b)90	Helena, Mont.	7.8	73	Mt. Washington, N.H.	35.3	231
Anchorage, Alas.	6.9	75	Honolulu, Ha.	11.4	(b)67	New Orleans, La.	8.2	(b)98
Atlanta, Ga.	9.1	60	Houston, Tex.	7.9	51	New York, N.Y.(c)	9.4	(b)70
Baltimore, Md.	9.2	80	Indianapolis, Ind.	9.6	46	Omaha, Neb.	10.6	109
Bismarck, N.D.	10.2	(b)72	Jacksonville, Fla.	8.0	(b)82	Philadelphia, Pa.	9.5	73
Boston, Mass.	12.5	(b)61	Kansas City, Mo.	10.8	(b)70	Phoenix, Ariz.	6.3	(b)86
Buffalo, N.Y.	12.0	91	Lexington, Ky.	9.3	46	Pittsburgh, Pa.	9.1	58
Cape Hatteras, N.C.	11.1	(b)110	Little Rock, Ark.	7.8	65	Portland, Ore.	7.9	88
Casper, Wyo.	12.9	81	Los Angeles, Cal.	6.2	49	St. Louis, Mo.	9.7	(b)60
Chicago, Ill.	10.3	58	Louisville, Ky.	8.3	(b)61	Salt Lake City, Ut.	8.9	71
Cleveland, Oh.	10.6	(b)74	Memphis, Tenn.	8.9	46	San Diego, Cal.	6.9	56
Dallas, Tex.	10.8	73	Miami, Fla.	9.3	(a)74	San Francisco, Cal.	8.7	47
Denver, Col.	8.7	(b)56	Milwaukee, Wis.	11.6	54	Seattle, Wash.	9.0	66
Detroit, Mich.	10.4	48	Minneapolis, Minn.	10.6	(b)92	Spokane, Wash.	8.9	59
Galveston, Tex.	11.0	(d)100	Mobile, Ala.	9.0	63	Washington, D.C.	9.4	(b)78

(a) Highest velocity ever recorded in Miami area was 132 mph, at former station in Miami Beach in September, 1926.
(b) Previous location. (c) Data for Central Park, Battery Place data through 1960, avg. 14.5, high 113. (d) Recorded before anemometer blew away. Estimated high 120.

The Meaning of "One Inch of Rain"

An acre of ground contains 43,560 square feet. Consequently, a rainfall of 1 inch over 1 acre of ground would mean a total of 6,272,640 cubic inches of water. This is equivalent of 3,630 cubic feet.

As a cubic foot of pure water weights about 62.4 pounds, the exact amount varying with the density, it follows that the weight of a uniform coating of 1 inch of rain over 1 acre of surface would be 226,512 pounds, or about 113 short tons. The weight of 1 U.S. gallon of pure water is about 8.345 pounds. Consequently a rainfall of 1 inch over 1 acre of ground would mean about 27,143 gallons of water.

1990: Warmest Year on Record

NASA's Goddard Inst. recorded the average global temperature in 1990 at **59.81 degrees**, the warmest since 1880. The British Meteorological Office reported that no year had been as warm since they began keeping records in 1850, and said that 6 of the 7 warmest years of the 20th century had occurred during the 1980s.

Tides and Their Causes

Source: NOAA, National Ocean Service, U.S. Department of Commerce

The tides are a natural phenomenon involving the alternating rise and fall in the large fluid bodies of the earth caused by the combined gravitational attraction of the sun and moon. The combination of these two variable force influences produces the complex recurrent cycle of the tides. Tides may occur in both oceans and seas, to a limited extent in large lakes, the atmosphere, and, to a very minute degree, in the earth itself. The period between succeeding tides varies as the result of many factors and force influences.

The tide-generating force represents the difference between (1) the centrifugal force produced by the revolution of the earth around the common center-of-gravity of the earth-moon system and (2) the gravitational attraction of the moon acting upon the earth's overlying waters. Since, on the average, the moon is only 238,852 miles from the earth compared with the sun's much greater distance of 92,956,000 miles, this closer distance outranks the much smaller mass of the moon compared with that of the sun, and the moon's tide-raising force is, accordingly, 2¹/₅ times that of the sun.

The effect of the tide-generating forces of the moon and sun acting tangentially to the earth's surface (the so-called "tractive force") tends to cause a maximum accumulation of the waters of the oceans at two diametrically opposite positions on the surface of the earth and to withdraw compensating amounts of water from all points 90° removed from the positions of these tidal bulges. As the earth rotates beneath the maxima and minima of these tide-generating forces, a sequence of two high tides, separated by two low tides, ideally is produced each day (semidiurnal tide).

Twice in each lunar month, when the sun, moon, and earth are directly aligned, with the moon between the earth and the sun (at new moon) or on the opposite side of the earth from the sun (at full moon), the sun and the moon exert their gravitational force in a mutual or additive fashion. The highest high tides and lowest low tides are produced. These are called *spring* tides. At two positions 90° in between, the gravitational forces of the moon and sun — imposed at right angles—tend to counteract each other to the greatest extent, and the range between high and low tides is reduced. These are called *neap* tides. This semi-monthly variation between the spring and neap tides is called the *phase inequality*.

The inclination of the moon's monthly orbit to the equator and the inclination of the sun during the earth's yearly orbit to the equator produce a difference in the height of succeeding high tides and in the extent of depression of succeeding low tides which is known as the diurnal inequality. In most cases, this produces a type of tide called a mixed tide. In extreme cases, these phenomena can result in only one high tide and one low each tide (diurnal tide). There are also other monthly and yearly variations in the tide due to the elliptical shape of the orbits themselves.

The datum for Charting and Predictions is (MLLW) Mean Lower Low Water. This became effective January 1989 according to the convention of 1980 which prescribed that datums on all United States coast lines would be the same. Namely (MHHW) Mean Higher High Water, (MHW) Mean High Water, (MTL) Mean Tide Level, (MSL) Mean Sea Level, (MLW) Mean Low Water, (MLLW) Mean Lower Low Water. Diurnal range of tide is the difference in height between mean higher high water and mean lower low water. Mean range of tide is the difference in height between mean high water and mean low water.

The actual range of tide in the waters of the open oceans may amount to only one to three feet. However, as the ocean tide approaches shoal waters and its effects are augmented the tidal range may be greatly increased. In Nova Scotia along the narrow channel of the Bay of Fundy, the range of tides or difference between high and low waters, may reach 43 1/2 feet or more (under spring tide conditions) due to resonant amplification.

At New Orleans, the periodic rise and fall of the diurnal tide is affected by the seasonal stages of the Mississippi River, being about 10 inches at low stage and zero at high. The Canadian Tide Tables for 1972 gave a maximum range of nearly 50 feet at Leaf Basin, Ungava Bay, Quebec.

In every case, actual high or low tide can vary considerably from the average, due to weather conditions such as strong winds, abrupt barometric pressure changes, or prolonged periods of extreme high or low pressure.

The Average Rise and Fall of Tides[1]

Places	Ft.	In.	Places	Ft.	In.	Places	Ft.	In.
Baltimore, Md.	1	8	Mobile, Ala.	1	6	San Diego, Cal.	5	9
Boston, Mass.	10	4	New London, Conn.	3	1	Sandy Hook, N.J.	5	2
Charleston, S.C.	5	10	Newport, R.I.	3	11	San Francisco, Cal.	5	10
Cristobal, Panama	1	1	New York, N.Y.	5	1	Savannah, Ga.	8	3
Eastport, Me.	19	4	Old Pt. Comfort, Va.	3	0	Seattle, Wash.	11	4
Galveston, Tex.	1	5	Philadelphia, Pa.	6	9	Tampa, Fla.	2	10
Halifax, N.S.	4	5[2]	Portland, Me.	9	11	Vancouver, B.C.	10	6
Key West, Fla.	1	10	St. John's, Nfld.	2	7[2]	Washington, D.C.	3	2

(1) Diurnal range. (2) Mean range.

Hurricane Names in 1992

Names assigned to Atlantic hurricanes, 1992 — Allen, Bonnie, Charley, Danielle, Earl, Frances, Georges, Hermine, Ivan, Jeanne, Karl, Lisa, Mitch, Nicole, Otto, Paula, Richard, Shary, Tomas, Virginie, Walter.

Names assigned to Eastern Pacific hurricanes, 1992 — Agatha, Blas, Celia, Darby, Estelle, Frank, Georgette, Howard, Isis, Javier, Kay, Lester, Madeline, Newton, Orlene, Paine, Roslyn, Seymour, Tina, Virgil, Winifred.

Explanation of Normal Temperatures

Normal temperatures listed in the tables on pages 207 and 208 are based on records of the National Weather Service for the 30-year period from 1951-1980 inclusive. To obtain the average maximum or minimum temperature for any month, the daily temperatures are added; the total is then divided by the number of days in that month.

The normal maximum temperature for January, for example, is obtained by adding the average maximums for Jan., 1951, Jan., 1952, etc., through Jan., 1980. The total is then divided by 30. The normal minimum temperature is obtained in a similar manner by adding the average minimums for each January in the 30-year period and dividing by 30. The normal temperature for January is one half of the sum for the normal maximum and minimum temperatures for that month. The mean temperature for any one day is one-half the total of the maximum and minimum temperatures for that day.

Monthly Normal Temperature and Precipitation

Source: Natl. Climatic Data Center, NESDIS, NOAA, U.S. Department of Commerce

These normals are based on records for the 30-year period 1951 to 1980 inclusive. (See explanation on page 206.) For stations that did not have continuous records from the same instrument site for the entire 30 years, the means have been adjusted to the record at the present site.

Airport station; *city office stations. T, temperature in Fahrenheit; P, precipitation in inches; L, less than .05 inch.

Station	Jan. T	Jan. P	Feb. T	Feb. P	Mar. T	Mar. P	Apr. T	Apr. P	May T	May P	June T	June P	July T	July P	Aug. T	Aug. P	Sept. T	Sept. P	Oct. T	Oct. P	Nov. T	Nov. P	Dec. T	Dec. P
Albany, N.Y.	21	2.4	23	2.3	34	3.0	47	2.9	58	3.3	67	3.3	71	3.0	69	3.3	61	3.2	51	2.9	39	3.0	26	3.0
Albuquerque, N.M.	35	0.4	39	0.4	46	0.5	55	0.4	64	0.5	75	0.5	79	1.3	76	1.5	69	0.9	57	0.9	44	0.4	36	0.5
Anchorage, Alas.	13	0.8	18	0.9	24	0.7	35	0.7	46	0.6	54	1.1	58	2.0	56	2.1	48	2.5	35	1.7	22	1.1	14	1.1
Asheville, N.C.	37	3.5	39	3.6	46	5.1	56	3.8	63	4.2	70	4.2	73	4.4	73	4.8	70	4.0	56	3.3	46	3.3	39	3.5
Atlanta, Ga.	42	4.9	45	4.4	53	5.9	62	4.4	69	4.0	76	3.4	79	4.7	78	3.4	73	3.2	62	2.5	52	3.4	45	4.2
Atlantic City, N.J.	34	3.3	35	3.2	42	3.7	51	3.1	60	2.9	68	2.9	74	3.9	74	4.5	68	2.7	58	2.8	48	3.5	38	3.5
Baltimore, Md.	33	3.0	35	3.0	43	3.7	54	3.4	63	3.4	72	3.8	77	3.9	76	4.6	69	3.5	57	3.1	46	3.1	37	3.4
Barrow, Alas.	-14	0.2	-20	0.2	-16	0.2	-2	0.2	19	0.2	33	0.4	39	0.9	38	1.0	31	0.6	14	0.6	-1	0.3	-13	0.2
Birmingham, Ala.	42	5.2	46	4.7	54	6.6	63	5.0	70	4.5	77	3.7	80	5.4	80	3.9	74	4.3	62	2.7	52	3.6	45	5.0
Bismarck, N.D.	7	0.5	15	0.5	26	0.7	43	1.5	55	2.2	64	3.0	70	2.0	69	1.7	57	1.4	46	0.8	29	0.5	15	0.5
Boise, Ida.	30	1.6	36	1.1	41	1.0	49	1.2	57	1.2	66	1.0	75	0.3	72	0.4	63	0.6	52	0.8	40	1.3	32	1.3
Boston, Mass.	30	4.0	31	3.7	38	4.1	49	3.7	59	3.5	68	2.9	74	2.7	72	3.7	65	3.4	55	3.4	45	4.2	34	4.9
Buffalo, N.Y.	24	3.0	25	2.4	33	3.0	45	3.0	56	2.9	66	2.7	71	3.0	69	4.2	62	3.4	52	2.9	40	3.6	29	3.4
Burlington, Vt.	17	1.9	18	1.7	29	2.2	43	2.8	55	3.0	65	3.6	70	3.4	67	3.9	59	3.2	48	2.8	37	2.8	23	2.4
Caribou, Me.	11	2.4	13	2.1	24	2.4	37	2.6	50	2.9	60	3.2	65	4.0	63	4.0	54	3.5	43	3.1	31	3.2	16	3.1
Charleston, S.C.	49	3.3	51	3.4	57	4.4	66	2.6	73	4.4	79	6.5	82	7.3	81	6.5	77	4.9	68	2.9	59	2.2	52	3.1
Chicago, Ill.	21	1.6	26	1.3	36	2.6	49	3.7	59	3.2	69	4.1	73	3.6	72	3.5	65	3.4	54	2.3	40	2.1	28	2.1
Cleveland, Oh.	26	2.5	27	2.2	37	3.0	48	3.3	58	3.3	68	3.5	72	3.4	70	3.4	64	2.9	53	2.5	42	2.8	31	2.8
Columbus, Oh.	27	2.8	30	2.2	40	3.2	51	3.4	61	3.8	70	4.0	74	4.0	72	3.7	66	2.8	54	1.9	42	2.6	32	2.6
Dallas-Ft. Worth, Tex.	44	1.7	49	1.9	56	2.4	66	3.6	74	4.3	82	2.6	86	2.0	86	1.8	79	3.3	68	2.5	56	1.8	48	1.7
Denver, Col.	30	0.5	34	0.7	38	1.2	47	1.8	57	2.5	67	1.6	73	1.9	71	1.5	63	1.2	52	1.0	39	0.8	33	0.6
Des Moines, Ia.	19	1.0	25	1.1	35	2.2	51	3.2	62	4.0	72	4.2	76	3.2	74	4.1	65	3.1	54	2.2	39	1.5	26	1.5
Detroit, Mich.	25	1.9	26	1.7	35	2.5	47	3.2	58	2.8	68	3.4	72	3.1	71	3.2	63	2.3	52	2.1	40	2.3	29	2.5
Dodge City, Kan.	30	0.5	35	0.5	42	1.5	54	1.8	64	3.3	75	3.0	80	3.1	78	2.5	69	1.9	58	1.3	43	0.8	34	0.5
Duluth, Minn.	6	1.2	12	0.9	23	1.8	38	2.2	50	3.2	59	4.0	65	4.0	63	4.1	54	3.3	44	2.2	28	1.7	14	1.3
Eureka, Cal.*	47	7.0	49	5.2	48	5.1	49	2.9	52	1.6	55	0.6	56	0.1	57	0.4	57	0.9	54	2.7	51	5.9	48	6.2
Fairbanks, Alas.	-13	0.5	-4	0.5	9	0.4	30	0.3	48	0.6	59	1.3	62	1.8	57	1.9	45	1.1	25	0.7	4	0.7	-10	0.7
Fresno, Cal.	46	2.0	51	1.9	54	1.6	60	1.2	68	0.3	75	0.1	81	L	79	L	74	0.2	65	0.4	53	1.2	45	1.6
Galveston, Tex.	54	3.0	56	2.3	62	2.1	69	2.6	76	3.3	81	3.5	83	3.8	83	4.4	80	5.8	73	2.6	63	3.2	57	3.6
Grand Junction, Col.	26	0.6	34	0.5	42	0.8	52	0.7	62	0.8	72	0.4	79	0.5	76	0.9	67	0.7	55	0.9	40	0.6	28	0.6
Gr. Rapids, Mich.	22	1.9	24	1.5	33	2.5	46	3.6	58	3.0	67	3.9	71	3.0	70	3.5	62	3.1	51	2.9	39	2.9	27	2.6
Hartford, Conn.	25	3.5	28	3.2	37	4.2	49	4.0	59	3.4	69	3.4	73	3.1	71	4.0	63	3.9	52	3.5	42	4.1	29	4.2
Helena, Mon.	18	0.7	26	0.4	32	0.7	42	1.0	52	1.7	60	2.0	68	1.0	66	1.2	56	0.8	45	0.7	31	0.5	23	0.6
Honolulu, Ha.	73	3.8	73	2.7	74	3.5	76	1.5	78	1.2	79	0.5	80	0.5	81	0.6	80	1.9	77	3.2	77	3.0	74	3.4
Houston, Tex.	51	3.2	55	3.3	61	2.7	69	4.2	75	4.7	81	4.0	83	3.3	83	3.7	78	4.9	70	3.7	60	3.4	54	3.7
Huron, S.D.	11	0.4	18	0.8	29	1.2	46	2.0	57	2.7	68	3.4	74	2.3	72	2.0	61	1.4	49	1.4	32	0.7	19	0.5
Indianapolis, Ind.	26	2.7	30	2.5	40	3.6	52	3.7	63	3.7	72	4.0	75	4.3	73	3.5	67	2.7	55	2.5	42	3.0	32	3.0
Jackson, Miss.	46	5.0	49	4.9	56	5.9	65	5.9	73	4.8	79	2.9	82	4.4	81	3.7	76	3.6	65	2.6	55	4.2	49	5.4
Jacksonville, Fla.	53	3.1	55	3.5	61	3.7	68	3.3	74	4.9	79	5.4	81	6.5	81	7.2	78	7.3	70	3.4	61	1.9	55	2.6
Juneau, Alas.	22	3.7	28	3.7	31	3.3	39	2.9	46	3.4	53	3.0	56	4.1	55	5.0	49	6.4	42	7.7	33	5.2	27	4.7
Kansas City, Mo.	26	1.0	32	1.0	42	2.1	55	2.7	65	3.4	76	4.1	79	3.5	77	3.2	68	3.3	58	2.5	43	1.2	32	1.1
Knoxville, Tenn.	38	4.7	42	4.2	50	5.5	60	3.9	67	3.7	74	4.0	78	4.3	77	3.0	72	3.0	60	2.7	49	3.8	41	4.6
Lander, Wyo.	20	0.5	26	0.6	32	1.1	42	2.2	53	2.7	62	1.5	71	0.7	69	0.5	58	0.9	47	1.2	31	0.8	23	0.5
Lexington, Ky.	32	3.6	35	3.3	44	4.8	55	4.0	64	4.2	72	4.3	76	5.0	75	4.0	69	3.3	57	2.3	45	3.3	36	3.8
Little Rock, Ark.	40	3.9	44	3.8	52	4.7	62	5.4	71	5.3	79	3.7	82	3.6	81	3.1	74	4.3	63	2.8	51	4.4	43	4.2
Los Angeles, Cal.*	57	3.7	59	3.0	60	2.4	62	1.2	65	0.2	69	L	74	L	75	0.1	73	0.3	69	0.2	63	1.9	58	2.0
Louisville, Ky.	33	3.4	36	3.2	45	4.7	57	4.1	65	4.2	74	3.6	78	4.1	76	3.3	70	3.6	58	2.6	46	3.7	37	3.5
Marquette, Mich.*	12	2.0	14	1.9	23	2.8	37	3.6	50	4.0	59	3.5	65	3.2	63	3.3	54	3.9	44	3.3	30	2.9	18	2.4
Memphis, Tenn.	40	4.4	44	4.3	52	5.4	63	5.8	71	5.1	79	3.6	82	4.0	81	3.7	74	3.6	63	2.4	51	4.3	42	4.9
Miami, Fla.	67	2.1	68	2.1	72	1.9	75	3.1	79	6.5	81	9.2	83	6.0	83	7.0	82	8.1	78	7.1	73	2.7	69	1.9
Milwaukee, Wis.	19	1.6	23	1.3	32	2.6	45	3.4	55	2.6	65	3.6	71	3.5	69	3.1	62	2.9	51	2.3	37	2.0	25	2.0
Minneapolis, Minn.	11	0.8	18	0.9	29	1.7	46	2.1	59	3.2	68	4.1	73	3.5	71	3.6	61	2.5	50	1.9	33	1.3	19	0.9
Mobile, Ala.	51	4.6	54	4.9	60	6.5	68	5.4	75	5.5	81	5.1	82	7.7	82	6.8	78	6.6	69	2.6	59	3.7	53	5.4
Moline, Ill.	20	1.6	25	1.3	36	2.8	50	4.0	61	4.2	71	4.3	75	4.9	73	3.6	65	3.7	54	2.7	39	2.0	26	1.9
Nashville, Tenn.	37	4.5	40	4.0	49	5.6	60	4.8	68	4.6	76	3.7	79	3.8	78	3.4	72	3.7	60	2.6	49	3.5	41	4.6
Newark, N.J.	31	3.1	33	3.1	41	4.2	52	3.6	62	3.6	72	2.9	77	3.9	76	4.3	68	3.7	57	3.1	47	3.6	36	3.4
New Orleans, La.	52	5.0	55	5.2	61	4.7	69	4.5	75	5.1	80	4.6	82	6.7	82	6.0	79	5.9	69	2.7	60	4.1	55	5.3
New York, N.Y.*	32	3.2	33	3.1	41	4.2	53	4.0	62	3.8	71	3.2	77	3.8	75	4.0	68	3.7	58	3.4	47	4.1	36	3.8
Nome, Alas.	9	0.8	3	0.5	7	0.6	18	0.6	36	0.5	45	1.2	51	2.2	50	3.1	42	2.3	28	1.3	16	0.9	4	0.7
Norfolk, Va.	40	3.7	41	3.3	49	3.9	58	2.9	67	3.8	76	3.5	78	5.2	78	5.3	72	4.4	61	3.4	52	2.9	44	3.2
Okla. City, Okla.	36	1.0	41	1.3	49	2.1	60	2.9	68	5.5	77	3.9	82	3.0	81	2.7	73	4.0	62	3.0	49	1.5	40	1.2
Omaha, Neb.	19	0.8	25	0.9	35	1.9	50	2.9	62	4.3	71	4.1	76	3.6	74	4.1	64	2.5	52	2.1	38	1.3	26	0.9
Pago Pago, Amer. Samoa.	81	13	81	11	81	11	80	11	80	8.6	79	6.5	79	7.1	79	6.7	80	11	80	11	81	11	81	14
Philadelphia, Pa.	31	3.2	33	2.8	42	3.9	53	3.5	63	3.2	72	3.9	77	3.9	75	4.1	68	3.4	57	2.8	46	3.3	36	3.5
Phoenix, Ariz.	52	0.7	56	0.6	61	0.8	68	0.3	77	0.1	87	0.2	92	0.7	90	1.0	85	0.6	73	0.6	61	0.5	53	0.8
Pittsburgh, Pa.	27	2.9	29	2.4	39	3.6	50	3.3	60	3.5	68	3.3	72	3.8	71	3.3	64	2.8	53	2.3	42	2.3	31	2.6
Portland, Me.	22	3.8	23	3.6	33	4.0	43	4.0	53	3.9	62	3.1	68	2.8	67	2.8	59	3.3	49	3.8	38	4.7	26	4.5
Portland, Ore.	39	6.2	43	3.9	46	3.6	50	2.3	57	2.1	63	1.5	67	0.5	67	1.1	63	1.6	54	3.1	46	5.2	42	6.4
Providence, R.I.	28	4.1	29	3.7	37	4.3	48	4.0	58	3.5	67	2.8	73	3.0	71	4.0	64	3.4	54	3.3	44	4.2	32	4.6
Raleigh, N.C.	40	3.6	42	3.4	49	3.7	59	2.9	67	3.7	74	3.4	78	4.4	77	4.4	71	3.3	60	2.7	50	2.9	42	3.1
Rapid City, S.D.	21	0.4	26	0.6	33	1.0	45	2.0	56	2.6	65	3.3	73	2.1	71	1.4	61	1.0	50	0.9	33	0.5	26	0.4
Reno, Nev.	32	1.2	37	1.0	41	0.7	46	0.4	54	0.7	61	0.4	69	0.3	67	0.3	61	0.3	52	0.4	42	0.5	33	1.2
Richmond, Va.	37	3.2	39	3.1	47	3.6	58	2.9	66	3.6	74	3.6	78	5.1	77	5.0	70	3.4	59	3.2	50	3.0	40	3.4
St. Louis, Mo.	29	1.7	34	2.1	43	3.3	56	3.6	66	3.5	75	3.7	79	3.9	78	2.6	69	2.7	58	2.3	45	2.5	33	2.4
Salt Lake City, Ut.	29	1.4	34	1.3	41	1.7	49	2.2	58	1.5	66	1.0	77	0.7	75	0.9	65	0.9	51	1.3	40	1.3	30	1.4
San Antonio, Tex.	50	1.6	54	1.9	62	1.3	70	2.7	76	3.7	82	3.0	85	1.9	84	2.7	79	3.8	70	2.9	60	2.2	53	1.5
San Diego, Cal.	57	2.1	58	1.4	59	1.6	61	0.8	63	0.2	66	0.1	70	L	72	0.1	71	0.2	67	0.3	63	1.1	57	1.4
San Francisco, Cal.	49	4.7	52	3.2	53	2.6	55	1.5	58	0.4	61	0.1	62	L	63	0.1	64	0.2	61	1.1	55	2.4	49	3.6
San Juan, P.R.	77	3.0	77	2.0	78	2.3	80	3.6	79	5.6	80	4.7	82	4.9	82	5.9	82	6.0	81	5.9	80	5.6	78	4.7
Sault Ste. Marie, Mich.*	13	2.2	14	1.7	24	2.0	38	2.4	50	2.9	58	3.3	64	3.0	63	3.5	54	3.9	45	2.9	33	2.8	20	2.6
Savannah, Ga.	49	3.1	52	3.2	58	3.8	66	3.2	73	4.6	79	5.7	81	7.4	81	6.7	77	5.2	67	2.3	58	1.9	51	2.8
Seattle, Wash.	39	6.0	43	4.2	44	3.6	49	2.4	55	1.6	60	1.4	65	0.7	64	1.3	60	2.0	53	3.4	45	5.9	41	6.3
Spokane, Wash.	26	2.5	32	1.6	38	1.4	46	1.1	54	1.4	62	1.2	70	0.5	68	0.7	60	0.7	48	1.1	35	2.1	29	2.5
Springfield, Mo.	32	1.6	36	2.1	45	3.4	56	4.0	65	4.3	73	4.7	78	3.6	77	3.8	70	4.2	58	3.2	45	3.2	35	2.2
Syracuse, N.Y.	23	2.6	24	2.7	33	3.1	46	3.3	57	3.1	66	3.6	71	3.8	69	3.8	62	3.3	51	3.1	41	3.5	28	3.2
Tampa, Fla.	60	2.2	61	3.0	66	3.5	72	1.8	77	3.4	81	5.3	82	7.4	82	7.6	81	6.2	74	2.3	67	1.9	61	2.1
Washington, D.C.	31	2.8	34	2.6	42	3.1	53	3.1	62	3.6	71	3.4	76	3.9	74	4.2	67	3.3	55	3.0	45	3.0	35	3.3
Wilmington, Del.	31	3.1	33	3.0	42	3.9	52	3.4	62	3.2	71	3.5	76	3.9	75	4.0	68	3.6	56	2.9	46	3.3	36	3.5

Normal Temperatures, Highs, Lows, Precipitation

Source: Natl. Climatic Data Center, NESDIS, NOAA, U.S. Department of Commerce

These normals are based on records for the thirty-year period 1951-1980. (See explanation on page 206.) The extreme temperatures (through 1990) are listed for the stations shown and may not agree with the states records shown on page 210-211.

Airport stations; * designates city office stations. The minus (−) sign indicates temperatures below zero. Fahrenheit thermometer registration.

State	Station	Normal temperature January Max.	January Min.	July Max.	July Min.	Extreme temperature Highest	Lowest	Normal annual precipitation (inches)
Alabama	Mobile	61	41	91	73	104	3	64.64
Alabama	Montgomery	57	36	92	72	105	0	49.16
Alaska	Juneau	27	16	64	47	90	−22	53.15
Arizona	Phoenix	65	39	105	80	118	17	7.11
Arkansas	Little Rock	50	30	93	71	112	−5	49.20
California	Los Angeles*	67	48	84	64	110	28	14.85
California	San Francisco	55	42	71	53	106	20	19.71
Colorado	Denver	43	16	88	59	104	−30	15.31
Connecticut	Hartford	34	17	85	62	102	−26	44.39
Delaware	Wilmington	39	23	86	66	102	−14	41.38
Dist. of Col.	Washington	43	28	88	70	104	−5	39.00
Florida	Jacksonville	65	42	91	72	105	7	52.76
Florida	Key West	72	66	89	80	95	41	39.42
Florida	Miami	75	59	89	76	98	30	57.55
Georgia	Atlanta	51	33	88	69	105	−8	48.61
Hawaii	Honolulu	80	65	87	73	94	53	23.47
Idaho	Boise	37	23	91	59	111	−23	11.71
Illinois	Chicago	29	14	83	63	104	−27	33.34
Indiana	Indianapolis	34	18	85	65	104	−23	39.12
Iowa	Des Moines	27	10	86	66	108	−24	30.83
Iowa	Dubuque	24	7	82	62	101	−28	38.59
Kansas	Wichita	40	19	93	70	113	−21	28.61
Kentucky	Louisville	41	24	88	68	105	−20	43.56
Louisiana	New Orleans	62	43	91	74	102	11	59.74
Maine	Portland	31	12	79	57	103	−39	43.52
Maryland	Baltimore	41	24	87	67	105	−7	41.84
Massachusetts	Boston	36	23	82	65	102	−12	43.84
Michigan	Detroit	31	16	83	61	104	−21	30.97
Michigan	Sault Ste. Marie*	21	5	75	52	98	−36	33.48
Minnesota	Minn.-St. Paul	20	2	83	63	105	−34	26.36
Mississippi	Jackson	57	35	93	68	106	2	52.82
Missouri	St. Louis	38	20	89	69	107	−18	33.91
Montana	Helena	28	8	84	52	105	−42	11.37
Nebraska	Omaha	30	10	89	67	114	−23	30.34
Nevada	Las Vegas	55	33	105	76	116	8	4.19
New Hampshire	Concord	31	9	83	56	102	−37	36.53
New Jersey	Atlantic City	41	23	84	65	106	−11	41.93
New Mexico	Albuquerque	47	22	93	65	105	−17	8.12
New Mexico	Roswell	55	27	94	69	109	−9	9.70
New York	Albany	30	12	83	60	100	−28	35.74
New York	New York-La Guardia	37	26	84	69	107	−3	42.82
No. Carolina	Charlotte	50	31	88	69	104	−5	43.16
No. Carolina	Raleigh	50	29	88	67	105	−9	41.76
No. Dakota	Bismarck	18	−4	84	56	109	−44	15.36
Ohio	Cincinnati-Greater	37	20	86	65	102	−25	40.14
Ohio	Cleveland	33	19	82	61	104	−19	35.40
Oklahoma	Oklahoma City	47	25	94	71	110	−8	30.89
Oregon	Portland	44	34	80	56	107	−3	37.39
Pennsylvania	Harrisburg	37	22	86	65	107	−9	39.09
Pennsylvania	Philadelphia	39	24	86	67	104	−7	41.42
Rhode Island	Block Island	37	25	76	64	92	−4	41.91
So. Carolina	Charleston	59	37	89	72	104	6	51.59
So. Dakota	Huron	22	0	87	61	112	−39	18.66
So. Dakota	Rapid City	32	9	87	59	110	−29	16.27
Tennessee	Nashville	46	28	90	69	107	−17	48.49
Texas	Amarillo	49	22	91	66	108	−14	19.10
Texas	Galveston*	59	48	87	79	101	8	40.24
Texas	Houston	62	41	94	73	107	7	44.76
Utah	Salt Lake City	37	20	93	62	107	−30	15.31
Vermont	Burlington	25	8	81	59	101	−30	33.69
Virginia	Norfolk	48	32	90	70	104	−3	45.22
Washington	Seattle-Tacoma	44	34	75	54	99	0	38.60
Washington	Spokane	31	20	84	55	108	−25	16.71
West Virginia	Huntington	41	25	86	65	102	−16	40.74
Wisconsin	Madison	25	7	83	58	104	−37	30.84
Wisconsin	Milwaukee	26	11	80	61	103	−26	30.94
Wyoming	Cheyenne	37	15	83	55	100	−34	13.31
Puerto Rico	San Juan	83	70	88	76	98	60	53.99

Mean Annual Snowfall (inches) based on record through 1980: Boston, Mass. 42; Sault Ste. Marie, Mich., 113; Albany, N.Y. 65.2; Rochester, N.Y. 89.2; Burlington, Vt., 78.6; Cheyenne, Wyo., 53.3; Juneau, Alas. 105.8.

Wettest Spot: Mount Waialeale, Ha., on the island of Kauai, is the rainiest place in the world, according to the National Geographic Society, with an average annual rainfall of 460 inches.

Highest Temperature: A temperature of 136° F. observed at Azizia, Tripolitania in Northern Africa on Sept. 13, 1922, is generally accepted as the world's highest temperature recorded under standard conditions.

The record high in the United States was 134° in Death Valley, Cal., July 10, 1913.

Lowest Temperature: A record low temperature of −128.6° F. was recorded at the Soviet Antarctica station Vostok on July 21, 1983.

The record low in the United States was −80° at Prospect Creek, Alas., Jan. 23, 1971.

The lowest official temperature on the North American continent was recorded at 81 degrees below zero in February, 1947, at a lonely airport in the Yukon called Snag.

These are the meteorological champions—the official temperature extremes—but there are plenty of other claimants to thermometer fame. However, sun readings are unofficial records, since meteorological data to qualify officially must be taken on instruments in a sheltered and ventilated location.

Annual Climatological Data

Source: Natl. Climatic Data Center, NESDIS, NOAA, U.S. Department of Commerce

1990

Station	Elev. ft.	Temperature °F — Highest	Date	Lowest	Date	Precipitation — Total (in.)	Greatest in 24 hrs.	Date	Sleet or snow — Total (in.)	Greatest in 24 hours	Date	Fastest Wind — MPH	Date	No. of days — Clear*	Cloudy*	Prec. .01 in. or more	Snow, sleet 1 in. or more
Albany, N.Y.	275	96	7/4	-7	2/26	46.01	2.62	10/23	56.9	9.7	1/29	33	3/26	54	202	133	13
Albuquerque, N.M.	5311	104	6/29	-7	12/23	10.25	1.15	7/13	15.4	3.8	12/22	52	7/14	155	105	80	5
Anchorage, Alas.	114	80	8/11	-24	12/1	19.01	1.12	9/22	95.9	5.8	11/17	35	11/9	75	238	125	28
Asheville, N.C.	2140	94	7/7	14	12/25	55.87	5.10	8/21	T	T	12/27	30	3/20	96	149	127	0
Atlanta, Ga.	1010	99	7/8	20	12/25	57.56	5.74	3/16	T	T	4/10	52	2/10	119	131	105	0
Baltimore, Md.	148	101	7/9	13	2/26	41.88	2.59	7/12	8.1	4.8	12/27	37	12/31	99	158	117	3
Barrow, Alas.	31	71	6/25	-43	2/24	4.61	.73	8/30	32.8	2.6	10/2	43	12/18	110	130	88	9
Birmingham, Ala.	678	103	8/19	16	12/25	47.46	3.27	12/22	T	T	12/24	—	—	—	—	101	0
Bismarck, N.D.	1647	97	8/16	-37	12/30	12.67	1.53	6/18	28.1	3.3	12/2	44	1/10	100	139	76	12
Boise, Ida.	2838	109	8/16	-25	12/22	12.07	2.05	5/28	27.9	5.3	12/19	33	5/30	122	146	83	13
Boston, Mass.	15	93	7/20	3	2/26	46.50	3.91	10/13	29.7	5.7	2/24	37	10/19	86	181	130	9
Buffalo, N.Y.	705	94	4/28	2	2/25	50.89	2.33	12/29	67.2	10.2	2/14	47	5/17	50	207	169	21
Burlington, Vt.	332	91	7/18	-6	2/18	42.18	2.48	11/10	68.0	10.2	2/15	39	2/13	54	217	168	17
Charleston, S.C.	40	100	7/6	29	2/26	45.13	4.92	10/10	0.0	0.0	—	35	6/23	103	160	94	0
Charleston, W. Va.	939	96	7/9	6	2/26	44.05	1.73	12/17	23.7	7.4	1/8	24	2/24	72	190	147	5
Chicago, Ill.	658	96	9/6	-6	12/26	43.12	3.34	5/9	21.4	9.7	2/14	40	3/15	88	185	128	7
Cincinnati, Oh.	869	96	7/9	5	12/24	57.58	2.85	5/16	19.1	7.5	12/27	35	6/6	93	169	135	4
Cleveland, Oh.	777	98	7/4	2	2/26	53.83	3.30	9/6	36.9	5.5	1/29	38	1/25	61	218	152	14
Columbus, Oh.	812	96	7/9	5	2/26	53.16	2.67	7/11	14.8	3.8	2/24	28	8/28	64	205	134	5
Concord, N.H.	342	93	7/18	-9	2/27	41.28	3.22	6/25	55.8	9.2	1/29	31	12/24	73	182	125	13
Dallas, Tex.	551	106	8/31	10	12/23	45.27	3.72	5/1	0.3	0.2	12/22	33	2/22	130	152	89	0
Denver, Co.	5283	102	7/1	-25	12/22	16.69	1.74	3/5	65.3	11.6	3/6	37	3/6	111	106	106	20
Des Moines, Ia.	938	97	9/6	-11	12/22	43.93	4.31	6/16	32.2	10.4	12/2	45	1/11	130	149	118	9
Detroit, Mich.	633	98	7/4	3	12/27	42.64	3.52	9/6	38.1	5.9	3/4	48	1/25	74	186	142	11
Dodge City, Kan.	2582	105	6/29	-7	12/22	20.88	2.21	5/29	27.8	11.8	1/18	45	3/11	148	119	85	6
Duluth, Minn.	1428	93	7/3	-27	2/17	33.39	3.12	9/5	56.9	8.9	2/15	37	3/15	87	166	125	14
Fairbanks, Alas.	436	90	7/4	-47	12/1	18.52	1.73	7/10	122.3	10.9	12/28	28	9/6	76	211	122	40
Fresno, Cal.	328	111	8/7	18	12/23	8.73	1.42	5/27	T	T	12/21	23	5/23	220	73	34	0
Galveston, Tex.	7	99	8/27	24	12/24	38.19	2.40	9/12	T	T	12/23	33	5/22	—	—	88	0
Grand Rapids, Mich.	784	95	7/8	-1	12/27	42.56	3.00	11/27	60.0	7.4	2/22	39	5/10	62	206	149	19
Hartford, Conn.	169	95	7/4	-4	2/26	53.17	3.07	10/23	33.4	8.1	12/28	32	11/12	80	176	131	9
Helena, Mont.	3828	103	8/6	-35	12/22	8.43	0.81	8/24	42.2	7.1	12/17	49	1/8	88	164	88	9
Honolulu, Ha.	7	93	9/4	57	12/30	19.84	3.52	2/24	0.0	0.0	—	35	2/7	97	92	109	0
Houston, Tex.	96	104	8/24	19	12/24	40.37	3.52	4/26	T	T	6/25	32	11/4	73	166	94	0
Huron, S.D.	1281	100	9/12	-30	12/23	22.98	3.74	5/18	26.9	11.7	2/15	44	6/11	121	147	80	10
Indianapolis, Ind.	792	97	7/9	-2	12/24	50.44	2.83	12/29	17.5	4.3	12/27	33	1/27	55	182	130	6
Jackson, Miss.	291	103	9/4	19	12/25	54.04	2.69	5/12	T	T	12/24	46	1/17	107	139	106	0
Jacksonville, Fla.	26	100	7/7	29	12/5	31.20	2.57	7/2	T	T	7/2	32	7/2	95	136	91	0
Kansas City, Mo.	1014	102	9/1	-6	12/22	40.61	3.23	5/15	16.0	9.2	3/23	48	6/6	142	137	106	4
Lander, Wyo.	5557	99	6/30	-35	12/22	11.57	1.27	7/20	71.6	12.7	11/5	37	7/23	109	140	67	18
Little Rock, Ark.	257	105	8/29	11	12/24	67.07	5.67	10/8	T	T	12/31	—	—	—	—	127	0
Los Angeles, Cal.	97	94	10/9	35	12/23	5.24	2.21	2/16	T	T	3/12	—	—	181	76	26	0
Louisville, Ky.	477	99	9/7	8	12/24	57.47	3.66	2/15	10.9	3.6	12/27	32	9/14	95	171	131	4
Marquette, Mich.	1415	89	7/3	-18	12/26	32.73	2.32	5/9	158.1	17.5	2/16	—	—	—	—	160	36
Memphis, Tenn.	258	101	9/6	12	12/24	59.79	3.65	12/20	0.4	0.4	12/22	37	7/22	121	151	112	0
Miami, Fla.	7	98	8/1	49	1/13	51.71	4.74	4/8	0.0	0.0	—	43	7/2	50	107	135	0
Milwaukee, Wis.	672	98	7/4	-7	12/26	40.86	3.69	8/17	53.3	13.8	1/25	39	3/15	79	177	124	15
Minneapolis, Minn.	834	100	7/3	-24	12/23	33.05	2.44	7/26	33.9	6.1	2/15	38	1/11	105	156	104	12
Mobile, Ala.	211	99	9/4	25	12/25	55.97	10.57	3/15	0.0	0.0	—	35	8/30	130	120	95	0
Moline, Ill.	582	99	7/4	-5	12/26	50.41	3.42	8/19	24.1	8.9	2/14	40	1/11	106	160	118	5
Nashville, Tenn.	590	103	8/28	11	12/25	47.09	2.60	2/3	0.7	0.4	3/19	35	6/6	91	154	113	0
Newark, N.J.	7	98	7/5	8	2/26	52.30	2.82	8/6	15.9	7.6	12/27	35	11/12	86	175	145	6
New Orleans, La.	4	100	8/5	30	12/25	61.05	6.81	12/2	T	T	4/22	40	9/4	92	154	92	0
New York, N.Y.	132	97	7/5	9	2/26	45.24	2.74	5/29	11.2	6.1	12/27	35	12/31	97	168	133	2
Norfolk, Va.	24	98	7/5	19	2/26	45.52	4.32	8/24	T	T	12/27	43	10/26	85	145	117	0
Oklahoma City, Okla.	1285	104	8/31	3	12/30	40.54	5.86	9/20	6.0	2.0	12/29	67	4/16	154	130	97	3
Omaha, Neb.	997	106	7/2	-13	12/23	26.28	2.80	7/25	27.2	6.1	12/2	44	1/11	114	153	100	8
Philadelphia, Pa.	5	97	7/5	10	2/26	35.79	2.25	5/29	13.5	6.4	12/27	40	10/18	83	164	128	4
Phoenix, Ariz.	1110	122	6/26	26	12/23	7.73	1.90	8/14	0.4	0.4	12/27	35	9/14	208	62	47	0
Pittsburgh, Pa.	1137	94	7/9	0	2/26	52.24	2.76	12/30	18.7	4.0	12/27	46	12/23	52	212	153	6
Portland, Me.	43	92	7/18	-3	2/27	52.69	4.70	11/10	56.2	11.4	2/4	31	11/6	78	194	133	11
Portland, Ore.	21	101	8/11	12	12/21	32.86	1.31	1/6	9.6	5.2	2/12	44	1/8	63	220	165	2
Providence, R.I.	51	91	7/19	4	2/27	44.78	2.50	4/3	39.3	6.9	12/28	36	4/11	85	178	126	11
Raleigh, N.C.	434	98	9/7	17	2/26	37.55	2.65	3/29	T	T	12/27	37	5/1	103	158	115	0
Rapid City, S.D.	3162	106	7/2	-30	12/30	16.45	1.82	9/5	29.5	4.0	3/6	54	6/11	106	127	95	10
Reno, Nev.	4404	103	8/6	-13	12/22	5.26	1.80	2/16	32.3	18.0	2/16	—	—	157	99	48	6
Richmond, Va.	164	101	7/6	16	2/26	41.93	4.15	8/9	0.2	0.2	4/7	31	6/22	105	165	115	0
Rochester, N.Y.	547	93	4/28	6	2/26	40.14	1.62	8/4	89.1	10.4	4/4	40	11/6	52	220	167	24
St. Louis, Mo.	535	102	7/4	0	12/24	45.09	3.62	5/15	28.7	8.4	3/23	46	5/15	97	180	116	8
Salt Lake City, Ut.	4221	103	8/8	-11	12/23	10.69	0.82	3/11	48.3	9.6	3/11	48	2/17	129	152	86	15
San Antonio, Tex.	788	102	8/27	16	12/23	38.31	5.42	7/15	T	T	12/23	31	2/9	90	165	83	0
San Diego, Cal.	13	94	6/26	36	12/23	7.29	0.85	2/17	0.0	0.0	—	26	11/26	139	107	33	0
San Francisco, Cal.	8	93	9/20	27	12/22	10.35	1.45	2/15	0.0	0.0	—	55	2/16	180	99	43	0
Sault Ste. Marie, Mich.	721	85	7/26	-19	2/25	35.06	1.52	11/21	129.6	8.6	1/25	38	10/27	59	227	161	44
Savannah, Ga.	46	102	7/1	27	1/14	43.08	5.79	10/10	0.0	0.0	—	35	10/4	116	125	95	0
Seattle, Wash.	400	94	8/11	12	12/29	44.75	3.58	11/23	13.6	9.8	2/16	—	—	55	233	163	3
Shreveport, La.	254	102	9/5	14	12/24	65.64	4.70	11/8	T	T	12/23	46	5/12	121	153	101	0
Sioux City, Ia.	1095	104	7/3	-14	12/23	24.63	2.20	6/15	26.2	4.4	12/2	—	—	121	155	92	9
Spokane, Wash.	2356	98	7/12	-16	12/29	19.61	1.80	7/24	49.9	8.4	2/15	47	12/18	95	187	112	16
Springfield, Mo.	1268	99	9/6	0	12/24	63.19	3.91	3/13	18.3	5.3	2/28	35	9/10	122	160	125	5
Syracuse, N.Y.	410	97	7/4	-10	2/26	49.47	2.98	8/28	117.0	10.4	1/29	38	11/25	57	215	184	31
Tampa, Fla.	19	97	6/29	40	12/25	34.39	2.92	7/14	0.0	0.0	—	32	4/2	137	78	95	0
Washington, D.C.	10	100	7/5	14	2/26	40.84	2.19	6/9	5.8	3.0	12/27	39	10/18	90	176	127	2
Wilmington, Del.	74	98	7/5	10	2/26	44.13	2.72	5/29	11.8	6.4	12/27	37	2/25	97	177	126	4

*To get partly cloudy days deduct the total of clear and cloudy days from 365 (1 yr.). T—trace. (1) Date shown is the starting date of the storm (in some cases it lasted more than one day).

Record Temperatures by States Through 1990

Source: Natl. Climatic Data Center, NESDIS, NOAA, U.S. Commerce Department

State	Lowest °F	Highest	Latest date	Station	Approximate elevation in feet
Alabama	−27		Jan. 30, 1966	New Market	760
		112	Sept. 5, 1925	Centerville	345
Alaska	−80		Jan. 23, 1971	Prospect Creek Camp	1,100
		100	June 27, 1915	Fort Yukon	419
Arizona	−40		Jan. 7, 1971	Hawley Lake	8,180
		127	July 7, 1905 [1]	Parker	345
Arkansas	−29		Feb. 13, 1905	Pond	1,250
		120	Aug. 10, 1936	Ozark	396
California	−45		Jan. 20, 1937	Boca	5,532
		134	July 10, 1913	Greenland Ranch	−178
Colorado	−61		Feb. 1, 1985	Maybell	5,920
		118	July 11, 1888	Bennett	5,484
Connecticut	−32		Feb. 16, 1943	Falls Village	585
		105	July 22, 1926	Waterbury	400
Delaware	−17		Jan. 17, 1893	Millsboro	20
		110	July 21, 1930	Millsboro	20
Dist. of Col.	−15		Feb. 11, 1899	Washington	112
		106	July 20, 1930	Washington	112
Florida	−2		Feb. 13, 1899	Tallahassee	193
		109	June 29, 1931	Monticello	207
Georgia	−17		Jan. 27, 1940	CCC Camp F-16	1,000
		112	Jul. 24, 1952	Louisville	132
Hawaii	12		May 17, 1979	Mauna Kea	13,770
		100	Apr. 27, 1931	Pahala	850
Idaho	−60		Jan. 16, 1943	Island Park Dam	6,285
		118	July 28, 1934	Orofino	1,027
Illinois	−35		Jan. 22, 1930	Mount Carroll	817
		117	July 14, 1954	E. St. Louis	410
Indiana	−35		Feb. 2, 1951	Greensburg	954
		116	July 14, 1936	Collegeville	672
Iowa	−47		Jan. 12, 1912	Washta	1,157
		118	July 20, 1934	Keokuk	614
Kansas	−40		Feb. 13, 1905	Lebanon	1,812
		121	July 24, 1936 [1]	Alton (near)	1,651
Kentucky	−34		Jan. 28, 1963	Cynthiana	684
		114	July 28, 1930	Greensburg	581
Louisiana	−16		Feb. 13, 1899	Minden	194
		114	Aug. 10, 1936	Plain Dealing	268
Maine	−48		Jan. 19, 1925	Van Buren	510
		105	July 10, 1911 [1]	North Bridgton	450
Maryland	−40		Jan. 13, 1912	Oakland	2,461
		109	July 10, 1936 [1]	Cumberland and Frederick	623-325
Massachusetts	−35		Jan. 12, 1981	Chester	640
		107	Aug. 2, 1975	Chester and New Bedford	120-640
Michigan	−51		Feb. 9, 1934	Vanderbilt	785
		112	July 13, 1936	Mio	963
Minnesota	−59		Feb. 16, 1903 [1]	Pokegama Dam	1,280
		114	July 6, 1936 [1]	Moorhead	904
Mississippi	−19		Jan. 30, 1966	Corinth	420
		115	July 29, 1930	Holly Springs	600
Missouri	−40		Feb. 13, 1905	Warsaw	700
		118	July 14, 1954 [1]	Warsaw and Union	687-560
Montana	−70		Jan. 20, 1954	Rogers Pass	5,470
		117	July 5, 1937	Medicine Lake	1,950
Nebraska	−47		Feb. 12, 1899	Camp Clarke	3,700
		118	July 24, 1936 [1]	Minden	2,169
Nevada	−50		Jan. 8, 1937	San Jacinto	5,200
		122	June 23, 1954 [1]	Overton	1,240
New Hampshire	−46		Jan. 28 1925	Pittsburgh	1,575
		106	July 4, 1911	Nashua	125
New Jersey	−34		Jan. 5, 1904	River Vale	70
		110	July 10, 1936	Runyon	18
New Mexico	−50		Feb. 1, 1951	Gavilan	7,350
		116	July 14, 1934 [1]	Orogrande	4,171
New York	−52		Feb. 18, 1979	Old Forge	1,720
		108	July 22, 1926	Troy	35
North Carolina	−34		Jan. 21, 1985	Mt. Mitchell	6,525
		110	Aug. 21, 1983	Fayetteville	213
North Dakota	−60		Feb. 15, 1936	Parshall	1,929
		121	July 6, 1936	Steele	1,857
Ohio	−39		Feb. 10, 1899	Milligan	800
		113	July 21, 1934 [1]	Gallipolis (near)	673
Oklahoma	−27		Jan. 18, 1930	Watts	958
		120	July 26, 1943 [1]	Tishmoningo	670
Oregon	−54		Feb. 10, 1933 [1]	Seneca	4,700
		119	Aug. 10, 1938	Pendleton	1,074
Pennsylvania	−42		Jan. 5, 1904	Smethport	1,469
		111	July 10, 1936 [1]	Phoenixville	100
Rhode Island	−23		Jan. 11, 1942	Kingston	100
		104	Aug. 2, 1975	Providence	51
South Carolina	−19		Jan. 21, 1985	Caesar's Head	3,100
		111	June 28, 1954 [1]	Camden	170
South Dakota	−58		Feb. 17, 1936	McIntosh	2,277
		120	July 5, 1936	Gannvalley	1,750

State	Lowest °F	Highest	Latest date	Station	Approximate elevation in feet
Tennessee	−32		Dec. 30, 1917	Mountain City	2,471
		113	Aug. 9, 1930 [1]	Perryville	377
Texas	−23		Feb. 8, 1933	Seminole	3,275
		120	Aug. 12, 1936	Seymour	1,291
Utah	−69		Feb. 1, 1985	Peter's Sink	8,092
		117	Jul. 5, 1985	Saint George	2,880
Vermont	−50		Dec. 30, 1933	Bloomfield	915
		105	July 4, 1911	Vernon	310
Virginia	−30		Jan. 22, 1985	Mtn. Lake Bio. Stn.	3,870
		110	July 15, 1954	Balcony Falls	725
Washington	−48		Dec. 30, 1968	Mazama	2,120
	−48		Dec. 30, 1968	Winthrop	1,765
		118	Aug. 5, 1961 [1]	Ice Harbor Dam	475
West Virginia	−37		Dec. 30, 1917	Lewisburg	2,200
		112	July 10, 1936 [1]	Martinsburg	435
Wisconsin	−54		Jan. 24, 1922	Danbury	908
		114	July 13, 1936	Wisconsin Dells	900
Wyoming	−63		Feb. 9, 1933	Moran	6,770
		114	July 12, 1900	Basin	3,500

(1) Also on earlier dates at the same or other places.

International Temperature and Precipitation

Source: Environmental Data Service, U.S. Commerce Department

A standard period of 30 years has been used to obtain the average daily maximum and minimum temperatures and precipitation. The length of record of extreme maximum and minimum temperatures includes all available years of data for a given location and is usually for a longer period.

Station	Elev. Ft.	Average Daily January Max.	January Min.	July Max.	July Min.	Extreme Max.	Extreme Min.	Average annual precipitation (inches)
Addis Ababa, Ethiopia	8,038	75	43	69	50	94	32	48.7
Algiers, Algeria	194	59	49	83	70	107	32	30.0
Amsterdam, Netherlands	5	40	34	69	59	95	3	25.6
Athens, Greece	351	54	42	90	72	109	20	15.8
Auckland, New Zealand	23	73	60	56	46	90	33	49.1
Bangkok, Thailand	53	89	67	90	76	104	50	57.8
Beirut, Lebanon	111	62	51	87	73	107	30	35.1
Belgrade, Yugoslavia	453	37	27	84	61	107	−14	24.6
Berlin, Germany	187	35	26	74	55	96	−15	23.1
Bogota, Colombia	8,355	67	48	64	50	75	30	41.8
Bombay, India	27	88	62	88	75	110	46	71.2
Bucharest, Romania	269	33	20	86	61	105	−18	22.8
Budapest, Hungary	394	35	26	82	61	103	−10	24.2
Buenos Aires, Argentina	89	85	63	57	42	104	22	37.4
Cairo, Egypt	381	65	47	96	70	117	34	1.1
Capetown, South Africa	56	78	60	63	45	103	28	20.0
Caracas, Venezuela	3,418	75	56	78	61	91	45	32.9
Casablanca, Morocco	164	63	45	79	65	110	31	15.9
Copenhagen, Denmark	43	36	29	72	55	91	−3	23.3
Damascus, Syria	2,362	53	36	96	64	113	21	8.6
Dublin, Ireland	155	47	35	67	51	86	8	29.7
Geneva, Switzerland	1,329	39	29	77	58	101	−1	33.9
Havana, Cuba	80	79	65	89	75	104	43	48.2
Hong Kong	109	64	56	87	78	97	32	85.1
Istanbul, Turkey	59	45	36	81	65	100	17	31.5
Jerusalem, Israel	2,654	55	41	87	63	107	26	19.7
Lagos, Nigeria	10	88	74	83	74	104	60	72.3
La Paz, Bolivia	12,001	63	43	62	33	80	26	22.6
Lima, Peru	394	82	66	67	57	93	49	1.6
London, England	149	44	35	73	55	99	9	22.9
Madrid, Spain	2,188	47	33	87	62	102	14	16.5
Manila, Philippines	49	86	69	88	75	101	58	82.0
Mexico City, Mexico	7,340	66	42	74	54	92	24	23.0
Moscow, U.S.S.R.	505	21	9	76	55	96	−27	24.8
Nairobi, Kenya	5,971	77	54	69	51	87	41	37.7
Oslo, Norway	308	30	20	73	56	93	−21	26.9
Paris, France	164	42	32	76	55	105	1	22.3
Prague, Czechoslovakia	662	34	25	74	58	98	−16	19.3
Reykjavik, Iceland	92	36	28	58	48	74	4	33.9
Rome, Italy	377	54	39	88	64	104	20	29.5
San Salvador, El Salvador	2,238	90	60	89	65	105	45	70.0
Santiago, Chile	1,706	85	53	59	37	99	24	14.2
Sao Paolo, Brazil	2,628	77	63	66	53	100	32	57.3
Shanghai, China	16	47	32	91	75	104	10	45.0
Singapore	33	86	73	88	75	97	66	95.0
Stockholm, Sweden	146	31	23	70	55	97	−26	22.4
Sydney, Australia	62	78	65	60	46	114	35	46.5
Teheran, Iran	3,937	45	27	99	72	109	−5	9.7
Tokyo, Japan	19	47	29	83	70	101	17	61.6
Tripoli, Libya	72	61	47	85	71	114	33	15.1
Vienna, Austria	664	34	26	75	59	98	−14	25.6
Warsaw, Poland	294	30	21	75	56	98	−22	22.0

Record Maximum 24-Hour Precipitation by State

(through 1990)

Source: Natl. Climatic Data Center, NESDIS, NOAA, U.S. Department of Commerce

State	Precip. (inches)	Date	Station	Elevation (feet)	State	Precip. (inches)	Date	Station	Elevation (feet)
Ala. . .	20.33	4/13/55	Axis	36	Mont. .	11.50	6/20/21	Circle	2,440
Alas. . .	15.20	10/12/82	Angoon	15	Neb. .	13.15	7/8-9/50	York	1,610
Ariz. . .	11.40	9/4-5/70	Workman Creek	6,970	Nev. . .	7.40	3/19/07	Lewer's Ranch	5,200
Ark. . .	14.06	12/3/82	Big Fork	1,100	N.H. .	10.38	2/10-11/70	Mount Washington	6,260
Cal. . .	26.12	1/22-23/43	Hoegees Camp	2,760	N.J. . .	14.81	8/19/39	Tuckerton	20
Colo. .	11.08	6/17/65	Holly	3,390	N.M. . .	11.28	5/18-19/55	Lake Maloya	7,400
Conn. .	12.77	8/19/55	Burlington	460	N.Y. . .	11.17	10/9/03	NYC Central Park	130
Del. . .	8.50	7/13/75	Dover	30	N.C. . .	22.22	7/15-16/16	Altapass	2,600
Fla. . . .	38.70	9/5/50	Yankeetown	5	N.D. . .	8.10	6/29/75	Litchville	1,470
Ga. . . .	18.00	8/28/11	St. George	77	Ohio . .	10.51	7/12/66	Sandusky	610
Ha. . . .	38.00	1/24-25/56	Kilauea Plantation	180	Okla. . .	15.50	9/3-4/40	Sapulpa	740
Id. . . .	7.17	11/23/09	Rattlesnake Creek	4,000	Ore. . .	10.17	12/21/15	Glenora	575
Ill. . . .	16.54	6/14-15/57	East St. Louis	410	Pa. . . .	34.50*	7/17/42	Smethport	1,510
Ind. . . .	10.50	8/6/05	Princeton	480	R.I. . . .	12.13	9/16-17/32	Westerly	40
Ia. . . .	16.70	8/5-6/59	Decatur Co.	1,110	S.C. . . .	13.25	7/14-15/16	Effingham	110
Kan. . .	12.59	5/31-6/1/41	Burlington	1,010	S.D. . .	8.00	9/10/00	Elk Point	1,127
Ky. . . .	10.40	6/28/60	Dunmor	610	Tenn. . .	11.00	3/28/02	McMinnville	900
La. . . .	22.00	8/28-29/62	Hackberry	10	Texas . .	43.00*	7/25-26/79	Alvin	50
Me. . . .	8.05	9/11/54	Brunswick	70	Utah . . .	6.00*	9/5/70	Bug Point	6,600
Md. . . .	14.75	7/26-27/97	Jewell	152	Vt.	8.77	11/3-4/27	Somerset	2,080
Mass. .	18.15	8/18-19/55	Westfield	220	Va. . . .	27.00*	8/20/69	Nelson Co.	est. 500
Mich. . .	9.78	8/31-9/1/14	Bloomingdale	750	Wash. . .	12.00	1/21/35	Quinault R.S.	220
Minn. . .	10.84	7/21-22/72	Fort Ripley	1,140	W.Va. . .	19.00*	7/18/89	Rockport	700
Miss. . .	15.68	7/9/68	Columbus	190	Wis. . . .	11.72	6/24/46	Mellen	1,150
Mo. . . .	18.18	7/20/65	Edgarton	850	Wyo. . .	6.06	8/1/85	Cheyenne	6,126

*Estimated

Wind Chill Table

Source: National Weather Service, NOAA, U.S. Commerce Department

Both temperature and wind cause heat loss from body surfaces. A combination of cold and wind makes a body feel colder than the actual temperature. The table shows, for example, that a temperature of 20 degrees Fahrenheit, plus a wind of 20 miles per hour, causes a body heat loss equal to that in minus 10 degrees with no wind. In other words, the wind makes 20 degrees feel like minus 10.

Top line of figures shows actual temperatures in degrees Fahrenheit. Column at left shows wind speeds.

MPH	35	30	25	20	15	10	5	0	−5	−10	−15	−20	−25	−30	−35	−40	−45
5	33	27	21	16	12	7	0	−5	−10	−15	−21	−26	−31	−36	−42	−47	−52
10	22	16	10	3	−3	−9	−15	−22	−27	−34	−40	−46	−52	−58	−64	−71	−77
15	16	9	2	−5	−11	−18	−25	−31	−38	−45	−51	−58	−65	−72	−78	−85	−92
20	12	4	−3	−10	−17	−24	−31	−39	−46	−53	−60	−67	−74	−81	−88	−95	−103
25	8	1	−7	−15	−22	−29	−36	−44	−51	−59	−66	−74	−81	−88	−96	−103	−110
30	6	−2	−10	−18	−25	−33	−41	−49	−56	−64	−71	−79	−86	−93	−101	−109	−116
35	4	−4	−12	−20	−27	−35	−43	−52	−58	−67	−74	−82	−89	−97	−105	−113	−120
40	3	−5	−13	−21	−29	−37	−45	−53	−60	−69	−76	−84	−92	−100	−107	−115	−123
45	2	−6	−14	−22	−30	−38	−46	−54	−62	−70	−78	−85	−93	−102	−109	−117	−125

(Wind speeds greater than 45 mph have little additional chilling effect.)

Heat Index

The index is a measure of the contribution that high humidity makes with abnormally high temperatures in reducing the body's ability to cool itself. For example, the index shows that for an actual air temperature of 100 degrees Fahrenheit and a relative humidity of 50 percent, the effect on the human body would be same as 120 degrees. Sunstroke and heat exhaustion are likely when the heat index reaches 105. This index is a measure of what hot weather "feels like" to the average person for various temperatures and relative humidities.

Relative Humidity	Air Temperature*										
	70	75	80	85	90	95	100	105	110	115	120
	Apparent Temperature*										
0%	64	69	73	78	83	87	91	95	99	103	107
10%	65	70	75	80	85	90	95	100	105	111	116
20%	66	72	77	82	87	93	99	105	112	120	130
30%	67	73	78	84	90	96	104	113	123	135	148
40%	68	74	79	86	93	101	110	123	137	151	
50%	69	75	81	88	96	107	120	135	150		
60%	70	76	82	90	100	114	132	149			
70%	70	77	85	93	106	124	144				
80%	71	78	86	97	113	136					
90%	71	79	88	102	122						
100%	72	80	91	108							

*Degrees Fahrenheit.

EDUCATION

Historical Summary of Public Elementary and Secondary Schools

Source: National Center for Education Statistics, U.S. Dept. of Education

Pupils and teachers (thousands)	1899-1900	1909-10	1919-20	1929-30	1939-40	1949-50	1959-60[1]	1969-70	1979-80	1988-89
Total U.S. population	75,995	90,492	104,512	121,770	130,880	148,665	179,323	203,212	224,567	245,807
Population 5-17 years of age	21,573	24,009	27,556	31,417	30,150	30,168	43,881	52,490	48,040	45,388
Percent aged 5-17 years	28.4	26.5	26.4	25.8	23.0	20.3	24.5	25.8	21.4	18.5
Enrollment (thousands)										
Elementary and secondary	15,503	17,814	21,578	25,678	25,434	25,111	36,087	45,619	41,645	40,189
Percent pop. 5-17 enrolled	71.9	74.2	78.3	81.7	84.4	83.2	82.2	86.9	86.7	88.5
Percent in high schools	3.3	5.1	10.2	17.1	26.0	22.7	23.5	28.5	32.9	29.1
High school graduates	62	111	231	592	1,143	1,063	1,627	2,589	2,748	2,395
Average school term (in days)	144.3	157.5	161.9	172.7	175.0	177.9	178.0	178.9	178.5	...
Total instructional staff	...	...	678	880	912	962	1,464	2,253	2,441	...
Teachers, librarians: Men	127	110	93	140	195	195	402	691	782[4]	...
Women	296	413	565	703	681	719	985	1,440	1,518[4]	...
Percent men	29.9	21.1	14.1	16.6	22.2	21.3	29.0	33.4	34.0[4]	...
Revenue & expenditures (millions)										
Total revenue	$219	$433	$970	$2,088	$2,260	$5,437	$14,746	$40,267	$96,881	$191,210
Total expenditures	214	426	1,036	2,316	2,344	5,837	15,613	40,683	95,962	189,800[4]
Current elem. and secondary	179	356	861	1,843	1,941	4,687	12,329	34,218	86,984[1]	172,932
Capital outlay	35	69	153	370	257	1,014	2,661	4,659	6,506	...
Interest on school debt	...	...	18	92	130	100	489	1,171	1,874	...
Other	...	...	3	9	13	35	132	636	598	...
Salaries and pupil cost						(Data in unadjusted dollars)				
Average annual teacher salary[2]	$325	$485	$871	$1,420	$1,441	$3,010	$5,174	$8,840	$16,715	$30,969
Expenditure per capita total pop.	2.83	4.71	9.91	19.03	17.91	39	87	200	424	772
Current expenditure per pupil ADA[3]	16.67	27.85	53.32	86.70	88.09	209	375	816	2,272	4,639

(1) Because of a modification of the scope, "current expenditures for elementary and secondary schools" data for 1959-60 and later years are not entirely comparable with data for prior years. (2) Includes supervisors, principals, teachers and other non-supervisory instructional staff. (3) "ADA" means average daily attendance in elementary and secondary day schools. (4) Estimated.

Years of School Completed, by Age, Race, and Hispanic Origin: 1989

Source: U.S. Bureau of the Census, unpublished data.

Sex, Age, Race, and Hispanic Origin	Population (1,000)	Elementary School 1 to 4 years	5 to 7 years	8 years	High School 1 to 3 years	4 years	College 1 to 3 years	4 years or more	Meridan years of school completed
Total persons	154,155	2.5	4.1	5.0	11.5	38.5	17.3	21.1	12.7
Male	73,225	2.8	4.3	4.8	11.0	35.4	17.4	24.5	12.8
Female	80,930	2.4	4.0	5.2	11.9	41.3	17.2	18.1	12.6
25 to 29 years old	21,478	1.0	1.5	1.6	10.4	41.7	20.4	23.4	12.9
30 to 34 years old	21,762	1.1	1.8	1.4	8.1	41.1	21.5	25.0	12.9
35 to 44 years old	35,873	1.4	2.1	1.8	7.9	37.3	21.5	27.9	13.0
45 to 54 years old	24,822	2.0	3.7	3.9	12.0	40.5	15.9	22.0	12.7
55 to 64 years old	21,399	3.5	6.5	6.6	15.3	39.8	13.3	16.2	12.5
65 years old and over	29,022	6.8	9.8	13.8	15.9	33.2	10.6	11.1	12.1
White	132,903	2.0	3.7	5.0	10.8	39.1	17.5	21.8	12.7
25 to 29 years old	17,973	0.9	1.7	1.5	9.9	41.2	20.4	24.4	12.9
30 to 34 years old	18,298	1.0	1.8	1.3	7.5	41.3	21.2	25.8	12.9
35 to 44 years old	30,687	1.4	1.9	1.8	7.0	37.3	21.9	28.8	13.1
45 to 54 years old	21,127	1.7	3.1	3.7	10.8	41.7	16.5	22.5	12.7
55 to 64 years old	18,818	2.7	4.7	6.6	14.2	41.1	13.7	17.1	12.5
65 years old and over	26,001	4.0	8.4	13.9	15.9	34.9	11.3	11.7	12.2
Black	16,395	5.3	7.1	4.9	18.1	38.5	18.3	11.8	12.4
25 to 29 years old	2,726	0.5	0.5	1.8	14.9	47.8	21.9	12.7	12.7
30 to 34 years old	2,662	0.5	0.9	1.4	13.8	44.1	25.0	13.9	12.7
35 to 44 years old	3,900	0.6	3.1	2.4	16.7	41.3	20.3	16.7	12.7
45 to 54 years old	2,565	2.9	8.1	6.0	22.9	35.9	12.4	11.8	12.3
55 to 64 years old	2,105	9.4	12.8	6.8	25.8	26.5	9.8	6.9	11.4
65 years old and over	2,436	21.8	22.0	13.5	18.1	15.8	4.1	4.5	8.5
Hispanic origin[1]	10,438	12.2	15.1	7.1	14.7	27.9	13.2	9.9	12.0
25 to 29 years old	2,152	5.4	10.9	4.4	18.4	34.0	17.0	10.1	12.3
30 to 34 years old	1,816	6.9	14.0	5.7	14.8	29.2	17.8	11.8	12.3
35 to 44 years old	2,669	10.8	14.1	6.1	12.9	30.2	14.9	10.9	12.2
45 to 54 years old	1,645	14.4	17.2	7.3	16.5	25.0	9.7	10.0	11.0
55 to 64 years old	1,151	20.0	17.2	10.7	15.4	22.2	7.4	7.2	9.4
65 years old and over	1,005	27.4	22.2	14.3	8.4	17.4	4.5	5.9	8.0

(1) Persons of Hispanic origin may be of any race.

Percent of Population With Less Than 12 Years of School and With 4 Years of College or More: 1970 to 1989

Source: U.S. Bureau of the Census.

Race	Less Than 12 Years of School 1970	1980	1989 Total	1989 35-44 yr.	1989 65 yr. and over	4 Years of College or More 1970	1980	1989 Total	1989 35-44 yr.	1989 65 yr. and over
All races[1]	47.7	33.5	23.1	13.4	45.1	10.7	16.2	21.1	27.9	11.1
White	45.5	31.2	21.6	12.1	42.1	11.3	17.1	21.8	28.8	11.7
Black	68.6	48.8	35.4	21.7	75.4	4.4	8.4	11.8	16.7	4.8
Hispanic origin[2]	67.9	58.0	49.1	43.9	72.3	4.5	7.6	9.8	10.9	5.9

(1) Includes races not shown separately. (2) Persons of Hispanic origin may be of any race.

Fall Enrollment and Teachers in Full-time Day Schools
Elementary and Secondary Day Schools, Fall 1989
Source: National Center for Education Statistics. U.S. Dept. of Education; National Education Assn.

	Local school districts	Classroom teachers	Total enrollment	Pupils per teacher	Teacher's average pay (1989-1990)	Instructional aides	Expenditure per pupil
United States	15,367	2,355,963	40,526,372	17.2	$31,304	373,221	$4,639
Alabama	129	39,928	723,343	18.1	25,500	3,138	3,197
Alaska	54	6,492	109,280	16.8	43,153	1,450	7,716
Arizona	238	32,134	607,615	18.9	29,600	4,792	3,902
Arkansas	329	25,585	434,960	17.0	22,009	3,709	3,273
California	1,074	212,687	4,771,978	22.4	38,996	52,963	4,121
Colorado	176	31,954	562,755	17.6	30,700	4,016	4,408
Connecticut.	166	35,308	461,560	13.1	40,496	6,048	6,857
Delaware	19	5,968	97,808	16.4	33,480	721	5,422
District of Columbia . . .	1	6,055	81,301	13.4	36,450	638	7,850
Florida	67	104,127	1,772,349	17.0	28,525	20,380	4,563
Georgia	186	61,487	1,126,535	18.3	27,892	16,029	3,852
Hawaii.	1	8,866	169,493	19.1	32,047	942	4,121
Idaho	115	10,715	214,932	20.1	23,494	1,123	2,838
Illinois	964	106,183	1,797,355	16.9	33,014	13,006	4,906
Indiana	303	54,486	954,165	17.5	30,493	11,174	4,284
Iowa.	431	30,423	478,486	15.7	26,747	3,288	4,285
Kansas	304	28,727	430,864	15.0	28,671	2,977	4,443
Kentucky	177	35,731	630,688	17.7	26,275	5,522	3,347
Louisiana	66	—	783,025	—	22,993	—	3,317
Maine	282	15,206	213,775	14.1	26,881	3,044	4,744
Maryland	24	41,646	698,806	16.8	36,092	5,585	5,758
Massachusetts.	352	59,040	825,588	14.0	34,225	9,046	5,979
Michigan	561	80,150	1,576,785	19.7	36,010	11,240	5,116
Minnesota	436	43,101	739,553	17.2	32,190	7,712	4,755
Mississippi	152	27,591	502,020	18.2	24,363	8,301	2,874
Missouri	543	51,227	807,934	15.8	27,229	4,136	4,263
Montana	548	9,627	151,265	15.7	25,081	1,131	4,293
Nebraska	838	18,464	270,920	14.7	24,751	2,563	4,360
Nevada	17	9,175	186,834	20.4	30,587	0	3,791
New Hampshire	170	10,572	171,696	16.2	28,939	1,926	4,807
New Jersey	603	79,597	1,076,005	13.5	36,030	9,371	7,549
New Mexico	88	16,150	296,057	18.3	25,120	3,438	3,473
New York.	721	174,610	2,565,841	14.7	38,800	24,490	7,663
North Carolina	134	63,160	1,080,744	17.1	27,814	18,388	3,874
North Dakota	280	7,809	117,816	15.1	23,016	1,033	3,952
Ohio.	613	101,627	1,767,159	17.4	31,170	8,386	4,649
Oklahoma	604	35,631	578,580	16.2	23,070	4,009	3,379
Oregon	303	25,630	472,394	18.4	30,563	4,191	5,182
Pennsylvania.	501	105,415	1,655,279	15.7	32,809	11,001	5,609
Rhode Island	37	9,369	135,729	14.5	36,057	1,003	5,976
South Carolina	91	36,337	616,177	17.0	27,076	4,816	3,736
South Dakota	185	8,191	127,329	15.5	21,300	1,298	3,581
Tennessee	141	42,824	819,660	19.1	27,052	8,555	3,491
Texas	1,062	199,397	3,328,514	16.7	27,502	29,762	3,877
Utah.	40	17,611	437,446	24.8	23,652	3,284	2,579
Vermont	276	6,852	94,779	13.8	28,798	1,128	5,481
Virginia	136	62,138	985,346	15.9	30,926	9,291	4,539
Washington	296	40,279	810,232	20.1	30,475	5,814	4,352
West Virginia	55	21,653	327,540	15.1	22,842	2,761	3,883
Wisconsin.	429	49,329	782,905	15.9	32,320	6,237	5,266
Wyoming	49	6,697	97,172	14.5	28,184	1,297	5,375

Programs for the Disabled
Source: Office of Special Educ. and Rehabilitative Services, U.S. Dept. of Education

Number of children 3 to 21 years old served annually in educational programs for the disabled.

Type of Handicapped	1982-83	1983-84	1984-85	1985-86	1986-87	1987-88	1988-89	1989-90
				Number Served, in Thousands				
All disabilities	4,255	4,298	4,315	4,317	4,374	4,446	4,544	4,252
Learning disabilities	1,741	1,806	1,832	1,862	1,914	1,928	1,987	2,060
Speech impairments.	1,131	1,128	1,126	1,125	1,136	953	967	974
Mental retardation	757	727	694	660	643	582	564	565
Serious emotional disturbance . . .	352	361	372	375	383	373	376	382
Hearing impairments	73	72	69	66	65	56	56	58
Orthopedic impairments.	57	56	56	57	57	47	47	48
Visual impairments.	28	29	28	27	26	22	23	23
Deaf-blindness	2	2	2	2	2	12	2	2

Note: Counts are based on reports from the 50 States, District of Columbia and Puerto Rico (i.e., figures from U.S. territories are not included). Details may not add to totals because of rounding.

School and Home Computer Use, 1989
Source: Bureau of the Census, U.S. Dept. of Commerce   (numbers in thousands)

Type of school and grade	All students	Use at school Number	Use at school Percent	Use at home Number	Use at home Percent	Use at home and school Number	Use at home and school Percent
Public school (K-12).	39,938	18,339	45.9	6,890	17.3	4,226	10.6
Grades K-4	16,697	7,239	43.4	2,140	12.8	1,402	8.4
Grades 5-8.	12,474	6,805	54.6	2,509	20.1	1,695	13.6
Grades 9-12	10,767	4,295	39.9	2,241	20.8	1,129	10.5
Private school (K-12)	4,068	2,028	49.9	1,140	28.0	717	17.6
Grades K-4	2,100	988	47.0	447	21.3	264	12.6
Grades 5-8.	1,213	717	59.1	411	33.9	296	24.4
Grades 9-12	755	323	42.8	282	37.4	157	20.8

Federal Funds for Education, 1980-1991

Source: U.S. Office of Management and Budget

Federal funds obligated for programs administered by the Department of Education: Fiscal years 1980 to 1990
(In thousands of dollars)

	1980	1984	1988	1989	1990	1991[1]
Total................	$14,102,165	$17,072,698	$20,697,311	$24,473,634	$25,214,653	$29,301,023
Elementary and secondary						
education.............	4,239,022	4,294,269	5,682,997	5,997,160	7,169,693	8,110,886
Grants for the disadvantaged	3,204,664	3,501,383	4,357,970	4,600,444	5,383,960	6,226,814
Special programs...........	788,918	549,117	1,067,213	1,129,444	1,524,001	1,610,678
Bilingual education..........	169,540	173,051	191,470	196,309	188,152	198,014
Indian education...........	75,900	70,718	66,344	70,963	73,580	75,380
School assistance in federally						
affected areas...........	812,873	608,791	731,241	731,768	815,573	808,286
Maintenance and operations	690,000	555,300	685,498	708,396	717,354	740,708
Construction.............	110,873	28,491	35,640	18,400	22,929	43,725
Disaster assistance.........	12,000	25,000	10,103	4,972	75,290	23,853
Education for the handicapped ...	1,555,253	2,416,799	3,075,456	3,814,846	3,480,122	5,091,091
State grant programs	815,805	1,082,180	1,115,333	1,642,647	1,258,871	2,407,086
Early childhood education[2]	38,745	53,164	210,752	319,012	280,341	612,914[2]
Special centers, projects, and						
research	55,075	54,871	78,600	102,141	72,966	94,343
Captioned films and media						
services.............	17,778	14,000	13,026	13,346	15,191	16,424
Personnel training	55,375	55,540	66,153	67,023	70,838	69,289
Handicapped rehabilitation						
Service and research	572,475	1,157,044	1,591,592	1,670,677	1,781,915	1,891,035
Vocational education and adult						
programs.............	1,153,743	954,320	1,000,055	1,052,470	1,138,674	1,317,000
Basic programs[3]	744,653	689,324	823,299	859,239	858,716	869,634
Consumer and homemaking	63,169	36,792	32,752	32,816	34,517	33,352
Program improvement and						
supportive services	162,512	117,249	—	—	—	—
State planning and advisory						
councils..............	13,423	11,200	7,681	7,945	7,923	9,128
Adult education, grants to States ..	153,724	99,755	129,183	139,771	188,280	268,903
Other................	16,262	—	7,140	12,699	49,238	135,983
Postsecondary student financial						
assistance	5,108,534	7,478,401	8,807,929	11,482,608	11,112,068	12,185,673
Educational opportunity grants[4]...	2,534378	3,565,209	4,620,133	5,379,725	4,919,264	6,154,696
Work-study	596,065	561,322	604,445	620,644	615,269	598,574
Direct student loans	322,749	191,962	216,963	202,904	157,415	173,589
Guaranteed student loans	1,597,877	3,130,939	3,297,305	5,203,843	5,341,039	5,164,932
Other student assistance						
programs	57,465	28,969	69,083	75,492	79,081	93,882
Direct aid to postsecondary						
institutions	277,068	311,221	341,063	398,318	341,634	433,300
Aid to minority and developing						
institutions.............	114,680	132,081	135,222	179,062	99,812	99,542
Special programs for the						
disadvantaged	147,389	164,740	205,841	219,256	241,822	333,758
Cooperative education	14,999	14,400	—	—	—	—
Higher education facilities	268,493	216,893	162,528	77,362	84,035	107,391
Construction loans and						
insurance	35,362	54,105	89,820	37,109	30,000	29,277
Interest subsidy grants........	24,626	23,925	24,466	22,524	38,471	43,064
College housing loans	208,505	138,863	48,242	17,729	15,564	35,050
Other higher education						
programs..............	34,927	82,410	79,305	73,574	188,999	225,603
International education and						
foreign languages	19,977	30,800	—	—	86,337	92,224
Fund for Improvement of						
Postsecondary Education.....	12,000	11,710	65,813	67,236	99,450	120,009
Other................	2,950	39,900	13,492	6,338	3,212	13,370
Public Library services	101,218	107,895	135,731	141,884	132,583	155,682
Public Library services........	66,451	65,000	78,922	80,944	82,505	83,898
Interlibrary cooperation	—	11,520	18,395	18,826	19,551	19,908
Public Library construction......	—	21,015	23,577	27,289	14,837	32,002
Research Libraries	5,992	6,000	5,744	5,675	6,593	6,831
Other................	28,775	880	9,093	9,150	9,097	13,043
Payments to special institutions ..	273,860	249,610	271,658	284,056	292,736	311,301
American Printing House for the						
Blind................	4,349	5,000	5,266	5,335	5,663	6,136
National Technical Institute for						
the Deaf..............	19,799	28,000	31,594	33,326	35,594	37,688
Gallaudet College	49,409	56,288	62,195	65,998	67,643	72,262
Howard University	200,303	160,322	172,603	179,397	183,836	195,215

(continued)

	1980	1984	1988	1989	1990	1991[1]
Departmental accounts.........	$277,174	$352,089	$409,348	$419,588	$458,536	$554,810
Educational research and improvement.............	51,415	57,165	68,147	78,263	87,074	135,215
Departmental management account...............	223,857	293,351	341,171	341,286	370,844	419,579
Other...................	1,875	1,401	—	—	—	—
Trust funds...............	27	172	30	39	618	16

(1) Estimated. (2) Includes preschool incentive grants. (3) Includes programs of national significance and special programs for the disadvantaged. (4) Includes Pell Grants, Supplemental Education Opportunity Grants and State Student Incentive Grants, and Income Contingent Loans. (—) Data are not available or not applicable.
NOTE: Because of rounding, details may not add to totals.

Public Libraries

Source: World Almanac questionnaire (1990)

City	No. bound Volumes	Circulation	Annual Acquisitions Expend.	City	No. bound Volumes	Circulation	Annual Acquisitions Expend.
Akron, Oh.[a] (18)	1,200,677	1,953,376	NA	Mesa, Ariz. (2)	517,012	2,301,346	954,245
Albuquerque, N.M.[a] (11)	610,502	2,283,512	$1,168,447	Miami, Fla.[a] (28)	2,386,204	4,200,000	$2,200,000
Anaheim, Cal.[a] (4)	383,000	1,361,538	611,212	Milwaukee, Wis.[a] (12)	2,051,114	3,382,982	1,360,814
Anchorage, Alas. (5)	395,700	1,099,780	662,790	Minneapolis, Minn. (14)	1,888,934	3,012,111	1,771,400
Arlington, Tex. (5)	321,487	1,238,631	307,336	Mobile, Ala.[a] (5)	363,511	949,993	460,513
Atlanta, Ga. (33)	1,678,750	2,303,681	3,011,362	Nashville, Tenn.[a] (16)	608,346	1,945,454	871,515
Baltimore, Md. (30)	2,289,857	1,532,279	2,418,089	New Orleans, La. (15)	1,039,264	1,159,303	750,063
Baton Rouge, La.[a] (10)	640,385	1,733,200	1,028,000	New York, N.Y. (research)	9,189,489	—	—
Birmingham, Ala.[a] (19)	1,092,285	2,072,444	916,174	Branches (81)	3,180,866	9,669,316	14,931,000
Boston, Mass.[a] (25)	4,916,277	1,454,414	NA	Brooklyn (58)	4,637,167	8,610,459	5,133,434
Buffalo, N.Y.[a] (53)	3,602,478	6,237,516	2,023,551	Queens (61)	5,500,000	11,320,000	5,500,000
Charlotte, N.C. (19)	1,200,000	2,700,000	1,400,000	Norfolk, Va. (11)	880,564	823,908	540,747
Cincinnati, Oh.[a] (39)	3,700,000	7,179,389	4,205,140	Oklahoma City, Okla. (11)	933,241	4,184,437	1,346,726
Cleveland, Oh. (29)	2,261,043	4,550,994	4,588,427	Oakland, Cal.[a] (16)	907,082	1,627,320	806,836
Colorado Springs, Col. (13)	743,898	1,649,441	7,945,110	Omaha, Neb.[a] (10)	588,013	1,860,728	892,109
Columbus, Oh. (20)	1,600,000	4,100,000	4,475,615	Philadelphia, Pa. (53)	3,458,700	4,800,000	6,200,000
Corpus Christi, Tex.[a](4)	293,452	750,138	284,750	Phoenix, Az. (10)	1,683,458	4,529,337	2,500,000
Dallas, Tex. (19)	2,409,864	4,364,027	17,201,527	Pittsburgh, Pa. (18)	1,880,241	2,841,120	13,764,737
Dayton, Oh. (19)	1,500,000	5,239,231	11,000,000	Portland, Ore. (15)	4,000,000	2,000,000	1,400,000
Denver, Col. (21)	2,239,106	3,396,268	1,856,485	Richmond, Va. (10)	780,000	858,213	450,000
Des Moines, Ia. (5)	487,444	1,246,350	292,163	Rochester, N.Y. (11)	500,000	1,587,691	7,200,000
Detroit, Mich. (25)	2,746,021	1,743,314	1,900,000	Sacramento, Cal. (24)	1,663,893	3,977,515	2,045,262
District of Columbia[a] (25)	1,507,556	1,843,098	1,530,000	St. Louis, Mo. (18)	1,903,218	7,915,559	2,700,000
El Paso, Tex. (10)	600,000	1,300,000	3,500,000	St. Paul, Minn. (12)	740,171	2,414,263	949,246
Fairfax, Va. (22)	1,761,264	8,454,714	3,387,721	San Diego, Cal.[a] (31)	1,561,232	4,568,116	1,862,547
Ft. Worth, Tex. (10)	1,126,931	3,356,148	1,157,965	San Francisco, Cal.[a] (26)	1,749,129	2,470,091	NA
Fresno, Cal. (33)	1,007,199	1,930,588	449,265	Shreveport, La.[a] (19)	376,069	956,907	394,686
Honolulu, Ha. (49)	2,310,843	6,454,824	2,886,133	Syracuse, N.Y.[a] (8)	509,386	1,189,319	NA
Indianapolis, Ind. (21)	1,500,000	5,376,388	2,170,167	Tampa, Fla. (17)	1,100,600	3,200,000	1,800,000
Jersey City, N.J.[a] (11)	744,383	395,266	447,465	Toledo, Oh.[a] (18)	1,500,000	4,400,000	NA
Kansas City, Mo.[a] (14)	1,346,364	875,040	NA	Tucson, Ariz.[a] (15)	760,000	3,900,000	NA
Los Angeles, Cal.[a] (62)	5,663,240	10,382,321	4,469,364	Tulsa, Okla. (20)	825,000	3,236,081	1,419,000
Louisville, Ky.[a] (14)	903,084	3,084,620	979,836	Wichita, Kan.[a] (12)	894,942	1,396,667	400,000
Memphis, Tenn. (23)	1,700,000	2,700,000	3,228,007	Yonkers, N.Y. (3)	233,532	865,901	481,286

(a) Has not provided up-to-date information. Figure in parentheses denotes number of branches. (NA) Not available.

Funding of Public Libraries

Source: National Center for Educational Statistics, U.S. Dept. of Education

States ranked by all money spent per capita for public libraries in 1989

1. New York..........	$29.48	18. California..........	15.89	35. Pennsylvania........	10.99
2. Dist. of Columbia.....	29.46	19. Kansas..........	15.85	36. North Carolina.......	10.55
3. Maryland...........	24.45	20. Oregon..........	14.74	37. Oklahoma..........	10.24
4. Alaska............	23.64	21. Arizona..........	14.53	38. Georgia...........	10.06
5. Ohio.............	23.34	22. New Hampshire......	14.46	39. Idaho............	9.84
6. Connecticut.........	22.10	23. Michigan..........	13.83	40. Nevada...........	9.65
7. New Jersey.........	21.16	24. Utah............	13.64	41. Texas............	8.94
8. Wyoming..........	19.83	25. Missouri..........	13.37	42. South Carolina......	8.72
9. Washington.........	19.81	26. Nebraska.........	13.16	43. Delaware..........	8.22
10. Illinois............	19.25	27. South Dakota.......	13.09	44. Alabama..........	8.13
11. Massachusetts.......	19.18	28. Maine...........	12.66	45. North Dakota.......	8.01
12. Minnesota..........	18.62	29. Vermont..........	12.37	46. Tennessee.........	7.70
13. Colorado..........	18.01	30. Florida...........	11.93	47. Montana..........	7.56
14. Indiana...........	17.95	31. Iowa............	11.85	48. West Virginia.......	7.46
15. Hawaii...........	17.23	32. Rhode Island.......	11.71	49. Kentucky..........	7.04
16. Wisconsin.........	16.53	33. Louisiana.........	11.53	50. Mississippi........	6.58
17. Virginia...........	16.29	34. New Mexico........	11.34	51. Arkansas.........	5.98

Preprimary School Enrollment of Children 3 to 5 Years Old: 1970 to 1989

Source: U.S. Bureau of the Census

Civilian noninstitutional population. Includes public and non-public nursery school and kindergarten programs. Excludes 5 year olds enrolled in elementary school.

	Number of children (1,000)						Enrollment rate				
	1970	1980	1985	1987	1988	1989	1970	1985	1987	1988	1989
Population, 3–5 years old	10,877	9,284	10,733	10,872	10,994	11,038	—	—	—	—	—
Total Enrolled[1]	4,075	4,878	5,865	5,932	5,977	6,026	37.5	54.6	54.6	54.4	54.6
Nursery	1,093	1,982	2,477	2,555	2,621	2,825	10.0	23.1	23.5	23.8	25.6
Kindergarten	2,982	2,896	3,388	3,377	3,356	3,201	27.4	31.6	31.1	30.5	29.0
White	3,414	3,994	4,757	4,748	4,891	4,911	37.8	54.7	54.1	55.4	55.0
Black	585	725	919	893	814	872	34.9	55.8	54.2	48.2	54.2
Hispanic origin[3]	NA	370	496	587	544	520	NA	43.3	45.5	44.2	41.6
3 years old	454	857	1,035	1,022	1,028	1,005	13.0	28.8	28.6	27.6	27.1
4 years old	1,003	1,423	1,765	1,717	1,768	1,882	27.9	49.1	47.7	49.1	51.0
5 years old	2,617	2,598	3,065	3,192	3,183	3,139	69.2	86.5	86.1	86.6	86.4
Labor Force Status of Mother											
All races:[2] With mother in labor force[4]	1,345	2,480	3,306	3,422	3,478	3,488	38.8	58.1	58.2	57.4	57.0
3 and 4 years old	526	1,252	1,656	1,568	1,619	1,708	23.5	43.6	41.6	41.1	41.8
5 years old	818	1,229	1,649	1,854	1,859	1,780	66.6	87.2	87.9	87.5	88.0
Employed	1,246	2,256	2,999	3,180	3,258	3,236	39.3	59.1	58.9	57.8	57.4
Full-time	770	1,445	1,969	2,085	2,140	2,152	38.6	57.4	57.9	57.6	55.3
Mother not in labor force	2,694	2,266	2,372	2,250	2,197	2,201	37.0	50.4	50.1	50.6	51.7

(NA) Not available. (1) Includes children with mothers whose labor force status is unknown and children with no mother present in household, not shown separately. (2) Includes other races not shown separately. (3) Person of Hispanic origin may be of any race. (4) Includes children with mothers who are unemployed, not shown separately.

Number of Private Schools and Their Enrollment in Grades K Through 12, 1987-1988

Source: National Center for Education Statistics, U.S. Dept. of Education

Selected Characteristics	Number of Schools				Enrollment			
	Total	Catholic	Other religious	Non-sectarian	Total	Catholic	Other religious	Non-sectarian
Total	26,836	9,527	12,132	5,177	5,226,096	2,822,585	1,590,632	812,879
School Size								
Less than 150	14,065	1,971	8,689	3,406	889,794	189,893	496,799	203,102
150 to 299	7,609	4,225	2,294	1,090	1,636,110	935,288	478,285	222,537
300 to 499	3,134	2,109	649	375	1,179,644	798,886	243,511	137,247
500 to 749	1,271	767	311	193	748,262	444,801	183,324	120,137
750 or more	758	455	188	—	772,287	453,717	188,714	—
Minority status								
Less than 5%	11,856	4,052	6,559	1,245	2,164,142	1,131,135	774,261	258,746
5 to 19%	7,877	2,507	3,413	1,957	1,620,981	811,080	501,486	308,415
20 to 49%	3,392	1,221	1,115	1,056	664,382	388,519	143,014	132,850
50% or more	3,712	1,748	1,046	918	776,592	491,851	171,871	112,869
Community								
Rural/farming	5,181	1,108	3,359	715	497,868	180,483	199,011	118,375
Small city/town	6,210	2,340	2,916	954	940,971	507,869	289,409	143,693
Suburban	5,257	1,925	2,137	1,194	1,358,717	749,503	401,839	207,376
Urban	10,150	4,141	3,717	2,292	2,412,844	1,383,368	700,102	329,374

Note: Details may not add to totals due to rounding or missing values in cells with too few sample cases. (—) Too few sample cases (fewer than 30) for a reliable estimate.

National Math Test, 1990

Source: U.S. Dept. of Education

Average score of students who participated in the national eighth grade mathematics exam. The best possible score was 350. Thirteen states chose not to participate.

The National Assessment Governing Board, a federal agency that conducted the test, cautioned against using the data as a simple ranking because of the many variables involved in the calculations and the overlapping performance of many states. Some who rank in the middle in overall average, for example, have groups of students who scored among among the highest in the nation.

	Average score						
National	261	13. Colorado	267	27. Texas	258
1. North Dakota	281	14. Indiana	267	28. Kentucky	256
2. Montana	280	15. Pennsylvania	266	29. California	256
3. Iowa	278	16. Michigan	264	30. New Mexico	256
4. Nebraska	276	17. Virginia	264	31. Arkansas	256
5. Minnesota	276	18. Ohio	264	32. West Virginia	256
6. Wisconsin	274	19. Oklahoma	263	33. Florida	255
7. New Hampshire	273	20. New York	261	34. Alabama	252
8. Wyoming	272	21. Delaware	261	35. Hawaii	251
9. Idaho	272	22. Maryland	260	36. North Carolina	250
10. Oregon	271	23. Illinois	260	37. Louisiana	246
11. Connecticut	270	24. Rhode Island	260	38. Guam	231
12. New Jersey	269	25. Arizona	259	39. D.C.	231
		26. Georgia	258	40. Virgin Islands	218

College Enrollment Rates

Source: American College Testing Program; U.S. Dept. of Labor

Enrollment in college as of October of each year for individuals age 16 to 24 who graduated from high school during the preceding 12 months.

Sixty percent of the 2.4 million high school graduates in 1990 were enrolled in college in October, a proportion equaling the record set in 1989. About 1.4 million members of the high school class of 1990 were attending college full time. The college enrollment rate of women (62 percent) exceeded that for men (58 percent), and the rate for whites (62 percent) remained well above that of blacks (46 percent) and Hispanics (47 percent). Overall, the percentage of high school graduates going on to college has risen 11 percent over the past decade.

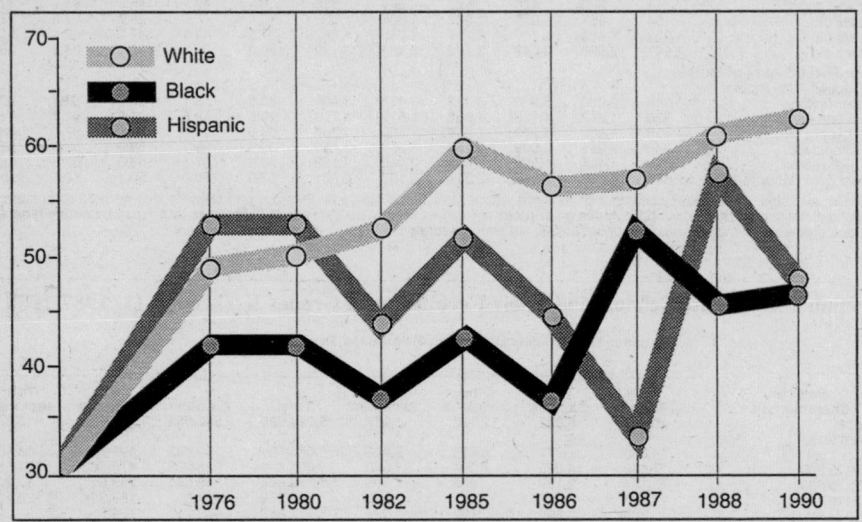

Scholastic Aptitude Test (SAT) Mean Scores and Characteristics of College Bound Seniors: 1970 to 1991

Source: College Entrance Examination Board

(For school year ending in year shown)

Type of Test and Characteristic	Unit	1970	1975	1980	1982	1984	1985	1987	1988	1989	1990	1991
Test Scores[1]												
Verbal, total[1]	Point	460	434	424	426	426	431	430	428	427	424	422
Male	Point	459	437	428	431	433	437	435	435	434	429	426
Female	Point	461	431	420	421	420	425	425	422	421	419	418
Math, total[2]	Point	488	472	466	467	471	475	476	476	476	476	474
Male	Point	509	495	491	493	495	499	500	498	500	499	497
Female	Point	465	449	443	443	449	452	453	455	454	455	453
Participants (thousands)												
Total		996	992	989	965	977	1,080	1,134	1,088	1,025	1,033	
Male	Percent	NA	49.9	48.2	48.1	48.2	48.3	48.0	48.0	48.0	48.0	48.0
White	Percent	NA	86.0	82.1	81.7	80.3	80.0	78.0	77.0	75.0	73.0	72.0
Black	Percent	NA	7.9	9.1	8.9	9.1	8.9	9.0	9.0	10.0	10.0	10.0
Obtaining scores[1] of—600 or above:												
Verbal	Percent	NA	7.9	7.2	7.1	7.0	7.0	8.0	7.0	7.8	7.0	7.0
Math	Percent	NA	15.6	15.1	15.3	17.0	17.0	18.0	17.0	18.0	18.0	17.0
Below 400:												
Verbal	Percent	NA	37.8	41.8	40.2	40.0	40.0	40.0	42.0	40.5	41.0	43.0
Math	Percent	NA	28.5	30.2	29.5	29.0	29.0	28.0	29.0	27.0	28.0	29.0

(NA) Not available. (1) Minimum score, 200; maximum score, 800. (2) 1967 and 1970 are estimates based on total number of persons taking SAT.

Note:
The 1991 averages represent the all-time verbal low and the first decline in math scores since 1980. Donald M. Stewart, president of the College Board, noted that some of this year's drop in SAT averages could be attributed to changes in the demographic backgrounds of students taking the test. He also emphasized that other factors were important when considering SAT averages, such as the kinds and numbers of rigorous academic courses taken by students. He also said that the scores reflect a "disturbing pattern of educational disparity" in academic preparation. "If this kind of dichotomy continues, we could evolve into a nation divided between a small class of educational elite and an underclass of students academically ill-prepared for the demands of college or the workplace."

American College Testing (ACT) Program Mean Scores and Characteristics of College-Bound Students: 1970 to 1990

Source: The American College Testing Program
Data for academic year ending in year shown.

Type of Test and Mean Test Scores[1]	Unit	1970	1975	1980	1982	1985	1986*	1987*	1988*	1989*	1990*
Composite	Point	19.9	18.6	18.5	18.4	18.6	20.8	20.8	20.8	20.6	20.6
Male	Point	20.3	19.5	19.3	19.2	19.4	19.6	19.5	19.6	19.3	21.0
Female	Point	19.4	17.8	17.9	17.8	17.9	18.1	18.1	18.1	18.0	20.3
English	Point	18.5	17.7	17.9	17.9	18.1	18.5	18.4	18.5	18.4	20.5
Male	Point	17.6	17.1	17.3	17.3	17.6	17.9	17.9	18.0	17.8	20.1
Female	Point	19.4	18.3	18.3	18.4	18.6	18.9	18.9	19.0	18.9	20.9
Math	Point	20.0	17.6	17.4	17.2	17.2	17.3	17.2	17.2	17.1	19.9
Male	Point	21.1	19.3	18.9	18.6	18.6	18.8	18.6	18.4	18.3	20.7
Female	Point	18.8	16.2	16.2	16.0	16.0	16.0	16.1	16.1	16.1	19.3
Participants											
Total	1,000	788	714	822	805	739	730	777	842	855	817
Male	Percent	52	46	45	45	46	46	46	46	46	46
White	Percent	(NA)	77	83	83	82	82	81	81	80	79
Black	Percent	4	7	8	8	8	8	8	8	9	9
Obtaining composite scores of—											
27** or above	Percent	14	14	13	13	14	14	14	14	14	12**
18** or below	Pecent	21	33	33	34	32	31	31	31	32	35**

*Beginning with the October 1989 test (1990 scores), an entirely new ACT Assessment was introduced. The Enhanced ACT Assessment increases the emphasis on rhetorical skills in the measurement of writing proficiency, increases the number of advanced math items, and includes a new reading test which features inferential and reasoning skills and a test designed to measure science reasoning. The Enhanced ACT also provides subscores in English, Mathematics, and Reading. The "Composite" scores for 1986-89 have been converted to provide a basis of comparison; all 1990 scores are for the Enhanced ACT. It is not possible to make direct comparisons between 1990 data and data from earlier years. **As of 1990.
(NA) Not available. (1) Minimum score, 1; maximum score, 36. (2) Test scores and characteristics of college-bound students based on a 10% sample through 1984. Begining in 1985, these data are now based on the performance of all ACT-tested students who graduated in the spring of a given school year and who took the ACT Assessment during junior or senior year of high school.

Public High School Graduation and Dropout Rates, 1989

Source: National Center for Education Statistics, U.S. Dept. of Education

	Graduation rate, rank		Dropout rate, rank			Graduation rate, rank		Dropout rate rank	
U.S.	71.4%		28.6%		Mo.	73.5%	(29)	26.5%	(23)
					Mont.	85.0	(6)	15.0	(46)
Ala.	67.7	(40)	22.3	(12)	Neb.	86.1	(5)	13.9	(47)
Alaska	64.2	(46)	35.8	(6)	Nev.	71.9	(31)	28.1	(21)
Ariz.	68.8	(38)	31.2	(14)	N.H.	74.1	(27)	25.9	(25)
Ark.	78.5	(15)	11.5	(37)	N.J.	79.6	(13)	20.4	(39)
Calif.	67.3	(41)	32.7	(11)	N.M.	71.5	(34)	28.5	(18)
Colo.	75.9	(23)	24.1	(29)	N.Y.	65.0	(43)	35.0	(9)
Conn.	83.2	(7)	16.8	(45)	N.C.	68.8	(37)	31.2	(15)
Del.	71.5	(33)	28.5	(19)	N.D.	87.9	(2)	12.1	(50)
D.C.	57.7	(50)	42.3	(2)	Ohio	75.6	(24)	24.4	(28)
Fla.	61.5	(48)	38.5	(4)	Okla.	74.4	(26)	25.6	(26)
Ga.	62.1	(47)	27.9	(5)	Ore.	70.8	(35)	29.2	(17)
Hawaii	81.7	(11)	18.3	(41)	Penn.	79.2	(14)	20.8	(38)
Idaho	78.2	(17)	21.8	(35)	R.I.	71.9	(32)	28.1	(20)
Ill.	78.5	(16)	21.5	(36)	S.C.	65.0	(44)	35.0	(8)
Ind.	76.2	(22)	13.8	(30)	S.D.	86.2	(4)	13.8	(48)
Iowa	86.4	(3)	13.6	(49)	Tenn.	68.7	(39)	21.3	(13)
Kan.	82.1	(8)	17.9	(44)	Tex.	64.2	(45)	35.8	(7)
Ky.	67.3	(41)	32.7	(11)	Utah	82.1	(9)	17.9	(43)
La.	56.9	(51)	43.1	(1)	Vt.	80.8	(12)	19.2	(40)
Me.	77.5	(18)	22.5	(34)	Va.	74.7	(25)	25.3	(27)
Md.	74.0	(28)	26.0	(24)	Wash.	76.4	(21)	23.6	(31)
Mass.	72.0	(30)	28.0	(22)	W.V.	76.7	(19)	23.3	(33)
Mich.	70.7	(36)	29.3	(16)	Wis.	81.8	(10)	18.2	(42)
Minn.	88.6	(1)	11.4	(51)	Wyo.	76.5	(20)	23.5	(32)
Miss.	60.1	(49)	39.9	(3)					

Institutions of Higher Education—Charges: 1970 to 1990

Source: National Center for Education Statistics, U.S. Dept. of Education.

Data are for the entire academic year ending in year shown. Figures for 1970 are average charges for full-time resident degree-credit students; figures for later years are average charges per full-time equivalent student. Room and board are based on full-time students.

Academic Control and year	Tuition and Required Fees			Board Rates			Dormitory Charges		
	All institutions	2-yr. colleges	4-yr. universities	All institutions	2-yr. colleges	4-yr. universities	All institutions	2-yr. colleges	4-yr. universities
Public:									
1970	$323	$178	$427	$511	$465	$540	$369	$308	$395
1980	583	355	840	867	894	898	715	572	749
1989	1,285	730	1,846	1,533	1,488	1,576	1,457	965	1,483
1990 est.	1,367	758	2,006	1,638	1,609	1,720	1,516	958	1,563
Private:									
1970	1,533	1,034	1,809	561	546	608	436	413	503
1980	3,130	2,062	3,811	955	924	1,078	827	769	999
1989	7,461	4,817	9,451	1,880	1,609	2,269	1,849	1,540	2,353
1990 est.	8,174	5,324	10,400	1,951	1,800	2,345	1,931	1,648	2,420

American Colleges and Universities
General Information for the 1990–91 Academic Year
Source: Peterson's Guides

These listings include all accredited undergraduate degree-granting institutions in the United States and U.S. territories that are classified as either four-year colleges with total institutional enrollments of 750 or more or two-year colleges with total institutional enrollments of 1,000 or more. Four-year colleges (those that award a bachelor's as their highest undergraduate degree) are listed first, followed by two-year colleges (those that award an associate as their highest or primary undergraduate degree).

All institutions are coeducational except those where the zip code is followed by: (1)–men only, (2)–primarily men, (3)–women only, (4)–primarily women.

Year is that of founding.

Governing official is the chief executive officer.

Institutional control: 1–independent (nonprofit), 2–independent-religious, 3–proprietary (profit making), 4–federal, 5–state, 7–commonwealth (Puerto Rico), 8–territory (U.S. territories), 9–county, 10–district, 11–city, 12–state and local, 13–state related.

Highest degree offered: B–bachelor's, M–master's, D–doctorate (includes first professional degrees).

Enrollment is the total number of matriculated undergraduate and (if applicable) graduate students.

Faculty is the total number of faculty members teaching undergraduate courses.

Any data not reported are indicated as NR.

Four-Year Colleges

Name, address	Year	Governing official, control, and highest degree offered		Enrollment	Faculty
Abilene Christian U, Abilene, TX 79699	1906	Dr. William J. Teague	2-D	4,053	255
Adams State Coll, Alamosa, CO 81102	1921	Dr. William M. Fulkerson, Jr.	5-M	2,447	121
Adelphi U, Garden City, NY 11530	1896	Dr. Peter Diamandopoulos	1-D	8,754	724
Adrian Coll, Adrian, MI 49221	1859	Dr. Stanley P. Caine	2-B	1,187	134
Alabama A&M U, Normal, AL 35762	1875	Dr. Carl Harris Marbury	5-D	4,886	353
Alabama State U, Montgomery, AL 36101	1874	Dr. C.C. Baker	5-M	4,525	270
Alaska Pacific U, Anchorage, AK 99508	1959	Dr. F. Thomas Trotter	2-D	817	58
Albany State Coll, Albany, GA 31705	1903	Dr. Billy C. Black	5-M	2,306	151
Albion Coll, Albion, MI 49224	1835	Dr. Melvin L. Vulgamore	2-B	1,643	133
Albright Coll, Reading, PA 19612	1856	Dr. David G. Ruffer	2-B	1,253	129
Alcorn State U, Lorman, MS 39096	1871	Dr. Walter Washington	5-M	2,890	183
Alderson-Broaddus Coll, Philippi, WV 26416	1871	Dr. W. Christian Sizemore	2-B	765	74
Alfred U, Alfred, NY 14802	1836	Dr. Edward G. Coll, Jr.	1-D	2,466	217
Allegheny Coll, Meadville, PA 16335	1815	Dr. Daniel F. Sullivan	2-M	1,798	203
Allentown Coll of St Francis de Sales, Center Valley, PA 18034-9568	1962	Very Rev. Daniel Gambet	2-M	1,700	99
Alma Coll, Alma, MI 48801	1886	Dr. Alan J. Stone	2-B	1,227	100
Alvernia Coll, Reading, PA 19607	1958	Dr. Daniel N. DeLucca	2-B	1,058	93
Alverno Coll, Milwaukee, WI 53215 (3)	1887	Joel Read	1-B	2,414	197
Amber U, Garland, TX 75041	1971	Dr. Douglas W. Warner	1-M	1,498	65
American International Coll, Springfield, MA 01109	1885	Dr. Harry J. Courniotes	1-D	1,831	124
American U, Washington, DC 20016	1893	Dr. Joseph D. Duffey	2-D	10,153	1,060
American U of Puerto Rico, Bayamón, PR 00621	1963	Juan B. Nazario-Negron	1-B	4,208	235
Amherst Coll, Amherst, MA 01002	1821	Peter R. Pouncey	1-B	1,580	189
Anderson Coll, Anderson, SC 29621	1911	Dr. Mark L. Hopkins	2-B	968	58
Anderson U, Anderson, IN 46012	1917	Dr. James L. Edwards	2-M	2,124	186
Andrews U, Berrien Springs, MI 49104	1874	Dr. W. Richard Lesher	2-D	2,869	282
Angelo State U, San Angelo, TX 76909	1928	Dr. Lloyd Drexell Vincent	5-M	6,298	206
Anna Maria Coll, Paxton, MA 01612	1946	Sr. Bernadette Madore	2-M	1,447	90
Appalachian State U, Boone, NC 28608	1899	Dr. John E. Thomas	5-D	11,483	715
Aquinas Coll, Grand Rapids, MI 49506	1886	Mr. R. Paul Nelson	2-M	2,633	169
Arizona State U, Tempe, AZ 85287	1885	Dr. Lattie F. Coor	5-D	42,952	1,861
Arkansas Coll, Batesville, AR 72503	1872	Dr. John V. Griffith	2-B	855	90
Arkansas State U, State University, AR 72467	1909	Dr. Eugene W. Smith	5-M	9,264	394
Arkansas Tech U, Russellville, AR 72801	1909	Dr. Kenneth G. Kersh	5-M	4,062	216
Armstrong State Coll, Savannah, GA 31419	1935	Dr. Robert A. Burnett	5-M	4,170	172
Art Ctr Coll of Design, Pasadena, CA 91103	1930	Mr. David R. Brown	1-M	1,183	208
Art Inst of Fort Lauderdale, Fort Lauderdale, FL 33316	1968	David P. Higley	3-B	2,200	150
Asbury Coll, Wilmore, KY 40390-1198	1890	Dr. Edwin G. Blue	2-B	1,053	97
Ashland U, Ashland, OH 44805	1878	Dr. Joseph Shultz	2-M	4,709	177
Assumption Coll, Worcester, MA 01615-0005	1904	Joseph H. Hagan	2-M	2,974	175
Atlantic Union Coll, South Lancaster, MA 01561	1882	Dr. Lawrence T. Geraty	2-B	1,228	61
Auburn U, Auburn University, AL 36849	1856	Dr. James E. Martin	5-D	21,537	1,208
Auburn U at Montgomery, Montgomery, AL 36117-3596	1967	Dr. James O. Williams	5-D	6,300	250
Augsburg Coll, Minneapolis, MN 55454	1869	Dr. Charles S. Anderson	2-M	2,965	169
Augusta Coll, Augusta, GA 30910	1925	Dr. Richard S. Wallace	5-M	5,580	165
Augustana Coll, Rock Island, IL 61201	1860	Dr. Thomas Tredway	2-B	2,253	170
Augustana Coll, Sioux Falls, SD 57197	1860	Dr. Lloyd Svendsbye	2-M	2,113	147
Aurora U, Aurora, IL 60506	1893	Thomas H. Zarle	2-M	2,116	240
Austin Coll, Sherman, TX 75091	1849	Dr. Harry E. Smith	2-M	1,230	99
Austin Peay State U, Clarksville, TN 37044	1927	Dr. Oscar Page	5-M	6,347	328
Averett Coll, Danville, VA 24541	1859	Dr. Frank R. Campbell	2-M	1,446	65
Avila Coll, Kansas City, MO 64145	1916	Dr. Larry Kramer	2-M	1,452	152
Azusa Pacific U, Azusa, CA 91702	1899	Dr. Richard E. Felix	2-M	3,072	252
Babson Coll, Babson Park, MA 02157	1919	Mr. William F. Glavin	1-M	3,040	160
Baker Coll of Flint, Flint, MI 48507	1911	Mr. Edward J. Kurtz	1-B	3,505	138
Baker Coll of Muskegon, Muskegon, MI 49442	1888	Mr. Robert D. Jewell	1-B	1,860	60
Baker Coll of Owosso, Owosso, MI 48867	1984	Dr. Rick Amidon	1-B	943	37
Baker U, Baldwin City, KS 66006	1858	Dr. Daniel M. Lambert	2-M	1,350	79
Baldwin-Wallace Coll, Berea, OH 44017	1845	Dr. Neal Malicky	2-M	4,863	357
Ball State U, Muncie, IN 47306	1918	Dr. John E. Worthen	5-D	19,344	1,011
Baptist Bible Coll, Springfield, MO 65803	1950	NR	2-M	840	37
Bard Coll, Annandale-on-Hudson, NY 12504	1860	Dr. Leon Botstein	1-M	1,169	112
Barnard Coll, New York, NY 10027-6598 (3)	1889	Ms. Ellen V. Futter	1-B	2,200	253
Barry U, Miami Shores, FL 33161	1940	Sr. Jeanne O'Laughlin	2-D	5,903	432

Name, address	Year	Governing official, control, and highest degree offered		Enrollment	Faculty
Barton Coll, Wilson, NC 27893	1902	Dr. James B. Hemby	2-B	1,719	106
Baruch Coll of the City U of New York, New York, NY 10010	1968	Dr. Joyce F. Brown	12-M	15,853	975
Bates Coll, Lewiston, ME 04240	1855	Dr. Donald W. Harward	1-B	1,500	150
Bayamón Central U, Bayamón, PR 00621	1970	Rev. Vincent A. M. Van Rooij, OP	2-M	2,830	121
Baylor U, Waco, TX 76798	1845	Dr. Herbert H. Reynolds	2-D	12,019	601
Beaver Coll, Glenside, PA 19038	1853	Dr. Bette E. Landman	2-M	2,252	130
Belhaven Coll, Jackson, MS 39202	1883	Dr. Newton Wilson	2-B	868	76
Bellarmine Coll, Louisville, KY 40205	1950	Dr. Joseph J. McGowan, Jr.	2-M	2,479	196
Bellevue Coll, Bellevue, NE 68005	1965	Dr. John B. Muller	1-M	2,048	66
Belmont Abbey Coll, Belmont, NC 28012	1876	Dr. Joseph Brosnan	2-B	1,023	88
Belmont U, Nashville, TN 37212	1951	Dr. William E. Troutt	2-M	2,812	261
Beloit Coll, Beloit, WI 53511	1846	Mr. Victor E. Ferrall, Jr.	1-M	1,065	120
Bemidji State U, Bemidji, MN 56601	1919	Dr. Leslie C. Duly	5-M	5,400	250
Benedict Coll, Columbia, SC 29204	1870	Dr. Marshall C. Grigsby	2-B	1,478	118
Benedictine Coll, Atchison, KS 66002	1859	Thomas O. James	2-M	827	88
Bentley Coll, Waltham, MA 02154	1917	Dr. Gregory H. Adamian	1-M	7,375	391
Berea Coll, Berea, KY 40404	1855	Dr. John B. Stephenson	1-B	1,535	130
Berean Coll of the Assemblies of God, Springfield, MO 65802	1948	Dr. Zenas J. Bicket	2-B	946	NR
Berklee Coll of Music, Boston, MA 02215	1945	Mr. Lee Eliot Berk	1-B	2,734	300
Berry Coll, Rome, GA 30149	1902	Dr. Gloria M. Shatto	1-M	1,805	146
Bethany Coll, Bethany, WV 26032	1840	Dr. D. Duane Cummins	2-B	859	73
Bethel Coll, St Paul, MN 55112	1871	Dr. George K. Brushaber	2-B	1,791	176
Bethune-Cookman Coll, Daytona Beach, FL 32115	1904	Dr. Oswald P. Bronson, Sr.	2-M	2,352	193
Biola U, La Mirada, CA 90639	1908	Dr. Clyde Cook	2-D	2,576	172
Birmingham-Southern Coll, Birmingham, AL 35254	1856	Dr. Neal R. Berte	2-M	1,902	156
Black Hills State U, Spearfish, SD 57799	1883	Dr. Clifford M. Trump	5-M	2,573	105
Bloomfield Coll, Bloomfield, NJ 07003	1868	Dr. John F. Noonan	2-B	1,701	124
Bloomsburg U of Pennsylvania, Bloomsburg, PA 17815	1839	Dr. Harry Ausprich	5-M	7,464	399
Bluefield State Coll, Bluefield, WV 24701	1895	Dr. Gregory D. Adkins	5-B	2,702	180
Bob Jones U, Greenville, SC 29614	1927	Dr. Bob Jones, III	2-D	4,281	348
Boise State U, Boise, ID 83725	1932	Dr. John H. Keiser	5-M	12,848	695
Boston Coll, Chestnut Hill, MA 02167	1863	Rev. J. Donald Monan, SJ	2-D	14,515	918
Boston U, Boston, MA 02215	1839	Jon Westling	1-D	24,071	1,801
Bowdoin Coll, Brunswick, ME 04011	1794	Mr. Robert H. Edwards	1-B	1,350	136
Bowie State U, Bowie, MD 20715	1865	Dr. James E. Lyons, Sr.	5-M	4,189	204
Bowling Green State U, Bowling Green, OH 43403	1910	Dr. Paul J. Olscamp	5-D	18,040	938
Bradley U, Peoria, IL 61625	1897	Dr. Martin G. Abegg	1-M	6,068	394
Brandeis U, Waltham, MA 02254	1948	Dr. Stuart H. Altman	1-D	3,793	486
Brenau Professional Coll, Gainesville, GA 30501	1878	Dr. John S. Burd	1-M	1,303	150
Brescia Coll, Owensboro, KY 42301	1950	Dr. Ruth Gehres	2-B	756	68
Briar Cliff Coll, Sioux City, IA 51104	1930	Sr. Margaret Wick	2-B	1,131	89
Bridgewater Coll, Bridgewater, VA 22812	1880	Dr. Wayne F. Geisert	2-B	1,007	77
Bridgewater State Coll, Bridgewater, MA 02324	1840	Dr. Adrian Tinsley	5-M	5,299	317
Brigham Young U, Provo, UT 84602	1875	Dr. Rex E. Lee	2-D	27,380	1,623
Brooklyn Coll of the City U of New York, Brooklyn, NY 11210	1930	Dr. Robert L. Hess	12-M	16,042	993
Brown U, Providence, RI 02912	1764	Vartan Gregorian	1-D	7,577	656
Bryant Coll, Smithfield, RI 02917	1863	Dr. William E. Trueheart	1-M	5,198	237
Bryn Mawr Coll, Bryn Mawr, PA 19010 (4)	1885	Mary Patterson McPherson	1-D	1,885	222
Bucknell U, Lewisburg, PA 17837	1846	Dr. Gary A. Sojka	1-M	3,634	255
Buena Vista Coll, Storm Lake, IA 50588	1891	Dr. Keith G. Briscoe	2-B	1,032	87
Butler U, Indianapolis, IN 46208	1855	Dr. Geoffrey Bannister	1-M	4,529	392
Cabrini Coll, Radnor, PA 19087-3699	1957	Sr. Eileen Currie, MSC	2-M	1,473	127
Caldwell Coll, Caldwell, NJ 07006	1939	Sr. Vivien Jennings	2-B	1,186	91
California Coll of Arts and Crafts, Oakland, CA 94618	1907	Mr. Neil J. Hoffman	1-M	1,115	167
California Inst of Tech, Pasadena, CA 91125	1891	Dr. Thomas E. Everhart	1-D	1,861	270
California Inst of the Arts, Valencia, CA 91355	1961	Dr. Steven D. Lavine	1-M	1,020	197
California Lutheran U, Thousand Oaks, CA 91360	1959	Dr. Jerry H. Miller	2-M	2,970	240
California Polytechnic State U, San Luis Obispo, San Luis Obispo, CA 93407	1901	Dr. Warren J. Baker	5-M	17,758	1,069
California State Polytechnic U, Pomona, Pomona, CA 91768	1938	Dr. Hugh O. La Bounty	5-M	19,472	1,082
California State U, Bakersfield, Bakersfield, CA 93311	1970	Dr. Tomas A. Arciniega	5-M	5,452	337
California State U, Chico, Chico, CA 95929	1887	Dr. Robin Wilson	5-M	16,641	1,051
California State U, Dominguez Hills, Carson, CA 90747	1960	Dr. Robert Detweiler	5-M	9,450	844
California State U, Fresno, Fresno, CA 93710	1911	Dr. Harold H. Haak	5-M	19,586	1,201
California State U, Fullerton, Fullerton, CA 92634	1957	Dr. Milton A. Gordon	5-M	25,602	1,540
California State U, Hayward, Hayward, CA 94542	1957	Dr. Norma Rees	5-M	13,000	628
California State U, Long Beach, Long Beach, CA 90840	1949	Dr. Curtis L. McCray	5-M	33,991	1,946
California State U, Los Angeles, Los Angeles, CA 90032	1947	Dr. James M. Rosser	5-D	21,596	1,270
California State U, Northridge, Northridge, CA 91330	1958	Dr. James Cleary	5-M	31,166	1,753
California State U, Sacramento, Sacramento, CA 95819	1947	Dr. Donald R. Gerth	5-M	26,339	1,378
California State U, San Bernardino, San Bernardino, CA 92407	1965	Dr. Anthony H. Evans	5-M	11,927	642
California State U, Stanislaus, Turlock, CA 95380	1957	Dr. John W. Moore	5-M	5,818	300
California U of Pennsylvania, California, PA 15419	1852	Dr. John Pierce Watkins	5-M	6,689	395
Calumet Coll of Saint Joseph, Whiting, IN 46394	1951	Dr. Dennis C. Rittenmeyer	2-B	976	110
Calvin Coll, Grand Rapids, MI 49546	1876	Dr. Anthony J. Diekema	2-M	4,270	297
Cameron U, Lawton, OK 73505	1908	Dr. Don Davis	5-M	5,039	306
Campbellsville Coll, Campbellsville, KY 42718	1906	Dr. Kenneth W. Winters	2-B	857	64
Campbell U, Buies Creek, NC 27506	1887	Dr. Norman A. Wiggins	2-D	4,997	289
Canisius Coll, Buffalo, NY 14208	1870	Rev. James M. Demske, SJ	2-M	4,693	348
Capital U, Columbus, OH 43209	1830	Josiah H. Blackmore	2-D	3,235	146
Capitol Coll, Laurel, MD 20708	1964	Dr. G. William Troxler	1-M	750	62
Cardinal Stritch Coll, Milwaukee, WI 53217-3985	1937	Dr. M. Lea Schneider	2-M	3,650	164
Caribbean U, Bayamón, PR 00619	1969	Dr. Angel E. Juan-Ortega	1-B	3,596	158
Carleton Coll, Northfield, MN 55057	1866	Dr. Stephen R. Lewis, Jr.	1-B	1,707	160
Carlow Coll, Pittsburgh, PA 15213 (4)	1929	Grace Ann Geibel, RSM	2-M	1,196	133
Carnegie Mellon U, Pittsburgh, PA 15213	1900	Dr. Robert Mehrabian	1-D	7,056	797
Carroll Coll, Helena, MT 59625	1909	Dr. Matthew Quinn	2-B	1,234	117
Carroll Coll, Waukesha, WI 53186	1846	Dr. Dan C. West	2-B	1,524	124
Carson-Newman Coll, Jefferson City, TN 37760	1851	Dr. J. Cordell Maddox	2-M	2,121	137
Carthage Coll, Kenosha, WI 53140	1847	Dr. F. Gregory Campbell	2-M	1,865	115
Case Western Reserve U, Cleveland, OH 44106	1826	Dr. Agnar Pytte	1-D	8,557	1,727

Name, address	Year	Governing official, control, and highest degree offered		Enrollment	Faculty
Castleton State Coll, Castleton, VT 05735	1787	Dr. Lyle A. Gray	5-M	1,975	165
Catawba Coll, Salisbury, NC 28144	1851	Dr. Stephen H. Wurster	2-M	973	77
Catholic U of America, Washington, DC 20064	1887	Rev. William J. Byron, SJ	2-D	6,600	570
Catholic U of Puerto Rico, Ponce, PR 00732	1948	Rev. F. Tosello Giangiacomo	2-M	12,613	498
Cedar Crest Coll, Allentown, PA 18104 (4)	1867	Dr. Dorothy G. Blaney	2-B	982	96
Cedarville Coll, Cedarville, OH 45314	1887	Dr. Paul H. Dixon	2-B	1,923	135
Centenary Coll, Hackettstown, NJ 07840	1867	Dr. Stephanie M. Bennett	2-B	820	88
Centenary Coll. of Louisiana, Shreveport, LA 71134	1825	Dr. Donald A. Webb	2-M	1,087	102
Ctr for Creative Studies—Coll of Art and Design, Detroit, MI 48202	1926	Josephine Kelsey	1-B	883	186
Central Bible Coll, Springfield, MO 65803	1922	H. Maurice Lednicky	2-B	1,043	51
Central Connecticut State U, New Britain, CT 06050	1849	Dr. John W. Shumaker	5-M	10,568	690
Central Methodist Coll, Fayette, MO 65248	1854	Dr. Joe A. Howell	2-B	801	70
Central Michigan U, Mount Pleasant, MI 48859	1892	Dr. Edward B. Jakubauskas	5-D	16,866	811
Central Missouri State U, Warrensburg, MO 64093	1871	Dr. Ed Elliott	5-M	11,429	502
Central State U, Wilberforce, OH 45384	1887	Dr. Arthur E. Thomas	5-B	2,886	140
Central U of Iowa, Pella, IA 50219	1853	Dr. William M. Wiebenga	2-B	1,695	123
Central Washington U, Ellensburg, WA 98926	1891	Dr. Donald L. Garrity	5-M	7,660	332
Central Wesleyan Coll, Central, SC 29630	1906	Dr. John M. Newby	2-M	1,005	106
Centre Coll, Danville, KY 40422	1819	Dr. Michael F. Adams	2-B	880	82
Chadron State Coll, Chadron, NE 69337	1911	Dr. Samuel H. Rankin	5-M	3,065	126
Chaminade U of Honolulu, Honolulu, HI 96816	1955	Mr. Kent M. Keith	2-M	2,624	195
Chapman Coll, Orange, CA 92666	1861	Dr. Allen E. Koenig	2-M	2,198	167
Charleston Southern U, Charleston, SC 29411	1964	Dr. Jairy C. Hunter, Jr.	2-M	2,158	121
Charter Oak Coll, Farmington, CT 06032	1973	Dr. Merle W. Harris	5-B	886	NR
Chestnut Hill Coll, Philadelphia, PA 19118 (3)	1924	Sr. Matthew Anita MacDonald	2-M	1,227	106
Cheyney U of Pennsylvania, Cheyney, PA 19319	1837	Dr. LeVerne McCummings	5-M	1,607	99
Chicago State U, Chicago, IL 60628	1867	Dr. Dolores Cross	5-M	7,152	397
Chowan Coll, Murfreesboro, NC 27855	1848	Dr. Jerry F. Jackson	2-B	892	71
Christian Brothers U, Memphis, TN 38104	1871	Br. Theodore Drahmann, FSC	2-M	1,765	140
Christopher Newport Coll, Newport News, VA 23606	1961	Dr. Anthony Santoro	5-M	4,861	198
The Citadel, The Military Coll of South Carolina, Charleston, SC 29409 (1)	1842	Lt. Gen. Claudius E. Watts, III	5-M	3,670	152
City Coll of the City U of New York, New York, NY 10031	1847	Bernard W. Harleston	12-D	14,090	1,334
City U, Bellevue, WA 98008	1973	Dr. Michael A. Pastore	1-M	4,627	375
Claflin Coll, Orangeburg, SC 29115	1869	Oscar A. Rogers	2-B	887	55
Claremont McKenna Coll, Claremont, CA 91711	1946	Mr. Jack L. Stark	1-B	847	109
Clarion U of Pennsylvania, Clarion, PA 16214	1867	Dr. Diane L. Reinhard	5-M	6,618	397
Clark Atlanta U, Atlanta, GA 30314	1869	Dr. Thomas Cole, Jr.	1-D	3,507	227
Clarke Coll, Dubuque, IA 52001	1843	Dr. Catherine Dunn, BVM	2-M	876	53
Clarkson U, Potsdam, NY 13699	1896	Dr. Richard H. Gallagher	1-D	3,329	238
Clark U, Worcester, MA 01610	1887	Dr. Richard P. Traina	1-D	2,909	271
Clayton State Coll, Morrow, GA 30260	1969	NR	5-B	4,142	191
Cleary Coll, Ypsilanti, MI 48197	1883	Mr. Thomas Sullivan	1-B	1,200	67
Clemson U, Clemson, SC 29634	1889	Dr. Max Lennon	5-D	16,303	1,075
Cleveland State U, Cleveland, OH 44115	1964	Dr. John A. Flower	5-D	19,220	666
Clinch Valley Coll of the U of Virginia, Wise, VA 24293	1954	Dr. Jimmy A. Knight	5-B	1,528	112
Coe Coll, Cedar Rapids, IA 52402	1851	Dr. John E. Brown	2-B	1,250	111
Coker Coll, Hartsville, SC 29550	1908	Dr. James D. Daniels	1-B	778	62
Colby Coll, Waterville, ME 04901	1813	William R. Cotter	1-B	1,741	195
Coleman Coll, La Mesa, CA 92042	1963	Dr. Bob Wall	1-M	991	105
Colgate U, Hamilton, NY 13346	1819	Dr. Neil R. Grabois	1-M	2,710	273
Coll for Human Services, New York, NY 10014	1964	Audrey C. Cohen	1-M	963	58
Coll Misericordia, Dallas, PA 18612	1924	Dr. Pasquale DiPasquale, Jr.	2-M	1,500	120
Coll of Aeronautics, Flushing, NY 11371 (2)	1932	Dr. Sam Frank	1-B	1,350	84
Coll of Boca Raton, Boca Raton, FL 33431	1962	Dr. Donald E. Ross	1-M	1,136	75
Coll of Charleston, Charleston, SC 29424	1770	Dr. Harry M. Lightsey, Jr.	5-M	7,726	423
Coll of Great Falls, Great Falls, MT 59405	1932	Dr. William A. Shields	2-M	1,108	82
Coll of Idaho, Caldwell, ID 83605	1891	Mr. Robert L. Hendren, Jr.	1-M	1,167	85
Coll of Insurance, New York, NY 10007	1962	Dr. Ellen Thrower	1-M	1,676	105
Coll of Mount St Joseph, Cincinnati, OH 45051	1920	Francis Marie Thrailkill, OSU	1-M	2,593	216
Coll of Mount Saint Vincent, Riverdale, NY 10471	1847	Sr. Doris Smith	1-M	1,063	91
Coll of New Rochelle, New Rochelle, NY 10805 (4)	1904	Sr. Dorothy A. Kelly, OSU	1-M	2,225	94
Coll of New Rochelle, New Resources Division, New Rochelle, NY 10805	1972	NR	1-B	3,459	398
Coll of Notre Dame, Belmont, CA 94002	1851	Sr. Veronica Skillin	2-M	1,171	101
Coll of Saint Benedict, Saint Joseph, MN 56374 (3)	1887	Sr. Colman O'Connell, OSB	2-B	1,916	166
Coll of St Catherine, St Paul, MN 55105 (3)	1905	Dr. Anita Pampusch	2-M	2,585	228
Coll of Saint Elizabeth, Convent Station, NJ 07961 (4)	1899	Sr. Jacqueline Burns	2-B	1,155	118
Coll of St Francis, Joliet, IL 60435	1920	Dr. John C. Orr	2-M	1,875	100
Coll of Saint Mary, Omaha, NE 68124 (4)	1923	Dr. Kenneth Nielsen	2-B	1,280	134
Coll of Saint Rose, Albany, NY 12203	1920	Dr. Louis C. Vaccaro	1-M	3,624	216
Coll of St Scholastica, Duluth, MN 55811	1906	Dr. Daniel H. Pilon	2-M	1,969	146
Coll of Santa Fe, Santa Fe, NM 87501	1947	Dr. James A. Fries	2-M	1,052	76
Coll of Staten Island of the City U of New York, Staten Island, NY 10314	1955	Dr. Edmond L. Volpe	12-M	12,185	707
Coll of the Holy Cross, Worcester, MA 01610	1843	Rev. John E. Brooks, SJ	2-B	2,738	248
Coll of the Ozarks, Point Lookout, MO 65726	1906	Dr. Jerry C. Davis	2-B	1,512	103
Coll of William and Mary, Williamsburg, VA 23185	1693	Dr. Paul R. Verkuil	5-D	7,672	716
The Coll of Wooster, Wooster, OH 44691	1866	Dr. Henry J. Copeland	2-B	1,804	160
Colorado Christian U, Lakewood, CO 80226	1914	Dr. Joe L. Wall	2-M	1,000	81
The Colorado Coll, Colorado Springs, CO 80903	1874	Dr. Gresham Riley	1-M	1,955	235
Colorado Sch of Mines, Golden, CO 80401	1874	Dr. George S. Ansell	5-D	2,446	215
Colorado State U, Fort Collins, CO 80523	1862	Dr. Albert C. Yates	5-D	20,795	1,804
Colorado Tech Coll, Colorado Springs, CO 80907	1965	Mr. David D. O'Donnell	3-M	1,246	76
Columbia Bible Coll and Sem, Columbia, SC 29230	1923	Dr. Johnny Miller	2-D	958	36
Columbia Coll, Chicago, IL 60605	1890	Mr. Mirron Alexandroff	1-M	6,795	741
Columbia Coll, Columbia, MO 65216	1851	Dr. Donald B. Ruthenberg	2-B	785	54
Columbia Coll, New York, NY 10027	1754	Dr. Jack Greenberg	1-B	3,243	420
Columbia Coll, Columbia, SC 29203 (3)	1854	Dr. Peter T. Mitchell	2-M	1,190	75
Columbia Union Coll, Takoma Park, MD 20912	1904	Dr. Clifford Sorensen	2-B	1,356	61
Columbia U, Sch of Engineering & Applied Sci, New York, NY 10027	1864	Dr. Ralph J. Schwarz	1-D	2,036	NR
Columbia U, Sch of General Studies, New York, NY 10027	1754	Ward H. Dennis	1-M	1,196	450
Columbia U, Sch of Nursing, New York, NY 10032 (4)	1935	Dr. Mary O. Mundinger	1-M	110	35
Columbus Coll, Columbus, GA 31993	1958	Dr. Frank D. Brown	5-M	4,167	180

Name, address	Year	Governing official, control, and highest degree offered		Enrollment	Faculty
Columbus Coll of Art and Design, Columbus, OH 43215	1879	Mr. Joseph V. Canzani	1-B	1,600	104
Concord Coll, Athens, WV 24712	1872	Dr. Jerry L. Beasley	5-B	2,651	144
Concordia Coll, Moorhead, MN 56562	1891	Dr. Paul J. Dovre	2-B	2,948	234
Concordia Coll, St Paul, MN 55104	1893	Dr. Robert Holst	2-M	1,235	91
Concordia Coll, Portland, OR 97211	1905	Dr. Charles E. Schlimpert	2-B	752	65
Concordia Teachers Coll, Seward, NE 68434	1894	Rev. Orville C. Walz	2-M	818	77
Concordia U, River Forest, IL 60305	1864	Dr. Eugene L. Krentz	2-M	1,364	132
Concordia U Wisconsin, Mequon, WI 53092-7699	1881	Dr. R. John Buuck	2-M	1,760	125
Connecticut Coll, New London, CT 06320	1911	Claire L. Gaudiani	1-M	1,978	220
Converse Coll, Spartanburg, SC 29302 (3)	1889	Dr. Ellen Wood Hall	1-M	1,224	90
Cooper Union for the Advancement of Science & Art, New York, NY 10003	1859	Mr. John Jay Iselin	1-M	1,036	167
Coppin State Coll, Baltimore, MD 21216	1900	Dr. Calvin W. Burnett	5-M	2,578	158
Cornell Coll, Mount Vernon, IA 52314	1853	Dr. David G. Marker	2-B	1,140	125
Cornell U, Ithaca, NY 14853	1865	Dr. Frank H. T. Rhodes	1-D	18,389	1,631
Corpus Christi State U, Corpus Christi, TX 78412	1971	Dr. Wallace Davis	5-M	3,815	188
Creighton U, Omaha, NE 68178	1878	Rev. Michael G. Morrison, SJ	2-D	6,168	1,221
Culver-Stockton Coll, Canton, MO 63435	1853	Dr. Walter S. Reuling	2-B	1,129	62
Cumberland Coll, Williamsburg, KY 40769	1889	Dr. James Taylor	2-M	1,812	117
Curry Coll, Milton, MA 02186	1879	Dr. William L. Boyle, Jr.	1-M	1,054	156
Daemen Coll, Amherst, NY 14226	1947	Dr. Robert S. Marshall	1-B	1,962	109
Dakota State U, Madison, SD 57042	1881	Dr. Jerald Tunheim	5-B	1,311	59
Dallas Baptist U, Dallas, TX 75211	1965	Dr. Gary R. Cook	2-M	2,333	141
Dartmouth Coll, Hanover, NH 03755	1769	James O. Freedman	1-D	5,500	311
Davenport Coll of Business, Grand Rapids, MI 49503	1866	Donald W. Maine	1-B	3,843	171
Davenport Coll of Business, Lansing Cmps, Lansing, MI 48933	1979	Don Colizzi	1-B	1,512	86
David Lipscomb U, Nashville, TN 37204	1891	Dr. Harold Hazelip	2-M	2,466	177
Davidson Coll, Davidson, NC 28036	1837	Dr. John W. Kuykendall	2-B	1,508	126
Davis & Elkins Coll, Elkins, WV 26241	1904	Dr. Dorothy I. MacConkey	2-B	890	77
The Defiance Coll, Defiance, OH 43512	1850	Dr. Marvin J. Ludwig	2-B	956	63
Delaware State Coll, Dover, DE 19901	1891	Dr. William B. DeLauder	5-M	2,606	177
Delaware Valley Coll, Doylestown, PA 18901	1896	Mr. Herman Silverman	1-B	1,100	80
Delta State U, Cleveland, MS 38733	1925	Dr. F. Kent Wyatt	5-D	3,995	258
Denison U, Granville, OH 43023	1831	Dr. Michele Tolela Myers	1-B	2,015	181
DePaul U, Chicago, IL 60604	1898	Rev. John T. Richardson, CM	2-D	15,718	930
DePauw U, Greencastle, IN 46135	1837	Dr. Robert Bottoms	2-B	2,347	236
Detroit Coll of Business, Dearborn, MI 48126	1962	Dr. James Mendola	1-B	4,700	84
Detroit Coll of Business, Warren Cmps, Warren, MI 48092	1975	Janet Guggenheim	1-B	1,028	89
DeVry Inst of Tech, Phoenix, AZ 85021	1967	James A. Dugan	3-B	2,647	69
DeVry Inst of Tech, City of Industry, CA 91746	1983	Paul R. McGuirk	3-B	1,886	66
DeVry Inst of Tech, Decatur, GA 30030	1969	Dr. Ronald Bush	3-B	3,121	74
DeVry Inst of Tech, Chicago, IL 60618	1931	Dr. E. Arthur Stunnard	3-M	3,300	78
DeVry Inst of Tech, Lombard, IL 60148	1982	Jerry R. Dill	3-M	2,507	83
DeVry Inst of Tech, Kansas City, MO 64131	1931	Mr. Charles R. Levalley	3-B	1,748	71
DeVry Inst of Tech, Columbus, OH 43209	1952	Mr. Richard A. Czerniak	3-B	2,715	81
DeVry Inst of Tech, Irving, TX 75038	1969	Mr. Thomas E. Colvin	3-B	2,293	85
Dickinson Coll, Carlisle, PA 17013	1773	Dr. A. Lee Fritschler	1-B	2,003	154
Dickinson State U, Dickinson, ND 58601-4896	1918	Dr. Albert A. Watrel	5-B	1,429	98
Dillard U, New Orleans, LA 70122	1869	Dr. Samuel DuBois Cook	2-B	1,668	NR
Doane Coll, Crete, NE 68333	1872	Dr. Fred D. Brown	2-B	751	73
Dominican Coll of Blauvelt, Orangeburg, NY 10962	1952	Sr. Kathleen Sullivan	1-B	1,495	122
Dordt Coll, Sioux Center, IA 51250	1955	Dr. John B. Hulst	2-B	1,054	87
Dowling Coll, Oakdale, NY 11769	1959	Dr. Victor P. Meskill	1-M	4,436	352
Drake U, Des Moines, IA 50311	1881	Dr. Michael R. Ferrari	1-D	8,028	266
Drew U, Madison, NJ 07940	1866	Mr. Thomas H. Kean	2-D	2,276	158
Drexel U, Philadelphia, PA 19104	1891	Dr. Richard D. Breslin	1-D	11,927	848
Drury Coll, Springfield, MO 65802	1873	Dr. John E. Moore, Jr.	2-M	1,454	111
Duke U, Durham, NC 27706	1838	Dr. H. Keith H. Brodie	2-D	11,178	1,530
Duquesne U, Pittsburgh, PA 15282	1878	Dr. John E. Murray, Jr.	2-D	6,975	575
D'Youville Coll, Buffalo, NY 14201	1908	Dr. Denise A. Roche, GNSH	1-M	1,482	97
Earlham Coll, Richmond, IN 47374	1847	Dr. Richard J. Wood	2-M	1,215	114
East Carolina U, Greenville, NC 27858	1907	Dr. Richard Eakin	5-D	16,500	1,069
East Central U, Ada, OK 74820	1909	Dr. Bill S. Cole	5-M	4,206	200
Eastern Coll, Saint Davids, PA 19087	1932	Dr. Roberta Hestenes	2-M	1,362	103
Eastern Connecticut State U, Willimantic, CT 06226	1889	David G. Carter	5-M	4,475	282
Eastern Illinois U, Charleston, IL 61920	1895	Dr. Stanley Rives	5-M	10,301	645
Eastern Kentucky U, Richmond, KY 40475	1906	Dr. Hanly Funderburk	5-M	15,371	847
Eastern Mennonite Coll, Harrisonburg, VA 22801	1917	Dr. Joseph L. Lapp	2-B	989	81
Eastern Michigan U, Ypsilanti, MI 48197	1849	Dr. William E. Shelton	5-M	26,031	1,037
Eastern Montana Coll, Billings, MT 59101	1927	Dr. Bruce H. Carpenter	5-M	3,989	242
Eastern Nazarene Coll, Quincy, MA 02170	1918	Dr. Cecil R. Paul	2-M	919	63
Eastern New Mexico U, Portales, NM 88130	1934	Dr. Thomas Bond	5-M	3,655	200
Eastern Oregon State Coll, La Grande, OR 97850	1929	David E. Gilbert	5-M	1,862	157
Eastern Washington U, Cheney, WA 99004	1882	Dr. Marshall Drummond	5-M	8,402	421
East Stroudsburg U of Pennsylvania, East Stroudsburg, PA 18301	1893	Dr. James Gilbert	5-M	5,537	269
East Tennessee State U, Johnson City, TN 37614	1911	Dr. Ronald E. Beller	5-D	11,750	600
East Texas Baptist U, Marshall, TX 75670-1498	1912	Dr. Robert E. Craig	2-B	924	68
East Texas State U, Commerce, TX 75429	1889	Dr. Jerry D. Morris	5-D	7,979	214
Eckerd Coll, St Petersburg, FL 33733	1958	Dr. Peter H. Armacost	2-B	1,370	114
Edgewood Coll, Madison, WI 53711	1927	Dr. James A. Ebben	2-M	1,435	96
Edinboro U of Pennsylvania, Edinboro, PA 16444	1857	Foster F. Diebold	5-M	8,131	410
Elizabeth City State U, Elizabeth City, NC 27909	1891	Dr. Jimmy R. Jenkins	5-B	1,746	128
Elizabethtown Coll, Elizabethtown, PA 17022	1899	Dr. Gerhard E. Spiegler	2-B	1,822	150
Elmhurst Coll, Elmhurst, IL 60126	1871	Dr. Ivan E. Frick	2-B	3,006	140
Elmira Coll, Elmira, NY 14901	1855	Dr. Thomas K. Meier	1-M	1,002	95
Elms Coll, Chicopee, MA 01013 (3)	1928	Sr. Mary A. Dooley	2-M	1,250	81
Elon Coll, Elon College, NC 27244	1889	Dr. J. Fred Young	2-M	3,263	186
Embry-Riddle Aeronautical U, Daytona Beach, FL 32114-3900	1926	Kenneth Tallman	1-M	5,075	259
Embry-Riddle Aeronautical U, Coll of Continuing Ed, Daytona Beach, FL 32114	1926	NR	1-M	3,808	NR
Embry-Riddle Aeronautical U, Western Cmps, Prescott, AZ 86301	1978	Paul S. Daly	1-B	1,676	102
Emerson Coll, Boston, MA 02116	1880	Dr. Kenneth J. McIlraith	1-D	2,423	238

Name, address	Year	Governing official, control, and highest degree offered		Enrollment	Faculty
Emmanuel Coll, Boston, MA 02115 (3)	1919	Sr. Janet Eisner	2-M	1,205	88
Emory & Henry Coll, Emory, VA 24327	1836	Dr. Charles W. Sydnor, Jr.	2-B	844	61
Emory U, Atlanta, GA 30322	1836	Dr. James T. Laney	2-D	9,390	533
Emporia State U, Emporia, KS 66801	1863	Dr. Robert E. Glennen	5-M	6,077	297
ETI Tech Coll, Cleveland, OH 44103	1929	Al Jablonski	3-B	1,000	38
Eugene Lang Coll, New Sch for Social Research, New York, NY 10011	1985	Donald Scott	1-B	360	60
Evangel Coll, Springfield, MO 65802	1955	Dr. Robert H. Spence	2-B	1,540	122
Evergreen State Coll, Olympia, WA 98505	1967	Dr. T. L. Purce	5-M	3,237	210
Fairfield U, Fairfield, CT 06430	1942	Rev. Aloysius P. Kelley	2-M	4,821	371
Fairleigh Dickinson U, Florham-Madison Cmps, Madison, NJ 07940	1958	Dr. Francis J. Mertz	1-M	3,826	188
Fairleigh Dickinson U, Rutherford Cmps, Rutherford, NJ 07070	1942	Dr. Francis J. Mertz	1-M	2,516	123
Fairleigh Dickinson U, Teaneck-Hackensack Cmps, Teaneck, NJ 07666	1954	Dr. Francis J. Mertz	1-D	5,468	276
Fairmont State Coll, Fairmont, WV 26554	1865	Dr. Robert Dillman	5-B	6,305	317
Fashion Inst of Tech, New York, NY 10001-5992	1944	Dr. Marvin J. Feldman	12-M	12,771	858
Faulkner U, Montgomery, AL 36109	1942	Dr. Billy D. Hilyer	2-D	1,852	92
Fayetteville State U, Fayetteville, NC 28301	1867	Dr. Lloyd V. Hackley	5-M	3,034	192
Felician Coll, Lodi, NJ 07644	1942	Sr. Theresa Martin	2-B	750	74
Ferris State U, Big Rapids, MI 49307	1884	Dr. J. William Wenrich	5-D	12,076	645
Ferrum Coll, Ferrum, VA 24088	1913	Dr. Jerry M. Boone	2-B	1,208	103
Fisk U, Nashville, TN 37208	1866	Dr. Henry Ponder	2-M	912	81
Fitchburg State Coll, Fitchburg, MA 01420	1894	Dr. Vincent J. Mara	5-M	6,179	274
Flagler Coll, St Augustine, FL 32085	1968	Dr. William L. Proctor	1-B	1,188	89
Florida A&M U, Tallahassee, FL 32307	1887	Dr. Frederick Humphries	5-D	8,355	670
Florida Atlantic U, Boca Raton, FL 33431	1961	Dr. Anthony James Catanese	5-D	12,758	568
Florida Inst of Tech, Melbourne, FL 32901	1958	Dr. Lynn E. Weaver	1-D	5,947	683
Florida International U, Miami, FL 33199	1965	Dr. Modesto A. Maidique	5-D	21,999	878
Florida Memorial Coll, Miami, FL 33054	1879	Dr. Lee E. Monroe	2-B	2,172	NR
Florida Southern Coll, Lakeland, FL 33801	1885	Dr. Robert A. Davis	2-M	1,797	134
Florida State U, Tallahassee, FL 32306	1857	Dr. Bernard F. Sliger	5-D	28,327	1,533
Fontbonne Coll, St Louis, MO 63105	1917	Dr. Meneve Dunham	2-M	1,146	140
Fordham U, New York, NY 10458	1841	Rev. Joseph A. O'Hare, SJ	2-D	13,158	594
Fort Hays State U, Hays, KS 67601	1902	Dr. Edward H. Hammond	5-M	5,501	229
Fort Lauderdale Coll, Fort Lauderdale, FL 33301	1940	Britt G. Dorman, Jr.	3-B	1,250	50
Fort Lewis Coll, Durango, CO 81301	1911	Joel M. Jones	5-B	4,001	223
Fort Valley State Coll, Fort Valley, GA 31030	1895	Dr. Oscar L. Prater	5-M	2,197	154
Framingham State Coll, Framingham, MA 01701	1839	Dr. Paul F. Weller	5-M	3,823	231
Franciscan U of Steubenville, Steubenville, OH 43952	1946	Rev. Michael Scanlan, TOR	2-M	1,575	89
Francis Marion Coll, Florence, SC 29501-0547	1970	Dr. Thomas C. Stanton	5-M	3,926	207
Franklin and Marshall Coll, Lancaster, PA 17604	1787	Dr. A. Richard Kneedler	1-B	1,807	180
Franklin Coll of Indiana, Franklin, IN 46131	1834	Mr. William Bryan Martin	2-B	880	86
Franklin Pierce Coll, Rindge, NH 03461	1962	Dr. Walter Peterson	1-B	1,341	110
Franklin U, Columbus, OH 43215	1902	Dr. Paul J. Otte	1-B	4,005	201
Freed-Hardeman U, Henderson, TN 38340	1869	Dr. Milton R. Sewell	2-M	1,194	82
Fresno Pacific U, Fresno, CA 93702	1944	Dr. Richard Kriegbaum	2-M	1,680	58
Friends U, Wichita, KS 67213	1898	Dr. Biff Green	2-M	1,540	100
Frostburg State U, Frostburg, MD 21532	1898	NR	5-M	5,019	300
Furman U, Greenville, SC 29613	1826	Dr. John E. Johns	2-M	2,703	199
Gallaudet U, Washington, DC 20002	1856	Dr. I. King Jordan	1-D	2,373	330
Gannon U, Erie, PA 16541	1925	Dr. M. Daniel Henry	2-M	4,585	342
Gardner-Webb Coll, Boiling Springs, NC 28017	1905	Dr. M. Christopher White	2-M	2,074	155
Geneva Coll, Beaver Falls, PA 15010	1848	Dr. Joseph McFarland	2-M	1,327	105
George Fox Coll, Newberg, OR 97132	1891	Dr. Edward F. Stevens	2-D	1,073	77
George Mason U, Fairfax, VA 22030	1957	Dr. George W. Johnson	5-D	20,308	1,007
Georgetown Coll, Georgetown, KY 40324	1829	Dr. Tom E. Benberg	2-M	1,595	94
Georgetown U, Washington, DC 20057	1789	Rev. Leo J. O'Donovan, SJ	2-D	11,525	765
George Washington U, Washington, DC 20052	1821	Mr. Stephen J. Trachtenberg	1-D	14,752	1,187
Georgia Coll, Milledgeville, GA 31061	1889	Dr. Edwin G. Speir	5-M	4,820	168
Georgia Inst of Tech, Atlanta, GA 30332	1885	Dr. John P. Crecine	5-D	12,241	580
Georgian Court Coll, Lakewood, NJ 08701 (4)	1908	Sr. Barbara Williams	2-M	1,729	147
Georgia Southern U, Statesboro, GA 30460	1906	Dr. Nicholas Henry	5-M	11,238	543
Georgia Southwestern Coll, Americus, GA 31709	1906	Dr. William H. Capitan	5-M	2,227	155
Georgia State U, Atlanta, GA 30303	1913	Dr. John M. Palms	5-D	23,386	1,135
Gettysburg Coll, Gettysburg, PA 17325	1832	Dr. Gordon A. Haaland	2-B	1,950	150
Glassboro State Coll, Glassboro, NJ 08028	1923	Dr. Herman D. James	5-M	9,650	420
Glenville State Coll, Glenville, WV 26351	1872	Dr. William K. Simmons	5-B	2,264	133
GMI Engineering & Management Inst, Flint, MI 48504	1919	Dr. William B. Cottingham	1-M	3,204	125
Golden Gate U, San Francisco, CA 94105	1901	Dr. Otto W. Butz	1-D	7,943	766
Goldey-Beacom Coll, Wilmington, DE 19808	1886	Mr. William R. Baldt	1-B	1,784	65
Gonzaga U, Spokane, WA 99258	1887	Rev. Bernard J. Coughlin, SJ	2-D	4,178	290
Gordon Coll, Wenham, MA 01984	1889	Dr. Richard F. Gross	2-B	1,150	101
Goshen Coll, Goshen, IN 46526	1894	Dr. Victor Stoltzfus	2-B	1,042	112
Goucher Coll, Baltimore, MD 21204	1885	Dr. Rhoda M. Dorsey	1-M	965	143
Governors State U, University Park, IL 60466	1969	Dr. Leo Goodman-Malamuth, II	5-M	5,595	321
Graceland Coll, Lamoni, IA 50140	1895	Dr. Barbara J. Higdon	2-B	935	82
Grambling State U, Grambling, LA 71245	1901	Dr. Joseph B. Johnson	5-D	6,485	282
Grand Canyon U, Phoenix, AZ 85017	1949	Dr. Bill Williams	2-M	1,846	161
Grand Rapids Baptist Coll and Sem, Grand Rapids, MI 49505	1941	Dr. Charles Wagner	2-M	895	60
Grand Valley State U, Allendale, MI 49401	1960	Mr. Arend D. Lubbers	5-M	11,726	581
Grand View Coll, Des Moines, IA 50316	1896	Dr. Arthur E. Puotinen	2-B	1,420	107
Grantham Coll of Engineering, Slidell, LA 70460	1951	Mr. Donald J. Grantham	3-B	900	4
Greensboro Coll, Greensboro, NC 27401	1838	Dr. William H. Likins	2-B	1,116	81
Greenville Coll, Greenville, IL 62246	1892	Dr. W. Richard Stephens	2-B	849	66
Griffin Coll, Seattle, WA 98121	1909	Peggy Jacobson	3-B	2,000	72
Grinnell Coll, Grinnell, IA 50112	1846	Dr. Pamela A. Ferguson	1-B	1,251	140
Grove City Coll, Grove City, PA 16127	1876	Dr. Charles S. MacKenzie	2-B	2,138	115
Guilford Coll, Greensboro, NC 27410	1837	Dr. William R. Rogers	2-B	1,368	108
Gustavus Adolphus Coll, St Peter, MN 56082	1862	Dr. John S. Kendall	2-B	2,320	194
Gwynedd-Mercy Coll, Gwynedd Valley, PA 19437 (4)	1948	Sr. Isabelle Keiss, RSM	2-M	1,994	168
Hahnemann U, Philadelphia, PA 19102	1848	Mr. Iqbal F. Paroo	1-D	1,325	430

Name, address	Year	Governing official, control, and highest degree offered	Enrollment	Faculty
Hamilton Coll, Clinton, NY 13323	1812	Dr. Harry C. Payne 1-B	1,668	206
Hamline U, St Paul, MN 55104	1854	Dr. Larry G. Osnes 2-D	2,514	151
Hampden-Sydney Coll, Hampden-Sydney, VA 23943 (1)	1776	Dr. James R. Leutze 2-B	956	93
Hampshire Coll, Amherst, MA 01002	1965	Mr. Gregory S. Prince, Jr. 1-B	1,263	100
Hampton U, Hampton, VA 23668	1868	Dr. William R. Harvey 1-M	5,468	390
Hannibal-LaGrange Coll, Hannibal, MO 63401	1858	Dr. Paul Brown 2-B	1,025	80
Hanover Coll, Hanover, IN 47243	1827	Dr. Russell L. Nichols 2-B	1,064	99
Harding U, Searcy, AR 72143	1924	Dr. David B. Burks, Jr. 2-M	3,311	190
Hardin-Simmons U, Abilene, TX 79698	1891	Dr. Edwin L. Hall 2-M	1,930	138
Hartwick Coll, Oneonta, NY 13820	1797	Dr. Philip S. Wilder, Jr. 1-B	1,498	161
Harvard U, Cambridge, MA 02138	1636	Neil Rudenstine 1-D	15,601	800
Hastings Coll, Hastings, NE 68902	1882	Dr. Thomas J. Reeves 2-M	962	85
Haverford Coll, Haverford, PA 19041	1833	Tom G. Kessinger 1-B	1,147	117
Hawaii Pacific U, Honolulu, HI 96813	1965	Mr. Chatt Wright 1-M	5,557	302
Heidelberg Coll, Tiffin, OH 44883	1850	Dr. William C. Cassell 2-M	1,426	113
Henderson State U, Arkadelphia, AR 71923	1890	Dr. Charles D. Dunn 5-M	3,526	163
Hendrix Coll, Conway, AR 72032-3080	1876	Dr. Joe B. Hatcher 2-B	1,006	76
Heritage Coll, Toppenish, WA 98948	1907	Dr. Kathleen Ross, SNJM 1-M	986	99
High Point Coll, High Point, NC 27261	1924	Dr. Jacob C. Martinson, Jr. 2-B	2,308	108
Hillsdale Coll, Hillsdale, MI 49242	1844	Dr. George C. Roche, III 1-B	1,110	102
Hiram Coll, Hiram, OH 44234	1850	Dr. G. Benjamin Oliver 2-B	900	93
Hobart Coll, Geneva, NY 14456 (1)	1822	NR 2-B	1,030	180
Hofstra U, Hempstead, NY 11550	1935	Dr. James M. Shuart 1-D	12,225	856
Hollins Coll, Roanoke, VA 24020 (3)	1842	Dr. Samuel R. Spencer, Jr. 1-M	1,137	108
Holy Family Coll, Philadelphia, PA 19114	1954	Sr. M. Francesca Onley 2-M	2,089	189
Holy Names Coll, Oakland, CA 94619-1699	1868	Sr. Lois MacGillivray, SNJM 2-M	894	91
Hood Coll, Frederick, MD 21701-9988 (4)	1893	Dr. Martha E. Church 2-M	1,995	93
Hope Coll, Holland, MI 49423	1862	Dr. John Jacobson, Jr. 2-B	2,813	237
Houghton Coll, Houghton, NY 14744	1883	Dr. Daniel R. Chamberlain 2-M	1,170	104
Houston Baptist U, Houston, TX 77074	1960	Dr. E. Douglas Hodo 2-M	2,255	145
Howard U, Washington, DC 20059	1867	Franklyn G. Jenifer 1-D	11,236	2,000
Humboldt State U, Arcata, CA 95521	1913	Dr. Alistair W. McCrone 5-M	7,654	551
Hunter Coll of the City U of New York, New York, NY 10021	1870	Dr. Paul Le Clerc 12-M	19,645	NR
Huntingdon Coll, Montgomery, AL 36106	1854	Dr. Allen K. Jackson 2-B	791	64
Husson Coll, Bangor, ME 04401	1898	Dr. William H. Beardsley 1-M	1,846	62
Idaho State U, Pocatello, ID 83209	1901	Dr. Richard Bowen 5-D	9,100	459
Illinois Benedictine Coll, Lisle, IL 60532	1887	Dr. Richard C. Becker 2-M	2,501	143
Illinois Coll, Jacksonville, IL 62650	1829	Dr. Donald C. Mundinger 2-B	888	85
Illinois Inst of Tech, Chicago, IL 60616	1892	Mr. Lewis Collens 1-D	6,504	510
Illinois State U, Normal, IL 61761	1857	Dr. Thomas P. Wallace 5-D	22,694	1,043
Illinois Wesleyan U, Bloomington, IL 61702	1850	Dr. Minor Myers, Jr. 2-B	1,767	178
Immaculata Coll, Immaculata, PA 19345 (4)	1920	Sr. Marian William 2-M	2,400	152
Incarnate Word Coll, San Antonio, TX 78209	1881	Dr. Louis J. Agnese, Jr. 2-M	2,579	159
Indiana Inst of Tech, Fort Wayne, IN 46803	1930	Donald J. Andorfer 1-B	961	42
Indiana State U, Terre Haute, IN 47809	1865	Dr. Richard G. Landini 5-D	11,783	814
Indiana U at South Bend, South Bend, IN 46634	1922	Dr. H. Daniel Cohen 5-M	7,215	469
Indiana U Bloomington, Bloomington, IN 47405	1820	Kenneth R. R. Gros Louis 5-D	35,453	1,653
Indiana U East, Richmond, IN 47374	1971	Dr. Charlie Nelms 5-B	2,053	138
Indiana U Northwest, Gary, IN 46408	1959	Dr. Peggy G. Elliott 5-M	5,078	333
Indiana U of Pennsylvania, Indiana, PA 15705	1875	Dr. John D. Welty 5-D	14,398	805
Indiana U–Purdue U at Fort Wayne, Fort Wayne, IN 46805-1499	1917	Dr. Joanne B. Lantz 5-M	11,879	667
Indiana U–Purdue U at Indianapolis, Indianapolis, IN 46202	1969	Gerald L. Bepko, Jr. 5-D	27,518	2,120
Indiana U Southeast, New Albany, IN 47150	1941	Dr. Leon Rand 5-M	5,642	325
Indiana Wesleyan U, Marion, IN 46953	1920	Dr. James Barnes 2-M	2,727	100
Iona Coll, New Rochelle, NY 10801	1940	Dr. John G. Driscoll, CFC 1-M	6,251	465
Iowa State U of Science and Tech, Ames, IA 50011	1858	Dr. Milton D. Glick 5-D	25,339	1,265
Iowa Wesleyan Coll, Mount Pleasant, IA 52641	1842	Robert J. Prins 2-B	914	44
Ithaca Coll, Ithaca, NY 14850	1892	Dr. James J. Whalen 1-M	6,433	592
ITT Tech Inst, Fort Wayne, IN 46825	1967	Jack B. Cozad 3-B	1,089	31
ITT Tech Inst, Indianapolis, IN 46268	1966	Alan Crews 3-B	1,085	42
Jackson State U, Jackson, MS 39217	1877	Dr. Herman Smith 5-D	6,838	424
Jacksonville State U, Jacksonville, AL 36265	1883	Dr. Harold J. McGee 5-M	8,448	283
Jacksonville U, Jacksonville, FL 32211	1934	Dr. James J. Brady 1-M	2,500	183
James Madison U, Harrisonburg, VA 22807	1908	Dr. Ronald E. Carrier 5-M	11,011	648
Jamestown Coll, Jamestown, ND 58401	1883	Dr. James Walker 2-B	899	63
Jersey City State Coll, Jersey City, NJ 07305	1927	Dr. William J. Maxwell 5-M	7,168	423
John Brown U, Siloam Springs, AR 72761	1919	Dr. John E. Brown, III 2-B	912	75
John Carroll U, University Heights, OH 44118	1886	Rev. Michael J. Lavelle, SJ 2-M	4,551	294
John Jay Coll of Criminal Justice of City U of NY, New York, NY 10019	1964	Dr. Gerald Lynch 12-D	8,695	508
Johns Hopkins U, Baltimore, MD 21218	1876	Dr. William C. Richardson 1-D	4,335	491
Johnson & Wales U, Providence, RI 02903	1914	Dr. John A. Yena 1-M	7,728	312
Johnson C Smith U, Charlotte, NC 28216	1867	Dr. Robert L. Albright 1-B	1,182	91
Johnson State Coll, Johnson, VT 05656	1828	Dr. Lynn Beach Sadler 5-M	1,680	139
Juilliard Sch, New York, NY 10023	1905	Dr. Joseph W. Polisi 1-D	843	220
Juniata Coll, Huntingdon, PA 16652	1876	Dr. Robert W. Neff 1-B	1,146	95
Kalamazoo Coll, Kalamazoo, MI 49007	1833	Dr. Lawrence Bryan 1-B	1,265	120
Kansas Newman Coll, Wichita, KS 67213	1933	Sr. Tarcisia Roths 2-B	956	158
Kansas State U, Manhattan, KS 66506	1863	Dr. Jon Wefald 5-D	21,137	1,843
Kansas Wesleyan U, Salina, KS 67401	1886	Dr. Marshall P. Stanton 2-B	803	48
Kean Coll of New Jersey, Union, NJ 07083	1855	Dr. Elsa Gomez 5-M	13,329	818
Keene State Coll, Keene, NH 03431	1909	Dr. Judith A. Sturnick 5-M	3,602	279
Kennesaw State Coll, Marietta, GA 30061	1966	Dr. Betty L. Siegel 5-M	10,030	438
Kent State U, Kent, OH 44242	1910	Dr. Michael Schwartz 5-D	24,434	1,343
Kentucky State U, Frankfort, KY 40601	1886	Dr. John T. Wolfe, Jr. 13-M	2,512	158
Kenyon Coll, Gambier, OH 43022	1824	Dr. Philip H. Jordan, Jr. 1-B	1,506	166
King's Coll, Wilkes-Barre, PA 18711-0801	1946	Rev. James Lackenmier, CSC 2-B	2,256	155
Knox Coll, Galesburg, IL 61401	1837	Dr. John P. McCall 1-B	1,029	88
Knoxville Coll, Knoxville, TN 37921	1875	Mr. John B. Turner 2-B	1,266	95
Kutztown U of Pennsylvania, Kutztown, PA 19530	1866	Dr. David E. McFarland 5-M	7,742	361
Lafayette Coll, Easton, PA 18042	1826	Dr. Robert I. Rotberg 2-B	1,960	195

Name, address	Year	Governing official, control, and highest degree offered		Enrollment	Faculty
LaGrange Coll, LaGrange, GA 30240	1831	Dr. Walter Y. Murphy	2-M	964	74
Lake Erie Coll, Painesville, OH 44077	1856	Dr. Clodus R. Smith	1-M	844	62
Lake Forest Coll, Lake Forest, IL 60045	1857	Dr. Eugene Hotchkiss, III	1-M	1,117	111
Lakeland Coll, Sheboygan, WI 53082	1862	Dr. David R. Black	2-M	1,994	96
Lake Superior State U, Sault Sainte Marie, MI 49783	1946	Dr. H. Erik Shaar	5-M	3,407	161
Lamar U–Beaumont, Beaumont, TX 77705	1923	Dr. Bill J. Franklin	5-D	11,848	725
Lambuth U, Jackson, TN 38301	1843	Dr. Thomas F. Boyd	2-B	819	65
Lander Coll, Greenwood, SC 29649	1872	Dr. Larry A. Jackson	5-M	2,677	166
Langston U, Langston, OK 73050	1897	Dr. Ernest L. Holloway	5-M	3,025	128
La Roche Coll, Pittsburgh, PA 15237	1963	Sr. Margaret Huber	2-M	1,858	129
La Salle U, Philadelphia, PA 19141	1863	Br. Patrick Ellis	2-M	6,478	326
Lawrence Tech U, Southfield, MI 48075	1932	Dr. Richard E. Marburger	1-M	5,469	292
Lawrence U, Appleton, WI 54912	1847	Dr. Richard Warch	1-B	1,235	121
Lebanon Valley Coll, Annville, PA 17003	1866	Mr. John A. Synodinos	2-M	830	97
Lee Coll, Cleveland, TN 37311	1918	Dr. Paul Conn	2-B	1,739	143
Lees-McRae Coll, Banner Elk, NC 28604	1900	Dr. Bradford L. Crain	2-B	863	70
Lehigh U, Bethlehem, PA 18015	1865	Dr. Peter Likins	1-D	6,663	488
Lehman Coll of the City U of New York, Bronx, NY 10468	1931	Dr. Ricardo R. Fernandez	12-M	8,123	615
Le Moyne Coll, Syracuse, NY 13214	1946	Rev. Kevin G. O'Connell, SJ	2-B	2,002	203
LeMoyne-Owen Coll, Memphis, TN 38126	1870	Dr. Doris W. Weathers	2-B	1,066	84
Lenoir-Rhyne Coll, Hickory, NC 28603	1891	Dr. John E. Trainer, Jr.	2-M	1,653	135
Lesley Coll, Cambridge, MA 02138 (3)	1909	Margaret A. McKenna	1-D	5,500	35
LeTourneau U, Longview, TX 75607	1946	Dr. Alvin O. Austin	2-B	788	59
Lewis and Clark Coll, Portland, OR 97219	1867	Dr. Michael J. Mooney	1-D	2,806	139
Lewis-Clark State Coll, Lewiston, ID 83501	1894	Dr. Lee A. Vickers	5-B	2,164	115
Lewis U, Romeoville, IL 60441	1932	Br. James Gaffney, FSC	2-M	3,666	160
Liberty U, Lynchburg, VA 24506	1971	Dr. A. Pierre Guillermin	2-D	5,198	242
Limestone Coll, Gaffney, SC 29340	1845	Dr. Dan Champion	1-B	860	77
Lincoln Memorial U, Harrogate, TN 37752	1897	Dr. Gary J. Burchett	1-M	1,819	103
Lincoln U, Jefferson City, MO 65102	1866	Dr. Wendell G. Rayburn	5-M	3,619	192
Lincoln U, Lincoln University, PA 19352	1854	Dr. Niara Sudarkasa	13-M	1,373	128
Lindenwood Coll, St Charles, MO 63301	1827	Dr. Dennis Spellmann	2-M	2,410	108
Lindsey Wilson Coll, Columbia, KY 42728	1903	Dr. John B. Begley	2-B	1,327	53
Linfield Coll, McMinnville, OR 97128	1849	Dr. Charles U. Walker	2-M	1,337	116
Livingston U, Livingston, AL 35470	1835	Dr. Asa N. Green	5-M	1,921	104
Lock Haven U of Pennsylvania, Lock Haven, PA 17745	1870	Dr. Craig Dean Willis	5-M	3,260	188
Loma Linda U Riverside, Riverside, CA 92515	1922	Dr. Fritz Guy	2-D	1,620	112
Long Island U, Brooklyn Cmps, Brooklyn, NY 11201	1926	Dr. David J. Steinberg	1-D	4,600	400
Long Island U, C W Post Cmps, Brookville, NY 11548	1954	Dr. David J. Steinberg	1-M	8,964	702
Long Island U, Southampton Cmps, Southampton, NY 11968	1963	Dr. David J. Steinberg	1-M	1,250	125
Longwood Coll, Farmville, VA 23901	1839	Dr. William F. Dorrill	5-M	2,990	190
Loras Coll, Dubuque, IA 52004	1839	Rev. Msgr. James Barta	2-M	1,905	166
Los Angeles Coll of Chiropractic, Whittier, CA 90609	1911	Dr. E. Maylon Drake	1-D	1,003	81
Louisiana Coll, Pineville, LA 71359	1906	Dr. Robert L. Lynn	2-B	1,075	80
Louisiana State U and A&M Coll, Baton Rouge, LA 70803	1860	Dr. William E. Davis	5-D	25,307	1,280
Louisiana State U in Shreveport, Shreveport, LA 71115	1965	Dr. John R. Darling	5-M	4,107	218
Louisiana State U Medical Ctr, New Orleans, LA 70112	1931	Dr. Perry G. Rigby	5-D	2,539	NR
Louisiana Tech U, Ruston, LA 71272	1894	Dr. Daniel D. Reneau	5-D	10,011	414
Lourdes Coll, Sylvania, OH 43560	1958	Sr. Ann Francis Klimkowski, OSF	2-B	1,049	106
Loyola Coll, Baltimore, MD 21210	1852	Rev. Joseph A. Sellinger, SJ	2-M	6,358	426
Loyola Marymount U, Los Angeles, CA 90045	1911	Rev. James N. Loughran, SJ	2-D	4,809	426
Loyola U Chicago, Chicago, IL 60611	1870	Rev. Raymond C. Baumhart, SJ	2-D	14,780	746
Loyola U, New Orleans, New Orleans, LA 70118	1912	Rev. James C. Carter, SJ	2-D	5,400	538
Lubbock Christian U, Lubbock, TX 79407	1957	Dr. Steven S. Lemley	2-M	1,035	110
Luther Coll, Decorah, IA 52101	1861	Dr. H. George Anderson	2-B	2,265	192
Lycoming Coll, Williamsport, PA 17701	1812	Dr. James E. Douthat	2-B	1,271	108
Lynchburg Coll, Lynchburg, VA 24501	1903	Dr. George N. Rainsford	2-M	2,446	173
Lyndon State Coll, Lyndonville, VT 05851	1911	Dr. Margaret R. Williams	5-M	1,166	85
Macalester Coll, St Paul, MN 55105	1874	Dr. Robert M. Gavin, Jr.	2-B	1,853	203
Madonna U, Livonia, MI 48150	1947	Sr. Mary Francilene	2-M	4,393	265
Malone Coll, Canton, OH 44709	1892	Dr. E. Arthur Self	2-M	1,563	115
Manchester Coll, North Manchester, IN 46962	1889	Dr. William P. Robinson	2-M	1,122	110
Manhattan Coll, Riverdale, NY 10471	1853	Br. Thomas J. Scanlan	1-M	3,782	309
Manhattan Sch of Music, New York, NY 10027	1917	Dr. Peter C. Simon	1-D	818	214
Manhattanville Coll, Purchase, NY 10577	1841	Dr. Marcia Savage	1-M	1,647	201
Mankato State U, Mankato, MN 56002-8400	1867	Dr. Margaret R. Preska	5-M	16,185	611
Mannes Coll of Music, New Sch for Social Research, New York, NY 10024	1916	Dr. Charles Kaufman	1-M	226	216
Mansfield U of Pennsylvania, Mansfield, PA 16933	1857	Mr. Rod C. Kelchner	5-M	3,182	176
Marian Coll, Indianapolis, IN 46222	1851	Dr. Daniel A. Felicetti	2-B	1,248	123
Marian Coll of Fond du Lac, Fond du Lac, WI 54935	1936	Matthew G. Flanigan	2-M	1,668	81
Marietta Coll, Marietta, OH 45750	1835	Dr. Patrick D. McDonough	1-M	1,387	127
Marist Coll, Poughkeepsie, NY 12601	1929	Dr. Dennis J. Murray	1-M	4,479	312
Marquette U, Milwaukee, WI 53233	1881	Rev. Albert J. DiVilio, SJ	2-D	11,775	925
Marshall U, Huntington, WV 25755	1837	Dr. Alan B. Gould	5-D	12,406	566
Mars Hill Coll, Mars Hill, NC 28754	1856	Dr. Fred B. Bentley	2-B	1,344	137
Marygrove Coll, Detroit, MI 48221	1910	Dr. John E. Shay, Jr.	2-M	1,299	67
Maryland Inst, Coll of Art, Baltimore, MD 21217	1826	Mr. Fred Lazarus	1-M	969	129
Marylhurst Coll, Marylhurst, OR 97036	1893	Nancy A. Wilgenbusch	2-M	1,031	274
Marymount Coll, Tarrytown, NY 10591-3796 (4)	1907	Sr. Brigid Driscoll	1-B	1,125	133
Marymount Manhattan Coll, New York, NY 10021 (4)	1936	Regina Peruggi	1-B	1,300	155
Marymount U, Arlington, VA 22207	1950	Sr. M. Majella Berg, RSHM	2-M	3,152	225
Maryville Coll–Saint Louis, St Louis, MO 63141	1872	Dr. Claudius Pritchard	1-M	3,337	205
Mary Washington Coll, Fredericksburg, VA 22401	1908	Dr. William M. Anderson, Jr.	5-M	3,450	227
Marywood Coll, Scranton, PA 18509	1915	Sr. Mary Reap, IHM	2-M	3,087	222
Massachusetts Coll of Art, Boston, MA 02115	1873	Dr. William F. O'Neil	5-M	1,201	91
Mass Coll of Pharmacy and Allied Health Sciences, Boston, MA 02115	1823	Dr. Louis P. Jeffrey	1-D	1,136	122
Massachusetts Inst of Tech, Cambridge, MA 02139	1861	Dr. Charles M. Vest	1-D	9,628	985
Master's Coll, Newhall, CA 91322	1927	Dr. John F. MacArthur, Jr.	2-M	1,008	87
Mayville State U, Mayville, ND 58257-1299	1889	Dr. James A. Schobel	5-B	763	52
McKendree Coll, Lebanon, IL 62254	1828	Dr. Gerrit J. TenBrink	2-B	1,229	74
McMurry U, Abilene, TX 79697	1923	Dr. Thomas K. Kim	2-B	1,633	117
McNeese State U, Lake Charles, LA 70609	1939	Dr. Robert D. Hebert	5-M	7,724	342

Name, address	Year	Governing official, control, and highest degree offered	Enrollment	Faculty
Medaille Coll, Buffalo, NY 14214	1875	Kevin I. Sullivan	1-B	1,105	70
Medgar Evers Coll of the City U of New York, Brooklyn, NY 11225	1969	Dr. Edison O. Jackson	12-B	3,800	272
Medical Coll of Georgia, Augusta, GA 30912	1828	Dr. Francis J. Tedesco	5-D	1,974	NR
Medical U of South Carolina, Charleston, SC 29425	1824	Dr. James B. Edwards	5-D	2,219	NR
Memphis State U, Memphis, TN 38152	1912	Dr. Thomas G. Carpenter	5-D	20,681	1,013
Mercer U, Macon, GA 31207	1833	Dr. R. Kirby Godsey	2-D	3,985	165
Mercer U Atlanta, Atlanta, GA 30341	1968	Dr. R. Kirby Godsey	2-M	892	59
Mercy Coll, Dobbs Ferry, NY 10522	1951	Dr. Jay Sexter	1-M	5,287	494
Mercyhurst Coll, Erie, PA 16546	1926	Dr. William P. Garvey	2-M	2,084	117
Meredith Coll, Raleigh, NC 27607 (3)	1891	Dr. John E. Weems	2-M	2,245	183
Merrimack Coll, North Andover, MA 01845	1947	Rev. John E. Deegan, OSA	2-B	2,395	176
Mesa State Coll, Grand Junction, CO 81502	1925	Dr. Ray N. Kieft	5-B	4,328	197
Messiah Coll, Grantham, PA 17027	1909	Dr. D. Ray Hostetter	2-B	2,252	203
Methodist Coll, Fayetteville, NC 28311	1956	Dr. M. Elton Hendricks	2-B	1,190	120
Metropolitan State Coll of Denver, Denver, CO 80217	1963	Dr. Thomas Brewer	5-B	17,341	887
Metropolitan State U, St Paul, MN 55101	1971	Dr. Tobin G. Barrozo	5-M	5,528	762
Miami U, Oxford, OH 45056	1809	Dr. Paul G. Pearson	5-D	15,841	873
Michigan State U, East Lansing, MI 48824	1855	Dr. John DiBiaggio	5-D	44,317	4,101
Michigan Tech U, Houghton, MI 49931	1885	Dr. Dale F. Stein	5-D	6,640	370
MidAmerica Nazarene Coll, Olathe, KS 66061	1966	Dr. Richard Spindle	2-M	1,249	94
Middlebury Coll, Middlebury, VT 05753	1800	Dr. Timothy Light	1-D	1,950	216
Middle Tennessee State U, Murfreesboro, TN 37132	1911	Dr. James E. Walker	5-D	14,865	653
Midland Lutheran Coll, Fremont, NE 68025	1883	Dr. Carl L. Hansen	2-B	960	65
Midwestern State U, Wichita Falls, TX 76308	1922	Dr. Louis J. Rodriguez	5-M	5,508	214
Millersville U of Pennsylvania, Millersville, PA 17551	1854	Dr. Joseph A. Caputo	5-M	7,789	419
Milligan Coll, Milligan College, TN 37682	1866	Dr. Marshall J. Leggett	2-M	811	65
Millikin U, Decatur, IL 62522	1901	Dr. J. Roger Miller	2-B	1,859	173
Millsaps Coll, Jackson, MS 39210	1890	Dr. George M. Harmon	2-M	1,410	105
Mills Coll, Oakland, CA 94613 (3)	1852	Dr. Virginia B. Smith	1-M	1,044	168
Milwaukee Sch of Engineering, Milwaukee, WI 53201	1903	Dr. Robert R. Spitzer	1-M	2,232	198
Minot State U, Minot, ND 58702	1913	Dr. Gordon B. Olson	5-M	3,637	189
Mississippi Coll, Clinton, MS 39058	1826	Dr. Lewis Nobles	2-D	3,620	234
Mississippi State U, Mississippi State, MS 39762	1878	Dr. Donald W. Zacharias	5-D	14,391	883
Mississippi U for Women, Columbus, MS 39701 (4)	1884	Dr. Clyda S. Rent	5-M	2,407	126
Missouri Baptist Coll, St Louis, MO 63141	1968	Dr. Patrick O. Copley	2-B	1,059	60
Missouri Southern State Coll, Joplin, MO 64801	1937	Dr. Julio Leon	5-B	6,012	293
Missouri Valley Coll, Marshall, MO 65340	1889	Dr. Earl J. Reeves	2-B	1,011	60
Missouri Western State Coll, St Joseph, MO 64507	1915	Dr. Janet Gorman Murphy	5-B	4,647	244
Mobile Coll, Mobile, AL 36613	1961	Dr. Michael A. Magnoli	2-M	1,325	113
Molloy Coll, Rockville Centre, NY 11570-1199	1955	Dr. Janet A. Fitzgerald, OP	1-M	1,633	180
Monmouth Coll, West Long Branch, NJ 07764	1933	Dr. Samuel H. Magill	1-M	4,276	329
Montana Coll of Mineral Science and Tech, Butte, MT 59701	1895	Dr. Lindsay D. Norman, Jr.	5-M	1,920	115
Montana State U, Bozeman, MT 59717	1893	Dr. William J. Tietz	5-D	10,392	550
Montclair State Coll, Upper Montclair, NJ 07043	1908	Dr. Irvin D. Reid	5-M	13,083	833
Moody Bible Inst, Chicago, IL 60610	1886	Dr. Joseph M. Stowell, III	2-M	1,480	78
Moorhead State U, Moorhead, MN 56563	1887	Dr. Roland Dille	5-M	8,900	456
Moravian Coll, Bethlehem, PA 18018	1742	Dr. Roger Harry Martin	2-M	1,802	135
Morehead State U, Morehead, KY 40351	1922	Dr. C. Nelson Grote	5-M	8,622	409
Morehouse Coll, Atlanta, GA 30314 (1)	1867	Dr. Leroy Keith, Jr.	1-B	2,720	150
Morgan State U, Baltimore, MD 21209	1867	Dr. Earl Richardson	5-D	4,689	336
Morningside Coll, Sioux City, IA 51106	1894	Dr. Miles Tommeraasen	2-M	1,366	103
Morris Brown Coll, Atlanta, GA 30314	1881	Dr. Calvert H. Smith	2-B	1,990	128
Morris Coll, Sumter, SC 29150	1908	Dr. Luns C. Richardson	2-B	760	59
Mount Holyoke Coll, South Hadley, MA 01075 (3)	1837	Mrs. Elizabeth T. Kennan	1-B	1,879	215
Mount Marty Coll, Yankton, SD 57078	1936	Sr. Jacquelyn Ernster	2-M	964	81
Mount Mary Coll, Milwaukee, WI 53222 (3)	1913	Sr. Ruth Hollenbach	2-M	1,452	134
Mount Mercy Coll, Cedar Rapids, IA 52402	1928	Dr. Thomas R. Feld	2-B	1,529	109
Mount Olive Coll, Mount Olive, NC 28365	1951	Dr. W. Burkette Raper	2-B	768	64
Mount Saint Mary Coll, Newburgh, NY 12550	1960	Dr. Ann Sakac	1-M	1,374	119
Mount St Mary's Coll, Los Angeles, CA 90049 (4)	1925	Sr. Karen Kennelly	2-M	1,179	146
Mount Saint Mary's Coll, Emmitsburg, MD 21727	1808	Dr. Robert J. Wickenheiser	2-M	1,866	143
Mount Senario Coll, Ladysmith, WI 54848	1962	Dr. John N. Cable	1-B	1,060	40
Mount Union Coll, Alliance, OH 44601	1846	Dr. Harold M. Kolenbrander	2-B	1,368	110
Mount Vernon Nazarene Coll, Mount Vernon, OH 43050	1964	Dr. E. LeBron Fairbanks	2-B	1,056	72
Muhlenberg Coll, Allentown, PA 18104	1848	Dr. Jonathan C. Messerli	2-B	1,638	157
Mundelein Coll, Chicago, IL 60660 (4)	1929	Carolyn Farrel, BVM	2-M	1,030	98
Murray State U, Murray, KY 42071	1922	Dr. Ronald J. Kurth	5-M	8,097	371
Muskingum Coll, New Concord, OH 43762	1837	Dr. Samuel W. Speck, Jr.	2-M	1,175	94
National Coll of Chiropractic, Lombard, IL 60148	1906	Dr. J. F. Winterstein	1-D	792	92
National–Louis U, Evanston, IL 60201	1886	NR	1-D	5,282	240
National U, San Diego, CA 92108	1971	Dr. Jerry C. Lee	1-D	9,059	1,673
Nazareth Coll of Rochester, Rochester, NY 14618-3790	1924	Dr. Rose Marie Beston	1-M	2,921	185
Nebraska Wesleyan U, Lincoln, NE 68504	1887	Dr. John W. White, Jr.	2-B	1,684	140
Neumann Coll, Aston, PA 19014	1965	Dr. Nan B. Hechenberger	2-M	1,263	104
New England Coll, Henniker, NH 03242-3293	1946	William R. O'Connell, Jr.	1-M	1,030	117
New England Inst of Tech, Warwick, RI 02886 (2)	1940	Dr. Richard I. Gouse	1-B	2,250	134
New Hampshire Coll, Manchester, NH 03104	1932	Richard A. Gustafson	1-M	3,049	77
New Jersey Inst of Tech, Newark, NJ 07102	1881	Dr. Saul K. Fenster	13-D	7,670	506
New Mexico Highlands U, Las Vegas, NM 87701	1893	Dr. Gilbert Sanchez	5-M	2,437	109
New Mexico Inst of Mining and Tech, Socorro, NM 87801	1889	Dr. Laurence H. Lattman	5-D	1,345	98
New Mexico State U, Las Cruces, NM 88003	1888	Dr. James E. Halligan	5-D	14,809	780
New Sch Bach of Arts, New Sch for Social Research, New York, NY 10011	1919	Gerald A. Heeger	1-B	265	545
New York Inst of Tech, Old Westbury, NY 11568	1955	Dr. Alexander Schure	1-M	12,744	1,340
New York U, New York, NY 10011	1831	Dr. John Brademas	1-D	32,756	4,160
Niagara U, Niagara University, NY 14109	1856	Rev. Brian J. O'Connell, CM	1-M	3,065	227
Nicholls State U, Thibodaux, LA 70310	1948	Dr. Donald J. Ayo	5-M	7,363	265
Nichols Coll, Dudley, MA 015701	1815	Dr. Lowell C. Smith	1-M	1,946	49
Norfolk State U, Norfolk, VA 23504	1935	Dr. Harrison B. Wilson	5-M	8,008	469
North Adams State Coll, North Adams, MA 01247	1894	Dr. Catherine Tisinger	5-M	2,341	127
North Carolina Ag and Tech State U, Greensboro, NC 27411	1891	Dr. Edward B. Fort	5-M	6,515	424
North Carolina Central U, Durham, NC 27707	1910	Dr. Tyronza R. Richmond	5-M	5,481	318
North Carolina State U, Raleigh, NC 27695	1887	Dr. Larry K. Monteith	5-D	26,683	1,448
North Carolina Wesleyan Coll, Rocky Mount, NC 27804	1956	Dr. Leslie H. Garner, Jr.	2-B	750	44

Name, address	Year	Governing official, control, and highest degree offered	Enrollment	Faculty
North Central Bible Coll, Minneapolis, MN 55404	1930	Dr. Don H. Argue 2-B	1,182	64
North Central Coll, Naperville, IL 60566	1861	Mr. Richard Luze 2-M	2,585	182
North Dakota State U, Fargo, ND 58105	1890	Dr. Jim Ozbun 5-D	8,707	420
Northeastern Illinois U, Chicago, IL 60625	1961	Dr. Gordon Lamb 5-M	10,453	535
Northeastern State U, Tahlequah, OK 74464	1846	Dr. W. Roger Webb 5-D	8,896	329
Northeastern U, Boston, MA 02115	1898	John A. Curry 1-D	30,515	2,368
Northeast Louisiana U, Monroe, LA 71209	1931	Dr. Dwight D. Vines 5-D	10,686	423
Northeast Missouri State U, Kirksville, MO 63501	1867	Dr. Russell G. Warren 5-M	5,819	453
Northern Arizona U, Flagstaff, AZ 86011	1899	Dr. Eugene M. Hughes . . . 5-D	16,994	927
Northern Illinois U, De Kalb, IL 60115	1895	Dr. John E. LaTourette . . . 5-D	24,509	1,293
Northern Kentucky U, Highland Heights, KY 41099	1968	Dr. Leon E. Boothe 5-D	11,254	609
Northern Michigan U, Marquette, MI 49855	1899	Dr. William E. Vandament . . 5-M	8,310	335
Northern Montana Coll, Havre, MT 59501	1929	Dr. William Daehling 5-M	1,770	113
Northern State U, Aberdeen, SD 57401	1901	Dr. Terence Brown 5-M	3,108	NR
North Georgia Coll, Dahlonega, GA 30597	1873	Dr. John H. Owen 5-M	2,518	147
Northland Coll, Ashland, WI 54806	1892	Dr. Robert Rue Parsonage . . 2-B	758	72
North Park Coll, Chicago, IL 60625	1891	Dr. David G. Horner 2-B	900	158
Northrop U, Los Angeles, CA 90045	1942	Dr. John R. Beljan 1-D	1,270	157
Northwestern Coll, Orange City, IA 51041	1882	Dr. James E. Bultman 2-M	1,064	88
Northwestern Coll, St Paul, MN 55113	1902	Dr. Donald Ericksen 2-B	1,115	85
Northwestern Oklahoma State U, Alva, OK 73717	1897	Dr. Joe J. Struckle 5-M	1,939	109
Northwestern State U of Louisiana, Natchitoches, LA 71497	1884	Dr. Robert A. Alost 5-M	7,334	210
Northwestern U, Evanston, IL 60208	1851	Dr. Arnold R. Weber 1-D	14,684	899
Northwest Missouri State U, Maryville, MO 64468	1905	Dr. Dean L. Hubbard 5-M	6,101	274
Northwest Nazarene Coll, Nampa, ID 83686	1913	Dr. A. Gordon Wetmore . . . 2-M	1,088	88
Northwood Inst, Midland, MI 48640	1959	Dr. David E. Fry 1-B	1,850	57
Norwich U, Northfield, VT 05663	1819	Lt. Gen. W. Russel Todd . . . 1-M	2,410	237
Notre Dame Coll, Manchester, NH 03104	1950	Dr. Carol J. Descoteaux, CSC 2-M	1,125	90
Notre Dame Coll of Ohio, South Euclid, OH 44121 (3)	1922	Sr. Marla Loehr, SND 2-B	849	87
Nova U, Fort Lauderdale, FL 33314	1964	Dr. Abraham S. Fischler . . . 1-D	9,562	251
Nyack Coll, Nyack, NY 10960	1882	Mr. Rexford A. Boda 2-M	814	77
Oakland U, Rochester, MI 48309	1957	Dr. Joseph E. Champagne . . 5-D	12,400	600
Oberlin Coll, Oberlin, OH 44074	1833	S. Frederick Starr 1-M	2,815	241
Occidental Coll, Los Angeles, CA 90041	1887	Dr. John B. Slaughter 1-M	1,677	154
Oglethorpe U, Atlanta, GA 30319	1835	Dr. Donald S. Stanton 1-M	1,092	87
Ohio Dominican Coll, Columbus, OH 43219	1871	Dr. Mary Andrew Matesich . . 2-B	1,365	95
Ohio Northern U, Ada, OH 45810	1871	Dr. DeBow Freed 2-D	2,651	175
Ohio State U, Columbus, OH 43210	1870	Dr. E. Gordon Gee 5-D	54,094	3,902
Ohio State U–Lima Cmps, Lima, OH 45804	1960	Dr. James J. Countryman . . 5-B	1,357	76
Ohio State U–Mansfield Cmps, Mansfield, OH 44906	1958	Dr. John O. Riedl, Jr. 5-B	1,309	75
Ohio State U–Marion Cmps, Marion, OH 43302	1957	Francis E. Hazard 5-B	1,100	70
Ohio State U–Newark Cmps, Newark, OH 43055	1957	Dr. Julius S. Greenstein . . . 5-B	1,567	74
Ohio U, Athens, OH 45701	1804	Dr. Charles J. Ping 5-D	17,000	950
Ohio U–Chillicothe, Chillicothe, OH 45601	1946	Dr. Delbert Meyer 5-M	1,614	67
Ohio U–Lancaster, Lancaster, OH 43130	1968	Dr. Raymond Wilkes 5-M	1,550	114
Ohio U–Zanesville, Zanesville, OH 43701	1946	Dr. Craig D. Laubenthal . . . 5-M	1,522	49
Ohio Wesleyan U, Delaware, OH 43015	1842	Dr. David L. Warren 2-B	2,040	161
Oklahoma Baptist U, Shawnee, OK 74801	1910	Dr. Bob R. Agee 2-B	2,208	137
Oklahoma Christian U of Science and Arts, Oklahoma City, OK 73136	1950	Dr. Terry Johnson 2-M	1,692	114
Oklahoma City U, Oklahoma City, OK 73106	1904	Dr. Jerald C. Walker 2-D	4,195	238
Oklahoma Panhandle State U, Goodwell, OK 73939	1909	Dr. Theodore W. Wischropp . . 5-B	1,400	71
Oklahoma State U, Stillwater, OK 74078	1890	Dr. John Campbell 5-D	19,591	681
Old Dominion U, Norfolk, VA 23529	1930	Dr. James V. Koch 5-D	16,729	949
Olivet Coll, Olivet, MI 49076	1844	Dr. Donald A. Morris 2-B	759	69
Olivet Nazarene U, Kankakee, IL 60901	1907	Dr. Leslie Parrott 2-M	1,700	116
Oral Roberts U, Tulsa, OK 74171	1963	Mr. G. Oral Roberts 2-D	3,550	390
Oregon Inst of Tech, Klamath Falls, OR 97601-8801	1947	Dr. Lawrence J. Wolf 5-B	3,023	144
Oregon State U, Corvallis, OR 97331	1868	Dr. John V. Byrne 5-D	16,024	2,431
Orlando Coll, Orlando, FL 32810	1918	Mrs. Ouida B. Kirby 3-M	1,220	44
Otis/Parsons Sch of Art and Design, Los Angeles, CA 90057	1917	Roger Workman 1-M	756	193
Otterbein Coll, Westerville, OH 43081	1847	Dr. C. Brent DeVore 2-M	2,479	173
Ouachita Baptist U, Arkadelphia, AR 71923	1886	Dr. Ben M. Elrod 2-B	1,255	101
Our Lady of Holy Cross Coll, New Orleans, LA 70131	1916	Rev. Thomas E. Chambers, CSC 2-M	1,036	63
Our Lady of the Lake U of San Antonio, San Antonio, TX 78207-4666	1911	Sr. Elizabeth Anne Sueltenfuss 2-D	2,693	146
Pace U, New York, NY 10038	1906	Dr. Patricia Ewers 1-D	8,355	1,212
Pace U, Pleasantville/Briarcliff Cmps, Pleasantville, NY 10570	1963	Dr. Richard Podgorski 1-M	3,937	1,212
Pace U, White Plains Cmps, White Plains, NY 10603	1923	Dr. Margaret R. Gotti 1-D	4,173	1,212
Pacific Lutheran U, Tacoma, WA 98447	1890	Dr. William O. Rieke 2-M	3,654	294
Pacific Union Coll, Angwin, CA 94508	1882	Dr. D. Malcolm Maxwell . . . 2-M	1,795	116
Pacific U, Forest Grove, OR 97116	1849	Dr. Robert F. Duvall 1-D	1,492	96
Palm Beach Atlantic Coll, West Palm Beach, FL 33402	1968	Dr. Paul R. Corts 2-M	1,500	100
Palmer Coll of Chiropractic, Davenport, IA 52803	1895	Donald P. Kern 1-D	1,680	129
Parks Coll of Saint Louis U, Cahokia, IL 62206	1927	Dr. Paul A. Whelan 2-B	1,137	60
Parsons Sch of Design, New Sch for Social Research, New York, NY 10011	1896	Charles S. Olton 1-M	1,900	332
Pembroke State U, Pembroke, NC 28372	1887	Dr. Joseph Oxendine 5-M	3,133	190
Penn State U at Erie, The Behrend Coll, Erie, PA 16563	1926	Dr. John M. Lilley 13-M	2,987	185
Penn State U at Harrisburg—The Capital Coll, Middletown, PA 17057	1966	Dr. Ruth Leventhal 13-D	3,416	203
Penn State U Univ Park Cmps, University Park, PA 16802	1855	Dr. Joab L. Thomas 13-D	38,864	2,141
Pepperdine U, Malibu, CA 90265	1937	Dr. David Davenport 2-D	3,486	292
Peru State Coll, Peru, NE 68421	1867	Dr. Robert L. Burns 5-M	1,835	82
Pfeiffer Coll, Misenheimer, NC 28109	1885	Dr. Zane E. Eargle 2-M	958	72
Philadelphia Coll of Pharmacy and Science, Philadelphia, PA 19104	1821	Dr. Allen Misher 1-D	1,657	161
Philadelphia Coll of Textiles and Science, Philadelphia, PA 19144	1884	Dr. James P. Gallagher . . . 1-M	3,320	113
Phillips U, Enid, OK 73701	1906	Dr. Robert Peck 2-M	931	74
Pikeville Coll, Pikeville, KY 41501	1889	Mr. William H. Owens 2-B	915	64

Name, address	Year	Governing official, control, and highest degree offered	Enrollment	Faculty
Pittsburg State U, Pittsburg, KS 66762	1903	Dr. Donald W. Wilson ... 5-M	5,918	288
Pitzer Coll, Claremont, CA 91711-6110	1963	Dr. Frank L. Ellsworth ... 1-B	750	88
Plymouth State Coll of the U System of NH, Plymouth, NH 03264	1871	Dr. William J. Farrell ... 5-M	4,000	200
Point Loma Nazarene Coll, San Diego, CA 92106	1902	Dr. Jim L. Bond ... 2-M	2,256	218
Point Park Coll, Pittsburgh, PA 15222	1960	Dr. J. Matthew Simon ... 1-M	2,977	185
Polytechnic U, Brooklyn Cmps, Brooklyn, NY 11201	1854	Dr. George Bugliarello ... 1-D	2,140	393
Polytechnic U, Farmingdale Cmps, Farmingdale, NY 11735	1854	Dr. Ernest Racz ... 1-D	1,095	393
Pomona Coll, Claremont, CA 91711	1887	Dr. David Alexander ... 1-B	1,375	154
Portland State U, Portland, OR 97207	1946	Dr. Judith Ramaley ... 5-D	14,758	713
Prairie View A&M U, Prairie View, TX 77446	1878	Mr. Julius W. Becton ... 5-M	4,990	306
Pratt Inst, Brooklyn, NY 11205	1887	Mr. Warren F. Ilehman ... 1-M	3,384	485
Presbyterian Coll, Clinton, SC 29325	1880	Dr. Kenneth B. Orr ... 2-B	1,136	99
Princeton U, Princeton, NJ 08544	1746	Harold T. Shapiro ... 1-D	6,321	832
Providence Coll, Providence, RI 02918	1917	Rev. John F. Cunningham, OP ... 2-D	5,917	287
Purdue U, West Lafayette, IN 47907	1869	Dr. Steven C. Beering ... 5-D	35,647	2,192
Purdue U Calumet, Hammond, IN 46323	1951	Dr. James W. Yackel ... 5-M	7,698	415
Purdue U North Central, Westville, IN 46391	1967	Dr. Dale W. Alspaugh ... 5-M	3,446	206
Queens Coll, Charlotte, NC 28274	1857	Dr. Billy O. Wireman ... 2-M	1,623	121
Queens Coll of the City U of New York, Flushing, NY 11367	1937	Dr. Shirley Strum Kenny ... 12-M	18,071	1,302
Quincy Coll, Quincy, IL 62301	1860	Rev. James Toal, OFM ... 2-M	1,607	107
Quinnipiac Coll, Hamden, CT 06518	1929	Dr. John L. Lahey ... 1-M	3,405	219
Radford U, Radford, VA 24142	1910	Dr. Donald N. Dedmon ... 5-M	8,863	496
Ramapo Coll of New Jersey, Mahwah, NJ 07430	1969	Dr. Robert A. Scott ... 5-B	4,525	238
Randolph-Macon Coll, Ashland, VA 23005	1830	Dr. Ladell Payne ... 2-B	1,141	137
Reed Coll, Portland, OR 97202	1909	NR ... 1-M	1,286	117
Regis Coll, Weston, MA 02193 (3)	1927	Sr. Therese Higgins, CSJ ... 2-B	1,163	106
Regis Coll of Regis U, Denver, CO 80221	1877	Rev. David M. Clarke, SJ ... 2-M	6,252	95
Rensselaer Polytechnic Inst, Troy, NY 12180	1824	Roland W. Schmitt ... 1-D	6,508	470
Rhode Island Coll, Providence, RI 02908	1854	Dr. John Nazarian ... 5-M	9,233	422
Rhode Island Sch of Design, Providence, RI 02903	1877	Dr. Thomas F. Schutte ... 1-M	1,912	284
Rhodes Coll, Memphis, TN 38112	1848	Dr. James H. Daughdrill, Jr. ... 2-B	1,407	156
Rice U, Houston, TX 77251	1912	Dr. George Rupp ... 1-D	4,016	584
Rider Coll, Lawrenceville, NJ 08648	1865	Dr. J. Barton Luedeke ... 1-M	5,510	300
Ripon Coll, Ripon, WI 54971	1851	Mr. William R. Stott, Jr. ... 1-B	854	97
Rivier Coll, Nashua, NH 03060	1933	Sr. Jeanne Perreault ... 2-M	2,806	186
Roanoke Coll, Salem, VA 24153	1842	Dr. David M. Gring ... 2-B	1,668	136
Robert Morris Coll, Coraopolis, PA 15108	1921	Dr. Edward A. Nicholson ... 1-M	5,279	213
Roberts Wesleyan Coll, Rochester, NY 14624	1866	Dr. William C. Crothers ... 2-B	969	66
Rochester Inst of Tech, Rochester, NY 14623	1829	Dr. M. Richard Rose ... 1-D	11,147	1,101
Rockford Coll, Rockford, IL 61108	1847	Dr. Gretchen Kreuter ... 1-M	1,474	123
Rockhurst Coll, Kansas City, MO 64110	1910	Rev. Thomas J. Savage, SJ ... 2-M	2,806	180
Roger Williams Coll, Bristol, RI 02809	1948	Dr. Natale A. Sicuro ... 1-B	2,111	229
Rollins Coll, Winter Park, FL 32789-4499	1885	Dr. Rita Bornstein ... 1-M	2,087	128
Roosevelt U, Chicago, IL 60605	1945	Dr. Theodore L. Gross ... 1-M	6,374	508
Rosary Coll, River Forest, IL 60305	1848	Jean Murray, OP ... 2-M	1,855	79
Rose-Hulman Inst of Tech, Terre Haute, IN 47803 (1)	1874	Dr. Samuel F. Hulbert ... 1-M	1,415	97
Rush U, Chicago, IL 60612	1969	Dr. Leo M. Henikoff ... 1-D	1,137	170
Russell Sage Coll, Troy, NY 12180 (3)	1916	Dr. Sara Chapman ... 1-M	2,227	174
Rust Coll, Holly Springs, MS 38635	1866	Dr. William A. McMillan ... 2-B	1,023	61
Rutgers, State U of NJ, Camden Coll of Arts & Scis, Camden, NJ 08101	1927	Dr. Walter K. Gordon ... 5-B	2,695	NR
Rutgers, State U of NJ, Coll of Engineering, New Brunswick, NJ 08903	1864	Dr. Ellis H. Dill ... 5-B	2,537	NR
Rutgers, State U of NJ, Coll of Nursing, Newark, NJ 07102	1956	Dorothy J. DeMaio ... 5-D	401	NR
Rutgers, State U of NJ, Coll of Pharmacy, New Brunswick, NJ 08903	1927	Dr. John Louis Colaizzi ... 5-D	747	NR
Rutgers, State U of NJ, Cook Coll, New Brunswick, NJ 08903	1921	Daryl B. Lund ... 5-B	2,874	NR
Rutgers, State U of NJ, Douglass Coll, New Brunswick, NJ 08903-0270 (3)	1918	Dr. Mary S. Hartman ... 5-B	3,227	NR
Rutgers, State U of NJ, Livingston Coll, New Brunswick, NJ 08903	1969	Walton Johnson ... 5-B	3,776	NR
Rutgers, State U of NJ, Mason Gross Sch of Arts, New Brunswick, NJ 08903	1976	Marilyn F. Somville ... 5-M	631	NR
Rutgers, State U of NJ, Newark Coll of Arts & Scis, Newark, NJ 07102	1946	David Hosford ... 5-B	3,396	NR
Rutgers, State U of NJ, Rutgers Coll, New Brunswick, NJ 08903	1766	James Reed ... 5-B	8,377	NR
Rutgers, State U of NJ, U Coll–Camden, Camden, NJ 08101	1950	Dr. Walter K. Gordon ... 5-B	872	NR
Rutgers, State U of NJ, U Coll–Newark, Newark, NJ 07102	1934	David Hosford ... 5-B	1,758	NR
Rutgers, State U of NJ, U Coll–New Brunswick, New Brunswick, NJ 08903	1934	Amy Cohen ... 5-B	3,087	NR
Sacred Heart U, Fairfield, CT 06432	1963	Dr. Anthony J. Cernera ... 2-M	4,500	271
Saginaw Valley State U, University Center, MI 48710	1963	Dr. Eric R. Gilbertson ... 5-M	6,212	368
St Ambrose U, Davenport, IA 52803	1882	Dr. Edward J. Rogalski ... 2-M	2,300	174
Saint Anselm Coll, Manchester, NH 03102	1889	Rev. Jonathan DeFelice ... 2-B	1,840	154
Saint Augustine's Coll, Raleigh, NC 27610-2298	1867	Dr. Prezell R. Robinson ... 2-B	1,900	92
St Bonaventure U, St Bonaventure, NY 14778	1854	Rev. Neil O'Connell, OFM ... 2-M	2,836	217
St Cloud State U, St Cloud, MN 56301-4498	1869	Dr. Brendan McDonald ... 5-M	17,076	797
St Edward's U, Austin, TX 78704	1885	Dr. Patricia Hayes ... 2-M	3,086	191
Saint Francis Coll, Fort Wayne, IN 46808	1890	Sr. M. JoEllen Scheetz ... 2-M	971	80
St Francis Coll, Brooklyn Heights, NY 11201	1858	Br. Donald Sullivan, OSF ... 1-B	1,743	109
Saint Francis Coll, Loretto, PA 15940	1847	Rev. Christian R. Oravec ... 2-M	1,172	80
St John Fisher Coll, Rochester, NY 14618	1948	Dr. William L. Pickett ... 2-M	2,137	162
Saint John's U, Collegeville, MN 56321 (1)	1857	Br. Dietrich Reinhart ... 2-M	2,035	183
St John's U, Jamaica, NY 11439	1870	Rev. Donald J. Harrington, CM ... 2-D	19,105	950
Saint Joseph Coll, West Hartford, CT 06117 (3)	1932	NR ... 2-M	1,090	127
Saint Joseph's Coll, Rensselaer, IN 47978	1889	Fr. Charles Banet ... 2-M	1,033	85
St Joseph's Coll, Brooklyn, NY 11205	1916	Sr. George Aquin O'Connor ... 1-B	827	91
St Joseph's Coll, Suffolk Cmps, Patchogue, NY 11772	1916	Sr. George Aquin O'Connor ... 1-B	1,936	169

Name, address	Year	Governing official, control, and highest degree offered		Enroll-ment	Faculty
Saint Joseph's U, Philadelphia, PA 19131	1851	Rev. Nicholas S. Rashford, SJ	2-M	6,619	368
St Lawrence U, Canton, NY 13617	1856	Patti McGill Peterson	1-M	2,235	197
Saint Leo Coll, Saint Leo, FL 33574	1889	Msgr. Frank Mouch	2-B	1,066	77
St Louis Coll of Pharmacy, St Louis, MO 63110	1864	Dr. Sumner M. Robinson	1-D	755	59
Saint Louis U, St Louis, MO 63103	1818	Rev. Lawrence Biondi, SJ	2-D	11,884	2,289
Saint Martin's Coll, Lacey, WA 98503	1895	Dr. David Spangler	2-M	1,078	50
Saint Mary Coll, Leavenworth, KS 66048-5082	1923	Dr. Peter Clifford, FSC	2-B	990	120
Saint Mary of the Plains Coll, Dodge City, KS 67801	1952	Dr. Bernard S. Parker	2-B	1,077	87
Saint Mary-of-the-Woods Coll, Saint Mary-of-the-Woods, IN 47876 (3)	1840	Barbara Doherty, SP	2-M	1,127	55
Saint Mary's Coll, Notre Dame, IN 46556 (3)	1844	Dr. William A. Hickey	2-B	1,798	192
Saint Mary's Coll of California, Moraga, CA 94575	1863	Br. Mel Anderson, FSC	2-M	3,605	180
St Mary's Coll of Maryland, St Mary's City, MD 20686	1840	Dr. Edward T. Lewis	5-B	1,330	147
Saint Mary's Coll of Minnesota, Winona, MN 55987-1399	1912	Br. Louis DeThomasis, FSC	2-M	3,754	121
St Mary's U of San Antonio, San Antonio, TX 78228	1852	Rev. John Moder, SM	2-D	4,000	179
Saint Michael's Coll, Colchester, VT 05439	1904	Dr. Paul J. Reiss	2-M	2,682	152
St Norbert Coll, De Pere, WI 54115	1898	Dr. Thomas A. Manion	2-M	1,934	154
St Olaf Coll, Northfield, MN 55057	1874	Dr. Melvin George	2-B	3,097	352
Saint Peter's Coll, Jersey City, NJ 07306	1872	Rev. Daniel A. Degnan, SJ	2-M	3,356	420
St Thomas Aquinas Coll, Sparkill, NY 10976	1958	Dr. Donald T. McNelis	1-M	2,075	115
St Thomas U, Miami, FL 33054	1961	Dr. Richard Greene	2-D	2,647	202
Saint Vincent Coll, Latrobe, PA 15650	1846	Rev. John F. Murtha, OSB	2-B	1,238	85
Saint Xavier Coll, Chicago, IL 60655	1847	Dr. Ronald Champagne	2-M	3,606	205
Salem State Coll, Salem, MA 01970	1854	Dr. Nancy D. Harrington	5-M	8,407	300
Salisbury State U, Salisbury, MD 21801	1925	Dr. Thomas A. Bellavance	5-M	5,742	325
Salve Regina U, Newport, RI 02840-4192	1934	Dr. M. Lucille McKillop, RSM	2-D	2,407	218
Samford U, Birmingham, AL 35229	1841	Dr. Thomas E. Corts	2-D	4,164	298
Sam Houston State U, Huntsville, TX 77341	1879	Dr. Martin J. Anisman	5-D	12,753	487
San Diego State U, San Diego, CA 92182	1897	Dr. Thomas B. Day	5-D	35,021	2,450
San Francisco Art Inst, San Francisco, CA 94133	1871	Mr. William O. Barrett	1-M	768	63
San Francisco State U, San Francisco, CA 94132	1899	Dr. Robert A. Corrigan	5-D	28,120	1,913
Sangamon State U, Springfield, IL 62794-9243	1969	Dr. A. Wayne Penn	5-M	4,347	234
San Jose State U, San Jose, CA 95192	1857	Dr. Gail Fullerton	5-M	30,338	1,850
Santa Clara U, Santa Clara, CA 95053	1851	Rev. Paul L. Locatelli, SJ	2-D	7,710	546
Sarah Lawrence Coll, Bronxville, NY 10708	1926	Dr. Alice Stone Ilchman	1-M	1,200	249
Savannah Coll of Art and Design, Savannah, GA 31401	1978	Richard G. Rowan	1-M	1,985	105
Savannah State Coll, Savannah, GA 31404	1890	Dr. Annette K. Brock	5-M	2,351	147
Sch of the Art Inst of Chicago, Chicago, IL 60603	1866	Mr. Anthony Jones	2-M	2,133	309
Sch of the Museum of Fine Arts, Boston, MA 02115	1876	Bruce K. MacDonald	3-M	750	54
Sch of Visual Arts, New York, NY 10010	1947	David Rhodes	1-M	2,200	800
Seattle Pacific U, Seattle, WA 98119	1891	Dr. David Le Shana	2-M	3,421	238
Seattle U, Seattle, WA 98122	1891	Rev. William J. Sullivan, SJ	2-D	4,640	376
Seton Hall U, South Orange, NJ 07079	1856	Rev. Thomas R. Peterson, OP	2-D	8,166	491
Seton Hill Coll, Greensburg, PA 15601 (4)	1883	JoAnne M. Boyle	2-M	1,037	105
Shawnee State U, Portsmouth, OH 45662	1986	Dr. Clive Veri	5-B	3,275	247
Shaw U, Raleigh, NC 27611	1865	Dr. Talbert O. Shaw	2-M	1,402	NR
Shenandoah U, Winchester, VA 22601	1875	Dr. James A. Davis	2-M	1,050	130
Shepherd Coll, Shepherdstown, WV 25443	1871	Dr. Michael P. Riccards	5-B	3,700	172
Shippensburg U of Pennsylvania, Shippensburg, PA 17257	1871	Dr. Anthony F. Ceddia	5-M	6,594	358
Shorter Coll, Rome, GA 30161	1873	Dr. James D. Jordan	2-M	558	92
Siena Coll, Loudonville, NY 12211	1937	Fr. William McConville, OFM	2-M	3,551	252
Siena Heights Coll, Adrian, MI 49221-1796	1919	Sr. Cathleen Real, CHM	2-M	1,224	110
Silver Lake Coll, Manitowoc, WI 54220	1869	Sr. Barbara Belinske	2-M	830	128
Simmons Coll, Boston, MA 02115 (3)	1899	William J. Holmes	1-D	2,819	186
Simpson Coll, Indianola, IA 50125	1860	Dr. Stephen G. Jennings	2-B	1,735	146
Sioux Falls Coll, Sioux Falls, SD 57105	1883	Dr. Thomas F. Johnson	2-M	937	66
Skidmore Coll, Saratoga Springs, NY 12866	1903	Dr. David H. Porter	1-B	2,139	220
Slippery Rock U of Pennsylvania, Slippery Rock, PA 16057	1889	Dr. Robert Aebersold	5-M	7,825	408
Smith Coll, Northampton, MA 01063 (3)	1871	Mary Maples Dunn	1-D	2,765	288
Sonoma State U, Rohnert Park, CA 94928	1961	Dr. David W. Benson	5-M	8,759	449
South Carolina State Coll, Orangeburg, SC 29117	1896	Dr. Albert E. Smith	5-D	5,026	253
South Dakota Sch of Mines and Tech, Rapid City, SD 57701	1885	Dr. Richard J. Gowen	5-D	2,253	143
South Dakota State U, Brookings, SD 57007	1881	Dr. Robert T. Wagner	5-D	7,642	454
Southeastern Coll of the Assemblies of God, Lakeland, FL 33801	1935	Dr. James Hennesy	2-B	1,192	80
Southeastern Louisiana U, Hammond, LA 70402	1925	Dr. G. Warren Smith	5-M	10,398	377
Southeastern Massachusetts U, North Dartmouth, MA 02747	1895	Dr. John R. Brazil	5-M	6,174	442
Southeastern Oklahoma State U, Durant, OK 74701	1909	Dr. Larry Williams	5-M	4,049	198
Southeastern U, Washington, DC 20024	1879	Dr. W. Robert Higgins	1-M	1,280	128
Southeast Missouri State U, Cape Girardeau, MO 63701	1873	Dr. Kala M. Stroup	5-M	8,816	432
Southern Arkansas U, Magnolia, AR 71753	1909	Dr. Harold T. Brinson	5-M	2,492	121
Southern California Coll, Costa Mesa, CA 92626	1920	Mr. Wayne E. Kraiss	2-M	919	81
Southern Coll of Seventh-day Adventists, Collegedale, TN 37315	1892	Dr. Donald R. Sahly	2-B	1,534	126
Southern Coll of Tech, Marietta, GA 30060-2896	1948	Dr. Stephen R. Cheshier	5-M	4,018	190
Southern Connecticut State U, New Haven, CT 06515	1893	Mr. Michael J. Adanti	5-M	13,618	671
Southern Illinois U at Carbondale, Carbondale, IL 62901	1869	Dr. John C. Guyon	5-D	24,083	1,369
Southern Illinois U at Edwardsville, Edwardsville, IL 62026	1957	Earl E. Lazerson	5-D	11,686	735
Southern Methodist U, Dallas, TX 75275	1911	Mr. A. Kenneth Pye	1-D	8,798	584
Southern Nazarene U, Bethany, OK 73008	1899	Dr. Loren P. Gresham	2-M	1,590	103
Southern Oregon State Coll, Ashland, OR 97520	1926	Dr. Joseph Cox	5-M	4,822	311
Southern U and A&M Coll, Baton Rouge, LA 70813	1880	Dr. Dolores R. Spiks	5-D	9,122	603
Southern Utah U, Cedar City, UT 84720	1897	Gerald R. Sherratt	5-M	4,200	145
Southwest Baptist U, Bolivar, MO 65613	1878	Dr. James L. Sells	2-M	1,834	195
Southwestern Adventist Coll, Keene, TX 76059	1894	Dr. Marvin E. Anderson	2-M	797	55
Southwestern Oklahoma State U, Weatherford, OK 73096	1903	Dr. Joe Anna Hibler	5-M	5,401	237
Southwestern U, Georgetown, TX 78626	1840	Dr. Roy B. Shilling, Jr.	2-B	1,239	102
Southwest Missouri State U, Springfield, MO 65804	1905	Dr. Marshall Gordon	5-M	19,480	861
Southwest State U, Marshall, MN 56258	1963	Mr. Gary DeCramer	5-B	3,035	128
Southwest Texas State U, San Marcos, TX 78666	1899	Dr. Jerome Supple	5-M	20,944	901
Spalding U, Louisville, KY 40203	1814	Dr. Eileen M. Egan	2-D	1,059	92
Spelman Coll, Atlanta, GA 30314 (3)	1881	Dr. Johnnetta B. Cole	1-B	1,708	160
Spring Arbor Coll, Spring Arbor, MI 49283	1873	Dr. Dorsey W. Brause	2-B	847	92
Springfield Coll, Springfield, MA 01109	1885	Dr. Frank S. Falcone	1-D	3,148	274

Name, address	Year	Governing official, control, and highest degree offered	Enrollment	Faculty
Spring Garden Coll, Philadelphia, PA 19119	1851	Dr. Daniel N. DeLucca . . . 1-B	1,465	100
Spring Hill Coll, Mobile, AL 36608	1830	Rev. William J. Rewak, SJ . . 2-M	1,232	82
Stanford U, Stanford, CA 94305	1891	Dr. Donald Kennedy 1-D	13,441	1,383
State U of NY at Albany, Albany, NY 12222	1844	Dr. H. Patrick Swaggert . . . 5-D	15,218	942
State U of NY at Binghamton, Binghamton, NY 13902-6000	1946	Dr. Lois B. DeFleur 5-D	12,202	729
State U of NY at Buffalo, Buffalo, NY 14260	1846	Dr. Steven B. Sample 5-D	24,678	2,036
State U of NY at Stony Brook, Stony Brook, NY 11794	1957	Dr. John H. Marburger, III . . 5-D	15,465	1,540
State U of NY Coll at Brockport, Brockport, NY 14420	1867	Dr. John E. Van de Wetering	5-M	8,138	500
State U of NY Coll at Buffalo, Buffalo, NY 14222	1867	Dr. F. C. Richardson 5-M	12,142	584
State U of NY Coll at Cortland, Cortland, NY 13045	1868	Dr. James M. Clark 5-M	6,170	412
State U of NY Coll at Fredonia, Fredonia, NY 14063	1826	Dr. Donald A. MacPhee . . . 5-M	5,041	326
State U of NY Coll at Geneseo, Geneseo, NY 14454	1867	Dr. Carol C. Harter 5-M	5,599	300
State U of NY Coll at New Paltz, New Paltz, NY 12561	1828	Alice Chandler 5-M	8,637	469
State U of NY Coll at Old Westbury, Old Westbury, NY 11568	1965	Dr. L. Eudora Pettigrew . . . 5-B	4,262	259
State U of NY Coll at Oneonta, Oneonta, NY 13820	1889	Dr. Alan B. Donovan 5-M	6,000	320
State U of NY Coll at Oswego, Oswego, NY 13126	1861	Dr. Stephen Weber 5-M	8,200	431
State U of NY Coll at Plattsburgh, Plattsburgh, NY 12901	1889	Dr. Charles Warren 5-M	6,555	404
State U of NY Coll at Potsdam, Potsdam, NY 13676	1816	Dr. William Merwin 5-M	4,826	269
State U of NY Coll at Purchase, Purchase, NY 10577	1967	Dr. Sheldon Grebstein 5-M	2,574	298
State U of NY Coll of Environ Sci and Forestry, Syracuse, NY 13210	1911	Dr. Ross S. Whaley 5-D	1,802	122
State U of NY Empire State Coll, Saratoga Springs, NY 12866-4391	1971	Dr. James W. Hall 5-M	6,522	354
State U of NY Health Science Ctr at Brooklyn, Brooklyn, NY 11203	1858	Dr. Donald J. Scherl 5-D	1,641	156
State U of NY Inst of Tech at Utica/Rome, Utica, NY 13504	1966	Dr. Peter J. Cayan 5-M	2,505	173
State U of NY Maritime Coll, Throgs Neck, NY 10465	1874	Rear Adm. Floyd Miller 5-M	784	109
Stephen F Austin State U, Nacogdoches, TX 75962	1923	Dr. Donald E. Bowen 5-D	12,815	629
Stephens Coll, Columbia, MO 65215 (3)	1833	Dr. Patsy H. Sampson 1-B	1,191	102
Stetson U, DeLand, FL 32720	1883	Dr. H. Douglas Lee 2-D	2,381	188
Stevens Inst of Tech, Hoboken, NJ 07030	1870	Dr. Harold J. Raveche 1-D	3,600	250
Stillman Coll, Tuscaloosa, AL 35403	1876	Dr. Cordell Wynn 2-B	770	63
Stockton State Coll, Pomona, NJ 08240	1971	Dr. Vera King Farris 5-B	5,639	287
Stonehill Coll, North Easton, MA 02357	1948	Rev. Bartley MacPhaidin . . 2-B	1,964	170
Suffolk U, Boston, MA 02108	1906	David J. Sargent 1-D	5,733	205
Sul Ross State U, Alpine, TX 79832	1920	Dr. R. Vic Morgan 5-M	2,265	112
Susquehanna U, Selinsgrove, PA 17870	1858	Dr. Joel L. Cunningham . . . 2-B	1,435	137
Swarthmore Coll, Swarthmore, PA 19081	1864	Dr. David W. Fraser 1-B	1,317	173
Syracuse U, Syracuse, NY 13244	1870	Dr. Melvin A. Eggers 1-D	16,700	1,667
Tampa Coll, Tampa, FL 33614	1890	Mr. David Zorn 3-M	985	45
Tarleton State U, Stephenville, TX 76402	1899	NR 5-M	6,250	302
Taylor U, Upland, IN 46989	1846	Dr. Jay L. Kesler 1-B	1,740	126
Teikyo Marycrest U, Davenport, IA 52804	1939	Dr. Wanda D. Bigham 1-M	1,969	83
Teikyo Post U, Waterbury, CT 06723-2540	1890	Dr. N. Patricia Yarborough . . 1-B	2,082	227
Temple U, Philadelphia, PA 19122	1884	Mr. Peter J. Liacouras 13-D	26,421	2,679
Temple U, Ambler Cmps, Ambler, PA 19002	1910	Mr. James Blackhurst 13-D	4,842	375
Tennessee State U, Nashville, TN 37209-1561	1912	Dr. George W. Cox 5-D	7,393	425
Tennessee Tech U, Cookeville, TN 38505	1915	Dr. Angelo A. Volpe 5-D	8,140	552
Tennessee Temple U, Chattanooga, TN 37404	1946	Dr. L.W. Nichols 2-D	1,071	82
Texas A&I U, Kingsville, TX 78363	1925	Dr. Manuel L. Ibanez 5-D	6,014	258
Texas A&M U, College Station, TX 77843	1876	Dr. William H. Mobley 5-D	41,171	2,306
Texas A&M U at Galveston, Galveston, TX 77553	1962	Dr. William J. Merrell 5-B	1,075	79
Texas Christian U, Fort Worth, TX 76129	1873	Dr. William Tucker 2-D	6,458	384
Texas Lutheran Coll, Seguin, TX 78155	1891	Dr. Charles H. Oestreich . . 2-B	982	79
Texas Southern U, Houston, TX 77004	1947	Dr. William H. Harris 5-D	9,198	448
Texas Tech U, Lubbock, TX 79409	1923	Robert W. Lawless 5-D	25,363	1,666
Texas Wesleyan U, Fort Worth, TX 76105	1890	Dr. W. L. Hailey 2-M	1,429	111
Texas Woman's U, Denton, TX 76204 (4)	1901	Dr. Shirley Sears Chater . . 5-D	9,850	555
Thiel Coll, Greenville, PA 16125	1866	Dr. C. Carlyle Haaland 2-B	931	100
Thomas A Edison State Coll, Trenton, NJ 08608	1972	Dr. George A. Pruitt 5-B	7,811	NR
Thomas Coll, Waterville, ME 04901	1894	Dr. George R. Spann 1-M	1,068	58
Thomas Jefferson U, Philadelphia, PA 19107	1824	Paul C. Brucker, MD 1-D	1,333	83
Thomas More Coll, Crestview Hills, KY 41017	1921	Dr. Charles J. Bensman . . . 2-B	1,297	138
Tiffin U, Tiffin, OH 44883	1888	Dr. George Kidd, Jr. 1-M	896	48
Toccoa Falls Coll, Toccoa Falls, GA 30598	1907	Dr. Paul L. Alford 2-B	840	63
Tougaloo Coll, Tougaloo, MS 39174	1869	Dr. Adib A. Shakir 2-B	948	62
Touro Coll, New York, NY 10001	1971	Dr. Bernard Lander 1-D	6,550	410
Towson State U, Towson, MD 21204	1866	Dr. Hoke L. Smith 5-M	15,034	907
Transylvania U, Lexington, KY 40508-1797	1780	Dr. Charles L. Shearer 2-B	1,091	104
Trenton State Coll, Trenton, NJ 08650-4700	1855	Dr. Harold Eickhoff 5-M	7,261	530
Trinity Coll, Hartford, CT 06106	1823	Tom Gerety, Jr. 1-M	2,137	194
Trinity Coll, Washington, DC 20017 (3)	1897	Patricia A. McGuire 2-M	1,108	85
Trinity Coll, Deerfield, IL 60015	1897	Dr. Kenneth M. Meyer 2-B	914	63
Trinity Coll of Vermont, Burlington, VT 05401 (4)	1925	Sr. Janice Ryan 2-B	1,116	99
Trinity U, San Antonio, TX 78212	1869	Dr. Ronald K. Calgaard . . . 2-M	2,538	264
Tri-State U, Angola, IN 46703	1884	Dr. Richard A. Kenyon 1-B	1,133	76
Troy State U, Troy, AL 36082	1887	Dr. Jack Hawkins, Jr. 5-M	4,275	205
Troy State U in Montgomery, Montgomery, AL 36103	1957	Dr. Millard E. Elrod 5-M	2,736	149
Tufts U, Medford, MA 02155	1852	Dr. Jean Mayer 1-D	7,634	565
Tulane U, New Orleans, LA 70118	1834	Dr. Eamon M. Kelly 1-D	11,485	734
Tuskegee U, Tuskegee, AL 36088	1881	Dr. Benjamin F. Payton . . . 1-D	3,627	318
Union Coll, Barbourville, KY 40906	1879	Dr. Jack C. Phillips 2-M	1,024	77
Union Coll, Schenectady, NY 12308	1795	Dr. John S. Morris 1-D	2,240	199
Union Inst, Cincinnati, OH 45206	1964	Robert T. Conley 1-D	1,180	697
Union U, Jackson, TN 38305	1823	Dr. Hyran E. Barefoot 2-M	1,672	112
United States Air Force Acad, Colorado Springs, CO 80840	1954	Lt. Gen. Charles R. Hamm . . 4-B	4,443	537
United States Coast Guard Acad, New London, CT 06320-4195	1876	Rear Adm. Thomas T. Matteson 4-B	951	105
United States International U, San Diego, CA 92131	1952	Dr. Kenneth McLennan 1-D	3,489	84
United States Merchant Marine Acad, Kings Point, NY 11024	1943	Rear Adm. P. L. Krinsky . . . 4-B	887	80
United States Military Acad, West Point, NY 10996	1802	Lt. Gen. Dave R. Palmer . . . 4-B	4,386	545
United States Naval Acad, Annapolis, MD 21402 (2)	1845	Rear Adm. Virgil L. Hill, Jr. . 4-B	4,420	600

Name, address	Year	Governing official, control, and highest degree offered	Enrollment	Faculty
Universidad Adventista de las Antillas, Mayagüez, PR 00709	1957	Mr. Moises Velazquez	2-B	775	58
Universidad Politécnica de Puerto Rico, Hato Rey, PR 00919	1974	Ernesto Vazquez-Torres	1-B	3,582	171
U of Akron, Akron, OH 44325	1870	William V. Muse	5-D	28,801	1,776
U of Alabama, Tuscaloosa, AL 35487-0132	1831	Dr. E. Roger Sayers	5-D	19,828	1,027
U of Alabama at Birmingham, Birmingham, AL 35294	1969	Dr. Charles A. McCallum	5-D	16,286	NR
U of Alabama in Huntsville, Huntsville, AL 35899	1950	Dr. Louis Padulo	5-D	8,139	471
U of Alaska Anchorage, Anchorage, AK 99508	1954	Dr. Donald F. Behrend	5-M	7,990	928
U of Alaska Fairbanks, Fairbanks, AK 99775	1917	Dr. Patrick J. O'Rourke	5-D	4,480	721
U of Arizona, Tucson, AZ 85721	1885	Dr. Manuel T. Pacheco	5-D	35,735	1,694
U of Arkansas, Fayetteville, AR 72701	1871	Dr. Daniel E. Ferritor	5-D	14,600	799
U of Arkansas at Little Rock, Little Rock, AR 72204	1927	Dr. James H. Young	5-D	11,362	659
U of Arkansas at Monticello, Monticello, AR 71655	1909	Dr. Fred J. Taylor	5-B	2,107	117
U of Arkansas at Pine Bluff, Pine Bluff, AR 71601	1873	Dr. Charles A. Walker	5-B	3,672	196
U of Arkansas for Medical Sciences, Little Rock, AR 72205	1879	Dr. Harry P. Ward	5-D	1,408	NR
U of Bridgeport, Bridgeport, CT 06601	1927	Dr. Janet D. Greenwood	1-D	4,278	322
U of California at Berkeley, Berkeley, CA 94720	1868	Chang-Lin Tien	5-D	30,638	NR
U of California, Davis, Davis, CA 95616	1906	Dr. Theodore L. Hullar	5-D	23,910	1,589
U of California, Irvine, Irvine, CA 92717	1965	Jack W. Peltason	5-D	16,761	728
U of California, Los Angeles, Los Angeles, CA 90024	1919	Charles E. Young	5-D	36,427	3,250
U of California, Riverside, Riverside, CA 92521	1954	Dr. Rosemary S. J. Schraer	5-D	8,716	681
U of California, San Diego, La Jolla, CA 92093	1959	Dr. Richard C. Atkinson	5-D	17,805	1,161
U of California, Santa Barbara, Santa Barbara, CA 93106	1891	Dr. Barbara S. Uehling	5-D	18,391	905
U of California, Santa Cruz, Santa Cruz, CA 95064	1965	Dr. Robert B. Stevens	5-D	10,052	559
U of Central Arkansas, Conway, AR 72032	1907	Winfred L. Thompson	5-M	8,396	421
U of Central Florida, Orlando, FL 32816	1963	Dr. Steven Altman	5-D	21,225	1,143
U of Central Oklahoma, Edmond, OK 73034	1890	Dr. Bill J. Lillard	5-M	14,501	562
U of Charleston, Charleston, WV 25304	1888	Dr. Edwin H. Welch	1-M	1,448	165
U of Chicago, Chicago, IL 60637	1891	Hanna Holborn Gray	1-D	11,063	1,200
U of Cincinnati, Cincinnati, OH 45221	1819	Dr. Joseph A. Steger	5-D	18,676	963
U of Colorado at Boulder, Boulder, CO 80309	1876	Dr. William Baughn	5-D	25,176	1,784
U of Colorado at Colorado Springs, Colorado Springs, CO 80933	1965	Dr. Dwayne C. Nuzum	5-D	4,901	358
U of Colorado at Denver, Denver, CO 80217	1912	John Buechner	5-D	9,137	516
U of Colorado Health Sciences Ctr, Denver, CO 80262	1883	Dr. Bernard W. Nelson	5-D	1,586	NR
U of Connecticut, Storrs, CT 06269	1881	Dr. Harry J. Hartley	5-D	17,867	947
U of Connecticut at Hartford, West Hartford, CT 06117	1946	Dr. Russell F. Farnen	5-B	1,294	91
U of Dallas, Irving, TX 75062	1956	Dr. Robert F. Sasseen	2-D	3,012	102
U of Dayton, Dayton, OH 45469	1850	Br. Raymond L. Fitz, SM	2-D	10,092	765
U of Delaware, Newark, DE 19716	1743	Dr. David P. Roselle	13-D	17,781	953
U of Denver, Denver, CO 80208	1864	Mr. Daniel Ritchie	1-D	7,609	379
U of Detroit Mercy, Detroit, MI 48221	1877	Rev. Robert A. Mitchell, SJ	2-D	7,758	546
U of Dubuque, Dubuque, IA 52001	1852	Dr. John J. Agria	2-M	1,138	79
U of Evansville, Evansville, IN 47722	1854	Dr. James S. Vinson	2-M	2,823	161
U of Findlay, Findlay, OH 45840	1882	Dr. Kenneth E. Zirkle	2-M	2,616	165
U of Florida, Gainesville, FL 32611	1853	Dr. John V. Lombardi	5-D	34,198	3,983
U of Georgia, Athens, GA 30602	1785	Dr. Charles B. Knapp	5-D	23,395	2,015
U of Guam, Mangilao, GU 96923	1952	Dr. Wilfred P. Leon Guerrero	8-M	2,391	244
U of Hartford, West Hartford, CT 06117	1877	Humphrey Tonkin	1-D	7,743	720
U of Hawaii at Hilo, Hilo, HI 96720	1970	Dr. Edward J. Kormondy	5-B	4,449	384
U of Hawaii at Manoa, Honolulu, HI 96822	1907	Dr. Albert J. Simone	5-D	18,874	4,940
U of Health Sciences/Chicago Medical Sch, North Chicago, IL 60064	1912	Dr. Myron Winick	1-D	906	20
U of Houston, Houston, TX 77004	1927	Dr. Marguerite Ross Barnett	5-D	32,289	2,280
U of Houston—Clear Lake, Houston, TX 77058	1971	Dr. Thomas M. Stauffer	5-M	7,560	321
U of Houston—Downtown, Houston, TX 77002	1974	Manuel T. Pacheco	5-B	8,702	361
U of Idaho, Moscow, ID 83843	1889	Dr. Elisabeth Zinser	5-D	9,533	570
U of Illinois at Chicago, Chicago, IL 60680	1965	Dr. James J. Stukel	5-D	25,182	2,037
U of Illinois at Urbana-Champaign, Champaign, IL 61820	1867	Dr. Morton W. Weir	5-D	35,766	2,967
U of Indianapolis, Indianapolis, IN 46227	1902	Dr. G. Benjamin Lantz, Jr.	2-M	3,391	276
U of Iowa, Iowa City, IA 52242	1847	Dr. Hunter R. Rawling, III	5-D	28,045	1,647
U of Kansas, Lawrence, KS 66045	1866	Gene A. Budig	5-D	28,909	1,236
U of Kentucky, Lexington, KY 40506-0032	1865	Dr. Charles T. Wethington, Jr.	5-D	23,100	1,879
U of La Verne, La Verne, CA 91750	1891	Dr. Stephen Morgan	1-D	5,933	572
U of Louisville, Louisville, KY 40292	1798	Dr. Donald C. Swain	5-D	23,600	1,650
U of Lowell, Lowell, MA 01854	1894	Dr. William T. Hogan	5-D	11,179	620
U of Maine, Orono, ME 04469	1865	Dr. Dale W. Lick	5-D	13,278	747
U of Maine at Farmington, Farmington, ME 04938	1864	Dr. J. Michael Orenduff	5-B	2,438	163
U of Maine at Machias, Machias, ME 04654	1909	Mr. Frederic A. Reynolds	5-B	1,008	63
U of Maine at Presque Isle, Presque Isle, ME 04769	1903	Dr. James R. Roach	5-M	1,458	105
U of Mary, Bismarck, ND 58504	1959	Sr. Thomas Welder	2-M	1,603	90
U of Mary Hardin-Baylor, Belton, TX 76513	1845	Dr. Jerry G. Bawcom	2-M	1,807	75
U of Maryland at Baltimore, Baltimore, MD 21201	1807	Dr. William J. Kinnard, Jr.	5-D	4,727	188
U of Maryland Baltimore County, Baltimore, MD 21228	1966	Dr. Michael K. Hooker	5-D	10,150	613
U of Maryland Coll Park, College Park, MD 20742	1856	Dr. William E. Kirwan	5-D	34,837	2,631
U of Maryland Eastern Shore, Princess Anne, MD 21853	1886	Dr. William P. Hytche	5-D	2,067	154
U of Maryland U Coll, College Park, MD 20742	1947	Dr. T. Benjamin Massey	5-M	40,385	2,263
U of Massachusetts at Amherst, Amherst, MA 01003	1863	Joseph Duffey	5-D	23,000	1,390
U of Massachusetts at Boston, Boston, MA 02125	1964	Dr. Sherry H. Penney	5-D	11,018	822
U of Miami, Coral Gables, FL 33124	1925	Edward T. Foote, II	1-D	13,686	1,143
U of Michigan, Ann Arbor, MI 48109	1817	Dr. James J. Duderstadt	5-D	36,306	3,619
U of Michigan—Dearborn, Dearborn, MI 48128	1959	Dr. Blenda Wilson	5-M	7,684	370
U of Michigan—Flint, Flint, MI 48502	1956	Dr. Clinton B. Jones	5-M	6,600	211
U of Minnesota, Duluth, Duluth, MN 55812	1948	Dr. Lawrence A. Ianni	5-M	7,916	415
U of Minnesota, Morris, Morris, MN 56267	1960	Dr. David C. Johnson	5-B	2,021	196
U of Minnesota, Twin Cities Cmps, Minneapolis, MN 55455	1851	Nils Hasselmo	5-D	40,972	2,939
U of Mississippi, University, MS 38677	1844	Dr. R. Gerald Turner	5-D	10,894	536
U of Mississippi Medical Ctr, Jackson, MS 39216	1955	Dr. Norman Crooks Nelson	5-D	1,637	108
U of Missouri—Columbia, Columbia, MO 65211	1839	Dr. Haskell Monroe	5-D	24,972	1,571
U of Missouri—Kansas City, Kansas City, MO 64110	1929	Dr. George A. Russell	5-D	11,357	983
U of Missouri—Rolla, Rolla, MO 65401	1870	Dr. Martin Jischke	5-D	5,439	381
U of Missouri—St Louis, St Louis, MO 63121	1963	Dr. Blance M. Touhill	5-D	13,161	635
U of Montana, Missoula, MT 59812	1893	George M. Dennison	5-D	10,055	501
U of Montevallo, Montevallo, AL 35115	1896	Dr. John W. Stewart	5-D	3,250	172
U of Nebraska at Kearney, Kearney, NE 68849	1903	Dr. William R. Nester	5-M	10,114	430
U of Nebraska at Omaha, Omaha, NE 68182	1908	Dr. Del D. Weber	5-M	16,661	690

Name, address	Year	Governing official, control, and highest degree offered		Enrollment	Faculty
U of Nebraska–Lincoln, Lincoln, NE 68588	1869	Dr. Martin A. Massengale	5-D	24,453	1,517
U of Nebraska Medical Ctr, Omaha, NE 68105	1869	Dr. Charles E. Andrews	5-D	2,444	155
U of Nevada, Las Vegas, Las Vegas, NV 89154	1957	Dr. Robert Maxson	5-D	18,216	831
U of Nevada, Reno, Reno, NV 89557	1874	Dr. Joseph N. Crowley	5-D	10,753	468
U of New England, Biddeford, ME 04005	1939	Dr. Charles W. Ford	1-D	1,210	106
U of New Hampshire, Durham, NH 03824	1866	Dr. Dale F. Nitzschke	5-D	11,468	825
U of New Haven, West Haven, CT 06516	1920	Dr. Phillip Kaplan	1-D	6,065	426
U of New Mexico, Albuquerque, NM 87131	1889	Richard E. Peck	5-D	24,600	1,543
U of New Orleans, New Orleans, LA 70148	1958	Dr. Gregory M. O'Brien	5-D	15,322	633
U of North Alabama, Florence, AL 35632	1872	Mr. Robert L. Potts	5-M	5,622	221
U of North Carolina at Asheville, Asheville, NC 28804	1927	Dr. Roy Carroll	5-M	3,310	229
U of North Carolina at Chapel Hill, Chapel Hill, NC 27599	1795	Paul Hardin, III	5-D	23,852	1,951
U of North Carolina at Charlotte, Charlotte, NC 28223	1946	Dr. James H. Woodward, Jr.	5-M	14,323	817
U of North Carolina at Greensboro, Greensboro, NC 27412	1891	Dr. William E. Moran	5-D	11,892	733
U of North Carolina at Wilmington, Wilmington, NC 28403	1947	Dr. James R. Leutze	5-M	6,978	412
U of North Dakota, Grand Forks, ND 58202	1883	Dr. Thomas J. Clifford	5-D	11,885	639
U of Northern Colorado, Greeley, CO 80639	1890	Dr. Robert C. Dickeson	5-D	10,239	514
U of Northern Iowa, Cedar Falls, IA 50614	1876	Dr. Constantine W. Curris	5-D	12,638	812
U of North Florida, Jacksonville, FL 32216	1965	Dr. Adam W. Herbert	5-D	8,021	214
U of North Texas, Denton, TX 76203	1890	Dr. Alfred F. Hurley	5-D	27,160	1,020
U of Notre Dame, Notre Dame, IN 46556	1842	Rev. Edward A. Malloy, CSC	2-D	9,900	800
U of Oklahoma, Norman, OK 73019	1890	Dr. Richard L. Van Horn	5-D	19,246	961
U of Oklahoma Health Sciences Ctr, Oklahoma City, OK 73190	1890	Dr. Clayton Rich	5-D	2,856	NR
U of Oregon, Eugene, OR 97403	1872	Myles Brand	5-D	18,043	1,133
U of Osteopathic Medicine and Health Sciences, Des Moines, IA 50312	1898	Dr. J. Leonard Azneer	1-D	1,002	108
U of Pennsylvania, Philadelphia, PA 19104	1740	Dr. F. Sheldon Hackney	1-D	21,903	3,951
U of Pittsburgh, Pittsburgh, PA 15260	1787	Dr. Wesley W. Posvar	13-D	28,120	3,060
U of Pittsburgh at Bradford, Bradford, PA 16701	1963	Dr. Richard E. McDowell	13-B	1,200	89
U of Pittsburgh at Greensburg, Greensburg, PA 15601	1963	Dr. George F. Chambers	13-B	1,563	101
U of Pittsburgh at Johnstown, Johnstown, PA 15904	1927	Dr. Frank H. Blackington, III	13-B	3,210	178
U of Portland, Portland, OR 97203	1901	Rev. David T. Tyson, CSC	2-M	2,460	192
U of Puerto Rico at Arecibo, Arecibo, PR 00613	1967	Prof. Ana J. Babilonia	7-B	3,350	158
U of Puerto Rico at Bayamón, Bayamón, PR 00619	1971	Aida Canals de Bird	7-B	3,697	174
U of Puerto Rico at Ponce, Ponce, PR 00732	1970	Mr. Pedro E. Laboy	7-B	2,128	125
U of Puerto Rico, Cayey, Cayey U Coll, Cayey, PR 00633	1967	Dr. Margarita Benítez	7-B	3,355	178
U of Puerto Rico, Humacao U Coll, Humacao, PR 00661	1962	Dr. Margarita Benítez	7-B	3,982	213
U of Puerto Rico Medical Sciences Cmps, San Juan, PR 00936	1950	Dr. Angel Roman	7-D	2,744	856
U of Puget Sound, Tacoma, WA 98416	1888	Dr. Philip M. Phibbs	2-M	3,334	230
U of Redlands, Redlands, CA 92373	1907	Dr. James R. Appleton	1-M	2,300	134
U of Rhode Island, Kingston, RI 02881	1892	Dr. Robert L. Carothers	5-D	12,111	761
U of Richmond, Richmond, VA 23173	1830	Dr. Richard L. Morrill	2-M	4,859	351
U of Rio Grande, Rio Grande, OH 45674	1876	Dr. Paul C. Hayes	1-M	2,013	108
U of Rochester, Rochester, NY 14627-0001	1850	G. Dennis O'Brien	1-D	8,376	655
U of St Thomas, St Paul, MN 55105	1885	Rev. Dennis Dease	2-D	9,805	570
U of St Thomas, Houston, TX 77006	1947	Joseph M. McFadden	2-D	1,964	148
U of San Diego, San Diego, CA 92110-2492	1949	Dr. Author E. Hughes	2-D	6,027	437
U of San Francisco, San Francisco, CA 94117-1080	1855	Rev. John P. Schlegel, SJ	2-D	6,331	517
U of Science and Arts of Oklahoma, Chickasha, OK 73018-0001	1908	Dr. Roy Troutt	5-B	1,451	75
U of Scranton, Scranton, PA 18510-4501	1888	Rev. J. A. Panuska, SJ	2-M	5,115	360
U of South Alabama, Mobile, AL 36688	1963	Dr. Frederick P. Whiddon	5-D	11,584	737
U of South Carolina, Columbia, SC 29208	1801	Dr. John M. Palms	5-D	25,613	1,436
U of South Carolina–Aiken, Aiken, SC 29801	1961	Dr. Robert E. Alexander	5-B	3,317	252
U of South Carolina at Spartanburg, Spartanburg, SC 29303	1967	Dr. Olin B. Sansbury, Jr.	5-B	3,501	231
U of South Carolina–Coastal Carolina Coll, Myrtle Beach, SC 29578	1954	Dr. Ronald G. Eaglin	5-B	4,080	230
U of South Dakota, Vermillion, SD 57069-2390	1862	Dr. Betty Turner Asher	5-D	6,816	416
U of Southern California, Los Angeles, CA 90089	1880	Dr. James H. Zumberge	1-D	28,895	3,406
U of Southern Colorado, Pueblo, CO 81001	1933	Dr. Robert Shirley	5-M	4,343	294
U of Southern Indiana, Evansville, IN 47712	1965	Dr. David L. Rice	5-M	6,480	273
U of Southern Maine, Portland, ME 04103	1878	Dr. Patricia Plante	5-D	10,487	502
U of Southern Mississippi, Hattiesburg, MS 39406	1910	Dr. Aubrey K. Lucas	5-D	11,912	684
U of South Florida, Tampa, FL 33620	1956	Dr. Francis T. Borkowski	5-D	32,360	1,422
U of Southwestern Louisiana, Lafayette, LA 70504	1898	Dr. Ray P. Authement	5-D	15,826	619
U of Tampa, Tampa, FL 33606	1931	Mr. Bruce A. Samson	1-M	2,503	200
U of Tennessee at Chattanooga, Chattanooga, TN 37403	1886	Dr. Frederick W. Obear	5-M	7,725	435
U of Tennessee at Martin, Martin, TN 38238	1927	Dr. Margaret N. Perry	5-M	5,369	263
U of Tennessee, Knoxville, Knoxville, TN 37996	1794	Dr. John J. Quinn	5-D	25,414	1,157
U of Tennessee, Memphis, Memphis, TN 38163	1911	Dr. James C. Hunt	5-D	1,785	913
U of Texas at Arlington, Arlington, TX 76019	1895	Dr. Wendell H. Nedderman	5-D	24,783	887
U of Texas at Austin, Austin, TX 78712	1883	Dr. William H. Cunningham	5-D	49,617	4,876
U of Texas at Dallas, Richardson, TX 75083	1961	Dr. Robert H. Rutford	5-D	8,685	255
U of Texas at El Paso, El Paso, TX 79968	1913	Dr. Diana Natalicio	5-D	16,524	729
U of Texas at San Antonio, San Antonio, TX 78285	1969	Dr. Samuel A. Kirkpatrick	5-D	15,489	660
U of Texas at Tyler, Tyler, TX 75701	1972	Dr. George F. Hamm	5-M	3,720	207
U of Texas Health Science Ctr at Houston, Houston, TX 77225	1943	Dr. M. David Low	5-D	3,016	79
U of Texas Health Science Ctr at San Antonio, San Antonio, TX 78284	1976	Dr. John P. Howe, III	5-D	2,456	137
U of Texas Medical Branch at Galveston, Galveston, TX 77550	1891	Dr. Thomas N. James	5-D	1,799	645
U of Texas of the Permian Basin, Odessa, TX 79762	1969	Dr. Duane M. Leach	5-M	2,041	105
U of Texas–Pan American, Edinburg, TX 78539	1927	Dr. Miguel A. Nevarez	5-M	12,220	450
U of Texas–Pan American at Brownsville, Brownsville, TX 78520	1973	NR	5-M	1,436	61
U of Texas Southwestern Medical Ctr at Dallas, Dallas, TX 75235	1943	Dr. C. Kern Wildenthal	5-D	1,529	270
U of the Arts, Philadelphia, PA 19102	1876	Peter Solmssen	1-M	1,310	382
U of the District of Columbia, Washington, DC 20008	1976	Dr. Rafael L. Cortada	10-M	11,990	697
U of the Pacific, Stockton, CA 95211	1851	Dr. Bill L. Atchley	1-D	6,000	356
U of the Sacred Heart, Santurce, PR 00914	1935	Jose Alberto Morales, Esq.	2-M	6,399	384
U of the South, Sewanee, TN 37375	1857	Dr. Samuel R. Williamson, Jr.	2-D	1,164	119
U of the State of NY, Regents Coll, Albany, NY 12203	1971	C. Wayne Williams	13-B	13,500	NR

Name, address	Year	Governing official, control, and highest degree offered	Enrollment	Faculty
U of the Virgin Islands, Charlotte Amalie, St Thomas, VI 00802	1962	Dr. Arthur A. Richards 8-M	2,466	175
U of Toledo, Toledo, OH 43606	1872	Mr. Frank E. Horton 5-D	24,781	1,354
U of Tulsa, Tulsa, OK 74104	1894	Dr. Robert H. Donaldson . . . 2-D	4,621	393
U of Utah, Salt Lake City, UT 84112	1850	Dr. Chase N. Peterson 5-D	24,311	924
U of Vermont, Burlington, VT 05405	1791	Dr. George H. Davis 5-D	9,466	1,005
U of Virginia, Charlottesville, VA 22906	1819	John T. Casteen, III 5-D	17,662	1,176
U of Washington, Seattle, WA 98195	1861	William P. Gerberding 5-D	33,536	2,834
U of West Florida, Pensacola, FL 32514-5750	1963	Dr. Morris L. Marx 5-M	7,844	255
U of Wisconsin–Eau Claire, Eau Claire, WI 54702	1916	Dr. Larry Schnack 5-M	10,644	564
U of Wisconsin–Green Bay, Green Bay, WI 54311	1968	Dr. David L. Outcalt 5-M	4,801	208
U of Wisconsin–La Crosse, La Crosse, WI 54601	1909	Dr. Noel J. Richards 5-M	8,759	452
U of Wisconsin–Madison, Madison, WI 53706	1848	Dr. Donna E. Shalala 5-D	40,905	2,396
U of Wisconsin–Milwaukee, Milwaukee, WI 53201	1956	Dr. John H. Schroeder, Jr. . . 5-D	25,380	1,263
U of Wisconsin–Oshkosh, Oshkosh, WI 54901	1871	Dr. John E. Kerrigan 5-M	11,093	538
U of Wisconsin–Parkside, Kenosha, WI 53141	1968	Dr. Sheila Kaplan 5-M	5,112	298
U of Wisconsin–Platteville, Platteville, WI 53818	1866	Dr. William W. Chmurny . . . 5-M	5,430	280
U of Wisconsin–River Falls, River Falls, WI 54022	1874	Dr. Gary A. Thibodeau 5-M	5,243	295
U of Wisconsin–Stevens Point, Stevens Point, WI 54481	1894	Dr. Keith R. Sanders 5-M	8,805	510
U of Wisconsin–Stout, Menomonie, WI 54751	1891	Dr. Charles Sorensen 5-M	7,445	416
U of Wisconsin–Superior, Superior, WI 54880	1893	Dr. Terrence MacTaggart . . 5-M	2,607	162
U of Wisconsin–Whitewater, Whitewater, WI 53190	1868	Dr. James R. Connor 5-M	10,185	672
U of Wyoming, Laramie, WY 82071	1886	Dr. Terry P. Roark 5-D	12,524	812
Upper Iowa U, Fayette, IA 52142	1857	Dr. James R. Rocheleau . . . 1-B	2,215	230
Upsala Coll, East Orange, NJ 07019	1893	Dr. Robert E. Karsten 2-M	990	107
Urbana U, Urbana, OH 43078	1850	Dr. Paul G. Bunnell 2-B	852	88
Ursinus Coll, Collegeville, PA 19426	1869	Dr. Richard P. Richter 2-B	1,073	123
Ursuline Coll, Pepper Pike, OH 44124 (4)	1871	Sr. Anne Marie Diederich, OSU 2-M	1,600	110
Utah State U, Logan, UT 84322	1888	Dr. Stanford Cazier 5-D	12,650	733
Utica Coll of Syracuse U, Utica, NY 13502	1946	Dr. Michael K. Simpson . . . 1-B	1,707	140
Valdosta State Coll, Valdosta, GA 31698	1906	Dr. Hugh C. Bailey 5-M	7,144	390
Valley City State U, Valley City, ND 58072	1890	Dr. Charles B. House, Jr. . . 5-B	1,082	66
Valparaiso U, Valparaiso, IN 46383	1859	Dr. Alan F. Harre 2-D	3,862	349
Vanderbilt U, Nashville, TN 37240	1873	Mr. Joe B. Wyatt 1-D	9,236	706
Vassar Coll, Poughkeepsie, NY 12601	1861	Frances D. Fergusson 1-M	2,459	243
Villa Julie Coll, Stevenson, MD 21153	1952	Dr. Carolyn Manuszak 1-B	1,596	114
Villanova U, Villanova, PA 19085	1842	Rev. Edmund J. Dobbin, OSA 2-D	11,265	935
Virginia Commonwealth U, Richmond, VA 23284	1838	Dr. Eugene P. Trani 5-D	21,764	2,143
Virginia Military Inst, Lexington, VA 24450 (1)	1839	Maj. Gen. John W. Knapp . . 5-B	1,320	98
Virginia Polytechnic Inst and State U, Blacksburg, VA 24061	1872	James D. McComas 5-D	23,365	1,932
Virginia State U, Petersburg, VA 23803	1882	Dr. Wesley C. McClure 5-M	3,988	247
Virginia Union U, Richmond, VA 23220	1865	Dr. S. Dallas Simmons 2-D	1,298	100
Virginia Wesleyan Coll, Norfolk, VA 23502	1961	Dr. Lambuth M. Clarke 2-B	1,390	85
Viterbo Coll, La Crosse, WI 54601	1890	Dr. Robert E. Gibbons 2-M	1,170	109
Wabash Coll, Crawfordsville, IN 47933 (1)	1832	Dr. F. Sheldon Wettack . . . 1-B	854	81
Wagner Coll, Staten Island, NY 10301	1883	Dr. Norman R. Smith 1-M	1,538	155
Wake Forest U, Winston-Salem, NC 27109	1834	Dr. Thomas K. Hearn, Jr. . . 1-D	5,505	326
Walla Walla Coll, College Place, WA 99324	1892	Dr. Neils-Eric Andreason . . 2-M	1,651	168
Walsh Coll, North Canton, OH 44720	1958	Dr. Francis Blouin 2-M	1,458	96
Walsh Coll of Accountancy and Business Admin, Troy, MI 48007	1922	Dr. Jeffery W. Barry 1-M	3,326	130
Wartburg Coll, Waverly, IA 50677	1852	Dr. Robert Vogel 2-B	1,440	122
Washburn U of Topeka, Topeka, KS 66621	1865	Dr. Hugh Thompson 11-D	6,492	376
Washington and Jefferson Coll, Washington, PA 15301	1781	Dr. Howard J. Burnett 1-B	1,205	108
Washington and Lee U, Lexington, VA 24450	1749	Dr. John D. Wilson 1-D	2,032	138
Washington Coll, Chestertown, MD 21620	1782	Dr. Charles Trout 1-M	1,003	79
Washington State U, Pullman, WA 99164	1890	Dr. Samuel H. Smith 5-D	17,494	925
Washington U, St Louis, MO 63130	1853	Dr. William H. Danforth . . . 1-D	9,701	2,982
Wayland Baptist U, Plainview, TX 79072	1908	NR	2,082	181
Waynesburg Coll, Waynesburg, PA 15370	1849	Mr. Timothy R. Thyreen . . . 2-M	1,244	71
Wayne State Coll, Wayne, NE 68787	1910	Dr. Donald J. Mash 5-M	3,512	172
Wayne State U, Detroit, MI 48202	1868	Dr. David Adamany 5-D	33,872	2,308
Weber State U, Ogden, UT 84408	1889	Dr. Paul H. Thompson 5-M	13,449	439
Webster U, St Louis, MO 63119	1915	Dr. Daniel H. Perlman 1-D	4,859	410
Wellesley Coll, Wellesley, MA 02181 (3)	1870	Dr. Nannerl Keohane 1-M	2,279	332
Wentworth Inst of Tech, Boston, MA 02115	1904	Dr. John F. Domelen 1-B	2,959	154
Wesleyan U, Middletown, CT 06459	1831	Mr. William M. Chace 1-D	3,417	341
Wesley Coll, Dover, DE 19901	1873	Dr. Reed M. Stewart 2-B	1,168	98
West Chester U of Pennsylvania, West Chester, PA 19383	1871	Dr. Kenneth L. Perrin 5-M	12,076	674
West Coast U, Los Angeles, CA 90020	1909	Dr. Robert M. L. Baker, Jr. . 1-M	1,600	250
Western Carolina U, Cullowhee, NC 28723	1889	Dr. Myron L. Coulter 5-M	6,222	398
Western Connecticut State U, Danbury, CT 06810	1903	Dr. Stephen Feldman 5-M	6,245	389
Western Illinois U, Macomb, IL 61455	1899	Dr. Ralph H. Wagoner 5-M	13,750	674
Western International U, Phoenix, AZ 85021	1978	Robert S. Webber 1-M	1,569	88
Western Kentucky U, Bowling Green, KY 42101	1906	Dr. Thomas C. Meredith . . . 5-M	15,240	786
Western Maryland Coll, Westminster, MD 21157	1867	Dr. Robert H. Chambers . . . 1-M	2,223	142
Western Michigan U, Kalamazoo, MI 49008	1903	Dr. Diether H. Haenicke . . . 5-D	26,995	1,043
Western Montana Coll of the U of Montana, Dillon, MT 59725	1893	Dr. W. Michael Easton 5-B	1,011	42
Western New England Coll, Springfield, MA 01119	1919	Dr. Beverly W. Miller 1-D	3,983	238
Western New Mexico U, Silver City, NM 88061	1893	Dr. Jerry L. Gallentine 5-M	1,878	103
Western Oregon State Coll, Monmouth, OR 97361	1856	Dr. Richard S. Meyers 5-M	4,017	347
Western State Coll of Colorado, Gunnison, CO 81230	1911	Dr. William T. Hamilton . . . 5-B	2,329	132
Western State U Coll of Law of Orange County, Fullerton, CA 92631	1966	NR 3-D	1,538	84
Western Washington U, Bellingham, WA 98225	1893	Dr. Kenneth P. Mortimer . . . 5-M	9,732	509
Westfield State Coll, Westfield, MA 01086	1838	Dr. Ronald L. Applbaum . . . 5-M	5,292	213
West Georgia Coll, Carrollton, GA 30118	1933	Dr. Maurice K. Townsend . . 5-M	7,072	309
West Liberty State Coll, West Liberty, WV 26074	1837	Dr. Clyde D. Campbell 5-B	2,386	144
Westminster Coll, Fulton, MO 65251-1299	1851	Dr. J. Harvey Saunders . . . 2-B	786	87
Westminster Coll, New Wilmington, PA 16172-0001	1852	Dr. Oscar E. Remick 2-M	1,500	114
Westminster Coll of Salt Lake City, Salt Lake City, UT 84105	1875	Dr. Charles H. Dick 1-M	2,054	165
Westmont Coll, Santa Barbara, CA 93108	1940	Dr. David K. Winter 2-B	1,264	109

Name, address	Year	Governing official, control, and highest degree offered	Enroll-ment	Faculty
West Texas State U, Canyon, TX 79016	1909	Dr. Barry B. Thompson 5-M	6,193	312
West Virginia Inst of Tech, Montgomery, WV 25136	1895	Dr. Robert C. Gillespie 5-M	2,898	198
West Virginia State Coll, Institute, WV 25112	1891	Hazo W. Carter 5-B	4,834	215
West Virginia U, Morgantown, WV 26506	1867	Dr. Neil S. Bucklew 5-D	20,854	1,440
West Virginia Wesleyan Coll, Buckhannon, WV 26201	1890	Dr. Thomas B. Courtice . . . 2-M	1,629	119
Wheaton Coll, Wheaton, IL 60187	1860	Dr. J. Richard Chase 2-M	2,533	240
Wheaton Coll, Norton, MA 02766	1834	Alice F. Emerson 1-B	1,264	126
Wheeling Jesuit Coll, Wheeling, WV 26003	1954	Fr. Thomas S. Acker, SJ . . 2-M	1,375	68
Wheelock Coll, Boston, MA 02215 (4)	1888	Dr. Daniel S. Cheever, Jr. . 1-M	1,208	152
Whitman Coll, Walla Walla, WA 99362	1859	Dr. David E. Maxwell 1-B	1,267	154
Whittier Coll, Whittier, CA 90608	1887	Dr. James L. Ash, Jr. 1-D	1,836	111
Whitworth Coll, Spokane, WA 99251	1890	Dr. Arthur J. De Jong 2-M	1,759	95
Wichita State U, Wichita, KS 67208	1895	Dr. Warren B. Armstrong . . 5-D	16,668	852
Widener U, Chester, PA 19013	1821	Mr. Robert J. Bruce 1-D	9,073	312
Wilberforce U, Wilberforce, OH 45384	1856	John L. Henderson 2-B	805	64
Wilkes U, Wilkes-Barre, PA 18766	1933	Dr. Christopher N. Breiseth . 1-M	3,629	237
Willamette U, Salem, OR 97301	1842	Dr. Jerry E. Hudson 2-D	2,225	143
William Jewell Coll, Liberty, MO 64068	1849	Dr. J. Gordon Kingsley . . . 2-B	1,477	143
William Paterson Coll of New Jersey, Wayne, NJ 07470	1855	Dr. Arnold Speert 5-M	10,041	649
Williams Coll, Williamstown, MA 01267	1793	Dr. Francis C. Oakley 1-M	2,120	268
William Smith Coll, Geneva, NY 14456 (3)	1908	Mr. Carroll W. Brewster . . . 1-B	808	185
William Woods Coll, Fulton, MO 65251 (3)	1870	Dr. Jahnae Barnett 2-B	750	69
Wilmington Coll, New Castle, DE 19720	1967	Dr. Audrey K. Doberstein . . 1-M	1,796	144
Wilmington Coll, Wilmington, OH 45177	1870	Neil Thorburn 2-B	920	62
Wilson Coll, Chambersburg, PA 17201 (4)	1869	Dr. Gwendolyn E. Jensen . . 2-B	853	82
Wingate Coll, Wingate, NC 28174	1895	NR 2-M	1,424	102
Winona State U, Winona, MN 55987	1858	Dr. Darrell Krueger 5-M	7,500	400
Winston-Salem State U, Winston-Salem, NC 27110	1892	Dr. Cleon F. Thompson, Jr. . 5-B	2,517	186
Winthrop Coll, Rock Hill, SC 29733	1886	Dr. Anthony DiGiorgio 5-M	5,106	424
Wittenberg U, Springfield, OH 45501	1845	Dr. William A. Kinnison . . . 2-B	2,350	182
Wofford Coll, Spartanburg, SC 29303	1854	Dr. Joab M. Lesesne 2-B	1,076	83
Woodbury U, Burbank, CA 91510	1884	Dr. Paul E. Sago 1-M	1,024	111
Worcester Polytechnic Inst, Worcester, MA 01609	1865	Dr. Jon C. Strauss 1-D	3,897	342
Worcester State Coll, Worcester, MA 01602	1874	Dr. Philip D. Vairo 5-M	5,246	206
Wright State U, Dayton, OH 45435	1964	Dr. Paige E. Mulhollan . . . 5-D	17,380	950
Xavier U, Cincinnati, OH 45207	1831	Mr. Michael Conaton 2-M	6,680	437
Xavier U of Louisiana, New Orleans, LA 70125	1925	Dr. Norman C. Francis . . . 2-D	2,960	253
Yale U, New Haven, CT 06520	1701	Benno C. Schmidt, Jr. . . . 1-D	10,842	749
Yeshiva U, New York, NY 10033	1886	Dr. Norman Lamm 1-D	4,670	164
York Coll of Pennsylvania, York, PA 17403	1787	Dr. George W. Waldner . . . 1-M	4,979	275
York Coll of the City U of New York, Jamaica, NY 11451	1967	Dr. Leo A. Corbie 12-B	5,729	200
Youngstown State U, Youngstown, OH 44555	1908	Dr. Neil D. Humphrey 5-M	15,454	976

Two-Year Colleges

The highest undergraduate degree offered for all two-year colleges is the associate degree.

Name, address	Year	Governing official, control, and highest degree offered	Enroll-ment	Faculty
Abraham Baldwin Ag Coll, Tifton, GA 31794	1933	Dr. Harold J. Loyd 5	2,500	89
Adirondack Comm Coll, Queensbury, NY 12804	1960	Dr. Roger Andersen 12	3,386	187
Aiken Tech Coll, Aiken, SC 29802	1972	Dr. Paul L. Blowers 12	1,900	175
Aims Comm Coll, Greeley, CO 80632	1967	Dr. George R. Conger . . . 10	8,836	376
Alamance Comm Coll, Haw River, NC 27258	1959	Dr. W. Ronald McCarter . . . 5	3,259	145
Allan Hancock Coll, Santa Maria, CA 93454	1920	Dr. Gary R. Edelbrock . . . 12	8,687	368
Allegany Comm Coll, Cumberland, MD 21502	1961	Dr. Donald L. Alexander . . 12	2,650	182
Allen County Comm Coll, Iola, KS 66749	1923	Dr. William A. Griffin, Jr. . . 12	1,537	125
Alpena Comm Coll, Alpena, MI 49707	1952	Dr. Donald L. Newport . . . 12	2,321	128
Alvin Comm Coll, Alvin, TX 77511	1949	Dr. A. Rodney Allbright . . . 12	3,892	203
Amarillo Coll, Amarillo, TX 79178	1929	Dr. George T. Miller 12	5,952	406
American Inst of Business, Des Moines, IA 50321	1921	Keith Fenton 1	1,053	60
American River Coll, Sacramento, CA 95841	1955	Dr. Queen F. Randall 10	23,335	700
Angelina Coll, Lufkin, TX 75902	1968	Dr. Larry M. Phillips 12	3,144	143
Anne Arundel Comm Coll, Arnold, MD 21012	1961	Dr. Thomas E. Florestano . 12	12,152	590
Anoka-Ramsey Comm Coll, Coon Rapids, MN 55433	1965	Dr. Patrick M. Johns 5	5,282	228
Antelope Valley Coll, Lancaster, CA 93536	1929	Dr. Allan W. Kurki 12	9,833	387
Arapahoe Comm Coll, Littleton, CO 80160	1965	Dr. James F. Weber 5	7,711	410
Arizona Western Coll, Yuma, AZ 85366	1962	Dr. James R. Carruthers . . 12	5,050	243
Arkansas State U–Beebe Branch, Beebe, AR 72012	1927	Mr. William H. Owen, Jr. . . 1	1,520	66
Art Inst of Atlanta, Atlanta, GA 30326	1949	Mark J. Fagan 3	1,283	108
Art Inst of Dallas, Dallas, TX 75231	1978	Ms. Deborah G. Wright . . . 3	1,170	84
Art Inst of Houston, Houston, TX 77006	1978	Steve R. Gregg 3	1,019	75
Art Inst of Philadelphia, Philadelphia, PA 19103	1966	Max R. Tudor 3	1,100	90
Art Inst of Pittsburgh, Pittsburgh, PA 15222	1921	Saundra M. Van Dyke 3	2,500	102
Art Inst of Seattle, Seattle, WA 98121	1982	David J. Pauldine 3	1,314	101
Asheville-Buncombe Tech Comm Coll, Asheville, NC 28801	1959	Mr. Harvey L. Haynes 5	3,476	224
Asnuntuck Comm Coll, Enfield, CT 06082	1972	Dr. Harvey S. Irlen 5	1,900	79
Atlanta Metropolitan Coll, Atlanta, GA 30310	1974	Dr. Edwin A. Thompson . . . 5	1,624	NR
Atlantic Comm Coll, Mays Landing, NJ 08330	1966	Dr. William Orth 9	5,044	215
Austin Comm Coll, Austin, MN 55912	1940	Mr. Steven R. Wallace . . . 5	1,244	73
Austin Comm Coll, Austin, TX 78714	1972	Dr. Dan Angel 10	24,019	1,334
Bakersfield Coll, Bakersfield, CA 93305	1913	Dr. Richard Wright 12	12,869	448
Barstow Coll, Barstow, CA 92311	1959	Dr. John C. Menzie 12	2,459	124
Barton County Comm Coll, Great Bend, KS 67530	1969	Dr. Jimmie L. Downing . . . 12	3,224	205
Bay de Noc Comm Coll, Escanaba, MI 49829	1963	Dr. Dwight E. Link 5	2,240	143
Beaufort County Comm Coll, Washington, NC 27889	1968	Mr. Ron Champion 5	1,302	95
Beckley Coll, Beckley, WV 25802	1933	Dr. Charles Polk 1	1,952	105
Bee County Coll, Beeville, TX 78102	1965	Dr. Norman Wallace 9	2,250	140
Belleville Area Coll, Belleville, IL 62221	1946	Dr. Joseph Cipfl 5	13,909	661
Bellevue Comm Coll, Bellevue, WA 98007	1966	B. Jean Floten 5	8,615	521
Belmont Tech Coll, St Clairsville, OH 43950	1971	Dr. Wesley R. Channell . . . 5	1,618	132
Bergen Comm Coll, Paramus, NJ 07652	1965	Dr. Jose Lopez-Isa 9	7,551	601
Berkshire Comm Coll, Pittsfield, MA 01201	1960	Dr. Cathryn L. Addy 5	2,150	126
Bessemer State Tech Coll, Bessemer, AL 35021	1966	Dr. W. Michael Bailey 5	1,793	102
Big Bend Comm Coll, Moses Lake, WA 98837	1962	Dr. Greg Fitch 5	1,146	124
Bishop State Comm Coll, Mobile, AL 36603	1965	Dr. Yvonne Kennedy 5	2,057	96

Name, address	Year	Governing official, control	Enrollment	Faculty
Bismarck State Coll, Bismarck, ND 58501	1939	Dr. Kermit Lidstrom ... 5	2,304	117
Black Hawk Coll–Quad-Cities Cmps, Moline, IL 61265	1946	Dr. Herbert C. Lyon ... 12	5,226	305
Blackhawk Tech Coll, Janesville, WI 53547	1968	Dr. James C. Catania ... 10	2,700	137
Blinn Coll, Brenham, TX 77833	1883	Walter C. Schwartz ... 12	6,930	205
Blue Mountain Comm Coll, Pendleton, OR 97801	1962	Mr. Ronald L. Daniels ... 9	4,500	189
Blue Ridge Comm Coll, Flat Rock, NC 28731	1969	Dr. David W. Sink ... 12	1,516	82
Blue Ridge Comm Coll, Weyers Cave, VA 24486	1965	Dr. James R. Perkins ... 5	2,740	159
Borough of Manhattan Comm Coll of City U of NY, New York, NY 10007	1963	Dr. Augusta Souza Kappner .. 12	15,266	1,108
Bossier Parish Comm Coll, Bossier City, LA 71111	1967	James M. Conerly ... 12	3,373	124
Bowling Green State U–Firelands Coll, Huron, OH 44839	1968	Dr. Robert DeBard ... 5	1,480	67
Brainerd Comm Coll, Brainerd, MN 56401	1938	Sally Jane Ihne ... 5	1,837	79
Bramson ORT Tech Inst, Forest Hills, NY 11375	1977	Dr. Howard J. Friedman ... 1	1,065	57
Brazosport Coll, Lake Jackson, TX 77566	1948	Dr. John R. Grable ... 12	3,600	146
Brevard Comm Coll, Cocoa, FL 32922	1960	Dr. Maxwell C. King ... 5	13,617	896
Brewer State Jr Coll, Fayette, AL 35555	1969	Dr. Wayland DeWitt ... 5	1,090	68
Bristol Comm Coll, Fall River, MA 02720	1965	Dr. Eileen Farley ... 5	2,809	183
Bronx Comm Coll of City U of NY, Bronx, NY 10453	1959	Ms. Eileen Farley ... 12	6,472	390
Brookdale Comm Coll, Lincroft, NJ 07738	1967	Dr. Peter Burnham ... 9	11,949	443
Brookhaven Coll, Farmers Branch, TX 75244	1978	NR ... 5	8,359	385
Broome Comm Coll, Binghamton, NY 13902	1946	Dr. Donald A. Dellow ... 12	6,400	466
Broward Comm Coll, Fort Lauderdale, FL 33301	1960	Dr. Willis N. Holcombe ... 5	25,081	744
Brunswick Coll, Brunswick, GA 31523	1961	NR ... 5	1,445	65
Bucks County Comm Coll, Newtown, PA 18940	1964	Dr. William E. Vincent ... 9	11,042	375
Burlington County Coll, Pemberton, NJ 08068	1966	Dr. Robert Messina ... 9	6,928	150
Butler County Comm Coll, El Dorado, KS 67042	1927	Dr. Rodney V. Cox, Jr. ... 12	4,688	299
Butler County Comm Coll, Butler, PA 16003	1965	NR ... 9	3,214	120
Caldwell Comm Coll and Tech Inst, Hudson, NC 28638	1964	Dr. Eric B. McKeithan ... 5	2,626	174
California Coll for Health Sciences, National City, CA 92050	1977	Charles Sinks ... 3	3,000	4
Camden County Coll, Blackwood, NJ 08012	1967	Dr. Robert W. Ramsay ... 12	12,014	385
Cañada Coll, Redwood City, CA 94061	1968	NR ... 10	7,500	263
Cape Cod Comm Coll, West Barnstable, MA 02668	1961	Dr. Vernon Beuke ... 5	2,011	164
Cape Fear Comm Coll, Wilmington, NC 28401	1959	Dr. Richard C. Conrath ... 5	2,900	153
Carl Albert State Coll, Poteau, OK 74953	1934	NR ... 5	1,676	160
Carl Sandburg Coll, Galesburg, IL 61401	1967	Jack W. Fuller ... 12	2,800	117
Carteret Comm Coll, Morehead City, NC 28557	1963	Dr. Donald W. Bryant ... 5	1,513	93
Casper Coll, Casper, WY 82601	1945	Dr. LeRoy Strausner ... 10	2,264	185
Catawba Valley Comm Coll, Hickory, NC 28602	1960	Dr. Cuyler A. Dunbar ... 5	3,300	175
Catonsville Comm Coll, Catonsville, MD 21228	1957	Dr. Frederick J. Walsh ... 9	10,580	534
Cayuga County Comm Coll, Auburn, NY 13021	1953	Dr. Lawrence H. Poole ... 12	2,792	144
Cazenovia Coll, Cazenovia, NY 13035	1824	Dr. Stephen M. Schneeweiss .. 1	1,071	145
Cecil Comm Coll, North East, MD 21901	1968	Dr. Robert L. Gell ... 5	1,574	95
Cedar Valley Coll, Lancaster, TX 75134	1977	Dr. Floyd S. Elkins ... 5	3,281	130
Central Alabama Comm Coll, Alexander City, AL 35010	1965	Dr. James H. Cornell ... 5	2,324	131
Central Arizona Coll, Coolidge, AZ 85228	1961	Dr. John J. Klein ... 9	8,514	NR
Central Carolina Comm Coll, Sanford, NC 27330	1962	Dr. Marvin R. Joyner ... 12	2,823	177
Central Comm Coll–Grand Island Cmps, Grand Island, NE 68802	1976	Donald Nelson ... 12	4,617	78
Central Comm Coll–Hastings Cmps, Hastings, NE 68902	1966	Dr. Judy Dresser ... 12	3,033	110
Central Comm Coll–Platte Cmps, Columbus, NE 68602	1968	Dr. Peter Rush ... 12	3,265	84
Central Florida Comm Coll, Ocala, FL 32678	1957	Dr. William J. Campion ... 12	5,400	202
Centralia Coll, Centralia, WA 98531	1925	Dr. Henry P. Kirk ... 5	1,375	112
Central Ohio Tech Coll, Newark, OH 43055	1971	Dr. Julius S. Greenstein ... 5	1,555	106
Central Oregon Comm Coll, Bend, OR 97701	1949	Dr. Robert L. Barber ... 10	3,036	201
Central Piedmont Comm Coll, Charlotte, NC 28235	1963	Dr. Ruth Shaw ... 12	16,772	949
Central Texas Coll, Killeen, TX 76542	1967	Dr. Luis M. Morton ... 12	5,303	NR
Central Virginia Comm Coll, Lynchburg, VA 24502	1966	Dr. J. E. Merritt ... 12	3,982	110
Central Wyoming Coll, Riverton, WY 82501	1966	Dr. JoAnne McFarland ... 12	1,457	135
Cerritos Coll, Norwalk, CA 90650	1956	Dr. Ernest Martinez ... 12	21,267	700
Cerro Coso Comm Coll, Ridgecrest, CA 93555	1973	Dr. Raymond A. McCue ... 5	4,118	241
Chabot Coll, Hayward, CA 94545	1961	Dr. Raul J. Cardoza ... 5	21,382	1,075
Chaffey Coll, Rancho Cucamonga, CA 91701	1883	Dr. Jerry W. Young ... 10	13,372	500
Champlain Coll, Burlington, VT 05401	1878	Dr. Robert A. Skiff ... 1	1,296	114
Charles County Comm Coll, La Plata, MD 20646	1958	Dr. John Sine ... 12	5,143	247
Charles Stewart Mott Comm Coll, Flint, MI 48502	1923	Mr. David G. Moore ... 9	9,965	405
Chattahoochee Valley State Comm Coll, Phenix City, AL 36869	1974	Dr. James E. Owen ... 5	1,621	71
Chattanooga State Tech Comm Coll, Chattanooga, TN 37406	1965	Dr. Harry D. Wagner ... 5	7,412	358
Chemeketa Comm Coll, Salem, OR 97309	1955	William Segura ... 12	9,807	893
Chesapeake Coll, Wye Mills, MD 21679	1965	Dr. Robert C. Schleiger ... 12	2,247	216
Chipola Jr Coll, Marianna, FL 32446	1947	Dr. Jerry W. Kandzer ... 5	2,751	110
Chippewa Valley Tech Coll, Eau Claire, WI 54701	1912	Mr. Norbert K. Wurtzel ... 10	3,750	400
Cincinnati Tech Coll, Cincinnati, OH 45223	1966	Dr. James P. Long ... 5	4,961	265
Cisco Jr Coll, Cisco, TX 76437	1940	Dr. Roger C. Schustereit ... 12	2,101	98
Citrus Coll, Glendora, CA 91740	1915	Dr. Louis F. Zellers ... 12	9,888	536
City Coll of San Francisco, San Francisco, CA 94112	1935	Dr. Willis F. Kirk ... 12	29,924	1,117
City Colls of Chicago, Chicago City-Wide Coll, Chicago, IL 60606	1975	Dr. Martha Bazik ... 12	2,874	116
City Colls of Chicago, Harold Washington Coll, Chicago, IL 60601	1962	Dr. Bernice Miller ... 12	7,466	195
City Colls of Chicago, Harry S Truman Coll, Chicago, IL 60640	1956	Dr. Wallace B. Appelson ... 12	6,111	170
City Colls of Chicago, Kennedy-King Coll, Chicago, IL 60621	1935	Dr. Harold Pates ... 12	3,127	147
City Colls of Chicago, Malcolm X Coll, Chicago, IL 60612	1911	Dr. Milton F. Brown ... 12	2,292	142
City Colls of Chicago, Olive-Harvey Coll, Chicago, IL 60628	1970	Mr. Homer D. Franklin ... 12	3,800	132
City Colls of Chicago, Richard J Daley Coll, Chicago, IL 60652	1960	Mr. William P. Conway ... 12	5,601	161
City Colls of Chicago, Wilbur Wright Coll, Chicago, IL 60634	1934	Mr. Raymond F. LeFevour ... 12	6,016	161
Clackamas Comm Coll, Oregon City, OR 97045	1966	Dr. John S. Keyser ... 9	6,437	514
Clark Coll, Vancouver, WA 98663	1933	Dr. Earl F. Johnson ... 5	9,100	320
Clark County Comm Coll, North Las Vegas, NV 89030	1971	Dr. Paul E. Meacham ... 5	19,555	670
Clatsop Comm Coll, Astoria, OR 97103	1958	Dr. Doreen Dailey ... 9	2,630	169
Cleveland Comm Coll, Shelby, NC 28150	1965	Dr. L. Steve Thornburg ... 5	1,642	92

Name, address	Year	Governing official, control	Enroll-ment	Faculty
Cleveland Inst of Electronics, Cleveland, OH 44114 (2)	1934	John R. Drinko ... 3	2,700	6
Cleveland State Comm Coll, Cleveland, TN 37320-3570	1967	Dr. James W. Ford ... 5	3,315	175
Clinton Comm Coll, Clinton, IA 52732	1946	Desna L. Wallin ... 5	1,240	75
Clinton Comm Coll, Plattsburgh, NY 12901	1969	Dr. Jay L. Fennell ... 12	2,106	156
Cloud County Comm Coll, Concordia, KS 66901	1965	Dr. James P. Ihrig ... 12	3,018	224
Coahoma Comm Coll, Clarksdale, MS 38614	1949	Dr. McKinley C. Martin ... 12	1,373	85
Coastal Carolina Comm Coll, Jacksonville, NC 28540	1964	Dr. Ronald K. Lingle, Jr. ... 12	3,737	170
Coastline Comm Coll, Fountain Valley, CA 92708	1976	Dr. William M. Vega ... 12	15,379	490
Cochise Coll, Douglas, AZ 85607	1962	Dr. Dan W. Rehurek ... 12	4,524	342
Coffeyville Comm Coll, Coffeyville, KS 67337	1923	Dr. Dan Kinney ... 12	2,015	86
Coll of Alameda, Alameda, CA 94501	1970	Ronald A. Kong ... 12	5,914	NR
Coll of DuPage, Glen Ellyn, IL 60137	1967	Dr. Harold D. McAninch ... 12	29,187	1,573
Coll of Eastern Utah, Price, UT 84501	1937	Dr. Michael A. Petersen ... 5	2,960	96
Coll of Lake County, Grayslake, IL 60030	1967	Dr. Daniel J. La Vista ... 10	14,885	753
Coll of Marin, Kentfield, CA 94904	1926	Ms. Myrna R. Miller ... 12	10,539	NR
Coll of San Mateo, San Mateo, CA 94402	1922	Dr. Lois A. Callahan ... 12	14,028	485
Coll of Southern Idaho, Twin Falls, ID 83303	1964	Mr. Gerald R. Meyerhoeffer ... 12	2,787	108
Coll of The Albemarle, Elizabeth City, NC 27906-2327	1960	Dr. Parker Chesson, Jr. ... 5	1,627	102
Coll of the Canyons, Santa Clarita, CA 91355	1969	Dr. Dianne G. Van Hook ... 12	6,104	228
Coll of the Desert, Palm Desert, CA 92260	1959	Dr. David A. George ... 12	12,000	315
Coll of the Mainland, Texas City, TX 77591	1967	Mr. Larry L. Stanley ... 12	3,764	180
Coll of the Redwoods, Eureka, CA 95501	1964	Dr. Cedric A. Sampson ... 12	7,638	449
Coll of the Sequoias, Visalia, CA 93277	1925	Dr. Lincoln H. Hall ... 12	9,086	380
Coll of the Siskiyous, Weed, CA 96094	1957	Dr. Eugene Schumacher ... 12	2,676	158
Collin County Comm Coll, McKinney, TX 75070	1985	Dr. John H. Anthony ... 12	9,059	420
Colorado Inst of Art, Denver, CO 80203	1952	Cheryl Murphy ... 3	1,328	77
Columbia Basin Coll, Pasco, WA 99301	1955	Dr. Marv Weiss ... 5	6,650	350
Columbia Coll, Columbia, CA 95310	1968	Dr. Dean Cunningham ... 12	3,600	104
Columbia-Greene Comm Coll, Hudson, NY 12534	1969	Dr. Terry A. Cline ... 12	1,696	110
Columbia State Comm Coll, Columbia, TN 38401	1966	Dr. Paul Sands ... 5	3,053	95
Columbus State Comm Coll, Columbus, OH 43216	1963	Dr. Harold M. Nestor ... 5	13,194	737
Comm Coll of Allegheny County Allegheny Cmps, Pittsburgh, PA 15212	1966	Dr. J. David Griffin ... 9	7,349	1,449
Comm Coll of Allegheny County Boyce Cmps, Monroeville, PA 15146	1966	Dr. Carl A. Di Sibio ... 9	4,700	190
Comm Coll of Allegheny County Coll Ctr-North, Pittsburgh, PA 15237	1972	Dr. Fred F. Bartok ... 9	3,382	1,394
Comm Coll of Allegheny County South Cmps, West Mifflin, PA 15122	1967	Dr. Thomas A. Juravich ... 9	5,294	760
Comm Coll of Aurora, Aurora, CO 80011	1983	Larry Carter ... 5	4,370	270
Comm Coll of Beaver County, Monaca, PA 15061	1966	Margaret Williams-Betlyn ... 5	2,800	150
Comm Coll of Denver, Denver, CO 80217	1970	Dr. Byron McClenney ... 5	5,975	195
Comm Coll of Philadelphia, Philadelphia, PA 19130	1964	Dr. Ronald J. Temple ... 12	15,151	989
Comm Coll of Rhode Island, Warwick, RI 02886	1964	Edward Liston ... 5	10,530	543
Comm Coll of the Air Force, Maxwell Air Force Base, AL 36112	1972	Col. R. A. Gregory, Jr. ... 4	382,826	10,000
Comm Coll of the Finger Lakes, Canandaigua, NY 14424	1965	Dr. Charles J. Meder ... 12	3,866	240
Comm Coll of Vermont, Waterbury, VT 05676	1970	Mr. Kenneth G. Kalb ... 5	1,496	475
Compton Comm Coll, Compton, CA 90221	1927	Dr. Warren A. Washington ... 12	5,248	347
Connors State Coll, Warner, OK 74469	1908	Dr. Carl O. Westbrook ... 5	2,035	92
Contra Costa Coll, San Pablo, CA 94806	1948	Dr. D. Candy Rose ... 12	9,725	281
Cooke County Coll, Gainesville, TX 76240	1924	Dr. Luther Bud Joyner ... 9	3,084	176
Copiah-Lincoln Comm Coll, Wesson, MS 39191	1928	Dr. Billy B. Thames ... 12	1,494	116
Corning Comm Coll, Corning, NY 14830	1956	Dr. Donald H. Hangen ... 12	3,077	135
Cosumnes River Coll, Sacramento, CA 95823	1970	Dr. Marc E. Hall ... 10	9,624	419
County Coll of Morris, Randolph, NJ 07869	1966	Dr. Edward J. Yaw ... 9	10,063	730
Cowley County Comm Coll and Voc-Tech Sch, Arkansas City, KS 67005	1922	Dr. Patrick J. McAtee ... 12	2,504	184
Crafton Hills Coll, Yucaipa, CA 92399	1972	Dr. Luis S. Gomez ... 12	5,240	232
Craven Comm Coll, New Bern, NC 28560	1965	Lewis S. Redd ... 5	2,193	372
Culinary Inst of America, Hyde Park, NY 12538-1499	1946	Mr. Ferdinand E. Metz ... 1	1,845	100
Cumberland County Coll, Vineland, NJ 08360	1963	Dr. Roland J. Chapdelaine ... 12	2,482	107
Cuyahoga Comm Coll, Eastern Cmps, Highland Hills Village, OH 44122	1971	Dr. Grace Carolyn Brown ... 12	5,764	225
Cuyahoga Comm Coll, Metropolitan Cmps, Cleveland, OH 44115	1963	Dr. Ronald R. Zambetti ... 12	6,268	474
Cuyahoga Comm Coll, Western Cmps, Parma, OH 44130	1966	Mr. John McNulty ... 12	11,884	552
Cypress Coll, Cypress, CA 90630	1966	Dr. Kirk Avery ... 12	14,792	434
Dabney S Lancaster Comm Coll, Clifton Forge, VA 24422	1964	Dr. John F. Backels ... 5	1,639	NR
Dalton Coll, Dalton, GA 30720	1963	Dr. Derrell C. Roberts ... 5	2,503	61
Danville Area Comm Coll, Danville, IL 61832	1946	Dr. Harry J. Braun ... 12	3,330	143
Danville Comm Coll, Danville, VA 24541	1967	Dr. Arnold R. Oliver ... 5	3,500	141
Darton Coll, Albany, GA 31707	1965	Dr. Peter J. Sireno ... 5	2,141	84
Davenport Coll of Business, Kalamazoo Cmps, Kalamazoo, MI 49007 (4)	1866	C. Dexter Rohm ... 1	1,548	104
Davidson County Comm Coll, Lexington, NC 27293	1958	Dr. J. Bryan Brooks ... 12	2,641	153
Daytona Beach Comm Coll, Daytona Beach, FL 32115	1958	Dr. Philip R. Day, Jr. ... 5	10,104	714
Dean Jr Coll, Franklin, MA 02038	1865	Mr. Frank B. Bruno ... 1	1,125	102
De Anza Coll, Cupertino, CA 95014	1967	Dr. A. Robert Dehart ... 12	26,269	977
DeKalb Coll, Decatur, GA 30034	1964	Dr. Marvin M. Cole ... 5	13,948	446
Delaware County Comm Coll, Media, PA 19063	1967	Dr. Richard D. De Cosmo ... 12	9,193	636
Delaware Tech & Comm Coll, Southern Cmps, Georgetown, DE 19947	1967	Mr. Jack F. Owens ... 5	2,989	160
Delaware Tech & Comm Coll, Stanton/Wilmington Cmps, Newark, DE 19702	1968	Dr. Orlando J. George, Jr. ... 5	5,983	342
Delaware Tech & Comm Coll, Terry Cmps, Dover, DE 19901	1972	Dr. Linda C. Jolly ... 5	1,856	104
Delgado Comm Coll, New Orleans, LA 70119	1921	Dr. James Caillier ... 5	9,100	484
Del Mar Coll, Corpus Christi, TX 78404	1935	Mr. B. R. Venters ... 12	10,538	480
Delta Coll, University Center, MI 48710	1961	Mr. Donald J. Carlyon ... 10	11,055	447
Des Moines Area Comm Coll, Ankeny, IA 50021	1966	Dr. Joseph Borgen ... 12	10,553	219
Diablo Valley Coll, Pleasant Hill, CA 94523	1949	Dr. Phyllis L. Peterson ... 12	23,000	800
Dixie Coll, St George, UT 84770	1911	Dr. Douglas Alder ... 5	2,528	107
Dodge City Comm Coll, Dodge City, KS 67801	1935	Dr. Thomas E. Gamble ... 12	2,428	84
Dundalk Comm Coll, Baltimore, MD 21222	1970	Dr. Martha A. Smith ... 9	3,410	205
Durham Tech Comm Coll, Durham, NC 27703	1961	Dr. Phail Wynn, Jr. ... 5	5,188	271

Name, address	Year	Governing official, control	Enrollment	Faculty
Dutchess Comm Coll, Poughkeepsie, NY 12601	1957	Dr. Jerry Lee 12	7,076	370
Dyersburg State Comm Coll, Dyersburg, TN 38025	1969	Dr. Karen A. Bowyer 5	1,374	132
East Central Coll, Union, MO 63084	1968	Dr. Dale Gibson 10	2,915	134
East Central Comm Coll, Decatur, MS 39327	1928	Dr. Eddie M. Smith 12	1,370	56
Eastern Arizona Coll, Thatcher, AZ 85552	1888	Mr. Gherald L. Hoopes, Jr. . . .12	3,367	230
Eastern New Mexico U–Roswell, Roswell, NM 88202	1958	Dr. Loyd R. Hughes 12	1,895	128
Eastern Oklahoma State Coll, Wilburton, OK 74578	1907	NR 12	2,623	89
Eastern Wyoming Coll, Torrington, WY 82240	1948	Dr. Roy Mason 12	1,740	53
Eastfield Coll, Mesquite, TX 75150	1970	Dr. Justus D. Sundermann . . .12	9,279	399
East Los Angeles Coll, Monterey Park, CA 91754	1945	Dr. Omero Suarez 12	14,587	450
Edgecombe Comm Coll, Tarboro, NC 27886	1968	Mr. Charles B. McIntyre 12	1,702	168
Edison Comm Coll, Fort Myers, FL 33906-6210	1962	Dr. Kenneth Walker 12	8,907	357
Edison State Comm Coll, Piqua, OH 45356	1973	Dr. Kenneth A. Yowell 5	3,416	160
Edmonds Comm Coll, Lynnwood, WA 98036	1967	Mr. Thomas C. Nielsen 12	5,738	285
El Camino Coll, Torrance, CA 90506	1947	Dr. Sam Schauerman 10	27,161	483
El Centro Coll, Dallas, TX 75202	1966	Dr. Wright L. Lassiter, Jr. . . .9	5,649	315
Elgin Comm Coll, Elgin, IL 60123	1949	Dr. Paul Heath 12	8,515	400
El Paso Comm Coll, El Paso, TX 79998	1969	Mr. Richard M. Rhodes 9	17,158	1,734
El Reno Jr Coll, El Reno, OK 73036	1938	Dr. Larry F. Devane 5	1,196	87
Enterprise State Jr Coll, Enterprise, AL 36331	1965	Dr. Joseph D. Talmadge 5	2,195	126
Erie Comm Coll, City Cmps, Buffalo, NY 14203	1971	Dr. Louis M. Ricci 12	3,681	190
Erie Comm Coll, North Cmps, Williamsville, NY 14221	1946	Dr. Louis M. Ricci 12	6,603	319
Erie Comm Coll, South Cmps, Orchard Park, NY 14127	1974	Dr. Louis M. Ricci 12	3,518	238
Essex Comm Coll, Baltimore, MD 21237	1957	Dr. Donald J. Slowinski 12	11,022	532
Essex County Coll, Newark, NJ 07102	1966	Dr. Zachary Yamba 9	6,710	269
Eugenio Maria de Hostos Comm Coll of City U of NY, Bronx, NY 10451	1968	Dr. I. Santiago 12	4,277	279
Everett Comm Coll, Everett, WA 98201	1941	Mr. Robert Drewel 5	3,175	231
Evergreen Valley Coll, San Jose, CA 95135	1975	NR 12	11,849	314
Fashion Inst of Design & Merchandising, LA Cmps, Los Angeles, CA 90015	1969	Ms. Tonian Hohberg 3	3,000	152
Fayetteville Tech Comm Coll, Fayetteville, NC 28303	1961	Dr. Craig Allen 12	5,600	396
Feather River Comm Coll District, Quincy, CA 95971	1968	Dr. Donald Donato 12	1,348	83
Fergus Falls Comm Coll, Fergus Falls, MN 56537	1960	Mr. Dan F. True 5	1,300	89
Fiorello H LaGuardia Comm Coll of City U of NY, Long Island City, NY 11101	1971	Raymond C. Bowen 12	9,170	633
Flathead Valley Comm Coll, Kalispell, MT 59901	1967	Dr. Howard L. Fryett 12	1,824	133
Florence-Darlington Tech Coll, Florence, SC 29501	1963	Dr. Michael B. McCall 5	2,324	201
Florida Comm Coll at Jacksonville, Jacksonville, FL 32202	1963	Dr. Charles C. Spence 5	18,415	1,458
Floyd Coll, Rome, GA 30162	1970	Dr. David B. McCorkle 5	2,019	66
Foothill Coll, Los Altos Hills, CA 94022	1958	Dr. Thomas H. Clements . . .12	21,800	500
Forsyth Tech Comm Coll, Winston-Salem, NC 27103	1964	Dr. Bob H. Greene 5	4,923	591
Fort Scott Comm Coll, Fort Scott, KS 66701	1919	NR 12	2,078	131
Fox Valley Tech Coll, Appleton, WI 54913	1967	Dr. Stanley J. Spanbauer . . .12	4,810	1,241
Frederick Comm Coll, Frederick, MD 21702	1957	Dr. Lee J. Betts 12	4,002	267
Fresno City Coll, Fresno, CA 93741	1910	Dr. Ernest R. Leach 12	17,943	835
Front Range Comm Coll, Westminster, CO 80030	1968	Dr. Cary Israel 5	9,746	450
Fullerton Coll, Fullerton, CA 92632	1913	Dr. Philip W. Borst 12	19,953	678
Fulton-Montgomery Comm Coll, Johnstown, NY 12095	1964	Mr. John G. Boshart 12	1,745	122
Gadsden State Comm Coll, Gadsden, AL 35902-0227	1965	Dr. Victor Ficker 5	5,426	237
Gainesville Coll, Gainesville, GA 30503	1964	Dr. J. Foster Watkins 12	2,489	106
Galveston Coll, Galveston, TX 77550	1967	John E. Pickelman 12	2,115	122
Garden City Comm Coll, Garden City, KS 67846	1919	Dr. James H. Tangeman 10	2,021	100
Garland County Comm Coll, Hot Springs, AR 71913	1973	NR 12	1,980	111
Gaston Coll, Dallas, NC 28034	1963	Dr. W. Wayne Scott 12	3,730	274
Gateway Tech Coll, Kenosha, WI 53144	1911	Dr. John R. Birkholz 12	7,844	755
Gavilan Coll, Gilroy, CA 95020	1919	Dr. John J. Holleman 12	4,029	185
Genesee Comm Coll, Batavia, NY 14020	1966	Dr. Stuart Steiner 12	3,414	212
George Corley Wallace State Comm Coll, Selma, AL 36702	1966	Dr. Julius Ray Brown 5	1,676	72
Georgia Military Coll, Milledgeville, GA 31061	1879	Maj. Gen. William Acker . . .12	1,918	160
Germanna Comm Coll, Locust Grove, VA 22508	1970	Dr. Francis S. Turnage 5	2,500	83
Glendale Comm Coll, Glendale, AZ 85302	1965	Dr. John R. Waltrip 12	18,240	590
Glendale Comm Coll, Glendale, CA 91208	1927	Dr. John A. Davitt 12	14,972	330
Glen Oaks Comm Coll, Centreville, MI 49032	1965	Dr. Philip G. Ward 12	1,467	81
Gloucester County Coll, Sewell, NJ 08080	1967	Dr. Richard N. Jones 12	4,373	188
Gogebic Comm Coll, Ironwood, MI 49938	1932	Dr. James R. Grote 12	1,340	89
Golden West Coll, Huntington Beach, CA 92647	1966	Ms. Judith Valles 12	13,442	459
Gordon Coll, Barnesville, GA 30204	1852	Dr. Jerry M. Williamson 5	1,483	85
Grand Rapids Comm Coll, Grand Rapids, MI 49503	1914	Mr. Richard Calkins 11	12,061	337
Grays Harbor Coll, Aberdeen, WA 98520	1930	Dr. Jewell Manspeaker 5	1,520	115
Greater Hartford Comm Coll, Hartford, CT 06105	1967	Dr. Conrad L. Mallett 5	3,065	185
Great Lakes Jr Coll of Business, Saginaw, MI 48607	1907	Angelo Guerriero 1	2,131	133
Greenfield Comm Coll, Greenfield, MA 01301	1962	Dr. Katherine H. Sloan 5	1,751	112
Greenville Tech Coll, Greenville, SC 29606	1962	Dr. Thomas E. Barton, Jr. 5	8,211	517
Grossmont Coll, El Cajon, CA 92020	1961	Dr. Richard M. Sanchez 12	17,241	640
Guilford Tech Comm Coll, Jamestown, NC 27282	1958	Mr. Don Cameron 12	7,550	539
Gulf Coast Comm Coll, Panama City, FL 32401	1957	Dr. Robert L. McSpadden 5	6,593	290
Hagerstown Jr Coll, Hagerstown, MD 21742-6590	1946	Dr. Norman P. Shea 9	3,353	183
Harford Comm Coll, Bel Air, MD 21014	1957	Dr. Richard J. Pappas 12	5,105	249
Harrisburg Area Comm Coll, Harrisburg, PA 17110	1964	Dr. Kenneth B. Woodbury, Jr. .12	9,667	424
Hartnell Coll, Salinas, CA 93901	1920	Dr. James R. Hardt 10	7,469	272
Hawkeye Inst of Tech, Waterloo, IA 50704	1967	Dr. John E. Hawse 12	1,820	151
Haywood Comm Coll, Clyde, NC 28721	1964	Dr. Dan W. Moore 12	1,284	86
Herkimer County Comm Coll, Herkimer, NY 13350	1966	Dr. Ronald F. Williams 12	2,400	110
Hesser Coll, Manchester, NH 03103	1900	Linwood W. Galeucia 3	2,200	60
Hibbing Comm Coll, Hibbing, MN 55746	1916	Dr. Anthony Kuznik 5	1,115	65
Highland Comm Coll, Freeport, IL 61032	1966	NR 10	3,258	169
Highland Comm Coll, Highland, KS 66035	1858	Dr. Eric M. Priest 12	1,744	162
Highline Comm Coll, Des Moines, WA 98198	1961	Dr. Edward M. Command 5	10,300	432
Hill Coll of the Hill Jr Coll District, Hillsboro, TX 76645	1923	Dr. W. R. Auvenshine 10	1,634	80
Hillsborough Comm Coll, Tampa, FL 33631-3127	1968	Dr. Andreas A. Paloumpis 5	18,079	575
Hinds Comm Coll, Raymond, MS 39154	1917	NR 12	8,762	656
Holmes Comm Coll, Goodman, MS 39079	1928	NR 12	2,073	125

Name, address	Year	Governing official, control	Enrollment	Faculty
Holyoke Comm Coll, Holyoke, MA 01040	1946	Dr. David M. Bartley 5	5,321	311
Horry-Georgetown Tech Coll, Conway, SC 29526	1965	Dr. D. Kent Sharples 12	1,659	113
Housatonic Comm Coll, Bridgeport, CT 06608	1966	Dr. Vincent S. Darnowski 5	2,485	98
Houston Comm Coll System, Houston, TX 77270	1971	Dr. Charles Green 12	36,437	1,349
Howard Coll, Big Spring, TX 79720	1945	Dr. Bob E. Riley 12	2,301	158
Howard Comm Coll, Columbia, MD 21044	1966	Dr. Dwight A. Burrill 12	4,777	285
Hudson County Comm Coll, Jersey City, NJ 07306	1974	Dr. Narcisa A. Polonio 12	2,708	170
Hudson Valley Comm Coll, Troy, NY 12180	1953	Dr. Joseph J. Bulmer 12	9,668	461
Hutchinson Comm Coll, Hutchinson, KS 67501	1928	Dr. Edward E. Berger 12	3,888	264
ICS Ctr for Degree Studies, Scranton, PA 18515	1975	Mr. Gary Keisling 3	28,090	5
Illinois Central Coll, East Peoria, IL 61635	1967	Dr. Thomas K. Thomas 12	13,218	576
Illinois Eastern Comm Colls, Frontier Comm Coll, Fairfield, IL 62837	1976	Richard Mason 12	2,387	139
Illinois Eastern Comm Colls, Olney Central Coll, Olney, IL 62450	1960	John E. Ravekes 12	1,606	86
Illinois Eastern Comm Colls, Wabash Valley Coll, Mount Carmel, IL 62863	1960	Dr. Harry K. Benson 12	3,609	80
Illinois Valley Comm Coll, Oglesby, IL 61348	1924	Dr. Alfred E. Wisgoski 10	4,502	NR
Imperial Valley Coll, Imperial, CA 92251-2663	1922	Dr. John A. DePaoli 12	4,971	224
Independence Comm Coll, Independence, KS 67301	1925	Dr. Jo Ann C. McDowell 10	1,605	153
Indiana Business Coll, Indianapolis, IN 46204	1902	Kenneth J. Konesco 3	1,700	NR
Indiana Vocational Tech Coll–Central Indiana, Indianapolis, IN 46206	1963	Dr. Meredith L. Carter 5	4,905	282
Indiana Vocational Tech Coll–Columbus, Columbus, IN 47203	1963	NR 5	2,523	146
Indiana Vocational Tech Coll–Eastcentral, Muncie, IN 47302	1968	NR 5	1,732	135
Indiana Vocational Tech Coll–Kokomo, Kokomo, IN 46901	1968	Dr. Ken Martin 5	1,466	105
Indiana Vocational Tech Coll–Lafayette, Lafayette, IN 47903	1968	Dr. Elizabeth J. Doversberger .5	1,628	118
Indiana Vocational Tech Coll–Northcentral, South Bend, IN 46619	1968	Dr. Carl F. Lutz 5	2,954	188
Indiana Vocational Tech Coll–Northeast, Fort Wayne, IN 46805	1969	Mr. Jon L. Rupright 5	3,304	196
Indiana Vocational Tech Coll–Northwest, Gary, IN 46409	1963	Mrs. Della Burt-Bradley 5	2,278	172
Indiana Vocational Tech Coll–Southcentral, Sellersburg, IN 47172	1968	Jonathan W. Thomas 5	1,719	107
Indiana Vocational Tech Coll–Southwest, Evansville, IN 47710	1963	Dr. H. Victor Baldi 5	2,292	156
Indiana Vocational Tech Coll–Wabash Valley, Terre Haute, IN 47802	1966	Mr. Sam E. Borden 5	2,080	128
Indiana Vocational Tech Coll–Whitewater, Richmond, IN 47374	1963	Dr. Judith A. Redwine 5	1,069	86
Indian Hills Comm Coll, Ottumwa, IA 52501	1966	Dr. Lyle A. Hellyer 12	3,003	139
Indian River Comm Coll, Fort Pierce, FL 34981	1960	Dr. Edwin R. Massey 5	12,774	786
Inver Hills Comm Coll, Inver Grove Heights, MN 55076	1969	Dr. Patrick A. Roche 5	5,207	236
Iona Coll–Sch of Associate Degree Studies, Yonkers, NY 10701	1940	Eileen Panetta 1	1,403	185
Iowa Central Comm Coll, Fort Dodge, IA 50501	1966	Dr. Jack L. Bottenfield 12	2,500	155
Iowa Lakes Comm Coll, Estherville, IA 51334	1967	Mr. Richard H. Blacker 12	1,574	40
Iowa Western Comm Coll, Council Bluffs, IA 51502	1966	Dr. Carl L. Heinrich 10	2,982	166
Irvine Valley Coll, Irvine, CA 92720	1979	Dr. Anna L. McFarlin 12	8,398	223
Isothermal Comm Coll, Spindale, NC 28160	1965	Dr. Willard L. Lewis 5	1,483	92
Itasca Comm Coll, Grand Rapids, MN 55744	1922	Dr. Lawrence N. Dukes 5	1,423	75
Itawamba Comm Coll, Fulton, MS 38843	1947	Dr. W. O. Benjamin 5	3,500	102
Jackson Comm Coll, Jackson, MI 49201	1928	Dr. Clyde LeTarte 9	7,000	440
Jackson State Comm Coll, Jackson, TN 38301	1967	Dr. Walter L. Nelms 5	3,252	163
James H Faulkner State Jr Coll, Bay Minette, AL 36507	1965	Dr. Gary L. Branch 5	3,109	151
Jamestown Comm Coll, Jamestown, NY 14701	1950	Dr. Timothy G. Davies 12	5,020	277
Jefferson Coll, Hillsboro, MO 63050	1963	Dr. Gery Hochanadel 12	4,013	163
Jefferson Comm Coll, Watertown, NY 13601	1961	Mr. John T. Henderson 12	2,100	180
Jefferson Davis State Jr Coll, Brewton, AL 36427	1965	Sandra K. McLeod 5	1,046	44
Jefferson State Comm Coll, Birmingham, AL 35215	1965	Dr. Judy M. Merritt 5	7,313	354
Jefferson Tech Coll, Steubenville, OH 43952	1966	Dr. Edward L. Florak 12	1,630	98
John A Logan Coll, Carterville, IL 62918	1967	Dr. Ray Hancock 12	4,364	223
John C Calhoun State Comm Coll, Decatur, AL 35609	1965	Dr. Jackson N. Sasser 5	7,833	378
Johnson County Comm Coll, Overland Park, KS 66210	1967	Dr. Charles J. Carlsen 12	13,744	632
Johnston Comm Coll, Smithfield, NC 27577	1969	Dr. John L. Tart 12	2,413	142
John Tyler Comm Coll, Chester, VA 23831	1967	Dr. Marshall W. Smith 12	5,343	215
John Wood Comm Coll, Quincy, IL 62301	1974	Dr. Robert C. Keys 10	4,005	143
Jones County Jr Coll, Ellisville, MS 39437	1928	Dr. T. Terrell Tisdale 12	4,126	153
Jordan Coll, Cedar Springs, MI 49319	1967	Lexie K. Coxon 2	2,322	191
J Sargeant Reynolds Comm Coll, Richmond, VA 23261	1972	Dr. S. A. Burnette 5	2,220	484
Kalamazoo Valley Comm Coll, Kalamazoo, MI 49009	1966	Dr. Marilyn J. Schlack 12	10,495	366
Kansas City Kansas Comm Coll, Kansas City, KS 66112	1923	Dr. Bill Spencer 9	5,016	284
Kaskaskia Coll, Centralia, IL 62801	1966	Mr. Raymond D. Woods 12	3,127	192
Kellogg Comm Coll, Battle Creek, MI 49017	1956	Dr. Paul R. Ohm 12	5,870	254
Kennebec Valley Tech Coll, Fairfield, ME 04937	1970	Barbara Woodlee 5	1,080	NR
Kent State U, Stark Cmps, Canton, OH 44720	1967	Dr. William G. Bittle 5	2,274	111
Kent State U, Trumbull Cmps, Warren, OH 44483	1954	David A. Allen, Jr. 5	1,704	89
Kent State U, Tuscarawas Cmps, New Philadelphia, OH 44663	1962	Harold D. Shade 5	1,261	84
Keystone Jr Coll, La Plume, PA 18440	1868	Dr. Robert E. Mooney, Jr. 1	1,244	113
Kilgore Coll, Kilgore, TX 75662	1935	NR 12	4,466	210
Kingsborough Comm Coll of City U of NY, Brooklyn, NY 11235	1963	Dr. Leon M. Goldstein 12	8,703	649
Kings River Comm Coll, Reedley, CA 93654	1926	Mr. Richard J. Giese 12	5,105	221
Kirkwood Comm Coll, Cedar Rapids, IA 52406	1966	Dr. Norm Nielsen 12	8,625	434
Kirtland Comm Coll, Roscommon, MI 48653	1966	Dorothy N. Franke 10	1,271	76
Labette Comm Coll, Parsons, KS 67357	1923	Dr. Joseph H. Roberts 12	2,465	261
Lake City Comm Coll, Lake City, FL 32055	1962	Dr. Muriel Kay Heimer 5	2,290	197
Lake Land Coll, Mattoon, IL 61938	1966	Dr. Robert K. Luther 12	4,437	264
Lakeland Comm Coll, Mentor, OH 44060	1967	Dr. Ralph R. Doty 12	8,807	427
Lake Michigan Coll, Benton Harbor, MI 49022	1946	Dr. Anne E. Mulder 10	3,422	240
Lakeshore Tech Coll, Cleveland, WI 53015	1967	Dr. Dennis Ladwig 12	2,749	344
Lake-Sumter Comm Coll, Leesburg, FL 34788	1961	Dr. Carl C. Andersen 12	2,380	97

Name, address	Year	Governing official, control	Enrollment	Faculty
Lake Tahoe Comm Coll, South Lake Tahoe, CA 95702	1975	Dr. Guy F. Lease 12	2,400	96
Lakewood Comm Coll, White Bear Lake, MN 55110	1967	Dr. Jerry Owens 5	6,217	165
Lamar U–Orange, Orange, TX 77630	1969	Dr. Steve Maradian 5	1,300	63
Lamar U–Port Arthur, Port Arthur, TX 77641	1909	Dr. Sam Monroe 5	2,053	98
Lane Comm Coll, Eugene, OR 97405	1964	Dr. Jerry Moskus 12	8,559	397
Laney Coll, Oakland, CA 94607	1953	Mr. Odell Johnson 5	11,208	379
Lansing Comm Coll, Lansing, MI 48901	1957	Dr. Abel B. Sykes, Jr. 12	23,390	1,000
Laramie County Comm Coll, Cheyenne, WY 82007	1968	Dr. Ed Boenisch 9	4,301	213
Laredo Jr Coll, Laredo, TX 78040	1946	Dr. Roger L. Worsley 12	5,123	297
Lassen Coll, Susanville, CA 96130	1925	Dr. Larry J. Blake 12	2,808	300
Lawson State Comm Coll, Birmingham, AL 35221	1965	Dr. Perry W. Ward 5	1,738	54
Lee Coll, Baytown, TX 77520-4796	1934	Dr. Vivian Bowling Blevins . 10	5,039	231
Lehigh County Comm Coll, Schnecksville, PA 18078	1967	Dr. Robert L. Barthlow 12	4,177	155
Lenoir Comm Coll, Kinston, NC 28502	1960	Dr. Lonnie H. Blizzard 5	2,250	159
Lewis and Clark Comm Coll, Godfrey, IL 62035	1970	Dr. J. Neil Admire 10	5,886	307
Lincoln Land Comm Coll, Springfield, IL 62794	1967	Dr. William D. Law, Jr. 10	7,877	401
Linn-Benton Comm Coll, Albany, OR 97321	1966	Mr. Jon Carnahan 12	13,151	462
Long Beach City Coll, Long Beach, CA 90808	1927	Dr. Beverly O'Neill 5	27,632	850
Longview Comm Coll, Lee's Summit, MO 64081	1969	Mr. Aldo W. Leker 12	9,625	457
Lorain County Comm Coll, Elyria, OH 44035	1963	Dr. Roy Church 12	6,616	330
Lord Fairfax Comm Coll, Middletown, VA 22645	1969	Dr. Marilyn C. Beck 12	2,599	120
Los Angeles City Coll, Los Angeles, CA 90029	1929	Dr. Edwin A. Young 10	16,374	614
Los Angeles Harbor Coll, Wilmington, CA 90744	1949	Mr. James L. Heinselman . . 12	8,908	350
Los Angeles Mission Coll, San Fernando, CA 91340	1974	Mr. Lowell J. Erickson 12	5,767	115
Los Angeles Pierce Coll, Woodland Hills, CA 91371	1947	Mr. Daniel Means 12	18,522	521
Los Angeles Southwest Coll, Los Angeles, CA 90047	1967	Dr. Thomas G. Lakin 12	6,100	228
Los Angeles Trade-Tech Coll, Los Angeles, CA 90015	1925	Mr. Thomas Stevens 12	12,940	250
Los Angeles Valley Coll, Van Nuys, CA 91401	1949	Dr. Mary E. Lee 12	19,838	311
Los Medanos Coll, Pittsburg, CA 94565	1974	Mr. Stanley H. Chin 10	7,369	225
Louisiana State U at Alexandria, Alexandria, LA 71302	1960	Dr. Ben F. Martin 5	2,404	88
Louisiana State U at Eunice, Eunice, LA 70535	1967	Dr. Michael Smith 5	2,284	85
Lurleen B Wallace State Jr Coll, Andalusia, AL 36420	1969	Mr. Seth Hammett 5	1,161	39
Luzerne County Comm Coll, Nanticoke, PA 18634	1966	Donald R. Bronsard 9	6,575	249
Macon Coll, Macon, GA 31297	1968	Dr. S. Aaron Hyatt 5	4,211	126
Madison Area Tech Coll, Madison, WI 53704	1911	Dr. Beverly S. Simone 10	12,411	1,950
Manatee Comm Coll, Bradenton, FL 34206	1957	Dr. Stephen J. Korcheck . . . 5	7,961	316
Manchester Comm Coll, Manchester, CT 06040	1963	Dr. Jonathan M. Daube 5	6,493	200
Maple Woods Comm Coll, Kansas City, MO 64156	1969	Dr. Stephen R. Brainard . . . 12	4,753	199
Marion Tech Coll, Marion, OH 43302-5694	1971	Dr. John Richard Bryson . . . 13	1,561	105
Marshalltown Comm Coll, Marshalltown, IA 50158	1927	Dr. William Simpson 10	1,415	93
Marymount Coll, Palos Verdes, California, Rancho Palos Verdes, CA 90274-6299	1932	Dr. Thomas D. Wood 2	1,076	91
Massachusetts Bay Comm Coll, Wellesley Hills, MA 02181	1961	Mr. Roger A. Van Winkle . . . 5	4,664	171
Massasoit Comm Coll, Brockton, MA 02402	1968	Dr. Gerard F. Burke 5	6,675	427
Mattatuck Comm Coll, Waterbury, CT 06708	1967	Dr. Richard L. Sanders 5	4,270	114
McHenry County Coll, Crystal Lake, IL 60012	1967	Mr. Robert C. Bartlett 12	3,768	165
McLennan Comm Coll, Waco, TX 76708	1965	Dr. Dennis F. Michaelis 9	5,630	230
Mendocino Coll, Ukiah, CA 95482	1973	Dr. Carl J. Ehmann 12	4,550	165
Merced Coll, Merced, CA 95348	1962	Dr. Tom K. Harris, Jr. 12	7,422	368
Mercer County Comm Coll, Trenton, NJ 08690	1966	Mr. John P. Hanley 12	7,005	354
Meridian Comm Coll, Meridian, MS 39307	1937	Dr. William F. Scaggs 12	2,952	236
Merritt Coll, Oakland, CA 94619	1953	Mr. Donald Hongisto 12	6,683	NR
Mesabi Comm Coll, Virginia, MN 55792	1918	Richard Kohlase 1	1,046	50
Mesa Comm Coll, Mesa, AZ 85202	1965	Dr. Larry K. Christiansen . . . 12	20,774	525
Metropolitan Comm Coll, Omaha, NE 68103	1974	Dr. J. Richard Gilliland 12	8,520	369
Miami-Dade Comm Coll, Miami, FL 33132	1960	Dr. Robert H. McCabe 12	52,063	2,112
Miami U–Hamilton Cmps, Hamilton, OH 45011	1968	Dr. Harriet V. Taylor 5	2,149	160
Miami U–Middletown Cmps, Middletown, OH 45042	1966	Dr. Michael P. Governanti . . 5	2,041	165
Middle Georgia Coll, Cochran, GA 31014	1884	Dr. Joe Ben Welch 5	1,540	81
Middlesex Comm Coll, Middletown, CT 06457	1966	Dr. Leila Gonzalez Sullivan . . 5	3,230	130
Middlesex Comm Coll, Bedford, MA 01730	1970	Dr. Carole A. Cowan 5	3,524	195
Middlesex County Coll, Edison, NJ 08818	1964	Dr. Flora M. Edwards 9	11,218	329
Midland Coll, Midland, TX 79705	1969	Dr. Jess H. Parrish 12	3,789	192
Midlands Tech Coll, Columbia, SC 29202	1974	Dr. James L. Hudgins 12	7,546	615
Mid Michigan Comm Coll, Harrison, MI 48625	1965	Dr. Eugene F. Schorzmann . . 12	1,925	199
Mid-Plains Comm Coll, North Platte, NE 69101	1965	Mr. Kenneth L. Aten 10	1,947	87
Mid-State Tech Coll, Wisconsin Rapids, WI 54494	1917	Dr. M. H. Schneeberg 10	2,219	86
Milwaukee Area Tech Coll, Milwaukee, WI 53233	1912	Dr. Barbara D. Holmes 10	21,900	1,604
Mineral Area Coll, Flat River, MO 63601	1922	Dr. Dixie A. Kohn 10	2,694	75
Minneapolis Comm Coll, Minneapolis, MN 55403	1965	Dr. Jacquelyn Belcher 5	4,064	175
MiraCosta Coll, Oceanside, CA 92056	1934	Dr. H. Deon Holt 10	9,951	460
Mission Coll, Santa Clara, CA 95054	1977	Dr. Betty M. Dean 5	11,557	315
Mississippi County Comm Coll, Blytheville, AR 72316-1109	1975	Dr. John P. Sullins 5	1,700	128
Mississippi Delta Comm Coll, Moorhead, MS 38761	1926	Dr. David W. Powe 10	2,122	128
Mississippi Gulf Coast Comm Coll, Perkinston, MS 39573	1911	Dr. Bobby S. Garvin 10	9,526	527
Mitchell Comm Coll, Statesville, NC 28677	1852	Dr. Douglas O. Eason 5	1,553	81
Moberly Area Comm Coll, Moberly, MO 65270	1927	Dr. Andrew Komar, Jr. 12	1,500	79
Modesto Jr Coll, Modesto, CA 95350	1921	Dr. Stanley L. Hodges 12	8,164	454
Mohave Comm Coll, Kingman, AZ 86401	1971	Dr. Charles W. Hall 5	5,059	294
Mohawk Valley Comm Coll, Utica, NY 13501	1946	Dr. Michael I. Schafer 12	6,500	343
Monroe Coll, Bronx, NY 10468	1933	Stephen J. Jerome 3	2,400	100
Monroe Comm Coll, Rochester, NY 14623	1961	Dr. Peter A. Spina 9	13,548	660
Monroe County Comm Coll, Monroe, MI 48161	1964	Mr. Gerald D. Welch 9	3,383	162
Montcalm Comm Coll, Sidney, MI 48885	1965	Dr. Donald C. Burns 12	2,040	112
Monterey Peninsula Coll, Monterey, CA 93940-4799	1947	Dr. David W. Hopkins, Jr. . . 5	8,500	235
Montgomery Coll–Germantown Cmps, Germantown, MD 20874	1975	Dr. Robert E. Parilla 12	3,436	130
Montgomery County Comm Coll, Blue Bell, PA 19422	1964	Dr. Edward M. Sweitzer . . . 9	8,172	410
Moorpark Coll, Moorpark, CA 93021	1967	Dr. Stanley L. Bowers 9	12,403	475
Moraine Park Tech Coll, Fond du Lac, WI 54936	1967	Dr. John J. Shanahan 12	5,513	284
Moraine Valley Comm Coll, Palos Hills, IL 60465	1967	Dr. Vernon O. Crawley 12	13,601	565
Morton Coll, Cicero, IL 60650	1924	Mr. Charles P. Ferro 12	4,603	239
Motlow State Comm Coll, Tullahoma, TN 37388	1969	Dr. A. Frank Glass 5	2,788	245
Mountain Empire Comm Coll, Big Stone Gap, VA 24219	1972	Dr. Ruth Mercedes Smith . . 5	2,900	133
Mountain View Coll, Dallas, TX 75211-6599	1970	Dr. William H. Jordan 9	6,027	224
Mt Hood Comm Coll, Gresham, OR 97030	1966	Dr. Paul Kreider 12	7,961	501
Mount Ida Coll, Newton Centre, MA 02159	1899	Dr. Bryan E. Carlson 1	1,800	140

Name, address	Year	Governing official, control	Enrollment	Faculty
Mt San Antonio Coll, Walnut, CA 91789	1946	Dr. John D. Randall ...10	22,676	925
Mt San Jacinto Coll, San Jacinto, CA 92383	1963	Dr. Richard H. Lowe ...12	6,100	181
Mount Wachusett Comm Coll, Gardner, MA 01440	1963	Daniel M. Asquino ...5	2,200	112
Murray State Coll, Tishomingo, OK 73460	1908	Dr. Clyde R. Kindell ...5	1,472	NR
Muscatine Comm Coll, Muscatine, IA 52761	1929	Dr. Victor G. McAvoy ...5	1,179	68
Muskegon Comm Coll, Muskegon, MI 49442	1926	Dr. James L. Stevenson ...12	5,009	150
Muskingum Area Tech Coll, Zanesville, OH 43701	1969	Dr. Lynn H. Willett ...12	2,400	104
Napa Valley Coll, Napa, CA 94558	1942	Dr. William H. Feddersen ...12	6,991	307
Nash Comm Coll, Rocky Mount, NC 27804	1967	Dr. J. Reid Parrott, Jr. ...5	1,578	92
Nashville State Tech Inst, Nashville, TN 37209	1970	Dr. Richard M. Turner, III ...5	5,974	320
Nassau Comm Coll, Garden City, NY 11530	1959	Dr. Sean A. Fanelli ...12	17,252	1,241
National Ed Ctr-Bauder Coll Cmps, Fort Lauderdale, FL 33334	1964	Mr. Dale Oakley ...3	1,000	41
National Ed Ctr-Brown Inst Cmps, Minneapolis, MN 55407	1946	Ralph H. Vieau ...3	1,400	65
National Ed Ctr-Spartan Sch of Aeronautics Cmps, Tulsa, OK 74158-2833 (2)	1928	Frank D. Iacobucci ...3	2,971	150
National Ed Ctr-Tampa Tech Inst Cmps, Tampa, FL 33610	1948	Mark W. Johnson ...3	1,036	34
National Sch of Tech, Inc, North Miami Beach, FL 33162	1977	NR ...3	1,100	30
Navajo Comm Coll, Tsaile, AZ 86556	1968	Mr. Laurence Gishey ...4	1,611	142
Navarro Coll, Corsicana, TX 75110	1946	Dr. Gerald Burson ...12	2,827	163
Neosho County Comm Coll, Chanute, KS 66720	1936	George H. VanAllen ...12	1,600	117
New Comm Coll of Baltimore, Baltimore, MD 21215	1947	Dr. Joseph T. Durham ...5	5,300	493
New England Banking Inst, Boston, MA 02111	1909	NR ...1	1,532	230
New Hampshire Tech Inst, Concord, NH 03302	1964	Dr. David E. Larrabee, Sr. ...5	1,261	114
New Mexico Jr Coll, Hobbs, NM 88240	1965	Dr. Charles D. Hays ...12	2,438	96
New Mexico State U-Alamogordo, Alamogordo, NM 88310	1958	Dr. Charles R. Reidlinger ...5	1,759	122
New Mexico State U-Carlsbad, Carlsbad, NM 88220	1950	Dr. Shelton W. Marlow ...5	1,077	74
New Orleans Baptist Theological Sem, New Orleans, LA 70126	1917	Dr. Landrum P. Leavell, II ...2	1,571	8
New River Comm Coll, Dublin, VA 24084	1969	Dr. Floyd M. Hogue ...5	2,224	186
New York City Tech Coll of City U of NY, Brooklyn, NY 11201	1946	Dr. Charles W. Merideth ...12	10,904	1,074
Niagara County Comm Coll, Sanborn, NY 14132	1962	Gerald L. Miller ...12	5,399	319
Nicolet Area Tech Coll, Rhinelander, WI 54501	1968	Dr. Patricia A. Travis ...12	1,250	64
Normandale Comm Coll, Bloomington, MN 55431	1968	Dr. Thomas J. Horak ...12	8,851	300
Northampton County Area Comm Coll, Bethlehem, PA 18017	1967	Dr. Robert J. Kopecek ...12	5,535	361
North Arkansas Comm Coll, Harrison, AR 72601	1974	Dr. Bill Baker ...12	1,171	75
North Central Michigan Coll, Petoskey, MI 49770	1958	Robert B. Graham ...9	1,776	93
North Central Tech Coll, Mansfield, OH 44901	1961	Dr. Byron E. Kee ...12	2,275	155
Northcentral Tech Coll, Wausau, WI 54401	1912	Dr. Donald Hagen ...10	4,453	211
North Country Comm Coll, Saranac Lake, NY 12983	1967	David W. Petty ...12	1,575	145
North Dakota State Coll of Science, Wahpeton, ND 58076	1903	Dr. Jerry Olson ...5	2,116	165
Northeast Alabama State Jr Coll, Rainsville, AL 35986	1963	Dr. Charles M. Pendley ...5	1,360	47
Northeast Comm Coll, Norfolk, NE 68702	1973	Dr. Robert P. Cox ...12	2,815	122
Northeastern Jr Coll, Sterling, CO 80751	1941	Dr. Henry M. Milander ...12	2,040	79
Northeastern Oklahoma A&M Coll, Miami, OK 74354	1919	Dr. Bobby R. Wright ...5	2,600	133
Northeast Iowa Comm Coll, Peosta Cmps, Peosta, IA 52068	1970	Karla Berns ...12	1,197	66
Northeast Mississippi Comm Coll, Booneville, MS 38829	1948	Joe M. Childers ...10	3,041	NR
Northeast State Tech Comm Coll, Blountville, TN 37617	1966	Dr. R. Wade Powers ...5	2,787	166
Northeast Texas Comm Coll, Mount Pleasant, TX 75455	1985	Michael C. Bruner ...12	1,782	88
Northeast Wisconsin Tech Coll, Green Bay, WI 54307	1913	Dr. Gerald D. Prindiville ...12	6,429	196
Northern Essex Comm Coll, Haverhill, MA 01830	1960	Dr. John R. Dimitry ...12	6,482	425
Northern Nevada Comm Coll, Elko, NV 89801	1967	Dr. Ronald K. Remington ...5	2,500	176
Northern New Mexico Comm Coll, Española, NM 87532	1909	Connie A. Valdez ...5	1,625	116
Northern Virginia Comm Coll, Annandale, VA 22003	1965	Dr. Richard J. Ernst ...5	35,831	1,291
North Florida Jr Coll, Madison, FL 32340	1958	Dr. William H. McCoy ...5	1,063	29
North Harris County Coll District, Houston, TX 77060	1972	Dr. John E. Pickelman ...12	15,822	713
North Hennepin Comm Coll, Minneapolis, MN 55445	1966	Dr. Frederick W. Capshaw ...5	6,163	212
North Idaho Coll, Coeur d'Alene, ID 83814	1933	Dr. Carl R. Bennett ...12	2,960	185
North Iowa Area Comm Coll, Mason City, IA 50401	1918	Dr. David Buettner ...12	2,771	88
North Lake Coll, Irving, TX 75038	1977	Dr. James F. Horton, Jr. ...9	6,552	270
Northland Pioneer Coll, Holbrook, AZ 86025	1974	Dr. John H. Anderson ...12	5,644	400
North Seattle Comm Coll, Seattle, WA 98103	1970	Arthur Binnie ...5	8,768	232
North Shore Comm Coll, Beverly, MA 01915	1965	Dr. George Traicoff ...5	3,236	200
Northwest Alabama Comm Coll, Phil Campbell, AL 35581	1961	Dr. Charles W. Britnell ...5	1,949	83
Northwest Coll, Powell, WY 82435	1946	NR ...12	2,048	169
Northwestern Coll, Lima, OH 45805	1920	Mr. Loren R. Jarvis ...3	1,216	64
Northwestern Connecticut Comm Coll, Winsted, CT 06098	1965	Dr. Booker T. DeVaughn ...5	2,204	78
Northwestern Michigan Coll, Traverse City, MI 49684	1951	Dr. Timothy G. Quinn ...12	4,394	234
Northwest Tech Coll, Archbold, OH 43502	1968	Dr. James O. Miller ...5	2,104	102
Norwalk Comm Coll, Norwalk, CT 06854	1961	Dr. William H. Schwab ...5	3,698	135
Oakland Comm Coll, Bloomfield Hills, MI 48013	1964	Dr. Patsy J. Fulton ...12	28,298	583
Oakton Comm Coll, Des Plaines, IL 60016	1969	Dr. Thomas TenHoeve ...10	10,794	495
Odessa Coll, Odessa, TX 79764	1946	Dr. Philip T. Speegle ...12	4,800	225
Ohio U-Ironton, Ironton, OH 45638	1956	Mr. Bill Dingus ...5	1,785	105
Ohlone Coll, Fremont, CA 94539	1967	Dr. Peter Blomerley ...12	8,851	434
Okaloosa-Walton Comm Coll, Niceville, FL 32578	1963	Dr. James R. Richburg ...12	5,618	353
Oklahoma State U Tech Branch, Oklahoma City, Oklahoma City, OK 73107	1961	Dr. James Hooper ...5	4,236	206
Oklahoma State U, Tech Branch, Okmulgee, Okmulgee, OK 74447	1946	Dr. Robert Klabenes ...5	2,109	137
Olympic Coll, Bremerton, WA 98310	1946	Dr. Wallace A. Simpson ...5	6,732	417
Onondaga Comm Coll, Syracuse, NY 13215	1962	Dr. Bruce H. Leslie ...12	8,000	400
Orangeburg-Calhoun Tech Coll, Orangeburg, SC 29115	1968	Dr. M. Rudolph Groomes ...5	1,506	120
Orange Coast Coll, Costa Mesa, CA 92628-5005	1947	Mr. David A. Grant ...12	24,468	868
Orange County Comm Coll, Middletown, NY 10940	1950	Dr. William F. Messner ...12	5,735	323
Owens Tech Coll, Toledo, OH 43699	1966	Daniel H. Brown ...5	6,857	370
Owens Tech Coll, Findlay Cmps, Findlay, OH 45840	1983	Kathleen Brubaker ...5	1,035	NR
Oxnard Coll, Oxnard, CA 93033	1975	Dr. Elise D. Schneider ...9	6,920	288
Palm Beach Comm Coll, Lake Worth, FL 33461	1933	Dr. Edward M. Eissey ...5	14,688	650
Palomar Coll, San Marcos, CA 92069	1946	Dr. George R. Boggs ...12	25,500	802
Palo Verde Coll, Blythe, CA 92225	1947	Dr. Wilford J. Beumel ...12	1,079	60
Panola Coll, Carthage, TX 75633	1947	Dr. Gary McDaniel ...12	1,457	61

Name, address	Year	Governing official, control	Enrollment	Faculty
Paris Jr Coll, Paris, TX 75460	1924	Mr. Bobby R. Walters	12	2,326	117
Parkland Coll, Champaign, IL 61821	1967	Dr. Zelema M. Harris	10	8,570	457
Parks Jr Coll, Denver, CO 80229	1895	Linda S. Bowman	3	1,087	73
Pasadena City Coll, Pasadena, CA 91106	1924	Dr. Jack A. Scott	10	21,242	924
Pasco-Hernando Comm Coll, Dade City, FL 33525	1972	Dr. Milton O. Jones	5	5,224	203
Passaic County Comm Coll, Paterson, NJ 07509	1968	Mr. Elliott Collins	9	3,274	249
Patrick Henry Comm Coll, Martinsville, VA 24115	1962	NR		1,086	88
Patrick Henry State Jr Coll, Monroeville, AL 36460	1965	Dr. John A. Johnson	5	1,160	71
Paul D Camp Comm Coll, Franklin, VA 23851	1971	Dr. Edwin L. Barnes	5	1,563	65
Pearl River Comm Coll, Poplarville, MS 39470	1909	Dr. Ted J. Alexander	12	2,741	150
Peirce Jr Coll, Philadelphia, PA 19102	1865	Dr. Raymond C. Lewin	1	1,133	64
Pellissippi State Tech Comm Coll, Knoxville, TN 37933	1974	Mr. J. L. Goins	6	6,000	289
Peninsula Coll, Port Angeles, WA 98362	1961	Dr. Paul G. Cornaby	5	1,177	133
Pennsylvania Coll of Tech, Williamsport, PA 17701	1965	Dr. Robert Breuder	12	4,383	349
Penn State U Altoona Cmps, Altoona, PA 16601	1929	Dr. James A. Duplass	13	2,509	129
Penn State U Beaver Cmps, Monaca, PA 15061	1964	David B. Otto	13	1,030	58
Penn State U Berks Cmps, Reading, PA 19610	1924	Dr. Frederick H. Gaige	13	1,665	89
Penn State U Delaware County Cmps, Media, PA 19063	1966	Edward S. J. Tomezsko	13	1,811	108
Penn State U DuBois Cmps, DuBois, PA 15801	1935	Dr. Donald T. Hartman	13	1,045	64
Penn State U Hazelton Cmps, Hazelton, PA 18201	1934	Dr. James J. Staudenmeier	13	1,308	70
Penn State U McKeesport Cmps, McKeesport, PA 15132	1947	Dr. Cash J. Kowalski	13	1,343	82
Penn State U New Kensington Cmps, New Kensington, PA 15068	1958	Dr. Robert D. Arbuckle	13	1,144	75
Penn State U Ogontz Cmps, Abington, PA 19001	1950	Dr. Anthony Fusaro	13	3,207	174
Penn State U Schuylkill Cmps, Schuylkill Haven, PA 17972	1934	Dr. Wayne Lammie	13	1,139	60
Penn State U Shenango Cmps, Sharon, PA 16146	1965	Mr. James Elder	13	1,192	84
Penn State U Worthington Scranton Cmps, Dunmore, PA 18512	1923	Dr. James D. Gallagher	13	1,364	82
Penn State U York Cmps, York, PA 17403	1926	Dr. John J. Romano	13	1,920	105
Penn Valley Comm Coll, Kansas City, MO 64111	1969	Dr. Wayne E. Giles	10	5,778	356
Pensacola Jr Coll, Pensacola, FL 32504	1948	Dr. Horace E. Hartsell	5	12,503	950
Phillips County Comm Coll, Helena, AR 72342	1965	Dr. Steven Jones	12	1,467	107
Phillips Jr Coll, Condie Cmps, Campbell, CA 95008	1968	Leslie E. Pritchard	3	1,000	45
Phoenix Coll, Phoenix, AZ 85013	1920	Ms. Myrna Harrison	12	12,930	770
Piedmont Comm Coll, Roxboro, NC 27573	1970	Dr. H. James Owen	5	1,072	56
Piedmont Tech Coll, Greenwood, SC 29648	1966	Dr. Lex D. Walters	5	2,144	127
Piedmont Virginia Comm Coll, Charlottesville, VA 22901	1972	Dr. Deborah M. DiCroce	5	4,249	262
Pierce Coll, Tacoma, WA 98498	1967	Dr. Frank Brouillet	5	9,050	429
Pikes Peak Comm Coll, Colorado Springs, CO 80906	1969	Dr. Marijane Axtell Paulsen	5	6,128	513
Pima Comm Coll, Tucson, AZ 85702	1966	Dr. Johnas F. Hockaday	5	28,766	1,509
Pitt Comm Coll, Greenville, NC 27835	1961	Dr. Charles E. Russell	12	4,276	221
Pittsburgh Inst of Aeronautics, Pittsburgh, PA 15236-0897 (2)	1929	Ivan D. Livi	1	1,012	56
Polk Comm Coll, Winter Haven, FL 33881	1964	Dr. Maryly VanLeer Peck	5	6,700	260
Porterville Coll, Porterville, CA 93257	1927	Dr. Paul D. Alcantra	5	2,823	130
Portland Comm Coll, Portland, OR 97219	1961	Dr. Daniel F. Moriarty	12	24,000	1,215
Potomac State Coll of West Virginia U, Keyser, WV 26726	1901	Dr. Joseph M. Gratto	5	1,348	83
Prairie State Coll, Chicago Heights, IL 60411	1958	Dr. W. Harold Garner	12	5,127	253
Prince George's Comm Coll, Largo, MD 20772	1958	Dr. Robert I. Bickford	9	13,087	600
Queensborough Comm Coll of City U of NY, Bayside, NY 11364	1958	Dr. Kurt R. Schmeller	12	12,185	628
Quincy Coll, Quincy, MA 02169	1958	Dr. O. Clayton Johnson	11	1,821	69
Quinebaug Valley Comm Coll, Danielson, CT 06239	1971	Dr. Robert E. Miller	5	1,270	59
Quinsigamond Comm Coll, Worcester, MA 01606	1963	Dr. Clifford S. Peterson	5	2,777	215
Rancho Santiago Coll, Santa Ana, CA 92706	1915	Dr. Robert D. Jensen	5	23,681	1,178
Randolph Comm Coll, Asheboro, NC 27204	1962	Dr. Larry K. Linker	5	1,427	80
Rappahannock Comm Coll, Glenns, VA 23149	1970	Dr. John H. Upton	12	1,952	131
Raritan Valley Comm Coll, Somerville, NJ 08876	1965	Dr. S. Charles Irace	9	5,388	276
Reading Area Comm Coll, Reading, PA 19603	1971	Dr. Gust Zogas	10	2,337	146
Red Rocks Comm Coll, Lakewood, CO 80401	1969	Ms. Dorothy A. Horrell	5	6,300	276
Rend Lake Coll, Ina, IL 62846	1967	Dr. Jonathan Astroth	5	4,322	201
Richard Bland Coll of the Coll of William and Mary, Petersburg, VA 23805	1961	Dr. Clarence Maze, Jr.	5	1,205	49
Richland Coll, Dallas, TX 75243	1972	Dr. Stephen Mittelstet	12	12,771	665
Richland Comm Coll, Decatur, IL 62521	1971	Dr. Charles R. Novak	10	3,801	185
Richmond Comm Coll, Hamlet, NC 28345	1964	Joseph W. Grimsley	5	1,002	100
Ricks Coll, Rexburg, ID 83460	1888	Dr. Steven D. Bennion	2	7,795	359
Rio Hondo Coll, Whittier, CA 90608	1960	Dr. Alex A. Sanchez	12	20,000	710
Rio Salado Comm Coll, Phoenix, AZ 85003	1978	Dr. Linda Thor	12	12,000	663
Riverside Comm Coll, Riverside, CA 92506	1916	Dr. Charles A. Kane	12	20,500	480
Roane State Comm Coll, Harriman, TN 37748	1971	Dr. Sherry L. Hoppe	5	4,928	264
Robert Morris Coll, Chicago Cmps, Chicago, IL 60601	1965	Richard D. Pickett	1	1,627	87
Robeson Comm Coll, Lumberton, NC 28359	1965	Fred W. Williams, Jr.	5	1,450	96
Rochester Comm Coll, Rochester, MN 55904	1915	Dr. Geraldine A. Evans	5	4,156	186
Rockingham Comm Coll, Wentworth, NC 27375	1964	Dr. N. J. Owens, Jr.	5	1,817	111
Rockland Comm Coll, Suffern, NY 10901	1959	Dr. F. Thomas Clark	12	8,023	710
Rock Valley Coll, Rockford, IL 61111	1964	Dr. Karl J. Jacobs	10	8,078	214
Rogers State Coll, Claremore, OK 74017-2099	1909	Dr. Richard H. Mosier	5	3,700	190
Rogue Comm Coll, Grants Pass, OR 97527	1970	Dr. Harvey Bennett	12	4,000	329
Rowan-Cabarrus Comm Coll, Salisbury, NC 28145	1963	Dr. Richard L. Brownell	5	3,062	130
Sacramento City Coll, Sacramento, CA 95822	1916	Dr. Robert M. Harris	12	17,229	420
Saddleback Coll, Mission Viejo, CA 92692	1967	Constance M. Carroll	12	22,230	645
Saint Augustine Coll, Chicago, IL 60640	1980	Fr. Carlos A. Plazas	1	1,455	126
Saint Charles County Comm Coll, St Charles, MO 63301	1986	Donald D. Shook	5	3,515	167
St Clair County Comm Coll, Port Huron, MI 48061	1923	Dr. R. Ernest Dear	9	4,528	252
St Johns River Comm Coll, Palatka, FL 32177	1958	Dr. R. L. McLendon, Jr.	5	3,282	143
St Louis Comm Coll at Florissant Valley, St Louis, MO 63135-1499	1963	Dr. Michael T. Murphy	10	10,619	402
St Louis Comm Coll at Forest Park, St Louis, MO 63110	1962	Dr. Vernon O. Crawley	10	7,142	81
St Louis Comm Coll at Meramec, Kirkwood, MO 63122	1963	Dr. Gwendolyn W. Stephenson	10	14,588	577
St Paul Tech Coll, St Paul, MN 55102	1922	Dr. Donovan Schwichtenberg	12	2,027	565
St Petersburg Jr Coll, St Petersburg, FL 33733	1927	Dr. Carl M. Kuttler, Jr.	12	18,719	543
St Philip's Coll, San Antonio, TX 78203	1898	Dr. Stephen R. Mitchell	10	5,556	347
Salem Comm Coll, Carneys Point, NJ 08069	1971	Dr. William Wenzel	9	1,356	75

Name, address	Year	Governing official, control	Enrollment	Faculty
Salt Lake Comm Coll, Salt Lake City, UT 84130	1948	Dr. Frank W. Budd 5	13,344	826
San Antonio Coll, San Antonio, TX 78212	1925	Dr. Max Castillo 12	20,653	854
Sandhills Comm Coll, Pinehurst, NC 28374	1963	Dr. John Dempsey 12	2,301	126
San Diego City Coll, San Diego, CA 92101	1914	Dr. Jeanne L. Atherton ...12	14,172	NR
San Diego Mesa Coll, San Diego, CA 92111	1962	Dr. Allen Brooks 10	27,000	766
San Diego Miramar Coll, San Diego, CA 92126	1969	Dr. Jerome Hunter 12	7,764	200
San Jacinto Coll-North Cmps, Houston, TX 77049	1974	Dr. Edwin E. Lehr 12	3,778	163
San Jacinto Coll-South Cmps, Houston, TX 77089	1979	Dr. Parker Williams 12	5,068	213
San Joaquin Delta Coll, Stockton, CA 95207	1935	Dr. L. H. Horton, Jr. 10	18,531	579
San Jose City Coll, San Jose, CA 95128	1921	Dr. Byron R. Skinner 10	11,102	416
San Juan Coll, Farmington, NM 87401	1958	Dr. James C. Henderson ...9	3,098	165
Santa Barbara City Coll, Santa Barbara, CA 93109	1908	Dr. Peter R. MacDougall ...10	11,741	481
Santa Fe Comm Coll, Gainesville, FL 32602	1966	Dr. Larry W. Tyree 12	10,261	539
Santa Fe Comm Coll, Santa Fe, NM 87502	1983	William C. Witter 12	2,964	198
Santa Monica Coll, Santa Monica, CA 90405	1929	Dr. Richard L. Moore 12	26,064	638
Santa Rosa Jr Coll, Santa Rosa, CA 95401	1918	Dr. Robert F. Agrella 12	28,464	NR
Sauk Valley Comm Coll, Dixon, IL 61021	1965	Dr. Richard L. Behrendt ...10	2,569	185
Schenectady County Comm Coll, Schenectady, NY 12305	1968	Dr. Peter F. Burnham 12	3,318	239
Schoolcraft Coll, Livonia, MI 48152	1961	Dr. Richard W. McDowell ...10	9,172	418
Scott Comm Coll, Bettendorf, IA 52722	1966	Lenny E. Stone 12	3,200	180
Scottsdale Comm Coll, Scottsdale, AZ 85250	1969	Dr. Arthur W. Decabooter ..12	9,347	380
Seattle Central Comm Coll, Seattle, WA 98122	1966	Dr. Charles H. Mitchell ...5	8,500	380
Seminole Comm Coll, Sanford, FL 32773	1966	Dr. Earl S. Weldon 12	6,404	512
Seminole Jr Coll, Seminole, OK 74868	1931	James J. Cook 5	1,493	80
Seward County Comm Coll, Liberal, KS 67905	1969	Donald E. Guild 12	1,800	147
Shasta Coll, Redding, CA 96049	1948	Dr. Margaret L. Dominici ..12	12,820	397
Shawnee Comm Coll, Ullin, IL 62992	1967	NR 12	2,500	111
Shelby State Comm Coll, Memphis, TN 38174	1972	Dr. Lawrence M. Cox 5	3,665	252
Shelton State Comm Coll, Tuscaloosa, AL 35405	1979	Dr. Tom Umphrey 5	3,435	NR
Sheridan Coll, Sheridan, WY 82801	1948	Dr. Stephen Maier 12	2,141	74
Shoreline Comm Coll, Seattle, WA 98133	1964	Dr. Ronald E. Bell 5	7,498	253
Sierra Coll, Rocklin, CA 95677	1936	Dr. Gerald C. Angove 5	13,774	507
Sinclair Comm Coll, Dayton, OH 45402	1887	Dr. David H. Ponitz 12	18,938	892
Skagit Valley Coll, Mount Vernon, WA 98273	1926	Dr. James M. Ford 5	2,823	319
Skyline Coll, San Bruno, CA 94066	1969	Ms. Linda Graef Salter 9	9,451	268
Snead State Jr Coll, Boaz, AL 35957	1935	Dr. William H. Osborn 5	1,691	66
Solano Comm Coll, Suisun City, CA 94585	1945	Dr. Virginia L. Holton 9	12,000	432
South Central Comm Coll, New Haven, CT 06511	1968	Dr. Antonio Perez 12	4,017	186
Southeast Comm Coll, Lincoln Cmps, Lincoln, NE 68520	1973	NR 10	4,409	568
Southeastern Comm Coll, Whiteville, NC 28472	1964	Dr. Stephen C. Scott 5	1,562	145
Southeastern Comm Coll, North Cmps, West Burlington, IA 52655	1968	Dr. R. Gene Gardner 12	2,018	94
Southeastern Illinois Coll, Harrisburg, IL 62946	1960	Dr. Harry W. Abell 5	3,445	163
Southern Maine Tech Coll, South Portland, ME 04106	1946	Dr. Wayne H. Ross 5	1,174	148
Southern State Comm Coll, Hillsboro, OH 45133	1975	Dr. George R. McCormick ...5	1,560	117
Southern U, Shreveport–Bossier City Cmps, Shreveport, LA 71107	1964	Dr. Robert H. Smith 5	1,020	75
Southern West Virginia Comm Coll, Logan, WV 25601	1971	Dr. Harry J. Boyer 5	2,950	127
South Florida Comm Coll, Avon Park, FL 33825	1965	Dr. Catherine P. Cornelius ..5	1,500	112
South Georgia Coll, Douglas, GA 31533-5098	1906	Dr. Edward D. Jackson, Jr. ..5	1,107	50
South Mountain Comm Coll, Phoenix, AZ 85040	1979	Raul Cardenas 12	3,288	124
South Plains Coll, Levelland, TX 79336	1958	Dr. Marvin L. Baker 12	5,137	321
South Puget Sound Comm Coll, Olympia, WA 98502	1970	Dr. Kenneth Minnaert 5	4,620	191
South Seattle Comm Coll, Seattle, WA 98106	1970	Mr. Jerry M. Brockey 5	6,700	234
Southside Virginia Comm Coll, Alberta, VA 23821	1970	Dr. John J. Cavan 5	1,399	167
Southwestern Baptist Theological Sem, Fort Worth, TX 76122	1908	Dr. Russell H. Dilday 2	3,740	183
Southwestern Coll, Chula Vista, CA 92010	1961	Joseph M. Conte 12	15,855	619
Southwestern Comm Coll, Creston, IA 50801	1966	Richard L. Byerly 5	1,136	65
Southwestern Michigan Coll, Dowagiac, MI 49047	1964	Mr. David C. Briegel 5	3,300	182
Southwestern Oregon Comm Coll, Coos Bay, OR 97420	1961	Dr. Stephen J. Kridelbaugh ..7	3,723	204
Southwest Mississippi Comm Coll, Summit, MS 39666	1918	NR 10	1,520	89
Southwest Texas Jr Coll, Uvalde, TX 78801	1946	Mr. Billy Word 12	2,658	149
Southwest Virginia Comm Coll, Richlands, VA 24641	1968	Dr. Charles R. King 5	7,293	273
Southwest Wisconsin Tech Coll, Fennimore, WI 53809	1967	Dr. Richard A. Rogers 12	1,273	117
Spartanburg Methodist Coll, Spartanburg, SC 29301	1911	Dr. George D. Fields 2	1,100	76
Spartanburg Tech Coll, Spartanburg, SC 29305	1961	Dr. Jack A. Powers 5	2,276	NR
Spokane Comm Coll, Spokane, WA 99207	1963	Dr. Joseph Rich 5	6,331	680
Spokane Falls Comm Coll, Spokane, WA 99204	1967	Dr. Vern Loland 5	5,813	646
Spoon River Coll, Canton, IL 61520	1959	Felix T. Haynes 5	2,300	133
Springfield Tech Comm Coll, Springfield, MA 01105	1967	Andrew M. Scibelli 5	3,424	202
Stanly Comm Coll, Albemarle, NC 28001	1971	Dr. Jan J. Crawford 5	1,301	76
Stark Tech Coll, Canton, OH 44720	1970	Dr. John J. McGrath 12	3,997	188
State Comm Coll of East St Louis, East St Louis, IL 62201	1969	Dr. Richard M. Bonner 5	1,236	83
State Fair Comm Coll, Sedalia, MO 65301	1966	Dr. Marvin Fielding 10	2,369	98
State Tech Inst at Memphis, Memphis, TN 38134	1967	Dr. Charles Temple 5	8,768	550
State U of NY Coll of A&T at Cobleskill, Cobleskill, NY 12043	1916	Dr. Neal V. Robbins 5	2,630	164
State U of NY Coll of A&T at Morrisville, Morrisville, NY 13408	1908	Dr. Frederick W. Woodward ..5	3,289	171
State U of NY Coll of Tech at Alfred, Alfred, NY 14802	1908	Dr. John O. Hunter 5	3,724	206
State U of NY Coll of Tech at Canton, Canton, NY 13617	1906	Dr. Earl W. MacArthur 5	2,662	124
State U of NY Coll of Tech at Delhi, Delhi, NY 13753	1913	Mr. Seldon M. Kruger 5	2,374	135
State U of NY Coll of Tech at Farmingdale, Farmingdale, NY 11735	1912	Dr. Frank A. Cipriani 5	11,106	530
Suffolk County Comm Coll-Ammerman Cmps, Selden, NY 11784	1962	Dr. John F. Cooper 12	11,857	471
Suffolk County Comm Coll-Eastern Cmps, Riverhead, NY 11901	1977	Steven T. Kenny 12	2,361	120
Suffolk County Comm Coll-Western Cmps, Brentwood, NY 11717	1974	Salvatore J. LaLima 12	5,039	275
Sullivan Coll, Louisville, KY 40232	1864	A. R. Sullivan 3	1,713	64
Sullivan County Comm Coll, Loch Sheldrake, NY 12759-4002	1962	Dr. John F. Walter 12	2,093	167
Sumter Area Tech Coll, Sumter, SC 29150	1963	Dr. Herbert C. Robbins 5	1,925	120
Surry Comm Coll, Dobson, NC 27017	1965	Dr. Swanson Richards 5	3,036	94
Tacoma Comm Coll, Tacoma, WA 98465	1965	Dr. Raymond Needham 5	4,603	292

Name, address	Year	Governing official, control	Enrollment	Faculty
Taft Coll, Taft, CA 93268	1922	Dr. David Cothrun 12	1,000	65
Tallahassee Comm Coll, Tallahassee, FL 32304	1966	Dr. James H. Hinson, Jr. 12	9,451	376
Tarrant County Jr Coll, Fort Worth, TX 76102	1967	Mr. C. A. Roberson 9	27,999	966
Tech Coll of the Lowcountry, Beaufort, SC 29902	1972	Dr. Anne S. McNutt 5	1,210	66
Temple Coll, Temple, TX 76504-7435	1926	Dr. Marvin R. Felder 10	2,352	118
Terra Tech Coll, Fremont, OH 43420-9670	1968	Dr. Richard M. Simon 5	2,397	148
Texarkana Coll, Texarkana, TX 75501	1927	Dr. Carl M. Nelson 12	3,894	185
Texas State Tech Inst–Harlingen Cmps, Harlingen, TX 78550-3697	1967	Dr. J. Gilbert Leal 5	2,889	182
Texas State Tech Inst–Waco Cmps, Waco, TX 76705	1965	Mr. Don E. Goodwin 5	3,803	362
Thomas Nelson Comm Coll, Hampton, VA 23670	1968	Dr. Robert G. Templin, Jr. 5	7,740	318
Three Rivers Comm Coll, Poplar Bluff, MO 63901	1966	Dr. Stephen M. Poort 5	2,062	67
Tidewater Comm Coll, Chesapeake Cmps, Chesapeake, VA 23320	1968	NR 5	2,633	120
Tidewater Comm Coll, Portsmouth Cmps, Portsmouth, VA 23703	1968	NR 5	3,836	175
Tidewater Comm Coll, Virginia Beach Cmps, Virginia Beach, VA 23456	1968	NR 5	11,257	440
Tompkins Cortland Comm Coll, Dryden, NY 13053	1968	Dr. Eduardo J. Marti 12	2,786	161
Treasure Valley Comm Coll, Ontario, OR 97914	1962	Dr. Glenn Mayle 12	2,559	121
Tri-County Tech Coll, Pendleton, SC 29670	1962	Dr. Don C. Garrison 5	2,935	NR
Trident Tech Coll, Charleston, SC 29411	1964	Dr. Charles W. Branch 12	6,939	375
Trinidad State Jr Coll, Trinidad, CO 81082	1925	Dr. Thomas E. Sullivan 5	1,714	100
Trinity Valley Comm Coll, Athens, TX 75751	1946	Mr. Ron Baugh 12	3,933	196
Triton Coll, River Grove, IL 60171	1964	Dr. Michael J. Bakalis 5	13,102	1,454
Truckee Meadows Comm Coll, Reno, NV 89512	1971	Dr. John Gwaltney 5	9,742	496
Tulsa Jr Coll, Tulsa, OK 74135	1968	Dr. Dean P. Van Trease 5	19,763	700
Tunxis Comm Coll, Farmington, CT 06032	1969	Ms. Marilyn Menack 5	2,592	184
Tyler Jr Coll, Tyler, TX 75711	1926	Dr. Raymond M. Hawkins 12	7,984	364
Ulster County Comm Coll, Stone Ridge, NY 12484	1962	Mr. Robert T. Brown 12	2,927	198
Umpqua Comm Coll, Roseburg, OR 97470	1964	Dr. James Kraby 12	1,931	120
Union County Coll, Cranford, NJ 07016	1933	Dr. Thomas H. Brown 12	9,981	421
U of Alaska Anchorage, Kenai Peninsula Coll, Soldotna, AK 99669	1964	Ginger Steffy 5	1,630	65
U of Alaska Anchorage, Matanuska-Susitna Coll, Palmer, AK 99645	1958	Mr. Glenn F. Massay 5	1,565	96
U of Alaska Southeast, Sitka Cmps, Sitka, AK 99835	1962	Mr. Richard M. Griffin 5	1,800	60
U of Cincinnati Clermont Coll, Batavia, OH 45103	1972	Dr. Roger J. Barry 5	1,463	107
U of Cincinnati Raymond Walters Coll, Cincinnati, OH 45236	1967	Dr. Neal A. Raisman 5	4,300	195
U of Hawaii–Honolulu Comm Coll, Honolulu, HI 96817	1920	Dr. Peter R. Kessinger 5	4,497	238
U of Hawaii–Kapiolani Comm Coll, Honolulu, HI 96816	1946	Dr. John F. Morton 5	6,399	239
U of Hawaii–Kauai Comm Coll, Lihue, HI 96766	1965	Mr. David Iha 5	1,413	129
U of Hawaii–Leeward Comm Coll, Pearl City, HI 96782	1968	Dr. Barbara B. Polk 5	5,805	264
U of Hawaii–Maui Comm Coll, Kahului, HI 96732	1967	Dr. Clyde Sakamoto 5	2,280	147
U of Hawaii–Windward Comm Coll, Kaneohe, HI 96744	1972	Dr. Peter T. Dyer 5	1,604	80
U of Kentucky, Ashland Comm Coll, Ashland, KY 41101	1937	Dr. Anthony Newberry 5	3,061	104
U of Kentucky, Elizabethtown Comm Coll, Elizabethtown, KY 42701	1964	Dr. Charles E. Stebbins 5	3,364	120
U of Kentucky, Hazard Comm Coll, Hazard, KY 41701	1968	Dr. G. Edward Hughes 5	1,318	76
U of Kentucky, Henderson Comm Coll, Henderson, KY 42420	1963	Dr. Patrick R. Lake 5	1,394	76
U of Kentucky, Hopkinsville Comm Coll, Hopkinsville, KY 42241-2100	1965	Dr. Thomas L. Riley 5	2,000	113
U of Kentucky, Jefferson Comm Coll, Louisville, KY 40202	1968	Dr. Ronald J. Horvath 5	7,599	365
U of Kentucky, Lexington Comm Coll, Lexington, KY 40506	1965	Dr. Allen G. Edwards 5	4,523	265
U of Kentucky, Madisonville Comm Coll, Madisonville, KY 42431	1968	Dr. Arthur D. Stumpf 5	2,136	127
U of Kentucky, Maysville Comm Coll, Maysville, KY 41056	1967	Dr. James C. Shires 5	1,043	77
U of Kentucky, Owensboro Comm Coll, Owensboro, KY 42303	1986	NR 5	2,462	122
U of Kentucky, Paducah Comm Coll, Paducah, KY 42002	1932	Dr. Leonard O'Hara 5	2,798	109
U of Kentucky, Prestonsburg Comm Coll, Prestonsburg, KY 41653	1964	NR 5	2,446	100
U of Kentucky, Somerset Comm Coll, Somerset, KY 42501	1965	Dr. Rollin J. Watson 5	2,200	122
U of Kentucky, Southeast Comm Coll, Cumberland, KY 40823	1960	Dr. W. Bruce Ayers 5	2,065	97
U of Maine at Augusta, Augusta, ME 04330	1965	Dr. George P. Connick 5	4,773	196
U of Minnesota, Crookston, Crookston, MN 56716	1966	Dr. Donald G. Sargeant 5	1,336	75
U of New Mexico–Gallup Branch, Gallup, NM 87301	1968	Dr. John M. Phillips 5	2,090	117
U of New Mexico–Valencia Cmps, Los Lunas, NM 87031	1981	Dr. Ralph Sigala 5	1,169	86
U of Puerto Rico, Carolina Regional Coll, Carolina, PR 00628	1974	Dr. Andres R. Rubio 7	1,700	85
U of South Carolina at Sumter, Sumter, SC 29150	1966	Mr. J. C. Anderson, Jr. 5	1,260	79
U of Wisconsin Ctr–Fox Valley, Menasha, WI 54952	1933	Dr. Robert E. Young 5	1,501	55
U of Wisconsin Ctr–Marathon County, Wausau, WI 54401	1933	NR 5	1,226	73
U of Wisconsin Ctr–Rock County, Janesville, WI 53546	1966	Dr. Jane Crisler 5	1,025	40
U of Wisconsin Ctr–Waukesha County, Waukesha, WI 53188	1966	Dr. Mary S. Knudten 5	2,293	86
Utah Valley Comm Coll, Orem, UT 84058	1941	Dr. Kerry D. Romesburg 5	7,886	407
Valencia Comm Coll, Orlando, FL 32802	1967	Dr. Paul C. Gianini, Jr. 5	18,420	883
Vance-Granville Comm Coll, Henderson, NC 27536	1969	Dr. Ben F. Currin 5	2,316	133
Ventura Coll, Ventura, CA 93003	1925	Dr. Robert W. Long 12	12,000	541
Vernon Regional Jr Coll, Vernon, TX 76384	1972	Dr. Wade Kirk 12	1,820	112
Victoria Coll, Victoria, TX 77901	1925	Dr. Jimmy Goodson 9	3,328	120
Victor Valley Coll, Victorville, CA 92392	1960	Dr. Ruth N. Johnson 5	7,000	359
Vincennes U, Vincennes, IN 47591	1801	Dr. Phillip M. Summers 5	6,139	400
Vincennes U–Jasper Ctr, Jasper, IN 47546	1970	Dr. Gerald J. Altstadt 5	1,111	61
Virginia Highlands Comm Coll, Abingdon, VA 24210	1967	Dr. N. DeWitt Moore, Jr. 5	2,236	122
Virginia Western Comm Coll, Roanoke, VA 24038	1966	Dr. Charles L. Downs 5	7,434	202
Vista Coll, Berkeley, CA 94704	1974	Dr. Barbara Beno 12	5,100	138
Volunteer State Comm Coll, Gallatin, TN 37066	1970	Dr. Hal R. Ramer 5	4,160	258
Wake Tech Comm Coll, Raleigh, NC 27603	1958	Dr. Bruce I. Howell 12	6,150	325
Wallace State Comm Coll, Hanceville, AL 35077	1966	Dr. James C. Bailey 5	4,043	211
Walla Walla Comm Coll, Walla Walla, WA 99362	1967	Dr. Steven L. VanAusdle 5	5,355	144

Name, address	Year	Governing official, control	Enrollment	Faculty
Walters State Comm Coll, Morristown, TN 37813	1970	Dr. Jack E. Campbell	5	4,567	205
Washington State Comm Coll, Marietta, OH 45750	1971	Dr. Carson K. Miller	5	1,833	79
Washtenaw Comm Coll, Ann Arbor, MI 48106	1965	Dr. Gunder A. Myran	12	10,909	677
Waterbury State Tech Coll, Waterbury, CT 06708	1964	Mr. Charles A. Ekstrom	5	1,378	45
Waubonsee Comm Coll, Sugar Grove, IL 60554	1966	Dr. John J. Swalec	10	6,838	438
Waukesha County Tech Coll, Pewaukee, WI 53072	1923	Dr. Richard T. Anderson	12	4,700	520
Wayne Comm Coll, Goldsboro, NC 27533-8002	1957	Dr. G. Herman Porter	12	2,406	126
Wayne County Comm Coll, Detroit, MI 48226	1967	Dr. Rafael Cortada	12	11,986	417
Weatherford Coll, Weatherford, TX 76086	1869	Dr. E. W. Mince	5	2,384	93
Wenatchee Valley Coll, Wenatchee, WA 98801	1939	Dr. Arnie Heuchert	12	2,789	168
Westark Comm Coll, Fort Smith, AR 72913	1928	Mr. Joel R. Stubblefield	12	5,240	230
Westchester Business Inst, White Plains, NY 10602	1915	Ernest H. Sutkowski	3	1,000	31
Westchester Comm Coll, Valhalla, NY. 10595	1946	Dr. Joseph N. Hankin	12	10,044	536
Western Iowa Tech Comm Coll, Sioux City, IA 51102	1966	Dr. Robert H. Kiser	5	1,200	157
Western Nebraska Comm Coll–Scottsbluff Cmps, Scottsbluff, NE 69361	1926	Dr. John N. Harms	12	1,569	51
Western Nevada Comm Coll, Carson City, NV 89703	1971	Dr. Anthony D. Calabro	5	5,320	316
Western Oklahoma State Coll, Altus, OK 73521	1926	Dr. Stephen R. Hensley	5	1,930	78
Western Piedmont Comm Coll, Morganton, NC 28655	1964	Dr. Jim A. Richardson	5	2,652	132
Western Texas Coll, Snyder, TX 79549	1969	Dr. Harry L. Krenek	12	1,060	55
Western Wisconsin Tech Coll, La Crosse, WI 54602	1911	Mr. James Lee Rasch	10	3,073	172
Western Wyoming Comm Coll, Rock Springs, WY 82902	1959	Dr. T. L. Boggs	12	2,506	100
West Hills Coll, Coalinga, CA 93210	1932	Stan R. Arterberry	5	2,197	139
West Los Angeles Coll, Culver City, CA 90230	1969	Dr. Linda M. Thor	12	9,714	292
Westmoreland County Comm Coll, Youngwood, PA 15697	1970	Dr. Daniel C. Krezenski	9	5,800	352
West Shore Comm Coll, Scottville, MI 49454	1967	Dr. William M. Anderson	12	1,305	71
West Valley Coll, Saratoga, CA 95070	1963	Dr. Leo Chavez	12	14,390	560
West Virginia Northern Comm Coll, Wheeling, WV 26003	1972	Dr. Ron Hutkin	5	2,882	162
Whatcom Comm Coll, Bellingham, WA 98226	1970	Dr. Harold G. Heiner	5	1,758	104
Wilkes Comm Coll, Wilkesboro, NC 28697	1965	Dr. James R. Randolph	5	2,023	108
William Rainey Harper Coll, Palatine, IL 60067	1965	Dr. Paul N. Thompson	12	19,826	919
Willmar Comm Coll, Willmar, MN 56201	1961	Harold G. Conradi	5	1,380	78
Willmar Tech Coll, Willmar, MN 56201	1961	Ronald Erpelding	12	1,345	98
Wilson Tech Comm Coll, Wilson, NC 27893	1958	Dr. Frank L. Eagles	5	1,404	87
Wisconsin Indianhead Tech Coll, Rice Lake Cmps, Rice Lake, WI 54868	1941	Mary Ellen Filkins	10	1,153	80
Wisconsin Indianhead Tech Coll, Superior Cmps, Superior, WI 54880	1912	Mr. Reid Haglin	10	1,390	74
Wytheville Comm Coll, Wytheville, VA 24382	1967	Dr. William F. Snyder	5	1,256	137
Yakima Valley Comm Coll, Yakima, WA 98907	1928	Dr. V. Philip Tullar	5	5,739	352
Yavapai Coll, Prescott, AZ 86301	1966	Dr. Paul Walker	12	7,046	351
York Tech Coll, Rock Hill, SC 29730	1961	Mr. Dennis F. Merrell	5	2,837	215
Yuba Coll, Marysville, CA 95901	1927	Dr. Patricia L. Wirth	12	12,979	267

Tuition and College Costs 1991-92

Based on the Peterson's Guides Annual Survey of Undergraduate Institutions, the average cost of tuition, mandatory fees, and college room and board at four-year private colleges is $12,656. The average cost at four-year public colleges is $5,561 for state residents and $8,916 for nonresidents. Two-year public colleges are the least expensive group of institutions; tuition and fees average $1,125 for state residents and $3,216 for nonresidents. Tuition and fees at two-year private colleges average $4,985.

The most expensive four-year institutions, including tuition, mandatory fees, and college room and board, are Bennington College ($23,200); Sarah Lawrence College ($23,150); Barnard College ($22,766); Brandeis University ($22,695); Bard College ($22,675); Boston University ($22,510); Tulane University ($22,485); Tufts University ($22,479); New York University ($22,444); Georgetown University ($22,236). Bennington College has the highest tuition of all four-year undergraduate institutions ($19,400). The least expensive are the U.S. service academies, which are all free.

College Freshman Attitudes

According to the 25th annual survey of college freshmen, conducted by the American Council on Education and the Univ. of California at Los Angeles, student activism is on the rise. A record 39.4 percent of the freshmen said they took part in demonstrations in high school. In the late 1960s, the figure was 15 to 16 percent.

Among incoming 1990 freshmen, 18.4 percent chose a business major, a substantial decrease from the 1987 survey's total of 24.6 percent.

Commitment to "being very well off financially" declined for the second straight year, to 73.7 percent, from 75.4 percent. The decreases followed 18 consecutive years of increases, from 39.1 percent in 1970 to 75.6 percent in 1987.

An all-time high of 43 percent said it was "essential" or "very important" to "influence social values."

The survey found that 79.4 percent of the freshmen believed that racial discrimination remained a major problem. Up from a low of 27.2 percent in 1986, 38 percent of the students said it was "essential" or "very important" to help promote racial understanding.

Almost 88 percent of the incoming freshmen agreed that the federal government was not doing enough to control environmental pollution.

The survey was based on responses from 194,182 freshmen at 382 of the nation's two- and four-year colleges and universities.

College Freshmen Goals

Become wealthy	74%	Help the less fortunate	62%	Clean up the environment	34%
Raise a family	70%	Develop a philosophy of life	43%	Create artistic work	12%
Become an expert in their field	65%	Promote racial understanding	38%		

HEALTH

Ethics on Care of the Terminally Ill

A book advising terminally ill people how to commit suicide was No. 1 in the hardcover advice category on the *New York Times* Best Seller List as of Aug. 18, 1991.

The Supreme Court heard its first ever "right-to-die" case on Dec. 6, 1989. *Cruzan v. Missouri Dept. of Health* concerned Nancy Beth Cruzan, 32, who had been unconscious since Jan. 1983, after a car accident. Her parents and a guardian appointed to represent her sought to stop the medical treatment sustaining her in a "persistent vegetative state." On June 25, 1990, the Supreme Court ruled, 5-4, that a person whose wishes were clearly known had a constitutional right to refuse life-sustaining medical treatment. However, the court held that "clear and convincing" evidence as to her wishes was absent in the case of Ms. Cruzan.

As of January, 1988, hospitals are required by the Joint Commission on Accreditation of Health Care Organizations to have formal policies specifying when doctors and nurses can refrain from trying to resuscitate terminally ill patients. The policy must be developed in consultation with the medical staff and the nursing staff, adopted by the medical staff and then approved by the hospital's governing body. The policy must define the roles of physicians, nursing personnel, and members of the patient's family in any decision to withhold resuscitation. It must also include "provisions designed to assure that a patient's rights are respected."

In March 1986, the American Medical Association announced that it would be ethical for doctors to withhold "all means of life prolonging medical treatment," including food and water, from permanently unconscious patients even if death was not imminent. The withholding of such therapy should occur only when a patient's unconscious state "is beyond doubt irreversible and there are adequate safeguards to confirm the accuracy of the diagnosis," the association's judicial council said.

In June 1991, the AMA adopted 2 reports of their Council on Ethical and Judicial Affairs. The first, "Decisions Near the End of Life," concludes: "the principle of patient autonomy requires that physicians must respect the decision to forego life-sustaining treatment of a patient who possesses decisionmaking capacity." Life-sustaining treatment is defined as "any treatment that serves to prolong life without reversing the underling medical condition," and includes "mechanical ventilation, renal dialysis, chemotherapy, antibiotics and artificial nutrition and hydration." The Council also reaffirmed its position that "physicians must not perform euthanasia or participate in assisted suicide." The second report, "Decisions to Forego Life-Sustaining Treatment for Incompetent Patients," encouraged the use of advance directives (living wills and the designation of durable power of attorney) by persons to ensure that their interests will be promoted in the event that they become incompetent. When there is no advance directive designating a proxy decisionmaker, the Council concludes, the patient's family should become the surrogate decisionmaker. Family is defined as "persons with whom the patient is closely associated." Surrogate decisionmakers should consider the patient's previous values and preferences and base decisions on what the patient would have likely decided had he or she been competent. When this is not possible, decisions should be based on what would objectively be in the best interests of the patient. The Council encouraged the establishment of ethics committees designed to facilitate sound decisionmaking, whose help should be solicited when there is no available surrogate, there is a conflict among family members, or a health care provider questions the decision of a surrogate.

A number of states have "living will" statutes that set out a procedure for a mentally competent person to declare that he or she does not wish to be subjected to a "death-prolonging" procedure. Information on living wills and health-care powers of attorney can be obtained from the American Bar Association's Commission on Legal Problems of the Elderly.

Immunization Schedule for Children

Source: American Academy of Pediatrics. Report of the Committee on Infectious Diseases. 1991 Red Book

Childhood immunization means protection against eight major diseases: polio, measles, mumps, rubella (German measles), whooping cough (pertussis), diphtheria, tetanus, and Haemophilus influenzae type b (Hib) infections. Check the table and ask your pediatrician if your child is up to date on vaccines. It could save a life or prevent disability. Measles, mumps, rubella, polio, pertussis, diphtheria, Haemophilus infections and tetanus are not just harmless childhood illnesses. All of them can cripple or kill.

All are preventable. In order to be completely protected against diphtheria, tetanus and pertussis, your child needs a shot of the combination diphtheria-tetanus-pertussis (DTP) vaccine at 2, 4, 6, 15 to 18 months, and a booster prior to school entry (4-6 years). At 15 months your child should have a shot for measles, mumps and rubella (MMR). A second MMR, primarily to boost measles and mumps immunity, should be given to children 11 years or older who have not had measles. In the event of measles outbreaks in the community, this MMR booster may be given on entry to kindergarten or at an earlier age. Children in high risk populations should be tested for tuberculosis in the first year. Hib conjugate vaccine is due at 2, 4, 6 and 15 months. At 14 to 16 years a tetanus-diphtheria booster shot should be given.

If you don't have a pediatrician or family physician, call your local public health department. It usually has supplies of vaccine and may give immunizations free.

*Note: The American College of Physicians recommends that adolescents and adults consult with their physicians about further vaccinations. Those without natural infection or proper immunization against childhood diseases like measles, mumps, rubella, and polio may be at increased risk for such disease and their complications as adults; in addition, tetanus and diphtheria should be boosted periodically; and various ages, occupations, lifestyles, environmental risks, and outbreaks of disease may call for adult immunization.

	DTP	Polio	TB Test*	Measles	Mumps	Rubella	Hib/ Conjugate	Tetanus- Diphtheria
2 months	X	X					X	
4 months	X	X					X	
6 months	X						X	
12-15 mos.			X					
15 months				X	X	X	X	
15-18 months	X	X						
4-6 years	X	X						
5-21 years				X	X	X		
14-16 years								X

*Only in high-prevalence populations.

Cancer's 7 Warning Signals*

Source: American Cancer Society

1. A change in bowel or bladder habits.
2. A sore that does not heal.
3. Unusual bleeding or discharge.
4. Thickening or lump in breast or elsewhere.
5. Indigestion or difficulty in swallowing.
6. Obvious change in wart or mole.
7. Nagging cough or hoarseness.
*If you have a warning signal, see your doctor.

Cancer Prevention

Source: American Cancer Society, 1991

PRIMARY PREVENTION: steps that might be taken to avoid those factors that might lead to the development of cancer.

Smoking

Cigarette smoking is responsible for 85% of lung cancer cases among men, 75% among women—about 83% overall. Smoking accounts for about 30% of all cancer deaths. Those who smoke two or more packs of cigarettes a day have lung cancer mortality rates 15-25 times greater than nonsmokers.

Nutrition

Risk for colon, breast and uterine cancers increases in obese people. High-fat diets may contribute to the development of cancers of the breast, colon and prostate. High-fiber foods may help reduce risk of colon cancer. A varied diet containing plenty of vegetables and fruits rich in vitamins A and C may reduce risk for a wide range of cancers. Salt-cured, smoked and nitrite-cured foods have been linked to esophageal and stomach cancer. The heavy use of alcohol, especially when accompanied by cigarette smoking or chewing tobacco, increases risk of cancers of the mouth, larynx, throat, esophagus, and liver.

Sunlight

Almost all of the more than 600,000 cases of non-melanoma skin cancer developed each year in the U.S. are considered to be sun-related. Such exposure is a major factor in the development of melanoma, and the incidence increases for those living near the equator.

Alcohol

Oral cancer and cancers of the larynx, throat, esophagus, and liver occur more frequently among heavy drinkers of alcohol.

Smokeless Tobacco

Use of chewing tobacco or snuff increases risk of cancers of the mouth, larynx, throat, and esophagus, and is highly habit-forming.

Estrogen

Estrogen treatment to control menopausal symptoms increases risk of endometrial cancer. Use of estrogen by menopausal women needs careful discussion by the woman and her physician.

Radiation

Excessive exposure to ionizing radiation can increase cancer risk. Most medical and dental X rays are adjusted to deliver the lowest dose possible without sacrificing image quality. Excessive radon exposure in the home may increase lung cancer, especially in cigarette smokers. If levels are found to be too high, remedial actions should be taken.

Occupational hazards

Exposure to a number of industrial agents (nickel, chromate, asbestos, vinyl chloride, etc.) increases risk of various cancers. Risk from asbestos is greatly increased when combined with smoking.

SECONDARY PREVENTION: steps to be taken to diagnose a cancer or precursor as early as possible after it has developed.

Colorectal tests

The ACS recommends 3 tests for the early detection of colon and rectum cancer in people without symptoms: The digital rectal examination performed by a physician during an office visit, every year after the age of 40; the stool blood test every year after 50; and the proctosigmoidoscopy examination every 3 to 5 years, based on the advice of a physician.

Pap test

For cervical cancer, women who are or have been sexually active, or have reached 18 years, should have an annual Pap test and pelvic examination. After a woman has had 3 or more consecutive satisfactory normal exams, the Pap test may be performed less frequently at the discretion of her physician.

Breast cancer detection

The ACS recommends the monthly practice of breast self-examination by women 20 years and older. Physical examination of the breast should be done every 3 years from ages 20-40 and then every year. The ACS recommends a mammogram every year for asymptomatic women age 50 and over, and a baseline mammogram between ages 35-39. Women 40-49 should have mammography every 1-2 years, depending on physical and mammographic findings.

Estimated New Cancer Cases and Deaths By Sex for Selected Sites, 1991*

Source: American Cancer Society

	Estimated New Cases			Estimated Deaths		
All Sites	**Total** 1,100,000	**Male** 545,000[1]	**Female** 555,000[1]	**Total** 514,000	**Male** 272,000	**Female** 242,000
Oral	30,800	20,600	10,200	8,150	5,275	2,875
Colon-Rectum	157,500	79,000	78,000	60,000	30,000	30,500
Lung	161,000	101,000	60,000	143,000	92,000	51,000
Skin	32,000+[2]	17,000+[2]	15,000+[2]	8,500[3]	5,400	3,100
Breast	175,900	900	175,000	44,800	300	44,500
Uterus	46,000[4]	—	46,000[4]	10,000	—	10,000

*Note: The estimates of new cancer cases are offered as a rough guide and should not be regarded as definitive. (1) Carcinoma in situ and non-melanoma skin cancers are not included in totals. Carcinoma in situ of the uterine cervix accounts for about 50,000 new cases annually, and carcinoma in situ of the female breast accounts for about 15,000 new cases annually. Non-melanoma skin cancer accounts for more than 600,000 new cases annually. (2) Melanoma only. (3) Melanoma 6,500; other skin 2,000. (4) Invasive cancer only.

Surviving Cancer After 5 Years

Source: National Cancer Institute

	1974-76	1977-80	1981-86
All Sites, Average	49.0%	49.4%	50.7%
Oral cavity and pharynx	52.9	52.0	50.9
Esophagus	4.7	5.2	8.0
Stomach	14.9	16.4	17.0
Colon	49.9	52.4	56.4
Rectum	48.1	49.6	53.4
Liver	3.8	2.9	4.5
Pancreas	2.7	2.6	3.1
Larynx	65.3	66.3	67.0
Lung and bronchus	12.2	13.1	13.1
Melanoma of skin	79.2	81.1	81.1
Breast	74.0	74.3	76.6
Cervix	68.3	67.3	65.8
Uterus	88.2	84.3	82.6
Ovary	36.5	38.0	38.9
Prostate gland	66.5	70.6	73.3
Testis	78.4	87.6	92.1
Urinary bladder	72.2	74.6	78.2
Kidney and renal pelvis	51.4	51.7	52.6
Brain and nervous system	22.1	24.2	24.8
Thyroid gland	91.8	92.5	94.2
Hodgkin's disease	70.9	73.1	75.9
Non-Hodgkin's lymphoma	46.9	48.2	50.8
Multiple myeloma	24.3	25.7	26.4
Leukemia	33.4	35.2	34.9

Heart and Blood Vessel Disease

Warning Signs

Source: American Heart Association, Dallas

Of Heart Attack
• Uncomfortable pressure, fullness, squeezing or pain in the center of the chest lasting two minutes or longer
• Pain may radiate to the shoulder, arm, neck or jaw
• Sweating may accompany pain or discomfort
• Nausea and vomiting may also occur
• Shortness of breath, dizziness, or fainting may accompany other signs

The American Heart Association advises immediate action at the onset of these symptoms. The Association points out that more than half of heart attack victims die before they reach the hospital and that the average victim waits 2 hours before seeking help.

Of Stroke
• Sudden temporary weakness or numbness of face or limbs on one side of the body
• Temporary loss of speech, or trouble speaking or understanding speech
• Temporary dimness or loss of vision, particularly in one eye
• Unexplained dizziness, unsteadiness, or sudden falls

Major Risk Factors

Blood pressure—High blood pressure increases the risk of stroke, heart attack, kidney failure and congestive heart failure.

Cholesterol—A cholesteral concentration over 240 mg/dl

approximately doubles the risk of coronary heart disease; about 25% of the U.S. adult population falls into this category. Blood cholesterol values between 200 and 240 mg/dl are in a zone of moderate and increasing risk.

Cigarettes—Cigarette smokers have more than twice the risk of heart attack and 2 to 4 times the risk of sudden cardiac death than nonsmokers. Young smokers have a higher risk for early death due to stroke.

Cardiovascular Diseases Statistical Summary

1989
Prevalence — 69,080,000 Americans have one or more forms of heart and blood vessel disease.
• hypertension — 62,770,000.
• coronary heart disease — 6,160,000
• rheumatic heart disease — 1,310,000.
• stroke — 2,980,000.

Mortality — 944,688 in 1989 (43.8% of all deaths).
• nearly one-fifth of all persons killed by CVD are under age 65.
Congenital or inborn heart defects —
• post-natal mortality from heart defects 5,800 in 1989.

Heart attack — caused 497,850 deaths in 1989.
• 6,160,000 alive today have history of heart attack and/or angina pectoris.
• As many as 1,500,000 Americans will have a heart attack this year and about 500,000 of them will die.

Stroke — killed about 147,470 in 1989; afflicts 2,980,000.

Hypertension (high blood pressure) — 62,770,000 Americans age 6 and above—nearly one in 3 adults.
Rheumatic heart disease — afflicts 1,310,000.
• killed 6,000 in 1989.
Note: 1989 mortality data are estimates based on 1989 provisional data published by the National Center for Health Statistics.

Drug Usage: America's High School Students

Source: National Institute on Drug Abuse/Univ. of Michigan Inst. for Social Research

Reporting on their 16th national survey of American high school seniors, University of Michigan researchers noted a significant downturn in the use of **cocaine**, which began to decline in 1986, but has dropped substantially since then. **Crack** use began to decline a year later and also has fallen appreciably.

In 1990, 33 percent of all high school seniors said they had taken at least one illicit drug during the past year, down from a peak of 54 percent in 1979.

While the study misses the 15 percent to 20 percent of a class group that drops out of school early, the investigators say there is little reason to think that trends would be different among them, although they would undoubtedly have higher rates of use overall.

The annual senior samples are comprised of roughly 17,000 seniors in 135 public and private high schools across the nation.

	Class of 1975	Class of 1980	Class of 1983	Class of 1984	Class of 1985	Class of 1986	Class of 1987	Class of 1988	Class of 1989	Class of 1990	'89-'90 change
Marijuana/Hashish	47.3	60.3	57.0	54.9	54.2	50.9	50.2	47.2	43.7	40.7	−3.0ss
Inhalants	NA	11.9	13.6	14.4	15.4	15.9	17.0	16.7	17.6	18.0	+0.4
Inhalants Adjusted[1]	NA	17.6	18.8	19.0	18.1	20.1	18.6	17.5	18.6	18.5	−0.1
Amyl & Butyl Nitrites	NA	11.1	8.4	8.1	7.9	8.6	4.7	3.2	3.3	2.1	−1.2s
Hallucinogens	16.3	13.3	11.9	10.7	10.3	9.7	10.3	8.9	9.4	9.4	0.0
Hallucinogens Adjusted[2]	NA	15.7	14.7	13.3	12.1	11.9	10.6	9.2	9.9	9.7	−0.2
LSD	11.3	9.3	8.9	8.0	7.5	7.2	8.4	7.7	8.3	8.7	+0.4
PCP	NA	9.6	5.6	5.0	4.9	4.8	3.0	2.9	3.9	2.8	−1.1
Cocaine	9.0	15.7	16.2	16.1	17.3	16.9[5]	15.2	12.1	10.3	9.4	−0.9
"Crack"	NA	NA	NA	NA	NA	NA	5.6	4.8	4.7	3.5	−1.2ss
Heroin	2.2	1.1	1.2	1.3	1.2	1.1	1.2	1.1	1.3	1.3	0.0
Other opiates[3]	9.0	9.8	9.4	9.7	10.2	9.0	9.2	8.6	8.3	8.3	0.0
Stimulants Adjusted[3,4]	NA	NA	26.9	27.9	26.2	23.4	21.6	19.8	19.1	17.5	−1.6s
Sedatives[3]	18.2	14.9	14.4	13.3	11.8	10.4	8.7	7.8	7.4	5.3	−2.1s
Barbiturates[3]	16.9	11.0	9.9	9.9	9.2	8.4	7.4	6.7	6.5	6.8	+0.3
Methaqualone[3]	8.1	9.5	10.1	8.3	6.7	5.2	4.0	3.3	2.7	2.3	−0.4
Tranquilizers[3]	17.0	15.2	13.3	12.4	11.9	10.9	10.9	9.4	7.6	7.2	−0.4
Alcohol	90.4	93.2	92.6	92.6	92.2	91.3	92.2	92.0	90.7	89.5	−1.2
Cigarettes	73.6	71.0	70.6	69.7	68.8	67.6	67.2	66.4	65.7	64.4	−1.3

NA=Not available. Level of significance between the two most recent classes: s=.05, ss=.01, sss=.001. (1) Adjusted for underreporting of amyl and butyl nitrites. (2) Adjusted for underreporting of PCP. (3) Only drug use which was not under a doctor's orders. (4) Adjusted for overreporting of the non-prescription stimulants. (5) In 1986, 12.6 percent of those who used cocaine used it in powder form, while 4.1 percent used the "crack" form.

Effects of Commonly Abused Drugs

Source: National Institute on Drug Abuse

Tobacco

Effects and dangers: Nicotine, the active ingredient in tobacco, acts as a stimulant on the heart and nervous system. When tobacco smoke is inhaled the immediate effects on the body are a faster heart beat and elevated blood pressure. These effects, however, are quickly dissipated. Tar (in the smoke) contains many carcinogens. These compounds, many of which are in polluted air but are found in vastly greater quantities in cigarette smoke, have been identified as major causes of cancer and respiratory difficulties. Even relatively young smokers can have shortness of breath, nagging cough, or develop cardiovascular and respiratory difficulties. A third principal component of cigarette smoke, carbon monoxide, is also a cause of some of the more serious health effects of smoking. Carbon monoxide can reduce the blood's ability to carry oxygen to body tissues and can promote the development of arteriosclerosis (hardening of the arteries). Long-term effects of smoking cigarettes are emphysema, chronic bronchitis, heart disease, lung cancer, and cancer in other parts of the body.

Risks during pregnancy: Women who smoke during pregnancy are more likely to have babies that weigh less.

Alcohol

Effects: Like sedatives, it is a central nervous system depressant. In small doses, it has a tranquilizing effect on most people, although it appears to stimulate others. Alcohol first acts on those parts of the brain which affect self-control and other learned behaviors, which often leads to the aggressive behavior associated with some people who drink.

Dangers: In large doses, alcohol can dull sensation and impair muscular coordination, memory, and judgment. Taken in larger quantities over a long period time, alcohol can damage the liver and heart and can cause permanent brain damage. A large dose of alcohol can interfere with the part of the brain that controls breathing. The respiratory failure which results can bring death. Delirium tremens, the most extreme manifestation of alcohol withdrawal, can also cause death.

Risks during pregnancy: Women who drink heavily during pregnancy (more than 3 ounces of alcohol per day or about 2 mixed drinks) run a higher risk of delivering babies with physical, mental and behavioral abnormalities.

Dependence: Repeated drinking produces tolerance to the drug's effects and dependence. The drinker's body then needs alcohol to function. Once dependent, drinkers experience withdrawal symptoms when they stop drinking.

Marijuana ("grass," "pot," "weed")

What is it?: A common plant (*Cannabis sativa*), its chief psychoactive ingredient is delta-9-tetrahydrocannabinol, or THC. The amount of THC in the marijuana cigarette (joint) primarily determines its psychoactive potential.

Effects: Most users experience an increase in heart rate, reddening of the eyes, and dryness in the mouth and throat. Studies indicate the drug temporarily impairs short-term memory, alters sense of time, and reduces the ability to perform tasks requiring concentration, swift reactions, and coordination. Many feel that their hearing, vision, and skin sensitivity are enhanced by the drug, but these reports have not been objectively confirmed by research. Feelings of euphoria, relaxation, altered sense of body image, and bouts of exaggerated laughter are also commonly reported.

Dangers: Scientists believe marijuana can be particularly harmful to lungs because users typically inhale the unfiltered smoke deeply and hold it in their lungs for prolonged periods of time. Marijuana smoke has been found to have more cancer-causing agents than are found in cigarette smoke (see above). Because marijuana use increases heart rate as much as 50% and brings on chest pain in people who have a poor blood supply to the heart (and more rapidly than tobacco smoke does), doctors believe people with heart conditions or who are at high risk for heart ailments, should not use marijuana. Findings also suggest that regular use may reduce fertility in women and that men with marginal fertility and endocrine functioning should avoid marijuana use.

Risks during pregnancy: Research is limited, but scientists believe marijuana which crosses the placental barrier, may

have a toxic effect on embryos and fetuses.

Dependence: Tolerance to marijuana, the need to take more and more of the drug over time to get the original effect, has been proven in humans and animals. Physical dependence has been demonstrated in research subjects who ingested an amount equal to smoking 10 to 20 joints a day. When the drug was discontinued, subjects experienced withdrawal symptoms—irritability, sleep disturbances, loss of appetite and weight, sweating, and stomach upset.

Bad reactions: Most commonly reported immediate adverse reaction to marijuana use is the "acute panic anxiety reaction," usually described as an exaggeration of normal marijuana effects in which intense fears of losing control accompany severe anxiety. The symptoms often disappear in a few hours when the acute drug effects have worn off.

Hallucinogens ("psychodelics")

What are they?: Drugs which affect perception, sensation, thinking, self-awareness, and emotion.

(1) **LSD (lysergic acid diethylamide),** a synthetic, is converted from lysergic acid which comes from fungus (ergot).

Effects: Vary greatly according to dosage, personality of the user, and conditions under which the drug is used. Basically, it causes changes in sensation. Vision alters; users describe changes in depth perception and in the meaning of the perceived object. Illusions and hallucinations often occur. Physical reactions range from minor changes such as dilated pupils, a rise in temperature and heartbeat, or a slight increase in blood pressure, to tremors. High doses can greatly alter the state of consciousness. Heavy use of the drug may produce flashbacks, recurrences of some features of a previous LSD experience days or months after the last dose.

Dangers: After taking LSD, a person loses control over normal thought processes. Although many perceptions are pleasant, others may cause panic or may make a person believe that he or she cannot be harmed. Longer-term harmful reactions include anxiety and depression, or "breaks from reality" which may last from a few days to months. Heavy users sometimes develop signs of organic brain damage, such as impaired memory and attention span, mental confusion, and difficulty with abstract thinking. It is not known yet whether such mental changes are permanent.

(2) **Mescaline:** Comes from peyote cactus and its effects are similar to those of LSD.

Phencyclidine (PCP or "angel dust")

What is it?: A drug that was developed as a surgical anesthetic for humans in the late 1950s. PCP was soon restricted to its only current legal use as a veterinary anesthetic and tranquilizer.

Effects: Vary according to dosage. Low doses may provide the usual releasing effects of many psychoactive drugs. A floaty euphoria is described, sometimes associated with a feeling of numbness (part of the drug's anesthetic effects). Increased doses produce an excited, confused intoxication, which may include muscle rigidity, loss of concentration and memory, visual disturbances, delirium, feelings of isolation, convulsions, speech impairment, violent behavior, fear of death, and changes in the user's perceptions of their bodies.

Dangers: PCP intoxication can produce violent and bizarre behavior even in people not otherwise prone to such behavior. Violent actions may be directed at themselves or others and often account for serious injuries and death. More people die from accidents caused by the erratic behavior produced by the drug than from the drug's direct effect on the body. A temporary, schizophrenic-like psychosis, which can last for days or weeks, has also occurred in users of moderate or higher doses.

Stimulants ("Uppers")

What are they?: A class of drugs which stimulate the central nervous system and produce an increase in alertness and activity.

(1) **Amphetamines** promote a feeling of alertness and increase in speech and general physical activity. Under medical supervision, the drugs are taken to control appetite.

Effects and dangers: Even small, infrequent doses can produce toxic effects in some people. Restlessness, anxiety, mood swings, panic, circulatory and cardiac disturbances, paranoid thoughts, hallucinations, convulsions, and coma

have all been reported. Heavy, frequent doses can produce brain damage which results in speed disturbances and difficulty in turning thoughts into words. Death can result from injected amphetamine overdose. Long-term users often have acne resembling a measles rash; trouble with teeth, gums and nails, and dry lifeless hair. As heavy users who inject amphetamines accumulate larger amounts of the drug in their bodies, the resulting toxicity can produce amphetamine psychosis. People in this extremely suspicious, paranoid state, frequently exhibit bizarre, sometimes violent behavior.
Dependence: People with a history of sustained low-dose use quite often become dependent and feel they need the drug to get by.
(2) Cocaine is a stimulant extracted from the leaves of the coca plant. It is available in many forms, the most available of which is cocaine hydrochloride. Cocaine hydrochloride is often used medically as a local anesthetic, but is also sold illegally on the street in large pieces called rocks. Street cocaine is a white, crystal-like powder that is most commonly inhaled or snorted, though some users ingest, inject, or smoke a form of the drug called freebase or crack.

Freebase and crack are formed by chemically converting street cocaine to a purified substance that is more suitable for smoking. Smoking freebase or crack produces a shorter, but more intense high than other ways of using the drug. It is the most direct and rapid means of getting the drug to the brain, and because larger amounts are reaching the brain more quickly, the effects of the drug are more intense and the dangers associated with its use are greater.

Ice, or crystal methamphetamine, is another stimulant that can be smoked and which has many of the same euphoric and adverse effects as crack.
Effects: The drug's usual effects are dilated pupils and increased blood pressure, heart rate, breathing rate, and body temperature. Even small doses may elicit feelings of euphoria; illusions of increased mental and physical strength and sensory awareness; and a decrease in hunger, pain, and the perceived need for sleep. Large doses significantly magnify these effects, sometimes causing irrational behavior and confusion.
Dangers: Paranoia is not an uncommon response to heavy doses. Psychosis may be triggered in users prone to mental instability. Repeated inhalation often results in nostril and nasal membrane irritation. Some regular users have reported feelings of restlessness, irritability, and anxiety. Others have experienced hallucinations of touch, sight, taste, or smell. When people stop using cocaine after taking it for a long time, they frequently become depressed. They tend to fight off this depression by taking more cocaine, just as in the up/down amphetamine cycle.
Cocaine is toxic. Although few people realize it, overdose deaths, though rare, have occurred as a result of injecting, ingesting and even snorting cocaine. The deaths are a result of seizures followed by respiratory arrest and coma, or sometimes by cardiac arrest. Other dangers associated with cocaine include the risk of infection, such as hepatitis, resulting from the use of unsterile needles and the risk of fire or explosion resulting from the use of volatile substances necessary for freebase preparation.
Dependence: Cocaine is not a narcotic; no evidence suggests that it produces a physical dependence. However, cocaine is psychologically a very dangerous, dependence-producing drug. Smoking freebase or crack increases this risk of dependence.
(3) Caffeine may be the world's most popular drug. It is primarily consumed in coffee and tea, but is also found in cocoa, cola and other soft drinks, as well as in many over-the-counter medicines.
Effects: Two to four cups of coffee increase heart rate, body temperature, urine production, and gastric juice secretion. Caffeine can also raise sugar levels and cause tremors, loss of coordination, decreased appetite, and postponement of fatigue. It can interfere with the depth of sleep and the amount of dream sleep by causing more rapid eye movement (REM) sleep at first, but less than average over an entire night. Extremely high doses may cause diarrhea, sleeplessness, trembling, severe headache, and nervousness.
Dependence: A form of physical dependence may result with regular consumption. In such cases, withdrawal symptoms may occur if caffeine use is stopped or interrupted. These symptoms include headache, irritability, and fatigue. Toler-

ance may develop with the use of six to eight cups or more a day. A regular user of caffeine who has developed a tolerance may also develop a craving for the drug's effects.
Dangers: Poisonous doses of caffeine have occurred occasionally and have resulted in convulsions, breathing failure, and even death. However, it is almost impossible to die from drinking too much coffee or tea. The deaths that have been reported have resulted from the misuse of tablets containing caffeine.

Sedatives (Tranquilizers, sleeping pills)
What are they?: Drugs which depress the central nervous system, more appropriately called sedative-hypnotics because they include drugs which calm the nerves (the sedation effect) and produce sleep (the hypnotic effect). Of drugs in this class, barbiturates ("barbs", "downers", "reds") have the highest rate of abuse and misuse. The most commonly abused barbiturates include pentobarbital (Nembutal), secobarbital (Seconal), and amobarbital (Amytal). These all have legitimate use as sedatives or sleeping aids. Among the most commonly abused nonbarbiturate drugs are glutethimide (Doriden), meprobamate (Miltown), methyprylon (Noludar), ethchlorvynol (Placidyl), and methaqualone (Sopor, Quaalude). These are prescribed to help people sleep. Benzodiazepines, especially diazepam (Valium), prescribed to relieve anxiety, are commonly abused, and their rate of abuse and misuse is increasing.
Dangers: These can kill. Barbiturate overdose is implicated in nearly one-third of all reported drug-induced deaths. Accidental deaths may occur when a user takes an unintended larger or repeated dose of sedatives because of confusion or impairment in judgment caused by initial intake of the drug. With lesser, but still large doses, users can go into coma. Moderately large doses often produce an intoxicated stupor. Users' speech is often slurred, memory vague, and judgment impaired. Taken along with alcohol, the combination can be fatal. Tranquilizers act somewhat differently from other sedatives and are considered less hazardous. But even by themselves, or in combination with other drugs (especially alcohol and other sedatives) they can be quite dangerous.
Dependence: Potential for dependence is greatest with barbiturates, but all sedatives, tranquilizers, can be addictive. Barbiturate withdrawal is often more severe than heroin withdrawal.

Narcotics
What they are?: Drugs that relieve pain and often induce sleep. The opiates, which are narcotics, include opium and drugs derived from opium, such as morphine, codeine, and heroin. Narcotics also include certain synthetic chemicals that have a morphine-like action, such as methadone.
Which are abused?: Heroin ("junk," "smack") accounts for 90% of narcotic abuse in the U.S. Sometimes medicinal narcotics are also abused, including paregoric containing codeine, and methadone, meperidine, and morphine.
Dependence: Anyone can become heroin dependent if he or she takes the drug regularly. Although environmental stress and problems of coping have often been considered as factors that lead to heroin addiction, physicians or psychologists do not agree that some people just have an "addictive personality" and are prone to dependence. All we know for certain is that continued use of heroin causes dependence.
Dangers: Physical dangers depend on the specific drug, its source, and the way it is used. Most medical problems are caused by the uncertain dosage level, use of unsterile needles and other paraphernalia, contamination of the drug, or combination of a narcotic with other drugs, rather than by the effects of the heroin (or another narcotic) itself. The life expectancy of a heroin addict who injects the drug intravenously is significantly lower than that of one who does not. An overdose can result in death. If, for example, an addict obtains pure heroin and is not tolerant of the dose, he or she may die minutes after injecting it. Infections from unsterile needles, solutions, syringes, cause many diseases. Serum hepatitis is common. Skin abscesses, inflammation of the veins and congestion of the lungs also occur.
Withdrawal: When a heroin-dependent person stops taking the drug, withdrawal begins within 4-6 hours after the last injection. Full-blown withdrawal symptoms—which include shaking, sweating, vomiting, a running nose and eyes, muscle aches, chills, abdominal pains, and diarrhea—begin some 12-16 hours after the last injection. The intensity of symptoms depends on the degree of dependence.

Basic First Aid

First aid experts stress that knowing what to do for an injured person until a doctor or trained person gets to an accident scene can save a life, especially in cases of stoppage of breath, severe bleeding, and shock.

People with special medical problems, such as diabetes, cardiovascular disease, epilepsy, or allergy, are also urged to wear some sort of emblem identifying it, as a safeguard against use of medication that might be injurious or fatal in an emergency. Emblems may be obtained from Medic Alert Foundation, Turlock, CA 95380.

Most accidents occur in homes. National Safety Council figures show that home accidents exceed those in other locations, such as in cars, at work, or in public places.

In all cases, get medical assistance as soon as possible.

Animal bite — Wound should be washed with soap under running water and animal should be caught alive for rabies test.

Asphyxiation — Start mouth-to-mouth resuscitation immediately after getting patient to fresh air.

Bleeding — Elevate the wound above the heart if possible. Press hard on wound with sterile compress until bleeding stops. Send for doctor if it is severe.

Burn — If mild, with skin unbroken and no blisters, plunge into ice water until pain subsides. Apply a dry dressing if necessary. Send for physician if burn is severe. Apply sterile compresses and keep patient quiet and comfortably warm until doctor's arrival. Do not try to clean burn, or to break blisters.

Chemical in eye — With patient lying down, pour cupsful of water immediately into corner of eye, letting it run to other side to remove chemicals thoroughly. Cover with sterile compress. Get medical attention immediately .

Choking — Do not use back slaps to dislodge obstruction. (See Abdominal Thrust)

Convulsions — Place person on back on bed or rug. Loosen clothing. Turn head to side. Do not place a blunt object between the victim's teeth. If convulsions do not stop, get medical attention immediately.

Cut (minor) — Apply mild antiseptic and sterile compress after washing with soap under warm running water.

Drowning — (See Mouth-to-Mouth Resuscitation) Artificial breathing must be started at once, before victim is out of the water, if possible. If the victim's stomach is bloated with water, put victim on stomach, place hands under stomach, and lift. If no pulse is felt, begin cardio-pulmonary resuscitation. This should only be done by those professionally trained. If necessary, treat for shock. (See Shock)

Electric shock — If possible, turn off power. Don't touch victim until contact is broken; pull him from contact with electrical source using rope, wooden pole, or loop of dry cloth. Start mouth-to-mouth resuscitation if breathing has stopped.

Foreign body in eye — Touch object with moistened corner of handkerchief if it can be seen. If it cannot be seen or does not come out after a few attempts, take patient to doctor. Do not rub eye.

Fainting — If victim feels faint, lower head to knees. Lay him down with head turned to side if he becomes unconscious. Loosen clothing and open windows. Keep patient lying quietly for at least 15 minutes after he regains consciousness. Call doctor if faint lasts for more than a few minutes.

Fall — Send for physician if patient has continued pain. Cover wound with sterile dressing and stop any severe bleeding. Do not move patient unless absolutely necessary — as in case of fire — if broken bone is suspected. Keep patient warm and comfortable.

Loss of Limb — If a limb is severed, it is important to properly protect the limb so that it can possibly be reattached to the victim. After the victim is cared for, the limb should be placed in a clean plastic bag, garbage can or other suitable container. Pack ice around the limb on the OUTSIDE of the bag to keep the limb cold. Call ahead to the hospital to alert them of the situation.

Poisoning — Call doctor. Use antidote listed on label if container is found. Call local Poison Control Center if possible. Except for lye, other caustics, and petroleum products, induce vomiting unless victim is unconscious. Give milk if poison or antidote is unknown.

Shock (injury-related) — Keep the victim lying down; if uncertain as to his injuries, keep him flat on his back. Maintain the victim's normal body temperature; if the weather is cold or damp, place blankets or extra clothing over and under the victim; if weather is hot, provide shade.

Snakebite — Immediately get victim to a hospital. If there is mild swelling or pain, apply a constricting band 2 to 4 inches above the bite.

Sting from insect — If possible, remove stinger and apply solution of ammonia and water, or paste of baking soda. Call physician immediately if body swells or patient collapses.

Unconsciousness — Send for doctor and place person on his back. Start resuscitation if he stops breathing. Never give food or liquids to an unconscious person.

Abdominal Thrust

The American Red Cross and the American Heart Association both agree that the recommended first aid for choking victims is the abdominal thrust, also known as the Heimlich maneuver, after its creator, Dr. Henry Heimlich. Slaps on the back are no longer advised and may even prove detrimental in an attempt to assist a choking victim.

- Get behind the victim and wrap your arms around him above his waist.
- Make a fist with one hand and place it, with the thumb knuckle pressing inward, just below the point of the "v" of the rib cage.
- Grasp the wrist with the other hand and give one or more upward thrusts or hugs.
- Start mouth-to-mouth resuscitation if breathing stops.

Mouth-to-Mouth Resuscitation

Stressing that your breath can save a life, the American Red Cross gives the following directions for mouth-to-mouth resuscitation if the victim is not breathing:

- Determine consciousness by tapping the victim on the shoulder and asking loudly, "Are you okay?"
- Tilt the victim's head back so that his chin is pointing upward. Do not press on the soft tissue under the chin, as this might obstruct the airway. If you suspect that an accident victim might have neck or back injuries, open the airway by placing the tips of your index and middle fingers on the corners of the victim's jaw to lift it forward without tilting the head.
- Place your cheek and ear close to the victim's mouth and nose. Look at the victim's chest to see if it rises and falls. Listen and feel for air to be exhaled for about 5 seconds.
- If there is no breathing, pinch the victim's nostrils shut with the thumb and index finger of your hand that is pressing on the victim's forehead. Another way to prevent leakage of air when the lungs are inflated is to press your cheek against the victim's nose.
- Blow air into victim's mouth by taking a deep breath and then sealing your mouth tightly around the victim's mouth. Initially, give two, quick (approx. 1.5 seconds each), full breaths without allowing the lungs to deflate completely between each breath.
- Watch the victim's chest to see if it rises.
- Stop blowing when the victim's chest is expanded. Raise your mouth; turn your head to the side and listen for exhalation.
- Watch the chest to see if it falls.
- Repeat the blowing cycle until the victim starts breathing.

Note: Infants (up to one year) and children (1 to 8 years) should be administered mouth-to-mouth resuscitation as described above, except for the following:

- Do not tilt the head as far back as an adult's head.
- Both the mouth and nose of the infant should be sealed by the mouth.
- Give breaths to a child once every four seconds.
- Blow into the infant's mouth and nose once every three seconds with less pressure and volume than for a child.

Stress: How Much Can Affect Your Health?

Source: Reprinted with permission from the *Journal of Psychosomatic Research*. Vol. 11, pp. 213-218, T.H. Holmes, M.D., R.H. Rahe, M.D.; The Social Readjustment Rating Scale © 1967, Pergamon Press, Ltd.

Change, both good and bad, can create stress and stress, if sufficiently severe, can lead to illness. Drs. Thomas Holmes and Richard Rahe, psychiatrists at the University of Washington in Seattle, developed the Social Readjustment Rating Scale. In their study, they gave a point value to stressful events. The psychiatrists discovered that in 79 percent of the persons studied, major illness followed the accumulation of stress-related changes totaling over 300 points in one year.

The Social Readjustment Rating Scale

Life Event	Value	Life Event	Value
Death of Spouse	100	In-law troubles	29
Divorce	73	Outstanding personal achievement	28
Marital separation from mate	65	Wife beginning or ceasing work outside the home	26
Detention in jail or other institution	63	Beginning or ceasing formal schooling	26
Death of a close family member	63	Major change in living conditions (e.g., building a new	
Major personal injury or illness	53	home, remodeling, deterioration of home or neigh-	
Marriage	50	borhood)	25
Being fired at work	47	Revision of personal habits (dress, manners, associa-	
Marital reconciliation with mate	45	tion, etc.)	24
Retirement from work	45	Troubles with the boss	23
Major change in the health or behavior of a family		Major change in working hours or conditions	20
member	44	Change in residence	20
Pregnancy	40	Changing to a new school	20
Sexual difficulties	39	Major change in usual type and/or amount of recrea-	
Gaining a new family member (e.g., through birth,		tion	19
adoption, moving in, etc.)	39	Major change in church activities (e.g., a lot more or a	
Major business readjustment (e.g., merger, reorgani-		lot less than usual)	19
zation, bankruptcy, etc.)	39	Major change in social activities (e.g., clubs, dancing,	
Major change in financial state (e.g., a lot worse off or		movies, visiting, etc.)	18
a lot better off than usual)	38	Taking out a mortgage or loan for a lesser purchase	
Death of a close friend	37	(e.g., for a car, TV, freezer, etc.)	17
Changing to a different line of work	36	Major change in sleeping habits (a lot more or a lot	
Major change in the number of arguments with spouse		less sleep, or change in part of day when asleep)	16
(e.g., either a lot more or a lot less than usual re-		Major change in number of family get-togethers (e.g.,	
garding child-rearing, personal habits, etc.)	35	a lot more or a lot less than usual)	15
Taking out a mortgage or loan for a major purchase		Major change in eating habits (a lot more or a lot less	
(e.g. for a home, business, etc.)	31	food intake, or very different meal hours or sur-	
Foreclosure on a mortgage or loan	30	roundings)	15
Major change in responsibilities at work (e.g., promo-		Vacation	13
tion, demotion, lateral transfer)	29	Christmas	12
Son or daughter leaving home (e.g., marriage, attend-		Minor violations of the law (e.g., traffic tickets, jay-	
ing college, etc.)	29	walking, disturbing the peace, etc.)	11

A Patient's Bill of Rights

Source: American Hospital Association. © copyright 1972.

Often, as a hospital patient, you feel you have little control over your circumstances. You do, however, have some important rights. They have been enumerated by the American Hospital Association.

1. The patient has the right to considerate and respectful care.

2. The patient has the right to obtain from his physician complete current information concerning his diagnosis, treatment, and prognosis in terms the patient can be expected to understand. When it is not medically advisable to give such information to the patient, the information should be made available to an appropriate person in his behalf. He has the right to know, by name, the physician responsible for coordinating his care.

3. The patient has the right to receive from his physician information necessary to give informed consent prior to the start of any procedure and/or treatment. Except in emergencies, such information for informed consent should include but not necessarily be limited to the specific procedure and/or treatment, the medically significant risks involved, and the probable duration of incapacitation. Where medically significant alternatives for care or treatment exist, or when the patient requests information concerning medical alternatives, the patient has the right to such information. The patient also has the right to know the name of the person responsible for the procedures and/or treatment.

4. The patient has the right to refuse treatment to the extent permitted by law and to be informed of the medical consequences of his action.

5. The patient has the right to every consideration of his privacy concerning his own medical care program. Case discussion, consultation, examination, and treatment are confidential and should be conducted discreetly. Those not directly involved in his care must have the permission of the patient to be present.

6. The patient has the right to expect that all communications and records pertaining to his care should be treated as confidential.

7. The patient has the right to expect that within its capacity a hospital must make reasonable response to the request of a patient for services. The hospital must provide evaluation, service, and/or referral as indicated by the urgency of the case. When medically permissible, a patient may be transferred to another facility only after he has received complete information and explanation concerning the need for and alternatives to such a transfer. The receiving institution must first have accepted the patient for transfer.

8. The patient has the right to obtain information as to any relationship of his hospital to other health care and education institutions insofar as this care is concerned. The patient has the right to obtain information as to the existence of any professional relationships among individuals, by name, who are treating him.

9. The patient has the right to be advised if the hospital proposes to engage in or perform human experimentation affecting his care or treatment. The patient has the right to refuse to participate in such research projects.

10. The patient has the right to expect reasonable continuity of care. He has the right to know in advance what appointment times and physicians are available and where. The patient has the right to expect that the hospital will provide a mechanism whereby he is informed by his physician of the patient's continuing health care requirements following discharge.

11. The patient has the right to examine and receive an explanation of his bill, regardless of the source of payment.

12. The patient has the right to know what hospital rules and regulations apply to his conduct as a patient.

Nutritive Value of Food (Calories, Proteins, etc.)

Source: Home and Garden Bulletin No. 72; available from Supt. of Documents. U. S. Government Printing Office, Washington, DC 20402

Food	Measure	Grams	Food Energy (calories)	Protein (grams)	Fat (grams)	Saturated fats (grams)	Carbohydrate (grams)	Calcium (milligrams)	Iron (milligrams)	Vitamin A (I.U.)	Thiamin (milligrams)	Riboflavin (milligrams)
Dairy products												
Cheese, cheddar	1 oz.	28	115	7	9	6.1	T	204	.2	300	.01	.11
Cheese, cottage, small curd	1 cup	210	220	26	9	6.0	6	126	.3	340	.04	.34
Cheese, cream	1 oz.	28	100	2	10	6.2	1	23	.3	400	T	.06
Cheese, Swiss	1 oz.	28	105	8	8	5.0	1	272	T	240	.01	.10
Half-and-Half	1 tbsp.	15	20	T	2	1.1	1	16	T	20	.01	.02
Cream, sour	1 tbsp.	15	25	T	3	1.6	1	14	T	90	T	.02
Milk, whole	1 cup	244	150	8	8	5.1	11	291	.1	310	.09	.40
Milk, nonfat (skim)	1 cup	244	85	8	T	.3	12	302	.1	500	.09	.37
Milkshake, chocolate	10.6 oz.	300	355	9	8	5.0	63	396	.9	260	.14	.67
Ice Cream, hardened	1 cup	133	270	5	14	8.9	32	176	.1	540	.05	.33
Sherbet	1 cup	193	270	2	4	2.4	59	103	.3	190	.03	.09
Yogurt, fruit-flavored	8 oz.	227	230	10	3	1.8	42	343	.2	120	.08	.40
Eggs												
Fried in butter	1	46	85	5	6	2.4	1	26	.9	290	.03	.13
Hard-cooked	1	50	80	6	6	1.7	1	28	1.0	260	.04	.14
Scrambled in butter (milk added)	1	64	95	6	7	2.8	1	47	.9	310	.04	.16
Fats & oils												
Butter	1 tbsp.	14	100	T	12	7.2	T	3	T	430	T	T
Margarine	1 tbsp.	14	100	T	12	2.1	T	3	T	470	T	T
Salad dressing, blue cheese	1 tbsp.	15	75	1	8	1.6	1	12	T	30	T	.02
Salad dressing, French	1 tbsp.	16	65	T	6	1.1	3	2	1	—	—	—
Salad dressing, Italian	1 tbsp.	15	85	T	9	1.6	1	2	T	T	T	T
Mayonnaise	1 tbsp.	14	100	T	11	2.0	T	3	.1	40	T	.01
Meat, poultry, fish												
Bluefish, baked with butter or margarine	3 oz.	85	135	22	4	—	0	25	0.6	40	.09	.08
Clams, raw, meat only	3 oz.	85	65	11	1	—	2	59	5.2	90	.08	.15
Crabmeat, white or king, canned	1 cup	135	135	24	3	.6	1	61	1.1	—	.11	.11
Fish sticks, breaded, cooked, frozen	1 oz.	28	50	5	3	—	2	3	.1	0	.01	.02
Salmon, pink, canned	3 oz.	85	120	17	5	.9	0	167	.7	60	.03	.16
Sardines, Atlantic, canned in oil	3 oz.	85	175	20	9	3.0	0	372	2.5	190	.02	.17
Shrimp, French fried	3 oz.	85	190	17	9	2.3	9	61	1.7	—	.03	.07
Tuna, canned in oil	3 oz.	85	170	24	7	1.7	0	7	1.6	70	.04	.10
Bacon, broiled or fried crisp	2 slices	15	85	4	8	2.5	T	2	.5	0	.08	.05
Ground beef, broiled, 10% fat	3 oz.	85	185	23	10	4.0	0	10	3.0	20	.08	.20
Roast beef, relatively lean	3 oz.	85	165	25	7	2.8	0	11	3.2	10	.06	.19
Beef steak, lean and fat	3 oz.	85	330	20	27	11.3	0	9	2.5	50	.05	.15
Beef & vegetable stew	1 cup	245	220	16	11	4.9	15	29	2.9	2,400	.15	.17
Lamb, chop, lean and fat	3.1 oz.	89	360	18	32	14.8	0	8	1.0	—	.11	.19
Liver, beef	3 oz.	85	195	22	9	2.5	5	9	7.5	45,390	.22	3.56
Ham, light cure, lean and fat	3 oz.	85	245	18	19	6.8	0	8	2.2	0	.40	.15
Pork, chop, lean and fat	2.7 oz	78	305	19	25	8.9	0	9	2.7	0	.75	.22
Bologna	1 slice	28	85	3	8	3.0	T	2	.5	—	.05	.06
Frankfurter, cooked	1	56	170	7	15	5.6	1	3	.8	—	.08	.11
Sausage, pork link, cooked	1 link	13	60	2	6	2.1	T	1	.3	0	.10	.04
Veal, cutlet, braised or broiled	3 oz.	85	185	23	9	4.0	0	9	2.7	—	.06	.21
Chicken, drumstick, fried, bones removed	1.3 oz.	38	90	12	4	1.1	1	6	.9	50	.03	.15
Chicken, half broiler, broiled, bones removed	6.2 oz.	176	240	42	7	2.2	0	16	3.0	160	.09	.34
Fruits & products												
Apple, 2-3/4 in. diam.	1	138	80	T	1	—	20	10	.4	120	.04	.03
Applejuice	1 cup	248	120	T	T	—	30	15	1.5	—	.02	.05
Apricots, raw	3	107	55	1	T	—	14	18	.5	2,890	.03	.04
Banana, raw	1	119	100	1	T	—	26	10	.8	230	.06	.07
Cherries, sweet, raw	10	68	45	1	T	—	12	15	.3	70	.03	.04
Fruit cocktail, canned, in heavy syrup	1 cup	255	195	1	T	—	50	23	1.0	360	.05	.03
Grapefruit, raw, medium, white	1/2	241	45	1	T	—	12	19	.5	10	.05	.02
Grapes, Thompson seedless	10	50	35	T	T	—	9	6	.2	50	.03	.02
Lemonade, frozen, diluted	1 cup	248	105	T	T	—	28	2	.1	10	.01	.02
Cantaloupe, 5-in. diam.	1/2	477	80	2	T	—	20	38	1.1	9,240	.11	.08
Orange, 2-5/8 in. diam.	1	131	65	1	T	—	16	54	.5	260	.13	.05
Orange juice, frozen, diluted	1 cup	249	120	2	T	—	29	25	.2	540	.23	.03
Peach, raw, 2-1/2 in. diam.	1	100	40	1	T	—	10	9	.5	1,330	.02	.05
Raisins, seedless	1 cup	145	420	4	T	—	112	90	5.1	30	.16	.12
Strawberries, raw	1 cup	149	55	1	1	—	13	31	1.5	90	.04	.10
Watermelon, 4 by 8 in. wedge	1 wedge	926	110	2	1	—	27	30	2.1	2,510	.13	.13
Grain products												
Bagel, egg	1	55	165	6	2	.5	28	9	1.2	30	.14	.10
Biscuit, 2 in. diam., from home recipe	1	28	105	2	5	1.2	13	34	.4	T	.08	.08
Bread, white, enriched, soft-crumb	1 slice	25	70	2	1	.2	13	21	.6	T	.10	.06
Bread, whole wheat, soft-crumb	1 slice	28	65	3	1	.1	14	24	.8	T	.09	.03
Oatmeal or rolled oats	1 cup	240	130	5	2	.4	23	22	1.4	0	.19	.05
Bran flakes (40% bran), added sugar, salt, iron, vitamins	1 cup	35	105	4	1	—	28	19	12.4	1,650	.41	.49
Corn flakes, added sugar, salt, iron, vitamins	1 cup	25	95	2	T	—	21	*	0.6	1,180	.29	.35
Rice, puffed, added iron, thiamin, niacin	1 cup	15	60	1	T	—	13	3	.3	0	.07	.01
Wheat, shredded, plain, 1 biscuit or 1/2 cup	1 serving	25	90	2	1	—	20	11	.9	0	.06	.03
Cake, angel food, 1/12 of cake	1	53	135	3	T	—	32	50	.2	0	.03	.08
Cupcake, 2-1/2 in. diam., with chocolate icing	1	36	130	2	5	2.0	21	47	.4	60	.05	.06
Boston cream pie with custard filling, 1/12 of cake	1	69	210	3	6	1.9	34	46	.7	140	.09	.11
Fruitcake, dark, 1/30 of loaf	1	15	55	1	2	.5	9	11	.4	20	.02	.02
Cake, pound, 1/17 of loaf	1	33	160	2	10	2.5	16	6	.5	80	.05	.06
Brownies, with nuts, from commercial recipe	1	20	85	1	4	.9	13	9	.4	20	.03	.02
Cookies, chocolate chip, from home recipe	4	40	205	2	12	3.5	24	14	.8	40	.06	.06
Crackers, graham	2	14	55	1	1	.3	10	6	.5	0	.02	.08

Food	Measure	Grams	Food Energy (calories)	Protein (grams)	Fat (grams)	Saturated fats (grams)	Carbohydrate (grams)	Calcium (milligrams)	Iron (milligrams)	Vitamin A (I.U.)	Thiamin (milligrams)	Riboflavin (milligrams)
Crackers, saltines	4	11	50	1	1	.3	8	2	.5	0	.05	.05
Danish pastry, round piece	1	65	275	*5	15	4.7	30	33	1.2	200	.18	.19
Doughnut, cake type	1	25	100	1	5	1.2	13	10	.4	20	.05	.05
Macaroni and cheese, from home recipe	1 cup	200	430	17	22	8.9	40	362	1.8	860	.20	.40
Muffin, corn	1	40	125	3	4	1.2	19	42	.7	120	.10	.10
Noodles, enriched, cooked	1 cup	160	200	7	2	—	37	16	1.4	110	.22	.13
Pie, apple, 1/7 of pie	1	135	345	3	15	3.9	51	11	.9	40	.15	.11
Pie, cherry, 1/7 of pie	1	135	350	4	15	4.0	52	19	.9	590	.16	.12
Pie, lemon meringue, 1/7 of pie	1	120	305	4	12	3.7	45	17	1.0	200	.09	.12
Pie, pecan, 1/7 of pie	1	118	495	6	27	4.0	61	55	3.7	190	.26	.14
Pizza, cheese, 1/6 of 12 in. diam. pie	1	60	145	6	4	1.7	22	86	1.1	230	.16	.18
Popcorn, popped, plain	1 cup	6	25	1	T	T	5	1	.2	—	—	.01
Pretzels, stick	10	3	10	T	T	—	2	1	T	0	.01	.01
Rolls, enriched, brown & serve	1	26	85	2	2	.4	14	20	.5	T	.10	.06
Rolls, frankfurter & hamburger	1	40	120	3	2	.5	21	30	.8	T	.16	.10
Spaghetti with meat balls & tomato sauce	1 cup	248	330	19	12	3.3	39	124	3.7	1,590	.25	.30
Legumes, nuts, seeds												
Beans, Great Northern, cooked	1 cup	180	210	14	1	—	38	90	4.9	0	.25	.13
Peanuts, roasted in oil, salted	1 cup	144	840	37	72	13.7	27	107	3.0	—	.46	.19
Peanut butter	1 tbsp.	16	95	4	8	1.5	3	9	.3	—	.02	.02
Sunflower seeds	1 cup	145	810	35	69	8.2	29	174	10.3	70	2.84	.33
Sugars & sweets												
Candy, caramels	1 oz.	28	115	1	3	1.6	22	42	.4	T	.01	.05
Candy, milk chocolate	1 oz.	28	145	2	9	5.5	16	65	.3	80	.02	.10
Fudge, chocolate	1 oz.	28	115	1	3	1.3	21	22	.3	T	.01	.03
Candy, hard	1 oz.	28	110	0	T	—	28	6	.5	0	0	0
Honey	1 tbsp.	21	65	T	0	0	17	1	.1	0	T	.01
Jams & Preserves	1 tbsp.	20	55	T	T	—	14	4	.2	T	T	.01
Sugar, white, granulated	1 tbsp.	12	45	0	0	0	12	0	T	0	0	0
Vegetables												
Asparagus, canned, spears	4 spears	80	15	2	T	—	3	15	1.5	640	.05	.08
Beans, green, from frozen, cuts	1 cup	135	35	2	T	—	8	54	.9	780	.09	.12
Broccoli, cooked	1 stalk	180	45	6	1	—	8	158	1.4	4,500	.16	.36
Cabbage, raw, coarsely shredded or sliced	1 cup	70	15	1	T	—	4	34	.3	90	.04	.04
Carrots, raw, 7-1/2 by 1-1/8 in.	1	72	30	1	T	—	7	27	.5	7,930	.04	.04
Celery, raw	1 stalk	40	5	T	T	—	2	16	.1	110	.01	.01
Collards, cooked	1 cup	190	65	7	1	—	10	357	1.5	14,820	.21	.38
Corn, sweet, cooked	1 ear	140	70	2	1	—	16	2	.5	310	.09	.08
Lettuce, iceberg, chopped	1 cup	55	5	T	T	—	2	11	.3	180	.03	.03
Mushrooms, raw	1 cup	70	20	2	T	—	3	4	.6	T	.07	.32
Onions, raw, chopped	1 cup	170	65	3	T	—	15	46	.9	T	.05	.07
Peas, frozen, cooked	1 cup	160	110	8	T	—	19	30	3.0	960	.43	.14
Potatoes, baked, peeled	1	156	145	4	T	—	33	14	1.1	T	.15	.07
Potatoes, frozen, French fried	10	50	110	2	4	1.1	17	5	.9	T	.07	.01
Potatoes, mashed, milk added	1 cup	210	135	4	2	.7	27	50	.8	40	.17	.11
Potato chips	10	20	115	1	8	2.1	10	8	.4	T	.04	.01
Potato salad	1 cup	250	250	7	7	2.0	41	80	1.5	350	.20	.18
Spinach, chopped, from frozen	1 cup	205	45	6	1	—	8	232	4.3	16,200	.14	.31
Sweet potatoes, baked in skin, peeled	1	114	160	2	1	—	37	46	1.0	9,230	.10	.08
Tomatoes, raw	1	135	25	1	T	—	6	16	.6	1,110	.07	.05
Miscellaneous												
Beer	12 fl. oz.	360	150	1	0	0	14	18	T	—	.01	.11
Gin, rum, vodka, whisky, 86 proof	1-1/2 fl. oz.	42	105	—	0	0	T	—	—	—	—	—
Wine, table	3-1/2 fl. oz.	102	85	T	0	0	4	9	.4	—	T	.01
Cola-type beverage	12 fl. oz.	369	145	0	0	0	37	—	—	0	0	0
Ginger ale	12 fl. oz	366	115	0	0	0	29	—	—	0	0	0
Gelatin dessert	1 cup	240	140	4	0	0	34	—	—	—	—	—
Olives, pickled, green	4 medium	16	15	T	2	.2	T	8	.2	40	—	—
Pickles, dill, whole	1	65	5	T	T	—	1	17	.7	70	T	.01
Popsicle, 3 fl. oz.	1	95	70	0	0	0	18	0	T	0	0	0
Soup, tomato, prepared with water	1 cup	245	90	2	3	.5	16	15	.7	1,000	.05	.05

T — Indicates trace   * — Varies by brand

Calories Used Per Minute According to Body Weight

Weight in Pounds

Activity	100	120	150	170	200	220
Volleyball (moderate)	2.3	2.7	3.4	3.9	4.6	5.0
Walking (3 mph)	2.7	3.2	4.0	4.6	5.4	5.9
Table tennis	2.7	3.2	4.0	4.6	5.4	5.9
Bicycling (5.5 mph)	3.1	3.8	4.7	5.3	6.3	6.9
Calisthenics	3.3	3.9	4.9	5.6	6.6	7.2
Skating (moderate)	3.6	4.3	5.4	6.1	7.2	7.9
Golf	3.6	4.3	5.4	6.1	7.2	7.9
Walking (4 mph)	3.9	4.6	5.8	6.6	7.8	8.5
Tennis	4.5	5.4	6.8	7.7	9.1	10.0
Canoeing (4 mph)	4.6	5.6	7.0	7.9	9.3	10.2
Swimming (breaststroke)	4.8	5.7	7.2	8.1	9.6	10.5
Bicycling (10 mph)	5.4	6.5	8.1	9.2	10.8	11.9
Swimming (crawl)	5.8	6.9	8.7	9.8	11.6	12.7
Jogging (11-min. mile)	6.1	7.3	9.1	10.4	12.2	13.4
Handball	6.3	7.6	9.5	10.7	12.7	13.9
Racquetball	6.3	7.6	9.5	10.7	12.7	13.9
Skiing (downhill)	6.3	7.6	9.5	10.7	12.7	13.9
Mountain climbing	6.6	8.0	10.0	11.3	13.3	14.6
Squash	6.8	8.1	10.2	11.5	13.6	14.9
Skiing (cross-country)	7.2	8.7	10.8	12.3	14.5	15.9
Running (8-min. mile)	9.4	11.3	14.1	16.0	18.8	20.7

Note: Many other factors, including air temperature, clothing, and the vigor with which a person exercises, can mean an increase or decrease in the number of calories used.

Food and Nutrition

Food contains proteins, carbohydrates, fats, water, vitamins and minerals. Nutrition is the way your body takes in and uses these ingredients to maintain proper functioning.

The U.S. Dept. of Health and Human Services and the Dept. of Agriculture issued dietary guidelines Nov. 5, 1990 that were the most specific ever, and covered children from age 2 as well as adults. Recommended were: (1) no more than 30 percent of calories from fat, or about 67 grams of fat in a 2,000-calorie daily diet; and no more than 10 percent or 22 grams of that from saturated fats high in cholesterol; (2) maximum alcohol consumption of about 1 drink a day for women, 2 for men; (3) daily consumption of vegetables of 3-5 servings; fruits, 2-4; pastas, cereals or breads, 6-11; milk, 2-3; meat, poultry, fish and eggs, 2-3. (For vegetables, 1 serving=about 1 cup raw leafy greens or one-half cup other kinds; fruit, 1 medium apple, banana, or orange; grains, 1 slice of bread or 1 oz. cereal; milk, 1 cup or 1.5 oz. of cheese; meat and poultry, 2-3 oz. cooked lean beef or chicken without skin.)

Protein

Proteins, composed of amino acids, are indispensable in the diet. They build, maintain, and repair the body. Best sources: eggs, milk, fish, meat, poultry, soybeans, nuts. High quality proteins such as eggs, meat, or fish supply all 8 amino acids needed in the diet.

Fats

Fats provide energy by furnishing calories to the body, and by carrying vitamins A, D, E, and K. They are the most concentrated source of energy in the diet. Best sources: butter, margarine, salad oils, nuts, cream, egg yolks, most cheeses, lard, meat.

Carbohydrates

Carbohydrates provide energy for body function and activity by supplying immediate calories. The carbohydrate group includes sugars, starches, fiber, and starchy vegetables. Best sources: grains, legumes, nuts, potatoes, fruits.

Water

Water dissolves and transports other nutrients throughout the body, aiding the processes of digestion, absorption, circulation, and excretion. It helps regulate body temperature.

Vitamins

Vitamin A—promotes good eyesight and helps keep the skin and mucous membranes resistant to infection. Best sources: liver, carrots, sweet potatoes, kale, collard greens, turnips, fortified milk.

Vitamin B1 (thiamine)—prevents beriberi. Essential to carbohydrate metabolism and health of nervous system.

Vitamin B2 (riboflavin)—protects skin, mouth, eye, eyelids, and mucous membranes. Essential to protein and energy metabolism. Best sources: liver, milk, meat, poultry, broccoli, mushrooms.

Vitamin B6 (pyridoxine)—important in the regulation of the central nervous system and in protein metabolism. Best sources: whole grains, meats, nuts, brewers' yeast.

Vitamin B12 (cobalamin)—needed to form red blood cells. Best sources: liver, meat, fish, eggs, soybeans.

Niacin—maintains the health of skin, tongue, and digestive system. Best sources: poultry, peanuts, fish, organ meats, enriched flour and bread.

Other B vitamins—biotin, choline, folic acid (folacin), inositol, PABA (para-aminobenzoic acid), pantothenic acid.

Vitamin C (ascorbic acid)—maintains collagen, a protein necessary for the formation of skin, ligaments, and bones. It helps heal wounds and mend fractures, and aids in resisting some types of virus and bacterial infections. Best sources: citrus fruits and juices, turnips, broccoli, Brussels sprouts, potatoes and sweet potatoes, tomatoes, cabbage.

Vitamin D—important for bone development. Best sources: sunlight, fortified milk and milk products, fish-liver oils, egg yolks, organ meats.

Vitamin E (tocopherol)—helps protect red blood cells. Best sources: vegetable oils, wheat germ, whole grains, eggs, peanuts, organ meats, margarine, green leafy vegetables.

Vitamin K—necessary for formation of prothrombin, which helps blood to clot. Also made by intestinal bacteria. Best dietary sources: green leafy vegetables, tomatoes.

Minerals

Calcium—the most abundant mineral in the body, works with phosphorus in building and maintaining bones and teeth. Best sources: milk and milk products, cheese, and blackstrap molasses.

Phosphorus—the 2d most abundant mineral, performs more functions than any other mineral, and plays a part in nearly every chemical reaction in the body. Best source: whole grains, cheese, milk.

Iron—Necessary for the formation of myoglobin, which transports oxygen to muscle tissue, and hemoglobin, which transports oxygen in the blood. Best sources: organ meats, beans, green leafy vegetables, and shellfish.

Other minerals—chromium, cobalt, copper, fluorine, iodine, magnesium, manganese, molybdenum, potassium, selenium, sodium, sulfur, and zinc.

Recommended Daily Dietary Allowances

Source: Food and Nutrition Board, Natl. Academy of Sciences—Natl. Research Council; 1989

Age (years) and sex group	Weight (lbs.)	Protein (grams)	Fat soluble vitamins					Water soluble vitamins						Minerals						
			Vitamin A[1]	Vitamin D[2]	Vitamin E[3]	Vitamin K	Vitamin C	Thiamin (mg.)	Riboflavin (mg.)	Niacin (mg.)[4]	Vitamin B6 (mg.)	Folate (micrograms)	Vitamin B12 (micrograms)	Calcium (mg.)	Phosphorus (mg.)	Magnesium (mg.)	Iron (mg.)	Zinc (mg.)	Iodine (micrograms)	Selenium (micrograms)
Infants... to 5 mos.	13	13	375	7.5	3	5	30	0.3	0.4	5	0.3	25	0.3	400	300	40	6	5	40	10
to 1 yr.	20	14	375	10	4	10	35	0.4	0.5	6	0.6	35	0.5	600	500	60	10	5	50	15
Children.. 1-3	29	16	400	10	6	15	40	0.7	0.8	9	1.0	50	0.7	800	800	80	10	10	70	20
4-6	44	24	500	10	7	20	45	0.9	1.1	12	1.1	75	1.0	800	800	120	10	10	90	20
7-10	62	28	700	10	7	30	45	1.0	1.2	13	1.4	100	1.4	800	800	170	10	10	120	30
Males ... 11-14	99	45	1000	10	10	45	50	1.3	1.5	17	1.7	150	2.0	1200	1200	270	12	15	150	40
15-18	145	59	1000	10	10	65	60	1.5	1.8	20	2.0	200	2.0	1200	1200	400	12	15	150	50
19-24	160	58	1000	10	10	70	60	1.5	1.7	19	2.0	200	2.0	1200	1200	350	10	15	150	70
25-50	174	63	1000	5	10	80	60	1.5	1.7	19	2.0	200	2.0	800	800	350	10	15	150	70
51+	170	63	1000	5	10	80	60	1.2	1.4	15	2.0	200	2.0	800	800	350	10	15	150	70
Females .. 11-14	101	46	800	10	8	45	50	1.1	1.3	15	1.4	150	2.0	1200	1200	280	15	12	150	45
15-18	120	44	800	10	8	55	60	1.1	1.3	15	1.5	180	2.0	1200	1200	300	15	12	150	50
19-24	128	46	800	10	8	60	60	1.1	1.3	15	1.6	180	2.0	1200	1200	280	15	12	150	55
25-50	138	50	800	5	8	65	60	1.1	1.3	15	1.6	180	2.0	800	800	280	15	12	150	55
51+	143	50	800	5	8	65	60	1.0	1.2	13	1.6	180	2.0	800	800	280	10	12	150	55

(1) Retinol equivalents. (2) Micrograms of cholecalciferol. (3) Milligrams alpha-tocopherol equivalents. (4) Niacin equivalents.

ASTRONOMY AND CALENDAR

Edited by Dr. Kenneth L. Franklin, Astronomer Emeritus
American Museum-Hayden Planetarium

Celestial Events Highlights, 1992

(Greenwich Mean Time, or as indicated)

This year the planets put on a show more like most years, in contrast to the 1991 summer spectacle. By Spring, Jupiter is in the sky all night, demonstrating its claim to be the "King of the Planets." While Jupiter is approaching the western horizon at dusk in late summer, Saturn takes its turn in the midnight sky. Indeed, except for a few weeks at the beginning of the year, Saturn is available for observation from mid-February to beyond the end of December. As February changes to March, there is triple encounter in the early morning sky, low in the southeast. Here, Venus passes faint Mars, then Saturn, and Mars catches Saturn in the first week of March. Two more encounters involve Venus, next with Jupiter in late August, and finally Saturn in late December, when Venus will be a dazzling "Christmas star." Venus and Mercury get together three times, but these meetings are hard to observe, as is almost anything to do with Mercury. We may have two possibilities to see this dizzy little planet in the evening sky, first in June and July, then in October and November. Mars, in the morning sky all year, brightens spectacularly by year's end, coming to opposition in January 1993.

None of the three solar eclipses involve much of the United States, but southern Alaska does catch two of them. In addition to Alaska, the western U.S., Canada, and most of Mexico can get a glimpse of the January eclipse, as it ends at sunset for much of this area. Most of the U.S. can see parts of both the partial lunar eclipse in June and the total lunar eclipse in December.

Although no bright stars are occulted by the Moon this year, all but two of the planets are hidden for some observers somewhere on the Earth. For Mercury, it is once; Venus, twice; Mars, twice; Uranus, once; and Neptune, ten times. Some of them occur in the daytime, and the east coast of the U.S. has a chance at only two of them: Neptune, June 16-17, and Mercury, October 27.

Regard the notices of other occultations as indications of a close approach of the Moon to the planet involved on the nights before and after the dates.

January

Mercury is a morning object all month, moving rapidly eastward across Sagittarius, passing successively Mars, Uranus, and Neptune.

Venus is the very bright "star" in the morning twilight, passed by the moon on the 1st and occulted by it on the 31st, for observers in the Antarctic.

Mars stays in the morning sky all year, very slowly brightening as the months pass, drifting from Sagittarius almost through Gemini by year's end.

Jupiter starts the year in the morning sky, but after opposition at the end of February is an evening object, in due time, leaving Leo for Virgo.

Saturn this month leaves the evening sky to pass beyond the sun, in conjunction January 29, thus unobservable until late February, hovering in Capricornus on the edge of Aquarius around opposition in August.

Moon passes Venus on the 1st, passes Mercury and occults Mars on the 3rd, annularly eclipses the Sun on the 4th, passes Saturn on the 6th, Jupiter on the 23rd, and occults Venus on the 31st.

Jan. 1—Moon passes 5° south of Venus.

Jan. 3—Moon passes 3° south of Mercury, and 0°.8 south of Mars, occulting Mars; Earth at perihelion, 91.4 million miles from the sun, closest this year.

Jan. 4—Annular eclipse of the Sun.

Jan. 5—Uranus in conjunction with the Sun.

Jan. 6—Moon passes 3° north of Saturn.

Jan. 7—Neptune in conjunction with the Sun; Venus passes 7° north of Antares.

Jan. 10—Mercury passes 0°.6 north of Mars.

Jan. 19—Sun enters Capricorn.

Jan. 20—Mercury passes 0°.6 south of Uranus.

Jan. 21—Mercury passes 1°.9 south of Neptune.

Jan. 23—Moon passes 7° south of Jupiter.

Jan. 29—Mars passes 0°.4 south of Uranus; Saturn in conjunction.

Jan. 31—Moon passes 1°.0 south of Venus, occulting it.

February

Mercury, in superior conjunction beyond the Sun on the 12th, passes into the evening sky.

Venus may be used to find Uranus and Neptune in the morning sky at the end of the first week of the month, and passes Mars on the 19th.

Mars, brightening almost imperceptibly, moves from Sagittarius into Capricornus, passing Venus near the border.

Jupiter dominates the night sky, achieving opposition to the Sun on the 29th.

Saturn, in Capricornus just south of eastern Aquarius, is brushed by Venus on the 29th.

Moon occults Uranus and passes Mars on the 1st, Jupiter and Venus on the 19th, Uranus, and Neptune, occulting the latter, on the 28th.

Feb. 1—Mars passes 1°.5 south of Neptune; Moon passes 0°.9 north of Uranus, occulting it, and passes 0°.03 south of Neptune, occulting it, and passes 1°.5 north of Mars.

Feb. 7—Venus passes 0°.9 north of Uranus.

Feb. 8—Venus passes 0°.3 south of Neptune.

Feb. 12—Mercury in superior conjunction.

Feb. 16—Sun enters Aquarius.

Feb. 19—Moon passes 6° south of Jupiter; Venus 0°.9 north of Mars.

Feb. 28—Pluto stationary in Libra; Moon passes 1°.2 north of Uranus, and 0°.2 north of Neptune, occulting it.

Feb. 29—Jupiter at opposition to the Sun; Venus passes 0°.1 north of Saturn.

March

Mercury may be visible in the evening twilight to the right of where the Sun sets before mid month.

Venus continues to be the bright object in the dawn twilight.

Mars, nearly as bright as a first magnitude star, enters Aquarius by the month's end, passing Saturn on the way.

Jupiter is still in retrograde near the hindquarters of Leo, the brightest "star" of the night sky.

Saturn, somewhat brighter than Mars, passes close to the ruddy planet on the 6th.

257

Moon passes Mars on the 1st, Saturn and Venus on the 2nd, Mercury on the 6th, Jupiter on the 17th, passes Uranus and occults Neptune on the 27th, passes Saturn on the 29th, and Mars on the 31st.

Mar. 1—Moon passes 4° north of Mars.

Mar. 2—Moon passes 4° north of Saturn, and 4° north of Venus.

Mar. 6—Moon passes 4° north of Mercury; Mars passes 0°.4 south of Saturn.

Mar. 9—Mercury at greatest elongation, 18° east of the Sun.

Mar. 11—Sun enters Pisces.

Mar. 16—Mercury stationary, beginning retrograde motion.

Mar. 17—Moon passes 6° south of Jupiter.

Mar. 20—Vernal equinox; Spring begins in the northern hemisphere at 08:48 GMT (3:48 AM EST), as the Sun crosses the equator from south to north.

Mar. 26—Mercury in inferior conjunction, between the Earth and the Sun.

Mar. 27—Moon passes 1°.5 north of Uranus, and 0°.5 north of Neptune, occulting it.

Mar. 29—Moon passes 4° north of Saturn.

Mar. 31—Moon passes 6° north of Mars.

April

Mercury brightens from about 3rd magnitude to nearly zero magnitude throughout April, showing itself to the right of the sunrise point in the morning twilight, slipping 2° north of still brilliant Venus on the 5th.

Venus moves deeper into the dawn twilight, but remains easy to find all month.

Mars, a reddish 1st magnitude "star," crosses from Aquarius into Pisces by the end of the month.

Jupiter slows its retrograde motion in Leo all month.

Saturn is slowly brightening in Capricornus.

Moon passes Venus on the 1st, Mercury on the 2nd, Jupiter on the 13th, passes Uranus and occults Neptune on the 23rd, passes Saturn on the 26th, Mars on the 29th, and Mercury, again, on the 30th.

Apr. 1—Moon passes 7° north of Venus.

Apr. 2—Moon passes 4° north of Mercury.

Apr. 5—Mercury passes 2° north of Venus.

Apr. 8—Mercury stationary, resuming direct, eastward motion against the background stars.

Apr. 13—Moon passes 6° south of Jupiter.

Apr. 18—Sun enters Aries.

Apr. 20—Neptune stationary in Sagittarius, beginning its retrograde, westward, motion among the stars.

Apr. 22—Uranus stationary in Sagittarius, beginning its retrograde motion.

Apr. 23—Moon passes 1°.8 north of Uranus, 0°.7 north of Neptune, occulting it; Mercury at greatest western elongation, 27° west of the Sun.

Apr. 26—Moon passes 5° north of Saturn.

Apr. 29—Moon passes 7° north of Mars.

Apr. 30—Moon passes 8° north of Mercury.

May

Mercury, brightening all month to nearly minus 2nd magnitude by the end, races through Pisces to catch Venus in Aries, both, heading for superior conjunction, now too deep in the rising Sun's glare for us to see their encounter.

Venus can be found deep in the dawn twilight at the beginning of the month, but it is effectively lost to sight by the third week.

Mars, in Pisces, marches across the fishes like an er-rant 1st magnitude star.

Jupiter begins its direct, eastward, motion across Leo on May Day.

Saturn continues to direct our eyes toward the faint constellation of Capricornus, the sea-goat, and begins its retrograde motion there on the 31st.

Moon passes Jupiter on the 10th, Uranus and Neptune on the 20th, occulting the latter, passes Saturn on the 23rd, and Mars on the 28th.

May 1—Jupiter stationary, beginning its direct motion.

May 10—Moon passes 6° south of Jupiter.

May 12—Pluto at opposition.

May 13—Sun enters Taurus.

May 20—Moon passes 2° north of Uranus and 0°.9 north of Neptune, occulting Neptune.

May 23—Moon passes 5° north of Saturn.

May 28—Moon passes 7° north of Mars.

May 29—Saturn stationary, beginning retrograde.

May 31—Mercury in superior conjunction, beyond the Sun.

June

Mercury leaves the evening twilight by the 2nd week, but stays close to the sunset point on the western horizon.

Venus is in superior conjunction, beyond the Sun, on the 13th, thus lost to view all month.

Mars, now about 1st magnitude, enters Aries this month.

Jupiter slowly speeds its eastward motion toward the eastern end of Leo.

Saturn is now moving westward in Capricornus, brightening a bit as it goes.

Moon passes Jupiter on the 7th, enters a way into the earth's shadow to experience a partial eclipse on the 15th, passes Uranus and Neptune, occulting the latter on the 17th, passes Saturn on the 19th, Mars on the 26th, and totally eclipses the Sun on the 30th.

Jun. 7—Moon passes 7° south of Jupiter.

Jun. 13—Venus in superior conjunction.

Jun. 15—Moon in partial eclipse.

Jun. 17—Moon passes 1°.9 north of Uranus and 0°.9 north of Neptune, occulting Neptune.

Jun. 19—Moon passes 5° north of Saturn.

Jun. 20—Sun enters Gemini.

Jun. 21—Summer solstice; Summer begins in the northern hemisphere at 03:14 GMT (10:14 PM on the 20th, EST), as the Sun stops its northward trek, now beginning to go south.

Jun. 23—Mercury 5° south of Pollux.

Jun. 26—Moon passes 6° north of Mars.

Jun. 30—Moon totally eclipses the Sun.

July

Mercury reaches its farthest east of the Sun, 26° on the 6th, but it has begun to fade, being difficult to see to the left of the Sun after sunset.

Venus is still in the evening glare of the Sun, but sharp eyes may find it after the middle of the month.

Mars, still brightening, moves into Taurus.

Jupiter is the bright evening star in the western sky after sunset.

Saturn is much brighter than a 1st magnitude star, an interloper in faint Capricornus.

Moon passes Mercury on the 2nd, Jupiter on the 4th, Uranus and Neptune on the 14th, again occulting Neptune, passes Saturn on the 16th, and Mars on the 25th.

Jul. 2—Moon passes 4° south of Mercury.

Jul. 3—Earth at aphelion, 94.4 million miles from the Sun, greatest distance this year.

Jul. 4—Moon passes 7° south of Jupiter.

Jul. 6—Mercury at greatest eastern elongation, 26° east of the Sun.

Jul. 7—Uranus at opposition in Sagittarius.

Jul. 9—Neptune at opposition in Sagittarius.

Jul. 14—Moon passes 1°.8 north of Uranus and 0°.8 north of Neptune, occulting the latter.

Jul. 16—Moon passes 5° north of Saturn.

Jul. 19—Mercury stationary, beginning retrograde motion.

Jul. 20—Sun enters Cancer.

Jul. 25—Moon passes 4° north of Mars; Mercury passes 6° south of Venus.

August

Mercury passes through inferior conjunction becoming a "morning star" on the 2nd, achieving greatest western elongation on the 21st, all the while brightening rapidly in the dawn twilight.

Venus has begun to crawl out of the western dusk into the darker sky of the evening, to have an encounter with Jupiter on the evening of the 22nd (EST).

Mars is quite prominent in Taurus all month.

Jupiter is the higher bright "evening star" until it has a tête-a-tête with Venus on the 22nd to exchange places.

Saturn rises in the southeast about sunset, staying in the sky all night, because it is in opposition to the Sun on the 7th.

Moon passes Jupiter on the 1st, Uranus and Neptune on the 10th, occulting the latter planet, passes Saturn on the 13th (the evening of the 12th, EST), Mars on the 22nd, and Mercury on the 27th.

Aug. 1—Moon passes 7° south of Jupiter.

Aug. 2—Mercury in inferior conjunction, between the Earth and the Sun.

Aug. 4—Pluto stationary, resuming direct motion.

Aug. 6—Venus passes 1°.1 north of Regulus.

Aug. 7—Saturn in opposition to the Sun.

Aug. 10—Moon passes 1°.8 north of Uranus, and 0°.8 north of Neptune, occulting it; Sun enters Leo.

Aug. 11—Mars passes 5° north of Aldebaran; nearly full Moon will seriously affect the annual Perseid meteor shower tonight and tomorrow night.

Aug. 12—Mercury stationary, resuming direct motion.

Aug. 13—Moon passes 5° north of Saturn.

Aug. 21—Mercury at greatest elongation, 18° west of the Sun.

Aug. 22—Moon passes 1°.4 north of Mars.

Aug. 23—Venus passes 0°.3 north of Jupiter.

Aug. 27—Moon passes 5° south of Mercury.

Aug. 29—Moon passes 7° south of Venus.

September

Mercury, now brighter than a 0 magnitude star, passes close to Regulus on the 2nd, before being lost in the solar glare, to pass through superior conjunction, beyond the Sun, on the 15th.

Venus becomes the sole "evening star" this month.

Mars, passing just north of El Nath, the right horn of the bull, enters Gemini in mid-month, brightening along the way.

Jupiter is lost in evening and morning twilight all month, passing beyond the Sun on the 17th.

Saturn, still solidly in Capricornus, continues its slow retrograde motion all month.

Moon passes Uranus and Neptune on the 6th, occulting Neptune on the way, passes Saturn on the 9th, occults Mars on the 20th, and passes Venus on the 28th.

Sep. 2—Mercury passes 1°.2 north of Regulus.

Sep. 6—Moon passes 1°.9 north of Uranus and 0°.9 north of Neptune, occulting the latter.

Sep. 9—Moon passes 5° north of Saturn.

Sep. 15—Mercury in superior conjunction, beyond the Sun.

Sep. 16—Sun enters Virgo.

Sep. 17—Jupiter in conjunction with the Sun.

Sep. 19—Venus passes 3° north of Spica.

Sep. 20—Moon passes 0°9 south of Mars, occulting the planet.

Sep. 22—Autumnal equinox; Autumn begins in the northern hemisphere at 18:43 GMT (1:43 PM EST), as the Sun crosses the equator, heading south.

Sep. 23—Uranus stationary in Sagittarius, resuming its direct motion.

Sep. 27—Neptune stationary in Sagittarius, resuming its direct motion.

Sep. 28—Moon passes 4° south of Venus.

October

Mercury is in the evening sky and brighter than 0 magnitude all month, providing a good chance to find it to the left of the point of sunset, especially on the 31st when it lies 24° to the Sun's east.

Venus is above Mercury and much brighter all month, with the crescent Moon below on the 27th and above on the 28th.

Mars, in Gemini all month, makes it to 0 magnitude at the end.

Jupiter enters Virgo this month, shining brightly in the dawn sky.

Saturn is still the bright interloper in Capricornus, about a quarter of the sky above Venus.

Moon passes Uranus on the 3rd, occults Neptune on the 4th, passes Saturn on the 6th, Mars on the 18th, Jupiter on the 24th, occults Mercury on the 27th, Venus on the 28th, and passes Uranus and Neptune (without occulting it) on the 31st.

Oct. 2—Mercury passes 2° north of Spica.

Oct. 3—Moon passes 2° north of Uranus.

Oct. 4—Moon passes 1°.2 north of Neptune, occulting it.

Oct. 6—Moon passes 5° north of Saturn.

Oct. 16—Saturn stationary, resuming direct motion.

Oct. 18—Moon passes 3° south of Mars.

Oct. 24—Moon passes 7° south of Jupiter.

Oct. 27—Venus passes 3° north of Antares; Moon passes 0°.5 north of Mercury, occulting it.

Oct. 28—Moon passes 0°.4 north of Venus, occulting it.

Oct. 30—Sun enters Libra.

Oct. 31—Moon passes 2° north of Uranus, and 1°.4 north of Neptune; Mercury at greatest elongation, 24° east of the Sun.

November

Mercury fades rapidly early this month, diving into the evening twilight before its inferior conjunction on the 21st, to become a morning object, thus lost to view.

Venus clearly dominates the evening western sky all month.

Mars brightens by more than a half magnitude this month, beginning its retrograde motion in Gemini on the 29th, after having passed Pollux on the 4th.

Jupiter, brighter than Mars, lies in Virgo, about 2 hours below the ruddy planet.

Saturn, no serious threat to the beauty of Venus, stays with Capricornus, as together, they approach still closer to the evening horizon.

Moon passes Saturn on the 2nd, Mars on the 15th, Jupiter on the 20th, Uranus, Neptune, and Venus on the 27th, and Saturn, again, on the 30th.

Nov. 2—Moon passes 5° north of Saturn.

Nov. 4—Mars passes 5° south of Pollux.

Nov. 11—Mercury stationary, beginning retrograde motion.

Nov. 15—Pluto in conjunction with the Sun; Moon passes 5° south of Mars.

Nov. 17—Last quarter moon can interfere with the sometimes surprising Leonid meteor shower tonight and tomorrow night.

Nov. 20—Moon passes 7° south of Jupiter.

Nov. 21—Mercury in inferior conjunction.

Nov. 22—Sun enters Scorpius.

Nov. 26—Venus passes 1°.9 south of Uranus.

Nov. 27—Venus passes 3° south of Neptune; Moon passes 3° north of Uranus, 1°.6 north of Neptune, and 5° north of Venus.

Nov. 29—Mars stationary, beginning retrograde motion; Sun enters Ophiuchus.

Nov. 30—Moon passes 5° north of Saturn.

December

Mercury can be quite bright to the right of the sunrise point these mornings.

Venus plays the part of the Christmas star this month, and is briefly visited by Saturn on the evenings of the 20th and 21st.

Mars, now strongly in retrograde motion in eastern Gemini, passing Pollux again, brightens perceptibly all month.

Jupiter continues to approach Spica, but will not make it.

Saturn passes Venus on the 21st, heading for the twilight, but still on the evening scene.

Moon enters the Earth's shadow to be totally eclipsed on the 9th-10th, passes Mars on the 12th, Jupiter on the 18th, Mercury on the 22nd, partially eclipses the Sun on the 24th, passes Saturn on the 27th, and Venus on the 28th.

Dec. 1—Mercury stationary, resuming its direct motion.

Dec. 9—Mercury at greatest elongation, 21° west of the Sun.

Dec. 10—Total lunar eclipse.

Dec. 12—Moon passes 6° south of Mars.

Dec. 14—Perhaps the Geminid meteor shower will show its occasional fireball after moon set tonight.

Dec. 16—Sun enters Sagittarius.

Dec. 18—Moon passes 7° south of Jupiter.

Dec. 19—Mercury passes 6° north of Antares.

Dec. 21—Winter solstice; winter begins in the northern hemisphere at 14:43 GMT (9:43 AM EST), to begin its journey toward the north; Venus passes 1°1 south of Saturn.

Dec. 22—Moon passes 1°.5 south of Mercury; Mars passes 3° south of Pollux.

Dec. 24—Partial solar eclipse.

Dec. 27—Moon passes 6° north of Saturn.

Dec. 28—Moon passes 7° north of Venus.

Planets and the Sun

The planets of the solar system, in order of their mean distance from the sun, are Mercury, Venus, Earth, Mars, Jupiter, Saturn, Uranus, Neptune and Pluto. Both Uranus and Neptune are visible through good field glasses, but Pluto is so distant and so small that only large telescopes or long exposure photographs can make it visible.

Since Mercury and Venus are nearer to the sun than is the earth, their motions about the sun are seen from the earth as wide swings first to one side of the sun and then to the other, although they are both passing continuously around the sun in orbits that are almost circular. When their passage takes them either between the earth and the sun, or beyond the sun as seen from the earth, they are invisible to us. Because of the laws which govern the motions of planets about the sun, both Mercury and Venus require much less time to pass between the earth and the sun than around the far side of the sun, so their periods of visibility and invisibility are unequal.

The planets that lie farther from the sun than does the earth may be seen for longer periods of time and are invisible only when they are so located in our sky that they rise and set about the same time as the sun when, of course, they are overwhelmed by the sun's great brilliance. None of the planets has any light of its own but each shines only by reflecting sunlight from its surface. Mercury and Venus, because they are between the earth and the sun, show phases very much as the moon does. The planets farther from the sun are always seen as full, although Mars does occasionally present a slightly gibbous phase — like the moon when not quite full.

The planets move rapidly among the stars because they are very much nearer to us. The stars are also in motion, some of them at tremendous speeds, but they are so far away that their motion does not change their apparent positions in the heavens sufficiently for anyone to perceive that change in a single lifetime. The very nearest star is about 7,000 times as far away as the most distant planet.

Planets of the Solar System

Mercury

Mercury, nearest planet to the sun, is the second smallest of the nine planets known to be orbiting the sun. Its diameter is 3,100 miles and its mean distance from the sun is 36,000,000 miles.

Mercury moves with great speed in its journey about the sun, averaging about 30 miles a second to complete its circuit in 88 of our days. Mercury rotates upon its axis over a period of nearly 59 days, thus exposing all

of its surface periodically to the sun. It is believed that the surface passing before the sun may have a temperature of about 800° F., while the temperature on the side turned temporarily away from the sun does not fall as low as might be expected. This night temperature has been described by Russian astronomers as "room temperature" — possibly about 70°. This would contradict the former belief that Mercury did not possess an atmosphere, for some sort of atmosphere would be needed to retain the fierce solar radiation that strikes Mercury. A shallow but dense layer of carbon dioxide would produce the "greenhouse" effect, in which heat accumulated during exposure to the sun would not completely escape at night. The actual presence of a carbon dioxide atmosphere is in dispute. Other research, however, has indicated a nighttime temperature approaching −300°.

This uncertainty about conditions upon Mercury and its motion arise from its shorter angular distance from the sun as seen from the earth, for Mercury is always too much in line with the sun to be observed against a dark sky, but is always seen during either morning or evening twilight.

Mariner 10 made 3 passes by Mercury in 1974 and 1975. A large fraction of the surface was photographed from varying distances, revealing a degree of cratering similar to that of the moon. An atmosphere of hydrogen and helium may be made up of gases of the solar wind temporarily concentrated by the presence of Mercury. The discovery of a weak but permanent magnetic field was a surprise. It has been held that both a fluid core and rapid rotation were necessary for the generation of a planetary magnetic field. Mercury may demonstrate these conditions to be unnecessary, or the field may reveal something about the history of Mercury.

Venus

Venus, slightly smaller than the earth, moves about the sun at a mean distance of 67,000,000 miles in 225 of our days. Its synodical revolution — its return to the same relationship with the earth and the sun, which is a result of the combination of its own motion and that of the earth — is 584 days. Every 19 months, then, Venus will be nearer to the earth than any other planet of the solar system. The planet is covered with a dense, white, cloudy atmosphere that conceals whatever is below it. This same cloud reflects sunlight efficiently so that when Venus is favorably situated, it is the third brightest object in the sky, exceeded only by the sun and the moon.

Spectral analysis of sunlight reflected from Venus' cloud tops has shown features that can best be explained by identifying the material of the clouds as sulphuric acid (oil of vitriol). Infrared spectroscopy from a balloon-borne telescope nearly 20 miles above the earth's surface gave indications of a small amount of water vapor present in the same region of the atmosphere of Venus. In 1956, radio astronomers at the Naval Research Laboratories in Washington, D. C., found a temperature for Venus of about 600° F., in marked contrast to minus 125° F., previously found at the cloud tops. Subsequent radio work confirmed a high temperature and produced evidence for this temperature to be associated with the solid body of Venus. With this peculiarity in mind, space scientists devised experiments for the U.S. space probe Mariner 2 to perform when it flew by in 1962. Mariner 2 confirmed the high temperature and the fact that it pertained to the ground rather than to some special activity of the atmosphere. In addition, Mariner 2 was unable to detect any radiation belts similar to the earth's so-called Van Allen belts. Nor was it able to detect the existence of a magnetic field even as weak as 1/100,000 of that of the earth.

In 1967, a Russian space probe, Venera 4, and the American Mariner 5 arrived at Venus within a few hours of each other. Venera 4 was designed to allow an instrument package to land gently on the planet's surface via parachute. It ceased transmission of information in about 75 minutes when the temperature it read went above 500° F. After considerable controversy, it was agreed that it still had 20 miles to go to reach the surface. The U.S. probe, Mariner 5, went around the dark side of Venus at a distance of about 6,000 miles. Again, it detected no significant magnetic field but its radio signals passed to earth through Venus' atmosphere twice — once on the night side and once on the day side. The results are startling. Venus' atmosphere is nearly all carbon dioxide and must exert a pressure at the planet's surface of up to 100 times the earth's normal sea-level pressure of one atmosphere. Since the earth and Venus are about the same size, and were presumably formed at the same time by the same general process from the same mixture of chemical elements, one is faced with the question: which is the planet with the unusual history — earth or Venus?

Radar astronomers using powerful transmitters as well as sensitive receivers and computers have succeeded in determining the rotation period of Venus. It turns out to be 243 days clockwise — in other words, contrary to the spin of most of the other planets and to its own motion around the sun. If it were exactly 243.16 days, Venus would always present the same face toward the earth at every inferior conjunction. This rate and sense of rotation allows a "day" on Venus of 117.4 earth days. Any part of Venus will receive sunlight on its clouds for over 58 days and will be in darkness for 58 days. Recent radar observations have shown surface features below the clouds. Large craters, continent-sized highlands, and extensive, dry "ocean" basins have been identified.

Mariner 10 passed Venus before traveling on to Mercury in 1974. The carbon dioxide molecule found in such abundance in the atmosphere is rather opaque to certain ultraviolet wavelengths, enabling sensitive television cameras to take pictures of the Venusian cloud cover. Photos radioed to earth show a spiral pattern in the clouds from equator to the poles.

In December, 1978, two U. S. Pioneer probes arrived at Venus. One went into orbit about Venus, the other split into 5 separate probes targeted for widely-spaced entry points to sample different conditions. The instrumentation ensemble was selected on the basis of previous missions that had shown the range of conditions to be studied. The probes confirmed expected high surface temperatures and high winds aloft. Winds of about 200 miles per hour, there, may account for the transfer of heat onto the night side in spite of the low rotation speed of the planet. Surface winds were light at the time, however. Atmosphere and cloud chemistries were examined in detail, providing much data for continued analysis. The probes detected 4 layers of clouds and more light on the surface than expected solely from sunlight. This light allowed Russian scientists to obtain at least two photos showing rocks on the surface. Sulphur seems to play a large role in the chemistry of Venus, and reactions involving sulphur may be responsible for the glow. To learn more about the weather and atmospheric circulation on Venus, the orbiter takes daily photos of the daylight side cloud cover. It confirms the cloud pattern and its circulation shown by Mariner 10. The ionosphere shows large variability. The orbiter's radar operates in 2 modes: one, for ground elevation variability, and the second for ground reflectivity in 2 dimensions, thus "imaging" the surface. Radar maps of the entire planet that show the features mentioned above have been produced.

The Venus orbiter, Magellan, was launched May 5, 1989. It was equipped to observe Venus by a side-scanning radar system, together with one to gather data on variations in elevations directly beneath the craft. By mid 1991, Magellan had mapped all of the planet but a small fraction near one of the poles.

Craters over 20 miles wide are believed to have been caused by impacting bodies. One 150 mile-wide crater, the largest found to date, has been named for Margaret Mead. Smaller craters are probably due to volcanic action. The largest such caldera has been named Sakajawea. Many lava flows have been seen, and some old craters and plains seem to be filled with lava.

Most of the surface is believed to be younger than 1000 to 500 million years old. Modifications of previously existing surface features have been due to tectonic actions such as faulting, and to weathering. Tectonic actions in general are distinctly different from such actions on Earth. The intense heat at the surface of Venus can prevent the surface materials from cooling to the same brittle condition as on Earth. The same actions on Earth, thus, may produce somewhat different results on Venus. Although there are deep regions, somewhat similar to our ocean basins, there is no water to fill them. There seems to be no activity on Venus similar to our moving tectonic plates, but there may be local stretching and compressing that produce rift valleys and higher plains and mountains. Although there is no weathering due to water on Venus, the action of winds is in evidence. Extensive sand dunes have been seen, and wind-blown deposits indicate stable wind patterns for very long periods of time.

Magellan has been changed to a different orbit in order to see the same surface from a different direction, thus getting better third-dimension relief of the Venusian features.

Mars

Mars is the first planet beyond the earth, away from the sun. Mars' diameter is about 4,200 miles, although a determination of the radius and mass of Mars by the space-probe, Mariner 4, which flew by Mars on July 14, 1965 at a distance of less than 6,000 miles, indicated that these dimensions were slightly larger than had been previously estimated. While Mars' orbit is also nearly circular, it is somewhat more eccentric than the orbits of many of the other planets, and Mars is more than 30 million miles farther from the sun in some parts of its year than it is at others. Mars takes 687 of our days to make one circuit of the sun, traveling at about 15 miles a second. Mars rotates upon its axis in almost the same period of time that the earth does — 24 hours and 37 minutes. Mars' mean distance from the sun is 141 million miles, so that the temperature on Mars would be lower than that on the earth even if Mars' atmosphere were about the same as ours. The atmosphere is not, however, for Mariner 4 reported that atmospheric pressure on Mars is between 1% and 2% of the earth's atmospheric pressure. This thin atmosphere appears to be largely carbon dioxide. No evidence of free water was found.

There appears to be no magnetic field about Mars. This would eliminate the previous conception of a dangerous radiation belt around Mars. The same lack of a magnetic field would expose the surface of Mars to an influx of cosmic radiation about 100 times as intense as that on earth.

Deductions from years of telescopic observation indicate that 5/8ths of the surface of Mars is a desert of reddish rock, sand, and soil. The rest of Mars is covered by irregular patches that appear generally green in hues that change through the Martian year. These were formerly held to be some sort of primitive vegetation, but with the findings of Mariner 4 of a complete lack of water and oxygen, such growth does not appear possible. The nature of the green areas is now unknown. They may be regions covered with volcanic salts whose color changes with changing temperatures

and atmospheric conditions, or they may be gray, rather than green. When large gray areas are placed beside large red areas, the gray areas will appear green to the eye.

Mars' axis of rotation is inclined from a vertical to the plane of its orbit about the sun by about 25° and therefore Mars has seasons as does the earth, except that the Martian seasons are longer because Mars' year is longer. White caps form about the winter pole of Mars, growing through the winter and shrinking in summer. These polar caps are now believed to be both water ice and carbon dioxide ice. It is the carbon dioxide that is seen to come and go with the seasons. The water ice is apparently in many layers with dust between them, indicating climatic cycles.

The canals of Mars have become more of a mystery than they were before the voyage of Mariner 4. Markings forming a network of fine lines crossing much of the surface of Mars have been seen there by men who have devoted much time to the study of the planet, but no canals have shown clearly enough in previous photographs to be universally accepted. A few of the 21 photographs sent back to earth by Mariner 4 covered areas crossed by canals. The pictures show faint, ill-defined, broad, dark markings, but no positive identification of the nature of the markings.

Mariners 6 & 7 in 1969 sent back many more photographs of higher quality than those of the pioneering Mariner 4. These pictures showed cratering similar to the earlier views, but in addition showed 2 other types of terrain. Some regions seemed featureless for many square miles, but others were chaotic, showing high relief without apparent organization into mountain chains or craters.

Mariner 9, the first artificial body to be placed in an orbit about Mars, has transmitted over 10,000 photographs covering 100% of the planet's surface. Preliminary study of these photos and other data shows that Mars resembles no other planet we know. Using terrestrial terms, however, scientists describe features that seem to be clearly of volcanic origin. One of these features is Nix Olympica, (now called Olympus Mons), apparently a shield volcano whose caldera is over 50 miles wide, and whose outer slopes are over 300 miles in diameter, and which stands about 90,000 feet above the surrounding plain. Some features may have been produced by cracking (faulting) of the surface and the sliding of one region over or past another. Many craters seem to have been produced by impacting bodies such as may have come from the nearby asteroid belt. Features near the south pole may have been produced by glaciers that are no longer present. Flowing water, non-existent on Mars at the present time, probably carved canyons, one 10 times longer and 3 times deeper than the Grand Canyon.

Although the Russians landed a probe on the Martian surface, it transmitted for only 20 seconds. In 1976, the U.S. landed 2 Viking spacecraft on the Martian surface. The landers had devices aboard to perform chemical analyses of the soil in search of evidence of life. The results have been inconclusive. The 2 Viking orbiters have returned the best pictures yet of Martian topographic features. Many features can be explained only if Mars once had large quantities of flowing water.

Mars' position in its orbit and its speed around that orbit in relation to the earth's position and speed bring Mars fairly close to the earth on occasions about two years apart and then move Mars and the earth too far apart for accurate observation and photography. Every 15-17 years, the close approaches are especially favorable to close observation.

Mars has 2 satellites, discovered in 1877 by Asaph Hall. The outer satellite, Deimos, revolves around Mars in about 31 hours. The inner satellite, Phobos, whips around Mars in a little more than 7 hours, making 3 trips around the planet each Martian day. Mariner and Viking photos show these bodies to be irregularly shaped and pitted with numerous craters. Phobos also shows a system of linear grooves, each about 1/3-mile across and roughly parallel. Phobos measures about 8 by 12 miles and Deimos about 5 by 7.5 miles in size.

Jupiter

Jupiter is the largest of the planets. Its equatorial diameter is 88,000 miles, 11 times the diameter of the earth. Its polar diameter is about 6,000 miles shorter. This is an equilibrium condition resulting from the liquidity of the planet and its extremely rapid rate of rotation: a Jupiter day is only 10 earth hours long. For a planet this size, this rotational speed is amazing, and it moves a point on Jupiter's equator at a speed of 22,000 miles an hour, as compared with 1,000 miles an hour for a point on the earth's equator. Jupiter is at an average distance of 480 million miles from the sun and takes almost 12 of our years to make one complete circuit of the sun.

The only directly observable chemical constituents of Jupiter's atmosphere are methane (CH_4) and ammonia (NH_3), but it is reasonable to assume the same mixture of elements available to make Jupiter as to make the sun. This would mean a large fraction of hydrogen and helium must be present also, as well as water (H_2O). The temperature at the tops of the clouds may be about minus 260° F. The clouds are probably ammonia ice crystals, becoming ammonia droplets lower down. There may be a space before water ice crystals show up as clouds: in turn, these become water droplets near the bottom of the entire cloud layer. The total atmosphere may be only a few hundred miles in depth, pulled down by the surface gravity (= 2.64 times earth's) to a relatively thin layer. Of course, the gases become denser with depth until they may turn into a slush or a slurry. Perhaps there is no surface — no real interface between the gaseous atmosphere and the body of Jupiter. Pioneers 10 and 11 provided evidence for considering Jupiter to be almost entirely liquid hydrogen. Long before a rocky core about the size of the earth is reached, hydrogen mixed with helium becomes a liquid metal at very high temperature and pressure. Jupiter's cloudy atmosphere is a fairly good reflector of sunlight and makes it appear far brighter than any of the stars.

Fourteen of Jupiter's 17 or more satellites have been found through earth-based observations. Four of the moons are large and bright, rivaling our own moon and the planet Mercury in diameter, and may be seen through a field glass. They move rapidly around Jupiter and their change of position from night to night is extremely interesting to watch. The other satellites are much smaller and in all but one instance much farther from Jupiter and cannot be seen except through powerful telescopes. The 4 outermost satellites are revolving around Jupiter clockwise as seen from the north, contrary to the motions of the great majority of the satellites in the solar system and to the direction of revolution of the planets around the sun. The reason for this retrograde motion is not known, but one theory is that Jupiter's tremendous gravitational power may have captured 4 of the minor planets or asteroids that move about the sun between Mars and Jupiter, and that these would necessarily revolve backward. At the great distance of these bodies from Jupiter — some 14 million miles — direct motion would result in decay of the orbits, while retrograde orbits would be stable. Jupiter's mass is more than twice the mass of all the other planets put together, and accounts for Jupiter's tremendous gravitational field and so, probably, for its numerous satellites and its dense atmosphere.

In December, 1973, Pioneer 10 passed about 80,000 miles from the equator of Jupiter and was whipped into a path taking it out of our solar system in about 50 years, and beyond the system of planets, on June 13, 1983. In December, 1974, Pioneer 11 passed within 30,000 miles of Jupiter, moving roughly from south to north, over the poles.

Photographs from both encounters were useful at the time but were far surpassed by those of Voyagers I and II. Thousands of high resolution multi-color pictures show rapid variations of features both large and small. The Great Red Spot exhibits internal counterclockwise rotation. Much turbulence is seen in adjacent material passing north or south of it. The satellites Amalthea, Io, Europa, Ganymede, and Callisto were photographed, some in great detail. Each is individual and unique, with no similarities to other known planets or satellites. Io has active volcanoes that probably have ejected material into a doughnut-shaped ring enveloping its orbit about Jupiter. This is not to be confused with the thin flat disk-like ring closer to Jupiter's surface. Now that such a ring has been seen by the Voyagers, older uncertain observations from Earth can be reinterpreted as early sightings of this structure.

Saturn

Saturn, last of the planets visible to the unaided eye, is almost twice as far from the sun as Jupiter, almost 900 million miles. It is second in size to Jupiter but its mass is much smaller. Saturn's specific gravity is less than that of water. Its diameter is about 71,000 miles at the equator; its rotational speed spins it completely around in a little more than 10 hours, and its atmosphere is much like that of Jupiter, except that its temperature at the top of its cloud layer is at least 100° lower. At about 300° F. below zero, the ammonia would be frozen out of Saturn's clouds. The theoretical construction of Saturn resembles that of Jupiter; it is either all gas, or it has a small dense center surrounded by a layer of liquid and a deep atmosphere.

Until Pioneer 11 passed Saturn in September 1979 only 10 satellites of Saturn were known. Since that time, the situation is quite confused. Added to data interpretations from the fly-by are earth-based observations using new techniques while the rings were edge-on and virtually invisible. It was hoped that the Voyager I and II fly-bys would help sort out the system. It is now believed that Saturn has at least 22 satellites, some sharing orbits. The Saturn satellite system is still confused.

Saturn's ring system begins about 7,000 miles above the visible disk of Saturn, lying above its equator and extending about 35,000 miles into space. The diameter of the ring system visible from Earth is about 170,000 miles; the rings are estimated to be no thicker than 10 miles. In 1973, radar observation showed the ring particles to be large chunks of material averaging a meter on a side.

Voyager I and II observations showed the rings to be considerably more complex than had been believed, so much so that interpretation will take much time. To the untrained eye, the Voyager photographs could be mistaken for pictures of a colorful phonograph record.

Uranus

Voyager II, after passing Saturn in August 1981, headed for a rendezvous with Uranus culminating in a fly-by January 24, 1986. This encounter answered many questions, and raised others.

Uranus, discovered by Sir William Herschel on Mar. 13, 1781, lies at a distance of 1.8 billion miles from the sun, taking 84 years to make its circuit around our star. Uranus has a diameter of about 32,000 miles and spins once in some 16.8 hours, according to fly-by data. One of the most fascinating features of Uranus is how far it is tipped over. Its north pole lies 98° from being directly up and down to its orbit plane. Thus, its seasons are extreme. When the sun rises at the north pole, it stays up for 42 years; then it sets and the north pole will be in darkness (and winter) for 42 years.

The satellite system of Uranus, consisting of at least 15 moons, (the 5 largest having been known before the fly-by) have orbits lying in the plane of the planet's equator. In that plane there is also a complex of rings, 9 of which were discovered in 1978. Invisible from Earth, the 9 original rings were found by observers watching Uranus pass before a star. As they waited, they saw their photoelectric equipment register several short eclipses of the star. Then the planet occulted the star as expected. After the star came out from behind Uranus, the star winked out several more times. Subsequent observations and analyses indicated the 9 narrow, nearly opaque rings circling Uranus. Evidence from the Voyager II fly-by has shown the ring particles to be predominantly a yard or so in diameter.

In addition to the 10 new, very small satellites, Voyager II returned detailed photos of the 5 large satellites. As in the case of other satellites newly observed in the Voyager program, these bodies proved to be entirely different from each other and any others. Miranda has grooved markings, reminiscent of Jupiter's Ganymede, but often arranged in a chevron pattern. Ariel shows rifts and channels. Umbriel is extremely dark, prompting some observers to regard its surface as among the oldest in the system. Titania has rifts and fractures, but not the evidence of flow found on Ariel. Oberon's main feature is its surface saturated with craters, unrelieved by other formations.

The structure of Uranus is subject to some debate. Basically, however, it may have a rocky core surrounded by a thick icy mantle on top of which is a crust of hydrogen and helium that gradually becomes an atmosphere. Perhaps continued analysis of the wealth of data returned by Voyager II will shed some light on this problem.

Neptune

Neptune, currently the most distant planet from the sun (until 1999), lies at an average distance of 2.8 billion miles. It was the last planet visited in Voyager II's epic 12 year trek from earth. While much new information was immediately perceived, much more must await further analysis of the tremendous amount of data returned from the spacecraft.

As with the other giant planets, there may be no solid surface to give real meaning to a measure of a diameter. However, a mean value of 30,600 miles may be assigned to a diameter between atmosphere levels where the pressure is about the same as sea level on earth, as determined by radio experimenters. A different radio observational technique gave evidence of a rotation period for the bulk of Neptune of 16.1 hours, a shorter value than the 18.2 hours given by the clouds seen in the blue atmosphere. Neptune orbits the sun in 164 years in nearly a circular orbit.

Voyager II, which passed 3000 miles from Neptune's north pole, found a magnetic field which is considerably asymmetric to the planet's structure, similar, but not so extreme, to that found at Uranus.

Neptune's atmosphere was seen to be quite blue, with quickly changing white clouds often suspended high above an apparent surface. In that apparent surface were found features, one of which was reminiscent of the Great Red Spot of Jupiter, even to the counterclockwise rotation expected in a high-pressure system in the southern hemisphere. Atmospheric constituents are mostly hydrocarbon compounds. Although lightning and auroras have been found on other giant planets, only the aurora phenomenon has been seen on Neptune.

Six new satellites were discerned around Neptune, one confirming a 1981 sighting that was then difficult to recover for proper identification. Five of these satellites orbit Neptune in a half day or less. Of the eight satellites of Neptune, the largest, Triton, is in a retrograde orbit suggesting that it was captured rather than being co-eval with Neptune. Triton is sufficiently large to raise significant tides on Neptune which will one day, say 100 million years from now, cause Triton to come close enough to Neptune for it to be torn apart. Nereid was found in 1949, and is in a long looping orbit suggesting it, too, was captured. Each of the satellites that has been photographed by the two Voyagers in the planetary encounters has been different from any of the other satellites, and certainly from any of the planets. Only about half of Triton has been observed, but its terrain shows cratering and a strange regional feature described as resembling the skin of a cantaloupe. Triton has a tenuous atmosphere of nitrogen with a trace of hydrocarbons, and evidence of active geysers injecting material into it. At minus 238 degrees Celsius, Triton is one of the coldest objects in the solar system observed by Voyager II.

In addition to the satellite system, Voyager II confirmed the existence of at least three rings composed of very fine particles. There may some clumpiness in their structure, but the known satellites may not contribute to the formation or maintenance of the rings, as they have in other systems.

As with the other giant planets, Neptune is emitting more energy than it receives from the sun, Voyager finding the excess to be 2.7 times the solar contribution. These excesses are thought to be cooling from internal heat sources and from the heat of formation of the planets.

Pluto

Although Pluto on the average stays about 3.6 billion miles from the sun, its orbit is so eccentric that its minimum distance of 2.7 billion miles is less than the current distance of Neptune. Thus Pluto, until 1999, is temporarily planet number 8 from the sun. At its mean distance, Pluto takes 247.7 years to circumnavigate the sun. Until recently that was about all that was known of Pluto.

About a century ago, a hypothetical planet was believed to lie beyond Neptune and Uranus because neither planet followed the paths predicted by astronomers even when all known gravitational influences were considered. Little more than a guess, a mass of one Earth was assigned to the mysterious body and mathematical searches were begun. Amid some controversy about the validity of the predictive process, Pluto was found nearly where it was predicted to be. It was found by Clyde Tombaugh at the Lowell Observatory in Flagstaff, Ariz., in 1930.

At the U.S. Naval Observatory, also in Flagstaff, on July 2, 1978, James Christy obtained a photograph of Pluto that was distinctly elongated. Repeated observations of this shape and its variation were convincing evidence of the discovery of a satellite of Pluto, now named Charon. Subsequent observations show it to be

750 miles across, at a distance of over 12,000 miles from Pluto, and taking 6.4 days to move around Pluto. In this same length of time Pluto and Charon each rotate once around their individual axes. The Pluto-Charon system thus appears to rotate as virtually a ridged body. Gravitational laws allow these interactions to give us the mass of Pluto as 0.003 of the Earth. This mass, together with a new diameter for Pluto of 1,430 miles makes the density about twice that of water. Theorists predict a rocky core for Pluto surrounded by a thick mantle of ice.

It is now clear that Pluto, the body found by Tombaugh, could not have influenced Neptune and Uranus to go astray. Theorists are again at work looking for a new planet X.

Because the rotational axis of the system is tipped from the reference plane of the solar system by about 98°.3, similar to that of Uranus, there is only a short interval every half solar period when Pluto and Charon alternately eclipse each other. Analysis of the variations in light in and out of the recent eclipses has led to the diameters quoted above, and to interesting knowledge of other aspects of the system. Each component is approximately spherical, but they are otherwise different. Pluto is red, Charon grey. Charon has a surface identified as water ice; Pluto's surface is frozen methane. There are large regions on Pluto that are dark, others, light; Pluto has spots, and, perhaps, polar caps. Although extremely cold, Pluto's methane surface produces a tenuous atmosphere that may be slowly escaping into space, perhaps going to Charon. When Pluto occulted a star, the star's light faded in such a way as to have passed through a haze layer lying above the planet's surface, indicating an inversion of temperatures, 110°K above, and 50°K below, suggesting Pluto has primitive weather.

There are tentative plans for a space-craft reconnaissance of the Pluto system, thus completing direct, close-up observation of each of the planets of the solar system.

Greenwich Sidereal Time for 0ʰ GMT, 1992

(Add 12 hours to obtain Right Ascension of Mean Sun)

Date		h	m	Date		h	m	Date		h	m	Date		h	m
Jan.	1	06	39.6		31	12	34.5	July	9	19	08.7		17	01	43.0
	11	07	19.1	Apr.	10	13	13.9		19	19	48.1		27	02	22.4
	21	07	58.5		20	13	53.3		29	20	27.6	Nov.	6	03	01.8
	31	08	37.9		30	14	32.7	Aug.	8	21	07.0		16	03	41.3
Feb.	10	09	17.3	May	10	15	12.2		18	21	46.4		26	04	20.7
	20	09	56.8		20	15	51.6		28	22	25.8	Dec.	6	05	00.1
Mar.	1	10	36.2		30	16	31.0	Sept.	7	23	05.3		16	05	39.5
	11	11	15.6	June	9	17	10.4		17	23	44.7		26	06	19.0
	21	11	55.0		19	17	49.9		27	00	24.1	1993 Jan. 5		06	58.4
					29	18	29.3	Oct.	7	01	03.5				

Astronomical Signs and Symbols

☉	The Sun	⊕	The Earth	♅	Uranus
☾	The Moon	♂	Mars	♆	Neptune
☿	Mercury	♃	Jupiter	♇	Pluto
♀	Venus	♄	Saturn	☌	Conjunction

☐	Quadrature
☍	Opposition
☊	Ascending Node
☋	Descending Node

Two heavenly bodies are in "conjunction" (☌) when they are due north and south of each other, either in Right Ascension (with respect to the north celestial pole) or in Celestial Longitude (with respect to the north ecliptic pole). If the bodies are seen near each other, they will rise and set at nearly the same time. They are in "opposition" (☍) when their Right Ascensions differ by exactly 12 hours, or their Celestial Longitudes differ by 180°. One of the two objects in opposition will rise while the other is setting. "Quadrature" (☐) refers to the arrangement when the coordinates of two bodies differ by exactly 90°. These terms may refer to the relative positions of any two bodies as seen from the earth, but one of the bodies is so frequently the sun that mention of the sun is omitted; otherwise both bodies are named. The geocentric angular separation between sun and object is termed "elongation." Elongation is limited only for Mercury and Venus; the "greatest elongation" for each of these bodies is noted in the appropriate tables and is approximately the time for longest observation. When a planet is in its "ascending" (☊) or "descending" (☋) node, it is passing northward or southward, respectively, through the plane of the earth's orbit, across the celestial circle called the ecliptic. The term "perihelion" means nearest to the sun, and "aphelion," farthest from the sun. An "occultation" of a planet or star is an eclipse of it by some other body, usually the moon.

Planetary Configurations, 1992

Greenwich Mean Time (0 designates midnight; 12 designates noon; * = star; ☾ = moon)

Mo.	d.	h.	m.		
Jan.	1	12	-	☌ ♀ ☾	♀ 5° N
	3	01	-	☌ ☿ ☾	☿ 3° N
	3	10	-	☌ ♂ ☾	♂ 0°.8 N; Occultation
	3	15	-		⊕ Perihelion
	4	23	-	☌ ☾ ☉	Annular Solar Eclipse

Mo.	d.	h.	m.		
	5	01	-	☌ ♅ ☉	
	6	23	-	☌ ♄ ☾	♄ 3° S
	7	13	-	☌ ♆ ☉	
	7	19	-	☌ ♀ *	♀ 7° N of Antares

(continued)

Mo.	d. h. m.		
	10 20	☌ ☿ ♂	☿ 0°.6 N
	20 03	☌ ☿ ♅	☿ 0°.6 S
	21 11	☌ ☿ ♆	☿ 1°.9 S
	23 01	☌ ♃ ☽	♃ 7° N
	29 21	☌ ♂ ♅	♂ 0°.4 S
	29 22	☌ ♄ ☉	
	31 17	☌ ♀ ☽	♀ 1°.0 N; Occultation
Feb.	1 08	☌ ♂ ♆	♂ 1°.5 S
	1 09	☌ ♅ ☽	♅ 0°.9 S; Occultation
	1 12	☌ ♆ ☽	♆ 0°.03 N; Occultation
	1 13	☌ ♂ ☽	♂ 1°.5 S
	7 07	☌ ♀ ♅	♀ 0°.9 N
	8 15	☌ ♀ ♆	♀ 0°.3 S
	12 09	☌ ☿ ☉	
	19 07	☌ ♃ ☽	♃ 6° N
	19 22	☌ ♀ ♂	♀ 0°.9 N
	28 02		♇ Stationary
	28 18	☌ ♅ ☽	♅ 1°.2 S
	28 21	☌ ♆ ☽	♆ 0°.2 S; Occultation
	29 01	☍ ♃ ☉	
	29 02	☌ ♀ ♄	♀ 0°.1 N
Mar.	1 18	☌ ♂ ☽	♂ 4° S
	2 01	☌ ♄ ☽	♄ 4° S
	2 06	☌ ♀ ☽	♀ 4° S
	6 06	☌ ☿ ☽	☿ 4° S
	6 13	☌ ♂ ♄	♂ 0°.4 S
	9 21		☿ Gr Elong 18° E of ☉
	16 15		☿ Stationary
	17 12	☌ ♃ ☽	♃ 6° N
	20 08 48		Vernal Equinox; Spring begins Northern Hemisphere
	26 15	☌ ☿ ☉	Inferior
	27 03	☌ ♅ ☽	♅ 1°.5 S
	27 05	☌ ♆ ☽	♆ 0°.5 S; Occultation
	29 14	☌ ♄ ☽	♄ 4° S
	31 01	☌ ♂ ☽	♂ 6° S
Apr.	1 19	☌ ♀ ☽	♀ 7° S
	2 08	☌ ☿ ☽	☿ 4° S
	5 23	☌ ☿ ♀	☿ 2° N
	8 01		☿ Stationary
	13 16	☌ ♃ ☽	♃ 6° N
	20 11		♆ Stationary
	22 01		♅ Stationary
	23 12	☌ ♅ ☽	♅ 1°.8 S
	23 14	☌ ♆ ☽	♆ 0°.7 S; Occultation
	23 15		☿ Gr Elong 27° W of ☉
	26 02	☌ ♄ ☽	♄ 5° S
	29 07	☌ ♂ ☽	♂ 7° S
	30 21	☌ ☿ ☽	☿ 8° S
May	1 05		♃ Stationary
	10 22	☌ ♃ ☽	♃ 6° N
	12 01	☍ ♇ ☉	
	20 20	☌ ♅ ☽	♅ 2° S
	20 21	☌ ♆ ☽	♆ 0°.9 S; Occultation
	23 12	☌ ♄ ☽	♄ 5° S
	28 09	☌ ♂ ☽	♂ 7° S
	29 03		♄ Stationary
	31 16	☌ ☿ ☉	☿ Superior
June	7 07	☌ ♃ ☽	♃ 7° N
	13 16	☌ ♀ ☉	Superior
	15 05	☍ ☽ ☉	Partial Lunar Eclipse
	17 01	☌ ♅ ☽	♅ 1°.9 S
	17 04	☌ ♆ ☽	♆ 0°.9 S; Occultation
	19 19	☌ ♄ ☽	♄ 5° S
	21 03 14		Summer Solstice; Summer begins Northern Hemisphere
	23 02	☌ ☿ ✶	☿ 5° S of Pollux
	26 08	☌ ♂ ☽	♂ 6° S
	30 12	☌ ☽ ☉	Total Solar Eclipse
July	2 10	☌ ☿ ☽	☿ 4° N
	3 12		⊕ at Aphelion
	4 20	☌ ♃ ☽	♃ 7° N
	6 01		☿ Gr Elong 26° E of ☉
	7 23	☍ ♅ ☉	
	9 13	☍ ♆ ☉	

Mo.	d. h. m.		
	14 06	☌ ♅ ☽	♅ 1°.8 S
	14 09	☌ ♆ ☽	♆ 0°.8 S; Occultation
	16 23	☌ ♄ ☽	♄ 5° S
	19 03		☿ Stationary
	25 04	☌ ♂ ☽	♂ 4° S
	25 15	☌ ☿ ♀	☿ 6° S
Aug.	1 12	☌ ♃ ☽	♃ 7° N
	2 21	☌ ☿ ☉	Inferior
	4 09		♇ Stationary
	6 18	☌ ♀ ✶	♀ 1°.1 N of Regulus
	7 10	☍ ♃ ☉	
	10 10	☌ ♅ ☽	♅ 1°.8 S
	10 14	☌ ♆ ☽	♆ 0°.8 S; Occultation
	11 09	☌ ♂ ✶	♂ 5° N of Aldebaran
	12 13		☿ Stationary
	13 01	☌ ♄ ☽	♄ 5° S
	21 02		☿ Gr Elong 18° W of ☉
	22 21	☌ ♂ ☽	♂ 1°.4 S
	23 03	☌ ♀ ☽	♀ 0°.3 N
	27 01	☌ ☿ ☽	☿ 5° N
	29 19	☌ ♀ ☽	♀ 7° N
Sept.	2 23	☌ ☿ ✶	☿ 1°.2 N of Regulus
	6 15	☌ ♅ ☽	♅ 1°.9 S
	6 19	☌ ♆ ☽	♆ 0°.9 S; Occultation
	9 03	☌ ♄ ☽	♄ 5° S
	15 04	☌ ☿ ☉	Superior
	17 19	☌ ♃ ☉	
	19 05	☌ ♀ ✶	♀ 3° N of Spica
	20 09	☌ ♂ ☽	♂ 0°.9 N; Occultation
	22 18 43		Autumnal Equinox; Autumn begins Northern Hemisphere
	23 00		♅ Stationary
	27 16		♆ Stationary
Oct.	2 22	☌ ☿ ✶	☿ 2° N of Spica
	3 22	☌ ♅ ☽	♅ 2° S
	4 02	☌ ♆ ☽	♆ 1°.2 S; Occultation
	6 08	☌ ♄ ☽	♄ 5° S
	16 04		♄ Stationary
	18 15	☌ ♂ ☽	♂ 3° N
	24 00	☌ ♃ ☽	♃ 7° N
	27 07	☌ ♀ ✶	♀ 3° N of Antares
	27 15	☌ ☿ ☽	☿ 0°.5 S; Occultation
	28 15	☌ ♀ ☽	♀ 0°.4 S; Occultation
	31 07	☌ ♅ ☽	♅ 2° S
	31 10	☌ ♆ ☽	♆ 1°.4 S
	31 16		☿ Gr. Elong 24° E of ☉
Nov.	2 16	☌ ♄ ☽	♄ 5° S
	4 21	☌ ♂ ✶	♂ 5° S of Pollux
	11 14		☿ Stationary
	15 00	☌ ♇ ☉	
	15 12	☌ ♂ ☽	♂ 5° N
	20 16	☌ ♃ ☽	♃ 7° N
	21 22	☌ ☿ ☉	Inferior
	26 12	☌ ♀ ☽	♀ 1°.9 S
	27 13	☌ ♀ ♀	♀ 3° S
	27 18	☌ ♅ ☽	♅ 3° S
	27 21	☌ ♆ ☽	♆ 1°.6 S
	27 21	☌ ♀ ☽	♀ 5° S
	29 16		♂ Stationary
	30 03	☌ ♄ ☽	♄ 5° S
Dec.	1 06		☿ Stationary
	9 14		☿ Gr Elong 21° W of ☉
	10 00	☍ ☽ ☉	Total Lunar Eclipse
	12 19	☌ ♂ ☽	♂ 6° N
	18 05	☌ ♃ ☽	♃ 7° N
	19 03	☌ ☿ ✶	☿ 6° N of Antares
	21 14 43		Winter Solstice; Winter begins Northern Hemisphere
	21 16	☌ ♀ ♄	♀ 1°.1 N
	22 14	☌ ☿ ☽	☿ 1°.5 N
	22 21	☌ ♂ ✶	♂ 3° S of Pollux
	24 01	☌ ☽ ☉	Partial Solar Eclipse
	27 17	☌ ♄ ☽	♄ 6° S
	28 07	☌ ♀ ☽	♀ 7° S

Rising and Setting of Planets, 1992

Greenwich Mean Time (0 designates midnight)

		20° N. Latitude Rise	Set	30° N. Latitude Rise	Set	40° N. Latitude Rise	Set	50° N. Latitude Rise	Set	60° N. Latitude Rise	Set
						Venus, 1992					
Jan.	1	3:40	14:51	3:56	14:35	4:16	14:15	4:44	13:47	5:29	13:02
	11	3:55	14:58	4:14	14:40	4:37	14:17	5:09	13:45	6:02	12:50
	21	4:10	15:08	4:30	14:48	4:55	14:24	5:30	13:49	6:30	12:48
	31	4:24	15:21	4:45	15:01	5:10	14:36	5:46	14:00	6:48	12:58
Feb.	10	4:37	15:36	4:56	15:17	5:21	14:53	5:55	14:18	6:53	13:20
	20	4:47	15:52	5:04	15:34	5:26	15:13	5:57	14:42	6:48	13:51
Mar.	1	4:54	16:08	5:09	15:53	5:27	15:35	5:53	15:09	6:34	14:28
	11	4:58	16:23	5:09	16:12	5:24	15:57	5:43	15:38	6:14	15:08
	21	4:59	16:37	5:07	16:30	5:17	16:20	5:30	16:08	5:50	15:48
	31	4:59	16:51	5:03	16:47	5:08	16:43	5:14	16:37	5:24	16:28
Apr.	10	4:58	17:04	4:58	17:04	4:58	17:05	4:57	17:06	4:56	17:08
	20	4:57	17:17	4:53	17:22	4:47	17:27	4:40	17:35	4:28	17:48
	30	4:57	17:30	4:48	17:39	4:38	17:50	4:23	18:05	4:00	18:28
May	10	4:58	17:45	4:45	17:58	4:30	18:13	4:08	18:35	3:34	19:10
	20	5:01	18:00	4:45	18:16	4:25	18:37	3:57	19:05	3:10	19:53
	30	5:07	18:16	4:48	18:36	4:24	19:00	3:50	19:34	2:51	20:34
June	9	5:16	18:33	4:55	18:54	4:28	19:21	3:49	20:00	2:40	21:11
	19	5:28	18:48	5:06	19:11	4:37	19:39	3:56	20:20	2:41	21:36
	29	5:43	19:02	5:21	19:24	4:52	19:52	4:12	20:33	2:57	21:47
July	9	5:59	19:13	5:38	19:34	5:12	20:00	4:34	20:37	3:28	21:43
	19	6:15	19:21	5:57	19:39	5:34	20:02	5:02	20:34	4:07	21:28
	29	6:31	19:26	6:16	19:41	5:58	19:59	5:32	20:25	4:49	21:06
Aug.	8	6:46	19:28	6:35	19:39	6:21	19:52	6:02	20:11	5:32	20:40
	18	7:00	19:28	6:53	19:34	6:45	19:43	6:33	19:54	6:15	20:12
	28	7:13	19:26	7:11	19:28	7:07	19:31	7:03	19:35	6:56	19:42
Sept.	7	7:26	19:24	7:28	19:22	7:30	19:19	7:33	19:16	7:37	19:11
	17	7:39	19:22	7:45	19:15	7:53	19:07	8:03	18:57	8:18	18:41
	27	7:52	19:21	8:03	19:10	8:16	18:57	8:33	18:39	9:01	18:11
Oct.	7	8:07	19:22	8:21	19:07	8:39	18:49	9:04	18:24	9:44	17:44
	17	8:22	19:26	8:41	19:07	9:03	18:45	9:35	18:13	10:28	17:19
	27	8:39	19:33	9:00	19:11	9:26	18:45	10:04	18:07	11:10	17:01
Nov.	6	8:55	19:43	9:18	19:20	9:47	18:51	10:29	18:09	11:45	16:52
	16	9:10	19:56	9:33	19:32	10:03	19:02	10:46	18:19	12:07	16:59
	26	9:22	20:10	9:45	19:47	10:14	19:19	10:55	18:37	12:11	17:22
Dec.	6	9:30	20:25	9:51	20:04	10:18	19:38	10:55	19:01	11:59	17:57
	16	9:35	20:39	9:53	20:21	10:15	19:59	10:46	19:28	11:38	18:37
	26	9:35	20:51	9:49	20:37	10:07	20:20	10:31	19:56	11:10	19:17
						Mars, 1992					
Jan.	1	5:27	16:18	5:49	15:57	6:16	15:29	6:55	14:51	8:04	13:41
	11	5:21	16:11	5:43	15:49	6:10	15:21	6:50	14:42	8:00	13:32
	21	5:13	16:05	5:35	15:43	6:03	15:15	6:42	14:37	7:51	13:27
	31	5:06	15:59	5:27	15:38	5:53	15:11	6:31	14:34	7:37	13:28
Feb.	10	4:57	15:54	5:17	15:34	5:42	15:09	6:17	14:34	7:18	13:33
	20	4:48	15:49	5:06	15:31	5:29	15:08	6:01	14:35	6:56	13:41
Mar.	1	4:37	15:44	4:54	15:28	5:14	15:07	5:43	14:38	6:31	13:51
	11	4:25	15:40	4:40	15:25	4:58	15:07	5:23	14:42	6:03	14:02
	21	4:13	15:34	4:25	15:22	4:40	15:07	5:01	14:46	5:34	14:14
	31	3:59	15:29	4:09	15:19	4:21	15:07	4:38	14:50	5:04	14:25
Apr.	10	3:45	15:23	3:52	15:16	4:01	15:07	4:14	14:55	4:33	14:36
	20	3:30	15:17	3:35	15:12	3:41	15:06	3:49	14:58	4:01	14:47
	30	3:15	15:10	3:17	15:08	3:20	15:05	3:23	15:02	3:29	14:57
May	10	2:59	15:03	2:59	15:04	2:58	15:04	2:58	15:05	2:56	15:07
	20	2:43	14:56	2:40	14:59	2:37	15:03	2:32	15:08	2:24	15:16
	30	2:27	14:49	2:22	14:55	2:15	15:02	2:06	15:11	1:52	15:26
June	9	2:12	14:42	2:04	14:50	1:54	15:00	1:41	15:13	1:20	15:35
	19	1:56	14:35	1:46	14:45	1:33	14:58	1:16	15:15	0:49	15:43
	29	1:41	14:27	1:29	14:40	1:13	14:55	0:52	15:17	0:18	15:51
July	9	1:26	14:19	1:12	14:34	0:54	14:52	0:29	15:17	23:45	15:59
	19	1:12	14:11	0:56	14:28	0:35	14:48	0:07	15:17	23:16	16:05
	29	0:58	14:03	0:40	14:21	0:18	14:43	23:44	15:15	22:49	16:10
Aug.	8	0:44	13:53	0:25	14:13	23:59	14:37	23:24	15:12	22:24	16:12
	18	0:31	13:43	0:10	14:04	23:43	14:30	23:06	15:07	22:00	16:12
	28	0:17	13:32	23:54	13:53	23:27	14:20	22:49	14:59	21:39	16:08
Sept.	7	0:03	13:19	23:40	13:41	23:12	14:09	22:32	14:48	21:20	16:00
	17	23:46	13:05	23:24	13:27	22:57	13:55	22:17	14:35	21:03	15:48
	27	23:30	12:49	23:08	13:11	22:41	13:39	22:00	14:19	20:47	15:32
Oct.	7	23:13	12:31	22:51	12:53	22:23	13:20	21:43	14:00	20:31	15:12
	17	22:53	12:10	22:31	12:32	22:04	12:59	21:25	13:38	20:14	14:49
	27	22:30	11:47	22:09	12:08	21:42	12:35	21:03	13:14	19:54	14:24
Nov.	6	22:04	11:21	21:43	11:42	21:16	12:09	20:38	12:47	19:29	13:56
	16	21:34	10:51	21:13	11:12	20:46	11:38	20:08	12:17	18:59	13:26
	26	20:58	10:16	20:37	10:38	20:10	11:05	19:31	11:44	18:21	12:54

(continued)

		20° N. Latitude		30° N. Latitude		40° N. Latitude		50° N. Latitude		60° N. Latitude	
		Rise	Set	Rise	Set	Rise	Set	Rise	Set	Rise	Set
Dec.	6	20:17	9:37	19:55	9:59	19:27	10:27	18:47	11:07	17:34	12:20
	16	19:29	8:52	19:06	9:15	18:37	9:44	17:55	10:26	16:36	11:44
	26	18:35	8:02	18:11	8:26	17:41	8:56	16:56	9:40	15:30	11:06

Jupiter, 1992

		20° N. Latitude		30° N. Latitude		40° N. Latitude		50° N. Latitude		60° N. Latitude	
		Rise	Set	Rise	Set	Rise	Set	Rise	Set	Rise	Set
Jan.	1	22:09	10:37	22:03	10:43	21:55	10:51	21:44	11:02	21:27	11:19
	11	21:29	9:57	21:22	10:03	21:14	10:11	21:03	10:22	20:46	10:39
	21	20:47	9:16	20:40	9:23	20:32	9:31	20:21	9:42	20:03	10:00
	31	20:04	8:34	19:57	8:41	19:49	8:50	19:37	9:02	19:18	9:20
Feb.	10	19:20	7:52	19:13	7:59	19:04	8:08	18:51	8:21	18:32	8:40
	20	18:36	7:09	18:28	7:16	18:18	7:26	18:05	7:39	17:44	8:00
Mar.	1	17:51	6:25	17:43	6:33	17:32	6:44	17:18	6:58	16:56	7:20
	11	17:06	5:42	16:57	5:51	16:47	6:01	16:32	6:16	16:09	6:39
	21	16:22	4:59	16:13	5:08	16:01	5:19	15:46	5:34	15:22	5:59
	31	15:38	4:16	15:29	4:26	15:17	4:37	15:01	4:53	14:36	5:18
Apr.	10	14:56	3:34	14:46	3:44	14:34	3:56	14:18	4:12	13:52	4:38
	20	14:14	2:53	14:04	3:03	13:52	3:15	13:36	3:22	13:10	3:58
	30	13:34	2:14	13:24	2:23	13:12	2:35	12:56	2:52	12:29	3:18
May	10	12:55	1:35	12:46	1:44	12:34	1:56	12:17	2:13	11:51	2:39
	20	12:18	0:56	12:09	1:06	11:57	1:18	11:40	1:34	11:15	2:00
	30	11:42	0:19	11:33	0:29	11:21	0:40	11:05	0:56	10:40	1:21
June	9	11:07	23:39	10:58	23:48	10:47	0:03	10:32	0:18	10:08	0:42
	19	10:33	23:04	10:24	23:12	10:13	23:23	9:59	23:37	9:36	0:04
	29	9:59	22:29	9:51	22:37	9:41	22:47	9:28	23:00	9:06	23:22
July	9	9:27	21:55	9:19	22:02	9:10	22:11	8:57	22:24	8:37	22:44
	19	8:55	21:21	8:48	21:28	8:39	21:36	8:28	21:48	8:09	22:06
	29	8:23	20:47	8:17	20:53	8:09	21:01	7:59	21:12	7:42	21:28
Aug.	8	7:52	20:14	7:47	20:19	7:40	20:26	7:30	20:36	7:15	20:51
	18	7:22	19:41	7:17	19:46	7:11	19:52	7:02	20:00	6:49	20:13
	28	6:51	19:08	6:47	19:12	6:42	19:17	6:35	19:25	6:23	19:36
Sept.	7	6:21	18:35	6:18	18:39	6:13	18:43	6:07	18:49	5:58	18:58
	17	5:51	18:03	5:48	18:05	5:45	18:09	5:40	18:14	5:32	18:21
	27	5:21	17:30	5:19	17:32	5:16	17:35	5:13	17:38	5:07	17:44
Oct.	7	4:50	16:57	4:49	16:59	4:47	17:00	4:45	17:03	4:41	17:06
	17	4:20	16:25	4:19	16:25	4:19	16:26	4:17	16:27	4:15	16:29
	27	3:49	15:52	3:49	15:51	3:49	15:51	3:49	15:51	3:49	15:52
Nov.	6	3:18	15:18	3:19	15:18	3:20	15:17	3:21	15:16	3:22	15:14
	16	2:47	14:45	2:48	14:43	2:50	14:42	2:52	14:40	2:55	14:37
	26	2:15	14:11	2:17	14:09	2:19	14:07	2:22	14:04	2:26	13:59
Dec.	6	1:42	13:36	1:44	13:34	1:47	13:31	1:51	13:27	1:56	13:22
	16	1:08	13:01	1:11	12:58	1:15	12:55	1:19	12:51	1:26	12:44
	26	0:34	12:25	0:37	12:22	0:41	12:18	0:46	12:13	0:53	12:06

Saturn, 1992

		20° N. Latitude		30° N. Latitude		40° N. Latitude		50° N. Latitude		60° N. Latitude	
		Rise	Set	Rise	Set	Rise	Set	Rise	Set	Rise	Set
Jan.	1	3:40	14:51	3:56	14:35	4:16	14:15	4:44	13:47	5:29	13:02
	11	3:55	14:58	4:14	14:40	4:37	14:17	5:09	13:45	6:02	12:50
	21	4:10	15:08	4:30	14:48	4:55	14:24	5:30	13:49	6:30	12:48
	31	4:24	15:21	4:45	15:01	5:10	14:36	5:46	14:00	6:48	12:58
Feb.	10	4:37	15:36	4:56	15:17	5:21	14:53	5:55	14:18	6:53	13:20
	20	4:47	15:52	5:04	15:34	5:26	15:13	5:57	14:42	6:48	13:51
Mar.	1	4:54	16:08	5:09	15:53	5:27	15:35	5:53	15:09	6:34	14:28
	11	4:58	16:23	5:09	16:12	5:24	15:57	5:43	15:38	6:14	15:08
	21	4:59	16:37	5:07	16:30	5:17	16:20	5:30	16:08	5:50	15:48
	31	4:59	16:51	5:03	16:47	5:08	16:43	5:14	16:37	5:24	16:28
Apr.	10	4:58	17:04	4:58	17:04	4:58	17:05	4:57	17:06	4:56	17:08
	20	4:57	17:17	4:53	17:22	4:47	17:27	4:40	17:35	4:28	17:48
	30	4:57	17:30	4:48	17:39	4:38	17:50	4:23	18:05	4:00	18:28
May	10	4:58	17:45	4:45	17:58	4:30	18:13	4:08	18:35	3:34	19:10
	20	5:01	18:00	4:45	18:16	4:25	18:37	3:57	19:05	3:10	19:53
	30	5:07	18:16	4:48	18:36	4:24	19:00	3:50	19:34	2:51	20:34
June	9	5:16	18:33	4:55	18:54	4:28	19:21	3:49	20:00	2:40	21:11
	19	5:28	18:48	5:06	19:11	4:37	19:39	3:56	20:20	2:41	21:36
	29	5:43	19:02	5:21	19:24	4:52	19:52	4:12	20:33	2:57	21:47
July	9	5:59	19:13	5:38	19:34	5:12	20:00	4:34	20:37	3:28	21:43
	19	6:15	19:21	5:57	19:39	5:34	20:02	5:02	20:34	4:07	21:28
	29	6:31	19:26	6:16	19:41	5:58	19:59	5:32	20:25	4:49	21:06
Aug.	8	6:46	19:28	6:35	19:39	6:21	19:52	6:02	20:11	5:32	20:40
	18	7:00	19:28	6:53	19:34	6:45	19:43	6:33	19:54	6:15	20:12
	28	7:13	19:26	7:11	19:28	7:07	19:31	7:03	19:35	6:56	19:42
Sept.	7	7:26	19:24	7:28	19:22	7:30	19:19	7:33	19:16	7:37	19:11
	17	7:39	19:22	7:45	19:15	7:53	19:07	8:03	18:57	8:18	18:41
	27	7:52	19:21	8:03	19:10	8:16	18:57	8:33	18:39	9:01	18:11
Oct.	7	8:07	19:22	8:21	19:07	8:39	18:49	9:04	18:24	9:44	17:44
	17	8:22	19:26	8:41	19:07	9:03	18:45	9:35	18:13	10:28	17:19
	27	8:39	19:33	9:00	19:11	9:26	18:45	10:04	18:07	11:10	17:01
Nov.	6	8:55	19:43	9:18	19:20	9:47	18:51	10:29	18:09	11:45	16:52
	16	9:10	19:56	9:33	19:32	10:03	19:02	10:46	18:19	12:07	16:59
	26	9:22	20:10	9:45	19:47	10:14	19:19	10:55	18:37	12:11	17:22
Dec.	6	9:30	20:25	9:51	20:04	10:18	19:38	10:55	19:01	11:59	17:57
	16	9:35	20:39	9:53	20:21	10:15	19:59	10:46	19:28	11:38	18:37
	26	9:35	20:51	9:49	20:37	10:07	20:20	10:31	19:56	11:10	19:17

Calculation of Risetimes

The *Daily Calendar* pages contain rise and set times for the Sun and Moon for the Greenwich Meridian at north latitudes 20°, 30°, 40°, 50°, and 60°. You probably live somewhere west of the Greenwich meridian, 0° longitude, and within the range of latitudes in the table. Notice that from day to day, the values for the sun at any particular latitude do not change very much. This slow variation for the sun means that no important correction needs to be made from one day to the next, once a proper correction for your latitude has been made. Thus, whenever it rises or sets at the 0° meridian, that will also be the time of that phenomenon at your Standard Time meridian. Any correction necessary for you to be able to observe that phenomenon from your location will be to account for your distance from the Standard Time meridian, and for your latitude.

The moon, however, moves its own diameter, about a half degree, in an hour, or about 12°.5 in one complete turn of the Earth—one day. Most of this is eastward against the background stars of the sky, but some is also north or south of the equator. If there is little change on the same day of the times over the range of latitudes, the moon is near the celestial equator. All of this motion considerably affects the times of rise or set, as you can see from the adjacent entries in the table. Thus, it is necessary also to take your longitude into account in addition to your latitude. If you have no need for total accuracy, simply note that the time will be between the four values you find surrounding your location and the dates of interest.

The process of finding more accurate corrections is called interpolation. In the example, linear interpolation, involving simple differences, is used four times: twice, once each in latitude and longitude for your location on the Earth; then twice for each moon rise, once each, again, for your latitude and your longitude. In extreme cases, higher order interpolation should be used. If such cases are important to you, it is suggested that you make a plot of the times, draw smooth curves through the plots, and interpolate by eye between the relevant curves. Some people find this exercise fun.

Let's find the time of the rise of the June Full Moon for Huntsville, Alabama.

First, where is Huntsville? Find the latitude and longitude on page 292.

I. Latitude: 34° 44′ 18″ N
    Longitude: 86° 35′ 19″ W

IA. Convert these values to decimals:
    $18″/60 = .3′$
    $44′ + 0′.3 = 44′.3$
    $44′.3/60 = 0°.7383$
    $34° + 0°.7383 = 34°.7383$
    $19″/60 = 0′.3167$
    $35′ + 0′.3167 = 35′.3167$
    $35′.3167/60 = 0°.5886$
    $86° + 0°.5886 = 86°.5886$

IB. Fraction Huntsville lies between 30° and 40°:
    $34.7383 - 30 = 4.7383$ or .474 of the way between 30° and 40°.

IC. Fraction the world must turn between Greenwich and Huntsville:
    $86.5886/360 = .2505$

ID. The CST meridian is 90°, thus $90 - 86.5886 = 3°.4114$ east. In 24 hours there are $24 \times 60 = 1440$ minutes; $1440/360 = 4$ minutes for every degree around the Earth. So events happen for Huntsville $4m \times 3°.4114 = 13.6$ minutes earlier than for the 90° meridian.

IE. The values in IB and IC are the interpolates for Huntsville; ID is the time correction from local to standard time for Huntsville. These three numbers never need to be calculated again.

II. Find the time of moonrise for the latitude of Huntsville at the Greenwich meridian on the 15th and 16th from the June calendar page.

	Lat. 30°		40°
June 15	19:29	28	19:57
diff	45		44
June 16	20:14	25	20:39

IIA. We want $28 \times .4738(IB) = 13.2672$ to be added to 19:29, or 19:42.3 for the 15th. And $25 \times .4738(IB) = 11.84$, added to 20:14, or 20:25.8 for the 16th.

IIB. Now $20:25.8 - 19:42.3 = 43.5$ minutes change of rise time at Greenwich from the 15th to the 16th. Only part of that happened while the Earth turned from Greenwich to Huntsville, namely, the .2505(IC) part of the 43.5 minutes. Thus, $43.5 \times .2505 = 10.9$ minutes.

IIC. The time of moonrise at Huntsville: $19:42.3 + 10.9 = 19:53.2$.

IID. The Standard time clock will read 13.6(ID) minutes earlier, or 19:39.6. But Daylight time is in effect in June, so the CDT clock will read 20:40 or 8:40 pm CDT when the June Full Moon rises in Huntsville.

Star Tables

These tables include stars of visual magnitude 2.5 and brighter. Co-ordinates are for mid-1992. Where no parallax figures are given, the trigonometric parallax figure is smaller than the margin for error and the distance given is obtained by indirect methods. Stars of variable magnitude designated by v.

To find the time when the star is on meridian, subtract R.A.M.S. of the sun table on page 265 from the star's right ascension, first adding 24h to the latter, if necessary. Mark this result P.M., if less than 12h; but if greater than 12, subtract 12h and mark the remainder A.M.

Star	Magnitude	Parallax ″	Light yrs.	Right ascen. h. m.	Declination ° ′
α Andromedae (Alpheratz)	2.06	0.02	90	0 08.0	29 03
β Cassiopeiae	2.27v	0.07	45	0 08.8	59 06
α Phoenicis	2.39	0.04	93	0 25.9	−42 20
α Cassiopeiae (Schedir)	2.23	0.01	150	0 40.1	56 30
β Ceti	2.04	0.06	57	0 43.2	−18 01
γ Cassiopeiae	2.47v	0.03	96	0 56.3	60 40
β Andromedae	2.06	0.04	76	1 09.3	35 35

(continued)

Star	Magni-tude	Paral-lax "	Light yrs.	Right ascen. h. m.	Decli-nation ° '
α Eridani (Achernar)	0.46	0.02	118	1 37.4	−57 16
γ Andromedae	2.26		260	2 03.4	42 18
α Arietis	2.00	0.04	76	2 06.8	23 26
ο Ceti	2.00v	0.01	103	2 19.0	−3 01
α Ursae Min. (Pole Star)	2.02v		680	2 23.3	89 14
β Persei (Algol)	2.12v	0.03	105	3 07.7	40 55
α Persei	1.80	0.03	570	3 23.8	49 50
α Tauri (Aldebaran)	0.85v	0.05	68	4 35.5	16 30
β Orionis (Rigel)	0.12v		900	5 14.2	−8 13
α Aurigae (Capella)	0.08	0.07	45	5 16.1	45 59
γ Orionis (Bellatrix)	1.64	0.03	470	5 24.7	6 21
β Tauri (El Nath)	1.65	0.02	300	5 25.8	28 36
δ Orionis	2.23v		1500	5 31.6	0 18
ε Orionis	1.70		1600	5 35.8	−1 12
ζ Orionis	2.05	0.02	1600	5 40.4	−1 57
κ Orionis	2.06	0.01	2100	5 47.4	−9 40
α Orionis (Betelgeuse)	0.50v		520	5 54.8	7 24
β Aurigae	1.90	0.04	88	5 59.0	44 57
β Canis Majoris	1.98	0.01	750	6 22.4	−17 57
α Carinae (Canopus)	−0.72	0.02	98	6 23.8	−52 41
γ Geminorum	1.93	0.03	105	6 37.3	16 24
α Canis Majoris (Sirius)	−1.46	0.38	8.7	6 44.8	−16 42
ε Canis Majoris	1.50		680	6 58.3	−28 58
δ Canis Majoris	1.86		2100	7 08.1	−26 23
η Canis Majoris	2.44		2700	7 23.8	−29 17
α Geminorum (Castor)	1.99	0.07	45	7 34.1	31 54
α Canis Minoris (Procyon)	0.38	0.29	11.3	7 38.9	5 15
β Geminorum (Pollux)	1.14	0.09	35	7 44.8	28 03
ζ Puppis	2.25		2400	8 03.3	−39 59
γ Velorum	1.82		520	8 09.3	−47 19
ε Carinae	1.86		340	8 22.3	−59 29
δ Velorum	1.96	0.04	76	8 44.5	−54 41
λ Velorum	2.21	0.02	750	9 07.7	−43 24
β Carinae	1.68	0.04	86	9 13.1	−69 41
ι Carinae	2.25		750	9 16.9	−59 15
κ Velorum	2.50	0.01	470	9 21.9	−54 59
α Hydrae	1.98	0.02	94	9 27.2	−8 38
α Leonis (Regulus)	1.35	0.04	84	10 08.0	12 00
γ Leonis	1.90	0.02	90	10 19.6	19 55
β Ursae Majoris (Merak)	2.37	0.04	78	11 01.4	56 26
α Ursae Majoris (Dubhe)	1.79	0.03	105	11 03.3	61 48

Star	Magni-tude	Paral-lax "	Light yrs.	Right ascen. h. m.	Decli-nation ° '
β Leonis (Denebola)	2.14	0.08	43	11 48.7	14 37
γ Ursae Majoris (Phecda)	2.44	0.02	90	11 53.5	53 44
α Crucis	1.58		370	12 26.2	−63 04
γ Crucis	1.63		220	12 30.8	−57 05
γ Centauri	2.17		160	12 41.1	−48 55
β Crucis	1.25v		490	12 47.3	−59 39
ε Ursae Majoris (Alioth)	1.77v	0.01	68	12 53.7	57 00
ζ Ursae Majoris (Mizar)	2.05	0.04	88	13 23.6	54 58
α Virginis (Spica)	0.97v	0.02	220	13 24.8	−11 07
ε Centauri	2.30v		570	13 39.4	−53 26
η Ursae Majoris (Alkaid)	1.86		210	13 47.3	49 21
β Centauri	0.61v	0.02	490	14 03.3	−60 21
θ Centauri	2.06	0.06	55	14 06.3	−36 20
α Bootis (Arcturus)	−0.04	0.09	36	14 15.3	19 13
η Centauri	2.31v		390	14 35.1	−42 08
α Centauri	−0.01	0.75	4.3	14 39.1	−60 49
α Lupi	2.30v		430	14 41.5	−47 22
ε Bootis	2.40	0.01	103	14 44.7	27 06
β Ursae Minoris	2.08	0.03	105	14 50.9	74 11
α Coronae Borealis	2.23v	0.04	76	15 34.4	26 44
δ Scorpii	2.32		590	15 59.9	−22 36
α Scorpii (Antares)	0.96v	0.02	520	16 29.0	−26 25
α Trianguli Australis	1.92	0.02	82	16 48.0	−69 01
ε Scorpii	2.29	0.05	66	16 49.7	−34 17
η Ophiuchi	2.43	0.05	69	17 10.0	−15 43
λ Scorpii	1.63v		310	17 33.1	−37 06
α Ophiuchi	2.08	0.06	58	17 34.6	12 34
θ Scorpii	1.87	0.02	650	17 36.8	−43 00
κ Scorpii	2.41v		470	17 42.0	−39 02
γ Draconis	2.23	0.02	108	17 56.5	51 29
ε Sagittarii	1.85	0.02	124	18 23.7	−34 23
α Lyrae (Vega)	0.03	0.12	26.5	18 36.7	38 47
σ Sagittarii	2.02		300	18 54.8	−26 18
α Aquilae (Altair)	0.77	0.20	16.5	19 50.5	8 51
γ Cygni	2.20		750	20 22.0	40 14
α Pavonis	1.94		310	20 25.1	−56 45
α Cygni (Deneb)	1.25		1600	20 41.2	45 15
γ Cygni	2.46	0.04	74	20 45.9	33 57
α Cephei	2.44	0.06	52	21 18.4	62 33
ε Pegasi	2.39		780	21 43.9	9 51
α Gruis	1.74	0.05	64	22 07.8	−47 00
β Gruis	2.11v		280	22 42.3	−46 55
α Piscis Austrinis (Fomalhaut)	1.16	0.14	22.6	22 57.3	−29 39
β Pegasi	2.42v	0.02	210	23 03.4	28 03
α Pegasi	2.49	0.03	109	23 04.4	15 10

Constellations

Culturally, constellations are imagined patterns among the stars that, in some cases, have been recognized through millenia in tradition. In the early days of astronomy, knowledge of the constellations was necessary in order to function as an astronomer. For today's astronomers, constellations are simply areas on the entire sky in which interesting objects await observation and interpretation.

Because western culture has prevailed in establishing modern science, equally viable and interesting constellations and celestial traditions of other cultures (of Asia or Africa, for example) are not well known outside of their regions of origin. Even the patterns with which we are most familiar today have undergone considerable change over the centuries, because the western heritage embraces teachings of cultures disparate in time as well as place.

Today, students of the sky the world over recognize 88 constellations that cover the entire celestial sphere. Many of these have their origins in ancient days; many are "modern," contrived out of unformed stars by astronomers a few centuries ago. Unformed stars were those usually too faint or inconveniently placed to be included in depicting the more prominent constellations. When astronomers began to travel to South Af-

rica in the 16th and 17th centuries, they found a sky that itself was unformed, and showing numerous brilliant stars. Thus, we find constellations in the southern hemisphere like the "air pump," the "microscope," the "furnace," and other technological marvels of the time, as well as some arguably traditional forms, such as the "fly."

Many of the commonly recognized constellations had their origins in ancient Asia Minor—Syria, Babylon, etc. These were adopted by the Greeks and Romans who translated their names and stories into their own languages, some details being modified in the process. After the declines of these cultures, most such knowledge entered oral tradition, or remained hidden in monastic libraries. Beginning in the 8th century, the Moslem explosion spread through the Mediterranean world. Wherever possible, everything was translated into Arabic to be taught in the universities the Moslems established all over their new-found world.

In the 13th century, Alphonsus XX of Spain, an avid student of astronomy, succeeded in having Claudius Ptolemy's *Almagest*, as its Arabian title was known, translated into Latin. It thus became widely available to European scholars. In the process, the constellation names were translated, but the star names were retained in their Arabic forms. Transliterating Arabic into the Roman alphabet has never been an exact art, so many of the star names we use today only "seem" Arabic to all but scholars.

Names of stars often indicated what parts of the traditional figures they represented: Deneb, the tail of the swan; Betelgeuse, the armpit of the giant. Thus, the names were an indication of the position in the sky of a particular star, provided one recognized the traditional form of the mythic figure.

In English, usage of the Latin names for the constellations couples often inconceivable creatures, represented in unimaginable configurations, with names that often seem unintelligible. Avoiding traditional names, astronomers may designate the brighter stars in a constellation with Greek letters, usually in order of brightness. Thus, the "alpha star" is often the brightest star of that constellation. The "of" implies possession, so the genetive (possessive) form of the constellation name is used, as in Alpha Orionis, the first star of Orion (Betelgeuse). Astronomers usually use a 3-letter form for the constellation name, understanding it to be read as either the nominative or genitive case of the name.

Until the 1920's, astronomers used curved boundaries for the constellation areas. As these were rather arbitrary at best, the International Astronomical Union adopted boundaries that ran due north-south and east-west, filling the sky much as the contiguous states fill up the area of the "lower 48" United States.

Within these boundaries, and occasionally crossing them, popular "asterisms" are recognized: the Big Dipper is a small part of Ursa Major, the big bear; the Sickle is the traditional head and mane of Leo, the lion; one of the horntips of Taurus, the bull, properly belongs to Auriga, the charioteer; the northeast star of the Great Square of Pegasus is Alpha Andromedae.

It is unlikely that further change will occur in the realm of the celestial constellations.

Name	Genitive	Abbreviation	Meaning
Andromeda	Andromedae	And	Chained Maiden
Antlia	Antliae	Ant	Air Pump
Apus	Apodis	Aps	Bird of Paradise
Aquarius	Aquarii	Aqr	Water Bearer
Aquila	Aquilae	Aql	Eagle
Ara	Arae	Ara	Altar
Aries	Arietis	Ari	Ram
Auriga	Aurigae	Aur	Charioteer
Bootes	Bootis	Boo	Herdsmen
Caelum	Caeli	Cae	Chisel
Camelopardalis	Camelopardalis	Cam	Giraffe
Cancer	Cancri	Cnc	Crab
Canes Venatici	Canum Venaticorum	CVn	Hunting Dogs
Canis Major	Canis Majoris	CMa	Great Dog
Canis Minor	Canis Minoris	CMi	Little Dog
Capricornus	Capricorni	Cap	Sea-goat
Carina	Carinae	Car	Keel
Cassiopeia	Cassiopeiae	Cas	Queen
Centaurus	Centauri	Cen	Centaur
Cepheus	Cephei	Cep	King

Name	Genitive	Abbreviation	Meaning
Cetus	Ceti	Cet	Whale
Chamaeleon	Chamaeleontis	Cha	Chameleon
Circinus	Circini	Cir	Compasses (art)
Columba	Columbae	Col	Dove
Coma Berenices	Comae Berenices	Com	Berenice's Hair
Corona Australis	Coronae Australis	CrA	Southern Crown
Corona Borealis	Coronae Borealis	CrB	Northern Crown
Corvus	Corvi	Crv	Crow
Crater	Crateris	Crt	Cup
Crux	Crucis	Cru	Cross (southern)
Cygnus	Cygni	Cyg	Swan
Delphinus	Delphini	Del	Dolphin
Dorado	Doradus	Dor	Goldfish
Draco	Draconis	Dra	Dragon
Equuleus	Equulei	Equ	Little Horse
Eridanus	Eridani	Eri	River
Fornax	Fornacis	For	Furnace
Gemini	Geminorum	Gem	Twins
Grus	Gruis	Gru	Crane (bird)
Hercules	Herculis	Her	Hercules
Horologium	Horologii	Hor	Clock
Hydra	Hydrae	Hya	Water Snake (female)
Hydrus	Hydri	Hyi	Water Snake (male)
Indus	Indi	Ind	Indian
Lacerta	Lacertae	Lac	Lizard
Leo	Leonis	Leo	Lion
Leo Minor	Leonis Minoris	LMi	Little Lion
Lepus	Leporis	Lep	Hare
Libra	Librae	Lib	Balance
Lupus	Lupi	Lup	Wolf
Lynx	Lyncis	Lyn	Lynx
Lyra	Lyrae	Lyr	Lyre
Mensa	Mensae	Men	Table Mountain
Microscopium	Microscopii	Mic	Microscope
Monoceros	Monocerotis	Mon	Unicorn
Musca	Muscae	Mus	Fly
Norma	Normae	Nor	Square (rule)
Octans	Octantis	Oct	Octant
Ophiuchus	Ophiuchi	Oph	Serpent Bearer
Orion	Orionis	Ori	Hunter
Pavo	Pavonis	Pav	Peacock
Pegasus	Pegasi	Peg	Flying Horse
Perseus	Persei	Per	Hero
Phoenix	Phoenicis	Phe	Phoenix
Pictor	Pictoris	Pic	Painter
Pisces	Piscium	Psc	Fishes
Piscis Austrinius	Piscis Austrini	PsA	Southern Fish
Puppis	Puppis	Pup	Stern (deck)
Pyxis	Pyxidis	Pyx	Compass (sea)
Reticulum	Reticuli	Ret	Reticle
Sagitta	Sagittae	Sge	Arrow
Sagittarius	Sagittarii	Sgr	Archer
Scorpius	Scorpii	Sco	Scorpion
Sculptor	Sculptoris	Scl	Sculptor
Scutum	Scuti	Sct	Shield
Serpens	Serpentis	Ser	Serpent
Sextans	Sextantis	Sex	Sextant
Taurus	Tauri	Tau	Bull
Telescopium	Telescopii	Tel	Telescope
Triangulum	Trianguli	Tri	Triangle
Triangulum Australe	Trianguli Australis	TrA	Southern Triangle
Tucana	Tucanae	Tuc	Toucan
Ursa Major	Ursae Majoris	UMa	Great Bear
Ursa Minor	Ursae Minoris	UMi	Little Bear
Vela	Velorum	Vel	Sail
Virgo	Virginis	Vir	Maiden
Volans	Volantis	Vol	Flying Fish
Vulpecula	Vulpeculae	Vul	Fox

Aurora Borealis and Aurora Australis

The Aurora Borealis, also called the Northern Lights, is a broad display of rather faint light in the northern skies at night. The Aurora Australis, a similar phenomenon, appears at the same time in southern skies. The aurora appears in a wide variety of forms. Sometimes it is seen as a quiet glow, almost foglike in character; sometimes as vertical streamers in which there may be considerable motion; sometimes as a series of luminous expanding arcs. There are many colors, with white, yellow, and red predominating.

The auroras are most vivid and most frequently seen at about 20 degrees from the magnetic poles, along the northern coast of the North American continent and the eastern part of the northern coast of Europe. They have been seen as far south as Key West and as far north as Australia and New Zealand, but rarely.

While the cause of the auroras is not known beyond question, there does seem to be a definite correlation between auroral displays and sun-spot activity. It is thought that atomic particles expelled from the sun by the forces that cause solar flares speed through space at velocities of 400 to 600 miles per second. These particles are entrapped by the earth's magnetic field, forming what are termed the Van Allen belts. The encounter of these clouds of the solar wind with the earth's magnetic field weakens the field so that previously trapped particles are allowed to impact the upper atmosphere. The collisions between solar and terrestrial atoms result in the glow in the upper atmosphere called the aurora. The glow may be vivid where the lines of magnetic force converge near the magnetic poles.

The auroral displays appear at heights ranging from 50 to about 600 miles and have given us a means of estimating the extent of the earth's atmosphere.

The auroras are often accompanied by magnetic storms whose forces, also guided by the lines of force of the earth's magnetic field, disrupt electrical communication.

Eclipses, 1992

(Greenwich Mean Time)

There are five eclipses in 1992, three of the sun and two of the moon.

I. Annular eclipse of the Sun, January, 4-5.

Partial phases are visible throughout the North Pacific Ocean, except the extreme western part, part of the northern South Pacific Ocean north of New Zealand, northeastern Australia, eastern New Guinea, Hawaiian Islands, and southwestern Alaska. The path of annularity is entirely in the Pacific Ocean.

Circumstances of the Eclipse

Event	Date	h	m
Eclipse begins	Jan 4	20	03.6
Central eclipse begins	4	21	16.0
Central eclipse at local noon	4	23	14.7
Central eclipse ends	5	0	53.1
Eclipse ends	5	2	05.6

Maximum duration of annularity: 11:36.2.

II. Partial eclipse of the Moon, June 15.

The beginning of the umbral phase is visible in South America, Central America, the United States except the northwest, southeastern Canada, Antarctica, the eastern South Pacific Ocean, extreme western Europe, Africa except the northeast, and the Atlantic Ocean. The end is visible in New Zealand, Hawaii, South America, Central America, North America except Alaska and northern Canada, Antarctica, extreme western Africa, the South Pacific Ocean, the southeastern North Pacific Ocean, and most of the Atlantic Ocean except the northeast.

Circumstances of the Eclipse

Event	Date	h	m
Moon enters penumbra	Jun 15	2	09.1
Moon enters umbra	15	3	26.6
Middle of eclipse	15	4	57.0
Moon leaves umbra	15	6	27.2
Moon leaves penumbra	15	7	44.9

Magnitude of the eclipse: 0.687.

III. Total eclipse of the sun, June 30.

Partial phases are visible in extreme eastern South America, the South Atlantic Ocean, South Africa, and the African coast parallel to the equator. Except for the southeastern tip of Uruguay, the path of totality passes entirely over the South Atlantic Ocean.

Circumstances of the Eclipse

Event	Date	h	m
Eclipse begins	Jun 30	09	50.9
Central eclipse begins	30	11	01.7
Central eclipse at noon	30	12	23.4
Central eclipse ends	30	13	18.9
Eclipse ends	30	14	29.7

Maximum duration of totality: 5:25.6.

IV. Total eclipse of the Moon, December 9-10.

The beginning of the umbral phase is visible in northeastern South America, eastern and northern North America, Greenland, the Arctic regions, Africa, Europe, most of Asia, most of the Atlantic Ocean, and the Indian Ocean. The end is visible in South America, Central America, most of North America, Greenland, the Arctic regions, Africa, Europe, northern and western Asia, the eastern Pacific Ocean, the Atlantic Ocean, and the western Indian Ocean.

Circumstances of the Eclipse

Event	Date	h	m
Moon enters penumbra	Dec 9	20	55.4
Moon enters umbra	9	21	59.4
Moon enters totality	9	23	06.8
Middle of eclipse	9	23	44.1
Moon leaves totality	10	0	21.5
Moon leaves umbra	10	1	28.8
Moon leaves penumbra	10	2	32.7

Magnitude of the eclipse: 1.276.

V. Partial eclipse of the Sun, December 23-24.

Partial phases are visible in Okinawa, Japan, Kuriles, Kamchatca, southeastern Alaska, and the northern North Pacific Ocean.

Circumstances of the Eclipse

Event	Date	h	m
Eclipse begins	Dec 23	22	20.7
Greatest eclipse	24	00	30.7
Eclipse ends	24	02	40.7

Magnitude of greatest eclipse: 0.843.

The Planets and the Solar System

Planet	Mean daily motion (")	Orbital velocity miles per sec.	Sidereal revolution days	Synodical revolution days	Dist. from sun in millions of mi. Max.	Min.	Dist. from Earth in millions of mi. Max.	Min.	Light at[1] perihelion	aphelion
Mercury . .	14732	29.75	88.0	115.9	43.4	28.6	136	50	10.58	4.59
Venus . . .	5768	21.76	224.7	583.9	67.7	66.8	161	25	1.94	1.89
Earth . . .	3548	18.51	365.3	—	94.6	91.4	—	—	1.03	0.97
Mars	1886	14.99	687.0	779.9	155.0	128.5	248	35	0.524	0.360
Jupiter . .	299	8.12	4332.1	398.9	507.0	460.6	600	368	0.0408	0.0336
Saturn . . .	120	5.99	10825.9	378.1	937.5	838.4	1031	745	0.01230	0.00984
Uranus . .	42	4.23	30676.1	369.7	1859.7	1669.3	1953	1606	0.00300	0.00250
Neptune . .	21	3.38	59911.1	367.5	2821.7	2760.4	2915	2667	0.00114	0.00109
Pluto	14	2.95	90824.2	366.7	4551.4	2756.4	4644	2663	0.00114	0.00042

1. Light at perihelion and aphelion is solar illumination in units of mean illumination at Earth.

Planet	Mean longitude of:* ascending node (° ' ")			perihelion (° ' ")			Inclination* of orbit to ecliptic (° ' ")			Mean* distance**	Eccentricity* of orbit	Mean longitude at the epoch* (° ' ")		
Mercury	48	12	58	77	18	25	7	00	25	0.387098	0.205635	146	49	38
Venus	76	35	35	131	11	24	3	23	40	0.723330	0.006761	263	5	28
Earth	—	—	—	102	47	31	—	—	—	0.999998	0.016678	206	50	19
Mars	49	29	33	335	48	25	1	50	59	1.523736	0.093455	297	52	24
Jupiter	100	23	13	15	31	41	1	18	18	5.20317	0.048207	99	44	26
Saturn	113	34	9	91	49	19	2	29	16	9.51632	0.055328	291	15	50
Uranus	73	58	1	169	47	35	0	46	19	19.1573	0.047694	271	31	4
Neptune	131	39	54	56	14	24	1	46	19	30.0022	0.010034	283	33	52
Pluto	110	05	49	223	35	53	17	09	44	39.4698	0.248646	224	33	30

* Consistent for the standard Epoch: 1990 Apr. 19 Ephemeris Time ** Astronomical units

Sun and planets	Semi-diameter at unit distance (' ")	Semi-diameter at mean least dist. (")	in miles mean s.d.	Volume ⊕=1.	Mass ⊕=1.	Density ⊕=1.	Sidereal period of rotation d.	h.	m.	s.	Gravity at surface ⊕=1.	Reflecting power Pct.	Probable temperature °F.
Sun	959.62		432560	1303730	332830	0.26	24	16	48		27.9		+ 10,000
Mercury . . .	3.37	5.5	1515	0.0559	0.0553	0.99	58	21	58		0.37	0.06	+ 620
Venus	8.34	30.1	3760	0.8541	0.8150	0.95	243	R			0.88	0.72	+ 900
Earth			3963	1.000	1.000	1.00		23	56	4.1	1.00	0.39	+ 72
Moon	2.40	932.4	1080	0.020	0.0123	0.62	27	7	43		0.17	0.07	± 72
Mars	4.69	8.95	2108.4	0.1506	0.1074	0.71		24	37	23	0.38	0.16	— 10
Jupiter	98.35	23.4	44362	1403	317.83	0.23		9	50	30	2.64	0.70	— 240
Saturn	82.83	9.7	37280	832	95.16	0.11		10	30		1.15	0.75	— 300
Uranus	35.4	1.9	15800	63	14.50	0.23		15	36	R	1.15	0.90	— 340
Neptune . . .	33.4	1.2	15300	55	17.20	0.31		16	7		1.12	0.82	— 370
Pluto	1.9	0.05	930	0.01	0.0025	0.25	6	9	17		0.04	0.14	?

(R) retrograde of Venus and Uranus.

The Sun

The sun, the controlling body of our solar system, is a star whose dimensions cause it to be classified among stars as average in size, temperature, and brightness. Its proximity to the earth makes it appear to us as tremendously large and bright. A series of thermo-nuclear reactions involving the atoms of the elements of which it is composed produces the heat and light that make life possible on earth.

The sun has a diameter of 864,000 miles and is distant, on the average, 92,900,000 miles from the earth. It is 1.41 times as dense as water. The light of the sun reaches the earth in 499.012 seconds or slightly more than 8 minutes. The average solar surface temperature has been measured by several indirect methods which agree closely on a value of 6,000° Kelvin or about 10,000° F. The interior temperature of the sun is about 35,000,000 F.°.

When sunlight is analyzed with a spectroscope, it is found to consist of a continuous spectrum composed of all the colors of the rainbow in order, crossed by many dark lines. The "absorption lines" are produced by gaseous materials in the atmosphere of the sun.

More than 60 of the natural terrestrial elements have been identified in the sun, all in gaseous form because of the intense heat of the sun.

Spheres and Corona

The radiating surface of the sun is called the photosphere, and just above it is the chromosphere. The chromosphere is visible to the naked eye only at times of total solar eclipses, appearing then to be a pinkish-violet layer with occasional great prominences projecting above its general level. With proper instruments the chromosphere can be seen or photographed whenever the sun is visible without waiting for a total eclipse. Above the chromosphere is the corona, also visible to the naked eye only at times of total eclipse. Instruments also permit the brighter portions of the corona to be studied whenever conditions are favorable. The pearly light of the corona surges millions of miles from the sun. Iron, nickel, and calcium are believed to be principal contributors to the composition of the corona, all in a state of extreme attenuation and high ionization that indicates temperatures on the order of a million degrees Fahrenheit.

Sunspots

There is an intimate connection between sunspots and the corona. At times of low sunspot activity, the fine streamers of the corona will be much longer above the sun's equator than over the polar regions of the sun, while during high sunspot activity, the corona extends fairly evenly outward from all regions of the sun, but to a much greater distance in space. Sunspots are dark, irregularly-shaped regions whose diameters may reach tens of thousands of miles. The average life of a sunspot group is from two to three weeks, but there have been groups that have lasted for more than a year, being carried repeatedly around as the sun rotated upon its axis. The record for the duration of a sunspot is 18 months. Sunspots reach a low point every 11.3 years, with a peak of activity occurring irregularly between two successive minima.

The sun is 400,000 times as bright as the full moon and gives the earth 6 million times as much light as do all the other stars put together. Actually, most of the stars that can be easily seen on any clear night are brighter than the sun.

The Zodiac

The sun's apparent yearly path among the stars is known as the ecliptic. The zone 16° wide, 8° on each side of the ecliptic, is known as the zodiac. Inside of this zone are the apparent paths of the sun, moon, earth, and major planets. Beginning at the point on the ecliptic which marks the position of the sun at the vernal equinox, and thence proceeding eastward, the zodiac is divided into twelve signs of 30° each, as shown herewith.

These signs are named from the twelve constellations of the zodiac with which the signs coincided in the time of the astronomer Hipparchus, about 2,000 years ago. Owing to the precession of the equinoxes, that is to say, to the retrograde motion of the equinoxes along the ecliptic, each sign in the zodiac has, in the course of 2,000 years, moved backward 30° into the constellation west of it; so that the sign Aries is now in the constellation Pisces, and so on. The vernal equinox will move from Pisces into Aquarius about the middle of the 26th century. The signs of the zodiac with their Latin and English names are as follows:

Spring	1.	♈ Aries.	The Ram.
	2.	♉ Taurus.	The Bull.
	3.	♊ Gemini.	The Twins.
Summer	4.	♋ Cancer.	The Crab.
	5.	♌ Leo.	The Lion.
	6.	♍ Virgo.	The Virgin.
Autumn	7.	♎ Libra.	The Balance.
	8.	♏ Scorpius.	The Scorpion.
	9.	♐ Sagittarius.	The Archer.
Winter	10.	♑ Capricorn.	The Goat.
	11.	♒ Aquarius.	The Water Bearer.
	12.	♓ Pisces.	The Fishes.

Moon's Perigee and Apogee, 1992

		Perigee							Apogee		
Month	Day	h	Month	Day	h	Month	Day	h	Month	Day	h
Jan...	19	22	July	30	8	Jan.	6	12	July	17	11
Feb...	17	11	Aug.....	27	18	Feb.....	2	12	Aug.....	13	16
Mar...	16	18	Sept.....	25	3	Feb.....	29	21	Sept.	9	19
Apr...	13	7	Oct.	23	5	Mar.....	28	14	Oct.	7	6
May...	8	12	Nov......	19	0	Apr.....	25	10	Nov......	3	23
June ..	4	2	Dec......	13	21	May.....	23	5	Dec.....	1	20
July...	2	1				June.....	19	22	Dec.....	29	17

		Perihelion					Aphelion	
Jan.	3	15				July	3	12

Astronomical Constants; Speed of Light

The following were adopted in 1968, in accordance with the resolutions and recommendations of the International Astronomical Union (Hamburg 1964): Speed of light, 299,792.5 kilometers per second, or about 186,282.3976 statute miles per second; solar parallax, 8″.794; constant of nutation, 9″.210; and constant of aberration, 20″.496.

The Moon

The moon completes a circuit around the earth in a period whose mean or average duration is 27 days 7 hours 43.2 minutes. This is the moon's sidereal period. Because of the motion of the moon in common with the earth around the sun, the mean duration of the lunar month — the period from one new moon to the next new moon — is 29 days 12 hours 44.05 minutes. This is the moon's synodical period.

The mean distance of the moon from the earth according to the American Ephemeris is 238,857 miles. Because the orbit of the moon about the earth is not circular but elliptical, however, the maximum distance from the earth that the moon may reach is 252,710 miles and the least distance is 221,463 miles. All distances are from the center of one object to the center of the other.

The moon's diameter is 2,160 miles. If we deduct the radius of the moon, 1,080 miles, and the radius of the earth, 3,963 miles from the minimum distance or perigee, given above, we shall have for the nearest approach of the bodies' surfaces 216,420 miles.

The moon rotates on its axis in a period of time exactly equal to its sidereal revolution about the earth — 27.321666 days. The moon's revolution about the earth is irregular because of its elliptical orbit. The moon's rotation, however, is regular and this, together with the irregular revolution, produces what is called "libration in longitude" which permits us to see first farther around the east side and then farther around the west side of the moon. The moon's variation north or south of the ecliptic permits us to see farther over first one pole and then the other of the moon and this is "libration in latitude." These two libration effects permit us to see a total of about 60% of the moon's surface over a period of time. The hidden side of the moon was photographed in 1959 by the Soviet space vehicle Lunik III. Since then many excellent pictures of nearly all of the moon's surface have been transmitted to earth by Lunar Orbiters launched by the U.S.

The tides are caused mainly by the moon, because of its proximity to the earth. The ratio of the tide-raising power of the moon to that of the sun is 11 to 5.

Harvest Moon and Hunter's Moon

The Harvest Moon, the full moon nearest the Autumnal Equinox, ushers in a period of several successive days when the moon rises soon after sunset. This phenomenon gives farmers in temperate latitudes extra hours of light in which to harvest their crops before frost and winter come. The 1992 Harvest Moon falls on Sept. 19 GMT. Harvest moon in the south temperate latitudes falls on Mar. 26.

The next full moon after Harvest Moon is called the Hunter's Moon, accompanied by a similar phenomenon but less marked; — Oct. 19, northern hemisphere; Apr. 24, southern hemisphere.

The Earth: Size, Computation of Time, Seasons

Size and Dimensions

The earth is the fifth largest planet and the third from the sun. Its mass is 6 sextillion, 588 quintillion short tons. Using the parameters of an ellipsoid adopted by the International Astronomical Union in 1964 and recognized by the International Union of Geodesy and Geophysics in 1967, the length of the equator is 24,901.55 miles, the length of a meridian is 24,859.82 miles, the equatorial diameter is 7,926.41 miles, and the area of this reference ellipsoid is approximately 196,938,800 square miles.

The earth is considered a solid, rigid mass with a dense core of magnetic, probably metallic material. The outer part of the core is probably liquid. Around the core is a thick shell or mantle of heavy crystalline rock which in turn is covered by a thin crust forming the solid granite and basalt base of the continents and ocean basins. Over broad areas of the earth's surface the crust has a thin cover of sedimentary rock such as sandstone, shale, and limestone formed by weathering of the earth's surface and deposition of sands, clays, and plant and animal remains.

The temperature in the earth increases about 1°F. with every 100 to 200 feet in depth, in the upper 100 kilometers of the earth, and the temperature near the core is believed to be near the melting point of the core materials under the conditions at that depth. The heat of the earth is believed to be derived from radioactivity in the rocks, pressures developed within the earth, and original heat (if the earth in fact was formed at high temperatures).

Atmosphere of the Earth

The earth's atmosphere is a blanket composed of nitrogen, oxygen, and argon, in amounts of about 78, 21, and 1% by volume. Also present in minute quantities are carbon dioxide, hydrogen, neon, helium, krypton, and xenon.

Water vapor displaces other gases and varies from nearly zero to about 4% by volume. The height of the ozone layer varies from approximately 12 to 21 miles above the earth. Traces exist as low as 6 miles and as high as 35 miles. Traces of methane have been found.

The atmosphere rests on the earth's surface with the weight equivalent to a layer of water 34 ft. deep. For about 300,000 ft. upward the gases remain in the proportions stated. Gravity holds the gases to the earth. The weight of the air compresses it at the bottom, so that the greatest density is at the earth's surface. Pressure, as well as density, decreases as height increases because the weight pressing upon any layer is always less than that pressing upon the layers below.

The temperature of the air drops with increased height until the tropopause is reached. This may vary from 25,000 to 60,000 ft. The atmosphere below the tropopause is the troposphere; the atmosphere for about twenty miles above the tropopause is the stratosphere, where the temperature generally increases with height except at high latitudes in winter. A temperature maximum near the 30-mile level is called the stratopause. Above this boundary is the mesosphere where the temperature decreases with height to a minimum, the mesopause, at a height of 50 miles. Extending above the mesosphere to the outer fringes of the atmosphere is the thermosphere, a region where temperature increases with height to a value measured in thousands of degrees Fahrenheit. The lower portion of this region, extending from 50 to about 400 miles in altitude, is characterized by a high ion density, and is thus called the ionosphere. The outer region is called exosphere; this is the region where gas molecules traveling at high speed may escape into outer space, above 600 miles.

Latitude, Longitude

Position on the globe is measured by means of meridians and parallels. Meridians, which are imaginary lines drawn around the earth through the poles, determine longitude. The meridian running through Greenwich, England, is the prime meridian of longitude, and all others are either east or west. Parallels, which are imaginary circles parallel with the equator, determine latitude. The length of a degree of longitude varies as the cosine of the latitude. At the equator a degree is 69.171 statute miles; this is gradually reduced toward the poles. Value of a longitude degree at the poles is zero.

Latitude is reckoned by the number of degrees north or south of the equator, an imaginary circle on the earth's surface everywhere equidistant between the two poles. According to the IAU Ellipsoid of 1964, the length of a degree of latitude is 68.708 statute miles at the equator and varies slightly north and south because of the oblate form of the globe; at the poles it is 69.403 statute miles.

Computation of Time

The earth rotates on its axis and follows an elliptical orbit around the sun. The rotation makes the sun appear to move across the sky from East to West. It determines day and night and the complete rotation, in relation to the sun, is called the apparent or true solar day. This varies but an average determines the mean solar day of 24 hours.

The mean solar day is in universal use for civil purposes. It may be obtained from apparent solar time by correcting observations of the sun for the equation of time, but when high precision is required, the mean solar time is calculated from its relation to sidereal time. These relations are extremely complicated, but for most practical uses, they may be considered as follows:

Sidereal time is the measure of time defined by the diurnal motion of the vernal equinox, and is determined from observation of the meridian transits of stars. One complete rotation of the earth relative to the equinox is called the **sidereal day**. The **mean sidereal day** is 23 hours, 56 minutes, 4.091 seconds of mean solar time.

The **Calendar Year** begins at 12 o'clock midnight precisely local clock time, on the night of Dec. 31-Jan. 1. The day and the calendar month also begin at midnight by the clock. The interval required for the earth to make one absolute revolution around the sun is a **sidereal year**; it consisted of 365 days, 6 hours, 9 minutes, and 9.5 seconds of mean solar time (approximately 24 hours per day) in 1900, and is increasing at the rate of 0.0001-second annually.

The **Tropical Year**, on which the return of the seasons depends, is the interval between two consecutive returns of the sun to the vernal equinox. The tropical year consists of 365 days, 5 hours, 48 minutes, and 46 seconds in 1900. It is decreasing at the rate of 0.530 seconds per century.

In 1956 the unit of time interval was defined to be identical with the second of **Ephemeris Time**, 1/31,556,925.9747 of the tropical year for 1900 January Od 12th hour E.T. A physical definition of the second based on a quantum transition of cesium (atomic second) was adopted in 1964. The atomic second is equal to 9,192,631,770 cycles of the emitted radiation. In 1967 this atomic second was adopted as the unit of time interval for the Intern'l System of Units.

The Zones and Seasons

The five zones of the earth's surface are Torrid, lying between the Tropics of Cancer and Capricorn; North Temperate, between Cancer and the Arctic Circle; South Temperate, between Capricorn and the Antarctic Circle; The Frigid Zones, between the polar Circles and the Poles.

The inclination or tilt of the earth's axis with respect to the sun determines the seasons. These are commonly marked in the North Temperate Zone, where spring begins at the vernal equinox, summer at the summer solstice, autumn at the autumnal equinox and winter at the winter solstice.

In the South Temperate Zone, the seasons are reversed. Spring begins at the autumnal equinox, summer at the winter solstice, etc.

If the earth's axis were perpendicular to the plane of the earth's orbit around the sun there would be no change of seasons. Day and night would be of nearly constant length and there would be equable conditions of temperature. But the axis is tilted 23° 27' away from a perpendicular to the orbit and only in March and September is the axis at right angles to the sun.

The points at which the sun crosses the equator are the equinoxes, when day and night are most nearly equal. The points at which the sun is at a maximum distance from the equator are the solstices. Days and nights are then most unequal.

In June the North Pole is tilted 23° 27' toward the sun and the days in the northern hemisphere are longer than the nights, while the days in the southern hemisphere are shorter than the nights. In December the North Pole is tilted 23° 27' away from the sun and the situation is reversed.

The Seasons in 1992

In 1992 the 4 seasons will begin as follows: add one hour to EST for Atlantic Time; subtract one hour for Central, two hours for Mountain, 3 hours for Pacific, 4 hours for Yukon, 5 hours for Alaska-Hawaii and six hours for Bering Time. Also shown in Greenwich Mean Time.

		Date	GMT	EST
Vernal Equinox	Spring	Mar. 20	8:48	3:48
Summer Solstice	Summer	June 21	3:14	10:14*
Autumnal Equinox	Autumn	Sept. 22	18:43	13:43
Winter Solstice	Winter	Dec. 21	14:43	9:43

* Previous Day

Poles of The Earth

The geographic (rotation) poles, or points where the earth's axis of rotation cuts the surface, are not absolutely fixed in the body of the earth. The pole of rotation describes an irregular curve about its mean position.

Two periods have been detected in this motion: (1) an annual period due to seasonal changes in barometric pressure, load of ice and snow on the surface and to other phenomena of seasonal character; (2) a period of about 14 months due to the shape and constitution of the earth.

In addition there are small but as yet unpredictable irregularities. The whole motion is so small that the actual pole at any time remains within a circle of 30 or 40 feet in radius centered at the mean position of the pole.

The pole of rotation for the time being is of course the pole having a latitude of 90° and an indeterminate longitude.

Magnetic Poles

The **north magnetic pole** of the earth is that region where the magnetic force is vertically downward and the **south magnetic pole** that region where the magnetic force is vertically upward. A compass placed at the magnetic poles experiences no directive force in azimuth.

There are slow changes in the distribution of the earth's magnetic field. These changes were at one time attributed in part to a periodic movement of the magnetic poles around the geographical poles, but later evidence refutes this theory and points, rather, to a slow migration of "disturbance" foci over the earth.

There appear shifts in position of the magnetic poles due to the changes in the earth's magnetic field. The center of the area designated as the north magnetic pole was estimated to be in about latitude 70.5° N and longitude 96° W in 1905; from recent nearby measurements and studies of the secular changes, the position in 1970 is estimated as latitude 76.2° N and longitude 101° W. Improved data rather than actual motion account for at least part of the change.

The position of the south magnetic pole in 1912 was near 71° S and longitude 150° E; the position in 1970 is estimated at latitude 66° S and longitude 139.1° E.

The direction of the horizontal components of the magnetic field at any point is known as magnetic north at that point, and the angle by which it deviates east or west of true north is known as the magnetic declination, or in the mariner's terminology, the **variation of the compass**.

A compass without error points in the direction of magnetic north. (In general this is *not* the direction of the magnetic north pole.) If one follows the direction indicated by the north end of the compass, he will travel along a rather irregular curve which eventually reaches the north magnetic pole (though not usually by a great-circle route). However, the action of the compass should not be thought of as due to any influence of the distant pole, but simply as an indication of the distribution of the earth's magnetism at the place of observation.

Rotation of The Earth

The speed of rotation of the earth about its axis has been found to be slightly variable. The variations may be classified as:

(A) **Secular.** Tidal friction acts as a brake on the rotation and causes a slow secular increase in the length of the day, about 1 millisecond per century.

(B) **Irregular.** The speed of rotation may increase for a number of years, about 5 to 10, and then start decreasing. The maximum difference from the mean in the length of the day during a century is about 5 milliseconds. The accumulated difference in time has amounted to approximately 44 seconds since 1900. The cause is probably motion in the interior of the earth.

(C) **Periodic.** Seasonal variations exist with periods of one year and six months. The cumulative effect is such that each year the earth is late about 30 milliseconds near June 1 and is ahead about 30 milliseconds near Oct. 1. The maximum seasonal variation in the length of the day is about 0.5 millisecond. It is believed that the principal cause of the annual variation is the seasonal change in the wind patterns of the Northern and Southern Hemispheres. The semiannual variation is due chiefly to tidal action of the sun, which distorts the shape of the earth slightly.

The secular and irregular variations were discovered by comparing time based on the rotation of the earth with time based on the orbital motion of the moon about the earth and of the planets about the sun. The periodic variation was determined largely with the aid of quartz-crystal clocks. The introduction of the cesium-beam atomic clock in 1955 made it possible to determine in greater detail than before the nature of the irregular and periodic variations.

Morning and Evening Stars, 1992

(GMT)

	Morning	Evening		Morning	Evening
Jan.	Mercury, Jan. 1	Saturn, Jan. 1 to Jan. 29	**June**		Neptune
	Venus, Jan. 1	Uranus, from Jan. 5			Pluto
	Mars, Jan. 1	Neptune, from Jan. 7	**July**	Mars	Mercury
	Jupiter, Jan. 1			Saturn	Venus
	Saturn, from Jan. 29			Uranus, from July 7	Jupiter
	Uranus, to Jan. 5			Neptune, from July 9	Pluto
	Neptune, to Jan. 7		**Aug.**	Mercury, from Aug. 2	Mercury, to Aug. 2
	Pluto, Jan. 1			Mars	Venus
Feb.	Mercury, to Feb. 12	Mercury, from Feb. 12		Saturn, to Aug. 7	Jupiter
	Venus	Jupiter, from Feb. 29		Uranus	Saturn, from Aug. 7
	Mars	Uranus		Neptune	Pluto
	Jupiter, to Feb. 29	Neptune	**Sept.**	Mercury, to Sept. 15	Mercury, from Sept. 15
	Saturn			Mars	Venus
	Pluto			Jupiter, from Sept. 17	Jupiter, to Sept. 17
Mar.	Mercury, from Mar. 26	Jupiter		Uranus	Saturn
	Venus	Uranus		Neptune	Pluto
	Mars	Neptune	**Oct.**	Mars	Mercury
	Saturn			Jupiter	Venus
	Pluto			Uranus	Saturn
Apr.	Mercury	Jupiter		Neptune	Pluto
	Venus	Uranus	**Nov.**	Mercury, from Nov. 21	Mercury, to Nov. 21
	Mars	Neptune		Mars	Venus
	Saturn	Pluto, from May 12		Jupiter	Saturn
	Pluto			Uranus	Pluto, to Nov. 15
May	Mercury, to May 31	Mercury, from May 31		Neptune	
	Venus	Jupiter		Pluto, from Nov. 15	
	Mars	Uranus	**Dec.**	Mercury	Venus
	Saturn	Neptune		Mars	Saturn
	Pluto, to May 12	Pluto		Jupiter	
June	Venus, to June 13	Mercury		Uranus	
	Mars	Venus, from June 13		Neptune	
	Saturn	Jupiter		Pluto	
		Uranus			

Chronological Eras, 1992

The year 1992 of the Christian Era comprises the latter part of the 216th and the beginning of the 217th year of the independence of the United States of America.

Era	Year	Begins in 1992	Era	Year	Begins in 1992
Byzantine	7501	Sept. 14	Japanese	2652	Jan. 1
Jewish	5753	Sept. 27 (sunset)	Grecian (Seleucidae)	2304	Sept. 14 or Oct. 14
Roman (Ab Urbe Condita)	2745	Jan. 14	Diocletian	1709	Sept. 11
Nabonassar (Babylonian)	2741	Apr. 25	Indian (Saka)	1914	Mar. 21
			Mohammedan (Hegira)	1413	July 1

Chronological Cycles, 1992

Dominical Letter.........	ED	Golden Number (Lunar Cycle). XVII	Roman Indiction......... 15
Epact.................	25*	Solar Cycle 13	Julian Period (year of) 6705

* Second Epact to be used as if it were 26.

Astronomical Twilight—Meridian of Greenwich

Date 1992	20° Begin	20° End	30° Begin	30° End	40° Begin	40° End	50° Begin	50° End	60° Begin	60° End
	h m	h m	h m	h m	h m	h m	h m	h m	h m	h m
Jan. 1	5 16	6 50	5 30	6 35	5 45	6 21	6 00	6 07	6 18	5 49
11	5 19	6 56	5 33	6 43	5 46	6 30	6 00	6 17	6 15	6 01
21	5 21	7 01	5 32	6 51	5 43	6 40	5 55	6 30	6 06	6 18
Feb. 1	5 21	7 07	5 29	6 58	5 38	6 51	5 45	6 44	5 51	6 38
11	5 18	7 11	5 24	7 05	5 29	7 01	5 32	6 59	5 32	7 01
21	5 13	7 15	5 17	7 12	5 17	7 12	5 16	7 14	5 09	7 23
Mar. 1	5 08	7 18	5 08	7 19	5 06	7 21	4 59	7 29	4 44	7 45
11	5 00	7 21	4 58	7 24	4 50	7 32	4 38	7 46	4 12	8 12
21	4 52	7 24	4 45	7 32	4 33	7 44	4 14	8 04	3 37	8 43
Apr. 1	4 42	7 28	4 31	7 39	4 14	7 57	3 47	8 25	2 53	9 21
11	4 32	7 32	4 18	7 47	3 56	8 09	3 20	8 47	2 03	10 10
21	4 23	7 38	4 04	7 54	3 37	8 23	2 52	9 11	0 37	11 47
May 1	4 14	7 41	3 52	8 04	3 19	8 37	2 22	9 39		
11	4 08	7 46	3 41	8 13	3 03	8 53	1 49	10 09		
21	4 02	7 52	3 32	8 22	2 48	9 07	1 13	10 46		
June 1	3 58	7 58	3 26	8 30	2 36	9 20	0 21	11 52		
11	3 56	8 03	3 22	8 36	2 29	9 30				
21	3 57	8 06	3 22	8 40	2 28	9 35				
July 1	3 59	8 07	3 25	8 41	2 30	9 35				
11	4 03	8 06	3 30	8 39	2 40	9 30				
21	4 08	8 03	3 39	8 33	2 52	9 18	1 12	11 23		
Aug. 1	4 15	7 56	3 48	8 23	3 09	9 01	1 49	10 20		
11	4 20	7 50	3 56	8 13	3 22	8 46	2 21	9 46		
21	4 24	7 41	4 05	8 01	3 34	8 27	2 47	9 15		
Sept. 1	4 29	7 31	4 14	7 46	3 51	8 08	3 13	8 43	1 40	10 02
11	4 32	7 20	4 20	7 33	4 02	7 50	3 33	8 16	2 36	9 12
21	4 35	7 11	4 26	7 19	4 14	7 31	3 52	7 52	3 11	8 31
Oct. 1	4 38	7 02	4 33	7 05	4 25	7 13	4 10	7 28	3 41	7 54
11	4 40	6 53	4 40	6 53	4 35	6 58	4 26	7 05	4 07	7 23
21	4 43	6 47	4 45	6 44	4 45	6 43	4 41	6 46	4 32	6 55
Nov. 1	4 46	6 41	4 52	6 34	4 56	6 30	4 58	6 27	4 56	6 27
11	4 50	6 38	4 59	6 28	5 06	6 21	5 13	6 14	5 17	6 08
21	4 55	6 36	5 06	6 25	5 16	6 15	5 26	6 04	5 37	5 52
Dec. 1	5 00	6 37	5 13	6 24	5 25	6 11	5 38	5 58	5 53	5 42
11	5 06	6 40	5 20	6 26	5 34	6 12	5 48	5 57	6 06	5 38
21	5 11	6 45	5 25	6 30	5 39	6 16	5 55	6 00	6 15	5 40
31	5 15	6 50	5 30	6 35	5 44	6 21	6 00	6 06	6 18	5 48

Telescopes

In the northern hemisphere the largest reflector is the 236-inch mirror at the Special Astrophysical Obs. in the Caucasus in the Soviet Union. The largest reflectors in the U.S. include 3 in California: at Palomar Mtn., 200 inches; at Lick Obs., Mt. Hamilton, 120 inches; and at Mt. Wilson Obs., 100 inches. The Whipple Obs. on the summit of Mauna Kea, Ha. is rapidly becoming the site of major instruments in the Northern hemisphere. Also in the U.S. are the Multiple Mirror Telescope (MMT) at Mt. Hopkins in Amado, AZ, which is a 176-inch single mirror reflector, a 158-inch reflector at Kitt Peak, Arizona, dedicated in June 1973, and a 107-inch telescope at the McDonald Obs. on Mt. Locke in Texas. A telescope at the Crimean Astrophysical Obs. in the Soviet Union has a 104-inch mirror. (In modern instruments, an electronic device responds to the light and directs the response to signal processors.)

Placed in service in 1975 were three large reflectors for the southern hemisphere. Associated Universities for Research in Astronomy (AURA), the operating organization of Kitt Peak National Obs., dedicated the 158-inch reflector (twin of the telescope on Kitt Peak) at Cerro Tololo International Obs., Chile; the European Southern Obs. has a 141-inch reflector at La Silla, Chile; and the Anglo-Australian telescope, 152 inches in diameter, is at Siding Spring Obs. Australia.

Optical Telescopes

Optical astronomical telescopes are of two kinds, refracting and reflecting. In the first, light passes through a lens which brings the light rays into focus, where the image may be examined after being magnified by a second lens, the eye-piece, or directly photographed.

The reflector usually consists of a concave parabolic mirror, generally of Pyrex or now of a relatively heat insensitive material, cervit, coated with silver or aluminum, which reflects the light rays back toward the upper end of the telescope, where they are either magnified and observed by the eye-piece or, as in the case of the refractors, photographed. In modern instruments, an electronic device responds to the light and directs the response to signal processors. In most reflecting telescopes, the light is reflected again by a secondary mirror and comes to a focus after passing through a hole in the side of the telescope, where the eye-piece or camera is located, or after passing through a hole in the center of the primary mirror.

1st Month   January, 1992   31 days

Greenwich Mean Time

NOTE: Light numbers indicate Sun. **Dark** numbers indicate **Moon**. *Degrees are North Latitude.*

FM = full moon; LQ = last quarter; NM = new moon; FQ = first quarter.

CAUTION: Must be converted to local time. For instructions see page 269.

Day of month / week / year	Sun on Meridian / Moon phase (h m s)	Sun's Declination (° ')	20° Rise Sun/Moon (h m)	20° Set Sun/Moon (h m)	30° Rise Sun/Moon (h m)	30° Set Sun/Moon (h m)	40° Rise Sun/Moon (h m)	40° Set Sun/Moon (h m)	50° Rise Sun/Moon (h m)	50° Set Sun/Moon (h m)	60° Rise Sun/Moon (h m)	60° Set Sun/Moon (h m)
1 We 1	12 3 17	−23 5	6 35	17 32	6 56	17 11	7 22	16 45	7 59	16 08	9 03	15 04
			3 36	14 44	3 58	14 21	4 26	13 52	5 07	13 11	6 20	11 56
2 Th 2	12 3 46	−22 60	6 35	17 32	6 56	17 12	7 22	16 46	7 59	16 09	9 02	15 06
			4 29	15 34	4 53	15 10	5 23	14 39	6 07	13 55	7 29	12 33
3 Fr 3	12 4 14	−22 55	6 36	17 33	6 56	17 12	7 22	16 47	7 58	16 10	9 02	15 07
			5 20	16 25	5 44	16 02	6 15	15 31	6 59	14 48	8 20	13 27
4 Sa 4	12 4 42 / 23 10 NM	−22 49	6 36	17 34	6 56	17 13	7 22	16 47	7 58	16 11	9 01	15 09
			6 09	17 18	6 31	16 56	7 00	16 28	7 41	15 48	8 54	14 36
5 Su 5	12 5 09	−22 43	6 36	17 34	6 57	17 14	7 22	16 48	7 58	16 12	9 00	15 10
			6 53	18 10	7 13	17 51	7 39	17 27	8 14	16 53	9 15	15 54
6 Mo 6	12 5 36	−22 36	6 36	17 35	6 57	17 15	7 22	16 49	7 58	16 14	8 59	15 12
			7 34	19 01	7 51	18 45	8 12	18 26	8 41	17 59	9 29	17 14
7 Tu 7	12 6 02	−22 29	6 37	17 36	6 57	17 15	7 22	16 50	7 58	16 15	8 59	15 14
			8 12	19 51	8 25	19 40	8 41	19 25	9 03	19 06	9 38	18 35
8 We 8	12 6 28	−22 22	6 37	17 36	6 57	17 16	7 22	16 51	7 57	16 16	8 58	15 16
			8 47	20 40	8 56	20 33	9 07	20 24	9 21	20 13	9 44	19 54
9 Th 9	12 6 54	−22 14	6 37	17 37	6 57	17 17	7 22	16 52	7 57	16 17	8 57	15 18
			9 21	21 29	9 25	21 26	9 31	21 23	9 38	21 19	9 50	21 13
10 Fr 10	12 7 19	−22 6	6 37	17 37	6 57	17 18	7 22	16 53	7 56	16 19	8 55	15 20
			9 54	22 18	9 54	22 20	9 54	22 23	9 54	22 26	9 54	22 32
11 Sa 11	12 7 43	−21 57	6 37	17 38	6 57	17 19	7 22	16 54	7 56	16 20	8 54	15 22
			10 28	23 08	10 23	23 15	10 18	23 23	10 10	23 35	9 59	23 54
12 Su 12	12 8 07	−21 48	6 38	17 39	6 57	17 19	7 21	16 55	7 55	16 21	8 53	15 24
			11 03	– –	10 54	– –	10 43	– –	10 28	– –	10 05	– –
13 Mo 13	12 8 30 / 2 32 FQ	−21 38	6 38	17 39	6 57	17 20	7 21	16 56	7 55	16 23	8 52	15 26
			11 42	0 01	11 29	0 12	11 12	0 27	10 49	0 47	10 13	1 19
14 Tu 14	12 8 52	−21 28	6 38	17 40	6 57	17 21	7 21	16 57	7 54	16 24	8 50	15 28
			12 26	0 56	12 08	1 13	11 46	1 33	11 15	2 01	10 25	2 48
15 We 15	12 9 14	−21 18	6 38	17 41	6 57	17 22	7 20	16 58	7 53	16 26	8 49	15 30
			13 15	1 56	12 54	2 16	12 27	2 41	11 49	3 17	10 44	4 20
16 Th 16	12 9 35	−21 7	6 38	17 41	6 57	17 23	7 20	16 59	7 53	16 27	8 47	15 32
			14 12	2 58	13 48	3 21	13 18	3 50	12 35	4 32	11 17	5 49
17 Fr 17	12 9 55	−20 56	6 38	17 42	6 56	17 24	7 20	17 01	7 52	16 29	8 46	15 35
			15 15	4 02	14 51	4 26	14 20	4 57	13 36	5 41	12 15	7 03
18 Sa 18	12 10 15	−20 44	6 38	17 43	6 56	17 24	7 19	17 02	7 51	16 30	8 44	15 37
			16 22	5 04	16 00	5 27	15 32	5 56	14 52	6 38	13 40	7 51
19 Su 19	12 10 34 / 21 28 FM	−20 32	6 38	17 43	6 56	17 25	7 19	17 03	7 50	16 32	8 42	15 39
			17 31	6 03	17 13	6 23	16 50	6 48	16 18	7 22	15 23	8 20
20 Mo 20	12 10 52	−20 20	6 38	17 44	6 56	17 26	7 18	17 04	7 49	16 33	8 41	15 42
			18 38	6 56	18 25	7 12	18 09	7 30	17 47	7 56	17 10	8 37
21 Tu 21	12 11 10	−20 7	6 38	17 45	6 56	17 27	7 18	17 05	7 48	16 35	8 39	15 44
			19 43	7 44	19 36	7 54	19 27	8 07	19 14	8 23	18 54	8 48
22 We 22	12 11 26	−19 54	6 38	17 45	6 55	17 28	7 17	17 06	7 47	16 36	8 37	15 47
			20 45	8 29	20 43	8 33	20 41	8 38	20 39	8 45	20 34	8 56
23 Th 23	12 11 42	−19 40	6 38	17 46	6 55	17 29	7 16	17 07	7 46	16 38	8 35	15 49
			21 44	9 10	21 48	9 09	21 53	9 08	22 00	9 06	22 10	9 03
24 Fr 24	12 11 58	−19 26	6 38	17 47	6 55	17 30	7 16	17 09	7 45	16 40	8 33	15 52
			22 42	9 50	22 51	9 44	23 03	9 36	23 19	9 26	23 44	9 09
25 Sa 25	12 12 12	−19 12	6 37	17 47	6 54	17 30	7 15	17 10	7 44	16 41	8 31	15 54
			23 39	10 31	23 53	10 19	– –	10 05	– –	9 46	– –	9 17
26 Su 26	12 12 26 / 15 27 LQ	−18 57	6 37	17 47	6 54	17 31	7 14	17 11	7 43	16 43	8 29	15 57
			– –	11 12	– –	10 56	0 11	10 37	0 35	10 10	1 15	9 26
27 Mo 27	12 12 39	−18 42	6 37	17 48	6 53	17 32	7 14	17 12	7 41	16 44	8 27	15 59
			0 35	11 56	0 53	11 36	1 16	11 12	1 49	10 38	2 44	9 40
28 Tu 28	12 12 51	−18 27	6 37	17 49	6 53	17 33	7 13	17 13	7 40	16 46	8 25	16 02
			1 31	12 42	1 52	12 20	2 19	11 51	2 58	11 11	4 08	10 00
29 We 29	12 13 02	−18 11	6 37	17 50	6 52	17 34	7 12	17 15	7 39	16 48	8 22	16 04
			2 25	13 31	2 48	13 07	3 18	12 36	4 01	11 53	5 21	10 32
30 Th 30	12 13 13	−17 55	6 36	17 50	6 52	17 35	7 11	17 16	7 37	16 50	8 20	16 07
			3 17	14 21	3 41	13 57	4 11	13 27	4 56	12 43	6 18	11 21
31 Fr 31	12 13 23	−17 39	6 36	17 51	6 51	17 36	7 10	17 17	7 36	16 51	8 18	16 10
			4 06	15 13	4 29	14 50	4 58	14 22	5 41	13 40	6 57	12 25

2nd Month — February, 1992 — 29 days

Greenwich Mean Time

NOTE: Light numbers indicate Sun. **Dark** numbers indicate **Moon.** *Degrees are North Latitude.*

FM = full moon; LQ = last quarter; NM = new moon; FQ = first quarter.

CAUTION: Must be converted to local time. For instructions see page 269.

Day of month / week / year	Sun on Meridian / Moon phase (h m s)	Sun's Declination (° ')	20° Rise	20° Set	30° Rise	30° Set	40° Rise	40° Set	50° Rise	50° Set	60° Rise	60° Set
1 Sa	12 13 31	−17 22	6 36	17 51	6 51	17 37	7 09	17 18	7 35	16 53	8 16	16 12
32			4 51	16 05	5 13	15 45	5 39	15 20	6 17	14 43	7 22	13 40
2 Su	12 13 40	−17 5	6 35	17 52	6 50	17 37	7 08	17 19	7 33	16 55	8 13	16 15
33			5 33	16 57	5 51	16 40	6 14	16 19	6 45	15 49	7 37	15 00
3 Mo	12 13 47	−16 48	6 35	17 53	6 50	17 38	7 07	17 21	7 32	16 56	8 11	16 17
34	19 00 NM		6 12	17 47	6 26	17 34	6 44	17 18	7 09	16 56	7 48	16 21
4 Tu	12 13 53	−16 30	6 35	17 53	6 49	17 39	7 06	17 22	7 30	16 58	8 09	16 20
35			6 48	18 37	6 59	18 28	7 11	18 18	7 28	18 03	7 55	17 41
5 We	12 13 59	−16 13	6 34	17 54	6 48	17 40	7 05	17 23	7 29	17 00	8 06	16 23
36			7 23	19 25	7 29	19 22	7 36	19 17	7 46	19 10	8 01	19 00
6 Th	12 14 4	−15 55	6 34	17 54	6 48	17 41	7 04	17 24	7 27	17 02	8 04	16 25
37			7 56	20 14	7 58	20 15	7 59	20 16	8 02	20 17	8 06	20 19
7 Fr	12 14 8	−15 36	6 34	17 55	6 47	17 42	7 03	17 25	7 26	17 03	8 01	16 28
38			8 30	21 04	8 27	21 10	8 23	21 16	8 18	21 25	8 11	21 39
8 Sa	12 14 11	−15 18	6 33	17 55	6 46	17 42	7 02	17 27	7 24	17 05	7 59	16 31
39			9 04	21 55	8 57	22 05	8 48	22 18	8 35	22 35	8 17	23 02
9 Su	12 14 14	−14 59	6 33	17 56	6 46	17 43	7 01	17 28	7 22	17 07	7 56	16 33
40			9 41	22 49	9 29	23 03	9 15	23 22	8 55	23 47	8 24	– –
10 Mo	12 14 15	−14 39	6 32	17 56	6 45	17 44	7 00	17 29	7 21	17 08	7 53	16 36
41			10 22	23 45	10 06	– –	9 46	– –	9 18	– –	8 34	0 28
11 Tu	12 14 16	−14 20	6 32	17 57	6 44	17 45	6 59	17 30	7 19	17 10	7 51	16 39
42	16 15 FQ		11 08	– –	10 48	0 04	10 23	0 27	9 48	1 00	8 49	1 56
12 We	12 14 16	−14 0	6 31	17 57	6 43	17 46	6 58	17 31	7 17	17 12	7 48	16 41
43			11 59	0 44	11 36	1 06	11 08	1 34	10 27	2 13	9 15	3 24
13 Th	12 14 15	−13 41	6 31	17 58	6 42	17 47	6 56	17 33	7 16	17 14	7 46	16 44
44			12 57	1 45	12 33	2 09	12 03	2 39	11 19	3 23	9 58	4 43
14 Fr	12 14 14	−13 21	6 30	17 58	6 41	17 47	6 55	17 34	7 14	17 15	7 43	16 47
45			14 00	2 46	13 37	3 10	13 07	3 40	12 25	4 23	11 08	5 41
15 Sa	12 14 12	−13 0	6 30	17 59	6 41	17 48	6 54	17 35	7 12	17 17	7 40	16 49
46			15 06	3 45	14 46	4 06	14 20	4 34	13 44	5 12	12 40	6 18
16 Su	12 14 9	−12 40	6 29	17 59	6 39	17 49	6 53	17 36	7 10	17 19	7 38	16 52
47			16 13	4 40	15 57	4 57	15 37	5 20	15 10	5 50	14 23	6 40
17 Mo	12 14 5	−12 19	6 28	18 00	6 39	17 50	6 51	17 37	7 08	17 21	7 35	16 54
48			17 19	5 30	17 09	5 43	16 56	5 59	16 37	6 20	16 09	6 54
18 Tu	12 14 0	−11 58	6 28	18 00	6 38	17 50	6 50	17 38	7 07	17 22	7 32	16 57
49	8 04 FM		18 23	6 16	18 18	6 24	18 12	6 33	18 04	6 45	17 52	7 04
19 We	12 13 55	−11 37	6 27	18 01	6 37	17 51	6 49	17 40	7 05	17 24	7 29	17 00
50			19 25	7 00	19 26	7 02	19 27	7 04	19 29	7 07	19 32	7 12
20 Th	12 13 49	−11 16	6 27	18 01	6 36	17 52	6 47	17 41	7 03	17 26	7 27	17 02
51			20 26	7 42	20 32	7 38	20 40	7 34	20 52	7 28	21 09	7 19
21 Fr	12 13 43	−10 54	6 26	18 02	6 35	17 53	6 46	17 42	7 01	17 27	7 24	17 05
52			21 25	8 24	21 37	8 15	21 52	8 04	22 12	7 49	22 45	7 26
22 Sa	12 13 36	−10 33	6 25	18 02	6 34	17 53	6 45	17 43	6 59	17 29	7 21	17 07
53			22 24	9 06	22 40	8 52	23 01	8 35	23 30	8 12	– –	7 35
23 Su	12 13 28	−10 11	6 25	18 02	6 33	17 54	6 43	17 44	6 57	17 31	7 18	17 10
54			23 21	9 50	23 42	9 32	– –	9 10	– –	8 39	0 18	7 48
24 Mo	12 13 20	− 9 49	6 24	18 03	6 32	17 55	6 42	17 45	6 55	17 32	7 15	17 13
55			– –	10 37	– –	10 16	0 07	9 49	0 43	9 11	1 46	8 06
25 Tu	12 13 11	− 9 27	6 23	18 03	6 31	17 56	6 41	17 46	6 53	17 34	7 12	17 15
56	7 56 LQ		0 17	11 26	0 40	11 02	1 09	10 33	1 50	9 51	3 06	8 34
26 We	12 13 1	− 9 5	6 23	18 04	6 30	17 56	6 39	17 48	6 51	17 36	7 09	17 17
57			1 11	12 16	1 35	11 52	2 05	11 22	2 49	10 38	4 10	9 17
27 Th	12 12 51	− 8 42	6 22	18 04	6 29	17 57	6 38	17 49	6 49	17 37	7 07	17 20
58			2 02	13 08	2 25	12 45	2 55	12 16	3 38	11 34	4 56	10 16
28 Fr	12 12 41	− 8 20	6 21	18 04	6 28	17 58	6 36	17 50	6 47	17 39	7 04	17 23
59			2 48	14 00	3 10	13 39	3 38	13 13	4 17	12 35	5 25	11 28
29 Sa	12 12 30	− 7 57	6 20	18 05	6 27	17 59	6 35	17 51	6 45	17 41	7 01	17 25
60			3 32	14 52	3 51	14 34	4 15	14 11	4 48	13 40	5 44	12 46

3rd Month   March, 1992   31 days

Greenwich Mean Time

NOTE: Light numbers indicate Sun. **Dark** numbers indicate **Moon.** *Degrees are North Latitude.*

FM = full moon; LQ = last quarter; NM = new moon; FQ = first quarter.

CAUTION: Must be converted to local time. For instructions see page 269.

Day of month / week / year	Sun on Meridian · Moon phase (h m s)	Sun's Declination (° ')	20° Rise Sun/Moon	20° Set Sun/Moon	30° Rise Sun/Moon	30° Set Sun/Moon	40° Rise Sun/Moon	40° Set Sun/Moon	50° Rise Sun/Moon	50° Set Sun/Moon	60° Rise Sun/Moon	60° Set Sun/Moon
1 Su 61	12 12 18	− 7 34	6 20	18 05	6 26	17 59	6 33	17 52	6 43	17 42	6 58	17 28
			4 11	15 42	4 27	15 28	4 46	15 11	5 13	14 46	5 56	14 06
2 Mo 62	12 12 6	− 7 11	6 19	18 06	6 25	18 00	6 32	17 53	6 41	17 44	6 55	17 30
			4 48	16 32	5 00	16 22	5 15	16 10	5 34	15 53	6 05	15 26
3 Tu 63	12 11 53	− 6 48	6 18	18 06	6 24	18 01	6 30	17 54	6 39	17 46	6 52	17 33
			5 24	17 22	5 31	17 16	5 40	17 09	5 53	17 00	6 12	16 45
4 We 64	12 11 40 · 13 22 NM	− 6 25	6 17	18 06	6 23	18 01	6 29	17 55	6 37	17 47	6 49	17 35
			5 58	18 11	6 01	18 10	6 04	18 09	6 10	18 07	6 17	18 05
5 Th 65	12 11 27	− 6 2	6 17	18 07	6 21	18 02	6 27	17 56	6 35	17 49	6 46	17 38
			6 31	19 01	6 30	19 05	6 28	19 09	6 26	19 16	6 23	19 25
6 Fr 66	12 11 13	− 5 39	6 16	18 07	6 20	18 03	6 26	17 57	6 33	17 51	6 43	17 40
			7 06	19 52	7 00	20 00	6 53	20 11	6 43	20 25	6 29	20 48
7 Sa 67	12 10 59	− 5 16	6 15	18 07	6 19	18 03	6 24	17 59	6 31	17 52	6 40	17 43
			7 43	20 45	7 32	20 58	7 20	21 14	7 02	21 37	6 36	22 13
8 Su 68	12 10 44	− 4 52	6 14	18 08	6 18	18 04	6 22	18 00	6 28	17 54	6 37	17 45
			8 23	21 41	8 08	21 58	7 50	22 19	7 25	22 50	6 45	23 40
9 Mo 69	12 10 29	− 4 29	6 13	18 08	6 17	18 05	6 21	18 01	6 26	17 56	6 34	17 48
			9 06	22 38	8 48	22 59	8 25	23 25	7 52	- -	6 59	- -
10 Tu 70	12 10 14	− 4 5	6 13	18 08	6 16	18 05	6 19	18 02	6 24	17 57	6 31	17 50
			9 55	23 37	9 34	- -	9 06	- -	8 28	0 02	7 21	1 07
11 We 71	12 9 58	− 3 42	6 12	18 08	6 14	18 06	6 18	18 03	6 22	17 59	6 28	17 53
			10 50	- -	10 26	0 00	9 56	0 30	9 14	1 11	7 57	2 28
12 Th 72	12 9 42 · 02 36 FQ	− 3 18	6 11	18 09	6 13	18 07	6 16	18 04	6 20	18 00	6 25	17 55
			11 49	0 37	11 25	1 00	10 56	1 30	10 13	2 13	8 55	3 32
13 Fr 73	12 9 26	− 2 55	6 10	18 09	6 12	18 07	6 15	18 05	6 18	18 02	6 22	17 58
			12 51	1 34	12 30	1 57	12 03	2 25	11 24	3 05	10 15	4 15
14 Sa 74	12 9 9	− 2 31	6 09	18 09	6 11	18 08	6 13	18 06	6 16	18 04	6 19	18 00
			13 56	2 28	13 38	2 48	13 15	3 12	12 44	3 46	11 50	4 42
15 Su 75	12 8 52	− 2 7	6 08	18 10	6 10	18 08	6 11	18 07	6 13	18 05	6 16	18 03
			15 00	3 19	14 47	3 34	14 30	3 53	14 08	4 18	13 31	4 59
16 Mo 76	12 8 35	− 1 44	6 07	18 10	6 09	18 09	6 10	18 08	6 11	18 07	6 13	18 05
			16 03	4 06	15 55	4 16	15 46	4 28	15 33	4 45	15 12	5 10
17 Tu 77	12 8 17	− 1 20	6 07	18 10	6 07	18 10	6 08	18 09	6 09	18 08	6 10	18 08
			17 05	4 50	17 03	4 54	17 00	5 00	16 57	5 08	16 52	5 19
18 We 78	12 7 60 · 18 18 FM	0 56	6 06	18 11	6 06	18 10	6 07	18 10	6 07	18 10	6 07	18 10
			18 06	5 32	18 09	5 31	18 14	5 30	18 20	5 29	18 30	5 27
19 Th 79	12 7 42	0 32	6 05	18 11	6 05	18 11	6 05	18 11	6 05	18 12	6 04	18 13
			19 06	6 14	19 15	6 08	19 27	6 00	19 42	5 50	20 07	5 35
20 Fr 80	12 7 24	0 9	6 04	18 11	6 04	18 12	6 03	18 12	6 03	18 13	6 01	18 15
			20 06	6 57	20 20	6 45	20 38	6 32	21 02	6 13	21 42	5 44
21 Sa 81	12 7 6	0 15	6 03	18 11	6 03	18 12	6 02	18 13	6 00	18 15	5 58	18 17
			21 06	7 41	21 24	7 25	21 47	7 06	22 20	6 39	23 15	5 55
22 Su 82	12 6 48	0 39	6 02	18 12	6 01	18 13	6 00	18 14	5 58	18 16	5 55	18 20
			22 04	8 28	22 26	8 08	22 53	7 44	23 32	7 09	- -	6 11
23 Mo 83	12 6 30	1 2	6 01	18 12	6 00	18 13	5 58	18 15	5 56	18 18	5 52	18 22
			23 01	9 17	23 24	8 55	23 53	8 26	- -	7 46	0 41	6 36
24 Tu 84	12 6 12	1 26	6 01	18 12	5 59	18 14	5 57	18 16	5 54	18 20	5 49	18 25
			23 54	10 08	- -	9 44	- -	9 15	0 36	8 32	1 54	7 13
25 We 85	12 5 54	1 50	6 00	18 12	5 58	18 15	5 55	18 17	5 52	18 21	5 46	18 27
			- -	11 00	0 17	10 37	0 47	10 08	1 30	9 15	2 49	8 07
26 Th 86	12 5 36 · 02 30 LQ	2 13	5 59	18 13	5 56	18 15	5 54	18 18	5 49	18 23	5 43	18 30
			0 43	11 53	1 05	11 31	1 33	11 04	2 13	10 25	3 25	9 15
27 Fr 87	12 5 17	2 37	5 58	18 13	5 55	18 16	5 52	18 19	5 47	18 24	5 40	18 32
			1 28	12 45	1 48	12 26	2 13	12 02	2 48	11 29	3 48	10 31
28 Sa 88	12 4 59	3 0	5 57	18 13	5 54	18 16	5 50	18 20	5 45	18 26	5 37	18 35
			2 09	13 36	2 26	13 21	2 46	13 01	3 15	12 35	4 02	11 50
29 Su 89	12 4 41	3 24	5 56	18 14	5 53	18 17	5 49	18 21	5 43	18 27	5 34	18 37
			2 47	14 26	3 00	14 15	3 16	14 01	3 38	13 41	4 13	13 10
30 Mo 90	12 4 23	3 47	5 55	18 14	5 52	18 18	5 47	18 22	5 41	18 29	5 31	18 39
			3 23	15 15	3 32	15 08	3 43	15 00	3 57	14 48	4 21	14 29
31 Tu 91	12 4 5	4 10	5 54	18 14	5 50	18 18	5 45	18 23	5 39	18 31	5 28	18 42
			3 57	16 05	4 02	16 02	4 07	15 59	4 15	15 55	4 27	15 48

4th Month

April, 1992

Greenwich Mean Time

30 days

NOTE: Light numbers indicate Sun. **Dark** numbers indicate **Moon.** *Degrees are North Latitude.*

FM = full moon; LQ = last quarter; NM = new moon; FQ = first quarter.

CAUTION: Must be converted to local time. For instructions see page 269.

Day of month week year	Sun on Meridian / Moon phase (h m s)	Sun's Declination (° ')	20° Rise Sun/Moon (h m)	20° Set Sun/Moon (h m)	30° Rise Sun/Moon (h m)	30° Set Sun/Moon (h m)	40° Rise Sun/Moon (h m)	40° Set Sun/Moon (h m)	50° Rise Sun/Moon (h m)	50° Set Sun/Moon (h m)	60° Rise Sun/Moon (h m)	60° Set Sun/Moon (h m)
1 We 92	12 03 47	4 33	5 54	18 14	5 49	18 19	5 44	18 24	5 36	18 32	5 25	18 44
			4 31	16 55	4 31	16 57	4 32	16 59	4 32	17 03	4 33	17 08
2 Th 93	12 03 30	4 56	5 53	18 15	5 48	18 19	5 42	18 25	5 34	18 34	5 22	18 47
			5 06	17 46	5 02	17 53	4 56	18 01	4 49	18 12	4 39	18 30
3 Fr 94	12 03 12 / 05 01 NM	5 19	5 52	18 15	5 47	18 20	5 41	18 26	5 32	18 35	5 19	18 49
			5 42	18 39	5 34	18 50	5 23	19 05	5 08	19 24	4 46	19 55
4 Sa 95	12 02 55	5 42	5 51	18 15	5 46	18 21	5 39	18 27	5 30	18 37	5 16	18 52
			6 22	19 35	6 08	19 50	5 52	20 10	5 30	20 38	4 55	21 23
5 Su 96	12 02 38	6 5	5 50	18 15	5 44	18 21	5 37	18 28	5 28	18 38	5 13	18 56
			7 05	20 32	6 48	20 52	6 26	21 17	5 56	21 51	5 08	22 51
6 Mo 97	12 02 21	6 28	5 49	18 16	5 43	18 22	5 36	18 29	5 26	18 40	5 10	18 57
			7 53	21 32	7 32	21 54	7 06	22 22	6 30	23 02	5 28	– –
7 Tu 98	12 02 4	6 51	5 48	18 16	5 42	18 22	5 34	18 30	5 24	18 42	5 07	18 59
			8 46	22 31	8 23	22 55	7 54	23 24	7 13	– –	6 00	0 15
8 We 99	12 01 47	7 13	5 48	18 16	5 41	18 23	5 33	18 32	5 21	18 43	5 04	19 01
			9 44	23 29	9 20	23 52	8 51	– –	8 08	0 07	6 51	1 24
9 Th 100	12 01 31	7 35	5 47	18 17	5 40	18 24	5 31	18 33	5 19	18 45	5 01	19 04
			10 45	– –	10 23	– –	9 55	0 20	9 15	1 01	8 04	2 13
10 Fr 101	12 01 15 / 10 06 FQ	7 58	5 46	18 17	5 39	18 24	5 30	18 34	5 17	18 46	4 58	19 06
			11 47	0 24	11 28	0 44	11 05	1 09	10 31	1 45	9 33	2 44
11 Sa 102	12 00 59	8 20	5 45	18 17	5 38	18 25	5 28	18 35	5 15	18 48	4 55	19 09
			12 50	1 14	12 35	1 30	12 17	1 51	11 51	2 19	11 10	3 04
12 Su 103	12 00 43	8 42	5 44	18 17	5 36	18 25	5 27	18 36	5 13	18 49	4 52	19 11
			13 51	2 00	13 41	2 12	13 29	2 27	13 13	2 47	12 47	3 17
13 Mo 104	12 00 28	9 4	5 44	18 18	5 35	18 26	5 25	18 37	5 11	18 51	4 49	19 14
			14 51	2 44	14 47	2 51	14 42	2 59	14 34	3 10	14 23	3 27
14 Tu 105	12 00 13	9 25	5 43	18 18	5 34	18 27	5 24	18 38	5 09	18 53	4 46	19 16
			15 51	3 25	15 52	3 27	15 53	3 29	15 55	3 31	15 58	3 35
15 We 106	11 59 58	9 47	5 42	18 18	5 33	18 27	5 22	18 39	5 07	18 54	4 43	19 19
			16 50	4 06	16 56	4 03	17 05	3 58	17 16	3 52	17 33	3 43
16 Th 107	11 59 44	10 8	5 41	18 19	5 32	18 28	5 21	18 40	5 05	18 56	4 40	19 21
			17 49	4 48	18 01	4 39	18 16	4 28	18 36	4 14	19 08	3 51
17 Fr 108	11 59 30 / 04 42 FM	10 29	5 40	18 19	5 31	18 29	5 19	18 41	5 03	18 57	4 37	19 24
			18 49	5 31	19 05	5 18	19 26	5 01	19 54	4 38	20 42	4 02
18 Sa 109	11 59 16	10 50	5 40	18 19	5 30	18 29	5 18	18 42	5 01	18 59	4 34	19 26
			19 49	6 17	20 09	5 59	20 34	5 37	21 10	5 06	22 12	4 16
19 Su 110	11 59 3	11 11	5 39	18 20	5 29	18 30	5 16	18 43	4 59	19 00	4 31	19 29
			20 47	7 06	21 09	6 45	21 38	6 18	22 18	5 41	23 32	4 37
20 Mo 111	11 58 50	11 32	5 38	18 20	5 28	18 30	5 15	18 44	4 57	19 02	4 28	19 31
			21 42	7 57	22 06	7 34	22 35	7 05	23 18	6 24	– –	5 09
21 Tu 112	11 58 38	11 52	5 37	18 20	5 27	18 31	5 13	18 45	4 55	19 03	4 25	19 33
			22 34	8 50	22 57	8 26	23 23	7 57	– –	7 14	0 36	5 56
22 We 113	11 58 26	12 13	5 37	18 20	5 26	18 32	5 12	18 46	4 53	19 05	4 23	19 36
			23 21	9 43	23 42	9 21	– –	8 53	0 06	8 13	1 20	7 00
23 Th 114	11 58 15	12 33	5 36	18 21	5 25	18 32	5 10	18 47	4 51	19 07	4 20	19 38
			– –	10 36	– –	10 16	0 08	9 51	0 45	9 16	1 48	8 14
24 Fr 115	11 58 4 / 21 40 LQ	12 52	5 35	18 21	5 24	18 33	5 09	18 48	4 49	19 08	4 17	19 41
			0 04	11 28	0 22	11 11	0 44	10 50	1 15	10 21	2 07	9 32
25 Sa 116	11 57 54	13 12	5 35	18 21	5 23	18 34	5 08	18 49	4 47	19 10	4 14	19 43
			0 43	12 18	0 58	12 06	1 16	11 50	1 40	11 28	2 19	10 52
26 Su 117	11 57 44	13 32	5 34	18 22	5 22	18 34	5 06	18 50	4 45	19 11	4 11	19 46
			1 20	13 08	1 30	12 59	1 43	12 48	2 01	12 34	2 28	12 10
27 Mo 118	11 57 34	13 51	5 33	18 22	5 21	18 35	5 05	18 51	4 43	19 13	4 08	19 48
			1 55	13 57	2 01	13 53	2 09	13 47	2 19	13 40	2 35	13 29
28 Tu 119	11 57 26	14 10	5 33	18 23	5 20	18 35	5 04	18 52	4 42	19 14	4 06	19 51
			2 29	14 46	2 31	14 46	2 33	14 47	2 36	14 47	2 41	14 48
29 We 120	11 57 17	14 29	5 32	18 23	5 19	18 36	5 02	18 53	4 40	19 16	4 03	19 53
			3 03	15 37	3 01	15 42	2 58	15 48	2 54	15 56	2 47	16 09
30 Th 121	11 57 9	14 47	5 31	18 23	5 18	18 37	5 01	18 54	4 38	19 17	4 00	19 56
			3 39	16 29	3 32	16 39	3 23	16 50	3 12	17 07	2 54	17 32

5th Month   May, 1992   31 days

Greenwich Mean Time

NOTE: Light numbers indicate Sun. **Dark** numbers indicate **Moon.** *Degrees are North Latitude.*

FM = full moon; LQ = last quarter; NM = new moon; FQ = first quarter.

CAUTION: Must be converted to local time. For instructions see page 269.

Day of month / week / year	Sun on Meridian / Moon phase (h m s)	Sun's Declination (° ')	20° Rise	20° Set	30° Rise	30° Set	40° Rise	40° Set	50° Rise	50° Set	60° Rise	60° Set
1 Fr	11 57 2	15 5	5 31	18 24	5 17	18 37	5 00	18 55	4 36	19 19	3 57	19 58
122			4 17	17 24	4 06	17 38	3 52	17 56	3 33	18 20	3 03	19 00
2 Sa	11 56 56	15 23	5 30	18 24	5 16	18 38	4 59	18 56	4 34	19 20	3 55	20 01
123	17 44 NM		5 00	18 22	4 44	18 40	4 24	19 03	3 58	19 35	3 15	20 29
3 Su	11 56 49	15 41	5 30	18 24	5 15	18 39	4 57	18 57	4 33	19 22	3 52	20 03
124			5 47	19 22	5 27	19 44	5 03	20 10	4 29	20 49	3 32	21 57
4 Mo	11 56 44	15 59	5 29	18 25	5 14	18 39	4 56	18 58	4 31	19 24	3 49	20 06
125			6 39	20 23	6 17	20 46	5 49	21 15	5 10	21 57	4 00	23 13
5 Tu	11 56 39	16 16	5 28	18 25	5 14	18 40	4 55	18 59	4 29	19 25	3 47	20 08
126			7 37	21 23	7 14	21 46	6 44	22 15	6 02	22 56	4 46	— —
6 We	11 56 34	16 33	5 28	18 25	5 13	18 41	4 54	19 00	4 28	19 27	3 44	20 11
127			8 38	22 19	8 16	22 40	7 47	23 07	7 07	23 44	5 54	0 10
7 Th	11 56 30	16 49	5 27	18 26	5 12	18 41	4 53	19 01	4 26	19 28	3 42	20 13
128			9 41	23 11	9 21	23 29	8 57	23 51	8 21	— —	7 20	0 47
8 Fr	11 56 27	17 6	5 27	18 26	5 11	18 42	4 52	19 02	4 24	19 30	3 39	20 16
129			10 44	23 59	10 28	— —	10 08	— —	9 41	0 21	8 55	1 09
9 Sa	11 56 24	17 22	5 26	18 27	5 11	18 43	4 51	19 03	4 23	19 31	3 36	20 18
130	15 43 FQ		11 45	— —	11 34	0 12	11 20	0 28	11 02	0 50	10 31	1 24
10 Su	11 56 22	17 38	5 26	18 27	5 10	18 43	4 50	19 04	4 21	19 32	3 34	20 20
131			12 45	0 43	12 39	0 51	12 32	1 01	12 22	1 15	12 06	1 35
11 Mo	11 56 20	17 53	5 26	18 27	5 09	18 44	4 49	19 05	4 20	19 34	3 32	20 23
132			13 43	1 24	13 42	1 27	13 42	1 31	13 41	1 36	13 39	1 44
12 Tu	11 56 19	18 9	5 25	18 28	5 08	18 45	4 48	19 06	4 18	19 35	3 29	20 25
133			14 41	2 04	14 45	2 02	14 51	2 00	14 59	1 56	15 12	1 51
13 We	11 56 18	18 24	5 25	18 28	5 08	18 45	4 47	19 07	4 17	19 37	3 27	20 28
134			15 39	2 44	15 48	2 37	16 00	2 29	16 17	2 17	16 44	1 59
14 Th	11 56 18	18 38	5 24	18 29	5 07	18 46	4 46	19 08	4 15	19 38	3 24	20 30
135			16 37	3 26	16 51	3 14	17 09	3 00	17 35	2 40	18 16	2 09
15 Fr	11 56 19	18 53	5 24	18 29	5 07	18 46	4 45	19 09	4 14	19 40	3 22	20 32
136			17 35	4 10	17 54	3 54	18 17	3 34	18 50	3 06	19 46	2 21
16 Sa	11 56 20	19 6	5 23	18 29	5 06	18 47	4 44	19 10	4 13	19 41	3 20	20 35
137	16 03 FM		18 34	4 57	18 55	4 37	19 22	4 12	20 01	3 38	21 10	2 39
17 Su	11 56 22	19 20	5 23	18 30	5 05	18 48	4 43	19 10	4 11	19 42	3 17	20 37
138			19 30	5 47	19 53	5 24	20 23	4 56	21 16	4 17	22 21	3 06
18 Mo	11 56 24	19 33	5 23	18 30	5 05	18 48	4 42	19 11	4 10	19 44	3 15	20 39
139			20 24	6 39	20 47	6 16	21 16	5 46	21 58	5 04	23 14	3 47
19 Tu	11 56 26	19 47	5 22	18 31	5 04	18 49	4 41	19 12	4 09	19 45	3 13	20 42
140			21 13	7 33	21 35	7 10	22 02	6 41	22 41	6 00	23 48	4 45
20 We	11 56 30	19 59	5 22	18 31	5 04	18 50	4 40	19 13	4 07	19 46	3 11	20 44
141			21 58	8 26	22 17	8 05	22 41	7 39	23 15	7 02	— —	5 56
21 Th	11 56 34	20 12	5 22	18 31	5 03	18 50	4 40	19 14	4 06	19 48	3 09	20 46
142			22 39	9 19	22 55	9 01	23 15	8 39	23 42	8 07	0 10	7 13
22 Fr	11 56 38	20 23	5 22	18 32	5 03	18 51	4 39	19 15	4 05	19 49	3 07	20 48
143			23 17	10 10	23 29	9 56	23 44	9 38	— —	9 13	0 25	8 33
23 Sa	11 56 43	20 35	5 21	18 32	5 02	18 51	4 38	19 16	4 04	19 50	3 05	20 50
144			23 52	11 00	— —	10 50	— —	10 37	0 04	10 20	0 35	9 52
24 Su	11 56 48	20 46	5 21	18 33	5 02	18 53	4 37	19 17	4 03	19 52	3 03	20 52
145	15 53 LQ		— —	11 49	— —	11 43	0 10	11 36	0 23	11 25	0 43	11 10
25 Mo	11 56 54	20 57	5 21	18 33	5 01	18 53	4 37	19 18	4 02	19 53	3 01	20 55
146			0 26	12 37	0 30	12 36	0 34	12 34	0 40	12 31	0 50	12 27
26 Tu	11 57 1	21 8	5 21	18 33	5 01	18 54	4 36	19 18	4 01	19 55	2 59	20 57
147			1 00	13 27	0 59	13 30	0 58	13 33	0 57	13 38	0 56	13 46
27 We	11 57 8	21 18	5 21	18 34	5 01	18 54	4 36	19 19	4 00	19 55	2 57	20 59
148			1 35	14 18	1 30	14 25	1 23	14 35	1 15	14 47	1 02	15 07
28 Th	11 57 15	21 28	5 20	18 34	5 00	18 54	4 35	19 20	3 59	19 56	2 55	21 01
149			2 12	15 11	2 02	15 23	1 50	15 38	1 34	15 59	1 10	16 32
29 Fr	11 57 23	21 37	5 20	18 35	5 00	18 55	4 34	19 21	3 58	19 57	2 54	21 02
150			2 52	16 07	2 38	16 24	2 21	16 44	1 57	17 13	1 20	18 01
30 Sa	11 57 31	21 46	5 20	18 35	5 00	18 55	4 34	19 21	3 57	19 58	2 52	21 04
151			3 37	17 07	3 19	17 27	2 56	17 52	2 26	18 28	1 35	19 30
31 Su	11 57 40	21 55	5 20	18 35	5 00	18 56	4 34	19 22	3 56	19 59	2 51	21 06
152			4 27	18 09	4 06	18 31	3 40	19 00	3 02	19 40	1 58	20 54

6th Month   June, 1992   30 days

Greenwich Mean Time

NOTE: Light numbers indicate Sun. **Dark** numbers indicate **Moon.** *Degrees are North Latitude.*

FM = full moon; LQ = last quarter; NM = new moon; FQ = first quarter.

CAUTION: Must be converted to local time. For instructions see page 269.

Day of month / week / year	Sun on Meridian Moon phase (h m s)	Sun's Declination (° ')	20° Rise Sun/Moon (h m)	20° Set Sun/Moon (h m)	30° Rise Sun/Moon (h m)	30° Set Sun/Moon (h m)	40° Rise Sun/Moon (h m)	40° Set Sun/Moon (h m)	50° Rise Sun/Moon (h m)	50° Set Sun/Moon (h m)	60° Rise Sun/Moon (h m)	60° Set Sun/Moon (h m)
1 Mo	11 57 49	22 4	5 20	18 36	4 59	18 57	4 33	19 23	3 56	20 00	2 49	21 08
153	03 57 NM		5 24	19 10	5 01	19 34	4 32	20 03	3 50	20 45	2 36	22 01
2 Tu	11 57 59	22 11	5 20	18 36	4 59	18 57	4 33	19 24	3 55	20 01	2 48	21 10
154			6 25	20 10	6 02	20 32	5 33	20 59	4 52	21 38	3 37	22 46
3 We	11 58 9	22 19	5 20	18 37	4 59	18 58	4 32	19 24	3 54	20 02	2 46	21 11
155			7 30	21 05	7 09	21 24	6 43	21 48	6 05	22 20	4 59	23 14
4 Th	11 58 19	22 26	5 20	18 37	4 59	18 58	4 32	19 25	3 54	20 03	2 45	21 13
156			8 35	21 56	8 18	22 10	7 56	22 28	7 26	22 53	6 35	23 31
5 Fr	11 58 30	22 33	5 20	18 37	4 59	18 59	4 32	19 25	3 53	20 04	2 44	21 14
157			9 38	22 42	9 26	22 51	9 10	23 03	8 48	23 19	8 14	23 44
6 Sa	11 58 41	22 39	5 20	18 38	4 59	18 59	4 32	19 26	3 53	20 05	2 43	21 16
158			10 39	23 24	10 32	23 29	10 23	23 34	10 10	23 42	9 51	23 53
7 Su	11 58 52	22 45	5 20	18 38	4 58	18 59	4 31	19 27	3 52	20 06	2 42	21 17
159	20 47 FQ		11 38	– –	11 36	– –	11 34	– –	11 30	– –	11 25	– –
8 Mo	11 59 3	22 51	5 20	18 38	4 58	19 00	4 31	19 27	3 52	20 07	2 41	21 18
160			12 36	0 04	12 39	0 04	12 43	0 03	12 49	0 02	12 57	0 01
9 Tu	11 59 15	22 56	5 20	18 39	4 58	19 00	4 31	19 28	3 51	20 07	2 40	21 20
161			13 33	0 44	13 41	0 39	13 52	0 32	14 06	0 23	14 28	0 09
10 We	11 59 27	23 1	5 20	18 39	4 58	19 01	4 31	19 28	3 51	20 08	2 39	21 21
162			14 30	1 25	14 43	1 14	15 00	1 02	15 22	0 44	15 59	0 18
11 Th	11 59 39	23 5	5 20	18 39	4 58	19 01	4 31	19 29	3 51	20 09	2 38	21 22
163			15 28	2 07	15 45	1 52	16 07	1 34	16 37	1 09	17 28	0 29
12 Fr	11 59 51	23 9	5 20	18 40	4 58	19 02	4 31	19 29	3 51	20 09	2 38	21 23
164			16 25	2 52	16 46	2 33	17 12	2 10	17 49	1 38	18 54	0 44
13 Sa	12 0 4	23 13	5 20	18 40	4 58	19 02	4 31	19 30	3 50	20 10	2 37	21 24
165			17 22	3 40	17 44	3 19	18 13	2 52	18 54	2 13	20 09	1 07
14 Su	12 0 16	23 16	5 20	18 40	4 58	19 02	4 31	19 30	3 50	20 10	2 37	21 25
166			18 16	4 31	18 39	4 08	19 08	3 39	19 51	2 57	21 08	1 42
15 Mo	12 0 29	23 19	5 20	18 41	4 58	19 03	4 31	19 31	3 50	20 11	2 36	21 25
167	04 50 FM		19 07	5 24	19 29	5 01	19 57	4 32	20 37	3 50	21 48	2 33
16 Tu	12 0 42	23 21	5 21	18 41	4 59	19 03	4 31	19 31	3 50	20 11	2 36	21 26
168			19 53	6 18	20 14	5 56	20 39	5 29	21 14	4 49	22 15	3 39
17 We	12 0 55	23 23	5 21	18 41	4 59	19 03	4 31	19 31	3 50	20 12	2 36	21 26
169			20 36	7 11	20 53	6 52	21 14	6 28	21 44	5 54	22 32	4 55
18 Th	12 1 8	23 24	5 21	18 41	4 59	19 03	4 31	19 32	3 50	20 12	2 36	21 27
170			21 15	8 03	21 28	7 47	21 45	7 27	22 08	7 00	22 43	6 15
19 Fr	12 1 21	23 25	5 21	18 42	4 59	19 04	4 31	19 32	3 50	20 12	2 36	21 27
171			21 51	8 53	22 00	8 41	22 12	8 27	22 28	8 06	22 52	7 34
20 Sa	12 1 34	23 26	5 21	18 42	4 59	19 04	4 31	19 32	3 50	20 13	2 36	21 28
172			22 25	9 42	22 30	9 35	22 37	9 25	22 46	9 12	22 59	8 52
21 Su	12 1 47	23 26	5 22	18 42	4 59	19 04	4 31	19 32	3 51	20 13	2 36	21 28
173			22 59	10 30	23 00	10 27	23 01	10 23	23 02	10 18	23 05	10 09
22 Mo	12 1 60	23 26	5 22	18 42	4 59	19 04	4 32	19 32	3 51	20 13	2 36	21 28
174			23 32	11 19	23 29	11 20	23 25	11 22	23 19	11 24	23 11	11 27
23 Tu	12 2 13	23 26	5 22	18 42	5 00	19 04	4 32	19 33	3 51	20 13	2 36	21 28
175	08 11 LQ		– –	12 08	24 00	12 14	23 50	12 21	23 37	12 30	23 18	12 45
24 We	12 2 25	23 25	5 22	18 43	5 00	19 05	4 32	19 33	3 51	20 13	2 37	21 28
176			0 07	12 59	– –	13 09	– –	13 22	23 58	13 39	23 27	14 07
25 Th	12 2 38	23 23	5 22	18 43	5 00	19 05	4 32	19 33	3 52	20 13	2 37	21 28
177			0 45	13 53	0 33	14 08	0 18	14 26	– –	14 51	23 39	15 32
26 Fr	12 2 51	23 22	5 23	18 43	5 01	19 05	4 33	19 33	3 52	20 13	2 38	21 27
178			1 27	14 50	1 11	15 09	0 51	15 32	0 23	16 04	23 57	17 00
27 Sa	12 3 3	23 19	5 23	18 43	5 01	19 05	4 33	19 33	3 53	20 13	2 39	21 27
179			2 14	15 50	1 54	16 12	1 30	16 39	0 55	17 18	– –	18 26
28 Su	12 3 16	23 17	5 23	18 43	5 01	19 05	4 34	19 33	3 53	20 13	2 39	21 27
180			3 07	16 52	2 45	17 15	2 17	17 45	1 37	18 26	0 27	19 42
29 Mo	12 3 28	23 14	5 24	18 43	5 02	19 05	4 34	19 33	3 54	20 13	2 40	21 26
181			4 07	17 54	3 43	18 16	3 14	18 45	2 32	19 26	1 16	20 39
30 Tu	12 3 40	23 10	5 24	18 43	5 02	19 05	4 34	19 33	3 54	20 14	2 41	21 25
182	12 18 NM		5 11	18 52	4 49	19 13	4 21	19 38	3 41	20 14	2 30	21 14

7th Month

July, 1992

Greenwich Mean Time

7th Month (left)   **31 days** (right)

NOTE: Light numbers indicate Sun. **Dark** numbers indicate **Moon**. *Degrees are North Latitude.*

FM = full moon; LQ = last quarter; NM = new moon; FQ = first quarter.

CAUTION: Must be converted to local time. For instructions see page 269.

Day of month / week / year	Sun on Meridian / Moon phase (h m s)	Sun's Declina-tion (° ')	20° Rise Sun/Moon (h m)	20° Set Sun/Moon (h m)	30° Rise Sun/Moon (h m)	30° Set Sun/Moon (h m)	40° Rise Sun/Moon (h m)	40° Set Sun/Moon (h m)	50° Rise Sun/Moon (h m)	50° Set Sun/Moon (h m)	60° Rise Sun/Moon (h m)	60° Set Sun/Moon (h m)
1 We — Sun	12 3 52	23 6	5 24	18 43	5 03	19 05	4 35	19 33	3 55	20 12	2 42	21 25
183 — Moon			5 03	18 43	5 34	19 05	5 01	20 23	5 01	20 51	4 03	21 36
2 Th — Sun	12 4 3	23 2	5 25	18 43	5 03	19 05	4 35	19 32	3 56	20 12	2 43	21 24
184 — Moon			5 25	18 44	5 04	19 05	6 51	21 02	6 25	21 21	5 44	21 51
3 Fr — Sun	12 4 14	22 57	5 26	18 44	5 04	19 05	4 36	19 32	3 56	20 12	2 45	21 23
185 — Moon			5 26	18 44	5 05	19 05	8 07	21 35	7 51	21 46	7 25	22 02
4 Sa — Sun	12 4 25	22 52	5 26	18 43	5 05	19 05	4 36	19 32	3 57	20 11	2 46	21 22
186 — Moon			5 27	18 43	5 06	19 04	9 21	22 06	9 14	22 08	9 04	22 11
5 Su — Sun	12 4 35	22 47	5 27	18 43	5 06	19 04	4 37	19 32	3 58	20 11	2 47	21 21
187 — Moon			5 27	18 43	5 07	19 04	10 33	22 35	10 35	22 29	10 39	22 19
6 Mo — Sun	12 4 46	22 41	5 28	18 43	5 07	19 04	4 38	19 32	3 59	20 10	2 49	21 20
188 — Moon			5 28	18 43	5 08	19 03	11 43	23 05	11 54	22 50	12 12	22 27
7 Tu — Sun	12 4 55	22 35	5 28	18 43	5 08	19 03	4 38	19 31	4 00	20 10	2 50	21 19
189 — Moon	02 43 FQ		5 29	18 43	5 09	19 03	12 52	23 37	13 12	23 14	13 44	22 38
8 We — Sun	12 5 4	22 28	5 29	18 43	5 09	19 02	4 39	19 31	4 01	20 09	2 52	21 17
190 — Moon			5 30	18 42	5 10	19 02	13 59	– –	14 27	23 41	15 14	22 51
9 Th — Sun	12 5 13	22 21	5 30	18 42	5 10	19 02	4 40	19 31	4 01	20 08	2 53	21 16
191 — Moon			5 30	18 42	5 11	19 01	15 05	0 11	15 40	– –	16 41	23 11
10 Fr — Sun	12 5 22	22 14	5 31	18 42	5 11	19 01	4 40	19 30	4 02	20 08	2 55	21 15
192 — Moon			5 31	18 41	5 12	19 00	16 06	0 51	16 47	0 14	17 59	23 42
11 Sa — Sun	12 5 30	22 6	5 31	18 41	5 13	19 00	4 41	19 30	4 03	20 07	2 57	21 13
193 — Moon			5 32	18 41	5 13	18 59	17 03	1 36	17 46	0 55	19 03	– –
12 Su — Sun	12 5 37	21 58	5 32	18 41	5 14	18 59	4 42	19 29	4 04	20 06	2 58	21 12
194 — Moon			5 33	18 40	5 14	18 58	17 54	2 26	18 35	1 44	19 49	0 26
13 Mo — Sun	12 5 44	21 49	5 33	18 40	5 15	18 58	4 42	19 29	4 05	20 05	3 00	21 10
195 — Moon			5 33	18 39	5 15	18 57	18 37	3 21	19 15	2 41	20 19	1 27
14 Tu — Sun	12 5 51	21 40	5 34	18 39	5 16	18 57	4 43	19 28	4 07	20 04	3 02	21 08
196 — Moon	19 06 FM		5 34	18 39	5 17	18 56	19 15	4 19	19 47	3 43	20 39	2 40
15 We — Sun	12 5 57	21 31	5 34	18 38	5 17	18 55	4 44	19 28	4 08	20 04	3 04	21 07
197 — Moon			5 35	18 38	5 18	18 55	19 47	5 19	20 12	4 49	20 52	3 59
16 Th — Sun	12 6 2	21 22	5 35	18 37	5 18	18 54	4 45	19 27	4 09	20 03	3 06	21 05
198 — Moon			19 51	6 48	20 02	6 35	20 15	6 18	20 34	5 55	21 02	5 18
17 Fr — Sun	12 6 7	21 12	5 41	18 27	5 29	18 39	4 45	19 26	4 10	20 02	3 08	21 03
199 — Moon			20 26	7 37	20 33	7 28	20 41	7 17	20 52	7 01	21 09	6 37
18 Sa — Sun	12 6 12	21 1	5 41	18 26	5 29	18 38	4 46	19 26	4 11	20 01	3 10	21 01
200 — Moon			20 59	8 26	21 02	8 21	21 05	8 15	21 09	8 07	21 16	7 54
19 Su — Sun	12 6 16	20 50	5 41	18 26	5 30	18 37	4 47	19 25	4 12	19 59	3 12	20 59
201 — Moon			21 33	9 14	21 31	9 13	21 29	9 13	21 26	9 12	21 22	9 11
20 Mo — Sun	12 6 19	20 39	5 41	18 25	5 30	18 36	4 48	19 24	4 14	19 58	3 14	20 57
202 — Moon			22 07	10 02	22 00	10 06	21 53	10 11	21 43	10 18	21 28	10 28
21 Tu — Sun	12 6 22	20 28	5 42	18 24	5 31	18 35	4 49	19 24	4 15	19 57	3 16	20 55
203 — Moon			22 42	10 52	22 32	11 00	22 19	11 11	22 02	11 25	21 36	11 47
22 We — Sun	12 6 25	20 16	5 42	18 23	5 31	18 34	4 49	19 23	4 16	19 56	3 18	20 53
204 — Moon	22 12 LQ		23 21	11 43	23 07	11 56	22 49	12 12	22 25	12 34	21 46	13 09
23 Th — Sun	12 6 26	20 4	5 42	18 23	5 32	18 33	4 50	19 22	4 17	19 55	3 20	20 51
205 — Moon			– –	12 38	23 47	12 54	23 24	13 15	22 53	13 45	22 01	14 34
24 Fr — Sun	12 6 27	19 52	5 42	18 22	5 33	18 31	4 51	19 21	4 19	19 53	3 23	20 49
206 — Moon			0 05	13 35	– –	13 55	– –	14 20	23 29	14 56	22 24	15 59
25 Sa — Sun	12 6 28	19 39	5 43	18 21	5 33	18 30	4 52	19 20	4 20	19 52	3 25	20 46
207 — Moon			0 54	14 34	0 32	14 57	0 06	15 25	– –	16 06	23 02	17 19
26 Su — Sun	12 6 28	19 26	5 43	18 20	5 34	18 29	4 53	19 19	4 21	19 51	3 27	20 44
208 — Moon			1 49	15 35	1 26	15 58	0 57	16 27	0 16	17 09	– –	18 24
27 Mo — Sun	12 6 28	19 12	5 43	18 19	5 34	18 28	4 54	19 18	4 23	19 49	3 29	20 42
209 — Moon			2 50	16 34	2 27	16 56	1 58	17 24	1 17	18 02	0 02	19 10
28 Tu — Sun	12 6 27	18 59	5 43	18 18	5 35	18 27	4 55	19 18	4 24	19 48	3 32	20 39
210 — Moon			3 55	17 31	3 34	17 50	3 08	18 13	2 31	18 45	1 25	19 38
29 We — Sun	12 6 25	18 45	5 44	18 18	5 35	18 26	4 56	19 17	4 25	19 47	3 34	20 37
211 — Moon	19 35 NM		5 02	18 23	4 45	18 37	4 24	18 55	3 54	19 19	3 04	19 57
30 Th — Sun	12 6 22	18 30	5 44	18 17	5 36	18 25	4 57	19 16	4 27	19 45	3 36	20 35
212 — Moon			6 08	19 11	5 56	19 21	5 41	19 32	5 20	19 47	4 47	20 09
31 Fr — Sun	12 6 20	18 15	5 44	18 16	5 36	18 23	4 58	19 15	4 28	19 44	3 39	20 33
213 — Moon			7 13	19 56	7 07	20 00	6 58	20 05	6 47	20 11	6 30	20 19

8th Month August, 1992 31 days

Greenwich Mean Time

NOTE: Light numbers indicate Sun. **Dark** numbers indicate **Moon**. *Degrees are North Latitude.*

FM = full moon; LQ = last quarter; NM = new moon; FQ = first quarter.

CAUTION: Must be converted to local time. For instructions see page 269.

Day of month / week / year	Sun on Meridian (h m s) / Moon phase	Sun's Declination (° ')	20° Rise	20° Set	30° Rise	30° Set	40° Rise	40° Set	50° Rise	50° Set	60° Rise	60° Set
1 Sa 214	12 6 16	18 1	5 35	18 37	5 19	18 53	4 58	19 14	4 29	19 42	3 41	20 30
	(Moon)		8 16	20 39	8 15	20 38	8 14	20 36	8 12	20 33	8 10	20 28
2 Su 215	12 6 12	17 45	5 36	18 36	5 20	18 52	4 59	19 12	4 31	19 41	3 43	20 27
	(Moon)		9 17	21 22	9 22	21 15	9 27	21 06	9 35	20 55	9 47	20 37
3 Mo 216	12 6 7	17 30	5 36	18 36	5 20	18 52	5 00	19 11	4 32	19 39	3 46	20 25
	(Moon)		10 17	22 05	10 27	21 53	10 39	21 38	10 56	21 18	11 22	20 47
4 Tu 217	12 6 2	17 14	5 37	18 35	5 21	18 51	5 01	19 10	4 34	19 37	3 48	20 22
	(Moon)		11 16	22 49	11 31	22 33	11 49	22 13	12 14	21 45	12 56	21 00
5 We 218	12 5 56	16 58	5 37	18 35	5 21	18 50	5 02	19 09	4 35	19 36	3 51	20 20
	10 58 FQ		12 14	23 35	12 33	23 16	12 56	22 51	13 29	22 16	14 25	21 18
6 Th 219	12 5 49	16 41	5 37	18 34	5 22	18 49	5 03	19 08	4 37	19 34	3 53	20 17
	(Moon)		13 12	– –	13 33	– –	14 00	23 34	14 38	22 55	15 47	21 45
7 Fr 220	12 5 42	16 25	5 38	18 34	5 23	18 48	5 04	19 07	4 38	19 32	3 55	20 14
	(Moon)		14 07	0 24	14 30	0 02	14 59	– –	15 40	23 41	16 56	22 25
8 Sa 221	12 5 34	16 8	5 38	18 33	5 23	18 47	5 05	19 05	4 40	19 31	3 58	20 12
	(Moon)		14 59	1 15	15 22	0 52	15 51	0 23	16 33	– –	17 48	23 20
9 Su 222	12 5 25	15 51	5 38	18 32	5 24	18 47	5 06	19 04	4 41	19 29	4 00	20 09
	(Moon)		15 48	2 08	16 09	1 45	16 37	1 16	17 15	0 35	18 23	– –
10 Mo 223	12 5 16	15 33	5 38	18 32	5 24	18 46	5 07	19 03	4 42	19 27	4 03	20 06
	(Moon)		16 33	3 00	16 52	2 40	17 16	2 13	17 49	1 36	18 46	0 29
11 Tu 224	12 5 7	15 16	5 39	18 31	5 25	18 45	5 08	19 02	4 44	19 25	4 05	20 04
	(Moon)		17 14	3 53	17 30	3 35	17 50	3 12	18 17	2 40	19 01	1 46
12 We 225	12 4 57	14 58	5 39	18 31	5 26	18 44	5 09	19 00	4 45	19 23	4 07	20 01
	(Moon)		17 52	4 44	18 04	4 29	18 19	4 11	18 40	3 46	19 12	3 05
13 Th 226	12 4 46	14 40	5 39	18 30	5 26	18 43	5 10	18 59	4 47	19 22	4 10	19 58
	10 27 FM		18 27	5 34	18 35	5 23	18 45	5 10	18 59	4 52	19 20	4 23
14 Fr 227	12 4 34	14 21	5 40	18 29	5 27	18 42	5 11	18 58	4 48	19 20	4 12	19 55
	(Moon)		19 01	6 22	19 05	6 16	19 10	6 08	19 17	5 58	19 27	5 41
15 Sa 228	12 4 23	14 3	5 40	18 28	5 27	18 41	5 12	18 56	4 50	19 18	4 15	19 52
	(Moon)		19 35	7 11	19 34	7 09	19 34	7 06	19 34	7 03	19 33	6 58
16 Su 229	12 4 10	13 44	5 40	18 28	5 28	18 40	5 13	18 55	4 51	19 16	4 17	19 50
	(Moon)		20 08	7 59	20 04	8 01	19 58	8 04	19 51	8 08	19 40	8 15
17 Mo 230	12 3 57	13 25	5 41	18 27	5 29	18 39	5 14	18 54	4 53	19 14	4 19	19 47
	(Moon)		20 43	8 48	20 34	8 55	20 24	9 03	20 09	9 15	19 47	9 33
18 Tu 231	12 3 44	13 5	5 41	18 26	5 29	18 38	5 15	18 52	4 54	19 12	4 22	19 44
	(Moon)		21 21	9 38	21 08	9 49	20 52	10 03	20 30	10 22	19 56	10 52
19 We 232	12 3 30	12 46	5 41	18 26	5 30	18 37	5 15	18 51	4 56	19 10	4 24	19 41
	(Moon)		22 01	10 31	21 45	10 46	21 24	11 05	20 55	11 31	20 09	12 15
20 Th 233	12 3 16	12 26	5 41	18 25	5 30	18 36	5 16	18 49	4 57	19 08	4 27	19 38
	(Moon)		22 47	11 25	22 27	11 44	22 02	12 08	21 27	12 41	20 28	13 38
21 Fr 234	12 3 1	12 6	5 42	18 24	5 31	18 35	5 17	18 48	4 59	19 06	4 29	19 35
	10 01 LQ		23 38	12 22	23 16	12 44	22 48	13 11	22 08	13 50	20 58	14 58
22 Sa 235	12 2 46	11 46	5 42	18 23	5 31	18 34	5 18	18 47	5 00	19 04	4 31	19 32
	(Moon)		– –	13 21	– –	13 43	23 42	14 12	23 01	14 54	21 46	16 08
23 Su 236	12 2 30	11 26	5 42	18 23	5 32	18 33	5 19	18 45	5 02	19 02	4 34	19 30
	(Moon)		0 34	14 19	0 11	14 41	– –	15 10	– –	15 50	22 56	17 01
24 Mo 237	12 2 14	11 6	5 42	18 22	5 33	18 31	5 20	18 44	5 03	19 00	4 36	19 27
	(Moon)		1 36	15 15	1 14	15 35	0 46	16 01	0 07	16 36	– –	17 36
25 Tu 238	12 1 58	10 45	5 43	18 21	5 33	18 31	5 21	18 42	5 05	18 58	4 39	19 24
	(Moon)		2 40	16 08	2 21	16 25	1 57	16 46	1 23	17 14	0 26	17 59
26 We 239	12 1 41	10 24	5 43	18 20	5 34	18 30	5 22	18 41	5 06	18 56	4 41	19 21
	(Moon)		3 46	16 58	3 31	17 10	3 13	17 25	2 47	17 44	2 05	18 15
27 Th 240	12 1 24	10 3	5 43	18 19	5 34	18 27	5 23	18 39	5 08	18 54	4 43	19 18
	(Moon)		4 51	17 45	4 42	17 52	4 30	18 00	4 14	18 10	3 48	18 26
28 Fr 241	12 1 7	9 42	5 43	18 18	5 35	18 27	5 24	18 37	5 09	18 52	4 46	19 15
	02 42 NM		5 56	18 30	5 52	18 31	5 47	18 32	5 40	18 34	5 30	18 36
29 Sa 242	12 0 49	9 21	5 44	18 18	5 35	18 26	5 25	18 36	5 11	18 50	4 48	19 12
	(Moon)		6 59	19 14	7 00	19 09	7 03	19 04	7 06	18 57	7 10	18 45
30 Su 243	12 0 30	8 59	5 44	18 17	5 36	18 25	5 26	18 34	5 12	18 48	4 51	19 09
	(Moon)		8 01	19 57	8 08	19 48	8 17	19 36	8 30	19 20	8 49	18 56
31 Mo 244	12 0 12	8 38	5 44	18 16	5 36	18 23	5 27	18 33	5 14	18 46	4 53	19 06
	(Moon)		9 02	20 43	9 15	20 28	9 30	20 11	9 52	19 46	10 26	19 08

9th Month   September, 1992   30 days

Greenwich Mean Time

NOTE: Light numbers indicate Sun. **Dark** numbers indicate **Moon.** *Degrees are North Latitude.*

FM = full moon; LQ = last quarter; NM = new moon; FQ = first quarter.

CAUTION: Must be converted to local time. For instructions see page 269.

In the table below, for each day the first (light) line gives the **Sun** values and the second (dark) line gives the **Moon** values. Times are h m.

Day / wk / year	Sun on Meridian / Moon phase (h m s)	Sun's Decl. °	20° Rise	20° Set	30° Rise	30° Set	40° Rise	40° Set	50° Rise	50° Set	60° Rise	60° Set
1 Tu 245	11 59 53	8 16	5 44	18 15	5 37	18 22	5 28	18 31	5 15	18 44	4 55	19 03
			10 03	21 30	10 20	21 11	10 41	20 49	11 11	20 17	12 00	19 25
2 We 246	11 59 34	7 54	5 45	18 14	5 38	18 21	5 29	18 30	5 17	18 41	4 58	19 00
			11 03	22 19	11 23	21 58	11 48	21 31	12 25	20 54	13 28	19 49
3 Th 247	11 59 14	7 32	5 45	18 13	5 38	18 20	5 30	18 28	5 18	18 39	5 00	18 57
	22 39 FQ		12 00	23 10	12 22	22 48	12 50	22 19	13 31	21 38	14 44	20 25
4 Fr 248	11 58 54	7 10	5 45	18 12	5 39	18 19	5 31	18 26	5 20	18 37	5 02	18 54
			12 54	– –	13 17	23 40	13 46	23 12	14 27	22 30	15 42	21 16
5 Sa 249	11 58 34	6 48	5 45	18 12	5 39	18 17	5 32	18 25	5 21	18 35	5 05	18 51
			13 44	0 03	14 06	– –	14 34	– –	15 14	23 29	16 23	22 21
6 Su 250	11 58 14	6 26	5 46	18 11	5 40	18 16	5 33	18 23	5 23	18 33	5 07	18 48
			14 31	0 56	14 51	0 35	15 16	0 08	15 51	– –	16 50	23 35
7 Mo 251	11 57 54	6 3	5 46	18 10	5 40	18 15	5 33	18 22	5 24	18 31	5 09	18 45
			15 13	1 48	15 30	1 30	15 51	1 06	16 20	0 32	17 08	– –
8 Tu 252	11 57 33	5 41	5 46	18 09	5 41	18 14	5 34	18 20	5 26	18 29	5 12	18 42
			15 52	2 40	16 05	2 24	16 22	2 05	16 45	1 37	17 20	0 52
9 We 253	11 57 12	5 18	5 46	18 08	5 41	18 13	5 35	18 18	5 27	18 26	5 14	18 39
			16 28	3 30	16 38	3 18	16 49	3 03	17 05	2 43	17 30	2 11
10 Th 254	11 56 51	4 56	5 46	18 07	5 42	18 11	5 36	18 17	5 29	18 24	5 16	18 36
			17 03	4 19	17 08	4 11	17 15	4 02	17 24	3 49	17 37	3 28
11 Fr 255	11 56 30	4 33	5 47	18 06	5 42	18 10	5 37	18 15	5 30	18 22	5 19	18 33
			17 36	5 08	17 38	5 04	17 39	5 00	17 41	4 54	17 44	4 45
12 Sa 256	11 56 9	4 10	5 47	18 05	5 43	18 09	5 38	18 13	5 32	18 20	5 21	18 30
	02 17 FM		18 10	5 56	18 07	5 57	18 03	5 58	17 58	6 00	17 51	6 02
13 Su 257	11 55 48	3 47	5 47	18 04	5 44	18 08	5 39	18 12	5 33	18 18	5 23	18 27
			18 45	6 45	18 38	6 50	18 29	6 57	18 17	7 06	17 58	7 20
14 Mo 258	11 55 26	3 24	5 47	18 03	5 44	18 06	5 39	18 10	5 35	18 15	5 26	18 24
			19 22	7 35	19 10	7 45	18 56	7 57	18 37	8 13	18 07	8 39
15 Tu 259	11 55 5	3 1	5 47	18 02	5 45	18 05	5 40	18 08	5 36	18 13	5 28	18 21
			20 02	8 27	19 46	8 41	19 27	8 58	19 01	9 22	18 19	10 00
16 We 260	11 54 43	2 38	5 48	18 02	5 45	18 04	5 41	18 07	5 38	18 11	5 31	18 17
			20 45	9 21	20 26	9 38	20 03	10 00	19 31	10 31	18 37	11 23
17 Th 261	11 54 22	2 15	5 48	18 01	5 46	18 03	5 43	18 05	5 41	18 07	5 33	18 14
			21 34	10 16	21 12	10 37	20 46	11 02	20 08	11 39	19 02	12 43
18 Fr 262	11 54 1	1 51	5 48	18 00	5 46	18 01	5 44	18 04	5 44	18 04	5 35	18 11
			22 27	11 13	22 04	11 35	21 36	12 03	20 55	12 43	19 43	13 55
19 Sa 263	11 53 39	1 28	5 48	17 59	5 47	18 00	5 45	18 02	5 42	18 04	5 38	18 08
	19 53 LQ		23 24	12 10	23 02	12 32	22 34	13 01	21 54	13 41	20 43	14 53
20 Su 264	11 53 18	1 5	5 48	17 58	5 47	17 59	5 46	18 00	5 44	18 02	5 40	18 05
			– –	13 05	– –	13 26	23 40	13 52	23 04	14 30	22 02	15 34
21 Mo 265	11 52 57	0 42	5 49	17 57	5 48	17 58	5 47	17 59	5 45	18 00	5 42	18 02
			0 26	13 57	0 05	14 16	– –	14 38	– –	15 09	23 34	16 01
22 Tu 266	11 52 36	0 18	5 49	17 56	5 48	17 56	5 48	17 57	5 47	17 58	5 45	17 59
			1 28	14 47	1 12	15 01	0 51	15 18	0 22	15 42	– –	16 19
23 We 267	11 52 15	0 5	5 49	17 55	5 49	17 55	5 49	17 55	5 48	17 56	5 47	17 56
			2 32	15 34	2 20	15 43	2 05	15 54	1 44	16 09	1 11	16 32
24 Th 268	11 51 54	0 29	5 49	17 54	5 49	17 54	5 50	17 54	5 50	17 53	5 49	17 53
			3 35	16 19	3 28	16 23	3 20	16 27	3 09	16 33	2 51	16 43
25 Fr 269	11 51 33	0 52	5 50	17 53	5 50	17 53	5 51	17 52	5 51	17 51	5 52	17 50
			4 38	17 03	4 37	17 01	4 35	16 59	4 33	16 57	4 30	16 53
26 Sa 270	11 51 13	– 1 15	5 50	17 52	5 51	17 51	5 51	17 50	5 53	17 49	5 54	17 47
	10 40 NM		5 41	17 47	5 45	17 40	5 50	17 31	5 58	17 20	6 09	17 03
27 Su 271	11 50 53	– 1 39	5 50	17 52	5 51	17 50	5 52	17 49	5 54	17 47	5 56	17 44
			6 43	18 32	6 52	18 20	7 05	18 05	7 21	17 45	7 48	17 14
28 Mo 272	11 50 33	– 2 2	5 50	17 51	5 52	17 49	5 53	17 47	5 56	17 45	5 59	17 41
			7 45	19 19	8 00	19 03	8 18	18 43	8 43	18 15	9 25	17 30
29 Tu 273	11 50 13	– 2 25	5 50	17 50	5 52	17 48	5 54	17 45	5 57	17 42	6 01	17 38
			8 47	20 09	9 06	19 49	9 29	19 25	10 02	18 50	10 58	17 51
30 We 274	11 49 53	– 2 49	5 51	17 49	5 53	17 46	5 55	17 44	5 59	17 40	6 03	17 35
			9 47	21 01	10 08	20 39	10 35	20 12	11 14	19 32	12 22	18 23

10th Month   October, 1992   31 days

Greenwich Mean Time

NOTE: Light numbers indicate Sun. **Dark** numbers indicate **Moon**. *Degrees are North Latitude.*

FM = full moon; LQ = last quarter; NM = new moon; FQ = first quarter.

CAUTION: Must be converted to local time. For instructions see page 269.

Day of month / week / year		Sun on Meridian / Moon phase (h m s)	Sun's Decl. (° ')	Rise 20°	Set 20°	Rise 30°	Set 30°	Rise 40°	Set 40°	Rise 50°	Set 50°	Rise 60°	Set 60°
1	Th	11 49 34	− 3 12	5 51	17 48	5 53	17 45	5 56	17 42	6 00	17 38	6 06	17 32
275				10 44	21 55	11 07	21 32	11 35	21 04	12 16	20 23	13 30	19 09
2	Fr	11 49 15	− 3 35	5 51	17 47	5 54	17 44	5 57	17 41	6 02	17 36	6 08	17 29
276				11 37	22 49	12 00	22 27	12 28	22 00	13 08	21 20	14 19	20 10
3	Sa	11 48 56	− 3 58	5 51	17 46	5 55	17 43	5 58	17 39	6 03	17 34	6 11	17 26
277		14 12 FQ		12 26	23 42	12 46	23 23	13 12	22 58	13 49	22 23	14 51	21 22
4	Su	11 48 38	− 4 22	5 52	17 45	5 55	17 42	5 59	17 37	6 05	17 32	6 13	17 23
278				13 10	− −	13 28	− −	13 50	23 57	14 21	23 28	15 12	22 39
5	Mo	11 48 20	− 4 45	5 52	17 44	5 56	17 40	6 00	17 36	6 06	17 29	6 15	17 20
279				13 50	0 34	14 05	0 18	14 23	− −	14 47	− −	15 27	23 57
6	Tu	11 48 2	− 5 8	5 52	17 44	5 56	17 39	6 01	17 34	6 08	17 27	6 18	17 17
280				14 27	1 25	14 38	1 12	14 52	0 56	15 10	0 33	15 38	− −
7	We	11 47 45	− 5 31	5 52	17 43	5 57	17 38	6 02	17 33	6 09	17 25	6 20	17 14
281				15 03	2 14	15 09	2 05	15 18	1 54	15 29	1 39	15 46	1 14
8	Th	11 47 28	− 5 54	5 53	17 42	5 58	17 37	6 03	17 31	6 11	17 23	6 23	17 11
282				15 37	3 03	15 39	2 58	15 43	2 52	15 47	2 44	15 53	2 31
9	Fr	11 47 12	− 6 17	5 53	17 41	5 58	17 36	6 04	17 29	6 13	17 21	6 25	17 08
283				16 11	3 51	16 09	3 51	16 07	3 50	16 04	3 49	16 01	3 48
10	Sa	11 46 56	− 6 39	5 53	17 40	5 59	17 35	6 05	17 28	6 14	17 19	6 28	17 05
284				16 45	4 40	16 39	4 44	16 32	4 49	16 23	4 55	16 08	5 05
11	Su	11 46 40	− 7 2	5 54	17 39	5 59	17 33	6 06	17 26	6 16	17 17	6 30	17 02
285		18 03 FM		17 22	5 30	17 12	5 38	16 59	5 49	16 43	6 02	16 17	6 24
12	Mo	11 46 25	− 7 25	5 54	17 39	6 00	17 32	6 07	17 25	6 17	17 15	6 32	16 59
286				18 01	6 22	17 47	6 34	17 30	6 50	17 06	7 11	16 29	7 45
13	Tu	11 46 10	− 7 47	5 54	17 38	6 01	17 31	6 08	17 23	6 19	17 13	6 35	16 56
287				18 44	7 16	18 27	7 32	18 05	7 52	17 34	8 21	16 45	9 08
14	We	11 45 56	− 8 9	5 55	17 37	6 01	17 30	6 10	17 22	6 21	17 11	6 37	16 53
288				19 32	8 11	19 11	8 31	18 45	8 55	18 10	9 30	17 08	10 30
15	Th	11 45 43	− 8 32	5 55	17 36	6 02	17 29	6 11	17 20	6 22	17 09	6 40	16 51
289				20 23	9 08	20 01	9 30	19 34	9 57	18 54	10 36	17 44	11 45
16	Fr	11 45 30	− 8 54	5 55	17 36	6 03	17 28	6 12	17 19	6 24	17 06	6 42	16 48
290				21 20	10 05	20 57	10 27	20 29	10 55	19 49	11 36	18 38	12 47
17	Sa	11 45 18	− 9 16	5 55	17 35	6 03	17 27	6 13	17 17	6 25	17 04	6 45	16 45
291				22 19	11 00	21 58	11 22	21 32	11 48	20 55	12 26	19 50	13 32
18	Su	11 45 6	− 9 38	5 56	17 34	6 04	17 26	6 14	17 16	6 27	17 02	6 47	16 42
292				23 20	11 52	23 02	12 11	22 40	12 35	22 09	13 08	21 16	14 03
19	Mo	11 44 55	− 9 59	5 56	17 33	6 05	17 25	6 15	17 14	6 29	17 00	6 50	16 39
293		04 12 LQ		− −	12 42	− −	12 57	23 50	13 16	23 27	13 42	22 49	14 23
20	Tu	11 44 45	−10 21	5 57	17 33	6 05	17 24	6 16	17 13	6 30	16 59	6 52	16 36
294				0 21	13 28	0 07	13 39	− −	13 52	− −	14 10	− −	14 38
21	We	11 44 35	−10 42	5 57	17 32	6 06	17 23	6 17	17 12	6 32	16 57	6 55	16 33
295				1 22	14 12	1 13	14 18	1 02	14 25	0 47	14 35	0 24	14 49
22	Th	11 44 26	−11 4	5 57	17 31	6 07	17 22	6 18	17 10	6 33	16 55	6 57	16 31
296				2 22	14 54	2 19	14 55	2 14	14 56	2 09	14 57	1 59	14 59
23	Fr	11 44 18	−11 25	5 58	17 31	6 07	17 21	6 19	17 09	6 35	16 53	7 00	16 28
297				3 23	15 37	3 25	15 33	3 27	15 27	3 30	15 20	3 35	15 09
24	Sa	11 44 10	−11 46	5 58	17 30	6 08	17 20	6 20	17 08	6 37	16 51	7 02	16 25
298				4 24	16 21	4 31	16 11	4 40	16 00	4 52	15 44	5 11	15 20
25	Su	11 44 4	−12 7	5 58	17 29	6 09	17 19	6 21	17 06	6 38	16 49	7 05	16 22
299		20 34 NM		5 26	17 07	5 38	16 53	5 53	16 35	6 14	16 12	6 48	15 34
26	Mo	11 43 57	−12 27	5 59	17 29	6 10	17 18	6 22	17 05	6 40	16 47	7 07	16 20
300				6 28	17 56	6 44	17 38	7 05	17 15	7 34	16 44	8 23	15 52
27	Tu	11 43 52	−12 48	5 59	17 28	6 10	17 17	6 24	17 04	6 42	16 45	7 10	16 17
301				7 29	18 48	7 49	18 27	8 15	18 01	8 50	17 24	9 53	16 19
28	We	11 43 47	−13 8	6 00	17 28	6 11	17 16	6 25	17 02	6 43	16 44	7 13	16 15
302				8 29	19 42	8 51	19 20	9 19	18 51	9 59	18 11	11 10	17 00
29	Th	11 43 43	−13 28	6 00	17 27	6 12	17 15	6 26	17 01	6 45	16 42	7 16	16 11
303				9 25	20 37	9 48	20 15	10 16	19 47	10 56	19 07	12 08	17 56
30	Fr	11 43 40	−13 48	6 01	17 26	6 12	17 14	6 27	17 00	6 47	16 40	7 18	16 09
304				10 17	21 32	10 38	21 12	11 05	20 46	11 43	20 09	12 48	19 05
31	Sa	11 43 38	−14 7	6 01	17 26	6 13	17 14	6 28	16 59	6 48	16 38	7 20	16 06
305				11 04	22 26	11 23	22 08	11 46	21 46	12 19	21 14	13 14	20 21

11th Month   November, 1992   30 days

Greenwich Mean Time

NOTE: Light numbers indicate Sun. **Dark** numbers indicate **Moon.** *Degrees are North Latitude.*

FM = full moon; LQ = last quarter; NM = new moon; FQ = first quarter.

CAUTION: Must be converted to local time. For instructions see page 269.

Day of month / week / year	Sun on Meridian / Moon phase (h m s)	Sun's Declination (° ')	20° Rise Sun/Moon	20° Set Sun/Moon	30° Rise Sun/Moon	30° Set Sun/Moon	40° Rise Sun/Moon	40° Set Sun/Moon	50° Rise Sun/Moon	50° Set Sun/Moon	60° Rise Sun/Moon	60° Set Sun/Moon
1 Su 306	11 43 36	−14 26	6 02	17 25	6 14	17 13	6 29	16 57	6 50	16 37	7 23	16 04
			11 46	23 17	12 02	23 03	12 21	22 45	12 48	22 20	13 32	21 40
2 Mo 307	11 43 36 09 11 FQ	−14 46	6 02	17 25	6 15	17 12	6 30	16 56	6 52	16 35	7 25	16 01
			12 25	− −	12 37	23 57	12 52	23 44	13 12	23 26	13 44	22 58
3 Tu 308	11 43 36	−15 4	6 03	17 24	6 16	17 11	6 32	16 55	6 53	16 33	7 28	15 58
			13 01	0 07	13 09	− −	13 19	− −	13 33	− −	13 54	− −
4 We 309	11 43 36	−15 23	6 03	17 24	6 16	17 11	6 33	16 54	6 55	16 32	7 30	15 56
			13 35	0 56	13 39	0 50	13 44	0 42	13 51	0 31	14 01	0 15
5 Th 310	11 43 38	−15 41	6 04	17 24	6 17	17 10	6 34	16 53	6 57	16 30	7 33	15 53
			14 09	1 44	14 09	1 42	14 09	1 40	14 09	1 36	14 09	1 31
6 Fr 311	11 43 40	−15 59	6 04	17 23	6 18	17 09	6 35	16 52	6 58	16 28	7 36	15 51
			14 43	2 33	14 39	2 35	14 34	2 38	14 27	2 42	14 16	2 47
7 Sa 312	11 43 44	−16 17	6 05	17 23	6 19	17 08	6 36	16 51	7 00	16 27	7 38	15 48
			15 19	3 22	15 11	3 29	15 00	3 37	14 46	3 48	14 25	4 05
8 Su 313	11 43 48	−16 35	6 05	17 22	6 19	17 08	6 37	16 50	7 02	16 25	7 41	15 46
			15 58	4 14	15 45	4 24	15 30	4 38	15 09	4 56	14 36	5 26
9 Mo 314	11 43 52	−16 52	6 06	17 22	6 20	17 07	6 38	16 49	7 03	16 24	7 43	15 44
			16 40	5 07	16 23	5 22	16 03	5 41	15 35	6 06	14 50	6 48
10 Tu 315	11 43 58 09 20 FM	−17 9	6 06	17 22	6 21	17 07	6 40	16 48	7 05	16 22	7 46	15 41
			17 26	6 03	17 07	6 21	16 43	6 44	16 09	7 17	15 11	8 12
11 We 316	11 44 5	−17 26	6 07	17 21	6 22	17 06	6 41	16 47	7 07	16 21	7 48	15 39
			18 18	7 01	17 56	7 21	17 29	7 48	16 51	8 25	15 44	9 31
12 Th 317	11 44 12	−17 42	6 07	17 21	6 23	17 05	6 42	16 46	7 08	16 20	7 51	15 37
			19 14	7 59	18 52	8 21	18 24	8 49	17 44	9 29	16 33	10 40
13 Fr 318	11 44 21	−17 58	6 08	17 21	6 24	17 05	6 43	16 45	7 10	16 18	7 53	15 34
			20 13	8 55	19 52	9 17	19 25	9 44	18 47	10 23	17 41	11 31
14 Sa 319	11 44 30	−18 14	6 08	17 20	6 24	17 04	6 44	16 44	7 11	16 17	7 56	15 32
			21 14	9 49	20 56	10 09	20 32	10 34	20 00	11 08	19 04	12 06
15 Su 320	11 44 40	−18 30	6 09	17 20	6 25	17 04	6 45	16 43	7 13	16 16	7 58	15 30
			22 15	10 40	22 01	10 56	21 42	11 16	21 17	11 44	20 35	12 29
16 Mo 321	11 44 51	−18 45	6 10	17 20	6 26	17 03	6 46	16 43	7 15	16 14	8 01	15 28
			23 16	11 26	23 05	11 38	22 53	11 53	22 36	12 14	22 08	12 45
17 Tu 322	11 45 2 11 39 LQ	−18 59	6 10	17 20	6 27	17 03	6 48	16 42	7 16	16 13	8 03	15 26
			− −	12 10	− −	12 17	− −	12 27	23 55	12 39	23 41	12 57
18 We 323	11 45 15	−19 14	6 11	17 20	6 28	17 03	6 49	16 41	7 18	16 12	8 06	15 24
			0 15	12 52	0 10	12 54	0 03	12 57	− −	13 01	− −	13 07
19 Th 324	11 45 28	−19 28	6 11	17 19	6 29	17 02	6 50	16 41	7 19	16 11	8 08	15 22
			1 14	13 33	1 14	13 31	1 14	13 27	1 14	13 23	1 14	13 17
20 Fr 325	11 45 43	−19 42	6 12	17 19	6 29	17 02	6 51	16 40	7 21	16 10	8 11	15 20
			2 12	14 15	2 18	14 08	2 24	13 58	2 33	13 46	2 47	13 27
21 Sa 326	11 45 58	−19 55	6 13	17 19	6 30	17 01	6 52	16 39	7 23	16 09	8 13	15 18
			3 12	14 59	3 22	14 47	3 35	14 32	3 52	14 11	4 20	13 39
22 Su 327	11 46 14	−20 8	6 13	17 19	6 31	17 01	6 53	16 39	7 24	16 08	8 16	15 16
			4 12	15 45	4 27	15 29	4 45	15 09	5 11	14 40	5 54	13 55
23 Mo 328	11 46 30	−20 21	6 14	17 19	6 32	17 01	6 54	16 38	7 26	16 07	8 18	15 14
			5 13	16 35	5 32	16 15	5 55	15 51	6 28	15 16	7 24	14 18
24 Tu 329	11 46 48 09 11 NM	−20 33	6 14	17 19	6 33	17 01	6 55	16 38	7 27	16 06	8 20	15 13
			6 13	17 28	6 34	17 06	7 01	16 39	7 39	16 00	8 47	14 51
25 We 330	11 47 6	−20 45	6 15	17 19	6 34	17 00	6 57	16 37	7 29	16 05	8 23	15 11
			7 11	18 23	7 34	18 01	8 02	17 33	8 42	16 52	9 54	15 40
26 Th 331	11 47 25	−20 57	6 16	17 19	6 35	17 00	6 58	16 37	7 30	16 04	8 25	15 10
			8 05	19 19	8 27	18 58	8 55	18 31	9 34	17 53	10 43	16 45
27 Fr 332	11 47 45	−21 8	6 16	17 19	6 35	17 00	6 59	16 37	7 32	16 03	8 27	15 08
			8 55	20 14	9 15	19 55	9 40	19 31	10 15	18 58	11 15	18 00
28 Sa 333	11 48 5	−21 19	6 17	17 19	6 36	17 00	7 00	16 37	7 33	16 02	8 29	15 07
			9 40	21 07	9 57	20 52	10 18	20 32	10 48	20 05	11 36	19 19
29 Su 334	11 48 26	−21 29	6 18	17 19	6 37	17 00	7 02	16 36	7 34	16 01	8 31	15 05
			10 21	21 59	10 34	21 47	10 51	21 32	11 14	21 11	11 50	20 38
30 Mo 335	11 48 48	−21 39	6 18	17 19	6 38	17 00	7 02	16 36	7 36	16 02	8 33	15 04
			10 58	22 48	11 08	22 40	11 20	22 30	11 36	22 17	12 01	21 56

12th Month   December, 1992   31 days

Greenwich Mean Time

NOTE: Light numbers indicate Sun. **Dark** numbers indicate **Moon**. *Degrees are North Latitude.*

FM = full moon; LQ = last quarter; NM = new moon; FQ = first quarter.

CAUTION: Must be converted to local time. For instructions see page 269.

Day of month / week / year	Sun on Meridian / Moon phase (h m s)	Sun's Declina-tion (°)	20° Rise Sun/Moon (h m)	20° Set Sun/Moon (h m)	30° Rise Sun/Moon (h m)	30° Set Sun/Moon (h m)	40° Rise Sun/Moon (h m)	40° Set Sun/Moon (h m)	50° Rise Sun/Moon (h m)	50° Set Sun/Moon (h m)	60° Rise Sun/Moon (h m)	60° Set Sun/Moon (h m)
1 Tu 336	11 49 11	−21 48	6 19	17 19	6 38	17 00	7 03	16 35	7 37	16 01	8 35	15 02
			11 33	23 37	11 39	23 33	11 46	23 28	11 55	23 22	12 09	23 12
2 We 337	11 49 34 06 17 FQ	−21 58	6 19	17 20	6 39	17 00	7 04	16 35	7 38	16 00	8 37	15 01
			12 07	– –	12 08	– –	12 10	– –	12 13	– –	12 17	– –
3 Th 338	11 49 57	−22 6	6 20	17 20	6 40	17 00	7 05	16 35	7 40	16 00	8 39	15 00
			12 40	0 25	12 38	0 25	12 35	0 26	12 31	0 26	12 24	0 28
4 Fr 339	11 50 21	−22 14	6 21	17 20	6 41	17 00	7 06	16 35	7 41	16 00	8 41	14 59
			13 15	1 13	13 08	1 18	13 00	1 24	12 49	1 32	12 32	1 44
5 Sa 340	11 50 46	−22 22	6 21	17 20	6 41	17 00	7 07	16 35	7 42	15 59	8 43	14 58
			13 52	2 03	13 41	2 12	13 28	2 23	13 10	2 38	12 42	3 03
6 Su 341	11 51 11	−22 30	6 22	17 20	6 42	17 00	7 08	16 35	7 43	15 59	8 45	14 57
			14 32	2 55	14 17	3 08	13 59	3 25	13 34	3 47	12 55	4 24
7 Mo 342	11 51 37	−22 37	6 23	17 21	6 43	17 00	7 08	16 35	7 44	15 59	8 46	14 56
			15 17	3 50	14 59	4 07	14 36	4 28	14 05	4 57	13 13	5 47
8 Tu 343	11 52 3	−22 43	6 23	17 21	6 44	17 00	7 09	16 35	7 45	15 58	8 48	14 56
			16 07	4 47	15 46	5 07	15 20	5 32	14 43	6 08	13 40	7 09
9 We 344	11 52 30 23 41 FM	−22 49	6 24	17 21	6 44	17 00	7 10	16 35	7 47	15 58	8 50	14 55
			17 02	5 46	16 40	6 07	16 12	6 35	15 32	7 14	14 22	8 24
10 Th 345	11 52 57	−22 55	6 24	17 21	6 45	17 01	7 11	16 35	7 48	15 58	8 51	14 55
			18 01	6 44	17 36	7 06	17 12	7 34	16 33	8 14	15 24	9 24
11 Fr 346	11 53 25	−23 0	6 25	17 22	6 46	17 01	7 12	16 35	7 49	15 58	8 53	14 54
			19 04	7 41	18 40	8 02	18 19	8 28	17 45	9 04	16 44	10 06
12 Sa 347	11 53 53	−23 5	6 26	17 22	6 46	17 01	7 13	16 35	7 50	15 58	8 54	14 54
			20 07	8 34	19 44	8 52	19 31	9 14	19 03	9 44	18 16	10 33
13 Su 348	11 54 21	−23 9	6 26	17 22	6 47	17 01	7 13	16 35	7 50	15 58	8 55	14 53
			21 09	9 24	20 51	9 37	20 43	9 54	20 23	10 17	19 51	10 52
14 Mo 349	11 54 49	−23 13	6 27	17 23	6 48	17 02	7 14	16 35	7 51	15 58	8 56	14 53
			22 10	10 09	22 57	10 18	21 55	10 29	21 44	10 43	21 26	11 06
15 Tu 350	11 55 17	−23 16	6 27	17 23	6 48	17 02	7 15	16 36	7 52	15 58	8 57	14 53
			23 09	10 52	23 03	10 56	23 06	11 01	23 03	11 07	22 59	11 17
16 We 351	11 55 47 19 13 LQ	−23 19	6 28	17 24	6 49	17 03	7 15	16 36	7 53	15 59	8 58	14 53
			– –	11 33	– –	11 32	– –	11 31	– –	11 29	– –	11 26
17 Th 352	11 56 17	−23 21	6 28	17 24	6 50	17 03	7 16	16 36	7 54	15 59	8 59	14 53
			0 07	12 14	0 11	12 08	0 15	12 01	0 22	11 51	0 32	11 36
18 Fr 353	11 56 46	−23 23	6 29	17 25	6 50	17 03	7 17	16 37	7 54	15 59	9 00	14 53
			1 05	12 57	1 14	12 46	1 25	12 33	1 40	12 15	2 03	11 47
19 Sa 354	11 57 16	−23 25	6 30	17 25	6 51	17 04	7 17	16 37	7 55	16 00	9 01	14 54
			2 04	13 41	2 17	13 26	2 34	13 07	2 57	12 42	3 35	12 01
20 Su 355	11 57 46	−23 26	6 30	17 25	6 51	17 04	7 18	16 38	7 56	16 00	9 02	14 54
			3 03	14 28	3 21	14 10	3 42	13 47	4 13	13 14	5 04	12 20
21 Mo 356	11 58 16	−23 26	6 31	17 26	6 52	17 05	7 18	16 38	7 56	16 00	9 02	14 54
			4 02	15 19	4 23	14 58	4 48	14 31	5 25	13 54	6 29	12 48
22 Tu 357	11 58 46	−23 26	6 31	17 26	6 52	17 05	7 19	16 39	7 57	16 01	9 03	14 55
			5 00	16 12	5 22	15 50	5 50	15 22	6 30	14 42	7 41	13 30
23 We 358	11 59 16	−23 26	6 32	17 27	6 53	17 06	7 19	16 39	7 57	16 02	9 03	14 56
			5 55	17 07	6 17	16 46	6 45	16 18	7 25	15 38	8 37	14 28
24 Th 359	11 59 46 00 43 NM	−23 25	6 32	17 28	6 53	17 06	7 20	16 40	7 57	16 02	9 03	14 56
			6 47	18 03	7 07	17 43	7 34	17 17	8 11	16 42	9 15	15 39
25 Fr 360	12 0 15	−23 24	6 32	17 28	6 54	17 07	7 20	16 40	7 58	16 03	9 03	14 57
			7 33	18 57	7 52	18 40	8 15	18 18	8 47	17 48	9 40	16 57
26 Sa 361	12 0 45	−23 22	6 33	17 29	6 54	17 07	7 21	16 41	7 58	16 04	9 04	14 58
			8 16	19 49	8 31	19 36	8 50	19 19	9 16	18 55	9 57	18 17
27 Su 362	12 1 15	−23 20	6 33	17 29	6 54	17 08	7 21	16 42	7 58	16 04	9 04	14 59
			8 55	20 40	9 06	20 30	9 20	20 18	9 39	20 02	10 09	19 36
28 Mo 363	12 1 44	−23 17	6 34	17 30	6 55	17 09	7 21	16 42	7 58	16 05	9 04	15 00
			9 31	21 29	9 38	21 24	9 47	21 17	10 00	21 07	10 18	20 53
29 Tu 364	12 2 14	−23 14	6 34	17 30	6 55	17 09	7 21	16 43	7 59	16 06	9 03	15 01
			10 05	22 17	10 08	22 16	10 13	22 14	10 18	22 12	10 26	22 09
30 We 365	12 2 43	−23 10	6 34	17 31	6 55	17 10	7 22	16 44	7 59	16 07	9 03	15 03
			10 39	23 05	10 38	23 08	10 37	23 12	10 36	23 16	10 34	23 24
31 Th 366	12 3 11	−23 6	6 35	17 32	6 56	17 11	7 22	16 45	7 59	16 08	9 03	15 04
			11 13	23 53	11 08	– –	11 02	– –	10 53	– –	10 41	– –

Julian and Gregorian Calendars; Leap Year; Century

Calendars based on the movements of sun and moon have been used since ancient times, but none has been perfect. The Julian calendar, under which western nations measured time until 1582 A.D., was authorized by Julius Caesar in 46 B.C., the year 709 of Rome. His expert was a Greek, Sosigenes. The Julian calendar, on the assumption that the true year was 365 1/4 days long, gave every fourth year 366 days. The Venerable Bede, an Anglo-Saxon monk, announced in 730 A.D. that the 365 1/4-day Julian year was 11 min., 14 sec. too long, making a cumulative error of about a day every 128 years, but nothing was done about it for over 800 years.

By 1582 the accumulated error was estimated to have amounted to 10 days. In that year Pope Gregory XIII decreed that the day following Oct. 4, 1582, should be called Oct. 15, thus dropping 10 days.

However, with common years 365 days and a 366-day leap year every fourth year, the error in the length of the year would have recurred at the rate of a little more than 3 days every 400 years. So 3 of every 4 centesimal years (ending in 00) were made common years, not leap years. Thus 1600 was a leap year, 1700, 1800 and 1900 were not, but 2000 will be. **Leap years** are those divisible by 4 except centesimal years, which are common unless divisible by 400.

The Gregorian calendar was adopted at once by France, Italy, Spain, Portugal and Luxembourg. Within 2 years most German Catholic states, Belgium and parts of Switzerland and the Netherlands were brought under the new calendar, and Hungary followed in 1587. The rest of the Netherlands, along with Denmark and the German Protestant states made the change in 1699-1700 (German Protestants retained the old reckoning of Easter until 1776).

The British Government imposed the Gregorian calendar on all its possessions, including the American colonies, in 1752. The British decreed that the day following Sept. 2, 1752, should be called Sept. 14, a loss of 11 days. All dates preceding were marked O.S., for Old Style. In addition New Year's Day was moved to Jan. 1 from Mar. 25. (e.g., under the old reckoning, Mar. 24, 1700 had been followed by Mar. 25, 1701.) George Washington's birth date, which was Feb. 11, 1731, O.S., became Feb. 22, 1732, N.S. In 1753 Sweden too went Gregorian, retaining the old Easter rules until 1844.

In 1793 the French Revolutionary Government adopted a calendar of 12 months of 30 days each with 5 extra days in September of each common year and a 6th extra day every 4th year. Napoleon reinstated the Gregorian calendar in 1806.

The Gregorian system later spread to non-European regions, first in the European colonies, then in the independent countries, replacing traditional calendars at least for official purposes. Japan in 1873, Egypt in 1875, China in 1912 and Turkey in 1917 made the change, usually in conjunction with political upheavals. In China, the republican government began reckoning years from its 1911 founding — e.g., 1948 was designated the year 37. After 1949, the Communists adopted the Common, or Christian Era year count, even for the traditional lunar calendar.

In 1918 the revolutionary government in Russia decreed that the day after Jan. 31, 1918, Old Style, would become Feb. 14, 1918, New Style. Greece followed in 1923. (In Russia the Orthodox Church has retained the Julian calendar, as have various Middle Eastern Christian sects.) For the first time in history, all major cultures have one calendar.

To change from the Julian to the Gregorian calendar, add 10 days to dates Oct. 5, 1582, through Feb. 28, 1700; after that date add 11 days through Feb. 28, 1800; 12 days through Feb. 28, 1900; and 13 days through Feb. 28, 2100.

A **century** consists of 100 consecutive calendar years. The 1st century consisted of the years 1 through 100. The 20th century consists of the years 1901 through 2000 and will end Dec. 31, 2000. The 21st century will begin Jan. 1, 2001.

Julian Calendar

To find which of the 14 calendars printed on pages 294-295 applies to any year, starting Jan. 1, under the Julian system, find the century for the desired year in the three left-hand columns below; read across. Then find the year in the four top rows; read down. The number in the intersection is the calendar designation for that year.

Year (last two figures of desired year)

```
      01 02 03 04   05 06 07 08   09 10 11 12   13 14 15 16   17 18 19 20   21 22 23 24   25 26 27 28
      29 30 31 32   33 34 35 36   37 38 39 40   41 42 43 44   45 46 47 48   49 50 51 52   53 54 55 56
      57 58 59 60   61 62 63 64   65 66 67 68   69 70 71 72   73 74 75 76   77 78 79 80   81 82 83 84
   00 85 86 87 88   89 90 91 92   93 94 95 96   97 98 99
```

Century	01	02	03	04	05	06	07	08	09	10	11	12	13	14	15	16	17	18	19	20	21	22	23	24	25	26	27	28
0 700 1400	12	7	1	2	10	5	6	7	3	4	5	13	1	2	3	11	6	7	1	9	4	5	6	14	2	3	4	12
100 800 1500	11	6	7	1	9	4	5	6	14	2	3	4	12	7	1	2	10	5	6	7	3	4	5	13	1	2	3	11
200 900 1600	10	5	6	7	8	3	4	5	13	1	2	3	11	6	7	1	9	4	5	6	14	2	3	4	12	7	1	2
300 1000 1700	9	4	5	6	14	2	3	4	12	7	1	2	10	5	6	7	8	3	4	5	13	1	2	3	11	6	7	1
400 1100 1800	8	3	4	5	13	1	2	3	11	6	7	1	9	4	5	6	14	2	3	4	12	7	1	2	10	5	6	7
500 1200 1900	14	2	3	4	12	7	1	2	10	5	6	7	8	3	4	5	13	1	2	3	11	6	7	1	9	4	5	6
600 1300 2000	13	1	2	3	11	6	7	1	9	4	5	6	14	2	3	4	12	7	1	2	10	5	6	7	8	3	4	5

Gregorian Calendar

Pick desired year from table below or on page 294 (for years 1800 to 2059). The number shown with each year shows which calendar to use for that year, as shown on pages 294-295. (The Gregorian calendar was inaugurated Oct. 15, 1582. From that date to Dec. 31, 1582, use calendar 6.)

1583-1802

1583..7	1603..4	1623..1	1643..5	1663..2	1683..6	1703..2	1723..6	1743..3	1763..7	1783..4
1584..8	1604..12	1624..9	1644..13	1664..10	1684..14	1704..10	1724..14	1744..11	1764..8	1784..12
1585..3	1605..7	1625..4	1645..1	1665..5	1685..2	1705..5	1725..2	1745..6	1765..3	1785..7
1586..4	1606..1	1626..5	1646..2	1666..6	1686..3	1706..6	1726..3	1746..7	1766..4	1786..1
1587..5	1607..2	1627..6	1647..3	1667..7	1687..4	1707..7	1727..4	1747..1	1767..5	1787..2
1588..13	1608..10	1628..14	1648..11	1668..8	1688..12	1708..8	1728..12	1748..9	1768..13	1788..10
1589..1	1609..5	1629..2	1649..6	1669..3	1689..7	1709..3	1729..7	1749..4	1769..1	1789..5
1590..2	1610..6	1630..3	1650..7	1670..4	1690..1	1710..4	1730..1	1750..5	1770..2	1790..6
1591..3	1611..7	1631..4	1651..1	1671..5	1691..2	1711..5	1731..2	1751..6	1771..3	1791..7
1592..11	1612..8	1632..12	1652..9	1672..13	1692..10	1712..13	1732..10	1752..14	1772..11	1792..8
1593..6	1613..3	1633..7	1653..4	1673..1	1693..5	1713..1	1733..5	1753..2	1773..6	1793..3
1594..7	1614..4	1634..1	1654..5	1674..2	1694..6	1714..2	1734..6	1754..3	1774..7	1794..4
1595..1	1615..5	1635..2	1655..6	1675..3	1695..7	1715..3	1735..7	1755..4	1775..1	1795..5
1596..9	1616..13	1636..10	1656..14	1676..11	1696..8	1716..11	1736..8	1756..12	1776..9	1796..13
1597..4	1617..1	1637..5	1657..2	1677..6	1697..3	1717..6	1737..3	1757..7	1777..4	1797..1
1598..5	1618..2	1638..6	1658..3	1678..7	1698..4	1718..7	1738..4	1758..1	1778..5	1798..2
1599..6	1619..3	1639..7	1659..4	1679..1	1699..5	1719..1	1739..5	1759..2	1779..6	1799..3
1600..14	1620..11	1640..8	1660..12	1680..9	1700..6	1720..9	1740..13	1760..10	1780..14	1800..11
1601..2	1621..6	1641..3	1661..7	1681..4	1701..1	1721..4	1741..1	1761..5	1781..2	1801..5
1602..3	1622..7	1642..4	1662..1	1682..5	1702..1	1722..5	1742..2	1762..6	1782..3	1802..6

Latitude, Longitude, and Altitude of North American Cities

Source: National Oceanic and Atmospheric Administration, U.S. Commerce Department for geographic positions.
Source for Canadian cities: Geodetic Survey of Canada, Dept. of Energy, Mines, and Resources.
Altitudes U.S. Geological Survey and various sources. * Approx. altitude at downtown business area U.S.; in Canada at city hall except where (a) is at tower of major airport.

City	Lat. N °	′	″	Long. W °	′	″	Alt.* feet
Abilene, Tex.	32	27	05	99	43	51	1710
Akron, Oh.	41	05	00	81	30	44	874
Albany, N.Y.	42	39	01	73	45	01	20
Albuquerque, N.M.	35	05	01	106	39	05	4,945
Allentown, Pa.	40	36	11	75	28	06	255
Alert, N.W.T.	82	29	50	62	21	15	95
Altoona, Pa.	40	30	55	78	24	03	1,180
Amarillo, Tex.	35	12	27	101	50	04	3,685
Anchorage, Alas.	61	10	00	149	59	00	118
Ann Arbor, Mich.	42	16	59	83	44	52	880
Asheville, N.C.	35	35	42	82	33	26	1,985
Ashland, Ky.	38	28	36	82	38	23	536
Atlanta, Ga.	33	45	10	84	23	37	1,050
Atlantic City, N.J.	39	21	32	74	25	53	10
Augusta, Ga.	33	28	20	81	58	00	143
Augusta, Me.	44	18	53	69	46	29	45
Austin, Tex.	30	16	09	97	44	37	505
Bakersfield, Cal.	35	22	31	119	01	18	400
Baltimore, Md.	39	17	26	76	36	45	20
Bangor, Me.	44	48	13	68	46	18	20
Baton Rouge, La.	30	26	58	91	11	00	57
Battle Creek, Mich.	42	18	58	85	10	48	820
Bay City, Mich.	43	36	04	83	53	15	595
Beaumont, Tex.	30	05	20	94	06	09	20
Belleville, Ont.	44	09	42	77	23	11	257
Bellingham, Wash.	48	45	34	122	28	36	60
Berkeley, Cal.	37	52	10	122	16	17	40
Bethlehem, Pa.	40	37	16	75	22	34	235
Billings, Mon.	45	47	00	108	30	04	3,120
Biloxi, Miss.	30	23	48	88	53	00	20
Binghamton, N.Y.	42	06	03	75	54	47	865
Birmingham, Ala.	33	31	01	86	48	36	600
Bismarck, N.D.	46	48	23	100	47	17	1,674
Bloomington, Ill.	40	28	58	88	59	96	800
Boise, Ida.	43	37	07	116	11	58	2,704
Boston, Mass.	42	21	24	71	03	25	21
Bowling Green, Ky.	36	59	41	86	26	33	510
Brandon, Man.	49	51	00	99	57	00	1,265(a)
Brantford, Ont.	43	08	34	80	15	39	705(a)
Brattleboro, Vt.	42	51	06	72	33	48	300
Bridgeport, Conn.	41	10	49	73	11	22	10
Brockton, Mass.	42	05	02	71	01	25	130
Brownsville, Tex.	25	54	07	97	29	58	35
Buffalo, N.Y.	42	52	52	78	52	21	585
Burlington, Ont.	43	19	33	79	47	57	284
Burlington, Vt.	44	28	34	73	12	46	110
Butte, Mon.	46	01	06	112	32	11	5,765
Calgary, Alta.	51	02	46	114	03	24	3,427
Cambridge, Mass.	42	22	01	71	06	22	20
Camden, N.J.	39	56	41	75	07	14	30
Canton, Oh.	40	47	50	81	22	37	1,030
Carson City, Nev.	39	10	00	119	46	00	4,680
Cedar Rapids, Ia.	41	58	01	91	39	53	730
Central Islip, N.Y.	40	47	24	73	12	00	80
Champaign, Ill.	40	07	05	88	14	48	740
Charleston, S.C.	32	46	35	79	55	53	9
Charleston, W.Va.	38	21	01	81	37	52	601
Charlotte, N.C.	35	13	44	80	50	45	720
Charlottetown, P.E.I.	46	14	07	63	07	49	31
Chattanooga, Tenn.	35	02	41	85	18	32	675
Cheyenne, Wy.	41	08	09	104	49	00	6,100
Chicago, Ill.	41	52	28	87	38	22	595
Churchill, Man.	58	45	15	94	10	00	94(a)
Cincinnati, Oh.	39	06	07	84	30	35	550
Cleveland, Oh.	41	29	51	81	41	50	660
Colorado Springs	38	50	07	104	49	16	5,980
Columbia, Mo.	38	57	03	92	19	46	730
Columbia, S.C.	34	00	02	81	02	00	190
Columbus, Ga.	32	28	07	84	59	24	265
Columbus, Oh.	39	57	47	83	00	17	780
Concord, N.H.	43	12	22	71	32	25	290
Corpus Christi, Tex.	27	47	51	97	23	45	35
Dallas, Tex.	32	47	09	96	47	37	435
Dartmouth, N.S.	44	39	50	63	34	08	24
Davenport, Ia.	41	31	19	90	34	33	590
Dawson, Yukon	64	03	30	139	26	00	1,211(a)
Dayton, Oh.	39	45	32	84	11	43	574
Daytona Beach, Fla.	29	12	44	81	01	10	7
Decatur, Ill.	39	50	42	88	56	47	682
Denver, Col.	39	44	58	104	59	22	5,280
Des Moines, Ia.	41	35	14	93	37	00	803
Detroit, Mich.	42	19	48	83	02	57	585
Dodge City, Kan.	37	45	17	100	01	09	2,480
Dubuque, Ia.	42	29	55	90	40	08	620
Duluth, Minn.	46	46	56	92	06	24	610
Durham, N.C.	36	00	00	78	54	45	405
Eau Claire, Wis.	44	48	31	91	29	49	790
Edmonton, Alta.	53	32	43	113	29	21	2,186
El Paso, Tex.	31	45	36	106	29	11	3,695
Elizabeth, N.J.	40	39	43	74	12	59	21
Enid, Okla.	36	23	40	97	52	35	1,240
Erie, Pa.	42	07	15	80	04	57	685
Eugene, Ore.	44	03	16	123	05	30	422
Eureka, Cal.	40	48	08	124	09	46	45
Evansville, Ind.	37	58	20	87	34	21	385
Fairbanks, Alas.	64	48	00	147	51	00	448
Fall River, Mass.	41	42	06	71	09	18	40
Fargo, N.D.	46	52	30	96	47	18	900
Flagstaff, Ariz.	35	11	36	111	39	06	6,900
Flint, Mich.	43	00	50	83	41	33	750
Ft. Smith, Ark.	35	23	10	94	25	36	440
Fort Wayne, Ind.	41	04	21	85	08	26	790
Fort Worth, Tex.	32	44	55	97	19	44	670
Fredericton, N.B.	45	57	47	66	38	38	29
Fresno, Cal.	36	44	12	119	47	11	285
Gadsden, Ala.	34	00	57	86	00	41	555
Gainesville, Fla.	29	38	56	82	19	19	175
Gallup, N.M.	35	31	30	108	44	30	6,540
Galveston, Tex.	29	18	10	94	47	43	5
Gary, Ind.	41	36	12	87	20	19	590
Grand Junction, Col.	39	04	06	108	33	54	4,590
Grand Rapids, Mich.	42	58	03	85	40	13	610
Great Falls, Mon.	47	29	33	111	18	23	3,340
Green Bay, Wis.	44	30	48	88	00	50	590
Greensboro, N.C.	36	04	17	79	47	25	839
Greenville, S.C.	34	50	52	82	24	01	966
Guelph, Ont.	43	32	35	80	14	54	1,065
Gulfport, Miss.	30	22	04	89	05	36	20
Halifax, N.S.	44	38	54	63	34	30	60
Hamilton, Ont.	43	15	20	79	52	30	329
Hamilton, Oh.	39	23	09	84	33	47	600
Harrisburg, Pa.	40	15	43	76	52	59	365
Hartford, Conn.	41	46	12	72	40	49	40
Helena, Mon.	46	35	33	112	02	24	4,155
Hilo, Hawaii	19	43	30	155	05	24	40
Holyoke, Mass.	42	12	29	72	36	36	115
Honolulu, Ha.	21	18	22	157	51	35	21
Houston, Tex.	29	45	26	95	21	37	40
Hull, Que.	45	25	42	75	42	41	185
Huntington, W.Va.	38	25	12	82	26	33	565
Huntsville, Ala.	34	44	18	86	35	19	640
Indianapolis, Ind.	39	46	07	86	09	46	710
Iowa City, Ia.	41	39	37	91	31	53	685
Jackson, Mich.	42	14	43	84	24	22	940
Jackson, Miss.	32	17	56	90	11	06	298
Jacksonville, Fla.	30	19	44	81	39	42	20
Jersey City, N.J.	40	43	50	74	03	56	20
Johnstown, Pa.	40	19	35	78	55	03	1,185
Joplin, Mo.	37	05	26	94	30	00	990
Juneau, Alas.	58	18	12	134	24	30	50
Kalamazoo, Mich.	42	17	29	85	35	14	755
Kansas City, Kan.	39	07	04	94	38	24	750
Kansas City, Mo.	39	04	56	94	35	20	750
Kenosha, Wis.	42	35	43	87	50	11	610
Key West, Fla.	24	33	30	81	48	12	5
Kingston, Ont.	44	13	53	76	28	48	264
Kitchener, Ont.	43	26	58	80	29	12	1,100
Knoxville, Tenn.	35	57	39	83	55	07	890
Lafayette, Ind.	40	25	11	86	53	39	550
Lancaster, Pa.	40	02	25	76	18	29	355
Lansing, Mich.	42	44	01	84	33	15	830
Laredo, Tex.	27	30	22	99	30	30	440
La Salle, Que.	45	25	30	73	39	30	110
Las Vegas, Nev.	36	10	20	115	08	37	2,030
Laval, Que.	45	33	05	73	44	42	140
Lawrence, Mass.	42	42	16	71	10	08	65
Lethbridge, Alta.	49	41	38	112	49	58	2,985
Lexington, Ky.	38	02	50	84	29	46	955
Lihue, Ha.	21	58	48	159	22	30	210
Lincoln, Neb.	40	48	59	96	42	15	1,150
Little Rock, Ark.	34	44	42	92	16	37	286
London, Ont.	42	59	17	81	14	03	822
Long Beach, Cal.	33	46	14	118	11	18	35
Lorain, Oh.	41	28	05	82	10	49	610
Los Angeles, Cal.	34	03	15	118	14	28	340
Louisville, Ky.	38	14	47	85	45	49	450
Lowell, Mass.	42	38	25	71	19	14	100
Lubbock, Tex.	33	35	05	101	50	33	3,195

City	Lat. N °	′	″	Long. W °	′	″	Alt.* feet
Macon, Ga.	32	50	12	83	37	36	335
Madison, Wis.	43	04	23	89	22	55	860
Manchester, N.H.	42	59	28	71	27	41	175
Marshall, Tex.	32	33	00	94	23	00	410
Memphis, Tenn.	35	08	46	90	03	13	275
Meriden, Conn.	41	32	06	72	47	30	190
Mexico City, Mexico.	19	25	45	99	07	00	7,347
Miami, Fla.	25	46	37	80	11	32	10
Milwaukee, Wis.	43	02	19	87	54	15	635
Minneapolis, Minn.	44	58	57	93	15	43	815
Minot, N.D.	48	14	09	101	17	38	1,550
Mississauga, Ont.	43	33	00	79	35	00	260(a)
Mobile, Ala.	30	41	36	88	02	33	5
Moline, Ill.	41	30	31	90	30	49	585
Moncton, N.B.	46	05	18	64	46	41	38
Montgomery, Ala.	32	22	33	86	18	31	160
Montpelier, Vt.	44	15	36	72	34	41	485
Montreal, Que.	45	30	33	73	33	14	90
Moose Jaw, Sask.	50	23	34	105	32	04	1,784
Muncie, Ind.	40	11	28	85	23	16	950
Nashville, Tenn.	36	09	33	86	46	55	450
Natchez, Miss.	31	33	48	91	23	30	210
Newark, N.J.	40	44	14	74	10	19	55
New Bedford, Mass.	41	38	13	70	55	41	15
New Britain, Conn.	41	40	08	72	46	59	200
New Haven, Conn.	41	18	25	72	55	30	40
New Orleans, La.	29	56	53	90	04	10	5
New York, N.Y.	40	45	06	73	59	39	55
Niagara Falls, N.Y.	43	05	34	79	03	26	570
Niagara Falls, Ont.	43	06	22	79	03	51	590
Nome, Alas.	64	30	00	165	25	00	25
Norfolk, Va.	36	51	10	76	17	21	10
North Bay, Ont.	46	18	35	79	27	45	670
Oakland, Cal.	37	48	03	122	15	54	25
Ogden, Ut.	41	13	31	111	58	21	4,295
Oklahoma City.	35	28	26	97	31	04	1,195
Omaha, Neb.	41	15	42	95	56	14	1,040
Orlando, Fla.	28	32	42	81	22	38	70
Oshawa, Ont.	43	53	46	78	51	57	350
Ottawa, Ont.	45	26	24	75	41	42	185
Paducah, Ky.	37	05	13	88	35	56	345
Pasadena, Cal.	34	08	44	118	08	41	830
Paterson, N.J.	40	55	01	74	10	21	100
Pensacola, Fla.	30	24	51	87	12	56	15
Peoria, Ill.	40	41	42	89	35	33	470
Peterborough, Ont.	44	18	32	78	19	13	673
Philadelphia, Pa.	39	56	58	75	09	21	100
Phoenix, Ariz.	33	27	12	112	04	28	1,090
Pierre, S.D.	44	22	18	100	20	54	1,480
Pittsburgh, Pa.	40	26	19	80	00	00	745
Pittsfield, Mass.	42	26	53	73	15	14	1,015
Pocatello, Ida.	42	51	38	112	27	01	4,460
Port Arthur, Tex.	29	52	30	93	56	15	10
Portland, Me.	43	39	33	70	15	19	25
Portland, Ore.	45	31	06	122	40	35	77
Portsmouth, N.H.	43	04	30	70	45	24	20
Portsmouth, Va.	36	50	07	76	18	14	10
Prince Rupert, B.C.	54	19	00	130	19	00	125(a)
Providence, R.I.	41	49	32	71	24	41	80
Provo, Ut.	40	14	06	111	39	24	4,550
Pueblo, Col.	38	16	17	104	36	33	4,690
Quebec City, Que.	46	48	51	71	12	30	163
Racine, Wis.	42	43	49	87	47	12	630
Rapid City, S.D.	44	04	52	103	13	11	3,230
Raleigh, N.C.	35	46	38	78	38	21	365
Reading, Pa.	40	20	09	75	55	40	265
Regina, Sask.	50	26	55	104	36	50	1,894(a)
Reno, Nev.	39	31	27	119	48	40	4,490
Richmond, Va.	37	32	15	77	26	09	160
Roanoke, Va.	37	16	13	79	56	44	905
Rochester, Minn.	44	01	21	92	28	03	990
Rochester, N.Y.	43	09	41	77	36	21	515
Rockford, Ill.	42	16	07	89	05	48	715
Sacramento, Cal.	38	34	57	121	29	41	30
Saginaw, Mich.	43	25	52	83	56	05	595
St. Catharines, Ont.	43	09	33	79	14	50	362(a)
St. Cloud, Minn.	45	34	00	94	10	24	1,040
Saint John, N.B.	45	16	12	66	03	48	27
St. John's, Nfld.	47	33	42	52	42	48	200(a)
St. Joseph, Mo.	39	45	57	94	51	02	850
St. Louis, Mo.	38	37	45	90	12	22	455
St. Paul, Minn.	44	57	19	93	06	07	780
St. Petersburg, Fla.	27	46	18	82	38	19	20
Salem, Ore.	44	56	24	123	01	59	155
Salina, Kan.	38	50	36	97	36	46	1,229
Salt Lake City, Ut.	40	45	23	111	53	26	4,390
San Angelo, Tex.	31	27	39	100	26	03	1,845
San Antonio, Tex.	29	25	37	98	29	06	650
San Bernardino, Cal.	34	06	30	117	17	28	1,080
San Diego, Cal.	32	42	53	117	09	21	20
San Francisco, Cal.	37	46	39	122	24	40	65
San Jose, Cal.	37	20	16	121	53	24	90
San Juan, P.R.	18	27	00	66	04	15	35
Santa Barbara, Cal.	34	25	18	119	41	55	100
Santa Cruz, Cal.	36	58	18	122	01	18	20
Santa Fe, N.M.	35	41	11	105	56	10	6,950
Sarasota, Fla.	27	20	05	82	32	30	20
Saskatoon, Sask.	52	07	49	106	39	35	1,587
Sault Ste. Marie, Ont.	46	30	24	84	20	04	589
Savannah, Ga.	32	04	42	81	05	37	20
Schenectady, N.Y.	42	48	42	73	55	42	245
Scranton, Pa.	41	24	32	75	39	46	725
Seattle, Wash.	47	36	32	122	20	12	10
Sheboygan, Wis.	43	45	03	87	42	52	630
Sherbrooke, Que.	45	24	27	71	51	07	535(a)
Sheridan, Wy.	44	47	55	106	57	10	3,740
Shreveport, La.	32	30	46	93	44	58	204
Sioux City, Ia.	42	29	46	96	24	30	1,110
Sioux Falls, S.D.	43	32	35	96	43	35	1,395
Somerville, Mass.	42	23	15	71	06	07	13
South Bend, Ind.	41	40	33	86	15	01	710
Spartanburg, S.C.	34	57	03	81	56	06	875
Spokane, Wash.	47	39	32	117	25	33	1,890
Springfield, Ill.	39	47	58	89	38	51	610
Springfield, Mass.	42	06	21	72	35	32	85
Springfield, Mo.	37	13	03	93	17	32	1,300
Springfield, Oh.	39	55	38	83	48	29	980
Stamford, Conn.	41	03	09	73	32	24	35
Steubenville, Oh.	40	21	42	80	36	53	660
Stockton, Cal.	37	57	30	121	17	16	20
Sudbury, Ont.	46	29	24	80	59	24	850(a)
Superior, Wis.	46	43	14	92	06	07	630
Sydney, N.S.	46	08	15	60	11	48	15
Syracuse, N.Y.	43	03	04	76	09	14	400
Tacoma, Wash.	47	14	59	122	26	15	110
Tallahassee, Fla.	30	26	30	84	16	56	150
Tampa, Fla.	27	56	58	82	27	25	15
Terre Haute, Ind.	39	28	03	87	24	26	496
Texarkana, Tex.	33	25	48	94	02	30	324
Thunder Bay, Ont.	48	22	54	89	14	42	616
Toledo, Oh.	41	39	14	83	32	39	585
Topeka, Kan.	39	03	16	95	40	23	930
Toronto, Ont.	43	39	10	79	23	00	300
Trenton, N.J.	40	13	14	74	46	13	35
Trois-Rivieres, Que.	46	20	36	72	32	37	115(a)
Troy, N.Y.	42	43	45	73	40	58	35
Tucson, Ariz.	32	13	15	110	58	08	2,390
Tulsa, Okla.	36	09	12	95	59	34	804
Urbana, Ill.	40	06	42	88	12	06	725
Utica, N.Y.	43	06	12	75	13	33	415
Vancouver, B.C.	49	18	56	123	04	44	141
Victoria, B.C.	48	25	43	123	21	49	57
Waco, Tex.	31	33	12	97	08	00	405
Walla Walla, Wash.	46	04	08	118	20	24	936
Washington, D.C.	38	53	51	77	00	33	25
Waterbury, Conn.	41	33	13	73	02	31	260
Waterloo, Ia.	42	29	40	92	20	20	850
West Palm Beach, Fla.	26	42	36	80	03	07	15
Wheeling, W. Va.	40	04	03	80	43	20	650
Whitehorse, Yukon	60	43	17	135	03	03	2,305(a)
White Plains, N.Y.	41	02	00	73	45	48	220
Wichita, Kan.	37	41	30	97	20	16	1,290
Wichita Falls, Tex.	33	54	34	98	29	28	945
Wilkes-Barre, Pa.	41	14	32	75	53	17	640
Wilmington, Del.	39	44	46	75	32	51	135
Wilmington, N.C.	34	14	14	77	56	58	35
Windsor, Ont.	42	18	56	83	02	10	603
Winnipeg, Man.	49	53	56	97	08	23	762
Winston-Salem, N.C.	36	05	52	80	14	42	860
Worcester, Mass.	42	15	37	71	48	17	475
Yakima, Wash.	46	36	09	120	30	39	1,060
Yellowknife, N.W.T.	62	27	16	114	22	33	674(a)
Yonkers, N.Y.	40	55	55	73	53	54	10
York, Pa.	39	57	35	76	43	36	370
Youngstown, Oh.	41	05	57	80	39	02	840
Yuma, Ariz.	32	42	54	114	37	24	160
Zanesville, Oh.	39	56	18	82	00	30	720

World Cities

City	Lat. N °	′	″	Long. W °	′	″	Alt.* feet
London, UK (Greenwich)	51	30	00N	0	0	0	245
Paris, France.	48	50	14N	2	20	14E	300
Berlin, Germany	52	32	00N	13	25	00E	110
Rome, Italy.	41	53	00N	12	30	00E	95
Warsaw, Poland	52	15	00N	21	00	00E	360
Moscow, USSR	55	45	00N	37	42	00E	394
Athens, Greece	37	58	00N	23	44	00E	300
Jerusalem, Israel	31	47	00N	35	13	00E	2,500
Johannesburg, So. Afr.	26	10	00S	28	02	00E	5,740
New Delhi, India	28	38	00N	77	12	00E	770
Peking, China	39	54	00N	116	28	00E	600
Rio de Janeiro, Brazil	22	53	43S	43	13	22W	30
Tokyo, Japan	35	45	00N	139	45	00E	30
Sydney, Australia	33	52	00S	151	12	00E	25

Perpetual Calendar

The number shown for each year indicates which Gregorian calendar to use. For 1583-1802, or for Julian calendar, see page 291. For years 1803-1820, use numbers for 1983-2000, respectively.

The page is a perpetual calendar grid. Each cell is labeled with an index number and contains twelve monthly calendars (JANUARY through DECEMBER) with columns S M T W T F S.

Calendar index numbers shown: 7, 8, 9, 10, 11, 1992, 12, 13, 14

The Julian Period

How many days have you lived? To determine this, you must multiply your age by 365, add the number of days since your last birthday until today, and account for all leap years. Chances are your answer would be wrong. Astronomers, however, find it convenient to express dates and long time intervals in days rather than in years, months and days. This is done by placing events within the Julian period.

The Julian period was devised in 1582 by Joseph Scaliger and named after his father Julius (not after the Julian calendar). Scaliger had Julian Day (JD) #1 begin at noon, Jan. 1, 4713 B. C., the most recent time that three major chronological cycles began on the same day — 1) the 28-year solar cycle, after which dates in the Julian calendar (e.g., Feb. 11) return to the same days of the week (e.g., Monday); 2) the 19-year lunar cycle, after which the phases of the moon return to the same dates of the year; and 3) the 15-year indiction cycle, used in ancient Rome to regulate taxes. It will take 7980 years to complete the period, the product of 28, 19, and 15.

Noon of Dec. 31, 1991, marks the beginning of JD 2,448,622; that many days will have passed since the start of the Julian period. The JD at noon of any date in 1992 may be found by adding to this figure the day of the year for that date, which is given in the left hand column in the chart below. Simple JD conversion tables are used by astronomers.

Days Between Two Dates

Table covers period of two ordinary years. Example—Days between Feb. 10, 1989 and Dec. 15, 1990; subtract 41 from 714; answer is 673 days. For leap year, such as 1992, one day must be added: final answer is 674.

Date	Jan.	Feb.	Mar.	April	May	June	July	Aug.	Sept.	Oct.	Nov.	Dec.
1	1	32	60	91	121	152	182	213	244	274	305	335
2	2	33	61	92	122	153	183	214	245	275	306	336
3	3	34	62	93	123	154	184	215	246	276	307	337
4	4	35	63	94	124	155	185	216	247	277	308	338
5	5	36	64	95	125	156	186	217	248	278	309	339
6	6	37	65	96	126	157	187	218	249	279	310	340
7	7	38	66	97	127	158	188	219	250	280	311	341
8	8	39	67	98	128	159	189	220	251	281	312	342
9	9	40	68	99	129	160	190	221	252	282	313	343
10	10	41	69	100	130	161	191	222	253	283	314	344
11	11	42	70	101	131	162	192	223	254	284	315	345
12	12	43	71	102	132	163	193	224	255	285	316	346
13	13	44	72	103	133	164	194	225	256	286	317	347
14	14	45	73	104	134	165	195	226	257	287	318	348
15	15	46	74	105	135	166	196	227	258	288	319	349
16	16	47	75	106	136	167	197	228	259	289	320	350
17	17	48	76	107	137	168	198	229	260	290	321	351
18	18	49	77	108	138	169	199	230	261	291	322	352
19	19	50	78	109	139	170	200	231	262	292	323	353
20	20	51	79	110	140	171	201	232	263	293	324	354
21	21	52	80	111	141	172	202	233	264	294	325	355
22	22	53	81	112	142	173	203	234	265	295	326	356
23	23	54	82	113	143	174	204	235	266	296	327	357
24	24	55	83	114	144	175	205	236	267	297	328	358
25	25	56	84	115	145	176	206	237	268	298	329	359
26	26	57	85	116	146	177	207	238	269	299	330	360
27	27	58	86	117	147	178	208	239	270	300	331	361
28	28	59	87	118	148	179	209	240	271	301	332	362
29	29	—	88	119	149	180	210	241	272	302	333	363
30	30	—	89	120	150	181	211	242	273	303	334	364
31	31	—	90	—	151	—	212	243	—	304	—	365

Date	Jan.	Feb.	Mar.	April	May	June	July	Aug.	Sept.	Oct.	Nov.	Dec.
1	366	397	425	456	486	517	547	578	609	639	670	700
2	367	398	426	457	487	518	548	579	610	640	671	701
3	368	399	427	458	488	519	549	580	611	641	672	702
4	369	400	428	459	489	520	550	581	612	642	673	703
5	370	401	429	460	490	521	551	582	613	643	674	704
6	371	402	430	461	491	522	552	583	614	644	675	705
7	372	403	431	462	492	523	553	584	615	645	676	706
8	373	404	432	463	493	524	554	585	616	646	677	707
9	374	405	433	464	494	525	555	586	617	647	678	708
10	375	406	434	465	495	526	556	587	618	648	679	709
11	376	407	435	466	496	527	557	588	619	649	680	710
12	377	408	436	467	497	528	558	589	620	650	681	711
13	378	409	437	468	498	529	559	590	621	651	682	712
14	379	410	438	469	499	530	560	591	622	652	683	713
15	380	411	439	470	500	531	561	592	623	653	684	714
16	381	412	440	471	501	532	562	593	624	654	685	715
17	382	413	441	472	502	533	563	594	625	655	686	716
18	383	414	442	473	503	534	564	595	626	656	687	717
19	384	415	443	474	504	535	565	596	627	657	688	718
20	385	416	444	475	505	536	566	597	628	658	689	719
21	386	417	445	476	506	537	567	598	629	659	690	720
22	387	418	446	477	507	538	568	599	630	660	691	721
23	388	419	447	478	508	539	569	600	631	661	692	722
24	389	420	448	479	509	540	570	601	632	662	693	723
25	390	421	449	480	510	541	571	602	633	663	694	724
26	391	422	450	481	511	542	572	603	634	664	695	725
27	392	423	451	482	512	543	573	604	635	665	696	726
28	393	424	452	483	513	544	574	605	636	666	697	727
29	394	—	453	484	514	545	575	606	637	667	698	728
30	395	—	454	485	515	546	576	607	638	668	699	729
31	396	—	455	—	516	—	577	608	—	669	—	730

Lunar Calendar, Chinese New Year, Vietnamese Tet

The ancient Chinese lunar calendar is divided into 12 months of either 29 or 30 days (compensating for the fact that the mean duration of the lunar month is 29 days, 12 hours, 44.05 minutes). The calendar is synchronized with the solar year by the addition of extra months at fixed intervals.

The Chinese calendar runs on a sexagenary cycle, i.e., 60 years. The cycles 1876-1935 and 1936-1995, with the years grouped under their twelve animal designations, are printed below. The Year 1992 (Lunar Year 4690) is found in the ninth column, under Monkey, and is known as a "Year of the Monkey." Readers can find the animal name for the year of their birth, marriage, etc., in the same chart. (Note: the first 3-7 weeks of each of the western years belong to the previous Chinese year and animal designation.)

Both the western (Gregorian) and traditional lunar calendars are used publicly in China, and two New Year's celebrations are held. On Taiwan, in overseas Chinese communities, and in Vietnam, the lunar calendar has been used only to set the dates for traditional festivals, with the Gregorian system in general use.

The four-day Chinese New Year, Hsin Nien, and the three-day Vietnamese New Year festival, Tet, begin at the first new moon after the sun enters Aquarius. The day may fall, therefore, between Jan. 21 and Feb. 19 of the Gregorian calendar. Feb. 4, 1992 marks the start of the new Chinese year. The date is fixed according to the date of the new moon in the Far East. Since this is west of the International Date Line the date may be one day later than that of the new moon in the United States.

Rat	Ox	Tiger	Hare (Rabbit)	Dragon	Snake	Horse	Sheep (Goat)	Monkey	Rooster	Dog	Pig
1876	1877	1878	1879	1880	1881	1882	1883	1884	1885	1886	1887
1888	1889	1890	1891	1892	1893	1894	1895	1896	1897	1898	1899
1900	1901	1902	1903	1904	1905	1906	1907	1908	1909	1910	1911
1912	1913	1914	1915	1916	1917	1918	1919	1920	1921	1922	1923
1924	1925	1926	1927	1928	1929	1930	1931	1932	1933	1934	1935
1936	1937	1938	1939	1940	1941	1942	1943	1944	1945	1946	1947
1948	1949	1950	1951	1952	1953	1954	1955	1956	1957	1958	1959
1960	1961	1962	1963	1964	1965	1966	1967	1968	1969	1970	1971
1972	1973	1974	1975	1976	1977	1978	1979	1980	1981	1982	1983
1984	1985	1986	1987	1988	1989	1990	1991	1992	1993	1994	1995

Standard Time, Daylight Saving Time, and Others

Source: Defense Mapping Agency Hydrographic/Topographic Center; U.S. Dept. of Transportation

Standard Time

Standard time is reckoned from Greenwich, England, recognized as the Prime Meridian of Longitude. The world is divided into 24 zones, each 15° of arc, or one hour in time apart. The Greenwich meridian (0°) extends through the center of the initial zone, and the zones to the east are numbered from 1 to 12 with the prefix "minus" indicating the number of hours to be subtracted to obtain Greenwich Time. Each zone extends 7½° on either side of its central meridian.

Westward zones are similarly numbered, but prefixed "plus" showing the number of hours that must be added to get Greenwich Time. While these zones apply generally to sea areas, it should be noted that the Standard Time maintained in many countries does not coincide with zone time. A graphical representation of the zones is shown on the Standard Time Zone Chart of the World published by the Defense Mapping Agency, Hydrographic/Topographic Center, Attn: PP Washington, DC 20315-0030.

The United States and possessions are divided into eight Standard Time zones, as set forth by the Uniform Time Act of 1966, which also provides for the use of Daylight Saving Time therein. Each zone is approximately 15° of longitude in width. All places in each zone use, instead of their own local time, the time counted from the transit of the "mean sun" across the Standard Time meridian which passes near the middle of that zone.

These time zones are designated as Atlantic, Eastern, Central, Mountain, Pacific, Yukon, Alaska-Hawaii, and Bering (Samoa), and the time in these zones is basically reckoned from the 60th, 75th, 90th, 105th, 120th, 135th, 150th and 165th meridians west of Greenwich. The line wanders to conform to local geographical regions. The time in the various zones is earlier than Greenwich Time by 4, 5, 6, 7, 8, 9, 10, and 11 hours respectively.

24-Hour Time

24-hour time is widely used in scientific work throughout the world. In the United States it is used also in operations of the Armed Forces. In Europe it is frequently used by the transportation networks in preference to the 12-hour a.m. and p.m. system. With the 24-hour system the day begins at midnight and is designated 0000 through 2359.

International Date Line

The Date Line is a zig-zag line that approximately coincides with the 180th meridian, and it is where the calendar dates are separated. The date must be advanced one day when crossing in a westerly direction and set back one day when crossing in an easterly direction.

The line is deflected eastward through the Bering Strait and westward of the Aleutians to prevent separating these areas by date. The line is again deflected eastward of the

Tonga and New Zealand Islands in the South Pacific for the same reason.

Daylight Saving Time

Daylight Saving Time is achieved by advancing the clock one hour. Under the Uniform Time Act, which became effective in 1967, all states, the District of Columbia, and U.S. possessions were to observe Daylight Saving Time beginning at 2 a.m. on the first Sunday in April and ending at 2 a.m. on the last Sunday in October. Any state could, by law, exempt itself; a 1972 amendment to the act authorized states split by time zones to take that into consideration in exempting themselves. Arizona, Hawaii, Puerto Rico, the Virgin Islands, American Samoa, and part of Indiana are now exempt. Some local zone boundaries in Kansas, Texas, Florida, Michigan, and Alaska have been modified in the last several years by the Dept. of Transportation, which oversees the act. To conserve energy Congress put most of the nation on year-round Daylight Saving Time for two years effective Jan. 6, 1974 through Oct. 26, 1975; but a further bill, signed in October, 1974, restored Standard Time from the last Sunday in that month to the last Sunday in February, 1975. At the end of 1975, Congress failed to renew this temporary legislation and the nation returned to the older end-of April to end-of October DST system.

On July 8, 1986, Pres. Ronald Reagan signed legislation moving up the start of daylight saving time to the first Sunday in April. Daylight Saving Time, which used to start the last Sunday in April, will still end the last Sunday in October. The Transportation Dept. estimated that the earlier starting date will help save more than $28 million in traffic accident costs and prevent more than 1,500 injuries and 20 deaths. The new law, opposed by some farm state lawmakers, took effect in 1987.

International

Adjusting clock time to be able to use the added daylight on summer evenings is common throughout the world.

Western Europe is on daylight saving time generally from the last Sunday in March to the last Sunday in September; however, the United Kingdom continues until the last Sunday in October.

The Soviet Union lies over 11 time zones, but maintains its standard time 1 hour fast of the zone designation. Additionally, it proclaims daylight saving time as does Europe.

China lies across 5 time zones, but has decreed that the entire country be placed on zone time minus 8 hours with daylight saving time from April 12 to September 12.

Many of the countries in the Southern Hemisphere maintain daylight saving time generally from October to March; however, most countries near the equator do not deviate from standard time.

Standard Time Differences—World Cities

The time indicated in the table is fixed by law and is called the legal time, or, more generally, Standard Time. Use of Daylight Saving Time varies widely. *Indicates morning of the following day. At 12:00 noon, Eastern Standard Time, the standard time (in 24-hour time) in foreign cities is as follows:

City	Time	City	Time	City	Time	City	Time
Addis Ababa	20 00	Cape Town	19 00	Leningrad	20 00	Santiago (Chile)	13 00
Alexandria	19 00	Caracas	13 00	Lima	12 00	Seoul	2 00*
Amsterdam	18 00	Casablanca	17 00	Lisbon	17 00	Shanghai	1 00*
Athens	19 00	Copenhagen	18 00	Liverpool	17 00	Singapore	1 00*
Auckland	5 00*	Dacca	23 00	London	17 00	Stockholm	18 00
Baghdad	20 00	Delhi	22 30	Madrid	18 00	Sydney (Australia)	3 00*
Bangkok	0 00	Dublin	17 00	Manila	1 00*	Tashkent	23 00
Beijing	1 00*	Gdansk	18 00	Mecca (Saudi Arabia)	20 00	Teheran	20 30
Belfast	17 00	Geneva	18 00	Melbourne	3 00*	Tel Aviv	19 00
Berlin	18 00	Havana	12 00	Mexico City	11 00	Tokyo	2 00*
Bogota	12 00	Helsinki	19 00	Montevideo	14 00	Valparaiso	13 00
Bombay	22 30	Ho Chi Minh City	0 00	Moscow	20 00	Vladivostok	3 00*
Bremen	18 00	Hong Kong	1 00*	Nagasaki	2 00*	Vienna	18 00
Brussels	18 00	Istanbul	19 00	Oslo	18 00	Warsaw	18 00
Bucharest	19 00	Jakarta	0 00	Paris	18 00	Wellington (N.Z.)	5 00*
Budapest	18 00	Jerusalem	19 00	Prague	18 00	Yokohama	2 00*
Buenos Aires	14 00	Johannesburg	19 00	Rangoon	23 30	Zurich	18 00
Cairo	19 00	Karachi	22 00	Rio De Janeiro	14 00		
Calcutta	22 30	Le Havre	18 00	Rome	18 00		

Standard Time Differences — North American Cities

At 12 o'clock noon, Eastern Standard Time, the standard time in N.A. cities is as follows:

City	Time		City	Time		City	Time	
Akron, Oh.	12.00	Noon	Frankfort, Ky.	12.00	Noon	*Phoenix, Ariz.	10.00	A.M.
Albuquerque, N.M.	10.00	A.M.	Galveston, Tex.	11.00	A.M.	Pierre, S.D.	11.00	A.M.
Atlanta, Ga.	12.00	Noon	Grand Rapids, Mich.	12.00	Noon	Pittsburgh, Pa.	12.00	Noon
Austin, Tex.	11.00	A.M.	Halifax, N.S.	1.00	P.M.	Portland, Me.	12.00	Noon
Baltimore, Md.	12.00	Noon	Hartford, Conn.	12.00	Noon	Portland, Ore.	9.00	A.M.
Birmingham, Ala.	11.00	A.M.	Helena, Mon.	10.00	A.M.	Providence, R.I.	12.00	Noon
Bismarck, N.D.	11.00	A.M.	*Honolulu, Ha.	7.00	A.M.	*Regina, Sask.	11.00	A.M.
Boise, Ida.	10.00	A.M.	Houston, Tex.	11.00	A.M.	Reno, Nev.	9.00	A.M.
Boston, Mass.	12.00	Noon	*Indianapolis, Ind.	12.00	Noon	Richmond, Va.	12.00	Noon
Buffalo, N.Y.	12.00	Noon	Jacksonville, Fla.	12.00	Noon	Rochester, N.Y.	12.00	Noon
Butte, Mon.	10.00	A.M.	Juneau, Alas.	8.00	A.M.	Sacramento, Cal.	9.00	A.M.
Calgary, Alta.	10.00	A.M.	Kansas City, Mo.	11.00	A.M.	St. John's, Nfld.	1.30	P.M.
Charleston, S.C.	12.00	Noon	Knoxville, Tenn.	12.00	Noon	St. Louis, Mo.	11.00	A.M.
Charleston, W.Va.	12.00	Noon	Lexington, Ky.	12.00	Noon	St. Paul, Minn.	11.00	A.M.
Charlotte, N.C.	12.00	Noon	Lincoln, Neb.	11.00	A.M.	Salt Lake City, Ut.	10.00	A.M.
Charlottetown, P.E.I.	1.00	P.M.	Little Rock, Ark.	11.00	A.M.	San Antonio, Tex.	11.00	A.M.
Chattanooga, Tenn.	12.00	Noon	Los Angeles, Cal.	9.00	A.M.	San Diego, Cal.	9.00	A.M.
Cheyenne, Wy.	10.00	A.M.	Louisville, Ky.	12.00	Noon	San Francisco, Cal.	9.00	A.M.
Chicago, Ill.	11.00	A.M.	*Mexico City	11.00	A.M.	Santa Fe, N.M.	10.00	A.M.
Cleveland, Oh.	12.00	Noon	Memphis, Tenn.	11.00	A.M.	Savannah, Ga.	12.00	Noon
Colorado Spr., Col.	10.00	A.M.	Miami, Fla.	12.00	Noon	Seattle, Wash.	9.00	A.M.
Columbus, Oh.	12.00	Noon	Milwaukee, Wis.	11.00	A.M.	Shreveport, La.	11.00	A.M.
Dallas, Tex.	11.00	A.M.	Minneapolis, Minn.	11.00	A.M.	Sioux Falls, S.D.	11.00	A.M.
*Dawson, Yuk.	9.00	A.M.	Mobile, Ala.	11.00	A.M.	Spokane, Wash.	9.00	A.M.
Dayton, Oh.	12.00	Noon	Montreal, Que.	12.00	Noon	Tampa, Fla.	12.00	Noon
Denver, Col.	10.00	A.M.	Nashville, Tenn.	11.00	A.M.	Toledo, Oh.	12.00	Noon
Des Moines, Ia.	11.00	A.M.	New Haven, Conn.	12.00	Noon	Topeka, Kan.	11.00	A.M.
Detroit, Mich.	12.00	Noon	New Orleans, La.	11.00	A.M.	Toronto, Ont.	12.00	Noon
Duluth, Minn.	11.00	A.M.	New York, N.Y.	12.00	Noon	*Tucson, Ariz.	10.00	A.M.
El Paso, Tex.	10.00	A.M.	Nome, Alas.	8.00	A.M.	Tulsa, Okla.	11.00	A.M.
Erie, Pa.	12.00	Noon	Norfolk, Va.	12.00	Noon	Vancouver, B.C.	9.00	A.M.
Evansville, Ind.	11.00	A.M.	Okla. City, Okla.	11.00	A.M.	Washington, D.C.	12.00	Noon
Fairbanks, Alas.	8.00	A.M.	Omaha, Neb.	11.00	A.M.	Wichita, Kan.	11.00	A.M.
Flint, Mich.	12.00	Noon	Peoria, Ill.	11.00	A.M.	Wilmington, Del.	12.00	Noon
*Fort Wayne, Ind.	12.00	Noon	Philadelphia, Pa.	12.00	Noon	Winnipeg, Man.	11.00	A.M.
Fort Worth, Tex.	11.00	A.M.						

* Cities with an asterisk do not observe daylight saving time. During much of the year, it is necessary to add one hour to the cities which do observe daylight savings time to get the proper time relation.

Legal or Public Holidays, 1992

Technically there are no national holidays in the United States; each state has jurisdiction over its holidays, which are designated by legislative enactment or executive proclamation. In practice, however, most states observe the federal legal public holidays, even though the President and Congress can legally designate holidays only for the District of Columbia and for federal employees. Federal legal public holidays are New Year's Day, Martin Luther King Day, Washington's Birthday, Memorial Day, Independence Day, Labor Day, Columbus Day, Veterans' Day, Thanksgiving, and Christmas.

Chief Legal or Public Holidays

When a holiday falls on a Sunday or a Saturday it is usually observed on the following Monday or the preceding Friday. For some holidays, government and business closing practices vary. In most states, the office of the Secretary of State can provide details for holiday closings. The following will be legal or public holidays in most states in 1992:

Jan. 1 (Wednesday) — New Year's Day.
Jan. 20 (Monday) — Martin Luther King Day.
Feb. 12 (Wednesday) — Lincoln's Birthday.
Feb. 17 (3d Mon. in Feb.) — Washington's Birthday, or Presidents' Day, or Washington-Lincoln Day.
May 25 (last Mon. in May) — Memorial Day, or Decoration Day.

July 4 (Saturday) — Independence Day.
Sept. 7 (1st Mon. in Sept.) — Labor Day.
Oct. 12 (2d Monday in Oct.) — Columbus Day, or Discoverers' Day, or Pioneers' Day.
Nov. 11 (Wednesday) — Veterans' Day.
Nov. 26 (4th Thursday in Nov.) — Thanksgiving Day.
Dec. 25 (Friday) — Christmas Day.
In some states, the following will be legal or public holidays in 1992:
Apr. 17 (Friday) — Good Friday. In some states, observed for half or part of day.
Nov. 3 (1st Tues. after 1st Mon. in Nov.) — Election Day.

Selected Foreign Holidays

Jan. 14 — Vinegrower's Day, Bulgaria.
Jan. 20 — St. Agnes Eve, England.
Feb. 3 — Setsubun (bean-throwing festival), Japan.
Feb. 8 — Narvik Sun Pageant, Norway.
Feb. 9-12 — Carnival, Brazil.
Mar. 28 — Teacher's Day, Czechoslovakia.
Apr. 8 — Buddha's Birthday, Korea, Japan.
Apr. 12 — Cosmonautics Day, USSR.
Apr. 22 — Independence Day, Israel.
Apr. 25 — ANZAC Day, Australia, New Zealand.
May 1 — Labor Day, most socialist countries.
May 5 — Cinco de Mayo, Mexico.
May 25 — African Freedom Day, Chad, Zambia.
June 22 — Midsummer Eve, Denmark.

July 1 — Canada Day, Canada.
July 14 — Bastille Day, France.
mid July — Feria de San Fermin, Spain.
July 24 — Simon Bolivar's Birthday, Venezuela.
Aug. 13 — Fox Hill Day, Bahamas.
Aug. 15 — Sour Herring Premiere, Sweden.
Sept. 19 — St. Gennaro, Italy.
Oct. 2 — Mahatma Gandhi's Birthday, India.
Oct. 6 — Ivy Day, Ireland.
Nov. 1 — All Saints' Day, Zaire.
Nov. 16 — Elephant Round-up, Thailand.
Nov. 17 — Volkstrauertag (Memorial Day), Germany.
Dec. 5 — Lover's Fair, Belgium.
Dec. 16-Jan. 6 — Christmas Observance, Philippines.

WEIGHTS AND MEASURES

Source: National Institute of Standards and Technology, U.S. Dept. of Commerce

The International System of Units

Two systems of weights and measures exist side by side in the United States today, with roughly equal but separate legislative sanction: the U.S. Customary System and the International (Metric) System. Throughout U.S. history, the Customary System (inherited from, but now different from, the British Imperial System) has been, as its name implies, customarily used; a plethora of federal and state legislation has given it, through implication, standing as our primary weights and measures system. However, the Metric System (incorporated in the scientists' new SI or Systeme International d'Unites) is the only system that has ever received specific legislative sanction by Congress. The "Law of 1866" reads:

It shall be lawful throughout the United States of America to employ the weights and measures of the metric system; and no contract or dealing, or pleading in any court, shall be deemed invalid or liable to objection because the weights or measures expressed or referred to therein are weights or measures of the metric system.

Over the last 100 years, the Metric System has seen slow, steadily increasing use in the United States. In science and also in the pharmaceutical industry, the use of metrics has for many years been predominant; today, the manufacturing industry is steadily increasing its use of the metric system largely motivated by the automotive industry, which is now predominantly metric.

On Feb. 10, 1964, the National Bureau of Standards issued the following bulletin:

Henceforth it shall be the policy of the National Bureau of Standards to use the units of the International System (SI), as adopted by the 11th General Conference on Weights and Measures (October 1960), except when the use of these units would obviously impair communication or reduce the usefulness of a report.

The Trade Act of 1988 calls for the federal government to adopt metric specifications by Dec. 31, 1992, and mandates the Commerce Dept. to oversee the program.

What had been the Metric System became the International System (SI), a more complete scientific system.

Seven units have been adopted to serve as the base for the International System as follows: **length**—meter; **mass**—kilogram; **time**—second; **electric current**—ampere; **thermodynamic temperature**—kelvin; **amount of substance**—mole; and **luminous intensity**—candela.

Prefixes

The following prefixes, in combination with the basic unit names, provide the multiples and submultiples in the International System. For example, the unit name "meter," with the prefix "kilo" added, produces "kilometer," meaning "1,000 meters."

Prefix	Symbol	Multiples	Equivalent	Prefix	Symbol	Submultiples	Equivalent
exa	E	10^{18}	quintillionfold	deci	d	10^{-1}	tenth part
peta	P	10^{15}	quadrillionfold	centi	c	10^{-2}	hundredth part
tera	T	10^{12}	trillionfold	milli	m	10^{-3}	thousandth part
giga	G	10^{9}	billionfold	micro	μ	10^{-6}	millionth part
mega	M	10^{6}	millionfold	nano	n	10^{-9}	billionth part
kilo	k	10^{3}	thousandfold	pico	p	10^{-12}	trillionth part
hecto	h	10^{2}	hundredfold	femto	f	10^{-15}	quadrillionth part
deka	da	10	tenfold	atto	a	10^{-18}	quintillionth part

Tables of Metric Weights and Measures

Linear Measure

10 millimeters (mm)	= 1 centimeter (cm)
10 centimeters	= 1 decimeter (dm) = 100 millimeters
10 decimeters	= 1 meter (m) = 1,000 millimeters
10 meters	= 1 dekameter (dam)
10 dekameters	= 1 hectometer (hm) = 100 meters
10 hectometers	= 1 kilometer (km) = 1,000 meters

Area Measure

100 square millimeters (mm²)	= 1 square centimeter (cm²)
10,000 square centimeters	= 1 square meter (m²) = 1,000,000 square millimeters
100 square meters	= 1 are (a)
100 ares	= 1 hectare (ha) = 10,000 square meters
100 hectares	= 1 square kilometer (km²) = 1,000,000 square meters

Fluid Volume Measure

10 milliliters (mL)	= 1 centiliter (cL)
10 centiliters	= 1 deciliter (dL) = 100 milliliters

10 deciliters	= 1 liter (L) = 1,000 milliliters
10 liters	= 1 dekaliter (daL)
10 dekaliters	= 1 hectoliter (hL) = 100 liters
10 hectoliters	= 1 kiloliter (kL) = 1,000 liters

Cubic Measure

1,000 cubic millimeters (mm³)	= 1 cubic centimeter (cm³)
1,000 cubic centimeters	= 1 cubic decimeter (dm³) = 1,000,000 cubic millimeters
1,000 cubic decimeters	= 1 cubic meter (m³) = 1 stere = 1,000,000 cubic millimeters = 1,000,000,000 cubic millimeters

Weight

10 milligrams (mg)	= 1 centigram (cg)
10 centigrams	= 1 decigram (dg) = 100 milligrams
10 decigrams	= 1 gram (g) = 1,000 milligrams
10 grams	= 1 dekagram (dag)
10 dekagrams	= 1 hectogram (hg) = 100 grams
10 hectograms	= 1 kilogram (kg) = 1,000 grams
1,000 kilograms	= 1 metric ton (t)

Table of U.S. Customary Weights and Measures

Linear Measure

12 inches (in)	= 1 foot (ft)
3 feet	= 1 yard (yd)
5 ½ yards	= 1 rod (rd), pole, or perch (16 ½ feet)

40 rods	= 1 furlong (fur) = 220 yards = 660 feet
8 furlongs	= 1 statute mile (mi) = 1,760 yards = 5,280 feet
3 miles	= 1 league = 5,280 yards = 15,840 feet
6076.11549 feet	= 1 International Nautical Mile

Liquid Measure

When necessary to distinguish the liquid pint or quart from the dry pint or quart, the word "liquid" or the abbreviation "liq" should be used in combination with the name or abbreviation of the liquid unit.

4 gills	= 1 pint (pt) = 28.875 cubic inches
2 pints	= 1 quart (qt) = 57.75 cubic inches
4 quarts	= 1 gallon (gal) = 231 cubic inches = 8 pints = 32 gills

Area Measure

Squares and cubes of units are sometimes abbreviated by using "superior" figures. For example. ft² means square foot, and ft³ means cubic foot.

144 square inches	= 1 square foot (ft²)
9 square feet	= 1 square yard (yd²) = 1,296 square inches
30 ¼ square yards	= 1 square rod (rd²) = 272 ¼ square feet
160 square rods	= 1 acre = 4,840 square yards = 43,560 square feet
640 acres	= 1 square mile (mi²)
1 mile square	= 1 section (of land)
6 miles square	= 1 township = 36 sections = 36 square miles

Cubic Measure

1 cubic foot (ft³)	= 1,728 cubic inches (in³)
27 cubic feet	= 1 cubic yard (yd³)

Gunter's or Surveyors' Chain Measure

7.92 inches (in)	= 1 link
100 links	= 1 chain (ch) = 4 rods = 66 feet
80 chains	= 1 survey mile (mi) = 320 rods = 5,280 feet

Troy Weight

24 grains	= 1 pennyweight (dwt)
20 pennyweights	= 1 ounce troy (oz t) = 480 grains
12 ounces troy	= 1 pound troy (lb t) = 240 pennyweights = 5,760 grains

Dry Measure

When necessary to distinguish the dry pint or quart from the liquid pint or quart, the word "dry" should be used in combination with the name or abbreviation of the dry unit.

2 pints (pt)	= 1 quart (qt) = 67.2006 cubic inches
8 quarts	= 1 peck (pk) = 537.605 cubic inches = 16 pints
4 pecks	= 1 bushel (bu) = 2,150.42 cubic inches = 32 quarts

Avoirdupois Weight

When necessary to distinguish the avoirdupois ounce or pound from the troy ounce or pound, the word "avoirdupois" or the abbreviation "avdp" should be used in combination with the name or abbreviation of the avoirdupois unit.

(The "grain" is the same in avoirdupois and troy weight.)

27 ¹¹⁄₃₂ grains	= 1 dram (dr)
16 drams	= 1 ounce (oz) = 437 ½ grains
16 ounces	= 1 pound (lb) = 256 drams = 7,000 grains
100 pounds	= 1 hundredweight (cwt)°
20 hundredweights	= 1 ton = 2,000 pounds°

In "gross" or "long" measure, the following values are recognized.

112 pounds	= 1 gross or long hundredweight°
20 gross or long hundredweights	= 1 gross or long ton = 2,240 pounds°

°When the terms "hundredweight" and "ton" are used unmodified, they are commonly understood to mean the 100-pound hundredweight and the 2,000-pound ton, respectively: these units may be designated "net" or "short" when necessary to distinguish them from the corresponding units in gross or long measure.

Tables of Equivalents

In this table it is necessary to distinguish between the "international" and the "survey" foot. The international foot, defined in 1959 as exactly equal to 0.3048 meter, is shorter than the old survey foot by exactly 2 parts in one million. The survey foot is still used in data expressed in feet in geodetic surveys within the U.S. In this table the survey foot is italicized.

When the name of a unit is enclosed in brackets thus, [1 hand], this indicates (1) that the unit is not in general current use in the United States, or (2) that the unit is believed to be based on "custom and usage" rather than on formal definition.

Equivalents involving decimals are, in most instances, rounded off to the third decimal place except where they are exact, in which cases these exact equivalents are so designated.

Lengths

1 angstrom (A)	0.1 nanometer (exactly) 0.000 1 micrometer (exactly) 0.000 000 1 millimeter (exactly) 0.000 000 004 inch
1 cable's length	120 fathoms (exactly) 720 *feet* (exactly) 219 meters
1 centimeter (cm)	0.3937 inch
1 chain (ch) (Gunter's or surveyors)	66 *feet* (exactly) 20.1168 meters
1 chain (engineers)	100 feet 30.48 meters (exactly)
1 decimeter (dm)	3.937 inches
1 degree (geographical)	364,566.929 feet 69.047 miles (avg.) 111.123 kilometers (avg.)
-of latitude	68.708 miles at equator 69.403 miles at poles
-of longitude	69.171 miles at equator
1 dekameter (dam)	32.808 feet
1 fathom	6 *feet* (exactly) 1.8288 meters (exactly)
1 foot (ft)	0.3048 meter (exactly)
1 furlong (fur)	10 chains (surveyors) (exactly) 660 *feet* (exactly) ⅛ statute mile (exactly) 201.168 meters
[1 hand] (height measure for horses from ground to top of shoulders)	4 inches
1 inch (in)	2.54 centimeters (exactly)
1 kilometer (km)	0.621 mile 3,281.5 feet

1 league (land)	3 survey miles (exactly) 4.828 kilometers
1 link (Gunter's or surveyors)	7.92 inches (exactly) 0.201 meter
1 link engineers	1 foot 0.305 meter
1 meter (m)	39.37 inches 1.094 yards
1 micrometer (μm) [the Greek letter mu]	0.001 millimeter (exactly) 0.000 039 37 inch
1 mil	0.001 inch (exactly) 0.025 4 millimeter (exactly)
1 mile (mi) (statute or land)	5,280 feet (exactly) 1.609 kilometers
1 international nautical mile (nmi)	1.852 kilometers (exactly) 1.150779 survey miles 6,076.11549 feet
1 millimeter (mm)	0.039 37 inch
1 nanometer (nm)	0.001 micrometer (exactly) 0.000 000 039 37 inch
1 pica (typography)	12 points
1 point (typography)	0.013 837 inch (exactly) 0.351 millimeter
1 rod (rd), pole, or perch	16 ½ *feet* (exactly) 5.029 meters
1 yard (yd)	0.9144 meter (exactly)

Areas or Surfaces

1 acre	43,560 square *feet* (exactly) 4,840 square yards 0.405 hectare
1 are (a)	119.599 square yards 0.025 acre

1 bolt (cloth measure):
length . . . . 100 yards (on modern looms)
width . . . . $\begin{cases} \text{42 inches (usually, for cotton)} \\ \text{60 inches (usually, for wool)} \end{cases}$
1 hectare (ha) . . . . 2.471 acres
[1 square (building)] . . . . 100 square feet
1 square centimeter (cm²) . . . . 0.155 square inch
1 square decimeter (dm²) . . . . 15.500 square inches
1 square foot (ft²) . . . . 929.030 square centimeters
1 square inch (in²) . . . . 6.4516 square centimeters (exactly)
1 square kilometer (km²) . . . $\begin{cases} \text{247.104 acres} \\ \text{0.386 square mile} \end{cases}$
1 square meter (m²) . . . . $\begin{cases} \text{1.196 square yards} \\ \text{10.764 square feet} \end{cases}$
1 square mile (mi²) . . . . 258.999 hectares
1 square millimeter (mm²) . . . . 0.002 square inch
1 square rod (rd²) sq. pole, or
sq. perch . . . . 25.293 square meters
1 square yard (yd²) . . . . 0.836 square meter

Capacities or Volumes

1 barrel (bbl) liquid . . . . 31 to 42 gallons°
°There are a variety of "barrels," established by law or usage. For example: federal taxes on fermented liquors are based on a barrel of 31 gallons; many state laws fix the "barrel for liquids" as 31 ½ gallons; one state fixes a 36-gallon barrel for cistern measurement; federal law recognizes a 40-gallon barrel for "proof spirits"; by custom, 42 gallons comprise a barrel of crude oil or petroleum products for statistical purposes, and this equivalent is recognized "for liquids" by 4 states.

1 barrel (bbl), standard, for fruits, vegetables, and other such commodities except dry cranberries . . . . $\begin{cases} \text{7,056 cubic inches} \\ \text{105 dry quarts} \\ \text{3.281 bushels, struck} \\ \text{measure} \end{cases}$
1 barrel (bbl), standard, cranberry . . . . $\begin{cases} \text{5,826 cubic inches} \\ \text{86}^{45}\text{/}_{64}\text{ dry quarts} \\ \text{2.709 bushels, struck} \\ \text{measure} \end{cases}$
1 board foot (lumber measure) . . . a foot-square board 1 inch thick
1 bushel (bu) (U.S.) (struck measure) . . . . $\begin{cases} \text{2,150.42 cubic inches} \\ \text{(exactly)} \\ \text{35.239 liters} \end{cases}$
[1 bushel, heaped (U.S.)] . . . $\begin{cases} \text{2,747.715 cubic inches} \\ \text{1.278 bushels, struck} \\ \text{measure*} \end{cases}$
*Frequently recognized as 1¼ bushels, struck measure.
[1 bushel (bu) (British Imperial) (struck measure)] . . $\begin{cases} \text{1.032 U.S. bushels} \\ \text{struck measure} \\ \text{2,219.36 cubic inches} \end{cases}$
1 cord (cd) firewood . . . . 128 cubic feet (exactly)
1 cubic centimeter (cm³) . . . . 0.061 cubic inch
1 cubic decimeter (dm³) . . . . 61.024 cubic inches
1 cubic inch (in³) . . . . . . $\begin{cases} \text{0.554 fluid ounce} \\ \text{4.433 fluid drams} \\ \text{16.387 cubic centimeters} \end{cases}$
1 cubic foot (ft³) . . . . $\begin{cases} \text{7.481 gallons} \\ \text{28.317 cubic decimeters} \end{cases}$
1 cubic meter (m³) . . . . 1.308 cubic yards
1 cubic yard (yd³) . . . . 0.765 cubic meter
1 cup, measuring . . . . $\begin{cases} \text{8 fluid ounces (exactly)} \\ \text{½ liquid pint (exactly)} \end{cases}$
[1 dram, fluid (fl dr) (British)] . . . . . . $\begin{cases} \text{0.961 U.S. fluid dram} \\ \text{0.217 cubic inch} \\ \text{3.552 milliliters} \end{cases}$
1 dekaliter (daL) . . . . $\begin{cases} \text{2.642 gallons} \\ \text{1.135 pecks} \end{cases}$
1 gallon (gal) (U.S.) . . . . . . $\begin{cases} \text{231 cubic inches (exactly)} \\ \text{3.785 liters} \\ \text{0.833 British gallon} \\ \text{128 U.S. fluid ounces (exactly)} \end{cases}$
[1 gallon (gal) British Imperial] . . . . . $\begin{cases} \text{277.42 cubic inches} \\ \text{1.201 U.S. gallons} \\ \text{4.546 liters} \\ \text{160 British fluid ounces (exactly)} \end{cases}$
1 gill (gi) . . . . $\begin{cases} \text{7.219 cubic inches} \\ \text{4 fluid ounces (exactly)} \\ \text{0.118 liter} \end{cases}$
1 hectoliter (hL) . . . . $\begin{cases} \text{26.418 gallons} \\ \text{2.838 bushels} \end{cases}$
1 liter (L) (1 cubic decimeter exactly) . . . . $\begin{cases} \text{1.057 liquid quarts} \\ \text{0.908 dry quart} \\ \text{61.025 cubic inches} \end{cases}$

1 milliliter (mL) (1 cu cm exactly) . . . . . $\begin{cases} \text{0.271 fluid dram} \\ \text{16.231 minims} \\ \text{0.061 cubic inch} \end{cases}$
1 ounce, liquid (U.S.) . . . . . . $\begin{cases} \text{1.805 cubic inches} \\ \text{29.573 milliliters} \\ \text{1.041 British fluid ounces} \end{cases}$
[1 ounce, fluid (fl oz) (British)] . . $\begin{cases} \text{0.961 U.S. fluid ounce} \\ \text{1.734 cubic inches} \\ \text{28.412 milliliters} \end{cases}$
1 peck (pk) . . . . 8.810 liters
1 pint (pt), dry . . . . $\begin{cases} \text{33.600 cubic inches} \\ \text{0.551 liter} \end{cases}$
1 pint (pt), liquid . . . . . . $\begin{cases} \text{28.875 cubic inches (exactly)} \\ \text{0.473 liter} \end{cases}$
1 quart (qt) dry (U.S.) . . . . $\begin{cases} \text{67.201 cubic inches} \\ \text{1.101 liters} \\ \text{0.969 British quart} \end{cases}$
1 quart (qt) liquid (U.S.) . . . $\begin{cases} \text{57.75 cubic in (exactly)} \\ \text{0.946 liter} \\ \text{0.833 British quart} \end{cases}$
[1 quart (qt) (British)] . . . . $\begin{cases} \text{69.354 cubic inches} \\ \text{1.032 U.S. dry quarts} \\ \text{1.201 U.S. liquid quarts} \end{cases}$
1 tablespoon . . . . $\begin{cases} \text{3 teaspoons*(exactly)} \\ \text{4 fluid drams} \\ \text{½ fluid ounce (exactly)} \end{cases}$
1 teaspoon . . . . $\begin{cases} \text{⅓ tablespoon*(exactly)} \\ \text{1⅓ fluid drams*} \end{cases}$
*The equivalent "1 teaspoon—1⅓ fluid drams" has been found by the bureau to correspond more closely with the actual capacities of "measuring" and silver teaspoons with the equivalent "1 teaspoon—1 fluid dram" which is given by many dictionaries.

Weights or Masses

1 assay ton°° (AT) . . . . 29.167 grams
°°Used in assaying. The assay ton bears the same relation to the milligram that a ton of 2,000 pounds avoirdupois bears to the ounce troy; hence the weight in milligrams of precious metal obtained from one assay ton of ore gives directly the number of troy ounces to the net ton.

1 bale (cotton measure) . . . . . . $\begin{cases} \text{500 pounds in U.S.} \\ \text{750 pounds in Egypt} \end{cases}$
1 carat (c) . . . . $\begin{cases} \text{200 milligrams (exactly)} \\ \text{3.086 grains} \end{cases}$
1 dram avoirdupois (dr avdp) gamma, see microgram $\begin{cases} 27^{11}\text{/}_{32}\ (=27.344)\text{ grains} \\ \text{1.772 grams} \end{cases}$
1 grain . . . . 64.799 milligrams
1 gram . . . . $\begin{cases} \text{15.432 grains} \\ \text{0.035 ounce, avoirdupois} \end{cases}$
1 hundredweight, gross or long°° (gross cwt) . . $\begin{cases} \text{112 pounds (exactly)} \\ \text{50.802 kilograms} \end{cases}$
1 hundredweight, net or short (cwt. or net cwt.) . . . $\begin{cases} \text{100 pounds (exactly)} \\ \text{45.359 kilograms} \end{cases}$
1 kilogram (kg) . . . . 2.205 pounds
1 microgram (µg [The Greek letter mu in combination with the letter g]) . . . . 0.000001 gram (exactly)
1 milligram (mg) . . . . 0.015 grain
1 ounce, avoirdupois (oz avdp) . . . . $\begin{cases} \text{437.5 grains (exactly)} \\ \text{0.911 troy ounce} \\ \text{28.350 grams} \end{cases}$
1 ounce, troy (oz t) . . . . . . $\begin{cases} \text{480 grains (exactly)} \\ \text{1.097 avoirdupois ounces} \\ \text{31.103 grams} \end{cases}$
1 pennyweight (dwt) . . . . . 1.555 grams
1 pound, avoirdupois (lb avdp) . . . . $\begin{cases} \text{7,000 grains (exactly)} \\ \text{1.215 troy pounds} \\ \text{453.592 37 grams (exactly)} \end{cases}$
1 pound, troy (lb t) . . . . . . $\begin{cases} \text{5,760 grains (exactly)} \\ \text{0.823 avoirdupois pound} \\ \text{373.242 grams} \end{cases}$
1 ton, gross or long°° (gross ton) . . . . $\begin{cases} \text{2,240 pounds (exactly)} \\ \text{1.12 net tons (exactly)} \\ \text{1.016 metric tons} \end{cases}$
°°°The gross or long ton and hundredweight are used commercially in the United States to only a limited extent, usually in restricted industrial fields. These units are the same as British "ton" and "hundredweight."

1 ton, metric (t) . . . . $\begin{cases} \text{2,204.623 pounds} \\ \text{0.984 gross ton} \\ \text{1.102 net tons} \end{cases}$
1 ton, net or short (sh ton) . . $\begin{cases} \text{2,000 pounds (exactly)} \\ \text{0.893 gross ton} \\ \text{0.907 metric ton} \end{cases}$

Tables of Interrelation of Units of Measurement

Units of length and area of the international and survey measures are included in the following tables. Units unique to the survey measure are italicized. See p. 300, Tables of Equivalents, 1st para.

1 international foot	= 0.999 998 survey foot (exactly)
1 survey foot	= 1200/3937 meter (exactly)
1 international foot	= 12 × 0.0254 meter (exactly)

Bold face type indicates exact values

Units of Length

Units	Inches	*Links*	Feet	Yards	*Rods*	*Chains*	Miles	cm	Meters
1 inch=	1	0.126 263	0.083 333	0.027 778	0.005 051	0.001 263	0.000 016	2.54	0.025 4
1 *link*=	7.92	1	0.66	0.22	0.04	0.01	0.000 125	20.117	0.201 168
1 foot=	12	1.515 152	1	0.333 333	0.060 606	0.015 152	0.000 189	30.48	0.304 8
1 yard=	36	4.545 45	3	1	0.181 818	0.045 455	0.000 568	91.44	0.914 4
1 *rod*=	198	25	16.5	5.5	1	0.25	0.003 125	502.92	5.029 2
1 *chain*=	792	100	66	22	4	1	0.012 5	2011.68	20.116 8
1 mile=	63 360	8000	5280	1760	320	80	1	160 934.4	1609.344
1 cm=	0.3937	0.049 710	0.032 808	0.010 936	0.001 988	0.000 497	0.000 006	1	0.01
1 meter=	39.37	4.970 960	3.280 840	1.093 613	0.198 838	0.049 710	0.000 621	100	1

Units of Area

Units	Sq. inches	*Sq. links*	Sq. feet	Sq. yards	*Sq. rods*	*Sq. chains*
1 sq. inch=	1	.015 942 3	0.006 944	0.000 771 605	0.000 025 5	0.000 001 594
1 sq. *link*=	62.726 4	1	0.435 6	0.0484	0.0016	0.000 1.
1 sq. foot=	144	2.295 684	1	0.111 111 1	0.003 673 09	0.000 229 568
1 sq. yard=	1296	20.661 16	9	1	0.033 057 85	0.002 066 12
1 sq. *rod*=	39 204	625	272.25	30.25	1	0.062 5
1 sq. *chain*=	627 264	10 000	4 356	484	16	1
1 *acre*=	6 272 640	100 000	43 560	4 840	160	10
1 sq. mile=	4 014 489 600	64 000 000	27 878 400	3 097 600	102 400	6400
1 sq. cm=	0.155 000 3	0.002 471 05	0.001 076	0.000 119 599	0.000 003 954	0.000 000 247
1 sq. meter=	1550.003	24.710 44	10.763 91	1.195 990	0.039 536 70	0.002 471 044
1 *hectare*=	15 500 031	247 104	107 639.1	11 959.90	395.367 0	24.710 44

Units	*Acres*	Sq. miles	Sq. cm	Sq. meters	*Hectares*
1 sq. inch=	0.000 000 159 423	0.000 000 000 249 10	6.451 6	0.000 645 16	0.000 000 065
1 sq. *link*=	0.000 01	0.000 000 015 625	404.685 642 24	0.040 468 56	0.000 004 047
1 sq. foot=	0.000 022 956 84	0.000 000 035 870 06	929.034 1	0.092 903 41	0.000 009 290
1 sq. yard=	0.000 206 611 6	0.000 000 322 830 6	8 361.273 6	0.836 127 36	0.000 083 613
1 sq. *rod*=	0.006 25	0.000 009 765 625	252 929.5	25.292 95	0.002 529 295
1 sq. *chain*=	0.1	0.000 156 25		4 046 873	404.687 3	0.040 468 73
1 *acre*=	1	0.001 562 5	40 468 73	4 046.873	0.404 687 3
1 sq. mile=	640	1	25 899 881 103	2 589 988.11	258.998 811 034
1 sq. cm=	0.000 000 024 711	0.000 000 000 038 610	1	0.000 1	0.000 000 01
1 sq. meter=	0.000 247 104 4	0.000 000 386 102 2	10 000	1	0.0001
1 *hectare*=	2.471 044	0.003 861 006	100 000 000	10 000	1

Units of Mass Not Greater than Pounds and Kilograms

Units	Grains	Pennyweights	Avdp drams	Avdp ounces
1 grain=	1	0.041 666 67	0.036 571 43	0.002 285 71
1 pennyweight=	24	1	0.877 714 3	0.054 857 14
1 dram avdp=	27.343 75	1.139 323	1	0.062 5
1 ounce avdp=	437.5	18.229 17	16	1
1 ounce troy=	480	20	17.554 29	1.097 143
1 pound troy=	5760	240	210.651 4	13.165 71
1 pound avdp=	7000	291.666 7	256	16
1 milligram=	0.015 432	0.000 643 015	0.000 564 383	0.000 035 274
1 gram=	15.432 36	0.643 014 9	0.564 383 4	0.035 273 96
1 kilogram=	15 432.36	643.014 9	564.383 4	35.273 96

Units	Troy ounces	Troy pounds	Avdp pounds	Milligrams	Grams	Kilograms
1 grain=	0.002 083 33	0.000 173 611	0.000 142 857	64.798 91	0.064 798 91	0.000 064 799
1 pennyw't.=	0.05	0.004 166 667	0.003 428 571	1555.173 84	1.555 173 84	0.001 555 174
1 dram avdp=	0.056 966 15	0.004 747 179	0.003 906 25	1771.845 195	1.771 845 195	0.001 771 845
1 oz avdp=	0.911 458 3	0.075 954 86	0.062 5	28 349.523 125	28.349 523 125	0.028 349 52
1 oz troy=	1	0.083 333 333	0.068 571 43	31 103.476 8	31.103 476 8	0.031 103 48
1 lb troy=	12	1	0.822 857 1	373 241.721 6	373.241 721 6	0.373 241 722
1 lb avdp=	14.583 33	1.215 278	1	453 592.37	453.592 37	0.453 592 37
1 milligram=	0.000 032 151	0.000 002 679	0.000 002 205	1	0.001	0.000 001
1 gram=	0.032 150 75	0.002 679 229	0.002 204 623	1000	1	0.001
1 kilogram=	32.150 75	2.679 229	2.204 623	1 000 000	1000	1

Units of Mass Not Less than Avoirdupois Ounces

Units	Avdp oz	Avdp lb	Short cwt	Short tons	Long tons	Kilograms	Metric tons
1 oz av=	1	0.0625	0.000 625	0.000 031 25	0.000 027 902	0.028 349 523	0.000 028 350
1 lb av=	16	1	0.01	0.000 5	0.000 446 429	0.453 592 37	0.000 453 592
1 sh cwt=	1 600	100	1	0.05	0.044 642 86	45.359 237	0.045 359 237
1 sh ton=	32 000	2000	20	1	0.892 857 1	907.184 74	0.907 184 74
1 long ton=	35 840	2240	22.4	1.12	1	1016.046 908 8	1.016 046 909
1 kg=	35.273 96	2.204 623	0.022 046 23	0.001 102 311	0.000 984 207	1	0.001
1 metric ton=	35 273.96	2 204.623	22.046 23	1.102 311	0.984 206 5	1000	1

Units of Volume

Units	Cubic inches	Cubic feet	Cubic yards	Cubic cm	Cubic dm	Cubic meters
1 cubic inch=	1	0.000 578 704	0.000 021 433	16.387 064	0.016 387	0.000 016 387
1 cubic foot=	1728	1	0.037 037 04	28 316.846 592	28.316 847	0.028 316 847
1 cubic yard=	46 656	27	1	764 554.857 984	764.554 858	0.764 554 858
1 cubic cm=	0.061 023 74	0.000 035 315	0.000 001 308	1	0.001	0.000 001
1 cubic dm=	61.023 74	0.035 314 67	0.001 307 951	1 000	1	0.001
1 cubic meter	61 023.74	35.314 67	1.307 951	1 000 000	1000	1

Units of Capacity (Liquid Measure)

Units	Minims	Fluid drams	Fluid ounces	Gills	Liquid pt
1 minim=	1	0.016 666 7	0.002 083 33	0.000 520 833	0.000 130 208
1 fluid dram=	60	1	0.125	0.031 25	0.007 812 5
1 fluid ounce=	480	8	1	0.25	0.062 5
1 gill=	1920	32	4	1	0.25
1 liquid pint=	7680	128	16	4	1
1 liquid quart=	15 360	256	32	8	2
1 gallon=	61 440	1024	128	32	8
1 cubic inch=	265.974	4.432 900	0.554 112 6	0.138 528 1	0.034 632 03
1 cubic foot=	459 603.1	7 660.052	957.506 5	239.376 6	59.844 16
1 milliliter=	16.230 73	0.270 512 18	0.033 814 02	0.008 453 506	.002 113 376
1 liter=	16 230.73	270.512 18	33.814 02	8.453 506	2.113 376

Units	Liquid quarts	Gallons	Cubic inches	Cubic feet	Liters
1 minim=	0.000 065 104 17	0.000 016 276 04	0.003 759 766	0.000 002 175 790	0.000 061 611 52
1 flu. dram=	0.003 906 25	0.000 976 562 5	0.225 585 9	0.000 130 547 4	0.003 696 691
1 fluid oz=	0.031 25	0.007 812 5	1.804 687 5	0.001 044 379	0.029 573 53
1 gill=	0.125	0.031 25	7.218 75	0.004 177 517	0.118 294 118
1 liquid pt=	0.5	0.125	28.875	0.016 710 07	0.473 176 473
1 liquid qt=	1	0.25	57.75	0.033 420 14	0.946 352 946
1 gallon=	4	1	231	0.133 680 6	3.785 411 784
1 cubic in.=	0.017 316 02	0.004 329 004	1	0.000 578 703 7	0.016 387 064
1 cubic foot=	29.922 08	7.480 519	1728	1	28.316 846 592
1 liter=	1.056 688	0.264 172 05	61.023 74	0.035 314 67	1

Units of Capacity (Dry Measure)

Units	Dry pints	Dry quarts	Pecks	Bushels	Cubic in.	Liters
1 dry pint=	1	0.5	0.062 5	0.015 625	33.600 312 5	0.550 610 47
1 dry quart=	2	1	0.125	0.031 25	67.200 625	1.101 220 9
1 peck=	16	8	1	0.25	537.605	8.809 767 5
1 bushel=	64	32	4	1	2150.42	35.239 07
1 cubic inch=	0.029 761 6	0.014 880 8	0.001 860 10	0.000 465 025	1	0.016 387 06
1 liter=	1.816 166	0.908 083	0.113 510 37	0.028 377 59	61.023 74	1

Miscellaneous Measures

Caliber—the diameter of a gun bore. In the U.S., caliber is traditionally expressed in hundredths of inches, eg. .22 or .30. In Britain, caliber is often expressed in thousandths of inches, eg. .270 or .465. Now, it is commonly expressed in millimeters, eg. the 7.62 mm. M14 rifle and the 5.56 mm. M16 rifle. Heavier weapons' caliber has long been expressed in millimeters, eg. the 81 mm. mortar, the 105 mm. howitzer (light), the 155 mm. howitzer (medium or heavy).

Naval guns' caliber refers to the barrel length as a multiple of the bore diameter. A 5-inch, 50-caliber naval gun has a 5-inch bore and a barrel length of 250 inches.

Carat, karat—a measure of the amount of alloy per 24 parts in gold. Thus 24-carat gold is pure; 18-carat gold is one-fourth alloy.

Decibel (dB)—a measure of the relative loudness or intensity of sound. A 20-decibel sound is 10 times louder than a 10-decibel sound; 30 decibels is 100 times louder; 40 decibels is 1,000 times louder, etc. One decibel is the smallest difference between sounds detectable by the human ear. A 120-decibel sound is painful.

10 decibels	– a light whisper
20	– quiet conversation
30	– normal conversation
40	– light traffic
50	– typewriter, loud conversation
60	– noisy office
70	– normal traffic, quiet train
80	– rock music, subway
90	– heavy traffic, thunder
100	– jet plane at takeoff

Em—a printer's measure designating the square width of any given type size. Thus, an em of 10-point type is 10 points. An en is half an em.

Gauge—a measure of shotgun bore diameter. Gauge numbers originally referred to the number of lead balls of the gun barrel diameter in a pound. Thus, a 16 gauge shotgun's bore was smaller than a 12-gauge shotgun's. Today, an international agreement assigns millimeter measures to each gauge, eg:

Gauge	Bore diameter in mm
6	23.34
10	19.67
12	18.52
14	17.60
16	16.81
20	15.90

Horsepower—the power needed to lift 550 pounds one foot in one second, or to lift 33,000 pounds one foot in one minute. Equivalent to 746 watts or 2,546.0756 Btu/h.

Quire—25 sheets of paper

Ream—500 sheets of paper

Electrical Units

The **watt** is the unit of power (electrical, mechanical, thermal, etc.). Electrical power is given by the product of the voltage and the current.

Energy is sold by the **joule**, but in common practice the billing of electrical energy is expressed in terms of the kilowatt-hour, which is 3,600,000 joules or 3.6 megajoules.

The **horsepower** is a non-metric unit sometimes used in mechanics. It is equal to 746 watts.

The **ohm** is the unit of electrical resistance and represents the physical property of a conductor that offers a resistance to the flow of electricity, permitting just 1 ampere to flow at 1 volt of pressure.

Compound Interest

Compounded Annually

Principal $100	Period	4%	5%	6%	7%	8%	9%	10%	12%	14%	16%
	1 day	0.011	0.014	0.016	0.019	0.022	0.025	0.027	0.033	0.038	0.044
	1 week	0.077	0.096	0.115	0.134	0.153	0.173	0.192	0.230	0.268	0.307
	6 mos.	2.00	2.50	3.00	3.50	4.00	4.50	5.00	6.00	7.00	8.00
	1 year	4.00	5.00	6.00	7.00	8.00	9.00	10.00	12.00	14.00	16.00
	2 years	8.16	10.25	12.36	14.49	16.64	18.81	21.00	25.44	29.96	34.56
	3 years	12.49	15.76	19.10	22.50	25.97	29.50	33.10	40.49	48.15	56.09
	4 years	16.99	21.55	26.25	31.08	36.05	41.16	46.41	57.35	68.90	81.06
	5 years	21.67	27.63	33.82	40.26	46.93	53.86	61.05	76.23	92.54	110.03
	6 years	26.53	34.01	41.85	50.07	58.69	67.71	77.16	97.38	119.50	143.64
	7 years	31.59	40.71	50.36	60.58	71.38	82.80	94.87	121.07	150.23	182.62
	8 years	36.86	47.75	59.38	71.82	85.09	99.26	114.36	147.60	185.26	227.84
	9 years	42.33	55.13	68.95	83.85	99.90	117.19	135.79	177.31	225.19	280.30
	10 years	48.02	62.89	79.08	96.72	115.89	136.74	159.37	210.58	270.72	341.14
	12 years	60.10	79.59	101.22	125.22	151.82	181.27	213.84	289.60	381.79	493.60
	15 years	80.09	107.89	139.66	175.90	217.22	264.25	317.72	447.36	613.79	826.55
	20 years	119.11	165.33	220.71	286.97	366.10	460.44	572.75	864.63	1,274.35	1,846.08

Ancient Measures

Biblical
Cubit	=	21.8 inches
Omer	=	0.45 peck
		3.964 liters
Ephah	=	10 omers
Shekel	=	0.497 ounce
		14.1 grams

Greek
Cubit	=	18.3 inches
Stadion	=	607.2 or 622 feet
Obolos	=	715.38 milligrams
Drachma	=	4.2923 grams
Mina	=	0.9463 pounds
Talent	=	60 mina

Roman
Cubit	=	17.5 inches
Stadium	=	202 yards
As, libra,	=	325.971 grams,
pondus		.71864 pounds

Weight of Water

1	cubic inch	.0360 pound	1	imperial gallon	10.0 pounds
12	cubic inches	.433 pound	11.2	imperial gallons	112.0 pounds
1	cubic foot	62.4 pounds	224	imperial gallons	2240.0 pounds
1	cubic foot	7.48052 U.S. gal	1	U.S. gallon	8.33 pounds
1.8	cubic feet	112.0 pounds	13.45	U.S. gallons	112.0 pounds
35.96	cubic feet	2240.0 pounds	269.0	U.S. gallons	2240.0 pounds

Density of Gases and Vapors

at 0°C and 760 mmHg

Source: National Institute of Standards and Technology (kilograms per cubic meter)

Gas	Wgt.	Gas	Wgt.	Gas	Wgt.
Acetylene	1.171	Ethylene	1.260	Methyl fluoride	1.545
Air	1.293	Fluorine	1.696	Mono methylamine	1.38
Ammonia	.759	Helium	.178	Neon	.900
Argon	1.784	Hydrogen	.090	Nitric oxide	1.341
Arsine	3.48	Hydrogen bromide	3.50	Nitrogen	1.250
Butane-iso	2.60	Hydrogen chloride	1.639	Nitrosyl chloride	2.99
Butane-n	2.519	Hydrogen iodide	5.724	Nitrous oxide	1.997
Carbon dioxide	1.977	Hydrogen selenide	3.66	Oxygen	1.429
Carbon monoxide	1.250	Hydrogen sulfide	1.539	Phosphine	1.48
Carbon oxysulfide	2.72	Krypton	3.745	Propane	2.020
Chlorine	3.214	Methane	.717	Silicon tetrafluoride	4.67
Chlorine monoxide	3.89	Methyl chloride	2.25	Sulfur dioxide	2.927
Ethane	1.356	Methyl ether	2.091	Xenon	5.897

Temperature Conversion Table

The numbers in bold face type refer to the temperature either in degrees Celsius or Fahrenheit which are to be converted. If converting from degrees Fahrenheit to Celsius, the equivalent will be found in the column on the left, while if converting from degrees Celsius to Fahrenheit the answer will be found in the column on the right.

For temperatures not shown. To convert Fahrenheit to Celsius subtract 32 degrees and multiply by 5, divide by 9; to convert Celsius to Fahrenheit, multiply by 9, divide by 5 and add 32 degrees.

Celsius		Fahrenheit	Celsius		Fahrenheit	Celsius		Fahrenheit
− 273.2	− 459.7		− 17.8	0	32	35.0	95	203
− 184	− 300		− 12.2	10	50	36.7	98	208.4
− 169	− 273	− 459.4	− 6.67	20	68	37.8	100	212
− 157	− 250	− 418	− 1.11	30	86	43	110	230
− 129	− 200	− 328	4.44	40	104	49	120	248
− 101	− 150	− 238	10.0	50	122	54	130	266
− 73.3	− 100	− 148	15.6	60	140	60	140	284
− 45.6	− 50	− 58	21.1	70	158	66	150	302
− 40.0	− 40	− 40	23.9	75	167	93	200	392
− 34.4	− 30	− 22	26.7	80	176	121	250	482
− 28.9	− 20	− 4	29.4	85	185	149	300	572
− 23.3	− 10	14	32.2	90	194			

Boiling and Freezing Points of Water

Water boils at 212°F at sea level. For every 550 feet above sea level, boiling point of water is lower by about 1°F. Methyl alcohol boils at 148°F. Average human oral temperature, 98.6°F. Water freezes at 32°F. Although "Centigrade" is still frequently used, the International Committee on Weights and Measures and the National Institute of Standards have recommended since 1948 that this scale be called "Celsius."

Breaking the Sound Barrier; Speed of Sound

The prefix Mach is used to describe supersonic speed. It derives from Ernst Mach, a Czech-born German physicist, who contributed to the study of sound. When a plane moves at the speed of sound it is Mach 1. When twice the speed of sound it is Mach 2. When it is near but below the speed of sound its speed can be designated at less than Mach 1, for example, Mach .90. Mach is defined as "in jet propulsion, the ratio of the velocity of a rocket or a jet to the velocity of sound in the medium being considered."

When a plane passes the sound barrier—flying faster than sound travels—listeners in the area hear thunderclaps, but pilots do not hear them.

Sound is produced by vibrations of an object and is transmitted by alternate increase and decrease in pressures that radiate outward through a material media of molecules —somewhat like waves spreading out on a pond after a rock has been tossed into it.

The frequency of sound is determined by the number of times the vibrating waves undulate per second, and is measured in cycles per second. The slower the cycle of waves, the lower the frequency. As frequencies increase, the sound is higher in pitch.

Sound is audible to human beings only if the frequency falls within a certain range. The human ear is usually not sensitive to frequencies of less than 20 vibrations per second, or more than about 20,000 vibrations per second—although this range varies among individuals. Anything at a pitch higher than the human ear can hear is termed ultrasonic.

Intensity or loudness is the strength of the pressure of these radiating waves, and is measured in decibels. The human ear responds to intensity in a range from zero to 120 decibels. Any sound with pressure over 120 decibels is painful.

The speed of sound is generally placed at 1,088 feet per second at sea level at 32°F. It varies in other temperatures and in different media. Sound travels faster in water than in air, and even faster in iron and steel. If in air it travels a mile in 5 seconds, it does a mile under water in 1 second, and through iron in $\frac{1}{3}$ of a second. It travels through ice cold vapor at approximately 4,708 feet per second, ice-cold water, 4,938; granite, 12,960; hardwood, 12,620; brick, 11,960; glass, 16,410 to 19,690; silver, 8,658; gold, 5,717.

Colors of the Spectrum

Color, an electromagnetic wave phenomenon, is a sensation produced through the excitation of the retina of the eye by rays of light. The colors of the spectrum may be produced by viewing a light beam refracted by passage through a prism, which breaks the light into its wave lenghts.

Customarily, the primary colors of the spectrum are thought of as those 6 monochromatic colors that occupy relatively large areas of the spectrum: red, orange, yellow, green, blue, and violet. However, Sir Isaac Newton named a 7th, indigo, situated between blue and violet on the spectrum. Aubert estimated (1865) the solar spectrum to contain approximately 1,000 distinguishable hues of which according to Rood (1881) 2 million tints and shades can be distinguished; Luckiesh stated (1915) that 55 distinctly different hues have been seen in a single spectrum.

Many physicists recognize only 3 primary colors: red, yellow, and blue (Mayer, 1775); red, green, and violet (Thomas Young, 1801); red, green, and blue (Clerk Maxwell, 1860).

The color sensation of black is due to complete lack of stimulation of the retina, that of white to complete stimulation. The infra-red and ultra-violet rays, below the red (long) end of the spectrum and above the violet (short) end respectively, are invisible to the naked eye. Heat is the principal effect of the infra-red rays and chemical action that of the ultra-violet rays.

Common Fractions Reduced to Decimals

8ths	16ths	32ds	64ths		8ths	16ths	32ds	64ths		8ths	16ths	32ds	64ths	
			1	.015625				23	.359375				45	.703125
		1	2	.03125	3	6	12	24	.375				46	.71875
			3	.046875				25	.390625				47	.734375
	1	2	4	.0625			13	26	.40625	6	12	24	48	.75
			5	.078125				27	.421875				49	.765625
		3	6	.09375		7	14	28	.4375			25	50	.78125
			7	.109375				29	.453125				51	.796875
1	2	4	8	.125			15	30	.46875		13	26	52	.8125
			9	.140625				31	.484375				53	.828125
		5	10	.15625	4	8	16	32	.5			27	54	.84375
			11	.171875				33	.515625				55	.859375
	3	6	12	.1875			17	34	.53125	7	14	28	56	.875
			13	.203125				35	.546875				57	.890625
		7	14	.21875		9	18	36	.5625			29	58	.90625
			15	.234375				37	.578125				59	.921875
2	4	8	16	.25			19	38	.59375		15	30	60	.9375
			17	.265625				39	.609375				61	.953125
		9	18	.28125	5	10	20	40	.625			31	62	.96875
			19	.296875				41	.640625				63	.984375
	5	10	20	.3125			21	42	.65625	8	16	32	64	1.
			21	.328125				43	.671875					
		11	22	.34375		11	22	44	.6875					

Spirits Measures

Pony . . . . 0.5 jigger

Shot . . . . { 0.666 jigger / 1.0 ounce

Jigger . . . . 1.5 shot

Pint . . . . { 16 shots / 0.625 fifth

Fifth . . . . { 25.6 shots / 1.6 pints / 0.8 quart / 0.75706 liter

Quart . . . . { 32 shots / 1.25 fifth

Magnum . . . . { 2 quarts / 2.49797 bottles (wine)

For champagne and brandy only:

Jeroboam . . . . . { 6.4 shots / 1.6 magnum / 0.8 gallon

For champagne only:

Rehoboam	. . . .	3 magnums
Methuselah	. . . .	4 magnums
Salmanazar	. . . .	6 magnums
Balthazar	. . . .	8 magnums
Nebuchadnezzar	.	10 magnums

Wine bottle (standard):

. . . . { 0.800633 quart / 0.7576778 liter

Mathematical Formulas

To find the CIRCUMFERENCE of a:

Circle — Multiply the diameter by 3.14159265 (usually 3.1416).

To find the AREA of a:

Circle — Multiply the square of the diameter by .785398 (usually .7854).

Rectangle — Multiply the length of the base by the height.

Sphere (surface) — Multiply the square of the radius by 3.1416 and multiply by 4.

Square — Square the length of one side.

Trapezoid — Add the two parallel sides, multiply by the height and divide by 2.

Triangle — Multiply the base by the height and divide by 2.

To find the VOLUME of a:

Cone — Multiply the square of the radius of the base by 3.1416, multiply by the height, and divide by 3.

Cube — Cube the length of one edge.

Cylinder — Multiply the square of the radius of the base by 3.1416 and multiply by the height.

Pyramid — Multiply the area of the base by the height and divide by 3.

Rectangular Prism — Multiply the length by the width by the height.

Sphere — Multiply the cube of the radius by 3.1416, multiply by 4 and divide by 3.

Playing Cards and Dice Chances

Poker Hands

Hand	Number possible	Odds against
Royal flush	4	649,739 to 1
Other straight flush	36	72,192 to 1
Four of a kind	624	4,164 to 1
Full house	3,744	693 to 1
Flush	5,108	508 to 1
Straight	10,200	254 to 1
Three of a kind	54,912	46 to 1
Two pairs	123,552	20 to 1
One pair	1,098,240	4 to 3 (1.37 to 1)
Nothing	1,302,540	1 to 1
Total	**2,598,960**	

Dice
(probabilities on 2 dice)

Total	Odds against (Single toss)	Total	Odds against (Single toss)
2	35 to 1	8	31 to 5
3	17 to 1	9	8 to 1
4	11 to 1	10	11 to 1
5	8 to 1	11	17 to 1
6	31 to 5	12	35 to 1
7	5 to 1		

Dice
(Probabilities of consecutive winning plays)

No. consecutive wins	By 7, 11 or point	No. consecutive wins	By 7, 11 or point
1	244 in 495	6	1 in 70
2	6 in 25	7	1 in 141
3	3 in 25	8	1 in 287
4	1 in 17	9	1 in 582
5	1 in 34		

Pinochle Auction
(Odds against finding in "widow" of 3 cards)

Open places	Odds against	Open places	Odds against
1	5 to 1	4	3 to 2 for
2	2 to 1	5	2 to 1 for
3	Even		

Bridge
The odds—against suit distribution in a hand of 4-4-3-2 are about 4 to 1, against 5-4-2-2 about 8 to 1, against 6-4-2-1 about 20 to 1, against 7-4-1-1 about 254 to 1, against 8-4-1-0 about 2,211 to 1, and against 13-0-0-0 about 158,753,389,899 to 1.

Measures of Force and Pressure

Dyne = force necessary to accelerate a 1-gram mass 1 centimeter per second squared = 0.000072 poundal

Poundal = force necessary to accelerate a 1-pound mass 1 foot per second squared = 13,825.5 dynes = 0.138255 newtons

Newton = force needed to accelerate a 1-kilogram mass 1 meter per second squared

Pascal (pressure) = 1 newton per square meter = 0.020885 pound per square foot

Atmosphere (air pressure at sea level) = 2,116.102 pounds per square foot = 14.6952 pounds per square inch = 1.0332 kilograms per square centimeter = 101,323 newtons per square meter.

Large Numbers

U.S.	Number of zeros	French British, German	U.S.	Number of zeros	French British, German
million	6	million	sextillion	21	1,000 trillion
billion	9	milliard	septillion	24	quadrillion
trillion	12	billion	octillion	27	1,000 quadrillion
quadrillion	15	1,000 billion	nonillion	30	quintillion
quintillion	18	trillion	decillion	33	1,000 quintillion

Roman Numerals

I	–	1	VI	–	6	XI	–	11	L	–	50	CD	–	400	$\overline{\text{X}}$ – 10,000
II	–	2	VII	–	7	XIX	–	19	LX	–	60	D	–	500	$\overline{\text{L}}$ – 50,000
III	–	3	VIII	–	8	XX	–	20	XC	–	90	CM	–	900	$\overline{\text{C}}$ – 100,000
IV	–	4	IX	–	9	XXX	–	30	C	–	100	M	–	1,000	$\overline{\text{D}}$ – 500,000
V	–	5	X	–	10	XL	–	40	CC	–	200	$\overline{\text{V}}$	–	5,000	$\overline{\text{M}}$ – 1,000,000

ARTS AND MEDIA

Notable Movies of the Year (Aug. 1990 to Aug. 1991)

Movie	Stars	Director
Alice	Mia Farrow, Alec Baldwin, William Hurt, Keye Luke	Woody Allen
Avalon	Armin Mueller-Stahl, Aiden Quinn, Elizabeth Perkins	Barry Levinson
Awakenings	Robert De Niro, Robin Williams	Penny Marshall
Backdraft	Kurt Russell, William Baldwin, Robert De Niro	Ron Howard
Bonfire of the Vanities	Tom Hanks, Bruce Willis, Melanie Griffin	Brian DePalma
Boyz N the Hood	Ice Cube, Cuba Gooding Jr., Morris Chestnut	John Singleton
City Slickers	Billy Crystal, Daniel Stern, Bruno Kirby	Ron Underwood
Dances with Wolves	Kevin Costner, Mary McDonnell	Kevin Costner
Defending Your Life	Albert Brooks, Meryl Streep	Albert Brooks
Dying Young	Julia Roberts, Campbell Scott	Joel Schumacher
GoodFellas	Robert De Niro, Ray Liotta, Joe Pesci	Martin Scorsese
Green Card	Gerald Depardieu, Andie MacDowell	Peter Weir
Havana	Robert Redford, Lena Olin, Alan Arkin	Sydney Pollack
Home Alone	Macaulay Culkin, Joe Pesci, Daniel Stern	Chris Columbus
Jungle Fever	Wesley Snipes, Annabella Sciorra, Spike Lee, Ossie Davis	Spike Lee
Kindergarten Cop	Arnold Schwarzenegger, Penelope Ann Miller	Ivan Reitman
L.A. Story	Steve Martin, Victoria Tennant, Marilu Henner	Mick Jackson
Memphis Belle	Matthew Modine, Eric Stoltz, D.B. Sweeney	Michael Caton-Jones
Mermaids	Cher, Winona Ryder, Bob Hoskins	Richard Benjamin
Miller's Crossing	Gabriel Byrne, Albert Finney, Marcia Gay Harden	Joel & Ethan Coen
Misery	James Caan, Kathy Bates	Rob Reiner
Mortal Thoughts	Demi Moore, Bruce Willis, Glenne Headly	Alan Rudolph
New Jack City	Wesley Snipes, Ice T, Judd Nelson	Mario Van Peebles
Once Around	Richard Dreyfuss, Holly Hunter, Danny Aiello	Lasse Hallstrom
Pacific Heights	Melanie Griffith, Matthew Modine, Michael Keaton	John Schlesinger
Postcards From the Edge	Meryl Streep, Shirley MacLaine, Dennis Quaid	Mike Nichols
Pump Up the Volume	Christian Slater, Ellen Greene, Scott Paulin	Allan Moyle
Reversal of Fortune	Glenn Close, Jeremy Irons, Ron Silver	Barbet Schroeder
Robin Hood: Prince of Thieves	Kevin Costner, Morgan Freeman, Alan Rickman	Kevin Reynolds
Rocky V	Sylvester Stallone, Talia Shire, Burt Young	John Avildsen
Sleeping With the Enemy	Julia Roberts, Patrick Bergin, Kevin Anderson	Joseph Ruben
State of Grace	Sean Penn, Ed Harris, Gary Oldman	Phil Joanou
Terminator 2: Judgement Day	Arnold Schwarzenegger, Linda Hamilton, Robert Patrick	James Cameron
Texasville	Jeff Bridges, Cybill Shepherd, Annie Potts, Cloris Leachman	Peter Bogdanovich
The Field	Richard Harris, Tom Berenger, John Hurt	Jim Sheridan
The Five Heartbeats	Robert Townsend, Michael Wright, Harry J. Lennix	Robert Townsend
The Godfather Part III	Al Pacino, Diane Keaton, Andy Garcia, Eli Wallach	Francis Coppola
The Grifters	Anjelica Huston, John Cusack, Annette Bening	Stephen Frears
The Naked Gun 2½	Leslie Nielsen, Priscilla Presley, George Kennedy	David Zucker
The Rocketeer	Bill Campbell, Jennifer Connelly, Alan Arkin	Joe Johnston
The Sheltering Sky	Debra Winger, John Malkovich	Bernardo Bertolucci
The Silence of the Lambs	Jodie Foster, Anthony Hopkins, Scott Glenn	Jonathan Demme
Thelma & Louise	Susan Sarandon, Geena Davis	Ridley Scott
Three Men and a Little Lady	Tom Selleck, Ted Danson, Steve Guttenberg	Emile Ardolino
Wild at Heart	Nicolas Cage, Laura Dern, Willem Dafoe	David Lynch

Notable New York Theater Openings, 1990-91 Season

Absent Friends, comedy by Alan Ayckbourn; with Brenda Blethyn, Peter Frechette, David Purdham, and Gillian Anderson.

Abundance, play by Beth Henley; with Tess Harper and Amanda Plummer.

Assassins, musical revue by Stephen Sondheim; with Victor Garber, Annie Golden, Terrence Mann, and Jace Alexander.

Mule Bone, production of a Langston Hughes and Zora Neale Hurston 1930s collaboration; with Leonard Jackson, Theresa Merritt, Reggie Montgomery, and Eric Ware.

Buddy, play based on the life and music of rock and roll legend Buddy Holly; with Paul Hipp.

Carnal Knowledge, play by Jules Feiffer; with Jon Cryer, Judd Nelson, Justine Bateman, and Karen Byers.

Fiddler on the Roof, revival of the Jerry Bock-Sheldon Harnick musical classic; with Topol.

I Hate Hamlet, comedy by Paul Rudnick; with Nicol Williamson, Evan Handler, and Celeste Holm.

Lost in Yonkers, play by Neil Simon; with Irene Worth, Mercedes Ruehl, and Kevin Spacey.

Lucifer's Child, play by William Luce; with Julie Harris.

Miss Saigon, musical by Claude-Michel Schonberg, Alain Boublil, and Richard Maltby Jr.; with Jonathan Pryce, Lea Salonga, Willy Falk, and Hinton Battle.

Oh, Kay!, revival of the 1926 George and Ira Gershwin musical; with Brian Mitchell, Angela Teek, and Gregg Burge.

Our Country's Good, play by Timberlake Wertenbaker based on a novel by Thomas Keneally; with Tracey Ellis, Peter Frechette, Cherry Jones, Ron McLarty, and Richard Poe.

Peter Pan, revival of the musical production by Moose Charlap and Carolyn Leigh based on the James M. Barry play; with Cathy Rigby and Stephen Hanen.

Shadowlands, play by William Nicholson; with Nigel Hawthorne, Jane Alexander, and Michael Allison.

Shogun; The Musical, by Paul Chihara and John Driver based on the James Clavell novel; with Philip Casnoff and June Angela.

States of Shock, drama by Sam Shepard; with John Malkovich and Michael Wincott.

The Big Love, play by Brooke Allen and Jay Presson; with Tracey Ullman.

The Country Girl, revival of the Clifford Odets drama; with Karen Allen, David Rasche, and Paul McCrane.

The Miser, revival of the Moliere classic; with Philip Bosco, Carole Shelley, and John Christopher Jones.

The Old Boy, by A.R. Gurney; with Stephen Collins, Matt McGrath, and Lizabeth Mackay.

The Secret Garden, musical by Lucy Simon and Marsha Norman based on the Frances Hodgson Burnett novel; with Mandy Patinkin and Daisy Eagan.

The Speed of Darkness, play by Steve Tesich; with Len Cariou, Stephen Lang, Lisa Eichhorn, and Kathryn Erbe.

The Will Rogers Follies, musical by Cy Coleman, Betty Comden, and Adolph Green; directed and choreographed by Tommy Tune; with Keith Carradine, Dee Hoty, and Candy Huffman.

Record Long Run Broadway Plays[1]

Source: *Variety*

Chorus Line	6,137	Hair	1,750	Funny Girl	1,348
Oh, Calcutta (revival)	5,959	*Les Miserables	1,732	Mumenschanz	1,326
*Cats	3,645	The Wiz	1,672	Oh! Calcutta! (original)	1,314
42d Street	3,486	Born Yesterday	1,642	Brighton Beach Memoirs	1,299
Grease	3,388	Ain't Misbehavin'	1,604	Angel Street	1,295
Fiddler on the Roof	3,242	Best Little Whorehouse in Texas	1,584	Lightnin'	1,291
Life With Father	3,224	Mary, Mary	1,572	Promises, Promises	1,281
Tobacco Road	3,182	Evita	1,567	The King and I	1,246
Hello Dolly	2,844	Voice of the Turtle	1,557	Cactus Flower	1,234
My Fair Lady	2,717	Barefoot in the Park	1,530	Sleuth	1,222
Annie	2,377	Dreamgirls	1,521	Torch Song Trilogy	1,222
Man of La Mancha	2,328	Mame	1,508	"1776"	1,217
Abie's Irish Rose	2,327	Same Time, Next Year	1,453	Equus	1,209
Oklahoma!	2,212	Arsenic and Old Lace	1,444	Sugar Babies	1,208
Pippin	1,944	The Sound of Music	1,443	Guys and Dolls	1,200
South Pacific	1,925	*Phantom of the Opera	1,431	Amadeus	1,181
Magic Show	1,920	How To Succeed in Business		Cabaret	1,165
Deathtrap	1,792	Without Really Trying	1,417	Mister Roberts	1,157
Gemini	1,788	Me and My Girl	1,412	Annie Get Your Gun	1,147
Harvey	1,775	Hellzapoppin	1,404	Seven Year Itch	1,141
Dancin'	1,774	The Music Man	1,375	Butterflies Are Free	1,128
La Cage aux Folles	1,761				

(1) Number of performances through June 30, 1991. * Still running June 30, 1991.

All-Time Top 50 American Movies

Source: *Variety*, Jan. 1991

Rental figures are in absolute dollars, reflecting actual amounts received by the distributors (estimated for movies in current release). Ticket price inflation favors recent films, but older films have the advantage of numerous reissues adding to their totals.

Rank/Title/Date	Total Rentals	Rank/Title/Date	Total Rentals	Rank/Title/Date	Total Rentals
1. E.T. The Extra-Terrestrial (1982)	$228,618,939	19. Superman (1978)	82,800,000	36. Honey, I Shrunk The Kids* (1989)	72,007,000
2. Star Wars (1977)	193,500,000	20. Close Encounters Of The Third Kind (1977/1980)	82,750,000	37. National Lampoon's Animal House (1978)	70,826,000
3. Return of the Jedi (1983)	168,002,414	21. **Pretty Woman** (1990)	81,903,000	38. Crocodile Dundee (1986)	70,227,000
4. Batman (1989)	150,500,000	22. Three Men And A Baby (1987)	81,356,000	39. Fatal Attraction (1987)	70,000,000
5. The Empire Strikes Back (1980)	141,600,000	23. Who Framed Roger Rabbit (1988)	81,244,000	40. Platoon (1986)	69,742,143
6. Ghostbusters* (1984)	132,720,000	24. Beverly Hills Cop II (1987)	80,857,776	41. **Look Who's Talking** (1989)	68,365,000
7. Jaws (1975)	129,549,325	25. Home Alone (1990)	80,000,000	42. Die Hard 2 (1990)	66,500,000
8. Raiders Of The Lost Ark (1981)	115,598,000	26. The Sound Of Music* (1965)	79,800,000	43. Rocky III (1982)	66,262,796
9. Indiana Jones and The Last Crusade (1989)	115,500,000	27. Gremlins (1984)	79,500,000	44. Superman II (1981)	65,100,000
10. Indiana Jones and The Temple Of Doom (1984)	109,000,000	27. Lethal Weapon 2 (1989)	79,500,000	45. Coming To America (1988)	65,000,000
11. Beverly Hills Cop (1984)	108,000,000	29. Top Gun (1986)	79,400,000	45. **Total Recall** (1990)	65,000,000
12. Back to the Future* (1985)	105,493,534	30. Gone With The Wind (1939)	79,375,077	47. **Teenage Mutant Ninja Turtles** (1990)	62,000,000
13. Grease (1978)	96,300,000	31. Rambo: First Blood Part II (1985)	78,919,250	48. Snow White And The Seven Dwarfs (1937)	61,752,000
14. Tootsie* (1982)	94,910,000	32. The Sting (1973)	78,212,000	49. On Golden Pond* (1981)	61,175,028
15. **Ghost** (1990)	94,000,000	33. Rocky IV (1985)	76,023,246	50. The Jungle Book (1967)	60,964,000
16. The Exorcist (1973)	89,000,000	34. Saturday Night Fever (1977)	74,100,000		
17. Rain Man* (1989)	86,813,000	35. Back To The Future, Part II* (1989)	72,285,899		
18. The Godfather (1972)	86,275,000				

Note: Boldface print = film new to list or significant improvement since previous year; * rentals adjusted since last report.

Top 50 Movies, 1990

Source: *Variety*, Jan. 1991

Figures represent U.S. and Canadian rentals accruing to distributors, not total ticket sales receipts taken in at theaters.

Rank/Title/Month Released	Total Rentals	Rank/Title/Month Released	Total Rentals	Rank/Title/Month Released	Total Rentals
1. Ghost; July	$94,000,000	10. Back To The Future, Part III; May	48,951,109	18. Dances With Wolves; Nov.	29,000,000
2. Pretty Woman; March	81,903,000	11. Presumed Innocent; August	43,800,000	19. Flatliners; August	28,800,000
3. Home Alone; 1990	80,000,000	12. Another 48 HRS.; June	40,100,000	20. The Godfather, Part III; Dec.	28,000,000
4. Die Hard 2; July	66,500,000	13. Days Of Thunder; June	40,000,000	21. Three Men And A Little Lady; Nov.	25,000,000
5. Total Recall; June	65,000,000	14. Bird On A Wire; May	38,402,931	22. Problem Child; July	24,368,353
6. Teenage Mutant Ninja Turtles; March	62,000,000	15. Born On The Fourth Of July; Dec. 1989	36,789,030	23. Robocop 2; June	22,317,000
7. Dick Tracy; June	59,526,000	16. Arachnophobia; July	31,019,000	24. The Jungle Book; June reissue	21,464,000
8. The Hunt For Red October; March	58,500,000	17. Hard To Kill; Feb.	30,000,000		
9. Driving Miss Daisy; 1990	49,500,000				

(continued)

Rank/Title/Month Released	Total Rentals
25. Gremlins 2: The New Batch; June	20,800,000
26. Marked For Death; Oct.	20,000,000
26. Misery; Nov.	20,000,000
26. Rocky V; Nov.	20,000,000
29. Young Guns II; August	19,700,000
30. Joe Versus The Volcano; March	18,900,000
31. Goodfellas; Sept.	18,200,000
32. Postcards From The Edge; Sept.	17,500,000
33. Darkman; August	16,011,825

Rank/Title/Month Released	Total Rentals
34. Kindergarten Cop; Dec.	16,000,000
35. Air America; August	15,000,000
36. Pacific Heights; Oct.	14,000,000
36. Steel Magnolias; continuing 1989	14,000,000
38. Look Who's Talking; continuing 1989	13,365,000
39. Tango & Cash; continuing 1989	13,100,000
40. Fantasia; reissue	13,000,000
40. Glory; Dec. 1989	13,000,000

Rank/Title/Month Released	Total Rentals
40. Edward Scissorhands; Dec.	13,000,000
40. Predator 2; Nov.	13,000,000
44. Cadillac Man; May	12,547,000
45. Child's Play 2; Nov.	12,507,550
46. Always; continuing 1989	12,260,000
47. House Party; 1990	12,000,000
47. Jacob's Ladder; Nov.	12,000,000
47. Look Who's Talking Too; Dec.	12,000,000
50. Memphis Belle; Oct.	11,700,000

National Film Registry

In accordance with the National Film Preservation Act passed by Congress in 1988, 25 films were placed on the National Film Registry in September 1989 as "culturally, historically, or esthetically significant." Another 25 were chosen in 1990, and 25 more will be chosen in 1991.

Films Chosen in 1989

The Best Years of Our Lives (1946)
Casablanca (1942)
Citizen Kane (1941)
The Crowd (1928)
Dr. Strangelove (or, How I Learned to Stop Worrying and Love the Bomb) (1964)
The General (1927)
Gone With the Wind (1939)
The Grapes of Wrath (1940)
High Noon (1952)
Intolerance (1916)
The Learning Tree (1969)
The Maltese Falcon (1941)
Mr. Smith Goes to Washington (1939)
Modern Times (1936)
Nanook of the North (1921)
On the Waterfront (1954)
The Searchers (1956)
Singin' in the Rain (1952)
Snow White and the Seven Dwarfs (1937)
Some Like It Hot (1959)
Star Wars (1977)
Sunrise (1927)
Sunset Boulevard (1950)
Vertigo (1958)
The Wizard of Oz (1939)

Films Chosen in 1990

All About Eve (1950)
All Quiet on the Western Front (1930)
Bringing Up Baby (1938)
Dodsworth (1936)
Duck Soup (1933)
Fantasia (1940)
The Freshman (1925)
The Godfather (1972)
The Great Train Robbery (1903)
Harlan County, U. S. A. (1976)
How Green Was My Valley (1941)
It's A Wonderful Life (1946)
Killer of Sheep (1977)
Love Me Tonight (1932)
Meshes of the Afternoon (1943)
Ninotchka (1939)
Primary (1960)
Raging Bull (1980)
Rebel Without a Cause (1955)
Red River (1948)
The River (1937)
Sullivan's Travels (1941)
Top Hat (1935)
The Treasure of the Sierra Madre (1948)
A Woman under the Influence (1974)

All-Time Top 50 Foreign-Language Movies in the U.S.

Source: *Variety*, Jan. 1991

(millions of dollars)

Rank/Title/Year of U.S. Distribution	Gross
1. I am Curious (Yellow) (1969)	$19.0
2. La Dolce Vita (1960)	18.0
3. La Cage aux Folles (1979)	17.0
4. Z (1969)	15.0
5. A Man and a Woman (1966)	13.0
6. Emmanuelle (1975)	11.5
7. Cinema Paradiso (1990)	11.3
8. Das Boot (1982)	11.0
9. Story of O (1975)	10.0
10. Eight and a Half (1963)	9.5
11. Yesterday, Today and Tomorrow (1964)	9.2
12. Marriage Italian Style (1964)	9.0
13. Elvira Madigan (1967)	9.0
14. Dear John (1964)	8.8
15. Cousin Cousine (1976)	8.5
16. My Life as a Dog (1987)	8.1
17. Fanny & Alexander (1983)	8.0
18. Women on the Verge of a Nervous Breakdown (1988)	7.5

Rank/Title/Year of U.S. Distribution	Gross
19. Ran (1985)	$7.1
20. Two Women (1961)	7.0
21. Without a Stitch (1970)	6.5
22. Diva (1982)	6.3
23. Swept Away (1975)	6.0
23. La Cage aux Folles II (1981)	6.0
25. Jean de Florette (1987)	5.5
26. King of Hearts (1967)	5.4
26. Au revoir, les enfants (1988)	5.4
28. Babette's Feast (1988)	5.3
29. Madame Rosa (1978)	5.2
30. The Garden of the Finzi-Continis (1971)	5.1
30. Manon of the Spring (1987)	5.1
32. Seven Beauties (1976)	5.0
32. Bread and Chocolate (1978)	5.0
34. Amarcord (1974)	4.7
35. The Emigrants (1972)	4.5
36. Get Out Your Handkerchiefs (1979)	4.3

Rank/Title/Year of U.S. Distribution	Gross
37. Autumn Sonata (1979)	$4.2
37. Entre Nous (1983)	4.2
39. The Innocent (1979)	4.1
39. Tie Me Up! Tie Me Down! (1990)	4.1
41. Satyricon (1970)	4.0
41. Cries and Whispers (1973)	4.0
41. Kagemusha (1980)	4.0
41. The Tin Drum (1980)	4.0
41. Return of Martin Guerre (1982)	4.0
46. Belle de Jour (1969)	3.9
46. Mephisto (1982)	3.9
48. Camille Claudel (1989)	3.8
49. La Traviata (1982)	3.7
50. The Last Metro (1981)	3.5
50. The Official Story (1985)	3.5

Bestselling Books of 1990

Source: *Publishers Weekly*, Jan. 4, 1991

Hardcover Fiction

1. *Oh, the Places You'll Go!*, Dr. Suess
2. *Clear and Present Danger*, Tom Clancy
3. *The Stand: The Complete and Uncut Edition*, Stephen King
   The Burden of Proof, Scott Turow
4. *The Bourne Ultimatum*, Robert Ludlum
5. *September*, Rosamunde Pilcher
6. *Message from Nam*, Danielle Steel
7. *Memories of Midnight*, Sidney Sheldon
   An Inconveniet Woman, Dominick Dunne
8. *Devices and Desires*, P.D. James
9. *Dragon*, Clive Cussler
   Tales from Margaritaville: Fictional Facts and Factual Fancies, Jimmy Buffett

Hardcover Nonfiction

1. *Wealth Without Risk*, Charles Givens
2. *Barbarians at the Gate: The Fall of RJR Nabisco*, Bryan Burrough and John Helyar
3. *Megatrends 2000*, John Naisbitt and Patricia Aburdene
4. *It Was on Fire When I Lay Down on It*, Robert Fulghum
5. *Liar's Poker: Rising Through the Wreckage on Wall Street*, Michael M. Lewis
6. *Men at Work*, George F. Will
7. *Dave Barry Turns 40*, Dave Barry
   You Just Don't Understand: Men and Women in Conversation, Deborah Tannen
8. *Homecoming: Reclaiming and Championing Your Inner Child*, John Bradshaw
   All I Really Needed to Know I Learned in Kindergarten, Robert Fulghum
9. *Secrets About Men Every Woman Should Know*, Barbara DeAngelis
10. *Beware the Naked Man Who Offers You His Shirt*, Harvey Mackay
11. *The Seven Habits of Highly Effective People*, Stephen R. Covey

Trade Paperback

1. *Codependent No More*, Melody Beattie
2. *The T-Factor Fat Gram Counter*, Jamie Pope-Cordle and Martin Katahn
3. *50 Simple Things You Can Do to Save the Earth*, Earthworks Group
4. *Weirdo from Another Planet!* Bill Watterson
5. *Dianetics: Revised Edition*, L. Ron Hubbard
6. *From Beirut to Jerusalem*, Thomas Friedman
7. *Happy Trails!*, Berke Breathed
   A Brief History of Time, Stephen W. Hawking
8. *The Road Less Traveled*, M. Scott Peck

9. *The Authoritative Calvin & Hobbes*, Bill Watterson
10. *Rand McNally Road Atlas 1990*
    50 Simple Things Kids Can Do to Save the Earth, Earthworks Group
    The Secret Diary of Laura Palmer, As Seen by Jennifer Lynch
11. *What to Expect When You're Expecting*, Eisenberg, Murkoff and Hathaway
    The Prehistory of the Far Side, Gary Larson
    The Language of Letting Go, Melody Beattie
    14,000 Things to Be Happy About, Barbar Ann Kipfer
    Liar's Poker, Michael Lewis

Mass Market Paperback

1. *All I Really Needed to Know I Learned in Kindergarten*, Robert Fulghum
2. *The Joy Luck Club*, Amy Tan
3. *Presumed Innocent*, Scott Turow
4. *Clear and Present Danger*, Tom Clancy
5. *The Pillars of the Earth*, Ken Follett
   The Hunt for Red October, Tom Clancy
6. *The Dark Half*, Stephen King
   Oldest Living Confederate Widow Tells All, Allen Gurganus
   While My Pretty One Sleeps, Mary Higgins Clark
   The Russia House, John Le Carre
   A Prayer for Owen Meany, John Irving
   When Rabbit Howls, The Troops for Truddi Chase
7. *The Shell Seekers*, Rosamunde Pilcher
   The Bonfire of the Vanities, Tom Wolfe
   Billy Bathgate, E.L. Doctorow
8. *Postcards from the Edge*, Carrie Fisher
   Garden of Lies, Eileen Goudge
   Star, Danielle Steel
   Web of Dreams, V.C. Andrews
   A Thief of Time, Tony Hillerman

Atlases, Annuals, and Almanacs

1. *The World Almanac & Book of Facts 1991*, Mark S. Hoffman, ed.
2. *J.K. Lasser's, Your Income Tax 1991*
3. *Ernst & Young's Arthur Young Tax Guide 1991*
4. *Old Farmer's Almanac 1991*
5. *The World Almanac & Book of Facts 1990*, Mark S. Hoffman, ed.
6. *Let's Go: Europe*
7. *The Universal Almanac, 1991 edition*, John W. Wright, gen. ed.
8. *1991 Mobil Road Atlas & Trip Planning Guide*, Susan Farewell
9. *Webster's New World Compact School & Office Dictionary*
10. *Old Farmer's Almanac 1990*

All-Time Bestselling Children's Books

Source: *Publishers Weekly*

(The number of copies sold is from the date of original publication through 1988, as estimated by each publisher, and does not include book club or international sales.)

Hardcover

1. *The Tale of Peter Rabbit*, Beatrix Potter, 1902; 9,000,000
2. *Pat the Bunny*, Dorothy Kunhardt, 1940; 4,857,417
3. *The Littlest Angel*, Charles Tazewell, 1946; 4,665,209
4. *The Cat in the Hat*, Dr. Seuss, 1957; 3,693,197
5. *Green Eggs and Ham*, Dr. Seuss, 1960; 3,683,097
6. *The Children's Bible*, 1965; 3,683,097

7. *The Real Mother Goose*, illus. Blanche F. Wright, 1916; 3,600,000
8. *Richard Scarry's Best Word Book Ever*, 1963; 3,303,583
9. *One Fish, Two Fish, Red Fish, Blue Fish*, Dr. Seuss, 1960; 2,970,833
10. *Hop on Pop*, Dr. Seuss, 1963; 2,953,324

Paperback

1. *The Outsiders*, S.E. Hinton, 1968; 5,855,085
2. *Are You There, God? It's Me, Margaret*, Judy Blume, 1974; 5,278,412
3. *Charlotte's Web*, E.B. White, illus. Garth Williams, 1973; 4,607,131
4. *Tales of a Fourth Grade Nothing*, Judy Blume, 1976; 4,582,039
5. *Little House on the Prairie*, Laura Ingalls Wilder, illus. Garth Williams, 1971; 3,803,209

6. *The Little Prince*, Antoine de Saint-Exupery, 1968; 3,667,861
7. *Little House in the Big Woods*, Laura Ingalls Wilder, illus. Garth Williams, 1971; 3,495,079
8. *That Was Then, This Is Now*, S.E. Hinton, 1972; 3,351,194
9. *Where the Red Fern Grows*, Wilson Rawls, 1974; 3,347,000
10. *Superfudge*, Judy Blume, 1981; 3,243,442

Notable Books of 1990

Source: American Library Association

Fiction

The Perez Family, Christine Bell
East Is East, T. Coraghessan Boyle
Possession, A.S. Byatt
Age of Iron, J.M. Coetzee
Seventh Heaven, Alice Hoffman
Animal Dreams, Barbara Kingsolver
Passing On, Penelope Lively
Palace Walk, Naguib Mahfouz

Family Pictures, Sue Miller
Friends of My Youth, Alice Munro
They Things They Carried, Tim O'Brien
Skywater, Melinda Worth Popham
Me and My Baby View the Eclipse, Lee Smith
Collected Stories of Wallace Stegner, Wallace Stegner
In a Father's Place, Christopher Tilghman

Nonfiction

The Natural History of the Senses, Diane Ackerman
Genome: The Story of the Most Astonishing Scientific Adventure of All Time, Jerry E. Bishop and Michael Waldholz
Black in Selma: The Uncommon Life of J.L. Chestnut, Jr., J.L. Chestnut and Julia Cass
Small Victories: The Real World of a Teacher, Her Students & Their High School: Samuel G. Freedman

Through a Window: My Thirty Years with the Chimpanzees of Gombe, Jane Goodall
Legacies: A Chinese Mosaic, Bette Bao Lord
My Traitor's Heart: A South African Exile Returns to Face His Country, His Tribe, and His Conscience, Rian Malan
Photography Until Now, John Szarkowski
Under God: Religion and American Politics, Garry Wills

Notable Children's Books of 1990

Source: American Library Association

Younger Readers

The Wall, Evé Bunting, illustrated by Ronald Himler
Ruby, Michael Emberley
The Day of Ahmed's Secret, Florence Parry Heide & Judith Heide Gilliland, il. Ted Lewin
Julius: The Baby of the World, Kevin Henkes
When I Am Old with You, Angela Johnson, il. David Soman
Aardvarks, Disembark!, Ann Jonas
Cowboy Dreams, Dayal Kaur Khalsa
The Little Dog Laughed, il. Lucy Cousins
Come a Tide, George Ella Lyon, il. Stephen Gammell
The Seven Chinese Brothers, Margaret Mahy, il. Jean Tseng
Fox Be Nimble, James Marshall

One Sun: A Book of Terse Verse, Bruce McMillan
Puss in Boots, Charles Perrault, il. Fred Marcellino
Henry and Mudge and the Happy Cat, Cynthia Rylant, il. Sucie Stevenson
July, James Stevenson
The Very Best of Friends, Margaret Wild, il. Julie Vivas
I Went Walking, Sue Williams, il. Julie Vivas
"More More More" Said the Baby: 3 Love Stories, Vera B. Williams
Sky Dogs, Jane Yolen, il. Barry Moser
The Wheels on the Bus: A Book with Parts That Move, Paul O. Zelinsky

Middle Readers

Two Short and One Long, Nina Ring Aamundsen
The Mousehole Cat, Antonia Barber, Nicola Bayley
Everywhere, Bruce Brooks
Bingo Brown, Gypsy Lover, Betsy Byars
The Midnight Horse, Sid Fleischman, il. Peter Sis
Insect Metamorphosis: From Egg to Adult, Ron and Nancy Goor
Cousins, Virginia Hamilton
Old John, Peter Hartling, trans. Elizabeth D. Crawford
Little Tricker the Squirrel Meets Big Double the Bear, Ken Kesey, il. Barry Moser
Seeing Earth from Space, Patricia Lauber
Further Tales of Uncle Remus, Julius Lester, il. Jerry Pinkney

Christopher Columbus: Voyager to the Unknown, Nancy Smiler Levinson
Mice Are Nice, compiled by Nancy Larrick, il. Ed Young
The Tale of the Mandarin Ducks, Katherine Paterson, il. Leo and Diane Dillon
Something Big Has Been Here, Jack Prelutsky, il. James Stevenson
Aída, Leontyne Price, il. Leo and Diane Dillon
Giraffes, the Sentinels of the Savannas, Helen Roney Sattler, il. Christopher Santoro
Good Queen Bess: The Story of Elizabeth I of England, Diane Stanley & Peter Vennema
Bird Watch, Jane Yolen, il. Ted Lewin

100 Bestselling U.S. Magazines

Source: Audit Bureau of Circulations. Schaumburg, Ill.

General magazines, exclusive of groups and comics; also exclusive of magazines that failed to file reports to ABC by press time. Based on total average paid circulation during the 6 months prior to Dec. 31, 1990.

Magazine	Circulation	Magazine	Circulation	Magazine	Circulation
1. NRTA/AARP Bulletin	22,103,887	11. Time	4,094,935	21. First for Women	2,649,810
2. Reader's Digest	16,264,547	12. Redbook	3,907,221	22. Cosmopolitan	2,600,971
3. TV Guide	15,604,267	13. National Enquirer	3,803,607	23. Southern Living	2,341,074
4. National Geographic	10,189,703	14. Playboy	3,488,006	24. U.S. News & World Report	2,311,534
5. Better Homes & Gardens	8,007,222	15. Star	3,431,453	25. Smithsonian	2,234,706
6. Family Circle	5,431,779	16. Sports Illustrated	3,220,016	26. Glamour	2,156,157
7. Good Housekeeping	5,152,521	17. Newsweek	3,211,958	27. Field & Stream	2,016,298
8. McCall's	5,020,127	18. People	3,208,668	28. VFW	2,103,256
9. Ladies' Home Journal	5,001,739	19. American Legion	2,956,342		(continued)
10. Woman's Day	4,802,842	20. Prevention	3,022,108		

(continued)

Magazine	Circulation	Magazine	Circulation	Magazine	Circulation
29. NEA Today	1,978,641	53. New Woman	1,340,540	77. Car and Driver	959,395
30. Money	1,905,053	54. Family Handyman	1,331,696	78. Home	942,159
31. Home & Away	1,877,949	55. US	1,326,410	79. Sport	925,984
32. Life	1,844,482	56. Changing Times	1,139,696	80. Cooking Light	924,499
33. Ebony	1,810,668	57. Sesame Street	1,249,565	81. Popular Photography	911,117
34. Popular Science	1,807,540	58. Rolling Stone	1,229,280	82. Gourmet	899,549
35. Country Living	1,803,867	59. Vogue	1,215,767	83. Business Week	894,053
36. Seventeen	1,772,362	60. Home Mechanix	1,215,178	84. Motor Trend	892,930
37. Parents	1,742,424	61. Discover	1,121,855	85. Health	878,994
38. 1,001 Home Ideas	1,662,102	62. Workbasket	1,215,175	86. Hot Rod	876,938
39. Popular Mechanics	1,651,064	63. Globe	1,200,484	87. Consumers Digest	873,704
40. Discovery	1,644,044	64. Mademoiselle	1,178,116	88. Workbench	862,985
41. Penthouse	1,612,574	65. Teen	1,175,037	89. Nation's Business	860,120
42. Outdoor Life	1,512,464	66. Leisure & Travel	1,117,897	90. Essence	850,607
43. Woman's World	1,505,312	67. Self	1,100,897	91. Omni	838,420
44. Adventure Road	1,493,624	68. Golf	1,088,999	92. Elle	836,556
45. Elks	1,472,652	69. Organic Gardening	1,034,842	93. Food & Wine	818,165
46. Soap Opera Digest	1,447,041	70. Weight Watchers	1,020,248	94. Weekly World News	816,676
47. Sunset	1,409,587	71. YM	1,008,522	95. Victoria	805,983
48. Bon Appetit	1,397,559	72. Yankee	1,000,784	96. National Examiner	805,307
49. American Hunter	1,380,230	73. Country Home	1,029,342	97. Endless Vacation	798,531
50. American Rifleman	1,378,042	74. House Beautiful	985,129	98. Homeowner	795,102
51. Golf Digest	1,357,433	75. Scouting	980,638	99. Vanity Fair	789,820
52. Boys' Life	1,357,173	76. Jet	968,545	100. PC	786,041

Top 100 U.S. Daily Newspapers

Source: *Editor & Publisher Yearbook.*

During 1990, the daily newspaper industry in the U.S. continued to follow the pattern started in the mid-70s—an increase in the number of morning newspapers, a decrease in the number of evening newspapers, and an increase in the number of daily newspapers publishing a Sunday edition. As of Feb. 1, 1990, there were 559 morning newspapers published in the U.S., and increase of 29 over the same date in 1989, and there was a decrease of 41 in the number of evening newspapers—from 1,125 to 1,084. During the same period, there was a decrease of 15 in the total number of daily newspapers (a.m. plus p.m.) being published—from 1,626 to 1,611. The number of all-day papers increased from 29 to 32. Average morning circulation for the 6-month period ending Sept. 30, 1990 increased from 40,759,016 to 41,311,167 compared with the same period in 1989, and evening circulation dropped to 21,016,795 from 21,890,202. Total daily circulation dropped .005%—from 62,649,218 to 62,327.962. Note: m = morning; e = evening.

		Circulation			Circulation
1. New York (NY) *Wall Street Journal*	(m)	1,857,131	37. Milwaukee (WI) *Journal*	(e)	265,461
2. Arlington (VA) *USA Today*	(m)	1,347,450	38. San Diego (CA) *Union*	(m)	265,246
3. Los Angeles (CA) *Times*	(m)	1,196,323	39. Sacramento (CA) *Bee*	(m)	264,462
4. New York (NY) *Times*	(m)	1,108,447	40. Columbus (OH) *Dispatch*	(m)	250,572
5. New York (NY) *Daily News*	(m)	1,097,693	41. Baltimore (MD) *Sun*	(m)	243,609
6. Washington (DC) *Post*	(m)	780,582	42. Denver (CO) *Post*	(m)	243,292
7. Chicago (IL) *Tribune*	(m)	721,067	43. Charlotte (NC) *Observer*	(m)	236,802
8. Long Island/New York (NY) *Newsday*	(all day)	714,128	44. Fort Lauderdale (FL) *Sun-Sentinel*	(m)	235,556
9. Detroit (MI) *Free Press*	(m)	636,182	45. Seattle (WA) *Times*	(e)	233,995
10. San Francisco (CA) *Chronicle*	(m)	562,887	46. Louisville (KY) *Courier-Journal*	(m)	233,714
11. Chicago (IL) *Sun-Times*	(m)	527,238	47. Pittsburgh (PA) *Press*	(m)	231,910
12. Boston (MA) *Globe*	(m)	521,354	48. Indianapolis (IN) *Star*	(m)	228,582
13. Philadelphia (PA) *Inquirer*	(m)	519,895	49. Hartford (CT) *Courant*	(m)	228,075
14. New York (NY) *Post*	(m)	510,219	50. Philadelphia (PA) *Daily News*	(e)	225,063
15. Detroit (MI) *News*	(e)	500,980	51. Oklahoma City (OK) *Daily Oklahoman*	(m)	221,595
16. Newark (NJ) *Star-Ledger*	(m)	476,257	52. Dallas (TX) *Times Herald*	(all day)	219,329
17. Houston (TX) *Chronicle*	(all day)	442,044	53. Memphis (TN) *Commercial Appeal*	(m)	210,477
18. Miami (FL) *Herald*	(m)	428,931	54. Des Moines (IA) *Register*	(m)	207,126
19. Cleveland (OH) *Plain Dealer*	(m)	428,012	55. Seattle (WA) *Seattle Post-Intelligencer*	(m)	205,357
20. Minneapolis (MN) *Star Tribune*	(m)	407,441	56. Providence (RI) *Journal*	(m)	204,337
21. Dallas (TX) *Morning News*	(m)	385,366	57. St. Paul (MN) *Pioneer Press*	(all day)	202,705
22. St. Louis (MO) *Post-Dispatch*	(m)	382,381	58. Los Angeles (CA) *Daily News*	(m)	199,589
23. Boston (MA) *Herald*	(m)	358,925	59. Cincinnati (OH) *Enquirer*	(m)	199,012
24. Orange County-Santa Ana (CA) *Register*	(all day)	353,637	60. Atlanta (GA) *Journal*	(e)	191,811
25. St. Petersburg (FL) *Times*	(m)	353,130	61. San Antonio (TX) *Express-News*	(all day)	185,589
26. Denver (CO) *Rocky Mountain News*	(m)	351,996	62. Dayton (OH) *Daily News*	(m)	183,633
27. Phoenix (AZ) *Arizona Republic*	(m)	330,706	63. Jacksonville (FL) *Florida Times-Union*	(m)	179,047
28. Houston (TX) *Post*	(m)	328,671	64. West Palm Beach (FL) *Post*	(m)	178,115
29. Portland (OR) *Oregonian*	(all day)	324,163	65. Milwaukee (WI) *Sentinel*	(m)	176,549
30. Atlanta (GA) *Constitution*	(m)	316,793	66. Austin (TX) *American-Statesman*	(m)	173,368
31. Buffalo (NY) *News*	(all day)	308,714	67. Birmingham (AL) *News*	(e)	169,660
32. Tampa (FL) *Tribune*	(m)	289,999	68. Baltimore (MD) *Evening Sun*	(e)	166,684
33. Kansas City (MO) *Star*	(m)	287,345	69. Pittsburgh (PA) *Post-Gazette*	(m)	162,520
34. Orlando (FL) *Sentinel*	(all day)	279,393			
35. New Orleans (LA) *Times-Picayune*	(all day)	278,990			
36. San Jose (CA) *Mercury News*	(all day)	278,676			

(continued)

			Circulation
70.	San Antonio (TX) *Light*. . .	(all day)	162,431
71.	Fort Worth (TX)		
	Star-Telegram	(m)	161,698
72.	Asbury Park (NJ) *Press* . .	(e)	159,629
73.	Hackensack (NJ) *Record* .	(e)	159,550
74.	Riverside (CA)		
	Press-Enterprise	(m)	154,764
75.	Akron (OH) *Beacon*		
	Journal	(m)	154,134
76.	Norfolk (VA) *Virginian-Pilot*	(m)	153,181
77.	Toledo (OH) *Blade*	(e)	153,023
78.	Raleigh (NC) *News &*		
	Observer	(m)	150,267
79.	Columbia (SC) *State*. . . .	(m)	145,528
80.	Fresno (CA) *Bee*	(m)	145,169
81.	Grand Rapids (MI) *Press* .	(e)	144,800
82.	Richmond (VA)		
	Times-Dispatch	(m)	143,141
83.	Allentown (PA) *Morning*		
	Call	(m)	136,435
84.	San Francisco (CA)		
	Examiner	(e)	136,346
85.	Las Vegas (NV)		
	Review-Journal	(m)	135,314

			Circulation
86.	Rochester (NY) *Democrat*		
	& Chronicle.	(m)	132,603
87.	Little Rock (AR) *Arkansas*		
	Democrat.	(m)	130,024
88.	Long Beach (CA)		
	Press-Telegram	(m)	129,195
89.	Nashville (TN) *Tennessean*	(m)	127,936
90.	Little Rock (AR) *Arkansas*		
	Gazette.	(m)	126,547
91.	Tulsa (OK) *World*.	(m)	125,037
92.	Lexington (KY)		
	Herald-Leader	(m)	124,000
93.	Omaha (NE) *World-Herald*	(m)	123,901
94.	Sarasota (FL)		
	Herald-Tribune	(m)	122,403
95.	Oakland (CA) *Tribune* . . .	(m)	121,537
96.	Albuquerque (NM) *Journal*	(m)	121,030
97.	Wichita (KS) *Eagle*.	(m)	120,828
98.	Wilmington (DE) *News*		
	Journal	(all day)	120,653
99.	Worcester (MA) *Telegram*		
	& Gazette.	(all day)	118,192
100.	Tacoma (WA) *Morning*		
	News-Tribune	(m)	117,881

Selected U.S. Daily Newspaper Circulation

Source: Audit Bureau of Circulations report of average paid circulation for 6 months to Mar. 31, 1991.

Newspaper	Daily	Newspaper	Daily	Newspaper	Daily
Akron Beacon Journal(m). . .	158,725	Evansville (Ind.) Courier(m) . .	63,926	Pensacola News-Journal(m) .	*†60,680
Albuquerque Journal(m). . . .	†123,481	Evansville (Ind.) Press(e) . . .	34,495	Peoria Journal Star(a)	*90,005
Albuquerque Tribune(e)	†40,812	Everett (Wash.) Herald(e). . .	53,174	Phoenix Gazette(e)	†96,642
Amarillo News(m)	44,165	Fargo (N.D.) Forum(m)	55,309	Portland (Me.) Press	
Amarillo Globe-Times(e) . . .	*22,144	Ft. Lauderdale News(e)	*7,827	Herald(m)	*†60,045
Anchorage Times(m)	*44,524	Ft. Myers (Fla.)		Reno Gazette Journal(m) . . .	66,781
Ann Arbor News(e)	†53,968	News-Press(m)	100,973	Roanoke Times & World	
Athens (Ga.) News(m).	*14,739	Ft. Wayne Journal-Gazette(m)	63,243	News(m&e)	*121,055
Athens (Ga.) Banner-Herald(e)	*13,723	Gary Post-Tribune(m)	70,411	Rockford (Ill.) Register-Star(m)	73,732
Augusta (Ga.) Chronicle(m). .	*71,442	Greenville (S.C.) News(m) . .	*91,219	Salem (Ore.)	
Augusta (Ga.) Herald(e) . . .	*11,961	Greenville (S.C.) Piedmont(e).	*25,846	Statesman-Journal(m) . . .	60,172
Bakersfield Californian(m). . .	†82,879	Honolulu Advertiser(m)	104,633	Salt Lake City Tribune(m) . . .	111,994
Bangor (Me.) News(m)	*76,290	Honolulu Star-Bulletin(e) . . .	88,755	San Bernardino Sun(m)	93,534
Baton Rouge Advocate(m) . .	*84,480	Huntington (W.Va.)		Sarasota Herald-Tribune(m) .	†142,598
Baton Rouge State-Times(m) .	*26,633	Herald-Dispatch(m)	†43,316	Savannah News(m)	*56,443
Bergen Co. (N.J.) Record(m) .	†172,667	Hyannis: Cape Cod Times(m) .	42,210	Savannah Press(e).	*18,019
Billings (Mont.) Gazette(m) . .	54,455	Jackson (Miss.)		Scranton Times(m)	*†46,345
Binghamton (N.Y.) Press &		Clarion-Ledger(m)	107,787	Scrantonian Tribune(m)	*†31,917
Sun Bulletin(m)	70,725	Jacksonville Times-Union(m) .	*184,394	Sioux City Journal(m)	*49,388
Birmingham Post-Herald(m) .	*64,163	Kalamazoo Gazette(e).	64,201	Spokane Chronicle(e)	*22,462
Bismark (N.D.) Tribune(m) . .	31,317	Knoxville News-Sentinel(m) . .	104,545	Springfield (Ill.) State Journal	
Bridgeport (Conn.) Post(m) . .	69,077	Lansing (Mich.) State		Register(m).	68,930
Bristol (Va.) Herald-Courier		Journal(m)	70,652	Springfield (Mass.) Union	
Tennessean(a)	*44,436	Las Vegas Review-Journal(a) .	*139,735	News(a)	113,719
Camden (N.J.) Courier-Post(e)	*102,189	Lynchburg (Va.) News &		Syracuse Herald-Journal(e) .	91,802
Casper (Wyo.) Star Tribune(m)	34,093	Advance(a)	*42,164	Syracuse Post-Standard(m) . .	88,874
Charleston (W.Va.) Gazette(m)	54,291	Macon (Ga.) Telegraph &		Tacoma News Tribune(m). . .	†121,049
Chattanooga News-Free		News(m)	75,263	Tallahassee Democrat(m) . . .	63,604
Press(e)	53,002	Madison (Wis.) State		Terre Haute Tribune Star(m) .	36,360
Cincinnati Post(e)	105,469	Journal(m)	*82,450	Toledo Blade(e)	153,062
Columbia (S.C.) State(m). . .	145,365	Middletown (N.Y.) Times		Topeka Capital-Journal(m) . .	67,706
Columbus (Ga.)		Herald Record(m)	†83,762	Tucson Star(m)	†98,793
Ledger-Enquirer(m)	55,976	Mobile Press(e).	*†44,018	Tulsa Tribune(e)	†69,044
Corpus Christi Caller-Times(m)	†69,671	Mobile Register(m)	*†62,269	Wilmington News Journal(a) .	†119,043
Daytona Beach		Modesto (Cal.) Bee(m)	*†85,020	Wilmington (N.C.) Star(m) . .	51,605
News-Journal(m)	100,668	Montgomery Advertiser(m) . .	*53,825	Winston-Salem Journal(m) . .	96,250
Dubuque Telegraph-Herald(e)	33,963	Montgomery Journal(e)	*15,127	Worcester Telegram	
El Paso Herald-Post(e)	†29,159	Nashville Banner(e)	62,675	Gazette(a)	†117,047
Erie (Pa.) News(m).	*30,881	Newport News (Va.) Press(m)	*†80,863	Yakima (Wash.)	
Erie (Pa.) Times(e).	*40,321	Newport News (Va.) Times		Herald-Republic(a)	†40,769
		Herald(e)	*†22,792	Youngstown Vindicator(e). . .	†88,325

(m) morning; (e) evening; (a) all day; * Mon.-Fri. average; † 3 months.

Some Notable U.S. Dance Companies

Source: Dance/USA, July 24, 1991

African-American Dance Ensemble, Durham, NC
Alvin Ailey American Dance Theater, New York, NY
Aman Folk Ensemble, Los Angeles, CA
American Ballet Theatre, New York, NY
Atlanta Ballet, GA
Avaz International Dance Theatre, Los Angeles, CA
Ballet Arizona, Phoenix, AZ

Ballet Chicago, IL
Ballet Hispanico of New York, New York, NY
BalletMet, Columbus, OH
Ballet Omaha, NE
Ballet West, Salt Lake City, UT

(continued)

Tandy Beal and Company, Santa Cruz, CA
Boston Ballet, Newton, MA
Trisha Brown Company, New York, NY
Donald Byrd/The Group, New York, NY
Caribbean Dance Company, St. Croix, VI
Chen & Dancers, New York, NY
Lucinda Childs Dance Company, New York, NY
Cincinnati/New Orleans City Ballet, Cincinnati, OH
Cleveland/San Jose Ballet, Cleveland, OH
Colorado Ballet, Denver, CO
Cunningham Dance Foundation, New York, NY
Dance Alloy, Pittsburgh, PA
Dance Exchange, Washington, DC
Dance Theatre of Harlem, New York, NY
Danceteller, Philadelphia, PA
Dayton Ballet Association, Dayton, OH
Dayton Contemporary Dance Company, Dayton, OH
Laura Dean Musicians and Dancers, New York, NY
Garth Fagan's Bucket Dance Theatre, Rochester, NY
Feld Ballets, New York, NY
Fort Worth Ballet, Fort Worth, TX
Joe Goode Performance Group, San Francisco, CA
David Gordon Pick Up Co., New York, NY
Martha Graham Dance Co., New York, NY
Hartford Ballet, Hartford, CT
Erick Hawkins Dance Co., New York, NY
Joseph Holmes Dance Theater, Chicago, IL
Houston Ballet, Houston, TX
Hubbard Street Dance Company, Chicago, IL
Jazz Tap Ensemble, Los Angeles, CA
Margaret Jenkins Dance Company, San Francisco, CA
Joffrey Ballet, New York, NY
Bill T. Jones/Arnie Zane Company, New York, NY
Rebecca Kelly Dance Company, New York, NY
KHADRA International Folk Ballet, San Francisco, CA
Zivili Kolo Ensemble, Granville, OH
Lewitzky Dance Foundation, Los Angeles, CA
Jose Limon Dance Company, New York, NY
Loretta Livingston & Dancers, Los Angeles, CA
Los Angeles Chamber Ballet, CA
Louisville Ballet, Louisville, KY
Lar Lubovitch Dance Company, New York, NY

Miami City Ballet, Miami Beach, FL
Bebe Miller and Company, New York, NY
Milwaukee Ballet, Milwaukee, WI
Monnaie Dance Group/Mark Morris, New York, NY
Elisa Monte Dance Company, New York, NY
Mordine & Company, Chicago, IL
Jennifer Muller/The Works, New York, NY
Muntu Dance Theater, Chicago, IL
New Dance Ensemble, Minneapolis, MN
New York City Ballet, New York, NY
Rosalind Newman and Dancers, New York, NY
Nikolais and Louis Dance, New York, NY
North Carolina Dance Theater, Winston Salem, NC
Oakland Ballet, Oakland, CA
ODC/San Francisco, San Francisco, CA
Ohio Ballet, Akron, OH
Pacific Northwest Ballet, Seattle, WA
Parsons Ballet Company, New York, NY
Pennsylvania Ballet, Philadelphia, PA
Philadanco, Philadelphia, PA
Pilobolus Dance Theater, Washington, CT
Stuart Pimsler Dance & Theater, Columbus, OH
Pittsburgh Ballet Theatre, Pittsburgh, PA
Pittsburgh Dance Alloy, Pittsburgh, PA
Repertory Dance Theatre, Salt Lake City, UT
Richmond Ballet, Richmond, VA
Ririe-Woodbury Dance Company, Salt Lake City, UT
Nicholas Rodriguez and Dance-Compass, Montclair, NJ
San Francisco Ballet, San Francisco, CA
Carlota Santana Spanish Dance Arts Co., New York, NY
Sarasota Ballet, FL
Solomons Company/Dance, New York, NY
Southern Ballet Theater, FL
State Ballet of Missouri, Kansas City, MO
Paul Taylor Dance Company, New York, NY
Joyce Trisler Danscompany, New York, NY
Tulsa Ballet Theatre, Tulsa, OK
Dan Wagoner and Dancers, New York, NY
Washington Ballet, Washington, DC
Nina Wiener Dance Company, New York, NY
Zenon Dance Company, Minneapolis, MN
ZeroMoving Dance Company, Philadelphia, PA

U.S. Opera Companies with Budgets of $500,000 or More

Source: OPERA America; June, 1991

Anchorage Opera; William F. Russell, gen. dir.
Arizona Opera Co. (Tucson); Glynn Ross, gen. dir.
Opera Theatre at Wildwood (Ariz.); Ann Chotard, art. dir.
Fullerton Civic Light Opera (Calif.); R. G. Duncan, gen. mgr.
Long Beach Opera (Calif.); Micheal Milenski, gen. dir.
Long Beach Civic Light Opera (Calif.); P. Logefeil, mng. dir.
Los Angeles Music Center Opera Assn.; Peter Hemmings, exec. dir.
Opera Pacific (Costa Mesa, Calif.); David DiChiera, gen. dir.
Sacramento Opera Assn. (Calif.); Marianne H. Oaks, gen. dir.
San Diego Civic Light Opera; Harris Goldman, gen mgr.
San Diego Opera Assn.; Ian Campbell, gen. mgr.
San Francisco Opera; Lotfi Mansouri, gen. dir.
San Francisco Opera Center (inc. Western Opera Theater); Christine Bullin, mgr.
Opera San José (Calif.); Irene Dalis, art. dir.
San José Civic Light Opera (Calif.); Stewart Slater, dir.
Central City Opera (Denver); Daniel Rule, gen. mgr.
Opera Colorado (Denver); Nathaniel Merrill, art. dir.

Connecticut Grand Opera & Stamford State Opera, John Hiddlestone, gen. mgr.
Connecticut Opera (Hartford); George Osborne, gen. dir.
Goodspeed Opera House (E. Haddam, Conn.); Michael Price, exec. dir.
Washington Opera (D.C.); Martin Feinstein, gen. dir.
Fort Lauderdale Opera; William H. Martin, gen. mgr.
Greater Miami Opera Assn.; Robert Heuer, gen. dir.
Orlando Opera Co. (Fla.); Robert Swedberg, gen. dir.
Palm Beach Opera; H. P. Benn, gen. dir.
Sarasota Opera Assn. (Fla.); Deane Allyn, exec. dir.
Atlanta Opera (Ga.); Alfred Kennedy, gen. mgr.
Augusta Opera (Ga.); Edward Bradberry, gen. dir.
Hawaii Opera Theatre; Marshall Turkins, gen. dir.
Chicago Opera Theater; Alan Stone, art. dir.
Lyric Opera of Chicago; Ardis Krainik, gen. mgr.
Indianapolis Opera; Durand L. Pope, gen. dir.
Des Moines Metro Opera (Indianola); Robert Larsen, art. dir.
Music Theatre of Wichita; Wayne Bryan, prod. dir.
Kentucky Opera Assn. (Louisville); Thomson Smillie, gen. dir.

New Orleans Opera Assn.; Arthur Cosenza, gen. dir.
Baltimore Opera Co.; Michael Harrison, gen. dir.
Opera Company of Boston; Sarah Caldwell, art. dir.
Boston Opera Theatre; Robert Canon, exec. dir.
Michigan Opera Theatre (Detroit); David DiChiera, gen. dir.
Opera Grand Rapids (Mich.); Robert Lyall, gen. dir.
Minnesota Opera Co. (St. Paul); Kevin Smith, gen. dir.
Lyric Opera of Kansas City (Missouri); Russell Patterson, gen. dir. & art. dir.
Opera Theatre of St. Louis (Missouri); Charles MacKay, gen. dir.
Opera/Omaha (Neb.); Mary Robert, gen. dir.
Nevada Opera (Reno); Ted Puffer, gen. dir.
June Opera Festival of N.J. (Princeton Junction); Deborah S. Sandler, exec. dir.
Metro Lyric Opera (Allenhurst, N.J.); Era M. Tognoli, gen. & art. dir.
New Jersey State Opera (Newark); Alfredo Silipigni, art. dir.
Albuquerque Civic Light Opera; Linda E. McVey, exec. dir.
Santa Fe Opera (New Mexico); John Crosby, gen. dir.
Tri-Cities Opera (Binghamton, N.Y.); P. Hibbitt & C. Savoca, art. dirs.
Chautauqua Opera (N.Y.); Linda Jackson, gen. mgr.
Glimmerglass Opera (Cooperstown, N.Y.); Paul Kellogg, gen. mgr.
Lake George Opera Festival (N.Y.); John Balme, art. dir.
Syracuse Opera; Julie Richard, mng. dir.
Light Opera of Manhattan; Raymond Allen, Jerry Gotham, art. dir.
Metropolitan Opera Assn. (New York City); Joseph Volpe, gen. mgr.
Music-Theatre Group (N.Y. & Stockbridge, Mass.); Lyn Austin, prod. dir.

New York City Opera; Christopher Keene, gen. dir.
New York City Opera Natl. Co.; Nancy Kelly, adm. dir.
Opera Orchestra of N.Y. (N.Y.C.); Eve Queler, art dir.
Opera Carolina (Charlotte, N.C.); James Wright, gen. dir.
Cincinnati Opera Assn.; James deBlasis, art. dir.
Cleveland Opera; David Bamberger, gen. dir.
Opera/Columbus (Oh.); John Gage, gen. dir.
Dayton Opera Assn. (Oh.); Jane Nelson, mng. dir.
Lyric Theatre of Oklahoma; Gayle Pearson, gen. mgr.
Tulsa Opera (Oklahoma); Myrna S. Ruffner, gen. mgr.
Portland Opera Assn. (Oregon); Robert Bailey, exec. dir.
American Music Theater Festival (Phila.); Marjorie Samoff, prod. dir.
Opera Company of Philadelphia; Robert B. Driver, gen. dir.
Pennsylvania Opera Theater (Phila.); Barbara Silverstein, art dir. & gen. mgr.
Pittsburgh Civic Light Opera; Charles Gray, exec. dir.
Pittsburgh Opera; Tito Capobianco, gen. dir.
Opera Memphis (Tenn.); Robert Driver, gen. & art. dir.
Austin Lyric Opera (Tex.) Walter Ducloux, art. dir.
Dallas Opera; Plato Karayanis, gen. dir.
Lyric Opera of Dallas (Tex.); John Burrows, art. dir.
Fort Worth Opera; Carl O. Johnson, art. dir.
Houston Grand Opera Assn.; R. David Gockley, gen. dir.
Texas Opera Theater (Houston); Ann Tomfohrde, dir.
Theatre Under the Stars (Houston); Frank Young, exec. dir.
Utah Opera (Salt Lake City); Anne Ewers, gen. dir.
Virginia Opera (Norfolk); Peter Mark, gen. dir.
Seattle Opera Assn.; Speight Jenkins, gen. dir.
Florentine Opera of Milwaukee; Dennis Hanthorn, gen. mgr.
Skylight Opera Theatre (Milwaukee); Jane Keegan, mng. dir.

Symphony Orchestras of the U.S.

Source: American Symphony Orchestra League. 777 14th St., N.W., Washington, DC 20005

(All orchestras listed had budgets in excess of $1.05 million in fiscal 1990.)

Symphony Orchestra[1]	Music Director[2]	Symphony Orchestra[1]	Music Director[2]
Alabama (Birmingham)	Paul Polivnick	Kansas City (Mo.)	William McGlaughlin
American (N.Y.C.)	Catherine Comet	Knoxville (Tenn.)	Kirk Trevor
Atlanta (Ga.)	Yoel Levi	Long Beach (Cal.)	JoAnn Falletta
Austin (Tex.)	Sung Kwak	Long Island Philharmonic (N.Y.)	Marin Alsop
Baltimore (Md.)	David Zinman	Los Angeles Chamber Or. (Cal.)	Iona Brown
Boston (Mass.)	Seiji Ozawa	Los Angeles Philharmonic (Cal.)	Esa-Pekka Salonen
Brooklyn Philharmonic (N.Y.)	Dennis Russell Davies	The Louisville Orchestra (Ky.)	Lawrence Leighton Smith
Buffalo Philharmonic (N.Y.)	Maximiano Valdez	Memphis (Tenn.)	Alan Balter
Cedar Rapids (Mich.)	Christian Tiemeyer	Milwaukee (Wis.)	Zdenek Macal
Charleston (S.C.)	David Stahl	The Minnesota Orchestra (Minneapolis)	Edo de Waart
Charlotte (N.C.)	Leo B. Driehuys	The Nashville Symphony (Tenn.)	Kenneth S. Schermerhorn
Chattanooga, & Opera Assn. (Tenn.)	Vakhtang Jordania	National (Washington, D.C.)	Mstislav Rostropovich
Chicago (Ill.)	Georg Solti	New Haven (Conn.)	Michael Palmer
Cincinnati (Oh.)	Jesus Lopez-Cobos	New Jersey (Newark)	Hugh Wolff
Cleveland (Oh.)	Christoph von Dohnanyi	New Mexico (Albuquerque)	Neal H. Stulberg
Colorado (Denver)	David T. Abosch	New Orleans (La.)	Maxim Shostakovich
Colorado Springs (Col.)	Christopher P. Wilkins	New World Symphony (Miami Beach, Fla.)	Michael Tilson Thomas
Columbus (Oh.)	Christian Badea	New York Philharmonic (N.Y.C.)	Zubin Mehta
Dallas (Tex.)	Eduardo Mata	North Carolina (Raleigh)	Gerhardt Zimmermann
Dayton Philharmonic (Oh.)	Isaiah Jackson	Oklahoma City Philharmonic (Okla.)	Joel A. Levine
Delaware (Wilmington)	Stephen Gunzenhauser	Omaha (Neb.)	Bruce B. Hangen
Detroit (Mich.)	Neeme Jarvi	Oregon (Portland)	James DePreist
Philharmonic Orchestra of Florida (Fort Lauderdale)	James Judd	Orpheus Chamber Or. (N.Y.C., N.Y.)	None
The Florida Orchestra (Tampa)	Jahja Ling	Pacific Symphony (Irvine, Cal.)	Carl St. Clair
Florida (Orlando)	Kenneth Jean	The Philadelphia Orchestra (Pa.)	Wolfgang Sowallisch
Florida Symphonic Pops (Boca Raton)	Mark S. Azzolina	Phoenix (Ariz.)	James L. Sedares
Fort Wayne Philharmonic (Ind.)	Ronald Ondrejka	Pittsburgh (Pa.)	Lorin Maazel
Fort Worth (Tex.)	John Giordano	Portland (Me.)	Toshi Shimada
Grand Rapids (Mich.)	Catherine Comet	Puerto Rico (Santurce)	Odon Alonso
Grant Park (Chicago, Ill.)	Zdenek Macal	Rhode Island Philharmonic Or. (Providence)	Andrew Massey
Hartford (Conn.)	Michael Lankester	The Richmond Symphony (Va.)	George Manahan
Honolulu (Ha.)	Donald Johanos	Rochester Philharmonic Or. (N.Y.)	Mark Elder
Houston (Tex.)	Christoph Eschenbach		
Hudson Valley Philharmonic (Poughkeepsie, N.Y.)	Imre Pallo		
Jacksonville (Fla.)	Roger Nierenberg		

(continued)

Symphony Orchestra[1]	Music Director[2]	Symphony Orchestra[1]	Music Director[2]
Sacramento (Cal.)	Carter Nice	Toldeo (Oh.)	Andrew Massey
St. Louis (Mo.)	Leonard Slatkin	Tucson (Ariz.)	Robert E. Bernhardt
St. Paul Chamber Or. (Minn.)	Hugh Wolff	Tulsa Philharmonic Or. (Okla.)	Bernard Rubenstein
San Antonio (Tex.)	Christopher P. Wilkins	Utah (Salt Lake City)	Joseph Silverstein
San Diego (Cal.)	Yoav Talmi	The Virginia Symphony (Norfolk)	Joseph Silverstein
San Francisco (Cal.)	Herbert Blomstedt	West Virginia (Charleston)	Thomas B. Conlin
San Jose (Cal.)	George Cleve	Wichita (Kan.)	Zuohuang Chen
Seattle (Wash.)	Gerard Schwarz		
Spokane (Wash.)	Bruce Ferden		
Springfield (Mass.)	Raymond C. Hervey		
Syracuse (N.Y.)	Kazuyoshi Akiyama		

(1) Orchestra name=place name + Symphony Orchestra, unless otherwise noted; (2) General title; listed is highest-ranking member of conducting personnel.

Recordings & Music Videos

The Recording Industry of America, Inc. confers Platinum Album Certification for a minimum sale of 1 million units in LP's, tapes and CD's with manufacturer's dollar volume at least $2 million, based on $33^1/3$% of suggested retail price for each record, tape, and CD sold. The requirement for a Multi-Platinum Certification for albums is the sale of 2 million units; awards are also given at subsequent million-unit sales marks. A further requirement is that the manufacturer's dollar volume total at least $4 million for sales of 2 million units based on $33^1/3$% of suggested retail price, $6 million for sales of 3 million units, etc. The sales of LP's, cassettes and CD configurations may be commingled to determine the number of albums sold. The requirement for a Platinum Single Certification is a minimal sale of 1 million units. The non-theatrical Platinum Music Video Single criterion is the sale of 50,000 units; and 100,000 units for a Platinum Music Video Long Form. The criterion for a Multi-Platinum Video Long Form Award changed on Apr. 1, 1991; before then, it was the sale of 200,000 units, but it was changed to the sale of 100,000 units; the criterion for a Multi-Platinum Music Video Single is 100,000, which may recertify in increments of 50,000 units. **Listed are 1990 Multi-Platinum and Platinum Awards for music released in 1990 and for music videos released at any time.**

Artists, Recording Titles

Albums, Platinum
(Number in parentheses—millions sold)
Bell Biv Devoe; Poison (3)
Garth Brooks; No Fences (2)
Mariah Carey; Mariah Carey (2)
M.C. Hammer; Please Hammer Don't Hurt 'Em (8)
Heart; Brigade (2)
Madonna; I'm Breathless (2)
Madonna; Vogue (2)
New Kids on the Block; Step by Step (3)
Sinead O'Connor; I Do Not Want What I Haven't Got (2)
Poison; Flesh & Blood (2)
Soundtrack; Pretty Woman (2)
Vanilla Ice; To the Extreme (6)
Wilson Phillips (3)

Albums, Platinum
Paula Abdul; Shut Up and Dance
AC/DC; The Razor's Edge
Anita Baker; Compositions
Depeche Mode; Violator
Digital Underground; Sex Packets
En Vogue; Born to Sing
Johnny Gill; Johnny Gill
Billy Idol; Charmed Life
Inxs; X
Led Zeppelin; Led Zeppelin (6 LP Box Set)
George Michael; Listen Without Prejudice
Bette Midler; Some People's Lives
Public Enemy; Fear of a Black Planet
Slaughter; Stick It to Ya
Soundtrack; Ghost
Soundtrack; Teenage Mutant Ninja Turtles
Lisa Stansfield; Affection
Keith Sweat; I'll Give All My Love to You
Vaughan Brothers; Family Style
Warrant; Cherry Pie

Singles, Multi-Platinum
(Number in parentheses—millions sold)
Madonna; Vogue (2)

Singles, Platinum
Bell Biv Devoe; Poison
Jon Bon Jovi; Blaze of Glory
Candyman; Knockin' Boots
En Vogue; Hold On

New Kids on the Block; Step by Step
Snap; The Power
Lisa Stansfield; All Around the World
Vanilla Ice; Ice Ice Baby

Music Videos, Multi-Platinum
(number in parentheses—units sold)
Paula Abdul; Straight Up (200,000)
Alabama; Pass It On Down (100,000)
Bon Jovi; New Jersey (100,000)
Bobby Brown; His Perogative (100,000)
Debbie Gibson; Live in Concert (100,000)
M.C. Hammer; Please Hammer Don't Hurt 'Em (150,000)
Janet Jackson; Rhythm Nation 1814 (200,000)
New Kids on the Block; Hangin' Tough-Live (1.2 million)
New Kids on the Block; Step by Step (1.05 million)
New Kids on the Block; Hangin' Tough (1.15 million)
Pink Floyd; Delicate Sound of Thunder (150,000)
Elvis Presley; Great Performances Vol. I: Center Stage (150,000)
Elvis Presley; Great Performances Vol. II: Man & Music (150,000)
The Rolling Stones; The Continuing Adventures (100,000)
Van Halen; Live Without a Net (100,000)

Music Videos, Platinum
Aerosmith; Things That Go Pump in the Night
Anita Baker; One Night of Rapture
B-52's; 1979-1989
Carman; Revival in the Land
Carreras, Domingo, Pavarotti; In Concert
Phil Collins; The Singles Collection
Phil Collins; Seriously Live
The Cure; The Cure in Orange
Depeche Mode; 101
Gloria Estefan & Miami Sound Machine; Evolution
Kenny G; Kenny G Live in Concert
Barry Manilow; Live on Broadway
Richard Marx; Richard Marx Volume I
Johnny Mathis; Home for Christmas
Motley Crue; Dr. Feelgood
David Lee Roth; David Lee Roth
Luther Vandross; Live at Wembley
Various; Kid's Praise V
The Who; The Who Live Featuring "Tommy"

Music Video Singles, Multi-Platinum
(number in parentheses-units sold)
Madonna; Justify My Love (400,000)

America's Favorite Prime-Time Television Programs, 1990

Source: Nielsen Media Research

(Percent of TV households and persons in TV households)

Regularly Scheduled Network Programs (February 1991)

(Nielsen People Meter Average Audience Estimates)

Program	TV House-holds	Women	Men	Teens	Chil-dren	Program	TV House-holds	Women	Men	Teens	Chil-dren
Cheers	21.4	16.6	13.4			NBC Sunday Night Movie			10.1		
60 Minutes	20.4	15.4	15.4			In the Heat of the Night			9.8		
CBS Sunday Movie	19.9	17.7	10.8			L.A. Law			9.4		
Roseanne	18.6	13.9	10.0	15.1	11.0	Rescue: 911			9.4		10.8
America's Funniest Home Videos	17.8	13.3	12.6	14.7	18.0	Wings			9.4		
Full House	17.8	13.1		13.5	19.8	Fresh Prince of Bel Air				18.2	12.4
A Different World	17.6	13.7		14.6	11.0	Simpsons				16.8	21.1
Family Matters	17.5			15.6	21.6	Blossom				15.6	
Empty Nest	17.4	14.6				In Living Color				14.7	
Murphy Brown	17.4	14.3	10.0			Wonder Years				13.9	11.8
America's Funniest People	17.3		12.3	18.7	18.0	Growing Pains				13.7	10.9
Designing Women	17.3	14.3	9.6			Doogie Howser, M.D.				13.3	
Murder, She Wrote	17.2	15.0	9.9			Who's The Boss?				12.4	10.6
Bill Cosby Show	16.7	13.6				Married With Children				12.3	
Golden Girls	16.7	14.0				Perfect Strangers					15.0
Major Dad		12.9				Babes					11.0
Matlock		12.9				Going Places					11.0
Unsolved Mysteries		12.9	10.3								

Note: Prime time = Mon.-Sat. 8pm-11pm & Sun. 7pm-11pm New York Time.

Favorite Syndicated Programs, 1990

Source: Nielsen Media Research, February, 1991

(Ratings based on Designated Market Area coverage as reported by Nielsen's Cassandra Report)

Program	TV house-holds	Women	Men	Teens	Chil-dren	Program	TV house-holds	Women	Men	Teens	Chil-dren
Wheel of Fortune	16.5	14.1	9.5	4.2	4.9	Cosby Show	8.4	6.1	3.9	9.0	8.5
Jeopardy	14.0	11.6	7.8	3.7	3.0	Golden Girls	8.0	6.3	3.7	4.6	3.4
Oprah Winfrey Show	11.6	9.9	3.4	4.0	1.4	Current Affair	8.0	6.1	4.6	2.6	1.8
Wheel of Fortune (wknd)	11.0	9.4	6.2	2.6	3.0	Cheers	7.4	5.0	5.1	4.2	2.5
Star Trek Next Generation	10.9	6.6	8.9	6.6	5.9	Inside Edition	7.4	5.8	4.0	1.8	1.3
Jeopardy (wknd)	9.8	8.3	5.5	2.3	2.5	Donahue	6.9	5.4	2.6	1.0	0.5
Entertainment Tonight	9.2	7.0	5.3	2.8	1.9	Who's The Boss?	6.7	4.4	3.0	7.6	6.9
						Night Court	6.4	4.2	4.0	5.8	4.2
						Family Feud	6.0	4.7	3.0	3.4	2.7

Average Television Viewing Time, 1990

Source: Nielsen Media Research, February 1991 (hours: minutes, per week)

		Mon.-Fri. 10am-4:30pm	Mon.-Fri. 4:30pm-7:30pm	Mon.-Sun. 8-11pm	Sat. 7am-1pm	Mon.-Fri. 11:30pm-1am
Total Persons	age 2+	5:01	4:25	8:40	:53	1:13
Total Women	age 18+	6:30	4:55	9:46	:46	1:24
	18-24	5:10	3:18	6:43	:35	1:11
	25-54	5:34	4:10	9:22	:43	1:25
	55+	8:49	6:59	11:49	:52	1:29
Total Men	age 18+	4:11	4:06	9:02	:47	1:25
	18-24	3:23	2:42	5:25	:32	1:13
	25-54	3:23	3:27	8:48	:47	1:26
	55+	6:32	6:26	11:37	:58	1:28
Female Teens	12-17	2:56	3:41	7:07	:49	:47
Male Teens	12-17	2:28	3:32	7:16	:59	:47
Children	2-5	6:47	4:40	5:31	1:35	:28
Children	6-11	2:34	4:04	5:53	1:26	:23

All-time Top Television Programs

Source: A.C. Nielsen estimates, Jan. 30, 1960 through Jan. 31, 1991, excluding unsponsored or joint network telecasts or programs under 30 minutes long. Ranked by percent of average audience.

Program	Date	Network	Households (000)	Program	Date	Network	Households (000)
1. M*A*S*H Special	2/28/83	CBS	50,150	16. Roots Pt. VI	1/28/77	ABC	32,680
2. Dallas	11/21/80	CBS	41,470	16. The Fugitive	8/29/67	ABC	25,700
3. Roots Pt. VIII	1/30/77	ABC	36,380	18. Super Bowl XXI	1/25/87	CBS	40,030
4. Super Bowl XVI	1/24/82	CBS	40,020	19. Roots Pt. V	1/27/77	ABC	32,540
5. Super Bowl XVII	1/30/83	NBC	40,480	20. Ed Sullivan	2/9/64	CBS	23,240
6. Super Bowl XX	1/26/86	NBC	41,490	21. Bob Hope Christmas Special	1/14/71	NBC	27,050
7. Gone With The Wind-Pt. 1	11/7/76	NBC	33,960	22. Roots Pt. III	1/25/77	ABC	31,900
8. Gone With The Wind-Pt. 2	11/8/76	NBC	33,750	23. Super Bowl XI	1/9/77	NBC	31,610
9. Super Bowl XII	1/15/78	CBS	34,410	23. Super Bowl XV	1/25/81	NBC	34,540
10. Super Bowl XIII	1/21/79	NBC	35,090	25. Super Bowl VI	1/16/72	CBS	27,450
11. Bob Hope Christmas Show	1/15/70	NBC	27,260	26. Roots Pt. II	1/24/77	ABC	31,400
12. Super Bowl XVIII	1/22/84	CBS	38,800	27. Beverly Hillbillies	1/8/64	CBS	22,570
12. Super Bowl XIX	1/20/85	ABC	39,390	28. Roots Pt. IV	1/26/77	ABC	31,190
14. Super Bowl XIV	1/20/80	CBS	35,330	28. Ed Sullivan	2/16/64	CBS	22,445
15. ABC Theater (The Day After)	11/20/83	ABC	38,550	30. Super Bowl XXIII	1/22/89	NBC	39,320

Top-Rated TV Shows of the Past

Source: A.C. Nielsen

1950s		Avg. rating over decade	1960s		Avg. rating over decade	1970s		Avg. rating over decade
Program	Network		Program	Network		Program	Network	
1. A. Godfrey's Talent Scouts	CBS	32.9	1. Bonanza	NBC	29.6	1. All in the Family	CBS	23.1
2. I Love Lucy	CBS	31.6	2. The Red Skelton Show	CBS	26.4	2. M*A*S*H	CBS	17.6
3. You Bet Your Life	NBC	30.1	3. The Andy Griffith Show	CBS	22.4	3. Hawaii Five-O	CBS	16.5
4. Dragnet	NBC	24.6	4. The Beverly Hillbillies	CBS	21.9	4. Happy Days	ABC	15.9
5. The Jack Benny Show	CBS	22.3	5. The Ed Sullivan Show	CBS	21.7	5. The Waltons	CBS	14.0
6. A. Godfrey and Friends	CBS	19.5	6. The Lucy Show/Here's Lucy	CBS	21.3	6. The Mary Tyler Moore Show	CBS	13.7
7. Gunsmoke	CBS	15.6	7. The Jackie Gleason Show	CBS	16.5	7. Sanford & Son	NBC	13.4
8. The Red Skelton Show	NBC	15.2	8. Bewitched	ABC	14.8	8. One Day at a Time	CBS	11.4
9. December Bride	CBS	13.8	9. Gomer Pyle	CBS	13.4	9. Three's Company	ABC	10.8
10. I've Got a Secret	CBS	12.9	10. Candid Camera	CBS	11.2	10. 60 Minutes	CBS	10.0
11. $64,000 Question	CBS	11.2	11. The Dick Van Dyke Show	CBS	11.1	11. Maude	CBS	9.8
12. Disneyland	ABC	10.8	12. The Danny Thomas Show	CBS	10.7	12. Gunsmoke	CBS	9.7
13. The Ed Sullivan Show	CBS	10.6	13. Family Affair	CBS	9.8	13. Charlie's Angels	ABC	9.6
14. Have Gun—Will Travel	CBS	10.3	14. Laugh-In	NBC	7.9	14. The Jeffersons	CBS	9.4
15. The Danny Thomas Show	CBS	9.9	15. Rawhide	CBS	7.5	15. Laverne & Shirley	ABC	9.3

U.S. Television Sets and Stations Received

Source: A.C. Nielsen

Set Ownership

(est. as of Jan. 1, 1991)

Total TV Households	93,100,000	
(98% of U.S. households own at least one TV set)		

Homes with:

Color TV sets	91,300,000	98%
B&W only	1,800,000	2%
2 or more sets	60,000,000	64%
One set	33,100,000	35%
Cable (May 1991)	56,072,270	60.3%

Total TV Households: 93,100,000
Total Persons 2+: 237,120,000
Total Women 18+: 95,570,000
Total Men 18+: 86,220,000
Total Teens 12-17: 19,750,000
Total Children 2-11: 35,580,000

Stations Receivable:
(September 1990)
% of TV homes receiving:

1-6	8%
7-10	36%
11-14	34%
15-19	16%
20-29	6%
30+	IFR

IFR = Less than 1%

100 Leading U.S. Advertisers, 1989

Source: *Advertising Age*, Sept. 26, 1990 © Crain Communications Inc. 1990

(millions of dollars)

Rank	Advertiser	Ad spending	Rank	Advertiser	Ad spending	Rank	Advertiser	Ad spending
1	Philip Morris	$2,072.0	36	U.S. Government	$309.5	70	Mobil	156.3
2	Procter & Gamble	1,779.3	37	Nissan Motor	300.6	71	Hasbro	$151.9
3	Sears, Roebuck	1,432.1	38	Honda Motor	298.8	72	Schering-Plough	150.2
4	General Motors	1,363.8	39	Campeau	294.9	73	Citicorp	146.3
5	Grand Metropolitan	823.3	40	Mars	293.3	74	Loews	143.0
6	PepsiCo	786.1	41	Hershey Foods	288.2	75	Paramount Communications	141.2
7	McDonald's	774.4	42	American Express	267.9	76	Hallmark Cards	138.2
8	Eastman Kodak	718.8	43	Colgate-Palmolive	246.3	77	Seagram	136.8
9	RJR Nabisco	703.5	44	General Electric	243.2	78	E.I. du Pont de Nemours	133.2
10	Kellogg	611.6	45	Pfizer	235.3	79	Bell Atlantic	132.0
11	Nestle	608.4	46	Tandy	232.7	80	Volkswagen	131.9
12	Unilever	604.1	47	American Stores	220.0	81	Circuit City Stores	131.2
13	Ford Motor	602.1	48	MCA	219.9	82	AMR	131.0
14	Anheuser-Busch	591.5	49	Montgomery Ward	213.6	83	News	128.9
15	Warner-Lambert	585.9	50	Hyundai	212.8	84	ITT	128.5
16	AT&T	567.7	51	ConAgra	211.3	85	UAL	127.3
17	Time Warner	567.5	52	U.S. Dairy Farmers	205.9	86	Wal-Mart	127.1
18	K mart	561.4	53	American Brands	204.2	87	Carter Hawley Hale	126.6
19	Chrysler	532.5	54	SmithKline Beecham	203.2	88	Kroger	125.5
20	Johnson & Johnson	487.1	55	Adolph Coors	201.0	89	Wm. Wrigley Jr.	124.3
21	General Mills	471.0	56	IBM	196.9	90	Levi Strauss	123.1
22	American Home Products	456.1	57	Cambpell Soup	196.7	91	Wendy's	122.4
23	Bristol-Myers Squibb	451.6	58	Revlon	196.7	92	United Telecommunications	121.3
24	Ralston Purina	429.5	59	B.A.T. Industries	196.4	93	Nynex	120.7
25	Toyota Motor	417.6	60	Mazda Motor	196.3	94	Continental Airlines Holdings	119.6
26	J.C. Penney	407.5	61	Gillette	185.1	95	Delta Air Lines	116.0
27	May Department Stores	385.7	62	Philips	182.3	96	Daimler-Benz	115.5
28	Coca-Cola	385.3	63	Clorox	179.9	97	Bayer	112.0
29	Sara Lee	357.9	64	Goodyear Tire & Rubber	168.3	98	Whitman	108.4
30	Quaker Oats	357.8	65	CPC	166.2	99	Nike	104.6
31	Sony	356.5	66	Marriot	162.0	100	Dr. Pepper/Seven Up	104.3
32	H.J. Heinz	342.3	67	Dow Chemical	160.2			
33	Walt Disney	338.7	68	S.C. Johnson & Son	160.1			
34	Dayton Hudson	314.2	69	Subaru	159.5			
35	R.H. Macy	312.7						

Total U.S. Ad Spending by Category and Medium, 1989

Source: *Advertising Age*, Sept. 26, 1990 © Crain Communications Inc. 1990

(millions of dollars)

Category	Total ad spending	Magazine	Sunday magazine	Newspaper	Network TV	Spot TV	Cable TV	Network radio
Retail	$6,028.7	$203.9	$110.2	$3,638.1	$294.8	$1,493.1	$30.4	$102.9
Automotive	5,519.9	883.6	29.1	881.8	1,520.0	1,656.4	85.9	85.2
Food	3,897.5	434.9	20.5	48.9	1,637.8	911.6	101.9	74.5
Business, consumer svcs.	3,891.4	524.4	40.3	1,405.5	625.0	804.8	96.4	93.8
Entertainment	2,753.2	24.3	2.1	517.5	837.0	1,154.6	51.5	9.3
Toiletries, cosmetics	2,212.2	650.0	32.2	9.7	921.5	301.6	32.3	19.7
Travel, hotels	2,133.1	367.6	40.1	982.4	180.9	273.4	31.1	42.3
Drugs & remedies	1,604.9	136.0	21.5	108.6	762.8	273.7	60.4	55.6
Beer, wine & liquor	1,184.6	256.6	13.7	32.0	380.9	220.9	38.4	9.2
Direct response cos.	1,150.9	507.5	226.4	109.6	62.7	123.0	62.6	31.6
Snacks & soft drinks	1,098.7	53.3	3.2	15.0	408.3	351.6	47.6	38.2
Apparel, footwear	891.1	391.4	30.2	11.3	232.2	89.8	36.4	3.4
Insurance & real estate	868.9	132.8	18.9	334.0	193.5	111.1	15.5	22.4
Publishing & media	763.2	192.6	4.6	248.3	11.3	152.5	18.6	15.2
Cigarettes, tobacco	675.1	401.5	45.7	31.6	0.2	4.9	0.7	2.1
Computers, office equip.	667.1	289.0	8.5	92.0	165.6	42.3	16.9	13.3
Household equip.	620.9	103.0	10.9	22.9	264.8	130.5	23.3	21.1
Soaps, cleansers	612.3	67.5	2.1	2.7	312.4	116.9	26.1	0.1
Sporting goods, toys	610.0	130.6	0.7	7.0	125.4	217.6	29.6	1.2
Jewelry, cameras	403.0	153.2	11.4	12.8	106.0	53.3	10.0	1.1
Building materials	379.7	81.3	7.8	56.5	92.0	85.3	18.0	10.8
Household furnishings	357.6	123.2	23.8	42.6	69.8	57.2	2.1	2.3
Electronic entertainment	349.6	102.5	2.8	11.0	58.7	84.6	30.5	17.3
Gasoline, lubricants	341.2	27.5	1.6	25.8	38.3	164.4	9.7	4.1
Pets, pet foods	275.2	45.8	4.4	4.3	133.9	40.9	10.7	4.2
Horticulture & farming	245.7	24.5	3.2	49.9	39.0	65.9	8.4	9.5
Freight, industrial	149.7	47.5	4.6	12.0	54.7	22.7	3.2	4.8
Industrial materials	109.8	62.8	0.7	7.7	24.0	11.0	2.0	NA
Business propositions	36.4	20.3	0.4	2.4	3.3	3.6	0.6	0.9
Airplanes, aviation	18.1	14.0	0.2	2.7	0.4	0.3	0.5	0.0
Miscellaneous	331.5	141.7	15.2	50.7	1.8	10.6	1.1	0.1
Total	$40,181.1	$6,594.9	$737.0	$8,777.3	$9,559.0	$9,030.4	$952.6	$696.2

Note: NA = Not available.

AWARDS — MEDALS — PRIZES

The Alfred B. Nobel Prize Winners

Alfred B. Nobel, inventor of dynamite, bequeathed $9,000,000, the interest to be distributed yearly to those who had most benefited mankind in physics, chemistry, medicine-physiology, literature, and peace. The first Nobel Memorial Prize in Economics was awarded in 1969. No awards given for years omitted. In 1990, each prize was worth approximately $710,000. (For 1991, see *Addenda*.)

Physics

1990 Richard E. Taylor, Can.; Jerome I. Friedman, Henry W. Kendall, both U.S.
1989 Norman F. Ramsey, U.S.; Hans G. Dehmelt, German-U.S. & Wolfgang Paul, German
1988 Leon M, Lederman, Melvin Schwartz, Jack Steinberger, all U.S.
1987 K. Alex Muller, Swiss; J. Georg Bednorz, W. German
1986 Ernest Ruska, German, Gerd Binnig, W. German, Heinrich Rohrer, Swiss
1985 Klaus von Klitzing, W. German
1984 Carlo Rubbia, Italian, Simon van der Meere, Dutch
1983 Subrahmanyan Chandrasekhar, William A. Fowler, both U.S.
1982 Kenneth G. Wilson, U.S.
1981 Nicolass Bloembergen, Arthur Schaalow, both U.S.; Kai M. Siegbahn, Swedish
1980 James W. Cronin, Val L. Fitch, U.S.
1979 Steven Weinberg, Sheldon L. Glashow, both U.S.; Abdus Salam, Pakistani
1978 Pyotr Kapitsa, USSR; Arno Penzias, Robert Wilson, both U.S.
1977 John H. Van Vleck, Philip W. Anderson, both U.S.; Nevill F. Mott, British
1976 Burton Richter, U.S. Samuel C.C. Ting, U.S.
1975 James Rainwater, U.S. Ben Mottelson, U.S.-Danish, Aage Bohr, Danish
1974 Martin Ryle, British Antony Hewish, British
1973 Ivar Giaever, U.S. Leo Esaki, Japan Brian D. Josephson, British
1972 John Bardeen, U.S. Leon N. Cooper, U.S. John R. Schrieffer, U.S.
1971 Dennis Gabor, British
1970 Louis Neel, French

Hannes Alfven, Swedish
1969 Murray Gell-Mann, U.S.
1968 Luis W. Alvarez, U.S.
1967 Hans A. Bethe, U.S.
1966 Alfred Kastler, French
1965 Richard P. Feynman, U.S. Julian S. Schwinger, U.S. Shinichiro Tomonaga, Japanese
1964 Nikolai G. Basov, USSR Aleksander M. Prochorov, USSR Charles H. Townes, U.S.
1963 Maria Goeppert-Mayer, U.S. J. Hans D. Jensen, German Eugene P. Wigner, U.S.
1962 Lev. D. Landau, USSR
1961 Robert Hofstadter, U.S. Rudolf L. Mossbauer, German
1960 Donald A. Glaser, U.S.
1959 Owen Chamberlain, U.S. Emilio G. Segre, U.S.
1958 Pavel Cherenkov, Ilya Frank, Igor Y. Tamm, all USSR
1957 Tsung-dao Lee, Chen Ning Yang, both U.S.
1956 John Bardeen, U.S. Walter H. Brattain, U.S. William Shockley, U.S.
1955 Polykarp Kusch, U.S. Willis E. Lamb, U.S.
1954 Max Born, British Walter Bothe, German
1953 Frits Zernike, Dutch
1952 Felix Bloch, U.S. Edward M. Purcell, U.S.
1951 Sir John D. Cockroft, British Ernest T. S. Walton, Irish
1950 Cecil F. Powell, British
1949 Hideki Yukawa, Japanese
1948 Patrick M. S. Blackett, British
1947 Sir Edward V. Appleton, British
1946 Percy Williams Bridgman, U.S.
1945 Wolfgang Pauli, U.S.
1944 Isidor Isaac Rabi, U.S.
1943 Otto Stern, U.S.
1939 Ernest O. Lawrence, U.S.
1938 Enrico Fermi, U.S.
1937 Clinton J. Davisson, U.S.

Sir George P. Thomson, British
1936 Carl D. Anderson, U.S. Victor F. Hess, Austrian
1935 Sir James Chadwick, British
1933 Paul A. M. Dirac, British Erwin Schrodinger, Austrian
1932 Werner Heisenberg, German
1930 Sir Chandrasekhara V. Raman, Indian
1929 Prince Louis-Victor de Broglie, French
1928 Owen W. Richardson, British
1927 Arthur H. Compton, U.S. Charles T. R. Wilson, British
1926 Jean B. Perrin, French
1925 James Franck, Gustav Hertz, both German
1924 Karl M. G. Siegbahn, Swedish
1923 Robert A. Millikan, U.S.
1922 Niels Bohr, Danish
1921 Albert Einstein, Ger.-U.S.
1920 Charles E. Guillaume, French
1919 Johannes Stark, German
1918 Max K. E. L. Planck, German
1917 Charles G. Barkla, British
1915 Sir William H. Bragg, British Sir William L. Bragg, British
1914 Max von Laue, German
1913 Heike Kamerlingh-Onnes, Dutch
1912 Nils G. Dalen, Swedish
1911 Wilhelm Wien, German
1910 Johannes D. van der Waals, Dutch
1909 Carl F. Braun, German Guglielmo Marconi, Italian
1908 Gabriel Lippmann, French
1907 Albert A. Michelson, U.S.
1906 Sir Joseph J. Thomson, British
1905 Philipp E. A. von Lenard, Ger.
1904 John W. Strutt, Lord Rayleigh, British
1903 Antoine Henri Becquerel, French Marie Curie, Polish-French Pierre Curie, French
1902 Hendrik A. Lorentz, Pieter Zeeman, both Dutch
1901 Wilhelm C. Roentgen, German

Chemistry

1990 Elias James Corey, U.S.
1989 Thomas R. Cech, Sidney Altman, both U.S.
1988 Johann Deisenhofer, Robert Huber, Hartmut Michel, all W. German
1987 Donald J. Cram, Charles J. Pederson, both U.S.; Jean-Marie Lehn, French
1986 Dudley Herschbach, Yuan T. Lee, both U.S.; John C. Polanyi, Canadian
1985 Herbert A. Hauptman, Jerome Karle, both U.S.
1984 Bruce Merrifield, U.S.
1983 Henry Taube, Canadian
1982 Aaron Klug, S. African
1981 Kenichi Fukui, Japan., Roald Hoffmann, U.S.
1980 Paul Berg, U.S.; Walter Gilbert, U.S., Frederick Sanger, U.K.
1979 Herbert C. Brown, U.S. George Wittig, German
1978 Peter Mitchell, British
1977 Ilya Prigogine, Belgian

1976 William N. Lipscomb, U.S.
1975 John Cornforth, Austral.-Brit., Vladimir Prelog, Yugo.-Switz.
1974 Paul J. Flory, U.S.
1973 Ernst Otto Fischer, W. German Geoffrey Wilkinson, British
1972 Christian B. Anfinsen, U.S. Stanford Moore, U.S. William H. Stein, U.S.
1971 Gerhard Herzberg, Canadian
1970 Luis F. Leloir, Arg.
1969 Derek H. R. Barton, British Odd Hassel, Norwegian
1968 Lars Onsager, U.S.
1967 Manfred Eigen, German Ronald G. W. Norrish, British George Porter, British
1966 Robert S. Mulliken, U.S.
1965 Robert B. Woodward, U.S.
1964 Dorothy C. Hodgkin, British
1963 Giulio Natta, Italian Karl Ziegler, German
1962 John C. Kendrew, British Max F. Perutz, British
1961 Melvin Calvin, U.S.

1960 Willard F. Libby, U.S.
1959 Jaroslav Heyrovsky, Czech
1958 Frederick Sanger, British
1957 Sir Alexander R. Todd, British
1956 Sir Cyril N. Hinshelwood, British Nikolai N. Semenov, USSR
1955 Vincent du Vigneaud, U.S.
1954 Linus C. Pauling, U.S.
1953 Hermann Staudinger, German
1952 Archer J. P. Martin, British Richard L. M. Synge, British
1951 Edwin M. McMillan, U.S. Glenn T. Seaborg, U.S.
1950 Kurt Alder, German Otto P. H. Diels, German
1949 William F. Giauque, U.S.
1948 Arne W. K. Tiselius, Swedish
1947 Sir Robert Robinson, British
1946 James B. Sumner, John H. Northrop, Wendell M. Stanley, U.S.
1945 Artturi I. Virtanen, Finnish
1944 Otto Hahn, German
1943 Georg de Hevesy, Hungarian
1939 Adolf F. J. Butenandt, German Leopold Ruzicka, Swiss

1938 Richard Kuhn, German
1937 Walter N. Haworth, British
     Paul Karrer, Swiss
1936 Peter J. W. Debye, Dutch
1935 Frederic Joliot-Curie, French
     Irene Joliot-Curie, French
1934 Harold C. Urey, U.S.
1932 Irving Langmuir, U.S.
1931 Friedrich Bergius, German
     Karl Bosch, German
1930 Hans Fischer, German
1929 Sir Arthur Harden, British
     Hans von Euler-Chelpin, Swed.

1928 Adolf O. R. Windaus, German
1927 Heinrich O. Wieland, German
1926 Theodor Svedberg, Swedish
1925 Richard A. Zsigmondy, German
1923 Fritz Pregl, Austrian
1922 Francis W. Aston, British
1921 Frederick Soddy, British
1920 Walther H. Nernst, German
1918 Fritz Haber, German
1915 Richard M. Willstatter, German
1914 Theodore W. Richards, U.S.
1913 Alfred Werner, Swiss
1912 Victor Grignard, French

     Paul Sabatier, French
1911 Marie Curie, Polish-French
1910 Otto Wallach, German
1909 Wilhelm Ostwald, German
1908 Ernest Rutherford, British
1907 Eduard Buchner, German
1906 Henri Moissan, French
1905 Adolf von Baeyer, German
1904 Sir William Ramsay, British
1903 Svante A. Arrhenius, Swedish
1902 Emil Fischer, German
1901 Jacobus H. van't Hoff, Dutch

Physiology or Medicine

1990 Joseph E. Murray, E. Donnall
     Thomas, both U.S.
1989 J. Michael Bishop, Harold E.
     Varmus, both U.S.
1988 Gertrude B. Elion, George H.
     Hitchings, both U.S; Sir James
     Black, Brit.
1987 Susumu Tonegawa, Japanese
1986 Rita Levi-Montalcini, It.-U.S.,
     Stanley Cohen, U.S.
1985 Michael S. Brown, Joseph L.
     Goldstein, both U.S.
1984 Cesar Milstein, Brit.-Argentina;
     Georges J. F. Koehler, German;
     Niels K. Jerne, Brit.-Danish
1983 Barbara McClintock, U.S.
1982 Sune Bergstrom, Bengt
     Samuelsson, both Swedish;
     John R. Vane, British.
1981 Roger W. Sperry,
     David H. Hubel, Tosten N. Wiesel,
     all U.S.
1980 Baruj Benacerraf, George Snell,
     both U.S.; Jean Dausset, France
1979 Alian M. Cormack, U.S.
     Geoffrey N. Hounsfield, British
1978 Daniel Nathans, Hamilton O. Smith,
     both U.S.; Werner Arber, Swiss
1977 Rosalyn S. Yalow, Roger C.L.
     Guillemin, Andrew V. Schally, U.S.
1976 Baruch S. Blumberg, U.S.
     Daniel Carleton Gajdusek, U.S.
1975 David Baltimore, Howard Temin,
     both U.S.; Renato Dulbecco,
     Ital.-U.S.
1974 Albert Claude, Lux.-U.S.; George
     Emil Palade, Rom.-U.S.; Christian
     Rene de Duve, Belg.
1973 Karl von Frisch, Ger.; Konrad
     Lorenz, Ger.-Austrian; Nikolaas
     Tinbergen, Brit.
1972 Gerald M. Edelman, U.S.
     Rodney R. Porter, British
1971 Earl W. Sutherland Jr., U.S.
1970 Julius Axelrod, U.S.
     Sir Bernard Katz, British
     Ulf von Euler, Swedish
1969 Max Delbruck,
     Alfred D. Hershey,

     Salvador Luria, all U.S.
1968 Robert W. Holley,
     H. Gobind Khorana,
     Marshall W. Nirenberg, all U.S.
1967 Ragnar Granit, Swedish
     Haldan Keffer Hartline, U.S.
     George Wald, U.S.
1966 Charles B. Huggins,
     Francis Peyton Rous, both U.S.
1965 Francois Jacob, Andre Lwoff,
     Jacques Monod, all French
1964 Konrad E. Bloch, U.S.
     Feodor Lynen, German
1963 Sir John C. Eccles, Australian
     Alan L. Hodgkin, British
     Andrew F. Huxley, British
1962 Francis H. C. Crick, British
     James D. Watson, U.S.
     Maurice H. F. Wilkins, British
1961 Georg von Bekesy, U.S.
1960 Sir F. MacFarlane Bumet,
     Australian
     Peter B. Medawar, British
1959 Arthur Kornberg, U.S.
     Severo Ochoa, U.S.
1958 George W. Beadle, U.S.
     Edward L. Tatum, U.S.
     Joshua Lederberg, U.S.
1957 Daniel Bovet, Italian
1956 Andre F. Cournand, U.S.
     Werner Forssmann, German
     Dickinson W. Richards, Jr., U.S.
1955 Alex H. T. Theorell, Swedish
1954 John F. Enders,
     Frederick C. Robbins,
     Thomas H. Weller, all U.S.
1953 Hans A. Krebs, British
     Fritz A. Lipmann, U.S.
1952 Selman A. Waksman, U.S.
1951 Max Theiler, U.S.
1950 Philip S. Hench,
     Edward C. Kendall, both U.S.
     Tadeus Reichstein, Swiss
1949 Walter R. Hess, Swiss
     Antonio Moniz, Portuguese
1948 Paul H. Müller, Swiss
1947 Carl F. Cori,
     Gerty T. Cori, both U.S.
     Bernardo A. Houssay, Arg.

1946 Hermann J. Muller, U.S.
1945 Ernst B. Chain, British
     Sir Alexander Fleming, British
     Sir Howard W. Florey, British
1944 Joseph Erlanger, U.S.
     Herbert S. Gasser, U.S.
1943 Henrik C. P. Dam, Danish
     Edward A. Doisy, U.S.
1939 Gerhard Domagk, German
1938 Corneille J. F. Heymans, Belg.
1937 Albert Szent-Gyorgyi, Hung.-U.S.
1936 Sir Henry H. Dale, British
     Otto Loewi, U.S.
1935 Hans Spemann, German
1934 George R. Minot, Wm. P. Murphy,
     G. H. Whipple, all U.S.
1933 Thomas H. Morgan, U.S.
1932 Edgar D. Adrian, British
     Sir Charles S. Sherrington, Brit.
1931 Otto H. Warburg, German
1930 Karl Landsteiner, U.S.
1929 Christiaan Eijkman, Dutch
     Sir Frederick G. Hopkins, British
1928 Charles J. H. Nicolle, French
1927 Julius Wagner-Jauregg, Aus.
1926 Johannes A. G. Fibiger, Danish
1924 Willem Einthoven, Dutch
1923 Frederick G. Banting, Canadian
     John J. R. Macleod, Scottish
1922 Archibald V. Hill, British
     Otto F. Meyerhof, German
1920 Schack A. S. Krogh, Danish
1919 Jules Bordet, Belgian
1914 Robert Barany, Austrian
1913 Charles R. Richet, French
1912 Alexis Carrel, French
1911 Allvar Gullstrand, Swedish
1910 Albrecht Kossel, German
1909 Emil T. Kocher, Swiss
1908 Paul Ehrlich, German
     Elie Metchnikoff, French
1907 Charles L. A. Laveran, French
1906 Camillo Golgi, Italian
     Santiago Ramon y Cajal, Sp.
1905 Robert Koch, German
1904 Ivan P. Pavlov, Russian
1903 Niels R. Finsen, Danish
1902 Sir Ronald Ross, British
1901 Emil A. von Behring, German

Literature

1990 Octavio Paz, Mexican
1989 Camilo José Cela, Spanish
1988 Naguib Mahfouz, Egyptian
1987 Joseph Brodsky, USSR-U.S.
1986 Wole Soyinka, Nigerian
1985 Claude Simon, French
1984 Jaroslav Siefert, Czech.
1983 William Golding, British
1982 Gabriel Garcia Marquez,
     Colombian-Mex.
1981 Elias Canetti, Bulgarian-British
1980 Czeslaw Milosz, Polish-U.S.
1979 Odysseus Elytis, Greek
1978 Isaac Bashevis Singer, U.S.
     (Yiddish)
1977 Vicente Aleixandre, Spanish
1976 Saul Bellow, U.S.
1975 Eugenio Montale, Ital.
1974 Eyvind Johnson, Harry Edmund
     Martinson, both Swedish
1973 Patrick White, Australian
1972 Heinrich Boll, W. German

1971 Pablo Neruda, Chilean
1970 Aleksandr I. Solzhenitsyn, Russ.
1969 Samuel Beckett, Irish
1968 Yasunari Kawabata, Japanese
1967 Miguel Angel Asturias, Guate.
1966 Samuel Joseph Agnon, Israeli
     Nelly Sachs, Swedish
1965 Mikhail Sholokhov, Russian
1964 Jean Paul Sartre, French
     (Prize declined)
1963 Giorgos Seferis, Greek
1962 John Steinbeck, U.S.
1961 Ivo Andric, Yugoslavian
1960 Saint-John Perse, French
1959 Salvatore Quasimodo, Italian
1958 Boris L. Pasternak, Russian
     (Prize declined)
1957 Albert Camus, French
1956 Juan Ramon Jimenez,
     Span.
1955 Halldor K. Laxness, Icelandic
1954 Ernest Hemingway, U.S.

1953 Sir Winston Churchill, British
1952 Francois Mauriac, French
1951 Par F. Lagerkvist, Swedish
1950 Bertrand Russell, British
1949 William Faulkner, U.S.
1948 T.S. Eliot, British
1947 Andre Gide, French
1946 Hermann Hesse, Swiss
1945 Gabriela Mistral, Chilean
1944 Johannes V. Jensen, Danish
1939 Frans E. Sillanpaa, Finnish
1938 Pearl S. Buck, U.S.
1937 Roger Martin du Gard, French
1936 Eugene O'Neill, U.S.
1934 Luigi Pirandello, Italian
1933 Ivan A. Bunin, French
1932 John Galsworthy, British
1931 Erik A. Karlfeldt, Swedish
1930 Sinclair Lewis, U.S.
1929 Thomas Mann, German
1928 Sigrid Undset, Norwegian
1927 Henri Bergson, French

1926 Grazia Deledda, Italian
1925 George Bernard Shaw, British
1924 Wladyslaw S. Reymont, Polish
1923 William Butler Yeats, Irish
1922 Jacinto Benavente, Spanish
1921 Anatole France, French
1920 Knut Hamsun, Norwegian
1919 Carl F. G. Spitteler, Swiss
1917 Karl A. Gjellerup, Danish

Henrik Pontoppidan, Danish
1916 Verner von Heidenstam, Swed.
1915 Romain Rolland, French
1913 Rabindranath Tagore, Indian
1912 Gerhart Hauptmann, German
1911 Maurice Maeterlinck, Belgian
1910 Paul J. L. Heyse, German
1909 Selma Lagerlof, Swedish
1908 Rudolf C. Eucken, German

1907 Rudyard Kipling, British
1906 Giosue Carducci, Italian
1905 Henryk Sienkiewicz, Polish
1904 Frederic Mistral, French
     Jose Echegaray, Spanish
1903 Bjornsterne Bjornson, Norw.
1902 Theodor Mommsen, German
1901 Rene F. A Sully Prudhomme,
     French

Nobel Memorial Prize in Economics

1990 Harry M. Markowitz, William F.
     Sharpe, Merton H. Miller, all U.S.
1989 Trygve Haavelmo, Norwegian
1988 Maurice Allais, French
1987 Robert M. Solow, U.S.
1986 James M. Buchanan, U.S.
1985 Franco Modigliani, It.-U.S.
1984 Richard Stone, British
1983 Gerard Debreu, Fr.-U.S.
1982 George J. Stigler, U.S.

1981 James Tobin, U.S.
1980 Lawrence R. Klein, U.S.
1979 Theodore W. Schultz, U.S.,
     Sir Arthur Lewis, British
1978 Herbert A. Simon, U.S.
1977 Bertil Ohlin, Swedish
     James E. Meade, British
1976 Milton Friedman, U.S.
1975 Tjalling Koopmans, Dutch-U.S.,
     Leonid Kantorovich, USSR

1974 Gunnar Myrdal, Swed.,
     Friedrich A. von Hayek, Austrian
1973 Wassily Leontief, U.S.
1972 Kenneth J. Arrow, U.S.
     John R. Hicks, British
1971 Simon Kuznets, U.S.
1970 Paul A. Samuelson, U.S.
1969 Ragnar Frisch, Norwegian
     Jan Tinbergen, Dutch

Peace

1990 Mikhail S. Gorbachev, USSR
1989 Dalai Lama, Tibet
1988 United Nations Peacekeeping
     Forces
1987 Oscar Arias Sanchez, Costa Rican
1986 Elie Wiesel, Romania-U.S.
1985 Intl. Physicians for the Prevention of
     Nuclear War, U.S.
1984 Bishop Desmond Tutu, So. African
1983 Lech Walesa, Polish
1982 Alva Myrdal, Swedish; Alfonso
     Garcia Robles, Mexican
1981 Office of U.N. High Commissioner
     for Refugees
1980 Adolfo Perez Esquivel, Argentine
1979 Mother Teresa of Calcutta,
     Albanian-Indian
1978 Anwar Sadat, Egyptian
     Menachem Begin, Israeli
1977 Amnesty International
1976 Mairead Corrigan, Betty Williams,
     N. Irish
1975 Andrei Sakharov, USSR
1974 Eisaku Sato, Japanese, Sean
     MacBride, Irish
1973 Henry Kissinger, U.S.
     Le Duc Tho, N. Vietnamese
     (Tho declined)
1971 Willy Brandt, W. German
1970 Norman E. Borlaug, U.S.
1969 Intl. Labor Organization
1968 Rene Cassin, French
1965 U.N. Children's Fund (UNICEF)
1964 Martin Luther King Jr., U.S.

1963 International Red Cross,
     League of Red Cross Societies
1962 Linus C. Pauling, U.S.
1961 Dag Hammarskjold, Swedish
1960 Albert J. Luthuli, South African
1959 Philip J. Noel-Baker, British
1958 Georges Pire, Belgian
1957 Lester B. Pearson, Canadian
1954 Office of the UN High
     Commissioner for Refugees
1953 George C. Marshall, U.S.
1952 Albert Schweitzer, French
1951 Leon Jouhaux, French
1950 Ralph J. Bunche, U.S.
1949 Lord John Boyd Orr of Brechin
     Mearns, British
1947 Friends Service Council, Brit.
     Amer. Friends Service Com.
1946 Emily G. Balch,
     John R. Mott, both U.S.
1945 Cordell Hull, U.S.
1944 International Red Cross
1938 Nansen International Office
     for Refugees
1937 Viscount Cecil of Chelwood, Brit.
1936 Carlos de Saavedra Lamas, Arg.
1935 Carl von Ossietzky, German
1934 Arthur Henderson, British
1933 Sir Norman Angell, British
1931 Jane Addams, U.S.
     Nicholas Murray Butler, U.S.
1930 Nathan Soderblom, Swedish
1929 Frank B. Kellogg, U.S.

1927 Ferdinand E. Buisson, French
     Ludwig Quidde, German
1926 Aristide Briand, French
     Gustav Stresemann, German
1925 Sir J. Austen Chamberlain, Brit.
     Charles G. Dawes, U.S.
1922 Fridtjof Nansen, Norwegian
1921 Karl H. Branting, Swedish
     Christian L. Lange, Norwegian
1920 Leon V.A. Bourgeois, French
1919 Woodrow Wilson, U.S.
1917 International Red Cross
1913 Henri La Fontaine, Belgian
1912 Elihu Root, U.S.
1911 Tobias M.C. Asser, Dutch
     Alfred H. Fried, Austrian
1910 Permanent Intl. Peace Bureau
1909 Auguste M. F. Beernaert, Belg.
     Paul H. B. B. d'Estournelles de
     Constant, French
1908 Klas P. Arnoldson, Swedish
     Fredrik Bajer, Danish
1907 Ernesto T. Moneta, Italian
     Louis Renault, French
1906 Theodore Roosevelt, U.S.
1905 Baroness Bertha von Suttner,
     Austrian
1904 Institute of International Law
1903 Sir William R. Cremer, British
1902 Elie Ducommun,
     Charles A. Gobat, both Swiss
1901 Jean H. Dunant, Swiss
     Frederic Passy, French

Pulitzer Prizes in Journalism, Letters, and Music

The Pulitzer Prizes were endowed by Joseph Pulitzer (1847-1911), publisher of The World, New York, N.Y., in a bequest to Columbia University, and are awarded annually by the president of the university on recommendation of the Pulitzer Prize Board for work done during the preceding year. The administrator is Robert C. Christopher of Columbia Univ. All prizes are $3,000 (originally $500) in each category, except Meritorious Public Service for which a gold medal is given.

Journalism

Meritorious Public Service

For distinguished and meritorious public service by a United States newspaper.
1918—New York Times. Also special award to Minna Lewinson and Henry Beetle Hough.
1919—Milwaukee Journal.
1921—Boston Post.
1922—New York World.
1923—Memphis (Tenn.) Commercial Appeal.
1924—New York World.
1926—Enquirer-Sun, Columbus, Ga.
1927—Canton (Oh.) Daily News.
1928—Indianapolis Times.
1929—Evening World, New York.
1931—Atlanta (Ga.) Constitution.
1932—Indianapolis (Ind.) News.
1933—New York World-Telegram.
1934—Medford (Ore.) Mail-Tribune.

1935—Sacramento (Cal.) Bee.
1936—Cedar Rapids (Ia.) Gazette.
1937—St.Louis Post-Dispatch.
1938—Bismarck (N.D.) Tribune.
1939—Miami (Fla.) Daily News.
1940—Waterbury (Conn.) Republican and American.
1941—St.Louis Post-Dispatch.
1942—Los Angeles Times.
1943—Omaha World Herald.
1944—New York Times.
1945—Detroit Free Press.
1946—Scranton (Pa.) Times.
1947—Baltimore Sun.
1948—St. Louis Post-Dispatch.
1949—Nebraska State Journal.
1950—Chicago Daily News; St. Louis Post-Dispatch.
1951—Miami (Fla.) Herald and Brooklyn Eagle.
1952—St. Louis Post-Dispatch.

1953—Whiteville (N.C.) News Reporter; Tabor City (N.C.) Tribune.
1954—Newsday (Long Island, N.Y.).
1955—Columbus (Ga.) Ledger and Sunday Ledger-Enquirer.
1956—Watsonville (Cal.) Register-Pajaronian.
1957—Chicago Daily News.
1958—Arkansas Gazette, Little Rock.
1959—Utica (N.Y.) Observer-Dispatch and Utica Daily Press.
1960—Los Angeles Times.
1961—Amarillo (Tex.) Globe-Times.
1962—Panama City (Fla.) News-Herald.
1963—Chicago Daily News.
1964—St.Petersburg (Fla.) Times.
1965—Hutchinson (Kan.) News.
1966—Boston Globe.
1967—The Louisville Courier-Journal; The Milwaukee Journal.
1968—Riverside (Cal.) Press-Enterprise.
1969—Los Angeles Times.
1970—Newsday (Long Island, N.Y.).
1971—Winston Salem (N.C.) Journal & Sentinel.
1972—New York Times.
1973—Washington Post.
1974—Newsday (Long Island, N.Y.).
1975—Boston Globe.
1976—Anchorage Daily News.
1977—Lufkin (Tex.) News.
1978—Philadelphia Inquirer.
1979—Point Reyes (Cal.) Light.
1980—Gannett News Service.
1981—Charlotte (N.C.) Observer.
1982—Detroit News.
1983—Jackson (Miss.) Clarion-Ledger.
1984—Los Angeles Times.
1985—Ft. Worth (Tex.) Star-Telegram.
1986—Denver Post.
1987—Pittsburgh Press.
1988—Charlotte Observer.
1989—Anchorage Daily News.
1990—The Philadelphia Inquirer, Gilbert M. Gaul; Washington (N.C.) Daily News.
1991—Des Moines Register, Jane Schorer.

Reporting

This category originally embraced all fields, local, national, and international. Later separate categories were created for the different fields of reporting.
1917—Herbert Bayard Swope, New York World.
1918—Harold A. Littledale, New York Evening Post.
1920—John J. Leary, Jr., New York World.
1921—Louis Seibold, New York World.
1922—Kirke L. Simpson, Associated Press.
1923—Alva Johnston, New York Times.
1924—Magner White, San Diego Sun.
1925—James W. Mulroy and Alvin H. Goldstein, Chicago Daily News.
1926—William Burke Miller, Louisville Courier-Journal.
1927—John T. Rogers, St. Louis Post-Dispatch.
1929—Paul Y. Anderson, St. Louis Post-Dispatch.
1930—Russell D. Owens, New York Times. Also $500 to W.O. Dapping, Auburn (N.Y.) Citizen.
1931—A.B. MacDonald, Kansas City (Mo.) Star.
1932—W.C. Richards, D.D. Martin, J.S. Pooler, F.D. Webb, J.N.W. Sloan, Detroit Free Press.
1933—Francis A. Jamieson, Associated Press.
1934—Royce Brier, San Francisco Chronicle.
1935—William H.Taylor, New York Herald Tribune.
1936—Lauren D.Lyman, New York Times.
1937—John J. O'Neill, N.Y.Herald Tribune; William L. Laurence, N.Y Times; Howard W. Blakeslee, A.P.; Gobind Behari Lal, Universal Service; and David Dietz, Scripps-Howard Newspapers.
1938—Raymond Sprigle, Pittsburgh Post-Gazette.
1939—Thomas L. Stokes, Scripps-Howard Newspaper Alliance.
1940—S.Burton Heath, New York World-Telegram.
1941—Westbrook Pegler, New York World-Telegram.
1942—Stanton Delaplane, San Francisco Chronicle.
1943—George Weller, Chicago Daily News.
1944—Paul Schoenstein, New York Journal-American.
1945—Jack S. McDowell, San Francisco Call-Bulletin.
1946—William L. Laurence, New York Times.
1947—Frederick Woltman, New York World-Telegram.
1948—George E. Goodwin, Atlanta Journal.
1949—Malcolm Johnson, New York Sun.
1950—Meyer Berger, New York Times.
1951—Edward S. Montgomery, San Francisco Examiner.
1952—Geo. de Carvalho, San Francisco Chronicle.

(1) General or Spot; (2) Special or Investigative

1953—(1) Providence (R.I.) Journal and Evening Bulletin; (2) Edward J. Mowery, New York World-Telegram & Sun.
1954—(1) Vicksburg (Miss.) Sunday Post-Herald; (2) Alvin Scott McCoy, Kansas City (Mo.) Star.
1955—(1) Mrs. Caro Brown, Alice (Tex.) Daily Echo; (2) Roland K. Towery, Cuero (Tex.) Record.
1956—(1) Lee Hills, Detroit Free Press; (2) Arthur Daley, New York Times.
1957—(1) Salt Lake Tribune, Salt Lake City, Ut.; (2) Wallace Turner and William Lambert, Portland Oregonian.
1958—(1) Fargo, (N.D.) Forum; (2) George Beveridge, Evening Star, Washington, D.C.
1959—(1) Mary Lou Werner, Washington Evening Star; (2) John Harold Brislin, Scranton (Pa.) Tribune, and The Scrantonian.
1960—(1) Jack Nelson, Atlanta Constitution; (2) Miriam Ottenberg, Washington Evening Star.
1961—(1) Sanche de Gramont, New York Herald Tribune; (2) Edgar May, Buffalo Evening News.
1962—(1) Robert D.Mullins, Deseret News, Salt Lake City; (2) George Bliss, Chicago Tribune.
1963—(1) Shared by Sylvan Fox, William Longgood, and Anthony Shannon, New York World-Telegram & Sun; (2) Oscar Griffin, Jr., Pecos (Tex.) Independent and Enterprise.
1964—(1) Norman C.Miller, Wall Street Journal; (2) Shared by James V. Magee, Albert V. Gaudiosi, and Frederick A. Meyer, Philadelphia Bulletin.
1965—(1) Melvin H.Ruder, Hungry Horse News (Columbia Falls, Mon.); (2) Gene Goltz, Houston Post.
1966—(1) Los Angeles Times Staff; (2) John A. Frasca, Tampa (Fla.) Tribune.
1967—(1) Robert V.Cox, Chambersburg (Pa.) Public Opinion; (2) Gene Miller, Miami Herald.
1968—Detroit Free Press Staff; (2) J. Anthony Lukas, New York Times.
1969—(1) John Fetterman, Louisville Courier-Journal and Times; (2) Albert L.Delugach, St. Louis Globe Democrat, and Denny Walsh, Life.
1970—(1) Thomas Fitzpatrick, Chicago Sun-Times; (2) Harold Eugene Martin, Montgomery Advertiser & Alabama Journal.
1971—(1) Akron Beacon Journal Staff; (2) William Hugh Jones, Chicago Tribune.
1972—(1) Richard Cooper and John Machacek, Rochester Times-Union; (2) Timothy Leland, Gerard M. O'Neill, Stephen A. Kurkjian and Anne De Santis, Boston Globe.
1973—(1) Chicago Tribune; (2) Sun Newspapers of Omaha.
1974—(1) Hugh F. Hough, Arthur M. Petacque, Chicago Sun-Times; (2) William Sherman, New York Daily News.
1975—(1) Xenia (Oh.) Daily Gazette; (2) Indianapolis Star.
1976—(1) Gene Miller, Miami Herald; (2) Chicago Tribune.
1977—(1) Margo Huston, Milwaukee Journal; (2) Acel Moore, Wendell Rawls Jr., Philadelphia Inquirer.
1978—(1) Richard Whitt, Louisville Courier-Journal; (2) Anthony R. Dolan, Stamford (Conn.) Advocate.
1979—(1) San Diego (Cal.) Evening Tribune; (2) Gilbert M. Gaul, Elliot G.Jaspin, Pottsville (Pa.) Republican.
1980—(1) Philadelphia Inquirer; (2) Stephen A. Kurkjian, Alexander B.Hawes Jr., Nils Bruzelius, Joan Vennochi, Robert M. Porterfield, Boston Globe.
1981—(1) Longview (Wash.) Daily News staff; (2) Clark Hallas and Robert B. Lowe, Arizona Daily Star.
1982—(1) Kansas City Star, Kansas City Times; (2) Paul Henderson, Seattle Times.
1983—(1) Fort Wayne (Ind.) News-Sentinel; (2) Loretta Tofani, Washington Post.
1984—(1) Newsday (N.Y.); (2) Boston Globe.
1985—(1) Thomas Turcol, Virginian-Pilot and Ledger-Star, Norfolk, Va.; (2) William K.Marimow, Philadelphia Inquirer; Lucy Morgan & Jack Reed, St. Petersburg (Fla.) Times.
1986—(1) Edna Buchanan, Miami Herald; (2) Jeffrey A. Marx & Michael M. York, Lexington (Ky.) Herald-Leader.
1987—(1) Akron Beacon Journal; (2) Daniel R. Biddle, H.G. Bissinger, Fredric N. Tulsky, Philadelphia Inquirer; John Woestendiek, Philadelphia Inquirer.
1988—(1) Alabama Journal; Lawrence (Mass.) Eagle-Tribune; (2) Walt Bogdanich, Wall Street Journal.
1989—(1) Louisville Courier-Journal; (2) Bill Dedman, Atlanta Journal and Constitution.
1990—(1) San Jose Mercury News; (2) Lon Kilzer, Chris Ison, Star Tribune, Minneapolis-St. Paul.
1991—(1) Miami Herald; (2) Joseph T. Hallinan, Susan M. Headden, Indianapolis Star.

Criticism or Commentary

(1) Criticism; (2) Commentary

1970—(1) Ada Louise Huxtable, New York Times; (2) Marquis W. Childs, St.Louis Post-Dispatch.
1971—(1) Harold C.Schonberg, New York Times; (2) William A. Caldwell, The Record, Hackensack, N.J.

1972—(1) Frank Peters Jr., St. Louis Post-Dispatch; (2) Mike Royko, Chicago Daily News.
1973—(1) Ronald Powers, Chicago Sun-Times; (2) David S. Broder, Washington Post.
1974—(1) Emily Genauer, Newsday, (N.Y.); (2) Edwin A. Roberts, Jr., National Observer.
1975—(1) Roger Ebert, Chicago Sun Times; (2) Mary McGrory, Washington Star.
1976—(1) Alan M.Kriegsman, Washington Post; (2) Walter W. (Red) Smith, New York Times.
1977—(1) William McPherson, Washington Post; (2) George F. Will, Wash. Post Writers Group.
1978—(1) Walter Kerr, New York Times; (2) William Safire, New York Times.
1979—(1) Paul Gapp, Chicago Tribune; (2) Russell Baker, New York Times.
1980—(1) William A. Henry III, Boston Globe; (2) Ellen Goodman, Boston Globe.
1981—(1) Jonathan Yardley, Washington Star; (2) Dave Anderson, New York Times.
1982—(1) Martin Bernheimer, Los Angeles Times; (2) Art Buchwald, Los Angeles Times Syndicate.
1983—(1) Manuela Hoelterhoff, Wall St. Journal; (2) Claude Sitton, Raleigh (N.C.) News & Observer.
1984—Paul Goldberger, New York Times; (2) Vermont Royster, Wall St. Journal.
1985—(1) Howard Rosenberg, Los Angeles Times; (2) Murray Kempton, Newsday (N.Y.).
1986—(1) Donal J. Henahan, New York Times; (2) Jimmy Breslin, New York Daily News.
1987—(1) Richard Eder, Los Angeles Times; (2) Charles Krauthammer, Washington Post.
1988—(1) Tom Shales, Washington Post; (2) Dave Barry, Miami Herald.
1989—(1) Michael Skube, News and Observer, Raleigh, N.C.; (2) Clarence Page, Chicago Tribune.
1990—(1) Allan Temko, San Francisco Chronicle; (2) Jim Murray, Los Angeles Times
1991—(1) David Shaw, Los Angeles Times; (2) Jim Hoagland, Washington Post.

National Reporting

1942—Louis Stark, New York Times.
1944—Dewey L. Fleming, Baltimore Sun.
1945—James B. Reston, New York Times.
1946—Edward A. Harris, St. Louis Post-Dispatch.
1947—Edward T. Folliard, Washington Post.
1948—Bert Andrews, New York Herald Tribune; Nat S. Finney, Minneapolis Tribune.
1949—Charles P. Trussell, New York Times.
1950—Edwin O. Guthman, Seattle Times.
1952—Anthony Leviero, New York Times.
1953—Don Whitehead, Associated Press.
1954—Richard Wilson, Des Moines Register.
1955—Anthony Lewis, Washington Daily News.
1956—Charles L. Bartlett, Chattanooga Times.
1957—James Reston, New York Times.
1958—Relman Morin, AP; Clark Mollenhoff, Des Moines Register & Tribune.
1959—Howard Van Smith, Miami (Fla.) News.
1960—Vance Trimble, Scripps-Howard, Washington, D.C.
1961—Edward R. Cony, Wall Street Journal.
1962—Nathan G. Caldwell and Gene S. Graham, Nashville Tennessean.
1963—Anthony Lewis, New York Times.
1964—Merriman Smith, UPI.
1965—Louis M. Kohlmeier, Wall Street Journal.
1966—Haynes Johnson, Washington Evening Star.
1967—Monroe Karmin and Stanley Penn, Wall Street Journal.
1968—Howard James, Christian Science Monitor; Nathan K. Kotz, Des Moines Register.
1969—Robert Cahn, Christian Science Monitor.
1970—William J. Eaton, Chicago Daily News.
1971—Lucinda Franks & Thomas Powers, UPI.
1972—Jack Anderson, United Feature Syndicate.
1973—Robert Boyd and Clark Hoyt, Knight Newspapers.
1974—James R. Polk, Washington Star-News; Jack White, Providence Journal-Bulletin.
1975—Donald L. Barlett and James B. Steele, Philadelphia Inquirer.
1976—James Risser, Des Moines Register.
1977—Walter Mears, Associated Press.
1978—Gaylord D. Shaw, Los Angeles Times.
1979—James Risser, Des Moines Register.
1980—Charles Stafford, Bette Swenson Orsini, St. Petersburg (Fla.) Times.
1981—John M. Crewdson, New York Times.
1982—Rick Atkinson, Kansas City Times.

1983—Boston Globe.
1984—John Noble Wilford, New York Times.
1985—Thomas J. Knudson, Des Moines (Ia.) Register.
1986—Craig Flournoy & George Rodrigue, Dallas Morning News; Arthur Howe, Philadelphia Inquirer.
1987—Miami Herald; and New York Times.
1988—Tim Weiner, Philadelphia Inquirer.
1989—Donald L. Barlett & James B. Steele, Philadelphia Inquirer.
1990—Ross Anderson, Bill Dietrich, Mary Ann Gwinn, Eric Nalder, The Seattle Times.
1991—Marjie Lundstrom, Rochelle Sharpe, Gannett News Service.

International Reporting

1942—Laurence Edmund Allen, Associated Press.
1943—Ira Wolfert, No. Am. Newspaper Alliance.
1944—Daniel DeLuce, Associated Press.
1945—Mark S. Watson, Baltimore Sun.
1946—Homer W. Bigart, New York Herald Tribune.
1947—Eddy Gilmore, Associated Press.
1948—Paul W. Ward, Baltimore Sun.
1949—Price Day, Baltimore Sun.
1950—Edmund Stevens, Christian Science Monitor.
1951—Keyes Beech and Fred Sparks, Chicago Daily News; Homer Bigart and Marguerite Higgins, New York Herald Tribune; Relman Morin and Don Whitehead, AP.
1952—John M. Hightower, Associated Press.
1953—Austin C. Wehrwein, Milwaukee Journal.
1954—Jim G. Lucas, Scripps-Howard Newspapers.
1955—Harrison Salisbury, New York Times.
1956—William Randolph Hearst, Jr., Frank Conniff, Hearst Newspapers; Kingsbury Smith, INS.
1957—Russell Jones, United Press.
1958—New York Times.
1959—Joseph Martin and Philip Santora, New York Daily News.
1960—A.M. Rosenthal, New York Times.
1961—Lynn Heinzerling, Associated Press.
1962—Walter Lippmann, New York Herald Tribune Synd.
1963—Hal Hendrix, Miami (Fla.) News.
1964—Malcolm W. Browne, AP; David Halberstam, New York Times.
1965—J.A. Livingston, Philadelphia Bulletin.
1966—Peter Arnett, AP.
1967—R. John Hughes, Christian Science Monitor.
1968—Alfred Friendly, Washington Post.
1969—William Tuohy, Los Angeles Times.
1970—Seymour M. Hersh, Dispatch News Service.
1971—Jimmie Lee Hoagland, Washington Post.
1972—Peter R. Kann, Wall Street Journal.
1973—Max Frankel, New York Times.
1974—Hedrick Smith, New York Times.
1975—William Mullen and Ovie Carter, Chicago Tribune.
1976—Sydney H. Schanberg, New York Times.
1978—Henry Kamm, New York Times.
1979—Richard Ben Cramer, Philadelphia Inquirer.
1980—Joel Brinkley, Jay Mather, Louisville (Ky.) Courier-Journal.
1981—Shirley Christian, Miami Herald.
1982—John Darnton, New York Times.
1983—Thomas L. Friedman, New York Times; Loren Jenkins, Washington Post.
1984—Karen Elliot House, Wall St. Journal
1985—Josh Friedman, Dennis Bell, Ozler Muhammad, Newsday (N.Y.).
1986—Lewis M. Simons, Pete Carey, Katherine Ellison, San Jose (Calif.) Mercury News.
1987—Michael Parks, Los Angeles Times.
1988—Thomas L. Friedman, New York Times.
1989—Glenn Frankel, Washington Post; Bill Keller, New York Times.
1990—Nicholas D. Kirstof, Sheryl WuDunn, New York Times.
1991—Caryle Murphy, Washington Post; Serge Schmemann, New York Times.

Correspondence

For Washington or foreign correspondence. Category was merged with those in national and international reporting in 1948.
1929—Paul Scott Mowrer, Chicago Daily News.
1930—Leland Stowe, New York Herald Tribune.
1931—H.R. Knickerbocker, Philadelphia Public Ledger and New York Evening Post.
1932—Walter Duranty, New York Times, and Charles G. Ross, St. Louis Post-Dispatch.
1933—Edgar Ansel Mowrer, Chicago Daily News.
1934—Frederick T. Birchall, New York Times.
1935—Arthur Krock, New York Times.

1936—Wilfred C. Barber, Chicago Tribune.
1937—Anne O'Hare McCormick, New York Times.
1938—Arthur Krock, New York Times.
1939—Louis P. Lochner, Associated Press.
1940—Otto D. Tolischus, New York Times.
1941—Bronze plaque to commemorate work of American correspondents on war fronts.
1942—Carlos P. Romulo, Philippines Herald.
1943—Hanson W. Baldwin, New York Times.
1944—Ernest Taylor Pyle, Scripps-Howard Newspaper Alliance.
1945—Harold V. (Hal) Boyle, Associated Press.
1946—Arnaldo Cortesi, New York Times.
1947—Brooks Atkinson, New York Times.

Editorial Writing

1917—New York Tribune.
1918—Louisville (Ky.) Courier-Journal.
1920—Harvey E. Newbranch, Omaha Evening World-Herald.
1922—Frank M. O'Brien, New York Herald.
1923—William Allen White, Emporia Gazette.
1924—Frank Buxton, Boston Herald, Special Prize. Frank I. Cobb, New York World.
1925—Robert Lathan, Charleston (S.C.) News and Courier.
1926—Edward M. Kingsbury, New York Times.
1927—F. Lauriston Bullard, Boston Herald.
1928—Grover C. Hall, Montgomery Advertiser.
1929—Louis Isaac Jaffe, Norfolk Virginian-Pilot.
1931—Chas. Ryckman, Fremont (Neb.) Tribune.
1933—Kansas City (Mo.) Star.
1934—E. P. Chase, Atlantic (Ia.) News Telegraph.
1936—Felix Morley, Washington Post. George B. Parker, Scripps-Howard Newspapers.
1937—John W. Owens, Baltimore Sun.
1938—W.W. Waymack, Des Moines (Ia.) Register and Tribune.
1939—Ronald G. Callvert, Portland Oregonian.
1940—Bart Howard, St. Louis Post-Dispatch.
1941—Reuben Maury, Daily News, N.Y.
1942—Geoffrey Parsons, New York Herald Tribune.
1943—Forrest W. Seymour, Des Moines (Ia.) Register and Tribune.
1944—Henry J. Haskell, Kansas City (Mo.) Star.
1945—George W. Potter, Providence (R.I.) Journal-Bulletin.
1946—Hodding Carter, Greenville (Miss.) Delta Democrat-Times.
1947—William H. Grimes, Wall Street Journal.
1948—Virginius Dabney, Richmond (Va.) Times-Dispatch.
1949—John H. Crider, Boston (Mass.) Herald, Herbert Elliston, Washington Post.
1950—Carl M. Saunders, Jackson (Mich.) Citizen-Patriot.
1951—William H. Fitzpatrick, New Orleans States.
1952—Louis LaCoss, St. Louis Globe Democrat.
1953—Vermont C. Royster, Wall Street Journal.
1954—Don Murray, Boston Herald.
1955—Royce Howes, Detroit Free Press.
1956—Lauren K. Soth, Des Moines (Ia.) Register and Tribune.
1957—Buford Boone, Tuscaloosa (Ala.) News.
1958—Harry S. Ashmore, Arkansas Gazette.
1959—Ralph McGill, Atlanta Constitution.
1960—Lenoir Chambers, Norfolk Virginian-Pilot.
1961—William J. Dorvillier, San Juan (Puerto Rico) Star.
1962—Thomas M. Storke, Santa Barbara (Cal.) News-Press.
1963—Ira B. Harkey, Jr., Pascagoula (Miss.) Chronicle.
1964—Hazel Brannon Smith, Lexington (Miss.) Advertiser.
1965—John R. Harrison, The Gainesville (Fla.) Sun.
1966—Robert Lasch, St. Louis Post-Dispatch.
1967—Eugene C. Patterson, Atlanta Constitution.
1968—John S. Knight, Knight Newspapers.
1969—Paul Greenberg, Pine Bluff (Ark.) Commercial.
1970—Philip L. Geyelin, Washington Post.
1971—Horance G. Davis, Jr., Gainesville (Fla.) Sun.
1972—John Strohmeyer, Bethlehem (Pa.) Globe-Times.
1973—Roger B. Linscott, Berkshire Eagle, Pittsfield, Mass.
1974—F. Gilman Spencer, Trenton (N.J.) Trentonian.
1975—John D. Maurice, Charleston (W. Va.) Daily Mail.
1976—Philip Kerby, Los Angeles Times.
1977—Warren L. Lerude, Foster Church, and Norman F. Cardoza, Reno (Nev.) Evening Gazette and Nevada State Journal.
1978—Meg Greenfield, Washington Post.
1979—Edwin M. Yoder, Washington Star.
1980—Robert L. Bartley, Wall Street Journal.
1982—Jack Rosenthal, New York Times.
1983—Editorial board, Miami Herald.
1984—Albert Scardino, Georgia Gazette.
1985—Richard Aregood, Philadelphia Daily News.
1986—Jack Fuller, Chicago Tribune.
1987—Jonathan Freedman, Tribune (San Diego).
1988—Jane Healy, Orlando Sentinel.

1989—Lois Wille, Chicago Tribune.
1990—Thomas J. Hylton, Pottstown (Pa.) Mercury.
1991—Ron Casey, Harold Jackson, Joey Kennedy, Birmingham (Ala.) News.

Editorial Cartooning

1922—Rollin Kirby, New York World.
1924—Jay N. Darling, Des Moines Register.
1925—Rollin Kirby, New York World.
1926—D. R. Fitzpatrick, St. Louis Post-Dispatch.
1927—Nelson Harding, Brooklyn Eagle.
1928—Nelson Harding, Brooklyn Eagle.
1929—Rollin Kirby, New York World.
1930—Charles Macauley, Brooklyn Eagle.
1931—Edmund Duffy, Baltimore Sun.
1932—John T. McCutcheon, Chicago Tribune.
1933—H. M. Talburt, Washington Daily News.
1934—Edmund Duffy, Baltimore Sun.
1935—Ross A. Lewis, Milwaukee Journal.
1937—C. D. Batchelor, New York Daily News.
1938—Vaughn Shoemaker, Chicago Daily News.
1939—Charles G. Werner, Daily Oklahoman.
1940—Edmund Duffy, Baltimore Sun.
1941—Jacob Burck, Chicago Times.
1942—Herbert L. Block, Newspaper Enterprise Assn.
1943—Jay N. Darling, Des Moines Register.
1944—Clifford K. Berryman, Washington Star.
1945—Bill Mauldin, United Feature Syndicate.
1946—Bruce Alexander Russell, Los Angeles Times.
1947—Vaughn Shoemaker, Chicago Daily News.
1948—Reuben L. (Rube) Goldberg, N. Y. Sun.
1950—James T. Berryman, Washington Star.
1951—Reginald W. Manning, Arizona Republic.
1952—Fred L. Packer, New York Mirror.
1953—Edward D. Kuekes, Cleveland Plain Dealer.
1954—Herbert L. Block, Washington Post & Times-Herald.
1955—Daniel R. Fitzpatrick, St. Louis Post-Dispatch.
1956—Robert York, Louisville (Ky.) Times.
1957—Tom Little, Nashville Tennessean.
1958—Bruce M. Shanks, Buffalo Evening News.
1959—Bill Mauldin, St. Louis Post-Dispatch.
1961—Carey Orr, Chicago Tribune.
1962—Edmund S. Valtman, Hartford Times.
1963—Frank Miller, Des Moines Register.
1964—Paul Conrad, Denver Post.
1966—Don Wright, Miami News.
1967—Patrick B. Oliphant, Denver Post.
1968—Eugene Gray Payne, Charlotte Observer.
1969—John Fischetti, Chicago Daily News.
1970—Thomas F. Darcy, Newsday.
1971—Paul Conrad, L. A. Times.
1972—Jeffrey K. MacNelly, Richmond News-Leader.
1974—Paul Szep, Boston Globe.
1975—Garry Trudeau, Universal Press Syndicate.
1976—Tony Auth, Philadelphia Inquirer.
1977—Paul Szep, Boston Globe.
1978—Jeffrey K. MacNelly, Richmond News Leader.
1979—Herbert L. Block, Washington Post.
1980—Don Wright, Miami (Fla.) News.
1981—Mike Peters, Dayton (Oh.) Daily News.
1982—Ben Sargent, Austin American-Statesman.
1983—Richard Lochner, Chicago Tribune.
1984—Paul Conrad, Los Angeles Times.
1985—Jeffrey K. MacNelly, Chicago Tribune.
1986—Jules Feiffer, Village Voice (N.Y. City)
1987—Berke Breathed, Washington Post.
1988—Doug Marlette, Atlanta Constitution, Charlotte Observer.
1989—Jack Higgins, Chicago Sun-Times.
1990—Tom Toles, The Buffalo News.
1991—Jim Borgman, Cincinnati Enquirer.

Spot News Photography

1942—Milton Brooks, Detroit News.
1943—Frank Noel, Associated Press.
1944—Frank Filan, AP; Earl L. Bunker, Omaha World-Herald,
1945—Joe Rosenthal, Associated Press, for photograph of planting American flag on Iwo Jima.
1947—Arnold Hardy, amateur, Atlanta, Ga.
1948—Frank Cushing, Boston Traveler.
1949—Nathaniel Fein, New York Herald Tribune.
1950—Bill Crouch, Oakland (Cal.) Tribune.
1951—Max Desfor, Associated Press.
1952—John Robinson and Don Ultang, Des Moines Register and Tribune.
1953—William M. Gallagher, Flint (Mich.) Journal.
1954—Mrs. Walter M. Schau, amateur.

1955—John L. Gaunt, Jr., Los Angeles Times.
1956—New York Daily News.
1957—Harry A. Trask, Boston Traveler.
1958—William C. Beall, Washington Daily News.
1959—William Seaman, Minneapolis Star.
1960—Andrew Lopez, UPI.
1961—Yasushi Nagao, Mainichi Newspapers, Tokyo.
1962—Paul Vathis, Associated Press.
1963—Hector Rondon, La Republica, Caracas, Venezuela.
1964—Robert H. Jackson, Dallas Times-Herald.
1965—Horst Faas, Associated Press.
1966—Kyoichi Sawada, UPI.
1967—Jack R. Thornell, Associated Press.
1968—Rocco Morabito, Jacksonville Journal.
1969—Edward Adams, AP.
1970—Steve Starr, AP.
1971—John Paul Filo, Valley Daily News & Daily Dispatch of Tarentum & New Kensington, Pa.
1972—Horst Faas and Michel Laurent, AP.
1973—Huynh Cong Ut, AP.
1974—Anthony K. Roberts, AP.
1975—Gerald H. Gay, Seattle Times.
1976—Stanley Forman, Boston Herald American.
1977—Neal Ulevich, Associated Press; Stanley Forman, Boston Herald American.
1978—John H. Blair, UPI.
1979—Thomas J. Kelly III, Pottstown (Pa.) Mercury.
1980—UPI.
1981—Larry C. Price, Ft. Worth (Tex.) Star-Telegram.
1982—Ron Edmonds, Associated Press.
1983—Bill Foley, AP.
1984—Stan Grossfeld, Boston Globe.
1985—The Register, Santa Ana, Calif.
1986—Carol Guzy & Michel duCille, Miami Herald.
1987—Kim Komenich, San Francisco Examiner.
1988—Scott Shaw, Odessa (Tex.) American.
1989—Ron Olshwanger, St. Louis Post-Dispatch.
1990—The Oakland (Calif.) Tribune photo staff.
1991—Greg Marinovich, Associated Press.

Feature Photography

1968—Toshio Sakai, UPI.
1969—Moneta Sleet Jr., Ebony.
1970—Dallas Kinney, Palm Beach Post.
1971—Jack Dykinga, Chicago Sun-Times.
1972—Dave Kennerly, UPI.
1973—Brian Lanker, Topeka Capitol-Journal.
1974—Slava Veder, AP.
1975—Matthew Lewis, Washington Post.
1976—Louisville Courier-Journal and Louisville Times.
1977—Robin Hood, Chattanooga News-Free Press.
1978—J. Ross Baughman, AP.
1979—Staff Photographers, Boston Herald American.
1980—Erwin H. Hagler, Dallas Times-Herald.
1981—Taro M. Yamasaki, Detroit Free Press.
1982—John H. White, Chicago Sun-Times.
1983—James B. Dickman, Dallas Times-Herald.
1984—Anthony Suad, Denver Post.
1985—Stan Grossfeld, Boston Globe; Larry C. Price, Philadelphia Inquirer.
1986—Tom Gralish, Philadelphia Inquirer.
1987—David Peterson, Des Moines Register.
1988—Michel duCille, Miami Herald.
1989—Manny Crisostomo, Detroit Free Press.
1990—David C. Turnley, Detroit Free Press.
1991—William Snyder, Dallas Morning News.

Special Citation

1938—Edmonton (Alberta) Journal, bronze plaque.

1941—New York Times.
1944—Byron Price and Mrs. William Allen White. Also to Richard Rodgers and Oscar Hammerstein 2d, for musical, Oklahoma!
1945—Press cartographers for war maps.
1947—(Pulitzer centennial year.) Columbia Univ. and the Graduate School of Journalism, and St. Louis Post-Dispatch.
1948—Dr. Frank Diehl Fackenthal.
1951—Cyrus L. Sulzberger, New York Times.
1952—Max Kase, New York Journal-American, Kansas City Star.
1953—The New York Times; Lester Markel.
1957—Kenneth Roberts, for his historical novels.
1958—Walter Lippmann, New York Herald Tribune.
1960—Garrett Mattingly, for The Armada.
1961—American Heritage Picture History of the Civil War.
1964—The Gannett Newspapers.
1973—James T. Flexner, for biography of George Washington.
1976—John Hohenberg, for services to American journalism.
1977—Alex Haley, for Roots.
1978—Richard Lee Strout, Christian Science Monitor and New Republic.
   —E.B. White.
1984—Theodore Geisel ("Dr. Seuss").
1985—William Schuman, composer, educational leader.
1987—Joseph Pulitzer Jr.

Feature Writing

1979—Jon D. Franklin, Baltimore Evening Sun.
1980—Madeleine Blais, Miami Herald Tropic Magazine. Janet Cooke, Washington Post.
1981—Teresa Carpenter, Village Voice, New York City.
1982—Saul Pett, Associated Press.
1984—Peter M. Rinearson, Seattle Times.
1985—Alice Steinbach, Baltimore Sun.
1986—John Camp, St. Paul Pioneer Press & Dispatch
1987—Steve Twomey, Philadelphia Inquirer.
1988—Jacqui Banaszynski, St. Paul Pioneer Press Dispatch.
1989—David Zucchino, Philadelphia Inquirer.
1990—Dave Curtin, Colorado Springs Gazette Telegraph.
1991—Sheryl James, St. Petersburg Times.

Explanatory Journalism

1985—Jon Franklin, Baltimore Evening Sun.
1986—New York Times Staff.
1987—Jeff Lyon & Peter Gorner, Chicago Tribune.
1988—Daniel Hertzberg, James B. Stewart, Wall Street Journal.
1989—David Hanners, William Snyder, Karen Blessen, Dallas Morning News.
1990—David A. Vise, Steve Coll, The Washington Post.
1991—Susan C. Faludi, Wall Street Journal.

Specialized Reporting

1985—Randall Savage, Jackie Crosby, Macon (Ga.) Telegraph and News.
1986—Andrew Schneider & Mary Pat Flaherty, Pittsburgh Press.
1987—Alex S. Jones, New York Times.
1988—Dean Baquet, William Gaines, Ann Marie Lipinski, Chicago Tribune.
1989—Edward Humes, Orange County (Calif.) Register.
1990—Tamar Stieber, Albuquerque Journal.
1991—Natalie Angier, New York Times.

Letters

Fiction

For fiction in book form by an American author, preferably dealing with American life.
1918—Ernest Poole, His Family.
1919—Booth Tarkington, The Magnificent Ambersons.
1921—Edith Wharton, The Age of Innocence.
1922—Booth Tarkington, Alice Adams.
1923—Willa Cather, One of Ours.
1924—Margaret Wilson, The Able McLaughlins.
1925—Edna Ferber, So Big.
1926—Sinclair Lewis, Arrowsmith. (Refused prize.)
1927—Louis Bromfield, Early Autumn.
1928—Thornton Wilder, Bridge of San Luis Rey.
1929—Julia M. Peterkin, Scarlet Sister Mary.

1930—Oliver LaFarge, Laughing Boy.
1931—Margaret Ayer Barnes, Years of Grace.
1932—Pearl S. Buck, The Good Earth.
1933—T. S. Stribling, The Store.
1934—Caroline Miller, Lamb in His Bosom.
1935—Josephine W. Johnson, Now in November.
1936—Harold L. Davis, Honey in the Horn.
1937—Margaret Mitchell, Gone with the Wind.
1938—John P. Marquand, The Late George Apley.
1939—Marjorie Kinnan Rawlings, The Yearling.
1940—John Steinbeck, The Grapes of Wrath.
1942—Ellen Glasgow, In This Our Life.
1943—Upton Sinclair, Dragon's Teeth.
1944—Martin Flavin, Journey in the Dark.
1945—John Hersey, A Bell for Adano.

1947—Robert Penn Warren, All the King's Men.
1948—James A Michener, Tales of the South Pacific.
1949—James Gould Cozzens, Guard of Honor.
1950—A. B. Guthrie Jr., The Way West.
1951—Conrad Richter, The Town.
1952—Herman Wouk, The Caine Mutiny.
1953—Ernest Hemingway, The Old Man and the Sea.
1955—William Faulkner, A Fable.
1956—MacKinlay Kantor, Andersonville.
1958—James Agee, A Death in the Family.
1959—Robert Lewis Taylor, The Travels of Jaimie McPheeters.
1960—Allen Drury, Advise and Consent.
1961—Harper Lee, To Kill a Mockingbird.
1962—Edwin O'Connor, The Edge of Sadness.
1963—William Faulkner, The Reivers.
1965—Shirley Ann Grau, The Keepers of the House.
1966—Katherine Anne Porter, Collected Stories of Katherine Anne Porter.
1967—Bernard Malamud, The Fixer.
1968—William Styron, The Confessions of Nat Turner.
1969—N. Scott Momaday, House Made of Dawn.
1970—Jean Stafford, Collected Stories.
1972—Wallace Stegner, Angle of Repose.
1973—Eudora Welty, The Optimist's Daughter.
1975—Michael Shaara, The Killer Angels.
1976—Saul Bellow, Humboldt's Gift.
1978—James Alan McPherson, Elbow Room.
1979—John Cheever, The Stories of John Cheever.
1980—Norman Mailer, The Executioner's Song.
1981—John Kennedy Toole, A Confederacy of Dunces.
1982—John Updike, Rabbit is Rich.
1983—Alice Walker, The Color Purple.
1984—William Kennedy, Ironweed.
1985—Alison Lurie, Foreign Affairs.
1986—Larry McMurtry, Lonesome Dove.
1987—Peter Taylor, A Summons to Memphis.
1988—Toni Morrison, Beloved.
1989—Anne Tyler, Breathing Lessons.
1990—Oscar Hijuelos, The Mambo Kings Play Songs of Love.
1991—John Updike, Rabbit at Rest.

Drama

For an American play, preferably original and dealing with American life.

1918—Jesse Lynch Williams, Why Marry?
1920—Eugene O'Neill, Beyond the Horizon.
1921—Zona Gale, Miss Lulu Bett.
1922—Eugene O'Neill, Anna Christie.
1923—Owen Davis, Icebound.
1924—Hatcher Hughes, Hell-Bent for Heaven.
1925—Sidney Howard, They Knew What They Wanted.
1926—George Kelly, Craig's Wife.
1927—Paul Green, In Abraham's Bosom.
1928—Eugene O'Neill, Strange Interlude.
1929—Elmer Rice, Street Scene.
1930—Marc Connelly, The Green Pastures.
1931—Susan Glaspell, Alison's House.
1932—George S. Kaufman, Morrie Ryskind and Ira Gershwin, Of Thee I Sing.
1933—Maxwell Anderson, Both Your Houses.
1934—Sidney Kingsley, Men in White.
1935—Zoe Akins, The Old Maid.
1936—Robert E. Sherwood, Idiot's Delight.
1937—George S. Kaufman and Moss Hart, You Can't Take It With You.
1938—Thornton Wilder, Our Town.
1939—Robert E. Sherwood, Abe Lincoln in Illinois.
1940—William Saroyan, The Time of Your Life.
1941—Robert E. Sherwood, There Shall Be No Night.
1943—Thornton Wilder, The Skin of Our Teeth.
1945—Mary Chase, Harvey.
1946—Russel Crouse and Howard Lindsay, State of the Union.
1948—Tennessee Williams, A Streetcar Named Desire.
1949—Arthur Miller, Death of a Salesman.
1950—Richard Rodgers, Oscar Hammerstein 2d, and Joshua Logan, South Pacific.
1952—Joseph Kramm, The Shrike.
1953—William Inge, Picnic.
1954—John Patrick, Teahouse of the August Moon.
1955—Tennessee Williams, Cat on a Hot Tin Roof.
1956—Frances Goodrich and Albert Hackett, The Diary of Anne Frank.
1957—Eugene O'Neill, Long Day's Journey Into Night.
1958—Ketti Frings, Look Homeward, Angel.
1959—Archibald MacLeish, J. B.
1960—George Abbott, Jerome Weidman, Sheldon Harnick and Jerry Bock, Fiorello.
1961—Tad Mosel, All the Way Home.

1962—Frank Loesser and Abe Burrows, How To Succeed In Business Without Really Trying.
1965—Frank D. Gilroy, The Subject Was Roses.
1967—Edward Albee, A Delicate Balance.
1969—Howard Sackler, The Great White Hope.
1970—Charles Gordone, No Place to Be Somebody.
1971—Paul Zindel, The Effect of Gamma Rays on Man-in-the-Moon Marigolds.
1973—Jason Miller, That Championship Season.
1975—Edward Albee, Seascape.
1976—Michael Bennett, James Kirkwood, Nicholas Dante, Marvin Hamlisch, Edward Kleban, A Chorus Line.
1977—Michael Cristofer, The Shadow Box.
1978—Donald L. Coburn, The Gin Game.
1979—Sam Shepard, Buried Child.
1980—Lanford Wilson, Talley's Folly.
1981—Beth Henley, Crimes of the Heart.
1982—Charles Fuller, A Soldier's Play.
1983—Marsha Norman, 'night, Mother.
1984—David Mamet, Glengarry Glen Ross.
1985—Stephen Sondheim, James Lapine, Sunday in the Park with George.
1987—August Wilson, Fences.
1988—Alfred Uhry, Driving Miss Daisy.
1989—Wendy Wasserstein, The Heidi Chronicles.
1990—August Wilson, The Piano Lesson.
1991—Neil Simon, Lost in Yonkers.

History

For a book on the history of the United States.

1917—J. J. Jusserand, With Americans of Past and Present Days.
1918—James Ford Rhodes, History of the Civil War.
1920—Justin H. Smith, The War with Mexico.
1921—William Sowden Sims, The Victory at Sea.
1922—James Truslow Adams, The Founding of New England.
1923—Charles Warren, The Supreme Court in United States History.
1924—Charles Howard McIlwain, The American Revolution: A Constitutional Interpretation.
1925—Frederick L. Paxton, A History of the American Frontier.
1926—Edward Channing, A History of the U.S.
1927—Samuel Flagg Bemis, Pinckney's Treaty.
1928—Vernon Louis Parrington, Main Currents in American Thought.
1929—Fred A. Shannon, The Organization and Administration of the Union Army, 1861-65.
1930—Claude H. Van Tyne, The War of Independence.
1931—Bernadotte E. Schmitt, The Coming of the War, 1914.
1932—Gen. John J. Pershing, My Experiences in the World War.
1933—Frederick J. Turner, The Significance of Sections in American History.
1934—Herbert Agar, The People's Choice.
1935—Charles McLean Andrews, The Colonial Period of American History.
1936—Andrew C. McLaughlin, The Constitutional History of the United States.
1937—Van Wyck Brooks, The Flowering of New England.
1938—Paul Herman Buck, The Road to Reunion, 1865-1900.
1939—Frank Luther Mott, A History of American Magazines.
1940—Carl Sandburg, Abraham Lincoln: The War Years.
1941—Marcus Lee Hansen, The Atlantic Migration, 1607-1860.
1942—Margaret Leech, Reveille in Washington.
1943—Esther Forbes, Paul Revere and the World He Lived In.
1944—Merle Curti, The Growth of American Thought.
1945—Stephen Bonsal, Unfinished Business.
1946—Arthur M. Schlesinger Jr., The Age of Jackson.
1947—James Phinney Baxter 3d, Scientists Against Time.
1948—Bernard De Voto, Across the Wide Missouri.
1949—Roy F. Nichols, The Disruption of American Democracy.
1950—O. W. Larkin, Art and Life in America.
1951—R. Carlyle Buley, The Old Northwest: Pioneer Period 1815-1840.
1952—Oscar Handlin, The Uprooted.
1953—George Dangerfield, The Era of Good Feelings.
1954—Bruce Catton, A Stillness at Appomattox.
1955—Paul Horgan, Great River: The Rio Grande in North American History.
1956—Richard Hofstadter, The Age of Reform.
1957—George F. Kennan, Russia Leaves the War.
1958—Bray Hammond, Banks and Politics in America—From the Revolution to the Civil War.
1959—Leonard D. White and Jean Schneider, The Republican Era; 1869-1901.
1960—Margaret Leech, In the Days of McKinley.
1961—Herbert Feis, Between War and Peace: The Potsdam Conference.

1962—Lawrence H. Gibson, The Triumphant Empire: Thunderclouds Gather in the West.
1963—Constance McLaughlin Green, Washington: Village and Capital, 1800-1878.
1964—Sumner Chilton Powell, Puritan Village: The Formation of A New England Town.
1965—Irwin Unger, The Greenback Era.
1966—Perry Miller, Life of the Mind in America.
1967—William H. Goetzmann, Exploration and Empire: the Explorer and Scientist in the Winning of the American West.
1968—Bernard Bailyn, The Ideological Origins of the American Revolution.
1969—Leonard W. Levy, Origin of the Fifth Amendment.
1970—Dean Acheson, Present at the Creation: My Years in the State Department.
1971—James McGregor Burns, Roosevelt: The Soldier of Freedom.
1972—Carl N. Degler, Neither Black Nor White.
1973—Michael Kammen, People of Paradox: An Inquiry Concerning the Origins of American Civilization.
1974—Daniel J. Boorstin, The Americans: The Democratic Experience.
1975—Dumas Malone, Jefferson and His Time.
1976—Paul Horgan, Lamy of Santa Fe.
1977—David M. Potter, The Impending Crisis.
1978—Alfred D. Chandler, Jr., The Visible Hand: The Managerial Revolution in American Business.
1979—Don E. Fehrenbacher, The Dred Scott Case: Its Significance in American Law and Politics.
1980—Leon F. Litwack, Been in the Storm So Long.
1981—Lawrence A. Cremin, American Education: The National Experience, 1783-1876.
1982—C. Vann Woodward, ed., Mary Chestnut's Civil War.
1983—Rhys L. Issac, The Transformation of Virginia, 1740-1790.
1985—Thomas K. McCraw, Prophets of Regulation.
1986—Walter A. McDougall, . . . The Heavens and the Earth.
1987—Bernard Bailyn, Voyagers to the West.
1988—Robert V. Bruce, The Launching of Modern American Science 1846-1876.
1989—Taylor Branch, Parting the Waters: America in the King Years, 1954-63; and James M. McPherson, Battle Cry of Freedom: The Civil War Era.
1990—Stanley Karnow, In Our Image: America's Empire in the Philippines.
1991—Laurel Thatcher Ulrich, A Midwife's Tale: The Life of Martha Ballard, based on her diary, 1785-1812.

Biography or Autobiography

For a distinguished biography or autobiography by an American author.
1917—Laura E. Richards and Maude Howe Elliott, assisted by Florence Howe Hall, Julia Ward Howe.
1918—William Cabell Bruce, Benjamin Franklin, Self-Revealed.
1919—Henry Adams, The Education of Henry Adams.
1920—Albert J. Beveridge, The Life of John Marshall.
1921—Edward Bok, The Americanization of Edward Bok.
1922—Hamlin Garland, A Daughter of the Middle Border.
1923—Burton J. Hendrick, The Life and Letters of Walter H. Page.
1924—Michael Pupin, From Immigrant to Inventor.
1925—M. A. DeWolfe Howe, Barrett Wendell and His Letters.
1926—Harvey Cushing, Life of Sir William Osler.
1927—Emory Holloway, Whitman: An Interpretation in Narrative.
1928—Charles Edward Russell, The American Orchestra and Theodore Thomas.
1929—Burton J. Hendrick, The Training of an American: The Earlier Life and Letters of Walter H. Page.
1930—Marquis James, The Raven (Sam Houston).
1931—Henry James, Charles W. Eliot.
1932—Henry F. Pringle, Theodore Roosevelt.
1933—Allan Nevins, Grover Cleveland.
1934—Tyler Dennett, John Hay.
1935—Douglas Southall Freeman, R. E. Lee
1936—Ralph Barton Perry, The Thought and Character of William James.
1937—Allan Nevins, Hamilton Fish: The Inner History of the Grant Administration.
1938—Divided between Odell Shepard, Pedlar's Progress; Marquis James, Andrew Jackson.
1939—Carl Van Doren, Benjamin Franklin.
1940—Ray Stannard Baker, Woodrow Wilson, Life and Letters.
1941—Ola Elizabeth Winslow, Jonathan Edwards.
1942—Forrest Wilson, Crusader in Crinoline.
1943—Samuel Eliot Morison, Admiral of the Ocean Sea (Columbus).
1944—Carleton Mabee, The American Leonardo: The Life of Samuel F. B. Morse.
1945—Russell Blaine Nye, George Bancroft; Brahmin Rebel.

1946—Linny Marsh Wolfe, Son of the Wilderness.
1947—William Allen White, The Autobiography of William Allen White.
1948—Margaret Clapp, Forgotten First Citizen: John Bigelow.
1949—Robert E. Sherwood, Roosevelt and Hopkins.
1950—Samuel Flag Bemis, John Quincy Adams and the Foundations of American Foreign Policy.
1951—Margaret Louise Colt, John C. Calhoun: American Portrait.
1952—Merlo J. Pusey, Charles Evans Hughes.
1953—David J. Mays, Edmund Pendleton, 1721-1803.
1954—Charles A. Lindbergh, The Spirit of St. Louis.
1955—William S. White, The Taft Story.
1956—Talbot F. Hamlin, Benjamin Henry Latrobe.
1957—John F. Kennedy, Profiles in Courage.
1958—Douglas Southall Freeman (decd. 1953), George Washington, Vols. I-VI: John Alexander Carroll and Mary Wells Ashworth, Vol. VII.
1959—Arthur Walworth, Woodrow Wilson: American Prophet.
1960—Samuel Eliot Morison, John Paul Jones.
1961—David Donald, Charles Sumner and The Coming of the Civil War.
1963—Leon Edel, Henry James: Vol. II. The Conquest of London, 1870-1881; Vol. III, The Middle Years, 1881-1895.
1964—Walter Jackson Bate, John Keats.
1965—Ernest Samuels, Henry Adams.
1966—Arthur M. Schlesinger Jr., A Thousand Days.
1967—Justin Kaplan, Mr. Clemens and Mark Twain.
1968—George F. Kennan, Memoirs (1925-1950).
1969—B. L. Reid, The Man from New York: John Quinn and his Friends.
1970—T. Harry Williams, Huey Long.
1971—Lawrence Thompson, Robert Frost: The Years of Triumph, 1915-1938.
1972—Joseph P. Lash, Eleanor and Franklin.
1973—W. A. Swanberg, Luce and His Empire.
1974—Louis Sheaffer, O'Neill, Son and Artist.
1975—Robert A. Caro, The Power Broker: Robert Moses and the Fall of New York.
1976—R.W.B. Lewis, Edith Wharton: A Biography.
1977—John E. Mack, A Prince of Our Disorder, The Life of T.E. Lawrence.
1978—Walter Jackson Bate, Samuel Johnson.
1979—Leonard Baker, Days of Sorrow and Pain: Leo Baeck and the Berlin Jews.
1980—Edmund Morris, The Rise of Theodore Roosevelt.
1981—Robert K. Massie, Peter the Great: His Life and World.
1982—William S. McFeely, Grant: A Biography.
1983—Russell Baker, Growing Up.
1984—Louis R. Harlan, Booker T. Washington.
1985—Kenneth Silverman, The Life and Times of Cotton Mather.
1986—Elizabeth Frank, Louise Bogan: A Portrait.
1987—David J. Garrow, Bearing the Cross: Martin Luther King Jr. and the Southern Christian Leadership Conference.
1988—David Herbert Donald, Look Homeward: A Life of Thomas Wolfe.
1989—Richard Ellmann, Oscar Wilde.
1990—Sebastian de Grazia, Machiavelli in Hell.
1991—Steven Naifeh, Gregory White Smith, Jackson Pollack: An American Saga.

American Poetry

Before this prize was established in 1922, awards were made from gifts provided by the Poetry Society: 1918—Love Songs, by Sara Teasdale. 1919—Old Road to Paradise, by Margaret Widemer; Corn Huskers, by Carl Sandburg.
1922—Edwin Arlington Robinson, Collected Poems.
1923—Edna St. Vincent Millay, The Ballad of the Harp-Weaver; A Few Figs from Thistles; Eight Sonnets in American Poetry, 1922; A Miscellany.
1924—Robert Frost, New Hampshire: A Poem with Notes and Grace Notes.
1925—Edwin Arlington Robinson, The Man Who Died Twice.
1926—Amy Lowell, What's O'Clock.
1927—Leonora Speyer, Fiddler's Farewell.
1928—Edwin Arlington Robinson, Tristram.
1929—Stephen Vincent Benet, John Brown's Body.
1930—Conrad Aiken, Selected Poems.
1931—Robert Frost, Collected Poems.
1932—George Dillon, The Flowering Stone.
1933—Archibald MacLeish, Conquistador.
1934—Robert Hillyer, Collected Verse.
1935—Audrey Wurdeman, Bright Ambush.
1936—Robert P. Tristram Coffin, Strange Holiness.
1937—Robert Frost, A Further Range.
1938—Marya Zaturenska, Cold Morning Sky.
1939—John Gould Fletcher, Selected Poems.

1940—Mark Van Doren, Collected Poems.
1941—Leonard Bacon, Sunderland Capture.
1942—William Rose Benet, The Dust Which Is God.
1943—Robert Frost, A Witness Tree.
1944—Stephen Vincent Benet, Western Star.
1945—Karl Shapiro, V-Letter and Other Poems.
1947—Robert Lowell, Lord Weary's Castle.
1948—W. H. Auden, The Age of Anxiety.
1949—Peter Viereck, Terror and Decorum.
1950—Gwendolyn Brooks, Annie Allen.
1951—Carl Sandburg, Complete Poems.
1952—Marianne Moore, Collected Poems.
1953—Archibald MacLeish, Collected Poems.
1954—Theodore Roethke, The Waking.
1955—Wallace Stevens, Collected Poems.
1956—Elizabeth Bishop, Poems, North and South.
1957—Richard Wilbur, Things of This World.
1958—Robert Penn Warren, Promises: Poems 1954-1956.
1959—Stanley Kunitz, Selected Poems 1928-1958.
1960—W. D. Snodgrass, Heart's Needle.
1961—Phyllis McGinley, Times Three: Selected Verse from Three Decades.
1962—Alan Dugan, Poems.
1963—William Carlos Williams, Pictures From Breughel.
1964—Louis Simpson, At the End of the Open Road.
1965—John Berryman, 77 Dream Songs.
1966—Richard Eberhart, Selected Poems.
1967—Anne Sexton, Live or Die.
1968—Anthony Hecht, The Hard Hours.
1969—George Oppen, Of Being Numerous.
1970—Richard Howard, Untitled Subjects.
1971—William S. Merwin, The Carrier of Ladders.
1972—James Wright, Collected Poems.
1973—Maxine Winokur Kumin, Up Country.
1975—Gary Snyder, Turtle Island.
1976—John Ashbery, Self-Portrait in a Convex Mirror.
1977—James Merrill, Divine Comedies.
1978—Howard Nemerov, Collected Poems.
1979—Robert Penn Warren, Now and Then: Poems 1976-1978.
1980—Donald Justice, Selected Poems.
1981—James Schuyler, The Morning of the Poem.
1982—Sylvia Plath, The Collected Poems.
1983—Galway Kinnell, Selected Poems.
1984—Mary Oliver, American Primitive.
1985—Carolyn Kizer, Yin.
1986—Henry Taylor, The Flying Change.
1987—Rita Dove, Thomas and Beulah.
1988—William Meredith, Partial Accounts: New and Selected Poems.

1989—Richard Wilbur, New and Collected Poems.
1990—Charles Simic, The World Doesn't End
1991—Mona Van Duyn, Near Changes.

General Non-Fiction

1962—Theodore H. White, The Making of the President 1960.
1963—Barbara W. Tuchman, The Guns of August.
1964—Richard Hofstadter, Anti-Intellectualism in American Life.
1965—Howard Mumford Jones, O Strange New World.
1966—Edwin Way Teale, Wandering Through Winter.
1967—David Brion Davis, The Problem of Slavery in Western Culture.
1968—Will and Ariel Durant, Rousseau and Revolution.
1969—Norman Mailer, The Armies of the Night; and Rene Jules Dubos, So Human an Animal: How We Are Shaped by Surroundings and Events.
1970—Eric H. Erikson, Gandhi's Truth.
1971—John Toland, The Rising Sun.
1972—Barbara W. Tuchman, Stilwell and the American Experience in China, 1911-1945.
1973—Frances FitzGerald, Fire in the Lake: The Vietnamese and the Americans in Vietnam; Robert Coles, Children of Crisis, Volumes II & III.
1974—Ernest Becker, The Denial of Death.
1975—Annie Dillard, Pilgrim at Tinker Creek.
1976—Robert N. Butler, Why Survive? Being Old in America.
1977—William W. Warner, Beautiful Swimmers.
1978—Carl Sagan, The Dragons of Eden.
1979—Edward O. Wilson, On Human Nature.
1980—Douglas R. Hofstadter, Gödel, Escher, Bach: An Eternal Golden Braid.
1981—Carl E. Schorske, Fin-de-Siecle Vienna: Politics and Culture.
1982—Tracy Kidder, The Soul of a New Machine.
1983—Susan Sheehan, Is There No Place on Earth for Me?
1984—Paul Starr, Social Transformation of American Medicine.
1985—Studs Terkel, The Good War.
1986—Joseph Lelyveld, Move Your Shadow; J. Anthony Lukas, Common Ground.
1987—David K. Shipler, Arab and Jew.
1988—Richard Rhodes, The Making of the Atomic Bomb.
1989—Neil Sheehan, A Bright Shining Lie: John Paul Vann and America in Vietnam.
1990—Dale Maharidge, Michael Williamson, And Their Children After Them.
1991—Bert Holldobler, Edward O. Wilson, The Ants.

Music

For composition by an American (before 1977, by a composer resident in the U.S.), in the larger forms of chamber, orchestra or choral music or for an operatic work including ballet. A special posthumous award was granted in 1976 to Scott Joplin.
1943—William Schuman, Secular Cantata No. 2, A Free Song.
1944—Howard Hanson, Symphony No. 4, Op. 34.
1945—Aaron Copland, Appalachian Spring.
1946—Leo Sowerby, The Canticle of the Sun.
1947—Charles E. Ives, Symphony No. 3.
1948—Walter Piston, Symphony No. 3.
1949—Virgil Thomson, Louisiana Story.
1950—Gian-Carlo Menotti, The Consul.
1951—Douglas Moore, Giants in the Earth.
1952—Gail Kubik, Symphony Concertante.
1954—Quincy Porter, Concerto for Two Pianos and Orchestra.
1955—Gian-Carlo Menotti, The Saint of Bleecker Street.
1956—Ernest Toch, Symphony No. 3.
1957—Norman Dello Joio, Meditations on Ecclesiastes.
1958—Samuel Barber, Vanessa.
1959—John La Montaine, Concerto for Piano and Orchestra.
1960—Elliott Carter, Second String Quartet.
1961—Walter Piston, Symphony No. 7.
1962—Robert Ward, The Crucible.
1963—Samuel Barber, Piano Concerto No. 1.
1966—Leslie Bassett, Variations for Orchestra.
1967—Leon Kirchner, Quartet No. 3.

1968—George Crumb, Echoes of Time and The River.
1969—Karel Husa, String Quartet No. 3.
1970—Charles W. Wuorinen, Time's Encomium.
1971—Mario Davidovsky, Synchronisms No. 6.
1972—Jacob Druckman, Windows.
1973—Elliott Carter, String Quartet No. 3.
1974—Donald Martino, Notturno. (Special citation) Roger Sessions.
1975—Dominick Argento, From the Diary of Virginia Woolf.
1976—Ned Rorem, Air Music.
1977—Richard Wernick, Visions of Terror and Wonder.
1978—Michael Colgrass, Deja Vu for Percussion and Orchestra.
1979—Joseph Schwantner, Aftertones of Infinity.
1980—David Del Tredici, In Memory of a Summer Day.
1982—Roger Sessions, Concerto For Orchestra. (Special Citation) Milton Babbitt.
1983—Ellen T. Zwilich, Three Movements for Orchestra.
1984—Bernard Rands, Canti del Sole.
1985—Stephen Albert, Symphony, RiverRun.
1986—George Perle, Wind Quintet IV.
1987—John Harbison, The Flight Into Egypt.
1988—William Bolcom, 12 New Etudes for Piano.
1989—Roger Reynolds, Whispers Out of Time.
1990—Mel Powell, Duplicates: A Concerto For Two Pianos and Orchestra.
1991—Shulamit Ran, Symphony.

Special Awards

Awarded in 1990 or 1991

Books, Allied Arts

Abby Award, by American Booksellers Association, for favorite book sold during year, $5,000: *The Education of Little Tree*, Forrest Carter.

American Academy and Institute of Arts and Letters: gold medal for poetry: Richard Wilbur; award of merit for the novel: Walter Abish; literature awards: Edgar Bowers,

Christopher Davis, Jaimy Gordon, Rachel Ingalls, Harry Mathews, J.D. McClatchy, Albert F. Moritz, James Schevill; Michael Braude Award for Light Verse: Gavin Ewart; Witter Bynner Prize for Poetry: Thylias Moss; E.M. Forster Award: Alan Hollinghurst; Sue Kaufman Prize for First Fiction: Charles Palliser; Rome Fellowship in Literature: Mary Caponegro; Richard and Hinda Rosenthal Foundation Award in Literature: Joanna Scott; Jean Stein Award for Fiction: Cormac McCarthy; Harold D. Vursell Memorial Award in Literature: Ursula K. Le Guin; Morton Dauwen Zabel Award in Poetry: Gordon Rogoff.

Randolph Caldecott Medal, by American Library Association, for most distinguished American picture book: David Macaulay, *Black and White.*

Christopher Awards, for books exemplifying highest values of human spirit: *Anton the Dove Fancier: And Other Tales of the Holocaust,* Bernard Gotfryd; *The Boy Who Felt No Pain,* Robert Marion; *Harvest of Hope: The Pilgrimage of a Mexican-American Physician,* Jorge Prieto; *House of Light,* Mary Oliver; *In Mysterious Ways: The Death and Life of a Parish Priest,* Paul Wilkes; *In the Lion's Den: The Life of Oswald Rufeisen,* Nechama Tec; *Inside Rikers Island: A Chaplain's Search for God,* Pierre Raphael; *Risking Hope: Fragile Faith in the Healing Process,* Kathleen O'Connell; *Road Song,* Natalie Kusz; *The Spiritual Life of Children,* Robert Coles; books for young people: *Mississippi Bridge,* Mildred D. Taylor; *Paul Revere's Ride,* Henry Wadsworth Longfellow, il. Ted Rand.

National Book Awards: fiction: *The Middle Passage,* Charles Johnson; nonfiction: *The House of Morgan: An American Banking Dynasty and the Rise of Modern Finance,* Ron Chernow.

National Book Critics Circle Awards: fiction: *Rabbit at Rest,* John Updike; biography: *Means of Ascent,* Robert A. Caro; nonfiction: *The Content of Our Character: A New Vision of Race in America,* Shelby Steele; poetry: *Bitter Angel,* Amy Gerstler; criticism: *Encounters and Reflections: Art in the Historical Present,* Arthur C. Danto; citation for excellence in reviewing: Molly Giles.

John Newbery Medal, by American Library Assn., for outstanding children's book: Jerry Spinelli, *Maniac Magee.*

PEN/Faulkner Award, $7,500: *Philadelphia Fire,* John Edgar Wideman.

Edgar Allan Poe Awards, by Mystery Writers of America: grandmaster: Tony Hillerman; novel: *New Orleans Mourning,* Julie Smith; first mystery novel: *Post Mortem,* Patricia Daniels Cornwell; original paperback: *The Man Who Would Be F. Scott Fitzgerald,* David Handler; fact crime: *In a Child's Name,* Peter Maas; critical: *Trouble Is Their Business: Private Eyes in Fiction, Films, and Television 1927-1988,* John Conquest; young adult: *Mote,* Chap Reaver; juvenile: *Stonewords,* Pam Conrad; short story: "Elvis Lives," Lynne Barrett, *Ellery Queen Mystery Magazine;* special award: *The Encyclopedia of World Crime,* Jay Robert Nash; Robert L. Fish Award: "Willie's Story," Jerry F. Skarky, *Alfred Hitchcock Mystery Magazine.*

Walt Whitman Award, by Academy of American Poets, for first book of poems, $1,000 and 2,000-copy purchase: Greg Gazner, *From the Iron Chair.*

Journalism Awards

National Journalism Awards, by Scripps Howard Foundation, $33,500 total (inc. broadcasting). Walker Stone Award for editorials: Lanny Keller, *Shreveport* (La.) *Journal;* Edward J. Meeman Award for environmental journalism: *The Alabama Journal; The Orlando* (Fla.) *Sentinel;* Charles E. Scripps Award for literacy: *Knoxville* (Tenn.) *News-Sentinel;* Ernie Pyle Award for human interest writing: Elizabeth Leland, *The Charlotte* (N.C.) *Observer;* Roy W. Howard Public Service Awards: Tom Shields, *The Tucson* (Ariz.) *Citizen; The Boston Globe;* Edward Willis Scripps Award for first amendment writing: Libby Averyt, *Corpus Christi* (Tex.) *Caller-Times;* Charles M. Schulz Award for promising cartoonist: Kerry Soper, Utah State College.

National Magazine Awards, by American Society of Magazine Editors: general excellence: *The New Republic; Interview; Condé Nast Traveler; Glamour;* special interest: *New York;* personal service: *New York;* reporting: *The New Yorker;* feature writing: *U.S. News & World Report;* public interest: *Family Circle;* design: *Condé Nast Traveler;* photography: *National Geographic;* fiction: *Esquire;* essay & criticism: *The Sciences;* single-topic issue: *The American Lawyer.*

Overseas Press Club of America Awards, $1,000 each. For print reporting: daily interpretation: Michael Dobbs, *The Washington Post;* Robert Capa Gold Medal for photography: Bruce Haley, Black Star, *U.S. News & World Report;* Olivier Rebbot Award for magazine and/or book photography: Christopher Morris, Black Star, *Time;* newspaper or wire service photography: Greg Marinovich, Associated Press; Ed Cunningham Award for magazine reporting: Peter McGrath and team, *Newsweek;* Hallie and Whit Burnett

Award for general magazine story: Louise Lief, *U.S. News & World Report;* cartooning: Mike Peters, *Dayton* (Oh.) *Daily News;* Morton Frank Award for business/economic reporting in magazines: Fiammetta Rocco, *Institutional Investor;* for business economic reporting in newspapers: James Risen, *Los Angeles Times;* Eric and Amy Burger Award, for human rights reporting: John Sawyer, *The St. Louis* (Mo.) *Post-Dispatch.*

George Polk Awards in Journalism, by Long Island University: foreign reporting: Caryle Murphy, *The Washington Post;* national reporting: Susan F. Rasky, David E. Rosenbaum, *The New York Times;* metropolitan reporting: Laurie Bennett, Robert Ourlian, *The Detroit News;* special publications prize: Joseph Belth, *The Insurance Forum;* local reporting: Heidi Evans, *The Daily News,* New York, N.Y.; regional reporting: Gayle Reaves, David Hanners, David McLemore, *The Dallas* (Tex.) *Morning News;* business reporting: Dianna Marder, *The Philadelphia Inquirer;* environmental reporting: Adam Seesel, *The Independent Weekly,* Durham, N.C.

Reuben Awards, by National Cartoonists Society: cartoonist: Gary Larson, "The Far Side," Universal Press Syndicate; comic strip: Art Sansom, "The Born Loser," Newspaper Enterprise Assn.; editorial cartoon: Pat Oliphant, Universal Press Syndicate; magazine: Harry Devlin; commercial: Steve DuQuette; electronic media: Chuck Jones.

John Peter Zenger Award, by University of Arizona, for service to freedom of the press and people's right to know: Terry Anderson.

Movie, Radio, TV, and Theater Awards

American Film Institute Life Achievement Award: Kirk Douglas.

Sarah Smith Blackburn Prize, for theater works by women, $5,000 and de Kooning lithograph: Cheryl West, Champaign, Ill., "Before It Hits Home"; Rona Monro, Edinburgh, Scotland, "Bold Girls."

Drama Desk Awards: musical: "The Will Rogers Follies"; play: "Lost in Yonkers," Neil Simon; actress: Mercedes Ruehl, "Lost in Yonkers"; actor: Ron Rifkin, "The Substance of Fire"; musical actress: Lea Salonga, "Miss Saigon"; musical actor: Jonathan Pryce, "Miss Saigon"; director: Jerry Zaks, "Six Degrees of Separation"; director of musical: Scott Ellis, "And the World Goes 'Round" and "A Little Night Music"; musical revue: "And the World Goes 'Round"; revival: "A Little Night Music."

Alfred I. Dupont-Columbia University Awards, for broadcast journalism: gold baton: "Inside Gorbachev's U.S.S.R.," PBS.

Emmy Awards, by Academy of Television Arts and Sciences, for primetime programs, 1990-91: Dramatic series: *L.A. Law,* NBC; actress: Patricia Wettig, *Thirtysomething,* ABC; actor: James Earl Jones, *Gabriel's Fire,* ABC; supporting actress: Madge Sinclair, *Gabriel's Fire,* ABC; supporting actor: Timothy Busfield, *Thirtysomething,* ABC; guest actress: Peggy McCay, *The Trials of Rosie O'Neill,* CBS; guest actor: David Opatoshu, *Gabriel's Fire;* directing: Thomas Carter, *Equal Justice,* ABC; writing: David E. Kelley, *L.A. Law.* Comedy series: *Cheers,* NBC; actress: Kirstie Alley, *Cheers;* actor: Burt Reynolds, *Evening Shade,* CBS; supporting actress: Bebe Neuwirth, *Cheers;* supporting actor: Jonathan Winters, *Davis Rules*, ABC; guest actress: Colleen Dewhurst, *Murphy Brown*, CBS; guest actor: Jay Thomas, *Murphy Brown;* directing: James Burrows, *Cheers;* writing: Gary Dontzig and Steven Peterman, *Murphy Brown.* Variety, music, or comedy program: *The 63rd Annual Academy Awards*, ABC; directing: *Late Night with David Letterman*, NBC; writing: *The 63rd Annual Academy Awards.* Individual performance, mini-series or special: Billy Crystal, *The 63rd Annual Academy Awards;* actress: Lynn Whitfield, *The Josephine Baker Story*, HBO; actor: John Gielgud, *Masterpiece Theater, Summer's Lease*, PBS; supporting actress: Ruby Dee, *Hallmark Hall of Fame, Decoration Day;* supporting actor: James Earl Jones, *Heatwave*, TNT.

Los Angeles Drama Critics Circle Awards: production: "The Beggar's Opera," Pacific Theatre Ensemble; "The Illusion," Los Angeles Theatre Center; "Present Laughter," Melrose Theatre; lead: Richard Doyle, "Holy Days"; Charles S. Dutton, "The Piano Lesson"; Ian Ogilvy, "Present Laughter"; Jeanne Paulsen, "Holy Days"; Brock Peters, "My Children! My Africa!"; Gordana Rashovich, "A Shayna Maidel"; featured: John Fleck, "The Illusion"; Nathan Lane, "The Lisbon Traviata"; ensemble: "The Beggar's Opera," Pacific Theatre Ensemble; direction: Martin Benson, "Holy Days"; Lisa James, "Palladium Is Moving"; Richard Kline, "Present Laughter"; Stephanie Shroyer, "The Beggar's Opera"; writing: Athol Fugard, "My Children! My Africa!" creation performance: Sheri Glaser, "Family Secrets"; special awards: Edward Parone & the Mark Taper Forum, "50/60 Vision"; Peter Sellars & the L.A. Festival.

National Journalism Awards, by Scripps Howard Foundation, $33,500 (inc. print); Jack R. Howard broadcast journalism awards: small market radio: Mark Urycki, WKSU-FM, Kent, Oh.; large market radio: Art Athens, WCBS, New York, N.Y.; broadcast-cable, small market TV: KVUE, Austin, Texas; large market TV: KCNC, Denver, Col.

New York Drama Critics Circle Awards: play: "Six Degrees of Separation," John Guare; musical: "The Will Rogers Follies"; foreign play: "Our Country's Good," Timberlake Wertenbaker; special citation: Eileen Atkins, "A Room of One's Own."

New York Film Critics Circle Awards: film: "Goodfellas"; director: Martin Scorsese, "Goodfellas"; actor: Robert

De Niro, "Goodfellas," "Awakenings"; actress: Joanne Woodward, "Mr. and Mrs. Bridge"; foreign film: "The Nasty Girl"; supporting actor: Bruce Davison, "Longtime Companion"; supporting actress: Jennifer Jason Leigh, "Miami Blues," "Last Exit to Brooklyn"; screenplay: Ruth Prawler Jhabvala, "Mr. and Mrs. Bridge"; cinematography: Vittorio Storaro, "The Sheltering Sky"; new director: Whit Stillman, "Metropolitan."

Overseas Press Club of America Awards, $1,000 each: President's Award, for lifetime achievement: Peter Arnett, CNN; Ben Grauer Award, daily spot radio news: Rich Lamb, WCBS, New York, N.Y.; Lowell Thomas Award, radio interpretation or documentary: Alex Chadwick, NPR; TV spot news: Bob Simon, CBS; Brian Ross, Ira Silverman, NBC; Edward R. Murrow Award, TV interpretation or documentary: Ted Koppel, Phyllis McGrady, "The Koppel Report"/ABC News; Madeline Dane Ross Award, concern for human condition: Tom Jarriel, Janice Tomlin, "20/20," ABC.

George Polk Awards in Journalism: broadcast journalism: special award: "South Africa Now," Globalvision; career award: Fred Friendly; network TV: Peter Jennings, Tom Yellin, Leslie Cockburn, ABC News; documentary TV: Hedrick Smith, Martin Smith, "Inside Gorbachev's U.S.S.R."; local TV: Kevin Kerrigan, Guam Cable TV.

Tony (Antoinette Perry) Awards: play: "Lost in Yonkers," Neil Simon; musical: "The Will Rogers Follies"; revival: "Fiddler on the Roof"; actor: Nigel Hawthorne, "Shadowlands"; actress: Mercedes Ruehl, "Lost in Yonkers"; musical actor: Jonathan Pryce, "Miss Saigon"; musical actress: Lea Salonga, "Miss Saigon"; featured actor: Kevin Spacey, "Lost in Yonkers"; featured actress: Irene Worth, "Lost in Yonkers"; featured musical actor: Hinton Battle, "Miss Saigon"; featured musical actress: Daisy Egan, "The Secret Garden"; direction: Jerry Zaks, "Six Degrees of Separation"; musical direction: Tommy Tune, "The Will Rogers Follies"; musical book: Marsha Norman, "The Secret Garden"; original musical score: Cy Coleman, Betty Comden and Adolph Green, "The Will Rogers Follies"; scenic design: Heidi Landesman, "The Secret Garden"; costumes: Willa Kim, "The Will Rogers Follies"; lighting: Jules Fisher, "The Will Rogers Follies"; choreography: Tommy Tune, "The Will Rogers Follies"; regional theater: Yale Repertory Theater.

Miscellaneous Awards

Louis Armstrong Trumpet Competition, by Thelonious Monk Institute of Jazz: first prize, $10,000: Ryan Kisor, Sioux City, Ia.

National Cowboy Hall of Fame: Barry Goldwater, Chuck Connors, James Drury; posthumous awards: Tim Holt, J. Ernest Browning.

National Medal of the Arts, by White House, for contribution to U.S. cultural life: Maurice Abravanel, Roy Acuff, Pietro Belluschi, J. Carter Brown, Charles "Honi" Coles, John O. Crosby, Richard Diebenkorn, R. Philip Hanes Jr., Kitty Carlisle Hart, Pearl Primus, Isaac Stern.

Rock-and-Roll Hall of Fame: La Vern Baker, the Byrds, John Lee Hooker, the Impressions, Wilson Pickett, Jimmy Reed, Ike and Tina Turner, Howlin' Wolf; Ralph Bass, producer; Dave Bartholomew, producer, writer, arranger.

Rostropovich Cello Competition, $12,000, recording contract, appearance on French TV, various recitals: Wendy

Warner, Evanston, Ill.; 2nd: Colin Carr, Britain; 3rd: Ann Gastinel and Xavier Phillips, France.

Samuel H. Scripps America Dance Festival Award, for contribution to modern dance, $25,000: Anna Sokolow.

Templeton Price, by John Marks Templeton, for progress in religion, $800,000: Rabbi Immanuel Jakobovits.

Westinghouse Science Talent Search: 1st prize, $40,000 college scholarship: Ashley Reiter, Charlotte, N.C.; 2nd, $30,000 scholarship: Dennis Lazarev, Fair Lawn, N.J.; 3rd, $20,000 scholarship: William Ching, New York, N.Y.; 4th, $15,000 scholarship; Dean Chung, Mountain Lakes, N.J.; 5th, $15,000 scholarship: Ciamac Moallemi, New York, N.Y.; 6th, $15,000 scholarship: Tessa Walters, San Dimas, Calif.; 7th, $10,000: Debbie Lin, New York, N.Y.; 8th, $10,000: Yves Jeanty, New York, N.Y.; 9th, $10,000: Jim Way Cheung, New York, N.Y.; 10th, $10,000: Rageshree Ramachandran, Fair Oaks, Calif.

The Spingarn Medal

The Spingarn Medal has been awarded annually since 1914 by the National Association for the Advancement of Colored People for the highest achievement by a black American.

1946	Dr. Percy L. Julian	1954	Carl Murphy	1961	Robert C. Weaver
1947	Channing H. Tobias	1955	Jack Roosevelt Robinson	1962	Medgar Wiley Evers
1948	Ralph J. Bunche	1956	Martin Luther King Jr.	1963	Roy Wilkins
1949	Charles Hamilton Houston	1957	Mrs. Daisy Bates and the Little	1964	Leontyne Price
1950	Mabel Keaton Staupers		Rock Nine	1965	John H. Johnson
1951	Harry T. Moore	1958	Edward Kennedy (Duke)	1966	Edward W. Brooke
1952	Paul R. Williams		Ellington	1967	Sammy Davis Jr.
1953	Theodore K. Lawless	1959	Langston Hughes	1968	Clarence M. Mitchell Jr.
		1960	Kenneth B. Clark	1969	Jacob Lawrence

1970 Leon Howard Sullivan	1977 Andrew Young	1984 Bill Cosby
1971 Gordon Parks	1978 Mrs. Rosa L. Parks	1985 Dr. Benjamin L. Hooks
1972 Wilson C. Riles	1979 Dr. Rayford W. Logan	1986 Percy E. Sutton
1973 Damon Keith	1980 Coleman Young	1987 Frederick Douglass Patterson
1974 Henry (Hank) Aaron	1981 Dr. Benjamin Elijah Mays	1988 Jesse Jackson
1975 Alvin Ailey	1982 Lena Horne	1989 L. Douglas Wilder
1976 Alex Haley	1983 Thomas Bradley	1990 Gen. Colin L. Powell

Miss America Winners

		1961	Nancy Fleming, Montague, Michigan
*921	Margaret Gorman, Washington, D.C.	1962	Maria Fletcher, Asheville, North Carolina
1922-23	Mary Campbell, Columbus, Ohio	1963	Jacquelyn Mayer, Sandusky, Ohio
1924	Ruth Malcolmson, Philadelphia, Pennsylvania	1964	Donna Axum, El Dorado, Arkansas
1925	Fay Lamphier, Oakland, California	1965	Vonda Kay Van Dyke, Phoenix, Arizona
1926	Norma Smallwood, Tulsa, Oklahoma	1966	Deborah Irene Bryant, Overland Park, Kansas
1927	Lois Delaner, Joliet, Illinois	1967	Jane Anne Jayroe, Laverne, Oklahoma
1933	Marion Bergeron, West Haven, Connecticut	1968	Debra Dene Barnes, Moran, Kansas
1935	Henrietta Leaver, Pittsburgh, Pennsylvania	1969	Judith Anne Ford, Belvidere, Illinois
1936	Rose Coyle, Philadelphia, Pennsylvania	1970	Pamela Anne Eldred, Birmingham, Michigan
1937	Bette Cooper, Bertrand Island, New Jersey	1971	Phyllis Ann George, Denton, Texas
1938	Marilyn Meseke, Marion, Ohio	1972	Laurie Lea Schaefer, Columbus, Ohio
1939	Patricia Donnelly, Detroit, Michigan	1973	Terry Anne Meeuwsen, DePere, Wisconsin
1940	Frances Marie Burke, Philadelphia, Pennsylvania	1974	Rebecca Ann King, Denver, Colorado
1941	Rosemary LaPlanche, Los Angeles, California	1975	Shirley Cothran, Fort Worth, Texas
1942	Jo-Caroll Dennison, Tyler, Texas	1976	Tawney Elaine Godin, Yonkers, N.Y.
1943	Jean Bartel, Los Angeles, California	1977	Dorothy Kathleen Benham, Edina, Minnesota
1944	Venus Ramey, Washington, D.C.	1978	Susan Perkins, Columbus, Ohio
1945	Bess Myerson, New York City, N.Y.	1979	Kylene Barker, Galax, Virginia
1946	Marilyn Buferd, Los Angeles, California	1980	Cheryl Prewitt, Ackerman, Mississippi
1947	Barbara Walker, Memphis, Tennessee	1981	Susan Powell, Elk City, Oklahoma
1948	BeBe Shopp, Hopkins, Minnesota	1982	Elizabeth Ward, Russellville, Arkansas
1949	Jacque Mercer, Litchfield, Arizona	1983	Debra Maffett, Anaheim, California
1951	Yolande Betbeze, Mobile, Alabama	1984	Vanessa Williams, Milwood, New York*
1952	Coleen Kay Hutchins, Salt Lake City, Utah		Suzette Charles, Mays Landing, New Jersey
1953	Neva Jane Langley, Macon, Georgia	1985	Sharlene Wells, Salt Lake City, Utah
1954	Evelyn Margaret Ay, Ephrata, Pennsylvania	1986	Susan Akin, Meridian, Mississippi
1955	Lee Meriwether, San Francisco, California	1987	Kellye Cash, Memphis, Tennessee
1956	Sharon Ritchie, Denver, Colorado	1988	Kaye Lani Rae Rafko, Monroe, Michigan
1957	Marian McKnight, Manning, South Carolina	1989	Gretchen Carlson, Anoka, Minnesota
1958	Marilyn Van Derbur, Denver, Colorado	1990	Debbye Turner, Columbia, Missouri
1959	Mary Ann Mobley, Brandon, Mississippi	1991	Marjorie Vincent, Illinois
1960	Lynda Lee Mead, Natchez, Mississippi	1992	Carolyn Suzanne Sapp, Hawaii

* Resigned July 23, 1984.

Motion Picture Academy Awards (Oscars)

1927-28
Actor: Emil Jannings, *The Way of All Flesh.*
Actress: Janet Gaynor, *Seventh Heaven.*
Director: Frank Borzage, *Seventh Heaven;* Lewis Milestone, *Two Arabian Knights.*
Picture: *Wings,* Paramount.

1928-29
Actor: Warner Baxter, *In Old Arizona.*
Actress: Mary Pickford, *Coquette.*
Director: Frank Lloyd, *The Divine Lady.*
Picture: *Broadway Melody,* MGM.

1929-30
Actor: George Arliss, *Disraeli.*
Actress: Norma Shearer, *The Divorcee.*
Director: Lewis Milestone, *All Quiet on the Western Front.*
Picture: *All Quiet on the Western Front,* Univ.

1930-31
Actor: Lionel Barrymore, *Free Soul.*
Actress: Marie Dressler, *Min and Bill.*
Director: Norman Taurog, *Skippy.*
Picture: *Cimarron,* RKO.

1931-32
Actor: Fredric March, *Dr. Jekyll and Mr. Hyde;* Wallace Beery, *The Champ* (tie).
Actress: Helen Hayes, *Sin of Madelon Claudet.*
Director: Frank Borzage, *Bad Girl.*
Picture: *Grand Hotel,* MGM.
Special: Walt Disney, *Mickey Mouse.*

1932-33
Actor: Charles Laughton, *Private Life of Henry VIII.*
Actress: Katharine Hepburn, *Morning Glory.*
Director: Frank Lloyd, *Cavalcade.*
Picture: *Cavalcade,* Fox.

1934
Actor: Clark Gable, *It Happened One Night.*
Actress: Claudette Colbert, *It Happened One Night.*
Director: Frank Capra, *It Happened One Night.*
Picture: *It Happened One Night,* Columbia.

1935
Actor: Victor McLaglen, *The Informer.*
Actress: Bette Davis, *Dangerous.*
Director: John Ford, *The Informer.*
Picture: *Mutiny on the Bounty,* MGM.

1936
Actor: Paul Muni, *Story of Louis Pasteur.*
Actress: Luise Rainer, *The Great Ziegfeld.*
Sup. Actor: Walter Brennan, *Come and Get It.*
Sup. Actress: Gale Sondergaard, *Anthony Adverse.*
Director: Frank Capra, *Mr. Deeds Goes to Town.*
Picture: *The Great Ziegfeld,* MGM.

1937
Actor: Spencer Tracy, *Captains Courageous.*
Actress: Luise Rainer, *The Good Earth.*
Sup. Actor: Joseph Schildkraut, *Life of Emile Zola.*
Sup. Actress: Alice Brady, *In Old Chicago.*
Director: Leo McCarey, *The Awful Truth.*
Picture: *Life of Emile Zola,* Warner.

1938
Actor: Spencer Tracy, *Boys Town.*
Actress: Bette Davis, *Jezebel.*
Sup. Actor: Walter Brennan, *Kentucky.*
Sup. Actress: Fay Bainter, *Jezebel.*
Director: Frank Capra, *You Can't Take It With You.*
Picture: *You Can't Take It With You,* Columbia.

1939
Actor: Robert Donat, *Goodbye Mr. Chips.*
Actress: Vivien Leigh, *Gone With the Wind.*
Sup. Actor: Thomas Mitchell, *Stage Coach.*
Sup. Actress: Hattie McDaniel, *Gone With the Wind.*
Director: Victor Fleming, *Gone With the Wind.*
Picture: *Gone With the Wind,* Selznick International.

1940
Actor: James Stewart, *The Philadelphia Story.*
Actress: Ginger Rogers, *Kitty Foyle.*

Sup. Actor: Walter Brennan, *The Westerner*.
Sup. Actress: Jane Darwell, *The Grapes of Wrath*.
Director: John Ford, *The Grapes of Wrath*.
Picture: *Rebecca*, Selznick International.
1941
Actor: Gary Cooper, *Sergeant York*.
Actress: Joan Fontaine, *Suspicion*.
Sup. Actor: Donald Crisp, *How Green Was My Valley*.
Sup. Actress: Mary Astor, *The Great Lie*.
Director: John Ford, *How Green Was My Valley*.
Picture: *How Green Was My Valley*, 20th Cent.-Fox.
1942
Actor: James Cagney, *Yankee Doodle Dandy*.
Actress: Greer Garson, *Mrs. Miniver*.
Sup. Actor: Van Heflin, *Johnny Eager*.
Sup. Actress: Teresa Wright, *Mrs. Miniver*.
Director: William Wyler, *Mrs. Miniver*.
Picture: *Mrs. Miniver*, MGM.
1943
Actor: Paul Lukas, *Watch on the Rhine*.
Actress: Jennifer Jones, *The Song of Bernadette*.
Sup. Actor: Charles Coburn, *The More the Merrier*.
Sup. Actress: Katina Paxinou, *For Whom the Bell Tolls*.
Director: Michael Curtiz, *Casablanca*.
Picture: *Casablanca*, Warner.
1944
Actor: Bing Crosby, *Going My Way*.
Actress: Ingrid Bergman, *Gaslight*.
Sup. Actor: Barry Fitzgerald, *Going My Way*.
Sup. Actress: Ethel Barrymore, *None But the Lonely Heart*.
Director: Leo McCarey, *Going My Way*.
Picture: *Going My Way*, Paramount.
1945
Actor: Ray Milland, *The Lost Weekend*.
Actress: Joan Crawford, *Mildred Pierce*.
Sup. Actor: James Dunn, *A Tree Grows in Brooklyn*.
Sup. Actress: Anne Revere, *National Velvet*.
Director: Billy Wilder, *The Lost Weekend*.
Picture: *The Lost Weekend*, Paramount.
1946
Actor: Fredric March, *Best Years of Our Lives*.
Actress: Olivia de Havilland, *To Each His Own*.
Sup. Actor: Harold Russell, *The Best Years of Our Lives*.
Sup. Actress: Anne Baxter, *The Razor's Edge*.
Director: William Wyler, *The Best Years of Our Lives*.
Picture: *The Best Years of Our Lives*, Goldwyn, RKO.
1947
Actor: Ronald Colman, *A Double Life*.
Actress: Loretta Young, *The Farmer's Daughter*.
Sup. Actor: Edmund Gwenn, *Miracle on 34th Street*.
Sup. Actress: Celeste Holm, *Gentleman's Agreement*.
Director: Elia Kazan, *Gentleman's Agreement*.
Picture: *Gentleman's Agreement*, 20th Cent.-Fox.
1948
Actor: Laurence Olivier, *Hamlet*.
Actress: Jane Wyman, *Johnny Belinda*.
Sup. Actor: Walter Huston, *Treasure of Sierra Madre*.
Sup. Actress: Claire Trevor, *Key Largo*.
Director: John Huston, *Treasure of Sierra Madre*.
Picture: *Hamlet*, Two Cities Film, Universal International.
1949
Actor: Broderick Crawford, *All the King's Men*.
Actress: Olivia de Havilland, *The Heiress*.
Sup. Actor: Dean Jagger, *Twelve O'Clock High*.
Sup. Actress: Mercedes McCambridge, *All the King's Men*.
Director: Joseph L. Mankiewicz, *Letter to Three Wives*.
Picture: *All the King's Men*, Columbia.
1950
Actor: Jose Ferrer, *Cyrano de Bergerac*.
Actress: Judy Holliday, *Born Yesterday*.
Sup. Actor: George Sanders, *All About Eve*.
Sup. Actress: Josephine Hull, *Harvey*.
Director: Joseph L. Mankiewicz, *All About Eve*.
Picture: *All About Eve*, 20th Century-Fox.
1951
Actor: Humphrey Bogart, *The African Queen*.
Actress: Vivien Leigh, *A Streetcar Named Desire*.
Sup. Actor: Karl Malden, *A Streetcar Named Desire*.
Sup. Actress: Kim Hunter, *A Streetcar Named Desire*.
Director: George Stevens, *A Place in the Sun*.
Picture: *An American in Paris*, MGM.
1952
Actor: Gary Cooper, *High Noon*.
Actress: Shirley Booth, *Come Back, Little Sheba*.
Sup. Actor: Anthony Quinn, *Viva Zapata!*.
Sup. Actress: Gloria Grahame, *The Bad and the Beautiful*.
Director: John Ford, *The Quiet Man*.
Picture: *Greatest Show on Earth*, C.B. DeMille, Paramount.

1953
Actor: William Holden, *Stalag 17*.
Actress: Audrey Hepburn, *Roman Holiday*.
Sup. Actor: Frank Sinatra, *From Here to Eternity*.
Sup. Actress: Donna Reed, *From Here to Eternity*.
Director: Fred Zinnemann, *From Here to Eternity*.
Picture: *From Here to Eternity*, Columbia.
1954
Actor: Marlon Brando, *On the Waterfront*.
Actress: Grace Kelly, *The Country Girl*.
Sup. Actor: Edmond O'Brien, *The Barefoot Contessa*.
Sup. Actress: Eva Marie Saint, *On the Waterfront*.
Director: Elia Kazan, *On the Waterfront*.
Picture: *On the Waterfront*, Horizon-American, Colum.
1955
Actor: Ernest Borgnine, *Marty*.
Actress: Anna Magnani, *The Rose Tattoo*.
Sup. Actor: Jack Lemmon, *Mister Roberts*.
Sup. Actress: Jo Van Fleet, *East of Eden*.
Director: Delbert Mann, *Marty*.
Picture: *Marty*, Hecht and Lancaster's Steven Prods., U.A.
1956
Actor: Yul Brynner, *The King and I*.
Actress: Ingrid Bergman, *Anastasia*.
Sup. Actor: Anthony Quinn, *Lust for Life*.
Sup. Actress: Dorothy Malone, *Written on the Wind*.
Director: George Stevens, *Giant*.
Picture: *Around the World in 80 Days*, Michael Todd, U.A.
1957
Actor: Alec Guinness, *The Bridge on the River Kwai*.
Actress: Joanne Woodward, *The Three Faces of Eve*.
Sup. Actor: Red Buttons, *Sayonara*.
Sup. Actress: Miyoshi Umeki, *Sayonara*.
Director: David Lean, *The Bridge on the River Kwai*.
Picture: *The Bridge on the River Kwai*, Columbia.
1958
Actor: David Niven, *Separate Tables*.
Actress: Susan Hayward, *I Want to Live*.
Sup. Actor: Burl Ives, *The Big Country*.
Sup. Actress: Wendy Hiller, *Separate Tables*.
Director: Vincente Minnelli, *Gigi*.
Picture: *Gigi*, Arthur Freed Production, MGM.
1959
Actor: Charlton Heston, *Ben-Hur*.
Actress: Simone Signoret, *Room at the Top*.
Sup. Actor: Hugh Griffith, *Ben-Hur*.
Sup. Actress: Shelley Winters, *Diary of Anne Frank*.
Director: William Wyler, *Ben-Hur*.
Picture: *Ben-Hur*, MGM.
1960
Actor: Burt Lancaster, *Elmer Gantry*.
Actress: Elizabeth Taylor, *Butterfield 8*.
Sup. Actor: Peter Ustinov, *Spartacus*.
Sup. Actress: Shirley Jones, *Elmer Gantry*.
Director: Billy Wilder, *The Apartment*.
Picture: *The Apartment*, Mirisch Co., U.A.
1961
Actor: Maximilian Schell, *Judgment at Nuremberg*.
Actress: Sophia Loren, *Two Women*.
Sup. Actor: George Chakiris, *West Side Story*.
Sup. Actress: Rita Moreno, *West Side Story*.
Director: Jerome Robbins, Robert Wise, *West Side Story*.
Picture: *West Side Story*, United Artists.
1962
Actor: Gregory Peck, *To Kill a Mockingbird*.
Actress: Anne Bancroft, *The Miracle Worker*.
Sup. Actor: Ed Begley, *Sweet Bird of Youth*.
Sup. Actress: Patty Duke, *The Miracle Worker*.
Director: David Lean, *Lawrence of Arabia*.
Picture: *Lawrence of Arabia*, Columbia.
1963
Actor: Sidney Poitier, *Lilies of the Field*.
Actress: Patricia Neal, *Hud*.
Sup. Actor: Melvyn Douglas, *Hud*.
Sup. Actress: Margaret Rutherford, *The V.I.P.s*.
Director: Tony Richardson, *Tom Jones*.
Picture: *Tom Jones*, Woodfall Prod., UA-Lopert Pictures.
1964
Actor: Rex Harrison, *My Fair Lady*.
Actress: Julie Andrews, *Mary Poppins*.
Sup. Actor: Peter Ustinov, *Topkapi*.
Sup. Actress: Lila Kedrova, *Zorba the Greek*.
Director: George Cukor, *My Fair Lady*.
Picture: *My Fair Lady*, Warner Bros.
1965
Actor: Lee Marvin, *Cat Ballou*.
Actress: Julie Christie, *Darling*.
Sup. Actor: Martin Balsam, *A Thousand Clowns*.
Sup. Actress: Shelley Winters, *A Patch of Blue*.

Director: Robert Wise, *The Sound of Music.*
Picture: *The Sound of Music,* 20th Century-Fox.

1966
Actor: Paul Scofield, *A Man for All Seasons.*
Actress: Elizabeth Taylor, *Who's Afraid of Virginia Woolf?*
Sup. Actor: Walter Matthau, *The Fortune Cookie.*
Sup. Actress: Sandy Dennis, *Who's Afraid of Virginia Woolf?*
Director: Fred Zinnemann, *A Man for All Seasons.*
Picture: *A Man for All Seasons,* Columbia.

1967
Actor: Rod Steiger, *In the Heat of the Night.*
Actress: Katharine Hepburn, *Guess Who's Coming to Dinner.*
Sup. Actor: George Kennedy, *Cool Hand Luke.*
Sup. Actress: Estelle Parsons, *Bonnie and Clyde.*
Director: Mike Nichols, *The Graduate.*
Picture: *In the Heat of the Night.*

1968
Actor: Cliff Robertson, *Charly.*
Actress: Katharine Hepburn, *The Lion in Winter;* Barbra
   Streisand, *Funny Girl* (tie).
Sup. Actor: Jack Albertson, *The Subject Was Roses.*
Sup. Actress: Ruth Gordon, *Rosemary's Baby.*
Director: Sir Carol Reed, *Oliver!*
Picture: *Oliver!*

1969
Actor: John Wayne, *True Grit.*
Actress: Maggie Smith, *The Prime of Miss Jean Brodie.*
Sup. Actor: Gig Young, *They Shoot Horses, Don't They?*
Sup. Actress: Goldie Hawn, *Cactus Flower.*
Director: John Schlesinger, *Midnight Cowboy.*
Picture: *Midnight Cowboy.*

1970
Actor: George C. Scott, *Patton* (refused).
Actress: Glenda Jackson, *Women in Love.*
Sup. Actor: John Mills, *Ryan's Daughter.*
Sup. Actress: Helen Hayes, *Airport.*
Director: Franklin Schaffner, *Patton.*
Picture: *Patton.*

1971
Actor: Gene Hackman, *The French Connection.*
Actress: Jane Fonda, *Klute.*
Sup. Actor: Ben Johnson, *The Last Picture Show.*
Sup. Actress: Cloris Leachman, *The Last Picture Show.*
Director: William Friedkin, *The French Connection.*
Picture: *The French Connection.*

1972
Actor: Marlon Brando, *The Godfather* (refused).
Actress: Liza Minnelli, *Cabaret.*
Sup. Actor: Joel Grey, *Cabaret.*
Sup. Actress: Eileen Heckart, *Butterflies are Free.*
Director: Bob Fosse, *Cabaret.*
Picture: *The Godfather.*

1973
Actor: Jack Lemmon, *Save the Tiger.*
Actress: Glenda Jackson, *A Touch of Class.*
Sup. Actor: John Houseman, *The Paper Chase.*
Sup. Actress: Tatum O'Neal, *Paper Moon.*
Director: George Roy Hill, *The Sting.*
Picture: *The Sting.*

1974
Actor: Art Carney, *Harry and Tonto.*
Actress: Ellen Burstyn, *Alice Doesn't Live Here Anymore.*
Sup. Actor: Robert DeNiro, *The Godfather, Part II.*
Sup. Actress: Ingrid Bergman, *Murder on the Orient Express.*
Director: Francis Ford Coppola, *The Godfather, Part II.*
Picture: *The Godfather, Part II.*

1975
Actor: Jack Nicholson, *One Flew Over the Cuckoo's Nest.*
Actress: Louise Fletcher, *One Flew Over the Cuckoo's Nest.*
Sup. Actor: George Burns, *The Sunshine Boys.*
Sup. Actress: Lee Grant, *Shampoo.*
Director: Milos Forman, *One Flew Over the Cuckoo's Nest.*
Picture: *One Flew Over the Cuckoo's Nest.*

1976
Actor: Peter Finch, *Network.*
Actress: Faye Dunaway, *Network.*
Sup. Actor: Jason Robards, *All the President's Men.*
Sup. Actress: Beatrice Straight, *Network.*
Director: John G. Avildsen, *Rocky.*
Picture: *Rocky.*

1977
Actor: Richard Dreyfuss, *The Goodbye Girl.*
Actress: Diane Keaton, *Annie Hall.*
Sup. Actor: Jason Robards, *Julia.*
Sup. Actress: Vanessa Redgrave, *Julia.*
Director: Woody Allen, *Annie Hall.*
Picture: *Annie Hall.*

1978
Actor: Jon Voight, *Coming Home.*

Actress: Jane Fonda, *Coming Home.*
Sup. Actor: Christopher Walken, *The Deer Hunter.*
Sup. Actress: Maggie Smith, *California Suite.*
Director: Michael Cimino, *The Deer Hunter.*
Picture: *The Deer Hunter.*

1979
Actor: Dustin Hoffman, *Kramer vs. Kramer.*
Actress: Sally Field, *Norma Rae.*
Sup. Actor: Melvyn Douglas, *Being There.*
Sup. Actress: Meryl Streep, *Kramer vs. Kramer.*
Director: Robert Benton, *Kramer vs. Kramer.*
Picture: *Kramer vs. Kramer.*

1980
Actor: Robert DeNiro, *Raging Bull.*
Actress: Sissy Spacek, *Coal Miner's Daughter.*
Sup. Actor: Timothy Hutton, *Ordinary People.*
Sup. Actress: Mary Steenburgen, *Melvin & Howard.*
Director: Robert Redford, *Ordinary People* .
Picture: *Ordinary People.*

1981
Actor: Henry Fonda, *On Golden Pond.*
Actress: Katharine Hepburn, *On Golden Pond.*
Sup. Actor: John Gielgud, *Arthur.*
Sup. Actress: Maureen Stapleton, *Reds.*
Director: Warren Beatty, *Reds.*
Picture: *Chariots of Fire.*

1982
Actor: Ben Kingsley, *Gandhi.*
Actress: Meryl Streep, *Sophie's Choice.*
Sup. Actor: Louis Gossett, Jr., *An Officer and a Gentleman.*
Sup. Actress: Jessica Lange, *Tootsie.*
Director: Richard Attenborough, *Gandhi.*
Picture: *Gandhi.*

1983
Actor: Robert Duvall, *Tender Mercies.*
Actress: Shirley MacLaine, *Terms of Endearment.*
Supporting Actor: Jack Nicholson, *Terms of Endearment.*
Supporting Actress: Linda Hunt, *The Year of Living Dangerously.*
Director: James L. Brooks, *Terms of Endearment.*
Picture: *Terms of Endearment.*

1984
Actor: F. Murray Abraham, *Amadeus.*
Actress: Sally Field, *Places in the Heart.*
Supporting Actor: Haing S. Ngor, *The Killing Fields.*
Supporting Actress: Peggy Ashcroft, *A Passage to India.*
Director: Milos Forman, *Amadeus.*
Picture: *Amadeus.*

1985
Actor: William Hurt, *Kiss of the Spider Woman.*
Actress: Geraldine Page, *The Trip to Bountiful.*
Supporting Actor: Don Ameche, *Cocoon.*
Supporting Actress: Anjelica Huston, *Prizzi's Honor.*
Director: Sydney Pollack, *Out of Africa.*
Picture: *Out of Africa.*

1986
Actor: Paul Newman, *The Color of Money.*
Actress: Marlee Matlin, *Children of a Lesser God.*
Supporting Actor: Michael Caine, *Hannah and Her Sisters.*
Supporting Actress: Dianne Wiest, *Hannah and Her Sisters.*
Director: Oliver Stone, *Platoon.*
Picture: *Platoon.*

1987
Actor: Michael Douglas, *Wall Street.*
Actress: Cher, *Moonstruck.*
Supporting Actor: Sean Connery, *The Untouchables.*
Supporting Actress: Olympia Dukakis, *Moonstruck.*
Director: Bernardo Bertolucci, *The Last Emperor.*
Picture: *The Last Emperor.*

1988
Actor: Dustin Hoffman, *Rain Man.*
Actress: Jodie Foster, *The Accused.*
Supporting Actor: Kevin Kline, *A Fish Called Wanda.*
Supporting Actress: Geena Davis, *The Accidental Tourist.*
Director: Barry Levinson, *Rain Man.*
Picture: *Rain Man.*

1989
Actor: Daniel Day-Lewis, *My Left Foot.*
Actress: Jessica Tandy, *Driving Miss Daisy.*
Supporting Actor: Denzel Washington, *Glory.*
Supporting Actress: Brenda Fricker, *My Left Foot.*
Director: Oliver Stone, *Born on the Fourth of July.*
Picture: *Driving Miss Daisy.*

1990
Picture: *Dances With Wolves.*
Actor: Jeremy Irons, *Reversal of Fortune.*
Actress: Kathy Bates, *Misery.*
Supporting Actor: Joe Pesci, *Goodfellas.*
Supporting Actress: Whoopi Goldberg, *Ghost.*
Director: Kevin Costner, *Dances With Wolves.*

Foreign Film: *Journey of Hope,* Switzerland
Art Direction: Jeffrey Bancroft; set decoration, Lisa Dean, both *Dick Tracy.*
Cinematography: Dean Semler, *Dances With Wolves.*
Costume Design: Franca Squarciapino, *Cyrano de Bergerac*
Feature Documentary: *American Dream.*
Short Subject Documentary: *Days of Waiting.*
Short Subject Live Action: *The Lunch Date.*

Editing: Neil Travis, *Dances With Wolves.*
Makeup: John Caglione Jr., Doug Drexler, *Dick Tracy.*
Original Score: John Barry, *Dances With Wolves.*
Original Song: Stephen Sondheim, "Sooner or Later" (I Always Get My Man) *Dick Tracy.*
Original Screenplay: Bruce Joel Rubin, *Ghost.*
Adapted Screenplay: Michael Blake, *Dances With Wolves.*

Grammy Awards

Source: National Academy of Recording Arts & Sciences

1958
Record: Domenico Modugno, *Nel Blu Dipinto Di Blu (Volare).*
Album: Henry Mancini, *The Music from Peter Gunn.*

1959
Record: Bobby Darin, *Mack the Knife.*
Album: Frank Sinatra, *Come Dance With Me.*

1960
Record: Percy Faith, *Theme From A Summer Place.*
Album: Bob Newhart, *Button Down Mind.*

1961
Record: Henry Mancini, *Moon River.*
Album: Judy Garland, *Judy At Carnegie Hall.*

1962
Record: Tony Bennett, *I Left My Heart in San Francisco.*
Album: Vaughn Meader, *The First Family.*

1963
Record: Henry Mancini, *The Days of Wine and Roses.*
Album: *The Barbra Streisand Album.*

1964
Record: Stan Getz and Astrud Gilberto, *The Girl From Ipanema.*
Album: *Getz/Gilberto.*

1965
Record: Herb Alpert, *A Taste Of Honey.*
Album: Frank Sinatra, *September of My Years.*

1966
Record: Frank Sinatra, *Strangers in the Night.*
Album: Frank Sinatra, *A Man and His Music.*

1967
Record: 5th Dimension, *Up, Up and Away.*
Album: The Beatles, *Sgt. Pepper's Lonely Hearts Club Band.*

1968
Record: Simon & Garfunkel, *Mrs. Robinson.*
Album: Glen Campbell, *By the Time I Get to Phoenix.*

1969
Record: 5th Dimension, *Aquarius/Let the Sunshine In.*
Album: *Blood, Sweat and Tears.*

1970
Record: Simon & Garfunkel, *Bridge Over Troubled Water.*
Album: *Bridge Over Troubled Water.*

1971
Record: Carole King, *It's Too Late.*
Album: Carole King, *Tapestry.*

1972
Record: Roberta Flack, *The First Time Ever I Saw Your Face.*
Album: *The Concert For Bangla Desh.*

1973
Record: Roberta Flack, *Killing Me Softly with His Song.*
Album: Stevie Wonder, *Innervisions.*

1974
Record: Olivia Newton-John, *I Honestly Love You.*
Album: Stevie Wonder, *Fulfullingness' First Finale.*

1975
Record: Captain & Tennille, *Love Will Keep Us Together.*
Album: Paul Simon, *Still Crazy After All These Years.*

1976
Record: George Benson, *This Masquerade.*
Album: Stevie Wonder, *Songs in the Key of Life.*

1977
Record: Eagles, *Hotel California.*
Album: Fleetwood Mac, *Rumours.*

1978
Record: Billy Joel, *Just the Way You Are.*
Album: Bee Gees, *Saturday Night Fever.*

1979
Record: The Doobie Brothers, *What a Fool Believes.*
Album: Billy Joel, *52nd Street.*

1980
Record: Christopher Cross, *Sailing.*
Album: Christopher Cross, *Christopher Cross.*

1981
Record: Kim Carnes, *Bette Davis Eyes.*
Album: John Lennon, Yoko Ono, *Double Fantasy.*

1982
Record: Toto, *Rosanna.*
Album: Toto, *Toto IV.*

1983
Record: Michael Jackson, *Beat It.*
Album: Michael Jackson, *Thriller.*

1984
Record: Tina Turner, *What's Love Got to Do With It.*
Album: Lionel Richie, *Can't Slow Down.*

1985
Record: USA for Africa, *We Are the World.*
Album: Phil Collins, *No Jacket Required.*

1986
Record: Steve Winwood, *Higher Love.*
Album: Paul Simon, *Graceland.*

1987
Record: Paul Simon, *Graceland.*
Album: U2, *The Joshua Tree.*

1988
Record: Bobby McFerrin, *Don't Worry, Be Happy.*
Album: George Michael, *Faith.*

1989
Record: Bette Midler, *Wind Beneath My Wings.*
Album: Bonnie Raitt, *Nick of Time.*

1990
Record: Phil Collins, *Another Day in Paradise.*
Album: Quincy Jones, *Back on the Block.*
Song: Julie Gold, *From a Distance.*
New Artist: Mariah Carey.
Pop Vocal, Female: Mariah Carey, *Vision of Love.*
Pop Vocal, Male: Roy Orbison, *Oh Pretty Woman.*
Pop Duo or Group with Vocal: Linda Ronstadt with Aaron Neville, *All My Life.*
Pop Instrumental: Angelo Badalamenti, *Twin Peaks Theme.*
Rock Vocal Female: Alannah Myles, *Black Velvet.*
Rock Vocal, Male: Eric Clapton, *Bad Love.*
Rock Duo or Group with Vocal: Aerosmith, *Janie's Got a Gun .*
Hard Rock: Living Colour, *Time's Up.*
Metal: Metallica, *Stone Cold Crazy.*
Alternative Music: Sinead O'Connor, *I Do Not Want What I Haven't Got.*
Rhythm-and-Blues-Vocal, Female: Anita Baker, *Compositions.*
Rhythm-and-Blues Vocal, Male: Luther Vandross, *Here and Now.*
Rhythm-and-Blues Duo or Group with Vocal: Ray Charles and Chaka Khan, *I'll Be Good to You.*
Rap Solo: M.C. Hammer, *You Can't Touch This.*
Rap Duo or Vocal: Ice-T, Melle Mel, Big Daddy Kane, Kool Moe Dee, *Back on the Block.*
Jazz Vocal, Female: Ella Fitzgerald, *All That Jazz.*
Jazz Vocal, Male: Harry Connick Jr., *We Are in Love.*
Jazz Instrumental, Soloist: Oscar Peterson, *The Legendary Oscar Peterson Trio Live at the Blue Note.*
Jazz Instrumental, Big Band: Count Basie Orchestra, *Basie's Bag.*
Country Vocal, Female: Kathy Mattea, *Where've You Been.*
Country Vocal, Male: Vince Gill, *When I Call Your Name.*
Country Duo or Group with Vocal: Kentucky Headhunters, *Pickin' on Nashville.*
Country Instrumental: Chet Atkins & Mark Knopfler, *So Soft, Your Goodbye.*
Traditional Soul Gospel Album: Tramaine Hawkins, *Tramaine Hawkins Live.*
Contemporary Soul Gospel Album: Take Six, *So Much 2 Say.*
Recording for Children: Howard Ashman & Alan Menken, *The Little Mermaid Soundtrack.*
Song for Movies or TV: Howard Ashman & Alan Menken, "Under the Sea."
Musical Cast Show Album: *Les Miserables: The Complete Symphonic Recording.*
Opera: Metropolitan Opera Orchestra, Cond. James Levine, Wagner's *Das Rheingold.*
Classical vocal: Jose Carrera, Placido Domingo, Luciano Pavarotti, *Carreras, Domingo, Pavarotti in Concert.*

NOTED PERSONALITIES

Widely Known Americans of the Present

Statesmen, authors of nonfiction, military men, and other prominent persons not listed in other categories; as of mid-1991.

Name (Birthplace)	Birthdate	Name (Birthplace)	Birthdate
Agnos, Art (Springfield, Mass.)	9/1/38	Fitzwater, Marlin (Salina, Kan.)	11/24/42
Ailes, Roger (Knoxville, Tenn.)	7/3/40	Florio, James J. (New York, N.Y.)	8/29/37
Arledge, Roone (Forest Hills, N.Y.)	7/8/31	Foley, Thomas S. (Spokane, Wash.)	3/6/29
Anderson, Jack (Long Beach, Cal.)	10/19/22	Ford, Betty (Chicago, Ill.)	4/8/18
Annenberg, Walter H. (Milwaukee, Wis.)	1908	Ford, Gerald R. (Omaha, Neb.)	7/14/13
Armstrong, Neil (Wapakoneta, Oh.)	8/5/30	Frank, Barney (Bayonne, N.J.)	3/31/40
Asimov, Isaac (Petrovichi, Russia)	1/2/20	Frankel, Max (Gera, Germany)	4/3/30
Ash, Mary Kay (Hot Wells, Tex.)	—	Friedan, Betty (Peoria, Ill.)	2/4/21
Aspin, Les (Milwaukee, Wis.)	7/21/38	Friedman, Milton (Brooklyn, N.Y.)	7/31/12
Baker, James A. (Houston, Tex.)	4/28/30	Galbraith, John Kenneth (Ontario, Can.)	10/15/08
Baker, Russell (Loudoun Co., Va.)	8/14/25	Gates, William (Seattle, Wash.)	10/28/55
Barnes, Clive (London, England)	5/13/27	Gephardt, Richard (St. Louis, Mo.)	1/31/41
Barthelmy, Sidney K. (New Orleans, La.)	3/17/42	Gibson, Charles (Evanston, Ill.)	3/9/43
Bennett, William J. (Salem, Oh.)	5/4/44	Gingrich, Newt (Harrisburg, Pa.)	6/17/43
Bentsen, Lloyd (Mission, Tex.)	2/11/21	Ginsberg, Allen (Paterson, N.J.)	6/3/21
Biden, Joseph R. Jr. (Scranton, Pa.)	11/20/42	Glenn, John (Cambridge, Oh.)	7/18/21
Blackmun, Harry (Nashville, Ill.)	11/12/08	Goldwater, Barry M. (Phoenix, Ariz.)	1/1/09
Blass, Bill (Ft. Wayne, Ind.)	6/22/22	Goodman, Ellen (Newton, Mass.)	4/11/41
Bombeck, Erma (Dayton, Oh.)	2/21/27	Gore, Albert Jr. (Washington, D.C.)	3/31/48
Boorstin, Daniel (Atlanta, Ga.)	10/1/14	Gottlieb, Robert A. (New York)	4/9/31
Bradlee, Ben (Boston, Mass.)	8/26/21	Gould, Stephen Jay (New York, N.Y.)	9/10/41
Bradley, Bill (Crystal City, Mo.)	7/28/43	Graham, Billy (Charlotte, N.C.)	11/7/18
Bradley, Ed (Philadelphia, Pa.)	6/22/41	Graham, Donald (Baltimore, Md.)	4/22/45
Bradley, Thomas (Calvert, Tex.)	12/29/17	Graham, Katharine (New York, N.Y.)	6/16/17
Brady, Nicholas (New York, N.Y.)	4/11/30	Gramm, Phil (Ft. Bennington, Ga.)	7/8/42
Brennan, William J. (Newark, N.J.)	4/25/06	Gray, William H. 3d (Baton Rouge, La.)	8/20/41
Breslin, Jimmy (Jamaica, N.Y.)	10/17/30	Greene, Bob (Columbus, Oh.)	5/10/47
Brinkley, David (Wilmington, N.C.)	7/10/20	Greenfield, Meg (Seattle, Wash.)	12/27/30
Broder, David (Chicago Heights, Ill.)	9/11/29	Greenspan, Alan (New York, N.Y.)	3/6/26
Brody, Jane (Brooklyn, N.Y.)	5/19/41	Gumble, Bryant (New Orleans, La.)	9/29/48
Brokaw, Tom (Webster, S. Dak.)	2/6/40	Halberstam, David (New York, N.Y.)	4/10/34
Brothers, Joyce (New York, N.Y.)	9/20/28	Harvey, Paul (Tulsa, Okla.)	9/4/18
Brown, Helen Gurley (Green Forest, Ark.)	2/18/22	Hatch, Orrin (Homestead, Pa.)	3/22/34
Buchanan, Pat (Washington, D.C.)	11/2/38	Hatfield, Mark O. (Dallas, Ore.)	7/12/22
Buchwald, Art (Mt. Vernon, N.Y.)	10/20/25	Heflin, Howell (Poulan, Ga.)	6/19/21
Buckley, William F. (New York, N.Y.)	11/24/25	Hefner, Hugh (Chicago, Ill.)	4/9/26
Buffet, Warren (Omaha, Neb.)	8/30/30	Helms, Jesse (Monroe, N.C.)	10/18/21
Bumpers, Dale (Charleston, Ark.)	8/12/25	Heloise (Waco, Tex.)	4/15/51
Buscaglia, Leo (Los Angeles, Cal.)	3/31/24	Hills, Carla (Los Angeles, Cal.)	1/3/34
Bush, Barbara (Rye, N.Y.)	6/8/25	Hollings, Ernest (Charleston, S.C.)	1/1/22
Byrd, Robert (N. Wilkesboro, N.C.)	11/20/17	Holtz, Lou (Fallansbee, W. Va.)	1/6/37
Canby, Vincent (Chicago, Ill.)	7/27/24	Iacocca, Lee A. (Allentown, Pa.)	10/15/24
Carter, Jimmy (Plains, Ga.)	10/1/24	Icahn, Carl (New York, N.Y.)	1936
Carter, Rosalynn (Plains, Ga.)	8/18/27	Iman (Somalia, Ethiopia)	7/25/55
Chancellor, John (Chicago, Ill.)	7/14/27	Inouye, Daniel K. (Honolulu, Ha.)	9/7/24
Chavez, Cesar (Yuma, Ariz.)	3/31/27	Jackson, Jesse (Greenville, S.C.)	10/8/41
Cheney, Richard B. (Lincoln, Neb.)	1/30/41	Jennings, Peter (Toronto, Ont.)	8/29/38
Child, Julia (Pasadena, Cal.)	8/15/12	Johnson, Lady Bird (Karnack, Tex.)	12/22/12
Chisholm, Shirley (Brooklyn, N.Y.)	11/30/24	Jordan, Barbara (Houston, Tex.)	2/21/36
Chung, Connie (Washington, D.C.)	8/20/46	Kael, Pauline (Petaluma, Calif.)	6/19/19
Claiborne, Craig (Sunflower, Miss.)	9/4/20	Kaplan, Justin (New York, N.Y.)	9/5/25
Claiborne, Liz (Brussels, Belg.)	3/31/29	Karan, Donna (Forest Hills, N.Y.)	10/2/48
Collins, Martha (Shelby Cty, Ky.)	12/7/36	Kassebaum, Nancy (Topeka, Kan.)	7/29/32
Commager, Henry Steele (Pittsburgh, Pa.)	10/25/02	Keillor, Garrison (Anoka, Minn.)	8/7/42
Cooney, Joan Ganz (Phoenix, Ariz.)	10/30/29	Kemp, Jack (Los Angeles, Cal.)	7/13/35
Cordesman, Anthony (Chicago, Ill.)	8/2/39	Kennedy, Anthony (Sacramento, Cal.)	7/23/36
Cosell, Howard (Winston-Salem, N.C.)	3/25/20	Kennedy, Edward M. (Brookline, Mass.)	2/22/32
Cousins, Norman (Union Hill, N.J.)	6/24/12	Kennedy, Rose (Boston, Mass.)	7/22/90
Cranston, Alan (Palo Alto, Cal.)	6/19/14	Kerr, Walter (Evanston, Ill.)	7/8/13
Crawford, Cindy (DeKalb, Ill.)	2/20/66	King, Coretta Scott (Marion, Ala.)	4/27/27
Crist, Judith (New York, N.Y.)	5/22/22	King, Larry (Brooklyn, N.Y.)	11/19/34
Cronkite, Walter (St. Joseph, Mo.)	11/4/16	Kinsley, Michael (Detroit, Mich.)	3/9/51
Cuomo, Mario (Queens, N.Y.)	6/15/32	Kirkland, Lane (Camden, S.C.)	3/12/22
Daley, Richard M. (Chicago, Ill.)	4/24/42	Kirkpatrick, Jeane (Duncan, Okla.)	11/19/26
Darman, Richard (Charlotte, N.C.)	5/10/43	Kissinger, Henry (Fuerth, Germany)	5/27/23
Dellums, Ronald (Oakland, Cal.)	11/24/35	Klein, Calvin (New York, N.Y.)	11/19/42
Dingell, John D. Jr. (Colorado Spngs., Col.)	7/8/26	Koch, Edward I. (New York, N.Y.)	12/12/24
Dinkins, David (Trenton, N.J.)	7/10/27	Koop, C. Everett (Brooklyn, N.Y.)	10/14/16
Dixon, Sharon Pratt (Washington, D.C.)	1/31/44	Koppel, Ted (Lancashire, Eng.)	2/8/40
Dodd, Christopher (Willimantic, Conn.)	5/27/44	Kouric, Katherine (Washington, D.C.)	1/7/57
Dole, Elizabeth (Salisbury, N.C.)	7/29/36	Kuhn, Maggie (Buffalo, N.Y.)	1905
Dole, Robert (Russell, Kan.)	7/22/23	Kunstler, William (New York, N.Y.)	7/7/19
Domenici, Pete (Albuquerque, N.M.)	5/7/32	Kuralt, Charles (Wilmington, N.C.)	9/10/34
Donaldson, Sam (El Paso, Tex.)	3/11/34	Landers, Ann (Sioux City, Ia.)	7/4/18
Drew, Elizabeth (Cincinnati, Oh.)	11/16/35	Lauder, Estee (New York, N.Y.)	—
Dukakis, Michael S. (Boston, Mass.)	11/3/33	Lauren, Ralph (Bronx, N.Y.)	10/14/39
Eisner, Michael (New York, N.Y.)	3/7/42	Leahy, Patrick (Montpelier, Vt.)	3/31/40
Ephron, Nora (New York, N.Y.)	5/19/41	Lear, Frances (Hudson, N.Y.)	7/14/23
Evangelista, Linda (St. Catherine's, Canada)	5/10/65	Lear, Norman (New Haven, Conn.)	7/27/22
Falwell, Jerry (Lynchburg, Va.)	8/11/33	Lehrer, Jim (Wichita, Kan.)	5/19/34
Feinstein, Dianne (San Francisco, Cal.)	6/22/33	Lewis, Anthony (New York, N.Y.)	3/27/27
Ferraro, Geraldine (Newburgh, N.Y.)	8/26/35	Lindbergh, Anne Morrow (Englewood, N.J.)	1906

Name (Birthplace)	Birthdate
Lorenzo, Frank (New York, N.Y.)	5/19/40
Lott, Trent (Grenada, Miss.)	10/9/41
Lugar, Richard G. (Indianapolis, Ind.)	4/4/32
Lukas, J. Anthony (New York, N.Y.)	4/25/33
Lunden, Joan (Sacramento, Calif.)	9/19/50
Lupica, Mike (Oneida, N.Y.)	5/11/52
MacNeil, Robert (Montreal, Que.)	1/19/31
Marshall, Thurgood (Baltimore, Md.)	7/2/08
Martin, Lynn (Evanston, Ill.)	12/26/39
Martinez, Bob (Tampa, Fla.)	12/25/34
McClendon, Sarah (Tyler, Tex.)	7/8/10
Metzenbaum, Howard (Cleveland, Oh.)	6/4/17
Michel, Robert H. (Peoria, Ill.)	3/2/23
Mikulski, Barbara (Baltimore, Md.)	7/20/36
Mitchell, George (Waterville, Me.)	8/20/33
Mondale, Walter (Ceylon, Minn.)	1/5/28
Mosbacher, Robert (Mt. Vernon, N.Y.)	3/11/27
Moyers, Bill (Hugo, Okla.)	6/5/34
Moynihan, Daniel P. (Tulsa, Okla.)	3/16/27
Mudd, Roger (Washington, D.C.)	2/9/28
Murdoch, Rupert (Melbourne, Austr.)	5/11/31
Nader, Ralph (Winsted, Conn.)	2/27/34
Nidetch, Jean (Brooklyn, N.Y.)	10/12/23
Nixon, Pat (Ely, Nev.)	3/16/12
Nixon, Richard (Yorba Linda, Cal.)	1/9/13
North, Oliver (San Antonio, Tex.)	10/7/43
Norton, Eleanor Holmes (Washington, D.C.)	6/13/37
Novak, Robert (Joliet, Ill.)	2/26/31
Novello, Antonia (Fajardo, P.R.)	8/23/44
Nunn, Sam (Perry, Ga.)	9/8/38
O'Connor, Cardinal John (Phila., Pa.)	1/15/20
O'Connor, Sandra Day (nr. Duncan, Ariz.)	3/26/30
Onassis, Jacqueline (Southampton, N.Y.)	7/28/29
O'Neill, Thomas P. (Cambridge, Mass.)	12/9/12
Packwood, Bob (Portland, Ore.)	9/11/32
Paley, William S. (Chicago, Ill.)	9/28/01
Pauley, Jane (Indianapolis, Ind.)	10/31/50
Pauling, Linus (Portland, Ore.)	2/28/01
Peretz, Martin (New York, N.Y.)	7/30/39
Phillips, Kevin (New York, N.Y.)	11/30/40
Pickens, T. Boone (Holdenville, Okla.)	5/22/28
Pickering, Thomas (Orange, N.J.)	11/5/31
Plimpton, George (New York, N.Y.)	3/18/27
Podhoretz, Norman (New York, N.Y.)	1/16/30
Porter, Sylvia (Patchogue, N.Y.)	6/18/13
Poussaint, Alvin F. (New York, N.Y.)	5/15/34
Powell, Colin (New York, N.Y.)	4/5/37
Quayle, Dan (Indianapolis, Ind.)	2/4/47
Quinn, Jane Bryant (Niagara Falls, N.Y.)	2/5/39
Rangel, Charles (New York, N.Y.)	6/11/30
Rather, Dan (Wharton, Tex.)	10/31/31
Reagan, Nancy (New York, N.Y.)	7/6/23
Reagan, Ronald (Tampico, Ill.)	2/6/11
Reasoner, Harry (Dakota City, Ia.)	4/17/23
Rehnquist, William (Milwaukee, Wis.)	10/1/24
Rich, Frank (Washington, D.C.)	6/2/49
Richards, Ann (Waco, Tex.)	9/3/33
Ride, Sally K. (Encino, Calif.)	1952
Roberts, Oral (nr. Ada, Okla.)	1/24/18
Robertson, Pat (Lexington, Va.)	3/22/30
Rockefeller, David (New York, N.Y.)	6/12/15
Rockefeller, John D. 4th "Jay" (New York, N.Y.)	6/18/37
Rockefeller, Laurance S. (New York, N.Y.)	5/26/10
Roemer, Charles E. "Buddy" (Shreveport, La.)	10/4/43
Rooney, Andy (Albany, N.Y.)	1/14/19
Rostenkowski, Dan (Chicago, Ill.)	1/2/28
Rozelle, Pete (S. Gate, Calif.)	3/1/26
Rukeyser, Louis (New York, N.Y.)	1/30/33
Safer, Morley (Toronto, Ontario)	11/8/31
Safire, William (New York, N.Y.)	12/17/29

Name (Birthplace)	Birthdate
Sagan, Carl (New York, N.Y.)	11/9/34
Salk, Jonas (New York, N.Y.)	10/28/14
Sawyer, Diane (Glasgow, Ky.)	12/22/45
Scalia, Antonin (Trenton, N.J.)	3/11/36
Schlesinger, Arthur Jr. (Columbus, Oh.)	10/15/17
Schroeder, Patricia (Portland, Ore.)	7/30/40
Schuller, Robert (Alton, Ia.)	9/16/26
H. Norman Schwarzkopf (Trenton, N.J.)	8/22/34
Scowcroft, Brent (Ogden, Ut.)	3/19/25
Sculley, John (New York, N.Y.)	4/6/39
Seaborg, Glenn T. (Ishpeming, Mich.)	4/19/12
Shanker, Albert (New York, N.Y.)	9/14/28
Shriver, Maria (Chicago, Ill.)	11/6/55
Shultz, George P. (New York, N.Y.)	12/13/20
Silver, Joan Micklin (Omaha, Neb.)	5/25/35
Silverstein, Shel (Chicago, Ill.)	1932
Simmons, Richard (New Orleans, La.)	7/12/48
Simon, Paul (Eugene, Ore.)	11/29/28
Simpson, Alan K. (Cody, Wyo.)	9/2/31
Smith, Liz (Ft. Worth, Tex.)	2/2/23
Solarz, Stephen J. (New York, N.Y.)	9/2/40
Souter, David H. (Melrose, Mass.)	9/17/39
Spock, Benjamin (New Haven, Conn.)	5/2/03
Stahl, Lesley (Lynn, Mass.)	12/16/41
Steinbrenner, George (Rocky River, Oh.)	7/4/30
Steinem, Gloria (Toledo, Oh.)	3/25/34
Stern, David J. (New York, N.Y.)	9/22/42
Stevens, John Paul (Chicago, Ill.)	4/20/20
Sullivan, Louis (Atlanta, Ga.)	11/3/33
Sulzberger, Arthur Ochs (New York, N.Y.)	2/5/26
Sununu, John H. (Havana, Cuba)	7/2/39
Tagliabue, Paul (Jersey City, N.J.)	11/24/40
Tarkanian, Jerry (Euclid, Oh.)	8/8/30
Tartikoff, Brandon (Long Island, N.Y.)	1949
Terkel, Studs (New York, N.Y.)	5/16/12
Thornburgh, Dick (Pittsburgh, Pa.)	7/16/32
Thurmond, J. Strom (Edgefield, S.C.)	12/5/02
Tiegs, Cheryl (Minnesota)	9/27/47
Tinker, Grant (Stamford, Conn.)	1/11/26
Tisch, Laurence (New York, N.Y.)	3/15/23
Toland, John (LaCrosse, Wis.)	6/29/12
Trillin, Calvin (Kansas City, Mo.)	12/5/35
Truman, Margaret (Independence, Mo.)	2/17/24
Trump, Donald (New York, N.Y.)	1946
Tsongas, Paul (Lowell, Mass.)	2/14/41
Turner, Ted (Cincinnati, Oh.)	1938
Udall, Morris K. (St. Johns, Ariz.)	6/15/22
Ueberroth, Peter (Chicago, Ill.)	9/2/37
Valenti, Jack (Houston, Tex.)	9/5/21
Van Buren, Abigail (Sioux City, Ia.)	7/4/18
Wallace, George (Clio, Ala.)	8/25/19
Wallace, Mike (Brookline, Mass.)	5/9/18
Walters, Barbara (Boston, Mass.)	9/25/31
Walton, Sam (Kingfisher, Okla.)	1920
Webster, William H. (St. Louis, Mo.)	3/6/24
Weicker, Lowell (Paris, France)	5/16/31
Wenner, Jann (New York, N.Y.)	1/7/46
Westheimer, Ruth (Germany)	1928
White, Bill (Lakewood, Fla.)	1/28/34
White, Byron (Ft. Collins, Col.)	6/8/17
Wicker, Tom (Hamlet, N.C.)	6/18/26
Wiesel, Elie (Sighet, Transyl.)	9/30/28
Wilder, L. Douglas (Richmond, Va.)	1/17/31
Will, George (Champaign, Ill.)	1941
Wilson, Pete (Lake Forest, Ill.)	8/23/33
Wright, James C. Jr. (Ft. Worth, Tex.)	12/22/22
Yard, Molly (Shanghai, China)	
Young, Andrew (New Orleans, La.)	3/12/32
Young, Coleman (Tuscaloosa, Ala.)	5/24/18
Ziegler, John (Grosse Point, Mich.)	2/9/34

Noted Black Americans

Names of black athletes and entertainers are not included here as they are listed elsewhere in The World Almanac.

The Rev. Dr. Ralph David Abernathy, 1926-1990, organizer, 1957, and president, 1968, of the Southern Christian Leadership Conference.

Crispus Attucks, c. 1723-1770, agitator who led group that precipitated the "Boston Massacre," Mar. 5, 1770.

James Baldwin, 1924-1987, author, playwright; The Fire Next Time, Blues for Mister Charlie, Just Above My Head.

Benjamin Banneker, 1731-1806, inventor, astronomer, mathematician, and gazetteer; served on commission that surveyed and laid out Washington, D. C.

Imamu Amiri Baraka, b. LeRoi Jones, 1934, poet, playwright.

James P. Beckwourth, 1798-c. 1867, western fur-trader, scout, after whom Beckwourth Pass in northern California is named.

Dr. Mary McCleod Bethune, 1875-1955, adviser to presidents Roosevelt, Truman; division administrator, Natl. Youth Administration, 1935; founder, pres. Bethune-Cookman College.

Henry Blair, 19th century, obtained patents (believed the first issued to a black) for a corn-planter, 1834, and for a cotton-planter, 1836.

Julian Bond, b. 1940, civil rights leader first elected to the Georgia state legislature, 1965; helped found Student Nonviolent Coordinating Committee.

Edward Bouchet, 1852-1918, first black to earn a Ph.D., Yale, 1876, at a U.S. university; first black elected to Phi Beta Kappa.

Thomas Bradley, b. 1917, elected mayor of Los Angeles, 1973.

Andrew F. Brimmer, b. 1926, first black member, 1966, Federal Reserve Board.

Edward W. Brooke, b. 1919, attorney general, 1962, of Massachusetts; first black elected to U. S. Senate, 1967, since 19th century Reconstruction.

Gwendolyn Brooks, b. 1917, poet, novelist; first black to win a Pulitzer Prize, 1950, for *Annie Allen.*

Sterling A. Brown, 1901-1989, poet, literature professor; helped establish Afro-American literary criticism.

William Wells Brown, 1815-1884, novelist, dramatist; first American black to publish a novel.

Dr. Ralph Bunche, 1904-1971, first black to win the Nobel Peace Prize, 1950; undersecretary of the UN, 1950.

Sherian Grace Cadoria, b. 1940, brigadier general; highest ranking black woman in U.S. armed forces as of 1990.

Alexa Canady, b. 1950, first black woman neurosurgeon in U.S.

George E. Carruthers, b. 1940, physicist developed the Apollo 16 lunar surface ultraviolet camera/spectograph.

George Washington Carver, 1861-1943, botanist, chemurgist, and educator; his extensive experiments in soil building and plant diseases revolutionized the economy of the South.

Charles Waddell Chestnutt, 1858-1932, author known primarily for his short stories, including *The Conjure Woman.*

Shirley Chisholm, b. 1924, first black woman elected to House of Representatives, Brooklyn, N. Y., 1968.

Bishop Philip R. Cousin, b. 1933, Pres., Natl. Council of Churches of Christ in the USA, 1985-.

Countee Cullen, 1903-1946, poet, played a prominent role in the "Harlem Renaissance" of the 1920s; "Heritage," *The Black Christ.*

Lt. Gen. Benjamin O. Davis Jr. b. 1912, West Point, 1936, first black Air Force general, 1954.

Brig. Gen. Benjamin O. Davis Sr., 1877-1970, first black general, 1940, in U. S. Army.

William L. Dawson, 1886-1970, Illinois congressman, first black chairman of a major House of Representatives committee.

David Dinkins, b. 1927, first black mayor of New York City, 1990-.

Sharon Pratt Dixon, b. 1944, mayor of Washington, D.C., 1990-.

Isaiah Dorman, 19th century, U. S. Army interpreter, killed with Custer, 1876, at Battle of the Little Big Horn.

Aaron Douglas, 1900-1979, painter; called father of black American art.

Frederick Douglass, 1817-1895, author, editor, orator, diplomat; edited the abolitionist weekly, The North Star, in Rochester, N. Y.; U.S. minister and consul general to Haiti.

St. Clair Drake, 1911-1990, black studies pioneer, *Black Metropolis* (1945, with Horace R. Cayton); first permanent director, African and Afro-American Studies, Stanford Univ.

Dr. Charles Richard Drew, 1904-1950, pioneer in development of blood banks; director of American Red Cross blood donor project in World War II.

William Edward Burghardt Du Bois, 1868-1963, historian, sociologist; a founder of the National Association for the Advancement of Colored People (NAACP), 1909, and founder of its magazine The Crisis; author, *The Souls of Black Folk.*

Paul Laurence Dunbar, 1872-1906, poet, novelist; won fame with *Lyrics of Lowly Life,* 1896.

Jean Baptiste Point du Sable, c. 1750-1818, pioneer trader and first settler of Chicago, 1779.

Marian Wright Edelman, b. 1939, founder, pres. of Children's Defense Fund.

Ralph Ellison, b. 1914, novelist, essayist, *Invisible Man.*

James Farmer, b. 1920, a founder of the Congress of Racial Equality, 1942; asst. secretary, Dept. of HEW, 1969.

Henry O. Flipper, 1856-1940, first black to graduate, 1877, from West Point.

Charles Fuller, b. 1939, Pulitzer Prize-winning playwright; *A Soldier's Play.*

Mary Hatwood Futrell, b. 1940, president, Natl. Education Assn., 1983-.

Marcus Garvey, 1887-1940, founded Universal Negro Improvement Assn., 1911.

Kenneth Gibson, b. 1932, Newark, N.J., mayor, 1970-1986.

Charles Gordone, b. 1925, won 1970 Pulitzer Prize in Drama, with *No Place to Be Somebody.*

Vice Adm. Samuel L. Gravely Jr. b. 1922, first black admiral, 1971, served in World War II, Korea, and Vietnam; commander, Third Fleet.

William H. Gray 3d, b. 1941, U.S. representative from Pa., 1979—; chairman, Budget Committee, 1985-88; chairman, House Democratic Caucus, 1988-89; majority whip, 1989-.

Ewart Guinier, 1911-1990, trade unionist, first chairman of Harvard Univ.'s Department of Afro-American Studies.

Alex Haley, b. 1921, Pulitzer Prize-winning author; *Roots, The Autobiography of Malcolm X.*

Jupiter Hammon, c. 1720-1800, poet; the first black American to have his works published, 1761.

Lorraine Hansberry, 1930-1965, playwright; won New York Drama Critics Circle Award, 1959, with *Raisin in the Sun.*

Barbara Harris, b. 1931, first woman Episcopal bishop.

Patricia Roberts Harris, 1924-1985, U. S. ambassador to Luxembourg, 1965-67; secretary, Dept. of HUD, 1977-1979, Dept. of HHS, 1979-1981.

William H. Hastie, 1904-1976 first black federal judge, appointed 1937; governor of Virgin Islands, 1946-49; judge, U.S. Circuit Court of Appeals, 1949.

Chester Himes, 1909-1984, novelist, *Cotton Comes to Harlem.*

Matthew A. Henson, 1866-1955, member of Peary's 1909 expedition to the North Pole; placed U.S. flag at the Pole.

Dr. William A. Hinton, 1883-1959, developed the Hinton and Davies-Hinton tests for detection of syphilis; first black professor, 1949, at Harvard Medical School.

Benjamin L. Hooks, b. 1925, first black member, 1972-1979, Federal Communications Comm.; exec. dir., NAACP, 1977—.

Nathan I. Huggins, 1927-1989, historian, scholar; Harvard professor from 1980, director of that university's Institute for Afro-American Research from 1981.

Langston Hughes, 1902-1967, poet; story, song lyric author, a major influence in the "Harlem Renaissance" of the 1920s; *The Weary Blues, Montage of a Dream Deferred.*

Charlayne Hunter-Gault, b. 1942, first black woman admitted to Univ. of Ga., 1961; ran *N.Y. Times* Harlem Bureau, 1968-1977; broadcast journalist, 1978—.

Rev. Jesse Jackson, b. 1941, national director, Operation Bread Basket; campaigned for Democratic presidential nomination, 1984, 1988; pres., founder, Rainbow Coalition; "shadow senator" for District of Columbia, 1991-.

Maynard Jackson, b. 1938, elected mayor of Atlanta, 1973.

Gen. Daniel James Jr. 1920-1978, first black 4-star general, 1975; Commander, North American Air Defense Command.

Pvt. Henry Johnson, 1897-1929, the first American decorated by France in World War I with the Croix de Guerre.

James Weldon Johnson, 1871-1938, poet, lyricist, novelist; first black admitted to Florida bar; U.S. consul in Venezuela and Nicaragua.

John H. Johnson, b. 1918, publisher, editor of Ebony, Jet, Ebony Jr. magazines, from 1942.

Barbara Jordan, b. 1936, former congresswoman from Texas; member, House Judiciary Committee.

Vernon E. Jordan, b. 1935, executive director, National Urban League, 1972.

Ernest Everett Just, 1883-1941, marine biologist, studied egg development; author, *Biology of Cell Surfaces,* 1941.

Leontine T.C. Kelly, b. 1920, United Methodist bishop; first black woman bishop of a major American denomination, 1989.

The Rev. Dr. Martin Luther King Jr., 1929-1968, led 382-day Montgomery, Ala., boycott that brought 1956 U.S. Supreme Court decision holding segregation on buses unconstitutional; founder, president, Southern Christian Leadership Conference, 1957; won Nobel Peace Prize, 1964.

Lewis H. Latimer, 1848-1928, associate of Edison; supervised installation of first electric street lighting in N.Y.C.

Mickey Leland, 1944-1989, U.S. representative from Texas, 1978 until death; chairman of Congressional Black Caucus, House Select Committee on Hunger.

Malcolm X, 1925-1965. Black Muslim leader and black nationalist whose ideas and oratory contributed to the black pride and black power movements in the 1960s.

Thurgood Marshall, b. 1908, first black U.S. solicitor general 1965; first black justice of the U. S. Supreme Court, 1967-1991; as a lawyer led the legal battery that won the Supreme Court decision declaring racial segregation of public schools unconstitutional, 1954.

Jan Matzeliger, 1852-1889, invented lasting machine, patented 1883, which revolutionized the shoe industry.

Benjamin Mays, 1895-1984, educator, civil rights leader; headed Morehouse College, 1940-1967.

Wade H. McCree Jr., 1920-1987, solicitor general of the U.S., 1977-1981.

Donald E. McHenry, b. 1936, U.S. ambassador to the United Nations, 1979-1981.

Ronald McNair, 1950-1986, physicist, first black astronaut; killed in *Challenger* explosion.

Dorie Miller, 1919-1943, Navy hero of Pearl Harbor attack; awarded the Navy Cross.

Ernest N. Morial, b. 1929, elected first black mayor of New Orleans, 1977.

Toni Morrison, b. 1931, novelist; *Song of Solomon, Sula, Tar Baby;* won 1988 Pulitzer Prize for *Beloved.*

Willard Motley, 1912-1965, novelist; *Knock on Any Door.*

Elijah Muhammad, 1897-1975, founded Black Muslims, 1931.

Pedro Alonzo Nino, navigator of the Nina, one of Columbus' 3 ships on his first voyage of discovery to the New World, 1492.

Rosa Parks, b. 1913, Montgomery Ala. citizen arrested for refusing to move to the back of the bus, Dec. 1, 1955, bringing a 382-day bus boycott led by Martin Luther King Jr.

Frederick D. Patterson, 1901-1988, founder of United Negro College Fund, 1944; Tuskegee Institute's third pres., 1935-1953.

Adam Clayton Powell, 1908-1972, early civil rights leader, congressman, 1945-1969; chairman, House Committee on Education and Labor, 1960-1967.

Colin Powell, b. 1937, first black Natl. Security Advisor, 1987-88; first black chairman of Joint Chiefs of Staff, 1989-.

Joseph H. Rainey, 1832-1887, first black elected to House of Representatives, 1869, from South Carolina.

A. Philip Randolph, 1889-1979, organized the Brotherhood of Sleeping Car Porters, 1925; organizer of 1941 and 1963 March on Washington movements; vice president, AFL-CIO.

Charles Rangel, b. 1930, congressman from N.Y.C. from 1970; member, Ways and Means Committee; chairman, Select Committee on Narcotics Abuse & Control.

Hiram R. Revels, 1822-1901, first black U.S. senator, elected in Mississippi, served 1870-1871.

Lloyd Richards, b. 1922(?), first black to direct a Broadway play, 1959; dean, Yale Univ. School of Drama & artistic director of Yale Repertory Theatre, 1979-1991.

Wilson C. Riles, b. 1917, elected, 1970, California State Superintendent of Public Instruction.

Norbert Rillieux, 1806-1894; invented a vacuum pan evaporator, 1846, revolutionizing the sugar-refining industry.

Paul Robeson, 1898-1976, actor and concert singer, graduated 1st in class at Rutgers, 1918, Phi Beta Kappa; grad. Columbia Univ. law school, 1923; associated with communist causes.

Max Robinson, 1939-1988, TV journalist, first black to anchor network news, 1978.

Carl T. Rowan, b. 1925, prize-winning journalist; director of the U.S. Information Agency, 1964, the first black to sit on the National Security Council; U. S. ambassador to Finland, 1963.

John B. Russwurm, 1799-1851, with **Samuel E. Cornish,** 1793-1858, founded, 1827, the nation's first black newspaper, Freedom's Journal, in N.Y.C.

Bayard Rustin, 1910-1987, organizer of the 1963 March on Washington; executive director, A. Philip Randolph Institute.

Peter Salem, at the Battle of Bunker Hill, June 17, 1775, shot and killed British commander Maj. John Pitcairn.

Ntozake Shange, b. 1948, writer, For Colored Girls Who Have Considered Suicide/When the Rainbow is Enuf.

Bishop Stephen Spottswood, 1897-1974, board chairman of NAACP, 1961-1974.

The Rev. Leon H. Sullivan, b. 1922, economic development planner, first black on General Motors Bd. of Directors.

Willard Townsend, 1895-1957, organized the United Transport Service Employees, 1935 (redcaps, etc.); vice pres. AFL-CIO.

Sojourner Truth, 1797-1883, born Isabella Baumfree; preacher, abolitionist; raised funds for Union in Civil War; worked for black educational opportunities.

Harriet Tubman, 1823-1913, Underground Railroad conductor served as nurse and spy for Union Army in the Civil War.

Nat Turner, 1800-1831, led the most significant of over 200 slave revolts in U.S., in Southampton, Va.; hanged.

Alice Walker, b. 1944, novelist, essayist, The Color Purple.

Booker T. Washington, 1856-1915, founder, 1881, and first president of Tuskegee Institute; author, Up From Slavery.

Harold Washington, 1922-1987, first black mayor of Chicago, from 1983 until death.

Dr. Robert C. Weaver, b. 1907, first black member of the U.S. Cabinet, secretary, Dept. of HUD, 1966.

Ida B. Wells (Barnett), 1862-1931, journalist who waged anti-lynching crusade.

Clifton R. Wharton Jr., b. 1926, first black pres. of major U.S. univ.; chancellor, nation's largest univ. system, 8 yrs.; chairman & CEO, country's largest pension fund, 1987—.

Phillis Wheatley, c. 1753-1784, poet; 2d American woman and first black woman to have her works published, 1770.

Bill White, b. 1934, first black baseball league president; named Natl. League head, 1989.

Walter White, 1893-1955, exec. secretary, NAACP, 1931-1955.

L. Douglas Wilder, first black governor, elected Virginia chief executive in 1989.

Roy Wilkins, 1901-1981, exec. director, NAACP, 1955-1977.

Dr. Daniel Hale Williams, 1858-1931, performed one of first 2 open-heart operations, 1893; founded Provident, Chicago's first Negro hospital; first black elected a fellow of the American College of Surgeons.

August Wilson, b. 1945, playwright, won 1987 Pulitzer Prize for Fences, 1990 Pulitzer for The Piano Lesson.

Granville T. Woods, 1856-1910, invented the third-rail system now used in subways, a complex railway telegraph device that helped reduce train accidents, and an automatic air brake.

Dr. Carter G. Woodson, 1875-1950, historian; founded Assn. for the Study of Negro Life and History, 1915, and Journal of Negro History, 1916.

Richard Wright, 1908-1960, novelist; Native Son, Black Boy.

Frank Yerby, b. 1916, first best-selling American black novelist; The Foxes of Harrow, Vixen.

Andrew Young, b. 1932, civil rights leader, congressman from Georgia, U.S. ambassador to the United Nations, 1977-79; mayor of Atlanta, 1982-89.

Whitney M. Young Jr., 1921-1971, exec. director, 1961, National Urban League; author, lecturer, newspaper columnist.

About 5,000 blacks served in the Continental Army during the **American Revolution,** mostly in integrated units, some in all-black combat units. Some 200,000 blacks served in the Union Army during the **Civil War;** 38,000 gave their lives; 22 won the Medal of Honor, the nation's highest award. Of 367,000 blacks in the armed forces during **World War I,** 100,000 served in France. More than 1,000,000 blacks served in the armed forces during **World War II;** all-black fighter and bomber AAF units and infantry divisions gave distinguished service. In 1954 the policy of all-black units was finally abolished. Of 274,937 blacks who served in the armed forces during the **Vietnam War** (1965-1974), 5,681 were killed in combat. During the **Persian Gulf War** (1990-1991), 104,000 blacks served in the Kuwaiti theater—20 percent of U.S. soldiers, compared with 8.7% during World War II and 9.8% in Vietnam.

As of Jan., 1990, there were 313 black mayors, 1 black governor, 6 state administrators, 317 state representatives, and 24 U.S. representatives. There were then 7,370 blacks holding elected office in the U.S. and Virgin Islands, an increase of 2% over the previous year, according to a survey by the Joint Center for Political Studies, Washington, D.C. The number of black women in politics was increasing at a faster rate than that of any other group in American politics, according to the Center. Between 1970 and April 1991, the overall number of black women elected to local, county, state, and congressional offices rose from 131 to 1,950; in the 1990 elections, 33 of the 70 newly elected black state legislators—nearly half—were women.

Notable Living American Fiction Writers and Playwrights

Name (Birthplace)	Birthdate	Name (Birthplace)	Birthdate
Adams, Alice (Fredericksburg, Va.)	8/14/26	Dailey, Janet (Storm Lake, Ia.)	5/21/44
Albee, Edward (Washington, D.C.)	3/12/28	De Vries, Peter (Chicago, Ill.)	2/27/10
Auchincloss, Louis (Lawrence, N.Y.)	9/27/17	Didion, Joan (Sacramento, Cal.)	12/5/34
Barth, John (Cambridge, Md.)	5/27/30	Doctorow, E. L. (New York, N.Y.)	1/6/31
Beattie, Ann (Washington, D.C.)	9/7/47	Dunne, John Gregory (Hartford, Conn.)	5/25/32
Bellow, Saul (Quebec, Canada)	7/10/15	Elkin, Stanley (New York, N.Y.)	5/11/30
Benchley, Peter (New York, N.Y.)	5/8/40	Ellison, Ralph (Oklahoma City, Okla.)	3/1/14
Berger, Thomas (Cincinnati, Oh.)	7/20/24	Fast, Howard (New York, N.Y.)	11/11/14
Blume, Judy (Elizabeth, N.J.)	2/12/38	Fox, Paula (New York, N.Y.)	4/22/23
Bradbury, Ray (Waukegan, Ill.)	8/22/20	French, Marilyn (New York, N.Y.)	11/21/29
Brooks, Gwendolyn (Topeka, Kan.)	6/7/17	Fuller, Charles (Philadelphia, Pa.)	3/5/39
Calisher, Hortense (New York, N.Y.)	12/20/11	Gaddis, William (New York, N.Y.)	1922
Clark, Mary Higgins (New York, N.Y.)	12/24/31	Geisel, Theodore ("Dr. Seuss,"	
Clavell, James (England)	10/10/24	Springfield, Mass.)	3/2/04
Cleary, Beverly (McMinnville, Ore.)	1916	Gilroy, Frank (New York, N.Y.)	10/13/25
Connell, Evan S. (Kansas City, Mo.)	8/17/24	Godwin, Gail (Birmingham, Ala.)	6/18/37
Conroy, Pat (Atlanta, Ga.)	10/26/45	Goldman, William (Chicago, Ill.)	8/12/31
Crews, Harry (Alma, Ga.)	6/6/35	Gordon, Mary (Long Island, N.Y.)	12/8/49
Crichton, Michael (Chicago, Ill.)	10/23/42	Grau, Shirley Ann (New Orleans, La.)	7/8/29

Name (Birthplace)	Birthdate
Guare, John (New York, N.Y.)	2/5/38
Hailey, Arthur (Luton, England)	4/5/20
Haley, Alex (Ithaca, N.Y.)	8/11/21
Hawkes, John (Stamford, Conn.)	8/17/25
Heller, Joseph (Brooklyn, N.Y.)	5/1/23
Helprin, Mark (New York, N.Y.)	6/28/47
Hersey, John (Tientsin, China)	6/17/14
Hinton, S.E. (Tulsa, Okla.)	1948
Irving, John (Exeter, N.H.)	3/2/42
Jong, Erica (New York, N.Y.)	3/26/42
Kennedy, William (Albany, N.Y.)	1/16/28
Kerr, Jean (Scranton, Pa.)	7/10/23
King, Stephen (Portland, Me.)	9/21/47
Kingston, Maxine Hong (Stockton, Cal.)	10/27/40
Knowles, John (Fairmont, W. Va.)	9/16/26
Krantz, Judith (New York, N.Y.)	1/9/28
LeGuin, Ursula (Berkeley, Cal.)	10/21/29
L'Engle, Madeleine (New York, N.Y.)	11/29/18
Leonard, Elmore (New Orleans, La.)	10/11/25
Levin, Ira (New York, N.Y.)	8/27/29
Ludlum, Robert (New York, N.Y.)	5/25/27
Lurie, Alison (Chicago, Ill.)	9/3/26
Mailer, Norman (Long Branch, N.J.)	1/31/23
Mamet, David (Chicago, Ill.)	11/30/47
McGuane, Thomas (Wyandotte, Mich.)	12/11/39
McMurtry, Larry (Wichita Falls, Tex.)	6/3/36
Michener, James A. (New York, N.Y.)	2/3/07
Miller, Arthur (New York, N.Y.)	10/17/15
Morris, Wright (Central City, Neb.)	1/6/10
Morrison, Toni (Lorain, Oh.)	2/18/31
Oates, Joyce Carol (Lockport, N.Y.)	6/16/38
Ozick, Cynthia (New York, N.Y.)	4/17/28
Paley, Grace (New York, N.Y.)	12/11/22
Piercy, Marge (Detroit, Mich.)	3/31/36
Potok, Chaim (New York, N.Y.)	2/17/29

Name (Birthplace)	Birthdate
Price, Reynolds (Macon, N.C.)	2/1/33
Puzo, Mario (New York, N.Y.)	10/15/20
Pynchon, Thomas (Glen Cove, N.Y.)	5/8/37
Rabe, David (Dubuque, Ia.)	3/10/40
Reed, Ishmael (Chattanooga, Tenn.)	2/22/38
Roth, Henry (Austria-Hungary)	2/8/06
Roth, Philip (Newark, N.J.)	3/19/33
Salinger, J. D. (New York, N.Y.)	1/1/19
Sanders, Lawrence (New York, N.Y.)	1920
Sendak, Maurice (New York, N.Y.)	6/10/28
Shepard, Sam (Ft. Sheridan, Ill.)	11/5/43
Simon, Neil (New York, N.Y.)	7/4/27
Singer, Isaac Bashevis (Radzymin, Poland)	7/14/04
Spillane, Mickey (Brooklyn, N.Y.)	3/9/18
Stegner, Wallace (Lake Mills, Ia.)	2/18/09
Stern, Richard (New York, N.Y.)	2/25/28
Stone, Robert (Brooklyn, N.Y.)	8/21/37
Styron, William (Newport News, Va.)	6/11/25
Taylor, Peter (Trenton, Tenn.)	1/8/17
Theroux, Paul (Medford, Mass.)	4/10/41
Tyler, Anne (Minneapolis, Minn.)	10/25/41
Updike, John (Shillington, Pa.)	3/18/32
Uris, Leon (Baltimore, Md.)	8/3/24
Vidal, Gore (West Point, N.Y.)	10/3/25
Vonnegut, Kurt Jr. (Indianapolis, Ind.)	11/11/22
Walker, Alice (Eatonton, Ga.)	2/9/44
Wambaugh, Joseph (East Pittsburgh, Pa.)	1/22/37
Wasserstein, Wendy (New York, N.Y.)	—
Welty, Eudora (Jackson, Miss.)	4/13/09
Wideman, John Edgar (Pittsburgh, Pa.)	6/14/41
Wilson, August (Pittsburgh, Pa.)	4/27/45
Wilson, Lanford (Lebanon, Mo.)	4/13/37
Wolfe, Tom (Richmond, Va.)	3/2/31
Wolff, Tobias (Birmingham, Ala.)	6/19/45
Wouk, Herman (New York, N.Y.)	5/27/15

American Architects and Some of Their Achievements

Max Abramovitz, b. 1908, Avery Fisher Hall, Lincoln Center, N.Y.C.

Henry Bacon, 1866-1924, Lincoln Memorial.

Pietro Belluschi, b. 1899, Juilliard School of Music, Lincoln Center, N.Y.C.

Marcel Breuer, 1902-1981, Whitney Museum of American Art, N.Y.C. (with Hamilton Smith).

Charles Bulfinch, 1763-1844, State House, Boston; Capitol, Wash. D.C., (part).

Gordon Bunshaft, b. 1909, Lever House, Park Ave, N.Y.C.; Hirshhorn Museum, Wash., D.C.

Daniel H. Burnham, 1846-1912, Union Station, Wash. D.C.; Flatiron, N.Y.C.

Irwin Chanin, 1892-1988, New York City theaters, skyscrapers.

Ralph Adams Cram, 1863-1942, Cathedral of St. John the Divine, N.Y.C.; U.S. Military Academy (part).

R. Buckminster Fuller, 1895-1983, U.S. Pavilion, Expo 67, Montreal (geodesic domes).

Cass Gilbert, 1859-1934, Custom House, Woolworth Bldg., N.Y.C.; Supreme Court bldg., Wash., D.C.

Bertram G. Goodhue, 1869-1924, Capitol, Lincoln, Neb.; St. Thomas, St. Bartholomew, N.Y.C.

Walter Gropius, 1883-1969, Pan Am Building, N.Y.C. (with Pietro Belluschi)

Peter Harrison, 1716-1775, Touro Synagogue, Redwood Library, Newport, R.I.

Wallace K. Harrison, 1895-1981, Metropolitan Opera House, Lincoln Center, N.Y.C.

Thomas Hastings, 1860-1929, Public Library, Frick Mansion, N.Y.C.

James Hoban, 1762-1831, The White House.

Raymond Hood, 1881-1934, Rockefeller Center, N.Y.C. (part); Daily News, N.Y.C.; Tribune, Chicago.

Richard M. Hunt, 1827-1895, Metropolitan Museum, N.Y.C. (part); Natl. Observatory, Wash., D.C.

William Le Baron Jenney, 1832-1907, Home Insurance, Chicago (demolished 1931).

Philip C. Johnson, b. 1906, N.Y. State Theater, Lincoln Center, N.Y.C.

Albert Kahn, 1869-1942, Athletic Club Bldg., General Motors Bldg., Detroit.

Louis Kahn, 1901-1974, Salk Laboratory, La Jolla, Cal.; Yale Art Gallery.

Christopher Grant LaFarge, 1862-1938, Roman Catholic Chapel, West Point.

Benjamin H. Latrobe, 1764-1820, U.S. Capitol (part).

William Lescaze, 1896-1969, Philadelphia Savings Fund Society; Borg-Warner Bldg., Chicago.

Bernard R. Maybeck, 1862-1957, Hearst Hall, Chick House, Univ. of Cal., First Church of Christ Scientist, Berkeley.

Charles F. McKim, 1847-1909, Public Library, Boston, Columbia Univ., N.Y.C. (part).

Charles M. McKim, b. 1920, KUHT-TV Transmitter Building, Houston; Lutheran Church of the Redeemer, Houston.

Ludwig Mies van der Rohe, 1886-1969, Seagram Building, N.Y.C. (with Philip C. Johnson); National Gallery, Berlin.

Robert Mills, 1781-1855, Washington Monument.

Richard J. Neutra, 1892-1970, Mathematics Park, Princeton; Orange Co. Courthouse, Santa Ana, Cal.

Gyo Obata, b. 1923, Natl. Air & Space Mus., Smithsonian Institution; Dallas-Ft. Worth Airport.

Frederick L. Olmsted, 1822-1903, Central Park, N.Y.C.; Fairmount Park, Philadelphia.

I(eoh) M(ing) Pei, b. 1917, National Center for Atmospheric Research, Boulder, Col.; East Wing, Natl. Gallery of Art, Wash., D.C.; Pyramid, The Louvre, Paris.

William Pereira, 1909-1985, Cape Canaveral; Transamerica Bldg., San Francisco.

John Russell Pope, 1874-1937, National Gallery.

George Browne Post, 1837-1913, New York Stock Exchange, Wisconsin state capitol.

John Portman, b. 1924, Peachtree Center, Atlanta.

James Renwick Jr., 1818-1895, Grace Church, St. Patrick's Cathedral, N.Y.C.; Smithsonian, Corcoran Galleries, Wash., D.C.

Henry H. Richardson, 1838-1886, Trinity Church, Boston.

Kevin Roche, b. 1922, Oakland Cal. Museum; Fine Arts Center, U. of Mass.

James Gamble Rogers, 1867-1947, Columbia-Presbyterian Medical Center, N.Y.C.; Northwestern Univ., Chicago.

John Wellborn Root, 1887-1963, Palmolive Building, Chicago; Hotel Statler, Washington; Hotel Tamanaco, Caracas.

Paul Rudolph, b. 1918, Jewitt Art Center, Wellesley College; Art & Architecture Bldg., Yale.

Charles M. Russell, 1866-1926, Western life.

Eero Saarinen, 1910-1961, Gateway to the West Arch, St. Louis; Trans World Flight Center, N.Y.C.

Louis Skidmore, 1897-1962, AEC town site, Oak Ridge, Tenn.; Terrace Plaza Hotel, Cincinnati.

Clarence S. Stein, 1882-1975, Temple Emanu-El, N.Y.C.

Edward Durell Stone, 1902-1978, U.S. Embassy, New Delhi, India; (H. Hartford) Gallery of Modern Art, N.Y.C.

Louis H. Sullivan, 1856-1924, Auditorium, Chicago.

Richard Upjohn, 1802-1878, Trinity Church, N.Y.C.

Ralph T. Walker, 1889-1973, N.Y. Telephone Hdqrs., N.Y.C.; IBM Research Lab., Poughkeepsie, N.Y.

Roland A. Wank, 1898-1970, Cincinnati Union Terminal; head architect TVA, 1933-44.

Stanford White, 1853-1906, Washington Arch; first Madison Square Garden, N.Y.C.

Frank Lloyd Wright, 1867 (or 1869)-1959, Imperial Hotel, Tokyo; Guggenheim Museum, N.Y.C.; Unity Church, Oak Park, Ill; Robie House, Chicago; Taliesin, Wis.

William Wurster, 1895-1973, Ghirardelli Sq., San Francisco; Cowell College, U. Cal., Berkeley.

Minoru Yamasaki, 1912-1986, World Trade Center, N.Y.C.

Noted American Cartoonists

Charles Addams, 1912-1988, macabre cartoons.

Brad Anderson, b. 1924, Marmaduke.

Peter Arno, 1904-1968, urban characterizations.

Tex Avery, 1908-1980, **Friz Freleng**, b. 1905?, **Chuck Jones**, b. 1912, animators of Bugs Bunny, Porky Pig, Daffy Duck.

George Baker, 1915-1975, The Sad Sack.

C. C. Beck, 1910-1989, Captain Marvel.

Jim Berry, b. 1932, Berry's World.

Herb Block (Herblock), b. 1909, leading political cartoonist.

George Booth, b. 1926, *New Yorker* cartoonist.

Berke Breathed, b. 1957, Bloom County.

Clare Briggs, 1875-1930, Mr. & Mrs.

Dik Browne, 1917-1989, Hi & Lois, Hagar the Horrible.

Ernie Bushmiller, 1905-1982, Nancy.

Milton Caniff, 1907-1988, Terry & the Pirates; Steve Canyon.

Al Capp, 1909-1979, Li'l Abner.

Paul Conrad, 1924, political cartoonist.

Roy Crane, 1901-1977, Captain Easy; Buz Sawyer.

Robert Crumb, b. 1943, "Underground" cartoonist.

Jay N. Darling (Ding), 1876-1962, political cartoonist.

Jim Davis, b. 1945, Garfield.

Billy DeBeck, 1890-1942, Barney Google.

Rudolph Dirks, 1877-1968, The Katzenjammer Kids.

Walt Disney, 1901-1966, producer of animated cartoons; created Mickey Mouse & Donald Duck.

Steve Ditko, b. 1927, Spider-Man.

Mort Drucker, b. 1929, *Mad* magazine.

Jules Feiffer, b. 1929, satirical *Village Voice* cartoonist.

Bud Fisher, 1884-1954, Mutt & Jeff.

Ham Fisher, 1900-1955, Joe Palooka.

James Montgomery Flagg, 1877-1960, illustrator; created the famous Uncle Sam recruiting poster during WWI.

Max Fleischer, 1883-1972, creator of Betty Boop, Popeye cartoons.

Hal Foster, 1892-1982, Tarzan; Prince Valiant.

Fontaine Fox, 1884-1964, Toonerville Folks.

Rube Goldberg, 1883-1970, Boob McNutt.

Chester Gould, 1900-1985, Dick Tracy.

Harold Gray, 1894-1968, Little Orphan Annie.

Matt Groening, b. 1954, Life is Hell, The Simpsons.

Cathy Guisewite, b. 1950, Cathy.

Bill Hanna, b. 1910, & **Joe Barbera**, b. 1911, animators of Tom & Jerry, Huckleberry Hound, Yogi Bear, Flintstones.

Johnny Hart, b. 1931, BC, Wizard of Id.

Jimmy Hatlo, 1898-1963, Little Iodine.

John Held Jr., 1889-1958, "Jazz Age" cartoonist.

George Herriman, 1881-1944, Krazy Kat.

Harry Hershfield, 1885-1974, Abie the Agent.

Al Hirschfeld, b. 1903, N.Y. Times theater caricaturist.

Burne Hogarth, b. 1911, Tarzan.

Helen Hokinson, 1900-1949, satirized clubwomen.

Bil Keane, b. 1922, The Family Circus.

Walt Kelly, 1913-1973, Pogo.

Hank Ketcham, b. 1920, Dennis the Menace.

Ted Key, b. 1912, Hazel.

Frank King, 1883-1969, Gasoline Alley.

Jack Kirby, b. 1917, Fantastic Four.

Rollin Kirby, 1875-1952, political cartoonist.

B(ernard) Kliban, b. 1935, cat books.

Edward Koren, b. 1935, New Yorker woolly characters.

Walter Lantz, b. 1900, Woody Woodpecker.

Gary Larson, b. 1950, The Far Side.

Mell Lazarus, b. 1929, Momma, Miss Peach.

Stan Lee, b. 1922, Marvel Comics.

Don Martin, b. 1931, *Mad* magazine.

Bill Mauldin, b. 1921, depicted squalid life of the G.I. in WWII.

Jeff MacNelly, b. 1947, political cartoonist, and strip Shoe.

Winsor McCay, 1872-1934, Little Nemo.

John T. McCutcheon, 1870-1949, midwestern rural life.

George McManus, 1884-1954, Bringing Up Father.

Dale Messick, b. 1906, Brenda Starr.

Norman Mingo, 1896-1980, Alfred E. Neuman.

Bob Montana, 1920-1975, Archie.

Dick Moores, 1909-1986, Gasoline Alley.

Willard Mullin, 1902-1978, sports cartoonist; created Dodgers "Bum" and Mets "Kid".

Russell Myers, b. 1938, Broom Hilda.

Thomas Nast, 1840-1902, political cartoonist; created the Democratic donkey and Republican elephant.

Pat Oliphant, b. 1935, political cartoonist.

Frederick Burr Opper, 1857-1937, Happy Hooligan.

Richard Outcault, 1863-1928, Yellow Kid; Buster Brown.

Mike Peters, b. 1943, editorial cartoons; Mother Goose & Grimm.

George Price, b. 1901, New Yorker lower-class life.

Alex Raymond, 1909-1956, Flash Gordon; Jungle Jim.

Art Sansom, b. 1920, The Born Loser.

Charles Schulz, b. 1922, Peanuts.

Elzie C. Segar, 1894-1938, Popeye.

Jerry Siegel, b. 1914, & **Joe Shuster**, b. 1914, Superman.

Sydney Smith, 1835-1935, The Gumps.

Otto Soglow, 1900-1975, Little King; Canyon Kiddies.

William Steig, b. 1907, *New Yorker* cartoonist.

James Swinnerton, 1875-1974, Little Jimmy.

Paul Terry, 1887-1971, animator of Mighty Mouse.

Bob Thaves, b. 1924, Frank and Ernest.

James Thurber, 1894-1961, *New Yorker* cartoonist.

Garry Trudeau, b. 1948, Doonesbury.

Mort Walker, b. 1923, Beetle Bailey.

Bill Watterson, b. 1958, Calvin and Hobbes.

Russ Westover, 1887-1966, Tillie the Toiler.

Frank Willard, 1893-1958, Moon Mullins.

J. R. Williams, 1888-1957, The Willets Family; Out Our Way.

Gahan Wilson, b. 1930, cartoonist of the macabre.

Tom Wilson, b. 1931, Ziggy.

Art Young, 1866-1943, political radical and satirist.

Chic Young, 1901-1973, Blondie.

Noted Political Leaders of the Past

(U.S. presidents and vice presidents, Supreme Court justices, signers of Declaration of Independence, listed elsewhere.)

Abu Bakr, 573-634, Mohammedan leader, first caliph, chosen successor to Mohammed.

Dean Acheson, 1893-1971, (U.S.) secretary of state, chief architect of cold war foreign policy.

Samuel Adams, 1722-1803, (U.S.) patriot, Boston Tea Party firebrand.

Konrad Adenauer, 1876-1967, (G.) West German chancellor.

Emilio Aguinaldo, 1869-1964, (Philip.) revolutionary, fought against Spain and the U.S.

Akbar, 1542-1605, greatest Mogul emperor of India.

Salvador Allende Gossens, 1908-1973, (Chil.) president, advocate of democratic socialism.

Herbert H. Asquith, 1852-1928, (Br.) Liberal prime minister, instituted an advanced program of social reform.

Atahualpa, ?-1533, Inca (ruling chief) of Peru.

Kemal Atatürk, 1881-1938, (Turk.) founded modern Turkey.

Clement Attlee, 1883-1967, (Br.) Labour party leader, prime minister, enacted national health, nationalized many industries.

Stephen F. Austin, 1793-1836, (U.S.) led Texas colonization.

Mikhail Bakunin, 1814-1876, (R.) revolutionary, leading exponent of anarchism.

Arthur J. Balfour, 1848-1930, (Br.) as foreign secretary under Lloyd George issued Balfour Declaration expressing official British approval of Zionism.

Bernard M. Baruch, 1870-1965, (U.S.) financier, gvt. adviser.

Fulgencio Batista y Zaldívar, 1901-1973, (Cub.) ruler overthrown by Castro.

Lord Beaverbrook, 1879-1964, (Br.) financier, statesman, newspaper owner.

Eduard Benes, 1884-1948, (Czech.) president during interwar and post-WW II eras.

David Ben-Gurion, 1886-1973, (Isr.) first premier of Israel.

Thomas Hart Benton, 1782-1858, (U.S.) Missouri senator, championed agrarian interests and westward expansion.

Lavrenti Beria, 1899-1953, (USSR) Communist leader prominent in political purges under Stalin.

Aneurin Bevan, 1897-1960, (Br.) Labour party leader.

Ernest Bevin, 1881-1951, (Br.) Labour party leader, foreign minister, helped lay foundation for NATO.

Otto von Bismarck, 1815-1898, (G.) statesman known as the Iron Chancellor, uniter of Germany, 1870.

James G. Blaine, 1830-1893, (U.S.) Republican politician, diplomat, influential in launching Pan-American movement.

Léon Blum, 1872-1950, (F.) socialist leader, writer, headed first Popular Front government.

Simón Bolívar, 1783-1830, (Venez.) South American revolutionary who liberated much of the continent from Spanish rule.

William E. Borah, 1865-1940, (U.S.) isolationist senator, instrumental in blocking U.S. membership in League of Nations and the World Court.

Cesare Borgia, 1476-1507, (It.) soldier, politician, an outstanding figure of the Italian Renaissance.

Leonid Brezhnev, 1906-1982, (USSR) leader of the Soviet Union, 1964-82.

Aristide Briand, 1862-1932, (F.) foreign minister, chief architect of Locarno Pact and anti-war Kellogg-Briand Pact.

William Jennings Bryan, 1860-1925, (U.S.) Democratic, populist leader, orator, 3 times lost race for presidency.

Nikolai Bukharin, 1888-1938, (USSR) communist leader.

William C. Bullitt, 1891-1967, (U.S.) diplomat, first ambassador to USSR, ambassador to France.

Ralph Bunche, 1904-1971, (U.S.) a founder and key diplomat of United Nations for more than 20 years.

John C. Calhoun, 1782-1850, (U.S.) political leader, champion of states' rights and a symbol of the Old South.

Robert Castlereagh, 1769-1822, (Br.) foreign secy, guided Grand Alliance against Napoleon.

Camillo Benso Cavour, 1810-1861, (It.) statesman, largely responsible for uniting Italy under the House of Savoy.

Nicolae Ceausescu, 1918-1989, Rumanian Communist leader, head of state from 1967-1989.

Austen Chamberlain, 1863-1937, (Br.) Conservative party leader, largely responsible for Locarno Pact of 1925.

Neville Chamberlain, 1869-1940, (Br.) Conservative prime minister whose appeasement of Hitler led to Munich Pact.

Salmon P. Chase, 1808-1873, (U.S.) public official, abolitionist, jurist, 6th Supreme Court chief justice.

Chiang Kai-shek, 1887-1975, (Chin.) Nationalist Chinese president whose govt. was driven from mainland to Taiwan.

Chou En-lai, 1898-1976, (Chin.) diplomat, prime minister, a leading figure of the Chinese Communist party.

Winston Churchill, 1874-1965, (Br.) prime minister, soldier, author, guided Britain through WW II.

Galeazzo Ciano, 1903-1944, (It.) fascist foreign minister, helped create Rome-Berlin Axis, executed by Mussolini.

Henry Clay, 1777-1852, (U.S.) "The Great Compromiser," one of most influential pre-Civil War political leaders.

Georges Clemenceau, 1841-1929, (F.) twice premier, Wilson's chief antagonist at Paris Peace Conference after WW I.

DeWitt Clinton, 1769-1828, (U.S.) political leader, responsible for promoting idea of the Erie Canal.

Robert Clive, 1725-1774, (Br.) first administrator of Bengal, laid foundation for British Empire in India.

Jean Baptiste Colbert, 1619-1683, (F.) statesman, influential under Louis XIV, created the French navy.

Oliver Cromwell, 1599-1658, (Br.) Lord Protector of England, led parliamentary forces during Civil War.

Curzon of Kedleston, 1859-1925, (Br.) viceroy of India, foreign secretary, major force in dealing with post-WW I problems in Europe and Far East.

Édouard Daladier, 1884-1970, (F.) radical socialist politician, arrested by Vichy, interned by Germans until liberation in 1945.

Georges Danton, 1759-1794, (F.) a leading figure in the French Revolution.

Jefferson Davis, 1808-1889, (U.S.) president of the Confederate States of America.

Charles G. Dawes, 1865-1951, (U.S.) statesman, banker, advanced Dawes Plan to stabilize post-WW I German finances.

Alcide De Gasperi, 1881-1954, (It.) premier, founder of the Christian Democratic party.

Charles DeGaulle, 1890-1970, (F.) general, statesman, and first president of the Fifth Republic.

Eamon De Valera, 1882-1975, (Ir.-U.S.) statesman, led fight for Irish independence.

Thomas E. Dewey, 1902-1971, (U.S.) New York governor, twice loser in try for presidency.

Ngo Dinh Diem, 1901-1963, (Viet.) South Vietnamese president, assassinated in government take-over.

Everett M. Dirksen, 1896-1969, (U.S.) Senate Republican minority leader, orator.

Benjamin Disraeli, 1804-1881, (Br.) prime minister, considered founder of modern Conservative party.

Engelbert Dollfuss, 1892-1934, (Aus.) chancellor, assassinated by Austrian Nazis.

Andrea Doria, 1466-1560, (It.) Genoese admiral, statesman, called "Father of Peace" and "Liberator of Genoa."

Stephen A. Douglas, 1813-1861, (U.S.) Democratic leader, orator, opposed Lincoln for the presidency.

John Foster Dulles, 1888-1959, (U.S.) secretary of state under Eisenhower, cold war policy maker.

Friedrich Ebert, 1871-1925, (G.) Social Democratic movement leader, instrumental in bringing about Weimar constitution.

Sir Anthony Eden, 1897-1977, (Br.) foreign secretary, prime minister during Suez invasion of 1956.

Ludwig Erhard, 1897-1977, (G.) economist, West German chancellor, led nation's economic rise after WW II.

Hamilton Fish, 1808-1893, (U.S.) secretary of state, successfully mediated disputes with Great Britain, Latin America.

James V. Forrestal, 1892-1949, (U.S.) secretary of navy, first secretary of defense.

Francisco Franco, 1892-1975, (Sp.) leader of rebel forces during Spanish Civil War and dictator of Spain.

Benjamin Franklin, 1706-1790, (U.S.) printer, publisher, author, inventor, scientist, diplomat.

Louis de Frontenac, 1620-1698, (F.) governor of New France (Canada); encouraged explorations, fought Iroquois.

Hugh Gaitskell, 1906-1963, (Br.) Labour party leader, major force in reversing its stand for unilateral disarmament.

Albert Gallatin, 1761-1849, (U.S.) secretary of treasury who was instrumental in negotiating end of War of 1812.

Léon Gambetta, 1838-1882, (F.) statesman, politician, one of the founders of the Third Republic.

Indira Gandhi, 1917-1984, (Ind.) succeeded father, Jawaharlal Nehru, as prime minister, assassinated.

Mohandas K. Gandhi, 1869-1948, (Ind.) political leader, ascetic, led nationalist movement against British rule.

Giuseppe Garibaldi, 1807-1882, (It.) patriot, soldier, a leading figure in the Risorgimento, the Italian unification movement.

Genghis Khan, c. 1167-1227, Mongol conqueror, ruler of vast Asian empire.

William E. Gladstone, 1809-1898, (Br.) prime minister 4 times, dominant force of Liberal party from 1868 to 1894.

Paul Joseph Goebbels, 1897-1945, (G.) Nazi propagandist, master of mass psychology.

Klement Gottwald, 1896-1953, (Czech.) communist leader ushered communism into his country.

Che (Ernesto) Guevara, 1928-1967, (Arg.) guerilla leader, prominent in Cuban revolution, killed in Bolivia.

Haile Selassie, 1891-1975, (Eth.) emperor, maintained monarchy through invasion, occupation, internal resistance.

Alexander Hamilton, 1755-1804, (U.S.) first treasury secretary, champion of strong central government.

Dag Hammarskjold, 1905-1961, (Swed.) statesman, UN secretary general.

John Hancock, 1737-1793, (U.S.) revolutionary leader, first signer of Declaration of Independence.

John Hay, 1838-1905, (U.S.) secretary of state, primarily associated with Open Door Policy toward China.

Patrick Henry, 1736-1799, (U.S.) major revolutionary figure, remarkable orator.

Édouard Herriot, 1872-1957, (F.) Radical Socialist leader, twice premier, president of National Assembly.

Theodor Herzl, 1860-1904, (Aus.) founder of modern Zionism.

Heinrich Himmler, 1900-1945, (G.) chief of Nazi SS and Gestapo, primarily responsible for the Holocaust.

Paul von Hindenburg, 1847-1934, (G.) field marshal, president.

Hirohito, 1902-1989; emperor of Japan from 1926.

Adolf Hitler, 1889-1945, (G.) dictator, founder of National Socialism; wrote *Mein Kampf*, strategy for world domination.

Ho Chi Minh, 1890-1969, (Viet.) North Vietnamese president, Vietnamese Communist leader, national hero.

Harry L. Hopkins, 1890-1946, (U.S.) New Deal administrator, closest adviser to FDR during WW II.

Edward M. House, 1858-1938, (U.S.) diplomat, confidential adviser to Woodrow Wilson.

Samuel Houston, 1793-1863, (U.S.) leader of struggle to win control of Texas from Mexico.

Cordell Hull, 1871-1955, (U.S.) secretary of state, initiated reciprocal trade to lower tariffs, helped organize UN.

Hubert H. Humphrey, 1911-1978, (U.S.) Minnesota Democrat, senator, vice president, spent 32 years in public service.

Ibn Saud, c. 1888-1953, (S. Arab.) founder of Saudi Arabia and its first king.

Jacob Javits, 1904-1986 (U.S.) U.S. senator from New York for 24 years.

Jinnah, Muhammed Ali, 1876-1948, (Pak.) founder, first governor-general of Pakistan.

Benito Juarez, 1806-1872, (Mex.) rallied countrymen against foreign threats, sought to create democratic, federal republic.

Kamehameha I, c. 1758-1819, (Haw.) founder, first monarch of unified Hawaii.

Frank B. Kellogg, 1856-1937, (U.S.) secretary of state, negotiated Kellogg-Briand Pact to outlaw war.

Robert F. Kennedy, 1925-1968, (U.S.) attorney general, senator, assassinated while seeking presidential nomination.

Aleksandr Kerensky, 1881-1970, (R.) revolutionary, served as premier after Feb. 1917 revolution until Bolshevik overthrow.

Ruhollah Khomeini, 1900-1989, (Iran), religious leader with Islamic title "ayatollah," directed overthrow of shah, 1979, became source of political authority in succeeding governments.

Nikita Khrushchev, 1894-1971, (USSR) premier, first secretary of Communist party, initiated de-Stalinization.

Lajos Kossuth, 1802-1894, (Hung.) principal figure in 1848 Hungarian revolution.

Pyotr Kropotkin, 1842-1921, (R.) anarchist, championed the peasants but opposed Bolshevism.

Kublai Khan, c. 1215-1294, Mongol emperor, founder of Yüan dynasty in China.

Béla Kun, 1886-c.1939, (Hung.) communist, member of 3d International, tried to foment worldwide revolution.

Robert M. LaFollette, 1855-1925, (U.S.) Wisconsin public official, leader of progressive movement.

Pierre Laval, 1883-1945, (F.) politician, Vichy foreign minister, executed for treason.

Andrew Bonar Law, 1858-1923, (Br.) Conservative party politician, led opposition to Irish home rule.

Vladimir Ilyich Lenin (Ulyanov), 1870-1924, (USSR) revolutionary, founder of Bolshevism, Soviet leader 1917-1924.

Ferdinand de Lesseps, 1805-1894, (F.) diplomat, engineer, conceived idea of Suez Canal.

Rene Levesque, 1922-1987 (Can.) Premier of Quebec, 1976-85; led unsuccessful fight to separate from Canada.

Liu Shao-ch'i, c.1898-1974, (Chin.) communist leader, fell from grace during "cultural revolution."

Maxim Litvinov, 1876-1951, (USSR) revolutionary, commissar of foreign affairs, favored cooperation with Western powers.

David Lloyd George, 1863-1945, (Br.) Liberal party prime minister, laid foundations for modern welfare state.

Henry Cabot Lodge, 1850-1924, (U.S.) Republican senator, led opposition to participation in League of Nations.

Huey P. Long, 1893-1935, (U.S.) Louisiana political demagogue, governor, assassinated.

Rosa Luxemburg, 1871-1919, (G.) revolutionary, leader of the German Social Democratic party and Spartacus party.

J. Ramsay MacDonald, 1866-1937, (Br.) first Labour party prime minister of Great Britain.

Harold Macmillan, 1895-1987 (Br.) prime minister of Great Britain, 1957-63.

Joseph R. McCarthy, 1908-1957, (U.S.) senator notorious for his witch hunt for communists in the government.

Makarios III, 1913-1977, (Cypr.) Greek Orthodox archbishop, first president of Cyprus.

Malcolm X (Malcolm Little), 1925-1965, (U.S.) black separatist leader, assassinated.

Mao Tse-tung, 1893-1976, (Chin.) chief Chinese Marxist theorist, soldier, led Chinese revolution establishing his nation as an important communist state.

Jean Paul Marat, 1743-1793, (F.) revolutionary, politician, identified with radical Jacobins, assassinated.

José Martí, 1853-1895, (Cub.) patriot, poet, leader of Cuban struggle for independence.

Jan Masaryk, 1886-1948, (Czech.) foreign minister, died by mysterious suicide following communist coup.

Thomas G. Masaryk, 1850-1937, (Czech.) statesman, philosopher, first president of Czechoslovak Republic.

Jules Mazarin, 1602-1661, (F.) cardinal, statesman, prime minister under Louis XIII and queen regent Anne of Austria.

Giuseppe Mazzini, 1805-1872, (It.) reformer dedicated to the Risorgimento, 19th-century movement for the political and social renewal of Italy.

Tom Mboya, 1930-1969, (Kenyan) political leader, instrumental in securing independence for his country.

Cosimo I de' Medici, 1519-1574, (It.) Duke of Florence, grand duke of Tuscany.

Lorenzo de' Medici, the Magnificent, 1449-1492, (It.) merchant prince, a towering figure in Italian Renaissance.

Catherine de Medicis, 1519-1589, (F.) queen consort of Henry II, regent of France, influential in Catholic-Huguenot wars.

Golda Meir, 1898-1979, (Isr.) prime minister, 1969-74.

Klemens W.N.L. Metternich, 1773-1859, (Aus.) statesman, arbiter of post-Napoleonic Europe.

Anastas Mikoyan, 1895-1978, (USSR) prominent Soviet leader from 1917; president 1964-65.

Guy Mollet, 1905-1975, (F.) social politician, resistance leader.

Henry Morgenthau Jr., 1891-1967, (U.S.) secretary of treasury, raised funds to finance New Deal and U.S. WW II activities.

Gouverneur Morris, 1752-1816, (U.S.) statesman, diplomat, financial expert who helped plan decimal coinage system.

Wayne Morse, 1900-1974, (U.S.) senator, long-time critic of Vietnam War.

Muhammad Ali, 1769?-1849, (Egypt) pasha, founder of dynasty that encouraged emergence of modern Egyptian state.

Benito Mussolini, 1883-1945, (It.) dictator and leader of the Italian fascist state.

Imre Nagy, c. 1895-1958, (Hung.) communist premier, assassinated after Soviets crushed 1956 uprising.

Gamal Abdel Nasser, 1918-1970, (Egypt.) leader of Arab unification, second Egyptian president.

Jawaharlal Nehru, 1889-1964, (Ind.) prime minister, guided India through its early years of independence.

Kwame Nkrumah, 1909-1972, (Ghan.) dictatorial prime minister, deposed in 1966.

Frederick North, 1732-1792, (Br.) prime minister, his inept policies led to loss of American colonies.

Daniel O'Connell, 1775-1847, (Ir.) political leader, known as The Liberator.

Omar, c.581-644, Mohammedan leader, 2d caliph, led Islam to become an imperial power.

Ignace Paderewski, 1860-1941, (Pol.) statesman, pianist, composer, briefly prime minister, an ardent patriot.

Viscount Palmerston, 1784-1865, (Br.) Whig-Liberal prime minister, foreign minister, embodied British nationalism.

George Papandreou, 1888-1968, (Gk.) Republican politician, served three times as prime minister.

Franz von Papen, 1879-1969, (G.) politician, played major role in overthrow of Weimar Republic and rise of Hitler.

Charles Stewart Parnell, 1846-1891, (Ir.) nationalist leader, "uncrowned king of Ireland."

Lester Pearson, 1897-1972, (Can.) diplomat, Liberal party leader, prime minister.

Robert Peel, 1788-1850, (Br.) reformist prime minister, founder of Conservative party.

Juan Perón, 1895-1974, (Arg.) president, dictator.

Joseph Pilsudski, 1867-1935, (Pol.) statesman, instrumental in re-establishing Polish state in the 20th century.

Charles Pinckney, 1757-1824, (U.S.) founding father, his Pinckney plan was largely incorporated into constitution.

William Pitt, the Elder, 1708-1778, (Br.) statesman, called the "Great Commoner," transformed Britain into imperial power.

William Pitt, the Younger, 1759-1806, (Br.) prime minister during French Revolutionary wars.

Georgi Plekhanov, 1857-1918, (R.) revolutionary, social philosopher, called "father of Russian Marxism."

Raymond Poincaré, 1860-1934, (F.) 9th president of the Republic, advocated harsh punishment of Germany after WW I.

Georges Pompidou, 1911-1974, (F.) Gaullist political leader, president from 1969 to 1974.

Grigori Potemkin, 1739-1791, (R.) field marshal, favorite of Catherine II.

Edmund Randolph, 1753-1813, (U.S.) attorney, prominent in drafting, ratification of constitution.

John Randolph, 1773-1833, (U.S.) southern planter, strong advocate of states' rights.

Jeannette Rankin, 1880-1973, (U.S.) pacifist, first woman member of U.S. Congress.

Walter Rathenau, 1867-1922, (G.) industrialist, social theorist, statesman.

Sam Rayburn, 1882-1961, (U.S.) Democratic leader, representative for 47 years, House speaker for 17.

Paul Reynaud, 1878-1966, (F.) statesman, premier in 1940 at the time of France's defeat by Germany.

Syngman Rhee, 1875-1965, (Kor.) first president of the Republic of Korea.

Cecil Rhodes, 1853-1902, (Br.) imperialist, industrial magnate, established Rhodes scholarships in his will.

Cardinal de Richelieu, 1585-1642, (F.) statesman, known as "red eminence," chief minister to Louis XIII.

Maximilien Robespierre, 1758-1794, (F.) leading figure of French Revolution, responsible for much of Reign of Terror.

Nelson Rockefeller, 1908-1979, (U.S.) Republican gov. of N.Y., 1959-73; U.S. vice president, 1974-77.

Eleanor Roosevelt, 1884-1962, (U.S.) humanitarian, United Nations diplomat.

Elihu Root, 1845-1937, (U.S.) lawyer, statesman, diplomat, leading Republican supporter of the League of Nations.

John Russell, 1792-1878, (Br.) Liberal prime minister during the Irish potato famine.

Anwar el-Sadat, 1918-1981, (Egypt) president, 1970-1981, promoted peace with Israel; assassinated.

António de O. Salazar, 1899-1970, (Port.) statesman, long-time dictator.

José de San Martin, 1778-1850, South American revolutionary, protector of Peru.

Eisaku Sato, 1901-1975, (Jap.) prime minister, presided over Japan's post-WW II emergence as major world power.

Philipp Scheidemann, 1865-1939, (G.) Social Democratic leader, first chancellor of the German republic.

Robert Schuman, 1886-1963, (F.) statesman, founded European Coal and Steel Community.

Carl Schurz, 1829-1906, (U.S.) German-American political leader, journalist, orator, dedicated reformer.

Kurt Schuschnigg, 1897-1977, (Aus.) chancellor, unsuccessful in stopping his country's annexation by Germany.

William H. Seward, 1801-1872, (U.S.) anti-slavery activist, as Lincoln's secretary of state purchased Alaska.

Carlo Sforza, 1872-1952, (It.) foreign minister, anti-fascist.

Sitting Bull, c. 1831-1890, (Native Amer.) Sioux leader in Battle of Little Bighorn over George A. Custer, 1876; fostered Ghost Dance religion.

Alfred E. Smith, 1873-1944, (U.S.) New York Democratic governor, first Roman Catholic to run for presidency.

Jan C. Smuts, 1870-1950, (S.Af.) statesman, philosopher, soldier, prime minister.

Paul Henri Spaak, 1899-1972, (Belg.) statesman, socialist leader.

Joseph Stalin, 1879-1953, (USSR) Soviet dictator, 1924-53.

Edwin M. Stanton, 1814-1869, (U.S.) Lincoln's secretary of war during the Civil War.

Edward R. Stettinius Jr., 1900-1949, (U.S.) industrialist, secretary of state who coordinated aid to WW II allies.

Adlai E. Stevenson, 1900-1965, (U.S.) Democratic leader, diplomat, Illinois governor, presidential candidate.

Henry L. Stimson, 1867-1950, (U.S.) statesman, served in 5 administrations, influenced foreign policy in 1930s and 1940s.

Gustav Stresemann, 1878-1929, (G.) chancellor, foreign minister, dedicated to regaining friendship for post-WW I Germany.

Sukarno, 1901-1970, (Indon.) dictatorial first president of the Indonesian republic.

Sun Yat-sen, 1866-1925, (Chin.) revolutionary, leader of Kuomintang, regarded as the father of modern China.

Robert A. Taft, 1889-1953, (U.S.) conservative Senate leader, called "Mr. Republican."

Charles de Talleyrand, 1754-1838, (F.) statesman, diplomat, the major force of the Congress of Vienna of 1814-15.

U Thant, 1909-1974 (Bur.) statesman, UN secretary-general.

Norman M. Thomas, 1884-1968, (U.S.) social reformer, 6 times unsuccessful Socialist party presidential candidate.

Josip Broz Tito, 1892-1980, (Yug.) president of Yugoslavia from 1953, World War II guerrilla chief, postwar rival of Stalin, leader of 3d world movement.

Palmiro Togliatti, 1893-1964, (It.) major leader of Italian Communist party.

Hideki Tojo, 1885-1948, (Jap.) statesman, soldier, prime minister during most of WW II.

François Toussaint L'Ouverture, c. 1744-1803, (Hait.) patriot, martyr, thwarted French colonial aims.

Leon Trotsky, 1879-1940, (USSR) revolutionary, founded Red Army, expelled from party in conflict with Stalin.

Rafael L. Trujillo Molina, 1891-1961, (Dom.) absolute dictator, assassinated.

Moise K. Tshombe, 1919-1969, (Cong.) politician, president of secessionist Katanga, premier of Republic of Congo (Zaire).

William M. Tweed, 1823-1878, (U.S.) politician, absolute leader of Tammany Hall, NYC's Democratic political machine.

Walter Ulbricht, 1893-1973, (G.) communist leader of German Democratic Republic.

Arthur H. Vandenberg, 1884-1951, (U.S.) senator, proponent of anti-communist bipartisan foreign policy after WW II.

Eleutherios Venizelos, 1864-1936, (Gk.) most prominent Greek statesman in early 20th century; expanded territory.

Hendrik F. Verwoerd, 1901-1966, (S.Af.) prime minister, rigorously applied apartheid policy despite protest.

Robert Walpole, 1676-1745, (Br.) statesman, generally considered Britain's first prime minister.

Daniel Webster, 1782-1852, (U.S.) orator, politician, advocate of business interests during Jacksonian agrarianism.

Chaim Weizmann, 1874-1952, Zionist leader, scientist, first Israeli president.

Wendell L. Willkie, 1892-1944, (U.S.) Republican who tried to unseat FDR when he ran for his 3d term.

Emiliano Zapata, c. 1879-1919, (Mex.) revolutionary, major influence on modern Mexico.

Notable Military and Naval Leaders of the Past

Creighton Abrams, 1914-1974, (U.S.) commanded forces in Vietnam, 1968-72.

Harold Alexander, 1891-1969, (Br.) led Allied invasion of Italy, WW2, 1943.

Ethan Allen, 1738-1789, (U.S.) headed Green Mountain Boys; captured Ft. Ticonderoga, 1775, Amer. Revolutionary War.

Edmund Allenby, 1861-1936, (Br.) in Boer War, WW1; led Egyptian expeditionary force, 1917-18.

Benedict Arnold, 1741-1801, (U.S.) victorious at Saratoga; tried to betray West Point to British, Amer. Revolutionary War.

Henry "Hap" Arnold, 1886-1950, (U.S.) commanded Army Air Force in WW2.

John Barry, 1745-1803, (U.S.) won numerous sea battles during Amer. Revolutionary War.

Pierre Beauregard, 1818-1893, (U.S.) Confederate general ordered bombardment of Ft. Sumter that began the Civil War.

Gebhard v. Blücher, 1742-1819, (G.) helped defeat Napoleon at Waterloo.

Napoleon Bonaparte, 1769-1821, (F.) defeated Russia and Austria at Austerlitz, 1805; invaded Russia, 1812; defeated at Waterloo, 1815.

Edward Braddock, 1695-1755, (Br.) commanded forces in French and Indian War.

Omar N. Bradley, 1893-1981, (U.S.) headed U.S. ground troops in Normandy invasion, WW2, 1944.

John Burgoyne, 1722-1792, (Br.) defeated at Saratoga, Amer. Revolutionary War.

Claire Chennault, 1890-1958, (U.S.) headed Flying Tigers in WW2.

Mark Clark, 1896-1984, (U.S.) led forces in WW2 and Korean War.

Karl v. Clausewitz, 1780-1831, (G.) wrote books on military theory.

Henry Clinton, 1738-1795, (Br.) commander of forces in American Revolutionary War, 1778-81.

Lucius D. Clay, 1897-1978, (U.S.) led Berlin airlift, 1948-49.

Cochise, c. 1815-1874, (Native Amer.) Chief of Chiricahua band of Apache Indians in Arizona.

Charles Cornwallis, 1738-1805, (Br.) victorious at Brandywine, 1777; surrendered at Yorktown, Amer. Revolutionary War.

Crazy Horse, 1849-1877, (U.S.) Sioux war chief victorious at Little Big Horn.

George A. Custer, 1839-1876, (U.S.) defeated and killed at Little Big Horn.

Moshe Dayan, 1915-1981, (Isr.) directed campaigns in the 1967, 1973 Arab-Israeli wars.

Stephen Decatur, 1779-1820, (U.S.) naval hero of Barbary wars, War of 1812.

Anton Denikin, 1872-1947, (R.) led White forces in Russian civil war.

George Dewey, 1837-1917, (U.S.) destroyed Spanish fleet at Manila, 1898, Spanish-American War.

Hugh C. Dowding, 1883-1970, (Br.) headed RAF, WW2, 1936-40.

Jubal Early, 1816-1894, (U.S.) Confederate general led raid on Washington, Civil War, 1864.

Dwight D. Eisenhower, 1890-1969, (U.S.) commanded Allied forces in Europe, WW2.

David Farragut, 1801-1870, (U.S.) Union admiral captured New Orleans, Mobile Bay, Civil War.

Ferdinand Foch, 1851-1929, (F.) headed victorious Allied armies, WW1, 1918.

Nathan Bedford Forrest, 1821-1877, (U.S.) Confederate general led cavalry raids against Union supply lines, Civil War.

Frederick the Great, 1712-1786, (G.) led Prussia in The Seven Years War.

Geronimo, 1829-1909 (Native Amer.) leader of Chiricahua band of Apache Indians.

Nathanael Greene, 1742-1786, (U.S.) defeated British in Southern campaign, 1780-81.

Charles G. Gordon, 1833-1885, (Br.) led forces in China, Crimean War; killed at Khartoum.

Horatio Gates, 1728-1806, (U.S.) commanded army at Saratoga, Amer. Revolutionary War.

Ulysses S. Grant, 1822-1885, (U.S.) headed Union army, Civil War, 1864-65; forced Lee's surrender, 1865.

Heinz Guderian, 1888-1953, (G.) tank theorist, led panzer forces in Poland, France, Russia, WW2.

Douglas Haig, 1861-1928, (Br.) led British armies in France, WW2, 1915-18.

William F. Halsey, 1882-1959, (U.S.) defeated Japanese fleet at Leyte Gulf, WW2, 1944.

Sir Arthur Travers Harris, 1895-1984, (Br.) led Britain's WW2 bomber command.

Richard Howe, 1726-1799, (Br.) commanded navy in Amer. Revolutionary War, 1776-78; June 1 victory against French, 1794.

William Howe, 1729-1814, (Br.) commanded forces in American Revolutionary War, 1776-78.

Isaac Hull, 1773-1843, (U.S.) sunk British frigate *Guerriere*, War of 1812.

Thomas (Stonewall) Jackson, 1824-1863, (U.S.) Confederate general led Shenandoah Valley campaign, Civil War.

Joseph Joffre, 1852-1931, (F.) headed Allied armies, won Battle of the Marne, WW1, 1914.

John Paul Jones, 1747-1792, (U.S.) commanded *Bonhomme Richard* in victory over Serapis, Amer. Revolutionary War, 1779.

Stephen Kearny, 1794-1848, (U.S.) headed Army of the West in Mexican War.

Ernest J. King, 1878-1956, (U.S.) chief naval strategist in WW2.

Horatio H. Kitchener, 1850-1916, (Br.) led forces in Boer War; victorious at Khartoum; organized army in WW1.

Lavrenti Kornilov, 1870-1918, (R.) Commander-in-Chief, 1917; led counter-revolutionary march on Petrograd.

Thaddeus Kosciusko, 1746-1817, (P.) aided American cause in Amer. Revolutionary War.

Mikhail Kutuzov, 1745-1813, (R.) fought French at Borodino, Napoleonic Wars, 1812; abandoned Moscow; forced French retreat.

Marquis de Lafayette, 1757-1834, (F.) aided American cause in Amer. Revolutionary War.

T(homas) E. Lawrence (of Arabia), 1888-1935, (Br.) organized revolt of Arabs against Turks in WW1.

Henry (Light-Horse Harry) Lee, 1756-1818, (U.S.) cavalry officer in Amer. Revolutionary War.

Robert E. Lee, 1807-1870, (U.S.) Confederate general defeated at Gettysburg, Civil War; surrendered to Grant, 1865.

Lyman Lemnitzer, 1899-1988, (U.S.) WWII hero, later general, chairman of Joint Chiefs of Staff.

James Longstreet, 1821-1904, (U.S.) aided Lee at Gettysburg, Civil War.

Douglas MacArthur, 1880-1964, (U.S.) commanded forces in SW Pacific in WW2; headed occupation forces in Japan, 1945-51; UN commander in Korean War.

Francis Marion, 1733-1795, (U.S.) led guerrilla actions in S.C. during Amer. Revolutionary War.

Duke of Marlborough, 1650-1722, (Br.) led forces against Louis XIV in War of the Spanish Succession.

George C. Marshall, 1880-1959, (U.S.) chief of staff in WW2; authored Marshall Plan.

George B. McClellan, 1826-1885, (U.S.) Union general, commanded Army of the Potomac, Civil War, 1861-62.

George Meade, 1815-1872; (U.S.) commanded Union forces at Gettysburg, Civil War.

Billy Mitchell, 1879-1936, (U.S.) WW1 air-power advocate; court-martialed for insubordination, later vindicated.

Helmuth v. Moltke, 1800-1891; (G.) victorious in Austro-Prussian, Franco-Prussian wars.

Louis de Montcalm, 1712-1759, (F.) headed troops in Canada, French and Indian War; defeated at Quebec, 1759.

Bernard Law Montgomery, 1887-1976, (Br.) stopped German offensive at Alamein, WW2, 1942; helped plan Normandy invasion.

Daniel Morgan, 1736-1802, (U.S.) victorious at Cowpens, 1781, Amer. Revolutionary War.

Louis Mountbatten, 1900-1979, (Br.) Supreme Allied Commander of SE Asia, WW2, 1943-46.

Joachim Murat, 1767-1815, (F.) leader of cavalry at Marengo, 1800; Austerlitz, 1805; and Jena, 1806, Napoleonic Wars.

Horatio Nelson, 1758-1805, (Br.) naval commander destroyed French fleet at Trafalgar.

Michel Ney, 1769-1815, (F.) commanded forces in Switzerland, Austria, Russia, Napoleonic Wars; defeated at Waterloo.

Chester Nimitz, 1885-1966, (U.S.) commander of naval forces in Pacific in WW2.

George S. Patton, 1885-1945, (U.S.) led assault on Sicily, 1943, 3d Army invasion of German-occupied Europe, WW2.

Oliver Perry, 1785-1819, (U.S.) won Battle of Lake Erie in War of 1812.

John Pershing, 1860-1948, (U.S.) commanded Mexican border campaign, 1916; American expeditionary forces in WW1.

Henri Philippe Pétain, 1856-1951, (F.) defended Verdun, 1916; headed Vichy government in WW2.

George E. Pickett, 1825-1875, (U.S.) Confederate general famed for "charge" at Gettysburg, Civil War.

Hyman Rickover, 1900-1986 (U.S.) father of the nuclear navy.

Erwin Rommel, 1891-1944, (G.) headed Afrika Korps, WW2.

Karl v. Rundstedt, 1875-1953, (G.) supreme commander in West, WW2, 1943-45.

Aleksandr Samsonov, 1859-1914, (R.) led invasion of E. Prussia, WW1, defeated at Tannenberg, 1914.

Winfield Scott, 1786-1866, (U.S.) hero of War of 1812; headed forces in Mexican war, took Mexico City.

Philip Sheridan, 1831-1888, (U.S.) Union cavalry officer, headed Army of the Shenandoah, Civil War, 1864-65.

William T. Sherman, 1820-1891, (U.S.) Union general, sacked Atlanta during "march to the sea," Civil War, 1864.

Carl Spaatz, 1891-1974, (U.S.) directed strategic bombing against Germany, later Japan, in WW2.

Raymond Spruance, 1886-1969, (U.S.) victorious at Midway Island, WW2, 1942.

Joseph W. Stilwell, 1883-1946, (U.S.) headed forces in the China, Burma, India theater in WW2.

J.E.B. Stuart, 1833-1864, (U.S.) Confederate cavalry commander, Civil War.

George H. Thomas, 1816-1870, (U.S.) saved Union army at Chattanooga, 1863; victorious at Nashville, 1864, Civil War.

Semyon Timoshenko, 1895-1970, (USSR) defended Moscow, Stalingrad, WW2; led winter offensive, 1942-43.

Alfred v. Tirpitz, 1849-1930, (G.) responsible for submarine blockade in WW1.

Jonathan M. Wainwright, 1883-1953, (U.S.) forced to surrender on Corregidor, WW2,4,942.

George Washington, 1732-1799, (U.S.) led Continental army, Amer. Revolutionary War, 1775-83.

Archibald Wavell, 1883-1950, (Br.) commanded forces in N. and E. Africa, and SE Asia in WW2.

Anthony Wayne, 1745-1796, (U.S.) captured Stony Point, 1779, Amer. Revolutionary War; defeated Indians at Fallen Timbers, 1794.

Duke of Wellington, 1769-1852, (Br.) defeated Napoleon at Waterloo.

James Wolfe, 1727-1759, (Br.) captured Quebec from French, French and Indian War, 1759.

Georgi Zhukov, 1895-1974, (USSR) defended Moscow, 1941, led assault on Berlin, WW2

Poets Laureate of England

There is no authentic record of the origin of the office of Poet Laureate of England. According to Warton, there was a Versificator Regis, or King's Poet, in the reign of Henry III (1216-1272), and he was paid 100 shillings a year. Geoffrey Chaucer (1340-1400) assumed the title of Poet Laureate, and in 1389 got a royal grant of a yearly allowance of wine. In the reign of Edward IV (1461-1483), John Kay held the post. Under Henry VII (1485-1509), Andrew Bernard was the Poet Laureate, and was succeeded under Henry VIII (1509-1547) by John Skelton. Next came Edmund Spenser, who died in 1599; then Samuel Daniel, appointed 1599, and then Ben Jonson, 1619. Sir William D'Avenant was appointed in 1637. He was a godson of William Shakespeare.

Others were John Dryden, 1670; Thomas Shadwell, 1688; Nahum Tate, 1692; Nicholas Rowe, 1715; the Rev. Laurence Eusden, 1718; Colley Cibber, 1730; William Whitehead, 1757, on the refusal of Gray; Rev. Thomas Warton, 1785, on the refusal of Mason; Henry J. Pye, 1790; Robert Southey, 1813, on the refusal of Sir Walter Scott; William Wordsworth, 1843; Alfred, Lord Tennyson, 1850; Alfred Austin, 1896; Robert Bridges, 1913; John Masefield, 1930; Cecil Day Lewis, 1967; Sir John Betjeman, 1972; Ted Hughes, 1984.

U.S. Poet Laureate

Robert Penn Warren, the poet, novelist, and essayist, was named the country's first official Poet Laureate on Feb. 26, 1986. The only writer to have won the Pulitzer Prize for fiction and poetry (twice), Warren was chosen by Daniel J. Boorstin, the Librarian of Congress. The appointment began

in September, 1986. On April 17, 1987, Richard Wilbur was named the second Poet Laureate; in May 1988, Howard Nemerov, the third, in May 1990 Mark Strand, the fourth; in May 1991, Joseph Brodsky, who came to the U.S. from the USSR in 1972, was named the fifth.

Noted Writers of the Past

George Ade, 1866-1944, (U.S.) humorist. *Fables in Slang.*

Conrad Aiken, 1889-1973, (U.S.) poet, critic. *Ushant.*

Louisa May Alcott, 1832-1888, (U.S.) novelist. *Little Women.*

Sholom Aleichem, 1859-1916, (R.) Yiddish writer. *Tevye's Daughter, Adventures of Mottel, The Old Country.*

Vicente Aleixandre, 1898-1984, (Sp.) poet. *La destrucción o el amor, Dialogolos del conocimiento.*

Horatio Alger, 1832-1899, (U.S.) "rags-to-riches" books.

Hans Christian Andersen, 1805-1875, (Den.) author of fairy tales. *The Princess and the Pea, The Ugly Duckling.*

Maxwell Anderson, 1888-1959, (U.S.) playwright. *What Price Glory?, High Tor, Winterset, Key Largo.*

Sherwood Anderson, 1876-1941, (U.S.) short-story writer. "Death in the Woods"; *Winesburg, Ohio* (collection).

Matthew Arnold, 1822-1888, (Br.) poet, critic. "Thrysis," "Dover Beach," "The Gypsy Scholar"; "Culture and Anarchy."

Jane Austen, 1775-1817, (Br.) novelist. *Pride and Prejudice, Sense and Sensibility, Emma, Mansfield Park, Persuasion.*

Isaac Babel, 1894-1941, (R.) short-story writer, playwright. *Odessa Tales, Red Cavalry.*

James M. Barrie, 1860-1937, (Br.) playwright, novelist. *Peter Pan, Dear Brutus, What Every Woman Knows.*

Honoré de Balzac, 1799-1850, (Fr.) novelist. *Le Père Goriot, Cousine Bette, Eugénie Grandet, The Human Comedy.*

Charles Baudelaire, 1821-1867, (Fr.) symbolist poet. *Les Fleurs du Mal.*

L. Frank Baum, 1856-1919, (U.S.) writer. *Wizard of Oz* series of children's books.

Simone de Beauvoir, 1908-1986, (Fr.) novelist, essayist. *The Second Sex, Memoirs of a Dutiful Daughter.*

Samuel Beckett, 1906-1989, (Ir.) novelist, playwright, in French and English. *Waiting for Godot, Endgame* (plays); *Murphy, Watt, Molloy* (novels).

Brendan Behan, 1923-1964, (Ir.) playwright. *The Quare Fellow, The Hostage, Borstal Boy.*

Robert Benchley, 1889-1945, (U.S.) humorist. *From Bed to Worse, My Ten Years in a Quandary.*

Stephen Vincent Benét, 1898-1943, (U.S.) poet, novelist. *John Brown's Body.*

John Berryman, 1914-1972, (U.S.) poet. *Homage to Mistress Bradstreet.*

Ambrose Bierce, 1842-1914, (U.S.) short-story writer, journalist. *In the Midst of Life, The Devil's Dictionary.*

William Blake, 1757-1827, (Br.) poet, artist. *Songs of Innocence, Songs of Experience, The Marriage of Heaven and Hell.*

Giovanni Boccaccio, 1313-1375, (It.) poet, storyteller. *Decameron, Filostrato.*

Jorge Luis Borges, 1900-1986 (Arg.) short-story writer, poet, essayist, *Labyrinths.*

James Boswell, 1740-1795, (Sc.) biographer. *The Life of Samuel Johnson, A Journal of a Tour of the Hebrides.*

Anne Bradstreet, c. 1612-1672, (U.S.) poet. *The Tenth Muse Lately Sprung Up in America.*

Bertolt Brecht, 1898-1956, (G.) dramatist, poet. *The Threepenny Opera, Mother Courage and Her Children.*

Charlotte Brontë, 1816-1855, (Br.) novelist. *Jane Eyre.*

Emily Brontë, 1818-1848, (Br.) novelist. *Wuthering Heights.*

Elizabeth Barrett Browning, 1806-1861, (Br.) poet. *Sonnets from the Portuguese, Aurora Leigh.*

Robert Browning, 1812-1889, (Br.) poet. "My Last Duchess," "Fra Lippo Lippi," *The Ring and The Book.*

Pearl Buck, 1892-1973, (U.S.) novelist. *The Good Earth.*

Mikhail Bulgakov, 1891-1940, (R.) novelist, playwright. *The Heart of a Dog, The Master and Margarita.*

John Bunyan, 1628-1688, (Br.) writer. *Pilgrim's Progress.*

Robert Burns, 1759-1796, (Sc.) poet. "Flow Gently, Sweet Afton," "My Heart's in the Highlands," "Auld Lang Syne."

Edgar Rice Burroughs, 1875-1950, (U.S.) novelist. *Tarzan of the Apes.*

George Gordon Lord Byron, 1788-1824, (Br.) poet. *Don Juan, Childe Harold, Manfred, Cain.*

Italo Calvino, 1923-1985 (It.) novelist, short story writer. *If on a Winter's Night a Traveler* . . .

Albert Camus, 1913-1960, (F.) novelist. *The Plague, The Stranger, Caligula, The Fall.*

Lewis Carroll, 1832-1898, (Br.) writer, mathematician. *Alice's Adventures in Wonderland, Through the Looking Glass.*

Karel Capek, 1890-1938, (Czech.) playwright, novelist, essayist. *R.U.R. (Rossum's Universal Robots).*

Giacomo Casanova, 1725-1798, (It.) adventurer, memoirist.

Willa Cather, 1876-1947, (U.S.) novelist, essayist. *O Pioneers!, My Ántonia, Death Comes for the Archbishop.*

Miguel de Cervantes Saavedra, 1547-1616, (Sp.) novelist, dramatist, poet. *Don Quixote de la Mancha.*

Raymond Chandler, 1888-1959, (U.S.) writer of detective fiction. Philip Marlowe series.

Geoffrey Chaucer, c. 1340-1400, (Br.) poet. *The Canterbury Tales, Troilus and Criseyde.*

John Cheever, 1912-1982, (U.S.) short story writer, novelist. *The Wapshot Scandal,* "The Country Husband."

Anton Chekhov, 1860-1904, (R.) short-story writer, dramatist. *Uncle Vanya, The Cherry Orchard, The Three Sisters.*

G.K. Chesterton, 1874-1936, (Br.) critic, novelist. Father Brown series of mysteries.

Kate Chopin, 1851-1904, (U.S.) novelist, short-story writer. *The Awakening.*

Agatha Christie, 1891-1976, (Br.) mystery writer. *And Then There Were None, Murder on the Orient Express.*

Jean Cocteau, 1889-1963, (F.) writer, visual artist, filmmaker. *The Beauty and the Beast, Enfants Terribles.*

Samuel Taylor Coleridge, 1772-1834, (Br.) poet, critic. "Kubla Khan," "The Rime of the Ancient Mariner," "Christabel."

(Sidonie) Colette, 1873-1954, (F.) novelist. *Claudine, Gigi.*

Joseph Conrad, 1857-1924, (Br.) novelist. *Lord Jim, Heart of Darkness, The Nigger of the Narcissus, Nostromo.*

James Fenimore Cooper, 1789-1851, (U.S.) novelist. *Leather-Stocking Tales.*

Pierre Corneille, 1606-1684, (F.) dramatist. *Medeé, Le Cid, Horace, Cinna, Polyeucte.*

Hart Crane, 1899-1932, (U.S.) poet. "The Bridge."

Stephen Crane, 1871-1900, (U.S.) novelist, short-story writer. *The Red Badge of Courage,* "The Open Boat."

e.e. cummings, 1894-1962, (U.S.) poet. *Tulips and Chimneys.*

Roald Dahl, (Br.) 1916-1990, (U.S.) writer. *Charlie and the Chocolate Factory.*

Gabriele D'Annunzio, 1863-1938, (It.) poet, novelist, dramatist. *The Child of Pleasure, The Intruder, The Victim.*

Dante Alighieri, 1265-1321, (It.) poet. *The Divine Comedy.*

Daniel Defoe, 1660-1731, (Br.) writer. *Robinson Crusoe, Moll Flanders, Journal of the Plague Year.*

Charles Dickens, 1812-1870, (Br.) novelist. *David Copperfield, Oliver Twist, Great Expectations, The Pickwick Papers.*

Emily Dickinson, 1830-1886, (U.S.) novelist.

Isak Dinesen (Karen Blixen), 1885-1962, (Dan.) author. *Out of Africa, Seven Gothic Tales, Winter's Tales.*

John Donne, 1573-1631, (Br.) poet. *Songs and Sonnets.*

John Dos Passos, 1896-1970, (U.S.) novelist. *U.S.A.*

Fyodor Dostoyevsky, 1821-1881, (R.) novelist. *Crime and Punishment, The Brothers Karamazov, The Possessed.*

Arthur Conan Doyle, 1859-1930, (Br.) novelist, created Sherlock Holmes mystery series.

Theodore Dreiser, 1871-1945, (U.S.) novelist. *An American Tragedy, Sister Carrie.*

John Dryden, 1631-1700, (Br.) poet, dramatist, critic. *All for Love, Mac Flecknoe, Absalom and Achitopel.*

Alexandre Dumas, 1802-1870, (F.) novelist, dramatist. *The Three Musketeers, The Count of Monte Cristo.*

Alexandre Dumas (fils), 1824-1895, (F.) dramatist, novelist. *La Dame aux camélias, Le Demi-Monde.*

Ilya G. Ehrenburg, 1891-1967, (R.) writer. *The Thaw.*

George Eliot (Mary Ann Evans or Marian Evans), 1819-1880, (Br.) novelist. *Adam Bede, Silas Marner, Middlemarch, The Mill on the Floss.*

T.S. Eliot, 1888-1965, (Br.) poet, critic. *The Waste Land,* "The Love Song of J. Alfred Prufrock," *Four Quartets.*

Ralph Waldo Emerson, 1803-1882, (U.S.) poet, essayist. "Brahma," "Nature," "The Over-Soul," "Self-Reliance."

James T. Farrell, 1904-1979, (U.S.) novelist. *Studs Lonigan.*

William Faulkner, 1897-1962, (U.S.) novelist. *Sanctuary, Light in August, The Sound and the Fury, Absalom, Absalom!*

Henry Fielding, 1707-1754, (Br.) novelist. *Tom Jones.*

F. Scott Fitzgerald, 1896-1940, (U.S.) short-story writer, novelist. *The Great Gatsby, Tender is the Night.*

Gustave Flaubert, 1821-1880, (F.) novelist. *Madame Bovary.*

C.S. Forester, 1899-1966, (Br.) novelist. Horatio Hornblower series.

E.M. Forster, 1879-1970, (Br.) novelist. *A Passage to India.*

Anatole France, 1844-1924. (F.) writer. *Penguin Island, My Friend's Book, Le Crime de Sylvestre Bonnard.*

Robert Frost, 1874-1963, (U.S.) poet. "Birches," "Fire and Ice," "Stopping by Woods on a Snowy Evening."

John Galsworthy, 1867-1933, (Br.) novelist, dramatist. *The Forsyte Saga, A Modern Comedy.*

Erle Stanley Gardner, 1889-1970, (U.S.) novelist. Perry Mason series of mysteries.

Jean Genet, 1911-1986, (Fr.) playwright, novelist. *The Blacks, The Maids, The Balcony.*

André Gide, 1869-1951, (F.) writer, *The Immoralist, The Pastoral Symphony, Strait is the Gate.*

Jean Giraudoux, 1882-1944, (F.) novelist, dramatist. *Electra, The Madwoman of Chaillot, Ondine, Tiger at the Gate.*

Johann W. von Goethe, 1749-1832, (G.) poet, dramatist, novelist. *Faust, The Sorrows of Young Werther.*

Nikolai Gogol, 1809-1852, (R.) short-story writer, dramatist, novelist. *Dead Souls, The Inspector General.*

Oliver Goldsmith, 1730?-1774, (Br.-Ir.) writer. *The Vicar of Wakefield, She Stoops to Conquer.*

Maxim Gorky, 1868-1936, (R.) writer. *The Lower Depths.*

Robert Graves, 1895-1985, (Br.) poet, classical scholar, novelist. *I, Claudius; The White Goddess.*

Thomas Gray, 1716-1771, (Br.) poet. "Elegy Written in a Country Churchyard," "The Progress of Poesy."

Graham Greene, 1904-1991, (Br.) novelist. *The Power and the Glory, The Heart of the Matter, The Ministry of Fear.*

Zane Grey, 1875-1939, (U.S.) writer of western stories.

Jakob Grimm, 1785-1863, (G.) philologist, folklorist. *German Methodology, Grimm's Fairy Tales.*

Wilhelm Grimm, 1786-1859, (G.) philologist, folklorist. *Grimm's Fairy Tales.*

Dashiell Hammett, 1894-1961, (U.S.) writer of detective fiction, created Sam Spade.

Knute Hamsun, 1859-1952 (Nor.) novelist. *Hunger.*

Thomas Hardy, 1840-1928, (Br.) novelist, poet. *The Return of the Native, Tess of the D'Urbervilles, Jude the Obscure.*

Joel Chandler Harris, 1848-1908, (U.S.) short-story writer. Uncle Remus series.

Moss Hart, 1904-1961, (U.S.) playwright. *Once in a Lifetime, You Can't Take It With You, The Man Who Came to Dinner.*

Bret Harte, 1836-1902, (U.S.) short-story writer, poet. *The Luck of Roaring Camp.*

Jaroslav Hasek, 1883-1923, (Czech.) writer. *The Good Soldier Schwelk.*

Nathaniel Hawthorne, 1804-1864, (U.S.) novelist, short story writer. *The Scarlet Letter,* "The Artist of the Beautiful."

Heinrich Heine, 1797-1856, (G.) poet. *Book of Songs.*

Lillian Hellman, 1905-1984, (U.S.) playwright, author of memoirs, "The Little Foxes," *An Unfinished Woman, Pentimento.*

Ernest Hemingway, 1899-1961, (U.S.) novelist, short-story writer. *A Farewell to Arms, For Whom the Bell Tolls.*

O. Henry (W.S. Porter), 1862-1910, (U.S.) short-story writer. "The Gift of the Magi."

Hermann Hesse, 1877-1962, (G.) novelist, poet. *Death and the Lover, Steppenwolf, Siddhartha.*

Oliver Wendell Holmes, 1809-1894, (U.S.) poet, novelist. *The Autocrat of the Breakfast-Table.*

Alfred E. Housman, 1859-1936, (Br.) poet. *A Shropshire Lad.*

William Dean Howells, 1837-1920, (U.S.) novelist, critic. *The Rise of Silas Lapham.*

Langston Hughes, 1902-1967, (U.S.) poet, playwright. *The Weary Blues, One-Way Ticket, Shakespeare in Harlem.*

Victor Hugo, 1802-1885, (F.) poet, dramatist, novelist. *Notre Dame de Paris, Les Misérables.*

Aldous Huxley 1894-1963, (Br.) writer. *Brave New World.*

Henrik Ibsen, 1828-1906, (Nor.) dramatist, poet. *A Doll's House, Ghosts, The Wild Duck, Hedda Gabler.*

Washington Irving, 1783-1859, (U.S.) writer. "Rip Van Winkle," "The Legend of Sleepy Hollow."

Shirley Jackson, 1919-1965, (U.S.) writer. "The Lottery."

Henry James, 1843-1916, (U.S.) novelist, short-story writer, critic. *The Portrait of a Lady, The American, Daisy Miller.*

Robinson Jeffers, 1887-1962, (U.S.) poet, dramatist. *Tamar and Other Poems, Medea.*

Samuel Johnson, 1709-1784, (Br.) author, scholar, critic. *Dictionary of the English Language.*

Ben Jonson, 1572-1637, (Br.) dramatist, poet. *Volpone.*

James Joyce, 1882-1941, (Ir.) writer. *Ulysses, Dubliners, A Portrait of the Artist as a Young Man, Finnegans Wake.*

Franz Kafka, 1883-1924, (G.) novelist, short-story writer. *The Trial, Amerika, The Castle, The Metamorphosis.*

George S. Kaufman, 1889-1961, (U.S.) playwright. *The Man Who Came to Dinner, You Can't Take It With You, Stage Door.*

Nikos Kazantzakis, 1883?-1957, (Gk.) novelist. *Zorba the Greek, A Greek Passion.*

John Keats, 1795-1821, (Br.) poet. "Ode on a Grecian Urn," "Ode to a Nightingale," "La Belle Dame Sans Merci."

Joyce Kilmer, 1886-1918, (U.S.) poet, "Trees."

Rudyard Kipling, 1865-1936, (Br.) author, poet. "The White Man's Burden," "Gunga Din," *The Jungle Book.*

Jean de la Fontaine, 1621-1695, (F.) poet. *Fables choisies.*

Pär Lagerkvist, 1891-1974, (Swed.) poet, dramatist, novelist. *Barabbas, The Sybil.*

Selma Lagerlöf, 1858-1940, (Swed.) novelist. *Jerusalem, The Ring of the Lowenskolds.*

Alphonse de Lamartine, 1790-1869, (F.) poet, novelist, statesman. *Méditations poétiques.*

Charles Lamb, 1775-1834, (Br.) essayist. *Specimens of English Dramatic Poets, Essays of Elia.*

Giuseppe di Lampedusa, 1896-1957, (It.) novelist. *The Leopard.*

Ring Lardner, 1885-1933, (U.S.) short story writer, humorist. *You Know Me, Al.*

D. H. Lawrence, 1885-1930, (Br.) novelist. *Sons and Lovers, Women in Love, Lady Chatterley's Lover.*

Mikhail Lermontov, 1814-1841, (R.) novelist, poet. "Demon," *Hero of Our Time.*

Alain-René Lesage, 1668-1747, (F.) novelist. *Gil Blas de Santillane.*

Gotthold Lessing, 1729-1781, (G.) dramatist, philosopher, critic. *Miss Sara Sampson, Minna von Barnhelm.*

Sinclair Lewis, 1885-1951, (U.S.) novelist. *Babbitt, Arrowsmith, Dodsworth, Main Street.*

Vachel Lindsay, 1879-1931, (U.S.) poet. *General William Booth Enters into Heaven, The Congo.*

Hugh Lofting, 1886-1947, (Br.) writer. Dr. Doolittle series of children's books.

Jack London, 1876-1916, (U.S.) novelist, journalist. *Call of the Wild, The Sea-Wolf.*

Henry Wadsworth Longfellow, 1807-1882, (U.S.) poet. *Evangeline, The Song of Hiawatha.*

Amy Lowell, 1874-1925, (U.S.) poet, critic. "Lilacs."

James Russell Lowell, 1819-1891, (U.S.) poet, editor. *Poems, The Bigelow Papers.*

Robert Lowell, 1917-1977, (U.S.) poet. "Lord Weary's Castle," "For the Union Dead."

Niccolò Machiavelli, 1469-1527, (It.) writer, statesman. *The Prince, Discourses on Livy.*

Bernard Malamud, 1914-1986, (U.S.) short story writer, novelist. "The Magic Barrel," *The Assistant, The Fixer.*

Stéphane Mallarmé, 1842-1898, (F.) poet. *The Afternoon of a Faun.*

Thomas Malory, ?-1471, (Br.) writer. *Morte d'Arthur.*

Andre Malraux, 1901-1976, (F.) novelist. *Man's Fate.*

Osip Mandelstam, 1891-1938, (R.) poet. *Stone, Tristia.*

Thomas Mann, 1875-1955, (G.) novelist, essayist. *Buddenbrooks, Death in Venice, The Magic Mountain.*

Katherine Mansfield, 1888-1923, (Br.) short story writer. "Bliss," "The Garden Party."

Christopher Marlowe, 1564-1593, (Br.) dramatist, poet. *Tamburlaine the Great, Dr. Faustus, The Jew of Malta.*

John Masefield, 1878-1967, (Br.) poet. "Sea Fever," "Cargoes," *Salt Water Ballads.*

Edgar Lee Masters, 1869-1950, (U.S.) poet, biographer. *Spoon River Anthology.*

W. Somerset Maugham, 1874-1965, (Br.) author. *Of Human Bondage, The Razor's Edge, The Moon and Sixpence.*

Guy de Maupassant, 1850-1893, (F.) novelist, short-story writer. "A Life," "Bel-Ami," "The Necklace."

François Mauriac, 1885-1970, (F.) novelist, dramatist. *Viper's Tangle, The Kiss to the Leper.*

Vladimir Mayakovsky, 1893-1930, (R.) poet, dramatist. *The Cloud in Trousers.*

Mary McCarthy, 1912-1989, (U.S.) critic, novelist. *Memories of a Catholic Girlhood.*

Carson McCullers, 1917-1967, (U.S.) novelist. *The Heart is a Lonely Hunter, Member of the Wedding.*

Herman Melville, 1819-1891, (U.S.) novelist, poet. *Moby Dick, Typee, Billy Budd, Omoo.*

H.L. Mencken, 1880-1956, (U.S.) author, critic, editor. *Prejudices, The American Language.*

George Meredith, 1828-1909, (Br.) novelist, poet. *The Ordeal of Richard Feverel, The Egoist.*

Prosper Mérimée, 1803-1870, (F.) author. *Carmen.*

Edna St. Vincent Millay, 1892-1950, (U.S.) poet. *The Harp Weaver and Other Poems, A Few Figs from Thistles.*

A.A. Milne, 1882-1956, (Br.) author. *Winnie-the-Pooh.*

John Milton, 1608-1674, (Br.) poet. *Paradise Lost.*

Mishima Yukio (Hiraoka Kimitake), 1925-1970, (Jap.) writer. *Confessions of a Mask.*

Gabriela Mistral, 1889-1957, (Chil.) poet. *Sonnets of Death, Desolación, Tala, Lagar.*

Margaret Mitchell, 1900-1949, (U.S.) novelist. *Gone With the Wind.*

Jean Baptiste Molière, 1622-1673, (F.) dramatist. *Le Tartuffe, Le Misanthrope, Le Bourgeois Gentilhomme.*

Ferenc Molnár, 1878-1952, (Hung.) dramatist, novelist. *Liliom, The Guardsman, The Swan.*

Michel de Montaigne, 1533-1592, (F.) essayist. *Essais.*

Eugenio Montale, 1896-1981, (It.) poet.

Clement C. Moore, 1779-1863, (U.S.) poet, educator. "A Visit from Saint Nicholas."

Marianne Moore, 1887-1972, (U.S.) poet. *O to Be a Dragon.*

Thomas More, 1478-1535, (Br.) writer. *Utopia.*

H.H. Munro (Saki), 1870-1916, (Br.) writer. *Reginald, The Chronicles of Clovis, Beasts and Super-Beasts.*

Murasaki (Shikibu), Lady, c. 978-1031?, (Jap.) novelist. *The Tale of Genji.*

Alfred de Musset, 1810-1857, (F.) poet, dramatist. *Confession d'un enfant du siècle.*

Vladimir Nabokov, 1899-1977, (Rus.-U.S.) novelist. *Lolita.*

Ogden Nash, 1902-1971, (U.S.) poet. *Hard Lines, I'm a Stranger Here Myself, The Private Dining Room.*

Pablo Neruda, 1904-1973, (Chil.) poet. *Twenty Love Poems and One Song of Despair, Toward the Splendid City.*

Sean O'Casey, 1884-1964, (Ir.) dramatist. *Juno and the Paycock, The Plough and the Stars.*

Flannery O'Connor, 1925-1964, (U.S.) novelist, short story writer. *Wise Blood,* "A Good Man Is Hard to Find."

Clifford Odets, 1906-1963, (U.S.) playwright. *Waiting for Lefty, Awake and Sing, Golden Boy, The Country Girl.*

John O'Hara, 1905-1970, (U.S.) novelist, short-story writer. *From the Terrace, Appointment in Samarra, Pal Joey.*

Omar Khayyam, c. 1028-1122, (Per.) poet. *Rubaiyat.*

Eugene O'Neill, 1888-1953, (U.S.) playwright. *Emperor Jones, Anna Christie, Long Day's Journey into Night.*

George Orwell, 1903-1950, (Br.) novelist, essayist. *Animal Farm, Nineteen Eighty-Four.*

Thomas (Tom) Paine, 1737-1809, (U.S.) writer, political theorist. *Common Sense.*

Dorothy Parker, 1893-1967, (U.S.) poet, short-story writer. *Enough Rope, Laments for the Living.*

Boris Pasternak, 1890-1960, (R.) poet, novelist. *Doctor Zhivago, My Sister, Life.*

Samuel Pepys, 1633-1703, (Br.) public official, diarist.

S. J. Perelman, 1904-1979, (U.S.) humorist. *The Road to Miltown, Under the Spreading Atrophy.*

Francesco Petrarca, 1304-1374, (It.) poet. *Africa, Trionfi, Canzoniere, On Solitude.*

Luigi Pirandello, 1867-1936, (It.) novelist, dramatist. *Six Characters in Search of an Author.*

Edgar Allan Poe, 1809-1849, (U.S.) poet, short-story writer, critic. "Annabel Lee," "The Raven," "The Purloined Letter."

Alexander Pope, 1688-1744, (Br.) poet. *The Rape of the Lock, An Essay on Man.*

Katherine Anne Porter, 1890-1980, (U.S.) novelist, short story writer. *Ship of Fools.*

Ezra Pound, 1885-1972, (U.S.) poet. *Cantos.*

Marcel Proust, 1871-1922, (F.) novelist. *A la recherche du temps perdu (Remembrance of Things Past).*

Aleksandr Pushkin, 1799-1837, (R.) poet, prose writer. *Boris Godunov, Eugene Onegin, The Bronze Horseman.*

François Rabelais, 1495-1553, (F.) writer. *Gargantua, Pantagruel.*

Jean Racine, 1639-1699, (F.) dramatist. *Andromaque, Phèdre, Bérénice, Britannicus.*

Ayn Rand, 1905-1982 (Rus.-U.S.) novelist, philosopher. *The Fountainhead, Atlas Shrugged.*

Erich Maria Remarque, 1898-1970, (Ger.-U.S.) novelist. *All Quiet on the Western Front.*

Samuel Richardson, 1689-1761, (Br.) novelist. *Clarissa Harlowe, Pamela; or, Virtue Rewarded.*

Rainer Maria Rilke, 1875-1926, (G.) poet. *Life and Songs, Divine Elegies, Poems from the Book of Hours.*

Arthur Rimbaud, 1854-1891, (F.) poet. *A Season in Hell.*

Edwin Arlington Robinson, 1869-1935, (U.S.) poet. "Richard Cory," "Miniver Cheevy."

Theodore Roethke, 1908-1963, (U.S.) poet. *Open House, The Waking, The Far Field.*

Romain Rolland, 1866-1944, (F.) novelist, biographer. *Jean-Christophe.*

Pierre de Ronsard, 1524-1585, (F.) poet. *Sonnets pour Hélène, La Franciade.*

Edmond Rostand, 1868-1918, (F.) poet, dramatist. *Cyrano de Bergerac.*

Damon Runyon, 1880-1946, (U.S.) short-story writer, journalist. *Guys and Dolls, Blue Plate Special.*

John Ruskin, 1819-1900, (Br.) critic, social theorist. *Modern Painters, The Seven Lamps of Architecture.*

Antoine de Saint-Exupery, 1900-1944, (F.) writer. *Wind, Sand and Stars, Le Petit Prince.*

George Sand (Amandine Aurore Dupine), 1804-1876, (F.) novelist. *Consuelo, The Haunted Pool, The Master Bell-Ringer.*

Carl Sandburg, 1878-1967, (U.S.) poet. *The People, Yes; Chicago Poems, Smoke and Steel, Harvest Poems.*

George Santayana, 1863-1952, (U.S.) poet, essayist, philosopher. *The Sense of Beauty, The Realms of Being.*

William Saroyan, 1908-1981, (U.S.) playwright, novelist. *The Time of Your Life, The Human Comedy.*

Jean-Paul Sartre, 1905-1980, (Fr.) philosopher, novelist, playwright. *Nausea, No Exit, Being and Nothingness.*

Friedrich von Schiller, 1759-1805, (G.) dramatist, poet, historian. *Don Carlos, Maria Stuart, Wilhelm Tell.*

Sir Walter Scott, 1771-1832, (Sc.) novelist, poet. *Ivanhoe.*

Jaroslav Seifert, 1902-1986, (Cz.) poet.

William Shakespeare, 1564-1616, (Br.) dramatist, poet. *Romeo and Juliet, Hamlet, King Lear, Julius Caesar, The Merchant of Venice, Othello, Macbeth, The Tempest;* sonnets.

George Bernard Shaw, 1856-1950, (Ir.-Br.) playwright, critic. *St. Joan, Pygmalion, Major Barbara, Man and Superman.*

Mary Wollstonecraft Shelley, 1797-1851, (Br.) novelist. *Frankenstein.*

Percy Bysshe Shelley, 1792-1822, (Br.) poet. *Prometheus Unbound, Adonais,* "Ode to the West Wind," "To a Skylark."

Richard B. Sheridan, 1751-1816, (Br.) dramatist. *The Rivals, School for Scandal.*

Mikhail Sholokhov, 1906-1984 (U.S.S.R.) writer. *And Quiet Flows the Don.*

Upton Sinclair, 1878-1968, (U.S.) novelist. *The Jungle.*

Edmund Spenser, 1552-1599, (Br.) poet. *The Faerie Queen.*

Christina Stead, 1903-1983 (Austral.) novelist, short-story writer. *The Man Who Loved Children.*

Richard Steele, 1672-1729, (Br.) essayist, playwright, began the *Tatler* and *Spectator. The Conscious Lovers.*

Lincoln Steffens, 1866-1936, (U.S.) editor, writer. *The Shame of the Cities.*

Gertrude Stein, 1874-1946, (U.S.) writer. *Three Lives.*

John Steinbeck, 1902-1968, (U.S.) novelist. *Grapes of Wrath, Of Mice and Men, Winter of Our Discontent.*

Stendhal (Marie Henri Beyle), 1783-1842, (F.) novelist. *The Red and the Black, The Charterhouse of Parma.*

Laurence Sterne, 1713-1768, (Br.) novelist. *Tristram Shandy.*

Wallace Stevens, 1879-1955, (U.S.) poet. *Harmonium, The Man With the Blue Guitar, Notes toward a Supreme Fiction.*

Robert Louis Stevenson, 1850-1894, (Br.) novelist, poet, essayist. *Treasure Island, A Child's Garden of Verses.*

Rex Stout, 1886-1975, (U.S.) novelist, created Nero Wolfe.

Harriet Beecher Stowe, 1811-1896, (U.S.) novelist. *Uncle Tom's Cabin.*

Lytton Strachey, 1880-1932, (Br.) biographer, critic. *Eminent Victorians, Queen Victoria, Elizabeth and Essex.*

August Strindberg, 1849-1912, (Swed.) dramatist, novelist. *The Father, Miss Julie, The Creditors.*

Jonathan Swift, 1667-1745, (Br.) writer. *Gulliver's Travels.*

Algernon C. Swinburne, 1837-1909, (Br.) poet, critic. *Atalanta.*

John M. Synge, 1871-1909, (Ir.) poet, dramatist. *Riders to the Sea, The Playboy of the Western World.*

Rabindranath Tagore, 1861-1941, (Ind.), author, poet. *Sadhana, The Realization of Life, Gitanjali.*

Booth Tarkington, 1869-1946, (U.S.) novelist. *Seventeen, Alice Adams, Penrod.*

Sara Teasdale, 1884-1933, (U.S.) poet. *Helen of Troy and Other Poems, Rivers to the Sea, Flame and Shadow.*

Alfred Lord Tennyson, 1809-1892, (Br.) poet. *Idylls of the King, In Memoriam,* "The Charge of the Light Brigade."

William Makepeace Thackeray, 1811-1863, (Br.) novelist. *Vanity Fair, Henry Esmond, Pendennis.*

Dylan Thomas, 1914-1953, (Welsh) poet. *Under Milk Wood, A Child's Christmas in Wales.*

Henry David Thoreau, 1817-1862, (U.S.) transcendentalist thinker, writer. *Walden.*

James Thurber, 1894-1961, (U.S.) humorist, cartoonist. "The Secret Life of Walter Mitty," *My Life and Hard Times.*

J.R.R. Tolkien, 1892-1973, (Br.) writer. *Lord of the Rings.*

Leo Tolstoy, 1828-1910, (R.) novelist, short-story writer. *War and Peace, Anna Karenina,* "The Death of Ivan Ilyich."

Anthony Trollope, 1815-1882, (Br.) novelist. *The Warden, Barchester Towers, The Palliser novels.*

Ivan Turgenev, 1818-1883, (R.) novelist, short-story writer. *Fathers and Sons, First Love, A Month in the Country.*

Mark Twain (Samuel Clemens), 1835-1910, (U.S.) novelist, humorist. *The Adventures of Huckleberry Finn, Tom Sawyer.*

Sigrid Undset, 1881-1949, (Nor.) novelist, poet. *Kristin Lavransdatter.*

Paul Valéry, 1871-1945, (F.) poet, critic. *La Jeune Parque, The Graveyard by the Sea.*

Jules Verne, 1828-1905, (F.) novelist. *Twenty Thousand Leagues Under the Sea.*

François Villon, 1431-1463?, (F.) poet. *Le petit et le Grand Testament.*

Evelyn Waugh, 1903-1966, (Br.) novelist. *The Loved One.*

H.G. Wells, 1866-1946, (Br.) novelist. *The Time Machine, The Invisible Man, The War of the Worlds.*

Rebecca West, 1893-1983 (Br.) critic. *Black Lamb and Grey Falcon.*

Edith Wharton, 1862-1937, (U.S.) novelist. *The Age of Innocence, The House of Mirth, Ethan Frome.*

E.B. White, 1899-1985 (U.S.), essayist, novelist. *Here is New York, Charlotte's Web, Stuart Little.*

T.H. White, 1906-1964, (Br.) author. *The Once and Future King, A Book of Beasts.*

Walt Whitman, 1819-1892, (U.S.) poet. *Leaves of Grass.*

John Greenleaf Whittier, 1807-1892, (U.S.) poet, journalist. *Snow-bound.*

Oscar Wilde, 1854-1900, (Ir.) playwright, story-writer. *The Picture of Dorian Gray, The Importance of Being Earnest.*

Laura Ingalls Wilder, 1867-1957, (U.S.) novelist. *Little House on the Prairie* series of children's books.

Thornton Wilder, 1897-1975, (U.S.) playwright. *Our Town, The Skin of Our Teeth, The Matchmaker.*

Tennessee Williams, 1912-1983 (U.S.) playwright. *A Streetcar Named Desire, Cat on a Hot Tin Roof, The Glass Menagerie.*

William Carlos Williams, 1883-1963, (U.S.) poet. *Tempers, Al Que Quiere!, Paterson.*

Edmund Wilson, 1895-1972, (U.S.) critic, novelist. *Axel's Castle, To the Finland Station.*

P.G. Wodehouse, 1881-1975, (U.S.) humorist. The "Jeeves" novels, *Anything Goes.*

Thomas Wolfe, 1900-1938, (U.S.) novelist. *Look Homeward, Angel, You Can't Go Home Again, Of Time and the River.*

Virginia Woolf, 1882-1941, (Br.) novelist, essayist. *Mrs. Dalloway, To the Lighthouse, The Waves, A Room of One's Own.*

William Wordsworth, 1770-1850, (Br.) poet. "Tintern Abbey," "Ode: Intimations of Immortality," *The Prelude.*

William Butler Yeats, 1865-1939, (Ir.) poet, playwright. *The Wild Swans at Coole, The Tower, Last Poems.*

Émile Zola, 1840-1902, (F.) novelist. *Nana, The Dram Shop.*

Noted Artists and Sculptors of the Past

Artists are painters unless otherwise indicated.

Washington Allston, 1779-1843, (U.S.) landscapist. Belshazzar's Feast.

Albrecht Altdorfer, 1480-1538, (Ger.) landscapist. Battle of Alexander.

Andrea del Sarto, 1486-1530, frescoes. Madonna of the Harpies.

Fra Angelico, c. 1400-1455, (It.) Renaissance muralist. Madonna of the Linen Drapers' Guild.

Alexsandr Archipenko, 1887-1964, (U.S.) sculptor. Boxing Match, Medranos.

John James Audubon, 1785-1851, (U.S.) Birds of America.

Hans Baldung Grien, 1484-1545, (Ger.) Todentanz.

Ernst Barlach, 1870-1938, (Ger.) Expressionist sculptor. Man Drawing a Sword.

Frederic-Auguste Bartholdi, 1834-1904, (Fr.) Liberty Enlightening the World, Lion of Belfort.

Fra Bartolommeo, 1472-1517, (It.) Vision of St. Bernard.

Aubrey Beardsley, 1872-1898, (Br.) illustrator. Salome, Lysistrata.

Max Beckmann, 1884-1950, (Ger.) Expressionist. The Descent from the Cross.

Gentile Bellini, 1426-1507, (It.) Renaissance. Procession in St. Mark's Square.

Giovanni Bellini, 1428-1516, (It.) St. Francis in Ecstasy.

Jacopo Bellini, 1400-1470, (It.) Crucifixion.

George Wesley Bellows, 1882-1925, (U.S.) sports artist. Stag at Sharkey's.

Thomas Hart Benton, 1889-1975, (U.S.) American regionalist. Threshing Wheat, Arts of the West.

Gianlorenzo Bernini, 1598-1680, (It.) Baroque sculpture. The Assumption.

Albert Bierstadt, 1830-1902, (U.S.) landscapist. The Rocky Mountains, Mount Corcoran.

George Caleb Bingham, 1811-1879, (U.S.) Fur Traders Descending the Missouri.

William Blake, 1752-1827, (Br.) engraver. Book of Job, Songs of Innocence, Songs of Experience.

Rosa Bonheur, 1822-1899, (Fr.) The Horse Fair.

Pierre Bonnard, 1867-1947, (Fr.) Intimist. The Breakfast Room.

Gutzon Borglum, 1871-1941, (U.S.) sculptor. Mt. Rushmore Memorial.

Hieronymus Bosch, 1450-1516, (Flem.) religious allegories. The Crowning with Thorns.

Sandro Botticelli, 1444-1510, (It.) Renaissance. Birth of Venus.

Constantin Brancusi, 1876-1957, (Rum.) Nonobjective sculptor. Flying Turtle, The Kiss.

Georges Braque, 1882-1963, (Fr.) Cubist. Violin and Palette.

Pieter Bruegel the Elder, c. 1525-1569, (Flem.) The Peasant Dance.

Pieter Bruegel the Younger, 1564-1638, (Flem.) Village Fair, The Crucifixion.

Edward Burne-Jones, 1833-1898, (Br.) Pre-Raphaelite artist-craftsman. The Mirror of Venus.

Alexander Calder, 1898-1976, (U.S.) sculptor. Lobster Trap and Fish Tail.

Michelangelo Merisi da Caravaggio, 1573-1610, (It.) Baroque. The Supper at Emmaus.

Emily Carr, 1871-1945, (Can.) landscapist. Blunden Harbour, Big Raven.

Carlo Carra, 1881-1966, (It.) Metaphysical school. Lot's Daughters.

Mary Cassatt, 1845-1926, (U.S.) Impressionist. Woman Bathing.

George Catlin, 1796-1872, (U.S.) American Indian life. Gallery of Indians.

Benvenuto Cellini, 1500-1571, (It.) Mannerist sculptor, goldsmith. Perseus.

Paul Cezanne, 1839-1906, (Fr.) Card Players, Mont-Sainte-Victoire with Large Pine Trees.

Marc Chagall, 1887-1985, (Rus.) Jewish life and folklore. I and the Village.

Jean Simeon Chardin, 1699-1779, (Fr.) still lifes. The Kiss, The Grace.

Frederic Church, 1826-1900, (U.S.) Hudson River school. Niagara, Andes of Ecuador.

Giovanni Cimabue, 1240-1302, (It.) Byzantine mosaicist. Madonna Enthroned with St. Francis.

Claude Lorrain, 1600-1682, (Fr.) ideal-landscapist. The Enchanted Castle.

Thomas Cole, 1801-1848, (U.S.) Hudson River school. The Ox-Bow.

John Constable, 1776-1837, (Br.) landscapist. Salisbury Cathedral from the Bishop's Grounds.

John Singleton Copley, 1738-1815, (U.S.) portraitist. Samuel Adams, Watson and the Shark.

Lovis Corinth, 1858-1925, (Ger.) Expressionist. Apocalypse.

Jean-Baptiste-Camille Corot, 1796-1875, (Fr.) landscapist. Souvenir de Mortefontaine, Pastorale.

Correggio, 1494-1534, (It.) Renaissance muralist. Mystic Marriages of St. Catherine.

Gustave Courbet, 1819-1877, (Fr.) Realist. The Artist's Studio.

Lucas Cranach the Elder, 1472-1553, (Ger.) Protestant Reformation portraitist. Luther.

Nathaniel Currier, 1813-1888, and **James M. Ives,** 1824-1895, (both U.S.) lithographers. A Midnight Race on the Mississippi.

John Steuart Curry, 1897-1946, (U.S.) Americana, murals. Baptism in Kansas.

Salvador Dali, 1904-1989, (Sp.) Surrealist. Persistence of Memory.

Honore Daumier, 1808-1879, (Fr.) caricaturist. The Third-Class Carriage.

Jacques-Louis David, 1748-1825, (Fr.) Neoclassicist. The Oath of the Horatii.

Arthur Davies, 1862-1928, (U.S.) Romantic landscapist. Unicorns.

Edgar Degas, 1834-1917, (Fr.) The Ballet Class.

Eugene Delacroix, 1789-1863, (Fr.) Romantic. Massacre at Chios.

Paul Delaroche, 1797-1856, (Fr.) historical themes. Children of Edward IV.

Luca Della Robbia, 1400-1482, (It.) Renaissance terracotta artist. Cantoria (singing gallery), Florence cathedral.

Donatello, 1386-1466, (It.) Renaissance sculptor. David, Gattamelata.

Jean Dubuffet, 1902-1985, (Fr.) painter, sculptor, printmaker. Group of Four Trees.

Marcel Duchamp, 1887-1968, (Fr.) Nude Descending a Staircase.

Raoul Dufy, 1877-1953, (Fr.) Fauvist. Chateau and Horses.

Asher Brown Durand, 1796-1886, (U.S.) Hudson River school. Kindred Spirits.

Albrecht Durer, 1471-1528, (Ger.) Renaissance engraver, woodcuts. St. Jerome in His Study, Melancholia I, Apocalypse.

Anthony van Dyck, 1599-1641, (Flem.) Baroque portraitist. Portrait of Charles I Hunting.

Thomas Eakins, 1844-1916, (U.S.) Realist. The Gross Clinic.

Jacob Epstein, 1880-1959, (Br.) religious and allegorical sculptor. Genesis, Ecce Homo.

Jan van Eyck, 1380-1441, (Flem.) naturalistic panels. Adoration of the Lamb.

Anselm Feuerbach, 1829-1880, (Ger.) Romantic Classicism. Judgement of Paris, Iphigenia.

John Bernard Flannagan, 1895-1942, (U.S.) animal sculptor. Triumph of the Egg.

Jean-Honore Fragonard, 1732-1806, (Fr.) Rococo. The Swing.

Daniel Chester French, 1850-1931, (U.S.) The Minute Man of Concord; seated Lincoln, Lincoln Memorial, Washington, D.C.

Caspar David Friedrich, 1774-1840, (Ger.) Romantic landscapes. Man and Woman Gazing at the Moon.

Thomas Gainsborough, 1727-1788, (Br.) portraitist. The Blue Boy.

Paul Gauguin, 1848-1903, (Fr.) Post-impressionist. The Tahitians.

Lorenzo Ghiberti, 1378-1455, (It.) Renaissance sculptor. Gates of Paradise baptistry doors, Florence.

Alberto Giacometti, 1901-1966, (It.) attenuated sculptures of solitary figures. Man Pointing.

Giorgione, c. 1477-1510, (It.) Renaissance. The Tempest.

Giotto di Bondone, 1267-1337, (It.) Renaissance. Presentation of Christ in the Temple.

Francois Girardon, 1628-1715, (Fr.) Baroque sculptor of classical themes. Apollo Tended by the Nymphs.

Vincent van Gogh, 1853-1890, (Dutch) The Starry Night, L'Arlesienne.

Arshile Gorky, 1905-1948, (U.S.) Surrealist. The Liver Is the Cock's Comb.

Francisco de Goya y Lucientes, 1746-1828, (Sp.) The Naked Maja, The Disasters of War (etchings).

El Greco, 1541-1614, View of Toledo.

Horatio Greenough, 1805-1852, (U.S.) Neo-classical sculptor. George Washington.

Matthias Grünewald, 1480-1528, (Ger.) mystical religious themes. The Resurrection.

Frans Hals, c. 1580-1666, (Dutch) portraitist. Laughing Cavalier, Gypsy Girl.

Childe Hassam, 1859-1935, (U.S.) Impressionist. Southwest Wind.

Edward Hicks, 1780-1849, (U.S.) folk painter. The Peaceable Kingdom.

Hans Hofmann, 1880-1966, (U.S.) early Abstract Expressionist. Spring. The Gate.

William Hogarth, 1697-1764, (Br.) caricaturist. The Rake's Progress.

Katsushika Hokusai, 1760-1849, (Jap.) printmaker. Crabs.

Hans Holbein the Elder, 1460-1524, (Ger.) late Gothic. Presentation of Christ in the Temple.

Hans Holbein the Younger, 1497-1543, (Ger.) portraitist. Henry VIII.

Winslow Homer, 1836-1910, (U.S.) marine themes. Marine Coast, High Cliff.

Edward Hopper, 1882-1967, (U.S.) realistic urban scenes. Sunlight in a Cafeteria.

Jean-Auguste-Dominique Ingres, 1780-1867, (Fr.) Classicist. Valpincon Bather.

George Inness, 1825-1894, (U.S.) luminous landscapist. Delaware Water Gap.

Vasily Kandinsky, 1866-1944, (Rus.) Abstractionist. Capricious Forms.

Paul Klee, 1879-1940, (Swiss) Abstractionist. Twittering Machine.

Oscar Kokoschka, 1886-1980, (Aus.) Expressionist. View of Prague.

Kathe Kollwitz, 1867-1945, (Ger.) printmaker, social justice themes. The Peasant War.

Gaston Lachaise, 1882-1935, (U.S.) figurative sculptor. Standing Woman.

John La Farge, 1835-1910, (U.S.) muralist. Red and White Peonies.

Fernand Leger, 1881-1955, (Fr.) machine art. The Cyclists.

Leonardo da Vinci, 1452-1519, (It.) Mona Lisa, Last Supper, The Annunciation.

Emanuel Leutze, 1816-1868, (U.S.) historical themes. Washington Crossing the Delaware.

Jacques Lipchitz, 1891-1973, (Fr.) Cubist sculptor. Harpist.

Filippino Lippi, 1457-1504, (It.) Renaissance. The Vision of St. Bernard.

Fra Filippo Lippi, 1406-1469, (It.) Renaissance. Coronation of the Virgin.

Morris Louis, 1912-1962, (U.S.) Abstract Expressionist. Signa, Stripes.

Aristide Maillol, 1861-1944, (Fr.) sculptor. The Mediterranean.

Edouard Manet, 1832-1883, (Fr.) forerunner of Impressionism. Luncheon on the Grass, Olympia.

Andrea Mantegna, 1431-1506, (It.) Renaissance frescoes. Triumph of Caesar.

Franz Marc, 1880-1916, (Ger.) Expressionist. Blue Horses.

John Marin, 1870-1953, (U.S.) expressionist seascapes. Maine Island.

Reginald Marsh, 1898-1954, (U.S.) satirical artist. Tattoo and Haircut.

Masaccio, 1401-1428, (It.) Renaissance. The Tribute Money.

Henri Matisse, 1869-1954, (Fr.) Fauvist. Woman with the Hat.

Michelangelo Buonarroti, 1475-1564, (It.) Pieta, David, Moses, The Last Judgment, Sistine Ceiling.

Jean-Francois Millet, 1814-1875, (Fr.) painter of peasant subjects. The Gleaners, The Man with a Hoe.

Joan Miró, 1893-1983, (Sp.) Exuberant colors, playful images. Catalan landscape, Dutch Interior.

Amedeo Modigliani, 1884-1920, (It.) Reclining Nude.

Piet Mondrian, 1872-1944, (Dutch) Abstractionist. Composition.

Claude Monet, 1840-1926, (Fr.) Impressionist. The Bridge at Argenteuil, Haystacks.

Henry Moore, 1898-1986, (Br.) sculptor of large-scale, abstract works. Reclining Figure (several).

Gustave Moreau, 1826-1898, (Fr.) Symbolist. The Apparition, Dance of Salome.

James Wilson Morrice, 1865-1924, (Can.) landscapist. The Ferry, Quebec, Venice, Looking Over the Lagoon.

Grandma Moses, 1860-1961, (U.S.) folk painter. Out for the Christmas Trees.

Edvard Munch, 1863-1944, (Nor.) Expressionist. The Cry.

Bartolome Murillo, 1618-1682, (Sp.) Baroque religious artist. Vision of St. Anthony. The Two Trinities.

Barnett Newman, 1905-1970, (U.S.) Abstract Expressionist. Stations of the Cross.

Isamu Noguchi, 1904-1988, (U.S.) trad. Japanese art, modern techniques.

Georgia O'Keeffe, 1887-1986, (U.S.) Southwest motifs. Cow's Skull.

Jose Clemente Orozco, 1883-1949, (Mex.) frescoes. House of Tears.

Charles Willson Peale, 1741-1827, (U.S.) American Revolutionary portraitist. Washington, Franklin, Jefferson, John Adams.

Rembrandt Peale, 1778-1860, (U.S.) portraitist. Thomas Jefferson.

Pietro Perugino, 1446-1523, (It.) Renaissance. Delivery of the Keys to St. Peter.

Pablo Picasso, 1881-1973, (Sp.) Guernica, Dove, Head of a Woman.

Piero della Francesca, c. 1415-1492, (It.) Renaissance. Duke of Urbino, Flagellation of Christ.

Camille Pissarro, 1830-1903, (Fr.) Impressionist. Morning Sunlight.

Jackson Pollock, 1912-1956, (U.S.) Abstract Expressionist. Autumn Rhythm.

Nicolas Poussin, 1594-1665, (Fr.) Baroque pictorial classicism. St. John on Patmos.

Maurice B. Prendergast, c. 1860-1924, (U.S.) Post-impressionist water colorist. Umbrellas in the Rain.

Pierre-Paul Prud'hon, 1758-1823, (Fr.) Romanticist. Crime pursued by Vengeance and Justice.

Pierre Cecile Puvis de Chavannes, 1824-1898, (Fr.) muralist. The Poor Fisherman.

Raphael Sanzio, 1483-1520, (It.) Renaissance. Disputa, School of Athens, Sistine Madonna.

Man Ray, 1890-1976, (U.S.) Dadaist. Observing Time, The Lovers.

Odilon Redon, 1840-1916, (Fr.) Symbolist lithographer. In the Dream.

Rembrandt van Rijn, 1606-1669, (Dutch) The Bridal Couple, The Night Watch.

Frederic Remington, 1861-1909, (U.S.) painter, sculptor, portrayer of the American West. Bronco Buster.

Pierre-Auguste Renoir, 1841-1919, (Fr.) Impressionist. The Luncheon of the Boating Party.

Joshua Reynolds, 1723-1792, (Br.) portraitist. Mrs. Siddons as the Tragic Muse.

Diego Rivera, 1886-1957, (Mex.) frescoes. The Fecund Earth.

Norman Rockwell, 1894-1978, (U.S.) illustrator. Saturday Evening Post covers.

Auguste Rodin, 1840-1917, (Fr.) sculptor. The Thinker, The Burghers of Calais.

Mark Rothko, 1903-1970, (U.S.) Abstract Expressionist. Light, Earth and Blue.

Georges Rouault, 1871-1958, (Fr.) Expressionist. The Old King.

Henri Rousseau, 1844-1910, (Fr.) primitive exotic themes. The Snake Charmer.

Theodore Rousseau, 1812-1867, (Swiss-Fr.) landscapist. Under the Birches, Evening.

Peter Paul Rubens, 1577-1640, (Flem.) Baroque. Mystic Marriage of St. Catherine.

Jacob van Ruisdael, c. 1628-1682, (Dutch) landscapist. Jewish Cemetery.

Salomon van Ruysdael, c. 1600-1670, (Dutch) landscapist. River with Ferry-Boat.

Albert Pinkham Ryder, 1847-1917, (U.S.) seascapes and allegories. Toilers of the Sea.

Augustus Saint-Gaudens, 1848-1907, (U.S.) memorial statues. Farragut, Mrs. Henry Adams (Grief).

Andrea Sansovino, 1460-1529, (It.) Renaissance sculptor. Baptism of Christ.

Jacopo Sansovino, 1486-1570, (It.) Renaissance sculptor. St. John the Baptist.

John Singer Sargent, 1856-1925, (U.S.) Edwardian society portraitist. The Wyndham Sisters, Madam X.

Georges Seurat, 1859-1891, (Fr.) Pointillist. Sunday Afternoon on the Island of Grande Jatte.

Gino Severini, 1883-1966, (It.) Futurist and Cubist. Dynamic Hieroglyph of the Bal Tabarin.

Ben Shahn, 1898-1969, (U.S.) social and political themes. Sacco and Vanzetti series, Seurat's Lunch, Handball.

Charles Sheeler, 1883-1965, (U.S.) Abstractionist. Upper Deck.

David Alfaro Siqueiros, 1896-1974, (Mex.) political muralist. March of Humanity.

John F. Sloan, 1871-1951, (U.S.) depictions of New York City. Wake of the Ferry.

David Smith, 1906-1965, (U.S.) welded metal sculpture. Hudson River Landscape, Zig, Cubi series.

Gilbert Stuart, 1755-1828, (U.S.) portraitist. George Washington.

Thomas Sully, 1783-1872, (U.S.) portraitist. Col. Thomas Handasyd Perkins, The Passage of the Delaware.

Yves Tanguy, 1900-1955, (Fr.) Surrealist. Rose of the Four Winds.

Giovanni Battista Tiepolo, 1696-1770, (It.) Rococo frescoes. The Crucifixion.

Jacopo Tintoretto, 1518-1594, (It.) Mannerist. The Last Supper.

Titian, c. 1485-1576, (It.) Renaissance. Venus and the Lute Player, The Bacchanal.

Henri de Toulouse-Lautrec, 1864-1901, (Fr.) At the Moulin Rouge.

John Trumbull, 1756-1843, (U.S.) historical themes. The Declaration of Independence.

J(oseph) M(allord) W(illiam) Turner, 1775-1851, (Br.) Romantic landscapist. Snow Storm.

Paolo Uccello, 1397-1475, (It.) Gothic-Renaissance. The Rout of San Romano.

Maurice Utrillo, 1883-1955, (Fr.) Impressionist. Sacre-Coeur de Montmartre.

John Vanderlyn, 1775-1852, (U.S.) Neo-classicist. Ariadne Asleep on the Island of Naxos.

Diego Velazquez, 1599-1660, (Sp.) Baroque. Las Meninas, Portrait of Juan de Pareja.

Jan Vermeer, 1632-1675, (Dutch) interior genre subjects. Young Woman with a Water Jug.

Paolo Veronese, 1528-1588, (It.) devotional themes, vastly peopled canvases. The Temptation of St. Anthony.

Andrea del Verrocchio, 1435-1488, (It.) Florentine sculptor. Colleoni.

Maurice de Vlaminck, 1876-1958, (Fr.) Fauvist landscapist. The Storm.

Andy Warhol, 1928-1987 (U.S.) Pop Art. Campbell's Soup Cans.

Antoine Watteau, 1684-1721, (Fr.) Rococo painter of "scenes of gallantry". The Embarkation for Cythera.

George Frederic Watts, 1817-1904, (Br.) painter and sculptor of grandiose allegorical themes. Hope, Physical Energy.

Benjamin West, 1738-1820, realistic historical themes. Death of General Wolfe.

James Abbott McNeill Whistler, 1834-1903, (U.S.) Arrangement in Grey and Black, No. 1: The Artist's Mother.

Archibald M. Willard, 1836-1918, (U.S.) The Spirit of '76.

Grant Wood, 1891-1942, (U.S.) Midwestern regionalist. American Gothic, Daughters of Revolution.

Ossip Zadkine, 1890-1967, (Rus.) School of Paris sculptor. The Destroyed City, Musicians, Christ.

Noted Philosophers and Religionists of the Past

Lyman Abbott, 1835-1922, (U.S.) clergyman, reformer; advocate of Christian Socialism.

Pierre Abelard, 1079-1142, (F.) philosopher, theologian, and teacher, used dialectic method to support Christian dogma.

Felix Adler, 1851-1933, (U.S.) German-born founder of the Ethical Culture Society.

St. Augustine, 354-430, Latin bishop considered the founder of formalized Christian theology.

Averroes, 1126-1198, (Sp.) Islamic philosopher.

Roger Bacon, c.1214-1294, (Br.) philosopher and scientist.

Bahaullah (Mirza Husayn Ali), 1817-1892, (Pers.) founder of Bahai faith.

Karl Barth, 1886-1968, (Sw.) theologian, a leading force in 20th-century Protestantism.

St. Benedict, c.480-547, (It.) founded the Benedictines.

Jeremy Bentham, 1748-1832, (Br.) philosopher, reformer, founder of Utilitarianism.

Henri Bergson, 1859-1941, (F.) philosopher of evolution.

George Berkeley, 1685-1753, (Ir.) philosopher, churchman.

John Biddle, 1615-1662, (Br.) founder of English Unitarianism.

Jakob Boehme, 1575-1624, (G.) theosophist and mystic.

William Brewster, 1567-1644, (Br.) headed Pilgrims, signed Mayflower Compact.

Emil Brunner, 1889-1966, (Sw.) Protestant theologian.

Giordano Bruno, 1548-1600, (It.) philosopher, first to state the cosmic theory.

Martin Buber, 1878-1965, (G.) Jewish philosopher, theologian, wrote I and Thou.

Buddha (Siddhartha Gautama), c.563-c.483 BC, (Ind.) philosopher, founded Buddhism.

John Calvin, 1509-1564, (F.) theologian, a key figure in the Protestant Reformation.

Rudolph Carnap, 1891-1970, (U.S.) German-born philosopher, a founder of logical positivism.

William Ellery Channing, 1780-1842, (U.S.) clergyman, early spokesman for Unitarianism.

Auguste Comte, 1798-1857, (F.) philosopher, the founder of positivism.

Confucius, 551-479 BC, (Chin.) founder of Confucianism.

John Cotton, 1584-1652, (Br.) Puritan theologian.

Thomas Cranmer, 1489-1556, (Br.) churchman, wrote much of Book of Common Prayer; promoter of English Reformation.

René Descartes, 1596-1650, (F.) philosopher, mathematician, "father of modern philosophy."

John Dewey, 1859-1952, (U.S.) philosopher, educator; helped inaugurate the progressive education movement.

Denis Diderot, 1713-1784, (F.) philosopher, creator of first modern encyclopedia.

Mary Baker Eddy, 1821-1910, (U.S.) founder of Christian Science, wrote Science and Health.

Jonathan Edwards, 1703-1758, (U.S.) preacher, theologian.

(Desiderius) Erasmus, c.1466-1536, (Du.) Renaissance humanist, wrote On the Freedom of the Will.

Johann Fichte, 1762-1814, (G.) philosopher, the first of the Transcendental Idealists.

George Fox, 1624-1691, (Br.) founder of Society of Friends.

St. Francis of Assisi, 1182-1226, (It.) founded Franciscans.

al Ghazali, 1058-1111, Islamic philosopher.

Georg W. Hegel, 1770-1831, (G.) Idealist philosopher.

Martin Heidegger, 1889-1976, (G.) existentialist philosopher, affected fields ranging from physics to literary criticism.

Johann G. Herder, 1744-1803, (G.) philosopher, cultural historian; a founder of German Romanticism.

David Hume, 1711-1776, (Sc.) philosopher, historian.

Jan Hus, 1369-1415, (Czech.) religious reformer.

Edmund Husserl, 1859-1938, (G.) philosopher, founded the Phenomenological movement.

Thomas Huxley, 1825-1895, (Br.) philosopher, educator.

Ignatius of Loyola, 1491-1556, (Sp.) founder of the Jesuits.

William Inge, 1860-1954, (Br.) theologian, explored the mystic aspects of Christianity.

William James, 1842-1910, (U.S.) philosopher, psychologist; advanced theory of the pragmatic nature of truth.

Karl Jaspers, 1883-1969, (G.) existentialist philosopher.

Immanuel Kant, 1724-1804, (G.) metaphysician, preeminent founder of modern critical philosophy; Critique of Pure Reason.

Soren Kierkegaard, 1813-1855, (Den.) philosopher, considered the father of Existentialism.

John Knox, 1505-1572, (Sc.) leader of the Protestant Reformation in Scotland.

Lao-Tzu, 604-531 BC, (Chin.) philosopher, considered the founder of the Taoist religion.

Gottfried von Leibniz, 1646-1716, (G.) philosopher, mathematician, influenced German Enlightenment.

Martin Luther, 1483-1546, (G.) leader of the Protestant Reformation, founded Lutheran church.

Maimonides, 1135-1204, (Sp.) Jewish philosopher.

Jacques Maritain, 1882-1973, (F.) Neo-Thomist philosopher.

Cotton Mather, 1663-1728, (U.S.) defender of orthodox Puritanism; founded Yale, 1701.

Philipp Melanchthon, 1497-1560, (G.) theologian, humanist; an important voice in the Reformation.

Thomas Merton, 1915-1968, (U.S.) Trappist monk, spiritual writer; The Seven Storey Mountain.

Mohammed, c.570-632, Arab prophet of the religion of Islam.

Dwight Moody, 1837-1899, (U.S.) evangelist.

George E. Moore, 1873-1958, (Br.) ethical theorist.

Elijah Muhammad, 1897-1975, (U.S.) leader of the Black Muslim sect.

Heinrich Muhlenberg, 1711-1787, (G.) organized the Lutheran Church in America.

John H. Newman, 1801-1890, (Br.) Roman Catholic cardinal, led Oxford Movement; Apologia pro Vita Sua.

Reinhold Niebuhr, 1892-1971, (U.S.) Protestant theologian, social and political critic.

Friedrich Nietzsche, 1844-1900, (G.) moral philosopher; The Birth of Tragedy, Thus Spake Zarathustra.

Blaise Pascal, 1623-1662, (F.) philosopher, mathematician.

St. Patrick, c.389-c.461, brought Christianity to Ireland.

St. Paul, ?-c.67, a founder of Christianity; his epistles are first Christian theological writing.

Charles S. Peirce, 1839-1914, (U.S.) philosopher, logician; originated concept of Pragmatism, 1878.

Josiah Royce 1855-1916, (U.S.) Idealist philosopher.

Charles T. Russell, 1852-1916, (U.S.) founder of Jehovah's Witnesses.

Fredrich von Schelling, 1775-1854, (G.) philosopher of romantic movement.

Friedrich Schleiermacher, 1768-1834, (G.) theologian, a founder of modern Protestant theology.

Arthur Schopenhauer, 1788-1860, (G.) philosopher.

Joseph Smith, 1805-1844, (U.S.) founded Latter Day Saints (Mormon) movement, 1830.

Herbert Spencer, 1820-1903, (Br.) philosopher of evolution.

Baruch Spinoza, 1632-1677, (Du.) rationalist philosopher.

Billy Sunday, 1862-1935, (U.S.) evangelist.

Daisetz Teitaro Suzuki, 1870-1966, (Jap.) Buddhist scholar.

Emanuel Swedenborg, 1688-1772, (Swed.) philosopher, mystic.

Thomas à Becket, 1118-1170, (Br.) archbishop of Canterbury, opposed Henry II.

Thomas à Kempis, c.1380-1471, (G.) theologian probably wrote *Imitation of Christ.*

Thomas Aquinas, 1225-1274, (It.) Roman Catholic saint, founder of system declared official Catholic philosophy; *Summa Theologica.*

Paul Tillich, 1886-1965, (U.S.) German-born philosopher and theologian; brought depth psychology to Protestantism.

John Wesley, 1703-1791, (Br.) theologian, evangelist; founded Methodism.

Alfred North Whitehead, 1861-1947, (Br.) philosopher, mathematician; *Principia Mathematica* (with Bertrand Russell).

William of Occam, c.1285-c.1349 (Br.) medieval scholastic philosopher.

Roger Williams, c.1603-1683, (U.S.) clergyman, championed religious freedom and separation of church and state.

Ludwig Wittgenstein, 1889-1951, (Aus.) philosopher, influenced language philosophy.

John Wycliffe, 1320-1384, (Br.) theologian, reformer.

Brigham Young, 1801-1877, (U.S.) Mormon leader after Smith's assassination, colonized Utah.

Huldrych Zwingli, 1484-1531, (Sw.) theologian, led Swiss Protestant Reformation.

Noted Social Reformers and Educators of the Past

Jane Addams, 1860-1935, (U.S.) co-founder of Hull House; won Nobel Peace Prize, 1931.

Susan B. Anthony, 1820-1906, (U.S.) a leader in temperance, anti-slavery, and women's suffrage movements.

Henry Barnard, 1811-1900, (U.S.) public school reformer.

Thomas Barnardo, 1845-1905, (Br.) social reformer, pioneered in the care of destitute children.

Clara Barton, 1821-1912, (U.S.) organizer of the American Red Cross.

Henry Ward Beecher, 1813-1887, (U.S.) clergyman, abolitionist.

Sarah G. Blanding, 1899-1985, (U.S.), head of Vassar College, 1946-64.

Amelia Bloomer, 1818-1894, (U.S.) social reformer, women's rights advocate.

William Booth, 1829-1912, (Br.) founded the Salvation Army.

John Brown, 1800-1859, (U.S.) abolitionist who led murder of 5 pro-slavery men, was hanged.

Nicholas Murray Butler, 1862-1947, (U.S.) educator headed Columbia Univ., 1902-45; won Nobel Peace Prize, 1931.

Frances X. (Mother) Cabrini, 1850-1917, (U.S.) Italian-born nun founded charitable institutions; first American canonized.

Carrie Chapman Catt, 1859-1947, (U.S.) suffragette, helped win passage of the 19th amendment.

Clarence Darrow, 1857-1938, (U.S.) lawyer, defender of "underdog," opponent of capital punishment.

Dorothy Day, 1897-1980, (U.S.) founder of Catholic Worker Movement.

Eugene V. Debs, 1855-1926, (U.S.) labor leader, led Pullman strike, 1894; 4-time Socialist presidential candidate.

Melvil Dewey, 1851-1931, (U.S.) devised decimal system of library-book classification.

Dorothea Dix, 1802-1887, (U.S.) crusader for humane care of mentally ill.

Frederick Douglass, 1817-1895, (U.S.) abolitionist.

W.E.B. DuBois, 1868-1963, (U.S.) Negro-rights leader, educator, and writer.

William Lloyd Garrison, 1805-1879, (U.S.) abolitionist, reformer.

Giovanni Gentile, 1875-1944, (It.) philosopher, educator; reformed Italian educational system.

Emma Goldman, 1869-1940, (Rus.-U.S.) published anarchist *Mother Earth,* birth control advocate.

Samuel Gompers, 1850-1924, (U.S.) labor leader; a founder and president of AFL.

William Green, 1873-1952, (U.S.) president of AFL, 1924-52.

Michael Harrington, 1928-1989, (U.S.) revealed poverty in affluent U.S. in *The Other America,* 1963.

Sidney Hillman, 1887-1946, (U.S.) labor leader, helped organize CIO.

John Holt, 1924-1985, (U.S.) educator and author, *How Children Fail.*

Samuel G. Howe, 1801-1876, (U.S.) social reformer, changed public attitudes toward the handicapped.

Helen Keller, 1880-1968, (U.S.) crusader for better treatment for the handicapped.

Martin Luther King Jr., 1929-1968, (U.S.) civil rights leader; won Nobel Peace Prize, 1964.

John L. Lewis, 1880-1969, (U.S.) labor leader, headed United Mine Workers, 1920-60.

Horace Mann, 1796-1859, (U.S.) pioneered modern public school system.

William H. McGuffey, 1800-1873, (U.S.) author of *Reader,* the mainstay of 19th century U.S. public education.

Alexander Meiklejohn, 1872-1964, (U.S.) British-born educator, championed academic freedom and experimental curricula.

Karl Menninger, 1893-1991, (U.S.) with brother William made Menninger Clinic, and Menninger Foundation in Topeka, Kans., the center of U.S. psychiatry.

Lucretia Mott, 1793-1880, (U.S.) reformer, pioneer feminist.

Philip Murray, 1886-1952, (U.S.) Scotch-born labor leader.

Florence Nightingale, 1820-1910, (Br.) founder of modern nursing.

Emmeline Pankhurst, 1858-1928, (Br.) woman suffragist.

Elizabeth P. Peabody, 1804-1894, (U.S.) education pioneer, founded 1st kindergarten in U.S., 1860.

Walter Reuther, 1907-1970, (U.S.) labor leader, headed UAW.

Jacob Riis, 1849-1914, (U.S.) crusader for urban reforms.

Margaret Sanger, 1883-1966, (U.S.) social reformer, pioneered the birth control movement.

Elizabeth Seton, 1774-1821, (U.S.) established parochial school education in U.S.

Earl of Shaftesbury (A.A. Cooper), 1801-1885, (Br.) social reformer.

Elizabeth Cady Stanton, 1815-1902, (U.S.) women's suffrage pioneer.

Lucy Stone, 1818-1893, (U.S.) feminist, abolitionist.

Harriet Tubman, c.1820-1913, (U.S.) abolitionist, ran Underground Railroad.

Booker T. Washington, 1856-1915, (U.S.) educator, reformer; championed vocational training for blacks.

Walter F. White, 1893-1955, (U.S.) headed NAACP, 1931-55.

William Wilberforce, 1759-1833, (Br.) social reformer, prominent in struggle to abolish the slave trade.

Emma Hart Willard, 1787-1870, (U.S.) pioneered higher education for women.

Frances E. Willard, 1839-1898, (U.S.) temperance, woman's rights leader.

Mary Wollstonecraft, 1759-1797 (Br.) wrote *Vindication of the Rights of Women.*

Whitney M. Young Jr., 1921-1971, (U.S.) civil rights leader, headed National Urban League, 1961-71.

Noted Historians, Economists, and Social Scientists of the Past

Brooks Adams, 1848-1927, (U.S.) historian, political theoretician; *The Law of Civilization and Decay.*

Henry Adams, 1838-1911, (U.S.) historian; *History of the United States of America, The Education of Henry Adams.*

Francis Bacon, 1561-1626, (Br.) philosopher, essayist, and statesman; applied scientific induction to philosophy.

George Bancroft, 1800-1891, (U.S.) historian, wrote 10-volume *History of the United States.*

Charles A. Beard, 1874-1948, (U.S.) historian; *The Economic Basis of Politics;* helped found New School for Social Research.

Bede (the Venerable), c.673-735, (Br.) scholar historian whose writings virtually comprise the learning of his time.

Ruth Benedict, 1887-1948, (U.S.) anthropologist, studied Indian tribes of the Southwest.

Bruno Bettelheim, 1903-1990, (Aust.-U.S.) psychoanalyst specializing in autistic children; *The Uses of Enchantment.*

Louis Blanc, 1811-1882, (F.) Socialist leader and historian whose ideas were a link between utopian and Marxist socialism.

Leonard Bloomfield, 1887-1949, (U.S.) linguist. *Language.*

Franz Boas, 1858-1942, (U.S.) German-born anthropologist, studied American Indians.

Van Wyck Brooks, 1886-1963, (U.S.) historian, critic of New England culture, esp. literature.

Edmund Burke, 1729-1797, (Ir.) British parliamentarian and political philosopher; influenced many Federalists.

Joseph Campbell, 1904-1987, (U.S.) wrote books on mythology, folklore.

Thomas Carlyle, 1795-1881, (Sc.) historian, critic; *Sartor Resartus, Past and Present, The French Revolution.*

Edward Channing, 1856-1931, (U.S.) historian, wrote 6-volume *A History of the United States.*

John R. Commons, 1862-1945, (U.S.) economist, labor historian; *Legal Foundations of Capitalism.*

Benedetto Croce, 1866-1952, (It.) philosopher, statesman, and historian; *Philosophy of the Spirit.*

Bernard A. De Voto, 1897-1955, (U.S.) historian; wrote trilogy on American West; edited Mark Twain manuscripts.

Ariel Durant, 1898-1981, (U.S.) historian, collaborated with husband on 11-volume *The Story of Civilization.*

Will Durant, 1885-1981, (U.S.) historian. *The Story of Civilization, The Story of Philosophy.*

Emile Durkheim, 1858-1917, (F.) a founder of modern sociology; *The Rules of Sociological Method.*

Friedrich Engels, 1820-1895, (G.) political writer, with Marx wrote the *Communist Manifesto.*

Irving Fisher, 1867-1947, (U.S.) economist, contributed to the development of modern monetary theory.

John Fiske, 1842-1901, (U.S.) historian and lecturer, popularized Darwinian theory of evolution.

Charles Fourier, 1772-1837, (F.) utopian socialist.

Henry George, 1839-1897, (U.S.) economist, reformer, led single-tax movement.

Edward Gibbon, 1737-1794, (Br.) historian, wrote *The History of the Decline and Fall of the Roman Empire.*

Francesco Guicciardini, 1483-1540, (It.) historian, wrote *Storia d'Italia,* principal historical work of the 16th-century.

Thomas Hobbes, 1588-1679, (Br.) political philosopher; *Leviathan.*

Richard Hofstadter, 1916-1970, (U.S.) historian; *The Age of Reform.*

John Maynard Keynes, 1883-1946, (Br.) economist, principal advocate of deficit spending.

Alfred L. Kroeber, 1876-1960, (U.S.) cultural anthropologist, studied Indians of North and South America.

James L. Laughlin, 1850-1933, (U.S.) economist, helped establish Federal Reserve System.

Lucien Lévy-Bruhl, 1857-1939, (F.) philosopher, studied the psychology of primitive societies; *Primitive Mentality.*

Kurt Lewin, 1890-1947, (U.S.) German-born psychologist, studied human motivation and group dynamics.

John Locke, 1632-1704, (Br.) philosopher; *Essay Concerning Human Understanding.*

Konrad Lorenz, 1904-1989, (Aus.) ethologist, pioneer in study of animal behavior.

Thomas B. Macauley, 1800-1859, (Br.) historian, statesman.

Bronislaw Malinowski, 1884-1942, (Pol.) considered the father of social anthropology.

Thomas R. Malthus, 1766-1834, (Br.) economist, famed for *Essay on the Principle of Population.*

Karl Mannheim, 1893-1947, (Hung.) sociologist, historian; *Ideology and Utopia.*

Karl Marx, 1818-1883, (G.) political philosopher, proponent of modern communism; *Communist Manifesto, Das Kapital.*

Giuseppe Mazzini, 1805-1872, (It.) political philosopher.

George H. Mead, 1863-1931, (U.S.) philosopher, social psychologist.

Margaret Mead, 1901-1978, (U.S.) cultural anthropologist, popularized field; *Coming of Age in Samoa.*

James Mill, 1773-1836, (Sc.) philosopher, historian, economist; a proponent of Utilitarianism.

John Stuart Mill, 1806-1873, (Br.) philosopher, political economist; *Essay on Liberty.*

Perry G. Miller, 1905-1963, (U.S.) historian, interpreted 17th-century New England.

Theodor Mommsen, 1817-1903, (G.) historian; *The History of Rome.*

Charles-Louis Montesquieu, 1689-1755, (F.) social philosopher; *The Spirit of Laws.*

Samuel Eliot Morison, 1887-1976, (U.S.) historian, chronicled voyages of early explorers.

Lewis Mumford, 1895-1990, (U.S.) sociologist, critic, *The Culture of Cities.*

Gunnar Myrdal, 1898-1987 (Swe.) economist, social scientist.

Allan Nevins, 1890-1971, (U.S.) historian, biographer; *The Ordeal of the Union.*

Jose Ortega y Gasset, 1883-1955, (Sp.) philosopher, advocated control by elite; *The Revolt of the Masses.*

Robert Owen, 1771-1858, (Br.) political philosopher, reformer; pioneer in cooperative movement.

Vilfredo Pareto, 1848-1923, (It.) economist, sociologist.

Francis Parkman, 1823-1893, (U.S.) historian; *France and England in North America, 1851-92.*

Marco Polo, c.1254-1324, (It.) narrated an account of his travels to China.

William Prescott, 1796-1859, (U.S.) early American historian; *The Conquest of Peru.*

Pierre Joseph Proudhon, 1809-1865, (F.) social theorist, the father of anarchism; *The Philosophy of Property.*

Francois Quesnay, 1694-1774, (F.) economic theorist, demonstrated circular flow of economic activity through society.

David Ricardo, 1772-1823, (Br.) economic theorist, advocated free international trade.

James H. Robinson, 1863-1936, (U.S.) historian, educator.

Carl Rogers, 1902-1987, (U.S.) psychotherapist, author.

Jean-Jacques Rousseau, 1712-1778, (F.) social philosopher, the father of romantic sensibility; *Confessions.*

Edward Sapir, 1884-1939 (Ger.-U.S.) anthropologist, studied ethnology and linguistics of some U.S. Indian groups.

Ferdinand de Saussure, 1857-1913, (Swiss) a founder of modern linguistics.

Hjalmar Schacht, 1877-1970, (G.) economist; Reichsbank president.

Joseph Schumpeter, 1883-1950, (U.S.) Czech.-born economist, championed big business, capitalism.

Albert Schweitzer, 1875-1965, (Alsatian) social philosopher, theologian, medical missionary.

George Simmel, 1858-1918, (G.) sociologist, philosopher; helped establish German sociology.

B.F. Skinner, 1904-1989, (U.S.) psychologist, championed behaviorism.

Adam Smith, 1723-1790, (Br.) economist, advocated laissez-faire economy and free trade.

Jared Sparks, 1789-1866, (U.S.) historian, educator, editor; *The Library of American Biography.*

Oswald Spengler, 1880-1936, (G.) philosopher and historian; *The Decline of the West.*

William G. Sumner, 1840-1910, (U.S.) social scientist, economist; championed laissez-faire economy, Social Darwinism.

Hippolyte Taine, 1828-1893, (F.) historian, basis of naturalistic school; *The Origins of Contemporary France.*

Frank W. Taussig, 1859-1940, (U.S.) economist, educator.

A(lan) J(ohn) P(ercivale) Taylor, 1906-1989, (Br.) historian, *The Origins of the Second World War.*

Nikolaas Tinbergen, 1907-1988, (Dutch-Br.) ethologist, pioneer in study of animal behavior.

Alexis de Tocqueville, 1805-1859, (F.) political scientist, historian; *Democracy in America.*

Francis E. Townsend, 1867-1960, (U.S.) led old-age pension movement, 1933.

Arnold Toynbee, 1889-1975, (Br.) historian; *A Study of History.*

Heinrich von Treitschke, 1834-1896, (G.) historian, political writer; *A History of Germany in the 19th Century.*

George Trevelyan, 1838-1928, (Br.) historian, statesman; favored "literary" over "scientific" history; *History of England.*

Barbara Tuchman, 1912-1989, (U.S.) author of popular history books, *The Guns of August, The March of Folly.*

Frederick J. Turner, 1861-1932, (U.S.) historian, educator; *The Frontier in American History.*

Thorstein B. Veblen, 1857-1929, (U.S.) economist, social philosopher; *The Theory of the Leisure Class.*

Giovanni Vico, 1668-1744, (It.) historian, philosopher, regarded by many as first modern historian. *New Science.*

Voltaire (F.M. Arouet), 1694-1778, (F.) philosopher, historian, writer of "philosophical romances; *Candide.*

Izaak Walton, 1593-1683, (Br.) wrote biographies, political-philosophical study of fishing, *The Compleat Angler.*

Sidney J., 1859-1947, and wife **Beatrice,** 1858-1943, **Webb** (Br.) leading figures in Fabian Society and British Labour Party.

Walter P. Webb, 1888-1963, (U.S.) historian of the West.

Max Weber, 1864-1920, (G.) sociologist. *The Protestant Ethic and the Spirit of Capitalism.*

Noted Scientists of the Past

Howard H. Aiken, 1900-1973, (U.S.) mathematician, credited with designing forerunner of digital computer.

Albertus Magnus, 1193-1280, (G.) theologian, philosopher, established medieval Christian study of natural science.

Andre-Marie Ampère, 1775-1836, (F.) scientist known for contributions to electrodynamics.

Amedeo Avogadro, 1776-1856, (It.) chemist, physicist, advanced important theories on properties of gases.

John Bardeen, 1908-1991, (U.S.) co-inventor of the transistor that led to modern electronics.

A.C. Becquerel, 1788-1878, (F.) physicist, pioneer in electrochemical science.

A.H. Becquerel, 1852-1908, (F.) physicist, discovered radioactivity in uranium.

Alexander Graham Bell, 1847-1922, (U.S.) inventor, first to patent and commercially exploit the telephone, 1876.

Daniel Bernoulli, 1700-1782, (Swiss) mathematician, advanced kinetic theory of gases and fluids.

Jöns Jakob Berzelius, 1779-1848, (Swed.) chemist, developed modern chemical symbols and formulas.

Henry Bessemer, 1813-1898, (Br.) engineer, invented Bessemer steel-making process.

Louis Blériot, 1872-1936, (F.) engineer, pioneer aviator, invented and constructed monoplanes.

Niels Bohr, 1885-1962, (Dan.) physicist, leading figure in the development of quantum theory.

Max Born, 1882-1970, (G.) physicist known for research in quantum mechanics.

Satyendranath Bose, 1894-1974, (In.) physicist, chemist, mathematician known for Bose statistics, forerunner of modern quantum theory.

Walter Brattain, 1902-1987, (U.S.) inventor, worked on invention of transistor.

Louis de Broglie, 1893-1987, (F.) physicist, best known for wave theory.

Robert Bunsen, 1811-1899, (G.) chemist, invented Bunsen burner.

Luther Burbank, 1849-1926, (U.S.) plant breeder whose work developed plant breeding into a modern science.

Vannevar Bush, 1890-1974, (U.S.) electrical engineer, developed differential analyzer, first electronic analogue computer.

Alexis Carrel, 1873-1944, (F.) surgeon, biologist, developed methods of suturing blood vessels and transplanting organs.

George Washington Carver, 1860?-1943, (U.S.) agricultural chemist at Tuskegee Institute, discovered hundreds of uses for peanut, sweet potato, soybean.

Henry Cavendish, 1731-1810, (Br.) chemist, physicist, discovered hydrogen.

James Chadwick, 1891-1974, (Br.) physicist, discovered the neutron.

Jean M. Charcot, 1825-1893, (F.) neurologist known for work on hysteria, hypnotism, sclerosis.

Albert Claude, 1899-1983, (Belg.) a founder of modern cell biology.

John D. Cockcroft, 1897-1967, (Br.) nuclear physicist, constructed first atomic particle accelerator with E.T.S. Walton.

Nicholas Copernicus, 1473-1543, (Pol.) astronomer who first described solar system, with earth as one of planets revolving around sun.

William Crookes, 1832-1919, (Br.) physicist, chemist, discovered thallium, invented a cathode-ray tube, radiometer.

Marie Curie, 1867-1934, (Pol.-F.) physical chemist known for work on radium and its compounds.

Pierre Curie, 1859-1906, (F.) physical chemist known for work with his wife on radioactivity.

Gottlieb Daimler, 1834-1900, (G.) engineer, inventor, pioneer automobile manufacturer.

John Dalton, 1766-1844, (Br.) chemist, physicist, formulated atomic theory, made first table of atomic weights.

Charles Darwin, 1809-1882, (Br.) naturalist, established theory of organic evolution; *Origin of Species.*

Humphry Davy, 1778-1829, (Br.) chemist, research in electrochemistry led to isolation of potassium, sodium, calcium, barium, boron, magnesium, and strontium.

Lee De Forest, 1873-1961, (U.S.) inventor, pioneer in development of wireless telegraphy, sound pictures, television.

Max Delbruck, 1907-1981, (U.S.) pioneer in modern molecular genetics.

Rudolf Diesel, 1858-1913, (G.) mechanical engineer, patented Diesel engine.

Thomas Dooley, 1927-1961, (U.S.) "jungle doctor," noted for efforts to supply medical aid to underdeveloped countries.

Christian Doppler, 1803-1853, (Aus.) physicist, demonstrated Doppler effect (change in energy wavelengths caused by motion).

Thomas A. Edison, 1847-1931, (U.S.) inventor, held over 1,000 patents, including incandescent electric lamp, phonograph.

Paul Ehrlich, 1854-1915, (G.) bacteriologist, pioneer in modern immunology and bacteriology.

Albert Einstein, 1879-1955, (Ger.-U.S.) theoretical physicist, known for formulation of relativity theory.

John F. Enders, 1897-1985, (U.S.) virologist who helped discover vaccines against polio, measles, and mumps.

Leonhard Euler, 1707-1783, (Swiss), mathematician, physicist, authored first calculus book.

Gabriel Fahrenheit, 1686-1736, (G.) physicist, introduced Fahrenheit scale for thermometers.

Michael Faraday, 1791-1867, (Br.) chemist, physicist, known for work in field of electricity.

Pierre de Fermat, 1601-1665, (F.) mathematician, discovered analytic geometry, founded modern theory of numbers and calculus of probabilities.

Enrico Fermi, 1901-1954, (It.) physicist, one of chief architects of the nuclear age.

Galileo Ferraris, 1847-1897, (It.) physicist, electrical engineer, discovered principle of rotary magnetic field.

Richard Feynman, 1918-1988, (U.S.) a leading theoretical physicist of the postwar generation.

Camille Flammarion, 1842-1925, (F.) astronomer, popularized study of astronomy.

Alexander Fleming, 1881-1955, (Br.) bacteriologist, discovered penicillin.

Jean B.J. Fourier, 1768-1830, (F.) mathematician, discovered theorem governing periodic oscillation.

James Franck, 1882-1964, (G.) physicist, proved value of quantum theory.

Sigmund Freud, 1856-1939, (Aus.) psychiatrist, founder of psychoanalysis.

Galileo Galilei, 1564-1642, (It.) astronomer, physicist, a founder of the experimental method.

Luigi Galvani, 1737-1798, (It.) physician, physicist, known as founder of galvanism.

Carl Friedrich Gauss, 1777-1855, (G.) mathematician, astronomer, physicist, made important contributions to almost every field of physical science, founded a number of new fields.

Joseph Gay-Lussac, 1778-1850, (F.) chemist, physicist, investigated behavior of gases, discovered law of combining volumes.

Josiah W. Gibbs, 1839-1903, (U.S.) theoretical physicist, chemist, founded chemical thermodynamics.

Robert H. Goddard, 1882-1945 (U.S.) physicist, father of modern rocketry.

George W. Goethals, 1858-1928, (U.S.) army engineer, built the Panama Canal.

William C. Gorgas, 1854-1920, (U.S.) sanitarian, U.S. army surgeon-general, his work to prevent yellow fever, malaria helped insure construction of Panama Canal.

Ernest Haeckel, 1834-1919, (G.) zoologist, evolutionist, a strong proponent of Darwin.

Otto Hahn, 1879-1968, (G.) chemist, worked on atomic fission.

J.B.S. Haldane, 1892-1964, (Sc.) scientist, known for work as geneticist and application of mathematics to science.

James Hall, 1761-1832, (Br.) geologist, chemist, founded experimental geology, geochemistry.

Edmund Halley, 1656-1742, (Br.) astronomer, calculated the orbits of many planets.

William Harvey, 1578-1657, (Br.) physician, anatomist, discovered circulation of the blood.

Hermann v. Helmholtz, 1821-1894, (G.) physicist, anatomist, physiologist, made fundamental contributions to physiology, optics, electrodynamics, mathematics, meteorology.

William Herschel, 1738-1822, (Br.) astronomer, discovered Uranus.

Heinrich Hertz, 1857-1894, (G.) physicist, his discoveries led to wireless telegraphy.

David Hilbert, 1862-1943, (G.) mathematician, formulated first satisfactory set of axioms for modern Euclidean geometry.

Edwin P. Hubble, 1889-1953, (U.S.) astronomer, produced first observational evidence of expanding universe.

Alexander v. Humboldt, 1769-1859, (G.) explorer, naturalist, propagator of earth sciences, originated ecology, geophysics.

Julian Huxley, 1887-1975, (Br.) biologist, a gifted exponent and philosopher of science.

Edward Jenner, 1749-1823, (Br.) physician, discovered vaccination.

William Jenner, 1815-1898, (Br.) physician, pathological anatomist.

Frederic Joliot-Curie, 1900-1958, (F.) physicist, with his wife continued work of Curies on radioactivity.

Irene Joliot-Curie, 1897-1956, (F.) physicist, continued work of Curies in radioactivity.

James P. Joule, 1818-1889, (Br.) physicist, determined relationship between heat and mechanical energy (conservation of energy).

Carl Jung, 1875-1961, (Sw.) psychiatrist, founder of analytical psychology.

Wm. Thomson Kelvin, 1824-1907, (Br.) mathematician, physicist, known for work on heat and electricity.

Sister Elizabeth Kenny, 1886-1952, (Austral.) nurse, developed method of treatment for polio.

Johannes Kepler, 1571-1630, (G.) astronomer, discovered important laws of planetary motion.

Joseph Lagrange, 1736-1813, (F.) geometer, astronomer, worked in all fields of analysis, and number theory, and analytical and celestial mechanics.

Jean B. Lamarck, 1744-1829, (F.) naturalist, forerunner of Darwin in evolutionary science.

Edwin Land, 1910-1991, (U.S.) invented Polaroid camera.

Irving Langmuir, 1881-1957, (U.S.) physical chemist, his studies of molecular films on solid and liquid surfaces opened new fields in colloid research and biochemistry.

Pierre S. Laplace, 1749-1827, (F.) astronomer, physicist, put forth nebular hypothesis of origin of solar system.

Antoine Lavoisier, 1743-1794, (F.) chemist, founder of modern chemistry.

Ernest O. Lawrence, 1901-1958, (U.S.) physicist, invented the cyclotron.

Louis Leakey, 1903-1972, (Br.) anthropologist, discovered important fossils, remains of early hominids.

Anton van Leeuwenhoek, 1632-1723, (Du.) microscopist, father of microbiology.

Gottfried Wilhelm Leibniz, 1646-1716, (G.) mathematician, developed theories of differential and integral calculus.

Justus von Liebig, 1803-1873, (G.) chemist, established quantitative organic chemical analysis.

Joseph Lister, 1827-1912, (Br.) pioneer of antiseptic surgery.

Percival Lowell, 1855-1916, (U.S.) astronomer, predicted the existence of Pluto.

Louis (1864-1984) and **Auguste Lumière,** 1862-1954, (Fr.) invented cinematograph, first mechanism to project moving pictures on screen.

Guglielmo Marconi, 1874-1937, (It.) physicist, known for his development of wireless telegraphy.

James Clerk Maxwell, 1831-1879, (Sc.) physicist, known especially for his work in electricity and magnetism.

Maria Goeppert Mayer, 1906-1972, (G.-U.S.) physicist, independently developed theory of structure of atomic nuclei.

Lise Meitner, 1878-1968, (Aus.) physicist whose work contributed to the development of the atomic bomb.

Gregor J. Mendel, 1822-1884, (Aus.) botanist, known for his experimental work on heredity.

Franz Mesmer, 1734-1815, (G.) physician, developed theory of animal magnetism.

Albert A. Michelson, 1852-1931, (U.S.) physicist, established speed of light as a fundamental constant.

Robert A. Millikan, 1868-1953, (U.S.) physicist, noted for study of elementary electronic charge and photoelectric effect.

Thomas Hunt Morgan, 1866-1945, (U.S.) geneticist, embryologist, established chromosome theory of heredity.

Isaac Newton, 1642-1727, (Br.) natural philosopher, mathematician, discovered law of gravitation, laws of motion.

Robert N. Noyce, 1927-1989, (U.S.) inventor of the microchip, which revolutionized the electronics industry.

J. Robert Oppenheimer, 1904-1967, (U.S.) physicist, director of Los Alamos during development of the atomic bomb.

Wilhelm Ostwald, 1853-1932, (G.) physical chemist, philosopher, chief founder of physical chemistry.

Louis Pasteur, 1822-1895, (F.) chemist, originated process of pasteurization.

Max Planck, 1858-1947, (G.) physicist, originated and developed quantum theory.

Henri Poincaré, 1854-1912, (F.) mathematician, physicist, influenced cosmology, relativity, and topology.

Joseph Priestley, 1733-1804, (Br.) chemist, one of the discoverers of oxygen.

Rabi, Isidor Isaac, 1899-1988 (U.S.) physicist, pioneered atom exploration.

Walter S. Reed, 1851-1902, (U.S.) army pathologist, bacteriologist, proved mosquitos transmit yellow fever.

Bernhard Riemann, 1826-1866, (G.) mathematician, contributed to development of calculus, complex variable theory, and mathematical physics.

Wilhelm Roentgen, 1845-1923, (G.) physicist, discovered X-rays.

Bertrand Russell, 1872-1970, (Br.) logician, philosopher, one of the founders of modern logic, wrote *Principia Mathematica*.

Ernest Rutherford, 1871-1937, (Br.) physicist, discovered the atomic nucleus.

Giovanni Schiaparelli, 1835-1910, (It.) astronomer, hypothesized canals on the surface of Mars.

Angelo Secchi, 1818-1878, (It.) astronomer, pioneer in classifying stars by their spectra.

Harlow Shapley, 1885-1972, (U.S.) astronomer, noted for his studies of the galaxy.

Charles P. Steinmetz, 1865-1923, (G.-U.S.) electrical engineer, developed basic ideas on alternating current systems.

Leo Szilard, 1898-1964, (Hung.-U.S.) physicist, helped create first sustained nuclear reaction.

Nikola Tesla, 1856-1943, (Croatia-U.S.) electrical engineer, contributed to most developments in electronics.

Rudolf Virchow, 1821-1902, (G.) pathologist, a founder of cellular pathology.

Alessandro Volta, 1745-1827, (It.) physicist, pioneer in electricity.

Alfred Russell Wallace, 1823-1913, (Br.) naturalist, proposed concept of evolution similar to Darwin.

August v. Wasserman, 1866-1925, (G.) bacteriologist, discovered reaction used as test for syphilis.

James E. Watt, 1736-1819, (Sc.) mechanical engineer, inventor, invented modern steam condensing engine.

Alfred L. Wegener, 1880-1930, (G.) meteorologist, geophysicist, postulated theory of continental drift.

Norbert Wiener, 1894-1964, (U.S.) mathematician, founder of the science of cybernetics.

Sewall Wright, 1889-1988 (U.S.) a leading evolutionary theorist.

Ferdinand v. Zeppelin, 1838-1917 (G.) soldier, aeronaut, airship designer.

Noted Business Leaders, Industrialists, and Philanthropists of the Past

Elizabeth Arden (F.N. Graham), 1884-1966, (U.S.) Canadian-born founder of cosmetics empire.

Philip D. Armour, 1832-1901, (U.S.) industrialist, streamlined meat packing.

John Jacob Astor, 1763-1848, (U.S.) German-born fur trader, banker, real estate magnate; at death, richest in U.S.

Francis W. Ayer, 1848-1923, (U.S.) ad industry pioneer.

August Belmont, 1816-1890, (U.S.) German-born financier.

James B. (Diamond Jim) Brady, 1856-1917, (U.S.) financier, philanthropist, legendary bon vivant.

Adolphus Busch, 1839-1913, (U.S.) German-born businessman, established brewery empire.

Asa Candler, 1851-1929, (U.S.) founded Coca-Cola Co.

Andrew Carnegie, 1835-1919, (U.S.) Scots-born industrialist, founded U.S. Steel; financed over 2,800 libraries.

Tom Carvel, 1908-1989, (Gr.-U.S.) founded ice cream chain.

William Colgate, 1783-1857, (U.S.) British-born businessman, philanthropist; founded soap-making empire.

Jay Cooke, 1821-1905, (U.S.) financier, sold $1 billion in Union bonds during Civil War.

Peter Cooper, 1791-1883, (U.S.) industrialist, inventor, philanthropist.

Ezra Cornell, 1807-1874, (U.S.) businessman, philanthropist; headed Western Union, established univ.

Erastus Corning, 1794-1872, (U.S.) financier, headed N.Y. Central.

Charles Crocker, 1822-1888, (U.S.) railroad builder, financier.

Samuel Cunard, 1787-1865, (Can.) pioneered trans-Atlantic steam navigation.

Marcus Daly, 1841-1900, (U.S.) Irish-born copper magnate.

George T. Delacorte, 1893-1991, (U.S.) publisher; Central Park donations included Alice in Wonderland statue.

Walt Disney, 1901-1966, (U.S.) pioneer in cinema animation, built entertainment empire.

Herbert H. Dow, 1866-1930, (U.S.) Canadian-born founder of chemical co.

James Duke, 1856-1925, (U.S.) founded American Tobacco, Duke Univ.

Eleuthere I. du Pont, 1771-1834, (U.S.) French-born gunpowder manufacturer; founded one of world's largest business empires.

Thomas C. Durant, 1820-1885, (U.S.) railroad official, financier.

William C. Durant, 1861-1947, (U.S.) industrialist, formed General Motors.

George Eastman, 1854-1932, (U.S.) inventor, manufacturer of photographic equipment.

Marshall Field, 1834-1906, (U.S.) merchant, founded Chicago's largest department store.

Harvey Firestone, 1868-1938, (U.S.) industrialist, founded tire co.

Henry M. Flagler, 1830-1913, (U.S.) financier, helped form Standard Oil; developed Florida as resort state.

Malcolm Forbes, 1919-1990, (U.S.) *Fortune* publisher.

Henry Ford, 1863-1947, (U.S.) auto maker, developed first popular low-priced car.

Henry Ford 2d, 1917-1987, (U.S.) headed auto company founded by grandfather.

Henry C. Frick, 1849-1919, (U.S.) industrialist, helped organize U.S. Steel.

Jakob Fugger (Jakob the Rich), 1459-1525, (G.) headed leading banking house, trading concern, in 16th-century Europe.

Alfred C. Fuller, 1885-1973, (U.S.) Canadian-born businessman, founded brush co.

Elbert H. Gary, 1846-1927, (U.S.) U.S. Steel head, 1903-27.

Amadeo P. Giannini, 1870-1949, (U.S.) founded Bank of America.

Stephen Girard, 1750-1831, (U.S.) French-born financier, philanthropist; richest man in U.S. at his death.

Jean Paul Getty, 1892-1976, (U.S.) founded oil empire.

Jay Gould, 1836-1892, (U.S.) railroad magnate, financier, speculator.

Hetty Green, 1834-1916, (U.S.) financier, the "witch of Wall St."; richest woman in U.S. in her day.

William Gregg, 1800-1867, (U.S.) launched textile industry in the South.

Meyer Guggenheim, 1828-1905, (U.S.) Swiss-born merchant, philanthropist; built merchandising, mining empires.

Armand Hammer, 1898-1990, (U.S.) headed Occidental Petroleum; promoted U.S.-Soviet ties.

Edward H. Harriman, 1848-1909, (U.S.) railroad financier, administrator; headed Union Pacific.

William Randolph Hearst, 1863-1951, (U.S.) a dominant figure in American journalism; built vast publishing empire.

Henry J. Heinz, 1844-1919, (U.S.) founded food empire.

James J. Hill, 1838-1916, (U.S.) Canadian-born railroad magnate, financier; founded Great Northern Railway.

Conrad N. Hilton, 1888-1979, (U.S.) intl. hotel chain founder.

Howard Hughes, 1905-1976, (U.S.) industrialist, financier, movie maker.

H.L. Hunt, 1889-1974, (U.S.) oil magnate.

Collis P. Huntington, 1821-1900, (U.S.) railroad magnate.

Henry E. Huntington, 1850-1927, (U.S.) railroad builder, philanthropist.

Walter L. Jacobs, 1898-1985, (U.S.) founder of the first rental car agency, which later became Hertz.

Howard Johnson, 1896-1972, (U.S.) founded restaurants.

Henry J. Kaiser, 1882-1967, (U.S.) industrialist, built empire in steel, aluminum.

Minor C. Keith, 1848-1929, (U.S.) railroad magnate; founded United Fruit Co.

Will K. Kellogg, 1860-1951, (U.S.) businessman, philanthropist, founded breakfast food co.

Richard King, 1825-1885, (U.S.) cattleman, founded half-million acre King Ranch in Texas.

William S. Knudsen, 1879-1948, (U.S.) Danish-born auto industry executive.

Samuel H. Kress, 1863-1955, (U.S.) businessman, art collector, philanthropist; founded "dime store" chain.

Ray A. Kroc, 1902-1984, (U.S.) builder of McDonald's fast food empire; owner, San Diego Padres baseball team.

Alfred Krupp, 1812-1887, (G.) armaments magnate.

Albert Lasker, 1880-1952, (U.S.) businessman, philanthropist.

Thomas Lipton, 1850-1931, (Scot.) merchant, built tea empire.

James McGill, 1744-1813, (Can.) Scots-born fur trader, founded univ.

Andrew W. Mellon, 1855-1937, (U.S.) financier, industrialist; benefactor of National Gallery of Art.

Charles E. Merrill, 1885-1956, (U.S.) financier, developed firm of Merrill Lynch.

John Pierpont Morgan, 1837-1913, (U.S.) most powerful figure in finance and industry at the turn-of-the-century.

Malcolm Muir, 1885-1979, (U.S.) created *Business Week* magazine; headed *Newsweek*, 1937-61.

Samuel Newhouse, 1895-1979, (U.S.) publishing and broadcasting magnate, built communications empire.

Aristotle Onassis, 1900-1975, (Gr.) shipping magnate.

William S. Paley, 1901-1989, (U.S.) built CBS communications empire.

George Peabody, 1795-1869, (U.S.) merchant, financier, philanthropist.

James C. Penney, 1875-1971, (U.S.) businessman, developed department store chain.

William C. Procter, 1862-1934, (U.S.) headed soap co.

John D. Rockefeller, 1839-1937, (U.S.) industrialist, established Standard Oil; became world's wealthiest person.

John D. Rockefeller Jr., 1874-1960, (U.S.) philanthropist, established foundation; provided land for United Nations.

Meyer A. Rothschild, 1743-1812, (G.) founded international banking house.

Thomas Fortune Ryan, 1851-1928, (U.S.) financier, dominated N.Y. City public transport; a founder of Amer. Tobacco.

Russell Sage, 1816-1906, (U.S.) financier.

David Sarnoff, 1891-1971, (U.S.) broadcasting pioneer, established first radio network, NBC.

Richard W. Sears, 1863-1914, (U.S.) founded mail-order co.

(Ernst) Werner von Siemens, 1816-1892, (G.) industrialist, inventor.

Alfred P. Sloan, 1875-1966, (U.S.) industrialist, philanthropist; headed General Motors.

A. Leland Stanford, 1824-1893, (U.S.) railroad official, philanthropist; founded univ.

Nathan Strauss, 1848-1931, (U.S.) German-born merchant, philanthropist; headed Macy's.

Levi Strauss, c.1829-1902, (U.S.) pants manufacturer.

Clement Studebaker, 1831-1901, (U.S.) wagon, carriage manufacturer.

Gustavus Swift, 1839-1903, (U.S.) pioneer meat-packer; promoted refrigerated railroad cars.

Gerard Swope, 1872-1957, (U.S.) industrialist, economist; headed General Electric.

James Walter Thompson, 1847-1928, (U.S.) ad executive.

Theodore N. Vail, 1845-1920, (U.S.) organized Bell Telephone system, headed ATT.

Cornelius Vanderbilt, 1794-1877, (U.S.) financier, established steamship, railroad empires.

Henry Villard, 1835-1900, (U.S.) German-born railroad executive, financier.

Charles R. Walgreen, 1873-1939, (U.S.) founded drugstore chain.

DeWitt Wallace, 1890-1981, (U.S.) and **Lila Wallace,** 1890-1984, (U.S.) co-founders of *Reader's Digest* magazine, philanthropists.

John Wanamaker, 1838-1922, (U.S.) pioneered department-store merchandising.

Aaron Montgomery Ward, 1843-1913, (U.S.) established first mail-order firm.

Thomas J. Watson, 1874-1956, (U.S.) headed IBM, 1924-49.

John Hay Whitney, 1905-1982, (U.S.) publisher, sportsman, philanthropist.

Charles E. Wilson, 1890-1961, (U.S.) auto industry executive; public official.

Frank W. Woolworth, 1852-1919, (U.S.) created 5 & 10 chain.

William Wrigley Jr., 1861-1932, (U.S.) founded chewing gum company.

Composers of the Western World

Carl Philipp Emanuel Bach, 1714-1788, (G.) Prussian and Wurtembergian Sonatas.

Johann Christian Bach, 1735-1782, (G.) Concertos; sonatas.

Johann Sebastian Bach, 1685-1750, (G.) St. Matthew Passion, The Well-Tempered Clavichord.

Samuel Barber, 1910-1981, (U.S.) Adagio for Strings, Vanessa.

Bela Bartok, 1881-1945, (Hung.) Concerto for Orchestra, The Miraculous Mandarin.

Ludwig Van Beethoven, 1770-1827, (G.) Concertos (Emperor); sonatas (Moonlight, Pastorale, Pathetique); symphonies (Eroica).

Vincenzo Bellini, 1801-1835, (It.) La Sonnambula, Norma, I Puritani.

Alban Berg, 1885-1935, (Aus.) Wozzeck, Lulu.

Hector Berlioz, 1803-1869, (F.) Damnation of Faust, Symphonie Fantastique, Requiem.

Leonard Bernstein, 1918-1990, (U.S.) Jeremiah, West Side Story.

Georges Bizet, 1838-1875, (F.) Carmen, Pearl Fishers.

Ernest Bloch, 1880-1959, (Swiss-U.S.) Schelomo, Voice in the Wilderness, Sacred Service.

Luigi Boccherini, 1743-1805, (It.) Cello Concerto in B Flat, Symphony in C.

Alexander Borodin, 1833-1887, (R.) Prince Igor, In the Steppes of Central Asia.

Johannes Brahms, 1833-1897, (G.) Liebeslieder Waltzes, Rhapsody in E Flat Major, Opus 119 for Piano, Academic Festival Overture; symphonies; quartets.

Benjamin Britten, 1913-1976, (Br.) Peter Grimes, Turn of the Screw, Ceremony of Carols, War Requiem.

Anton Bruckner, 1824-1896, (Aus.) Symphonies (Romantic), Intermezzo for String Quintet.

Ferruccio Busoni, 1866-1924, (It.) Doctor Faust, Comedy Overture.

Dietrich Buxtehude, 1637-1707, (D.) Cantatas, trio sonatas.

William Byrd, 1543-1623, (Br.) Masses, sacred songs.

(Alexis-) Emmanuel Chabrier, 1841-1894, (Fr.) Le Roi Malgre Lui, Espana.

Gustave Charpentier, 1860-1956, (F.) Louise.

Frederic Chopin, 1810-1849, (P.) Polonaises, mazurkas, waltzes, etudes, nocturnes. Polonaise No. 6 in A Flat Major (Heroic); sonatas.

Aaron Copland, 1900-1990, (U.S.) Appalachian Spring.

(Achille-) Claude Debussy, 1862-1918, (F.) Pelleas et Melisande, La Mer, Prelude to the Afternoon of a Faun.

C.P. Leo Delibes, 1836-1891, (F.) Lakme, Coppelia, Sylvia.

Norman Dello Joio, b. 1913, (U.S.), Triumph of St. Joan, Psalm of David.

Gaetano Donizetti, 1797-1848, (It.) Elixir of Love, Lucia Di Lammermoor, Daughter of the Regiment.

Paul Dukas, 1865-1935, (Fr.) Sorcerer's Apprentice.

Antonin Dvorak, 1841-1904, (C.) Symphony in E Minor (From the New World).

Edward Elgar, 1857-1934, (Br.) Pomp and Circumstance.

Manuel de Falla, 1876-1946, (Sp.) La Vide Breve, El Amor Brujo.

Gabriel Faure, 1845-1924, (Fr.) Requiem, Ballade.

Friedrich von Flotow, 1812-1883, (G.) Martha.

Cesar Franck, 1822-1890, (Belg.) D Minor Symphony.

George Gershwin, 1898-1937, (U.S.) Rhapsody in Blue, American in Paris, Porgy and Bess.

Umberto Giordano, 1867-1948, (It.) Andrea Chenier.

Alexander K. Glazunoff, 1865-1936, (R.) Symphonies, Stenka Razin.

Mikhail Glinka, 1804-1857, (R.) Ruslan and Ludmilla.

Christoph W. Gluck, 1714-1787, (G.) Alceste, Iphigenie en Tauride.

Charles Gounod, 1818-1893, (F.) Faust, Romeo and Juliet.

Edvard Grieg, 1843-1907, (Nor.) Peer Gynt Suite, Concerto in A Minor.

George Frederick Handel, 1685-1759, (G., Br.) Messiah, Xerxes, Berenice.

Howard Hanson, 1896-1981, (U.S.) Symphonies No. 1 (Nordic) and 2 (Romantic).

Roy Harris, 1898-1979, (U.S.) Symphonies. Amer. Portraits.

Joseph Haydn, 1732-1809, (Aus.) Symphonies (Clock); oratorios; chamber music.

Paul Hindemith, 1895-1963, (U.S.) Mathis Der Maler.

Gustav Holst, 1874-1934, (Br.) The Planets.

Arthur Honegger, 1892-1955, (Swiss) Judith, Le Roi David, Pacific 231.

Alan Hovhaness, b. 1911, (U.S.) Symphonies, Magnificat.

Engelbert Humperdinck, 1854-1921, (G.) Hansel and Gretel.

Charles Ives, 1874-1954, (U.S.) Third Symphony.

Aram Khachaturian, 1903-1978, (Armen.) Gayane (ballet), symphonies.

Zoltan Kodaly, 1882-1967, (Hung.) Hary Janos, Psalmus Hungaricus.

Fritz Kreisler, 1875-1962, (Aus.) Caprice Viennois, Tambourin Chinois.

Rodolphe Kreutzer, 1766-1831, (F.) 40 etudes for violin.

Edouard V.A. Lalo, 1823-1892, (F.) Symphonie Espagnole.

Ruggiero Leoncavallo, 1857-1919, (It.) Pagliacci.

Franz Liszt, 1811-1886, (Hung.) 20 Hungarian rhapsodies; symphonic poems.

Edward MacDowell, 1861-1908, (U.S.) To a Wild Rose.

Gustav Mahler, 1860-1911, (Aus.) Lied von der Erde.

Pietro Mascagni, 1863-1945, (It.) Cavalleria Rusticana.

Jules Massenet, 1842-1912, (F.) Manon, Le Cid, Thais.

Felix Mendelssohn, 1809-1847, (G.) Midsummer Night's Dream, Songs Without Words.

Gian-Carlo Menotti, b. 1911, (It.-U.S.) The Medium, The Consul, Amahl and the Night Visitors.

Giacomo Meyerbeer, 1791-1864, (G.) Robert le Diable, Les Huguenots.

Claudio Monteverdi, 1567-1643, (It.) Opera; masses; madrigals.

Wolfgang Amadeus Mozart, 1756-1791, (Aus.) Magic Flute, Marriage of Figaro; concertos; symphonies, etc.

Modest Moussorgsky, 1835-1881, (R.) Boris Godunov, Pictures at an Exhibition.

Jacques Offenbach, 1819-1880, (F.) Tales of Hoffmann.

Carl Orff, 1895-1982, (G.) Carmina Burana.

Ignace Paderewski, 1860-1941, (P.) Minuet in G.

Niccolo Paganini, 1782-1840, (It.) Violinist, many bravura variations for violin.

Giovanni P. da Palestrina, c. 1525-1594, (It.) Masses; madrigals.

Amilcare Ponchielli, 1834-1886, (It.) La Gioconda.

Francis Poulenc, 1899-1963, (F.) Dialogues des Carmelites.

Serge Prokofiev, 1891-1953, (R.) Love for Three Oranges, Lt. Kije, Peter and the Wolf.

Giacomo Puccini, 1858-1924, (It.) La Boheme, Manon Lescaut, Tosca, Madame Butterfly.

Sergei Rachmaninov, 1873-1943, (R.) 24 preludes, 4 concerti, 4 symphonies. Prelude in C Sharp Minor.

Maurice Ravel, 1875-1937, (Fr.) Bolero, Daphnis et Chloe, Rapsodie Espagnole.

Nikolai Rimsky-Korsakov, 1844-1908, (R.) Golden Cockerel, Capriccio Espagnol, Scheherazade, Russian Easter Overture.

Gioacchino Rossini, 1792-1868, (It.) Barber of Seville, Semiramide, William Tell.

Chas. Camille Saint-Saens, 1835-1921, (F.) Samson and Delilah, Danse Macabre.

Alessandro Scarlatti, 1660-1725, (It.) Cantatas; concertos.

Domenico Scarlatti, 1685-1757, (It.) Harpsichord sonatas.

Arnold Schoenberg, 1874-1951, (Aus.) Pelleas and Melisande, Transfigured Night, De Profundis.

Franz Schubert, 1797-1828, (A.) Lieder; symphonies (Unfinished); overtures (Rosamunde).

William Schuman, b. 1910, (U.S.) Credendum, New England Triptych.

Robert Schumann, 1810-1856, (G.) Symphonies, songs.

Aleksandr Scriabin, 1872-1915, (R.) Prometheus.

Dimitri Shostakovich, 1906-1975, (R.) Symphonies, Lady Macbeth of Mzensk, The Nose.

Jean Sibelius, 1865-1957, (Finn.) Finlandia, Karelia.

Bedrich Smetana, 1824-1884, (Cz.) The Bartered Bride.

Karlheinz Stockhausen, b. 1928, (G.) Kontrapunkte, Kontakte.

Richard Strauss, 1864-1949, (G.) Salome, Elektra, Der Rosenkavalier, Thus Spake Zarathustra.

Igor F. Stravinsky, 1882-1971, (R.-U.S.) Oedipus Rex, Le Sacre du Printemps, Petrushka.

Peter I. Tchaikovsky, 1840-1893, (R.) Nutcracker Suite, Swan Lake, Eugene Onegin.

Ambroise Thomas, 1811-1896, (F.) Mignon.

Virgil Thomson, 1896-1989, (U.S.) Opera, ballet; Four Saints in Three Acts.

Ralph Vaughan Williams, 1872-1958, (Br.) Job, London Symphony, Symphony No. 7 (Antartica).

Giuseppe Verdi, 1813-1901, (It.) Aida, Rigoletto, Don Carlo, Il Trovatore, La Traviata, Falstaff, Macbeth.

Heitor Villa-Lobos, 1887-1959, (Brazil) Choros.

Antonio Vivaldi, 1678-1741, (It.) Concerti, The Four Seasons.

Richard Wagner, 1813-1883, (G.) Rienzi, Tannhauser, Lohengrin, Tristan and Isolde.

Carl Maria von Weber, 1786-1826, (G.) Der Freischutz.

Composers of Operettas, Musicals, and Popular Music

Richard Adler, b. 1921, (U.S.) *Pajama Game; Damn Yankees.*

Milton Ager, 1893-1979, (U.S.) I Wonder What's Become of Sally; Hard Hearted Hannah; Ain't She Sweet?

Leroy Anderson, 1908-1975, (U.S.) Syncopated Clock.

Paul Anka, b. 1941, (Can.) My Way; She's a Lady; Tonight Show theme.

Harold Arlen, 1905-1986, (U.S.) Stormy Weather; Over the Rainbow; Blues in the Night; That Old Black Magic.

Burt Bacharach, b. 1928, (U.S.) Raindrops Keep Fallin' on My Head; Walk on By; What the World Needs Now is Love.

Ernest Ball, 1878-1927, (U.S.) Mother Machree; When Irish Eyes Are Smiling.

Irving Berlin, 1888-1989 (U.S.) *This is the Army; Annie Get Your Gun; Call Me Madam;* God Bless America; White Christmas.

Leonard Bernstein, 1918-1990, (U.S.) *On the Town; Wonderful Town; Candide; West Side Story.*

Eubie Blake, 1883-1983, (U.S.) *Shuffle Along;* I'm Just Wild about Harry.

Jerry Bock, b. 1928, (U.S.) *Mr. Wonderful; Fiorello; Fiddler on the Roof; The Rothschilds.*

Carrie Jacobs Bond, 1862-1946, (U.S.) I Love You Truly.

Nacio Herb Brown, 1896-1964, (U.S.) Singing in the Rain; You Were Meant for Me; All I Do Is Dream of You.

Hoagy Carmichael, 1899-1981, (U.S.) Stardust; Georgia on My Mind; Old Buttermilk Sky.

George M. Cohan, 1878-1942, (U.S.) Give My Regards to Broadway; You're A Grand Old Flag; Over There.

Cy Coleman, b. 1929, (U.S.) *Sweet Charity; Witchcraft.*

Noel Coward, 1899-1973 (Br.) *Bitter Sweet;* Mad Dogs and Englishmen; Mad About the Boy.

Walter Donaldson, 1893-1947, (U.S.) My Buddy; Carolina in the Morning; You're Driving Me Crazy; Makin' Whoopee.

Neil Diamond, b. 1941, (U.S.) I'm a Believer; Sweet Caroline.

Vernon Duke, 1903-1969, (U.S.) April in Paris.

Bob Dylan, b. 1941, (U.S.) Blowin' in the Wind.

Gus Edwards, 1879-1945, (U.S.) School Days; By the Light of the Silvery Moon; In My Merry Oldsmobile.

Sherman Edwards, 1919-1981, (U.S.) See You in September; Wonderful! Wonderful!

Duke Ellington, 1899-1974, (U.S.) Sophisticated Lady; Satin Doll; It Don't Mean a Thing; Solitude.

Sammy Fain, 1902-1989, (U.S.) I'll Be Seeing You; Love Is a Many-Splendored Thing.

Fred Fisher, 1875-1942, (U.S.) Peg O' My Heart; Chicago.

Stephen Collins Foster, 1826-1864, (U.S.) My Old Kentucky Home; Old Folks At Home.

Rudolf Friml, 1879-1972, (naturalized U.S.) *The Firefly; Rose Marie; Vagabond King; Bird of Paradise.*

John Gay, 1685-1732, (Br.) *The Beggar's Opera.*

George Gershwin, 1898-1937, (U.S.) Someone to Watch Over Me; I've Got a Crush on You; Embraceable You.

Ferde Grofe, 1892-1972, (U.S.) Grand Canyon Suite.

Marvin Hamlisch, b. 1944, (U.S.) The Way We Were; Nobody Does It Better, *A Chorus Line.*

W. C. Handy, 1873-1958, (U.S.) St. Louis Blues.

Ray Henderson, 1896-1970, (U.S.) *George White's Scandals;* That Old Gang of Mine; Five Foot Two, Eyes of Blue.

Victor Herbert, 1859-1924, (Ir.-U.S.) *Mlle. Modiste; Babes in Toyland; The Red Mill; Naughty Marietta; Sweethearts.*

Jerry Herman, b. 1932, (U.S.) *Hello Dolly; Mame.*

Brian Holland, b. 1941, Lamont Dozier, b. 1941, Eddie Holland, b. 1939, (all U.S.) Heat Wave; Stop! In the Name of Love; Baby, I Need Your Loving.

Scott Joplin, 1868-1917, (U.S.) *Treemonisha.*

John Kander, b. 1927, (U.S.) *Cabaret; Chicago; Funny Lady.*

Jerome Kern, 1885-1945, (U.S.) *Sally; Sunny; Show Boat.*

Carole King, b. 1942, (U.S.) Will You Love Me Tomorrow?; Natural Woman; One Fine Day; Up on the Roof.

Burton Lane, b. 1912, (U.S.) *Finian's Rainbow.*

Franz Lehar, 1870-1948, (Hung.) *Merry Widow.*

Jerry Leiber & Mike Stoller, both b. 1933, (both U.S.) Hound Dog; Searchin'; Yakety Yak; Love Me Tender.

Mitch Leigh, b. 1928, (U.S.) *Man of La Mancha.*

John Lennon, 1940-1980, & Paul McCartney, b. 1942, (both Br.) I Want to Hold Your Hand; She Loves You; Hard Day's Night; Can't Buy Me Love; And I Love Her.

Frank Loesser, 1910-1969, (U.S.) *Guys and Dolls; Where's Charley?; The Most Happy Fella; How to Succeed . . . .*

Frederick Loewe, 1901-1988, (Aust.-U.S.) *The Day Before Spring; Brigadoon; Paint Your Wagon; My Fair Lady; Camelot.*

Henry Mancini, b. 1924, (U.S.) *Moon River; Days of Wine and Roses; Pink Panther Theme.*

Barry Mann, b. 1939, & **Cynthia Weil,** b. 1937, (both U.S.) You've Lost That Loving Feeling, Saturday Night at the Movies.

Jimmy McHugh, 1894-1969 (U.S.) *Don't Blame Me; I'm in the Mood for Love; I Feel a Song Coming On.*

Alan Menken, b. 1950, (U.S.) *Little Shop of Horrors.*

Joseph Meyer, 1894-1987, (U.S.) If You Knew Susie; California, Here I Come; Crazy Rhythm.

Chauncey Olcott, 1860-1932, (U.S.) *Mother Machree.*

Jerome "Doc" Pomus, 1926-1991, (U.S.) Save the Last Dance for Me, A Teenager in Love.

Cole Porter, 1893-1964, (U.S.) *Anything Goes; Kiss Me Kate; Can Can; Silk Stockings.*

Richard Rodgers, 1902-1979, (U.S.) *Connecticut Yankee; Oklahoma!; Carousel; South Pacific; The King and I; The Sound of Music.*

Smokey Robinson, b. 1940, (U.S.) Shop Around; My Guy; My Girl; Get Ready.

Sigmund Romberg, 1887-1951, (Hung.) *Maytime; The Student Prince; Desert Song; Blossom Time.*

Harold Rome, b. 1908, (U.S.) *Pins and Needles; Call Me Mister; Wish You Were Here; Fanny; Destry Rides Again.*

Vincent Rose. b. 1880-1944, (U.S.) *Avalon; Whispering; Blueberry Hill.*

Harry Ruby, 1895-1974, (U.S.) *Three Little Words; Who's Sorry Now?*

Arthur Schwartz, 1900-1984, (U.S.) *The Band Wagon; Dancing in the Dark; By Myself; That's Entertainment.*

Neil Sedaka, b. 1939, (U.S.) Breaking Up Is Hard to Do.

Paul Simon, b. 1942, (U.S.) Sounds of Silence; I Am a Rock; Mrs. Robinson; Bridge Over Troubled Waters.

Stephen Sondheim, b. 1930, (U.S.) *A Little Night Music; Company; Sweeney Todd; Sunday in the Park with George.*

John Philip Sousa. 1854-1932, (U.S.) *El Capitan;* Stars and Stripes Forever.

Oskar Straus, 1870-1954, (Aus.) *Chocolate Soldier.*

Johann Strauss, 1825-1899, (Aus.) *Gypsy Baron; Die Fledermaus;* waltzes: Blue Danube, Artist's Life.

Charles Strouse, b. 1928, (U.S.) *Bye Bye, Birdie; Annie.*

Jule Styne, b. 1905, (b. Br.-U.S.) *Gentlemen Prefer Blondes; Bells Are Ringing; Gypsy; Funny Girl.*

Arthur S. Sullivan, 1842-1900, (Br.) *H.M.S. Pinafore, Pirates of Penzance; The Mikado.*

Deems Taylor, 1885-1966, (U.S.) *Peter Ibbetson.*

Egbert van Alstyne, 1882-1951, (U.S.) In the Shade of the Old Apple Tree; Memories; Pretty Baby.

Jimmy Van Heusen, 1913-1990, (U.S.) Moonlight Becomes You; Swinging on a Star; All the Way; Love and Marriage.

Albert von Tilzer, 1878-1956, (U.S.) I'll Be With You in Apple Blossom Time; Take Me Out to the Ball Game.

Harry von Tilzer, 1872-1946, (U.S.) Only a Bird in a Gilded Cage; On a Sunday Afternoon.

Fats Waller, 1904-1943, (U.S.) Honeysuckle Rose; Ain't Misbehavin'.

Harry Warren, 1893-1981, (U.S.) You're My Everything; We're in the Money; I Only Have Eyes for You.

Jimmy Webb, b. 1946, (U.S.) Up, Up and Away; By the Time I Get to Phoenix; Didn't We?; Wichita Lineman.

Andrew Lloyd Webber, b. 1948, (Br.) *Jesus Christ Superstar, Evita, Cats, The Phantom of the Opera.*

Kurt Weill, 1900-1950, (G.-U.S.) *Threepenny Opera; Lady in the Dark; Knickerbocker Holiday; One Touch of Venus.*

Percy Wenrich, 1887-1952, (U.S.) When You Wore a Tulip; Moonlight Bay; Put On Your Old Gray Bonnet.

Richard A. Whiting, 1891-1938, (U.S.) Till We Meet Again; Sleepytime Gal; Beyond the Blue Horizon; My Ideal.

John Williams, b. 1932, (U.S.) *Jaws, E.T., Star Wars* series, *Raiders of the Lost Ark* series.

Meredith Willson, 1902-1984, (U.S.) *The Music Man.*

Stevie Wonder, b. 1950, (U.S.) You Are the Sunshine of My Life; Signed, Sealed, Delivered, I'm Yours.

Vincent Youmans, 1898-1946, (U.S.) *Two Little Girls in Blue; Wildflower; No, No, Nanette; Hit the Deck; Rainbow; Smiles.*

Lyricists

Howard Ashman, 1951-1991, (U.S.) *Little Shop of Horrors, The Little Mermaid.*

Johnny Burke, 1908-1984, (U.S.) What's New?; Misty; Imagination; Polka Dots and Moonbeams.

Sammy Cahn, b. 1913, (U.S.) High Hopes; Love and Marriage; The Second Time Around; It's Magic.

Betty Comden, b. 1919 (U.S.) and **Adolph Green,** b. 1915 (U.S.) The Party's Over; Just in Time; New York, New York.

Hal David, b. 1921 (U.S.) What the World Needs Now Is Love; Close to You.

Buddy De Sylva, 1895-1950, (U.S.) When Day is Done; Look for the Silver Lining; April Showers.

Howard Dietz, 1896-1983, (U.S.) Dancing in the Dark; You and the Night and the Music; That's Entertainment.

Al Dubin, 1891-1945, (U.S.) Tiptoe Through the Tulips; Anniversary Waltz; Lullaby of Broadway.

Fred Ebb, b. 1936 (U.S.) *Cabaret, Zorba, Woman of the Year.*

Dorothy Fields, 1905-1974, (U.S.) On the Sunny Side of the Street; Don't Blame Me; The Way You Look Tonight.

Ira Gershwin, 1896-1983, (U.S.) The Man I Love; Fascinating Rhythm; S'Wonderful; Embraceable You.

William S. Gilbert, 1836-1911, (Br.) *The Mikado; H.M.S. Pinafore, Pirates of Penzance.*

Gerry Goffin, b. 1939, (U.S.) Will You Love Me Tomorrow, Take Good Care of My Baby, Up on the Roof, One Fine Day.

Mack Gordon, 1905-1959, (Pol.-U.S.) You'll Never Know; The More I See You; Chattanooga Choo-Choo.

Oscar Hammerstein II, 1895-1960, (U.S.) *Ol' Man River; Oklahoma; Carousel.*

E. Y. (Yip) Harburg, 1898-1981, (U.S.) Brother, Can You Spare a Dime; April in Paris; Over the Rainbow.

Lorenz Hart, 1895-1943, (U.S.) Isn't It Romantic; Blue Moon; Lover; Manhattan; My Funny Valentine; Mountain Greenery.

DuBose Heyward, 1885-1940, (U.S.) Summertime; A Woman Is A Sometime Thing.

Gus Kahn, 1886-1941, (U.S.) Memories; Ain't We Got Fun.

Alan J. Lerner, 1918-1986, (U.S.) *Brigadoon; My Fair Lady; Camelot; Gigi; On a Clear Day You Can See Forever.*

Johnny Mercer, 1909-1976, (U.S.) Blues in the Night; Come Rain or Come Shine; Laura; That Old Black Magic.

Bob Merrill, b. 1921, (U.S.) People; Don't Rain on My Parade.

Jack Norworth, 1879-1959, (U.S.) Take Me Out to the Ball Game; Shine On Harvest Moon.

Mitchell Parish, b. 1901, (U.S.) Stairway to the Stars; Stardust.

Andy Razaf, 1895-1973, (U.S.) Honeysuckle Rose, Ain't Misbehavin', S'posin'.

Leo Robin, 1900-1984, (U.S.) Thanks for the Memory; Hooray for Love; Diamonds are a Girl's Best Friend.

Paul Francis Webster, 1907-1984, (U.S.) I Got It Bad and That Ain't Good, Secret Love, The Shadow of Your Smile, Love Is a Many-Splendored Thing.

Jack Yellen, 1892-1991, (U.S.) Down by the O-Hi-O; Ain't She Sweet; Happy Days Are Here Again.

Noted Jazz Artists

Jazz has been called America's only completely unique contribution to Western culture. The following individuals have made major contributions in this field:

Julian "Cannonball" Adderley, 1928-1975: alto sax.

Louis "Satchmo" Armstrong, 1900-1971: trumpet, singer; originated the "scat" vocal.

Mildred Bailey, 1907-1951: blues singer.

Chet Baker, 1929-1988: trumpet.

Count Basie, 1904-1984: orchestra leader, piano.

Sidney Bechet, 1897-1959: early innovator, soprano sax.

Bix Beiderbecke, 1903-1931: cornet, piano, composer.

Bunny Berigan, 1909-1942: trumpet, singer.

Barney Bigard, 1906-1980: clarinet.

Art Blakey, b. 1919: drums, leader.

Jimmy Blanton, 1921-1942: bass.

Charles "Buddy" Bolden, 1868-1931: cornet; formed the first jazz band in the 1890s.

Big Bill Broonzy, 1893-1958: blues singer, guitar.

Clifford Brown, 1930-1956: trumpet.

Ray Brown, b. 1926: bass.

Dave Brubeck, b. 1920: piano, combo leader.

Don Byas, 1912-1972: tenor sax.

Harry Carney, 1910-1974: baritone sax.

Benny Carter, b. 1907: alto sax, trumpet, clarinet.

Ron Carter, b. 1937: bass, cello.

Sidney Catlett, 1910-1951: drums.

Charlie Christian, 1919-1942: guitar.

Kenny Clarke, 1914-1985: pioneer of modern drums.

Buck Clayton, b. 1911: trumpet, arranger.

Al Cohn, 1925-1988: tenor sax, composer.

Cozy Cole, 1909-1981: drums.

Ornette Coleman, b. 1930: saxophone; unorthodox style.

John Coltrane, 1926-1967: tenor sax innovator.

Eddie Condon, 1904-1973: guitar, band leader; promoter of Dixieland.

Chick Corea, b. 1941: pianist, composer.

Tadd Dameron, 1917-1965: piano, composer.

Eddie "Lockjaw" Davis, 1921-1986: tenor sax.

Miles Davis, b. 1926: trumpet; pioneer of cool jazz.

Wild Bill Davison, 1906-1989: cornet, leader; prominent in early Chicago jazz.

Buddy De Franco, b. 1933: clarinet.

Paul Desmond, 1924-1977: alto sax.

Vic Dickenson, 1906-1984: trombone, composer.

Warren "Baby" Dodds, 1898-1959: Dixieland drummer.

Johnny Dodds, 1892-1940: clarinet.

Eric Dolphy, 1928-1964: alto sax, composer.

Jimmy Dorsey, 1904-1957: clarinet, alto sax; band leader.

Tommy Dorsey, 1905-1956: trombone; band leader.

Roy Eldridge, 1911-1989: trumpet, drums, singer.

Duke Ellington, 1899-1974: piano, band leader, composer.

Bill Evans, 1929-1980: piano.

Gil Evans, 1912-1988: composer, arranger, piano.

Ella Fitzgerald, b. 1918: singer.

"Red" Garland, 1923-1984; piano.

Erroll Garner, 1921-1977: piano, composer, "Misty."

Stan Getz, 1927-1991: tenor sax.

Dizzy Gillespie, b. 1917: trumpet, composer; bop developer.

Benny Goodman, 1909-1986: clarinet, band and combo leader.

Dexter Gordon, 1923-1990: tenor sax; bop-derived style.

Stephane Grappelli, b. 1908: violin.

Bobby Hackett, 1915-1976: trumpet, cornet.

Lionel Hampton, b. 1913: vibes, drums, piano, combo leader.

Herbie Hancock, b. 1940: piano, composer.

W. C. Handy, 1873-1958: composer, "St. Louis Blues."

Coleman Hawkins, 1904-1969: tenor sax; 1939 recording of "Body and Soul" a classic.

Roy Haynes, b. 1926: drums.

Fletcher Henderson, 1898-1952: orchestra leader, arranger; pioneered jazz and dance bands of the 30s.

Woody Herman, 1913-87: clarinet, alto sax, band leader.

Jay C. Higginbotham, 1906-1973: trombone.

Earl "Fatha" Hines, 1905-1983: piano, songwriter.

Johnny Hodges, 1906-1971: alto sax.

Billie Holiday, 1915-1959: blues singer, "Strange Fruit."

Sam "Lightnin' " Hopkins, 1912-1982: blues singer, guitar.

Mahalia Jackson, 1911-1972: gospel singer.

Milt Jackson, b. 1923: vibes, piano, guitar.

Illinois Jacquet, b. 1922: tenor sax.

Keith Jarrett, b. 1945: technically phenomenal pianist.

Blind Lemon Jefferson, 1897-1930: blues singer, guitar.

Bunk Johnson, 1879-1949: cornet, trumpet.

James P. Johnson, 1891-1955: piano, composer.

J. J. Johnson, b. 1924: trombone, composer.

Elvin Jones, b. 1927: drums.

Jo Jones, 1911-1985: drums.

Philly Joe Jones, 1923-1985: drums.

Quincy Jones, b. 1933: arranger.

Thad Jones, 1923-1986: trumpet, cornet.

Scott Joplin, 1868-1917: composer; "Maple Leaf Rag."

Stan Kenton, 1912-1979: orchestra leader, composer, piano.

Barney Kessel, b. 1923: guitar.

Lee Konitz, b. 1927: alto sax.

Gene Krupa, 1909-1973: drums, band and combo leader.

Scott LaFaro, 1936-1961: bass.

Huddie Ledbetter (Leadbelly), 1888-1949: blues singer, guitar.

John Lewis, b. 1920: composer, piano, combo leader.

Mel Lewis, 1929-1990: drummer, orchestra leader.

Jimmie Lunceford, 1902-1947: band leader, sax.

Herbie Mann, b. 1930: flute.

Wynton Marsalis, b. 1961: trumpet.

Jimmy McPartland, b. 1907: trumpet.

Marian McPartland, b. 1920: piano.

Glenn Miller, 1904-1944: trombone, dance band leader.

Charles Mingus, 1922-1979: bass, composer, band leader.

Thelonious Monk, 1920-1982: piano, composer, combo leader; a developer of bop.

Wes Montgomery, 1925-1968: guitar.

"Jelly Roll" Morton, 1885-1941: composer, piano, singer.

Bennie Moten, 1894-1935: piano; an early organizer of large jazz orchestras.

Gerry Mulligan, b. 1927: baritone sax, arranger, leader.

Turk Murphy, 1915-1987: trombone, band leader.

Theodore "Fats" Navarro, 1923-1950: trumpet.

Red Nichols, 1905-1965: cornet, combo leader.

Red Norvo, b. 1908: vibes, band leader.

Anita O'Day, b. 1919: singer.

King Oliver, 1885-1938: cornet, band leader; teacher of Louis Armstrong.

Sy Oliver, 1910-1988: Swing Era arranger, composer, conductor.

Kid Ory, 1886-1973: trombone, "Muskrat Ramble".

Charlie "Bird" Parker, 1920-1955: alto sax, composer; rated by many as the greatest jazz improviser.

Art Pepper, 1925-1982: alto sax.

Oscar Peterson, b. 1925: piano, composer, combo leader.

Oscar Pettiford, 1922-1960: a leading bassist in the bop era.

Bud Powell, 1924-1966: piano; modern jazz pioneer.

Tito Puente, b. 1923: band leader.

Sun Ra, b. 1915?: big band leader, pianist, composer.

Gertrude "Ma" Rainey, 1886-1939: blues singer.

Don Redman, 1900-1964: composer, arranger; pioneer in the evolution of the large orchestra.

Django Reinhardt, 1910-1953: guitar; Belgian gypsy, first European to influence American jazz.

Buddy Rich, 1917-1987: drums, band leader.

Max Roach, b. 1925: drums.

Sonny Rollins, b. 1929: tenor sax.

Frank Rosolino, 1926-1978: trombone.

Jimmy Rushing, 1903-1972: blues singer.

George Russell, b. 1923: composer, piano.

Pee Wee Russell, 1906-1969: clarinet.

Artie Shaw, b. 1910: clarinet, combo leader.

George Shearing, b. 1919: piano, composer.

Horace Silver, b. 1928: piano, combo leader.

Zoot Sims, 1925-1985: tenor, alto sax; clarinet.

Zutty Singleton, 1898-1975: Dixieland drummer.

Bessie Smith, 1894-1937: blues singer.

Clarence "Pinetop" Smith, 1904-1929: piano, singer; pioneer of boogie woogie.

Willie "The Lion" Smith, 1897-1973: stride style pianist.

Muggsy Spanier, 1906-1967: cornet, band leader.

Billy Strayhorn, 1915-67: composer, piano.

Sonny Stitt, 1924-1982: alto, tenor sax.

Art Tatum, 1910-1956: piano; technical virtuoso.

Billy Taylor, b. 1921: piano, composer.

Cecil Taylor, b. 1933: piano, composer.

Jack Teagarden, 1905-1964: trombone, singer.

Dave Tough, 1908-1948: drums.

Lennie Tristano, 1919-1978: piano, composer.

Joe Turner, 1911-1985: blues singer.

McCoy Tyner, b. 1938: piano, composer.

Sarah Vaughan, 1924-1990: singer.

Joe Venuti, 1904-1978: first great jazz violinist.

Thomas "Fats" Waller, 1904-1943: piano, singer, composer. "Ain't Misbehavin' ".

Dinah Washington, 1924-1963: singer.

Chick Webb, 1902-1939: band leader, drums.

Ben Webster, 1909-1973: tenor sax.

Paul Whiteman, 1890-1967: orchestra leader; a major figure in the introduction of jazz to a large audience.

Charles "Cootie" Williams, 1908-1985: trumpet, band leader.

Mary Lou Williams, 1914-1981: piano, composer.

Teddy Wilson, 1912-1986: piano, composer.

Kai Winding, 1922-1983: trombone, composer.

Jimmy Yancey, 1894-1951: piano.

Lester "Pres" Young, 1909-1959: tenor sax, composer: a bop pioneer.

Rock & Roll Notables

For more than a quarter of a century, rock & roll has been an important force in American popular culture. The following individuals or groups have made a significant impact. Next to each is an associated single record or record album.

Paula Abdul: "Forever Your Girl"

The Allman Brothers Band: "Ramblin' Man"

The Animals: "House of the Rising Sun"

Paul Anka: "Lonely Boy"

The Association: "Cherish"

Frankie Avalon: "Venus"

The Band: "The Weight"

The Beach Boys: "Surfin' U.S.A."

The Beatles: "Hey Jude"

The Bee Gees: "Stayin' Alive"

Pat Benatar: "Hit Me With Your Best Shot"

Chuck Berry: "Johnny B. Goode"

The Big Bopper: "Chantilly Lace"

Black Sabbath: "Paranoid"

Blind Faith: "Can't Find My Way Home"

Blondie: "Heart of Glass"

Blood, Sweat and Tears: "Spinning Wheel"
Bon Jovi: *Slippery When Wet*
Gary "U.S." Bonds: "Quarter to Three"
Booker T. and the MGs: "Green Onions"
Earl Bostic: "Flamingo"
David Bowie: "Let's Dance"
James Brown: "Papa's Got a Brand New Bag"
Jackson Browne: "Doctor My Eyes"
Buffalo Springfield: "For What It's Worth"
The Byrds: "Turn! Turn! Turn!"

Canned Heat: "Going Up the Country"
The Cars: "Shake It Up"
Tracy Chapman: "Fast Car"
Ray Charles: "Georgia on My Mind"
Chubby Checker: "The Twist"
Chicago: "Saturday in the Park"
Eric Clapton: "Layla"
The Coasters: "Yakety Yak"
Eddie Cochran: "Summertime Blues"
Phil Collins: "Another Day in Paradise"
Sam Cooke: "You Send Me"
Alice Cooper: "School's Out"
Elvis Costello: "Alison"
Cream: "Sunshine of Your Love"
Credence Clearwater Revival: "Proud Mary"
Crosby, Stills, Nash and Young: "Suite: Judy Blue Eyes"
The Crystals: "Da Doo Ron Ron"

Danny and the Juniors: "At the Hop"
Bobby Darin: "Splish Splash"
Spencer Davis Group: "Gimme Some Lovin' "
Bo Diddley: "Who Do You Love?"
Dion and the Belmonts: "A Teenager in Love"
Dire Straits: *Brothers in Arms*
Fats Domino: "Blueberry Hill"
The Doobie Brothers: "What a Fool Believes"
The Doors: "Light My Fire"
The Drifters: "Save the Last Dance for Me"
Duran Duran: "Hungry Like the Wolf"
Bob Dylan: "Like a Rolling Stone"

The Eagles: "Hotel California"
Earth, Wind and Fire: "Shining Star"
Emerson, Lake and Palmer: "From the Beginning"
The Eurythmics: "Sweet Dreams (Are Made of This)"
Everly Brothers: "Wake Up Little Susie"

Jose Feliciano: "Light My Fire"
The Five Satins: "In the Still of the Night"
Fleetwood Mac: *Rumours*
Dan Fogelberg: "Missing You"
The Four Seasons: "Sherry"
The Four Tops: "I Can't Help Myself"
Aretha Franklin: "Respect"

Marvin Gaye: "I Heard It through the Grapevine"
Grand Funk Railroad: "We're an American Band"
The Grateful Dead: "Truckin' "

Bill Haley and the Comets: "Rock Around the Clock"
Hall and Oates: "Rich Girl"
M.C. Hammer: "U Can't Touch This"
Jimi Hendrix: *Are You Experienced?*
Buddy Holly and the Crickets: "That'll Be the Day"
Whitney Houston: "The Greatest Love"

Janis Ian: "At Seventeen"
The Isley Brothers: "It's Your Thing"

The Jackson 5/The Jacksons: "ABC"
Janet Jackson: "Control"
Michael Jackson: "Beat It"
Tommy James & The Shondells: "Crimson and Clover"
Jay and the Americans: "This Magic Moment"
The Jefferson Airplane/Jefferson Starship: "White Rabbit"
Jethro Tull: *Aqualung*
Joan Jett: "I Love Rock n' Roll"
Billy Joel: "Uptown Girl"
Elton John: "Sad Songs"
Janis Joplin: "Me and Bobby McGee"

Chaka Khan: "I Feel for You"
B.B. King: "The Thrill Is Gone"
Carole King: *Tapestry*
The Kinks: "You Really Got Me"
Kiss: "Rock n' Roll All Night"
Gladys Knight and the Pips: "Midnight Train to Georgia"

Cyndi Lauper: "Girls Just Want to Have Fun"
Led Zeppelin: "Stairway to Heaven"

Brenda Lee: "I'm Sorry"
Huey Lewis and the News: *Sports*
Jerry Lee Lewis: "Whole Lotta Shakin' Going On"
Little Anthony and the Imperials: "Tears on My Pillow"
Little Richard: "Tutti Frutti"
Lovin Spoonful: "Do You Believe in Magic?"
Frankie Lymon: "Why Do Fools Fall in Love?"
Lynyrd Skynyrd: "Freebird"

Madonna: "Material Girl"
The Mamas and the Papas: "Monday, Monday"
Bob Marley: "Jamming"
Martha and the Vandellas: "Dancin' in the Streets"
The Marvelettes: "Please Mr. Postman"
Clyde McPhatter: "Money Honey"
John Cougar Mellencamp: "Hurt So Good"
George Michael: "I Want Your Sex"
Steve Miller Band: "Abracadabra"
Joni Mitchell: "Big Yellow Taxi"
The Monkees: "I'm a Believer"
Moody Blues: "Nights in White Satin"

Rick Nelson: "Hello Mary Lou"
Roy Orbison: "Oh Pretty Woman"

Carl Perkins: "Blue Suede Shoes"
Tom Petty and the Heartbreakers: "Refugee"
Pink Floyd: *Dark Side of the Moon*
Poco: *Deliverin'*
The Police: "Every Breath You Take"
Iggy Pop: "Lust for Life"
Elvis Presley: "Love Me Tender"
The Pretenders: *Learning to Crawl*
Lloyd Price: "Stagger Lee"
Prince: "Purple Rain"
Procul Harum: "A Whiter Shade of Pale"

Queen: "Bohemian Rhapsody"
The Rascals: "Good Lovin' "
Otis Redding: "The Dock of the Bay"
Lou Reed: "Walk on the Wild Side"
Righteous Brothers: "You've Lost that Lovin' Feeling"
Johnny Rivers: "Poor Side of Town"
Smokey Robinson and the Miracles: "Ooh Baby Baby"
The Rolling Stones: "Satisfaction"
The Ronettes: "Be My Baby"
Linda Ronstadt: "You're No Good"
Run D.M.C.: "Raisin' Hell"

Sam and Dave: "Soul Man"
Santana: "Black Magic Woman"
Neil Sedaka: "Breaking Up is Hard to Do"
Del Shannon: "Runaway"
The Shirelles: "Soldier Boy"
Simon and Garfunkel: "Bridge Over Troubled Water"
Carly Simon: "You're So Vain"
Sly and the Family Stone: "Everyday People"
Patti Smith: "Because the Night"
Southside Johnny and the Asbury Jukes: *This Time*
Dusty Springfield: "You Don't Have to Say You Love Me"
Bruce Springsteen: "Born in the U.S.A."
Steely Dan: "Rikki Don't Lose That Number"
Steppenwolf: "Born to Be Wild"
Rod Stewart: "Maggie Mae"
Sting: "If You Love Somebody, Set Them Free"
Donna Summer: "Bad Girls"
The Supremes: "Stop! In the Name of Love"

Talking Heads: "Wild Wild Life"
James Taylor: "You've Got a Friend"
The Temptations: "My Girl"
Three Dog Night: "Joy to the World"
Traffic: "Feelin' Alright"
Big Joe Turner: "Shake, Rattle & Roll"
Tina Turner: "What's Love Got to Do with It?"

U2: "With or Without You"
Van Halen: "Jump"

Dionne Warwick: "I'll Never Fall in Love Again"
Muddy Waters: "Rollin' Stone"'
Mary Wells: "My Guy"
The Who: "My Generation"
Jackie Wilson: "That's Why"
Stevie Wonder: "You Are the Sunshine of My Life"

The Yardbirds: "For Your Love"
Yes: "Owner of a Lonely Heart"
Frank Zappa/Mothers of Invention: *Sheik Yerbouti*

Entertainment Personalities — Where and When Born

Actors, Actresses, Dancers, Musicians, Producers, Radio-TV Performers, Singers
(As of Aug., 1991)

Name	Birthplace	Born	Name	Birthplace	Born
Abbado, Claudio	Milan, Italy	6/26/33	Astin, John	Baltimore, Md.	3/30/30
Abbott, George	Forestville, N.Y.	6/25/87	Atherton, William	New Haven, Conn.	7/30/47
Abdul, Paula	San Fernando, Cal.	6/19/62	Atkins, Chet	Luttrell, Tenn.	6/20/24
Abraham, F. Murray	Pittsburgh, Pa.	10/24/39	Attenborough, Richard	Cambridge, England	8/29/23
Acuff, Roy	Maynardville, Tenn.	9/15/03	Auberjonois, Rene.	New York, N.Y.	6/1/40
Adams, Don	New York, N.Y.	4/19/26	Aumont, Jean-Pierre	Paris, France	1/5/09
Adams, Edie	Kingston, Pa.	4/16/29	Austin, Patti	New York, N.Y.	8/10/48
Adams, Joey	New York, N.Y.	1/6/11	Autry, Alan	Shreveport, La.	7/31/-
Adams, Mason	New York, N.Y.	2/26/19	Autry, Gene	Tioga, Tex.	9/29/07
Adams, Maud	Lulea, Sweden	2/12/45	Avalon, Frankie	Philadelphia, Pa.	9/18/39
Adjani, Isabelle	W. Germany	6/27/55	Ax, Emmanuel	Lvov, USSR	6/8/49
Adler, Larry	Baltimore, Md.	2/10/14	Axton, Hoyt	Duncan, Okla.	3/25/38
Agutter, Jenny	London, England	12/20/52	Aykroyd, Dan	Ottawa, Ont.	7/1/52
Aiello, Danny	New York, N.Y.	6/20/33	Ayres, Lew	Minneapolis, Minn.	12/28/08
Aimee, Anouk	Paris, France	4/27/32	Aznavour, Charles	Paris, France	5/22/24
Akins, Claude	Nelson, Ga.	5/25/18			
Albanese, Licia	Bari, Italy	7/22/13	Bacall, Lauren	New York, N.Y.	9/16/24
Alberghetti, Anna Maria.	Pesaro, Italy	5/15/36	Bacon, Kevin	Philadelphia, Pa.	7/8/58
Albert, Eddie	Rock Island, Ill.	4/22/08	Baez, Joan	Staten Island, N.Y.	1/9/41
Albright, Lola	Akron, Oh.	7/20/24	Bain, Conrad	Lethbridge, Alta.	2/4/23
Alda, Alan	New York, N.Y.	1/28/36	Baio, Scott	Brooklyn, N.Y.	9/22/61
Alexander, Jane	Boston, Mass.	10/28/39	Baker, Anita	Toledo, Oh.	1/26/57
Alexander, Jason	Newark, N.J.	9/23/59	Baker, Carroll	Johnstown, Pa.	5/28/31
Allen, Debbie	Houston, Tex.	1/16/51	Baker, Joe Don	Groesbeck, Tex.	2/12/36
Allen, Joan	Rochelle, Ill.	8/20/56	Bakula, Scott	St. Louis, Mo.	10/9/-
Allen, Karen	Carrollton, Ill.	10/5/51	Baldwin, Alec	Massapequa, N.Y.	4/3/58
Allen, Mel	Birmingham, Ala.	2/14/13	Baldwin, William	Massapequa, N.Y.	1963
Allen, Nancy	New York, N.Y.	6/24/50	Ballard, Kaye	Cleveland, Oh.	11/20/26
Allen, Peter	Tenderfield, Australia.	2/10/44	Balsam, Martin	New York, N.Y.	11/4/19
Allen, Steve	New York, N.Y.	12/26/21	Bancroft, Anne	New York, N.Y.	9/17/31
Allen, Woody	Brooklyn, N.Y.	12/1/35	Banks, Jonathan	Washington, D.C.	1/31/47
Alley, Kirstie	Wichita, Kan.	1/12/55	Bannon, Jack	Los Angeles, Cal.	6/14/40
Allman, Gregg	Nashville, Tenn.	12/7/47	Barber, Red	Columbus, Miss.	2/17/08
Allyson, June	New York, N.Y.	10/7/17	Bardot, Brigitte	Paris, France	9/28/34
Alonso, Maria Conchita.	Cuba	1957	Barker, Bob	Darrington, Wash.	12/12/23
Alpert, Herb	Los Angeles, Cal.	3/31/35	Barkin, Ellen	New York, N.Y.	4/16/55
Altman, Robert	Kansas City, Mo.	2/20/25	Barr, Roseanne	Salt Lake City, Ut.	11/3/52
Ameche, Don	Kenosha, Wis.	5/31/08	Barrault, Jean-Louis.	Vesinet, France	9/8/10
Ames, Ed.	Boston, Mass.	7/9/27	Barrie, Barbara	Chicago, Ill.	5/23/31
Ames, Leon	Portland, Ind.	1/20/03	Barrie, Mona	London, England	12/18/09
Amos, John	Newark, N.J.	12/27/41	Barry, Gene	New York, N.Y.	6/14/19
Amsterdam, Morey	Chicago, Ill.	12/14/14	Bartholomew, Freddie	London, England	3/28/24
Anderson, Harry	Newport, R.I.	10/14/49	Barty, Billy	Millsboro, Pa.	10/25/24
Anderson, Ian	Dunfermline, Scotland	8/10/47	Baryshnikov, Mikhail	Riga, Latvia	1/28/48
Anderson, Judith	Adelaide, Australia	2/10/98	Basinger, Kim	Athens, Ga.	12/8/53
Anderson, Loni	St. Paul, Minn.	8/5/46	Bassey, Shirley	Cardiff, Wales.	1/8/37
Anderson, Lynn	Grand Forks, N.D.	9/26/47	Bateman, Jason	Rye, N.Y.	1/14/69
Anderson, Marian	Philadelphia, Pa.	2/17/02	Bateman, Justine	Rye, N.Y.	2/19/66
Anderson, Melissa Sue.	Berkeley, Cal.	9/26/62	Bates, Alan	Ailestree, England	2/17/34
Anderson, Richard	Long Branch, N.J.	8/8/26	Battle, Kathleen	Portsmouth, Oh.	
Anderson, Richard Dean	Minneapolis, Minn.	1/23/53	Baxter, Meredith	Los Angeles, Cal.	6/21/47
Andersson, Bibi	Stockholm, Sweden	11/11/35	Beal, John	Joplin, Mo.	8/13/09
Andress, Ursula	Bern, Switzerland	3/19/36	Bean, Orson	Burlington, Vt.	7/22/28
Andrews, Anthony	London, England	1948	Beasley, Allyce	New York, N.Y.	7/6/54
Andrews, Dana	Collins, Miss.	1/1/09	Beatty, Ned	Louisville, Ky.	7/6/37
Andrews, Julie	Walton, England	10/1/35	Beatty, Warren	Richmond, Va.	3/30/37
Andrews, Maxene	Minneapolis, Minn.	1/3/18	Beck, John	Chicago, Ill.	1/28/43
Andrews, Patty	Minneapolis, Minn.	2/16/20	Bedelia, Bonnie	New York, N.Y.	3/25/48
Anka, Paul	Ottawa, Ont.	7/30/41	Bee Gees		
Ann-Margret	Stockholm, Sweden	4/28/41	Gibb, Barry	Isle of Man, England	9/1/46
Anspach, Susan	New York, N.Y.	11/23/39	Gibb, Robin	" "	12/22/49
Ant, Adam	London, England	11/3/54	Gibb, Maurice	" "	12/22/49
Anton, Susan	Oak Glen, Cal.	10/12/50	Beery, Noah Jr.	New York, N.Y.	8/10/13
Applegate, Christina	Los Angeles, Cal.	11/25/62	Begley, Ed Jr.	Los Angeles, Cal.	9/16/49
Archer, Anne	Los Angeles, Cal.	8/25/50	Belafonte, Harry	New York, N.Y.	3/1/27
Arkin, Alan	New York, N.Y.	3/26/34	Bel Geddes, Barbara	New York, N.Y.	10/31/22
Arnaz, Desi Jr.	Los Angeles, Cal.	1/19/53	Bellamy, Ralph	Chicago, Ill.	6/17/04
Arnaz, Lucie	Hollywood, Cal.	7/17/51	Belmondo, Jean-Paul	Neuilly-sur-Seine, France	4/9/33
Arness, James	Minneapolis, Minn.	5/26/23	Belushi, Jim	Chicago, Ill.	6/15/54
Arnold, Eddy	Henderson, Tenn.	5/15/18	Benatar, Pat	Brooklyn, N.Y.	1/10/53
Arquette, Rosanna	New York, N.Y.	8/10/59	Benedict, Dirk	Helena, Mont.	3/1/45
Arroyo, Martina	New York, N.Y.	2/2/37	Bening, Annette	Topeka, Kan.	1958
Arthur, Beatrice	New York, N.Y.	5/13/26	Benjamin, Richard.	New York, N.Y.	5/22/38
Ashcroft, Peggy	Croyden, England	12/22/07	Bennett, Tony	New York, N.Y.	8/3/26
Ashley, Elizabeth	Ocala, Fla.	8/30/41	Benson, George	Pittsburgh, Pa.	3/22/43
Asner, Ed.	Kansas City, Mo.	11/15/29	Benson, Robby	Dallas, Tex.	1/21/55
Assante, Armand	New York, N.Y.	10/4/49	Beradino, John	Los Angeles, Cal.	5/1/17

Name	Birthplace	Born
Berenger, Tom	Chicago, Ill.	5/31/50
Bergen, Candice	Beverly Hills, Cal.	5/9/46
Bergen, Polly	Knoxville, Tenn.	7/14/30
Bergerac, Jacques	Biarritz, France	5/26/27
Bergman, Ingmar	Uppsala, Sweden	7/14/18
Berle, Milton	New York, N.Y.	7/12/08
Berlinger, Warren	Brooklyn, N.Y.	8/31/37
Berman, Lazar	Leningrad, USSR	2/26/30
Berman, Shelley	Chicago, Ill.	2/3/26
Bernsen, Corbin	No. Hollywood, Cal.	9/7/54
Berry, Chuck	St. Louis, Mo.	10/18/26
Berry, Ken	Moline, Ill.	11/3/33
Bertinelli, Valerie	Wilmington, Del.	4/23/60
Bikel, Theodore	Vienna, Austria	5/2/24
Birney, David	Washington, D.C.	4/23/39
Bishop, Joey	Bronx, N.Y.	2/3/18
Bisoglio, Val	New York, N.Y.	5/7/26
Bisset, Jacqueline	Weybridge, England	9/13/44
Bixby, Bill	San Francisco, Cal.	1/22/34
Black, Clint	Katy, Tex.	1962
Black, Karen	Park Ridge, Ill.	7/1/42
Blackstone Jr., Harry	Three Rivers, Mich.	6/30/34
Blades, Ruben	Panama	1948
Blaine, Vivian	Newark, N.J.	11/21/21
Blair, Linda	St. Louis, Mo.	1/22/59
Blake, Robert	Nutley, N.J.	9/18/33
Bledsoe, Tempestt	Chicago, Ill.	8/1/73
Bloom, Claire	London, England	2/15/31
Blyth, Ann	Mt. Kisco, N.Y.	8/16/28
Bochco, Steven	New York, N.Y.	12/16/43
Bogarde, Dirk	London, England	3/28/20
Bogdanovich, Peter	Kingston, N.Y.	7/30/39
Bonet, Lisa	San Francisco, Cal.	11/16/67
Bonham-Carter, Helena	London, England	5/26/66
Bon Jovi, Jon	Sayreville, N.J.	3/2/61
Bono, Sonny	Detroit, Mich.	2/16/35
Booke, Sorrell	Buffalo, N.Y.	1/4/30
Boone, Debby	Hackensack, N.J.	9/22/56
Boone, Pat	Jacksonville, Fla.	6/1/34
Booth, Shirley	New York, N.Y.	8/30/07
Borge, Victor	Copenhagen, Denmark	1/3/09
Borgnine, Ernest	Hamden, Conn.	1/24/17
Bosco, Philip	Jersey City, N.J.	9/26/30
Bosley, Tom	Chicago, Ill.	10/1/27
Bosson, Barbara	Charleroi, Pa.	11/1/39
Bostwick, Barry	San Mateo, Cal.	2/24/46
Bottoms, Joseph	Santa Barbara, Cal.	4/22/54
Bottoms, Timothy	Santa Barbara, Cal.	8/30/51
Boucher, Hart	Toronto, Ont.	12/3/56
Bowie, David	London, England	1/8/47
Boxleitner, Bruce	Elgin, Ill.	5/12/50
Boy George	London, England	6/14/61
Boyle, Peter	Philadelphia, Pa.	10/18/33
Bracco, Lorraine	New York, N.Y.	1955
Bracken, Eddie	New York, N.Y.	2/7/20
Branagh, Kenneth	Belfast, No. Ireland	1961
Brand, Neville	Kewanee, Ill.	8/13/21
Brando, Marlon	Omaha, Neb.	4/3/24
Brazzi, Rossano	Bologna, Italy	9/18/16
Brendel, Alfred	Wiesenberg, Austria	1/5/31
Brennan, Eileen	Los Angeles, Cal.	9/3/35
Brenner, David	Philadelphia, Pa.	2/4/45
Brewer, Teresa	Toledo, Oh.	5/7/31
Bridges, Beau	Hollywood, Cal.	12/9/41
Bridges, Jeff	Los Angeles, Cal.	12/4/49
Bridges, Lloyd	San Leandro, Cal.	1/15/13
Brimley, Wilford	Salt Lake City, Ut.	9/27/34
Broderick, Matthew	New York, N.Y.	3/21/62
Brolin, James	Los Angeles, Cal.	7/18/40
Bronson, Charles	Ehrenfeld, Pa.	11/3/22
Brooks, Albert	Beverly Hills, Cal.	7/22/47
Brooks, Avery	Evansville, Ind.	10/2/-
Brooks, Garth	Tulsa, Okla.	2/7/62
Brooks, Mel	New York, N.Y.	6/28/26
Brooks, Stephen	Columbus, Oh.	1942
Brosnan, Pierce	Co. Meath, Ireland	5/15/53
Brown, Blair	Washington, D.C.	1948
Brown, Bryan	Australia	1947
Brown, James	Pulaski, Tenn.	6/17/28
Brown, Jim	St. Simons Island, Ga.	2/17/36
Brown, Les	Reinerton, Pa.	3/14/12
Brown, Ray	Pittsburgh, Pa.	10/13/26
Browne, Roscoe Lee	Woodbury, N.J.	5/2/25
Bryant, Anita	Barnsdall, Okla.	3/25/40
Buckley, Betty	Ft. Worth, Tex.	7/3/47
Bujold, Genevieve	Montreal, Que.	7/1/42
Bumbry, Grace	St. Louis, Mo.	1/4/37
Burghoff, Gary	Bristol, Conn.	5/24/40
Burke, Delta	Orlando, Fla.	7/30/56
Burke, Paul	New Orleans, La.	7/21/26
Burnett, Carol	San Antonio, Tex.	4/26/33
Burns, George	New York, N.Y.	1/20/96
Burr, Raymond	New Westminster, B.C.	5/21/17
Burstyn, Ellen	Detroit, Mich.	12/7/32
Burton, LeVar	Landsthul, W. Germany	2/16/57
Busey, Gary	Goose Creek, Tex.	6/29/44
Busfield, Timothy	Lansing, Mich.	6/12/57
Butkus, Dick	Chicago, Ill.	12/9/42
Button, Dick	Englewood, N.J.	7/18/29
Buttons, Red	New York, N.Y.	2/5/19
Buzzi, Ruth	Westerly, R.I.	7/24/36
Byrne, David	Dumbarton, Scotland.	5/14/52
Caan, James	New York, N.Y.	3/26/39
Caballe, Montserrat	Barcelona, Spain	4/12/33
Caesar, Sid	Yonkers, N.Y.	9/8/22
Cage, Nicolas	Long Beach, Cal.	1/7/64
Caine, Michael	London, England	3/14/33
Caldwell, Sarah	Maryville, Mo.	3/6/24
Caldwell, Zoe	Melbourne, Australia	9/14/33
Calhoun, Rory	Los Angeles, Cal.	8/8/23
Callas, Charlie	Brooklyn, N.Y.	12/20/-
Calloway, Cab	Rochester, N.Y.	12/25/07
Cameron, Kirk	Panorama City, Cal.	10/12/70
Camp, Hamilton	London, England	10/30/34
Campanella, Joseph	New York, N.Y.	11/21/27
Campbell, Glen	Billstown, Ark.	4/22/36
Candy, John	Toronto, Ont.	10/31/50
Cannell, Stephen J.	Los Angeles, Cal.	2/5/42
Cannon, Dyan	Tacoma, Wash.	1/4/37
Cantrell, Lana	Sydney, Australia.	8/7/43
Capra, Frank	Palermo, Italy	5/18/97
Cara, Irene	New York, N.Y.	3/18/59
Carey, Macdonald	Sioux City, Ia.	3/15/13
Carey, Mariah	Huntington, N.Y.	1970
Cariou, Len	Winnipeg, Canada	9/30/39
Carle, Frankie	Providence, R.I.	3/25/03
Carlin, George	New York, N.Y.	5/12/38
Carlisle, Kitty	New Orleans, La	9/3/15
Carmen, Eric	Cleveland, Oh.	8/11/49
Carmichael, Ian	Hull, England	6/18/20
Carnes, Kim	California	7/20/45
Carney, Art	Mt. Vernon, N.Y.	11/4/18
Carnovsky, Morris	St. Louis, Mo.	9/5/97
Caron, Leslie	Boulogne, France.	7/1/31
Carpenter, John	Carthage, N.Y.	1/16/48
Carr, Vikki	El Paso, Tex.	7/19/41
Carradine, David	Hollywood, Cal.	10/8/36
Carradine, Keith	San Mateo, Cal.	8/8/49
Carreras, Jose	Barcelona, Spain	12/5/47
Carroll, Diahann	Bronx, N.Y.	7/17/35
Carroll, Pat	Shreveport, La.	5/5/27
Carson, Johnny	Corning, Ia.	10/23/25
Carter, Dixie	McLemoresville, Tenn.	5/25/39
Carter, Jack	New York, N.Y.	6/24/23
Carter, June	Maces Spring, Va.	6/23/29
Carter, Lynda	Phoenix, Ariz.	7/24/51
Carter, Nell	Birmingham, Ala.	9/13/48
Carvey, Dana	Missoula, Mont.	6/6/55
Casadesus, Gaby	Marseilles, France	1902
Cash, Johnny	Kingsland, Ark.	2/26/32
Cash, Rosanne	Memphis, Tenn.	5/24/55
Cass, Peggy	Boston, Mass.	5/21/24
Cassidy, David	New York, N.Y.	4/12/50
Cassidy, Shaun	Los Angeles, Cal.	9/27/58
Cates, Phoebe	New York, N.Y.	1964
Cavallaro, Carmen	New York, N.Y.	5/6/13
Cavett, Dick	Gibbon, Neb.	11/19/36
Chamberlain, Richard.	Beverly Hills, Cal..	3/31/35
Champion, Marge	Los Angeles, Cal.	9/2/23
Channing, Carol	Seattle, Wash.	1/31/23
Channing, Stockard	New York, N.Y.	2/13/44
Chaplin, Geraldine	Santa Monica, Cal.	7/31/44
Chapman, Tracy	Cleveland, OH.	1965
Charisse, Cyd	Amarillo, Tex.	3/8/21
Charles, Ray	Albany, Ga.	9/23/30
Charo	Murcia, Spain	1/15/51
Chase, Chevy	New York, N.Y.	10/8/43
Checker, Chubby	Philadelphia, Pa.	10/3/41
Cher	El Centro, Cal.	5/20/46
Chong, Rae Dawn	California	1961
Chong, Thomas	Edmonton, Alta.	5/24/38
Christie, Julie	Assam, India	4/14/40
Christopher, William	Evanston, Ill.	10/20/32
Clapton, Eric	Surrey, England.	3/30/45
Clark, Dane	New York, N.Y.	2/18/13
Clark, Dick	Mt. Vernon, N.Y.	11/30/29

Name	Birthplace	Born
Clark, Petula	Ewell, Surrey, England	11/15/32
Clark, Roy	Meherrin, Va.	4/15/33
Clark, Susan	Sarnia, Ont.	3/8/40
Clary, Robert	Paris, France	3/1/26
Clayburgh, Jill	New York, N.Y.	4/30/44
Cleese, John	England	10/27/39
Cliburn, Van	Shreveport, La.	7/12/34
Clooney, Rosemary	Maysville, Ky.	5/23/28
Close, Glenn	Greenwich, Conn.	3/19/47
Coburn, James	Laurel, Neb.	8/31/28
Coca, Imogene	Philadelphia, Pa.	11/18/08
Cohn, Mindy	Los Angeles, Cal.	5/20/66
Colbert, Claudette	Paris, France	9/18/05
Cole, Gary	Park Ridge, Ill.	9/20/57
Cole, Natalie	Los Angeles, Cal.	2/6/50
Cole, Olivia	Memphis, Tenn.	11/26/42
Coleman, Dabney	Austin, Tex.	1/3/32
Coleman, Gary	Zion, Ill.	2/8/68
Collins, Joan	London, England	5/23/33
Collins, Judy	Seattle, Wash.	5/1/39
Collins, Pauline	Exmouth, England	9/3/40
Collins, Phil	London, England	1/30/51
Comden, Betty	Brooklyn, N.Y.	5/3/19
Como, Perry	Canonsburg, Pa.	5/18/12
Conner, Nadine	Compton, Cal.	2/20/13
Connery, Sean	Edinburgh, Scotland	8/25/30
Connick Jr., Harry	New Orleans, La.	1967
Conniff, Ray	Attleboro, Mass.	11/6/16
Connors, Chuck	Brooklyn, N.Y.	4/10/21
Connors, Mike	Fresno, Cal.	8/15/25
Conrad, Robert	Chicago, Ill.	3/1/35
Conrad, William	Louisville, Ky.	9/27/20
Constantine, Michael	Reading, Pa.	5/22/27
Conti, Tom	Paisley, Scotland	11/22/41
Conway, Tim	Willoughby, Oh.	12/15/33
Cook, Barbara	Atlanta, Ga.	10/25/27
Cook, Peter	Torquay, England.	11/17/37
Cooke, Alistair	Manchester, England.	11/20/08
Coolidge, Rita	Nashville, Tenn.	5/1/45
Cooper, Alice	Detroit, Mich.	2/4/48
Cooper, Jackie	Los Angeles, Cal.	9/15/21
Copperfield, David	Metuchen, N.J.	9/16/56
Coppola, Francis	Detroit, Mich.	4/7/39
Corby, Ellen	Racine, Wis.	6/3/13
Cord, Alex	New York, N.Y.	8/3/31
Corea, Chick	Chelsea, Mass.	6/12/41
Corelli, Franco	Ancona, Italy	4/8/23
Corey, Jeff	New York, N.Y.	8/10/14
Cosby, Bill	Philadelphia, Pa.	7/12/37
Costas, Bob	New York, N.Y.	3/22/52
Costello, Elvis	London, England	8/25/54
Costner, Kevin	Los Angeles, Cal.	1/18/55
Cotten, Joseph	Petersburg, Va.	5/15/05
Cougar, John	Seymour, Ind.	10/7/51
Courtenay, Tom	Hull, England	2/25/37
Cox, Ronny	Cloudcroft, N.M.	8/23/38
Craddock, Crash	Greensboro, N.C.	6/16/40
Crain, Jeanne	Barstow, Cal.	5/25/25
Crawford, Michael	Salisbury, England	1/19/42
Crenna, Richard	Los Angeles, Cal.	11/30/26
Crespin, Regine	Marseilles, France	2/23/26
Cronyn, Hume	London, Ont.	7/18/11
Crosby, Bob	Spokane, Wash.	8/23/13
Crosby, David	Los Angeles, Cal.	8/14/41
Crosby, Norm	Boston, Mass.	9/15/27
Cross, Ben	London, England	12/16/47
Crouse, Lindsay	New York, N.Y.	5/12/48
Crowell, Rodney	Houston, Tex.	8/17/50
Cruise, Tom	Syracuse, N.Y.	7/3/62
Crystal, Billy	Long Beach, N.Y.	3/14/47
Cullum, John	Knoxville, Tenn.	3/2/30
Culp, Robert	Oakland, Cal.	8/16/30
Cummings, Constance	Seattle, Wash.	5/15/10
Curtin, Jane	Cambridge, Mass.	9/6/47
Curtis, Jamie Lee	Los Angeles, Cal.	11/22/58
Curtis, Keene	Salt Lake City, Ut.	2/15/23
Curtis, Tony	New York, N.Y.	6/3/25
Cusack, Cyril	Durban, S. Africa	11/26/10
Cusack, Joan	Evanston, Ill.	10/11/62
Cusack, John	Chicago, Ill.	6/28/66
Cushing, Peter	Surrey, England.	5/26/13
Dafoe, Willem	Appleton, Wis.	7/22/55
Dahl, Arlene	Minneapolis, Minn.	8/11/28
Dale, Jim	Rothwell, England	8/15/35
Dalton, Abby	Las Vegas, Nev.	8/15/32
Dalton, Timothy	Wales	3/21/44
Daltrey, Roger	London, England	3/1/44
Daly, Tyne	Madison, Wis.	2/21/47

Name	Birthplace	Born
Damone, Vic	Brooklyn, N.Y.	6/12/28
D'Angelo, Beverly	Columbus, Oh.	1954
Dangerfield, Rodney	Babylon, N.Y.	11/22/22
Daniels, Charlie	Wilmington, N.C.	10/28/36
Daniels, Jeff	Georgia	1955
Daniels, William	Brooklyn, N.Y.	3/31/27
Danner, Blythe	Philadelphia, Pa.	2/3/44
Danson, Ted	San Diego, Cal.	12/29/47
Danza, Tony	New York, N.Y.	4/21/50
Darby, Kim	Hollywood, Cal.	7/8/48
D'Arby, Terence Trent	New York, N.Y.	3/15/62
Darren, James	Philadelphia, Pa.	6/8/36
Davidson, John	Pittsburgh, Pa.	12/13/41
Davis, Ann B.	Schenectady, N.Y.	5/5/26
Davis, Clifton	Chicago, Ill.	10/4/45
Davis, Geena	Ware, Mass.	1/21/57
Davis, Judy	Perth, Australia	1956
Davis, Mac	Lubbock, Tex.	1/21/42
Davis, Ossie	Cogdell, Ga.	12/18/17
Davis, Skeeter	Dry Ridge, Ky.	12/30/31
Dawber, Pam	Farmington Hills, Mich.	10/18/51
Dawson, Richard	Hampshire, England	11/20/32
Day, Doris	Cincinnati, Oh.	4/3/24
Day, Laraine	Roosevelt, Ut.	10/13/20
Day-Lewis, Daniel	England	4/29/58
Dean, Jimmy	Plainview, Tex.	8/10/28
De Camp, Rosemary	Prescott, Ariz.	11/14/10
DeCarlo, Yvonne	Vancouver, B.C.	9/1/22
Dee, Frances	Los Angeles, Cal.	11/26/07
Dee, Ruby	Cleveland, Oh.	10/27/23
Dee, Sandra	Bayonne, N.J.	4/23/42
Defore, Don	Cedar Rapids, Ia.	8/25/17
DeHaven, Gloria	Los Angeles, Cal.	7/23/25
De Havilland, Olivia	Tokyo, Japan	7/1/16
Delany, Dana	New York, N.Y.	3/13/56
Della Chiesa, Vivienne	Chicago, Ill.	10/9/20
Delon, Alain	Sceaux, France.	11/8/35
DeLuise, Dom	Brooklyn, N.Y.	8/1/33
De Mille, Agnes	New York, N.Y.	9/18/05
De Mornay, Rebecca	Santa Rosa, Cal.	1962
Deneuve, Catherine	Paris, France	10/22/43
De Niro, Robert	New York, N.Y.	8/17/43
Dennehy, Brian	Bridgeport, Conn.	7/9/38
Dennis, Sandy	Hastings, Neb.	4/27/37
Denver, Bob	New Rochelle, N.Y.	1/9/35
Denver, John	Roswell, N.M.	12/31/43
DePalma, Brian	Newark, N.J.	9/11/40
Depardieu, Gerard	Chateauroux, France.	12/27/48
Depp, Johnny	Owensboro, KY.	6/9/63
Derek, Bo	Long Beach, Cal.	11/20/56
Derek, John	Hollywood, Cal.	8/12/26
Dern, Bruce	Chicago, Ill.	6/4/36
Dern, Laura	Los Angeles, Cal.	1966
Devane, William	Albany, N.Y.	9/5/37
DeVito, Danny	Neptune, N.J.	11/17/44
DeWitt, Joyce	Wheeling, W.Va.	4/23/49
Dey, Susan	Pekin, Ill.	12/10/52
Diamond, Neil	Brooklyn, N.Y.	1/24/41
Dickinson, Angie	Kulm, N.D.	9/30/31
Diddley, Bo	McComb, Miss.	12/20/28
Dietrich, Marlene	Berlin, Germany	12/27/01
Diller, Phyllis	Lima, Oh.	7/17/17
Dillman, Bradford	San Francisco, Cal.	4/14/30
Dillon, Matt	New Rochelle, N.Y.	2/18/64
Dixon, Ivan	New York, N.Y.	4/6/31
Dobson, Kevin	New York, N.Y.	3/18/44
Domingo, Placido	Madrid, Spain	1/21/41
Domino, Fats	New Orleans, La.	2/26/28
Donahue, Phil	Cleveland, Oh.	12/21/35
Donahue, Troy	New York, N.Y.	1/27/36
Donovan	Glasgow, Scotland	5/10/43
Dotrice, Roy	Guernsey, England	5/26/23
Douglas, Kirk	Amsterdam, N.Y.	12/9/18
Douglas, Michael	New Brunswick, N.J.	9/25/44
Douglas, Mike	Chicago, Ill.	8/11/25
Down, Leslie-Ann	London, England	3/17/54
Downey, Robert Jr.	New York, N.Y.	4/4/65
Downs, Hugh	Akron, Oh.	2/14/21
Doyle, David	Lincoln, Neb.	12/1/29
Dragon, Daryl	Los Angeles, Cal.	8/27/42
Drake, Alfred	Bronx, N.Y.	10/7/14
Drake, Larry	Tulsa, Okla.	2/21/-
Drew, Ellen	Kansas City, Mo.	11/23/15
Dryer, Fred	Hawthorne, Cal.	7/6/46
Dreyfuss, Richard	Brooklyn, N.Y.	10/29/47
Dru, Joanne	Logan, W.Va.	1/31/23
Duchin, Peter	New York, N.Y.	7/28/37
Duffy, Julia	Minneapolis, Minn.	6/27/51

Name	Birthplace	Born
Duffy, Patrick	Townsend, Mont.	3/17/49
Dufour, Val	New Orleans, La.	2/5/27
Dukakis, Olympia	Lowell, Mass.	6/20/31
Duke, Patty	New York, N.Y.	12/14/46
Dukes, David	San Francisco, Cal.	6/6/45
Dullea, Keir	Cleveland, Oh.	5/30/36
Dunaway, Faye	Bascom, Fla.	1/14/41
Duncan, Sandy	Henderson, Tex.	2/20/46
Dunham, Katherine	Joliet, Ill.	6/22/10
Dunn, Nora	Chicago, Ill.	4/29/52
Dunne, Griffin	California	6/8/55
Durbin, Deanna	Winnipeg, Man.	12/4/21
Durning, Charles	Highland Falls, N.Y.	2/28/23
Dussault, Nancy	Pensacola, Fla.	6/30/36
Duvall, Robert	San Diego, Cal.	1/5/31
Duvall, Shelley	Houston, Tex.	7/7/49
Dylan, Bob	Duluth, Minn.	5/24/41
Dysart, Richard	Augusta, Me.	3/30/-
Dzundza, George	Rosenheim, Germany	7/19/45
Easton, Sheena	Bellshill, Scotland.	4/27/59
Eastwood, Clint	San Francisco, Cal.	5/31/30
Ebert, Roger	Urbana, Ill.	6/18/42
Ebsen, Buddy	Belleville, Ill.	4/2/08
Eckstine, Billy	Pittsburgh, Pa.	7/8/14
Edelman, Herb.	Brooklyn, N.Y.	11/5/33
Eden, Barbara	Tucson, Ariz.	8/23/34
Edwards, Anthony	Santa Barbara, Cal.	1/19/62
Edwards, Blake	Tulsa, Okla.	7/26/22
Edwards, Ralph	Merino, Col.	6/13/13
Eggar, Samantha	London, England	3/5/39
Eichhorn, Lisa	Reading, Pa.	2/4/52
Eikenberry, Jill	New Haven, Conn.	1/21/47
Ekberg, Anita	Malmo, Sweden	9/29/31
Ekland, Britt	Stockholm, Sweden	10/6/42
Elam, Jack	Miami, Ariz.	11/13/16
Elizondo, Hector	New York, N.Y.	12/22/36
Elliott, Bob	Boston, Mass.	3/26/23
Elliott, Denholm	London, England	5/31/22
Elliott, Sam	Sacramento, Cal.	8/9/44
Elvira (Cassandra Peterson)	Manhattan, Kan.	9/17/51
Estefan, Gloria	Cuba	9/1/57
Estevez, Emilio	New York, N.Y.	5/12/62
Estrada, Erik	New York, N.Y.	3/16/49
Evans, Dale	Uvalde, Tex.	10/31/12
Evans, Gene	Holbrook, Ariz.	7/11/24
Evans, Linda	Hartford, Conn.	11/18/42
Evans, Robert	New York, N.Y.	6/29/30
Everett, Chad	South Bend, Ind.	6/11/36
Everly, Don.	Brownie, Ky.	2/1/37
Everly, Phil	Chicago, Ill.	1/19/38
Evigan, Greg	S. Amboy, N.J.	10/14/53
Ewell, Tom	Owensboro, Ky.	4/29/09
Fabares, Shelley	Santa Monica, Cal.	1/19/42
Fabian (Forte)	Philadelphia, Pa.	2/6/43
Fabray, Nanette	San Diego, Cal.	10/27/20
Fairbanks, Douglas Jr.	New York, N.Y.	12/9/09
Fairchild, Morgan	Dallas, Tex.	2/3/50
Falana, Lola	Philadelphia, Pa.	9/11/46
Falk, Peter	New York, N.Y.	9/16/27
Farentino, James	Brooklyn, N.Y.	2/24/38
Fargo, Donna	Mt. Airy, N.C.	11/10/45
Farr, Jamie	Toledo, Oh.	7/1/34
Farrell, Eileen	Willimantic, Conn.	2/13/20
Farrell, Mike	St. Paul, Minn.	2/6/39
Farrow, Mia	Los Angeles, Cal.	2/9/45
Faustino, David	California	3/3/74
Fawcett, Farrah	Corpus Christi, Tex.	2/2/47
Faye, Alice	New York, N.Y.	5/5/12
Feld, Fritz	Berlin, Germany	10/15/00
Feldon, Barbara	Pittsburgh, Pa.	3/12/41
Feldshuh, Tovah	New York, N.Y.	12/27/52
Feliciano, Jose	Lares, Puerto Rico	9/10/45
Fell, Norman	Philadelphia, Pa.	3/24/24
Fellini, Federico	Rimini, Italy	1/20/20
Fender, Freddy	San Benito, Tex.	6/4/37
Ferrell, Conchata	Charleston, W. Va.	3/28/43
Ferrer, Jose	Santurce, P.R.	1/8/12
Ferrer, Mel	Elberon, N.J.	8/25/17
Fiedler, John	Platville, Wis.	2/3/25
Field, Sally	Pasadena, Cal.	11/6/46
Fields, Kim	Los Angeles, Cal.	5/12/69
Finney, Albert	Salford, England	5/9/36
Firkusny, Rudolf	Napajedla, Czechoslovakia	2/11/12
Firth, Peter	Yorkshire, England	10/27/53
Fischer-Dieskau, Dietrich	Berlin, Germany	5/28/25
Fisher, Carrie	Beverly Hills, Cal.	10/21/56
Fisher, Eddie	Philadelphia, Pa.	8/10/28
Fitzgerald, Ella	Newport News, Va.	4/25/18
Fitzgerald, Geraldine	Dublin, Ireland.	11/24/13
Flack, Roberta	Black Mountain, N.C.	2/10/39
Flanagan, Fionnula	Dublin, Ireland.	12/10/41
Flanders, Ed	Minneapolis, Minn.	12/29/34
Fleming, Rhonda	Hollywood, Cal.	8/10/23
Fletcher, Louise	Birmingham, Ala.	1936
Foch, Nina	Leyden, Netherlands.	4/20/24
Fogelberg, Dan	Peoria, Ill.	8/13/51
Fonda, Jane	New York, N.Y.	12/21/37
Fonda, Peter	New York, N.Y.	2/23/39
Fontaine, Joan	Tokyo, Japan	10/22/17
Ford (Tenn.), Ernie	Bristol, Tenn.	2/13/19
Ford, Faith	Alexandria, La.	9/14/-
Ford, Glenn	Quebec, Canada	5/1/16
Ford, Harrison	Chicago, Ill.	7/13/42
Forrest, Steve	Huntsville, Tex.	9/29/24
Forsythe, John	Penns Grove, N.J.	1/29/18
Foster, Jodie	New York, N.Y.	11/19/62
Fox, James	London, England	5/19/39
Fox, Michael J.	Edmonton, Alta.	6/9/61
Foxworth, Robert	Houston, Tex.	11/1/41
Foxx, Redd	St. Louis, Mo.	12/9/22
Frampton, Peter	Kent, England	4/22/50
Francescatti, Zino	Marseilles, France	8/9/05
Franciosa, Anthony	New York, N.Y.	10/25/28
Francis, Anne	Ossining, N.Y.	9/16/30
Francis, Arlene	Boston, Mass.	10/20/08
Francis, Connie	Newark, N.J.	12/12/38
Francis, Genie	Los Angeles, Cal.	5/26/62
Frankenheimer, John	Malba, N.Y.	2/19/30
Franklin, Aretha	Memphis, Tenn.	3/25/42
Franklin, Bonnie	Santa Monica, Cal.	1/6/44
Franklin, Joe	New York, N.Y.	1929
Frann, Mary	St. Louis, Mo.	2/27/43
Franz, Dennis	Chicago, Ill.	10/28/44
Freeman Jr., Al	San Antonio, Tex.	3/21/34
Freeman, Morgan	Memphis, Tenn.	6/1/37
Frick, Mr. (W. Groebli)	Basel, Switzerland	4/21/15
Friedkin, William	Chicago, Ill.	8/29/39
Frost, David	Tenterden, England	4/7/39
Funicello, Annette	Utica, N.Y.	10/22/42
Funt, Allen	New York, N.Y.	9/16/14
Gabor, Eva	Hungary	1921
Gabor, Zsa Zsa	Hungary	—
Gabriel, John	Niagara Falls, N.Y.	5/25/31
Gabriel, Peter	London, England	5/13/50
Gail, Max	Detroit, Mich.	4/5/43
Gallagher, Megan	Reading, Pa.	2/6/-
Galway, James	Belfast, Ireland	12/8/39
Garagiola, Joe	St. Louis, Mo.	2/12/26
Garcia, Andy	Havana, Cuba.	1956
Gardenia, Vincent	Naples, Italy	1/7/22
Garfunkel, Art	New York, N.Y.	10/13/41
Garland, Beverly	Santa Cruz, Cal.	10/17/26
Garner, James	Norman, Okla.	4/7/28
Garr, Teri	Lakewood, Oh.	12/11/49
Garrett, Betty	St. Joseph, Mo.	5/23/19
Garson, Greer	Co. Down, N. Ireland.	9/29/08
Gatlin, Larry	Seminole, Tex.	5/2/48
Gayle, Crystal	Paintsville, Ky.	1/9/51
Gaynor, Mitzi	Chicago, Ill.	9/4/30
Gazzara, Ben	New York, N.Y.	8/28/30
Gedda, Nicolai	Stockholm, Sweden	7/11/25
Geldof, Bob	Co. Dublin, Ire.	10/5/51
Gere, Richard	Philadelphia, Pa.	8/31/49
Getty, Estelle	New York, N.Y.	7/25/24
Ghostley, Alice	Eve, Mo.	8/14/26
Giannini, Giancarlo	Spezia, Italy	8/1/42
Gibb, Cynthia	Bennington, Vt.	12/14/63
Gibbs, Marla	Chicago, Ill.	6/14/31
Gibson, Debbie	Merrick, N.Y.	8/31/70
Gibson, Henry	Germantown, Pa.	9/21/35
Gibson, Mel	Peerskill, N.Y.	1/3/56
Gielgud, John	London, England	4/14/04
Gifford, Frank	Santa Monica, Cal.	8/16/30
Gilbert, Melissa	Los Angeles, Cal.	5/8/64
Gilberto, Astrud	Salvador, Brazil.	3/30/40
Gillette, Anita	Baltimore, Md.	8/16/38
Gilley, Mickey	Natchez, Miss.	3/9/36
Ginty, Robert.	New York, N.Y.	11/14/48
Gish, Lillian.	Springfield, Oh.	10/14/96
Givens, Robin	New York, N.Y.	11/27/64
Glaser, Paul Michael	Cambridge, Mass.	3/25/43
Glass, Ron	Evansville, Ind.	7/10/45
Glenn, Scott	Pittsburgh, Pa.	1/26/42
Gless, Sharon	Los Angeles, Cal.	5/31/43

Name	Birthplace	Born	Name	Birthplace	Born
Glover, Danny	San Francisco, Cal.	1947	Harris, Ed	Englewood, N.J.	11/28/50
Glynn, Carlin	Cleveland, Oh.	2/19/40	Harris, Emmylou	Birmingham, Ala.	4/2/47
Godard, Jean Luc	Paris, France	12/3/30	Harris, Julie	Grosse Pte. Park, Mich.	12/2/25
Godunov, Alexander	Sakhalin Is., USSR	11/28/49	Harris, Neil Patrick	Albuquerque, N.M.	6/15/73
Goldberg, Whoopi	New York, N.Y.	11/13/49	Harris, Phil	Linton, Ind.	6/24/04
Goldblum, Jeff	Pittsburgh, Pa.	10/22/52	Harris, Richard	Co. Limerick, Ireland	10/1/33
Goldsboro, Bobby	Marianna, Fla.	1/18/42	Harris, Rosemary	Ashby, England	9/19/30
Goldthwait, Bob	Syracuse, N.Y.	1962	Harrison, George	Liverpool, England	2/25/43
Goodman, John	St. Louis, Mo.	6/20/53	Harrison, Gregory	Avalon, Cal.	5/31/50
Gordon, Gale	New York, N.Y.	2/2/06	Harry, Deborah	Miami, Fla.	7/1/45
Gorman, Cliff.	New York, N.Y.	10/13/36	Hart, Mary	Sioux Falls, S.D.	11/8/51
Gorme, Eydie	Bronx, N.Y.	8/16/32	Hartley, Mariette.	New York, N.Y.	6/21/40
Gorshin, Frank	Pittsburgh, Pa.	4/5/34	Hartman, David	Pawtucket, R.I.	5/19/35
Gossett Jr., Louis	Brooklyn, N.Y.	5/27/36	Hartman, Lisa	Houston, Tex.	6/1/56
Gould, Elliott	Brooklyn, N.Y.	8/29/38	Hartman, Phil	Ontario, Canada	9/24/48
Gould, Harold	Schenectady, N.Y.	12/10/23	Hasselhoff, David	Baltimore, Md.	7/17/52
Gould, Morton	Richmond Hill, N.Y.	12/10/13	Hasso, Signe.	Stockholm, Sweden	8/15/10
Goulet, Robert	Lawrence, Mass.	11/26/33	Hauer, Rutger	Netherlands	1/23/44
Gowdy, Curt	Green River, Wyo.	7/31/19	Haver, June	Rock Island, Ill.	6/10/26
Graham, Virginia.	Chicago, Ill.	7/4/12	Havoc, June	Seattle, Wash.	11/8/16
Grammer, Kelsey	Virgin Islands	2/20/-	Hawn, Goldie	Washington, D.C.	11/21/45
Granger, Farley	San Jose, Cal.	7/1/25	Hayden, Melissa.	Toronto, Ont.	4/25/23
Granger, Stewart	London, England	5/6/13	Hayes, Helen	Washington, D.C.	10/10/00
Grant, Amy.	Augusta, Ga.	12/25/60	Hayes, Isaac	Covington, Tenn.	8/20/42
Grant, Lee	New York, N.Y.	10/31/29	Hays, Robert.	Bethesda, Md.	7/24/47
Graves, Peter	Minneapolis, Minn.	3/18/26	Heard, John	Washington, D.C.	5/7/47
Gray, Coleen	Staplehurst, Neb.	10/23/22	Hearn, George.	Memphis, Tenn.	1935
Gray, Erin	Honolulu, Ha.	1/7/52	Heatherton, Joey	Rockville Centre, N.Y.	9/14/44
Gray, Linda.	Santa Monica, Cal.	9/12/40	Heckart, Eileen	Columbus, Oh.	3/29/19
Grayson, Kathryn	Winston-Salem, N.C.	2/9/22	Helmond, Katherine	Galveston, Tex.	7/5/34
Greco, Buddy	Philadelphia, Pa.	8/14/26	Hemingway, Margaux.	Portland, Ore.	2/19/55
Greco, Jose	Abruzzi, Italy	12/23/18	Hemingway, Mariel	Mill Valley, Cal.	11/21/61
Green, Adolph	New York, N.Y.	12/2/15	Hemmings, David	Guildford, England	11/18/41
Green, Al	Forest City, Ark.	4/13/46	Hemsley, Sherman	Philadelphia, Pa.	2/1/38
Greene, Ellen	New York, N.Y.	1950	Henderson, Florence	Dale, Ind.	2/14/34
Greene, Michele	Las Vegas, Nev.	2/3/-	Henderson, Skitch.	Halstad, Minn.	1/27/18
Greene, Shecky	Chicago, Ill.	4/8/26	Henner, Marilu	Chicago, Ill.	4/6/52
Gregory, Cynthia	Los Angeles, Cal.	7/8/46	Henning, Doug.	Ft. Garry, Man.	5/3/47
Gregory, Dick	St. Louis, Mo.	10/12/32	Henreid, Paul	Trieste, Austria	1/10/08
Gregory, James	Bronx, N.Y.	12/23/11	Hepburn, Audrey	Brussels, Belgium	5/4/29
Grey, Joel	Cleveland, Oh.	4/11/32	Hepburn, Katharine	Hartford, Conn.	11/8/09
Griffin, Merv	San Mateo, Cal.	7/6/25	Herman, Pee-wee.	Peekskill, N.Y.	8/27/52
Griffith, Andy	Mount Airy, N.C.	6/1/26	Herrmann, Edward	Washington, D.C.	7/21/43
Griffith, Melanie	New York, N.Y.	8/9/57	Hershey, Barbara	Los Angeles, Cal.	2/5/48
Grimes, Tammy	Lynn, Mass.	1/30/34	Hesseman, Howard.	Lebanon, Ore.	2/27/40
Grizzard, George	Roanoke Rapids, N.C.	4/1/28	Heston, Charlton	Evanston, Ill.	10/4/24
Grodin, Charles	Pittsburgh, Pa.	4/21/35	Hewitt, Christopher.	Sussex, England	4/5/-
Groh, David	New York, N.Y.	5/21/41	Higgins, Joel	Bloomington, Ill.	9/28/43
Grosbard, Ulu	Antwerp, Belgium	1/19/29	Hildegarde	Adell, Wis.	2/1/06
Gross, Michael.	Chicago, Ill.	6/21/47	Hill, Arthur	Melfort, Sask.	8/1/22
Guardino, Harry	New York, N.Y.	12/23/25	Hill, Benny	Southampton, England.	1/21/25
Guillaume, Robert.	St. Louis, Mo.	11/30/37	Hill, George Roy	Minneapolis, Minn.	12/20/22
Guinness, Alec.	London, England	4/2/14	Hiller, Wendy	Stockport, England	8/15/12
Gumbel, Greg	New Orleans, La.	5/3/46	Hillerman, John	Denison, Tex.	12/30/32
Guthrie, Arlo	New York, N.Y.	7/10/47	Hines, Gregory	New York, N.Y.	2/14/46
Guttenberg, Steve.	New York, N.Y.	8/24/58	Hines, Jerome	Hollywood, Cal.	11/8/21
Guy, Jasmine	Boston, Mass.	3/10/64	Hingle, Pat	Miami, Fla.	7/19/24
Gwynne, Fred	New York, N.Y.	7/10/26	Hirsch, Judd	New York, N.Y.	3/15/35
Hackett, Buddy	Brooklyn, N.Y.	8/31/24	Hirt, Al	New Orleans, La.	11/7/22
Hackman, Gene	San Bernardino, Cal.	1/30/30	Ho, Don.	Kakaako, Oahu, Ha.	8/13/30
Hagen, Uta.	Gottingen, Germany	6/12/19	Hoffman, Dustin	Los Angeles, Cal.	8/8/37
Haggard, Merle	Bakersfield, Cal.	4/6/37	Hogan, Paul	New South Wales, Australia.	10/8/39
Hagman, Larry.	Weatherford, Tex.	9/21/31	Holbrook, Hal	Cleveland, Oh.	2/17/25
Hague, Albert	Berlin, Germany	10/13/20	Holder, Geoffrey.	Trinidad	8/1/30
Haid, Charles	San Francisco, Cal.	6/2/43	Holliday, Polly	Jasper, Ala.	7/2/37
Hale, Barbara	DeKalb, Ill.	4/18/22	Holliman, Earl	Delhi, La.	9/11/28
Hall, Arsenio	Cleveland, Oh.	2/12/58	Holloway, Sterling	Cedartown, Ga.	1/4/05
Hall, Daryl	Pottstown, Pa.	10/11/49	Holm, Celeste	New York, N.Y.	4/29/19
Hall, Deidre	Milwaukee, Wis.	10/31/48	Hooks, Jan.	Decatur, Ga.	4/23/57
Hall, Huntz	New York, N.Y.	8/15/19	Hooks, Robert.	Washington, D.C.	4/18/37
Hall, Monty	Winnipeg, Man.	8/25/25	Hope, Bob	London, England	5/29/03
Hall, Tom T.	Olive Hill, Ky.	5/25/36	Hopkins, Anthony	Wales	12/31/37
Hamel, Veronica.	Philadelphia, Pa.	11/20/43	Hopkins, Telma	Louisville, Ky.	10/28/48
Hamill, Mark	Oakland, Cal.	9/25/51	Hopper, Dennis	Dodge City, Kan.	5/17/36
Hamilton, George	Memphis, Tenn.	8/12/39	Horne, Lena	Brooklyn, N.Y.	6/30/17
Hamlin, Harry	Pasadena, Cal.	10/30/51	Horne, Marilyn	Bradford, Pa.	1/16/34
Hampton, Lionel	Birmingham, Ala.	4/12/13	Horsley, Lee.	Muleshoe, Tex.	5/15/55
Hancock, Herbie.	Chicago, Ill.	4/12/40	Horton, Robert.	Los Angeles, Cal.	7/29/24
Hanks, Tom	Oakland, Cal.	7/9/56	Hoskins, Bob.	Suffolk, England	10/26/42
Hannah, Daryl	Chicago, Ill.	1961	Houston, Whitney	E. Orange, N.J.	8/9/63
Hardison, Kadeem	New York, N.Y.	7/24/-	Howard, Ken.	El Centro, Cal.	3/28/44
Harmon, Mark	Burbank, Cal.	9/2/51	Howard, Ron.	Duncan, Okla.	3/1/53
Harper, Jessica	Chicago, Ill.	1949	Howell, C. Thomas	Los Angeles, Cal.	12/7/66
Harper, Tess.	Mammoth Springs, Ark.	8/15/50	Howes, Sally Ann	London, England	7/20/30
Harper, Valerie	Suffern, N.Y.	8/22/40	Hughes, Barnard	Bedford Hills, N.Y.	7/16/15
Harrelson, Woody.	Midland, Tex.	7/23/61	Hulce, Tom.	Whitewater, Wis.	12/6/53
Harrington, Pat Jr...	New York, N.Y.	8/13/29	Humperdinck, Engelbert	Madras, India	5/3/36
Harris, Barbara	Evanston, Ill.	7/25/35			

Name	Birthplace	Born
Hunt, Linda	Morristown, N.J.	4/2/45
Hunter, Holly	Conyers, Ga.	3/20/58
Hunter, Kim	Detroit, Mich.	11/12/22
Hunter, Ross	Cleveland, Oh.	5/6/21
Hunter, Tab	New York, N.Y.	7/11/31
Hurt, John	Chesterfield, England	1/22/40
Hurt, Mary Beth	Marshalltown, Ia.	9/26/46
Hurt, William	Washington, D.C.	3/20/50
Hussey, Ruth	Providence, R.I.	10/30/14
Huston, Anjelica	Ireland	7/8/51
Hutton, Betty	Battle Creek, Mich.	2/26/21
Hutton, Lauren	Charleston, S.C.	11/17/43
Hutton, Timothy	Malibu, Cal.	8/16/61
Hyman, Earle	Rocky Mount, N.C.	10/11/26
Ian, Janis	New York, N.Y.	4/7/51
Idol, Billy	London, England	11/30/55
Iglesias, Julio	Madrid, Spain	9/23/43
Ireland, John	Vancouver, B.C.	1/30/14
Irons, Jeremy	Cowes, England	9/19/48
Irving, Amy	Palo Alto, Cal.	9/10/53
Irving, George S.	Springfield, Mass.	11/1/22
Ives, Burl	Hunt Township, Ill.	6/14/09
Ivey, Judith	El Paso, Tex.	9/4/51
Jackee	Winston-Salem, N.C.	8/14/-
Jackson, Anne	Allegheny, Pa.	9/3/25
Jackson, Glenda	Liverpool, England	5/9/36
Jackson, Janet	Gary, Ind.	5/16/66
Jackson, Jermaine	Gary, Ind.	12/11/54
Jackson, La Toya	Gary, Ind.	1/29/56
Jackson, Kate	Birmingham, Ala.	10/29/48
Jackson, Michael	Gary, Ind.	8/29/58
Jackson, Victoria	Miami, Fla.	8/2/59
Jacobi, Derek	London, England	10/22/38
Jaeckel, Richard	Long Beach, N.Y.	10/10/26
Jagger, Mick	Dartford, England	7/26/43
James, Dennis	Jersey City, N.J.	8/24/17
James, John	Minneapolis, Minn.	4/18/56
Janis, Conrad	New York, N.Y.	2/11/28
Jarreau, Al	Milwaukee, Wis.	3/12/40
Jason-Leigh, Jennifer	Los Angeles, Cal.	1958
Jeffreys, Anne	Goldsboro, N.C.	1/26/23
Jennings, Waylon	Littlefield, Tex.	6/15/37
Jett, Joan	Philadelphia, Pa.	9/22/60
Jewison, Norman	Toronto, Ont.	7/21/26
Jillian, Ann	Cambridge, Mass.	1/29/50
Joel, Billy	Bronx, N.Y.	5/9/49
John, Elton	Middlesex, England.	3/25/47
Johns, Glynis	Durban, S. Africa	10/5/23
Johnson, Anne-Marie	Los Angeles, Cal.	7/18/-
Johnson, Arte	Benton Harbor, Mich.	1/20/29
Johnson, Ben	Foraker, Okla.	6/13/18
Johnson, Don	Flatt Creek, Mo.	12/15/49
Johnson, Van	Newport, R.I.	8/25/16
Jones, Allan	Scranton, Pa.	10/14/07
Jones, Charlie	Ft. Smith, Ark.	11/9/30
Jones, Dean	Morgan City, Ala.	1/25/35
Jones, George	Saratoga, Tex.	9/12/31
Jones, Grace	Spanishtown, Jamaica	5/19/52
Jones, Grandpa	Niagara, Ky.	10/20/13
Jones, Henry	Philadelphia, Pa.	8/1/12
Jones, Jack	Hollywood, Cal.	1/14/38
Jones, James Earl	Tate Co., Miss.	1/17/31
Jones, Jennifer	Tulsa, Okla.	3/2/19
Jones, Shirley	Smithton, Pa.	3/31/34
Jones, Tom	Pontypridd, Wales	6/7/40
Jones, Tommy Lee	San Saba, Tex.	9/15/46
Jordan, Richard	New York, N.Y.	7/19/38
Jourdan, Louis	Marseilles, France	6/19/19
Julia, Raul	San Juan, P.R.	3/9/40
Jump, Gordon	Dayton, Oh.	4/1/32
Kahn, Madeline	Boston, Mass.	9/29/42
Kanaly, Steve	Burbank, Cal.	3/14/46
Kane, Carol	Cleveland, Oh.	6/18/52
Karlen, John	New York, N.Y.	5/28/33
Karras, Alex	Gary, Ind.	7/15/35
Kasem, Casey	Detroit, Mich.	1933
Katt, William	Los Angeles, Cal.	2/16/51
Kavner, Julie	Los Angeles, Cal.	9/7/51
Kazan, Elia	Istanbul, Turkey.	9/7/09
Kazan, Lainie	New York, N.Y.	5/15/42
Keach, Stacy	Savannah, Ga.	6/2/41
Keaton, Diane	Santa Ana, Cal.	1/5/46
Keaton, Michael	Pittsburgh, Pa.	9/9/51
Keel, Howard	Gillespie, Ill.	4/13/17
Keeler, Ruby	Halifax, N.S.	8/25/09
Keeshan, Bob	Lynbrook, N.Y.	6/27/27
Keitel, Harvey	Brooklyn, N.Y.	1947
Keith, Brian	Bayonne, N.J.	11/14/21
Keith, David	Knoxville, Tenn.	5/8/54
Kellerman, Sally	Long Beach, Cal.	6/2/37
Kelley, DeForest	Atlanta, Ga.	1/20/20
Kelly, Gene	Pittsburgh, Pa.	8/23/12
Kelly, Nancy	Lowell, Mass.	3/25/21
Kennedy, George	New York, N.Y.	2/18/25
Kennedy, Jayne	Washington, D.C.	11/27/51
Kent, Allegra	Los Angeles, Cal.	8/11/37
Kercheval, Ken	Wolcottville, Ind.	7/15/35
Kerns, Joanna	San Francisco, Cal.	2/12/53
Kerr, Deborah	Helensburgh, Scotland.	9/30/21
Kerr, John	New York, N.Y.	11/15/31
Khan, Chaka	Great Lakes, Ill.	3/23/53
Kidder, Margot	Yellowknife, N.W.T.	10/17/48
Kiley, Richard	Chicago, Ill.	3/31/22
King, Alan	Brooklyn, N.Y.	12/26/27
King, B. B.	Itta Bena, Miss.	9/16/25
King, Carole	Brooklyn, N.Y.	2/9/42
King, Larry	New York, N.Y.	11/19/33
King, Perry	Alliance, Oh.	4/30/48
Kingsley, Ben	Yorkshire, England	12/31/43
Kinski, Klaus	Sopot, Poland.	10/8/26
Kinski, Nastassia	Berlin, W. Germany.	1/24/60
Kirby, Bruno	New York, N.Y.	1949
Kirby, Durward	Covington, Ky.	8/24/12
Kirkland, Geisey	Bethlehem, Pa.	12/29/53
Kirsten, Dorothy	Montclair, N.J.	7/6/19
Kitt, Eartha	North, S.C.	1/26/28
Klein, Robert	New York, N.Y.	2/8/42
Klemperer, Werner	Cologne, Germany	3/22/19
Kline, Kevin	St. Louis, Mo.	10/24/47
Klugman, Jack	Philadelphia, Pa.	4/27/22
Knight, Gladys	Atlanta, Ga.	5/28/44
Knotts, Don	Morgantown, W. Va.	7/21/24
Kopell, Bernie	New York, N.Y.	6/21/33
Korman, Harvey	Chicago, Ill.	2/15/27
Kotto, Yaphet	New York, N.Y.	11/15/37
Kramer, Stanley	New York, N.Y.	9/29/13
Kramer, Stepfanie	Los Angeles, Cal.	8/6/56
Kristofferson, Kris	Brownsville, Tex.	6/22/36
Kubelik, Rafael	Bychori, Czechoslovakia.	6/29/14
Kubrick, Stanley	Bronx, N.Y.	7/26/28
Kurtz, Swoosie	Omaha, Neb.	9/6/44
LaBelle, Patti	Philadelphia, Pa.	10/4/44
Ladd, Cheryl	Huron, S.D.	7/12/51
Ladd, Diane	Meridian, Miss.	11/29/32
Lahti, Christine	Detroit, Mich.	4/5/50
Laine, Cleo	Middlesex, England.	10/28/27
Laine, Frankie	Chicago, Ill.	3/30/13
Lamarr, Hedy	Vienna, Austria	11/9/13
Lamas, Lorenzo	Santa Monica, Cal.	1/20/58
Lamb, Gil	Minneapolis, Minn.	6/14/06
Lamour, Dorothy	New Orleans, La.	12/10/14
Lancaster, Burt	New York, N.Y.	11/2/13
Landau, Martin	New York, N.Y.	6/20/34
Landesberg, Steve	New York, N.Y.	11/23/45
Landis, John	Chicago, Ill.	8/3/50
Lane, Abbe	Brooklyn, N.Y.	12/14/32
Lane, Diane	New York, N.Y.	1/22/63
Lane, Priscilla	Indianola, Ia.	6/12/17
Lang, K.D.	Consort, Alberta	11/2/61
Lang, Stephen	New York, N.Y.	7/11/52
Lange, Hope	Redding Ridge, Conn.	11/28/31
Lange, Jessica	Cloquet, Minn.	4/20/49
Langella, Frank	Bayonne, N.J.	1/1/40
Langford, Frances	Lakeland, Fla.	4/4/13
Lansbury, Angela	London, England	10/16/25
Lansing, Robert	San Diego, Cal.	6/5/28
Laredo, Ruth	Detroit, Mich.	11/20/37
Larroquette, John	New Orleans, La.	11/25/47
Lasser, Louise	New York, N.Y.	4/11/39
Lauper, Cyndi	New York, N.Y.	6/20/53
Laurie, Piper	Detroit, Mich.	1/22/32
Lauter, Ed	Long Beach, N.Y.	10/30/40
Lavin, Linda	Portland, Me.	10/15/37
Lawrence, Carol	Melrose Park, Ill.	9/5/34
Lawrence, Steve	Brooklyn, N.Y.	7/8/35
Lawrence, Vicki	Inglewood, Cal.	3/26/49
Leach, Robin	London, England	8/29/41
Leachman, Cloris	Des Moines, Ia.	4/4/26
Lear, Norman	New Haven, Conn.	7/27/22
Learned, Michael	Washington, D.C.	4/9/39
LeBon, Simon	Bushey, England	10/27/58
Lee, Brenda	Atlanta, Ga.	12/11/44
Lee, Christopher	London, England	5/27/22
Lee, Michele	Los Angeles, Cal.	6/24/42
Lee, Peggy	Jamestown, N.D.	5/26/20

Name	Birthplace	Born
Lee, Spike	Atlanta, Ga.	3/20/57
Legrand, Michel	Paris, France	2/24/32
Leibman, Ron	New York, N.Y.	10/11/37
Leifer, Carol	E. Williston, N.Y.	1956
Leigh, Janet	Merced, Cal.	7/6/27
Leinsdorf, Erich	Vienna, Austria	2/4/12
Leisure, David	San Diego, Cal.	11/16/-
Lemmon, Chris	Los Angeles, Cal.	1/22/54
Lemmon, Jack	Boston, Mass.	2/8/25
Lennon, Julian	London, England	4/8/63
Lennon Sisters		
Dianne	Los Angeles, Cal.	12/1/39
Janet	Culver City, Cal.	11/15/46
Kathy	Santa Monica, Cal.	8/22/42
Peggy	Los Angeles, Cal.	4/8/41
Leno, Jay	New Rochelle, N.Y.	4/28/50
Lenz, Kay	Los Angeles, Cal.	3/4/53
Leonard, Sheldon	New York, N.Y.	2/22/07
Leontovich, Eugenie	Moscow, Russia	3/21/00
Leslie, Joan	Detroit, Mich.	1/26/25
Letterman, David	Indianapolis, Ind.	4/12/47
Levine, James	Cincinnati, Oh.	6/23/43
Levinson, Barry	Baltimore, Md.	1932
Lewis, Emmanuel	New York, N.Y.	3/9/71
Lewis, Dawnn	New York, N.Y.	8/13/60
Lewis, Huey	New York, N.Y.	7/5/51
Lewis, Jerry	Newark, N.J.	3/16/26
Lewis, Jerry Lee	Ferriday, La.	9/29/35
Lewis, Richard	New York, N.Y.	6/29/47
Lewis, Shari	New York, N.Y.	1/17/34
Light, Judith	Trenton, N.J.	2/9/50
Lightfoot, Gordon	Orillia, Ont.	11/17/38
Linden, Hal	New York, N.Y.	3/20/31
Lindfors, Viveca	Uppsala, Sweden.	12/29/20
Linkletter, Art	Saskatchewan, Canada	7/17/12
Linn-Baker, Mark	St. Louis, Mo.	6/17/53
Liotta, Ray	Newark, N.J.	12/18/-
Lithgow, John	Rochester, N.Y.	10/19/45
Little, Cleavon	Chickasha, Okla.	6/1/39
Little, Rich	Ottawa, Ont.	11/26/38
Little Richard	Macon, Ga.	12/5/32
Lloyd, Christopher	Stamford, Conn.	10/22/38
Lloyd, Emily	England	9/29/70
Locke, Sondra	Shelbyville, Tenn.	5/28/47
Lockhart, June	New York, N.Y.	6/25/25
Locklear, Heather	Los Angeles, Cal.	9/25/61
Loggia, Robert	New York, N.Y.	1/3/30
Loggins, Kenny	Everett, Wash.	1/17/47
Lollobrigida, Gina	Subiaco, Italy	7/4/27
Lom, Herbert	Prague, Czechoslovakia	1/9/17
London, Julie	Santa Rosa, Cal.	9/26/26
Long, Shelley	Ft. Wayne, Ind.	8/23/49
Lord, Jack	New York, N.Y.	12/30/22
Loren, Sophia	Rome, Italy	9/20/34
Loring, Gloria	New York, N.Y.	12/10/46
Loudon, Dorothy	Boston, Mass.	9/17/33
Louise, Tina	New York, N.Y.	2/11/34
Lovitz, Jon	Tarzana, Cal.	7/21/57
Lowe, Rob	Charlottesville, Va.	3/17/64
Loy, Myrna	Helena, Mon.	8/2/05
Lucas, George	Modesto, Cal.	5/14/44
Lucci, Susan	Westchester Co., N.Y.	12/23/49
Luckinbill, Laurence	Ft. Smith, Ark.	11/21/34
Ludwig, Christa	Berlin, Germany	3/16/28
Lumet, Sidney	Philadelphia, Pa.	6/25/24
Lupino, Ida	London, England	2/4/14
LuPone, Patti	Northport, N.Y.	4/21/49
Lynch, David	Missoula, Mont.	1/20/46
Lynn, Jeffrey	Auburn, Mass.	2/16/09
Lynn, Loretta	Butcher Hollow, Ky.	4/14/-
Maazel, Lorin	Paris, France	3/6/30
MacArthur, James	Los Angeles, Cal.	12/8/37
MacCorkindale, Simon	Cambridge, England	2/12/52
MacDowell, Andie	Gaffney, S.C.	4/21/58
MacGraw, Ali	Pound Ridge, N.Y.	4/1/38
Mac Lachlan, Kyle	Yakima, Wash.	1960
MacLaine, Shirley	Richmond, Va.	4/24/34
MacLeod, Gavin	Mt. Kisco, N.Y.	2/28/30
MacMurray, Fred	Kankakee, Ill.	8/30/08
MacNee, Patrick	London, England	2/6/22
MacNeil, Cornell	Minneapolis, Minn.	9/24/22
Macchio, Ralph	Long Island, N.Y.	11/4/61
Macy, Bill	Revere, Mass.	5/18/22
Madden, John	Austin, Minn.	4/10/36
Madigan, Amy	Chicago, Ill.	9/11/57
Madonna (Ciccone)	Bay City, Mich.	8/16/58
Majors, Lee	Wyandotte, Mich.	4/23/40
Malbin, Elaine	New York, N.Y.	5/24/32
Malden, Karl	Chicago, Ill.	3/22/13
Malfitano, Catherine	New York, N.Y.	4/18/48
Malkovich, John	Christopher, Ill.	12/9/53
Malle, Louis	Thumeries, France	10/30/32
Malone, Dorothy	Chicago, Ill.	1/30/25
Manchester, Melissa	Bronx, N.Y.	2/15/51
Mancini, Henry	Cleveland, Oh.	4/16/24
Mandel, Howie	Toronto, Ont.	11/29/-
Mandrell, Barbara	Houston, Tex.	12/25/48
Mangione, Chuck	Rochester, N.Y.	11/29/40
Manilow, Barry	New York, N.Y.	6/17/46
Mann, Herbie	New York, N.Y.	4/16/30
Manoff, Dinah	New York, N.Y.	1/25/58
Mantegna, Joe	Chicago, Ill.	11/13/47
Marceau, Marcel	Strasbourg, France	3/22/23
Marsalis, Wynton	New Orleans, La.	10/18/61
Marchand, Nancy	Buffalo, N.Y.	6/19/28
Margolin, Janet	New York, N.Y.	7/25/43
Marin, Cheech	Los Angeles, Cal.	7/13/46
Markova, Alicia	London, England	12/1/10
Marriner, Neville	Lincoln, England	4/15/24
Marsh, Jean	London, England	7/1/34
Marshall, E. G.	Owatonna, Minn.	6/18/10
Marshall, Penny	New York, N.Y.	10/15/43
Marshall, Peter	Huntington, W.Va.	3/30/27
Martin, Dean	Steubenville, Oh.	6/17/17
Martin, Dick	Detroit, Mich.	1/30/23
Martin, Steve	Waco, Tex.	4/14/45
Martin, Tony	San Francisco, Cal.	12/25/13
Martins, Peter	Copenhagen, Denmark	10/27/46
Mason, Jackie	Sheboygan, Wis.	6/9/31
Mason, Marsha	St. Louis, Mo.	4/3/42
Masterson, Mary Stuart	New York, N.Y.	1967
Mastrantonio, Mary Eliz.	Lombard, Ill.	11/17/58
Mastroianni, Marcello	Rome, Italy	9/28/23
Matheson, Tim	Glendale, Cal.	12/31/47
Mathis, Johnny	San Francisco, Cal.	9/30/35
Matthau, Walter	New York, N.Y.	10/1/20
Mature, Victor	Louisville, Ky.	1/29/16
May, Elaine	Philadelphia, Pa.	4/21/32
Mayfield, Curtis	Chicago, Ill.	6/3/42
Mayo, Virginia	St. Louis, Mo.	11/30/20
Mazursky, Paul	Brooklyn, N.Y.	4/25/30
McArdle, Andrea	Philadelphia, Pa.	11/5/63
McBride, Patricia	Teaneck, N.J.	8/23/42
McCallum, David	Glasgow, Scotland	9/19/33
McCambridge, Mercedes	Joliet, Ill.	3/17/18
McCarthy, Andrew	New York, N.Y.	1963
McCarthy, Kevin	Seattle, Wash.	2/15/14
McCartney, Paul	Liverpool, England	6/18/42
McCarver, Tim	Memphis, Tenn.	10/16/41
McClanahan, Rue	Healdton, Okla.	2/21/36
McClure, Doug	Glendale, Cal.	5/11/35
McClurg, Edie	Kansas City, Mo.	7/23/51
McCoo, Marilyn	Jersey City, N.J.	9/30/43
McDowall, Roddy	London, England	9/28/28
McDowell, Malcolm	Leeds, England	6/13/43
McEntire, Reba	McAlester, Okla.	3/28/54
McFarland, Spanky	Dallas, Tex.	10/2/28
McFerrin, Bobby	New York, N.Y.	3/11/50
McGavin, Darren	Spokane, Wash.	5/7/22
McGillis, Kelly	Newport, Cal.	1957
McGoohan, Patrick	New York, N.Y.	3/19/28
McGovern, Elizabeth	Evanston, Ill.	7/18/61
McGovern, Maureen	Youngstown, Oh.	7/27/49
McGuire, Al	New York, N.Y.	9/7/31
McGuire, Dorothy	Omaha, Neb.	6/14/19
McKechnie, Donna	Pontiac, Mich.	11/16/42
McKee, Lonette	Detroit, Mich.	1954
McKellen, Ian	Burnley, England	5/25/39
McKeon, Nancy	Westbury, N.Y.	4/4/66
McLean, Don	New Rochelle, N.Y.	10/2/45
McLerie, Allyn	Grand Mere, Que.	12/1/26
McMahon, Ed	Detroit, Mich.	3/6/23
McNichol, Kristy	Los Angeles, Cal.	9/11/62
McQueen, Butterfly	Tampa, Fla.	1/7/11
McRaney, Gerald	Collins, Miss.	8/19/47
Meadows, Audrey	Wu Chang, China.	2/8/24
Meadows, Jayne	Wu Chang, China.	9/27/20
Meara, Anne	New York, N.Y.	9/20/29
Mehta, Zubin	Bombay, India.	4/29/36
Melanie	New York, N.Y.	2/3/47
Mendes, Sergio	Niteroi, Brazil	2/11/41
Menuhin, Yehudi	New York, N.Y.	4/22/16
Mercer, Marian	Akron, Oh.	11/26/35
Mercouri, Melina	Athens, Greece	10/18/25
Meredith, Burgess	Cleveland, Oh.	11/16/08

Name	Birthplace	Born
Merrick, David	Hong Kong	11/27/12
Merrill, Dina	New York, N.Y.	12/9/25
Merrill, Robert	Brooklyn, N.Y.	6/4/19
Messina, Jim	Maywood, Cal.	12/5/47
Metcalf, Laurie	Carbonville, Ill.	6/16/55
Meyers, Ari	San Juan, Puerto Rico	4/6/69
Michael, George	Watford, England	6/26/63
Michaels, Al	New York, N.Y.	11/12/44
Midler, Bette	Paterson, N.J.	12/1/45
Milano, Alyssa	New York, N.Y.	12/19/72
Miles, Sarah	Ingatestone, England	12/31/41
Miles, Vera	near Boise City, Okla.	8/23/29
Miller, Ann	Houston, Tex.	4/12/19
Miller, Dennis	Pittsburgh, Pa.	11/3/53
Miller, Mitch	Rochester, N.Y.	7/4/11
Miller, Roger	Ft. Worth, Tex.	1/2/36
Mills, Donna	Chicago, Ill.	12/11/42
Mills, John	Suffolk, England	2/22/08
Mills, Juliet	London, England	11/21/41
Milner, Martin	Detroit, Mich.	12/28/27
Milnes, Sherrill	Downers Grove, Ill.	1/10/35
Milsap, Ronnie	Robinsville, N.C.	1/16/44
Milstein, Nathan	Odessa, Russia	12/31/04
Minnelli, Liza	Los Angeles, Cal.	3/12/46
Mitchell, Cameron	Dallastown, Pa.	4/11/18
Mitchell, James	Sacramento, Cal.	2/29/20
Mitchell, Joni	McLeod, Alta.	11/7/43
Mitchum, Robert	Bridgeport, Conn.	8/6/17
Modine, Matthew	Loma Linda, Cal.	3/22/59
Moffat, Donald	Plymouth, England	12/26/30
Moffo, Anna	Wayne, Pa.	6/27/27
Molinaro, Al	Kenosha, Wis.	6/24/19
Moll, Richard	Pasadena, Cal.	1/13/43
Montalban, Ricardo	Mexico City, Mexico	11/25/20
Montand, Yves	Monsumagno, Italy	10/13/21
Montgomery, Elizabeth	Hollywood, Cal.	4/15/33
Moody, Ron	London, England	1/8/24
Moore, Clayton	Chicago, Ill.	9/14/08
Moore, Constance	Sioux City, Ia.	1/18/22
Moore, Demi	Roswell, N.M.	11/11/62
Moore, Dudley	London, England	4/19/35
Moore, Garry	Baltimore, Md.	1/31/15
Moore, Mary Tyler	Brooklyn, N.Y.	12/29/37
Moore, Melba	New York, N.Y.	10/29/45
Moore, Roger	London, England	10/14/27
Moore, Terry	Los Angeles, Cal.	1/1/29
Moranis, Rick	Toronto, Ont.	4/18/53
Moreau, Jeanne	Paris, France	1/23/28
Moreno, Rita	Humacao, P.R.	12/11/31
Morgan, Dennis	Prentice, Wis.	12/10/10
Morgan, Harry	Detroit, Mich.	4/10/15
Morgan, Henry	New York, N.Y.	3/31/15
Moriarty, Michael	Detroit, Mich.	4/5/41
Morini, Erika	Vienna, Austria	1/5/10
Morita, Pat	Isleton, Cal.	6/28/32
Morley, Robert	Wiltshire, England	5/26/08
Morris, Greg	Cleveland, Oh.	9/27/34
Morris, Howard	New York, N.Y.	9/4/25
Morse, Robert	Newton, Mass.	5/18/31
Morton, Joe	New York, N.Y.	10/18/47
Moses, William	Los Angeles, Cal.	11/17/59
Muldaur, Diana	New York, N.Y.	8/19/38
Mulgrew, Kate	Dubuque, Ia.	4/29/55
Mulhare, Edward	Ireland	4/8/23
Mull, Martin	Chicago, Ill.	8/18/43
Mulligan, Richard	New York, N.Y.	11/13/32
Munsel, Patrice	Spokane, Wash.	5/14/25
Murphy, Ben	Jonesboro, Ark.	3/6/42
Murphy, Eddie	Brooklyn, N.Y.	4/3/61
Murphy, George	New Haven, Conn.	7/4/02
Murphy, Michael	Los Angeles, Cal.	5/5/38
Murray, Anne	Springhill, Nova Scotia	6/20/45
Murray, Bill	Evanston, Ill.	9/21/50
Murray, Don	Hollywood, Cal.	7/31/29
Murray, Kathryn	Jersey City, N.J.	9/15/06
Musante, Tony	Bridgeport, Conn.	6/30/36
Musburger, Brent	Portland, Ore.	5/26/39
Muti, Riccardo	Naples, Italy	7/28/41
Nabors, Jim	Sylacauga, Ala.	6/12/33
Nash, Graham	Blackpool, England	2/2/42
Natwick, Mildred	Baltimore, Md.	6/19/08
Naughton, James	Middletown, Conn.	7/6/46
Neal, Patricia	Packard, Ky.	1/20/26
Nealon, Kevin	Bridgeport, Conn.	11/18/53
Neill, Sam	New Zealand	1948
Nelligan, Kate	London, Ontario	3/16/51
Nelson, Craig T.	Spokane, Wash.	4/4/46
Nelson, Ed	New Orleans, La.	12/21/28
Nelson, Gene	Seattle, Wash.	3/24/20
Nelson, Harriet (Hilliard)	Des Moines, Ia.	7/18/14
Nelson, Judd	Portland, Me.	11/28/59
Nelson, Tracy	Santa Monica, Cal.	10/25/63
Nelson, Willie	Abbott, Tex.	4/30/33
Nero, Peter	New York, N.Y.	5/22/34
Neuwirth, Bebe	Princeton, N.J.	12/31/-
New Kids On The Block		
Knight, Jonathan	Worcester, Mass.	11/29/68
Knight, Jordan	Worcester, Mass.	5/17/70
McIntyre, Joe	Needham, Mass.	12/31/72
Wahlberg, Donnie	Boston, Mass.	8/17/69
Wood, Danny	Boston, Mass.	5/14/69
Newhart, Bob	Oak Park, Ill.	9/29/29
Newley, Anthony	Hackney, England	9/24/31
Newman, Paul	Cleveland, Oh.	1/26/25
Newman, Randy	Los Angeles, Cal.	11/28/43
Newton, Wayne	Norfolk, Va.	4/3/42
Newton-John, Olivia	Cambridge, England	9/26/47
Nicholas, Fayard	Philadelphia, Pa.	10/20/14
Nicholas, Harold	Philadelphia, Pa.	3/27/24
Nichols, Mike	Berlin, Germany	11/6/31
Nicholson, Jack	Neptune, N.J.	4/28/37
Nicks, Stevie	Phoenix, Ariz.	5/26/48
Nielsen, Leslie	Regina, Sask	2/11/26
Nilsson, Birgit	Karup, Sweden	5/17/18
Nimoy, Leonard	Boston, Mass.	3/26/31
Noble, James	Dallas, Tex.	3/5/22
Nolte, Nick	Omaha, Neb.	2/8/40
Norman, Jessye	Augusta, Ga.	9/15/45
Norris, Chuck	Ryan, Okla.	3/10/40
North, Sheree	Los Angeles, Cal.	1/17/33
Novak, Kim	Chicago, Ill.	2/13/33
Nureyev, Rudolf	Russia	3/17/38
Oates, John	New York, N.Y.	4/7/48
O'Brian, Hugh	Rochester, N.Y.	4/19/25
O'Brien, Margaret	San Diego, Cal.	1/15/37
Ocean, Billy	Trinidad	1/21/50
O'Connell, Helen	Lima, Oh.	5/23/20
O'Connor, Carroll	New York, N.Y.	8/2/24
O'Connor, Donald	Chicago, Ill.	8/28/25
O'Connor, Sinead	Dublin, Ireland.	12/8/67
Odetta	Birmingham, Ala.	12/31/30
O'Hara, Maureen	Dublin, Ireland.	8/17/20
O'Herlihy, Dan	Wexford, Ireland	5/1/19
Oldman, Gary	London, England	3/21/58
Olin, Ken	Chicago, Ill.	7/30/54
Olin, Lena	Sweden	1955
Olmos, Edward James	E. Los Angeles, Cal.	2/24/47
Olsen, Merlin	Logan, Ut.	9/15/40
O'Neal, Patrick	Ocala, Fla.	9/26/27
O'Neal, Ryan	Los Angeles, Cal.	4/20/41
O'Neal, Tatum	Los Angeles, Cal.	11/5/63
O'Neill, Ed	Youngstown, Oh.	1946
O'Neill, Jennifer	Brazil.	2/20/47
Ontkean, Michael	Vancouver, B.C.	1/24/46
Opatoshu, David.	New York, N.Y.	1/30/18
Orbach, Jerry	New York, N.Y.	10/20/35
Orlando, Tony	New York, N.Y.	4/3/44
Osbourne, Ozzy	Birmingham, England.	12/3/46
O'Shea, Milo	Ireland	1926
Oslin, K.T.	Arkansas	1942
Osmond, Donny	Ogden, Ut.	12/9/57
Osmond, Marie	Ogden, Ut.	10/13/59
O'Sullivan, Maureen	Boyle, Ireland	5/17/11
O'Toole, Annette	Houston, Tex.	4/1/53
O'Toole, Peter	Connemara, Ireland	8/2/32
Owens, Buck	Sherman, Tex.	8/12/29
Oz, Frank	Herford, England	5/25/44
Ozawa, Seiji	Shenyang, China	9/1/35
Paar, Jack	Canton, Oh.	5/1/18
Pacino, Al	New York, N.Y.	4/25/40
Packer, Billy	Wellsville, N.Y.	2/25/40
Page, Patti	Claremore, Okla.	11/8/27
Paige, Janis	Tacoma, Wash.	9/16/22
Palance, Jack	Lattimer, Pa.	2/18/20
Palin, Michael	England	5/5/43
Palmer, Betsy	East Chicago, Ind.	11/1/29
Papas, Irene	Greece.	3/9/26
Papp, Joseph	Brooklyn, N.Y.	6/22/21
Parker, Alan	London, England	2/14/44
Parker, Eleanor	Cedarville, Oh.	6/26/22
Parker, Fess	Ft. Worth, Tex.	8/16/27
Parker, Jameson	Baltimore, Md.	11/18/47
Parker, Jean	Deer Lodge, Mon.	8/11/12
Parker, Sarah Jessica	Nelsonville, Oh.	3/25/65
Parks, Bert	Atlanta, Ga.	12/30/14
Parsons, Estelle	Lynn, Mass.	11/20/27

Name	Birthplace	Born
Parton, Dolly	Sevierville, Tenn.	1/19/46
Pasternak, Joseph	Hungary	9/19/01
Patinkin, Mandy	Chicago, Ill.	11/30/52
Pavarotti, Luciano	Modena, Italy	10/12/35
Paycheck, Johnny	Greenfield, Oh.	5/31/41
Pearl, Minnie	Centerville, Tenn.	10/25/12
Peck, Gregory	La Jolla, Cal.	4/5/16
Pendergrass, Teddy	Philadelphia, Pa.	3/26/50
Penn, Arthur	Philadelphia, Pa.	9/27/22
Penn, Sean	Burbank, Cal.	8/17/60
Penny, Joe	London, England	9/14/56
Peppard, George	Detroit, Mich.	10/1/28
Perkins, Elizabeth	Vermont	1961
Perkins, Anthony	New York, N.Y.	4/4/32
Perlman, Itzhak	Tel Aviv, Israel	8/31/45
Perlman, Rhea	Brooklyn, N.Y.	3/31/48
Perlman, Ron	New York, N.Y.	4/13/-
Perrine, Valerie	Galveston, Tex.	9/3/43
Persoff, Nehemiah	Jerusalem, Palestine	8/14/20
Pesci, Joe	Newark, N.J.	2/9/43
Peters, Bernadette	New York, N.Y.	2/28/48
Peters, Brock	New York, N.Y.	7/2/27
Peters, Jean	Canton, Oh.	10/15/26
Peters, Roberta	New York, N.Y.	5/4/30
Petty, Tom	Gainesville, Fla.	10/20/53
Pfeiffer, Michelle.	Santa Ana, Cal.	4/29/57
Phillips, MacKenzie	Alexandria, Va.	11/10/59
Phillips, Michelle	Long Beach, Cal.	6/4/44
Phoenix, River	Madras, Ore.	8/23/70
Pickett, Cindy	Norman, Okla.	4/18/47
Picon, Molly	New York, N.Y.	6/1/98
Pinchot, Bronson	New York, N.Y.	5/20/59
Piscopo, Joe	Passaic, N.J.	6/17/51
Pleasence, Donald	Worksop, England	10/5/19
Pleshette, Suzanne	New York, N.Y.	1/31/37
Plowright, Joan	Brigg, England	10/28/29
Plummer, Amanda	New York, N.Y.	3/23/57
Plummer, Christopher.	Toronto, Ont.	12/13/27
Poitier, Sidney	Miami, Fla.	2/20/27
Polanski, Roman	Paris, France	8/18/33
Pollack, Sidney	Lafayette, Ind.	7/1/34
Ponti, Carlo	Milan, Italy	12/11/13
Post, Markie	Palo Alto, Cal.	11/4/50
Poston, Tom	Columbus, Oh.	10/17/27
Potts, Annie	Nashville, Tenn.	10/28/-
Powell, Jane	Portland, Ore.	4/1/28
Powers, Stefanie	Hollywood, Cal.	11/2/42
Prentiss, Paula	San Antonio, Tex.	3/4/39
Presley, Priscilla	New York, N.Y.	5/24/45
Preston, Billy	Houston, Tex.	9/9/46
Previn, Andre	Berlin, Germany	4/6/29
Price, Leontyne	Laurel, Miss.	2/10/27
Price, Ray	Perryville, Tex.	1/12/26
Price, Vincent	St. Louis, Mo.	5/27/11
Pride, Charlie	Sledge, Miss.	3/18/39
Prince	Minneapolis, Minn.	6/7/58
Principal, Victoria	Japan	—
Prosky, Robert.	Philadelphia, Pa.	12/13/30
Prowse, Juliet	Bombay, India.	9/25/37
Pryce, Jonathan	Wales	6/1/47
Pryor, Richard	Peoria, Ill.	12/1/40
Pulliam, Keshia Knight	Newark, N.J.	4/9/79
Pyle, Denver	Bethune, Col.	5/11/20
Quaid, Dennis	Houston, Tex.	4/9/54
Quaid, Randy	Houston, Tex.	10/1/50
Quinn, Aidan	Chicago, Ill.	3/8/59
Quinn, Anthony	Chihuahua, Mexico	4/21/15
Quinn, Martha	Albany, N.Y.	5/11/59
Rabb, Ellis	Memphis, Tenn.	6/20/30
Rabbitt, Eddie	Brooklyn, N.Y.	11/27/41
Rachins, Alan	Cambridge, Mass.	10/10/47
Rae, Charlotte	Milwaukee, Wis.	4/22/26
Raffin, Deborah	Los Angeles, Cal.	3/13/53
Rainer, Luise	Vienna, Austria	1/12/09
Raitt, Bonnie	Burbank, Cal.	11/8/49
Raitt, John	Santa Ana, Cal.	1/19/17
Ralston, Esther	Bar Harbor, Me.	9/17/02
Ralston, Vera Hruba	Prague, Czechoslovakia	6/12/19
Rambo, Dack	Delano, Cal.	11/13/41
Ramey, Samuel	Colby, Kan.	3/28/42
Rampal, Jean-Pierre	Marseilles, France	1/7/22
Randall, Tony	Tulsa, Okla.	2/26/20
Randolph, John	New York, N.Y.	6/1/15
Randolph, Joyce.	Detroit, Mich.	10/21/25
Rashad, Phylicia	Houston, Tex.	6/17/48
Ratzenberger, John.	Bridgeport, Conn.	4/6/47
Rawls, Lou	Chicago, Ill.	12/1/36
Rayburn, Gene	Christopher, Ill.	12/22/17
Raye, Martha	Butte, Mon.	8/27/16
Raymond, Gene	New York, N.Y.	8/13/08
Reddy, Helen	Melbourne, Australia	10/25/41
Redford, Robert	Santa Monica, Cal.	8/18/37
Redgrave, Lynn	London, England	3/8/43
Redgrave, Vanessa	London, England	1/30/37
Reed, Jerry	Atlanta, Ga.	3/20/37
Reed, Oliver	London, England	2/13/38
Reed, Rex	Ft. Worth, Tex.	10/2/38
Reed, Robert	Highland Park, Ill.	10/19/32
Reese, Della	Detroit, Mich.	7/6/31
Reeve, Christopher	New York, N.Y.	9/25/52
Regalbuto, Joe	New York, N.Y.	8/24/-
Reid, Kate	London, England	11/4/30
Reid, Tim	Norfolk, Va.	12/19/44
Reilly, Charles Nelson	New York, N.Y.	1/13/31
Reiner, Carl	Bronx, N.Y.	3/20/22
Reiner, Rob	Bronx, N.Y.	3/6/45
Reinhold, Judge	Wilmington, Del.	5/21/56
Reinking, Ann	Seattle, Wash.	11/10/50
Resnik, Regina	New York, N.Y.	8/30/24
Reynolds, Burt.	Waycross, Ga.	2/11/36
Reynolds, Debbie	El Paso, Tex.	4/1/32
Rhue, Madlyn	Washington, D.C.	10/3/34
Rich, Charlie	Forest City, Ark.	12/14/32
Richards, Keith	Kent, England.	12/18/43
Richardson, Tony	Shipley, England	6/5/28
Richie, Lionel	Tuskegee, Ala.	6/20/50
Rickles, Don	New York, N.Y.	5/8/26
Riegert, Peter	New York, N.Y.	4/11/47
Rigg, Diana	Doncaster, England	7/20/38
Ringwald, Molly	Rosewood, Cal.	2/14/68
Ritter, John	Burbank, Cal.	9/17/48
Rivera, Chita	Washington, D.C.	1/23/33
Rivera, Geraldo	New York, N.Y.	7/4/43
Rivers, Joan	Brooklyn, N.Y.	6/8/33
Robards, Jason Jr.	Chicago, Ill.	7/26/22
Robbins, Jerome	New York, N.Y.	10/11/18
Robbins, Tim	W. Covina, Cal.	10/16/58
Roberts, Doris	St. Louis, Mo.	11/4/29
Roberts, Eric	Biloxi, Miss.	4/18/56
Roberts, Julia	Smyrna, Ga.	1967
Roberts, Pernell	Waycross, Ga.	5/18/30
Roberts, Tony	New York, N.Y.	10/22/39
Robertson, Cliff	La Jolla, Cal.	9/9/25
Robertson, Dale	Harrah, Okla.	7/14/23
Robinson, Charles	Houston, Tex.	11/9/-
Robinson, Holly	Philadelphia, Pa.	1965
Robinson, Smokey	Detroit, Mich.	2/19/40
Roche, Eugene	Boston, Mass.	9/22/28
Rodgers, Jimmie	Camas, Wash.	1933
Rodrigues, Percy	Montreal, Que.	6/13/24
Rodriquez, Johnny	Sabinal, Tex.	12/10/51
Rogers, Chas. (Buddy)	Olathe, Kan.	8/13/04
Rogers, Fred	Latrobe, Pa.	3/20/28
Rogers, Ginger	Independence, Mo.	7/16/11
Rogers, Kenny	Houston, Tex.	8/21/38
Rogers, Mimi	Coral Gables, Fla.	1/27/-
Rogers, Roy	Cincinnati, Oh.	11/5/12
Rogers, Wayne	Birmingham, Ala.	4/7/33
Roland, Gilbert.	Juarez, Mexico	12/11/05
Rolle, Esther	Pompano Beach, Fla.	11/8/33
Rollins, Howard	Baltimore, Md.	10/17/50
Romero, Cesar	New York, N.Y.	2/15/07
Ronstadt, Linda	Tucson, Ariz.	7/15/46
Rooney, Mickey	Brooklyn, N.Y.	9/23/20
Rose Marie	New York, N.Y.	8/15/25
Ross, Diana	Detroit, Mich.	3/26/44
Ross, Katharine	Hollywood, Cal.	1/29/42
Ross, Marion	Albert Lea, Minn.	10/25/28
Rosselini, Isabella	Rome, Italy	6/18/52
Rostropovich, Mstislav	Baku, USSR.	3/12/27
Roth, David Lee	Bloomington, Ind.	10/10/55
Rourke, Mickey	Miami, Fla.	1956
Rowlands, Gena	Cambria, Wis.	6/19/34
Rubinstein, John	Los Angeles, Cal.	12/8/46
Rush, Barbara	Denver, Col.	1/4/30
Russell, Jane	Bemidji, Minn.	6/21/21
Russell, Ken	Southampton, England.	7/3/27
Russell, Kurt	Springfield, Mass.	3/17/51
Russell, Mark	Buffalo, N.Y.	8/23/32
Russell, Nipsey	Atlanta, Ga.	10/13/24
Russell, Theresa	San Diego, Cal.	1957
Rutherford, Ann	Toronto, Ont.	11/2/20
Ruttan, Susan	Oregon City, Ore.	9/16/50
Ryan, Meg	Fairfield, Conn.	11/19/63
Ryan, Peggy	Long Beach, Cal.	8/28/24
Ryan, Roz	Detroit, Mich.	7/7/51

Name	Birthplace	Born
Rydell, Bobby	Philadelphia, Pa.	4/26/42
Ryder, Winona	Winona, Minn.	1971
Saget, Bob	Philadelphia, Pa.	5/17/56
Sahl, Mort	Montreal, Que.	5/11/27
Saint, Eva Marie	Newark, N.J.	7/4/24
St. James, Susan	Los Angeles, Cal.	8/14/46
St. John, Jill	Los Angeles, Cal.	8/19/40
Sainte-Marie, Buffy	Maine	2/20/41
Sajak, Pat	Chicago, Ill.	10/26/47
Saks, Gene	New York, N.Y.	11/8/21
Sales, Soupy	Franklinton, N.C.	1/8/26
Samms, Emma	London, England	8/28/60
Sanderson, William	Memphis, Tenn.	1/10/48
Sandy, Gary	Dayton, Oh.	12/25/45
Sanford, Isabel	New York, N.Y.	8/29/17
Santana, Carlos	Mexico	7/20/47
Sarandon, Chris	Beckley, W.Va.	7/24/42
Sarandon, Susan	New York, N.Y.	10/4/46
Sarnoff, Dorothy	New York, N.Y.	5/25/17
Sarrazin, Michael	Quebec City, Que.	5/22/40
Savage, Fred	Highland Park, Ill.	7/9/76
Savalas, Telly	Garden City, N.Y.	1/21/24
Saxon, John	Brooklyn, N.Y.	8/5/35
Sayles, John	Schenetady, N.Y.	9/28/50
Scaggs, Boz	Dallas, Tex.	6/8/44
Schallert, William	Los Angeles, Cal.	7/6/22
Scheider, Roy	Orange, N.J.	11/10/32
Schell, Maria	Vienna, Austria	1/15/26
Schell, Maximilian	Vienna, Austria	12/8/30
Schenkel, Chris	Bippus, Ind.	8/21/23
Schnabel, Stefan	Berlin, Germany	2/2/12
Schneider, Alexander	Vilna, Poland	10/21/08
Schneider, John	Mt. Kisco, N.Y.	4/8/54
Schreiber, Avery	Chicago, Ill.	4/9/35
Schroder, Rick	Staten Island, N.Y.	4/3/70
Schwarzenegger, Arnold	Graz, Austria	7/30/47
Schwarzkopf, Elisabeth	Jarotschin, Poland	12/9/15
Scofield, Paul	Hurst, Pierpont, England.	1/21/22
Scolari, Peter	New Rochelle, Ill.	9/12/54
Scorsese, Martin	New York, N.Y.	11/17/42
Scott, George C.	Wise, Va.	10/18/27
Scott, Lizabeth	Scranton, Pa.	9/29/22
Scott, Martha	Jamesport, Mo.	9/22/14
Scotto, Renata	Savona, Italy	2/24/35
Scully, Vin	New York, N.Y.	11/29/27
Sebastian, John	New York N.Y.	3/17/44
Sedaka, Neil	New York, N.Y.	3/13/39
Seeger, Pete	New York, N.Y.	5/3/19
Segal, George	Great Neck, N.Y.	2/13/34
Segal, Vivienne	Philadelphia, Pa.	4/19/97
Seidelman, Susan	Philadelphia, Pa.	12/11/52
Seinfeld, Jerry	New York, N.Y.	1954
Sellecca, Connie	New York, N.Y.	5/25/55
Selleck, Tom	Detroit, Mich.	1/29/45
Severinsen, Doc	Arlington, Ore.	7/7/27
Seymour, Jane	Middlesex, England.	2/15/51
Shackelford, Ted	Oklahoma City, Okla.	6/23/46
Shaffer, Paul	Thunder Bay, Ont.	11/28/49
Shandling, Garry	Tucson, Ariz.	11/29/49
Shankar, Ravi	India	4/7/20
Sharif, Omar	Alexandria, Egypt.	4/10/32
Shatner, William	Montreal, Que.	3/22/31
Shea, John	N. Conway, N.H.	4/14/49
Shearer, Moira	Scotland	1/17/26
Sheedy, Ally	New York, N.Y.	6/12/62
Sheen, Charlie	Santa Monica, Cal.	9/3/65
Sheen, Martin	Dayton, Oh.	8/3/40
Shelley, Carole	London, England	8/16/39
Shepard, Sam	Ft. Sheridan, Ill.	11/5/43
Shepherd, Cybill	Memphis, Tenn.	2/18/49
Shields, Brooke	New York, N.Y.	5/31/65
Shire, Talia	New York, N.Y.	4/25/46
Shore, Dinah	Winchester, Tenn.	3/1/17
Short, Bobby	Danville, Ill.	9/15/24
Short, Martin	Hamilton, Ont.	3/26/51
Shull, Richard B.	Evanston, Ill.	2/24/29
Sidney, Sylvia	New York, N.Y.	8/8/10
Siepi, Cesare	Milan, Italy	2/10/23
Sikking, James B.	Los Angeles, Cal.	3/5/34
Sills, Beverly	Brooklyn, N.Y.	5/25/29
Silver, Ron	New York, N.Y.	7/2/46
Simmons, Gene	Haifa, Israel	8/25/49
Simmons, Jean	London, England	1/31/29
Simon, Carly	New York, N.Y.	6/25/45
Simon, Paul	Newark, N.J.	11/5/42
Simone, Nina	Tyron, N.C.	2/21/33
Sinatra, Frank	Hoboken, N.J.	12/12/15
Sinbad	Benton Harbor, Mich.	11/10/-
Sinclair, Madge	Kingston, Jamaica	4/28/38
Siskel, Gene	Chicago, Ill.	1/26/46
Skelton, Red (Richard)	Vincennes, Ind.	7/18/13
Skerritt, Tom	Detroit, Mich.	8/25/33
Slater, Helen	Massapequa, N.Y.	12/14/63
Slezak, Erika	Hollywood, Cal.	8/5/46
Slick, Grace	Chicago, Ill.	10/30/39
Smirnoff, Yakov	Odessa, USSR	1/24/51
Smith, Allison	New York, N.Y.	12/9/69
Smith, Alexis	Penticton, B.C.	6/8/21
Smith, Buffalo Bob	Buffalo, N.Y.	11/27/17
Smith, Connie	Elkhart, Ind.	8/14/41
Smith, Jaclyn	Houston, Tex.	10/26/47
Smith, Keely	Norfolk, Va.	3/9/35
Smith, Maggie	Ilford, England.	12/28/34
Smits, Jimmy	New York, N.Y.	7/9/55
Smothers, Dick	New York, N.Y.	11/20/39
Smothers, Tom	New York, N.Y.	2/2/37
Snipes, Wesley	Orlando, Fla.	1962
Snow, Hank	Nova Scotia, Canada	5/9/14
Snyder, Tom	Milwaukee, Wis.	5/12/36
Solti, Georg	Budapest, Hungary.	10/21/12
Somers, Suzanne	San Bruno, Cal.	10/16/46
Somes, Michael	nr. Stroud, England.	9/28/17
Sommer, Elke	Berlin, Germany	11/5/41
Sorvino, Paul	New York, N.Y.	1939
Sothern, Ann	Valley City, N.D.	1/22/09
Soul, David	Chicago, Ill.	8/28/43
Spacek, Sissy	Quitman, Tex.	12/25/49
Spacey, Kevin	S. Orange, N.J.	1960
Spader, James	Boston, Mass.	1961
Spano, Joe	San Francisco, Cal.	7/7/46
Spelling, Aaron	Dallas, Tex.	4/22/28
Spencer, John	New Jersey	1946
Spielberg, Steven	Cincinnati, Oh.	12/18/47
Springfield, Dusty	London, England	4/16/39
Springfield, Rick	Sydney, Australia.	8/23/49
Springsteen, Bruce	Freehold, N.J.	9/23/49
Stack, Robert	Los Angeles, Cal.	1/13/19
Stafford, Jo	Coalinga, Cal.	11/12/18
Stahl, Richard	Detroit, Mich.	1/4/32
Stallone, Sylvester	New York, N.Y.	7/6/46
Stamos, John	Cypress, Cal.	8/19/63
Stamp, Terence	Stepney, England.	7/22/39
Stander, Lionel	New York, N.Y.	1/11/08
Stang, Arnold	New York, N.Y.	9/28/25
Stanley, Kim	Tularosa, N.M.	2/11/25
Stanton, Harry Dean	Kentucky	7/14/26
Stapleton, Jean	New York, N.Y.	1/19/23
Stapleton, Maureen	Troy, N.Y.	6/21/25
Starr, Kay	Dougherty, Okla.	7/21/22
Starr, Ringo	Liverpool, England	7/7/40
Steenburgen, Mary	Little Rock, Ark.	1953
Steiger, Rod	W. Hampton, N.Y.	4/14/25
Stephens, James	Mt. Kisco, N.Y.	5/18/51
Sterling, Jan	New York, N.Y.	4/3/23
Sterling, Robert	New Castle, Pa.	11/13/17
Stern, Howard	New York, N.Y.	1954
Stern, Isaac	Kreminiecz, Russia	7/21/20
Sternhagen, Frances	Washington, D.C.	1/13/30
Stevens, Andrew	Memphis, Tenn.	6/10/55
Stevens, Cat	London, England	7/21/48
Stevens, Connie	Brooklyn, N.Y.	8/8/38
Stevens, Kaye	E. Cleveland, Oh.	7/21/35
Stevens, Rise	New York, N.Y.	6/11/13
Stevens, Stella	Yazoo City, Miss.	10/1/36
Stevenson, McLean	Normal, Ill.	11/14/29
Stevenson, Parker	Philadelphia, Pa.	6/4/52
Stewart, James	Indiana, Pa.	5/20/08
Stewart, Rod	London, England	1/10/45
Stickney, Dorothy	Dickinson, N.D.	6/21/00
Stiers, David Ogden	Peoria, Ill.	10/31/42
Stiller, Jerry	New York, N.Y.	6/8/29
Stills, Stephen	Dallas, Tex.	1/3/45
Sting (G. Sumner)	Newcastle, England	10/2/51
Stockwell, Dean	Hollywood, Cal.	3/5/36
Stoltz, Eric	American Somoa	1961
Stone, Oliver	New York, N.Y.	9/15/46
Stookey, Paul	Baltimore, Md.	12/30/37
Storch, Larry	New York, N.Y.	1/8/23
Storm, Gale	Bloomington, Tex.	4/5/22
Straight, Beatrice	Old Westbury, N.Y.	8/2/18
Strasser, Robin	New York, N.Y.	5/7/45
Stratas, Teresa	Toronto, Ont.	5/26/38
Strauss, Peter	New York, N.Y.	2/20/47
Streep, Meryl	Summit, N.J.	6/22/49
Streisand, Barbra	Brooklyn, N.Y.	4/24/42

Name	Birthplace	Born
Stritch, Elaine	Detroit, Mich.	2/2/26
Struthers, Sally	Portland, Ore.	7/28/48
Stuarti, Enzo	Rome, Italy	3/3/25
Sullivan, Barry	New York, N.Y.	8/29/12
Sullivan, Susan	New York, N.Y.	11/18/44
Sumac, Yma	Ichocan, Peru	9/10/27
Summer, Donna	Boston, Mass.	12/31/48
Sutherland, Donald	St. John, New Brunswick	7/17/34
Sutherland, Joan	Sydney, Australia.	11/7/26
Sutherland, Kiefer	London, England	12/20/66
Swayze, Patrick	Houston, Tex.	8/18/54
Swenson, Inga	Omaha, Neb.	12/29/34
Swit, Loretta	Passaic, N.J.	11/4/37
Mr. T (Lawrence Tero)	Chicago, Ill.	5/21/52
Tallchief, Maria	Fairfax, Okla.	1/24/25
Tandy, Jessica	London, England	6/7/09
Tarkenton, Fran	Richmond, Va.	2/3/40
Taylor, Elizabeth	London, England	2/27/32
Taylor, James	Boston, Mass.	3/12/48
Taylor, Rod	Sydney, Australia.	1/11/29
Te Kanawa, Kiri	Gisborne, New Zealand	3/6/44
Tebaldi, Renata	Pesaro, Italy.	2/1/22
Temple, Shirley	Santa Monica, Cal.	4/23/28
Tennant, Victoria	London, England	9/30/50
Tennille, Toni.	Montgomery, Ala.	5/8/43
Tharp, Twyla	Portland, Ind.	7/1/41
Thaxter, Phyllis	Portland, Me.	11/20/19
Thicke, Alan	Kirkland Lake, Ont.	3/1/47
Thomas, B.J.	Hugo, Okla.	8/7/42
Thomas, Heather	Greenwich, Conn.	9/8/57
Thomas, Marlo.	Detroit, Mich.	11/21/43
Thomas, Philip Michael	Columbus, Oh.	5/26/49
Thomas, Richard	New York, N.Y.	6/13/51
Thompson, Jack.	Sydney, Australia.	8/31/40
Thompson, Lea	Rochester, Minn.	5/31/61
Thompson, Sada	Des Moines, Ia.	9/27/29
Thulin, Ingrid	Sweden	1/27/29
Tiegs, Cheryl	Minnesota	9/27/47
Tierney, Gene	Brooklyn, N.Y.	11/20/20
Tiffany	Norwalk, Cal.	10/2/71
Tillis, Mel	Tampa, Fla.	8/8/32
Tiny Tim	New York, N.Y.	4/12/23
Todd, Richard	Dublin, Ireland.	6/11/19
Tomlin, Lily	Detroit, Mich.	9/1/39
Tomlinson, David	Scotland	5/7/17
Toomey, Regis.	Pittsburgh, Pa.	8/13/02
Torme, Mel	Chicago, Ill.	9/13/25
Torn, Rip	Temple, Tex.	2/6/31
Townsend, Robert.	Chicago, Ill.	2/6/57
Travanti, Daniel J.	Kenosha, Wis.	3/7/40
Travers, Mary	Louisville, Ky.	11/9/36
Travis, Randy	Marshville, N.C.	5/4/59
Travolta, John	Englewood, N.J.	2/18/54
Trebek, Alex	Sudbury, Ont.	7/22/40
Trevor, Claire	New York, N.Y.	3/8/09
Troyanos, Tatiana	New York, N.Y.	9/12/38
Tucker, Michael	Baltimore, Md.	2/6/44
Tucker, Tanya	Seminole, Tex.	10/10/58
Tune, Tommy	Wichita Falls, Tex.	2/28/39
Turner, Kathleen.	Springfield, Mo.	6/19/54
Turner, Lana	Wallace, Ida.	2/8/20
Turner, Tina	Nutbush, Tenn.	11/26/39
Tushingham, Rita	Liverpool, England	3/14/40
Twiggy (Leslie Hornby)	London, England	9/19/46
Twitty, Conway	Friar's Point, Miss.	9/1/33
Tyson, Cicely	New York, N.Y.	12/19/33
Uecker, Bob	Milwaukee, Wis.	1/26/35
Uggams, Leslie	New York, N.Y.	5/25/43
Ullman, Tracey	Slough, England	12/30/59
Ullmann, Liv	Tokyo, Japan.	12/16/38
Underwood, Blair	Tacoma, Wash.	8/25/-
Urich, Robert.	Toronto, Oh.	12/19/46
Ustinov, Peter	London, England	4/16/21
Vaccaro, Brenda	Brooklyn, N.Y.	11/18/39
Vale, Jerry	New York, N.Y.	7/8/31
Valente, Caterina	Paris, France	1/14/31
Valli, Frankie	Newark, N.J.	5/3/37
Van Ark, Joan	New York, N.Y.	6/16/43
Van Doren, Mamie	Rowena, S.D.	2/6/33
Vandross, Luther	New York, N.Y.	4/20/51
Van Dyke, Dick	West Plains, Mo.	12/13/25
Van Dyke, Jerry	Danville, Ill.	7/27/31
Van Fleet, Jo.	Oakland, Cal.	12/30/22
Van Halen, Eddie	Nijmegan, Netherlands.	1/26/57
Van Pallandt, Nina.	Copenhagen, Denmark	7/15/32
Van Patten, Dick.	New York, N.Y.	12/9/28
Van Peebles, Mario	Mexico.	1/15/57
Vaughn, Robert	New York, N.Y.	11/22/32
Venuta, Benay	San Francisco, Cal.	1/27/11
Verdon, Gwen	Los Angeles, Cal.	1/13/25
Vereen, Ben	Miami, Fla.	10/10/46
Verrett, Shirley.	New Orleans, La.	5/31/31
Vickers, Jon	Prince Albert, Sask.	10/26/26
Vigoda, Abe	New York, N.Y.	2/24/21
Villella, Edward	Long Island, N.Y.	10/1/36
Vincent, Jan-Michael	Denver, Col.	7/15/44
Vinson, Helen	Beaumont, Tex.	9/17/07
Vinton, Bobby	Canonsburg, Pa.	4/16/35
Vitale, Dick.	E. Rutherford, N.J.	6/9/40
Voight, Jon	Yonkers, N.Y.	12/29/38
Von Stade, Frederica	Somerville, N.J.	6/1/45
Von Sydow, Max	Lund, Sweden.	4/10/29
Wagner, Lindsay.	Los Angeles, Cal.	6/22/49
Wagner, Robert	Detroit, Mich.	2/10/30
Wagoner, Porter.	West Plains, Mo.	8/12/27
Wahl, Ken	Chicago, Ill.	2/14/56
Wain, Bea	Bronx, N.Y.	4/30/17
Waite, Ralph	White Plains, N.Y.	6/22/29
Walden, Robert	New York, N.Y.	9/25/43
Walken, Christopher	New York, N.Y.	3/31/43
Walker, Clint	Hartford, Ill.	5/30/27
Walker, Nancy	Philadelphia, Pa.	5/10/22
Wallach, Eli.	Brooklyn, N.Y.	12/7/15
Walston, Ray	Laurel, Miss.	11/2/24
Walter, Jessica	New York, N.Y.	1/31/44
Wanamaker, Sam	Chicago, Ill.	6/14/19
Ward, Fred	San Diego, Cal.	1943
Ward, Rachel	London, England	1957
Ward, Simon	London, England	10/19/41
Warden, Jack	Newark, N.J.	9/18/20
Warfield, William.	W. Helena, Ark.	1/22/20
Warner, Malcolm-Jamal	Jersey City, N.J.	8/18/70
Warren, Lesley Ann	New York, N.Y.	8/16/46
Warrick, Ruth	St. Joseph, Mo.	6/29/16
Warwick, Dionne.	E. Orange, N.J.	12/12/41
Washington, Denzel	Mt. Vernon, N.Y.	12/28/54
Waterston, Sam	Cambridge, Mass.	11/15/40
Watkins, Carlene	Hartford, Conn.	6/4/52
Watts, Andre.	Nuremberg, Germany	6/20/46
Wayans, Keenan Ivory	New York, N.Y.	—
Wayne, David	Traverse City, Mich.	1/30/14
Waxman, Al	Toronto, Ont.	3/2/35
Weaver, Dennis	Joplin, Mo.	6/4/24
Weaver, Fritz.	Pittsburgh, Pa.	1/19/26
Weaver, Sigourney	New York, N.Y.	10/8/49
Weir, Peter.	Sydney, Australia.	8/8/44
Weitz, Bruce	Norwalk, Conn.	5/27/43
Welch, Raquel	Chicago, Ill.	9/5/40
Weld, Tuesday	New York, N.Y.	8/27/43
Welk, Lawrence	nr. Strasburg, N.D.	3/11/03
Wells, Kitty	Nashville, Tenn.	8/30/19
Wendt, George	Chicago, Ill.	10/17/48
Weston, Jack	Cleveland, Oh.	8/21/24
White, Barry	Galveston, Tex.	9/12/44
White, Betty	Oak Park, Ill.	1/17/22
White, Jesse	Buffalo, N.Y.	1/3/19
White, Vanna	N. Myrtle Beach, S.C.	2/18/57
Whiting, Margaret	Detroit, Mich.	7/22/24
Whitmore, James	White Plains, N.Y.	10/1/21
Widmark, Richard	Sunrise, Minn.	12/26/14
Wiest, Dianne	Kansas City, Mo.	3/28/48
Wilder, Billy	Vienna, Austria	6/22/06
Wilder, Gene	Milwaukee, Wis.	6/11/35
Williams, Andy	Wall Lake, Ia.	12/3/30
Williams, Billy Dee	New York, N.Y.	4/6/37
Williams, Cindy	Van Nuys, Cal.	8/22/47
Williams, Esther	Los Angeles, Cal.	8/8/23
Williams, Hal	Columbus, Oh.	12/14/38
Williams Jr., Hank	Shreveport, La.	5/26/49
Williams, Joe.	Cordele, Ga.	12/12/18
Williams, JoBeth	Houston, Tex.	1953
Williams, Paul	Omaha, Neb.	9/19/40
Williams, Robin	Chicago, Ill.	7/21/52
Williams, Treat.	Rowayton, Conn.	12/1/51
Williamson, Nicol	Hamilton, Scotland	9/14/38
Willis, Bruce	W. Germany.	3/19/55
Wilson, Demond	Valdosta, Ga.	10/13/46
Wilson, Elizabeth	Grand Rapids, Mich.	4/4/25
Wilson, Flip.	Jersey City, N.J.	12/8/33
Wilson, Nancy	Chillicothe, Oh.	2/20/37
Windom, William.	New York, N.Y.	9/28/23
Winfield, Paul	Los Angeles, Cal.	5/22/41
Winfrey, Oprah	Kosciusko, Miss.	1/29/54
Winger, Debra	Cleveland, Oh.	5/16/55
Winkler, Henry	New York, N.Y.	10/30/45

Name	Birthplace	Born
Winters, Jonathan	Dayton, Oh.	11/11/25
Winters, Shelley	St. Louis, Mo.	8/18/22
Winwood, Steve	Birmingham, England.	5/12/48
Wiseman, Joseph	Montreal, Que.	5/15/18
Withers, Jane	Atlanta, Ga.	4/12/26
Wonder, Stevie	Saginaw, Mich.	5/13/50
Woodard, Alfre	Tulsa, Okla.	11/2/53
Woods, James	Vernal, N.J.	4/18/47
Woodward, Edward	Croyden, England	6/1/30
Woodward, Joanne	Thomasville, Ga.	2/27/30
Worth, Irene	Nebraska	6/23/16
Wray, Fay	Alberta, Canada	9/10/07
Wright, Martha	Seattle, Wash.	3/23/26
Wright, Max	Detroit, Mich.	8/2/-
Wright, Steven	New York, N.Y.	12/6/55
Wright, Teresa	New York, N.Y.	10/27/18
Wyatt, Jane	Campgaw, N.J.	8/10/11
Wyman, Jane	St. Joseph, Mo.	1/4/14

Name	Birthplace	Born
Wynette, Tammy	Red Bay, Ala.	5/5/42
Yarborough, Glenn	Milwaukee, Wis.	1/12/30
Yarrow, Peter	New York, N.Y.	5/31/38
York, Michael	Fulmer, England	3/27/42
York, Susannah	London, England	1/9/42
Young, Alan	Northumberland, England	11/19/19
Young, Burt	New York, N.Y.	4/30/40
Young, Loretta	Salt Lake City, Ut.	1/6/13
Young, Neil	Toronto, Ont.	11/12/45
Young, Robert	Chicago, Ill.	2/22/07
Youngman, Henny	Liverpool, England	1/12/06
Zappa, Frank	Baltimore, Md.	12/21/40
Zeffirelli, Franco	Florence, Italy.	2/12/23
Zerbe, Anthony	Long Beach, Cal.	5/20/36
Zimbalist, Efrem Jr.	New York, N.Y.	11/30/23
Zmed, Adrian	Chicago, Ill.	3/14/54
Zukerman, Pinchas	Tel Aviv, Israel	7/16/48

Entertainment Personalities of the Past

(as of mid-1991)

Born	Died	Name
1895	1974	Abbott, Bud
1872	1953	Adams, Maude
1855	1926	Adler, Jacob P.
1903	1984	Adler, Luther
1898	1933	Adoree, Renee
1902	1986	Aherne, Brian
1931	1989	Ailey, Alvin
1909	1964	Albertson, Frank
1907	1981	Albertson, Jack
1894	1956	Allen, Fred
1906	1964	Allen, Gracie
1883	1950	Allgood, Sara
1913	1967	Andrews, Laverne
1876	1958	Anglin, Margaret
1887	1933	Arbuckle, Fatty (Roscoe)
1908	1990	Arden, Eve
1900	1976	Arlen, Richard
1868	1946	Arliss, George
1888	1945	Armetta, Henry
1900	1971	Armstrong, Louis
1917	1986	Arnaz, Desi
1890	1956	Arnold, Edward
1905	1974	Arquette, Cliff
1900	1991	Arthur, Jean
1899	1987	Astaire, Fred
1906	1987	Astor, Mary
1885	1946	Atwill, Lionel
1845	1930	Auer, Leopold
1905	1967	Auer, Mischa
1900	1972	Austin, Gene
1898	1940	Ayres, Agnes
1913	1989	Backus, Jim
1918	1990	Bailey, Pearl
1892	1968	Bainter, Fay
1906	1975	Baker, Josephine
1904	1983	Balanchine, George
1911	1989	Ball, Lucille
1882	1956	Bancroft, George
1902	1968	Bankhead, Tallulah
1890	1952	Banks, Leslie
1890	1955	Bara, Theda
1810	1891	Barnum, Phineas T.
1879	1959	Barrymore, Ethel
1882	1942	Barrymore, John
1878	1954	Barrymore, Lionel
1848	1905	Barrymore, Maurice
1897	1963	Barthelmess, Richard
1890	1962	Barton, James
1914	1984	Basehart, Richard
1904	1984	Basie, Count
1923	1985	Baxter, Anne
1889	1951	Baxter, Warner
1880	1928	Bayes, Nora
1904	1965	Beatty, Clyde
1902	1962	Beavers, Louise
1884	1946	Beery, Noah
1889	1949	Beery, Wallace
1901	1970	Begley, Ed
1854	1931	Belasco, David
1949	1982	Belushi, John

Born	Died	Name
1906	1968	Benaderet, Bea
1906	1964	Bendix, William
1904	1965	Bennett, Constance
1910	1990	Bennett, Joan
1943	1987	Bennett, Michael
1894	1974	Benny, Jack
1924	1970	Benzell, Mimi
1899	1966	Berg, Gertrude
1903	1978	Bergen, Edgar
1915	1982	Bergman, Ingrid
1895	1976	Berkeley, Busby
1923	1986	Bernardi, Herschel
1844	1923	Bernhardt, Sarah
1893	1943	Bernie, Ben
1889	1967	Bickford, Charles
1911	1960	Bjoerling, Jussi
1895	1973	Blackmer, Sidney
1908	1989	Blanc, Mel
1900	1943	Bledsoe, Jules
1928	1972	Blocker, Dan
1909	1979	Blondell, Joan
1888	1959	Blore, Eric
1901	1975	Blue, Ben
1899	1957	Bogart, Humphrey
1880	1965	Boland, Mary
1895	1969	Boles, John
1904	1987	Bolger, Ray
1903	1960	Bond, Ward
1892	1981	Bondi, Beulah
1917	1981	Boone, Richard
1833	1893	Booth, Edwin
1796	1852	Booth, Junius Brutus
1894	1953	Bordoni, Irene
1888	1960	Bori, Lucrezia
1905	1965	Bow, Clara
1874	1946	Bowes, Maj. Edward
1928	1977	Boyd, Stephen
1898	1972	Boyd, William
1899	1978	Boyer, Charles
1893	1939	Brady, Alice
1894	1974	Brennan, Walter
1904	1979	Brent, George
1891	1951	Brice, Fanny
1891	1959	Broderick, Helen
1904	1951	Bromberg, J. Edward
1892	1973	Brown, Joe E.
1926	1966	Bruce, Lenny
1895	1953	Bruce, Nigel
1910	1982	Bruce, Virginia
1915	1985	Brynner, Yul
1903	1979	Buchanan, Edgar
1891	1957	Buchanan, Jack
1885	1957	Buck, Gene
1938	1982	Buono, Victor
1885	1970	Burke, Billie
1911	1967	Burnette, Smiley
1902	1971	Burns, David
1925	1984	Burton, Richard
1897	1946	Busch, Mae
1883	1966	Bushman, Francis X.
1896	1946	Butterworth, Charles

Born	Died	Name
1893	1971	Byington, Spring
1904	1972	Cabot, Bruce
1918	1977	Cabot, Sebastian
1899	1986	Cagney, James
1895	1956	Calhern, Louis
1923	1977	Callas, Maria
1933	1976	Cambridge, Godfrey
1865	1940	Campbell, Mrs. Patrick
1892	1964	Cantor, Eddie
1878	1947	Carey, Harry
1950	1983	Carpenter, Karen
1906	1988	Carradine, John
1880	1961	Carrillo, Leo
1892	1972	Carroll, Leo G.
1905	1965	Carroll, Nancy
1910	1963	Carson, Jack
1862	1937	Carter, Mrs. Leslie
1873	1921	Caruso, Enrico
1876	1973	Casals, Pablo
1929	1989	Cassavetes, John
1893	1969	Castle, Irene
1887	1918	Castle, Vernon
1889	1960	Catlett, Walter
1873	1938	Cavanaugh, Hobart
1919	1980	Chaliapin, Feodor
1918	1961	Champion, Gower
1883	1930	Chandler, Jeff
1905	1973	Chaney, Lon
1942	1981	Chaney Jr., Lon
1889	1977	Chapin, Harry
1893	1940	Chaplin, Charles
1893	1961	Chase, Charlie
1888	1972	Chatterton, Ruth
1888	1960	Chevalier, Maurice
1914	1968	Clark, Bobby
1920	1966	Clark, Fred
1932	1963	Clift, Montgomery
1898	1937	Cline, Patsy
1892	1967	Clive, Colin
1911	1976	Clyde, Andy
1877	1961	Cobb, Lee J.
1878	1942	Coburn, Charles
1902	1986	Cohan, George M.
1919	1965	Cohen, Myron
1890	1965	Cole, Nat (King)
1891	1958	Collins, Ray
1908	1934	Colman, Ronald
1907	1944	Columbo, Russ
1887	1940	Compton, Betty
1917	1982	Connolly, Walter
1911	1975	Conried, Hans
1914	1984	Conte, Richard
1935	1964	Coogan, Jackie
1901	1961	Cooke, Sam
1888	1971	Cooper, Gary
1896	1973	Cooper, Gladys
1914	1968	Cooper, Melville
1893	1974	Corey, Wendell
1890	1972	Cornell, Katherine
		Correll, Charles (Andy)

Born	Died	Name
1905	1979	Costello, Dolores
1904	1957	Costello, Helene
1906	1959	Costello, Lou
1877	1950	Costello, Maurice
1899	1973	Coward, Noel
1924	1973	Cox, Wally
1908	1983	Crabbe, Buster
1847	1924	Crabtree, Lotta
1928	1978	Crane, Bob
1911	1986	Crawford, Broderick
1908	1977	Crawford, Joan
1916	1944	Cregar, Laird
1880	1942	Crews, Laura Hope
1880	1974	Crisp, Donald
1942	1973	Croce, Jim
1903	1977	Crosby, Bing
1897	1975	Cross, Milton
1910	1986	Crothers, Scatman
1908	1990	Cummings, Robert
1878	1968	Currie, Finlay
1914	1978	Dailey, Dan
1923	1965	Dandridge, Dorothy
1869	1941	Danforth, William
1894	1963	Daniell, Henry
1901	1971	Daniels, Bebe
1936	1973	Darin, Bobby
1921	1965	Darnell, Linda
1879	1967	Darwell, Jane
1909	1986	Da Silva, Howard
1866	1949	Davenport, Harry
1908	1989	Davis, Bette
1907	1961	Davis, Joan
1925	1990	Davis Jr., Sammy
1931	1955	Dean, James
1905	1968	Dekker, Albert
1908	1983	Del Rio, Dolores
1892	1983	Demarest, William
1881	1959	DeMille, Cecil B.
1891	1967	Denny, Reginald
1901	1974	DeSica, Vittorio
1905	1977	Devine, Andy
1942	1972	De Wilde, Brandon
1907	1974	De Wolfe, Billy
1920	1985	Diamond, Selma
1879	1947	Digges, Dudley
1901	1966	Disney, Walt
1894	1949	Dix, Richard
1905	1958	Donat, Robert
1889	1972	Donlevy, Brian
1901	1981	Douglas, Melvyn
1907	1959	Douglas, Paul
1889	1956	Draper, Ruth
1881	1965	Dresser, Louise
1869	1934	Dressler, Marie
1820	1897	Drew, Mrs. John
1853	1927	Drew, John (son)
1909	1951	Duchin, Eddy
1890	1974	Dumbrille, Douglass
1889	1965	Dumont, Margaret
1878	1927	Duncan, Isadora
1905	1967	Dunn, James
1935	1973	Dunn, Michael
1898	1990	Dunne, Irene
1893	1980	Durante, Jimmy
1907	1968	Duryea, Dan
1858	1924	Duse, Eleanora
1894	1929	Eagels, Jeanne
1901	1967	Eddy, Nelson
1897	1971	Edwards, Cliff
1879	1945	Edwards, Gus
1899	1974	Ellington, Duke
1941	1974	Elliot, Cass
1891	1967	Elman, Mischa
1881	1951	Errol, Leon
1888	1976	Evans, Edith
1901	1989	Evans, Maurice
1913	1967	Evelyn, Judith
1883	1939	Fairbanks, Douglas
1914	1970	Farmer, Frances
1870	1929	Farnum, Dustin
1876	1953	Farnum, William
1882	1967	Farrar, Geraldine
1904	1971	Farrell, Glenda
1868	1940	Faversham, William
1861	1939	Fawcett, George
1897	1961	Fay, Frank

Born	Died	Name
1895	1962	Fazenda, Louise
1933	1982	Feldman, Marty
1898	1985	Fetchit, Stepin
1894	1979	Fiedler, Arthur
1918	1973	Field, Betty
1898	1979	Fields, Gracie
1879	1946	Fields, W.C.
1931	1978	Fields, Totie
1902	1977	Finch, Peter
1902	1975	Fine, Larry
1865	1932	Fiske, Minnie Maddern
1888	1961	Fitzgerald, Barry
1895	1962	Flagstad, Kirsten
1900	1971	Flippen, Jay C.
1909	1959	Flynn, Errol
1925	1974	Flynn, Joe
1880	1942	Fokine, Michel
1910	1968	Foley, Red
1905	1982	Fonda, Henry
1920	1978	Fontaine, Frank
1887	1983	Fontanne, Lynn
1919	1991	Fonteyn, Margot
1895	1973	Ford, John
1901	1976	Ford, Paul
1899	1966	Ford, Wallace
1927	1987	Fosse, Bob
1901	1970	Foster, Preston
1857	1928	Foy, Eddie
1903	1968	Francis, Kay
1887	1966	Frawley, William
1885	1938	Frederick, Pauline
1870	1955	Friganza, Trixie
1890	1958	Frisco, Joe
1901	1960	Gable, Clark
1889	1963	Galli-Curci, Amelita
1905	1990	Garbo, Greta
1877	1967	Garden, Mary
1922	1990	Gardner, Ava
1913	1952	Garfield, John
1922	1969	Garland, Judy
1939	1984	Gaye, Marvin
1906	1984	Gaynor, Janet
1902	1978	Geer, Will
1900	1954	George, Gladys
1892	1962	Gibson, Hoot
1894	1971	Gilbert, Billy
1895	1936	Gilbert, John
1855	1937	Gillette, William
1879	1939	Gilpin, Charles
1897	1987	Gingold, Hermione
1898	1968	Gish, Dorothy
1916	1987	Gleason, Jackie
1886	1959	Gleason, James
1884	1938	Gluck, Alma
1905	1990	Goddard, Paulette
1903	1983	Godfrey, Arthur
1874	1955	Golden, John
1882	1974	Goldwyn, Samuel
1909	1986	Goodman, Benny
1915	1969	Gorcey, Leo
1896	1985	Gordon, Ruth
1899	1982	Gosden, Freeman (Amos)
1904	1944	Gottschalk, Ferdinand
1829	1869	Gottschalk, Louis
1916	1973	Grable, Betty
1894	1991	Graham, Martha
1925	1981	Grahame, Gloria
1904	1986	Grant, Cary
1915	1987	Greene, Lorne
1879	1954	Greenstreet, Sydney
1874	1948	Griffith, David Wark
1912	1980	Griffith, Hugh
1912	1967	Guthrie, Woody
1875	1959	Gwenn, Edmund
1888	1942	Hackett, Charles
1902	1958	Hackett, Raymond
1892	1950	Hale, Alan
1925	1981	Haley, Bill
1899	1979	Haley, Jack
1902	1985	Hamilton, Margaret
1847	1919	Hammerstein, Oscar
1893	1964	Hardwicke, Cedric
1892	1957	Hardy, Oliver
1911	1937	Harlow, Jean
1844	1911	Harrigan, Edward
1908	1990	Harrison, Rex
1870	1946	Hart, William S.

Born	Died	Name
1928	1973	Harvey, Laurence
1910	1973	Hawkins, Jack
1890	1973	Hayakawa, Sessue
1885	1969	Hayes, Gabby
1902	1971	Hayward, Leland
1917	1975	Hayward, Susan
1918	1987	Hayworth, Rita
1896	1937	Healy, Ted
1910	1971	Heflin, Van
1901	1987	Heifetz, Jascha
1873	1918	Held, Anna
1942	1970	Hendrix, Jimi
1936	1990	Henson, Jim
1910	1969	Henie, Sonja
1879	1942	Herbert, Henry
1887	1951	Herbert, Hugh
1886	1956	Hersholt, Jean
1899	1980	Hitchcock, Alfred
1914	1974	Hodiak, John
1894	1973	Holden, Fay
1918	1981	Holden, William
1922	1965	Holliday, Judy
1936	1959	Holly, Buddy
1888	1951	Holt, Jack
1918	1973	Holt, Tim
1898	1978	Homolka, Oscar
1902	1972	Hopkins, Miriam
1858	1935	Hopper, DeWolf
1874	1959	Hopper, Edna Wallace
1915	1970	Hopper, William
1904	1989	Horowitz, Vladimir
1886	1970	Horton, Edward Everett
1874	1926	Houdini, Harry
1902	1988	Houseman, John
1906	1952	Howard, Curly
1881	1965	Howard, Eugene
1867	1961	Howard, Joe
1890	1943	Howard, Leslie
1897	1975	Howard, Moe
1891	1955	Howard, Shemp
1885	1955	Howard, Tom
1916	1988	Howard, Trevor
1885	1949	Howard, Willie
1925	1985	Hudson, Rock
1890	1977	Hull, Henry
1886	1957	Hull, Josephine
1895	1958	Humphrey, Doris
1925	1969	Hunter, Jeffrey
1901	1962	Husing, Ted
1906	1987	Huston, John
1884	1950	Huston, Walter
1892	1950	Ingram, Rex
1895	1969	Ingram, Rex
1895	1980	Iturbi, Jose
1838	1905	Irving, Henry
1871	1944	Irving, Isabel
1872	1914	Irving, Laurence
1875	1942	Jackson, Joe
1911	1972	Jackson, Mahalia
1891	1984	Jaffe, Sam
1903	1991	Jagger, Dean
1916	1983	James, Harry
1889	1956	Janis, Elsie
1886	1950	Jannings, Emil
1930	1980	Janssen, David
1900	1974	Jenkins, Allen
1898	1981	Jessel, George
1892	1962	Johnson, Chic
1886	1950	Jolson, Al
1889	1942	Jones, Buck
1933	1983	Jones, Carolyn
1911	1965	Jones, Spike
1943	1970	Joplin, Janis
1902	1982	Jory, Victor
1905	1981	Joslyn, Allyn
1910	1966	Kane, Helen
1887	1969	Karloff, Boris
1893	1970	Karns, Roscoe
1913	1987	Kaye, Danny
1811	1868	Kean, Charles
1806	1880	Kean, Mrs. Charles
1787	1833	Kean, Edmund
1895	1966	Keaton, Buster
1899	1960	Keith, Ian
1894	1973	Kellaway, Cecil
1898	1979	Kelly, Emmett

Born	Died	Name	Born	Died	Name	Born	Died	Name
1928	1982	Kelly, Grace	1924	1987	Marvin, Lee	1860	1941	Paderewski, Ignace
1910	1981	Kelly, Patsy	1888	1964	Marx, Arthur (Harpo)	1924	1987	Page, Geraldine
1907	1968	Kelton, Pert	1901	1979	Marx, Herbert (Zeppo)	1889	1954	Pallette, Eugene
1823	1895	Kemble, Agnes	1890	1977	Marx, Julius (Groucho)	1914	1986	Palmer, Lilli
1775	1854	Kemble, Charles	1886	1961	Marx, Leonard (Chico)	1894	1958	Pangborn, Franklin
1809	1893	Kemble, Fannie	1893	1977	Marx, Milton (Gummo)	1914	1975	Parks, Larry
1926	1959	Kendall, Kay	1909	1984	Mason, James	1881	1940	Pasternack, Josef A.
1914	1990	Kennedy, Arthur	1896	1983	Massey, Raymond	1837	1908	Pastor, Tony
1890	1948	Kennedy, Edgar	1879	1948	May, Edna	1843	1919	Patti, Adelina
1886	1956	Kibbee, Guy	1885	1957	Mayer, Louis B.	1840	1889	Patti, Carlotta
1888	1964	Kilbride, Percy	1895	1973	Maynard, Ken	1885	1931	Pavlova, Anna
1923	1986	Knight, Ted	1884	1945	McCormack, John	1904	1984	Peerce, Jan
1901	1980	Kostelanetz, Andre	1905	1990	McCrea, Joel	1885	1950	Pemberton, Brock
1919	1962	Kovacs, Ernie	1899	1952	McDaniel, Hattie	1899	1967	Pendleton, Nat
1885	1974	Kruger, Otto	1899	1981	McHugh, Frank	1905	1941	Penner, Joe
1921	1991	Kulp, Nancy	1907	1991	McIntire, John	1892	1937	Perkins, Osgood
			1883	1959	McLaglen, Victor	1915	1963	Piaf, Edith
1913	1964	Ladd, Alan	1907	1971	McMahon, Horace	1893	1979	Pickford, Mary
1895	1967	Lahr, Bert	1930	1980	McQueen, Steve	1897	1984	Pidgeon, Walter
1919	1973	Lake, Veronica	1920	1980	Medford, Kay	1892	1957	Pinza, Ezio
1915	1982	Lamas, Fernando	1880	1946	Meek, Donald	1898	1963	Pitts, Zasu
1902	1986	Lanchester, Elsa	1861	1931	Melba, Nellie	1904	1976	Pons, Lily
1919	1948	Landis, Carole	1890	1973	Melchior, Lauritz	1897	1981	Ponselle, Rosa
1904	1972	Landis, Jessie Royce	1904	1961	Melton, James	1904	1963	Powell, Dick
1936	1991	Landon, Michael	1890	1963	Menjou, Adolphe	1912	1982	Powell, Eleanor
1884	1944	Langdon, Harry	1902	1966	Menken, Helen	1892	1984	Powell, William
1853	1929	Langtry, Lillie	1908	1984	Merman, Ethel	1913	1958	Power, Tyrone
1921	1959	Lanza, Mario	1905	1986	Milland, Ray	1905	1986	Preminger, Otto
1870	1950	Lauder, Harry	1904	1944	Miller, Glenn	1935	1977	Presley, Elvis
1899	1962	Laughton, Charles	1860	1926	Miller, Henry	1918	1987	Preston, Robert
1890	1965	Laurel, Stan	1898	1936	Miller, Marilyn	1911	1978	Prima, Louis
1923	1984	Lawford, Peter	1903	1955	Minnevitch, Borrah	1954	1977	Prinze, Freddie
1898	1952	Lawrence, Gertrude	1913	1955	Miranda, Carmen			
1908	1991	Lean, David	1892	1962	Mitchell, Thomas	1946	1989	Radner, Gilda
1940	1973	Lee, Bruce	1880	1940	Mix, Tom	1895	1980	Raft, George
1907	1952	Lee, Canada	1926	1962	Monroe, Marilyn	1890	1967	Rains, Claude
1914	1970	Lee, Gypsy Rose	1911	1973	Monroe, Vaughn	1889	1970	Rambeau, Marjorie
1888	1976	Lehmann, Lotte	1917	1951	Montez, Maria	1892	1967	Rathbone, Basil
1913	1967	Leigh, Vivien	1904	1981	Montgomery, Robert	1897	1960	Ratoff, Gregory
1922	1976	Leighton, Margaret	1901	1947	Moore, Grace	1891	1943	Ray, Charles
1940	1980	Lennon, John	1876	1962	Moore, Victor	1941	1967	Redding, Otis
1898	1981	Lenya, Lotte	1906	1974	Moorehead, Agnes	1908	1985	Redgrave, Michael
1870	1941	Leonard, Eddie	1890	1949	Morgan, Frank	1921	1986	Reed, Donna
1900	1987	LeRoy Mervyn	1900	1941	Morgan, Helen	1914	1959	Reeves, George
1906	1972	Levant, Oscar	1901	1970	Morris, Chester	1923	1964	Reeves, Jim
1905	1980	Levene, Sam	1914	1959	Morris, Wayne	1892	1923	Reid, Wallace
1902	1971	Lewis, Joe E.	1943	1971	Morrison, Jim	1873	1943	Reinhardt, Max
1892	1971	Lewis, Ted	1932	1982	Morrow, Vic	1935	1991	Remick, Lee
1919	1987	Liberace	1915	1977	Mostel, Zero	1909	1971	Rennie, Michael
1820	1887	Lind, Jenny	1897	1969	Mowbray, Alan	1902	1983	Richardson, Ralph
1894	1989	Lillie, Beatrice	1895	1967	Muni, Paul	1921	1985	Riddle, Nelson
1889	1968	Lindsay, Howard	1915	1970	Munshin, Jules	1898	1977	Ritchard, Cyril
1893	1971	Lloyd, Harold	1924	1971	Murphy, Audie	1907	1974	Ritter, Tex
1870	1922	Lloyd, Marie	1885	1965	Murray, Mae	1905	1969	Ritter, Thelma
1891	1957	Lockhart, Gene				1901	1965	Ritz, Al
1913	1969	Logan, Ella	1896	1970	Nagel, Conrad	1906	1986	Ritz, Harry
1909	1942	Lombard, Carole	1900	1973	Naish, J. Carroll	1903	1985	Ritz, Jimmy
1902	1977	Lombardo, Guy	1898	1961	Naldi, Nita	1925	1982	Robbins, Marty
1927	1974	Long, Richard	1906	1975	Nelson, Ozzie	1898	1976	Robeson, Paul
1895	1975	Lopez, Vincent	1940	1985	Nelson, Rick	1878	1949	Robinson, Bill
1888	1968	Lorne, Marion	1885	1967	Nesbit, Evelyn	1893	1973	Robinson, Edward G.
1904	1964	Lorre, Peter	1909	1983	Niven, David	1865	1942	Robson, May
1912	1962	Lovejoy, Frank	1890	1950	Nijinsky, Vaslav	1905	1977	Rochester (E. Anderson)
1890	1971	Lowe, Edmund	1893	1974	Nilsson, Anna Q.	1897	1933	Rodgers, Jimmy
1892	1947	Lubitsch, Ernst	1902	1985	Nolan, Lloyd	1879	1935	Rogers, Will
1882	1956	Lugosi, Bela	1894	1930	Normand, Mabel	1880	1962	Rooney, Pat
1894	1971	Lukas, Paul	1899	1968	Novarro, Ramon	1899	1966	Rose, Billy
1892	1977	Lunt, Alfred	1893	1951	Novello, Ivor	1910	1980	Roth, Lillian
1853	1932	Lupino, George				1922	1987	Rowan, Dan
1893	1942	Lupino, Stanley	1903	1978	Oakie, Jack	1887	1982	Rubinstein, Artur
1926	1982	Lynde, Paul	1860	1926	Oakley, Annie	1878	1953	Ruffo, Titta
1926	1971	Lynn, Diana	1928	1982	Oates, Warren	1886	1970	Ruggles, Charles
			1911	1979	Oberon, Merle	1924	1961	Russell, Gail
1903	1965	MacDonald, Jeanette	1915	1985	O'Brien, Edmond	1861	1922	Russell, Lillian
1902	1969	MacLane, Barton	1899	1983	O'Brien, Pat	1911	1976	Russell, Rosalind
1921	1986	MacRae, Gordon	1908	1981	O'Connell, Arthur	1892	1972	Rutherford, Margaret
1909	1973	Macready, George	1880	1959	O'Connor, Una	1903	1973	Ryan, Irene
1908	1973	Magnani, Anna	1908	1968	O'Keefe, Dennis	1909	1973	Ryan, Robert
1896	1967	Mahoney, Will	1880	1938	Oland, Warner			
1890	1975	Main, Marjorie	1860	1932	Olcott, Chauncey	1924	1963	Sabu (Dastagir)
1932	1967	Mansfield, Jayne	1883	1942	Oliver, Edna May	1877	1968	St. Denis, Ruth
1854	1897	Mansfield, Richard	1907	1989	Olivier, Laurence	1884	1955	Sakall, S.Z.
1905	1980	Mantovani, Annunzio	1892	1963	Olsen, Ole	1885	1936	Sale (Chic), Charles
1897	1975	March, Fredric	1849	1920	O'Neill, James	1906	1972	Sanders, George
1945	1981	Marley, Bob	1936	1988	Orbison, Roy	1896	1960	Savo, Jimmy
1890	1966	Marshall, Herbert	1899	1985	Ormandy, Eugene	1895	1964	Schildkraut, Joseph
1913	1990	Martin, Mary	1876	1949	Ouspenskaya, Maria	1865	1930	Schildkraut, Rudolph
1920	1981	Martin, Ross	1887	1972	Owen, Reginald	1889	1965	Schipa, Tito
1885	1969	Martinelli, Giovanni				1882	1951	Schnabel, Artur

Born	Died	Name	Born	Died	Name	Born	Died	Name
1920	1981	Scott, Hazel	1878	1947	Tanguay, Eva	1887	1969	Walburn, Raymond
1898	1987	Scott, Randolph	1885	1966	Taylor, Deems	1914	1951	Walker, Robert
1914	1965	Scott, Zachary	1899	1958	Taylor, Estelle	1898	1983	Wallenstein, Alfred
1843	1896	Scott-Siddons, Mrs.	1887	1946	Taylor, Laurette	1887	1980	Walsh, Raoul
1938	1979	Seberg, Jean	1911	1969	Taylor, Robert	1876	1962	Walter, Bruno
1892	1974	Seeley, Blossom	1878	1938	Tearle, Conway	1876	1958	Warner, H. B.
1893	1987	Segovia, Andres	1884	1953	Tearle, Godfrey	1924	1963	Washington, Dinah
1925	1980	Sellers, Peter	1892	1937	Tell, Alma	1900	1977	Waters, Ethel
1902	1965	Selznick, David O.	1864	1942	Tempest, Marie	1907	1979	Wayne, John
1884	1960	Sennett, Mack	1847	1928	Terry, Ellen	1891	1966	Webb, Clifton
1927	1978	Shaw, Robert	1871	1940	Tetrazzini, Luisa	1920	1982	Webb, Jack
1891	1972	Shawn, Ted	1899	1936	Thalberg, Irving	1867	1942	Weber, Joe
1868	1949	Shean, Al	1912	1991	Thomas, Danny	1905	1973	Webster, Margaret
1902	1983	Shearer, Norma	1892	1960	Thomas, John Charles	1915	1985	Welles, Orson
1915	1967	Sheridan, Ann	1882	1976	Thorndike, Sybil	1896	1975	Wellman, William
1875	1953	Shubert, Lee	1896	1960	Tibbett, Lawrence	1892	1980	West, Mae
1755	1831	Siddons, Mrs. Sarah	1909	1958	Todd, Michael	1895	1968	Wheeler, Bert
1921	1985	Signoret, Simone	1874	1967	Toler, Sidney	1889	1938	White, Pearl
1912	1985	Silvers, Phil	1903	1968	Tone, Franchot	1891	1967	Whiteman, Paul
1900	1976	Sim, Alastair	1867	1957	Toscanini, Arturo	1865	1948	Whitty, May
1858	1942	Skinner, Otis	1898	1968	Tracy, Lee	1912	1979	Wilding, Michael
1863	1948	Smith, C. Aubrey	1900	1967	Tracy, Spencer	1895	1948	William, Warren
1907	1986	Smith, Kate	1903	1972	Traubel, Helen	1877	1922	Williams, Bert
1917	1979	Soo, Jack	1894	1975	Treacher, Arthur	1923	1953	Williams, Hank
1854	1932	Sousa, John Philip	1853	1917	Tree, Herbert Beerbohm	1905	1975	Wills, Bob
1884	1957	Sparks, Ned	1890	1973	Truex, Ernest	1903	1978	Wills, Chill
1876	1948	Speaks, Oley	1932	1984	Truffaut, Francois	1894	1953	Wilson, Dooley
1873	1937	Standing, Guy	1919	1986	Tucker, Forrest	1917	1972	Wilson, Marie
1907	1990	Stanwyck, Barbara	1915	1975	Tucker, Richard	1884	1969	Winninger, Charles
1934	1970	Stevens, Inger	1884	1966	Tucker, Sophie	1904	1959	Withers, Grant
1882	1977	Stokowski, Leopold	1874	1940	Turpin, Ben	1907	1961	Wong, Anna May
1873	1959	Stone, Fred	1908	1959	Twelvetrees, Helen	1938	1981	Wood, Natalie
1879	1953	Stone, Lewis				1892	1978	Wood, Peggy
1904	1980	Stone, Milburn	1894	1970	Ulric, Lenore	1888	1963	Woolley, Monty
1898	1959	Sturges, Preston	1933	1975	Ure, Mary	1902	1981	Wyler, William
1911	1960	Sullavan, Margaret				1886	1966	Wynn, Ed
1902	1974	Sullivan, Ed	1895	1926	Valentino, Rudolph	1916	1986	Wynn, Keenan
1903	1956	Sullivan, Francis L.	1901	1986	Vallee, Rudy			
1892	1946	Summerville, Slim	1911	1979	Vance, Vivian	1890	1960	Young, Clara Kimball
1899	1983	Swanson, Gloria	1924	1990	Vaughan, Sarah	1913	1978	Young, Gig
1904	1969	Swarthout, Gladys	1893	1943	Veidt, Conrad	1887	1953	Young, Roland
			1926	1981	Vera-Ellen			
1893	1957	Talmadge, Norma	1885	1957	Von Stroheim, Erich	1902	1979	Zanuck, Darryl F.
1899	1972	Tamiroff, Akim	1906	1981	Von Zell, Harry	1869	1932	Ziegfeld, Florenz
						1873	1976	Zukor, Adolph

Original Names of Selected Entertainers

Edie Adams: Elizabeth Edith Enke
Eddie Albert: Edward Albert Heimberger
Alan Alda: Alphonso D'Abruzzo
Jane Alexander: Jane Quigley
Fred Allen: John Sullivan
Woody Allen: Allen Konigsberg
Julie Andrews: Julia Wells
Eve Arden: Eunice Quedens
Beatrice Arthur: Bernice Frankel
Jean Arthur: Gladys Greene
Fred Astaire: Frederick Austerlitz
Lauren Bacall: Betty Joan Perske
Anne Bancroft: Anna Maria Italiano
Brigitte Bardot: Camille Javal
Gene Barry: Eugene Klass
Orson Bean: Dallas Burrows
Pat Benatar: Patricia Andrejewski
Robbie Benson: Robert Segal
Tony Bennett: Anthony Benedetto
Busby Berkeley: William Berkeley Enos
Jack Benny: Benjamin Kubelsky
Joey Bishop: Joseph Gottlieb
Robert Blake: Michael Gubitosi
Victor Borge: Borge Rosenbaum
David Bowie: David Robert Jones
Boy George: George Alan O'Dowd
Fanny Brice: Fanny Borach
Morgan Brittany: Suzanne Cupito
Charles Bronson: Charles Buchinski
Albert Brooks: Albert Einstein
Mel Brooks: Melvin Kaminsky
George Burns: Nathan Birnbaum
Ellen Burstyn: Edna Gilhooley
Richard Burton: Richard Jenkins
Red Buttons: Aaron Chwatt
Nicolas Cage: Nicholas Coppola
Michael Caine: Maurice Micklewhite
Maria Callas: Maria Kalogeropoulos
Vikki Carr: Florencia Casillas
Diahann Carroll: Carol Diahann Johnson

Cyd Charisse: Tula Finklea
Ray Charles: Ray Charles Robinson
Cher: Cherilyn Sarkisian
Patsy Cline: Virginia Patterson Hensley
Lee J. Cobb: Leo Jacoby
Claudette Colbert: Lily Chauchoin
Michael Connors: Kreker Ohanian
Robert Conrad: Conrad Robert Falk
Alice Cooper: Vincent Furnier
David Copperfield: David Kotkin
Howard Cosell: Howard Cohen
Elvis Costello: Declan Patrick McManus
Lou Costello: Louis Cristillo
Joan Crawford: Lucille Le Sueur
Michael Crawford: Michael Dumbell-Smith
Tom Cruise: Thomas Mapother
Tony Curtis: Bernard Schwartz
Vic Damone: Vito Farinola
Rodney Dangerfield: Jacob Cohen
Bobby Darin: Walden Waldo Cassotto
Doris Day: Doris von Kappelhoff
Yvonne De Carlo: Peggy Middleton
Sandra Dee: Alexandra Zuck
John Denver: Henry John Deutschendorf Jr.
Bo Derek: Cathleen Collins
John Derek: Derek Harris
Angie Dickinson: Angeline Brown
Bo Diddley: Elias Bates
Phyllis Diller: Phyllis Driver
Diana Dors: Diana Fluck
Melvyn Douglas: Melvyn Hesselberg
Bob Dylan: Robert Zimmerman
Sheena Easton: Sheena Shirley Orr
Barbara Eden: Barbara Huffman
Ron Ely: Ronald Pierce
Chad Everett: Raymond Cramton
Tom Ewell: S. Yewell Tompkins
Douglas Fairbanks: Douglas Ullman
Morgan Fairchild: Patsy McClenny
Alice Faye: Ann Leppert

Stepin Fetchit: Lincoln Perry
Sally Field: Sally Mahoney
W.C. Fields: William Claude Dukenfield
Peter Finch: William Mitchell
Barry Fitzgerald: William Joseph Shields
Joan Fontaine: Joan de Havilland
John Ford: Sean O'Fearna
John Forsythe: John Freund
Redd Foxx : John Sanford
Anthony Franciosa: Anthony Papaleo
Arlene Francis: Arlene Kazanjian
Connie Francis: Concetta Franconero
Greta Garbo: Greta Gustafsson
Vincent Gardenia: Vincent Scognamiglio
John Garfield: Julius Garfinkle
Judy Garland: Frances Gumm
James Garner: James Bumgarner
Crystal Gayle: Brenda Gayle Webb
Paulette Goddard: Marion Levy
Whoopi Goldberg: Caryn Johnson
Eydie Gorme: Edith Gormezano
Stewart Granger: James Stewart
Cary Grant: Archibald Leach
Lee Grant: Lyova Rosenthal
Joel Grey: Joe Katz
Buddy Hackett: Leonard Hacker
Jean Harlow: Harlean Carpentier
Rex Harrison: Reginald Carey
Laurence Harvey: Larushka Skikne
Helen Hayes: Helen Brown
Susan Hayward: Edythe Marriner
Rita Hayworth: Margarita Cansino
Pee-Wee Herman: Paul Rubenfeld
Barbara Hershey: Barbara Herzstine
William Holden: William Beedle
Judy Holliday: Judith Tuvim
Harry Houdini: Ehrich Weiss
Leslie Howard: Leslie Stainer
Moe Howard: Moses Horowitz
Rock Hudson: Roy Scherer Jr. (later Fitzgerald)
Engelbert Humperdinck: Arnold Dorsey
Kim Hunter: Janet Cole
Mary Beth Hurt: Mary Supinger
Betty Hutton: Betty Thornberg
David Janssen: David Meyer
Elton John: Reginald Dwight
Don Johnson: Donald Wayne
Jennifer Jones: Phyllis Isley
Tom Jones: Thomas Woodward
Louis Jourdan: Louis Gendre
Boris Karloff: William Henry Pratt
Danny Kaye: David Kaminsky
Diane Keaton: Diane Hall
Michael Keaton: Michael Douglas
Howard Keel: Harold Leek
Chaka Khan: Yvette Stevens
Carole King: Carole Klein
Ben Kingsley: Krishna Banji
Nastassja Kinski: Nastassja Naksyznyski
Ted Knight: Tadeus Wladyslaw Konopka
Cheryl Ladd: Cheryl Stoppelmoor
Veronica Lake: Constance Ockleman
Dorothy Lamour: Mary Kaumeyer
Michael Landon: Eugene Orowitz
Mario Lanza: Alfredo Cocozza
Stan Laurel: Arthur Jefferson
Steve Lawrence: Sidney Leibowitz
Brenda Lee: Brenda Mae Tarpley
Bruce Lee: Lee Yuen Kam
Gypsy Rose Lee: Rose Louise Hovick
Michelle Lee: Michelle Dusiak
Peggy Lee: Norma Egstrom
Janet Leigh: Jeanette Morrison
Vivien Leigh: Vivien Hartley
Huey Lewis: Hugh Cregg
Jerry Lewis: Joseph Levitch
Hal Linden: Harold Lipshitz
Carole Lombard: Jane Peters
Jack Lord: John Joseph Ryan
Sophia Loren: Sophia Scicoloni
Peter Lorre: Laszio Lowenstein
Myrna Loy: Myrna Williams
Bela Lugosi: Bela Ferenc Blasko
Moms Mabley: Loretta Mary Aitken
Shirley MacLaine: Shirley Beaty
Madonna: Madonna Louise Ciccone

Lee Majors: Harvey Lee Yeary 2d
Karl Malden: Malden Sekulovich
Jayne Mansfield: Vera Jane Palmer
Fredric March: Frederick Bickel
Peter Marshall: Pierre LaCock
Dean Martin: Dino Crocetti
Ethel Merman: Ethel Zimmerman
Ray Milland: Reginald Truscott-Jones
Ann Miller: Lucille Collier
Joni Mitchell: Roberta Joan Anderson
Marilyn Monroe: Norma Jean Mortenson, (later) Baker
Yves Montand: Ivo Levi
Ron Moody: Ronald Moodnick
Demi Moore: Demi Guynes
Garry Moore: Thomas Garrison Morfit
Rita Moreno: Rosita Alverio
Harry Morgan: Harry Bratsburg
Paul Muni: Muni Weisenfreund
Mike Nichols: Michael Igor Peschowsky
Chuck Norris: Carlos Ray
Sheree North: Dawn Bethel
Hugh O'Brian: Hugh Krampke
Maureen O'Hara: Maureen Fitzsimmons
Patti Page: Clara Ann Fowler
Jack Palance: Walter Palanuik
Lilli Palmer: Lilli Peiser
Bert Parks: Bert Jacobson
Minnie Pearl: Sarah Ophelia Cannon
Bernadette Peters: Bernadette Lazzaro
Edith Piaf: Edith Gassion
Slim Pickens: Louis Lindley
Mary Pickford: Gladys Smith
Stephanie Powers: Stefania Federkiewcz
Paula Prentiss: Paula Ragusa
Robert Preston: Robert Preston Meservey
Prince: Prince Rogers Nelson
Tony Randall: Leonard Rosenberg
Martha Raye: Margaret O'Reed
Donna Reed: Donna Belle Mullenger
Della Reese: Delloreese Patricia Early
Joan Rivers: Joan Sandra Molinsky
Edward G. Robinson: Emmanuel Goldenberg
Ginger Rogers: Virginia McMath
Roy Rogers: Leonard Slye
Mickey Rooney: Joe Yule Jr.
Lillian Russell: Helen Leonard
Theresa Russell: Theresa Paup
Winona Ryder: Winona Horowitz
Susan St. James: Susan Miller
Soupy Sales: Milton Hines
Susan Sarandon: Susan Tomaling
Randolph Scott: George Randolph Crane
Jane Seymour: Joyce Frankenberg
Omar Sharif: Michael Shalhoub
Martin Sheen: Ramon Estevez
Beverly Sills: Belle Silverman
Talia Shire: Talia Coppola
Phil Silvers: Philip Silversmith
Suzanne Somers: Suzanne Mahoney
Ann Sothern: Harriette Lake
Robert Stack: Robert Modini
Barbara Stanwyck: Ruby Stevens
Jean Stapleton: Jeanne Murray
Ringo Starr: Richard Starkey
Connie Stevens: Concetta Ingolia
Sting: Gordon Sumner
Donna Summers: LaDonna Gaines
Robert Taylor: Spangler Arlington Brugh
Danny Thomas: Muzyad Yakhoob, later Amos Jacobs
Randy Travis: Randy Traywick
Sophie Tucker: Sophia Kalish
Tina Turner: Annie Mae Bullock
Conway Twitty: Harold Lloyd Jenkins
Rudolph Valentino: Rudolpho D'Antonguolla
Frankie Valli: Frank Castelluccio
David Wayne: Wayne McMeekan
John Wayne: Marion Morrison
Clifton Webb: Webb Parmalee Hollenbeck
Raquel Welch: Raquel Tejada
Gene Wilder: Jerome Silberman
Shelly Winters: Shirley Schrift
Stevie Wonder: Stevland Morris
Natalie Wood: Natasha Gurdin
Jane Wyman: Sarah Jane Fulks
Gig Young: Byron Barr

CABINETS OF THE U. S.

Secretaries of State

The Department of Foreign Affairs was created by act of Congress July 27, 1789, and the name changed to Department of State on Sept. 15.

President	Secretary	Home	Apptd.
Washington	Thomas Jefferson	Va.	1789
"	Edmund Randolph	"	1794
"	Timothy Pickering	Pa.	1795
Adams, J.	"	"	1797
"	John Marshall	Va.	1800
Jefferson	James Madison	"	1801
Madison	Robert Smith	Md.	1809
"	James Monroe	Va.	1811
Monroe	John Quincy Adams	Mass.	1817
Adams, J.Q.	Henry Clay	Ky.	1825
Jackson	Martin Van Buren	N.Y.	1829
"	Edward Livingston	La.	1831
"	Louis McLane	Del.	1833
"	John Forsyth	Ga.	1834
Van Buren	"	"	1837
Harrison, W.H.	Daniel Webster	Mass.	1841
Tyler	"	"	1841
"	Abel P. Upshur	Va.	1843
"	John C. Calhoun	S.C.	1844
Polk	"	"	1845
"	James Buchanan	Pa.	1845
Taylor	"	"	1849
"	John M. Clayton	Del.	1849
Fillmore	"	"	1850
"	Daniel Webster	Mass.	1850
"	Edward Everett	"	1852
Pierce	William L. Marcy	N.Y.	1853
Buchanan	"	"	1857
"	Lewis Cass	Mich.	1857
"	Jeremiah S. Black	Pa.	1860
Lincoln	"	"	1861
"	William H. Seward	N.Y.	1861
Johnson, A.	"	"	1865
Grant	Elihu B. Washburne	Ill.	1869
"	Hamilton Fish	N.Y.	1869
Hayes	"	"	1877
"	William M. Evarts	"	1877
Garfield	"	"	1881
"	James G. Blaine	Me.	1881
Arthur	"	"	1881
"	F.T. Frelinghuysen	N.J.	1881
Cleveland	F.T. Frelinghuysen	N.J.	1885
"	Thomas F. Bayard	Del.	1885
Harrison, B.	"	"	1889
"	James G. Blaine	Me.	1889
Harrison, B.	John W. Foster	Ind.	1892
Cleveland	Walter Q. Gresham	Ind.	1893
"	Richard Olney	Mass.	1895
McKinley	"	"	1897
"	John Sherman	Oh.	1897
"	William R. Day	"	1898
"	John Hay	D.C.	1898
Roosevelt, T.	"	"	1901
"	Elihu Root	N.Y.	1905
"	Robert Bacon	"	1909
Taft	"	"	1909
"	Philander C. Knox	Pa.	1909
Wilson	"	"	1913
"	William J. Bryan	Neb.	1913
"	Robert Lansing	N.Y.	1915
"	Bainbridge Colby	"	1920
Harding	Charles E. Hughes	"	1921
Coolidge	"	"	1923
"	Frank B. Kellogg	Minn.	1925
Hoover	"	"	1929
"	Henry L. Stimson	N.Y.	1929
Roosevelt, F.D.	Cordell Hull	Tenn.	1933
"	E.R. Stettinius Jr.	Va.	1944
Truman	"	"	1945
"	James F. Byrnes	S.C.	1945
"	George C. Marshall	Pa.	1947
"	Dean G. Acheson	Conn.	1949
Eisenhower	John Foster Dulles	N.Y.	1953
"	Christian A. Herter	Mass.	1959
Kennedy	Dean Rusk	N.Y.	1961
Johnson, L.B.	"	"	1963
Nixon	William P. Rogers	N.Y.	1969
"	Henry A. Kissinger	D.C.	1973
Ford	"	"	1974
Carter	Cyrus R. Vance	N.Y.	1977
"	Edmund S. Muskie	Me.	1980
Reagan	Alexander M. Haig Jr.	Conn.	1981
"	George P. Shultz	Cal.	1982
Bush	James A. Baker 3d	Tex.	1989

Secretaries of the Treasury

The Treasury Department was organized by act of Congress Sept. 2, 1789.

President	Secretary	Home	Apptd.
Washington	Alexander Hamilton	N.Y.	1789
"	Oliver Wolcott	Conn.	1795
Adams, J.	"	"	1797
"	Samuel Dexter	Mass.	1801
Jefferson	"	"	1801
"	Albert Gallatin	Pa.	1801
Madison	"	"	1809
"	George W. Campbell	Tenn.	1814
"	Alexander J. Dallas	Pa.	1814
"	William H. Crawford	Ga.	1816
Monroe	"	"	1817
Adams, J.Q.	Richard Rush	Pa.	1825
Jackson	Samuel D. Ingham	"	1829
"	Louis McLane	Del.	1831
"	William J. Duane	Pa.	1833
"	Roger B. Taney	Md.	1833
"	Levi Woodbury	N.H.	1834
Van Buren	"	"	1837
Harrison, W.H.	Thomas Ewing	Oh.	1841
Tyler	"	"	1841
"	Walter Forward	Pa.	1841
"	John C. Spencer	N.Y.	1843
Tyler	George M. Bibb	Ky.	1844
Polk	Robert J. Walker	Miss.	1845
Taylor	William M. Meredith	Pa.	1849
Fillmore	Thomas Corwin	Oh.	1850
Pierce	James Guthrie	Ky.	1853
Buchanan	Howell Cobb	Ga.	1857
"	Phillip F. Thomas	Md.	1860
"	John A. Dix	N.Y.	1861
Lincoln	Salmon P. Chase	Oh.	1861
Lincoln	William P. Fessenden	Me.	1864
"	Hugh McCulloch	Ind.	1865
Johnson, A.	"	"	1865
Grant	George S. Boutwell	Mass.	1869
"	William A. Richardson	Mass.	1873
"	Benjamin H. Bristow	Ky.	1874
"	Lot M. Morrill	Me.	1876
Hayes	John Sherman	Oh.	1877
Garfield	William Windom	Minn.	1881
Arthur	Charles J. Folger	N.Y.	1881
"	Walter Q. Gresham	Ind.	1884
"	Hugh McCulloch	Ind.	1884
Cleveland	Daniel Manning	N.Y.	1885
Cleveland	Charles S. Fairchild	"	1887
Harrison, B.	William Windom	Minn.	1889
"	Charles Foster	Oh.	1891
Cleveland	John G. Carlisle	Ky.	1893
McKinley	Lyman J. Gage	Ill.	1897
Roosevelt, T.	"	"	1901
"	Leslie M. Shaw	Ia.	1902
"	George B. Cortelyou	N.Y.	1907
Taft	Franklin MacVeagh	Ill.	1909
Wilson	William G. McAdoo	N.Y.	1913
"	Carter Glass	Va.	1918
"	David F. Houston	Mo.	1920
Harding	Andrew W. Mellon	Pa.	1921
Coolidge	"	"	1923
Hoover	"	"	1929
"	Ogden L. Mills	N.Y.	1932
Roosevelt, F.D.	William H. Woodin	"	1933
"	Henry Morgenthau, Jr.	"	1934

President	Secretary	Home	Apptd.
Truman	Fred M. Vinson	Ky.	1945
"	John W. Snyder	Mo.	1946
Eisenhower	George M. Humphrey	Oh.	1953
"	Robert B. Anderson	Conn.	1957
Kennedy	C. Douglas Dillon	N.J.	1961
Johnson, L.B.	"		1963
"	Henry H. Fowler	Va.	1965
"	Joseph W. Barr	Ind.	1968
Nixon	David M. Kennedy	Ill.	1969
"	John B. Connally	Tex.	1971
Nixon	George P. Shultz	Ill.	1972
"	William E. Simon	N.J.	1974
Ford	"		1974
Carter	W. Michael Blumenthal	Mich.	1977
"	G. William Miller	R.I.	1979
Reagan	Donald T. Regan	N.Y.	1981
"	James A. Baker 3d	Tex.	1985
"	Nicholas F. Brady	N.J.	1988
Bush	"		1989

Secretaries of Defense

The Department of Defense, originally designated the National Military Establishment, was created Sept. 18, 1947. It is headed by the secretary of defense, who is a member of the president's cabinet.

The departments of the army, of the navy, and of the air force function within the Department of Defense, and their respective secretaries are no longer members of the president's cabinet.

President	Secretary	Home	Apptd.
Truman	James V. Forrestal	N.Y.	1947
"	Louis A. Johnson	W.Va.	1949
"	George C. Marshall	Pa.	1950
"	Robert A. Lovett	N.Y.	1951
Eisenhower	Charles E. Wilson	Mich.	1953
"	Neil H. McElroy	Oh.	1957
"	Thomas S. Gates Jr.	Pa.	1959
Kennedy	Robert S. McNamara	Mich.	1961
Johnson, L.B.	"		1963
"	Clark M. Clifford	Md.	1968
Nixon	Melvin R. Laird	Wis.	1969
"	Elliot L. Richardson	Mass.	1973
"	James R. Schlesinger	Va.	1973
Ford	"		1974
"	Donald H. Rumsfeld	Ill.	1975
Carter	Harold Brown	Cal.	1977
Reagan	Caspar W. Weinberger	Cal.	1981
"	Frank C. Carlucci	Pa.	1987
Bush	Richard B. Cheney	Wyo.	1989

Secretaries of War

The War (and Navy) Department was created by act of Congress Aug. 7, 1789, and Gen. Henry Knox was commissioned secretary of war under that act Sept. 12, 1789.

President	Secretary	Home	Apptd.
Washington	Henry Knox	Mass.	1789
"	Timothy Pickering	Pa.	1795
"	James McHenry	Md.	1796
Adams, J.	"	"	1797
"	Samuel Dexter	Mass.	1800
Jefferson	Henry Dearborn	Mass.	1801
Madison	William Eustis	Mass.	1809
"	John Armstrong	N.Y.	1813
Madison	James Monroe	Va.	1814
"	William H. Crawford	Ga.	1815
Monroe	John C. Calhoun	S.C.	1817
Adams, J.Q.	James Barbour	Va.	1825
"	Peter B. Porter	N.Y.	1828
Jackson	John H. Eaton	Tenn.	1829
"	Lewis Cass	Mich.	1831
"	Benjamin F. Butler	N.Y.	1837
Van Buren	Joel R. Poinsett	S.C.	1837
Harrison, W.H.	John Bell	Tenn.	1841
Tyler	John Bell	Tenn	1841
Tyler	John C. Spencer	N.Y.	1841
"	James M. Porter	Pa.	1843
"	William Wilkins	"	1844
Polk	William L. Marcy	N.Y.	1845
Taylor	George W. Crawford	Ga.	1849
Fillmore	Charles M. Conrad	La.	1850
Pierce	Jefferson Davis	Miss.	1853
Buchanan	John B. Floyd	Va.	1857
"	Joseph Holt	Ky.	1861
Lincoln	Simon Cameron	Pa.	1861
"	Edwin M. Stanton	Pa.	1862
Johnson, A.	"	"	1865
"	John M. Schofield	Ill.	1868
Grant	John A. Rawlins	Ill.	1869
"	William T. Sherman	Oh.	1869
"	William W. Belknap	Ia.	1869
"	Alphonso Taft	Oh.	1876
"	James D. Cameron	Pa.	1876
Hayes	George W. McCrary	Ia.	1877
"	Alexander Ramsey	Minn.	1879
Garfield	Robert T. Lincoln	Ill.	1881
Arthur	"	"	1881
Cleveland	William C. Endicott	Mass.	1885
Harrison, B.	Redfield Proctor	Vt.	1889
"	Stephen B. Elkins	W.Va.	1891
Cleveland	Daniel S. Lamont	N.Y.	1893
McKinley	Russel A. Alger	Mich.	1897
"	Elihu Root	N.Y.	1899
Roosevelt, T.	"		1901
"	William H. Taft	Oh.	1904
"	Luke E. Wright	Tenn.	1908
Taft	Jacob M. Dickinson	Tenn.	1909
"	Henry L. Stimson	N.Y.	1911
Wilson	Lindley M. Garrison	N.J.	1913
"	Newton D. Baker	Oh.	1916
Harding	John W. Weeks	Mass.	1921
Coolidge	"	"	1923
"	Dwight F. Davis	Mo.	1925
Hoover	James W. Good	Ill.	1929
Hoover	Patrick J. Hurley	Okla.	1929
Roosevelt, F.D.	George H. Dern	Ut.	1933
"	Harry H. Woodring	Kan.	1937
Roosevelt, F.D.	Henry L. Stimson	N.Y.	1940
Truman	Robert P. Patterson	N.Y.	1945
"	*Kenneth C. Royall	N.C.	1947

Secretaries of the Navy

The Navy Department was created by act of Congress Apr. 30, 1798.

President	Secretary	Home	Apptd.
Adams, J.	Benjamin Stoddert	Md.	1798
Jefferson	"	"	1801
"	Robert Smith	"	1801
Madison	Paul Hamilton	S.C.	1809
"	William Jones	Pa.	1813
"	Benjamin Williams Crowninshield	Mass.	1814
Monroe	"		1817
"	Smith Thompson	N.Y.	1818
"	Samuel L. Southard	N.J.	1823
Adams, J.Q.	"	"	1825
Jackson	John Branch	N.C.	1829
"	Levi Woodbury	N.H.	1831
"	Mahlon Dickerson	N.J.	1834
Van Buren	Mahlon Dickerson	N.J.	1837
"	James K. Paulding	N.Y.	1838
Harrison, W.H.	George E. Badger	N.C.	1841
Tyler	"		1841
"	Abel P. Upshur	Va.	1841
"	David Henshaw	Mass.	1843
"	Thomas W. Gilmer	Va.	1844
"	John Y. Mason	Va.	1844
Polk	George Bancroft	Mass.	1845
"	John Y. Mason	Va.	1846
Taylor	William B. Preston	Va.	1849
Fillmore	William A. Graham	N.C.	1850
"	John P. Kennedy	Md.	1852
Pierce	James C. Dobbin	N.C.	1853

President	Secretary	Home	Apptd.	President	Secretary	Home	Apptd.
Buchanan	Isaac Toucey	Conn.	1857	Roosevelt, T.	Paul Morton	Ill.	1904
Lincoln	Gideon Welles	Conn.	1861	"	Charles J. Bonaparte	Md.	1905
Johnson, A.	"	"	1865	"	Victor H. Metcalf	Cal.	1906
Grant	Adolph E. Borie	Pa.	1869	"	Truman H. Newberry	Mich.	1908
"	George M. Robeson	N.J.	1869	Taft	George von L. Meyer	Mass.	1909
Hayes	Richard W. Thompson	Ind.	1877	Wilson	Josephus Daniels	N.C.	1913
"	Nathan Goff Jr.	W.Va.	1881	Harding	Edwin Denby	Mich.	1921
Garfield	William H. Hunt	La.	1881	Coolidge	"	"	1923
Arthur	William E. Chandler	N.H.	1882	"	Curtis D. Wilbur	Cal.	1924
Cleveland	William C. Whitney	N.Y.	1885	Hoover	Charles Francis Adams	Mass.	1929
Harrison, B.	Benjamin F. Tracy	N.Y.	1889	Roosevelt, F.D.	Claude A. Swanson	Va.	1933
Cleveland	Hilary A. Herbert	Ala.	1893	"	Charles Edison	N.J.	1940
McKinley	John D. Long	Mass.	1897	"	Frank Knox	Ill.	1940
Roosevelt, T.	"	"	1901	"	*James V. Forrestal	N.Y.	1944
"	William H. Moody	"	1902	Truman	"	"	1945

*Last members of Cabinet. The War Department became the Department of the Army and it and the Navy Department became branches of the Department of Defense, created Sept. 18, 1947.

Attorneys General

The office of attorney general was organized by act of Congress Sept. 24, 1789. The Department of Justice was created June 22, 1870.

President	Attorney General	Home	Apptd.	President	Attorney General	Home	Apptd.
Washington	Edmund Randolph	Va.	1789	Cleveland	Augustus Garland	Ark.	1885
"	William Bradford	Pa.	1794	Harrison, B.	William H. H. Miller	Ind.	1889
"	Charles Lee	Va.	1795	Cleveland	Richard Olney	Mass.	1893
Adams, J.	"	"	1797	"	Judson Harmon	Oh.	1895
Jefferson	Levi Lincoln	Mass.	1801	McKinley	Joseph McKenna	Cal.	1897
"	John Breckenridge	Ky.	1805	"	John W. Griggs	N.J.	1898
"	Caesar A. Rodney	Del.	1807	"	Philander C. Knox	Pa.	1901
Madison	"	"	1809	Roosevelt, T.	"	"	1901
"	William Pinkney	Md.	1811	"	William H. Moody	Mass.	1904
"	Richard Rush	Pa.	1814	"	Charles J. Bonaparte	Md.	1906
Monroe	"	"	1817	Taft	George W. Wickersham	N.Y.	1909
"	William Wirt	Va.	1817	Wilson	J.C. McReynolds	Tenn.	1913
Adams, J.Q.	"	"	1825	"	Thomas W. Gregory	Tex.	1914
Jackson	John M. Berrien	Ga.	1829	"	A. Mitchell Palmer	Pa.	1919
"	Roger B. Taney	Md.	1831	Harding	Harry M. Daugherty	Oh.	1921
"	Benjamin F. Butler	N.Y.	1833	Coolidge	"	"	1923
Van Buren	"	"	1837	"	Harlan F. Stone	N.Y.	1924
"	Felix Grundy	Tenn.	1838	"	John G. Sargent	Vt.	1925
"	Henry D. Gilpin	Pa.	1840	Hoover	William D. Mitchell	Minn.	1929
Harrison, W.H.	John J. Crittenden	Ky.	1841	Roosevelt, F.D.	Homer S. Cummings	Conn.	1933
Tyler	"	"	1841	"	Frank Murphy	Mich.	1939
"	Hugh S. Legare	S.C.	1841	"	Robert H. Jackson	N.Y.	1940
"	John Nelson	Md.	1843	"	Francis Biddle	Pa.	1941
Polk	John Y. Mason	Va.	1845	Truman	Thomas C. Clark	Tex.	1945
"	Nathan Clifford	Me.	1846	"	J. Howard McGrath	R.I.	1949
"	Isaac Toucey	Conn.	1848	"	J.P. McGranery	Pa.	1952
Taylor	Reverdy Johnson	Md.	1849	Eisenhower	Herbert Brownell Jr.	N.Y.	1953
Fillmore	John J. Crittenden	Ky.	1850	"	William P. Rogers	Md.	1957
Pierce	Caleb Cushing	Mass.	1853	Kennedy	Robert F. Kennedy	Mass.	1961
Buchanan	Jeremiah S. Black	Pa.	1857	Johnson, L.B.	"	"	1963
"	Edwin M. Stanton	Pa.	1860	"	N. de B. Katzenbach	Ill.	1964
Lincoln	Edward Bates	Mo.	1861	"	Ramsey Clark	Tex.	1967
"	James Speed	Ky.	1864	Nixon	John N. Mitchell	N.Y.	1969
Johnson, A.	"	"	1865	"	Richard G. Kleindienst	Ariz.	1972
"	Henry Stanbery	Oh.	1866	"	Elliot L. Richardson	Mass.	1973
"	William M. Evarts	N.Y.	1868	"	William B. Saxbe	Oh.	1974
Grant	Ebenezer R. Hoar	Mass.	1869	Ford	"	"	1974
"	Amos T. Akerman	Ga.	1870	"	Edward H. Levi	Ill.	1975
"	George H. Williams	Ore.	1871	Carter	Griffin B. Bell	Ga.	1977
"	Edwards Pierrepont	N.Y.	1875	"	Benjamin R. Civiletti	Md.	1979
"	Alphonso Taft	Oh.	1876	Reagan	William French Smith	Cal.	1981
Hayes	Charles Devens	Mass.	1877	"	Edwin Meese 3d	Cal.	1985
Garfield	Wayne MacVeagh	Pa.	1881	"	Richard Thornburgh	Pa	1988
Arthur	Benjamin H. Brewster	"	1881	Bush	"	"	1989

Secretaries of the Interior

The Department of Interior was created by act of Congress Mar. 3, 1849.

President	Secretary	Home	Apptd.	President	Secretary	Home	Apptd.
Taylor	Thomas Ewing	Oh.	1849	Grant	Jacob D. Cox	Oh.	1869
Fillmore	Thomas M. T. McKennan	Pa.	1850	"	Columbus Delano	"	1870
Fillmore	Alex H. H. Stuart	Va.	1850	"	Zachariah Chandler	Mich.	1875
Pierce	Robert McClelland	Mich.	1853	Hayes	Carl Schurz	Mo.	1877
Buchanan	Jacob Thompson	Miss.	1857	Garfield	Samuel J. Kirkwood	Ia.	1881
Lincoln	Caleb B. Smith	Ind.	1861	Arthur	Henry M. Teller	Col.	1882
"	John P. Usher	"	1863	Cleveland	Lucius Q.C. Lamar	Miss.	1885
Johnson, A.	"	"	1865	"	William F. Vilas	Wis.	1888
"	James Harlan	Ia.	1865	Harrison, B.	John W. Noble	Mo.	1889
"	Orville H. Browning	Ill.	1866	Cleveland	Hoke Smith	Ga.	1893

President	Secretary	Home	Apptd.	President	Secretary	Home	Apptd.
Cleveland	David R. Francis	Mo.	1896	Truman	Julius A. Krug	Wis.	1946
McKinley	Cornelius N. Bliss	N.Y.	1897	"	Oscar L. Chapman	Col.	1949
"	Ethan A. Hitchcock	Mo.	1898	Eisenhower	Douglas McKay	Ore.	1953
Roosevelt, T.	"	"	1901	"	Fred A. Seaton	Neb.	1956
"	James R. Garfield	Oh.	1907	Kennedy	Stewart L. Udall	Ariz.	1961
Taft	Richard A. Ballinger	Wash.	1909	Johnson, L.B.	"	"	1963
"	Walter L. Fisher	Ill.	1911	Nixon	Walter J. Hickel	Alas.	1969
Wilson	Franklin K. Lane	Cal.	1913	"	Rogers C.B. Morton	Md.	1971
"	John B. Payne	Ill.	1920	Ford	"	"	1974
Harding	Albert B. Fall	N.M.	1921	"	Stanley K. Hathaway	Wyo.	1975
"	Hubert Work	Col.	1923	"	Thomas S. Kleppe	N.D.	1975
Coolidge	"	"	1923	Carter	Cecil D. Andrus	Ida.	1977
"	Roy O. West	Ill.	1929	Reagan	James G. Watt	Col.	1981
Hoover	Ray Lyman Wilbur	Cal.	1929	"	William P. Clark	Cal.	1983
Roosevelt, F.D.	Harold L. Ickes	Ill.	1933	"	Donald P. Hodel	Ore.	1985
Truman	"	"	1945	Bush	Manuel Lujan	N.M.	1989

Secretaries of Agriculture

The Department of Agriculture was created by act of Congress May 15, 1862. On Feb. 8, 1889, its commissioner was renamed secretary of agriculture and became a member of the cabinet.

President	Secretary	Home	Apptd.	President	Secretary	Home	Apptd.
Cleveland	Norman J. Colman	Mo.	1889	Truman	Clinton P. Anderson	N.M.	1945
Harrison, B.	Jeremiah M. Rusk	Wis.	1889	"	Charles F. Brannan	Col.	1948
Cleveland	J. Sterling Morton	Neb.	1893	Eisenhower	Ezra Taft Benson	Ut.	1953
McKinley	James Wilson	Ia.	1897	Kennedy	Orville L. Freeman	Minn.	1961
Roosevelt, T.	"	"	1901	Johnson, L.B.	"	"	1963
Taft	"	"	1909	Nixon	Clifford M. Hardin	Ind.	1969
Wilson	David F. Houston	Mo.	1913	"	Earl L. Butz	Ind.	1971
"	Edwin T. Meredith	Ia.	1920	Ford	"	"	1974
Harding	Henry C. Wallace	Ia.	1921	"	John A. Knebel	Va.	1976
Coolidge	"	"	1923	Carter	Bob Bergland	Minn.	1977
"	Howard M. Gore	W.Va.	1924	Reagan	John R. Block	Ill.	1981
"	William M. Jardine	Kan.	1925	"	Richard E. Lyng	Cal.	1986
Hoover	Arthur M. Hyde	Mo.	1929	Bush	Clayton K. Yeutter	Neb.	1989
Roosevelt, F.D.	Henry A. Wallace	Ia.	1933	Bush	Edward Madigan	Ill.	1991
"	Claude R. Wickard	Ind.	1940				

Secretaries of Commerce and Labor

The Department of Commerce and Labor, created by Congress Feb. 14, 1903, was divided by Congress Mar. 4, 1913, into separate departments of Commerce and Labor. The secretary of each was made a cabinet member.

Secretaries of Commerce and Labor

President	Secretary	Home	Apptd.
Roosevelt, T.	George B. Cortelyou	N.Y.	1903
"	Victor H. Metcalf	Cal.	1904
"	Oscar S. Straus	N.Y.	1906
Taft	Charles Nagel	Mo.	1909

Secretaries of Labor

President	Secretary	Home	Apptd.
Wilson	William B. Wilson	Pa.	1913
Harding	James J. Davis	Pa.	1921
Coolidge	"	"	1923
Hoover	"	"	1929
"	William N. Doak	Va.	1930
Roosevelt, F.D.	Frances Perkins	N.Y.	1933
Truman	L.B. Schwellenbach	Wash.	1945
"	Maurice J. Tobin	Mass.	1949
Eisenhower	Martin P. Durkin	Ill.	1953
"	James P. Mitchell	N.J.	1953
Kennedy	Arthur J. Goldberg	Ill.	1961
"	W. Willard Wirtz	Ill.	1962
Johnson, L.B.	"	"	1963
Nixon	George P. Shultz	Ill	1969
"	James D. Hodgson	Cal.	1970
"	Peter J. Brennan	N.Y.	1973
Ford	"	"	1974
"	John T. Dunlop	Cal.	1975
"	W.J. Usery Jr.	Ga.	1976
Carter	F. Ray Marshall	Tex.	1977
Reagan	Raymond J. Donovan	N.J.	1981
"	William E. Brock	Tenn.	1985
"	Ann D. McLaughlin	D.C.	1987
Bush	Elizabeth Hanford Dole	N.C.	1989
Bush	Lynn Martin	Ill.	1991

Secretaries of Commerce

President	Secretary	Home	Apptd.
Wilson	William C. Redfield	N.Y.	1913
"	Joshua W. Alexander	Mo.	1919
Harding	Herbert C. Hoover	Cal.	1921
Coolidge	"	"	1923
"	William F. Whiting	Mass.	1928
Hoover	Robert P. Lamont	Ill.	1929
"	Roy D. Chapin	Mich.	1932
Roosevelt, F.D.	Daniel C. Roper	S.C.	1933
"	Harry L. Hopkins	N.Y.	1939
"	Jesse Jones	Tex.	1940
"	Henry A. Wallace	Ia.	1945
Truman	"	"	1945
"	W. Averell Harriman	N.Y.	1947
"	Charles Sawyer	Oh.	1948
Eisenhower	Sinclair Weeks	Mass.	1953
"	Lewis L. Strauss	N.Y.	1958
"	Frederick H. Mueller	Mich.	1959
Kennedy	Luther H. Hodges	N.C.	1961
Johnson, L.B.	"	"	1963
"	John T. Connor	N.J.	1965
"	Alex B. Trowbridge	N.J.	1967
"	Cyrus R. Smith	N.Y.	1968
Nixon	Maurice H. Stans	Minn.	1969
"	Peter G. Peterson	Ill.	1972
"	Frederick B. Dent	S.C.	1973
Ford	"	"	1974
"	Rogers C.B. Morton	Md.	1975
"	Elliot L. Richardson	Mass.	1975
Carter	Juanita M. Kreps	N.C.	1977
"	Philip M. Klutznick	Ill.	1979
Reagan	Malcolm Baldrige	Conn.	1981
"	C. William Verity Jr.	Oh.	1987
Bush	Robert A. Mosbacher	Tex.	1989

Secretaries of Housing and Urban Development

The Department of Housing and Urban Development was created by act of Congress Sept. 9, 1965.

President	Secretary	Home	Apptd.	President	Secretary	Home	Apptd.
Johnson, L.B.	Robert C. Weaver	Wash.	1966	Ford	Carla Anderson Hills	Cal.	1975
"	Robert C. Wood	Mass.	1969	Carter	Patricia Roberts Harris	D.C.	1977
Nixon	George W. Romney	Mich.	1969	"	Moon Landrieu	La.	1979
"	James T. Lynn	Oh.	1973	Reagan	Samuel R. Pierce Jr.	N.Y.	1981
Ford	"	"	1974	Bush	Jack F. Kemp	N.Y.	1989

Secretaries of Transportation

The Department of Transportation was created by act of Congress Oct. 15, 1966.

President	Secretary	Home	Apptd.	President	Secretary	Home	Apptd.
Johnson, L.B.	Alan S. Boyd	Fla.	1966	Carter	Neil E. Goldschmidt	Ore.	1979
Nixon	John A. Volpe	Mass.	1969	Reagan	Andrew L. Lewis Jr.	Pa.	1981
"	Claude S. Brinegar	Cal.	1973	"	Elizabeth Hanford Dole	N.C.	1983
Ford	Claude S. Brinegar	Cal.	1974	"	James H. Burnley	N.C.	1987
"	William T. Coleman Jr.	Pa.	1975	Bush	Samuel K. Skinner	Ill.	1989
Carter	Brock Adams	Wash.	1977				

Secretaries of Energy

The Department of Energy was created by federal law Aug. 4, 1977.

President	Secretary	Home	Apptd.	President	Secretary	Home	Apptd.
Carter	James R. Schlesinger	Va.	1977	Reagan	Donald P. Hodel	Ore.	1982
"	Charles Duncan Jr.	Wyo.	1979	"	John S. Herrington	Cal.	1985
Reagan	James B. Edwards	S.C.	1981	Bush	James D. Watkins	Cal.	1989

Secretaries of Health, Education, and Welfare

The Department of Health, Education and Welfare, created by Congress Apr. 11, 1953, was divided by Congress Sept. 27, 1979, into separate departments of Education, and Health and Human Services. The secretary of each is a cabinet member.

President	Secretary	Home	Apptd.	President	Secretary	Home	Apptd.
Eisenhower	Oveta Culp Hobby	Tex.	1953	Nixon	Robert H. Finch	Cal.	1969
"	Marion B. Folsom	N.Y.	1955	"	Elliot L. Richardson	Mass.	1970
"	Arthur S. Flemming	Oh.	1958	"	Caspar W. Weinberger	Cal.	1973
Kennedy	Abraham A. Ribicoff	Conn.	1961	Ford	"	"	1974
"	Anthony J. Celebrezze	Oh.	1962	"	Forrest D. Mathews	Ala.	1975
Johnson, L.B.	"	"	1963	Carter	Joseph A. Califano, Jr.	D.C.	1977
"	John W. Gardner	N.Y.	1965	"	Patricia Roberts Harris	D.C.	1979
Johnson, L.B.	Wilbur J. Cohen	Mich.	1968				

Secretaries of Health and Human Services

President	Secretary	Home	Apptd.	President	Secretary	Home	Apptd.
Carter	Patricia Roberts Harris	D.C.	1979	Reagan	Otis R. Bowen	Ind.	1985
Reagan	Richard S. Schweiker	Pa.	1981	Bush	Louis W. Sullivan	Ga.	1989
"	Margaret M. Heckler	Mass.	1983				

Secretaries of Education

President	Secretary	Home	Apptd.	President	Secretary	Home	Apptd.
Carter	Shirley Hufstedler	Cal.	1979	Reagan	Lauro F. Cavazos	Tex.	1988
Reagan	Terrel Bell	Ut.	1981	Bush	"	"	1989
Reagan	William J. Bennett	N.Y.	1985	"	Lamar Alexander	Tenn.	1991

Secretaries of Veterans Affairs

The Department of Veterans Affairs was created Oct. 25, 1988 when Pres. Reagan signed a bill which made the Veterans Administration into a cabinet post as of Mar. 15, 1989.

President	Secretary	Home	Apptd.
Bush	Edward J. Derwinski	Ill.	1989

Librarians of Congress

Librarian	Served	Appointed by President	Librarian	Served	Appointed by President
John J. Beckley	1802-1807	Jefferson	Herbert Putnam	1899-1939	McKinley
Patrick Magruder	1807-1815	Jefferson	Archibald MacLeish	1939-1944	F. Roosevelt
George Watterston	1815-1829	Madison	Luther H. Evans	1945-1953	Truman
John Silva Meehan	1829-1861	Jackson	L. Quincy Mumford	1954-1974	Eisenhower
John G. Stephenson	1861-1864	Lincoln	Daniel J. Boorstin	1975-1987	Ford
Ainsworth Rand Spofford	1864-1897	Lincoln	James H. Billington	1987-	Reagan
John Russell Young	1897-1899	McKinley			

Speakers of the House of Representatives

Party designations: A, American; D, Democratic; DR, Democratic Republican; F, Federalist;
R, Republican; W, Whig. *Served only one day.

Name	Party	State	Tenure	Name	Party	State	Tenure
Frederick Muhlenberg	F	Pa.	1789-1791	*Theodore M. Pomeroy	R	N.Y.	1869-1869
Jonathan Trumbull	F	Conn.	1791-1793	James G. Blaine	R	Me.	1869-1875
Frederick Muhlenberg	F	Pa.	1793-1795	Michael C. Kerr	D	Ind.	1875-1876
Jonathan Dayton	F	N.J.	1795-1799	Samuel J. Randall	D	Pa.	1876-1881
Theodore Sedgwick	F	Mass.	1799-1801	Joseph W. Keifer	R	Oh.	1881-1883
Nathaniel Macon	DR	N.C.	1801-1807	John G. Carlisle	D	Ky.	1883-1889
Joseph B. Varnum	DR	Mass.	1807-1811	Thomas B. Reed	R	Me.	1889-1891
Henry Clay	DR	Ky.	1811-1814	Charles F. Crisp	D	Ga.	1891-1895
Langdon Cheves	DR	S.C.	1814-1815	Thomas B. Reed	R	Me.	1895-1899
Henry Clay	DR	Ky.	1815-1820	David B. Henderson	R	Ia.	1899-1903
John W. Taylor	DR	N.Y.	1820-1821	Joseph G. Cannon	R	Ill.	1903-1911
Philip P. Barbour	DR	Va.	1821-1823	Champ Clark	D	Mo.	1911-1919
Henry Clay	DR	Ky.	1823-1825	Frederick H. Gillett	R	Mass.	1919-1925
John W. Taylor	D	N.Y.	1825-1827	Nicholas Longworth	R	Oh.	1925-1931
Andrew Stevenson	D	Va.	1827-1834	John N. Garner	D	Tex.	1931-1933
John Bell	D	Tenn.	1834-1835	Henry T. Rainey	D	Ill.	1933-1935
James K. Polk	D	Tenn.	1835-1839	Joseph W. Byrns	D	Tenn.	1935-1936
Robert M. T. Hunter	D	Va.	1839-1841	William B. Bankhead	D	Ala.	1936-1940
John White	W	Ky.	1841-1843	Sam Rayburn	D	Tex.	1940-1947
John W. Jones	D	Va.	1843-1845	Joseph W. Martin Jr.	R	Mass.	1947-1949
John W. Davis	D	Ind.	1845-1847	Sam Rayburn	D	Tex.	1949-1953
Robert C. Winthrop	W	Mass.	1847-1849	Joseph W. Martin Jr.	R	Mass.	1953-1955
Howell Cobb	D	Ga.	1849-1851	Sam Rayburn	D	Tex.	1955-1961
Linn Boyd	D	Ky.	1851-1855	John W. McCormack	D	Mass.	1962-1971
Nathaniel P. Banks	A	Mass.	1856-1857	Carl Albert	D	Okla.	1971-1977
James L. Orr	D	S.C.	1857-1859	Thomas P. O'Neill Jr.	D	Mass.	1977-1987
William Pennington	R	N.J.	1860-1861	James Wright	D	Tex.	1987-1989
Galusha A. Grow	R	Pa.	1861-1863	Thomas S. Foley	D	Wash.	1989-
Schuyler Colfax	R	Ind.	1863-1869				

Floor Leaders in the U.S. Senate

Majority Leaders

Name	State	Party	Tenure
Charles Curtis	Kan.	R	1925-1929
James E. Watson	Ind.	R	1929-1933
Joseph T. Robinson	Ark.	D	1933-1937
Alben W. Barkley	Ky.	D	1937-1947
Wallace H. White	Me.	R	1947-1949
Scott W. Lucas	Ill.	D	1949-1951
Ernest W. McFarland	Ariz.	D	1951-1953
Robert A. Taft	Oh.	R	1953
William F. Knowland	Cal.	R	1953-1955
Lyndon B. Johnson	Tex.	D	1955-1961
Mike Mansfield	Mont.	D	1961-1977
Robert C. Byrd	W.Va.	D	1977-1981
Howard H. Baker Jr.	Tenn.	R	1981-1985
Robert J. Dole	Kan.	R	1985-1987
Robert C. Byrd	W.Va.	D	1987-1989
George J. Mitchell	Me.	D	1989-

Minority Leaders

Name	State	Party	Tenure
Oscar W. Underwood	Ala.	D	1920-1923
Joseph T. Robinson	Ark.	D	1923-1933
Charles L. McNary	Ore.	R	1933-1944
Wallace H. White	Me.	R	1944-1947
Alben W. Barkley	Ky.	D	1947-1949
Kenneth S. Wherry	Neb.	R	1949-1951
Henry Styles Bridges	N.H.	R	1952-1953
Lyndon B. Johnson	Tex.	D	1953-1955
William F. Knowland	Cal.	R	1955-1959
Everett M. Dirksen	Ill.	R	1959-1969
Hugh D. Scott	Penn.	R	1969-1977
Howard H. Baker Jr.	Tenn.	R	1977-1981
Robert C. Byrd	W.Va.	D	1981-1987
Robert J. Dole	Kan.	R	1987-

Federal Bureau of Investigation

The Federal Bureau of Investigation was created July 26, 1908 and was referred to as Office of Chief Examiner. It became the Bureau of Investigation (Mar. 26, 1909), United States Bureau of Investigation (July 1, 1932), Division of Investigation (Aug. 10, 1933), and Federal Bureau of Investigation (July 1, 1935).

Director	Assumed office	Director	Assumed office
Stanley W. Finch	July 26, 1908	L. Patrick Gray, act.	May 3, 1972
A(lexander) Bruce Bielaski	Apr. 30, 1912	William D. Ruckelshaus, act.	Apr. 27, 1973
William E. Allen, act.	Feb. 10, 1919	Clarence M. Kelley	July 9, 1973
William J. Flynn	July 1, 1919	William H. Webster	Feb. 23, 1978
William J. Burns	Aug. 22, 1921	John E. Otto, act.	May 27, 1987
J. Edgar Hoover, act.	May 10, 1924	William S. Sessions	Nov. 2, 1987
J. Edgar Hoover	Dec. 10, 1924		

Central Intelligence Agency

On June 13, 1942 President Roosevelt established the Office of Strategic Services (OSS) and named William J. Donovan as its director. The OSS was disbanded Oct. 1, 1945 and its functions absorbed by the State and War departments. President Truman, Jan. 22, 1946, established the Central Intelligence Agency Group (CIG) to operate under the direction of the National Intelligence Authority (NIA). The National Security Act of 1947 replaced the NIA with the National Security Council and the CIG with the Central Intelligence Agency.

Director	Served	Appointed by President	Director	Served	Appointed by President
Adm. Sidney W. Souers	1946	Truman	Richard Helms	1966-1973	Johnson
Gen. Hoyt S. Vandenberg	1946-1947	Truman	James R. Schlesinger	1973	Nixon
Adm. Roscoe H. Hillenkoetter	1947-1950	Truman	William E. Colby	1973-1976	Nixon
Gen. Walter Bedell Smith	1950-1953	Truman	George Bush	1976-1977	Ford
Allen W. Dulles	1953-1961	Eisenhower	Adm. Stansfield Turner	1977-1981	Carter
John A. McCone	1961-1965	Kennedy	William J. Casey	1981-1987	Reagan
Adm. William F. Raborn Jr.	1965-1966	Johnson	William H. Webster[1]	1987-	Reagan

(1) Pres. Bush nominated Robert M. Gates to replace Webster. (See *Chronology* and *Index*.)

Voting Age Population Turnout in Presidential Elections

Source: Committee for the Study of the American Electorate

	1988 % VAP Voted	1984 % VAP Voted	+/− 88-84		1988 % VAP Voted	1984 % VAP Voted	+/− 88-84		1988 % VAP Voted	1984 % VAP Voted	+/− 88-84
Ala.	45.80	49.85	−4.06	Ky.	48.16	50.77	−2.61	N.D.	61.54	62.67	−1.13
Alas.	51.98	59.15	−7.17	La.	51.28	54.55	−3.27	Oh.	55.13	58.20	−3.07
Ariz.	44.99	45.23	−.25	Me.	62.15	64.77	−2.62	Okla.	48.17	52.15	−3.43
Ark.	47.00	51.84	−4.84	Md.	49.11	51.41	−2.30	Ore.	58.59	61.82	−3.23
Cal.	47.36	49.56	−2.19	Mass.	58.06	57.60	.45	Pa.	50.07	53.98	−3.91
Col.	55.14	55.05	.09	Mich.	54.03	57.90	−3.87	R.I.	52.95	55.85	−2.89
Conn.	57.92	61.10	−3.17	Minn.	66.33	68.16	−1.83	S.C.	38.91	40.66	−1.75
Del.	51.00	55.46	−4.46	Miss.	51.02	52.23	−1.21	S.D.	61.49	62.57	−1.08
D.C.	39.44	43.21	−3.77	Mo.	54.80	57.25	−2.45	Tenn.	44.69	49.05	−4.36
Fla.	44.75	48.24	−3.49	Mon.	62.41	65.04	−2.63	Tex.	44.23	47.20	−2.96
Ga.	38.79	41.98	−3.19	Neb.	56.68	55.64	1.04	Ut.	60.02	61.55	−1.53
Ha.	43.02	44.31	−1.29	Nev.	44.88	41.49	3.39	Vt.	59.06	59.84	−.78
Ida.	58.34	59.93	−1.59	N.H.	54.74	52.98	1.76	Va.	48.23	50.69	−2.46
Ill.	53.32	57.11	−3.79	N.J.	52.06	56.68	−4.52	Wash.	54.59	58.09	−3.51
Ind.	53.31	55.92	−2.62	N.M.	47.35	51.33	−3.99	W.Va.	46.73	51.74	−5.01
Ia.	59.72	62.25	−2.99	N.Y.	48.11	51.18	−3.06	Wis.	61.98	63.46	−1.48
Kan.	54.29	56.84	−2.55	N.C.	43.44	47.36	−3.92	Wy.	50.30	53.38	−3.08

Voter Turnout in 1990

The Committee for the Study of the American Electorate estimated that about 67.7 million Americans, or 36 percent of the 186 million eligible voters, participated in the 1990 midterm elections. This was about equal to the percentage voting in the 1986 midterm elections, which was itself the lowest national turnout since World War II. Turnout was highest in Maine and Montana, where 55 percent of those eligible voted.

National Political Parties

As of mid-1991

Republican Party

National Headquarters—310 First St., SE, Washington, DC 20003.
Chairman—Clayton Yeutter.
Co-Chairman—Jeanie Austin.
Vice Chairmen—Bernard M. Shanley, Jack Londen, Martha Moore, Nelda Barton, Ernest Angelo Jr., Kay Riddle, Elsie Vartanian, Duane Acklie.
Secretary—Kit Mehrtens.
Treasurer—William J. McManus.
General Counsel—Jan Baran.

Democratic Party

National Headquarters—430 South Capitol St., SE, Washington, DC 20003.
Chairman—Ronald H. Brown.
Vice Chairpersons—Lynn Cutler, Jack Otero, Carmen Perez, James Brady, Lottie Shackelford.
Secretary—Kathleen M. Vick.
Treasurer—Robert Farmer.

America's Third Parties

Since 1860, there have been only 4 presidential elections in which all "third parties" together polled more than 10% of the vote: the Populists (James Baird Weaver) in 1892, the National Progressives (Theodore Roosevelt) in 1912, the La Follette Progressives in 1924, and George Wallace's American Party in 1968. In 1948, the combined "third parties" (Henry Wallace's Progressives, Strom Thurmond's States' Rights party or Dixiecrats, Prohibition, Socialists, and others) received only 5.75% of the vote. In most elections since 1860, fewer than one vote in 20 has been cast for a third party. The only successful third party in American history was the Republican Party in the election of Abraham Lincoln in 1860.

Notable Third Parties

Party	Presidential nominee	Year	Issues	Strength in
Anti-Masonic	William Wirt	1832	Against secret societies and oaths	Pa., Vt.
Liberty	James G. Birney	1844	Anti-slavery	North
Free Soil	Martin Van Buren	1848	Anti-slavery	New York, Ohio
American (Know Nothing)	Millard Fillmore	1856	Anti-immigrant	Northeast, South
Greenback	Peter Cooper	1876	For "cheap money,"	
Greenback	James B. Weaver	1880	labor rights	National
Prohibition	John P. St. John	1884	Anti-liquor	National
Populist	James B. Weaver	1892	For "cheap money," end of national banks	South, West
Socialist	Eugene V. Debs	1900-20	For public ownership	National
Progressive (Bull Moose)	Theodore Roosevelt	1912	Against high tariffs	Midwest, West
Progressive	Robert M. LaFollette	1924	Farmer & labor rights	Midwest, West
Socialist	Norman Thomas	1928-48	Liberal reforms	National
Union	William Lemke	1936	Anti "New Deal"	National
States' Rights	Strom Thurmond	1948	For states' rights	South
Progressive	Henry Wallace	1948	Anti-cold war	New York, California
American Independent	George Wallace	1968	For states' rights	South
American	John G. Schmitz	1972	For "law and order"	Far West, Oh., La.
None (Independent)	John B. Anderson	1980	A 3d choice	National

UNITED STATES FACTS
Superlative U.S. Statistics
Source: U.S. Geological Survey; U.S. Bureau of the Census

Area for 50 states and D. of C.	Total	3,618,770 sq. mi.
	Land 3,539,289 sq. mi.—Water 79,481 sq. mi.	
Largest state	Alaska	591,004 sq. mi.
Smallest state	Rhode Island	1,212 sq. mi.
Largest county (excludes Alaska)	San Bernardino County, California	20,064 sq. mi.
Smallest county	Kalawo, Hawaii	14 sq. mi.
Northernmost city	Barrow, Alaska	71°17'N.
Northernmost point	Point Barrow, Alaska	71°23'N.
Southernmost city	Hilo, Hawaii	19°43'N.
Southernmost settlement	Naalehu, Hawaii	19°03'N.
Southernmost point	Ka Lae (South Cape), Island of Hawaii	18°55'N. (155°41'W.)
Easternmost city	Eastport, Maine	66°59'02"W.
Easternmost settlement	Lubec, Maine	66°58'49"W.
Easternmost point	West Quoddy Head, Maine	66°57'W.
Westernmost city	West Unalaska, Alaska	166°32'W.
Westernmost settlement	Adak, Alaska	176°39'W.
Westernmost point	Cape Wrangell, Alaska	172°27'E.
Highest settlement	Climax, Colorado	11,560 ft.
Lowest settlement	Calipatria, California	−185 ft.
Highest point on Atlantic coast	Cadillac Mountain, Mount Desert Is., Maine	1,530 ft.
Oldest national park	Yellowstone National Park (1872), Wyoming, Montana, Idaho	3,468 sq. mi.
Largest national park	Wrangell-St. Elias, Alaska	13,018 sq. mi.
Largest national monument	Death Valley, California, Nevada	3,231 sq. mi.
Highest waterfall	Yosemite Falls—Total in three sections	2,425 ft.
	Upper Yosemite Fall	1,430 ft.
	Cascades in middle section	675 ft.
	Lower Yosemite Fall	320 ft.
Longest river	Mississippi-Missouri	3,710 mi.
Highest mountain	Mount McKinley, Alaska	20,320 ft.
Lowest point	Death Valley, California	−282 ft.
Deepest lake	Crater Lake, Oregon	1,932 ft.
Rainiest spot	Mt. Waialeale, Hawaii	Annual aver. rainfall 460 inches
Largest gorge	Grand Canyon, Colorado River, Arizona	277 miles long, 600 ft. to 18 miles wide, 1 mile deep
Deepest gorge	Hell's Canyon, Snake River, Idaho-Oregon	7,900 ft.
Strongest surface wind	Mount Washington, New Hampshire recorded 1934	231 mph
Biggest dam	New Cornelia Tailings, Ten Mile Wash, Arizona	274,026,000 cu. yds. material used
Tallest building	Sears Tower, Chicago, Illinois	1,454 ft.
Largest building	Boeing 747 Manufacturing Plant, Everett, Washington	205,600,000 cu. ft.; covers 47 acres.
Tallest structure	TV tower, Blanchard, North Dakota	2,063 ft.
Longest bridge span	Verrazano-Narrows, New York	4,260 ft.
Highest bridge	Royal Gorge, Colorado	1,053 ft. above water
Deepest well	Gas well, Washita County, Oklahoma	31,441 ft.

The 48 Contiguous States

Area for 48 states	Total	3,021,295 sq. mi.
	Land 2,962,031 sq. mi.—Water 59,264 sq. mi.	
Largest state	Texas	266,807 sq. mi
Northernmost city	International Falls, Minnesota	48°36'N.
Northernmost settlement	Angle Inlet, Minnesota	49°21'N.
Northernmost point	Northwest Angle, Minnesota	49°23'N.
Southernmost city	Key West, Florida	24°33'N.
Southernmost mainland city	Florida City, Florida	25°27'N.
Southernmost point	Key West, Florida	24°33'N.
Westernmost town	La Push, Washington	124°38'W.
Westernmost point	Cape Alava, Washington	124°44'W.
Highest mountain	Mount Whitney, California	14,494 ft.

Note to users: The distinction between cities and towns varies from state to state. In this table the U.S. Bureau of the Census usage is followed.

Geodetic Datum of North America

In July 1986, the National Oceanic and Atmospheric Administration's National Geodetic Survey (NGS) completed the readjustment and redefinition of the North American Datum. This new datum is known as the North American Datum of 1983. Rapid advances in economic growth and scientific exploration in the United States after World War II resulted in an increasing need for accurate coordinate information. To facilitate the use of satellite surveying and navigation systems, the new datum was redefined using the Geodetic Reference System 1980 as the reference ellipsoid because this model more closely approximates the true size and shape of the Earth. The readjustment of the datum resulted in position changes of as much as 330 feet in the Continental United States and as much as 1/4 mile in Hawaii, the Aleutian Islands, Puerto Rico, and the Virgin Islands.

Statistical Information about the U.S.

In the *Statistical Abstract of the United States* the Bureau of the Census, U.S. Dept. of Commerce, annually publishes a summary of social, political, and economic information. A book of almost 1,000 pages, it presents in 31 sections comprehensive data on population, housing, health, education, employment, income, prices, business, banking, energy, science, defense, trade, government finance, foreign country comparison, and other subjects. Special features include data from the 1990 Census, sections on State Rankings and Metropolitan Statistical Areas and a new section on computer technology in the office. The book is prepared under the direction of Glenn W. King, Chief, Statistical Compendia Staff, Bureau of the Census. Supplements to the *Statistical Abstract* are *County and City Data Book, 1988; Historical Statistics of the United States, Colonial Times to 1970;* and *State and Metropolitan Area Data Book, 1991.* Information concerning these and other publications may be obtained from the Supt. of Documents, Government Printing Office, Wash., D.C. 20402, or from the U.S. Bureau of the Census, Data User Services Division, Wash., D.C. 20233.

Highest and Lowest Altitudes in the U.S. and Territories

Source: U.S. Geological Survey (Minus sign means below sea level; elevations are in feet.)

State	Highest Point Name	County	Elev.	Lowest Point Name	County	Elev.
Alabama	Cheaha Mountain	Cleburne	2,405	Gulf of Mexico		Sea level
Alaska	Mount McKinley		20,320	Pacific Ocean		Sea level
Arizona	Humphreys Peak	Coconino	12,633	Colorado R.	Yuma	70
Arkansas	Magazine Mountain	Logan	2,753	Ouachita R.	Ashley-Union	55
California	Mount Whitney	Inyo-Tulare	14,494	Death Valley	Inyo	−282
Colorado	Mount Elbert	Lake	14,433	Arkansas R.	Prowers	3,350
Connecticut	Mount Frissell	Litchfield	2,380	L.I. Sound		Sea level
Delaware	On Ebright Road	New Castle	442	Atlantic Ocean		Sea level
Dist. of Col.	Tenleytown	N. W. part	410	Potomac R.		1
Florida	Sec. 30, T 6N, R 20W.	Walton	345	Atlantic Ocean		Sea level
Georgia	Brasstown Bald	Towns-Union	4,784	Atlantic Ocean		Sea level
Guam	Mount Lamlam	Agat District	1,332	Pacific Ocean		Sea level
Hawaii	Mauna Kea	Hawaii	13,796	Pacific Ocean		Sea level
Idaho	Borah Peak	Custer	12,662	Snake R.	Nez Perce	710
Illinois	Charles Mound	Jo Daviess	1,235	Mississippi R.	Alexander	279
Indiana	Franklin Township	Wayne	1,257	Ohio R.	Posey	320
Iowa	Sec. 29, T 100N, R 41W.	Osceola	1,670	Mississippi R.	Lee	480
Kansas	Mount Sunflower	Wallace	4,039	Verdigris R.	Montgomery	679
Kentucky	Black Mountain	Harlan	4,139	Mississippi R.	Fulton	257
Louisiana	Driskill Mountain	Bienville	535	New Orleans	Orleans	−8
Maine	Mount Katahdin	Piscataquis	5,267	Atlantic Ocean		Sea level
Maryland	Backbone Mountain	Garrett	3,360	Atlantic Ocean		Sea level
Massachusetts	Mount Greylock	Berkshire	3,487	Atlantic Ocean		Sea level
Michigan	Mount Arvon	Baraga	1,979	Lake Erie	Monroe	571
Minnesota	Eagle Mountain	Cook	2,301	Lake Superior		600
Mississippi	Woodall Mountain	Tishomingo	806	Gulf of Mexico		Sea level
Missouri	Taum Sauk Mt.	Iron	1,772	St. Francis R.	Dunklin	230
Montana	Granite Peak	Park	12,799	Kootenai R.	Lincoln	1,800
Nebraska	Johnson Township	Kimball	5,426	Missouri R.	Richardson	840
Nevada	Boundary Peak	Esmeralda	13,140	Mount Manchester	Clark	479
New Hamp.	Mt. Washington	Coos	6,288	Atlantic Ocean	Rockingham	Sea level
New Jersey	High Point	Sussex	1,803	Atlantic Ocean		Sea level
New Mexico	Wheeler Peak	Taos	13,161	Red Bluff Res.	Eddy	2,842
New York	Mount Marcy	Essex	5,344	Atlantic Ocean		Sea level
North Carolina	Mount Mitchell	Yancey	6,684	Atlantic Ocean		Sea level
North Dakota	White Butte	Slope	3,506	Red R.	Pembina	750
Ohio	Campbell Hill	Logan	1,549	Ohio R.	Hamilton	455
Oklahoma	Black Mesa	Cimarron	4,973	Little R.	McCurtain	289
Oregon	Mount Hood	Clackamas-Hood R.	11,239	Pacific Ocean		Sea level
Pennsylvania	Mt. Davis	Somerset	3,213	Delaware R.	Delaware	Sea level
Puerto Rico	Cerro de Punta	Ponce District	4,390	Atlantic Ocean		Sea level
Rhode Island	Jerimoth Hill	Providence	812	Atlantic Ocean		Sea level
Samoa	Lata Mountain	Tau Island	3,160	Pacific Ocean		Sea level
South Carolina	Sassafras Mountain	Pickens	3,560	Atlantic Ocean		Sea level
South Dakota	Harney Peak	Pennington	7,242	Big Stone Lake	Roberts	966
Tennessee	Clingmans Dome	Sevier	6,643	Mississippi R.	Shelby	178
Texas	Guadalupe Peak	Culberson	8,749	Gulf of Mexico		Sea level
Utah	Kings Peak	Duchesne	13,528	Beaverdam Wash.	Washington	2,000
Vermont	Mount Mansfield	Lamoille	4,393	Lake Champlain		95
Virginia	Mount Rogers	Grayson-Smyth	5,729	Atlantic Ocean		Sea level
Virgin Islands	Crown Mountain	St. Thomas Island	1,556	Atlantic Ocean		Sea level
Washington	Mount Rainier	Pierce	14,410	Pacific Ocean		Sea level
West Virginia	Spruce Knob	Pendleton	4,861	Potomac R.	Jefferson	240
Wisconsin	Timms Hill	Price	1,951	Lake Michigan		579
Wyoming	Gannett Peak	Fremont	13,804	B. Fourche R.	Crook	3,099

U.S. Coastline by States

Source: NOAA, U.S. Dept. of Commerce
(statute miles)

State	Coastline[1]	Shoreline[2]	State	Coastline[1]	Shoreline[2]
Atlantic coast	2,069	28,673	**Gulf coast**	1,631	17,141
Connecticut	0	618	Alabama	53	607
Delaware	28	381	Florida	770	5,095
Florida	580	3,331	Louisiana	397	7,721
Georgia	100	2,344	Mississippi	44	359
Maine	228	3,478	Texas	367	3,359
Maryland	31	3,190			
Massachusetts	192	1,519	**Pacific coast**	7,623	40,298
New Hampshire	13	131	Alaska	5,580	31,383
New Jersey	130	1,792	California	840	3,427
New York	127	1,850	Hawaii	750	1,052
North Carolina	301	3,375	Oregon	296	1,410
Pennsylvania	0	89	Washington	157	3,026
Rhode Island	40	384			
South Carolina	187	2,876	**Arctic coast, Alaska**	1,060	2,521
Virginia	112	3,315	**United States**	12,383	88,633

(1) Figures are lengths of general outline of seacoast. Measurements were made with a unit measure of 30 minutes of latitude on charts as near the scale of 1:1,200,000 as possible. Coastline of sounds and bays is included to a point where they narrow to width of unit measure. and includes the distance across at such point. (2) Figures obtained in 1939-40 with a recording instrument on the largest-scale charts and maps then available. Shoreline of outer coast, offshore islands, sounds, bays, rivers, and creeks is included to the head of tidewater or to a point where tidal waters narrow to a width of 100 feet.

States: Settled, Capitals, Entry into Union, Area, Rank

The original 13 states—The 13 colonies that seceded from Great Britain and fought the War of Independence (American Revolution) became the 13 original states. They were: Delaware, Pennsylvania, New Jersey, Georgia, Connecticut, Massachusetts, Maryland, South Carolina, New Hampshire, Virginia, New York, North Carolina, and Rhode Island. The order for the original 13 states is the order in which they ratified the Constitution.

State	Set- tled*	Capital	Entered Union Date	Order	Extent in miles Long (approx. mean)	Wide	Area in square miles Land	Inland Water	Total	Rank in area
Ala.	1702	Montgomery	Dec. 14, 1819	22	330	190	50,767	938	51,705	29
Alas.	1784	Juneau	Jan. 3, 1959	49	(a)1,480	810	570,833	20,171	591,004	1
Ariz.	1776	Phoenix	Feb. 14, 1912	48	400	310	113,508	492	114,000	6
Ark.	1686	Little Rock	June 15, 1836	25	260	240	52,078	1,109	53,187	27
Cal.	1769	Sacramento	Sept. 9, 1850	31	770	250	156,299	2,407	158,706	3
Col.	1858	Denver	Aug. 1, 1876	38	380	280	103,595	496	104,091	8
Conn.	1634	Hartford	Jan. 9, 1788	5	110	70	4,872	147	5,018	48
Del.	1638	Dover	Dec. 7, 1787	1	100	30	1,932	112	2,045	49
D.C.		Washington					63	6	69	51
Fla.	1565	Tallahassee	Mar. 3, 1845	27	500	160	54,153	4,511	58,664	22
Ga.	1733	Atlanta	Jan. 2, 1788	4	300	230	58,056	854	58,910	21
Ha.	1820	Honolulu	Aug. 21, 1959	50	...	...	6,425	46	6,471	47
Ida.	1842	Boise	July 3, 1890	43	570	300	82,412	1,153	83,564	13
Ill.	1720	Springfield	Dec. 3, 1818	21	390	210	55,645	700	56,345	24
Ind.	1733	Indianapolis	Dec. 11, 1816	19	270	140	35,932	253	36,185	38
Ia.	1788	Des Moines	Dec. 28, 1846	29	310	200	55,965	310	56,275	25
Kan.	1727	Topeka	Jan. 29, 1861	34	400	210	81,778	499	82,277	14
Ky.	1774	Frankfort	June 1, 1792	15	380	140	39,669	740	40,410	37
La.	1699	Baton Rouge	Apr. 30, 1812	18	380	130	44,521	3,230	47,752	31
Me.	1624	Augusta	Mar. 15, 1820	23	320	190	30,995	2,270	33,265	39
Md.	1634	Annapolis	Apr. 28, 1788	7	250	90	9,837	623	10,460	42
Mass.	1620	Boston	Feb. 6, 1788	6	190	50	7,824	460	8,284	45
Mich.	1668	Lansing	Jan. 26, 1837	26	490	240	56,954	1,573	58,527	23
Minn.	1805	St. Paul	May 11, 1858	32	400	250	79,548	4,854	84,402	12
Miss.	1699	Jackson	Dec. 10, 1817	20	340	170	47,233	457	47,689	32
Mo.	1735	Jefferson City	Aug. 10, 1821	24	300	240	68,945	752	69,697	19
Mon.	1809	Helena	Nov. 8, 1889	41	630	280	145,388	1,658	147,046	4
Neb.	1823	Lincoln	Mar. 1, 1867	37	430	210	76,644	711	77,355	15
Nev.	1849	Carson City	Oct. 31, 1864	36	490	320	109,894	667	110,561	7
N.H.	1623	Concord	June 21, 1788	9	190	70	8,993	286	9,279	44
N.J.	1660	Trenton	Dec. 18, 1787	3	150	70	7,468	319	7,787	46
N.M.	1610	Santa Fe	Jan. 6, 1912	47	370	343	121,335	258	121,593	5
N.Y.	1614	Albany	July 26, 1788	11	330	283	47,377	1,731	49,108	30
N.C.	1660	Raleigh	Nov. 21, 1789	12	500	150	48,843	3,826	52,669	28
N.D.	1812	Bismarck	Nov. 2, 1889	39	340	211	69,300	1,403	70,702	17
Oh.	1788	Columbus	Mar. 1, 1803	17	220	220	41,004	325	41,330	35
Okla.	1889	Oklahoma City	Nov. 16, 1907	46	400	220	68,655	1,301	69,956	18
Ore.	1811	Salem	Feb. 14, 1859	33	360	261	96,184	889	97,073	10
Pa.	1682	Harrisburg	Dec. 12, 1787	2	283	160	44,888	420	45,308	33
R.I.	1636	Providence	May 29, 1790	13	40	30	1,055	158	1,212	50
S.C.	1670	Columbia	May 23, 1788	8	260	200	30,203	909	31,113	40
S.D.	1859	Pierre	Nov. 2, 1889	40	380	210	75,952	1,164	77,116	16
Tenn.	1769	Nashville	June 1, 1796	16	440	120	41,155	989	42,144	34
Tex.	1682	Austin	Dec. 29, 1845	28	790	660	262,017	4,790	266,807	2
Ut.	1847	Salt Lake City	Jan. 4, 1896	45	350	270	82,073	2,826	84,899	11
Vt.	1724	Montpelier	Mar. 4, 1791	14	160	80	9,273	341	9,614	43
Va.	1607	Richmond	June 25, 1788	10	430	200	39,704	1,063	40,767	36
Wash.	1811	Olympia	Nov. 11, 1889	42	360	240	66,511	1,627	68,139	20
W.Va.	1727	Charleston	June 20, 1863	35	240	130	24,119	112	24,232	41
Wis.	1766	Madison	May 29, 1848	30	310	260	54,426	1,727	56,153	26
Wy.	1834	Cheyenne	July 10, 1890	44	360	280	96,989	820	97,809	9

* First European permanent settlement. (a) Aleutian Islands and Alexander Archipelago are not considered in these lengths.

The Continental Divide

The Continental Divide: watershed, created by mountain ranges or table-lands of the Rocky Mountains, from which the drainage is easterly or westerly; the easterly flowing waters reaching the Atlantic Ocean chiefly through the Gulf of Mexico, and the westerly flowing waters reaching the Pacific Ocean through the Columbia River, or through the Colorado River, which flows into the Gulf of California.

The location and route of the Continental Divide across the United States may briefly be described as follows:

Beginning at point of crossing the United States-Mexican boundary, near long. 108°45'W., the Divide, in a northerly direction, crosses New Mexico along the western edge of the Rio Grande drainage basin, entering Colorado near long. 106°41'W.

Thence by a very irregular route northerly across Colorado along the western summits of the Rio Grande and of the Arkansas, the South Platte, and the North Platte River basins, and across Rocky Mountain National Park, entering Wyoming near long. 106°52'W.

Thence in a northwesterly direction, forming the western rims of the North Platte, Big Horn, and Yellowstone River basins, crossing the southwestern portion of Yellowstone National Park.

Thence in a westerly and then a northerly direction forming the common boundary of Idaho and Montana, to a point on said boundary near long. 114°00'W.

Thence northeasterly and northwesterly through Montana and the Glacier National Park, entering Canada near long. 114°04'W.

Chronological List of Territories

Source: National Archives and Records Service

Name of territory	Date of Organic Act			Organic Act effective			Admission as state			Yrs. terr.
Northwest Territory(a)	July	13,	1787	No fixed date			Mar.	1,	1803(b)	16
Territory southwest of River Ohio	May	26,	1790	No fixed date			June	1,	1796(c)	6
Mississippi	Apr.	7,	1798	When president acted			Dec.	10,	1817	19
Indiana	May	7,	1800	July 4, 1800			Dec.	11,	1816	16
Orleans	Mar.	26,	1804	Oct. 1, 1804			Apr.	30,	1812(d)	7
Michigan	Jan.	11,	1805	June 30, 1805			Jan.	26,	1837	31
Louisiana-Missouri(e)	Mar.	3,	1805	July 4, 1805			Aug.	10,	1821	16
Illinois	Feb.	3,	1809	Mar. 1, 1809			Dec.	3,	1818	9
Alabama	Mar.	3,	1817	When Miss. became a state			Dec.	14,	1819	2
Arkansas	Mar.	2,	1819	July 4, 1819			June	15,	1836	17
Florida	Mar.	30,	1822	No fixed date			Mar.	3,	1845	23
Wisconsin	Apr.	20,	1836	July 3, 1836			May	29,	1848	12
Iowa	June	12,	1838	July 3, 1838			Dec.	28,	1846	7
Oregon	Aug.	14,	1848	Date of act			Feb.	14,	1859	10
Minnesota	Mar.	3,	1849	Date of act			May	11,	1858	9
New Mexico	Sept.	9,	1850	On president's proclamation			Jan.	6,	1912	61
Utah	Sept.	9,	1850	Date of act			Jan.	4,	1896	44
Washington	Mar.	2,	1853	Date of act			Nov.	11,	1889	36
Nebraska	May	30,	1854	Date of act			Mar.	1,	1867	12
Kansas	May	30,	1854	Date of act			Jan.	29,	1861	6
Colorado	Feb.	28,	1861	Date of act			Aug.	1,	1876	15
Nevada	Mar.	2,	1861	Date of act			Oct.	31,	1864	3
Dakota	Mar.	2,	1861	Date of act			Nov.	2,	1889	28
Arizona	Feb.	24,	1863	Date of act			Feb.	14,	1912	49
Idaho	Mar.	3,	1863	Date of act			July	3,	1890	27
Montana	May	26,	1864	Date of act			Nov.	8,	1889	25
Wyoming	July	25,	1868	When officers were qualified			July	10,	1890	22
Alaska(f)	May	17,	1884	No fixed date			Jan.	3,	1959	75
Oklahoma	May	2,	1890	Date of act			Nov.	16,	1907	17
Hawaii	Apr.	30,	1900	June 14, 1900			Aug.	21,	1959	59

(a) Included Ohio, Indiana, Illinois, Michigan, Wisconsin, eastern Minnesota; (b) as the state of Ohio; (c) as the state of Tennessee; (d) as the state of Louisiana; (e) organic act for Missouri Territory of June 4, 1812, became effective Dec. 7, 1812; (f) Although the May 17, 1884 act actually constituted Alaska as a district, it was often referred to as a territory, and unofficially administered as such. The Territory of Alaska was legally and formally organized by an act of Aug. 24, 1912.

Geographic Centers, U.S. and Each State

Source: U.S. Geological Survey

United States, including Alaska and Hawaii — South Dakota; Butte County, W of Castle Rock, Approx. lat. 44°58′N. long. 103°46′W.

Contiguous U. S. (48 states) — Near Lebanon, Smith Co., Kansas, lat. 39°50′N. long. 98°35′W.

North American continent — The geographic center is in Pierce County, North Dakota, 6 miles W of Balta, latitude 48°10′, longitude 100°10′W.

State—county, locality

Alabama—Chilton, 12 miles SW of Clanton.
Alaska—lat. 63°50′N. long. 152°W. Approx. 60 mi. NW of Mt. McKinley.
Arizona—Yavapai, 55 miles ESE of Prescott.
Arkansas—Pulaski, 12 miles NW of Little Rock.
California—Madera, 38 miles E of Madera.
Colorado—Park, 30 miles NW of Pikes Peak.
Connecticut—Hartford, at East Berlin.
Delaware—Kent, 11 miles S of Dover.
District of Columbia—Near 4th and L Sts., NW.
Florida—Hernando, 12 miles NNW of Brooksville.
Georgia—Twiggs, 18 miles SE of Macon.
Hawaii—Hawaii, 20°15′N, 156°20′W, off Maui Island.
Idaho—Custer, at Custer, SW of Challis.
Illinois—Logan, 28 miles NE of Springfield.
Indiana—Boone, 14 miles NNW of Indianapolis.
Iowa—Story, 5 miles NE of Ames.
Kansas—Barton, 15 miles NE of Great Bend.
Kentucky—Marion, 3 miles NNW of Lebanon.
Louisiana—Avoyelles, 3 miles SE of Marksville.
Maine—Piscataquis, 18 miles north of Dover.
Maryland—Prince Georges, 4.5 miles NW of Davidsonville.
Massachusetts—Worcester, north part of city.
Michigan—Wexford, 5 miles NNW of Cadillac.
Minnesota—Crow Wing, 10 miles SW of Brainerd.
Mississippi—Leake, 9 miles WNW of Carthage.
Missouri—Miller, 20 miles SW of Jefferson City.
Montana—Fergus, 11 miles west of Lewistown.
Nebraska—Custer, 10 miles NW of Broken Bow.
Nevada—Lander, 26 miles SE of Austin.
New Hampshire—Belknap, 3 miles E of Ashland.
New Jersey—Mercer, 5 miles SE of Trenton.
New Mexico—Torrance, 12 miles SSW of Willard.
New York—Madison, 12 miles S of Oneida and 26 miles SW of Utica.
North Carolina—Chatham, 10 miles NW of Sanford.
North Dakota—Sheridan, 5 miles SW of McClusky.
Ohio—Delaware, 25 miles NNE of Columbus.
Oklahoma—Oklahoma, 8 miles N of Oklahoma City.
Oregon—Crook, 25 miles SSE of Prineville.
Pennsylvania—Centre, 2.5 miles SW of Bellefonte.
Rhode Island—Kent, 1 mile SSW of Crompton.
South Carolina—Richland, 13 miles SE of Columbia.
South Dakota—Hughes, 8 miles NE of Pierre.
Tennessee—Rutherford, 5 mi. NE of Murfreesboro.
Texas—McCulloch, 15 miles NE of Brady.
Utah—Sanpete, 3 miles N of Manti.
Vermont—Washington, 3 miles E of Roxbury.
Virginia—Buckingham, 5 miles SW of Buckingham.
Washington—Chelan, 10 mi. WSW of Wenatchee.
West Virginia—Braxton, 4 miles E of Sutton.
Wisconsin—Wood, 9 miles SE of Marshfield.
Wyoming—Fremont, 58 miles ENE of Lander.

There is no generally accepted definition of geographic center, and no satisfactory method for determining it. The geographic center of an area may be defined as the center of gravity of the surface, or that point on which the surface of the area would balance if it were a plane of uniform thickness.

No marked or monumented point has been established by any government agency as the geographic center of either the 50 states, the contiguous United States, or the North American continent. A monument was erected in Lebanon, Kan., contiguous U.S. center, by a group of citizens. A cairn in Rugby, N.D. marks the center of the North American continent.

International Boundary Lines of the U.S.

The length of the northern boundary of the contiguous U.S. — the U.S.-Canadian border, excluding Alaska — is 3,987 miles according to the U.S. Geological Survey, Dept. of the Interior. The length of the Alaskan-Canadian border is 1,538 miles. The length of the U.S.-Mexican border, from the Gulf of Mexico to the Pacific Ocean, is approximately 1,933 miles (1963 boundary agreement).

Origin of the Names of U.S. States

Source: State officials, the Smithsonian Institution, and the Topographic Division, U.S. Geological Survey.

Alabama—Indian for tribal town, later a tribe (Alabamas or Alibamons) of the Creek confederacy.

Alaska—Russian version of Aleutian (Eskimo) word, alakshak, for "peninsula," "great lands," or "land that is not an island."

Arizona—Spanish version of Pima Indian word for "little spring place," or Aztec arizuma, meaning "silver-bearing."

Arkansas—French variant of Quapaw, a Siouan people meaning "downstream people."

California—Bestowed by the Spanish conquistadors (possibly by Cortez). It was the name of an imaginary island, an earthly paradise, in "Las Serges de Esplandian," a Spanish romance written by Montalvo in 1510. Baja California (Lower California, in Mexico) was first visited by Spanish in 1533. The present U.S. state was called Alta (Upper) California.

Colorado—Spanish, red, first applied to Colorado River.

Connecticut—From Mohican and other Algonquin words meaning "long river place."

Delaware—Named for Lord De La Warr, early governor of Virginia; first applied to river, then to Indian tribe (Lenni-Lenape), and the state.

District of Columbia—For Columbus, 1791.

Florida—Named by Ponce de Leon on Pascua Florida, "Flowery Easter," on Easter Sunday, 1513.

Georgia—For King George II of England by James Oglethorpe, colonial administrator, 1732.

Hawaii—Possibly derived from native word for homeland, Hawaiki or Owhyhee.

Idaho—A coined name with an invented Indian meaning: "gem of the mountains;" originally suggested for the Pike's Peak mining territory (Colorado), then applied to the new mining territory of the Pacific Northwest. Another theory suggests Idaho may be a Kiowa Apache term for the Comanche.

Illinois—French for Illini or land of Illini, Algonquin word meaning men or warriors.

Indiana—Means "land of the Indians."

Iowa—Indian word variously translated as "one who puts to sleep" or "beautiful land."

Kansas—Sioux word for "south wind people."

Kentucky—Indian word variously translated as "dark and bloody ground," "meadow land" and "land of tomorrow."

Louisiana—Part of territory called Louisiana by Sieur de La Salle for French King Louis XIV.

Maine—From Maine, ancient French province. Also: descriptive, referring to the mainland as distinct from the many coastal islands.

Maryland—For Queen Henrietta Maria, wife of Charles I of England.

Massachusetts—From Indian tribe named after "large hill place" identified by Capt. John Smith as being near Milton, Mass.

Michigan—From Chippewa words mici gama meaning "great water," after the lake of the same name.

Minnesota—From Dakota Sioux word meaning "cloudy water" or "sky-tinted water" of the Minnesota River.

Mississippi—Probably Chippewa; mici zibi, "great river" or "gathering-in of all the waters." Also: Algonquin word, "Messipi."

Missouri—Algonquin Indian tribe named after Missouri River, meaning "muddy water."

Montana—Latin or Spanish for "mountainous."

Nebraska—From Omaha or Otos Indian word meaning "broad water" or "flat river," describing the Platte River.

Nevada—Spanish, meaning snow-clad.

New Hampshire—Named 1629 by Capt. John Mason of Plymouth Council for his home county in England.

New Jersey—The Duke of York, 1664, gave a patent to John Berkeley and Sir George Carteret to be called Nova Caesaria, or New Jersey, after England's Isle of Jersey.

New Mexico—Spaniards in Mexico applied term to land north and west of Rio Grande in the 16th century.

New York—For Duke of York and Albany who received patent to New Netherland from his brother Charles II and sent an expedition to capture it, 1664.

North Carolina—In 1619 Charles I gave a large patent to Sir Robert Heath to be called Province of Carolana, from Carolus, Latin name for Charles. A new patent was granted by Charles II to Earl of Clarendon and others. Divided into North and South Carolina, 1710.

North Dakota—Dakota is Sioux for friend or ally.

Ohio—Iroquois word for "fine or good river."

Oklahoma—Choctaw coined word meaning red man, proposed by Rev. Allen Wright, Choctaw-speaking Indian.

Oregon—Origin unknown. One theory holds that the name may have been derived from that of the Wisconsin River shown on a 1715 French map as "Ouaricon-sint."

Pennsylvania—William Penn, the Quaker, who was made full proprietor by King Charles II in 1681, suggested Sylvania, or woodland, for his tract. The king's government owed Penn's father, Admiral William Penn, £16,000, and the land was granted as partial settlement. Charles II added the Penn to Sylvania, against the desires of the modest proprietor, in honor of the admiral.

Puerto Rico—Spanish for Rich Port.

Rhode Island—Exact origin is unknown. One theory notes that Giovanni de Verrazano recorded an island about the size of Rhodes in the Mediterranean in 1524, but others believe the state was named Roode Eylandt by Adriaen Block, Dutch explorer, because of its red clay.

South Carolina—See North Carolina.

South Dakota—See North Dakota.

Tennessee—Tanasi was the name of Cherokee villages on the Little Tennessee River. From 1784 to 1788 this was the State of Franklin, or Frankland.

Texas—Variant of word used by Caddo and other Indians meaning friends or allies, and applied to them by the Spanish in eastern Texas. Also written texias, tejas, teysas.

Utah—From a Navajo word meaning upper, or higher up, as applied to a Shoshone tribe called Ute. Spanish form is Yutta, English Uta or Utah. Proposed name Deseret, "land of honeybees," from Book of Mormon, was rejected by Congress.

Vermont—From French words vert (green) and mont (mountain). The Green Mountains were said to have been named by Samuel de Champlain. When the state was formed, 1777, Dr. Thomas Young suggested combining vert and mont into Vermont.

Virginia—Named by Sir Walter Raleigh, who fitted out the expedition of 1584, in honor of Queen Elizabeth, the Virgin Queen of England.

Washington—Named after George Washington. When the bill creating the Territory of Columbia was introduced in the 32d Congress, the name was changed to Washington because of the existence of the District of Columbia.

West Virginia—So named when western counties of Virginia refused to secede from the United States, 1863.

Wisconsin—An Indian name, spelled Ouisconsin and Mesconsing by early chroniclers. Believed to mean "grassy place" in Chippewa. Congress made it Wisconsin.

Wyoming—The word was taken from Wyoming Valley, Pa., which was the site of an Indian massacre and became widely known by Campbell's poem, "Gertrude of Wyoming." In Algonquin it means "large prairie place."

Territorial Sea of the U.S.

According to a December 27, 1988 proclamation by Pres. Ronald Reagan: "The territorial sea of the United States henceforth extends to 12 nautical miles from the baselines of the United States determined in accordance with international law. In accordance with international law, as reflected in the applicable provisions of the 1982 United Nations Convention on the Law of the Sea, within the territorial sea of the United States, the ships of all countries enjoy the right of innocent passage and the ships and aircraft of all countries enjoy the right of transit passage through international straits."

Accession of Territory by the U.S.

Source: Bureau of the Census, U.S. Dept. of Commerce

	Acquisition date	Gross Area (Land and water) Sq. mi.		Acquisition date	Gross Area (Land and water) Sq. mi.		Acquisition date	Gross Area (Land and water) Sq. mi.
Total U.S.	(x)	3,623,434	Gadsden Purchase	1853	29,640	Virgin Islands of		
United States. . . .	(x)	3,618,770	Alaska	1867	591,004	the U.S..	1917	132
Territory in 1790[1].	(x)	891,364	Hawaii	1898	6,471	Pacific Islands,		
Louisiana Purchase	1803	831,321	Other areas:			Trust Territory		
Purchase of Florida	1819	69,866	Puerto Rico	[2]1898	3,515	of the[5]	1947	533
Texas.	1845	384,958	Guam.	[3]1898	209	No. Mariana Islands[5]	1947	184
Oregon.	1846	283,439	American Samoa .	[4]1899	77	All other[6]	(x)	14
Mexican Cession .	1848	530,706						

(x) Not applicable. (1) Includes that part of drainage basin of Red River of the North, south of 49th parallel, sometimes considered part of Louisiana Purchase. (2) Ceded by Spain in 1898, ratified in 1899, and became Commonwealth of Puerto Rico by Act of Congress on July 25, 1952. (3) Acquired 1898; ratified 1899. (4) Acquired 1899; ratified 1900. (5) Land area only. (6) Comprises the following islands with gross areas as indicated, in sq. mi.: Midway (2), Wake (3), Palmyra (4), Navassa (2), Baker, Howland, and Jarvis (combined area, 3), Johnston Atoll (combined area, less than .5), and Kingman Reef (less than .5). Excludes Canton and Enderbury Islands (combined area 27 sq. mi.), which are considered to be under the jurisdiction of Kiribati since 1979, and Swan Islands (1 sq. mi.), which were returned to Honduras in 1972.

Public Lands of the U. S.

Source: Bureau of Land Management, U.S. Dept. of the Interior

Disposition of Public Lands 1781 to 1988

Disposition by methods not elsewhere classified[1]	Acres	Granted to states for:	Acres
	303,500,000	Support of common schools	77,630,000
Granted or sold to homesteaders	287,500,000	Reclamation of swampland	64,920,000
Granted to railroad corporations	94,400,000	Construction of railroads	37,130,000
Granted to veterans as military bounties. .	61,000,000	Support of misc. institutions[6]	21,700,000
Confirmed as private land claims[2]	34,000,000	Purposes not elsewhere classified[7] . . .	117,600,000
Sold under timber and stone law[3]	13,900,000	Canals and rivers	6,100,000
Granted or sold under timber culture law[4].	10,900,000	Construction of wagon roads	3,400,000
Sold under desert land law[5]	10,700,000	**Total granted to states . . . . . .**	**328,480,000**

(1) Chiefly public, private, and preemption sales, but includes mineral entries, scrip locations, sales of townsites and townlots. (2) The Government has confirmed title to lands claimed under valid grants made by foreign governments prior to the acquisition of the public domain by the United States. (3) The law provided for the sale of lands valuable for timber or stone and unfit for cultivation. (4) The law provided for the granting of public lands to settlers on condition that they plant and cultivate trees on the lands granted. (5) The law provided for the sale of arid agricultural public lands to settlers who irrigate them and bring them under cultivation. (6) Universities, hospitals, asylums, etc. (7) For construction of various public improvements (individual items not specified in the granting act) reclamation of desert lands, construction of water reservoirs, etc.

Public Lands Administered by Federal Agencies

Agency (Acres, Sept. 30, 1989)	Public domain	Acquired	Total
Forest Service	161,038,854.3	28,341,223.5	189,380,077.8
Bureau of Land Management.	268,093,335.0	2,324,840.0	270,418,175.0
Bureau of Reclamation	3,533,817.5	1,969,275.9	5,503,093.4
Fish and Wildlife Service	81,321,344	10,097,347	91,318,691
National Park Service	64,325,741.0	8,517,114.8	72,842,855.8
Bureau of Indian Affairs	2,554,358.7	193,079.6	2,747,438.3
Tennessee Valley Authority.	0	1,040,231.3	1,040,231.3
Corps of Engineers	604,971.2	4,869,200.0	5,474,171.2
U.S. Army.	3,187,901.0	6,495,173.0	9,683,074.0
U.S. Navy.	618,005.6	1,743,750.2	2,361,755.8
U.S. Air Force	6,858,510.0	1,255,022.0	8,113,532.0
Department of Energy.	1,465,862.4	700,478.8	2,166,341.2
Total, all agencies (incl. those not shown) . .	**660,976,655.8**	**63,089,515.1**	**724,066,170.9**

National Recreation Areas Administered by Forest Service

			Acreage				Acreage
Allegheny	Pa.	1984	23,063	Oregon Dunes	Ore..	1972	31,566
Arapaho.	Col.	1978	34,928	Rattlesnake.	Mon.	1980	61,000
Flaming Gorge	Ut.-Wyo. . .	1968	201,114	Sawtooth	Ida.	1972	756,019
Grand Island	Mich.	1990	13,048	Smith River	Col.	1990	339,400
Hell's Canyon	Ida.-Ore. . .	1975	538,115	Spruce Knob-Seneca Rocks .	W. Va. . . .	1965	100,000
Mount Baker	Wash.. . . .	1984	8,473	Whiskeytown Shasta-Trinity . . .	Cal.	1965	203,587
Mount Rogers	Va.	1966	154,816	White Rocks	Vt.	1984	36,400

National Parks, Other Areas Administered by Nat'l. Park Service

Figures given are date area initially protected by Congress or presidential proclamation, date given current designation, and gross area in acres 12/31/90.

National Parks

Acadia, Me. (1916/1929) 41,888. Includes Mount Desert Island, half of Isle au Haut, Schoodic Point on mainland. Highest elevation on Eastern seaboard.

Arches, Ut. (1929/1971) 73,379. Contains giant red sandstone arches and other products of erosion.

Badlands, S.D. (1929/1978) 242,756; eroded prairie, bison, bighorn and antelope. Contains animal fossils of 40 million years ago.

Big Bend, Tex. (1935/1944) 801,163. Rio Grande, Chisos Mts.

Biscayne, Fla. (1968/1980) 173,467. Aquatic park encompasses chain of islands south of Miami.

Bryce Canyon, Ut. (1923/1928) 35,835. Spectacularly colorful and unusual display of erosion effects.

Canyonlands, Ut. (1964) 337,570. At junction of Colorado and Green rivers, extensive evidence of prehistoric Indians.

Capitol Reef, Ut. (1937/1971) 241,904. A 60-mile uplift of sandstone cliffs dissected by high-walled gorges.

Carlsbad Caverns, N.M. (1923/1930) 46,775. Largest known caverns; not yet fully explored.

Channel Islands, Cal. (1938/1980) 249,354. Seal lion breeding place, nesting sea birds, unique plants.

Crater Lake, Ore. (1902) 183,224. Extraordinary blue lake in crater of extinct volcano encircled by lava walls 500 to 2,000 feet high.

Denali, Alas. (1917/1980) 4,716,726. Name changed from Mt. McKinley NP. Contains highest mountain in U.S.; wildlife.

Everglades, Fla. (1934) 1,506,499. Largest remaining subtropical wilderness in continental U.S.

Gates of the Arctic, Alas. (1978/1980) 7,523,888. Vast wilderness in north central region.

Glacier, Mon. (1910) 1,013,572. Superb Rocky Mt. scenery, numerous glaciers and glacial lakes. Part of Waterton-Glacier Intl. Peace Park established by U.S. and Canada in 1932.

Glacier Bay, Alas. (1925/1980) 3,225,284. Great tidewater glaciers that move down mountain sides and break up into the sea; much wildlife.

Grand Canyon, Ariz. (1908/1919) 1,218,375. Most spectacular part of Colorado River's greatest canyon.

Grand Teton, Wy. (1929) 309,994. Most impressive part of the Teton Mountains, winter feeding ground of largest American elk herd.

Great Basin, Nev. (1922/1986) 77,100. Wide basins and high mountain ranges.

Great Smoky Mountains, N.C.-Tenn. (1926/1934) 520,269. Largest eastern mountain range, magnificent forests.

Guadalupe Mountains, Tex. (1966/1972) 86,416. Extensive Permian limestone fossil reef; tremendous earth fault.

Haleakala, Ha. (1916/1960) 28,655. Dormant volcano on Maui with large colorful craters.

Hawaii Volcanoes, Ha. (1916/1961) 229,177. Contains Kilauea and Mauna Loa, active volcanoes.

Hot Springs, Ark. (1832/1921) 5,839. Government supervised bath houses use waters of 45 of the 47 natural hot springs.

Isle Royale, Mich. (1931) 571,790. Largest island in Lake Superior, noted for its wilderness area and wildlife.

Katmai, Alas. (1918/1980) 3,716,000. Valley of Ten Thousand Smokes, scene of 1912 volcanic eruption.

Kenai Fjords, Alas. (1978/1980) 669,541. Abundant mountain goats, marine mammals, birdlife; the Harding Icefield, one of the major icecaps in U.S.

Kings Canyon, Cal. (1890/1940) 461,901. Mountain wilderness, dominated by Kings River Canyons and High Sierra; contains giant sequoias.

Kobuk Valley, Alas. (1978/1980) 1,750,421. Broad river is core of native culture.

Lake Clark, Alas. (1978/1980) 2,636,839. Across Cook Inlet from Anchorage. A scenic wilderness rich in fish and wildlife.

Lassen Volcanic, Cal. (1907/1916) 106,372. Contains Lassen Peak, recently active volcano, and other volcanic phenomena.

Mammoth Cave, Ky. (1926/1941) 52,419. 144 miles of surveyed underground passages, beautiful natural formations, river 300 feet below surface.

Mesa Verde, Col. (1906) 52,122. Most notable and best preserved prehistoric cliff dwellings in the United States.

Mount Rainier, Wash. (1899) 235,612. Greatest single-peak glacial system in the lower 48 states.

North Cascades, Wash. (1968) 504,781. Spectacular mountainous region with many glaciers, lakes.

Olympic, Wash. (1909/1938) 922,654. Mountain wilderness containing finest remnant of Pacific Northwest rain forest, active glaciers, Pacific shoreline, rare elk.

Petrified Forest, Ariz. (1906/1962) 93,533. Extensive petrified wood and Indian artifacts. Contains part of Painted Desert.

Redwood, Cal. (1968) 110,132. Forty miles of Pacific coastline, groves of ancient redwoods and world's tallest trees.

Rocky Mountain, Col. (1915) 265,198. On the continental divide, includes 107 named peaks over 11,000 feet.

Samoa, American Samoa (1988) 9,000. Features the only paleotropical rain forest.

Sequoia, Cal. (1890) 402,482. Groves of giant sequoias, highest mountain in contiguous United States — Mount Whitney (14,494 feet). World's largest tree.

Shenandoah, Va. (1926/1935) 195,039. Portion of the Blue Ridge Mountains; overlooks Shenandoah Valley; Skyline Drive.

Theodore Roosevelt, N.D. (1947/1978) 70,447. Contains part of T.R.'s ranch and scenic badlands.

Virgin Islands, V.I. (1956) 14,689. Covers 75% of St. John Island, lush growth, lovely beaches, Indian relics, evidence of colonial Danes.

Voyageurs, Minn. (1971/1975) 218,035. Abundant lakes, forests, wildlife, canoeing, boating.

Wind Cave, S.D. (1903) 28,295. Limestone caverns in Black Hills. Extensive wildlife includes a herd of bison.

Wrangell-St. Elias, Alas. (1978/1980) 8,331,604. Largest area in park system, most peaks over 16,000 feet, abundant wildlife; day's drive east of Anchorage.

Yellowstone, Ida., Mon., Wy., (1872) 2,219,791. Oldest national park. World's greatest geyser area has about 3,000 geysers and hot springs; spectacular falls and impressive canyons of the Yellowstone River; grizzly bear, moose, and bison.

Yosemite, Cal. (1890) 761,170. Yosemite Valley, the nation's highest waterfall, 3 groves of sequoias, and mountainous.

Zion, Ut. (1909/1919) 146,598. Unusual shapes and landscapes have resulted from erosion and faulting; Zion Canyon, with sheer walls ranging up to 2,500 feet, is readily accessible.

National Historical Parks

Appomattox Court House, Va. (1930/1954) 1,325. Where Lee surrendered to Grant.

Boston, Mass. (1974) 41. Includes Faneuil Hall, Old North Church, Bunker Hill, Paul Revere House.

Chaco Culture, N.M. (1907/1980) 33,974. Ruins of pueblos built by prehistoric Indians.

Chesapeake and Ohio Canal, Md.-W.Va.-D.C. (1961/1971) 20,781. 184 mile historic canal; D.C. to Cumberland, Md.

Colonial, Va. (1930/1936) 9,327. Includes most of Jamestown Island, site of first successful English colony; Yorktown, site of Cornwallis' surrender to George Washington; and the Colonial Parkway.

Cumberland Gap, Ky.-Tenn.-Va. (1940) 20,274. Mountain pass of the Wilderness Road which carried the first great migration of pioneers into America's interior.

George Rogers Clark, Vincennes, Ind. (1966) 26. Commemorates American defeat of British in west during Revolution.

Harpers Ferry, Md., W. Va. (1944/1963) 2,239. At the confluence of the Shenandoah and Potomac rivers, the site of John Brown's 1859 raid on the Army arsenal.

Independence, Pa. (1948/1956) 45. Contains several properties in Philadelphia associated with the Revolutionary War and the founding of the U.S. Includes Independence Hall.

Jean Laffite (and preserve), La. (1939/1978) 20,020. Includes Chalmette, site of 1815 Battle of New Orleans; French Quarter.

Kalaupapa, Ha. (1980) 10,779. Molokai's former leper colony site and other historic areas.

Kaloko-Honokohau, Ha. (1978) 1,161. Culture center has 234 historic features and grave of first king, Kamehameha.

Klondike Gold Rush, Alas.-Wash. (1976) 13,191. Alaskan Trails in 1898 Gold Rush. Museum in Seattle.

Lowell, Mass. (1978) 137. Seven mills, canal, 19th C. structures, park to show planned city of Industrial Revolution.

Lyndon B. Johnson, Tex. (1969/1980) 1,571. President's birthplace, boyhood home, ranch.

Minute Man, Mass. (1959) 750. Where the colonial Minute Men battled the British, April 19, 1775. Also contains Nathaniel Hawthorne's home.

Morristown, N.J. (1933) 1,671. Sites of important military encampments during the Revolutionary War; Washington's headquarters 1777, 1779-80.

Natchez, Miss. (1988) 80. Mansions, townhouses, and villas concerning history of Natchez, Miss.

Nez Perce, Ida. (1965) 2,109. Illustrates the history and culture of the Nez Perce Indian country. 20 separate sites.

Pecos, N.M. (1965/1990) 6,547. Ruins of ancient 15th century Pueblo of Pecos, archeological sites, and 2 associated Spanish colonial missions from the 17th and 18th centuries.

Pu'uhonua o Honaunau, Ha. (1955/1978) 182. Until 1819, a sanctuary for Hawaiians vanquished in battle, and those guilty of crimes or breaking taboos.

San Antonio Missions, Tex. (1978/1983) 493. Four of finest Spanish missions in U.S., 18th C. irrigation system.

San Francisco Maritime (1988) 50. Artifacts, photographs, and historic vessels related to the development of the Pacific Coast.

San Juan Island, Wash. (1966) 1,752. Commemorates peaceful relations of the U.S., Canada and Great Britain since the 1872 boundary disputes.

Saratoga, N.Y. (1938) 3,393. Scene of a major battle which became a turning point in the War of Independence.

Sitka, Alas. (1910/1972) 107. Scene of last major resistance of the Tlingit Indians to the Russians, 1804.

Tumacacori, Ariz. (1908/1990) 17. Historic Spanish Catholic mission building stands near the site first visited by Jesuit Father Kino in 1691.

Valley Forge, Pa. (1976) 3,468. Continental Army campsite in 1777-78 winter.

War in the Pacific, Guam (1978) 1,960. Scenic park memorial for WWII combatants in Pacific.

Women's Rights, N.Y. (1980) 6. Seneca Falls site where Susan B. Anthony, Elizabeth Cady Stanton began rights movement in 1848.

Zuni-Cibola, N. Mex. (1988) 800. Historical, archeological, and cultural site associated with the Zuni Tribe over its 1700-year cultural continuum.

National Battlefields

Antietam, Md. (1890/1978) 3,244. Battle ended first Confederate invasion of North, Sept. 17, 1862.

Big Hole, Mon. (1910/1963) 656. Site of major battle with Nez Perce Indians.

Cowpens, S.C. (1929/1972) 842. Revolutionary War battlefield.

Fort Donelson, Tenn. (1928/1985) 536. Site of first major Union victory.

Fort Necessity, Pa. (1931/1961) 903. First battle of French and Indian War.

Monocacy, Md. (1934/1976) 1,647. Civil War battle in defense of Wash., D.C., July 9, 1864.

Moores Creek, N.C. (1926/1980) 87. 1776 battle between Patriots and Loyalists commemorated here.

Petersburg, Va. (1926/1962) 2,735. Scene of 10-month Union campaign 1864-65.

Stones River, Tenn. (1927/1960) 403. Civil War battle leading to Sherman's "March to the Sea."

Tupelo, Miss. (1929/1961) 1. Crucial battle over Sherman's supply line.

Wilson's Creek, Mo. (1960/1970) 1,750. Civil War battle for control of Missouri.

National Battlefield Parks

Kennesaw Mountain, Ga. (1917/1935) 2,885. Two major battles of Atlanta campaign in Civil War.

Manassas, Va. (1940) 5,072. Two battles of Bull Run in Civil War, 1861 and 1862.

Richmond, Va. (1936) 769. Site of battles defending Confederate capital.

National Battlefield Site

Brices Cross Roads, Miss. (1929) 1. Civil War battlefield.

National Military Parks

Chickamauga and Chattanooga, Ga.-Tenn. (1890) 8,106. Four Civil War battlefields.

Fredericksburg and Spotsylvania County, Va. (1927) 7,688. Sites of several major Civil War battles and campaigns.

Gettysburg, Pa. (1895) 3,942. Site of decisive Confederate defeat in North. Gettysburg Address.

Guilford Courthouse, N.C. (1917) 220. Revolutionary War battle site.

Horseshoe Bend, Ala. (1956) 2,040. On Tallapoosa River, where Gen. Andrew Jackson broke the power of the Creek Indian Confederacy.

Kings Mountain, S.C. (1931) 3,945. Revolutionary War battle.

Pea Ridge, Ark. (1956) 4,300. Civil War battle.

Shiloh, Tenn. (1894) 3,838. Major Civil War battle; site includes some well-preserved Indian burial mounds.

Vicksburg, Miss. (1899) 1,620. Union victory gave North control of the Mississippi and split the Confederacy in two.

National Memorials

Arkansas Post, Ark. (1960) 389. First permanent French settlement in the lower Mississippi River valley.

Arlington House, the Robert E. Lee Memorial, Va. (1925/1972) 28. Lee's home overlooking the Potomac.

Chamizal, El Paso, Tex. (1966/1974) 55. Commemorates 1963 settlement of 99-year border dispute with Mexico.

Coronado, Ariz. (1941/1952) 4,750. Commemorates first European exploration of the Southwest.

DeSoto, Fla. (1948) 27. Commemorates 16th-century Spanish explorations.

Federal Hall, N.Y. (1939/1955) 0.45. First seat of U.S. government under the Constitution.

Fort Caroline, Fla. (1950) 138. On St. Johns River, overlooks site of second attempt by French Huguenots to colonize North America.

Fort Clatsop, Ore. (1958) 125. Lewis and Clark encampment 1805-06.

General Grant, N.Y. (1958) 0.76. Tombs of Pres. and wife.

Hamilton Grange, N.Y. (1962) 0.11. Home of Alexander Hamilton.

Jefferson National Expansion, St. Louis, Mo. (1935/1969) 191. Commemorates westward expansion.

John F. Kennedy Center for the Performing Arts, D.C. (1958/1964) 18.

Johnstown Flood, Pa. (1964) 164. Commemorates tragic flood of 1889.

Lincoln Boyhood, Ind. (1962) 200. Lincoln grew up here.

Lincoln Memorial, D.C. (1911) 110.

Lyndon B. Johnson Grove on the Potomac, D.C. (1973) 17.

Mount Rushmore, S.D. (1925) 1,278. World famous sculpture of 4 presidents.

Perry's Victory and International Peace Memorial, Put-in-Bay, Oh. (1936/1978) 25. The world's most massive Doric column, constructed 1912-15, to inculcate the lessons of international peace by arbitration and disarmament.

Roger Williams, R.I. (1965) 5. Memorial to founder of Rhode Island.

Thaddeus Kosciuszko, Pa. (1972) 0.02. Memorial to Polish hero of American Revolution.

Theodore Roosevelt Island, D.C. (1932) 89.

Thomas Jefferson Memorial, D.C. (1934) 18.

USS Arizona, Ha. (1980). 00. Memorializes American losses at Pearl Harbor.

Vietnam Veterans, D.C. (1980) 2. Black granite wall inscribed with names of killed in action and missing in the Vietnam War.

Washington Monument, D.C. (1848) 106.

Wright Brothers, N.C. (1927/1953) 431. Site of first powered flight.

National Historic Sites

Abraham Lincoln Birthplace, Hodgenville, Ky. (1916/1959) 117.

Adams, Quincy, Mass. (1946/1952) 10. Home of Presidents John Adams, John Quincy Adams, and celebrated descendants.

Allegheny Portage Railroad, Pa. (1964) 1,247. Part of the Pennsylvania Canal system.

Andersonville, Andersonville, Ga. (1970) 495. Noted Civil War prison.

Andrew Johnson, Greeneville, Tenn. (1935/1963) 17. Home of the President.

Bent's Old Fort, Col. (1960) 800. Old West fur-trading post.

Boston African American (1980) Pre-Civil War black history structures.

Carl Sandburg Home, N.C. (1968/1972) 264. Poet's home.

Charles Pinckney, S.C. (1988) 8.

Christiansted, St. Croix; V.I. (1952/1961) 27. Commemorates Danish colony.

Clara Barton, Md. (1974) 9. Home of founder of American Red Cross.

Edgar Allan Poe, Pa. (1978/1980) 1. Poet's home.

Edison, West Orange, N.J. (1955/1962) 21. Home and laboratory.

Eisenhower, Gettysburg, Pa. (1967/1969) 690. Home of 34th president.

Eleanor Roosevelt, Hyde Park, N.Y. (1977) 181. Personal retreat.

Eugene O'Neill, Danville, Cal. (1976) 13. Playwright's home.

Ford's Theatre, Washington, D.C. (1866/1970) 0.29. Includes theater, now restored, where Lincoln was assassinated, house where he died, and Lincoln Museum.

Fort Bowie, Ariz. (1964/1972) 1,000. Focal point of operations against Geronimo and the Apaches.

Fort Davis, Tex. (1961/1963) 460. Frontier outpost battled Comanches and Apaches.

Fort Laramie, Wy. (1938/1960) 833. Military post on Oregon Trail.

Fort Larned, Kan. (1964/1966) 718. Military post on Santa Fe Trail.

Fort Point, San Francisco, Cal. (1970) 29. Largest West Coast fortification.

Fort Raleigh, N.C. (1941) 157. First English settlement.

Fort Scott, Kan. (1965/1978) 17. Commemorates U.S. frontier of 1840-50.

Fort Smith, Ark. (1961) 75. Active post from 1817 to 1890.

Fort Union Trading Post, Mon., N.D. (1966) 442. Principal fur-trading post on upper Missouri, 1829-1867.

Fort Vancouver, Wash. (1948/1961) 209. Hdqts. for Hudson's Bay Company in 1825. Early military and political seat.

Frederick Douglass Home, D.C. (1962/1988) 9. Home of nation's leading black spokesman.

Frederick Law Olmsted, Mass. (1979) 2. Home of famous park planner (1822-1903).

Friendship Hill, Pa. (1978) 675. Home of Albert Gallatin, Jefferson's Sec'y of Treasury. Not open to public.

Golden Spike, Utah (1957) 2,735. Commemorates completion of first transcontinental railroad in 1869.

Grant-Kohrs Ranch, Mon. (1972) 1,498. Ranch house and part of 19th century ranch.

Hampton, Md. (1948) 62. 18th-century Georgian mansion.

Harry S. Truman, Mo. (1983). 0.78. Home of Pres. Truman after 1919.

Herbert Hoover, West Branch, Ia. (1965) 187. Birthplace and boyhood home of 31st president.

Home of Franklin D. Roosevelt, Hyde Park, N.Y. (1944) 290. Birthplace, home and "Summer White House".

Hopewell Furnace, Pa. (1938/1985) 848. 19th-century iron making village.

Hubbell Trading Post, Ariz. (1965) 160. Indian trading post.

James A. Garfield, Mentor, Oh. (1980) 8. President's home.

Jimmy Carter, Ga. (1987) 70. Birthplace and home of 39th president.

John Fitzgerald Kennedy, Brookline, Mass. (1967) 0.09. Birthplace and childhood home of the President.

John Muir, Martinez, Cal. (1964) 340. Home of early conservationist and writer.

Knife River Indian Villages, N.D. (1974) 1,293. Remnants of 5 Hidatsa villages.

Lincoln Home, Springfield, Ill. (1971) 12. Lincoln's residence when he was elected President, 1860.

Longfellow, Cambridge, Mass. (1972) 2. Longfellow's home, 1837-82, and Washington's hq. during Boston Siege, 1775-76.

Maggie L. Walker, Va. (1978) 1. Richmond home of black leader and 1903 founder of bank.

Martin Luther King, Jr., Atlanta, Ga. (1980) 23. Birthplace, grave.

Martin Van Buren, N.Y. (1974) 40. Lindenwald, home of 8th president, near Kinderhook.

Ninety Six, S.C. (1976) 989. Colonial trading village.

Palo Alto Battlefield, Tex. (1978) 50. One of 2 Mexican War battles fought in U.S.

Pennsylvania Avenue, D.C. (1965) NA. Includes area between Capitol and White House, Ford's Theatre.

Puukohola Heiau, Ha. (1972) 80. Ruins of temple built by King Kamehameha.

Sagamore Hill, Oyster Bay, N.Y. (1962) 83. Home of President Theodore Roosevelt from 1885 until his death in 1919.

Saint-Gaudens, Cornish, N.H. (1964/1977) 148. Home, studio and gardens of American sculptor Augustus Saint-Gaudens.

Saint Paul's Church, N.Y. (1943/1978) 6. Eighteenth Century site of John Peter Zenger's "freedom of press" trial.

Salem Maritime, Mass. (1938) 9. Only port never seized from the patriots by the British. Major fishing and whaling port.

San Juan, P.R. (1949) 75. 16th-century Spanish fortifications.

Saugus Iron Works, Mass. (1968) 9. Reconstructed 17th-century colonial ironworks.

Springfield Armory, Mass. (1974) 55. Small arms manufacturing center for nearly 200 years.

Steamtown, Pa. (1986) 44. Railyard, roadhouse and repair shops of former Delaware, Lackawanna and Western Railroad.

Theodore Roosevelt Birthplace, N.Y., N.Y. (1962) 0.11.

Theodore Roosevelt Inaugural, Buffalo, N.Y. (1966) 1. Wilcox House where he took oath of office, 1901.

Thomas Stone, Md. (1978) 328. Home of signer of Declaration, built in 1771. Not open to public.

Tuskegee Institute, Ala. (1974) 68. College founded by Booker T. Washington in 1881 for blacks.

Ulysses S. Grant, St. Louis Co., Mo. (1989) 10. Home of Grant during pre-Civil War years.

Vanderbilt Mansion, Hyde Park, N.Y. (1940) 212. Mansion of 19th-century financier.

Weir Farm, Witon, Conn. (1990) 62. Home and studios of American impressionist painter J. Alden Weir.

Whitman Mission, Wash. (1936/1963) 98. Site where Dr. and Mrs. Marcus Whitman ministered to the Indians until slain by them in 1847.

William Howard Taft, Cincinnati, Oh. (1969) 3. Birthplace and early home of the 27th president.

National Monuments

Name	State	Year	Acreage
Agate Fossil Beds	Neb.	1965	3,055
Alibates Flint Quarries	N.M.-Tex.	1965	1,371
Aniakchak	Alas.	1978	17
Aztec Ruins	N.M.	1923	319
Bandelier	N.M.	1916	32,737
Black Canyon of the Gunnison	Col.	1933	20,766
Booker T. Washington	Va.	1956	224
Buck Island Reef	V.I.	1961	880
Cabrillo	Cal.	1913	137
Canyon de Chelly	Ariz.	1931	83,840
Cape Krusenstern	Alas.	1978	659,807
Capulin Volcano	N.M.	1916	793
Casa Grande Ruins	Ariz.	1892	473
Castillo de San Marcos	Fla.	1924	20
Castle Clinton	N.Y.	1946	1
Cedar Breaks	Ut.	1933	6,155
Chiricahua	Ariz.	1924	11,985
Colorado	Col.	1911	20,454
Congaree Swamp	S.C.	1976	22,200
Craters of the Moon	Ida.	1924	53,545
Custer Battlefield	Mon.	1879	765
Death Valley	Cal.-Nev.	1933	2,067,628
Devils Postpile	Cal.	1911	798
Devils Tower	Wy.	1906	1,347
Dinosaur	Col.-Ut.	1915	210,844
Effigy Mounds	Ia.	1949	1,481
El Malpais	N.M.	1987	114,335
El Morro	N.M.	1906	1,279
Florissant Fossil Beds**	Col.	1969	5,998
Fort Frederica	Ga.	1936	216
Fort Jefferson	Fla.	1935	64,700
Fort Matanzas	Fla.	1924	228
Fort McHenry National Monument and Historic Shrine	Md.	1925	43
Fort Pulaski	Ga.	1924	5,623
Fort Stanwix	N.Y.	1935	16
Fort Sumter	S.C.	1948	194
Fort Union	N.M.	1954	721
Fossil Butte	Wy.	1972	8,198
G. Washington Birthplace	Va.	1930	533
George Washington Carver	Mo.	1943	210
Gila Cliff Dwellings	N.M.	1907	533
Grand Portage	Minn.	1951	710
Great Sand Dunes	Col.	1932	38,662
Hagerman Fossil Beds	Ida.	1988	4,280
Hohokam Pima*	Ariz.	1972	1,690
Homestead Nat'l. Monument of America	Neb.	1936	195
Hovenweep	Col.-Ut.	1923	785
Jewel Cave	S.D.	1908	1,274
John Day Fossil Beds	Ore.	1974	14,014
Joshua Tree	Cal.	1936	559,955
Lava Beds	Cal.	1925	46,560
Montezuma Castle	Ariz.	1906	858
Mound City Group	Oh.	1923	270
Muir Woods	Cal.	1908	554
Natural Bridges	Ut.	1908	7,636
Navajo	Ariz.	1909	360
Ocmulgee	Ga.	1934	683
Oregon Caves	Ore.	1909	488
Organ Pipe Cactus	Ariz.	1937	330,689
Petroglyph	N.M.	1990	5,207
Pinnacles	Cal.	1908	16,265
Pipe Spring	Ariz.	1923	40
Pipestone	Minn.	1937	282
Poverty Point	La.	1988	911
Rainbow Bridge	Ut.	1910	160
Russell Cave	Ala.	1961	310
Saguaro	Ariz.	1933	83,574
Salinas	N.M.	1909	1,077
Scotts Bluff	Neb.	1919	2,997
Statue of Liberty	N.J.-N.Y.	1924	58
Sunset Crater	Ariz.	1930	3,040
Timpanogos Cave	Ut.	1922	250
Tonto	Ariz.	1907	1,120
Tuzigoot	Ariz.	1939	801
Walnut Canyon	Ariz.	1915	2,249
White Sands	N.M.	1933	143,733
Wupatki	Ariz.	1924	35,253
Yucca House*	Col.	1919	10

National Preserves

Aniakchak	Alas.	1978	465,603

Name	State	Year	Acreage
Bering Land Bridge	Alas.	1978	2,784,960
Big Cypress	Fla.	1974	716,000
Big Thicket	Tex.	1974	85,736
Denali	Alas.	1917	1,311,365
Gates of the Arctic	Alas.	1978	948,629
Glacier Bay	Alas.	1925	57,884
Katmai	Alas.	1918	374,000
Lake Clark	Alas.	1978	1,407,293
Noatak	Alas.	1978	6,574,481
Timucuan Ecological & Historic Preserve	Fla.	1988	46,000
Wrangell-St. Elias	Alas.	1978	4,856,721
Yukon-Charley Rivers	Alas.	1978	2,523,509

National Seashores

Assateague Island	Md.-Va.	1965	39,631
Canaveral	Fla.	1975	57,662
Cape Cod	Mass.	1961	43,558
Cape Hatteras	N.C.	1937	30,319
Cape Lookout**	N.C.	1966	28,243
Cumberland Island	Ga.	1972	36,415
Fire Island	N.Y.	1964	19,579
Gulf Islands	Fla.-Miss.	1971	135,618
Padre Island	Tex.	1962	130,434
Point Reyes	Cal.	1962	71,050

National Parkways

Blue Ridge	Va.-N.C.	1936	86,941
George Washington Memorial	Va.-Md.	1930	7,159
John D. Rockefeller Jr. Mem.	Wy.	1972	23,777
Natchez Trace	Ala.-Miss.-Tenn.	1938	51,742

National Lakeshores

Apostle Islands	Wis.	1970	69,372
Indiana Dunes	Ind.	1966	13,845
Pictured Rocks	Mich.	1966	72,903
Sleeping Bear Dunes	Mich.	1970	71,188

National Reserve

City of Rocks	Ida.	1988	14,407

National Rivers

Big South Fork Natl. R. and Recreation	Tenn.-Ky.	1976	122,960
Buffalo	Ark.	1972	94,219
New River Gorge	W.Va.	1978	62,144
Ozark	Mo.	1964	80,791
Mississippi Natl. R. and Recreation	Minn.	1988	50,000

National Wild and Scenic Rivers

Name	State	Year	Acreage
Alagnak Wild	Alas.	1980	24,038
Bluestone	W.Va.	1988	N.A.
Delaware	N.Y.-N.J.-Pa.	1978	1,973
Lower Saint Croix	Minn.-Wis.	1972	9,475
Missouri Natl. Recreational River.	Neb.	1978	0
Obed Wild	Tenn.	1976	5,075
Rio Grande	Tex.	1978	9,600
Saint Croix	Minn.-Wis.	1968	67,379
Upper Delaware	N.Y.-N.J.	1978	75,000

Parks (no other classification)

Catoctin Mountain	Md.	1954	5,770
Constitution Gardens	D.C.	1978	52
Fort Washington	Md.	1930	341
Greenbelt	Md.	1950	1,176
Piscataway	Md.	1961	4,263
Prince William Forest	Va.	1948	18,572
Rock Creek	D.C.	1890	1,754
Wolf Trap Farm Park for the Performing Arts	Va.	1966	130

National Recreation Areas

Amistad	Tex.	1965	57,292
Bighorn Canyon	Mon.-Wy.	1966	120,296
Chattahoochee R.	Ga.	1978	9,257
Chickasaw	Okla.	1902	9,522
Coulee Dam	Wash.	1946	100,390
Curecanti	Col.	1965	42,114
Cuyahoga Valley	Oh.	1974	32,525
Delaware Water Gap	N.J.-Pa.	1965	66,652
Gateway	N.Y.-N.J.	1972	26,311
Gauley R.	W.Va.	1988	10,300
Glen Canyon	Ariz.-Ut.	1958	1,236,880
Golden Gate	Cal.	1972	73,122
Lake Chelan	Wash.	1968	61,883
Lake Mead	Ariz.-Nev.	1936	1,495,666
Lake Meredith	Tex.	1965	44,978
Ross Lake	Wash.	1968	117,575
Santa Monica Mts.	Cal.	1978	150,050
Whiskeytown	Cal.	1965	42,503

National Mall

National Mall	D.C.	1933	146

National Scenic Trails

Appalachian	Me. to Ga.	1968	161,382
Natchez Trace	Ala.-Miss.-Tenn.	1983	10,995
Potomac Heritage	Md.-D.C.-Va.-Pa.	1983	***

International Historic Sites

Saint Croix Island	Me.	1949	35

* Not open to the public. ** No federal facilities. *** Undetermined.

National Park Service Recreation Visits

Source: National Park Service

The following places had more than 2.5 million recreation visits in 1990:

Park	Recreation Visits	Park	Recreation Visits
Blue Ridge Parkway	16,854,602	Grand Canyon Natl. Park	3,776,685
Golden Gate Natl. Recreation Area	14,650,213	JFK Center for the Performing Arts	3,733,509
Lake Mead Natl. Recreation Area	8,582,223	Independence Natl. Historical Park	3,347,163
Great Smoky Mountains Natl. Park	8,151,769	Yosemite Natl. Park	3,124,939
Gateway Natl. Recreation Area	5,790,221	Yellowstone Natl. Park	2,823,872
Natchez Trace Parkway	5,505,253	Olympic Natl. Park	2,794,903
Cape Cod Natl. Seashore	5,449,380	Rocky Mountain Natl. Park	2,647,323
George Washington Memorial Parkway	5,328,436		

Attendance at all areas administered by the National Park Service in 1990 was 256,908,909 recreation visits.

Federal Indian Reservations and Trust Lands[1]

Source: Bureau of Indian Affairs, U.S. Dept. of the Interior (data as of 1990)

The total American Indian population according to the 1990 Census is 1.959 million.

State	No of Reser.	Tribally-owned acreage[2]	Individually-owned acreage[2]	No. of persons[3]	Major tribes and/or nations
Alabama	1	230	0	16,504	Poarch Creek
Alaska	1[4]	86,773	1,265,432	85,698	Aleut, Eskimo, Athapascan,[5] Haida, Tlingit, Tsimpshian
Arizona	23	19,775,959	256,879	203,527	Navajo, Apache, Papago, Hopi, Yavapai, Pima
California	96	520,049	66,769	242,164	Hoopa, Paiute, Yurok, Karok, Mission Bands
Colorado	2	764,120	2,805	27,776	Ute
Connecticut	1	1,638	0	6,654	Mashantucket Pequot
Florida	4	153,874	0	36,335	Seminole, Miccosukee
Idaho	4	464,077	327,301	13,780	Shoshone, Bannock, Nez Perce
Iowa	1	3,550	0	7,349	Sac and Fox
Kansas	4	7,219	23,763	21,965	Potawatomi, Kickapoo, Iowa
Louisiana	3	415	0	18,541	Chitimacha, Coushatta, Tunica-Biloxi
Maine	3	191,511	0	5,998	Passamaquoddy, Penobscot, Maliseet
Michigan	8	14,411	9,276	55,638	Chippewa, Potawatomi, Ottawa
Minnesota	14	779,138	50,338	49,909	Chippewa, Sioux
Mississippi	1	20,486	0	8,825	Choctaw
Montana	7	2,663,385	2,911,450	47,679	Blackfeet, Crow, Sioux, Assiniboine, Cheyenne
Nebraska	3	21,742	43,208	12,410	Omaha, Winnebago, Santee Sioux
Nevada	19	1,147,088	78,529	19,637	Paiute, Shoshone, Washoe
New Mexico	25	7,119,982	621,715	134,355	Zuni, Apache, Navajo
New York	8	118,199	0	62,651	Seneca, Mohawk, Onondaga, Oneida
North Carolina	1	56,509	0	80,155	Cherokee
North Dakota	3	214,006	627,289	25,917	Sioux, Chippewa, Mandan, Arikara, Hidatsa
Oklahoma	1[6]	96,839	1,000,165	252,420	Cherokee, Creek, Choctaw, Chickasaw, Osage, Cheyenne, Arapahoe, Kiowa, Comanche
Oregon	7	660,367	135,053	38,496	Warm Springs, Wasco, Paiute, Umatilla, Siletz
Rhode Island	1	1,800	0	4,071	Narragansett
South Dakota	9	2,399,531	2,121,188	50,573	Sioux
Texas	3	4,726	0	65,877	Alabama-Coushatta, Tiwa, Kickapoo
Utah	4	2,284,766	32,838	24,283	Ute, Goshute, Southern Paiute
Washington	27	2,250,731	467,785	81,483	Yakima, Lummi, Quinault
Wisconsin	11	338,097	80,345	39,387	Chippewa, Oneida, Winnebago
Wyoming	1	1,958,095	101,537	9,479	Shoshone, Arapahoe

(1) As of 1988 the federal government recognized and acknowledged that it had a special relationship with, and a trust responsibility for, 307 federally recognized Indian entities in the continental U.S., plus some 200 tribal entities in Alaska. The term "Indian entities" encompasses Indian tribes, bands, villages, groups, pueblos, Eskimos, and Aleuts, eligible for federal services and classified in the following 3 categories: (a) Officially approved Indian organizations pursuant to federal statutory authority (Indian Reorganization Act; Oklahoma Indian Welfare Act and Alaska Native Act.) (b) Officially approved Indian organizations outside of specified federal statutory authority. (c) Traditional Indian organizations recognized without formal federal approval of organizational structure. Some reservation boundaries transcend state boundaries (e.g., Navajo which is in Arizona, New Mexico, and Utah). For statistical convenience under "Number of Reservations," such reservations are counted in the state where population is predominant and/or tribal headquarters is located. (2) The acreages refer only to Indian lands which are either owned by the tribes or individual Indians, and held in trust by the U.S. government. Many of these parcels are located off reservations. Not all lands within reservation boundaries are necessarily trust lands. Many parcels are privately-owned by tribes, individual Indians, and non-Indians. Also, some internal lands are the property of various governmental agencies. (3) Total Indian population in each state with reservation/trust lands, including those persons living outside of the BIA Service area. (4) Alaskan Indian Affairs are carried out under the Alaska Native Claims Settlement Act (Dec. 18, 1971). The Act provided for the establishment of regional and village corporations to conduct business for profit and non-profit purposes. There are 13 such regional corporations, each one with organized village corporations. The Annette Island Reservation remains the only federally recognized reservation in Alaska in the sense of specific reservation boundaries, trust lands, etc. (5) Aleuts and Eskimos are racially and linguistically related. Athapascans are related to the Navaho and Apache Indians. (6) Indian land status in Oklahoma is unique and there are no reservations except for Osage in the sense that the term is used elsewhere in the U.S. Likewise, many of the Oklahoma tribes are unique in their high degree of assimilation to the white culture.

American Indian Population: States Without Federal Reservations and Trust Lands, 1990

Source: Bureau of the Census, U.S. Dept. of Commerce

State	No. of Persons	State	No. of Persons	State	No. of Persons
Arkansas	12,773	Indiana	12,972	Ohio	20,358
Delaware	2,019	Kentucky	5,769	Pennsylvania	14,733
District of Columbia	1,466	Maryland	12,972	South Carolina	8,246
Georgia	13,348	Massachusetts	12,241	Tennessee	10,039
Hawaii	5,099	Missouri	19,835	Vermont	1,696
Illinois	21,836	New Hampshire	2,134	Virginia	15,282
		New Jersey	14,970	West Virginia	2,458

PRESIDENTIAL ELECTIONS

Popular and Electoral Vote, 1984 and 1988

Source: News Election Service

States	1988 Electoral Vote Dukakis	1988 Electoral Vote Bush	1988 Democrat Dukakis	1988 Republican Bush	1984 Electoral Vote Mondale	1984 Electoral Vote Reagan	1984 Democrat Mondale	1984 Republican Reagan
Ala.. . . .	0	9	549,506	815,576	0	9	551,899	872,849
Alas. . . .	0	3	72,584	119,251	0	3	62,007	138,377
Ariz. . . .	0	7	454,029	702,541	0	7	333,854	681,416
Ark.. . . .	0	6	349,237	466,578	0	6	338,646	534,774
Cal.. . . .	0	47	4,702,233	5,054,917	0	47	3,815,947	5,305,410
Col.. . . .	0	8	621,453	728,177	0	8	454,975	821,817
Conn. . .	0	8	676,584	750,241	0	8	569,597	890,877
Del.. . . .	0	3	108,647	139,639	0	3	101,656	152,190
D.C. . . .	3	0	159,407	27,590	3	0	180,408	29,009
Fla.. . . .	0	21	1,655,851	2,616,597	0	21	1,448,344	2,728,775
Ga.. . . .	0	12	714,792	1,081,331	0	12	706,628	1,068,722
Ha.. . . .	4	0	192,364	158,625	0	4	147,098	184,934
Ida.. . . .	0	4	147,272	253,881	0	4	108,510	297,523
Ill..	0	24	2,215,940	2,310,939	0	24	2,086,499	2,707,103
Ind.. . . .	0	12	860,643	1,297,763	0	12	841,481	1,377,230
Ia..	8	0	670,557	545,355	0	8	605,620	703,088
Kan. . . .	0	7	422,636	554,049	0	7	332,471	674,646
Ky.. . . .	0	9	580,368	734,281	0	9	536,756	815,345
La.	0	10	717,460	883,702	0	10	651,586	1,037,299
Me.. . . .	0	4	243,569	307,131	0	4	214,515	336,500
Md.. . . .	0	10	826,304	876,167	0	10	787,935	879,918
Mass. . .	13	0	1,401,415	1,194,635	0	13	1,239,606	1,310,936
Mich.. . .	0	20	1,675,783	1,965,486	0	20	1,529,638	2,251,571
Minn.. . .	10	0	1,109,471	962,337	10	0	1,036,364	1,032,603
Miss. . . .	0	7	363,921	557,890	0	7	352,192	582,377
Mo.. . . .	0	11	1,001,619	1,084,953	0	11	848,583	1,274,188
Mon. . . .	0	4	168,936	190,412	0	4	146,742	232,450
Neb. . . .	0	5	259,235	397,956	0	5	187,475	459,135
Nev. . . .	0	4	132,738	206,040	0	4	91,655	188,770
N.H. . . .	0	4	163,696	281,537	0	4	120,377	267,051
N.J.. . . .	0	16	1,317,541	1,740,604	0	16	1,261,323	1,933,630
N.M. . . .	0	5	244,497	270,341	0	5	201,769	307,101
N.Y. . . .	36	0	3,347,882	3,081,871	0	36	3,119,609	3,664,763
N.C. . . .	0	13	890,167	1,237,258	0	13	824,287	1,346,481
N.D. . . .	0	3	127,739	166,559	0	3	104,429	200,336
Oh.. . . .	0	23	1,939,629	2,416,549	0	23	1,825,440	2,678,559
Okla.. . .	0	8	483,423	678,367	0	8	385,080	861,530
Ore.. . .	7	0	616,206	560,126	0	7	536,479	685,700
Pa.. . . .	0	25	2,194,944	2,300,087	0	25	2,228,131	2,584,323
R.I.. . . .	4	0	225,123	177,761	0	4	197,106	212,080
S.C. . . .	0	8	370,554	606,443	0	8	344,459	615,539
S.D. . . .	0	3	145,560	165,415	0	3	116,113	200,267
Tenn.. . .	0	11	679,794	947,233	0	11	711,714	990,212
Tex. . . .	0	29	2,352,748	3,036,829	0	29	1,949,276	3,433,428
Ut.	0	5	207,352	428,442	0	5	155,369	469,105
Vt.	0	3	115,775	124,331	0	3	95,730	135,865
Va.. . . .	0	12	859,799	1,309,162	0	12	796,250	1,337,078
Wash.. . .	10	0	933,516	903,835	0	10	798,352	1,051,670
W.Va.. . .	6	0	341,016	310,065	0	6	328,125	405,483
Wis. . . .	11	0	1,126,794	1,047,499	0	11	995,740	1,198,584
Wyo.. . .	0	3	67,113	106,867	0	3	53,370	133,241
Total. . .	112	426	41,805,422	48,881,221	13	525	37,457,215	54,281,858

Presidential Election Returns by Counties

All results are official. Results for New England states are for selected cities or towns due to unavailability of county results. Totals are always statewide.

Source: News Election Service

Alabama

County	1988 Dukakis (D)	Bush (R)	1984 Mondale (D)	Reagan (R)
Autauga	3,667	7,828	3,366	8,350
Baldwin	9,271	25,933	7,272	24,964
Barbour	3,836	4,958	4,591	5,459
Bibb	2,244	2,885	2,167	3,487
Blount	4,485	8,754	3,738	8,508
Bullock	3,122	1,421	3,537	1,697
Butler	3,465	3,923	3,641	4,941
Calhoun	12,451	19,806	12,752	23,291
Chambers	5,103	7,694	5,302	8,024
Cherokee	3,176	2,868	3,029	3,225
Chilton	3,820	8,761	3,924	8,243
Choctaw	3,491	3,629	3,373	3,960
Clarke	4,217	5,708	4,452	6,282
Clay	1,602	3,496	1,456	3,432
Cleburne	1,383	3,071	1,238	3,259
Coffee	4,319	8,890	4,370	10,558
Colbert	10,397	7,775	11,008	9,530
Conecuh	3,022	3,256	2,737	3,538
Coosa	1,860	2,405	1,781	2,585
Covington	3,845	8,130	3,812	9,944
Crenshaw	1,836	2,617	1,904	3,261
Cullman	8,517	14,351	7,989	14,782
Dale	3,476	9,266	3,215	10,319
Dallas	9,660	7,630	10,955	9,585
DeKalb	7,333	11,478	7,212	12,098
Elmore	4,501	10,852	4,198	11,694
Escambia	4,020	6,807	3,853	8,694
Etowah	17,762	17,828	19,074	19,243
Fayette	3,186	4,338	2,533	4,654
Franklin	4,961	5,146	4,601	5,304
Geneva	2,685	5,703	2,330	6,308
Greene	3,295	1,048	3,675	1,361
Hale	3,187	2,414	3,289	2,691
Henry	2,206	3,613	2,231	3,952
Houston	7,001	19,989	6,488	20,834
Jackson	7,418	6,090	7,635	6,730
Jefferson	107,766	148,879	107,506	158,362
Lamar	2,274	3,214	1,910	3,943
Lauderdale	12,862	12,942	12,907	15,354
Lawrence	4,646	3,616	4,866	4,466
Lee	9,078	17,180	9,077	16,757
Limestone	5,455	9,086	5,410	8,423
Lowndes	3,328	1,405	3,567	1,629
Macon	6,351	1,304	7,857	1,543
Madison	25,800	53,575	26,889	50,428
Marengo	4,402	4,241	4,811	5,261
Marion	4,505	5,955	3,918	6,771
Marshall	7,357	12,148	7,704	12,330
Mobile	45,524	72,203	47,252	81,923
Monroe	3,509	5,379	3,725	5,917
Montgomery	28,709	41,131	31,206	43,328
Morgan	10,594	18,679	11,324	24,103
Perry	3,574	2,107	3,731	2,600
Pickens	3,107	3,851	3,586	4,685
Pike	3,813	5,897	3,541	6,231
Randolph	2,462	4,625	2,438	4,940
Russell	6,589	6,333	7,610	6,654
St. Clair	4,335	10,604	4,000	10,408
Shelby	7,138	27,052	5,884	21,858
Sumter	4,390	2,212	4,478	2,493
Talladega	8,291	12,973	8,490	14,467
Tallapoosa	4,598	8,502	4,458	9,045
Tuscaloosa	18,166	27,396	16,066	28,075
Walker	11,338	11,011	10,591	12,852
Washington	3,402	3,741	3,081	4,434
Wilcox	3,369	1,739	2,663	2,337
Winston	2,954	6,235	2,624	6,845
Totals	549,506	815,576	551,899	872,849

Alabama Vote Since 1940

1940, Roosevelt, Dem., 250,726; Willkie, Rep., 42,174; Babson, Proh., 698; Browder, Com., 509; Thomas, Soc., 100.

1944, Roosevelt, Dem., 198,918; Dewey, Rep., 44,540; Watson, Proh., 1,095; Thomas, Soc., 190.

1948, Thurmond, States' Rights, 171,443; Dewey, Rep., 40,930; Wallace, Prog., 1,522; Watson, Proh., 1,085.

1952, Eisenhower, Rep., 149,231; Stevenson, Dem., 275,075; Hamblen, Proh., 1,814.

1956, Stevenson, Dem., 290,844; Eisenhower, Rep. 195,694; Independent electors, 20,323.

1960, Kennedy, Dem., 324,050; Nixon, Rep., 237,981; Faubus, States' Rights, 4,367; Decker, Proh., 2,106; King, Afro-Americans, 1,485; scattering, 236.

1964, Dem. 209,848 (electors unpledged); Goldwater, Rep., 479,085; scattering, 105.

1968, Nixon, Rep., 146,923; Humphrey, Dem., 196,579; Wallace, 3d party, 691,425; Munn, Proh., 4,022.

1972, Nixon, Rep., 728,701; McGovern, Dem., 219,108 plus 37,815 Natl. Demo. Party of Alabama; Schmitz, Conservative, 11,918; Munn., Proh., 8,551.

1976, Carter, Dem., 659,170; Ford, Rep., 504,070; Maddox, Am. Ind., 9,198; Bubar, Proh., 6,669; Hall, Com., 1,954; MacBride, Libertarian, 1,481.

1980, Reagan, Rep., 654,192; Carter, Dem., 636,730; Anderson, Independent, 16,481; Rarick, Amer. Ind., 15,010; Clark, Libertarian, 13,318; Bubar, Statesman, 1,743; Hall, Com., 1,629; DeBerry, Soc. Work., 1,303; McReynolds, Socialist, 1,006; Commoner, Citizens, 517.

1984, Reagan, Rep., 872,849; Mondale, Dem., 551,899; Bergland, Libertarian, 9,504.

1988, Bush, Rep., 815,576; Dukakis, Dem., 549,506; Paul, Lib., 8,460; Fulani, Ind., 3,311.

Alaska

Election District	1988 Dukakis (D)	Bush (R)	1984 Mondale (D)	Reagan (R)
No. 1	3,167	4,564	2,937	5,256
No. 2	1,879	2,274	1,857	2,645
No. 3	1,884	2,313	1,561	2,540
No. 4	6,057	5,963	5,293	7,322
No. 5	3,696	6,874	2,896	8,188
No. 6	1,543	2,347	1,261	2,883
No. 7	2,088	3,806	1,539	4,363
No. 8	3,815	7,629	2,752	8,603
No. 9	3,980	6,876	3,186	8,361
No. 10	3,786	6,241	3,034	7,634
No. 11	2,590	3,189	2,621	5,176
No. 12	3,733	3,511	4,063	5,348
No. 13	2,643	4,968	2,616	6,106
No. 14	3,387	6,164	2,843	7,465
No. 15	3,726	8,949	2,749	8,993
No. 16	4,174	8,851	2,935	9,942
No. 17	1,302	3,093	1,014	3,793
No. 18	1,674	5,998	967	4,858
No. 19	2,737	4,485	1,905	3,880
No. 20	3,389	5,225	2,914	6,538
No. 21	2,816	3,127	2,433	3,629
No. 22	1,377	1,861	1,319	2,075
No. 23	1,390	1,898	1,546	2,165
No. 24	1,381	1,818	1,473	2,321
No. 25	1,430	1,611	1,825	2,004
No. 26	1,568	2,959	1,216	3,019
No. 27	1,372	2,657	1,252	3,270
Totals	72,584	119,251	62,007	138,377

Alaska Vote Since 1960

1960, Kennedy, Dem., 29,809; Nixon, Rep. 30,953.

1964, Johnson, Dem., 44,329; Goldwater, Rep., 22,930.

1968, Nixon, Rep., 37,600; Humphrey, Dem., 35,411; Wallace, 3d party, 10,024.

1972, Nixon, Rep., 55,349; McGovern, Dem., 32,967; Schmitz, American, 6,903.

1976, Carter, Dem., 44,058; Ford, Rep., 71,555; MacBride, Libertarian, 6,785.

1980, Reagan, Rep., 86,112; Carter, Dem., 41,842; Clark, Libertarian, 18,479; Anderson, Ind., 11,155; Write-in, 857.

1984, Reagan, Rep., 138,377; Mondale, Dem., 62,007; Bergland, Libertarian, 6,378.

1988, Bush, Rep., 119,251; Dukakis, Dem., 72,584; Paul, Lib., 5,484; Fulani, New. Alliance, 1,024.

Arizona

County	1988 Dukakis (D)	Bush (R)	1984 Mondale (D)	Reagan (R)
Apache	8,944	5,347	7,277	5,638
Cochise	11,812	15,815	9,671	16,405
Coconino	14,660	16,649	11,528	17,581
Gila	7,147	7,861	6,509	8,543
Graham	3,407	5,120	3,080	5,247
Greenlee	1,733	1,526	1,963	1,801

La Paz	1,746	2,562	1,502	2,757
Maricopa	230,952	442,337	154,833	411,902
Mohave	10,197	17,651	7,436	17,364
Navajo	9,023	10,393	8,017	11,379
Pima	113,824	117,899	91,585	123,830
Pinal	13,850	14,966	11,923	16,464
Santa Cruz	3,268	3,320	2,463	3,855
Yavapai	14,514	27,842	9,609	24,802
Yuma	8,952	13,253	6,458	13,848
Totals	454,029	702,541	333,854	681,416

Arizona Vote Since 1940

1940, Roosevelt, Dem., 95,267; Willkie, Rep., 54,030; Babson, Proh., 742.

1944, Roosevelt, Dem., 80,926; Dewey, Rep., 56,287; Watson, Proh., 421.

1948, Truman, Dem., 95,251; Dewey, Rep., 77,597; Wallace, Prog., 3,310; Watson, Proh., 786; Teichert, Soc. Labor, 121.

1952, Eisenhower, Rep., 152,042; Stevenson, Dem., 108,528.

1956, Eisenhower, Rep., 176,990; Stevenson, Dem., 112,880; Andrews, Ind. 303.

1960, Kennedy, Dem., 176,781; Nixon, Rep., 221,241; Hass, Soc. Labor, 469.

1964, Johnson, Dem., 237,753; Goldwater, Rep., 242,535; Hass, Soc. Labor, 482.

1968, Nixon, Rep., 266,721; Humphrey, Dem., 170,514; Wallace, 3d party, 46,573; McCarthy, New Party, 2,751; Halstead, Soc. Worker, 85; Cleaver, Peace and Freedom, 217; Blomen, Soc. Labor, 75.

1972, Nixon, Rep., 402,812; McGovern, Dem., 198,540; Schmitz, Amer., 21,208; Soc. Workers, 30,945. (Due to ballot peculiarities in 3 counties (particularly Pima), thousands of voters cast ballots for the Socialist Workers Party *and* one of the major candidates. Court ordered both votes counted as official.

1976, Carter, Dem., 295,602; Ford, Rep., 418,642; McCarthy, Ind., 19,229; MacBride, Libertarian, 7,647; Camejo, Soc. Workers, 928; Anderson, Amer., 564; Maddox, Am. Ind., 85.

1980, Reagan, Rep., 529,688; Carter, Dem., 246,843; Anderson, Ind., 76,952; Clark, Libertarian, 18,784; De Berry, Soc. Workers, 1,100; Commoner, Citizens, 551; Hall, Com., 25; Griswold, Workers World, 2.

1984, Reagan, Rep., 681,416; Mondale, Dem., 333,854; Bergland, Libertarian, 10,585.

1988, Bush, Rep., 702,541; Dukakis, Dem., 454,029; Paul, Lib., 13,351; Fulani, New Alliance, 1,662.

Arkansas

	1988		1984	
County	Dukakis (D)	Bush (R)	Mondale (D)	Reagan (R)
Arkansas	3,075	4,007	3,153	4,804
Ashley	4,466	4,111	3,373	5,675
Baxter	4,808	8,614	4,528	10,870
Benton	9,399	24,295	7,306	24,296
Boone	3,998	7,567	3,356	7,961
Bradley	2,167	2,089	2,313	2,690
Calhoun	1,024	1,316	1,058	1,474
Carroll	2,632	4,553	2,263	5,041
Chicot	2,426	1,901	3,407	2,502
Clark	4,675	3,389	4,638	4,185
Clay	3,442	2,766	3,279	3,767
Cleburne	3,404	4,932	3,172	5,769
Cleveland	1,404	1,462	1,378	1,773
Columbia	3,706	5,810	3,680	6,526
Conway	4,134	4,066	3,742	5,049
Craighead	9,083	11,887	8,035	14,047
Crawford	3,582	9,092	3,071	9,551
Crittenden	6,702	7,441	6,520	6,663
Cross	2,989	3,186	2,701	3,917
Dallas	1,990	1,947	2,035	2,361
Desha	2,859	2,334	2,918	2,696
Drew	2,578	2,995	2,638	3,407
Faulkner	7,302	10,678	7,169	11,595
Franklin	2,458	3,588	2,399	4,382
Fulton	2,018	1,918	1,864	2,329
Garland	11,406	19,281	11,484	21,213
Grant	2,142	2,717	2,148	3,167
Greene	5,065	5,161	4,730	6,179
Hempstead	3,841	3,938	3,327	4,904
Hot Spring	5,090	4,181	5,836	5,629
Howard	1,818	2,510	1,746	3,079
Independence	4,523	6,637	4,415	7,428
Izard	2,652	2,824	2,346	2,726
Jackson	4,199	3,049	4,038	3,901
Jefferson	16,664	12,520	18,082	14,514
Johnson	2,818	4,046	3,056	4,720
Lafayette	1,915	1,860	1,695	2,290
Lawrence	3,179	3,205	2,594	4,039
Lee	2,878	1,863	2,541	2,101
Lincoln	2,204	1,557	2,406	1,860
Little River	2,740	2,347	2,090	3,155
Logan	1,254	2,203	3,206	5,663
Lonoke	4,786	7,215	4,636	8,425
Madison	2,106	3,067	2,133	3,516
Marion	2,033	2,993	1,945	3,545
Miller	5,437	7,110	4,686	8,302
Mississippi	6,759	7,841	7,548	10,180
Monroe	2,052	1,862	2,413	2,508
Montgomery	1,362	1,752	1,497	2,221
Nevada	1,732	1,714	1,783	2,352
Newton	1,489	2,504	1,414	2,749
Ouachita	5,229	6,297	5,858	6,700
Perry	1,470	1,627	1,404	2,047
Phillips	5,580	3,892	5,946	4,686
Pike	1,681	2,105	1,443	2,665
Poinsett	3,873	3,644	3,906	5,622
Polk	2,390	4,099	2,101	5,181
Pope	4,941	10,084	5,082	10,667
Prairie	1,688	1,947	1,437	2,407
Pulaski	55,857	70,562	54,237	77,651
Randolph	2,781	2,590	2,557	3,188
St. Francis	4,656	4,298	4,866	5,379
Saline	8,436	12,353	5,977	11,709
Scott	1,707	2,507	1,609	3,066
Searcy	1,340	2,743	1,313	2,819
Sebastian	9,684	24,426	8,688	27,595
Sevier	2,037	2,254	1,942	3,302
Sharp	2,955	3,623	2,492	4,392
Stone	1,728	2,186	1,654	2,325
Union	5,931	10,581	6,208	12,333
Van Buren	2,607	3,562	2,529	4,060
Washington	12,557	23,601	11,319	24,993
White	6,957	11,094	6,603	12,566
Woodruff	1,924	1,097	2,055	1,675
Yell	2,763	3,535	2,679	4,051
Totals	349,237	466,578	338,646	534,774

Arkansas Vote Since 1940

1940, Roosevelt, Dem., 158,622; Willkie, Rep., 42,121; Babson, Proh., 793; Thomas, Soc., 305.

1944, Roosevelt, Dem., 148,965; Dewey, Rep., 63,551; Thomas, Soc. 438.

1948, Truman, Dem., 149,659; Dewey, Rep., 50,959; Thurmond, States' Rights, 40,068; Thomas, Soc., 1,037; Wallace, Prog., 751; Watson, Proh., 1.

1952, Eisenhower, Rep., 177,155; Stevenson, Dem., 226,300; Hamblen, Proh., 886; MacArthur, Christian Nationalist, 458; Hass, Soc. Labor, 1.

1956, Stevenson, Dem., 213,277; Eisenhower, Rep., 186,287; Andrews, Ind., 7,008.

1960, Kennedy, Dem., 215,049; Nixon, Rep., 184,508; Nat'l. States' Rights, 28,952.

1964, Johnson, Dem., 314,197; Goldwater, Rep., 243,264; Kasper, Nat'l. States Rights, 2,965.

1968, Nixon, Rep., 189,062; Humphrey, Dem., 184,901; Wallace, 3d party, 235,627.

1972, Nixon, Rep., 445,751; McGovern, Dem., 198,899; Schmitz, Amer. , 3,016.

1976, Carter, Dem., 498,604; Ford, Rep., 267,903; McCarthy, Ind., 639; Anderson, Amer., 389.

1980, Reagan, Rep., 403,164; Carter, Dem., 398,041; Anderson, Ind., 22,468; Clark, Libertarian, 8,970; Commoner, Citizens, 2,345; Bubar, Statesman, 1,350; Hall, Comm., 1,244.

1984, Reagan, Rep., 534,774; Mondale, Dem., 338,646; Bergland, Libertarian, 2,220.

1988, Bush, Rep., 466,578; Dukakis, Dem., 349,237; Duke, Chr. Pop., 5,146; Paul, Lib., 3,297.

California

	1988		1984	
County	Dukakis (D)	Bush (R)	Mondale (D)	Reagan (R)
Alameda	310,283	162,815	279,281	190,029
Alpine	230	306	194	264
Amador	5,197	6,893	4,166	6,970
Butte	30,406	40,143	25,126	44,836
Calaveras	5,674	7,640	3,919	7,339
Colusa	2,022	3,077	1,715	3,362
Contra Costa	169,411	158,652	137,941	167,797
Del Norte	3,587	3,714	2,693	3,989
El Dorado	19,801	30,021	13,969	26,900
Fresno	92,635	94,835	83,416	101,156
Glenn	2,894	4,944	2,480	5,994
Humboldt	29,781	21,460	24,870	27,495
Imperial	10,243	12,889	8,231	13,816
Inyo	2,653	5,042	2,348	5,811

Kern	55,083	90,550	44,523	85,872
Kings	9,142	12,118	7,317	13,357
Lake	9,828	9,366	8,292	10,291
Lassen	3,446	5,157	3,253	5,338
Los Angeles	1,372,352	1,239,716	1,114,578	1,370,813
Madera	10,642	13,255	8,701	13,853
Marin	69,394	46,855	56,796	55,845
Mariposa	2,998	3,768	2,121	3,571
Mendocino	17,152	12,979	14,172	16,107
Merced	20,105	21,717	16,875	25,003
Modoc	1,416	2,518	1,219	2,995
Mono	1,284	2,177	944	2,630
Monterey	48,998	50,022	39,676	54,440
Napa	22,283	23,235	18,234	25,715
Nevada	14,980	21,383	10,941	19,440
Orange	269,013	586,230	200,477	615,099
Placer	27,516	42,096	20,527	36,565
Plumas	4,251	4,603	3,709	5,079
Riverside	133,122	199,979	99,853	178,397
Sacramento	186,557	201,832	153,450	197,957
San Benito	4,559	5,578	3,454	5,530
San Bernardino	151,118	235,167	114,710	217,556
San Diego	333,264	523,143	251,134	487,362
San Francisco	201,887	72,503	190,396	88,683
San Joaquin	61,699	75,309	53,441	81,084
San Luis Obispo	35,667	46,613	26,626	48,331
San Mateo	141,859	109,261	120,853	133,912
Santa Barbara	63,586	77,524	49,505	85,458
Santa Clara	277,810	254,442	224,032	280,425
Santa Cruz	63,133	37,728	47,240	39,862
Shasta	21,171	32,402	19,178	32,854
Sierra	791	860	781	1,078
Siskiyou	8,365	9,056	7,130	10,544
Solano	54,344	50,314	41,435	50,867
Sonoma	91,262	67,725	69,383	74,014
Stanislaus	44,685	51,648	36,599	54,085
Sutter	6,557	14,100	5,526	14,425
Tehama	7,213	9,854	6,511	11,536
Trinity	2,518	3,267	2,204	3,525
Tulare	30,711	46,891	27,707	50,262
Tuolumne	8,717	10,646	7,212	10,376
Ventura	89,065	147,604	64,623	146,647
Yolo	30,429	22,358	25,264	23,604
Yuba	5,444	8,937	4,996	9,265
Totals	4,702,233	5,054,917	3,815,947	5,305,410

California Vote Since 1940

1940, Roosevelt, Dem., 1,877,618; Willkie, Rep., 1,351,419; Thomas, Prog., 16,506; Browder, Com., 13,586; Babson, Proh., 9,400.

1944, Roosevelt, Dem., 1,988,564; Dewey, Rep., 1,512,965; Watson, Proh., 14,770; Thomas, Soc., 3,923; Teichert, Soc. Labor, 327.

1948, Truman, Dem., 1,913,134; Dewey, Rep., 1,895,269; Wallace, Prog., 190,381; Watson, Proh., 16,926; Thomas, Soc., 3,459; Thurmond, States' Rights, 1,228; Teichert, Soc. Labor, 195; Dobbs, Soc. Workers, 133.

1952, Eisenhower, Rep., 2,897,310; Stevenson, Dem., 2,197,548; Hallinan, Prog., 24,106; Hamblen, Proh., 15,653; MacArthur, (Tenny Ticket), 3,326; (Kellems Ticket) 178; Hass, Soc. Labor, 273; Hoopes, Soc., 206; scattered, 3,249.

1956, Eisenhower, Rep., 3,027,668; Stevenson, Dem., 2,420,136; Holtwick, Proh., 11,119; Andrews, Constitution, 6,087; Hass, Soc. Labor, 300; Hoopes, Soc., 123; Dobbs, Soc. Workers, 96; Smith, Christian Nat'l., 8.

1960, Kennedy, Dem., 3,224,099; Nixon, Rep., 3,259,722; Decker, Proh., 21,706; Hass, Soc. Labor, 1,051.

1964, Johnson, Dem., 4,171,877; Goldwater, Rep., 2,879,108; Hass, Soc. Labor, 489; DeBerry, Soc. Worker, 378; Munn, Proh., 305; Hensley, Universal, 19.

1968, Nixon, Rep., 3,467,664; Humphrey, Dem., 3,244,318; Wallace, 3d party, 487,270; Peace and Freedom party, 27,707; McCarthy, Alternative, 20,721; Gregory, write-in, 3,230; Mitchell, Com., 260; Munn, Proh., 59; Blomen, Soc. Labor, 341; Soeters, Defense, 17.

1972, Nixon, Rep., 4,602,096; McGovern, Dem., 3,475,847; Schmitz, Amer., 232,554; Spock, Peace and Freedom, 55,167; Hall, Com., 373; Hospers, Libertarian, 980; Munn, Proh., 53; Fisher, Soc. Labor, 197; Jenness, Soc. Workers, 574; Green, Universal, 21.

1976, Carter, Dem., 3,742,284; Ford, Rep., 3,882,244; Mac-Bride, Libertarian, 56,388; Maddox, Am. Ind., 51,098; Wright, People's, 41,731; Camejo, Soc. Workers, 17,259; Hall, Com., 12,766; write-in, McCarthy, 58,412; other write-in, 4,935.

1980, Reagan, Rep. 4,524,858; Carter, Dem., 3,083,661; Anderson, Ind., 739,833; Clark, Libertarian, 148,434; Com-

moner, Ind. 61,063; Smith, Peace & Freedom, 18,116; Rarick, Amer. Ind., 9,856.

1984, Reagan, Rep. 5,305,410; Mondale, Dem., 3,815,947; Bergland, Libertarian, 48,400.

1988, Bush, Rep., 5,054,917; Dukakis, Dem., 4,702,233; Paul, Lib., 70,105; Fulani, Ind., 31,181.

Colorado

	1988		1984	
	Dukakis	Bush	Mondale	Reagan
County	(D)	(R)	(D)	(R)
Adams	49,464	43,163	35,285	55,092
Alamosa	2,146	2,567	1,720	2,953
Arapahoe	61,113	95,926	39,891	107,556
Archuleta	795	1,440	584	1,557
Baca	851	1,670	580	1,903
Bent	1,088	1,032	859	1,314
Boulder	57,265	48,174	42,195	53,535
Chaffee	2,548	3,080	1,779	3,680
Cheyenne	399	760	307	892
Clear Creek	1,698	1,820	1,089	2,151
Conejos	1,976	1,445	1,553	1,669
Costilla	1,120	454	997	621
Crowley	630	862	517	993
Custer	310	753	241	832
Delta	3,521	5,449	2,835	6,678
Denver	127,173	77,753	110,200	105,096
Dolores	230	488	173	667
Douglas	6,931	17,035	3,011	12,249
Eagle	3,314	4,366	2,032	4,500
Elbert	1,566	2,805	802	2,605
El Paso	39,995	96,965	28,185	88,377
Fremont	5,278	7,623	3,895	8,250
Garfield	4,620	6,358	3,076	7,111
Gilpin	804	728	634	896
Grand	1,451	2,306	1,017	2,865
Gunnison	1,897	2,520	1,424	3,100
Hinsdale	111	295	98	310
Huerfano	1,876	1,079	1,602	1,581
Jackson	294	584	191	722
Jefferson	81,824	110,820	53,700	124,496
Kiowa	398	645	265	850
Kit Carson	1,196	2,262	778	2,762
Lake	1,516	969	1,324	1,364
La Plata	5,443	7,714	4,040	8,719
Larimer	35,703	45,967	23,896	49,883
Las Animas	4,075	2,162	3,670	2,992
Lincoln	874	1,356	587	1,661
Logan	3,382	4,485	2,155	5,883
Mesa	14,372	22,150	9,938	23,736
Mineral	174	217	117	333
Moffat	1,634	2,757	1,228	3,630
Montezuma	2,233	4,208	1,665	4,753
Montrose	3,748	6,012	2,864	7,162
Morgan	3,728	4,795	2,331	6,097
Otero	3,910	4,265	3,005	5,373
Ouray	439	814	366	914
Park	1,343	1,909	782	2,041
Philips	923	1,317	651	1,689
Pitkin	3,420	2,801	2,293	3,117
Prowers	2,207	2,978	1,467	3,501
Pueblo	32,788	20,119	27,126	24,634
Rio Blanco	803	1,821	484	2,131
Rio Grande	1,545	2,626	1,104	3,122
Routt	2,922	3,264	2,051	4,239
Saguache	1,033	945	867	1,201
San Juan	192	210	183	320
San Miguel	961	798	654	833
Sedgwick	611	921	429	1,146
Summit	2,595	2,893	1,588	3,253
Teller	1,656	3,760	1,043	3,460
Washington	958	1,707	568	2,060
Weld	20,548	26,497	13,863	31,293
Yuma	1,835	2,513	1,121	3,394
Total	621,453	728,177	454,975	821,817

Colorado Vote Since 1940

1940, Roosevelt, Dem., 265,554; Willkie, Rep., 279,576; Thomas, Soc., 1,899; Babson, Proh., 1,597; Browder, Com., 378.

1944, Roosevelt, Dem., 234,331; Dewey, Rep., 268,731; Thomas, Soc., 1,977.

1948, Truman, Dem., 267,288; Dewey, Rep., 239,714; Wallace, Prog., 6,115; Thomas, Soc., 1,678; Dobbs, Soc. Workers, 228; Teichert, Soc. Labor, 214.

1952, Eisenhower, Rep., 379,782; Stevenson, Dem., 245,504; MacArthur, Constitution, 2,181; Hallinan, Prog., 1,919; Hoopes, Soc., 365; Hass, Soc. Labor, 352.

1956, Eisenhower, Rep., 394,479; Stevenson, Dem., 263,997; Hass, Soc. Lab., 3,308; Andrews, Ind., 759; Hoopes, Soc., 531.

1960, Kennedy, Dem., 330,629; Nixon, Rep., 402,242; Hass, Soc. Labor, 2,803; Dobbs, Soc. Workers, 572.

1964, Johnson, Dem., 476,024; Goldwater, Rep., 296,767; Hass, Soc. Labor, 302; DeBerry, Soc. Worker, 2,537; Munn, Proh., 1,356.

1968, Nixon, Rep., 409,345; Humphrey, Dem., 335,174; Wallace, 3d party, 60,813; Blomen, Soc. Labor, 3,016; Gregory, New-party, 1,393; Munn, Proh., 275; Halstead, Soc. Worker, 235.

1972, Nixon, Rep., 597,189; McGovern, Dem., 329,980; Fisher, Soc. Labor, 4,361; Hospers, Libertarian, 1,111; Hall, Com., 432; Jenness, Soc. Workers, 555; Munn, Proh., 467; Schmitz, Amer., 17,269; Spock, Peoples, 2,403.

1976, Carter, Dem., 460,353; Ford, Rep., 584,367; McCarthy, Ind., 26,107; MacBride, Libertarian, 5,330; Bubar, Proh., 2,882.

1980, Reagan, Rep., 652,264; Carter, Dem., 367,973; Anderson, Ind., 130,633; Clark, Libertarian, 25,744; Commoner, Citizens, 5,614; Bubar, Statesman, 1,180; Pulley, Socialist, 520; Hall, Com., 487.

1984, Reagan, Rep., 821,817; Mondale, Dem., 454,975; Bergland, Libertarian, 11,257.

1988, Bush, Rep., 728,177; Dukakis, Dem., 621,453; Paul, Lib., 15,482; Dodge, Proh., 4,604.

Connecticut

City	1988 Dukakis (D)	Bush (R)	1984 Mondale (D)	Reagan (R)
Bridgeport	23,831	17,084	24,332	24,256
Hartford	27,295	8,100	29,327	11,821
New Britain	15,843	9,569	14,608	13,723
New Haven	31,951	11,616	32,518	16,483
Norwalk	14,518	18,618	12,509	22,447
Stamford	20,773	24,877	19,432	29,167
Waterbury	18,202	20,018	18,217	24,764
West Hartford	19,311	16,482	16,882	20,517
Totals	676,584	750,241	569,597	890,877

Connecticut Vote Since 1940

1940, Roosevelt, Dem., 417,621; Willkie, Rep., 361,021; Browder, Com., 1,091; Aiken, Soc. Labor, 971; Willkie, Union, 798.

1944, Roosevelt, Dem., 435,146; Dewey, Rep., 390,527; Thomas, Soc., 5,097; Teichert, Soc. Labor, 1,220.

1948, Truman, Dem., 423,297; Dewey, Rep., 437,754; Wallace, Prog., 13,713; Thomas, Soc., 6,964; Teichert, Soc. Labor, 1,184; Dobbs, Soc. Workers, 606.

1952, Eisenhower, Rep., 611,012; Stevenson, Dem., 481,649; Hoopes, Soc., 2,244; Hallinan, Peoples, 1,466; Hass, Soc. Labor, 535; write-in, 5.

1956, Eisenhower, Rep., 711,837; Stevenson, Dem., 405,079; scattered, 205.

1960, Kennedy, Dem., 657,055; Nixon, Rep., 565,813.

1964, Johnson, Dem., 826,269; Goldwater, Rep., 390,996; scattered, 1,313.

1968, Nixon, Rep., 556,721; Humphrey, Dem., 621,561; Wallace, 3d party, 76,650; scattered, 1,300.

1972, Nixon, Rep., 810,763; McGovern, Dem., 555,498; Schmitz, Amer., 17,239; scattered, 777.

1976, Carter, Dem., 647,895; Ford, Rep., 719,261; Maddox, George Wallace Party, 7,101; LaRouche, U.S. Labor, 1,789.

1980, Reagan, Rep., 677,210; Carter, Dem., 541,732; Anderson, Ind., 171,807; Clark, Libertarian, 8,570; Commoner, Citizens, 6,130; scattered, 836.

1984, Reagan, Rep., 890,877; Mondale, Dem., 569,597.

1988, Bush, Rep., 750,241; Dukakis, Dem., 676,584; Paul, Lib., 14,071; Fulani, New Alliance, 2,491.

Delaware

County	1988 Dukakis (D)	Bush (R)	1984 Mondale (D)	Reagan (R)
Kent	12,996	19,923	11,789	21,531
New Castle	79,147	92,587	76,238	102,322
Sussex	16,504	27,129	13,629	28,337
Totals	108,647	139,639	101,656	152,190

Delaware Vote Since 1940

1940, Roosevelt, Dem., 74,559; Willkie, Rep., 61,440; Babson, Proh., 220; Thomas, Soc., 115.

1944, Roosevelt, Dem., 68,166; Dewey, Rep., 56,747; Watson, Proh., 294; Thomas, Soc., 154.

1948, Truman, Dem., 67,813; Dewey, Rep., 69,688; Wallace, Prog., 1,050; Watson, Proh., 343; Thomas, Soc., 250; Teichert, Soc. Labor, 29.

1952, Eisenhower, Rep., 90,059; Stevenson, Dem., 83,315; Hass, Soc. Labor, 242; Hamblen, Proh., 234; Hallinan, Prog., 155; Hoopes, Soc., 20.

1956, Eisenhower, Rep., 98,057; Stevenson, Dem., 79,421; Oltwick, Proh., 400; Hass, Soc. Labor, 110.

1960, Kennedy, Dem., 99,590; Nixon, Rep., 96,373; Faubus, States' Rights, 354; Decker, Proh., 284; Hass, Soc. Labor, 82.

1964, Johnson, Dem., 122,704; Goldwater, Rep., 78,078; Hass, Soc. Labor, 113; Munn, Proh., 425.

1968, Nixon, Rep., 96,714; Humphrey, Dem., 89,194; Wallace, 3d party, 28,459.

1972, Nixon, Rep., 140,357; McGovern, Dem., 92,283; Schmitz, Amer., 2,638; Munn, Proh., 238.

1976, Carter, Dem., 122,596; Ford, Rep., 109,831; McCarthy, non-partisan, 2,437; Anderson, Amer., 645; LaRouche, U.S. Labor, 136; Bubar, Proh., 103; Levin, Soc. Labor, 86.

1980, Reagan, Rep., 111,252; Carter, Dem., 105,754; Anderson, Ind., 16,288; Clark, Libertarian, 1,974; Greaves, American, 400.

1984, Reagan, Rep., 152,190; Mondale, Dem., 101,656; Bergland, Libertarian, 268.

1988, Bush, Rep., 139,639; Dukakis, Dem., 108,647; Paul, Lib., 1,162; Fulani, New Alliance, 443.

District of Columbia

County	1988 Dukakis (D)	Bush (R)	1984 Mondale (D)	Reagan (R)
Totals	159,407	27,590	180,408	29,009

District of Columbia Vote Since 1964

1964, Johnson, Dem., 169,796; Goldwater, Rep., 28,801.

1968, Nixon, Rep., 31,012; Humphrey, Dem., 139,566.

1972, Nixon, Rep., 35,226; McGovern, Dem., 127,627; Reed, Soc. Workers, 316; Hall, Com., 252.

1976, Carter, Dem., 137,818; Ford, Rep., 27,873; Camejo, Soc. Workers, 545; MacBride, Libertarian, 274; Hall, Com., 219; LaRouche, U.S. Labor, 157.

1980, Reagan, Rep., 23,313; Carter, Dem., 130,231; Anderson, Ind., 16,131; Commoner, Citizens, 1,826; Clark, Libertarian, 1,104; Hall, Com., 369; De Berry, Soc. Work., 173; Griswold, Workers World, 52; write-ins, 690.

1984, Mondale, Dem., 180,408; Reagan, Rep., 29,009; Bergland, Libertarian, 279.

1988, Bush, Rep., 27,590; Dukakis, Dem., 159,407; Fulani, New Alliance, 2,901; Paul, Lib., 554.

Florida

County	1988 Dukakis (D)	Bush (R)	1984 Mondale (D)	Reagan (R)
Alachua	29,375	30,124	26,551	30,582
Baker	1,353	3,414	1,381	3,485
Bay	11,582	31,712	9,381	29,322
Bradford	2,386	4,218	2,341	4,128
Brevard	42,967	104,721	36,963	102,339
Broward	218,211	220,196	194,542	254,501
Calhoun	1,329	2,420	1,312	2,493
Charlotte	15,967	28,879	11,303	27,464
Citrus	12,177	21,052	10,463	20,754
Clay	7,766	25,882	5,488	21,545
Collier	12,768	38,910	9,065	33,603
Columbia	4,072	7,759	4,261	8,807
Dade	216,847	270,672	223,793	324,216
De Soto	2,181	4,237	2,302	4,822
Dixie	1,366	2,027	1,224	2,204
Duval	74,832	127,875	77,459	128,653
Escambia	29,934	64,774	26,798	66,638
Flagler	4,241	6,494	2,999	4,907
Franklin	1,283	1,911	1,089	2,218
Gadsden	6,368	5,987	7,399	5,805
Gilchrist	1,137	1,854	1,051	2,056
Glades	1,034	1,546	1,070	1,987
Gulf	1,687	3,040	1,783	3,573
Hamilton	1,314	2,062	1,401	1,921
Hardee	1,688	3,636	1,536	3,957
Hendry	2,036	3,962	2,018	4,524
Hernando	15,432	21,179	12,204	21,273
Highlands	8,087	16,713	7,217	16,465
Hillsborough	98,969	150,065	86,189	157,827
Holmes	1,639	4,221	1,231	4,547

Indian River	10,447	24,619	8,731	23,694
Jackson	5,002	8,392	4,956	9,086
Jefferson	2,055	2,326	2,055	2,244
Lafayette	722	1,450	862	1,513
Lake	16,762	37,314	12,215	35,304
Lee	40,709	87,247	30,011	85,006
Leon	33,446	36,032	29,654	36,301
Levy	3,433	5,250	3,103	5,561
Liberty	709	1,419	649	1,409
Madison	1,950	2,556	2,101	2,816
Manatee	26,618	51,160	20,887	55,775
Marion	20,679	41,488	16,221	37,796
Martin	11,486	31,270	8,976	28,897
Monroe	10,151	15,919	7,771	16,316
Nassau	4,138	8,366	3,483	8,033
Okaloosa	9,726	40,295	7,289	36,963
Okeechobee	3,007	4,733	2,226	4,447
Orange	53,991	117,141	48,737	122,007
Osceola	9,811	21,350	6,627	18,344
Palm Beach	144,143	181,408	116,071	186,755
Pasco	50,369	63,788	40,961	66,609
Pinellas	152,371	210,971	128,547	240,535
Polk	38,236	77,065	35,505	84,174
Putnam	8,569	11,621	7,821	11,424
St. Johns	7,999	19,166	6,652	16,493
St. Lucie	17,427	32,241	13,039	28,189
Santa Rosa	5,251	18,948	4,646	21,237
Sarasota	42,095	84,585	30,512	87,713
Seminole	22,627	60,328	17,789	56,229
Sumter	3,900	5,933	3,460	6,252
Suwannee	3,126	5,859	2,788	6,079
Taylor	1,762	4,054	1,728	4,030
Union	691	1,643	761	1,804
Volusia	55,437	74,116	43,811	68,317
Wakulla	1,605	3,157	1,469	3,087
Walton	3,231	7,481	2,500	7,117
Washington	2,139	4,366	1,916	4,603
Totals	1,655,851	2,616,597	1,448,344	2,728,775

Florida Vote Since 1940

1940, Roosevelt, Dem., 359,334; Willkie, Rep., 126,158.

1944, Roosevelt, Dem., 339,377; Dewey, Rep., 143,215.

1948, Truman, Dem., 281,988; Dewey, Rep., 194,280; Thurmond, States' Rights, 89,755; Wallace, Prog., 11,620.

1952, Eisenhower, Rep., 544,036; Stevenson, Dem., 444,950; scattered, 351.

1956, Eisenhower, Rep., 643,849; Stevenson, Dem., 480,371.

1960, Kennedy, Dem., 748,700; Nixon, Rep., 795,476.

1964, Johnson, Dem., 948,540; Goldwater, Rep., 905,941.

1968, Nixon, Rep., 886,804; Humphrey, Dem., 676,794; Wallace, 3d party, 624,207.

1972, Nixon, Rep., 1,857,759; McGovern, Dem., 718,117; scattered, 7,407.

1976, Carter, Dem., 1,636,000; Ford, Rep., 1,469,531; McCarthy, Ind., 23,643; Anderson, Amer., 21,325.

1980, Reagan, Rep., 2,046,951; Carter, Dem., 1,419,475; Anderson, Ind., 189,692; Clark, Libertarian, 30,524; write-ins, 285.

1984, Reagan, Rep., 2,728,775; Mondale, Dem., 1,448,344.

1988, Bush, Rep., 2,616,597; Dukakis, Dem., 1,655,851; Paul, Lib., 19,796, Fulani, New Alliance, 6,655.

Georgia

County	1988 Dukakis (D)	Bush (R)	1984 Mondale (D)	Reagan (R)
Appling	1,837	3,000	1,958	2,929
Atkinson	887	1,126	901	944
Bacon	780	1,407	1,010	1,778
Baker	707	629	691	675
Baldwin	4,008	5,852	3,853	5,717
Banks	984	1,590	1,063	1,549
Barrow	2,442	4,738	2,367	4,123
Bartow	4,884	8,039	4,780	7,104
Ben Hill	1,867	2,005	1,859	2,313
Berrien	1,381	2,030	1,670	2,395
Bibb	22,084	22,179	26,427	24,170
Bleckley	1,175	1,950	1,465	1,912
Brantley	1,450	1,539	1,517	1,679
Brooks	1,500	2,136	1,661	2,229
Bryan	1,423	2,802	1,398	2,265
Bulloch	3,417	6,354	3,644	6,117
Burke	2,861	2,988	3,127	3,137
Butts	1,730	2,184	1,820	2,141
Calhoun	901	644	1,077	776
Camden	2,090	2,913	2,164	2,841
Candler	677	1,261	1,014	1,497
Carroll	4,706	10,754	5,590	11,436
Catoosa	3,588	9,319	3,089	7,908
Charlton	943	1,327	1,111	1,366
Chatham	25,063	35,623	28,271	38,482
Chattahoochee	362	454	428	459
Chattooga	2,206	3,665	2,576	2,953
Cherokee	4,378	14,593	3,499	11,146
Clarke	11,154	11,150	10,132	11,503
Clay	595	398	750	419
Clayton	14,689	28,225	11,763	31,553
Clinch	594	863	625	862
Cobb	39,297	106,621	28,414	97,429
Coffee	2,777	4,019	2,633	4,200
Colquitt	2,998	5,653	3,208	5,815
Columbia	4,617	16,401	3,727	12,294
Cook	1,226	1,555	1,510	1,860
Coweta	4,212	9,668	3,650	7,981
Crawford	1,340	1,235	1,423	1,298
Crisp	1,690	2,916	2,128	2,895
Dade	1,120	2,539	1,150	2,750
Dawson	761	1,908	643	1,322
Decatur	2,348	3,866	2,656	4,134
DeKalb	92,521	90,179	77,329	104,697
Dodge	2,164	2,677	2,513	2,765
Dooly	1,613	1,386	1,726	1,435
Dougherty	12,579	15,520	12,904	16,920
Douglas	5,086	13,493	4,371	12,428
Early	1,359	1,918	1,494	2,239
Echols	245	422	227	453
Effingham	1,905	3,933	2,055	4,266
Elbert	2,118	2,796	2,670	3,366
Emanuel	2,387	3,530	2,458	3,920
Evans	1,023	1,707	1,193	1,601
Fannin	2,123	4,271	1,965	4,159
Fayette	4,593	16,443	2,861	12,575
Floyd	8,548	14,697	8,873	15,437
Forsyth	2,347	7,947	2,275	6,841
Franklin	1,842	2,615	1,838	2,549
Fulton	120,752	91,785	125,567	95,149
Gilmer	1,363	3,353	1,234	2,972
Glascock	210	580	317	827
Glynn	6,339	11,126	6,574	11,724
Gordon	2,369	6,051	2,607	5,566
Grady	1,883	2,989	2,261	3,886
Greene	1,818	1,432	1,992	1,599
Gwinnett	20,948	66,372	14,139	54,749
Habersham	2,114	4,871	2,125	4,647
Hall	7,782	17,415	7,421	15,076
Hancock	1,947	621	2,109	644
Haralson	2,404	4,529	1,938	3,945
Harris	1,905	3,414	2,096	3,138
Hart	2,476	3,044	2,496	2,842
Heard	874	1,551	810	1,492
Henry	4,348	10,882	4,096	9,142
Houston	8,664	15,748	9,226	14,255
Irwin	918	1,226	905	1,330
Jackson	2,607	4,407	2,717	4,202
Jasper	1,188	1,474	1,122	1,431
Jeff Davis	1,242	2,050	1,380	2,233
Jefferson	2,346	2,788	2,816	2,999
Jenkins	953	1,286	1,108	1,399
Johnson	927	1,567	1,199	1,733
Jones	2,662	3,618	2,781	3,401
Lamar	1,416	2,035	1,605	2,198
Lanier	698	725	741	852
Laurens	4,879	6,929	5,471	7,181
Lee	995	2,875	1,284	2,972
Liberty	2,906	3,100	2,803	3,229
Lincoln	893	1,417	1,115	1,357
Long	681	858	816	1,099
Lowndes	6,427	10,855	6,167	10,437
Lumpkin	1,286	2,688	1,110	1,991
McDuffie	1,704	3,231	2,006	3,284
McIntosh	1,527	1,273	1,796	1,512
Macon	2,268	1,412	2,521	1,515
Madison	1,639	3,724	1,690	3,768
Marion	844	804	951	846
Meriwether	2,934	3,101	2,864	3,195
Miller	515	1,105	526	1,348
Mitchell	2,260	2,590	2,791	2,737
Monroe	1,970	2,570	2,189	2,420
Montgomery	903	1,228	950	1,365
Morgan	1,508	2,108	1,714	2,301
Murray	1,679	3,996	1,649	3,521
Muscogee	18,772	23,058	20,835	23,816
Newton	3,111	5,809	3,389	5,810
Oconee	1,990	4,265	1,467	3,471
Oglethorpe	1,154	1,951	1,238	2,122
Paulding	2,717	7,329	2,621	6,048
Peach	2,972	2,782	3,369	2,652
Pickens	1,430	3,021	1,329	2,801
Pierce	1,558	1,947	1,501	1,978
Pike	1,176	2,074	1,203	1,855
Polk	2,977	5,454	3,262	5,435
Pulaski	1,476	1,400	1,440	1,509
Putnam	1,532	2,111	1,336	1,830
Quitman	436	296	490	361
Rabun	1,301	2,278	1,267	2,191
Randolph	1,369	1,319	1,454	1,578
Richmond	20,489	27,566	21,208	29,869
Rockdale	4,330	12,413	3,291	10,121
Schley	439	635	403	614
Screven	1,461	2,178	1,747	2,583
Seminole	1,171	1,469	1,350	1,636
Spalding	4,318	7,730	4,878	8,571
Stephens	2,185	4,329	2,272	4,057
Stewart	1,136	832	1,308	805

Sumter........	3,332	4,289	3,725	4,607
Talbot	1,248	802	1,494	778
Taliaferro	469	306	550	318
Tattnall........	1,694	3,172	1,954	3,641
Taylor	1,134	1,145	1,340	1,292
Telfair	1,765	1,805	2,049	1,980
Terrell	1,383	1,517	1,598	1,744
Thomas	3,530	6,572	4,039	6,427
Tift	2,446	4,760	2,736	4,429
Toombs	1,152	4,433	2,385	4,470
Towns	942	1,783	1,007	1,960
Treutlen	726	970	843	1,086
Troup.........	4,562	9,484	5,272	9,340
Turner	1,122	1,312	1,270	1,329
Twiggs	1,730	1,261	1,755	1,143
Union.........	1,258	2,396	1,112	1,914
Upson	2,666	4,614	2,943	4,803
Walker	4,753	10,487	5,000	10,734
Walton	3,091	5,974	2,481	4,995
Ware	4,292	4,819	4,435	5,547
Warren........	1,091	897	1,258	1,087
Washington	2,615	2,752	3,034	2,887
Wayne	2,417	3,340	2,434	3,698
Webster	427	361	534	402
Wheeler	658	709	774	833
White.........	1,028	2,648	1,090	2,369
Whitfield	4,618	12,761	5,284	11,957
Wilcox........	1,079	1,235	1,212	1,218
Wilkes	1,549	1,810	1,586	1,837
Wilkinson......	1,831	1,546	2,102	1,756
Worth.........	1,311	2,668	1,685	2,910
Totals	**714,792**	**1,081,331**	**706,628**	**1,068,722**

Georgia Vote Since 1940

1940, Roosevelt, Dem., 265,194; Willkie, Rep., 23,934; Ind. Dem., 22,428; total, 46,362; Babson, Proh., 983.

1944, Roosevelt, Dem., 268,187; Dewey, Rep., 56,506; Watson, Proh., 36.

1948, Truman, Dem. 254,646; Dewey, Rep., 76,691; Thurmond, States' Rights, 85,055; Wallace, Prog., 1,636; Watson, Proh., 732.

1952, Eisenhower, Rep., 198,979; Stevenson, Dem., 456,823; Liberty Party, 1.

1956, Stevenson, Dem., 444,388; Eisenhower, Rep., 222,778; Andrews, Ind., write-in, 1,754.

1960, Kennedy, Dem., 458,638; Nixon, Rep., 274,472; write-in, 239.

1964, Johnson, Dem., 522,557; Goldwater, Rep., 616,600.

1968, Nixon, Rep., 380,111; Humphrey, Dem., 334,440; Wallace, 3d party, 535,550; write-in, 162.

1972, Nixon, Rep., 881,496; McGovern, Dem., 289,529; Schmitz, Amer., 2,288; scattered.

1976, Carter, Dem., 979,409; Ford, Rep., 483,743; write-in, 4,306.

1980, Reagan, Rep., 654,168; Carter, Dem., 890,955; Anderson, Ind., 36,055; Clark, Libertarian, 15,627.

1984, Reagan, Rep., 1,068,722; Mondale, Dem., 706,628.

1988, Bush, Rep., 1,081,331; Dukakis, Dem., 714,792; Paul, Lib., 8,435; Fulani, New Alliance, 5,099.

Hawaii

	1988		1984	
	Dukakis	Bush	Mondale	Reagan
County	(D)	(R)	(D)	(R)
Hawaii	24,091	17,125	17,866	20,707
Honolulu.......	138,971	120,258	107,404	140,258
Kauai.........	11,770	8,298	8,862	9,249
Maui	17,532	12,944	12,966	14,720
Totals	**192,364**	**158,625**	**147,098**	**184,934**

Hawaii Vote Since 1960

1960, Kennedy, Dem., 92,410; Nixon, Rep., 92,295.

1964, Johnson, Dem., 163,249; Goldwater, Rep., 44,022.

1968, Nixon, Rep., 91,425; Humphrey, Dem., 141,324; Wallace, 3d party, 3,469.

1972, Nixon, Rep., 168,865; McGovern, Dem., 101,409.

1976, Carter, Dem., 147,375; Ford, Rep., 140,003; MacBride, Libertarian, 3,923.

1980, Reagan, Rep., 130,112; Carter, Dem., 135,879; Anderson, Ind., 32,021; Clark, Libertarian, 3,269; Commoner, Citizens, 1,548; Hall, Com., 458.

1984, Reagan, Rep., 184,934; Mondale, Dem., 147,098; Bergland, Libertarian, 2,167.

1988, Bush, Rep., 158,625; Dukakis, Dem., 192,364; Paul, Lib., 1,999; Fulani, New Alliance, 1,003.

Idaho

	1988		1984	
	Dukakis	Bush	Mondale	Reagan
County	(D)	(R)	(D)	(R)
Ada..........	30,525	54,951	21,760	60,036
Adams	643	1,107	540	1,381
Bannock.......	13,074	14,986	9,399	18,742
Bear Lake	867	2,084	481	2,760
Benewah.	1,518	1,650	1,447	2,039
Bingham.......	4,346	10,131	3,064	11,900
Blaine	2,498	3,130	1,971	3,603
Boise	620	1,044	436	1,249
Bonner........	5,555	5,721	4,628	6,889
Bonneville......	7,032	22,613	4,877	24,392
Boundary	1,336	1,800	1,158	2,159
Butte	521	899	429	1,245
Camas	136	288	123	364
Canyon........	10,207	21,426	7,527	24,613
Caribou	867	2,239	535	3,032
Cassias	1,833	5,345	1,036	6,503
Clark.........	133	281	59	353
Clearwater.....	1,861	1,659	1,608	2,176
Custer	616	1,253	461	1,653
Elmore	2,078	3,756	1,458	4,595
Franklin	806	2,992	439	3,261
Fremont	1,178	3,401	818	4,006
Gem	2,064	2,926	1,607	3,644
Gooding	1,872	2,908	1,247	3,819
Idaho.........	2,198	3,541	1,996	4,219
Jefferson......	1,198	5,295	743	5,770
Jerome........	1,985	3,830	1,284	4,913
Kootenai	11,621	15,093	9,004	17,330
Latah	6,544	6,367	5,571	7,709
Lemhi........	1,157	2,378	852	2,810
Lewis	807	786	648	1,000
Lincoln	574	918	386	1,211
Madison	1,009	6,197	483	6,798
Minidoka......	2,290	4,623	1,368	5,938
Nez Perce	7,754	7,027	5,981	8,153
Oneida	508	1,269	360	1,526
Owyhee	848	1,707	574	2,141
Payette.	1,900	3,786	1,410	4,605
Power	1,095	1,838	678	2,298
Shoshone	3,379	2,134	3,033	3,156
Teton........	531	982	370	1,242
Twin Falls	7,078	13,243	4,567	16,974
Valley	1,251	1,897	945	2,299
Washington	1,359	2,380	1,119	3,015
Totals	**147,272**	**253,881**	**108,510**	**297,523**

Idaho Vote Since 1940

1940, Roosevelt, Dem., 127,842; Willkie, Rep., 106,553; Thomas, Soc., 497; Browder, Com., 276.

1944, Roosevelt, Dem., 107,399; Dewey, Rep., 100,137; Watson, Proh., 503; Thomas, Soc., 282.

1948, Truman, Dem., 107,370; Dewey, Rep., 101,514; Wallace, Prog., 4,972; Watson, Proh., 628; Thomas, Soc., 332.

1952, Eisenhower, Rep., 180,707; Stevenson Dem., 95,081; Hallinan, Prog., 443; write-in, 23.

1956, Eisenhower, Rep., 166,979; Stevenson, Dem., 105,868; Andrews, Ind., 126; write-in, 16.

1960, Kennedy, Dem., 138,853; Nixon, Rep., 161,597.

1964, Johnson, Dem., 148,920; Goldwater, Rep., 143,557.

1968, Nixon, Rep., 165,369; Humphrey, Dem., 89,273; Wallace, 3d party, 36,541.

1972, Nixon, Rep., 199,384; McGovern, Dem., 80,826; Schmitz, Amer., 28,869; Spock, Peoples, 903.

1976, Carter, Dem., 126,549; Ford, Rep., 204,151; Maddox, Amer., 5,935; MacBride, Libertarian, 3,558; LaRouche, U.S. Labor, 739.

1980, Reagan, Rep., 290,699; Carter, Dem., 110,192; Anderson, Ind., 27,058; Clark, Libertarian, 8,425; Rarick, Amer., 1,057.

1984, Reagan, Rep., 297,523; Mondale, Dem., 108,510; Bergland, Libertarian, 2,823.

1988, Bush, Rep., 253,881; Dukakis, Dem., 147,272; Paul, Lib., 5,313; Fulani, Ind., 2,502.

Illinois

	1988		1984	
	Dukakis	Bush	Mondale	Reagan
County	(D)	(R)	(D)	(R)
Adams	13,768	15,831	10,336	20,225
Alexander	2,693	1,954	2,872	2,574
Bond	3,459	3,608	2,870	4,240
Boone	4,234	6,923	3,717	7,536
Brown	1,267	1,373	959	1,478
Bureau	7,354	8,896	6,925	11,741
Calhoun	1,544	1,238	1,443	1,648

Carroll	2,990	4,464	2,398	5,237
Cass	3,316	2,916	2,937	3,435
Champaign	29,733	33,247	27,266	39,224
Christian	8,295	7,040	7,541	8,534
Clark	3,275	4,508	3,032	5,318
Clay	2,761	3,494	2,524	4,562
Clinton	5,935	7,681	4,628	9,233
Coles	8,327	11,043	7,156	14,044
Cook	1,129,973	878,582	1,112,641	1,055,558
Crawford	3,555	4,951	3,130	6,261
Cumberland	1,904	2,667	1,733	3,002
DeKalb	11,811	17,182	10,942	20,294
DeWitt	2,660	3,942	2,352	4,534
Douglas	3,184	4,378	2,886	5,691
DuPage	94,285	217,907	71,430	227,141
Edgar	3,880	5,538	3,241	6,821
Edwards	1,218	2,212	1,057	2,778
Effingham	4,553	8,431	3,841	9,617
Fayette	4,632	5,452	3,844	6,607
Ford	2,026	4,059	1,763	4,871
Franklin	11,023	7,677	10,667	9,656
Fulton	9,046	6,999	9,131	9,147
Gallatin	2,455	1,580	2,164	1,939
Greene	3,020	3,136	2,563	4,057
Grundy	5,525	8,743	4,671	9,595
Hamilton	2,618	2,622	2,251	3,074
Hancock	4,740	4,568	3,713	6,251
Hardin	1,308	1,504	1,205	1,689
Henderson	2,085	1,726	1,969	2,289
Henry	11,594	11,358	10,679	14,504
Iroquois	4,221	9,596	3,300	11,327
Jackson	11,334	9,687	12,105	13,609
Jasper	2,135	3,024	1,750	3,673
Jefferson	7,729	7,624	7,200	9,642
Jersey	4,376	4,343	3,762	5,146
JoDaviess	4,141	4,923	3,348	5,877
Johnson	1,872	2,797	1,647	3,424
Kane	36,366	66,283	31,875	72,655
Kankakee	15,147	20,316	15,246	23,807
Kendall	4,347	10,653	3,789	10,872
Knox	12,752	10,842	12,027	14,974
Lake	64,327	114,115	53,947	118,401
LaSalle	22,271	22,166	20,532	27,388
Lawrence	3,140	3,655	2,924	4,686
Lee	4,608	8,903	3,919	11,178
Livingston	5,009	10,324	4,567	12,291
Logan	4,727	8,490	4,052	9,932
McDonough	5,247	7,173	4,561	9,383
McHenry	18,919	46,135	14,420	47,282
McLean	18,659	30,572	15,880	32,221
Macon	25,364	23,862	25,463	30,457
Macoupin	12,195	9,362	10,602	12,282
Madison	54,175	44,907	48,352	57,021
Marion	8,592	8,695	7,599	11,300
Marshall	2,742	3,588	2,386	4,060
Mason	3,406	3,424	3,354	4,109
Massac	3,227	3,507	3,194	3,827
Menard	2,103	3,560	1,826	3,925
Mercer	4,204	3,683	3,982	4,907
Monroe	4,529	6,275	3,256	6,936
Montgomery	7,293	6,388	6,360	8,191
Morgan	6,032	8,808	5,361	10,683
Moultrie	3,013	3,167	2,458	3,593
Ogle	5,641	11,644	4,803	13,503
Peoria	35,253	37,605	36,830	45,607
Perry	5,167	4,576	4,584	5,852
Piatt	3,099	4,137	2,840	5,000
Pike	4,614	3,965	3,965	5,295
Pope	996	1,202	940	1,545
Pulaski	1,793	1,666	1,724	1,923
Putnam	1,601	1,516	1,487	1,912
Randolph	7,844	7,396	6,355	9,415
Richland	2,863	4,264	2,182	5,665
Rock Island	40,174	27,412	40,208	35,121
St. Clair	55,465	41,439	52,294	51,046
Saline	6,676	5,798	6,038	7,176
Sangamon	37,729	50,175	34,059	54,086
Schuyler	1,866	2,178	1,533	2,515
Scott	1,243	1,535	943	1,976
Shelby	4,650	5,370	4,317	6,372
Stark	1,274	1,841	1,072	2,228
Stephenson	7,460	11,342	6,723	14,237
Tazewell	24,603	28,861	23,095	33,782
Union	4,197	4,244	3,815	4,721
Vermilion	17,918	16,943	16,530	22,932
Wabash	2,241	3,453	1,795	3,639
Warren	3,617	4,584	3,318	5,846
Washington	2,689	4,127	2,363	5,129
Wayne	3,135	5,481	2,621	6,298
White	4,144	4,354	3,457	5,500
Whiteside	11,328	12,978	11,226	16,743
Will	49,816	73,129	45,193	78,684
Williamson	12,712	12,274	11,614	14,430
Winnebago	45,280	55,699	44,629	64,203
Woodford	4,604	9,474	4,425	10,758
Totals	2,215,940	2,310,939	2,086,499	2,707,103

Illinois Vote Since 1940

1940, Roosevelt, Dem., 2,149,934; Willkie, Rep., 2,047,240; Thomas, Soc., 10,914; Babson, Proh., 9,190.

1944, Roosevelt, Dem., 2,079,479; Dewey, Rep., 1,939,314; Teichert, Soc. Labor, 9,677; Watson, Proh., 7,411; Thomas, Soc., 180.

1948, Truman, Dem., 1,994,715; Dewey, Rep., 1,961,103; Watson, Proh., 11,959; Thomas, Soc., 11,522; Teichert, Soc. Labor, 3,118.

1952, Eisenhower, Rep., 2,457,327; Stevenson, Dem., 2,013,920; Hass, Soc. Labor, 9,363; write-in, 448.

1956, Eisenhower, Rep., 2,623,327; Stevenson, Dem., 1,775,682; Hass, Soc. Labor, 8,342; write-in, 56.

1960, Kennedy, Dem., 2,377,846; Nixon, Rep., 2,368,988; Hass, Soc. Labor, 10,560; write-in, 15.

1964, Johnson, Dem., 2,796,833; Goldwater, Rep., 1,905,946; write-in, 62.

1968, Nixon, Rep., 2,174,774; Humphrey, Dem., 2,039,814; Wallace, 3d party, 390,958; Blomen, Soc. Labor, 13,878; write-in, 325.

1972, Nixon, Rep. 2,788,179; McGovern, Dem., 1,913,472; Fisher, Soc. Labor, 12,344; Schmitz, Amer., 2,471; Hall, Com., 4,541; others, 2,229.

1976, Carter, Dem., 2,271,295; Ford, Rep., 2,364,269; McCarthy, Ind., 55,939; Hall, Com., 9,250; MacBride, Libertarian, 8,057; Camejo, Soc. Workers, 3,615; Levin, Soc. Labor, 2,422; LaRouche, U.S. Labor, 2,018; write-in, 1,968.

1980, Reagan, Rep., 2,358,049; Carter, Dem., 1,981,413; Anderson, Ind., 346,754; Clark, Libertarian, 38,939; Commoner, Citizens, 10,692; Hall, Com., 9,711; Griswold, Workers World, 2,257; DeBerry, Socialist Workers, 1,302; write-ins, 604.

1984, Reagan, Rep., 2,707,103; Mondale, Dem., 2,086,499; Bergland, Libertarian, 10,086.

1988, Bush, Rep., 2,310,939; Dukakis, Dem., 2,215,940; Paul, Lib., 14,944; Fulani, Solid., 10,276.

Indiana

County	1988		1984	
	Dukakis (D)	Bush (R)	Mondale (D)	Reagan (R)
Adams	3,811	8,137	3,923	7,958
Allen	39,238	74,638	38,462	75,505
Bartholomew	8,804	17,364	8,075	18,704
Benton	1,349	2,698	1,357	3,281
Blackford	2,253	3,336	2,395	3,787
Boone	4,168	11,608	3,982	11,790
Brown	2,115	3,348	2,657	3,517
Carroll	2,952	4,981	2,774	5,528
Cass	5,784	10,970	5,521	12,355
Clark	14,528	16,544	14,138	19,419
Clay	3,724	5,852	3,707	6,957
Clinton	4,412	8,570	4,329	8,969
Crawford	2,036	2,532	2,256	2,633
Daviess	3,483	6,768	3,545	7,721
Dearborn	5,066	8,195	4,920	9,149
Decatur	2,979	6,245	2,766	6,551
Dekalb	4,657	9,018	4,617	8,769
Delaware	20,548	27,348	29,791	30,092
Dubois	5,954	9,995	5,423	9,391
Elkhart	14,236	33,793	13,240	34,660
Fayette	4,118	5,949	4,122	7,142
Floyd	11,024	14,291	10,616	15,466
Fountain	3,279	5,113	2,897	5,450
Franklin	2,472	4,777	2,225	5,202
Fulton	2,788	5,234	2,527	6,057
Gibson	7,031	7,610	7,082	8,618
Grant	10,799	18,441	9,986	20,482
Greene	5,979	7,689	5,267	8,438
Hamilton	8,853	36,654	6,364	30,254
Hancock	5,355	13,374	4,550	12,880
Harrison	4,933	6,702	4,634	7,255
Hendricks	7,643	22,090	6,659	21,307
Henry	7,779	11,280	7,064	11,926
Howard	11,518	19,971	10,458	22,386
Huntington	3,873	11,675	4,598	10,805
Jackson	5,550	9,470	5,163	9,879
Jasper	3,237	6,009	2,821	6,537
Jay	3,212	5,363	3,174	5,975
Jefferson	5,221	6,949	4,952	7,482
Jennings	3,667	5,636	3,264	6,356
Johnson	9,001	24,654	7,715	23,482
Knox	7,006	9,813	6,417	10,872
Kosciusko	5,321	17,761	4,877	17,560
LaGrange	2,029	4,495	1,884	4,772
Lake	105,026	79,929	117,984	94,870
LaPorte	17,585	20,537	15,904	23,346
Lawrence	5,787	10,742	5,608	11,440
Madison	24,443	32,596	22,254	36,510
Marion	128,627	184,519	130,185	184,880
Marshall	5,488	10,490	4,931	11,100
Martin	2,132	3,066	1,937	3,363

Miami	4,613	8,533	4,224	9,551	Black Hawk	31,657	24,112	31,467	32,262
Monroe	15,855	20,756	14,719	21,772	Boone	7,232	4,381	6,485	5,746
Montgomery	3,623	10,793	3,626	11,119	Bremer	4,961	5,079	4,084	6,895
Morgan	5,375	14,284	4,627	14,884	Buchanan	4,778	3,495	4,129	4,965
Newton	1,744	3,274	1,596	3,560	Buena Vista	4,580	4,170	4,109	5,193
Noble	4,143	7,889	4,237	8,459	Butler	2,593	3,523	2,323	4,570
Ohio	1,113	1,412	1,068	1,503	Calhoun	2,990	2,474	2,541	3,311
Orange	2,739	5,245	D2,571	5,909	Carroll	5,437	3,701	4,960	5,021
Owen	2,484	3,837	2,082	4,204	Cass	2,934	3,962	2,417	5,053
Parke	2,563	4,458	2,205	5,052	Cedar	4,032	3,373	3,086	4,617
Perry	4,804	4,720	4,760	4,785	Cerro Gordo	12,857	9,358	11,570	11,214
Pike	3,037	3,294	3,231	3,689	Cherokee	3,574	3,218	3,349	4,046
Porter	19,390	29,790	17,862	32,505	Chickasaw	3,530	2,549	3,186	3,661
Posey	4,468	5,987	4,452	6,472	Clarke	2,262	1,631	2,030	2,262
Pulaski	2,213	3,677	2,008	4,167	Clay	4,173	3,641	3,774	4,450
Putnam	3,850	7,119	3,392	7,820	Clayton	4,320	3,839	3,446	5,029
Randolph	3,990	6,856	3,805	7,793	Clinton	12,549	10,243	11,240	13,914
Ripley	3,605	6,414	3,336	7,143	Crawford	3,868	3,375	3,396	4,552
Rush	2,451	5,112	2,307	5,429	Dallas	7,501	4,858	6,564	6,080
St. Joseph	48,056	49,481	47,513	54,404	Davis	2,246	1,563	2,187	1,956
Scott	3,378	3,455	3,460	4,110	Decatur	2,192	1,406	2,098	2,104
Shelby	5,382	10,176	5,357	11,056	Delaware	3,947	3,425	3,158	4,769
Spencer	4,061	4,964	4,005	5,816	Des Moines	11,593	7,652	11,173	9,559
Starke	4,104	4,458	3,674	5,104	Dickinson	3,342	3,678	3,025	4,064
Steuben	3,114	6,855	2,441	6,424	Dubuque	23,797	14,530	21,876	19,239
Sullivan	4,320	4,246	4,006	4,771	Emmet	2,778	2,173	2,746	2,946
Switzerland	1,479	1,572	1,484	1,857	Fayette	5,304	4,921	4,677	6,505
Tippecanoe	16,256	27,897	15,789	29,706	Floyd	4,377	3,266	4,154	4,341
Tipton	2,485	5,148	2,328	5,687	Franklin	2,594	2,320	2,349	3,129
Union	946	1,814	816	1,970	Fremont	1,547	1,946	1,426	2,686
Vanderburgh	31,270	38,928	31,049	40,994	Greene	3,011	2,091	2,831	2,579
Vermillion	4,044	3,674	3,666	4,428	Grundy	2,211	3,433	1,915	4,527
Vigo	19,192	21,929	18,429	26,259	Guthrie	2,910	2,005	2,517	2,783
Wabash	4,168	9,153	4,077	9,862	Hamilton	4,156	3,277	3,330	4,279
Warren	1,542	2,243	1,309	2,525	Hancock	2,831	2,731	2,539	3,362
Warrick	7,999	10,504	6,345	10,202	Hardin	5,088	3,856	4,477	5,195
Washington	3,370	4,998	3,334	5,874	Harrison	2,883	3,108	2,495	4,352
Wayne	10,209	16,388	10,173	18,955	Henry	3,754	3,951	3,377	4,516
Wells	3,437	7,712	3,274	7,579	Howard	2,330	1,970	2,135	2,718
White	3,256	6,220	3,157	7,279	Humboldt	2,713	2,584	2,406	3,396
Whitley	3,642	7,679	3,690	7,763	Ida	1,787	1,951	1,559	2,618
Totals	860,643	1,297,763	841,481	1,377,230	Iowa	3,338	3,247	2,815	4,352
					Jackson	4,864	3,237	4,400	4,811
					Jasper	8,940	6,703	8,023	8,576
					Jefferson	3,594	3,614	2,961	4,727
					Johnson	28,759	15,453	26,000	18,667
					Jones	4,641	3,496	3,825	4,907
					Keokuk	2,899	2,278	2,649	2,913
					Kossuth	5,088	3,938	4,838	4,872
					Lee	10,911	6,228	8,912	8,756
					Linn	42,993	33,129	38,528	41,061
					Louisa	2,268	2,060	1,927	2,623
					Lucas	2,454	1,776	2,422	2,630
					Lyon	1,706	3,517	1,401	4,178
					Madison	3,421	2,410	3,067	3,168
					Mahaska	4,451	4,798	4,107	6,086
					Marion	6,922	5,914	6,313	7,259
					Marshall	9,760	7,657	8,809	10,839
					Mills	2,092	3,212	1,434	3,994
					Mitchell	2,870	2,338	2,531	3,144
					Monona	2,408	2,068	2,159	2,746
					Monroe	2,338	1,313	2,342	1,927
					Montgomery	1,898	3,166	1,661	4,224
					Muscatine	7,059	6,904	5,986	9,069
					O'Brien	2,768	4,241	2,479	5,008
					Osceola	1,277	1,951	1,146	2,285
					Page	2,185	4,583	1,914	5,876
					Palo Alto	3,377	2,041	3,018	2,715
					Plymouth	4,220	5,316	3,464	6,482
					Pocahontas	2,722	1,871	2,481	2,627
					Polk	84,476	57,854	75,413	71,413
					Pottawattamie	14,958	17,193	12,329	21,527
					Poweshiek	4,876	3,683	4,103	4,715
					Ringgold	1,609	1,110	1,593	1,512
					Sac	2,613	2,411	2,363	3,298
					Scott	34,415	31,025	32,550	38,034
					Shelby	2,806	3,019	2,291	4,200
					Sioux	2,923	10,270	2,585	11,665
					Story	19,051	13,782	18,277	19,804
					Tama	4,584	3,362	4,061	4,882
					Taylor	1,671	1,647	1,499	2,496
					Union	3,236	2,751	2,875	3,583
					Van Buren	1,612	1,692	1,606	2,138
					Wapello	10,177	5,350	10,545	7,098
					Warren	9,627	6,424	8,171	8,277
					Washington	3,776	3,741	3,079	4,613
					Wayne	1,988	1,467	1,927	2,061
					Webster	10,267	6,926	9,930	9,619
					Winnebago	2,804	2,863	2,669	3,616
					Winneshiek	4,443	4,194	3,724	5,277
					Woodbury	20,153	18,790	18,951	23,002
					Worth	2,440	1,488	2,263	1,985
					Wright	3,353	2,658	2,980	3,675
					Totals	670,557	545,355	605,620	703,088

Indiana Vote Since 1940

1940, Roosevelt, Dem., 874,063; Willkie, Rep., 899,466; Babson, Proh., 6,437; Thomas, Soc., 2,075; Aiken, Soc. Labor, 706.

1944, Roosevelt, Dem., 781,403; Dewey, Rep., 875,891; Watson, Proh., 12,574; Thomas, Soc., 2,223.

1948, Truman, Dem., 807,833; Dewey, Rep., 821,079; Watson, Proh., 14,711; Wallace, Prog., 9,649; Thomas, Soc., 2,179; Teichert, Soc. Labor, 763.

1952, Eisenhower, Rep., 1,136,259; Stevenson, Dem., 801,530; Hamblen, Proh., 15,335; Hallinan, Prog., 1,222; Hass, Soc. Labor, 979.

1956, Eisenhower, Rep., 1,182,811; Stevenson, Dem., 783,908; Holtwick, Proh., 6,554; Hass, Soc. Labor, 1,334.

1960, Kennedy, Dem., 952,358; Nixon, Rep., 1,175,120; Decker, Proh., 6,746; Hass, Soc. Labor, 1,136.

1964, Johnson, Dem., 1,170,848; Goldwater, Rep., 911,118; Munn, Proh., 8,266; Hass, Soc. Labor, 1,374.

1968, Nixon, Rep., 1,067,885; Humphrey, Dem., 806,659; Wallace, 3d party, 243,108; Munn, Proh., 4,616; Halstead, Soc. Worker, 1,293; Gregory, write-in, 36.

1972, Nixon, Rep., 1,405,154; McGovern, Dem., 708,568; Reed, Soc. Workers, 5,575; Fisher, Soc. Labor, 1,688; Spock, Peace & Freedom, 4,544.

1976, Carter, Dem., 1,014,714; Ford, Rep., 1,185,958; Anderson, Amer., 14,048; Camejo, Soc. Workers, 5,695; LaRouche, U.S. Labor, 1,947.

1980 Reagan, Rep., 1,255,656; Carter, Dem., 844,197; Anderson, Ind., 111,639; Clark, Libertarian, 19,627; Commoner, Citizens, 4,852; Greaves, American, 4,750; Hall, Com., 702; DeBerry, Soc., 610.

1984 Reagan, Rep., 1,377,230; Mondale, Dem., 841,481; Bergland, Libertarian, 6,741.

1988, Bush, Rep., 1,297,763; Dukakis, Dem., 860,643; Fulani, New Alliance, 10,215.

Iowa

County	1988		1984	
	Dukakis (D)	Bush (R)	Mondale (D)	Reagan (R)
Adair	2,261	1,833	1,979	2,615
Adams	1,283	1,080	1,221	1,706
Allamakee	2,768	3,186	2,282	3,997
Appanoose	3,209	2,779	3,289	3,412
Audubon	1,863	1,478	1,854	2,306
Benton	5,873	4,011	4,993	5,566

Iowa Vote Since 1940

1940, Roosevelt, Dem., 578,800; Willkie, Rep., 632,370; Babson, Proh., 2,284; Browder, Com., 1,524; Aiken, Soc. Labor, 452.

1944, Roosevelt, Dem., 499,876; Dewey, Rep., 547,267; Watson, Proh., 3,752; Thomas, Soc., 1,511; Teichert, Soc. Labor, 193.

1948, Truman, Dem., 522,380; Dewey, Rep., 494,018; Wallace, Prog., 12,125; Teichert, Soc. Labor, 4,274; Watson, Proh., 3,382; Thomas, Soc., 1,829; Dobbs, Soc. Workers, 26.

1952, Eisenhower, Rep., 808,906; Stevenson, Dem., 451,513; Hallinan, Prog., 5,085; Hamblen, Proh., 2,882; Hoopes, Soc., 219; Hass, Soc. Labor, 139; scattering 29.

1956, Eisenhower, Rep., 729,187; Stevenson, Dem., 501,858; Andrews (A.C.P. of Iowa), 3,202; Hoopes, Soc., 192; Hass, Soc. Labor, 125.

1960, Kennedy, Dem., 550,565; Nixon, Rep., 722,381; Hass, Soc. Labor, 230; write-in, 634.

1964, Johnson, Dem., 733,030; Goldwater, Rep., 449,148; Hass, Soc. Labor, 182; DeBerry, Soc. Worker, 159; Munn, Proh., 1,902.

1968, Nixon, Rep., 619,106; Humphrey, Dem., 476,699; Wallace, 3d party, 66,422; Munn, Proh., 362; Halstead, Soc. Worker, 3,377; Cleaver, Peace and Freedom, 1,332; Blomen, Soc. Labor, 241.

1972, Nixon, Rep., 706,207; McGovern, Dem., 496,206; Schmitz, Amer., 22,056; Jenness, Soc. Workers, 488; Fisher, Soc. Labor, 195; Hall, Com. 272; Green, Universal, 199; scattered, 321.

1976, Carter, Dem., 619,931; Ford, Rep., 632,863; McCarthy, Ind., 20,051; Anderson, Amer., 3,040; MacBride, Libertarian, 1,452.

1980, Reagan, Rep., 676,026; Carter, Dem., 508,672; Anderson, Ind., 115,633; Clark, Libertarian, 13,123; Commoner, Citizens, 2,273; McReynolds, Socialist, 534; Hall Com., 298; DeBerry, Soc. Work., 244; Greaves, American, 189; Bubar, Statesman, 150; scattering, 519.

1984, Reagan, Rep., 703,088; Mondale, Dem., 605,620; Bergland, Libertarian, 1,844.

1988, Bush, Rep., 545,355; Dukakis, Dem., 670,557; LaRouche, Ind., 3,526; Paul, Lib., 2,494.

Kansas

County	1988 Dukakis (D)	1988 Bush (R)	1984 Mondale (D)	1984 Reagan (R)
Allen	2,392	3,429	1,779	4,266
Anderson	1,466	1,781	1,155	2,462
Atchison	3,177	3,243	2,641	4,536
Barber	1,118	1,539	805	2,111
Barton	5,024	7,741	3,111	10,234
Bourbon	2,623	3,660	2,174	4,856
Brown	1,719	3,059	1,303	3,894
Butler	7,690	10,976	6,352	12,920
Chase	538	884	393	1,162
Chautauqua	661	1,247	497	1,688
Cherokee	4,069	4,281	3,663	5,081
Cheyenne	594	1,105	356	1,442
Clark	409	876	324	1,075
Clay	1,112	2,997	919	3,559
Cloud	2,022	3,043	1,878	3,856
Coffey	1,246	2,581	1,037	3,063
Comanche	375	738	285	993
Cowley	6,186	7,778	5,153	9,930
Crawford	7,783	6,940	6,722	9,518
Decatur	793	1,291	467	1,769
Dickinson	2,870	5,121	2,168	6,487
Doniphan	1,312	2,162	962	2,818
Douglas	15,752	16,149	12,877	18,804
Edwards	792	993	606	1,352
Elk	608	1,075	452	1,301
Ellis	5,289	5,194	3,457	7,509
Ellsworth	1,219	1,711	905	2,353
Finney	3,408	5,381	2,398	6,943
Ford	3,817	5,685	2,914	6,738
Franklin	3,592	4,777	2,524	6,283
Geary	2,721	3,782	2,301	4,475
Gove	663	966	426	1,310
Graham	702	1,139	480	1,423
Grant	907	1,654	615	2,043
Gray	696	1,180	514	1,580
Greeley	317	506	227	699
Greenwood	1,421	2,217	1,173	2,900
Hamilton	517	801	408	1,037
Harper	1,235	1,941	893	2,696
Harvey	5,503	6,893	4,599	8,507
Haskell	427	964	281	1,151
Hodgeman	439	732	306	939
Jackson	2,261	2,759	1,667	3,464
Jefferson	2,810	3,605	1,990	4,524
Jewell	684	1,546	583	1,992
Johnson	55,183	95,591	37,782	101,042

Kearny	524	1,073	321	1,214
Kingman	1,420	2,205	1,047	2,826
Kiowa	485	1,276	361	1,537
Labette	4,433	5,125	3,631	6,542
Lane	450	768	282	1,008
Leavenworth	8,797	9,913	6,583	11,018
Lincoln	796	1,229	551	1,723
Linn	1,497	2,163	1,152	2,794
Logan	503	988	331	1,235
Lyon	5,314	6,820	4,188	9,796
McPherson	4,354	6,563	3,185	8,630
Marion	2,024	3,685	1,633	4,407
Marshall	2,560	3,140	1,813	4,097
Meade	664	1,322	491	1,804
Miami	4,427	4,807	3,076	5,877
Mitchell	1,145	2,257	919	3,036
Montgomery	5,429	9,067	4,933	12,023
Morris	1,165	1,682	820	2,240
Morton	569	1,074	322	1,353
Nemaha	2,261	2,849	1,761	3,653
Neosho	3,402	3,739	2,679	4,968
Ness	887	1,230	539	1,779
Norton	855	1,923	611	2,515
Osage	2,840	3,496	2,072	4,288
Osborne	943	1,541	686	2,171
Ottawa	953	1,836	698	2,343
Pawnee	1,474	1,825	1,092	2,570
Phillips	960	2,316	626	2,810
Pottawatomie	2,544	3,897	1,798	4,596
Pratt	1,651	2,505	1,253	3,240
Rawlins	612	1,318	412	1,625
Reno	11,545	12,753	9,229	16,621
Republic	1,069	2,346	966	2,974
Rice	2,033	2,503	1,559	3,598
Riley	7,283	9,507	5,974	11,306
Rooks	1,012	1,938	699	2,604
Rush	1,020	1,045	718	1,758
Russell	1,448	2,403	1,055	3,673
Saline	7,998	11,371	6,527	15,242
Scott	717	1,590	427	2,017
Sedgwick	65,618	86,124	55,060	95,972
Seward	1,655	4,089	1,198	5,047
Shawnee	33,940	35,489	26,307	43,435
Sheridan	600	901	429	1,274
Sherman	1,082	1,929	714	2,702
Smith	1,004	1,951	684	2,330
Stafford	1,121	1,532	844	2,062
Stanton	310	592	205	783
Stevens	612	1,642	386	1,862
Summer	4,417	5,394	3,713	6,942
Thomas	1,408	2,342	887	3,106
Trego	795	979	598	1,491
Wabaunsee	1,166	1,737	805	2,276
Wallace	257	655	152	838
Washington	1,063	2,269	889	2,979
Wichita	399	721	232	916
Wilson	1,545	2,743	1,343	3,660
Woodson	761	1,062	596	1,408
Wyandotte	38,678	19,097	35,887	27,267
Totals	422,636	554,049	332,471	674,646

Kansas Vote Since 1940

1940, Roosevelt, Dem., 364,725; Willkie, Rep., 489,169; Babson, Proh., 4,056; Thomas, Soc., 2,347.

1944, Roosevelt, Dem., 287,458; Dewey, Rep., 442,096; Watson, Proh., 2,609; Thomas, Soc., 1,613.

1948, Truman, Dem., 351,902; Dewey, Rep., 423,039; Watson, Proh., 6,468; Wallace, Prog., 4,603; Thomas, Soc., 2,807.

1952, Eisenhower, Rep., 616,302; Stevenson, Dem., 273,296; Hamblen, Proh., 6,038; Hoopes, Soc., 530.

1956, Eisenhower, Rep., 566,878; Stevenson, Dem., 296,317; Holtwick, Proh., 3,048.

1960, Kennedy, Dem., 363,213; Nixon, Rep., 561,474; Decker, Proh., 4,138.

1964, Johnson, Dem., 464,028; Goldwater, Rep., 386,579; Munn, Proh., 5,393; Hass, Soc. Labor, 1,901.

1968, Nixon, Rep., 478,674; Humphrey, Dem., 302,996; Wallace, 3d, 88,921; Munn, Proh., 2,192.

1972, Nixon, Rep., 619,812; McGovern, Dem., 270,287; Schmitz, Cons., 21,808; Munn, Proh., 4,188.

1976, Carter, Dem., 430,421; Ford, Rep., 502,752; McCarthy, Ind., 13,185; Anderson, Amer., 4,724; MacBride, Libertarian, 3,242; Maddox, Cons., 2,118; Bubar, Proh., 1,403.

1980, Reagan, Rep., 566,812; Carter, Dem., 326,150; Anderson, Ind., 68,231; Clark, Libertarian, 14,470; Shelton, American, 1,555; Hall, Com., 967; Bubar, Statesman, 821; Rarick, Conservative, 789.

1984, Reagan, Rep., 674,646; Mondale, Dem., 332,471; Bergland, Libertarian, 3,585.

1988, Bush, Rep., 554,049; Dukakis, Dem., 422,636; Paul, Ind., 12,553; Fulani, Ind., 3,806.

Kentucky

	1988		1984	
County	Dukakis (D)	Bush (R)	Mondale (D)	Reagan (R)
Adair	1,723	4,346	1,812	4,500
Allen	1,573	3,342	1,521	3,427
Anderson	2,176	3,225	1,717	3,425
Ballard	2,162	1,460	2,002	1,663
Barren	4,799	6,653	4,503	7,717
Bath	2,099	1,614	1,781	2,020
Bell	5,182	5,759	5,490	7,249
Boone	5,382	12,667	4,853	12,690
Bourbon	2,793	3,308	2,649	3,836
Boyd	9,552	9,379	9,601	10,925
Boyle	3,575	4,746	3,378	5,675
Bracken	1,176	1,630	1,136	1,812
Breathitt	3,387	2,149	3,435	2,855
Breckinridge	2,765	3,841	2,669	4,432
Bullitt	6,005	8,859	5,005	9,556
Butler	1,245	3,278	1,055	3,121
Caldwell	2,564	2,952	2,427	3,162
Calloway	5,287	6,225	5,028	6,442
Campbell	9,553	19,387	9,068	21,473
Carlisle	1,428	1,104	1,277	1,308
Carroll	1,913	1,702	1,564	1,824
Carter	4,570	4,325	3,985	4,656
Casey	1,216	3,857	1,122	4,356
Christian	5,704	9,250	5,432	10,708
Clark	4,252	5,329	3,595	6,130
Clay	1,709	4,156	1,634	4,772
Clinton	899	3,248	838	3,459
Crittenden	1,443	2,211	1,483	2,167
Cumberland	753	2,231	766	2,729
Daviess	14,815	17,356	13,347	19,495
Edmonson	1,243	2,555	1,200	3,001
Elliott	1,797	550	1,683	601
Estill	1,692	3,077	1,593	3,512
Fayette	32,554	48,065	28,961	51,993
Fleming	2,086	2,409	1,616	2,824
Floyd	12,327	5,296	10,259	5,218
Franklin	9,271	9,805	7,790	11,057
Fulton	1,531	1,474	1,534	1,780
Gallatin	1,060	881	1,042	1,042
Garrard	1,710	2,661	1,566	3,284
Grant	1,896	2,835	1,685	2,840
Graves	7,153	6,274	6,759	7,287
Grayson	2,575	5,186	2,200	5,524
Green	1,595	3,139	1,611	3,210
Greenup	6,956	6,559	6,923	7,451
Hancock	1,478	1,733	1,287	1,967
Hardin	7,262	13,240	6,329	14,293
Harlan	7,341	5,166	7,663	6,959
Harrison	2,748	2,983	2,405	3,467
Hart	2,519	2,927	2,278	3,065
Henderson	7,648	6,911	6,795	7,389
Henry	2,544	2,286	2,279	2,802
Hickman	1,158	1,142	1,049	1,380
Hopkins	7,453	7,979	6,743	9,368
Jackson	678	3,926	542	3,806
Jefferson	127,936	139,711	119,350	161,283
Jessamine	2,955	7,057	2,379	7,081
Johnson	3,538	4,619	3,078	5,225
Kenton	14,838	30,738	14,642	34,304
Knott	5,185	1,691	4,487	1,728
Knox	2,919	4,903	2,932	5,730
Larue	1,822	2,590	1,514	2,873
Laurel	3,620	9,296	3,267	9,621
Lawrence	2,198	2,294	2,223	2,713
Lee	984	1,588	768	1,862
Leslie	1,105	3,280	1,075	3,385
Letcher	4,697	3,601	4,153	3,676
Lewis	1,568	3,108	1,484	3,445
Lincoln	2,677	3,530	2,498	3,996
Livingston	2,052	1,834	2,007	1,866
Logan	3,379	4,295	3,347	4,889
Lyon	1,337	1,077	1,272	969
McCracken	12,208	12,160	12,535	12,903
McCreary	1,644	3,477	1,609	4,028
McLean	2,269	1,829	1,917	1,942
Madison	6,672	9,958	6,509	11,309
Magoffin	2,895	2,158	2,942	2,343
Marion	3,152	2,500	2,835	3,305
Marshall	5,888	5,256	5,725	5,152
Martin	1,581	2,587	1,471	3,248
Mason	2,721	3,158	2,663	2,751
Meade	3,079	3,441	2,503	3,820
Menifee	1,096	670	956	785
Mercer	2,832	3,904	2,516	4,592
Metcalfe	1,705	2,179	1,575	2,349
Monroe	1,025	4,214	1,052	4,670
Montgomery	3,082	3,435	2,490	3,864
Morgan	2,329	1,452	2,481	1,834
Muhlenberg	6,912	5,369	6,157	6,094
Nelson	4,788	5,283	4,199	6,044
Nicholas	1,242	1,271	1,107	1,535
Ohio	3,612	4,910	3,253	5,119
Oldham	4,025	8,716	2,857	8,112
Owen	1,823	1,468	1,575	1,735
Owsley	345	1,266	375	1,466
Pendleton	1,576	2,487	1,529	2,767
Perry	5,557	5,154	5,258	5,218
Pike	16,339	9,976	15,817	11,869
Powell	2,113	2,128	1,575	2,269
Pulaski	4,788	13,482	4,384	14,434
Robertson	515	511	467	567
Rockcastle	1,041	3,880	1,089	4,328
Rowan	2,968	3,093	2,748	3,698
Russell	1,455	4,292	1,448	4,476
Scott	3,380	4,482	2,606	4,461
Shelby	3,834	4,998	3,326	5,390
Simpson	2,138	2,699	2,140	3,073
Spencer	1,121	1,368	910	1,456
Taylor	2,879	5,362	3,286	5,932
Todd	1,632	2,262	1,505	2,364
Trigg	1,991	2,427	1,905	2,512
Trimble	1,342	1,083	1,088	1,389
Union	3,316	2,292	3,090	2,524
Warren	9,684	16,703	7,937	16,167
Washington	1,950	2,445	1,786	2,804
Wayne	2,057	3,672	2,277	4,449
Webster	3,019	2,159	3,042	2,504
Whitley	3,794	7,337	3,575	7,851
Wolfe	1,516	916	1,394	1,257
Woodford	2,653	4,512	2,290	4,746
Totals	580,368	734,281	536,756	815,345

Kentucky Vote Since 1940

1940, Roosevelt, Dem., 557,222; Willkie, Rep., 410,384; Babson, Proh., 1,443; Thomas, Soc., 1,014.

1944, Roosevelt, Dem., 472,589; Dewey, Rep., 392,448; Watson, Proh., 2,023; Thomas, Soc., 535; Teichert, Soc. Labor, 326.

1948, Truman, Dem., 466,756; Dewey, Rep., 341,210; Thurmond, States' Rights, 10,411; Wallace, Prog., 1,567; Thomas, Soc., 1,284; Watson, Proh., 1,245; Teichert, Soc. Labor, 185.

1952, Eisenhower, Rep., 495,029; Stevenson, Dem., 495,729; Hamblen, Proh., 1,161; Hass, Soc. Labor, 893; Hallinan, Proh., 336.

1956, Eisenhower, Rep., 572,192; Stevenson, Dem., 476,453; Byrd, States' Rights, 2,657; Holtwick, Proh., 2,145; Hass, Soc. Labor, 358.

1960, Kennedy, Dem., 521,855; Nixon, Rep., 602,607.

1964, Johnson, Dem., 669,659; Goldwater, Rep., 372,977; John Kasper, Nat'l. States Rights, 3,469.

1968, Nixon, Rep., 462,411; Humphrey, Dem., 397,547; Wallace, 3d p., 193,098; Halstead, Soc. Worker, 2,843.

1972, Nixon, Rep., 676,446; McGovern, Dem., 371,159; Schmitz, Amer., 17,627; Jenness, Soc. Workers, 685; Hall, Com., 464; Spock, Peoples, 1,118.

1976, Carter, Dem., 615,717; Ford, Rep., 531,852; Anderson, Amer., 8,308; McCarthy, Ind., 6,837; Maddox, Amer. Ind., 2,328; MacBride, Libertarian, 814.

1980, Reagan, Rep., 635,274; Carter, Dem., 616,417; Anderson, Ind., 31,127; Clark, Libertarian, 5,531; McCormack, Respect For Life, 4,233; Commoner, Citizens, 1,304; Pulley, Socialist, 393; Hall, Com., 348.

1984, Reagan, Rep., 815,345; Mondale, Dem., 536,756.

1988, Bush, Rep., 734,281; Dukakis, Dem., 580,368; Duke, Pop., 4,494; Paul, Lib., 2,118.

Louisiana

	1988		1984	
Parish	Dukakis (D)	Bush (R)	Mondale (D)	Reagan (R)
Acadia	11,510	11,319	9,262	14,906
Allen	5,204	3,674	4,842	4,474
Ascension	12,147	10,726	11,048	11,945
Assumption	5,610	4,017	4,660	5,433
Avoyelles	7,353	7,659	6,808	9,402
Beauregard	4,704	6,466	4,199	7,353
Bienville	3,705	3,680	3,530	4,587
Bossier	9,035	20,807	7,006	22,638
Caddo	39,204	54,498	35,727	63,429
Calcasieu	33,932	29,649	33,214	35,566
Caldwell	1,423	2,997	1,348	3,341
Cameron	2,257	1,775	1,608	2,265
Catahoula	1,916	2,862	1,649	3,640
Claiborne	3,158	3,756	2,788	4,349
Concordia	3,461	5,037	3,332	6,177
DeSoto	5,366	5,022	4,642	5,989
E. Baton Rouge	59,270	86,791	56,673	95,704
East Carroll	1,809	1,536	2,089	1,974
East Feliciana	3,659	3,527	4,122	4,166
Evangeline	7,693	7,437	6,981	8,680
Franklin	3,043	5,520	2,937	6,708

Grant	2,628	4,402	2,588	5,334
Iberia	12,166	15,438	10,170	17,727
Iberville	8,678	5,855	8,587	6,455
Jackson	2,842	4,251	2,568	5,034
Jefferson	53,035	110,942	41,183	123,997
Jefferson Davis	6,799	5,851	5,962	8,296
Lafayette	24,133	36,648	19,265	44,344
Lafourche	15,013	16,152	10,186	20,930
LaSalle	1,622	4,559	1,318	5,404
Lincoln	5,427	8,853	5,432	9,087
Livingston	9,659	15,779	8,913	17,465
Madison	2,416	2,334	2,906	2,849
Morehouse	4,496	7,335	4,829	8,585
Natchitoches	6,151	7,224	5,806	8,836
Orleans	116,851	64,763	119,478	86,316
Ouachita	15,429	33,858	15,525	37,270
Plaquemines	3,997	6,084	3,261	7,655
Pointe Coupee	6,308	4,333	6,732	5,477
Rapides	17,928	29,977	16,121	32,879
Red River	2,254	2,266	1,958	3,060
Richland	2,833	5,226	2,918	5,980
Sabine	3,532	4,767	2,980	6,295
St. Bernard	11,406	19,609	8,076	24,428
St. Charles	7,973	9,685	6,784	10,185
St. Helena	3,013	2,006	2,956	2,366
St. James	6,707	3,799	5,989	4,627
St. John The Baptist	8,366	7,464	7,646	9,093
St. Landry	19,091	15,790	17,950	19,055
St. Martin	10,148	7,541	8,589	9,698
St. Mary	10,364	11,540	9,411	15,275
St. Tammany	15,638	38,334	11,719	38,664
Tangipahoa	13,527	16,669	12,799	19,580
Tensas	1,556	1,645	1,628	1,956
Terrebonne	12,686	18,745	9,640	23,696
Union	3,210	5,900	2,916	6,585
Vermilion	12,180	9,224	9,033	12,721
Vernon	4,998	7,453	4,076	9,035
Washington	8,369	9,374	7,680	11,185
Webster	7,434	10,204	6,509	12,055
W. Baton Rouge	4,686	3,972	4,631	4,189
West Carroll	1,607	3,077	1,474	3,874
West Feliciana	2,146	1,854	2,296	2,097
Winn	2,699	4,165	2,633	4,934
Totals	717,460	883,702	651,586	1,037,299

Louisiana Vote Since 1940

1940, Roosevelt, Dem., 319,751; Willkie, Rep., 52,446.

1944, Roosevelt, Dem., 281,564; Dewey, Rep., 67,750.

1948, Thurmond, States' Rights, 204,290; Truman, Dem., 136,344; Dewey, Rep., 72,657; Wallace, Prog., 3,035.

1952, Eisenhower, Rep., 306,925, Stevenson, Dem., 345,027.

1956, Eisenhower, Rep., 329,047; Stevenson, Dem., 243,977; Andrews, States' Rights, 44,520.

1960, Kennedy, Dem., 407,339; Nixon, Rep., 230,890; States' Rights (unpledged) 169,572.

1964, Johnson, Dem., 387,068; Goldwater, Rep., 509,225.

1968, Nixon, Rep., 257,535; Humphrey, Dem., 309,615; Wallace, 3d party, 530,300.

1972, Nixon, Rep., 686,852; McGovern, Dem., 298,142; Schmitz, Amer., 52,099; Jenness, Soc. Workers, 14,398.

1976, Carter, Dem., 661,365; Ford, Rep., 587,446; Maddox, Amer., 10,058; Hall, Com., 7,417; McCarthy, Ind., 6,588; MacBride, Libertarian, 3,325.

1980, Reagan, Rep., 792,853; Carter, Dem., 708,453; Anderson, Ind., 26,345; Rarick, Amer. Ind., 10,333; Clark, Libertarian, 8,240; Commoner, Citizens, 1,584; DeBerry, Soc. Work., 783.

1984, Reagan, Rep., 1,037,299; Mondale, Dem., 651,586; Bergland, Libertarian, 1,876.

1988, Bush, Rep., 883,702; Dukakis, Dem., 717,460; Duke, Pop., 18,612; Paul, Lib., 4,115.

Maine

City	1988 Dukakis (D)	Bush (R)	1984 Mondale (D)	Reagan (R)
Auburn	4,629	5,947	4,430	6,994
Augusta	4,576	5,182	4,451	5,995
Bangor	6,534	7,194	6,155	8,389
Bath	1,838	2,543	1,714	2,899
Biddeford	5,017	4,375	5,489	4,147
Brewer	1,784	2,908	1,461	3,093
Gardiner	1,395	1,609	1,216	1,942
Lewiston	9,225	7,265	9,853	9,480
Old Town	2,220	1,640	2,217	2,087
Portland	18,234	11,676	17,543	13,315
Rockland	1,198	1,850	1,051	2,169
Saco	3,159	3,852	3,094	3,761
Sanford	3,456	4,541	3,517	4,578
South Portland	5,820	5,744	5,377	6,653
Waterville	4,031	3,158	4,075	3,873

Westbrook	3,648	4,086	3,345	4,456
Totals	243,569	307,131	214,515	336,500

Maine Vote Since 1940

1940, Roosevelt, Dem., 156,478; Willkie, Rep., 165,951; Browder, Com., 411.

1944, Roosevelt, Dem., 140,631; Dewey, Rep., 155,434; Teichert, Soc. Labor, 335.

1948, Truman, Dem., 111,916; Dewey, Rep., 150,234; Wallace, Prog., 1,884; Thomas, Soc., 547; Teichert, Soc. Labor, 206.

1952, Eisenhower, Rep., 232,353; Stevenson, Dem., 118,806; Hallinan, Prog., 332; Hass, Soc. Labor, 156; Hoopes, Soc., 138; scattered, 1.

1956, Eisenhower, Rep., 249,238; Stevenson, Dem., 102,468.

1960, Kennedy, Dem., 181,159; Nixon, Rep., 240,608.

1964, Johnson, Dem., 262,264; Goldwater, Rep., 118,701.

1968, Nixon, Rep., 169,254; Humphrey, Dem., 217,312; Wallace, 3d party, 6,370.

1972, Nixon, Rep., 256,458; McGovern, Dem., 160,584; scattered, 229.

1976, Carter, Dem., 232,279; Ford, Rep., 236,320; McCarthy, Ind., 10,874; Bubar, Proh., 3,495.

1980, Reagan, Rep., 238,522; Carter, Dem., 220,974; Anderson, Ind., 53,327; Clark, Libertarian, 5,119; Commoner, Citizens, 4,394; Hall, Com., 591; write-ins, 84.

1984, Reagan, Rep., 336,500; Mondale, Dem., 214,515.

1988, Bush, Rep., 307,131; Dukakis, Dem., 243,569; Paul, Lib., 2,700; Fulani, New Alliance, 1,405.

Maryland

County	1988 Dukakis (D)	Bush (R)	1984 Mondale (D)	Reagan (R)
Allegany	11,844	17,462	11,143	19,763
Anne Arundel	55,440	98,540	47,565	94,171
Baltimore	121,570	163,881	106,908	171,929
Calvert	6,376	10,956	5,455	8,303
Caroline	2,440	4,661	2,198	4,876
Carroll	12,368	31,224	8,898	27,230
Cecil	7,807	13,224	6,681	13,111
Charles	11,823	20,828	10,264	16,132
Dorchester	3,709	6,343	3,160	6,699
Frederick	17,061	32,575	13,411	29,606
Garrett	2,557	6,665	2,386	7,042
Harford	19,803	38,493	17,133	37,382
Howard	34,007	44,153	25,713	35,641
Kent	2,925	3,761	2,390	3,897
Montgomery	165,187	154,191	146,036	146,924
Prince George's	133,816	86,545	136,063	95,121
Queen Anne's	3,857	7,803	2,938	6,784
St. Mary's	7,434	12,767	6,420	11,201
Somerset	2,911	4,222	2,439	4,508
Talbot	3,948	8,170	3,198	8,028
Washington	14,408	25,912	13,329	27,118
Wicomico	9,413	16,272	8,160	16,124
Worcester	4,787	8,430	3,770	8,208
Totals	826,304	876,167	787,935	879,918

Maryland Vote Since 1940

1940, Roosevelt, Dem., 384,546; Willkie, Rep., 269,534; Thomas, Soc., 4,093; Browder, Com., 1,274; Aiken, Soc. Labor, 657.

1944, Roosevelt, Dem., 315,490; Dewey, Rep., 292,949.

1948, Truman, Dem., 286,521; Dewey, Rep., 294,814; Wallace, Prog., 9,983; Thomas, Soc., 2,941; Thurmond, States' Rights, 2,476; Wright, write-in, 2,294.

1952, Eisenhower, Rep., 499,424; Stevenson, Dem., 395,337; Hallinan, Prog., 7,313.

1956, Eisenhower, Rep., 559,738; Stevenson, Dem., 372,613.

1960, Kennedy, Dem., 565,800; Nixon, Rep., 489,538.

1964, Johnson, Dem., 730,912; Goldwater, Rep., 385,495; write-in, 50.

1968, Nixon, Rep., 517,995; Humphrey, Dem., 538,310; Wallace, 3d party, 178,734.

1972, Nixon, Rep., 829,305; McGovern, Dem., 505,781; Schmitz, Amer., 18,726.

1976, Carter, Dem., 759,612; Ford, Rep., 672,661.

1980, Reagan, Rep., 680,606; Carter, Dem., 726,161; Anderson, Ind., 119,537; Clark, Libertarian, 14,192.

1984, Reagan, Rep., 879,918; Mondale, Dem., 787,935; Bergland, Libertarian, 5,721.

1988, Bush, Rep., 876,167; Dukakis, Dem., 826,304; Paul, Lib., 6,748; Fulani, Alliance, 5,115.

Massachusetts

City	Dukakis (D) 1988	Bush (R) 1988	Mondale (D) 1984	Reagan (R) 1984
Boston	122,349	62,202	131,745	75,311
Brockton	14,776	16,056	14,130	17,161
Cambridge	32,027	8,770	32,582	10,007
Fall River	20,184	8,394	20,722	11,463
Framingham	15,826	12,745	14,368	15,074
Lawrence	9,255	8,265	10,986	9,877
Lowell	16,391	13,998	15,042	16,834
Lynn	18,540	12,182	17,103	14,445
New Bedford	22,609	9,901	22,070	13,147
Newton	29,039	13,892	27,343	16,184
Quincy	20,911	18,403	18,971	20,123
Somerville	21,612	8,931	21,065	11,318
Springfield	30,113	16,244	29,376	21,431
Worcester	34,369	24,355	32,525	27,348
Totals	1,401,415	1,194,635	1,239,606	1,310,936

Massachusetts Vote Since 1940

1940, Roosevelt, Dem., 1,076,522; Willkie, Rep., 939,700; Thomas, Soc., 4,091; Browder, Com., 3,806; Aiken, Soc. Labor, 1,492; Babson, Proh., 1,370.

1944, Roosevelt, Dem., 1,035,296; Dewey, Rep., 921,350; Teichert, Soc. Labor, 2,780; Watson, Proh., 973.

1948, Truman, Dem., 1,151,788; Dewey, Rep., 909,370; Wallace, Prog., 38,157; Teichert, Soc. Labor, 5,535; Watson, Proh., 1,663.

1952, Eisenhower, Rep., 1,292,325; Stevenson, Dem., 1,083,525; Hallinan, Prog., 4,636; Hass, Soc. Labor, 1,957; Hamblen, Proh., 886; scattered, 69; blanks, 41,150.

1956, Eisenhower, Rep., 1,393,197; Stevenson, Dem., 948,190; Hass, Soc. Labor, 5,573; Holtwick, Proh., 1,205; others, 341.

1960, Kennedy, Dem., 1,487,174; Nixon, Rep., 976,750; Hass, Soc. Labor, 3,892; Decker, Proh., 1,633; others, 31; blank and void, 26,024.

1964, Johnson, Dem., 1,786,422; Goldwater, Rep., 549,727; Hass, Soc. Labor, 4,755; Munn, Proh., 3,735; scattered, 159; blank, 48,104.

1968, Nixon, Rep., 766,844; Humphrey, Dem., 1,469,218; Wallace, 3d party, 87,088; Blomen, Soc. Labor, 6,180; Munn, Proh., 2,369; scattered, 53; blanks, 25,394.

1972, Nixon, Rep., 1,112,078; McGovern, Dem., 1,332,540; Jenness, Soc. Workers, 10,600; Fisher, Soc. Labor, 129; Schmitz, Amer., 2,877; Spock, Peoples, 101; Hall, Com., 46; Hospers, Libertarian, 43; scattered, 342.

1976, Carter, Dem., 1,429,475; Ford, Rep., 1,030,276; McCarthy, Ind., 65,637; Camejo, Soc. Workers, 8,138; Anderson, Amer., 7,555; La Rouche, U.S. Labor, 4,922; MacBride, Libertarian, 135.

1980, Reagan, Rep., 1,057,631; Carter, Dem., 1,053,802; Anderson, Ind., 382,539; Clark, Libertarian, 22,038; DeBerry, Soc. Workers, 3,735; Commoner, Citizens, 2,056; McReynolds, Socialist, 62; Bubar, Statesman, 34; Griswold, Workers World, 19; scattered, 2,382.

1984, Reagan, Rep., 1,310,936; Mondale, Dem., 1,239,606.

1988, Bush, Rep., 1,194,635; Dukakis, Dem., 1,401,415; Paul, Lib., 24,251; Fulani, New Alliance, 9,561.

Michigan

County	Dukakis (D) 1988	Bush (R) 1988	Mondale (D) 1984	Reagan (R) 1984
Alcona	1,918	2,966	1,616	3,223
Alger	2,210	1,830	2,018	2,175
Allegan	10,785	22,163	8,389	23,762
Alpena	6,341	6,664	5,136	8,212
Antrim	3,159	5,231	2,507	5,726
Arenac	3,211	3,064	2,436	3,483
Baraga	1,753	1,630	1,818	1,965
Barry	7,983	12,546	5,898	14,245
Bay	28,225	20,710	22,597	26,198
Benzie	2,437	3,240	1,866	3,590
Berrien	21,948	37,799	21,228	43,160
Branch	5,231	9,225	3,860	11,004
Calhoun	22,717	26,771	20,313	34,470
Cass	7,444	10,229	6,634	11,647
Charlevoix	3,875	5,802	3,175	6,355
Cheboygan	3,943	5,395	3,358	6,053
Chippewa	5,222	6,786	4,575	8,135
Clare	4,710	5,661	3,764	6,587
Clinton	9,225	15,497	6,226	17,387
Crawford	1,825	3,097	1,558	3,303
Delta	8,891	7,114	7,934	8,952
Dickinson	6,129	6,158	5,614	6,880
Eaton	15,322	24,193	10,290	27,720
Emmet	4,170	7,105	3,254	7,760
Genesee	104,880	70,922	89,491	92,943
Gladwin	4,164	4,746	3,368	5,401
Gogebic	5,151	3,509	5,554	4,006
Grand Traverse	10,098	17,191	7,271	18,036
Gratiot	5,719	8,447	4,000	10,456
Hillsdale	4,763	10,571	3,616	12,063
Houghton	6,510	7,098	6,434	8,652
Huron	5,714	9,419	3,966	11,073
Ingham	55,984	58,363	46,411	68,753
Ionia	8,160	12,028	5,735	14,162
Iosco	4,929	7,234	3,850	7,907
Iron	3,774	2,866	3,559	3,468
Isabella	7,960	10,362	6,435	12,215
Jackson	21,865	33,885	18,340	40,133
Kalamazoo	39,457	50,205	32,460	58,327
Kalkaska	2,092	3,369	1,595	3,623
Kent	73,467	131,910	66,238	137,417
Keweenaw	631	536	628	599
Lake	1,958	1,713	1,845	2,125
Lapeer	10,736	16,670	7,800	19,222
Leelanau	3,331	5,215	2,498	5,356
Lenawee	13,690	19,115	11,012	22,409
Livingston	13,749	31,331	10,720	31,846
Luce	864	1,528	833	1,715
Mackinac	2,093	3,127	1,949	3,627
Macomb	112,856	175,632	97,816	194,300
Manistee	4,765	5,368	3,917	6,328
Marquette	15,418	11,704	14,074	14,196
Mason	4,531	6,800	3,803	8,202
Mecosta	4,736	8,181	4,048	9,023
Menominee	4,918	5,440	4,425	6,618
Midland	13,452	19,994	10,769	21,521
Missaukee	1,621	3,566	1,256	3,970
Monroe	21,847	26,189	19,617	29,419
Montcalm	7,664	10,963	5,491	13,109
Montmorency	1,563	2,514	1,387	2,913
Muskegon	28,977	33,567	25,247	39,355
Newaygo	5,389	9,896	4,496	10,636
Oakland	174,745	283,359	150,286	306,050
Oceana	3,356	5,693	2,865	6,405
Ogemaw	4,012	4,091	3,132	4,901
Ontonagon	2,517	2,023	2,350	2,464
Osceola	2,860	5,218	2,127	5,923
Oscoda	1,170	1,972	951	2,239
Otsego	2,635	4,620	2,117	4,639
Ottawa	18,769	61,515	15,000	60,142
Presque Isle	3,025	3,614	2,481	4,207
Roscommon	4,394	5,866	3,359	6,419
Saginaw	45,616	42,401	38,420	51,495
St. Clair	20,909	32,336	16,998	36,114
St. Joseph	7,017	13,084	5,795	15,405
Sanilac	5,445	10,653	4,126	12,627
Schoolcraft	2,071	1,802	1,920	2,139
Shiawassee	13,056	15,506	9,514	18,756
Tuscola	9,060	12,093	6,212	14,698
Van Buren	10,668	14,522	8,853	16,426
Washtenaw	61,799	55,029	55,084	58,736
Wayne	450,222	291,996	496,632	367,391
Wexford	4,287	6,043	3,398	7,279
Totals	1,675,783	1,965,486	1,529,638	2,251,571

Michigan Vote Since 1940

1940, Roosevelt, Dem., 1,032,991; Willkie, Rep., 1,039,917; Thomas, Soc., 7,593; Browder, Com., 2,834; Babson, Proh., 1,795; Aiken, Soc. Labor, 795.

1944, Roosevelt, Dem., 1,106,899; Dewey, Rep., 1,084,423; Watson, Proh., 6,503; Thomas, Soc., 4,598; Smith, America First, 1,530; Teichert, Soc. Labor, 1,264.

1948, Truman, Dem., 1,003,448; Dewey, Rep., 1,038,595; Wallace, Prog., 46,515; Watson, Proh., 13,052; Thomas, Soc., 6,063; Teichert, Soc. Labor, 1,263; Dobbs, Soc. Workers, 672.

1952, Eisenhower, Rep., 1,551,529; Stevenson, Dem., 1,230,657; Hamblen, Proh., 10,331; Hallinan, Prog., 3,922; Hass, Soc. Labor, 1,495; Dobbs, Soc. Workers, 655; scattered, 3.

1956, Eisenhower, Rep., 1,713,647; Stevenson, Dem., 1,359,898; Holtwick, Proh., 6,923.

1960, Kennedy, Dem., 1,687,269; Nixon, Rep., 1,620,428; Dobbs, Soc. Workers, 4,347; Decker, Proh., 2,029; Daly, Tax Cut, 1,767; Hass, Soc. Labor, 1,718; Ind. American, 539.

1964, Johnson, Dem., 2,136,615; Goldwater, Rep., 1,060,152; DeBerry, Soc. Workers, 3,817; Hass, Soc. Labor, 1,704; Proh. (no candidate listed), 699, scattering, 145.

1968, Nixon, Rep., 1,370,665; Humphrey, Dem., 1,593,082; Wallace, 3d party, 331,968; Halstead, Soc. Worker, 4,099; Blomen, Soc. Labor, 1,762; Cleaver, New Politics, 4,585; Munn, Proh., 60; scattering, 29.

1972, Nixon, Rep., 1,961,721; McGovern, Dem., 1,459,435; Schmitz, Amer., 63,321; Fisher, Soc. Labor, 2,437; Jenness, Soc. Workers, 1,603; Hall, Com., 1,210.

1976, Carter, Dem., 1,696,714; Ford, Rep., 1,893,742; McCarthy, Ind., 47,905; MacBride, Libertarian, 5,406; Wright, People's, 3,504, Camejo, Soc. Workers, 1,804; LaRouche, U.S. Labor, 1,366; Levin, Soc. Labor, 1,148; scattering, 2,160.

1980, Reagan, Rep., 1,915,225; Carter, Dem., 1,661,532; Anderson, Ind., 275,223; Clark, Libertarian, 41,597; Commoner, Citizens, 11,930; Hall, Com., 3,262; Griswold, Workers World, 30; Greaves, American, 21; Bubar, Statesman, 9.

1984, Reagan, Rep., 2,251,571; Mondale, Dem., 1,529,638; Bergland, Libertarian, 10,055.

1988, Bush, Rep., 1,965,486; Dukakis, Dem., 1,675,783; Paul, Lib., 18,336; Fulani, Ind., 2,513.

Minnesota

County	1988 Dukakis (D)	Bush (R)	1984 Mondale (D)	Reagan (R)
Aitkin	3,863	3,011	3,943	3,422
Anoka	57,953	46,853	50,305	46,578
Becker	5,787	6,738	5,456	7,553
Beltrami	7,566	6,652	7,481	7,414
Benton	5,861	6,060	4,922	6,830
Big Stone	2,026	1,469	1,994	1,821
Blue Earth	12,375	11,959	11,877	14,298
Brown	5,109	6,898	4,469	8,399
Carlton	8,790	4,626	9,189	4,877
Carver	8,439	12,560	6,725	11,963
Cass	5,127	5,895	4,773	6,619
Chippewa	3,238	3,190	3,047	3,964
Chisago	7,875	6,163	6,683	6,279
Clay	11,186	10,380	10,294	11,565
Clearwater	1,769	1,763	1,917	2,066
Cook	1,080	1,078	1,129	1,219
Cottonwood	3,095	3,390	3,073	4,275
Crow Wing	9,674	11,017	8,719	11,362
Dakota	61,942	61,606	49,125	55,119
Dodge	2,925	3,848	2,786	4,428
Douglas	5,803	7,898	5,444	9,005
Faribault	3,879	4,846	3,993	5,690
Fillmore	4,114	5,004	4,351	6,342
Freeborn	8,836	7,226	9,338	8,413
Goodhue	9,438	9,455	8,679	11,171
Grant	1,950	1,693	1,867	2,111
Hennepin	292,909	240,209	272,401	253,921
Houston	3,936	4,777	3,512	5,645
Hubbard	3,306	4,365	2,806	4,621
Isanti	6,075	5,246	5,378	5,660
Itasca	10,517	8,358	11,455	9,306
Jackson	3,275	2,629	3,437	3,131
Kanabec	2,970	2,571	2,660	3,027
Kandiyohi	8,962	8,634	8,402	9,539
Kittson	1,650	1,381	1,610	1,716
Koochiching	3,867	2,842	4,238	3,466
LacQuiParle	2,805	2,116	2,685	2,731
Lake	3,887	1,838	4,468	2,003
Lake O'Woods	798	984	824	1,094
Le Sueur	5,410	5,415	5,070	6,033
Lincoln	1,891	1,479	1,827	1,905
Lyon	5,657	5,969	5,389	7,170
McLeod	5,736	7,967	4,864	8,728
Mahnomen	1,277	1,051	1,241	1,328
Marshall	3,001	2,752	2,705	3,433
Martin	4,922	5,724	4,673	7,308
Meeker	4,544	4,999	4,156	5,511
Mille Lacs	4,327	3,862	4,011	4,307
Morrison	6,469	6,598	6,225	7,556
Mower	11,893	6,969	12,498	8,054
Murray	2,840	2,316	2,741	2,780
Nicollet	6,786	6,878	5,789	7,472
Nobles	4,953	4,348	4,619	4,876
Norman	2,149	1,789	2,202	2,152
Olmsted	19,423	27,683	16,335	28,129
Otter Tail	10,373	14,015	9,714	15,664
Pennington	3,105	2,920	2,913	3,536
Pine	5,540	3,857	5,223	4,493
Pipestone	2,382	2,760	2,391	3,043
Polk	7,523	7,032	7,033	8,617
Pope	3,074	2,627	2,757	3,064
Ramsey	143,767	88,736	141,623	95,667
Red Lake	1,229	918	1,294	1,184
Redwood	3,178	5,076	2,957	6,020
Renville	4,454	4,356	3,972	5,571
Rice	11,570	9,460	10,880	10,456
Rock	2,435	2,737	2,188	2,971
Roseau	2,630	3,500	2,319	3,445
St. Louis	70,344	31,799	77,683	34,162
Scott	11,405	13,050	9,452	12,573
Sherburne	7,959	8,360	6,140	7,738
Sibley	3,154	3,655	2,761	4,638
Stearns	23,798	27,529	20,944	30,216
Steele	5,496	7,981	5,060	8,780
Stevens	2,721	2,679	2,451	3,251
Swift	3,579	2,156	3,531	2,893
Todd	5,023	5,633	4,657	6,585
Traverse	1,399	1,061	1,325	1,399
Wabasha	4,442	4,681	3,872	5,299
Wadena	2,484	3,733	2,454	4,306
Waseca	3,721	4,471	3,527	5,509
Washington	34,952	30,850	28,527	29,046
Watonwan	2,544	2,821	2,425	3,526
Wilkin	1,486	1,933	1,410	2,367
Winona	10,310	11,012	9,577	11,981
Wright	14,177	14,987	12,486	15,399
Yellow Med	3,282	2,925	3,018	3,819
Totals	1,109,471	962,337	1,036,364	1,032,603

Minnesota Vote Since 1940

1940, Roosevelt, Dem., 644,196; Willkie, Rep., 596,274; Thomas, Soc., 5,454; Browder, Com., 2,711; Aiken, Ind., 2,553.

1944, Roosevelt, Dem., 589,864; Dewey, Rep., 527,416; Thomas, Soc., 5,073; Teichert, Ind. Gov't., 3,176.

1948, Truman, Dem., 692,966; Dewey, Rep., 483,617; Wallace, Prog., 27,866; Thomas, Soc., 4,646; Teichert, Soc. Labor, 2,525; Dobbs, Soc. Workers, 606.

1952, Eisenhower, Rep., 763,211; Stevenson, Dem., 608,458; Hallinan, Prog., 2,666; Hass, Soc. Labor, 2,383; Hamblen, Proh., 2,147; Dobbs, Soc. Workers, 618.

1956, Eisenhower, Rep., 719,302; Stevenson, Dem., 617,525; Hass, Soc. Labor (Ind. Gov.), 2,080; Dobbs, Soc. Workers, 1,098.

1960, Kennedy, Dem., 779,933; Nixon, Rep., 757,915; Dobbs, Soc. Workers, 3,077; Industrial Gov., 962.

1964, Johnson, Dem., 991,117; Goldwater, Rep., 559,624; DeBerry, Soc. Workers, 1,177; Hass, Industrial Gov., 2,544.

1968, Nixon, Rep., 658,643; Humphrey, Dem., 857,738; Wallace, 3d party, 68,931; scattered, 2,443; Halstead, Soc. Worker, 808; Blomen, Ind. Gov't., 285; Mitchell, Com., 415; Cleaver, Peace, 935; McCarthy, write-in, 585; scattered, 170.

1972, Nixon, Rep., 898,269; McGovern, Dem., 802,346; Schmitz, Amer., 31,407; Spock, Peoples, 2,805; Fisher, Soc. Labor, 4,261; Jenness, Soc. Workers, 940; Hall, Com., 662; scattered, 962.

1976, Carter, Dem., 1,070,440; Ford, Rep., 819,395; McCarthy, Ind., 35,490; Anderson, Amer., 13,592; Camejo, Soc. Workers, 4,149; MacBride, Libertarian, 3,529; Hall, Com., 1,092.

1980, Reagan, Rep., 873,268; Carter, Dem., 954,173; Anderson, Ind., 174,997; Clark, Libertarian, 31,593; Commoner, Citizens, 8,406; Hall, Com., 1,117; DeBerry, Soc. Workers, 711; Griswold, Workers World, 698; McReynolds, Socialist, 536; write-ins, 281.

1984, Mondale, Dem., 1,036,364; Reagan, Rep., 1,032,603; Bergland, Libertarian, 2,996.

1988, Bush., 962,337; Dukakis, Dem., 1,109,471; McCarthy, Minn. Prog., 5,403; Paul, Lib., 5,109.

Mississippi

County	1988 Dukakis (D)	Bush (R)	1984 Mondale (D)	Reagan (R)
Adams	7,732	8,116	7,849	9,440
Alcorn	5,335	6,641	4,862	7,203
Amite	2,834	3,333	2,569	3,463
Attala	2,997	4,524	3,327	4,670
Benton	1,718	1,565	1,715	1,737
Bolivar	7,606	6,105	8,769	6,939
Calhoun	2,086	3,375	1,749	3,579
Carroll	1,560	2,628	1,462	2,823
Chickasaw	2,713	3,390	2,329	3,605
Choctaw	1,335	2,297	1,166	2,491
Claiborne	3,083	1,233	3,179	1,294
Clarke	2,576	4,522	2,262	4,551
Clay	3,849	3,645	4,046	4,112
Coahoma	6,139	4,939	6,839	5,759
Copiah	4,175	5,100	4,591	5,806
Covington	2,591	4,005	2,219	4,165
DeSoto	5,449	14,681	4,369	12,576
Forrest	6,953	14,249	6,786	15,719
Franklin	1,563	2,376	1,494	2,564
George	2,435	4,545	1,655	4,346
Greene	1,637	2,837	1,297	2,744
Grenada	3,683	5,352	3,325	5,181
Hancock	3,760	7,763	2,630	7,662
Harrison	14,439	32,892	12,495	33,995
Hinds	41,058	52,749	42,373	56,953

Holmes	5,350	2,737	5,641	3,102
Humphreys	2,644	2,018	2,596	2,309
Issaquena	511	424	501	512
Itawamba	3,143	4,535	2,674	4,587
Jackson	10,328	29,830	8,821	29,585
Jasper	3,184	3,368	3,104	3,727
Jefferson	2,693	702	3,049	856
Jefferson Davis	2,948	2,745	2,644	2,884
Jones	7,383	16,764	7,298	17,586
Kemper	2,069	2,128	2,089	2,354
Lafayette	3,967	5,841	3,646	6,006
Lamar	2,535	9,145	1,964	7,929
Lauderdale	7,967	18,302	7,534	18,807
Lawrence	2,517	3,682	2,274	3,970
Leake	2,787	4,168	2,845	4,663
Lee	6,604	13,767	6,208	13,312
Leflore	5,830	6,409	7,443	7,550
Lincoln	4,534	8,710	4,458	8,898
Lowndes	5,993	11,258	6,078	12,049
Madison	8,242	11,399	8,002	9,298
Marion	4,240	7,019	3,757	7,355
Marshall	6,982	4,668	5,845	4,389
Monroe	4,669	6,447	4,437	7,387
Montgomery	1,893	2,504	1,881	3,093
Neshoba	2,942	6,363	2,630	6,715
Newton	2,332	5,658	2,127	5,911
Noxubee	2,722	1,870	2,928	2,123
Oktibbeha	5,100	7,126	5,097	7,574
Panola	5,227	5,382	5,465	5,850
Pearl River	3,939	10,220	3,695	9,978
Perry	1,326	2,983	1,415	3,098
Pike	6,531	7,637	6,137	8,254
Pontotoc	2,772	4,939	2,434	5,182
Prentiss	3,429	4,348	2,897	4,821
Quitman	2,497	1,832	2,343	2,198
Rankin	6,201	22,937	5,874	22,393
Scott	2,939	5,522	3,274	5,763
Sharkey	1,609	1,277	1,723	1,487
Simpson	3,016	6,151	2,894	5,983
Smith	1,660	4,573	1,573	5,116
Stone	1,452	3,007	1,185	2,980
Sunflower	4,898	4,362	4,913	5,178
Tallahatchie	2,881	2,633	2,725	2,901
Tate	2,872	4,553	2,846	4,677
Tippah	2,958	4,593	2,566	4,706
Tishomingo	3,378	3,646	2,879	3,527
Tunica	1,510	896	1,621	1,109
Union	3,044	5,511	2,766	5,837
Walthall	2,354	3,103	2,219	3,305
Warren	7,437	12,507	8,054	12,959
Washington	10,222	10,229	10,617	12,454
Wayne	2,889	4,496	2,818	5,000
Webster	1,550	3,061	1,397	3,390
Wilkinson	2,678	1,528	2,627	1,722
Winston	3,851	5,317	3,543	5,192
Yalobusha	2,402	2,660	2,337	2,934
Yazoo	4,989	5,538	5,037	6,275
Totals	363,921	557,890	352,192	582,377

Mississippi Vote Since 1940

1940, Roosevelt, Dem., 168,252; Willkie, Ind. Rep., 4,550; Rep., 2,814; total, 7,364; Thomas, Soc., 103.

1944, Roosevelt, Dem., 158,515; Dewey, Rep., 3,742; Reg. Dem., 9,964; Ind. Rep., 7,859.

1948, Thurmond, States' Rights, 167,538; Truman, Dem., 19,384; Dewey, Rep., 5,043; Wallace, Prog., 225.

1952, Eisenhower, Ind. vote pledged to Rep. candidate, 112,966; Stevenson, Dem., 172,566.

1956, Stevenson, Dem., 144,498; Eisenhower, Rep., 56,372; Black and Tan Grand Old Party, 4,313; total, 60,685; Byrd, Ind., 42,966.

1960, Democratic unpledged electors, 116,248; Kennedy, Dem., 108,362; Nixon, Rep., 73,561. Mississippi's victorious slate of 8 unpledged Democratic electors cast their votes for Sen. Harry F. Byrd (D-Va.).

1964, Johnson, Dem., 52,618; Goldwater, Rep., 356,528.

1968, Nixon, Rep., 88,516; Humphrey, Dem., 150,644; Wallace, 3d party, 415,349.

1972, Nixon, Rep., 505,125; McGovern, Dem., 126,782; Schmitz, Amer., 11,598; Jenness, Soc. Workers, 2,458.

1976, Carter, Dem., 381,309; Ford, Rep., 366,846; Anderson, Amer., 6,678; McCarthy, Ind., 4,074; Maddox, Ind., 4,049; Camejo, Soc. Workers, 2,805; MacBride, Libertarian, 2,609.

1980, Reagan, Rep., 441,089; Carter, Dem., 429,281; Anderson, Ind., 12,036; Clark, Libertarian, 5,465; Griswold, Workers World, 2,402; Pulley, Soc. Worker, 2,347.

1984, Reagan, Rep., 582,377; Mondale, Dem., 352,192; Bergland, Libertarian, 2,336.

1988, Bush, Rep., 557,890; Dukakis, Dem., 363,921; Duke, Ind., 4,232; Paul, Lib., 3,329.

Missouri

	1988		1984	
County	Dukakis (D)	Bush (R)	Mondale (D)	Reagan (R)
Adair	3,571	5,721	3,119	6,430
Andrew	3,108	3,407	2,457	4,252
Atchison	1,468	1,761	1,219	2,277
Audrain	5,226	5,072	4,662	7,261
Barry	4,210	7,231	3,483	7,683
Barton	1,603	3,339	1,348	3,996
Bates	3,332	3,574	2,889	4,223
Benton	2,654	3,467	2,251	3,805
Bollinger	1,883	2,710	1,923	2,778
Boone	24,370	22,948	19,364	26,600
Buchanan	18,601	15,336	15,369	19,735
Butler	5,751	7,968	4,699	8,712
Caldwell	1,726	2,074	1,382	2,678
Callaway	5,209	6,687	4,327	8,262
Camden	3,930	7,773	3,088	8,057
Cape Girardeau	7,904	16,583	7,346	17,404
Carroll	2,330	2,811	1,980	3,495
Carter	1,087	1,429	916	1,402
Cass	10,092	12,799	7,517	14,456
Cedar	1,774	2,966	1,440	3,539
Chariton	2,347	2,193	2,244	2,744
Christian	4,724	7,670	3,223	7,634
Clark	1,925	1,493	1,627	2,068
Clay	29,620	30,293	22,586	36,529
Clinton	3,653	3,282	2,778	4,226
Cole	8,359	18,023	6,702	20,366
Cooper	2,510	3,737	2,219	4,603
Crawford	3,107	3,856	2,913	4,716
Dade	1,315	2,154	1,100	2,600
Dallas	2,293	2,859	1,902	3,577
Daviess	1,743	1,765	1,526	2,414
DeKalb	1,970	1,863	1,464	2,188
Dent	2,421	2,975	2,544	3,490
Douglas	1,735	3,225	1,536	3,662
Dunklin	5,281	5,026	4,967	6,092
Franklin	11,891	16,611	8,319	18,669
Gasconade	1,621	4,216	1,130	4,678
Gentry	1,872	1,554	1,600	2,047
Greene	35,475	52,211	27,965	57,250
Grundy	2,052	2,668	1,861	3,156
Harrison	1,776	2,271	1,649	2,844
Henry	4,135	4,167	3,741	5,419
Hickory	1,677	2,043	1,212	2,190
Holt	1,258	1,583	1,026	2,087
Howard	2,446	1,865	2,014	2,360
Howell	4,324	7,277	3,767	8,204
Iron	2,283	1,877	2,023	2,316
Jackson	147,964	107,810	135,067	132,271
Jasper	11,159	19,934	9,259	23,066
Jefferson	27,738	29,279	20,026	34,525
Johnson	5,373	7,512	4,238	8,413
Knox	1,255	1,212	1,097	1,513
Laclede	3,442	6,070	2,665	6,406
Lafayette	5,654	6,825	4,848	8,581
Lawrence	4,432	6,911	3,720	8,370
Lewis	2,460	1,803	1,977	2,438
Lincoln	4,605	5,305	3,290	6,137
Linn	3,150	3,061	3,112	3,822
Livingston	3,077	3,462	2,699	4,090
McDonald	2,299	3,812	2,109	4,521
Macon	3,215	3,406	3,037	4,542
Madison	2,167	2,528	1,862	2,808
Maries	1,552	1,919	1,388	2,267
Marion	5,617	5,034	4,666	6,831
Mercer	877	875	875	1,229
Miller	2,555	5,662	2,054	6,706
Mississippi	2,814	2,218	2,524	2,502
Moniteau	1,936	3,502	1,614	4,197
Monroe	2,461	1,542	1,992	2,163
Montgomery	2,064	2,714	1,668	3,261
Morgan	2,604	3,958	2,169	4,392
New Madrid	3,812	3,387	3,776	4,323
Newton	5,798	10,617	4,623	11,709
Nodaway	4,240	4,103	3,615	5,471
Oregon	2,042	1,717	2,026	1,979
Osage	1,771	3,885	1,343	4,381
Ozark	1,329	2,404	1,110	2,614
Pemiscot	3,288	3,066	3,293	3,733
Perry	2,136	3,836	1,837	4,493
Pettis	5,486	9,648	5,413	10,991
Phelps	5,867	8,329	5,074	9,012
Pike	3,816	3,271	3,313	3,933
Platte	11,225	11,838	7,668	12,859
Polk	3,419	5,030	2,819	5,467
Pulaski	3,446	4,642	2,865	5,330
Putnam	803	1,365	797	1,542
Ralls	2,499	1,494	2,011	2,067
Randolph	5,291	4,384	4,471	5,735
Ray	4,879	3,763	3,979	4,875
Reynolds	1,864	1,162	2,026	1,330
Ripley	1,961	2,647	1,883	2,927
St. Charles	29,286	50,005	17,617	47,784
St. Clair	1,864	2,312	1,655	2,667
St. Francois	8,158	7,923	7,137	9,792
Ste. Genevieve	3,612	2,532	2,723	3,245

St. Louis	216,534	262,784	173,144	307,684	Powell	1,174	1,574	1,066	1,877
Saline	5,039	4,625	4,281	6,042	Prairie	343	541	289	693
Schuyler	1,013	1,063	1,141	1,250	Ravalli	4,763	7,418	3,825	8,161
Scotland	1,117	1,248	1,075	1,485	Richland	1,824	2,628	1,362	3,847
Scott	5,914	8,013	5,569	8,727	Roosevelt	2,083	1,957	1,962	2,431
Shannon	1,796	1,696	1,580	1,779	Rosebud	1,869	1,822	1,920	2,413
Shelby	1,818	1,586	1,573	2,243	Sanders	1,959	2,152	1,654	2,467
Stoddard	4,701	5,822	4,294	6,701	Sheridan	1,354	1,381	1,087	1,774
Stone	2,889	5,080	2,119	5,706	Silver Bow	11,422	5,043	11,095	6,637
Sullivan	1,562	1,897	1,784	2,306	Stillwater	1,407	1,920	1,100	2,118
Taney	3,888	7,043	2,912	7,082	Sweet Grass	462	1,242	378	1,417
Texas	3,887	4,584	3,662	5,591	Teton	1,303	1,876	1,102	2,257
Vernon	3,402	4,149	2,984	5,181	Toole	1,070	1,505	789	1,949
Warren	2,935	4,452	1,964	5,150	Treasure	231	291	209	353
Washington	3,744	3,240	2,987	3,755	Valley	2,163	2,467	1,849	3,123
Wayne	2,456	2,648	2,363	2,867	Wheatland	443	667	407	753
Webster	3,890	5,123	2,982	5,529	Wibaux	258	358	216	423
Worth	732	677	734	921	Yellowstone	21,987	28,069	19,437	34,124
Wright	2,232	4,151	1,973	4,687	Totals	168,936	190,412	146,742	232,450
Totals	1,001,619	1,084,953	848,583	1,274,188					

Missouri Vote Since 1940

1940, Roosevelt, Dem., 958,476; Willkie, Rep., 871,009; Thomas, Soc., 2,226; Babson, Proh., 1,809; Aiken, Soc. Labor, 209.

1944, Roosevelt, Dem., 807,357; Dewey, Rep., 761,175; Thomas, Soc., 1,750; Watson, Proh., 1,175; Teichert, Soc. Labor, 221.

1948, Truman, Dem., 917,315; Dewey, Rep., 655,039; Wallace, Prog., 3,998; Thomas, Soc., 2,222.

1952, Eisenhower, Rep., 959,429; Stevenson, Dem., 929,830; Hallinan, Prog., 987; Hamblen, Proh., 885; MacArthur, Christian Nationalist, 302; America First, 233; Hoopes, Soc., 227; Hass, Soc. Labor, 169.

1956, Stevenson, Dem., 918,273; Eisenhower, Rep., 914,299.

1960, Kennedy, Dem., 972,201; Nixon, Rep., 962,221.

1964, Johnson, Dem., 1,164,344; Goldwater, Rep., 653,535.

1968, Nixon, Rep., 811,932; Humphrey, Dem., 791,444; Wallace, 3d party, 206,126.

1972, Nixon, Rep., 1,154,058; McGovern, Dem., 698,531.

1976, Carter, Dem., 999,163; Ford, Rep., 928,808; McCarthy, Ind., 24,329.

1980, Reagan, Rep., 1,074,181; Carter, Dem., 931,182; Anderson, Ind., 77,920; Clark, Libertarian, 14,422; DeBerry, Soc. Workers, 1,515; Commoner, Citizens, 573; write-ins, 31.

1984, Reagan, Rep., 1,274,188; Mondale, Dem., 848,583.

1988, Bush, Rep., 1,084,953; Dukakis, Dem., 1,001,619; Fulani, New Alliance, 6,656; Paul, write-in, 434.

Montana Vote Since 1940

1940, Roosevelt, Dem., 145,698; Willkie, Rep., 99,579; Thomas, Soc., 1,443; Babson, Proh., 664; Browder, Com., 489.

1944, Roosevelt, Dem., 112,556; Dewey, Rep., 93,163; Thomas, Soc., 1,296; Watson, Proh., 340.

1948, Truman, Dem., 119,071; Dewey, Rep., 96,770; Wallace, Prog.; 7,313; Thomas, Soc., 695; Watson, Proh., 429.

1952, Eisenhower, Rep., 157,394; Stevenson, Dem., 106,213; Hallinan, Prog., 723; Hamblen, Proh., 548; Hoopes, Soc., 159.

1956, Eisenhower, Rep., 154,933; Stevenson, Dem., 116,238.

1960, Kennedy, Dem., 134,891; Nixon, Rep., 141,841; Decker, Proh., 456; Dobbs, Soc. Workers, 391.

1964, Johnson, Dem., 164,246; Goldwater, Rep., 113,032; Kasper, Nat'l States Rights, 519; Munn, Proh., 499; DeBerry, Soc. Worker, 332.

1968, Nixon, Rep., 138,835; Humphrey, Dem., 114,117; Wallace, 3d party, 20,015; Halstead, Soc. Worker, 457; Munn, Proh., 510; Caton, New Reform, 470.

1972, Nixon, Rep., 183,976; McGovern, Dem., 120,197; Schmitz, Amer., 13,430.

1976, Carter, Dem., 149,259; Ford, Rep., 173,703; Anderson, Amer., 5,772.

1980, Reagan, Rep., 206,814; Carter, Dem., 118,032; Anderson, Ind., 29,281; Clark, Libertarian, 9,825.

1984, Reagan, Rep., 232,450; Mondale, Dem., 146,742; Bergland, Libertarian, 5,185.

1988, Bush, Rep., 190,412; Dukakis, Dem., 168,936; Paul, Lib., 5,047; Fulani, New Alliance, 1,279.

Montana

	1988		1984	
County	Dukakis (D)	Bush (R)	Mondale (D)	Reagan (R)
Beaverhead	1,274	2,668	942	3,044
Big Horn	2,233	1,711	2,681	2,390
Blaine	1,460	1,402	1,229	1,736
Broadwater	592	1,054	458	1,345
Carbon	2,039	2,360	1,657	2,877
Carter	242	686	194	823
Cascade	15,718	15,946	14,252	19,846
Chouteau	1,166	1,980	896	2,425
Custer	2,343	3,007	1,982	3,879
Daniels	571	802	473	984
Dawson	2,120	2,658	1,776	3,468
Deer Lodge	3,185	1,168	3,539	1,901
Fallon	612	1,002	569	1,237
Fergus	2,052	3,948	1,804	4,585
Flathead	10,202	14,461	8,310	17,012
Gallatin	9,527	13,214	8,163	15,643
Garfield	196	631	134	770
Glacier	2,151	1,728	2,167	2,228
Golden Valley	203	335	211	384
Granite	511	789	417	880
Hill	4,219	3,467	3,657	4,635
Jefferson	1,746	2,007	1,324	2,226
Judith Basin	590	902	483	1,050
Lake	4,109	4,883	3,473	5,754
Lewis & Clark	11,932	10,946	8,768	13,569
Liberty	418	771	323	895
Lincoln	3,601	3,500	2,959	4,090
Madison	878	2,045	708	2,308
McCone	567	814	459	1,015
Meagher	337	656	283	771
Mineral	789	616	718	943
Missoula	19,178	15,965	16,540	19,777
Musselshell	898	1,280	781	1,541
Park	2,526	3,823	2,387	4,115
Petroleum	91	204	86	258
Phillips	905	1,462	787	1,934
Pondera	1,245	1,795	1,039	2,239
Powder River	395	815	346	1,066

Nebraska

	1988		1984	
County	Dukakis (D)	Bush (R)	Mondale (D)	Reagan (R)
Adams	4,145	8,063	2,940	9,092
Antelope	933	2,626	697	3,222
Arthur	58	210	33	248
Banner	112	361	58	457
Blaine	72	338	48	363
Boone	976	2,160	690	2,508
Box Butte	2,466	3,253	1,471	4,011
Boyd	480	967	308	1,173
Brown	435	1,335	312	1,513
Buffalo	4,700	9,980	3,083	11,343
Burt	1,458	2,050	1,054	2,645
Butler	1,715	2,083	1,192	2,555
Cass	3,674	4,658	2,495	5,451
Cedar	1,759	2,462	1,201	3,298
Chase	597	1,446	367	1,687
Cherry	642	2,240	463	2,720
Cheyenne	1,333	2,862	857	3,159
Clay	1,097	2,352	811	2,919
Colfax	1,542	2,329	981	2,998
Cuming	1,238	3,201	779	3,931
Custer	1,496	4,202	1,090	4,749
Dakota	2,941	2,744	2,510	3,467
Dawes	1,122	2,618	864	3,325
Dawson	2,184	5,529	1,487	6,678
Deuel	302	769	198	961
Dixon	1,166	1,802	985	2,154
Dodge	6,116	8,412	4,259	10,167
Douglas	76,444	99,806	58,867	112,557
Dundy	333	828	225	992
Fillmore	1,433	1,952	1,009	2,474
Franklin	768	1,294	522	1,597
Frontier	384	1,057	258	1,351
Furnas	791	1,830	579	2,363
Gage	4,008	5,114	2,699	6,102
Garden	366	986	180	1,158

County	1988 Dukakis (D)	Bush (R)	1984 Mondale (D)	Reagan (R)
Garfield	234	803	196	899
Gosper	331	694	201	802
Grant	89	301	51	404
Greeley	670	763	485	948
Hall	6,822	12,020	4,615	13,082
Hamilton	1,289	3,019	840	3,417
Harlan	725	1,403	493	1,692
Hayes	160	512	100	591
Hitchcock	480	1,132	341	1,391
Holt	1,327	4,081	893	4,611
Hooker	91	378	55	433
Howard	1,186	1,526	887	1,899
Jefferson	1,819	2,470	1,366	3,114
Johnson	1,162	1,182	821	1,536
Kearney	1,056	2,120	726	2,505
Keith	1,067	2,879	631	3,423
Keya Paha	145	446	126	505
Kimball	540	1,321	339	1,732
Knox	1,477	2,644	1,149	3,364
Lancaster	44,260	44,605	32,780	48,627
Lincoln	6,070	8,395	4,483	10,692
Logan	93	373	66	445
Loup	97	295	79	323
McPherson	60	229	57	295
Madison	2,779	9,135	1,755	9,786
Merrick	1,192	2,376	818	2,696
Morrill	753	1,554	463	1,888
Nance	794	1,185	524	1,391
Nemaha	1,457	2,293	1,004	2,752
Nuckolls	1,114	1,750	947	2,132
Otoe	2,616	3,724	1,868	4,679
Pawnee	767	975	552	1,306
Perkins	467	1,117	307	1,418
Phelps	1,047	3,316	739	3,739
Pierce	914	2,474	545	3,016
Platte	3,285	9,029	2,057	10,035
Polk	944	1,768	610	2,149
Red Willow	1,505	3,325	1,022	4,101
Richardson	1,926	2,702	1,422	3,634
Rock	198	756	147	873
Saline	3,119	2,352	2,385	2,941
Sarpy	10,936	20,179	6,831	20,155
Saunders	3,524	4,454	2,467	5,217
Scotts Bluff	4,454	8,594	3,060	10,676
Seward	2,682	3,467	1,905	3,969
Sheridan	612	2,251	377	2,661
Sherman	839	914	701	1,144
Sioux	194	568	121	732
Stanton	637	1,709	410	2,080
Thayer	1,322	1,981	946	2,578
Thomas	81	383	73	298
Thurston	1,225	1,105	1,077	1,410
Valley	873	1,603	739	2,052
Washington	2,552	4,567	1,561	5,163
Wayne	1,111	2,473	833	3,075
Webster	891	1,314	645	1,694
Wheeler	141	309	97	365
York	1,748	4,744	1,114	5,012
Totals	259,235	397,956	187,475	459,135

Nebraska Vote Since 1940

1940, Roosevelt, Dem., 263,677; Willkie, Rep., 352,201.

1944, Roosevelt, Dem., 233,246; Dewey, Rep., 329,880.

1948, Truman, Dem., 224,165; Dewey, Rep., 264,774.

1952, Eisenhower, Rep., 421,603; Stevenson Dem., 188,057.

1956, Eisenhower, Rep., 378,108; Stevenson, Dem., 199,029.

1960, Kennedy, Dem., 232,542; Nixon, Rep., 380,553.

1964, Johnson, Dem., 307,307; Goldwater, Rep., 276,847.

1968, Nixon, Rep., 321,163; Humphrey, Dem., 170,784; Wallace, 3d party, 44,904.

1972, Nixon, Rep., 406,298; McGovern, Dem., 169,991; scattered 817.

1976, Carter, Dem., 233,287; Ford, Rep., 359,219; McCarthy, Ind., 9,383; Maddox, Amer. Ind., 3,378; MacBride, Libertarian, 1,476.

1980, Reagan, Rep., 419,214; Carter, Dem., 166,424; Anderson, Ind., 44,854; Clark, Libertarian, 9,041.

1984, Reagan, Rep., 459,135; Mondale, Dem., 187,475; Bergland, Libertarian, 2,075.

1988, Bush, Rep., 397,956; Dukakis, Dem., 259,235; Paul, Lib., 2,534; Fulani, New Alliance, 1,740.

Nevada

County	1988 Dukakis (D)	Bush (R)	1984 Mondale (D)	Reagan (R)
Churchill	1,481	4,578	1,304	4,479
Clark	78,359	108,110	53,386	94,133
Douglas	3,107	7,074	1,877	6,385
Elko	2,310	5,722	1,566	5,110
Esmeralda	143	380	158	453
Eureka	151	413	124	439
Humboldt	1,024	2,378	862	2,498
Lander	439	1,214	301	1,222
Lincoln	466	1,035	397	1,175
Lyon	2,301	4,390	1,673	4,370
Mineral	978	1,480	766	1,645
Nye	1,748	3,619	1,269	3,573
Pershing	458	867	333	956
Storey	432	651	252	570
Washoe	32,902	52,654	22,321	50,418
White Pine	1,351	1,774	1,276	1,917
Totals	132,738	206,040	91,655	188,770

Nevada Vote Since 1940

1940, Roosevelt, Dem., 31,945; Willkie, Rep., 21,229.

1944, Roosevelt, Dem., 29,623; Dewey, Rep., 24,611.

1948, Truman, Dem., 31,291; Dewey, Rep., 29,357; Wallace, Prog., 1,469.

1952, Eisenhower, Rep., 50,502; Stevenson, Dem., 31,688.

1956, Eisenhower, Rep., 56,049; Stevenson, Dem., 40,640.

1960, Kennedy, Dem., 54,880; Nixon, Rep., 52,387.

1964, Johnson, Dem., 79,339; Goldwater, Rep., 56,094.

1968, Nixon, Rep., 73,188; Humphrey, Dem., 60,598; Wallace, 3d party, 20,432.

1972, Nixon, Rep., 115,750; McGovern, Dem. 66,016.

1976, Carter Dem., 92,479; Ford, Rep., 101,273; MacBride, Libertarian, 1,519; Maddox, Amer. Ind., 1,497; scattered 5,108.

1980, Reagan, Rep., 155,017; Carter, Dem., 66,666; Anderson, Ind., 17,651; Clark, Libertarian, 4,358.

1984, Reagan, Rep., 188,770; Mondale, Dem., 91,655; Bergland, Libertarian, 2,292.

1988, Bush, Rep., 206,040; Dukakis, Dem., 132,738; Paul, Lib., 3,520; Fulani, New Alliance, 835.

New Hampshire

City	1988 Dukakis (D)	Bush (R)	1984 Mondale (D)	Reagan (R)
Berlin City	2,271	2,529	1,863	3,261
Claremont	2,254	2,513	2,006	2,868
Concord	6,698	7,439	5,172	7,190
Dover	4,803	5,357	3,826	5,397
Keene	4,466	4,535	3,238	4,975
Laconia	2,111	3,835	1,552	4,151
Manchester	12,567	23,893	10,283	24,780
Nashua	12,833	19,369	9,305	16,961
Portsmith	5,377	4,827	4,418	4,967
Rochester	3,591	5,368	2,622	5,457
Totals	163,696	281,537	120,377	267,051

New Hampshire Vote Since 1940

1940, Roosevelt, Dem., 125,292; Willkie, Rep., 110,127.

1944, Roosevelt, Dem., 119,663; Dewey, Rep., 109,916; Thomas, Soc., 46.

1948, Truman, Dem., 107,995; Dewey, Rep., 121,299; Wallace, Prog., 1,970; Thomas, Soc., 86; Teichert, Soc. Labor, 83; Thurmond, States' Rights, 7.

1952, Eisenhower, Rep., 166,287; Stevenson, Dem., 106,663.

1956, Eisenhower, Rep., 176,519; Stevenson, Dem., 90,364; Andrews, Const., 111.

1960, Kennedy, Dem., 137,772; Nixon, Rep., 157,989.

1964, Johnson, Dem., 182,065; Goldwater, Rep., 104,029.

1968, Nixon, Rep., 154,903; Humphrey, Dem., 130,589; Wallace, 3d party, 11,173; New Party, 421; Halstead, Soc. Worker, 104.

1972, Nixon, Rep., 213,724; McGovern, Dem., 116,435; Schmitz, Amer., 3,386; Jenness, Soc. Workers, 368; scattered, 142.

1976, Carter, Dem., 147,645; Ford, Rep., 185,935; McCarthy, Ind., 4,095; MacBride, Libertarian, 936; Reagan, write-in, 388; La Rouche, U.S. Labor, 186; Camejo, Soc. Workers, 161; Levin, Soc. Labor, 66; scattered, 215.

1980, Reagan, Rep., 221,705; Carter, Dem., 108,864; Anderson, Ind., 49,693; Clark, Libertarian, 2,067; Commoner, Citizens, 1,325; Hall, Com., 129; Griswold, Workers World, 76; DeBerry, Soc. Workers, 72; scattered, 68.

1984, Reagan, Rep., 267,051; Mondale, Dem., 120,377; Bergland, Libertarian, 735.

1988, Bush, Rep., 281,537; Dukakis, Dem., 163,696; Paul, Lib., 4,502; Fulani, New Alliance, 790.

New Jersey

	1988		1984	
County	Dukakis (D)	Bush (R)	Mondale (D)	Reagan (R)
Atlantic	34,047	44,748	33,240	49,158
Bergen	160,655	226,885	155,039	268,507
Burlington	61,140	87,416	57,467	89,815
Camden	90,704	100,072	90,233	109,749
Cape May	15,105	28,738	13,378	28,768
Cumberland	21,869	26,024	21,141	29,398
Essex	156,098	111,491	173,295	136,798
Gloucester	35,479	51,708	32,702	54,041
Hudson	95,696	81,807	94,304	112,834
Hunterdon	13,758	31,907	10,972	29,737
Mercer	68,712	65,384	66,398	71,195
Middlesex	117,149	143,361	104,905	160,221
Monmouth	91,844	147,320	79,382	152,595
Morris	58,721	127,420	53,201	137,719
Ocean	64,474	124,587	51,012	124,391
Passaic	66,254	88,070	69,590	101,593
Salem	9,956	15,240	8,935	17,368
Somerset	37,406	67,658	31,924	66,303
Sussex	13,676	36,086	11,502	35,680
Union	93,158	112,967	92,056	135,446
Warren	11,640	21,715	10,647	21,938
Totals	1,317,541	1,740,604	1,261,323	1,933,630

New Jersey Vote Since 1940

1940, Roosevelt, Dem., 1,016,404; Willkie, Rep., 944,876; Browder, Com., 8,814; Thomas, Soc., 2,823; Babson, Proh., 851; Aiken, Soc. Labor, 446.

1944, Roosevelt, Dem., 987,874; Dewey, Rep., 961,335; Teichert, Soc. Labor, 6,939; Watson, Nat'l. Proh., 4,255; Thomas, Soc., 3,385.

1948, Truman, Dem., 895,455; Dewey, Rep., 981,124; Wallace, Prog., 42,683; Watson, Proh., 10,593; Thomas, Soc., 10,521; Dobbs, Soc. Workers, 5,825; Teichert, Soc. Labor, 3,354.

1952, Eisenhower, Rep., 1,373,613; Stevenson, Dem., 1,015,902; Hoopes, Soc., 8,593; Hass, Soc. Labor, 5,815; Hallinan, Prog., 5,589; Krajewski, Poor Man's, 4,203; Dobbs, Soc. Workers, 3,850; Hamblen, Proh., 989.

1956, Eisenhower, Rep., 1,606,942; Stevenson Dem., 850,337; Holtwick, Proh., 9,147; Hass, Soc. Labor, 6,736; Andrews, Conservative, 5,317; Dobbs, Soc. Workers, 4,004; Krajewski, American Third Party, 1,829.

1960, Kennedy, Dem., 1,385,415; Nixon, Rep., 1,363,324; Dobbs, Soc. Workers, 11,402; Lee, Conservative, 8,708; Hass, Soc. Labor, 4,262.

1964, Johnson, Dem., 1,867,671; Goldwater, Rep., 963,843; DeBerry, Soc. Workers, 8,181; Hass, Soc. Labor, 7,075.

1968, Nixon, Rep., 1,325,467; Humphrey, Dem., 1,264,206; Wallace, 3d party, 262,187; Halstead, Soc. Worker, 8,667; Gregory, Peace Freedom, 8,084; Blomen, Soc. Labor, 6,784.

1972, Nixon, Rep., 1,845,502; McGovern, Dem., 1,102,211; Schmitz, Amer., 34,378; Spock, Peoples, 5,355; Fisher, Soc. Labor, 4,544; Jenness, Soc. Workers, 2,233; Mahalchik, Amer. First, 1,743; Hall, Com., 1,263.

1976, Carter, Dem., 1,444,653; Ford, Rep., 1,509,688; McCarthy, Ind., 32,717; MacBride, Libertarian, 9,449; Maddox, Amer., 7,716; Levin, Soc. Labor, 3,686; Hall, Com., 1,662; LaRouche, U.S. Labor, 1,650; Camejo, Soc. Workers, 1,184; Wright, People's, 1,044; Bubar, Proh., 554; Zeidler, Soc., 469.

1980, Reagan, Rep., 1,546,557; Carter, Dem., 1,147,364; Anderson, Ind., 234,632; Clark, Libertarian, 20,652; Commoner, Citizens, 8,203; McCormack, Right to Life, 3,927; Lynen, Middle Class, 3,694; Hall, Com., 2,555; Pulley, Soc. Workers, 2,198; McReynolds, Soc., 1,973; Gahres, Down With Lawyers, 1,718; Griswold, Workers World, 1,288; Wendelken, Ind., 923.

1984, Reagan, Rep., 1,933,630; Mondale, Dem., 1,261,323; Bergland, Libertarian, 6,416.

1988, Bush, Rep., 1,740,604; Dukakis, Dem., 1,317,541; Lewin, Peace & Freedom, 9,953; Paul, Lib., 8,421.

New Mexico

	1988		1984	
County	Dukakis (D)	Bush (R)	Mondale (D)	Reagan (R)
Bernalillo	78,346	92,830	67,789	104,694
Catron	490	925	418	970
Chaves	6,730	13,367	5,332	15,248
Cibola	3,458	2,640	3,140	3,578
Colfax	2,785	2,256	2,435	2,994
Curry	3,995	8,032	3,108	9,188
De Baca	480	643	386	756
Dona Ana	19,608	21,582	13,878	22,153
Eddy	8,544	9,805	7,364	11,810
Grant	5,443	4,196	5,755	4,979
Guadalupe	1,243	861	946	990
Harding	291	377	224	401
Hidalgo	901	1,100	860	1,282
Lea	5,879	11,309	4,558	14,569
Lincoln	1,690	3,511	1,134	3,992
Los Alamos	3,275	6,622	2,859	6,882
Luna	3,066	3,415	2,557	4,145
McKinley	9,595	5,694	7,915	6,557
Mora	1,601	923	1,235	1,017
Otero	5,284	9,984	4,167	9,751
Quay	1,901	2,454	1,368	2,842
Rio Arriba	7,503	3,024	6,938	4,116
Roosevelt	2,033	3,589	1,696	4,598
Sandoval	9,332	9,411	7,080	9,005
San Juan	11,094	16,202	8,963	18,690
San Miguel	6,131	2,763	5,227	3,485
Santa Fe	23,581	12,891	18,262	15,886
Sierra	1,595	2,507	1,335	2,663
Socorro	2,960	3,114	2,541	3,403
Taos	6,271	2,897	5,144	4,154
Torrance	1,618	2,252	1,274	2,326
Union	638	1,291	488	1,503
Valencia	7,136	7,874	5,393	8,474
Totals	244,497	270,341	201,769	307,101

New Mexico Vote Since 1940

1940, Roosevelt, Dem., 103,699; Willkie, Rep., 79,315.

1944, Roosevelt, Dem., 81,389; Dewey, Rep., 70,688; Watson, Proh., 148.

1948, Truman, Dem., 105,464; Dewey, Rep., 80,303; Wallace, Prog., 1,037; Watson, Proh., 127; Thomas, Soc., 83; Teichert, Soc. Labor, 49.

1952, Eisenhower, Rep., 132,170; Stevenson, Dem., 105,661; Hamblen, Proh., 297; Hallinan, Ind. Prog., 225; MacArthur, Christian National, 220; Hass, Soc. Labor, 35.

1956, Eisenhower, Rep., 146,788; Stevenson, Dem., 106,098; Holtwick, Proh., 607; Andrews, Ind., 364; Hass, Soc. Labor, 69.

1960, Kennedy, Dem., 156,027; Nixon, Rep., 153,733; Decker, Proh., 777; Hass, Soc. Labor, 570.

1964, Johnson, Dem., 194,017; Goldwater, Rep., 131,838; Hass, Soc. Labor, 1,217; Munn, Proh., 543.

1968, Nixon, Rep., 169,692; Humphrey, Dem., 130,081; Wallace, 3d party, 25,737; Chavez, 1,519; Halstead, Soc. Worker, 252.

1972, Nixon, Rep., 235,606; McGovern, Dem., 141,084; Schmitz, Amer., 8,767; Jenness, Soc. Workers, 474.

1976, Carter, Dem., 201,148; Ford, Rep., 211,419; Camejo, Soc. Workers, 2,462; MacBride, Libertarian, 1,110; Zeidler, Soc., 240; Bubar, Proh., 211.

1980, Reagan, Rep., 250,779; Carter, Dem., 167,826; Anderson, Ind., 29,459; Clark, Libertarian, 4,365; Commoner, Citizens, 2,202; Bubar, Statesman, 1,281; Pulley, Soc. Worker, 325.

1984, Reagan, Rep., 307,101; Mondale, Dem., 201,769; Bergland, Libertarian, 4,459.

1988, Bush, Rep., 270,341; Dukakis, Dem., 244,497; Paul, Lib., 3,268; Fulani, New Alliance, 2,237.

New York

	1988		1984	
County	Dukakis (D)	Bush (R)	Mondale (D)	Reagan (R)
Albany	86,564	59,534	75,447	74,542
Allegany	5,614	11,880	4,720	14,527
Bronx	218,245	76,043	223,112	109,308
Broome	48,130	47,610	37,658	58,109
Cattaraugus	12,447	19,691	10,194	24,162
Cayuga	15,044	16,934	12,207	21,451
Chautauqua	25,814	31,642	22,986	39,597
Chemung	15,966	20,951	14,638	24,909
Chenango	8,021	11,727	6,343	14,254
Clinton	12,670	15,702	10,804	19,549
Columbia	11,585	15,111	8,960	18,814
Cortland	7,673	10,934	6,438	13,691
Delaware	7,463	11,391	5,745	14,002
Dutchess	38,968	62,165	32,867	70,324
Erie	238,779	188,796	237,631	222,882
Essex	6,623	10,350	5,119	12,114
Franklin	7,928	9,135	6,400	10,617
Fulton	9,012	11,757	7,644	14,887
Genesee	9,945	14,182	8,549	16,582
Greene	7,265	11,874	5,858	14,150

Hamilton	976	2,320	737	2,637
Herkimer	12,694	15,104	10,346	18,827
Jefferson	14,137	19,304	10,960	23,445
Kings	363,916	178,961	368,518	230,064
Lewis	4,252	5,787	2,757	7,069
Livingston	9,506	14,004	7,399	16,389
Madison	10,665	14,902	8,291	17,568
Monroe	153,650	155,271	132,109	182,696
Montgomery	11,371	11,128	9,044	14,398
Nassau	250,130	337,430	240,697	392,017
New York	385,675	115,927	379,521	144,281
Niagara	43,801	42,537	41,368	51,289
Oneida	47,665	55,039	42,603	65,377
Onondaga	94,751	104,080	81,777	121,857
Ontario	17,341	21,780	12,844	24,507
Orange	38,465	65,446	32,663	69,413
Orleans	5,913	9,028	4,429	10,453
Oswego	18,430	25,362	14,437	31,481
Otsego	11,069	13,021	9,582	16,777
Putnam	12,158	24,086	9,473	25,707
Queens	325,147	217,049	328,379	285,477
Rensselaer	33,066	35,412	26,755	43,892
Richmond	47,812	77,427	44,345	83,187
Rockland	47,634	63,825	44,687	70,020
St. Lawrence	18,921	20,290	15,963	26,062
Saratoga	31,584	43,498	22,166	47,394
Schenectady	36,483	33,364	30,612	42,808
Schoharie	5,389	7,008	3,996	8,692
Schuyler	2,900	4,291	2,422	5,207
Seneca	6,215	7,221	4,825	9,420
Steuben	12,824	25,359	10,471	28,848
Suffolk	199,215	311,242	171,295	335,485
Sullivan	11,635	15,713	10,475	18,037
Tioga	8,102	12,670	5,860	14,856
Tompkins	21,455	14,932	19,357	18,255
Ulster	30,744	41,173	26,445	47,372
Warren	8,580	15,860	5,886	17,616
Washington	8,201	14,103	5,909	16,580
Wayne	12,959	20,613	9,700	24,171
Westchester	169,860	197,956	160,225	229,005
Wyoming	5,228	9,451	4,381	11,199
Yates	3,507	5,488	2,670	6,367
Totals	3,347,882	3,081,871	3,119,609	3,664,763

New York Vote Since 1940

1940, Roosevelt, Dem., 2,834,500; American Lab., 417,418; total, 3,251,918; Willkie, Rep., 3,027,478; Thomas, Soc., 18,950; Babson, Proh., 3,250.

1944, Roosevelt, Dem., 2,478,598; American Lab., 496,405; Liberal, 329,325; total, 3,304,238; Dewey, Rep., 2,987,647; Teichert, Ind. Gov't., 14,352; Thomas, Soc., 10,553.

1948, Truman, Dem., 2,557,642; Liberal, 222,562; total, 2,780,204; Dewey, Rep., 2,841,163; Wallace, Amer. Lab., 509,559; Thomas, Soc., 40,879; Teichert, Ind. Gov't., 2,729; Dobbs, Soc. Workers, 2,675.

1952, Eisenhower, Rep., 3,952,815; Stevenson, Dem., 2,687,890, Liberal, 416,711; total, 3,104,601; Hallinan, American Lab., 64,211; Hoopes, Soc., 2,664; Dobbs, Soc. Workers, 2,212; Hass, Ind. Gov't., 1,560; scattering, 178; blank and void, 87,813.

1956, Eisenhower, Rep., 4,340,340; Stevenson, Dem., 2,458,212; Liberal, 292,557; total, 2,750,769; write-in votes for Andrews, 1,027; Werdel, 492; Hass, 150; Hoopes, 82; others, 476.

1960, Kennedy, Dem., 3,423,909; Liberal, 406,176; total, 3,830,085; Nixon, Rep., 3,446,419; Dobbs, Soc. Workers, 14,319; scattering, 256; blank and void, 88,896.

1964, Johnson, Dem., 4,913,156; Goldwater, Rep., 2,243,559; Hass, Soc. Labor, 6,085; DeBerry, Soc. Workers, 3,215; scattering, 188; blank and void, 151,383.

1968, Nixon, Rep., 3,007,932; Humphrey, Dem., 3,378,470; Wallace, 3d party, 358,864; Blomen, Soc. Labor, 8,432; Halstead, Soc. Worker, 11,851; Gregory, Freedom and Peace, 24,517; blank, void, and scattering, 171,624.

1972, Nixon, Rep., 3,824,642; Conservative, 368,136; McGovern, Dem., 2,767,956; Liberal, 183,128; Reed, Soc. Workers, 7,797; Fisher, Soc. Labor, 4,530; Hall, Com., 5,641; blank, void, or scattered, 161,641.

1976, Carter, Dem., 3,389,558; Ford, Rep., 3,100,791; MacBride, Libertarian, 12,197; Hall, Com., 10,270; Camejo, Soc. Workers, 6,996; LaRouche, U.S. Labor, 5,413; blank, void, or scattered, 143,037.

1980, Reagan, Rep., 2,893,831; Carter, Dem., 2,728,372; Anderson, Lib., 467,801; Clark, Libertarian, 52,648; McCormack, Right To Life, 24,159; Commoner, Citizens, 23,186; Hall, Com., 7,414; DeBerry, Soc. Workers, 2,068; Griswold, Workers World, 1,416; scattering, 1,064.

1984, Reagan, Rep., 3,664,763; Mondale, Dem., 3,119,609; Bergland, Libertarian, 11,949.

1988, Bush, Rep., 3,081,871; Dukakis, Dem., 3,347,882; Marra, Right to Life, 20,497; Fulani, New Alliance, 15,845.

North Carolina

	1988		1984	
	Dukakis	Bush	Mondale	Reagan
County	(D)	(R)	(D)	(R)
Alamance	12,642	24,131	11,230	26,063
Alexander	4,148	7,968	3,581	8,502
Alleghany	2,087	2,174	2,013	2,589
Anson	4,831	2,782	5,015	3,719
Ashe	4,034	6,019	4,009	6,611
Avery	1,367	4,277	1,159	4,702
Beaufort	5,352	8,150	5,987	9,284
Bertie	3,762	2,145	3,953	2,879
Bladen	5,031	3,770	5,064	4,701
Brunswick	7,881	10,007	6,774	9,673
Buncombe	26,964	36,828	23,337	37,698
Burke	10,848	15,933	10,353	18,766
Cabarrus	10,686	22,524	8,477	22,528
Caldwell	7,862	15,176	7,311	17,024
Camden	1,081	1,144	1,075	1,282
Carteret	6,859	11,076	5,882	11,637
Caswell	4,189	3,299	4,157	3,992
Catawba	12,922	28,872	11,700	31,476
Chatham	7,600	6,999	7,458	8,595
Cherokee	2,567	4,557	2,776	4,894
Chowan	1,756	1,884	1,736	2,171
Clay	1,289	2,174	1,340	2,259
Cleveland	10,321	14,039	10,288	17,095
Columbus	9,172	6,659	8,728	9,150
Craven	7,313	12,057	7,186	12,893
Cumberland	23,789	27,057	22,614	31,602
Currituck	1,555	2,443	1,668	2,885
Dare	2,806	5,234	1,839	4,738
Davidson	13,215	28,374	11,469	30,471
Davie	3,166	7,988	2,911	8,201
Duplin	5,945	5,774	6,830	7,708
Durham	35,441	29,928	32,244	29,185
Edgecombe	9,044	6,831	10,545	9,635
Forsyth	39,726	57,688	36,814	59,208
Franklin	5,438	5,499	4,766	5,984
Gaston	14,582	34,775	14,142	39,167
Gates	2,024	1,451	2,225	1,694
Graham	1,313	2,091	1,494	2,514
Granville	5,280	4,880	5,217	6,302
Greene	2,729	2,498	2,772	3,195
Guilford	50,351	66,060	46,027	73,096
Halifax	8,726	7,462	9,278	8,832
Harnett	7,259	9,749	7,106	11,198
Haywood	9,010	8,957	7,958	10,146
Henderson	9,338	19,711	7,222	19,369
Hertford	4,943	2,977	4,498	3,176
Hoke	3,281	2,020	3,214	2,449
Hyde	1,316	940	1,004	1,195
Iredell	10,530	21,536	9,999	23,641
Jackson	4,933	5,166	4,367	5,582
Johnston	8,717	15,563	7,833	16,210
Jones	1,946	1,649	2,025	2,062
Lee	4,231	7,104	3,925	8,198
Lenoir	7,649	10,669	8,556	13,321
Lincoln	6,444	11,651	5,996	12,621
McDowell	4,449	6,526	4,076	7,639
Macon	3,773	6,026	3,570	6,661
Madison	3,033	3,453	2,988	3,666
Martin	3,598	3,149	3,870	4,266
Mecklenburg	71,907	106,236	63,190	106,754
Mitchell	1,377	4,620	1,286	4,737
Montgomery	3,995	4,504	3,831	5,109
Moore	7,642	14,543	7,063	14,681
Nash	8,740	15,906	8,588	17,295
New Hanover	15,401	23,807	12,591	23,771
Northampton	4,599	2,415	5,094	3,198
Onslow	7,162	12,253	5,713	13,928
Orange	22,326	14,503	20,564	15,585
Pamlico	2,188	2,297	2,152	2,554
Pasquotank	3,860	4,006	3,854	4,646
Pender	4,377	4,826	4,354	5,079
Perquimans	1,543	1,781	1,441	1,939
Person	3,777	4,832	3,528	5,854
Pitt	14,777	18,245	13,481	18,983
Polk	2,534	3,874	2,169	4,046
Randolph	8,641	23,881	7,511	25,759
Richmond	7,151	5,073	7,494	6,807
Robeson	16,988	9,908	15,257	12,947
Rockingham	11,551	14,591	10,605	17,895
Rowan	12,127	23,192	10,643	25,207
Rutherford	6,926	10,337	6,862	11,369
Sampson	8,009	8,524	9,115	10,665
Scotland	3,865	3,199	4,028	4,077
Stanly	6,627	11,885	6,138	13,116
Stokes	5,319	8,661	4,950	9,515
Surry	7,245	11,393	7,188	13,340
Swain	1,821	1,795	2,000	2,012
Transylvania	4,280	7,009	3,733	6,956

Tyrrell	785	637	807	774	Wells	1,317	1,901	1,036	2,426
Union	8,820	17,015	7,048	16,885	Williams	4,004	5,653	3,177	8,166
Vance	5,631	5,625	5,880	6,836	Totals	127,739	166,559	104,429	200,336
Wake	61,352	81,613	50,323	81,251					
Warren	4,249	2,163	3,946	2,664					
Washington	2,806	2,186	3,114	2,731					
Watauga	6,048	8,662	5,163	9,370					
Wayne	9,135	15,292	10,011	17,961					
Wilkes	7,230	15,231	6,852	18,670					
Wilson	8,214	10,997	8,343	12,243					
Yadkin	3,195	7,918	3,075	8,976					
Yancey	3,803	4,160	3,651	4,296					
Totals	890,167	1,237,258	824,287	1,346,481					

North Carolina Vote Since 1940

1940, Roosevelt, Dem., 609,015; Willkie, Rep., 213,633.

1944, Roosevelt, Dem., 527,399; Dewey, Rep., 263,155.

1948, Truman, Dem., 459,070; Dewey, Rep., 258,572; Thurmond, States' Rights, 69,652; Wallace, Prog., 3,915.

1952, Eisenhower, Rep., 558,107; Stevenson, Dem., 652,803.

1956, Eisenhower, Rep., 575,062; Stevenson, Dem., 590,530.

1960, Kennedy, Dem., 713,136; Nixon, Rep., 655,420.

1964, Johnson, Dem., 800,139; Goldwater Rep., 624,844.

1968, Nixon, Rep., 627,192; Humphrey, Dem., 464,113; Wallace, 3d party, 496,188.

1972, Nixon, Rep., 1,054,889; McGovern, Dem., 438,705; Schmitz, Amer., 25,018.

1976, Dem., 927,365; Ford, Rep., 741,960; Anderson, Amer., 5,607; MacBride, Libertarian, 2,219; LaRouche, U.S. Labor, 755.

1980, Reagan, Rep., 915,018; Carter, Dem., 875,635; Anderson, Ind., 52,800; Clark, Libertarian, 9,677; Commoner, Citizens, 2,287; DeBerry, Soc. Workers, 416.

1984, Reagan, Rep., 1,346,481; Mondale, Dem., 824,287; Bergland, Libertarian, 3,794.

1988, Bush, Rep., 1,237,258; Dukakis, Dem., 890,167; Fulani, New Alliance, 5,682; Paul, write-in, 1,263.

North Dakota

	1988		1984	
County	Dukakis (D)	Bush (R)	Mondale (D)	Reagan (R)
Adams	708	1,018	530	1,343
Barnes	2,858	3,631	2,507	4,348
Benson	1,691	1,316	1,599	1,729
Billings	211	437	133	505
Bottineau	1,684	2,530	1,279	3,356
Bowman	737	1,111	562	1,559
Burke	693	971	543	1,298
Burleigh	10,760	18,000	8,781	19,913
Cass	22,107	26,699	18,054	29,221
Cavalier	1,333	2,096	1,110	2,661
Dickey	1,249	2,064	1,051	2,460
Divide	875	869	626	1,165
Dunn	842	1,263	716	1,583
Eddy	748	891	796	1,049
Emmons	925	1,634	620	1,885
Foster	837	1,218	765	1,422
Golden Valley	388	781	325	964
Grand Forks	12,494	14,801	10,050	15,898
Grant	654	1,351	507	1,607
Griggs	846	1,020	828	1,254
Hettinger	698	1,395	524	1,646
Kidder	678	1,039	506	1,240
La Moure	1,223	1,642	1,086	1,978
Logan	540	1,111	401	1,222
McHenry	1,665	1,888	1,283	2,485
McIntosh	598	1,726	427	2,047
McKenzie	1,273	1,949	974	2,610
McLean	2,428	2,906	2,062	3,673
Mercer	1,843	3,013	1,729	3,705
Morton	4,708	5,588	3,996	7,146
Mountrail	1,977	1,443	1,565	1,959
Nelson	1,151	1,078	1,026	1,445
Oliver	526	696	419	915
Pembina	1,616	2,471	1,367	2,895
Pierce	1,008	1,422	691	1,883
Ramsey	2,665	3,103	2,304	4,150
Ransom	1,459	1,362	1,222	1,706
Renville	837	893	592	1,163
Richland	3,523	4,670	3,047	5,980
Rolette	2,426	1,126	2,179	1,479
Sargent	1,306	1,119	1,295	1,385
Sheridan	428	885	306	1,075
Sioux	701	325	655	442
Slope	202	315	174	419
Stark	3,678	6,137	2,759	7,641
Steele	895	690	781	941
Stutsman	4,214	5,375	3,495	6,591
Towner	970	946	789	1,242
Traill	1,940	2,562	1,580	3,037
Walsh	2,646	3,250	2,264	4,347
Ward	9,906	13,179	7,336	16,077

North Dakota Vote Since 1940

1940, Roosevelt, Dem., 124,036; Willkie, Rep., 154,590; Thomas, Soc., 1,279; Knutson, Com., 545; Babson, Proh., 325.

1944, Roosevelt, Dem., 100,144; Dewey, Rep., 118,535; Thomas, Soc., 943; Watson, Proh., 549.

1948, Truman, Dem., 95,812; Dewey, Rep., 115,139; Wallace, Prog., 8,391; Thomas, Soc., 1,000, Thurmond, States' Rights, 374.

1952, Eisenhower, Rep., 191,712; Stevenson, Dem., 76,694; MacArthur, Christian Nationalist, 1,075; Hallinan, Prog., 344; Hamblen, Proh., 302.

1956, Eisenhower, Rep., 156,766; Stevenson, Dem., 96,742; Andrews, Amer., 483.

1960, Kennedy, Dem., 123,963; Nixon, Rep., 154,310; Dobbs, Soc. Workers, 158.

1964, Johnson, Dem., 149,784; Goldwater, Rep., 108,207; DeBerry, Soc. Worker, 224; Munn, Proh., 174.

1968, Nixon, Rep., 138,669; Humphrey, Dem., 94,769; Wallace, 3d party, 14,244; Halstead, Soc. Worker, 128; Munn, Prohibition, 38; Troxell, Ind., 34.

1972, Nixon, Rep., 174,109; McGovern, Dem., 100,384; Jenness, Soc. Workers, 288; Hall, Com., 87; Schmitz, Amer., 5,646.

1976, Carter, Dem., 136,078; Ford, Rep., 153,470; Anderson, Amer., 3,698; McCarthy, Ind., 2,952; Maddox, Amer. Ind., 269; MacBride, Libertarian, 256; scattering, 371.

1980, Reagan, Rep., 193,695; Carter, Dem., 79,189; Anderson, Ind., 23,640; Clark, Libertarian, 3,743; Commoner, Libertarian, 429; McLain, Nat'l People's League, 296; Greaves, American, 235; Hall, Com., 93; DeBerry, Soc. Workers, 89; McReynolds, Soc., 82; Bubar, Statesman, 54.

1984, Reagan, Rep., 200,336; Mondale, Dem., 104,429; Bergland, Libertarian, 703.

1988, Bush, Rep., 166,559; Dukakis, Dem., 127,739; Paul, Lib., 1,315; LaRouche, Natl. Econ. Recovery, 905.

Ohio

	1988		1984	
County	Dukakis (D)	Bush (R)	Mondale (D)	Reagan (R)
Adams	3,740	5,916	3,534	6,113
Allen	13,727	31,021	12,176	33,506
Ashland	6,072	12,726	4,786	14,339
Ashtabula	20,536	17,654	19,344	21,669
Athens	10,795	9,314	10,201	11,548
Auglaize	4,756	13,562	4,102	14,766
Belmont	19,515	12,214	19,458	15,170
Brown	5,047	7,539	4,067	8,221
Butler	33,770	75,725	27,700	76,216
Carroll	4,667	6,179	3,771	6,703
Champaign	4,272	8,995	3,544	9,935
Clark	23,247	32,729	21,154	35,831
Clermont	15,352	37,417	11,713	35,316
Clinton	3,746	8,856	3,332	9,603
Columbiana	21,581	21,175	20,155	24,552
Coshocton	6,020	8,282	4,392	9,842
Crawford	6,018	12,472	4,932	14,682
Cuyahoga	353,401	242,439	362,626	284,094
Darke	6,851	14,914	5,904	16,379
Defiance	5,448	9,566	5,004	10,951
Delaware	7,590	20,693	5,773	19,050
Erie	15,097	16,670	13,508	19,174
Fairfield	12,504	29,208	9,817	30,843
Fayette	2,623	6,186	2,126	6,838
Franklin	147,585	226,265	131,530	250,360
Fulton	5,076	10,230	4,217	11,412
Gallia	4,834	7,399	4,251	8,194
Geauga	11,874	22,339	9,954	22,369
Greene	18,025	34,432	17,129	34,267
Guernsey	5,926	8,507	4,967	10,252
Hamilton	140,354	227,004	140,350	246,288
Hancock	7,435	19,896	5,758	22,169
Hardin	4,145	7,291	3,813	8,722
Harrison	3,881	3,298	3,370	4,276
Henry	3,764	8,618	2,779	9,317
Highland	4,278	8,776	3,784	9,000
Hocking	3,706	5,426	3,280	6,071
Holmes	2,179	5,064	1,737	5,146
Huron	7,794	12,633	6,609	14,388
Jackson	4,505	6,671	4,369	7,411
Jefferson	22,095	14,141	22,832	17,105
Knox	6,882	12,180	5,730	14,062

County	Lake			
Lake	39,667	52,963	36,711	54,587
Lawrence	11,628	12,937	11,431	14,973
Licking	16,793	34,540	13,995	37,560
Logan	4,484	11,099	3,645	12,230
Lorain	55,600	50,410	52,970	57,379
Lucas	99,755	83,788	97,293	100,285
Madison	3,421	8,303	2,928	8,979
Mahoning	75,524	43,722	76,514	53,424
Marion	9,596	14,864	8,827	17,392
Medina	19,505	29,962	15,897	30,690
Meigs	3,699	5,486	3,549	6,307
Mercer	4,978	11,162	4,422	11,542
Miami	11,138	24,915	9,695	26,300
Monroe	4,269	2,557	3,611	3,302
Montgomery	95,737	131,596	94,016	137,053
Morgan	2,085	3,713	1,868	3,994
Morrow	3,515	7,130	2,839	8,116
Muskingum	11,691	19,736	10,037	21,821
Noble	2,079	3,155	1,777	3,853
Ottawa	8,038	9,352	7,053	10,920
Paulding	3,114	5,381	2,811	5,545
Perry	5,011	6,602	3,961	7,548
Pickaway	4,905	10,796	4,110	11,942
Pike	5,191	5,611	4,895	6,318
Portage	25,607	26,334	21,719	29,536
Preble	4,937	10,297	4,198	11,065
Putnam	4,004	11,183	3,194	11,936
Richland	19,617	30,047	16,141	35,299
Ross	9,271	14,563	8,020	17,015
Sandusky	9,709	14,203	8,564	17,214
Scioto	14,442	16,029	14,120	18,818
Seneca	9,504	13,704	7,905	16,520
Shelby	5,065	12,198	4,315	13,509
Stark	69,639	87,087	65,157	98,434
Summit	112,612	101,155	109,569	115,637
Trumbull	58,674	38,815	56,902	45,623
Tuscarawas	14,185	17,145	13,149	19,366
Union	3,130	8,846	2,579	9,336
Van Wert	3,848	9,410	3,338	9,570
Vinton	2,385	2,652	1,990	3,041
Warren	11,145	31,419	9,031	29,848
Washington	9,967	14,767	7,920	16,529
Wayne	13,571	22,320	11,323	24,475
Williams	4,666	10,782	3,624	10,804
Wood	18,579	26,013	15,907	29,750
Wyandot	2,936	6,178	2,342	7,204
Totals	1,939,629	2,416,549	1,825,440	2,678,559

Ohio Vote Since 1940

1940, Roosevelt, Dem., 1,733,139; Willkie, Rep., 1,586,773.

1944, Roosevelt, Dem., 1,570,763; Dewey, Rep., 1,582,293.

1948, Truman, Dem., 1,452,791; Dewey, Rep., 1,445,684; Wallace, Prog., 37,596.

1952, Eisenhower, Rep., 2,100,391; Stevenson, Dem., 1,600,367.

1956, Eisenhower, Rep., 2,262,610; Stevenson, Dem., 1,439,655.

1960, Kennedy, Dem., 1,944,248; Nixon, Rep., 2,217,611.

1964, Johnson, Dem., 2,498,331; Goldwater, Rep., 1,470,865.

1968, Nixon, Rep., 1,791,014; Humphrey, Dem., 1,700,586; Wallace, 3d party, 467,495; Gregory, 372; Munn, Proh., 19; Blomen, Soc. Labor, 120; Halstead, Soc. Worker, 69; Mitchell, Com., 23.

1972, Nixon, Rep., 2,441,827; McGovern, Dem., 1,558,889; Fisher, Soc. Labor, 7,107; Hall, Com., 6,437; Schmitz, Amer., 80,067; Wallace, Ind., 460.

1976, Carter, Dem., 2,011,621; Ford, Rep., 2,000,505; McCarthy, Ind., 58,258; Maddox, Amer. Ind., 15,529; MacBride, Libertarian, 8,961; Hall, Com., 7,817; Camejo, Soc. Workers, 4,717; LaRouche, U.S. Labor, 4,335; scattered, 130.

1980, Reagan, Rep., 2,206,545; Carter, Dem., 1,752,414; Anderson, Ind., 254,472; Clark, Libertarian, 49,033; Commoner, Citizens, 8,564; Hall, Com., 4,729; Congress, Ind. 4,029; Griswold, Workers World, 3,790; Bubar, Statesman, 27.

1984, Reagan, Rep., 2,678,559; Mondale, Dem., 1,825,440; Bergland, Libertarian, 5,886.

1988, Bush, Rep., 2,416,549; Dukakis, Dem., 1,939,629; Fulani, Ind., 12,017; Paul, Ind., 11,926.

Oklahoma

	1988		1984	
County	Dukakis (D)	Bush (R)	Mondale (D)	Reagan (R)
Adair	2,624	3,558	2,266	4,423
Alfalfa	1,117	1,960	866	2,715
Atoka	2,565	1,971	2,047	2,361

County	Beaver			
Beaver	777	2,013	536	2,689
Beckham	3,388	3,463	2,601	5,005
Blaine	1,775	2,889	1,484	4,037
Bryan	6,849	4,615	5,475	6,246
Caddo	5,387	4,689	4,463	6,811
Canadian	7,453	17,872	5,245	20,929
Carter	7,988	8,430	6,161	11,578
Cherokee	6,483	5,838	5,307	7,614
Choctaw	3,362	2,217	2,801	3,155
Cimarron	470	1,153	359	1,420
Cleveland	22,067	36,313	16,512	42,806
Coal	1,365	891	1,284	1,259
Comanche	11,441	17,464	8,890	21,382
Cotton	1,482	1,266	1,264	1,796
Craig	2,940	2,463	2,515	3,629
Creek	9,512	11,308	7,465	15,011
Custer	3,697	6,735	2,700	8,191
Delaware	4,889	5,248	3,789	6,690
Dewey	963	1,543	664	2,098
Ellis	786	1,422	562	1,881
Garfield	8,067	15,248	5,730	19,642
Garvin	5,438	5,109	4,215	7,505
Grady	6,689	7,994	4,846	11,042
Grant	1,249	1,690	825	2,470
Greer	1,256	1,225	1,220	1,664
Harmon	890	611	785	1,009
Harper	593	1,281	373	1,748
Haskell	2,963	1,822	2,535	2,417
Hughes	3,259	2,037	2,901	2,663
Jackson	3,542	4,423	2,996	5,773
Jefferson	1,767	1,063	1,496	1,656
Johnston	2,042	1,518	1,820	2,195
Kay	7,751	12,646	6,044	16,731
Kingfisher	1,777	4,011	1,125	5,528
Kiowa	2,296	2,030	2,016	2,951
Latimer	2,365	1,830	1,858	2,210
Le Flore	6,594	6,964	5,990	8,604
Lincoln	4,225	6,409	3,020	8,088
Logan	4,603	6,947	3,551	8,356
Love	1,889	1,361	1,359	1,833
McClain	3,594	4,771	2,549	6,056
McCurtain	4,928	4,920	3,994	6,381
McIntosh	4,041	2,665	3,479	3,646
Major	982	2,638	619	3,385
Marshall	2,730	1,911	2,039	2,488
Mayes	6,691	6,115	5,154	8,585
Murray	2,697	2,056	2,229	3,073
Muskogee	13,760	11,147	12,343	14,652
Noble	1,661	3,015	1,238	4,018
Nowata	2,203	2,000	1,687	3,030
Okfuskee	2,209	1,851	1,684	2,443
Oklahoma	75,812	135,376	60,235	159,974
Okmulgee	8,262	5,674	7,380	8,704
Osage	7,778	7,162	6,095	10,083
Ottawa	6,658	5,026	5,781	7,666
Pawnee	2,781	3,324	2,165	4,699
Payne	10,568	16,027	7,653	20,811
Pittsburg	8,623	7,594	6,860	9,778
Pontotoc	6,484	6,609	5,526	8,301
Pottawatomie	8,873	12,099	6,966	16,143
Pushmataha	2,430	1,841	2,079	2,499
Roger Mills	866	1,132	680	1,550
Rogers	8,771	12,940	6,013	16,137
Seminole	4,911	4,078	3,957	6,009
Sequoyah	4,951	5,710	4,202	7,042
Stephens	7,833	9,844	6,359	12,871
Texas	1,717	4,971	1,033	5,968
Tillman	2,148	1,754	1,674	2,637
Tulsa	69,044	127,512	58,274	159,549
Wagoner	7,378	10,219	5,271	12,534
Washington	6,971	14,613	5,476	19,043
Washita	2,290	2,402	1,547	3,847
Woods	1,735	2,835	1,231	3,741
Woodward	2,408	4,996	1,647	6,376
Totals	483,423	678,367	385,080	861,530

Oklahoma Vote Since 1940

1940, Roosevelt, Dem., 474,313; Willkie, Rep., 348,872; Babson, Proh., 3,027.

1944, Roosevelt, Dem., 401,549; Dewey, Rep., 319,424; Watson, Proh., 1,663.

1948, Truman, Dem., 452,782; Dewey, Rep., 268,817.

1952, Eisenhower, Rep., 518,045; Stevenson, Dem., 430,939.

1956, Eisenhower, Rep., 473,769; Stevenson, Dem., 385,581.

1960, Kennedy, Dem., 370,111; Nixon, Rep., 533,039.

1964, Johnson, Dem., 519,834; Goldwater, Rep. 412,665.

1968, Nixon, Rep., 449,697; Humphrey, Dem., 301,658; Wallace, 3d party, 191,731.

1972, Nixon, Rep. 759,025; McGovern, Dem., 247,147; Schmitz, Amer., 23,728.

1976, Carter, Dem., 532,442; Ford, Rep., 545,708; McCarthy, Ind., 14,101.

1980, Reagan, Rep., 695,570; Carter, Dem., 402,026; Anderson, Ind., 38,284; Clark, Libertarian, 13,828.

1984, Reagan, Rep., 861,530; Mondale, Dem., 385,080; Bergland, Libertarian, 9,066.

1988, Bush, Rep., 678,367; Dukakis, Dem., 483,423; Paul., Lib., 6,261; Fulani, New Alliance, 2,985.

Oregon

County	1988 Dukakis (D)	1988 Bush (R)	1984 Mondale (D)	1984 Reagan (R)
Baker.........	2,896	3,696	2,591	5,204
Benton........	16,930	14,004	16,073	17,836
Clackamas.....	59,799	61,381	47,254	68,630
Clatsop........	8,074	5,956	7,525	7,522
Columbia.......	8,983	6,424	8,219	7,811
Coos.........	13,996	10,153	13,582	13,637
Crook........	2,719	3,049	2,268	3,773
Curry........	4,015	4,761	3,423	5,363
Deschutes.....	14,264	16,425	11,671	19,323
Douglas.......	17,255	20,120	14,609	25,243
Gilliam.......	417	470	369	700
Grant........	1,437	2,264	1,344	2,695
Harney.......	1,379	1,833	1,290	2,197
Hood River....	3,275	3,257	3,022	4,531
Jackson.......	28,028	32,516	22,230	37,895
Jefferson......	2,346	2,509	1,920	3,283
Josephine......	10,646	15,876	8,539	19,470
Klamath......	8,429	13,484	7,575	17,686
Lake.........	1,237	2,161	1,184	2,466
Lane.........	69,883	47,563	63,999	61,493
Lincoln.......	9,598	7,364	8,637	9,110
Linn.........	17,007	18,312	16,161	23,463
Malheur.......	2,965	6,285	2,611	8,441
Marion.......	41,193	45,292	36,440	54,535
Morrow.......	1,375	1,529	1,254	2,130
Multnomah.....	161,361	95,561	144,179	119,932
Polk.........	9,626	10,553	8,709	12,678
Sherman......	435	555	398	828
Tillamook.....	5,529	4,297	4,988	5,267
Umatilla......	8,327	10,254	8,246	14,211
Union........	4,682	5,061	4,134	6,645
Wallowa......	1,425	1,993	1,204	2,619
Wasco.......	5,141	4,462	5,526	6,905
Washington....	59,837	67,018	44,602	75,877
Wheeler......	274	367	253	504
Yamhill......	11,423	13,321	9,450	15,797
Totals........	616,206	560,126	536,479	685,700

Oregon Vote Since 1940

1940, Roosevelt, Dem., 258,415; Willkie, Rep., 219,555; Aiken, Soc. Labor, 2,487; Thomas, Soc., 398; Browder, Com., 191; Babson, Proh., 154.

1944, Roosevelt, Dem., 248,635; Dewey, Rep., 225,365; Thomas, Soc., 3,785; Watson, Proh., 2,362.

1948, Truman, Dem., 243,147; Dewey, Rep., 260,904; Wallace, Prog., 14,978; Thomas, Soc., 5,051.

1952, Eisenhower, Rep., 420,815; Stevenson, Dem., 270,579; Hallinan, Ind., 3,665.

1956, Eisenhower, Rep., 406,393; Stevenson, Dem., 329,204.

1960, Kennedy, Dem., 367,402; Nixon, Rep., 408,060.

1964, Johnson, Dem., 501,017; Goldwater, Rep., 282,779; write-in, 2,509.

1968, Nixon, Rep., 408,433; Humphrey, Dem., 358,866; Wallace, 3d party, 49,683; write-in, McCarthy, 1,496; N. Rockefeller, 69; others, 1,075.

1972, Nixon, Rep., 486,686; McGovern, Dem., 392,760; Schmitz, Amer., 46,211; write-in, 2,289.

1976, Carter, Dem., 490,407; Ford, Rep., 492,120; McCarthy, Ind., 40,207; write-in, 7,142.

1980, Reagan, Rep., 571,044; Carter, Dem., 456,890; Anderson, Ind., 112,389; Clark, Libertarian, 25,838; Commoner, Citizens, 13,642; scattered, 1,713.

1984, Reagan, Rep., 658,700; Mondale, Dem., 536,479.

1988, Bush, Rep., 560,126; Dukakis, Dem., 616,206; Paul, Lib., 14,811; Fulani, Ind., 6,487.

Pennsylvania

County	1988 Dukakis (D)	1988 Bush (R)	1984 Mondale (D)	1984 Reagan (R)
Adams........	8,299	15,650	7,289	16,786
Allegheny.....	348,814	231,137	372,576	284,692
Armstrong.....	13,892	11,509	14,525	13,709
Beaver.......	50,327	25,764	54,765	32,052
Bedford.......	5,754	11,123	5,424	13,085
Berks........	41,040	70,153	37,849	74,605
Blair........	15,588	25,823	15,651	30,104
Bradford......	6,635	13,568	5,474	14,808
Bucks........	82,472	127,563	74,568	130,119
Butler.......	22,341	27,777	24,735	31,676
Cambria......	38,517	25,626	39,865	32,173

County	1988 Dukakis (D)	1988 Bush (R)	1984 Mondale (D)	1984 Reagan (R)
Cameron......	901	1,731	990	2,031
Carbon........	9,104	10,232	8,836	10,701
Centre.......	18,357	23,875	16,194	27,802
Chester.......	44,853	93,522	38,870	92,221
Clarion.......	5,616	8,026	5,407	9,836
Clearfield......	12,235	14,296	11,963	18,653
Clinton.......	5,759	5,735	4,525	6,678
Columbia......	7,767	12,114	8,254	14,402
Crawford......	13,021	17,249	12,792	20,181
Cumberland....	24,613	47,292	21,374	49,282
Dauphin......	35,079	48,917	33,576	54,330
Delaware.....	96,144	147,656	98,207	161,754
Elk.........	5,879	6,737	5,486	8,470
Erie.........	53,913	48,306	52,471	55,860
Fayette.......	33,098	16,915	35,098	21,314
Forest.......	895	1,159	839	1,468
Franklin......	12,368	27,086	11,480	27,243
Fulton.......	1,532	3,086	1,309	3,254
Greene.......	9,126	4,879	9,365	6,376
Huntingdon....	4,752	8,800	4,430	10,220
Indiana.......	16,514	14,983	15,791	18,845
Jefferson......	6,235	9,743	5,950	11,334
Juniata.......	2,834	4,881	2,624	5,059
Lackawanna....	45,591	42,083	45,851	48,132
Lancaster.....	38,982	96,979	31,308	99,090
Lawrence.....	21,884	15,829	23,981	19,277
Lebanon......	11,912	24,415	10,520	27,008
Lehigh.......	42,801	56,363	41,089	61,799
Luzerne......	58,553	59,059	58,482	69,169
Lycoming.....	13,528	24,792	13,147	28,498
McKean......	5,300	9,323	4,818	10,963
Mercer.......	24,278	21,301	24,658	24,211
Mifflin.......	4,790	8,170	5,178	9,106
Monroe.......	9,859	17,185	8,193	16,109
Montgomery...	109,834	170,294	99,741	181,426
Montour......	2,031	3,617	2,055	4,174
Northampton...	39,264	42,748	37,979	44,648
Northumberland...	14,255	20,207	13,748	22,109
Perry........	3,910	8,545	3,692	9,365
Philadelphia....	449,566	219,053	501,369	267,178
Pike.........	3,097	6,659	2,503	6,343
Potter.......	2,119	4,432	1,789	5,164
Schuylkill.....	24,797	32,666	25,758	37,330
Snyder.......	2,658	9,054	2,383	8,968
Somerset.....	13,815	16,809	13,900	19,502
Sullivan......	1,091	1,808	952	1,926
Susquehanna...	4,871	9,077	4,471	10,566
Tioga........	4,807	9,471	4,060	10,532
Union........	3,163	7,912	2,747	7,792
Venango......	8,624	11,468	9,114	13,507
Warren.......	6,790	8,991	6,244	10,838
Washington....	47,527	28,651	50,911	34,782
Wayne.......	3,775	9,926	3,155	10,061
Westmoreland...	76,710	61,472	79,906	71,377
Wyoming.....	2,797	6,607	2,518	7,230
York........	37,691	72,408	33,359	75,020
Totals........	2,194,944	2,300,087	2,228,131	2,584,323

Pennsylvania Vote Since 1940

1940, Roosevelt, Dem., 2,171,035; Willkie, Rep., 1,889,848; Thomas, Soc., 10,967; Browder, Com., 4,519; Aiken, Ind. Gov., 1,518.

1944, Roosevelt, Dem., 1,940,479; Dewey, Rep., 1,835,054; Thomas, Soc., 11,721; Watson, Proh., 5,750; Teichert, Ind. Gov., 1,789.

1948, Truman, Dem., 1,752,426; Dewey, Rep., 1,902,197; Wallace, Prog., 55,161; Thomas, Soc., 11,325; Watson, Proh., 10,338; Dobbs, Militant Workers, 2,133; Teichert, Ind. Gov., 1,461.

1952, Eisenhower, Rep., 2,415,789; Stevenson, Dem., 2,146,269; Hamblen, Proh., 8,771; Hallinan, Prog., 4,200; Hoopes, Soc., 2,684; Dobbs, Militant Workers, 1,502; Hass, Ind. Gov., 1,347; scattered, 155.

1956, Eisenhower, Rep., 2,585,252; Stevenson, Dem., 1,981,769; Hass, Soc. Labor, 7,447; Dobbs, Militant Workers, 2,035.

1960, Kennedy, Dem., 2,556,282; Nixon, Rep., 2,439,956; Hass, Soc. Labor, 7,185; Dobbs, Soc. Workers, 2,678; scattering, 440.

1964, Johnson, Dem., 3,130,954; Goldwater, Rep., 1,673,657; DeBerry, Soc. Workers, 10,456; Hass, Soc. Labor, 5,092; scattering, 2,531.

1968, Nixon, Rep., 2,090,017; Humphrey, Dem., 2,259,405; Wallace, 3d party, 378,582; Blomen, Soc. Labor, 4,977; Halstead, Soc. Workers, 4,862; Gregory, 7,821; others, 2,264.

1972, Nixon, Rep., 2,714,521; McGovern, Dem., 1,796,951; Schmitz, Amer., 70,593; Jenness, Soc. Workers, 4,639; Hall, Com., 2,686; others, 2,715.

1976, Carter, Dem., 2,328,677; Ford, Rep., 2,205,604; McCarthy, Ind., 50,584; Maddox, Constitution, 25,344;

Camejo, Soc. Workers, 3,009; LaRouche, U.S. Labor, 2,744; Hall, Com., 1,891; others, 2,934.

1980, Reagan, Rep., 2,261,872; Carter, Dem., 1,937,540; Anderson, Ind., 292,921; Clark, Libertarian, 33,263; DeBerry, Soc. Workers, 20,291; Commoner, Consumer, 10,430; Hall, Com., 5,184.

1984, Reagan, Rep., 2,584,323; Mondale, Dem., 2,228,131; Bergland, Libertarian, 6,982.

1988, Bush, Rep., 2,300,087; Dukakis, Dem., 2,194,944; McCarthy, Consumer, 19,158; Paul, Lib., 12,051.

Rhode Island

City	1988 Dukakis (D)	1988 Bush (R)	1984 Mondale (D)	1984 Reagan (R)
Cranston	19,711	17,129	17,742	19,517
East Providence	11,948	8,181	11,064	10,332
Pawtucket	15,985	9,359	14,109	12,460
Providence	34,806	15,310	35,751	19,748
Warwick	21,662	18,052	19,278	22,276
Totals	225,123	177,761	197,106	212,080

Rhode Island Vote Since 1940

1940, Roosevelt, Dem., 182,182; Willkie, Rep., 138,653; Browder, Com., 239; Babson, Proh., 74.

1944, Roosevelt, Dem., 175,356; Dewey, Rep., 123,487; Watson, Proh., 433.

1948, Truman, Dem., 188,736; Dewey, Rep., 135,787; Wallace, Prog., 2,619; Thomas, Soc., 429; Teichert, Soc. Labor, 131.

1952, Eisenhower, Rep., 210,935; Stevenson, Dem., 203,293; Hallinan, Prog., 187; Hass, Soc. Labor, 83.

1956, Eisenhower, Rep., 225,819; Stevenson, Dem., 161,790.

1960, Kennedy, Dem., 258,032; Nixon, Rep., 147,502.

1964, Johnson, Dem., 315,463; Goldwater, Rep., 74,615.

1968, Nixon, Rep., 122,359; Humphrey, Dem., 246,518; Wallace, 3d party, 15,678; Halstead, Soc. Worker, 383.

1972, Nixon, Rep., 220,383; McGovern, Dem., 194,645; Jenness, Soc. Workers, 729.

1976, Carter, Dem., 227,636; Ford, Rep., 181,249; MacBride, Libertarian, 715; Camejo, Soc. Workers, 462; Hall, Com., 334; Levin, Soc. Labor, 188.

1980, Reagan, Rep., 154,793; Carter, Dem., 198,342; Anderson, Ind., 59,819; Clark, Libertarian, 2,458; Hall, Com., 218; McReynolds, Socialist, 170; DeBerry, Soc. Worker, 90; Griswold, Workers World, 77.

1984, Reagan, Rep., 212,080; Mondale, Dem., 197,106; Bergland, Libertarian, 277.

1988, Bush, Rep., 177,761; Dukakis, Dem., 225,123; Paul, Lib., 825; Fulani, New Alliance, 280.

South Carolina

County	1988 Dukakis (D)	1988 Bush (R)	1984 Mondale (D)	1984 Reagan (R)
Abbeville	3,629	3,738	3,051	3,798
Aiken	10,598	27,665	9,872	25,872
Allendale	1,796	1,295	2,170	1,570
Anderson	12,281	25,939	10,324	24,123
Bamberg	2,830	2,403	2,892	2,908
Barnwell	2,564	4,467	2,811	4,346
Beaufort	8,691	16,184	7,347	13,668
Berkeley	9,312	16,779	7,380	16,972
Calhoun	2,175	2,585	2,513	2,742
Charleston	32,977	49,149	29,470	53,779
Cherokee	4,322	7,763	4,101	8,655
Chester	3,737	3,968	3,559	4,441
Chesterfield	4,699	4,999	4,593	5,451
Clarendon	5,030	4,337	5,591	5,102
Colleton	4,508	4,962	4,910	6,200
Darlington	7,625	9,854	7,456	11,100
Dillon	3,251	3,793	3,360	4,646
Dorchester	7,371	14,756	7,037	15,289
Edgefield	3,020	3,814	3,227	3,224
Fairfield	3,827	2,714	4,117	3,147
Florence	12,531	19,490	14,639	22,753
Georgetown	5,402	7,032	6,392	7,370
Greenville	27,188	67,371	24,137	66,766
Greenwood	6,511	9,096	6,339	10,887
Hampton	3,435	2,826	3,736	3,464
Horry	13,316	24,843	8,940	20,396
Jasper	2,894	2,004	3,753	3,102
Kershaw	4,494	8,877	4,323	8,822
Lancaster	6,181	9,152	5,804	10,383
Laurens	5,930	9,731	5,312	9,729
Lee	3,423	2,936	3,912	3,548
Lexington	11,366	41,467	8,828	38,628
McCormick	1,722	1,172	1,526	1,186
Marion	5,008	4,403	5,043	4,698
Marlboro	3,937	2,921	4,294	3,951
Newberry	3,825	6,427	3,790	7,176
Oconee	4,299	10,184	3,333	8,625
Orangeburg	14,655	13,281	15,121	14,286
Pickens	6,103	17,448	4,481	15,155
Richland	36,420	43,841	32,212	46,773
Saluda	1,984	3,225	1,962	3,515
Spartanburg	22,964	40,801	20,130	41,553
Sumter	9,502	13,161	9,566	12,909
Union	4,420	6,019	4,424	6,331
Williamsburg	7,343	5,914	7,586	6,492
York	11,458	21,657	9,273	20,008
Totals	370,554	606,443	344,459	615,539

South Carolina Vote Since 1940

1940, Roosevelt, Dem., 95,470; Willkie, Rep., 1,727.

1944, Roosevelt, Dem., 90,601; Dewey, Rep., 4,547; Southern Democrats, 7,799; Watson, Proh., 365; Rep. Tolbert faction, 63.

1948, Thurmond, States' Rights, 102,607; Truman, Dem., 34,423; Dewey, Rep., 5,386; Wallace, Prog., 154; Thomas, Soc., 1.

1952, Eisenhower ran on two tickets. Under state law vote cast for two Eisenhower slates of electors could not be combined. Eisenhower, Ind., 158,289; Rep., 9,793; total, 168,082; Stevenson, Dem., 173,004; Hamblen, Proh., 1.

1956, Stevenson, Dem., 136,372; Byrd, Ind., 88,509; Eisenhower, Rep., 75,700; Andrews, Ind., 2.

1960, Kennedy, Dem., 198,129; Nixon, Rep., 188,558; write-in, 1.

1964, Johnson, Dem., 215,700; Goldwater, Rep., 309,048; write-ins: Nixon, 1; Wallace, 5; Powell, 1; Thurmond, 1.

1968, Nixon, Rep., 254,062; Humphrey, Dem., 197,486; Wallace, 3d party, 215,430.

1972, Nixon, Rep., 477,044; McGovern, Dem., 184,559; United Citizens, 2,265; Schmitz, Amer., 10,075; write-in, 17.

1976, Carter, Dem., 450,807; Ford, Rep., 346,149; Anderson, Amer., 2,996; Maddox, Amer. Ind., 1,950; write-in, 681.

1980, Reagan, Rep., 439,277; Carter, Dem., 428,220; Anderson, Ind., 13,868; Clark, Libertarian, 4,807; Rarick, Amer. Ind., 2,086.

1984, Reagan, Rep., 615,539; Mondale, Dem., 344,459; Bergland, Libertarian, 4,359.

1988, Bush, Rep., 606,443; Dukakis, Dem., 370,554; Paul, Lib., 4,935; Fulani, United Citizens, 4,077.

South Dakota

County	1988 Dukakis (D)	1988 Bush (R)	1984 Mondale (D)	1984 Reagan (R)
Aurora	987	856	840	1,029
Beadle	4,523	4,611	3,523	5,876
Bennett	579	663	453	856
Bon Homme	1,574	1,826	1,408	2,478
Brookings	4,860	5,394	4,089	6,679
Brown	8,673	8,537	6,852	10,541
Brule	991	971	961	1,578
Buffalo	334	151	236	253
Butte	1,256	2,291	784	2,865
Campbell	334	909	214	1,035
Chas. Mix	2,205	1,966	1,879	2,660
Clark	1,164	1,247	960	1,748
Clay	2,859	2,307	2,711	3,057
Codington	4,570	5,050	3,528	6,108
Corson	722	710	792	955
Custer	1,180	1,806	858	2,183
Davison	3,705	4,024	3,248	4,783
Day	2,137	1,616	1,932	2,150
Deuel	1,246	1,251	941	1,537
Dewey	1,007	765	772	941
Douglas	695	1,438	536	1,713
Edmunds	1,259	1,327	1,007	1,553
Fall River	1,380	2,002	1,135	2,748
Faulk	714	842	579	1,124
Grant	1,988	2,148	1,606	2,738
Gregory	1,138	1,566	780	1,777
Haakon	379	958	237	1,168
Hamlin	1,258	1,380	963	1,762
Hand	1,101	1,461	846	2,030
Hanson	776	786	625	898
Harding	259	633	186	716
Hughes	2,853	4,545	2,072	4,985
Hutchinson	1,594	2,700	1,237	3,372
Hyde	436	546	350	797
Jackson	450	671	365	903
Jerauld	751	777	542	1,012
Jones	261	521	206	689

Kingsbury	1,472	1,592	1,249	2,121
Lake	2,663	2,439	2,367	3,027
Lawrence	3,705	5,570	2,565	5,949
Lincoln	3,190	3,537	2,626	3,988
Lyman	631	843	478	1,120
McCook	1,492	1,501	1,448	1,902
McPherson	571	1,358	418	1,813
Marshall	1,372	1,142	1,111	1,529
Meade	3,212	5,189	2,093	5,908
Mellette	385	460	303	616
Miner	955	795	960	1,004
Minnehaha	29,135	26,765	23,042	29,908
Moody	1,715	1,161	1,586	1,633
Pennington	12,068	19,510	8,224	21,947
Perkins	851	1,326	714	1,686
Potter	701	1,175	482	1,551
Roberts	2,267	2,012	2,063	2,767
Sanborn	770	815	611	1,080
Shannon	1,206	256	1,489	324
Spink	2,071	1,969	1,680	2,627
Stanley	511	698	351	942
Sully	393	571	266	836
Todd	1,117	535	1,022	679
Tripp	1,219	2,113	935	2,483
Turner	1,780	2,436	1,486	3,086
Union	2,612	1,907	2,221	2,431
Walworth	1,094	1,940	779	2,396
Yankton	3,777	4,186	2,932	5,161
Ziebach	427	362	359	429
Totals	145,560	165,415	116,113	200,267

South Dakota Vote Since 1940

1940, Roosevelt, Dem., 131,862; Willkie, Rep., 177,065.

1944, Roosevelt, Dem., 96,711; Dewey, Rep., 135,365.

1948, Truman, Dem., 117,653; Dewey, Rep., 129,651; Wallace, Prog., 2,801.

1952, Eisenhower, Rep., 203,857; Stevenson, Dem., 90,426.

1956, Eisenhower, Rep., 171,569; Stevenson, Dem., 122,288.

1960, Kennedy, Dem., 128,070; Nixon, Rep., 178,417.

1964, Johnson, Dem., 163,010; Goldwater, Rep., 130,108.

1968, Nixon, Rep., 149,841; Humphrey, Dem., 118,023; Wallace, 3d party, 13,400.

1972, Nixon, Rep., 166,476; McGovern, Dem., 139,945; Jenness, Soc. Workers, 994.

1976, Carter, Dem., 147,068; Ford, Rep., 151,505; MacBride, Libertarian, 1,619; Hall, Com., 318; Camejo, Soc. Workers, 168.

1980, Reagan, Rep., 198,343; Carter, Dem., 103,855; Anderson, Ind., 21,431; Clark, Libertarian, 3,824; Pulley, Soc. Workers, 250.

1984, Reagan, Rep., 200,267; Mondale, Dem., 116,113.

1988, Bush, Rep., 165,415; Dukakis, Dem., 145,560; Paul, Lib., 1,060; Fulani, New Alliance, 730.

Tennessee

	1988 Dukakis (D)	Bush (R)	1984 Mondale (D)	Reagan (R)
County				
Anderson	9,589	15,056	10,415	16,783
Bedford	4,046	4,856	4,499	4,699
Benton	2,826	2,167	3,398	2,481
Bledsoe	1,274	1,858	1,316	1,950
Blount	9,602	20,027	9,188	20,525
Bradley	6,122	15,829	6,085	16,322
Campbell	4,188	5,197	4,692	5,685
Cannon	1,726	1,604	1,846	1,669
Carroll	4,151	5,635	4,568	6,017
Carter	4,634	12,036	4,642	13,153
Cheatham	3,067	4,132	3,007	4,109
Chester	1,757	2,781	1,854	2,793
Claiborne	2,977	4,071	2,870	4,474
Clay	1,183	1,291	1,281	1,338
Cocke	2,115	5,430	2,068	6,665
Coffee	5,686	7,837	5,691	7,695
Crockett	1,742	2,214	1,937	2,479
Cumberland	3,964	7,557	3,605	7,083
Davidson	89,270	98,599	89,498	98,115
Decatur	1,880	2,286	2,031	2,390
De Kalb	2,452	2,098	2,645	2,337
Dickson	5,129	5,343	5,809	5,846
Dyer	3,690	6,508	3,991	6,610
Fayette	3,292	3,573	3,634	3,733
Fentress	1,856	3,103	1,755	2,922
Franklin	5,442	5,381	5,846	5,705
Gibson	7,542	8,415	8,334	9,484
Giles	3,918	3,518	3,812	3,875
Grainger	1,423	2,734	1,565	3,212
Greene	5,077	11,947	4,763	13,215
Grundy	2,415	1,429	2,596	1,396
Hamblen	5,061	10,418	4,922	11,144
Hamilton	40,990	68,111	41,449	69,626
Hancock	737	1,303	619	1,491

Hardeman	3,526	3,547	3,797	3,712
Hardin	2,808	4,252	3,051	4,632
Hawkins	5,212	9,356	4,802	9,863
Haywood	2,923	2,687	3,308	2,839
Henderson	2,296	5,418	2,426	5,362
Henry	5,138	4,784	5,407	5,376
Hickman	2,643	2,246	2,941	2,370
Houston	1,467	882	1,716	882
Humphreys	3,037	2,132	3,668	2,249
Jackson	1,962	1,168	2,894	1,544
Jefferson	3,168	6,832	3,185	7,721
Johnson	1,329	3,715	999	3,853
Knox	41,829	73,092	43,448	76,965
Lake	935	806	1,191	878
Lauderdale	3,296	3,308	3,506	3,566
Lawrence	4,903	6,273	5,458	6,034
Lewis	1,419	1,324	1,556	1,733
Lincoln	3,672	4,288	4,103	3,982
Loudon	3,480	7,122	3,227	7,113
McMinn	4,568	8,462	5,141	9,604
McNairy	3,510	4,625	3,825	4,776
Macon	1,538	2,962	1,747	3,330
Madison	11,001	16,952	12,006	17,819
Marion	4,175	4,407	3,942	4,337
Marshall	2,795	2,975	2,935	3,416
Maury	6,280	8,397	6,950	9,008
Meigs	1,048	1,507	1,012	1,575
Monroe	4,000	6,355	4,223	6,665
Montgomery	9,145	12,599	9,939	13,228
Moore	731	786	808	863
Morgan	1,941	2,576	2,121	2,903
Obion	4,785	6,037	4,769	6,384
Overton	2,511	1,873	2,749	2,054
Perry	1,208	854	1,316	948
Pickett	634	1,118	706	1,246
Polk	2,073	2,297	2,112	2,785
Putnam	6,606	9,547	7,443	8,999
Rhea	2,595	5,144	2,804	5,692
Roane	6,535	10,881	6,623	11,882
Robertson	5,884	5,714	5,756	5,445
Rutherford	12,245	20,397	11,618	19,503
Scott	1,611	2,562	1,810	3,107
Sequatchie	1,196	1,659	1,238	1,785
Sevier	3,643	11,920	3,384	12,517
Shelby	149,759	157,457	169,717	165,947
Smith	2,522	2,138	3,258	2,393
Stewart	1,979	1,302	2,174	1,285
Sullivan	17,396	32,996	16,925	36,516
Sumner	11,702	19,523	11,535	18,442
Tipton	3,824	6,052	3,895	5,945
Trousdale	1,193	969	1,142	781
Unicoi	1,794	3,664	1,696	4,249
Union	1,431	2,110	1,495	2,447
Van Buren	796	780	810	718
Warren	4,646	4,529	4,813	4,811
Washington	10,087	19,615	9,452	21,762
Wayne	1,516	3,405	1,534	3,332
Weakley	4,239	5,701	4,752	6,480
White	2,562	2,646	3,033	2,895
Williamson	7,864	20,847	6,929	17,975
Wilson	8,360	13,317	8,433	12,858
Totals	679,794	947,233	711,714	990,212

Tennessee Vote Since 1940

1940, Roosevelt, Dem., 351,601; Willkie, Rep., 169,153; Babson, Proh., 1,606; Thomas, Soc., 463.

1944, Roosevelt, Dem., 308,707; Dewey, Rep., 200,311; Watson, Proh., 882; Thomas, Soc., 892.

1948, Truman, Dem., 270,402; Dewey, Rep., 202,914; Thurmond, States' Rights, 73,815; Wallace, Prog., 1,864; Thomas, Soc., 1,288.

1952, Eisenhower, Rep., 446,147; Stevenson, Dem., 443,710; Hamblen, Proh., 1,432; Hallinan, Prog., 885; MacArthur, Christian Nationalist, 379.

1956, Eisenhower, Rep., 462,288; Stevenson, Dem., 456,507; Andrews, Ind., 19,820; Holtwick, Proh., 789.

1960, Kennedy, Dem., 481,453; Nixon, Rep., 556,577; Faubus, States' Rights, 11,304; Decker, Proh., 2,458.

1964, Johnson, Dem. 635,047; Goldwater, Rep., 508,965; write-in, 34.

1968, Nixon, Rep., 472,592; Humphrey, Dem., 351,233; Wallace, 3d party, 424,792.

1972, Nixon, Rep., 813,147; McGovern, Dem., 357,293; Schmitz, Amer., 30,373; write-in, 369.

1976, Carter, Dem., 825,879; Ford, Rep., 633,969; Anderson, Amer., 5,769; McCarthy, Ind., 5,004; Maddox, Am. Ind., 2,303; MacBride, Libertarian, 1,375; Hall, Com., 547; LaRouche, U.S. Labor, 512; Bubar, Proh., 442; Miller, Ind., 316; write-in, 230.

1980, Reagan, Rep., 787,761; Carter, Dem., 783,051; Anderson, Ind., 35,991; Clark, Libertarian, 7,116; Commoner, Citizens, 1,112; Bubar, Statesman, 521; McReynolds, So-

cialist, 519; Hall, Com., 503; DeBerry, Soc. Worker, 490;
Griswold, Workers World, 400; write-ins, 152.
1984, Reagan, Rep., 990,212; Mondale, Dem., 711,714;
Bergland, Libertarian, 3,072.
1988, Bush, Rep., 947,233; Dukakis, Dem., 679,794; Paul,
Ind., 2,041; Duke, Ind., 1,807.

Texas

County	1988 Dukakis (D)	Bush (R)	1984 Mondale (D)	Reagan (R)
Anderson	6,128	7,858	4,747	8,634
Andrews	1,122	3,052	820	3,918
Angelina	10,849	12,738	9,054	14,685
Aransas	2,305	3,858	1,696	4,352
Archer	1,627	2,010	1,089	2,487
Armstrong	314	720	238	791
Atascosa	4,657	4,777	3,547	5,279
Austin	2,593	4,524	1,941	4,872
Bailey	876	1,459	684	1,888
Bandera	1,251	3,435	771	3,152
Bastrop	8,004	5,991	4,744	6,439
Baylor	1,153	914	1,019	1,314
Bee	4,616	4,620	3,659	5,377
Bell	17,751	29,382	13,322	31,117
Bexar	174,036	193,192	136,947	203,319
Blanco	1,012	1,680	700	1,957
Borden	169	283	140	325
Bosque	2,670	3,458	2,046	3,923
Bowie	12,331	15,454	10,077	18,244
Brazoria	23,436	34,028	18,609	39,166
Brazos	14,885	29,369	12,348	34,733
Brewster	1,569	1,708	1,462	2,066
Briscoe	574	464	471	538
Brooks	2,859	608	2,702	896
Brown	4,763	6,810	4,070	8,468
Burleson	3,085	2,242	2,578	3,076
Burnet	4,343	5,120	2,983	5,895
Caldwell	4,649	3,553	3,461	4,315
Calhoun	3,314	3,183	2,586	4,434
Callahan	2,017	2,887	1,305	3,538
Cameron	30,972	24,263	26,394	29,545
Camp	2,121	1,908	1,917	2,238
Carson	1,034	2,100	826	2,412
Cass	5,941	5,305	5,053	6,677
Castro	1,436	1,604	1,009	2,026
Chambers	3,035	3,694	2,632	4,322
Cherokee	5,604	7,520	4,494	8,187
Childress	1,060	1,201	900	1,574
Clay	2,288	2,043	1,844	2,569
Cochran	681	771	557	1,117
Coke	674	863	532	1,060
Coleman	1,978	2,340	1,420	2,790
Collin	22,934	67,776	13,604	61,095
Collingsworth	809	872	742	1,396
Colorado	2,847	3,723	2,428	4,528
Comal	5,716	13,994	4,179	13,452
Comanche	2,622	2,120	2,248	2,678
Concho	643	617	580	821
Cooke	4,217	7,196	3,278	8,260
Coryell	4,026	7,461	3,113	9,056
Cottle	690	379	623	507
Crane	596	1,219	392	1,473
Crockett	881	932	589	1,094
Crosby	1,435	1,121	1,212	1,376
Culberson	557	417	407	509
Dallam	645	1,205	496	1,594
Dallas	243,198	347,094	203,592	405,444
Dawson	2,155	3,154	1,781	3,685
Deaf Smith	1,930	3,744	1,485	4,762
Delta	1,244	849	973	1,024
Denton	26,204	57,444	16,772	52,865
DeWitt	2,579	3,628	1,882	4,401
Dickens	696	435	692	594
Dimmit	2,735	900	2,546	1,338
Donley	661	1,043	529	1,297
Duval	4,177	907	3,748	1,201
Eastland	3,215	3,929	2,522	4,841
Ector	10,825	23,155	8,913	31,228
Edwards	368	556	159	626
Ellis	11,169	16,422	8,029	16,873
El Paso	62,622	55,573	51,917	66,114
Erath	4,113	5,427	3,234	6,122
Falls	2,877	2,344	2,834	3,133
Fannin	5,163	4,024	4,399	4,692
Fayette	3,390	4,551	2,379	5,711
Fisher	1,516	721	1,384	965
Floyd	1,391	1,741	1,023	2,092
Foard	513	306	448	472
Fort Bend	23,351	39,818	18,729	41,370
Franklin	1,453	1,439	1,104	1,836
Freestone	2,916	3,159	2,489	3,624
Frio	3,016	1,505	2,656	2,003
Gaines	1,310	2,265	797	2,714
Galveston	38,633	34,913	36,092	40,262
Garza	989	1,183	521	1,219
Gillespie	1,588	5,662	1,137	5,496
Glasscock	143	384	128	403
Goliad	1,358	1,427	836	1,540
Gonzales	2,897	2,983	2,196	3,962
Gray	2,460	7,259	2,003	8,955
Grayson	14,347	18,825	11,803	22,554
Gregg	12,486	26,465	10,700	29,697
Grimes	2,735	2,820	2,370	3,365
Guadalupe	7,111	13,265	5,060	14,382
Hale	3,502	6,284	3,202	7,670
Hall	1,029	714	984	1,058
Hamilton	1,355	1,718	1,130	2,118
Hansford	443	1,967	259	2,213
Hardeman	1,143	855	927	1,238
Hardin	8,245	6,897	6,782	8,380
Harris	342,919	464,217	334,135	536,029
Harrison	8,974	11,957	7,773	12,618
Hartley	505	1,229	356	1,419
Haskell	1,715	1,193	1,434	1,701
Hays	11,187	11,716	6,663	12,467
Hemphill	527	1,170	413	1,650
Henderson	9,819	11,005	7,302	12,725
Hidalgo	54,330	29,246	44,147	35,059
Hill	4,381	4,796	3,420	5,344
Hockley	2,850	4,368	2,044	5,462
Hood	4,255	7,400	3,063	6,817
Hopkins	4,984	5,133	3,707	5,772
Houston	3,846	3,882	3,275	4,542
Howard	4,445	6,024	4,115	7,519
Hudspeth	406	405	362	557
Hunt	8,820	12,331	6,971	14,303
Hutchinson	2,950	7,526	2,052	9,078
Irion	326	539	199	619
Jack	1,521	1,542	945	1,825
Jackson	2,141	2,954	1,804	3,661
Jasper	6,613	4,985	5,787	5,965
Jeff Davis	325	524	299	511
Jefferson	55,649	35,754	54,846	45,124
Jim Hogg	1,630	510	1,703	608
Jim Wells	8,495	4,335	7,795	5,896
Johnson	12,507	17,509	9,148	18,254
Jones	2,898	3,000	2,343	4,017
Karnes	2,529	2,383	1,802	3,068
Kaufman	7,358	8,466	5,554	9,343
Kendall	1,446	4,875	938	4,568
Kenedy	119	76	110	96
Kent	398	274	253	332
Kerr	3,587	11,207	3,102	11,829
Kimble	551	1,061	442	1,333
King	64	111	53	141
Kinney	669	771	486	774
Kleberg	5,367	4,443	4,924	5,712
Knox	1,013	765	921	1,027
Lamar	7,553	8,021	5,504	9,273
Lamb	2,230	3,064	1,919	3,692
Lampasas	1,954	3,000	1,356	3,285
LaSalle	1,651	693	1,604	1,007
Lavaca	3,531	4,377	2,464	5,058
Lee	2,527	2,513	1,659	2,967
Leon	2,316	2,778	1,821	3,207
Liberty	8,343	8,524	6,292	10,504
Limestone	3,476	3,257	3,228	4,063
Lipscomb	377	1,111	241	1,461
Live Oak	1,573	2,277	1,260	2,481
Llano	2,629	3,550	1,894	4,042
Loving	23	54	16	57
Lubbock	22,202	50,760	18,793	57,151
Lynn	1,086	1,279	1,009	1,617
McCulloch	1,665	1,618	1,433	2,060
McLennan	27,545	38,606	23,206	42,232
McMullen	94	302	61	337
Madison	1,835	1,896	1,384	2,158
Marion	2,255	1,857	2,111	2,336
Martin	632	1,017	512	1,218
Mason	671	975	570	1,168
Matagorda	5,675	6,787	5,201	8,452
Maverick	4,395	1,592	3,063	1,783
Medina	4,227	5,722	3,053	5,737
Menard	614	552	394	725
Midland	8,487	30,618	7,214	33,706
Milam	4,865	3,512	3,734	4,384
Mills	842	1,043	688	1,262
Mitchell	1,773	1,596	1,332	2,007
Montague	3,689	3,475	2,602	4,406
Montgomery	18,394	40,360	13,293	41,230
Moore	1,537	3,710	1,129	4,649
Morris	3,522	2,104	2,925	2,778
Motley	262	429	282	533
Nacogdoches	6,886	11,767	5,694	13,063
Navarro	6,749	6,445	5,672	7,816
Newton	3,640	1,659	3,296	2,123
Nolan	2,853	2,734	2,524	3,608
Nueces	49,209	46,337	46,721	54,333
Ochiltree	579	2,928	419	3,492
Oldham	303	691	226	762
Orange	17,834	11,059	16,816	15,386
Palo Pinto	3,930	4,649	3,349	5,701
Panola	4,123	4,642	3,179	5,676
Parker	8,517	14,090	6,050	13,647
Parmer	764	2,061	567	2,524
Pecos	1,960	2,483	1,596	3,451
Polk	5,943	5,831	3,898	5,987
Potter	9,563	16,400	8,365	20,396

Presidio	1,176	586	992	837
Rains	1,448	1,281	1,027	1,560
Randall	8,492	27,986	6,044	30,249
Reagan	418	935	243	1,079
Real	483	795	360	1,004
Red River	3,165	2,475	2,518	2,979
Reeves	2,812	1,724	2,396	2,461
Refugio	1,831	1,883	1,559	2,421
Roberts	135	441	106	539
Robertson	3,630	2,184	3,339	2,663
Rockwall	2,659	7,214	1,639	6,688
Runnels	1,720	2,417	1,179	2,968
Rusk	5,140	9,117	4,599	11,081
Sabine	2,053	1,925	1,940	2,045
San Augustine	2,118	1,946	1,583	1,937
San Jacinto	2,972	2,691	2,466	3,174
San Patricio	9,920	9,159	8,838	11,074
San Saba	1,165	1,099	1,070	1,566
Schleicher	494	653	326	854
Scurry	2,119	3,749	1,564	5,028
Shackelford	681	865	415	1,181
Shelby	4,261	3,999	3,610	4,863
Sherman	340	1,145	246	1,269
Smith	18,719	34,658	15,227	40,740
Somervell	983	1,304	635	1,422
Starr	6,958	1,218	5,047	1,658
Stephens	1,519	2,342	1,046	2,898
Sterling	188	464	129	577
Stonewall	724	421	643	599
Sutton	571	996	465	1,251
Swisher	1,893	1,271	1,642	1,611
Tarrant	151,310	242,660	120,147	248,050
Taylor	13,073	28,563	9,628	34,444
Terrell	390	296	289	407
Terry	1,941	2,645	1,535	3,181
Throckmorton	534	455	388	586
Titus	4,357	4,247	3,631	5,069
Tom Green	12,283	21,463	8,981	23,847
Travis	127,783	105,915	94,124	124,944
Trinity	2,657	2,448	2,115	2,599
Tyler	4,198	3,070	3,119	3,638
Upshur	5,242	5,991	4,614	7,325
Upton	544	1,189	380	1,603
Uvalde	3,684	4,266	2,482	4,790
Val Verde	5,044	5,109	3,857	5,909
Van Zandt	6,153	7,371	4,506	8,474
Victoria	8,923	15,056	7,037	18,787
Walker	5,826	8,473	4,263	8,809
Waller	3,957	3,607	3,828	4,116
Ward	1,858	2,709	1,188	3,474
Washington	2,960	6,041	2,483	6,506
Webb	16,227	7,528	12,308	8,582
Wharton	5,935	6,978	5,072	8,495
Wheeler	1,067	1,703	805	2,251
Wichita	17,956	23,324	16,009	28,932
Wilbarger	2,248	2,669	2,011	3,644
Willacy	3,165	1,750	3,037	2,340
Williamson	19,589	27,322	9,911	25,774
Wilson	3,953	4,436	2,829	4,588
Winkler	947	1,656	752	2,213
Wise	5,288	6,064	3,856	6,958
Wood	4,553	6,216	3,449	7,144
Yoakum	727	1,762	456	2,204
Young	3,007	4,156	2,203	5,282
Zapata	2,171	958	1,577	1,214
Zavala	3,338	628	2,937	924
Totals	2,352,748	3,036,829	1,949,276	3,433,428

Texas Vote Since 1940

1940, Roosevelt, Dem., 840,151; Willkie, Rep., 199,152; Babson, Proh., 925; Thomas, Soc., 728; Browder, Com., 212.

1944, Roosevelt, Dem., 821,605; Dewey, Rep., 191,425; Texas Regulars, 135,439; Watson, Proh., 1,017; Thomas, Soc., 594; America First, 250.

1948, Truman, Dem., 750,700; Dewey, Rep., 282,240; Thurmond, States' Rights, 106,909; Wallace, Prog., 3,764; Watson, Proh., 2,758; Thomas, Soc., 874.

1952, Eisenhower, Rep., 1,102,878; Stevenson, Dem., 969,228; Hamblen, Proh., 1,983; MacArthur, Christian Nationalist, 833; MacArthur, Constitution, 730; Hallinan, Prog., 294.

1956, Eisenhower, Rep., 1,080,619; Stevenson, Dem., 859,958; Andrews, Ind., 14,591.

1960, Kennedy, Dem., 1,167,932; Nixon, Rep., 1,121,699; Sullivan, Constitution, 18,169; Decker, Proh., 3,870; write-in, 15.

1964, Johnson, Dem., 1,663,185; Goldwater, Rep., 958,566; Lightburn, Constitution, 5,060.

1968, Nixon, Rep., 1,227,844; Humphrey, Dem., 1,266,804; Wallace, 3d party, 584,269; write-in, 489.

1972, Nixon, Rep., 2,298,896; McGovern, Dem., 1,154,289; Schmitz, Amer., 6,039; Jenness, Soc. Workers, 8,664; others, 3,393.

1976, Carter, Dem., 2,082,319; Ford, Rep., 1,953,300; McCarthy, Ind., 20,118; Anderson, Amer., 11,442; Camejo, Soc. Workers, 1,723; write-in, 2,982.

1980, Reagan, Rep., 2,510,705; Carter, Dem., 1,881,147; Anderson, Ind., 111,613; Clark, Libertarian, 37,643; write-in, 528.

1984, Reagan, Rep., 3,433,428; Mondale, Dem., 1,949,276.

1988, Bush, Rep., 3,036,829; Dukakis, Dem., 2,352,748; Paul, Lib., 30,355; Fulani, New Alliance, 7,208.

Utah

	1988		1984	
County	Dukakis (D)	Bush (R)	Mondale (D)	Reagan (R)
Beaver	816	1,286	708	1,516
Box Elder	2,736	12,585	1,983	13,243
Cache	5,871	21,766	4,123	22,127
Carbon	5,521	3,019	4,357	4,393
Daggett	132	272	227	296
Davis	16,868	50,469	11,727	49,863
Duchesne	1,227	3,118	746	4,437
Emery	1,788	2,322	1,326	3,081
Garfield	370	1,470	315	1,609
Grand	1,287	1,265	876	2,463
Iron	1,736	6,038	1,342	6,856
Juab	974	1,505	917	1,902
Kane	398	1,788	294	1,710
Millard	1,124	3,515	1,192	4,345
Morgan	647	1,889	481	1,934
Piute	206	476	151	606
Rich	234	621	131	797
Salt Lake	107,453	163,557	78,488	183,536
San Juan	1,407	2,377	1,145	2,598
Sanpete	1,822	4,579	1,227	5,507
Sevier	1,403	4,747	1,072	5,736
Summit	2,545	3,881	1,539	4,093
Tooele	4,166	5,539	3,584	6,478
Uintah	1,799	5,341	1,186	7,337
Utah	18,533	68,134	14,801	72,284
Wasatch	1,451	2,487	1,015	2,789
Washington	3,054	13,306	1,846	12,049
Wayne	353	784	224	930
Weber	21,431	39,676	18,346	44,590
Totals	207,352	428,442	155,369	469,105

Utah Vote Since 1940

1940, Roosevelt, Dem., 154,277; Willkie, Rep., 93,151; Thomas, Soc., 200; Browder, Com., 191.

1944, Roosevelt, Dem., 150,088; Dewey, Rep., 97,891; Thomas, Soc., 340.

1948, Truman, Dem., 149,151; Dewey, Rep., 124,402; Wallace, Prog., 2,679; Dobbs, Soc. Workers, 73.

1952, Eisenhower, Rep., 194,190; Stevenson, Dem., 135,364.

1956, Eisenhower, Rep., 215,631; Stevenson, Dem., 118,364.

1960, Kennedy, Dem., 169,248; Nixon, Rep., 205,361; Dobbs, Soc. Workers, 100.

1964, Johnson, Dem., 219,628; Goldwater, Rep., 181,785.

1968, Nixon, Rep., 238,728; Humphrey, Dem., 156,665; Wallace, 3d party, 26,906; Halstead, Soc. Worker, 89; Peace and Freedom, 180.

1972, Nixon, Rep., 323,643; McGovern, Dem., 126,284; Schmitz, Amer., 28,549.

1976, Carter, Dem., 182,110; Ford, Rep., 337,908; Anderson, Amer., 13,304; McCarthy, Ind., 3,907; MacBride, Libertarian, 2,438; Maddox, Am. Ind., 1,162; Camejo, Soc. Workers, 268; Hall, Com., 121.

1980, Reagan, Rep., 439,687; Carter, Dem., 124,266; Anderson, Ind., 30,284; Clark, Libertarian, 7,226; Commoner, Citizens, 1,009; Greaves, American, 965; Rarick, Amer. Ind., 522; Hall, Com., 139; DeBerry, Soc. Worker, 124.

1984, Reagan, Rep., 469,105; Mondale, Dem., 155,369; Bergland, Libertarian, 2,447.

1988, Bush, Rep., 428,442; Dukakis, Dem., 207,352; Paul, Lib., 7,473; Dennis, American, 2,158.

Vermont

	1988		1984	
City	Dukakis (D)	Bush (R)	Mondale (D)	Reagan (R)
Barre City	2,132	2,100	1,903	2,195
Bennington	3,180	2,748	2,879	3,237
Brattleboro	3,136	2,044	2,741	2,645
Burlington	9,748	6,382	10,080	7,857
Montpelier	2,351	2,013	2,120	2,257

Rutland City....	3,590	3,631	3,298	3,970
St. Albans City ...	1,441	1,295	1,346	1,748
St. Johnsbury...	1,188	1,974	915	2,152
South Burlington .	3,373	3,136	2,728	3,443
Winooski.......	1,426	1,014	1,361	1,264
Totals........	115,775	124,331	95,730	135,865

Vermont Vote Since 1940

1940, Roosevelt, Dem., 64,269; Willkie, Rep., 78,371; Browder, Com., 411.

1944, Roosevelt, Dem., 53,820; Dewey, Rep., 71,527.

1948, Truman, Dem., 45,557; Dewey, Rep., 75,926; Wallace, Prog., 1,279; Thomas, Soc., 585.

1952, Eisenhower, Rep., 109,717; Stevenson, Dem., 43,355; Hallinan, Prog., 282; Hoopes, Soc., 185.

1956, Eisenhower, Rep., 110,390; Stevenson, Dem., 42,549; scattered, 39.

1960, Kennedy, Dem., 69,186; Nixon, Rep., 98,131.

1964, Johnson, Dem., 107,674; Goldwater, Rep., 54,868.

1968, Nixon, Rep., 85,142; Humphrey, Dem., 70,255; Wallace, 3d party, 5,104; Halstead, Soc. Worker, 295; Gregory, New Party, 579.

1972, Nixon, Rep., 117,149; McGovern, Dem., 68,174; Spock, Liberty Union, 1,010; Jenness, Soc. Workers, 296; scattered, 318.

1976, Carter, Dem., 77,798; Carter, Ind. Vermonter, 991; Ford, Rep., 100,387; McCarthy, Ind., 4,001; Camejo, Soc. Workers, 430; LaRouche, U.S. Labor, 196; scattered, 99.

1980, Reagan, Rep., 94,598; Carter, Dem., 81,891; Anderson, Ind., 31,760; Commoner, Citizens, 2,316; Clark, Libertarian, 1,900; McReynolds, Liberty Union, 136; Hall, Com. 118; DeBerry, Soc. Worker, 75; scattered, 413.

1984, Reagan, Rep., 135,865; Mondale, Dem., 95,730; Bergland, Libertarian, 1,002.

1988, Bush, Rep., 124,331; Dukakis, Dem., 115,775; Paul, Lib., 1,000; LaRouche, Ind., 275.

Virginia

	1988		1984	
County	Dukakis (D)	Bush (R)	Mondale (D)	Reagan (R)
Accomack....	4,443	6,926	4,355	8,047
Albemarle......	10,363	15,117	7,982	14,455
Alleghany......	2,316	2,555	1,932	3,067
Amelia.......	1,359	2,187	1,432	2,336
Amherst.......	3,567	6,507	3,409	7,004
Appomattox....	1,740	3,205	1,498	3,386
Arlington.......	40,314	34,191	37,031	34,848
Augusta.......	4,170	13,251	3,899	15,308
Bath........	881	1,273	727	1,434
Bedford.......	5,406	10,702	4,754	10,371
Bland.......	937	1,556	867	1,812
Botetourt.......	3,763	5,687	3,243	5,959
Brunswick....	3,070	2,742	3,040	2,950
Buchanan.......	6,935	3,912	7,828	5,053
Buckingham....	1,941	2,481	1,879	2,627
Campbell.......	4,574	12,713	4,380	13,388
Caroline.......	3,186	3,065	3,111	2,949
Carroll.......	3,190	6,377	2,914	7,056
Charles City.....	1,839	826	1,776	776
Charlotte.......	1,923	2,699	1,811	2,999
Chesterfield....	18,723	58,828	13,739	54,896
Clarke.......	1,478	2,502	1,215	2,529
Craig........	864	1,112	845	1,173
Culpeper.......	2,555	5,896	2,255	5,596
Cumberland....	1,132	1,978	1,237	2,027
Dickenson......	4,461	3,091	4,848	3,921
Dinwiddie......	3,405	4,165	3,485	4,547
Essex.......	1,294	2,038	1,300	2,120
Fairfax........	125,711	200,631	107,295	183,181
Fauquier.......	4,837	11,733	4,056	10,319
Floyd.......	1,727	2,921	1,599	3,431
Fluvanna.......	1,562	2,447	1,332	2,247
Franklin.......	5,734	7,391	4,903	7,684
Frederick.......	3,707	9,921	2,671	9,542
Giles........	3,042	3,490	3,047	4,340
Gloucester......	3,372	7,646	2,830	7,109
Goochland......	2,209	3,765	2,178	3,404
Grayson.......	2,441	3,968	2,319	4,508
Greene.......	899	2,234	760	2,216
Greensville....	2,083	1,610	2,352	2,304
Halifax.......	4,282	5,671	4,231	6,726
Hanover.......	5,985	20,570	4,831	18,800
Henrico........	26,980	62,284	21,336	63,864
Henry........	7,536	10,871	6,976	12,693
Highland.......	456	807	398	997
Isle of Wight.....	3,747	5,779	3,650	5,664
James City......	4,642	8,945	3,486	7,104
King George.....	1,519	2,587	1,450	2,356
King and Queen...	1,309	1,376	1,201	1,449
King William.....	1,561	2,735	1,448	2,803
Lancaster......	1,551	3,380	1,559	3,416
Lee........	4,906	4,080	5,085	5,365
Loudoun...	10,101	20,448	8,227	17,765
Louisa.......	2,789	3,831	2,703	3,789
Lunenburg....	1,870	2,530	1,754	2,713
Madison........	1,427	2,501	1,302	2,723
Mathews........	1,235	2,752	1,106	2,868
Mecklenburg....	3,275	5,887	3,438	6,777
Middlesex....	1,361	2,571	1,206	2,612
Montgomery....	8,909	12,326	7,202	12,428
Nelson........	2,272	2,502	2,021	2,777
New Kent.......	1,427	2,917	1,204	2,679
Northampton...	2,242	2,562	2,226	2,906
Northumberland...	1,506	2,984	1,407	3,166
Nottoway.......	2,217	3,161	2,296	3,418
Orange........	2,592	4,319	2,285	4,483
Page........	2,499	5,013	2,437	5,021
Patrick........	2,093	3,990	1,908	4,703
Pittsylvania....	6,612	12,229	7,791	15,743
Powhatan....	1,467	4,040	1,381	3,921
Prince Edward....	2,434	3,147	2,589	3,454
Prince George....	2,469	4,982	2,136	4,999
Prince William....	19,198	39,654	15,631	34,992
Pulaski........	4,686	6,844	4,364	8,242
Rappahannock....	1,003	1,657	999	1,696
Richmond.......	924	1,862	830	1,869
Roanoke.......	12,938	22,011	10,569	23,348
Rockbridge....	2,412	3,541	2,098	4,067
Rockingham....	4,716	13,241	4,220	13,480
Russell........	6,222	4,374	6,760	5,738
Scott........	3,616	4,986	3,904	5,804
Shenandoah....	3,276	8,612	2,771	9,048
Smyth........	3,989	7,446	4,102	8,593
Southampton....	3,000	3,439	3,300	4,669
Spotsylvania....	5,486	10,978	4,012	8,207
Stafford.......	5,380	12,234	4,429	10,283
Surry........	1,602	1,246	1,875	1,462
Sussex........	1,958	1,822	2,408	2,183
Tazewell.......	8,098	7,165	8,014	9,645
Warren........	2,769	4,700	2,551	5,016
Washington....	5,819	10,722	5,573	12,132
Westmoreland....	2,311	2,974	2,363	3,219
Wise........	7,017	6,189	7,303	7,909
Wythe........	3,201	5,827	2,996	6,773
York........	4,639	11,103	4,063	10,214
City				
Alexandria......	24,358	20,913	23,552	21,166
Bedford........	960	1,322	997	1,553
Bristol........	2,446	4,407	2,429	5,012
Buena Vista......	828	1,121	724	1,335
Charlottesville....	7,671	5,817	7,317	6,947
Chesapeake....	18,828	29,738	16,740	27,542
Clifton Forge....	961	759	896	965
Colonial Heights....	1,581	6,001	1,218	6,387
Covington.......	1,567	1,274	1,391	1,722
Danville.......	7,353	12,221	5,846	12,141
Emporia.......	977	1,289	807	1,252
Fairfax........	3,430	5,576	3,263	6,234
Falls Church....	2,484	2,470	2,398	2,684
Franklin.......	1,630	1,557	1,537	1,561
Fredericksburg ...	2,683	3,401	2,439	3,500
Galax........	907	1,278	814	1,548
Hampton.......	19,106	24,034	18,180	25,537
Harrisonburg....	2,799	5,376	2,384	5,221
Hopewell.......	2,566	4,672	2,564	5,661
Lexington.......	997	994	946	1,197
Lynchburg....	8,279	15,323	8,542	17,447
Manassas.......	2,658	5,980	1,824	4,615
Manassas Park....	434	993	375	975
Martinsville....	2,794	3,360	2,942	4,234
Newport News....	21,413	32,570	21,834	33,614
Norfolk........	37,778	30,538	38,913	36,360
Norton........	795	608	842	806
Petersburg....	8,177	4,231	9,248	5,753
Poquoson.......	877	3,840	647	3,667
Portsmouth....	19,698	16,087	21,623	18,940
Radford.......	1,855	2,481	1,781	2,855
Richmond.......	42,155	31,586	49,408	38,754
Roanoke.......	17,185	15,389	17,300	19,008
Salem........	3,760	5,694	3,347	6,419
South Boston....	936	1,694	974	1,899
Staunton.......	2,457	5,775	2,012	6,137
Suffolk........	8,080	9,742	8,842	10,128
Virginia Beach....	33,780	76,481	24,703	72,571
Waynesboro....	2,038	4,672	1,579	4,465
Williamsburg....	1,534	1,648	1,469	1,913
Winchester....	2,300	4,497	2,064	5,055
Total........	859,799	1,309,162	796,250	1,337,078

Virginia Vote Since 1940

1940, Roosevelt, Dem., 235,961; Willkie, Rep., 109,363; Babson, Proh., 882; Thomas, Soc., 282; Browder, Com., 71; Aiken, Soc. Labor, 48.

1944, Roosevelt, Dem., 242,276; Dewey, Rep., 145,243; Watson, Proh., 459; Thomas, Soc., 417; Teichert, Soc. Labor, 90.

1948, Truman, Dem., 200,786; Dewey, Rep., 172,070; Thurmond, States' Rights, 43,393; Wallace, Prog., 2,047; Thomas, Soc., 726; Teichert, Soc. Labor, 234.

1952, Eisenhower, Rep., 349,037; Stevenson, Dem., 268,677; Hass, Soc. Labor, 1,160; Hoopes, Social Dem., 504; Hallinan, Prog., 311.

1956, Eisenhower, Rep., 386,459; Stevenson, Dem., 267,760; Andrews, States' Rights, 42,964; Hoopes, Soc. Dem., 444; Hass, Soc. Labor, 351.

1960, Kennedy, Dem., 362,327; Nixon, Rep., 404,521; Coiner, Conservative, 4,204; Hass, Soc. Labor, 397.

1964, Johnson, Dem., 558,038; Goldwater, Rep., 481,334; Hass, Soc. Labor, 2,895.

1968, Nixon, Rep., 590,319; Humphrey, Dem., 442,387; Wallace, 3d party, *320,272; Blomen, Soc. Labor, 4,671; Munn, Proh., 601; Gregory, Peace and Freedom, 1,680.

*10,561 votes for Wallace were omitted in the count.

1972, Nixon, Rep., 988,493; McGovern, Dem., 438,887; Schmitz, Amer., 19,721; Fisher, Soc. Labor, 9,918.

1976, Carter, Dem., 813,896; Ford, Rep., 836,554; Camejo, Soc. Workers, 17,802; Anderson, Amer., 16,686; LaRouche, U.S. Labor, 7,508; MacBride, Libertarian, 4,648.

1980, Reagan, Rep., 989,609; Carter, Dem., 752,174; Anderson, Ind., 95,418; Commoner, Citizens, 14,024; Clark, Libertarian, 12,821; DeBerry, Soc. Worker, 1,986.

1984, Reagan, Rep., 1,337,078; Mondale, Dem., 796,250.

1988, Bush, Rep., 1,309,162; Dukakis, Dem., 859,799; Fulani, Ind., 14,312; Paul, Lib., 8,336.

Washington

County	1988		1984	
	Dukakis (D)	Bush (R)	Mondale (D)	Reagan (R)
Adams	1,612	2,612	1,311	3,449
Asotin	3,422	2,874	3,042	3,876
Benton	14,817	28,698	13,784	32,307
Chelan	8,183	11,601	6,978	13,667
Clallam	11,123	11,200	9,701	13,605
Clark	40,021	37,285	35,248	40,681
Columbia	730	1,172	673	1,404
Cowlitz	16,090	12,009	15,361	14,858
Douglas	3,760	5,378	3,127	6,443
Ferry	972	972	935	1,232
Franklin	4,772	6,488	4,328	7,724
Garfield	593	714	493	913
Grant	7,564	10,859	6,298	12,888
Grays Harbor	14,097	8,860	14,050	11,286
Island	8,510	12,552	6,850	13,548
Jefferson	5,270	4,184	4,602	4,543
King	349,663	290,574	289,620	332,987
Kitsap	33,748	34,743	29,681	36,101
Kittitas	5,318	5,048	4,830	6,580
Klickitat	2,991	2,920	2,712	3,910
Lewis	8,629	14,184	7,634	15,846
Lincoln	1,884	2,689	1,671	3,474
Mason	7,826	7,426	7,007	8,410
Okanogan	5,630	5,856	5,330	7,476
Pacific	5,017	3,073	4,679	3,613
Pend Oreille	1,925	1,802	1,655	2,374
Pierce	96,688	94,167	79,498	112,877
San Juan	3,008	2,660	2,514	2,900
Skagit	15,159	16,550	13,947	18,840
Skamania	1,748	1,356	1,552	1,736
Snohomish	80,694	84,158	66,728	90,362
Spokane	68,520	68,787	59,620	88,043
Stevens	5,068	6,576	4,304	8,211
Thurston	33,860	31,990	26,840	34,442
Wahkiakum	961	629	930	776
Walla Walla	7,448	9,683	6,804	12,361
Whatcom	25,571	23,820	22,670	27,228
Whitman	7,403	7,680	6,621	10,021
Yakima	23,221	30,026	24,724	40,678
Totals	933,516	903,835	798,352	1,051,670

Washington Vote Since 1940

1940, Roosevelt, Dem., 462,145; Willkie, Rep., 322,123; Thomas, Soc., 4,586; Browder, Com., 2,626; Babson, Proh., 1,686; Aiken, Soc. Labor, 667.

1944, Roosevelt, Dem., 486,774; Dewey, Rep., 361,689; Thomas, Soc., 3,824; Watson, Proh., 2,396; Teichert, Soc. Labor, 1,645.

1948, Truman, Dem., 476,165; Dewey, Rep., 386,315; Wallace, Prog., 31,692; Watson, Proh., 6,117; Thomas, Soc., 3,534; Teichert, Soc. Labor, 1,133; Dobbs, Soc. Workers, 103.

1952, Eisenhower, Rep., 599,107; Stevenson, Dem., 492,845; MacArthur, Christian Nationalist, 7,290; Hallinan, Prog.,

2,460; Hass, Soc. Labor, 633; Hoopes, Soc., 254; Dobbs, Soc. Workers, 119.

1956, Eisenhower, Rep., 620,430; Stevenson, Dem., 523,002; Hass, Soc. Labor, 7,457.

1960, Kennedy, Dem., 599,298; Nixon, Rep., 629,273; Hass, Soc. Labor, 10,895; Curtis, Constitution, 1,401; Dobbs, Soc. Workers, 705.

1964, Johnson, Dem., 779,699; Goldwater, Rep., 470,366; Hass, Soc. Labor, 7,772; DeBerry, Freedom Soc., 537.

1968, Nixon, Rep., 588,510; Humphrey, Dem., 616,037; Wallace, 3d party, 96,990; Blomen, Soc. Labor, 488; Cleaver, Peace and Freedom, 1,609; Halstead, Soc. Worker, 270; Mitchell, Free Ballot, 377.

1972, Nixon, Rep., 837,135; McGovern, Dem., 568,334; Schmitz, Amer., 58,906; Spock, Ind., 2,644; Fisher, Soc. Labor, 1,102; Jenness, Soc. Worker, 623; Hall, Com., 566; Hospers, Libertarian, 1,537.

1976, Carter, Dem., 717,323; Ford, Rep., 777,732; McCarthy, Ind., 36,986; Maddox, Amer. Ind., 8,585; Anderson, Amer., 5,046; MacBride, Libertarian, 5,042; Wright, People's, 1,124; Camejo, Soc. Workers, 905; LaRouche, U.S. Labor, 903; Hall, Com., 817; Levin, Soc. Labor, 713; Zeidler, Soc., 358.

1980, Reagan, Rep., 865,244; Carter, Dem., 650,193; Anderson, Ind., 185,073; Clark, Libertarian, 29,213; Commoner, Citizens, 9,403; DeBerry, Soc. Worker, 1,137; McReynolds, Socialist, 956; Hall, Com., 834; Griswold, Workers World, 341.

1984, Reagan, Rep., 1,051,670; Mondale, Dem., 798,352; Bergland, Libertarian, 8,844.

1988, Bush, Rep., 903,835; Dukakis, Dem., 933,516; Paul, Lib., 17,240; LaRouche, Ind., 4,412.

West Virginia

County	1988		1984	
	Dukakis (D)	Bush (R)	Mondale (D)	Reagan (R)
Barbour	3,221	3,023	3,108	3,877
Berkeley	6,313	10,761	6,181	12,887
Boone	6,539	2,786	7,121	4,656
Braxton	3,377	2,024	3,350	2,902
Brooke	6,258	4,006	6,636	4,819
Cabell	15,368	17,197	15,513	21,815
Calhoun	1,644	1,395	1,473	1,765
Clay	2,263	1,536	2,117	1,667
Doddridge	955	1,880	836	2,343
Fayette	11,009	5,143	11,650	7,360
Gilmer	1,661	1,387	1,494	1,953
Grant	893	3,215	828	3,715
Greenbrier	6,091	5,395	5,599	7,337
Hampshire	2,085	3,253	2,102	4,065
Hancock	8,338	5,882	8,708	7,326
Hardy	1,689	2,581	1,641	2,938
Harrison	17,005	13,364	14,969	19,400
Jackson	4,573	5,696	4,147	7,117
Jefferson	4,334	5,349	4,216	5,884
Kanawha	41,144	38,140	37,832	51,499
Lewis	3,272	3,602	2,693	5,297
Lincoln	5,049	3,457	5,467	4,405
Logan	11,317	4,244	10,892	6,425
McDowell	7,204	2,463	8,546	4,284
Marion	14,441	9,229	13,833	13,106
Marshall	7,903	6,793	7,947	8,615
Mason	5,468	5,332	5,701	6,648
Mercer	10,152	10,221	9,164	13,910
Mineral	4,059	6,015	3,832	7,291
Mingo	7,429	2,896	8,434	4,275
Monongalia	14,178	12,091	13,236	14,972
Monroe	2,427	2,719	2,333	3,612
Morgan	1,545	3,002	1,457	3,469
Nicholas	5,173	3,731	4,588	4,656
Ohio	10,121	10,341	10,163	13,447
Pendleton	1,595	1,901	1,464	2,047
Pleasants	1,421	1,761	1,458	2,255
Pocahontas	1,958	1,876	1,903	2,479
Preston	4,357	5,804	4,054	6,955
Putnam	6,640	8,163	5,208	9,238
Raleigh	14,302	10,395	14,442	14,571
Randolph	5,233	4,746	4,839	6,100
Ritchie	1,446	2,874	1,231	3,355
Roane	2,447	2,861	2,468	3,751
Summers	3,072	2,231	2,670	2,975
Taylor	2,852	2,816	2,754	4,007
Tucker	1,869	1,699	1,766	2,240
Tyler	1,501	2,365	1,395	3,170
Upshur	3,065	4,813	2,468	5,951
Wayne	8,521	7,123	8,378	8,811
Webster	2,185	1,016	2,355	1,565
Wetzel	3,928	3,381	3,549	4,626
Wirt	929	1,125	868	1,450
Wood	12,959	19,450	11,357	24,821

Wyoming.......	6,138	3,516	5,691	5,379
Totals........	341,016	310,065	328,125	405,483

West Virginia Vote Since 1940

1940, Roosevelt, Dem., 495,662; Willkie, Rep., 372,414.

1944, Roosevelt, Dem., 392,777; Dewey, Rep., 322,819.

1948, Truman, Dem., 429,188; Dewey, Rep., 316,251; Wallace, Prog., 3,311.

1952, Eisenhower, Rep., 419,970; Stevenson, Dem., 453,578.

1956, Eisenhower, Rep., 449,297; Stevenson, Dem., 381,534.

1960, Kennedy, Dem., 441,786; Nixon, Rep., 395,995.

1964, Johnson, Dem., 538,087; Goldwater, Rep., 253,953.

1968, Nixon, Rep., 307,555; Humphrey, Dem., 374,091; Wallace, 3d party, 72,560.

1972, Nixon, Rep., 484,964; McGovern, Dem., 277,435.

1976, Carter, Dem., 435,864; Ford, Rep., 314,726.

1980, Reagan, Rep., 334,206; Carter, Dem., 367,462; Anderson, Ind., 31,691; Clark, Libertarian, 4,356.

1984, Reagan, Rep., 405,483; Mondale, Dem., 328,125.

1988, Bush, Rep., 310,065; Dukakis, Dem., 341,016; Fulani, New Alliance, 2,230.

Wisconsin

	1988		1984	
County	Dukakis (D)	Bush (R)	Mondale (D)	Reagan (R)
Adams........	3,598	3,258	2,713	3,644
Ashland.......	4,526	2,926	4,680	3,517
Barron........	8,951	8,527	8,060	9,587
Bayfield.......	4,323	3,095	4,034	3,474
Brown........	41,788	43,625	30,208	51,186
Buffalo.......	3,481	2,783	2,921	3,325
Burnet........	3,537	2,884	3,328	3,528
Calumet......	6,481	8,107	4,735	8,969
Chippewa.....	11,447	9,757	10,200	10,983
Clark........	6,642	6,296	5,647	8,098
Columbia.....	9,132	10,475	8,124	11,658
Crawford......	3,608	3,238	3,435	4,411
Dane........	105,414	69,143	94,638	74,009
Dodge.......	12,663	17,003	11,052	20,455
Door........	5,425	6,907	3,915	8,264
Douglas......	13,907	6,440	14,290	7,066
Dunn........	9,205	7,273	7,709	8,472
Eau Claire....	21,150	17,664	19,344	20,394
Florence......	1,018	1,106	870	1,227
Fond duLac...	15,887	21,985	13,982	26,067
Forest.......	2,142	1,845	2,213	2,296
Grant.......	9,421	10,049	7,890	13,427
Green.......	5,153	6,636	4,367	7,826
Green Lake....	3,033	5,205	2,441	6,198
Iowa........	4,268	4,240	3,842	4,982
Iron........	2,090	1,599	1,967	1,667
Jackson......	3,924	3,555	3,427	4,383
Jefferson.....	11,816	14,309	10,788	17,779
Juneau.......	3,734	4,869	3,151	5,627
Kenosha......	30,089	21,661	29,233	26,112
Kewaunee.....	4,786	4,330	3,444	5,705
La Crosse.....	22,204	21,548	17,787	25,717
La Fayette....	3,521	3,665	2,959	4,582
Langlade.....	4,254	4,884	3,675	5,828
Lincoln......	5,819	5,257	5,352	6,681
Manitowoc....	19,680	16,020	17,249	19,635
Marathon.....	24,658	24,482	20,126	27,077
Marinette.....	8,030	9,637	6,798	11,439
Marquette....	2,463	3,059	2,031	3,404
Menominee....	1,028	381	832	392
Milwaukee.....	268,287	168,363	259,134	196,259
Monroe......	6,437	7,073	5,564	8,225
Oconto......	6,549	7,084	5,288	8,713
Oneida......	7,414	8,130	6,416	9,782
Outagamie....	27,771	33,113	19,789	36,765
Ozaukee......	12,661	22,899	10,763	23,896
Pepin.......	1,906	1,311	1,629	1,555
Pierce.......	8,659	6,045	7,285	7,611
Polk........	8,981	6,866	8,033	8,101
Portage......	16,317	12,057	14,399	13,603
Price........	3,987	3,450	3,479	4,286
Racine.......	39,631	36,342	36,953	42,085
Richland.....	3,643	4,026	2,844	4,857
Rock........	29,576	28,178	26,430	32,483
Rusk........	3,888	3,063	3,843	4,061
St. Croix.....	11,392	9,960	10,126	11,365
Sauk........	8,324	10,225	7,157	11,067
Sawyer......	3,231	3,260	2,981	3,911
Shawano.....	6,587	8,362	5,469	10,635
Sheboygan....	23,429	23,471	21,111	26,343
Taylor.......	3,785	4,254	3,271	4,918
Trempealeau...	6,212	4,902	5,405	6,007
Vernon......	5,754	5,226	5,051	6,468
Vilas........	3,781	5,842	2,940	5,963
Walworth.....	12,203	18,259	9,876	20,590
Washburn.....	3,393	3,074	3,188	3,847
Washington...	15,907	24,328	12,966	25,278

Waukesha......	57,598	90,467	47,308	92,415
Waupaca.......	7,078	11,559	5,894	13,097
Waushara......	3,535	4,953	2,782	5,768
Winnebago.....	28,508	35,085	22,791	39,014
Wood........	16,074	16,549	12,118	20,525
Totals	1,126,794	1,047,499	995,740	1,198,584

Wisconsin Vote Since 1940

1940, Roosevelt, Dem., 704,821; Willkie, Rep., 679,260; Thomas, Soc., 15,071; Browder, Com., 2,394; Babson, Proh., 2,148; Aiken, Soc. Labor, 1,882.

1944, Roosevelt, Dem., 650,413; Dewey, Rep., 674,532; Thomas, Soc., 13,205; Teichert, Soc. Labor, 1,002.

1948, Truman, Dem., 647,310; Dewey, Rep., 590,959; Wallace, Prog., 25,282; Thomas, Soc., 12,547; Teichert, Soc. Labor, 399; Dobbs, Soc. Workers, 303.

1952, Eisenhower, Rep., 979,744; Stevenson, Dem., 622,175; Hallinan, Ind., 2,174; Dobbs, Ind., 1,350; Hoopes, Ind., 1,157; Hass, Ind., 770.

1956, Eisenhower, Rep., 954,844; Stevenson, Dem., 586,768; Andrews, Ind., 6,918; Hoopes, Soc., 754; Hass, Soc. Labor, 710; Dobbs, Soc. Workers, 564.

1960, Kennedy, Dem., 830,805; Nixon, Rep., 895,175; Dobbs, Soc. Workers, 1,792; Hass, Soc. Labor, 1,310.

1964, Johnson, Dem., 1,050,424; Goldwater, Rep., 638,495; DeBerry, Soc. Worker, 1,692; Hass, Soc. Labor, 1,204.

1968, Nixon, Rep., 809,997; Humphrey, Dem., 748,804; Wallace, 3d party, 127,835; Blomen, Soc. Labor, 1,338; Halstead, Soc. Worker, 1,222; scattered, 2,342.

1972, Nixon, Rep., 989,430; McGovern, Dem., 810,174; Schmitz, Amer., 47,525; Spock, Ind., 2,701; Fisher, Soc. Labor, 998; Hall, Com., 663; Reed, Ind., 506; scattered, 893.

1976, Carter, Dem., 1,040,232; Ford, Rep., 1,004,987; McCarthy, Ind., 34,943; Maddox, Amer. Ind., 8,552; Zeidler, Soc., 4,298; MacBride, Libertarian, 3,814; Camejo, Soc. Workers, 1,691; Wright, People's, 943; Hall, Com., 749; LaRouche, U.S. Lab., 738; Levin, Soc. Labor, 389; scattered, 2,839.

1980, Reagan, Rep., 1,088,845; Carter, Dem., 981,584; Anderson, Ind., 160,657; Clark, Libertarian, 29,135; Commoner, Citizens, 7,767; Rarick, Constitution, 1,519; McReynolds, Socialist, 808; Hall, Com., 772; Griswold, Workers World, 414; DeBerry, Soc. Workers, 383; scattered, 1,337.

1984, Reagan, Rep., 1,198,584; Mondale, Dem., 995,740; Bergland, Libertarian, 4,883.

1988, Bush, Rep., 1,047,499; Dukakis, Dem., 1,126,794; Paul, Lib., 5,157; Duke, Pop., 3,056.

Wyoming

	1988		1984	
County	Dukakis (D)	Bush (R)	Mondale (D)	Reagan (R)
Albany........	5,486	5,653	4,708	7,452
Big Horn......	1,469	3,258	1,175	4,019
Campbell......	2,288	6,702	1,525	8,387
Carbon.......	2,555	3,336	2,295	4,557
Converse......	1,301	2,885	929	3,542
Crook........	553	1,939	450	2,286
Fremont......	5,020	7,681	3,969	9,885
Goshen.......	1,875	3,075	1,364	3,776
Hot Springs....	800	1,490	672	1,943
Johnson......	707	2,081	558	2,634
Laramie......	11,851	15,561	10,110	19,348
Lincoln......	1,592	3,237	1,021	3,854
Natrona......	9,148	14,005	7,598	18,488
Niobrara.....	354	825	239	1,098
Park........	2,646	6,884	1,965	7,994
Platte.......	1,482	2,253	1,232	2,813
Sheridan.....	4,655	5,980	3,648	7,460
Sublette......	576	1,636	389	1,976
Sweetwater....	6,720	6,780	5,230	8,308
Teton.......	2,217	3,616	1,565	3,487
Uinta.......	1,922	3,464	1,276	4,075
Washakie.....	1,197	2,538	970	3,245
Weston.......	699	1,988	482	2,614
Totals	67,113	106,867	53,370	133,241

Wyoming Vote Since 1940

1940, Roosevelt, Dem., 59,287; Willkie, Rep., 52,633; Babson, Proh., 172; Thomas, Soc., 148.

1944, Roosevelt, Dem., 49,419; Dewey, Rep., 51,921.

1948, Truman, Dem., 52,354; Dewey, Rep., 47,947; Wallace, Prog., 931; Thomas, Soc., 137; Teichert, Soc. Labor, 56.

1952, Eisenhower, Rep., 81,047; Stevenson, Dem., 47,934; Hamblen, Proh., 194; Hoopes, Soc., 40; Haas, Soc. Labor, 36.

1956, Eisenhower, Rep., 74,573; Stevenson, Dem., 49,554.

1960, Kennedy, Dem., 63,331; Nixon, Rep., 77,451.

1964, Johnson, Dem., 80,718; Goldwater, Rep., 61,998.

1968, Nixon, Rep., 70,927; Humphrey, Dem., 45,173; Wallace, 3d party, 11,105.

1972, Nixon, Rep., 100,464; McGovern, Dem., 44,358; Schmitz, Amer., 748.

1976, Carter, Dem., 62,239; Ford, Rep., 92,717; McCarthy, Ind., 624; Reagan, Ind., 307; Anderson, Amer., 290; MacBride, Libertarian, 89; Brown, Ind., 47; Maddox, Amer. Ind., 30.

1980, Reagan, Rep., 110,700; Carter, Dem., 49,427; Anderson, Ind., 12,072; Clark, Libertarian, 4,514.

1984, Reagan, Rep., 133,241; Mondale, Dem., 53,370; Bergland, Libertarian, 2,357.

1988, Bush, Rep., 106,867; Dukakis, Dem., 67,113; Paul, Lib., 2,026; Fulani, New Alliance, 545.

Official 1988 Presidential General Election Results

Source: Federal Election Commission

Candidate	Party[1]	Official Popular Vote Total	Percent of Total Vote
George Bush	Republican	48,886,097	53.37
Michael S. Dukakis	Democratic	41,809,074	45.65
Delmar Dennis	American	3,475	0.00
Earl Dodge	Prohibition	8,002	0.01
David Duke	Populist	47,047	0.05
Lenora B. Fulani	New Alliance	217,219	0.24
James C. Griffin	American Independent	27,818	0.03
Jack Herer	GrassRoots	1,949	0.00
Larry Holmes	Workers World	7,846	0.01
Willa Kenoyer	Socialist	3,882	0.00
Lyndon H. LaRouche	National Economic	25,542	0.03
Herbert Lewin	Peace & Freedom	10,370	0.01
William A. Marra	Right to Life	20,504	0.02
John G. Martin	Third World Assembly	236	0.00
Eugene J. McCarthy	Consumer	30,905	0.03
Ronald E. Paul	Libertarian	432,116	0.47
James Mac Warren	Socialist Workers	15,604	0.02
Edward Winn	Workers League	18,662	0.02
Louie G. Youngkeit	Independent	372	0.00
Write-In		21,039	0.02
None of Above	(Nevada Option)	6,934	0.01
Total Votes		**91,594,693**	

Voting Age Population: 182,628,000
(Census Bureau Estimate)

1 Party designations may vary from one state to another.

Electoral Votes for President

(based on 1990 Census)

Major Parties' Popular and Electoral Vote for President

(F) Federalist; (D) Democrat; (R) Republican; (DR) Democrat Republican; (NR) National Republican;
(W) Whig; (P) People's; (PR) Progressive; (SR) States' Rights; (LR) Liberal Republican; Asterisk (*)—See notes.

Year	President elected	Popular	Elec.	Losing candidate	Popular	Elec.
1789	George Washington (F)	Unknown	69	No opposition.	—	—
1792	George Washington (F)	Unknown	132	No opposition.	—	—
1796	John Adams (F).	Unknown	71	Thomas Jefferson (DR)	Unknown	68
1800*	Thomas Jefferson (DR)	Unknown	73	Aaron Burr (DR)	Unknown	73
1804	Thomas Jefferson (DR)	Unknown	162	Charles Pinckney (F)	Unknown	14
1808	James Madison (DR).	Unknown	122	Charles Pinckney (F)	Unknown	47
1812	James Madison (DR).	Unknown	128	DeWitt Clinton (F)	Unknown	89
1816	James Monroe (DR)	Unknown	183	Rufus King (F)	Unknown	34
1820	James Monroe (DR)	Unknown	231	John Quincy Adams (DR). . . .	Unknown	1
1824*	John Quincy Adams (DR) . . .	105,321	84	Andrew Jackson (DR)	155,872	99
				Henry Clay (DR)	46,587	37
				William H. Crawford (DR). . . .	44,282	41
1828	Andrew Jackson (D)	647,231	178	John Quincy Adams (NR). . . .	509,097	83
1832	Andrew Jackson (D)	687,502	219	Henry Clay (NR)	530,189	49
1836	Martin Van Buren (D).	762,678	170	William H. Harrison (W)	548,007	73
1840	William H. Harrison (W)	1,275,017	234	Martin Van Buren (D)	1,128,702	60
1844	James K. Polk (D)	1,337,243	170	Henry Clay (W).	1,299,068	105
1848	Zachary Taylor (W).	1,360,101	163	Lewis Cass (D)	1,220,544	127
1852	Franklin Pierce (D)	1,601,474	254	Winfield Scott (W)	1,386,578	42
1856	James Buchanan (D).	1,927,995	174	John C. Fremont (R).	1,391,555	114
1860	Abraham Lincoln (R)	1,866,352	180	Stephen A. Douglas (D)	1,375,157	12
				John C. Breckinridge (D)	845,763	72
				John Bell (Const. Union). . . .	589,581	39
1864	Abraham Lincoln (R)	2,216,067	212	George McClellan (D)	1,808,725	21
1868	Ulysses S. Grant (R)	3,015,071	214	Horatio Seymour (D).	2,709,615	80
1872*	Ulysses S. Grant (R)	3,597,070	286	Horace Greeley (D-LR)	2,834,079	—
1876*	Rutherford B. Hayes (R). . . .	4,033,950	185	Samuel J. Tilden (D)	4,284,757	184
1880	James A. Garfield (R)	4,449,053	214	Winfield S. Hancock (D). . . .	4,442,030	155
1884	Grover Cleveland (D)	4,911,017	219	James G. Blaine (R).	4,848,334	182
1888*	Benjamin Harrison (R)	5,444,337	233	Grover Cleveland (D)	5,540,050	168
1892	Grover Cleveland (D)	5,554,414	277	Benjamin Harrison (R).	5,190,802	145
				James Weaver (P)	1,027,329	22
1896	William McKinley (R)	7,035,638	271	William J. Bryan (D-P)	6,467,946	176
1900	William McKinley (R)	7,219,530	292	William J. Bryan (D).	6,358,071	155
1904	Theodore Roosevelt (R)	7,628,834	336	Alton B. Parker (D)	5,084,491	140
1908	William H. Taft (R)	7,679,006	321	William J. Bryan (D).	6,409,106	162
1912	Woodrow Wilson (D)	6,286,214	435	Theodore Roosevelt (PR)	4,216,020	88
				William H. Taft (R)	3,483,922	8
1916	Woodrow Wilson (D)	9,129,606	277	Charles E. Hughes (R).	8,538,221	254
1920	Warren G. Harding (R)	16,152,200	404	James M. Cox (D)	9,147,353	127
1924	Calvin Coolidge (R).	15,725,016	382	John W. Davis	8,385,586	136
				Robert M. LaFollette (PR). . . .	4,822,856	13
1928	Herbert Hoover (R).	21,392,190	444	Alfred E. Smith (D)	15,016,443	87
1932	Franklin D. Roosevelt (D) . . .	22,821,857	472	Herbert Hoover (R)	15,761,841	59
				Norman Thomas (Socialist) . . .	884,781	—
1936	Franklin D. Roosevelt (D) . . .	27,751,597	523	Alfred Landon (R)	16,679,583	8
1940	Franklin D. Roosevelt (D) . . .	27,243,466	449	Wendell Willkie (R).	22,304,755	82
1944	Franklin D. Roosevelt (D) . . .	25,602,505	432	Thomas E. Dewey (R)	22,006,278	99
1948	Harry S. Truman (D)	24,105,812	303	Thomas E. Dewey (R)	21,970,065	189
				J. Strom Thurmond (SR)	1,169,021	39
				Henry A. Wallace (PR)	1,157,172	—
1952	Dwight D. Eisenhower (R) . . .	33,936,252	442	Adlai E. Stevenson (D)	27,314,992	89
1956*	Dwight D. Eisenhower (R) . . .	35,585,316	457	Adlai E. Stevenson (D)	26,031,322	73
1960*	John F. Kennedy (D)	34,227,096	303	Richard M. Nixon (R).	34,108,546	219
1964	Lyndon B. Johnson (D).	43,126,506	486	Barry M. Goldwater (R)	27,176,799	52
1968	Richard M. Nixon (R)	31,785,480	301	Hubert H. Humphrey (D)	31,275,166	191
				George C. Wallace (3d party) .	9,906,473	46
1972*	Richard M. Nixon (R)	47,165,234	520	George S. McGovern (D)	29,170,774	17
1976*	Jimmy Carter (D)	40,828,929	297	Gerald R. Ford (R)	39,148,940	240
1980	Ronald Reagan (R).	43,899,248	489	Jimmy Carter (D).	35,481,435	49
				John B. Anderson (independent)	5,719,437	—
1984	Ronald Reagan (R).	54,281,858	525	Walter F. Mondale (D).	37,457,215	13
1988*	George Bush (R)	48,881,221	426	Michael S. Dukakis (D)	41,805,422	111

1800—Elected by House of Representatives because of tied electoral vote. **1824**—Elected by House of Representatives. No candidate polled a majority. In 1824, the Democrat Republicans had become a loose coalition of competing political groups. By 1828, the supporters of Jackson were known as Democrats, and the J.Q. Adams and Henry Clay supporters as National Republicans. **1872**—Greeley died Nov. 29, 1872. His electoral votes were split among 4 individuals. **1876**—Fla., La., Ore., and S. C. election returns were disputed. Congress in joint session (Mar. 2, 1877) declared Hayes and Wheeler elected President and Vice-President. **1888**—Cleveland had more votes than Harrison but the 233 electoral votes cast for Harrison against the 168 for Cleveland elected Harrison president. **1956**—Democrats elected 74 electors but one from Alabama refused to vote for Stevenson. **1960**—Sen. Harry F. Byrd (D-Va.) received 15 electoral votes. **1972**—John Hospers of Cal. and Theodora Nathan of Ore. received one vote from an elector of Virginia. **1976**—Ronald Reagan of Cal. received one vote from an elector of Washington. **1988**—Sen. Lloyd Bentsen (D.-Tex.) received 1 electoral vote.

The Electoral College

The president and the vice president of the United States are the only elective federal officials not elected by direct vote of the people. They are elected by the members of the Electoral College, an institution that has survived since the founding of the nation despite repeated attempts in Congress to alter or abolish it. In the elections of 1824, 1876 and 1888 the presidential candidate receiving the largest popular vote failed to win a majority of the electoral votes.

On presidential election day, the first Tuesday after the first Monday in November of every 4th year, each state chooses as many electors as it has senators and representatives in Congress. In 1964, for the first time, as provided by the 23d Amendment to the Constitution, the District of Columbia voted for 3 electors. Thus, with 100 senators and 435 representatives, there are 538 members of the Electoral College, with a majority of 270 electoral votes needed to elect the president and vice president.

Political parties customarily nominate their lists of electors at their respective state conventions. An elector cannot be a member of Congress or any person holding federal office.

Some states print the names of the candidates for president and vice president at the top of the November ballot while others list only the names of the electors. In either case, the electors of the party receiving the highest vote are elected. The electors meet on the first Monday after the 2d Wednesday in December in their respective state capitals or in some other place prescribed by state legislatures. By long-established custom they vote for their party nominees, although the Constitution does not require them to do so. All of the state's electoral votes are then awarded to the winners. The only Constitutional requirement is that at least one of the persons each elector votes for shall not be an inhabitant of that elector's home state.

Certified and sealed lists of the votes of the electors in each state are mailed to the president of the U.S. Senate. He opens them in the presence of the members of the Senate and House of Representatives in a joint session held on Jan. 6 (the next day if that falls on a Sunday), and the electoral votes of all the states are then counted. If no candidate for president has a majority, the House of Representatives chooses a president from among the 3 highest candidates, with all representatives from each state combining to cast one vote for that state. If no candidate for vice president has a majority, the Senate chooses from the top 2, with the senators voting as individuals.

Voting for President

Source: Federal Election Commission; Commission for Study of American Electorate

Candidates		Voter Participation (% of voting-age population)	Candidates		Voter Participation (% of voting-age population)
1932	Roosevelt-Hoover	52.4	1964	Johnson-Goldwater	61.9
1936	Roosevelt-Landon	56.0	1968	Humphrey-Nixon	60.9
1940	Roosevelt-Willkie	58.9	1972	McGovern-Nixon	55.2(a)
1944	Roosevelt-Dewey	56.0	1976	Carter-Ford	53.5
1948	Truman-Dewey	51.1	1980	Carter-Reagan	54.0
1952	Stevenson-Eisenhower	61.6	1984	Mondale-Reagan	53.1
1956	Stevenson-Eisenhower	59.3	1988	Dukakis-Bush	50.1
1960	Kennedy-Nixon	62.8			

(a) The sharp drop in 1972 reflects the expansion of eligibility with the enfranchisement of 18 to 21 year olds.

Party Nominees for President and Vice President

Asterisk (*) denotes winning ticket

Year	Democratic President	Democratic Vice President	Republican President	Republican Vice President
1844	James K. Polk*	George M. Dallas	Henry Clay (Whig)	Theo. Frelinghuysen
1848	Lewis Cass	William Butler	Zachary Taylor*(Whig)	Millard Fillmore
1852	Franklin Pierce*	William King	Winfield Scott (Whig)	William Graham
1856	James Buchanan*	John Breckinridge	John Freemont	William Dayton
1860	John Breckinridge	Joseph Lane	Abraham Lincoln*	Hannibal Hamlin
1864	George McClellan	G.H. Pendleton	Abraham Lincoln*	Andrew Johnson
1868	Horatio Seymour	Francis Blair	Ulysses S. Grant*	Schuyler Colfax
1872	Horace Greeley	B. Gratz Brown	Ulysses S. Grant*	Henry Wilson
1876	Samuel J. Tilden	Thomas Hendricks	Rutherford B. Hayes*	William Wheeler
1880	Winfield Hancock	William English	James A. Garfield*	Chester A. Arthur
1884	Grover Cleveland*	Thomas Hendricks	James Blaine	John Logan
1888	Grover Cleveland	A.G. Thurman	Benjamin Harrison*	Levi Morton
1892	Grover Cleveland*	Adlai Stevenson	Benjamin Harrison	Whitelaw Reid
1896	William J. Bryan	Arthur Sewall	William McKinley*	Garret Hobart
1900	William J. Bryan	Adlai Stevenson	William McKinley*	Theodore Roosevelt
1904	Alton Parker	Henry Davis	Theodore Roosevelt*	Charles Fairbanks
1908	William J. Bryan	John Kern	William H. Taft*	James Sherman
1912	Woodrow Wilson*	Thomas Marshall	William H. Taft	James Sherman[1]
1916	Woodrow Wilson*	Thomas Marshall	Charles Hughes	Charles Fairbanks
1920	James M. Cox	Franklin D. Roosevelt	Warren G. Harding*	Calvin Coolidge
1924	John W. Davis	Charles W. Bryan	Calvin Coolidge*	Charles G. Dawes
1928	Alfred E. Smith	Joseph T. Robinson	Herbert Hoover*	Charles Curtis
1932	Franklin D. Roosevelt*	John N. Garner	Herbert Hoover	Charles Curtis
1936	Franklin D. Roosevelt*	John N. Garner	Alfred M. Landon	Frank Knox
1940	Franklin D. Roosevelt*	Henry A. Wallace	Wendell L. Willkie	Charles McNary
1944	Franklin D. Roosevelt*	Harry S. Truman	Thomas E. Dewey	John W. Bricker
1948	Harry S. Truman*	Alben W. Barkley	Thomas E. Dewey	Earl Warren
1952	Adlai E. Stevenson	John J. Sparkman	Dwight D. Eisenhower*	Richard M. Nixon
1956	Adlai E. Stevenson	Estes Kefauver	Dwight D. Eisenhower*	Richard M. Nixon
1960	John F. Kennedy*	Lyndon B. Johnson	Richard M. Nixon	Henry Cabot Lodge
1964	Lyndon B. Johnson*	Hubert H. Humphrey	Barry M. Goldwater	William E. Miller
1968	Hubert H. Humphrey	Edmund S. Muskie	Richard M. Nixon*	Spiro T. Agnew
1972	George S. McGovern	R. Sargent Shriver Jr.	Richard M. Nixon*	Spiro T. Agnew
1976	Jimmy Carter*	Walter F. Mondale	Gerald R. Ford	Robert J. Dole
1980	Jimmy Carter	Walter F. Mondale	Ronald Reagan*	George Bush
1984	Walter F. Mondale	Geraldine Ferraro	Ronald Reagan*	George Bush
1988	Michael S. Dukakis	Lloyd Bentsen	George Bush*	J. Danforth "Dan" Quayle

(1) Died Oct. 30; replaced on ballot by Nicholas Butler.

Presidents of the U.S.

No.	Name	Politics	Born	in	Inaug.	at age	Died	at age
1	George Washington	Fed.	1732, Feb. 22	Va.	1789	57	1799, Dec. 14	67
2	John Adams	Fed.	1735, Oct. 30	Mass.	1797	61	1826, July 4	90
3	Thomas Jefferson	Dem.-Rep.	1743, Apr. 13	Va.	1801	57	1826, July 4	83
4	James Madison	Dem.-Rep.	1751, Mar. 16	Va.	1809	57	1836, June 28	85
5	James Monroe	Dem.-Rep.	1758, Apr. 28	Va.	1817	58	1831, July 4	73
6	John Quincy Adams	Dem.-Rep.	1767, July 11	Mass.	1825	57	1848, Feb. 23	80
7	Andrew Jackson	Dem.	1767, Mar. 15	S.C.	1829	61	1845, June 8	78
8	Martin Van Buren	Dem.	1782, Dec. 5	N.Y.	1837	54	1862, July 24	79
9	William Henry Harrison	Whig	1773, Feb. 9	Va.	1841	68	1841, Apr. 4	68
10	John Tyler	Whig	1790, Mar. 29	Va.	1841	51	1862, Jan. 18	71
11	James Knox Polk	Dem.	1795, Nov. 2	N.C.	1845	49	1849, June 15	53
12	Zachary Taylor	Whig	1784, Nov. 24	Va.	1849	64	1850, July 9	65
13	Millard Fillmore	Whig	1800, Jan. 7	N.Y.	1850	50	1874, Mar. 8	74
14	Franklin Pierce	Dem.	1804, Nov. 23	N.H.	1853	48	1869, Oct. 8	64
15	James Buchanan	Dem.	1791, Apr. 23	Pa.	1857	65	1868, June 1	77
16	Abraham Lincoln	Rep.	1809, Feb. 12	Ky.	1861	52	1865, Apr. 15	56
17	Andrew Johnson	(1)	1808, Dec. 29	N.C.	1865	56	1875, July 31	66
18	Ulysses Simpson Grant	Rep.	1822, Apr. 27	Oh.	1869	46	1885, July 23	63
19	Rutherford Birchard Hayes	Rep.	1822, Oct. 4	Oh.	1877	54	1893, Jan. 17	70
20	James Abram Garfield	Rep.	1831, Nov. 19	Oh.	1881	49	1881, Sept. 19	49
21	Chester Alan Arthur	Rep.	1829, Oct. 5	Vt.	1881	51	1886, Nov. 18	57
22	Grover Cleveland	Dem.	1837, Mar. 18	N.J.	1885	47	1908, June 24	71
23	Benjamin Harrison	Rep.	1833, Aug. 20	Oh.	1889	55	1901, Mar. 13	67
24	Grover Cleveland	Dem.	1837, Mar. 18	N.J.	1893	55	1908, June 24	71
25	William McKinley	Rep.	1843, Jan. 29	Oh.	1897	54	1901, Sept. 14	58
26	Theodore Roosevelt	Rep.	1858, Oct. 27	N.Y.	1901	42	1919, Jan. 6	60
27	William Howard Taft	Rep.	1857, Sept. 15	Oh.	1909	51	1930, Mar. 8	72
28	Woodrow Wilson	Dem.	1856, Dec. 28	Va.	1913	56	1924, Feb. 3	67
29	Warren Gamaliel Harding	Rep.	1865, Nov. 2	Oh.	1921	55	1923, Aug. 2	57
30	Calvin Coolidge	Rep.	1872, July 4	Vt.	1923	51	1933, Jan. 5	60
31	Herbert Clark Hoover	Rep.	1874, Aug. 10	Ia.	1929	54	1964, Oct. 20	90
32	Franklin Delano Roosevelt	Dem.	1882, Jan. 30	N.Y.	1933	51	1945, Apr. 12	63
33	Harry S. Truman	Dem.	1884, May 8	Mo.	1945	60	1972, Dec. 26	88
34	Dwight David Eisenhower	Rep.	1890, Oct. 14	Tex.	1953	62	1969, Mar. 28	78
35	John Fitzgerald Kennedy	Dem.	1917, May 29	Mass.	1961	43	1963, Nov. 22	46
36	Lyndon Baines Johnson	Dem.	1908, Aug. 27	Tex.	1963	55	1973, Jan. 22	64
37	Richard Milhous Nixon (2)	Rep.	1913, Jan. 9	Cal.	1969	56		
38	Gerald Rudolph Ford	Rep.	1913, July 14	Neb.	1974	61		
39	Jimmy (James Earl) Carter	Dem.	1924, Oct. 1	Ga.	1977	52		
40	Ronald Reagan	Rep.	1911, Feb. 6	Ill.	1981	69		
41	George Bush	Rep.	1924, June 12	Mass.	1989	64		

(1) Andrew Johnson — a Democrat, nominated vice president by Republicans and elected with Lincoln on National Union ticket. (2) Resigned Aug. 9, 1974.

Presidents, Vice Presidents, Congresses

President	Service	Vice President	Congress
1 George Washington	Apr. 30, 1789—Mar. 3, 1797	1 John Adams	1, 2, 3, 4
2 John Adams	Mar. 4, 1797—Mar. 3, 1801	2 Thomas Jefferson	5, 6
3 Thomas Jefferson	Mar. 4, 1801—Mar. 3, 1805	3 Aaron Burr	7, 8
"	Mar. 4, 1805—Mar. 3, 1809	4 George Clinton	9, 10
4 James Madison	Mar. 4, 1809—Mar. 3, 1813	"(1)	11, 12
"	Mar. 4, 1813—Mar. 3, 1817	5 Elbridge Gerry (2)	13, 14
5 James Monroe	Mar. 4, 1817—Mar. 3, 1825	6 Daniel D. Tompkins	15, 16, 17, 18
6 John Quincy Adams	Mar. 4, 1825—Mar. 3, 1829	7 John C. Calhoun	19, 20
7 Andrew Jackson	Mar. 4, 1829—Mar. 3, 1833	"(3)	21, 22
"	Mar. 4, 1833—Mar. 3, 1837	8 Martin Van Buren	23, 24
8 Martin Van Buren	Mar. 4, 1837—Mar. 3, 1841	9 Richard M. Johnson	25, 26
9 William Henry Harrison (4)	Mar. 4, 1841—Apr. 4, 1841	10 John Tyler	27
10 John Tyler	Apr. 6, 1841—Mar. 3, 1845		27, 28
11 James K. Polk	Mar. 4, 1845—Mar. 3, 1849	11 George M. Dallas	29, 30
12 Zachary Taylor (4)	Mar. 5, 1849—July 9, 1850	12 Millard Fillmore	31
13 Millard Fillmore	July 10, 1850—Mar. 3, 1853		31, 32
14 Franklin Pierce	Mar. 4, 1853—Mar. 3, 1857	13 William R. King (5)	33, 34
15 James Buchanan	Mar. 4, 1857—Mar. 3, 1861	14 John C. Breckinridge	35, 36
16 Abraham Lincoln	Mar. 4, 1861—Mar. 3, 1865	15 Hannibal Hamlin	37, 38
"(4)	Mar. 4, 1865—Apr. 15, 1865	16 Andrew Johnson	39
17 Andrew Johnson	Apr. 15, 1865—Mar. 3, 1869		39, 40
18 Ulysses S. Grant	Mar. 4, 1869—Mar. 3, 1873	17 Schuyler Colfax	41, 42
"	Mar. 4, 1873—Mar. 3, 1877	18 Henry Wilson (6)	43, 44
19 Rutherford B. Hayes	Mar. 4, 1877—Mar. 3, 1881	19 William A. Wheeler	45, 46
20 James A. Garfield (4)	Mar. 4, 1881—Sept. 19, 1881	20 Chester A. Arthur	47
21 Chester A. Arthur	Sept. 20, 1881—Mar. 3, 1885		47, 48
22 Grover Cleveland (7)	Mar. 4, 1885—Mar. 3, 1889	21 Thomas A. Hendricks (8)	49, 50
23 Benjamin Harrison	Mar. 4, 1889—Mar. 3, 1893	22 Levi P. Morton	51, 52
24 Grover Cleveland (7)	Mar. 4, 1893—Mar. 3, 1897	23 Adlai E. Stevenson	53, 54
25 William McKinley	Mar. 4, 1897—Mar. 3, 1901	24 Garret A. Hobart (9)	55, 56
"(4)	Mar. 4, 1901—Sept. 14, 1901	25 Theodore Roosevelt	57
26 Theodore Roosevelt	Sept. 14, 1901—Mar. 3, 1905		57, 58
"	Mar. 4, 1905—Mar. 3, 1909	26 Charles W. Fairbanks	59, 60
27 William H. Taft	Mar. 4, 1909—Mar. 3, 1913	27 James S. Sherman (10)	61, 62
28 Woodrow Wilson	Mar. 4, 1913—Mar. 3, 1921	28 Thomas R. Marshall	63, 64, 65, 66
29 Warren G. Harding (4)	Mar. 4, 1921—Aug. 2, 1923	29 Calvin Coolidge	67

(continued)

Presidents, Vice Presidents, Congresses

President	Service	Vice President	Congress
30 Calvin Coolidge	Aug. 3, 1923—Mar. 3, 1925		68
"	Mar. 4, 1925—Mar. 3, 1929	30 Charles G. Dawes	69, 70
31 Herbert C. Hoover	Mar. 4, 1929—Mar. 3, 1933	31 Charles Curtis	71, 72
32 Franklin D. Roosevelt (16)	Mar. 4, 1933—Jan. 20, 1941	32 John N. Garner	73, 74, 75, 76
"	Jan. 20, 1941—Jan. 20, 1945	33 Henry A. Wallace	77, 78
"(4)	Jan. 20, 1945—Apr. 12, 1945	34 Harry S. Truman	79
33 Harry S. Truman	Apr. 12, 1945—Jan. 20, 1949		79, 80
"	Jan. 20, 1949—Jan. 20, 1953	35 Alben W. Barkley	81, 82
34 Dwight D. Eisenhower	Jan. 20, 1953—Jan. 20, 1961	36 Richard M. Nixon	83, 84, 85, 86
35 John F. Kennedy (4)	Jan. 20, 1961—Nov. 22, 1963	37 Lyndon B. Johnson	87, 88
36 Lyndon B. Johnson	Nov. 22, 1963—Jan. 20, 1965		88
"	Jan. 20, 1965—Jan. 20, 1969	38 Hubert H. Humphrey	89, 90
37 Richard M. Nixon	Jan. 20, 1969—Jan. 20, 1973	39 Spiro T. Agnew (11)	91, 92, 93
"(12)	Jan. 20, 1973—Aug. 9, 1974	40 Gerald R. Ford (13)	93
38 Gerald R. Ford (14)	Aug. 9, 1974—Jan. 20, 1977	41 Nelson A. Rockefeller (15)	93, 94
39 Jimmy (James Earl)Carter	Jan. 20, 1977—Jan. 20, 1981	42 Walter F. Mondale	95, 96
40 Ronald Reagan	Jan. 20, 1981—Jan. 20, 1989	43 George Bush	97, 98, 99, 100
41 George Bush	Jan. 20, 1989—	44 Dan Quayle	101, 102

(1) Died Apr. 20, 1812. (2) Died Nov. 23, 1814. (3) Resigned Dec. 28, 1832, to become U.S. Senator. (4) Died in office. (5) Died Apr. 18, 1853. (6) Died Nov. 22, 1875. (7) Terms not consecutive. (8) Died Nov. 25, 1885. (9) Died Nov. 21, 1899. (10) Died Oct. 30, 1912. (11) Resigned Oct. 10, 1973. (12) Resigned Aug. 9, 1974. (13) First non-elected vice president, chosen under 25th Amendment procedure. (14) First non-elected president. (15) 2d non-elected vice president. (16) First president to be inaugurated under 20th Amendment, Jan. 20, 1937.

Vice Presidents of the U.S.

The numerals given vice presidents do not coincide with those given presidents, because some presidents had none and some had more than one.

Name	Birthplace	Year	Home	Inaug.	Politics	Place of death	Year	Age
1 John Adams	Quincy, Mass.	1735	Mass.	1789	Fed.	Quincy, Mass.	1826	90
2 Thomas Jefferson	Shadwell, Va.	1743	Va.	1797	Dem.-Rep.	Monticello, Va.	1826	83
3 Aaron Burr	Newark, N.J.	1756	N.Y.	1801	Dem.-Rep.	Staten Island, N.Y.	1836	80
4 George Clinton	Ulster Co., N.Y.	1739	N.Y.	1805	Dem.-Rep.	Washington, D.C.	1812	73
5 Elbridge Gerry	Marblehead, Mass.	1744	Mass.	1813	Dem.-Rep.	Washington, D.C.	1814	70
6 Daniel D. Tompkins	Scarsdale, N.Y.	1774	N.Y.	1817	Dem.-Rep.	Staten Island, N.Y.	1825	51
7 John C. Calhoun (1)	Abbeville, S.C.	1782	S.C.	1825	Dem.-Rep.	Washington, D.C.	1850	68
8 Martin Van Buren	Kinderhook, N.Y.	1782	N.Y.	1833	Dem.	Kinderhook, N.Y.	1862	79
9 Richard M. Johnson	Louisville, Ky.	1780	Ky.	1837	Dem.	Frankfort, Ky.	1850	70
10 John Tyler	Greenway, Va.	1790	Va.	1841	Whig	Richmond, Va.	1862	71
11 George M. Dallas	Philadelphia, Pa.	1792	Pa.	1845	Dem.	Philadelphia, Pa.	1864	72
12 Millard Fillmore	Summerhill, N.Y.	1800	N.Y.	1849	Whig	Buffalo, N.Y.	1874	74
13 William R. King	Sampson Co., N.C.	1786	Ala.	1853	Dem.	Dallas Co., Ala.	1853	67
14 John C. Breckinridge	Lexington, Ky.	1821	Ky.	1857	Dem.	Lexington, Ky.	1875	54
15 Hannibal Hamlin	Paris, Me.	1809	Me.	1861	Rep.	Bangor, Me.	1891	81
16 Andrew Johnson	Raleigh, N.C.	1808	Tenn.	1865	(2)	Carter Co., Tenn.	1875	66
17 Schuyler Colfax	New York, N.Y.	1823	Ind.	1869	Rep.	Mankato, Minn.	1885	62
18 Henry Wilson	Farmington, N.H.	1812	Mass.	1873	Rep.	Washington, D.C.	1875	63
19 William A. Wheeler	Malone, N.Y.	1819	N.Y.	1877	Rep.	Malone, N.Y.	1887	68
20 Chester A. Arthur	Fairfield, Vt.	1829	N.Y.	1881	Rep.	New York, N.Y.	1886	57
21 Thomas A. Hendricks	Muskingum Co., Oh.	1819	Ind.	1885	Dem.	Indianapolis, Ind.	1885	66
22 Levi P. Morton	Shoreham, Vt.	1824	N.Y.	1889	Rep.	Rhinebeck, N.Y.	1920	96
23 Adlai E. Stevenson (3)	Christian Co., Ky.	1835	Ill.	1893	Dem.	Chicago, Ill.	1914	78
24 Garret A. Hobart	Long Branch, N.J.	1844	N.J.	1897	Rep.	Paterson, N.J.	1899	55
25 Theodore Roosevelt	New York, N.Y.	1858	N.Y.	1901	Rep.	Oyster Bay, N.Y.	1919	60
26 Charles W. Fairbanks	Unionville Centre, Oh.	1852	Ind.	1905	Rep.	Indianapolis, Ind.	1918	66
27 James S. Sherman	Utica, N.Y.	1855	N.Y.	1909	Rep.	Utica, N.Y.	1912	57
28 Thomas R. Marshall	N. Manchester, Ind.	1854	Ind.	1913	Dem.	Washington, D.C.	1925	71
29 Calvin Coolidge	Plymouth, Vt.	1872	Mass.	1921	Rep.	Northampton, Mass.	1933	60
30 Charles G. Dawes	Marietta, Oh.	1865	Ill.	1925	Rep.	Evanston, Ill.	1951	85
31 Charles Curtis	Topeka, Kan.	1860	Kan.	1929	Rep.	Washington, D.C.	1936	76
32 John Nance Garner	Red River Co., Tex.	1868	Tex.	1933	Dem.	Uvalde, Tex.	1967	98
33 Henry Agard Wallace	Adair County, Ia.	1888	Iowa	1941	Dem.	Danbury, Conn.	1965	77
34 Harry S. Truman	Lamar, Mo.	1884	Mo.	1945	Dem.	Kansas City, Mo.	1972	88
35 Alben W. Barkley	Graves County, Ky.	1877	Ky.	1949	Dem.	Lexington, Va.	1956	78
36 Richard M. Nixon	Yorba Linda, Cal.	1913	Cal.	1953	Rep.			
37 Lyndon B. Johnson	Johnson City, Tex.	1908	Tex.	1961	Dem.	San Antonio, Tex.	1973	64
38 Hubert H. Humphrey	Wallace, S.D.	1911	Minn.	1965	Dem.	Waverly, Minn.	1978	66
39 Spiro T. Agnew (4)	Baltimore, Md.	1918	Md.	1969	Rep.			
40 Gerald R. Ford	Omaha, Neb.	1913	Mich.	1973	Rep.			
41 Nelson A. Rockefeller	Bar Harbor, Me.	1908	N.Y.	1974	Rep.	New York, N.Y.	1979	70
42 Walter F. Mondale	Ceylon, Minn.	1928	Minn.	1977	Dem.			
43 George Bush	Milton, Mass.	1924	Tex.	1981	Rep.			
44 Dan Quayle	Indianapolis, Ind.	1947	Ind.	1989	Rep.			

(1) John C. Calhoun resigned Dec. 28, 1832, having been elected to the Senate to fill a vacancy. (2) Andrew Johnson — a Democrat nominated by Republicans and elected with Lincoln on the National Union Ticket. (3) Adlai E. Stevenson, 23d vice president, was grandfather of Democratic candidate for president, 1952 and 1956. (4) Resigned Oct. 10, 1973.

BIOGRAPHIES OF U.S. PRESIDENTS

George Washington (1789-1797)

George Washington, first president, was born Feb. 22, 1732 (Feb. 11, 1731, old style), the son of Augustine Washington and Mary Ball, at Wakefield on Pope's Creek, Westmoreland Co., Va. His early childhood was spent on a farm, near Fredericksburg. His father died when George was 11. He studied mathematics and surveying and when 16 went to live with his half brother Lawrence, who built and named Mount Vernon. George surveyed the lands of William Fairfax in the Shenandoah Valley, keeping a diary. He accompanied Lawrence to Barbados, West Indies, contracted small pox, and was deeply scarred. Lawrence died in 1752 and George acquired his property by inheritance. He valued land and when he died owned 70,000 acres in Virginia and 40,000 acres in what is now West Virginia.

Washington's military service began in 1753 when Gov. Dinwiddie of Virginia sent him on missions deep into Ohio country. He clashed with the French and had to surrender Fort Necessity July 3, 1754. He was an aide to Braddock and at his side when the army was ambushed and defeated on a march to Ft. Duquesne, July 9, 1755. He helped take Fort Duquesne from the French in 1758.

After his marriage to Martha Dandridge Custis, a widow, in 1759, Washington managed his family estate at Mount Vernon. Although not at first for independence, he opposed British exactions and took charge of the Virginia troops before war broke out. He was made commander-in-chief by the Continental Congress June 15, 1775.

The successful issue of a war filled with hardships was due to his leadership. He was resourceful, a stern disciplinarian, and the one strong, dependable force for unity. He favored a federal government and became chairman of the Constitutional Convention of 1787. He helped get the Constitution ratified and was unanimously elected president by the electoral college and inaugurated, Apr. 30, 1789, on the balcony of New York's Federal Hall.

He was reelected 1792, but refused to consider a 3d term and retired to Mount Vernon. He suffered acute laryngitis after a ride in snow and rain around his estate, was bled profusely, and died Dec. 14, 1799.

John Adams (1797-1801)

John Adams, 2d president, Federalist, was born in Braintree (Quincy), Mass., Oct. 30, 1735 (Oct. 19, o. s.), the son of John Adams, a farmer, and Susanna Boylston. He was a great-grandson of Henry Adams who came from England in 1636. He graduated from Harvard, 1755, taught school, studied law. In 1765 he argued against taxation without representation before the royal governor. In 1770 he defended in court the British soldiers who fired on civilians in the "Boston Massacre." He was a delegate to the first Continental Congress, and signed the Declaration of Independence. He was a commissioner to France, 1778, with Benjamin Franklin and Arthur Lee; won recognition of the U.S. by The Hague, 1782; was first American minister to England, 1785-1788, and was elected vice president, 1788 and 1792.

In 1796 Adams was chosen president by the electors. Intense antagonism to America by France caused agitation for war, led by Alexander Hamilton. Adams, breaking with Hamilton, opposed war.

To fight alien influence and muzzle criticism Adams supported the Alien and Sedition laws of 1798, which led to his defeat for reelection. He died July 4, 1826, on the same day as Jefferson (the 50th anniversary of the Declaration of Independence).

Thomas Jefferson (1801-1809)

Thomas Jefferson, 3d president, was born Apr. 13, 1743 (Apr. 2, o. s.), at Shadwell, Va., the son of Peter Jefferson, a civil engineer of Welsh descent who raised tobacco, and Jane Randolph. His father died when he was 14, leaving him 2,750 acres and his slaves. Jefferson attended the College of William and Mary, 1760-1762, read classics in Greek and Latin and played the violin. In 1769 he was elected to the House of Burgesses. In 1770 he began building Monticello, near Charlottesville. He was a member of the Virginia Committee of Correspondence and the Continental Congress. Named a member of the committee to draw up a Declaration of Independence, he wrote the basic draft. He was a member of the Virginia House of Delegates, 1776-79, elected governor to succeed Patrick Henry, 1779, reelected 1780, resigned June 1781, amid charges of ineffectual military preparation. During his term he wrote the statute on religious freedom. In the Continental Congress, 1783, he drew up an ordinance for the Northwest Territory forbidding slavery after 1800; its terms were put into the Ordinance of 1787. He was sent to Paris with Benjamin Franklin and John Adams to negotiate commercial treaties, 1784; made minister to France, 1785.

Washington appointed him secretary of state, 1789. Jefferson's strong faith in the consent of the governed, as opposed to executive control favored by Hamilton, secretary of the treasury, often led to conflict: Dec. 31, 1793, he resigned. He was the Democrat Republican candidate for president in 1796; beaten by John Adams, he became vice president. In 1800, Jefferson and Aaron Burr received equal electoral college votes for president. The House of Representatives elected Jefferson. Major events of his administration were the Louisiana Purchase, 1803, and the Lewis and Clark Expedition. He established the Univ. of Virginia and designed its buildings. He died July 4, 1826, on the same day as John Adams.

James Madison (1809-1817)

James Madison, 4th president, Democrat Republican, was born Mar. 16, 1751 (Mar. 5, 1750, o. s.) at Port Conway, King George Co., Va., eldest son of James Madison and Eleanor Rose Conway. Madison was graduated from Princeton, 1771; studied theology, 1772; sat in the Virginia Constitutional Convention, 1776. He was a member of the Continental Congress. He was chief recorder at the Constitutional Convention in 1787, and supported ratification in the Federalist Papers, written with Alexander Hamilton and John Jay. He was elected to the House of Representatives in 1789, helped frame the Bill of Rights and fought the Alien and Sedition Acts. He became Jefferson's secretary of state, 1801.

Elected president in 1808, Madison was a "strict constructionist," opposed to the free interpretation of the Constitution by the Federalists. He was reelected in 1812 by the votes of the agrarian South and recently admitted western states. Caught between British and French maritime restrictions, the U.S. drifted into war, declared June 18, 1812. The war ended in a stalemate. He retired in 1817 to his estate at Montpelier. There he edited his famous papers on the Constitutional Convention. He became rector of the Univ. of Virginia, 1826. He died June 28, 1836.

James Monroe (1817-1825)

James Monroe, 5th president, Democrat Republican, was born Apr. 28, 1758, in Westmoreland Co., Va., the son of Spence Monroe and Eliza Jones, who were of Scottish and Welsh descent, respectively. He attended the College of William and Mary, fought in the 3d Virginia Regiment at White Plains, Brandywine, Monmouth, and was wounded at Trenton. He studied law with Thomas Jefferson, 1780, was a member of the Virginia House of Delegates and of Congress, 1783-86. He opposed ratification of the Constitution because it lacked a bill of rights; was U.S. senator, 1790; minister to France, 1794-96; governor of Virginia, 1799-1802, and 1811. Jefferson sent him to France as minister, 1803. He helped Robert Livingston negotiate the Louisiana Purchase, 1803. He ran against Madison for president in 1808. He was elected to the Virginia Assembly, 1810-1811; was secretary of state under Madison, 1811-1817.

In 1816 Monroe was elected president; in 1820 reelected with all but one electoral college vote. Monroe's administration became the "Era of Good Feeling." He obtained Florida from Spain; settled boundaries with Canada, and eliminated border forts. He supported the anti-slavery position that led to the Missouri Compromise. His most significant contribution was the "Monroe Doctrine," which became a cornerstone of U.S. foreign policy. Monroe retired to Oak Hill, Va. Financial problems forced him to sell his property. He moved to New York City to live with a daughter. He died there July 4, 1831.

John Quincy Adams (1825-1829)

John Quincy Adams, 6th president, independent Federalist, was born July 11, 1767, at Braintree (Quincy), Mass., the son of John and Abigail Adams. His father was the 2d president. He was educated in Paris, Leyden, and Harvard, graduating in 1787. He served as American minister in various European capitals, and helped draft the War of 1812 peace treaty. He was U.S. Senator, 1803-08. President Monroe made him secretary of state, 1817, and he negotiated the cession of the Floridas from Spain, supported exclusion of slavery in the Missouri Compromise, and helped formulate the Monroe Doctrine. In 1824 he was elected president by the House after he failed to win an electoral college majority. His expansion of executive powers was strongly opposed and he was beaten in 1828 by Jackson. In 1831 he entered Congress and served 17 years with distinction. He opposed slavery, the annexation of Texas, and the Mexican War. He helped establish the Smithsonian Institution. He had a stroke in the House and died in the Speaker's Room, Feb. 23, 1848.

Andrew Jackson (1829-1837)

Andrew Jackson, 7th president, was a Jeffersonian-Republican, later a Democrat. He was born in the Waxhaws district, New Lancaster Co., S.C., Mar. 15, 1767, the posthumous son of Andrew Jackson and Elizabeth Hutchinson, who were Irish immigrants. At 13, he joined the militia in the Revolution and was captured.

He read law in Salisbury, N.C., moved to Nashville, Tenn., speculated in land, married, and practiced law. In 1796 he helped draft the constitution of Tennessee and for a year occupied its one seat in Congress. He was in the Senate in 1797, and again in 1823. He defeated the Creek Indians at Horseshoe Bend, Ala., 1814. With 6,000 backwoods fighters he defeated Pakenham's 12,000 British troops at the Chalmette, outside New Orleans, Jan. 8, 1815. In 1818 he briefly invaded Spanish Florida to quell Seminoles and outlaws who harassed frontier settlements. In 1824 he ran for president against John Quincy Adams and had the most popular and electoral votes but not a majority; the election was decided by the House, which chose Adams. In 1828 he defeated Adams, carrying the West and South. He was a noisy debater and a duelist and introduced rotation in office called the "spoils system." Suspicious of privilege, he ruined the Bank of the United States by depositing federal funds with state banks. Though "Let the people rule" was his slogan, he at times supported strict constructionist policies against the expansionist West. He killed the congressional caucus for nominating presidential candidates and substituted the national convention, 1832. When South Carolina refused to collect imports under his protective tariff he ordered army and naval forces to Charleston. Jackson recognized the Republic of Texas, 1836. He died at the Hermitage, June 8, 1845.

Martin Van Buren (1837-1841)

Martin Van Buren, 8th president, Democrat, was born Dec. 5, 1782, at Kinderhook, N.Y., the son of Abraham Van Buren, a Dutch farmer, and Mary Hoes. He was surrogate of Columbia County, N.Y., state senator and attorney general. He was U.S. senator 1821, reelected, 1827, elected governor of New York, 1828. He helped swing eastern support to Jackson in 1828 and was his secretary of state 1829-31. In 1832 he was elected vice president. He was a consummate politician, known as "the little magician," and influenced Jackson's policies. In 1836 he defeated William Henry Harrison for president and took office as the Panic of 1837 initiated a 5-year nationwide depression. He inaugurated the independent treasury system. His refusal to spend land revenues led to his defeat by Harrison in 1840. He lost the Democratic nomination in 1844 to Polk. In 1848 he ran for president on the Free Soil ticket and lost. He died July 24, 1862, at Kinderhook.

William Henry Harrison (1841)

William Henry Harrison, 9th president, Whig, who served only 31 days, was born in Berkeley, Charles City Co., Va., Feb. 9, 1773, the 3d son of Benjamin Harrison, signer of the Declaration of Independence. He attended Hampden Sydney College. He was secretary of the Northwest Territory, 1798; its delegate in Congress, 1799; first governor of Indiana Territory, 1800; and superintendent of Indian affairs. With 900 men he routed Tecumseh's Indians at Tippecanoe, Nov. 7, 1811. A major general, he defeated British and Indians at Battle of the Thames, Oct. 5, 1813. He served in Congress, 1816-19; Senate, 1825-28. In 1840, he was elected president with a "log cabin and hard cider" slogan. He caught pneumonia during the inauguration and died Apr. 4, 1841.

John Tyler (1841-1845)

John Tyler, 10th president, independent Whig, was born Mar. 29, 1790, in Greenway, Charles City Co., Va., son of John Tyler and Mary Armistead. His father was governor of Virginia, 1808-11. Tyler was graduated from William and Mary, 1807; member of the House of Delegates, 1811; in congress, 1816-21; in Virginia legislature, 1823-25; governor of Virginia, 1825-26; U.S. senator, 1827-36. In 1840 he was elected vice president and, on Harrison's death, succeeded him. He favored pre-emption, allowing settlers to get government land; rejected a national bank bill and thus alienated most Whig supporters; refused to honor the spoils system. He signed the resolution annexing Texas, Mar. 1, 1845. He accepted renomination, 1844, but withdrew before election. In 1861, he chaired an unsuccessful Washington conference called to avert civil war. After its failure he supported secession, sat in the provisional Confederate Congress, became a member of the Confederate House, but died in Richmond, Jan. 18, 1862, before it met.

James Knox Polk (1845-1849)

James Knox Polk, 11th president, Democrat, was born in Mecklenburg Co., N.C., Nov. 2, 1795, the son of Samuel Polk, farmer and surveyor of Scotch-Irish descent, and Jane Knox. He graduated from the Univ. of North Carolina, 1818; member of the Tennessee state legislature, 1823-25. He served in Congress 1825-39 and as speaker 1835-39. He was governor of Tennessee 1839-41, but was defeated 1841 and 1843. In 1844, when both Clay and Van Buren announced opposition to annexing Texas, the Democrats made Polk the first dark horse nominee because he demanded control of all Oregon and annexation of Texas. Polk re-established the independent treasury system originated by Van Buren. His expansionist policy was opposed by Clay, Webster, Calhoun; he sent troops under Zachary Taylor to the Mexican border and, when Mexicans attacked, declared war existed. The Mexican war ended with the annexation of California and much of the Southwest as part of America's "manifest destiny." He compromised on the Oregon boundary ("54-40 or fight!") by accepting the 49th parallel and giving Vancouver to the British. Polk died in Nashville, June 15, 1849.

Zachary Taylor (1849-1850)

Zachary Taylor, 12th president, Whig, who served only 16 months, was born Nov. 24, 1784, in Orange Co., Va., the son of Richard Taylor, later collector of the port of Louisville, Ky., and Sarah Strother. Taylor was commissioned first lieutenant, 1808; fought in the War of 1812; the Black Hawk War, 1832; and the second Seminole War, 1837. He was called Old Rough and Ready. He settled on a plantation near Baton Rouge, La. In 1845 Polk sent him with an army to the Rio Grande. When the Mexicans attacked him, Polk declared war. Taylor was successful at Palo Alto and Resaca de la Palma, 1846; occupied Monterrey. Polk made him major general but sent many of his troops to Gen. Winfield Scott. Outnumbered 4-1, he defeated Santa Anna at Buena Vista, 1847. A national hero, he received the Whig nomination in 1848, and was elected president. He resumed the spoils system and though once a slave-holder worked to have California admitted as a free state. He died in office July 9, 1850.

Millard Fillmore (1850-1853)

Millard Fillmore, 13th president, Whig, was born Jan. 7, 1800, in Cayuga Co., N.Y., the son of Nathaniel Fillmore and Phoebe Millard. He taught school and studied law; admitted to the bar, 1823. He was a member of the state assembly, 1829-32; in Congress, 1833-35 and again 1837-43. He opposed the entrance of Texas as slave territory and voted for a protective tariff. In 1844 he was defeated for governor of New York. In 1848 he was elected vice president and succeeded as president July 10, 1850, after Taylor's death. Fillmore favored the Compromise of 1850 and signed the Fugitive Slave Law. His policies pleased neither expansionists nor slave-holders and he was not renominated in 1852. In 1856 he was nominated by the American (Know-Nothing) party and accepted by the Whigs, but defeated by Buchanan. He died in Buffalo, Mar. 8, 1874.

Franklin Pierce (1853-1857)

Franklin Pierce, 14th president, Democrat, was born in Hillsboro, N. H., Nov. 23, 1804, the son of Benjamin Pierce, veteran of the Revolution and governor of New Hampshire, 1827. He graduated from Bowdoin, 1824. A lawyer, he served in the state legislature 1829-33; in Congress, supporting Jackson, 1833-37; U.S. senator, 1837-42. He enlisted in the Mexican War, became brigadier general under Gen. Winfield Scott. In 1852 Pierce was nominated on the 49th ballot over Lewis Cass, Stephen A. Douglas, and James Buchanan, and defeated Gen. Scott, Whig. Though against slavery, Pierce was influenced by pro-slavery Southerners. He approved the Kansas-Nebraska Act, leaving slavery to popular vote ("squatter sovereignty"), 1854. He signed a reciprocity treaty with Canada and approved the Gadsden Purchase from Mexico, 1853. Denied renomination by the Democrats, he spent most of his remaining years in Concord, N.H., where he died Oct. 8, 1869.

James Buchanan (1857-1861)

James Buchanan, 15th president, Federalist, later Democrat, was born of Scottish descent near Mercersburg, Pa., Apr. 23, 1791, the son of James Buchanan, merchant, and Elizabeth Speer. He graduated from Dickinson, 1809; was a volunteer in the War of 1812; member, Pennsylvania legislature, 1814-16, Congress, 1820-31; Jackson's minister to Russia, 1831-33; U.S. senator 1834-45. As Polk's secretary of state, 1845-49, he ended the Oregon dispute with Britain, supported the Mexican War and annexation of Texas. As minister to Britain, 1853, he signed the Ostend Manifesto. Nominated by Democrats, he was elected, 1856, over John C. Fremont (Republican) and Millard Fillmore (American Know-Nothing and Whig tickets). On slavery he favored popular sovereignty and choice by state constitutions; he accepted the pro-slavery Dred Scott decision as binding. He denied the right of states to secede. A strict constructionist, he desired to keep peace and found no authority for using force. He died at Wheatland, near Lancaster, Pa., June 1, 1868.

Abraham Lincoln (1861-1865)

Abraham Lincoln, 16th president, Republican, was born Feb. 12, 1809, in a log cabin on a farm then in Hardin Co., Ky., now in Larue. He was the son of Thomas Lincoln, a carpenter, and Nancy Hanks.

The Lincolns moved to Spencer Co., Ind., near Gentryville, when Abe was 7. When his mother died his father married Mrs. Sarah Bush Johnston, 1819; she had a favorable influence on Abe. In 1830 the family moved to Macon Co., Ill. Lincoln lost election to the Illinois General Assembly, 1832, but later won 4 times, beginning in 1834. He enlisted in the militia for the Black Hawk War, 1832. In New Salem he ran a store, surveyed land, and was postmaster.

In 1837 Lincoln was admitted to the bar and became partner in a Springfield, Ill., law office. He was elected to Congress, 1847-49. He opposed the Mexican War. He supported Zachary Taylor, 1848. He opposed the Kansas-Nebraska Act and extension of slavery, 1854. He failed in his bid for the Senate, 1855. He supported John C. Fremont, 1856.

In 1858 Lincoln had Republican support in the Illinois legislature for the Senate but was defeated by Stephen A. Douglas, Dem., who had sponsored the Kansas-Nebraska Act.

Lincoln was nominated for president by the Republican party on an anti-slavery platform, 1860. He ran against Douglas, a northern Democrat; John C. Breckinridge, southern pro-slavery Democrat; John Bell,

Constitutional Union party. When he won the election, South Carolina seceded from the Union Dec. 20, 1860, followed in 1861 by 10 Southern states.

The Civil War erupted when Fort Sumter was attacked Apr. 12, 1861. On Sept. 22, 1862, 5 days after the battle of Antietam, he announced that slaves in territory then in rebellion would be free Jan. 1, 1863, date of the Emancipation Proclamation, His speeches, including his Gettysburg and Inaugural addresses, are remembered for their eloquence.

Lincoln was reelected, 1864, over Gen. George B. McClellan, Democrat. Lee surrendered Apr. 9, 1865. On Apr. 14, Lincoln was shot by actor John Wilkes Booth in Ford's Theatre, Washington. He died the next day.

Andrew Johnson (1865-1869)

Andrew Johnson, 17th president, Democrat, was born in Raleigh, N.C., Dec. 29, 1808, the son of Jacob Johnson, porter at an inn and church sexton, and Mary McDonough. He was apprenticed to a tailor but ran away and eventually settled in Greeneville, Tenn. He became an alderman, 1828; mayor, 1830; state representative and senator, 1835-43; member of Congress, 1843-53; governor of Tennessee, 1853-57; U.S. senator, 1857-62. He supported John C. Breckinridge against Lincoln in 1860. He had held slaves, but opposed secession and tried to prevent his home state, Tennessee, from seceding. In Mar. 1862, Lincoln appointed him military governor of occupied Tennessee. In 1864 he was nominated for vice president with Lincoln on the National Union ticket to win Democratic support. He succeeded Lincoln as president Apr. 15, 1865. In a controversy with Congress over the president's power over the South, he proclaimed, May 26, 1865, an amnesty to all Confederates except certain leaders if they would ratify the 13th Amendment abolishing slavery. States doing so added anti-Negro provisions that enraged Congress, which restored military control over the South. When Johnson removed Edwin M. Stanton, secretary of war, without notifying the Senate, thus repudiating the Tenure of Office Act, the House impeached him for this and other reasons. He was tried by the Senate, and acquitted by only one vote, May 26, 1868. He returned to the Senate in 1875. Johnson died July 31, 1875.

Ulysses Simpson Grant (1869-1877)

Ulysses S. Grant, 18th president, Republican, was born at Point Pleasant, Oh., Apr. 27, 1822, son of Jesse R. Grant, a tanner, and Hannah Simpson. The next year the family moved to Georgetown, Oh. Grant was named Hiram Ulysses, but on entering West Point, 1839, his name was entered as Ulysses Simpson and he adopted it. He was graduated in 1843; served under Gens. Taylor and Scott in the Mexican War; resigned, 1854; worked in St. Louis until 1860, then went to Galena, Ill. With the start of the Civil War, he was named colonel of the 21st Illinois Vols., 1861, then brigadier general; took Forts Henry and Donelson; fought at Shiloh, took Vicksburg. After his victory at Chattanooga, Lincoln placed him in command of the Union Armies. He accepted Lee's surrender at Appomattox, Apr., 1865. President Johnson appointed Grant secretary of war when he suspended Stanton, but Grant was not confirmed. He was nominated for president by the Republicans in 1868 and elected over Horatio Seymour, Democrat. The 15th Amendment, amnesty bill, and civil service reform were events of his administration. The Liberal Republicans and Democrats opposed him with Horace Greeley, 1872, but he was reelected. An attempt by the Stalwarts (Old Guard) to nominate him in 1880 failed. In 1884 the collapse of Grant & Ward, investment house, left him penniless. He wrote his personal memoirs while ill with cancer and completed them 4 days before his death at Mt. McGregor, N.Y., July 23, 1885. The book realized over $450,000.

Rutherford Birchard Hayes (1877-1881)

Rutherford B. Hayes, 19th president, Republican, was born in Delaware, Oh., Oct. 4, 1822, the posthumous son of Rutherford Hayes, a farmer, and Sophia Birchard. He was raised by his uncle Sardis Birchard. He graduated from Kenyon College, 1842, and Harvard Law School, 1845. He practiced law in Lower Sandusky, Oh., now Fremont; was city solicitor of Cincinnati, 1858-61. In the Civil War, he was major of the 23d Ohio Vols., was wounded several times, and rose to the rank of brevet major general, 1864. He served in Congress 1864-67, supporting Reconstruction and Johnson's impeachment. He was elected governor of Ohio, 1867 and 1869; beaten in the race for Congress, 1872; reelected governor, 1875. In 1876 he was nominated for president and believed he had lost the election to Samuel J. Tilden, Democrat. But a few Southern states submitted 2 different sets of electoral votes and the result was in dispute. An electoral commission, appointed by Congress, 8 Republicans and 7 Democrats, awarded all disputed votes to Hayes allowing him to become president by one electoral vote. Hayes, keeping a promise to southerners, withdrew troops from areas still occupied in the South, ending the era of Reconstruction. He proceeded to reform the civil service, alienating political spoilsmen. He advocated repeal of the Tenure of Office Act. He supported sound money and specie payments. Hayes died in Fremont, Oh., Jan. 17, 1893.

James Abram Garfield (1881)

James A. Garfield, 20th president, Republican, was born Nov. 19, 1831, in Orange, Cuyahoga Co., Oh., the son of Abram Garfield and Eliza Ballou. His father died in 1833. He worked as a canal bargeman, farmer, and carpenter; attended Western Reserve Eclectic, later Hiram College, and was graduated from Williams in 1856. He taught at Hiram, and later became principal. He was in the Ohio senate in 1859. Anti-slavery and anti-secession, he volunteered for the war, became colonel of the 42d Ohio Infantry and brigadier in 1862. He fought at Shiloh, was chief of staff for Rosecrans and was made major general for gallantry at Chickamauga. He entered Congress as a radical Republican in 1863; supported specie payment as against paper money (greenbacks). On the electoral commission in 1877 he voted for Hayes against Tilden on strict party lines. He was senator-elect in 1880 when he became the Republican nominee for president. He was chosen as a compromise over Gen. Grant, James G. Blaine, and John Sherman. This alienated the Grant following but Garfield was elected. On July 2, 1881, Garfield was shot by mentally disturbed office-seeker, Charles J. Guiteau, while entering a railroad station in Washington. He died Sept. 19, 1881, at Elberon, N.J.

Chester Alan Arthur (1881-1885)

Chester A. Arthur, 21st president, Republican, was born at Fairfield, Vt., Oct. 5, 1829, the son of the Rev. William Arthur, from County Antrim, Ireland, and Malvina Stone. He graduated from Union College, 1848, taught school at Pownall, Vt., studied law in New York. In 1853 he argued in a fugitive slave case that slaves transported through N.Y. State were thereby freed. He was made collector of the Port of New York, 1871. President Hayes, reforming the civil service, forced Arthur to resign, 1879. This made the

New York machine stalwarts enemies of Hayes. Arthur and the stalwarts tried to nominate Grant for a 3d term in 1880. When Garfield was nominated, Arthur received 2d place in the interests of harmony. When Garfield died, Arthur became president. He supported civil service reform and the tariff of 1883. He was defeated for renomination by James G. Blaine. He died in New York City Nov. 18, 1886.

Grover Cleveland (1885-1889) (1893-1897)

(According to a ruling of the State Dept., Grover Cleveland is both the 22d and the 24th president, because his 2 terms were not consecutive. By individuals, he is only the 22d.)

Grover Cleveland, 22d and 24th president, Democrat, was born in Caldwell, N.J. Mar. 18, 1837, the son of Richard F. Cleveland, a Presbyterian minister, and Ann Neale. He was named Stephen Grover, but dropped the Stephen. He clerked in Clinton and Buffalo, N.Y., taught at the N.Y. City Institution for the Blind; was admitted to the bar in Buffalo, 1859; became assistant district attorney, 1863; sheriff, 1871; mayor, 1881; governor of New York, 1882. He was an independent, honest administrator who hated corruption. He was nominated for president over Tammany Hall opposition, 1884, and defeated Republican James G. Blaine. He enlarged the civil service, vetoed many pension raids on the Treasury. In 1888 he was defeated by Benjamin Harrison, although his popular vote was larger. Reelected over Harrison in 1892, he faced a money crisis brought about by lowering of the gold reserve, circulation of paper and exorbitant silver purchases under the Sherman Act; obtained a repeal of the latter and a reduced tariff. A severe depression and labor troubles racked his administration but he refused to interfere in business matters and rejected Jacob Coxey's demand for unemployment relief. He broke the Pullman strike, 1894. In 1896, the Democrats repudiated his administration and chose silverite William Jennings Bryan as their candidate. Cleveland died in Princeton, N.J., June 24, 1908.

Benjamin Harrison (1889-1893)

Benjamin Harrison, 23d president, Republican, was born at North Bend, Oh., Aug. 20, 1833. His great-grandfather, Benjamin Harrison, was a signer of the Declaration of Independence; his grandfather, William Henry Harrison, was 9th President; his father, John Scott Harrison, was a member of Congress. His mother was Elizabeth F. Irwin. He attended school on his father's farm; graduated from Miami Univ. at Oxford, Oh., 1852; admitted to the bar, 1853, and practiced in Indianapolis. In the Civil War, he rose to the rank of brevet brigadier general, fought at Kennesaw Mountain, Peachtree Creek, Nashville, and in the Atlanta campaign. He failed to be elected governor of Indiana, 1876; but became senator, 1881. In 1888 he defeated Cleveland for president despite having fewer popular votes. He expanded the pension list, signed the McKinley high tariff bill, the Sherman Antitrust Act, and the Sherman Silver Purchase Act. During his administration, 6 states were admitted to the union. He was defeated for reelection, 1892. He represented Venezuela in a boundary arbitration with Great Britain in Paris, 1899. He died in Indianapolis, Mar. 13, 1901.

William McKinley (1897-1901)

William McKinley, 25th president, Republican, was born in Niles, Oh., Jan. 29, 1843, the son of William McKinley, an ironmaker, and Nancy Allison. McKinley attended school in Poland, Oh., and Allegheny College, Meadville, Pa., and enlisted for the Civil War at 18 in the 23d Ohio, in which Rutherford B. Hayes was a major. He rose to captain and in 1865 was made brevet major. He studied law in the Albany, N.Y., law school; opened an office in Canton, Oh., in 1867, and campaigned for Grant and Hayes. He served in the House of Representatives, 1877-83, 1885-91, and led the fight for passage of the McKinley Tariff, 1890. Defeated for reelection on the tariff issue in 1890, he was governor of Ohio, 1892-96. He had support for president in the convention that nominated Benjamin Harrison in 1892. In 1896 he was elected president on a protective tariff, sound money (gold standard) platform over William Jennings Bryan, Democratic proponent of free silver. McKinley was reluctant to intervene in Cuba but the loss of the battleship Maine at Havana crystallized opinion. He demanded Spain's withdrawal from Cuba; Spain made some concessions but Congress announced state of war as of Apr. 21. He was reelected in the 1900 campaign, defeating Bryan's anti-imperialist arguments with the promise of a "full dinner pail." McKinley was respected for his conciliatory nature, but conservative on business issues. On Sept. 6, 1901, while welcoming citizens at the Pan-American Exposition, Buffalo, N.Y., he was shot by Leon Czolgosz, an anarchist. He died Sept. 14.

Theodore Roosevelt (1901-1909)

Theodore Roosevelt, 26th president, Republican, was born in N.Y. City, Oct. 27, 1858, the son of Theodore Roosevelt, a glass importer, and Martha Bulloch. He was a 5th cousin of Franklin D. Roosevelt and an uncle of Eleanor Roosevelt. Roosevelt graduated from Harvard, 1880; attended Columbia Law School briefly; sat in the N.Y. State Assembly, 1882-84; ranched in North Dakota, 1884-86; failed election as mayor of N.Y. City, 1886; member of U.S. Civil Service Commission, 1889; president, N.Y. Police Board, 1895, supporting the merit system; assistant secretary of the Navy under McKinley, 1897-98. In the war with Spain, he organized the 1st U.S. Volunteer Cavalry (Rough Riders) as lieutenant colonel; led the charge up Kettle Hill at San Juan. Elected New York governor, 1898-1900, he fought the spoils system and achieved taxation of corporation franchises. Nominated for vice president, 1900, he became nation's youngest president when McKinley died. He was reelected in 1904. As president he fought corruption of politics by big business; dissolved Northern Securities Co. and others for violating, anti-trust laws; intervened in coal strike on behalf of the public, 1902; obtained Elkins Law forbidding rebates to favored corporations, 1903; Hepburn Law regulating railroad rates, 1906; Pure Food and Drugs Act, 1906, Reclamation Act and employers' liability laws. He organized conservation, mediated the peace between Japan and Russia, 1905; won the Nobel Peace Prize. He was the first to use the Hague Court of International Arbitration. By recognizing the new Republic of Panama he made Panama Canal possible.

In 1908 he obtained the nomination of William H. Taft, who was elected. Feeling that Taft had abandoned his policies, Roosevelt unsuccessfully sought the nomination in 1912. He bolted the party and ran on the Progressive "Bull Moose" ticket against Taft and Woodrow Wilson, splitting the Republicans and insuring Wilson's election. He was shot during the campaign but recovered. In 1916 he supported Charles E. Hughes, Republican. A strong friend of Britain, he fought American isolation in World War I. He wrote some 40 books on many topics; his *Winning of the West* is best known. He died Jan. 6, 1919, at Sagamore Hill, Oyster Bay, N.Y.

William Howard Taft (1909-1913)

William Howard Taft, 27th president, Republican, was born in Cincinnati, Oh., Sept. 15, 1857, the son of Alphonso Taft and Louisa Maria Torrey. His father was secretary of war and attorney general in Grant's cabinet; minister to Austria and Russia under Arthur. Taft was graduated from Yale, 1878; Cincinnati Law School, 1880; became law reporter for Cincinnati newspapers; was assistant prosecuting attorney, 1881-83; assistant county solicitor, 1885; judge, superior court, 1887; U.S. solicitor-general, 1890; federal circuit judge, 1892. In 1900 he became head of the U.S. Philippines Commission and was first civil governor of the Philippines, 1901-04; secretary of war, 1904; provisional governor of Cuba, 1906. He was groomed for president by Roosevelt and elected over Bryan, 1908. His administration dissolved Standard Oil and tobacco trusts; instituted Dept. of Labor; drafted direct election of senators and income tax amendments. His tariff and conservation policies angered progressives; though renominated he was opposed by Roosevelt; the result was Democrat Woodrow Wilson's election. Taft, with some reservations, supported the League of Nations. He was professor of constitutional law, Yale, 1913-21; chief justice of the U.S. Supreme Court, 1921-30; illness forced him to resign. He died in Washington, Mar. 8, 1930.

Woodrow Wilson (1913-1921)

Woodrow Wilson, 28th president, Democrat, was born at Staunton, Va., Dec. 28, 1856, as Thomas Woodrow Wilson, son of a Presbyterian minister, the Rev. Joseph Ruggles Wilson and Janet (Jessie) Woodrow. In his youth Wilson lived in Augusta, Ga., Columbia, S.C., and Wilmington, N.C. He attended Davidson College, 1873-74; was graduated from Princeton, A.B., 1879; A.M., 1882; read law at the Univ. of Virginia, 1881; practiced law, Atlanta, 1882-83; Ph.D., Johns Hopkins, 1886. He taught at Bryn Mawr, 1885-88; at Wesleyan, 1888-90; was professor of jurisprudence and political economy at Princeton, 1890-1910; president of Princeton, 1902-1910; governor of New Jersey, 1911-13. In 1912 he was nominated for president with the aid of William Jennings Bryan, who sought to block James "Champ" Clark and Tammany Hall. Wilson won the election because the Republican vote for Taft was split by the Progressives under Roosevelt.

Wilson protected American interests in revolutionary Mexico and fought for American rights on the high seas. His sharp warnings to Germany led to the resignation of his secretary of state, Bryan, a pacifist. In 1916 he was reelected by a slim margin with the slogan, "He kept us out of war." Wilson's attempts to mediate in the war failed. After 4 American ships had been sunk by the Germans, he secured a declaration of war against Germany on Apr. 6, 1917.

Wilson proposed peace Jan. 8, 1918, on the basis of his "Fourteen Points," a state paper with worldwide influence. His doctrine of self-determination continues to play a major role in territorial disputes. The Germans accepted his terms and an armistice, Nov. 11.

Wilson went to Paris to help negotiate the peace treaty, the crux of which he considered the League of Nations. The Senate demanded reservations that would not make the U.S. subordinate to the votes of other nations in case of war. Wilson refused to consider any reservations and toured the country to get support. He suffered a stroke, Oct., 1919. An invalid for months, he clung to his executive powers while his wife and doctor sought to shield him from affairs which would tire him.

He was awarded the 1919 Nobel Peace Prize, but the treaty embodying the League of Nations was rejected by the Senate, 1920. He died in Washington, Feb. 3, 1924.

Warren Gamaliel Harding (1921-1923)

Warren Gamaliel Harding, 29th president, Republican, was born near Corsica, now Blooming Grove, Oh., Nov. 2, 1865, the son of Dr. George Tyron Harding, a physician, and Phoebe Elizabeth Dickerson. He attended Ohio Central College. He was state senator, 1900-04; lieutenant governor, 1904-06; defeated for governor, 1910; chosen U.S. senator, 1915. He supported Taft, opposed federal control of food and fuel; voted for anti-strike legislation, woman's suffrage, and the Volstead prohibition enforcement act over President Wilson's veto; and opposed the League of Nations. In 1920 he was nominated for president and defeated James M. Cox in the election. The Republicans capitalized on war weariness and fear that Wilson's League of Nations would curtail U.S. sovereignty. Harding stressed a return to "normalcy"; worked for tariff revision and repeal of excess profits law and high income taxes. Two Harding appointees, Albert B. Fall (interior) and Harry Daugherty (attorney general), became involved in the Teapot Dome scandal that embittered Harding's last days. He called the International Conference on Limitation of Armaments, 1921-22. Returning from a trip to Alaska he became ill and died in San Francisco, Aug. 2, 1923.

Calvin Coolidge (1923-1929)

Calvin Coolidge, 30th president, Republican, was born in Plymouth, Vt., July 4, 1872, the son of John Calvin Coolidge, a storekeeper, and Victoria J. Moor, and named John Calvin Coolidge. Coolidge graduated from Amherst in 1895. He entered Republican state politics and served as mayor of Northampton, Mass., state senator, lieutenant governor, and, in 1919, governor. In Sept., 1919, Coolidge attained national prominence by calling out the state guard in the Boston police strike. He declared: "There is no right to strike against the public safety by anybody, anywhere, anytime." This brought his name before the Republican convention of 1920, where he was nominated for vice president. He succeeded to the presidency on Harding's death. He opposed the League of Nations; approved the World Court; vetoed the soldiers' bonus bill, which was passed over his veto. In 1924 he was elected by a huge majority. He reduced the national debt by $2 billion in 3 years. He twice vetoed the McNary-Haugen farm bill, which would have provided relief to financially hard-pressed farmers. With Republicans eager to renominate him he announced, Aug. 2, 1927: "I do not choose to run for president in 1928." He died in Northampton, Jan. 5, 1933.

Herbert Clark Hoover (1929-1933)

Herbert C. Hoover, 31st president, Republican, was born at West Branch, Ia., Aug. 10, 1874, son of Jesse Clark Hoover, a blacksmith, and Hulda Randall Minthorn. Hoover grew up in Indian Territory (now Oklahoma) and Oregon; won his A.B. in engineering at Stanford, 1891. He worked briefly with U.S. Geological Survey and western mines; then was a mining engineer in Australia, Asia, Europe, Africa, U.S. While chief engineer, imperial mines, China, he directed food relief for victims of Boxer Rebellion, 1900. He directed American Relief Committee, London, 1914-15; U.S. Comm. for Relief in Belgium, 1915-1919; was U.S. Food Administrator, 1917-1919; American Relief Administrator, 1918-1923, feeding children in defeated nations; Russian Relief, 1918-1923. He was secy. of commerce, 1921-28. He was elected president over Alfred E. Smith, 1928. In 1929 the stock market crashed and the economy collapsed. During the depression, Hoover opposed federal aid to the unemployed. He was defeated in the 1932 election by Franklin D. Roosevelt. President Truman made him coordinator of European Food Program, 1947, chairman of the Commission for Reorganization of the Executive Branch, 1947-49. He founded the Hoover Institution on War, Revolution, and Peace at Stanford Univ. He died in N.Y. City, Oct. 20, 1964.

Franklin Delano Roosevelt (1933-1945)

Franklin D. Roosevelt, 32d president, Democrat, was born near Hyde Park, N.Y., Jan. 30, 1882, the son of James Roosevelt and Sara Delano. He graduated from Harvard, 1904; attended Columbia Law School; was admitted to the bar. He went to the N.Y. Senate, 1910 and 1913. In 1913 President Wilson made him assistant secretary of the navy.

Roosevelt ran for vice president, 1920, with James Cox and was defeated. From 1920 to 1928 he was a N.Y. lawyer and vice president of Fidelity & Deposit Co. In Aug., 1921, polio paralyzed his legs. He learned to walk with leg braces and a cane.

Roosevelt was elected governor of New York, 1928 and 1930. In 1932, W. G. McAdoo, pledged to John N. Garner, threw his votes to Roosevelt, who was nominated. The depression and the promise to repeal prohibition insured his election. He asked emergency powers, proclaimed the New Deal, and put into effect a vast number of administrative changes. Foremost was the use of public funds for relief and public works, resulting in deficit financing. He greatly expanded the controls of the central government over business, and by an excess profits tax and progressive income taxes produced a redistribution of earnings on an unprecedented scale. The Wagner Act gave labor many advantages in organizing and collective bargaining. He was the last president inaugurated on Mar. 4 (1933) and the first inaugurated on Jan. 20 (1937).

Roosevelt was the first president to use radio for "fireside chats." When the Supreme Court nullified some New Deal laws, he sought power to "pack" the court with additional justices, but Congress refused to give him the authority. He was the first president to break the "no 3d term" tradition (1940) and was elected to a 4th term, 1944, despite failing health. He was openly hostile to fascist governments before World War II and launched a lend-lease program on behalf of the Allies. He wrote the principles of fair dealing into the Atlantic Charter, Aug. 14, 1941 (with Winston Churchill), and urged the Four Freedoms (freedom of speech, of worship, from want, from fear) Jan. 6, 1941. When Japan attacked Pearl Harbor, Dec. 7, 1941, the U.S. entered the war. He conferred with allied heads of state at Casablanca, Jan., 1943; Quebec, Aug., 1943; Teheran, Nov.-Dec., 1943; Cairo, Dec., 1943; Yalta, Feb., 1945. He died at Warm Springs, Ga., Apr. 12, 1945.

Harry S. Truman (1945-1953)

Harry S. Truman, 33d president, Democrat, was born at Lamar, Mo., May 8, 1884, the son of John Anderson Truman and Martha Ellen Young. A family disagreement on whether his middle name was Shippe or Solomon, after names of 2 grandfathers, resulted in his using only the middle initial S. He attended public schools in Independence, Mo., worked for the Kansas City Star, 1901, and as railroad timekeeper, and helper in Kansas City banks up to 1905. He ran his family's farm, 1906-17. He was commissioned a first lieutenant and took part in the Vosges, Meuse-Argonne, and St.

Mihiel actions in World War I. After the war he ran a haberdashery, became judge of Jackson Co. Court, 1922-24; attended Kansas City School of Law, 1923-25.

Truman was elected U.S. senator in 1934; reelected 1940. In 1944 with Roosevelt's backing he was nominated for vice president and elected. On Roosevelt's death Truman became president. In 1948 he was elected president.

Truman authorized the first uses of the atomic bomb (Hiroshima and Nagasaki, Aug. 6 and 9, 1945), bringing World War II to a rapid end. He was responsible for creating NATO, the Marshall Plan, and what came to be called the Truman Doctrine (to aid nations such as Greece and Turkey, threatened by Russian or other communist takeover). He broke a Russian blockade of West Berlin with a massive airlift, 1948-49. When communist North Korea invaded South Korea, June, 1950, he won UN approval for a "police action" and sent in forces under Gen. Douglas MacArthur. When MacArthur opposed his policy of limited objectives, Truman removed him from command.

Truman was responsible for higher minimum-wage, increased social-security, and aid-for-housing laws. Truman died Dec. 26, 1972, in Kansas City, Mo.

Dwight David Eisenhower (1953-1961)

Dwight D. Eisenhower, 34th president, Republican, was born Oct. 14, 1890, at Denison, Tex., the son of David Jacob Eisenhower and Ida Elizabeth Stover. The next year, the family moved to Abilene, Kan. He graduated from West Point, 1915. He was on the American military mission to the Philippines, 1935-39 and during 4 of those years on the staff of Gen. Douglas MacArthur. He was made commander of Allied forces landing in North Africa, 1942, full general, 1943. He became supreme Allied commander in Europe, 1943, and as such led the Normandy invasion June 6, 1944. He was given the rank of general of the army Dec. 20, 1944, made permanent in 1946. On May 7, 1945, he received the surrender of the Germans at Rheims. He returned to the U.S. to serve as chief of staff, 1945-1948. In 1948, Eisenhower published *Crusade in Europe*, his war memoirs, which quickly became a best seller. From 1948 to 1953, he was president of Columbia Univ., but took leave of absence in 1950, to command NATO forces.

Eisenhower resigned from the army and was nominated for president by the Republicans, 1952. He defeated Adlai E. Stevenson in the election. He again defeated Stevenson, 1956. He called himself a moderate, favored "free market system" vs. government price and wage controls; kept government out of labor disputes; reorganized defense establishment; promoted missile programs. He continued foreign aid; sped end of Korean fighting; endorsed Taiwan and SE Asia defense treaties; backed UN in condemning Anglo-French raid on Egypt; advocated "open skies" policy of mutual inspection to USSR. He sent U.S. troops into Little Rock, Ark., Sept., 1957, during the segregation crisis and ordered Marines into Lebanon July-Aug., 1958.

During his retirement at his farm near Gettysburg, Pa., Eisenhower took up the role of elder statesman, counseling his 3 successors in the White House. He died Mar. 28, 1969, in Washington.

John Fitzgerald Kennedy (1961-1963)

John F. Kennedy, 35th president, Democrat, was born May 29, 1917, in Brookline, Mass., the son of Joseph P. Kennedy, financier, who later became ambassador to Great Britain, and Rose Fitzgerald. He entered Harvard, attended the London School of

Economics briefly in 1935, received a B.S., from Harvard, 1940. He served in the Navy, 1941-1945, commanded a PT boat in the Solomons and won the Navy and Marine Corps Medal. He wrote *Profiles in Courage*, which won a Pulitzer prize. He served as representative in Congress, 1947-1953; was elected to the Senate in 1952, reelected 1958. He nearly won the vice presidential nomination in 1956.

In 1960, Kennedy won the Democratic nomination for president and defeated Richard M. Nixon, Republican. He was the first Roman Catholic president.

In Apr. 1961, Kennedy's new administration suffered a severe setback when an invasion force of anti-Castro Cubans, trained and directed by the U.S. Central Intelligence Agency, failed to establish a beachhead at the Bay of Pigs in Cuba.

Kennedy's most important act was his successful demand Oct. 22, 1962, that the Soviet Union dismantle its missile bases in Cuba. He established a quarantine of arms shipments to Cuba and continued surveillance by air. He defied Soviet attempts to force the Allies out of Berlin. He made the steel industry rescind a price rise. He backed civil rights, a mental health program, arbitration of railroad disputes, and expanded medical care for the aged. Astronaut flights and satellite orbiting were greatly developed during his administration.

On Nov. 22, 1963, Kennedy was assassinated in Dallas, Tex.

Lyndon Baines Johnson (1963-1969)

Lyndon B. Johnson, 36th president, Democrat, was born near Stonewall, Tex., Aug. 27, 1908, son of Sam Ealy Johnson and Rebekah Baines. He graduated from Southwest Texas State Teachers College, 1930, attended Georgetown Univ. Law School, Washington, 1935. He taught public speaking in Houston, 1930-32; served as secretary to Rep. R. M. Kleberg, 1932-35. In 1937 Johnson won a contest to fill the vacancy caused by the death of a representative and in 1938 was elected to the full term, after which he returned for 4 terms. He was elected U.S. senator in 1948 and reelected in 1954. He became Democratic leader, 1953. Johnson had strong support for the Democratic presidential nomination in at the 1960 convention, where the nominee, John F. Kennedy, asked him to run for vice president. His campaigning helped overcome religious bias against Kennedy in the South.

Johnson became president when Kennedy was assassinated. Johnson worked hard for welfare legislation, signed civil rights, anti-poverty, and tax reduction laws. He was elected to a full term, 1964. The war in Vietnam overshadowed other developments during his administration, such as the "Great Society" social programs.

In face of increasing division in the nation and his own party over his handling of the war, Johnson announced that he would not seek another term, Mar. 31, 1968.

Retiring to his ranch near Johnson City, Tex., Johnson wrote his memoirs and oversaw the construction of the Lyndon Baines Johnson Library. He died Jan. 22, 1973.

Richard Milhous Nixon (1969-1974)

Richard M. Nixon, 37th president, Republican, was the only president to resign without completing an elected term. He was born in Yorba Linda, Cal., Jan. 9, 1913, the son of Francis Anthony Nixon and Hannah Milhous. Nixon graduated from Whittier College, 1934; Duke Univ. Law School, 1937. After practicing law in Whittier and serving briefly in the Office of Price Administration in 1942, he entered the navy, and served in the South Pacific.

Nixon was elected to the House of Representatives in 1946 and 1948. He achieved prominence as the House Un-American Activities Committee member who forced the showdown that resulted in the Alger Hiss perjury conviction. In 1950 Nixon was elected to the Senate.

He was elected vice president in the Eisenhower landslides of 1952 and 1956. With Eisenhower's endorsement, Nixon won the Republican nomination in 1960. He was defeated by Democrat John F. Kennedy, returned to Cal. and was defeated in his race for governor, 1962.

In 1968, he won the presidential nomination and went on to defeat Democrat Hubert H. Humphrey.

Nixon was the first U.S. president to visit China and Russia (1972). He and his foreign affairs advisor, Henry A. Kissinger, achieved a detente with China. Nixon appointed 4 Supreme Court justices, including the chief justice, thus altering the court's balance in favor of a more conservative view.

Reelected 1972, Nixon secured a cease-fire agreement in Vietnam and completed the withdrawal of U.S. troops.

Nixon's 2d term was cut short by a series of scandals beginning with the burglary of Democratic party national headquarters in the Watergate office complex on June 17, 1972. On July 16, 1973, a White House aide, under questioning by a Senate committee, revealed that most of Nixon's office conversations and phone calls had been recorded. Nixon claimed executive privilege to keep the tapes secret and the courts and Congress sought the tapes for criminal proceedings against former White House aides and for a House inquiry into possible impeachment.

On July 24, 1974, the Supreme Court ruled that Nixon's claim of executive privilege must fall before the special prosecutor's subpoenas of tapes relevant to criminal trial proceedings. That same day, the House Judiciary Committee opened debate on impeachment. On July 30, the committee recommended House adoption of 3 articles of impeachment charging Nixon with obstruction of justice, abuse of power, and contempt of Congress.

On Aug. 5, Nixon released transcripts of conversations held 6 days after the Watergate break-in showing that Nixon had known of, approved, and directed Watergate cover-up activities. Nixon resigned from office Aug. 9.

Gerald Rudolph Ford (1974-1977)

Gerald R. Ford, 38th president, Republican, was born July 14, 1913, in Omaha, Neb., son of Leslie King and Dorothy Gardner, and was named Leslie Jr. When he was 2, his parents were divorced and his mother moved with the boy to Grand Rapids, Mich. There she met and married Gerald R. Ford, who formally adopted the boy and gave him his own name.

He graduated from the Univ. of Michigan, 1935 and Yale Law School, 1941.

He began practicing law in Grand Rapids, but in 1942 joined the navy and served in the Pacific, leaving the service in 1946 as a lieutenant commander.

He entered congress in 1949 and spent 25 years in the House, 8 of them as Republican leader.

On Oct. 12, 1973, after Vice President Spiro T. Agnew resigned, Ford was nominated by President Nixon to replace him. It was the first use of the procedures set out in the 25th Amendment.

When Nixon resigned Aug. 9, 1974, Ford became president, the first to serve without being chosen in a national election. On Sept. 8 he pardoned Nixon for any federal crimes he might have committed as president. Ford vetoed 48 bills in his first 21 months in office, saying most would prove too costly. He visited China. In 1976, he was defeated in the election by Democrat Jimmy Carter.

Jimmy (James Earl) Carter (1977-1981)

Jimmy (James Earl) Carter, 39th president, Democrat, was the first president from the Deep South since before the Civil War. He was born Oct. 1, 1924, at Plains, Ga., where his parents, James and Lillian Gordy Carter, had a farm and several businesses.

He attended Georgia Tech, and graduated from the U.S. Naval Academy. He entered the Navy's nuclear submarine program as an aide to Adm. Hyman Rickover, and studied nuclear physics at Union College.

His father died in 1953 and Carter left the Navy to take over the family businesses — peanut-raising, warehousing, and cotton-ginning. He was elected to the Georgia state senate, was defeated for governor, 1966, but elected in 1970.

Carter won the Democratic nomination and defeated President Gerald R. Ford in the election of 1976. He played a major role in the peace negotiations between Israel and Egypt. In Nov. 1979, Iranian student militants attacked the U.S. embassy in Teheran and held members of the embassy staff hostage.

Carter was widely criticized for the poor state of the economy and high inflation. He was also viewed as weak in his handling of foreign policy. He reacted to the Soviet invasion of Afghanistan by imposing a grain embargo and boycotting the Moscow Olympic games. His failure to obtain the release of the remaining 52 hostages held in Iran plagued Carter to the end of his term. He was defeated by Ronald Reagan in the 1980 election. Carter finally succeeded in obtaining the release of the hostages on Inauguration Day, as the new president was taking the oath of office.

Ronald Wilson Reagan (1981-1989)

Ronald Wilson Reagan, 40th president, Republican, was born Feb. 6, 1911, in Tampico, Ill., the son of John Edward Reagan and Nellie Wilson. Reagan graduated from Eureka (Ill.) College in 1932. Following his graduation, he worked as a sports announcer in Des Moines, Ia.

Reagan began a successful career as a film actor in 1937, and starred in numerous movies, and later television, until the 1960s. He was a captain in the Army Air Force during World War II.

He served as president of the Screen Actors Guild from 1947 to 1952, and in 1959.

Once a liberal Democrat, Reagan became active in Republican politics during the 1964 presidential campaign of Barry Goldwater. He was elected governor of California in 1966, and reelected in 1970.

In 1980, he gained the Republican nomination and won a landslide victory over Jimmy Carter. He was easily reelected in 1984. Reagan, at 73, was the oldest man ever elected president.

Reagan successfully forged a bipartisan coalition in Congress which led to enactment of an economic program which included the largest budget and tax cuts in U.S. history, and a Social Security reform bill designed to insure the long-term solvency of the system. In 1986, he signed into law a revolutionary tax-reform bill. He was shot in an assassination attempt in 1981, and had major surgery in 1985 and 1987.

In 1983, Reagan sent a task force to lead the invasion of Grenada, and joined 3 European nations in

maintaining a peacekeeping force in Beirut, Lebanon. His opposition to international terrorism led to the U.S. bombing of Libyan military installations in 1986. He strongly supported El Salvador, the Nicaraguan contras, and other anti-communist governments and forces throughout the world. Aid was sent to the rebels fighting Soviet troops in Afghanistan. When the Iran/Iraq war threatened freedom of the seas, U.S. Navy ships were sent to the Persian Gulf.

Reagan held summit meetings with Soviet leader Gorbachev in 1985 in Geneva, 1986 in Iceland, 1987 in Washington, D.C. where an historic treaty eliminating short and medium-range missiles from Europe was signed, and 1988 in Moscow where Reagan criticized the Soviet record on human rights, and met with Soviet dissidents.

Reagan faced a major crisis in 1986-1987, when it was revealed that the U.S. had sold weapons to Iran in exchange for the release of U.S. hostages being held in Lebanon; and that subsequently some of the money was diverted to the Nicaraguan contras. The scandal led to the resignation of leading White House aides; some were indicted and convicted of criminal charges.

As Reagan left office, the nation was experiencing its 6th consecutive year of economic prosperity. Along with the strong economy, the nation enjoyed low unemployment, energy costs, and inflation. Reagan, however, was unable to control the high budget deficits which plagued him throughout his administration.

George Herbert Walker Bush (1989-   )

George Herbert Walker Bush, 41st president, Republican, was born June 12, 1924, in Milton, Mass., the son of Prescott Bush, U.S. senator from Connecticut, and Dorothy Walker. He served as a U.S. Navy pilot in World War II, earning the Distinguished Flying Cross and three Air Medals for service in the Pacific. After graduating from Yale Univ. (1948), he settled in Texas where, in 1953, he helped found an oil company.

After losing a bid for a U.S. Senate seat in Texas, 1964, he was elected to the House of Representatives in 1966 and 1968. He lost a 2d U.S. Senate race in 1970. He served as U.S. ambassador to the United Nations, 1971-73, headed the U.S. Liaison Office in Beijing, 1974-75, and was director of the Central Intelligence Agency, 1976-77.

Following an unsuccessful bid for the 1980 Republican presidential nomination, Bush was chosen by Ronald Reagan as his vice presidential running mate. He served as U.S. vice president, 1981-89.

In 1988, he gained the Republican presidential nomination and defeated Democrat Michael Dukakis in the election. Calling on Americans "to make kinder the face of the nation and gentler the face of the world," Bush took office faced with the ongoing U.S. budget and trade deficits as well as the rescue of insolvent U.S. savings and loan institutions.

Bush has made no major changes from Reagan's policies in his first 2 years in office. He continued to face a severe budget deficit, struggled with military cutbacks in light of reduced "cold war" tensions, and vetoed congressional actions favorable to abortion and a minimum-wage law that didn't reflect his own views.

Bush has supported Soviet reforms and eastern Europe democratization. He was criticized for his failure to support strongly enough the independence efforts of the Baltic republics and for his soft reaction to the quelling of the China democratic movement. He held summit meetings with Soviet leader Gorbachev in 1989 and 1990.

In Dec. 1989, Bush sent military forces to Panama which overthrew the government and captured military strongman Gen. Manuel Noriega.

Bush reacted to Iraq's Aug. 1990 invasion of Kuwait by sending U.S. forces to the Persian Gulf area and assembling a U.N. backed coalition among NATO and Arab League members. A U.S.-led international force launched air and missile attacks on Iraq, Jan. 1991, after a U.N. deadline for withdrawal from Kuwait had passed. In Feb., Allied forces retook Kuwait after a 4-day ground assault. The quick victory gave Bush one of the highest presidential approval ratings in history despite some criticism of his domestic policy.

Wives and Children of the Presidents

Listed in order of presidential administrations.

Name (Born–died, married)	State	Sons/ daughters
Martha Dandridge Custis Washington (1732-1802, 1759)	Va.	None
Abigail Smith Adams (1744-1818, 1764).	Mass.	3/2
Martha Wayles Skelton Jefferson (1748-1782, 1772)	Va.	1/5
Dorothea "Dolley" Payne Todd Madison (1768-1849, 1794)	N.C.	None
Elizabeth Kortright Monroe (1768-1830, 1786)	N.Y.	../2 (A)
Louisa Catherine Johnson Adams (1775-1852, 1797)	Md.(B)	3/1
Rachel Donelson Robards Jackson (1767-1828, 1791)	Va.	None
Hannah Hoes Van Buren (1783-1819, 1807)	N.Y.	4/ ...
Anna Symmes Harrison (1775-1864, 1795)	N.J.	6/4
Letitia Christian Tyler (1790-1842, 1813)	Va.	3/5
Julia Gardiner Tyler (1820-1889, 1844)	N.Y.	5/2
Sarah Childress Polk (1803-1891, 1824)	Tenn.	None
Margaret Smith Taylor (1788-1852, 1810)	Md.	1/5
Abigail Powers Fillmore (1798-1853, 1826)	N.Y.	1/1
Caroline Carmichael McIntosh Fillmore (1813-1881, 1858)	N.J.	None
Jane Means Appleton Pierce (1806-1863, 1834)	N.H.	3/ ...
Mary Todd Lincoln (1818-1882, 1842)	Ky.	4/ ...
Eliza McCardle Johnson (1810-1876, 1827)	Tenn.	3/2
Julia Dent Grant (1826-1902, 1848)	Mo.	3/1
Lucy Ware Webb Hayes (1831-1889, 1852)	Oh.	7/1
Lucretia Rudolph Garfield (1832-1918, 1858)	Oh.	4/1
Ellen Lewis Herndon Arthur (1837-1880, 1859)	Va.	2/1
Frances Folsom Cleveland (1864-1947, 1886)	N.Y.	2/3

Name (Born–died, married)	State	Sons/ daughters
Caroline Lavinia Scott Harrison (1832-1892, 1853)	Oh.	1/1
Mary Scott Lord Dimmick Harrison (1858-1948, 1896)	Pa.	../1
Ida Saxton McKinley (1847-1907, 1871).	Oh.	../2
Alice Hathaway Lee Roosevelt (1861-1884, 1880)	Mass.	../1
Edith Kermit Carow Roosevelt (1861-1948, 1886)	Conn.	4/1
Helen Herron Taft (1861-1943, 1886)	Oh.	2/1
Ellen Louise Axson Wilson (1860-1914, 1885)	Ga.	../3
Edith Bolling Galt Wilson (1872-1961, 1915)	Va.	None
Florence Kling De Wolfe Harding (1860-1924, 1891)	Oh.	None
Grace Anna Goodhue Coolidge (1879-1957, 1905)	Vt.	2/ ...
Lou Henry Hoover (1875-1944, 1899)	Ia.	2/ ...
Anna Eleanor Roosevelt Roosevelt (1884-1962, 1905)	N.Y.	4/1 (A)
Bess Wallace Truman (1885-1982, 1919)	Mo.	../1
Mamie Geneva Doud Eisenhower (1896-1979, 1916)	Ia.	1/ ...(A)
Jacqueline Lee Bouvier Kennedy (b. 1929, 1953)	N.Y.	1/1 (A)
Claudia "Lady Bird" Alta Taylor Johnson (b. 1912, 1934)	Tex.	../2
Thelma Catherine Patricia Ryan Nixon (b. 1912, 1940)	Nev.	../2
Elizabeth Bloomer Warren Ford (b. 1918, 1948)	Ill.	3/1
Rosalynn Smith Carter (b. 1927, 1946)	Ga.	3/1
Anne Frances "Nancy" Robbins Davis Reagan (b. 1921, 1952)	N.Y.	1/1 (C)
Barbara Pierce Bush (b. 1925, 1945).	N.Y.	4/2

James Buchanan, 15th president, was unmarried. (A) plus one infant, deceased. (B) Born London, father a Md. citizen. (C) President Reagan married and divorced Jane Wyman. They had a son and a daughter.

First Lady: Barbara Bush

The first lady was born Barbara Pierce in Rye, N.Y. on June 8, 1925; the daughter of Marvin and Pauline (Robinson) Pierce. She attended Smith College, 1943-44. She married George Bush, Jan. 6, 1945. They have four sons and a daughter (another daughter died in childhood). Mrs. Bush has had a lifelong involvement in a number of causes, especially the promotion of literacy.

Burial Places of the Presidents

Washington	Mt. Vernon, Va.	Fillmore	Buffalo, N.Y.	T. Roosevelt	Oyster Bay, N.Y.
J. Adams	Quincy, Mass.	Pierce	Concord, N.H.	Taft	Arlington Nat'l. Cem'y.
Jefferson	Charlottesville, Va.	Buchanan	Lancaster, Pa.	Wilson	Washington Cathedral
Madison	Montpelier Station, Va.	Lincoln	Springfield, Ill.	Harding	Marion, Oh.
Monroe	Richmond, Va.	A. Johnson	Greeneville, Tenn.	Coolidge	Plymouth, Vt.
J.Q. Adams	Quincy, Mass.	Grant	New York City	Hoover	West Branch, Ia.
Jackson	Nashville, Tenn.	Hayes	Fremont, Oh.	F.D. Roosevelt	Hyde Park, N.Y.
Van Buren	Kinderhook, N.Y.	Garfield	Cleveland, Oh.	Truman	Independence, Mo.
W.H. Harrison	North Bend, Oh.	Arthur	Albany, N.Y.	Eisenhower	Abilene, Kan.
Tyler	Richmond, Va.	Cleveland	Princeton, N.J.	Kennedy	Arlington Nat'l. Cem'y.
Polk	Nashville, Tenn.	B. Harrison	Indianapolis, Ind.	L.B. Johnson	Stonewall, Tex.
Taylor	Louisville, Ky.	McKinley	Canton, Oh.		

1492
Christopher Columbus and crew sighted land Oct. 12 in the present-day Bahamas.

1497
John Cabot explored northeast coast to Delaware.

1513
Juan Ponce de Leon explored Florida coast.

1524
Giovanni da Verrazano led French expedition along coast from Carolina north to Nova Scotia; entered New York harbor.

1539
Hernando de Soto landed in Florida May 28; crossed Mississippi River, 1541.

1540
Francisco Vazquez de Coronado explored Southwest north of Rio Grande. Hernando de Alarcon reached Colorado River, Don Garcia Lopez de Cardenas reached Grand Canyon. Others explored California coast.

1565
St. Augustine, Fla. founded by Pedro Menendez. Razed by Francis Drake 1586.

1579
Francis Drake claimed California for Britain. Metal plate, found 1936, thought to be left by Drake, termed probable hoax 1979.

1607
Capt. John Smith and 105 cavaliers in 3 ships landed on Virginia coast, started first permanent English settlement in New World at Jamestown in May.

1609
Henry Hudson, English explorer of Northwest Passage, employed by Dutch, sailed into New York harbor in Sept., and up Hudson to Albany. The same year, Samuel de Champlain explored Lake Champlain just to the north.
Spaniards settled Santa Fe, N.M.

1619
House of Burgesses, first representative assembly in New World, elected July 30 at Jamestown, Va.
First black laborers — indentured servants — in English N. American colonies, landed by Dutch at Jamestown in Aug. Chattel slavery legally recognized, 1650.

1620
Plymouth Pilgrims, Puritan separatists from Church of England, some living in Holland, left Plymouth, England Sept. 16 on Mayflower. Original destination Virginia, they reached Cape Cod Nov. 19, explored coast; 103 passengers landed Dec. 26 at Plymouth. Mayflower Compact was agreement to form a government and abide by its laws. Half of colony died during harsh winter.

1624
Dutch left 8 men from ship New Netherland on Manhattan Island in May. Rest sailed to Albany.

1626
Peter Minuit bought Manhattan for Dutch from Man-a-hat-a Indians May 6 for trinkets valued at $24.

1634
Maryland founded as Catholic colony with religious tolerance.

1636
Roger Williams founded Providence, R.I., June, as a democratically ruled colony with separation of church and state. Charter was granted, 1644.
Harvard College founded Oct. 28, now oldest in U.S.; Grammar school, compulsory education established at Boston.

1654
First Jews arrived in New Amsterdam.

1660
British Parliament passed Navigation Act, regulating colonial commerce to suit English needs.

1664
Three hundred British troops Sept. 8 seized New Netherland from Dutch, who yield peacefully. Charles II granted province of New Netherland and city of New Amsterdam to brother, Duke of York; both renamed New York. The Dutch recaptured the colony Aug. 9, 1673, but ceded it to Britain Nov. 10, 1674.

1676
Nathaniel Bacon led planters against autocratic British Gov. Berkeley, burned Jamestown, Va. Bacon died, 23 followers executed.
Bloody Indian war in New England ended Aug. 12. King Philip, Wampanoag chief, and many Narragansett Indians killed.

1682
Robert Cavelier, Sieur de La Salle, claimed lower Mississippi River country for France, called it Louisiana Apr. 9. Had French outposts built in Illinois and Texas, 1684. Killed during mutiny Mar. 19, 1687.

1683
William Penn signed treaty with Delaware Indians and made payment for Pennsylvania lands.

1692
Witchcraft delusion at Salem (now Danvers) Mass. inspired by preaching; 19 persons executed.

1696
Capt. William Kidd, who was born in Scotland and settled in America, was hired by British to fight pirates and take booty, but himself became a pirate. Arrested and sent to England, he was hanged 1701.

1699
French settlements made in Mississippi, Louisiana.

1704
Indians attacked Deerfield, Mass. Feb. 28-29, killed 40, carried off 100.
Boston News Letter, first regular newspaper, started by John Campbell, postmaster. (*Publick Occurences* was suppressed after one issue 1690.)

1709
British-Colonial troops captured French fort, Port Royal, Nova Scotia, in Queen Anne's War 1701-13. France yielded Nova Scotia by treaty 1713.

1712
Slaves revolted in New York Apr. 6. Six committed suicide, 21 were executed. Second rising, 1741; 13 slaves hanged, 13 burned, 71 deported.

1716
First theater in colonies opened in Williamsburg, Va.

1728
Pennsylvania Gazette founded by Samuel Keimer in Philadelphia. Benjamin Franklin bought interest 1729.

1732
Benjamin Franklin published first *Poor Richard's Almanac;* published annually to 1757.

1735
Freedom of the press recognized in New York by acquittal of John Peter Zenger, editor of *Weekly Journal,* on charge of libeling British Gov. Cosby by criticizing his conduct in office.

1740-41
Capt. Vitus Bering, Dane employed by Russians, reached Alaska.

1744
King George's War pitted British and colonials vs. French. Colonials captured Louisburg, Cape Breton Is. June 17, 1745. Returned to France 1748 by Treaty of Aix-la-Chapelle.

1752
Benjamin Franklin, flying kite in thunderstorm, proved lightning is electricity June 15; invented lightning rod.

1754
French and Indian War (in Europe called 7 Years War, started 1756) began when French occupied Ft. Duquesne (Pittsburgh). British moved Acadian French from Nova Scotia to Louisiana Oct. 8, 1755. British captured Quebec Sept. 18, 1759 in battles in which French Gen. Montcalm and

British Gen. Wolfe were killed. Peace signed **Feb. 10 1763.** French lost Canada and American Midwest. British tightened colonial administration in North America.

1764
Sugar Act placed duties on lumber, foodstuffs, molasses and rum in colonies, to pay French and Indian War debts.

1765
Stamp Act required revenue stamps to help defray cost of royal troops. Nine colonies, led by New York and Massachusetts at Stamp Act Congress in New York **Oct. 7-25, 1765,** adopted Declaration of Rights opposing taxation without representation in Parliament and trial without jury by admiralty courts. Stamp Act repealed **Mar. 17, 1766.**

1767
Townshend Acts levied taxes on glass, painter's lead, paper, and tea. In 1770 all duties except on tea were repealed.

1770
British troops fired **Mar. 5** into Boston mob, killed 5 including **Crispus Attucks,** a black man, reportedly leader of group; later called **Boston Massacre.**

1773
East India Co. tea ships turned back at Boston, New York, Philadelphia in May. Cargo ship burned at Annapolis **Oct. 14,** cargo thrown overboard at **Boston Tea Party Dec. 16,** to protest the Tea Act.

1774
"Intolerable Acts" of Parliament curtailed Massachusetts self-rule; barred use of Boston harbor till tea was paid for.
First Continental Congress held in Philadelphia **Sept. 5-Oct. 26;** protested British measures, called for civil disobedience.
Rhode Island abolished slavery.

1775
Patrick Henry addressed Virginia convention, **Mar. 23** said "Give me liberty or give me death."
Paul Revere and William Dawes on night of **Apr. 18** rode to alert patriots that British were on way to Concord to destroy arms. At Lexington, Mass. **Apr. 19** Minutemen lost 8. On return from Concord British took 273 casualties.
Col. Ethan Allen (joined by Col. Benedict Arnold) captured **Ft. Ticonderoga, N.Y. May 10;** also Crown Point. Colonials headed for **Bunker Hill,** fortified Breed's Hill, Charlestown, Mass., repulsed British under Gen. William Howe twice before retreating **June 17;** British casualties 1,000; called Battle of Bunker Hill. Continental Congress **June 15** named **George Washington** commander-in-chief.

1776
France and Spain each agreed **May 2** to provide one million livres in arms to Americans.
In Continental Congress **June 7,** Richard Henry Lee (Va.) moved "that these united colonies are and of right ought to be free and independent states." Resolution adopted July 2. **Declaration of Independence** approved July 4.
Col. Moultrie's batteries at **Charleston, S.C.** repulsed British sea attack **June 28.**
Washington, with 10,000 men, lost **Battle of Long Island Aug. 27,** evacuated New York.
Nathan Hale executed as spy by British **Sept. 22.**
Brig. Gen. Arnold's Lake Champlain fleet was defeated at Valcour **Oct. 11,** but British returned to Canada. Howe failed to destroy Washington's army at **White Plains Oct. 28.** Hessians captured Ft. Washington, Manhattan, and 3,000 men **Nov. 16;** Ft. Lee, N.J. **Nov. 18.**
Washington in Pennsylvania, recrossed **Delaware River Dec. 25-26,** defeated 1,400 Hessians at Trenton, N.J. **Dec. 26.**

1777
Washington defeated Lord Cornwallis at **Princeton Jan. 3.** Continental Congress adopted Stars and Stripes. *See Flag article.*
Maj. Gen. John Burgoyne with 8,000 from Canada captured **Ft. Ticonderoga July 6.** Americans beat back Burgoyne at Bemis Heights **Oct. 7** and cut off British escape route. Burgoyne surrendered 5,000 men at **Saratoga N.Y. Oct. 17.**
Marquis de Lafayette, aged 20, made major general.
Articles of Confederation and Perpetual Union adopted by Continental Congress **Nov. 15**
France recognized independence of 13 colonies **Dec. 17.**

1778
France signed treaty of aid with U.S. **Feb. 6.** Sent fleet; British evacuated Philadelphia in consequence **June 18.**

1779
John Paul Jones on the *Bonhomme Richard* defeated *Serapis* in British North Sea waters **Sept. 23.**

1780
Charleston, S.C. fell to the British **May 12,** but a British force was defeated near **Kings Mountain, N.C. Oct. 7** by militiamen.
Benedict Arnold found to be a traitor **Sept. 23.** Arnold escaped, made brigadier general in British army.

1781
Bank of North America incorporated in Philadelphia **May 26.**
Cornwallis, sapped by patriot victories, retired to **Yorktown, Va.** Adm. De Grasse landed 3,000 French and stopped British fleet in Hampton Roads. Washington and Rochambeau joined forces, arrived near Williamsburg **Sept. 26.** When siege of Cornwallis began **Oct. 6,** British had 6,000, Americans 8,846, French 7,800. **Cornwallis surrendered Oct. 19.**

1782
New British cabinet agreed in March to recognize U.S. independence. Preliminary agreement signed in Paris **Nov. 30.**

1783
Massachusetts Supreme Court **outlawed slavery** in that state, noting the words in the state Bill of Rights "all men are born free and equal."
Britain, U.S. signed **peace treaty Sept. 3** (Congress ratified it **Jan. 14, 1784).**
Washington ordered army disbanded **Nov. 3,** bade farewell to his officers at Fraunces Tavern, N.Y. City **Dec. 4.**
Noah Webster published *American Spelling Book,* great bestseller.

1784
Jefferson's proposal to **ban slavery** in new territory after 1802 is narrowly defeated **Mar. 1.**
First successful daily newspaper, **Pennsylvania Packet & General Advertiser,** published **Sept. 21.**

1786
Delegates from 5 states at **Annapolis, Md. Sept. 11-14** asked Congress to call convention in Philadelphia to write practical constitution for the 13 states.

1787
Shays's Rebellion, of debt-ridden farmers in Massachusetts, failed **Jan. 25.**
Northwest Ordinance adopted **July 13** by Continental Congress. Determined government of Northwest Territory north of Ohio River, west of New York; 60,000 inhabitants could get statehood. Guaranteed freedom of religion, support for schools, no slavery.
Constitutional convention opened at Philadelphia **May 25** with George Washington presiding. Constitution adopted by delegates **Sept. 17;** ratification by 9th state, New Hampshire, **June 21, 1788,** meant adoption; declared in effect **Mar. 4, 1789.**

1789
George Washington chosen president by all electors voting (73 eligible, 69 voting, 4 absent); John Adams, vice president, 34 votes. **Feb. 4.** First Congress met at Federal Hall, N.Y. City; regular sessions began **Apr. 6.** Washington inaugurated there **Apr. 30.** Supreme Court created by Federal Judiciary Act **Sept. 24.** Congress submitted Bill of Rights to states **Sept. 25.**

1790
Congress passed **Census Act Mar. 1; Naturalization Act** (2-year residency) **Mar. 26.**

Congress met in Phila. **Dec. 6,** new temporary Capital.
1791
Bill of Rights went into effect **Dec. 15.**
1792
Coinage Act established **U.S. Mint** in Philadelphia **Apr. 2.**
Gen. **"Mad" Anthony Wayne** made commander in Ohio-Indiana area, trained "American Legion"; established string of forts. Routed Indians at Fallen Timbers on Maumee River **Aug. 20, 1794,** checked British at Fort Miami, Ohio.
White House cornerstone laid **Oct. 13.**
1793
Eli Whitney invented **cotton gin,** reviving southern slavery.

1794
Whiskey Rebellion, west Pennsylvania farmers protesting liquor tax of **1791,** was suppressed by 15,000 militiamen **Sept. 1794.** Alexander Hamilton used incident to establish authority of the new federal government in enforcing its laws.
1795
U.S. bought peace from **Algiers and Tunis** by paying $800,000, supplying a frigate and annual tribute of $25,000 **Nov. 28.**
Gen. **Wayne** signed peace with Indians at Fort Greenville.
Univ. of North Carolina became first operating state university.

1796
Washington's Farewell Address as president delivered **Sept. 19.** Gave strong warnings against permanent alliances with foreign powers, big public debt, large military establishment and devices of "small, artful, enterprising minority" to control or change government.
1797
U.S. **frigate United States** launched at Philadelphia **July 10; Constellation** at Baltimore **Sept. 7; Constitution (Old Ironsides)** at Boston **Sept. 20.**
1798
Alien & Sedition Acts passed by Federalists; intended to silence political opposition **June-July.**
War with France threatened over French raids on U.S. shipping and rejection of U.S. diplomats. Congress voided all treaties with France, ordered Navy to capture French armed ships. Navy (45 ships) and 365 privateers captured 84 French ships. USS Constellation took French warship Insurgente **1799.** Napoleon stopped French raids after becoming First Consul.
1800
Federal gvt. moves from Philadelphia to **Washington, D.C.**
1801
Tripoli declared war **June 10** against U.S., which refused added tribute to commerce-raiding Arab corsairs. Land and naval campaigns forced Tripoli to conclude **peace June 4, 1805.**
1803
Supreme Court, in **Marbury v. Madison** case, for the first time overturned a U.S. law **Feb. 24.**
Napoleon, who had recovered **Louisiana** from Spain by secret treaty, sold all of **Louisiana,** stretching to Canadian border, to U.S., for $11,250,000 in bonds, plus $3,750,000 indemnities to American citizens with claims against France. U.S. took title **Dec. 20.** Purchases doubled U.S. area.
1804
Lewis and Clark expedition ordered by Pres. Jefferson to explore what is now northwest U.S. Started from St. Louis **May 14;** ended **Sept. 23, 1806.** Sacagawea, an Indian woman, served as guide.
Vice Pres. **Aaron Burr,** after long political rivalry, **shot Alexander Hamilton** in a duel **July 11** in Weehawken, N.J.; Hamilton died the next day.
1807
Robert Fulton made first practical steamboat trip; left N.Y. City **Aug. 17,** reached Albany, 150 mi., in 32 hrs.
Embargo Act bans all trade with foreign countries, forbids ships to set sail for foreign ports **Dec. 22.**

1808
Slave importation outlawed. Some 250,000 slaves were illegally imported **1808-1860.**
1811
William Henry Harrison, governor of Indiana, defeated Indians under the Prophet, in battle of Tippecanoe **Nov. 7.**
Cumberland Road begun at Cumberland, Md.; became important route to West.
1812
War of 1812 had 3 main causes: Britain seized U.S. ships trading with France; Britain seized 4,000 naturalized U.S. sailors by 1810; Britain armed Indians who raided western border. U.S. stopped trade with Europe **1807** and **1809.** Trade with Britain only was stopped, **1810.**
Unaware that Britain had raised the blockade against France 2 days before, Congress declared war **June 18** by a small majority. The West favored war, New England opposed it. The British were handicapped by war with France.
U.S. naval victories in 1812 included: USS Essex captured Alert **Aug. 13;** USS Constitution destroyed Guerriere **Aug. 19;** USS Wasp took Frolic **Oct. 18;** USS United States defeated Macedonian off Azores **Oct. 25;** Constitution beat Java **Dec. 29.** British captured Detroit **Aug. 16.**
1813
Oliver H. Perry defeated British fleet at Battle of Lake Erie, **Sept. 10.** U.S. victory at Battle of the Thames, Ont., **Oct. 5,** broke Indian allies of Britain, and made Detroit frontier safe for U.S. But Americans failed in Canadian invasion attempts. York (Toronto) and Buffalo were burned.
1814
British landed in Maryland in August, defeated U.S. force **Aug. 24, burned Capitol** and **White House.** Maryland militia stopped British advance **Sept. 12.** Bombardment of Ft. McHenry, Baltimore, for 25 hours, **Sept. 13-14,** by British fleet failed; Francis Scott Key wrote words to **Star Spangled Banner.**
U.S. won naval **Battle of Lake Champlain Sept. 11.** Peace treaty signed at Ghent **Dec. 24.**
1815
Some 5,300 British, unaware of peace treaty, attacked U.S. entrenchments near **New Orleans, Jan. 8.** British had over 2,000 casualties, Americans lost 71.
U.S. flotilla finally ended piracy by **Algiers, Tunis, Tripoli** by **Aug. 6.**
1816
Second Bank of the U.S. chartered.
1817
Rush-Bagot treaty signed **Apr. 28-29;** limited U.S., British armaments on the Great Lakes.
1819
Spain cedes **Florida** to U.S. **Feb. 22.**
American steamship **Savannah** made first part steam-powered, part sail-powered crossing of Atlantic, Savannah, Ga. to Liverpool, Eng., 29 days.
1820
First organized **immigration of blacks to Africa** from U.S. began with 86 free blacks sailing **Feb.** to Sierra Leone, Brit. Colony.
Henry Clay's **Missouri Compromise** bill passed by Congress **March 3.** Slavery was allowed in Missouri, but not elsewhere west of the Mississippi River north of 36° 30′ latitude (the southern line of Missouri). Repealed **1854.**
1821
Emma Willard founded Troy Female Seminary, first U.S. women's college.
1823
Monroe Doctrine enunciated **Dec. 2,** opposing European intervention in the Americas.
1824
Pawtucket, R.I. **weavers strike** in first such action by women.
1825
Erie Canal opened; first boat left Buffalo **Oct. 26,** reached N.Y. City **Nov. 4.** Canal cost $7 million but cut travel time

one-third, shipping costs nine-tenths; opened Great Lakes area, made N.Y. City chief Atlantic port.

John Stevens, of Hoboken, N.J., built and operated first experimental **steam locomotive** in U.S.

1828

South Carolina **Dec. 19** declared the right of state **nullification of federal laws,** opposing the "Tariff of Abominations."

Noah Webster published his *American Dictionary of the English Language.*

Baltimore & Ohio 1st U.S. passenger RR, was begun **July 4.**

1830

Mormon church organized by Joseph Smith in Fayette, N.Y. **Apr. 6.**

1831

William Lloyd Garrison began abolitionist newspaper *The Liberator* **Jan. 1.**

Nat Turner, black slave in Virginia, led local slave rebellion, killed 57 whites in **Aug.** Troops called in, Turner captured, tried, and hanged.

1832

Black Hawk War (Ill.-Wis.) **Apr.-Sept.** pushed Sauk and Fox Indians west across Mississippi.

South Carolina convention passed **Ordinance of Nullification** in **Nov.** against permanent tariff, threatening to withdraw from the Union. Congress **Feb. 1833** passed a compromise tariff act, whereupon South Carolina repealed its act.

1833

Oberlin College, first in U.S. to adopt coeducation; refused to bar students on account of race, **1835.**

1835

Seminole Indians in Florida under Osceola began attacks **Nov. 1,** protesting forced removal. The unpopular 8-year war ended **Aug. 14, 1842;** Indians were sent to Oklahoma. War cost the U.S. 1,500 soldiers.

Texas proclaimed right to secede from Mexico; Sam Houston put in command of Texas army, **Nov. 2-4.**

Gold discovered on **Cherokee land** in Georgia. Indians forced to cede lands **Dec. 20** and to cross Mississippi.

1836

Texans besieged in Alamo in San Antonio by Mexicans under Santa Anna **Feb. 23-Mar. 6;** entire garrison killed. Texas independence declared, **Mar. 2.** At San Jacinto **Apr. 21** Sam Houston and Texans defeated Mexicans.

Marcus Whitman, H.H. Spaulding and wives reached Fort Walla Walla on Columbia River, Oregon. **First white women to cross plains.**

1838

Cherokee Indians made **"Trail of Tears,"** removed from Georgia to Oklahoma starting **Oct.**

1841

First emigrant **wagon train for California,** 47 persons, left Independence, Mo. **May 1,** reached Cal. **Nov. 4.**

Brook Farm commune set up by New England Transcendentalist intellectuals. Lasts to **1846.**

1842

Webster-Ashburton Treaty signed **Aug. 9,** fixing the U.S.-Canada border in Maine and Minnesota.

First use of **anesthetic** (sulphuric ether gas).

Settlement of Oregon begins via **Oregon Trail.**

1843

More than 1,000 settlers left Independence, Mo. for Oregon **May 22,** arrived **Oct.**

1844

First message over first **telegraph line** sent **May 24** by inventor Samuel F.B. Morse from Washington to Baltimore: "What hath God wrought!"

1845

Texas Congress voted for annexation to U.S. **July 4.** U.S. Congress admits Texas to Union **Dec. 29.**

1846

Mexican War. Pres. James K. Polk ordered Gen. Zachary Taylor to seize disputed Texan land settled by Mexicans.

After border clash, U.S. declared war **May 13; Mexico May 23.** Northern Whigs opposed war, southerners backed it.

Bear flag of Republic of California raised by American settlers at Sonoma **June 14.**

About 12,000 U.S. troops took Vera Cruz Mar. 27, 1847, Mexico City Sept. 14, 1847. By **treaty, Feb. 1848,** Mexico ceded claims to Texas, California, Arizona, New Mexico, Nevada, Utah, part of Colorado. U.S. assumed $3 million American claims and paid Mexico $15 million.

Treaty with Great Britain **June 15** set **boundary in Oregon** territory at 49th parallel (extension of existing line). Expansionists had used slogan "54' 40' or fight."

Mormons, after violent clashes with settlers over polygamy, left Nauvoo, Ill. for West under Brigham Young, settled **July 1847** at Salt Lake City, Utah.

Elias Howe invented **sewing machine.**

1847

First **adhesive U.S. postage stamps** on sale **July 1;** Benjamin Franklin 5¢, Washington 10¢.

Ralph Waldo Emerson published first book of poems; **Henry Wadsworth Longfellow** published *Evangeline.*

1848

Gold discovered Jan. 24 in California; 80,000 prospectors emigrate in **1849.**

Lucretia Mott and Elizabeth Cady Stanton lead **Seneca Falls, N.Y. Women's Rights Convention July 19-20.**

1850

Sen. Henry Clay's **Compromise of 1850** admitted California as 31st state **Sept. 9,** slavery forbidden; made Utah and New Mexico territories without decision on slavery; made Fugitive Slave Law more harsh; ended District of Columbia slave trade.

1851

Herman Melville's *Moby Dick,* **Nathaniel Hawthorne's** *House of the Seven Gables* published.

1852

Uncle Tom's Cabin, by **Harriet Beecher Stowe,** published.

1853

Commodore Matthew C. Perry, U.S.N., received by Lord of Toda, Japan **July 14; negotiated treaty to open Japan** to U.S. ships.

1854

Republican party formed at Ripon, Wis. **Feb. 28.** Opposed Kansas-Nebraska Act (became law **May 30**) which left issue of slavery to vote of settlers.

Henry David Thoreau published *Walden.*

1855

Walt Whitman published *Leaves of Grass.*

First railroad train crossed Mississippi on the river's first bridge, Rock Island, Ill.-Davenport, Ia. **Apr. 21.**

1856

Republican party's first nominee for president, **John C. Fremont,** defeated. Abraham Lincoln made 50 speeches for him.

Lawrence, Kan. sacked **May 21** by slavery party; abolitionist **John Brown** led anti-slavery men against Missourians at **Osawatomie, Kan. Aug. 30**

1857

Dred Scott decision by U.S. Supreme Court **Mar. 6** held, 6-3, that a slave did not become free when taken into a free state, Congress could not bar slavery from a territory, and blacks could not be citizens.

1858

First **Atlantic cable** completed by Cyrus W. Field **Aug. 5;** cable failed **Sept. 1.**

Lincoln-Douglas debates in Illinois **Aug. 21-Oct. 15.**

1859

First commercially productive **oil well,** drilled near Titusville, Pa., by Edwin L. Drake **Aug. 27.**

Abolitionist **John Brown** with 21 men seized U.S. Armory at Harpers Ferry (then Va.) **Oct. 16.** U.S. Marines captured raiders, killing several. Brown was hanged for treason by Virginia **Dec. 2.**

1860

New England shoe-workers, 20,000, strike Feb. 22 win higher wages.

Abraham Lincoln, Republican, elected president in 4-way race.

First Pony Express between Sacramento, Cal. and St. Joseph, Mo. started Apr. 3; service ended Oct. 24, 1861 when first transcontinental telegraph line was completed.

1861

Seven southern states set up Confederate States of America Feb. 8, with Jefferson Davis as president, captured Federal arsenals and forts. Civil War began as Confederates fired on Ft. Sumter in Charleston, S.C. Apr. 12; they captured it Apr. 14.

President Lincoln called for 75,000 volunteers Apr. 15. By May, 11 states had seceded. Lincoln blockaded southern ports Apr. 19, cutting off vital exports, aid.

Confederates repelled Union forces at first Battle of Bull Run July 21.

First transcontinental telegraph was put in operation.

1862

Homestead Act was approved May 20; it granted free family farms to settlers.

Land Grant Act approved July 7, providing for public land sale to benefit agricultural education; eventually led to establishment of state university systems.

Union forces were victorious in western campaigns, took New Orleans. Battles in East were inconclusive.

1863

Lincoln issued Emancipation Proclamation Jan. 1, freeing "all slaves in areas still in rebellion."

The entire Mississippi River was in Union hands by July 4. Union forces won a major victory at Gettysburg, Pa. July 1-July 4. Lincoln read his Gettysburg Address Nov. 19.

Draft riots in N.Y. City killed about 1,000, including blacks who were hanged by mobs July 13-16. Rioters protested provision allowing money payment in place of service. Such payments were ended 1864.

1864

Gen. Sherman marched through Georgia, taking Atlanta Sept. 1, Savannah Dec. 22.

Sand Creek massacre of Cheyenne and Arapaho Indians Nov. 29 in a raid by 900 cavalrymen who killed 150-500 men, women, and children; 9 soldiers died. The tribes were awaiting surrender terms when attacked.

1865

Robert E. Lee surrendered 27,800 Confederate troops to Grant at Appomattox Court House, Va. Apr. 9. J.E. Johnston surrendered 31,200 to Sherman at Durham Station, N.C. Apr. 18. Last rebel troops surrendered May 26.

President Lincoln was shot Apr. 14 by John Wilkes Booth in Ford's Theater, Washington; died the following morning. Booth was reported dead Apr. 26. Four co-conspirators were hanged July 7.

Thirteenth Amendment, abolishing slavery, took effect Dec. 18.

1866

Ku Klux Klan formed secretly in South to terrorize blacks who voted. Disbanded 1869-71. A second Klan was organized 1915.

Congress took control of southern Reconstruction, backed freedmen's rights.

1867

Alaska sold to U.S. by Russia for $7.2 million Mar. 30 through efforts of Sec. of State William H. Seward.

Horatio Alger published first book, Ragged Dick.

The Grange was organized Dec 4, to protect farmer interests.

1868

The World Almanac, a publication of the New York World, appeared for the first time.

Pres. Andrew Johnson tried to remove Edwin M. Stanton, secretary of war; was impeached by House Feb. 24 for violation of Tenure of Office Act; acquitted by Senate March-May. Stanton resigned.

1869

Financial "Black Friday" in New York Sept. 24; caused by attempt to "corner" gold.

Transcontinental railroad completed; golden spike driven at Promontory, Utah May 10 marking the junction of Central Pacific and Union Pacific.

Knights of Labor formed in Philadelphia. By 1886, it had 700,000 members nationally.

Woman suffrage law passed in Territory of Wyoming Dec. 10.

1871

Great fire destroyed Chicago Oct. 8-11; loss est. at $196 million.

1872

Amnesty Act restored civil rights to citizens of the South May 22 except for 500 Confederate leaders.

Congress founded first national park — Yellowstone in Wyoming.

1873

First U.S. postal card issued May 1.

Banks failed, panic began in Sept. Depression lasted 5 years.

"Boss" William Tweed of N.Y. City convicted of stealing public funds. He died in jail in 1878.

Bellevue Hospital in N.Y. City started the first school of nursing.

1875

Congress passed Civil Rights Act Mar. 1 giving equal rights to blacks in public accommodations and jury duty. Act invalidated in 1883 by Supreme Court.

First Kentucky Derby held May 17 at Churchill Downs, Louisville, Ky.

1876

Samuel J. Tilden, Democrat, received majority of popular votes for president over Rutherford B. Hayes, Republican, but 22 electoral votes were in dispute; issue left to Congress. Hayes given presidency in Feb., 1877 after Republicans agree to end Reconstruction of South.

Col. George A. Custer and 264 soldiers of the 7th Cavalry killed June 25 in "last stand," Battle of the Little Big Horn, Mont., in Sioux Indian War.

Mark Twain published Tom Sawyer.

1877

Molly Maguires, Irish terrorist society in Scranton, Pa. mining areas, broken up by hanging of 11 leaders for murders of mine officials and police.

Pres. Hayes sent troops in violent national railroad strike.

1878

First commercial telephone exchange opened, New Haven, Conn. Jan. 28.

Thomas A. Edison founded Edison Electric Light Co. Oct. 15.

1879

F.W. Woolworth opened his first five-and-ten store in Utica, N.Y. Feb. 22.

Henry George published Progress & Poverty, advocating single tax on land.

1881

Pres. James A. Garfield shot in Washington, D.C. July 2; died Sept. 19.

Booker T. Washington founded Tuskegee Institute for blacks.

Helen Hunt Jackson published A Century of Dishonor about mistreatment of Indians.

1883

Pendleton Act, passed Jan. 16, reformed federal civil service.

Brooklyn Bridge opened May 24.

1886

Haymarket riot and bombing, evening of May 4, followed bitter labor battles for 8-hour day in Chicago; 7 police and 4 workers died, 66 wounded. Eight anarchists found guilty. Gov. John P. Altgeld denounced trial as unfair.

Geronimo, Apache Indian, finally surrendered Sept. 4.

The Statue of Liberty was dedicated Oct. 28.

American Federation of Labor (AFL) formed **Dec. 8** by 25 craft unions.

1888

Great blizzard in eastern U.S. **Mar. 11-14; 400** deaths.

1889

U.S. declared Oklahoma open to white settlement **Apr. 22;** within 24 hours claims for 2 mln. acres were staked by 50,000 settlers.

Johnstown, Pa. flood May 31; 2,200 lives lost.

1890

First execution by **electrocution:** William Kemmler **Aug. 6** at Auburn Prison, Auburn, N.Y., for murder.

Battle of **Wounded Knee,** S.D. **Dec. 29,** the last major conflict between Indians and U.S. troops. About 200 Indian men, women, and children, and 29 soldiers were killed.

Castle Garden closed as N.Y. immigration depot; **Ellis Island** opened **Dec. 31,** closed **1954.**

Sherman Antitrust Act begins federal effort to curb monopolies.

Jacob Riis published *How the Other Half Lives,* about city slums.

1891

Forest Reserve Act Mar. 3 let Pres. close public forest land to settlement for establishment of national parks.

1892

Homestead, Pa., strike at Carnegie steel mills; 7 guards and 11 strikers and spectators shot to death **July 6;** setback for unions.

1893

Financial panic began, led to 4-year depression.

1894

Thomas A. **Edison's kinetoscope** (motion pictures) (invented **1887**) given first public showing **Apr. 14.**

Jacob S. **Coxey** led 500 unemployed from the Midwest into Washington, D.C. **Apr. 30.** Coxey was arrested for trespassing on Capitol grounds.

1896

William Jennings Bryan delivered "Cross of Gold" speech **July 7;** wins Democratic Party nomination.

Supreme Court, in **Plessy v. Ferguson,** approved racial segregation under the "separate but equal" doctrine.

1898

U.S. **battleship Maine** blown up **Feb. 15** at Havana, 260 killed.

U.S. **blockaded Cuba Apr. 22** in aid of independence forces. U.S. declared war on Spain, **Apr. 24,** destroyed Spanish fleet in Philippines **May 1,** took Guam **June 20.**

Puerto Rico taken by U.S. **July 25-Aug. 12.** Spain agreed **Dec. 10** to cede Philippines, Puerto Rico, and Guam, and approved independence for Cuba.

U.S. annexed independent republic of **Hawaii.**

1899

Filipino insurgents, unable to get recognition of independence from U.S., started guerrilla war **Feb. 4.** Crushed with capture **May 23, 1901** of leader, Emilio Aguinaldo.

U.S. declared **Open Door Policy** to make China an open international market and to preserve its integrity as a nation.

John Dewey published *School and Society,* backing progressive education.

1900

Carry Nation, Kansas anti-saloon agitator, began raiding with hatchet.

U.S. helped suppress **"Boxers"** in Peking.

International Ladies' Garment Workers Union was founded in NYC in **Nov.**

1901

Texas had its first significant oil strike, near Beaumont **Jan. 10.**

Pres. William **McKinley was shot Sept. 6** by an anarchist, Leon Czolgosz; died **Sept. 14.**

1903

Treaty between U.S. and Colombia to have U.S. dig **Panama Canal** signed **Jan. 22,** rejected by Colombia. Panama declared independence with U.S. support **Nov. 3;** recognized

by Pres. Theodore Roosevelt **Nov. 6.** U.S., Panama signed canal treaty **Nov. 18.**

Wisconsin set first **direct primary** voting system **May 23.**

First **automobile trip** across U.S. from San Francisco to New York **May 23-Aug. 1.**

First successful flight in heavier-than-air mechanically propelled airplane by **Orville Wright Dec. 17** near Kitty Hawk, N.C., 120 ft. in 12 seconds. Fourth flight same day by **Wilbur Wright,** 852 ft. in 59 seconds. Improved plane patented **May 22, 1906.**

Jack London published *Call of the Wild.*

Great Train Robbery, pioneering film, produced.

1904

Ida Tarbell published muckraking *History of Standard Oil.*

1905

First **Rotary Club** founded in Chicago **Dec.**

1906

San Francisco earthquake and fire **Apr. 18-19** left 503 dead, $350 million damages.

Pure Food and Drug Act and Meat Inspection Act both passed **June 30.**

1907

Financial panic and depression started **Mar. 13.**

First round-world cruise of U.S. **"Great White Fleet";** 16 battleships, 12,000 men.

1908

Henry Ford introduced **Model T** car, priced at $850 **Oct. 1.**

1909

Adm. Robert E. Peary reached **North Pole Apr. 6** on 6th attempt, accompanied by Matthew Henson, a black man, and 4 Eskimos.

National Conference on the Negro convened **May 30,** leading to founding of the National Association for the Advancement of Colored People.

1910

Boy Scouts of America founded **Feb. 8.**

1911

Supreme Court dissolved **Standard Oil Co. May 15.**

NYC's **Triangle Waist Sweatshop** caught fire, trapping and killing 146, mostly young women **Mar. 25.**

First **transcontinental airplane flight** (with numerous stops) by C.P. Rodgers, New York to Pasadena, **Sept. 17-Nov. 5;** time in air 82 hrs., 4 min.

1912

Amer. **Girl Guides** founded **Mar. 12;** name changed in 1913 to **Girl Scouts.**

U.S. sent marines **Aug. 14** to **Nicaragua,** which was in default of loans to U.S. and Europe.

1913

N.Y. Armory Show brought modern art to U.S. **Feb. 17.**

U.S. **blockaded Mexico** in support of revolutionaries.

Charles Beard published his *Economic Interpretation of the Constitution.*

Federal Reserve System was authorized **Dec. 23,** in a major reform of U.S. banking and finance.

1914

Ford Motor Co. raised basic wage rates from $2.40 for 9-hr. day to $5 for 8-hr. day **Jan. 5.**

When U.S. sailors were arrested at Tampico **Apr. 9,** Atlantic fleet was sent to **Veracruz,** occupied city.

Pres. Wilson proclaimed U.S. **neutrality** in the European war **Aug. 4.**

Panama Canal was officially opened **Aug. 15.**

The **Clayton Antitrust Act** was passed **Oct. 15,** strengthening federal anti-monopoly powers.

1915

First **telephone talk,** New York to San Francisco, **Jan. 25** by Alexander Graham Bell and Thomas A. Watson.

British ship **Lusitania** sunk **May 7** by German submarine; 128 American passengers lost (Germany had warned passengers in advance). As a result of U.S. campaign, Germany issued apology and promise of payments **Oct. 5.** Pres. Wilson asked for a military fund increase **Dec. 7.**

U.S. troops landed in **Haiti** July 28. Haiti became a virtual U.S. protectorate under **Sept. 16** treaty.

1916

Gen. John J. **Pershing entered Mexico** to pursue Francisco (Pancho) Villa, who had raided U.S. border areas. Forces withdrawn **Feb. 5, 1917.**

Rural Credits Act passed **July 17,** followed by Warehouse Act. **Aug. 11;** both provided financial aid to farmers.

Bomb exploded during **San Francisco** Preparedness Day parade **July 22,** killed 10. Thomas J. Mooney, labor organizer, and Warren K. Billings, shoe worker, were convicted; both pardoned in 1939.

U.S. bought **Virgin Islands** from Denmark **Aug. 4.**

Jeannette Rankin, 1st U.S. Congresswoman (R-Montana) elected.

U.S. established military government in the **Dominican Republic** Nov. 29.

Trade and loans to **European Allies** soared during the year.

John Dewey published *Democracy and Education.*

Carl Sandburg published *Chicago Poems.*

1917

Germany, suffering from British blockade, declared almost unrestricted **submarine warfare** Jan. 31. U.S. cut diplomatic ties with Germany **Feb. 3,** and formally declared war **Apr. 6.**

Conscription law was passed **May 18.** First U.S. troops arrived in Europe **June 26.**

The 18th **(Prohibition)** Amendment to the Constitution was submitted to the states by Congress **Dec. 18.** On **Jan. 16, 1919,** the 36th state (Nevada) ratified it. Franklin D. Roosevelt, as 1932 presidential candidate, endorsed repeal; 21st Amendment repealed 18th; ratification completed **Dec. 5, 1933.**

1918

Pres. Wilson set out his **14 Points** as basis for peace **Jan. 8.**

Over one million **American troops** were in Europe by July. War ended **Nov. 11.**

Influenza epidemic killed an estimated 20 million worldwide, 548,000 in U.S.

1919

First **transatlantic flight,** by U.S. Navy seaplane, left Rockaway, N.Y. **May 8,** stopped at Newfoundland, Azores, Lisbon **May 27.**

Boston police strike Sept. 9; National Guard breaks strike.

Sherwood Anderson published *Winesburg, Ohio.*

About 250 **alien radicals** were deported **Dec. 22.**

1920

In national **Red Scare,** some 2,700 Communists, anarchists, and other radicals were arrested **Jan.-May.**

Senate refused **Mar. 19** to ratify the **League of Nations** Covenant.

Nicola Sacco, 29, shoe factory employee and radical agitator, and **Bartolomeo Vanzetti,** 32, fish peddler and anarchist, accused of killing 2 men in Mass. payroll holdup **Apr. 15.** Found guilty **1921.** A 6-year worldwide campaign for release on grounds of want of conclusive evidence and prejudice failed. Both were executed **Aug. 23, 1927.** Vindicated July 19, 1977 by proclamation of Mass. Gov. Dukakis.

First regular licensed **radio broadcasting** begun **Aug. 20.**

19th Amendment ratified **Aug. 26,** giving women right to vote.

League of Women Voters founded.

Wall St., N.Y. City, **bomb** explosion killed 30, injured 100, did $2 million damage **Sept. 16.**

Sinclair Lewis's *Main Street,* **F. Scott Fitzgerald's** *This Side of Paradise* published.

1921

Congress sharply curbed **immigration,** set national quota system **May 19.**

Joint Congressional resolution declaring **peace with Germany, Austria, and Hungary** signed **July 2** by Pres. Harding; treaties were signed in **Aug.**

Limitation of Armaments Conference met in Washington Nov. 12 to **Feb. 6, 1922.** Major powers agreed to curtail naval construction, outlaw poison gas, restrict submarine attack on merchantmen, respect integrity of China.

Ku Klux Klan began revival with violence against blacks in North, South, and Midwest.

1922

Violence during **coal-mine strike** at Herrin, Ill., **June 22-23** cost 36 lives, 21 of them non-union miners.

Reader's Digest founded.

1923

First **sound-on-film motion picture,** "Phonofilm" was shown by Lee de Forest at Rivoli Theater, N.Y. City, beginning in **April.**

1924

Law approved by Congress **June 15** making all **Indians** citizens.

Nellie Tayloe Ross elected governor of Wyoming **Nov. 9** after death of her husband **Oct. 2;** installed **Jan. 5, 1925,** first woman governor. **Miriam (Ma) Ferguson** was elected governor of Texas **Nov. 9;** installed **Jan. 20, 1925.**

George Gershwin wrote *Rhapsody in Blue.*

1925

John T. Scopes found guilty of having taught evolution in Dayton, Tenn. high school, fined $100 and costs **July 24.**

1926

Dr. **Robert H. Goddard** demonstrated practicality of **rockets Mar. 16** at Auburn, Mass. with first liquid fuel rocket; rocket traveled 184 ft. in 2.5 secs.

Congress established **Army Air Corps July 2.**

Air Commerce Act passed **Nov. 2,** providing federal aid for airlines and airports.

1927

About 1,000 **marines landed in China Mar. 5** to protect property in civil war.

Capt. **Charles A. Lindbergh** left Roosevelt Field, N.Y. **May 20** alone in plane Spirit of St. Louis on first New York-Paris nonstop flight. Reached Le Bourget airfield **May 21,** 3,610 miles in 33 ¹/₂ hours.

The Jazz Singer, with **Al Jolson,** demonstrated part-talking pictures in N.Y. City **Oct. 6.**

Show Boat opened in New York **Dec. 27.**

O. E. Rolvaag published *Giants in the Earth.*

1928

Herbert Hoover elected president against **Alfred E. Smith,** the Catholic governor of New York.

Amelia Earhart became first woman to fly the Atlantic **June 17.**

1929

"**St. Valentine's Day massacre**" in Chicago **Feb. 14;** gangsters killed 7 rivals.

Farm price stability aided by **Agricultural Marketing Act,** passed **June 15.**

Albert B. Fall, former sec. of the interior, was convicted of accepting a bribe of $100,000 in the leasing of the **Elk Hills (Teapot Dome)** naval oil reserve; sentenced **Nov. 1** to $100,000 fine and year in prison.

Stock Market crash Oct. 29 marked end of postwar prosperity as stock prices plummeted. Stock losses for 1929-31 estimated at $50 billion; worst American depression began.

Thomas Wolfe published *Look Homeward, Angel.* **William Faulkner** published *The Sound and the Fury.*

1930

London Naval Reduction Treaty signed by U.S., Britain, Italy, France, and Japan **Apr. 22;** in effect **Jan. 1, 1931;** expired **Dec. 31, 1936.**

Hawley-Smoot Tariff signed; rate hikes slash world trade.

1931

Empire State Building opened in N.Y. City **May 1.**

Al Capone was convicted of tax evasion **Oct. 17.**

Pearl Buck published *The Good Earth.*

1932

Reconstruction Finance Corp. established **Jan. 22** to stimulate banking and business. Unemployment at 12 million.

Charles Lindbergh Jr. kidnaped Mar. 1, found dead May 12.

Bonus March on Washington May 29 by World War I veterans demanding Congress pay their bonus in full.

1933

FDR named Frances Perkins U.S. Secy of Labor; 1st woman in U.S. Cabinet.

All banks in the U.S. were ordered closed by Pres. Roosevelt Mar. 6.

In the "100 days" special session, Mar. 9—June 16, Congress passed New Deal social and economic measures.

Gold standard dropped by U.S.; announced by Pres. Roosevelt Apr. 19, ratified by Congress June 5.

Prohibition ended in the U.S. as 36th state ratified 21st Amendment Dec. 5.

U.S. foreswore armed intervention in Western Hemisphere nations Dec. 26.

1934

U.S. troops pull out of Haiti Aug. 6.

1935

Comedian Will Rogers and aviator Wiley Post killed Aug. 15 in Alaska plane crash.

Social Security Act passed by Congress Aug. 14.

Huey Long, Senator from Louisiana and national political leader, was assassinated Sept. 8.

Porgy and Bess, George Gershwin opera on American theme, opened Oct. 10 in N.Y. City.

Committee for Industrial Organization (CIO) formed to expand industrial unionism Nov. 9.

1936

Boulder Dam completed.

Margaret Mitchell published Gone With the Wind.

1937

Joe Louis knocked out James J. Braddock, became world heavyweight champ June 22.

Amelia Earhart, aviator, and co-pilot Fred Noonan lost July 2 near Howland Is. in the Pacific.

Pres. Roosevelt asked for 6 additional Supreme Court justices; "packing" plan defeated.

Auto, steel labor unions won first big contracts.

1938

Naval Expansion Act passed May 17.

National minimum wage enacted June 25.

Orson Welles radio dramatization of War of the Worlds caused nationwide scare Oct. 30.

1939

Pres. Roosevelt asked defense budget hike Jan. 5, 12.

N.Y. World's Fair opened Apr. 30, closed Oct. 31; reopened May 11, 1940, and finally closed Oct. 21.

Einstein alerts FDR to A-bomb opportunity in Aug. 2 letter.

U.S. declares its neutrality in European war Sept. 5.

Roosevelt proclaimed a limited national emergency Sept. 8, an unlimited emergency May 27, 1941. Both ended by Pres. Truman Apr. 28, 1952.

John Steinbeck published Grapes of Wrath.

1940

U.S. okayed sale of surplus war material to Britain June 3; announced transfer of 50 overaged destroyers Sept. 3.

First peacetime draft approved Sept. 14.

Richard Wright published Native Son.

1941

The Four Freedoms termed essential by Pres. Roosevelt in speech to Congress Jan. 6: freedom of speech and religion, freedom from want and fear.

Lend-Lease Act signed Mar. 11, providing $7 billion in military credits for Britain. Lend-Lease for USSR approved in Nov.

U.S. occupied Iceland July 7.

The Atlantic Charter, 8-point declaration of principles, issued by Roosevelt and Winston Churchill Aug. 14.

Japan attacked Pearl Harbor, Hawaii, 7:55 a.m. Hawaiian time, Dec. 7, 19 ships sunk or damaged, 2,300 dead. U.S. declared war on Japan Dec. 8, on Germany and Italy Dec. 11 after those countries declared war.

1942

Federal government forcibly moved 110,000 Japanese-Americans (including 75,000 U.S. citizens) from West Coast to detention camps. Exclusion lasted 3 years.

Battle of Midway June 4-7 was Japan's first major defeat.

Marines landed on Guadalcanal Aug. 7; last Japanese not expelled until Feb. 9, 1943.

U.S., Britain invaded North Africa Nov. 8.

First nuclear chain reaction (fission of uranium isotope U-235) produced at Univ. of Chicago, under physicists Arthur Compton, Enrico Fermi, others Dec. 2.

1943

All war contractors barred from racial discrimination May 27.

Pres. Roosevelt signed June 10 the pay-as-you-go income tax bill. Starting July 1 wage and salary earners were subject to a paycheck withholding tax.

Race riot in Detroit June 21; 34 dead, 700 injured. Riot in Harlem section of N.Y. City; 6 killed.

U.S. troops invaded Italy Sept. 9.

Marines advanced in Gilbert Is. in Nov.

1944

U.S., Allied forces invaded Europe at Normandy June 6.

G.I. Bill of Rights signed June 22, providing veterans benefits.

U.S. forces landed on Leyte, Philippines Oct. 20.

1945

Yalta Conference met in the Crimea, USSR, Feb. 3-11. Roosevelt, Churchill, and Stalin agreed Russia would enter war against Japan.

Marines landed on Iwo Jima Feb. 19; U.S. forces invaded Okinawa Apr. 1.

Pres. Roosevelt, 63, died of cerebral hemorrhage in Warm Springs, Ga. Apr. 12; V.P. Harry S. Truman became pres.

Germany surrendered May 7.

First atomic bomb, produced at Los Alamos, N.M., exploded at Alamogordo, N.M. July 16. Bomb dropped on Hiroshima Aug. 6, on Nagasaki Aug. 9. Japan surrendered Aug. 15.

U.S. forces entered Korea south of 38th parallel to displace Japanese Sept. 8.

Gen. Douglas MacArthur took over supervision of Japan Sept. 9.

1946

Strike by 400,000 mine workers began Apr. 1; other industries followed.

Philippines given independence by U.S. July 4.

1947

Truman Doctrine: Pres. Truman asked Congress to aid Greece and Turkey to combat Communist terrorism Mar. 12. Approved May 15.

United Nations Security Council voted unanimously Apr. 2 to place under U.S. trusteeship the Pacific islands formerly mandated to Japan.

Jackie Robinson on Brooklyn Dodgers Apr. 11, broke the color barrier in major league baseball.

Taft-Hartley Labor Act curbing strikes was vetoed by Truman June 20; Congress overrode the veto.

Proposals later known as the Marshall Plan, under which the U.S. would extend aid to European countries, were made by Sec. of State George C. Marshall June 5. Congress authorized some $12 billion in next 4 years.

1948

USSR began a land blockade of Berlin's Allied sectors Apr. 1. This blockade and Western counter-blockade were lifted Sept. 30, 1949, after British and U.S. planes had lifted 2,343,315 tons of food and coal into the city.

Organization of American States founded Apr. 30.

Alger Hiss, former State Dept. official, indicted Dec. 15 for perjury, after denying he had passed secret documents to Whittaker Chambers for transmission to a communist spy ring. His second trial ended in conviction Jan. 21, 1950, and a sentence of 5 years in prison.

Kinsey Report on Sexuality in the Human Male published.

1949

U.S. troops withdrawn from **Korea June 29.**

North Atlantic Treaty Organization (**NATO**) established **Aug. 24** by U.S., Canada, and 10 West European nations, agreeing that an armed attack against one or more of them would be considered an attack against all.

Mrs. I. Toguri D'Aquino (**Tokyo Rose** of Japanese wartime broadcasts) was sentenced **Oct. 7** to 10 years in prison for treason. Paroled **1956,** pardoned **1977.**

Eleven leaders of U.S. **Communist party** convicted **Oct. 14,** after 9-month trial in N.Y. City, of advocating violent overthrow of U.S. government. Ten defendants sentenced to 5 years in prison each and the 11th to 3 years. Supreme Court upheld the convictions **June 4, 1951.**

1950

U.S. **Jan 14** recalled all consular officials from China after the latter seized the American consulate general in Peking.

Masked bandits robbed **Brink's Inc.,** Boston express office, **Jan. 17** of $2.8 million, of which $1.2 million was in cash. Case solved **1956,** 8 sentenced to life.

Pres. Truman authorized production of **H-bomb Jan. 31.**

United Nations asked for troops to restore Korea peace **June 25.**

Truman ordered Air Force and Navy to **Korea June 27** after North Korea invaded South. Truman approved ground forces, air strikes against North **June 30.**

U.S. sent 35 military advisers to **South Vietnam June 27,** and agreed to provide military and economic aid to anti-Communist government.

Army seized all railroads **Aug. 27** on Truman's order to prevent a general strike; roads returned to owners in **1952.**

U.S. forces landed at **Inchon Sept. 15;** UN force took Pyongyang **Oct. 20,** reached China border **Nov. 20,** China sent troops across border **Nov. 26.**

Two members of a **Puerto Rican nationalist** movement tried to kill Pres. Truman **Nov. 1.** (see Assassinations)

U.S. **Dec. 8** banned shipments to **Communist China** and to Asiatic ports trading with it.

1951

Sen. **Estes Kefauver** led Senate investigation into organized crime. Preliminary report **Feb. 28** said gambling take was over $20 billion a year.

Julius Rosenberg, his wife, Ethel, and Morton Sobell, all U.S. citizens, were found guilty **Mar. 29** of conspiracy to commit wartime espionage. Rosenbergs sentenced to death, Sobell to 30 years. Rosenbergs executed **June 19, 1953.** Sobell released **Jan. 14, 1969.**

Gen. **Douglas MacArthur** was removed from his Korea command **Apr. 11** for unauthorized policy statements.

Korea cease-fire talks began in July; lasted 2 years. **Fighting ended July 27, 1953.**

Tariff concessions by the U.S. to the Soviet Union, Communist China, and all communist-dominated lands were suspended **Aug. 1.**

The U.S., **Australia,** and **New Zealand** signed a mutual security pact **Sept. 1.**

Transcontinental television inaugurated **Sept. 4** with Pres. Truman's address at the Japanese Peace Treaty Conference in San Francisco.

Japanese Peace Treaty signed in San Francisco **Sept. 8** by U.S., Japan, and 47 other nations.

J.D. **Salinger** published *Catcher in the Rye.*

1952

U.S. **seizure of nation's steel mills** was ordered by Pres. Truman **Apr. 8** to avert a strike. Ruled illegal by Supreme Court **June 2.**

Peace contract between West Germany, U.S., Great Britain, and France was signed **May 26.**

The last racial and ethnic barriers to naturalization were removed, **June 26-27,** with the passage of the **Immigration and Naturalization Act of 1952.**

First **hydrogen device** explosion **Nov. 1** at Eniwetok Atoll in Pacific.

1953

Pres. Eisenhower announced **May 8** that U.S. had given France $60 million for **Indochina War.** More aid was announced in **Sept.** In **1954** it was reported that three fourths of the war's costs were met by U.S.

1954

Nautilus, first atomic-powered submarine, was launched at Groton, Conn. **Jan. 21.**

Five members of Congress were wounded in the House **Mar. 1** by 4 **Puerto Rican independence supporters** who fired at random from a spectators' gallery.

Sen. **Joseph McCarthy** led televised hearings **Apr. 22-June 17** into alleged Communist influence in the Army.

Racial segregation in public schools was unanimously ruled unconstitutional by the Supreme Court **May 17,** as a violation of the 14th Amendment clause guaranteeing equal protection of the laws.

Southeast Asia Treaty Organization (**SEATO**) formed by collective defense pact signed in Manila **Sept. 8** by the U.S., Britain, France, Australia, New Zealand, Philippines, Pakistan, and Thailand.

Condemnation of Sen. **Joseph R. McCarthy** (R., Wis.) voted by Senate, 67-22 **Dec. 2** for contempt of a Senate elections subcommittee, for abuse of its members, and for insults to the Senate during his Army investigation hearings.

1955

U.S. agreed **Feb. 12** to help train **South Vietnamese** army.

Supreme Court ordered "**all deliberate speed**" in integration of public schools **May 31.**

A **summit meeting** of leaders of U.S., Britain, France, and USSR took place **July 18-23** in Geneva, Switzerland.

Rosa Parks refused **Dec. 1** to give her seat to a white man on a bus in Montgomery, Ala. Bus segregation ordinance declared unconstitutional by a federal court following boycott and NAACP protest.

Merger of America's 2 largest labor organizations was effected **Dec. 5** under the name American Federation of Labor and Congress of Industrial Organizations. The merged **AFL-CIO** had a membership estimated at 15 million.

1956

Massive resistance to Supreme Court desegregation rulings was called for **Mar. 12** by 101 Southern congressmen.

Federal-Aid **Highway Act** signed **June 29,** inaugurating interstate highway system.

First transatlantic **telephone cable** went into operation **Sept. 25.**

1957

Congress approved first **civil rights bill** for blacks since Reconstruction **Apr. 29,** to protect voting rights.

National Guardsmen, called out by Arkansas Gov. Orval Faubus **Sept. 4,** barred 9 black students from entering previously all-white Central High School in **Little Rock.** Faubus complied **Sept. 21** with a federal court order to remove the National Guardsmen. The blacks entered school **Sept. 23** but were ordered to withdraw by local authorities because of fear of mob violence. Pres. Eisenhower sent federal troops **Sept. 24** to enforce the court's order.

Jack **Kerouac** published *On the Road.*

1958

First U.S. earth satellite to go into orbit, **Explorer I,** launched by Army **Jan. 31** at Cape Canaveral, Fla.; discovered Van Allen radiation belt.

Five thousand U.S. Marines sent to **Lebanon** to protect elected government from threatened overthrow **July-Oct.**

First domestic **jet airline** passenger service in U.S. opened by National Airlines **Dec. 10** between N.Y. and Miami.

1959

Alaska admitted as 49th state **Jan. 3; Hawaii** admitted **Aug. 21.**

St. Lawrence Seaway opened **Apr. 25.**

The **George Washington,** first U.S. ballistic-missile submarine, launched at Groton, Conn. **June 9.**

N.S. **Savannah,** world's first atomic-powered merchant ship, launched **July 21** at Camden, N.J.

Soviet Premier **Khrushchev** paid unprecedented visit to U.S. **Sept. 15-27,** made transcontinental tour.

1960

Sit-ins began **Feb. 1** when 4 black college students in Greensboro, N.C. refused to move from a Woolworth lunch counter when denied service. By **Sept. 1961** more than 70,000 students, whites and blacks, had participated in sit-ins.

U.S. launched first **weather satellite,** Tiros I, **Apr. 1.**

Congress approved a strong **voting rights act Apr. 21.**

A **U-2 reconnaisance plane** of the U.S. was shot down in the Soviet Union **May 1.** The incident led to cancellation of an imminent Paris summit conference.

Mobs attacked U.S. embassy in **Panama Sept. 17** in dispute over flying of U.S. and Panamanian flags.

U.S. announced **Dec. 15** it backed rightist group in **Laos,** which took power the next day.

1961

The U.S. severed diplomatic and consular relations with **Cuba Jan. 3,** after disputes over nationalizations of U.S. firms, U.S. military presence at Guantanamo base, etc.

Invasion of Cuba's **"Bay of Pigs" Apr. 17** by Cuban exiles trained, armed, and directed by the U.S., attempting to overthrow the regime of Premier Fidel Castro, was repulsed.

Commander Alan B. Shepard Jr. was rocketed from Cape Canaveral, Fla., 116.5 mi. above the earth in a Mercury capsule **May 5** in the first U.S. manned sub-orbital space flight.

1962

Lt. Col. John H. Glenn Jr. became the first American in orbit **Feb. 20** when he circled the earth 3 times in the Mercury capsule **Friendship 7.**

Pres. Kennedy said **Feb. 14** U.S. military advisers in Vietnam would fire if fired upon.

Supreme Court **Mar. 26** backed **one-man one-vote** apportionment of seats in state legislatures.

First U.S. **communications satellite** launched in **July.**

James Meredith became first black student at Univ. of Mississippi **Oct. 1** after 3,000 troops put down riots.

A Soviet **offensive missile buildup** in Cuba was revealed **Oct. 22** by Pres. Kennedy, who ordered a naval and air quarantine on shipment of offensive military equipment to the island. Kennedy and Soviet Premier Khrushchev reached agreement **Oct. 28** on a formula to end the crisis. Kennedy announced **Nov. 2** that Soviet missile bases in Cuba were being dismantled.

Rachel Carson's *Silent Spring* launched environmentalist movement.

1963

Supreme Court ruled **Mar. 18** that all **criminal defendants** must have counsel and that illegally acquired evidence was not admissible in state as well as federal courts.

Supreme Court ruled, 8-1, **June 17** that laws requiring **recitation of the Lord's Prayer** or Bible verses in public schools were unconstitutional.

A limited **nuclear test-ban treaty** was agreed upon **July 25** by the U.S., Soviet Union and Britain, barring all nuclear tests except underground.

Washington demonstration by 200,000 persons **Aug. 28** in support of **black demands** for equal rights. Highlight was speech in which Dr. Martin Luther King said: "I have a dream that this nation will rise up and live out the true meaning of its creed, 'We hold these truths to be self-evident: that all men are created equal.' "

South Vietnam Pres. **Ngo Dinh Diem assassinated Nov. 2;** U.S. had earlier withdrawn support.

Pres. **John F. Kennedy was shot** and fatally wounded by an assassin **Nov. 22** as he rode in a motorcade through downtown Dallas, Tex. Vice Pres. Lyndon B. Johnson was inaugurated president shortly after in Dallas. Lee Harvey Oswald was arrested and charged with the murder. Oswald was shot and fatally wounded **Nov. 24** by Jack Ruby, 52, a Dallas nightclub owner, who was convicted of murder **Mar. 14, 1964** and sentenced to death. Ruby died of natural causes **Jan. 3, 1967** while awaiting retrial.

U.S. troops in **Vietnam** totalled over 15,000 by year-end; aid to South Vietnam was over $500 million in **1963.**

1964

Panama suspended relations with U.S. **Jan. 9** after riots. U.S. offered **Dec. 18** to negotiate a new canal treaty.

Supreme Court ordered **Feb. 17** that **congressional districts** have equal populations.

U.S. reported **May 27** it was sending military planes to **Laos.**

Omnibus **civil rights bill** passed **June 29** banning discrimination in voting, jobs, public accommodations, etc.

Three **civil rights workers** were reported missing in Mississippi **June 22;** found buried **Aug. 4.** Twenty-one white men were arrested. On **Oct. 20, 1967,** an all-white federal jury convicted 7 of conspiracy in the slayings.

U.S. **Congress Aug. 7** passed **Tonkin Resolution,** authorizing presidential action in Vietnam, after North Vietnam boats reportedly attacked 2 U.S. destroyers **Aug. 2.**

Congress approved **War on Poverty** bill **Aug. 11.**

The **Warren Commission** released **Sept. 27** a report concluding that Lee Harvey Oswald was solely responsible for the Kennedy assassination.

1965

Pres. Johnson in **Feb.** ordered continuous **bombing of North Vietnam** below 20th parallel.

Some 14,000 U.S. troops sent to **Dominican Republic** during civil war **Apr. 28.** All troops withdrawn by next year.

New **Voting Rights Act** signed **Aug. 6.**

Los Angeles riot by blacks living in **Watts** area resulted in death of 34 persons and property damage est. at $200 million **Aug. 11-16.**

Water Quality Act passed **Sept. 21** to meet pollution, shortage problems.

National origins quota system of **immigration** abolished **Oct. 3.**

Electric power failure blacked out most of northeastern U.S., parts of 2 Canadian provinces the night of **Nov. 9-10.**

U.S. forces in S. **Vietnam** reached 184,300 by year-end.

1966

U.S. forces began firing into **Cambodia May 1.**

Bombing of Hanoi area of North Vietnam by U.S. planes began **June 29.** By **Dec. 31,** 385,300 U.S. troops were stationed in South Vietnam, plus 60,000 offshore and 33,000 in Thailand.

Medicare, government program to pay part of the medical expenses of citizens over 65, began **July 1.**

Edward Brooke (R, Mass.) elected **Nov. 8** as first black U.S. senator in 85 years.

1967

Black representative **Adam Clayton Powell** (D, N.Y.) was denied **Mar. 1** his seat in Congress because of charges he misused gvt. funds. Reelected in 1968, he was seated, but fined $25,000 and stripped of his 22 years' seniority.

Pres. Johnson and Soviet Premier Aleksei Kosygin met **June 23 and 25** at **Glassboro State College** in N.J.; agreed not to let any crisis push them into war.

Black riots in **Newark, N.J. July 12-17** killed 26, injured 1,500; over 1,000 arrested. In Detroit, Mich., **July 23-30** at least 40 died; 2,000 injured, 5,000 left homeless by rioting, looting, burning in city's black ghetto. Quelled by 4,700 federal paratroopers and 8,000 National Guardsmen.

Thurgood Marshall sworn in **Oct. 2** as first black U.S. Supreme Court Justice. Carl B. Stokes (D, Cleveland) and Richard G. Hatcher (D, Gary, Ind.) were elected first black mayors of major U.S. cities **Nov. 7.**

By **December** 475,000 U.S. troops were in **South Vietnam,** all North Vietnam was subject to bombing. Protests against the war mounted in U.S. during year.

1968

USS Pueblo and 83-man crew seized in Sea of Japan **Jan. 23** by North Koreans; 82 men released **Dec. 22.**

"Tet offensive": Communist troops attacked Saigon, 30 province capitals **Jan. 30,** suffer heavy casualties.

Pres. Johnson curbed bombing of North Vietnam Mar. 31. Peace talks began in Paris May 10. All bombing of North halted Oct. 31.

Martin Luther King Jr., 39, assassinated Apr. 4 in Memphis, Tenn. James Earl Ray, an escaped convict, pleaded guilty to the slaying, was sentenced to 99 years.

Sen. Robert F. Kennedy (D, N.Y.) 42, shot June 5 in Hotel Ambassador, Los Angeles, after celebrating presidential primary victories. Died June 6. Sirhan Bishara Sirhan, Jordanian, convicted of murder.

Rep. Shirley Chisholm (D., N.Y.) became the first black woman elected to Congress.

1969

Expanded four-party Vietnam peace talks began Jan. 18. U.S. force peaked at 543,400 in April. Withdrawal started July 8. Pres. Nixon set Vietnamization policy Nov. 3.

U.S. astronaut Neil A. Armstrong, 38, commander of the Apollo 11 mission, became the first man to set foot on the moon July 20. Air Force Col. Edwin E. Aldrin Jr. accompanied Armstrong.

Anti-Vietnam War demonstrations reached peak in U.S.; some 250,000 marched in Washington, D.C. Nov. 15.

Massacre of hundreds of civilians at Mylai, South Vietnam in 1968 incident was reported Nov. 16.

1970

United Mine Workers official Joseph A. Yablonski, his wife, and their daughter were found shot Jan. 5 in their Clarksville, Pa. home. UMW chief W. A. (Tony) Boyle was later convicted of the killing.

A federal jury Feb. 18 found the "Chicago 7" innocent of conspiring to incite riots during the 1968 Democratic National Convention. However, 5 were convicted of crossing state lines with intent to incite riots.

Millions of Americans participated in anti-pollution demonstrations Apr. 22 to mark the first Earth Day.

U.S. and South Vietnamese forces crossed Cambodian borders Apr. 30 to get at enemy bases. Four students were killed May 4 at Kent St. Univ. in Ohio by National Guardsmen during a protest against the war.

Two women generals, the first in U.S. history, were named by Pres. Nixon May 15.

A postal reform measure was signed Aug. 12, creating an independent U.S. Postal Service, thus relinquishing governmental control of the U.S. mails after almost 2 centuries.

1971

Charles Manson, 36, and 3 of his followers were found guilty Jan. 26 of first-degree murder in the 1969 slaying of actress Sharon Tate and 6 others.

U.S. air and artillery forces aided a 44-day incursion by South Vietnam forces into Laos starting Feb. 8.

A Constitutional Amendment lowering the voting age to 18 in all elections was approved in the Senate by a vote of 94-0 Mar. 10. The proposed 26th Amendment got House approval by a 400-19 vote Mar. 23. Thirty-eighth state ratified June 30.

A court-martial jury Mar. 29, convicted Lt. William L. Calley Jr. of premeditated murder of 22 South Vietnamese at Mylai on Mar. 16, 1968. He was sentenced to life imprisonment Mar. 31. Sentence was reduced to 20 years Aug. 20.

Publication of classified Pentagon papers on the U.S. involvement in Vietnam was begun June 13 by the New York Times. In a 6-3 vote, the U.S. Supreme Court June 30 upheld the right of the Times and the Washington Post to publish the documents under the protection of the First Amendment.

U.S. bombers struck massively in North Vietnam for 5 days starting Dec. 26, in retaliation for alleged violations of agreements reached prior to the 1968 bombing halt. U.S. forces at year-end were down to 140,000.

1972

Pres. Nixon arrived in Peking Feb. 21 for an 8-day visit to China, which he called a "journey for peace." The unprecedented visit ended with a joint communique pledging that both powers would work for "a normalization of relations."

By a vote of 84 to 8, the Senate approved Mar. 22 a Constitutional Amendment banning discrimination against women because of their sex and sent the measure to the states for ratification.

North Vietnamese forces launched the biggest attacks in 4 years across the demilitarized zone Mar. 30. The U.S. responded Apr. 15 by resumption of bombing of Hanoi and Haiphong after a 4-year lull.

Nixon announced May 8 the mining of North Vietnam ports. Last U.S. combat troops left Aug. 11.

Alabama Gov. George C. Wallace, campaigning at a Laurel, Md. shopping center May 15, was shot and seriously wounded as he greeted a large crowd. Arthur H. Bremer, 21, was sentenced Aug. 4 to 63 years for shooting Wallace and 3 bystanders.

In the first visit of a U.S. president to Moscow, Nixon arrived May 22 for a week of summit talks with Kremlin leaders which culminated in a landmark strategic arms pact.

Five men were arrested June 17 for breaking into the offices of the Democratic National Committee in the Watergate office complex in Washington, D.C.

The White House announced July 8 that the U.S. would sell to the USSR at least $750 million of American wheat, corn, and other grains over a period of 3 years.

Full-scale bombing of North Vietnam resumed after Paris peace negotiations reached an impasse Dec. 18.

1973

Five of seven defendants in the Watergate break-in trial pleaded guilty Jan. 11 and 15, and the other 2 were convicted Jan. 30.

The Supreme Court ruled 7-2, Jan. 22, that a state may not prevent a woman from having an abortion during the first 6 months of pregnancy, invalidating abortion laws in Texas and Georgia, and, by implication, overturning restrictive abortion laws in 44 other states.

Four-party Vietnam peace pacts were signed in Paris Jan. 27, and North Vietnam released some 590 U.S. prisoners by Apr. 1. Last U.S. troops left Mar. 29.

The end of the military draft was announced Jan. 27.

China and the U.S. agreed Feb. 22 to set up permanent liaison offices in each other's country.

Top Nixon aides H.R. Haldeman, John D. Ehrlichman, and John W. Dean, and Attorney General Richard Kleindienst resigned Apr. 30 amid charges of White House efforts to obstruct justice in the Watergate case.

The Senate Armed Services Committee July 16 began a probe into allegations that the U.S. Air Force had made 3,500 secret B-52 raids into Cambodia in 1969 and 1970.

John Dean, former Nixon counsel, told Senate hearings June 25 that Nixon, his staff and campaign aides, and the Justice Department all had conspired to cover up Watergate facts. Nixon refused July 23 to release tapes of relevant White House conversations. Some tapes were turned over to the court Nov. 26.

The U.S. officially ceased bombing in Cambodia at midnight Aug. 14 in accord with a June Congressional action.

Vice Pres. Spiro T. Agnew Oct. 10 resigned and pleaded "nolo contendere" (no contest) to charges of tax evasion on payments made to him by Maryland contractors when he was governor of that state. Gerald Rudolph Ford Oct. 12 became first appointed vice president under the 25th Amendment; sworn in Dec. 6.

A total ban on oil exports to the U.S. was imposed by Arab oil-producing nations Oct. 19-21 after the outbreak of an Arab-Israeli war. The ban was lifted Mar. 18, 1974.

Atty. Gen. Elliot Richardson resigned, and his deputy William D. Ruckelshaus and Watergate Special Prosecutor Archibald Cox were fired by Pres. Nixon Oct. 20 when Cox threatened to secure a judicial ruling that Nixon was violating a court order to turn tapes over to Watergate case Judge John Sirica.

Leon Jaworski, conservative Texas Democrat, was named Nov. 1 by the Nixon administration to be special prosecutor to succeed Archibald Cox.

Congress overrode Nov. 7 Nixon's veto of the war powers bill which curbed the president's power to commit armed forces to hostilities abroad without Congressional approval.

1974

Impeachment hearings were opened May 9 against Nixon by the House Judiciary Committee.

John D. Ehrlichman and 3 White House "plumbers" were found guilty July 12 of conspiring to violate the civil rights of Dr. Lewis Fielding, formerly psychiatrist to Pentagon Papers leaker Daniel Ellsberg, by breaking into his Beverly Hills, Cal. office.

The U.S. Supreme Court ruled, 8-0, July 24 that Nixon had to turn over 64 tapes of White House conversations sought by Watergate Special Prosecutor Leon Jaworski.

The House Judiciary Committee, in televised hearings July 24-30, recommended 3 articles of impeachment against Nixon. The first, voted 27-11 July 27, charged Nixon with taking part in a criminal conspiracy to obstruct justice in the Watergate cover-up. The second, voted 28-10 July 29, charged he "repeatedly" failed to carry out his constitutional oath in a series of alleged abuses of power. The third, voted 27-17 July 30, accused him of unconstitutional defiance of committee subpoenas. The House of Representatives voted without debate Aug. 20, by 412-3, to accept the committee report, which included the recommended impeachment articles.

Nixon resigned Aug. 9. His support began eroding Aug. 5 when he released 3 tapes, admitting he originated plans to have the FBI stop its probe of the Watergate break-in for political as well as national security reasons. Vice President Gerald R. Ford was sworn in as the 38th U.S. president on Aug. 9.

An unconditional pardon to ex-Pres. Nixon for all federal crimes that he "committed or may have committed" while president was issued by Pres. Gerald Ford Sept. 8.

1975

Found guilty of Watergate cover-up charges Jan. 1 were ex-Atty. Gen. John N. Mitchell, ex-presidential advisers H.R. Haldeman and John D. Ehrlichman.

U.S. civilians were evacuated from Saigon Apr. 29 as communist forces completed takeover of South Vietnam.

U.S. merchant ship Mayaguez and crew of 39 seized by Cambodian forces in Gulf of Siam May 12. In rescue operation, U.S. Marines attacked Tang Is., planes bombed air base; Cambodia surrendered ship and crew.

Congress voted $405 million for South Vietnam refugees May 16; 140,000 were flown to the U.S.

Illegal CIA operations, including records on 300,000 persons and groups, and infiltration of agents into black, antiwar and political movements, were described by a "blue-ribbon" panel headed by Vice Pres. Rockefeller June 10.

FBI agents captured Patricia (Patty) Hearst, kidnaped Feb. 4, 1974, in San Francisco Sept. 18 with others. She was indicted for bank robbery; a San Francisco jury convicted her Mar. 20, 1976.

1976

Payments abroad of $22 million in bribes by Lockheed Aircraft Corp. to sell its planes were revealed Feb. 4 by a Senate subcommittee. Lockheed admitted payments in Japan, Turkey, Italy, and Holland.

The U.S. celebrated its Bicentennial July 4, marking the 200th anniversary of its independence with festivals, parades, and N.Y. City's Operation Sail, a gathering of tall ships from around the world viewed by 6 million persons.

A mystery ailment "legionnaire's disease" killed 29 persons who attended an American Legion convention July 21-24 in Philadelphia. The cause was found to be a bacterium, it was reported June 18, 1977.

The Viking II set down on Mars' Utopia Plains Sept. 3, following the successful landing by Viking I July 20.

1977

Pres. Jimmy Carter Jan. 21 pardoned most Vietnam War draft evaders, who numbered some 10,000.

Convicted murderer Gary Gilmore was executed by a Utah firing squad Jan. 17, in the first exercise of capital punishment anywhere in the U.S. since 1967. Gilmore had opposed all attempts to delay the execution.

Carter signed an act Aug. 4 creating a new Cabinet-level Energy Department.

1978

U.S. Senate voted Apr. 18 to turn over the Panama Canal to Panama on Dec. 31, 1999; Mar. 16 vote had given approval to a treaty guaranteeing the area's neutrality after the year 2000.

The U.S. Supreme Court June 28 voted 5-4 not to allow a firm quota system in affirmative action plans; the Court did uphold programs that were more "flexible" in nature.

The House Select Committee on Assassinations opened hearings Sept. 6 into assassinations of Pres. Kennedy and Martin Luther King Jr.; the committee recessed Dec. 30 after concluding conspiracies likely in both cases, but with no further hard evidence for further prosecutions.

Congress passed the Humphrey-Hawkins "full employment" Bill Oct. 15, which set national goal of reducing unemployment to 4% by 1983, while reducing inflation to 3% in same period; Pres. Carter signed bill, Oct. 27.

1979

A major accident occurred, Mar. 28, at a nuclear reactor on Three Mile Island near Middletown, Pa.

The federal government announced, Nov. 1, a $1.5 billion loan-guarantee plan to aid the nation's 3d largest automaker, Chrysler Corp., which had reported a loss of $460.6 million for the 3d quarter of 1979.

Some 90 people, including 63 Americans, were taken hostage, Nov. 4, at the American embassy in Teheran, Iran, by militant student followers of Ayatollah Khomeini who demanded the return of former Shah Mohammad Reza Pahlavi, who was undergoing medical treatment in New York City.

1980

Pres. Carter announced, Jan. 4, punitive measures against the USSR, inc. an embargo on the sale of grain and high technology, in retaliation for the Soviet invasion of Afghanistan. At Carter's request, the U.S. Olympic Committee voted, Apr. 12, not to attend the Moscow Summer Olympics.

Eight Americans were killed and 5 wounded, Apr. 24, in an ill-fated attempt to rescue the hostages held by Iranian militants at the U.S. Embassy in Teheran.

In Washington, Mt. St. Helens erupted, May 18, in a violent blast estimated to be 500 times as powerful as the Hiroshima atomic bomb. The blast, followed by others on May 25 and June 12, left about 60 dead, and economic losses estimated at nearly $3 billion.

In a sweeping victory, Nov. 4, Ronald Wilson Reagan was elected 40th President of the United States, defeating incumbent Jimmy Carter. The stunning GOP victory extended to the U.S. Congress where Republicans gained control of the Senate and wrested 33 House seats from the Democrats.

Former Beatle John Lennon was shot and killed, Dec. 8, outside his apartment building in New York City.

1981

Minutes after the inauguration of Pres. Ronald Reagan, Jan. 20, the 52 Americans who had been held hostage in Iran for 444 days were flown to freedom following an agreement in which the U.S. agreed to return to Iran $8 billion in frozen assets.

President Reagan was shot in the chest by a would-be assassin, Mar. 30, in Washington, D.C., as he walked to his limousine following an address.

The world's first reusable spacecraft, the Space Shuttle Columbia, was sent into space, Apr. 12, and completed its successful mission 2 days later.

Both houses of Congress passed, July 29, President Reagan's tax-cut legislation. The largest tax cut in the nation's history was expected to reduce taxes by $37.6 bln. in fiscal 1982, and to save taxpayers $750 bln. over the next 5 years.

Federal air traffic controllers, Aug. 3, began an illegal nationwide strike after their union rejected the government's final offer for a new contract. Most of the 13,000 striking controllers defied the back-to-work order, and were dismissed by President Reagan Aug. 5.

In a 99-0 vote, the Senate confirmed, Sept. 21, the appointment of Sandra Day O'Connor as an associate justice of the U.S. Supreme Court. She was the first woman appointed to that body.

President Reagan ordered sanctions against the new Polish military government, Dec. 23, in response to the imposition of martial law in that country.

1982

The 13-year-old lawsuit against AT&T by the Justice Dept. was settled Jan. 8. AT&T agreed to give up the 22 Bell System companies but in return was allowed to expand into previously prohibited areas inc. data processing, telephone and computer equipment sales, and computer communication devices.

On Mar. 2, the Senate voted 57-37 for a bill that virtually eliminated busing for the purposes of racial integration.

On June 12, in N.Y.'s Central Park, hundreds of thousands demonstrated against nuclear arms.

The Equal Rights Amendment was defeated after a 10-year struggle for ratification.

The elections on Nov. 2 resulted in gains for the Democrats—the margin in the new House was 269-166. In the Senate elections, Democrats won 20 out of 33 seats, but were still the minority, 54-46.

The highest unemployment rate since 1940, 10.4%, was reported on Nov. 5. The rate for Nov. reached 10.8%, with over 11 million unemployed.

Lech Walesa, former leader of Solidarity, the Polish labor union, was freed Nov. 13, after 11 months of internment following the imposition of martial law and the outlawing of Solidarity. Pres. Reagan lifted the U.S. embargo on sales of oil and gas equipment to the Soviet Union.

The Space Shuttle Columbia completed its first operational flight Nov. 16.

A retired dentist, Dr. Barney B. Clark, 61, became the first recipient of a permanent artificial heart during a 7½ hour operation in Salt Lake City Dec. 2. The heart was designed by Dr. Robert Jarvik, also on the surgical team.

1983

On Apr. 20, Pres. Reagan signed a compromise, bipartisan bill designed to rescue the Social Security System from bankruptcy.

In an 8-1 decision, the U.S. Supreme Court held, May 24, that the Internal Revenue Service could deny tax exemptions to private schools that practiced racial discrimination.

Sally Ride became the first American woman to travel in space, June 18, when the space shuttle Challenger was launched from Cape Canaveral, Fla.

On Oct. 23, 241 U.S. Marines and sailors, members of the multinational peacekeeping force in Lebanon, were killed when a TNT-laden suicide terrorist blew up Marine headquarters at Beirut Intl. Airport. Almost simultaneously, a second truck bomb blew up a French paratroop barracks two miles away, killing more than 40.

U.S. Marines and Rangers and a small force from 6 Caribbean nations invaded the island of Grenada on Oct. 25, in response to a request from the Organization of Eastern Caribbean States. After a few days, Grenadian militia and Cuban "construction workers" were overcome, hundreds of U.S. citizens evacuated safely, and the Marxist regime deposed. The U.S. Congress applied the War Powers Resolution, requiring U.S. troops to leave Grenada by Dec. 24.

1984

In his State of the Union address, Jan. 25, Pres. Reagan called for budget cuts of $100 billion over 3 years, but opposed increased taxes.

On Feb. 26, as the position of Pres. Amin Gemayel of Lebanon deteriorated and his army crumbled, Pres. Reagan removed U.S. Marines from Beirut and placed them on U.S. ships offshore.

The space shuttle Challenger was launched on its 4th trip into space, Feb. 3. On Feb. 7, Navy Capt. Bruce McCandless, followed by Army Lt. Colonel Robert Stewart, became the first humans to fly free of a spacecraft.

During March, the U.S. Senate rejected 2 Constitutional amendments that would have permitted prayer in the public schools.

The Central Intelligence Agency (CIA) acknowledged in April that it had participated in the mining of Nicaraguan harbors. This touched off a controversy in Congress, and the Senate, Apr. 10, adopted a nonbinding resolution condemning U.S. participation in the mining.

From Apr. 26 to May 1, Pres. Reagan visited China for the first time, holding discussions with Chinese leaders.

On May 7, American veterans of the Vietnam war reached an out-of-court settlement with 7 chemical companies in their class-action suit the herbicide Agent Orange.

A federal judge in Salt Lake City held, May 10, that the U.S. government had been negligent in its above-ground testing of nuclear weapons in Nevada from 1951 to 1962.

On June 6, former vice president Walter Mondale won the Democratic presidental nomination. In a historic move, July 12, Mondale chose a woman, Rep. Geraldine Ferraro (N.Y.) as candidate for vice president.

Pres. Reagan, Aug. 11, signed a law prohibiting public high schools from barring students who wished to assemble for religious or political activities outside of school hours.

Ronald Reagan was reelected U.S. President Nov. 6 in the greatest Republican landslide in history, carrying 49 states against Walter F. Mondale.

1985

The controversial MX missile survived critical votes in the Senate and House. The Senate, Mar. 19 and 21, voted to authorize the missiles and to appropriate $1.5 million for the construction of 21 missiles. The House gave its endorsement Mar. 26 and 28.

E.F. Hutton, one of the nation's largest brokerage companies, pleaded guilty, May 2, to 2,000 federal charges related to the manipulation of its checking accounts. The company agreed to pay $2 million in fines and to pay back up to $8 million to banks it had defrauded.

"Live Aid," a 17-hour rock concert broadcast July 13 on radio and TV from London and Phila. to 152 countries, raised $70 million for the starving peoples of Africa.

On Oct. 7, 5 hijackers seized an Italian cruise ship, the Achille Lauro, in the open sea as it approached Port Said, Egypt. Some 400 persons were aboard, including about 340 crew. The hijackers, members of the Palestine Liberation Front, a faction broken from the PLO, demanded the release of 50 Palestinians held by Israel.

In November, for the first time in 6 years, the leaders of the U.S. and the Soviet Union met at a summit conference. In Geneva, Switzerland, Pres. Reagan and Mikhail Gorbachev, the general secretary of the Soviet Communist Party, talked privately for 5 hours, Nov. 19 and 20.

1986

On Jan. 20, for the 1st time, the U.S. officially observed Martin Luther King Day.

Moments after liftoff, Jan. 28, the space shuttle Challenger exploded, killing 6 astronauts and Christa McAuliffe, a New Hampshire teacher. Subsequent investigations found that NASA had abandoned "good judgment and common sense" regarding safety problems that caused the explosion.

U.S. warplanes struck targets in Tripoli and Benghazi, Libya, Apr. 14—retaliation against the Libyan bombing of a W. Berlin disco that killed 2, injured 200, Apr. 5. On Jan. 7, Pres. Reagan had said that the U.S. had aborted 26 "terrorist missions" in 1985. In an executive order, he banned trade with and travel to Libya, ordering Americans out. A 2nd executive order, Jan. 8, had frozen all Libyan government assets in the U.S. and U.S. bank branches abroad.

U.S. officials said, June 12, that AIDS cases and deaths would increase tenfold in the next 5 years. At that time, the government had recorded 21,517 cases, 11,713 deaths. An anti-viral drug, azidothymidine (AZT) was found to improve the health of some AIDS patient, but was not a cure.

Because of the mounting abuse of illegal drugs in the U.S., specifically cocaine as "crack," Congress passed anti-drug laws and the U.S. joined Bolivia in raids against cocaine processing hideouts.

The U.S., via Congress's Sept. override of Pres. Reagan's veto, joined other nations in imposing economic sanctions on So. Africa, pressuring the Botha gvt. to end apartheid.

The U.S. Senate confirmed, Sept. 17, Pres. Reagan's nomination of William Rehnquist as chief justice, Antonin Scalia as associate justice of the Supreme Court.

Congress passed, in late Sept., the comprehensive Tax Reform Law. In effect in 1987, it simplified the system, drastically changing tax brackets, deductions, and more.

The U.S. and USSR reached tentative agreement on a world-wide ban of medium-range missiles, Sept. 18. But hopes of reducing strategic long-range missiles ended in Iceland in Oct., when Gorbachev called for a limit on the development of "Star Wars," and Reagan refused it.

One day before the 1986 Congressional elections, it was reported that the U.S. had sent spare parts and ammunition to Iran. Over the next months it was revealed that additional arms sales had been made to Iran, and profits diverted to a fund for Nicaraguan contras.

In the Congressional races, Nov. 4, Democrats won a 55-45 Senate majority, after 6 yrs. of a Republican majority, and enlarged their House majority by 5, to 258-177.

The most scandalous year in Wall Street history ended with Ivan Boesky's agreeing, Nov. 14, to plead guilty to an unspecified criminal count, pay a $100 million fine, and return profits; he was barred for life from trading securities.

1987

Pres. Reagan produced the nation's first trillion-dollar budget, Jan. 5.

The stock market continued its phenomenal rise. The Dow closed at 2002.25, Jan. 8, its first finish above 2000. The Dow advanced for 13 consecutive trading days, another record; Jan. 20; the average soared 51.60 points, Jan. 22, a one-day record. At month's end, the cumulative advance was more than 250 points, yet another record.

Condom ads became prominent in the U.S. media in Jan., reflecting concern for "safe sex" to prevent AIDS.

The Tower Commission Report, Feb. 27, found Pres. Reagan confused and uninformed; and further faulted White House Chief of Staff Donald Regan; former Natl. Security Adviser Robert McFarlane; his successor Adm. John Poindexter; and CIA Director William Casey. Casey had resigned, Feb. 2, on doctors' discovery of a brain tumor; McFarlane attempted suicide, Feb. 9; Regan resigned, Feb. 27.

An Iraqi warplane missile killed 37 sailors on the frigate U.S.S. Stark in the Persian Gulf, May 17. Iraq called it an accident. The Stark's officers were found negligent, June 14. The U.S. escorted Kuwaiti oil tankers to the Gulf, reflagging them for the U.S.

Public hearings by the Senate and House committees investigating the Iran-contra affair went on from May-Aug. Former CIA Director Casey died, May 6, 5 months after brain surgery; Lt. Col. Oliver North, a media sensation, said he had believed all his activities authorized by his superiors; Poindexter said his own purpose had been "to provide some future deniability for the president . . ."; Shultz said Casey, McFarlane, and Poindexter had lied to him and deceived Pres. Reagan. Pres. Reagan, Aug. 12, said he had been "stubborn in pursuit of a policy that went astray," but again denied knowing of the funds' diversion to the contras.

Wall Street crashed, Oct. 19, the Dow plummeting a record 508 points—22.6 percent—after a record high of 2722.42, Aug. 25; a 200-point drop by Oct., called a correction by most; and drops of 91.55, Oct. 6; 95.46, Oct. 14; and 108.36, Oct. 16.

Pres. Reagan and Soviet leader Gorbachev met in Wash., Dec. 8, and signed an unprecedented agreement calling for the dismantling of all 1,752 U.S. and 859 Soviet missiles with a 300-3,400-mile range. The leaders agreed to meet in Moscow in 1988.

1988

Federal grand juries in Miami and Tampa returned indictments, Feb. 4, against Gen. Manuel Noriega, the effective ruler of Panama, charging that he had protected and otherwise assisted the Medellin drug cartel. Attempts by the U.S. to oust Noriega plunged Panama into political and economic turmoil.

Nearly 1.4 million illegal aliens met the May 4 deadline for applying for amnesty under a U.S. Immigration and Naturalization Service policy. It was estimated that more than half the applications were in Calif., and that, nationwide, about 71 percent of the aliens had entered the U.S. from Mexico.

Much of the U.S. suffered the worst drought in more than 50 years. By June 23, half of the nation's agricultural counties had been designated disaster areas.

A missile, fired from the U.S. Navy warship Vincennes, in the Persian Gulf, struck and destroyed a commercial Iranian airliner, July 3, killing all 290 persons on the plane. Navy personnel had mistaken the airliner for an Iranian F-14 jet fighter. Although the Pentagon first said that the plane was outside its designated commercial air corridor, headed directly for the Vincennes, and descending, this was subsequently disproven.

Fire destroyed about 4 million acres of forest land throughout the west, including Alaska, during the late summer. Property damage was also considerable.

Failures at nuclear-power plants posed problems across the U.S., according to congressional testimony, starting Sept. 30. Problems cited including aging equipment, poor management and training, and lax safety standards.

George Bush, vice president under Ronald Reagan, was elected 41st U.S. president, Nov. 8. Bush defeated the Democratic nominee, Gov. Michael Dukakis (Mass.), by 54 to 46 percent of the popular vote, and 426 electoral votes to Dukakis's 112. Sen. Dan Quayle (Ind.) was the successful vice presidential nominee; Sen. Lloyd Bentsen (Tex.) was the Democratic nominee for v.p. Democrats continued to control both houses of Congress.

The securities co. Drexel Burnham Lambert agreed, Dec. 21, to plead guilty to 6 violations of federal law, inc. insider trading, stock manipulation, and falsified records; and to pay penalties of $650 million, by far the largest such settlement.

1989

The Labor Dept. reported, Jan. 6, that unemployment was 5.3%, a 14-year low, at the end of 1988. For the whole year, the economy grew 3.8%, the most in 4 years.

The largest oil spill in U.S. history occurred after the Exxon Valdez struck Bligh Reef in Alaska's Prince William Sound, Mar. 24. The off-course tanker was being piloted by the third mate instead of by the captain. Exxon Corp. announced, Mar. 25, that it accepted full financial responsibility for the spill, initially estimated at 240,000 barrels, then announced that the spill could not be contained; as of Mar. 29, it extended 45 miles.

Former Natl. Security Council staff member Oliver North became the first person, May 4, convicted in a jury trial in connection with the Iran-contra scandal. The jury acquitted North on 9 charges, found him guilty of 3: aiding and abetting the obstruction of Congress; altering, destroying, removing, or concealing NSC documents; receiving as an illegal gratuity a $13,800 security system for his home. North received, July 6, a 3-year suspended prison sentence, 2 years' probation, a $150,000 fine, and an order to perform 1,200 hours of community service.

House speaker Jim Wright (D. Tex.), who faced 69 ethical charges, announced his resignation as speaker and from the House, May 31. Rep. Tony Coehlho (D. Calif.), also under scrutiny, announced his **resignation as majority whip** and from the House.

The **U.S. Supreme Court** announced, **July 3**, its 5-4 decision to put new **restraints on a woman's right to have an abortion**, although it did not overturn Roe v. Wade.

Jack Kemp, secy. of **Housing and Urban Development**, acknowledged, **July 11**, that an estimated **$2 billion** had been lost due to **fraud and mismanagement** during the tenure of his predecessor **Samuel Pierce.**

Legislation passed by Congress to **rescue the savings and loan industry** was signed into law, **Aug. 9**, by Pres. George Bush. The bill provided $166 billion over 10 years to close or merge insolvent S&Ls. The total cost was put at $400 billion over 30 years, most to be paid by taxpayers.

Army Gen. Colin Powell was nominated by Pres. Bush, **Aug. 10**, to serve as **chairman of the Joint Chiefs of Staff;** he became the first black to hold the post.

Stock prices, advancing fairly steadily since their big plunge in Oct. 1987, **suddenly fell again in Oct. 1989**, the Dow Jones dropping 190.58 points to a close of 2,569.26, the 2d highest one-day decline in points ever.

Minutes before the start of the 3d game of the 1989 World Series between the San Francisco Giants and the Oakland Athletics, **Oct. 17**, an **earthquake struck the San Francisco Bay area,** causing at least 59 deaths and massive property damage.

Democrats won most of the **top offices** at stake and **black candidates scored major breakthroughs,** in off-year elections, **Nov. 7.** Lt. Gov. L. Douglas Wilder, a Democrat, was elected governor of Virginia, the nation's first black governor since Reconstruction; Manhattan Borough Pres. David Dinkins, also a Democrat, became the first black elected mayor of New York City.

Pennsylvania became the first state, **Nov. 18,** to **restrict abortions,** after the U.S. Supreme Court gave states the right to do so in July.

Pres. Bush signed into law, **Nov. 19,** an **increase in the minimum wage.** Currently $3.35, the wage would rise to **$4.25** an hour by 1991, with a training wage of $3.35 for 16- to 19-year-olds in their first 3 months on a job.

U.S. troops invaded Panama, Dec. 20, overthrowing the government of Manuel Noriega, who eluded capture, took refuge in the Vatican mission, then surrendered to the U.S. Jan. 3, 1990.

1990

A proposed **Constitutional amendment** to permit the federal government or the states to prosecute those who dese-

crated the American flag failed to win approval in the House, June 21, and the Senate, June 26.

The **Dow Jones Industrial average** pushed to an **all-time high** on Wall Street, **July 16 and 17,** finishing at 2,999.75 and averaging above 3,000.

Pres. Bush signed a bill that would bar **discrimination** against people with **physical or mental disabilities, July 26.**

Justice William Brennan announced, **July 20,** his immediate resignation from the U.S. Supreme Court, due to illness; Pres. Bush nominated **Judge David Souter** of the U.S. Court of Appeals for the First Circuit in Boston, **July 23,** and the Senate voted to endorse him, **Sept. 27.**

Operation Desert Shield forces left for **Saudi Arabia, Aug. 7,** to defend that country following the **invasion** of its neighbor **Kuwait by Iraq.** The American Auto Assn. reported, **Aug. 9,** that the retail price for gas had risen 18 cents per gallon in the week since Iraq's action.

Pres. Bush **vetoed, Oct. 22,** a **civil rights bill** that sought in effect to reverse 6 recent Supreme Court decisions that civil rights organizations contended had weakened anti-discrimination laws on hiring and promoting.

The Democratic Party made small gains in the Senate and House in **elections, Nov. 6.** Democrats gained one seat in the Senate, for a 56-44 margin over Republicans, and gained 8 seats in the House for a 267-167 margin. One independent was elected in Vermont. About 96 percent of incumbents seeking re-election were successful; only 15 lost. In gubernatorial elections, 14 statehouses changed parties, Democrats emerging with a 28-19 margin, compared with 29-21 before the election. Independents won in Alaska and Connecticut, and a runoff would be required in Arizona.

Pres. Bush signed, **Nov. 15,** a bill designed to **reduce budget deficits** by nearly $500 billion over 5 years. The top tax rate would rise from 28 to 31 percent and exemptions for upper-income Americans would be phased out; gas, cigarette, liquor taxes would increase; a luxury tax would be imposed on some planes, cars, boats, furs, and jewelry.

Pres. Bush signed, **Nov. 15,** the 1990 **Clean Air Act,** a comprehensive updating of the original Clean Air Act of 1970. It called for reductions by more than 50% of the overall annual level of sulfur dioxide emissions from power plants and a one-third cut in nitrogen oxide emissions; oil companies would be required to develop cleaner-burning gasoline, cities to reduce the concentration of the smog-component ozone, and production of chemicals that threatened the earth's ozone shield would be halted.

Some Figures in American Folklore

Johnny Appleseed: John Chapman, 1774-1845; according to legend, wandered through Ohio, Indiana, and W. Pennsylvania for 40 years, sowing seeds that produced the Midwest orchards.

Billy the Kid: William H. Bonney, 1859-1881; range war gunman and cattle rustler accused of 21 murders, the first before he reached his teens.

Daniel Boone: 1734-1820; frontiersman who blazed the Wilderness Road and founded Boonesboro, Kentucky, which he helped defend against the Indians in 1779; many legendary adventures were disproved.

Paul Bunyan: legendary lumberjack of fantastic size and strength, the hero of many tall tales popular in the Western timber country.

Kit Carson: Christopher Carson, 1809-1868; frontiersman, soldier, and Indian agent who guided John C. Fremont's expeditions into Wyoming and California, 1842-46.

Casey Jones: John Luther Jones, 1864-1900; locomotive engineer celebrated in song; driving the Cannon Ball express from Memphis to Canton, Mississippi, he applied the brakes in time to save the lives of the passengers in a wreck at Vaughn, Mississippi, but he was killed.

Davey Crockett: 1786-1836; a hero of frontier America, he fought in the Creek War under Andrew Jackson, was elected to the Tennessee legislature and the U.S. Congress, joined Texas independence forces, was killed at the Alamo.

John Henry: legendary black man celebrated for his strength; in one version of his story, he succeeded in outworking a steam drill but died from the strain.

Hiawatha: c. 1550; chief of the Onandaga Indians, credited with founding the Iroquois Confederacy, and the hero of a well-known poem by Henry Wadsworth Longfellow.

Jesse James: 1847-1882; outlaw who led his gang in daring bank and train robberies in the Midwest from 1866. He was murdered by Robert Ford, one of his gang.

Annie Oakley: Phoebe Anne Oakley Mozee, 1860-1926; rifle and shotgun markswoman who was the star attraction of Buffalo Bill's Wild West Show, 1885-1902.

Pocahontas: c. 1595-1617; daughter of Chief Powhatan, she was said to have saved the life of Capt. John Smith at Jamestown as Powhatan was about to execute him.

Betsy Ross: 1752-1846; seamstress who made flags during the American Revolution; however, the legend that she designed and made the first American national flag is generally discredited.

Uncle Remus: main character in *Uncle Remus: His Songs and His Sayings,* by Joel Chandler Harris, 1880, based on oral tales of southern blacks. Uncle Remus is depicted as a benign autocratic figure spinning animal fables to a white boy on a plantation.

Declaration of Independence

The Declaration of Independence was adopted by the Continental Congress in Philadelphia, on July 4, 1776. John Hancock was president of the Congress and Charles Thomson was secretary. A copy of the Declaration, engrossed on parchment, was signed by members of Congress on and after Aug. 2, 1776. On Jan. 18, 1777, Congress ordered that "an authenticated copy, with the names of the members of Congress subscribing the same, be sent to each of the United States, and that they be desired to have the same put upon record." Authenticated copies were printed in broadside form in Baltimore, where the Continental Congress was then in session. The following text is that of the original printed by John Dunlap at Philadelphia for the Continental Congress.

IN CONGRESS, July 4, 1776.

A DECLARATION

By the REPRESENTATIVES of the

UNITED STATES OF AMERICA,

In GENERAL CONGRESS assembled

When in the Course of human Events, it becomes necessary for one People to dissolve the Political Bands which have connected them with another, and to assume among the Powers of the Earth, the separate and equal Station to which the Laws of Nature and of Nature's God entitle them, a decent Respect to the Opinions of Mankind requires that they should declare the causes which impel them to the Separation.

We hold these Truths to be self-evident, that all Men are created equal, that they are endowed by their Creator with certain unalienable Rights, that among these are Life, Liberty, and the Pursuit of Happiness—That to secure these Rights, Governments are instituted among Men, deriving their just Powers from the Consent of the Governed, that whenever any Form of Government becomes destructive of these Ends, it is the Right of the People to alter or to abolish it, and to institute new Government, laying its Foundation on such Principles, and organizing its Powers in such Form, as to them shall seem most likely to effect their Safety and Happiness. Prudence, indeed, will dictate that Governments long established should not be changed for light and transient Causes; and accordingly all Experience hath shewn, that Mankind are more disposed to suffer, while Evils are sufferable, than to right themselves by abolishing the Forms to which they are accustomed. But when a long Train of Abuses and Usurpations, pursuing invariably the same Object, evinces a Design to reduce them under absolute Despotism, it is their Right, it is their Duty, to throw off such Government, and to provide new Guards for their future Security. Such has been the patient Sufferance of these Colonies; and such is now the Necessity which constrains them to alter their former Systems of Government. The History of the present King of Great-Britain is a History of repeated Injuries and Usurpations, all having in direct Object the Establishment of an absolute Tyranny over these States. To prove this, let Facts be submitted to a candid World.

He has refused his Assent to Laws, the most wholesome and necessary for the public Good.

He has forbidden his Governors to pass Laws of immediate and pressing Importance, unless suspended in their Operation till his Assent should be obtained; and when so suspended, he has utterly neglected to attend to them.

He has refused to pass other Laws for the Accommodation of large Districts of People, unless those People would relinquish the Right of Representation in the Legislature, a Right inestimable to them, and formidable to Tyrants only.

He has called together Legislative Bodies at Places unusual, uncomfortable, and distant from the Depository of their Public Records, for the sole Purpose of fatiguing them into Compliance with his Measures.

He has dissolved Representative Houses repeatedly, for opposing with manly Firmness his Invasions on the Rights of the People.

He has refused for a long Time, after such Dissolutions, to cause others to be elected; whereby the Legislative Powers, incapable of Annihilation, have returned to the People at large for their exercise; the State remaining in the mean time exposed to all the Dangers of Invasion from without, and Convulsions within.

He has endeavoured to prevent the Population of these States; for that Purpose obstructing the Laws for Naturalization of Foreigners; refusing to pass others to encourage their Migrations hither, and raising the Conditions of new Appropriations of Lands.

He has obstructed the Administration of Justice, by refusing his Assent to Laws for establishing Judiciary Powers.

He has made Judges dependent on his Will alone, for the Tenure of their Offices, and the Amount and payment of their Salaries.

He has erected a Multitude of new Offices, and sent hither Swarms of Officers to harrass our People, and eat out their Substance.

He has kept among us, in Times of Peace, Standing Armies, without the consent of our Legislatures.

He has affected to render the Military independent of, and superior to the Civil Power.

He has combined with others to subject us to a Jurisdiction foreign to our Constitution, and unacknowledged by our Laws; giving his Assent to their Acts of pretended Legislation:

For quartering large Bodies of Armed Troops among us:

For protecting them, by a mock Trial, from Punishment for any Murders which they should commit on the Inhabitants of these States:

For cutting off our Trade with all Parts of the World:

For imposing Taxes on us without our Consent:

For depriving us, in many Cases, of the Benefits of Trial by Jury:

For transporting us beyond Seas to be tried for pretended Offences:

For abolishing the free System of English Laws in a neighbouring Province, establishing therein an arbitrary Government, and enlarging its Boundaries, so as to render it at once an Example and fit Instrument for introducing the same absolute Rule into these Colonies:

For taking away our Charters, abolishing our most valuable Laws, and altering fundamentally the Forms of our Governments:

For suspending our own Legislatures, and declaring themselves invested with Power to legislate for us in all Cases whatsoever.

He has abdicated Government here, by declaring us out of his Protection and waging War against us.

He has plundered our Seas, ravaged our Coasts, burnt our towns, and destroyed the Lives of our People.

He is, at this Time, transporting large Armies of foreign Mercenaries to complete the works of Death, Desolation, and Tyranny, already begun with circumstances of Cruelty and Perfidy, scarcely paralleled in the most barbarous Ages, and totally unworthy the Head of a civilized Nation.

He has constrained our fellow Citizens taken Captive on the high Seas to bear Arms against their Country, to become the Executioners of their Friends and Brethren, or to fall themselves by their Hands.

He has excited domestic Insurrections amongst us, and has endeavoured to bring on the Inhabitants of our Frontiers, the merciless Indian Savages, whose known Rule of Warfare, is an undistinguished Destruction, of all Ages, Sexes and Conditions.

In every stage of these Oppressions we have Petitioned for Redress in the most humble Terms: Our repeated Petitions have been answered only by repeated Injury. A Prince, whose Character is thus marked by every act which may deine a Tyrant, is unfit to be the Ruler of a free People.

Nor have we been wanting in Attentions to our British Brethren. We have warned them from Time to Time of Attempts by their Legislature to extend an unwarrantable Jurisdiction over us. We have reminded them of the Circumstances of our Emigration and Settlement here. We have appealed to their native Justice and Magnanimity, and we have conjured them by the Ties of our common Kindred to disavow these Usurpations, which, would inevitably interrupt our Connections and Correspondence. They too have been deaf to the Voice of Justice and of Consanguinity. We must, therefore, acquiesce in the Necessity, which denounces our Separation, and hold them, as we hold the rest of Mankind, Enemies in War, in Peace, Friends.

We, therefore, the Representatives of the UNITED STATES OF AMERICA, in General Congress, Assembled, appealing to the Supreme Judge of the World for the Rectitude of our Intentions, do, in the Name, and by Authority of the good People of these Colonies, solemnly Publish and Declare, That these United Colonies are, and of Right ought to be, Free and Independent States; that they are absolved from all Allegiance to the British Crown, and that all political Connection between them and the State of Great-Britain, is and ought to be totally dissolved; and that as Free and Independent States, they have full Power to levy War, conclude Peace, contract Alliances, establish Commerce, and to do all other Acts and Things which Independent States may of right do. And for the support of this declaration, with a firm Reliance on the Protection of divine Providence, we mutually pledge to each other our lives, our Fortunes, and our sacred Honor.

JOHN HANCOCK, President

Attest.
CHARLES THOMSON, Secretary.

Signers of the Declaration of Independence

Delegate and state	Vocation	Birthplace	Born	Died
Adams, John (Mass.)	Lawyer	Braintree (Quincy), Mass.	Oct. 30, 1735	July 4, 1826
Adams, Samuel (Mass.)	Political leader	Boston, Mass.	Sept. 27, 1722	Oct. 2, 1803
Bartlett, Josiah (N.H.)	Physician, judge	Amesbury, Mass.	Nov. 21, 1729	May 19, 1795
Braxton, Carter (Va.)	Farmer	Newington Plantation, Va.	Sept. 10, 1736	Oct. 10, 1797
Carroll, Chas. of Carrollton (Md.)	Lawyer	Annapolis, Md.	Sept. 19, 1737	Nov. 14, 1832
Chase, Samuel (Md.)	Judge	Princess Anne, Md.	Apr. 17, 1741	June 19, 1811
Clark, Abraham (N.J.)	Surveyor	Roselle, N.J.	Feb. 15, 1726	Sept. 15, 1794
Clymer, George (Pa.)	Merchant	Philadelphia, Pa.	Mar. 16, 1739	Jan. 23, 1813
Ellery, William (R.I.)	Lawyer	Newport, R.I.	Dec. 22, 1727	Feb. 15, 1820
Floyd, William (N.Y.)	Soldier	Brookhaven, N.Y.	Dec. 17, 1734	Aug. 4, 1821
Franklin, Benjamin (Pa.)	Printer, publisher.	Boston, Mass.	Jan. 17, 1706	Apr. 17, 1790
Gerry, Elbridge (Mass.)	Merchant	Marblehead, Mass.	July 17, 1744	Nov. 23, 1814
Gwinnett, Button (Ga.)	Merchant	Down Hatherly, England.	c. 1735	May 19, 1777
Hall, Lyman (Ga.)	Physician	Wallingford, Conn.	Apr. 12, 1724	Oct. 19, 1790
Hancock, John (Mass.)	Merchant	Braintree (Quincy), Mass.	Jan. 12, 1737	Oct. 8, 1793
Harrison, Benjamin (Va.)	Farmer	Berkeley, Va.	Apr. 5, 1726	Apr. 24, 1791
Hart, John (N.J.)	Farmer	Stonington, Conn.	c. 1711	May 11, 1779
Hewes, Joseph (N.C.)	Merchant	Princeton, N.J.	Jan. 23, 1730	Nov. 10, 1779
Heyward, Thos. Jr. (S.C.)	Lawyer, farmer.	St. Luke's Parish, S.C.	July 28, 1746	Mar. 6, 1809
Hooper, William (N.C.)	Lawyer	Boston, Mass.	June 28, 1742	Oct. 14, 1790
Hopkins, Stephen (R.I.)	Judge, educator	Providence, R.I.	Mar. 7, 1707	July 13, 1785
Hopkinson, Francis (N.J.)	Judge, author.	Philadelphia, Pa.	Sept. 21, 1737	May 9, 1791
Huntington, Samuel (Conn.)	Judge	Windham County, Conn.	July 3, 1731	Jan. 5, 1796
Jefferson, Thomas (Va.)	Lawyer	Shadwell, Va.	Apr. 13, 1743	July 4, 1826
Lee, Francis Lightfoot (Va.)	Farmer	Westmoreland County, Va.	Oct. 14, 1734	Jan. 11, 1797
Lee, Richard Henry (Va.)	Farmer	Westmoreland County, Va.	Jan. 20, 1732	June 19, 1794
Lewis, Francis (N.Y.)	Merchant	Llandaff, Wales	Mar., 1713	Dec. 31, 1802
Livingston, Philip (N.Y.)	Merchant	Albany, N.Y.	Jan. 15, 1716	June 12, 1778
Lynch, Thomas Jr. (S.C.)	Farmer	Winyah, S.C.	Aug. 5, 1749	(at sea) 1779
McKean, Thomas (Del.)	Lawyer	New London, Pa.	Mar. 19, 1734	June 24, 1817
Middleton, Arthur (S.C.)	Farmer	Charleston, S.C.	June 26, 1742	Jan. 1, 1787
Morris, Lewis (N.Y.)	Farmer	Morrisania (Bronx County), N.Y.	Apr. 8, 1726	Jan. 22, 1798
Morris, Robert (Pa.)	Merchant	Liverpool, England	Jan. 20, 1734	May 9, 1806
Morton, John (Pa.)	Judge	Ridley, Pa.	1724	Apr., 1777
Nelson, Thos. Jr. (Va.)	Farmer	Yorktown, Va.	Dec. 26, 1738	Jan. 4, 1789
Paca, William (Md.)	Judge	Abingdon, Md.	Oct. 31, 1740	Oct. 23, 1799
Paine, Robert Treat (Mass.)	Judge	Boston, Mass.	Mar. 11, 1731	May 12, 1814
Penn, John (N.C.)	Lawyer	Near Port Royal, Va.	May 17, 1741	Sept. 14, 1788
Read, George (Del.)	Judge	Near North East, Md.	Sept. 18, 1733	Sept. 21, 1798
Rodney, Caesar (Del.)	Judge	Dover, Del.	Oct. 7, 1728	June 29, 1784
Ross, George (Pa.)	Judge	New Castle, Del.	May 10, 1730	July 14, 1779
Rush, Benjamin (Pa.)	Physician	Byberry, Pa. (Philadelphia).	Dec. 24, 1745	Apr. 19, 1813
Rutledge, Edward (S.C.)	Lawyer	Charleston, S.C.	Nov. 23, 1749	Jan. 23, 1800
Sherman, Roger (Conn.)	Lawyer	Newton, Mass.	Apr. 19, 1721	July 23, 1793
Smith, James (Pa.)	Lawyer	Dublin, Ireland	c. 1719	July 11, 1806
Stockton, Richard (N.J.)	Lawyer	Near Princeton, N.J.	Oct. 1, 1730	Feb. 28, 1781
Stone, Thomas (Md.)	Lawyer	Charles County, Md.	1743	Oct. 5, 1787
Taylor, George (Pa.)	Ironmaster	Ireland.	1716	Feb. 23, 1781
Thornton, Matthew (N.H.)	Physician	Ireland.	1714	June 24, 1803
Walton, George (Ga.)	Judge	Prince Edward County, Va.	1741	Feb. 2, 1804
Whipple, William (N.H.)	Merchant, judge.	Kittery, Me.	Jan. 14, 1730	Nov. 28, 1785
Williams, William (Conn.)	Merchant	Lebanon, Conn.	Apr. 23, 1731	Aug. 2, 1811
Wilson, James (Pa.)	Judge	Carskerdo, Scotland	Sept. 14, 1742	Aug. 28, 1798
Witherspoon, John (N.J.)	Clergyman, educator.	Gifford, Scotland	Feb. 5, 1723	Nov. 15, 1794
Wolcott, Oliver (Conn.)	Judge	Windsor, Conn.	Dec. 1, 1726	Dec. 1, 1797
Wythe, George (Va.)	Lawyer	Elizabeth City Co. (Hampton), Va.	1726	June 8, 1806

Constitution of the United States
The Original 7 Articles

PREAMBLE

We, the people of the United States, in order to form a more perfect Union, establish justice, insure domestic tranquility, provide for the common defense, promote the general welfare, and secure the blessings of liberty to ourselves and our posterity do ordain and establish this Constitution for the United States of America.

ARTICLE I.

Section 1—Legislative powers; in whom vested:

All legislative powers herein granted shall be vested in a Congress of the United States, which shall consist of a Senate and House of Representatives.

Section 2—House of Representatives, how and by whom chosen. Qualifications of a Representative. Representatives and direct taxes, how apportioned. Enumeration. Vacancies to be filled. Power of choosing officers, and of impeachment.

1. The House of Representatives shall be composed of members chosen every second year by the people of the several States, and the electors in each State shall have the qualifications requisite for electors of the most numerous branch of the State Legislature.

2. No person shall be a Representative who shall not have attained to the age of twenty-five years, and been seven years a citizen of the United States, and who shall not, when elected, be an inhabitant of that State in which he shall be chosen.

3. *(Representatives and direct taxes shall be apportioned among the several States which may be included within this Union, according to their respective numbers, which shall be determined by adding to the whole number of free persons, including those bound to service for a term of years, and excluding Indians not taxed, three-fifths of all other persons.) (The previous sentence was superseded by Amendment XIV, section 2.)* The actual enumeration shall be made within three years after the first meeting of the Congress of the United States, and within every subsequent term of ten years, in such manner as they shall by law direct. The number of Representatives shall not exceed one for every thirty thousand, but each State shall have at least one Representative; and until such enumeration shall be made, the State of New Hampshire shall be entitled to choose three, Massachusetts eight, Rhode Island and Providence Plantations one, Connecticut five, New York six, New Jersey four, Pennsylvania eight, Delaware one, Maryland six, Virginia ten, North Carolina five, South Carolina five, and Georgia three.

4. When vacancies happen in the representation from any State, the Executive Authority thereof shall issue writs of election to fill such vacancies.

5. The House of Representatives shall choose their Speaker and other officers; and shall have the sole power of impeachment.

Section 3—Senators, how and by whom chosen. How classified. Qualifications of a Senator. President of the Senate, his right to vote. President pro tem., and other officers of the Senate, how chosen. Power to try impeachments. When President is tried, Chief Justice to preside. Sentence.

1. The Senate of the United States shall be composed of two Senators from each State, *(chosen by the Legislature thereof), (The preceding five words were superseded by Amendment XVII, section 1.)* for six years; and each Senator shall have one vote.

2. Immediately after they shall be assembled in consequence of the first election, they shall be divided as equally as may be into three classes. The seats of the Senators of the first class shall be vacated at the expiration of the second year, of the second class at the expiration of the fourth year, and of the third class at the expiration of the sixth year, so that one-third may be chosen every second year; *(and if vacancies happen by resignation, or otherwise, during the recess of the Legislature of any State, the Executive thereof may make temporary appointments until the next meeting of the Legislature, which shall then fill such vacancies.) (The words*

in parentheses were superseded by Amendment XVII, section 2.)

3. No person shall be a Senator who shall not have attained to the age of thirty years, and been nine years a citizen of the United States, and who shall not, when elected, be an inhabitant of that State for which he shall be chosen.

4. The Vice President of the United States shall be President of the Senate, but shall have no vote, unless they be equally dividing.

5. The Senate shall choose their other officers, and also a President pro tempore, in the absence of the Vice President, or when he shall exercise the office of President of the United States.

6. The Senate shall have the sole power to try all impeachments. When sitting for that purpose, they shall be on oath or affirmation. When the President of the United States is tried, the Chief Justice shall preside: and no person shall be convicted without the concurrence of two-thirds of the members present.

7. Judgment in cases of impeachment shall not extend further than to removal from office, and disqualification to hold and enjoy any office of honor, trust or profit under the United States: but the party convicted shall nevertheless be liable and subject to indictment, trial, judgment and punishment, according to law.

Section 4—Times, etc., of holding elections, how prescribed. One session each year.

1. The times, places and manner of holding elections for Senators and Representatives, shall be prescribed in each State by the Legislature thereof; but the Congress may at any time by law make or alter such regulations, except as to the places of choosing Senators.

2. The Congress shall assemble at least once in every year, and such meeting shall *(be on the first Monday in December,) (The words in parentheses were superseded by Amendment XX, section 2).* unless they shall by law appoint a different day.

Section 5—Membership, quorum, adjournments, rules. Power to punish or expel. Journal. Time of adjournments, how limited, etc.

1. Each House shall be the judge of the elections, returns and qualifications of its own members, and a majority of each shall constitute a quorum to do business; but a smaller number may adjourn from day to day, and may be authorized to compel the attendance of absent members, in such manner, and under such penalties as each House may provide.

2. Each House may determine the rules of its proceedings, punish its members for disorderly behavior, and, with the concurrence of two-thirds, expel a member.

3. Each House shall keep a journal of its proceedings, and from time to time publish the same, excepting such parts as may in their judgment require secrecy; and the yeas and nays of the members of either House on any question shall, at the desire of one-fifth of those present, be entered on the journal.

4. Neither House, during the session of Congress, shall, without the consent of the other, adjourn for more than three days, nor to any other place than that in which the two Houses shall be sitting.

Section 6—Compensation, privileges, disqualifications in certain cases.

1. The Senators and Representatives shall receive a compensation for their services, to be ascertained by law, and paid out of the Treasury of the United States. They shall in all cases, except treason, felony and breach of the peace, be privileged from arrest during their attendance at the session of their respective Houses, and in going to and returning from the same; and for any speech or debate in either House, they shall not be questioned in any other place.

2. No Senator or Representative shall, during the time for which he was elected, be appointed to any civil office under the authority of the United States, which shall have been created, or the emoluments whereof shall have been increased during such time; and no person holding any office under the United States, shall be a member of either House

during his continuance in office.

Section 7—House to originate all revenue bills. Veto. Bill may be passed by two-thirds of each House, notwithstanding, etc. Bill, not returned in ten days, to become a law. Provisions as to orders, concurrent resolutions, etc.

1. All bills for raising revenue shall originate in the House of Representatives; but the Senate may propose or concur with amendments as on other bills.

2. Every bill which shall have passed the House of Representatives and the Senate, shall, before it becomes a law, be presented to the President of the United States; if he approves he shall sign it, but if not he shall return it, with his objections to that House in which it shall have originated, who shall enter the objections at large on their journal, and proceed to reconsider it. If after such reconsideration two-thirds of that House shall agree to pass the bill, it shall be sent, together with the objections, to the other House, by which it shall likewise be reconsidered, and if approved by two-thirds of that House, it shall become a law. But in all such cases the votes of both Houses shall be determined by yeas and nays, and the names of the persons voting for and against the bill shall be entered on the journal of each House respectively. If any bill shall not be returned by the President within ten days (Sundays excepted) after it shall have been presented to him, the same shall be a law, in like manner as if he had signed it, unless the Congress by their adjournment prevent its return, in which case it shall not be a law.

3. Every order, resolution, or vote to which the concurrence of the Senate and House of Representatives may be necessary (except on a question of adjournment) shall be presented to the President of the United States; and before the same shall take effect, shall be approved by him, or being disapproved by him, shall be repassed by two-thirds of the Senate and House of Representatives, according to the rules and limitations prescribed in the case of a bill.

Section 8—Powers of Congress.

The Congress shall have power

1. To lay and collect taxes, duties, imposts and excises, to pay the debts and provide for the common defense and general welfare of the United States; but all duties, imposts and excises shall be uniform throughout the United States;

2. To borrow money on the credit of the United States;

3. To regulate commerce with foreign nations, and among the several States, and with the Indian tribes;

4. To establish a uniform rule of naturalization, and uniform laws on the subject of bankruptcies throughout the United States;

5. To coin money, regulate the value thereof, and of foreign coin, and fix the standard of weights and measures;

6. To provide for the punishment of counterfeiting the securities and current coin of the United States;

7. To establish post-offices and post-roads;

8. To promote the progress of science and useful arts, by securing for limited times to authors and inventors the exclusive right to their respective writings and discoveries;

9. To constitute tribunals inferior to the Supreme Court;

10. To define and punish piracies and felonies committed on the high seas, and offenses against the law of nations;

11. To declare war, grant letters of marque and reprisal, and make rules concerning captures on land and water;

12. To raise and support armies, but no appropriation of money to that use shall be for a longer term than two years;

13. To provide and maintain a navy;

14. To make rules for the government and regulation of the land and naval forces;

15. To provide for calling forth the militia to execute the laws of the Union, suppress insurrections and repel invasions;

16. To provide for organizing, arming, and disciplining the militia, and for governing such part of them as may be employed in the service of the United States, reserving to the States respectively, the appointment of the officers, and the authority of training the militia according to the discipline prescribed by Congress;

17. To exercise exclusive legislation in all cases whatsoever, over such district (not exceeding ten miles square) as may, by cession of particular States, and the acceptance of Congress, become the seat of the Government of the United States, and to exercise like authority over all places purchased by the consent of the Legislature of the State in which the same shall be, for the erection of forts, magazines, arsenals, dockyards, and other needful buildings;—And

18. To make all laws which shall be necessary and proper for carrying into execution the foregoing powers, and all other powers vested by this Constitution in the Government of the United States, or in any department or officer thereof.

Section 9—Provision as to migration or importation of certain persons. Habeas corpus, bills of attainder, etc. Taxes, how apportioned. No export duty. No commercial preference. Money, how drawn from Treasury, etc. No titular nobility. Officers not to receive presents, etc.

1. The migration or importation of such persons as any of the States now existing shall think proper to admit, shall not be prohibited by the Congress prior to the year one thousand eight hundred and eight, but a tax or duty may be imposed on such importation, not exceeding ten dollars for each person.

2. The privilege of the writ of habeas corpus shall not be suspended, unless when in cases of rebellion or invasion the public safety may require it.

3. No bill of attainder or ex post facto law shall be passed.

4. No capitation, or other direct, tax shall be laid, unless in proportion to the census or enumeration herein before directed to be taken. *(Modified by Amendment XVI.)*

5. No tax or duty shall be laid on articles exported from any State.

6. No preference shall be given by any regulation of commerce or revenue to the ports of one State over those of another: nor shall vessels bound to, or from, one State, be obliged to enter, clear, or pay duties in another.

7. No money shall be drawn from the Treasury, but in consequence of appropriations made by law; and a regular statement and account of the receipts and expenditures of all public money shall be published from time to time.

8. No title of nobility shall be granted by the United States: and no person holding any office of profit or trust under them, shall, without the consent of the Congress, accept of any present, emolument, office, or title, of any kind whatever, from any king, prince, or foreign state.

Section 10—States prohibited from the exercise of certain powers.

1. No State shall enter into any treaty, alliance, or confederation; grant letters of marque and reprisal; coin money; emit bills of credit; make anything but gold and silver coin a tender in payment of debts; pass any bill of attainder, ex post facto law, or law impairing the obligation of contracts, or grant any title of nobility.

2. No State shall, without the consent of the Congress, lay any imposts or duties on imports or exports, except what may be absolutely necessary for executing its inspection laws: and the net produce of all duties and imposts, laid by any State on imports or exports, shall be for the use of the Treasury of the United States; and all such laws shall be subject to the revision and control of Congress.

3. No State shall, without the consent of Congress, lay any duty of tonnage, keep troops, or ships of war in time of peace, enter into any agreement or compact with another State, or with a foreign power, or engage in war, unless actually invaded, or in such imminent danger as will not admit of delay.

ARTICLE II.

Section 1—President: his term of office. Electors of President; number and how appointed. Electors to vote on same day. Qualification of President. On whom his duties devolve in case of his removal, death, etc. President's compensation. His oath of office.

1. The Executive power shall be vested in a President of the United States of America. He shall hold his office during the term of four years, and together with the Vice President, chosen for the same term, be elected as follows

2. Each State shall appoint, in such manner as the Legis-

lature thereof may direct, a number of electors, equal to the whole number of Senators and Representatives to which the State may be entitled in the Congress: but no Senator or Representative, or person holding an office of trust or profit under the United States, shall be appointed an elector.

(The electors shall meet in their respective States, and vote by ballot for two persons, of whom one at least shall not be an inhabitant of the same State with themselves. And they shall make a list of all the persons voted for, and of the number of votes for each; which list they shall sign and certify, and transmit sealed to the seat of the Government of the United States, directed to the President of the Senate. The President of the Senate shall, in the presence of the Senate and House of Representatives, open all the certificates, and the votes shall then be counted. The person having the greatest number of votes shall be the President, if such number be a majority of the whole number of electors appointed; and if there be more than one who have such majority, and have an equal number of votes, then the House of Representatives shall immediately choose by ballot one of them for President; and if no person have a majority, then from the five highest on the list the said House shall in like manner choose the President. But in choosing the President, the votes shall be taken by States, the representation from each State having one vote; a quorum for this purpose shall consist of a member or members from two-thirds of the States, and a majority of all the States shall be necessary to a choice. In every case, after the choice of the President, the person having the greatest number of votes of the electors shall be the Vice President. But if there should remain two or more who have equal votes, the Senate shall choose from them by ballot the Vice President.)

(This clause was superseded by Amendment XII.)

3. The Congress may determine the time of choosing the electors, and the day on which they shall give their votes; which day shall be the same throughout the United States.

4. No person except a natural born citizen, or a citizen of the United States, at the time of the adoption of this Constitution, shall be eligible to the office of President; neither shall any person be eligible to that office who shall not have attained to the age of thirty-five years, and been fourteen years a resident within the United States.

(For qualification of the Vice President, see Amendment XII.)

5. In case of the removal of the President from office, or of his death, resignation, or inability to discharge the powers and duties of the said office, the same shall devolve on the Vice President, and the Congress may by law provide for the case of removal, death, resignation or inability, both of the President and Vice President, declaring what officer shall then act as President, and such officer shall act accordingly, until the disability be removed, or a President shall be elected.

(This clause has been modified by Amendments XX and XXV.)

6. The President shall, at stated times, receive for his services, a compensation, which shall neither be increased nor diminished during the period for which he shall have been elected, and he shall not receive within that period any other emolument from the United States, or any of them.

7. Before he enter on the execution of his office, he shall take the following oath or affirmation:

"I do solemnly swear (or affirm) that I will faithfully execute the office of President of the United States, and will to the best of my ability, preserve, protect and defend the Constitution of the United States."

Section 2—President to be Commander-in-Chief. He may require opinions of cabinet officers, etc., may pardon. Treaty-making power. Nomination of certain officers. When President may fill vacancies.

1. The President shall be Commander-in-Chief of the Army and Navy of the United States, and of the militia of the several States, when called into the actual service of the United States; he may require the opinion, in writing, of the principal officer in each of the executive departments, upon any subject relating to the duties of their respective offices, and he shall have power to grant reprieves and pardons for offenses against the United States, except in cases of impeachment.

2. He shall have power, by and with the advice and consent of the Senate, to make treaties, provided two-thirds of the Senators present concur; and he shall nominate, and by and with the advice and consent of the Senate, shall appoint ambassadors, other public ministers and consuls, judges of the Supreme Court, and all other officers of the United States, whose appointments are not herein otherwise provided for, and which shall be established by law: but the Congress may by law vest the appointment of such inferior officers, as they think proper, in the President alone, in the courts of law, or in the heads of departments.

3. The President shall have power to fill up all vacancies that may happen during the recess of the Senate, by granting commissions, which shall expire at the end of their next session.

Section 3—President shall communicate to Congress. He may convene and adjourn Congress, in case of disagreement, etc. Shall receive ambassadors, execute laws, and commission officers.

He shall from time to time give to the Congress information of the state of the Union, and recommend to their consideration such measures as he shall judge necessary and expedient; he may, on extraordinary occasions, convene both Houses, or either of them, and in case of disagreement between them, with respect to the time of adjournment, he may adjourn them to such time as he shall think proper; he shall receive ambassadors and other public ministers; he shall take care that the laws be faithfully executed, and shall commission all the officers of the United States.

Section 4—All civil offices forfeited for certain crimes.

The President, Vice President, and all civil officers of the United States, shall be removed from office on impeachment for, and conviction of, treason, bribery, or other high crimes and misdemeanors.

ARTICLE III.

Section 1—Judicial powers, Tenure. Compensation.

The judicial power of the United States, shall be vested in one Supreme Court, and in such inferior courts as the Congress may from time to time ordain and establish. The judges, both of the Supreme and inferior courts, shall hold their offices during good behavior, and shall at stated times, receive for their services, a compensation, which shall not be diminished during their continuance in office.

Section 2—Judicial power; to what cases it extends. Original jurisdiction of Supreme Court; appellate jurisdiction. Trial by jury, etc. Trial, where.

1. The judicial power shall extend to all cases, in law and equity, arising under this Constitution, the laws of the United States, and treaties made, or which shall be made, under their authority; to all cases affecting ambassadors, other public ministers and consuls; to all cases of admiralty and maritime jurisdiction; to controversies to which the United States shall be a party; to controversies between two or more States; between a State and citizens of another State; between citizens of different States, between citizens of the same State claiming lands under grants of different States, and between a State, or the citizens thereof, and foreign states, citizens or subjects.

(This section is modified by Amendment XI.)

2. In all cases affecting ambassadors, other public ministers and consuls, and those in which a State shall be party, the Supreme Court shall have original jurisdiction. In all the other cases before mentioned, the Supreme Court shall have appellate jurisdiction, both as to law and fact, with such exceptions, and under such regulations as the Congress shall make.

3. The trial of all crimes, except in cases of impeachment, shall be by jury; and such trial shall be held in the State where the said crimes shall have been committed; but when not committed within any State, the trial shall be at such place or places as the Congress may by law have directed.

Section 3—Treason Defined, Proof of, Punishment of.

1. Treason against the United States, shall consist only in levying war against them, or in adhering to their enemies,

giving them aid and comfort. No person shall be convicted of treason unless on the testimony of two witnesses to the same overt act, or on confession in open court.

2. The Congress shall have power to declare the punishment of treason, but no attainder of treason shall work corruption of blood, or forfeiture except during the life of the person attainted.

ARTICLE IV.

Section 1—Each State to give credit to the public acts, etc., of every other State.

Full faith and credit shall be given in each State to the public acts, records, and judicial proceedings of every other State. And the Congress may by general laws prescribe the manner in which such acts, records and proceedings shall be proved, and the effect thereof.

Section 2—Privileges of citizens of each State. Fugitives from justice to be delivered up. Persons held to service having escaped, to be delivered up.

1. The citizens of each State shall be entitled to all privileges and immunities of citizens in the several States.

2. A person charged in any State with treason, felony, or other crime, who shall flee from justice, and be found in another State, shall on demand of the Executive authority of the State from which he fled, be delivered up, to be removed to the State having jurisdiction of the crime.

(3. No person held to service or labor in one State, under the laws thereof, escaping into another, shall in consequence of any law or regulation therein, be discharged from such service or labor, but shall be delivered up on claim of the party to whom such service or labor may be due.) (This clause was superseded by Amendment XIII.)

Section 3—Admission of new States. Power of Congress over territory and other property.

1. New States may be admitted by the Congress into this Union; but no new State shall be formed or erected within the jurisdiction of any other State; nor any State be formed by the junction of two or more States, or parts of States, without the consent of the Legislatures of the States concerned as well as of the Congress.

2. The Congress shall have power to dispose of and make all needful rules and regulations respecting the territory or other property belonging to the United States; and nothing in this Constitution shall be so construed as to prejudice any claims of the United States, or of any particular State.

Section 4—Republican form of government guaranteed. Each state to be protected.

The United States shall guarantee to every State in this Union a Republican form of government, and shall protect each of them against invasion; and on application of the Legislature, or of the Executive (when the Legislature cannot be convened) against domestic violence.

ARTICLE V.

Constitution: how amended; proviso.

The Congress, whenever two-thirds of both Houses shall deem it necessary, shall propose amendments to this Constitution, or, on the application of the Legislatures of two-thirds of the several States, shall call a convention for proposing amendments, which, in either case, shall be valid to all intents and purposes, as part of this Constitution, when ratified by the Legislatures of three-fourths of the several States, or by conventions in three-fourths thereof, as the one

or the other mode of ratification may be proposed by the Congress; provided that no amendment which may be made prior to the year one thousand eight hundred and eight shall in any manner affect the first and fourth clauses in the Ninth Section of the First Article; and that no State, without its consent, shall be deprived of its equal suffrage in the Senate.

ARTICLE VI.

Certain debts, etc., declared valid. Supremacy of Constitution, treaties, and laws of the United States. Oath to support Constitution, by whom taken. No religious test.

1. All debts contracted and engagements entered into, before the adoption of this Constitution, shall be as valid against the United States under this Constitution, as under the Confederation.

2. This Constitution, and the laws of the United States which shall be made in pursuance thereof; and all treaties made, or which shall be made, under the authority of the United States, shall be the supreme law of the land; and the judges in every State shall be bound thereby, any thing in the Constitution or laws of any State to the contrary notwithstanding.

3. The Senators and Representatives before mentioned, and the members of the several State Legislatures, and all executive and judicial officers, both of the United States and of the several States, shall be bound by oath or affirmation, to support this Constitution; but no religious test shall ever be required as a qualification to any office or public trust under the United States.

ARTICLE VII.

What ratification shall establish Constitution.

The ratification of the Conventions of nine States, shall be sufficient for the establishment of this Constitution between the States so ratifying the same.

Done in convention by the unanimous consent of the States present the Seventeenth day of September in the year of our Lord one thousand seven hundred and eighty seven, and of the independence of the United States of America the Twelfth. In witness whereof we have hereunto subscribed our names.

George Washington, President and deputy from Virginia.

New Hampshire—John Langdon, Nicholas Gilman.

Massachusetts—Nathaniel Gorham, Rufus King.

Connecticut—Wm. Saml. Johnson, Roger Sherman.

New York—Alexander Hamilton.

New Jersey—Wil: Livingston, David Brearley, Wm. Paterson, Jona: Dayton.

Pennsylvania—B. Franklin, Thomas Mifflin, Robt. Morris, Geo. Clymer, Thos. FitzSimons, Jared Ingersoll, James Wilson, Gouv. Morris.

Delaware—Geo: Read, Gunning Bedford Jun., John Dickinson, Richard Bassett, Jaco: Broom.

Maryland—James McHenry, Daniel of Saint Thomas' Jenifer, Danl. Carroll.

Virginia—John Blair, James Madison Jr.

North Carolina—Wm. Blount, Rich'd. Dobbs Spaight, Hugh Williamson.

South Carolina—J. Rutledge, Charles Cotesworth Pinckney, Charles Pinckney, Pierce Butler.

Georgia—William Few, Abr. Baldwin.

Attest: William Jackson, Secretary.

Ten Original Amendments: The Bill of Rights
In force Dec. 15, 1791

(The First Congress, at its first session in the City of New York, Sept. 25, 1789, submitted to the states 12 amendments to clarify certain individual and state rights not named in the Constitution. They are generally called the Bill of Rights.

(Influential in framing these amendments was the Declaration of Rights of Virginia, written by George Mason (1725-1792) in 1776. Mason, a Virginia delegate to the Constitutional Convention, did not sign the Constitution and opposed its ratification on the ground that it did not sufficiently oppose slavery or safeguard individual rights.

(In the preamble to the resolution offering the proposed amendments, Congress said: "The conventions of a number of the States having at the time of their adopting the Constitution, expressed a desire, in order to prevent misconstruction or abuse of its powers, that further declaratory and restrictive clauses should be added, and as extending the ground of public confidence in the government will best insure the beneficent ends of its institution, be it resolved," etc.

(Ten of these amendments now commonly known as one to 10 inclusive, but originally 3 to 12 inclusive, were ratified by the states as follows: New Jersey, Nov. 20, 1789; Maryland, Dec. 19, 1789; North Carolina, Dec. 22, 1789; South Carolina, Jan. 19, 1790; New Hampshire, Jan 25, 1790; Delaware, Jan 28, 1790; New York, Feb. 27, 1790; Pennsylvania, Mar. 10, 1790; Rhode

Island, June 7, 1790; Vermont, Nov 3, 1791; Virginia, Dec. 15, 1791; Massachusetts, Mar. 2, 1939; Georgia, Mar. 18, 1939; Connecticut, Apr. 19, 1939. These original 10 ratified amendments follow as Amendments I to X inclusive.

(Of the two original proposed amendments which were not ratified by the necessary number of states, the first related to apportionment of Representatives; the second, to compensation of members. See p. 465.)

AMENDMENT I.
Religious establishment prohibited. Freedom of speech, of the press, and right to petition.

Congress shall make no law respecting an establishment of religion, or prohibiting the free exercise thereof; or abridging the freedom of speech, or of the press; or the right of the people peaceably to assemble, and to petition the Government for a redress of grievances.

AMENDMENT II.
Right to keep and bear arms.

A well-regulated militia, being necessary to the security of a free State, the right of the people to keep and bear arms, shall not be infringed.

AMENDMENT III.
Conditions for quarters for soldiers.

No soldier shall, in time of peace be quartered in any house, without the consent of the owner, nor in time of war, but in a manner to be prescribed by law.

AMENDMENT IV.
Right of search and seizure regulated.

The right of the people to be secure in their persons, houses, papers, and effects, against unreasonable searches and seizures, shall not be violated, and no warrants shall issue, but upon probable cause, supported by oath or affirmation, and particularly describing the place to be searched, and the persons or things to be seized.

AMENDMENT V.
Provisions concerning prosecution. Trial and punishment—private property not to be taken for public use without compensation.

No person shall be held to answer for a capital, or otherwise infamous crime, unless on a presentment or indictment of a Grand Jury, except in cases arising in the land and naval forces, or in the militia, when in actual service in time of war or public danger; nor shall any person be subject for the same offense to be twice put in jeopardy of life or limb; nor shall be compelled in any criminal case to be a witness against himself, nor be deprived of life, liberty, or property, without due process of law; nor shall private property be taken for public use without just compensation.

AMENDMENT VI.
Right to speedy trial, witnesses, etc.

In all criminal prosecutions, the accused shall enjoy the right to a speedy and public trial, by an impartial jury of the State and district wherein the crime shall have been committed, which district shall have been previously ascertained by law, and to be informed of the nature and cause of the accusation; to be confronted with the witnesses against him; to have compulsory process for obtaining witnesses in his favor, and to have the assistance of counsel for his defense.

AMENDMENT VII.
Right of trial by jury.

In suits at common law, where the value in controversy shall exceed twenty dollars, the right of trial by jury shall be preserved, and no fact tried by a jury shall be otherwise reexamined in any court of the United States, than according to the rules of the common law.

AMENDMENT VIII.
Excessive bail or fines and cruel punishment prohibited.

Excessive bail shall not be required, nor excessive fines imposed, nor cruel and unusual punishments inflicted.

AMENDMENT IX.
Rule of construction of Constitution.

The enumeration in the Constitution, of certain rights, shall not be construed to deny or disparage others retained by the people.

AMENDMENT X.
Rights of States under Constitution.

The powers not delegated to the United States by the Constitution, nor prohibited by it to the States, are reserved to the States respectively, or to the people.

Amendments Since the Bill of Rights

AMENDMENT XI.
Judicial powers construed.

The judicial power of the United States shall not be construed to extend to any suit in law or equity, commenced or prosecuted against one of the United States by citizens of another State, or by citizens or subjects of any foreign state.

(This amendment was proposed to the Legislatures of the several States by the Third Congress on March 4, 1794, and was declared to have been ratified in a message from the President to Congress, dated Jan. 8, 1798.

(It was on Jan 5, 1798, that Secretary of State Pickering received from 12 of the States authenticated ratifications, and informed President John Adams of that fact.

(As a result of later research in the Department of State, it is now established that Amendment XI became part of the Constitution on Feb. 7, 1795, for on that date it had been ratified by 12 States as follows:

(1. New York, Mar. 27, 1794. 2. Rhode Island, Mar. 31, 1794. 3. Connecticut, May 8, 1794. 4. New Hampshire, June 16, 1794. 5. Massachusetts, June 26, 1794. 6. Vermont, between Oct 9, 1794, and Nov. 9, 1794. 7. Virginia, Nov. 18, 1794. 8. Georgia, Nov. 29, 1794. 9. Kentucky, Dec. 7, 1794. 10. Maryland, Dec. 26, 1794. 11. Delaware, Jan 23, 1795. 12. North Carolina, Feb. 7, 1795.

(On June 1, 1796, more than a year after Amendment XI had become a part of the Constitution (but before anyone was officially aware of this), Tennessee had been admitted as a State; but not until Oct. 16, 1797, was a certified copy of the resolution of Congress proposing the amendment sent to the Governor of Tennessee (John Sevier) by Secretary of State Pickering, whose office was then at Trenton, New Jersey, because of the epidemic of yellow fever at Philadelphia; it seems, however, that the Legislature of Tennessee took no action on Amendment XI, owing doubtless to the fact that public announcement of its adoption was made soon thereafter.

(Besides the necessary 12 States, one other, South Carolina, ratified Amendment XI, but this action was not taken until Dec. 4, 1797; the two remaining States, New Jersey and Pennsylvania, failed to ratify.)

AMENDMENT XII.
Manner of choosing President and Vice-President.

(Proposed by Congress Dec. 9, 1803; ratification completed June 15, 1804.)

The Electors shall meet in their respective States and vote by ballot for President and Vice-President, one of whom, at least, shall not be an inhabitant of the same State with themselves; they shall name in their ballots the person voted for as President, and in distinct ballots the person voted for as Vice-President, and they shall make distinct lists of all persons voted for as President, and of all persons voted for as Vice-President, and of the number of votes for each, which lists they shall sign and certify, and transmit sealed to the seat of the Government of the United States, directed to the President of the Senate; the President of the Senate shall, in the presence of the Senate and House of Representatives, open all the certificates and the votes shall then be counted;—The person having the greatest number of votes for President, shall be the President, if such number be a majority of the whole number of Electors appointed; and if no person have such majority, then from the persons having the highest numbers not exceeding three on the list of those voted for as President, the House of Representatives shall choose immediately, by ballot, the President. But in choosing the President, the votes shall be taken by States, the representation from each State having one vote; a quorum for this purpose shall consist of a member or members from two-thirds of the States, and a majority of all the States shall be necessary to a choice. *(And if the House of Representatives shall not choose a President whenever the right of choice shall devolve upon them, before the fourth day of March next following, then the Vice-President shall act as President, as in the case of the death or other constitutional disability of the President.) (The words in parentheses were superseded by Amendment XX, section 3.)* The person having the greatest number of votes as Vice-President, shall be the Vice-President, if such number be a majority of the whole number of Electors appointed, and if no person have a majority, then from the two highest numbers on the list, the Senate shall choose the Vice-President; a quorum for the purpose shall consist of two-thirds of the whole number of Senators, and a majority of the whole number shall be necessary to a choice. But no person constitutionally ineligible to the office of President shall be eligible to that of Vice-President of the United States.

THE RECONSTRUCTION AMENDMENTS

(Amendments XIII, XIV, and XV are commonly known as the Reconstruction Amendments, inasmuch as they followed the Civil War, and were drafted by Republicans who were bent on imposing their own policy of reconstruction on the South. Post-bellum legislatures there—Mississippi, South Carolina, Georgia, for example—had set up laws which, it was charged, were contrived to perpetuate Negro slavery under other names.)

AMENDMENT XIII.
Slavery abolished.

(Proposed by Congress Jan. 31, 1865; ratification completed Dec. 18, 1865. The amendment, when first proposed by a resolution in Congress, was passed by the Senate, 38 to 6, on Apr. 8, 1864, but was defeated in the House, 95 to 66 on June 15, 1864. On reconsideration by the House, on Jan. 31, 1865, the resolution passed, 119 to 56. It was approved by President Lincoln on Feb. 1, 1865, although the Supreme Court had decided in 1798 that the President has nothing to do with the proposing of amendments to the Constitution, or their adoption.)

1. Neither slavery nor involuntary servitude, except as a punishment for crime whereof the party shall have been duly convicted, shall exist within the United States or any place subject to their jurisdiction.

2. Congress shall have power to enforce this article by appropriate legislation.

AMENDMENT XIV.
Citizenship rights not to be abridged.

(The following amendment was proposed to the Legislatures of the several states by the 39th Congress, June 13, 1866, and was declared to have been ratified in a proclamation by the Secretary of State, July 28, 1868.

(The 14th amendment was adopted only by virtue of ratification subsequent to earlier rejections. Newly constituted legislatures in both North Carolina and South Carolina (respectively July 4 and 9, 1868), ratified the proposed amendment, although earlier legislatures had rejected the proposal. The Secretary of State issued a proclamation, which, though doubtful as to the effect of attempted withdrawals by Ohio and New Jersey, entertained no doubt as to the validity of the ratification by North and South Carolina. The following day (July 21, 1868), Congress passed a resolution which declared the 14th Amendment to be a part of the Constitution and directed the Secretary of State so to promulgate it. The Secretary waited, however, until the newly constituted Legislature of Georgia had ratified the amendment, subsequent to an earlier rejection, before the promulgation of the ratification of the new amendment.)

1. All persons born or naturalized in the United States, and subject to the jurisdiction thereof, are citizens of the United States and of the State wherein they reside. No State shall make or enforce any law which shall abridge the privileges or immunities of citizens of the United States; nor shall

any State deprive any person of life, liberty, or property, without due process of law; nor deny to any person within its jurisdiction the equal protection of the laws.

2. Representatives shall be apportioned among the several States according to their respective numbers, counting the whole number of persons in each State, excluding Indians not taxed. But when the right to vote at any election for the choice of Electors for President and Vice-President of the United States, Representatives in Congress, the executive and judicial officers of a State, or the members of the Legislature thereof, is denied to any of the male inhabitants of such State, being twenty-one years of age, and, citizens of the United States, or in any way abridged, except for participation in rebellion, or other crime, the basis of representation therein shall be reduced in the proportion which the number of such male citizens shall bear to the whole number of male citizens twenty-one years of age in such State.

3. No person shall be a Senator or Representative in Congress, or Elector of President and Vice-President, or hold any office, civil or military, under the United States, or under any State, who, having previously taken an oath, as a member of Congress, or as an officer of the United States, or as a member of any State Legislature, or as an executive or judicial officer of any State, to support the Constitution of the United States, shall have engaged in insurrection or rebellion against the same, or given aid or comfort to the enemies thereof. But Congress may by a vote of two-thirds of each House, remove such disability.

4. The validity of the public debt of the United States, authorized by law, including debts incurred for payment of pensions and bounties for services in suppressing insurrection or rebellion, shall not be questioned. But neither the United States nor any State shall assume or pay any debt or obligation incurred in aid of insurrection or rebellion against the United States, or any claim for the loss or emancipation of any slave; but all such debts, obligations and claims, shall be held illegal and void.

5. The Congress shall have power to enforce, by appropriate legislation, the provisions of this article.

AMENDMENT XV.
Race no bar to voting rights.

(The following amendment was proposed to the legislatures of the several States by the 40th Congress, Feb. 26, 1869, and was declared to have been ratified in a proclamation by the Secretary of State, Mar. 30, 1870.)

1. The right of citizens of the United States to vote shall not be denied or abridged by the United States or by any State on account of race, color, or previous condition of servitude.

2. The Congress shall have power to enforce this article by appropriate legislation.

AMENDMENT XVI.
Income taxes authorized.

(Proposed by Congress July 12, 1909; ratification declared by the Secretary of State Feb. 25, 1913.)

The Congress shall have power to lay and collect taxes on incomes, from whatever source derived, without apportionment among the several States, and without regard to any census or enumeration.

AMENDMENT XVII.
United States Senators to be elected by direct popular vote.

(Proposed by Congress May 13, 1912; ratification declared by the Secretary of State May 31, 1913.)

1. The Senate of the United States shall be composed of two Senators from each State, elected by the people thereof, for six years; and each Senator shall have one vote. The electors in each State shall have the qualifications requisite for electors of the most numerous branch of the State Legislatures.

2. When vacancies happen in the representation of any State in the Senate, the executive authority of such State shall issue writs of election to fill such vacancies: Provided, That the Legislature of any State may empower the Executive thereof to make temporary appointments until the peo-

ple fill the vacancies by election as the Legislature may direct.

3. This amendment shall not be so construed as to affect the election or term of any Senator chosen before it becomes valid as part of the Constitution.

AMENDMENT XVIII.

Liquor prohibition amendment.

(Proposed by Congress Dec. 18, 1917; ratification completed Jan. 16, 1919. Repealed by Amendment XXI, effective Dec. 5, 1933.)

(1. After one year from the ratification of this article the manufacture, sale, or transportation of intoxicating liquors within, the importation thereof into, or the exportation thereof from the United States and all territory subject to the jurisdiction thereof for beverage purposes is hereby prohibited.

(2. The Congress and the several States shall have concurrent power to enforce this article by appropriate legislation.

(3. This article shall be inoperative unless it shall have been ratified as an amendment to the Constitution by the Legislatures of the several States, as provided in the Constitution, within seven years from the date of the submission hereof to the States by the Congress.)

(The total vote in the Senates of the various States was 1,310 for, 237 against—84.6% dry. In the lower houses of the States the vote was 3,782 for, 1,035 against—78.5% dry.

(The amendment ultimately was adopted by all the States except Connecticut and Rhode Island.)

AMENDMENT XIX.

Giving nationwide suffrage to women.

(Proposed by Congress June 4, 1919; ratification certified by Secretary of State Aug. 26, 1920.)

1. The right of citizens of the United States to vote shall not be denied or abridged by the United States or by any State on account of sex.

2. Congress shall have power to enforce this Article by appropriate legislation.

AMENDMENT XX.

Terms of President and Vice President to begin on Jan. 20; those of Senators, Representatives, Jan. 3.

(Proposed by Congress Mar. 2, 1932; ratification completed Jan. 23, 1933.)

1. The terms of the President and Vice President shall end at noon on the 20th day of January, and the terms of Senators and Representatives at noon on the 3rd day of January, of the years in which such terms would have ended if this article had not been ratified; and the terms of their successors shall then begin.

2. The Congress shall assemble at least once in every year, and such meeting shall begin at noon on the 3rd day of January, unless they shall by law appoint a different day.

3. If, at the time fixed for the beginning of the term of the President, the President elect shall have died, the Vice President elect shall become President. If a President shall not have been chosen before the time fixed for the beginning of his term, or if the President elect shall have failed to qualify, then the Vice President elect shall act as President until a President shall have qualified; and the Congress may by law provide for the case wherein neither a President elect nor a Vice President elect shall have qualified, declaring who shall then act as President, or the manner in which one who is to act shall be selected, and such person shall act accordingly until a President or Vice President shall have qualified.

4. The Congress may by law provide for the case of the death of any of the persons from whom the House of Representatives may choose a President whenever the right of choice shall have devolved upon them, and for the case of the death of any of the persons from whom the Senate may choose a Vice President whenever the right of choice shall have devolved upon them.

5. Sections 1 and 2 shall take effect on the 15th day of October following the ratification of this article (Oct., 1933).

6. This article shall be inoperative unless it shall have been ratified as an amendment to the Constitution by the

Legislatures of three-fourths of the several States within seven years from the date of its submission.

AMENDMENT XXI.

Repeal of Amendment XVIII.

(Proposed by Congress Feb. 20, 1933; ratification completed Dec. 5, 1933.)

1. The eighteenth article of amendment to the Constitution of the United States is hereby repealed.

2. The transportation or importation into any State, Territory, or Possession of the United States for delivery or use therein of intoxicating liquors, in violation of the laws thereof, is hereby prohibited.

3. This article shall be inoperative unless it shall have been ratified as an amendment to the Constitution by conventions in the several States, as provided in the Constitution, within seven years from the date of the submission hereof to the States by the Congress.

AMENDMENT XXII.

Limiting Presidential terms of office.

(Proposed by Congress Mar. 24, 1947; ratification completed Feb. 27, 1951.)

1. No person shall be elected to the office of the President more than twice, and no person who has held the office of President, or acted as President, for more than two years of a term to which some other person was elected President shall be elected to the office of the President more than once. But this Article shall not apply to any person holding the office of President when this Article was proposed by the Congress, and shall not prevent any person who may be holding the office of President, or acting as President, during the term within which this Article becomes operative from holding the office of President or acting as President during the remainder of such term.

2. This article shall be inoperative unless it shall have been ratified as an amendment to the Constitution by the Legislatures of three-fourths of the several States within seven years from the date of its submission to the States by the Congress.

AMENDMENT XXIII.

Presidential vote for District of Columbia.

(Proposed by Congress June 16, 1960; ratification completed Mar. 29, 1961.)

1. The District constituting the seat of Government of the United States shall appoint in such manner as the Congress may direct:

A number of electors of President and Vice President equal to the whole number of Senators and Representatives in Congress to which the District would be entitled if it were a State, but in no event more than the least populous State; they shall be in addition to those appointed by the States, but they shall be considered, for the purposes of the election of President and Vice President, to be electors appointed by a State; and they shall meet in the District and perform such duties as provided by the twelfth article of amendment.

2. The Congress shall have power to enforce this article by appropriate legislation.

AMENDMENT XXIV.

Barring poll tax in federal elections.

(Proposed by Congress Aug. 27, 1962; ratification completed Jan. 23, 1964.)

1. The right of citizens of the United States to vote in any primary or other election for President or Vice President, for electors for President or Vice President, or for Senator or Representative in Congress, shall not be denied or abridged by the United States or any State by reason of failure to pay any poll tax or other tax.

2. The Congress shall have power to enforce this article by appropriate legislation.

AMENDMENT XXV.

Presidential disability and succession.

(Proposed by Congress July 6, 1965; ratification completed Feb. 10, 1967.)

1. In case of the removal of the President from office or of his death or resignation, the Vice President shall become President.

2. Whenever there is a vacancy in the office of the Vice President, the President shall nominate a Vice President who shall take office upon confirmation by a majority vote of both houses of Congress.

3. Whenever the President transmits to the President pro tempore of the Senate and the Speaker of the House of Representatives his written declaration that he is unable to discharge the powers and duties of his office, and until he transmits to them a written declaration to the contrary, such powers and duties shall be discharged by the Vice President as Acting President.

4. Whenever the Vice President and a majority of either the principal officers of the executive departments or of such other body as Congress may by law provide, transmit to the President pro tempore of the Senate and the Speaker of the House of Representatives their written declaration that the President is unable to discharge the powers and duties of his office, the Vice President shall immediately assume the powers and duties of the office as Acting President.

Thereafter, when the President transmits to the President pro tempore of the Senate and the Speaker of the House of Representatives his written declaration that no inability exists, he shall resume the powers and duties of his office unless the Vice President and a majority of either the principal officers of the executive department or of such other body as Congress may by law provide, transmit within four days to the President pro tempore of the Senate and the Speaker of the House of Representatives their written declaration that the President is unable to discharge the powers and duties of his office. Thereupon Congress shall decide the issue, assembling within forty-eight hours for that purpose if not in session. If the Congress, within twenty-one days after receipt of the latter written declaration, or, if Congress is not in session, within twenty-one days after Congress is required to assemble, determines by two-thirds vote of both houses that the President is unable to discharge the powers and duties of his office, the Vice President shall continue to discharge the same as Acting President; otherwise, the President shall resume the powers and duties of his office.

AMENDMENT XXVI.

Lowering voting age to 18 years.

(Proposed by Congress Mar. 23, 1971; ratification completed July 1, 1971.)

1. The right of citizens of the United States, who are 18 years of age or older, to vote shall not be denied or abridged by the United States or any state on account of age.

2. The Congress shall have the power to enforce this article by appropriate legislation.

PROPOSED AMENDMENT RELATING TO CONGRESSIONAL PAY

(Proposed by the first Congress Sept. 25, 1789 as one of the 12 amendments to the Constitution, the 10 that were accepted became the Bill of Rights; ratified as of May 1991 by 35 states: Maryland, North Carolina, South Carolina, Delaware, Vermont, Virginia 1789-1791; Ohio 1873; Wyoming 1978; Maine 1983; Colorado 1984; South Dakota, New Hampshire, Arizona, Tennessee, Oklahoma 1985; New Mexico, Indiana, Utah 1986; Montana, Connecticut, Wisconsin, Arkansas 1987; Georgia, W. Virginia, Louisiana 1988; Iowa, Idaho, Nevada, Alaska, Oregon, Minnesota, Texas 1989; Kansas, Florida 1990; N. Dakota 1991. An additional 3 ratifications are needed to attain the requisite three-quarters of the States.)

No law, varying the compensation for the services of the Senators and Representatives, shall take effect, until an election of Representatives shall have intervened.

Origin of the Constitution

The War of Independence was conducted by delegates from the original 13 states, called the Congress of the United States of America and generally known as the Continental Congress. In 1777 the Congress submitted to the legislatures of the states the Articles of Confederation and Perpetual Union, which were ratified by New Hampshire, Massachusetts, Rhode Island, Connecticut, New York, New Jersey, Pennsylvania, Delaware, Virginia, North Carolina, South Carolina, and Georgia, and finally, in 1781, by Maryland.

The first article of the instrument read: "The stile of this confederacy shall be the United States of America." This did not signify a sovereign nation, because the states delegated only those powers they could not handle individually, such as power to wage war, establish a uniform currency, make treaties with foreign nations and contract debts for general expenses (such as paying the army). Taxes for the payment of such debts were levied by the individual states. The president under the Articles signed himself "President of the United States in Congress assembled," but here the United States were considered in the plural, a cooperating group. Canada was invited to join the union on equal terms but did not act.

When the war was won it became evident that a stronger federal union was needed to protect the mutual interests of the states. The Congress left the initiative to the legislatures. Virginia in Jan. 1786 appointed commissioners to meet with representatives of other states, with the result that delegates from Virginia, Delaware, New York, New Jersey, and Pennsylvania met at Annapolis. Alexander Hamilton prepared for their call by asking delegates from all states to meet in Philadelphia in May 1787 "to render the Constitution of the Federal government adequate to the exigencies of the union." Congress endorsed the plan Feb. 21, 1787. Delegates were appointed by all states except Rhode Island.

The convention met May 14, 1787. George Washington was chosen president (presiding officer). The states certified 65 delegates, but 10 did not attend. The work was done by 55, not all of whom were present at all sessions. Of the 55 attending delegates, 16 failed to sign, and 39 actually signed Sept. 17, 1787, some with reservations. Some historians have said 74 delegates (9 more than the 65 actually certified) were named and 19 failed to attend. These 9 additional persons refused the appointment, were never delegates and never counted as absentees. Washington sent the Constitution to Congress with a covering letter and that body, Sept. 28, 1787, ordered it sent to the legislatures, "in order to be submitted to a convention of delegates chosen in each state by the people thereof."

The Constitution was ratified by votes of state conventions as follows: Delaware, Dec. 7, 1787, unanimous; Pennsylvania, Dec. 12, 1787, 43 to 23; New Jersey, Dec. 18, 1787, unanimous; Georgia, Jan 2, 1788, unanimous; Connecticut, Jan. 9, 1788, 128 to 40; Massachusetts, Feb. 6, 1788, 187 to 168; Maryland, Apr. 28, 1788, 63 to 11; South Carolina, May 23, 1788, 149 to 73; New Hampshire, June 21, 1788, 57 to 46; Virginia, June 25, 1788, 89 to 79; New York, July 26, 1788, 30 to 27. Nine states were needed to establish the operation of the Constitution "between the states so ratifying the same" and New Hampshire was the 9th state. The government did not declare the Constitution in effect until the first Wednesday in Mar. 1789 which was Mar. 4. After that North Carolina ratified it Nov. 21, 1789, 194 to 77; and Rhode Island, May 29, 1790, 34 to 32. Vermont in convention ratified it Jan. 10, 1791, and by act of Congress approved Feb. 18, 1791, was admitted into the Union as the 14th state, Mar. 4, 1791.

On Sept. 17, 1987, the nation began a four-year celebration of the 200th anniversary of the signing of the Constitution of the United States.

As of April 1987, 32 states have voted to issue convention calls to hold a second constitutional convention. Convention bills are pending before 11 more state legislatures, while bills to rescind previous calls are under consideration in four states. When the total reaches 34, the Constitution stipulates that a convention must be held. The convention drive began in the mid 1970s to bring about the consideration of an amendment requiring a balanced federal budget.

Selected Landmark Decisions of the U.S. Supreme Court

1803: Marbury v. Madison. The Court ruled that Congress exceeded its power in the Judiciary Act of 1789; thus, the Court established its power to review acts of Congress and declare invalid those it found in conflict with the Constitution.

1819: McCulloch v. Maryland. The Court ruled that Congress had the authority to charter a national bank, under the Constitution's granting of the power to enact all laws "necessary and proper" to exact the responsibilities of government. The Court also held that the national bank was immune to state taxation.

1819: Trustees of Dartmouth College v. Woodward. The Court ruled that a state could not arbitrarily alter the terms of a college's contract. (In later years the Court widened the implications by using the same principle to limit the states' ability to interfere with business contracts.)

1857: Dred Scott v. Sanford. The Court declared unconstitutional the already-repealed Missouri Compromise of 1820 because it deprived a person of his property—a slave—without due process of law. The Court also ruled that slaves were not citizens of any state nor of the U.S. (The latter part of the decision was overturned by ratification of the 14th Amendment in 1868.)

1896: Plessy v. Ferguson. The Court ruled that a state law requiring federal railroad trains to provide separate but equal facilities for black and white passengers neither infringed upon federal authority to regulate interstate commerce nor violated the 13th and 14th Amendments. (The "separate but equal" doctrine remained effective until the 1954 Brown v. Board of Education decision.)

1904: Northern Securities Co. v. U.S. The Court ruled that a holding company formed solely to eliminate competition between two railroad lines was a combination in restraint of trade, thus a violation of the federal antitrust act.

1908: Muller v. Oregon. The Court ruled to uphold a state law limiting the maximum working hours of women. (Instead of presenting legal arguments, Louis D. Brandeis, counsel for the state, brought forth evidence from social workers, physicians, and factory inspectors that the number of hours women worked affected their health and morals.)

1911: Standard Oil. Co. of New Jersey et al. v. U.S. The Court ruled that the Standard Oil Trust must be dissolved because of its unreasonable restraint of trade, not because of its size.

1919: Schenck v. U.S. In its first decision regarding the extent of protection afforded by the First Amendment, the Court sustained the Espionage Act of 1917, maintaining that freedom of speech and press could be constrained if "the words used are in such circumstances and are of such a nature as to create a clear and present danger. . ."

1925: Gitlow v. New York. The Court ruled that the First Amendment prohibition against government abridgement of the freedom of speech applied to the states as well as to the federal government. The decision was the first of a number of rulings holding that the 14th Amendment extended the guarantees of the Bill of Rights to state action.

1935: Schechter Poultry Corp. v. U.S. The Court ruled that Congress exceeded its authority to delegate legislative powers and to regulate interstate commerce when it enacted the National Industrial Recovery Act, which afforded the U.S. president too much discretionary power.

1951: Dennis et al. v. U.S. The Court upheld convictions under the Smith Act of 1940 for speaking about communist theory that advocated the forcible overthrow of the government. (In the 1957 Yates v. U.S. decision, the Court moderated this ruling by allowing such advocacy in the abstract, if not connected to action to achieve the goal.)

1954: Brown v. Board of Education of Topeka. The Court ruled that separate public schools for black and white students were inherently unequal, thus state-sanctioned segregation in public schools violated the equal protection guar-

antee of the 14th Amendment. And in **Bolling v. Sharpe** the Court ruled that the congressionally-mandated segregated public school system in the District of Columbia violated the Fifth Amendment's due process guarantee of personal liberty. (The Brown ruling also led to the abolition of state-sponsored segregation in other public facilities.)

1957: Roth v. U.S., Alberts v. California. The Court ruled that obscene material was not protected by the First Amendment guarantees of freedom of speech and press, defining obscene as "utterly without redeeming social value" and appealing to "prurient interests" in the view of the average person. (This definition, the first offered by the Court, was modified in several subsequent decisions, and the "average person" standard was replaced by the "local community" standard in the 1973 Miller v. California case.)

1961: Mapp v. Ohio. The Court ruled that evidence obtained in violation of the 4th Amendment guarantee against unreasonable search and seizure must be excluded from use at state as well as federal trials.

1962: Engel v. Vitale. The Court ruled that public school officials could not require pupils to recite a state-composed prayer at the start of each school day, even if the prayer was non-denominational and pupils who so desired could be excused from reciting it, because such official state sanction of religious utterances was an unconstitutional attempt to establish religion.

1962: Baker v. Carr. The Court held that the constitutional challenges to the unequal distribution of voters among legislative districts could be resolved by federal courts, rejecting the doctrine set out in Colegrove v. Green in 1946 that such apportionment challenges were "political questions."

1963: Gideon v. Wainwright. The Court ruled that the due process clause of the 14th Amendment extended to state as well as federal defendants, thus all persons charged with serious crimes must be provided with an attorney, and states were required to appoint counsel for defendants unable to pay their own attorneys' fees.

1964: New York Times Co. v. Sullivan. The Court ruled that the First Amendment guarantee of freedom of the press protected the press from libel suits for defamatory reports on public officials unless the officials proved that the reports were made from actual malice. The Court defined malice as "with knowledge that (the defamatory statement) was false or with reckless disregard of whether it was false or not."

1965: Griswold v. Conn. The Court ruled that a state unconstitutionally interfered with personal privacy in the marriage relationship when it prohibited anyone, including married couples, from using contraceptives.

1966: Miranda v. Arizona. The Court ruled that the guarantee of due process required that before any questioning of suspects in police custody, the suspects must be informed of their right to remain silent, that anything they say may be used against them, and that they have the right to counsel.

1973: Roe v. Wade, Doe v. Bolton. The Court ruled that the right to privacy inherent in the 14th Amendment's due process guarantee of personal liberty protected a woman's decision whether or not to bear a child, and was impermissibly abridged by state laws that made abortion a crime. During the first trimester of pregnancy, the Court maintained, the decision to have an abortion should be left entirely to a woman and her physician.

1974: U.S. v. Nixon. The Court ruled that neither the separation of powers nor the need to preserve the confidentiality of presidential communications could alone justify an absolute executive privilege of immunity from judicial demands for evidence to be used in a criminal trial.

1976: Gregg v. Georgia, Profitt v. Fla, Jurek v. Texas. The Court held that death, as a punishment for persons convicted of first degree murder, was not in and of itself cruel and unusual punishment in violation of the 8th Amendment.

The Court also ruled that the Amendment required the sentencing judge and jury to consider the individual character of the offender and the circumstances of the particular crime before deciding whether or not to impose the death sentence. In the associated **Woodson v. N.C., Roberts v. LA.,** the Court ruled that states could not make death the mandatory penalty for first-degree murder, since that would fail to meet the constitutional requirement for the consideration of the individual offender and offense.

1978: Regents of Univ. of Calif. v. Bakke. The Court ruled that a special admissions program for a state medical school under which a set number of places were set aside for minority group members, with white applicants denied the opportunity to compete for those seats, violated Title XIV of the 1964 Civil Rights Act, which forbids the exclusion of anyone, because of race, from participation in a federally-funded program. The Court also ruled that admissions programs that considered race as one of a complex of factors involved in the decision to admit or reject an applicant were not unconstitutional.

1979: United Steelworkers of America v. Weber, Kaiser Aluminum v. Weber, U.S. v. Weber. The Court ruled that Title VII of the 1964 Civil Rights Act, which forbids racial discrimination in employment, did not forbid employers to adopt voluntarily race-conscious affirmative action programs to encourage minority participation in areas in which they traditionally were underrepresented.

1986: Bowers v. Hardwick. The Court refused to extend the right of privacy inherent in the Constitution to homosexual activity, upholding a Georgia law that made sodomy a crime. (Although the Georgia law covered heterosexual sodomy as well as homosexual sodomy, enforcement in Georgia and most other states had been confined to homosexual activity.)

1989: Webster v. Reproductive Health Services. The Court upheld a Missouri abortion law that prohibited public employees from performing abortions unless the mother's life was in danger, barred the use of public buildings for performing abortions, and required physicians, before performing abortions of fetuses more than 20 weeks old, to perform tests to discover whether the fetus could live outside the womb.

Patrick Henry's Speech to the Virginia Convention

The following is an excerpt from Patrick Henry's speech to the Virginia Convention on Mar. 23, 1775:

Gentlemen may cry, peace, peace—but there is no peace. The war is actually begun! The next gale that sweeps from the north will bring to our ears the clash of resounding arms! Our brethren are already in the field! Why stand we here idle? What is it that gentlemen wish? What would they have? Is life so dear, or peace so sweet, as to be purchased at the price of chains and slavery? Forbid it, Almighty God! I know not what course others may take; but as for me, give me liberty, or give me death!

Common Sense

The following is an excerpt from Thomas Paine's *Common Sense.* Paine adopted the doctrine of separation from Britain after the battles of Lexington and Concord, and published his pamphlet in Jan. 1776.

The cause of America is in great measure the cause of all mankind. Many circumstances hath, and will arise, which are not local, but universal, and through which principles of all Lovers of Mankind are affected, and in the Event of which, their Affections are interested. The laying a Country desolate with Fire and Sword, declaring war against natural rights of all Mankind, and extirpating the Defenders thereof from the Face of the Earth, is the Concern of every Man to whom Nature hath given the Power of feeling; ... It is repugnant to reason, to the universal order of things, to all examples from former ages, to suppose, that this continent can longer remain subject to any external power ...

The last cord is now broken, the people of England are presenting addresses against us. There are injuries which nature cannot forgive; she would cease to be nature if she did ...

O ye that love mankind! Ye that dare oppose, not only the tyranny, but the tyrant, stand forth! Every spot of the old world is overrun with oppression. Freedom hath been hunted round the globe. Asia, and Africa, have long expelled her—Europe regards her like a stranger, and England hath given her warning to depart. O! Receive the fugitive, and prepare in time an asylum for mankind.

Law on Succession to the Presidency

If by reason of death, resignation, removal from office, inability, or failure to qualify there is neither a president nor vice president to discharge the powers and duties of the office of president, then the speaker of the House of Representatives shall upon his resignation as speaker and as representative, act as president. The same rule shall apply in the case of the death, resignation, removal from office, or inability of an individual acting as president.

If at the time when a speaker is to begin the discharge of the powers and duties of the office of president there is no speaker, or the speaker fails to qualify as acting president, then the president pro tempore of the Senate, upon his resignation as president pro tempore and as senator, shall act as president.

An individual acting as president shall continue to act until the expiration of the then current presidential term, except that (1) if his discharge of the powers and duties of the office is founded in whole or in part in the failure of both the president-elect and the vice president-elect to qualify, then he shall act only until a president or vice president qualifies, and (2) if his discharge of the powers and duties of the office is founded in whole or in part on the inability of the president or vice president, then he shall act only until the removal of the disability of one of such individuals.

If, by reason of death, resignation, removal from office, or failure to qualify, there is no president pro tempore to act as president, then the officer of the United States who is highest on the following list, and who is not under any disability to discharge the powers and duties of president shall act as president; the secretaries of state, treasury, defense, attorney general; secretaries of interior, agriculture, commerce, labor, health and human services, housing and urban development, transportation, energy, education.

(Legislation approved July 18, 1947; amended Sept. 9, 1965, Oct. 15, 1966, Aug. 4, 1977, and Sept. 27, 1979. (See also Constitutional Amendment XXV.)

Presidential Oath of Office

The Constitution (Article II) directs that the President shall take the following oath or affirmation: "I do solemnly swear (affirm) that I will faithfully execute the office of President of the United States, and will, to the best of my ability, preserve, protect, and defend the Constitution of the United States." (Custom decrees the use of the words "So help me God" at the end of the oath when taken by the President-elect, his/her left hand on the Bible for the duration of the oath, with his/her right hand slightly raised.)

How the Declaration of Independence Was Adopted

On June 7, 1776, Richard Henry Lee, who had issued the first call for a congress of the colonies, introduced in the Continental Congress at Philadelphia a resolution declaring "that these United Colonies are, and of right ought to be, free and independent states, that they are absolved from all allegiance to the British Crown, and that all political connection between them and the state of Great Britain is, and ought to be, totally dissolved."

The resolution, seconded by John Adams on behalf of the Massachusetts delegation, came up again June 10 when a committee of 5, headed by Thomas Jefferson, was appointed to express the purpose of the resolution in a declaration of independence. The others on the committee were John Adams, Benjamin Franklin, Robert R. Livingston, and Roger Sherman.

Drafting the Declaration was assigned to Jefferson, who worked on a portable desk of his own construction in a room at Market and 7th Sts. The committee reported the result June 28, 1776. The members of the Congress suggested a number of changes, which Jefferson called "deplorable." They didn't approve Jefferson's arraignment of the British people and King George III for encouraging and fostering the slave trade, which Jefferson called "an execrable commerce." They made 86 changes, eliminating 480 words and leaving 1,337. In the final form capitalization was erratic. Jefferson had written that men were endowed with "inalienable" rights; in the final copy it came out as "unalienable" and has been thus ever since.

The Lee-Adams resolution of independence was adopted by 12 yeas July 2 — the actual date of the act of independence. The Declaration, which explains the act, was adopted July 4, in the evening.

After the Declaration was adopted, July 4, 1776, it was turned over to John Dunlap, printer, to be printed on broadsides. The original copy was lost and one of his broadsides

was attached to a page in the journal of the Congress. It was read aloud July 8 in Philadelphia, Easton, Pa., and Trenton, N.J. On July 9 at 6 p.m. it was read by order of Gen. George Washington to the troops assembled on the Common in New York City (City Hall Park).

The Continental Congress of July 19, 1776, adopted the following resolution:

"Resolved, That the Declaration passed on the 4th, be fairly engrossed on parchment with the title and stile of 'The Unanimous Declaration of the thirteen United States of America' and that the same, when engrossed, be signed by every member of Congress."

Not all delegates who signed the engrossed Declaration were present on July 4. Robert Morris (Pa.), William Williams (Conn.) and Samuel Chase (Md.) signed on Aug. 2, Oliver Wolcott (Conn.), George Wythe (Va.), Richard Henry Lee (Va.) and Elbridge Gerry (Mass.) signed in August and September, Matthew Thornton (N. H.) joined the Congress Nov. 4 and signed later. Thomas McKean (Del.) rejoined Washington's Army before signing and said later that he signed in 1781.

Charles Carroll of Carrollton was appointed a delegate by Maryland on July 4, 1776, presented his credentials July 18, and signed the engrossed Declaration Aug. 2. Born Sept. 19, 1737, he was 95 years old and the last surviving signer when he died Nov. 14, 1832.

Two Pennsylvania delegates who did not support the Declaration on July 4 were replaced.

The 4 New York delegates did not have authority from their state to vote on July 4. On July 9 the New York state convention authorized its delegates to approve the Declaration and the Congress was so notified on July 15, 1776. The 4 signed the Declaration on Aug. 2.

The original engrossed Declaration is preserved in the National Archives Building in Washington.

The Continental Congress: Meetings, Presidents

Meeting places	Dates of meetings	Congress presidents	Date elected
Philadelphia	Sept. 5 to Oct. 26, 1774	Peyton Randolph, Va. (1)	Sept. 5, 1774
"	"	Henry Middleton, S.C.	Oct. 22, 1774
Philadelphia	May 10, 1775 to Dec. 12, 1776	Peyton Randolph, Va.	May 10, 1775
"	"	John Hancock, Mass.	May 24, 1775
Baltimore	Dec. 20, 1776 to Mar. 4, 1777	"	
Philadelphia	Mar. 5 to Sept. 18, 1777		
Lancaster, Pa.	Sept. 27, 1777 (one day)		
York, Pa.	Sept. 30, 1777 to June 27, 1778	Henry Laurens, S.C.	Nov. 1, 1777(4)
Philadelphia	July 2, 1778 to June 21, 1783	John Jay, N.Y.	Dec. 10, 1778
"	"	Samuel Huntington, Conn.	Sept. 28, 1779
"	"	Thomas McKean, Del.	July 10, 1781
"	"	John Hanson, Md. (2)	Nov. 5, 1781
"	"	Elias Boudinot, N.J.	Nov. 4, 1782
Princeton, N.J.	June 30 to Nov. 4, 1783	Thomas Mifflin, Pa.	Nov. 3, 1783
Annapolis, Md.	Nov. 26, 1783 to June 3, 1784		
Trenton, N.J.	Nov. 1 to Dec. 24, 1784	Richard Henry Lee, Va.	Nov. 30, 1784
New York City	Jan. 11 to Nov. 4, 1785		
"	Nov. 7, 1785 to Nov. 3, 1786	John Hancock, Mass. (3)	Nov. 23, 1785
"		Nathaniel Gorham, Mass.	June 6, 1786
"	Nov. 6, 1786 to Oct. 30, 1787	Arthur St. Clair, Pa.	Feb. 2, 1787
"	Nov. 5, 1787 to Oct. 21, 1788	Cyrus Griffin, Va.	Jan. 22, 1788
"	Nov. 3, 1788 to Mar. 2, 1789	"	

(1) Resigned Oct. 22, 1774. (2) Titled "President of the United States in Congress Assembled," John Hanson is considered by some to be the first U.S. President as he was the first to serve under the Articles of Confederation. He was, however, little more than presiding officer of the Congress, which retained full executive power. He could be considered the head of government, but not head of state. (3) Resigned May 29, 1786, without serving, because of illness. (4) Articles of Confederation agreed upon, Nov. 15, 1777; last ratification from Maryland, Mar. 1, 1781.

Origin of the United States National Motto

In God We Trust, designated as the U. S. National Motto by Congress in 1956, originated during the Civil War as an inscription for U. S. coins, although it was used by Francis Scott Key in a slightly different form when he wrote The Star Spangled Banner in 1814. On Nov. 13, 1861, when Union morale had been shaken by battlefield defeats, the Rev. M. R. Watkinson, of Ridleyville, Pa., wrote to Secy. of the Treasury Salmon P. Chase. "From my heart I have felt our national shame in disowning God as not the least of our present national disasters," the minister wrote, suggesting "recognition of the Almighty God in some form on our coins." Secy. Chase ordered designs prepared with the inscription *In God We Trust* and backed coinage legislation which authorized use of this slogan. It first appeared on some U. S. coins in 1864, disappeared and reappeared on various coins until 1955, when Congress ordered it placed on all paper money and all coins.

The Great Seal of the U.S.

On July 4, 1776, the Continental Congress appointed a committee consisting of Benjamin Franklin, John Adams and Thomas Jefferson "to bring in a device for a seal of the United States of America." After many delays, a verbal description of a design by William Barton was finally approved by Congress on June 20, 1782. The seal shows an American bald eagle with a ribbon in its mouth bearing the device E pluribus unum (One out of many). In its talons are the arrows of war and an olive branch of peace. On the reverse side it shows an unfinished pyramid with an eye (the eye of Providence) above it.

The American's Creed

William Tyler Page, Clerk of the U.S. House of Representatives, wrote "The American's Creed" in 1917. It was accepted by the House on behalf of the American people on April 3, 1918.

"I believe in the United States of America as a government of the people, by the people, for the people; whose just powers are derived from the consent of the governed; a democracy in a republic; a sovereign Nation of many sovereign States; a perfect union, one and inseparable; established upon those principles of freedom, equality, justice, and humanity for which American patriots sacrificed their lives and fortunes.

"I therefore believe it is my duty to my country to love it, to support its Constitution, to obey its laws, to respect its flag, and to defend it against all enemies."

The Flag of the U.S.—The Stars and Stripes

The 50-star flag of the United States was raised for the first time officially at 12:01 a.m. on July 4, 1960, at Fort McHenry National Monument in Baltimore, Md. The 50th star had been added for Hawaii; a year earlier the 49th, for Alaska. Before that, no star had been added since 1912, when N.M. and Ariz. were admitted to the Union.

The true history of the Stars and Stripes has become so cluttered by a volume of myth and tradition that the facts are difficult, and in some cases impossible, to establish. For example, it is not certain who designed the Stars and Stripes, who made the first such flag, or even whether it ever flew in any sea fight or land battle of the American Revolution.

One thing all agree on is that the Stars and Stripes originated as the result of a resolution offered by the Marine Committee of the Second Continental Congress at Philadelphia and adopted June 14, 1777. It read:

Resolved: that the flag of the United States be thirteen stripes, alternate red and white; that the union be thirteen stars, white in a blue field, representing a new constellation.

Congress gave no hint as to the designer of the flag, no instructions as to the arrangement of the stars, and no information on its appropriate uses. Historians have been unable to find the original flag law.

The resolution establishing the flag was not even published until Sept. 2, 1777. Despite repeated requests, Washington did not get the flags until 1783, after the Revolutionary War was over. And there is no certainty that they were the Stars and Stripes.

Early Flags

Although it was never officially adopted by the Continental Congress, many historians consider the first flag of the U.S. to have been the Grand Union (sometimes called Great Union) flag. This was a modification of the British Meteor flag, which had the red cross of St. George and the white cross of St. Andrew combined in the blue canton. For the Grand Union flag, 6 horizontal stripes were imposed on the red field, dividing it into 13 alternate red and white stripes. On Jan. 1, 1776, when the Continental Army came into formal existence, this flag was unfurled on Prospect Hill, Somerville, Mass. Washington wrote that "we hoisted the Union Flag in compliment to the United Colonies."

One of several flags about which controversy has raged for years is at Easton, Pa. Containing the devices of the national flag in reversed order, this has been in the public library at Easton for over 150 years. Some contend that this flag was actually the first Stars and Stripes, first displayed on July 8, 1776. This flag has 13 red and white stripes in the canton, 13 white stars centered in a blue field.

A flag was hastily improvised from garments by the defenders of Fort Schuyler at Rome, N.Y., Aug. 3-22, 1777. Historians believe it was the Grand Union Flag.

The Sons of Liberty had a flag of 9 red and white stripes, to signify 9 colonies, when they met in New York in 1765 to oppose the Stamp Tax. By 1775, the flag had grown to 13 red and white stripes, with a rattlesnake on it.

At Concord, Apr. 19, 1775, the minute men from Bedford, Mass., are said to have carried a flag having a silver arm with sword on a red field.

At Cambridge, Mass., the Sons of Liberty used a plain red flag with a green pine tree on it.

In June 1775, Washington went from Philadelphia to Boston to take command of the army, escorted to New York by the Philadelphia Light Horse Troop. It carried a yellow flag which had an elaborate coat of arms — the shield charged with 13 knots, the motto "For These We Strive" — and a canton of 13 blue and silver stripes.

In Feb., 1776, Col. Christopher Gadsden, member of the Continental Congress, gave the S. Carolina Provincial Congress a flag "such as is to be used by the commander-in-chief of the American Navy." It had a yellow field, with a rattlesnake about to strike and the words "Don't Tread on Me."

At the battle of Bennington, Aug. 16, 1777, patriots used a flag of 7 white and 6 red stripes with a blue canton extending down 9 stripes and showing an arch of 11 white stars over the figure 76 and a star in each of the upper corners. The stars are seven-pointed. This flag is preserved in the Historical Museum at Bennington, Vt.

At the Battle of Cowpens, Jan. 17, 1781, the 3d Maryland Regt. is said to have carried a flag of 13 red and white stripes, with a blue canton containing 12 stars in a circle around one star.

Who Designed the Flag? No one knows for certain. Francis Hopkinson, designer of a naval flag, declared he also designed the flag and in 1781 asked Congress to reimburse him for his services. Congress did not do so. Dumas Malone of Columbia Univ. wrote: "This talented man . . . designed the American flag."

Who Called the Flag Old Glory? — The flag is said to have been named Old Glory by William Driver, a sea captain of Salem, Mass. One legend has it that when he raised the flag on his brig, the Charles Doggett, in 1824, he said: "I name thee Old Glory." But his daughter, who presented the flag to the Smithsonian Institution, said he named it at his 21st birthday celebration Mar. 17, 1824, when his mother presented the homemade flag to him.

The Betsy Ross Legend — The widely publicized legend that Mrs. Betsy Ross made the first Stars and Stripes in June 1776, at the request of a committee composed of George Washington, Robert Morris, and George Ross, an uncle, was first made public in 1870, by a grandson of Mrs. Ross. Historians have been unable to find a historical record of such a meeting or committee.

Adding New Stars

The flag of 1777 was used until 1795. Then, on the admission of Vermont and Kentucky to the Union, Congress passed and Pres. Washington signed an act that after May 1, 1795, the flag should have 15 stripes, alternate red and white, and 15 white stars on a blue field in the union.

When new states were admitted it became evident that the flag would become burdened with stripes. Congress thereupon ordered that after July 4, 1818, the flag should have 13 stripes, symbolizing the 13 original states; that the union have 20 stars, and that whenever a new state was admitted a new star should be added on the July 4 following admission. No law designates the permanent arrangement of the stars. However, since 1912 when a new state has been admitted, the new design has been announced by executive order. No star is specifically identified with any state.

Code of Etiquette for Display and Use of the U.S. Flag

Although the Stars and Stripes originated in 1777, it was not until 146 years later that there was a serious attempt to establish a uniform code of etiquette for the U.S. flag. The War Department issued Feb. 15, 1923, a circular on the rules of flag usage. These were adopted almost in their entirety June 14, 1923, by a conference of 68 patriotic organizations in Washington. Finally, on June 22, 1942, a joint resolution of Congress, amended by Public Law 94-344 July 7, 1976, codified "existing rules and customs pertaining to the display and use of the flag . . ."

When to Display the Flag—The flag should be displayed on all days, especially on legal holidays and other special occasions, on official buildings when in use, in or near polling places on election days, and in or near schools when in session. A citizen may fly the flag at any time he wishes. It is customary to display the flag only from sunrise to sunset on buildings and on stationary flagstaffs in the open. However, it may be displayed at night on special occasions, preferably lighted. In Washington, the flag now flies over the White House both day and night. It flies over the Senate wing of the Capitol when the Senate is in session and over the House wing when that body is in session. It flies day and night over the east and west fronts of the Capitol, without floodlights at night but receiving light from the illuminated Capitol Dome. It flies 24 hours a day at several other places, including the Fort McHenry Nat'l Monument in Baltimore, where it inspired Francis Scott Key to write The Star Spangled Banner.

How to Fly the Flag—The flag should be hoisted briskly and lowered ceremoniously, and should never be allowed to touch the ground or the floor. When hung over a sidewalk from a rope extending from a building to a pole, the union should be away from the building. When hung over the center of a street it should have the union to the north in an east-west street and to the east in a north-south street. No other flag may be flown above or, if on the same level, to the right of the U.S. flag, except that at the United Nations Headquarters the UN flag may be placed above flags of all member nations and other national flags may be flown with equal prominence or honor with the flag of the U.S. At services by Navy chaplains at sea, the church pennant may be flown above the flag.

When two flags are placed against a wall with crossed staffs, the U.S. flag should be at right—its own right, and its staff should be in front of the staff of the other flag; when a number of flags are grouped and displayed from staffs, it should be at the center and highest point of the group.

Church and Platform Use—In an auditorium, the flag may be displayed flat, above and behind the speaker. When displayed from a staff in a church or public auditorium, the flag should hold the position of superior prominence, in advance of the audience, and in the position of honor at the clergyman's or speaker's right as he faces the audience. Any other flag so displayed should be placed on the left of the clergyman or speaker or to the right of the audience.

When the flag is displayed horizontally or vertically against a wall, the stars should be uppermost and at the observer's left.

How to Dispose of Worn Flags—The flag, when it is in such condition that it is no longer a fitting emblem for display, should be destroyed in a dignified way, preferably by burning.

When to Salute the Flag—All persons present should face the flag, stand at attention and salute on the following occasions: (1) When the flag is passing in a parade or in a review, (2) During the ceremony of hoisting or lowering, (3) When the National Anthem is played, and (4) During the Pledge of Allegiance. Those present in uniform should render the military salute. When not in uniform, men should remove the hat with the right hand holding it at the left shoulder, the hand being over the heart. Men without hats should salute in the same manner. Aliens should stand at attention. Women should salute by placing the right hand over the heart.

On Memorial Day, the flag should fly at half-staff until noon, then be raised to the peak.

As provided by Presidential proclamation the flag should fly at half-staff for 30 days from the day of death of a president or former president; for 10 days from the day of death of a vice president, chief justice or retired chief justice of the U.S., or speaker of the House of Representatives; from day of death until burial of an associate justice of the Supreme Court, cabinet member, former vice president, or Senate president pro tempore, majority or minority Senate leader, or majority or minority House leader; for a U.S. senator, representative, territorial delegate, or the resident commissioner of Puerto Rico, on day of death and the following day within the metropolitan area of the District of Columbia and from day of death until burial within the decedent's state, congressional district, territory or commonwealth; and for the death of the governor of a state, territory, or possession of the U.S., from day of death until burial within that state, territory, or possession.

When used to cover a casket, the flag should be placed so that the union is at the head and over the left shoulder. It should not be lowered into the grave nor touch the ground.

Prohibited Uses of the Flag—The flag should not be dipped to any person or thing. (An exception—customarily, ships salute by dipping their colors.) It should never be displayed with the union down save as a distress signal. It should never be carried flat or horizontally, but always aloft and free.

It should not be displayed on a float, motor car or boat except from a staff.

It should never be used as a covering for a ceiling, nor have placed upon it any word, design, or drawing. It should never be used as a receptacle for carrying anything. It should not be used to cover a statue or a monument.

The flag should never be used for advertising purposes, nor be embroidered on such articles as cushions or hankerchiefs, printed or otherwise impressed on boxes or anything that is designed for temporary use and discard; or used as a costume or athletic uniform. Advertising signs should not be fastened to its staff or halyard.

The flag should never be used as drapery of any sort, never festooned, drawn back, nor up, in folds, but always allowed to fall free. Bunting of blue, white and red always arranged with the blue above and the white in the middle, should be used for covering a speaker's desk, draping the front of a platform, and for decoration in general.

An Act of Congress approved Feb. 8, 1917, provided certain penalties for the desecration, mutilation or improper use of the flag within the District of Columbia. A 1968 federal law provided penalties of up to a year's imprisonment or a $1,000 fine or both, for publicly burning or otherwise desecrating any flag of the United States. In addition, many states have laws against flag desecration. In 1989, the Supreme Court ruled that no laws could prohibit political protesters from burning the flag. The decision had the effect of declaring unconstitutional the flag desecration laws of 48 states, as well as a similar Federal statute, in cases of peaceful political expression.

The Supreme Court, June 1990, declared that a new Federal law making it a crime to burn or deface the American flag violates the free-speech guarantee of the First Amendment. The 5-4 decision led to renewed calls in Congress for a constitutional amendment to make it possible to prosecute flag burning.

Pledge of Allegiance to the Flag

I pledge allegiance to the flag of the United States of America and to the republic for which it stands, one nation under God, indivisible, with liberty and justice for all.

This, the current official version of the Pledge of Allegiance, has developed from the original pledge, which was first published in the Sept. 8, 1892, issue of the Youth's Companion, a weekly magazine then published in Boston. The original pledge contained the phrase "my flag," which was changed more than 30 years later to "flag of the United States of America." An act of Congress in 1954 added the words "under God."

The authorship of the pledge had been in dispute for many years. The Youth's Companion stated in 1917 that the original draft was written by James B. Upham, an executive of the magazine who died in 1910. A leaflet circulated by the magazine later named Upham as the originator of the draft "afterwards condensed and perfected by him and his associates of the Companion force."

Francis Bellamy, a former member of the Youth's Companion editorial staff, publicly claimed authorship of the pledge in 1923. The United States Flag Assn., acting on the advice of a committee named to study the controversy, upheld in 1939 the claim of Bellamy, who had died 8 years earlier. The Library of Congress issued in 1957 a report attributing the authorship to Bellamy.

The National Anthem — The Star-Spangled Banner

The Star-Spangled Banner was ordered played by the military and naval services by President Woodrow Wilson in 1916. It was designated the National Anthem by Act of Congress, Mar. 3, 1931. It was written by Francis Scott Key, of Georgetown, D. C., during the bombardment of Fort McHenry, Baltimore, Md., Sept. 13-14, 1814. Key was a lawyer, a graduate of St. John's College, Annapolis, and a volunteer in a light artillery company. When a friend, Dr. Beanes, a physician of Upper Marlborough, Md., was taken aboard Admiral Cockburn's British squadron for interfering with ground troops, Key and J. S. Skinner, carrying a note from President Madison, went to the fleet under a flag of truce on a cartel ship to ask Beanes' release. Admiral Cockburn consented, but as the fleet was about to sail up the Patapsco to bombard Fort McHenry he detained them, first on H. M. S. Surprise, and then on a supply ship.

Key witnessed the bombardment from his own vessel. It began at 7 a.m., Sept. 13, 1814, and lasted, with intermissions, for 25 hours. The British fired over 1,500 shells, each weighing as much as 220 lbs. They were unable to approach closely because the Americans had sunk 22 vessels in the channel. Only four Americans were killed and 24 wounded. A British bomb-ship was disabled.

During the bombardment Key wrote a stanza on the back of an envelope. Next day at Indian Queen Inn, Baltimore, he wrote out the poem and gave it to his brother-in-law, Judge J. H. Nicholson. Nicholson suggested the tune. Anacreon in Heaven, and had the poem printed on broadsides, of which two survive. On Sept. 20 it appeared in the "Baltimore American." Later Key made 3 copies; one is in the Library of Congress and one in the Pennsylvania Historical Society.

The copy that Key wrote in his hotel Sept. 14, 1814, remained in the Nicholson family for 93 years. In 1907 it was sold to Henry Walters of Baltimore. In 1934 it was bought at auction in New York from the Walters estate by the Walters Art Gallery, Baltimore, for $26,400. The Walters Gallery in 1953 sold the manuscript to the Maryland Historical Society for the same price.

The flag that Key saw during the bombardment is preserved in the Smithsonian Institution, Washington. It is 30 by 42 ft., and has 15 alternate red and white stripes and 15 stars, for the original 13 states plus Kentucky and Vermont. It was made by Mary Young Pickersgill. The Baltimore Flag House, a museum, occupies her premises, which were restored in 1953.

The Star-Spangled Banner

I

Oh, say can you see by the dawn's early light
  What so proudly we hailed at the twilight's last gleaming?
Whose broad stripes and bright stars thru the perilous fight,
  O'er the ramparts we watched were so gallantly streaming?
And the rocket's red glare, the bombs bursting in air,
  Gave proof through the night that our flag was still there.
Oh, say does that star-spangled banner yet wave
  O'er the land of the free and the home of the brave?

II

On the shore, dimly seen through the mists of the deep,
  Where the foe's haughty host in dread silence reposes,
What is that which the breeze, o'er the towering steep,
  As it fitfully blows, half conceals, half discloses?
Now it catches the gleam of the morning's first beam,
  In full glory reflected now shines in the stream:
Tis the star-spangled banner! Oh long may it wave
  O'er the land of the free and the home of the brave!

III

And where is that band who so vauntingly swore
  That the havoc of war and the battle's confusion,
A home and a country should leave us no more!
  Their blood has washed out their foul footsteps' pollution.
No refuge could save the hireling and slave
  From the terror of flight, or the gloom of the grave:
And the star-spangled banner in triumph doth wave
  O'er the land of the free and the home of the brave!

IV

Oh! thus be it ever, when freemen shall stand
  Between their loved home and the war's desolation!
Blest with victory and peace, may the heav'n rescued land
  Praise the Power that hath made and preserved us a nation.
Then conquer we must, when our cause it is just,
  And this be our motto: "In God is our trust."
And the star-spangled banner in triumph shall wave
  O'er the land of the free and the home of the brave!

America
(My Country 'Tis of Thee)

First sung in public on July 4, 1831, at a service in the Park Street Church, Boston, the words were written by Rev. Samuel Francis Smith, a Baptist clergyman, who set them to a melody he found in a German songbook, unaware that it was the tune for the British anthem, "God Save the King/Queen."

My country, 'tis of thee,
Sweet land of liberty, Of thee I sing.
Land where my fathers died!
Land of the Pilgrims' pride!
From ev'ry mountainside,
Let freedom ring!

My native country, thee,
Land of the noble free,
Thy name I love.
I love thy rocks and rills,
Thy woods and templed hills;
My heart with rapture thrills
Like that above.

Let music swell the breeze,
And ring from all the trees
Sweet freedom's song.
Let mortal tongues awake;
Let all that breathe partake;
Let rocks their silence break,
The sound prolong.

Our fathers' God, to Thee,
Author of liberty,
To Thee we sing.
Long may our land be bright
With freedom's holy light;
Protect us by Thy might,
Great God, our King!

America, the Beautiful

Composed by Katherine Lee Bates, a Massachusetts educator and author, in 1893. It was inspired by the view Bates experienced atop Pike's Peak. Its final form was established in 1911 and is set to the music of Samuel A. Ward's "Materna."

O beautiful for spacious skies,
For amber waves of grain,
For purple mountain majesties
Above the fruited plain.
America! America!
God shed His grace on thee,
And crown thy good with brotherhood
From sea to shining sea.
    O beautiful for pilgrim feet
Whose stern impassion'd stress
A thorough-fare for freedom beat
Across the wilderness.
America! America!
God mend thine ev'ry flaw,
Confirm thy soul in self control,
Thy liberty in law.

O beautiful for heroes prov'd
In liberating strife,
Who more than self their country lov'd
And mercy more than life.
America! America!
May God thy gold refine
Till all success be nobleness,
And ev'ry gain divine.
    O beautiful for patriot dream
That sees beyond the years,
Thine alabaster cities gleam,
Undimmed by human tears.
America! America!
God shed His grace on thee,
And crown thy good with brotherhood
From sea to shining sea.

The Liberty Bell: Its History and Significance

The Liberty Bell, in Independence Hall, Philadelphia, is an object of great reverence to Americans because of its association with the historic events of the War of Independence.

The original Province bell, ordered to commemorate the 50th anniversary of the Commonwealth of Pennsylvania, was cast by Thomas Lister, Whitechapel, London, and reached Philadelphia in Aug. 1752. It bore an inscription from Leviticus XXV, 10: "Proclaim liberty throughout all the land unto all the inhabitants thereof."

The bell was cracked by a stroke of its clapper in Sept. 1752 while it hung on a truss in the State House yard for testing. Pass & Stow, Philadelphia founders, recast the bell, adding 1 1/2 ounces of copper to a pound of the original metal to reduce brittleness. It was found that the bell contained too much copper, injuring its tone, so Pass & Stow recast it again, this time successfully.

In June 1753 the bell was hung in the wooden steeple of the State House, erected on top of the brick tower. In use while the Continental Congress was in session in the State House, it rang out in defiance of British tax and trade restrictions, and proclaimed the Boston Tea Party and the first public reading of the Declaration of Independence.

On Sept. 18, 1777, when the British Army was about to occupy Philadelphia, the bell was moved in a baggage train of the American Army to Allentown, Pa. where it was hidden in the Zion Reformed Church until June 27, 1778. It was moved back to Philadelphia after the British left.

In July 1781 the wooden steeple became insecure and had to be taken down. The bell was lowered into the brick section of the tower. Here it was hanging in July, 1835, when it cracked while tolling for the funeral of John Marshall, chief justice of the United States. Because of its association with the War of Independence it was not recast but remained mute in this location until 1846, the year of the Mexican War, when it was placed on exhibition in the Declaration Chamber of Independence Hall.

In 1876, when many thousands of Americans visited Philadelphia for the Centennial Exposition, it was placed in its old walnut frame in the tower hallway. In 1877 it was hung from the ceiling of the tower by a chain of 13 links. It was returned again to the Declaration Chamber and in 1896 taken back to the tower hall, where it occupied a glass case. In 1915 the case was removed so that the public might touch it. On Jan. 1, 1976, just after midnight to mark the opening of the Bicentennial Year, the bell was moved to a new glass and steel pavilion behind Independence Hall for easier viewing by the larger number of visitors expected during the year.

The measurements of the bell follow: circumference around the lip, 12 ft.; circumference around the crown, 7 ft. 6 in.; lip to the crown, 3 ft.; height over the crown, 2 ft. 3 in.; thickness at lip, 3 in.; thickness at crown, 1 1/4 in.; weight, 2080 lbs.; length of clapper, 3 ft. 2 in.; cost, £60 14s 5d.

Statue of Liberty National Monument

Since 1886, the Statue of Liberty Enlightening the World has stood as a symbol of freedom in New York harbor. It also commemorates French-American friendship for it was given by the people of France, designed by Frederic Auguste Bartholdi (1834-1904). A $2.5 million building housing the American Museum of Immigration was opened by Pres. Nixon Sept. 26, 1972, at the base of the statue. It houses a permanent exhibition of photos, posters, and artifacts tracing the history of American immigration. The Monument is administered by the National Park Service.

Nearby Ellis Island, gateway to America for more than 12 million immigrants between 1892 and 1954, was proclaimed part of the National Monument in 1965 by Pres. Johnson.

Edouard de Laboulaye, French historian and admirer of American political institutions, suggested that the French present a monument to the United States, the latter to provide pedestal and site. Bartholdi visualized a colossal statue at the entrance of New York harbor, welcoming the peoples of the world with the torch of liberty.

On Washington's birthday, Feb. 22, 1877, Congress approved the use of a site on Bedloe's Island suggested by Bartholdi. This island of 12 acres had been owned in the 17th century by a Walloon named Isaac Bedloe. It was called Bedloe's until Aug. 3, 1956, when Pres. Eisenhower approved a resolution of Congress changing the name to Liberty Island.

The statue was finished May 21, 1884, and formally presented to U.S. Minister Morton July 4, 1884, by Ferdinand de Lesseps, head of the Franco-American Union, promoter of the Panama Canal, and builder of the Suez Canal.

On Aug. 5, 1884, the Americans laid the cornerstone for the pedestal. This was to be built on the foundations of Fort Wood, which had been erected by the Government in 1811. The American committee had raised $125,000, but this was found to be inadequate. Joseph Pulitzer, owner of the New York World, appealed on Mar. 16, 1885, for general donations. By Aug. 11, 1885, he had raised $100,000.

The statue arrived dismantled, in 214 packing cases, from Rouen, France, in June, 1885. The last rivet of the statue was driven Oct. 28, 1886, when Pres. Grover Cleveland dedicated the monument.

The statue weighs 450,000 lbs. or 225 tons. The copper sheeting weighs 200,000 lbs. There are 167 steps from the land level to the top of the pedestal, 168 steps inside the statue to the head, and 54 rungs on the ladder leading to the arm that holds the torch.

Two years of restoration work was completed before the statue's centennial celebration on July 4, 1986. Among other repairs, the multi-million dollar project included replacing the 1,600 wrought iron bands that hold its copper skin to its frame, replacing its torch, and installing an elevator.

A four-day extravaganza of concerts, tall ships, ethnic festivals, and fireworks celebrated the 100th anniversary. The festivities included Chief Justice Warren E. Burger's swearing-in of 5,000 new citizens on Ellis Island, while 20,000 others across the country were simultaneously sworn in through a satellite telecast.

The ceremonies were followed by others on Oct. 28, 1986, the statue's 100th birthday.

Emma Lazarus' Famous Poem

A poem by Emma Lazarus is graven on a tablet within the pedestal on which the statue stands.

The New Colossus

Not like the brazen giant of Greek fame,
With conquering limbs astride from land to land;
Here at our sea-washed, sunset gates shall stand
A mighty woman with a torch, whose flame
Is the imprisoned lightning, and her name
Mother of Exiles. From her beacon-hand
Glows world-wide welcome; her mild eyes command
The air-bridged harbor that twin cities frame.
"Keep ancient lands, your storied pomp!" cries she
With silent lips. "Give me your tired, your poor,
Your huddled masses yearning to breathe free,
The wretched refuse of your teeming shore.
Send these, the homeless, tempest-tost to me,
I lift my lamp beside the golden door!"

Dimensions of the Statue	Ft.	In.
Height from base to torch (45.3 meters)	151	1
Foundation of pedestal to torch (91.5 meters)	305	1
Heel to top of head	111	1
Length of hand	16	5
Index finger	8	0
Circumference at second joint	3	6
Size of finger nail . . . . 13x10 in.		
Head from chin to cranium	17	3
Head thickness from ear to ear	10	0
Distance across the eye	2	6
Length of nose	4	6
Right arm, length	42	0
Right arm, greatest thickness	12	0
Thickness of waist	35	0
Width of mouth	3	0
Tablet, length	23	7
Tablet, width	13	7
Tablet, thickness	2	0

Lincoln's Address at Gettysburg, 1863

Fourscore and seven years ago our fathers brought forth on this continent a new nation, conceived in liberty and dedicated to the proposition that all men are created equal.

Now we are engaged in a great civil war, testing whether that nation or any nation so conceived and so dedicated can long endure. We are met on a great battle field of that war. We have come to dedicate a portion of that field, as a final resting-place for those who here gave their lives that that nation might live. It is altogether fitting and proper that we should do this.

But, in a larger sense, we can not dedicate — we can not consecrate — we can not hallow — this ground. The brave men, living and dead, who struggled here, have consecrated it, far above our poor power to add or detract. The world will little note, nor long remember, what we say here, but it can never forget what they did here. It is for us the living, rather, to be dedicated here to the unfinished work which they who fought here have thus far so nobly advanced. It is rather for us to be here dedicated to the great task remaining before us — that from these honored dead we take increased devotion to that cause for which they gave the last full measure of devotion — that we here highly resolve that these dead shall not have died in vain — that this nation, under God, shall have a new birth of freedom — and that government of the people, by the people, for the people, shall not perish from the earth.

Confederate States and Secession

The American Civil War, 1861-65, grew out of sectional disputes over the continued existence of slavery in the South and the contention of Southern legislators that the states retained many sovereign rights, including the right to secede from the Union.

The war was not fought by state against state but by one federal regime against another, the Confederate government in Richmond assuming control over the economic, political, and military life of the South, under protest from Georgia and South Carolina.

South Carolina voted an ordinance of secession from the Union, repealing its 1788 ratification of the U.S. Constitution on Dec. 20, 1860, to take effect Dec. 24. Other states seceded in 1861. Their votes in conventions were:

Mississippi, Jan. 9, 84-15; Florida, Jan. 10, 62-7; Alabama, Jan. 11, 61-39; Georgia, Jan. 19, 208-89; Louisiana, Jan. 26, 113-17; Texas, Feb. 1, 166-7, ratified by popular vote Feb. 23 (for 34,794, against 11,325); Virginia, Apr. 17, 88-55, ratified by popular vote May 23 (for 128,884; against

32,134); Arkansas, May 6, 69-1; Tennessee, May 7, ratified by popular vote June 8 (for 104,019, against 47,238); North Carolina, May 21.

Missouri Unionists stopped secession in conventions Feb. 28 and Mar. 9. The legislature condemned secession Mar. 7. Under the protection of Confederate troops, secessionist members of the legislature adopted a resolution of secession at Neosho, Oct. 31. The Confederate Congress seated the secessionists' representatives.

Kentucky did not secede and its government remained Unionist. In a part occupied by Confederate troops, Kentuckians approved secession and the Confederate Congress admitted their representatives.

The Maryland legislature voted against secession Apr. 27, 53-13. Delaware did not secede. Western Virginia held conventions at Wheeling, named a pro-Union governor June 11, 1861; admitted to Union as West Virginia June 20, 1863; its constitution provided for gradual abolition of slavery.

Confederate Government

Forty-two delegates from South Carolina, Georgia, Alabama, Mississippi, Louisiana, and Florida met in convention at Montgomery, Ala., Feb. 4, 1861. They adopted a provisional constitution of the Confederate States of America, and elected Jefferson Davis (Miss.) provisional president, and Alexander H. Stephens (Ga.) provisional vice president.

A permanent constitution was adopted Mar. 11; it abolished the African slave trade. The Congress moved to Richmond, Va. July 20. Davis was elected president in October,

and was inaugurated Feb. 22, 1862.

The Congress adopted a flag, consisting of a red field with a white stripe, and a blue jack with a circle of white stars. Later the more popular flag was the red field with blue diagonal cross bars that held 13 white stars. The stars represented the 11 states actually in the Confederacy plus Kentucky and Missouri.

(See also Civil War, U.S., in Index)

The Mayflower Compact

The threat of James I to "harry them out of the land" sent a little band of religious dissenters from England to Holland in 1608. They were known as "Separatists" because they wished to cut all ties with the Established Church. In 1620, some of them, known now as the Pilgrims, joined with a larger group in England to set sail on the *Mayflower* for the New World. A joint stock company financed their venture.

In November, they sighted Cape Cod and decided to land an exploring party at Plymouth Harbor. However, a rebellious group picked up at Southampton and London troubled the Pilgrim leaders, and to control their actions forty-one of the Pilgrims drew up the "Mayflower Compact," which was signed before going ashore. The voluntary agreement to govern themselves was America's first written constitution.

In the name of God, Amen. We, whose names are underwritten, the Loyal Subjects of our dread Sovereign Lord, King *James*, by the Grace of God, of *Great Britain, France and Ireland*, King, *Defender of the Faith*, etc.

Having undertaken for the Glory of God, and Advancement of the Christian Faith, and the Honour of our King and Country, a voyage to plant the first colony in the northern Parts of Virginia; do by these Presents, solemnly and mutually in the Presence of God and one of another, covenant and combine ouselves together into a civil Body Politick, for our better Ordering and Preservation, and Further-

ance of the Ends aforesaid; And by Virtue hereof to enact, constitute, and frame, such just and equal Laws, Ordinances, Acts, Constitutions and Offices, from time to time, as shall be thought most meet and convenient for the General good of the Colony; unto which we promise all due Submission and Obedience.

In Witness whereof we have hereunto subscribed our names at *Cape Cod* the eleventh of *November*, in the Reign of our Sovereign Lord, King *James* of *England, France* and *Ireland*, the eighteenth, and of *Scotland* the fifty-fourth. *Anno Domini, 1620.*

Forms of Address for Persons of Rank and Public Office

In these examples John Smith is used as a representative American name. The salutation Dear Sir or Dear Madam is always permissible when addressing a person not known to the writer. Female equivalents should be substituted where appropriate.

President of the United States

Address: The President, The White House, Washington, DC 20500. Also, The President and Mrs. _____.
Salutation: Dear Sir or Mr. President or Dear Mr. President. More intimately: My dear Mr. President. Also: Dear Mr. President and Mrs. _____.
The vice president takes the same forms.

Cabinet Officers

Address: Mr. John Smith, Secretary of State, Washington, D.C. or The Hon. John Smith. Similar addresses for other members of the cabinet. Also: Secretary and Mrs. John Smith.
Salutation: Dear Sir, or Dear Mr. Secretary. Also: Dear Mr. and Mrs. Smith.

The Bench

Address: The Hon. John Smith, Chief Justice of the United States. The Hon. John Smith, Associate Justice of the Supreme Court of the United States. The Hon. John Smith, Associate Judge, U.S. District Court.
Salutation: Dear Sir, or Dear Mr. Chief Justice. Dear Mr. Justice. Dear Judge Smith.

Members of Congress

Address: The Hon. John Smith, United States Senate, Washington, DC 20510, or Sen. John Smith, etc. Also The Hon. John Smith, House of Representatives, Washington, DC 20515, or Rep. John Smith, etc.
Salutation: Dear Mr. Senator or Dear Mr. Smith; for Representative, Dear Mr. Smith.

Officers of Armed Forces

Address: Careful attention should be given to the precise rank, thus: General of the Army John Smith, Fleet Admiral John Smith. The rules for Air Force are same as Army.
Salutation: Dear Sir, or Dear General. All general officers, whatever rank, are entitled to be addressed as generals. Likewise a lieutenant colonel is addressed as colonel and first and second lieutenants are addressed as lieutenant.

Warrant officers and flight officers are addressed as Mister. Chaplains are addressed as Chaplain. A Catholic chaplain may be addressed as Father. Students of the U.S. Military Academy and Air Force Academy are addressed as Cadet, students of the U.S. Naval Academy are addressed as Midshipman/woman. Noncommissioned officers are addressed by their titles.

Ambassador, Governor, Mayor

Address: The Hon. John Smith, followed by his or her title. They can be addressed either at their embassy, or at the Department of State, Washington, D.C. An ambassador from a foreign nation may be addressed as His or Her Excellency. An American is not to be so addressed.
Salutation: Dear Mr. or Madam Ambassador. An ambassador from a foreign nation may be called Your Excellency.

Governors and mayors are often addressed as The Hon. Jane Smith, Governor of _____, or The Hon. John Smith, Mayor of _____; also Governor John Smith, State House, Albany, N.Y., or Mayor Jane Smith, City Hall, Erie, Pa.

The Clergy

Address: His Holiness, the Pope, or His Holiness Pope (name), State of Vatican City, Italy.
Salutation: Your Holiness or Most Holy Father.

Also: His Eminence, John, Cardinal Smith; salutation: Your Eminence. An archbishop or a bishop is addressed The Most Reverend, and the salutation is Your Excellency. A monsignor who is a papal chamberlain is The Very Reverend Monsignor and the salutation is Dear Sir or Very Reverend Monsignor; a monsignor who is a domestic prelate is The Right Reverend Monsignor and salutation is Right Reverend Monsignor. A priest is addressed Reverend John Smith. A brother of an order is addressed Brother ——. A sister takes the same form.

A bishop of the Episcopal Church is The Right Reverend John Smith; salutation is Right Reverend Sir, or Dear Bishop Smith. If a clergyman is a doctor of divinity, he is addressed: The Reverend John Smith, D.D., and the salutation is Reverend Sir, or Dear Dr. Smith. When a clergyman does not have the degree the salutation is Dear Mr. Smith.

A bishop of the Methodist Church is addressed Bishop John Smith with titles following.

Royalty and Nobility

An emperor is to be addressed in a letter as Sir, or Your Imperial Majesty.

A king or queen is addressed as His Majesty (Name), King of (Name), or Her Majesty (Name), Queen of (Name), Salutation: Sir, or Madam, or May it please Your Majesty.

Princes and princesses and other persons of royal blood are addressed as His (or Her) Royal Highness, and saluted with May it please Your Royal Highness.

A duke or marquis is My Lord Duke (or Marquis), a duke is His (or Your) Grace.

AFGHANISTAN	ALBANIA	ALGERIA	ANGOLA	ANTIGUA AND BARBUDA
ARGENTINA	AUSTRALIA	AUSTRIA	THE BAHAMAS	BAHRAIN
BANGLADESH	BARBADOS	BELGIUM	BELIZE	BENIN
BHUTAN	BOLIVIA	BOTSWANA	BRAZIL	BRUNEI DARUSSALAM
BULGARIA	BURKINA FASO	BURUNDI	CAMBODIA	CAMEROON
CANADA	CAPE VERDE	CENTRAL AFRICAN REPUBLIC	CHAD	CHILE
CHINA	COLOMBIA	COMOROS	CONGO	COSTA RICA
COTE D'IVOIRE	CUBA	CYPRUS	CZECHOSLOVAKIA	DENMARK
DJIBOUTI	DOMINICA	DOMINICAN REPUBLIC	ECUADOR	EGYPT
EL SALVADOR	EQUATORIAL GUINEA	ETHIOPIA	FIJI	FINLAND
FRANCE	GABON	THE GAMBIA	GERMANY	GHANA

F2

GREECE GRENADA GUATEMALA GUINEA GUINEA-BISSAU

GUYANA HAITI HONDURAS HUNGARY ICELAND

INDIA INDONESIA IRAN IRAQ IRELAND

ISRAEL ITALY JAMAICA JAPAN JORDAN

KENYA NORTH KOREA SOUTH KOREA KUWAIT LAOS

LEBANON LESOTHO LIBERIA LIBYA LIECHTENSTEIN

LUXEMBOURG MADAGASCAR MALAWI MALAYSIA MALDIVES

MALI MALTA MAURITANIA MAURITIUS MEXICO

MONACO MONGOLIA MOROCCO MOZAMBIQUE MYANMAR (BURMA)

NAMIBIA NEPAL NETHERLANDS NEW ZEALAND NICARAGUA

NIGER NIGERIA NORWAY OMAN PAKISTAN

PANAMA — PAPUA NEW GUINEA — PARAGUAY — PERU — PHILIPPINES

POLAND — PORTUGAL — QATAR — ROMANIA — RWANDA

ST. KITTS AND NEVIS — SAINT LUCIA — ST. VINCENT AND THE GRENADINES — SAN MARINO — SAO TOME AND PRINCIPE

SAUDI ARABIA — SENEGAL — SEYCHELLES — SIERRA LEONE — SINGAPORE

SOLOMON ISLANDS — SOMALIA — SOUTH AFRICA — SPAIN — SRI LANKA

SUDAN — SURINAME — SWAZILAND — SWEDEN — SWITZERLAND

SYRIA — TAIWAN — TANZANIA — THAILAND — TOGO

TONGA — TRINIDAD AND TOBAGO — TUNISIA — TURKEY — UGANDA

U.S.S.R. (SOVIET UNION) — UNITED ARAB EMIRATES — UNITED KINGDOM — UNITED STATES — URUGUAY

VANUATU — VATICAN CITY — VENEZUELA — VIETNAM — WESTERN SAMOA

YEMEN — YUGOSLAVIA — ZAIRE — ZAMBIA — ZIMBABWE

M4

INTERNATIONAL TIME ZONES

The world is divided into 24 time zones, each 15° longitude wide. The longitudinal meridian passing through Greenwich, England, is the starting point, and is called the *prime meridian*. The 12th zone is divided by the 180th meridian (International Date Line). When the line is crossed going west, the date is advanced one day; when crossed going east, the date becomes a day earlier.

© The World Almanac and Book of Facts, 1992

NORTH AMERICA

M5

SOVIET UNION

ARCTIC OCEAN

ICELAND

Greenland (Kalaallit Nunaat) (Denmark)

CANADA

UNITED STATES

PACIFIC OCEAN

ATLANTIC OCEAN

MEXICO

Gulf of Mexico

CUBA

Caribbean Sea

SOUTH AMERICA

Elevation

Meters	Feet
4,000	13,120
2,000	6,560
500	1,640
200	656
0	0
Below Sea Level	Below Sea Level

0   250   500   750   1000 Miles

0   250   500   1000 1200 Kilometers

© The World Almanac and Book of Facts, 1992

Tropic of Cancer

ATLANTIC

OCEAN

Equator

THE
BAHAMAS

Turks & Caicos Is. (U.K.)

Virgin
Islands (U.S., U.K.)
Anguilla (U.K.)
ANTIGUA & BARBUDA
Guadeloupe (Fr.)
DOMINICA
Martinique (Fr.)
SAINT LUCIA
BARBADOS
ST. VINCENT &
THE GRENADINES
GRENADA
TRINIDAD
& TOBAGO

Havana
CUBA
Santa Clara
Camaguey
Holguin
Guantanamo
Cap-Haitien
DOMINICAN
REPUBLIC
Pico Duarte
10,417
San
Juan
Ponce
Puerto
Rico
(U.S.)

Isle of
Youth
Cienfuegos
Santiago de Cuba
Montego Bay
JAMAICA
Kingston
Santiago
HAITI
Port-au-Prince
Santo
Domingo

Cayman
Is. (U.K.)

Caribbean
Sea

Curaçao
(Neth.)
Aruba
(Neth.)
Bonaire
(Neth.)

Pico Cristobal Colon
18,947

Maracaibo

Lake
Maracaibo

Coro
Maracay
Valencia
Caracas
Barquisimeto
Barcelona
Cumaná
Maturín
El Tigre
Ciudad
Guayana
Ciudad
Bolívar

Port-of-
Spain

Margarita
Island

Georgetown
New Amsterdam
Paramaribo
GUYANA
SURINAME
French
Guiana
(Fr.)
Cayenne
Kourou

Mt. Roraima
9,094

VENEZUELA

GUIANA
HIGHLANDS

Angel Falls

Orinoco

Puerto
Ayacucho

San Fernando
de Apure

Boa Vista

Macapá

Marajó
Island

BRAZIL

Belém

Santarém

Manaus

Amazon

SELVAS

MATO
GROSSO

Xingu

Tapajós

Madeira

São Luis

Parnaiba

Teresina

Fortaleza

Natal
Joao
Pessoa
Recife
Maceió
Aracaju
Salvador

Feira de Santana

Vitoria da

Juazeiro do Norte
Campina Grande

BRAZILIAN

Gurupi

Imperatriz

Tocantins

São Francisco

MEXICO
BELIZE
Belize City
Belmopan
Volcan
Tajumulco
13,845
GUATEMALA
Guatemala
Santa Ana El
Esquintla
SALVADOR
San Salvador
HONDURAS
Gulf of
Honduras
San Pedro Sula
Cerro Las Minas 9,347
Tegucigalpa
NICARAGUA
Leon
Managua
Granada
Lake
Nicaragua
Volcan Irazu 11,260
COSTA RICA
San Jose
Puntarenas
Volcan Baru
11,401
David
Limon
PANAMA
Panama
Colon
MOSQUITO
COAST
ISTHMUS OF
PANAMA
Gulf of
Panama

Buenaventura
COLOMBIA
Cali
Pasto
Quito
ECUADOR

Esmeraldas
Portoviejo
Manta
Guayaquil
Machala
Cuenca
Ambato
Cotopaxi 19,347
Chimborazo 20,561

Galapagos
Islands
(Ecuador)

Equator

PACIFIC

Medellín
Manizales
Pereira
Armenia
Cartagena
Barranquilla
Santa Marta
Sincelejo
Monteria
Cúcuta
Barrancabermeja
Valledupar
Bucaramanga
San Cristóbal
Mérida
Valera
Bogotá
Tunja
Villavicencio
Ibague
Palmira
Neiva
Popayan
Nevada del Huila
18,865

A N D E S

Cajamarca
Trujillo
Chiclayo
Talara
Sullana
Piura
Tumbes
Aguja
Point
Chimbote
Nev. Huascaran
22,205
Nev. Yerupaja
21,709
Callao
Lima
PERU
LA MONTAÑA
Iquitos
Yurimaguas
Moyobamba
Pucallpa
Huánuco
Cerro
de Pasco
Huancayo
Ayacucho
Cuzco
Ica

Marañón
Ucayali
Putumayo
Napo
Juruá
Purus

Cruzeiro do Sul
Benjamin
Constant
Rio Branco
Porto Velho
Guajara-Mirim
Riberalta
Cobija
Puerto
Maldonado
Trinidad

Madre
Beni
Mamore

Negro

Manicore

M10

EUROPE

Elevation

Meters	Feet
4,000	13,120
2,000	6,560
500	1,640
200	656
0	0
Below Sea Level	Below Sea Level

ATLANTIC OCEAN

Greenland (Den.)

Keflavik · Akureyri
Reykjavik · ICELAND
Hekla 4,892

Norwegian Sea

Faeroe Is. (Den.)

Shetland Is. (U.K.)

Orkney Is.

Hebrides

Inverness
Aberdeen
Dundee
Edinburgh
Glasgow
Belfast · **UNITED**
IRELAND · Newcastle
Dublin · **KINGDOM**
Liverpool · Leeds
Cork · Limerick · **Manchester** · Sheffield
Birmingham
Cardiff · **London**
Bristol
Land's End · Portsmouth
English Channel · Channel Is. (U.K.)
Plymouth · Le Havre · Rouen
Brest · Nantes · **Paris**
Tours · Orleans
FRANCE · Dijon
Limoges
Bordeaux · Lyon
Grenoble
Toulouse
Marseille · Nice
PYRENEES

North Cape
Hammerfest
Tromso
Ivalo
LAPLAND
Bodo · Kiruna · Rovaniemi
Lulea · Oulu
NORWAY
Trondheim · Ostersund · Umea · Vaasa · Kuopio
Alesund · **FINLAND**
SWEDEN · Tampere
Bergen · Glittertind 8,113 · Gavle · Aland Is. (Fin.) · Turku · **Helsinki**
Oslo · Uppsala
Skien · **Stockholm**
Stavanger · Kristiansand · Linkoping · Jonkoping · Gotland (Swe.)
Goteborg
Alborg · Jutland · Helsingborg
Copenhagen · Malmo
DENMARK · Odense · Bornholm (Den.)
Rostock · Gdansk
Hamburg · Szczecin · **POLAND** · Bialystok
NETHERLANDS · Bremen · **Berlin** · Poznan · **Warsaw**
Amsterdam · Hannover · Magdeburg · Leipzig
Hague · **Essen** · **Cologne** · Dresden · Wroclaw · **Katowice** · Lublin
Brussels · Bonn · **GERMANY** · Prague · Ostrava · **Kracow**
BELGIUM · Frankfurt · Nurnberg · **CZECHO.** · Brno · Kosice
Luxembourg · **LUX.** · Mannheim
Strasbourg · **Stuttgart** · **Munich** · Linz · **Vienna** · Bratislava · Miskolc
Basel · Zurich · Salzburg · **AUSTRIA** · Debrecen · Iasi
Bern · **SWITZ.** · Graz · **HUNGARY** · **Budapest** · Cluj-Napoca · **ROMANIA**
Geneva · Mt. Blanc · Matterhorn 14,690 · Ljubljana · Zagreb · Pecs · Timisoara · Brasov
Turin · **Milan** · Trieste · **Belgrade** · **Bucharest**
Genoa · Verona · Venice · **YUGOSLAVIA** · **BALKAN** · Ruse · Constanta
Bologna · Sarajevo · Danube · Varna
SAN MARINO · Split · Drubrovnik · **Skopje** · **Sofia** · Plovdiv · Burgas
Florence · **APENNINES** · Tirana · **BULGARIA**
Rome · Bari · **ALBANIA** · Olympus 9,570 · **Thessaloniki**
Naples · Vesuvius 4,202 · Vlore · Larisa · Volos · **TURKEY**
ITALY · Corfu · **GREECE** · **Athens**
Palermo · Messina · Etna 11,053 · Catania
Sicily · **MALTA** · Ionian Sea · Patras · Peloponnesus · Rhodes
Sardinia (It.) · Cagliari · *Tyrrhenian Sea*
Corsica (Fr.) · Ajaccio · Elba · MONACO
Iraklion · Crete

North Sea

Baltic Sea
Gulf of Bothnia
Gulf of Finland

SOVIET UNION

CARPATHIAN MOUNTAINS
DINARIC ALPS

Bay of Biscay

La Coruna · Gijon
Vigo
Oporto
Coimbra · Valladolid · San Sebastian · Bilbao · Pico de Aneto 11,168 · **ANDORRA**
PORTUGAL · IBERIAN · **Madrid** · Zaragoza · **Barcelona**
Lisbon · Tagus · **SPAIN** · PENINSULA
Cape St. Vincent · Cordoba · **Valencia** · Palma · Balearic Is. (Sp.)
Seville · Granada · Alicante
Cadiz · **Malaga** · Gibraltar (U.K.)
Strait of Gibraltar

AFRICA

Mediterranean Sea

1. Slovenia
2. Croatia
3. Bosnia and Hercegovina
4. Serbia
5. Montenegro
6. Macedonia

© The World Almanac and Book of Facts, 1992

0 · 250 · 500 Miles
0 · 250 · 500 · 750 Kilometers

SOVIET UNION & BALTIC STATES

M11

© The World Almanac and Book of Facts, 1992

M12

Istanbul
Izmir •Bursa
Ankara
Konya •Samsun
TURKEY •Trabzon
Nicosia •Adana •Erzurum
Mersin
CYPRUS
Latakia •Diyarbakir
Beirut Mt. Ararat 16,804
ISRAEL• LEBANON
Tel Aviv–SYRIA Mosul
Yafo Damascus •Arbil
Jerusalem• SYRIAN Karkuk
Amman JORDAN DESERT
Dead Sea
1,312 IRAQ
Lowest Aqaba Baghdad Bakhtaran
point in •Tabuk Al Hillah Al Hilah
Asia

Tabriz
Lake Van
Lake Urmia

Rasht

Mt. Damavand 18,606

Teheran
Qom •Gorgan
Esfahan
Yazd

SOVIET UNION

Yining
Urumqi
Pobedy Peak 24,406
Kashi
Shache TAKLIMAKAN DESERT

KUNLUN MOUNTA

AN NAFUD
•Hail
Medina
Buraydah
Jidda
Mecca
At Taif
SAUDI
ARABIA
Abha

Basra
Abadan
Kuwait
KUWAIT
Shiraz
Riyadh
Ad Dammam
BAHRAIN
Al Hufuf
QATAR
Abu Dhabi Doha
UNITED Dubai
ARAB
EMIRATES Muscat
Sanaa
Al Hudaydah
YEMEN
Aden Al Mukalla

ZAGROS MOUNTAINS

DASHT-E
KAVIR
Mashhad
DASHT-E LUT

IRAN

Birjand

Kerman

Zahedan

Bandar Abbas
OMAN
Gulf
Ras al Hadd Sur
Gulf of Oman

OMAN

Salalah

Herat
Mazar-e
Sharif
AFGHANISTAN
Farah
Kabul
Qandahar
Quetta

Chitral
Peshawar
Islamabad
Rawalpindi Srinagar
Faisalabad
PAKISTAN Lahore
Multan Chandigarh
Sukkur Indus
Turbat THAR
DESERT
Jaipur
Karachi Jodhpur Agra
Hyderabad
Ahmedabad Allahabad
Indore Bhopal
Rajkot
Surat DECCAN
Nagpur PLATEAU
Bombay Poona INDIA
Sholapur Hyderabad
Panaji
Hubli
WESTERN GHATS Vijayawada
Bangalore
Mysore
Coimbatore
Cochin Madurai
Trivandrum
Cape Comorin
Male
MALDIVES

K2 28,250
PLATEAU OF TIBE
HIMALAY
Delhi
New
Delhi NEPAL Pokhara
Kanpur Mt. Everest 2
Lucknow Kathmandu
Varanasi Darj
Patna
Jabalpur Asansol
Ranchi
Raipur Khulna
Calcutta
Cuttack
Vishakhapatnam
EASTERN GHATS
Madras
Trincomalee
SRI LANKA
Colombo
Galle

Mediterranean Sea

Red Sea

RUB AL KHALI

Gulf of Aden

AFRICA

Socotra
(Yemen)

Arabian
Sea

10°

Euphrates

Persian Gulf

Black Sea

ASIA MINOR

30°

40°

60°

70°

80°

ELBURZ MTS.

Caspian Sea

HINDU KUSH

Tropic of Cancer

Bay of
Bengal

Chagos
Archipelago
(U.K.)

Equator

INDIAN

OCEAN

SOUTH ASIA

Elevation

Meters		Feet
4,000		13,120
2,000		6,560
500		1,640
200		656
0		0
Below Sea Level		Below Sea Level

0	250	500	750	1,000 Miles
0	250	500	750	1,000	1,250 Kilometers

0°

70°

20°

60°

70°

80°

90°

© The World Almanac and Book of Facts, 1992

M14

EUROPE

A S I A

Azores
(Portugal)

Madeira
Islands
(Portugal)
Funchal

Canary Islands
(Sp.) Santa Cruz
Las Palmas

Mediterranean Sea

Cape
Bón

Strait of Gibraltar
Ceuta (Sp.)
Tangier Tetouan
Melilla
Kenitra Oujda
Rabat Fes
Casablanca
Safi Khouribga
Agadir Marrakech
Jebel Toubkal 13,661

ATLAS MOUNTAINS

Bechar

MOROCCO

El Djazair
(Algiers)
Wahran El Asnam
Béjaïa Batna
Sidi Bel Abbes Biskra
Ghardaia
Djebel Chelia 7,631
Touggourt

Annaba
Skikda Tunis
Qacentina TUNISIA
Tébessa Sfax
Tripoli
Misratah

In-Amenas

I-n-Salah

ALGERIA

Western
Sahara
(Occ. by
Morocco)
El Aaiun

Nouadhibou

Atar

Nouakchott

MAURITANIA

Ayoun el Atrous

Kayes
Kaédi
Saint-
Louis
SENEGAL
Dakar THE
Thies GAMBIA
Kaolack Banjul
GUINEA-
BISSAU Labé
Bissau GUINEA
Conakry
Freetown
SIERRA
LEONE Monrovia
LIBERIA
Abidjan

Tombouctou

Mopti
MALI
Ségou
Bamako
Sikasso

Nioro

Korhogo
CÔTE
Bouaké D'IVOIRE
Yamoussoukro
Gao

Niamey
NIGER
BURKINA
FASO
Bobo- Ouagadougou
Dioulasso
Tamale
GHANA
Kumasi TOGO
Accra Lomé

Gulf of Sidra

Ghadamis

SAHARA

HOGGAR
Mt. Tahat 9,573
Tamanrasset

AÏR
Agadez

Maradi
Zinder
Sokoto
Zaria
Katsina Kano
NIGERIA
Abuja
Minna
Ilorin Enugu
Oshogbo
Ibadan Onitsha
Abeokuta
Ogbomosho
BENIN Porto-Novo
Ogbomosho
Lagos

LIBYA

Banghazi

Al Bayda
Tobruk

Waha

Al Jawf

LIBYAN DESERT

TIBESTI
Emi Koussi 11,204

CHAD
Faya-Largeau
Abeche
N'Djamena
Lake Chad
Maroua
Garoua

Maiduguri
Kumo
Makurdi

Maradi
Maradi Benue

Mt. Greboun 6,378

Tropic of Cancer

Port
Said Suez
Suez Canal Cairo
Alexandria Tanta
Al Jizah
Al Fayyum
SINAI
EGYPT
Asyut
Siwah Al Kharijah
Al Khariyah

Nile

Luxor
Aswan

NUBIAN DESERT
Port Sudan

Marawi

Atbarah
Kassala
Omdurman
Khartoum Wad Madani
Al Ubayyid SUDAN
Al Fashir
El Obeid
Nyala
Sarh
Mundou
Waw
Rumbek
Bambari
Baoussam

CENTRAL AFRICAN
REPUBLIC
Bouar

Red Sea

Lake
Nasser

White Nile
Blue Nile
Kushi

Ras Dashan 15,158

Lake Tana
Bahir Dar

Misiwa
Asmera
Mekele
Al Dadani

Gonder

Gulf of Aden
Lowest point
in Africa
Lake Assai (−512)
Djibouti
DJIBOUTI Cape
Guardafui

Berbera
Hargeysa

Dire Dawa
Harer
Nazret
ETHIOPIA
Addis Ababa
Jima Batu 14,131

ETHIOPIAN
HIGHLANDS

SOMALI
PENINSULA

Malakal

© The World Almanac and Book of Facts, 1992

AFRICA

Elevation

Meters	Feet
4,000	13,120
2,000	6,560
500	1,640
200	656
0	0
Below Sea Level	Below Sea Level

750 Miles
1,000 Kilometers
500   750
250   500
0   250
0

ATLANTIC OCEAN

INDIAN OCEAN

SEYCHELLES

COMOROS
Moroni

MADAGASCAR
Antananarivo
Antsirabe
Antsiranana
Mahajanga
Toamasina
Fianarantsoa
Toliara
Tolanaro
Maromokotro 9,436

Mozambique Channel

Mogadishu
Merca
KENYA
Marsabit
Meru
Eldoret
Nakuru Mt. Kenya 17,058
Nairobi
Machakos
Kismaayo
UGANDA
Kampala Jinja
Kisumu
RWANDA
Kigali
BURUNDI
Bujumbura
Kindu
Bukavu
Goma
Kisangani Beni
Bumba
Marghenta 16,763
Mt. Meru
Arusha
Moshi
Kilimanjaro 19,340
Highest point in Africa
Mombasa
Tanga
Zanzibar
Zanzibar I.
Pemba I.
Dar-es-Salaam
SERENGETI PLAIN
Lake Victoria
TANZANIA
Dodoma
Morogoro
Iringa
Tabora
Kigoma
Mwanza
Tabora
Mbeya
Songea
Mtwara
Nacala
Nampula
MOZAMBIQUE
Quelimane
Beira
Chimoio
Tete
MALAWI
Lilongwe
Blantyre
Lake Malawi
Chinde
ZAIRE
CONGO BASIN
Kinshasa
Mbandaka
Kikwit
Kananga
Mbuji-Mayi
Tshikapa
Kabinda
Ilebo
Mwene-Ditu
Kamina
Kalemie
Kabalo
Kolwezi
KATANGA PLATEAU
Likasi
Lubumbashi
Ndola
Kitwe
Luanshya
Kabwe
Chingola
ZAMBIA
Lusaka
Lake Kariba
Zambezi
Livingstone
Victoria Falls
ZIMBABWE
Harare
Mutare
Gweru
Kwekwe
Bulawayo
Francistown
Messina
ANGOLA
Luanda
Malanje
Menongue
Lobito
Benguela
Namibe
Lubango
Huambo
GABON
Libreville
Port-Gentil
Lambarene
EQUATORIAL GUINEA
SAO TOME AND PRINCIPE
Sao Tome
Principe
Annobon (Eq. Guinea)
Douala
Brazzaville
Pointe-Noire
Loubomo
Cabinda (Angola)
Mbanza-Ngungu
Matadi
Francville
Bandundu
CONGO
NAMIBIA
Windhoek
Walvis Bay (S. Africa)
KALAHARI DESERT
NAMIB DESERT
Luderitz
Keetmanshoop
Grootfontein
Ruacana Falls
Cunene
Augrabies Falls
Orange
BOTSWANA
Gaborone
Serowe
SOUTH AFRICA
Johannesburg
Pretoria
Vereeniging
Klerksdorp
Welkom
Kimberley
Bloemfontein
Upington
Springbok
Worcester
Cape Town
Cape of Good Hope
Cape Agulhas
Middelburg
Biaho
Umtata
East London
Port Elizabeth
Durban
Pietermaritzburg
Newcastle
SWAZILAND
Mbabane
Manzini
LESOTHO
Maseru
Maputo
Xai-Xai
Inhambane
Thabazimbi
Palapye
Limpopo
Marico
Nossob
Okavango
Equator
Tropic of Capricorn
Tropic of Cancer
Lake Albert
Lake Tanganyika
Lake Mweru
Lake Kivu
Kasai
Congo
Boyoma Falls
Zambezi
0°   10°   20°   30°

AUSTRALIA &
THE PACIFIC

Elevation

Meters	Feet
2,000	6,560
1,000	3,280
200	656
0	0
Below Sea Level	Below Sea Level

WORLD HISTORY

Prehistory: Our Ancestors Take Over

Homo sapiens. The precise origins of *homo sapiens*, the species to which all humans belong, are subject to broad speculation based on a small number of fossils, genetic and anatomical studies, and the geological record. But most scientists agree that we evolved from ape-like primate ancestors in a process that began millions of years ago.

Current theories say the first hominid (human-like primate) was *Ramapithecus*, who emerged 12 million years ago. Its remains have been found in Asia, Europe, and Africa. Further development was apparently limited to Africa, where 2 lines of hominids appeared some 5 or 6 million years ago. One was *Australopithecus*, a tool-maker and social animal, who lived from perhaps 4 to 3 million years ago, and then apparently became extinct.

The 2nd was a human line, *Homo habilis*, a large-brained specimen that walked upright and had a dextrous hand. *Homo habilis* lived in semi-permanent camps and had a food-gathering and sharing economy.

Homo erectus, our nearest ancestor, appeared in Africa perhaps 1.75 million years ago, and began spreading into Asia and Europe soon after. It had a fairly large brain and a skeletal structure similar to ours. *Homo erectus* learned to control fire, and probably had primitive language skills. The final brain development to *Homo sapiens* and then to our sub-species *Homo sapiens sapiens* occurred between 500,000 and 50,000 years ago, either in one place — probably Africa — or virtually simultaneously and independently in different places in Africa, Europe, and Asia. There is no question that all modern races are members of the same species, *Homo sapiens sapiens*.

The spread of mankind into the remaining habitable continents probably took place during the last ice age up to 100,000 years ago: to the Americas across a land bridge from Asia, and to Australia across the Timor Straits.

Earliest cultures. A variety of cultural modes — in tool-making, diet, shelter, and possibly social arrangements and spiritual expression, arose as early mankind adapted to different geographic and climatic zones.

Three basic tool-making traditions are recognized by archeologists as arising and often coexisting from one million years ago to the near past: the *chopper tradition*, found largely in E. Asia, with crude chopping tools and simple flake tools; the *flake tradition*, found in Africa and W. Europe, with a variety of small cutting and flaking tools, and the *biface tradition*, found in all of Africa, W. and S. Europe, and S. Asia, producing pointed hand axes chipped on both faces. Later biface sites yield more refined axes and a variety of other tools, weapons, and ornaments using bone, antler, and wood as well as stone.

Only sketchy evidence remains for the different stages in man's increasing control over the environment. Traces of 400,000-year-old covered wood shelters have been found at Nice, France. Scraping tools at Neanderthal sites (200,000-30,000 BC in Europe, N. Africa, the Middle East and Central Asia) suggest the treatment of skins for clothing. Sites from all parts of the world show seasonal migration patterns and exploitation of a wide range of plant and animal food sources.

Painting and decoration, for which there is evidence at the Nice site, flourished along with stone and ivory sculpture after 30,000 years ago; 60 caves in France and 30 in Spain show remarkable examples of wall painting. Other examples have been found in Africa. Proto-religious rites are suggested by these works, and by evidence of ritual cannibalism by Peking Man, 500,000 BC, and of ritual burial with medicinal plants and flowers by Neanderthals at Shanidar in Iraq.

The Neolithic Revolution. Sometime after 10,000 BC, among widely separated human communities, a series of dramatic technological and social changes occurred that are summed up as the Neolithic Revolution. The cultivation of previously wild plants encouraged the growth of permanent settlements. Animals were domesticated as a work force and food source. The manufacture of pottery and cloth began. These techniques permitted a huge increase in world population and in human control over the earth.

No region can safely claim priority as the "inventor" of these techniques. Dispersed sites in Cen. and S. America, S.E. Europe, and the Middle East show roughly contemporaneous (10-8,000 BC) evidence of one or another "neolithic" trait. Dates near 6-3,000 BC have been given for E. and S. Asian, W. European, and sub-Saharan African neolithic remains. The variety of crops — field grains, rice, maize, and roots, and the varying mix of other traits suggest that the revolution occurred independently in all these regions.

History Begins: 4000 - 1000 BC

Near Eastern cradle. If history began with writing, the first chapter opened in Mesopotamia, the Tigris-Euphrates river valley. Clay tablets with pictographs were used by the Sumerians to keep records after 4000 BC. A **cuneiform** (wedge shaped) script evolved by 3000 BC as a full syllabic alphabet. Neighboring peoples adapted the script to their own language.

Sumerian life centered, from 4000 BC, on large cities (Eridu, Ur, Uruk, Nippur, Kish, Lagash) organized around temples and priestly bureaucracies, with the surrounding plains watered by vast irrigation works and worked with traction plows. Sailboats, wheeled vehicles, potters wheels, and kilns were used. Copper was smelted and tempered in Sumeria from c4000 BC and bronze was produced not long after. Ores, as well as precious stones and metals were obtained through long-distance ship and caravan trade. Iron was used from c2000 BC. Improved ironworking, developed partly by the **Hittites**, became widespread by 1200 BC.

Sumerian political primacy passed among cities and their kingly dynasties. Semitic-speaking peoples, with cultures derived from the Sumerian, founded a succession of dynasties that ruled in Mesopotamia and neighboring areas for most of 1800 years; among them the **Akkadians** (first under Sargon c2350 BC), the Amorites (whose laws, codified by **Hammurabi**, c1792-1750 BC, have Biblical parallels), and the Assyrians, with interludes of rule by the Hittites, Kassites, and Mitanni, all possibly Indo-Europeans. The political and cultural center of gravity shifted northwest with each successive empire.

Mesopotamian learning, maintained by scribes and preserved by successive rulers in vast libraries, was not abstract or theoretical. Algebraic and geometric problems could be solved on a practical basis in construction, commerce, or administration. Systematic lists of astronomical phenomena, plants, animals and stones were kept; medical texts listed ailments and their herbal cures.

The Sumerians worshipped anthropomorphic gods representing natural forces — Anu, god of heaven; Enlil (Ea), god of water. Epic poetry related these and other gods in a hierarchy. Sacrifices were made at **ziggurats** — huge stepped temples. Gods were thought to control all events, which could be foretold using oracular materials. This religious pattern persisted into the first millenium BC.

The Syria-Palestine area, site of some of the earliest urban remains (Jericho, 7000 BC), and of the recently uncovered **Ebla** civilization (fl. 2500 BC), experienced Egyptian cultural and political influence along with Mesopotamian. The **Phoenician** coast was an active commercial center. A phonetic alphabet was invented here before 1600 BC. It became the ancestor of all European, Middle Eastern, Indian, S.E.

4500

Thai bronzes

3500

Bronze Age begins

1st pyramids — Sumerian cities

Indus Valley civilization

Egypt unified

2500

2500 BC

Ebla civilization

Bronze-age Minoan civilization emerges on Crete

Egyptian literature begins

Peruvian neolithic ceremonial centers

1750 — Hammurabi

Phonetic alphabet invented before 1600

Aryans invade India

Mt. Sinai revelations to Moses

Chinese Shang dynasty

Mexican Olmec civilization established

1000 BC

Asian, Ethiopian, and Korean alphabets.

Regional commerce and diplomacy were aided by the use of Akkadian as a *lingua franca*, later replaced by Aramaic.

Egypt. Agricultural villages along the Nile were united by 3300 BC into two kingdoms, Upper and Lower Egypt, unified under the Pharaoh Menes c3100 BC; Nubia to the south was added 2600 BC. A national bureaucracy supervised construction of canals and monuments (**pyramids** starting 2700 BC). Brilliant First Dynasty achievements in architecture, sculpture and painting, set the standards and forms for all subsequent Egyptian civilization and are still admired. **Hieroglyphic writing** appeared by 3400 BC, recording a sophisticated literature including romantic and philosophical modes after 2300 BC.

An ordered hierarchy of gods, including totemistic animal elements, was served by a powerful priesthood in Memphis. The pharaoh was identified with the falcon god Horus. Later trends were the belief in an afterlife, and the quasi-monotheistic reforms of **Akhenaton** (c1379-1362 BC).

After a period of conquest by Semitic Hyksos from Asia (c1700-1500 BC), the New Kingdom established an empire in Syria. Egypt became increasingly embroiled in Asiatic wars and diplomacy. Eventually it was conquered by Persia in 525 BC, and it faded away as an independent culture.

India. An urban civilization with a so-far-undeciphered writing system stretched across the Indus Valley and along the Arabian Sea c3000-1500 BC. Major sites were Harappa and **Mohenjo-Daro** in Pakistan, well-planned geometric cities with underground sewers and vast granaries. The entire region (600,000 sq. mi.) may have been ruled as a single state. Bronze was used, and arts and crafts were highly developed. Religious life apparently took the form of fertility cults.

Indus civilization was probably in decline when it was destroyed by **Aryan invaders** from the northwest, speaking an Indo-European language from which all the languages of Pakistan, north India and Bangladesh descend. Led by a warrior aristocracy whose legendary deeds are recorded in the **Rig Veda**, the Aryans spread east and south, bringing their pantheon of sky gods, elaborate priestly (Brahmin) ritual, and the beginnings of the caste system; local customs and beliefs were assimilated by the conquerors.

Europe. On Crete, the bronze-age **Minoan civilization** emerged c2500 BC. A prosperous economy and richly decorative art (e.g. at Knossos palace) was supported by seaborne commerce. Mycenae and other cities in Greece and Asia Minor (e.g. **Troy**) preserved elements of the culture to c1100 BC. Cretan Linear A script, c2000-1700 BC, is undeciphered; Linear B, c1300-1200 BC, records a Greek dialect.

Possible connection between Minoan-Mycenaean monumental stonework, and the great megalithic monuments and tombs of W. Europe, Iberia, and Malta (c4000-1500 BC) is unclear.

China. Proto-Chinese neolithic cultures had long covered northern and southeastern China when the first large political state was organized in the north by the **Shang dynasty** c1500 BC. Shang kings called themselves Sons of Heaven, and presided over a cult of human and animal sacrifice to ancestors and nature gods. The Chou dynasty, starting c1100 BC, expanded the area of the Son of Heaven's dominion, but feudal states exercised most temporal power.

A writing system with 2,000 different characters was already in use under the Shang, with **pictographs** later supplemented by phonetic characters. The system, with modifications, is still in use, despite changes in spoken Chinese.

Technical advances allowed urban specialists to create fine ceramic and jade products, and bronze casting after 1500 BC was the most advanced in the world.

Bronze artifacts have recently been discovered in northern Thailand dating to 3600 BC, hundreds of years before similar Middle Eastern finds.

Americas. Olmecs settled on the Gulf coast of Mexico, 1500 BC, and soon developed the first civilization in the Western Hemisphere. Temple cities and huge stone sculpture date to 1200 BC. A rudimentary calendar and writing system existed. Olmec religion, centering on a jaguar god, and art forms influenced all later Meso-American cultures.

Neolithic ceremonial centers were built on the Peruvian desert coast, c2000 BC.

Classical Era of Old World Civilizations

Greece. After a period of decline during the Dorian Greek invasions (1200-1000 BC), Greece and the Aegean area developed a unique civilization. Drawing upon Mycenaean traditions, Mesopotamian learning (weights and measures, lunisolar calendar, astronomy, musical scales), the Phoenician alphabet (modified for Greek), and Egyptian art, the revived **Greek city-states** saw a rich elaboration of intellectual life. Long-range commerce was aided by metal coinage (introduced by the Lydians in Asia Minor before 700 BC); colonies were founded around the Mediterranean and Black Sea shores (Cumae in Italy 760 BC, Massalia in France c600 BC).

Philosophy, starting with Ionian speculation on the nature of matter and the universe (Thales c634-546), and including mathematical speculation (Pythagoras c580-c500), culminated in Athens in the rationalist idealism of **Plato** (c428-347) and **Socrates** (c470-399); the latter was executed for alleged impiety. **Aristotle** (384-322) united all fields of study in his system. The arts were highly valued. Architecture culminated in the **Parthenon** in Athens (438, sculpture by Phidias); poetry and drama (Aeschylus 525-456) thrived. Male beauty and strength, a chief artistic theme, were enhanced at the gymnasium and the national games at Olympia.

Ruled by local tyrants or oligarchies, the Greeks were never politically united, but managed to resist inclusion in the Persian Empire (Darius defeated at Marathon 490 BC, Xerxes at Salamis, Plataea 479 BC). Local warfare was common; the **Peloponnesian Wars**, 431-404 BC, ended in Sparta's victory over Athens. Greek political power waned, but classical Greek cultural forms spread throughout the ancient world from the Atlantic to India.

Hebrews. Nomadic Hebrew tribes entered Canaan before 1200 BC, settling among other Semitic peoples speaking the same language. They brought from the desert a **monotheistic faith** said to have been revealed to Abraham in Canaan c1800 BC and to Moses at Mt. Sinai c1250 BC, after the Hebrews' escape from bondage in Egypt. David (ruled 1000-961 BC) and Solomon (ruled 961-922 BC) united the Hebrews in a kingdom that briefly dominated the area. Phoenicians to the north established colonies

Paleontology: The History of Life

All dates are approximate, and are subject to change based on new fossil finds or new dating techniques; but the sequence of events is generally accepted. Dates are in years before the present.

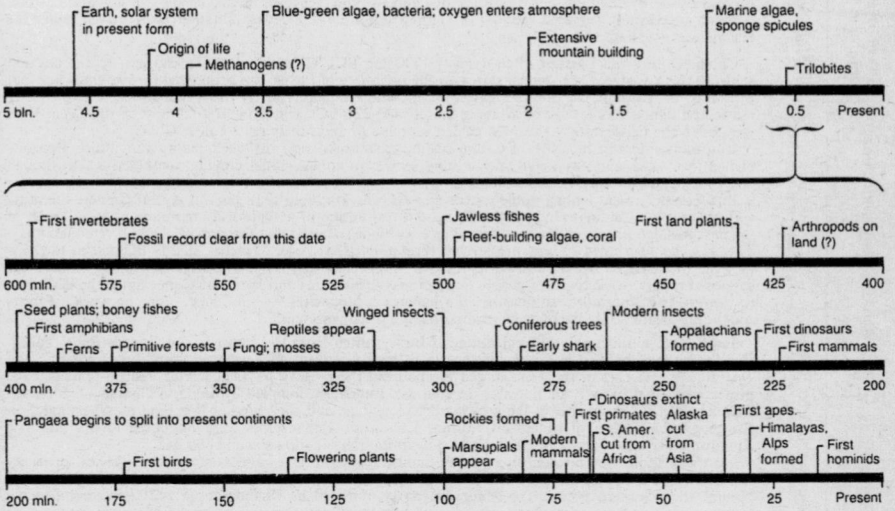

Earth, solar system in present form — Blue-green algae, bacteria; oxygen enters atmosphere — Marine algae, sponge spicules — Origin of life — Methanogens (?) — Extensive mountain building — Trilobites

5 bln. 4.5 4 3.5 3 2.5 2 1.5 1 0.5 Present

First invertebrates — Fossil record clear from this date — Jawless fishes — Reef-building algae, coral — First land plants — Arthropods on land (?)

600 mln. 575 550 525 500 475 450 425 400

Seed plants; boney fishes — First amphibians — Ferns — Primitive forests — Fungi; mosses — Reptiles appear — Winged insects — Coniferous trees — Early shark — Modern insects — Appalachians formed — First dinosaurs — First mammals

400 mln. 375 350 325 300 275 250 225 200

Pangaea begins to split into present continents — First birds — Flowering plants — Rockies formed — Marsupials appear — Modern mammals — First primates — S. Amer. cut from Africa — Dinosaurs extinct — Alaska cut from Asia — First apes. — Himalayas, Alps formed — First hominids

200 mln. 175 150 125 100 75 50 25 Present

Ancient Near Eastern Civilizations
4000 B.C.-500 B.C.

Scythians
Danube R.
LIBYA Black Sea
MACEDON
LYDIA PHRYGIA HITTITES Kushshar
Sardis
MINOANS CILICIA ARMENIA
Mediterranean Sea ASSYRIA
Nineveh
Ebla Ashur MEDES
Damascus Mari Ecbatana
Sidon BABYLONIA
Jerusalem Tyre ELAM
Babylon Susa
Memphis Ur
EGYPT SUMER Persepolis
Tel el Amarna PERSIS
Thebes Persian Gulf
Red Sea
NUBIA
SABAEANS
Caspian Sea
Aral Sea
Jaxartes River
Samarkand
SOGDIANA
Oxus River
BACTRIA
PARTHIA
Taxila
Harappa
INDUS VALLEY CIV.
Mohenjo-Daro
Sutkagen Dor
Arabian Sea

— Persian Empire c. 500 B.C.

Timeline (1000 BC – 400 BC):

- 1000 BC
- Chavin dynasty begins in Peru
- Hebrew kingdom divided
- Chou dynasty begins in China
- Carthage established
- 800
- Nubia begins rule of Egypt
- Metal coins in Asia Minor
- Isaiah d.
- Zoroaster b.
- Pythagoras b.
- 600
- Indian Buddhism, Jainism begin
- Confucius b.
- Siddarta b.
- Aeschylus b.
- Socrates b.
- Plato b.
- Parthenon
- Peloponnesian Wars
- 400 BC

around the E. and W. Mediterranean (**Carthage** c814 BC) and sailed into the Atlantic.

A temple in Jerusalem became the national religious center, with sacrifices performed by a hereditary priesthood. Polytheistic influences, especially of the fertility cult of Baal, were opposed by **prophets** (Elijah, Amos, Isaiah).

Divided into **two kingdoms** after Solomon, the Hebrews were unable to resist the revived Assyrian empire, which conquered Israel, the northern kingdom in 722 BC. Judah, the southern kingdom, was conquered in 586 BC by the Babylonians under Nebuchadnezzar II. But with the fixing of most of the Biblical canon by the mid-fourth century BC, and the emergence of rabbis, arbiters of law and custom, Judaism successfully survived the loss of Hebrew autonomy. A Jewish kingdom was revived under the Hasmoneans (168-42 BC).

China. During the **Eastern Chou** dynasty (770-256 BC), Chinese culture spread east to the sea and south to the Yangtze. Large feudal states on the periphery of the empire contended for pre-eminence, but continued to recognize the Son of Heaven (king), who retained a purely ritual role enriched with courtly music and dance. In the Age of Warring States (403-221 BC), when the first sections of the **Great Wall** were built, the Ch'in state in the West gained supremacy, and finally united all of China.

Iron tools entered China c500 BC, and casting techniques were advanced, aiding agriculture. Peasants owned their land, and owed civil and military service to nobles. Cities grew in number and size, though barter remained the chief trade medium.

Intellectual ferment among noble scribes and officials produced the Classical Age of Chinese literature and philosophy. **Confucius** (551-479 BC) urged a restoration of a supposedly harmonious social order of the past through proper conduct in accordance with one's station and through filial and ceremonial piety. The *Analects*, attributed to him, are revered throughout East Asia. **Mencius** (d. 289 BC) added the view that the Mandate of Heaven can be removed from an unjust dynasty. The Legalists sought to curb the supposed natural wickedness of people through new institutions and harsh laws; they aided the Ch'in rise to power. The Naturalists emphasized the balance of opposites — yin, yang — in the world. **Taoists** sought mystical knowledge through meditation and disengagement.

India. The political and cultural center of India shifted from the Indus to the Ganges River Valley. Buddhism, Jainism, and mystical revisions of orthodox Vedism all developed around 500-300 BC. The *Upanishads*, last part of the *Veda*, urged escape from the illusory physical world. Vedism remained the preserve of the priestly Brahmin caste. In contrast, **Buddhism**, founded by Siddarta Gautama (c563-c483 BC), appealed to merchants in the growing urban centers, and took hold at first (and most lastingly) on the geographic fringes of Indian civilization. The classic Indian epics were composed in this era: The *Ramayana* perhaps around 300 BC, the *Mahabharata* over a period starting 400 BC.

Northern India was divided into a large number of monarchies and aristocratic republics, probably derived from tribal groupings, when the Magadha kingdom was formed in Bihar c542 BC. It soon became the dominant power. The **Maurya dynasty**, founded by Chandragupta c321 BC, expanded the kingdom, uniting most of N. India in a centralized bureaucratic empire. The third Mauryan king, **Asoka** (ruled c274-236) conquered most of the subcontinent; he converted to Buddhism, and inscribed its tenets on pillars throughout India. He downplayed the caste system and tried to end expensive sacrificial rites.

Before its final decline in India, Buddhism developed the popular worship of heavenly Bodhisatvas (enlightened beings), and produced a refined architecture (stupa—shrine—at Sanchi 100 AD) and sculpture (Gandhara reliefs 1-400 AD).

Persia. Aryan peoples (Persians, Medes) dominated the area of present Iran by the beginning of the first millenium BC. The prophet **Zoroaster** (born c628 BC) introduced a dualistic religion in which the forces of good (Ahura Mazda, Lord of Wisdom) and evil (Ahiram) battle for dominance; individuals are judged by their actions and earn damnation or salvation. Zoroaster's hymns (*Gathas*) are included in the *Avesta*, the Zoroastrian scriptures. A version of this faith became the established religion of the Persian Empire, and probably influenced later monotheistic religions.

Africa. Nubia, periodically occupied by Egypt since the third millenium, ruled Egypt c750-661, and survived as an independent Egyptianized kingdom (**Kush**; capital Meroe) for 1,000 years.

The Iron Age Nok culture flourished c500 BC-200 AD on the Benue Plateau of **Nigeria**.

Americas. The Chavin culture controlled north Peru from 900-200 BC. Its ceremonial centers, featuring the jaguar god, survived long after. Chavin architecture, ceramics, and textiles influenced other Peruvian cultures.

Mayan civilization began to develop in Central America in the 5th century BC.

Great Empires Unite the Civilized World: 400 BC - 400 AD

Persia and Alexander. Cyrus, ruler of a small kingdom in Persia from 559 BC, united the Persians and Medes within 10 years, conquered Asia Minor and Babylonia in another 10. His son Cambyses followed by Darius (ruled 522-486) added vast lands to the east and north as far as the Indus Valley and Central Asia, as well as Egypt and Thrace. The whole empire was ruled by an international bureaucracy and army, with Persians holding the chief positions. The resources and styles of all the subject civilizations were exploited to create a rich syncretic art.

The Hellenized kingdom of Macedon, which under Phillip II dominated Greece, passed to his son **Alexander** in 336 BC. Within 13 years, Alexander conquered all the Persian dominions. Imbued by his tutor Aristotle with Greek ideals, Alexander encouraged Greek colonization, and Greek-style cities were founded throughout the empire (e.g. Alexandria, Egypt). After his death in 323 BC, wars of succession divided the empire into three parts — Macedon, Egypt (ruled by the **Ptolemies**), and the **Seleucid** Empire.

In the ensuing 300 years (the **Hellenistic Era**), a cosmopolitan Greek-oriented culture permeated the ancient world from W. Europe to the borders of India, absorbing native elites everywhere.

Hellenistic philosophy stressed the private individual's search for happiness. The Cynics followed Diogenes (c372-287), who stressed satisfaction of animal needs and contempt for social convention. Zeno (c335-c263) and the Stoics exalted reason, identified it with virtue, and counseled an ascetic disregard for misfortune. The Epicureans tried to build lives of moderate pleasure without political or emotional

The Rise of the Roman Empire

GERMANIA

SARMATIA

BELGICA

GAUL   RAETIA

TARRACONENSIS

LUSITANIA

BAETICA

ILLYRICUM

DACIA

Rome

THRACE   Constantinople

BITHYNIA   PONTUS

ARMENIA

ASIA

GALATIA

ACHAEA   CILICIA

MESOPOTAMIA

MAURETANIA

Carthage

AFRICA

SYRIA

TRIPOLI

JUDEA

CYRENAICA   ARABIA

EGYPT

238 B.C.E.
133 B.C.E.
44 B.C.E.
A.D. 14
A.D. 117

Ancient Asian Empires

Caspian Sea

GOBI DESERT

ALTAI MTS.

Great Wall

PAMIR MTS.

TARIM BASIN

Sea of Japan

East China Sea

HIMALAYA MTS.

Tibet

Lo-yang
Chang-an

Han Empire
100 B.C.

Asoka's
Empire
250 B.C.

Pataliputra

Arabian Sea

Bay of Bengal

South China Sea

Khmer Empire
Angkor
A.D. 1000
1250

- - - Approximate Borders

involvement. Hellenistic arts imitated life realistically, especially in sculpture and literature (comedies of Menander, 342-292).

The sciences thrived, especially at Alexandria, where the Ptolemies financed a great library and museum. Fields of study included mathematics (Euclid's geometry, c300 BC; Menelaus' non-Euclidean geometry, c100 AD); astronomy (heliocentric theory of Aristarchus, 310-230 BC; Julian calendar 45 BC; Ptolemy's *Almagest*, c150 AD); geography (world map of Eratosthenes, 276-194 BC); hydraulics (Archimedes, 287-212 BC); medicine (Galen, 130-200 AD), and chemistry. Inventors refined uses for siphons, valves, gears, springs, screws, levers, cams, and pulleys.

A restored Persian empire under the Parthians (N. Iranian tribesmen) controlled the eastern Hellenistic world 250 BC-229 AD. The Parthians and the succeeding Sassanian dynasty (229-651) fought with Rome periodically. The Sassanians revived Zoroastrianism as a state religion, and patronized a nationalistic artistic and scholarly renaissance.

Rome. The city of Rome was founded, according to legend, by Romulus in 753 BC. Through military expansion and colonization, and by granting citizenship to conquered tribes, the city annexed all of Italy south of the Po in the 100-year period before 268 BC. The Latin and other Italic tribes were annexed first, followed by the Etruscans (a civilized people north of Rome) and the Greek colonies in the south. With a large standing army and reserve forces of several hundred thousand, Rome was able to defeat Carthage in the 3 Punic Wars, 264-241, 218-201, 149-146 (despite the invasion of Italy by Hannibal, 218), thus gaining Sicily and territory in Spain and North Africa.

New provinces were added in the East, as Rome exploited local disputes to conquer Greece and Asia Minor in the 2d century BC, and Egypt in the first (after the defeat and suicide of Antony and Cleopatra, 30 BC). All the Mediterranean civilized world up to the disputed Parthian border was now Roman, and remained so for 500 years. Less civilized regions were added to the Empire: Gaul (conquered by Julius Caesar, 56-49 BC), Britain (43 AD) and Dacia NE of the Danube (117 AD).

The original aristocratic republican government, with democratic features added in the fifth and fourth centuries BC, deteriorated under the pressures of empire and class conflict (Gracchus brothers, social reformers, murdered 133, 121; slave revolts 135, 73). After a series of civil wars (Marius vs. Sulla 88-82, Caesar vs. Pompey 49-45, triumvirate vs. Caesar's assassins 44-43, Antony vs. Octavian 32-30), the empire came under the rule of a deified monarch (first emperor, Augustus, 27 BC-14 AD). Provincials (nearly all granted citizenship by Caracalla, 212 AD) came to dominate the army and civil service. Traditional Roman law, systematized and interpreted by independent jurists, and local self-rule in provincial cities were supplanted by a vast tax-collecting bureaucracy in the 3d and 4th centuries. The legal rights of women, children, and slaves were strengthened.

Roman innovations in civil engineering included water mills, windmills, and rotary mills, and the use of cement that hardened under water. Monumental architecture (baths, theaters, apartment houses) relied on the arch and the dome. The network of roads (some still standing) stretched 53,000 miles, passing through mountain tunnels as long as 3.5 miles. Aqueducts brought water to cities, underground sewers removed waste.

Roman art and literature were derivative of Greek models. Innovations were made in sculpture (naturalistic busts and equestrian statues), decorative wall painting (as at Pompeii), satire (Juvenal, 60-127), history (Tacitus 56-120), prose romance (Petronius, d. 66 AD). Violence and torture dominated mass public amusements, which were supported by the state.

India. The Gupta monarchs reunited N. India c320 AD. Their peaceful and prosperous reign saw a revival of Hindu religious thought and Brahmin power. The old Vedic traditions were combined with devotion to a plethora of indigenous deities (who were seen as manifestations of Vedic gods). Caste lines were reinforced, and Buddhism gradually disappeared. The art (often erotic), architecture, and literature of the period, patronized by the Gupta court, are considered to be among India's finest achievements (Kalidasa, poet and dramatist, fl. c400). Mathematical innovations included the use of zero and decimal numbers. Invasions by White Huns from the NW destroyed the empire c550.

Rich cultures also developed in S. India in this era. Emotional Tamil religious poetry aided the Hindu revival. The Pallava kingdom controlled much of S. India c350-880, and helped spread Indian civilization to S.E. Asia.

China. The Ch'in ruler Shih Huang Ti (ruled 221-210 BC), known as the First Emperor, centralized political authority in China, standardized the written language, laws, weights, measures, and coinage, and conducted a census, but tried to destroy most philosophical texts. The Han dynasty (206 BC-220 AD) instituted the Mandarin bureaucracy, which lasted for 2,000 years. Local officials were selected by examination in the Confucian classics and trained at the imperial university and at provincial schools. The invention of paper facilitated this bureaucratic system. Agriculture was promoted, but the peasants bore most of the tax burden. Irrigation was improved; water clocks and sundials were used; astronomy and mathematics thrived; landscape painting was perfected.

With the expansion south and west to (nearly the present borders of today's China), trade was opened with India, S.E. Asia, and the Middle East, over sea and caravan routes. Indian missionaries brought Mahayana Buddhism to China by the first century AD, and spawned a variety of sects. Taoism was revived, and merged with popular superstitions. Taoist and Buddhist monasteries and convents multiplied in the turbulent centuries after the collapse of the Han dynasty.

The One God Triumphs: 1-750 AD

Christianity. Religions indigenous to particular Middle Eastern nations became international in the first 3 centuries of the Roman Empire. Roman citizens worshipped Isis of Egypt, Mithras of Persia, Demeter of Greece, and the great mother Cybele of Phrygia. Their cults centered on mysteries (secret ceremonies) and the promise of an afterlife, symbolized by the death and rebirth of the god. Judaism, which had begun as the national cult of Judea, also spread by emigration and conversion. It was the only ancient religion west of India to survive.

Christians, who emerged as a distinct sect in the second half of the 1st century AD, revered Jesus, a Jewish preacher killed by the Romans at the request of Jewish authorities in Jerusalem c30 AD. They considered him the Savior (Messiah, or Christ) who rose from the dead and could grant eternal life to the faithful, despite their sinfulness. They believed he was an incarnation of the one god worshipped by the Jews, and that he would return soon to pass final judgment on the world. The missionary activities of such early leaders as **Paul of Tarsus** spread the faith, at first mostly among Jews or among quasi-Jews attracted by the Pauline rejection of such difficult Jewish laws as circumcision. Intermittent persecution, as in Rome under Nero in 64 AD, on grounds of suspected disloyalty, failed to disrupt the Christian communities. Each congregation, generally urban and of plebeian character, was tightly organized under a leader (bishop) elders (presbyters or priests), and assistants (deacons). Stories about Jesus (the Gospels) and the early church (Acts) were written down in the late first and early 2d centuries, and circulated along with letters of Paul. An authoritative canon of these writings was not fixed until the 4th century.

A school for priests was established at Alexandria in the second century. Its teachers (**Origen** c182-251) helped define Christian doctrine and promote the faith in Greek-style philosophical works. Pagan Neoplatonism was given Christian coloration in the works of Church Fathers such as Augustine (354-430). Christian hermits, often drawn from the lower classes, began to associate in monasteries, first in Egypt (St. Pachomius c290-345), then in other eastern lands, then in the West (**St. Benedict's rule,** 529). Popular devotion to saints, especially Mary, mother of Jesus, spread.

Under **Constantine** (ruled 306-337), Christianity became in effect the established religion of the Empire. Pagan temples were expropriated, state funds were used to build huge churches and support the hierarchy, and laws were adjusted in accordance with Christian notions. Pagan worship was banned by the end of the fourth century, and severe restrictions were placed on Judaism.

The newly established church was rocked by doctrinal disputes, often exacerbated by regional rivalries both within and outside the Empire. Chief heresies (as defined by church councils backed by imperial authority) were **Arianism,** which denied the divinity of Jesus; **Donatism,** which rejected the convergence of church and state and denied the validity of sacraments performed by sinful clergy; and the **Monophysite** position denying the dual nature of Christ.

Judaism. First century Judaism embraced several sects, including: the **Sadducees,** mostly drawn from the Temple priesthood, who were culturally Hellenized; the **Pharisees,** who upheld the full range of traditional customs and practices of equal weight to literal scriptural law, and elaborated synagogue worship; and the **Essenes,** an ascetic, millenarian sect. Messianic fervor led to repeated, unsuccessful rebellions against Rome (66-70, 135). As a result, the Temple was destroyed, and the population decimated.

To avoid the dissolution of the faith, a program of codification of law was begun at the academy of Yavneh. The work continued for some 500 years in Palestine and Babylonia, ending in the final redaction of the **Talmud** (c600), a huge collection of legal and moral debates, rulings, liturgy, Biblical exegesis, and legendary materials.

Islam. The earliest Arab civilization emerged by the end of the 2d millenium BC in the watered highlands of Yemen. Seaborne and caravan trade in frankincense and myrrh connected the area with the Nile and Fertile Crescent. The Minaean, Sabean (Sheba), and Himyarite states successively held sway. By Mohammed's time (7th century AD), the region was a province of Sassanian Persia. In the North, the Nabataean kingdom at Petra and the kingdom of Palmyra were first Aramaicized and then Romanized, and finally absorbed like neighboring Judea into the Roman Empire. Nomads shared the central region with a few trading towns and oases. Wars between tribes and raids on settled communities were common, and were celebrated in a poetic tradition that by the 6th century helped establish a classic literary Arabic.

In 611 Mohammed, an 40-year-old Arab of Mecca, announced a revelation from the one true God, calling on him to repudiate pagan idolatry. Drawing on elements of Judaism and Christianity, and eventually incorporating some Arab pagan traditions (such as reverence for the black stone at the kaaba shrine in Mecca), Mohammed's teachings, recorded in the **Koran,** forged a new religion, Islam (submission to Allah). Opposed by the leaders of Mecca, Mohammed made a *hejira* (migration) to Medina to the north in 622, the beginning of the Moslem lunar calendar. He and his followers defeated the Meccans in 624 in the first *jihad* (holy war), and by his death (632), nearly all the Arabian peninsula accepted his religious and secular leadership.

Under the first two **caliphs** (successors) Abu Bakr (632-34) and Oman (634-44), Moslem rule was confirmed over Arabia. Raiding parties into Byzantine and Persian border areas developed into campaigns of conquest against the two empires, which had been weakened by wars and by disaffection among subject peoples (including Coptic and Syriac Christians opposed to the Byzantine orthodox church). Syria, Palestine, Egypt, Iraq, and Persia all fell to the inspired Arab armies. The Arabs at first remained a distinct minority, using non-Moslems in the new administrative system, and tolerating Christians, Jews, and Zoroastrians as self-governing "Peoples of the Book," whose taxes supported the empire.

Disputes over the succession, and puritan reaction to the wealth and refinement that empire brought to the ruling strata, led to the growth of schismatic movements. The followers of Mohammed's son-in-law Ali (assassinated 661) and his descendants became the founders of the more mystical **Shi'ite** sect, still the largest non-orthodox Moslem sect. The **Karijites,** puritanical, militant, and egalitarian, persist as a minor sect to the present.

Under the **Ummayad** caliphs (661-750), the boundaries of Islam were extended across N. Africa and into Spain. Arab armies in the West were stopped at Tours in 732 by the Frank **Charles Martel.** Asia Minor, the Indus Valley, and Transoxiana were conquered in the East. The vast majority of the subject population gradually converted to Islam, encouraged by tax and career privileges. The Arab language supplanted the local tongues in the central and western areas, but Arab soldiers and rulers in the East eventually became assimilated to the indigenous languages.

New Peoples Enter History: 400-900

Barbarian invasions. Germanic tribes infiltrated S and E from their Baltic homeland during the 1st millenium BC, reaching S. Germany by 100 BC and the Black Sea by 214 AD. Organized into large federated tribes under elected kings, most resisted Roman domination and raided the empire in time of civil war (Goths took Dacia 214, raided Thrace 251-269). German troops and commanders came to dominate the Roman armies by the end of the 4th century. Huns, invaders from Asia, entered Europe 372, driving more Germans into the western empire. Emperor Valens allowed Visigoths to cross the Danube 376. Huns under Attila (d. 453) raided Gaul, Italy, Balkans. The western empire, weakened by overtaxation and social stagnation, was overrun in the 5th century. Gaul was effectively lost 406-7, Spain 409, Britain 410, Africa 429-39. Rome was sacked 410 by Visigoths under Alaric, 455 by Vandals. The last western emperor, Romulus Augustulus, was deposed 476 by the Germanic chief Odoacer.

Celts. Celtic cultures, which in pre-Roman times covered most of W. Europe, were confined almost entirely to the British Isles after the Germanic invasions. **St. Patrick** completed the conversion of Ireland (c457-92). A strong monastic tradition took hold. Irish monastic missionaries in Scotland, England, and the continent (Columba c521-597; Columban c543-615) helped restore Christianity after the Germanic invasions. The monasteries became renowned centers of classic and Christian learning, and presided over the recording of a Christianized Celtic mythology, elaborated by secular writers and bards. An intricate decorative art style developed, especially in book illumination (Lindisfarne Gospels, c700, Book of Kells, 8th century).

Successor states. The Visigoth kingdom in Spain (from 419) and much of France (to 507) saw a continuation of much Roman administration, language, and law (Breviary of Alaric 506), until its destruction by the Moslems, 711. The Vandal kingdom in Africa, from 429, was conquered by the Byzantines, 533. Italy was ruled in succession by an Ostrogothic kingdom under Byzantine suzerainty 489-554, direct Byzantine government, and the German Lombards (568-774). The latter divided the peninsula with the Byzantines and the papacy under the dynamic reformer Pope Gregory the Great (590-604) and his successors.

King Clovis (ruled 481-511) united the Franks on both sides of the Rhine, and after his conversion to orthodox Christianity, defeated the Arian Burgundians (after 500) and Visigoths (507) with the support of the native clergy and the papacy. Under the **Merovingian** kings a feudal system emerged: power was fragmented among hierarchies of military landowners. Social stratification, which in late Roman times had acquired legal, hereditary sanction, was reinforced. The Carolingians (747-987) expanded the kingdom and restored central power. **Charlemagne** (ruled 768-814) conquered nearly all the Germanic lands, including Lombard Italy, and was crowned Emperor by Pope Leo III in Rome in 800. A centuries-long decline in commerce and the arts was reversed under Charlemagne's patronage. He welcomed Jews to his kingdom, which became a center of Jewish learning (Rashi 1040-1105). He sponsored the "Carolingian Renaissance" of learning under the Anglo-Latin scholar Alcuin (c732-804), who reformed church liturgy.

Byzantine Empire. Under Diocletian (ruled 284-305) the empire had been divided into 2 parts to facilitate administration and defense. Constantine founded **Constantinople**, 330, (at old Byzantium) as a fully Christian city. Commerce and taxation financed a sumptuous, orientalized court, a class of hereditary bureaucratic families, and magnificent urban construction (Hagia Sophia, 532-37). The city's fortifications and naval innovations (Greek fire) repelled assaults by Goths, Huns, Slavs, Bulgars, Avars, Arabs, and Scandinavians. Greek replaced Latin as the official language by c700. Byzantine art, a solemn, sacral, and stylized variation of late classical styles (mosaics at S. Vitale, Ravenna, 526-48) was a starting point for medieval art in E. and W. Europe.

Justinian (ruled 527-65) reconquered parts of Spain, N. Africa, and Italy, codified Roman law (*codex Justinianus*, 529, was medieval Europe's chief legal text), closed the Platonic Academy at Athens and ordered all pagans to convert. Lombards in Italy, Arabs in Africa retook most of his conquests. The Isaurian dynasty from Anatolia (from 717) and the Macedonian dynasty (867-1054) restored military and commercial power. The Iconoclast controversy (726-843) over the permissibility of images, helped alienate the Eastern Church from the papacy.

Arab Empire. Baghdad, founded 762, became the seat of the **Abbasid** Caliphate (founded 750), while Ummayads continued to rule in Spain. A brilliant cosmopolitan civilization emerged, inaugurating an Arab-Moslem golden age. Arab lyric poetry revived; Greek, Syriac, Persian, and Sanskrit books were translated into Arabic, often by Syriac Christians and Jews, whose theology and Talmudic law, respectively, influenced Islam. The arts and music flourished at the court of **Harun al-Rashid** (786-809), celebrated in *The Arabian Nights.* The sciences, medicine, and mathematics were pursued at Baghdad, Cordova, and Cairo (founded 969). Science and Aristotelian philosophy culminated in the systems of Avicenna (980-1037), Averroes (1126-98), and Maimonides (1135-1204), a Jew; all influenced later Christian scholarship and theology. The Islamic ban on images encouraged a sinuous, geometric decorative tradition, applied to architecture and illumination. A gradual loss of Arab control in Persia (from 874) led to the capture of Baghdad by Persians, 945. By the next century, Spain and N. Africa were ruled by Berbers, while Turks prevailed in Asia Minor and the Levant. The loss of political power by the caliphs allowed for the growth of non-orthodox trends, especially the mystical **Sufi** tradition (theologian Ghazali, 1058-1111).

Africa. Immigrants from Saba in S. Arabia helped set up the **Axum** kingdom in Ethiopia in the 2d century (their language, Ge'ez, is preserved by the Ethiopian Church). In the 4th century, when the kingdom became Christianized, it defeated Kushite Meroe and expanded into Yemen. Axum was the center of a vast ivory trade; it controlled the Red Sea coast until c1100. Arab conquest in Egypt cut Axum's political and economic ties with Byzantium.

The Iron Age entered W. Africa by the end of the 1st millenium BC. **Ghana,** the first known sub-Saharan state, ruled in the upper Senegal-Niger region c400-1240, controlling the trade of gold from mines in the S to trans-Sahara caravan routes to the N. The **Bantu** peoples, probably of W. African origin, began to spread E and S perhaps 2000 years ago, displacing the Pygmies and Bushmen of central and southern Africa over a 1,500-year period.

Japan. The advanced Neolithic Yayoi period, when irrigation, rice farming, and iron and bronze casting techniques were introduced from China or Korea, persisted to c400 AD. The myriad Japanese states were then united by the **Yamato** clan, under an emperor who acted as the chief priest of the animistic **Shinto** cult. Japanese political and military intervention in Korea by the 6th century quickened a Chinese cultural invasion, bringing Buddhism, the Chinese language (which long remained a literary and governmental medium), Chinese ideographs and Buddhist styles in painting, sculpture, literature, and architecture (7th c. Horyu-ji temple at Nara). The Taika Reforms, 646, tried to centralize Japan according to Chinese bureaucratic and Buddhist philosophical values, but failed to curb traditional Japanese decentralization. A nativist reaction against the Buddhist **Nara period** (710-94) ushered in the

Heian period (794-1185) centered at the new capital, Kyoto. Japanese elegance and simplicity modified Chinese styles in architecture, scroll painting, and literature; the writing system was also simplified. The courtly novel *Tale of Genji* (1010-20) testifies to the enhanced role of women.

Southeast Asia. The historic peoples of southeast Asia began arriving some 2500 years ago from China and Tibet, displacing scattered aborigines. Their agriculture relied on rice and tubers (yams), which they may have introduced to Africa. Indian cultural influences were strongest; literacy and Hindu and Buddhist ideas followed the southern India-China trade route. From the southern tip of Indochina, the kingdom of **Funan** (1st-7th centuries) traded as far west as Persia. It was absorbed by Chenla, itself conquered by the **Khmer Empire** (600-1300). The Khmers, under Hindu god-kings (Suryavarman II, 1113-c1150), built the monumental Angkor Wat temple center for the royal phallic cult. The **Nam-Viet** kingdom in Annam, dominated by China and Chinese culture for 1,000 years, emerged in the 10th century, growing at the expense of the Khmers, who also lost ground in the NW to the new, highly-organized **Thai** kingdom. On Sumatra, the **Srivijaya** Empire at Palembang controlled vital sea lanes (7th to 10th centuries). A Buddhist dynasty, the Sailendras, ruled central **Java** (8th-9th centuries), building at Borobudur one of the largest stupas in the world.

China. The short-lived Sui dynasty (581-618) ushered in a period of commercial, artistic, and scientific achievement in China, continuing under the **T'ang** dynasty (618-906). Such inventions as the magnetic compass, gunpowder, the abacus, and printing were introduced or perfected. Medical innovations included cataract surgery. The state, from the cosmopolitan capital, Ch'ang-an, supervised foreign trade which exchanged Chinese silks, porcelains, and art works for spices, ivory, etc., over Central Asian caravan routes and sea routes reaching Africa. A golden age of poetry bequeathed tens of thousands of works to later generations (Tu Fu 712-70, Li Po 701-62). Landscape painting flourished. Commercial and industrial expansion continued under the **Northern Sung** dynasty (960-1126), facilitated by paper money and credit notes. But commerce never achieved respectability; government monopolies expropriated successful merchants. The population, long stable at 50 million, doubled in 200 years with the introduction of early-ripening rice and the double harvest. In art, native Chinese styles were revived.

Americas. An Indian empire stretched from the Valley of Mexico to Guatemala, 300-600, centering on the huge city **Teotihuacan** (founded 100 BC). To the S, in Guatemala, a high **Mayan** civilization developed, 150-900, around hundreds of rural ceremonial centers. The Mayans improved on Olmec writing and the calendar, and pursued astronomy and mathematics (using the idea of zero). In S. America, a widespread pre-Inca culture grew from **Tiahuanaco** near Lake Titicaca (Gateway of the Sun, c700).

Christian Europe Regroups and Expands: 900-1300

Scandinavians. Pagan Danish and Norse (**Viking**) adventurers, traders, and pirates raided the coasts of the British Isles (Dublin founded c831), France, and even the Mediterranean for over 200 years beginning in the late 8th century. Inland settlement in the W was limited to Great Britain (King Canute, 994-1035) and Normandy, settled under Rollo, 911, as a fief of France. Other Vikings reached Iceland (874), Greenland (c986), and probably N. America (Leif Eriksson c1000). Norse traders (**Varangians**) developed Russian river commerce from the 8th-11th centuries, and helped set up a state at Kiev in the late 9th century. Conversion to Christianity occurred during the 10th century, reaching Sweden 100 years later. Eleventh century Norman bands conquered S. Italy and Sicily. Duke **William of Normandy** conquered England, 1066, bringing continental feudalism and the French language, essential elements in later English civilization.

East Europe. Slavs inhabited areas of E. Central Europe in prehistoric times, and reached most of their present limits by c850. The first Slavic states were in the Balkans (Slav-Turk **Bulgarian Empire**, 680-1018) and Moravia (628). Missions of St. Cyril (whose Greek-based Cyrillic alphabet is still used by S. and E. Slavs) converted Moravia, 863. The Eastern Slavs, part-civilized under the overlordship of the Turkish-Jewish **Khazar** trading empire (7th-10th centuries), gravitated toward Constantinople by the 9th century. The **Kievan state** adopted Eastern Christianity under Prince Vladimir, 989. King Boleslav I (992-1025) began **Poland's** long history of eastern conquest. The Magyars (**Hungarians**) in Europe since 896, accepted Latin Christianity, 1001.

Germany. The German kingdom that emerged after the breakup of Charlemagne's Empire remained a confederation of largely autonomous states. The Saxon Otto I, king from 936, established the **Holy Roman Empire** of Germany and Italy in alliance with Pope John XII, who crowned him emperor, 962; he defeated the Magyars, 955. Imperial power was greatest under the **Hohenstaufens** (1138-1254), despite the growing opposition of the papacy, which ruled central Italy, and the Lombard League cities. Frederick II (1194-1250) improved administration, patronized the arts; after his death German influence was removed from Italy.

Christian Spain. From its northern mountain redoubts, Christian rule slowly migrated south through the 11th century, when Moslem unity collapsed. After the capture of **Toledo** (1085), the kingdoms of Portugal, Castile, and Aragon undertook repeated crusades of reconquest, finally completed in 1492. Elements of Islamic civilization persisted in recaptured areas, influencing all W. Europe.

Crusades. Pope Urban II called, 1095, for a crusade to restore Asia Minor to Byzantium and conquer the Holy Land from the Turks. Some 10 crusades (to 1291) succeeded only in founding 4 temporary Frankish states in the Levant. The 4th crusade sacked Constantinople, 1204. In Rhineland (1096), England (1290), France (1306), Jews were massacred or expelled, and wars were launched against Christian heretics (**Albigensian** crusade in France, 1229). Trade in eastern luxuries expanded, led by the Venetian naval empire.

Economy. The agricultural base of European life benefitted from improvements in **plow design** c1000, and by draining of lowlands and clearing of forests, leading to a rural population increase. Towns grew in N. Italy, Flanders, and N. Germany (Hanseatic League). Improvements in **loom design** permitted factory textile production. **Guilds** dominated urban trades from the 12th century. Banking (centered in Italy, 12th-15th century) facilitated long-distance trade.

The Church. The split between the Eastern and Western churches was formalized in 1054. W. and

950
— Otto I emperor
— Cairo founded
— Leif Eriksson
— Leif Eriksson reaches Amer.
— Poland begins eastern conquest
— Kiev Christian under Vladimir
— Tales of Genji in Japan
— Choir of St. Denis
1050
— Sufi mystic Ghazali b.
— E. W Church split
— Jewish scholar Rashi b.
— Christians capture Toledo
— Seljuk Turks take Baghdad
— Angkor Wat temple built
— Univ. Bologna founded
— Maimonides b.
— German Frederick II born
— Zen comes to Japan
1150
— Ghengis Khan b.
— Sultanate of Delhi founded
— Crusades
— Magna Carta
— Aquinas b.
— Dominicans, Franciscans founded
— Mali replaces Ghana
1250

Central Europe was divided into 500 bishoprics under one united hierarchy, but conflicts between secular and church authorities were frequent (German **Investiture Controversy**, 1075-1122). Clerical power was first strengthened through the international monastic reform begun at Cluny, 910. Popular religious enthusiasm often expressed itself in heretical movements (Waldensians from 1173), but was channelled by the **Dominican** (1215) and **Franciscan** (1223) friars into the religious mainstream.

Arts. Romanesque architecture (11th-12th centuries) expanded on late Roman models, using the rounded arch and massed stone to support enlarged basilicas. Painting and sculpture followed Byzantine models. The literature of chivalry was exemplified by the epic (Chanson de Roland, c1100) and by courtly love poems of the troubadours of Provence and minnesingers of Germany. **Gothic architecture** emerged in France (choir of St. Denis, c1040) and spread as French cultural influence predominated in Europe. Rib vaulting and pointed arches were used to combine soaring heights with delicacy, and freed walls for display of stained glass. Exteriors were covered with painted relief sculpture and elaborate architectural detail.

Learning. Law, medicine, and philosophy were advanced at independent **universities** (Bologna, late 11th century), originally corporations of students and masters. Twelfth century translations of Greek classics, especially Aristotle, encouraged an analytic approach. Scholastic philosophy, from Anselm (1033-1109) to Aquinas (1225-74) attempted to reconcile reason and revelation.

Apogee of Central Asian Power; Islam Grows: 1250-1500

Turks. Turkic peoples, of Central Asian ancestry, were a military threat to the Byzantine and Persian Empires from the 6th century. After several waves of invasions, during which most of the Turks adopted Islam, the **Seljuk Turks** took Baghdad, 1055. They ruled Persia, Iraq, and, after 1071, Asia Minor, where massive numbers of Turks settled. The empire was divided in the 12th century into smaller states ruled by Seljuks, Kurds (**Saladin** c1137-93), and Mamelukes (a military caste of former Turk, Kurd, and Circassian slaves), which governed Egypt and the Middle East until the Ottoman era (c1290-1922).

Osman I (ruled c1290-1326) and succeeding sultans united Anatolian Turkish warriors in a militaristic state that waged holy war against Byzantium and Balkan Christians. Most of the Balkans had been subdued, and Anatolia united, when **Constantinople fell**, 1453. By the mid-16th century, Hungary, the Middle East, and North Africa had been conquered. The Turkish advance was stopped at Vienna, 1529, and at the naval battle of Lepanto, 1571, by Spain, Venice, and the papacy.

The Ottoman state was governed in accordance with orthodox Moslem law. Greek, Armenian, and Jewish communities were segregated, and ruled by religious leaders responsible for taxation; they dominated trade. State offices and most army ranks were filled by slaves through a system of child conscription among Christians.

India. Mahmud of Ghazni (971-1030) led repeated Turkish raids into N. India. Turkish power was consolidated in 1206 with the start of the **Sultanate at Delhi.** Centralization of state power under the early Delhi sultans went far beyond traditional Indian practice. Moslem rule of most of the subcontinent lasted until the British conquest some 600 years later.

Mongols. Genghis Khan (c1162-1227) first united the feuding Mongol tribes, and built their armies into an effective offensive force around a core of highly mobile cavalry. He and his immediate successors created the largest land empire in history; by 1279 it stretched from the east coast of Asia to the Danube, from the Siberian steppes to the Arabian Sea. East-West trade and contacts were facilitated (Marco Polo c1254-1324). The western Mongols were Islamized by 1295; successor states soon lost their Mongol character by assimilation. They were briefly reunited under the Turk Tamerlane (1336-1405).

Kublai Khan ruled China from his new capital Peking (founded 1264). Naval campaigns against Japan (1274, 1281) and Java (1293) were defeated, the latter by the Hindu-Buddhist maritime kingdom of Majapahit. The **Yuan** dynasty made use of Mongols and other foreigners (including Europeans) in official posts, and tolerated the return of Nestorian Christianity (suppressed 841-45) and the spread of Islam in the South and West. A native reaction expelled the Mongols, 1367-68.

Russia. The Kievan state in Russia, weakened by the decline of Byzantium and the rise of the Catholic Polish-Lithuanian state, was overrun by the Mongols, 1238-40. Only the northern trading republic of Novgorod remained independent. The grand dukes of Moscow emerged as leaders of a coalition of princes that eventually defeated the Mongols, by 1481. With the fall of Constantinople, the **Tsars** (Caesars) at Moscow (from Ivan III, ruled 1462-1505) set up an independent Russian Orthodox Church. Commerce failed to revive. The isolated Russian state remained agrarian, with the peasant class falling into serfdom.

Persia. A revival of Persian literature, using the Arab alphabet and literary forms, began in the 10th century (epic of Firdausi, 935-1020). An art revival, influenced by Chinese styles, began in the 12th. Persian cultural and political forms, and often the Persian language, were used for centuries by Turkish and Mongol elites from the Balkans to India. Persian mystics from Rumi (1207-73) to Jami (1414-92) promoted **Sufism** in their poetry.

Africa. Two Berber dynasties, imbued with Islamic militance, emerged from the Sahara to carve out empires from the Sahel to central Spain — the **Almoravids**, c1050-1140, and the fanatical **Almohads**, c1125-1269. The Ghanaian empire was replaced in the upper Niger by Mali, c1230-c1340, whose Moslem rulers imported Egyptians to help make **Timbuktu** a center of commerce (in gold, leather, slaves) and learning. The Songhay empire (to 1590) replaced Mali. To the S, forest kingdoms produced refined art works (Ife terra cotta, **Benin** bronzes). Other Moslem states in Nigeria (Hausas) and Chad originated in the 11th century, and continued in some form until the 19th century European conquest. Less developed Bantu kingdoms existed across central Africa.

Some 40 Moslem Arab-Persian trading colonies and city-states were established all along the E. African coast from the 10th century (Kilwa, Mogadishu). The interchange with Bantu peoples produced the **Swahili** language and culture. Gold, palm oil, and slaves were brought from the interior, stimulating the growth of the Monamatapa kingdom of the Zambezi (15th century). The Christian Ethiopian empire (from 13th century) continued the traditions of Axum.

Southeast Asia. Islam was introduced into Malaya and the Indonesian islands by Arab, Persian, and

Indian traders. Coastal Moslem cities and states (starting before 1300), enriched by trade, soon dominated the interior. Chief among these was the **Malacca** state, on the Malay peninsula, c1400-1511.

Arts and Statecraft Thrive in Europe: 1350-1600

Italian Renaissance & humanism. Distinctive Italian achievements in the arts in the late Middle Ages (Dante, 1265-1321, Giotto, 1276-1337) led to the vigorous new styles of the Renaissance (14th-16th centuries). Patronized by the rulers of the quarreling petty states of Italy (Medicis in Florence and the papacy, c1400-1737), the plastic arts perfected realistic techniques, including **perspective** (Masaccio, 1401-28, Leonardo 1452-1519). Classical motifs were used in architecture and increased talent and expense were put into secular buildings. The Florentine dialect was refined as a national literary language (Petrarch, 1304-74). Greek refugees from the E strengthened the respect of humanist scholars for the classic sources (Bruni 1370-1444). Soon an international movement aided by the spread of **printing** (Gutenberg c1400-1468), **humanism** was optimistic about the power of human reason (Erasmus of Rotterdam, 1466-1536, Thomas More's *Utopia*, 1516) and valued individual effort in the arts and in politics (Machiavelli, 1469-1527).

France. The French monarchy, strengthened in its repeated struggles with powerful nobles (Burgundy, Flanders, Aquitaine) by alliances with the growing commercial towns, consolidated bureaucratic control under Philip IV (ruled 1285-1314) and extended French influence into Germany and Italy (popes at Avignon, France, 1309-1417). The **Hundred Years War,** 1337-1453, ended English dynastic claims in France (battles of Crécy, 1346, Poitiers, 1356; Joan of Arc executed, 1431). A French Renaissance, dating from royal invasions of Italy, 1494, 1499, was encouraged at the court of Francis I (ruled 1515-47), who centralized taxation and law. French vernacular literature consciously asserted its independence (La Pleiade, 1549).

England. The evolution of England's unique political institutions began with the Magna Carta, 1215, by which King John guaranteed the privileges of nobles and church against the monarchy and assured jury trial. After the Wars of the Roses (1455-85), the **Tudor dynasty** reasserted royal prerogatives (Henry VIII, ruled 1509-47), but the trend toward independent departments and ministerial government also continued. English trade (wool exports from c1340) was protected by the nation's growing maritime power (**Spanish Armada** destroyed, 1588).

English replaced French and Latin in the late 14th century in law and literature (Chaucer, 1340-1400) and English translation of the Bible began (Wycliffe, 1380s). Elizabeth I (ruled 1558-1603) presided over a confident flowering of poetry (Spenser, 1552-99), drama (**Shakespeare**, 1564-1616), and music.

German Empire. From among a welter of minor feudal states, church lands, and independent cities, the Hapsburgs assembled a far-flung territorial domain, based in Austria from 1276. The family held the title Holy Roman Emperor from 1452 to the Empire's dissolution in 1806, but failed to centralize its domains, leaving Germany disunited for centuries. Resistance to Turkish expansion brought Hungary under Austrian control from the 16th century. The Netherlands, Luxembourg, and Burgundy were added in 1477, curbing French expansion.

The Flemish painting tradition of naturalism, technical proficiency, and bourgeois subject matter began in the 15th century (Jan Van Eyck, 1366-1440), the earliest northern manifestation of the Renaissance. Durer (1471-1528) typified the merging of late Gothic and Italian trends in 16th century German art. Imposing civic architecture flourished in the prosperous commercial cities.

Spain. Despite the unification of Castile and Aragon in 1479, the 2 countries retained separate governments, and the nobility, especially in Aragon and Catalonia, retained many privileges. Spanish lands in Italy (Naples, Sicily) and the Netherlands entangled the country in European wars through the mid-17th century, while explorers, traders, and conquerors built up a Spanish empire in the Americas and the Philippines.

From the late 15th century, a **golden age** of literature and art produced works of social satire (plays of Lope de Vega, 1562-1635; Cervantes, 1547-1616), as well as spiritual intensity (El Greco, 1541-1614; Velazquez, 1599-1660).

Black Death. The bubonic plague reached Europe from the E in 1348, killing as much as half the population by 1350. Labor scarcity forced a rise in wages and brought greater freedom to the peasantry, making possible **peasant uprisings** (Jacquerie in France, 1358, Wat Tyler's rebellion in England, 1381). In the *ciompi* revolt, 1378, Florentine wage earners demanded a say in economic and political power.

Explorations. Organized European maritime exploration began, seeking to evade the Venice-Ottoman monopoly of eastern trade and to promote Christianity. Expeditions from Portugal beginning 1418 explored the west coast of Africa, until **Vasco da Gama** rounded the Cape of Good Hope in 1497 and reached India. A Portuguese trading empire was consolidated by the seizure of Goa, 1510, and Malacca, 1551. Japan was reached in 1542. Spanish voyages (**Columbus**, 1492-1504) uncovered a new world, which Spain hastened to subdue. Navigation schools in Spain and Portugal, the development of large sailing ships (carracks), and the invention of the rifle, c1475, aided European penetration.

Mughals and Safavids. East of the Ottoman empire, two Moslem dynasties ruled unchallenged in the 16th and 17th centuries. The Mughal empire in India, founded by Persianized Turkish invaders from the NW under Babur, dates from their 1526 conquest of Delhi. The dynasty ruled most of India for over 200 years, surviving nominally until 1857. **Akbar** (ruled 1556-1605) consolidated administration at his glorious court, where Urdu (Persian-influenced Hindi) developed. Trade relations with Europe increased. Under Shah Jahan (1629-58), a secularized art fusing Hindu and Moslem elements flourished in miniature painting and architecture (**Taj Mahal**). Sikhism, founded c1519, combined elements of both faiths. Suppression of Hindus and Shi'ite Moslems in S India in the late 17th century weakened the empire.

Fanatical devotion to the Shi'ite sect characterized the Safavids of Persia, 1502-1736, and led to hostilities with the Sunni Ottomans for over a century. The prosperity and strength of the empire are evidenced by the mosques at its capital, **Isfahan.** The dynasty enhanced Iranian national consciousness.

China. The Ming emperors, 1368-1644, the last native dynasty in China, wielded unprecedented personal power, while the Confucian bureaucracy began to suffer from inertia. European trade (Portugese

1500 — Brazil discovered — Calvin b. — Watch invented

Vesalius b. — St. Theresa of Avila b. — Luther's 95 Theses — Persian Safavids rule

Aztecs — Cortes conquers Aztecs — Mughal empire starts — So. Ger. peasants rise

Pizarro conquers Incas — Jesuits founded

Council of Trent — 1550

Dutch republic founded

Velazquez b. — Japan persecutes Christians — Civil War in France — Descartes b.

1600

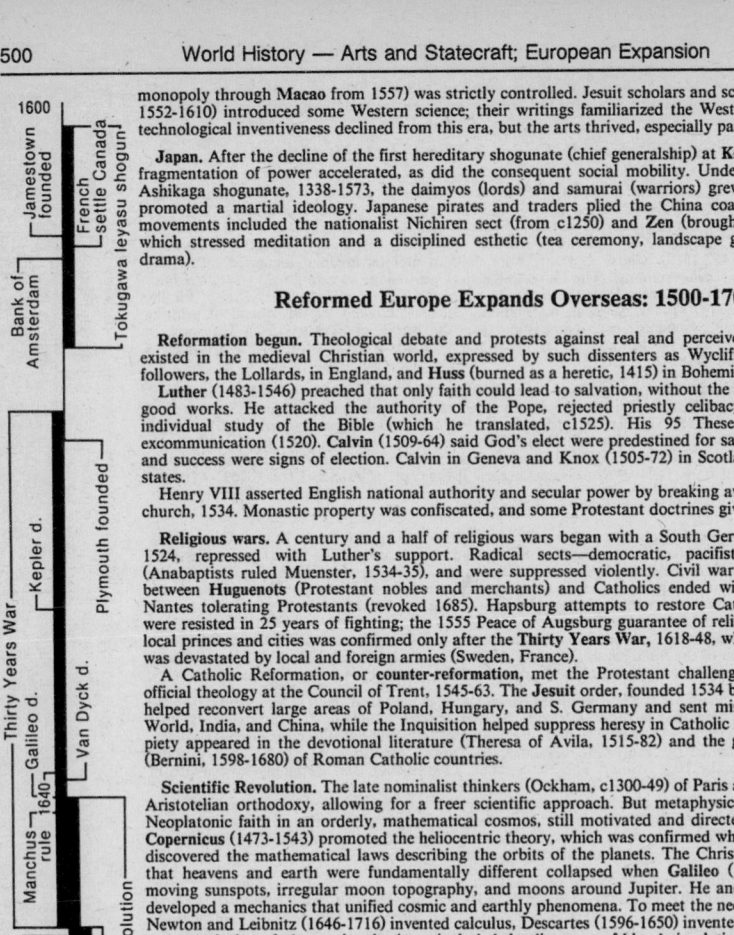

monopoly through **Macao** from 1557) was strictly controlled. Jesuit scholars and scientists (Matteo Ricci 1552-1610) introduced some Western science; their writings familiarized the West with China. Chinese technological inventiveness declined from this era, but the arts thrived, especially painting and ceramics.

Japan. After the decline of the first hereditary shogunate (chief generalship) at **Kamakura** (1185-1333), fragmentation of power accelerated, as did the consequent social mobility. Under Kamakura and the Ashikaga shogunate, 1338-1573, the daimyos (lords) and samurai (warriors) grew more powerful and promoted a martial ideology. Japanese pirates and traders plied the China coast. Popular Buddhist movements included the nationalist Nichiren sect (from c1250) and Zen (brought from China, 1191), which stressed meditation and a disciplined esthetic (tea ceremony, landscape gardening, judo, Noh drama).

Reformed Europe Expands Overseas: 1500-1700

Reformation begun. Theological debate and protests against real and perceived clerical corruption existed in the medieval Christian world, expressed by such dissenters as Wycliffe (c1320-84) and his followers, the Lollards, in England, and **Huss** (burned as a heretic, 1415) in Bohemia.

Luther (1483-1546) preached that only faith could lead to salvation, without the mediation of clergy or good works. He attacked the authority of the Pope, rejected priestly celibacy, and recommended individual study of the Bible (which he translated, c1525). His 95 Theses (1517) led to his excommunication (1520). **Calvin** (1509-64) said God's elect were predestined for salvation; good conduct and success were signs of election. Calvin in Geneva and Knox (1505-72) in Scotland erected theocratic states.

Henry VIII asserted English national authority and secular power by breaking away from the Catholic church, 1534. Monastic property was confiscated, and some Protestant doctrines given official sanction.

Religious wars. A century and a half of religious wars began with a South German peasant uprising, 1524, repressed with Luther's support. Radical sects—democratic, pacifist, milennarian—arose (Anabaptists ruled Muenster, 1534-35), and were suppressed violently. Civil war in France from 1562 between **Huguenots** (Protestant nobles and merchants) and Catholics ended with the 1598 Edict of Nantes tolerating Protestants (revoked 1685). Hapsburg attempts to restore Catholicism in Germany were resisted in 25 years of fighting; the 1555 Peace of Augsburg guarantee of religious independence to local princes and cities was confirmed only after the **Thirty Years War**, 1618-48, when much of Germany was devastated by local and foreign armies (Sweden, France).

A Catholic Reformation, or **counter-reformation**, met the Protestant challenge, clearly defining an official theology at the Council of Trent, 1545-63. The **Jesuit** order, founded 1534 by Loyola (1491-1556), helped reconvert large areas of Poland, Hungary, and S. Germany and sent missionaries to the New World, India, and China, while the Inquisition helped suppress heresy in Catholic countries. A revival of piety appeared in the devotional literature (Theresa of Avila, 1515-82) and the grandiose Baroque art (Bernini, 1598-1680) of Roman Catholic countries.

Scientific Revolution. The late nominalist thinkers (Ockham, c1300-49) of Paris and Oxford challenged Aristotelian orthodoxy, allowing for a freer scientific approach. But metaphysical values, such as the Neoplatonic faith in an orderly, mathematical cosmos, still motivated and directed subsequent inquiry. **Copernicus** (1473-1543) promoted the heliocentric theory, which was confirmed when Kepler (1571-1630) discovered the mathematical laws describing the orbits of the planets. The Christian-Aristotelian belief that heavens and earth were fundamentally different collapsed when Galileo (1564-1642) discovered moving sunspots, irregular moon topography, and moons around Jupiter. He and Newton (1642-1727) developed a mechanics that unified cosmic and earthly phenomena. To meet the needs of the new physics, Newton and Leibnitz (1646-1716) invented calculus, Descartes (1596-1650) invented analytic geometry.

An explosion of observational science included the discovery of blood circulation (Harvey, 1578-1657) and microscopic life (Leeuwenhoek, 1632-1723), and advances in anatomy (Vesalius, 1514-64, dissected corpses) and chemistry (Boyle, 1627-91). Scientific research institutes were founded: Florence, 1657, London (**Royal Society**), 1660, Paris, 1666. Inventions proliferated (Savery's steam engine, 1696).

Arts. Mannerist trends of the high Renaissance (Michelangelo, 1475-1564) exploited virtuosity, grace, novelty, and exotic subjects and poses. The notion of artistic genius was promoted, in contrast to the anonymous medieval artisan. Private connoisseurs entered the art market. These trends were elaborated in the 17th century **Baroque** era, on a grander scale. Dynamic movement in painting and sculpture was emphasized by sharp lighting effects, use of rich materials (colored marble, gilt), realistic details. Curved facades, broken lines, rich, deep-cut detail, and ceiling decoration characterized Baroque architecture, especially in Germany. Monarchs, princes, and prelates, usually Catholic, used Baroque art to enhance and embellish their authority, as in royal portraits by Velazquez (1599-1660) and Van Dyck (1599-1641).

National styles emerged. In France, a taste for rectilinear order and serenity (Poussin, 1594-1665), linked to the new rational philosophy, was expressed in classical forms. The influence of **classical values** in French literature (tragedies of Racine, 1639-99) gave rise to the "battle of the Ancients and Moderns." New forms included the essay (Montaigne, 1533-92) and novel (*Princesse de Cleves*, La Fayette, 1678).

Dutch painting of the 17th century was unique in its wide social distribution. The Flemish tradition of undemonstrative realism reached its peak in Rembrandt (1606-69) and Vermeer (1632-75).

Economy. European economic expansion was stimulated by the new trade with the East, New World gold and silver, and a doubling of population (50 mln. in 1450, 100 mln. in 1600). New business and financial techniques were developed and refined, such as joint-stock companies, insurance, and letters of credit and exchange. The Bank of Amsterdam, 1609, and the Bank of England, 1694, broke the old monopoly of private banking families. The rise of a business mentality was typified by the spread of clock towers in cities in the 14th century. By the mid-15th century, portable clocks were available; the first watch was invented in 1502.

By 1650, most governments had adopted the **mercantile system**, in which they sought to amass metallic wealth by protecting their merchants' foreign and colonial trade monopolies. The rise in prices and the new coin-based economy undermined the craft guild and feudal manorial systems. Expanding industries, such as clothweaving and mining, benefitted from technical advances. Coal replaced disappearing wood as the chief fuel; it was used to fuel new 16th century blast furnaces making cast iron.

New World. The **Aztecs** united much of the Mesoamerican culture area in a militarist empire by 1519, from their capital, Tenochtitlan (pop. 300,000), which was the center of a cult requiring enormous levels of ritual human sacrifice. Most of the civilized areas of S. America were ruled by the centralized **Inca Empire** (1476-1534), stretching 2,000 miles from Ecuador to N.W. Argentina. Lavish and sophisticated traditions in pottery, weaving, sculpture, and architecture were maintained in both regions.

These empires, beset by revolts, fell in 2 short campaigns to gold-seeking Spanish forces based in the Antilles and Panama. **Cortes** took Mexico, 1519-21; **Pizarro** Peru, 1531-35. From these centers, land and sea expeditions claimed most of N. and S. America for Spain. The Indian high cultures did not survive the impact of Christian missionaries and the new upper class of whites and mestizos. In turn, New World silver, and such Indian products as potatoes, tobacco, corn, peanuts, chocolate, and rubber exercised a major economic influence on Europe. While the Spanish administration intermittently concerned itself with the welfare of Indians, the population remained impoverished at most levels, despite the growth of a distinct South American civilization. European diseases reduced the native population.

Brazil, which the Portuguese discovered in 1500 and settled after 1530, and the Caribbean colonies of several European nations developed a plantation economy where sugar cane, tobacco, cotton, coffee, rice, indigo, and lumber were grown commercially by slaves. From the early 16th to the late 19th centuries, some 10 million Africans were transported to slavery in the New World.

Netherlands. The urban, Calvinist northern provinces of the Netherlands rebelled against Hapsburg Spain, 1568, and founded an oligarchic mercantile republic. Their strategic control of the Baltic grain market enabled them to exploit Mediterranean food shortages. Religious refugees — French and Belgian Protestants, Iberian Jews — added to the cosmopolitan commercial talent pool. After Spain absorbed Portugal in 1580, the Dutch seized Portuguese possessions and created a vast, though generally short-lived commercial empire in Brazil, the Antilles, Africa, India, Ceylon, Malacca, Indonesia, and Taiwan, and challenged or supplanted Portuguese traders in China and Japan.

England. Anglicanism became firmly established under Elizabeth I after a brief Catholic interlude under "Bloody Mary," 1553-58. But religious and political conflicts led to a rebellion by Parliament, 1642. Roundheads (Puritans) defeated Cavaliers (Royalists); Charles I was beheaded, 1649. The new **Commonwealth** was ruled as a military dictatorship by Cromwell, who also brutally crushed an Irish rebellion, 1649-51. Conflicts within the Puritan camp (democratic Levelers defeated 1649) aided the Stuart restoration, 1660, but Parliament was permanently strengthened and the peaceful **"Glorious Revolution"**, 1688, advanced political and religious liberties (writings of Locke, 1632-1704). British privateers (Drake, 1540-96) challenged Spanish control of the New World, and penetrated Asian trade routes (Madras taken, 1639). N. American colonies (Jamestown, 1607, Plymouth, 1620) provided an outlet for religious dissenters.

France. Emerging from the religious civil wars in 1628, France regained military and commercial great power status under the ministries of **Richelieu** (1624-42), Mazarin (1643-61), and Colbert (1662-83). Under Louis XIV (ruled 1643-1715) royal absolutism triumphed over nobles and local *parlements* (defeat of Fronde, 1648-53). Permanent colonies were founded in Canada (1608), the Caribbean (1626), and India (1674).

Sweden. Sweden seceded from the Scandinavian Union in 1523. The thinly-populated agrarian state (with copper, iron, and timber exports) was united by the Vasa kings, whose conquests by the mid-17th century made Sweden the dominant Baltic power. The empire collapsed in the Great Northern War (1700-21).

Poland. After the union with Lithuania in 1447, Poland ruled vast territories from the Baltic to the Black Sea, resisting German and Turkish incursions. Catholic nobles failed to gain the loyalty of the Orthodox Christian peasantry in the East; commerce and trades were practiced by German and Jewish immigrants. The bloody 1648-49 cossack uprising began the kingdom's dismemberment.

China. A new dynasty, the **Manchus**, invaded from the NE and seized power in 1644, and expanded Chinese control to its greatest extent in Central and Southeast Asia. Trade and diplomatic contact with Europe grew, carefully controlled by China. New crops (sweet potato, maize, peanut) allowed an economic and population growth (300 million pop. in 1800). Traditional arts and literature were pursued with increased sophistication (*Dream of the Red Chamber*, novel, mid-18th century).

Japan. Tokugawa Ieyasu, shogun from 1603, finally unified and pacified feudal Japan. Hereditary daimyos and samurai monopolized government office and the professions. An urban merchant class grew, literacy spread, and a cultural renaissance occurred (haiku of Basho, 1644-94). Fear of European domination led to persecution of Christian converts from 1597, and stringent isolation from outside contact from 1640.

Philosophy, Industry, and Revolution: 1700-1800

Science and Reason. Faith in human reason and science as the source of truth and a means to improve the physical and social environment, espoused since the Renaissance (Francis Bacon, 1561-1626), was bolstered by scientific discoveries in spite of theological opposition (**Galileo's forced retraction**, 1633). Descartes applied the logical method of mathematics to discover "self-evident" scientific and philosophical truths, while Newton emphasized induction from experimental observation.

The challenge of reason to traditional religious and political values and institutions began with **Spinoza** (1632-77), who interpreted the Bible historically and called for political and intellectual freedom.

French philosophes assumed leadership of the **"Enlightenment"** in the 18th century. Montesquieu (1689-1755) used British history to support his notions of limited government. Voltaire's (1694-1778) diaries and novels of exotic travel illustrated the intellectual trends toward secular ethics and relativism. Rousseau's (1712-1778) radical concepts of the **social contract** and of the inherent goodness of the common man gave impetus to anti-monarchical republicanism. The *Encyclopedia*, 1751-72, edited by Diderot and d'Alembert, designed as a monument to reason, was largely devoted to practical technology.

In England, ideals of political and religious liberty were connected with empiricist philosophy and science in the followers of Locke. But the extreme **empiricism of Hume** (1711-76) and Berkeley

1680

Savery's steam engine

Glorious Revolution

Bank of England

Edict of Nantes revoked

Racine d.

Locke d.

St. Petersburg founded

Great Northern War

Newcomen engine

Spectator

Louis XIV d.

1715

Newton d.

Voltaire's *Lettres philosophiques*

Watteau d.

Maria Theresa rule

Frederick II,

Montesquieu's *Spirit of Laws*

Poor Richard's Almanack

Vico d.

Hume's *Human Understanding*

1750

(1685-1753) posed limits to the identification of reason with absolute truth, as did the evolutionary approach to law and politics of Burke (1729-97) and the utilitarianism of Bentham (1748-1832). Adam Smith (1723-90) and other **physiocrats** called for a rationalization of economic activity by removing artificial barriers to a supposedly natural free exchange of goods.

Despite the political disunity and backwardness of most of Germany, German writers participated in the new philosophical trends popularized by Wolff (1679-1754). **Kant's** (1724-1804) **idealism**, unifying an empirical epistemology with *a priori* moral and logical concepts, directed German thought away from skepticism. Italian contributions included work on electricity by Galvani (1737-98) and Volta (1745-1827), the pioneer **historiography of Vico** (1668-1744), and writings on penal reform by Beccaria (1738-94). The American Franklin (1706-90) was celebrated in Europe for his varied achievements.

The growth of the **press** (*Spectator*, 1711-14) and the wide distribution of realistic but sentimental **novels** attested to the increase of a large bourgeois public.

Arts. Rococo art, characterized by extravagant decorative effects, asymmetries copied from organic models, and artificial pastoral subjects, was favored by the continental aristocracy for most of the century (Watteau, 1684-1721), and had musical analogies in the ornamentalized polyphony of late Baroque. The **Neoclassical** art after 1750, associated with the new scientific archeology, was more streamlined, and infused with the supposed moral and geometric rectitude of the Roman Republic (David, 1748-1825). In England, **town planning** on a grand scale began (Edinburgh, 1767).

Industrial Revolution in England. Agricultural improvements, such as the sowing drill (1701) and livestock breeding, were implemented on the large fields provided by enclosure of common lands by private owners. Profits from agriculture and from colonial and foreign trade (1800 volume, £ 54 million) were channelled through hundreds of banks and the **Stock Exchange** (founded 1773) into new industrial processes.

The Newcomen steam pump (1712) aided coal mining. Coal fueled the new efficient steam engines patented by Watt in 1769, and coke-smelting made cheap, sturdy iron for machinery by the 1730s. The **flying shuttle** (1733) and **spinning jenny** (1764) were used in the large new cotton textile factories, where women and children were much of the work force. Goods were transported cheaply over **canals** (2,000 miles built 1760-1800).

American Revolution. The British colonies in N. America attracted a mass immigration of religious dissenters and poor people throughout the 17th and 18th centuries, coming from all parts of the British Isles, Germany, the Netherlands, and other countries. The population reached 3 million whites and blacks by the 1770s. The small native population was decimated by European diseases and wars with and between the various colonies. British attempts to control colonial trade, and to tax the colonists to pay for the costs of colonial administration and defense clashed with traditions of local self government, and eventually provoked the colonies to rebellion. (*See American Revolution in Index.*)

Central and East Europe. The monarchs of the three states that dominated eastern Europe — Austria, Prussia, and Russia — accepted the advice and legitimation of philosophes in creating more modern, centralized institutions in their kingdoms, enlarged by the division of Poland (1772-95).

Under Frederick II (ruled 1740-86) Prussia, with its efficient modern army, doubled in size. State monopolies and tariff protection fostered industry, and some legal reforms were introduced. Austria's heterogeneous realms were legally unified under **Maria Theresa** (ruled 1740-80) and **Joseph II** (1780-90). Reforms in education, law, and religion were enacted, and the Austrian serfs were freed (1781). With its defeat in the Seven Years' War in 1763, Austria lost Silesia and ceased its active role in Germany, but was compensated by expansion to the E and S (Hungary, Slavonia, 1699, Galicia, 1772).

Russia, whose borders continued to expand in all directions, adopted some Western bureaucratic and economic policies under **Peter I** (ruled 1682-1725) and Catherine II (ruled 1762-96). Trade and cultural contacts with the West multiplied from the new Baltic Sea capital, **St. Petersburg** (founded 1703).

French Revolution. The growing French middle class lacked political power, and resented aristocratic tax privileges, especially in light of liberal political ideals popularized by the American Revolution. Peasants lacked adequate land and were burdened with feudal obligations to nobles. Wars with Britain drained the treasury, finally forcing the king to call the **Estates-General** in 1789 (first time since 1614), in an atmosphere of food riots (poor crop in 1788).

Aristocratic resistance to absolutism was soon overshadowed by the reformist Third Estate (middle class), which proclaimed itself the **National Constituent Assembly** June 17 and took the "Tennis Court oath" on June 20 to secure a constitution. The storming of the Bastille July 14 by Parisian artisans was followed by looting and seizure of aristocratic property throughout France. Assembly reforms included abolition of class and regional privileges, a Declaration of Rights, suffrage by taxpayers (75% of males), and the **Civil Constitution of the Clergy** providing for election and loyalty oaths for priests. A republic was declared Sept. 22, 1792, in spite of royalist pressure from Austria and Prussia, which had declared war in April (joined by Britain the next year). Louis XVI was beheaded Jan. 21, 1793, Queen Marie Antoinette was beheaded Oct. 16, 1793.

Royalist uprisings in La Vendee in the S and military reverses led to a **reign of terror** in which tens of thousands of opponents of the Revolution and criminals were executed. Radical reforms in the **Convention** period (Sept. 1793-Oct. 1795) included the abolition of colonial slavery, economic measures to aid the poor, support of public education, and a short-lived de-Christianization.

Division among radicals (execution of Hebert, March 1794, Danton, April, and Robespierre, July) aided the ascendance of a moderate **Directory**, which consolidated military victories. **Napoleon Bonaparte** (1769-1821), a popular young general, exploited political divisions and participated in a coup Nov. 9, 1799, making himself first consul (dictator).

India. Sikh and Hindu rebels (Rajputs, Marathas) and Afghans destroyed the power of the Mughals during the 18th century. After France's defeat in the Seven Years War, 1763, Britain was the chief European trade power in India. Its control of inland **Bengal and Bihar** was recognized by the Mughal shah in 1765, who granted the **British East India Co.** (under Clive, 1727-74) the right to collect land revenue there. Despite objections from Parliament (1784 India Act) the company's involvement in local wars and politics led to repeated acquisitions of new territory. The company exported Indian textiles, sugar, and indigo.

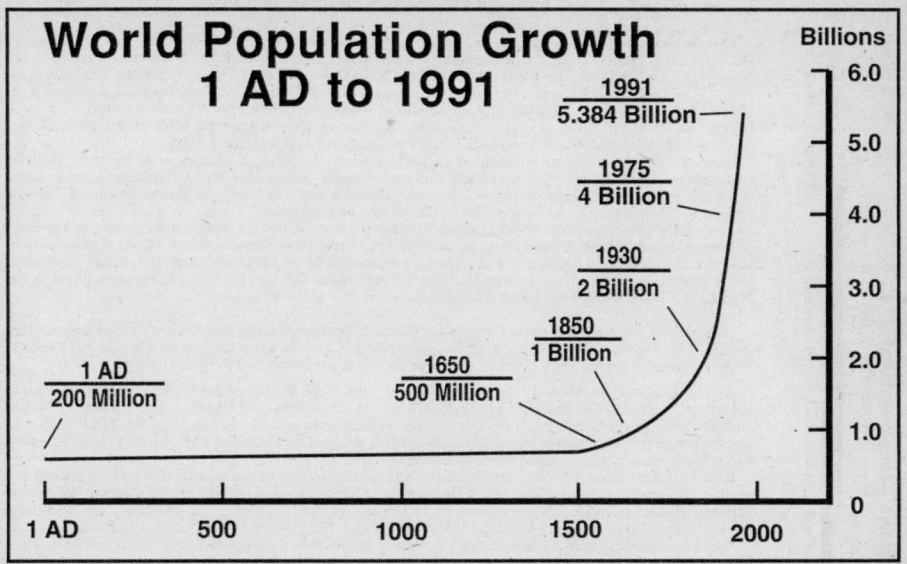

World Population Growth
1 AD to 1991

Billions

6.0

1991
5.384 Billion

5.0

1975
4 Billion

4.0

1930
2 Billion

3.0

1850
1 Billion

2.0

1 AD
200 Million

1650
500 Million

1.0

0

1 AD   500   1000   1500   2000

RUSSIAN EMPIRE

Lake Baikal

MANCHURIA

OTTOMAN EMPIRE

JAPAN

Jerusalem

MONGOLIA

KOREA

Baghdad

Teheran

Peking

SINKIANG

PERSIA   AFGHANISTAN

CHINESE EMPIRE

Shanghai

Kabul

KASHMIR

Mecca

TIBET

CHINA

Pacific Ocean

PUNJAB

Lhasa

Chungking

ARABIA

BALUCHISTAN

Delhi

NEPAL

TAIWAN

OMAN

Karachi

BHUTAN

Canton

PHILIPPINE ISLANDS

BRITISH INDIA

Mandalay

Hong Kong

Calcutta

TONGKING

HAINAN

Bombay

BURMA

LAOS

South China Sea

Arabian Sea

Rangoon

SIAM

Bangkok

Madras

CAMBODIA

Bay of Bengal

Saigon

CEYLON

ASIA CIRCA 1900

0   600   1200

Singapore

BORNEO

CELEBES

Scale of Miles

SUMATRA

Indian Ocean

JAVA

Change Gathers Steam: 1800-1840

Timeline (1800–1845):

- 1800
- Haiti indep.
- Mill b.
- Hugo b.
- Dix b.
- Lamarck's *Philosophie Zoologique*
- Napoleon emperor
- Congress of Vienna
- 1815
- Scott's *Ivanhoe*
- Brazil indep.
- Grimm's *Fairy Tales*
- S. Amer. colonies win indep.
- Greek indep. movement
- Byron d.
- Decembrist uprising
- Blake d.
- 1830
- Volta d.
- Beethoven d.
- Belgian indep.
- 1st Eng. reform bill
- 1st Brit. Factory Act.
- Brit. Emp. slavery banned
- Brook Farm, Mass.
- Opium War
- Telegraph perfected by Morse
- 1845

French ideals and empire spread. Inspired by the ideals of the French Revolution, and supported by the expanding French armies, new republican regimes arose near France: the **Batavian** Republic in the Netherlands (1795-1806), the **Helvetic** Republic in Switzerland (1798-1803), the **Cisalpine** Republic in N. Italy (1797-1805), the **Ligurian** Republic in Genoa (1797-1805), and the **Parthenopean** Republic in S. Italy (1799). A Roman Republic existed briefly in 1798 after Pope Pius VI was arrested by French troops. In Italy and Germany, new nationalist sentiments were stimulated both in imitation of and reaction to France (anti-French and anti-Jacobin peasant uprisings in Italy, 1796-9).

From 1804, when Napoleon declared himself emperor, to 1812, a succession of military victories (Austerlitz, 1805, Jena, 1806) extended his control over most of Europe, through puppet states (**Confederation of the Rhine** united W. German states for the first time and **Grand Duchy of Warsaw** revived Polish national hopes), expansion of the empire, and alliances.

Among the lasting reforms initiated under Napoleon's absolutist reign were: establishment of the Bank of France, centralization of tax collection, codification of law along Roman models (*Code Napoleon*), and reform and extension of secondary and university education. In an 1801 concordat, the papacy recognized the effective autonomy of the French Catholic Church. Some 400,000 French soldiers were killed in the Napoleonic Wars, along with 600,000 foreign troops.

Last gasp of old regime. France's coastal blockade of Europe (**Continental System**) failed to neutralize Britain. The disastrous 1812 invasion of Russia exposed Napoleon's overextension. After an 1814 exile at Elba, Napoleon's armies were defeated at **Waterloo**, 1815, by British and Prussian troops.

At the **Congress of Vienna**, the monarchs and princes of Europe redrew their boundaries, to the advantage of Prussia (in Saxony and the Ruhr), Austria (in Illyria and Venetia), and Russia (in Poland and Finland). British conquest of Dutch and French colonies (S. Africa, Ceylon, Mauritius) was recognized, and France, under the restored Bourbons, retained its expanded 1792 borders. The settlement brought 50 years of international peace to Europe.

But the Congress was unable to check the advance of liberal ideals and of nationalism among the smaller European nations. The 1825 **Decembrist uprising** by liberal officers in Russia was easily suppressed. But an independence movement in **Greece**, stirred by commercial prosperity and a cultural revival, succeeded in expelling Ottoman rule by 1831, with the aid of Britain, France, and Russia.

A constitutional monarchy was secured in France by an **1830 revolution**; Louis Philippe became king. The revolutionary contagion spread to **Belgium**, which gained its independence from the Dutch monarchy, 1830; to **Poland**, whose rebellion was defeated by Russia, 1830-31; and to Germany.

Romanticism. A new style in intellectual and artistic life began to replace Neo-classicism and Rococo after the mid-18th century. By the early 19th, this style, Romanticism, had prevailed in the European world.

Rousseau had begun the reaction against excessive rationalism and skepticism; in education (*Emile*, 1762) he stressed subjective spontaneity over regularized instruction. In Germany, Lessing (1729-81) and Herder (1744-1803) favorably compared the German folk song to classical forms, and began a cult of Shakespeare, whose passion and "natural" wisdom was a model for the Romantic *Sturm und Drang* (storm and stress) movement. **Goethe's** *Sorrows of Young Werther* (1774) set the model for the tragic, passionate genius.

A new interest in **Gothic architecture** in England after 1760 (Walpole, 1717-97) spread through Europe, associated with an aesthetic Christian and mystic revival (Blake, 1757-1827). Celtic, Norse, and German mythology and folk tales were revived or imitated (Macpherson's Ossian translation, 1762, Grimm's *Fairy Tales*, 1812-22). The medieval revival (Scott's *Ivanhoe*, 1819) led to a new interest in history, stressing national differences and organic growth (Carlyle, 1795-1881; Michelet, 1798-1874), corresponding to theories of natural evolution (Lamarck's *Philosophie zoologique*, 1809, Lyell's *Geology*, 1830-33).

Revolution and war fed an obsession with freedom and conflict, expressed by poets (**Byron**, 1788-1824, **Hugo**, 1802-85) and philosophers (**Hegel**, 1770-1831).

Wild gardens replaced the formal French variety, and painters favored rural, stormy, and mountainous landscapes (**Turner**, 1775-1851; **Constable**, 1776-1837). Clothing became freer, with wigs, hoops, and ruffles discarded. Originality and genius were expected in the life as well as the work of inspired artists (Murger's *Scenes from Bohemian Life*, 1847-49). Exotic locales and themes (as in "Gothic" horror stories) were used in art and literature (Delacroix, 1798-1863, Poe, 1809-49).

Music exhibited the new dramatic style and a breakdown of classical forms (Beethoven, 1770-1827). The use of folk melodies and modes aided the growth of distinct national traditions (Glinka in Russia, 1804-57).

Latin America. Haiti, under the former slave **Toussaint L'Ouverture**, was the first Latin American independent state, 1800. All the mainland Spanish colonies won their independence 1810-24, under such leaders as **Bolívar** (1783-1830). Brazil became an independent empire under the Portuguese prince regent, 1822. A new class of military officers divided power with large landholders and the church.

United States. Heavy immigration and exploitation of ample natural resources fueled rapid economic growth. The spread of the franchise, public education, and antislavery sentiment were signs of a widespread democratic ethic.

China. Failure to keep pace with Western arms technology exposed China to greater European influence, and hampered efforts to bar imports of opium, which had damaged Chinese society and drained wealth overseas. In the **Opium War**, 1839-42, Britain forced China to expand trade opportunities and to cede Hong Kong.

Triumph of Progress: 1840-80

Idea of Progress. As a result of the cumulative scientific, economic, and political changes of the preceding eras, the idea took hold among literate people in the West that continuing growth and improvement was the natural state of human and natural life.

Darwin's statement of the **theory of evolution** and survival of the fittest (*Origin of Species*, 1859), defended by intellectuals and scientists against theological objections, was taken as confirmation that progress was the natural direction of life. The controversy helped define popular ideas of the dedicated scientist and ever-expanding human knowledge of and control over the world (Foucault's demonstration of earth's rotation, 1851, Pasteur's germ theory, 1861).

Liberals following Ricardo (1772-1823) in their faith that unrestrained competition would bring continuous economic expansion sought to adjust political life to the new social realities, and believed that unregulated competition of ideas would yield truth (Mill, 1806-73). In England, successive reform bills (1832, 1867, 1884) gave representation to the new industrial towns, and extended the franchise to the middle and lower classes and to Catholics, Dissenters, and Jews. On both sides of the Atlantic, reformists tried to improve conditions for the mentally ill (Dix, 1802-87), women (Anthony, 1820-1906), and prisoners. Slavery was barred in the British Empire, 1833; the United States, 1865; and Brazil, 1888.

Socialist theories based on ideas of human perfectibility or historical progress were widely disseminated. Utopian socialists like Saint-Simon (1760-1825) envisaged an orderly, just society directed by a technocratic elite. A model factory town, New Lanark, Scotland, was set up by utopian Robert Owen (1771-1858), and utopian communal experiments were tried in the U.S. (Brook Farm, Mass., 1841-7). Bakunin's (1814-76) anarchism represented the opposite utopian extreme of total freedom. Marx (1818-83) posited the inevitable triumph of socialism in the industrial countries through a historical process of class conflict.

Spread of industry. The technical processes and managerial innovations of the English industrial revolution spread to Europe (especially Germany) and the U.S., causing an explosion of industrial production, demand for raw materials, and competition for markets. Inventors, both trained and self-educated, provided the means for larger-scale production (Bessemer steel, 1856, sewing machine, 1846). Many inventions were shown at the 1851 London Great Exhibition at the Crystal Palace, whose theme was universal prosperity.

Local specialization and long-distance trade were aided by a revolution in transportation and communication. Railroads were first introduced in the 1820s in England and the U.S. Over 150,000 miles of track had been laid worldwide by 1880, with another 100,000 miles laid in the next decade. Steamships were improved (*Savannah* crossed Atlantic, 1819). The telegraph, perfected by 1844 (Morse), connected the Old and New Worlds by cable in 1866, and quickened the pace of international commerce and politics. The first commercial telephone exchange went into operation in the U.S. in 1878.

The new class of industrial workers, uprooted from their rural homes, lacked job security, and suffered from dangerous overcrowded conditions at work and at home. Many responded by organizing trade unions (legalized in England, 1824; France, 1884). The U.S. Knights of Labor had 700,000 members by 1886. The First International, 1864-76, tried to unite workers internationally around a Marxist program. The quasi-Socialist Paris Commune uprising, 1871, was violently suppressed. Factory Acts to reduce child labor and regulate conditions were passed (1833-50 in England). Social security measures were introduced by the Bismarck regime in Germany, 1883-89.

Revolutions of 1848. Among the causes of the continent-wide revolutions were an international collapse of credit and resulting unemployment, bad harvests in 1845-7, and a cholera epidemic. The new urban proletariat and expanding bourgeoisie demanded a greater political role. Republics were proclaimed in France, Rome, and Venice. Nationalist feelings reached fever pitch in the Hapsburg empire, as Hungary declared independence under Kossuth, a Slav Congress demanded equality, and Piedmont tried to drive Austria from Lombardy. A national liberal assembly at Frankfurt called for German unification.

But riots fueled bourgeois fears of socialism (Marx and Engels' 1848 *Communist Manifesto*) and peasants remained conservative. The old establishment — The Papacy, the Hapsburgs (using Croats and Romanians against Hungary), the Russian army — was able to rout the revolutionaries by 1849. The French Republic succumbed to a renewed monarchy by 1852 (Emperor Napoleon III).

Great nations unified. Using the "blood and iron" tactics of Bismarck from 1862, Prussia controlled N. Germany by 1867 (war with Denmark, 1864, Austria, 1866). After defeating France in 1870 (loss of Alsace-Lorraine), it won the allegiance of S. German states. A new **German Empire** was proclaimed, 1871. **Italy**, inspired by Mazzini (1805-72) and Garibaldi (1807-82), was unified by the reformed Piedmont kingdom through uprisings, plebiscites, and war.

The U.S., its area expanded after the 1846-47 Mexican War, defeated a secession attempt by slave states, 1861-65. The Canadian provinces were united in an autonomous **Dominion of Canada**, 1867. Control in India was removed from the East India Co. and centralized under British administration after the 1857-58 Sepoy rebellion, laying the groundwork for the modern Indian State. Queen Victoria was named Empress of India, 1876.

Europe dominates Asia. The Ottoman Empire began to collapse in the face of Balkan nationalisms and European imperial incursions in N. Africa (Suez Canal, 1869). The Turks had lost control of most of both regions by 1882. Russia completed its expansion south by 1884 (despite the temporary setback of the Crimean War with Turkey, Britain, and France, 1853-56) taking Turkestan, all the Caucasus, and Chinese areas in the East and sponsoring Balkan Slavs against the Turks. A succession of reformist and reactionary regimes presided over a slow modernization (serfs freed, 1861). Persian independence suffered as Russia and British India competed for influence.

China was forced to sign a series of unequal treaties with European powers and Japan. Overpopulation and an inefficient dynasty brought misery and caused rebellions (Taiping, Moslems) leaving tens of millions dead. Japan was forced by the U.S. (Commodore Perry's visits, 1853-54) and Europe to end its isolation. The Meiji restoration, 1868, gave power to a Westernizing oligarchy. Intensified empire-building gave Burma to Britain, 1824-86, and Indo-China to France, 1862-95. Christian missionary activity followed imperial and trade expansion in Asia.

Respectability. The fine arts were expected to reflect and encourage the progress of morals and

1845 —

Communist Manifesto

Sewing machine

Mexican War begins

Freud b.

Perry in Japan

Second Empire in France

U.S. Civil War

1860 —

Bessemer steel

Sepoy rebellion

Overseas cable

Canada united

Marxist 1st International

1870 —

Paris commune

German empire founded

Mazzini d.

1st telephone

1880 —

The Seven Wonders of the World

These ancient works of art and architecture were considered awe-inspiring in splendor and/or size by the Greek and Roman world of the Alexandrian epoch and later. Classical writers disagreed as to which works made up the list of Wonders, but the following were usually included:

The Pyramids of Egypt: The only surviving Wonder, these monumental structures of masonry located on the west bank of the Nile River above Cairo were built from 3000 to 1800 B.C. as royal tombs. Three—Khufu, Khafra, and Menkaura—were often grouped as the first Wonder of the World. The largest, **The Great Pyramid of Khufu,** or Cheops, is a solid mass of limestone blocks covering 13 acres. It is estimated to contain 2.3 million blocks of stone, the stones themselves averaging 2½ tons and some weighing 30 tons. Its construction reputedly took 100,000 laborers 20 years.

The Hanging Gardens of Babylon: These gardens were laid out on a brick terrace about 400 feet square and 75 feet above the ground. To irrigate the trees, shrubs, and flowers, screws were turned to lift water from the Euphrates River. The gardens were probably built by King Nebuchandnezzar II around 600 B.C. **The Walls of Babylon,** long, thick, and made of colorfully glazed brick, were considered by some to be among the Seven Wonders.

The Statue of Zeus (Jupiter) at Olympia: This statue of the king of the gods showed him seated on a throne. His flesh was made of ivory, his robe and ornaments of gold. Reputedly 40 feet high, the statue was made by Phidias and was placed in the great temple of Zeus in the sacred grove of Olympia around 457 B.C.

The Colossus of Rhodes: A bronze statue of the sun god Helios, the Colossus was worked on for 12 years in the early 200's B.C. by the sculptor Chares. It was probably 120 feet high. A symbol of the city of Rhodes at its height, the statue stood on a promontory overlooking the harbor.

The Temple of Artemis (Diana) at Ephesus: This largest and most complex temple of ancient times was built around 550 B.C. and was made of marble except for its tile-covered wooden roof. It was begun in honor of a non-Hellenic goddess who later became identified with the Greek goddess of the same name. Ephesus was one of the greatest of the Ionian cities.

The Mausoleum at Halicarnassus: The source of our word "mausoleum," this marble tomb was built in what is now southeastern Turkey by Artemisia for her husband Mausolus, an official of the Persian Empire who died in 353 B.C. About 135 feet high, it was adorned with the works of 4 sculptors.

The Pharos (Lighthouse) of Alexandria: This sculpture was designed around 270 B.C., during the reign of King Ptolemy II, by the Greek architect Sostratos. Estimates of its height range from 200 to 600 feet.

Africa 1914

- British
- French
- German
- Belgian
- Italian
- Portuguese
- Spanish
- Independent

manners among the different classes. "Victorian" prudery, exaggerated delicacy, and familial piety were heralded by **Bowdler's** expurgated edition of Shakespeare (1818). Government-supported mass education inculcated a work ethic as a means to escape poverty (Horatio Alger, 1832-99).

The official **Beaux Arts** school in Paris set an international style of imposing public buildings (Paris Opera, 1861-74, Vienna Opera, 1861-69) and uplifting statues (Bartholdi's *Statue of Liberty*, 1885). Realist painting, influenced by photography (Daguerre, 1837), appealed to a new mass audience with social or historical narrative (Wilkie, 1785-1841, Poynter, 1836-1919) or with serious religious, moral, or social messages (pre-Raphaelites, Millet's *Angelus*, 1858) often drawn from ordinary life. The **Impressionists** (Pissarro, 1830-1903, Renoir, 1841-1919) rejected the central role of serious subject matter in favor of a colorful and sensual depiction of a moment, but their sunny, placid depictions of bourgeois scenes kept them within the respectable consensus.

Realistic **novelists** presented the full panorama of social classes and personalities, but retained sentimentality and moral judgment (Dickens, 1812-70, Eliot, 1819-80, Tolstoy, 1828-1910, Balzac, 1799-1850).

Veneer of Stability: 1880-1900

Imperialism triumphant. The vast **African** interior, visited by European explorers (Barth, 1821-65, Livingstone, 1813-73) was conquered by the European powers in rapid, competitive thrusts from their coastal bases after 1880, mostly for domestic political and international strategic reasons. W. African Moslem kingdoms (Fulani), Arab slave traders (Zanzibar), and Bantu military confederations (Zulu) were alike subdued. Only Christian Ethiopia (defeat of Italy, 1896) and Liberia resisted successfully. France (W. Africa) and Britain ("Cape to Cairo," Boer War, 1899-1902) were the major beneficiaries. The ideology of "the white man's burden" (Kipling, *Barrack Room Ballads*, 1892) or of a "civilizing mission" (France) justified the conquests.

West European foreign capital investments soared to nearly $40 billion by 1914, but most was in E. Europe (France, Germany) the Americas (Britain) and the white colonies. The foundation of the modern interdependent world economy was laid, with cartels dominating raw material trade.

An industrious world. Industrial and technological proficiency characterized the 2 new great powers — Germany and the U.S. Coal and iron deposits enabled Germany to reach second or third place status in iron, steel, and shipbuilding by the 1900s. German electrical and chemical industries were world leaders. The U.S. post-civil war boom (interrupted by "panics," 1884, 1893, 1896) was shaped by massive immigration from S. and E. Europe from 1880, government subsidy of railroads, and huge private monopolies (Standard Oil, 1870, U.S. Steel, 1901). The **Spanish-American War,** 1898 (Philippine rebellion, 1899-1901) and the Open Door policy in China (1899) made the U.S. a world power.

England led in **urbanization** (72% by 1890), with **London** the world capital of finance, insurance, and shipping. Electric subways (London, 1890), sewer systems (Paris, 1850s), parks, and bargain department stores helped improve living standards for most of the urban population of the industrial world.

Asians assimilate. Asian reaction to European economic, military, and religious incursions took the form of imitation of Western techniques and adoption of Western ideas of progress and freedom. The Chinese "self-strengthening" movement of the 1860s and 70s included rail, port, and arsenal improvements and metal and textile mills. Reformers like **K'ang Yu-wei** (1858-1927) won liberalizing reforms in 1898, right after the European and Japanese "scramble for concessions."

A universal education system in Japan and importation of foreign industrial, scientific, and military experts aided Japan's unprecedented rapid modernization after 1868, under the authoritarian Meiji regime. Japan's victory in the **Sino-Japanese War,** 1894-95, put Formosa and Korea in its power.

In India, the British alliance with the remaining princely states masked reform sentiment among the Westernized urban elite; higher education had been conducted largely in English for 50 years. The **Indian National Congress,** founded in 1885, demanded a larger government role for Indians.

"Fin-de-siecle" sophistication. Naturalist writers pushed realism to its extreme limits, adopting a quasi-scientific attitude and writing about formerly taboo subjects like sex, crime, extreme poverty, and corruption (Flaubert, 1821-80, Zola, 1840-1902, Hardy, 1840-1928). Unseen or repressed psychological motivations were explored in the clinical and theoretical works of **Freud** (1856-1939) and in the fiction of Dostoevsky (1821-81), James (1843-1916), Schnitzler (1862-1931) and others.

A contempt for bourgeois life or a desire to shock a complacent audience was shared by the French **symbolist** poets (Verlaine, 1844-96, Rimbaud, 1854-91), neo-pagan English writers (Swinburne, 1837-1909), continental dramatists (Ibsen, 1828-1906) and satirists (Wilde, 1854-1900). **Nietzsche** (1844-1900) was influential in his elitism and pessimism.

Post-impressionist art neglected long-cherished conventions of representation (Cezanne, 1839-1906) and showed a willingness to learn from primitive and non-European art (Gauguin, 1848-1903, Japanese prints).

Racism. Gobineau (1816-82) gave a pseudo-biological foundation to modern racist theories, which spread in the latter 19th century along with **Social Darwinism,** the belief that societies are and should be organized as a struggle for survival of the fittest. The Medieval period was interpreted as an era of natural Germanic rule (Chamberlain, 1855-1927) and notions of superiority were associated with German national aspirations (Treitschke, 1834-96). **Anti-Semitism,** with a new racist rationale, became a significant political force in Germany (Anti-Semitic Petition, 1880), Austria (Lueger, 1844-1910), and France (Dreyfus case, 1894-1906).

Last Respite: 1900-1909

Alliances. While the peace of Europe (and its dependencies) continued to hold (1907 **Hague Conference** extended the rules of war and international arbitration procedures), imperial rivalries, protectionist trade practices (in Germany and France), and the escalating arms race (British *Dreadnought* battleship launched, Germany widens Kiel canal, 1906) exacerbated minor disputes (German-French Moroccan "crises", 1905, 1911).

Security was sought through alliances: **Triple Alliance** (Germany, Austria-Hungary, Italy) renewed

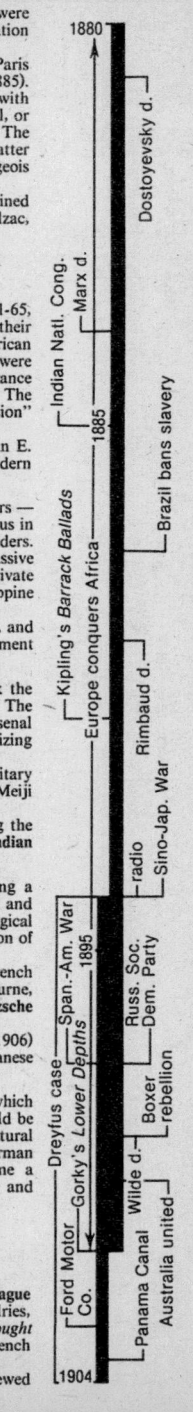

1880

Dostoyevsky d.

Indian Natl. Cong.
Marx d.
1885
Brazil bans slavery

Kipling's *Barrack Room Ballads*
Europe conquers Africa
Rimbaud d.
radio
Sino-Jap. War

Span.-Am. War
1895
Russ. Soc.
Dem. Party

Dreyfus case
Gorky's *Lower Depths*
Wilde d.
Boxer rebellion

Ford Motor Co.
Panama Canal
Australia united

1904

1904

1916

1910

Pure Food & Drug Act

Rev. in Russia

Russo-Jap. War

Labour Party

Ibsen d.

Young Turks rev.

Dreadnought launched

Hague Conf.

Robie House

Futurist Manifesto

Japan annexes Korea

Mex. rev. starts

Portugal rev. starts

2d Morocco crisis

Diaz Mex. rule ends

Chinese repub.

Ottomans lose Europe

Theory of Relativity

Maugham's "Of Human Bondage"

World War I

1902, 1907; Anglo-Japanese Alliance, 1902; Franco-Russian Alliance, 1899; **Entente Cordiale** (Britain, France) 1904; Anglo-Russian Treaty, 1907; German-Ottoman friendship.

Ottomans decline. The inefficient, corrupt Ottoman government was unable to resist further loss of territory. Nearly all European lands were lost in 1912 to Serbia, Greece, Montenegro, and Bulgaria. Italy took Libya and the Dodecanese islands the same year, and Britain took Kuwait, 1899, and the Sinai, 1906. The **Young Turk** revolution in 1908 forced the sultan to restore a constitution, introduced some social reform, industrialization, and secularization.

British Empire. British trade and cultural influence remained dominant in the empire, but constitutional reforms presaged its eventual dissolution: the colonies of **Australia** were united in 1901 under a self-governing commonwealth. **New Zealand** acquired dominion status in 1907. The old Boer republics joined Cape Colony and Natal in the self-governing **Union of South Africa** in 1910.
  The 1909 Indian Councils Act enhanced the role of elected province legislatures in **India.** The Moslem League, founded 1906, sought separate communal representation.

East Asia. Japan exploited its growing industrial power to expand its empire. Victory in the 1904-05 war against Russia (naval battle of Tsushima, 1905) assured Japan's domination of **Korea** (annexed 1910) and Manchuria (took Port Arthur 1905).
  In China, central authority began to crumble (empress died, 1908). Reforms (Confucian exam system ended 1905, modernization of the army, building of railroads) were inadequate and secret societies of reformers and nationalists, inspired by the Westernized **Sun Yat-sen** (1866-1925) fomented periodic uprisings in the south.
  Siam, whose independence had been guaranteed by Britain and France in 1896, was split into spheres of influence by those countries in 1907.

Russia. The population of the Russian Empire approached 150 million in 1900. Reforms in education, law, and local institutions (*zemstvos*), and an industrial boom starting in the 1880s (oil, railroads) created the beginnings of a modern state, despite the autocratic tsarist regime. Liberals (1903 Union of Liberation), Socialists (Social Democrats founded 1898, Bolsheviks split off 1903), and populists (Social Revolutionaries founded 1901) were periodically repressed, and national minorities persecuted (anti-Jewish pogroms, 1903, 1905-6).
  An industrial crisis after 1900 and harvest failures aggravated poverty in the urban proletariat, and the 1904-05 defeat by Japan (which checked Russia's Asian expansion) sparked the revolution of 1905-06. A **Duma** (parliament) was created, and an agricultural reform (under Stolypin, prime minister 1906-11) created a large class of landowning peasants (kulaks).

The world shrinks. Developments in transportation and communication and mass population movements helped create an awareness of an interdependent world. Early **automobiles** (Daimler, Benz, 1885) were experimental, or designed as luxuries. Assembly-line mass production (Ford Motor Co., 1903) made the invention practicable, and by 1910 nearly 500,000 motor vehicles were registered in the U.S. alone. **Heavier-than-air flights** began in 1903 in the U.S. (Wright brothers), preceded by glider, balloon, and model plane advances in several countries. Trade was advanced by improvements in **ship design** (gyrocompass, 1907), speed (Lusitania crossed Atlantic in 5 days, 1907), and reach (Panama Canal begun, 1904).
  The first transatlantic **radio** telegraphic transmission occurred in 1901, 6 years after Marconi discovered radio. Radio transmission of human speech had been made in 1900. Telegraphic transmission of photos was achieved in 1904, lending immediacy to news reports. **Phonographs,** popularized by Caruso's recordings (starting 1902) made for quick international spread of musical styles (ragtime). **Motion pictures,** perfected in the 1890s (Dickson, Lumiere brothers), became a popular and artistic medium after 1900; newsreels appeared in 1909.
  Emigration from overcrowded European centers soared in the decade: 9 million migrated to the U.S., and millions more went to Siberia, Canada, Argentina, Australia, South Africa, and Algeria. Some 70 million Europeans emigrated in the century before 1914. Several million Chinese, Indians, and Japanese migrated to Southeast Asia, where their urban skills often enabled them to take a predominant economic role.

Social reform. The social and economic problems of the poor were kept in the public eye by realist fiction writers (Dreiser's *Sister Carrie,* 1900; Gorky's *Lower Depths,* 1902; Sinclair's *Jungle,* 1906), journalists (U.S. **muckrakers** — Steffens, Tarbell) and artists (Ashcan school). Frequent labor strikes and occasional assassinations by anarchists or radicals (Austrian Empress, 1898; King Umberto I of Italy, 1900; U.S. Pres. McKinley, 1901; Russian Interior Minister Plehve, 1904; Portugal's King Carlos, 1908) added to social tension and fear of revolution.
  But democratic reformism prevailed. In Germany, Bernstein's (1850-1932) **revisionist Marxism,** downgrading revolution, was accepted by the powerful Social Democrats and trade unions. The British Fabian Society (the Webbs, Shaw) and the Labour Party (founded 1906) worked for reforms such as social security and union rights (1906), while women's suffragists grew more militant. U.S. **progressives** fought big business (Pure Food and Drug Act, 1906). In France, the 10-hour work day (1904) and separation of church and state (1905) were reform victories, as was universal suffrage in Austria (1907).

  Arts. An unprecedented period of experimentation, centered in France, produced several new **painting** styles: fauvism exploited bold color areas (Matisse, *Woman with Hat,* 1905); expressionism reflected powerful inner emotions (the Brücke group, 1905); cubism combined several views of an object on one flat surface (Picasso's *Demoiselles,* 1906-07); futurism tried to depict speed and motion (Italian Futurist Manifesto, 1910). **Architects** explored new uses of steel structures, with facades either neo-classical (Adler and Sullivan in U.S.); curvilinear Art Nouveau (Gaudi's Casa Mila, 1905-10); or functionally streamlined (Wright's Robie House, 1909).
  Music and **Dance** shared the experimental spirit. Ruth St. Denis (1877-1968) and Isadora Duncan (1878-1927) pioneered modern dance, while Diaghilev in Paris revitalized classic ballet from 1909. Composers explored atonal music (Debussy, 1862-1918) and dissonance (Schönberg, 1874-1951), or revolutionized classical forms (Stravinsky, 1882-1971), often showing jazz or folk music influences.

War and Revolution: 1910-1919

War threatens. Germany under Wilhelm II sought a political and imperial role consonant with its industrial strength, challenging Britain's world supremacy and threatening France, still resenting the loss of Alsace-Lorraine. Austria wanted to curb an expanded Serbia (after 1912) and the threat it posed to its own Slav lands. Russia feared Austrian and German political and economic aims in the Balkans and Turkey. An accelerated arms race resulted: the German standing army rose to over 2 million men by 1914. Russia and France had over a million each, Austria and the British Empire nearly a million each. Dozens of enormous battleships were built by the powers after 1906.

The **assassination of Austrian Archduke Franz Ferdinand** by a Serbian, June 28, 1914, was the pretext for war. The system of alliances made the conflict Europe-wide; Germany's invasion of Belgium to outflank France forced Britain to enter the war. Patriotic fervor was nearly unanimous among all classes in most countries.

World War I. German forces were stopped in France in one month. The rival armies dug **trench networks**. Artillery and improved machine guns prevented either side from any lasting advance despite repeated assaults (600,000 dead at **Verdun**, Feb.-July 1916). Poison gas, used by Germany in 1915, proved ineffective. Over one million U.S. troops tipped the balance after mid-1917, forcing Germany to sue for peace.

In the East, the Russian armies were thrown back (battle of **Tannenberg**, Aug. 20, 1914) and the war grew unpopular. An allied attempt to relieve Russia through Turkey failed (**Gallipoli** 1915). The new Bolshevik regime signed the capitulatory Brest-Litovsk peace in March, 1918. Italy entered the war on the allied side, May 1915, but was pushed back by Oct. 1917. A renewed offensive with Allied aid in Oct.-Nov. 1918 forced Austria to surrender.

The British Navy successfully blockaded Germany, which responded with submarine U-boat attacks; **unrestricted submarine warfare** against neutrals after Jan. 1917 helped bring the U.S. into the war. Other battlefields included Palestine and Mesopotamia, both of which Britain wrested from the Turks in 1917, and the African and Pacific colonies of Germany, most of which fell to Britain, France, Australia, Japan, and South Africa.

From 1916, the civilian population and economy of both sides were mobilized to an unprecedented degree. Over 10 million soldiers died (May 1917 French mutiny crushed).

Settlement. At the **Versailles conference** (Jan.-June 1919) and in subsequent negotiations and local wars (Russian-Polish War 1920), the map of Europe was redrawn with a nod to U.S. Pres. Wilson's principle of self-determination. Austria and Hungary were separated and much of their land was given to Yugoslavia (formerly Serbia), Romania, Italy, and the newly independent Poland and Czechoslovakia. Germany lost territory in the West, North, and East, while Finland and the Baltic states were detached from Russia. Turkey lost nearly all its Arab lands to British-sponsored Arab states or to direct French and British rule.

A huge **reparations** burden and partial demilitarization were imposed on Germany. Wilson obtained approval for a League of Nations, but the U.S. Senate refused to allow the U.S. to join.

Russian revolution. Military defeats and high casualties caused a contagious lack of confidence in Tsar Nicholas, who was forced to abdicate, Mar. 1917. A liberal provisional government failed to end the war, and massive desertions, riots, and fighting between factions followed. A moderate socialist government under Kerensky was overthrown in a violent **coup by the Bolsheviks** in Petrograd under Lenin, who disbanded the elected Constituent Assembly, Nov. 1917.

The Bolsheviks brutally suppressed all opposition and ended the war with Germany, Mar. 1918. **Civil war** broke out in the summer between the Red Army, including the Bolsheviks and their supporters, and monarchists, anarchists, nationalities (Ukrainians, Georgians, Poles) and others. Small U.S., British, French and Japanese units also opposed the Bolsheviks, 1918-19 (Japan in Vladivostok to 1922). The civil war, anarchy, and pogroms devastated the country until the 1920 Red Army victory. The wartime total monopoly of political, economic, and police power by the Communist Party leadership was retained.

Other European revolutions. An unpopular monarchy in **Portugal** was overthrown in 1910. The new republic took severe anti-clerical measures, 1911.

After a century of Home Rule agitation, during which **Ireland** was devastated by famine (one million dead, 1846-47) and emigration, republican militants staged an unsuccessful uprising in Dublin, Easter 1916. The execution of the leaders and mass arrests by the British won popular support for the rebels. The Irish Free State, comprising all but the 6 northern counties, achieved dominion status in 1922.

In the aftermath of the world war, radical revolutions were attempted in Germany (**Spartacist** uprising Jan. 1919), **Hungary** (Kun regime 1919), and elsewhere. All were suppressed or failed for lack of support.

Chinese revolution. The Manchu Dynasty was overthrown and a republic proclaimed, Oct. 1911. First president Sun Yat-sen resigned in favor of strongman Yuan Shih-k'ai. Sun organized the parliamentarian **Kuomintang** party.

Students launched protests May 4, 1919 against League of Nations concessions in China to Japan. Nationalist, liberal, and socialist ideas and political groups spread. The **Communist Party** was founded 1921. A communist regime took power in Mongolia with Soviet support in 1921.

India restive. Indian objections to British rule erupted in nationalist riots as well as in the non-violent tactics of Gandhi (1869-1948). Nearly 400 unarmed demonstrators were shot at **Amritsar**, Apr. 1919. Britain approved limited self-rule that year.

Mexican revolution. Under the long Diaz dictatorship (1876-1911) the economy advanced, but Indian and mestizo lands were confiscated, and concessions to foreigners (mostly U.S.) damaged the middle class. A **revolution in 1910** led to civil wars and U.S. intervention (1914, 1916-17). Land reform and a more democratic constitution (1917) were achieved.

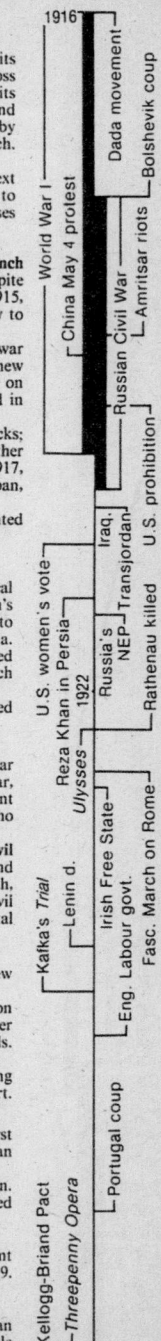

1916

World War I
China May 4 protest
Dada movement
Bolshevik coup
Amritsar riots
Russian Civil War
U.S. prohibition
U.S. women's vote
Reza Khan in Persia
Russia's NEP
1922
Iraq; Transjordan
Rathenau killed
Kafka's Trial
Lenin d.
Ulysses
Irish Free State
Eng. Labour govt.
Fasc. March on Rome
Portugal coup
Kellogg-Briand Pact
Threepenny Opera
1928

Timeline (left margin, top to bottom): 1928 · India salt march · Stock market crash · Smoot-Hawley Tariff · Alfonso leaves Spain · Japan seizes Manchuria · Gandhi's fast · 1933 · Hitler dictator · International Style · FDR in office · Hitler takes Rhineland · Nuremberg Laws · Long March in China · Fr. Popular Front · Italy takes Ethiopia · Japan invades China · Civil War in Spain · 1938

The Aftermath of War: 1920-29

U.S. Easy credit, technological ingenuity, and war-related industrial decline in Europe caused a long economic boom, in which ownership of the new products — autos, phones, radios — became democratized. Prosperity, an increase in women workers, women's suffrage (1920) and drastic change in fashion (flappers, mannish bob for women, clean-shaven men), created a wide perception of social change, despite prohibition of alcoholic beverages (1919-33). Union membership and strikes increased. Fear of radicals led to Palmer raids (1919-20) and Sacco/Vanzetti case (1921-27).

Europe sorts itself out. Germany's liberal **Weimar constitution** (1919) could not guarantee a stable government in the face of rightist violence (Rathenau assassinated 1922) and Communist refusal to cooperate with Socialists. Reparations and allied occupation of the Rhineland caused staggering inflation which destroyed middle class savings, but economic expansion resumed after mid-decade, aided by U.S. loans. A sophisticated, innovative culture developed in architecture and design (Bauhaus, 1919-28), film (Lang, *M*, 1931), painting (Grosz), music (Weill, *Threepenny Opera*, 1928), theater (Brecht, *A Man's a Man*, 1926), criticism (Benjamin), philosophy (Jung), and fashion. This culture was considered decadent and socially disruptive by rightists.

England elected its first labor governments (Jan. 1924, June 1929). A 10-day general strike in support of coal miners failed, May 1926. In **Italy**, strikes, political chaos and violence by small Fascist bands culminated in the Oct. 1922 Fascist March on Rome, which established Mussolini's dictatorship. Strikes were outlawed (1926), and Italian influence was pressed in the Balkans (Albania a protectorate 1926). A conservative dictatorship was also established in **Portugal** in a 1926 military coup.

Czechoslovakia, the only stable democracy to emerge from the war in Central or East Europe, faced opposition from Germans (in the Sudetenland), Ruthenians, and some Slovaks. As the industrial heartland of the old Hapsburg empire, it remained fairly prosperous. With French backing, it formed the Little Entente with Yugoslavia (1920) and **Romania** (1921) to block Austrian or Hungarian irredentism. **Hungary** remained dominated by the landholding classes and expansionist feeling. Croats and Slovenes in **Yugoslavia** demanded a federal state until King Alexander proclaimed a dictatorship (1929). Poland faced nationality problems as well (Germans, Ukrainians, Jews); Pilsudski ruled as dictator from 1926. The Baltic states were threatened by traditionally dominant ethnic Germans and by Soviet-supported communists.

An economic collapse and famine in **Russia**, 1921-22, claimed 5 million lives. The New Economic Policy (1921) allowed land ownership by peasants and some private commerce and industry. Stalin was absolute ruler within 4 years of Lenin's 1924 death. He inaugurated a brutal collectivization program 1929-32, and used foreign communist parties for Soviet state advantage.

Internationalism. Revulsion against World War I led to pacifist agitation, the Kellogg-Briand Pact renouncing aggressive war (1928), and **naval disarmament** pacts (Washington, 1922, London, 1930). But the League of Nations was able to arbitrate only minor disputes (Greece-Bulgaria, 1925).

Middle East. Mustafa Kemal (Ataturk) led **Turkish** nationalists in resisting Italian, French, and Greek military advances, 1919-23. The sultanate was abolished 1922, and elaborate reforms passed, including secularization of law and adoption of the Latin alphabet. Ethnic conflict led to persecution of **Armenians** (over 1 million dead in 1915, 1 million expelled), Greeks (forced Greek-Turk population exchange, 1923), and Kurds (1925 uprising).

With evacuation of the Turks from **Arab** lands, the puritanical Wahabi dynasty of eastern Arabia conquered present Saudi Arabia, 1919-25. British, French, and Arab dynastic and nationalist maneuvering resulted in the creation of two more Arab monarchies in 1921: Iraq and Transjordan (both under British control), and two French mandates: Syria and Lebanon. Jewish immigration into British-mandated **Palestine**, inspired by the Zionist movement, was resisted by Arabs, at times violently (1921, 1929 massacres).

Reza Khan ruled **Persia** after his 1921 coup (shah from 1925), centralized control, and created the trappings of a modern state.

China. The Kuomintang under **Chiang Kai-shek** (1887-1975) subdued the warlords by 1928. The Communists were brutally suppressed after their alliance with the Kuomintang was broken in 1927. Relative peace thereafter allowed for industrial and financial improvements, with some Russian, British, and U.S. cooperation.

Arts. Nearly all bounds of subject matter, style, and attitude were broken in the arts of the period. Abstract art first took inspiration from natural forms or narrative themes (Kandinsky from 1911), then worked free of any representational aims (Malevich's suprematism, 1915-19, Mondrian's geometric style from 1917). The **Dada** movement from 1916 mocked artistic pretension with absurd collages and constructions (Arp, Tzara, from 1916). Paradox, illusion, and psychological taboos were exploited by **surrealists** by the latter 1920s (Dali, Magritte). Architectural schools celebrated industrial values, whether vigorous abstract constructivism (Tatlin, *Monument to 3rd International*, 1919) or the machined, streamlined **Bauhaus** style, which was extended to many design fields (Helvetica type face).

Prose writers explored revolutionary narrative modes related to dreams (Kafka's *Trial*, 1925), internal monologue (Joyce's *Ulysses*, 1922), and word play (Stein's *Making of Americans*, 1925). Poets and novelists wrote of modern alienation (Eliot's *Waste Land*, 1922) and aimlessness (Lost Generation).

Sciences. Scientific specialization prevailed by the 20th century. Advances in knowledge and technological aptitude increased with the geometric increase in the number of practitioners. Physicists challenged common-sense views of causality, observation, and a mechanistic universe, putting science further beyond popular grasp (Einstein's general theory of relativity, 1915; Bohr's quantum mechanics, 1913; Heisenberg's uncertainty principle, 1927).

Rise of the Totalitarians: 1930-39

Depression. A worldwide financial panic and economic depression began with the Oct. 1929 U.S. stock market crash and the May 1931 failure of the Austrian Credit-Anstalt. A credit crunch caused international bankruptcies and **unemployment:** 12 million jobless by 1932 in the U.S., 5.6 million in Germany, 2.7 million in England. Governments responded with **tariff restrictions** (Smoot-Hawley Act 1930; Ottawa Imperial Conference, 1932) which dried up world trade. Government public works programs were vitiated by deflationary budget balancing.

Germany. Years of agitation by violent extremists was brought to a head by the Depression. Nazi leader **Hitler** was named chancellor by Pres. Hindenburg Jan. 1933, and given dictatorial power by the Reichstag in Mar. Opposition parties were disbanded, strikes banned, and all aspects of economic, cultural, and religious life brought under central government and Nazi party control and manipulated by sophisticated propaganda. Severe persecution of Jews began (**Nuremberg Laws** Sept. 1935). Many Jews, political opponents and others were sent to concentration camps (Dachau, 1933) where thousands died or were killed. Public works, renewed conscription (1935), arms production, and a 4-year plan (1936) ended unemployment.

Hitler's expansionism started with reincorporation of the Saar (1935), occupation of the **Rhineland** (Mar. 1936), and annexation of Austria (Mar. 1938). At **Munich,** Sept. 1938, an indecisive Britain and France sanctioned German dismemberment of Czechoslovakia.

Russia. Urbanization and education advanced. Rapid industrialization was achieved through successive **5-year-plans** starting 1928, using severe labor discipline and mass forced labor. Industry was financed by a decline in living standards and exploitation of agriculture, which was almost totally collectivized by the early 1930s (*kolkhoz,* collective farm; *sovkhoz,* state farm, often in newly-worked lands). Successive **purges** increased the role of professionals and management at the expense of workers. Millions perished in a series of man-made disasters: elimination of kulaks (peasant land-owners), 1929-34; severe famine, 1932-33; party purges (Great Purge, 1936-38); suppression of nationalities; and poor conditions in labor camps.

Spain. An industrial revolution during World War I created an urban proletariat, which was attracted to socialism and anarchism; Catalan nationalists challenged central authority. The 5 years after King Alfonso left Spain, Apr. 1931, were dominated by tension between intermittent leftist and anti-clerical governments and clericals, monarchists and other rightists. Anarchist and communist rebellions were crushed, but a July, 1936, extreme right rebellion led by Gen. Francisco Franco and aided by Nazi Germany and Fascist Italy succeeded, after a 3-year **civil war** (over 1 million dead in battles and atrocities). The war polarized international public opinion.

Italy. Despite propaganda for the ideal of the Corporate State, few domestic reforms were attempted. An entente with Hungary and Austria, Mar. 1934, a pact with Germany and Japan, Nov. 1937, and intervention by 50-75,000 troops in Spain, 1936-39, sealed Italy's identification with the fascist bloc (anti-Semitic laws after Mar. 1938). Ethiopia was conquered, 1935-37, and **Albania** annexed, Jan. 1939, in conscious imitation of ancient Rome.

East Europe. Repressive regimes fought for power against an active opposition (liberals, socialists, communists, peasants, Nazis). Minority groups and Jews were restricted within national boundaries that did not coincide with ethnic population patterns. In the destruction of Czechoslovakia, **Hungary** occupied southern Slovakia (Nov. 1938) and Ruthenia (Mar. 1939), and a pro-Nazi regime took power in the rest of Slovakia. Other boundary disputes (e.g. Poland-Lithuania, Yugoslavia-Bulgaria, Romania-Hungary) doomed attempts to build joint fronts against Germany or Russia. Economic depression was severe.

East Asia. After a period of liberalism in **Japan,** nativist militarists dominated the government with peasant support. Manchuria was seized, Sept. 1931-Feb. 1932, and a puppet state set up (Manchukuo). Adjacent Jehol (inner Mongolia) was occupied in 1933. China proper was invaded July 1937; large areas were conquered by Oct. 1938.

In **China** Communist forces left Kuomintang-besieged strongholds in the South in a Long March (1934-35) to the North. The Kuomintang-Communist civil war was suspended Jan. 1937 in the face of threatening Japan.

The democracies. The Roosevelt Administration, in office Mar. 1933, embarked on an extensive program of social reform and economic stimulation, including protection for labor unions (heavy industries organized), social security, public works, wages and hours laws, assistance to farmers. Isolationist sentiment (1937 Neutrality Act) prevented U.S. intervention in Europe, but military expenditures were increased in 1939.

French political instability and polarization prevented resolution of economic and international security questions. The **Popular Front** government under Blum (June 1936-Apr. 1938) passed social reforms (40-hour week) and raised arms spending. National coalition governments ruled Britain from Aug. 1931, brought some economic recovery, but failed to define a consistent foreign policy until Chamberlain's government (from May 1937), which practiced deliberate **appeasement** of Germany and Italy.

India. Twenty years of agitation for autonomy and then for independence (Gandhi's **salt march,** 1930) achieved some constitutional reform (extended provincial powers, 1935) despite Moslem-Hindu strife. Social issues assumed prominence with peasant uprisings (1921), strikes (1928), Gandhi's efforts for untouchables (1932 "fast unto death"), and social and agrarian reform by the provinces after 1937.

Arts. The streamlined, geometric design motifs of Art Deco (from 1925) prevailed through the 1930s. Abstract art flourished (Moore sculptures from 1931) alongside a new realism related to social and political concerns (**Socialist Realism** the official Soviet style from 1934; Mexican muralists Rivera, 1886-1957, and Orozco, 1883-1949), which was also expressed in fiction and poetry (Steinbeck's *Grapes of Wrath,* 1939; Sandburg's *The People, Yes,* 1936). Modern architecture (*International Style,* 1932) was unchallenged in its use of man-made materials (concrete, glass), lack of decoration, and monumentality (Rockefeller Center, 1929-40). U.S.-made films captured a world-wide audience with their larger-than-life fantasies (*Gone with the Wind,* 1939).

War, Hot and Cold: 1940-49

War in Europe. The Nazi-Soviet non-aggression pact (Aug. '39) freed Germany to attack Poland (Sept.). Britain and France, who had guaranteed Polish independence, declared war on Germany. Russia seized East Poland (Sept.), attacked Finland (Nov.) and took the Baltic states (July '40). Mobile German forces staged "blitzkrieg" attacks Apr.-June, '40, conquering neutral Denmark, Norway, and the low countries and defeating France; 350,000 British and French troops were evacuated at Dunkirk (May). The Battle of Britain, June-Dec. '40, denied Germany air superiority, German-Italian campaigns won the Balkans by Apr. '41. Three million Axis troops invaded Russia June '41, marching through the Ukraine to the Caucasus, and through White Russia and the Baltic republics to Moscow and Leningrad.

Russian winter counterthrusts, '41-'42 and '42-'43 stopped the German advance (Stalingrad Sept. '42-Feb. '43). With British and U.S. Lend-Lease aid and sustaining great casualties, the Russians drove the Axis from all E. Europe and the Balkans in the next 2 years. Invasions of N. Africa (Nov. '42), Italy (Sept. '43), and Normandy (June '44) brought U.S., British, Free French and allied troops to Germany by spring '45. Germany surrendered May 7, 1945.

War in Asia-Pacific. Japan occupied Indochina Sept. '40, dominated Thailand Dec. '41, attacked Hawaii, the Philippines, Hong Kong, Malaya Dec. 7, 1941. Indonesia was attacked Jan. '42, Burma conquered Mar. 42. Battle of Midway (June '42) turned back the Japanese advance. "Island-hopping" battles (Guadalcanal Aug. '42-Jan. '43, Leyte Gulf Oct. '44, Iwo Jima Feb.-Mar. '45, Okinawa Apr. '45) and massive bombing raids on Japan from June '44 wore out Japanese defenses. Two U.S. atom bombs, dropped Aug. 6 and 9, forced Japan to surrender Aug. 14, 1945.

Atrocities. The war brought 20th-century cruelty to its peak. Nazi murder camps (Auschwitz) systematically killed 6 million Jews. Gypsies, political opponents, sick and retarded people, and others deemed undesirable were murdered by the Nazis, as were vast numbers of Slavs, especially leaders.

Civilian deaths. German bombs killed 70,000 English civilians. Some 100,000 Chinese civilians were killed by Japanese forces in the capture of Nanking. Severe retaliation by the Soviet army, E. European partisans, Free French and others took a heavy toll. U.S. and British bombing of Germany killed hundreds of thousands, as did U.S. bombing of Japan (80-200,000 at Hiroshima alone). Some 45 million people lost their lives in the war.

Settlement. The United Nations charter was signed in San Francisco June 26, 1945 by 50 nations. The International Tribunal at Nuremberg convicted 22 German leaders for war crimes Sept. '46, 23 Japanese leaders were convicted Nov. '48. Postwar border changes included large gains in territory for the USSR, losses for Germany, a shift westward in Polish borders, and minor losses for Italy. Communist regimes, supported by Soviet troops, took power in most of E. Europe, including Soviet-occupied Germany (GDR proclaimed Oct. '49). Japan lost all overseas lands.

Recovery. Basic political and social changes were imposed on Japan and W. Germany by the western allies (Japan constitution Nov. '46, W. German basic law May '49). U.S. Marshall Plan aid ($12 billion '47-'51) spurred W. European economic recovery after a period of severe inflation and strikes in Europe and the U.S. The British Labour Party introduced a national health service and nationalized basic industries in 1946.

Cold War. Western fears of further Soviet advances (Cominform formed Oct. '47, Czechoslovakia coup, Feb. '48, Berlin blockade Apr.'48-Sept. '49) led to formation of NATO. Civil War in Greece and Soviet pressure on Turkey led to U.S. aid under the Truman Doctrine (Mar. '47). Other anti-communist security pacts were the Org. of American States (Apr. '48) and Southeast Asia Treaty Org. (Sept. '54). A new wave of Soviet purges and repression intensified in the last years of Stalin's rule, extending to E. Europe (Slansky trial in Czechoslovakia, 1951). Only Yugoslavia resisted Soviet control (expelled by Cominform, June '48; U.S. aid, June '49).

China, Korea. Communist forces emerged from World War II strengthened by the Soviet takeover of industrial Manchuria. In 4 years of fighting, the Kuomintang was driven from the mainland; the People's Republic was proclaimed Oct. 1, 1949. Korea was divided by Russian and U.S. occupation forces. Separate republics were proclaimed in the 2 zones Aug.-Sept. '48.

India. India and Pakistan became independent dominions Aug. 15, 1947. Millions of Hindu and Moslem refugees were created by the partition; riots, 1946-47, took hundreds of thousands of lives; Gandhi himself was assassinated Jan. '48. Burma became completely independent Jan. '48; Ceylon took dominion status in Feb.

Middle East. The UN approved partition of Palestine into Jewish and Arab states. Israel was proclaimed May 14, 1948. Arabs rejected partition, but failed to defeat Israel in war, May '48-July '49. Immigration from Europe and the Middle East swelled Israel's Jewish population. British and French forces left Lebanon and Syria, 1946. Transjordan occupied most of Arab Palestine.

Southeast Asia. Communists and others fought against restoration of French rule in Indochina from 1946; a non-communist government was recognized by France Mar. '49, but fighting continued. Both Indonesia and the Philippines became independent, the former in 1949 after 4 years of war with Netherlands, the latter in 1946. Philippine economic and military ties with the U.S. remained strong; a communist-led peasant rising was checked in '48.

Arts. New York became the center of the world art market; abstract expressionism was the chief mode (Pollock from '43, de Kooning from '47). Literature and philosophy explored existentialism (Camus' Stranger, 1942, Sartre's Being and Nothingness, 1943). Non-western attempts to revive or create regional styles (Senghor's Negritude, Mishima's novels) only confirmed the emergence of a universal culture. Radio and phonograph records spread American popular music (swing, bebop) around the world.

Timeline (1948–1958):
- 1948
- Israel indep.
- China People's Rep.
- Gandhi killed
- Burma independent
- Ger. Dem. Rep.
- Lonely Crowd
- Indonesia indep.
- Indochina War
- H-bomb
- Egypt rev.
- Korean War
- Stalin d.
- Ghana indep.
- Sputnik
- EEC Treaty
- Suez War
- Hungary rev.
- Bandung conf.
- On the Road
- SEATO founded
- McCarthy censured
- Peron ousted
- 1958

The American Decade: 1950-59

Polite decolonization. The peaceful decline of European political and military power in Asia and Africa accelerated in the 1950s. Nearly all of N. Africa was freed by 1956, but France fought a bitter war to retain Algeria, with its large European minority, until 1962. **Ghana,** independent 1957, led a parade of new black African nations (over 2 dozen by 1962) which altered the political character of the UN. Ethnic disputes often exploded in the new nations after decolonization (UN troops in Cyprus 1964; **Nigeria** civil war 1967-70). Leaders of the new states, mostly sharing socialist ideologies, tried to create an Afro-Asian bloc (Bandung Conf. 1955), but Western economic influence and U.S. political ties remained strong (Baghdad Pact, 1955).

Trade. World trade volume soared, in an atmosphere of monetary stability assured by international accords (**Bretton Woods** 1944). In Europe, economic integration advanced (**European Economic Community** 1957, European Free Trade Association 1960). Comecon (1949) coordinated the economies of Soviet-bloc countries.

U.S. Economic growth produced an abundance of consumer goods (9.3 million motor vehicles sold, 1955). Suburban housing tracts changed life patterns for middle and working classes (Levittown 1946-51). **Eisenhower's** landslide election victories (1952, 1956) reflected consensus politics. Censure of McCarthy (Dec. '54) curbed the political abuse of anti-communism. A system of alliances and military bases bolstered U.S. influence on all continents. Trade and payments surpluses were balanced by overseas investments and foreign aid ($50 billion, 1950-59).

USSR. In the "thaw" after Stalin's death in 1953, relations with the West improved (evacuation of Vienna, Geneva summit conf., both 1955). Repression of scientific and cultural life eased, and many prisoners were freed or rehabilitated culminating in **de-Stalinization** (1956). Khrushchev's leadership aimed at consumer sector growth, but farm production lagged, despite the virgin lands program (from 1954). The 1956 Hungarian revolution, the 1960 U-2 spy plane episode, and other incidents renewed East-West tension and domestic curbs.

East Europe. Resentment of Russian domination and Stalinist repression combined with nationalist, economic and religious factors to produce periodic violence. East Berlin workers rioted in 1953, Polish workers rioted in Poznan, June 1956, and a broad-based revolution broke out in Hungary, Oct. 1956. All were suppressed by Soviet force or threats (at least 7,000 dead in Hungary). But Poland was allowed to restore private ownership of farms, and a degree of personal and economic freedom returned to Hungary. Yugoslavia experimented with worker self-management and a market economy.

Korea. The 1945 division of Korea left industry in the North, which was organized into a militant regime and armed by Russia. The South was politically disunited. Over 60,000 North Korean troops invaded the South June 25, 1950. The U.S., backed by the UN Security Council, sent troops. UN forces reached the Chinese border in Nov. Some 200,000 Chinese troops crossed the Yalu River and drove back UN forces. Cease-fire in July 1951 found the opposing forces near the original 38th parallel border. After 2 years of sporadic fighting, an armistice was signed July 27, 1953. U.S. troops remained in the South, and U.S. economic and military aid continued. The war stimulated rapid economic recovery in Japan.

China. Starting in 1952, industry, agriculture, and social institutions were forcibly collectivized. As many as several million people were executed as Kuomintang supporters or as class and political enemies. The Great Leap Forward, 1958-60, unsuccessfully tried to force the pace of development by substituting labor for investment.

Indochina. Ho's forces, aided by Russia and the new Chinese Communist government, fought French and pro-French Vietnamese forces to a standstill, and captured the strategic Dienbienphu camp in May, 1954. The Geneva Agreements divided Vietnam in half pending elections (never held), and recognized Laos and Cambodia as independent. The U.S. aided the anti-Communist Republic of Vietnam in the South.

Middle East. Arab revolutions placed leftist, militantly nationalist regimes in power in Egypt (1952) and Iraq (1958). But Arab unity attempts failed (United Arab Republic joined Egypt, Syria, Yemen 1958-61). Arab refusal to recognize Israel (Arab League economic blockade began Sept. 1951) led to a permanent state of war, with repeated incidents (Gaza, 1955). Israel occupied Sinai, Britain and France took the Suez Canal, Oct. 1956, but were replaced by the UN Emergency Force. The Mossadegh government in Iran nationalized the British-owned oil industry May 1951, but was overthrown in a U.S.-aided coup Aug. 1953.

Latin America. Dictator Juan Peron, in office 1946, enforced land reform, some nationalization, welfare state measures, and curbs on the Roman Catholic Church, but crushed opposition. A Sept. 1955 coup deposed Peron. The 1952 revolution in Bolivia brought land reform, nationalization of tin mines, and improvement in the status of Indians, who nevertheless remained poor. The Batista regime in Cuba was overthrown, Jan. 1959, by Fidel Castro, who imposed a communist dictatorship, aligned Cuba with Russia, improved education and health care. A U.S.-backed anti-Castro invasion (Bay of Pigs, Apr. 1961) was crushed. Self-government advanced in the British Caribbean.

Technology. Large outlays on research and development in the U.S. and USSR focused on military applications (H-bomb in U.S. 1952, USSR 1953, Britain 1957, intercontinental missiles late 1950s). Soviet launching of the Sputnik satellite, Oct. 1957, spurred increases in U.S. science education funds (National Defense Education Act).

Literature and letters. Alienation from social and literary conventions reached an extreme in the theater of the absurd (Beckett's *Waiting for Godot* 1952), the "new novel" (Robbe-Grillet's *Voyeur* 1955), and avant-garde film (Antonioni's *L'Avventura* 1960). U.S. Beatniks (Kerouac's *On the Road* 1957) and others rejected the supposed conformism of Americans (Riesman's *Lonely Crowd* 1950).

1958 — Castro in Cuba — Sino-Soviet split begins — Berlin Wall — Man in Space — Algeria indep. — Silent Spring — March on Wash. — Feminine Mystique — JFK killed — Diem deposed — Tonkin Gulf res. — Indonesia coup — China Cult. Rev. — GATT — Mideast War — U.S. in Vietnam — 1968

1968

Sino-Soviet fighting
First Earth Day
Woodstock festival
Men on moon
Pentagon Papers published
U.S. SST barred
Bangladesh indep.
Roe v. Wade abortion ruling
Nixon in Peking
Israel-Arab 6-Day War
Worldwide recession
Nixon resigns
Indochina War ends
1 mln. die in Cambodia
Franco d.
Mao d.
U.S. hostages taken in Iran
Khomeini govt. in Iran
Egypt-Israel treaty
3 Mile Island
USSR invades Afghanistan
18% inflation rate in U.S.

1980

Rising Expectations: 1960-69

Economic boom. The longest sustained economic boom on record spanned almost the entire decade in the capitalist world; the closely-watched GNP figure doubled in the U.S. 1960-70, fueled by Vietnam War-related budget deficits. The **General Agreement on Tariffs and Trade,** 1967, stimulated West European prosperity, which spread to peripheral areas (Spain, Italy, E. Germany). Japan became a top economic power ($20 billion exports 1970). Foreign investment aided the industrialization of Brazil. Soviet 1965 economic reform attempts (decentralization, material incentives) were limited; but growth continued.

Reform and radicalization. Pres. John F. Kennedy, inaugurated 1961, emphasized youthful idealism, vigor; he was assassinated Nov. 22, 1963. A series of political and social reform movements took root in the U.S., later spreading to other countries with the help of ubiquitous U.S. film and television programs and heavy overseas travel (2.2 million U.S. passports issued 1970). Blacks agitated peaceably and with partial success against segregation and poverty (1963 March on Washington, 1964 **Civil Rights Act);** but some urban ghettos erupted in extensive riots (Watts, 1965; Detroit, 1967; King assassination, Apr. 4, 1968). New concern for the poor (Harrington's *Other America,* 1963) led to Pres. Johnson's **"Great Society"** programs (Medicare, Water Quality Act, Higher Education Act, all 1965). Concern with the environment surged (Carson's *Silent Spring,* 1962). **Feminism** revived as a cultural and political movement (Friedan's *Feminine Mystique,* 1963, National Organization for Women founded 1966) and a movement for homosexual rights emerged (Stonewall riot, in NYC, 1969). Pope John XXIII called Vatican II, 1962-65, which liberalized Roman Catholic liturgy.

Opposition to U.S. involvement in Vietnam, especially among university students (**Moratorium** protest Nov. '69) turned violent (Weatherman Chicago riots Oct. '69). New Left and Marxist theories became popular, and membership in radical groups swelled (Students for a Democratic Society, Black Panthers). Maoist groups, especially in Europe, called for total transformation of society. In France, students sparked a nationwide strike affecting 10 million workers May-June '68, but an electoral reaction barred revolutionary change.

Arts and styles. The boundary between fine and popular arts were blurred by Pop Art (Warhol) and rock musicals (Hair, 1968). Informality and exaggeration prevailed in fashion (beards, miniskirts). A non-political "counterculture" developed, rejecting traditional bourgeois life goals and personal habits, and use of marijuana and hallucinogens spread (Woodstock festival Aug. '69). Indian influence was felt in music (Beatles), religion (Ram Dass), and fashion.

Science. Achievements in space (men on moon July '69) and electronics (lasers, integrated circuits) encouraged a faith in scientific solutions to problems in agriculture ("green revolution"), medicine (heart transplants 1967) and other areas. The harmful effects of science, it was believed, could be controlled (1963 nuclear weapon test ban treaty, 1968 non-proliferation treaty).

China. Mao's revolutionary militance caused disputes with Russia under "revisionist" Khrushchev, starting 1960. The two powers exchanged fire in 1969 border disputes. China used force to capture areas disputed with India 1962. The "Great Proletarian Cultural Revolution" tried to impose a utopian egalitarian program in China and spread revolution abroad; political struggle, often violent, convulsed China 1965-68.

Indochina. Communist-led guerrillas aided by N. Vietnam fought from 1960 against the S. Vietnam government of Ngo Dinh Diem (killed 1963). The U.S. military role increased after the 1964 Tonkin Gulf incident. U.S. forces peaked at 543,400, Apr. '69. Massive numbers of N. Viet troops also fought. Laotian and Cambodian neutrality were threatened by communist insurgencies, with N. Vietnamese aid, and U.S. intrigues.

Third World. A bloc of authoritarian leftist regimes among the newly independent nations emerged in political opposition to the U.S.-led Western alliance, and came to dominate the conference of nonaligned nations (Belgrade 1961, Cairo 1964, Lusaka 1970). Soviet political ties and military bases were established in Cuba, Egypt, Algeria, Guinea, and other countries, whose leaders were regarded as revolutionary heros by opposition groups in pro-Western or colonial countries. Some leaders were ousted in coups by pro-Western groups—Zaire's Lumumba (killed 1961), Ghana's Nkrumah (exiled 1966), and Indonesia's Sukarno (effectively ousted 1965 after a Communist coup failed).

Middle East. Arab-Israeli tension erupted into a brief war June 1967. Israel emerged as a major regional power. Military shipments before and after the war brought much of the Arab world into the Soviet political sphere. Most Arab states broke U.S. diplomatic ties, while Communist countries cut their ties to Israel. Intra-Arab disputes continued: Egypt and Saudi Arabia supported rival factions in a bloody Yemen civil war 1962-70; Lebanese troops fought Palestinian commandos 1969.

East Europe. To stop the large-scale exodus of citizens, E. German authorities built a fortified wall across Berlin Aug. '61. Soviet sway in the Balkans was weakened by Albania's support of China (USSR broke ties Dec. '61) and Romania's assertion of industrial and foreign policy autonomy 1964. Liberalization in Czechoslovakia, spring 1968, was crushed by troops of 5 Warsaw Pact countries. West German treaties with Russia and Poland, 1970, facilitated the transfer of German technology and confirmed post-war boundaries.

Disillusionment: 1970-79

U.S.: Caution and neoconservatism. A relatively sluggish economy, energy and resource shortages (natural gas crunch 1975, gasoline shortage 1979) and environmental problems contributed to a "**limits of growth**" philosophy. Suspicion of science and technology killed or delayed major projects (supersonic transport dropped 1971, DNA recombination curbed 1976, Seabrook A-plant protests 1977-78) and was fed by the Three Mile Island nuclear reactor accident Mar. '79.

Mistrust of big government weakened support for government reform plans among liberals. School busing and racial quotas were opposed (**Bakke decision** June '78); the Equal Rights Amendment for women languished; civil rights for homosexuals was opposed (Dade County referendum June '77).

Completion of communist forces' takeover of S. Vietnam (evacuation of U.S. civilians Apr. '75), revelations of Central Intelligence Agency misdeeds (Rockefeller Commission report June '75), and **Watergate** scandals (Nixon quit Aug. '74) reduced faith in U.S. moral and material capacity to influence world affairs. Revelations of Soviet crimes (Solzhenitsyn's *Gulag Archipelago* from 1974) and Russian intervention in Africa aided a revival of anti-Communist sentiment.

Economy sluggish. The 1960s boom faltered in the 1970s; a severe recession in the U.S. and Europe 1974-75 followed a huge oil price hike Dec. '73. Monetary instability (U.S. cut ties to gold Aug. '71), the decline of the dollar, and **protectionist** moves by industrial countries (1977-78) threatened trade. Business investment and spending for research declined. Severe inflation plagued many countries (25% in Britain 1975; 18% in U.S. 1979).

China picks up pieces. After the 1976 deaths of Mao and Chou, a power struggle for the leadership succession was won by pragmatists. A nationwide purge of orthodox Maoists was carried out and the "**Gang of Four**" led by Mao's widow Chiang Ching was arrested.

The new leaders freed over 100,000 political prisoners, and reduced public adulation of Mao. Political and trade ties were expanded with Japan, Europe, and U.S. in the late 1970's, as relations worsened with Russia, Cuba, and Vietnam (4-week invasion by China 1979). Ideological guidelines in industry, science, education, and the armed forces, which the ruling faction said had caused chaos and decline, were reversed (bonuses to workers Dec. '77; exams for college entrance Oct. '77). Severe restrictions on cultural expression were eased (Beethoven ban lifted Mar. '77).

Europe. European unity moves (EEC-EFTA trade accord 1972) faltered as economic problems appeared (Britain floated pound 1972; France floated franc 1974). Germany and Switzerland curbed guest workers from S. Europe. Greece and Turkey quarreled over Cyprus (Turks intervened 1974), Aegean oil rights.

All non-Communist Europe was under democratic rule after free elections were held in **Spain** June '76, 7 months after the death of Franco. The conservative, colonialist regime in **Portugal** was overthrown Apr. '74. In **Greece**, the 7-year-old military dictatorship yielded power in 1974. Northern Europe, though ruled mostly by Socialists (**Swedish** Socialists unseated 1976, after 44 years in power), turned conservative. The **British** Labour government imposed wage curbs 1975, and suspended nationalization schemes. Terrorism in **Germany** (1972 Munich Olympics killings) led to laws curbing some civil liberties. **French** "new philosophers" rejected leftist ideologies and the shaky Socialist-Communist coalition lost a 1978 election bid.

Religion back in politics. The improvement in Moslem countries' political fortunes by the 1950s (with the exception of Central Asia under Soviet and Chinese rule) and the growth of Arab oil wealth, was followed by a resurgence of traditional piety. **Libyan** dictator Qaddafy mixed strict Islamic laws with socialism in his militant ideology, called for an eventual Moslem return to Spain and Sicily. The illegal Moslem Brotherhood in **Egypt** was accused of violence, while extreme Moslem groups bombed theaters, 1977, to protest secular values.

In **Turkey**, the National Salvation Party was the first Islamic group to share power (1974) since secularization in the 1920s. Religious authorities, such as Ayatollah Ruholla Khomeini, led the **Iranian** revolution and religiously motivated Moslems took part in the insurrection in Saudi Arabia that briefly seized the Grand Mosque in Mecca 1979. Moslem puritan opposition to **Pakistan** Pres. Bhutto helped lead to his overthrow July '77. However, Moslem solidarity could not prevent Pakistan's eastern province (**Bangladesh**) from declaring independence, Dec. '71, after a bloody civil war.

Moslem and Hindu resentment against coerced sterilization in **India** helped defeat the Gandhi government, which was replaced Mar. '77 by a coalition including religious Hindu parties and led by devout Hindu Desai. Moslems in the southern **Philippines**, aided by Libya, conducted a long rebellion against central rule from 1973.

Evangelical Protestant groups grew in numbers and prosperity in the U.S. A revival of interest in Orthodox Christianity occurred among **Russian** intellectuals (Solzhenitsyn). The secularist **Israeli** Labor party, after decades of rule, was ousted in 1977 by conservatives led by Begin, an observant Jew; religious militants founded settlements on the disputed West Bank, part of Biblically-promised Israel. U.S. Reform Judaism revived many previously discarded traditional practices.

The Buddhist Soka Gakkai movement launched the Komeito party in Japan 1964, which became a major opposition party in 1972 and 1976 elections.

Old-fashioned religious wars raged intermittently in **N. Ireland** (Catholic vs. Protestant 1969-   ) and **Lebanon** (Christian vs. Moslem 1975-   ) while religious militancy complicated the Israel-Arab dispute (1973 Israel-Arab war). In spite of a **1979 peace treaty between Egypt and Israel** which looked forward to a resolution of the Palestinian issue, increased religious militancy on the West Bank made a resolution unlikely.

Latin America. Repressive conservative regimes strengthened their hold on most of the continent, with the violent coup against the elected Allende government in Chile, Sept. '73, the 1976 military coup in Argentina, and coups against reformist regimes in Bolivia, 1971 and 1979, and Peru, 1976. In Central America, increasing liberal and leftist militancy led to the ouster of the Somoza regime of Nicaragua in 1979 and civil conflict in El Salvador.

Indochina. Communist victory in Vietnam, Cambodia, and Laos by May '75 did not bring peace. Attempts at radical social reorganization left over one million dead in Cambodia 1975-78 and caused hundreds of thousands of ethnic Chinese and others to flee Vietnam ("boat people" 1979). The Vietnamese invasion of Cambodia swelled the refugee population and contributed to widespread starvation in that devastated country.

Russian expansion. Soviet influence, checked in some countries (troops ousted by Egypt 1972) was projected further afield, often with the use of Cuban troops (Angola 1975-89, Ethiopia 1977-88) and aided by a growing navy, merchant fleet, and international banking ability. Detente with the West — 1972 Berlin pact, 1972 strategic arms pact (**SALT**) — gave way to a more antagonistic relationship in the late 1970s, exacerbated by the Soviet invasion of Afghanistan 1979.

Africa. The last remaining European colonies were granted independence (**Spanish Sahara** 1976, **Djibouti** 1977) and, after 10 years of civil war and many negotiation sessions, a black government took over Zimbabwe (Rhodesia) 1979; white domination remained in **S. Africa**. Great power involvement in local wars (Russia in Angola, Ethiopia; France in Chad, Zaire, Mauritania) and the use of tens of thousands of Cuban troops was denounced by some African leaders as neocolonialism. Ethnic or tribal clashes made Africa the chief world locus of sustained warfare in the late 1970s.

Arts. Traditional modes in painting, architecture, and music, pursued in relative obscurity for much of the 20th century, returned to popular and critical attention in the 1970s. The pictorial emphasis in neorealist and photorealist painting, the return of many architects to detail, decoration, and traditional natural materials, and the concern with ordered structure in musical composition were, ironically, novel experiences for artistic consumers after the exhaustion of experimental possibilities. However, these more conservative styles coexisted with modernist works in an atmosphere of variety and tolerance.

Timeline (right margin, 1980–1990):

- 1980
- Iran-Iraq War begins
- Solidarity founded
- U.S. hostages held in Iran
- ERA defeated
- Israel invades Lebanon
- U.S. Congress O.K.'s tax cut
- U.S.-led boycott of Moscow Olympics
- S. Africa gives voice to Coloureds, Asians
- U.S. invades Grenada
- U.S. mines Nicaragua ports
- Gorbachev made USSR Gen-Secy
- Reagan landslide re-election
- Achille Lauro terrorism
- Challenger explodes
- 150 mln. Africans near famine
- U.S. Tax Reform Law
- U.S. stock market crash
- U.S. bombs Libya
- Iran-contra scandal
- Nicaragua cease-fire
- USSR withdraws from Afghanistan
- Iran-Iraq cease-fire
- "evolutionary change" S. Africa
- Poland free election
- Tiananmen Sq. protests crushed
- Berlin Wall opens
- Eastern Europe Marxist economies fall
- 1990

Revitalization of Capitalism, Demand for Democracy: 1980-89

USSR, Eastern Europe. A troublesome 1980-85 for the USSR was followed by 5 years of astonishing change: the surrender of the Communist monopoly, remaking of the Soviet state, and disintegration of the Soviet empire. After deaths of Brezhnev 1982, Andropov 1984, Chernenko 1985; harsh treatment of dissent; restriction of emigration; invasion of Afghanistan Dec.'79; Gen. Secy. **Mikhail Gorbachev** (1985-) promoted **glasnost, perestroika,** economic and social reform (Jan.'87), supported by Communist Party (July '88); signed **INF treaty** (Dec.'87). Gorbachev pledged to cut the military budget (1988); military withdrawal from Afghanistan was completed Feb.'89; democratization was not hindered in Poland, Hungary; the Soviet people chose part of the new Congress from competing candidates Mar.'89. At decade's end, Gorbachev was widely considered responsible for the **1989 ending of the Cold War.**

Poland. Solidarity, the labor union founded 1980 by Lech Walesa, outlawed 1982, was legalized 1988, after years of unrest. Poland's first free election since the Communist takeover brought Solidarity victory (June '89); Tadeusz Mazowiecki, a Walesa advisor, became Prime Minister in a government with the Communists (Aug.'89).

In the fall of 1989 the failure of Marxist economies in **Hungary, E. Germany, Czechoslovakia, Bulgaria,** and **Romania** brought the fall of the Communist monopoly, the demand for democracy. The Berlin Wall was opened Nov.'89.

U.S. "The Reagan Years" (1981-88) brought the **longest economic boom** in U.S. history via budget and tax cuts, deregulation, "junk bond" financing, leveraged buyouts, mergers and takeovers; a **strong anti-Communist stance,** via increased defense spending, aid to anti-communists in Central America, invasion of Cuba-threatened Grenada, championing of MX missile system and "Star Wars." Four Reagan-Gorbachev summits, 1985-88, climaxed in INF treaty 1987. Financial scandals mounted (E.F. Hutton 1985, Ivan Boesky 1986), the stock market crashed Oct.'87, the trade imbalance grew (esp. with Japan), the budget deficit soared ($3.2 trillion 1988); homelessness, drug abuse (esp. "crack") grew. The Iran-contra affair (North TV testimony July'87) was the low point, but V.P. Bush was elected pres. 1988.

Middle East. This area remained militarily unstable, with sharp divisions on economic, political, racial, and religious lines. In **Iran,** the revolution (1979-80) and violent political upheavals after, brought strong anti-U.S. stance. A dispute with **Iraq** over the Shatt al-Arab waterway became warfare Sept.'80-July'88, with millions killed.

Libya's support for international terrorism caused the U.S. to close the diplomatic mission (May'81), embargo oil (Mar.'82); U.S. accused Muammar al-Qadaffy of aiding terrorists in Dec.'85 Rome, Vienna airport attacks, retaliated by bombing Libya Apr.'86.

Israel affirmed all Jerusalem as its capital (July'80); destroyed an Iraqi atomic reactor 1981; invaded Lebanon 1982, bringing the PLO to agree to withdraw. A **Palestinian uprising,** inc. women, children hurling rocks, bottles at troops, began Dec.'87 in Israeli-occupied Gaza, spread to the West Bank; troops responded with force, killing 300 by 1988's end, with 6,000 more in detention camps.

Israeli withdrawal from **Lebanon** began Feb.'85, ended June'85, as Lebanon continued torn with military and political conflict between rival factions. Premier Karami was assassinated June'87. Artillery duels between Christian East Beirut and Moslem West Beirut, Mar.-Apr.'89, left 200 dead, 700 wounded. At 80s end, violence still dominated.

Central America. In Nicaragua, the leftist Sandinista National Liberation Front, in power after the 1979 civil war, faced problems due to Nicaragua's military aid to leftist guerrillas in El Salvador, U.S. backing of anti-government contras. The U.S. CIA admitted directing the mining of Nicaraguan ports 1984; U.S. sent aid, humanitarian 1985, military 1986. Profits from secret arms sales to Iran were found diverted to contras 1987. Cease-fire talks between Sandinista government and contras came in 1988, elections in Feb.'90.

In **El Salvador,** a military coup (Oct.'79) failed to halt extreme right-wing violence and left-wing activity. Archbishop Oscar Romero was assassinated Mar.'80; Jan.-June some 4,000 civilians reportedly were killed. In 1984, newly-elected Pres. Duarte decreased rights abuses. Leftist guerrillas continued their offensive 1989.

Africa. 1980-85 marked the rapid decline of the economies of virtually all Africa's 61 countries, due to accelerating desertification, the world economic recession, heavy indebtedness to overseas creditors, rapid population growth, political instability. Some 60 million Africans, almost one-fifth of the population, faced prolonged hunger 1981; much of Africa had one of the worst droughts ever 1983, and by year's end **150 million faced near-famine.** "Live Aid" marathon rock concert (July'85), U.S. and Western nations sent aid Sept.'85. Economic hardship fueled political unrest, coups. Wars in Ethiopia, Sudan, military strife in 6 other nations continued through 1989. AIDS took a heavy toll.

South Africa. Anti-apartheid sentiment gathered force, demonstrations and violent police response grew. South African white voters approved (Nov.'83) the first constitution to give "Coloureds" Asians a voice, while still excluding blacks—70% of the population. The U.S. imposed economic sanctions Aug.'85, 11 Western nations followed in Sept. P.W. Botha, 80s president, was succeeded by F.W. deClerk, Sept.'89, on a platform of "evolutionary" change via negotiation with the black population.

China. From 1980 through mid-1989 the Communist Party, under Chairman Deng Xiaoping, pursued far-reaching changes in political and economic institutions, expanding commercial and technical ties to the industrialized world, increasing the role of market forces in stimulating urban economic development. But Apr.'89, brought the demand for more changes: students camped out in Tiananmen Sq., Beijing; some 100,000 students and workers marched, at least 20 other cities saw protests. Martial law was imposed; Army troops crushed protests in Tiananmen Sq., June 3-4 with death toll estimates 500-7,000, up to 10,000 injured, up to 10,000 dissidents arrested, 31 tried and executed. The conciliatory Communist Party chief was ousted; the Politburo adopted reforms against official corruption (July).

Japan. Relations with other nations, esp. U.S., 1980-89, were dominated by **trade imbalances favoring Japan.** In 1985 the U.S. trade deficit with Japan was $49.7 billion, one-third of the total U.S. trade deficit. After Japan was found to sell semiconductors, computer memory chips below cost (Apr.'86), the U.S. was assured a "fair share" of the market, but charged Japan with failing to live up to the agreement Mar.'87. The Omnibus Trade Bill, Aug.'88, provided for retaliation; Pres. Bush called Japan's practices "unjustifiable," the law gave Japan 18 months to stop or face trade restrictions.

European Community. With the addition of Greece, Portugal, and Spain, the EC became a **common market of over 300 million people,** the West's largest trading entity. **Margaret Thatcher** became the first British prime minister in this century to win 3 consecutive terms 1987. France elected its first socialist president, **Francois Mitterand** 1981, re-elected 1988. Italy elected its first socialist premier, Bettino Craxi 1983.

International Terrorism. With the 1979 overthrow of the Shah of Iran, terrorism became a prominent political tactic that increased through the 80s, but with fewer "spectacular" attacks after 1985. Iranian militants held 52 Americans hostage in Iran for 444 days, 1979-81; a TNT-laden suicide terrorist blew up U.S. Marine headquarters in Beirut, killing 241 Americans, while a truck bomb blew up a French paratroop barracks, killing 58, 1984; the Achille Lauro was hijacked, an American passenger killed, and the U.S. subsequently intercepted the Egyptian plane flying the terrorists to safety 1985. Incidents rose to 700 in 1985, 1,000+ in 1988. The Pentagon reported 52 terrorist groups Jan.'89.

Assassinations included Egypt's Pres. **Anwar el-Sadat** 1981; India's Prime Minister **Indira Gandhi** 1984; Lebanese Premier **Rashid Karami** 1987; Pakistan's Pres. **Mohammed Zia-ul Haz** 1988.

HISTORICAL FIGURES

Ancient Greeks and Latins

Greeks

Aeschines, orator, 389-314BC.
Aeschylus, dramatist, 525-456BC.
Aesop, fableist, c620-c560BC.
Alcibiades, politician, 450-404BC.
Anacreon, poet, c582-c485BC.
Anaxagoras, philosopher, c500-428BC.
Anaximander, philosopher, 611-546BC.
Antiphon, speechwriter, c480-411BC.
Apollonius, mathematician, c265-170BC.
Archimedes, math. c287-212BC.
Aristophanes, dramatist, c448-380BC.
Aristotle, philosopher, 384-322BC.
Athenaeus, scholar, fl.c200.
Callicrates, architect, fl.5th cent.BC.
Callimachus, poet, c305-240BC.
Cratinus, comic dramatist, 520-421BC.
Democritus, philosopher, c460-370BC.
Demosthenes, orator, 384-322BC.
Diodorus, historian, fl.20BC.
Diogenes, philosopher, c372-c287BC.

Dionysius, historian, d.c7BC.
Empedocles, philosopher, c490-430BC.
Epicharmus, dramatist, c530-440BC.
Epictetus, philosopher, c55-c135.
Epicurus, philosopher, 341-270BC.
Eratosthenes, scientist, c276-194BC.
Euclid, mathematician, fl.c300BC.
Euripides, dramatist, c484-406BC.
Galen, physician, c129-199.
Heraclitus, philosopher, c535-c475BC.
Herodotus, historian, c484-420BC.
Hesiod, poet, 8th cent. BC.
Hippocrates, physician, c460-377BC.
Homer, poet, believed lived c850BC.
Isocrates, orator, 436-338BC.
Menander, dramatist, 342-292BC.
Phidias, sculptor, c500-435BC.
Pindar, poet, c518-c438BC.
Plato, philosopher, c428-c347BC.
Plutarch, biographer, c46-120.

Polybius, historian, c200-c118BC.
Praxiteles, sculptor, 400-330BC.
Pythagoras, phil., math., c580-c500BC.
Sappho, poet, c610-c580BC.
Simonides, poet, 556-c468BC.
Socrates, philosopher, c470-399BC.
Solon, statesman, 640-560BC.
Sophocles, dramatist, C496-406BC.
Strabo, geographer, c63BC-AD24.
Thales, philosopher, c634-c546BC.
Themistocles, politician, c524-c460BC.
Theocritus, poet, c310-250BC.
Theophrastus, phil. c372-c287BC.
Thucydides, historian, fl.5th cent.BC.
Timon, philosopher, c320-c230BC.
Xenophon, historian, c434-c355BC.
Zeno, philosopher, c495-c430BC.

Latins

Ammianus, historian, c330-395.
Apuleius, satirist, c124-c170.
Boethius, scholar, c480-524
Caesar, Julius, general, 100-44BC.
Catilina, politician, c108-62BC.
Cato(Elder), statesman, 234-149BC.
Catullus, poet, c84-54BC.
Cicero, orator, 106-43BC.
Claudian, poet, c370-c404.
Ennius, poet, 239-170BC.
Gellius, author, c130-c165.
Horace, poet, 65-8BC.

Juvenal, satirist, c60-c127.
Livy, historian, 59BC-AD17.
Lucan, poet, 39-65.
Lucilius, poet, c180-c102BC.
Lucretius, poet, c99-c55BC.
Martial, epigrammatist, c38-c103.
Nepos, historian, c100-c25BC.
Ovid,poet, 43BC-AD17.
Persius, satirist, 34-62.
Plautus, dramatist, c254-c184BC.
Pliny, scholar, 23-79.
Pliny(Younger), author, 62-113.

Quintilian, rhetorician, c35-c97.
Sallust, historian, 86-34BC.
Seneca, philosopher, 4BC-AD65.
Silius, poet, c25-101.
Statius, poet, c45-c96.
Suetonius, biographer, c69-c122.
Tacitus, historian, c56-c120.
Terence, dramatist, 185-c159BC.
Tibullus, poet, c55-c19BC.
Virgil, poet, 70-19BC.
Vitruvius, architect, fl.1st cent.BC.

Rulers of England and Great Britain

Name	England	Began	Died	Age	Rgd
Saxons and Danes					
Egbert	King of Wessex, won allegiance of all English	829	839	—	10
Ethelwulf	Son, King of Wessex, Sussex, Kent, Essex	839	858	—	19
Ethelbald	Son of Ethelwulf, displaced father in Wessex	858	860	—	2
Ethelbert	2d son of Ethelwulf, united Kent and Wessex	860	866	—	6
Ethelred I	3d son, King of Wessex, fought Danes	866	871	—	5
Alfred	The Great, 4th son, defeated Danes, fortified London	871	899	52	28
Edward	The Elder, Alfred's son, united English, claimed Scotland	899	924	55	25
Athelstan	The Glorious, Edward's son, King of Mercia, Wessex	924	940	45	16
Edmund I	3d son of Edward, King of Wessex, Mercia	940	946	25	6
Edred	4th son of Edward	946	955	32	9
Edwy	The Fair, eldest son of Edmund, King of Wessex	955	959	18	3
Edgar	The Peaceful, 2d son of Edmund, ruled all English	959	975	32	17
Edward	The Martyr, eldest son of Edgar, murdered by stepmother	975	978	17	4
Ethelred II	The Unready, 2d son of Edgar, married Emma of Normandy	978	1016	48	37
Edmund II	Ironside, son of Ethelred II, King of London	1016	1016	27	0
Canute	The Dane, gave Wessex to Edmund, married Emma	1016	1035	40	19
Harold I	Harefoot, natural son of Canute	1035	1040	—	5
Hardecanute	Son of Canute by Emma, Danish King	1040	1042	24	2
Edward	The Confessor, son of Ethelred II (Canonized 1161)	1042	1066	62	24
Harold II	Edward's brother-in-law, last Saxon King	1066	1066	44	0
House of Normandy					
William I	The Conqueror, defeated Harold at Hastings	1066	1087	60	21
William II	Rufus, 3d son of William I, killed by arrow	1087	1100	43	13
Henry I	Beauclerc, youngest son of William I	1100	1135	67	35
House of Blois					
Stephen	Son of Adela, daughter of William I, and Count of Blois	1135	1154	50	19
House of Plantagenet					
Henry II	Son of Geoffrey Plantagenet (Angevin) by Matilda, dau. of Henry I	1154	1189	56	35
Richard I	Coeur de Lion, son of Henry II, crusader	1189	1199	42	10
John	Lackland, son of Henry II, signed Magna Carta, 1215	1199	1216	50	17
Henry III	Son of John, acceded at 9, under regency until 1227	1216	1272	65	56
Edward I	Longshanks, son of Henry III	1272	1307	68	35
Edward II	Son of Edward I, deposed by Parliament, 1327	1307	1327	43	20
Edward III	Of Windsor, son of Edward II	1327	1377	65	50
Richard II	Grandson of Edw. III, minor until 1389, deposed 1399	1377	1400	33	22
House of Lancaster					
Henry IV	Son of John of Gaunt, Duke of Lancaster, son of Edw. III	1399	1413	47	13
Henry V	Son of Henry IV, victor of Agincourt	1413	1422	34	9
Henry VI	Son of Henry V, deposed 1461, died in Tower	1422	1471	49	39

Name		Began	Died	Age	Rgd
	House of York				
Edward IV	Great-great-grandson of Edward III, son of Duke of York	1461	1483	41	22
Edward V	Son of Edward IV, murdered in Tower of London	1483	1483	13	0
Richard III	Crookback, bro. of Edward IV, fell at Bosworth Field	1483	1485	35	2
	House of Tudor				
Henry VII	Son of Edmund Tudor, Earl of Richmond, whose father had married the widow of Henry V; descended from Edward III through his mother, Margaret Beaufort via John of Gaunt. By marriage with dau. of Edward IV he united Lancaster and York	1485	1509	53	24
Henry VIII	Son of Henry VII by Elizabeth, dau. of Edward IV.	1509	1547	56	38
Edward VI	Son of Henry VIII, by Jane Seymour, his 3d queen. Ruled under regents. Was forced to name Lady Jane Grey his successor. Council of State proclaimed her queen July 10, 1553. Mary Tudor won Council, was proclaimed queen July 19, 1553. Mary had Lady Jane Grey beheaded for treason, Feb., 1554	1547	1553	16	6
Mary I	Daughter of Henry VIII, by Catherine of Aragon	1553	1558	43	5
Elizabeth I	Daughter of Henry VIII, by Anne Boleyn	1558	1603	69	44

Great Britain
House of Stuart

Name		Began	Died	Age	Rgd
James I	James VI of Scotland, son of Mary, Queen of Scots. *First to call himself King of Great Britain. This became official with the Act of Union, 1707*	1603	1625	59	22
Charles I	Only surviving son of James I; beheaded Jan. 30, 1649	1625	1649	48	24

Commonwealth, 1649-1660
Council of State, 1649; Protectorate, 1653

Name		Began	Died	Age	Rgd
The Cromwells	Oliver Cromwell, Lord Protector	1653	1658	59	—
	Richard Cromwell, son, Lord Protector, resigned May 25, 1659	1658	1712	86	—

House of Stuart (Restored)

Name		Began	Died	Age	Rgd
Charles II	Eldest son of Charles I, died without issue	1660	1685	55	25
James II	2d son of Charles I. Deposed 1688. Interregnum Dec. 11, 1688, to Feb. 13, 1689	1685	1701	68	3
William III	Son of William, Prince of Orange, by Mary, dau. of Charles I	1689	1702	51	13
and Mary II	Eldest daughter of James II and wife of William III		1694	33	6
Anne	2d daughter of James II	1702	1714	49	12

House of Hanover

Name		Began	Died	Age	Rgd
George I	Son of Elector of Hanover, by Sophia, grand-dau. of James I	1714	1727	67	13
George II	Only son of George I, married Caroline of Brandenburg	1727	1760	77	33
George III	Grandson of George II, married Charlotte of Mecklenburg	1760	1820	81	59
George IV	Eldest son of George III, Prince Regent, from Feb., 1811	1820	1830	67	10
William IV	3d son of George III, married Adelaide of Saxe-Meiningen	1830	1837	71	7
Victoria	Dau. of Edward, 4th son of George III; married (1840) Prince Albert of Saxe-Coburg and Gotha, who became Prince Consort	1837	1901	81	63

House of Saxe-Coburg and Gotha

Name		Began	Died	Age	Rgd
Edward VII	Eldest son of Victoria, married Alexandra, Princess of Denmark	1901	1910	68	9

House of Windsor
Name Adopted July 17, 1917

Name		Began	Died	Age	Rgd
George V	2d son of Edward VII, married Princess Mary of Teck	1910	1936	70	25
Edward VIII	Eldest son of George V; acceded Jan. 20, 1936, abdicated Dec. 11	1936	1972	77	1
George VI	2d son of George V; married Lady Elizabeth Bowes-Lyon	1936	1952	56	15
Elizabeth II	Elder daughter of George VI, acceded Feb. 6, 1952	1952	—	—	—

Rulers of Scotland

Kenneth I MacAlpin was the first Scot to rule both Scots and Picts, 846 AD.

Duncan I was the first general ruler, 1034. Macbeth seized the kingdom 1040, was slain by Duncan's son, Malcolm III MacDuncan (Canmore), 1057.

Malcolm married Margaret, Saxon princess who had fled from the Normans. Queen Margaret introduced English language and English monastic customs. She was canonized, 1250. Her son Edgar, 1097, moved the court to Edinburgh. His brothers Alexander I and David I succeeded. Malcolm IV, the Maiden, 1153, grandson of David I, was followed by his brother, William the Lion, 1165, whose son was Alexander II, 1214. The latter's son, Alexander III, 1249, defeated the Norse and regained the Hebrides. When he died, 1286, his granddaughter, Margaret, child of Eric of Norway and grandniece of Edward I of England, known as the Maid of Norway, was chosen ruler, but died 1290, aged 8.

John Baliol, 1292-1296. (Interregnum, 10 years).

Robert Bruce (The Bruce), 1306-1329, victor at Bannockburn, 1314.

David II, only son of Robert Bruce, ruled 1329-1371.

Robert II, 1371-1390, grandson of Robert Bruce, son of Walter, the Steward of Scotland, was called The Steward, first of the so-called Stuart line.

Robert III, son of Robert II, 1390-1406.

James I, son of Robert III, 1406-1437.

James II, son of James I, 1437-1460.

James III, eldest son of James II, 1460-1488.

James IV, eldest son of James III, 1488-1513.

James V, eldest son of James IV, 1513-1542.

Mary, daughter of James V, born 1542, became queen when one week old; was crowned 1543. Married, 1558, Francis, son of Henry II of France, who became king 1559, died 1560. Mary ruled Scots 1561 until abdication, 1567. She also married (2) Henry Stewart, Lord Darnley, and (3) James, Earl of Bothwell. Imprisoned by Elizabeth I, Mary was beheaded 1587.

James VI, 1566-1625, son of Mary and Lord Darnley, became King of England on death of Elizabeth in 1603. Although the thrones were thus united, the legislative union of Scotland and England was not effected until the Act of Union, May 1, 1707.

Prime Ministers of Great Britain

(W=Whig; T=Tory; Cl=Coalition; P=Peelite; L=Liberal; C=Conservative; La=Labour)

Sir Robert Walpole (W)	1721-1742	Viscount Goderich (T)	1827-1828	Herbert H. Asquith	1915-1916
Earl of Wilmington (W)	1742-1743	Duke of Wellington (T)	1828-1830	David Lloyd George (Cl)	1916-1922
Henry Pelham (W)	1743-1754	Earl Grey (W)	1830-1834	Andrew Bonar Law (C)	1922-1923
Duke of Newcastle (W)	1754-1756	Viscount Melbourne (W)	1834	Stanley Baldwin (C)	1923-1924
Duke of Devonshire (W)	1756-1757	Sir Robert Peel (T)	1834-1835	James Ramsay MacDonald	
Duke of Newcastle (W)	1757-1762	Viscount Melbourne (W)	1835-1841	(La)	1924
Earl of Bute (T)	1762-1763	Sir Robert Peel (T)	1841-1846	Stanley Baldwin (C)	1924-1929
George Grenville (W)	1763-1765	Lord John Russell (later		James Ramsay MacDonald	
Marquess of Rockingham		Earl) (W)	1846-1852	(La)	1929-1931
(W)	1765-1766	Earl of Derby (T)	1852	James Ramsay MacDonald	
William Pitt the Elder		Earl of Aberdeen (P)	1852-1855	(Cl)	1931-1935
(Earl of Chatham) (W)	1766-1768	Viscount Palmerston (L)	1855-1858	Stanley Baldwin (Cl)	1935-1937
Duke of Grafton (W)	1768-1770	Earl of Derby (T)	1858-1859	Neville Chamberlain (Cl)	1937-1940
Frederick North (Lord		Viscount Palmerston (L)	1859-1865	Winston Churchill (Cl)	1940-1945
North) (T)	1770-1782	Earl Russell (L)	1865-1866	Winston Churchill (C)	1945
Marquess of Rockingham		Earl of Derby (C)	1866-1868	Clement Attlee (La)	1945-1951
(W)	1782	Benjamin Disraeli (C)	1868	Sir Winston Churchill	1951-1955
Earl of Shelburne (W)	1782-1783	William E. Gladstone (L)	1868-1874	Sir Anthony Eden (C)	1955-1957
Duke of Portland (Cl)	1783	Benjamin Disraeli (C)	1874-1880	Harold Macmillan (C)	1957-1963
William Pitt the Younger		William E. Gladstone (L)	1880-1885	Sir Alec Douglas-Home	
(T)	1783-1801	Marquess of Salisbury (C)	1885-1886		1963-1964
Henry Addington (T)	1801-1804	William E. Gladstone (L)	1886	Harold Wilson (La)	1964-1970
William Pitt the Younger		Marquess of Salisbury (C)	1886-1892	Edward Heath (C)	1970-1974
(T)	1804-1806	William E. Gladstone (L)	1892-1894	Harold Wilson (La)	1974-1976
William Wyndham Grenville,		Earl of Rosebery (L)	1894-1895	James Callaghan (La)	1976-1979
Baron Grenville (W)	1806-1807	Marquess of Salisbury (C)	1895-1902	Margaret Thatcher (C)	1979-1990
Duke of Portland (T)	1807-1809	Arthur J. Balfour (C)	1902-1905	John Major (C)	1990-
Spencer Perceval (T)	1809-1812	Sir Henry			
Earl of Liverpool (T)	1812-1827	Campbell-Bannerman (L)	1905-1908		
George Canning (T)	1827	Herbert H. Asquith (L)	1908-1915		

Historical Periods of Japan

Yamato	c.300-592	Conquest of Yamato plain c. 300 A.D.	Ashikaga	1338-1573	Ashikaga Takauji becomes shogun, 1338.
Asuka	592-710	Accession of Empress Suiko, 592.	Muromachi	1392-1573	Unification of Southern and Northern Courts, 1392.
Nara	710-794	Completion of Heijo (Nara), 710; capital moves to Naga-oka, 784.	Sengoku	1467-1600	Beginning of the Onin war, 1467
Heian	794-1192	Completion of Heian (Kyoto), 794	Momoyama	1573-1603	Oda Nobunaga enters Kyoto, 1568; Nobunaga deposes last Ashikaga shogun, 1573;
Fujiwara	858-1160	Fujiwara-no-Yoshifusa becomes regent, 858.			Tokugawa Ieyasu victor at Sekigahara, 1600.
Taira	1160-1185	Taira-no-Kiyomori assumes control, 1160; Minamoto-no-Yoritomo victor over Taira, 1185.	Edo	1603-1867	Ieyasu becomes shogun, 1603.
			Meiji	1868-1912	Enthronement of Emperor Mutsuhito (Meiji), 1867; Meiji Restoration and Charter Oath, 1868.
Kamakura	1192-1333	Yoritomo becomes shogun, 1192.	Taisho	1912-1926	Accession of Emperor Yoshihito, 1912.
Namboku	1334-1392	Restoration of Emperor Godaigo, 1334; Southern Court established by Godaigo at Yoshino, 1336.	Showa	1926-1989	Accession of Emperor Hirohito, 1926.
			Heisei	1989-	Accession of Emperor Akihito, 1989

Rulers of France: Kings, Queens, Presidents

Caesar to Charlemagne

Julius Caesar subdued the Gauls, native tribes of Gaul (France) 57 to 52 BC. The Romans ruled 500 years. The Franks, a Teutonic tribe, reached the Somme from the East ca. 250 AD. By the 5th century the Merovingian Franks ousted the Romans. In 451 AD, with the help of Visigoths, Burgundians and others, they defeated Attila and the Huns at Chalons-sur-Marne.

Childeric I became leader of the Merovingians 458 AD. His son Clovis I (Chlodwig, Ludwig, Louis), crowned 481, founded the dynasty. After defeating the Alemanni (Germans) 496, he was baptized a Christian and made Paris his capital. His line ruled until Childeric III was deposed, 751.

The West Merovingians were called Neustrians, the eastern Austrasians. Pepin of Herstal (687-714) major domus, or head of the palace, of Austrasia, took over Neustria as dux (leader) of the Franks. Pepin's son, Charles, called Martel (the Hammer) defeated the Saracens at Tours-Poitiers, 732; was succeeded by his son, Pepin the Short, 741, who deposed Childeric III and ruled as king until 768.

His son, Charlemagne, or Charles the Great (742-814) became king of the Franks, 768, with his brother Carloman, who died 771. He ruled France, Germany, parts of Italy, Spain, Austria, and enforced Christianity. Crowned Emperor of the Romans by Pope Leo III in St. Peter's, Rome, Dec. 25, 800 AD. Succeeded by son, Louis I the Pious, 814. At death, 840, Louis left empire to sons, Lothair (Roman emperor); Pepin I (king of Aquitaine); Louis II (of Germany); Charles the Bald (France). They quarreled and by the peace of Verdun, 843, divided the empire.

(continued)

AD Name, year of accession

The Carolingians

843 Charles I (the Bald), Roman Emperor, 875
877 Louis II (the Stammerer), son
879 Louis III (died 882) and Carloman, brothers
885 Charles II (the Fat), Roman Emperor, 881
888 Eudes (Odo) elected by nobles
898 Charles III (the Simple), son of Louis II, defeated by
922 Robert, brother of Eudes, killed in war
923 Rudolph (Raoul) Duke of Burgundy
936 Louis IV, son of Charles III
954 Lothair, son, aged 13, defeated by Capet
986 Louis V (the Sluggard), left no heirs

The Capets

987 Hugh Capet, son of Hugh the Great
996 Robert II (the Wise), his son
1031 Henry I, his son
1060 Philip I (the Fair), son
1108 Louis VI (the Fat), son
1137 Louis VII (the Younger), son
1180 Philip II (Augustus), son, crowned at Reims
1223 Louis VIII (the Lion), son
1226 Louis IX, son, crusader; Louis IX (1214-1270) reigned 44
years, arbitrated disputes with English King Henry III; led
crusades, 1248 (captured in Egypt 1250) and 1270, when
he died of plague in Tunis. Canonized 1297 as St. Louis.
1270 Philip III (the Hardy), son
1285 Philip IV (the Fair), son, king at 17
1314 Louis X (the Headstrong), son. His posthumous son, John
I, lived only 7 days
1316 Philip V (the Tall), brother of Louis X
1322 Charles IV (the Fair), brother of Louis X

House of Valois

1328 Philip VI (of Valois), grandson of Philip III
1350 John II (the Good), his son, retired to England
1364 Charles V (the Wise), son
1380 Charles VI (the Beloved), son
1422 Charles VII (the Victorious), son. In 1429 Joan of Arc
(Jeanne d'Arc) promised Charles to oust the English, who
occupied northern France. Joan won at Orleans and
Patay and had Charles crowned at Reims July 17, 1429.
Joan was captured May 24, 1430, and executed May 30,
1431, at Rouen for heresy. Charles ordered her rehabilitation, effected 1455.
1461 Louis XI (the Cruel), son, civil reformer
1483 Charles VIII (the Affable), son
1498 Louis XII, great-grandson of Charles V
1515 Francis I, of Angouleme, nephew, son-in-law. Francis I
(1494-1547) reigned 32 years, fought 4 big wars, was
patron of the arts, aided Cellini, del Sarto, Leonardo da
Vinci, Rabelais, embellished Fontainebleau.
1547 Henry II, son, killed at a joust in a tournament. He was
the husband of Catherine de Medicis (1519-1589) and
the lover of Diane de Poitiers (1499-1566). Catherine was
born in Florence, daughter of Lorenzo de Medicis. By her
marriage to Henry II she became the mother of Francis II,
Charles IX, Henry III and Queen Margaret (Reine Margot)
wife of Henry IV. She persuaded Charles IX to order the
massacre of Huguenots on the Feast of St. Bartholomew,
Aug. 24, 1572, the day her daughter was married to
Henry of Navarre.
1559 Francis II, son. In 1548, Mary, Queen of Scots since infancy, was betrothed when 6 to Francis, aged 4. They
were married 1558. Francis died 1560, aged 16; Mary
ruled Scotland, abdicated 1567.
1560 Charles IX, brother
1574 Henry III, brother, assassinated

House of Bourbon

1589 Henry IV, of Navarre, assassinated. Henry IV made enemies when he gave tolerance to Protestants by Edict of
Nantes, 1598. He was grandson of Queen Margaret of
Navarre, literary patron. He married Margaret of Valois,
daughter of Henry II and Catherine de Medicis; was divorced; in 1600 married Marie de Medicis, who became
Regent of France, 1610-17 for her son, Louis XIII, but
was exiled by Richelieu, 1631.

1610 Louis XIII (the Just), son. Louis XIII (1601-1643) married
Anne of Austria. His ministers were Cardinals Richelieu
and Mazarin.
1643 Louis XIV (The Grand Monarch), son. Louis XIV was king
72 years. He exhausted a prosperous country in wars for
thrones and territory. By revoking the Edict of Nantes
(1685) he caused the emigration of the Huguenots. He
said: "I am the state."
1715 Louis XV, great-grandson. Louis XV married a Polish princess; lost Canada to the English. His favorites, Mme.
Pompadour and Mme. Du Barry, influenced policies.
Noted for saying "After me, the deluge".
1774 Louis XVI, grandson; married Marie Antoinette, daughter
of Empress Maria Therese of Austria. King and queen
beheaded by Revolution, 1793. Their son, called Louis
XVII, died in prison, never ruled.

First Republic

1792 National Convention of the French Revolution
1795 Directory, under Barras and others
1799 Consulate, Napoleon Bonaparte, first consul. Elected
consul for life, 1802.

First Empire

1804 Napoleon I, emperor. Josephine (de Beauharnais) empress, 1804-09; Marie Louise, empress, 1810-1814. Her
son, Francois (1811-1832), titular King of Rome, later
Duke de Reichstadt and "Napoleon II," never ruled. Napoleon abdicated 1814, died 1821.

Bourbons Restored

1814 Louis XVIII king; brother of Louis XVI.
1824 Charles X, brother; reactionary; deposed by the July
Revolution, 1830.

House of Orleans

1830 Louis-Philippe, the "citizen king."

Second Republic

1848 Louis Napoleon Bonaparte, president, nephew of Napoleon I. He became:

Second Empire

1852 Napoleon III, emperor; Eugenie (de Montijo) empress.
Lost Franco-Prussian war, deposed 1870. Son, Prince
Imperial (1856-79), died in Zulu War. Eugenie died 1920.

Third Republic—Presidents

1871 Thiers, Louis Adolphe (1797-1877)
1873 MacMahon, Marshal Patrice M. de (1808-1893)
1879 Grevy, Paul J. (1807-1891)
1887 Sadi-Carnot, M. (1837-1894), assassinated
1894 Casimir-Perier, Jean P. P. (1847-1907)
1895 Faure, Francois Felix (1841-1899)
1899 Loubet, Emile (1838-1929)
1906 Fallieres, C. Armand (1841-1931)
1913 Poincare, Raymond (1860-1934)
1920 Deschanel, Paul (1856-1922)
1920 Millerand, Alexandre (1859-1943)
1924 Doumergue, Gaston (1863-1937)
1931 Doumer, Paul (1857-1932), assassinated
1932 Lebrun, Albert (1871-1950), resigned 1940
1940 Vichy govt. under German armistice: Henri Philippe Pe-
tain (1856-1951) Chief of State, 1940-1944.
Provisional govt. after liberation: Charles de Gaulle
(1890-1970) Oct. 1944-Jan. 21, 1946; Felix Gouin
(1884-1977) Jan. 23, 1946; Georges Bidault (1899-1983)
June 24, 1946.

Fourth Republic—Presidents

1947 Auriol, Vincent (1884-1966)
1954 Coty, Rene (1882-1962)

Fifth Republic—Presidents

1959 de Gaulle, Charles Andre J. M. (1890-1970)
1969 Pompidou, Georges (1911-1974)
1974 Giscard d'Estaing, Valery (1926-   )
1981 Mitterrand, Francois (1916-   )

Rulers of Middle Europe; Rise and Fall of Dynasties

Carolingian Dynasty

Charles the Great, or Charlemagne, ruled France, Italy, and
Middle Europe; established Ostmark (later Austria); crowned
Roman emperor by pope in Rome, 800 AD; died 814.
Louis I (Ludwig) the Pious, son; crowned by Charlemagne 814,
d. 840.

Louis II, the German, son; succeeded to East Francia (Germany) 843-876.

Charles the Fat, son; inherited East Francia and West Francia
(France) 876, reunited empire, crowned emperor by pope, 881,
deposed 887.

Arnulf, nephew, 887-899. Partition of empire.

Louis the Child, 899-911, last direct descendant of Charlemagne.

Conrad I, duke of Franconia, first elected German king, 911-918, founded House of Franconia.

Saxon Dynasty; First Reich

Henry I, the Fowler, duke of Saxony, 919-936.

Otto I, the Great, 936-973, son; crowned Holy Roman Emperor by pope, 962.

Otto II, 973-983, son; failed to oust Greeks and Arabs from Sicily.

Otto III, 983-1002, son; crowned emperor at 16.

Henry II, the Saint, duke of Bavaria, 1002-1024, great-grandson of Otto the Great.

House of Franconia

Conrad II, 1024-1039, elected king of Germany.

Henry III, the Black, 1039-1056, son; deposed 3 popes; annexed Burgundy.

Henry IV, 1056-1106, son; regency by his mother, Agnes of Poitou. Banned by Pope Gregory VII, he did penance at Canossa.

Henry V, 1106-1125, son; last of Salic House.

Lothair, duke of Saxony, 1125-1137. Crowned emperor in Rome, 1134.

House of Hohenstaufen

Conrad III, duke of Swabia, 1138-1152. In 2d Crusade.

Frederick I, Barbarossa, 1152-1190; Conrad's nephew.

Henry VI, 1190-1196, took lower Italy from Normans. Son became king of Sicily.

Philip of Swabia, 1197-1208, brother.

Otto IV, of House of Welf, 1198-1215; deposed.

Frederick II, 1215-1250, son of Henry VI; king of Sicily; crowned king of Jerusalem; in 5th Crusade.

Conrad IV, 1250-1254, son; lost lower Italy to Charles of Anjou.

Conradin (1252-1268) son, king of Jerusalem and Sicily, beheaded. Last Hohenstaufen.

Interregnum, 1254-1273, Rise of the Electors.

Transition

Rudolph I of Hapsburg, 1273-1291, defeated King Ottocar II of Bohemia. Bequeathed duchy of Austria to eldest son, Albert.

Adolph of Nassau, 1292-1298, killed in war with Albert of Austria.

Albert I, king of Germany, 1298-1308, son of Rudolph.

Henry VII, of Luxemburg, 1308-1313, crowned emperor in Rome. Seized Bohemia, 1310.

Louis IV of Bavaria (Wittelsbach), 1314-1347. Also elected was Frederick of Austria, 1314-1330 (Hapsburg). Abolition of papal sanction for election of Holy Roman Emperor.

Charles IV, of Luxemburg, 1347-1378, grandson of Henry VII, German emperor and king of Bohemia, Lombardy, Burgundy; took Mark of Brandenburg.

Wenceslaus, 1378-1400, deposed.

Rupert, Duke of Palatine, 1400-1410.

Hungary

Stephen I, house of Arpad, 997-1038. Crowned king 1000; converted Magyars; canonized 1083. After several centuries of feuds Charles Robert of Anjou became Charles I, 1308-1342.

Louis I, the Great, son, 1342-1382; joint ruler of Poland with Casimir III, 1370. Defeated Turks.

Mary, daughter, 1382-1395, ruled with husband. Sigismund of Luxemburg, 1387-1437, also king of Bohemia. As bro. of Wenceslaus he succeeded Rupert as Holy Roman Emperor, 1410.

Albert II, 1438-1439, son-in-law of Sigismund; also Roman emperor. *(see under Hapsburg.)*

Ulaszlo I of Poland, 1440-1444.

Ladislaus V, posthumous son of Albert II, 1444-1457. John Hunyadi (Hunyadi Janos) governor (1446-1452), fought Turks, Czechs; died 1456.

Matthias I (Corvinus) son of Hunyadi, 1458-1490. Shared rule of Bohemia, captured Vienna, 1485, annexed Austria, Styria, Carinthia.

Ladislas II (king of Bohemia), 1490-1516.

Louis II, son, aged 10, 1516-1526. Wars with Suleiman, Turk. In 1527 Hungary was split between Ferdinand I, Archduke of

Austria, bro.-in-law of Louis II, and John Zapolya of Transylvania. After Turkish invasion, 1547, Hungary was split between Ferdinand, Prince John Sigismund (Transylvania) and the Turks.

House of Hapsburg

Albert V of Austria, Hapsburg, crowned king of Hungary, Jan. 1438, Roman emperor, March, 1438, as Albert II; died 1439.

Frederick III, cousin, 1440-1493. Fought Turks.

Maximilian I, son, 1493-1519. Assumed title of Holy Roman Emperor (German), 1493.

Charles V, grandson, 1519-1556. King of Spain with mother co-regent; crowned Roman emperor at Aix, 1520. Confronted Luther at Worms; attempted church reform and religious conciliation; abdicated 1556.

Ferdinand I, king of Bohemia, 1526, of Hungary, 1527; disputed. German king, 1531. Crowned Roman emperor on abdication of brother Charles V, 1556.

Maximilian II, son, 1564-1576.

Rudolph II, son, 1576-1612.

Matthias, brother, 1612-1619, king of Bohemia and Hungary.

Ferdinand II of Styria, king of Bohemia, 1617, of Hungary, 1618, Roman emperor, 1619. Bohemian Protestants deposed him, elected Frederick V of Palatine, starting Thirty Years War.

Ferdinand III, son, king of Hungary, 1625, Bohemia, 1627, Roman emperor, 1637. Peace of Westphalia, 1648, ended war. Leopold I, 1658-1705; Joseph I, 1705-1711; Charles VI, 1711-1740.

Maria Theresa, daughter, 1740-1780, Archduchess of Austria, queen of Hungary; ousted pretender, Charles VII, crowned 1742; in 1745 obtained election of her husband Francis I as Roman emperor and co-regent (d. 1765). Fought Seven Years' War with Frederick II (the Great) of Prussia. Mother of Marie Antoinette, Queen of France.

Joseph II, son 1765-1790, Roman emperor, reformer; powers restricted by Empress Maria Theresa until her death, 1780. First partition of Poland. Leopold II, 1790-1792.

Francis II, son, 1792-1835. Fought Napoleon. Proclaimed first hereditary emperor of Austria, 1804. Forced to abdicate as Roman emperor, 1806; last use of title. Ferdinand I, son, 1835-1848, abdicated during revolution.

Austro-Hungarian Monarchy

Francis Joseph I, nephew, 1848-1916, emperor of Austria, king of Hungary. Dual monarchy of Austria-Hungary formed, 1867. After assassination of heir, Archduke Francis Ferdinand, June 28, 1914, Austrian diplomacy precipitated World War I.

Charles I, grand-nephew, 1916-1918, last emperor of Austria and king of Hungary. Abdicated Nov. 11-13, 1918, died 1922.

Rulers of Prussia

Nucleus of Prussia was the Mark of Brandenburg. First margrave was Albert the Bear (Albrecht), 1134-1170. First Hohenzollern margrave was Frederick, burgrave of Nuremberg, 1417-1440.

Frederick William, 1640-1688, the Great Elector. Son, Frederick III, 1688-1713, was crowned King Frederick of Prussia, 1701.

Frederick William I, son, 1713-1740.

Frederick II, the Great, son, 1740-1786, annexed Silesia part of Austria.

Frederick William II, nephew, 1786-1797.

Frederick William III, son, 1797-1840. Napoleonic wars.

Frederick William IV, son, 1840-1861. Uprising of 1848 and first parliament and constitution.

Second and Third Reich

William I, 1861-1888, brother. Annexation of Schleswig and Hanover; Franco-Prussian war, 1870-71, proclamation of German Reich, Jan. 18, 1871, at Versailles; William, German emperor (Deutscher Kaiser), Bismarck, chancellor.

Frederick III, son, 1888.

William II, son, 1888-1918. Led Germany in World War I, abdicated as German emperor and king of Prussia, Nov. 9, 1918. Died in exile in Netherlands June 4, 1941. Minor rulers of Bavaria, Saxony, Wurttemberg also abdicated.

Germany proclaimed a republic at Weimar, July 1, 1919. Presidents: Frederick Ebert, 1919-1925, Paul von Hindenburg-Beneckendorff, 1925, reelected 1932, d. Aug. 2, 1934. Adolf Hitler, chancellor, chosen successor as Leader-Chancellor (Fuehrer & Reichskanzler) of Third Reich. Annexed Austria, March, 1938. Precipitated World War II, 1939-1945. Committed suicide April 30, 1945.

Rulers of Poland

House of Piasts

Miesko I, 962?-992; Poland Christianized 966. Expansion under 3 Boleslavs: I, 992-1025, son, crowned king 1024; II,

1058-1079, great-grandson, exiled after killing bishop Stanislav who became chief patron saint of Poland: III, 1106-1138, nephew, divided Poland among 4 sons eldest suzerain.

(continued)

1138-1306, feudal division. 1226 founding in Prussia of military order Teutonic Knights. 1226 invasion by Tartars/Mongols.

Vladislav I, 1306-1333, reunited most Polish territories, crowned king 1320. Casimir III the Great, 1333-1370, son, developed economic, cultural life, foreign policy.

House of Anjou

Louis I, 1370-1382, nephew/identical with Louis I of Hungary. Jadwiga, 1384-1399, daughter, married 1386 Jagiello, Grand Duke of Lituania.

House of Jagelloneans

Vladislav II, 1386-1434, Christianized Lituania, founded personal union between Poland & Lituania. Defeated 1410 Teutonic Knights at Grunwald.

Vladislav III, 1434-1444, son, simultaneously king of Hungary. Fought Turks, killed 1444 in battle of Varna.

Casimir IV, 1446-1492, brother, competed with Hapsburgs, put son Vladislav on throne of Bohemia, later also of Hungary.

Sigismund I, 1506-1548, brother, patronized science & arts, his & son's reign "Golden Age."

Sigismund II, 1548-1572, son, established 1569 real union of Poland and Lituania (lasted until 1795).

Elective kings

Polish nobles proclaimed 1572 Poland a Republic headed by king to be elected by whole nobility.

Stephen Batory, 1576-1586, duke of Transylvania, married Ann, sister of Sigismund II August. Fought Russians.

Sigismund III Vasa, 1587-1632, nephew of Sigismund II. 1592-1598 also king of Sweden. His generals fought Russians, Turks.

Vladislav II Vasa, 1632-1648, son. Fought Russians.

John II Casimir Vasa, 1648-1668, brother. Fought Cossacks, Swedes, Russians, Turks, Tartars (the "Deluge"). Abdicated 1668.

John III Sobieski, 1674-1696. Won Vienna from Turks, 1683.

Stanislav II, 1764-1795, last king. Encouraged reforms; 1791 1st modern Constitution in Europe. 1772, 1793, 1795 Poland partitioned among Russia, Prussia, Austria. Unsuccessful insurrection against foreign invasion 1794 under Kosciuszko, Amer-Polish gen.

1795-1918 Poland under foreign rule

1807-1815 Grand Duchy of Warsaw created by Napoleon I, Frederick August of Saxony grand duke.

1815 Congress of Vienna proclaimed part of Poland "Kingdom" in personal union with Russia.

Polish uprisings: 1830 against Russia, 1846, 1848 against Austria, 1863 against Russia—all repressed.

1918-1939 Second Republic

1918-1922 Head of State Jozef Pilsudski. Presidents: Gabriel Narutowicz 1922, assassinated. Stanislav Wojsiechowski 1922-1926, had to abdicate after Pilsudski's coup d'état. Ignacy Mosciecki, 1926-1939, ruled with Pilsudski as (until 1935) virtual dictator.

1939-1945 Poland under foreign occupation

Nazi aggression Sept. 1939. Polish govt.-in-exile, first in France, then in England. Vladislav Raczkiewicz pres., Gen. Vladislav Sikorski, then Stanislav Mikolajczyk, prime ministers. Polish Committee of Natl. Liberation proclaimed at Lublin July 1944, transformed into govt. Jan. 1, 1945.

Rulers of Denmark, Sweden, Norway

Denmark

Earliest rulers invaded Britain; King Canute, who ruled in London 1016-1035, was most famous. The Valdemars furnished kings until the 15th century. In 1282 the Danes won the first national assembly, Danehof, from King Erik V.

Most redoubtable medieval character was Margaret, daughter of Valdemar IV, born 1353, married at 10 to King Haakon VI of Norway. In 1376 she had her first infant son Olaf made king of Denmark. After his death, 1387, she was regent of Denmark and Norway. In 1388 Sweden accepted her as sovereign. In 1389 she made her grand-nephew, Duke Erik of Pomerania, titular king of Denmark, Sweden, and Norway, with herself as regent. In 1397 she effected the Union of Kalmar of the three kingdoms and had Erik VII crowned. In 1439 the three kingdoms deposed him and elected, 1440, Christopher of Bavaria king (Christopher III). On his death, 1448, the union broke up.

Succeeding rulers were unable to enforce their claims as rulers of Sweden until 1520, when Christian II conquered Sweden. He was thrown out 1522, and in 1523 Gustavus Vasa united Sweden. Denmark continued to dominate Norway until the Napoleonic wars, when Frederick VI, 1808-1839, joined the Napoleonic cause after Britain had destroyed the Danish fleet, 1807. In 1814 he was forced to cede Norway to Sweden and Helgoland to Britain, receiving Lauenburg. Successors Christian VIII, 1839; Frederick VII, 1848; Christian IX, 1863; Frederick VIII, 1906; Christian X, 1912; Frederick IX, 1947; Margrethe II, 1972.

Sweden

Early kings ruled at Uppsala, but did not dominate the country. Sverker, c1130-c1156, united the Swedes and Goths. In 1435 Sweden obtained the Riksdag, or parliament. After the Union of Kalmar, 1397, the Danes either ruled or harried the country until Christian II of Denmark conquered it anew, 1520. This led to a rising under Gustavus Vasa, who ruled Sweden 1523-1560, and established an independent kingdom. Charles IX, 1599-1611, crowned 1604, conquered Moscow. Gustavus II Adolphus, 1611-1632, was called the Lion of the North. Later rulers: Christina, 1632; Charles X, Gustavus 1654; Charles XI, 1660; Charles XII (invader of Russia and Poland, defeated at Poltava, June 28, 1709), 1697; Ulrika Eleanora, sister, elected queen 1718; Frederick I (of Hesse), her husband, 1720; Adolphus Frederick, 1751; Gustavus III, 1771; Gustavus IV Adolphus, 1792; Charles XIII, 1809. (Union with Norway began 1814.) Charles XIV John, 1818. He was Jean Bernadotte, Napoleon's Prince of Ponte Corvo, elected 1810 to succeed Charles XIII. He founded the present dynasty: Oscar I, 1844; Charles XV, 1859; Oscar II, 1872; Gustavus V, 1907; Gustav VI Adolf, 1950; Carl XVI Gustaf, 1973.

Norway

Overcoming many rivals, Harald Haarfager, 872-930, conquered Norway, Orkneys, and Shetlands; Olaf I, great-grandson, 995-1000, brought Christianity into Norway, Iceland, and Greenland. In 1035 Magnus the Good also became king of Denmark. Haakon V, 1299-1319, had married his daughter to Erik of Sweden. Their son, Magnus, became ruler of Norway and Sweden at 6. His son, Haakon VI, married Margaret of Denmark; their son Olaf IV became king of Norway and Denmark, followed by Margaret's regency and the Union of Kalmar, 1397.

In 1450 Norway became subservient to Denmark. Christian IV, 1588-1648, founded Christiania, now Oslo. After Napoleonic wars, when Denmark ceded Norway to Sweden, a strong nationalist movement forced recognition of Norway as an independent kingdom united with Sweden under the Swedish kings, 1814-1905. In 1905 the union was dissolved and Prince Carl of Denmark became Haakon VII. He died Sept. 21, 1957, aged 85; succeeded by son, Olav V, 1957.

Rulers of the Netherlands and Belgium

The Netherlands (Holland)

William Frederick, Prince of Orange, led a revolt against French rule, 1813, and was crowned King of the Netherlands, 1815. Belgium seceded Oct. 4, 1830, after a revolt, and formed a separate government. The change was ratified by the two kingdoms by treaty Apr. 19, 1839.

Succession: William II, son, 1840; William III, son, 1849; Wilhelmina, daughter of William III and his 2d wife Princess Emma of Waldeck, 1890; Wilhelmina abdicated, Sept. 4, 1948, in favor of daughter, Juliana. Juliana abdicated Apr. 30, 1980, in favor of daughter, Beatrix.

Belgium

A national congress elected Prince Leopold of Saxe-Coburg King; he took the throne July 21, 1831, as Leopold I. Succession: Leopold II, son 1865; Albert I, nephew of Leopold II, 1909; Leopold III, son of Albert, 1934; Prince Charles, Regent 1944; Leopold returned 1950, yielded powers to son Baudouin, Prince Royal, Aug. 6, 1950, abdicated July 16, 1951. Baudouin I took throne July 17, 1951.

For political history prior to 1830 see articles on the Netherlands and Belgium.

Roman Rulers

From Romulus to the end of the Empire in the West. Rulers of the Roman Empire in the East sat in Constantinople and for a brief period in Nicaea, until the capture of Constantinople by the Turks in 1453, when Byzantium was succeeded by the Ottoman Empire.

BC	Name	AD	Name	AD	Name
	The Kingdom	98	Trajanus	324	Constantinus I (the Great)
753	Romulus (Quirinus)	117	Hadrianus	337	Constantinus II, Constans I,
716	Numa Pompilius	138	Antoninus Pius		Constantius II
673	Tullus Hostilius	161	Marcus Aurelius and Lucius Verus	340	Constantinus II and Constans I
640	Ancus Marcius	169	Marcus Aurelius (alone)	350	Constantius II
616	L. Tarquinius Priscus	180	Commodus	361	Julianus II (the Apostate)
578	Servius Tullius	193	Pertinax; Julianus I	363	Jovianus
534	L. Tarquinius Superbus	193	Septimius Severus		**West (Rome) and East**
	The Republic	211	Caracalla and Geta		**(Constantinople)**
509	Consulate established	212	Caracalla (alone)	364	Valentinianus I (West) and Valens
509	Quaestorship instituted	217	Macrinus		(East)
498	Dictatorship introduced	218	Elagabalus (Heliogabalus)	367	Valentinianus I with
494	Plebeian Tribunate created	222	Alexander Severus		Gratianus (West) and Valens (East)
494	Plebeian Aedileship created	235	Maximinus I (the Thracian)	375	Gratianus with Valentinianus
444	Consular Tribunate organized	238	Gordianus I and Gordianus II;		II (West) and Valens (East)
435	Censorship instituted		Pupienus and Balbinus	378	Gratianus with Valentinianus II
366	Praetorship established	238	Gordianus III		(West) Theodosius I (East)
366	Curule Aedileship created	244	Philippus (the Arabian)	383	Valentinianus II (West) and
362	Military Tribunate elected	249	Decius		Theodosius I (East)
326	Proconsulate introduced	251	Gallus and Volusianus	394	Theodosius I (the Great)
311	Naval Duumvirate elected	253	Aemilianus	395	Honorius (West) and Arcadius
217	Dictatorship of Fabius Maximus	253	Valerianus and Gallienus		(East)
133	Tribunate of Tiberius Gracchus	258	Gallienus (alone)	408	Honorius (West) and Theodosius II
123	Tribunate of Gaius Gracchus	268	Claudius Gothicus		(East)
82	Dictatorship of Sulla	270	Quintillus	423	Valentinianus III (West) and
60	First Triumvirate formed	270	Aurelianus		Theodosius II (East)
	(Caesar, Pompeius, Crassus)	275	Tacitus	450	Valentinianus III (West)
46	Dictatorship of Caesar	276	Florianus		and Marcianus (East)
43	Second Triumvirate formed	276	Probus	455	Maximus (West), Avitus
	(Octavianus, Antonius, Lepidus)	282	Carus		(West); Marcianus (East)
	The Empire	283	Carinus and Numerianus	456	Avitus (West), Marcianus (East)
27	Augustus (Gaius Julius	284	Diocletianus	457	Majorianus (West), Leo I (East)
	Caesar Octavianus)	286	Diocletianus and Maximianus	461	Severus II (West), Leo I (East)
14	Tiberius I	305	Galerius and Constantius I	467	Anthemius (West), Leo I (East)
37	Gaius Caesar (Caligula)	306	Galerius, Maximinus II, Severus I	472	Olybrius (West), Leo I (East)
41	Claudius I	307	Galerius, Maximinus	473	Glycerius (West), Leo I (East)
54	Nero		II, Constantinus I, Licinius,	474	Julius Nepos (West), Leo II (East)
68	Galba		Maxentius	475	Romulus Augustulus (West) and
69	Galba; Otho, Vitellius	311	Maximinus II, Constantinus I,		Zeno (East)
69	Vespasianus		Licinius, Maxentius	476	End of Empire in West; Odovacar,
79	Titus	314	Maximinus II, Constantinus I,		King, drops title of Emperor;
81	Domitianus		Licinius		murdered by King Theodoric of
96	Nerva	314	Constantinus I and Licinius		Ostrogoths 493 AD

Rulers of Modern Italy

After the fall of Napoleon in 1814, the Congress of Vienna, 1815, restored Italy as a political patchwork, comprising the Kingdom of Naples and Sicily, the Papal States, and smaller units. Piedmont and Genoa were awarded to Sardinia, ruled by King Victor Emmanuel I of Savoy.

United Italy emerged under the leadership of Camillo, Count di Cavour (1810-1861), Sardinian prime minister. Agitation was led by Giuseppe Mazzini (1805-1872) and Giuseppe Garibaldi (1807-1882), soldier, Victor Emmanuel I abdicated 1821. After a brief regency for a brother, Charles Albert was King 1831-1849, abdicating when defeated by the Austrians at Novara. Succeeded by Victor Emmanuel II, 1849-1861.

In 1859 France forced Austria to cede Lombardy to Sardinia, which gave rights to Savoy and Nice to France. In 1860 Garibaldi led 1,000 volunteers in a spectacular campaign, took Sicily and expelled the King of Naples. In 1860 the House of Savoy annexed Tuscany, Parma, Modena, Romagna, the Two Sicilies, the Marches, and Umbria. Victor Emmanuel assumed the title of King of Italy at Turin Mar. 17, 1861. In 1866 he allied with Prussia in the Austro-Prussian War, with Prussia's victory received Venetia. On Sept. 20, 1870, his troops under Gen. Raffaele Cadorna entered Rome and took over the Papal States, ending the temporal power of the Roman Catholic Church.

Succession: Umberto I; 1878, assassinated 1900; Victor Emmanuel III, 1900, abdicated 1946, died 1947; Umberto II, 1946, ruled a month. In 1921 Benito Mussolini (1883-1945) formed the Fascist party and became prime minister Oct. 31, 1922. He made the King Emperor of Ethiopia, 1937; entered World War II as ally of Hitler. He was deposed July 25, 1943.

At a plebiscite June 2, 1946, Italy voted for a republic; Premier Alcide de Gasperi became chief of state June 13, 1946. On June 28, 1946, the Constituent Assembly elected Enrico de Nicola, Liberal, provisional president. Successive presidents: Luigi Einaudi, elected May 11, 1948, Giovanni Gronchi, Apr. 29, 1955; Antonio Segni, May 6, 1962; Giuseppe Saragat, Dec. 28, 1964; Giovanni Leone, Dec. 29, 1971; Alessandro Pertini, July 9, 1978; Francesco Cossiga, July 9, 1985.

Rulers of Spain

From 8th to 11th centuries Spain was dominated by the Moors (Arabs and Berbers). The Christian reconquest established small kingdoms (Asturias, Aragon, Castile, Catalonia, Leon, Navarre, and Valencia). In 1474 Isabella, b. 1451, became Queen of Castile & Leon. Her husband, Ferdinand, b. 1452, inherited Aragon 1479, with Catalonia, Valencia, and the Balearic Islands, became Ferdinand V of Castile. By Isabella's request Pope Sixtus IV established the Inquisition, 1478. Last Moorish kingdom, Granada, fell 1492. Columbus opened New World of colonies, 1492. Isabella died 1504, succeeded by her daughter, Juana "the Mad," but Ferdinand ruled until his death 1516.

Charles I, b. 1500, son of Juana and grandson of Ferdinand and Isabella, and of Maximilian I of Hapsburg; succeeded later as Holy Roman Emperor, Charles V, 1520; abdicated 1556. Philip II, son, 1556-1598, inherited only Spanish throne; conquered Portugal, fought Turks, persecuted non-Catholics, sent Armada against England. Was married to Mary I of England, 1554-1558. Succession: Philip III, 1598-1621; Philip IV, 1621-1665; Charles II, 1665-1700, left Spain to Philip of Anjou, grandson of Louis XIV, who as Philip V, 1700-1746, founded Bourbon dynasty. Ferdinand VI, 1746-1759; Charles III, 1759-1788; Charles IV, 1788-1808, abdicated.

Napoleon now dominated politics and made his brother Joseph King of Spain 1808, but the Spanish ousted him in 1813. Ferdinand VII, 1808, 1814-1833, lost American colonies; succeeded by daughter Isabella II, aged 3, with wife Maria Christina of Naples regent until 1843. Isabella deposed by revolution 1868. Elected king by the Cortes, Amadeo of Savoy, 1870; abdicated 1873. First republic, 1873-74. Alphonso XII, son of Isabella, 1875-85. His posthumous son was Alphonso XIII, with his mother, Queen Maria Christina regent; Spanish-American war, Spain lost Cuba, gave up Puerto Rico, Philippines, Sulu Is., Marianas. Alphonso took throne 1902, aged 16, married British Princess Victoria Eugenia of Battenberg. The dictatorship of Primo de Rivera, 1923-30, precipitated the revolution of 1931. Alphonso agreed to leave without formal abdication. The monarchy was abolished and the second republic established, with socialist backing. Presidents were Niceto Alcala Zamora, to 1936, when Manuel Azaña was chosen.

In July, 1936, the army in Morocco revolted against the government and General Francisco Franco led the troops into Spain. The revolution succeeded by Feb., 1939, when Azaña resigned. Franco became chief of state, with provisions that if he was incapacitated the Regency Council by two-thirds vote may propose a king to the Cortes, which must have a two-thirds majority to elect him.

Alphonso XIII died in Rome Feb. 28, 1941, aged 54. His property and citizenship had been restored.

A succession law restoring the monarchy was approved in a 1947 referendum. Prince Juan Carlos, son of the pretender to the throne, was designated by Franco and the Cortes in 1969 as the future king and chief of state. Upon Franco's death, Nov. 20, 1975, Juan Carlos was proclaimed king, Nov. 22, 1975.

Leaders in the South American Wars of Liberation

Simon Bolivar (1783-1830), Jose Francisco de San Martin (1778-1850), and Francisco Antonio Gabriel Miranda (1750-1816), are among the heroes of the early 19th century struggles of South American nations to free themselves from Spain. All three, and their contemporaries, operated in periods of factional strife, during which soldiers and civilians suffered.

Miranda, a Venezuelan, who had served with the French in the American Revolution and commanded parts of the French Revolutionary armies in the Netherlands, attempted to start a revolt in Venezuela in 1806 and failed. In 1810, with British and American backing, he returned and was briefly a dictator, until the British withdrew their support. In 1812 he was overcome by the royalists in Venezuela and taken prisoner, dying in a Spanish prison in 1816.

San Martin was born in Argentina and during 1789-1811 served in campaigns of the Spanish armies in Europe and Africa. He first joined the independence movement in Argentina in 1812 and in 1817 invaded Chile with 4,000 men over the mountain passes. Here he and Gen. Bernardo O'Higgins (1778-1842) defeated the Spaniards at Chacabuco, 1817, and O'Higgins was named Liberator and became first director of Chile, 1817-23. In 1821 San Martin occupied Lima and Callao, Peru, and became protector of Peru.

Bolivar, the greatest leader of South American liberation from Spain, was born in Venezuela, the son of an aristocratic family. He first served under Miranda in 1812 and in 1813 captured Caracas, where he was named Liberator. Forced out next year by civil strife, he led a campaign that captured Bogota in 1814. In 1817 he was again in control of Venezuela and was named dictator. He organized Nueva Granada with the help of General Francisco de Paula Santander (1792-1840). By joining Nueva Granada, Venezuela, and the present terrain of Panama and Ecuador, the republic of Colombia was formed with Bolivar president. After numerous setbacks he decisively defeated the Spaniards in the second battle of Carabobo, Venezuela, June 24, 1821.

In May, 1822, Gen. Antonio Jose de Sucre, Bolivar's lieutenant, took Quito. Bolivar went to Guayaquil to confer with San Martin, who resigned as protector of Peru and withdrew from politics. With a new army of Colombians and Peruvians Bolivar defeated the Spaniards in a battle at Junín in 1824 and cleared Peru.

De Sucre organized Charcas (Upper Peru) as Republica Bolivar (now Bolivia) and acted as president in place of Bolivar, who wrote its constitution. De Sucre defeated the Spanish faction of Peru at Ayacucho, Dec. 19, 1824.

Continued civil strife finally caused the Colombian federation to break apart. Santander turned against Bolivar, but the latter defeated him and banished him. In 1828 Bolivar gave up the presidency he had held precariously for 14 years. He became ill from tuberculosis and died Dec. 17, 1830. He is buried in the national pantheon in Caracas.

Rulers of Russia; Premiers of the USSR

First ruler to consolidate Slavic tribes was Rurik, leader of the Russians who established himself at Novgorod, 862 A.D. He and his immediate successors had Scandinavian affiliations. They moved to Kiev after 972 AD and ruled as Dukes of Kiev. In 988 Vladimir was converted and adopted the Byzantine Greek Orthodox service, later modified by Slav influences. Important as organizer and lawgiver was Yaroslav, 1019-1054, whose daughters married kings of Norway, Hungary, and France. His grandson, Vladimir II (Monomakh), 1113-1125, was progenitor of several rulers, but in 1169 Andrew Bogolubski overthrew Kiev and began the line known as Grand Dukes of Vladimir.

Of the Grand Dukes of Vladimir, Alexander Nevsky, 1246-1263, had a son, Daniel, first to be called Duke of Muscovy (Moscow) who ruled 1294-1303. His successors became Grand Dukes of Muscovy. After Dmitri III Donskoi defeated the Tartars in 1380, they also became Grand Dukes of all Russia. Independence of the Tartars and considerable territorial expansion were achieved under Ivan III, 1462-1505.

Tsars of Muscovy—Ivan III was referred to in church ritual as Tsar. He married Sofia, niece of the last Byzantine emperor. His successor, Basil III, died in 1533 when Basil's son Ivan was only 3. He became Ivan IV, "the Terrible"; crowned 1547 as Tsar of all the Russias, ruled till 1584. Under the weak rule of his son, Feodor I, 1584-1598, Boris Godunov had control. The dynasty died, and after years of tribal strife and intervention by Polish and Swedish armies, the Russians united under 17-year-old Michael Romanov, distantly related to the first wife of Ivan IV. He ruled 1613-1645 and established the Romanov line. Fourth ruler after Michael was Peter I.

Tsars, or Emperors of Russia (Romanovs)—Peter I, 1682-1725, known as Peter the Great, took title of Emperor in 1721. His successors and dates of accession were: Catherine, his widow, 1725; Peter II, his grandson, 1727; Anne, Duchess of Courland, 1730, daughter of Peter the Great's brother, Tsar Ivan V; Ivan VI, 1740, great-grandson of Ivan V, child, kept in prison and murdered 1764; Elizabeth, daughter of Peter I, 1741; Peter III, grandson of Peter I, 1761, deposed 1762 for his consort, Catherine II, former princess of Anhalt Zerbst (Germany) who is known as Catherine the Great; Paul I, her son, 1796, killed 1801; Alexander I, son of Paul, 1801, defeated Napoleon; Nicholas I, his brother, 1825; Alexander II, son of Nicholas, 1855, assassinated 1881 by terrorists; Alexander III, son, 1881.

Nicholas II, son, 1894-1917, last Tsar of Russia, was forced to abdicate by the Revolution that followed losses to Germany in WWI. The Tsar, the Empress, the Tsesarevich (Crown Prince) and the Tsar's 4 daughters were murdered by the Bolsheviks in Ekaterinburg, July 16, 1918.

Provisional Government—Prince Georgi Lvov and Alexander Kerensky, premiers, 1917.

Union of Soviet Socialist Republics

Bolshevik Revolution, Nov. 7, 1917, displaced Kerensky; council of People's Commissars formed, Lenin (Vladimir Ilyich Ulyanov), premier. Lenin died Jan. 21, 1924. Aleksei Rykov (executed 1938) and V. M. Molotov held the office, but actual ruler was Joseph Stalin (Joseph Vissarionovich Djugashvili), general secretary of the Central Committee of the Communist Party. Stalin became president of the Council of Ministers (premier) May 7, 1941, died Mar. 5, 1953. Succeeded by Georgi M. Malenkov, as head of the Council and premier and Nikita S. Khrushchev, first secretary of the Central Committee. Malenkov resigned Feb. 8, 1955, became deputy premier, was dropped July 3, 1957. Marshal Nikolai A. Bulganin became premier Feb. 8, 1955; was demoted and Khrushchev became premier Mar. 27 1958. Khrushchev was ousted Oct. 14-15, 1964, replaced by Leonid I. Brezhnev as first secretary of the party and by Aleksei N. Kosygin as premier. On June 16, 1977, Brezhnev took office as president. Brezhnev died Nov. 10, 1982; 2 days later the Central Committee unanimously elected former KGB head Yuri V. Andropov president. Andropov died Feb. 9, 1984; on Feb. 13, Konstantin U. Chernenko was chosen by Central Committee as its general secretary. Chernenko died Mar. 10, 1985. On Mar. 11, he was succeeded as general secretary by Mikhail Gorbachev, who replaced Andrei Gromyko as president on Oct. 1, 1988.

Governments of China

(Until 221 BC and frequently thereafter, China was not a unified state. Where dynastic dates overlap, the rulers or events referred to appeared in different areas of China.)

Hsia	c1994BC	-	c1523BC	Tang (a golden age of Chinese culture; capital: Sian)	618	-	906
Shang	c1523	-	c1028	Five Dynasties (Yellow River basin)	902	-	960
Western Chou	c1027	-	770	Ten Kingdoms (southern China)	907	-	979
Eastern Chou	770	-	256	Liao (Khitan Mongols; capital: Peking)	947	-	1125
Warring States	403	-	222	Sung	960	-	1279
Ch'in (first unified empire)	221	-	206	Northern Sung (reunified central and southern China)	960	-	1126
Han	202BC	-	220AD	Western Hsai (non-Chinese rulers in northwest)	990	-	1227
Western Han (expanded Chinese state beyond the Yellow and Yangtze River valleys)	202BC	-	9AD	Chin (Tartars; drove Sung out of central China)	1115	-	1234
Hsin (Wang Mang, usurper)	9AD	-	23AD	Yuan (Mongols; Kublai Khan made Peking his capital in 1267)	1271	-	1368
Eastern Han (expanded Chinese state into Indo-China and Turkestan)	25	-	220	Ming (China reunified under Chinese rule; capital: Nanking, then Peking in 1420)	1368	-	1644
Three Kingdoms (Wei, Shu, Wu)	220	-	265	Ch'ing (Manchus, descendents of Tartars)	1644	-	1911
Chin (western)	265	-	317	Republic (disunity; provincial rulers, warlords)	1912	-	1949
(eastern)	317	-	420	People's Republic of China	1949	-	—
Northern Dynasties (followed several short-lived governments by Turks, Mongols, etc.)	386	-	581				
Southern Dynasties (capital: Nanking)	420	-	589				
Sui (reunified China)	581	-	618				

Leaders Since 1949

Mao Zedong	Chairman, Central People's Administrative Council, Communist Party (CPC), 1949-1976	Hua Guofeng	Premier, 1976-1980; CPC Chairman, 1976-1981
		Zhao Ziyong	Premier, 1980-88; CPC Chairman, 1987-89
Zhou Enlai	Premier, foreign minister, 1949-1976	Hu Yaobang	CPC Chairman, 1981-1987
Deng Xiaoping	Vice Premier, 1949-1976; 1977-1987	Li Xiannian	President, 1983-1988
		Yong Shang-Kun	President, 1988-
Liu Shaoqi	President, 1959-1969	Li Peng	Premier, 1988-

Chronological List of Popes

Source: Annuario Pontificio. Table lists year of accession of each Pope.

The Roman Catholic Church names the Apostle Peter as founder of the Church in Rome. He arrived there c. 42, was martyred there c. 67, and raised to sainthood.

The Pope's temporal title is: Sovereign of the State of Vatican City.

The Pope's spiritual titles are: Bishop of Rome, Vicar of Jesus Christ, Successor of St. Peter, Prince of the Apostles, Supreme Pontiff of the Universal Church, Patriarch of the West, Primate of Italy, Archbishop and Metropolitan of the Roman Province.

Anti-Popes are in *Italics*. Anti-Popes were illegitimate claimants of or pretenders to the papal throne.

Year	Pope
See above	St. Peter
67	St. Linus
76	St. Anacletus or Cletus
88	St. Clement I
97	St. Evaristus
105	St. Alexander I
115	St. Sixtus I
125	St. Telesphorus
136	St. Hyginus
140	St. Pius I
155	St. Anicetus
166	St. Soter
175	St. Eleutherius
189	St. Victor I
199	St. Zephyrinus
217	St. Callistus I
217	*St. Hippolytus*
222	St. Urban I
230	St. Pontian
235	St. Anterus
236	St. Fabian
251	St. Cornelius
251	*Novatian*
253	St. Lucius I
254	St. Stephen I
257	St. Sixtus II
259	St. Dionysius
269	St. Felix I
275	St. Eutychian
283	St. Caius
296	St. Marcellinus
308	St. Marcellus I
309	St. Eusebius
311	St. Melchiades
314	St. Sylvester I
336	St. Marcus
337	St. Julius I
352	Liberius
355	*Felix II*
366	St. Damasus I
366	*Ursinus*
384	St. Siricius
399	St. Anastasius I
401	St. Innocent I
417	St. Zosimus
418	St. Boniface I
418	*Eulalius*
422	St. Celestine I
432	St. Sixtus III
440	St. Leo I
461	St. Hilary
468	St. Simplicius
483	St. Felix III (II)
492	St. Gelasius I
496	Anastasius II
498	St. Symmachus
498	*Lawrence*
	(501-505)
514	St. Hormisdas
523	St. John I, Martyr
526	St. Felix IV (III)
530	Boniface II
530	*Dioscorus*
533	John II
535	St. Agapitus I
536	St. Silverius, Martyr
537	Vigilius
556	Pelagius I
561	John III
575	Benedict I
579	Pelagius II
590	St. Gregory I
604	Sabinian
607	Boniface III
608	St. Boniface IV
615	St. Deusdedit or Adeodatus
619	Boniface V
625	Honorius I
640	Severinus
642	Theodore I
649	St. Martin I, Martyr
654	St. Eugene I
657	St. Vitalian
672	Adeodatus II
676	Donus
678	St. Agatho
682	St. Leo II
684	St. Benedict II
685	John V
686	Conon
687	*Theodore*
687	*Paschal*
687	St. Sergius I
701	John VI
705	John VII
708	Sisinnius
708	Constantine
715	St. Gregory II
731	St. Gregory III
741	St. Zachary
752	Stephen II (III)
757	St. Paul I
767	*Constantine*
768	*Philip*
768	Stephen III (IV)
772	Adrian I
795	St. Leo III
816	Stephen IV (V)
817	St. Paschal I
824	Eugene II
827	Valentine
827	Gregory IV
844	*John*
844	Sergius II
847	St. Leo IV
855	Benedict III
855	*Anastasius*
858	St. Nicholas I
867	Adrian II
872	John VIII
882	Marinus I
884	St. Adrian III
885	Stephen V (VI)
891	Formosus
896	Boniface VI
896	Stephen VI (VII)
897	Romanus
897	Theodore II
898	John IX
900	Benedict IV
903	Leo V
903	*Christopher*
904	Sergius III
911	Anastasius III
913	Landus
914	John X
928	Leo VI
928	Stephen VII (VIII)
931	John XI
936	Leo VII
939	Stephen VIII (IX)
942	Marinus II
946	Agapitus II
955	John XII
963	Leo VIII
964	Benedict V
965	John XIII
973	Benedict VI
974	*Boniface VII*
974	Benedict VII
983	John XIV
985	John XV
996	Gregory V
997	*John XVI*
999	Sylvester II
1003	John XVII
1004	John XVIII
1009	Sergius IV
1012	Benedict VIII
1012	*Gregory*
1024	John XIX
1032	Benedict IX
1045	Sylvester III
1045	Benedict IX
1045	Gregory VI
1046	Clement II
1047	Benedict IX
1048	Damasus II
1049	St. Leo IX
1055	Victor II
1057	Stephen IX (X)
1058	*Benedict X*
1059	Nicholas II
1061	Alexander II
1061	*Honorius II*
1073	St. Gregory VII
1080	*Clement III*
1086	Bl. Victor III
1088	Bl. Urban II
1099	Paschal II
1100	*Theodoric*
1102	*Albert*
1105	*Sylvester IV*
1118	Gelasius II
1118	*Gregory VIII*
1119	Callistus II
1124	Honorius II
1124	*Celestine II*
1130	Innocent II
1130	*Anacletus II*
1138	*Victor IV*
1143	Celestine II
1144	Lucius II
1145	Bl. Eugene III
1153	Anastasius IV
1154	Adrian IV
1159	Alexander III
1159	*Victor IV*
1164	*Paschal III*
1168	*Callistus III*
1179	*Innocent III*
1181	Lucius III
1185	Urban III
1187	Gregory VIII
1187	Clement III
1191	Celestine III
1198	Innocent III
1216	Honorius III
1227	Gregory IX
1241	Celestine IV
1243	Innocent IV
1254	Alexander IV
1261	Urban IV
1265	Clement IV
1271	Bl. Gregory X
1276	Bl. Innocent V
1276	Adrian V
1276	John XXI
1277	Nicholas III
1281	Martin IV
1285	Honorius IV
1288	Nicholas IV
1294	St. Celestine V
1294	Boniface VIII
1303	Bl. Benedict XI
1305	Clement V
1316	John XXII
1328	*Nicholas V*
1334	Benedict XII
1342	Clement VI
1352	Innocent VI
1362	Bl. Urban V
1370	Gregory XI
1378	Urban VI
1378	*Clement VII*
1389	Boniface IX
1394	*Benedict XIII*
1404	Innocent VII
1406	Gregory XII
1409	*Alexander V*
1410	*John XXIII*
1417	Martin V
1431	Eugene IV
1439	*Felix V*
1447	Nicholas V
1455	Callistus III
1458	Pius II
1464	Paul II
1471	Sixtus IV
1484	Innocent VIII
1492	Alexander VI
1503	Pius III
1503	Julius II
1513	Leo X
1522	Adrian VI
1523	Clement VII
1534	Paul III
1550	Julius III
1555	Marcellus II
1555	Paul IV
1559	Pius IV
1566	St. Pius V
1572	Gregory XIII
1585	Sixtus V
1590	Urban VII
1590	Gregory XIV
1591	Innocent IX
1592	Clement VIII
1605	Leo XI
1605	Paul V
1621	Gregory XV
1623	Urban VIII
1644	Innocent X
1655	Alexander VII
1667	Clement IX
1670	Clement X
1676	Bl. Innocent XI
1689	Alexander VIII
1691	Innocent XII
1700	Clement XI
1721	Innocent XIII
1724	Benedict XIII
1730	Clement XII
1740	Benedict XIV
1758	Clement XIII
1769	Clement XIV
1775	Pius VI
1800	Pius VII
1823	Leo XII
1829	Pius VIII
1831	Gregory XVI
1846	Pius IX
1878	Leo XIII
1903	St. Pius X
1914	Benedict XV
1922	Pius XI
1939	Pius XII
1958	John XXIII
1963	Paul VI
1978	John Paul I
1978	John Paul II

WORLD EXPLORATION AND GEOGRAPHY

Early Explorers of the Western Hemisphere

The first men to discover the New World or Western Hemisphere are believed to have walked across a "land bridge" from Siberia to Alaska, an isthmus since broken by the Bering Strait. From Alaska, these ancestors of the Indians spread through North, Central, and South America. Anthropologists have placed these crossings at between 18,000 and 14,000 B.C.; but evidence found in 1967 near Puebla, Mex., indicates mankind reached there as early as 35,000-40,000 years ago.

At first, these people were hunters using flint weapons and tools. In Mexico, about 7000-6000 B.C., they founded farming cultures, developing corn, squash, etc. Eventually, they created complex civilizations — Olmec, Toltec, Aztec,

and Maya and, in South America, Inca. Carbon-14 tests show men lived about 8000 B.C. near what are now Front Royal, Va., Kanawha, W. Va., and Dutchess Quarry, N.Y. The Hopewell Culture, based on farming, flourished about 1000 B.C.; remains of it are seen today in large mounds in Ohio and other states.

Norsemen (Norwegian Vikings sailing out of Iceland and Greenland) are credited by most scholars with being the first Europeans to discover America, with at least 5 voyages around 1000 A.D. to areas they called Helluland, Markland, Vinland—possibly Labrador, Nova Scotia or Newfoundland, and New England.

(For information on Christopher Columbus see Index).

Year	Explorer	Nationality and employer	Discovery or exploration
1497	John Cabot	Italian-English	Newfoundland or Nova Scotia
1498	John and Sebastian Cabot	Italian-English	Labrador to Hatteras
1499	Alonso de Ojeda	Spanish	South American coast, Venezuela
1500, Feb.	Vicente y Pinzon	Spanish	South American coast, Amazon River
1500, Apr.	Pedro Alvarez Cabral	Portuguese	Brazil (for Portugal)
1500-02	Gaspar Corte-Real	Portuguese	Labrador
1501	Rodrigo de Bastidas	Spanish	Central America
1513	Vasco Nunez de Balboa	Spanish	Pacific Ocean
1513	Juan Ponce de Leon	Spanish	Florida
1515	Juan de Solis	Spanish	Rio de la Plata
1519	Alonso de Pineda	Spanish	Mouth of Mississippi River
1519	Hernando Cortes	Spanish	Mexico
1520	Ferdinand Magellan	Portuguese-Spanish	Straits of Magellan, Tierra del Fuego
1524	Giovanni da Verrazano	Italian-French	Atlantic coast-New York harbor
1532	Francisco Pizarro	Spanish	Peru
1534	Jacques Cartier	French	Canada, Gulf of St. Lawrence
1536	Pedro de Mendoza	Spanish	Buenos Aires
1536	A.N. Cabeza de Vaca	Spanish	Texas coast and interior
1539	Francisco de Ulloa	Spanish	California coast
1539-41	Hernando de Soto	Spanish	Mississippi River near Memphis
1539	Marcos de Niza	Italian-Spanish	Southwest (now U.S.)
1540	Francisco V. de Coronado	Spanish	Southwest (now U.S.)
1540	Hernando Alarcon	Spanish	Colorado River
1540	Garcia de L. Cardenas	Spanish	Grand Canyon of the Colorado
1541	Francisco de Orellana	Spanish	Amazon River
1542	Juan Rodriguez Cabrillo	Portuguese-Spanish	San Diego harbor
1565	Pedro Menendez de Aviles	Spanish	St. Augustine
1576	Martin Frobisher	English	Frobisher's Bay, Canada
1577-80	Francis Drake	English	California coast
1582	Antonio de Espejo	Spanish	Southwest (named New Mexico)
1584	Amadas & Barlow (for Raleigh)	English	Virginia
1585-87	Sir Walter Raleigh's men	English	Roanoke Is., N.C.
1595	Sir Walter Raleigh	English	Orinoco River
1603-09	Samuel de Champlain	French	Canadian interior, Lake Champlain
1607	Capt. John Smith	English	Atlantic coast
1609-10	Henry Hudson	English-Dutch	Hudson River, Hudson Bay
1634	Jean Nicolet	French	Lake Michigan; Wisconsin
1673	Jacques Marquette, Louis Jolliet	French	Mississippi S to Arkansas
1682	Sieur de La Salle	French	Mississippi S to Gulf of Mexico
1789	Alexander Mackenzie	Canadian	Canadian Northwest

Arctic Exploration

Early Explorers

1587 — John Davis (England). Davis Strait to Sanderson's Hope, 72° 12′ N.

1596 — Willem Barents and Jacob van Heemskerck (Holland). Discovered Bear Island, touched northwest tip of Spitsbergen, 79° 49′ N, rounded Novaya Zemlya, wintered at Ice Haven.

1607 — Henry Hudson (England). North along Greenland's east coast to Cape Hold-with-Hope, 73° 30′, then north of Spitsbergen to 80° 23′. Returning he discovered Hudson's Touches (Jan Mayen).

1616 — William Baffin and Robert Bylot (England). Baffin Bay to Smith Sound.

1728 — Vitus Bering (Russia). Proved Asia and America were separated by sailing through strait.

1733-40 — Great Northern Expedition (Russia). Surveyed

Siberian Arctic coast.

1741 — Vitus Bering (Russia). Sighted Alaska from sea, named Mount St. Elias. His lieutenant, Chirikof, discovered coast.

1771 — Samuel Hearne (Hudson's Bay Co.). Overland from Prince of Wales Fort (Churchill) on Hudson Bay to mouth of Coppermine River.

1778 — James Cook (Britain). Through Bering Strait to Icy Cape, Alaska, and North Cape, Siberia.

1789 — Alexander Mackenzie (North West Co., Britain). Montreal to mouth of Mackenzie River.

1806 — William Scoresby (Britain). N. of Spitsbergen to 81° 30′.

1820-3 — Ferdinand von Wrangel (Russia). Completed a survey of Siberian Arctic coast. His exploration joined that

(continued)

of James Cook at North Cape, confirming separation of the continents.

1845 — Sir John Franklin (Britain) was one of many to seek the Northwest Passage—an ocean route connecting the Atlantic and Pacific via the Arctic. His 2 ships (the *Erebus* and *Terror*) were last seen entering Lancaster Sound July, 26.

1881 — The steamer *Jeanette* on an expedition led by Lt. Cmdr. George W. DeLong was trapped in ice and crushed, June 1881. DeLong and 11 crewmen died; 12 others survived.

1888 — Fridtjof Nansen (Norway) crossed Greenland's icecap, 1893-96 — Nansen in Fram drifted from New Siberian Is. to Spitsbergen; tried polar dash in 1895, reached Franz Josef Land.

1897 — Salomon A. Andree (Sweden) and 2 others started in balloon from Danes, Is., Spitsbergen, July 11, to drift across pole to America, and disappeared. Over 33 years later, Aug. 6, 1930, their frozen bodies were found on White Is., 82° 57′ N 29° 52′ E.

1903-06 — Roald Amundsen (Norway) first sailed Northwest Passage.

Discovery of North Pole

Robert E. Peary explored Greenland's coast, 1891-92, tried for North Pole, 1893. In 1900 he reached northern limit of Greenland and 83° 50′ N; in 1902 he reached 84° 06′ N; in 1906 he went from Ellesmere Is. to 87° 06′ N. He sailed in the *Roosevelt*, July, 1908, to winter off Cape Sheridan, Grant Land. The dash for the North Pole began Mar. 1 from Cape Columbia, Ellesmere Land. Peary reached the pole, 90° N, Apr. 6, 1909.

Peary had several supporting groups carrying supplies until the last group turned back at 87° 47′ N. Peary, Matthew Henson, and 4 Eskimos proceeded with dog teams and sleds. They crossed the pole several times, finally built an igloo at 90°, remained 36 hours. Started south, Apr. 7 at 4 p.m., for Cape Columbia. The Eskimos were Coqueeh, Ootah, Eginwah, and Seegloo.

1914 — Donald MacMillan (U.S.). Northwest, 200 miles, from Axel Heiberg Island to seek Peary's Crocker Land.

1915-17 — Vihjalmur Stefansson (Canada) discovered Borden, Brock, Meighen, and Lougheed Islands.

1918-20 — Roald Amundsen sailed Northeast Passage.

Antarctic Exploration

Early History

Antarctica has been approached since 1773-75, when Capt. James Cook (Britain) reached 71° 10′ S. Many sea and landmarks bear names of early explorers. Bellingshausen (Russia) discovered Peter I and Alexander I Islands, 1819-21. Nathaniel Palmer (U.S.) discovered Palmer Peninsula, 60° W, 1820, without realizing that this was a continent. James Weddell (Britain) found Weddell Sea, 74° 15′ S, 1823.

First to announce existence of the continent of Antarctica was Charles Wilkes (U.S.), who followed the coast for 1,500 mi., 1840. Adelie Coast, 140° E, was found by Dumont d'Urville (France), 1840. Ross Ice Shelf was found by James Clark Ross (Britain), 1841-42.

1895 — Leonard Kristensen (Norway) landed a party on the coast of Victoria Land. They were the first ashore on the main continental mass. C.E. Borchgrevink, a member of that party, returned in 1899 with a British expedition, first to winter on Antarctica.

1902-04 — Robert F. Scott (Britain) discovered Edward VII Peninsula. He reached 82° 17′ S, 146° 33′ E from McMurdo Sound.

1908-09 — Ernest Shackleton (Britain) introduced the use of Manchurian ponies in Antarctic sledging. He reached 88° 23′ S, discovering a route on to the plateau by way of the Beardmore Glacier and pioneering the way to the pole.

Discovery of South Pole

1911 — Roald Amundsen (Norway) with 4 men and dog teams reached the pole, Dec. 14.

1925 — Amundsen and Lincoln Ellsworth (U.S.) reached 87° 44′ N in attempt to fly to North Pole from Spitsbergen.

1926 — Richard E. Byrd and Floyd Bennett (U.S.) first over North Pole by air, May 9.

1926 — Amundsen, Ellsworth, and Umberto Nobile (Italy) flew from Spitsbergen over North Pole May 12, to Teller, Alaska, in dirigible *Norge*.

1928 — Nobile crossed North Pole in airship, May 24, crashed, May 25. Amundsen lost while trying to effect rescue by plane.

North Pole Exploration Records

On Aug. 3, 1958, the *Nautilus*, under Comdr. William R. Anderson, became the first ship to cross the North Pole beneath the Arctic ice.

The nuclear-powered U.S. submarine *Seadragon*, Comdr. George P. Steele 2d, made the first east-west underwater transit through the Northwest Passage during August, 1960. It sailed from Portsmouth N.H., headed between Greenland and Labrador through Baffin Bay, then west through Lancaster Sound and McClure Strait to the Beaufort Sea. Traveling submerged for the most part, the submarine made 850 miles from Baffin Bay to the Beaufort Sea in 6 days.

On Aug. 16, 1977, the Soviet nuclear icebreaker *Arktika* reached the North Pole and became the first surface ship to break through the Arctic ice pack to the top of the world.

On April 30, 1978, Naomi Uemura, a Japanese explorer, became the first man to reach the North Pole alone by dog sled. During the 54-day, 600-mile trek over the frozen Arctic, Uemura survived attacks by a marauding polar bear.

In April, 1982, Sir Ranulph Fiennes and Charles Burton, British explorers, reached the North Pole and became the first to circle the earth from pole to pole. They had reached the South Pole 16 months earlier. The 52,000-mile trek took 3 years, involved 23 people, and cost an estimated $18 million. The expedition was also the first to travel down the Scott Glacier and the first to journey up the Yukon and through the Northwest Passage in a single season.

On May 2, 1986, 6 American and Canadian explorers reached the North Pole assisted only by dogs. They became the first to reach the Pole without mechanical assistance since Robert E. Peary planted a flag there in 1909. The explorers, Americans Will Steger, Paul Schurke, Anne Bancroft, and Geoff Carroll, and Canadians Brent Boddy and Richard Weber completed the 500-mile journey in 56 days.

1912 — Capt. Scott reached the pole from Ross Island, Jan. 18, with 4 companions. They found Amundsen's tent. None of Scott's party survived. They were found, Nov. 12.

1928 — First man to use an airplane over Antarctica was Hubert Wilkins (Britain).

1929 — Richard E. Byrd (U.S.) established Little America on Bay of Whales. On 1,600-mi. airplane flight begun, Nov. 28, he crossed South Pole, Nov. 29 with 3 others.

1934-35 — Byrd led 2d expedition to Little America, explored 450,000 sq. mi., wintered alone at weather station, 80° 08′ S.

1934-37 — John Rymill led British Graham Land expedition; discovered that Palmer Peninsula is part of Antarctic mainland.

1935 — Lincoln Ellsworth (U.S.) flew south along Palmer Peninsula's east coast, then crossed continent to Little America, making 4 landings on unprepared terrain in bad weather.

1939-41 — U.S. Antarctic Service built West Base on Ross Ice Shelf under Paul Siple, and East Base on Palmer Peninsula under Richard Black. U.S. Navy plane flights discovered about 150,000 sq. miles of new land.

1940 — Byrd charted most of coast between Ross Sea and Palmer Peninsula.

1946-47 — U.S. Navy undertook Operation High-jump under Byrd. Expedition included 13 ships and 4,000 men. Airplanes photomapped coastline and penetrated beyond pole.

1946-48 — Ronne Antarctic Research Expedition, Comdr. Finn Ronne, USNR, determined the Antarctic to be only one continent with no strait between Weddell Sea and Ross Sea; discovered 250,000 sq. miles of land by flights to 79° S Lat., and made 14,000 aerial photographs over 450,000 sq. miles of land. Mrs. Ronne and Mrs. H. Darlington were the first women to winter on Antarctica.

1955-57 — U.S. Navy's Operation Deep Freeze led by Adm. Byrd. Supporting U.S. scientific efforts for the International Geophysical Year, the operation was commanded by Rear Adm. George Dufek. It established 5 coastal stations fronting the Indian, Pacific, and Atlantic oceans and also 3 interior stations; explored more than 1,000,000 sq. miles in Wilkes Land.

1957-58 — During the International Geophysical year, July 1957, through Dec. 1958, scientists from 12 countries conducted ambitious programs of Antarctic research. A network of some 60 stations on the continent and sub-Arctic islands studied oceanography, glaciology, meteorology, seismology, geomagnetism, the ionosphere, cosmic rays, aurora, and airglow.

Dr. V.E. Fuchs led a 12-man Trans-Antarctic Expedition on the first land crossing of Antarctica. Starting from the Weddell Sea, they reached Scott Station, Mar. 2, 1958, after traveling 2,158 miles in 98 days.

1958 — A group of 5 U.S. scientists led by Edward C. Thiel, seismologist, moving by tractor from Ellsworth Station on Weddell Sea, identified a huge mountain range, 5,000 ft. above the ice sheet and 9,000 ft. above sea level. The range, originally seen by a Navy plane, was named the Dufek Massif, for Rear Adm. George Dufek.

1959 — Twelve nations — Argentina, Australia, Belgium, Chile, France, Japan, New Zealand, Norway, South Africa, the Soviet Union, the United Kingdom, and the U.S. — signed a treaty suspending any territorial claims for 30 years and reserving the continent for research.

1961-62 — Scientists discovered a trough, the Bentley Trench, running from Ross Ice Shelf, Pacific, into Marie Byrd Land, around the end of the Ellsworth Mtns., toward the Weddell Sea.

1962 — First nuclear power plant began operation at McMurdo Sound.

1963 — On Feb. 22 a U.S. plane made the longest non-stop flight ever made in the S. Pole area, covering 3,600 miles in 10 hours. The flight was from McMurdo Station south past the geographical S. Pole to Shackleton Mtns., southeast to the "Area of Inaccessibility" and back to McMurdo Station.

1964 — A British survey team was landed by helicopter on Cook Island, the first recorded visit since its discovery in 1775.

1964 — New Zealanders completed one of the last and most important surveys when they mapped the mountain area from Cape Adare west some 400 miles to Pennell Glacier.

1989 — Two Americans, Victoria Murden and Shirley Metz, became the first women to reach the South Pole overland when they arrived with 9 others on Jan. 17, 1989. The 51-day trek on skis covered 740 miles.

Volcanoes

Source: Global Volcanism Network, Smithsonian Institution

More than 75 per cent of the world's 850 active volcanoes lie within the "Ring of Fire," a zone running along the west coast of the Americas from Chile to Alaska and down the east coast of Asia from Siberia to New Zealand. Twenty per cent of these volcanoes are located in Indonesia. Other prominent groupings are located in Japan, the Aleutian Islands, and Central America. Almost all active regions are found at the boundaries of the large moving plates which comprise the earth's surface. The "Ring of Fire" marks the boundary between the plates underlying the Pacific Ocean and those underlying the surrounding continents. Other active regions, such as the Mediterranean Sea and Iceland, are located on plate boundaries.

Major Historical Eruptions

Approximately 7,000 years ago, Mazama, a 9,900-feet-high volcano in southern Oregon, erupted violently, ejecting ash and lava. The ash spread over the entire northwestern United States and as far away as Saskatchewan, Canada. During the eruption, the top of the mountain collapsed, leaving a caldera 6 miles across and about a half mile deep, which filled with rain water to form what is now called Crater Lake.

In 79 A.D., Vesuvio, or Vesuvius, a 4,190 feet volcano overlooking Naples Bay became active after several centuries of quiescence. On Aug. 24 of that year, a heated mud and ash flow swept down the mountain engulfing the cities of Pompeii, Herculaneum, and Stabiae with debris over 60 feet deep. About 10 percent of the population of the 3 towns was killed.

The largest eruptions in recent centuries have been in Indonesia. In 1883, an eruption similar to the Mazama eruption occurred on the island of Krakatau. On August 27, the 2,640-feet-high peak of the volcano collapsed to 1,000 feet below sea level, leaving only a small portion of the island standing above the sea. Ash from the eruption colored sunsets around the world for 2 years. A tsunami ("tidal wave") generated by the collapse killed 36,000 people in nearby Java and Sumatra and eventually reached England. A similar, but even more powerful, eruption had taken place 68 years earlier at Tambora volcano on the Indonesian island of Sumbawa.

Notable Active Volcanoes

Name, latest activity	Location	Height (feet)	Name, latest activity	Location	Height (feet)
Africa			**Asia-Oceania**		
			Klyuchevskaya (1990)	USSR	15,584
Cameroon (1982)	Cameroon	13,354	Kerinci (1987)	Sumatra	12,467
Nyirangongo (1977)	Zaire	11,400	Rindjani (1966)	Indonesia	12,224
Nyamuragira (1988)	Zaire	10,028	Semeru (1989)	Java	12,060
Karthala (1977)	Comoro Is.	8,000	Slamet (1988)	Java	11,247
Piton de la Fournaise (1990)	Reunion Is.	5,981	Raung (1990)	Java	10,932
Erta-Ale (1973)	Ethiopia	1,650	Agung (1964)	Bali	10,308
			On-Take (1991)	Japan	10,049
Antarctica			Mayon (1988)	Philippines	9,991
			Merapi (1988)	Java	9,551
Erebus (1991)	Ross Island	12,450	Bezymianny (1986)	USSR	9,514
Big Ben (1960)	Heard Island	9,007	Marapi (1988)	Sumatra	9,485
Deception Island (1970)	South Shetland Islands	1,890	Ruapehu (1990)	New Zealand	9,175
			Asama (1991)	Japan	8,300

(continued)

Name, latest activity	Location	Height (feet)
Niigata Yakeyama (1989)	Japan	8,111
Canlaon (1989)	Philippines	8,070
Yake Dake (1963)	Japan	8,064
Alaid (1972)	Kuril Is.	7,662
Ulawun (1990)	New Britain	7,532
Ngauruhoe (1975)	New Zealand	7,515
Chokai (1974)	Japan	7,300
Galunggung (1982)	Java	7,113
Amburombu (1969)	Indonesia	7,051
Azuma (1978)	Japan	6,700
Pinatubo (1991)	Philippines	5,770
Tangkuban Prahu (1967)	Java	6,637
Sangeang Api (1988)	Indonesia	6,351
Nasu (1977)	Japan	6,210
Tiatia (1973)	Kuril Islands	6,013
Manam (1991)	Papua New Guinea	6,000
Soputan (1989)	Indonesia	5,994
Siau (1976)	Indonesia	5,853
Kelud (1990)	Java	5,679
Batur (1968)	Bali	5,636
Kirisima (1982)	Japan	5,577
Bagana (1989)	Papua New Guinea	6,558
Keli Mutu (1968)	Indonesia	5,460
Akita Komaga take (1970)	Japan	5,449
Gamkonora (1981)	Indonesia	5,364
Aso (1991)	Japan	5,223
Lewotobi Laki-Laki (1968)	Indonesia	5,217
Lokon-Empung (1988)	Indonesia	5,187
Bulusan (1988)	Philippines	5,115
Sarycheva (1976)	Kuril Islands	4,960
Karkar (1981)	Papua New Guinea	4,920
Karymsky (1985)	USSR	4,869
Lopevi (1982)	New Hebrides	4,755
Unzen (1991)	Japan	4,462
Ambrym (1979)	New Hebrides	4,376
Awu (1968)	Indonesia	4,350
Sakurajima (1991)	Japan	3,668
Langila (1991)	New Britain	3,586
Dukono (1971)	Indonesia	3,566
Suwanosezima (1991)	Japan	2,640
Oshima (1990)	Japan	2,550
Usu (1978)	Japan	2,400
Pagan (1990)	Mariana Is.	1,870
White Island (1991)	New Zealand	1,075
Taal (1988)	Philippines	984

Central America—Caribbean

Name, latest activity	Location	Height (feet)
Acatenango (1972)	Guatemala	12,992
Fuego (1991)	Guatemala	12,582
Tacana (1988)	Guatemala	12,400
Santiaguito (Santa Maria) (1991)	Guatemala	12,362
Irazu (1991)	Costa Rica	11,260
Poas (1991)	Costa Rica	8,930
Pacaya (1991)	Costa Rica	8,346
Izalco (1966)	El Salvador	7,749
San Miguel (1986)	El Salvador	6,994
Rincon de la Vieja (1987)	Costa Rica	6,234
El Viejo (San Cristobal) (1991)	Nicaragua	5,840

Name, latest activity	Location	Height (feet)
Ometepe (Concepcion) (1986)	Nicaragua	5,106
Arenal (1991)	Costa Rica	5,092
Momotombo (1982)	Nicaragua	4,199
Soufriere (1979)	St. Vincent	4,048
Telica (1987)	Nicaragua	3,409

South America

Name, latest activity	Location	Height (feet)
Guallatiri (1987)	Chile	19,882
Lascar (1991)	Chile	19,652
Cotopaxi (1975)	Ecuador	19,347
Tupungatito (1986)	Chile	18,504
Ruiz (1991)	Colombia	17,716
Sangay (1988)	Ecuador	17,159
Guagua Pichincha (1988)	Ecuador	15,696
Purace (1977)	Colombia	15,601
Galeras (1991)	Colombia	13,996
Llaima (1990)	Chile	10,239
Villarica (1984)	Chile	9,318
Hudson (1973)	Chile	8,580
Alcedo (1970)	Galapagos Is.	3,599

Mid-Pacific

Name, latest activity	Location	Height (feet)
Mauna Loa (1987)	Hawaii	13,680
Kilauea (1991)	Hawaii	4,077

Mid-Atlantic Ridge

Name, latest activity	Location	Height (feet)
Beerenberg (1985)	Jan Mayen Is.	7,470
Hekla (1991)	Iceland	4,892
Leirhnukur (1975)	Iceland	2,145
Krafla (1984)	Iceland	2,145

Europe

Name, latest activity	Location	Height (feet)
Etna (1990)	Italy	11,053
Stromboli (1990)	Italy	3,038

North America

Name, latest activity	Location	Height (feet)
Colima (1991)	Mexico	14,003
Redoubt (1991)	Alaska	10,197
Iliamna (1978)	Alaska	10,016
Shishaldin (1987)	Aleutian Is.	9,387
Mt. St. Helens (1991)	Washington	8,300+
Pavlof (1988)	Aleutian Is.	8,261
Veniaminof (1987)	Alaska	8,225
El Chichon (1983)	Mexico	7,300
Katmai (1974)	Alaska	6,715
Makushin (1987)	Aleutian Is.	6,680
Pogromni (1964)	Alaska	6,568
Trident (1963)	Alaska	6,010
Great Sitkin (1974)	Aleutian Is.	5,710
Cleveland (1987)	Aleutian Is.	5,675
Gareloi (1982)	Aleutian Is.	5,334
Korovin (1987)	Aleutian Is.	4,852
Akutan (1990)	Aleutian Is.	4,275
Kiska (1990)	Aleutian Is.	4,275
Augustine (1988)	Alaska	3,999
Okmok (1988)	Aleutian Is.	3,519
Seguam (1977)	Alaska	3,458

Notable Volcanic Eruptions

Date	Volcano	Deaths	Date	Volcano	Deaths
79 A.D.	Mt. Vesuvius, Italy	16,000	May 8, 1902	Mt. Pelée, Martinique	30,000
1169	Mt. Etna, Sicily	15,000	1911	Mt. Taal, Philippines	1,400
1631	Mt. Vesuvius, Italy	4,000	1919	Mt. Kelud, Java	5,000
1669	Mt. Etna, Sicily	20,000	Jan. 18-21, 1951	Mt. Lamington, New Guinea	3,000
1772	Mt. Papandayan, Java	3,000	Apr. 26, 1966	Mt. Kelud, Java	1,000
1792	Mt. Unzen-Dake, Japan	10,400	May 18, 1980	Mt. St. Helens, U.S.	60
1815	Tamboro, Java	12,000	Nov. 13, 1985	Nevado del Ruiz, Colombia	22,940
Aug. 26-28, 1883	Krakatau, Indonesia	35,000	Aug. 24, 1986	NW Cameroon	1,700+
Apr. 8, 1902	Santa Maria, Guatemala	1,000			

Mountains

Height of Mount Everest

Mt. Everest was considered to be 29,002 ft. tall when Edmund Hillary and Tenzing Norgay scaled it in 1953. This triangulation figure had been accepted since 1850. In 1954 the Surveyor General of the Republic of India set the height at 29,028 ft., plus or minus 10 ft. because of snow. The National Geographic Society accepts the new figure, but many mountaineering groups still use 29,002 ft.

In 1987, new calculations based on satellite measurements indicate that the Himalayan peak K-2 rose 29,064 feet above sea level and that Mt. Everest is 800 feet higher. The National Geographic Society has not accepted the revised figure.

United States, Canada, Mexico

Name	Place	Height (feet)	Name	Place	Height (feet)	Name	Place	Height (feet)
McKinley	Alaska	20,320	Alverstone	Alas-Yukon	14,565	Princeton	Col	14,197
Logan	Yukon	19,850	Browne Tower	Alaska	14,530	Crestone Needle	Col	14,197
Citlaltepec (Orizaba)	Mexico	18,700	Whitney	Cal	14,494	Yale	Col	14,196
St. Elias	Alas-Yukon	18,008	Elbert	Col	14,433	Bross	Col	14,172
Popocatepetl	Mexico	17,887	Massive	Col	14,421	Kit Carson	Col	14,165
Foraker	Alaska	17,400	Harvard	Col	14,420	Wrangell	Alaska	14,163
Iztaccihuatl	Mexico	17,343	Rainier	Wash	14,410	Shasta	Cal	14,162
Lucania	Yukon	17,147	Williamson	Cal	14,375	Sill	Cal	14,162
King	Can	16,971	Blanca Peak	Col	14,345	El Diente	Col	14,159
Steele	Can	16,644	La Plata	Col	14,336	Maroon	Col	14,156
Bona	Alaska	16,550	Uncompahgre	Col	14,309	Tabeguache	Col	14,155
Blackburn	Alaska	16,390	Crestone	Col	14,294	Oxford	Col	14,153
Kennedy	Alaska	16,286	Lincoln	Col	14,286	Sneffels	Col	14,150
Sanford	Alaska	16,237	Grays Peak	Col	14,270	Point Success	Wash	14,150
South Buttress	Alaska	15,885	Antero	Col	14,269	Democrat	Col	14,148
Wood	Yukon	15,885	Torreys	Col	14,267	Capitol	Col	14,130
Vancouver	Alas-Yukon	15,700	Castle	Col	14,265	Liberty Cap	Wash	14,112
Churchill	Alaska	15,638	Quandary	Col	14,265	Pikes Peak	Col	14,110
Fairweather	Alas-Yukon	15,300	Evans	Col	14,264	Snowmass	Col	14,092
Zinantecatl (Toluca)	Mexico	15,016	Longs Peak	Col	14,256	Windom	Col	14,087
Hubbard	Alas-Yukon	15,015	McArthur	Yukon	14,253	Russell	Cal	14,086
Bear	Alaska	14,831	Wilson	Col	14,246	Eolus	Col	14,084
Walsh	Yukon	14,780	White	Cal	14,246	Columbia	Col	14,073
East Buttress	Alaska	14,730	North Palisade	Cal	14,242	Augusta	Alas-Yukon	14,070
Matlalcueyetl	Mexico	14,636	Shavano	Col	14,229	Missouri	Col	14,067
Hunter	Alaska	14,573	Belford	Col	14,197	Humboldt	Col	14,064

South America

Peak, country	Height (feet)	Peak, country	Height (feet)	Peak, country	Height (feet)
Aconcagua, Argentina	22,834	Laudo, Argentina	20,997	Polleras, Argentina	20,456
Ojos del Salado, Arg.-Chile	22,572	Ancohuma, Bolivia	20,958	Pular, Chile	20,423
Bonete, Argentina	22,546	Ausangate, Peru	20,945	Chani, Argentina	20,341
Tupungato, Argentina-Chile	22,310	Toro, Argentina-Chile	20,932	Aucanquilcha, Chile	20,295
Pissis, Argentina	22,241	Illampu, Bolivia	20,873	Juncal, Argentina-Chile	20,276
Mercedario, Argentina	22,211	Tres Cruces, Argentina-Chile	20,853	Negro, Argentina	20,184
Huascaran, Peru	22,205	Huandoy, Peru	20,852	Quela, Argentina	20,128
Llullaillaco, Argentina-Chile	22,057	Parinacota, Bolivia-Chile	20,768	Condoriri, Bolivia	20,095
El Libertador, Argentina	22,047	Tortolas, Argentina-Chile	20,745	Palermo, Argentina	20,079
Cachi, Argentina	22,047	Ampato, Peru	20,702	Solimana, Peru	20,068
Yerupaja, Peru	21,709	Condor, Argentina	20,669	San Juan, Argentina-Chile	20,049
Galan, Argentina	21,654	Salcantay, Peru	20,574	Sierra Nevada, Arg.-Chile	20,023
El Muerto, Argentina-Chile	21,457	Chimborazo, Ecuador	20,561	Antofalla, Argentina	20,013
Sajama, Bolivia	21,391	Huancarhuas, Peru	20,531	Marmolejo, Argentina-Chile	20,013
Nacimiento, Argentina	21,302	Farnatina, Argentina	20,505	Chachani, Peru	19,931
Illimani, Bolivia	21,201	Pumasillo, Peru	20,492	Licancabur, Argentina-Chile	19,425
Coropuna, Peru	21,083	Solo, Argentina	20,492		

The highest point in the West Indies is in the Dominican Republic, Pico Duarte (10,417 ft.)

Africa, Australia, and Oceania

Peak, country	Height (feet)	Peak, country	Height (feet)	Peak, country	Height (feet)
Kilimanjaro, Tanzania	19,340	Meru, Tanzania	14,979	Toubkal, Morocco	13,661
Kenya, Kenya	17,058	Wilhelm, Papua New Guinea	14,793	Kinabalu, Malaysia	13,455
Margherita Pk., Uganda-Zaire	16,763	Karisimbi, Zaire-Rwanda	14,787	Kerinci, Sumatra	12,467
Jaja, New Guinea	16,500	Elgon, Kenya-Uganda	14,178	Cook, New Zealand	12,349
Trikora, New Guinea	15,585	Batu, Ethiopia	14,131	Teide, Canary Islands	12,198
Mandala, New Guinea	15,420	Guna, Ethiopia	13,881	Semeru, Java	12,060
Ras Dashan, Ethiopia	15,158	Gughe, Ethiopia	13,780	Kosciusko, Australia	7,310

Europe

Peak, country	Height (feet)	Peak, country	Height (feet)	Peak, country	Height (feet)
Alps		Nadelhorn, Switz.	14,196	Dent D'Herens, Switz.	13,686
		Grand Combin, Switz.	14,154	Breithorn, It., Switz.	13,665
Mont Blanc, Fr., It.	15,771	Lenzpitze, Switz.	14,088	Bishorn, Switz.	13,645
Monte Rosa (high-		Finsteraarhorn, Switz.	14,022	Jungfrau, Switz.	13,642
est peak of group), Switz.	15,203	Castor, Switz.	13,865	Ecrins, Fr.	13,461
Dom, Switz.	14,911	Zinalrothorn, Switz.	13,849	Monch, Switz.	13,448
Liskamm, It., Switz.	14,852	Hohberghorn, Switz.	13,842	Pollux, Switz.	13,422
Weisshorn, Switz.	14,780	Alphubel, Switz.	13,799	Schreckhorn, Switz.	13,379
Taschhorn, Switz.	14,733	Rimpfischhorn, Switz.	13,776	Ober Gabelhorn, Switz.	13,330
Matterhorn, It., Switz.	14,690	Aletschorn, Switz.	13,763	Gran Paradiso, It.	13,323
Dent Blanche, Switz.	14,293	Strahlhorn, Switz.	13,747	*(continued)*

(continued)

Peak, country	Height (feet)	Peak, country	Height (feet)	Peak, country	Height (feet)
Bernina, It., Switz.	13,284	Schalihorn, Switz.	13,040	Long, Sp.	10,479
Fiescherhorn, Switz.	13,283	Scerscen, Switz.	13,028	Estats, Sp.	10,304
Grunhorn, Switz.	13,266	Eiger, Switz.	13,025	Montcalm, Sp.	10,105
Lauteraarhorn, Switz.	13,261	Jagerhorn, Switz.	13,024		
Durrenhorn, Switz.	13,238	Rottalhorn, Switz.	13,022	**Caucasus (Europe-Asia)**	
Allalinhorn, Switz.	13,213				
Weissmies, Switz.	13,199	**Pyrenees**		El'brus, USSR	18,510
Lagginhorn, Switz.	13,156			Shkara, USSR	17,064
Zupo, Switz.	13,120	Aneto, Sp.	11,168	Dykh Tau, USSR	17,054
Fletschhorn, Switz.	13,110	Posets, Sp.	11,073	Kashtan Tau, USSR	16,877
Adlerhorn, Switz.	13,081	Perdido, Sp.	11,007	Dzhangi Tau, USSR	16,565
Gletscherhorn, Switz.	13,068	Vignemale, Fr., Sp.	10,820	Kazbek, USSR	16,558

Asia

Peak	Country	Height (feet)	Peak	Country	Height (feet)	Peak	Country	Height (feet)
Everest	Nepal-Tibet.	29,028	Kungur.	Sinkiang.	25,325	Badrinath	India.	23,420
K2 (Godwin Austen)	Kashmir.	28,250	Tirich Mir	Pakistan.	25,230	Nunkun	Kashmir.	23,410
Kanchenjunga	India-Nepal.	28,208	Makalu II.	Nepal-Tibet.	25,120	Lenina Peak.	USSR.	23,405
Lhotse I (Everest)	Nepal-Tibet.	27,923	Minya Konka	China.	24,900	Pyramid	India-Nepal.	23,400
Makalu I	Nepal-Tibet.	27,824	Kula Gangri	Bhutan-Tibet	24,784	Api	Nepal.	23,399
Lhotse II (Everest)	Nepal-Tibet.	27,560	Changtzu (Everest)	Nepal-Tibet.	24,780	Pauhunri.	India-Tibet.	23,385
Dhaulagiri	Nepal.	26,810	Muz Tagh Ata.	Sinkiang.	24,757	Trisul.	India.	23,360
Manaslu I	Nepal.	26,760	Skyang Kangri	Kashmir.	24,750	Kangto.	India-Tibet.	23,260
Cho Oyu.	Nepal-Tibet.	26,750	Communism Peak	USSR.	24,590	Nyenchhen Thanglha.	Tibet.	23,255
Nanga Parbat.	Kashmir.	26,660	Jongsang Peak.	India-Nepal.	24,472	Trisuli	India.	23,210
Annapurna I.	Nepal.	26,504	Pobedy Peak.	Sinkiang-USSR.	24,406	Pumori.	Nepal-Tibet.	23,190
Gasherbrum	Kashmir.	26,470	Sia Kangri.	Kashmir.	24,350	Dunagiri.	India.	23,184
Broad.	Kashmir.	26,400	Haramosh Peak	Pakistan.	24,270	Lombo Kangra.	Tibet.	23,165
Gosainthan	Tibet.	26,287	Istoro Nal	Pakistan.	24,240	Saipal.	Nepal.	23,100
Annapurna II	Nepal.	26,041	Tent Peak.	India-Nepal.	24,165	Macha Pucchare.	Nepal.	22,958
Gyachung Kang	Nepal-Tibet.	25,910	Chomo Lhari	Bhutan-Tibet	24,040	Numbar.	Nepal.	22,817
Disteghil Sar	Kashmir.	25,868	Chamlang.	Nepal.	24,012	Kanjiroba.	Nepal.	22,580
Himalchuli	Nepal.	25,801	Kabru.	India-Nepal.	24,002	Ama Dablam.	Nepal.	22,350
Nuptse (Everest).	Nepal-Tibet.	25,726	Alung Gangri	Tibet.	24,000	Cho Polu.	Nepal.	22,093
Masherbrum.	Kashmir.	25,660	Baltoro Kangri	Kashmir.	23,990	Lingtren.	Nepal-Tibet.	21,972
Nanda Devi.	India.	25,645	Mussu Shan.	Sinkiang.	23,890	Khumbutse.	Nepal-Tibet.	21,785
Rakaposhi.	Kashmir.	25,550	Mana.	India.	23,860	Hlako Gangri.	Tibet.	21,266
Kamet.	India-Tibet.	25,447	Baruntse.	Nepal.	23,688	Mt. Grosvenor.	China.	21,190
Namcha Barwa.	Tibet.	25,445	Nepal Peak.	India-Nepal.	23,500	Thagchhab Gangri	Tibet.	20,970
Gurla Mandhata.	Tibet.	25,355	Amne Machin.	China.	23,490	Damavand.	Iran.	18,606
Ulugh Muz Tagh	Sinkiang-Tibet.	25,340	Gauri Sankar.	Nepal-Tibet.	23,440	Ararat.	Turkey.	16,804

Antarctica

Peak	Height (feet)	Peak	Height (feet)	Peak	Height (feet)	Peak	Height (feet)
Vinson Massif	16,864	Andrew Jackson	13,750	Shear	13,100	Campbell	12,434
Tyree.	16,290	Sidley	13,720	Odishaw.	13,008	Don Pedro Christophersen.	12,355
Shinn.	15,750	Ostenso	13,710	Donaldson.	12,894	Lysaght	12,326
Gardner	15,375	Minto.	13,668	Ray.	12,808	Huggins	12,247
Epperly	15,100	Miller.	13,650	Sellery.	12,779	Sabine.	12,200
Kirkpatrick.	14,855	Long Gables.	13,620	Waterman.	12,730	Astor.	12,175
Elizabeth.	14,698	Dickerson.	13,517	Anne.	12,703	Mohl.	12,172
Markham.	14,290	Giovinetto.	13,412	Press.	12,566	Frankes.	12,064
Bell.	14,117	Wade.	13,400	Falla.	12,549	Jones.	12,040
Mackellar.	14,098	Fisher.	13,386	Rucker.	12,520	Gjelsvik.	12,008
Anderson.	13,957	Fridtjof Nansen.	13,350	Goldthwait.	12,510	Coman.	12,000
Bentley.	13,934	Wexler.	13,202	Morris.	12,500		
Kaplan.	13,878	Lister.	13,200	Erebus.	12,450		

Some Notable U.S. Mountains

Name	Place	Height (feet)	Name	Place	Height (feet)	Name	Place	Height (feet)
Gannett Peak	Wyo.	13,804	San Gorgonio	Cal.	11,502	Clingmans Dome	N.C.-Tenn.	6,643
Grand Teton	Wyo.	13,766	Hood	Ore.	11,235	Washington	N.H.	6,288
Kings	Utah	13,528	Lassen	Cal.	10,457	Rogers	Va.	5,927
Cloud	Wyo.	13,175	Granite	Mont.	10,321	Marcy	N.Y.	5,344
Boundary	Nevada	13,140	Guadalupe	Texas	8,751	Katahdin	Maine	5,268
Wheeler	N.M.	13,065	Olympus	Wash.	7,965	Spruce Knob	W. Va.	4,862
Borah	Idaho	12,662	Harney	S.D.	7,242	Mansfield	Vt.	4,393
Humphreys	Ariz.	12,633	Mitchell	N.C.	6,684	Black Mountain	Ky.	4,145
Adams	Wash.	12,307						

Ocean Areas and Average Depths

Four major bodies of water are recognized by geographers and mapmakers: the Pacific, Atlantic, Indian, and Arctic oceans. The Atlantic and Pacific oceans are considered divided at the equator into the No. and So. Atlantic; the No. and So. Pacific. The Arctic Ocean is the name for waters north of the continental land masses in the region of the Arctic Circle.

	Sq. miles	Avg. depth (feet)		Sq. miles	Avg. depth (feet)
Pacific Ocean	64,186,300	12,925	Hudson Bay	281,900	305
Atlantic Ocean	33,420,000	11,730	East China Sea	256,600	620
Indian Ocean	28,350,500	12,598	Andaman Sea	218,100	3,667
Arctic Ocean	5,105,700	3,407	Black Sea	196,100	3,906
South China Sea	1,148,500	4,802	Red Sea	174,900	1,764
Caribbean Sea	971,400	8,448	North Sea	164,900	308
Mediterranean Sea	969,100	4,926	Baltic Sea	147,500	.180
Bering Sea	873,000	4,893	Yellow Sea	113,500	121
Gulf of Mexico	582,100	5,297	Persian Gulf	88,800	328
Sea of Okhotsk	537,500	3,192	Gulf of California	59,100	2,375
Sea of Japan	391,100	5,468			

Principal Ocean Depths

Source: Defense Mapping Agency Hydrographic/Topographic Center, U.S. Dept. of Defense

Name of area	Location	Depth Meters	Depth Fathoms	Feet
Pacific Ocean				
Mariana Trench	11°22′N 142°36′E	10,924	5,973	35,840
Tonga Trench	23°16′S 174°44′W	10,800	5,906	35,433
Philippine Trench	10°38′N 126°36′E	10,057	5,499	32,995
Kermadec Trench	31°53′S 177°21′W	10,047	5,494	32,963
Bonin Trench	24°30′N 143°24′E	9,994	5,464	32,788
Kuril Trench	44°15′N 150°34′E	9,750	5,331	31,988
Izu Trench	31°05′N 142°10′E	9,695	5,301	31,808
New Britain Trench	06°19′S 153°45′E	8,940	4,888	29,331
Yap Trench	08°33′N 138°02′E	8,527	4,663	27,976
Japan Trench	36°08′N 142°43′E	8,412	4,600	27,599
Peru-Chile Trench	23°18′S 71°14′W	8,064	4,409	26,457
Palau Trench	07°52′N 134°56′E	8,054	4,404	26,424
Aleutian Trench	50°51′N 177°11′E	7,679	4,199	25,194
New Hebrides Trench	20°36′S 168°37′E	7,570	4,139	24,836
North Ryukyu Trench	24°00′N 126°48′E	7,181	3,927	23,560
Mid. America Trench	14°02′N 93°39′W	6,662	3,643	21,857
Atlantic Ocean				
Puerto Rico Trench	19°55′N 65°27′W	8,605	4,705	28,232
So. Sandwich Trench	55°42′S 25°56′E	8,325	4,552	27,313
Romanche Gap	0°13′S 18°26′W	7,728	4,226	25,354
Cayman Trench	19°12′N 80°00′W	7,535	4,120	24,721
Brazil Basin	09°10′S 23°02′W	6,119	3,346	20,076
Indian Ocean				
Java Trench	10°19′S 109°58′E	7,125	3,896	23,376
Ob′ Trench	09°45′S 67°18′E	6,874	3,759	22,553
Diamantina Trench	35°50′S 105°14′E	6,602	3,610	21,660
Vema Trench	09°08′S 67°15′E	6,402	3,501	21,004
Agulhas Basin	45°20′S 26°50′E	6,195	3,387	20,325
Arctic Ocean				
Eurasia Basin	82°23′N 19°31′E	5,450	2,980	17,881
Mediterranean Sea				
Ionian Basin	36°32′N 21°06′E	5,150	2,816	16,896

Note: Deeper depths have been reported in some of the above areas. However, they are not official unless confirmed by research vessels.

Principal World Rivers

Source: Geological Survey, U.S. Dept. of the Interior

River	Outflow	Length (Feet)	River	Outflow	Length (Feet)	River	Outflow	Length (Feet)
Albany	James Bay	610	Chang Jiang	E. China Sea	3,964	Dvina, North	White Sea	824
Amazon	Atlantic Ocean	4,000	Churchill, Man.	Hudson Bay	1,000	Dvina, West	Gulf of Riga	634
Amu	Aral Sea	1,578	Churchill, Que.	Atlantic Ocean	532	Ebro	Mediterranean	565
Amur	Tatar Strait	2,744	Colorado	Gulf of Calif.	1,450	Elbe	North Sea	724
Angara	Yenisey River	1,151	Columbia	Pacific Ocean	1,243	Euphrates	Shatt al-Arab.	1,700
Arkansas	Mississippi	1,459	Congo	Atlantic Ocean	2,718	Fraser	Str. of Georgia	850
Back	Arctic Ocean	605	Danube	Black Sea	1,776	Gambia	Atlantic Ocean	700
Brahmaputra	Bay of Bengal	1,800	Dnieper	Black Sea	1,420	Ganges	Bay of Bengal	1,560
Bug, Southern	Dnieper River	532	Dniester	Black Sea	877	Garonne	Bay of Biscay	357
Bug, Western	Wisla River	481	Don	Sea of Azov	1,224	Huang	Yellow Sea	2,903
Canadian	Arkansas River	906	Drava	Danube River	447			*(continued)*

(continued)

River	Outflow	Length (Feet)
Indus	Arabian Sea	1,800
Irrawaddy	Bay of Bengal	1,337
Japura	Amazon River	1,750
Jordan	Dead Sea	200
Kootenay	Columbia River	485
Lena	Laptev Sea	2,734
Loire	Bay of Biscay	634
Mackenzie	Arctic Ocean	2,635
Madeira	Amazon River	2,013
Magdalena	Caribbean Sea	956
Marne	Seine River	326
Mekong	S. China Sea	2,600
Meuse	North Sea	580
Mississippi	Gulf of Mexico	2,340
Missouri	Mississippi	2,540
Murray-Darling	Indian Ocean	2,310
Negro	Amazon	1,400
Nelson	Hudson Bay	410
Niger	Gulf of Guinea	2,590
Nile	Mediterranean	4,160
Ob-Irtysh	Gulf of Ob	3,362
Oder	Baltic Sea	567
Ohio	Mississippi	1,310
Orange	Atlantic Ocean	1,300
Orinoco	Atantic Ocean	1,600
Ottawa	St. Lawrence R.	790
Paraguay	Parana River	1,584
Parana	Rio de la Plata	2,485
Peace	Slave River	1,210
Pilcomayo	Paraguay River	1,000
Po	Adriatic Sea	405
Purus	Amazon River	2,100
Red	Mississippi	1,290
Red River of N.	Lake Winnipeg	545
Rhine	North Sea	820
Rhone	Gulf of Lions	505
Rio de la Plata	Atlantic Ocean	150
Rio Grande	Gulf of Mexico	1,900
Rio Roosevelt	Aripuana	400
Saguenay	St. Lawrence R.	434
St. John	Bay of Fundy	418
St. Lawrence	Gulf of St. Law.	800
Salween	Andaman Sea	1,500
Sao Francisco	Atlantic Ocean	1,988
Saskatchewan	Lake Winnipeg	1,205
Seine	English Chan.	496
Shannon	Atlantic Ocean	230
Snake	Columbia River	1,038
Songhua	Amur River	1,150
Syr	Aral Sea	1,370
Tajo, Tagus	Atlantic Ocean	626
Tennessee	Ohio River	652
Thames	North Sea	236
Tiber	Tyrrhenian Sea	252
Tigris	Shatt al-Arab	1,180
Tisza	Danube River	600
Tocantins	Para River	1,677
Ural	Caspian Sea	1,575
Uruguay	Rio de la Plata	1,000
Volga	Caspian Sea	2,194
Weser	North Sea	454
Wisla	Bay of Danzig	675
Xi	S. China Sea	1,200
Yellow (See Huang)		
Yenisei	Kara Sea	2,543
Yukon	Bering Sea	1,979
Zambezi	Indian Ocean	1,700

Major Rivers in North America

Source: Geological Survey, U.S. Dept. of the Interior

River	Source or Upper Limit of Length	Outflow	Miles
Alabama	Gilmer County, Ga.	Mobile River	729
Albany	Lake St. Joseph, Ontario	James Bay	610
Allegheny	Potter County, Pa.	Ohio River	325
Altamaha-Ocmulgee	Junction of Yellow and South Rivers, Newton County, Ga.	Atlantic Ocean	392
Apalachicola-Chattahoochee	Towns County, Ga.	Gulf of Mexico	524
Arkansas	Lake County, Col.	Mississippi River	1,459
Assiniboine	Eastern Saskatchewan	Red River	450
Attawapiskat	Attawapiskat, Ontario	James Bay	465
Back (N.W.T.)	Contwoyto Lake	Chantrey Inlet	605
Big Black (Miss.)	Webster County, Miss.	Mississippi River	330
Brazos	Junction of Salt and Double Mountain Forks, Stonewall County, Tex.	Gulf of Mexico	923
Canadian	Las Animas County, Col.	Arkansas River	906
Cedar (Iowa)	Dodge County, Minn.	Iowa River	329
Cheyenne	Junction of Antelope Creek and Dry Fork, Converse County, Wyo.	Missouri River	290
Churchill	Methy Lake, Saskatchewan	Hudson Bay	1,000
Cimarron	Colfax County, N.M.	Arkansas River	600
Colorado (Ariz.)	Rocky Mountain National Park, Col. (90 miles in Mexico)	Gulf of Cal.	1,450
Colorado (Texas)	West Texas	Matagorda Bay	862
Columbia	Columbia Lake, British Columbia	Pacific Ocean, bet. Ore. and Wash.	1,243
Columbia, Upper	Columbia Lake, British Columbia	To mouth of Snake River	890
Connecticut	Third Connecticut Lake, N.H.	L.I. Sound, Conn.	407
Coppermine (N.W.T.)	Lac de Gras	Coronation Gulf (Arctic Ocean)	525
Cumberland	Letcher County, Ky.	Ohio River	720
Delaware	Schoharie County, N.Y.	Liston Point, Delaware Bay	390
Fraser	Near Mount Robson (on Continental Divide)	Strait of Georgia	850
Gila	Catron County, N.M.	Colorado River	649
Green (Ut.-Wyo.)	Junction of Wells and Trail Creeks, Sublette County, Wyo.	Colorado River	730
Hamilton (Lab.)	Lake Ashuanipi	Atlantic Ocean	532
Hudson	Henderson Lake, Essex County, N.Y.	Upper N.Y. Bay	306
Illinois	St. Joseph County, Ind.	Mississippi River	420
James (N.D.-S.D.)	Wells County, N.D.	Missouri River	710
James (Va.)	Junction of Jackson and Cowpasture Rivers, Botetourt County, Va.	Hampton Roads	340
Kanawha-New	Junction of North and South Forks of New River, N.C.	Ohio River	352
Kentucky	Junction of North and Middle Forks, Lee County, Ky.	Ohio River	259
Klamath	Lake Ewauna, Klamath Falls, Ore.	Pacific Ocean	250
Koyukuk	Endicott Mountains, Alaska	Yukon River	470
Kuskokwim	Alaska Range	Kuskokwim Bay	724
Liard	Southern Yukon, Alaska	Mackenzie River	693
Little Missouri	Crook County, Wyo.	Missouri River	560
Mackenzie	Great Slave Lake, N.W.T.	Arctic Ocean	2,635
Milk	Junction of North and South Forks, Alberta	Missouri River	625
Minnesota	Big Stone Lake, Minn.	Mississippi River	332
Mississippi	Lake Itasca, Minn.	Mouth of Southwest Pass	2,340
Mississippi, Upper	Lake Itasca, Minn.	To mouth of Missouri River	1,171
Mississippi-Missouri-Red Rock	Source of Red Rock, Beaverhead Co., Mon.	Mouth of Southwest Pass	3,710
Missouri	Junction of Jefferson, Madison, and Gallatin rivers, Madison County, Mon.	Mississippi River	2,315
Missouri-Red Rock	Source of Red Rock, Beaverhead Co., Mon.	Mississippi River	2,540
Mobile-Alabama-Coosa	Gilmer County, Ga.	Mobile Bay	774
Nelson (Manitoba)	Lake Winnipeg	Hudson Bay	410

River	Source or Upper Limit of Length	Outflow	Miles
Neosho	Morris County, Kan.	Arkansas River, Okla.	460
Niobrara	Niobrara County, Wyo.	Missouri River, Neb.	431
North Canadian	Union County, N.M.	Canadian River, Okla.	800
North Platte	Junction of Grizzly and Little Grizzly creeks, Jackson County, Col.	Platte River, Neb.	618
Ohio	Junction of Allegheny and Monongahela rivers, Pittsburgh, Pa.	Mississippi River	981
Ohio-Allegheny	Potter County, Pa.	Mississippi River	1,306
Osage	East-central Kansas	Missouri River	500
Ottawa	Lake Capimitchigama	St. Lawrence River	790
Ouachita	Polk County, Ark.	Red River	605
Peace	Stikine Mountains, B.C.	Slave River	1,210
Pearl	Neshoba County, Miss.	Gulf of Mexico	411
Pecos	Mora County, N.M.	Rio Grande	926
Pee Dee-Yadkin	Watauga County, N.C.	Winyah Bay	435
Pend Oreille-Clark Fork	Near Butte, Mon.	Columbia River	531
Platte	Junction of North and South Platte Rivers, Neb.	Missouri River	310
Porcupine	Ogilvie Mountains, Alaska	Yukon River, Alaska	569
Potomac	Garrett County, Md.	Chesapeake Bay	383
Powder	Junction of South and Middle Forks, Wyo.	Yellowstone River	375
Red (Okla.-Tex.-La.)	Curry County, N.M.	Mississippi River	1,290
Red River of the North	Junction of Otter Tail and Bois de Sioux Rivers, Wilkin County, Minn.	Lake Winnipeg	545
Republican	Junction of North Fork and Arikaree River, Neb.	Kansas River	445
Rio Grande	San Juan County, Col.	Gulf of Mexico	1,900
Roanoke	Junction of North and South Forks, Montgomery County, Va.	Albemarle Sound	380
Rock (Ill.-Wis.)	Dodge County, Wis.	Mississippi River	300
Sabine	Junction of South and Caddo Forks, Hunt County, Tex.	Sabine Lake	380
Sacramento	Siskiyou County, Cal.	Suisun Bay	377
St. Francis	Iron County, Mo.	Mississippi River	425
St. Lawrence	Lake Ontario	Gulf of St. Lawrence (Atlantic Ocean)	800
Salmon (Idaho)	Custer County, Ida.	Snake River	420
San Joaquin	Junction of South and Middle Forks, Madera County, Cal.	Suisun Bay	350
San Juan	Silver Lake, Archuleta County, Col.	Colorado River	360
Santee-Wateree-Catawba	McDowell County, N.C.	Atlantic Ocean	538
Saskatchewan, North	Rocky Mountains	Saskatchewan R.	800
Saskatchewan, South	Rocky Mountains	Saskatchewan R.	865
Savannah	Junction of Seneca and Tugaloo rivers, Anderson County, S.C.	Atlantic Ocean, Ga.-S.C.	314
Severn (Ontario)	Sandy Lake	Hudson Bay	610
Smoky Hill	Cheyenne County, Col.	Kansas River, Kan.	540
Snake	Teton County, Wyo.	Columbia River, Wash.	1,038
South Platte	Junction of South and Middle Forks, Park County, Col.	Platte River	424
Susitna	Alaska Range	Cook Inlet	313
Susquehanna	Otsego Lake, Otsego County, N.Y.	Chesapeake Bay	444
Tallahatchie	Tippah County, Miss.	Yazoo River	301
Tanana	Wrangell Mountains, Alaska	Yukon River	659
Tennessee	Junction of French Broad and Holston Rivers	Ohio River	652
Tennessee-French Broad	Transylvania County, N.C.	Ohio River	883
Tombigbee	Prentiss County, Miss.	Mobile River	525
Trinity	North of Dallas, Tex.	Galveston Bay	360
Wabash	Darke County, Oh.	Ohio River	512
Washita	Hemphill County, Tex.	Red River, Okla.	500
White (Ark.-Mo.)	Madison County, Ark.	Mississippi River	722
Willamette	Douglas County, Ore.	Columbia River	309
Wind-Bighorn	Junction of Wind and Little Wind Rivers, Fremont Co., Wyo. (Source of Wind R. is Togwotee Pass, Teton Co., Wyo.)	Yellowstone River	336
Wisconsin	Lac Vieux Desert, Vilas County, Wis.	Mississippi River	430
Yellowstone	Park County, Wyo.	Missouri River	692
Yukon	Coast Mountains of British Columbia	Bering Sea	1,979

Lakes of the World

Source: Geological Survey, U.S. Dept. of the Interior

A lake is a body of water surrounded by land. Although some lakes are called seas, they are lakes by definition. The Caspian Sea is bounded by the Soviet Union and Iran and is fed by eight rivers.

Name	Continent	Area (sq. mi.)	Length (miles)	Depth (feet)	Elevation (feet)
Caspian Sea	Asia-Europe	143,244	760	3,363	-92
Superior	North America	31,700	350	1,330	600
Victoria	Africa	26,828	250	270	3,720
Aral Sea	Asia	24,904(A)	280	220	174
Huron	North America	23,000	206	750	579
Michigan	North America	22,300	307	923	579
Tanganyika	Africa	12,700	420	4,823	2,534
Baykal	Asia	12,162	395	5,315	1,493
Great Bear	North America	12,096	192	1,463	512
Nyasa	Africa	11,150	360	2,280	1,550

(continued)

Name	Continent	Area (sq. mi.)	Length (miles)	Depth (feet)	Elevation (feet)
Great Slave	North America	11,031	298	2,015	513
Erie	North America	9,910	241	210	570
Winnipeg	North America	9,417	266	60	713
Ontario	North America	7,550	193	802	245
Balkhash	Asia	7,115	376	85	1,115
Ladoga	Europe	6,835	124	738	13
Chad	Africa	6,300	175	24	787
Maracaibo	South America	5,217	133	115	Sea level
Onega	Europe	3,710	145	328	108
Eyre	Australia	3,600	90	4	−52
Volta	Africa	3,276	250	....	....
Titicaca	South America	3,200	122	922	12,500
Nicaragua	North America	3,100	102	230	102
Athabasca	North America	3,064	208	407	700
Reindeer	North America	2,568	143	720	1,106
Rudolf	Africa	2,473	154	240	1,230
Issyk Kul	Asia	2,355	115	2,303	5,279
Torrens	Australia	2,230	130	....	92
Vanern	Europe	2,156	91	328	144
Nettilling	North America	2,140	67	....	95
Winnipegosis	North America	2,075	141	38	830
Albert	Africa	2,075	100	168	2,030
Kariba	Africa	2,050	175	390	1,590
Nipigon	North America	1,872	72	540	1,050
Gairdner	Australia	1,840	90	....	112
Urmia	Asia	1,815	90	49	4,180
Manitoba	North America	1,799	140	12	813

(A) Probably less because of the diversion of feeder rivers.

The Great Lakes

Source: National Ocean Service, U.S. Dept. of Commerce

The Great Lakes form the largest body of fresh water in the world and with their connecting waterways are the largest inland water transportation unit. Draining the great North Central basin of the U.S., they enable shipping to reach the Atlantic via their outlet, the St. Lawrence R., and also the Gulf of Mexico via the Illinois Waterway, from Lake Michigan to the Mississippi R. A third outlet connects with the Hudson R. and thence the Atlantic via the N. Y. State Barge Canal System. Traffic on the Illinois Waterway and the N.Y. State Barge Canal System is limited to recreational boating and small shipping vessels.

Only one of the lakes, Lake Michigan, is wholly in the United States; the others are shared with Canada. Ships move from the shores of Lake Superior to Whitefish Bay at the east end of the lake, thence through the Soo (Sault Ste. Marie) locks, through the St. Mary's River and into Lake Huron. To reach Gary, and Port of Indiana and South Chicago, Ill., ships move west from Lake Huron to Lake Michigan through the Straits of Mackinac.

Lake Superior is 600 feet above mean water level at Point-au-Pere, Quebec, on the International Great Lakes Datum (1955). From Duluth, Minn., to the eastern end of Lake Ontario is 1,156 mi.

	Superior	Michigan	Huron	Erie	Ontario
Length in miles	350	307	206	241	193
Breadth in miles	160	118	183	57	53
Deepest soundings in feet	1,330	923	750	210	802
Volume of water in cubic miles	2,900	1,180	850	116	393
Area (sq. miles) water surface—U.S.	20,600	22,300	9,100	4,980	3,560
Canada	11,100	......	13,900	4,930	3,990
Area (sq. miles) entire drainage basin—U.S.	16,900	45,600	16,200	18,000	15,200
Canada	32,400	......	35,500	4,720	12,100
Total Area (sq. miles) U.S. and Canada	81,000	67,900	74,700	32,630	34,850
Mean surface above mean water level at Point-au-Pere, Quebec, aver. level in feet (1900-1988)	600.61	578.34	578.34	570.53	244.74
Latitude, North	46° 25'	41° 37'	43° 00'	41° 23'	43° 11'
	49° 00'	46° 06'	46° 17'	42° 52'	44° 15'
Longitude, West	84° 22'	84° 45'	79° 43'	78° 51'	76° 03'
	92° 06'	88° 02'	84° 45'	83° 29'	79° 53'
National boundary line in miles	282.8	None	260.8	251.5	174.6
United States shore line (mainland only) miles	863	1,400	580	431	300

Highest and Lowest Continental Altitudes

Source: National Geographic Society

Continent	Highest point	Elevation (feet)	Lowest point	Elevation (feet) below sea level
Asia	Mount Everest, Nepal-Tibet	29,028	Dead Sea, Israel-Jordan	1,312
South America	Mount Aconcagua, Argentina	22,834	Valdes Peninsula, Argentina	131
North America	Mount McKinley, Alaska	20,320	Death Valley, California	282
Africa	Kilimanjaro, Tanzania	19,340	Lake Assal, Djibouti	512
Europe	Mount El'brus, USSR	18,510	Caspian Sea, USSR	92
Antarctica	Vinson Massif	16,864	Unknown	...
Australia	Mount Kosciusko, New South Wales	7,310	Lake Eyre, South Australia	52

Famous Waterfalls
Source: National Geographic Society

The earth has thousands of waterfalls, some of considerable magnitude. Their importance is determined not only by height but volume of flow, steadiness of flow, crest width, whether the water drops sheerly or over a sloping surface, and in one leap or a succession of leaps. A series of low falls flowing over a considerable distance is known as a cascade.

Sete Quedas or Guaira is the world's greatest waterfall when its mean annual flow (estimated at 470,000 cubic feet per second) is combined with height. A greater volume of water passes over Boyoma Falls (Stanley Falls), though not one of its seven cataracts, spread over nearly 60 miles of the Congo River, exceeds 10 feet.

Estimated mean annual flow, in cubic feet per second, of other major waterfalls are: Niagara, 212,200; Paulo Afonso, 100,000; Urubupunga, 97,000; Iguazu, 61,000; Patos-Maribondo, 53,000; Victoria, 35,400; and Kaieteur, 23,400.

Height = total drop in feet in one or more leaps. † = falls of more than one leap; * = falls that diminish greatly seasonally; ** = falls that reduce to a trickle or are dry for part of each year. If river names not shown, they are the same as the falls. R. = river; L. = lake; (C) = cascade type.

Name and location	Elevation (Feet)	Name and location	Elevation (Feet)	Name and location	Elevation (Feet)
Africa		Wales		Kentucky	
		Rhaiadr	240	Cumberland	68
		Italy—Frua, Toce R. (C)	470	Maryland	
Angola		Norway		*Great, Potomac R. (C)	71
Ruacana, Cuene R.	406	Mardalsfossen (Northern)	1,535	Minnesota	
Ethiopia		† Mardalsfossen (Southern)	2,149	**Minnehaha	53
Fincha	508	† **Skjeggedal, Nybuai R.	1,378	New Jersey	
Lesotho		**Skykje	984	Passaic	70
*Maletsunyane	630	Vetti, Morka-Koldedola R.	900	New York	
Zimbabwe-Zambia		Sweden		*Taughannock	215
*Victoria, Zambezi R.	343	† Handol	427	Oregon	
South Africa		Switzerland		† Multnomah	620
*Augrabies, Orange R.	480	Giessbach (C)	984	Tennessee	
† Tugela	2,014	† Reichenbach	656	Fall Creek	256
Tanzania-Zambia		† Simmen	459	Washington	
*Kalambo	726	Staubbach	984	Mt. Rainier Natl. Park	
		† Trummelbach	1,312	Sluiskin, Paradise R.	300
Asia				**Snoqualmie	268
		North America		Wisconsin	
				*Big Manitou, Black R. (C)	165
India—*Cauvery	330	**Canada**		Wyoming	
*Jog (Gersoppa), Sharavathi R.	830	Alberta		Yellowstone Natl. Pk. Tower.	132
Japan		Panther, Nigel Cr.	600	*Yellowstone (upper)	109
*Kegon, Daiya R.	330	British Columbia		*Yellowstone (lower)	308
		† Della	1,443	**Mexico**	
Australasia		† Takakkaw, Daly Glacier	1,200	El Salto	218
		Quebec			
		Montmorency	274		
Australia		**Canada—United States**		**South America**	
New South Wales		Niagara: American	182		
Wentworth	614	Horseshoe	173	**Argentina-Brazil**	
Wollomombi	1,100	**United States**		Iguazu	230
Queensland		California		**Brazil**	
Tully	885	*Feather, Fall R.	640	Glass	1,325
† Wallaman, Stony Cr.	1,137	Yosemite National Park		Patos-Maribondo, Grande R.	115
New Zealand		*Bridalveil	620	Paulo Afonso, Sao Francisco R.	275
Helena	890	*Illilouette	370	**Colombia**	
† Sutherland, Arthur R.	1,904	*Nevada, Merced R.	594	Catarata de Candelas,	
		**Ribbon	1,612	Cusiana R.	984
Europe		**Silver Strand, Meadow Br.	1,170	*Tequendama, Bogota R.	427
		*Vernal, Merced R.	317	**Ecuador**	
		† **Yosemite	2,425	*Agoyan, Pastaza R.	200
Austria—† Gastein	492	Colorado		**Guyana**	
† Krimml	1,312	† Seven, South Cheyenne Cr.	300	Kaieteur, Potaro R.	741
France—*Gavarnie	1,385	Hawaii		Great, Kamarang R.	1,600
Great Britain—Scotland		Akaka, Kolekole Str.	442	† Marina, Ipobe R.	500
Glomach	370	Idaho		**Venezuela—**	
		**Shoshone, Snake R.	212	† *Angel	3,212
				Cuquenan	2,000

Notable Deserts of the World

Arabian (Eastern), 70,000 sq. mi. in Egypt between the Nile river and Red Sea, extending southward into Sudan.

Atacama, 600 mi. long area rich in nitrate and copper deposits in N. Chile.

Chihuahuan, 140,000 sq. mi. in Tex., N.M., Ariz., and Mexico.

Death Valley, 3,300 sq. mi. in E. Cal. and SW Nev. Contains lowest point below sea level (282 ft.) in Western Hemisphere.

Gibson, 120,000 sq. mi. in the interior of W. Australia.

Gobi, 500,000 sq. mi. in Mongolia and China.

Great Sandy, 150,000 sq. mi. in W. Australia.

Great Victoria, 150,000 sq. mi. in W. and S. Australia.

Kalahari, 225,000 sq. mi. in southern Africa.

Kara-Kum, 120,000 sq. mi. in Turkmen SSR.

Kyzyl Kum, 100,000 sq. mi. in Kazakh and Uzbek SSRs.

Libyan, 450,000 sq. mi. in the Sahara extending from Lybia through SW Egypt into Sudan.

Lut (Dasht-e Lut), 20,000 sq. mi. in E. Iran.

Mojave, 15,000 sq. mi. in S. Cal.

Namib, long narrow area extending 800 miles along SW coast of Africa.

Nubian, 100,000 sq. mi. in the Sahara in NE Sudan.

Painted Desert, section of high plateau in N. Ariz. extending 150 mi.

Rub al Khali (Empty Quarter), 250,000 sq. mi. in the south Arabian Peninsula.

Sahara, 3,500,000 sq. mi. in N. Africa extending westward to the Atlantic. Largest desert in the world.

Sonoran, 70,000 sq. mi. in SW Ariz. and SE Cal. extending into Mexico.

Syrian, 100,000 sq. mi. arid wasteland extending over much of N. Saudi Arabia, E. Jordan, S. Syria, and W. Iraq.

Taklimakan, 140,000 sq. mi. in Sinkiang Province, China.

Thar (Great Indian), 100,000 sq. mi. arid area extending 400 mi. along India-Pakistan border.

Important Islands and Their Areas

Figure in parentheses shows rank among the world's 10 largest islands; some islands have not been surveyed accurately; in such cases estimated areas are shown.

Location-Ownership
Area in square miles

Arctic Ocean
Canadian

Axel Heiberg	16,671
Baffin (5)	195,928
Banks	27,038
Bathurst	6,194
Devon	21,331
Ellesmere (10)	75,767
Melville	16,274
Prince of Wales	12,872
Somerset	9,570
Southampton	15,913
Victoria (9)	83,896

USSR

Franz Josef Land	8,000
Novaya Zemlya (two is.)	35,000
Wrangel	2,800

Norwegian

Svalbard	23,940
Nordaustlandet	5,410
Spitsbergen	15,060

Atlantic Ocean

Anticosti, Canada	3,066
Ascension, UK	34
Azores, Portugal	888
Faial	67
Sao Miguel	291
Bahamas	5,353
Bermuda Is., UK	20
Block, Rhode Island	10
Canary Is., Spain	2,808
Fuerteventura	668
Gran Canaria	592
Tenerife	795
Cape Breton, Canada	3,981
Cape Verde Is.	1,750
Faeroe Is., Denmark	540
Falkland Is., UK	4,700
Fernando de Noronha Archipelago, Brazil	7
Greenland, Denmark (1)	840,000
Iceland	39,769
Long Island, N.Y.	1,396
Bioko Is. Equatorial Guinea	785
Madeira Is., Portugal	307
Marajo, Brazil	15,528
Martha's Vineyard, Mass.	91
Mount Desert, Me.	108
Nantucket, Mass.	46
Newfoundland, Canada	42,030
Prince Edward, Canada	2,184
St. Helena, UK	47
South Georgia, UK	1,450
Tierra del Fuego, Chile and Argentina	18,800
Tristan da Cunha, UK	40

British Isles

Great Britain, mainland (8)	84,200
Channel Islands	75
Guernsey	24
Jersey	45
Sark	2
Hebrides	2,744
Ireland	32,599
Irish Republic	27,136
Northern Ireland	5,463
Man	227
Orkney Is.	390
Scilly Is.	6
Shetland Is.	567
Skye	670
Wight	147

Baltic Sea

Aland Is., Finland	581
Bornholm, Denmark	227
Gotland, Sweden	1,164

Caribbean Sea

Antigua	108
Aruba, Netherlands	75
Barbados	166
Cuba	44,218
Isle of Youth	1,182
Curacao, Netherlands	171
Dominica	290
Guadeloupe, France	687
Hispaniola, Haiti and Dominican Republic	29,530
Jamaica	4,244
Martinique, France	425
Puerto Rico, U.S.	3,515
Tobago	116
Trinidad	1,864
Virgin Is., UK	59
Virgin Is., U.S.	132

Indian Ocean

Andaman Is., India	2,500
Madagascar (4)	226,658
Mauritius	720
Pemba, Tanzania	380
Reunion, France	969
Seychelles	171
Sri Lanka	25,332
Zanzibar, Tanzania	640

Persian Gulf

Bahrain	258

Mediterranean Sea

Balearic Is., Spain	1,936
Corfu, Greece	229
Corsica, France	3,369
Crete, Greece	3,186
Cyprus	3,572
Elba, Italy	86
Euboea, Greece	1,409
Malta	122
Rhodes, Greece	542
Sardinia, Italy	9,262
Sicily, Italy	9,822

Pacific Ocean

Aleutian Is., U.S.	6,821
Adak	289
Amchitka	121
Attu	388
Kanaga	135
Kiska	110
Tanaga	209
Umnak	675
Unalaska	1,064
Unimak	1,600
Canton, Kiribati*	4
Caroline Is., U.S. trust terr.	472
Christmas, Kiribati*	94
Clipperton, France	2
Diomede, Big, USSR	11
Diomede, Little, U.S.	2
Easter, Chile	69
Fiji	7,056
Vanua Levu	2,242
Viti Levu	4,109
Funafuti, Tuvalu*	2
Galapagos Is., Ecuador	3,043
Guadalcanal	2,500
Guam	209
Hainan, China	13,000
Hawaiian Is., U.S.	6,450
Hawaii	4,037
Oahu	593
Hong Kong, UK	29
Japan	145,809
Hokkaido	30,144
Honshu (7)	87,805
Iwo Jima	8
Kyushu	14,114
Okinawa	459
Shikoku	7,049
Kodiak, U.S.	3,670
Marquesas Is., France	492
Marshall Is., U.S. trust terr.	70
Bikini*	2
Nauru	8
New Caledonia, France	6,530
New Guinea (2)	306,000
New Zealand	103,883
Chatham	372
North	44,035
South	58,305
Stewart	674
Northern Mariana Is.	184
Philippines	115,831
Leyte	2,787
Luzon	40,880
Mindanao	36,775
Mindoro	3,790
Negros	4,907
Palawan	4,554
Panay	4,446
Samar	5,050
Quemoy	56
Sakhalin, USSR	29,500
Samoa Is.	1,177
American Samoa	77
Tutuila	52
Samoa (Western)	1,133
Savaii	670
Upolu	429
Santa Catalina, U.S.	72
Tahiti, France	402
Taiwan	13,823
Tasmania, Australia	26,178
Tonga Is.	270
Vancouver, Canada	12,079
Vanuatu	5,700

East Indies

Bali, Indonesia	2,147
Borneo, Indonesia-Malaysia, UK (3)	280,100
Celebes, Indonesia	69,000
Java, Indonesia	48,900
Madura, Indonesia	2,113
Moluccas, Indonesia	28,766
New Britain, Papua New Guinea	14,093
New Ireland, Papua New Guinea	3,707
Sumatra, Indonesia (6)	165,000
Timor, Indonesia	11,570

* Atolls: Bikini (lagoon area, 230 sq. mi., land area 2 sq. mi.), U.S. Trust Territory of the Pacific Islands; Canton (lagoon 20 sq. mi., land 4 sq. mi.), Kiribati; Christmas (lagoon 140 sq. mi., land 94 sq. mi.), Kiribati; Funafuti (lagoon 84 sq. mi., land 2 sq. mi.), Tuvalu. **Australia**, often called an island, is a continent. Its mainland area is 2,939,975 sq. mi.

Islands in minor waters; Manhattan (22 sq mi.) Staten (59 sq. mi.) and Governors (173 acres), all in New York Harbor, U.S.; Isle Royale (209 sq. mi.), Lake Superior, U.S.; Manitoulin (1,068 sq. mi.), Lake Huron, Canada; Pinang (110 sq. mi.), Strait of Malacca, Malaysia; Singapore (239 sq. mi.), Singapore Strait, Singapore.

DISASTERS
Some Notable Shipwrecks Since 1850
(Figures indicate estimated lives lost; as of mid-1991)

1854, Mar.—City of Glasgow; British steamer missing in North Atlantic; 480.

1854, Sept. 27—Arctic; U.S. (Collins Line) steamer sunk in collision with French steamer Vesta near Cape Race; 285-351.

1856, Jan. 23—Pacific; U.S. (Collins Line) steamer missing in North Atlantic; 186-286.

1858, Sept. 23—Austria; German steamer destroyed by fire in North Atlantic; 471.

1863, Apr. 27—Anglo-Saxon; British steamer wrecked at Cape Race; 238.

1865, Apr. 27—Sultana; a Mississippi River steamer blew up near Memphis, Tenn; 1,450.

1869, Oct. 27—Stonewall; steamer burned on Mississippi River below Cairo, Ill.; 200.

1870, Jan. 25—City of Boston; British (Inman Line) steamer vanished between New York and Liverpool; 177.

1870, Oct 19—Cambria; British steamer wrecked off northern Ireland; 196.

1872, Nov. 7—Mary Celeste; U.S. half-brig sailed from New York for Genoa; found abandoned in Atlantic 4 weeks later in mystery of sea; crew never heard from; loss of life unknown.

1873, Jan. 22—Northfleet; British steamer foundered off Dungeness, England; 300.

1873, Apr. 1—Atlantic; British (White Star) steamer wrecked off Nova Scotia; 585.

1873, Nov. 23—Ville du Havre; French steamer, sunk after collision with British sailing ship Loch Earn; 226.

1875, May 7—Schiller; German steamer wrecked off Scilly Isles; 312.

1875, Nov. 4—Pacific; U.S. steamer sunk after collision off Cape Flattery; 236.

1878, Sept. 3—Princess Alice; British steamer sank after collision in Thames River; 700.

1878, Dec. 18—Byzantin; French steamer sank after Dardanelles collision; 210.

1881, May 24—Victoria; steamer capsized in Thames River, Canada; 200.

1883, Jan. 19—Cimbria; German steamer sunk in collision with British steamer Sultan in North Sea; 389.

1887, Nov. 15—Wah Yeung; British steamer burned at sea; 400.

1890, Feb. 17—Duburg; British steamer wrecked, China Sea; 400.

1890, Sept. 19—Ertogrul; Turkish frigate foundered off Japan; 540.

1891, Mar. 17—Utopia; British steamer sank in collision with British ironclad Anson off Gibraltar; 562.

1895, Jan. 30—Elbe; German steamer sank in collision with British steamer Craithie in North Sea; 332.

1895, Mar. 11—Reina Regenta; Spanish cruiser foundered near Gibraltar; 400.

1898, Feb. 15—Maine; U.S. battleship blown up in Havana Harbor; 260.

1898, July 4—La Bourgogne; French steamer sunk in collision with British sailing ship Cromartyshire off Nova Scotia; 549.

1898, Nov. 26—Portland; U.S. steamer wrecked off Cape Cod; 157.

1904, June 15—General Slocum; excursion steamer burned in East River, New York City; 1,030.

1904, June 28—Norge; Danish steamer wrecked on Rockall Island, Scotland; 620.

1906, Aug. 4—Sirio; Italian steamer wrecked off Cape Palos, Spain; 350.

1908, Mar. 23—Matsu Maru; Japanese steamer sank in collision near Hakodate, Japan; 300.

1909, Aug. 1—Waratah; British steamer, Sydney to London, vanished; 300.

1910, Feb. 9—General Chanzy; French steamer wrecked off Minorca, Spain; 200.

1911, Sept. 25—Liberté; French battleship exploded at Toulon; 285.

1912, Mar. 5—Principe de Asturias; Spanish steamer wrecked off Spain; 500.

1912, Apr. 14-15—Titanic; British (White Star) steamer hit iceberg in North Atlantic; 1,503.

1912, Sept. 28—Kichemaru; Japanese steamer sank off Japanese coast; 1,000.

1914, May 29—Empress of Ireland; British (Canadian Pacific) steamer sunk in collision with Norwegian collier in St. Lawrence River; 1,014.

1915, May 7—Lusitania; British (Cunard Line) steamer torpedoed and sunk by German submarine off Ireland; 1,198.

1915, July 24—Eastland; excursion steamer capsized in Chicago River; 812.

1916, Feb. 26—Provence; French cruiser sank in Mediterranean; 3,100.

1916, Mar. 3—Principe de Asturias; Spanish steamer wrecked near Santos, Brazil; 558.

1916, Aug. 29—Hsin Yu; Chinese steamer sank off Chinese coast; 1,000.

1917, Dec. 6—Mont Blanc, Imo; French ammunition ship and Belgian steamer collided in Halifax Harbor; 1,600.

1918, Apr. 25—Kiang-Kwan Chinese steamer sank in collision off Hankow; 500.

1918, July 12—Kawachi; Japanese battleship blew up in Tokayama Bay; 500.

1918, Oct. 25—Princess Sophia; Canadian steamer sank off Alaskan coast; 398.

1919, Jan. 17—Chaonia; French steamer lost in Straits of Messina, Italy; 460.

1919, Sept. 9—Valbanera; Spanish steamer lost off Florida coast; 500.

1921, Mar. 18—Hong Kong; steamer wrecked in South China Sea; 1,000.

1922, Aug. 26—Niitaka; Japanese cruiser sank in storm off Kamchatka, USSR; 300.

1927, Oct. 25—Principessa Mafalda; Italian steamer blew up, sank off Porto Seguro, Brazil; 314.

1928, Nov. 12—Vestris; British steamer sank in gale off Virginia; 113.

1934, Sept. 8—Morro Castle; U.S. steamer, Havana to New York, burned off Asbury Park, N.J.; 134.

1939, May 23—Squalus; U.S. submarine sank off Portsmouth, N.H.; 26.

1939, June 1—Thetis; British submarine, sank in Liverpool Bay; 99.

1942, Feb. 18—Truxtun and Pollux; U.S. destroyer and cargo ship ran aground, sank off Newfoundland; 204.

1942, Oct. 2—Curacao; British cruiser sank after collision with liner Queen Mary; 338.

1944, Dec. 17-18—3 U.S. Third Fleet destroyers sank during typhoon in Philippine Sea; 790.

1947, Jan. 19—Himera; Greek steamer hit a mine off Athens; 392.

1947, Apr. 16—Grandcamp; French freighter exploded in Texas City, Tex., Harbor, starting fires; 510.

1948, Nov.—Chinese army evacuation ship exploded and sunk off S. Manchuria; 6,000.

1948, Dec. 3—Kiangya; Chinese refugee ship wrecked in explosion S. of Shanghai; 1,100+.

1949, Sept. 17—Noronic; Canadian Great Lakes Cruiser burned at Toronto dock; 130.

1952, Apr. 26—Hobson and Wasp; U.S. destroyer and aircraft carrier collided in Atlantic; 176.

1953, Jan. 31—Princess Victoria; British ferry sank in storm off northern Irish coast; 134.

1954, Sept. 26—Toya Maru; Japanese ferry sank in Tsugaru Strait, Japan; 1,172.

1956, July 26—Andrea Doria and Stockholm; Italian liner and Swedish liner collided off Nantucket; 51.

1957, July 14—Eshghabad; Soviet ship ran aground in Caspian Sea; 270.

1961, July 8—Save; Portuguese ship ran aground off Mozambique; 259.

1962, Apr. 8—Dara; British liner exploded and sunk in Persian Gulf; 236.

1963, Apr. 10—Thresher; U.S. Navy atomic submarine sank in North Atlantic; 129.

1964, Feb. 10—Voyager, Melbourne; Australian destroyer sank after collision with Australian aircraft carrier Melbourne off New South Wales; 82.

1965, Nov. 13—Yarmouth Castle; Panamanian registered cruise ship burned and sank off Nassau; 90.

1967, July 29—Forrestal; U.S. aircraft carrier caught fire off N. Vietnam; 134.

1968, Jan. 25—Dakar; Israeli submarine vanished in Mediterranean Sea; 69.

1968, Jan. 27—Minerve; French submarine vanished in Mediterranean; 52.

1968, late May—Scorpion; U.S. nuclear submarine sank in Atlantic near Azores; 99 (located Oct. 31).

1969, June 2—Evans; U.S. destroyer cut in half by Australian carrier Melbourne, S. China Sea; 74.

1970, Mar. 4—Eurydice; French submarine sank in Mediterranean near Toulon; 57.

1970, Dec. 15—Namyong-Ho; South Korean ferry sank in Korea Strait; 308.

1974, May 1— Motor launch capsized off Bangladesh; 250.

1974, Sept. 26— Soviet destroyer burned and sank in Black Sea; 200+.

1976, Oct. 20—George Prince and Frosta; ferryboat and Norwegian tanker collided on Mississippi R. at Luling, La.; 77.

1976, Dec. 25—Patria; Egyptian liner caught fire and sank in the Red Sea; c. 100.

1977, Jan. 11—Grand Zenith; Panamanian-registered tanker sank off Cape Cod, Mass.; 38.

1979, Aug. 14—23 yachts competing in Fastnet yacht race sunk or abandoned during storm in S. Irish Sea; 18.

1981, Jan. 27—Tamponas II; Indonesian passenger ship caught fire and sank in Java Sea; 580.

1981, May 26—Nimitz; U.S. Marine combat jet crashed on deck of U.S. aircraft carrier; 14.

1983, Feb. 12—Marine Electric; coal freighter sank during storm off Chincoteague, Va.; 33.

1983, May 25—10th of Ramadan; Nile steamer caught fire and sank in L. Nassar; 357.

1986, Aug. 31—Admiral Nakhimov; Soviet passenger ship and **Pyotr Vasev,** Soviet freighter, collided in the Black Sea; 398.

1987, Mar. 6—British ferry capsized off Zeebrugge, Belgium; 188.

1987, Dec. 20—Philippine ferry *Dona Paz* and oil tanker *Victor* collided in the Tablas Strait; 3,000+.

1988, Aug. 6—Indian ferry capsized on Ganges R.; 400+.

1989, Apr. 7—Soviet submarine caught fire and sank off Norway; 42.

1989, Apr. 19—USS Iowa; U.S. battleship; explosion in gun turret; 47.

1989, Aug. 20—British barge *Bowbelle* struck British pleasure cruiser *Marchioness* on Thames R. in central London; 56.

1989, Sept. 10—Romanian pleasure boat and Bulgarian barge collided on Danube R.; 161.

1991, Apr. 10—Auto ferry and oil tanker collided outside Livorno Harbor, Italy; 140.

Some Notable Aircraft Disasters Since 1937

Date			Aircraft	Site of accident	Deaths
1937	May	6	German zeppelin Hindenburg	Burned at mooring, Lakehurst, N.J.	36
1944	Aug.	23	U.S. Air Force B-24	Hit school, Freckelton, England	76[1]
1945	July	28	U.S. Army B-25	Hit Empire State bldg., N.Y.C.	14[1]
1947	May	30	Eastern Air Lines DC-4	Crashed near Port Deposit, Md.	53
1952	Dec.	20	U.S. Air Force C-124	Fell, burned, Moses Lake, Wash.	87
1953	Mar.	3	Canadian Pacific Comet Jet	Karachi, Pakistan	11[2]
1953	June	18	U.S. Air Force C-124	Crashed, burned near Tokyo	129
1955	Nov.	1	United Air Lines DC-6B	Exploded, crashed near Longmont, Col.	44[3]
1956	June	20	Venezuelan Super-Constellation	Crashed in Atlantic off Asbury Park, N.J.	74
1956	June	30	TWA Super-Const., United DC-7	Collided over Grand Canyon, Arizona	128
1960	Dec.	16	United DC-8 jet, TWA Super-Const.	Collided over N.Y. City	134[4]
1962	Mar.	16	Flying Tiger Super-Const.	Vanished in Western Pacific	107
1962	June	3	Air France Boeing 707 jet	Crashed on takeoff from Paris	130
1962	June	22	Air France Boeing 707 jet	Crashed in storm, Guadeloupe, W.I.	113
1963	June	3	Chartered Northw. Airlines DC-7	Crashed in Pacific off British Columbia	101
1963	Nov.	29	Trans-Canada Airlines DC-8F	Crashed after takeoff from Montreal	118
1965	May	20	Pakistani Boeing 720-B	Crashed at Cairo, Egypt, airport	121
1966	Jan.	24	Air India Boeing 707 jetliner	Crashed on Mont Blanc, France-Italy	117
1966	Feb.	4	All-Nippon Boeing 727	Plunged into Tokyo Bay	133
1966	Mar.	5	BOAC Boeing 707 jetliner	Crashed on Mount Fuji, Japan	124
1966	Dec.	24	U.S. military-chartered CL-44	Crashed into village in So. Vietnam	129[1]
1967	Apr.	20	Swiss Britannia turboprop	Crashed at Nicosia, Cyprus	126
1967	July	19	Piedmont Boeing 727, Cessna 310	Collided in air, Hendersonville, N.C.	82
1968	Apr.	20	S. African Airways Boeing 707	Crashed on takeoff, Windhoek, SW Africa	122
1968	May	3	Braniff International Electra	Crashed in storm near Dawson, Tex.	85
1969	Mar.	16	Venezuelan DC-9	Crashed after takeoff from Maracaibo, Venezuela	155[5]
1969	Dec.	8	Olympia Airways DC-6B	Crashed near Athens in storm	93
1970	Feb.	15	Dominican DC-9	Crashed into sea on takeoff from Santo Domingo	102
1970	July	3	British chartered jetliner	Crashed near Barcelona, Spain	112
1970	July	5	Air Canada DC-8	Crashed near Toronto International Airport	108
1970	Aug.	9	Peruvian turbojet	Crashed after takeoff from Cuzco, Peru	101[1]
1970	Nov.	14	Southern Airways DC-9	Crashed in mountains near Huntington, W. Va.	75[6]
1971	July	30	All-Nippon Boeing 727 and Japanese Air Force F-86	Collided over Morioka, Japan	162[7]
1971	Sept.	4	Alaska Airlines Boeing 727	Crashed into mountain near Juneau, Alaska	111
1972	Aug.	14	E. German Ilyushin-62	Crashed on take-off East Berlin	156
1972	Oct.	13	Aeroflot Ilyushin-62	E. German airline crashed near Moscow	176
1972	Dec.	3	Chartered Spanish airliner	Crashed on take-off, Canary Islands	155
1972	Dec.	29	Eastern Airlines Lockheed Tristar	Crashed on approach to Miami Int'l. Airport	101
1973	Jan.	22	Chartered Boeing 707	Burst into flames during landing, Kano Airport, Nigeria	176
1973	Feb.	21	Libyan jetliner	Shot down by Israeli fighter planes over Sinai	108
1973	Apr.	10	British Vanguard turboprop	Crashed during snowstorm at Basel, Switzerland	104
1973	June	3	Soviet Supersonic TU-144	Crashed near Goussainville, France	14[8]
1973	July	11	Brazilian Boeing 707	Crashed on approach to Orly Airport, Paris	122
1973	July	31	Delta Airlines jetliner	Crashed, landing in fog at Logan Airport, Boston	89
1973	Dec.	23	French Caravelle jet	Crashed in Morocco	106
1974	Mar.	3	Turkish DC-10 jet	Crashed at Ermenonville near Paris	346
1974	Apr.	23	Pan American 707 jet	Crashed in Bali, Indonesia	107
1974	Dec.	1	TWA-727	Crashed in storm, Upperville, Va.	92
1974	Dec.	4	Dutch-chartered DC-8	Crashed in storm near Colombo, Sri Lanka	191
1975	Apr.	4	Air Force Galaxy C-5B	Crashed near Saigon, So. Vietnam, after takeoff with load of orphans	172
1975	June	24	Eastern Airlines Boeing 727 jet	Crashed in storm, JFK Airport, N.Y. City	113
1975	Aug.	3	Chartered 707	Hit mountainside, Agadir, Morocco	188
1976	Sept.	10	British Airways Trident, Yugoslav DC-9	Collided near Zagreb, Yugoslavia	176
1976	Sept.	19	Turkish 727	Hit mountain, southern Turkey	155
1976	Oct.	13	Bolivian 707 cargo jet	Crashed in Santa Cruz, Bolivia	100[9]
1977	Jan.	13	Aeroflot TU-104	Exploded and crashed at Alma-Ata, Central Asia	90
1977	Mar.	27	KLM 747, Pan American 747	Collided on runway, Tenerife, Canary Islands	582
1977	Nov.	19	TAP Boeing 727	Crashed on Madeira	130
1977	Dec.	4	Malaysian Boeing 737	Hijacked, then exploded in mid-air over Straits of Johore	100
1977	Dec.	13	U.S. DC-3	Crashed after takeoff at Evansville, Ind.	29[10]
1978	Jan.	1	Air India 747	Exploded, crashed into sea off Bombay	213
1978	Sept.	25	Boeing 727, Cessna 172	Collided in air, San Diego, Cal.	150
1978	Nov.	15	Chartered DC-8	Crashed near Colombo, Sri Lanka	183
1979	May	25	American Airlines DC-10	Crashed after takeoff at O'Hare Intl. Airport, Chicago	275[11]
1979	Aug.	17	Two Soviet Aeroflot jetliners	Collided over Ukraine	173

Date			Aircraft	Site of accident	Deaths
1979	Oct.	31	Western Airlines DC-10	Mexico City Airport	74
1979	Nov.	26	Pakistani Boeing 707	Crashed near Jidda, Saudi Arabia	156
1979	Nov.	28	New Zealand DC-10	Crashed into mountain in Antarctica	257
1980	Mar.	14	Polish Ilyushin 62	Crashed making emergency landing, Warsaw	87[12]
1980	Aug.	19	Saudi Arabian Tristar	Burned after emergency landing, Riyadh	301
1981	Dec.	1	Yugoslavian DC-9	Crashed into mountain in Corsica	174
1982	Jan.	13	Air Florida Boeing 737	Crashed into Potomac River after takeoff	78
1982	July	9	Pan-Am Boeing 727	Crashed after takeoff in Kenner, La.	153[13]
1982	Sept.	11	U.S. Army CH-47 Chinook helicopter	Crashed during air show in Mannheim, W. Germany	46
1983	Sept.	1	S. Korean Boeing 747	Shot down after violating Soviet airspace	269
1983	Nov.	27	Colombian Boeing 747	Crashed near Barajas Airport, Madrid	183
1985	Feb.	19	Spanish Boeing 727	Crashed into Mt. Oiz, Spain	148
1985	June	23	Air-India Boeing 747	Crashed into Atlantic Ocean S. of Ireland	329
1985	Aug.	2	Delta Air Lines jumbo jet	Crashed at Dallas-Ft. Worth Intl. Airport	133
1985	Aug.	12	Japan Air Lines Boeing 747	Crashed into Mt. Ogura, Japan	520[14]
1985	Dec.	12	Arrow Air DC 8	Crashed after takeoff in Gander, Newfoundland	256[15]
1986	Mar.	31	Mexican Boeing 727	Crashed NW of Mexico City	166
1986	Aug.	31	Aeromexico DC-9	Collided with Piper PA-28 over Cerritos, Cal.	82[16]
1987	May	9	Ilyushin 62M	Crashed after takeoff in Warsaw, Poland	183
1987	Aug.	16	Northwest Airlines MD-82	Crashed after takeoff in Romulus, Mich.	156
1988	July	3	Iranian A300 Airbus	Shot down by U.S. Navy warship *Vincennes* over Persian Gulf	290
1988	Dec.	21	Pan Am Boeing 747	Exploded and crashed in Lockerbie, Scotland	270[17]
1989	Feb.	8	Boeing 707	Crashed into mountain in Azores Islands off Portugal	144
1989	June	7	Suriname DC-8	Crashed near Paramaribo Airport, Suriname	168
1989	July	19	United Airlines DC-10	Crashed while landing with a disabled hydrolic system, Sioux City, Ia.	111
1989	Sept.	19	French DC-10	Exploded in air over Niger	171
1991	May	26	Austrian Boeing 767-300	Exploded over rural Thailand	223

(1) Including those on the ground and in buildings. (2) First fatal crash of commercial jet plane. (3) Caused by bomb planted by John G. Graham in insurance plot to kill his mother, a passenger. (4) Including all 128 aboard the planes and 6 on ground. (5) Killed 84 on plane and 71 on ground. (6) Including 43 Marshall U. football players and coaches. (7) Airliner-fighter crash, pilot of fighter parachuted to safety, was arrested for negligence. (8) First supersonic plane crash killed 6 crewmen and 8 on the ground; there were no passengers. (9) Crew of 3 killed; 97, mostly children, killed on ground. (10) Including U. of Evansville basketball team. (11) Highest death toll in U.S. aviation history. (12) Including 22 members of U.S. boxing team. (13) Including 8 on ground. (14) Worst single-plane disaster. (15) Incl. 248 members of U.S. 101st Airborne Division. (16) Incl. 15 on the ground. (17) Incl. 11 on the ground.

Notable Railroad Disasters

Date			Location	Deaths	Date			Location	Deaths
1876	Dec.	29	Ashtabula, Oh.	92	1937	July	16	Nr. Patna, India	107
1880	Aug.	11	Mays Landing, N. J.	40	1938	June	19	Saugus, Mont.	47
1887	Aug.	10	Chatsworth, Ill.	81	1939	Aug.	12	Nr. Harney, Nev.	24
1888	Oct.	10	Mud Run, Pa.	55	1939	Dec.	22	Nr. Magdeburg, Germany	132
1891	June	14	Nr. Basel, Switzerland	100	1939	Dec.	22	Nr. Friedrichshafen, Germany	99
1896	July	30	Atlantic City, N. J.	60	1940	Apr.	19	Little Falls, N. Y.	31
1903	Dec.	23	Laurel Run, Pa.	53	1940	July	31	Cuyahoga Falls, Oh.	43
1904	Aug.	7	Eden, Col.	96	1943	Aug.	29	Wayland, N. Y.	27
1904	Sept.	24	New Market Tenn.	56	1943	Sept.	6	Frankford Junction, Philadelphia, Pa.	79
1906	Mar.	16	Florence, Col.	35	1943	Dec.	16	Between Rennert and Buie, N. C.	72
1906	Oct.	28	Atlantic City, N. J.	40	1944	Jan.	16	Leon Province, Spain	500
1906	Dec.	30	Washington, D. C.	53	1944	Mar.	2	Salerno, Italy.	521
1907	Jan.	2	Volland, Kan.	33	1944	July	6	High Bluff, Tenn.	35
1907	Jan.	19	Fowler, Ind.	29	1944	Aug.	4	Near Stockton, Ga.	47
1907	Feb.	16	New York, N.Y.	22	1944	Sept.	14	Dewey, Ind.	29
1907	Feb.	23	Colton, Cal.	26	1944	Dec.	31	Bagley, Utah	50
1907	May	11	Lompoc, Cal.	36	1945	Aug.	9	Michigan, N. D.	34
1907	July	20	Salem, Mich.	33	1946	Mar.	20	Aracaju, Mexico	185
1910	Mar.	1	Wellington, Wash.	96	1946	Apr.	25	Naperville, Ill.	45
1910	Mar.	21	Green Mountain, Ia.	55	1947	Feb.	18	Gallitzin, Pa.	24
1911	Aug.	25	Manchester, N. Y.	29	1949	Oct.	22	Nr. Dwor, Poland	200+
1912	July	4	East Corning, N. Y.	39	1950	Feb.	17	Rockville Centre, N. Y.	31
1912	July	5	Ligonier, Pa.	23	1950	Sept.	11	Coshocton, Oh.	33
1914	Aug.	5	Tipton Ford, Mo.	43	1950	Nov.	22	Richmond Hill, N. Y.	79
1914	Sept.	15	Lebanon, Mo.	28	1951	Feb.	6	Woodbridge, N. J.	84
1915	May	22	Nr. Gretna, Scotland	227	1951	Nov.	12	Wyuta, Wyo.	17
1916	Mar.	29	Amherst, Oh.	27	1951	Nov.	25	Woodstock, Ala.	17
1917	Sept.	28	Kellyville, Okla.	23	1952	Mar.	4	Nr. Rio de Janeiro, Brazil	119
1917	Dec.	12	Modane, France	543[(1)]	1952	July	9	Rzepin, Poland	160
1917	Dec.	20	Shepherdsville, Ky.	46	1952	Oct.	8	Harrow, England	112
1918	June	22	Ivanhoe, Ind.	68	1953	Mar.	27	Conneaut, Oh.	21
1918	July	9	Nashville, Tenn.	101	1955	Apr.	3	Guadalajara, Mexico	300
1918	Nov.	1	Brooklyn, N. Y.	97	1956	Jan.	19	Los Angeles, Cal.	30
1919	Jan.	12	South Byron, N. Y.	22	1956	Feb.	28	Swampscott, Mass.	13
1919	July	1	Dunkirk, N. Y.	12	1956	Sept.	5	Springer, N. M.	20
1919	Dec.	20	Onawa, Maine	23	1957	June	11	Vroman, Col.	12
1921	Feb.	27	Porter, Ind.	37	1957	Sept.	1	Kendal, Jamaica.	178
1921	Dec.	5	Woodmont, Pa.	27	1957	Sept.	29	Montgomery, W. Pakistan	250
1922	Aug.	5	Sulphur Spring, Mo.	34	1957	Dec.	4	London, England	90
1922	Dec.	13	Humble, Tex.	22	1958	May	8	Rio de Janeiro, Brazil	128
1923	Sept.	27	Lockett, Wy.	31	1958	Sept.	15	Elizabethport, N. J.	48
1925	June	16	Hackettstown, N. J.	50	1960	Mar.	14	Bakersfield, Cal.	14
1925	Oct.	27	Victoria, Miss.	21	1960	Nov.	14	Pardubice, Czech.	110
1926	Sept.	5	Waco, Col.	30	1962	Jan.	8	Woerden, Netherlands	91
1928	Aug.	24	I.R.T. subway, Times Sq., N. Y.	18	1962	May	3	Tokyo, Japan	163

(continued)

Date			Location	Deaths	Date			Location	Deaths
1962	July	28	Steelton, Pa.	19	1977	Feb.	4	Chicago, Ill., elevated train	11
1964	July	26	Oporto, Portugal	94	1981	June	6	Bihar, India	500+
1966	Dec.	28	Everett, Mass.	13	1982	Jan.	27	El Asnam, Algeria	130
1970	Feb.	1	Buenos Aires, Argentina	236	1982	July	11	Tepic, Mexico	120
1971	June	10	Salem, Ill.	11	1983	Feb.	19	Empalme, Mexico	100
1972	June	16	Vierzy, France	107	1987	Jan.	4	Essex, Md.	16
1972	July	21	Seville, Spain	76	1988	Dec.	12	London, England	115
1972	Oct.	6	Saltillo, Mexico	208	1989	Jan.	15	Maizdi Khan, Bangladesh.	110+
1972	Oct.	30	Chicago, Ill.	45	1990	Jan.	4	Sindh Province, Pakistan	210+
1974	Aug.	30	Zagreb, Yugoslavia	153	1991	May	14	Shigaraki, Japan.	42
1977	Jan.	18	Granville, Australia	82					

(1) World's worst train wreck; passenger train derailed.

Principal U.S. Mine Disasters Since 1900

Source: Bureau of Mines, U.S. Interior Department.

Note: Prior to 1968, only disasters with losses of 60 or more lives are listed; since 1968, all disasters in which 5 or more people were killed are listed. Only fatalities to mining company employees are included. All bituminous-coal mines unless otherwise noted.

Date		Location	Deaths	Date		Location	Deaths
1900	May 1	Scofield, Ut.	200	1923	Feb. 8	Dawson, N.M.	120
1902	May 19	Coal Creek, Tenn.	184	1923	Aug. 14	Kemmerer, Wy.	99
1902	July 10	Johnstown, Pa.	112	1924	Mar. 8	Castle Gate, Ut.	171
1903	June 30	Hanna, Wy.	169	1924	Apr. 28	Benwood, W. Va.	119
1904	Jan. 25	Cheswick, Pa.	179	1926	Jan. 13	Wilburton, Okla.	91
1905	Feb. 20	Virginia City, Ala.	112	1926[2]	Nov. 3	Ishpeming, Mich.	51
1907	Jan. 29	Stuart W. Va.	84	1927	Apr. 30	Everettville, W. Va.	97
1907	Dec. 6	Monongah, W. Va.	361	1928	May 19	Mather, Pa.	195
1907	Dec. 19	Jacobs Creek, Pa.	239	1929	Dec. 17	McAlester, Okla.	61
1908	Nov. 28	Marianna, Pa.	154	1930	Nov. 5	Millfield, Oh.	79
1909	Jan. 12	Switchback, W. Va.	67	1940	Jan. 10	Bartley, W. Va.	91
1909	Nov. 13	Cherry, Ill.	259	1940	Mar. 16	St. Clairsville, Oh.	72
1910	Jan. 31	Primero, Col.	75	1940	July 15	Portage, Pa.	63
1910	May 5	Palos, Ala.	90	1943	Feb. 27	Washoe, Mon.	74
1910	Nov. 8	Delagua, Col.	79	1944	July 5	Belmont, Oh.	66
1911[1]	Apr. 7	Throop, Pa.	72	1947	Mar. 25	Centralia, Ill.	111
1911	Apr. 8	Littleton, Ala.	128	1951	Dec. 21	West Frankfort, Ill.	119
1911	Dec. 9	Briceville, Tenn.	84	1968[3]	Mar. 6	Calumet, La.	21
1912	Mar. 20	McCurtain, Okla.	73	1968	Nov. 20	Farmington, W. Va.	78
1912	Mar. 26	Jed, W. Va.	83	1970	Dec. 30	Hyden, Ky.	38
1913	Apr. 23	Finleyville, Pa.	96	1972[2]	May 2	Kellogg, Ida.	91
1913	Oct. 22	Dawson, N.M.	263	1976	Mar. 9, 11	Oven Fork, Ky.	26
1914	Apr. 28	Eccles, W. Va.	181	1977	Mar. 1	Tower City, Pa.	9
1915	Mar. 2	Layland, W. Va.	112	1981	Apr. 15	Redstone, Col.	15
1917	Apr. 27	Hastings, Col.	121	1981	Dec. 7	Topmost, Ky.	8
1917[2]	June 8	Butte, Mon.	163	1981	Dec. 8	nr. Chattanooga, Tenn.	13
1917	Aug. 4	Clay, Ky.	62	1982	Jan. 20	Floyd County, Ky.	7
1919[1]	June 5	Wilkes-Barre, Pa.	92	1983	June 21	McClure, Va	7
1922	Nov. 6	Spangler, Pa.	77	1984	Dec. 19	Huntington, Ut.	27
1922	Nov. 22	Dolomite, Ala.	90	1989	Sept. 13	Wheatcroft, Ky.	10

(1) Anthracite mine. (2) Metal mine. (3) Nonmetal mine.
World's worst mine disaster killed 1,549 workers in Honkeiko Colliery in Manchuria Apr. 25, 1942.

Some Notable Tornadoes In U.S. Since 1925

Date			Location	Deaths	Date			Location	Deaths
1925	Mar.	18	Mo., Ill. Ind.	689	1960	May	5, 6	SE Oklahoma, Arkansas	30
1927	Apr.	12	Rock Springs, Tex.	74	1965	Apr.	11	Ind., Ill., Oh., Mich., Wis.	271
1927	May	9	Arkansas, Poplar Bluff, Mo.	92	1966	Mar.	3	Jackson, Miss.	57
1927	Sept.	29	St. Louis, Mo.	90	1966	Mar.	3	Mississippi, Alabama.	61
1930	May	6	Hill, Navarro, Ellis Co., Tex.	41	1967	Apr.	21	Ill., Mich.	33
1932	Mar.	21	Ala. (series of tornadoes)	268	1968	May	15	Midwest	71
1936	Apr.	5	Miss., Ga.	455	1969	Jan.	23	Mississippi.	32
1936	Apr.	6	Gainesville, Ga.	203	1971	Feb.	21	Mississippi delta	110
1938	Sept.	29	Charleston, S.C.	32	1973	May	26-27	South, Midwest (series)	47
1942	Mar.	16	Central to NE Miss.	75	1974	Apr.	3-4	Ala., Ga., Tenn., Ky., Oh.	350
1942	Apr.	27	Rogers & Mayes Co., Okla.	52	1977	Apr.	4	Ala., Miss., Ga.	22
1944	June	23	Oh., Pa., W. Va., Md.	150	1979	Apr.	10	Tex., Okla.	60
1945	Apr.	12	Okla.-Ark.	102	1980	June	3	Grand Island, Neb. (series)	4
1947	Apr.	9	Tex., Okla. & Kan.	169	1982	Mar.	2-4	South, Midwest (series)	17
1948	Mar.	19	Bunker Hill & Gillespie, Ill.	33	1982	May	29	So. Ill.	10
1949	Jan.	3	La. & Ark.	58	1983	May	18-22	Tex.	12
1952	Mar.	21	Ark., Mo., Tenn. (series)	208	1984	Mar.	28	N. Carolina; S. Carolina	67
1953	May	11	Waco, Tex.	114	1984	Apr.	21-22	Mississippi	15
1953	June	8	Mich., Oh.	142	1984	Apr.	26	Series Okla to Minn.	17
1953	June	9	Worcester and vicinity, Mass.	90	1985	May	31	N.Y., Pa., Oh., Ont. (series)	90
1953	Dec.	5	Vicksburg, Miss.	38	1987	May	22	Saragosa, Tex.	29
1955	May	25	Kan., Mo., Okla., Tex.	115	1990	June	2-3	Midwest, Great Lakes	13
1957	May	20	Kan., Mo.	48	1990	Aug.	28	N. Ill.	25
1958	June	4	Northwestern Wisconsin	30	1991	Apr.	26	Kan., Okla.	23
1959	Feb.	10	St. Louis, Mo.	21					

Hurricanes, Typhoons, Blizzards, Other Storms

Names of hurricanes and typhoons in italics—H.—hurricane; T.—typhoon

Date	Location	Deaths
1888 Mar. 11-14	Blizzard, Eastern U.S..	400
1900 Aug.-Sept.	H., Galveston, Tex.	6,000
1906 Sept. 21	H., La., Miss.	350
1906 Sept. 18	Typhoon, Hong Kong	10,000
1926 Sept. 11-22	H., Fla., Ala.	243
1926 Oct. 20	H., Cuba	600
1928 Sept. 6-20	H., So. Fla.	1,836
1930 Sept. 3	H., Dominican Rep.	2,000
1938 Sept. 21	H., Long Island N.Y., New England	600
1940 Nov. 11-12	Blizzard, U.S. NE, Midwest	144
1942 Oct. 15-16	H., Bengal, India	40,000
1944 Sept. 9-16	H., N.C. to New Eng.	46
1952 Oct. 22	Typhoon, Philippines	0,300
1954 Aug. 30	H. Carol, Northeast U.S.	68
1954 Oct. 5-18	H. Hazel, Eastern, U.S., Haiti.	347
1955 Aug. 12-13	H. Connie, Carolinas, Va., Md.	43
1955 Aug. 7-21	H. Diane, Eastern U.S.	400
1955 Sept. 19	H. Hilda, Mexico	200
1955 Sept. 22-28	H. Janet, Caribbean	500
1956 Feb. 1-29	Blizzard, Western Europe.	1,000
1957 June 25-30	H. Audrey, Tex. to Ala.	390
1958 Feb. 15-16	Blizzard, NE U.S.	171
1959 Sept. 17-19	T. Sarah, Japan, S. Korea	2,000
1959 Sept. 26-27	T. Vera, Honshu, Japan.	4,466
1960 Sept. 4-12	H. Donna, Caribbean, E. U.S.	148
1961 Sept. 11-14	H. Carla, Tex.	46
1961 Oct. 31	H. Hattie, Br. Honduras.	400
1963 May 28-29	Windstorm, Bangladesh.	22,000
1963 Oct. 4-8	H. Flora, Caribbean	6,000
1964 Oct. 4-7	H. Hilda, La., Miss., Ga.	38
1964 June 30	T. Winnie, N. Philippines	107
1964 Sept. 5	T. Ruby, Hong Kong and China	735
1965 May 11-12	Windstorm, Bangladesh.	17,000
1965 June 1-2	Windstorm, Bangladesh.	30,000
1965 Sept. 7-12	H. Betsy, Fla., Miss., La.	74
1965 Dec. 15	Windstorm, Bangladesh.	10,000
1966 June 4-10	H. Alma, Honduras, SE U.S.	51
1966 Sept. 24-30	H. Inez, Carib., Fla., Mex..	293

Date	Location	Deaths
1967 July 9	T. Billie, SW Japan	347
1967 Sept. 5-23	H. Beulah, Carib., Mex., Tex.	54
1967 Dec. 12-20	Blizzard, Southwest, U.S..	51
1968 Nov. 18-28	T. Nina, Philippines	63
1969 Aug. 17-18	H. Camille, Miss., La.	256
1970 July 30-		
Aug. 5	H. Celia, Cuba, Fla., Tex.	31
1970 Aug. 20-21	H. Dorothy, Martinique	42
1970 Sept. 15	T. Georgia, Philippines	300
1970 Oct. 14	T. Sening, Philippines	583
1970 Oct. 15	T. Titang, Philippines	526
1970 Nov. 13	Cyclone, Bangladesh	300,000
1971 Aug. 1	T. Rose, Hong Kong.	130
1972 June 19-29	H. Agnes, Fla. to N.Y.	118
1972 Dec. 3	T. Theresa, Philippines	169
1973 June-Aug.	Monsoon rains in India	1,217
1974 June 11	Storm Dinah, Luzon Is., Philip.	71
1974 July 11	T. Gilda, Japan, S. Korea.	108
1974 Sept. 19-20	H. Fifi, Honduras.	2,000
1974 Dec. 25	Cyclone leveled Darwin, Aus.	50
1975 Sept. 13-27	H. Eloise, Caribbean, NE U.S.	71
1976 May 20	T. Olga, floods, Philippines	215
1977 July 25, 31	T. Thelma, T. Vera, Taiwan.	39
1978 Oct. 27	T. Rita, Philippines.	c. 400
1979 Aug. 30-		
Sept. 7	H. David, Caribbean, East. U.S.	1,100
1980 Aug. 4-11	H. Allen, Caribbean, Texas	272
1981 Nov. 25	T. Irma, Luzon Is., Philippines.	176
1983 June	Monsoon rains in India	900
1983 Aug. 18	H. Alicia, southern Texas	17
1984 Sept. 2	T. Ike, southern Philippines	1,363
1985 May 25	Cyclone, Bangladesh	10,000
1985 Oct. 26-		
Nov. 6	H. Juan, SE U.S..	97
1987 Nov. 25	T. Nina, Philippines	650
1989 Sept. 16-22	H. Hugo, Caribbean, SE U.S.	504
1990 May 6-11	Cyclones, SE India	450
1991 Apr. 30	Cyclone, Bangladesh	200,000+

Floods, Tidal Waves

Date		Location	Deaths
1228	....	Holland	100,000
1642	....	China	300,000
1887	....	Huang He River, China	900,000
1889	May 31	Johnstown, Pa..	2,200
1900	Sept. 8	Galveston, Tex.	5,000
1903	June 15	Heppner, Ore.	325
1911	....	Chang Jiang River, China.	100,000
1913	Mar. 25-27	Ohio, Indiana	732
1915	Aug. 17	Galveston, Tex.	275
1928	Mar. 13	Collapse of St. Francis	
		Dam, Saugus, Cal.	450
1928	Sept. 13	Lake Okeechobee, Fla.	2,000
1931	Aug.	Huang He River, China	3,700,000
1937	Jan. 22	Ohio, Miss. Valleys	250
1939	....	Northern China.	200,000
1946	Apr. 1	Hawaii, Alaska	159
1947	....	Honshu Island, Japan.	1,900
1951	Aug.	Manchuria	1,800
1953	Jan. 31	Western Europe	2,000
1954	Aug. 17	Farahzad, Iran	2,000
1955	Oct. 7-12	India, Pakistan	1,700
1959	Nov. 1	Western Mexico	2,000
1959	Dec. 2	Frejus, France	412
1960	Oct. 10	Bangladesh.	6,000
1960	Oct. 31	Bangladesh.	4,000
1962	Feb. 17	German North Sea coast	343
1962	Sept. 27	Barcelona, Spain	445
1963	Oct. 9	Dam collapse, Vaiont, Italy	1,800
1966	Nov. 3-4	Florence, Venice, Italy.	113
1967	Jan. 18-24	Eastern Brazil	894
1967	Mar. 19	Rio de Janeiro, Brazil	436
1967	Nov. 26	Lisbon, Portugal	464
1968	Aug. 7-14	Gujarat State, India	1,000
1968	Oct. 7	Northeastern India.	780
1969	Jan. 18-26	So. Cal.	100
1969	Mar. 17	Mundau Valley, Alagoas, Brazil	218

Date		Location	Deaths
1969	Aug. 20-22	Western Virginia	189
1969	Sept. 15	South Korea	250
1969	Oct. 1-8	Tunisia	500
1970	May 20	Central Romania.	160
1970	July 22	Himalayas, India.	500
1971	Feb. 26	Rio de Janeiro, Brazil	130
1972	Feb. 26	Buffalo Creek, W. Va.	118
1972	June 9	Rapid City, S.D.	236
1972	Aug. 7	Luzon Is., Philippines	454
1973	Aug. 19-31	Pakistan	1,500
1974	Mar. 29	Tubaro, Brazil	1,000
1974	Aug. 12	Monty-Long, Bangladesh.	2,500
1976	June 5	Teton Dam collapse, Ida.	11
1976	July 31	Big Thompson Canyon, Col.	139
1976	Nov. 17	East Java, Indonesia	136
1977	July 19-20	Johnstown, Pa.	68
1978	June-Sept.	Northern India	1,200
1979	Jan.-Feb.	Brazil	204
1979	July 17	Lomblen Is., Indonesia	539
1979	Aug. 11	Morvi, India.	5,000-15,000
1980	Feb. 13-22	So. Cal., Ariz.	26
1981	Apr.	Northern China.	550
1981	July	Sichuan, Hubei Prov., China	1,300
1982	Jan. 23	Nr. Lima, Peru	600
1982	May 12	Guangdong, China.	430
1982	June 6	So. Conn.	12
1982	Sept. 17-21	El Salvador, Guatemala.	1,300+
1982	Dec. 2-9	Ill., Mo., Ark.	22
1983	Feb.-Mar.	Cal. coast.	13
1983	Apr. 6-12	Ala., La., Miss., Tenn.	15
1984	May 27	Tulsa, Okla.	13
1984	Aug.-Sept.	S. Korea	200+
1985	July 19	Northern Italy, dam burst	361
1987	Aug.-Sept.	Northern Bangladesh	1,000+
1988	Sept.	Northern India	1,000+
1990	June 14	Shadyside, Oh..	23

Fires

Date		Location	Deaths
1835	Dec. 16	New York City, 500 bldgs. destroyed	—

Date		Location	Deaths
1845	May	Canton, China, theater.	1,670

(continued)

Date			Location	Deaths	Date			Location	Deaths
1871	Oct.	8	Chicago, $196 million loss	250	1966	Oct.	17	N. Y. City bldg. (firemen)	12
1871	Oct.	8	Peshtigo, Wis., forest fire	1,182	1966	Dec.	7	Erzurum, Turkey, barracks	68
1872	Nov.	9	Boston, 800 bldgs. destroyed	—	1967	Feb.	7	Montgomery, Ala., restaurant	25
1876	Dec.	5	Brooklyn (N.Y.), theater	295	1967	May	22	Brussels, Belgium, store	322
1877	June	20	St. John, N. B., Canada	100	1967	July	16	Jay, Fla., state prison	37
1881	Dec.	8	Ring Theater, Vienna	850	1968	Feb.	26	Shrewsbury, England, hospital	22
1887	May	25	Opera Comique, Paris	200	1968	May	11	Vijayawada, India, wedding hall	58
1887	Sept.	4	Exeter, England, theater	200	1968	Nov.	18	Glasgow, Scotland, factory	24
1894	Sept.	1	Minn., forest fire	413	1969	Jan.	26	Victoria Hotel, Dunnville, Ont.	13
1897	May	4	Paris, charity bazaar	150	1969	Dec.	2	Notre Dame, Can., nursing home	54
1900	June	30	Hoboken, N. J., docks	326	1970	Jan.	9	Marietta, Oh., nursing home	27
1902	Sept.	20	Birmingham, Ala., church	115	1970	Mar.	20	Seattle, Wash., hotel	19
1903	Dec.	30	Iroquois Theater, Chicago	602	1970	Nov.	1	Grenoble, France, dance hall	145
1908	Jan.	13	Rhoads Theater, Boyertown, Pa.	170	1970	Dec.	20	Tucson, Arizona, hotel	28
1908	Mar.	4	Collinwood, Oh., school	176	1971	Mar.	6	Burghoezli, Switzerland,	
1911	Mar.	25	Triangle factory, N. Y. City	145				psychiatric clinic	28
1913	Oct.	14	Mid Glamorgan, Wales, colliery	439	1971	Apr.	20	Hotel, Bangkok, Thailand	24
1918	Apr.	13	Norman Okla., state hospital	38	1971	Oct.	19	Honesdale, Pa., nursing home	15
1918	Oct.	12	Cloquet, Minn., forest fire	400	1971	Dec.	25	Hotel, Seoul, So. Korea	162
1919	June	20	Mayaguez Theater, San Juan	150	1972	May	13	Osaka, Japan, nightclub	116
1923	May	17	Camden, S. C., school	76	1972	July	5	Sherborne, England, hospital	30
1924	Dec.	24	Hobart, Okla., school	35	1973	Feb.	6	Paris, France, school	21
1929	May	15	Cleveland, Oh., clinic	125	1973	Nov.	6	Fukui, Japan, train	28
1930	Apr.	21	Columbus, Oh., penitentiary	320	1973	Nov.	29	Kumamoto, Japan, department	
1931	July	24	Pittsburgh, Pa., home for aged	48				store	107
1934	Dec.	11	Hotel Kerns, Lansing, Mich.	34	1973	Dec.	2	Seoul, Korea, theater	50
1938	May	16	Atlanta, Ga., Terminal Hotel	35	1974	Feb.	1	Sao Paulo, Brazil, bank building	189
1940	Apr.	23	Natchez, Miss., dance hall	198	1974	June	30	Port Chester, N. Y., discotheque	24
1942	Nov.	28	Cocoanut Grove, Boston	491	1974	Nov.	3	Seoul, So. Korea, hotel discotheque	88
1942			St. John's, Newfoundland, hostel	100	1975	Dec.	12	Mina, Saudi Arabia, tent city	138
1943	Sept.	7	Gulf Hotel, Houston	55	1976	Oct.	24	Bronx, N.Y., social club	25
1944	July	6	Ringling Circus, Hartford	168	1977	Feb.	25	Moscow, Rossiya hotel	45
1946	June	5	LaSalle Hotel, Chicago	61	1977	May	28	Southgate, Ky., nightclub	164
1946	Dec.	7	Winecoff Hotel, Atlanta	119	1977	June	9	Abidjan, Ivory Coast, nightclub	41
1946	Dec.	12	New York, ice plant, tenement	37	1977	June	26	Columbia, Tenn., jail	42
1949	Apr.	5	Effingham, Ill., hospital	77	1977	Nov.	14	Manila, PI, hotel	47
1950	Jan.	7	Davenport, Ia., Mercy Hospital	41	1978	Jan.	28	Kansas City, Coates House Hotel	16
1953	Mar.	29	Largo, Fla., nursing home	35	1979	July	14	Saragossa, Spain, hotel	80
1953	Apr.	16	Chicago, metalworking plant	35	1979	Dec.	31	Chapais, Quebec, social club	42
1957	Feb.	17	Warrenton, Mo., home for aged	72	1980	May	20	Kingston, Jamaica, nursing home	157
1958	Mar.	19	New York City, loft building	24	1980	Nov.	21	MGM Grand Hotel, Las Vegas	84
1958	Dec.	1	Chicago, parochial school	95	1980	Dec.	4	Stouffer Inn, Harrison, N.Y.	26
1958	Dec.	16	Bogota, Colombia, store	83	1981	Jan.	9	Keansburg, N.J., boarding home	30
1959	June	23	Stalheim, Norway, resort hotel	34	1981	Feb.	10	Las Vegas Hilton	8
1960	Mar.	12	Pusan, Korea, chemical plant	68	1981	Feb.	14	Dublin, Ireland, discotheque	44
1960	July	14	Guatemala City, mental hospital	225	1982	Sept.	4	Los Angeles, apartment house	24
1960	Nov.	13	Amude, Syria, movie theater	152	1982	Nov.	8	Biloxi, Miss., county jail	29
1961	Jan.	6	Thomas Hotel, San Francisco	20	1983	Feb.	13	Turin, Italy, movie theater	64
1961	Dec.	8	Hartford, Conn., hospital	16	1983	Dec.	17	Madrid, Spain, discotheque	83
1961	Dec.	17	Niteroi, Brazil, circus	323	1984	May	11	Great Adventure Amusement Park,	
1963	May	4	Diourbel, Senegal, theater	64				N.J.	8
1963	Nov.	16	Surfside Hotel, Atlantic City, N.J.	25	1985	Apr.	21	Tabaco, Philippines, movie theater	44
1963	Nov.	23	Fitchville, Oh., rest home	63	1985	Apr.	26	Buenos Aires, Argentina hospital	79
1963	Dec.	29	Roosevelt Hotel, Jacksonville, Fla.	22	1985	May	11	Bradford, England, soccer stadium	53
1964	May	8	Manila, apartment bldg	30	1986	Dec.	31	Puerto Rico, Dupont Plaza Hotel	96
1964	Dec.	18	Fountaintown, Ind., nursing home	20	1987	May 6-			
1965	Mar.	1	LaSalle, Canada, apartment	28		June 2		Northern China forest fire	193
1966	Mar.	11	Numata, Japan, 2 ski resorts	31	1987	Nov.	17	London, England subway	30
1966	Aug.	13	Melbourne, Australia, hotel	29	1990	Mar.	25	N.Y. City social club	87
1966	Sept.	12	Anchorage, Alaska, hotel	14					

Explosions

Date			Location	Deaths	Date			Location	Deaths
1910	Oct.	1	Los Angeles Times Bldg.,	21	1958	May	22	Nike missiles, Leonardo, N.J.	10
1913	Mar.	7	Dynamite, Baltimore harbor	55	1959	Jan.	10	World War II bomb, Philippines	38
1915	Sept.	27	Gasoline tank car, Ardmore, Okla.	47	1959	June	28	Rail tank cars, Meldrin, Ga.	25
1917	Apr.	10	Munitions plant, Eddystone, Pa.	133	1959	Aug.	7	Dynamite truck, Roseburg, Ore.	13
1917	Dec.	6	Halifax Harbor, Canada	1,654	1959	Nov.	2	Jamuri Bazar, India, explosives	46
1918	May	18	Chemical plant, Oakdale, Pa.	193	1959	Dec.	13	Dortmund, Ger., 2 apt. bldgs.	26
1918	July	2	Explosives, Split Rock, N.Y.	50	1960	Mar.	4	Belgian munitions ship, Havana	100
1918	Oct.	4	Shell plant, Morgan Station, N.J.	64	1960	Oct.	25	Gas, Windsor, Ont., store	11
1919	May	22	Food plant, Cedar Rapids, Ia.	44	1962	Jan.	16	Gas pipeline, Edson, Alberta, Canada	8
1920	Sept.	16	Wall Street, New York, bomb	30	1962	Oct.	3	Telephone Co. office, N. Y. City	23
1924	Jan.	3	Food plant, Pekin, Ill.	42	1963	Jan.	2	Packing plant, Terre Haute, Ind.	16
1928	April	13	Dance hall, West Plains, Mo.	40	1963	Mar.	9	Dynamite plant, S. Africa	45
1937	Mar.	18	New London, Tex., school	413	1963	Aug.	13	Explosives dump, Gauhiti, India	32
1940	Sept.	12	Hercules Powder, Kenvil, N.J.	55	1963	Oct.	31	State Fair Coliseum, Indianapolis	73
1942	June	5	Ordnance plant, Elwood, Ill.	49	1964	July	23	Bone, Algeria, harbor munitions	100
1944	Apr.	14	Bombay, India, harbor	700	1965	Apr.	4	Gas pipeline, Natchitoches, La.	17
1944	July	17	Port Chicago, Cal., pier	322	1965	Aug.	9	Missile silo, Searcy, Ark.	53
1944	Oct.	21	Liquid gas tank, Cleveland	135	1965	Oct.	21	Bridge, Tila Bund, Pakistan	80
1947	Apr.	16	Texas City, Tex., pier	561	1965	Oct.	30	Cartagena, Colombia	48
1948	July	28	Farben works, Ludwigshafen, Ger.	184	1965	Nov.	24	Armory, Keokuk, Ia.	20
1950	May	19	Munitions barges, S. Amboy, N. J.	30	1966	Oct.	13	Chemical plant, La Salle, Que.	11
1956	Aug.	7	Dynamite trucks, Cali, Colombia	1,100	1967	Feb.	17	Chemical plant, Hawthorne, N.J.	11
1958	Apr.	18	Sunken munitions ship, Okinawa	40	1967	Dec.	25	Apartment bldg., Moscow	20

Date		Location	Deaths	Date		Location	Deaths
1968	Apr. 6	Sports store, Richmond, Ind.	43	1981	Feb. 13	Sewer system, Louisville, Ky.	0
1970	Apr. 8	Subway construction, Osaka, Japan	73	1982	Apr. 7	Tanker truck, tunnel, Oakland, Cal. .	7
1971	June 24	Tunnel, Sylmar, Cal.	17	1982	Apr. 25	Antiques exhibition, Todi, Italy	33
1971	June 28	School, fireworks, Pueblo, Mex. . . .	13	1982	Nov. 2	Salang Tunnel, Afghanistan. . 1,000-3,000	
1971	Oct. 21	Shopping center, Glasgow, Scot. . .	20	1984	Feb. 25	Oil pipeline, Cubatao, Brazil	508
1973	Feb. 10	Liquified gas tank, Staten Is., N.Y. . .	40	1984	June 21	Naval supply depot, Severomorsk,	
1975	Dec. 27	Chasnala, India, mine.	431			USSR	200+
1976	Apr. 13	Lapua, Finland, munitions works . .	40	1984	Nov. 19	Gas storage area, NE Mexico City .	334
1977	Nov. 11	Freight train, Iri, S. Korea.	57	1984	Dec. 5	Coal mine, Taipei, Taiwan	94
1977	Dec. 22	Grain elevator, Westwego, La. . . .	35	1985	June 25	Fireworks factory, Hallett, Okla. . . .	21
1978	Feb. 24	Derailed tank car, Waverly, Tenn. . .	12	1988	July 6	Oil rig, North Sea	167
1978	July 11	Propylene tank truck, Spanish		1989	June 3	Gas pipeline, between Ufa, Asha,	
		coastal campsite.	150			USSR	650+
1980	Oct. 23	School, Ortuella, Spain.	64				

Notable Nuclear Accidents

Oct. 7, 1957 — A fire in the Windscale plutonium production reactor north of Liverpool, England spread radioactive material throughout the countryside. In 1983, the British government said that 39 people probably died of cancer as a result.

1957 — A chemical explosion in Kasli, USSR, in tanks containing nuclear waste, spread radioactive material and forced a major evacuation.

Jan. 3, 1961 — An experimental reactor at a federal installation near Idaho Falls, Id. killed three workers—the only deaths in U.S. reactor operations. The plant had high radiation levels but damage was contained.

Oct. 5, 1966 — A sodium cooling system malfunction caused a partial core meltdown at the Enrico Fermi demonstration breeder reactor near Detroit, Mich. Radiation was contained.

Jan. 21, 1969 — A coolant malfunction from an experimental underground reactor in Lucens Vad, Switzerland resulted in the release of a large amount of radiation into a cavern, which was then sealed.

Nov. 19, 1971 — The water-storage space at the Northern States Power Co.'s reactor in Monticello, Minn. filled to capacity and spilled over, dumping about 50,000 gallons of radioactive waste water into the Mississippi River. Some was taken into the St. Paul water system.

Mar. 22, 1975 — A technician checking for air leaks with a lighted candle caused a $100 million fire at the Brown's Ferry reactor in Decatur, Ala. The fire burned out electrical controls, lowering the cooling water to dangerous levels.

Mar. 28, 1979 — The worst commercial nuclear accident in the U.S. occured as equipment failures and human mistakes led to a loss of coolant, and partial core meltdown at the Three Mile Island reactor in Middletown, Pa.

Aug. 7, 1979 — Highly enriched uranium was released from a top-secret nuclear fuel plant near Erwin, Tenn. About 1,000 people were contaminated with up to 5 times as much radiation as would normally be received in a year.

Feb. 11, 1981 — Eight workers were contaminated when over 100,000 gallons of radioactive coolant leaked into the containment building of the TVA's Sequoyah 1 plant in Tennessee.

Apr. 25, 1981 — Some 100 workers were exposed to radioactive material during repairs of a nuclear plant at Tsuruga, Japan.

Jan. 25, 1982 — A steam-generator pipe broke at the Rochester Gas & Electric Co's Ginna plant near Rochester, N.Y. Small amounts of radioactive steam escaped into the air.

Jan. 6, 1986 — A cylinder of nuclear material burst after being improperly heated at a Kerr-McGee plant at Gore, Okla. One worker died and 100 were hospitalized.

Apr., 1986 — A serious accident at the Chernobyl nuclear plant about 60 miles from Kiev in the Soviet Union spewed clouds of radiation that spread over several European nations.

Record Oil Spills

As a rule, the number of tons can be multiplied by 7 to estimate the number of barrels spilled; the exact number of barrels in a ton varies with the type of oil. Each barrel contains 42 gallons.

Name, place	Date	Cause	Tons
Ixtoc I oil well, southern Gulf of Mexico	June 3, 1979	Blowout	600,000
Nowruz oil field, Persian Gulf.	Feb., 1983	Blowout	600,000 (est.)
Atlantic Empress & Aegean Captain, off Trinidad & Tobago	July 19, 1979.	Collision	300,000
Castillo de Bellver, off Cape Town, South Africa.	Aug. 6, 1983	Fire.	250,000
Amoco Cadiz, near Portsall, France.	March 16, 1978	Grounding	223,000
Torrey Canyon, off Land's End, England	March 18, 1967	Grounding	119,000
Sea Star, Gulf of Oman.	Dec. 19, 1972	Collision	115,000
Urquiola, La Coruna, Spain.	May 12, 1976.	Grounding	100,000
Hawaiian Patriot, northern Pacific	Feb. 25, 1977.	Fire.	99,000
Othello, Tralhavet Bay, Sweden.	March 20, 1970	Collision	60,000-100,000

Other Notable Oil Spills

Name, place	Date	Cause	Gallons
Persian Gulf	Jan. 23, 1991 (began)	Spillage by Iraq. . . .	130,000,000*
World Glory, off South Africa.	June 13, 1968	Hull failure.	13,524,000
Burmah Agate, Galveston Bay, Tex..	Nov. 1, 1979	Collision	10,700,000
Exxon Valdez, Prince William Sound, Alas.	Mar. 24, 1989	Grounding	10,080,000
Keo, off Massachusetts	Nov. 5, 1969	Hull failure.	8,820,000
Storage tank, Sewaren, N.J.	Nov. 4, 1969	Tank rupture	8,400,000
Ekofisk oil field, North Sea	Apr. 22, 1977.	Well blowout	8,200,000
Argo Merchant, Nantucket, Mass.	Dec. 15, 1976	Grounding	7,700,000
Pipeline, West Delta, La.	Oct. 15, 1967.	Dragging anchor . . .	6,720,000
Tanker off Japan.	Nov. 30, 1971	Ship broke in half. . .	6,258,000
Storage tank, Monongahela River	Jan. 2, 1988	Tank rupture	3,800,000

* Estimated by Saudi Arabia. Some estimates are as low as 25,000,000 gallons.

Notable Recent Oil Spills

Date	Place	Cause	Gallons
1990, Sept. 16	Saginaw River, Mich.	Unloading difficulties	1,500,000
Aug. 6	Mediterranean Sea, Spain	Collision	3,000,000
July 28	Galveston Bay, Tex.	Collision	700,000
June 28	Suez Canal, Egypt	Ran aground	2,000,000
June 9	Gulf of Mexico	Explosion on tanker.	3,900,000
June 7	Kill Van Kull, N.J.	Ran aground	260,000
Apr. 26	Gorman, Tex.	Pipeline rupture	150,000
Apr. 2	Syzran, USSR	Not available	2,000,000
Mar. 6	Arthur Kill Waterway, N.Y.-N.J.	Explosion on barge	130,000
Mar. 3	Allegheny River, Pa.	Ruptured pipeline	75,000
Feb. 7	Huntington Beach, Cal.	Hull puncture	400,000

Major Earthquakes

Magnitude of earthquakes (Mag.), distinct from deaths or damage caused, is measured on the Richter scale, on which each higher number represents a tenfold increase in energy measured in ground motion. Adopted in 1935, the scale has been applied in the following table to earthquakes as far back as reliable seismograms are available.

Date	Location	Deaths	Mag.	Date	Location	Deaths	Mag.
526 May 20	Syria, Antioch	250,000	N.A.	1962 Sept. 1	Northwestern Iran	12,230	7.1
856	Greece, Corinth	45,000	"	1963 July 26	Yugoslavia, Skopje	1,100	6.0
1057	China, Chihli	25,000	"	1964 Mar. 27	Alaska	131	8.4
1268	Asia Minor, Cilicia	60,000	"	1966 Aug. 19	Eastern Turkey	2,520	6.9
1290 Sept. 27	China, Chihli	100,000	"	1968 Aug. 31	Northeastern Iran	12,000	7.4
1293 May 20	Japan, Kamakura	30,000	"	1970 Jan. 5	Yunnan Province, China	10,000	7.7
1531 Jan. 26	Portugal, Lisbon	30,000	"	1970 Mar. 28	Western Turkey	1,086	7.4
1556 Jan. 24	China, Shaanxi.	830,000	"	1970 May 31	Northern Peru	66,794	7.7
1667 Nov.	Caucasia, Shemaka.	80,000	"	1971 Feb. 9	San Fernando Val-		
1693 Jan. 11	Italy, Catania.	60,000	"		ley, Cal.	65	6.6
1730 Dec. 30	Japan, Hokkaido.	137,000	"	1972 Apr. 10	Southern Iran	5,057	6.9
1737 Oct. 11	India, Calcutta	300,000	"	1972 Dec. 23	Nicaragua	5,000	6.2
1755 June 7	Northern Persia	40,000	"	1974 Dec. 28	Pakistan (9 towns)	5,200	6.3
1755 Nov. 1	Portugal, Lisbon	60,000	8.75*	1975 Sept. 6	Turkey (Lice, etc.).	2,312	6.8
1783 Feb. 4	Italy, Calabria	30,000	N.A.	1976 Feb. 4	Guatemala	22,778	7.5
1797 Feb. 4	Ecuador, Quito.	41,000	"	1976 May 6	Northeast Italy	946	6.5
1811-12	New Madrid, Mo. (series).	—	8.7*	1976 June 26	New Guinea, Irian Jaya.	443	7.1
1822 Sept. 5	Asia Minor, Aleppo	22,000	"	1976 July 28	China, Tangshan.	242,000	8.2
1828 Dec. 28	Japan, Echigo	30,000	"	1976 Aug. 17	Philippines, Mindanao.	8,000	7.8
1868 Aug. 13-15	Peru and Ecuador	40,000	"	1976 Nov. 24	E. Turkey.	4,000	7.9
1875 May 16	Venezuela, Colombia.	16,000	"	1977 Mar. 4	Romania	1,541	7.5
1886 Aug. 31	Charleston, S.C.	60	6.6	1977 Aug. 19	Indonesia	200	8.0
1896 June 15	Japan, sea wave	27,120	N.A.	1977 Nov. 23	Northwestern Argentina	100	8.2
1906 Apr. 18-19	San Francisco, Cal.	503	8.3	1978 June 12	Japan, Sendai	21	7.5
1906 Aug. 16	Chile, Valparaiso	20,000	8.6	1978 Sept. 16	Northeast Iran	25,000	7.7
1908 Dec. 28	Italy, Messina	83,000	7.5	1979 Sept. 12	Indonesia.	100	8.1
1915 Jan. 13	Italy, Avezzano	29,980	7.5	1979 Dec. 12	Colombia, Ecuador	800	7.9
1920 Dec. 16	China, Gansu	100,000	8.6	1980 Oct. 10	Northwestern Algeria	4,500	7.3
1923 Sept. 1	Japan, Yokohama.	200,000	8.3	1980 Nov. 23	Southern Italy	4,800	7.2
1927 May 22	China, Nan-Shan	200,000	8.3	1982 Dec. 13	North Yemen.	2,800	6.0
1932 Dec. 26	China, Gansu	70,000	7.6	1983 Mar. 31	Southern Colombia	250	5.5
1933 Mar. 2	Japan.	2,990	8.9	1983 May 26	N. Honshu, Japan.	81	7.7
1933 Mar. 10	Long Beach, Cal.	115	6.2	1983 Oct. 30	Eastern Turkey	1,300	7.1
1934 Jan. 15	India, Bihar-Nepal.	10,700	8.4	1985 Mar. 3	Chile	146	7.8
1935 May 31	India, Quetta	50,000	7.5	1985 Sept. 19, 21	Mexico City.	4,200+	8.1
1939 Jan. 24	Chile, Chillan.	28,000	8.3	1987 Mar. 5-6	NE Ecuador	4,000+	7.3
1939 Dec. 26	Turkey, Erzincan.	30,000	7.9	1988 Aug. 20	India/Nepal border	1,000+	6.5
1946 Dec. 21	Japan, Honshu.	2,000	8.4	1988 Nov. 6	China/Burma border	1,000	7.3
1948 June 28	Japan, Fukui.	5,131	7.3	1988 Dec. 7	NW Armenia	55,000+	6.8
1949 Aug. 5	Ecuador, Pelileo.	6,000	6.8	1989 Oct. 17	San Francisco Bay area	62	6.9
1950 Aug. 15	India, Assam.	1,530	8.7	1990 May 30	N. Peru	115	6.3
1953 Mar. 18	NW Turkey.	1,200	7.2	1990 May 30	Romania	8	6.5
1956 June 10-17	N. Afghanistan.	2,000	7.7	1990 June 21	NW Iran.	40,000+	7.7
1957 July 2	Northern Iran.	2,500	7.4	1990 July 16	Luzon, Philippines	1,621	7.7
1957 Dec. 13	Western Iran	2,000	7.1	1991 Feb. 1	Pakistan, Afghanistan		
1960 Feb. 29	Morocco, Agadir.	12,000	5.8		border	1,200	6.8
1960 May 21-30	Southern Chile.	5,000	8.3	(*) estimated from earthquake intensity. (N.A.) not available.			

Some Recent Earthquakes

Source: Global Volcanism Network, Smithsonian Institution

Date	Location	Magnitude	Date	Location	Magnitude
May 30, 1991	S. Alaska	6.8	Nov. 6	S. Iran	6.8
May 24	S. Peru	6.8	Oct. 17	W. Brazil	6.7
May 19	Indonesia	6.9	Sept. 2	W. Equador	6.1
Apr. 29	Georgia, USSR	7.2	Aug. 3	N.W. China	6.1
Apr. 22	Costa Rica, Panama	7.4	July 9	Sudan	6.5
Feb. 9	Solomon Islands	6.9	June 20	N. Iran	7.6
Jan. 5	Burma	7.1	June 14	Kazakhstan, USSR	6.8
Dec. 30, 1990	New Britain	6.7	June 14	Panay Is., Philippines	7.1
Nov. 15	Indonesia	6.8	June 7	Papua New Guinea	6.5

Historic Assassinations Since 1865

1865—Apr. 14. U. S. Pres. Abraham Lincoln, shot by John Wilkes Booth in Washington, D. C.; died Apr. 15.

1881—Mar. 13. Alexander II, of Russia—July 2. U. S. Pres. James A. Garfield, shot by Charles J. Guiteau, Washington D.C.; died Sept. 19.

1900—July 29. Umberto I, king of Italy.

1901—Sept. 6. U. S. Pres. William McKinley in Buffalo, N. Y., died Sept. 14. Leon Czolgosz executed for the crime Oct. 29.

1913—Feb. 23. Mexican Pres. Francisco I, Madero and Vice Pres. Jose Pino Suarez.—Mar. 18. George, king of Greece.

1914—June 28. Archduke Francis Ferdinand of Austria-Hungary and his wife in Sarajevo, Bosnia (later part of Yugoslavia), by Gavrilo Princip.

1916—Dec. 30. Grigori Rasputin, politically powerful Russian monk.

1918—July 12. Grand Duke Michael of Russia, at Perm.—July 16. Nicholas II, abdicated as czar of Russia; his wife, the Czarina Alexandra, their son, Czarevitch Alexis, and their daughters, Grand Duchesses Olga, Tatiana, Marie, Anastasia, and 4 members of their household were executed by Bolsheviks at Ekaterinburg.

1920—May 20. Mexican Pres. Gen. Venustiano Carranza in Tlaxcalantongo.

1922—Aug. 22. Michael Collins, Irish revolutionary.—Dec. 16. Polish President Gabriel Narutowicz in Warsaw by an anarchist.

1923—July 20. Gen. Francisco "Pancho" Villa, ex-rebel leader, in Parral, Mexico.

1928—July 17. Gen. Alvaro Obregon, president-elect of Mexico, in San Angel, Mexico.

1933—Feb. 15. In Miami, Fla. Joseph Zangara, anarchist, shot at Pres.-elect Franklin D. Roosevelt, but a woman seized his arm, and the bullet fatally wounded Mayor Anton J. Cermak, of Chicago, who died Mar. 6. Zangara was electrocuted on Mar. 20, 1933.

1934—July 25. In Vienna, Austrian Chancellor Engelbert Dollfuss by Nazis.

1935—Sept. 8. U. S. Sen. Huey P. Long, shot in Baton Rouge, La., by Dr. Carl Austin Weiss, who was slain by Long's bodyguards.

1940—Aug. 20. Leon Trotsky (Lev Bronstein), 63, exiled Russian war minister, near Mexico City. Killer identified as Ramon Mercador del Rio, a Spaniard, served 20 years in Mexican prison.

1948—Jan. 30. Mohandas K. Gandhi, 78, shot in New Delhi, India, by Nathuran Vinayak Godse.—Sept. 17. Count Folke Bernadotte, UN mediator for Palestine, ambushed in Jerusalem.

1951—July 20. King Abdullah ibn Hussein of Jordan. Oct. 27. Prime Min. Liaquat Ali Khan of Pakistan shot in Rawalpindi.

1956—Sept. 21. Pres. Anastasio Somoza of Nicaragua, in Leon; died Sept. 29.

1957—July 26. Pres. Carlos Castillo Armas of Guatemala, in Guatemala City by one of his own guards.

1958—July 14. King Faisal of Iraq; his uncle, Crown Prince Abdul Illah, and July 15, Premier Nuri as-Said, by rebels in Baghdad.

1959—Sept. 25. Prime Minister Solomon Bandaranaike of Ceylon, by Buddhist monk in Colombo.

1961—Jan. 17. Ex-Premier Patrice Lumumba of the Congo, in Katanga Province—May 30. Dominican dictator Rafael Leonidas Trujillo Molina shot to death by assassins near Ciudad Trujillo.

1963—June 12. Medgar W. Evers, NAACP's Mississippi field secretary, in Jackson, Miss.—Nov. 2. Pres. Ngo Dinh Diem of the Republic of Vietnam and his brother, Ngo Dinh Nhu, in a military coup.—Nov. 22. U. S. Pres. John F. Kennedy fatally shot in Dallas, Tex.; accused Lee Harvey Oswald murdered by Jack Ruby while awaiting trial.

1965—Jan. 21. Iranian premier Hassan Ali Mansour fatally wounded by assassin in Teheran; 4 executed.—Feb. 21. Malcolm X, black nationalist, fatally shot in N. Y. City.

1966—Sept. 6. Prime Minister Hendrik F. Verwoerd of South Africa stabbed to death in parliament at Capetown.

1968—Apr. 4. Rev. Dr. Martin Luther King Jr. fatally shot in Memphis, Tenn. by James Earl Ray.—June 5. Sen. Robert F. Kennedy (D-N. Y.) fatally shot in Los Angeles; Sirhan Sirhan, resident alien, convicted of murder.

1971—Nov. 28. Jordan Prime Minister Wasfi Tal, in Cairo, by Palestinian guerrillas.

1973—Mar. 2. U. S. Ambassador Cleo A. Noel Jr., U. S. Charge d'Affaires George C. Moore and Belgian Charge d'Affaires Guy Eid killed by Palestinian guerrillas in Khartoum, Sudan.

1974—Aug. 15. Mrs. Park Chung Hee, wife of president of So. Korea, hit by bullet meant for her husband.—Aug. 19. U. S. Ambassador to Cyprus, Rodger P. Davies, killed by sniper's bullet in Nicosia.

1975—Feb. 11. Pres. Richard Ratsimandrava, of Madagascar, shot in Tananarive.—Mar. 25. King Faisal of Saudi Arabia shot by nephew Prince Musad Abdel Aziz, in royal palace, Riyadh.—Aug. 15. Bangladesh Pres. Sheik Mujibur Rahman killed in coup.

1976—Feb. 13. Nigerian head of state, Gen. Murtala Ramat Mohammed, slain by self-styled "young revolutionaries."

1977—Mar. 16. Kamal Jumblat, Lebanese Druse chieftain, was shot near Beirut.—Mar. 18. Congo Pres. Marien Ngouabi shot in Brazzaville.

1978—July 9. Former Iraqi Premier Abdul Razak Al-Naif shot in London.

1979—Feb. 14. U.S. Ambassador Adolph Dubs shot and killed by Afghan Moslem extremists in Kabul.—Aug. 27. Lord Mountbatten, WW2 hero, and 2 others were killed when a bomb exploded on his fishing boat off the coast of Co. Sligo, Ire. The IRA claimed responsibility.—Oct. 26. So. Korean President Park Chung Hee and 6 bodyguards fatally shot by Kim Jae Kyu, head of Korean CIA, and 5 aides in Seoul.

1980—Apr. 12. Liberian President William R. Tolbert slain in military coup.—Sept. 17. Former Nicaraguan President Anastasio Somoza Debayle and 2 others shot in Paraguay.

1981—Oct. 6. Egyptian President Anwar El-Sadat fatally shot by a band of commandos while reviewing a military parade in Cairo.

1982—Sept. 14. Lebanese President-elect Bishir Gemayel killed by bomb in east Beirut.

1983—Aug. 21. Philippine opposition political leader Benigno Aquino Jr. fatally shot by a gunman at Manila International Airport.—Oct. 9. Four S. Korea cabinet ministers and 15 others killed by bomb blast in Rangoon, Burma.

1984—Oct. 31. Indian Prime Minister Indira Gandhi shot and killed by 2 of her bodyguards, who were members of the minority Sikh sect, in New Delhi.

1986—Feb. 28. Swedish Premier Olof Palme shot and killed by a gunman in Stockholm.

1988—June 1. Lebanese Premier Rashid Karami killed when a bomb exploded aboard a helicopter in which he was traveling. —Apr. 16. PLO military chief Khalil Wazir (Abu Jihad) was gunned down by Israeli commandos in Tunisia.

1989—Aug. 18. Columbian Liberal Party presidential candidate Luis Carlos Galan was killed by Medellin cartel drug traffickers at a campaign rally in Bogota.—Nov. 22. Lebanese president Rene Moawad was killed when a bomb exploded next to his motorcade.

1990—Mar. 22. Columbian Patriotic Union presidential candidate Bernando Jamamillo Ossa was shot by a gunman at an airport in Bogota.

1991—May 21. Rajiv Gandhi, former prime minister of India, was killed when a bomb exploded during an election rally in Madras.

Assassination Attempts

1910—Aug. 6. N. Y. City Mayor William J. Gaynor shot and seriously wounded by discharged city employee.

1912—Oct. 14. Former U. S. President Theodore Roosevelt shot and seriously wounded by demented man in Milwaukee, Wis.

1950—Nov. 1. In an attempt to assassinate President Truman, 2 members of a Puerto Rican nationalist movement—Griselio Torresola and Oscar Collazo—tried to shoot their way into Blair House. Torresola was killed, and a guard, Pvt. Leslie Coffelt was fatally shot. Collazo was convicted Mar. 7, 1951 for the murder of Coffelt.

1970—Nov. 27. Pope Paul VI unharmed by knife-wielding assailant who attempted to attack him in Manila airport.

1972—May 15. Alabama Gov. George Wallace shot in Laurel, Md. by Arthur Bremer; seriously crippled.

1972—Dec. 7. Mrs. Ferdinand E. Marcos, wife of the Philippine president, was stabbed and seriously injured in Pasay City, Philippines.

1975—Sept. 5. Pres. Gerald R. Ford was unharmed when a Secret Service agent grabbed a pistol aimed at him by Lynette (Squeaky) Fromme, a Charles Manson follower, in Sacramento.

1975—Sept. 22. Pres. Gerald R. Ford escaped unharmed when Sara Jane Moore, a political activist, fired a revolver at him.

1980—Apr. 14. Indian Prime Minister Indira Gandhi was unharmed when a man threw a knife at her in New Delhi.

1980—May 29. Civil rights leader Vernon E. Jordan Jr. shot and wounded in Ft. Wayne, Ind.

1981—Jan. 16. Irish political activist Bernadette Devlin McAliskey and her husband were shot and seriously wounded by 3 members of a protestant paramilitary group in Co. Tyrone, Ire.

1981—Mar. 30. Pres. Ronald Reagan, Press Secy. James Brady, Secret Service agent Timothy J. McCarthy, and Washington, D.C. policeman Thomas Delahanty were shot and seriously wounded by John W. Hinckley Jr. in Washington, D.C.

1981—May 13. Pope John Paul II and 2 bystanders were shot and wounded by Mehmet Ali Agca, an escaped Turkish murderer, in St. Peter's Square, Rome.

1982—May 12. Pope John Paul II was unharmed when a man with a knife was overpowered by guards, in Fatima, Portugal.

1982—June 3. Israel's ambassador to Britain Shlomo Argov was shot and seriously wounded by Arab terrorists in London.

1986—Sept. 7. Chile President Gen. Augusto Pinochet Ugarte escaped unharmed when his motorcade was attacked by rebels using rockets, bazookas, grenades, and rifles.

Notable Kidnapings in the U.S.

Edward A. Cudahy Jr., 16, in Omaha, Neb., **Dec. 18, 1900.** Returned Dec. 20 after $25,000 paid. Pat Crowe confessed.

Robert Franks, 13, in Chicago, **May 22, 1924**, by 2 youths, Richard Loeb and Nathan Leopold, who killed boy. Demand for $10,000 ignored. Loeb died in prison, Leopold paroled 1958.

Charles A. Lindbergh Jr., 20 mos. old, in Hopewell, N.J., **Mar. 1, 1932**; found dead May 12. Ransom of $50,000 was paid to man identified as Bruno Richard Hauptmann, 35, paroled German convict who entered U.S. illegally. Hauptmann was convicted after spectacular trial at Flemington, and electrocuted in Trenton, N.J. prison, Apr. 3, 1936.

William A. Hamm Jr., 39, in St. Paul, **June 15, 1933.** $100,000 paid. Alvin Karpis given life, paroled in 1969.

Charles F. Urschel, in Oklahoma City, **July 22, 1933.** Released July 31 after $200,000 paid. George (Machine Gun) Kelly and 5 others given life.

Brooke L. Hart, 22, in San Jose, Cal. Thomas Thurmond and John Holmes arrested after demanding $40,000 ransom. When Hart's body was found in San Francisco Bay, **Nov. 26, 1933,** a mob attacked the jail at San Jose and lynched the 2 kidnapers.

George Weyerhaeuser, 9, in Tacoma, Wash., **May 24, 1935.** Returned home June 1 after $200,000 paid. Kidnapers given 20 to 60 years.

Charles Mattson, 10, in Tacoma, Wash., **Dec. 27, 1936.** Found dead Jan. 11, 1937. Kidnaper asked $28,000, failed to contact.

Arthur Fried, in White Plains, N.Y., **Dec. 4, 1937.** Body not found. Two kidnapers executed.

Robert C. Greenlease, 6, taken from Kansas City, Mo. school **Sept. 28, 1953,** and held for $600,000. Body found Oct. 7. Mrs. Bonnie Brown Heady and Carl A. Hall pleaded guilty and were executed.

Peter Weinberger, 32 days old, Westbury, N.Y., **July 4, 1956,** for $2,000 ransom, not paid. Child found dead. Angelo John LaMarca, 31, convicted, executed.

Cynthia Ruotolo, 6 wks old, taken from carriage in front of Hamden, Conn. store **Sept. 1, 1956.** Body found in lake.

Lee Crary, 8 in Everett, Wash., **Sept. 22, 1957,** $10,000 ransom, not paid. He escaped after 3 days, led police to George E. Collins, who was convicted.

Frank Sinatra Jr., 19, from hotel room in Lake Tahoe, Cal., **Dec. 8, 1963.** Released Dec. 11 after his father paid $240,000 ransom. Three men sentenced to prison; most of ransom recovered.

Barbara Jane Mackle, 20, abducted **Dec. 17, 1968,** from Atlanta, Ga., motel, was found unharmed 3 days later, buried in a coffin-like wooden box 18 inches underground, after her father had paid $500,000 ransom; Gary Steven Krist sentenced to life, Ruth Eisenmann-Schier to 7 years; most of ransom recovered.

Mrs. Roy Fuchs, 35, and 3 children held hostage 2 hours, **May 14, 1969,** in Long Island, N. Y., released after her husband, a bank manager, paid kidnapers $129,000 in bank funds; 4 men arrested, ransom recovered.

Mrs. Virginia Piper, 49 abducted **July 27, 1972,** from her home in suburban Minneapolis; found unharmed near Duluth 2 days later after her husband paid $1 million ransom to the kidnapers.

Patricia (Patty) Hearst, 19, taken from her Berkeley, Cal., apartment **Feb. 4, 1974.** Symbionese Liberation Army demanded her father, Randolph A. Hearst, give millions to poor. She was identified by FBI as taking part in a San Francisco bank holdup, **Apr. 15.** FBI, **Sept. 18, 1975,** captured Patricia and others in San Francisco; they were indicted on various charges. Patricia for bank robbery. Convicted, **Mar. 20, 1976.** She was released from prison under executive clemency, **Feb. 1, 1979.** In 1978, William and Emily Harris were sentenced to 10 years to life for the Hearst kidnaping. Both were paroled in 1983.

J. Reginald Murphy, 40, an editor of *Atlanta* (Ga.) *Constitution*, kidnaped **Feb. 20, 1974,** freed **Feb. 22** after payment of $700,000 ransom by the newspaper. Police arrested William A. H. Williams, a contractor; most of the money was recovered.

E. B. Reville, Hepzibah, Ga., banker, and wife Jean, kidnaped **Sept. 30, 1974.** Ransom of $30,000 paid. He was found alive; Mrs. Reville was found dead in car trunk **Oct. 2.**

Jack Teich, Kings Point, N.Y., steel executive, seized **Nov. 12, 1974;** released **Nov. 19** after payment of $750,000.

Source: World Almanac questionnaire

Arranged according to key words in titles. Founding year of organization in parentheses; last figure after ZIP code indicates membership.

AFS Intercultural Programs (1917), 313 E. 43rd Street, N.Y., NY 10017; approx. 7,000.

ASM International (1913), 9639 Kinsman Rd., Materials Park, OH 44073-0002; 54,000.

Aaron Burr Assn. (1946), 4520 King Edward Ct., Annandle, VA 22003; 600.

Abortion Federation, Natl. (1977), 1436 U St. NW, Suite 103, Washington, DC 20009; 300 organizations.

Accountants, Amer. Institute of Certified Public (1887), 1211 Ave. of the Americas, N.Y., NY 10036; 305,465.

Accountants, Natl. Assn. of (1919), 10 Paragon Dr., Box 433, Montvale, NJ 07645-1760; 85,000.

Accountants, Natl. Society of Public (1945), 1010 N. Fairfax St., Alexandria, VA 22314.

Accountants for Cooperatives, Natl. Soc. of (1936), 6320 Augusta Dr., Ste. 802-C, Springfield, VA 22150; 2,000.

Acoustical Society of America (1929), 500 Sunnyside Blvd., Woodbury, NY 11797; 6,500.

Actors' Equity Assn. (1913), 165 W. 46 St., N.Y., NY 10036.

Actors' Fund of America (1882), 1501 Broadway, N.Y., NY 10036; 3,500.

Actuaries, American Academy of (1965), 1720 I St. NW, Wash., DC 20006; 9,500.

Actuaries, Society of (1949), 475 N. Martingale Rd., Suite 800, Schaumburg, IL 60173-2226; 12,925.

Adirondack Mountain Club (1922), RR 3, Box 3055, Lake George, NY 12845; 18,000.

Advertisers, Assn. of Natl. (1910), 155 E. 44th St., N.Y., NY 10017.

Advertising Agencies, Amer. Assn. of (1917), 666 Third Ave., N.Y., NY 10017; 765 agencies.

Aeronautic Assn., Natl. (1905), 1815 N. Fort Myer Dr., Ste. 700, Arlington, VA 22209; 5,000.

Aeronautics and Astronautics, Amer. Institute of (1963), 1633 Broadway, N.Y., NY 10019; 38,000.

Aerospace Industries Assn. of America (1919), 1250 Eye St. NW, Wash., DC 20005; 56 cos.

Aerospace Medical Assn. (1929), 320 S. Henry St., Alexandria, VA 22314-3524; 4,350.

Afro-American Life and History, Assn. for the Study of (1915), 1401 14th St. NW, Wash., DC 20005; 1,800.

Aging Assn., Amer. (1970), 600 South 42nd St., Omaha, NE 68198-4635; 400.

Agricultural Chemicals Assn., Natl. (1933), 1155 15th St. NW, Wash., DC 20005; 80 cos.

Agricultural Economics Assn., Amer. (1910), 80 Heady Hall, Iowa State Univ., Ames, IA 50011; 4,500.

Agricultural History Society (1919), Room 928, 1301 New York Ave. NW, Wash., DC 20250; 1,400.

Agronomy, Amer. Society of (1907), 677 S. Segoe Rd., Madison, WI 53711; 12,500.

Aircraft Assn., Experimental (1953), EAA Aviation Center, Oshkosh, WI 54903-3086; 125,000.

Aircraft Owners and Pilots Assn. (1939), 421 Aviation Way, Frederick, MD 21701; 300,000.

Air Force Assn. (1946), 1501 Lee Hwy., Arlington, VA 22209.

Air Force Sergeants Assn. (1961), P.O. Box 31050, Temple Hills, MD 20748.

Air Line Employees Assn. (1948), 5600 S. Central Ave., Chicago, IL 60638; 3,679.

Air Line Pilots Assn. (1931), 1625 Massachusetts Ave. NW, Wash., DC 20036; 41,000.

Air Pollution Control Assn. (1907), P.O. Box 2861, Pittsburgh, PA 15230; 8,500.

Air Transport Assn. of America (1936), 1709 New York Ave. NW, Wash., DC 20006; 20 airlines.

Air & Waste Management Assn. (1907), P.O. Box 2861, Pittsburgh, PA 15230; 12,000.

Al-Anon Family Groups (1950), P.O. Box 862, Midtown Sta., N.Y., NY 10018; 24,918.

Alcohol Problems, Amer. Council on (1895), 3426 Bridgeland Dr., Bridgeton, MO 63044.

Alcoholics Anonymous (1935), 468 Park Ave. So., N.Y., NY 10016; 1 mln.+.

Alcoholism and Drug Dependence, Natl. Council on (1944), 12 W. 21st St., N.Y., NY 10010; 200 affiliates.

All-Terrain Vehicle Owners Assn., Natl. (1972), P.O. Box 1272, Bensalem, PA 19020; 2,514.

Allergy and Immunology, Amer. Academy of (1943), 611 E. Wells St., Milwaukee, WI 53202; 4,200.

Alpine Club, Amer. (1902), 113 E. 90th St., N.Y., NY 10028.

Altrusa Intl. (1917), 332 S. Michigan Ave., Chicago, IL 60604.

Alzheimer's Assn. (1980), 70 E. Lake St., Chicago, IL 60601-5997; 35,000

Amer. Indian Affairs, Assn. on (1922), 245 Fifth Ave., N.Y., NY, 10016; 15,000.

American Legion, The (1919), 700 N. Pennsylvania St., Indianapolis, IN 46204; 3.0 mln. **American Legion Auxiliary** (1920), 777 N. Meridian St., Indianapolis, IN 46204; 897,156.

Amer. States, Organization of (1890), 17th & Constitution Ave. NW, Wash., DC 20006; 35 countries.

Amer. Veterans of World War II, Korea & Vietnam (AMVETS), (1947); AMVETS Auxiliary (1946), 4647 Forbes Blvd., Lanham, MD 20706.

Amideast (Amer. Mideast Educational & Training Services) (1951), 1100 17th St. NW, Suite 300, Wash., DC 20036.

Amnesty Intl. USA (1961), 322 Eighth Ave., N.Y., NY 10001.

Amputation Foundation, Natl. (1923), 12-45 150th St., Whitestone, NY.11357; 2,500.

Anderson, Inc., Historic (1955), P.O. Box 268, Anderson, TX 77830; 35.

Andersonville, Natl. Soc. of (1975), P.O. Box 65, Andersonville, GA 31711; 140.

Animal Protection Institute of America (1968), 2831 Fruitridge Rd., P.O. Box 95822, Sacramento, CA 95822; 135,000.

Animal Welfare Institute (1951), 1686 34th St. NW, Wash., DC 20007; 8,000.

Animals, Amer. Society for Prevention of Cruelty to (ASPCA) (1866), 441 E. 92d St., N.Y., NY 10128; 400,000.

Animals, The Fund for (1967), 200 W. 57th St., N.Y., NY 10019; 200,000.

Animals, People for the Ethical Treatment of (1980), P.O. Box 42516, Wash., DC 20015; 350,000.

Antelopes, Grand United Order of (1925), 162 Fourth Ave., E. Orange, NJ 01017; 499.

Anthropological Assn., Amer. (1902), 1703 New Hampshire Ave. NW, Wash., DC 20009; 10,000.

Antiquarian Society, Amer. (1812), 185 Salisbury St., Worcester, MA 01609-1634; 543.

Anti-Vivisection Society, Amer. (1883), Suite 204, 801 Old York Rd., Jenkintown, PA 19046; 10,000+.

Appalachian Mountain Club (1876), 5 Joy St., Boston, MA 02138; 02138-1433.

Appalachian Trail Conference (1925), Washington & Jackson Sts., Harpers Ferry, WV 25425; 23,000.

Appraisers, Amer. Society of (1936), 535 Herndon Pkwy., #150, Herndon, VA 22070; 6,000.

Arab Americans, Natl. Assn. of (1972), 2033 M St. NW, Wash., DC 20036.

Arbitration Assn., Amer. (1926), 140 W. 51st St., N.Y., NY 10020-1203; 6,523.

Arboriculture, Intl. Society of (1924), 5 Lincoln Sq., Urbana, IL 61801; 4,500.

Archaeological Institute of America (1879), 675 Commonwealth Ave., Boston, MA 02215; 10,000.

Archaeology, Institute of Nautical (1976), P.O. Drawer HG, College Station, TX 77841; 800.

Archery Assn., Natl. (1879), 1750 E. Boulder St., Colorado Springs, CO 80909; 3,900.

Architects, Amer. Institute of (1857), 1735 New York Ave. NW, Wash., DC 20006; 51,000.

Architectural Historians, Society of (1940), 1232 Pine Street, Phila., PA 19107-5944; 3,600.

Armed Forces Communications and Electronics Assn. (1946), 4400 Fair Lakes Ct., Fairfax, VA 22033; 40,000.

Army, Assn. of the United States (1950), 2425 Wilson Blvd., Arlington, VA 22201; 150,000.

Arts, Amer. Council for the (1960), 1285 Avenue of the Americas, N.Y., NY 10019; 2,300.

Arts, Amer. Federation of (1909), 41 E. 65th St., N.Y., NY 10021; 1,100.

Arts and Letters, Amer. Academy and Institute of (1898), 633 W. 155th St., N.Y., NY 10032; 250.

Arts and Letters, Natl. Society of (1944), 2800 Quebec St. NW, Washington, DC 20008; 1,700.

Arts & Sciences, Amer. Academy of (1780), Norton's Woods, 136 Irving St., Cambridge, MA 02138; 3,500.

Asbestos Council, Natl. (1983), 1777 NE Expressway, Ste. 150, Atlanta, GA 30329; 4,300.

Assistance League, Natl. (1949), 5627 Fernwood Ave., Los Angeles, CA 90038; 17,000.

Association Executives, American Society of (1920), 1575 Eye St. NW, Wash., DC 20005; 18,000.

Association Publications, Society of Natl. (1963), 3299 K St. NW, Suite 700, Wash., DC 20007; 210 publications.

Astrologers, Amer. Federation of (1938), 6535 S. Rural Rd., Tempe, AZ 85283; 4,500.

Astronautical Society, Amer. (1954), 6352 Rolling Mill Pl., Suite 102, Springfield, VA 22152; 1,737.

Astronomical Society, Amer. (1899), 2000 Florida Ave., NW, Suite 300, Wash., DC 20009; 5,700.

Ataxia Foundation, Natl. (1957), 600 Twelve Oaks Cntr., 15500 Wayzata Blvd., Wayzata MN 55391; 1,400.

Atheist Assn. (1925), 910 E Street, San Diego, CA 92101.

Atheists, Amer. (1959), P.O. Box 140195, Austin, TX 78714.

Atheists, United World (1972), 7215 Cameron Rd., Austin, TX 78752; 30 org.

Athetic Assn., Natl. Jr. College (1939), P.O. Box 7305, Colorado Springs, CO 80933-7305; 556.

Athletic Assn., Natl. Scholastic (1985), 6991 Simson St., Oakland, CA 94605-2226.

Athletic Associations, Natl. Federation of State H. S. (1920), 11724 Plaza Circle, Box 20626, Kansas City, MO 64195.

Athletic Union of the U.S., Amateur (1888), 3400 W. 86th St., Indianapolis, IN 46268.

Athletics Congress/USA, The (1979), One Hoosier Dome, Indianapolis, IN 46225; 125,000.

Auctioneers Assn., Natl. (1949), 8880 Ballentine, Overland Park, KS 66214; 5,000.

Audubon Society, Natl. (1905), 950 Third Ave., N.Y., NY 10022; 600,000.

Authors Guild, Inc., The (1921), 330 W. 42nd St., 29th Fl., New York, NY 10036-6902; 6,500

Authors League of America (1912), 234 W. 44th St., N.Y., NY 10036; 15,000.

Autism, Society of America, (1965), 8601 Georgia Ave., Ste. 503, Silver Springs, MD 20910; 10,000.

Autograph Collectors Club, Universal (1965), P.O. Box 6181, Wash., DC 20044-6181; 2,447.

Automobile Assn., Amer. (1902), 8111 Gatehouse Rd., Falls Church, VA 22047; 28 million+.

Automobile Club, Natl. (1924), One Market Plaza, San Francisco, CA 94105; 316,000.

Automobile Club of America, Antique (1935), 501 W. Governor Rd., Hershey, PA 17033; 53,000.

Automobile Dealers Assn., Natl. (1917), 8400 Westpark Dr., McLean, VA 22102; 20,000.

Automobile License Plate Collectors' Assn. (1954), P.O. Box 712, Weston, W. VA 26452; 2,218.

Automotive Hall of Fame (1939), 3225 Cook Rd., Midland, MI 48641; 2,500.

Automotive Testers, Society of (1950), 461 Stuart Ln., Palatine, IL 60067; 326.

Avon Collectors, Inc., Natl. Assn. of (1971), P.O. Box 68, W. Newton, IN 46183; 100 clubs.

Badminton Assn., U.S. (1936), 920 O Street, Lincoln, NE 68508; 1,974.

Bald-Headed Men of America (1973), 1 Bald Drive, Morehead City, N.C. 28557; approx. 20,000.

Ball Players of Amer., Assn. of Professional (1924), 12062 Valley View St., #211, Garden Grove, CA 92645; 12,000.

Band & Choral Directors Hall of Fame, Natl. (1985), 519 N. Halifax Ave., Daytona Beach, FL 32118.

Bankers Assn., Amer. (1875), 1120 Connecticut Ave. NW, Wash., DC 20036.

Bankers Assn. of America, Independent (1930), One Thomas Circle NW, Suite 950, Wash. DC 20005; 6,400 banks.

Bar Assn., Federal (1920), 1815 H St. NW, Wash., DC 20006; 15,000.

Barbershop Quartet Singing in Amer., Soc. for Preservation & Encouragement of (1938), 6315 Third Ave., Kenosha, WI 53140-5199; 38,000.

Baseball Congress, Amer. Amateur (1935), 118-19 Redfield Plaza, Marshall, MI 49068; 14,200 teams.

Baseball Congress, Natl. (1931), P.O. Box 1420, Wichita, KS 67201.

Baseball Research, Society for Amer. (1971), P.O. Box 93183, Cleveland, OH 44101; 5,000+.

Basketball Assn., Natl. (1946), 645 Fifth Ave., N.Y., NY 10022.

Battleship Assn., Amer. (1964), P.O. Box 711247, San Diego, CA 92171; 2,500.

Beer Can Collectors of America (1970), 747 Merus Ct., Fenton, MO 63026-2092; 4,000.

Beta Gamma Sigma (1913), 605 Old Ballas Rd., Suite 200, St. Louis, MO 63141; 300,000.

Beta Sigma Phi (1931), 1800 W. 91st Place, Kansas City, MO 64114; 250,000.

Bible Society, Amer. (1816), 1865 Broadway, N.Y., NY 10023; 300,000.

Biblical Literature, Society of (1880), 1549 Clairmont Rd., Ste. 204, Decatur, GA 30033; 5,500.

Bibliographical Society of America (1904), P.O. Box 397, Grand Central Sta., N.Y., NY 10163; 1,300.

Big Brothers/Big Sisters of America (1902), 230 No. 13th St., Philadelphia, PA 19107; 494 agencies.

Biochemistry and Molecular Biology, Amer. Society for (1906), 9650 Rockville Pike, Bethesda, MD 20814; 8,100.

Blind, Amer. Council of the (1961) 1155 15th St. NW, Suite 720, Wash., DC 20005; 45,000.

Blind, Amer. Foundation for the (1921), 15 W. 16th St., N.Y., NY 10011; 250.

Blind, Natl. Federation of the (1940), 1800 Johnson St., Baltimore, MD 21230.

Blindness, Natl. Society to Prevent (1908), 500 E. Remington Rd., Schaumburg, IL 60173; 26 affiliates.

Blindness, Research to Prevent (1960), 598 Madison Ave., N.Y., NY 10023; 1,400.

Blue Angels Assn. (1982), 4600 Twin Oaks Dr., Apt. 702, Warrington, FL 32506; 250.

Blue Cross and Blue Shield Assn. (1946), 676 St. Clair, Chicago, IL 60611; 74 plans.

Blueberry Council, No. Amer. (1965), P.O. Box 166, Marmora, NJ 08223; 65.

Bluebird Society, No. Amer. (1978), 2 Countryside Ct., Silver Spring, MD 20906; 5,000.

B'nai B'rith Intl. (1853), 1640 Rhode Island Ave. NW, Wash., DC 20036; 500,000.

Boat Assn., Amer. Power (1903), 17640 E. Nine Mile Rd., E. Detroit, MI 48021; 5,000.

Boat Club, Chris Craft Antique (1973), 217 S. Adams St., Tallahassee, FL 32301; 1,896.

Boat Owners Assn. of the U.S. (1966), 880 S. Pickett St., Alexandria, VA 22304; 350,000.

Bodybuilders Assn., Amer. (1981), 6991 Simson St., Oakland, CA 94605-2226; 854.

Bookplate Collectors and Designers, Amer. Soc. of (1922), 605 N. Stoneman Ave. #F, Alhambra, CA 91801; 250.

Booksellers Assn., Amer. (1900), 122 E. 42d St., N.Y., NY 10168; 5,557.

Botanical Gardens & Arboreta, Amer. Assn. of (1940), 786 Church Rd, Wayne, PA 19087; 1,800.

Bottle Clubs, Federation of Historical (1969), 5001 Queen Ave. N., Minneapolis, MN 55430; 90 clubs.

Bowling Congress, Amer. (1895), 5301 S. 76th St., Greendale, WI 53129; 3.03 mln.

Boys' Brigades of America, United (1893), 2803 Glendale Ave., Baltimore, MD 21234; 150.

Boys' Clubs of America (1906), 771 First Ave., N.Y., NY 10017; 1.2 mln.

Boy Scouts of America (1910), 1325 Walnut Hill Lane, Irving, TX 75015-2079; 3.8 mln.

Bread for the World (1975), 802 Rhode Island Ave. NE, Washington, DC 20018; 43,000.

Bridge, Tunnel and Turnpike Assn., Intl. (1932), 2120 L St. NW, Suite 305, Wash., DC 20037; 260 organizations.

Brith Sholom, Natl. (1905), 3939 Conshohocken Ave., Philadelphia, PA 19131; 5,000.

Broadcasters, Natl. Assn. of (1922), 1771 N St. NW, Wash., DC 20036; 6,170 radio & TV stations.

Burroughs Bibliophiles, The (1960), 454 Elaine Dr., Pittsburgh, PA 15236; 417.

Bus Assn., Amer. (1928), 1015 15th St. NW, Suite 250, Wash., DC 20005; 3,000.

Business Bureaus, Council of Better (1970), 4200 Wilson Blvd., Arlington, VA 22203; 180 bureaus.

Business Clubs, Natl. Assn. of Amer. (1922), 3315 No. Main St., High Point, NC 27262; 7,250.

Business Communication, Assn. for (1935), Univ. of North Texas, Denton, TX 76203; 2,400.

Business Communicators, Intl. Assn. of (1970), One Hallidie Pl., Suite 600, San Francisco, CA 94102; 11,500.

Business Education Assn., Natl. (1946), 1906 Association Dr., Reston, VA 22091; 18,000.

Business Real Estate & Law Assn., Amer. (1923), Dept. of Legal Studies, Univ. of Georgia, Athens, GA 30602; 1,200.

Business-Professional Advertising Assn. (1922), 100 Metroplex Dr., Edison, NJ 08817; 4,500.

Button Society, Natl. (1938), 2733 Juno Pl., Akron, OH 44313; 2,500.

Byron Society, The (1971 England, 1973 in U.S.), 259 New Jersey Ave., Collingswood, NJ 08108; 300.

CARE (1945), 660 First Ave., N.Y., NY 10016.

CB Radio Patrol of Amer., Federation of Police (1977), 1100 NE 125th St., N. Miami, FL 33161; 35,000.

CLU & CHFC, Amer. Soc. of (1928), 270 Bryn Mawr Ave., Bryn Mawr, PA 19010; 32,000.

CORE (Congress of Racial Equality) (1942), 1457 Flatbush Ave., Brooklyn, NY 11210.

CPCU, The Society of (1944), 720 Providence Rd., Malvern, PA 19355; 18,000.

Campers & Hikers Assn., Natl. (1954), 4804 Transit Rd., Bld. 2, Depew, NY 14043; 24,000 families.

Camp Fire Boys & Girls (1910), 4601 Madison Ave., Kansas City, MO 64112; 600,000.

Campers & Hikers Assn., Inc. (1954), 7172 Transit Rd., Buffalo, NY 14221; 30,000.

Camping Assn., Amer. (1910), 5000 SR 67 N., Martinsville, IN 46151; 5,200.

Cancer Society, Amer. (1913), 90 Park Ave., N.Y., NY 10017; 257.

Canoe Assn., U.S. (1968), 606 Ross St., Middletown, OH 45044; 1,000.

Carillonneurs in North America, Guild of (1936), 3718 Settle Rd., Cincinnati, OH 45227; 483.

Carnegie Hero Fund Commission (1904), 2307 Oliver Bldg., Pittsburgh, PA 15222; 21 members.

Cartoonists Society, Natl. (1946), 157 W. 57th St., Suite 904, N.Y., NY 10019; 500.

Cat Fanciers' Assn. (1906), 1309 Allaire Ave., Ocean, NJ 07712; 600 member clubs.

Catholic Bishops, Natl. Conference of/U.S. Cath. Conference (1966), 1312 Massachusetts Ave. NW, Wash., DC 20005.

Catholic Charities, USA (1910), 1731 King St., Ste 200, Alexandria, VA 22314; 3,400.

Catholic Church Extension Society of the U.S.A. (1905), 35 E. Wacker Dr., Chicago, IL 60601.

Catholic Daughters of the Americas (1903), 10 W. 71st St., N.Y., NY 10023; 150,000.

Catholic Educational Assn., Natl. (1904), 1077-30th St. NW, Suite 100, Wash, DC 20007; 18,353.

Catholic Historical Soc., Amer. (1884), 263 S. Fourth St., P.O. Box 84, Philadelphia, PA 19106; 850.

Catholic Library Assn. (1921), 461 W. Lancaster Ave., Haverford, PA 19041; 1,518.

Catholic Press Assn. of U.S. and Canada (1911), 119 N. Park Ave., Rockville Centre, NY 11570.

Catholic Rural Life Conference, Natl. (1923), 4625 NW Beaver Ave., Des Moines, IA 50310; 2,000.

Catholic War Veterans of the U.S.A. (1935), 419 North Lee Street, Alexandria, VA 22314; 35,000.

Celiac Sprue Assn./USA (1986), 2313 Rocklyn Dr., Suite 1, Des Moines, IA 50322; 1,800.

Cemetery Assn., Amer. (1887), 5201 Leesburg Pike, Falls Church, VA 22041; 3,000.

Ceramic Society, Amer. (1898), 757 Brooksedge Plaza Dr., Westerville, OH 43081; 14,000.

Cerebral Palsy Assns., United (1949), 7 Penn Plaza, N.Y., NY 10001; 180 affiliates.

Chamber of Commerce of the U.S.A. (1912), 1615 H St. NW, Wash., DC 20062; 200,000.

Chamber Music Players, Amateur (1948), 545 Eighth Ave., N.Y., NY 10018; 4,000.

Chaplain's Intl. Assn. (1960), Adjutant General Office, 5045 N. Robberson, Springfield, MO 65803; 824.

Chaplains Assn. of the U.S.A., The Military (1925), P.O. Box 645, Riverdale, MD 20737-0645; 1,500.

Checker Federation, Amer., (1948), 3475 Belmont Ave., Baton Rouge, LA 70808; 1,000.

Chemical Manufacturers Assn. (1872), 2501 M St. NW, Wash., DC 20037; 171 companies.

Chemical Society, Amer. (1876), 1155 16th St. NW, Wash., DC 20036; 135,000.

Chemistry, Amer. Assn. for Clinical (1947), 2029 K St. NW, 7th fl. Wash., DC 20006; 10,000.

Chemists, Amer. Institute of (1923), 7315 Wisconsin Ave., Bethesda, Md. 20814; 5,000

Chemists, Amer. Society of Brewing (1934), 3340 Pilot Knob Rd., St. Paul MN 55121.

Chemists, Amer. Assn. of Cereal (1915), 3340 Pilot Knob Rd., St. Paul, MN 55121; 3,523.

Chess Federation, U.S. (1939), 186 Rte. 9W, New Windsor, NY 12553; 56,000.

Chess League of Amer., Correspondence (1897), P.O. Box 416, Warrenville, IL 60555; 1,000.

Child Welfare League of America (1920), 440 First St. NW, Wash., DC 20001; 600 agencies.

Childbirth Without Pain Education Assn. (1959), 20134 Snowden, Detroit, MI 48235; 3,000.

Childhood Education Intl., Assn. for (1892), 11141 Georgia Ave., Suite 200, Wheaton, MD 20902; 14,000.

Children of the Amer. Revolution, Natl. Society of the (1895), 1776 D St. NW, Wash., DC 20006; 10,000.

Children's Aid Society (1853), 105 E. 22d St., N.Y., NY 10010; 1,207.

Children's Book Council (1945), 568 Broadway, Suite 404, N.Y., NY 10012; 62 publishing houses.

Chiropractic Assn., Amer. (1930), 1916 Wilson Blvd., Arlington, VA 22201; 20,000.

Chiropractors Assn., Intl. (1926), 1901 L St. NW, Wash., DC 20036; 7,000.

Christian Endeavor, Intl. Society of (1881), 1221 E. Broad St., P.O. Box 1110, Columbus, OH 43216.

Christian Laity Counseling Board (1970), 5901 Plainfield Dr., Charlotte, NC 28215; 38 min.

Christians and Jews, Natl. Conference of (1927), 71 Fifth Ave., Suite 1100 N.Y., NY 10003.

Church Business Administration, Natl. Assn. of (1956), 7001 Grapevine Hwy., Suite 324, Ft. Worth, TX 76180; 1,500.

Church Federation, Ecumenical (1982), 13014-270, N. Dalemabry, Tampa, FL 33618-2808.

Churches, U.S. Conference for the World Council of (1948), 475 Riverside Dr., N.Y., NY 10115; 27 churches.

Church Women United (1941), The Interchurch Center, 475 Riverside Dr., Rm. 812, N.Y., NY 10115.

Cinematographers, Am. Society of (1919), 1782 N. Orange Dr., Hollywood, CA 90028; 266.

Cincinnati, Society of the (1783), 2118 Massachusetts Ave. NW, Wash., DC 20008; 3,200.

Circulation Managers Assn., Intl. (1889), 11600 Sunrise Valley Dr., Reston, VA 22091; 1,705.

Circus Fans Assn. of America (1926), P.O. Box 3187, Flint, MI 48502; 2,400.

Cities, Natl. League of (1924), 1301 Pennsyivania Ave. NW, Wash., DC 20004; 15,000 cities.

Citizens Band Radio Patrol (1977), 1100 NE 125th St., N. Miami, FL 33161; 35,000.

City Management Assn., Intl. (1914), 777 North Capitol St., Ste. 500, Wash., DC 20002; 6,000.

Civic League, Natl. (1894), 1601 Grant St., Suite 250, Denver, CO 80203; 1,500.

Civil Air Patrol, (1941), Bldg. 714, Maxwell AFB, AL 36112-5572; 63,000.

Civil Engineers, Amer. Society of (1852), 345 E. 47th St., N.Y., NY 10017; 104,000.

Civil Liberties Union, Amer. (1920), 132 W. 43rd St., N.Y. NY 10036; 250,000.

Civil War Round Table of New York (1951), P.O. Box 3485, N.Y., NY 10185; 150+.

Civic League, Natl. (1894), 55 West 44th St., N.Y., NY 10036; 3,000.

Civitan Internatl. (1920), 1401 52nd St. S., Birmingham, AL 35213-1903; 35,000.

Classical League, Amer. (1919), Hall, Miami Univ., Oxford, OH 45056; 3,604.

Clinical Pastoral Education, Assn. for (1967), 1549 Clairmont Rd., Decatur, GA 30033; 3,500.

Clinical Pathologists, Amer. Society of (1922), 2100 W. Harrison St., Chicago, IL 60612; 50,000.

Clinical Social Work, Inc., Natl. Fed. of Soc. for (1971), P.O. Box 3740, Arlington, VA 22203; 10,000+.

Coal Association, Natl. (1917), 1130 17th St. NW, Wash., DC 20036; 150 corporate members.

College Athletic Conference, Eastern (1938), 1311 Craigville Beach Rd., P.O. Box 3, Centerville, MA 02632.

College Board, The (1900), 45 Columbus Ave., N.Y., NY 10023; 2,800 institutions.

College Music Society (1958), 202 W. Spruce St., Missoula, MT 59802; 6,500.

College Physical Education Assn. for Men, Natl. (1897), 108 Cooke Hall, Univ. of Minnesota, Minneapolis, MN 55455.

College Placement Council (1956), 62 Highland Ave., Bethlehem, PA 18017; 3,100.

Colleges, Amer. Assn. of Community and Jr. (1921), One Dupont Circle NW, Suite 410, Wash., DC 20036.

Colleges, Assn. of Amer. (1915), 1818 R St. NW, Wash., DC 20009; 620 institutions.

Colleges and Universities, Assn. of Intl. (1973), I301 S. Noland Rd., Independence, MO 64055; 11,415.

Collegiate Athletic Assn., Natl. (1906), 6201 College Blvd., Overland Park, KS 66211-2422; 827 inst.

Collegiate Body-Building Assn., Natl. (1983), 6991 Simson St., Oakland, CA 94605; 683.

Collegiate Schools of Business, Amer. Assembly of (1916), 605 Old Ballas Rd., St. Louis, MO 63141-7077.

Colonial Dames of Amer. (1899), 421 E. 61 St., N.Y., NY 10021; 2,049.

Colonial Dames XVII Century, Natl. Society (1915), 1300 New Hampshire Ave. NW, Wash., DC 20036; 13,000.

Colonial Wars, General Society of (1892), 840 Woodbine Ave., Glendale, OH 45246; 4,300.

Colorado Alumni Assn., U.S.S. (1984), P.O. Box 9862, McLean, VA 22102-0062; 755.

Commerce, U.S. Junior Chamber of (1920), 4 W. 21st St., Tulsa, OK 74114-1116; 230,000.

Commercial Collectors Assn., Amer. (1970), 4040 W. 70th St., Minneapolis, MN 55435; 3,225.

Commercial Law League of America (1895), 175 W. Jackson, #1541, Chicago, IL 60604; 5,300.

Commercial Travelers of America, Order of United (1888), 632 N. Park St., Columbus, OH 43215; 186,000.

Common Cause (1970), 2030 M St. NW, Wash., DC 20036.

Communication, Intl. Training In (1938), 2519 Woodland Dr., Anaheim, CA 92801; 18,000.

Communication, Soc. for Technical (1953), 815 15th St. NW, Wash., DC 20005; 15,000.

Communication Administration, Assn. for (1971), 5105 Backlick Rd., Annadale, VA 22003; 700.

Communities, Federation of Egalitarian (1976), E. Wind, Rt. 3WA, Box 6B2, Tecumseh, MO 65760; 140.

Community Cultural Center Assoc., Amer. (1978), 19 Foothills Dr., Pompton Plains, NJ 07444.

Composers/USA, Natl. Assn. of (1932), P.O. Box 49652, Barrington Sta., Los Angeles, CA 90049; 600.

Composers, Authors & Publishers, Amer. Society of (ASCAP) (1914), One Lincoln Plaza, N.Y., NY 10023; 24,000.

Computing Machinery, Assn. for (1947), 11 W. 42nd St., N.Y., NY 10036; 55,000.

Concrete Institute, Amer. (1904), 22400 W. Seven Mile Rd., Detroit, MI 48219-1849; 16,770.

Conscientious Objection, Central Committee for (1948), 2208 South St., Phila., PA 19146; 20,000.

Conservation Engineers, Assn. of (1961), Alabama Dept. of Conservation, 64 N. Union St., Montgomery, AL 36130; 225.

Constantian Society, The (1970), 123 Orr Rd., Pittsburgh, PA 15241; 500.

Construction Industry Manufacturers Assn. (1911), 111 E. Wisconsin Ave., Milwaukee, WI 53202; 150 companies.

Construction Specifications Institute (1948), 601 Madison St., Alexandria, VA 22314-1791; 19,200.

Consumer Credit Assn., Intl. (1912), 243 N. Lindbergh, St. Louis, MO 63141; 20,000.

Consumer Federation of America (1968), 1314 14th St. NW, Wash., DC 20005; 200+.

Consumer Interests, Amer. Council on (1953), 240 Stanley Hall, Univ. of Missouri, Columbia, MO 65211; 1,680.

Consumer Protection Institute (1970), 5901 Plainfield Dr., Charlotte, NC 28215.

Consumers League, Natl. (1899), 815 15th St. NW, Suite 928-N, Wash., DC 20009; 8,000.

Consumers Union of the U.S. (1936), 101 Truman Ave., Yonkers, NY 10703; 405,990.

Contraception, Assn. for Voluntary Surgical (1943), 122 E. 42nd St., New York, NY 10168; 5,000.

Contract Bridge League, Amer. (1937), 2200 Democrat Rd., Memphis, TN 38132; 190,000.

Contract Management Assn., Natl. (1959), 6728 Old McLean Village Dr., McLean, VA 22101; 20,176.

Contractors, Natl. Assn. of Education and Training (1989), 50 E St. SE, Wash., DC 20003; 18.

Contractors of Amer., General (1919), 1957 E St. NW, Wash., DC 20006; 32,000.

Cooperative Business Assn., Natl. (1916), 1401 New York Ave. NW, #1100, Wash., DC 20005; 180 organizations.

Cooperative League of the U.S.A. (1916), 1401 New York Ave. NW, Suite 1100, Wash., DC 20005; 285 co-ops.

Correctional Assn., Amer. (1870), 8025 Laurel Lakes Court, Laurel, MD 20707; 24,000.

Correctional Officers, Intl. Assn. of (1977), P.O. Box 7051, Marquette, MI 49855; 10,000.

Cosmetology Assn., Natl. (1921), 3510 Olive St., St. Louis, MO 63103; 47,000.

Cosmopolitan Intl. (1914), 7341 W. 80th, Overland Park, KS 66204; 3,057.

Cotton Council of America, Natl. (1938), 1918 North Parkway, Memphis, TN 38112; 297 delegates.

Counseling and Development, Amer. Assn. for (1952), 5999 Stevenson Ave., Alexandria, VA 22304; 58,000.

Counselors and Family Therapists, Natl. Academy of (1970), 55 Morris Ave., Springfield, NJ 07081-1422; 500.

Country Music Assn. (1958), One Music Circle S., Nashville, TN 37203; 6,588.

Creative Children and Adults, Natl. Assn. for (1974), 8080 Springvalley Dr., Cincinnati, OH 45236; 1,500.

Credit Assn., International (1912), 243 N. Lindberg, St. Louis, MO 63141; 13,500.

Credit Management, Nat. Assn. of (1896), 8815 Centre Park Dr., Columbia, MD 21045.

Credit Union Natl. Assn. (1934), 5710 Mineral Point Rd., Madison, WI 53705; 52 state credit union leagues.

Crime and Delinquency, Natl. Council on (1907), 685 Market St., Suite 620, San Francisco, CA 94105; 500.

Criminal Investigators Assn., Intl. (1970), P.O. Box 15350, Chevy Chase, MD 20815; 1,000.

Criminology, Amer. Society of (1941), 1314 Kinnear Rd., Suite 212, Columbus, OH 43212; 2,800.

Crop Science Society of America (1955), 677 S. Segoe Rd., Madison, WI 53711; 5,400.

Cross-Examination Debate Assn. (1971), California State Univ.-Northridge, Northridge, CA 91330; 310.

Cryptogram Assn., Amer. (1929) 4 Hawthorne Dr., Cherry Hill, NJ 08003; 1,100.

Customs Brokers & Forwarders Assn. of Am., Natl. (1897), One World Trade Center, Ste. 1153, N.Y., NY 10048.

Cyprus, Sovereign Order of (1192, 1964 in U.S.), 853 Seventh Ave., N.Y., NY 10019; 474.

Dairy Council, Natl. (1915), 6300 N. River Rd., Rosemont, IL 60018.

Dairy and Food Industries Supply Assn. (1912), 6245 Executive Blvd., Rockville, MD 20852; 832.

Dairy Goat Assn., American (1904), 209 W. Main St., Spindale, NC 28160; 12,000.

Dairylea Cooperative (1907), 831 James St., Syracuse, NY13203; 3,000.

Danish Brotherhood in America (1882), 3717 Harney St., Omaha, NE 68131; 9,534.

Daughters of the American Revolution, Natl. Society, (1890), 1776 D St. NW, Wash., DC 20006-5392; 202,197.

Daughters of the Confederacy, United (1894), 328 N. Blvd., Richmond, VA 23220-4057; 26,000.

Daughters of 1812, Natl. Society, U.S. (1892), 1461 Rhode Island Ave. NW, Wash., DC 20005; 4,700.

Daughters of the Republic of Texas (1891), 5758 Balcones Dr., Ste. 201, Austin, TX 78731; 6,008.

Daughters of Union Veterans of the Civil War (1885), 503 S. Walnut St., Springfield, IL 62704; 4,000.

Deaf, Alexander Graham Bell Assn. for the (1890), 3417 Volta Pl. NW, Wash., DC 20007; 5,000.

Deaf, Natl. Assn. of the (1880), 814 Thayer Ave., Silver Spring, MD 20910; 20,000.

Death and Dying, Natl. Council on (1990), 250 W. 50th St., N.Y., NY 10019; 120,000.

Defense Preparedness Assn., Amer. (1919), 2101 Wilson Blvd., Ste. 400, Arlington, VA 22201; 40,000.

Delta Kappa Gamma Society Intl. (1929), 416 W. 12th St., Austin, TX 78701; 165,000.

Deltiologists of America (1960), P.O. Box 8, Norwood, PA 19074; 1,600.

Democratic Natl. Committee, (1792), 430 S. Capitol St. SE, Wash., DC 20003; 408.

DeMolay, Intl. Council, Order of (1919), 10200 N. Executive Hills Blvd., Kansas City, MO 64153; 50,000.

Dental Assn., Amer. (1859), 211 E. Chicago Ave., Chicago, IL 60611; 140,000.

Descendants of the Colonial Clergy, Society of the (1933), 30 Leewood Rd., Wellesley, MA 02181; 1,400.

Descendants of the Signers of the Declaration of Independence (1907), 1300 Locust St., Phila., PA 19107; 937.

Descendants of Washington's Army at Valley Forge, Society of (1976), P.O. Box 915, Valley Forge, PA 19482-0915.

Diabetes Assn., Amer. (1940), 1660 Duke St., Alexandria, VA 22314; 259,000.

Dialect Society, Amer. (1889), c/o Allan Metcalf, English Dept., MacMurray College, Jacksonville, IL 62650; 550.

Direct Marketing Assn. (1917), 6 E. 43d St., N.Y., NY 10017.

Directors Guild of America (1936), 7950 Sunset Blvd., Los Angeles, CA 90046; 7,800.

Disabled Amer. Veterans (1920), P.O. Box 14301, Cincinnati, OH 45250; 1.1 mln.

Disc Sports, U.S. (1983), 180 Norman Rd., Rochester, NY 14623; 6,500.

Dogs on Stamps Study Unit, Amer. Topical Assn. (1979), 3208 Hana Rd., Edison, NJ 08817; 250.

Dowsers, Amer. Society of (1961), Brainerd St., Danville, VT 05828; 3,500.

Dozenal Society of America (1945), Math Dept., Nassau Community College, Garden City, NY 11530; 300.

Dracula Society, Count (1962), 334 W. 54th St., Los Angeles, CA 90037; 500.

Drug, Chemical and Allied Trades Assn. (1890), 2 Roosevelt Ave., Syosset, NY 11791; 2,000.

Ducks Unlimited (1937), One Waterfowl Way at Gilmer Rd., Long Grove, IL 60014; 640,000.

Dutch Settlers Soc. of Albany (1924), 6 DeLucia Terr., Loudonville, NY 12211; 300.

Eagles, Fraternal Order of (1898), 12660 West Capitol Dr., Brookfield, WI 53055; 1.1 mln.

Earth, Friends of the (1969), 530 7th St. SE, Washington, DC 20003; 20,000.

Easter Seal Society, Natl. (1919), 70 E. Lake St., Chicago, IL 60601.

Eastern Star, General Grand Chapter, Order of the (1876), 1618 New Hampshire Ave. NW, Wash., DC 20009; 1.7 mln.

Economic Assn., Amer. (1885), 2014 Broadway, Ste. 305, Nashville, TN 37203; 27,260.

Economic Development, Committee for (1942), 1700 K St., NW, Suite 700, Washington, DC 20006; 365.

Edison Electric Institute (1933), 701 Pennsylvania Ave. NW, Wash., DC 20004-2696; 180 corporations.

Education, Amer. Assn. for Adult and Continuing (1982), 1112 16th St. NW, Suite 420, Wash., DC 20036; 3,000.

Education, Amer. Council on (1918), One Dupont Circle NW, #800, Wash., DC 20036; 1,848 schools.

Education, Amer. Soc. for Engineering (1893), 11 Dupont Circle NW, Suite 200, Washington, DC 20036; 10,000+.

Education, Council for Advancement & Support of (1974), 11 Dupont Circle NW, Wash., DC 20036; 2,950 schools.

Education, Council for Basic (1956), 725 15th St. NW, Wash., DC 20005; 10,000.

Education, Institute of Intl. (1919), 809 United Nations Plaza, N.Y., NY 10017; 700 U.S. colleges, univ.

Education, Natl. Committee for Citizens in (1973), 10840 Little Patuxent Pwky., Suite 301, Columbia, MD 21044; 650.

Education, Natl. Society for the Study of (1901), 5835 Kimbark Ave., Chicago, IL 60637; 2,400.

Education Assn., Natl. (1857), 1201 16th St. NW, Wash., DC 20036; 2 mln.

Education Society, Comparative and Intl. (1956), Univ. of S. California, Univ. Park, Los Angeles, CA 90089; 2,500.

Education of Young Children, Natl. Assn. for the (1926), 1834 Connecticut Ave. NW, Wash., DC 20009; 70,000.

Educational Exchange, Council on Intl. (1947), 205 E. 42d St., N.Y., NY 10017; 200 organizations.

Educational Research Assn., Amer. (1916), 1230 17th St. NW, Wash., DC 20036; 16,000.

8th Air Force Historical Society (1975), P.O. Box 7215, St. Paul, MN 55107; 18,000.

82nd Airborne Division Assn., Inc. (1944), 2670 W. Stansifer Ct., Bloomington, IN 47403; 21,200.

88th Infantry Division Assn., Inc. (1948), P.O. Box 925, Havertown, PA 19083; 5,152.

Electrical and Electronics Engineers, Institute of (1884), 345 E. 47th St., N.Y., NY 10017; 300,000.

Electrical Manufacturers Assn., Natl. (1926), 2101 L St. NW, Wash., DC 20037; 560 companies.

Electrochemical Society (1902), 10 S. Main St., Pennington, NJ 08534-2896; 6,000.

Electronic Industries Assn. (1924), 2001 Pennsylvania Ave., Wash., DC 20006-1813; 1,058 companies.

Electronics Sales & Service Dealers Assn., Natl. (1973), 2708 W. Berry, Ft. Worth, TX 76109; 1,400.

Electronics Technicians, Intl. Society of Certified (1970), 2708 W. Berry, Ft. Worth, TX 76109; 1,400.

Electroplaters' and Surface Finishers' Society, Amer. (1909), 12644 Research Pkwy, Orlando, FL 32826; 8,200.

Elks of the U.S.A., Benevolent and Protective Order of (1868), 2750 Lakeview Ave., Chicago, IL 60614; 1.5 mln.

Energy Research Institute, Clean (1974), 1251 Memorial Dr., 219 MacArthur Engineering Bldg., Coral Gables, FL, 33146.

Energy, Intl. Assn. for Hydrogen (1975), P.O. Box 242866, Miami, FL 33124-8266; 2,500.

Engine and Boat Manufacturers, Natl. Assn. of (1904), 401 N. Michigan Ave., Chicago, IL 60611.

Engineering, Natl. Academy of (1964), 2101 Constitution Ave. NW, Wash., DC 20418; 1,535.

Engineering, Soc. for the Advancement of Material & Process (1944), P.O. Box 2459, Covina, CA 91722; 10,000.

Engineering Societies, Amer. Assn. of (1979), 345 E. 47th St., N.Y., NY 10017; 38 societies.

Engineering Society of N. Amer, Illuminating (1906), 345 E. 47th St., N.Y., NY 10017; 10,000.

Engineering Trustees, United (1904), 345 E. 47th St., N.Y., NY 10017.

Engineers, Amer. Inst. of Chemical (1908), 345 E. 47th St., N.Y., N.Y. 10003; 52,000.

Engineers, Amer. Institute of Mining, Metallurgical and Petroleum (1871), 345 E. 47th St., N.Y., NY 10017.

Engineers, Amer. Soc. of Agricultural (1907), 2950 Niles Rd., St. Joseph, MI 49085-9659; 10,000.

Engineers, Amer. Soc. of Civil (1852), 345 E. 47th St., N.Y., NY 10017; 111,112.

Engineers, Amer. Soc. of Naval (1888), 1452 Duke St., Alexandria, VA 22314; 8,500.

Engineers, Amer. Soc. of Plumbing (1964), 3617 Thousand Oaks Blvd., #210, Westlake Vlge, CA 91362-3625; 4,500.

Engineers, Amer. Soc. of Safety (1911), 1800 E. Oakton St., Des Plains, IL 60018; 25,000.

Engineers, Assn. of Energy (1977), 4025 Pleasantdale Rd., Suite 420, Atlanta, GA 30340; 7,500.

Engineers, Inst. of Industrial (1948), 25 Technology Park, Atlanta, GA 30092; 43,000.

Engineers, Inst. of Transportation (1930), Suite 410, 525 School St. NW, Wash., DC 20024, 7,700.

Engineers, Natl. Society of Professional (1934), 1420 King St., Alexandria, VA 22314; 75,000.

Engineers, Soc. of Fire Protection (1950), 60 Batterymarch St., Boston, MA 02110; 3,750.

Engineers, Soc. of Logistics (1966), 125 W. Park Loop, Suite 201, Huntsville, AL 35806; 10,000.

Engineers, Soc. of Manufacturing (1932), One SME Drive, P.O. Box 930, Dearborn, MI 48121; 80,000.

Engineers, Society of Mining (1871), 8307 Shaffer Pkwy., Littleton, CO 80127; 23,058.

Engineers, Society of Plastics (1942), 14 Fairfield Dr., Brookfield Ctr., CT 06805; 25,000.

Engineers, Society of Tribologists & Lubrication (1944), 838 Busse Hwy., Park Ridge, IL 60068; 4,100.

English Assn., College (1939), English Dept., Nazareth College, 4245 East Ave., Rochester, NY 14610; 1,450.

English-Speaking Union of the U.S. (1920), 16 E. 69th St., N.Y., NY 10021; 27,000.

Entomological Society of America (1889), 9301 Annapolis Rd., Lanham, MD 20706; 8,500.

Environmental Health Assn., Natl. (1937), 720 S. Colorado Blvd., Suite 970, Denver, CO 80222; 5,000.

Epigraphic Society, Inc., The (1974), 6625 Bamburgh Dr., San Diego, CA 92117; 1,120.

Esperanto League for North America (1952), P.O. Box 1129, El Cerrito, CA 94530; 1,014.

European Council, Ltd., Eastern (1990), 11 John St., Ste. 406, N.Y., NY 10038; 1,000.

Evangelism Crusades, Intl. (1959), 14617 Victory Blvd., Van Nuys, CA 91411; 500.

Exchange Club, Natl. (1911), 3050 Central Ave., Toledo, OH 43606-1757; 44,000.

Executive Management Services Corp. (1973), P.O. Box 58, Atlantic Beach, NY 11509.

Experiment in Intl. Living/School for Intl. Training (1932), P.O. Box 676, Kipling Rd., Brattleboro, VT 05302; 70,000.

Fairs & Expositions, Intl. Assn. of (1919), P.O. Box 985, Springfield, MO 65801; 1,500.

Family Life, Natl. Alliance for, Inc. (1973), Ste. 4, 225 Jericho Tpk., Floral Park, NY 11001; 499.

Family Relations, Natl. Council on (1938), 3989 Central Ave. NE, Suite 550, Minneapolis, MN 55421; 3,592.

Family Service Assn. of America (1911), 11700 W. Lake Park Dr., Park Pl, Milwaukee, WI 53224; 286 agencies.

Farm Bureau Federation, Amer. (1919), 225 Touhy Ave., Park Ridge, IL 60068; 3.8 mln. families.

Farmers of America Organization, Natl. Future (1928), 5632 Mt. Vernon Memorial Hwy., Alexandria, VA 22309-0160.

Farmers Union, Natl. (1902), Denver, CO 80251; 250,000.

Farmers' Educational and Co-Operative Union of America (1902), 10065 E. Harvard Ave., Denver, CO 80231; 250,000.

Fast Draw Assn., World (1975), 1026 Llagas Rd., Morgan Hill, CA 95037; 320.

Fat Acceptance, Natl. Assn. to Advance (NAAFA) (1969), P.O. Box 188620, Sacramento, CA 95818; 3,000.

Federal Employees, Natl. Fed. of (1917), 1016 16th St. NW, Wash., DC 20036.

Federal Employees Veterans Assn. (1954), Leslie Harris, 1024 E. Cliveden St., Phila., PA 19119; 4,562.

Feminists for Life of America (1972), 811 E. 47th St., Kansas City, MO 64110; 3,000.

Film Library Assn., Educational (1943), 45 John St., Suite 301, N.Y., NY 10038; 1,600.

Financial Analysts Federation (1945), #5 Boar's Head Lane, Charlottesville, VA 22901; 17,000.

Financial Executives Institute (1931), 10 Madison Ave., P.O. Box 1938, Morristown, NJ 07962-1938, 13,500.

Financiers, Intl. Soc. of (1979), P.O. Box 18508, Asheville, NC 28814; 300+.

Fire Chiefs, Intl. Assn. of (1873), 1329 18th St. NW, Wash., DC 20036; 9,500.

Fire Marshals Assn. of No. America (1906), NFPA, Batterymarch Pk., Quincy, MA 02269-9101.

Fire Protection Assn., Natl. (1896), Batterymarch Park, Quincy MA 02269; 38,000.

Fish Assn., Intl. Game (1939), 3000 E. Las Olas Blvd., Ft. Lauderdale, FL 33316; 25,000.

Fisheries Institute, Natl. (1945), 2000 M St., Washington, DC 20036; 1,250.

Fishes, Soc. for the Protection of Old (1967), School of Fisheries, WH-10 Univ. of Washington, Seattle, WA 98195; 250.

Fishing Institute, Sport (1949), 1010 Massachusetts Ave. NW, Suite 320, Wash., DC 20001; 214.

Fishing Tackle Manufacturers Assn., Amer. (1950), 1250 Grove Ave., Barrington, IL 60010.

Flag Research Center, The (1962), 3 Edgehill Rd., Winchester, MA 01890; 1,200.

Flight Attendants, Assn. of (1973), 1625 Massachusetts Ave. NW, Wash., DC 20036; 28,000.

Florida Tobacco & Candy Assn. (1976), 217 S. Adams St., Tallahassee, FL 32302; 35.

Fly Fishers, Fed. of (1965), Box 1088, 200 Yellowstone Ave., W. Yellowstone, MT 59758; 12,000.

Flying Disc Fed., World (1985), Gnejsvägen 24, 85240; Sundsvall, Sweden; 15,000.

Food Brokers Assn., Natl. (1904), 1010 Massachusetts Ave. NW, Wash., DC 20001; 1,800 companies.

Food Institute, Amer. Frozen (1942), 1764 Old Meadow Ln., Suite 350, McLean, VA 22102; 500 firms.

Footwear Industries Assn., Amer. (1871), 3700 Market St., Philadelphia, PA 19104; 180.

Foreign Relations, Council on (1921), 58 E. 68th St., N.Y., NY 10021; 2,500.

Foreign Student Affairs, Natl. Assn. for (1948), 1860 19th St. NW, Wash., DC 20009; 5,500.

Foreign Study, Amer. Institute for (1964), 102 Greenwich Ave., Greenwich, CT 06830; 300,000.

Foreign Trade Council, Inc., Natl. (1914), 1625 K St. NW, Washington, DC 20006; 500 companies.

Forensic Sciences, Amer. Academy of (1948), 218 E. Cache La Poudre, Colorado Springs, CO 80903; 3,500.

Forest Council (1932), 1250 Connecticut Ave. NW, Suite 320, Washington, DC 20036.

Forest History Society (1946), 701 Vickers Ave., Durham, NC 27701; 2,000.

Forest Products Assn., Natl. (1902), 1250 Connecticut Ave. NW, Wash., DC 20036; 700 companies.

Forest Products Research Society (1947), 2801 Marshall Ct., Madison, WI 53705; 3,600.

Foresters, Society of Amer. (1900), 5400 Grosvenor La., Bethesda, MD 20814; 19,500.

Forestry Assn., Amer. (1875), 1516 P St. NW, Wash., DC 20005; 40,000.

Fortean Organization, Intl. (1965), P.O. Box 367, Arlington, VA 22210; 1,000.

Founders and Patriots of Amer., The Order of the (1896), 3813 Acapulco Ct., Irving, TX 75062; 1,250.

Foundrymen's Society, Amer. (1896), Golf & Wolf Rds., Des Plaines, IL 60016; 13,255.

4-H Clubs (1901-1905), Extension Service, U.S. Dept of Agriculture, Wash., DC 20250; 5.8 mln.

Franklin D. Roosevelt Philatelic Society (1963), 154 Laguna St., St. Augustine Shores, FL 32086; 696.

Freedom, Young Americans for (1960), Box 1002, Woodland Rd. Sterling, VA 22170; 80,000.

Freedom of Information Center (1958), 20 Walter Williams Hall, Univ. of Missouri, Columbia, MO 65211.

Freedoms Foundation at Valley Forge (1949), Valley Forge, PA 19481; 5,000.

Friedreich's Ataxia Group in America (1969), P.O. Box 11116, Oakland, CA 94611; 2,100+.

French Institute (1911), 22 E. 60th St., N.Y., NY 10022.

Friendship and Good Will, Intl. Soc. of (1978), 211 W. 4th Ave., P.O. Box 2637, Gastonia, NC 28053-2637; 3,926.

Frisbee Assn., Intl. (1967), 900 E. El Monte, San Gabriel, CA 91776; 110,000.

Funeral and Memorial Societies, Continental Assn. of (1963), 2001 S. St. NW, Suite 530, Washington, DC 20009.

GASP (Group Against Smokers' Pollution) (1971), P.O. Box 632, College Park, MD 20741-0632; 10,000.

Gamblers Anonymous (1957), 3255 Wilshire Blvd., #610, Los Angeles, CA 90010; 1,200 groups.

Garden Club of Amer. (1913), 598 Madison Ave., N.Y., NY 10022; 15,000.

Garden Clubs, Natl. Council of State (1929), 4401 Magnolia Ave., St. Louis, MO 63110; 308,623.

Garden Clubs of America, Men's (1932), 5560 Merle Hay Rd., Johnston, IA 50131; 9,500.

Gas Appliance Manufacturers Assn. (1935), 1901 N. Moore St., Arlington, VA 22209; 210 companies.

Gas Assn., Amer. (1918), 1515 Wilson Blvd., Arlington, VA 22209; 229 companies; 3,000 individuals.

Gay and Lesbian Task Force, Natl. (1973), 1734 14th St. NW, Washington, DC 20009; 17,000.

Genealogical Society, Natl. (1903), 4527 17th St. N., Arlington, VA 22207; 9,500.

Genetic Assn., Amer. (1903), P.O. Box 39, Buckeystown, MD 21701; 1,600.

Geographers, Assn. of Amer. (1904), 1710 16th St. NW, Wash., DC 20009-3198; 6,300.

Geographic Education, Natl. Council for (1915), 16A Leonard Hall, IUPA, Indiana, PA 15705; 3,500.

Geographic Society, Natl. (1888), 1600 M St. NW, Wash., DC 20036; 10 mln.

Geographical Society, Amer. (1851), 156 Fifth Ave., Suite 600, N.Y., NY 10010-7002; 5,000.

Geolinguistics, Amer. Society of (1965), University of Rhode Island, Kingston, RI 02892; 70.

Geological Institute, Amer. (1948), 4220 King St., Alexandria, VA 22302; 20 societies.

Geological Society of America (1888), 3300 Penrose Pl., P.O. Box 9140, Boulder, CO 80301; 17,000.

Geologists, Assn. of Engineering (1960), 323 Boston Post Rd. Suite 2D, Sudbury, MA 01776; 2,800.

Geologists, Amer. Assn. of Petroleum (1917), 1444 S. Boulder, Tulsa, OK 74119; 34,500.

Geophysicists, Society of Exploration (1930), 8801 S. Yale Ave., Tulsa OK 74137; 14,854.

Geriatrics Society, Amer. (1942), 770 Lexington Ave., Suite 300, N.Y., NY 10021; 6,100.

Gideons Intl. (1899), 2900 Lebanon Rd., Nashville, TN 37214; 104,000.

Gifted & Talented Club, Natl. (1987), 4049 Ross Park Dr., San Jose, CA 95118; 200.

Gifted Children, Amer. Assn. for (1946), 15 Gramercy Park, N.Y., NY 10003.

Gifted Children, Natl. Assn. for (1957), 1155 15th St. NW, Ste. 1002, Wash., DC 20005; 6,500.

Girls Clubs of America (1945), 30 E. 33d St., N.Y., NY 10016; 250,000+.

Girl Scouts of the U.S.A. (1912), 830 Third Ave., N.Y., NY 10022; 3.2 mln.

Gladiolus Council, No. Amer. (1945), 9338 Manzanita Dr., Sun City, AZ 85373; 1,275.

Gold Star Mothers, Amer. (1928), 2128 Leroy Pl. NW, Wash., DC 20008; 3,000.

Golf Association, U.S. (1894), Box 708, Far Hills, NJ 07931.

Goose Island Bird & Girl Watching Society (1960), 301 Arthur Ave., Park Ridge, IL 60068; 757.

Gospel Music Assn. (1964), 38 Music Square W., Nashville, TN 37203; 3,000.

Governing Boards, Assn. of (1922), 1 Dupont Circle, Ste. 400, Washington, DC 20036; 1,107.

Government Finance Officers Assn. (1906), 180 N. Michigan Ave., Suite 800, Chicago, IL 60601; 12,500.

Gov't. Funding of Soc. Serv., Greater Wash. Organizations for (1981), 6612 Virginia View Ct. NW, Wash., DC 20816.

Graduate Schools in the U.S., Council of (1961), One Dupont Circle NW, Wash., DC 20036; 365 institutions.

Grandmother Clubs of America, Natl. Federation of (1934), 203 N. Wabash Ave., Chicago, IL 60601; 10,000.

Grange, Natl. (1867), 1616 H St. NW, Wash., DC 20006.

Graphic Artists, Society of Amer. (1915), 32 Union Sq., East, N.Y., NY 10003; 203.

Graphic Arts, Amer. Institute of (1914), 1059 Third Ave., N.Y., NY 10021; 6,000.

Gray Panthers (1970), 1424 16th St. NW, Suite 602, Wash., DC 20036; 30,000.

Greek-Amer. War Veterans in America, Natl. Legion of (1938), 739 W. 186th St., N.Y., NY 10033; 11.

Green Mountain Club, The (1910), 43 State St., Box 889, Montpelier, VT 05601; 5,500.

Grocers, Natl. Assn. of (1893), 1825 Samuel Morse Dr., Reston, VA 22090.

Grocery Manufacturers of America (1908), 1010 Wisconsin Ave., Suite 800, Wash., DC 20007; 137 companies.

Guide Dog Foundation for the Blind (1946), 371 E. Jericho Tpke., Smithtown, NY 11787-2976.

Gyro Intl. (1912), 1096 Mentor Ave., Painesville, OH 44077.

HIAS (Hebrew Immigrant Aid Society) (1880), 200 Park Ave. S, N.Y., NY 10003; 6,000.

Hadassah, the Women's Zionist Organization of America (1912), 50 W. 58th St., N.Y., NY 10019; 385,000.

Hairdressers and Cosmetologists Assn., Natl. (1921), 3510 Olive St., St. Louis, MO 63103; 50,406.

Handball Assn., U.S. (1951), 930 N. Benton Ave., Tucson, AZ 85711; 10,000.

Handgun, Intl. Metallic Silhouette Assn. (1976), P.O. Box 368, Burlington, IA 52601; 1,300.

Handicapped, Federation of the (1935), 211 W. 14th St., N.Y., NY 10011; 650.

Handicapped, Natl. Assn. of the Physically (1958), Bethesda Scarlet Oaks, #117, 440 Lafayette Ave., Cincinnati, OH 45220-1000; 700.

Health Council, Natl. (1920), 350 Fifth Ave., Suite 1118, N.Y., NY 10118; 107 natl. organizations.

Health, Physical Education, Recreation and Dance, Amer. Alliance for (1885), 1900 Association Dr., Reston, VA 22091.

Health Professions, Am. Soc. of Allied (1967), 1101 Connecticut Ave. NW, Ste. 700, Wash., DC 20036-4387; 500.

Hearing Aid Society, Natl. (1951), 20361 Middlebelt Rd., Livonia, MI 48152; 2,700.

Hearing and Speech Action, Natl. Assn. for (1910), 10801 Rockville Pike, Rockville, MD 20852; 3,500.

Heart Assn., Amer. (1924), 7320 Greenville Ave., Dallas TX 75231; 200,000.

Hearts, Mended (1951), 7320 Greenville Ave., Dallas TX 75231; 20,000.

Heating, Refrigerating & Air Conditioning Engineers, Amer. Soc. of (1894), 1791 Tullie Circle NE, Atlanta, GA 30329.

Helicopter Assn. Intl. (1948), 1619 Duke St., Alexandria, VA 22314; 1,500.

Helicopter Society, Amer. (1943), 217 N. Washington St., Alexandria VA 22314; 8,000.

Hemispheric Affairs, Council on (1975), 724 9th St. NW, Wash., DC 20001; 2,500.

High School Assns., Natl. Federation of State (1920), P.O. Box 20626, Kansas City, MO 64153; 51.

High Twelve Internatl. (1921), 11155-B2 South Towne Square, St. Louis, MO 63123; 25,000.

Hiking Society, Amer. (1977), 1015 31st St. NW, Wash., DC 20007-4490; 5,000.

Historians, Organization of Amer. (1907), 112 N. Bryan St., Bloomington, IN 47408; 12,000.

Historical Assn., Amer. (1884), 400 A St. SE, Wash., DC 20003; 14,000.

Historic Preservation, Natl. Trust for (1966), 1785 Massachusetts Ave. NW, Wash., DC 20036; 240,000.

Hockey, U.S.A. (1937), 2997 Broadmoor Valley Rd., Colorado Springs, CO 80906; 250,000.

Holy Cross of Jerusalem, Order of (1965), 853 Seventh Ave., N.Y., NY 10019; 2,225.

Home Builders, Natl. Assn. of (1942), 15th & M Sts. NW, Wash., DC 20005; 157,479.

Home Economics Assn., Amer. (1909), 1555 King St., Alexandria, VA 22314; 23,000.

Homemakers of America, Future (1945), 1910 Association Dr., Reston, VA 22091; 281,000+.

Homemakers Council, Natl. Extension (1936), 4089 Snake Island Rd., Sturgeon Bay, WI 54235; 355,000.

Honor Society, Natl. (1921), 1904 Association Dr., Reston, VA 22091; 22,000.

Hospital Marketing and Public Relations of the Amer. Hospital, Amer. Soc. for (1964), 840 N. Lake Shore Dr., 9E, Chicago, IL 60611; 3,100.

Horatio Alger Soc. (1965), 4907 Allison Dr., Lansing, MI 48910; 300.

Horse Council, American (1969), 1700 K St. NW, #300, Washington, DC 20006; 2,100.

Horse Protection Assn., Amer. (1966), 1000 29th St. NW, Suite T-100, Wash., DC 20007; 8,000.

Horse Show Assn. of America Ltd., Natl. (1883), 680 5th Ave., #1602, N.Y., NY 10019.

Horse Shows Assn., Amer. (1917), 220 E. 42 St., N.Y., NY 10017-5806; 54,000+.

Hospital Association, Amer. (1899), 840 N. Lake Shore Dr., Chicago, IL 60611; 40,000.

Hospital Marketing and Public Relations, Amer. Society for (1964), 840 N. Lake Shore Dr., Chicago, IL 60611; 3,167.

Hot Rod Assn., Natl. (1951), 2035 Financial Way, Glendora, CA 91740; 74,524.

Hotel & Motel Assn., Amer. (1910), 1201 New York Ave., NW, Washington, DC; 10,000.

Human Resource Management, Society for (1948), 606 N. Washington St., Alexandria, VA 22314; 45,000.

Human Rights and Social Justice, Americans for (1977), P.O. Box 6258, Ft. Worth, TX 76115.

Humane Society of the U.S. (1954), 2100 L St. NW, Wash., DC 20037; 1.3 mln.+.

Humanics, American (1948), 4601 Madison Ave., Kansas City, MO 64112; 600.

Hydrogen Energy, Intl. Assn. for (1975), P.O. Box 248266, Coral Gables, FL 33124; 2,000.

Idaho, U.S.S. (BB-42) Assn. (1957), P.O. Box 711247, San Diego, CA 92171; 850.

Identification, Intl. Assn. for (1916), P.O. Box 2423, Alameda, CA 94501; 2,850.

Illustrators, Society of (1901), 128 E. 63 St., N.Y., NY 10021; 965.

Industrial Democracy, League for (1905), 181 Hudson St., N.Y., NY 10013; 1,500.

Industrial Designers Society of America (1965), 1142-E Walker Rd., Great Falls, VA 22066; 2,030.

Industrial Engineers, Amer. Institute of (1948), 25 Technology Park, Norcross, GA 30092; 40,000.

Industrial Health Foundation (1935), 34 Penn Circle West, Pittsburgh, PA 15206; 170 companies.

Industrial Security, Amer. Soc. for (1955), 1655 N. Ft. Myer Dr., Suite 1200, Arlington, VA 22209; 25,000.

Information, Freedom of, Center (1958), P.O. Box 858, Columbia, MO 65205.

Information and Image Management, Assn. for (1943), 1100 Wayne Ave., Ste. 1100, Silver Springs, MD 20910; 7,808.

Information Industry Assn. (1968), 555 New Jersey Ave. NW, Suite 800, Wash., DC 20001; 600 companies.

Insurance Assn., Amer. (1964), 1130 Connecticut Ave. NW, Suite 1000, Wash., DC 20036; 220 companies.

Insurance Society, Inc., Intl. (1965), Box 870224, Rm. 328, Farrah Hall, Tuscaloosa, AL 35487; 1,000 indv., 150 corporate.

Intelligence Officers, Assn. of Former (1975), 6723 Whittier Ave., Suite 303A, McLean, VA 22101; 3,500.

Intercollegiate Athletics, Natl. Assn. of (1940), 1221 Baltimore Ave., Kansas City, MO 64105; 500 schools.

Interior Designers, Amer. Society of (1975), 1430 Broadway, N.Y., NY 10018; 28,000.

International Interculture Programs, AFS (1947), 313 E. 43rd St., N.Y., NY 10017; 100,000.

Intertel, Inc. (1966), P.O. Box 150580, Lakewood, CO 80215.

Inventors, Amer. Assn. of (1891), 2020 Pennsylvania Ave. NW, Wash., DC 20006; 5,727.

Investment Clubs, Natl. Assn. of (1951), 1515 E. Eleven Mile Rd., Royal Oak, MI 44067; 140,000.

Investment Management and Research, Assn. for (1990), 5 Boar's Head Ln., Charlottesville, VA 22901; 21,000.

Investors Corp., Natl. Assn. of (1951), 1515 E. Eleven Mile Rd., Royal Oak, MI 48067; 115,000.

Irish-American Cultural Inst. (1962), 2115 Summit Ave., Univ. of St. Thomas, St. Paul, MN 55105; 7,000.

Iron Castings Society (1897), 455 State St., Des Plaines, IL 60016; 200 firms.

Iron and Steel Engineers, Assn. of (1907), Three Gateway Center, Suite 2350, Pittsburgh, PA 15222; 11,856.

Iron and Steel Institute, Amer. (1905), 1133 15th St. NW, Wash., DC 20005-2701; 55 cos.

Italian Historical Society of America (1949), 111 Columbia Heights, Bklyn., NY 11201.

Italy-America Chamber of Commerce (1887), 350 Fifth Ave., N.Y., NY 10118; 850.

Izaak Walton League of America, The (1922), 1401 Wilson Blvd., Level B, Arlington, VA 22209; 53,000.

(Jesse) James Farm, Friends of, (1979), Rt. 2, Box 236, Kearney, MO 64060; 300.

Jamestowne Society (1936), P.O. Box 14523, Richmond, VA 23221; 2,721.

Jane Austen Society of N. Amer. (1979), 4169 Lions Ave., N. Vancouver, B.C., Canada, V7R 352; 2,300.

Japanese Amer. Citizens League (1929), 1765 Sutter St., San Francisco, CA 94115; 26,000.

Jewish Appeal, United (1939), 99 Park Avenue, N.Y., NY 10016.

Jewish Book Council (1943), 15 E. 26th St., N.Y., NY 10010.

Jewish Committee, Amer. (1906), 165 E. 56th St., N.Y., NY 10022; 50,000.

Jewish Congress, Amer. (1918), 15 E. 84th St., N.Y., NY 10028; 50,000.

Jewish Federations, Council of (1932), 730 Broadway, N.Y., NY 10003; 200 agencies.

Jewish Historical Society, Amer. (1892), 2 Thornton Rd., Waltham, MA 02154; 3,300.

Jewish War Veterans of the U.S.A. (1896), 1811 R St. NW, Wash., DC 20009; 100,000.

Jewish Welfare Bd. Natl. (1917), 15 E. 26th St., N.Y., NY 10010.

Jewish Women, Natl. Council of (1893), 53 W. 23rd St., N.Y., NY 10010; 100,000.

Job's Daughters, Internatl. Order of (1920), 233 W. 6th St., Papillion, NE 68046; 32,000.

Jockey Club (1894), 380 Madison Ave., N.Y., NY 10017; 90.

John Birch Society (1958), 395 Concord Ave., Belmont, MA 02178; 25,000.

John Pelham Historical Assn. (1982), 7 Carmel Terr., Hampton, VA 23666; 125.

Joseph Diseases Foundation, Intl. (1977), P.O. Box 2550, Livermore, CA 94550; 3,800.

Journalists, Society of Professional (Sigma Delta Chi) (1909), 53 W. Jackson Blvd., Suite 731, Chicago, IL 60604.

Journalists and Authors, Amer. Society of (1948), 1501 Broadway, Suite 1907, N.Y., NY 10036; 750+.

Judaism, Amer. Council for (1943), 298 Fifth Ave., N.Y., NY 10001; 20,000.

Judicature Society, Amer. (1913), 25 E. Washington, Chicago, IL 60602; 20,000.

Juggler's Assn., Intl. (1947), P.O. Box 3707, Akron, OH 44314-3707; 3,000.

Junior Achievement (1919), 550 Summer St., Stamford, CT 06901; 300,000.

Junior Auxiliaries, Natl. Assn. of (1941), 845 S. Main, Greenville, MS 38701; 9,000.

Junior Colleges, Amer. Assn. of Community and (1920), One Dupont Circle NW, Wash., DC 20036; 900.

Junior Leagues, Assn. of (1921), 660 First Ave., N.Y., NY 10016; 189,000.

Kennel Club, Amer. (1884), 51 Madison Ave., N.Y., NY 10010; 130 clubs.

Kidney Fund, Amer. (1971), 6110 Executive Blvd., #1010, Rockville, MD 20852.

Kiwanis Intl. (1915), 3636 Woodview Trace, Indianapolis, IN 46268-3196; 329,000.

Klinefelter's Syndrome Assn. of Canada (1988), P.O. Box 5000, Penetanguishene, Ontario, Canada L0K 1P0.

Knights of Columbus (1882), One Columbus Plaza, New Haven, CT 06507; 1.4 mln.

Knights of Pythias (1864), 2785 E. Desert Inn Rd., #150, Las Vegas, NV 89121; 96,000.

Knights Templar U.S.A., Grand Encampment (1816), 14 E. Jackson Blvd., Suite 1700, Chicago, IL 60604-2293; 295,000.

Krishna Consciousness, Intl. Soc. for (ISKON) (1966) 3764 Watseka Ave., Los Angeles, CA 92109; 1 mln.

La Leche League Intl. (1956), 9616 Minneapolis Ave., P.O. Box 1209, Franklin Park, IL 60131; 50,000.

Lambs, The (1874), 3 W. 51st St., N.Y., NY 10019; 194.

Landscape Architects, Amer. Society of (1899), 1733 Connecticut Ave., NW, Wash., DC 20009; 7,000.

Law, Amer. Society of International (1906), 2223 Massachusetts Ave. NW, Washington, DC 20008; 4,300.

Law Enforcement Officers Assn., Amer. (1966), 1000 Connecticut Ave. NW, Suite 9, Wash., DC 20036; 50,000.

Law Libraries, Amer. Assn. of (1906), 53 W. Jackson Blvd., Chicago, IL 60604; 4,630.

Law and Social Policy, Center for (1969), 1751 N St. NW, Wash., DC 20036.

Learned Societies, Amer. Council of (1919), 228 E. 45th St., N.Y., NY 10017; 45 societies.

Lefthanders, League of (1975), P.O. Box 89, New Milford, NJ 07646; 1,200.

Lefthanders Intl. (1975), P.O. Box 8249, Topeka, KS 66608.

Legal Administrators, Assn. of (1971), 175 E. Hawthorn Pkwy. #325, Vernon Hills, IL 60061-1428; 8,000.

Legion of Valor of the U.S.A. (1890), 92 Oak Leaf Lane, Chapel Hill, NC 27516; 780.

Leif Ericson Society (1962), Box 301, Chicago, IL 60690-0301; 1,200.

Leprosy Missions, Amer. (1906), One Alm Way, Greenville, SC 29601.

Leukemia Society of America (1949), 733 Third Ave., N.Y., NY 10017; 57 chapters.

Lewis and Clark Trail Heritage Foundation, Inc. (1969), P.O. Box 3434, Great Falls, MT 59403; 1,373.

Lewis Carroll Society of N. America (1974), 617 Rockford Rd., Silver Spring, MD 20902; 325.

Liberty Lobby (1955), 300 Independence Ave. SE, Wash., DC 20003; 25,000.

Libraries Assn., Special (1909), 1700 18th St., NW, Wash., DC 20009; 12,500.

Library Administration & Management Assn. (1957), 50 E. Huron St., Chicago, IL 60611; 5,074.

Library Assn., Amer. (1876), 50 E. Huron St., Chicago, IL 60611; 50,000.

Library Assn., Medical (1861), 6 N. Michigan Ave., Suite 300, Chicago, IL 60602; 5,000+.

Library Assn., Am. Theological (1947), 820 Church St., Ste. 300, Evanston, IL 60201; 463.

Life, Americans United for (1971), 343 S. Dearborn St., Ste. 1804, Chicago, IL 60604.

Life Insurance, Amer. Council of (1976), 1001 Pennsylvania Ave., NW, Wash., DC 20004; 616 firms.

Life Office Management Assn. (1924), 5770 Powers Ferry Rd., Atlanta, GA 30327; 870 companies.

Life Underwriters, Amer. Soc. of Certified (1929), 270 Bryn Mawr Ave., Byrn Mawr, PA 19010; 28,000.

Life Underwriters, Natl. Assn. of (1890), 1922 F St. NW, Wash., DC 20006; 135,000.

Lighter-Than-Air Society (1952), 1800 Triplett Blvd., Akron, OH 44306; 1,200.

Lions Clubs, Intl. Assn. of (1917), 300 22d St., Oak Brook, IL 60521-8842; 1,363,000.

Litchfield Institute, The (1984), P.O. Box 483, Bristol, CT 06010-0483; 52.

Literacy Intl., Laubach (1955), 1320 Jamesville Ave., Box 131, Syracuse, NY 13210.

Literacy Volunteers of America (1962), 5795 Widewaters Parkway, Syracuse, NY 13214; 100,000.

Little League Baseball (1939), P.O. Box 3485, Williamsport, PA 17701; 16,450 leagues.

Little People of America (1957), P.O. Box 9897, Washington, DC 20016; 5,000.

London Club (1975), Rt. One, Big Springs, KS 66050; 200.

Longwave Club of America (1974), 45 Wildflower Rd., Levittown, PA 19057; 536.

Lung Assn., Amer. (1904), 1740 Broadway, N.Y., NY 10019.

Lutheran Education Assn. (1942), 7400 Augusta St., River Forest, IL 60305; 3,750.

Magazine Photographers, Am. Soc. of (1944), 419 Park Ave. South, N.Y., NY 10016; 5,000+.

Magazine Publishers Assn. (1919), 575 Lexington Ave., N.Y., NY 10022; 312 publishers.

Magicians, Intl. Brotherhood of (1926), 103 N. Main St., Bluffton, OH 45817; 15,000.

Magicians Assn. Worldwide, Amateur (1988), 325 Maple St., Lynne, MA 01904-0073; 18,000.

Magicians, Society of Amer. (1902), 1333 Cory St., Yellow Springs, OH 45387; 5,500.

Management Assn., Amer. (1923), 135 W. 50th St., N.Y., NY 10020; 70,000.

Management Consultants, Institute of (1968), 230 Park Ave., Suite 544, N.Y., NY 10169; 2,200.

Management Consulting Firms, Assn. of (1929), 230 Park Ave., N.Y., NY 10169; 53 firms.

Manufacturers, Natl. Assn. of (1897), 1776 F St. NW, Wash., DC 20006; 13,000 companies.

Manufacturers' Agents Natl. Assn. (1947), 23016 Mill Creek Rd., P.O. Box 3467, Laguna Hills, CA 92654; 10,000.

March of Dimes Birth Defects Foundation (1938), 1275 Mamaroneck Ave., White Plains, NY 10605.

Marijuana Laws, Natl. Organization for the Reform of (NORML) (1970), 1636 R St. NW, #3, Wash., DC 20009.

Marine Corps League (1923), P.O. Box 3070, Merrifield, VA 22116-3070; 34,000.

Marine Manufacturers Assn., Natl. (1904), 401 N. Michigan Ave., Chicago, IL 60611; 1,650 companies.

Marine Technology Society (1963), 1825 K St. NW, Suite 218, Wash., DC 20006; 2,800.

Marketing Assn., Amer. (1934), 250 S. Wacker Dr., Chicago, IL 60606; 49,122.

Masonic Relief Assn. of U.S. and Canada (1885), 32613 Seidel Dr., Burlington, WS 53105; 14,700.

Masonic Service Assn. of the U.S. (1919), 8120 Fenton St., Silver Spring, MD 20910; 43 Grand Lodges.

Masons, Ancient and Accepted Scottish Rite, Southern Jurisdiction, Supreme Council (1801), 1733 16th St. NW, Wash., DC 20009; 551,878.

Masons, Supreme Council 33°, Ancient and Accepted Scottish Rite, Northern Masonic Jurisdiction (1813), 33 Marrett Rd., Lexington, MA 02173; 412,612.

Masons, Royal Arch, General Grand Chapter (1797), 1084 New Circle Rd. NE, Lexington, KY 40805; 290,500.

Mathematical Assn. of America (1915), 1529 Eighteenth Street, NW, Wash., DC 20036; 26,000.

Mathematical Society, Amer. (1888), 201 Charles St., Providence, RI 02904; 28,700.

Mathematical Statistics, Institute of (1935), 3401 Investment Blvd., #7, Hayward, CA 94545; 3,788.

Mathematics, Society for Industrial and Applied (1952), 3600 University City Science Ctr., Phila., PA 19104-2688; 8,200.

Mayflower Descendants, General Society of (1897), 4 Winslow St., P.O. Box 3297, Plymouth, MA 02361; 25,000.

Mayors, U.S. Conference of (1932), 1620 Eye St. NW, Wash., DC 20006; 946 cities.

Mechanical Engineers, Amer. Society of (1880), 345 E. 47th St., N.Y., NY 10017; 120,000.

Mechanics, Amer. Academy of (1969), Dept. of Civil Engineering, Northwestern Univ., Evanston, IL 60201; 1,200.

Medical Assn., Amer. (1847), 535 N. Dearborn St., Chicago, IL 60610; 290,000.

Medical Assn., Natl. (1895), 1012 Tenth St. NW, Wash., DC 20001; 16,000.

Medical Record Assn., Amer. (1928), 919 N. Michigan Ave., Chicago, IL 60611; 31,000.

Medical Technologists, Amer. College of (1942), 5608 Lane, Raytown, MO 64133; 368.

Medieval Academy of America (1926), 1430 Massachusetts Ave., Cambridge, MA 02138; 3,700.

Mensa, Amer. (1960), 2626 E. 14th St., Brooklyn, NY 11235.

Mental Health Assn., Natl. (1909), 1021 Prince St., Alexandria, VA 22314; 1 min.

Mental Health Program Directors, Natl. Assn. of State (1963), 1101 King St., Suite 160, Alexandria, VA 22314; 55.

Mentally Ill, Natl. Alliance for the (1979), 2101 Wilson Blvd., Suite 302, Arlington, VA 22201; 80,000.

Merchant Marine Library Assn., Amer. (1921), One World Trade Center, Suite 1365, N.Y., NY 10048.

Merchant Marine Veterans, Amer. (1983), 905 Cape Coral Pkwy., Cape Coral, FL 33904; 1,734.

Merchant Marine Veterans of WWII, U.S. (1944), P.O. Box 629, San Pedro, CA 90731; 7,126.

Merchants Assn., Natl. Retail (1911), 100 W. 31st St., N.Y., NY 10001; 45,000.

Merrill's Marauders Assn. (1946), 11244 N. 33rd St., Phoenix, AZ 85028-2723; 1,695.

Metal Finishers, Natl. Assn. of (1950), 111 E. Wacker Dr., Suite 600, Chicago, IL 60601; 900.

Metallurgy Institute, Amer. Powder (1959), 105 College Rd. East, Princeton, NJ 08540; 2,800.

Metal Powder Industries Federation, (1943), 105 College Rd. East, Princeton, NJ 08540; 260 cos.

Metals, Amer. Society for (ASM Internatl.) (1913), Metals Park, OH 44073; 53,000.

Meteorological Society, Amer. (1919), 45 Beacon St., Boston, MA 02108; 10,200.

Metric Assn., U.S. (1916), 10245 Andasol Ave., Northridge, CA 91325; 2,000.

Microbiology, Amer. Society for (1899), 1325 Massachusetts Ave. NW, Wash. DC 20005; 37,000.

Mideast Educational and Training Services, America-, (1951), 1100 17th Street, NW, Wash., DC 20036.

Military Order of the Loyal Legion of the U.S.A. (1865), 1805 Pine St., Phila., PA 19103; 800.

Military Order of the Purple Heart of the USA (1932), 5413-B Backlick Rd., Springfield, VA 22151; 23,500.

Military Order of the World Wars (1919), 435 N. Lee St., Alexandria, VA 22314; 15,000.

Mining and Metallurgical Society of America (1908), 275 Madison Ave., N.Y., NY 10016; 295.

Mining, Metallurgy and Exploration, Inc., Society for (1871), 8307 Shaffer Pkwy., Littleton, CO 80127; 20,279.

Ministerial Assn., Amer. (1929), 2210 Wilshire Blvd., Suite 582, Santa Monica, CA 90403; 3,000.

Missouri Alliance for Historic Preservation (1970), P.O. Box 895, Jefferson City, MO 65102; 250.

Model Railroad Assn., Natl. (1935), 4121 Cromwell Rd., Chattanooga, TN 37421; 25,000.

Modern Language Assn. of America (1883), 10 Astor Pl., N.Y., NY 10003; 32,000.

Modern Language Teachers Assns., Natl. Federation of (1916), Gannon Univ., Erie, PA 16541; 7,200.

Moose, Loyal Order of (1888), Mooseheart, IL 60539.

Mothers, American (1935), 301 Park Ave., N.Y., NY 10022; 4,000.

Mothers-in-Law Club Intl. (1970), 420 Adelberg Ln., Cedarhurst, NY 11516; 5,000.

Mothers of Twins Clubs, Natl. Organization of (1960), P.O. Box 23188, Albuquerque, NM 87192-1188; 14,000.

Motion Picture Arts & Sciences, Academy of (1927), 8949 Wilshire Blvd., Beverly Hills, CA 90211; 5,300.

Motion Pictures, Natl. Board of Review of (1909), P.O. Box 589, Lenox Hill Sta., N.Y., NY 10021.

Motion Picture & Television Engineers, Society of (1916), 595 West Hartsdale Ave., White Plains, NY 10607; 9,500.

Motor Vehicle Administrators, Amer. Assn. of (1933), 4200 Wilson Blvd.; Suite 600, Arlington, VA 22203; 173.

Motor Vehicle Manufacturers Assn. (1903), 7430 2nd Ave., Suite 300, Detroit, MI 48202; 7 companies.

Motorcyclist Assn., American (1924), 33 Collegeview Rd., Westerville, OH 43081; 160,000.

Multiethnic Americans, Assn. of, 1060 Tennessee St., San Francisco, CA 94107.

Multiple Sclerosis Society, Natl. (1946), 205 E. 42d St., N.Y., NY 10017; 400,000.

Murray Hill Assn., The (1940), 237 Madison Ave., The Morgan Hotel, N.Y., NY 10016; 100.

Muscular Dystrophy Assn. (1950), 810 Seventh Ave., N.Y., NY 10019.

Museums, Amer. Assn. of (1906), 1225 Eye St. NW, Ste. 200, Wash., DC 20005; 11,500.

Music Center, Amer. (1939), 30 W. 26th St., N.Y., NY 10010.

Music Council, Natl. (1940), 40 W. 37th St., N.Y., NY 10018; 50 organizations.

Music Educators Natl. Conference (1907), 1902 Association Dr., Reston, VA 22090; 54,069.

Music Scholarship Assn., Amer. (1956), 1826 Carew Tower, Cincinnati, OH 45202; 1,400.

Music Teachers Natl. Assn. (1876), 617 Vine St., Suite 1432, Cincinnati, OH 45202-2439; 22,000+.

Musicological Society, Amer. (1934), 201 S. 34th St., Phila., PA 19104-6313, 3,500.

Music Publishers' Assn., Natl. (1917), 205 E. 42nd St., N.Y., NY 10017; 300.

Muzzle Loading Rifle Assn., Natl. (1933), P.O. Box 67, Friendship, IN 47021; 26,000.

NAACP (Natl. Assn. for the Advancement of Colored People) (1909), 4805 Mt. Hope Drive, Baltimore, MD 21215.

NOT-SAFE (1981), Box 5743-WA, Montecito, CA 93150.

Na'amat USA (1925), 200 Madison Ave., N.Y., NY 10016.

Narcolepsy and Cataplexy Foundation of Amer. (1975), 1410 York Ave., Suite 2D, N.Y. NY 10021; 3,991.

Narcolepsy Assoc., Amer. (1975), 335 Quarry Rd., Belmont, CA 94002; 4,500.

Narcotics Anonymous (1953), P.O. Box 9999, Van Nuys, CA 91409; 1 million.

National Guard Assn. of the U.S. (1878), One Massachusetts Ave. NW, Wash., DC 20001; 54,000.

Nature Conservancy (1951), 1815 N. Lynn St., Arlington, VA 22209; 575,000.

Naturist Society, The (1980), P.O. Box 132, Oshkosh, WI 54902; 15,000.

Naturopathy Institute, The (1984), P.O. Box 56, Malverne, NY 11565.

Navajo Code Talkers Assn. (1971), Box 1182, Window Rock, AZ 86515; 295.

Naval Architects & Marine Engineers, The Society of (1893), 601 Pavonia Ave., Ste. 400, Jersey City, NJ 07306.

Naval Institute, U.S. (1873), Preble Hall, U.S. Naval Academy, Annapolis, MD 21402; 100,000.

Naval Reserve Assn. (1954), 1619 King St., Alexandria, VA 22314; 24,500.

Navigation, Institute of (1945), 1026 16th St. NW, Suite 104, Wash., DC 20036; 3,200.

Navy Club of the U.S.A. Auxiliary (1941), 418 W. Pontiac St., Ft. Wayne, IN 46807; 1,000.

Navy League of the U.S. (1902); 2300 Wilson Blvd., Arlington, VA 22201; 71,000.

Needlework Guild of America (1885), 1007-B St. Road, Southhampton, PA 18966.

Negro College Fund, United (1944), 500 E. 62d St., N.Y., NY 10021; 42 institutions.

Neurofibromatosis Foundation, Natl. (1978), 141 Fifth Ave., Suite 7-S, N.Y., NY 10010; 25,000.

New Age Walkers (1982), 3301 Bellaire Dr., Altadena, CA 91001; 4,500.

Newspaper Editors, Amer. Society of (1922), 11600 Sunrise Valley Dr., Reston, VA 22091; 1,000.

Newspaper Marketing Assn., Intl. (1930), 11600 Sunrise Valley Dr., Reston, VA 22091; 1,300+.

Newspaper Publishers Assn., Amer. (1887), The Newspaper Center, Box 17407 Dulles Airport, Wash., DC 20041.

Newswomen's Club of N.Y. (1922), 15 Gramercy Park S., N.Y., NY 10003; 200.

Nikola Tesla Walkers (1982), 745 S. Brightview Dr., Glendora, CA 91740; 4,600.

Ninety-Nines (Intl. Organization of Women Pilots) (1929), P.O. Box 59965, Will Rogers Airport, Oklahoma City, OK 73159.

Nobel Laureate Center, Amer. (1941), 1 Morningside Dr. N., Westport, CT 06880; 625.

Non-Commissioned Officers Assn. (1960), 10635 IH 35 No., San Antonio, TX 78233; 162,000.

Northern Cross Society (1983), Route One, Lecompton, KS 66050; 100.

Notaries, Amer. Society of (1965), 918 16th St. NW, Wash., DC 20006; 26,013.

Nuclear Society, Amer. (1954), 555 N. Kensington Ave., La Grange Park, IL 60525; 15,000.

Numismatic Assn., Amer. (1891), 818 N. Cascade Ave., Colorado Springs, CO 80903-3279; 30,528.

Numismatic Society, Amer. (1858), Broadway at 155th St., N.Y., NY 10032; 2,390.

Nurses' Assn., Amer. (1896), 2420 Pershing Rd., Kansas City, MO 64108.

Nursing, Natl. League for (1952), 350 Hudson St., N.Y., NY 10014; 18,000.

Nutrition, Amer. Institute of (1928), 9650 Rockville Pike, Bethesda, MD 20814; 3,000.

ORT Federation, Amer. (Org. for Rehabilitation through Training) (1922), 817 Broadway, N.Y., NY 10003; 17,000.

Odd Fellows, Independent Order of (1819), 422 N. Trade St., Winston Salem, NC 27101; 494,145.

Old Crows, Assn. of (1964), 1000 N. Payne St., Alexandria, VA 22314-1696; 25,000.

Olympic Committee, U.S. (1921), 1750 E. Boulder St., Colorado Springs, CO 80909; 70 organizations.

Omnibus Soc. of Am. (1961), 3440 W. Evergreen, Chicago, IL 60651; 110.

One Shoe Crew, The, 86 Clavela Ave., Sacramento, CA 95828.

Opthalmology, Amer. Academy of (1979), 655 Beach St., San Francisco, CA 94109; 16,250.

Optical Society of America (1916), 2010 Massachusetts Ave. NW, Wash., DC 20036; 11,208.

Optimist Intl. (1919), 4494 Lindell Blvd., St. Louis, MO 63108.

Optometric Assn., Amer. (1898), 243 N. Lindbergh Blvd., St. Louis, MO 63141; 27,800.

Oral and Maxillofacial Surgeons, Amer. Assn. of (1918), 9700 W. Bryn Mawr Ave., Rosemont, IL 60018; 5,302.

Organists, Amer. Guild of (1896), 475 Riverside Dr., Suite 1260, N.Y., NY 10115; 24,300.

Oriental Society, Amer. (1842), 329 Sterling Memorial Library, Yale Sta., New Haven, CT 06520; 1,440.

Ornithologists' Union, Amer. (1883), c/o National Museum of Natural History, Smithsonian, Wash., DC 20560; 4,200.

Osteopathic Assn., Amer. (1887), 212 E. Ohio St., Chicago, IL 60611; 23,292.

Ostomy Assn., United (1970), 36 Executive Park, Suite 120, Irving, CA 92714, 45,000.

Outlaw and Lawman History, Natl. Organization for (1974), 615-C N. 8th St., Killeen, TX 76541; 559.

Overeaters Anonymous (1960), 4025 Spencer St., #203, Torrance, CA 90503; 120,000.

PTA (Natl. Congress of Parents and Teachers), Natl. (1897), 700 N. Rush St., Chicago, IL 60611; 6.6 mln.

Paleontological Research Institution (1932), 1259 Trumansburg Rd., Ithaca, NY 14850; 700+.

Paper Industry, Technical Assn. of the Pulp and (1915), 15 Technology Pkwy. S., Norcross, GA 30084; 29,950.

Paper Institute, Amer. (1964), 260 Madison Ave., N.Y., NY 10016; 166 companies.

Parasitologists, Amer. Society of (1924), 1041 New Hampshire St., Box 368, Lawrence, KS 66044; 1,491.

Parents Without Partners (1957), 8807 Colesville Rd., Silver Spring, MD 20910; 125,000.

Parkinson's Disease Foundation (1957), 650 W. 168th St., N.Y., NY 10032; 66,000.

Parliamentarians, Amer. Institute of (1958), 203 W. Wayne, Ft. Wayne, IN 46802; 1,350.

Parliamentarians, Natl. Assn. of (1930), 6601 Winchester, Kansas City, MO 64133-4600; 4,400.

Parliamentary Law, Intl. Organization of Professionals in (1977), 3611 Victoria Ave., Los Angeles, CA 90016; 200.

Pasta Assn., Natl. (1904), 2101 Wilson Blvd., Suite 920, Arlington, VA 22201; 100 companies.

Pathologists, Amer. Assn. of (1976), 9650 Rockville Pike, Bethesda, MD 20814; 2,000.

Patriotism, Natl. Committee for Responsible (1967), P.O. Box 665, Grand Central Sta., N.Y., NY 10163; 160.

Pearl Harbor History Associates (1982), P.O. Box 205, Sperryville, VA 22740-0205; 375.

Pearl Harbor Survivors Assn. (1958), 3215 Albert St., Orlando, FL 32806.

PEN Amer. Center (1922), 568 Broadway, N.Y., NY 10012.

PEN Women, Natl. League of Amer. (1897), 1300 17th St. NW, Wash., DC 20036-1973; 5,000.

Pennsylvania Society of New York (1899), 80 N. Main St., Sellersville, PA 18960; 1,800.

Pension Actuaries, Amer. Society of (1966), 2029 K St. NW, Wash., DC 20006; 3,052.

Pension Plan, Committee for a Natl. (1979), P.O. Box 27851, Las Vegas, NV 89126; 2,000.

P.E.O. (Philanthropic Educational Organization) Sisterhood (1869), 3700 Grand Ave., Des Moines, IA 50312; 242,000.

Personnel Administration, Amer. Society for (1948), 606 N. Washington St., Alexandria, VA 22314; 40,000.

Petroleum Equipment Inst. (1951), 3739 E. 31st St., Tulsa, OK 74135; 1,200 member companies.

Petroleum Institute, Amer. (1919), 1220 L St. NW, Wash., DC 20005; 250 corporations.

Petroleum Landmen, Amer. Assn. of (1955), 777 Main St., Suite 1470, Fort Worth, TX 76102; 11,200.

Pharmaceutical Assn., Amer. (1852), 2215 Constitution Ave. NW, Wash., DC 20037; 40,000.

Phi Delta Kappa (1906), 8th & Union, Box 789, Bloomington, IN 47401-0789; 132,000.

Philatelic Pages & Panels, Amer. Soc. for (1984), 1138 Princeton Dr., Richardson, TX 75081-3615; 679.

Philatelic Society, Amer. (1886), 100 Oakwood Ave., State College, PA 16803; 57,000.

Philological Assn., Amer. (1869), Dept. of Classics, Fordham Univ., Bronx, NY 10458; 2,500.

Philosophical Assn., Amer. (1900), Univ. of Delaware, Newark, DE 19716; 8,000.

Philosophical Enquiry, Intl. Society for (1974), c/o Betty Hansen, 227 Wash. Blvd., Hudson, NY 12534; 478.

Philosophical Society, Amer. (1743), 104 S. 5th St., Phila., PA 19106; 700.

Photogrammetry and Remote Sensing, Amer. Society of (1934), 5410 Grosvenor Ln., Ste. 210, Bethesda, MD 20814.

Photographers of America, Professional (1880), 1090 Executive Way, Des Plaines, IL 60018; 15,000.

Photographic Society of Amer. (1934), 3000 United Founders Blvd. #103, Oklahoma City, OK 73112.

Physical Therapy Assn., Amer. (1921), 1111 N. Fairfax St., Alexandria, VA 22314; 50,000.

Physicians, Amer. Academy of Family (1947), 8880 Ward Pkwy., Kansas City, MO 64114; 70,000.

Physics, Amer. Inst. of (1931), 335 E. 45th St., N.Y., NY 10017-3483.

Physiological Society, Amer. (1887), 9650 Rockville Pike, Bethesda, MD 20814; 7,000.

Phytopathological Soc., The Amer. (1908), 3340 Pilot Knob Rd., St. Paul, MN 55121; 4,300+.

Pilgrim Society (1820), 75 Court St., Plymouth, MA 02360-3891; 900.

Pilgrims of the U.S. (1903), 80 Broadway, N.Y., NY 10005.

Pilot Club Intl. (1921), P.O. Box 4844, 244 College St., Macon, GA 31213-0599; 20,000.

Planetary Society (1979), 65 N. Catalina Ave., Pasadena, CA 91106; 120,000.

Planned Parenthood Federation of America (1916), 810 Seventh Ave., N.Y., NY 10019; 187 affiliates.

Planning Assn., Amer. (1909), 1776 Massachusetts Ave. NW, Wash., DC 20036; 26,000.

Plastic Modelers Society, Intl. (1965), P.O. Box 2890, Sacramento, CA 95812; 3,568.

Plastics Industry, Society of (1937), 1275 K St. NW, Suite 400, Washington, DC 20005; 2,100.

Platform Assn., Intl. (1831), Box 250, Winnetka, IL 60093.

Poetry Day Committee, Natl. (1947), 1110 N. Venetian Dr., Miami, FL 33139-1019; 17,500.

Poetry Society of America (1910), 15 Gramercy Park, N.Y., NY 10003; 1,700.

Poets, Academy of Amer. (1934), 177 E. 87th St., N.Y., NY 10121; 3,000.

Polar Society, Amer. (1934), c/o Byrd Polar Research Ctr., 125 S. Oval Mall, Columbus, OH 43210; 2,000.

Police, Internatl. Assn. of Chiefs of (1893), 1110 N. Glebe Rd., Suite 200, Arlington, VA 22201; 13,500.

Police Officers Assn., Natl. Police Reserve Officers Assn., Natl. (1955/1967), 1316 Gardiner Lane, Louisville, KY 40213; 6,000.

Polish Army Veterans Assn. of America (1921), 19 Irving Pl., N.Y., NY 10003; 9,762.

Polish Cultural Society of America (1940), P.O. Box 31, Wall Street, N.Y., NY 10005; 105,981.

Polish Genealogical Society of CT (1984), 8 Lyle Rd., New Britain, CT 06053; 250.

Polish Legion of American Veterans (1921), 3024 N. Laramie Ave., Chicago, IL 60641; 15,000.

Political Items Collectors, Amer. (1945), P.O. Box 340339, San Antonio, TX 78234; 2,600.

Political Science, Academy of (1880), 475 Riverside Dr., Suite 1274, N.Y., NY 10115-0012; 9,000.

Political Science Assn., Amer. (1903), 1527 New Hampshire Ave. NW, Wash., DC 20036; 13,000.

Political & Social Science, Amer. Academy of (1891), 3937 Chestnut St., Phila., PA 19104; 15,000.

Pollution Control, Internatl. Assn. for (1970), 444 N. Capital St. NW, Wash. DC 20001; 500.

Polo Assn., U.S. (1890), 4059 Iron Works Pike, Lexington, KY, 40511; 3,000.

Population Assn. of America (1931), 1429 Duke St., Alexandria, VA 22314-3402; 2,700.

Portuguese Continental Union of the U.S.A. (1925), 899 Boylston St., Boston, MA 02115; 7,457.

Postmasters of the U.S., Natl. Assn. of (1898), 8 Herbert St., Arlington, VA 22305; 43,000.

Postmasters of the U.S., Natl. League of (1904), 1023 N. Royal St., Alexandria, VA 22314; 21,874.

Poultry Science Assn. (1921), 309 W. Clark St., Champaign, IL 61820; 2,000.

Power Boat Assn., Amer. (1903), 17640 E. Nine Mile Rd., P.O. Box 377, E. Detroit, MI 48021; 10,000.

Precancel Collectors, Natl. Assn. of (1950), 5121 Park Blvd., Wildwood, NJ 08260; 7,000+.

Press, Associated (1848), 50 Rockefeller Plaza, N.Y., NY 10020; 1,365 newspapers & 3,600 broadcast stations.

Press Club, Natl. (1908), 529 14th St. NW, Wash., DC 20045.

Press Intl., United (1907), 1400 I St. NW, Wash. DC 20005.

Press and Radio Club (1948), P.O. Box 70023, Montgomery, AL 36107; 799.

Press Women, Natl. Federation of (1937), 1105 Main St., Box 99, Blue Springs, MD 64015; 5,000.

Printing Industries of America (1887), 100 Dangerfield Rd., Alexandria, VA 22314; 13,000+ companies.

Prisoners of War, Amer. Ex- (1942), 3201 E. Pioneer Pkwy. #40, Arlington, TX 76010-5396; 34,000.

Procrastinators Club of America (1956), Box 712, Bryn Athyn, PA 19009; 6,500.

Propeller Club of the U.S. (1927), 3927 Old Lee Highway, Ste. 101A, Fairfax, VA 22030; 13,000.

Psychiatric Assn., Amer. (1844), 1400 K St. NW, Wash., DC 20005; 37,500.

Psychical Research, Amer. Society for (1907), 5 W. 73d St., N.Y., NY 10025; 1,500.

Psychoanalytic Assn., Amer. (1911), 309 E. 49th St., N.Y., NY 10017; 3,050.

Psychological Assn., Amer. (1892), 1200 17th St. NW, Wash., DC 20036; 60,000.

Psychological Assn. for Psychoanalysis, Natl. (1948), 150 W. 13th St., N.Y., NY 10011; 342.

Psychological Minorities, Society for the Aid of (1953), 42-25 Hampton St., Elmhurst, NY 11373; 543.

Psychotherapy Assn., Amer. Group (1942), 25 E. 21st St., N.Y., NY 10010; 3,400.

Psoriasis Foundation, Natl (1968), 6443 SW Beaverton Hwy., #210, Portland, OR 97221; 14,000.

Public Administration, Amer. Soc. for (1939), 1120 G St. NW, Wash, DC 20005; 14,800.

Public Health Assn., World Fed. of (1967), 1015 15th St. NW, Wash., DC 20005; 48 natl. assn.

Public Relations Soc. of Amer. (1947), 33 Irving Pl. N.Y., NY 10003; 15,357.

Publicly Traded Cos., Assn. of (1973), 1707 L St. NW, Suite 950, Wash., DC 20036; 791.

Publishers, Assn. of Amer. (1970), One Park Ave., N.Y., NY 10016; 330 publishing houses.

Puppeteers of Amer. (1937), 5 Cricklewood Path, Pasadena, CA 91107; 2,200.

Quality Control, Amer. Society for (1946), 310 W. Wisconsin Ave., Milwaukee, WI 53203; 60,000.

Quota Internatl. (1919), 1420 21st St. NW, Wash., DC 20036.

Rabbinical Alliance of America (1942), 3 W. 16th St. N.Y., NY 10011; 500.

Rabbinical Assembly (1900), 3080 Broadway, N.Y., NY 10027; 1,265.

Rabbis, Central Conference of Amer. (1889), 192 Lexington Ave., N.Y., NY 10016; 1,540.

Racial Equality, Congress of (1942), 1457 Flatbush Ave., Brooklyn, NY 11210.

Radio, Natl. Assn. of Business and Educational (1965), 1501 Duke St., Suite 200, Alexandria, VA 22314; 4,873.

Radio Union, Intl. Amateur (1925), P.O. Box AAA, Newington, CT 06111; 126 societies.

Radio and TV Society, Intl. (1939), 420 Lexington Ave., N.Y., NY 10170; 1,900.

Radio Relay League, Amer. (1914), 225 Main St., Newington, CT 06111; 160,000.

Railroad Club of Chicago, The (1934), 506 5th St., Wilmette, IL 60091; 100.

Railroad Passengers, Natl. Assn. of (1967), 900 2nd St. NE, Suite 308, Wash., DC 20002; 12,800.

Railroads, Assn. of Amer. (1934), 50 F St. NW, Wash., DC 20001; 113.

Railway Historical Society, Natl. (1935), P.O. Box 58153, Phila., PA 19102-8153; 19,000+.

Railway Progress Institute (1908), 700 N. Fairfax St., Suite 601, Alexandria, VA 22314-2098; 130 companies.

Rainbow Walkers (1982), 4370 Fairlawn Dr., Lake Canada, CA 91011; 1,444.

Range Management, Society for (1948), 1839 York Street, Denver, CO 80206; 5,000.

Rape, Feminist Alliance Against (1974), P.O. Box 21033, Wash., DC 20009.

Reading Assn., Intl. (1956), P.O. Box 8139, 800 Barksdale Rd., Newark, DE 19714-8139; 94,000.

Real Estate Institute, Intl. (1975), 8383 E. Evans Rd., Scottsdale, AZ 85260; 3,000.

Rebekah Assemblies, Intl. Assn. of (1916), 422 N. Trade St., Suite "R" Winston-Salem, NC 27101; 218,901.

Reconciliation, Fellowship of (1915), 523 N. Broadway, Nyack, NY 10960; 35,000.

Records Managers & Administrators, Assn. of (1975), 4200 Somerset Dr., Suite 215, Prairie Village, KS 66208; 10,500.

Recreation and Park Assn., Natl. (1965), 3101 Park Ctr. Dr., 12th Fl., Alexandria, VA 22302; 21,000.

Recycling Coalition, Natl., 1101 30th St. NW, Ste. 305, Wash., DC 20007.

Red Cross, American (1881), 17th & D Sts. NW, Wash., DC 20006; 1.2 mln. volunteers.

Red Men, Improved Order of (1765), 4007 W. Waco Dr., Waco, TX, 76710; 33,000.

Redwoods League, Save-the- (1918), 114 Sansome St., Rm. 605, San Francisco, CA 94104; 45,000.

Reed Organ Society, Inc. (1982), The Musical Museum, Deansboro, NY 13328; 800.

Regional Plan Assn. (1929), 1040 Ave. of the Americas, N.Y., NY 10018; 1,000.

Rehabilitation Assn., Natl. (1925), 633 S. Washington St., Alexandria, VA 22314; 16,000.

Religion, Amer. Academy of (1909), 501 Hall of Languages, Syracuse Univ., Syracuse, NY 13244-1170; 5,600.

Religion Foundation, Freedom from (1978), P.O. Box 750, Madison, WI 53701; 3,100.

Remodeling Industry, Natl. Assn. of the (1956), 1901 N. Moore St., Suite 808, Arlington, VA 22209.

Renaissance Society of America (1954), 1161 Amsterdam Ave., N.Y., NY 10027; 3,000.

Republican National Committee (1856), 310 1st Street SE, Washington, DC 20003-1801.

Reserve Officers Assn. of the U.S. (1922), One Constitution Ave., NE, Wash., DC 20002; 123,000.

Restaurant Assn., Natl. (1919), 1200 17th St. NW, Wash., DC 20036; 20,000.

Retarded Citizens of the U.S., Assn. for (1950), 500 E. Border St., Ste. 300, Arlington, TX 76006; 140,000.

Retired Credit Union People, Natl. Assn. for (1978), P.O. Box 391, 5910 Mineral Pt. Rd., Madison, WI 53705; 71,036.

Retired Federal Employees, Natl. Assn. of (1921), 1533 New Hampshire Ave. NW, Wash., DC 20036; 500,000.

Retired Officers Assn. (1929), 201 N. Washington St., Alexandria, VA 22314-2529; 365,000.

Retired Persons, Amer. Assn. of (1958), 1909 K St. NW, Wash., DC 20049; 32 mln.

Retired Teachers Assn., Natl. (1947), 1909 K St. NW, Wash., DC 20049; 540,000.

Revolver Assn., U.S. (1900), 96 W. Union St., Ashland, MA 01721; 1,510.

Reye's Syndrome Foundation, Natl. (1974), 426 N. Lewis, Bryan, OH 43506; 4,000+.

Richard III Society (1969), P.O. Box 13787, New Orleans, LA 70185; 700.

Rifle Assn., Natl. (1871), 1600 Rhode Island Ave. NW, Wash., DC 20036; 2.8 mln.

Road & Transportation Builders' Assn., Amer. (1902), 501 School St. SW, Wash., DC 20024-2713; 3,600.

Rodeo Cowboys Assn., Professional (1936), 101 Pro Rodeo Dr., Colorado Springs, CO 80921; 8,983.

Roller Skating, U.S. Amateur Confederation of (1937), 4730 South St., P.O. Box 6579, Lincoln, NE 68506; 20,000.

Roller Skating Rink Operators Assn. (1937), 7700 A St., P.O. Box 81846, Lincoln, NE 68501; 1,150 rinks.

Rose Society, Amer. (1899), 8877 Jefferson Paige Rd., Shreveport, LA 71119; 20,000.

Rotary Intl. (1905), One Rotary Center, Evanston, IL 60201.

Running and Fitness Assn., Amer. (1968), 9310 Old Georgetown Rd., Bethesda, MD 20814; 18,000.

Ruritan Natl. (1928), Ruritan Natl. Rd., Dublin, VA 24084.

SANE/FREEZE (1987), 1819 H St. NW, Suite 640, Wash., DC 20006-3603; 170,000.

Safety and Fairness Everywhere, Natl. Assn. Taunting (1980), P.O. Box 5743WA, Montecito, CA 93150; 12,000.

Safety Council, Natl. (1913), 444 N. Michigan Ave., Chicago, IL 60611; 12,500.

Sailors, Tin Can (1976), Battleship Cove, Fall River, MA 02721; 14,000.

St. Andrew the Apostle, The Soc. of (1983), Route 3, Sylvester, WV 25193; 450.

St. Dennis of Zante, Sovereign Greek Order of (1050; 1953 in U.S.), 739 W. 186th St., N.Y., NY 10033; 93.

St. George the Martyr, Knightly Assn. of (1980), State Route #3, Sylvester, WV 25193; 10,000.

St. John of Damascus Assn. of Orthodox Iconographers, Iconologists and Architects (1979), Rt. 711 North, P.O. Box 638, Ligonier, PA 15658-0638; 400.

St. Luke, Physician of Amer., Order of (1952), 2210 Wilshire Blvd., Santa Monica, CA 90403; 300+.

St. Paul, Natl. Guild of (1937), 601 Hill 'n Dale, Lexington, KY 40503; 13,652.

Salespersons, Natl. Assn. of Professional (1970), P.O. Box 76461, Atlanta, GA 30358; 35,000.

Salt Institute (1914), 700 N. Fairfax St., Ste. 600, Alexandria, VA, 22314-2040; 23 companies.

Sane Nuclear Policy, Committee for a (1957), 711 G St. SE, Wash., DC 20003; 130,000.

Savings Institutions, Natl. Council of (1983), 1101 15th St. NW, Wash., DC 20005; 550 members.

Savings & Loan League, Natl. (1943), 1101 15th St. NW, Wash., DC 20005; 300 associations.

School Administrators, Amer. Assn. of (1865), 1801 N. Moore St., Arlington, VA 22209; 18,500.

School Boards Assn., Natl. (1940), 1680 Duke St., Alexandria, VA 22314.

School Counselor Assn., Amer. (1953), 5999 Stevenson Ave., Alexandria, VA 22304; 13,000.

Schools of Art, Natl. Assn. of (also: School of Art and Design, School of Dance, Music, and Theater) (1944), 11250 Roger Bacon Dr., Reston, VA 22090; 161.

Schools & Colleges, Amer. Council on (1927), 13014 Dale Mabry Hwy., Ste. 270-B, Tampa, FL 33180-2808; 137.

Science, Amer. Assn. for the Advancement of (1848), 1333 H St. NW, Wash., DC 20005; 130,000.

Science Fiction Society, World (1939), P.O. Box 1270, Kendall Sq. Sta., Cambridge, MA 02142; 5,000.

Science Service (1921), 1719 N St. NW, Wash., DC 20036.

Science Teachers Assn., Natl. (1985), 1742 Connecticut Ave. NW, Wash., DC 20009; 50,000.

Science Writers, Natl. Assn. of (1934), P.O. Box 294, Greenlawn, NY 11740; 1,650.

Sciences, Natl. Academy of (1863), 2101 Constitution Ave. NW, Wash., DC 20418; 1,936.

Scientists, Federation of American (1945), 307 Massachusetts Ave. NE, Wash., DC 20002; 5,000.

Screen Actors Guild (1933), 7065 Hollywood Blvd. Hollywood, CA 90028; 75,000.

Screen Printing Assn. Intl. (1948), 10015 Main St., Fairfax, VA 22031; 3,000 corporations.

Sculpture Soc., Natl. (1893), 15 E. 26th St., N.Y., NY 10010.

Seamen's Service, United (1942), One World Trade Ctr., Suite 1365, N.Y., NY 10048.

2d Air Division Assn. (1947), 1 Jeffrey's Neck Rd., Ipswich, MA 01938; 7,852.

Secondary School Principals, Natl. Assn. of (1916), 1904 Association Dr., Reston, VA 22091; 42,000.

Secretaries Intl., Professional (1942), 10502 NW Ambassador Dr., P.O. Box 20404, Kansas City, MO 64195-0404; 41,000.

Secretaries, Natl. Assn. of Legal (1950), 2250 E 73, Ste. 550, Tulsa, OK 74136-6805; 16,000.

Securities Industry Assn. (1972), 120 Broadway, N.Y., NY 10271; 600 firms.

Semantics, Inst. of General (1938), 163 Engle St., Englewood, NJ 07631; 300.

Separation of Church & State, Americans United for (1947), 8120 Fenton St., Silver Spring, MD 20910; 50,000.

Separationists, Inc., Society of (1959), 7215 Cameron Rd., Austin, TX 78752; 30,000.

Sertoma Internatl. (1912), 1912 E. Meyer Blvd., Kansas City, MO 64132; 35,000.

Sex Information & Education Council of the U.S. (SIECUS) (1964), New York University, 32 Washington Place, Rm. 52, N.Y., NY 10003; 2,600.

Shakespeare Assn. of America (1972), Dept. of English, SMU, Dallas, TX 75275; 750.

Sheet Metal & Air Conditioning Contractor's Natl. Assn., Inc. (1943), 8224 Old Courthouse Rd., Vienna, VA 22182; 2,290.

Shipbuilders Council of America (1921), 1110 Vermont Ave. NW, Wash., DC 20005; 50 organizations.

Ships in Bottles Assn. of Amer. (1983), P.O. Box 180550, Coronado, CA 92178; 425.

Shore & Beach Preservation Assn., Amer. (1926), 3000 Citrus Circle, Suite 230, Walnut Creek, CA 94598; 1,000.

Shrine, Ancient Arabic Order of the Nobles of the Mystic (1872), 2900 Rocky Pt. Dr., Tampa, FL 33607; 799,000.

Shut-Ins, Natl. Society for (1970), 237 Franklin St., Reading, PA 19602; 85.

Sierra Club (1892), 730 Polk St., San Francisco, CA 94109.

Silurians, Soc. of the (1924), 164 Lexington Ave., N.Y., NY 10016; 500.

Skating Union of the U.S., Amateur (1927), 1033 Shady Lane, Glen Ellyn, IL 60137; 3,000.

Skeet Shooting Assn., Natl. (1946), P.O. Box 680007, San Antonio, TX 78268; 15,800.

Ski Assn., U.S. (1904), P.O. Box 100, Park City, UT 84060.

Small Business, Amer. Federation of (1938), 407 S. Dearborn St., Chicago, IL 60605; 24,000.

Small Business United, Natl. (1986), 1155 15th St. NW, Suite 710, Wash., DC 20005; 50,000.

Smoking & Health, Natl. Clearinghouse for (1965), Center for Disease Control, 1600 Clifton Road NE, Atlanta, GA 30333.

Soccer Federation, U.S. (1913), Viscount Hotel, 40 JFK Intl. Airport, Jamaica, NY 11430; 700,000.

Social Biology, Society for the Study of (1926), Medical Dept., Brookhaven Natl. Laboratory, Upton, NY 11973; 415.

Social Sciences, Natl. Institute of (1865), 444 Madison Ave., Ste. 2901, N.Y., NY 10022; 300.

Social Work Education, Council on (1952), 1600 Duke Street, Alexandria, VA 22314; 2,500.

Social Workers, Natl. Assn. of (1955), 7981 Eastern Ave., Silver Spring, MD 20910; 127,000.

Socialists of America, Democratic (1981), 15 Dutch St., Suite 500, N.Y., NY 10038; 5,500.

Sociological Assn., Amer. (1905), 1722 N St. NW, Wash., DC 20036; 12,666.

Softball Association, Amateur (1933), 2801 N.E. 50th St., Oklahoma City, OK 73111; 226,000 teams.

Softball League, Cinderella (1958), P.O. Box 1411, Corning, NY 14830.

Soft Drink Assn., Natl. (1921), 1101 16th St. NW, Wash., DC 20036; 1,000.

Soil Conservation Society of America (1945), 7515 N.E. Ankeny Rd., Ankeny, IA 50021; 12,000.

Soil Science Society of America (1936), 677 S. Segoe Rd., Madison, WI 53711; 6,200.

Sojourners, Natl. (1919), 8301 E. Boulevard Dr., Alexandria, VA 22308; 9,500.

Soldier's, Sailor's and Airmen's Club (1919), 283 Lexington Ave., N.Y., NY 10016.

Songwriters Guild of America, The (1931), 276 Fifth Ave., Ste. 306, N.Y., NY 10001; 5,000.

Sons of the Amer. Legion (1932), Box 1055, Indianapolis, IN 46206; 124,925.

Sons of the American Revolution, Natl. Society of (1889), 1000 S. 4th, Louisville, KY 40203; 27,000.

Sons of Confederate Veterans (1896), Southern Station, Box 5164, Hattiesburg, MS 39406-5164; 12,500.

Sons of the Desert (1965), P.O. Box 8341, Universal City, CA 91608; 10,000.

Sons of Italy in America, The Order (1905), 219 E. St., NE, Wash. DC 20002; 450,000.

Sons of Norway (1895), 1455 W. Lake St., Minneapolis, MN 55408; 85,000.

Sons of Poland, Assn. of the (1903), 591 Summit Ave., Rm. 702, Jersey City, NJ 07306; 10,000.

Sons of the Republic of Texas, The (1922), 5942 Abrams Rd., #222, Dallas, TX 75231; 3,500.

Sons of the Revolution, General Society of the/Fraunces Tavern Museum (1890), 54 Pearl St., N.Y., NY 10004; 5,600.

Sons of St. Patrick, Society of the Friendly (1784), 80 Wall St., N.Y., NY 10005; 1,400.

Sons of Sherman's March to the Sea (1966), 1725 Farmers Ave., Tempe, AZ 85281; 675.

Sons of Union Veterans of the Civil War (1881), 411 Bartlett St., Lansing, MI 48915; 2,500.

Soroptimist Intl. of the Americas (1921), 1616 Walnut St., Phila., PA 19103; 50,000.

Southern Christian Leadership Conference (1957), 334 Auburn Ave. NE, Atlanta, GA 30303; 1 mln.

Space Education Assoc., U.S. (1973), 746 Turnpike Rd., Elizabethtown, PA 17022-1161; 1,500.

Speech Communication Assn. (1914), 5105 Backlick Rd., Annandale, VA 22003; 6,700.

Speech-Language-Hearing Assn., Amer. (1925), 10801 Rockville Pike, Rockville, MD 20852; 64,000.

Speleological Society, Natl. (1941), 2813 Cave Ave., Huntsville, AL 35810; 9,200.

Spiritual Awareness, Assn. for (1984), P.O. Box 224, Clifton Hill, MO 65244; 2,050.

Sports Car Club of America (1944), P.O. Box 3278, Englewood, CO 80155-3278; 51,081.

Sports Club, Indoor (1930), 1145 Highland St., Napoleon, OH 43545.

Sportscasters Assn., Amer. (1979), 5 Beekman St., N.Y., NY 10038; 550.

Standards Institute, Amer. Natl. (1918), 1430 Broadway, N.Y., NY 10018; 1,000.

State Communities Aid Assn. (1872), 151 Chestnut St., Albany, NY 12210; 95.

State Governments, Council of (1933), P.O. Box 11910, Iron Works Pike, Lexington, KY 40578; 50 states, 4 territories.

State & Local History, Amer. Assn. for (1940), 172 Second Ave. N., Nashville, TN 37201; 5,800.

Statistical Assn., Amer. (1839), 1429 Duke St., Alexandria, VA 22314-3402; 15,000.

Steamship Historical Society of America (1935), 300 Ray Dr., Ste 4, Providence, RI 02906; 3,300.

Steel Construction, Amer. Institute of (1921), 400 N. Michigan Ave., Chicago, IL 60611-4185; 2,600+.

Stock Car Auto Racing, Natl. Assn. for (NASCAR) (1948), 1801 Speedway Blvd., Daytona Beach, FL 32015; 17,000.

Stock Exchange, Amer. (1911), 86 Trinity Pl., N.Y., NY 10006; 871.

Stock Exchange, N.Y. (1792), 11 Wall St., N.Y., NY 10005.

Stock Exchange, Phila. (1790), 1900 Market St., Phila., PA 19103; 505.

Structural Stability Research Council (1944), Fritz Engineering Laboratory No. 13, Lehigh Univ., Bethlehem, PA 18015.

Student Assn., U.S. (1947), 1012 14th St. NW, Suite 403, Wash., DC 20005.

Student Councils, Natl. Assn. of (1931), 1904 Association Dr., Reston, VA 22091; 9,000 schools.

Stuttering Project, Natl. (1977), 4601 Irving St., San Francisco, CA 94122-1020; 3,600.

Sudden Infant Death Syndrome Alliance, Natl. (1987), 10500 Little Patuxent Pkwy., Ste. 420, Columbia, MD 21044.

Sugar Brokers Assn., Natl. (1903), 1 World Trade Center, N.Y., NY 10047; 100.

Sunbathing Assn., Amer. (1931), 1703 N. Main St., Kissimmee, FL 34744; 38,000.

Sunday League (1933), 279 Highland Ave., Newark, NJ 07104; 25,000.

Surgeons, Amer. College of (1913), 55 E. Erie St., Chicago IL 60611-2797; 50,904.

Surgeons, Intl. College of (1935), 1516 N. Lake Shore Dr., Chicago IL 60610; 6,800.

Surgeons of the U.S., Assn. of Military (1891), 9320 Old Georgetown Rd., Bethesda, MD 20814; 14,500.

Surveying & Mapping, Amer. Congress on (1941), 210 Little Falls, Falls Church, VA 22046; 10,800.

Symphony Orchestra League, Amer. (1942), 777 14th St. NW, Wash., DC 20005; 899 orchestras.

Systems Management, Assn. for (1947), 1433 West Bagley Rd., Berea, OH 44017; 8,000.

Table Tennis Assn., U.S. (1933), Olympic Complex, 1750 E. Boulder St., Colorado Springs, CO 80909; 7,000.

Tailhook Assn., The (1957), P.O. Box 40, Bonita, CA 91908.

Tall Buildings and Urban Habitat, Council on (1969), Lehigh Univ., Bethlehem, PA 18015; 2,500.

Tax Accountants, Natl. Assn. of Enrolled Federal (1960), 6108 N. Harding Ave., Chicago, IL 60659-3108; 450.

Tax Administrators, Federation of (1937), 444 N. Capitol St. NW, Wash., DC 20001.

Tax Assn., Natl.–Tax Institute of America (1907), 5310 E. Main St., Suite 104, Columbus, OH 43213; 1,800.

Tax Foundation, Inc. (1937), 470 L'Enfant Plaza SW, Suite 7112, Wash., DC 20024; 10,000.

Tax Free America (1986), 11015 Cumpston St., N. Hollywood, CA 91601; 400,000.

Taxpayers Union, Natl. (1969), 713 Maryland Ave. NE, Wash., DC 20002; 200,000.

Tea Assn. of the U.S.A. (1899), 230 Park Ave., N.Y., NY 10169; 179.

Teachers Assn., Amer. String (1946), UGA Sta. Box 2066, Athens, GA 30612-0066; 6,800.

Teachers of English, Natl. Council of (1911), 1111 Kenyon Rd., Urbana, IL 61801; 125,000.

Teachers of English to Speakers of Other Languages (1966), 1600 Cameron St., Suite 300, Alexandria, VA 22314.

Teachers of French, Amer. Assn. of (1927), 57 E. Armory Ave., Champaign, IL 61820; 11,000.

Teachers of German, American Assn. of (1926), 112 Haddontowne Court #104, Cherry Hill, NJ 08034; 6,500.

Teachers of Mathematics, Natl. Council of (1920), 1906 Association Dr., Reston, VA 22091; 56,000.

Teachers of Singing, Natl. Assn. of (1944), 2800 Univ. Blvd. N, J.U. Sta., Jacksonville, FL 32211; 4,600.

Teachers of Spanish & Portuguese, Amer. Assn. of (1917), P.O. Box 6349, 218 Lee Hall, MSU., MS 39762-6349.

Telephone Pioneers of Amer. (1911), 22 Cortland, St., 25th fl., N.Y., NY 10007; 780,000.

Television Arts & Sciences, Natl. Academy of (1947), 111 W. 57th St., Suite 1020, N.Y., NY 10019; 12,000.

Television Bureau of Advertising (1954), 485 Lexington Ave., N.Y., NY 10017.

Television & Radio Artists, Amer. Federation of (1937), 1350 Ave. of the Americas, N.Y., NY 10019; 66,000.

Telluride Assn. (1911), 217 West Ave., Ithaca, NY 14850.

Tennis Assn., U.S. (1881), 1212 Ave. of Americas, N.Y., NY 10036.

Terraplane Club, Hudson-Essex (1959), 100 E. Cross St., Ypsilanti, MI 48197; 3,100.

Tesla Memorial Soc., Inc. (1979), 453 Martin Rd., Lackawanna, NY 14218; 1,100.

Testing & Materials, Amer. Society for (1898), 1916 Race St., Phila., PA 19103; 32,000.

Texas State Genealogical Society (1960), 2507 Tannehill, Houston, TX 77008-3052; 1,000.

Textile Assn., Northern (1854), 230 Congress St., Boston, MA 02110; 150.

Textile Manufacturers Institute, Amer. (1949), 1801 K St. NW, Suite 900, Wash., DC 20006.

Theatre Organ Society, Amer. (1955), P.O. Box 3043, Olivenhain, CA 92024; 6,000.

Theodore Roosevelt Assn. (1919), P.O. Box 720, Oyster Bay, NY 11771; 1,985.

Theological Schools in the U.S. and Canada, Assn. of (1918), 42 E. National Rd., Vandalia, OH 45377; 204.

Theosophical Society in America, The (1875), 1926 N. Main St., Wheaton, IL 60187; 5,486.

Thoreau Society (1941), 156 Belknap St., Concord, MA 01742; 1,400.

Thoroughbred Racing Assns. (1942), 3000 Marcus Ave., Lake Success, NY 11042; 55 racing associations.

Titanic Historical Society (1963), 207 Centre St., Indian Orchard, MA 01151-0053; 4,300.

Toastmasters Intl. (1924), 23182 Arroyo Vista, Rancho Santa Margarita, CA 92688; 155,000.

Topical Assn., Amer. (1949), P.O. Box 630, Johnstown, PA 15907; 7,000.

Torch Clubs, Internatl. Assn. of (1924), 435 N. Michigan Ave., #1717, Chicago, IL 60611; 3,250.

Toy Manufacturers of America (1916), 200 Fifth Ave., N.Y., NY 10010; 240.

Traffic and Transportation, Amer. Society of (1946), 1816 Norris Pl. #4, Louisville, KY 40205; 2,400.

Trail Association, North Country (1980), 2780 Mundy Ave., White Cloud, MI 49349; 200.

Transit Assn., Amer. Public (1974), 1201 New York Ave. NW, Wash., DC 20005; 1,060.

Translators Assn., Amer. (1960), 109 Croton Ave., Ossining, NY 10562; 3,000.

Transportation and Logistics, Inc., Amer. Society of (1946), P.O. Box 33095, Louisville, KY 40232; 1,700.

Trapshooting Assn., Amateur (1923), 601 W. National Rd. Vandalia, OH 45371; 100,000+.

Traumatic Stress Studies, Inc., The Intl. Soc. for (1985), 435 N. Michigan Ave., Ste. 1717, Chicago, IL 60611; 1,675.

Travel Agents, Amer. Society of (1931), 1101 King St., Alexandria, VA 22314; 29,000.

Travel Industry Assn. of America (1941), 1133 21st St. NW, Wash., DC 20036; 1,700.

Travelers Protective Assn. of America (1890), 3755 Lindell Blvd., St. Louis, MO 63108; 180,383.

Trilateral Commission, The (1973), 345 E. 46th St., N.Y., NY 10017; 325.

Triple Nine Society (1979), 2119 College St., Cedar Falls, IA 50613; 700.

Trucking Assn., Amer. (1933), 2200 Mill Rd., Alexandria, VA 22314; 150.

True Sisters, United Order (1846), 212 Fifth Ave., N.Y., NY 10010; 8,500.

Truth Seeker Co., Inc. (1873), 910 E Street, San Diego, CA 92101; 3,000.

Tuberous Sclerosis Assn. of Amer. (1970), P.O. Box 44, Rockland, MA 02370; 2,500.

UFOs, Natl. Investigation Committee on (1967), 14617 Victory Blvd., Suite 4, Van Nuys, CA 91411.

UNICEF, U.S. Committee for (1947), 333 E. 38th St., N.Y., NY 10016.

USO (United Service Organizations) (1941), 601 Indiana Ave., NW, Wash., DC 20004.

Underwriters, Amer. Soc. of Chartered Life (1927), 270 Bryn Mawr Ave., Bryn Mawr, PA 19010; 30,000.

Underwriters, Soc. of Chartered Property and Casualty (1944), Kahler Hall, 720 Providence Rd., Malvern, PA 19355.

Uniformed Services Society of Military Widows, Natl. Assn. for (1968), 5535 Hempstead Way, Springfield, VA 22151.

United Nations Assn. of the U.S.A. (1923, as League of Nations Assn.) 485 Fifth Ave., N.Y., NY 10017; 28,000.

U.S., Amer. Assn. for Study of the, in World Affairs (1948), 3813 Annandale Rd., Annandale, VA 22003; 1,500.

United Way of America (1918), 801 N. Fairfax St., Alexandria, VA 22309; 1,200.

Universities, Assn. of Amer. (1914), One Dupont Circle, Suite 730, Wash., DC 20036; 58 institutions.

Universities & Colleges, Assn. of Governing Bds. of (1921), One Dupont Circle NW, Suite 400, Wash., DC 20036.

University Continuing Education Assn., Natl. (1915), One Dupont Circle, Ste. 615, Wash., DC 20036; 2,000.

University Extension Assn., Natl. (1915), One Dupont Circle, Suite 400, NW, Wash., DC 20036; 1,100.

University Foundation, Intl. (1973), 1301 S. Noland Rd., Independence, MO 64055; 11,275.

University Professors, Amer. Assn. of (1915), 1012 14th St. NW, Suite 500, Wash., DC 20005; 41,000.

University Women, Amer. Assn. of (1881), 2401 Virginia Ave. NW, Wash., DC 20037; 140,000.

Urban Coalition, Natl. (1967), 1120 G St. NW, Suite 900, Wash., DC 20005; 42 affiliates.

Urban League, Natl. (1910), 500 E. 62d St., N.Y., NY 10020.

Utility Commissioners, Natl. Assn. of Regulatory (1889), 1102 Interstate Commerce Commission Bldg., 12th & Constitution Ave. NW, Wash., DC 20044-0684; 373.

Vampire Research Center (1972), P.O. Box 252, Elmhurst, NY 11373; 500.

Variety Clubs Intl. (1928), 1560 Bdway., N.Y., NY 10036.

VASA Order of America (1896), 65 Bryant Rd., Cranston, R.I. 02910; 30,000.

Ventriloquists, No. American Assn. of (1944), 800 W. Littleton Blvd., Box 420, Littleton, CO 80120; 1,428.

Veterans Assn., Blinded (1945), 477 H St. NW, Wash., DC 20001; 7,007.

Veterans Assn., China-Burma-India (1948), 750 N. Lincoln Memorial Dr., Milwaukee, WI 53202; 7,000.

Veterans Committee, Amer. (1944), 6309 Bannockurn Dr., Bethesda, MD 20817; 15,000.

Veterans of Foreign Wars of the U.S. (1899) **& Ladies Auxiliary** (1914), 406 W. 34th St., Kansas City, MO 64111.

Veterans of the Vietnam War (1980), 760 Jumper Rd., Wilkes-Barre, PA 18702-9699; 35,000.

Veterans of World War I (1958), 941 N. Capitol St. NE, Room 1201-C, Wash., DC 20002-4234; 45,000.

Veterans of WWII, Submarine (1955), 6523 San Joaquin St., Sacramento, CA 95820; 8,000.

Veterinary Medical Assn., Amer. (1863), 930 N. Meacham Rd., Schaumburg, IL 60196; 50,718.

Victorian Society in America (1966), 219 S. Sixth St., Phila., PA 19106; 4,000.

Volleyball Assn., U.S. (1928), 3595 E. Fountain Blvd., Ste. I-2, Colorado Springs, CO 80910; 65,000.

Walking Society, American (1980), Viana House, Box 1315, Beverly Hills, CA 90213; 2.8 mln.

War Mothers, Amer. (1917), 2615 Woodley Pl. NW, Wash., DC 20008; 3,000.

Warrant and Warrant Officers' Assn., Chief, U.S. Coast Guard (1929), c/o Fort McNair Yacht Basin, 200 V Street, SW, Wash., DC 20024; 3,346.

Washington, DC Area Trucking Assn. (1933), 2200 Mill Rd., Alexandria, VA 22314; 130 companies.

Watch & Clock Collectors, Natl. Assn. of (1940), 514 Poplar St., Columbia, PA 17512; 34,000.

Watercolor Soc., American (1867), 47 Fifth Ave., N.Y., NY 10003; 487.

Water Pollution Control Admin., Assn. of State and Interstate (1961), 444 N. Capital St. NW, Suite 330, Wash., DC 20001.

Water Pollution Control Federation (1928), 601 Wythe St., Alexandria, VA 22314-1994; 32,000.

Water Resources Assn., Amer. (1964), 5410 Grosvenor Ln., Suite 220, Bethesda, MD 20814-2192; 3,600.

Water Ski Assn., Amer. (1939), 799 Overlook Dr. SE, Winter Haven, FL 33884; 25,000.

Water Well Assn., Natl. (1948), 6375 Riverside Drive, Dublin, OH 43017; 22,000.

Water Works Assn., Amer. (1881), 6666 W. Quincy Ave., Denver, CO 80235; 52,000.

Watts Family Assn. (1969), 12401 Burton St., N. Hollywood, CA 91605; 12 branches.

Welding Society, Amer. (1919), 550 NW LeJeune Rd., Miami, FL 33126; 38,000.

Wheelchair Athletic Assn., Natl. (1957), 3595 E. Fountain Blvd., Suite L-1, Colorado Springs, CO 80916; 1,500.

Widows, Society of Military (1968), 5535 Hemstead Way, Springfield, VA 22151; 2,000.

Wilderness Society (1935), 900 17th St. NW, Wash., DC 20006; 350,000.

Wild Horse Organized Assistance (WHOA!) (1971), 140 Greenstone Dr., Reno, NV 89512; 10,000.

Wildlife, Defenders of (1947), 1244 19th St. NW, Wash., DC 20036; 80,000.

Wildlife Federation, Natl. (1936), 1400 16th St. NW, Wash., DC 20036; 5.1 mln.

Wildlife Foundation, No. Amer. (1929), 102 Wilmot Rd., #410, Deerfield, IL 60015; 6,000.

Wildlife Fund, World (1961), 1250 24th St. NW, Wash., DC 20037; 1 mln.

Wildlife Management Institute (1911), 1101-14th St., Suite 725, NW, Wash., DC 20005.

William Penn Assn. (1886), 709 Brighton Rd., Pittsburgh, PA 15233; 90,000.

Wireless Pioneers, Society of (1968), 146 Coleen St., Livermore, CA 94550; 5,340.

Wizard of Oz Club, Intl. (1957), Box 95, Kinderhook, IL 62345; 2,500.

Women, Natl. Assn. of Bank (1920), 500 No. Michigan Ave., Suite 1400, Chicago, IL 60611; 30,000.

Women, Natl. Council of (1888), 777 United Nations Plaza, N.Y., NY 10017; approx. 800.

Women, Natl. Organization for (NOW) (1966), 1000 16th St., NW, Ste. 700 Wash., DC 20036; 250,000.

Women Artists, Natl. Assn. of (1889), 41 Union Sq., N.Y., NY 10003; 700.

Women Engineers, Society of (1950), 345 E. 47th St., N.Y., NY 10017; 14,000.

Women in Communications (1909), 2101 Wilson Blvd., Ste. 417, Arlington, VA 22201; 12,000.

Women in Radio and TV, Inc. (1951), 1321 Connecticut Ave. NW, Washington, DC 20036; 3,000.

Women Geographers, Society of (1925), 1619 New Hampshire Ave. NW, Wash., DC 20009; 500.

Women Intl., Financial (1921), 500 N. Michigan Ave., Ste. 1400, Chicago, IL 60611; 20,000.

Women Marines Assn. (1960), P.O. Box 387, Quantico, VA 22134; 3,172.

Women Strike for Peace (1961), 105 2nd St. NE, Washington, DC 20002; 10,000.

Women of the U.S., Natl. Council of (1888), 777 U.N. Plaza, N.Y., NY 10017; 28 organizations.

Women Voters of the U.S., League of (1920), 1730 M St. NW, Wash., DC 20036; 120,000.

Women World War Veterans (1919), 237 Madison Ave., N.Y., NY 10016; 35,000.

Women's Army Corps Veterans Assn. (1947), Hwy. 21, Anniston, AL 36206; 3,500.

Women's Association, American Business (1949), 9100 Ward Parkway, P.O. Box 8728, Kansas City, MO 64114.

Women's Christian Temperance Union, Natl. (1874), 1730 Chicago Ave., Evanston, IL 60201; 40,000.

Women's Clubs, General Federation of (1890), 1734 N St. NW., Wash., DC 20036.

Women's Clubs, Natl. Federation of Business & Professional (1919), 2012 Massachusetts Ave. NW, Wash., DC 20036.

Women's Educational & Industrial Union (1877), 356 Boylston St., Boston, MA 02116; 1,131.

Women's Intl. League for Peace & Freedom (1915), 1213 Race St., Phila., PA 19107; 50,000.

Women's Legal Defense Fund (1971), 2000 P St. NW, Suite 400, Washington, DC 20036; 1,900.

Women's Overseas Service League (1921), P.O. Box 39058, Friendship Station, Washington, DC 20016; 1,450.

Woodmen of America, Modern (1883), 1701 1st Ave., Rock Island, IL 61201; 648,711.

Woodmen of the World Life Insurance Soc. (1890), 1700 Farnam St., Omaha, NE 68102; 953,000.

Workmen's Circle (1900), 45 E. 33d St., N.Y., NY 10016.

World Federalist Assn. (1975), 418 7th St. SE, Washington, DC 20003; 8,900.

World Future Society (1966), 4916 St. Elmo Ave., Bethesda, MD 20814; 30,000.

World Health, Amer. Assn. for (1953), 2001 S St., NW, Suite 530, Washington, DC 20009; 1,100.

World Peace, Intl. Assn. of Educators for (1969), P.O. Box 3282, Mastin Lake Sta., Huntsville, AL 35810-0282; 20,500.

World's Fair Collectors Soc. (1968), P.O. Box 20806, Sarasota, FL 34276; 400.

Writers Guild of America, West (1933), 8955 Beverly Blvd., W. Hollywood, CA 90048; 7,500+.

Yeoman F. Natl. (1936), 223 El Camino Real, Vallejo, CA 94590; 800.

Young Men's Christian Assns. of the U.S.A., (1851), 101 N. Wacker Dr., Chicago, IL 60606; 13 mln.

YM-YMHAs of Greater New York, Associated (1957), 130 E. 59th St., N.Y., NY 10020; 55,100.

Young Women's Christian Assn. of the U.S.A. (1906), 726 Broadway, N.Y., NY 10003; 1.6 mln.

Youth Hostels, American (1934), P.O. Box 37613, Wash., DC 20013; 124,000+.

Zero Population Growth (1968), 1400 16th St. NW, Suite 320, Wash., DC 20036; 32,000.

Ziegfeld Club (1936), 593 Park Ave., N.Y., NY 10021; 303.

Zionist Organization of America (1897), 4 E. 34th St., N.Y., NY 10016; 140,000.

Zoological Parks & Aquariums, Amer. Assn. of (1924), Oglebay Park, Wheeling, WV 26003; 5,800.

Zoologists, Amer. Society of (1890), 104 Sirius Circle, Thousand Oaks, CA 91360; 3,709.

POSTAL INFORMATION

U.S. Postal Service

The Postal Reorganization Act, creating a government-owned postal service under the executive branch and replacing the old Post Office Department, was signed into law by President Nixon on Aug. 12, 1970. The service officially came into being on July 1, 1971.

The U.S. Postal Service is governed by an 11-person Board of Governors. Nine members are appointed to 9-year terms by the president with Senate approval. These 9, in turn, choose a postmaster general, who is no longer a member of the president's cabinet. The board and the new postmaster general choose the 11th member, who serves as deputy postmaster general. An independent Postal Rate Commission of 5 members, appointed by the president, recommends postal rates to the governors for their approval.

As of Sept. 30, 1990, there were 28,959 post offices throughout the U.S. and possessions.

U.S. Domestic Rates

Postal rates and fees shown below were implemented on Feb. 3, 1991. Domestic rates apply to the U.S., its territories and possessions and APOs and FPOs.

First Class

Letters written, and matter sealed against inspection, 29¢ for 1st oz. or fraction, 23¢ for each additional oz. or fraction. U.S. Postal cards; single 19¢; double 38¢; private postcards, same.

First class includes written matter, namely letters, postal cards, postcards (private mailing cards) and all other matter wholly or partly in writing, whether sealed or unsealed, except manuscripts for books, periodical articles and music, manuscript copy accompanying proofsheets or corrected proofsheets of the same and the writing authorized by law on matter of other classes. Also matter sealed or closed against inspection, bills and statements of accounts.

Express Mail

Express Mail Service is available for any mailable article up to 70 pounds, and guarantees delivery between major U.S. cities or your money back. Articles received by the acceptance time authorized by the postmaster at a postal facility offering Express Mail will be delivered by 3 p.m. the next day to some locations or will be delivered by noon the next day to other destinations. Or, if you prefer, your shipment can be picked up as early as 10 a.m. the next business day. Second day service is available to locations not on the Next Day Delivery Network. Rates include insurance, Shipment Receipt, and Record of Delivery at the destination post office.

Consult Postmaster for other Express Mail Services and rates. (The Postal Service will refund, upon application to originating office, the postage for any Express Mail shipments not meeting the service standard except for those delayed by strike or work stoppage, delay or cancellation of flights, or governmental action beyond the control of the Postal Service.)

Third Class

Third class (limit up to but not including 16 ounces): Mailable matter not in 1st and 2d classes.

Single mailing: Publications, small parcels, printed matter, booklets and catalogs, 29¢ the first ounce, 52¢ for over 1 to 2 ozs., 75¢ for over 2 to 3 ozs., 98¢ for over 3 to 4 ozs., $1.21 for over 4 to 6 ozs., $1.33 for over 6 to 8 ozs., $1.44 for over 8 to 10 ozs., $1.56 for over 10 to 12 ozs., $1.67 for over 12 to 14 ozs., $1.79 for over 14 but less than 16 ozs.

Bulk mailing: At least 200 pieces or 50 pounds of such items as solicitations, newsletters, advertising materials, books and cassettes, each item of which individually weighs less than one pound. Minimum rate per piece: Basic presort, $0.198 for pieces weighing 3.3067 ounces or less; for pieces weighing more than 3.3067 ounces, the rate is $0.109 per piece + $0.600 per pound. Contact your post office for the discounts offered for presorted, destination entry and automation compatible mail.

Separate rates for some nonprofit organizations. Bulk mailing fee, $60 per calendar year. Apply to postmaster for permit. One-time fee for permit imprint, $60.

Parcel Post—Fourth Class

Fourth class or parcel post (16 ounces and over): merchandise, printed matter, etc., may be sealed, subject to inspection.

Priority Mail

First class mail of more than 11 ounces can be sent "Priority Mail" service. The most expeditious handling and transportation available will be used for fastest delivery.

A new pickup service has been initiated for Priority Mail. It costs $4.50 for each stop by the Postal Service. There is also a new flat rate Priority Mail envelope, applicable at the 2-pound rate for matter sent in the Special Postal Service-provided envelope.

Forwarding Addresses

The mailer, in order to obtain a forwarding address, must endorse the envelope or cover "Address Correction Requested." The destination post office then will determine whether a forwarding address has been left on file and provide it for a fee of 35¢ per manual correction and 20¢ per automated correction.

Priority Mail

Packages weighing up to 70 pounds and not exceeding 108 inches in length and girth combined, including written and other material of the first class, whether sealed or unsealed, fractions of a pound being charged as a full pound.

Rates according to zone apply between the U.S. and Puerto Rico and Virgin Islands.

Parcels weighing less than 15 pounds, measuring over 84 inches but not exceeding 108 inches in length and girth combined are chargeable with a minimum rate equal to that for a 15 pound parcel for the zone to which addressed.

Zones	To 2	3	4	5	Zones	To 2	3	4	5
1, 2, 3, ...	$2.90	$4.10	$4.65	$5.45	6.	$2.90	$4.10	$4.65	$5.45
4.	2.90	4.10	4.65	5.45	7.	2.90	4.10	4.65	5.45
5.	2.90	4.10	4.65	5.45	8.	2.90	4.10	4.65	5.45

*Consult postmaster for parcels over 5 lbs.

Special Handling

Third and fourth class parcels will be handled and delivered as expeditiously as practicable (but not special delivery) upon payment, in addition to the regular postage: up to 10 lbs., $1.80; over 10 lbs., $2.50. Such parcels must be endorsed, Special Handling.

Special Delivery

First class mail up to 2 lbs. $7.65, over 2 lbs. and up to 10 lbs., $7.95; over 10 lbs. $7.25. All other classes up to 2 lbs. $8.05, over 2 and up to 10 lbs., $8.65, over 10 lbs. $9.30.

Bound Printed Matter Rates
(Single Piece Zone Rate)

Fourth-Class Mail: Single-Piece Bound Printed Matter

Weight lbs.	Local	1&2	3	Rate Zones 4	5	6	7	8
1.5	$0.93	$1.27	$1.30	$1.36	$1.45	$1.54	$1.65	$1.75
2	0.94	1.30	1.34	1.42	1.53	1.66	1.81	1.93
2.5	0.96	1.33	1.38	1.48	1.62	1.78	1.97	2.12
3	0.98	1.35	1.42	1.54	1.71	1.90	2.12	2.31
3.5	0.99	1.38	1.46	1.60	1.80	2.02	2.28	2.50
4	1.01	1.41	1.50	1.66	1.89	2.14	2.44	2.69
4.5	1.02	1.44	1.54	1.72	1.98	2.26	2.59	2.88
5	1.04	1.47	1.58	1.78	2.07	2.38	2.75	3.07
6	1.07	1.53	1.66	1.89	2.24	2.61	3.06	3.44
7	1.10	1.59	1.74	2.01	2.42	2.85	3.38	3.82
8	1.14	1.64	1.82	2.13	2.60	3.09	3.69	4.20
9	1.17	1.70	1.90	2.25	2.77	3.33	4.01	4.57
10	1.20	1.76	1.98	2.37	2.95	3.57	4.32	4.95

(Includes both catalogs and similar bound printed matter.)

(Bound printed matter must weigh at least 1 pound and not more than 10 pounds. Bound printed matter includes catalogs, directories and books not eligible for special fourth-class rates.)

Domestic Mail Special Services

Registry — Only matter prepaid with postage at First-class postage rates may be registered. Stamps or meter stamps must be attached. The face of the article must be at least 5" long, 3½" high. The mailer is required to declare the value of mail presented for registration.

Registered Mail

Value	Insured	Uninsured
$0.00 to $100	$4.50	$4.40
$100.01 to $500 . .	4.85	4.70
$500.01 to $1,000 . .	5.25	5.05
$1,000.01 to $2,000 .	5.70	5.40
$2,000.01 to $3,000 .	6.15	5.75
$3,000.01 to $4,000 .	6.60	6.10
$4,000.01 to $5,000 .	7.05	6.45
$5,000.01 to $6,000 .	7.50	6.80
$6,000.01 to $7,000 .	7.95	7.15
$7,000.01 to $8,000 .	8.40	7.50
$8,000.01 to $9,000 .	8.85	7.85
$9,000.01 to $10,000	9.30	8.20

Consult postmaster for registry rates above $10,000.

C.O.D.: Unregistered — is applicable to first-, third-, fourth-class, and express mail matter. Such mail must be based on bona fide orders or be in conformity with agreements between senders and addressees. **Registered** — for details consult postmaster.

Insurance — is applicable to third and fourth class matter. Matter for sale addressed to prospective purchasers who have not ordered it or authorized its sending will not be insured.

Insured Mail

$0.01 to $50	$0.75
50.01 to $100.	1.60
100.01 to $150.	2.40
150.01 to $200.	2.40
200.01 to $300.	3.50
300.01 to $400.	4.60
400.01 to $500.	5.40
500.01 to $600.	6.20

Liability for insured mail is limited to $600.

Certified mail — service is available for any matter having no intrinsic value on which 1st class or air mail postage is paid. Receipt is furnished at time of mailing and evidence of delivery obtained. The fee is $1.00 in addition to postage. Return receipt, restricted delivery, and special delivery are available upon payment of additional fees. No indemnity.

Special Fourth Class Rate
(limit 70 lbs.)

First pound or fraction, $1.05 (59¢ if 500 pieces or more of special rate matter are presorted to 5 digit ZIP code or 88¢ if 500 pieces or more are presorted to Bulk Mail Cntrs.); each additional pound or fraction through 7 pounds, 43¢; each additional pound, 25¢. Only the following specific articles: Books of at least 8 printed pages consisting wholly of reading matter or scholarly bibliography, or reading matter with incidental blank spaces for notations and containing no advertising matter other than incidental announcements of books; 16-millimeter or narrower width films in final form and catalogs of such films of 24 pages or more (at least 22 of which are printed) except films and film catalogs sent to or from commercial theaters; printed music in bound or sheet form; printed objective test materials; sound recordings, playscripts and manuscripts for books, periodicals, and music; printed educational reference charts; loose-leaf pages and binders thereof consisting of medical information for distribution to doctors, hospitals, medical schools, and medical students; computer-readable media containing prerecorded information and guides for use with such media. Package must be marked "Special 4th Class Rate" stating item contained.

Library Rate (limit 70 lbs.)

First pound 65¢, each additional pound through 7 pounds, 24¢; each additional pound, 12¢. Books when loaned or exchanged between and sent to or from schools, colleges, public libraries, and certain non-profit organizations; books, printed music, bound academic theses, periodicals, sound recordings, other library materials, museum materials (specimens, collections), scientific or mathematical kits, instruments or other devices; also catalogs, guides or scripts for some of these materials. Must be marked "Library Rate".

Also qualifying for library rate are: Books mailed from publishers or distributors to schools, libraries, colleges or universities or to bookstores owned, operated and controlled by schools, colleges or universities.

Parcel Post Rate Schedule
(Inter BMC/ASF Zip Codes Only, Machinable Parcels, No Discount, No Surcharge)

Weight up to but not exceeding—(pounds)	1 and 2	3	4	Zones 5	6	7	8
2.	$2.19	$2.32	$2.46	$2.74	$2.85	$2.85	$2.85
3.	2.29	2.49	2.70	3.12	3.54	4.00	4.05
4.	2.39	2.65	2.94	3.50	4.06	4.35	4.60
5.	2.49	2.81	3.17	3.88	4.58	5.20	5.40
6.	2.59	2.98	3.41	4.26	5.10	6.33	8.55
7.	2.68	3.14	3.65	4.64	5.62	7.06	9.60
8.	2.78	3.31	3.89	5.02	6.14	7.78	10.65
9.	2.88	3.47	4.12	5.40	6.67	8.51	11.70
10.	2.98	3.63	4.36	5.78	7.19	9.24	12.75
11.	3.08	3.80	4.60	6.16	7.71	9.97	13.75
12.	3.18	3.96	4.83	6.54	8.23	10.69	14.80

Weight up to but not exceeding—(pounds)	1 and 2	3	4	5	6	7	8
				Zones			
13.	3.25	4.08	4.99	6.79	8.57	11.17	15.85
14.	3.32	4.19	5.16	7.04	8.92	11.65	16.90
15.	3.38	4.28	5.27	7.23	9.17	11.99	17.95
16.	3.43	4.36	5.39	7.40	9.40	12.31	19.00
17.	3.48	4.44	5.49	7.56	9.62	12.61	19.91
18.	3.53	4.51	5.60	7.72	9.83	12.90	20.38
19.	3.58	4.59	5.69	7.87	10.03	13.17	20.83
20.	3.63	4.65	5.79	8.01	10.22	13.43	21.26
21.	3.68	4.72	5.88	8.15	10.40	13.68	21.66
22.	3.72	4.79	5.97	8.28	10.57	13.91	22.05
23.	3.77	4.85	6.05	8.40	10.74	14.14	22.43
24.	3.81	4.91	6.13	8.52	10.90	14.36	22.78
25.	3.85	4.97	6.21	8.64	11.05	14.57	23.13

Postal Union Mail Special Services

Registration — available to practically all countries. Fee $4.40. The maximum indemnity payable — generally only in case of complete loss (of both contents and wrapper) — is $24.60. To Canada only the fee is $4.50 providing indemnity for loss up to $100, $4.85 for loss up to $500, and $5.25 for loss up to $1,000.

Return receipt — showing to whom and date deliv'd, 90¢.

Special delivery — Available to most countries. Consult post office. Fees for International Special Delivery same for air or surface: for letters, letter packages and post cards not over 2 pounds, $5.60. If over 2 pounds, $6.00, for printed matter, matter for the blind, or small packets, $5.90 if not over 2 pounds; if over 2 pounds, $6.75.

Marking — an article intended for special delivery service must have affixed to the cover near the name of the country of destination "EXPRES" (special delivery) label, obtainable at the post office, or it may be marked on the cover boldly in red "EXPRES" (special delivery).

Special handling — entitles AO surface packages to priority handling between mailing point and U.S. point of dispatch. Fees: $1.80 for packages to 10 pounds, and $2.50 for packages over 10 pounds.

Airmail — there is daily air service to practically all countries.

Prepayment of replies from other countries — a mailer who wishes to prepay a reply by letter from another country may do so by sending his correspondent one or more international reply coupons, which may be purchased at United States post offices. One coupon should be accepted in any country in exchange for stamps to prepay a surface letter of the first unit of weight to the U.S.

Additional international special services: Insurance: Available to many countries for loss of or damage to items paid at parcel post rate. Consult postmaster for indemnity limits for individual countries.

Limit of Indemnity Not Over	Fees Canada	All other Countries
$50	$0.75	$1.60
100	1.60	2.40
200	2.40	3.50
300	3.50	4.60
400	4.60	5.40
500	5.40	6.20
600	6.20	6.60
700		6.90
800		7.20
900		7.50
1,000		7.80
1,100		8.10
1,200		8.40

Restricted Delivery: Available to many countries for registered mail, limits who may receive an item. Fee: $2.50.

Post Office-Authorized 2-Letter State Abbreviations

The abbreviations below are approved by the U.S. Postal Service for use in addresses only. They do not replace the traditional abbreviations in other contexts. The official list follows, including the District of Columbia, Guam, Puerto Rico, the Canal Zone, and the Virgin Islands (all capital letters are used):

Alabama	AL	Hawaii	HI	Mississippi	MS
Alaska	AK	Idaho	ID	Montana	MT
American Samoa	AS	Illinois	IL	Nebraska	NE
Arizona	AZ	Indiana	IN	Nevada	NV
Arkansas	AR	Iowa	IA	New Hampshire	NH
California	CA	Kansas	KS	New Jersey	NJ
Colorado	CO	Kentucky	KY	New Mexico	NM
Connecticut	CT	Louisiana	LA	New York	NY
Delaware	DE	Maine	ME	North Carolina	NC
Dist. of Col.	DC	Marshall Islands	MH	North Dakota	ND
Federated States of		Maryland	MD	Northern Mariana Is.	MP
Micronesia	FM	Massachusetts	MA	Ohio	OH
Florida	FL	Michigan	MI	Oklahoma	OK
Georgia	GA	Minnesota	MN	Oregon	OR
Guam	GU	Missouri	MO	Pennsylvania	PA

Puerto Rico	PR				
Rhode Island	RI				
South Carolina	SC				
South Dakota	SD				
Tennessee	TN				
Texas	TX				
Utah	UT				
Vermont	VT				
Virginia	VA				
Virgin Islands	VI				
Washington	WA				
West Virginia	WV				
Wisconsin	WI				
Wyoming	WY				

Also approved for use in addressing mail are the following abbreviations:

Alley	Aly	Court	Ct	Grove	Grv	Rural	R
Arcade	Arc	Courts	Cts	Heights	Hts	Square	Sq
Avenue	Ave	Crescent	Cres	Highway	Hwy	Street	St
Boulevard	Blvd	Drive	Dr	Lane	Ln	Terrace	Ter
Branch	Br	Expressway	Expy	Manor	Mnr	Trail	Trl
Bypass	Byp	Extended	Ext	Place	Pl	Turnpike	Tpke
Causeway	Cswy	Extension	Ext	Plaza	Plz	Viaduct	Via
Center	Ctr	Freeway	Fwy	Point	Pt	Vista	Vis
Circle	Cir	Gardens	Gdns	Road	Rd		

Size Standards for Domestic Mail

Minimum Size

Pieces which do not meet the following requirements are prohibited from the mails:

a. All pieces must be at least .007 of an inch thick, and
b. All pieces (except keys and identification devices) which are ¼ inch or less thick must be:
  (1) Rectangular in shape,

(continued)

(2) At least 3½ inches high, and
(3) At least 5 inches long.

Note: Pieces greater than ¼ inch thick can be mailed even if they measure less than 3½ by 5 inches.

Nonstandard Mail

All First-Class Mail, except presort and carrier route First-Class mail, weighing one ounce or less and all single-piece rate Third-Class mail weighing one ounce or less is nonstandard (and subject to a 10¢ surcharge in addition to the applicable postage and fees) if:

1. Any of the following dimensions are exceeded:
   Length—11½ inches,
   Height—6⅛ inches,
   Thickness—¼ inch, or
2. The length divided by the height is not between 1.3 and 2.5, inclusive. The nonstandard surcharge for presort and carrier route First-Class mail is 5¢.

Air Mail, Parcel Post International Rates

Aerogrammes — 45¢ each to all countries.
Air mail postcards (single) - 40¢ to all countries except Canada and Mexico (30¢ each)

Weight steps	A	B	C	D	E
			Parcel post rate groups		
First 1 pound	$6.00	$7.75	$9.25	$10.70	$12.30
Each additional pound or fraction up to 5 pounds	3.00	4.25	5.00	6.00	7.00
Each additional pound or fraction over 5 pounds	2.00	3.00	4.00	5.00	6.00

Parcel Post Rate Groups

Country	Rate group	Maximum weight limits for air parcel post	Country	Rate group	Maximum weight limits for air parcel post
Afghanistan	D	44	Eat Timor	No Parcel Post Service.	
Albania	C	44	Ecuador	C	44
Algeria	D	44	Egypt	D	44
Andorra	B	44	El Salvador	B	44
Angola	E	22	Equatorial Guinea	D	44
Anguilla	A	22	Estonia	E	22
Antigua & Barbuda	A	22	Ethiopia	D	44
Argentina	D	44	Falkland Islands	D	44
Aruba	A	44	Faroe Islands	C	44
Ascension	No Air Service		Fiji	B	44
Australia	D	44	Finland	D	44
Austria	B	44	France	E	44
Azores	C	44	French Guiana	C	44
Bahamas	A	22	French Polynesia	D	44
Bahrain	D	22	Gabon	D	44
Bangladesh	E	22	Gambia	B	22
Barbados	B	44	Germany	C	44
Belgium	D	44	Ghana	D	22
Belize	A	44	Gibraltar	C	44
Benin	C	44	Great Britain and Northern Ireland	C	50
Bermuda	A	44	Greece	C	44
Bhutan	E	22	Greenland	D	44
Bolivia	B	44	Grenada	A	44
Botswana	E	22	Guadeloupe	A	44
Brazil	E	44	Guatemala	A	44
British Virgin Islands	A	44	Guinea	B	44
Brunei	D	22	Guinea-Bissau	B	22
Bulgaria	D	44	Guyana	B	44
Burkina Faso	D	44	Haiti	A	44
Burma	D	22	Honduras	B	44
Burundi	E	44	Hong Kong	C	44
Cameroon	D	44	Hungary	C	44
Canada	Separate Rate Group.	66	Iceland	C	44
Cape Verde	D	22	India	D	44
Cayman Islands	A	44	Indonesia	E	22
Central African Rep.	E	44	Iran	D	44
Chad	D	44	Iraq	D	44
Chile	D	22	Ireland (Eire)	C	50
China (Peoples Republic of)	D	44	Israel	C	33
Colombia	B	44	Italy (incl. San Marino)	C	44
Comoros	E	44	Jamaica	A	22
Congo	D	44	Japan	E	44
Corsica	E	44	Jordan	C	44
Costa Rica	A	44	Kampuchea (Cambodia)	No Parcel Post Service.	
Cote d'Ivoire (Ivory Coast)	D	44	Kenya	D	44
Cuba	No Parcel Post Service.		Kiribati	B	44
Cyprus	C	44	Korea, Democratic People's Republic	No Parcel Post Service.	
Czecholovakia	C	33	Korea, Republic of (South)	C	44
Denmark	C	44	Kuwait	C	44
Djibouti	D	44	Lao	E	44
Dominica	A	22	Latvia	E	22
Dominican Rep.	A	44			

Country	Rate group	Maximum weight limits for air parcel post	Country	Rate group	Maximum weight limits for air parcel post
Lebanon	C	11	Saint Pierre & Miquelon	A	44
Lesotho	E	22	Saint Vincent & the Grenadines	A	22
Liberia	C	22	San Marino	C	44
Libya	D	44	Sao Tome & Principe	D	44
Liechtenstein	B	44	Saudia Arabia	D	22
Lithuania	E	22	Senegal	D	44
Luxembourg	B	44	Seychelles	D	22
Macao	C	44	Sierre Leone	D	44
Madagascar	E	44	Singapore	D	22
Madeira Islands	B	44	Solomon Islands	C	44
Malawi	D	22	Somalia	D	44
Malaysia	D	22	South Africa (including South West Africa & Namibia)	D	22
Maldives	D	22			
Mali	C	44	Spain	C	44
Malta	C	22	Sri Lanka	D	44
Martinique	A	44	Sudan	D	44
Mauritania	D	44	Suriname	B	44
Mauritius	E	22	Swaziland	D	44
Mexico	A	44	Sweden	D	44
Monaco	E	44	Switzerland	B	44
Mongolia	No Parcel Post Service.		Syria	C	44
Montserrat	A	44	Taiwan	C	44
Morocco	C	44	Tanzania	E	22
Mozambique	E	22	Thailand	D	44
Nauru	C	44	Togo	D	44
Nepal	D	44	Tonga	B	22
Netherlands	C	44	Trinidad & Tobago	B	22
Netherlands Antilles	A	44	Tristan da Cunha	E	22
New Caledonia	D	44	Tunisia	C	44
New Zealand	D	44	Turkey	C	44
Nicaragua	B	44	Turks and Caicos Islands	A	22
Niger	D	44	Tuvalu	B	44
Nigeria	C	22	Uganda	D	22
Norway	D	44	Union of Soviet Socialist Republics	E	22
Oman	D	22	United Arab Emirates	D	44
Pakistan	D	22	Uruguay	B	44
Panama	A	44	Vanuatu	B	44
Papua New Guinea	D	44	Vatican City State	C	44
Paraguay	D	44	Venezuela	B	44
Peru	B	44	Vietnam	No Parcel Post Service.	
Philippines	D	44	Wallis & Futuna Islands	D	44
Pitcairn Islands	B	22	Western Samoa	B	22
Poland	B	33	Yemen, Republic of	E	44
Portugal	C	22	Yugoslavia	C	33
Qatar	C	44	Zaire	E	33
Reunion	E	44	Zambia	E	44
Romania	C	44	Zimbabwe	E	44
Rwanda	D	44			
Saint Christopher & Nevis	A	44			
Saint Helena	C	44			
Saint Lucia	A	44			

Postcards

Surface rates to Canada and Mexico, 30¢; to all other countries, 35¢. By air, Canada and Mexico, 30¢; to all other countries, 40¢. Maximum size permitted, 6 x 4¼ in.; minimum, 5½ x 3½.

Gross Postal Revenues at Large Cities

Fiscal year	Boston	Chicago	L.A.	New York	Phila.	St. Louis	Wash., D.C.
1975	$136,453,079	$365,378,795	$193,229,077	$453,905,277	$134,571,376	$85,591,774	$115,489,343
1980	224,428,760	528,233,991	271,136,828	666,377,778	221,161,624	127,427,555	187,334,312
1981	256,524,082	551,988,015	301,159,594	741,286,845	235,116,018	142,548,957	201,191,995
1982	292,971,572	597,246,568	338,798,409	848,507,590	265,242,959	160,596,946	215,772,861
1983	294,932,399	589,476,264	330,734,928	856,569,717	273,210,529	165,000,437	212,117,368
1984	314,230,399	598,141,605	338,760,060	907,426,500	295,917,848	177,041,331	225,378,646
1985	339,550,469	563,693,370	358,859,412	938,829,064	300,811,081	194,786,119	236,131,464
1986	378,861,842	579,432,633	381,254,469	960,987,314	330,671,509	211,134,497	253,607,563
1987	405,124,317	612,014,066	389,819,485	962,000,684	367,123,549	221,972,462	290,840,099
1988	428,049,178	618,237,375	415,847,750	999,747,864	384,189,378	245,040,401	341,131,117
1989	421,170,296	610,124,516	439,708,491	1,052,810,676	374,566,877	264,109,672	307,918,572
1990	426,200,044	593,027,761	434,305,082	1,224,750,953	325,928,242	267,125,823	307,899,289

Other cities for fiscal year 1990: Dallas, $494,597,086; Atlanta, $411,841,358; Houston, $355,802,355; Minneapolis, $290,651,288; San Francisco, $275,519,620; Baltimore, $258,563,894; Hartford, CT, $256,474,744; Columbus, OH, $297,384,914.

LANGUAGE

Sources for this section: *The World Almanac Guide to Good Word Usage; The Columbia Encyclopedia; Webster's Third New International Dictionary; The Oxford English Dictionary, 2nd ed.; The Associated Press Stylebook and Libel Manual; The Encyclopedia Americana.*

Neologisms

("New" words; from the Second Edition of the *Oxford English Dictionary*. Oxford Univ. Press. 1989.)

antiquark: the antiparticle of a quark.

arcade game: a (mechanical or electronic) game of a type orig. popularized in amusement arcades.

assertiveness training: a technique by which diffident persons are trained to behave (more) assuredly.

astroturfed: carpeted with astroturf.

birth parent: a natural (as opposed to an adoptive) parent.

build-down: a systematic reduction of nuclear armaments, by destroying two or more for each new one deployed.

bulimarexic: suffering from or characteristic of bulimia nervosa; one who suffers from bulimia nervosa.

camp-on: a facility of some telephone systems by which the caller of an engaged number can arrange for the system to ring it automatically as soon as it becomes free (in some cases ringing the caller also if he has replaced his receiver).

car-phone: a radio-telephone designed for use in a motor vehicle.

designer drug: a drug synthesized to mimic a legally restricted or prohibited drug without itself being subject to restriction.

fast tracker: a high-flyer; an ambitious or thrusting person.

foodie: also foody. One who is particular about food, a gourmet.

gender gap: the difference in (esp. political) attitudes between men and women.

hate mail: letters (often anonymous) in which the senders express their hostility towards the recipient.

Jazzercise: a proprietary name for a program of physical exercises arranged to be carried out in a class to the accompaniment of jazz music; also, exercise of this kind.

microwavable: of food and food containers: suitable for cooking or heating in a microwave oven.

NIMBY, nimby: "not in my backyard," a slogan expressing objection to the siting of something considered unpleasant, such as nuclear waste, in one's own locality.

passive smoking: the inhalation of smoke involuntarily from the tobacco being smoked by others, considered as a health risk.

rainbow coalition: a political grouping of minority peoples and other disadvantaged elements, esp. for the purpose of electing a candidate.

right to die: the alleged right of a brain-damaged or otherwise incurably ill person to the termination of life-sustaining treatment.

skanking: a style of West Indian dancing to reggae music, in which the body bends forward at the waist, and the knees are raised and the hands claw the air in time to the beat; dancing in this style.

street credibility: popularity with, or accessibility to, ordinary people, esp. those involved in urban street culture; the appearance or fact of being "street-wise"; hence (apparent) familiarity with contemporary trends, fashions, social issues.

yuppiedom: the condition or fact of being a yuppie; the domain of yuppies; yuppies as a class.

Eponyms (words named for people)

Bloody Mary—a vodka and tomato juice drink; after the nickname of Mary I, Queen of England, 1553-58, notorious for her persecution of Protestants.

Bloomers—full, loose trousers gathered at the knee; after Mrs. Amelia Bloomer, an American social reformer who advocated such clothing, 1851.

Bobbies—in Great Britain, police officers; after Sir Robert Peel, the statesman who organized the London police force, 1850.

Bowdlerize—to delete written matter considered indelicate; after Thomas Bowdler, British editor of an expurgated Shakespeare, 1825.

Boycott—to combine against in a policy of nonintercourse for economic or political reasons; after Charles C. Boycott, an English land agent in County Mayo, Ireland, ostracized in 1880 for refusing to reduce rents.

Braille—a system of writing for the blind; after Louis Braille, the French teacher of the blind who invented it, 1852.

Caesarean section—surgical removal of a child from the uterus through an abdominal incision; after Julius Caesar, born c. 102 B.C., in this manner, according to legend.

Casanova—a man who is a promiscuous and unscrupulous lover; after Giovanni Casanova, an Italian adventurer, 1725-98.

Chauvinist—excessively patriotic; after Nicolas Chauvin, a legendary French soldier devoted to Napoleon.

Derby—a stiff felt hat with a dome-shaped crown and rather narrow rolled brim; after Edward Stanley, 12th Earl of Derby, who in 1780 founded the Derby horse race at Epsom Downs, England, to which these hats are worn.

Gerrymander—to divide an election district in an unnatural way, to favor one political party; after Elbridge Gerry, and the salamander, for the salamander-like shape of a Mass. election district created, 1812, during Gerry's governorship.

Guillotine—a machine for beheading; after Joseph Guillotine, a French physician who proposed its use in 1789 as more humane than hanging.

Leotard—a close-fitting garment for the torso, worn by dancers, acrobats, and the like; after Julius Leotard, a 19th-century French aerial gymnast.

Silhouette—an outline image; from Etienne de Silhouette, the French finance minister, 1757, who advocated economies that included buying such paper portraits instead of painted miniatures.

Foreign Words and Phrases

(L = Latin; F = French; Y = Yiddish; R = Russian; G = Greek; I = Italian; S = Spanish)

ad hoc (L; ad HOK): for the particular end or purpose at hand

ad infinitum (L; ad in-FI-NITE-UM): endless

ad nauseum (L; ad NAWZ-ee-um): to a sickening degree

apropos (L; ap-ruh-POH): to the point; appropriate

bête noire (F; BET NWAHR): a thing or person viewed with particular dislike.

bon appetit (F; BOH nap-uh-teet): good appetite

bona fide (L; BOH nuh-feyed): genuine

carte blanche (F; kahrt BLANNSH): full discretionary power

cause celebre (F; kawz suh-LEB-ruh): a notorious incident

C'est la vie (F; se lah VEE): That's life

chutzpah (Y; KHOOT-spuh): amazing nerve bordering on arrogance

coup de grace (F; kooh duh GRAHS): the final blow

coup d'etat (F; kooh duh tah): forceful overthrow of a government

creme de la creme (F; KREM duh luh KREM): the best of the best

cum laude/magna cum laude/summa cum laude (L; KUHM loud-ay; MAHN-ya ...; SOO-ma ...): with praise or honor; with great praise or honor; with the highest praise or honor

de facto (L; di FAK-toh): in fact; generally agreed to without a formal decision

deja vu (F; DAY-zhah VOOH): the sensation that something happening has happened before

de jure (L; dee JOOR-ee, day YOOR-ay): determined by law, as opposed to de facto

de rigueur (F; duh ree-GUR): necessary according to convention

detente (F; day-TAHNT): an easing or relaxation of strained relations

éminence grise (F; ay-meh-NAHNN-suh GREEZ): one who wields power behind the scenes

enfant terrible (F; ahnn-FAHNN te-REE-bluh): one whose unconventional behavior causes embarrassment

en masse (F; ahn MAHS): in a large body

ergo (L; ER-goh): therefore

esprit de corps (F; es-PREE duh KAWR): group spirit; feeling of camaraderie

Eureka (G; YOOR-EE-kuh): I have found it

ex post facto (L; eks pohst FAK-toh): an explanation or regulation concocted after the event

fait accompli (F; fayt uh-kom-PLEE): an accomplished fact

faux pas (F; fowe PAH): a social blunder

glasnost (R; glahs-nust): openness, candor

hoi polloi (G; hoy puh-LOY): the masses

in loco parentis (L; in LO H-Koh puh-REN-tis): in place of a parent

in memoriam (L; in muh-MAWR-ee-uhm): in memory of

in situ (L; in SEYE-tyooh): in the original arrangement

in toto (L; in TOH-toh): totally

je ne sais quoi (F; zhuh nuh say KWAH): I don't know what; the little something that eludes description

joie de vivre (F; zhwah duh VEEV-ruh): joy of living, love of life

mea culpa (L; MAY-uh CUL-puh): my fault

meshugga (Y; meh-SHOOG-uh): crazy

modus operandi (L; MOH-duhs op-uh-RAN-dee): method of operation

noblesse oblige (F; noh-BLES uh-BLEEZH); the obligation of nobility to help the less fortunate

non compos mentis (L; non KOM-puhs MEN-tis): out of control of the mind; insane

nouveau riche (L; nooh-voh REESH): pejorative for recent rich who spend money conspicuously

perestroika (R; PAIR-es TROY-kuh): restructuring

persona non grata (L; per-SOH-nah non GRAH-tah): unacceptable person

post-mortem (L; pohst-MORE-tuhm): after death; autopsy; analysis after event

prima donna (I; pree-muh DAH-nuh): temperamental person

pro tempore (L; proh TEM-puh-ree): for the time being

que sera sera (S; keh sair-ah sair-AH): what will be, will be

quid pro quo (L; kwid proh KWOH): something given or received for something else

raison d'etre (F; RAY-zohnn DET-ruh): reason for being

shlemiel (Y; shleh-MEEL): an unlucky bungling person

savoir-faire (F; sav-wahr-FAIR): dexterity in social and practical affairs

semper fidelis (L; SEM-puhr fee-DAY-lis): always faithful

status quo (L; STAY-tus QWOH): existing order of things

tour de force (L; TOOR duh FAWRS): feat accomplished through great skill

terra firma (L; TER-uh FUR-muh): solid ground

verbatim (L; ver-BAY-tuhm): word for word

vis-a-vis (F; vee-ZUH-VEE): compared with

Esperanto

In 1887, Dr. L. L. Zamenhof, a linguist and physician, published a slim textbook on his "Internacia Lingvo" (International Language) under the pseudonym "Doktoro Esperanto." The term "Esperanto" became attached to the language itself as it gained adherents rapidly until the outbreak of World War I. Hardly recovered from the effects of the war, Esperanto was savaged by Nazism, Stalinism, Fascism, the Japanese militarists of the 1930's, and chauvinistic groups in many other countries. Not until the late 1950's did the number of speakers begin to show the steady increase which continues as Esperanto begins its second century.

Controlled experiments show that because of its logical structure, phonemic spelling, and regular grammar Esperanto can be learned to a given criterion of performance in from one-twentieth to one-fifth the time needed for the learning of a typical national language.

Inteligenta persono lernas la lingvon Esperanto rapide kaj facile. Esperanto estas la moderna, kultura lingvo por la tuta mondo.

Some Foreign Idioms

English
Naked as a jaybird
A bird in the hand is worth two in the bush.

To kill two birds with one stone

To eat crow
To eat like a pig
Don't bite off more than you can chew.

Pride goes before a fall.

To go by fits and starts
There is honor among thieves.
Once in a blue moon

Italian
Naked as a worm (Nudo come un verme)
Better a finch in hand than a thrush on a branch. (Meglio fringuello in man che tordo in frasca.)
To catch two pigeons with one bean (Pigliare due piccioni con una fava)
To swallow the toad (Inghiottire el rospo)
To eat like a buffalo (Mangiare come un bufalo)
Don't take a step longer than your leg. (Non fare il passo piu lungo della gamba.)
Pride rode out on horseback and came back on foot. (La superbia andò a cavallo e tornò a piedi.)
To go by hiccups (Andare a singbiozzo)
A dog doesn't eat a dog. (Cane non mangia cane.)
Every death of a pope (Ad oogni morte di papa)

English
Don't waste your breath!
To turn up like a bad penny

To talk to yourself
Let's get back to the subject.
To pull a long face
He laughs in your face.
By rule of thumb
To be knock-kneed
Put that in your pipe and smoke it!

It's Greek to me!

French
Save your saliva! (Espargne ta salive!)
To arrive like a hair in the soup. (Arriver comme un cheveu sun la soupe.)
To talk to angels (Parler aux anges)
Let's get back to our sheep. (Revenons à nos moutons.)
To make a funny nose (Faire un drole de nez)
He laughs in your nose. (Il vous rit au nez.)
From the view of the nose (A vue de nez)
To have your legs in an X (Avoir les james en X)
Put this in your pocket with your handkerchief on top! (Mets-le dans ta poche avec ton mouchoir dessus!)
It's Chinese! (C'est de chinois!)

English
To hit the ceiling
Go fly a kite!
There's always room for one more.

To have the tables turned

To cut off your nose to spite your face

To slam the door in your face

Give him an inch, he'll take a mile.

To be alive and kicking
You can't make a silk purse out of a sow's ear.

To swear a blue streak

Spanish
To scream at the sky (Poner el grito en el cielo)
Go fry asparagus! (Véte a freír esparragos!)
Where six can eat, seven can eat. (Donde come seis, comen siete.)
To go out for wool and come home shorn (Ir por lana y volver esquilado)
To throw stones at your own roof (Tirar piedras contra su propio tejado)
To slam the door on your nostrils (Cerrarle la puerta en la narices)
Give him a hand and he takes a foot. (Le da la mano y se toma el pie.)
To be alive and wagging your tail (Estar vivo y coleando)
A monkey dressed in silk is still a monkey. (Aunque la mona se vista de seda, mona se queda.)
To toss our toads and snakes (Echar sapos y culebras)

English
Go jump in the lake!
You can only do one thing at a time.

He's as slow as molasses.
He repeats himself.
Where there's smoke, there's fire.

Are you in a hurry?
Drop dead!
He makes a lot of trouble for me.

Go fight City Hall.
Thanks for nothing.

Yiddish
Go whistle in the ocean! (Gai feifen ahfenyam!)
You can't dance at two weddings at the same time. (Me ken nit tantzen auf tsvai chassenes mit ain mol.)
He creeps like a bedbug. (Er kricht vi a vantz.)
He grinds ground flour. (Er molt gemolen mel.)
When bells ring, it's usually a holiday. (Az es klingt, iz misstomeh chogeh.)
Are you standing on one leg? (Bist ahf ain fus?)
You should live in the earth! (Zolst ligen in drerd!)
He makes my wedding black. (Er macht mir a shvartzeh chasseneh.)
Go fight with God. (Shlog zich mit Got arum.)
Many thanks in your belly button. (A shainem dank dir ir pupik.)

Names of the Days

English	French	Italian	Spanish	German
Sunday	Dimanche	domenica	domingo	Sonntag
Monday	Lundi	lunedi	lunes	Montag
Tuesday	Mardi	martedi	martes	Dienstag
Wednesday	Mercredi	mercoledi	miércoles	Mittwoch
Thursday	Jeudi	giovedi	jueves	Donnerstag
Friday	Vendredi	venedri	viernes	Freitag
Saturday	Samedi	sabato	sábado	Sonnabend

Commonly Confused English Words

adverse: unfavorable
averse: opposed

affect: to influence
effect: to cause

aggravate: to make worse
annoy: to irritate

allusion: an indirect reference
illusion: an unreal impression

anxious: apprehensive
eager: avid

censor: to subject to examination by an official empowered to demand alteration or withdrawal
censure: a judgment involving condemnation

complement: to make complete; something that completes
compliment: to praise; praise

capital: the seat of government
capitol: the building in which a legislative body meets

emigrate: to leave for another place of residence

immigrate: to come to another place of residence

elicit: to draw or bring out
illicit: illegal

denote: to mean
connote: to suggest beyond the explicit meaning

farther: more distant in space
further: an extension of time or degree

historic: an important occurrence
historical: any occurrence in the past

imply: to relay information but not explicitly
infer: to understand information that is not relayed explicitly

imminent: ready to take place
eminent: standing out

incredible: unbelievable
incredulous: skeptical

include: used when the items following are part of a whole

comprise: used when the items following are all of a whole

ingenious: clever
ingenuous: innocent

insidious: intended to trick
invidious: detrimental to reputation

literally: actually
figuratively: metaphorically

oral: spoken, as opposed to written
verbal: referring to skill with language, as opposed to other skills

prevaricate: to lie
procrastinate: to put off

pestilence: a contagious or infectious epidemic disease
petulance: rudeness

prostrate: stretched out flat, face down
prostate: of or relating to the prostate gland

qualitative: relating to quality
quantitative: relating to number

National Spelling Bee Champions

The Scripps Howard National Spelling Bee, conducted by Scripps Howard Newspapers and other leading newspapers since 1939, was instituted by the Louisville (Ky.) Courier-Journal in 1925. Children under 16 years of age and not beyond the eighth grade are eligible to compete for cash prizes at the finals, which are held annually in Washington, D.C. The 1991 winners are: first prize, **Joanne Lagatia**, Clintonville, Wis. (*The Wisconsin State Journal*); second prize, **Maria Roshini Mathew**, Sterling, Ill. (*The Daily Gazette*); third prize, **Todd Erik Wallace**, Blackfoot, Ida. (*The Morning News*), tied with **Eric Herman**, Trenton, N.J. (*The Trenton Times*).

Winning Words

These were the last words given in each of the years 1965-1991 at the Scripps Howard National Spelling Bee. They were all correctly spelled, thereby determining the national champion.

1965 — eczema	1972 — macerate	1979 — maculature	1986 — odontalgia
1966 — ratoon	1973 — vouchsafe	1980 — elucubrate	1987 — staphylococci
1967 — chihuahua	1974 — hydrophyte	1981 — sarcophagus	1988 — elegiacal
1968 — abalone	1975 — incisor	1982 — psoriasis	1989 — spoliator
1969 — interlocutory	1976 — narcolepsy	1983 — purim	1990 — fibranne
1970 — croissant	1977 — cambist	1984 — luge	1991 — antipyretic
1971 — shalloon	1978 — deification	1985 — milieu	

Commonly Misspelled English Words

accidentally	convenience	government	miniature
accommodate	deceive	grammar	mysterious
acquainted	describe	humorous	necessary
all right	description	hurrying	opportunity
already	desirable	incidentally	optimistic
amateur	despair	independent	performance
appearance	desperate	inoculate	permanent
appropriate	eliminate	irresistible	rhythm
bureau	embarrass	laboratory	ridiculous
character	fascinating	lightning	similar
commitment	finally	maintenance	sincerely
conscious	foreign	marriage	transferred
conscientious	forty		

Some Common Abbreviations

Usage of periods after abbreviations varies, but recently the tendency has been toward omission. Definitions preceding those in parentheses are in Latin.

A.A. = Alcoholics Anonymous
A.A.A. = American Automobile Association
AC = alternating current
A.D. = anno Domini (in the year of the Lord)
A.M. = ante meridiem (before noon)
A.F.L. = American Federation of Labor
A.M.A. = American Medical Association
anon. = anonymous
ASAP = as soon as possible
ASCAP = American Society of Composers, Authors, and Publishers
B.A. = Bachelor of Arts
bbl. = barrel(s)
B.C. = before Christ
B.C.E. = before the Christian era
B.S. = Bachelor of Science
B.T.U. = British thermal unit
bu. = bushel
C. = centrigrade, Celsius
c. = copyright
c. (or ca.) = circa (about)
C.I.A. = Central Intelligence Agency
C.E.O. = chief executive officer
C.I.O. = Congress of Industrial Organizations
cm = centimeter
C.O.D. = cash (or collect) on delivery
C.P. = Communist Party
C.P.A. = Certified Public Accountant
C.P.R. = cardio-pulomonary resuscitation
D.A. = District Attorney
D.A.R. = Daughters of the American Revolution
DC = direct current
D.D. = Doctor of Divinity
D.D.S. = Doctor of Dental Surgery

DNA = deoxyribonucleic acid
DOA = dead on arrival
ed. = edited, edition, editor
e.g. = exempli gratia (for example)
esp. = especially
et. al. = et alii (and others)
etc. = et cetera (and so forth)
F. = Fahrenheit
F.B.I. = Federal Bureau of Investigation
f.o.b. = freight on board
FYI = for your information
g.n.p. = gross national product
G.O.P. = Grand Old party (Republican)
Hon. = the Honorable
H.R.H. = His (Her) Royal Highness
i.e. = id est (that is)
I.Q. = Intelligence Quotient
I.R.A. = Irish Republican Army
I.R.S. = Internal Revenue Service
J.D. = Juris Doctor (Doctor of Laws)
J.P. = Justice of the Peace
K = 1,000
k. = karat
kg. = kilogram
km. = kilometer
l = liter
lb. = libra (pound)
M.A. = Master of Arts
M.D. = Medicineae Doctor (Doctor of Medicine)
mfg. = manufacturing
ml = milliliter
mm = millimeter
M.S. = Master of Science

mph = miles per hour
MS = manuscript
MSG = monosodium glutamate
Msgr. = Monsignor
NCO = Noncommissioned Officer
No. = numero (number)
op. = opus (work)
oz. = ounce
p. = page
P.M. = post meridiem (afternoon)
POW = prisoner of war
P.S. = post scriptum (postscript)
pt. = pint(s), part, point
qt. = quart(s)
REM = rapid eye movement
R.F.D. = rural free delivery
R.I.P. = Requiescat in pace (May he rest in peace)
R.N. = Registered Nurse
ROTC = Reserve Officers' Training Corps
rpm = revolutions per minute
RR = railroad
R.S.V.P. = Répondez, s'il, vous plait (Please answer)
S.A.S.E. = self-addressed stamped envelope
S.P.C.A. = Society for the Prevention of Cruelty to Animals
St. = saint, street
T. = ton
T.N.T. = trinitrotoluene
UFO = unidentified flying object
UHF = ultra high frequency
U.S.S. = United States Ship
v. (or vs.) = versus (against)
VHF = very high frequency
w = watt

Latin and Greek Prefixes and Suffixes

Latin prefix/English meaning
a, abs/from
alti, alto/high
ambi/both
ante/before
aqui/water
arbori/tree
audio/hearing
avi/bird
brevi/short
centi/hundred
cerebro/brain
circum/around
ferri, ferro/iron
fissi/split
igni/fire
inter/between
juxta/close
lacto/milk
luni/moon
magni/great
mal/bad
multi/many
naso/nose
nati/birth
oculo/eye
oleo/oil
omni/all
ovi, ovo/egg
plano/flat
post/after

pre/before
pro/for
pulmo/lung
re/again
recti/straight
retro/backward
somni/sleep
stelli/star
sub/under
super/above
terri/land
trans/through
ultra/beyond
uni/one
Latin suffix/
English meaning
cide, cidal/kill
fid/split
fuge, fugal/flee from
grade/walking
pennale/wing
vorous/eating
Greek prefix/
English meaning
a/not
anti/against
astro/star
auto/self
biblio/book
bio/life
cardio/heart

chloro/green
chrono/time
cosmo/universe
ex/outside
geo/earth
geronto/old age
gluc/sweet
grapho/writing
helio/sun
hemi/half
hetero/different
homeo/similar
homo/same
hydro/water
hyper/above
kinesi/movement
litho/stone
logo/word
macro/large
mega/great
meso/middle
meta/beyond
micro/small
mono/one
necro/dead body
neo/new
ornitho/bird
osteo/bone
pan/all
para/close
phono/sound

photo/light
poly/many
proto/first
pseudo/false
psycho/mind, spirit
pyro/fire
rhino/nose
theo/god
thermo/heat
toxico/poison
zoo/living
Greek suffix/
English meaning
algia/pain
archy/government
gamy/marriage
gnomy/knowledge
iasis/disease
itis/inflammation
lepsy/seizure
logy/science of
machy/battle
meter/measure
oid/like
oma/tumor
phobe/fear
scope/observation
sect/cutting
soma/body
sophy/wisdom

A Collection of Animal Collectives

The English language boasts an abundance of names to describe groups of things, particularly pairs or aggregations of animals. Some of these words have fallen into comparative disuse, but many of them are still in service, helping to enrich the vocabularies of those who like their language to be precise, who tire of hearing a group referred to as "a bunch of," or who enjoy the sound of words that aren't overworked.

bale of turtles
band of gorillas
bed of clams, oysters
bevy of quail, swans
brace of ducks
brood of chicks
cast of hawks
cete of badgers
charm of goldfinches
cloud of gnats
clowder of cats
clutch of chicks
clutter of cats
colony of ants
congregation of plovers
covey of quail, partridge

crash of rhinoceri
cry of hounds
down of hares
drift of swine
drove of cattle, sheep
exaltation of larks
flight of birds
flock of sheep, geese
gaggle of geese
gam of whales
gang of elks
grist of bees
herd of elephants
horde of gnats
husk of hares
kindle or kendle of kittens

knot of toads
leap of leopards
leash of greyhounds, foxes
litter of pigs
mob of kangaroos
murder of crows
muster of peacocks
mute of hounds
nest of vipers
nest, nide of pheasants
pack of hounds, wolves
pair of horses
pod of whales, seals
pride of lions
school of fish
sedge or siege of cranes

shoal of fish, pilchards
skein of geese
skulk of foxes
sleuth of bears
sounder of boars, swine
span of mules
spring of teals
swarm of bees
team of ducks, horses
tribe or trip of goats
troop of kangaroos,
    monkeys
volery of birds
watch of nightingales
wing of plovers
yoke of oxen

Young of Animals Have Special Names

The young of many animals, birds and fish have come to be called by special names. A young eel, for example, is an elver. Many young animals, of course, are often referred to simply as infants, babies, younglets, or younglings.

bunny: rabbit.
calf: cattle, elephant, antelope, rhino, hippo, whale, etc.
cheeper: grouse, partridge, quail.
chick, chicken: fowl.
cockerel: rooster.
codling, sprag: codfish.
colt: horse (male).
cub: lion, bear, shark, fox, etc.
cygnet: swan.
duckling: duck.
eaglet: eagle.
elver: eel.
eyas: hawk, others.
fawn: deer.

filly: horse (female).
fingerling: fish generally.
flapper: wild fowl.
fledgling: birds generally.
foal: horse, zebra, others.
fry: fish generally.
gosling: goose.
heifer: cow.
joey: kangaroo, others.
kid: goat.
kit: fox, beaver, rabbit, cat.
kitten, kitty, catling: cats, other fur-bearers.
lamb, lambkin, cosset, hog: sheep.
leveret: hare.

nestling: birds generally.
owlet: owl.
parr, smolt, grilse: salmon.
piglet, shoat, farrow, suckling: pig.
polliwog, tadpole: frog.
poult: turkey.
pullet: hen.
pup: dog, seal, sea lion, fox.
puss, pussy: cat.
spike, blinker, tinker: mackerel.
squab: pigeon.
squeaker: pigeon, others.
whelp: dog, tiger, beasts of prey.
yearling: cattle, sheep, horse, etc.

The Principal Languages of the World

Source: Sidney S. Culbert, Guthrie Hall NI-25 — University of Washington, Seattle, Wash. 98195

Total number of speakers (native plus non-native) of languages spoken by at least one million persons (midyear 1991)

Language	Millions	Language	Millions	Language	Millions
Achinese (N Sumatra, Indonesia)	3	Cantonese (or Yue) (China; Hong-kong)	64	Fon (SC Benin; S Togo)	1
Afrikaans (So. Africa)	10	Catalan (NE Spain; S France; Andorra)	9	French	122
Akan (or Twi-Fante) Ghana	7			Fula (or Peulh) (Cameroon; Nigeria)	13
Albanian (Albania; Yugoslavia)	5	Cebuano (Bohol Sea area, Philippines)	12	Fulakundu (Senegambia; Guinea Bissau)	2
Amharic (Ethiopia)	17	Chagga (Kilimanjaro area, Tanzania)	1	Futa Jalon (NW Guinea; Sierra Leone)	3
Arabic	202	Chiga (Ankole, Uganda)	1	Galician (Galicia, NW Spain)	3
Armenian (USSR)	5	Chinese[3]		Galla (see Oromo)	
Assamese[1] (Assam, India; Bangladesh)	22	Chuvash (Chuvash ASSR, USSR)	2	Ganda (or Luganda) (S Uganda)	3
Aymara (Bolivia; Peru)	2	Czech (Czechoslovakia)	12	Georgian (Georgian SSR, USSR)	4
Azerbaijani (Iran; Azer. SSR, USSR)	14	Danish (Denmark)	5	German	118
Balinese (Indonesia)	3	Dimli (EC Turkey)	1	Gilaki (Gilan, NW Iran)	2
Baluchi (Baluchistan, Pakistan)	4	Dogri (Jammu-Kashmir, C and E India)	1	Gogo (Riff Valley; Tanzania)	1
Bashkir (Bashkir ASSR, USSR)	1			Gondi (Central India)	2
Batak Toda (including Anakola) Indonesia (see also Karo-Dairi)	4	Dong (Guizhou, Hunan, Guangxi, China)	2	Greek (Greece)	12
Baule (Côte d' Ivoire)	2	Dutch-Flemish (Netherlands; Belgium)	21	Guarani (Paraguay)	3
Beja (Kassala, Sudan; Ethiopia)	1	Dyerma (SW Niger)	2	Gujarati[1] (W and C India; S Pakistan)	39
Bemba (Zambia)	2	Edo (Bendel, S Nigeria)	1	Gusii (Kisii District, Nyanza, Kenya)	2
Bengali[1]	187	Efik (incl. Ibibio) (SE Nigeria; W. Cam.)	6	Hadiyya (Arusi, Ethiopia)	2
Berber[2]				Hakka (or Kejia) (SE China)	32
Beti (Cameroon; Gabon; Eq. Guinea)	2	English	450	Hani (S China)	1
Bhili (India)	3	Esperanto	2	Hausa (N Nigeria; Niger; Cameroon)	35
Bikol (SE Luzon, Philippines)	4	Estonian (Estonian SSR, USSR)	1	Haya (Kagera, NW Tanzania)	1
Brahui (Pakistan; Afghan.; Iran)	1	Ewe (SE Ghana; S Togo)	3	Hebrew (Israel)	4
Bugis (Indonesia, Malaysia)	4	Fang-Bulu (Dialects of Beti, q. v.)		Hindi[1,4]	367
Bulgarian (Bulgaria)	9	Farsi (Iranian form of Persian, q. v.)		Ho (Bihar and Orissa States, India)	1
Burmese (Burma)	30	Finnish (Finland; Sweden)	6	Hungarian (or Magyar) (Hungary)	14
Buyi (S Guizhou, S China)	2	Flemish (see Dutch-Flemish)		Iban (Kalimantan, Indonesia; Malaysia)	1
Byelorussian (Byelorussian SSR, USSR)	10			Ibibio (see Efik)	

Language	Millions
Igbo (or Ibo) (lower Niger R., Nigeria)	16
Ijaw (Niger River delta, Nigeria)	2
Ilocano (NW Luzon, Philippines)	7
Indonesian (see Malay-Indonesian)	
Italian (Italy)	63
Japanese	126
Javanese (Java, Indonesia)	60
Kabyle (W Kabylia, N Algeria)	3
Kamba (E Kenya)	3
Kannada[1] (S India)	42
Kanuri (Nigeria; Niger; Chad; Cam.)	4
Karen (see Pho and Sgaw)	
Karo-Dairi (N Sumatra, Indonesia)	2
Kashmiri[1] (N India; NE Pakistan)	4
Kazakh (Kazakh SSR, USSR)	8
Kenuzi-Dongola (S Egypt; Sudan)	1
Khalka (see Mongolian)	
Khmer (Kampuchea; Vietnam; Thailand)	7
Khmer, Northern (Thailand)	1
Kikuyu (or Gekoyo) (W and C Kenya)	5
Kirghiz (Kirghiz SSR, USSR)	2
Kituba (Bas-Zaire, Bandundu, Zaire)	
Kongo (W Zaire; S Congo; NW Angola)	3
Konkani (Maharashtra and SW India)	4
Korean (So., No. Korea; China; Japan)	72
Kurdish (south-west of Caspian Sea)	9
Kurukh (or Oraon) (C and E India)	2
Lao[5] (Laos)	4
Lampung (Sumatra, Indonesia)	
Latvian (Latvian SSR, USSR)	2
Lingala (including Bangala) (Zaire)	6
Lithuanian (Lithuanian SSR, USSR)	3
Luba-Lulua (or Chiluba) (Kasai, Zaire)	6
Luba-Shaba (Shaba, Zaire)	1
Lubu (E Sumatra, Indonesia)	1
Luhya (W Kenya)	3
Luo (Kenya; Nyanza, Tanzania)	3
Luri (SW Iran; Iraq)	3
Lwena (E Angola; W Zambia)	1
Macedonian (Macedonia, Yugoslavia)	2
Madurese (Madura, Indonesia)	10
Magindanaon (Moro Gulf, S Philippines)	1
Makassar (S Sulawesi, Indonesia)	2
Makua (S Tanzania; N Mozambique)	3
Malagasy (Madagascar)	11
Malay-Indonesian	145
Malay, Pattani (SE penninsular Thailand)	1
Malayalam[1] (Kerala, India)	34
Malinke-Bambara-Dyula (W Africa)	9
Mandarin	885
Marathi[1] (Maharashtra, India)	65
Mazandarani (S Mazandaran, N Iran)	2
Mbundu (or Umbundu) (Benguela, Angola)	3
Mbundu (or Kimbundu) (Luanda, Angola)	3

Language	Millions
Meithei (NE India; Bangladesh)	1
Mende (Central, S and E Sierra Leone)	2
Meru (Eastern Province, C Tanzania)	1
Miao (or Hmong) (S China; SE Asia)	5
Mien (China; Viet.; Laos; Thailand)	2
Min (SE China; Taiwan; Malaysia)	49
Minangkabau (W Sumatra, Indonesia)	6
Moldavian (included with Romanian)	
Mongolian (Mongolia; NE China)	5
Mordvin (in and near Mord. SSR, USSR)	
Moré (central part of Burkina Faso)	4
Nepali (Nepal; NE India; Bhutan)	13
Ngulu (Zambezia, Mozambique; Malawi)	2
Nkole (Western Prov., Uganda)	1
Norwegian (Norway)	5
Nung (NE of Hanoi, Vietnam; China)	1
Nupe (Kwara, Niger States, Nigeria)	1
Nyamwezi-Sukuma (NW Tanzania)	4
Nyanja (Malawi; Zambia; N Zimbabwe)	4
Oriya[1] (Central and E India)	30
Oromo (W Ethiopia; N Kenya)	10
Pampangan (NW of Manila, Philippines)	2
Panay-Hiligaynon (Philippines)	6
Pangasinan (Lingayen G., Philippines)	2
Pashtu (Pakistan; Afghanistan; Iran)	21
Pedi (see Sotho, Northern)	
Persian (Iran; Afghanistan)	33
Polish (Poland)	43
Portuguese	175
Provençal (S France)	4
Punjabi[1] (Punjab, Pakistan; NW India)	87
Pushto (see Pashtu) (many spellings)	
Quechua (Peru; Bol. Ec.; Arg.)	8
Rejang (SW Sumatra, Indonesia)	1
Riff (N Morocco; Algerian coast)	1
Romanian (Romania; Moldavia, USSR)	25
Romany (Vlach only) (Europe; Amer.)	1
Ruanda (Rwanda; S Uganda; E Zaire)	8
Rundi (Burundi)	6
Russian	294
Samar-Leyte (Central E Philippines)	3
Sango (Central African Republic)	3
Santali (E India; Nepal)	5
Sasak (Lombok, Alas Strait, Indonesia)	1
Serbo-Croatian (Yugoslavia)	20
Sgaw (SW W N of Rangoon, SW Burma)	1
Shan (Shan, E Burma)	3
Shilha (W Algeria; S Morocco)	3
Shona (Zimbabwe)	7
Sidamo (Sidamo, S Ethiopia)	1
Sindhi[1] (SE Pakistan; W India)	17

Language	Millions
Sinhalese (Sri Lanka)	13
Slovak (Czechoslovakia)	5
Slovene (Slovenia, NW Yugoslavia)	2
Soga (Busoga, Uganda)	1
Somali (Somalia; Eth.; Ken.; Djibouti)	7
Songye (Kasai Or., NW Shala, Zaire)	1
Soninke (Mali; countries to W S E)	1
Sotho, Northern (So. Africa)	3
Sotho, Southern (So. Africa; Lesotho)	4
Spanish	352
Sundanese (Sunda Strait, Indonesia)	24
Swahili (Kenya; Tanz.; Zaire; Uganda)	45
Swati (Swaziland; So. Africa)	1
Swedish (Sweden; Finland)	9
Sylhetti (Bangladesh)	5
Tagalog (Philippines)	39
Tajiki (Tajik Uzbek Kirghiz SSRs, USSR)	4
Tamazight (N Morocco; W Algeria)	3
Tamil[1] (Tamil Nadu, India; Sri Lanka)	66
Tatar (Tatar SSR, USSR)	7
Tausug (Philippines; Malaysia)	1
Telugu[1] (Andhra Pradesh, SE India)	69
Temne (central Sierra Leone)	1
Thai[5] (Thailand)	48
Tho (N Vietnam; S China)	1
Thonga (Mozambique; So. Africa)	3
Tibetan (SW China; N India; Nepal)	5
Tigrinya (S Eritrea, Tigre, Ethiopia)	4
Tiv (SE Nigeria; Cameroon)	2
Tong (see Dong)	
Tonga (SW Zambia; NW Zimbabwe)	2
Tswana (Botswana; So. Africa)	3
Tudza (N Vietnam; S China)	1
Tulu (S India)	2
Tumbuka (N Malawi; NE Zambia)	2
Turkish (Turkey)	56
Turkmen (S USSR; NE Iran; Afghanistan)	3
Twi-Fante (see Akan)	
Uighur (Xinjiang, NW China; SC USSR)	7
Ukrainian (Ukraine, USSR; Poland)	46
Urdu[1,4] (Pakistan; India)	94
Uzbek (Uzbek SSR, USSR)	13
Vietnamese (Vietnam)	59
Wolaytta (SW Ethiopia)	2
Wolof (Senegal)	6
Wu (Shanghai and nearby prov., China)	63
Xhosa (SW Cape Province, So. Africa)	7
Yao (see Mien)	
Yao (Malawi; Tanzania; Mozambique)	1
Yi (S and SW China)	6
Yiddish[6]	
Yoruba (SW Nigeria; Zou, Benin)	18
Zande (NE Zaire; SW Sudan)	1
Zhuang (S China)	14
Zulu (N Natal, So. Africa; Lesotho)	7

(1) One of the fifteen languages of the Constitution of India. (2) See Kabyle, Riff, Shilha, and Tamazight. (3) See Mandarin, Cantonese, Wu, Min, and Hakka. The "common speech" (Putonghua) or the "national language" (Guoyu) is a standardized form of Mandarin as spoken in the area of Beijing. (4) Hindi and Urdu are essentially the same language, Hindustani. As the official language of Pakistan it is written in a modified Arabic script and called Urdu. As the official language of India it is written in the Devanagari script and called Hindi. (5) The distinctions between some Thai dialects and Lao is political rather than linguistic. (6) Yiddish is usually considered a variant of German, though it has its own standard grammar, dictionaries, a highly developed literature, and is written in Hebrew characters.

Computer Language

Source: Electronic Computer Glossary by Alan Freedman, The Computer Language Co. Inc., 1992

access: (used as a verb) to store data on and retrieve data from a disk or other device connected to the computer.

acoustic coupler: a device that connects a terminal or computer to the handset of a telephone. It may also include the modem.

address: a number of a particular memory or disk location. Like a post office box.

analog: a representation of an object that resembles the original. For example, the telephone system converts sound waves into analogous electrical waves.

artificial intelligence: a broad range of computer applications that resemble human intelligence and behavior, such as expert systems and robots.

ASCII: acronym for American Standard Code for Information Interchange. A widely-used code for storing data.

assembly language: a machine oriented language using mnemonics to represent each machine-language instruction. Each CPU has its own assembly language.

authorization code: an identification number or password used to gain access to a computer system.

backup file: a copy of a current file used if the current file is destroyed.

BASIC: Beginner's All-purpose Symbolic Instruction Code; a computer language used by many small and personal computer systems.

baud rate: the switching speed of a line. One baud equals one bit per second or more.

binary: refers to the base-2 number system in which the only allowable digits are 0 and 1.

bit: short for binary digit, the smallest unit of information stored in a computer. It always has the binary value of "O" or "1."

bubble memory: a memory that circulates tiny bubble-like magnetic bits in a solid state structure. Not widely used.

buffer: a temporary place to put information for processing.

bug: a mistake that occurs in a program within a computer or in the unit's electrical system. When a mistake is found and corrected, it's called debugging.

byte: an 8-bit sequence of binary digits. Each byte corresponds to 1 character of data, representing a single letter, number, or symbol. Bytes are the most common unit for measuring computer and disk storage capacity.

c: a high-level programming language often used to write commercial products due to its transportability to many different computer systems.

CAD/CAM: abbreviation for computer-aided design/computer-aided manufacturing.

cathode ray tube terminal: a device used as a computer terminal which contains a television-like screen for displaying data. Most CRT terminals also have a typewriter-like keyboard.

CD-ROM: Information is retrieved by a laser beam that scans tracks of microscopic holes in a rotating compact disk. They can store 550 million characters, but cannot store new information.

COBOL: Common Business Oriented Language; one of the most widely used business programming languages.

chip: a common term for an integrated circuit, a collection of interconnected microminiature electronic components.

code: lines of programming statements written by a programmer.

command: an action statement or order to the computer.

compiler: a program that translates a high-level language, such as BASIC, into machine language.

connect time: the time a user at a terminal (a work station away from the main computer) is logged-on to a computer system.

CPU: the Central Processing Unit within the computer that executes the instructions the user gives the system.

cursor: the symbol on the computer monitor that marks the place where the operator is working.

database: a large amount of data stored in a well organized format. A database management system is a program that allows access to the information.

dedicated: designed for a single use.

density: the number of bits that can be stored in a linear inch.

desktop publishing: using a personal computer to produce high-quality printed output camera ready for the printer.

diagnostics: software programs that test the operational capability of hardware components.

directory: an index to the location of files on a disk.

disk: a revolving plate on which information and programs are stored. See also **Floppy disk.**

disk drive: a peripheral machine that stores information on disks.

documentation: user or operator instructions that come with some hardware and software that tells how to use the material.

DOS: a single-user operating system commonly used on PCs.

download: to transmit data from a central to a remote computer or from a file server to a personal computer.

dump: a printout of the contents of memory or a file.

error message: a statement by the computer indicating that the user has done something incorrectly.

fax: facsimile, the communication of a printed page between remote locations.

field: the physical unit of data in a record.

file: any collection of data treated as a single unit.

file server: a computer that stores data and programs that are shared by many users in a network.

floppy disk: a small inexpensive disk used to record and store information. It must be used in conjunction with a disk drive.

font: a set of characters of a particular design and size.

foreground/background: an operating system prioritizing method in multitasking computer systems. Programs running in the foreground have highest priority.

format: the arrangement by which information is stored.

function: in programming, a routine, or set of instructions, that performs a particular task.

gigabyte: one billion bytes.

hacker: a very technical person in the computer field; the term is sometimes used in a derogatory manner to refer to people who gain unauthorized access into computer systems and data banks.

hardware: the physical apparatus that makes up a computer, silicon chips, transformers, boards and wires. Also used to describe various pieces of equipment including the CPU, printer, modem, CRT (cathode ray tube).

hexadecimal: refers to the base-16 number system, which is used as a shorthand for referencing machine codes.

intelligent terminal: a terminal with built-in processing capability. It has memory, but no disk or tape storage.

interface: the hardware or software necessary to connect one device or system to another.

K: abbreviation for Kilo-byte used to denote 1,024 units of stored matter.

language: any set of compiled, unified, or related commands or instructions that are acceptable to a computer.

laptop computer: a portable computer that usually weighs less than 12 pounds and has a self-contained power supply.

light pen: an input device that uses a light-sensitive stylus connected by a wire to a video terminal.

load: the actual operation of putting information and data into the computer or memory.

loop: in programming, the repetition of some function within the program.

machine readable: any paper form or storage medium that can be automatically read by the computer.

master file: a collection of records pertaining to one of the main subjects of an information system.

megabyte: one million bytes.

memory: the computer's internal work space.

menu: programs, functions or other choices displayed on the monitor for user selection.

microcomputer: a computer that uses a microprocessor for its CPU. All personal computers are microcomputers.

microprocessor: a complete CPU on a single chip.

minicomputer: an intermediate computer system sized between the very small microcomputer and the large computer.

modem: stands for Modulator-Demodulator. A device that adapts a terminal or computer to an analog telephone line.

mouse: a puck-like object that is used as a pointing and drawing device.

multitasking: the ability to run more than one program at the same time.

network: in communications, the path between terminals and computers. In database management, a database design.

noise: random disturbances that degrade or disrupt data communications.

object-oriented programming: development method that reuses existing code and provides more flexibility.

operating system: a master control program that runs the computer and acts as a scheduler and traffic cop.

OS/2: a single-user, multitasking operating system that was designed to be the successor to DOS.

password: a word or code used to identify an authorized user.

PC: microcomputer that serves one user.

peripheral: any hardware device connected to a computer, such as printers or joy sticks.

pixel: picture element, the smallest display element on a video display screen.

program: coded instructions telling a computer how to perform a specific function.

RAM: stands for Random Access Memory. Same as memory.

random access: the ability to retrieve records in a file without reading any previous records.

record: a group of related fields that are used to store data about a subject. A collection of records is a *file*, and a collection of files is a *database*.

ROM: stands for Read Only Memory. A permanent memory.

semiconductor: a solid state substance that can be electrically altered, such as a transistor.

software: the programs, or sets of instructions, that tell the computer what to do.

spreadsheet: a software program that simulates a paper spreadsheet, or worksheet, in which columns of numbers are totaled.

superconductor: a material that has almost no resistance to

the flow of electricity.

telecommuting: working at home and communicating via computer with the office.

user friendly: hardware or software that is easy to use.

user interface: hardware and software that provide the interface between the user and the computer.

virus: a program that infects a computer system. It is secretly attached to a program and does its dirty work after the program has been run once.

voice recognition: the understanding of spoken words by a machine.

window: a separate viewing area on a display screen.

word processor: a text–editing program or system that allows electronic writing and correcting of articles, etc.

Economic and Financial Glossary

Acquisition: The purchase of one company by another.

Balanced Budget: The federal government budget is balanced when receipts are equal to current expenditure.

Balance of payments: The difference between all payments made to and from foreign countries over a set period of time. A *favorable* balance exists when more payments are coming in than going out; an *unfavorable* balance, when the reverse is true. Payments include gold, the cost of merchandise and services, interest and dividend payments, money spent by travelers, and repayment of principal on loans.

Balance of trade (trade gap): The difference between exports and imports, both in actual funds and credit. A nation's balance of trade is *favorable* when exports exceed imports and *unfavorable* when the reverse is true.

Bear Market: A market in which prices are falling.

Bearer Bond: A bond issued in bearer form rather than being registered in the owner's name. Ownership is determined by possession.

Bond: A written promise or IOU by the issuer to repay a fixed amount of borrowed money on a specified date and to pay a set annual rate of interest in the meantime, usually at semi-annual intervals. Bonds are generally considered safe because the borrower (whether a company or the government) usually must make interest payments before the money is spent on anything else.

Bull Market: A market in which prices are on the rise.

Commercial Paper: An extremely short-term corporate IOU, generally due in 270 days or less. Available in face amounts of $100,000, $250,000, $500,000, $1,000,000 and combinations thereof.

Convertible Bond: A corporate bond (see below) which may be converted into a stated number of shares of common stock. Its price tends to fluctuate along with fluctuations in the price of the stock and with changes in interest rates.

Corporate Bond: Evidence of debt by a corporation. The bond normally has a stated life and pays a fixed rate of interest. Considered safer than the common or preferred stock of the same company.

Cost of living: The cost of maintaining a standard of living measured in terms of purchased goods and services. A rise in the cost of living mirrors the rate of inflation.

Cost-of-living benefits: Benefits that go to those persons whose money receipts increase automatically as prices rise.

Credit crunch (liquidity crisis): The period when cash for lending to business and consumers is in short supply.

Debenture: An unsecured long-term debt obligation backed only by the general credit of the issuing corporation.

Deficit spending: The practice whereby a government goes into debt to finance some of its expenditures.

Depression: A long period of economic decline when prices are low, unemployment is high, and there are many business failures.

Devaluation: The official lowering of a nation's currency, decreasing its value in relation to foreign currencies.

Discount Rate: The rate of interest set by the Federal Reserve that member banks are charged when borrowing money through the Federal Reserve System.

Disposable income: Income after taxes which is available to persons for spending and saving.

Dividend: Payment by a corporation to its shareholders, usually in the form of cash, stock shares, or other property.

Dow-Jones Industrial Average: A measure of stock market prices, based on 30 leading companies on the New York Stock Exchange.

Econometrics: The application of mathematical and statistical methods to the study of economic and financial data.

Economic Growth: The steady process of increasing productive capacity of the economy, and hence of increasing national income.

Federal Deposit Insurance Corporation (FDIC): A government-sponsored corporation that insures accounts in national banks and other qualified institutions.

Federal Reserve System: The entire banking system of the U.S., incorporating 12 Federal Reserve banks (one in each of 12 Federal Reserve districts), and 24 Federal Reserve branch banks, all national banks and state-chartered commercial banks and trust companies that have been admitted to its membership. The system greatly influences the nation's monetary and credit policies.

Full employment: The economy is said to be at full employment when only fractional unemployment exists. That is, everyone who wishes to work at the going wage-rate for his type of labor is employed. Since it takes time to switch from one job to another, there will be at any given time a small amount of unemployment.

Golden Parachute: Provisions in the employment contracts of executives guaranteeing substantial severance benefits if they lose their position in a corporate takeover.

Government Bond: An IOU of the U.S. Treasury, considered the safest security in the investment world. They are divided into two categories, those that are not marketable and those that are. *Savings Bonds* cannot be bought and sold once the original purchase is made. These include the familiar Series EE bonds. You buy them at 50 percent of their face value and when they mature, 12 years later, they will pay you back 100 percent of face value if you cash them in. Another type, Series H, are not discounted, but issued in amounts of $500, $1,000, $5,000, and $10,000 and pay their interest in semiannual checks. Marketable bonds fall into 12 categories. *Treasury Bills* are short-term U.S. obligations, maturing in 3, 6, or 12 months. They are sold at a discount of the face value, and the minimum denomination is $10,000. *Treasury Notes* mature in up to 10 years. Denominations range from $500, $1,000 to $5,000, $10,000 and up. *Treasury Bonds* mature in 10 to 30 years. The minimum investment is $1,000.

Greenmail: A company buys back its own shares from a suitor for more than the going market price to avoid a hostile takeover.

Gross National Product (GNP): The market value of all goods and services that have been bought for final use during a year. The GNP is generally considered to be the most comprehensive measure of a nation's economic activity. The *Real* GNP is the GNP adjusted for inflation.

Individual Retirement Account (IRA): A self-funded retirement plan that allows employed individuals to contribute a maximum yearly sum toward their retirement. Interest earned in the account is tax deferred.

Inflation: An increase in the average level of prices; double-digit inflation occurs when the percent increase rises above 9.9.

Insider Information: Important facts about the condition or plans of a corporation that have not been released to the general public.

Junk Bonds: Debt securities that sell at relatively low prices, because of the low credit rating of their issuers. They pay significantly higher yields than top-grade bonds to reflect their added risk. In the 1980s, they have been used to finance hostile takeovers.

Key leading indicators: A series of eleven indicators from different segments of the economy used by the Commerce Department to foretell what will happen in the economy in the near future.

Leveraged Buy-Out: An acquisition of a public company by a small group, often including the company's management, which takes the company private. Much of the purchase price is borrowed with the debt repaid from company profits or by selling company assets.

Liquid Assets: Assets that include cash or those items that are easily converted into cash.

Margin Account: A brokerage account that allows a person to trade securities on credit.

Money supply: The currency held by the public plus checking accounts in commercial banks and savings institutions.

Mortgage-Backed Securities: Created when a bank, builder or government agency gathers together a group of mortgages and then sells bonds to other institutions and the public. The investors receive their proportionate share of the interest payments on the loans as well as the principal payments. Usually, these mortgages are guaranteed by the government, making them a fairly safe investment despite the fact that their market value does fluctuate.

Municipal Bond: Issued by governmental units such as states, cities, local taxing authorities and other agencies. Interest is exempt from U.S. — and sometimes state and local — income tax. *Municipal Bond Unit Investment Trusts* allow you to invest with as little as $1,000 in a portfolio of many different municipal bonds chosen by professionals. The income is exempt from federal income taxes.

Mutual Fund: A portfolio, or selection, of professionally bought and managed stocks in which you pool your money along with thousands of other people. A share price is based on net asset value, or the value of all the investments owned by the funds, less any debt, and divided by the total number of shares. The major advantage is less risk — it is spread out over many stocks and, if one or two do badly, the remainder may shield you from the losses. *Bond Funds* are mutual funds that deal in the bond market exclusively. *Money Market Mutual Funds* buy in the so-called "Money Market" — institutions that need to borrow large sums of money for short terms. Usually the individual investor cannot afford the denominations required in the "Money Market" (i.e. treasury bills, commercial paper, certificates of deposit), but through a money market mutual fund he can take advantage of these instruments when interest rates are high. These funds offer special checking account advantages. The minimum investment is generally $1,000.

National debt: The debt of the national government as distinguished from the debts of the political subdivisions of the nation and private business and individuals.

National debt ceiling: Limit set by Congress beyond which the national debt cannot rise. This limit is periodically raised by congressional vote.

Option: A contractual agreement between a buyer and a seller to buy or sell shares of a security. A *Call* option contract gives the right to purchase shares of a specific stock at a stated price within a given period of time. A *Put* option contract gives the buyer the right to sell shares of a specific stock at a stated price within a given period of time.

Per capita income: The nation's total income divided by the number of people in the nation.

Prime interest rate: The rate charged by banks on short-term loans to large commercial customers with the highest credit rating.

Producer price index: A statistical measure of the change in the price of wholesale goods. It is reported for 3 different stages of the production chain: crude, intermediate, and finished goods.

Program Trading: A term used for trading techniques involving large numbers and large blocks of stocks, usually used in conjunction with computer programs. Techniques include *Index Arbitrage* in which traders profit from price differences between stocks and futures contracts on stock indexes, and *Portfolio Insurance* which is the use of stock-index futures to protect stock investors from large losses when the market drops.

Public debt: The total of the nation's debts owed by state, local, and national government. This is considered a good measure of how much of the nation's spending is financed by borrowing rather than taxation.

Recession: A mild decrease in economic activity marked by a decline in real GNP, employment, and trade, usually lasting 6 months to a year, and marked by widespread decline in many sectors of the economy.

Savings Association Insurance Fund (SAIF): Created in 1989 to insure accounts in savings and loan associations up to $100,000.

Seasonal adjustment: Statistical changes made to compensate for regular fluctuations in data that are so great they tend to distort the statistics and make comparisons meaningless. For instance, seasonal adjustments are made in midwinter for a slowdown in housing construction and for the rise in farm income in the fall after the summer crops are harvested.

Stagnation: A period of economic slowdown in which there is little growth in GNP, capital investment, and real income.

Stock: *Common Stocks* are shares of ownership in a corporation; they are the most direct way to participate in the fortunes of a company. There can be wide swings in the prices of this kind of stock. *Preferred Stock* is a type of stock on which a fixed dividend must be paid before holders of common stock are issued their share of the issuing corporation's earnings. Prices are higher and yields lower than comparable bonds. However, they are attractive to corporate investors because 85 percent of preferred dividends are tax exempt to corporations. *Convertible Preferred Stock* can be converted into the common stock of the company that issued the preferred. This stock has the advantage of producing a higher yield than common stock and it also has appreciation potential. *Over-the-Counter Stock* is not traded on the major or regional exchanges, but rather through dealers from whom you buy directly. These stocks tend to belong to smaller companies. Prices of OTC stocks are based on the dealer's supply and demand. *Blue Chip* stocks are so called because they have been leading stocks for a long time. *Growth* stocks are stocks whose earnings have grown over several years.

Stock-index Futures: A futures contract is an agreement to buy or sell a specific amount of a commodity or financial instrument at a particular price at a set date. Futures on a stock index (such as the Standard & Poor's 500) are bets on the future price of that group of stocks.

Supply-side economics: The school of economic thinking which stresses the importance of the costs of production as a means of revitalizing the economy. Advocates policies that raise capital and labor output by increasing the incentives to produce.

Takeover: The passing of control of one company by another company or group by sale or merger. A friendly takeover occurs when the acquired company's management is agreeable to the merger; when management is opposed to the merger it is an unfriendly takeover. Takeover *arbitrage* is the purchase and/or selling of the securities of companies involved in takeover situations in order to realize a profit.

Tender Offer: A public offer to buy a company's stock; usually priced at a premium above the market.

Unit Investment Trust: A portfolio of many different corporate bonds, preferred stocks, government-backed securities or utility common stocks in which you can invest with as little as $1,000. Professional managers choose the securities, arrange for safe-keeping and collect the income. You receive your pro rata share of income every month.

Zero Coupon Bond: A corporate or government bond that is issued at a deep discount from the maturity value and pays no interest during the life of the bond. It is redeemable at face value.

CONGRESS

The One Hundred and Second Congress
With 1990 Election Results
The Senate

Terms are for 6 years and end Jan. 3 of the year preceding name. Annual salary $135,100; President Pro Tempore, Majority Leader, and Minority Leader $113,400. To be eligible for the U.S. Senate a person must be at least 30 years of age, a citizen of the United States for at least 9 years, and a resident of the state from which he is chosen. The Congress must meet annually on Jan. 3, unless it has, by law, appointed a different day.

The ZIP code of the Senate is 20510, the telephone number is 202-224-3121.

Senate officials: President Pro Tempore, Robert Byrd; Majority Leader, George Mitchell; Majority Whip, Alan Cranston; Minority Leader, Bob Dole; Minority Whip, Alan Simpson.

Dem., 57; Rep., 43; Total, 100. *Incumbent. Bold face denotes winner.

Official Totals (Source: News Election Service)

Term ends	Senator (Party)/Service from[1]	1990 Election	Term ends	Senator (Party)/Service from[1]	1990 Election
	Alabama			**Indiana**	
1997	**Howell Heflin*** (D)/1979	717,814	1997	**Dan Coats*** (R)/1989	806,048
	Bill Cabaniss (R)	467,190		Baron P. Hill (D)	696,639
1993	Richard C. Shelby (D)/1987		1995	Richard G. Lugar* (R)/1977	
	Alaska			**Iowa**	
1997	**Ted Stevens*** (R)/12/24/68	125,806	1997	**Tom Harkin*** (D)/1985	535,975
	Michael Beasley (D)	61,152		Tom Tauke (R)	446,869
1993	Frank Murkowski (R)/1981		1993	Charles E. Grassley (R)/1981	
	Arizona			**Kansas**	
1993	John S. McCain (R)/1987		1997	**Nancy L. Kassebaum*** (R)/12/23/78	578,605
1995	Dennis DeConcini* (D)/1977			Dick Williams (D)	207,491
			1993	Robert J. Dole (R)/1969	
	Arkansas			**Kentucky**	
1997	**David Pryor*** (D)/1979	Unopposed	1997	**Mitch McConnell*** (R)/1985	478,034
1993	Dale Bumpers (D)/1975			G. Harvey I. Sloane (D)	437,976
			1993	Wendell H. Ford (D)/12/28/74	
	California			**Louisiana**	
1993	Alan Cranston (D)/1969		1997	**J. Bennett Johnston*** (D)/11/14/72	
1995	John Seymour (R)/1/10/91[2]		1993	John B. Breaux (D)/1987	
	Colorado			**Maine**	
1997	**Hank Brown** (R)	569,048	1997	**William S. Cohen*** (R)/1979	319,167
	Josie Heath (D)	425,746		Neil Rolde (D)	201,053
1993	Timothy E. Wirth (D)/1987		1995	George J. Mitchell* (D)/5/17/80	
	Connecticut			**Maryland**	
1993	Christopher J. Dodd (D)/1981		1993	Barbara A. Mikulski (D)/1987	
1995	Joe Lieberman (D)/1989		1995	Paul S. Sarbanes* (D)/1977	
	Delaware			**Massachusetts**	
1997	**Joseph R. Biden Jr.*** (D)/1973	112,918	1997	**John F. Kerry*** (D)/1/2/85	1,321,712
	M. Jane Brady (R)	64,554		Jim Rappaport (R)	992,917
1995	William V. Roth Jr.* (R)/1/1/71		1995	Edward M. Kennedy* (D)/11/7/62	
	Florida			**Michigan**	
1993	Bob Graham (D)/1987		1997	**Carl Levin*** (D)/1979	1,471,753
1995	Connie Mack (R)/1989			Bill Schuette (R)	1,055,695
			1995	Donald W. Riegle Jr.* (D)/12/30/76	
	Georgia			**Minnesota**	
1997	**Sam Nunn*** (D)/1972	Unopposed	1997	**Paul David Wellstone** (D)	911,999
1993	Wyche Fowler Jr. (D)/1987			Rudy Boschwitz* (R)/12/30/78	864,375
			1995	David Durenberger* (R)/11/8/78	
	Hawaii			**Mississippi**	
1993	Daniel K. Inouye (D)/1963		1997	**Thad Cochran*** (R)/12/27/78	
1995	**Daniel K. Akaka*** (D)/5/16/90	188,901	1995	Trent Lott (R)/3/3/89	
	Patricia Saiki (R)	155,978			
	Ken Schoolland (B)	4,787		**Missouri**	
	Idaho		1993	Christopher S. Bond (R)/1987	
1997	**Larry E. Craig*** (R)	193,641	1995	John C. Danforth* (R)/12/27/76	
	Ron J. Twilegar (D)	122,295			
1993	Steven D. Symms (R)/1981			**Montana**	
	Illinois		1997	**Max Baucus*** (D)/12/15/78	217,563
1997	**Paul Simon*** (D)/1985	2,115,377		Allen Kolstad (R)	93,836
	Lynn Martin (R)	1,135,628	1995	Conrad Burns (R)/1989	
1993	Alan J. Dixon (D)/1981				

Term ends	Senator (Party)/Service from[1]	1990 Election	Term ends	Senator (Party)/Service from[1]	1990 Election
	Nebraska			**Rhode Island**	
1997	**J. James Exon*** (D)/1979	**349,779**	1997	**Claiborne Pell** (D)/1961	**225,105**
	Hal Daub (R)	243,013		Claudine Schneider (R)	138,947
1995	J. Robert Kerrey (D)/1989		1995	John H. Chafee* (R)/12/29/76	
	Nevada			**South Carolina**	
1993	Harry M. Reid (D)/1987		1997	**Strom Thurmond*** (R)/11/7/56	**482,032**
1995	Richard H. Bryan (D)/1989			Bob Cunningham (D)	244,112
			1993	Ernest Fritz Hollings* (D)/11/9/66	
	New Hampshire			**South Dakota**	
1997	**Robert Smith** (R)	**189,630**	1997	**Larry Pressler*** (R)/1979	**135,682**
	John Durkin (D)	91,262		Ted Muenster (D)	116,727
1993	Warren Rudman (R)/12/31/80			Dean L. Sinclair (I)	
			1993	Thomas A. Daschle (D)/1987	
	New Jersey			**Tennessee**	
1997	**Bill Bradley*** (D)/1979	**977,810**	1997	**Albert Gore Jr.*** (D)/1985	**530,897**
	Christine Todd Whitman (R)	918,874		William R. Hawkins (R)	233,702
1995	Frank R. Lautenberg* (D)/12/27/82		1995	James R. Sasser* (D)/1977	
	New Mexico			**Texas**	
1997	**Pete V. Domenici*** (R)/1973	**296,712**	1997	**Phil Gramm*** (R)/1985	**2,302,357**
	Tom R. Benavides (D)	110,033		Hugh Parmer (D)	1,429,986
1995	Jeff Bingaman* (D)/1983		1995	Lloyd Bentsen* (D)/1971	
	New York			**Utah**	
1993	Alfonse M. D'Amato (R)/1981		1993	Jake Garn (R)/12/21/74	
1995	Daniel Patrick Moynihan* (D)/1977		1995	Orrin G. Hatch* (R)/1977	
	North Carolina			**Vermont**	
1997	**Jesse Helms*** (R)/1973	**1,088,331**	1993	Patrick J. Leahy (D)/1975	
	Harvey Gantt (D)	981,573	1995	James M. Jeffords (R)/1989	
1993	Terry Sanford (D) 11/5/86			**Virginia**	
	North Dakota		1997	**John W. Warner*** (R)/1/2/79	**876,782**
1993	Kent Conrad (D)/1987			Nancy Spanaus (I)	196,755
1995	Quentin N. Burdick* (D)/8/8/60		1995	Charles S. Robb (D)/1989	
	Ohio			**Washington**	
1993	John Glenn (D)/12/24/74		1993	Brock Adams (D)/1987	
1995	Howard M. Metzenbaum* (D)/12/29/76		1995	Slade Gorton (R)/1981	
	Oklahoma			**West Virginia**	
1997	**David L. Boren*** (D)/1979	**735,684**	1997	**John D. Rockefeller IV*** (D)/1/15/85	**276,234**
	Stephen Jones (R)	148,814		John Yoder (R)	128,071
1993	Don Nickles (R)/1981		1995	Robert C. Byrd* (D)/1959	
	Oregon			**Wisconsin**	
1997	**Mark O. Hatfield*** (R)/1/10/67	**590,095**	1993	Robert W. Kasten Jr. (R)/1981	
	Harry Lonsdale (D)	507,743	1995	Herbert H. Kohl (D)/1989	
1993	Bob Packwood (R)/1969			**Wyoming**	
	Pennsylvania		1997	**Alan K. Simpson*** (R)/1979	**100,784**
1993	Arlen Specter (R)/1981			Kathy Helling (D)	56,848
1995	Harris Wofford (D)[3]		1995	Malcolm Wallop* (R)/1977	

(1) Jan. 3, unless otherwise noted. (2) Pete Wilson was elected governor in 1990; he appointed John Seymour to his Senate seat until the Nov. 3, 1992 election. (3) John Heinz died; Harris Wofford was appointed to fill his term until Nov. 5, 1991 election.

The House of Representatives

Members' terms to Jan. 3, 1993. Annual salary $125,100; Speaker of the House, $160,000; Majority Leader and Minority Leader $138,900. To be eligible for membership, a person must be at least 25, a U.S. citizen for at least 7 years, and a resident of the state from which he or she is chosen. The ZIP code of the House is 20515, the telephone number is 202-225-3121.

House Officials: Speaker, Thomas S. Foley; Majority Leader, Richard A. Gephardt; Majority Whip, David E. Bonior; Minority Leader, Robert H. Michel; Minority Whip, Newt Gingrich.

D-Democrat; R-Republican; AI-American Independent; ASI-Amer. System Independent; B-Libertarian; C-Conservative; I-Independent; IC-Ind. Conservative; IS-Illinois Solidarity; JW-Jim Wham; L-Liberal; LP-Liberty Party; LU-Liberty Union; NA-New Alliance; PO-Populist; PF-Peace & Freedom; T-Right to Life; TB-Tax Break; TC-Tax Cut.

Dem., 267, Rep., 167, Ind., 1. Total 435. *Incumbent. Bold face denotes winner.

Official Totals. (Source: News Election Service)

Dist.	Representative (Party)	1990 Election	Dist.	Representative (Party)	1990 Election
	Alabama			Faye Baggiano (D)	83,243
1.	**H.L."Sonny" Callahan*** (R)	**Unopposed**	3.	**Glen Browder*** (D)	**101,923**
2.	**William L. Dickinson*** (R)	**87,649**			

Dist.	Representative (Party)	1990 Election
	Don Sledge (R)	36,731
4.	Tom Bevill* (D)	Unopposed
5.	Bud Cramer (D)	113,047
	Albert McDonald (R)	55,326
6.	Ben Erdreich* (D)	134,412
	David A. Alvarez (I)	8,640
	Nathaniel Ivory (NA)	1,745
7.	Claude Harris Jr.* (D)	127,490
	Michael D. Barker (R)	53,258

Alaska At Large

Dist.	Representative (Party)	1990 Election
	Don Young* (R)	99,003
	John C. Devens (D)	91,677

Arizona

Dist.	Representative (Party)	1990 Election
1.	John J. Rhodes III (R)	Unopposed
2.	Morris K. Udall* (D)[1]	76,549
	Joseph D. Sweeney (R)	39,586
3.	Bob Stump* (R)	134,279
	Roger Hartstone (D)	103,018
4.	John Kyl* (R)	141,843
	Mark Ivey Jr. (D)	89,395
5.	Jim Kolbe* (R)	138,975
	Chuck Phillips (D)	75,642

Arkansas

Dist.	Representative (Party)	1990 Election
1.	Bill Alexander* (D)	101,007
	Terry Hayes (R)	56,067
2.	Ray Thornton (D)	103,455
	Jim Keet (R)	67,786
3.	John Paul Hammerschmidt* (R)	129,850
	Dan Ivy (D)	54,330
4.	Beryl Anthony Jr.* (D)	110,352
	Roy Rood (R)	42,122

California

Dist.	Representative (Party)	1990 Election
1.	Frank Riggs (R)	99,782
	Douglas H. Bosco* (D)	96,468
	Darlene G. Comingore (PF)	34,011
2.	Wally Herger* (R)	133,315
	Erwin E. "Bill" Rush (D)	65,333
	Ross Crain (B)	10,753
3.	Robert T. Matsui* (D)	132,143
	Lowell Patrick Landowski (R)	76,148
	David M. McCann (B)	10,797
4.	Vic Fazio* (D)	115,090
	Mark Baughman (R)	82,738
	Bryce Bigwood (B)	12,626
5.	Nancy Pelosi* (D)	120,633
	Alan Nichols (R)	35,671
6.	Barbara Boxer* (D)	137,306
	Bill Boerum (R)	64,402
7.	George Miller* (D)	121,080
	Roger A. Payton (R)	79,031
8.	Ronald V. Dellums* (D)	119,645
	Barbara Galewski (R)	75,544
9.	Fortney H. "Pete" Stark* (D)	94,739
	Victor Romero (R)	67,412
10.	Don Edwards* (D)	81,875
	Mark Patrosso (R)	48,747
11.	Tom Lantos* (D)	105,029
	G.M. "Bill" Quraishi (R)	45,818
	June R. Genis (B)	8,518
12.	Tom Campbell* (R)	125,157
	Robert Palmer (D)	69,270
	Chuck Olson (B)	11,271
13.	Norman Y. Mineta* (D)	97,286
	David E. Smith (R)	59,773
	John H. Webster (B)	10,587
14.	John T. Doolittle (R)	128,039
	Patricia Malberg (D)	120,742
15.	Gary A. Condit* (D)	97,147
	Cliff Burris (R)	49,634
16.	Leon E. Panetta* (D)	134,236
	Jerry M. Reiss (R)	39,885
	Brian H. Tucker (B)	6,881
17.	Calvin Dooley (D)	82,611
	Charles "Chip" Pashayan* (R)	68,848

Dist.	Representative (Party)	1990 Election
18.	Richard H. Lehman* (D)	Unopposed
19.	Robert J. "Bob" Lagomarsino* (R)	94,599
	Anita Perez Ferguson (D)	76,991
20.	Bill Thomas* (R)	112,962
	Michael A. Thomas (D)	65,101
	William H. Dilbeck (B)	10,555
21.	Elton Gallegly* (R)	118,326
	Richard D. Freiman (D)	68,921
	Peggy Christensen (B)	15,364
22.	Carlos J. Moorhead* (R)	108,634
	David Bayer (D)	61,630
	William H. Wilson (B)	6,702
	Jan B. Tucker (PF)	3,963
23.	Anthony C. Beilenson* (D)	103,141
	Jim Salomon (R)	57,118
	John Honigsfeld (PF)	6,834
24.	Henry A. Waxman* (D)	71,562
	John N. Cowles (R)	26,607
	Maggie Phair (PF)	5,706
25.	Edward R. Roybal* (D)	48,120
	Steven J. Renshaw (R)	17,021
	Robert H. Scott (B)	3,576
26.	Howard L. Berman* (D)	78,031
	Roy Dahlson (R)	44,492
	Bernard Zimring (B)	5,268
27.	Mel Levine* (D)	90,857
	David Barrett Cohen (R)	58,140
	Edward E. Ferrer (PF)	7,101
28.	Julian C. Dixon* (D)	69,482
	George Zandivar Adams (R)	21,245
	William R. Williams (PF)	2,723
	Bob Weber (B)	2,150
29.	Maxine Waters (D)	51,350
	Bill De Witt (R)	12,054
	Waheed R. Boctor (B)	1,268
30.	Matthew G. Martinez* (D)	45,456
	Reuben D. Franco (R)	28,914
	G. Curtis Feger (B)	3,713
31.	Mervyn M. Dymally* (D)	56,394
	Eunice N. Sato (R)	27,593
32.	Glenn M. Anderson* (D)	68,268
	Sanford W. Kahn (R)	42,692
33.	David Dreier* (R)	101,336
	Georgia Houston Webb (D)	49,981
	Gail Lightfoot (B)	7,840
34.	Esteban E. Torres* (D)	55,646
	John Eastman (R)	36,024
35.	Jerry Lewis* (R)	121,602
	Barry Norton (D)	66,100
	Jerry Johnson (B)	13,020
36.	George E. Brown Jr.* (D)	72,409
	Bob Hammock (R)	64,961
37.	Al McCandless* (R)	115,469
	Ralph Waite (D)	103,961
	Gary R. Odom (AI)	6,474
	Bonnie Flickinger (B)	6,178
38.	Robert K. "Bob" Dornan* (R)	60,561
	Barbara Jackson (D)	43,693
39.	William E. "Bill" Dannemeyer* (R)	113,849
	Francis X. "Frank" Hoffman (D)	53,670
	Maxine B. Quirk (PF)	6,709
40.	Christopher Cox (R)	142,299
	Eugene C. Gratz (D)	68,087
41.	Bill Lowery* (R)	105,723
	Dan Kripke (D)	93,586
	Karen S.R. Works (PF)	15,428
42.	Dana Rohrabacher* (R)	109,353
	Guy C. Kimbrough (D)	67,189
	Richard Gibb Martin (B)	7,744
43.	Ron Packard* (R)	151,206
	Doug Hansen (PF)	40,212
	Richard L. "Rick" Arnold (D)	30,720
44.	Randy "Duke" Cunningham (R)	50,377
	Jim Bates* (D)	48,712
	Donna White (PF)	5,237
	John Wallner (B)	4,385
45.	Duncan Hunter* (R)	112,591
	Joe Shea (D)	46,068

Dist.	Representative (Party)	1990 Election
Colorado		
1.	**Patricia Schroeder*** (D)	**82,176**
	Gloria Gonzales Roemer (R)	46,802
2.	**David E. Skaggs*** (D)	**105,248**
	Jason Lewis (R)	68,226
3.	**Ben Nighthorse Campbell*** (D)	**124,487**
	Bob Ellis (R)	49,961
4.	**Wayne Allard** (R)	**89,285**
	Richard R. "Dick" Bond (D)	75,901
5.	**Joel Hefley*** (R)	**127,740**
	Cal Johnston (D)	57,776
6.	**Daniel Schaefer*** (R)	**105,312**
	Don Jarrett (D)	57,961
Connecticut		
1.	**Barbara Bailey Kennelly*** (D)	**126,566**
	James P. Garvey (R)	50,690
2.	**Samuel Gejdenson*** (D)	**105,085**
	John M. Ragsdale (R)	70,922
3.	**Rosa L. De Lauro** (D)	**90,772**
	Thomas Scott (R)	83,440
4.	**Christopher Shays*** (R)	**105,683**
	Al Smith (D)	32,352
5.	**Gary A. Franks** (R)	**93,912**
	Anthony "Toby" Moffett (D)	85,803
	William G. Hare (LP)	1,888
6.	**Nancy L. Johnson*** (R)	**141,105**
	Paul Kulas (D)	48,628
Delaware At Large		
	Thomas R. Carper* (D)	**116,274**
	Ralph O. Williams (R)	58,037
Florida		
1.	**Earl Hutto*** (D)	**88,354**
	Terry Ketchel (R)	80,788
2.	**Pete Peterson** (D)	**103,007**
	Bill Grant* (R)	77,897
3.	**Charles E. Bennett*** (D)	**84,261**
	Rod Sullivan (R)	31,703
4.	**Craig T. James*** (R)	**120,804**
	Reid Hughes (D)	95,293
5.	**Bill McCollum*** (R)	**94,417**
	Bob Fletcher (D)	63,243
6.	**Cliff Stearns*** (R)	**138,547**
	Art Johnson (D)	95,410
7.	**Sam M. Gibbons*** (D)	**99,454**
	Charles D. Prout (IS)	47,754
8.	**C. W. Bill Young*** (R)	**Unopposed**
9.	**Michael Bilirakis*** (R)	**142,145**
	Cheryl Davis Knapp (D)	102,495
10.	**Andy Ireland*** (R)	**Unopposed**
11.	**Jim Bacchus** (D)	**120,974**
	Bill Tolley (R)	111,916
12.	**Tom Lewis*** (R)	**Unopposed**
13.	**Porter J. Goss*** (R)	**Unopposed**
14.	**Harry A. Johnston*** (D)	**156,050**
	Scott Shore (R)	80,239
15.	**E. Clay Shaw Jr.*** (R)	**Unopposed**
16.	**Larry Smith*** (D)	**Unopposed**
17.	**William Lehman*** (D)	**79,560**
	Earl Rodney (R)	22,027
18.	**Ileana Ros-Lehtinen*** (R)	**56,354**
	Bernard "Bernie" Anscher (D)	36,967
19.	**Dante B. Fascell*** (D)	**87,677**
	Bob Alien (R)	53,774
Georgia		
1.	**Lindsay Thomas*** (D)	**80,515**
	Chris Meredith (R)	32,532
2.	**Charles Hatcher*** (D)	**77,910**
	Jonathan Perry Waters (R)	28,781
3.	**Richard Ray*** (D)	**72,961**
	Paul Broun (R)	42,561
4.	**Ben Jones*** (D)	**96,526**
	John Linder (R)	87,569

Dist.	Representative (Party)	1990 Election
5.	**John Lewis*** (D)	**86,037**
	J. W. Tibbs Jr. (R)	27,781
6.	**Newt Gingrich*** (R)	**78,768**
	Dave Worley (D)	77,794
7.	**George "Buddy" Darden*** (D)	**95,817**
	Al Beverly (R)	63,588
8.	**J. Roy Rowland*** (D)	**81,344**
	Robert F. "Bob" Cunningham (R)	36,980
9.	**Ed Jenkins*** (D)	**96,197**
	Joe Hoffman (R)	76,121
10.	**Doug Barnard Jr.*** (D)	**89,683**
	Sam Jones (R)	64,184
Hawaii		
1.	**Neil Abercrombie** (D)	**97,622**
	Mike Liu (R)	62,982
2.	**Patsy Takemoto Mink*** (D)	**118,155**
	Andy Poepoe (R)	54,605
Idaho		
1.	**Larry LaRocco** (D)	**85,054**
	C.A. "Skip" Smyser (R)	75,406
2.	**Richard Stallings*** (D)	**98,008**
	Sean McDevitt (R)	56,044
Illinois		
1.	**Charles A. Hayes*** (D)	**100,890**
	Babette Peyton (R)	6,708
2.	**Gus Savage*** (D)	**80,245**
	William T. Hespel (R)	22,350
3.	**Martin A. Russo*** (D)	**110,512**
	Carl L. Klein (R)	45,299
4.	**George E. Sangmeister*** (D)	**77,290**
	Manny Hoffman (R)	53,258
5.	**William O. Lipinski*** (D)	**73,805**
	David J. Shestokas (R)	34,440
6.	**Henry J. Hyde*** (R)	**96,410**
	Robert J. Cassidy (D)	48,155
7.	**Cardiss Collins*** (D)	**80,021**
	Michael Dooley (R)	20,099
8.	**Dan Rostenkowski*** (D)	**70,151**
	Robert Marshall (B)	18,529
9.	**Sidney R. Yates*** (D)	**96,557**
	Herbert Sohn (R)	39,031
10.	**John E. Porter*** (R)	**104,070**
	Peg McNamara (D)	47,286
11.	**Frank Annunzio*** (D)	**82,703**
	Walter W. Dudycz (R)	68,850
12.	**Philip M. Crane*** (R)	**113,081**
	Steve Pedersen (IS)	24,450
13.	**Harris W. Fawell*** (R)	**116,048**
	Steven K. Thomas (D)	60,305
14.	**J. Dennis Hastert*** (R)	**112,383**
	Donald J. Westphal (D)	55,592
15.	**Edward R. Madigan*** (R)	**Unopposed**
16.	**John W. Cox Jr.** (D)	**83,061**
	John W. Hallock Jr. (R)	69,105
17.	**Lane Evans*** (D)	**102,062**
	Dan Lee (R)	51,380
18.	**Robert H. Michel*** (R)	**Unopposed**
19.	**Terry L. Bruce*** (D)	**113,958**
	Robert F. Kerans (R)	55,680
	Brian James O'Neill II (IS)	2,250
20.	**Richard J. Durbin*** (D)	**130,114**
	Paul Jurgens (R)	66,433
21.	**Jerry F. Costello*** (D)	**95,208**
	Robert H. Gaffner (R)	48,949
22.	**Glenn Poshard*** (D)	**138,425**
	Jim Wham (JW)	26,896
Indiana		
1.	**Peter J. Visclosky*** (D)	**68,920**
	William "Bill" Costas (R)	35,450
2.	**Philip R. Sharp*** (D)	**93,495**
	Mike Pence (R)	63,980
3.	**Timothy J. Roemer** (D)	**80,740**
	John Hiler* (R)	77,911
4.	**Jill L. Long*** (D)	**99,347**
	Richard Walter Hawks (R)	64,415

Dist.	Representative (Party)	1990 Election
5.	James Jontz* (D)	81,373
	John Johnson (R)	71,750
6.	Dan Burton* (R)	116,470
	James Philip Fadely (D)	67,024
7.	John T. Myers* (R)	88,598
	John William Riley Sr. (D)	65,248
8.	Francis X. McCloskey* (D)	97,465
	Richard E. Mourdock (R)	80,645
9.	Lee H. Hamilton* (D)	107,526
	Floyd Coates (R)	48,325
10.	Andrew Jacobs Jr.* (D)	69,362
	Janos Horvath (R)	35,049

Iowa

Dist.	Representative (Party)	1990 Election
1.	Jim Leach* (R)	Unopposed
2.	Jim Nussle (R)	82,650
	Eric Tabor (D)	81,008
3.	David R. Nagle* (D)	Unopposed
4.	Neal Smith* (D)	Unopposed
5.	Jim Ross Lightfoot* (R)	99,978
	Rod Powell (D)	47,022
6.	Fred Grandy* (R)	112,333
	Mike D. Earll (D)	44,063

Kansas

Dist.	Representative (Party)	1990 Election
1.	Pat Roberts* (R)	102,974
	Duane E. West (D)	61,396
2.	Jim Slattery* (D)	99,093
	Scott Morgan (R)	58,643
3.	Jan Meyers* (R)	88,725
	Leroy Jones (D)	58,923
4.	Dan Glickman* (D)	112,015
	Roger M. Grund Sr. (R)	46,283
5.	Dick Nichols (R)	90,555
	George D. Wingert (D)	62,244

Kentucky

Dist.	Representative (Party)	1990 Election
1.	Carroll Hubbard Jr.* (D)	85,323
	Marvin Seat (PO)	12,879
2.	William H. Natcher* (D)	77,057
	Martin A. Tori (R)	39,624
3.	Romano L. Mazzoli* (D)	84,750
	Al Brown (R)	55,188
4.	Jim Bunning* (R)	101,680
	Galen Martin (D)	44,979
5.	Harold Rogers* (R)	Unopposed
6.	Larry J. Hopkins* (R)	Unopposed
7.	Carl C. Perkins* (D)	61,330
	William T. "Will" Scott (R)	59,377

Louisiana

Dist.	Representative (Party)	1990 Election
1.	Bob Livingston* (R)	Declared Elected
2.	William J. Jefferson (D)	55,361
	Marc H. Morial (D)	50,004
3.	Billy Tauzin* (D)	Declared Elected
4.	Jim McCrery* (R)	Declared Elected
5.	Jerry Huckaby* (D)	Declared Elected
6.	Richard Baker* (R)	Unopposed
7.	James A. "Jimmy" Hayes* (D)	Declared Elected
8.	Clyde C. Holloway* (R)	Declared Elected

In Louisiana, all candidates of all parties run against each other in an open primary, unless they're unopposed incumbents in which case they are declared elected. All candidates who receive more than 50 percent of the primary vote are also declared elected, and do not appear on the General Election ballot.

Maine

Dist.	Representative (Party)	1990 Election
1.	Thomas H. Andrews (D)	167,623
	David F. Emery (R)	110,836
2.	Olympia J. Snowe* (R)	121,704
	Patrick K. McGowan (D)	116,798

Dist.	Representative (Party)	1990 Election
	Maryland	
1.	Wayne T. Gilchrest (R)	88,920
	Roy Dyson* (D)	67,518
2.	Helen Delich Bentley* (R)	115,398
	Ronald P. Bowers (D)	39,785
3.	Benjamin L. Cardin* (D)	82,545
	Harwood Nichols (R)	35,841
4.	Thomas McMillen* (D)	85,601
	Robert P. Duckworth (R)	59,846
5.	Steny H. Hoyer* (D)	84,747
	Lee F. Breuer (R)	20,314
6.	Beverly B. Byron* (D)	105,502
	Christopher P. Fiotes Jr. (R)	56,479
7.	Kweisi Mfume* (D)	59,628
	Kenneth Kondner (R)	10,529
8.	Constance A. Morella (R)	130,059
	James Walker Jr. (D)	39,343

Massachusetts

Dist.	Representative (Party)	1990 Election
1.	Silvio O. Conte* (R)	150,748
	John R. Arden (D)	43,611
2.	Richard E. Neal* (D)	Unopposed
3.	Joseph D. Early* (D)	Unopposed
4.	Barney Frank* (D)	143,473
	John R. Soto (R)	75,454
5.	Chester G. Atkins* (D)	110,232
	John F. MacGovern (R)	101,017
6.	Nicholas Mavroules* (D)	149,284
	Edgar L. Kelley (R)	80,177
7.	Edward J. Markey* (D)	Unopposed
8.	Joseph P. Kennedy II (D)	125,479
	Glenn W. Fiscus (R)	39,310
9.	John Joseph Moakley* (D)	124,534
	Robert Horan (I)	52,660
10.	Gerry E. Studds* (D)	137,805
	Jon L. Bryan (R)	120,217
11.	Brian J. Donnelly* (D)	Unopposed

Michigan

Dist.	Representative (Party)	1990 Election
1.	John Conyers Jr.* (D)	76,556
	Ray Shoulders (R)	7,298
2.	Carl D. Pursell* (R)	95,962
	Elmer White (D)	49,678
3.	Howard Wolpe* (D)	82,376
	Brad Haskins (R)	60,007
4.	Fred Upton* (R)	75,850
	JoAnne McFarland (D)	55,449
5.	Paul B. Henry* (R)	126,308
	Thomas Trzybinski (D)	41,170
6.	Bob Carr* (D)	Unopposed
7.	Dale E. Kildee* (D)	90,307
	David J. Morrill (R)	41,759
8.	Bob Traxler* (D)	98,903
	James White (R)	45,259
9.	Guy Vander Jagt* (R)	89,078
	Geraldine Greene (D)	73,604
10.	Dave Camp (R)	99,952
	Joan Louise Dennison (D)	50,923
11.	Robert W. Davis* (R)	94,555
	Marcia Gould (D)	59,759
12.	David E. Bonior* (D)	98,232
	Jim Dingeman (R)	51,119
13.	Barbara-Rose Collins (D)	54,345
	Carl R. Edwards Sr. (R)	11,203
14.	Dennis M. Hertel* (D)	78,506
	Kenneth C. McNealy (R)	40,499
15.	William D. Ford* (D)	68,742
	Burl C. Adkins (R)	41,092
16.	John D. Dingell* (D)	88,962
	Frank Beaumont (R)	42,629
17.	Sander Levin* (D)	92,205
	Blaine L. Lankford (R)	40,100
18.	William S. Broomfield* (R)	126,629
	Walter O. Briggs IV (D)	64,185

Minnesota

Dist.	Representative (Party)	1990 Election
1.	Timothy J. "Tim" Penny* (D)	156,749
	Doug Anderson (R)	43,856
2.	Vin Weber* (R)	126,367
	Jim Stone (D)	77,935

Dist.	Representative (Party)	1990 Election
3.	Jim Ramstad (R)	195,833
	Lou Demars (D)	96,395
4.	Bruce F. Vento* (D)	143,353
	Ian Maitland (R)	77,639
5.	Martin Olav Sabo* (D)	144,682
	Raymond C. "Buzz" Gilbertson (R)	53,720
6.	Gerry Sikorski* (D)	164,816
	Bruce D. Anderson (R)	90,138
7.	Collin C. Peterson (D)	107,126
	Arlan Strangeland* (R)	92,876
8.	James L. Oberstar* (D)	151,145
	Jerry Shuster (R)	56,068

Mississippi

Dist.	Representative (Party)	1990 Election
1.	Jamie L. Whitten* (D)	43,668
	Bill Bowlin (R)	23,650
2.	Mike Espy* (D)	59,393
	Dorothy Benford (R)	11,224
3.	G. V. "Sonny" Montgomery* (D)	Unopposed
4.	Mike Parker* (D)	57,137
	Jerry "Rev" Parks (R)	13,754
5.	Gene Taylor* (D)	89,926
	Sheila Smith (R)	20,588

Missouri

Dist.	Representative (Party)	1990 Election
1.	William "Bill" Clay* (D)	62,550
	Wayne G. Piotrowski (R)	40,160
2.	Joan Kelly Horn (D)	94,308
	Jack Buechner* (R)	94,260
3.	Richard A. Gephardt* (D)	88,950
	Malcolm L. "Mack" Holekamp (R)	67,659
4.	Ike Skelton* (D)	105,527
	David Eyerly (R)	65,095
5.	Alan Wheat* (D)	71,890
	Robert H. Gardner (R)	43,897
6.	E. Thomas Coleman* (R)	78,956
	Bob McClure (D)	73,093
7.	Melton D. "Mel" Hancock* (R)	83,609
	Thomas Patrick "Pat" Deaton (D)	76,725
8.	Bill Emerson* (R)	81,452
	Russ Carnahan (D)	60,751
9.	Harold L. Volkmer* (D)	94,156
	Don Curtis (R)	69,514

Montana

Dist.	Representative (Party)	1990 Election
1.	Pat Williams* (D)	100,409
	Brad Johnson (R)	63,837
2.	Ron Marlenee* (R)	96,449
	Don Burris (D)	56,739

Nebraska

Dist.	Representative (Party)	1990 Election
1.	Douglas K. Bereuter* (R)	129,654
	Larry Hall (D)	70,587
2.	Peter Hoagland* (D)	111,903
	Ally Milder (R)	80,845
3.	Bill Barrett (R)	98,607
	Sandra K. Scofield (D)	94,234

Nevada

Dist.	Representative (Party)	1990 Election
1.	James H. Bilbray* (D)	84,650
	Bob Dickinson (R)	47,377
2.	Barbara F. Vucanovich* (R)	103,508
	Jane Wisdom (D)	59,581

New Hampshire

Dist.	Representative (Party)	1990 Election
1.	"Bill" Zeliff (R)	81,684
	Joseph F. Keefe (D)	66,176
2.	"Dick" Swett (D)	74,829
	Chuck Douglas* (R)	67,063

New Jersey

Dist.	Representative (Party)	1990 Election
1.	Robert E. Andrews (D)	73,522
	Daniel J. Mangini (R)	57,801
2.	William J. Hughes* (D)	98,734
	William A. Kanengiser (PO)	13,246
3.	Frank Pallone Jr.* (D)	77,709
	Paul A. Kapalko (R)	73,451
4.	Christopher H. Smith* (R)	101,508
	Mark Setaro (D)	55,454
5.	Marge Roukema* (R)	118,101
	Lawrence Wayne Olsen (D)	35,010
6.	Bernard J. Dwyer* (D)	63,696
	Paul "Daniels" Danielczyk (R)	58,209
7.	Matthew J. Rinaldo* (R)	100,274
	Bruce H. Bergen (D)	31,114
8.	Robert A. Roe* (D)	55,212
	Stephen Sibilia (IC)	13,239
	Bruce Eden (PO)	3,347
9.	Robert G. Torricelli* (D)	82,736
	Peter J. Russo (R)	59,759
10.	Donald M. Payne* (D)	46,616
	Howard E. Berkeley (R)	9,072
11.	Dean A. Gallo* (R)	95,198
	Michael Gordon (D)	47,782
12.	Dick Zimmer (R)	108,173
	Marguerite Chandler (D)	52,498
13.	H. James Saxton* (R)	100,537
	John H. Adler (D)	68,286
14.	Frank J. Guarini* (D)	57,581
	Fred J. Theemling Jr. (R)	25,473

New Mexico

Dist.	Representative (Party)	1990 Election
1.	Steven H. Schiff* (R)	97,374
	Rebecca Vigil-Giron (D)	41,306
2.	Joe Skeen* (R)	Unopposed
3.	Bill Richardson* (D)	104,225
	Phil T. Archuletta (R)	35,751

New York

Dist.	Representative (Party)	1990 Election
1.	George J. Hochbrueckner* (D,TB)	75,211
	Francis W. Creighton (R)	46,380
	Clayton Baldwin Jr. (C)	6,883
	Peter J. O'Hara (T)	5,111
2.	Thomas J. Downey* (D)	56,722
	John W. Bugler (R,T,TC)	36,859
	Dominic A. Curcio (C)	8,150
3.	Robert J. Mrazek* (D,L)	73,029
	Robert Previdi (R,C)	59,089
	Francis A. Dreger (T)	4,915
4.	Norman F. Lent* (R,C)	79,304
	Francis T. Goban (D)	41,308
	John J. Dunkle (T)	6,706
	Ben-Zion J. Heyman (L)	2,343
5.	Raymond J. McGrath* (R,C)	71,948
	Mark S. Edstein (D,L)	53,920
	Edward K. Kitt (T)	6,000
6.	Floyd H. Flake* (D,L)	44,306
	William Sampol (R)	13,224
	John Cronin (T)	3,111
7.	Gary L. Ackerman* (D,L)	Unopposed
8.	James H. Scheuer* (D,L)	56,396
	Gustave Reifenkugel (R,C)	21,646
9.	Thomas J. Manton* (D)	35,177
	Ann Pfoser Darby (R)	13,330
	Thomas V. Ognibene (C)	6,137
10.	Charles E. Schumer* (D,L)	61,468
	Patrick J. Kinsella (R,C)	14,963
11.	Edolphus Towns* (D,L)	36,286
	Ernest Johnson (C)	1,676
	Lorraine Stevens (NA)	1,094
12.	Major R. Owens* (D,L)	40,570
	Joseph N.O. Caesar (C)	1,159
	Mamie Moore (NA)	1,021
13.	Stephen J. Solarz* (D,L)	47,446
	Edwin Ramos (R,C)	11,557
14.	Susan Molinari* (R,C)	58,616
	Anthony J. Pocchia (D,L)	34,625
	Christine Sacchi (T)	4,370
15.	Bill Green* (R,IN)	52,919
	Frances L. Reiter (D,L)	33,464
	Michael T. Berns (C)	3,654
16.	Charles B. Rangel* (D,R,L)	55,882
	Alvaader Frazier (NA)	1,592
17.	Ted Weiss* (D,L)	79,161
	William W. Koeppel Jr. (R)	15,219
	Mark Goret (C)	2,928
	John Patterson (NA)	1,087

Dist.	Representative (Party)	1990 Election
18.	**Jose Serrano*** (D,L)	38,024
	Joseph Chiavaro (R)	1,189
19.	**Eliot L. Engel*** (D,L)	45,758
	William J. Gouldman (R)	17,135
	Kevin Brawley (C,T)	11,868
20.	**Nita M. Lowey*** (D)	82,203
	Glenn D. Bellitto (R)	35,575
	John M. Schafer (C,T)	13,030
21.	**Hamilton Fish Jr.*** (R,C)	99,866
	Richard L. Barbuto (D)	34,128
	Richard S. Curtin (T)	5,925
22.	**Benjamin A. Gilman*** (R)	95,495
	John G. Dow (D)	37,034
	Margaret M. Beirne (T)	6,656
23.	**Michael R. McNulty*** (D,C)	117,239
	Margaret B. Burhmaster (R)	65,760
24.	**Gerald B. Solomon*** (R,C,T)	121,206
	Bob Lawrence (D)	56,671
25.	**Sherwood L. Boehlert*** (R)	91,348
	William L. Griffin (L)	17,481
26.	**David O'B. Martin*** (R,C)	Unopposed
27.	**James T. Walsh*** (R,C)	95,220
	Peggy L. Murray (D,L)	52,438
	Stephen K. Hoff (T)	3,097
28.	**Matthew F. McHugh*** (D)	97,815
	Seymour Krieger (R)	53,077
29.	**Frank Horton*** (R)	89,105
	Alton F. Eber (D)	34,835
	Peter DeMauro (C)	12,599
	Donald M. Peters (T)	4,878
30.	**Louise M. Slaughter*** (D)	97,280
	John M. Regan Jr. (R,C,T)	67,534
31.	**William Paxon*** (R,C,T)	90,237
	Kevin P. Gaughan (D,L)	69,328
32.	**John J. LaFalce*** (D,L)	68,367
	Michael T. Waring (R)	39,053
	Kenneth J. Kowalski (C,T)	16,853
33.	**Henry J. Nowak*** (D,L)	84,905
	Thomas K. Kepfer (R)	18,181
	Louis P. Corrigan Jr. (C)	6,460
34.	**Amory Houghton Jr.*** (R,C)	89,831
	Joseph P. Leahey (D)	37,421
	Nevin K. Eklund (L)	1,807

North Carolina

Dist.	Representative (Party)	1990 Election
1.	**Walter B. Jones*** (D)	105,832
	Howard D. Moye (R)	57,526
2.	**I.T. "Tim" Valentine Jr.*** (D)	130,979
	Hal C. Sharpe (R)	44,263
3.	**Martin Lancaster*** (D)	83,930
	Don Davis (R)	57,605
4.	**David E. Price*** (D)	139,396
	John Carrington (R)	100,661
5.	**Stephen Neal*** (D)	113,814
	Ken Bell (R)	78,747
6.	**Howard Coble*** (R)	125,392
	Helen R. Allegrone (D)	62,913
7.	**Charles G. Rose III*** (D)	94,946
	Robert C. Anderson (R)	49,681
8.	**W. G. "Bill" Hefner*** (D)	98,700
	Ted Blanton (R)	80,852
9.	**J. Alex McMillan*** (R)	131,936
	David P. McKnight (D)	80,802
10.	**T. Cass Ballenger*** (R)	106,400
	Daniel R. Green Jr. (D)	65,710
11.	**Charles H. Taylor** (R)	101,991
	James McClure Clarke* (D)	99,318

North Dakota At Large

Dist.	Representative (Party)	1990 Election
	Byron L. Dorgan* (D)	152,520
	Edward T. Schafer (R)	81,443

Ohio

Dist.	Representative (Party)	1990 Election
1.	**Charles Luken** (D)	83,932
	J. Kenneth Blackwell (R)	80,362
2.	**Willis D. Gradison Jr.*** (R)	103,817
	Tyrone K. Yates (D)	57,345
3.	**Tony P. Hall*** (D)	Unopposed
4.	**Michael G. Oxley*** (R)	103,397
	Thomas E. Burkhart (D)	64,467
5.	**Paul E. Gillmor*** (R)	113,615
	P. Scott Mange (D)	41,693
6.	**Bob McEwen*** (R)	117,220
	Ray Mitchell (D)	47,415
7.	**David L. Hobson** (R)	97,123
	Jack Schira (D)	59,349
8.	**John A. Boehner** (R)	99,955
	Gregory V. Jolivette (D)	63,584
9.	**Marcy Kaptur*** (D)	117,681
	Jerry D. Lammers (R)	33,791
10.	**Clarence E. Miller*** (R)	106,009
	John M. Buchanan (D)	61,656
11.	**Dennis E. Eckart*** (D)	111,923
	Margaret R. Mueller (R)	58,372
12.	**John R. Kasich*** (R)	130,495
	Mike Gelpi (D)	50,784
13.	**Donald J. Pease*** (D)	93,431
	William D. Nielsen (R)	60,925
14.	**Thomas C. Sawyer*** (D)	97,875
	Jean E. Bender (R)	66,460
15.	**Chalmers P. Wylie*** (R)	99,251
	Thomas V. Erney (D)	68,510
16.	**Ralph Regula*** (R)	101,097
	Warner D. Mendenhall (D)	70,516
17.	**James A. Traficant Jr.*** (D)	133,207
	Robert R. DeJulio Jr. (R)	38,199
18.	**Douglas Applegate*** (D)	120,782
	John A. Hales (R)	41,823
19.	**Edward F. Feighan*** (D)	132,951
	Susan M. Lawko (R)	72,315
20.	**Mary Rose Oakar*** (D)	109,390
	Bill Smith (R)	39,749
21.	**Louis Stokes*** (D)	103,338
	Franklin H. Roski (R)	25,906

Oklahoma

Dist.	Representative (Party)	1990 Election
1.	**James M. Inhofe*** (R)	75,618
	Kurt G. Glassco (D)	59,521
2.	**Mike Synar*** (D)	90,820
	Terry M. Gorham (R)	57,331
3.	**Bill Brewster** (D)	107,641
	Patrick K. Miller (R)	26,261
4.	**Dave McCurdy*** (D)	100,879
	Howard Bell (R)	36,232
5.	**Mickey Edwards*** (R)	114,608
	Bryce Baggett (D)	50,086
6.	**Glenn English*** (D)	110,100
	Robert Burns (R)	27,540

Oregon

Dist.	Representative (Party)	1990 Election
1.	**Les AuCoin*** (D)	150,292
	Earl Molander (R)	72,382
	Rick Livingston (I)	15,585
2.	**Bob Smith*** (R)	127,998
	Jim Smiley (D)	60,131
3.	**Ron Wyden*** (D)	169,731
	Phil Mooney (R)	40,216
4.	**Peter A. DeFazio*** (D)	162,494
	Tonie Nathan (B)	26,432
5.	**Mike Kopetski** (D)	124,610
	Denny Smith* (R)	101,650

Pennsylvania

Dist.	Representative (Party)	1990 Election
1.	**Thomas M. Foglietta*** (D)	73,423
	James Love Jackson (R)	19,018
2.	**William H. Gray** (D)[2]	94,584
	Donald Bakove (R)	8,118
3.	**Robert A. Borski*** (D)	89,908
	Joseph Marc McColgan (R)	59,901
4.	**Joseph P. Kolter*** (D)	74,105
	Gordon R. Johnson (R)	58,481
5.	**Richard T. Schulze*** (R)	75,097
	Samuel C. Stretton (D)	50,597
	Lewis duPont Smith (ASI)	5,795
6.	**Gus Yatron*** (D)	74,394
	John F. Hicks (R)	56,093

Dist.	Representative (Party)	1990 Election
7.	Curt Weldon* (R)	105,868
	John Innelli (D)	56,292
8.	Peter H. Kostmayer* (D)	85,015
	Audrie Zettick Schaller (R)	65,100
9.	Bud Shuster* (R, D)	Unopposed
10.	Joseph M. McDade* (R,D)	Unopposed
11.	Paul E. Kanjorski* (D)	Unopposed
12.	John P. Murtha* (D)	80,686
	Willeam A. Choby (R)	50,007
13.	Lawrence Coughlin* (R)	89,577
	Bernard Tomkin (D)	58,967
14.	William J. Coyne* (D)	77,636
	Richard E. Caligiuri (R)	30,497
15.	Don Ritter* (R)	77,178
	Richard J. Orloski (D)	50,233
16.	Robert S. Walker* (R)	85,596
	Ernest Eric Guyll (D)	43,849
17.	George W. Gekas* (R, D)	Unopposed
18.	Rick Santorum (R)	85,697
	Doug Walgren* (D)	80,880
19.	William F. Goodling* (R)	Unopposed
20.	Joseph M. Gaydos* (D)	82,080
	Robert C. Lee (R)	43,054
21.	Thomas J. Ridge* (R)	Unopposed
22.	Austin J. Murphy* (D)	78,375
	Suzanne Hayden (R)	45,509
23.	William F. Clinger Jr.* (R)	78,189
	Daniel J. Shannon (D)	53,465

Rhode Island

Dist.	Representative (Party)	1990 Election
1.	Ronald K. Machtley* (R)	89,963
	J. Scott Wolf (D)	73,131
2.	John F. Reed (D)	108,818
	Gertrude M. Coxe (R)	74,953

South Carolina

Dist.	Representative (Party)	1990 Election
1.	Arthur Ravenel Jr.* (R)	80,839
	Eugene Platt (D)	42,555
2.	Floyd D. Spence* (R)	90,054
	Geb Sommer (B)	11,101
3.	Butler Derrick* (D)	72,561
	Ray Haskett (R)	52,419
4.	Liz J. Patterson* (D)	81,927
	Terry E. Haskins (R)	51,338
5.	John Spratt* (D)	Unopposed
6.	Robin Tallon* (D)	Unopposed

South Dakota At Large

Dist.	Representative (Party)	1990 Election
	Tim Johnson* (D)	173,814
	Donald Frankenfeld (R)	83,484

Tennessee

Dist.	Representative (Party)	1990 Election
1.	James H. "Jimmy" Quillen* (R)	Unopposed
2.	John J. Duncan Jr.* (R)	62,797
	Peter Hebert (D)	15,127
3.	Marilyn Lloyd* (D)	49,662
	Grady L. Rhoden (R)	36,855
4.	Jim Cooper* (D)	52,101
	Claiborne "Clay" Sanders (R)	22,890
5.	Bob Clement* (D)	55,101
	Tom Stone (I)	13,577
	Al Borgman (I)	5,383
	Maurice C. Kuttab (I)	2,192
6.	Bart Gordon* (D)	60,538
	Gregory Cochran (R)	26,424
7.	Don Sundquist* (R)	66,141
	Ken Bloodworth (D)	40,516
8.	John Tanner* (D)	Unopposed
9.	Harold E. Ford* (D)	48,629
	Aaron C. Davis (R)	25,730

Texas

Dist.	Representative (Party)	1990 Election
1.	Jim Chapman* (D)	89,241
	Hamp Hodges (R)	56,954
2.	Charles Wilson* (D)	76,974
	Donna Peterson (R)	61,555
3.	Steve Bartlett* (R)	Unopposed
4.	Ralph M. Hall* (D)	Unopposed
5.	John Bryant* (D)	65,228
	Jerry Rucker (R)	41,307
6.	Joe Barton* (R)	125,049
	John E. Welch (D)	62,344
7.	Bill Archer* (R)	Unopposed
8.	Jack Fields* (R)	Unopposed
9.	Jack Brooks* (D)	79,786
	Maury Meyers (R)	58,399
10.	J. J. "Jake" Pickle* (D)	152,784
	David Beilharz (R)	73,766
11.	Chet Edwards (D)	73,810
	Hugh D. Shine (R)	64,269
12.	Pete Geren* (D)	98,026
	Mike McGinn (R)	39,438
13.	Bill Sarpalius* (D)	81,815
	Dick Waterfield (R)	63,045
14.	Greg Laughlin* (D)	89,251
	Joe Dial (R)	75,098
15.	E. "Kika" de la Garza* (D)	Unopposed
16.	Ronald Coleman* (D)	Unopposed
17.	Charles W. Stenholm* (D)	Unopposed
18.	Craig A. Washington* (D)	Unopposed
19.	Larry Combest* (R)	Unopposed
20.	Henry B. Gonzalez* (D)	Unopposed
21.	Lamar Smith* (R)	144,570
	Kirby J. Roberts (D)	48,585
22.	Tom DeLay* (R)	93,425
	Bruce Director (D)	37,721
23.	Albert G. Bustamente* (D)	71,052
	Jerome L. "Jerry" Gonzales (R)	40,856
24.	Martin Frost* (D)	Unopposed
25.	Mike Andrews* (D)	Unopposed
26.	Dick Armey* (R)	147,856
	John Wayne Caton (D)	62,158
27.	Solomon P. Ortiz* (D)	Unopposed

Utah

Dist.	Representative (Party)	1990 Election
1.	James V. Hansen* (R)	82,746
	Kenley Brunsdale (D)	69,491
2.	Wayne Owens (D)	85,167
	Genevieve Atwood (R)	58,869
3.	Bill Orton (D)	79,163
	Karl Snow (R)	49,452

Vermont At Large

Dist.	Representative (Party)	1990 Election
	Bernie Sanders (I)	117,522
	Peter Smith* (R)	82,938
	Dolores Sandoval (D)	6,315
	Peter Diamondstone (LU)	1,965

Virginia

Dist.	Representative (Party)	1990 Election
1.	Herbert H. "Herb" Bateman* (R)	72,000
	Fox (D)	69,194
2.	Owen B. Pickett (D)	55,179
	Broskie (I)	15,915
3.	Thomas J. "Tom" Bliley Jr.* (R)	77,125
	Starke (D)	36,253
	Simpson (I)	4,317
4.	Norman Sisisky* (D)	71,051
	McReynolds (I)	12,295
	Chandler (I)	7,102
5.	L. F. Payne Jr.* (D)	Unopposed
6.	James R. "Jim" Olin* (D)	92,968
	Berg (I)	18,148
7.	D. French Slaughter* (R)	81,688
	Smith (D)	58,684
8.	Moran (D)	88,475
	Stan Parris* (R)	76,367
	Murphy (I)	5,958
9.	Frederick C. "Rick" Boucher* (D)	Unopposed
10.	Frank R. Wolf* (R)	103,761
	Canter (D)	57,249
	Minnich (I)	5,273
	LaRouche (I)	2,293

Washington

Dist.	Representative (Party)	1990 Election
1.	John Miller* (R)	100,339
	Cynthia Sullivan (D)	92,447

Dist.	Representative (Party)	1990 Election
2.	Al Swift* (D)	92,837
	Doug Smith (R)	75,669
3.	Jolene Unsoeld* (D)	95,645
	Bob Williams (R)	82,269
4.	Sid Morrison* (R)	106,545
	Ole H. Hougen (D)	44,241
5.	Thomas S. Foley* (D)	110,234
	Marlyn Derby (R)	49,965
6.	Norman D. Dicks* (D)	79,079
	Norbert "Bert" Mueller (R)	49,786
7.	Jim McDermott* (D)	106,761
	Larry Penberthy (R)	35,511
8.	Rod Chandler* (R)	96,323
	David Giles (D)	75,031

West Virginia

Dist.	Representative (Party)	1990 Election
1.	Alan B. Mollohan* (D)	72,849
	Howard K. Tuck (R)	35,657
2.	Harley O. Staggers Jr.* (D)	63,174
	Oliver Luck (R)	50,708
3.	Bob Wise* (D)	Unopposed
4.	Nick J. Rahall II * (D)	39,948
	Marianne R. Brewster (R)	36,946

Wisconsin

Dist.	Representative (Party)	1990 Election
1.	Les Aspin* (D)	Unopposed
2.	Scott L. Klug (R)	96,938
	Robert W. Kastenmeier* (D)	85,156
3.	Steven C. Gunderson* (R)	94,509
	James L. Ziegeweid (D)	60,409
4.	Gerald D. Kleczka* (D)	96,981
	Joseph L. Cook (R)	43,001
5.	Jim Moody* (D)	77,557
	Donalda Arnell Hammersmith (R)	31,255
6.	Thomas E. Petri* (R)	Unopposed
7.	David R. Obey* (D)	100,069
	John L. McEwen (R)	60,961
8.	Toby Roth* (R)	95,902
	Jerome Van Sistine (D)	83,199
9.	F. James Sensenbrenner Jr.* (R)	Unopposed

Wyoming At Large

Craig Thomas* (R)		87,078
Pete Maxfield (D)		70,977

(1) Rep. Udall resigned in May, 1991; a special election was set for Sept. (2) Rep. Gray resigned in June, 1991; a special election was to be set by no later than Sept. 22.

Resident Commissioner (Non-Voting)
Puerto Rico
Jaime B. Fuster* (PDP)

Non-Voting Delegates

District of Columbia
Eleanor Holmes Norton (D)

Guam
Ben G. Blaz* (R)

Virgin Islands
Ron de Lugo* (D)

American Samoa
Eni F.H. Faleomavaega* (D)

Political Divisions of the U.S. Senate and House of Representatives From 1927 (70th Cong.) to 1993 (102nd Cong.)

Source: Clerk of the House of Representatives; Secretary of the Senate; as of May 10, 1991

Congress	Years	Senate Number of Senators	Democrats	Republicans	Other parties	Vacant	House of Representatives Number of Representatives	Democrats	Republicans	Other parties	Vacant
70th	1927-29	96	47	48	1		435	195	237	3	
71st	1929-31	96	39	56	1		435	163	267	1	4
72d	1931-33	96	47	48	1		435	[2]216	218	1	
73d	1933-35	96	59	36	1		435	313	117	5	
74th	1935-37	96	69	25	2		435	322	103	10	
75th	1937-39	96	75	17	4		435	333	89	13	
76th	1939-41	96	69	23	4		435	262	169	4	
77th	1941-43	96	66	28	2		435	267	162	6	
78th	1943-45	96	57	38	1		435	222	209	4	
79th	1945-47	96	57	38	1		435	243	190	2	
80th	1947-49	96	45	51			435	188	246	1	
81st	1949-51	96	54	42			435	263	171	1	
82d	1951-53	96	48	47	1		435	234	199	2	
83d	1953-55	96	46	48	2		435	213	221	1	
84th	1955-57	96	48	47	1		435	232	203		
85th	1957-59	96	49	47			435	234	201		
86th	1959-61	98	64	34			[3]436	283	153		
87th	1961-63	100	64	36			[4]437	262	175		
88th	1963-65	100	67	33			435	258	176		1
89th	1965-67	100	68	32			435	295	140		
90th	1967-69	100	64	36			435	248	187		
91st	1969-71	100	58	42			435	243	192		
92d	1971-73	100	54	44	2		435	255	180		
93d	1973-75	100	56	42	2		435	242	192	1	
94th	1975-77	100	61	37	2		435	291	144		
95th	1977-79	100	61	38	1		435	292	143		
96th	1979-81	100	58	41	1		435	277	158		
97th	1981-83	100	46	53	1		435	242	190		3
98th	1983-85	100	46	54			435	269	166		
99th	1985-87	100	47	53			435	253	182		
100th	1987-89	100	54	46			435	258	177		
101st	1989-91	100	57	43			435	262	173		
102nd	1991-93	100	57	43			435	266	164	1	4

(2) Democrats organized House due to Republican deaths. (3) Proclamation declaring Alaska a State issued Jan. 3, 1959. (4) Proclamation declaring Hawaii a State issued Aug. 21, 1959.

Congressional Committees

Senate Standing Committees
(As of May 20, 1991)

Agriculture, Nutrition, and Forestry
Chairman: Patrick J. Leahy, Vt.
Ranking Rep.: Richard G. Lugar, Ind.

Appropriations
Chairman: Robert C. Byrd, W.V.
Ranking Rep.: Mark O. Hatfield, Ore.

Armed Services
Chairman: Sam Nunn, Ga.
Ranking Rep.: John W. Warner, Va.

Banking, Housing, and Urban Affairs
Chairman: Donald W. Riegle Jr., Mich.
Ranking Rep.: Jake Garn, Utah

Budget
Chairman: Jim Sasser, Tenn.
Ranking Rep.: Pete V. Dominici, N.M.

Commerce, Science, and Transportation
Chairman: Ernest F. Hollings, S.C.
Ranking Rep.: John C. Danforth, Mo.

Energy and Natural Resources
Chairman: J. Bennett Johnston, La.
Ranking Rep.: Malcolm Wallop, Wyo.

Environment and Public Works
Chairman: Quentin N. Burdick, N.D.
Ranking Rep.: John H. Chafee, R.I.

Finance
Chairman: Lloyd Bentsen, Tex.
Ranking Rep.: Bob Packwood, Ore.

Foreign Relations
Chairman: Claiborne Pell, R.I.
Ranking Rep.: Jesse Helms, N.C.

Governmental Affairs
Chairman: John Glenn, Ohio
Ranking Rep.: William V. Roth Jr., Del.

Judiciary
Chairman: Joseph R. Biden Jr., Del.
Ranking Rep.: Strom Thurmond, S.C.

Labor and Human Resources
Chairman: Edward M. Kennedy, Mass.
Ranking Rep.: Orrin G. Hatch, Utah

Rules and Administration
Chairman: Wendell H. Ford, Ky.
Ranking Rep.: Ted Stevens, Alas.

Small Business
Chairman: Dale Bumpers, Ark.
Ranking Rep.: Robert W. Kasten Jr., Wis.

Veterans' Affairs
Chairman: Alan Cranston, Cal.
Ranking Rep.: Arlen Specter, Pa.

Senate Select and Special Committees
(As of May 20, 1991)

Aging
Chairman: David H. Pryor, Ark.
Ranking Rep.: William S. Cohen, Me.

Ethics
Chairman: Howell Heflin, Ala.
Ranking Rep.: Warren Rudman, N.H.

Indian Affairs
Chairman: Daniel K. Inouye, Ha.
Ranking Rep.: John McCain, Ariz.

Intelligence
Chairman: David L. Boren, Okla.
V. Chairman: Frank H. Murkowski, Alas.

Joint Committees of Congress

Economic
Chairman: Sen. Paul S. Sarbanes, Md.
V. Chairman: Rep. Lee H. Hamilton, Ind.

Library
Chairman: Sen. Claiborne Pell, R.I.
V. Chairman: Rep. Charlie Rose, N.C.

Printing
Chairman: Rep. Charlie Rose, N.C.
V. Chairman: Sen. Wendell H. Ford, Ky.

Taxation
Chairman: Rep. Dan Rostenkowski (D), Ill.
V. Chairman: Sen. Lloyd Bentsen (D), Tex.

House Standing Committees
(As of May 20, 1991)

Agriculture
Chairman: E de la Garza, Tex.
Ranking Rep.: E. Thomas Coleman, Mo.

Appropriations
Chairman: Jamie L. Whitten, Miss.
Ranking Rep.: Joseph M. McDade, Pa.

Armed Services
Chairman: Les Aspin, Wis.
Ranking Rep.: William L. Dickinson, Ala.

Banking, Finance, and Urban Affairs
Chairman: Henry B. Gonzalez, Tex.
Ranking Rep.: Chalmers P. Wylie, Oh.

Budget
Chairman: Leon E. Panetta, Cal.
Ranking Rep.: Willis D. Gradison Jr., Oh.

District of Columbia
Chairman: Ronald V. Dellums, Cal.
Ranking Rep.: Thomas J. Bliley Jr., Va.

Education and Labor
Chairman: William D. Ford, Mich.
Ranking Rep.: William F. Goodling, Pa.

Energy and Commerce
Chairman: John D. Dingell, Mich.
Ranking Rep.: Norman F. Lent, N.Y.

Foreign Affairs
Chairman: Dante B. Fascell, Fla.
Ranking Rep.: William S. Broomfield, Mich.

Government Operations
Chairman: John Conyers Jr., Mich.
Ranking Rep.: Frank Horton, N.Y.

House Administration
Chairman: Charlie Rose, N.C.
Ranking Rep.: William M. Thomas, Cal.

Interior and Insular Affairs
Chairman: George Miller, Cal.
Ranking Rep.: Don Young, Alas.

Judiciary
Chairman: Jack Brooks, Tex.
Ranking Rep.: Hamilton Fish Jr., N.Y.

Merchant Marine and Fisheries
Chairman: Walter B. Jones, N.C.
Ranking Rep.: Robert W. Davis, Mich.

Post Office and Civil Service
Chairman: William (Bill) Clay, Mo.
Ranking Rep.: Benjamin A. Gilman, N.Y.

Public Works and Transportation
Chairman: Robert A. Roe, N.J.
Ranking Rep.: John Paul Hammerschmidt, Ark.

Rules
Chairman: John Moakley, Mass.
Ranking Rep.: Gerald B.H. Solomon, N.Y.

Science, Space, and Technology
Chairman: George E. Brown Jr., Cal.
Ranking Rep.: Robert S. Walker, Pa.

Small Business
Chairman: John J. LaFalce, N.Y.
Ranking Rep.: Andy Ireland, Fla.

Standards of Official Conduct
Chairman: Louis Stokes, Oh.
Ranking Rep.: James V. Hansen, Ut.

Veterans' Affairs
Chairman: G.V. Montgomery, Miss.
Ranking Rep.: Bob Stump, Ariz.

Ways and Means
Chairman: Dan Rostenkowski, Ill.
Ranking Rep.: Bill Archer, Tex.

House Select Committees

Aging
Chairman: Edward R. Roybal, Cal.

(continued)

Ranking Rep.: Matthew J. Rinaldo, N.J.
Children, Youth, and Families
  Chairman: Patricia Schroeder, Col.
  Ranking Rep.: Frank R. Wolf, Va.
Hunger
  Chairman: Tony P. Hall, Ohio
  Ranking Rep.: Bill Emerson, Mo.

Intelligence
  Chairman: Dave McCurdy, Okla.
  Ranking Rep.: Bud Shuster, Pa.
Narcotics Abuse and Control
  Chairman: Charles B. Rangel, N.Y.
  Ranking Rep.: Lawrence Coughlin, Pa.

Congressional Bills Vetoed, 1789-1991

Source: Senate Library

	Regular vetoes	Pocket vetoes	Total vetoes	Vetoes over-ridden		Regular vetoes	Pocket vetoes	Total vetoes	Vetoes over-ridden
Washington	2	—	2	—	Benjamin Harrison	19	25	44	1
John Adams	—	—	—	—	Cleveland	42	128	170	5
Jefferson	—	—	—	—	McKinley	6	36	42	—
Madison	5	2	7	—	Theodore Roosevelt	42	40	82	1
Monroe	1	—	1	—	Taft	30	9	39	1
John Q. Adams	—	—	—	—	Wilson	33	11	44	6
Jackson	5	7	12	—	Harding	5	1	6	—
Van Buren	—	1	1	—	Coolidge	20	30	50	4
William Harrison	—	—	—	—	Hoover	21	16	37	3
Tyler	6	4	10	1	Franklin Roosevelt	372	263	635	9
Polk	2	1	3	—	Truman	180	70	250	12
Taylor	—	—	—	—	Eisenhower	73	108	181	2
Fillmore	—	—	—	—	Kennedy	12	9	21	—
Pierce	9	—	9	5	Lyndon Johnson	16	14	30	—
Buchanan	4	3	7	—	Nixon	26	17	43	7
Lincoln	2	5	7	—	Ford	48	18	66	12
Andrew Johnson	21	8	29	15	Carter	13	18	31	2
Grant	45	48	93	4	Reagan	39	39	78	9
Hayes	12	1	13	1	Bush[1]	15	6	21	0
Garfield	—	—	—	—					
Arthur	4	8	12	1	**Total**	**1,453**	**1,057**	**2,491**	**103**
Cleveland	304	110	414	2					

(1) As of May 23, 1991.

Congressional Reapportionment for the 103rd Congress

Source: Bureau of the Census, U.S. Dept. of Commerce

As a result of population changes from 1980 to 1990, as reported in the 1990 Census, 8 states will have more representatives in the 103rd Congress, which will convene in January 1993. The states with the largest gains will be California (+7), Florida (+4), and Texas (+3), while Washington, Arizona, Georgia, North Carolina, and Virginia will each gain a seat. Thirteen states will have fewer representatives.

New York will lose 3 seats, while Illinois, Michigan, Ohio, and Pennsylvania will lose 2 seats each. West Virginia, Kentucky, Louisiana, Kansas, Massachusetts, New Jersey, Iowa, and Montana will lose one seat.

The population shifts will give the West 8, and the South 7 additional seats. The Midwest will lose 8, and the Northeast 7 seats.

How a Bill Becomes a Law

1. A Senator or Representative introduces a bill by sending it to the clerk of the House, who assigns it a number and title. This procedure is termed the *first reading*. The clerk then refers the bill to the appropriate Senate or House committee.

2. If the committee opposes the bill, they immediately *table*, or kill it. Otherwise, the committee holds hearings to listen to opinions and facts offered by members and other interested people. The committee then debates the bill and possibly offers amendments. A vote is taken, and if favorable, the bill is sent back to the clerk of the House.

3. The clerk reads the bill to the House. This is termed the *second reading*. Members may then debate the bill and suggest amendments.

4. *The third reading* is simply by title, and the bill is put to a voice or roll call vote.

5. The bill then goes to the other house, where it may be defeated, or passed with or without amendments. If defeated, the bill dies. If passed with amendments, a

joint Congressional committee works out the differences and arrives at a compromise.

6. After its final passage by both houses, the bill is sent to the President. If he signs it, the bill becomes a law. However, he may *veto* the bill by refusing to sign it and sending it back to the house where it originated, with his reasons for the veto.

7. The President's objections are then read and debated, and a roll-call vote taken. If the bill receives less than a two-thirds vote, it is defeated. If it receives at least two-thirds, it is sent to the other house. If that house also passes it by at least two-thirds, the President's veto is *overridden*, and the bill becomes a law.

8. If the President wishes neither to sign nor to veto the bill, he may retain it for 10 days—not including Sunday—after which it automatically becomes a law even without his signature. However, if Congress has adjourned within those 10 days, the bill is automatically killed; this indirect rejection is termed a *pocket veto*.

UNITED STATES GOVERNMENT

LEGISLATIVE BRANCH	EXECUTIVE BRANCH	JUDICIAL BRANCH
CONGRESS	**PRESIDENT**	**Supreme Court of the United States**
Senate House	Vice President Cabinet	Courts of Appeals
		District Courts
Architect of the Capitol	**Executive Office of the President**	Claims Court
U.S Botanic Garden		Court of Appeals for the Federal Circuit
General Accounting Office	White House Office	Court of International Trade
Government Printing Office	Office of Management and Budget	Territorial Courts
Library of Congress	Council of Economic Advisors	Court of Military Appeals
Office of Technology Assessment	National Security Council	Court of Veterans Appeals
Congressional Budget Office	Office of Policy Development	Administrative Office of the Courts
Copyright Royalty Tribunal	Office of the U.S.Trade Representative	Federal Judicial Center
U.S. Tax Court	Council on Environmental Quality	
	Office of Science and Technology Policy	
	Office of Administration	
	Office of National Drug Control Policy	
	National Critical Materials Council	
	National Space Council	

The Bush Administration
As of mid-1991

Terms of office of the president and vice president, from Jan. 20, 1989 to Jan. 20, 1993. No person may be elected president of the United States for more than two 4-year terms.

President — George Bush of Texas receives salary of $200,000 a year taxable; in addition an expense allowance of $50,000 to assist in defraying expenses resulting from his official duties. Also there may be expended not exceeding $100,000, nontaxable, a year for travel expenses and $20,000 for official entertainment available for allocation within the Executive Office of the President. Congress has provided lifetime pensions of $69,630 a year, free mailing privileges, free office space, and up to $96,000 a year for office help for former Presidents except for the first 30 month period during which a former President is entitled to staff assistance for which an amount up to $150,000 a year may be paid, and $20,000 annually for their widows.

Vice President — Dan Quayle of Indiana receives salary of $160,600 a year and $10,000 for expenses, all of which is taxable.

For succession to presidency, see Succession in Index.

The Cabinet
(Salary: $138,900 per annum)

Secretary of State — James A. Baker 3d, Tex.
Secretary of Treasury — Nicholas F. Brady, N.J.
Secretary of Defense — Richard B. Cheney, Wyo.
Attorney General — vacant.
Secretary of Interior — Manuel Lujan, N.M.
Secretary of Agriculture — Edward Madigan, Ill.
Secretary of Commerce — Robert A. Mosbacher, Tex.
Secretary of Labor — Lynn Martin, Ill.
Secretary of Health and Human Services — Louis W. Sullivan, Ga.
Secretary of Housing and Urban Development — Jack F. Kemp, N.Y.
Secretary of Transportation — Samuel K. Skinner, Ill.
Secretary of Energy — James D. Watkins, Cal.
Secretary of Education — Lamar Alexander, Tenn.
Secretary of Veterans Affairs — Edward J. Derwinski, Ill.

The White House Staff
1600 Pennsylvania Ave. NW 20500

Chief of Staff — John H. Sununu.

Asst. to the President & Deputy Chief of Staff — Andrew Card Jr.
Assistants to the President:
  Counsel to the President — C. Boyden Gray.
  Presidential Personnel — Charles G. Untermeyer.
  Public Events & Initiatives — Sigmund A. Rogich.
  Science & Technology — D. Allan Bromley.
  Press Secretary — Max Marlin Fitzwater.
  Legislative Affairs — Frederick D. McClure.
  Communications — David Demarest Jr.
  Economic & Domestic Affairs — Roger B. Porter.
  Management & Admin. — vacant.
  Cabinet Secy. — Edith Holiday.
  National Security — Brent Scowcroft.
  Staff Secretary — Philip Brady.
  National Service — C. Gregg Petersmeyer.
  Media Affairs — J. Dorrance Smith.

Executive Agencies

Council of Economic Advisers — Michael J. Boskin.
Central Intelligence Agency — William H. Webster, dir.
Office of National Drug Control Policy — Robert Martinez.
Office of Management and Budget — Richard G. Darman.
U.S. Trade Representative — Carla Hills.
Council on Environmental Quality — Michael Deland, chmn.

Department of State
2201 C St. NW 20520

Secretary of State — James A. Baker 3d.
Deputy Secretary — Lawrence S. Eagleburger.
Under Sec. for Political Affairs — Robert M. Kimmitt.
Under Sec. for Security Assistance, Science and Technology — Reginald Bartholomew.
Under Secretary for Management — Ivan Selin.
Legal Advisor — Edwin Williamson.
Assistant Secretaries for:

Administration — Arthur W. Forte.
African Affairs — Herman J. Cohen.
East Asian & Pacific Affairs — Richard H. Solomon.
Consular Affairs — Elizabeth Tamposi.
Diplomatic Security — Sheldon Krys.
Economic & Business Affairs — Eugene J. McAllister.
European & Canadian Affairs — James Dobbins, act.
Human Rights & Humanitarian Affairs — Richard Schifter.
Intelligence & Research — Douglas P. Mulholland.
Legislative Affairs — Janet Mullins.
Inter-American Affairs — Bernard Aronson.
International Narcotics Matters — Melvin Levitsky.
International Organizations — John R. Bolton.
Near-Eastern & S. Asian Affairs — John H. Kelly.
Political-Military Affairs — Richard Clarke.
Public Affairs & Spokesman — Margaret DeB. Tutwiler.
Oceans, International Environmental & Scientific Affairs — Frederick M. Bernthal.

Department of the Treasury
1500 Pennsylvania Ave. NW 20220
Secretary of the Treasury — Nicholas F. Brady.
Deputy Sec. of the Treasury — John E. Robson.
Under Sec. for Finance — Robert R. Glauber.
Under Sec. for International Affairs — David C. Mulford.
General Counsel — Jeanne Archibald.
Assistant Secretaries: — Desiree Tucker Sorini (Public Affairs & Public Liaison); vacant (Intl. Affairs); Jerome Powell (Domestic Finance); Peter Nunez (Enforcement); Gerald Murphy (Fiscal); Kenneth W. Gideon (Tax Policy); Mary C. Sophos (Legislative Affairs); Sidney Jones (Economic Policy); Hollis S. McLoughlin (Policy Management).
Bureaus:
Alcohol, Tobacco & Firearms — Stephen E. Higgins, dir.
Comptroller of the Currency — Robert Clarke.
Customs — Carol Hallett, comm.
Engraving & Printing — Peter H. Daley, dir.
Federal Law Enforcement Training Center — Charles F. Rinkevich, dir.
Financial Management Service — William E. Douglas, comm.
Internal Revenue Service — Fred T. Goldberg, comm.
Mint — Donna Pope, dir.
Public Debt — Richard L. Gregg, comm.
Treasurer of the U.S. — Catalina Villalpando.
U.S. Savings Bond Division — Jerrold B. Speers, dir.
U.S. Secret Service — John R. Simpson, dir.

Department of Defense
The Pentagon 20301
Secretary of Defense — Richard B. Cheney.
Deputy Secretary — Donald J. Atwood Jr.
Special Assistant — David S. Addington.
Under Secy. for Acquisition — Donald Yockey, act.
Under Secy. for Policy — Paul Wolfowitz.
Asst. Secretaries:
Command Control Communications & Intelligence — Duane P. Andrews.
Force Management & Personnel — Christopher Jehn.
Health Affairs — Enrique Mendez Jr.
International Security Affairs — Henry S. Rowen.
International Security Policy — Stephen J. Hadley.
Legislative Affairs — David Gribbin 3d.
Products & Logistics — Colin R. McMillan.
Program Analysis & Evaluation — David S.C. Chu.
Public Affairs — Pete Williams.
Reserve Affairs — Stephen M. Duncan.
Special Operations & Low Intensity Conflict— J.R. Locher 3d.
Comptroller— Sean O'Keefe.
General Counsel — Terrance O'Donnell.
Admin. & Management — David O. Cooke, dir.

Operational Test & Evaluation — Robert C. Duncan, dir.
Chairman, Joint Chiefs of Staff — Gen. Colin L. Powell, USA.

Department of the Army
The Pentagon 20310
Secretary of the Army — Michael P.W. Stone.
Under Secretary — John W. Shannon.
Assistant Secretaries for:
Civil Works — Robert W. Page.
Installations & Logistics — Susan Livingstone.
Financial Management — Douglas A. Brook.
Research, Development and Acquisition — Stephen Conver.
Manpower & Reserve Affairs — G. Kim Wincup.
Chief of Public Affairs — Brig. Gen. Charles W. McClain, Jr.
Chief of Staff — Gen. Gordon R. Sullivan.
Inspector General — Lt. Gen. J.H. Corns.
Deputy Chiefs of Staff:
Logistics — Lt. Gen. Jimmy D. Ross.
Operations & Plans — Lt. Gen. Dennis J. Reymer.
Personnel — Maj. Gen. William H. Reno.
Intelligence — Lt. Gen. Charles B. Eichelberger.
Commanders:
U.S. Army Materiel Command — Gen. William G.T. Tuttle Jr.
U.S. Army Forces Command — Gen. Edwin Burba.
U.S. Army Training and Doctrine Command — Gen. John W. Foss.
First U.S. Army — Lt. Gen. James E. Thompson.
Second U.S. Army — Lt. Gen. James W. Crysel.
Third U.S. Army — Lt. Gen. John J. Yeosock.
Fourth U.S. Army — Lt. Gen. James R. Hall.
Fifth U.S. Army — Lt. Gen. George R. Stotser.
Sixth U.S. Army — Lt. Gen. William H. Harrison.

Department of the Navy
The Pentagon 20350
Secretary of the Navy — H. Lawrence Garrett 3d.
Under Secretary — J. Daniel Howard.
Assistant Secretaries for:
Financial Management — Robert C. McCormack.
Installations & Environment — Jacqueline Schafer.
Manpower, Reserve Affairs — Barbara Spyridon Pope.
Research, Development & Acquisition — Gerald Cann.
Judge Advocate General — RADM John E. Gorden.
Chief of Naval Operations — ADM Frank B. Kelso 2d.
Chief of Information — RADM Brent Baker.
Military Sealift Command — VADM Francis R. Donovan.
Chief of Naval Personnel — VADM Jeremy M. Boorda.

U.S. Marine Corps:
(Arlington Annex 20380)

Commandant — Gen. Carl E. Mundy Jr.
Asst. Commandant — Gen. John R. Dailey.

Department of the Air Force
The Pentagon 20330
Secretary of the Air Force — Donald B. Rice.
Under Secretary — Anne N. Foreman.
Assistant Secretaries for:
Financial Management — Michael B. Donley.
Space — Martin C. Faga.
Manpower & Reserve Affairs — Jerome G. Cooper.
Acquisition — John J. Welch Jr.
Public Affairs — Brig. Gen. Hallie E. Robertson.
Chief of Staff — Gen. Merrill McPeak.

Department of Justice
Constitution Ave. & 10th St. NW 20530
Attorney General — vacant.
Deputy Attorney General — William P. Barr.

Solicitor General — Kenneth W. Starr.
Liaison Services —William Lucas.
Intelligence Policy & Review — Mary Lawton.
Professional Responsibility —Michael E. Shaheen Jr.
Assistants:
  Antitrust Division — James F. Rill.
  Civil Division — Stuart M. Gerson.
  Civil Rights Division — John R. Dunne.
  Criminal Division — Robert S. Mueller.
  Justice Programs —Richard Abell.
  Justice Management Division — Harry H. Flickinger.
  Environment & Natural Resources Division — Richard B. Stewart.
  Policy Development — Steven R. Schlesinger.
  Legal Counsel — J. Michael Luttis.
  Legislative Affairs — W. Lee Rawls.
  Tax Division — Shirley D. Peterson.
Fed. Bureau of Investigation — William S. Sessions, dir.
Exec. Off. for Immigration Review — David L. Milhollan, dir.
Bureau of Prisons — Michael W. Huggins.
Comm. Relations Service — Grace F. Hughes.
Office of Inspector General — Richard J. Hankinson.
Office of Justice Programs — Jimmy Gurulé.
Drug Enforcement Adm. — Robert C. Bonner.
Office of Special Counsel for Immigration Related Unfair Employment Practices — Andrew Strotny, act.
Exec. Off. for U.S. Trustees — John Logan.
Exec. Off. for U.S. Attorneys — Laurence S. McWhorter.
Public Affairs — Daniel G. Eramian, dir.
Immigration and Naturalization Service — Gene McNary.
Pardon Attorney — Margaret Love.
U.S. Parole Commission — Carol Pavilack Getty, chmn.
U.S. Marshals Service — K. Michael Moore, dir.
Foreign Claims Settlement Comm. — Stanley J. Glod.
Interpol, U.S. Natl. Central Bureau — Darrell W. Mills, chief.

Department of the Interior
C St. between 18th & 19th Sts. NW 20240
Secretary of the Interior — Manuel Lujan.
Deputy Secretary — Frank A. Bracken.
Assistant Secretaries for:
  Fish, Wildlife and Parks — Mike Hayden.
  Policy, Budget, and Administration — John Schrote.
  Indian Affairs — Eddie Frank Brown.
  Territorial & Intl. Affairs — Stella Guerra.
  Land & Minerals — David C. O'Neal.
  Water & Science — John M. Sayre.
Bureau of Land Management — Cy Jamison, dir.
Bureau of Mines — T.S. Ary, dir.
Bureau of Reclamation — Dennis C. Underwood, comm.
Fish & Wildlife Service — John F. Turner, dir.
Geological Survey — Dallas L. Peck, dir.
National Park Service — James M. Ridenour, dir.
Public Affairs — I. Stephen Goldstein, dir.
Office of Congressional and Legislative Affairs — James M. Hughes.
Solicitor — Thomas L. Sansonetti.

Department of Agriculture
The Mall, 12th & 14th Sts. 20250
Secretary of Agriculture — Edward Madigan.
Deputy Secretary — Ann M. Veneman.
Administration — vacant.
Internatl. Affairs & Commodity Programs — Richard T. Crowder.
Food & Consumer Services — Catherine A. Bertini.
Marketing & Inspection Services — Jo Ann Smith.
Small Community & Rural Development — Roland Vautour.

Economics — Bruce Gardner.
Congressional Relations — Franklin E. Bailey.
Natural Resources & Environment — James Moseley.
General Counsel — Alan Raul.
Science & Education — Charles Hess.
Inspector General — Leon Snead.
Public Affairs — Cameron Bruemmer, act.

Department of Commerce
14th St. between Constitution & E St. NW 20230
Secretary of Commerce — Robert Mosbacher.
Deputy Secretary — Rockwell Schnabel.
Chief of Staff — Thomas Collamore.
General Counsel — Wendell Willkie.
Assistant Secretaries:
  Administration — Preston Moore.
  Economic Development Adm. — L. Joyce Hampers.
  Intl. Economic Policy — Thomas Duesterberg.
  Import Administration — Eric I. Garfinkel.
  Legislative Affairs — Craig Helsing.
  Natl. Telecommunications Information Adm. — Janice Obuchowski.
  Patent & Trademark Office — Harry F. Manbeck.
  Trade Development — Timothy McBride.
Bureau of the Census — Dr. Barbara E. Bryant, dir.
Bureau of Economic Analysis — Allan H. Young, dir.
Under Secy. for International Trade — J. Michael Farren.
Under Secy. for Econ. Affairs — Michael Darby.
Under Secy. for Technology — Robert M. White.
Natl. Oceanic & Atmospheric Admin. — John A. Knauss.
Natl. Technical Info. Service — Joseph F. Caponio, dir.
Natl. Institute For Standards & Technology — John W. Lyons.
Minority Business Development Agency — Joe Lira.
Public Affairs — William Fritts, dir.
Consumer Affairs — vacant.

Department of Labor
200 Constitution Ave. NW 20210
Secretary of Labor — Lynn Martin.
Deputy Secretary — vacant.
Assistant Secretaries for:
  Administration and Management — Thomas C. Komarek.
  Congressional Affairs — Kathleen M. Harrington.
  Employment & Training — Roberts Jones.
  Employment Standards — vacant.
  Labor-Management Standards — vacant.
  Mine Safety & Health — William Tattersall.
  Occupational Safety & Health — Gerard F. Scannell.
  Pension & Welfare Benefit Programs — David Ball.
  Policy — vacant.
  Public and Intergovernmental Affairs — Dale Triber Tate.
  Veterans Employment — Thomas E. Collins 3d.
Solicitor of Labor — vacant.
Dep. Under Secy. for International Affairs — Shellyn Gae McCaffrey.
Dep. Under Secy. for Labor-Management Relations & Co-operative Programs — vacant.
Office of Information & Public Affairs — Johanna Schneider, dir.
Women's Bureau — Elsie Vartanian.
Inspector General — Julian De La Rosa.
Comm. of Labor Statistics — Janet L. Norwood.

Department of Health and Human Services
200 Independence Ave. SW 20201
Secretary of HHS — Louis W. Sullivan.
Under Secretary — Constance Horner.
Assistant Secretaries for:

Adm. for Children & Families — Jo Anne Barnhart.
Management & Budget — Kevin E. Moley.
Public Affairs — Alixe Glen.
Health — James Mason, M.D.
Planning & Evaluation — Martin Gerry.
Legislation — Steven Kelmar.
Personnel Administration — Thomas McFee.

General Counsel — Michael Astrue.
Inspector General — Richard P. Kusserow.
Office of Civil Rights — Edward Mercado, dir.
Surgeon General — Antonia C. Novello.
Social Security Adm. — Gwendolyn S. King.
Office of Consumer Affairs — Ann Windham Wallace, dir.
Health Care Financing Adm. — Gail Wilensky, adm.

Department of Housing and Urban Development

451 7th St. SW 20410

Secretary of Housing & Urban Development — Jack Kemp.
Deputy Secretary — Alfred A. DelliBovi.
Deputies — Edwin I. Gardner, Stephen A. Glaude.
Assistant Secretaries for:

Administration — Jim E. Tarro.
Community Planning & Development — S. Anna Kondratas.
Fair Housing & Equal Opportunity — Gordon H. Mansfield.
Field Mgt. — Linda Marston.
Housing & Federal Housing Commissioner — Arthur J. Hill.
Legislation & Congressional Relations — Ivan Ransopher.
Policy Development & Research — John Weicher.
Public Affairs — Mary S. Brunette.
Public & Indian Housing — Joseph G. Schiff.

President, Govt. Natl. Mortgage Assn. — Raoul Carrol.
General Counsel — Francis A. Keating 2d.
Inspector General — Paul A. Adams.

Department of Transportation

400 7th St. SW 20590

Secretary of Transportation — Samuel K. Skinner.
Deputy Secretary — Elaine Chao.
Assistant Secretaries — Jeffrey Shane (Policy and International Affairs); Kate Moore (Budget and Programs); John H. Seymour (Administration); Marion Blakey (Public Affairs); Galen Reser (Governmental Affairs).
National Highway Traffic Safety Admin. — Jerry Curry.
U. S. Coast Guard Commandant — Adm. John W. King.
Federal Aviation Admin. — James Busey.
Federal Highway Admin. — Thomas Larson.
Federal Railroad Admin. — Gilbert Carmichael.
Maritime Admin. — Capt. Warren LeBack.
Urban Mass Transportation Admin. — Brian Clymer.
Research & Special Programs Admin. — Travis Dungan.
Saint Lawrence Seaway Development Corp. — Stan E. Parris.

Department of Energy

1000 Independence Ave. SW 20585

Secretary of Energy — James D. Watkins.
Deputy Secy. — W. Henson Moore.

Under Secretary — John C. Tuck.
General Counsel — Stephen A. Wakefield.
Inspector General — John C. Layton.
Assistant Secretaries — Jacqueline Knox Brown (Congressional & Intergovernmental Affairs); Richard A Claytor (Defense Programs); John J. Easton Jr. (International Affairs & Energy Emergencies); William H. Young (Nuclear Energy); Robert H. Gentile (Fossil Energy); J. Michael Davis (Conservation & Renewable Energy); Paul L. Ziemer (Environment, Safety & Health).

Energy Information Adm. — Calvin A. Kent.
Economic Regulatory Adm. — C. L. van Orman, act.
Federal Energy Regulatory Comm. — Martin L. Allday, chmn.

Hearings & Appeals — George B. Breznay, dir.
Energy Research — James F. Decker, act. dir.
Civilian Radioactive Waste Management — John W. Bartlett, dir.

Minority Economic Impact — Melva G. Wray, dir.
Board of Contract Appeals — E. Barclay van Doren, chmn.
Public Affairs — M.J. Jameson, dir.

Department of Education

400 Maryland Ave. SW 20202

Secretary of Education — Lamar Alexander.
Deputy Secretary — David Kearns.
Under Secretary — John Theodore Sanders.
Chief of Staff — Stephen I. Danzansky.
Inspector General — James B. Thomas Jr.
Deputy Under Secretaries — Gary Rasmussen, William Smith.

General Counsel — Stephen Winnick, act.
Assistant Secretaries:
Legislation & Congressional Affairs — William Hansen, act.

Elementary and Secondary Education — John T. MacDonald.

Postsecondary Education — Michael Farrell, act.
Educational Research and Improvement — Bruno V. Manno, act.

Adult & Vocational Education — Betsy Brand.
Special Education and Rehabilitative Services — Robert Davila.

Civil Rights — Michael L. Williams.
Bilingual & Minority Language Affairs — Rita Esquivel.

Department of Veterans Affairs

810 Vermont Ave. NW 20420

Secretary of Veterans Affairs — Edward J. Derwinski.
Deputy — Anthony J. Principi.
Asst. Secy. For:
Finance & Information Resources Mgmt. — S. Anthony McCann.
Human Resources Adm. — Ronald E. Ray.
Acquisition & Facilities — David Lewis.
Public & Intergovernmental Affairs — Edward T. Timberlake.

Inspector General — Stephen Trodden.
Veterans Benefits Adm. — D'Wayne Gray, dir.
Veterans Health Adm. — James W. Holsinger Jr., dir.
General Counsel — vacant.
Board of Veterans Appeals — Charles L. Cragin, chmn.

Judiciary of the U.S.

Data as of mid-1991

Justices of the United States Supreme Court

The Supreme Court comprises the chief justice of the United States and 8 associate justices, all appointed by the president with advice and consent of the Senate. Salaries: chief justice $160,600 annually, associate justice $153,600. The Supreme Court is located at the U.S. Supreme Court Bldg., 1 First St. NE, Wash., DC 20543.

Name; apptd from *Chief Justices in italics*	Service Term	Yrs.	Born	Died
John Jay, N. Y.	1789-1795	5	1745	1829
John Rutledge, S. C.	1789-1791	1	1739	1800
William Cushing, Mass.	1789-1810	20	1732	1810
James Wilson, Pa.	1789-1798	8	1742	1798
John Blair, Va.	1789-1796	6	1732	1800
James Iredell, N. C.	1790-1799	9	1751	1799
Thomas Johnson, Md.	1791-1793	1	1732	1819
William Paterson, N. J.	1793-1806	13	1745	1806
John Rutledge, S.C.	1795(a)	—	1739	1800
Samuel Chase, Md.	1796-1811	15	1741	1811
Oliver Ellsworth, Conn.	1796-1800	4	1745	1807
Bushrod Washington, Va.	1798-1829	31	1762	1829
Alfred Moore, N. C.	1799-1804	4	1755	1810
John Marshall, Va.	1801-1835	34	1755	1835
William Johnson, S. C.	1804-1834	30	1771	1834
Henry B. Livingston, N. Y.	1806-1823	16	1757	1823
Thomas Todd, Ky.	1807-1826	18	1765	1826
Joseph Story, Mass.	1811-1845	33	1779	1845
Gabriel Duval, Md.	1811-1835	22	1752	1844
Smith Thompson, N. Y.	1823-1843	20	1768	1843
Robert Trimble, Ky.	1826-1828	2	1777	1828
John McLean, Oh.	1829-1861	32	1785	1861
Henry Baldwin, Pa.	1830-1844	14	1780	1844
James M. Wayne, Ga.	1835-1867	32	1790	1867
Roger B. Taney, Md.	1836-1864	28	1777	1864
Philip P. Barbour, Va.	1836-1841	4	1783	1841
John Catron, Tenn.	1837-1865	28	1786	1865
John McKinley, Ala.	1837-1852	15	1780	1852
Peter V. Daniel, Va.	1841-1860	19	1784	1860
Samuel Nelson, N. Y.	1845-1872	27	1792	1873
Levi Woodbury, N. H.	1845-1851	5	1789	1851
Robert C. Grier, Pa.	1846-1870	23	1794	1870
Benjamin R. Curtis, Mass.	1851-1857	6	1809	1874
John A. Campbell, Ala.	1853-1861	8	1811	1889
Nathan Clifford, Me.	1858-1881	23	1803	1881
Noah H. Swayne, Oh.	1862-1881	18	1804	1884
Samuel F. Miller, Ia.	1862-1890	28	1816	1890
David Davis, Ill.	1862-1877	14	1815	1886
Stephen J. Field, Cal.	1863-1897	34	1816	1899
Salmon P. Chase, Oh.	1864-1873	8	1808	1873
William Strong, Pa.	1870-1880	10	1808	1895
Joseph P. Bradley, N. J.	1870-1892	21	1813	1892
Ward Hunt, N. Y.	1872-1882	9	1810	1886
Morrison R. Waite, Oh.	1874-1888	14	1816	1888
John M. Harlan, Ky.	1877-1911	34	1833	1911
William B. Woods, Ga.	1880-1887	6	1824	1887
Stanley Matthews, Oh.	1881-1889	7	1824	1889
Horace Gray, Mass.	1881-1902	20	1828	1902
Samuel Blatchford, N. Y.	1882-1893	11	1820	1893
Lucius Q. C. Lamar, Miss.	1888-1893	5	1825	1893
Melville W. Fuller, Ill.	1888-1910	21	1833	1910
David J. Brewer, Kan.	1889-1910	20	1837	1910
Henry B. Brown, Mich.	1890-1906	15	1836	1913
George Shiras Jr., Pa.	1892-1903	10	1832	1924
Howell E. Jackson, Tenn.	1893-1895	2	1832	1895
Edward D. White, La.	1894-1910	16	1845	1921
Rufus W. Peckham, N. Y.	1895-1909	13	1838	1909
Joseph McKenna, Cal.	1898-1925	26	1843	1926
Oliver W. Holmes, Mass.	1902-1932	29	1841	1935
William R. Day, Oh.	1903-1922	19	1849	1923

(a) Rejected Dec. 15, 1795. (b) nominated.

Name; apptd from *Chief Justices in italics*	Service Term	Yrs.	Born	Died
William H. Moody, Mass.	1906-1910	3	1853	1917
Horace H. Lurton, Tenn.	1909-1914	4	1844	1914
Charles E. Hughes, N. Y.	1910-1916	5	1862	1948
Willis Van Devanter, Wy.	1910-1937	26	1859	1941
Joseph R. Lamar, Ga.	1910-1916	5	1857	1916
Edward D. White, La.	1910-1921	10	1845	1921
Mahlon Pitney, N. J.	1912-1922	10	1858	1924
James C. McReynolds, Tenn.	1914-1941	26	1862	1946
Louis D. Brandeis, Mass.	1916-1939	22	1856	1941
John H. Clarke, Oh.	1916-1922	5	1857	1945
William H. Taft, Conn.	1921-1930	8	1857	1930
George Sutherland, Ut.	1922-1938	15	1862	1942
Pierce Butler, Minn.	1922-1939	16	1866	1939
Edward T. Sanford, Tenn.	1923-1930	7	1865	1930
Harlan F. Stone, N. Y.	1925-1941	16	1872	1946
Charles E. Hughes, N. Y.	1930-1941	11	1862	1948
Owen J. Roberts, Pa.	1930-1945	15	1875	1955
Benjamin N. Cardozo, N.Y.	1932-1938	6	1870	1938
Hugo L. Black, Ala.	1937-1971	34	1886	1971
Stanley F. Reed, Ky.	1938-1957	19	1884	1980
Felix Frankfurter, Mass.	1939-1962	23	1882	1965
William O. Douglas, Conn.	1939-1975	36	1898	1980
Frank Murphy, Mich.	1940-1949	9	1890	1949
Harlan F. Stone, N. Y.	1941-1946	5	1872	1946
James F. Byrnes, S. C.	1941-1942	1	1879	1972
Robert H. Jackson, N. Y.	1941-1954	12	1892	1954
Wiley B. Rutledge, Ia.	1943-1949	6	1894	1949
Harold H. Burton, Oh.	1945-1958	13	1888	1964
Fred M. Vinson, Ky.	1946-1953	7	1890	1953
Tom C. Clark, Tex.	1949-1967	18	1899	1977
Sherman Minton, Ind.	1949-1956	7	1890	1965
Earl Warren, Cal.	1953-1969	16	1891	1974
John Marshall Harlan, N. Y.	1955-1971	16	1899	1971
William J. Brennan Jr., N. J.	1956-1990	33	1906	—
Charles E. Whittaker, Mo.	1957-1962	5	1901	1973
Potter Stewart, Oh.	1958-1981	23	1915	1985
Byron R. White, Col.	1962 —		1917	—
Arthur J. Goldberg, Ill.	1962-1965	3	1908	1990
Abe Fortas, Tenn.	1965-1969	4	1910	1982
Thurgood Marshall, N.Y.	1967-1991	24	1908	—
Warren E. Burger, Va.	1969-1986	17	1907	—
Harry A. Blackmun, Minn.	1970 —		1908	—
Lewis F. Powell Jr., Va.	1972-1987	15	1907	—
William H. Rehnquist, Ariz.	1972-1986	14	1924	—
John Paul Stevens, Ill.	1975 —		1920	—
Sandra Day O'Connor, Ariz.	1981 —		1930	—
William H. Rehnquist, Ariz.	1986 —		1924	—
Antonin Scalia, Va.	1986 —		1936	—
Anthony M. Kennedy, Cal.	1988 —		1936	—
David H. Souter, N.H.	1990 —		1939	—
Clarence Thomas, D.C.	1991(b)		1948	—

U.S. Court of International Trade

New York, NY 10007 (Salaries, $125,000)

Chief Judge — Gregory W. Carman, act.

Judges — Jane A. Restani, Dominick L. DiCarlo, Thomas J. Aquilino Jr., Nicholas Tsoucalas, R. Kenton Musgrave, Richard W. Goldberg.

U.S. Claims Court

Washington, D.C. 20005 (Salaries, $125,000)

Chief Judge — Loren A. Smith.
Judges — James F. Merow, John P. Wiese, Robert J. Yock, Reginald W. Gibson, Lawrence S. Margolis, Christine C. Nettesheim, Moody R. Tidwell 3d, Marian Blank Horn, Eric G. Bruggink, Bohdan A. Futey, Wilkes C. Robinson, Roger B. Andewelt, James T. Turner, Robert H. Hodges Jr.

U.S. Tax Court

Washington DC 20217 (Salaries, $125,000)

Chief Judge — Arthur L. Nims 3d.
Judges — Herbert L. Chabot, Edna G. Parker, Jules J. Korner 3d, Mary Ann Cohen, John O. Colvin, Perry Shields, Charles E. Clapp 2d, Lapsley W. Hamblen Jr., Stephen J. Swift, Joel Gerber, Julien I. Jacobs, Lawrence A. Wright, Carolyn Miller Parr, Robert P. Ruwe, Thomas B. Wells, Laurence J. Whalen, B. John Williams Jr., James S. Halpern.

U.S. Courts of Appeals

(Salaries, $132,700. CJ means Chief Judge)

Federal Circuit — Helen W. Nies, CJ; Giles S. Rich, Pauline Newman, Glenn L. Archer Jr., H. Robert Mayer, Paul R. Michel, S. Jay Plager; Alan D. Lourie, Raymond C. Clevenger 3d, Randall F. Rader; Clerk's Office, Washington, DC 20439.
District of Columbia — Abner J. Mikva, CJ; Patricia M. Wald, Harry T. Edwards, Ruth Bader Ginsburg, Laurence H. Silberman; James L. Buckley, Stephen F. Williams, Douglas Ginsburg, David B. Sentelle; Karen LeCraft Henderson, A. Raymond Randolph; Clerk's Office, Washington, DC 20001.
First Circuit (Me., Mass., N.H., R.I., Puerto Rico) — Stephen Breyer, CJ; Levin H. Campbell, Juan R. Torruella, Bruce M. Selya, Conrad K. Cyr; Clerk's Office, Boston, MA 02109.
Second Circuit (Conn., N.Y., Vt.) — James L. Oakes, CJ; Thomas J. Meskill, Jon O. Newman, Amalya Lyle Kearse, Richard J. Cardamone, Ralph K. Winter Jr., George C. Pratt, Roger J. Miner, Frank X. Altimari, J. Daniel Mahoney, John M. Walker; Joseph M. McLaughlin. Clerk's Office, New York, NY 10007.
Third Circuit (Del., N.J., Pa., Virgin Is.) — Dolores K. Sloviter, CJ; Edward R. Becker, Carol Los Mansmann, Walter K. Stapleton, Morton I. Ginsberg, Anthony J. Scirica, William D. Hutchinson, Robert E. Cowen, Richard L. Nygaard, Samuel A. Alito Jr.; Clerk's Office, Philadelphia, PA 19106.
Fourth Circuit (Md., N.C., S.C., Va., W.Va.) — Sam J. Ervin 3d, CJ; Kenneth K. Hall, Donald Stuart Russell, H. Emory Widener Jr., James D. Phillips Jr., Francis D. Murnaghan Jr., James M. Sprouse, J. Harvie Wilkinson 3d, William W. Wilkins Jr., Paul V. Niemeyer; Clerk's Office, Richmond, VA 23219.
Fifth Circuit (La., Miss., Tex.) — Charles Clark, CJ; Henry A. Politz, Carolyn D. King, Will Garwood, E. Grady Jolly, Patrick E. Higginbotham, W. Eugene Davis, Jerry E. Smith, Edith Hollan Jones, John M. Duhe Jr., Rhesa A. Barksdale, Jacques L. Wiener Jr., Emilio M. Garza; Clerk's Office, New Orleans, LA 70130.
Sixth Circuit (Ky., Mich., Ohio, Tenn.) — Gilbert S. Merritt, CJ; Damon J. Keith, Boyce F. Martin Jr., Nathaniel R. Jones, Robert B. Krupansky, Cornelia G. Kennedy, H. Ted Milburn, Ralph B. Guy Jr., David A. Nelson, James L. Ryan, Danny J. Boggs, Alan E. Norris, Richard H. Suhrheinrich; Clerk's Office, Cincinnati, OH 45202.
Seventh Circuit (Ill., Ind., Wis.) — William J. Bauer, CJ; Walter J. Cummings, Harlington Wood Jr., Richard D. Cudahy, Richard A. Posner, John L. Coffey, Joel M. Flaum, Frank H. Easterbrook, Kenneth F. Ripple, Daniel A. Manion, Michael S. Kanne; Clerk's Office, Chicago, IL 60604.
Eighth Circuit (Ark., Ia., Minn., Mo., Neb., N.D., S.D.) — Donald P. Lay, CJ; Theodore McMillian, Richard S. Arnold, John R. Gibson, George C. Fagg, Pasco M. Bowman 2d, Roger L. Wollman, Frank J. Magill, C. Arlen Beam, James B. Loken; Clerk's Office, St. Louis, MO 63101.
Ninth Circuit (Alaska, Ariz., Cal., Ha., Ida., Mont., Nev., Ore., Wash., Guam, N. Mariana Islands) — J. Clifford Wallace, CJ; James R. Browning, Procter Hug Jr., Thomas Tang, Jerome Farris, Betty B. Fletcher, Mary M. Schroeder, Harry Pregerson, Arthur L. Alarcon, Cecil F. Poole, Dorothy W. Nelson, William C. Canby Jr., William A. Norris, Stephen Reinhardt, Robert R. Beezer, Cynthia M. Hall, Charles E. Wiggins, Melvin Brunetti, Alex Kozinski, David R. Thompson, John T. Noonan, Diarmuid F. O'Scannlain, Edward Leavy, Stephen S. Trout, Ferdinand F. Fernandez, Pamela Ann Rymer, Thomas G. Nelson; Clerk's Office, San Francisco, CA 94101.
Tenth Circuit (Col., Kan., N.M., Okla., Ut., Wy.) — William J. Holloway Jr., CJ; Monroe G. McKay, James K. Logan, Stephanie K. Seymour, John P. Moore, Stephen H. Anderson, Deanell R.

Tacha, Bobby R. Baldock, Wade Brorby, David M. Ebel; Clerk's Office, Denver, CO 80294.
Eleventh Circuit (Ala. Fla., Ga.)— Gerald B. Tjoflat, CJ; Peter T. Fay, Phyllis A. Kravitch, Frank M. Johnson Jr., Joseph W. Hatchett, R. Lanier Anderson 3d, Thomas A. Clark, J.L. Edmondson, Emmett R. Cox, Stanley F. Birch Jr., Joel F. Dubina; Clerk's Office, Atlanta GA 30303.
Temporary Emergency Court of Appeals — Reynaldo G. Garza, CJ; Clerk's Office, Washington, DC 20001 .

U.S. District Courts

(Salaries, $125,000. CJ means Chief Judge)

Alabama — Northern: Sam C. Pointer Jr., CJ; James Hughes Hancock, Robert B. Propst, E. B. Haltom Jr., U. W. Clemon, William M. Acker Jr., Edwin L. Nelson; Clerk's Office, Birmingham 35203. **Middle:** Myron H. Thompson, CJ; William H. Albritton; Clerk's Office, Montgomery 36101. **Southern:** Alex T. Howard Jr., CJ; Charles R. Butler Jr., Richard W. Vollmer Jr.; Clerk's Office, Mobile 36602.

Alaska — H. Russel Holland, CJ; Andrew J. Kleinfeld, John Singleton; Clerk's Office, Anchorage 99513.

Arizona — William D. Browning, CJ; Richard M. Bilby, Alfredo C. Marquez, Earl H. Carroll, Paul G. Rosenblat, Robert C. Bloomfield, Roger G. Strand, Stephen M. McNamee; Clerk's Office, Phoenix 85025.

Arkansas — Eastern: Garnett Thomas Eisele, CJ; Henry Woods, George Howard Jr., Stephen M. Reasoner, Susan Weber Wright; Clerk's Office, Little Rock 72203. **Western:** H. Franklin Waters, CJ; George Howard Jr., Morris S. Arnold; Clerk's Office, Fort Smith 72902.

California — Northern: Thelton E. Henderson, CJ; Robert P. Aguilar, Marilyn H. Patel, Eugene F. Lynch, John P. Vukasin Jr, Charles A. Legge, D. Lowell Jensen, Fern M. Smith, Vaughn R. Walker, James Ware; Clerk's Office, San Francisco 94102. **Eastern:** Robert E. Coyle, CJ; Lawrence K. Karlton, Edward J. Garcia, William B. Shubb, David F. Levi, Oliver W. Wanger; Clerk's Office, Sacramento 95814. **Central:** Manuel L. Real, CJ; Wm. Matthew Byrne Jr., Robert M. Takasugi, Mariana R. Pfaelzer, Terry J. Hatter Jr., A. Wallace Tashima, Consuelo Bland Marshall, David V. Kenyon, Richard A. Gadbois, Edward Rafeedie, Harry L. Hupp, Alicemarie H. Stotler, James M. Ideman, William J. Rea, William D. Keller, Stephen V. Wilson, J. Spencer Letts, Dickran M. Tevrizian Jr., John G. Davies, Ronald S.W. Lew, Gary L. Taylor; Clerk's Office, Los Angeles 90012. **Southern:** Judith N. Keep, CJ; Gordon Thompson Jr., Earl B. Gilliam, Rudi M. Brewster, John S. Rhoades Sr., Marilyn L. Huff; Clerk's Office, San Diego 92189.

Colorado — Sherman G. Finesilver, CJ; Richard P. Matsch, Jim R. Carrigan, Zita L. Weinshienk, Lewis T. Babcock, Edward W. Nottingham, Daniel B. Sparr; Clerk's Office, Denver 80294.

Connecticut — Ellen B. Burns, CJ; T.F. Gilroy Daly, Warren W. Eginton, Jose A. Cabranes, Peter C. Dorsey, Alan H. Nevas; Clerk's Office, New Haven 06510.

Delaware — Joseph J. Longobardi, CJ; Joseph J. Farnan Jr., Jane R. Roth; Clerk's Office, Wilmington 19801.

District of Columbia — Aubrey E. Robinson Jr., CJ; Gerhard A. Gesell, Charles R. Richey, Louis F. Oberdorfer, Harold H. Greene, John Garrett Penn, Joyce Hens Green, Norma H. Johnson, Thomas P. Jackson, Thomas F. Hogan, Stanley S. Harris, George H. Revercomb, Stanley Sporkin, Royce C. Lamberth, Michael Boudin; Clerk's Office, Washington DC 20001.

Florida — Northern: William H. Stafford Jr., CJ; Maurice M. Paul, C. Roger Vinson; Clerk's Office, Tallahassee 32301. **Middle:** Susan H. Black, CJ; William Terrell Hodges, William J. Castagna; John H. Moore 2d, Elizabeth A. Kovachevich, George K. Sharp, Patricia C. Fawsett; Clerk's Office, Jacksonville 32201. **Southern:** James Lawrence King, CJ; Norman C. Roettiger Jr.; Jose A. Gonzalez Jr., James C. Paine, James W. Kehoe, Eugene P. Spellman, Edward B. Davis, Lenore C. Nesbitt, Stanley Marcus, William J. Zloch, Kenneth L. Ryskamp, Federico A. Moreno; Clerk's Office, Miami 33128.

Georgia — Northern: William C. O'Kelley, CJ; Richard C. Freeman, Harold L. Murphy, Marvin H. Shoob, G. Ernest Tidwell, Orinda Dale Evans, Robert L. Vining Jr., Robert H. Hall, Harold T. Ward, J. Owen Forrester, Jack T. Camp, Charles A. Moye Jr.; Clerk's Office, Atlanta 30335. **Middle:** Wilbur D. Owens Jr., CJ; J. Robert Elliott, Duross Fitzpatrick; Clerk's Office, Macon 31202. **Southern:** B. Avant Edenfield, CJ; Anthony A. Alaimo, Dudley H. Bowen Jr.; Clerk's Office, Savannah 31412.

Hawaii — Harold M. Fong, CJ, Alan C. Kay, David A. Ezra; Clerk's Office, Honolulu 96850.

Idaho — Harold L. Ryan, CJ; Edward J. Lodge; Clerk's Office; Boise, 83724.

Illinois — **Northern:** James B. Moran, CJ; John F. Grady, Nicholas J. Bua, Marvin E. Aspen, Milton I. Shadur, Charles P. Kocoras, John A. Nordberg, William T. Hart, Paul E. Plunkett, Ilana Diamond Rovner, Charles R. Norgle Sr., James F. Holderman Jr., Ann C. Williams, Brian Barnett Duff, Harry D. Lienenweber, James B. Zagel, James H. Alesia, Suzanne B. Conlon, George M. Marovich, George W. Lindberg; Clerk's Office, Chicago 60604. **Central:** Harold Albert Baker, CJ; Michael M. Mihm, Richard Mills; Clerk's Office, Springfield 62705. **Southern:** James L. Foreman, CJ; William L. Beatty, William D. Stiehl; Clerk's Office, E. St. Louis 62202.

Indiana — **Northern:** Allen Sharp, CJ; William C. Lee, James T. Moody, Robert L. Miller Jr., Rudy Lozano; Clerk's Office, South Bend 46601. **Southern:** Gene E. Brooks, CJ; S. Hugh Dillin, Sarah E. Barker, Larry J. McKinney, John D. Tinder; Clerk's Office, Indianapolis 46204.

Iowa — **Northern:** Donald E. O'Brien, CJ, David R. Hansen; Clerk's Office, Cedar Rapids 52401. **Southern:** Harold D. Vietor, CJ; Charles R. Wolle; Clerk's Office, Des Moines 50309.

Kansas — Earl E. O'Connor, CJ; Patrick F. Kelly, Sam A. Crow, C. Thomas Van Bebber; Clerk's Office, Wichita 67202.

Kentucky — **Eastern:** Eugene E. Siler Jr., CJ; William Bertelsman, Henry R. Wilhoit Jr., Karl S. Forester, Joseph M. Hood; Clerk's Office, Lexington 40586. **Western:** Thomas A. Ballantine, CJ; Ronald E. Meredith, Charles R. Simpson 3d, Edward H. Johnstone; Clerk's Office, Louisville 40202.

Louisiana — **Eastern:** Frederick J. R. Heebe, CJ; Morley L. Sear, Adrian A. Duplantier, Robert F. Collins, George Arceneaux Jr., Veronica D. Wicker, Patrick E. Carr, Peter Beer, A J. McNamara, Henry A. Mentz Jr., Martin L. C. Feldman, Marcel Livaudais Jr.; Clerk's Office, New Orleans 70130. **Middle:** John V. Parker, CJ; Frank J. Polozola; Clerk's Office, Baton Rouge 70821. **Western:** John M. Shaw, CJ; Tom Stagg, F. A. Little Jr., Donald E. Walter, Richard Haiks; Clerk's Office, Shreveport 71101.

Maine — Gene Carter, CJ; D. Brock Hornby; Clerk's Office, Portland 04112.

Maryland — William E. Black Jr., CJ; Joseph C. Howard, Norman P. Ramsey, John R. Hargrove, J. Frederick Motz, Frederic N. Smalkin, William M. Nickerson, Marvin J. Garbis; Clerk's Office, Baltimore 21201.

Massachusetts — Frank H. Freedman, CJ; Joseph L. Tauro, Walter Jay Skinner, A. David Mazzone, Robert E. Keeton, Rya W. Zobel, David S. Nelson, William G. Young, Mark L. Wolf, Douglas P. Woodlock, Edward F. Harrington; Clerk's Office, Boston 02109.

Michigan — **Eastern:** Julian A. Cook Jr., CJ; Stewart A. Newblatt, Avern Cohn, Anna Diggs Taylor, George E. Woods, George La Plata, Barbara K. Hackett, Lawrence P. Zatkoff, Patrick J. Duggan, Bernard A. Friedman, Paul V. Gadola, Gerald E. Rosen, Robert H. Cleland; Clerk's Office, Detroit 48226. **Western:** Benjamin F. Gibson, CJ; Richard A. Enslen, Robert H. Bell; Clerk's Office, Grand Rapids 49503.

Minnesota — Donald D. Alsop, CJ; Harry H. MacLaughlin, Robert G. Renner, Diana E. Murphy, Paul A. Magnuson, James M. Rosenbaum, David S. Doty; Edward J. Devitt, Earl R. Larson; Clerk's Office, St. Paul 55101.

Mississippi — **Northern:** L. T. Senter Jr., CJ; Neal Biggers, Glen H. Davidson; Clerk's Office, Oxford 38655. **Southern:** William H. Barbour Jr., CJ; Harry T. Wingate, Tom S. Lee, Walter J. Gex 3d, Charles W. Pickering Sr.; Clerk's Office, Jackson 39201.

Missouri — **Eastern:** Edward D. Filippine, CJ; William L. Hungate, Clyde S. Cahill Jr., Stephen N. Limbaugh, George F. Gunn Jr., Jean Hamilton; Clerk's Office, St. Louis 63101. **Western:** Howard F. Sachs, CJ; Scott O. Wright, Russell G. Clark, Howard F. Sachs, Joseph E. Stevens Jr., D. Brook Bartlett, Dean Whipple; Clerk's Office, Kansas City 64106.

Montana — Paul G. Hatfield, CJ; Charles C. Lovell, Jack D. Shanstrom; Clerk's Office, Billings 59101.

Nebraska — Lyle E. Strom, CJ; William G. Cambridge; Clerk's Office, Omaha 68101.

Nevada — Edward C. Reed Jr., CJ; Lloyd D. George, Howard D. McKibben, Philip M. Pro; Clerk's Office, Las Vegas 89101.

New Hampshire — Shane Devine, CJ; Norman H. Stahl; Clerk's Office, Concord 03301.

New Jersey — John F. Gerry, CJ; Anne E. Thompson, D. R. Debevoise, H. Lee Sarokin, Harold A. Ackerman, John W. Bissell, Maryanne Trump Barry, Joseph H. Rodriguez, Garrett E. Brown Jr., Alfred J. Lechner Jr., Nicholas H. Politan, Alfred M. Wolin, John C. Lifland; Clerk's Office, Newark 07102.

New Mexico — Juan G. Burciaga, CJ; Santiago E. Campos, John E. Conway, James A. Parker; Clerk's Office, Albuquerque 87103.

New York — **Northern:** Neal P. McCurn, CJ; Thomas J. McAvoy, Con G. Cholakis; Clerk's Office, Albany 12201. **Eastern:** Thomas C. Platt Jr., CJ; Jack B. Weinstein, Charles P. Sifton, Eugene H. Nickerson, Israel Leo Glasser, Raymond J. Dearie, Leonard D. Wexler, Edward R. Korman, Reena Raggi; Arthur D. Spatt, Carol Bagley Amon; Clerk's Office, Brooklyn 11201. **Southern:** Charles L. Brieant, CJ; David N. Edelstein, Thomas P. Griesa, Kevin Thomas Duffy, Leonard B. Sand, Mary Johnson Lowe, Gerard L. Goettel, Charles S. Haight Jr., Pierre N. Leval, John E. Sprizzo, Shirley Wohl Kram, John F. Keenan, Peter K. Leisure, Louis L. Stanton, Miriam G. Cedarbaum, Michael B. Mukasey, Kenneth Conboy, Kimba Wood, Robert P. Patterson Jr.; Lawrence McKenna, John S. Martin Jr.; Clerk's Office N. Y. City 10007. **Western:** Michael A. Telesca, CJ; Richard J. Arcara, David G. Larimer, William M. Skretny; Clerk's Office, Buffalo 14202.

North Carolina — **Eastern:** James C. Fox, CJ; W. Earl Britt, Terrence W. Boyle, Malcolm J. Howard; Clerk's Office, Raleigh 27611. **Middle:** Richard C. Erwin, CJ; Frank W. Bullock, N. Carlton Tilley Jr.; Clerk's Office, Greensboro 27402. **Western:** Richard L. Woorhees, CJ; Robert D. Potter, Graham C. Mullen; Clerk's Office Asheville 28801.

North Dakota — Patrick A. Conmy, CJ, Rodney S. Webb; Clerk's Office, Bismarck 58502.

Ohio — **Northern:** Thomas D. Lambros, CJ; Frank J. Battisti, George W. White, Ann Aldrich, Alvin I. Krenzler, John W. Potter, David D. Dowd Jr., Sam H. Bell, Alice M. Batchelder; Clerk's Office, Cleveland 44114. **Southern:** John D. Holschuh, CJ; Carl B. Rubin, Walter H. Rice, S. Arthur Spiegel, Herman J. Weber, James L. Graham, George C. Smith; Clerk's Office, Columbus 43215.

Oklahoma — **Northern:** H. Dale Cook, CJ; James O. Ellison, Thomas R. Brett, David L. Russell; Clerk's Office, Tulsa 74103. **Eastern:** Frank H. Shey, CJ; Clerk's Office, Muskogee 74401. **Western:** Ralph G. Thompson, CJ; Wayne Alley, Lee R. West, Robin Cauthron; Clerk's Office, Oklahoma City 73102.

Oregon — James A. Redden, CJ; Owen M. Panner, Helen J. Frye, Malcolm F. Marsh, Robert E. Jones; Clerk's Office, Portland 97205.

Pennsylvania — **Eastern:** Louis Charles Bechtle, CJ; Edward N. Cahn, Norma L. Shapiro, James T. Giles, James McGirr Kelly, Thomas N. O'Neill Jr., Marvin Katz, Edmund V. Ludwig, Robert F. Kelly, Franklin S. Van Antwerpen, Robert S. Gawthrop, Lowell A. Reed Jr., Jan E. Dubois, Herbert J. Hutton, Jay C. Waldman, Ronald L. Buckwalter; Clerk's Office, Philadelphia 19106. **Middle:** Richard P. Conaboy, CJ; Sylvia H. Rambo, William W. Caldwell, Edward M. Kosik, James F. McClure Jr.; Clerk's Office, Scranton 18501. **Western:** Maurice B. Cohill Jr., CJ; Gustave Diamond, Donald E. Ziegler, Alan N. Bloch, Glenn E. Mencer, William L. Standish, D. Brooks Smith, Donald J. Lee, Timothy K. Lewis; Clerk's Office, Pittsburgh 15230.

Rhode Island — Francis J. Boyle, CJ; Ronald R. Lagueux, Ernest C. Torres; Clerk's Office, Providence 02903.

South Carolina — Falcon B. Hawkins, CJ; C. Weston Houck, Matthew J. Perry Jr., George R. Anderson Jr., Clyde H. Hamilton, Joseph F. Anderson Jr., David C. Norton, Dennis W. Shedd, Henry M. Herlong Jr.; Clerk's Office, Columbia 29202.

South Dakota — John Baily Jones, CJ; Richard H. Battey, Donald J. Potter; Clerk's Office, Sioux Falls 57102.

Tennessee — **Eastern:** Thomas G. Hull, CJ; James H. Jarvis, R. Allan Edgar, Leon Jordan; Clerk's Office, Knoxville 37901. **Middle:** Thomas A. Wiseman Jr., CJ; Thomas A. Higgins, John T. Nixon; Clerk's Office, Nashville 37203. **Western:** Odell Horton, CJ; Julia S. Gibbons, James D. Todd, Jerome Turner; Clerk's Office, Memphis 38103.

Texas — Northern: Barefoot Sanders, CJ; Mary Lou Robinson, Jerry Buchmeyer, A. Joe Fish, Robert B. Maloney, Sidney A. Fitzwater, Samuel R. Cummings, John H. McBryde; Clerk's Office, Dallas 75242. **Southern:** James De Anda, CJ; Norman W. Black, George P. Kazen, Filemon B. Vela, Hayden W. Head Jr., Ricardo H. Hinojosa, Lynn N. Hughes, David Hittner, Kenneth M. Hoyt, Simeon T. Lake 3d, Melinda Harmon, John Rainey, Samuel B. Kent; Clerk's Office, Houston 77208. **Eastern:** Robert M. Parker, CJ; William Wayne Justice, Howell Cobb, Sam B. Hall Jr., Paul N. Brown, Richard A. Schell; Clerk's Office, Tyler 75702. **Western:** Lucius D. Bunton 3d, CJ; Harry Lee Hudspeth, Hipolito F. Garcia, James R. Nowlin, Edward C. Prado, Walter S. Smith Jr.; Clerk's Office, San Antonio 78206.

Utah — Bruce S. Jenkins, CJ; J. Thomas Greene, David Sam, David K. Winder; Clerk's Office, Salt Lake City 84101.

Vermont — Franklin S. Billings Jr., CJ; Fred I. Parker; Clerk's Office, Burlington 05402.

Virginia — Eastern: Albert V. Bryan Jr., CJ; J. Calvitt Clarke, Richard L. Williams, James C. Cacheris, Robert G. Doumar, Claude M. Hilton, James R. Spencer, Thomas S. Ellis 3d, Rebecca Beach Smith; Clerk's Office, Alexandria 22320. **Western:** James C. Turk, CJ; James H. Michael Jr., Jackson L. Kiser, Samuel G. Wilson; Clerk's Office, Roanoke 24006.

Washington — Eastern: Justin L. Quackenbush, CJ; Alan A. McDonald; Fred Van Sickle; Clerk's Office, Spokane 99210. **Western:** Barbara J. Rothstein, CJ; John C. Coughenour, Carolyn R. Dimmick, Robert J. Bryan, William L. Dwyer, Thomas Zilly; Clerk's Office, Seattle 98104.

West Virginia — Northern: Robert Earl Maxwell, CJ; Frederick P. Stamp Jr.; Clerk's Office, Elkins 26241. **Southern:** Charles H. Haden 2d, CJ; Robert J. Staker, John T. Copenhaver Jr., Elizabeth V. Hallanan; Clerk's Office, Charleston 25329.

Wisconsin — Eastern: Robert W. Warren, CJ; Terence T. Evans, Thomas J. Curran, J.P. Stadtmueller; Clerk's Office, Milwaukee 53202. **Western:** Barbara B. Crabb, CJ; John C. Shabaz; Clerk's Office, Madison 53701.

Wyoming — Clarence A. Brimmer, CJ; Alan B. Johnson; Clerk's Office, Cheyenne 82001.

U.S. Territorial District Courts

Guam — vacancy; Clerk's Office, Agana 96910.

Puerto Rico — Juan M. Perez-Gimenez, CJ; Gilberto Gierbolini, Carmen Consuelo Cerezo, Jaime Pieras Jr., Raymond L. Acosta, Hector M. Laffitte, Jose Antonio Fuste; Clerk's Office, San Juan 00904.

Virgin Islands — vacancy CJ; Clerk's Office, Charlotte Amalie, St. Thomas 00801.

U.S. Court of Veterans Appeals

Washington, D.C. 20004 (Salaries, $125,000)
Chief Judge — Frank Q. Nebeker.
Judges — Kenneth B. Kramer, John J. Farley 3d, Hart T. Mankin, Ronald M. Holdaway, Donald L. Ivers, Jonathan R. Steinberg.

State Officials, Salaries, Party Membership

As of mid-1991; † Ind. or other party.

Alabama

Governor — Guy Hunt, R., $87,913.
Lt. Gov. — Jim Folsom Jr., D., $52 per legislative day, plus annual salary of $1,900 per month plus $1,500 per month for expenses.
Sec. of State — Billy Joe Camp, D., $57,203.
Atty. Gen. — Jimmy Evans, D., $90,474.
Treasurer — George Wallace Jr., D., $57,203.
Legislature: meets annually the 3d Tuesday in Apr. (first year of term of office, first Tuesday in Feb. (2d and 3d years), 2d Tuesday in Jan. (4th year) at Montgomery. Members receive $50 a day salary, plus $1,900 per month expenses and mileage of 10c per mile.
Senate — Dem., 28; Rep., 7. Total, 35.
House — Dem., 82; Rep., 23. Total, 105.

Alaska

Governor — Walter Hickel, † $81,648.
Lt. Gov. — Stephen McAlpine, †, $76,188.
Atty. General — Charles Cole, R., $79,860.
Legislature: meets annually in January at Juneau, for 120 days with a 10-day extension possible upon ⅔ vote. First session in odd years. Members receive $22,140 per year plus $80 a day per diem.
Senate — Dem., 10; Rep., 10. Total, 20.
House — Dem., 23; Rep., 17. Total, 40.

Arizona

Governor — Fife Symington(A), R., $75,000.
Sec. of State — Richard Mahoney, D., $52,000.
Atty. Gen. — Grant Woods, R., $72,800.
Treasurer — Tony West, R., $52,000.
Legislature: meets annually in January at Phoenix. Each member receives an annual salary of $15,000.
Senate — Dem., 17; Rep., 13. Total, 30.
House — Dem., 27; Rep., 33. Total, 60.
(A) Won runoff 2/26/91

Arkansas

Governor — Bill Clinton, D., $35,000.
Lt. Gov. — Jim Guy Tucker, D., $14,000.
Sec. of State — W. J. "Bill" McCuen, D., $22,500.
Atty. Gen. — Winston Bryant, D., $26,500.
Treasurer — Jimmie Lou Fisher Lumpkin, D., $22,500.
Auditor — Julia Hughes Jones, D., $22,500.
General Assembly: meets odd years in January at Little Rock. Members receive $7,500 per year, $74 a day while in regular session, plus 21 cents a mile travel expenses.
Senate — Dem., 31; Rep., 4. Total, 35.
House — Dem., 88; Rep. 11; 1 ind. Total, 100.

California

Governor — Pete Wilson, R., $120,000.
Lt. Gov. — Leo T. McCarthy, D., $90,000.
Sec. of State — March Fong Eu, D., $90,000.
Controller — Gray Davis, D., $90,000.
Atty. Gen. — Dan Lungren, R., $102,000.
Legislature: meets at Sacramento; regular sessions commence on the first Monday in Dec. of every even-numbered year; each session lasts 2 years. Members receive $44,898 per year plus mileage and $65 per diem.
Senate — Dem., 26; Rep., 11, 1 ind., 2 vac.; Total, 40.
Assembly — Dem., 46; Rep., 32, 2 vac.; Total, 80.

Colorado

Governor — Roy Romer, D., $70,000.
Lt. Gov. — Mike Callihan, D., $48,500.
Secy. of State — Natalie Meyer, R., $48,500.
Atty. Gen. — Gale Norton, R., $60,000.
Treasurer — Gail Schoettler, D., $48,500.
General Assembly: meets annually in January at Denver. Members receive $17,500 annually.
Senate — Dem., 11; Rep., 24. Total, 35.
House — Dem., 26; Rep., 39. Total, 65.

Connecticut

Governor — Lowell Weicker, †, $78,000.
Lt. Gov. — Eunice S. Groark, †, $55,000.
Sec. of State — Pauline R. Kezer, R., $50,000.
Treasurer — Francisco Borges, D., $50,000.
Comptroller — William E. Curry Jr., D., $50,000.
Atty. Gen. — Richard Blumenthal, D., $60,000.
General Assembly: meets annually odd years in January and even years in February at Hartford. Salary $15,200 per year plus $4,500 (senator), $3,500 (representative) per year for expenses, plus travel allowance.
Senate — Dem., 20; Rep., 16. Total, 36.
House — Dem., 88; Rep., 63. Total, 151.

Delaware

Governor — Michael N. Castle, R., $80,000.
Lt. Gov. — Dale E. Wolf, R., $35,000.
Sec. of State — Michael Harkins, R., $69,900.
Atty. Gen. — Charles Oberly 3d, D., $81,400.
Treasurer — Janet C. Rzewnicki, R., $63,000.
General Assembly: 55 day session beginning the 2d Tuesday in January until June 30. Members receive $23,000 base salary, plus $5,500 expense account.
Senate — Dem., 15; Rep., 6. Total, 21.
House — Dem., 17; Rep., 24. Total, 41.

Florida

Governor — Lawton Chiles, D., $103,909.
Lt. Gov. — Buddy MacKay, D., $94,040.
Sec. of State — Jim Smith, R., $94,040.
Comptroller — Gerald Lewis, D., $94,040.
Atty. Gen. — Robert Butterworth, D., $94,040.
Treasurer — Tom Gallagher, R., $94,040.

Legislature: meets annually at Tallahassee. Members receive $22,560 per year plus expense allowance while on official business.
Senate — Dem., 23; Rep., 17. Total, 40.
House — Dem., 74; Rep., 46. Total, 120.

Georgia

Governor — Zell Miller, D., $91,092.
Lt. Gov. — Pierre Howard, D., $59,145.
Sec. of State — Max Cleland, D., $72,966.
Insurance Comm. — Tim Ryles, D., $72,954.
Atty. Gen. — Michael J. Bowers, $74,645.
General Assembly: meets annually at Atlanta. Members receive $10,509 per year, $59 per diem, and $4,800 expense reimbursement. During session $59 per day for expenses.
Senate — Dem., 45; Rep., 11. Total, 56.
House — Dem., 145; Rep., 35. Total, 180.

Hawaii

Governor — John Waihee, D., $94,780.
Lt. Gov. — Benjamin Cayetano, D., $90,041.
Atty. Gen. — Warren Price, $85,302.
Comptroller — Russel Nagata, $85,302.
Dir. of Budget & Finance — Yukio Takemoto, $85,302.
Legislature: meets annually on 3d Wednesday in January at Honolulu. Members receive $27,000 per year plus expenses.
Senate — Dem., 22. Rep., 3. Total, 25.
House — Dem., 45. Rep. 6. Total, 51.

Idaho

Governor — Cecil D. Andrus, D., $75,000.
Lt. Gov. — C. L. "Butch" Otter, R., $20,000.
Sec. of State — Pete T. Cenarrusa, R., $62,500.
Treasurer — Lydia Justice Edwards, R., $62,500.
Atty. Gen. — Larry EchoHawk, D., $67,500.
Legislature: meets annually the Monday on or nearest the 9th of January at Boise. Members receive $70 per day during session, $50 per day when not in session, plus certain travel and living allowances.
Senate — Dem., 22; Rep., 22. Total, 44.
House — Dem., 28; Rep., 56 Total, 84.

Illinois

Governor — Jim Edgar, R., $97,370.
Lt. Gov. — Bob Kustra, R., $68,732.
Sec. of State — George H. Ryan, R., $85,915.
Comptroller — D.C. Netsch, D., $74,459.
Atty. Gen. — Roland W. Burris, D., $85,915.
Treasurer — Patrick Quinn, D., $74,459.
General Assembly: meets annually in January at Springfield. Members receive $35,661 per annum.
Senate — Dem., 31; Rep., 28. Total, 59.
House — Dem., 72; Rep., 46. Total, 118.

Indiana

Governor — Evan Bayh, D., $77,200 plus discretionary expenses.
Lt. Gov. — Frank O'Bannon, D., $64,000 plus discretionary expenses.
Sec. of State — Joseph Hogsett D., $46,000.
Atty. Gen. — Linley E. Pearson, D., $59,200.
Treasurer — Marjorie H. O'Laughlin, D., $46,000.
Auditor — Ann G. DeVore, D., $46,000.
General Assembly: meets annually in January. Members receive $11,600 per year plus $83 per day while in session, $25 per day while not in session.
Senate — Dem., 24; Rep., 26. Total, 50.
House — Dem., 52; Rep., 48. Total, 100.

Iowa

Governor — Terry E. Branstad, R., $76,900.
Lt. Gov. — Joy Corning, R., $60,000.
Sec. of State — Elaine Baxter, D., $60,000.
Atty. Gen. — Bonnie Campbell, D., $73,600.
Treasurer — Michael L. Fitzgerald, D., $60,000.
Auditor — Richard D. Johnson, R., $60,000.
Secy. of Agriculture — Dale M. Cochran, D., $60,000.
General Assembly: meets annually in January at Des Moines. Members receive $16,600 annually plus maximum expense allowance of $40 per day for first 110 days of first session, and first 100 days of 2d session; mileage expenses at 21c a mile.
Senate — Dem., 30; Rep., 20. Total, 50.
House — Dem., 61; Rep., 39. Total, 100.

Kansas

Governor — Joan Finney, D., $74,235.
Lt. Gov. — James Francisco, D., $20,998.
Sec. of State — Bill Graves, R., $57,668.
Atty. Gen. — Robert T. Stephan, R., $66,324.

Treasurer — Sally Thompson, D., $57,668.
Legislature: meets annually in January at Topeka. Members receive $60 a day plus $70 a day expenses while in session, plus $600 per month while not in session.
Senate — Dem., 18; Rep., 22. Total. 40.
House — Dem., 63; Rep., 62. Total, 125.

Kentucky

Governor — Wallace G. Wilkinson, D., $69,730.
Lt. Gov. — Brereton Jones, D., $59,262.
Sec. of State — Bremer Ehrler, D., $59,262.
Atty. Gen. — Fred Cowan, D., $59,262.
Treasurer — Robert Meade, D., $59,262.
Auditor — Bob Babbage, D., $59,262.
General Assembly: meets even years in January at Frankfort. Members receive $100 per day and $100 per day during session and $950 per month for expenses for interim.
Senate — Dem., 27; Rep., 11. Total, 38.
House — Dem., 68; Rep., 32. Total, 100.

Louisiana

Governor — Charles "Buddy" Roemer, R., $73,440.
Lt. Gov. — Paul Hardy, R., $63,367.
Sec. of State — Fox McKeithen, D., $60,169.
Atty. Gen. — William J. Guste Jr., D., $60,169.
Treasurer — Mary Landrieu, D., $60,169.
Legislature: meets annually for 60 legislative days commencing on 3d Monday in April. Members receive $75 per day and mileage plus annual salary of $16,800.
Senate — Dem., 33; Rep., 6. Total, 39.
House — Dem., 87; Rep., 18. Total, 105.

Maine

Governor — John R. McKernan Jr., R., $70,000.
Sec. of State — G. William Diamond, D., $48,152.
Atty. Gen. — Michael E. Carpenter, D., $61,152.
Treasurer — Samuel Shapiro, D., $61,200.
Legislature: meets annually the first Wednesday in December at Augusta, and the Wednesday after the first Tuesday in Jan. in even numbered years. Members receive $10,500 for first regular sessions, $7,500 for second regular session plus expenses; presiding officers receive 50% more.
Senate — Dem., 22; Rep., 13. Total, 35.
House — Dem., 97; Rep., 54. Total, 151.

Maryland

Governor — William Donald Schaefer, D., $120,000.
Lt. Gov. — Melvin Steinberg, D., $100,000.
Comptroller — Louis L. Goldstein, D., $100,000.
Atty. Gen. — J. Joseph Curran Jr., D., $100,000.
Sec. of State — Winfield M. Kelly Jr., D., $70,000.
Treasurer — Lucille Maurer, D., $100,000.
General Assembly: meets 90 consecutive days annually beginning on the 2d Wednesday in January at Annapolis. Members receive $27,000 per year plus expenses.
Senate — Dem., 38; Rep., 9. Total, 47.
House — Dem., 117; Rep., 24. Total, 141.

Massachusetts

Governor — William Weld, R., $75,000.
Lt. Gov. — A. Paul Cellucci, R., $60,000.
Sec. of State — Michael Joseph Connolly, D., $60,000.
Atty. Gen. — L. Scott Harshbarger, D., $65,000.
Treasurer — Joseph Malone, R., $60,000.
Auditor — A. Joseph DeNucci, D., $60,000.
General Court (Legislature): meets each January in Boston. Salaries $30,000 per annum.
Senate — Dem., 24; Rep., 16. Total, 40.
House — Dem., 122; Rep., 37; ind., 1. Total, 160.

Michigan

Governor — John Engler, R., $106,700.
Lt. Gov. — Connie Binsfeld, R., $80,300.
Sec. of State — Richard H. Austin, D., $109,000.
Atty. Gen. — Frank J. Kelley, D., $109,000.
Treasurer — Doug Roberts, N-P, $83,100.
Legislature: meets annually in January at Lansing. Members receive $45,450 per year, plus $8,500 expense allowance.
Senate — Dem., 18; Rep., 20. Total, 38.
House — Dem., 61; Rep., 49. Total, 110.

Minnesota

Governor — Arne Carlson, R., $109,053.
Lt. Gov. — Joanell Dyrstad, IR, $59,981.
Sec. of State — Joan Anderson Growe, DFL, $59,981.
Atty. Gen. — Hubert H. Humphrey 3d, DFL, $85,194.
Treasurer — Michael McGrath, DFL, $59,981.
Auditor — Mark Dayton, IR, $65,437.

Legislature: meets for a total of 120 days within every 2 years at St. Paul. Members receive $27,979 per year, plus expense allowance during session.
Senate — DFL, 46; IR, 21. Total, 67.
House — DFL., 79; IR, 55. Total, 134.
(DFL means Democratic-Farmer-Labor. IR means Independent Republican.)

Mississippi

Governor — Ray Mabus, D., $75,600.
Lt. Gov. — Brad Dye, D., $40,800.
Sec. of State — Dick Molpus, D., $54,000.
Atty. Gen. — Mike Moore, D., $61,200.
Treasurer — Marshall Bennett, D., $54,000.
Legislature: meets annually in January at Jackson. Members receive $10,100 per regular session plus travel allowance, and $500 per month while not in session.
Senate — Dem., 43; Rep., 9. Total, 52.
House — Dem., 103; Rep., 19. Total, 122.

Missouri

Governor — John D. Ashcroft, R., $88,541.
Lt. Gov. — Mel Carnahan, D., $53,277.
Sec. of State — Roy D. Blunt, R., $70,909.
Atty. Gen. — William L. Webster, R., $76,786.
Treasurer — Wendell Bailey, R., $70,909.
State Auditor — Margaret Kelly, R., $70,909.
General Assembly: meets annually in Jefferson City on the first Wednesday after first Monday in January. Members receive $22,414 annually.
Senate — Dem., 23; Rep., 11. Total, 34.
House — Dem., 98; Rep., 65. Total, 163.

Montana

Governor — Stan Stephens, R., $53,006.
Lt. Gov. — Alan Kolstad, R., $37,970.
Sec. of State — Mike Cooney, D., $35,030.
Atty. Gen. — Marc Racicot, R., $48,345.
Legislative Assembly: meets odd years in January at Helena. Members receive $59.12 per legislative day plus $50 per day for expenses while in session.
Senate — Dem., 29; Rep., 21. Total, 50.
House — Dem., 61; Rep., 39. Total, 100.

Nebraska

Governor — Ben Nelson, D., $65,000.
Lt. Gov. — Maxine Moul, D., $47,000.
Sec. of State — Allen J. Beermann, R., $52,000.
Atty. Gen. — Don Stenberg, R., $64,500.
Treasurer — Dawn Rockey, D., $49,500.
Legislature: meets annually in January at Lincoln. Members receive salary of $12,000 annually plus travelling expenses.
Unicameral body composed of 49 members who are elected on a nonpartisan ballot and are classed as senators.

Nevada

Governor — Robert Miller, D., $90,000.
Lt. Gov. — Sue Wagner, R., $20,000.
Sec. of State — Cheryl Lau, R., $62,500.
Comptroller — Darrel Daines, R., $62,500.
Atty. Gen. — Frankie Sue Del Papa, D., $85,000.
Treasurer — Bob Seale, R., $62,500.
Legislature: meets odd years in January at Carson City. Members receive $130 per day for 60 days (20 days for special sessions).
Senate — Dem., 11; Rep., 10. Total, 21.
Assembly — Dem., 22; Rep., 20. Total, 42.

New Hampshire

Governor — Judd Gregg, R., $72,146.
Sec. of State — William M. Gardner, D., $57,533.
Atty. Gen. — John Arnold, $64,405.
Treasurer — Georgie A. Thomas, R., $57,533.
General Court (Legislature): meets every year in January at Concord. Members receive $200; presiding officers $250.
Senate — Dem., 11; Rep., 13. Total, 24.
House — Rep., 269; Dem., 127., ind. 2, vac. 2; Total, 400.

New Jersey

Governor — James J. Florio, D., $85,000.
Sec. of State — Joan Haberle, D., $95,000.
Atty. Gen. — Robert J. Del Tuso, D., $95,000.
Treasurer — Douglas C. Berman, D., $95,000.
Legislature: meets throughout the year at Trenton. Members receive $25,000 per year, except president of Senate and speaker of Assembly who receive 1/3 more.
Senate — Dem., 23; Rep., 17. Total, 40.
Assembly — Dem., 43; Rep. 36, 1 vacancy; Total, 80.

New Mexico

Governor — Bruce King, D., $90,000.
Lt. Gov. — Casey Luna, D., $65,000.
Sec. of State — Stephanie Gonzales, D., $65,000.
Atty. Gen. — Tom Udall, D., $72,500.
Treasurer — David King, D., $65,000.
Legislature: meets on the 3d Tuesday in January at Santa Fe; odd years for 60 days, even years for 30 days. Members receive $75 per day while in session.
Senate — Dem., 26; Rep., 16. Total, 42.
House — Dem., 45; Rep., 25. Total, 70.

New York

Governor — Mario M. Cuomo, D., $130,000.
Lt. Gov. — Stan Lundine, D., $110,000.
Sec. of State — Gail S. Shaffer, D., $87,338.
Comptroller — Edward V. Regan, R., $110,000.
Atty. Gen. — Robert Abrams, D., $110,000.
Legislature: meets annually in January at Albany. Members receive $57,500 per year.
Senate — Dem., 27; Rep., 34. Total, 61.
Assembly — Dem., 92; Rep., 58. Total, 150.

North Carolina

Governor — James G. Martin, R., $123,300 plus $11,500 per year expenses.
Lt. Gov. — James C. Gardner, R., $75,252 plus expenses.
Sec. of State — Rufus L. Edmisten, D., $75,252.
Atty. Gen. — Lacy Thornberg, D., $75,252.
Treasurer — Harlan E. Boyles, D., $75,252.
General Assembly: meets odd years in January at Raleigh. Members receive $11,124 annual salary and $5,500 annual expense allowance, plus $81 per diem subsistence and travel allowance while in session.
Senate — Dem., 37; Rep., 13. Total, 50.
House — Dem., 74; Rep., 46. Total, 120.

North Dakota

Governor — George A. Sinner, D., $65,200.
Lt. Gov. — Lloyd B. Omdahl, D., $53,500.
Sec. of State — Jim Kusler, D., $49,300.
Atty. Gen. — Nicholas Spaeth, D., $55,700.
Treasurer — Robert Hanson, D., $49,300.
Legislative Assembly: meets odd years in January at Bismarck. Members receive $90 per day expenses during session and $180 per month when not in session.
Senate — Dem., 27; Rep., 26. Total, 53.
House — Dem., 48; Rep., 58. Total, 106.

Ohio

Governor — George Voinovich, R., $100,000.
Lt. Gov. — Michael DeWine, R., $51,710.
Sec. of State — Bob Taft, R., $73,872.
Atty. Gen. — Lee Fisher, D., $73,872.
Treasurer — Mary Ellen Withrow, D., $73,872.
Auditor — Thomas E. Ferguson, D., $73,872.
General Assembly: meets odd years at Columbus on first Monday in January; no limit on session. Members receive $38,482 per annum.
Senate — Dem., 12; Rep., 21. Total, 33.
House — Dem., 61; Rep., 38. Total, 99.

Oklahoma

Governor — David Walters, D., $70,000.
Lt. Gov. — Jack Mildren, D., $40,000.
Sec. of State — John Kennedy, D., $37,500.
Atty. Gen. — Robert H. Henry, D., $55,000.
Treasurer — Claudette Henry, R., $50,000.
Auditor — Clifton Scott, D., $44,800.
Legislature: meets annually in May at Oklahoma City. Members receive $32,000 annually.
Senate — Dem., 37; Rep., 11. Total, 48.
House — Dem., 69; Rep., 32. Total, 101.

Oregon

Governor — Barbara Roberts, D., $80,000.
Sec. of State — Phil Keisling, D., $61,500.
Atty. Gen. — David B. Frohnmayer, D., $66,000.
Treasurer — Tony Meeker, R., $61,500.
Legislative Assembly: meets odd years in January at Salem. Members receive $1,029 monthly and $73 expenses per day both during & out of session.
Senate — Dem., 20; Rep. 10. Total, 30.
House — Dem., 32; Rep., 28. Total, 60.

Pennsylvania

Governor — Robert Casey, D., $105,000.
Lt. Gov. — Mark S. Singel, D., $83,000.
Sec. of the Commonwealth — Christopher Lewis, D., $72,000.

Atty. Gen. — Ernest R. Preate, R., $84,000.
Treasurer — Catherine Baker Knoll, D., $84,000.
General Assembly — convenes annually in January at Harrisburg. Members receive $47,000 per year plus expenses.
Senate — Dem., 24; Rep., 26. Total, 50.
House — Dem., 107; Rep., 96. Total, 203.

Rhode Island

Governor — Bruce Sundlun, D., $69,000.
Lt. Gov. — Roger N. Begin, D., $52,000.
Sec. of State — Kathleen S. Connell, D., $52,000.
Atty. Gen. — James E. O'Neil, D., $55,000.
Treasurer — Anthony J. Solomon, D., $52,000.
General Assembly: meets annually in January at Providence. Members receive $5 per day for 60 days, and travel allowance of 8c per mile.
Senate — Dem., 45; Rep., 5. Total, 50.
House — Dem., 89; Rep., 11. Total, 100.

South Carolina

Governor — Carroll A. Campbell Jr.; R., $98,000.
Lt. Gov. — Nick Theodore, D., $43,000.
Sec. of State — Jim Miles, R., $85,000.
Comptroller Gen. — Earle E. Morris Jr., D., $85,000.
Atty. Gen. — T.T. Medlock, D., $85,000.
Treasurer — G.L. Patterson Jr., D., $85,000.
General Assembly: meets annually in January at Columbia. Members receive $10,400 per year and expense allowance of $79 per day, plus travel and postage allowance.
Senate — Dem., 34; Rep., 11, 1 vac. Total, 46.
House — Dem. 74; Rep., 42; 1 ind., 7 vac. Total, 124.

South Dakota

Governor — George S. Mickelson, R., $60,819.
Lt. Gov. — Walter Miller, R., $52,915.
Sec. of State — Joyce Hazeltine, R., $41,308.
Treasurer — G. Homer Harding, R., $41,308.
Atty. Gen. — Mark Bennett, R., $51,625.
Auditor — Vernon Larson, R., $41,308.
Legislature: meets annually in January at Pierre. Members receive $4,267 for 40-day session in odd-numbered years, and $3,733 for 35-day session in even-numbered years, plus $75 per legislative day.
Senate — Dem., 17; Rep., 18. Total, 35.
House — Dem., 25. Rep., 45. Total, 70.

Tennessee

Governor — Ned Ray McWherter, D., $85,000.
Lt. Gov. — John S. Wilder, D., $49,500.
Sec. of State — Bryant Millsaps, D., $73,140.
Comptroller — William Snodgrass, D., $73,140.
Atty. Gen. — Charles W. Burson, D., $85,500.
General Assembly: meets annually in January at Nashville. Members receive $16,500 yearly plus $78.00 per diem plus office expenses.
Senate — Dem., 20; Rep., 13. Total, 33.
House — Dem., 57; Rep., 42. Total, 99.

Texas

Governor — Ann Richards, D., $93,342.
Lt. Gov. — Bob Bullock, D., $7,200.
Sec. of State — John Hannah, D., $64,890.
Comptroller — John Sharp, D., $74,698.
Atty. Gen. — Dan Morales, D., $74,698.
Treasurer — Kay Bailey Hutchison, R., $74,698.
Legislature: meets odd years in January at Austin. Members receive annual salary not exceeding $7,200, per diem while in session, and travel allowance.
Senate — Dem., 24; Rep., 7. Total, 31.
House — Dem., 93; Rep., 150. Total, 150.

Utah

Governor — Norman Bangerter, R., $70,000.
Lt. Gov. — W. Val Oveson, R., $52,500.
Atty. Gen. — R. Paul Van Dam, D., $56,000.
Treasurer — Edward T. Alter, D., $53,000.
Legislature: convenes for 45 days on 2d Monday in January each year; members receive $25 per day, $15 daily expenses, and mileage.
Senate — Dem., 10; Rep., 19. Total, 29.
House — Dem., 31; Rep., 44. Total, 75.

Vermont

Governor — Howard Dean, D., $80,730.
Lt. Gov. — vacant, $33,655.
Sec. of State — James H. Douglas, R., $50,800.
Atty. Gen. — Jeffrey Amestoy, R., $61,025.
Treasurer — Paul W. Ruse Jr., D., $50,800.
Auditor of Accounts — Alexander V. Acebo, R., $50,800.
General Assembly: meets odd years in January at Montpelier. Members receive $480 per week while in session plus $95 per day for special session, plus specified expenses.
Senate — Dem., 15; Rep., 15. Total, 30.
House — Dem., 73; Rep., 75., ind. 2. Total, 150.

Virginia

Governor — L. Douglas Wilder, D., $108,000.
Lt. Gov. — Donald S. Beyer Jr., $29,550.
Atty. Gen. — Mary Sue Terry, D., $95,000.
Sec. of the Commonwealth — Pamela Womack, D., $56,603.
Treasurer — Eddie N. Moore Jr., $85,881.
General Assembly: meets annually in January at Richmond. Members receive $18,000 annually plus expense and mileage allowances.
Senate — Dem., 30; Rep., 10. Total, 40.
House — Dem., 59; Rep., 39; Ind., 2. Total, 100.

Washington

Governor — Booth Gardner, D., $96,700.
Lt. Gov. — Joel Pritchard, D., $51,100.
Sec. of State — Ralph Munro, R., $52,600.
Atty. Gen. — Ken Eikenberry, R., $75,700.
Treasurer — Daniel K. Grimm, D., $65,000.
Legislature: meets annually in January at Olympia. Members receive $17,900 annually plus per diem of $66 per diem and 24¢ per mile while in session, and $66 per diem for attending meetings during interim.
Senate — Dem., 24; Rep., 25. Total, 49.
House — Dem., 63; Rep., 35. Total, 98.

West Virginia

Governor — Gaston Caperton, D., $72,000.
Sec. of State — Ken Hechler, D., $43,200.
Atty. Gen. — Mario Palumbo, D., $50,400.
Treasurer — Larrie Bailey, D., $50,400.
Comm. of Agric. — Cleve Benedict, R., $46,800.
Auditor — Glen B. Gainer Jr., D., $46,800.
Legislature: meets annually in January at Charleston. Members receive $6,500.
Senate — Dem., 33; Rep., 1. Total, 34.
House — Dem., 74; Rep., 26. Total, 100.

Wisconsin

Governor — Tommy G. Thompson, R., $86,149.
Lt. Gov. — Scott McCallum, R., $46,360.
Sec, of State — Douglas La Follette, D., $42,089.
Treasurer — Cathy S. Zeuske, R., $42,089.
Atty. Gen. — James E. Doyle, D., $73,930.
Superintendent of Public Instruction — Herbert J. Grover, $66,536.
Legislature: meets in January at Madison. Members receive $31,236 annually plus $55 per day expenses.
Senate — Dem., 18; Rep., 15. Total, 33.
Assembly — Dem., 57; Rep., 42. Total, 99.

Wyoming

Governor — Mike Sullivan, D., $70,000.
Sec. of State — Kathy Karpan, D., $52,500.
Atty. Gen. — Joseph Meyer, $52,500.
Treasurer — Stan Smith, R., $52,500.
Auditor — Dave Ferrari, R., $52,500.
Legislature: meets odd years in January, even years in February, at Cheyenne. Members receive $75 per day while in session, plus $60 per day for expenses.
Senate — Dem., 10; Rep., 20. Total, 30.
House — Dem., 22; Rep. 42. Total, 64.

Puerto Rico

Governor — Rafael Hernández-Colón.
Legislature: composed of a Senate of 27 members and a House of Representatives of 53 members. Majority of the members of both chambers belongs to the Popular Democratic Party. They meet annually on the 2d Monday in January at San Juan.

U.S. Government Independent Agencies

Source: National Archives & Records Administration

Address: Washington, DC. Location and ZIP codes of agencies in parentheses; as of mid-1991.

ACTION — Jane A. Kenny, dir. (1100 Vermont Ave., NW, 20525).

Administrative Conference of the United States — Marshall J. Breger, chmn. (2120 L St. NW, 20037).

African Development Foundation — Gregory Robeson Smith, pres. (1400 Eye St. NW, 20005).

Central Intelligence Agency — vacant, dir. (Wash., DC 20505).

Commission on Civil Rights — Arthur A. Fletcher, chmn. (1121 Vermont Ave. NW, 20425).

Commodity Futures Trading Commission — Wendy L. Gramm, chmn. (2033 K St. NW, 20581).

Consumer Product Safety Commission — Jacquline Jones-Smith, chmn. (5401 Westbard Ave., Bethesda, MD 20207).

Environmental Protection Agency — William K. Reilly, adm. (401 M St., SW, 20460).

Equal Employment Opportunity Commission — Evan J. Kemp. Jr., chmn. (1801 L St. NW., 20507).

Export-Import Bank of the United States — John D. Macomber, pres. and chmn. (811 Vermont Ave. NW 20571).

Farm Credit Administration — Harold B. Steele, chmn., Federal Farm Credit Board (1501 Farm Credit Drive, McLean, VA 22102).

Federal Communications Commission — Alfred C. Sikes, chmn. (1919 M St. NW, 20554).

Federal Deposit Insurance Corporation — L. William Seidman, chmn. (550 17th St. NW, 20429).

Federal Election Commission — John Warren McGarry, chmn. (999 E. St. NW, 20463).

Federal Emergency Management Agency — Wallace E. Stickney, dir. (500 C St. SW, 20472).

Federal Housing Finance Board — Daniel F. Evans Jr., chmn. (1777 F St. NW., 20006).

Federal Labor Relations Authority — Jean McKee, chmn. (500 C St. SW, 20424).

Federal Maritime Commission — Christopher L. Koch, chmn. (1100 L St. NW 20573).

Federal Mediation and Conciliation Service — Bernard E. DeLury, dir. (2100 K St. NW, 20427).

Federal Mine Safety & Health Review Commission — Ford B. Ford, chmn. (1730 K St. NW, 20006).

Federal Reserve System — Chairman, board of governors: Alan Greenspan. (20th St. & Constitution Ave. NW, 20551).

Federal Retirement Thrift Investment Board — Roger W. Mehle, chmn. (805 15th St. NW, 20005).

Federal Trade Commission — Janet D. Steiger, chmn. (Pennsylvania Ave. at 6th St. NW, 20580).

General Accounting Office — Comptroller General of the U.S.; Charles A. Bowsher (441 G St. NW, 20548).

General Services Administration — Richard G. Austin, act. adm. (18th & F Sts. NW, 20405).

Government Printing Office — Public printer: Robert W. Houk. (North Capitol and H Sts. NW, 20401).

Inter-American Foundation — Frank D. Yturria, chmn. (1515 Wilson Blvd., Rosslyn, VA 22209).

Interstate Commerce Commission — Edward J. Philbin, chmn. (12th St. & Constitution Ave. NW, 20423).

Library of Congress — James H. Billington, librarian of Congress (101 Independence Ave. SE, 20540).

Merit Systems Protection Board — Daniel R. Levinson, chmn. (1120 Vermont Ave. NW, 20419).

National Aeronautics and Space Administration — Richard H. Truly, adm. (600 Independence Ave., SW 20546).

National Archives & Records Administration — Don W. Wilson archivist (7th & Pennsylvania Ave. NW, 20408).

National Credit Union Administration — Roger W. Jepsen, chmn. (1776 G St. NW, 20456).

National Foundation on the Arts and the Humanities — John E. Frohnmayer, (arts) 1100 Pennsylvania Ave. NW, 20506; Lynne V. Cheney, chmn. (humanities) same address. Institute of Museum Services: Susannah S. Kent, dir., same address.

National Labor Relations Board — James M. Stephens, chmn. (1717 Pennsylvania Ave. NW, 20570).

National Mediation Board — Patrick J. Cleary, chmn. (1425 K St. NW, 20572).

National Railroad Passenger Corporation (Amtrak) — W. Graham Claytor Jr., chmn. (60 Massachusetts Ave. NE, 20002).

National Science Foundation — Mary L. Good, chmn., National Science Board (1800 G St. NW, 20550).

National Transportation Safety Board — James L. Kolstad, chmn. (800 Independence Ave. SW, 20594).

Nuclear Regulatory Commission — Kenneth M. Carr, chmn. (1717 H St. NW, 20555).

Occupational Safety and Health Review Commission — Edwin G. Foulke Jr., chmn. (1825 K St. NW, 20006).

Office of Personnel Management — Constance B. Newman, dir., (1900 E St. NW, 20415).

Peace Corps — Paul D. Coverdell, dir. (1990 K St. NW, 20526).

Postal Rate Commission — George W. Haley, chmn. (1333 H. St. NW, 20268-0001).

Railroad Retirement Board — Glen L. Bower, chmn. (2000 L. St. NW, 20036), Main Office (844 Rush St., Chicago, IL 60611).

Securities and Exchange Commission — Richard C. Breeden, chmn. (450 5th St. NW, 20549).

Selective Service System — Robert W. Gambino, dir. (1023 31st St. NW, 20435).

Small Business Administration — Patricia F. Saiki, adm. (409 Third St. SW, 20416).

Smithsonian Institution — Robert McC. Adams, secy. (1000 Jefferson Dr. SW, 20560).

Tennessee Valley Authority — Chairman, board of directors: Marvin Runyon. (400 W. Summit Hill Dr., Knoxville, TN 37902 and Room 300, 412 1st St. SE, Washington, DC 20444).

United States Arms Control & Disarmament Agency — Ronald F. Lehman 2d, dir. (320 21st St. NW 20451).

United States Information Agency — Eugene P. Kopp, act. dir. (301 4th St. SW, 20547).

United States International Development Cooperation Agency — Ronald W. Roskens, act. dir. (320 21st St. NW 20523).

United States International Trade Commission — (vacancy), chmn. (500 E St. NW, 20436).

United States Postal Service — Anthony M. Frank, postmaster general (475 L'Enfant Plaza SW, 20260).

Governors of States and Possessions

(as of mid-1991)

State	Capital	Governor	Party	Term years	Term expires	Annual salary
Alabama	Montgomery	Guy Hunt	Rep.	4	Jan. 1995	$87,913
Alaska	Juneau	Walter Hickel	Ind.	4	Dec. 1994	81,648
Arizona	Phoenix	Fife Symington	Rep.	4	Jan. 1995	75,000

State	Capital	Governor	Party	Term	Date	Salary
Arkansas	Little Rock	Bill Clinton	Dem.	4	Jan. 1995	35,000
California	Sacramento	Pete Wilson	Rep.	4	Jan. 1995	120,000
Colorado	Denver	Roy Romer	Dem.	4	Jan. 1995	70,000
Connecticut	Hartford	Lowell Weicker	Ind.	4	Jan. 1995	78,000
Delaware	Dover	Michael N. Castle	Rep.	4	Jan. 1993	80,000
Florida	Tallahassee	Lawton Chiles	Dem.	4	Jan. 1995	103,909
Georgia	Atlanta	Zell Miller	Dem.	4	Jan. 1995	91,092
Hawaii	Honolulu	John Waihee	Dem.	4	Dec. 1994	94,780
Idaho	Boise	Cecil D. Andrus	Dem.	4	Jan. 1995	75,000
Illinois	Springfield	Jim Edgar	Rep.	4	Jan. 1995	97,370
Indiana	Indianapolis	Evan Bayh	Dem.	4	Jan. 1993	77,200
Iowa	Des Moines	Terry E. Branstad	Rep.	4	Jan. 1995	76,900
Kansas	Topeka	Joan Finney	Dem.	4	Jan. 1995	74,235
Kentucky	Frankfort	Wallace G. Wilkinson	Dem.	4	Dec. 1991	69,730
Louisiana	Baton Rouge	Charles "Buddy" Roemer	Rep.	4	May 1992	73,440
Maine	Augusta	John McKernan Jr.	Rep.	4	Jan. 1995	70,000
Maryland	Annapolis	William Donald Schaefer	Dem.	4	Jan. 1995	120,000
Massachusetts	Boston	William Weld	Rep.	4	Jan. 1995	75,000
Michigan	Lansing	John Engler	Rep.	4	Jan. 1995	106,700
Minnesota	St. Paul	Arne Carlson	Rep.	4	Jan. 1995	109,053
Mississippi	Jackson	Ray Mabus	Dem.	4	Jan. 1992	75,600
Missouri	Jefferson City	John D. Ashcroft	Rep.	4	Jan. 1993	88,541
Montana	Helena	Stan Stephens	Rep.	4	Jan. 1993	53,006
Nebraska	Lincoln	Ben Nelson	Dem.	4	Jan. 1995	65,000
Nevada	Carson City	Robert Miller	Dem.	4	Jan. 1995	90,000
New Hampshire	Concord	Judd Gregg	Rep.	2	Jan. 1993	72,146
New Jersey	Trenton	James Florio	Dem.	4	Jan. 1994	85,000
New Mexico	Santa Fe	Bruce King	Dem.	4	Jan. 1995	90,000
New York	Albany	Mario M. Cuomo	Dem.	4	Jan. 1995	130,000
North Carolina	Raleigh	James G. Martin	Rep.	4	Jan. 1993	123,300
North Dakota	Bismarck	George A. Sinner	Dem.	4	Jan. 1993	65,200
Ohio	Columbus	George Voinovich	Rep.	4	Jan. 1995	100,000
Oklahoma	Oklahoma City	David Walters	Dem.	4	Jan. 1995	70,000
Oregon	Salem	Barbara Roberts	Dem.	4	Jan. 1995	80,000
Pennsylvania	Harrisburg	Robert Casey	Dem.	4	Jan. 1995	105,000
Rhode Island	Providence	Bruce Sundlun	Dem.	2	Jan. 1993	69,000
South Carolina	Columbia	Carroll A. Campbell Jr.	Rep.	4	Jan. 1995	98,000
South Dakota	Pierre	George S. Mickelson	Rep.	4	Jan. 1995	60,819
Tennessee	Nashville	Ned Ray McWherter	Dem.	4	Jan. 1995	85,000
Texas	Austin	Ann Richards	Dem.	4	Jan. 1995	93,342
Utah	Salt Lake City	Norman Bangerter	Rep.	4	Jan. 1993	70,000
Vermont	Montpelier	Howard Dean	Dem.	2	Jan. 1993	80,730
Virginia	Richmond	L. Douglas Wilder	Dem.	4	Jan. 1994	108,000
Washington	Olympia	Booth Gardner	Dem.	4	Jan. 1993	96,700
West Virginia	Charleston	Gaston Caperton	Dem.	4	Jan. 1993	72,000
Wisconsin	Madison	Tommy G. Thompson	Rep.	4	Jan. 1995	86,149
Wyoming	Cheyenne	Mike Sullivan	Dem.	4	Jan. 1995	70,000
Puerto Rico	San Juan	Rafael Hernandez Colón	P.D.	4	Jan. 1993	—

Mayors and City Managers of Selected U.S. Cities

As of mid-1991

* Asterisk before name denotes city manager. All others are mayors. For mayors, dates are those of next election; for city managers, they are dates of appointment.

D, Democrat; R, Republican; N-P, Non-Partisan

City	Name	Term	City	Name	Term
Abilene, Tex.	Gary McCaleb, N-P	1993, May.	Anderson, S.C.	*Richard Burnette	1976, Sept.
Abington, Pa.	*Albert Herrmann	1978, May	Ann Arbor, Mich.	*vacant	
Akron, Oh.	D.L. Plusquellic, D	1991, Nov.	Appleton, Wis.	Dorothy Johnson, N-P	1992, Apr.
Alameda, Cal.	E. William Withrow, R.	1995, Apr.	Arcadia, Cal.	*George J. Watts	1981, Feb.
Albany, Ga.	*Roy Lane	1991, Mar.	Arlington, Mass.	*Donald R. Marquis	1966, Nov.
Albany, N.Y.	Thomas M. Whalen,3d,D	1993, Nov.	Arlington, Tex.	*George Campbell	1991, Feb.
Albuquerque, N.M.	Louis Saavedra, N-P	1993, Nov.	Arlington Hts., Ill.	William Maki, N-P	1993, Apr.
Alexandria, La.	Edward Randolph Jr., D	1994, Oct.	Arvada, Col.	*Neal G. Berlin	1986, Mar.
Alexandria, Va.	*Vola Lawson	1985, Sept.	Asheville, N.C.	*Douglas Bean	1986, Apr.
Alhambra, Cal.	*Kevin J. Murphy	1983, May	Athens, Ga.	Gwen O'Looney, D	1995, Nov.
Allentown, Pa.	Joseph S. Daddona, D	1993, Nov.	Atlanta, Ga.	Maynard Jackson, D	1993, Oct.
Altoona, Pa.	Alan Mikula, D	1991, Nov.	Atlantic City, N.J.	Jim Whelan, N-P.	1994, May
Amarillo, Tex.	*John Ward	1983, June	Augusta, Ga.	Charles Devaney, D.	1993, Nov.
Ames, Ia.	*Steven L. Schainker	1982, Oct.	Aurora, Col.	*James Griesemer	1984, Jan.
Anaheim, Cal.	*James Roth	1990, May	Aurora, Ill.	David L. Pierce, N-P.	1993, Apr.
Anchorage, Alas.	Tom Fink, R	1994, Apr.	Austin, Tex.	*Camille Barnett.	1989, Mar.
Anderson, Ind.	J. Mark Lawler, D	1991, Nov.	Bakersfield, Cal.	*J. Dale Hawley	1988, Jan.

City	Name	Term
Baldwin Park, Cal.	*Donald Penman	1990, Jan.
Baltimore, Md.	Kurt Schmoke, D	1991, Nov.
Baton Rouge, La.	Tom Ed McHugh, D	1992, Oct.
Battle Creek, Mich.	*Rance L. Leaders	1988, June
Bayonne, N.J.	Richard Rutkowski, N-P	1994, May
Baytown, Tex.	*Bobby Rountree	1989, May
Beaumont, Tex.	*Ray A. Riley	1989, Feb.
Belleville, Ill.	Richard Brauer, N-P	1993, Apr.
Bellevue, Wash.	*Phillip Kushlan	1985, Feb.
Bellflower, Cal.	*Jack Simpson	1980, July
Berkeley, Cal.	*Michael Brown	1990, Jan.
Bethlehem, Pa.	Kenneth Smith, R.	1993, Nov.
Beverly Hills, Cal.	*Edward Kreins	1979, Oct.
Billings, Mont.	*Alan Tandy	1985, May
Biloxi, Miss.	Peter Halat, D	1993, May
Binghamton, N.Y.	Juanita M. Crabb, D	1993, Nov.
Birmingham, Ala.	Richard Arrington Jr., D.	1991, Oct.
Bismarck, N.D.	Bill Sorensen, N-P	1994, Apr.
Bloomfield, N.J.	James Gasparini, D	1993, Nov.
Bloomington, Ill.	Jesse Smart, D	1993, Apr.
Bloomington, Ind.	Tomilea Allison, D	1991, Nov.
Bloomington, Minn.	*Mark Bernhardson	1991, May
Boca Raton, Fla.	Emil Danciu, N-P	1995, Mar.
Boise, Ida.	Dirk Kempthorne, R	1993, Nov.
Boston, Mass.	Raymond L. Flynn, D	1991 Nov.
Boulder, Col.	*Joseph deRaines.	1989, Apr.
Bridgeport, Conn.	Mary Moran, R.	1991, Nov.
Bristol, Conn.	William Stortz, D.	1991, Nov.
Brockton, Mass.	Carl Pitaro, D	1991, Nov.
Brooklyn Park, Minn.	*Craig R. Rapp	1989, Nov.
Brownsville, Tex.	*Steve Fitzgibbons	1987, Jan.
Bryan, Tex.	*Ernest R. Clark.	1979, Feb.
Buena Park, Cal.	*Kevin O'Rourke	1985, Nov.
Buffalo, N.Y.	James D. Griffin, D	1993, Nov.
Burbank, Cal.	*Bud Ovrom	1985, June
Burlington, Vt.	Peter Clavelle, N-P	1995, Mar.
Calumet City, Ill.	Robert C. Stefaniak, D	1993, Apr.
Cambridge, Mass.	*Robert Healy.	1981, July
Camden, N.J.	Aaron Thompson, D.	1993, May
Canton, Oh.	Sam Purses, D.	1991, Nov.
Carlsbad, Cal.	*Ray Patchett	1987, Sept.
Carson, Cal.	*Jack Smith	1988, Dec.
Casper, Wyo.	*Thomas Forslund	1988, June
Cedar Rapids, Ia.	Donald Canney, N-P	1991, Nov.
Champaign, Ill.	*Steven C. Carter.	1985, Feb.
Charleston, S.C.	Joseph P. Riley Jr., D.	1991, Nov.
Charleston, W. Va.	Kent S. Hall, R.	1995, Apr.
Charlotte, N.C.	Sue Myrick, R	1991, Nov.
Charlottesville, Va.	*Cole Hendrix	1970, Jan.
Chattanooga, Tenn.	Gene Roberts, R	1993, Apr.
Chesapeake, Va.	*James W. Rein.	1987, Mar.
Chester, Pa.	Willie Mae James Leake, R	1991, Nov.
Cheyenne, Wyo.	Gary Schaeffer, R.	1992, Nov.
Chicago, Ill.	Richard M. Daley, D.	1995, Apr.
Chicopee, Mass.	Joseph Chessey, D	1991, Nov.
Chino, Cal.	*Richard Rowe	1985, Feb.
Chula Vista, Cal.	*John Goss	1983, Jan.
Cincinnati, Oh.	*Gerald Newfarmer	1990, Sept.
Clearwater, Fla.	*Michael Wright	1991, Mar.
Cleveland, Oh.	Michael Wight, N-P.	1993, Nov.
Cleveland Hgts., Oh.	*Robert Downey.	1985, Jan.
Clifton, N.J.	*Roger Kemp	1987, Nov.
Col. Spgs., Col.	*Marty Zickefoose.	1990, May
Columbia, Mo.	*Raymond A. Beck	1985, Aug.
Columbia, S.C.	*Miles Hadley	1989, Dec.
Columbus, Ga.	Frank Martin, D	1994, Nov.
Columbus, Oh.	Dana Rinehart, R	1991, Nov.
Commerce, Cal.	*Robert Hinderliter	1973, Aug.
Compton, Cal.	*Howard Caldwell.	1989, June
Concord, Cal.	*Rita Hardin	1991, June
Coon Rapids., Minn.	*Richard Thistle	1979, July
Coral Gables, Fla.	*H.C. Eads Jr.	1988, May
Corona, Cal.	*William Garrett	1989, Dec.
Corpus Christi, Tex.	*Juan Garza	1988, Apr.
Costa Mesa, Cal.	*Allan L. Roeder.	1985, Oct.
Council Bluffs, Ia.	Tom Hanafan, N-P	1993, Nov.
Covington, Ky.	*Greg Jarvis	1989, Nov.
Cranston, R.I.	Michael Traficante, R	1994, Nov.
Crystal, Minn.	*John Irving	1963, Jan.
Culver City, Cal.	*Dale Jones	1967, Sept.
Cuyahoga Falls, Oh.	Don L. Robart, R	1993, Nov.
Dallas, Tex.	*Jan Hart.	1990, Apr.
Daly City, Cal.	*David R. Rowe	1969, Sept.
Danbury, Conn.	Gene Eriquez, N-P	1991, Nov.
Danville, Va.	*Charles Church	1981, June
Davenport, Ia.	Thomas W. Hart, D	1991, Nov.
Dayton, Oh.	Richard Clay Dixon, D.	1993, Nov.
Daytona Bch., Fla.	*Howard D. Tipton	1978, Oct.
Dearborn, Mich.	Michael Guido, N-P	1993, Nov.
Dearborn Hts., Mich.	Lyle Van Houton, R	1993, Nov.
Decatur, Ill.	*James Bacon Jr.	1988, Oct.
Delray Beach, Fla.	*David Handen	1990, May
Denton, Tex.	*Larry Harrell	1986, Feb.
Denver, Col.	Wellington Webb, D	1995, May
Des Moines, Ia.	John Dorrian, D	1991, Nov.
Des Plaines, Ill.	Michael Albrecht, R	1993, Apr.
Detroit, Mich.	Coleman A. Young, N-P	1993, Nov.
Dotham, Ala.	*Don J. Marnon	1987, May
Downey, Cal.	*Gerald Caton	1989, Oct.
Dubuque, Ia.	*W. Kenneth Gearhart	1979, Aug.
Duluth, Minn.	John Fedo, N-P	1991, Nov.
Durham, N.C.	*Orville Powell.	1983, Mar.
E. Chicago, Ind.	Robert A. Pastrick, D	1991, Nov.
E. Hartford, Conn.	Susan Kniep, R.	1991, Nov.
E. Lansing, Mich.	Liz Schweitzer, N-P	1991, Nov.
E. Orange, N.J.	Cardell Cooper, D.	1993, Nov.
Eau Claire, Wis.	*Eric Anderson	1984, Jan.
Edina, Minn.	*Kenneth Rosland.	1977, Nov.
Edison, N.J.	Thomas Paterniti, D	1993, Nov.
Edmond, Okla.	*C. Max Speegle	1987, Sept.
El Cajon, Cal.	Joan Shoemaker, R.	1994, June
El Monte, Cal.	Don McMillen, N-P	1994, Apr.
El Paso, Tex.	William Tilney, N-P	1993, May
Elgin, Ill.	*Larry L. Rice	1989, Oct.
Elizabeth, N.J.	Thomas G. Dunn, D	1992, Nov.
Elkhart, Ind.	James Perron, D	1991, Nov.
Elyria, Oh.	Michael Keys, D	1991, Nov.
Enfield, Conn.	*Robert J. Mulready.	1983, Feb.
Enid, Okla.	*Jim Ferree	1990, May
Erie, Pa.	Joyce Savocchio, D	1994, Nov.
Escondido, Cal.	*Douglas Clark	1989, June
Euclid, Oh.	David Lynch, R	1991, Nov.
Eugene, Ore.	*Michael Gleason	1981, Jan.
Evanston, Ill.	*Eric Anderson	1991, June
Evansville, Ind.	Frank McDonald, D	1991, Nov.
Everett, Mass.	John McCarthy, D.	1991, Nov.
Everett, Wash.	Pete Kinch, N-P	1993, Nov.
Fairfield, Cal.	*Charles Long	1988, Sept.
Fall River, Mass.	Carlton Viveiros, N-P	1991, Nov.
Fargo, N.D.	Jon Lindgren, D	1994, Apr.
Farmington Hills, Mich.	*William M. Costick	1981, Jan.
Fayetteville, N.C.	*John P. Smith.	1981, Jan.
Fitchburg, Mass.	Jeffrey Bean, D	1991, Nov.
Flagstaff, Ariz.	*Frank Abeyta	1981, Jan.
Flint, Mich.	Matthew Collier, N-P	1991, Nov.
Florissant, Mo.	James J. Eagan, N-P	1995, Apr.
Fontana, Cal.	*Russell Carlsen	1991, Feb.
Ft. Collins, Col.	*Steven Burkett	1986, Apr.
Ft. Lauderdale, Fla.	*George Hanbury 2d	1990, Apr.
Ft. Lee, N.J.	Nicholas Corbiscello, R	1991, Nov.
Ft. Smith, Ark.	Ray Baker, N-P	1994, Dec.
Ft. Wayne, Ind.	Paul Helmke, R	1991, Nov.
Ft. Worth, Tex.	Kay Granger, N-P	1993, May
Fountain Valley, Cal.	*Judy Kelsey.	1984, May
Fremont, Cal.	*Charles Kent McClain .	1981, May
Fresno, Cal.	*Michael Bierman	1990, Nov.
Fullerton, Cal.	*William C. Winter .	1979, Oct.
Gadsden, Ala.	David Nolen, D.	1994, July
Gainesville, Fla.	*W.D. Higginbotham Jr..	1984, Sept.
Galveston, Tex.	*Douglas W. Matthews	1985, Mar.
Gardena, Cal.	*Kenneth Landau	1985, Apr.
Garden Grove, Cal.	*George Tindall	1988, June
Garland, Tex.	*James K. Spore	1985, Mar.
Gary, Ind.	Thomas Barnes, D	1991, Nov.
Gastonia, N.C.	*Gary Hicks	1973, Dec.
Glendale, Ariz.	*Martin Vanacour	1985, Mar.
Glendale, Cal.	*David Ramsay	1988, May
Grand Forks, N.D.	Michael Polovitz, D	1992, Apr.
Gr. Prairie, Tex.	*vacant	
Gr. Rapids, Mich.	*Kurt Kimball.	1987, Apr.
Great Falls, Mont.	*G. Allen Johnson .	1981, Jan.
Greeley, Col.	William Morton, N-P	1991, Nov.
Green Bay, Wis.	Samuel Halloin, N-P	1995, Apr.
Greenville, S.C.	*John Dullea	1971, Oct.
Greenwich, Conn.	John Margenot, D, first selectman	1991, Nov.
Groton, Conn.	Catherine Kolnaski, D.	1995, May
Gulfport, Miss.	Ken Combs, R.	1993, Apr.
Hamden, Conn.	John L. Carusone, D	1991, Nov.
Hamilton, Oh.	*Hal Shepherd	1989, Apr.
Hammond, Ind.	Thomas McDermott, R	1991, Nov.
Hampton, Va.	James Eason, D.	1992, May
Harlingen, Tex.	*Mike Perez	1989, July
Harrisburg, Pa.	Stephen Reed, D	1993, Nov.

City	Name	Term
Hartford, Conn.	Carrie Saxon Perry, D	1991, Nov.
Haverhill, Mass.	Theodore Pelosi, R	1991, Nov.
Hawthorne, Cal.	*James Mitsch.	1990, Dec.
Hayward, Cal.	*Louis Garcia	1989, Jan.
Henderson, Nev.	*Philip Speight.	1988, Aug.
Hesperia, Cal.	*Robert Rizzo	1988, July
High Point, N.C.	*H. Lewis Price	1983, July
Hollywood, Fla.	*vacant	
Holyoke, Mass.	Michael Dunn, D	1991, Nov.
Honolulu, Ha.	Frank Fasi, R	1992, Nov.
Houston, Tex.	Kathryn Whitmire, N-P	1991, Nov.
Huntington, W. Va.	Robert Nelson, D	1993, June
Huntington Beach, Cal.	*Michael Ubervaga	1990, Feb.
Huntsville, Ala.	Steve Hettinger, N-P	1992, Aug.
Idaho Falls, Ida.	Thomas Campbell, N-P.	1993, Nov.
Independence, Mo.	*L.C. Kaufman.	1990, Aug.
Indianapolis, Ind.	William Hudnut, R	1991, Nov.
Inglewood, Cal.	*Paul Eckles.	1975, Nov.
Iowa City, Ia.	*Stephen Atkins	1986, July
Irving, Tex.	*Jack Huffman.	1974, Jan.
Irvington, N.J.	Michael Steele, D	1994, May
Jackson, Mich.	*William P. Buchanan.	1985, Nov.
Jackson, Miss.	Kane Ditto, D.	1993, May
Jacksonville, Fla.	Ed Austin, D	1995, May
Janesville, Wis.	*Steven Sheiffer.	1987, May
Jersey City, N.J.	Gerald McCann, N-P	1993, May
Johnson City, Tenn.	*John G. Campbell	1984, June
Joliet, Ill.	*John M. Mezera.	1987, Jan.
Kalamazoo, Mich.	*James Holgersson.	1989, June
Kansas City, Kan.	*David Isabell	1985, June
Kansas City, Mo.	Emanuel Cleaver, D.	1995, Apr.
Kenner, La.	Aaron Broussard, N-P	1994, June
Kenosha, Wis.	Patrick Moran, N-P	1992, Apr.
Kettering, Oh.	Richard Hartmann, R.	1993, Nov.
Killeen, Tex.	*Daniel Hobbs	1990, Jan.
Knoxville, Tenn.	Victor Ashe, R	1991, Nov.
Kokomo, Ind.	Robert Sargent, D.	1991, Nov.
LaCrosse, Wis.	Patrick Zielke, N-P	1993, Apr.
La Habra, Cal.	*Lee Risner	1970, Nov.
La Mesa, Cal.	*David Wear.	1990, Apr.
La Mirada, Cal.	*Gary K. Sloan	1981, Apr.
Lafayette, Ind.	James Riehle, D.	1991, Nov.
Lafayette, La.	Dud Lastrapes, R	1992, Mar.
Lake Charles, La.	James Sudduth, D.	1993, Apr.
Lakeland, Fla.	*E.S. Strickland	1986, Feb.
Lakewood, Cal.	*Howard L. Chambers	1976, June
Lakewood, Col.	*Walter Kane	1991, Aug.
Lakewood, Oh.	David Harbarger, R	1991, Nov.
Lancaster, Pa.	Janice Stork, D.	1993, Nov.
Lansing, Mich.	Terry John McKane, N-P	1993, Nov.
Laredo, Tex.	*Marvin Townsend	1982, June
Largo, Fla.	*Stephen Bonczek	1988, July
Las Cruces, N.M.	*Dana Miller	1983, Feb.
Las Vegas, Nev.	Jan Laverty Jones, N-P	1995, June
Lauderhill, Fla.	Ilene Lieberman, D.	1992, Mar.
Lawrence, Kan.	*Mike Wildgen	1990, Apr.
Lawrence, Mass.	Kevin Sullivan, N-P	1993, Nov.
Lawton, Okla.	*Robert Hopkins.	1990, Jan.
Lexington, Ky.	Scotty Baesler, N-P	1993, Nov.
Lima, Oh.	David Berger, N-P	1993, Nov.
Lincoln, Neb.	Mike Johanns, R.	1995, May
Little Rock, Ark.	*Thomas Dalton	1986, June
Livermore, Cal.	*Leland Horner	1978, Oct.
Livonia, Mich.	Robert Bennett, N-P	1991, Nov.
Long Beach, Cal.	*James Hankla	1987, Mar.
Longmont, Col.	*Geoff Dolan.	1987, Jan.
Longview, Tex.	*C. Ray Jackson	1980, Apr.
Lorain, Oh.	Alex Olejko, D.	1991, Nov.
Los Angeles, Cal.	Thomas Bradley, N-P	1993, June
Louisville, Ky.	Jerry Abramson, D	1993, Nov.
Lowell, Mass.	*James Campbell	1987, Jan.
L. Merion, Pa.	*Thomas B. Fulweiler	1968, Jan.
Lubbock, Tex.	*Larry Cunningham	1976, Sept.
Lynchburg, Va.	*E. Allen Culverhouse	1979, June
Lynn, Mass.	Albert DiVirgilio, D.	1991, Nov.
Lynwood, Cal.	*Charles Gomez	1982, Mar.
Macon, Ga.	Lee Robinson, D.	1991, Nov.
Madison, Wis.	Paul Soglin, R	1995, Apr.
Malden, Mass.	James S. Conway, D	1991, Nov.
Manchester, N.H.	Ray Wieczorek, R.	1991, Nov.
Mansfield, Oh.	Edward Meehan, R	1991, Nov.
Marietta, Ga.	Joe Mack Wilson, D.	1993, Nov.
McAllen, Tex.	Othal Brand, R.	1993, Apr.
Medford, Mass.	Michael McGlynn, N-P	1991, Nov.
Medford, Ore.	*Harold Anderson.	1987, Sept.
Melbourne, Fla.	*Samuel Halter	1978, July
Memphis, Tenn.	Richard C. Hackett, N-P	1991, Oct.
Mentor, Oh.	*Julian Suso	1990, Mar.
Meriden, Conn.	*Michael Aldi.	1988, Jan.
Meridian, Miss.	Jimmy Kemp, R	1993, June
Mesa, Ariz.	*C.K. Luster	1979, June
Mesquite, Tex.	*James Prugel.	1987, Dec.
Miami, Fla.	Xavier Suarez, N-P	1993, Nov.
Miami Beach, Fla.	*vacant	
Middletown, Oh.	*William Klosterman	1988, July
Midland, Tex.	Carroll M. Thomas, N-P	1992, May
Midwest City, Okla.	*Charles Johnson	1984, Nov.
Milford, Conn.	Frederick Lisman, R.	1991, Nov.
Milwaukee, Wis.	John Norquist, D.	1992, Apr.
Minneapolis, Minn.	Donald Fraser, D	1993, Nov.
Minnetonka, Minn.	*James F. Miller.	1980, Jan.
Mobile, Ala.	Michael Dow, N-P	1993, Aug.
Modesto, Cal.	*Garth Lipsky	1974, Jan.
Monroe, La.	Robert Powell, D	1992, Apr.
Montclair, N.J.	*Bertrand Kendall	1980, Sept.
Montebello, Cal.	*Richard Torres	1989, May
Monterey Park, Cal.	*Mark Lewis	1988, July
Montgomery, Ala.	Emory Folmar, R	1991, Nov.
Mt. Prospect, Ill.	*John F. Dixon.	1987, Mar.
Mt. Vernon, N.Y.	Roland Blackwood, D.	1991, Nov.
Mountain View, Cal.	*Bruce Liedstrand.	1976, June
Muncie, Ind.	James Carey, D.	1991, Nov.
Muskogee, Okla.	*Walter Beckham	1984, Feb.
Napa, Cal.	*Patricia Thompson	1989, Oct.
Naperville, Ill.	Samuel McCrane, N-P	1995, Apr.
Nashua, N.H.	James Donchess, N-P	1991, Nov.
Nashville, Tenn.	Bill Boner, D	1991, Aug.
National City, Cal.	*Tom McCabe.	1979, Mar.
New Bedford, Mass.	John Bullard, D	1991, Nov.
New Britain, Conn.	Donald DeFronzo, D	1991, Nov.
New Haven, Conn.	John Daniels, D	1991, Nov.
New London, Conn.	*C.F. Driscoll.	1969, May
New Orleans, La.	Sidney Barthelemy, D.	1994, Mar.
New Rochelle, N.Y.	*C. Samuel Kissinger	1975, Apr.
New York, N.Y.	David Dinkins, D.	1993, Nov.
Newark, N.J.	Sharpe James, D	1994, May
Newark, Oh.	William Moore, R	1991, Nov.
Newport, R.I.	*Francis Edwards	1987, Jan.
Newport Beach, Cal.	*Robert L. Wynn.	1971, Aug.
Newport News, Va.	*Ed Maroney.	1987, Jan.
Newton, Mass.	Theodore Mann, R	1993, Nov.
Niagara Falls, N.Y.	Michael O'Laughlin, D	1991, Nov.
Norfolk, Va.	*James B. Oliver Jr.	1987, Jan.
Norman, Okla.	Dick Reynolds, N-P	1992, Mar.
North Charleston, S.C.	John Bourne Jr., R	1994, May
North Las Vegas	*Michael Dyal	1982, May
No. Little Rock, Ark.	Patrick Hayes, D	1992, Nov.
Norwalk, Cal.	*Richard Powers	1988, July
Norwalk, Conn.	Frank Esposito, R	1991, Nov.
Novato, Cal.	*Phillip J. Brown.	1975, May
Oak Park, Ill.	*J.N. Nielsen.	1986, July
Oak Ridge, Tenn.	*Jeffrey J. Broughton.	1986, Sept.
Oakland, Cal.	*Henry L. Gardner	1981, June
Oceanside, Cal.	*James Turner.	1990, Aug.
Odessa, Tex.	*Raymond Kendall	1991, Apr.
Ogden, Ut.	Scott Sneddon, N-P	1991, Nov.
Oklahoma City, Okla.	*Paula Hearn	1989, Oct.
Omaha, Neb.	P.J. Morgan, D.	1993, May
Ontario, Cal.	*Roger Hughbanks, N-P	1975, July
Orange, Cal.	*J. William Little	1984, Jan.
Orlando, Fla.	Bill Frederick, N-P	1992, Sept.
Oshkosh, Wis.	*W. O. Frueh.	1976, Aug.
Overland Park, Kan.	*Donald Pipes	1977, June
Owensboro, Ky.	*Max Rhoads	1959, Sept.
Oxnard, Cal.	*Vernon Hazen	1990, Aug.
Pacifica, Cal.	*Daniel Pincetich	1985, Dec.
Palm Springs, Cal.	*Dallas Flicek	1990, Aug.
Palo Alto, Cal.	*William Zaner.	1979, Sept.
Parma, Oh.	Michael Ries, D	1991, Nov.
Pasadena, Cal.	Jeff Hughston, N-P	1992, May
Pasadena, Tex.	John Ray Harrison	1993, May
Paterson, N.J.	William Pascrell, D	1994, May
Pawtucket, R.I.	Brian Sarault, D.	1991, Nov.
Peabody, Mass.	Peter Torigian, D	1991, Nov.
Pembroke Pines, Fla.	*Charles Dodge	1989, Aug.
Pensacola, Fla.	*Steve Garman	1986, June
Peoria, Ill.	*Thomas Mikulecky	1987, July
Petersburg, Va.	*Richard M. Brown	1984, Oct.
Philadelphia, Pa.	W. Wilson Goode, D	1991, Nov.
Phoenix, Ariz.	Paul Johnson, N-P	1991, Oct.
Pico Rivera, Cal.	*Dennis Courtemarche.	1984, Nov.
Pine Bluff, Ark	Carolyn Robinson, D	1992, Nov.
Pittsburgh, Pa.	Sophie Masloff, D	1993, Nov.
Pittsfield, Mass.	Anne E. Wojtkowski, D.	1991, Nov.
Plainfield, N.J.	*Jewel Thompson-Chin.	1990, Sept.

City	Name	Term
Plano, Tex.	*Thomas Muehlenbeck	1987, Dec.
Pocatello, Ida.	Peter Angstadt, N-P	1993, Nov.
Pomona, Cal.	*Julio Fuentes	1989, Dec.
Pompano Beach, Fla.	*Roy Stype	1989, Oct.
Pontiac, Mich.	Wallace Holland, N-P	1993, Nov.
Port Arthur, Tex.	*Cornelius Boganey	1990, Apr.
Portland, Me.	*Robert Ganley	1986, Sept.
Portland, Ore.	Bud Clark, N-P	1992, Nov.
Portsmouth, Oh.	Franklin Gerlach, N-P	1993, Nov.
Portsmouth, Va.	*George Hanbury	1982, June
Poughkeepsie, N.Y.	*William J. Theysohn	1982, Mar.
Providence, R.I.	Vincent Cianci Jr., N-P	1994, Nov.
Provo, Ut.	Joseph Jenkins, R	1993, Nov.
Pueblo, Col.	*Lewis A. Quigley	1987, Jan.
Quincy, Ill.	Verne Hagstorm, D	1993, Apr.
Quincy, Mass.	James Sheets, N-P	1991, Nov.
Racine, Wis.	N. Owen Davies, N-P	1995, Apr.
Raleigh, N.C.	*Dempsey Benton	1983, Dec.
Rancho Palos Verdes, Cal.	*Paul Bussey	1990, June
Rapid City, S.D.	Edward McLaughlin, R	1993, May
Reading, Pa.	Warren Haggerty Jr., D	1991, Nov.
Redding, Cal.	*Robert Christofferson	1987, Jan.
Redlands, Cal.	*James Wheaton	1991, Mar.
Redondo Beach, Cal.	*R.H. Griest	1990, July
Redwood City, Cal.	*James M. Smith	1982, Feb.
Reno, Nev.	*Clay Holstine	1991, May
Revere, Mass.	George V. Colella, D	1992, Nov.
Rialto, Cal.	*Gerald Johnson	1988, July
Richardson, Tex.	*Bob Hughey	1974, Jan.
Richmond, Cal.	*Larry Moore	1987, Aug.
Richmond, Va.	*Robert C. Bobb	1986, July
Riverside, Cal.	*John E. Holmes	1990, Oct.
Roanoke, Va.	*W.R. Herbert	1985, Nov.
Rochester, Minn.	*Steven Kvenvold	1979, June
Rochester, N.Y.	Thomas Ryan Jr., D	1993, Nov.
Rock Hill, S.C.	*Joe Lanford	1979, July
Rock Island, Ill.	*John Phillips	1986, Nov.
Rockford, Ill.	Charles Box, D	1993, Apr.
Rockville, Md.	*Bruce Romer	1988, Sept.
Rome, N.Y.	Carl Eilenberg, R	1991, Nov.
Roseville, Mich.	Jeanne Riesterer, N-P	1993, Nov.
Roswell, N.M.	*Ralph Fresquez	1986, Jan.
Royal Oak, Mich.	*William Baldridge	1975, Sept.
Sacramento, Cal.	*Walter Slipe	1976, Mar.
Saginaw, Mich.	*Vernon E. Stoner	1987, Feb.
St. Clair Shores, Mich.	*Mark Wollenweber	1990, Jan.
St. Cloud, Minn.	Charles Winkleman, N-P	1993, Nov.
St. Joseph, Mo.	Glenda Kelly, N-P	1994, Apr.
St. Louis, Mo.	Vincent Schoemehl, D	1993, Apr.
St. Louis Park, Minn.	*William C. Dixon	1988, Oct.
St. Paul, Minn.	James Scheibel, N-P	1993, Nov.
St. Petersburg, Fla.	*Robert Obering	1985, Oct.
Salem, Ore.	*Gary Eide	1988, Jan.
Salina, Kan.	*Dennis Kissinger	1988, Jan.
Salinas, Cal.	*Roy Herte	1988, Sept.
Salt Lake City, Ut.	Palmer DePaulis, D	1991, Nov.
San Angelo, Tex.	*Stephen Brown	1982, May
San Antonio, Tex.	Nelson Wolff, N-P	1995, Apr.
San Bernardino, Cal.	Bob Holcomb, D	1993, May
San Bruno, Cal.	*Lew Pond	1990, May
San Diego, Cal.	Maureen O'Connor, N-P	1992, Nov.
San Francisco, Cal.	Art Agnos, D	1991, Nov.
San Jose, Cal.	*Leslie White	1989, May
San Leandro, Cal.	*Richard H. Randall	1986, July
San Mateo, Cal.	*Richard Delong	1976, Sept.
San Rafael, Cal.	*Pamela Nicolai	1985, Dec.
Sandy, Ut.	Larry Smith, N-P	1992, Nov.
Santa Ana, Cal.	*David Ream	1986, July
Santa Barbara, Cal.	*Richard Thomas	1977, Jan.
Santa Clara, Cal.	*Jennifer Sparacino	1987, Mar.
Santa Cruz, Cal.	*Richard Wilson	1981, June
Santa Fe, N.M.	Sam Pick, D	1994, Mar.
Santa Maria, Cal.	*Wayne Schwammel	1989, June
Santa Monica, Cal.	*John Jalili	1984, Dec.
Santa Rosa, Cal.	*Kenneth Blackman	1970, July
Sarasota, Fla.	*David Sollenberger	1987, July
Savannah, Ga.	*Arthur A. Mendonsa	1962, July
Schenectady, N.Y.	Karen Johnson, D	1991, Nov.
Scottsdale, Ariz.	*Jorge Carrasco	1988, Oct.
Scranton, Pa.	James Connors, R	1993, Nov.
Seattle, Wash.	Norman Rice, N-P	1993, Nov.
Shaker Heights, Oh.	Stephen Alfred, N-P	1991, Nov.
Sheboygan, Wis.	Richard Schneider, N-P	1993, Apr.
Shreveport, La.	*Newton Bruce	1990, May
Simi Valley, Cal.	*M.L. Koester	1979, Sept.
Sioux City, Ia.	Robert Scott, N-P	1991, Nov.
Sioux Falls, S.D.	Jack White, R	1995, June
Skokie, Ill.	*Albert Rigoni	1987, Jan.
Somerville, Mass.	Michael Capuano, D	1991, Nov.
South Bend, Ind.	Joseph Kernan, D	1991, Nov.
Southfield, Mich.	*Robert Block	1985, Jan.
Sparks, Nev.	*Patricia Thompson	1983, Sept.
Spartanburg, S.C.	*Wayne Bowers	1984, Sept.
Spokane, Wash.	*Terry Novak	1978, July
Springfield, Ill.	Ossie Langfelder, D	1995, Apr.
Springfield, Mass	Mary Hurley, D	1991, Nov.
Springfield, Mo.	*Thomas Finnie	1990, Apr.
Springfield, Oh.	*Matthew Kridler	1988, Oct.
Stamford, Conn.	Thom Serrani, D	1991, Nov.
Sterling Hts., Mich.	*Steve Duchane	1987, Nov.
Stockton, Cal.	*Alan N. Harvey	1988, Aug.
Stratford, Conn.	*Ronald Owens	1984, July
Sunnyvale, Cal.	*Thomas Lewcock	1980, Apr.
Suffolk, Va.	*Richard-Hedrick	1991, July
Sunrise, Fla.	*Patrick Salerno	1990, Dec.
Syracuse, N.Y.	Thomas G. Young, D	1993, Nov.
Tacoma, Wash.	*Ray Corpuz Jr.	1990, Jan.
Tallahassee, Fla.	*Daniel A. Kleman	1974, Aug.
Tampa, Fla.	Sandra Friedman, N-P	1995, Mar.
Taunton, Mass.	Richard Johnson, D	1991, Nov.
Taylor, Mich.	Cameron Priebe, D	1993, Nov.
Tempe, Ariz.	Harry E. Mitchell, D	1992, Mar.
Temple, Tex.	*vacant	
Terre Haute, Ind.	P. Pete Chalos, D	1991, Nov.
Thornton, Col.	*Jack Ethredge	1985, Jan.
Thousand Oaks, Cal.	*Grant Brimhall	1978, Jan.
Titusville, Fla.	*Norman Hickey	1974, June
Toledo, Oh.	*Thomas Hoover	1990, Sept.
Topeka, Kan.	Butch Felker, N-P	1993, Apr.
Torrance, Cal.	*Leroy J. Jackson	1983, Jan.
Trenton, N.J.	Douglas Palmer, N-P	1994, May
Troy, Mich.	*Frank Gerstenecker	1970, Feb
Troy, N.Y.	*Steven Dworsky	1986, July
Tucson, Ariz.	*Thomas Wilson	1990, July
Tulsa, Okla.	Rodger Randle, D	1994, Apr.
Tuscaloosa, Ala.	Alvin DuPont, D	1993, Oct.
Tyler, Tex.	*Gary Gwyn	1982, Nov.
Union City, N.J.	Robert Menendez, D	1994, May
Univ. City, Mo.	*Frank Ollendorff	1980, Mar.
Upland, Cal.	*Ray Silver	1988, Dec.
Utica, N.Y.	Louis La Polla, R	1991, Nov.
Vallejo, Cal.	*Edward Wohlenberg	1989, Apr.
Vancouver, Wash.	*Thomas Fischbach	1990, Aug.
Ventura, Cal.	*John Baker	1986, Nov.
Vineland, N.J.	Harry Curley, R	1992, May
Virginia Beach, Va.	*Aubrey Watts Jr.	1988, Nov.
Waco, Tex.	*John Harrison	1977, Sept.
Walnut Creek, Cal.	*Donald Blubaugh	1988, Apr.
Waltham, Mass.	William Stanley, D	1991, Nov.
Warner Robins, Ga.	Ed Martin, D	1992, Oct.
Warren, Mich.	Ronald Bonkowski, N-P.	1991, Nov.
Warren, Oh.	Daniel Sferra, D	1991, Nov.
Warwick, R.I.	Charles Donovan, N-P	1394, Nov.
Wash, D.C.	Sharon Dixon, D	1994, Nov.
Waterbury, Conn.	Joseph Santopietro, R	1991, Nov.
Waterloo, Ia.	Bernard L. McKinley, N-P	1991, Nov.
Waukegan, Ill.	Haig Paravonian, R	1993, Apr.
Waukesha, Wis.	Paul Vrakas, N-P	1994, Apr.
Wauwatosa, Wis.	James Brundahl, N-P	1992, Apr.
W. Allis, Wis.	Fred Cashmore, N-P	1992, Apr.
W. Covina, Cal.	*Herman Fast	1976, Aug.
W. Hartford, Conn.	Sandy Klebanoff, D	1991, Nov.
W. Haven, Conn.	Clemente Evangeliste, R	1991, Nov.
W. Palm Beach, Fla.	*Paul Steinbrenner	1986, Jan.
Westland, Mich.	Robert Thomas, D	1993, Nov.
Westminster, Cal.	*Jerry Kenny	1989, Jan.
Westminster, Col.	*William Christopher	1978, May
Wheaton, Ill.	*Donald Rose	1980, Nov.
White Plains, N.Y.	Alfred Del Vecchio, R	1993, Nov.
Whittier, Cal.	Thomas Sawyer, N-P	1992, Apr.
Wichita, Kan.	*Chris Cherches	1985, Oct.
Wichita Falls, Tex.	*James Berzina	1983, June
Wilkes-Barre, Pa.	Lee Namey, D	1991, Nov.
Wilmington, Del.	Daniel Frawley, D	1992, Nov.
Wilmington, N.C.	*William B. Farris	1983, May
Winston-Salem, N.C.	*Bryce A. Stuart	1980, Jan.
Woonsocket, R.I.	Francis Lanctot, D	1991, Nov.
Worcester, Mass.	*William Mulford	1985, Nov.
Wyandotte, Mich.	James R. DeSana, D	1995, Apr.
Wyoming, Mich.	*James Sheeran	1976, Nov.
Yakima, Wash.	*Richard Zais Jr.	1979, Jan.
Yonkers, N.Y.	*Neil De Luca	1988, Jan.
York, Pa.	William Althaus, R	1993, Nov.
Youngstown, Oh.	Patrick Ungaro, D	1993, Nov.
Yuma, Ariz.	*Doug Lowe, R	1984, Jan.
Zanesville, Oh.	Donald Lewis Mason, R	1991, Nov.

CITIES OF THE U.S.[1]

Sources: Bureau of the Census: population (1990 Census); population growth (1980-1990). Geography Division, Bureau of the Census: population density (1990); area (1990). Bureau of Labor Statistics: employment (Jan. 1991). Bureau of Economic Analysis: per capita personal income (MSA, 1989).

Akron, Ohio

Population: 223,019; **Pop. density:** 4,055 per sq. mi.; **Pop. growth:** −6.0%. **Area:** 55 sq. mi. **Employment:** 100,656 employed, 8.2% unemployed; **Per capita income:** $16,805; % change 1988-89: 5.7.

History: settled 1825; inc. as city 1865; located on Ohio-Erie Canal and is a port of entry; since 1870 the rubber capital of the U.S.

Transportation: 1 airport; major trucking industry; Conrail; metro transit system. **Communications:** 4 TV, 7 radio stations; CATV. **Medical facilities:** 11 hospitals; specialized children's treatment center. **Educational facilities:** 13 univ. and colleges; 68 public schools. **Further information:** Akron Regional Development Board or Akron-Summit Convention and Visitors Bureau, Cascade Plaza, Akron, OH 44308.

Albuquerque, New Mexico

Population: 384,736; **Pop. density:** 4,050 per sq. mi.; **Pop. growth:** 15.6%. **Area:** 95 sq. mi. **Employment:** 203,448 employed, 5.2% unemployed; **Per capita income:** $15,806; % change 1988-89: 5.1.

History: founded 1706 by the Spanish; inc. 1890.

Transportation: 1 international airport; 2 railroads; 2 bus lines. **Communications:** 5 TV, 31 radio stations; CATV. **Medical facilities:** 10 major hospitals. **Educational facilities:** 1 university. **Further information:** Convention & Visitors Bureau, 625 Silver S.W., Albuquerque, NM 87125.

Anaheim, California

Population: 266,406; **Pop. density:** 6,498 per sq. mi.; **Pop. growth:** 21.4%. **Area:** 41 sq. mi. **Employment:** 153,183 employed, 5.3% unemployed; **Per capita income:** $24,298; % change 1988-89: 6.6.

History: founded 1858; inc. 1876; now known as home of Disneyland (since 1955).

Transportation: 3 municipal airports; 4 railroads; Greyhound buses. **Communications:** 12 TV, 4 radio stations; CATV. **Medical facilities:** 6 general hospitals. **Educational facilities:** 3 colleges, 5 junior colleges; 62 elementary, 8 junior high, 8 high schools. **Further information:** Chamber of Commerce, 100 South Anaheim Blvd., Suite 300, Anaheim, CA 92805.

Anchorage, Alaska

Population: 226,338 **Pop. density:** 131 per sq. mi.; **Pop. growth:** 29.8% . **Area:** 1,732 sq. mi.. **Employment:** 110,058 employed, 6.1% unemployed; **Per capita income:** $24,773; % change 1988-89: 14.2.

History: founded 1914 as a construction camp for railroad; HQ of Alaska Defense Command, WWII; severely damaged in earthquake 1964.

Transportation: 1 international airport, 3 other airports. **Communications:** 6 TV, 16 radio stations. **Medical facilities:** 3 hospitals. **Educational facilities:** 2 univ., 1 comm. college. **Further information:** Chamber of Commerce, 437 E St., Anchorage, AK 99501.

Arlington, Texas

Population: 261,721; **Pop. density:** 3,313 per sq. mi.; **Pop. growth:** 63.5%. **Area:** 79 sq. mi.; **Employment:** 124,636 employed, 5.0% unemployed; **Per capita income:** $17,259; % change 1988-89: 4.5.

History: settled in 1840s between Dallas & Ft. Worth; inc. 1884.

Transportation: Dallas/Ft. Worth airport is 20 minutes away; 11 railway lines; intercity transport system in planning stage. **Communications:** 13 TV, 53 radio stations; CATV. **Medical facilities:** 4 hospitals. **Educational facilities:** 51 public schools; 1 univ. **Further information:** Chamber of Commerce, 316 W. Main St., Arlington, TX 76010.

Atlanta, Georgia

Population: 394,017; **Pop. density:** 3,008 per sq. mi.; **Pop. growth:** −7.3%. **Area:** 131 sq. mi. **Employment:** 209,818 employed, 7.6% unemployed; **Per capita income:** $19,055; % change 1988-89: 3.4.

History: founded as "Terminus" 1837; renamed Atlanta 1845 after Atlantis; inc. 1847; played major role in Civil War and burned during Gen. Sherman's "March to the Sea."

Transportation: 1 international airport; 7 railroad lines, 2 systems; 2 bus terminals; rapid rail. **Communications:** 9 TV, 41 radio stations; 21 cable TV companies. **Medical facilities:** 60 hospitals; VA hospital; Natl. Centers for Disease Control; Natl. Cancer Center. **Educational facilities:** 37 colleges, universities, seminaries, junior colleges. **Further information:** Chamber of Commerce, 235 International Blvd., Atlanta, GA 30303.

Aurora, Colorado

Population: 222,103; **Pop. density:** 3,702 per sq. mi.; **Pop. growth:** 40.1%. **Area:** 60 sq. mi. **Employment:** 110,993 employed, 4.9% unemployed; **Per capita income:** $18,155 (1988); % change 1983-88: 22.4.

History: residential suburb 5 mi. east of Denver; fast-growing trade center for large livestock and farm area.

Transportation: 1 international airport; 4 railroads; 2 bus lines; city bus system. **Further information:** ECO Aurora, Inc., 1470 S. Havana, Ste. 708, Aurora, CO 80012.

Austin, Texas

Population: 465,622; **Pop. density:** 4,014 per sq. mi.; **Pop. growth:** 34.6%. **Area:** 116 sq. mi.. **Employment:** 264,978 employed, 5.2% unemployed; **Per capita income:** $16,113; % change 1988-89: 5.2.

History: first permanent settlement 1835; capital of Rep. of Texas 1838; named after Stephen Austin; inc. 1840.

Transportation: 1 international airport; 4 railroads. **Communications:** 5 TV, 18 radio stations. **Medical facilities:** 15 hospitals. **Educational facilities:** 7 universities and colleges. **Further information:** Chamber of Commerce, P.O. Box 1967, Austin, TX 78767.

Bakersfield, California

Population: 174,820; **Pop. density:** 2,033 per sq. mi.; **Pop. growth:** 65.5%. **Area:** 86 sq. mi.. **Employment:** 63,374 employed, 7.7% unemployed; **Per capita income:** $14,856; % change 1988-89: 2.9.

History: incorporated in 1898.

Transportation: 1 airport; 3 railroads; Greyhound buses; local bus system. **Medical facilities:** 4 major hospitals; 9 convalescent; 2 psychiatric; 3 physical rehab.

---

(1) Based on 1990 census, the 100 most populated cities (inc.=incorporated; est.=established; NA=not available).

centers; 3 clinics; 2 urgent care centers. **Educational facilities:** 58 public schools; 1 community college; 1 university; 9 vocational schools; 1 adult school; 1 college of law. **Further information:** Greater Bakersfield Chamber of Commerce, 1033 Truxtun Avenue, Bakersfield, CA 93301.

Baltimore, Maryland

Population: 736,014; **Pop. density:** 9,200 per sq. mi.; **Pop. growth:** −6.4%. **Area:** 80 sq. mi.. **Employment:** 307,068 employed, 9.1% unemployed; **Per capita income:** $20,267; % change 1988-89: 6.6.
History: founded by Maryland legislature 1729; inc. 1797; bombing of its Ft. McHenry 1814 inspired Francis Scott Key to write "Star-Spangled Banner;" rebuilt after fire 1904.
Transportation: 1 major airport; 3 railroads, bus system; subway system, 2 underwater tunnels. **Communications:** 6 TV, 33 radio stations. **Medical facilities:** 29 hospitals; 2 major medical centers. **Educational facilities:** 189 public schools; over 30 universities and colleges. **Further information:** Greater Baltimore Committee, Suite 900, Two Hopkins Plaza, Baltimore, MD 21202.

Baton Rouge, Louisiana

Population: 219,531; **Pop. density:** 3,599 per sq. mi.; **Pop. growth:** −0.4%. **Area:** 61 sq. mi.. **Employment:** 112,723 employed, 5.6% unemployed; **Per capita income:** $14,757; % change 1988-89: 7.5.
History: claimed by Spain at time of La. Purchase 1803; est. independence by rebellion 1810; inc. as town 1817; held by Union during most of Civil War.
Transportation: 1 airport, 7 airlines; 1 bus line; 3 railroad trunk lines. **Communications:** 5 TV, 19 radio stations; CATV. **Medical facilities:** 7 hospitals. **Educational facilities:** 96 public, 46 private schools; 2 univ. **Further information:** Chamber of Commerce, P.O. Box 3217, Baton Rouge, LA 70821.

Birmingham, Alabama

Population: 265,968; **Pop. density:** 2,687 per sq. mi.; **Pop. growth:** −6.5%. **Area:** 99 sq. mi.. **Employment:** 120,955 employed, 6.1% unemployed; **Per capita income:** $15,833; % change 1988-89: 6.6.
History: settled due to discovery of elements needed for steel production; inc. 1871; named after Great Britain's steel making center.
Transportation: 1 airport; 4 major rail freight lines, Amtrak; 1 bus line; 75 truck line terminals; 4 interstate highways. **Communications:** 5 TV, 22 radio stations; 1 educational TV, 1 educational radio station. **Medical facilities:** Univ. of Alabama in Birmingham Medical Center; VA hospital with organ transplant program; 15 other hospitals. **Educational facilities:** 1 university, 2 colleges, 2 junior colleges. **Further information:** Chamber of Commerce, 2027 First Ave. N., Birmingham, AL 35202.

Boston, Massachusetts

Population: 574,283; **Pop. density:** 12,484 per sq. mi.; **Pop. growth:** 2.0%. **Area:** 46 sq. mi.. **Employment:** 268,909 employed, 7.8% unemployed; **Per capita income:** $23,746; % change 1988-89: 6.2.
History: settled 1630 by John Winthrop; capital of Mass. Bay Colony; figured strongly in Am. Revolution, earning distinction as the "Cradle of Liberty;" inc. 1822.
Transportation: 1 major airport; 2 railroads; city rail and subway system; 2 underwater tunnels. **Communications:** 8 TV, 17 radio stations; CATV. **Medical facilities:** 16 hospitals; 8 major medical research centers. **Educational facilities:** 11 universities and colleges. **Further information:** Chamber of Commerce, Federal Reserve Bank, 600 Atlantic Ave., 13th Fl., Boston, MA 02106.

Buffalo, New York

Population: 328,123; **Pop. density:** 7,812 per sq. mi.; **Pop. growth:** −8.3%. **Area:** 42 sq. mi.. **Employment:** 129,997 employed, 10.7% unemployed; **Per capita income:** $17,724; % change 1988-89: 7.8.
History: founded 1790 by the Dutch; raided twice by British during War of 1812; as western terminus for Erie Canal became a center for trade and manufacturing; inc. 1832.
Transportation: 1 international airport; 6 major railroads; metro rail system; water service to Great Lakes-St. Lawrence seaways system, and Atlantic seaboard. **Communications:** 5 TV, 23 radio stations, 2 cable systems. **Medical facilities:** 21 hospitals. **Educational facilities:** 2 universities, 9 colleges; 78 public schools. **Further information:** Greater Buffalo Chamber of Commerce, 107 Delaware Ave., Buffalo, NY 14202.

Charlotte, North Carolina

Population: 395,934; **Pop. density:** 2,869 per sq. mi.; **Pop. growth:** 25.5%. **Area:** 138 sq. mi. **Employment:** 208,374 employed, 4.3% unemployed; **Per capita income:** $17,377; % change 1988-89: 5.9.
History: settled by Scotch-Irish immigrants 1740s; inc. 1767 and named after Queen Charlotte, George III's wife; scene of first major U.S. gold discovery 1799.
Transportation: 1 airport; 2 major railway lines; 2 bus lines; 200 trucking firms. **Communications:** 6 TV, 20 radio stations. **Medical facilities:** 12 hospitals, 1 medical center. **Educational facilities:** 2 universities, 5 colleges. **Further information:** Chamber of Commerce, P.O. Box 32785, Charlotte, NC 28232.

Chicago, Illinois

Population: 2,783,726; **Pop. density:** 12,209 per sq. mi.; **Pop. growth:** −7.4%. **Area:** 228 sq. mi. **Employment:** 1,312,114 employed, 8.0% unemployed; **Per capita income:** $20,349; % change 1988-89: 6.6.
History: site acquired from Indians 1795; area began settlement with opening of Erie Canal 1825; chartered as city 1837; boomed with arrival of railroads from east and canal to Mississippi R.; much of city destroyed by fire 1871; major grain & livestock market.
Transportation: 3 airports; major railroad system; major trucking industry. **Communications:** 9 TV, 31 radio stations. **Medical facilities:** over 123 hospitals. **Educational facilities:** 95 institutions of higher learning. **Further information:** Association of Commerce and Industry, 200 N. LaSalle St., Chicago, IL 60601.

Cincinnati, Ohio

Population: 364,040; **Pop. density:** 4,667 per sq. mi.; **Pop. growth:** −5.5%. **Area:** 78 sq. mi.. **Employment:** 189,744 employed, 5.9% unemployed; **Per capita income:** $17,624; % change 1988-89: 6.0.
History: founded 1788 and named after the Society of Cincinnati, an organization of Revolutionary War officers; chartered as village 1802; inc. as city 1819.
Transportation: 1 international airport; 3 railroads; 1 bus system. **Communications:** 6 TV, 3 CATV systems; 27 radio stations. **Medical facilities:** 32 hospitals; Children's Hospital Medical Center; VA hospital. **Educational facilities:** 4 universities; 5 colleges, 8 technical & 2-year colleges. **Further information:** Chamber of Commerce, 300 Carew Tower, 441 Vine St., Cincinnati, OH 45202.

Cleveland, Ohio

Population: 505,616; **Pop. density:** 6,400 per sq. mi.; **Pop. growth:** −11.9%. **Area:** 79 sq. mi.. **Employment:**

218,727 employed, 9.0% unemployed; **Per capita income: $19,395; % change 1988-89:** 7.2.

History: surveyed in 1796; inc. as village 1814, as city 1836; annexed Ohio City 1854.

Transportation: 1 intl. airport; rail service; major port; rapid transit system. **Communications:** 7 TV, 20 radio stations. **Medical facilities:** numerous hospitals; major medical research center. **Educational facilities:** 124 public schools; 8 universities and colleges. **Further information:** Convention & Visitor's Bureau, 3100 Terminal Tower, Cleveland, OH 44115.

Colorado Springs, Colorado

Population: 281,140; **Pop. density:** 2,730 per sq. mi.; **Pop. growth:** 30.7%. **Area:** 103 sq. mi.. **Employment:** 131,780 employed, 7.5% unemployed; **Per capita income:** $16,105; % change 1988-89: 4.5.

History: founded 1859 at the foot of Pikes Peak; inc. 1886.

Transportation: 1 municipal airport; 2 railroads; Greyhound-Trailways bus line. **Communications:** 5 TV, 22 radio stations. **Medical facilities:** 9 hospitals. **Educational facilities:** 3 universities, 7 colleges. **Further information:** Chamber of Commerce, P.O. Drawer B, Colorado Springs, CO 80901.

Columbus, Georgia

Population: 179,278; **Pop. density:** 822 per sq. mi.; **Pop. growth:** 5.4%. **Area:** 218 sq. mi. **Employment:** 71,659 employed, 6.1% unemployed; **Per capita income:** $13,459; % change 1988-89: 5.9.

History: settled and inc. 1828; a port city on Chattahouchee R.

Transportation: 1 airport; metro bus system; 2 bus lines; 2 railroads. **Communications:** 5 TV, 11 radio stations. **Medical facilities:** 5 hospitals. **Educational facilities:** 53 public schools; 1 college. **Further information:** Chamber of Commerce, P.O. Box 1200, Columbus, GA 31902.

Columbus, Ohio

Population: 632,910; **Pop. density:** 3,497 per sq. mi.; **Pop. growth:** 12.0%. **Area:** 181 sq. mi.. **Employment:** 318,383 employed, 5.1% unemployed; **Per capita income:** $17,178; % change 1988-89: 5.7.

History: first settlement 1797; laid out as new capital 1812 with current name; became city 1834.

Transportation: 2 airports; 3 railroads; 4 intercity bus lines. **Communications:** 5 TV, 19 radio stations. **Medical facilities:** 22 hospitals. **Educational facilities:** 12 universities and colleges. **Further information:** Chamber of Commerce, P.O. Box 1527, Columbus, OH 43216.

Corpus Christi, Texas

Population: 257,453; **Pop. density:** 2,476 per sq. mi.; **Pop. growth:** 10.9%. **Area:** 104 sq. mi.. **Employment:** 113,292 employed, 7.5% unemployed; **Per capita income:** $13,272; % change 1988-89: 5.8.

History: settled 1839 and inc. 1852.

Transportation: 1 international airport; 2 bus lines; metro bus system; 3 freight railroads. **Communications:** 6 TV, 17 radio stations. **Medical facilities:** 14 ,hospitals including a children's center. **Educational facilities:** 54 public schools; 1 univ., 1 college. **Futher information:** Chamber of Commerce, PO Box 640, Corpus Christi, TX 78403.

Dallas, Texas

Population: 1,006,877; **Pop. density:** 3,024 per sq. mi.; **Pop. growth:** 11.3%. **Area:** 333 sq. mi.. **Employment:** 591,699 employed, 6.7% unemployed; **Per capita income:** $19,485; % change 1988-89: 5.0.

History: first settled 1841; platted 1846; inc. 1871; developed as the financial and commercial center of Southwest; known for its oil industry and cotton market.

Transportation: 1 international airport; Amtrak; major transit system. **Communications:** 10 TV, 49 radio stations. **Medical facilities:** 70 hospitals; major medical center. **Educational facilities:** 7 univ., 2 colleges. **Further information:** Chamber of Commerce, 1507 Pacific Ave., Dallas, TX 75201.

Dayton, Ohio

Population: 182,044; **Pop. density:** 3,793 per sq, mi.; **Pop. growth:** −5.9%. **Area:** 48 sq. mi. **Employment:** 80,439 employed, 9.1% unemployed; **Per capita income:** $16,919; % change 1988-89: 5.3.

History: settled 1796; inc. 1805; disastrous flood 1913; site where Wright Bros. invented first airplane to sustain flight 1903.

Transportation: 1 international airport, 12 airlines, 2 railroads; 4 bus lines; countywide Dayton Regional Transit Authority. **Communications:** 5 TV, 8 radio stations. **Medical facilities:** 15 hospitals including VA facility. **Educational facilities:** 26 institutions of higher learning. **Further information:** Dayton Area Chamber of Commerce, Fifth and Main, Chamber Plaza, Dayton, OH 45402.

Denver, Colorado

Population: 467,610; **Pop. density:** 4,213 per sq. mi.; **Pop. growth:** −5.1%. **Area:** 111 sq. mi. **Employment:** 253,023 employed, 6.2% unemployed; **Per capita income:** $19,231; % change 1988-89: 6.2.

History: settled 1858 by gold prospectors and miners; inc. 1861; growth spurred by gold and silver boom; the financial and industrial center of Rocky Mt. region.

Transportation: 1 international airport; 5 major rail freight lines, Amtrak; 2 bus lines. **Communications:** 7 TV, 35 radio stations. **Medical facilities:** 34 hospitals. **Educational facilities:** 2 universities; 3 colleges. **Further information:** Chamber of Commerce, 1301 Welton St., Denver, CO 80204.

Des Moines, Iowa

Population: 193,187 **Pop. density:** 2,927 per sq. mi.; **Pop. growth:** 1.1%. **Area:** 66 sq. mi.. **Employment:** 118,187 employed, 4.8% unemployed; **Per capita income:** $18,039; % change 1988-89: 6.4.

History: Fort Des Moines built 1843; settled and inc. 1851; chartered as city 1857.

Transportation: 1 international airport; 3 bus lines; 4 railroads; metro bus system. **Communications:** 5 TV, 18 radio stations; CATV. **Medical facilities:** 8 hospitals. **Educational facilities:** 1 univ., 2 colleges. **Further information:** Chamber of Commerce, 8th & High Sts., Des Moines, IA 50309.

Detroit, Michigan

Population: 1,027,974; **Pop. density:** 7,559 per sq. mi.; **Pop. growth:** −14.6%. **Area:** 136 sq. mi. **Employment:** 388,956 employed, 12.6% unemployed; **Per capita income:** $19,660; % change 1988-89: 6.7.

History: founded by French 1701; controlled by British 1760; acquired by U.S. 1796; destroyed by fire 1805; capital of state 1837-47; inc. as city 1824; auto manufacturing began 1899.

Transportation: 1 international airport; 10 railroads; major international port; public transit system. **Communications:** 9 TV, 37 radio stations. **Medical facilities:** 28 hospitals, major medical center. **Educational facilities:** 13 universities and colleges. **Further information:** Chamber of Commerce, 150 Michigan Avenue, Detroit, MI 48226.

El Paso, Texas

Population: 515,342; **Pop. density:** 2,156 per sq. mi.. **Pop. growth:** 21.2%. **Area:** 239 sq. mi. **Employment:** 205,478 employed, 11.8% unemployed; **Per capita income:** $10,735; % change 1988-89: 7.2.

History: first settled 1827; inc. 1873; arrival of railroad 1881 boosted city's population and industries.

Transportation: International airport; 5 major rail lines; 8 bus lines; 9 major highways; gateway to Mexico. **Communications:** 6 TV, 23 radio stations. **Medical facilities:** 16 hospitals; cancer treatment center. **Educational facilities:** 2 colleges and universities. **Further information:** Convention and Visitors Bureau, 5 Civic Center Plaza, El Paso, TX 79901.

Fort Wayne, Indiana

Population: 173,072; **Pop. density:** 3,328 per sq. mi.; **Pop. growth:** 0.4%. **Area:** 52 sq. mi. **Employment:** 88,072 employed, 7.9% unemployed; **Per capita income:** $17,236; % change 1988-89: 5.8.

History: French fort 1680; U.S. fort 1794; settled by 1832; inc. 1840 prior to Wabash-Erie canal completion 1843.

Transportation: 1 airport, 9 airlines; 3 railroads; 5 bus lines. **Communications:** 5 TV stations; 13 radio stations. **Medical facilities:** 3 major hospitals; VA hospital. **Educational facilities:** 82 public schools; 5 colleges. **Further information:** Chamber of Commerce, 826 Ewing Street, Fort Wayne, IN 46802.

Fort Worth, Texas

Population: 447,619; **Pop. density:** 1,865 per sq. mi.; **Pop. growth:** 16.2%. **Area:** 240 sq. mi. **Employment:** 257,370 employed, 7.4% unemployed; **Per capita income:** $17,259; % change 1988-89: 4.5.

History: est. as military post 1849; inc. 1873; oil discovered 1917; Fort Worth is a sister city to Dallas.

Transportation: 1 intl. airport; 8 major railroads, Amtrak; local bus service; 2 transcontinental, 2 intrastate bus lines. **Communications:** 9 TV, 37 radio stations. **Medical facilities:** 35 hospitals; 2 children's hospitals; 4 government hospitals. **Educational facilities:** 8 colleges & universities. **Further information:** Chamber of Commerce; 700 Throckmorton, Fort Worth, TX 76102.

Fremont, California

Population: 173,339; **Pop. density:** 2,211 per sq. mi.; **Pop. growth:** 31.4%. **Area:** 78.4 sq. mi. **Employment:** 83,579 employed, 4.5% unemployed; **Per capita income:** $20,967.

History: area first settled by Spanish 1769; during 1800s a collection of towns formed the area; inc. 1956.

Transportation: intracity bus line; Bay Area Rapid Transit System (southern terminal). **Communications:** NA **Medical facilities:** 1 hospital. **Educational facilities:** 43 public schools; 1 jr. college. **Further information:** Chamber of Commerce, One Fremont Pl., 39650 Liberty St., Ste. 130, Fremont, CA 94538.

Fresno, California

Population: 354,202; **Pop. density:** 5,449 per sq. mi.; **Pop. growth:** 62.9%. **Area:** 65 sq. mi. **Employment:** 120,386 employed, 12.0% unemployed; **Per capita income:** $15,927; % change 1988-89: 5.7.

History: founded 1872; inc. as city 1885.

Transportation: 2 municipal airports; Amtrak; 1 bus line; intracity bus system. **Communications:** 11 TV stations, 5 CATV services; 58 radio stations. **Medical facilities:** 6 general hospitals including a VA facility. **Educational facilities:** 8 colleges and univ.; 85 public schools. **Further information:** Chamber of Commerce, P.O. Box 1469, Fresno, CA 93721.

Garland, Texas

Population: 180,650; **Pop. density:** 3,226 per sq. mi.; **Pop. growth:** 30.1%. **Area:** 56 sq. mi. **Employment:** 93,678 employed, 4.7% unemployed; **Per capita income:** $19,602; % change 1988-89: 5.5.

History: city in Dallas co., 14 mi. NE of Dallas.

Transportation: 45 miles from Dallas/Ft. Worth airport; 2 railroads. **Communications:** 3 TV stations (from Dallas). **Medical facilities:** total of 306 hospital beds. **Educational facilities:** 53 public schools; 1 univ., 2 community colleges. **Further information:** Chamber of Commerce, P.O. Box 460939, Garland, TX 75046.

Glendale, California

Population: 180,038; **Pop. density:** 5,886 per sq. mi.; **Pop. growth:** 29%. **Area:** 30.59 sq. mi. **Employment:** 81,562 employed, 5.8% unemployed; **Per capita income:** $19,906; % change 1983-1988: 5.6.

History: Township in 1887, incorporated in 1906. Adjacent to Los Angeles.

Transportation: 1 airport; 1 railroad; in triangle surrounded by 3 freeways; Southern California Rapid Transit system; Glendale Beeline bus. **Communications:** 2 radio stations, 1 cable company. **Medical facilities:** 1,100 beds in three hospitals. **Educational facilities:** 1 community college. **Further information:** Chamber of Commerce, 200 S. Louise, Glendale, CA 91205.

Grand Rapids, Michigan

Population: 189,126; **Pop. density:** 4,358 per sq. mi.; **Pop. growth:** 4.0%. **Area:** 43.4 sq. mi. **Employment:** 98,370 employed, 8.0% unemployed; **Per capita income:** $17,766; % change 1988-89: 6.8.

History: originally site of Ottowa Indian village; trading post 1826; became lumbering center and chartered as town 1850.

Transportation: 1 international airport; 4 railroads; 5 bus lines; transit bus system. **Communications:** 6 TV, 25 radio stations. **Medical facilities:** 10 hospitals. **Educational facilities:** 64 public schools; 8 colleges. **Further information:** Chamber of Commerce, 17 Fountain St., NW, Grand Rapids, MI 49503.

Greensboro, North Carolina

Population: 183,521; **Pop. density:** 3,059 per sq. mi.; **Pop. growth:** 17.9%. **Area:** 60 sq. mi.; **Employment:** 86,749 employed, 7.0% unemployed; **Per capita income:** $17,652; % change 1988-89: 6.0.

History: settled 1749; site of Revolutionary War conflict 1781 between Nathanael Greene and Cornwallis; inc. 1807.

Transportation: 1 regional airport; 2 railroads; Trailways/Greyhound bus service. **Communications:** all cable TV stations; 11 radio stations. **Medical facilities:** 4 hospitals. **Educational facilities:** 38 public schools; 2

univ., 1 college. **Further information:** Chamber of Commerce, P.O. Box 3246, Greensboro, NC 27402.

Hialeah, Florida

Population: 188,004; **Pop. density:** 9,691 per sq. mi.; **Pop. growth:** 29.4%. **Area:** 19.4 sq. mi.; **Employment:** NA. **Per capita income:** $17,963; % change 1988-89: 6.9.

History: inc. 1925; built over drained swamplands NW of Miami.

Transportation: Miami Int'l. airport is 5 miles away; Amtrak; 2 rail freight lines. **Communications:** NA. **Medical facilities:** 3 hospitals. **Educational facilities:** 2 universities. **Further information:** Hialeah Dept. of Eco. Development, Office of the Mayor, 501 Palm Ave., Hialeah, FL 33010.

Honolulu, Hawaii

Population: 365,272; **Pop. density:** 613 per sq. mi.; **Pop. growth:** 0.1%. **Area:** 596 sq. mi.; **Employment:** 384,430 employed, 2.5% unemployed (MSA); **Per capita income:** $19,171; % change 1988-89: 9.3.

History: harbor first discovered 1794; city began 1816; became capital 1816.

Transportation: 1 major airport; large, active port for passengers and cargo. **Communications:** 10 TV, 28 radio stations. **Medical facilities:** 33 hospitals. **Educational facilities:** 163 public schools (state); 102 private schools (state); 4 univ., 1 college. **Further information:** Visitors Bureau, 2270 Kalakaua Avenue, Honolulu, HI 96815.

Houston, Texas

Population: 1,630,553; **Pop. density:** 2,933 per sq. mi.; **Pop. growth:** 2.2%. **Area:** 556 sq. mi.. **Employment:** 964,965 employed, 6.1% unemployed; **Per capita income:** $17,598; % change 1988-89: 8.6.

History: founded 1836; inc. 1837; capital of Rep. of Texas 1837-39, 1842-45; developed rapidly after completion of canal to Gulf of Mexico 1914; important oil center.

Transportation: 2 commercial airports; 5 railroads; major bus transit system; major international port. **Communications:** 9 TV, 45 radio stations. **Medical facilities:** 59 hospitals; major medical center. **Educational facilities:** 27 universities and colleges. **Further information:** Chamber of Commerce, 1100 Milam, Houston, TX 77002.

Huntington Beach, California

Population: 181,519; **Pop. density:** 6,723 per sq. mi.; **Pop. growth:** 6.5%. **Area:** 27 sq. mi.. **Employment:** 121,263 employed, 4.6% unemployed; **Per capita income:** $24,288; % change 1988-89: 6.7.

History: settled in early 1880s; inc. 1909; oil discovered 1920, led to city's development.

Transportation: 1 airport; 1 railroad; 2 bus lines. **Communications:** 1 TV station; CATV. **Medical facilities:** 2 hospitals. **Educational facilities:** 45 public schools; 1 junior college. **Further information:** Chamber of Commerce, Seacliff Village, 2213 Main #32, Huntington Beach, CA 92648.

Indianapolis, Indiana

Population: 741,952; **Pop. density:** 2,108 per sq. mi.; **Pop. growth:** 4.3%. **Area:** 352 sq. mi.. **Employment:** 377,992 employed, 6.1% unemployed; **Per capita income:** $18,080; % change 1988-89: 6.6.

History: settled in 1820, made into capital 1825.

Transportation: 1 international airport; 5 railroads; 3 interstate bus lines. **Communications:** 7 TV, 25 radio stations. **Medical facilities:** 17 hospitals; 1 major medical and research center. **Educational facilities:** 6 universities and colleges; major public library system. **Further information:** Chamber of Commerce, 320 N. Meridian Street, Indianapolis, IN 46204.

Jackson, Mississippi

Population: 196,637; **Pop. density:** 1,852 per sq. mi.; **Pop. growth:** −3.1%. **Area:** 106.2 sq. mi.. **Employment:** 98,400 employed, 6.0% unemployed; **Per capita income:** $14,479; % change 1988-89: 7.2.

History: originally known as Le Fleur's Bluff, selected as capital 1821 and named for Andrew Jackson; inc. 1833; scene of secession convention 1861; captured by Sherman 1863.

Transportation: 5 airlines; 2 bus lines; Ill. Central railroad. **Communications:** 5 TV, 25 radio stations. **Medical facilities:** 12 hospitals including a VA facility. **Educational facilities:** 1 univ., 5 colleges. **Further information:** Chamber of Commerce, P.O. Box 22548, Jackson, MS 39225.

Jacksonville, Florida

Population: 672,971; **Pop. density:** 885 per sq. mi.; **Pop. growth:** 17.9%. **Area:** 760 sq. mi.. **Employment:** 304,648 employed, 6.1% unemployed; **Per capita income:** $16,215; % change 1988-89: 5.0.

History: settled 1816 as Cowford; renamed after Andrew Jackson 1822; inc. 1832; rechartered 1851; scene of conflicts in Seminole and Civil Wars.

Transportation: 1 international airport; 3 railroads; 2 interstate bus lines. **Communications:** 6 TV, 21 radio stations. **Medical facilities:** 14 hospitals. **Educational facilities:** 5 universities and colleges. **Further information:** Chamber of Commerce, 3 Independent Drive, P.O. Box 329, Jacksonville, FL 32201.

Jersey City, New Jersey

Population: 228,537; **Pop. density:** 17,313 per sq. mi.; **Pop. growth:** 2.2%. **Area:** 13.2 sq. mi. **Employment:** 89,205 employed, 11.1% unemployed; **Per capita income:** $18,440; % change 1988-89: 8.7

History: bought from Indians 1830; chartered as town by British 1668; scene of Revolutionary War conflict 1779; chartered under present name 1838; important station on Underground Railroad.

Transportation: bus and subway system. **Medical facilities:** 10 hospitals. **Educational facilities:** 3 colleges. **Further information:** Chamber of Commerce & Industry of Hudson County, 911 Bergen Ave., Jersey City, NJ 07303.

Kansas City, Missouri

Population: 435,146; **Pop. density:** 1,377 per sq. mi.; **Pop. growth:** −2.9%. **Area:** 316 sq. mi. **Employment:** 233,164 employed, 6.7% unemployed; **Per capita income:** $17,899; % change 1988-89: 4.8.

History: settled by 1838 at confluence of the Missouri and Kansas rivers; inc. 1851.

Transportation: 1 international airport; a major rail center; 191 trunk lines; several barge companies. **Communications:** 7 TV, 29 radio stations. **Medical facilities:** 14 hospitals; VA facility. **Educational facilities:** 9 colleges & universities. **Further information:** Chamber of Commerce, 600 Boatmen's Center, 920 Main St., Kansas City, MO 64105.

Las Vegas, Nevada

Population: 258,295; **Pop. density:** 4,696 per sq. mi.; **Pop. growth:** 56.9%. **Area:** 55 sq. mi. **Employment:** 134,496 employed, 6.1% unemployed; **Per capita income:** $18,508; % change 1988-89: 8.6.

History: occupied by Mormons 1855-57; bought by railroad 1903; city of Las Vegas inc. 1911; gambling legalized 1931.

Transportation: 1 international airport; 2 railroads; bus system. **Communcations:** 7 TV and 28 radio stations. **Medical facilities:** 8 hospitals. **Educational facilities:** 130 public schools; 1 college; 1 univ. **Further information:** Chamber of Commerce, 2301 E. Sahara Ave., Las Vegas, NV, 89104.

Lexington–Fayette, Kentucky

Population: 225,366; **Pop. density:** 794 per sq. mi.; **Pop. growth:** 10.4%. **Area:** 284 sq. mi.. **Employment:** 120,742 employed, 3.5% unemployed; **Per capita income:** $16,760; % change 1988-89: 6.0.

History: site was founded and named 1775 by hunters who heard of the Revolutionary War battle at Lexington, Mass.; settled 1779; inc. 1832.

Transportation: 8 airlines, 2 railroads; city buses. **Communications:** 5 TV stations, CATV; 9 radio stations. **Medical facilities:** 5 general, 5 specialized hospitals. **Educational facilities:** 2 univ., 2 colleges. **Further information:** Chamber of Commerce, 330 East Main, Lexington, KY 40507.

Lincoln, Nebraska

Population: 191,972; **Pop. density:** 3,200 per sq. mi.; **Pop. growth:** 11.7%. **Area:** 60 sq. mi.. **Employment:** 114,795 employed, 2.1% unemployed; **Per capita income:** $16,067; % change 1988-89: 6.9.

History: originally called Lancaster, chosen state capital 1867 and renamed after Abraham Lincoln; inc. 1869.

Transportation: 1 airport; Greyhound, Amtrak, 2 railroads. **Communications:** 1 TV, 13 radio stations. **Medical facilities:** 4 hospitals including a VA facility. **Educational facilities:** 2 univ., 1 college, 46 public, 15 private schools. **Further information:** Chamber of Commerce, 1221 N St., Lincoln, NE 68508.

Little Rock, Arkansas

Population: 175,795; **Pop. density:** 2,225 per sq. mi.; **Pop. growth:** 10.5%. **Area:** 79 sq. mi. **Employment:** 88,836 employed, 5.8% unemployed; **Per capita income:** $15,657; % change 1988-89: 6.5.

History: founded 1821; inc. as city 1835.

Transportation: 1 airport, 7 airlines; 3 railroads; 1 bus line. **Communications:** 7 TV stations; 34 radio stations. **Medical facilities:** 16 hospitals; veterans' medical center. **Educational facilities:** 49 public schools; 8 colleges and universities; Univ. of Arkansas. **Further information:** Chamber of Commerce, One Spring St., Little Rock, AR 72201.

Long Beach, California

Population: 429,433; **Pop. density:** 8,589 per sq. mi.; **Pop. growth:** 18.8%. **Area:** 50 sq. mi.. **Employment:** 191,295 employed, 6.3% unemployed; **Per capita income:** $19,906; % change 1988-89: 5.6.

History: settled as early as 1769 by Spanish; by 1884 present site developed due to its harbor; inc. 1888; oil discovered 1921.

Transportation: 1 airport; 3 railroads; major international port; 6 bus lines, "lite" rail service. **Communications:** CATV; 4 radio stations. **Medical facilities:** 10 hospitals. **Educational facilities:** 78 public schools; 1 university, 1 college. **Further information:** Chamber of Commerce, One World Trade Center, Long Beach, CA 90831.

Los Angeles, California

Population: 3,485,398; **Pop. density:** 7,495 per sq. mi.; **Pop. growth:** 17.4%. **Area:** 465 sq. mi.. **Employment:** 1,638,825 employed, 7.3% unemployed; **Per capita income:** $19,906; % change 1988-89: 5.6.

History: founded by Spanish 1781; captured by U.S. 1846; inc. 1850; Hollywood a district of L.A.

Transportation: 1 intl. airport; 4 railroads; major freeway system; intracity transit system. **Communications:** 19 TV, 71 radio stations. **Medical facilities:** 822 hospitals and clinics. **Educational facilities:** 11 universities and colleges; 1,642 public schools; 800 private schools. **Further information:** Chamber of Commerce, 404 S. Bixel St., P.O. Box 3696, Los Angeles, CA 90051.

Louisville, Kentucky

Population: 269,063; **Pop. density:** 4,484 per sq. mi.; **Pop. growth:** −9.9%. **Area:** 60 sq. mi. **Employment:** 128,892 employed, 8.3% unemployed. **Per capita income:** $16,768; % change 1988-89: 6.9.

History: settled 1778; named for Louis XVI of France; inc. 1828; base for Union forces in Civil War.

Transportation: 2 municipal airports; 1 terminal, 6 trunk-line railroads; 3 bus lines; 5 barge lines. **Communications:** 4 TV, 20 radio stations, 2 educational, CATV. **Medical facilities:** 21 hospitals. **Educational facilities:** 10 colleges & universities, 9 business colleges & technical schools. **Further information:** Chamber of Commerce, One Riverfront Plaza, Louisville, KY 40202.

Lubbock, Texas

Population: 186,206; **Pop. density:** 2,069 per sq. mi.; **Pop. growth:** 6.8%. **Area:** 90 sq. mi. **Employment:** 91,137 employed, 5.3% unemployed; **Per capita income:** $14,208; % change 1988-89: 6.0.

History: settled 1879; inc. in 1909 through merger of two towns.

Transportation: 1 international airport; 2 railroads, bus line. **Communications:** 5 TV, 18 radio stations. **Medical facilities:** 7 hospitals. **Educational facilities:** 51 public schools; 2 univ., 1 college. **Further information:** Chamber of Commerce, P.O. Box 561, Lubbock, TX 79408.

Madison, Wisconsin

Population: 191,262; **Pop. density:** 3,188 per sq. mi.; **Pop. growth:** 12.1%. **Area:** 60 sq. mi. **Employment:** 112,759 employed, 2.8% unemployed; **Per capita income:** $19,023; % change 1988-98: 6.9.

History: first white settlement 1832; named after James Madison who died in 1836; chartered 1856.

Transportation: 1 airport, 8 airlines; 2 railroads; intracity bus system. **Communications:** 6 TV, 18 radio stations. **Medical facilities:** 6 hospitals. **Educational facilities:** 39 public schools; 3 colleges and universities; Univ. of Wisconsin. **Further information:** Chamber of Commerce, P.O. Box 71, Madison, WI 53701.

Memphis, Tennessee

Population: 610,337; **Pop. density:** 2,312 per sq. mi.; **Pop. growth:** −5.5%. **Area:** 264 sq. mi.. **Employment:** 312,097 employed, 5.5% unemployed; **Per capita income:** $16,484; % change 1988-89: 6.4.

History: French, Spanish and U.S. forts by 1797; settled by 1819; inc. as town 1826, as city 1840; surrendered charter to state 1879 after yellow fever epidemics; re-chartered as city 1893.

Transportation: 1 international airport; 6 railroads; bus system. **Communications:** 6 TV, 29 radio stations. **Medical facilities:** 21 hospitals. **Educational facilities:** 12 universities and colleges; 205 public, 76 private schools. **Further information:** Memphis Area Chamber of Commerce, 22 N. Front St., Box 224, Memphis TN 38101.

Mesa, Arizona

Population: 288,091; **Pop. density:** 4,237 per sq. mi.; **Pop. growth:** 89.0%. **Area:** 68 sq. mi. **Employment:** 102,295 employed, 3.6% unemployed; **Per capita income:** $17,705; % change 1988-89: 5.3.

History: founded by Mormons 1878; inc. 1883; 15 mi. from Phoenix; population boomed fivefold from 1960-80.

Transportation: 1 intl. airports; 2 railroads; trolley and bus lines. **Medical facilities:** 4 major hospitals. **Educational facilities:** 49 public schools; 1 college, 1 univ. **Further information:** Convention and Visitor's Bureau, 120 N. Center, Mesa, AZ 85201.

Miami, Florida

Population: 358,548; **Pop. density:** 10,546 per sq. mi.; **Pop. growth:** 3.4%. **Area:** 34 sq. mi.. **Employment:** 188,285 employed; 8.4% unemployed; **Per capita income:** $17,963; % change 1988-89: 6.9.

History: site of fort 1836; settlement began 1870; inc. 1896 and modern city developed into resort and recreation center; land speculation 1920s added to city's growth, as did Cuban immigration in 1970s and 1980s.

Transportation: 1 international airport; 2 passenger railroads, 1 all-freight; 2 bus lines; 65 truck lines. **Communications:** 6 commercial, 5 educational TV stations; 31 radio stations. **Medical facilities:** 41 hospitals, VA Hospital. **Educational facilities:** 6 colleges & universities. **Further information:** Metro-Dade Department of Tourism, 234 W. Flagler St., Miami, FL 33130.

Milwaukee, Wisconsin

Population: 628,088; **Pop. density:** 6,543 per sq. mi.; **Pop. growth:** −1.3%. **Area:** 96 sq. mi. **Employment:** 294,302 employed, 5.2% unemployed; **Per capita income:** $18,842; % change 1988-89: 6.3.

History: Indian trading post by 1674; settlement began 1835; inc. as city 1848; beer industry is famous.

Transportation: 1 international airport; 2 railroads; major port; 4 bus lines. **Communications:** 12 TV, 33 radio stations. **Medical facilities:** 25 hospitals; major medical center. **Educational facilities:** 12 universities and colleges. **Further information:** Association of Commerce, 756 N. Milwaukee Street, Milwaukee, WI 53202.

Minneapolis, Minnesota

Population: 368,383; **Pop. density:** 6,698 per sq. mi.; **Pop. growth:** −0.7%. **Area:** 55 sq. mi.. **Employment:** 197,775 employed, 4.0% unemployed; **Per capita income:** $20,227; % change 1988-89: 5.5.

History: site visited by Hennepin 1680; included in area of military reservations 1819; inc. 1867.

Transportation: 1 international airport; 6 railroads; mass transit systems; 5 major barge lines. **Communications:** 6 TV, 39 radio stations. **Medical facilities:** 36 hospitals, including leading heart hospital at Univ. of Minnesota. **Educational facilities:** 48 public school districts; 13 colleges and universities. **Further information:** Greater Minneapolis Chamber of Commerce, 81 S. 9th St., Ste. 200, Minneapolis, MN 55402.

Mobile, Alabama

Population: 196,278; **Pop. density:** 1,596 per sq. mi.; **Pop. growth:** −2.1%. **Area:** 123 sq. mi. **Employment:** 88,236 employed, 5.8% unemployed; **Per capita income:** $12,985; % change 1988-89: 6.0.

History: settled by French 1711; later occupied by U.S. 1813; inc. as town 1814, as city 1819; only seaport of Alabama.

Transportation: 4 rail freight lines, Amtrak, 4 major airlines, 65 truck lines; leading river system. **Communications:** 7 TV, 19 radio stations; CATV. **Medical facilities:** 7 hospitals. **Educational facilities:** 1 univ., 2 colleges. **Further information:** Chamber of Commerce, P.O. Box 2187, Mobile, AL 36652.

Montgomery, Alabama

Population: 187,106; **Pop. density:** 1,462 per sq. mi.; **Pop. growth:** 5.2%. **Area:** 128 sq. mi.. **Employment:** 84,877 employed, 5.4% unemployed; **Per capita income:** $14,962; % change 1988-89: 6.3.

History: inc. as town 1819, as city 1837; first capital of Confederacy 1861.

Transportation: 12 airlines; 2 railroads; 1 bus line; Alabama River is navigable to Gulf of Mexico. **Communications:** 5 TV, 6 radio stations; CATV. **Medical facilities:** 16 hospitals; VA and 32 clinics. **Educational facilities:** 48 public, 28 private schools, 5 universities. **Further information:** Chamber of Commerce, P.O. Box 79, Montgomery, AL 36101.

Nashville-Davidson, Tennessee

Population: 510,784; **Pop. density:** 1,064 per sq. mi.; **Pop. growth:** 6.9%. **Area:** 480 sq. mi.. **Employment:** 259,285 employed, 4.2% unemployed; **Per capita income:** $17,134; % change 1988-89: 4.4.

History: settled 1779; first chartered 1806; important Union base during Civil War.

Transportation: 1 airport, 2 railroads; 3 bus lines; transit system. **Communications:** 7 TV, 30 radio stations. **Medical facilities:** 14 hospitals; VA Hospital, speech-hearing center. **Educational facilities:** 16 colleges & universities. **Further information:** Chamber of Commerce, 161 4th Ave., Nashville, TN 37219.

Newark, New Jersey

Population: 275,221; **Pop. density:** 11,468 per sq. mi.; **Pop. growth:** −16.4%. **Area:** 24 sq. mi.. **Employment:** 110,570 employed, 13.3% unemployed; **Per capita income:** $24,729; % change 1988-89: 7.3.

History: settled by Puritans 1666; used as supply base by Washington 1776; inc. as town 1833, as city 1836.

Transportation: 1 international airport; 2 railroads; bus system; 2 subways. **Communications:** 3 TV, 5 radio stations. **Medical facilities:** 6 hospitals. **Educational facilities:** 5 universities and colleges; 71 public schools. **Further information:** Metro Newark Chamber of Commerce, 40 Clinton St., Newark, NJ 07102.

Newport News, Virginia

Population: 170,045; **Pop. density:** 2,464 per sq. mi.; **Pop. growth:** 17.4%. **Area:** 69 sq. mi. **Employment:** 72,259 employed, 5.9% unemployed; **Per capita income:** $15,721; % change 1988-89: 4.1.

History: the cities of Warwick and Newport News consolidated in 1958 into the larger city of Newport News; one of the world's major shipbuilding centers.

Transportation: 1 international airport; 2 railroads; Greyhound buses; local bus system. **Communications:** 7 TV, 20 radio stations received in area. **Medical facilities:** 3 hospitals; adolescent psychiatry hospital. **Educational**

facilities: 33 public schools. **Further information:** Peninsula Chamber of Commerce, A-12, Coliseum Mall, 1800 West Mercury Blvd., Hampton, VA 23666.

New Orleans, Louisiana

Population: 496,938; **Pop. density:** 2,497 per sq. mi.; **Pop. growth:** −10.9%. **Area:** 199 sq. mi.. **Employment:** 208,014 employed, 5.3% unemployed; **Per capita income:** $14,745; % change 1988-89: 5.5.
History: founded by French 1718, became major seaport on Mississippi R.; acquired by U.S. as part of La. Purchase 1803; inc. as city 1805; 29-day Battle of New Orleans fought during War of 1812.
Transportation: 2 airports; major railroad center; major international port. **Communications:** 7 TV, 18 radio stations. **Medical facilities:** numerous hospitals; major medical research center. **Educational facilities:** 13 universities and colleges. **Further information:** Chamber of Commerce, 301 Camp Street, New Orleans, LA 70130.

New York City, New York

Population: 7,322,564; **Pop. density:** 24,327 per sq. mi.; **Pop. growth:** 3.5%. **Area:** 301 sq. mi.. **Employment:** 3,118,000 employed, 7.4% unemployed; **Per capita income:** $22,064; % change 1988-89: 7.1.
History: trading post established by H. Hudson 1609; British took control from Dutch 1664 and named New York; briefly capital of U.S.; Washington inaugurated as president 1789; comprised of 5 boroughs: The Bronx, Brooklyn, Manhattan, Queens, Staten Island.
Transportation: 2 airports; 2 rail terminals; major subway network; ferry system; 4 underwater tunnels. **Communications:** 13 TV stations, 117 radio stations. **Medical facilities:** 100 hospitals; 5 medical research centers. **Educational facilities:** 94 universities and colleges; 976 public schools, 914 private schools. **Further information:** Convention and Visitors Bureau, 2 Columbus Circle, New York, NY 10019.

Norfolk, Virginia

Population: 261,229; **Pop. density:** 4,929 per sq. mi.; **Pop. growth:** −2.2%. **Area:** 53 sq. mi.. **Employment:** 91,406 employed, 5.5% unemployed; **Per capita income:** $15,721; % change 1988-89: 4.1.
History: founded 1682; burned by patriots to prevent capture by British during Revolutionary War; rebuilt and inc. as town 1805, as city 1845; location of world's largest naval base.
Transportation: 1 international airport; 4 major railroad systems in area. **Communications:** 7 TV, 38 radio stations. **Medical facilities:** 11 hospitals. **Educational facilities:** 53 public schools; 2 universities, 1 college. **Further information:** Hampton Roads Chamber of Commerce, 480 Bank St., Norfolk, VA 23510.

Oakland, California

Population: 372,242; **Pop. density:** 6,893 per sq. mi.; **Pop. growth:** 9.7%. **Area:** 54 sq. mi.. **Employment:** 177,604 employed, 7.4% unemployed; **Per capita income:** $22,249; % change 1988-89: 5.4.
History: area settled by Spanish 1820; inc. as city under present name 1854.
Transportation: 1 international airport; western terminus for 3 railroads; underground, underwater 75-mile subway. **Communications:** 1 TV, 3 radio stations. **Medical facilities:** 7 hospitals, including Children's Hospital Medical Center, VA hospital. **Educational facilities:** 94 public schools; 8 "eastbay" colleges and universities. **Further information:** Chamber of Commerce, 475 14th St., Oakland, CA 94612-1903.

Oklahoma City, Oklahoma

Population: 444,719; **Pop. density:** 736 per sq. mi.; **Pop. growth:** 10.1%. **Area:** 604 sq. mi.. **Employment:** 212,225 employed, 8.1% unemployed; **Per capita income:** $15,536; % change 1988-89: 6.7.
History: settled during landrush in Midwest 1889; inc. 1890; oil discovered 1928.
Transportation: 1 international airport; 3 railroads; public transit system; 5 major bus lines. **Communications:** 8 TV, 24 radio stations; cable TV. **Medical facilities:** 12 hospitals, VA hospital. **Educational facilities:** 87 public schools; 17 colleges and universities. **Further information:** Chamber of Commerce, One Santa Fe Plaza, Oklahoma City, OK 73102.

Omaha, Nebraska

Population: 335,795; **Pop. density:** 3,690 per sq. mi.; **Pop. growth:** 7.0%. **Area:** 91 sq. mi.. **Employment:** 182,892 employed, 3.0% unemployed; **Per capita income:** $16,753; % change 1988-89: 6.3.
History: founded 1854; inc. 1857; large livestock market; home for U.S. Strategic Air Command.
Transportation: 8 major airlines; 4 major railroads; intercity bus line. **Communications:** 8 TV, 22 radio stations. **Medical facilities:** 17 hospitals; institute for cancer research. **Educational facilities:** 229 public, 138 private schools; 3 universities, 6 colleges. **Further information:** Chamber of Commerce, 1301 Harney St., Omaha, NE 68102.

Philadelphia, Pennsylvania

Population: 1,585,577; **Pop. density:** 11,659 per sq. mi.; **Pop. growth:** −6.1%. **Area:** 136 sq. mi.. **Employment:** 670,436 employed, 7.4% unemployed; **Per capita income:** $19,750; % change 1988-89: 6.6.
History: first settled by Swedes 1636; by English 1681; named Philadelphia 1682; chartered 1701; Continental Congress met 1774, 1775; Dec. of Independence signed 1776; national capital 1790-1800; cap. of Penn. 1683-1799.
Transportation: 1 major airport; 3 railroads; major freshwater port; subway, el, rail commuter, bus, and streetcar system. **Communications:** 6 TV stations; 53 radio stations. **Medical facilities:** 124 hospitals. **Educational facilities:** 88 degree-granting institutions. **Further information:** Office of City Representative, 1660 Municipal Services Bldg., Philadelphia, PA 19107.

Phoenix, Arizona

Population: 983,403; **Pop. density:** 3,035 per sq. mi.; **Pop. growth:** 24.5%. **Area:** 324 sq. mi.. **Employment:** 572,775 employed, 4.6% unemployed; **Per capita income:** $17,705; % change 1988-89: 5.3.
History: settled in 1870; inc. as city 1881.
Transportation: 1 intl. airport; 2 railroads; 2 transcontinental bus lines; public transit system. **Communications:** 8 TV, 35 radio stations; CATV. **Medical facilities:** 42 hospitals, 1 medical research center. **Educational facilities:** 411 public schools; 11 institutions of higher learning. **Further information:** Chamber of Commerce, 34 W. Monroe, Suite 900, Phoenix, AZ 85003.

Pittsburgh, Pennsylvania

Population: 369,879; **Pop. density:** 6,725 per sq. mi.; **Pop. growth:** −12.8%. **Area:** 55 sq. mi.. **Employment:** 161,232 employed, 5.3% unemployed; **Per capita income:** $17,763; % change 1988-89: 7.8.
History: settled around Ft. Pitt 1758; inc. as city 1816; has one of largest inland ports; by Civil War, already a center for iron production.

Transportation: 1 international airport; 20 railroads; 2 bus lines; trolley/subway system. Communications: 6 TV, 25 radio stations. Medical facilities: 32 hospitals; VA installation. Educational facilities: 86 public schools; 3 universities, 6 colleges. Further information: Chamber of Commerce, 3 Gateway Ctr., Pittsburgh, PA 15222.

Portland, Oregon

Population: 437,319; Pop. density: 4,246 per sq. mi.; Pop. growth: 18.8%. Area: 103 sq. mi.. Employment: 199,741 employed, 5.3% unemployed; Per capita income: $18,163; % change 1988-89: 8.0.

History: settled by pioneers 1845, developed as trading center, aided by California Gold Rush 1849; chartered as city 1851.

Transportation: 1 international airport; 3 major rail freight lines, Amtrak; 2 intercity bus lines; 27-mi. frontage freshwater port; mass transit bus and rail system. Communications: 5 TV, 23 radio stations. Medical facilities: 32 hospitals; VA hospital. Educational facilities: 11 colleges and universities, 3 community colleges. Further information: Chamber of Commerce, 221 N.W. 2nd Ave., Portland, OR 97209.

Raleigh, North Carolina

Population: 207,951; Pop. density: 3,851 per sq. mi.; Pop. growth: 38.4%. Area: 54 sq. mi. Employment: 114,337 employed, 4.6% unemployed; Per capita income: $18,945; % change 1988-89: 6.7.

History: named after Sir Walter Raleigh, site chosen for capital 1788; laid out 1792; inc. 1795; occupied by Gen. Sherman 1865.

Transportation: 1 airport, 7 airlines; 3 railroads; 1 bus line. Communications: 6 TV stations; 20 radio stations. Medical facilities: 11 hospitals. Educational facilities: 4 colleges and universities, 4 junior colleges; 82 public schools. Further information: Chamber of Commerce, 800 S. Salisbury St., P.O. Box 2978, Raleigh, NC 27602.

Richmond, Virginia

Population: 203,056; Pop. density: 3,384 per sq. mi.; Pop. growth: −7.4%. Area: 60 sq. mi. Employment: 108,571 employed, 6.0% unemployed; Per capita income: $20,164; % change 1988-89: 7.8.

History: first settled 1607; attacked by British under Benedict Arnold 1781; inc. as city 1782; capital of Confederate States of America, 1861.

Transportation: 1 international airport; 4 railroads, 3 intracity bus lines; deepwater terminal accessible to ocean-going ships. Communications: 6 TV, 26 radio stations; CATV. Medical facilities: Medical Coll. of Virginia renowned for heart and kidney transplants; 19 other hospitals including VA facility. Educational facilities: 173 public, 45 private schools; 9 colleges and universities. Further information: Chamber of Commerce, P.O. Box 12324, Richmond, VA 23241.

Riverside, California

Population: 226,505; Pop. density: 3,190 per sq. mi.; Pop. growth: 32.8%. Area: 71 sq. mi.. Employment: 128,211 employed, 9.8% unemployed; Per capita income: $16,238; % change 1988-89: 3.1.

History: founded 1870; inc. 1886; known for its citrus industry.

Communications: 11 TV, 13 radio stations. Educational facilities: 1 univ., 1 college. Further information: Chamber of Commerce, 4261 Main St., Riverside, CA 92501.

Rochester, New York

Population: 231,636; Pop. density: 6,813 per sq. mi.; Pop. growth: −4.2%. Area: 34 sq. mi.. Employment: 106,307 employed, 7.9% unemployed; Per capita income: $19,858; % change 1988-89: 8.3.

History: first permanent white settlement 1812; inc. as village 1817, as city 1834; developed as Erie Canal town.

Transportation: 1 airport; Amtrak; 3 bus lines; intracity transit service; Port of Rochester. Communications: 5 TV, 18 radio stations. Medical facilities: 8 general hospitals. Educational facilities: 10 colleges, 3 community colleges. Further information: Chamber of Commerce, 55 St. Paul St., Rochester, NY 14604.

Sacramento, California

Population: 369,365; Pop. density: 3,848 per sq. mi.; Pop. growth: 34.0%. Area: 96 sq. mi.. Employment: 163,167 employed, 7.6% unemployed; Per capita income: $18,299; % change 1988-89: 6.8.

History: settled 1839; important trading center during California Gold Rush 1840s.

Transportation: metropolitan airport; 2 mainline transcontinental rail carriers; bus and light rail system. Communications: 7 TV, 25 radio stations. Medical facilities: 8 hospitals. Educational facilities: 2 universities, 4 community colleges. Further information: Chamber of Commerce, 917 7th St., P.O. Box 1017, Sacramento, CA 95805.

St. Louis, Missouri

Population: 396,685; Pop. density: 6,503 per sq. mi.; Pop. growth: −12.4%. Area: 61 sq. mi.. Employment: 169,227 employed, 8.0% unemployed; Per capita income: $18,957; % change 1988-89: 6.5.

History: founded 1764 as a fur trading post by French; acquired by U.S. 1803; chartered as city 1822; gateway to Missouri R.

Transportation: 1 international airport; major rail center, 17 trunk line railroads; major inland port; 14 bus lines; 14 barge lines. Communications: 6 TV, 35 radio stations. Medical facilities: 65 hospitals. Educational facilities: 5 universities, 26 colleges and seminaries. Further information: Regional Commerce and Growth Assoc., Ten Broadway, St. Louis, MO 63102.

St. Paul, Minnesota

Population: 272,235; Pop. density: 5,235 per sq. mi.; Pop. growth: 0.7%. Area: 52 sq. mi.. Employment: 138,275 employed, 4.4% unemployed; Per capita income: $20,227; % change 1988-89: 5.5.

History: founded in early 1840s as "Pig's Eye Landing;" became capital of the Minnesota territory 1849 and chartered as St. Paul.

Transportation: 1 international airport; 6 major rail lines; 3 interstate bus lines; public transit system. Communications: 6 TV, 35 radio stations; CATV. Medical facilities: 7 hospitals. Educational facilities: 2 univ., 5 colleges. Further information: Chamber of Commerce, 600 N. Central Tower, 445 Minnesota St., St. Paul, MN 55101.

St. Petersburg, Florida

Population: 238,629; Pop. density: 4,186 per sq. mi.; Pop. growth: 0.0%. Area: 57 sq. mi.. Employment: 129,752 employed, 6.6% unemployed; Per capita income: $17,675; % change 1988-89: 7.5.

History: settled in 1888; inc. 1892.

Transportation: 1 international airport; bus system; 1 full-service port. Communications: 9 TV, 49 radio stations. Medical facilities: 9 hospitals. Educational facilities: 128 public schools; 6 colleges. Further information:

Chamber of Commerce, P.O. Box 1371, St. Petersburg, FL 33731.

San Antonio, Texas

Population: 935,933; **Pop. density:** 3,559 per sq. mi.; **Pop. growth:** 19.1%. **Area:** 263 sq. mi.. **Employment:** 403,314 employed, 8.1% unemployed; **Per capita income:** $14,144; % change 1988-89: 5.0.

History: first Spanish garrison 1718; Battle at the Alamo fought here 1835; city subsequently captured by Texans; inc. 1837.

Transportation: 1 intl. airport; 4 railroads; 6 bus lines; public transit system. **Communications:** 7 TV, 31 radio stations. **Medical facilities:** 26 hospitals; major medical center. **Educational facilities:** 14 universities and colleges. **Further information:** Chamber of Commerce, 602 E. Commerce, P.O. Box 1628, San Antonio, TX 78296.

San Diego, California

Population: 1,110,549; **Pop. density:** 3,470 per sq. mi.; **Pop. growth:** 26.8%. **Area:** 320 sq. mi.. **Employment:** 520,108 employed, 6.3% unemployed; **Per capita income:** $18,651; % change 1988-89: 5.6.

History: claimed by the Spanish 1542, first mission est. 1769; scene of conflict during Mexican-American War 1846; inc. 1850.

Transportation: 1 major airport; 1 railroad; major freeway system; bus system; trolley system. **Communications:** 8 TV, 22 radio stations. **Medical facilities:** 31 hospitals. **Educational facilities:** 5 universities, 7 colleges. **Further information:** Greater SD Chamber of Commerce, 402 W. Broadway, Suite 1000, San Diego, CA 92101-3585.

San Francisco, California

Population: 723,959, **Pop. density:** 15,934 per sq. mi.; **Pop. growth:** 6.6%. **Area:** 46 sq. mi.. **Employment:** 372,694 employed, 5.1% unemployed; **Per capita income:** $28,170; % change 1988-89: 6.5.

History: sited by Spanish 1542, settled by 1776; claimed by U.S. 1846; became a major city during California Gold Rush 1849; inc. as city 1850; earthquake devasted city 1906.

Transportation: 1 major airport; intracity railway system; 2 railway transit systems; bus and railroad service; ferry system; 1 underwater tunnel. **Communications:** 14 TV and cable stations; 69 radio stations. **Medical facilities:** 23 hospitals; 1 major medical center. **Educational facilities:** 4 universities and colleges. **Further information:** Chamber of Commerce, 465 California Street, San Francisco, CA 94104.

San Jose, California

Population: 782,248; **Pop. density:** 4,951 per sq. mi.; **Pop. growth:** 24.3%. **Area:** 158 sq. mi.. **Employment:** 355,348 employed, 6.5% unemployed; **Per capita income:** $24,581; % change 1988-89: 6.3.

History: founded by the Spanish 1777 between San Francisco and Monterey; briefly capital of Calif. 1849-51; inc. 1850.

Transportation: 1 international airport; 2 railroads; bus system. **Communications:** 4 TV, 14 radio stations. **Medical facilities:** 6 hospitals. **Educational facilities:** 3 universities and colleges. **Further information:** Chamber of Commerce, 180 S. Market St., San Jose, CA 95113.

Santa Ana, California

Population: 293,742, **Pop. density:** 10,879 per sq. mi.; **Pop. growth:** 44.0%. **Area:** 27 sq. mi.. **Employment:** 128,908 employed, 6.1% unemployed (county); **Per capita income:** $24,288; % change 1988-89: 6.6.

History: founded 1869; inc. as city 1886.

Transportation: 1 airport; 5 major freeways including main Los Angeles-San Diego artery; Amtrak. **Communications:** CATV system. **Medical facilities:** 4 hospitals. **Educational facilities:** 1 university, 1 community college. **Further information:** Chamber of Commerce, 600 W. Santa Ana Blvd., P.O. Box 205, Santa Ana, CA 92702.

Seattle, Washington

Population: 516,259; **Pop. density:** 6,146 per sq. mi.; **Pop. growth:** 4.5%. **Area:** 84 sq. mi.. **Employment:** 331,316 employed, 4.8% unemployed; **Per capita income:** $21,137; % change 1988-89: 7.8.

History: settled 1851; inc. 1869; suffered severe fire 1889; played prominent role during Alaska Gold Rush 1897; growth followed opening of Panama Canal 1914; center of aircraft industry WWII.

Transportation: 1 international airport; 2 railroads; ferries serve Puget Sound, Alaska, Canada. **Communications:** 7 TV, 42 radio stations. **Medical facilities:** 27 hospitals. **Educational facilities:** 4 colleges; 11 community colleges. **Further information:** Greater Seattle Chamber of Commerce, 600 University St., Ste. 1200, Seattle, WA 98101-3186.

Shreveport, Louisiana

Population: 198,525; **Pop. density:** 2,482 per sq. mi.; **Pop. growth:** −4.1%. **Area:** 80 sq. mi.. **Employment:** 88,967 employed, 7.0% unemployed; **Per capita income:** $13,744; % change 1988-89: 4.7.

History: founded 1833 near site of a 160-mile log jam cleared by Capt. Henry Shreve; inc. 1839; oil discovered 1906.

Transportation: 1 airport; 2 bus lines. **Communications:** 5 TV, 16 radio stations; CATV. **Medical facilities:** 11 hospitals. **Educational facilities:** 3 univ., 3 colleges. **Further information:** Chamber of Commerce, P.O. Box 20074, Shreveport, LA 71120.

Spokane, Washington

Population: 177,196; **Pop. density:** 3,408 per sq. mi.; **Pop. growth:** 3.4%. **Area:** 52 sq. mi. **Employment:** 81,471 employed, 7.3% unemployed; **Per capita income:** $15,507; % change 1988-89: 8.5.

History: settled 1872; inc. as village of Spokane Falls 1881 but destroyed in fire 1889; reinc. as city of Spokane 1891.

Transportation: 1 international airport; 2 railroads; bus system. **Communications:** 5 TV and 25 radio stations. **Medical facilities:** 6 major hospitals. **Educational facilities:** 8 colleges and universities; 14 public school districts, 11 high schools. **Further information:** Chamber of Commerce, W. 1020 Riverside Ave., P.O. Box 2147, Spokane, WA 99210.

Stockton, California

Population: 210,943; **Pop. density:** 5,274 per sq. mi.; **Pop. growth:** 42.3%. **Area:** 40 sq. mi. **Employment:** 73,064 employed, 6.5% unemployed; **Per capita income:** $14,861; % change 1988-89: 4.2.

History: site purchased 1842; settled 1847; inc. 1850; chief distributing point for agricultural products of San Joaquin Valley.

Transportation: 1 airport, 7 railroads; 2 bus lines, city bus system. **Communications:** 5 TV stations. **Medical**

facilities: 4 hospitals; regional burn center. **Educational facilities:** 45 public schools; 4 colleges and universities. **Further information:** Chamber of Commerce, 445 W. Weber Ave., Suite 220, Stockton, CA 95203.

Tacoma, Washington

Population: 176,664; **Pop. density:** 3,696 per sq. mi.; **Pop. growth:** 11.5%. **Area:** 47.8 sq. mi. **Employment:** 77,637 employed, 7.0% unemployed; **Per capita income:** $15,546; % change 1988-89: 6.2.

History: discovered 1792 by the British; first permanent settlement 1864; terminus for the Northern Pacific Railroad; inc. 1884.

Transportation: 1 airport; 1 railroad; transit system; Port of Tacoma. **Communications:** NA. **Medical facilities:** 6 hospitals, VA facility. **Educational facilities:** 2 univ., 2 colleges. **Further information:** Chamber of Commerce, P.O. Box 1933, Tacoma, WA 98401-1933.

Tampa, Florida

Population: 280,015; **Pop. density:** 3,334 per sq. mi.; **Pop. growth:** 3.1%. **Area:** 84 sq. mi.. **Employment:** 176,711 employed, 5.7% unemployed; **Per capita income:** $17,675; % change 1988-89: 7.5

History: U.S. army fort on site 1824; inc. 1855.

Transportation: 1 international airport; Port of Tampa, 140 steamship lines; 2 bus lines. **Communications:** 7 TV, 27 radio stations. **Medical facilities:** 19 hospitals. **Educational facilities:** 131 public schools; 4 colleges and universities. **Further information:** Chamber of Commerce, 801 E. Kennedy Blvd., P.O. Box 420, Tampa, FL 33601.

Toledo, Ohio

Population: 332,943; **Pop. density:** 3,964 per sq. mi.; **Pop. growth:** −6.1%. **Area:** 84 sq. mi.. **Employment:** 152,709 employed, 11.8% unemployed; **Per capita income:** $16,893; % change 1988-89: 5.3.

History: site of Ft. Industry, 1794; settled 1817; figured in "Toledo War" 1835-36 between Ohio and Michigan over their borders; inc. 1837.

Transportation: 10 major airlines; 9 railroads; 100 motor freight lines; 2 interstate bus lines. **Communications:** 5 TV, 17 radio stations; 4 cablevision cos. **Medical facilities:** 9 major hospital complexes. **Educational facilities:** 7 colleges and universities. **Further information:** Office of Tourism and Conventions, 218 Huron, Toledo, OH 43604.

Tucson, Arizona

Population: 405,390; **Pop. density:** 4,095 per sq. mi.; **Pop. growth:** 22.6%. **Area:** 99 sq. mi.. **Employment:** 196,205 employed, 3.9% unemployed; **Per capita income:** $15,203; % change 1988-89: 5.7.

History: settled 1775 by Spanish as a presidio; acquired by U.S. in Gadsen Purchase 1853; inc. 1877.

Transportation: 1 international airport; 3 railroads; bus system. **Communications:** 6 TV, 27 radio stations; CATV. **Medical facilities:** 15 hospitals. **Educational facilities:** 2 univ., 1 college; 165 public schools. **Further information:** Chamber of Commerce, P.O. Box 991, Tucson, AZ 85702.

Tulsa, Oklahoma

Population: 367,302; **Pop. density:** 1,979 per sq. mi.; **Pop. growth:** 1.8%. **Area:** 185.6 sq. mi.. **Employment:** 186,103 employed, 5.6% unemployed; **Per capita income:** $16,016; % change 1988-89: 6.8.

History: settled in 1830s by Creek Indians; modern town founded 1882 and inc. 1898; oil discovered early 20th century.

Transportation: 1 international airport; 5 rail lines; 2 bus lines; transit bus system. **Communications:** 7 TV, 23 radio stations. **Medical facilities:** 6 hospitals. **Educational facilities:** 57 public and 23 private schools; 6 colleges and universities. **Further information:** Chamber of Commerce, 616 S. Boston Ave., Tulsa, OK 74119.

Virginia Beach, Virginia

Population: 393,069; **Pop. density:** 1,541 per sq. mi.; **Pop. growth:** 49.9%. **Area:** 255 sq. mi.. **Employment:** 161,142 employed, 5.0% unemployed; **Per capita income:** $17,383; % change 1988-89: 4.1.

History: area founded by Capt. John Smith 1607; formed by merger with Princess Anne co. 1963.

Transportation: 1 airport; 2 railroads; 2 bus lines; public transit system. **Communications:** 6 TV, 40 radio stations. **Medical facilities:** 2 hospitals. **Educational facilities:** 62 public schools; 1 university, 2 colleges. **Further information:** Chamber of Commerce, 4512 Virginia Beach Blvd., Virginia Beach, VA 23462.

Washington, District of Columbia

Population: 606,900; **Pop. density:** 9,633 per sq. mi.; **Pop. growth:** −4.9%. **Area:** 63 sq. mi.. **Employment:** 265,754 employed, 7.6% unemployed; **Per capita income:** $24,845; % change 1988-89: 6.9.

History: capital of the U.S.; 10-mile-square diamond at Potomac R. chosen by George Washington 1790 on land ceded from Va. and Md.; Congress first met 1800; inc. 1802; sacked by British, War of 1812.

Transportation: 2 airports; rail transit system; extensive local bus service; 1 bus, 2 rail lines. **Communications:** 5 TV, 61 radio stations. **Medical facilities:** 43 hospitals; major medical research center. **Educational facilities:** 6 universities and colleges. **Further information:** Convention and Visitors Association, 1411 K St. NW, Suite 500, Washington, DC 20005.

Wichita, Kansas

Population: 304,011; **Pop. density:** 3,010 per sq. mi.; **Pop. growth:** 8.6%. **Area:** 101 sq. mi.. **Employment:** 161,230 employed, 5.5% unemployed; **Per capita income:** $17,387; % change 1988-89: 5.6.

History: founded 1864; inc. 1871.

Transportation: 1 airport; 3 major rail freight lines; 2 bus lines. **Communications:** 5 TV, 23 radio stations. **Medical facilities:** 7 hospitals. **Educational facilities:** 95 public schools; 2 univ., 2 colleges. **Further information:** Chamber of Commerce, 350 W. Douglas, Wichita, KS 67202.

Yonkers, New York

Population: 188,082; **Pop. density:** 10,449 per sq. mi.; **Pop. growth:** −3.7%. **Area:** 18 sq. mi.. **Employment:** 96,287 employed, 7.1% unemployed; **Per capita income:** $20,396 (1988).

History: founded 1641 by the Dutch; inc. as town 1855; chartered as city 1872; borders NYC to the North.

Transportation: intracity bus system; rail service. **Communications:** see New York City. **Medical facilities:** 3 hospitals. **Educational facilities:** 30 public schools; 3 colleges. **Further information:** Chamber of Commerce, 480 N. Broadway, Yonkers, NY 10701.

Notable Tall Buildings in North American Cities

Height from sidewalk to roof, including penthouse and tower if enclosed as integral part of structure; actual number of stories beginning at street level. Asterisks (*) denote buildings still under construction Jan. 1992. Year is date of completion

City	Hgt. ft.	Stories
Akron, Oh.		
First National Tower	330	28
National City Center	301	23
Albany, N.Y.		
Erastus Corning II Tower	589	44
State Office Building	388	34
Agency (4 bldgs.), So. Mall	310	23
Atlanta, Ga.		
*C & S Plaza, 600 Peachtree St.	1,063	57
*One Peachtree Center	855	63
Atlantic Center/IBM (1988)	828	52
191 Peachtree (1990)	770	54
Westin Peachtree Plaza (1973)	723	71
Georgia Pacific Tower (1981)	697	51
Promenade II/AT&T (1989)	691	40
Southern Bell Telephone, (1980)	677	47
*GLG Center	602	51
Concourse Tower #5 (1988)	570	32
First Atlanta Bank, 2 Peachtree (1968)	556	44
Marriott Marquis (1985)	554	52
*Concourse Tower #6	553	32
Equitable Building, 100 Peachtree (1967)	453	34
101 Marietta Tower, 101 Marietta (1975)	446	36
Ravinia #3 (1991)	444	34
Bell South Enterprises (1990)	428	28
Atlanta Plaza I (1986)	425	32
Park Place, 2660 Peachtree (1986)	420	40
Club Towers Apts. (1989)	410	38
First American Bank (1961)	409	32
Peachtree Summit (1975)	406	31
North Avenue Tower, (1979)	403	26
Tower Place, 3361 Piedmont Rd. (1974)	401	29
First Union Bank, (1987)	396	30
Richard B. Russell, Federal Bldg. (1978)	383	26
Atlanta Hilton Hotel (1974)	383	32
Peachtree Center, Harris Bldg. (1975)	382	31
AT&T Long Line Bldg. (1975)	380	
Marquis One (1985)	378	30
Marquis Two, (1987)	378	30
Trust Company Bank (1968)	377	28
Coastal States Insurance (1971)	377	27
Peachtree Center Cain Building (1972)	376	30
Peachtree Center Building (1966)	374	31
One Georgia Center (1966)	371	29
The Campanile, 1145 Peachtree (1987)	367	25
Riverwood Tower (1989)	362	26
Austin, Tex.		
One American Center, 600 Congress	395	32
One Congress Plaza, 111 Congress	391	30
First RepublicBank Tower, 515 Congress	328	26
Baltimore, Md.		
U.S. Fidelity & Guaranty Co.	529	40
Maryland National Bank Bldg.	509	34
6 St. Paul Place	493	37
World Trade Center Bldg.	395	32
Tremont Plaza Hotel	395	37
250 W. Pratt St.	360	26
Harbor Court	356	28
Blaustein Bldg.	342	30
Union Trust Tower	335	24
Central Savings Bank Bldg.	330	28
Charles Center South	330	26
Baton Rouge, La.		
State Capitol (1932)	460	34
Hancock Bank Bldg. (1974)	315	24
Birmingham, Ala.		
Southtrust Tower	454	34
Am South/Sonat Tower	390	30
South Central Bell Hdqts. Bldg.	390	30
City Federal Bldg.	325	27
Boston, Mass.		
John Hancock Tower	790	60
Prudential Center	750	52
Boston Co. Bldg., Court St.	605	41

City	Hgt. ft.	Stories
Federal Reserve Bldg.	604	32
International Place, 100 Oliver St.	600	46
First National Bank of Boston	591	37
One Financial Center	590	46
Shawmut Bank Bldg.	520	38
Exchange Place, 53 State St.	510	39
Sixty State St.	509	38
One Post Office Sq.	507	40
One Beacon St.	507	40
New England Merch. Bank Bldg.	500	40
U.S. Custom House	496	32
John Hancock Bldg.	495	26
State St. Bank Bldg.	477	34
125 High St. (1990)	455	30
One Hundred Summer St.	450	33
McCormack Bldg.	401	22
Keystone Custodian Funds.	400	32
Saltonstall Office Bldg.	396	22
Devonshire, 250 Wash. St.	396	40
Harbor Towers (2 bldgs.)	396	40
Westin Hotel, Copley Place	395	36
Federal Center (1988)	393	28
75 State St. (1988)	390	31
John F. Kennedy Bldg.	387	24
Marriott Hotel, Copley Place	383	39
101 Federal St. (1988)	382	31
Longfellow Towers (2 bldgs.)	380	38
Buffalo, N.Y.		
Marine Midland Center (1971)	529	40
City Hall (1926)	378	32
Rand Bldg., not incl. 40-ft. beacon (1929)	351	29
Main Place Tower (1969)	350	26
Calgary, Alta.		
Petro-Canada Tower #2	689	52
Benkers Hall (1989)	645	50
Calgary Tower	626	
Canterra Tower (1988)	580	46
First Canadian Centre	547	44
Scotia Centre	504	38
Nova Bldg., 801 7th Ave. SW	500	37
Petro-Canada Tower #1	469	33
Two Bow Valley Square	468	39
Fifth & Fifth Bldg.	460	35
Home Oil Tower	463	34
Canada Trust Tower (1991)	462	40
Shell Tower	460	34
Dome Oil Tower	449	33
Four Bow Valley Square	441	37
Esso Plaza (twin towers)	435	34
Oxford Square	421	33
Family Life Bldg.	410	33
Pan Canadian Bldg., 150 9th Ave. SW	410	28
Norcen Tower	408	33
Alberta Stock Exchange Bldg.	407	33
Amoco Centre (1988)	396	30
Western Centre	385	40
Calgary Place	385	30
Three Bow Valley Square	382	33
Charlotte, N.C.		
One First Union Center (1988)	580	42
NCNB Plaza (1974)	503	40
Interstate Tower (1990)	462	32
Two First Union Center (1971)	433	32
Wachovia Center (1974)	420	32
Charlotte Plaza (1982)	388	27
First Citizens Plaza (1987)	320	23
Chicago, Ill.		
Sears Tower (world's tallest)	1,454	110
Amoco	1,136	80
John Hancock Center	1,127	100
311 S. Wacker	970	65
Two Prudential Plaza	901	64
AT&T Corporate Center (1989)	891	60
900 N. Michigan	871	66
Water Tower Place	859	74
First Natl. Bank	852	60
Three First National Plaza	775	57
Olympia Centre	727	63

City	Hgt. ft.	Stories
Leo Burnett Bldg. (1989)	700	46
600 N. Lakeshore Dr.	697	75
IBM Plaza	695	52
One Magnificent Mile	673	58
Daley Center.	662	31
1,000 Lake Shore Plaza	648	55
Lake Point Tower	645	70
Board of Trade, incl. 81 ft. statue	605	44
Prudential Bldg., 130 E. Randolph.	601	41
Antenna tower, 311 ft., makes total. . .	912	...
CNA Plaza	600	44
Huron Apts.	599	56
Marina City Apts., 2 buildings	588	61
Mid Continental Plaza, 55 E. Monroe . . .	580	50
Associates Center.	575	41
Pittsfield, 55 E. Washington St..	572	38
Onterie Center (1985)	570	58
Civic Opera Bldg.	555	45
Newberry Plaza, State & Oak	553	56
One South Wacker Dr.	550	40
Harbor Point.	550	54
Madison Plaza	551	45
190 S. LaSalle	550	40
LaSalle Natl. Bank, 135 S. LaSalle St. . .	535	44
One LaSalle Street	530	49
111 E. Chestnut St.	529	56
Chicago Mercantile Exchange (2 Bldgs) .	525	40
River Plaza, Rush & Hubbard	524	56
35 E. Wacker Drive	523	40
United Ins. Bldg., 1 E. Wacker Dr.	522	41
Lincoln Tower, 75 E. Wacker Dr.	519	42
Quaker Tower	518	35
Carbide & Carbon, 230 N. Mich.	503	37
Walton Colonnade.	500	44
Xerox Center.	500	40
One Financial Place	498	40
LaSalle-Wacker, 221 N. LaSalle St.	491	41
Amer. Nat'l. Bank, 33 N. LaSalle St. . . .	479	40
Bankers, 105 W. Adams St.	476	41
Brunswick Bldg.	475	37
310 Center	475	37
American Furniture Mart	474	24
333 Wacker Dr.	472	36
Sheraton Hotel, 505 N. Mich. Ave.	471	42
Playboy Bldg., 919 N. Mich. Ave.	468	37

Cincinnati, Oh.

City	Hgt. ft.	Stories
Carew Tower (1931)	568	49
Central Trust Tower (1979)	504	33
Dubois Tower, 5th & Walnut (1969)	423	32
Netherland Plaza	372	31
Central Trust Center	355	27
Atrium Two (1984).	350	30
Star Bank Center (1981)	351	26
Clarion North Tower.	350	33
Cinn. Commerce Center (1984)	346	29

Cleveland, Oh.

City	Hgt. ft.	Stories
Society Center.	948	57
Terminal Tower	708	52
BP America	658	46
Plaza Tower at Erieview	529	40
One Cleveland Center	450	31
Bank One Center	446	28
Justice Center, 1250 Ontario.	420	26
Federal Bldg..	419	32
National City Center.	410	35
Ameritrust	383	29
Cleveland St. J. F. Rhodes Tower.	373	20
Eaton Center.	360	28
Ohio-Bell..	360	22

Columbus, Oh.

City	Hgt. ft.	Stories
James A. Rhodes (State Office Tower). .	629	41
LeVeque Tower, 50 W. Broad	555	47
Ohio Bureau of Worker's Compensation & Ind. Comm. (1990)	530	33
Huntington Center, 41 S. High St.	512	37
Verne-Riffe State Office Tower	503	33
One Nationwide Plaza	482	40
One Riverside Plaza	456	31
Borden Bldg., 180 E. Broad	438	34
Three Nationwide Plaza (1989)	408	27
One Columbus.	366	26
Columbus Center, 100 E. Broad.	357	24

Dallas, Tex.

City	Hgt. ft.	Stories
First RepublicBank Plaza, 901 Main St.. .	939	73
Momentum Place	787	61

City	Hgt. ft.	Stories
Texas Commerce Tower	738	55
Allied Bank Tower.	721	60
Renaissance Tower.	710	56
Trammell Crow Center	686	50
Arco Tower, 1601 Bryan St.	660	49
First City Center	655	49
Thanksgiving Tower, 1600 Pacific Ave. . .	645	50
First National Bank	625	52
Republic Bank Tower	598	50
SW Bell Admin. Tower	580	37
One Lincoln Plaza	579	45
Olympia York, 1999 Bryan St.	562	37
Reunion Tower.	560	50
Southland Life Tower	550	42
Maxus Energy, 717 N. Harwood St.	550	34
2001 Bryan St.	512	40
San Jacinto Tower	456	33
Republic Bank Bldg., not incl. 150-ft. ornamental tower	452	36
Stouffer Hotel	451	29
Skyway Tower, ...	448	31
One Main Place	445	34
1600 Pacific Bldg.	434	31
Mercantile Natl. Bank Bldg., not incl. 115-ft. weather beacon	430	31
Magnolia Bldg.	430	31
Mart Hotel	400	29
Complex Union Tower	400	33
One Dallas Centre	386	30
Southwestern Bell Toll Bldg.	372	22

Dayton, Oh.

City	Hgt. ft.	Stories
Kettering Tower, 2d & Main (1970)	405	30
Dayton Arcade Centre (1989)	400	20
Mead World Hqtrs, 10 W. 2d St. (1976). .	385	28

Denver, Col.

City	Hgt. ft.	Stories
Republic Plaza.	714	56
Mountain Bell Center	709	54
United Bank of Denver	698	52
1999 Broadway	544	43
Arco Tower.	527	41
Anaconda Tower	507	40
Amoco Bldg., 17th Ave. & Broadway . . .	448	36
17th Street Plaza	438	35
Stellar Plaza	437	31
First Interstate Tower North	434	32
One Denver Place.	428	34
Brooks Towers, 1020 15th St.	420	42
Tabor Center, #1	408	32
Manville Plaza	404	29
Colorado Nat'l. Bank, 17th & Curtis	389	26
First Interstate Tower South	385	28
Security Life Bldg.	384	33
Mellon Financial Center.	374	31
Dominion Plaza	368	30
Lincoln Center	366	30
Denver Natl. Bank Plaza	363	29
Bank Western	357	27
Colorado State Bank	352	26

Des Moines, Ia.

City	Hgt. ft.	Stories
Principal Financial Group Bldg. (1990) . .	630	44
Ruan Center (1974)	457	35
Financial Center, 7th & Walnut (1973) . .	345	25
Marriott Hotel, 700 Grand Ave. (1981) . .	340	33
Plaza, 3d & Walnut (1984)	340	25

Detroit, Mich.

City	Hgt. ft.	Stories
Westin Hotel	720	71
Penobscot Bldg.	557	47
1 Detroit Center	491	40
Guardian	485	40
Renaissance Center (4 bldgs).	479	39
Book Tower	472	35
150 W. Jefferson Bldg.	470	29
Prudential 3000 Town Center	448	32
Cadillac Tower.	437	40
David Stott	436	38
ANR Bldg.	430	32
Fisher.	420	28
J. L. Hudson Bldg.	397	28
McNamara Federal Office Bldg.	393	27
2000 Prudential Town Ctr.	392	28
American Center	374	27
Top of Troy Bldg.	374	27
Comerica Bldg., 211 N. Fort	370	28
Edison Plaza	365	25
David Broderick Tower	358	34

City	Hgt. ft.	Stories
1st National Bldg.	350	25
Buhl, 535 Griswold	350	26

Edmonton, Alta.

City	Hgt. ft.	Stories
Manulife Place, 10170-101 St.	479	39
Royal Trust Tower.	476	30
AGT Tower, 10020-100 St.	441	34
Canada Trust Tower, 10124-103 Ave.	440	34
Metropolitan Place, 10303 Jasper Ave.	370	30
Scotia Place, 10060 Jasper Ave.	366	30
CN Tower, 1004-104 Ave.	365	26
Phipps McKinnon	359	21

Fort Wayne, Ind.

City	Hgt. ft.	Stories
One Summit Square, (1981)	442	26
Ft. Wayne Natl. Bank (1970).	339	26

Fort Worth, Tex.

City	Hgt. ft.	Stories
City Center Tower II (1984)	546	38
Burnett Plaza (1983)	538	40
Continental Plaza (1982)	520	40
1st City Bank Tower (1982)	475	33
Team Bank-Ft. Worth (1974).	457	37
Texas Bldg. (1955)	420	31

Harrisburg, Pa.

City	Hgt. ft.	Stories
State Office Tower #2.	334	21
333 Market St. (incl. tower).	327	19

Hartford, Conn.

City	Hgt. ft.	Stories
City Place	535	38
Travelers Ins. Co. Bldg.	527	34
Goodwin Square.	522	30
Hartford Plaza.	420	22
Hartford Natl. Bank & Trust	360	26
One Commercial Plaza	349	27
Bushnell Tower	349	27

Honolulu, Hi.

City	Hgt. ft.	Stories
Waterfront Towers (1990)	400	46
Ala Moana Hotel.	396	38
Pacific Tower.	350	30
Franklin Towers	350	41
Honolulu Tower	350	40
Discovery Bay	350	42
Hyatt Regency Waikiki	350	39
Maile Court Hotel	350	43
Regency Tower, 2525 Date St.	350	42
Pearlridge Square.	350	43
Yacht Harbor Towers.	350	40
Canterbury Place	350	40
Royal Iolani.	350	38
Island Colony	350	44
Century Center	350	41
Pacific Beach Hotel	350	43
Hawaiian Monarch Hotel	350	43
Waikiki Hobron.	350	43
Honolulu Tower 2	350	40
Tapa Tower, 2005 Kalia Rd.	350	36
Executive Center, 1088 Bishop St.	350	41
1001 Bishop	350	28

Houston, Tex.

City	Hgt. ft.	Stories
Texas Commerce Tower.	1,002	75
Allied Bank Plaza, 1000 Louisiana.	992	71
Transco Tower.	901	64
RepublicBank Center	780	56
Heritage Plaza, 1111 Bagby	762	53
interFirst Plaza.	744	55
1600 Smith St.	729	54
Gulf Tower, 1301 McKinney	725	52
One Shell Plaza (not incl. 285 ft. TV tower)	714	50
Four Allen Center	692	50
Capital Natl. Bank Plaza	685	50
One Houston Center	678	47
First City Tower	662	47
1100 Milam Bldg.	651	47
San Felipe Plaza.	620	45
Exxon Bldg.	606	44
The America Tower.	577	42
Marathon Oil Tower.	572	41
Two Houston Center	570	40
Dresser Tower.	550	40
1415 Louisiana Tower.	550	44
Pennzoil, 700 Milam (2 bldgs.)	523	36
Two Allen Center	521	36
Entex Bldg.	518	35
Huntington	506	34

City	Hgt. ft.	Stories
Tenneco Bldg.	502	33
Conoco Tower.	465	32
One Allen Center	452	34
Summit Tower West	441	31
Coastal Tower.	441	31
Four Leafs Towers (2 bldgs.).	439	40
Phoenix Tower.	434	34
Gulf Bldg.	428	37
The Spires	426	41
Central Tower (4 Oaks Place)	420	30
First City Natl. Bank.	410	32
Houston Lighting & Power	410	27
Niels Esperson Bldg.	409	31
Hyatt Regency Houston	401	34

Indianapolis, Ind.

City	Hgt. ft.	Stories
Bank One Tower (1989)	728	51
AUL Tower (1981).	533	38
Market Tower (1988)	515	32
Indiana Natl. Bank Tower (1969).	504	35
Riley Towers (2 bldgs.) (1963).	427	30
300 N. Meridian Bldg. (1988).	408	28
First Indiana Plaza (1988)	396	31
City-County Bldg. (1962)	375	28

Jacksonville, Fla.

City	Hgt. ft.	Stories
Barnett Tower	631	43
Independent Life & Acccident Ins. Co.	535	37
Southern Bell (1983)	447	32
Gulf Life Tower	435	27
American Heritage Ins. Bldg.	357	23
Blue Cross-Blue Shield (1973).	350	22

Kansas City, Mo.

City	Hgt. ft.	Stories
One Kansas City Place	626	42
AT&T Town Pavilion.	590	38
Hyatt Regency.	504	40
Kansas City Power and Light Bldg.	476	32
City Hall	443	29
Federal Office Bldg.	413	35
Commerce Tower.	402	32
City Center Sq.	402	30
Southwest Bell Telephone Bldg.	394	27
Pershing Road Associates	352	28

Las Vegas, Nev.

City	Hgt. ft.	Stories
Fitzgerald Casino-Hotel.	400	34
Landmark Hotel	356	31
Las Vegas Hilton	345	30

Lexington, Ky.

City	Hgt. ft.	Stories
Lexington Financial Center (1986).	410	30
Kincaid Tower (1980)	333	22

Little Rock, Ark.

City	Hgt. ft.	Stories
TCBY Towers (1986)	546	40
First Commercial Bank (1975)	454	30
Worthen Bank & Trust (1969)	375	24
Stephens Bldg. (1985)	365	25
Tower Bldg. (1960)	350	18
Union National Bank (1968)	331	21

Los Angeles, Cal.

City	Hgt. ft.	Stories
First Interstate World Center (1989).	1,017	73
First Interstate Bank.	858	62
Cal. Plaza 11A.	750	57
Wells Fargo Tower	750	54
Security Pacific Plaza	735	55
So. Cal. Gas Center (1990)	733	55
777 Tower.	725	52
Mitsui Fudoson (1990)	716	52
Atlantic Richfield Tower.	699	52
Bank of America Tower.	699	52
444 S. Flower St.	625	48
AT&T Bldg.	620	42
One California Plaza	578	42
Century Plaza Towers (2 bldgs.).	571	44
IBM Tower	560	45
Citicorp Plaza	534	42
1999 Ave. of the Stars (1989)	533	39
Manulife Tower (1990)	517	37
Union Bank Square	516	41
MCA-Getty	506	36
WTC Bldg.	496	36
Fox Plaza.	492	34
ARCO Center	462	33
City Hall	454	28
Equitable Life Bldg.	454	34
Transamerica Center.	452	32

City	Hgt. ft.	Stories
Mutual Benefit Life Ins. Bldg.	435	31
Warner Center Plaza III	415	25
Broadway Plaza	414	33
1900 Ave. of Stars	398	27
1 Wilshire Bldg.	395	28
The Evian.	390	31
400 S. Hope St.	375	26
Westin Bonaventure Hotel	367	35
Beaudry Center	365	29
Cal. Fed. Savings & Loan Bldg.	363	28
Century City North	363	26
Home Savings Tower	356	25

Louisville, Ky.

City	Hgt. ft.	Stories
First Natl. Bank	512	40
Citizen's Plaza	420	30
Humana Bldg.	350	27
Meindinger Tower	338	26
Brown & Williamson Tower.	338	26

Memphis, Tenn.

City	Hgt. ft.	Stories
100 N. Main Bldg.	430	37
Commerce Square	396	31
Sterick Bldg.	365	31
Clark, 5100 Poplar	365	32
Morgan Keegan Tower, 50 Front St. . . .	341	23
First Natl. Bank Bldg.	332	25

Miami, Fla.

City	Hgt. ft.	Stories
Southeast Financial Center (1983)	764	55
Centrust Tower (1987)	562	35
Metro-Dade Administration Bldg.	510	30
Florida National Tower (1986)	484	35
One Biscayne Corp..	456	40
Amerifirst Bldg. (1973)	375	32
Hotel Inter-Continental Miami	366	35
Venitia, 1635 Bayshore Dr.	365	42
Dade County Court House	357	28

Milwaukee, Wis.

City	Hgt. ft.	Stories
First Wis. Center & Office Tower	625	42
Milwaukee Center	422	28
Faison Bldg. (1989)	417	34
411 Bldg.	385	30
Northwestern Mutual Insurance (1989) . .	359	19
City Hall	350	9
Allen-Bradley Co.	333	17

Minneapolis, Minn.

City	Hgt. ft.	Stories
IDS Center (1973)	787	51
Norwest (1988)	777	57
*First Bank Place	774	53
Multifoods Tower (1983)	651	52
Piper Jaffray Tower (1984).	627	42
*Dain Bosworth Plaza.	550	40
Pillsbury Center, 200 S. 6th St. (1981) . .	545	40
Lincoln Centre, 333 S. 7th (1987)	496	31
Foshay Tower, not including 163-ft.		
antenna tower (1929).	496	32
Plaza VII, 45 S. 7th (1987)	494	36
100 South Fifth (1987)	490	36
Telephone Bldg. (1931).	423	27
Hennepin Co. Govt. Center (1974)	413	24
First Bank Place West (1960)	386	26
Marriott Hotel (1983)	379	31

Montreal, Que.

City	Hgt. ft.	Stories
Place Victoria	624	47
Place Ville Marie.	616	42
Canadian Imperial Bank		
of Commerce	604	43
Le Complexe Desjardins		
La Tour du Sud	498	40
La Tour du L'Est.	428	32
La Tour du Nord	355	27
Trust Royal Bldg.	429	32
Chateau Champlain Hotel	420	38
Port Royal Apts.	400	33
Royal Park Tower.	397	22
Sun Life Bldg.	390	26
500 Place d'Armes	390	32

Nashville, Tenn.

City	Hgt. ft.	Stories
Third National Financial Center	490	30
American General Center	452	31
Landmark Center	409	30
James K. Polk State Office Bldg.	392	32
Stouffer Hotel (1987)	385	35
First American N.A. Bank.	354	28

City	Hgt. ft.	Stories
One Nashville Plaza.	346	23

Newark, N.J.

City	Hgt. ft.	Stories
Natl. Newark & Essex Bldg.	465	36
Raymond-Commerce	448	37
Park Plaza Bldg.	400	26
Prudential Plaza	370	24
Public Service Elec. & Gas	360	26
Prudential Ins. Co., 753 Broad St.	360	26
AT&T Bldg.	359	31
Gateway 1	355	28

New Orleans, La.

City	Hgt. ft.	Stories
One Shell Square	697	51
Place St. Charles	645	53
Plaza Tower	531	45
Energy Centre	530	39
LL&E Tower, 901 Poydras	481	36
Sheraton Hotel.	478	47
Marriott Hotel	450	42
Texaco Bldg..	442	33
Canal Place One	439	32
1010 Common.	438	31
Int'l. Trade Mart Bldg.	407	33
225 Baronne St.	362	28
One Poydras Plaza	360	28
Hyatt-Regency Hotel, Poydras Plaza . . .	360	25
Hibernia Bank Bldg.	355	23

New York, N.Y.

City	Hgt. ft.	Stories
World Trade Center (2 towers) (1973) . .	1,368/	110/110
	1,362	
Empire State, 34th St. & 5th Ave.	1,250	102
TV tower, 164 ft., makes total (1931). .	1,414	. . .
Chrysler, Lexington & 43d (1930)	1,046	77
Amer. International, 70 Pine (1932)	950	67
40 Wall Tower (1929).	927	71
Citicorp Center (1977)	914	46
G.E. Bldg., Rockefeller Center (1933). . .	850	70
Chase Manhattan Plaza (1960)	813	60
Pan Am Bldg., 200 Park Ave. (1963) . . .	808	59
Cityspire (1989)	802	72
Woolworth, 233 Broadway (1913).	792	60
1 Worldwide Plaza	778	47
1 Penn Plaza (1972)	764	57
Carnegie Tower	756	59
Exxon, 1251 Ave. of Americas (1971). . .	750	54
Equitable Center Tower West (1985) . . .	750	54
60 Wall St. (1989).	745	50
1 Liberty Plaza (1972)	743	50
Citibank (1907)	741	57
World Financial Center, Tower C (1988) .	739	54
One Astor Plaza (1969).	730	54
Solow Bldg. (1979)	725	50
Marine Midland	724	52
Metropolitan Tower (1988)	716	66
Union Carbide Bldg. (1960).	707	52
General Motors Bldg. (1968).	705	50
Metropolitan Life, (1909)	700	50
500 5th Ave. (1928).	697	58
Chem. Bank, N.Y. Trust Bldg. (1963) . . .	687	50
55 Water St.	687	53
1585 Broadway	685	42
Chanin, Lexington & 42d (1929)	680	56
15 Columbus Circle (1970).	679	44
McGraw Hill, 1221 Ave. of Am. (1972) . .	674	51
Citicorp (Queens) (1990)	673	50
Lincoln, 60 E. 42d Street (1939)	673	53
1633 Broadway	670	48
Trump Tower, 725 5th Ave. (1983)	664	68
599 Lexington Ave. (1988)	653	47
Museum Tower Apts. (1985)	650	58
712 5th Ave. (1990)	650	52
American Brands, 245 Park Ave.	648	47
A. T. & T. Tower, (1983)	648	37
World Financial Center Tower B (1986). .	645	50
General Electric, 570 Lexington (1931) . .	640	50
Irving Trust, 1 Wall St. (1932)	640	50
345 Park Ave.	634	44
Grace Plaza, 1114 Ave. of Am.	630	50
1 New York Plaza (1969).	630	50
Home Insurance Co. Bldg.	630	44
N.Y. Telephone, 1095 Ave. of Am..	630	40
Central Park Place (1988)	628	56
888 7th Ave.	628	42
1 Hammarskjold Plaza	628	50
Waldorf-Astoria, 301 Park Ave. (1931) . .	625	47
Burlington House, (1970)	625	50
Olympic Tower, 645 5th Ave. (1976) . . .	620	51

City	Hgt. ft.	Stories
10 E. 40th St.	620	48
101 Park Ave.	618	50
750 7th Ave.	615	35
New York Life, 51 Madison Ave. (1928)	615	40
Ringa Royal Hotel	610	54
17 State St.	610	41
Penney Bldg., 1301 Ave. of Am.	609	46
IBM, 590 Madison Ave. (1983)	603	41
780 3rd Ave.	600	50
560 Lexington Ave.	600	22
Celanese Bldg. (1973)	592	45
U.S. Court House, 505 Pearl St. (1976).	590	37
*Kalikow Hotel.	588	58
Federal Bldg., Foley Square	587	41
Time & Life, 1271 Ave. of Am. (1959)	587	47
Cooper Bregstein Bldg., 1250 Bway.	580	40
Stevens Tower, 1185 Ave. of Am.	580	42
Municipal, Bldg. (1919)	580	34
520 Madison Ave. (1983)	577	42
1 Madison Square Plaza (1968)	576	42
World Financial Center Tower A (1986)	575	42
One Financial Sq. (1987)	575	37
Park Ave. Plaza (1981)	575	44
Westvaco Bldg. 299 Park Ave..	574	42
Marriott Marquis Hotel (1985)	574	42
Socony Mobil Bldg., East 42d St.	572	45
Sperry Rand Bldg., 1290 Ave. of Am.	570	43
600 3d Ave.	570	42
Helmsley Bldg., 230 Park (1929)	565	35
1 Bankers Trust Plaza	565	40
Hemsley Palace Hotel (1980)	563	51
30 Broad St.	562	48
Park Ave Tower (1986).	561	36
Sherry-Netherland, 5th Ave. & 59th St.	560	40
Continental Can, 633 3d Ave. (1983)	557	39
Sperry & Hutchinson, 330 Madison	555	39
Continental Corp., 180 Maiden Lane	555	41
Galleria, 117 E. 57th St. (1975)	552	57
Interchem Bldg., 1133 Ave. of Am.	552	45
151 E. 44th St.	550	44
N.Y. Telephone, 323 Bway. (1979)	550	45
919 3d Ave.	550	45
Burroughs Bldg., 605 3d Ave.	550	47
Bankers Trust, 33 E. 48 St. (1963)	547	44
Transportation Bldg., 225 Bway.	546	41
Equitable, 120 Broadway (1915).	545	45
1 Brooklyn Bridge Plaza (1976)	540	42
Paine Webber Bldg. (1961).	540	42
Ritz Tower, Park Ave. & 57th St.	540	42
Bankers Trust, 6 Wall St.	540	41
1166 Ave. of Americas	540	39
1700 Broadway	533	44
Downtown Athletic Club, 19 West St.	530	41
Nelson Towers, 7th Ave. & 34th St.	525	45
767 3d Ave.	525	45
Hotel Pierre, 5th Ave. & 61st St. (1928).	525	39
House of Seagram, (1958)	525	44
7 World Trade Center (1985)	525	38
Random House, 825 3d Ave.	522	44
3 Park Ave.	522	40
North American Plywood, 800 3d Ave.	520	42
Du Mont Bldg., 515 Madison Ave.	520	41
26 Broadway.	520	42
Newsweek Bldg., 444 Madison Ave.	518	31
Sterling Drug Bldg., 90 Park Ave.	515	43
First National City Bank.	515	41
Bank of New York, 48 Wall St.	513	41
Navarre, 512 7th Ave.	513	32
Manhattan Savings Bank, Bklyn.	512	43
ITT—American, 437 Madison Ave.	512	42
International, Rockefeller Ctr.	512	40
1407 Broadway Realty Corp.	512	44
United Nations, 405 E. 42 St. (1953)	505	39

Oakland, Cal.

City	Hgt. ft.	Stories
Ordway Bldg., 2150 Valdez St.	404	28
Kaiser Bldg.	390	28
Lake Merritt Plaza	371	27
American President Lines (1990)	360	29
Raymond Kaiser Engineer Bldg.	336	25
Clorox Bldg.	330	24

Oklahoma City, Okla.

City	Hgt. ft.	Stories
Liberty Tower (1971)	500	36
First National Center (1974)	493	33
City Place (1935)	440	32
First Oklahoma Tower (1982)	425	31
Kerr-McGee Center	393	30
Mid America Tower (1981)	362	19

Omaha, Neb.

City	Hgt. ft.	Stories
Woodmen Tower	469	30
Northwestern Bell Telephone Hdqrs.	334	16
Masonic Manor	320	22
First Natl. Center	320	22

Orlando, Fla.

City	Hgt. ft.	Stories
Sun Bank Center Tower (1988)	441	31
First F.A. Bldg. (1988).	409	28

Ottawa, Ont.

City	Hgt. ft.	Stories
Place de Ville, Tower C.	368	29
R.H. Coats Bldg..	326	27

Philadelphia, Pa.

City	Hgt. ft.	Stories
One Liberty Place (1987)	960	61
Two Liberty Place (1989)	845	52
Mellon Bank Center (1989)	795	54
Bell Atlantic Tower (1991)	739	53
Blue Cross Tower (1990)	700	50
Commerce Sq., #1 (1990)	572	40
City Hall Tower, incl. 37-ft. statue of Wm. Penn. (1901)	548	7
1818 Market St. (1974)	500	40
Provident Mutual Life (1983)	491	40
Meridan Bank (1972)	492	38
Phila. Saving Fund Society (1932)	492	39
Central Penn Natl. Bank (1970)	490	36
Centre Square (2 towers) (1973)	490/416	38/32
Industrial Valley Bank (1968).	482	32
Philadelphia National Bank (1930).	475	25
Two Mellon Plaza (1930)	450	30
2000 Market St. (1973)	435	29
Two Logan Square (1987)	435	34
2 Girard Plaza (1930)	412	30
Fidelity Bank Bldg. (1927)	405	30
Lewis Tower, 15th & Locust (1929)	400	33
One Logan Square (1982)	400	32
1500 Locust St. (1973)	390	44
Philadelphia Electric Co. (1970)	384	29
Academy House, 1420 Locust St.	377	37
Penn Mutual Life (1931)	375	20
The Drake, 15th & Spruce (1928)	375	33
INA Annex	369	27
Medical Tower, 255 So. 17th (1931)	364	33
United Engineers, 17th & Ludlow (1976)	344	22
Inquirer Building (1924)	340	18

Phoenix, Ariz.

City	Hgt. ft.	Stories
Valley National Bank (1972)	483	40
Arizona Bank Downtown(1976)	407	31
Phoenix Plaza (1989)	397	25
First Interstate Bank Plaza (1971)	372	27
Phoenix Center (1979)	361	27
Citibank Plaza (1964)	356	27
One Renaissance Sq. (1987)	347	26
Two Renaissance Sq. (1989)	347	26
Merabank Tower	341	26

Pittsburgh, Pa.

City	Hgt. ft.	Stories
USX Towers	841	64
One Mellon Bank Center	725	54
One PPG Place	635	40
Fifth Avenue Place (1987)	616	32
One Oxford Centre	615	46
Gulf, 7th Ave. and Grant St.	582	44
University of Pittsburgh	535	42
Mellon Bank Bldg.	520	41
1 Oliver Plaza	511	39
Grant, Grant St. at 3rd Ave.	485	40
Koppers, 7th Ave. and Grant.	475	34
Equibank Bldg.	445	34
CNG Tower (1987)	430	32
Pittsburgh National Bldg.	424	30
Alcoa Bldg., 425 Sixth Ave..	410	30
Liberty Tower	358	29
Westinghouse Bldg.	355	23
Oliver, 535 Smithfield St.	347	25
Gateway Bldg. No. 3	344	24
Centre City Tower.	341	26
Federal Bldg., 1000 Liberty Ave..	340	23
Bell Telephone, 416 7th Ave.	339	21
Hilton Hotel.	333	22
Frick, 437 Grant St.	330	20

Portland, Ore.

City	Hgt. ft.	Stories
First Interstate Tower	546	41
U.S. Bancorp Tower.	536	39
Koin Tower Plaza	509	35

City	Hgt. ft.	Stories
Standard Insurance Center.	367	27
Pacwest Center	356	31

Providence, R.I.

City	Hgt. ft.	Stories
Fleet National Bank	420	26
Rhode Island Hospital Trust Tower	410	30
40 Westminster Bldg.	301	24

Raleigh, N.C.

City	Hgt. ft.	Stories
2 Hanover Sq. (1991)	431	29
First Union (1991)	390	29

Richmond, Va.

City	Hgt. ft.	Stories
James Monroe Bldg.	450	29
City Hall (incl. penthouse)	425	17
Crestar Bank Hdqt. Bldg.	400	24
Federal Reserve Bank	393	26
Sovran Center	333	25

Rochester, N.Y.

City	Hgt. ft.	Stories
Xerox Tower	443	30
Lincoln First Tower	390	26
Eastman Kodak Bldg.	360	19

Sacramento, Cal.

City	Hgt. ft.	Stories
Wells Fargo Center	405	30
Park Plaza Tower	373	26
Renaissance Tower	372	28

St. Louis, Mo.

City	Hgt. ft.	Stories
Gateway Arch	630	...
Metropolitan Square Tower	591	42
S.W. Bell Telephone Bldg.	587	44
Mercantile Center Tower	550	37
Centerre Plaza.	433	31
Laclede Gas. Bldg., 8th & Olive	400	31
S.W. Bell Telephone Bldg.	398	31
Civil Courts.	387	13
Queeny Tower.	321	24
Counsel Tower.	320	30

St. Paul, Minn.

City	Hgt. ft.	Stories
First Natl. Bank Bldg., incl. 100-ft. sign.	517	32
Minn. World Trade Center	471	36
Galtier Plaza's Jackson Tower.	440	46
Osborn Bldg., 320 Wabasha.	368	20
Kellogg Square Apts.	366	32
Northwestern Bell Telephone (2 bldgs.).	340	16
Pointe of St. Paul	340	34
American National Bank Bldg.	335	25
North Central Tower, 445 Minn.	328	27
Amhoist/Park Tower	324	26

Salt Lake City, Ut.

City	Hgt. ft.	Stories
L.D.S. Church Office Bldg.	420	30
Beneficial Life Tower	351	21
Amer. Towers (2 bldgs.)	324	27

San Antonio, Tex.

City	Hgt. ft.	Stories
Tower of the Americas (1968)	622	...
Marriott Rivercenter (1988).	546	38
NBC Plaza (1988).	444	32
Tower Life (1929)	404	30
NCNB Plaza (1983)	387	28
Nix Professional Bldg. (1931)	375	23

San Diego, Cal.

City	Hgt. ft.	Stories
Symphony Tower (1989)	499	34
First Interstate Bank (1985)	398	23
Union Bank (1969).	388	27
First National Bank (1982)	379	27
The Meridan	375	27
Imperial Bank	355	24
Executive Complex (1963)	350	25
Wells Fargo Bldg. (1982)	348	20
Great American Bldg. (1974).	339	24

San Francisco, Cal.

City	Hgt. ft.	Stories
Transamerica Pyramid	853	48
Bank of America.	778	52
101 California St.	600	48
5 Fremont Center	600	43
Embarcadero Center, No. 4	570	45
Security Pacific Bank	569	45
One Market Plaza, Spear St.	565	43
Wells Fargo Bldg.	561	43
Standard Oil, 575 Market St.	551	39
One Sansome-Citicorp	550	39
Shaklee Bldg., 444 Market	537	38

City	Hgt. ft.	Stories
Aetna Life	529	38
First & Market Bldg.	529	38
Metropolitan Life.	524	38
Crocker National Bank	500	38
Hilton Hotel.	493	46
Pacific Gas & Electric	492	34
Union Bank.	487	37
Pacific Insurance.	476	34
Bechtel Bldg., Fremont St.	475	33
333 Market Bldg.	474	33
Hartford Bldg.	465	33
Mutual Benefit Life.	438	32
Russ Bldg.	435	31
Pacific Telephone Bldg.	435	26
Pacific Gateway	416	30
Embarcadero Center, No. 3	412	31
Embarcadero Center, No. 2	412	31
595 Market Bldg.	410	31
101 Montgomery St.	405	28
Cal. State Automobile Assn.	399	29
Alcoa Bldg.	398	27
St. Francis Hotel.	395	32
Shell Bldg.	386	29
Del Monte	378	28
Pacific 3-Apparel Mart	376	30
Meridien Hotel	374	34

Seattle, Wash.

City	Hgt. ft.	Stories
Columbia Seafirst Center (1985)	954	76
Two Union Square (1989)	740	56
Washington Mutual Tower (1988)	730	55
AT&T Gateway Tower (1990)	722	62
1001 4th Pl. (1969)	609	50
Space Needle (1962)	605	...
Pacific First Center (1989)	580	44
First Interstate Center (1983)	574	48
Seafirst 5th Ave. Plaza (1981)	543	42
Security Pacific Bank Tower (1977)	514	42
Smith Tower (1914)	500	42
520 Pike Tower (1984)	498	29
Key Tower (1986)	493	40
Federal Office Bldg.	487	37
US West Communications	466	33
One Union Square (1981)	456	38
1111 3d Ave. Bldg. (1980)	454	35
Westin Bldg., 2001 6th Ave. (1981)	409	34
Westin Hotel	397	40
Unigard Financial Center (1973)	389	27
Century Square (1986)	379	30
Sheraton Seattle Hotel	371	34
Fourth & Blanchard Bldg. (1979)	360	24
Crown Plaza Hotel	352	33

Tampa, Fla.

City	Hgt. ft.	Stories
Barnett Plaza (1986)	577	42
Tampa City Center (1981)	537	39
First Financial Tower (1973)	458	36
NCNB Plaza (1988)	454	33

Toledo, Oh.

City	Hgt. ft.	Stories
Owens-Illinois Corp. Headquarters	411	32
Owens-Corning Fiberglas Tower	400	30
Ohio Citizens Bank Bldg.	368	27
Toledo Govt. Center.	327	22

Toronto, Ont.

City	Hgt. ft.	Stories
CN Tower, World's tallest self-supporting structure (1976)	1,821	...
First Canadian Place (1979)	970	72
Bay/Adelaide Project (1991)	951	57
Scotia Plaza (1988)	902	68
Canada Trust Tower (1990)	869	52
Bay-Wellington Tower (1990)	705	47
Commerce Court West (1972)	784	57
Toronto-Dominion Tower (TD Centre) (1967)	758	56
Royal Trust Tower (TD Centre) (1969)	600	46
Royal Bank Plaza—South Tower (1977)	589	41
Manulife Centre (1975)	545	53
IBM Tower (TD Centre) (1986).	520	36
Two Bloor West (1974)	488	34
Exchange Tower (1981)	480	36
Commerce Court North (1930)	476	34
Simpson Tower (1968)	473	33
Eaton Tower (1990).	471	34
Cadillac-Fairview Tower (1982)	466	36
Palace Point (1991)	455	46
Palace Pier (1978).	453	46
Continental Bank Bldg. (1980)	450	35

City	Hgt. ft.	Stories	City	Hgt. ft.	Stories
Sheraton Centre (1972)	443	43	City of Faith Hospital	348	30
Hudson's Bay Centre (1974)	442	35	Philtower	343	24
Royal York Hotel (1929)	439	26			
Ernst & Yonge Tower (1990)	438	31	**Vancouver, B.C.**		
Old Toronto Exchange Bldg. (1990)	436	31	Royal Centre Tower (1973)	460	36
Leaside Towers (2 bldgs.) (1970)	423	44	Canada Trust Tower, 1055 Melville	454	35
Metro Hall (1991)	420	27	Scotiabank Tower	451	36
Commercial Union Tower (1974)	420	32	Bentall IV (1981)	450	35
Maple Leaf Mills Tower	419	30	Vancouver Center (1977)	450	36
Plaza 2 Hotel	415	41	Park Place (1984)	450	35
Sun Life Bldg., (1981)	410	28	T-D Bank Tower (1978)	440	30
			200 Granville Square (1973)	438	28
Tulsa, Okla.			Harbour Centre (1977)	428	21
Bank of Oklahoma Tower	667	52	Bentall III (1974)	399	31
City of Faith Clinic Tower	640	60			
1st National Tower	516	41	**Winston-Salem, N.C.**		
Mid-Continent Tower	513	36	Wachovia Bldg. (1965)	410	30
4th Natl. Bank of Tulsa	412	33	One Triad Park (1987)	340	20
320 South Boston Bldg.	400	24	Reynolds Bldg. (1924)	315	21
Occidental Place	388	28			
Univ. Club Tower	377	32			

Other Notable Tall Buildings in U.S.

Cape Canaveral, Fla., Vehicle Assembly Bldg., 40 (552); Amarillo, Tex., American Natl. Bank, 33 (374); Atlantic City, N.J., Taj Mahal, 51 (429); Charleston, W. Va., Kanawha Valley Bldg., 20 (384); Galveston, Tex., American National Ins., 20 (358); Hamilton, Ont., Century Twenty One, 43 (418); Knoxville, Tenn., United American Bank, 30 (400); Lincoln, Neb., State Capitol (432); Mobile, Ala., First Natl. Bank, 33 (420); Niagara Falls, Ont., Skylon, (520); Shreveport La., Commercial National Tower, 24 (365); Springfield, Mass., Valley Bank Tower, 29 (370); Tallahassee, Fla., State Capitol Tower, 22 (345).

Some Notable Foreign Structures

Structure	Hgt. ft.	Stories	Structure	Hgt. ft.	Stories
Bank of China, Hong Kong	1,209	72	Shinjuku Nomura, Tokyo	666	53
Moscow State Univ (incl. spire)	994	32	Overseas-Chinese Banking Corp., Singapore	660	52
Eiffel Tower, Paris	984	-	Shinjuku Sumitomo, Tokyo	656	52
MesseTurm. Bldg. Frankfurt	832	70	Parque Central Torre Oficinas, Caracas	656	56
One Canada Sq, London	800	56	Ukraine Hotel, Moscow	650	60
Palace of Science & Culture, Warsaw	790	42	Natwest Tower, London	600	50
M.L.C. Centre, Sydney	786	70	Tour Elf Aquitaine, Paris	578	48
Ikebukuro Office Tower, Tokyo	742	60	Ulm Cathedral, W. Germany	530	-
Carlton Centre, Johannesburg	722	50	Cologne Cathedral, W. Germany	515	-
Shinjuku Center, Tokyo	709	55	Tour du Cite Administrative, Brussels	492	36
Shinjuku Mitsui, Tokyo	696	55			
Tour Maine Montparnasse, Paris	688	56			

Notable Bridges in North America

Source: Survey of State Highway Engineers (1991)

Asterisk (*) designates railroad bridge. Span of a bridge is distance (in feet) between its supports.

Year	Bridge	Location	Longest span	Year	Bridge	Location	Longest span
				1964	Vincent Thomas	Los Angeles Harbor	1,500
				1909	Manhattan	East R., N.Y.C.	1,470
Suspension				1936	Triboro	East R., N.Y.C.	1,380
1964	Verrazano-Narrows	New York, N.Y.	4,260	1931	St. Johns	Portland, Ore.	1,207
1937	Golden Gate	San Fran. Bay, Cal.	4,200	1929	Mount Hope	Rhode Island	1,200
1957	Mackinac	Sts. of Mackinac	3,800	1960	Ogdensburg, N.Y.	St. Lawrence R.	1,150
1931	Geo. Washington	Hudson River, N.Y.-N.J.	3,500	1939	Deer Isle	Maine	1,080
1950	Tacoma Narrows	Washington	2,800	1931	Maysville (Ky.)	Ohio River	1,060
1936	¹Transbay	San Fran. Bay, Cal.	2,310	1867	Cincinnati	Ohio River	1,057
1939	Bronx-Whitestone	East R., N.Y.C.	2,300	1971	Dent	Clearwater Co., Ida.	1,050
1970	Pierre Laporte	Quebec	2,190	1900	Miampimi	Mexico	1,030
1951	Del. Memorial	Wilmington, Del.	2,150	1849	Wheeling, W. Va.	Ohio River	1,010
1968	Del. Mem. (new)	Wilmington, Del.	2,150				
1957	Walt Whitman	Phila., Pa.	2,000	**Cantilever**			
1929	Ambassador	Detroit-Canada	1,850	1917	Quebec	Quebec	1,800
1961	Throgs Neck	Long Is. Sound	1,800	1981	Ravenswood	W. Va.	1,723
1926	Benjamin Franklin	Philadelphia	1,750	1974	Commodore Barry	Chester, Pa.	1,622
1924	Bear Mt., N.Y.	Hudson River	1,632	1958	Mississippi R.	New Orleans, La.	1,575
1952	²Wm. Preston Lane Mem.	Sandy Point, Md.	1,600	1988	Mississippi R.	New Orleans, La	1,575
1903	Williamsburg	East R., N.Y.C.	1,600	1936	Transbay	San Fran. Bay.	1,400
1969	Newport	Narragansett Bay, R.I.	1,600	1968	W. 17th St.	Huntington, W. Va.	1,312
1883	Brooklyn	East R., N.Y.C.	1,595	1968	Mississippi R.	Baton Rouge, La.	1,235
1939	Lion's Gate	Burrard Inlet, B.C.	1,550	1955	Tappan Zee	Hudson River	1,212
1930	Mid-Hudson, N.Y.	Poughkeepsie	1,500	1930	Lewis and Clark	Longview, Wash.	1,200
				1909	Queensboro	East R., N.Y.C.	1,182

Year	Bridge	Location	Longest span
1927	Carquinez Strait	California	1,100
1958	Parallel Span	"	1,100
1930	Jacques Cartier	Montreal, P.Q.	1,097
1968	Isaiah D. Hart	Jacksonville, Fla.	1,088
1957	[3]Richmond	San Fran. Bay, Cal.	1,070
1929	Grace Memorial	Charleston, S.C.	1,050
1980	Newburgh-Beacon	Hudson R., N.Y.	1,000
1963	Newburgh-Beacon	Hudson R., N.Y.	1,000
1949	Martin Luther King	St. Louis, Mo.	962
1982	Yeager	Charleston, W. Va.	947
1975	Caruthersville, Mo.	Mississippi R.	920
1977	Saint Marys	Saint Marys, W. Va.	900
1969	Silver Memorial	Pt. Pleasant, W. Va.	900
1987	Carl Perkins	Ohio River/So. Portsmouth, Ky.	900
1986	Mississippi River	Natchez, Miss.	875
1940	Mississippi River	Natchez, Miss.	875
1938	Blue Water	Pt. Huron, Mich.	871
1972	Mississippi River	Vicksburg, Miss	870
1972	N. Fork American R.	Auburn, Cal.	862
1940	[3]Baton Rouge	Mississippi R.	848
1899	*Cornwall	St. Lawrence R.	843
1940	Mississippi River	Greenville, Miss.	840
1961	Helena, Ark.	Mississippi R.	840
1963	Brent Spence	Covington, Ky.	831
1963	Cincinnati, Oh.	Ohio River	830
1963	Mississippi, R.	Donaldsonville, La.	825
1940	Mississippi River	Vicksburg, Miss.	825
1929	Louisville	Ohio River	820
1961	Campbellton-Cross Point	New Brunswick-Quebec.	815
1950	Maurice J. Tobin	Boston, Mass.	800
1935	Rip Van Winkle	Catskill, N.Y.	800
1938	Cairo	Ohio River, Ill.-Ky.	800
1932	Washington Mem.	Seattle, Wash.	800
1936	McCullough	Coos Bay, Ore.	793
1935	[4]Huey P Long	New Orleans	790
1916	*Memphis (Harahan)	Mississippi R.	790
1892	*Memphis	Mississippi R.	790
1949	Memphis-Arkansas	Mississippi R.	790
1904	*Mingo Jct., W. Va.	Ohio River	769
1910	*Beaver, Pa.	Ohio River	767

Simple Truss

Year	Bridge	Location	Longest span
1976	Chester	Chester, W. Va.	745
1917	*Metropolis	Ohio River	720
1929	Irvin S. Cobb	Ohio River-Ill.-Ky.	716
1922	*Tanana River	Nenana, Alaska	700
1933	*Henderson	Ohio River-Ind.-Ky.	665
1967	I-77, Ohio River	Williamstown, W. Va.	650
1917	4 MacArthur, Ill.-Mo.	St. Louis	647
1919	Louisville	Ohio River	644
1933	Atchafalaya	Morgan City, La.	608
1924	*Castleton	Hudson River	598
1937	Delaware R.	Easton, Pa.	550
1930	Swindell Bridge	Pittsburgh, Pa.	545
1889	*Cincinnati	Ohio River	542
1952	Allegheny R., Tpk.	Pittsburgh, Pa.	534
1930	*Martinez	California	528
1951	Rankin	Pittsburgh, Pa.	525
1914	Old Brownsville	Brownsville, Pa.	520
1906	Donora-Webster	Donora-Webster, Pa.	515
1909	Hulton	Pittsburgh, Pa.	505
1967	Tanana River	Alaska	500

Steel Truss

Year	Bridge	Location	Longest span
1988	Glade Creek	Raleigh Co., W.Va.	784
1973	Atchafalaya R.	Krotz Springs, La.	780
1972	Atchafalaya R.	Simmesport, La.	720
1957	SR-3, Rappahannock	Middlesex Co., Va.	648
1940	Jamestown	Jamestown, R.I.	640
1949	Memphis	Mississippi R., Ark.	621
1978	Atchafalaya R.	Morgan City, La.	607
1938	US-22	Delaware River, N.J.	540
1955	Interstate (I-5)	Columbia River, Ore.-Wash.	531
1910	[4]McKinley, St. Louis	Mississippi River.	517
1972	Mississippi River	Muscatine, Ia.	512
1896	Newport	Ohio River, Ky.	511
1970	Lake Koocanusa	Lincoln Co., Mon.	500
1931	US-60	Cumberland R., Ky.	500
1958	Lake Oahe	Mobridge, S.D.	500
1958	Lake Oahe	Gettysburg, S.D.	500

Continuous Truss

Year	Bridge	Location	Longest span
1966	Columbia R. (Astoria)	Ore.-Wash.	1,232
1977	Francis Scott Key	Baltimore, Md.	1,200

Year	Bridge	Location	Longest span
1943	Dubuque, Ia.	Mississippi R.	845
1956	[7]Earl C. Clements	Ohio R., Ill.-Ky.	825
1953	John E. Mathews	Jacksonville, Fla.	810
1940	Gov. Nice Mem.	Potomac River, Md.	800
1957	Kingston-Rhinecliff	Hudson R., N.Y.	800
1986	Rochester-Monaca	Rochester-Monaca, Pa.	780
1918	*Sciotoville	Ohio River	775
1976	I-275, Lawrenceburg Bridge	Ohio River	750
1981	Sewickley	Sewickley, Pa.	750
1984	13th St. Bridge, Ohio R.	Ashland, Ky.	740
1959	Monaca-E. Rochester	Monaca-East Rochester, Pa.	730
1976	Betsy Ross	Philadelphia, Pa.	729
1929	Madison-Milton	Ohio River	727
1977	I-275, Brent Bridge	Ohio River	720
1970	Vanport	Vanport, Pa.	715
1966	[5]Matthew E. Welsh	Mauckport	707
1962	Champlain	Montreal, P.Q.	707
1973	Girard Point	Philadelphia, Pa.	700
1954	Pa. Tpk., Delaware R.	Philadephia, Pa.	682
1949	George Platt	Philadelphia, Pa.	680
1938	Port Arthur-Orange	Texas	680
1929	*Cincinnati	Ohio River	675
1928	Cape Girardeau, Mo.	Mississippi R.	672
1946	Chester, Ill.	Mississippi R.	670
1970	Gulfgate	Port Arthur, Tex.	664
1953	Jefferson City	Missouri River	640
1930	Quincy, Ill.	Mississippi R.	628
1961	Shippingport	Shippingport, Pa.	620
1959	US 181, over harbor	Corpus Christi, Tex.	620
1934	Bourne	Cape Cod Canal	616
1935	Sagamore	Cape Cod Canal	616
1965	Clarion R. (I-80)	Clarion, Pa.	612
1975	Donora-Monesson	Donora-Monesson, Pa.	608
1957	Blatnik	Duluth, Minn.	600
1965	Rio Grande Gorge	Taos, N.M.	600
1941	Columbia River	Kettle Falls, Wash.	600
1954	Columbia River	Umatilla, Ore.	600
1954	Columbia River	The Dalles, Ore.	576
1962	W. Br. Feather River	Oroville, Cal.	576
1967	Glenwood	Pittsburgh, Pa.	567
1936	Meredosia	Illinois River	567
1936	Mark Twain Mem.	Hannibal, Mo.	562
1957	Mackinac	Mackinac Straits, Mich.	560

Continuous Box and Plate Girder

Year	Bridge	Location	Longest span
1988	Piney Creek-US19	Beckley, W. Va.	1,760
1973	Danville-US119	Danville, W. Va.	1,545
1983	Mississippi R.	Luling, La.	1,222
1974	Dunbar-S. Charleston	South Charleston, W. Va.	842
1988	Beaver Creek-I-64	Beckley, W. Va.	764
1982	Houston Ship Chan.	Houston, Tex.	750
1967	San Mateo-Hayward No. 2	San Fran. Bay, Cal.	750
1977	Intracoastal Canal	Gibbstown, La.	750
1976	Intracoastal Canal	Forked Is., La.	750
1969	[6]San Diego-Coronado	San Diego Bay, Cal.	660
1987	Columbia R.	Umatilla Ore.	629
1981	Douglas	Juneau, Alaska	620
1976	Wax L. Outlet	Calumet, La.	618
1975	S. Charleston-I-64	South Charleston, W. Va.	612
1981	Glenn Jackson (I-205)	Columbia R., Ore.-Wash.	600
1967	Poplar St.	St. Louis, Mo.	600
1982	Illinois R.	Pekin, Ill.	550
1982	I-440	Arkansas R.	540
1977	US-64, Tennessee R.	Savannah, Tenn.	525
1988	Mon City	Monongahela, Pa.	520
1965	McDonald-Cartier	Ottawa, Ont.	520
1986	Veterans	Pittsburgh, Pa.	440
1986	SR 76, Cumberland R.	Dover, Tenn.	440
1985	SR 20, Tennessee R.	Perryville, Tenn.	440
1970	Willamette R., I-205.	West Linn, Ore.	430
1974	I-430	Arkansas R.	430
1985	I-435	Missouri R., Ks.-Mo.	425
1984	US-36	Missouri R., Ks.-Mo.	425
1972	I-635, Kansas City	Missouri R., Kan.-Mo.	425
1985	FAU 3456, Tennessee R.	Chattanooga, Tenn.	420
1967	I-24, Tennessee R.	Marion Co., Tenn.	420
1978	Snake River	Clarkston, Wash.	420
1975	36th St.	Charleston, W.Va.	420

Year	Bridge	Location	Longest span
1976	35th St. Bridge, Kanawha	Charleston, W. Va.	415
1986	SR 1, Tennessee R.	New Johnsonville, Tenn.	411
1979	Arkansas R.	Clarksville, Ark.	410
1975	Yukon River	Alaska	410

Continuous Plate

Year	Bridge	Location	Longest span
1973	Ship Channel (I-610)	Houston, Tex.	630
1971	W. Atchafalaya	Henderson, La.	573
1981	Illinois 23	Illinois R., Ill.	510
1968	Trinity R.	Dallas, Tex.	480
1978	San Joaquin R.	Antioch, Cal.	460
1977	Thomas Johnson Mem.	Solomons, Md.	451
1975	Lewis Bridge	St. Louis, Mo.	450
1975	I-129	Missouri R., Ia.	450
1967	Mississippi River	LaCrescent, Minn.	450
1972	Whiskey Bay Pilot Channel	Ramah, La.	425
1966	I-480	Missouri R., Ia.-Neb.	425
1970	I-435	Missouri R., Mo.	425
1972	I-80	Missouri R., Ia.-Neb.	425
1978	I-24	Cumberland R., Ky.	420

Cable-Stayed

Year	Bridge	Location	Longest span
1991	Talmadge Mem'l	Savannah, Ga.	1,100
1979	Intercity	Pasco-Kennewick, Wash.	970
1985	E. Huntington	Huntington, W. Va.	900
1985	Mississippi R.	Quincy, Ill.	900
1980	Veterans Mem'l	Weirton, W. Va.-Steubenville, Oh.	820
1991	Neches R.	Port Arthur - Orange, Tex.	640
1990	James River	Middlesex Co., Va.	630
1972	Sitka Harbor	Sitka, Alaska	450
1976	Capt. William Moore	Skagway, Alaska	250

I-Beam Girder

Year	Bridge	Location	Longest span
1980	Shreveport Int.	Louisiana	438
1948	US-27	Licking River, Ky.	316
1947	US-31E	Green River, Ky.	316
1941	US-62	Rolling Fork, Ky.	240
1942	Licking River	Owingsville, Ky.	240
1954	Fuller Warren	Jacksonville, Fla.	224

Steel Arch

Year	Bridge	Location	Longest span
1977	New River Gorge	Fayetteville, W. Va.	1,700
1931	Bayonne, N.J.	Kill Van Kull	1,652
1973	Fremont	Portland, Ore.	1,255
1964	Port Mann	British Columbia.	1,200
1916	*Hell Gate	East R., N.Y.C.	1,038
1959	Glen Canyon	Colorado River	1,028
1967	Trois-Rivieres	St. Lawrence R., P.Q.	1,100
1962	Lewiston-Queenston	Niagara River, Ont.	1,000
1976	Perrine	Twin Falls, Ida.	993
1941	Rainbow	Niagara Falls	984
1986	Moundsville Bridge, Ohio R.	Moundsville, W. Va.	912
1984	I-255	Mississippi R., Mo.	909
1972	9I-40, Mississippi R.	Memphis, Tenn.	900
1970	Lake Quinsigamond	Worcester, Mass.	849
1966	Charles Braga.	Somerset, Mass.	840
1936	Henry Hudson	Harlem River, N.Y.C.	840
1967	Lincoln Trail	Ohio R., Ind.-Ky.	825
1978	I-57, Cairo, Ill.	Mississippi R.	821
1980	I-65 Mobile River	Mobile, Ala.	800
1961	Sherman Minton	Louisville, Ky.	800
1936	French King	Conn. R. (Rt. 2, Mass.)	782
1978	I-470 Bridge, Ohio R.	Wheeling, W. Va.	780
1930	West End	Pittsburgh	780

Concrete Arch

Year	Bridge	Location	Longest span
1971	Selah Creek (twin)	Selah, Wash.	549
1968	Cowlitz River	Mossyrock, Wash.	520
1931	Westinghouse	Pittsburgh	460
1923	Cappelen	Minneapolis	400

Twin Concrete Trestle

Year	Bridge	Location	Longest span
1979	I-55/I-10	Manchae, La.	181,157
1969	L. Pontchartrain Cswy.	Mandeville, La.	126,720
1972	Atchafalaya Flwy.	Baton Rouge, La.	93,984
1963	8L. Pontchartrain	Slidell, La.	28,547

Concrete Slab Dam

Year	Bridge	Location	Longest span
1927	Conowingo Dam	Maryland	4,611
1952	SR-4, Roanoke R.	Mecklenburg Co., Va.	2,785
1936	Hoover Dam	Boulder City, Nev.	1,324

Drawbridges

Vertical Lift

Year	Bridge	Location	Longest span
1959	*Arthur Kill	N.Y.-N.J.	558
1965	Pennsylvania Railroad	Kirkwood-Mt. Pleasant, Del.	548
1935	*Cape Cod Canal.	Massachusetts	544
1960	*Delair, N.J.	Delaware River	542
1937	Marine Parkway	Jamaica Bay, N.Y.C.	540
1931	Burlington, N.J.	Delaware R.	534
1968	Second Narrows	Vancouver, B.C.	493
1912	*A-S-B Fratt	Kansas City	428
1945	*Harry S. Truman	Kansas City	427
1955	Roosevelt Island	East River, N.Y.C.	418
1980	US-17, James R.	Isle of Wight, Co., Va.	415
1932	*M-K-T R.R.	Missouri R.	414
1969	Wilm'gtn Mem.	Wilmington, N.C.	408
1930	Aerial.	Duluth, Minn.	386
1941	Main St.	Jacksonville, Fla.	386
1962	Burlington	Ontario	370
1941	Acosta	St. Johns R., Fla.	365
1922	*Cincinnati	Ohio River	365
1967	SR-156, James R.	Prince George Co., Va.	364
1964	Red R.	Alexandria, La.	360
1957	Industrial Canal	New Orleans, La.	360
1950	Red R.	Moncla, La.	360
1936	Tribo	Harlem River, N.Y.C.	344
1961	4Corpus Christi Harbor.	Corpus Christi, Tex.	344
1939	U.S. 1&9, Passaic R.	Newark, N.J.	333
1929	Carlton	Bath-Woolwich, Me.	328
1930	*Martinez	California.	328
1960	St. Andrews Bay	Panama City, Fla.	327
1929	*Penn-Lehigh	Newark Bay	322
1987	Industrial Canal Bridge.	New Orleans, La.	320
1920	*Chattanooga	Tennessee R.	310

Bascule

Year	Bridge	Location	Longest span
1969	E. Pearl River	Slidell, La.	482
1955	Chehalis R.	Aberdeen, Wash.	340
1917	SR-8, Tennessee River	Chattanooga, Tenn.	306
1940	Lorain, Ohio.	Black River	300
1968	Elizabeth River	Chesapeake, Va.	280
1913	Broadway	Portland, Ore.	278
1982	Columbus Drive.	Chicago R.	269
1954	Fuller Warren	St. Johns R., Fla.	267
1958	Morrison	Portland, Ore.	262
1926	Burnside	Portland, Ore.	252

Swing Bridges

Year	Bridge	Location	Longest span
1926	4Fort Madison	Mississippi R.	525
1930	Rigolets Pass	New Orleans, La.	400
1950	Douglass Memorial	Wash. D.C.	386
1945	Lord Delaware	Mattaponi River, Va.	252
1957	Eltham	Pamunkey River, Va.	237

Swing Span

Year	Bridge	Location	Longest span
1908	*Willamette R.	Portland, Ore.	521
1903	*East Omaha	Missouri R.	519
1952	US-17	York River, Va.	500
1897	*Duluth, Minn.	St. Louis Bay	486
1899	*C.M.&N.R.R.	Chicago	474
1913	Rt. 82, Conn-R.	E. Haddam, Ct.	465
1914	*Coos Bay	Oregon	458

Floating Pontoon

Year	Bridge	Location	Longest span
1963	Evergreen Pt.	Seattle, Wash.	7,518
1961	Hood Canal	Pt. Gamble, Wash.	6,471
1989	3rd Lake Washington Bridge	Seattle, Wash.	6,130

(1) The Transbay Bridge has 2 spans of 2,310 ft. each. (2) A second bridge in parallel was completed in 1973. (3) The Richmond Bridge has twin spans, 1,070 ft. each. (4) Railroad and vehicular bridge. (5) Two spans each 707 ft. (6) Two spans each 660 ft. (7) Two spans each 825 ft. (8) Total length of bridge. (9) Two spans each 900 ft.

Notable International Bridges

Angostura, suspension type, span 2,336 feet, 1967 at Ciudad Bolivar, Venezuela. Total length, 5,507.

(continued)

Bendorf Bridge on the Rhine River, 5 mi. n. of Coblenz, completed 1965, is a 3-span cement girder bridge, 3,378 ft. overall length, 101 ft. wide, with the main span 682 ft.

Bosporus Bridge linking Europe and Asia opened at Istanbul in 1973, at 3,524 ft. is the fifth longest suspension bridge in the world.

Gladesville Bridge at Sydney, Australia, has the longest concrete arch in the world (1,000 ft. span).

Humber Bridge, with a suspension span of 4,626 ft., the longest in the world, crosses the Humber estuary 5 miles west of the city of Kingston upon Hull, England. Unique in a large suspension bridge are the towers of reinforced concrete instead of steel.

Second Narrow's Bridge, Canada's longest railway lift span connecting Vancouver and North Vancouver over Burrard Inlet.

Oland Island Bridge in Sweden was completed in 1972. It is 19,882 feet long, Europe's longest.

Oosterscheldebrug, opened Dec. 15, 1965, is a 3.125-mile causeway for automobiles over a sea arm in Zeeland, the Netherlands. It completes a direct connection between Flushing and Rotterdam.

Rio-Niteroi, Guanabara Bay, Brazil, completed in 1972, is world's longest continuous box and plate girder bridge, 8 miles, 3,363 feet long, with a center span of 984 feet and a span on each side of 656 feet.

Tagus River Bridge near Lisbon, Portugal, has a 3,323-ft. main span. Opened Aug. 6, 1966, it was named Salazar Bridge for the former premier.

Zoo Bridge across the Rhine at Cologne, with steel box girders, has a main span of 850 ft.

Oldest Bridge in Continuous Use

Completed in 1841, the 178 ft. long, wood truss (with orthotropic steel deck) covered bridge spans the Housatonic River on Rt. 128 in West Cornwall, Connecticut.

Underwater Vehicular Tunnels in North America

(3,000 feet in length or more)

Name	Location	Waterway	Lgth. Ft.
Bart Trans-Bay Tubes (Rapid Transit)	San Francisco, Cal.	S.F. Bay	3.6 miles
Brooklyn-Battery	New York, N.Y.	East River	9,117
Holland Tunnel	New York, N.Y.	Hudson River	8,557
Lincoln Tunnel	New York, N.Y.	Hudson River	8,216
Thimble Shoal Channel	Northampton Co., Va.	Chesapeake Bay	8,187
Chesapeake Channel	Northampton Co., Va.	Chesapeake Bay	7,941
Baltimore Harbor Tunnel	Baltimore, Md.	Patapsco River	7,650
Hampton Roads (twin)	Hampton, Va.	Hampton Roads.	7,479
Fort McHenry Tunnel (2)	Baltimore, Md.	Baltimore Harbor	7,200
Queens Midtown	New York, N.Y.	East River	6,414
Sumner Tunnel	Boston, Mass.	Boston Harbor.	5,650
Louis-Hippolyte Lafontaine Tunnel	Montreal, Que.	St. Lawrence River	5,280
Detroit-Windsor	Detroit, Mich.	Detroit River	5,135
Callahan Tunnel	Boston, Mass.	Boston Harbor.	5,046

Land Vehicular Tunnels in U.S.

(over 2,000 feet in length.)

Name	Location	Lgth. Ft.	Name	Location	Lgth. Ft.
			Blue Mountain (twin)	Penna. Turnpike	4,435
E. Johnson Memorial	I-70, Col.	8,959	Lehigh	Penna. Turnpike	4,379
Eisenhower Memorial	I-70, Col.	8,941	Wawona	Yosemite Natl. Park	4,233
Allegheny (twin)	Penna. Turnpike	6,072	Big Walker Mt.	Bland Co., Va.	4,229
Liberty Tubes.	Pittsburgh, Pa.	5,920	Fort Pitt	Pittsburgh, Pa.	3,560
Zion Natl. Park	Rte. 9, Utah.	5,766	Dingess Tunnel.	Mingo Co., W.Va.	3,400
East River Mt. (twin)	Bland Co., Va.	5,412	Mall Tunnel	Dist. of Columbia.	3,400
Tuscarora (twin)	Penna. Turnpike	5,400	Caldecott	Oakland, Cal.	3,371
Kittatinny (twin)	Penna. Turnpike	4,660	Cody No. 1	U.S. 14, 16, 20, Wyo.	3,202

World's Longest Railway Tunnels

Source: Railway Directory & Year Book. Tunnels over 5 miles in length.

Tunnel	Date	Miles	Operating railway	Country
Seikan	1985	33.5	Japanese Railway	Japan
Dai-shimizu	1979	14	Japanese Railway	Japan
Simplon No. 1 and 2	1906, 1922	12	Swiss Fed. & Italian St.	Switz.-Italy
Kanmon	1975	12	Japanese Railway	Japan
Apennine.	1934	11	Italian State.	Italy
Rokko	1972	10	Japanese Railway	Japan
Mt. MacDonald	1989	9.1	Canadian Pacific	Canada
Gotthard	1882	9	Swiss Federal	Switzerland
Lotschberg	1913	9	Bern-Lotschberg-Simplon.	Switzerland
Hokuriku	1962	9	Japanese Railway	Japan
Mont Cenis (Frejus)	1871	8	Italian State.	France-Italy
Shin-Shimizu	1961	8	Japanese Railway	Japan
Aki	1975	8	Japanese Railway	Japan
Cascade	1929	8	Burlington Northern	U.S.
Flathead	1970	8	Burlington Northern	U.S.

STATES AND OTHER AREAS OF THE U.S.

Sources: Population: Commerce Dept., Bureau of the Census (1990 census, inc. armed forces personnel in each state but excluding such personnel stationed overseas); area: Bureau of the Census, Geography Division; forested land: Agriculture Dept., Forest Service; lumber production: Bureau of the Census, Industry Division; mineral production: Interior Dept., Bureau of Mines; commercial fishing: Commerce Dept., Natl. Marine Fisheries Service; value of construction: McGraw-Hill Information Systems Co., F.W. Dodge Division; per capita income: Commerce Dept., Bureau of Economic Analysis; unemployment: Labor Dept., Bureau of Labor Statistics; finance: Federal Deposit Insurance Corp., U.S. League of Savings Institutions; federal employees: Labor Dept., Office of Personnel Management; energy: Energy Dept., Energy Information Administration; education: Education Dept., National Education Assn. Other information from sources in individual states, usually Commerce Dept.

Alabama

Heart of Dixie, Camellia State

People. Population (1990): 4,040,587; **rank:** 22. **Pop. density:** 79.6 per sq. mi. **Racial distrib.:** 73.6% White; 25.3% Black; 0.6% Hispanic. **Net change** (1980-90): 3.8%.

Geography. Total area: 51,705 sq. mi.; **rank:** 29. **Land area:** 50,750 sq. mi. **Acres forested land:** 21,725,000. **Location:** in the east south central U.S., extending N-S from Tenn. to the Gulf of Mexico; east of the Mississippi River. **Climate:** long, hot summers; mild winters; generally abundant rainfall. **Topography:** coastal plains inc. Prairie Black Belt give way to hills, broken terrain; highest elevation, 2,407 ft. **Capital:** Montgomery.

Economy. Principal industries: pulp and paper, chemicals, electronics, apparel, textiles, primary metals, lumber and wood, food processing, fabricated metals, automotive tires. **Principal manufactured goods** (1988-1989): electronics, cast iron and plastic pipe, fabricated steel prods., ships, paper products, chemicals, steel, mobile homes, fabrics, poultry processing. **Agriculture:** Chief crops (1988-89): peanuts, cotton, soybeans, hay, corn, wheat, potatoes, pecans, sweet potatoes, cottonseed, catfish. **Livestock** (1989): 1.8 mln. cattle; 345,000 hogs/pigs; 16.3 mln. poultry. **Timber/lumber** (1989): pine, hardwoods; 1.9 bln. bd. ft. **Nonfuel Minerals** (1990): $562 mln., mostly cement, clays, lime, sand & gravel, stone. **Commercial fishing** (1990): $35.9 mln. **Chief ports:** Mobile. **Value of construction** (1990): $3.0 bln. **Employment distribution** (1990): 24% mfg.; 21.9% trade; 18.4% serv. **Per capita income** (1990): $14,826. **Unemployment** (1990): 6.8%. **Tourism** (1988): tourists spent $2.3 bln. **Sales Tax** (1990): 4%.

Finance. FDIC-insured commercial banks & trust companies (1990): 221. **Deposits:** $29.7 bln. **Savings institutions** (1990): 36. **Assets:** $9.3 bln.

Federal government. No. federal civilian employees (Mar. 1990): 48,176. **Avg. salary:** $30,808. **Notable federal facilities:** George C. Marshall NASA Space Center, Huntsville; Gunter & Maxwell AFB, Montgomery; Ft. Rucker, Ozark; Ft. McClellan, Anniston; Natl. Fertilizer Development Center, Muscle Shoals; Navy Station & U.S. Corps of Engineers, Mobile; Redstone Arsenal, Huntsville.

Energy. Electricity production (1990, mwh, by source): Hydroelectric: 10.4 mln. Mineral: 58.1 mln. Nuclear: 12.1 mln.

Education. Student-teacher ratio (1989): 18.1. **Avg. salary, public school teachers** (1990-91): $27,300.

State data. Motto: We dare defend our rights. **Flower:** Camellia. **Bird:** Yellowhammer. **Tree:** Southern Pine. **Song:** Alabama. **Entered union** Dec. 14, 1819; **rank,** 22d. **State fair** at: Birmingham; early Oct.

History. First Europeans were Spanish explorers in the early 1500s. The French made the first permanent settlement, on Mobile Bay, 1701-02; later, English settled in the northern areas. France ceded the entire region to England at the end of the French and Indian War, 1763, but Spanish Florida claimed the Mobile Bay area until U. S. troops took it, 1813. Gen. Andrew Jackson broke the power of the Creek Indians, 1814, and they were removed to Oklahoma. The Confederate States were organized Feb. 4, 1861, at Montgomery, the first capital.

Tourist attractions. Jefferson Davis' "first White House" of the Confederacy; Ivy Green, Helen Keller's birthplace, Tuscumbia; statue of Vulcan, Birmingham; George Washington Carver Museum, Tuskegee Univ.; W.C. Handy Home & Museum, Florence; Alabama Space and Rocket Center, Huntsville; Alabama Shakespeare Festival, Montgomery; Moundville State Monument, Moundville; Pike Pioneer Museum, Troy, USS Alabama Memorial Park, Mobile; 28 hunting areas, 24 public lakes, 82 campgrounds, 21 state parks.

At Russell Cave National Monument, near Bridgeport: a detailed record of occupancy by humans from about 10,000 BC to 1650 AD.

Famous Alabamians include Hank Aaron, Tallulah Bankhead, Hugo L. Black, Paul "Bear" Bryant, George Washington Carver, Nat King Cole, William C. Handy, Bo Jackson, Helen Keller, Harper Lee, Joe Louis, Willie Mays, John Hunt Morgan, Jesse Owens, George Wallace, Booker T. Washington, Hank Williams.

Alabama Business Council (State Chamber of Commerce). 468 S. Perry St., P.O. Box 76, Montgomery, AL 36195; 1-800-248-5033.

Toll-free travel information. 1-800-392-8096; 1-800-ALABAMA out of state.

Alaska

Unofficial nickname: "The Last Frontier"

People. Population (1990): 550,043; **rank:** 49. **Racial distrib.:** 75.5% White; 4.1% Black; 3.2% Hispanic; 15.6% Amer. Ind., Eskimo or Aleut; 3.6% Asian or Pacific Is. **Pop. density:** 0.96 per sq. mi., **Net change** (1980-90): 36.9%.

Geography. Total area: 591,000 sq. mi.; **rank:** 1. **Land area:** 570,373 sq. mi. **Acres forested land:** 129,045,000. **Location:** NW corner of North America, bordered on east by Canada. **Climate:** SE, SW, and central regions, moist and mild; far north extremely dry. Extended summer days, winter nights, throughout. **Topography:** includes Pacific and Arctic mountain systems, central plateau, and Arctic slope. Mt. McKinley, 20,320 ft., is the highest point in North America. **Capital:** Juneau.

Economy. Principal industries: oil, gas, tourism, commercial fishing. **Principal manufactured goods:** fish products, lumber and pulp, furs. **Agriculture** (1988): Chief crops: barley, hay, greenhouse nursery prods., potatoes, lettuce, milk. **Livestock** (1988): 9,500 cattle; 2,400 sheep; 6,000 poultry; 23,000 reindeer. **Timber/lumber:** spruce, yellow cedar, hemlock. **Nonfuel minerals** (1990): $641.4 mln.; gold, sand & gravel, crushed and broken stone. **Commercial fishing** (1990): $1.5 bln. **Chief ports:** Anchorage, Dutch Harbor, Kodiak, Seward, Skagway, Juneau, Sitka, Valdez, Wrangell. **International airports at:** Anchorage, Fairbanks, Ketchikan, Juneau. **Value of construction** (1990): $1.9 bln. **Employment distribution** (1989): 30.8% gvt.; 20.3% serv.; 19.9% trade. **Per capita income** (1990): $21,761. **Unemployment** (1990): 6.9%. **Tourism** (1987-88): $500 mln.

Finance. FDIC-insured commercial banks & trust companies (1990): 7. **Deposits:** $3.3 bln. **Commercial bank deposits, per capita** (1990): $7,475. **Savings institutions** (1990): 3. **Assets:** $287 mln.

Federal government. No. federal civilian employees (Mar. 1990): 11,612. **Avg. salary:** $35,020.

Energy. Electricity production (1990, mwh, by source): Hydroelectric: 975,000. Mineral: 35.2 mln.

Education. Student-teacher ratio (1989): 16.8. **Avg. salary, public school teachers** (1990-91): $43,861.

State data. Motto: North to the future. **Flower:** Forget-Me-Not. **Bird:** Willow Ptarmigan. **Tree:** Sitka Spruce. **Song:** Alaska's Flag. **Entered union:** Jan. 3, 1959; rank, 49th. **State fair at:** Palmer; late Aug.—early Sept.

History. Vitus Bering, a Danish explorer working for Russia, was the first European to land in Alaska, 1741. Alexander Baranov, first governor of Russian America, set up headquarters at Archangel, near present Sitka, in 1799. Secretary of State William H. Seward in 1867 bought Alaska from Russia for $7.2 million, a bargain some called "Seward's Folly." In 1896 gold was discovered and the famed Gold Rush was on.

Tourist attractions: Portage Glacier, Mendenhall Glacier, Glacier Bay National Park, Katmai National Park & Preserve, Denali National Park, one of North America's great wildlife sanctuaries, surrounding Mt. McKinley, No. America's highest peak. Pribilof Islands fur seal rookeries, restored St. Michael's Russian Orthodox Cathedral, Sitka.

Famous Alaskans include Tom Bodett, Susan Butcher, Ernest Gruening, Sydney Laurence, Libby Riddles, Jefferson "Soapy" Smith.

Tourist information. Alaska Division of Tourism, P.O. Box E, Juneau, AK 99811-0800.

Arizona

Grand Canyon State

People. Population (1990): 3,665,228; **rank:** 24. **Pop. density:** 32.3 per sq. mi. **Racial distrib.:** 80.8% White; 3.0% Black; 5.6% American Indian; 18.8% Hispanic. **Net change** (1980-90): 34.8%.

Geography. Total area: 114,000 sq. mi.; **rank:** 6. **Land area:** 113,642 sq. mi. **Acres forested land:** 19,384,000. **Location:** in the southwestern U.S. **Climate:** clear and dry in the southern regions and northern plateau; high central areas have heavy winter snows. **Topography:** Colorado plateau in the N, containing the Grand Canyon; Mexican Highlands running diagonally NW to SE; Sonoran Desert in the SW. **Capital:** Phoenix.

Economy. Principal industries: manufacturing, tourism, mining, agriculture. **Principal manufactured goods:** electronics, printing and publishing, foods, primary and fabricated metals, aircraft and missiles, apparel. **Agriculture:** Chief crops: cotton, sorghum, barley, corn, wheat, sugar beets, citrus fruits. **Livestock** (1989): 830,000 cattle; 100,000 hogs/pigs; 262,000 sheep; 320,000 poultry. **Timber/lumber** (1989): pine, fir, spruce; 439 mln. bd. ft. **Nonfuel Minerals** (1990): $3.1 bln.; copper, molybdenum, gold, silver. **International airports at:** Phoenix, Tucson, Yuma. **Value of construction** (1990): $4.5 bln. **Employment distribution** (1989): 26.7% services; 25.2% trade; 16.9% gvt.; 12.9% mfg. **Per capita income** (1990): $16,297. **Unemployment** (1990): 5.3%. **Tourism** (1989): tourists spent $5.6 bln. **Sales tax:** 5.0% (Maricopa, Pinal Countries, 5.5%).

Finance. FDIC-insured commercial bank & trust **companies** (1990): 39. **Deposits:** $25.9 bln. **Savings institutions** (1990): 12. **Assets:** $20.4 bln.

Federal government: No. federal civilian employees (Mar. 1990): 28,494. **Avg. salary:** $28,674. **Notable federal facilities:** Williams, Luke, Davis-Monthan AF bases; Ft. Huachuca Army Base; Yuma Proving Grounds.

Energy. Electricity production (1989, mwh, by source): Hydroelectric: 7.7 mln.; Mineral: 34.0; Nuclear: 20.1.

Education. Student-teacher ratio (1989): 18.9. **Avg. salary, public school teachers** (1990-91): $30,780.

State data. Motto: Ditat Deus (God enriches). **Flower:** Blossom of the Saguaro cactus. **Bird:** Cactus wren. **Tree:** Paloverde. **Song:** Arizona. **Entered union** Feb. 14, 1912; rank, 48th. **State fair at:** Phoenix; late Oct.—early Nov.

History. Marcos de Niza, a Franciscan, and Estevan, a black slave, explored the area, 1539. Eusebio Francisco Kino, Jesuit missionary, taught Indians Christianity and farming, 1690-1711, left a chain of missions. Spain ceded Arizona to Mexico, 1821. The U. S. took over at the end of the Mexican War, 1848. The area below the Gila River was obtained from Mexico in the Gadsden Purchase,

1854. Long Apache wars did not end until 1886, with Geronimo's surrender.

Tourist attractions. The Grand Canyon of the Colorado, an immense, vari-colored fissure 217 mi. long, 4 to 13 mi. wide at the brim, 4,000 to 5,500 ft. deep; the Painted Desert, extending for 30 mi. along U.S. 66; the Petrified Forest; Canyon Diablo, 225 ft. deep and 500 ft. wide; Meteor Crater, 4,150 ft. across, 570 ft. deep, made by a prehistoric meteor. Also, London Bridge at Lake Havasu City.

Famous Arizonans include Cochise, Geronimo, Barry Goldwater, Zane Grey, Carl Hayden, George W. P. Hunt, Helen Jacobs, Percival Lowell, Sandra Day O'Connor, William H. Pickering, John J. Rhodes, Morris Udall, Stewart Udall, Frank Lloyd Wright.

Tourist information. Phoenix & Valley of the Sun Visitor and Convention Bureau, 1-602-254-6500.

Arkansas

Land of Opportunity

People. Population (1990): 2,350,725; **rank:** 33. **Pop. density:** 45.1 per sq. mi. **Racial distrib.:** 82.7% White; 15.9% Black; 0.8% Hispanic. **Net change** (1980-90): 2.8%.

Geography. Total area: 53,187 sq. mi.; **rank:** 27. **Land area:** 52,075 sq. mi. **Acres forested land:** 16,987,000. **Location:** in the west south-central U.S. **Climate:** long, hot summers, mild winters; generally abundant rainfall. **Topography:** eastern delta and prairie, southern lowland forests, and the northwestern highlands, which include the Ozark Plateaus. **Capital:** Little Rock.

Economy. Principal industries: manufacturing, agriculture, tourism, forestry. **Principal manufactured goods:** food prods., chemicals, lumber, paper, electric motors, furniture, home appliances, auto components, airplane parts, apparel, machinery, petroleum prods. **Agriculture: Chief crops:** soybeans, rice, cotton, tomatoes, watermelons, grapes, blueberries, apples, commercial vegetables, peaches, wheat. **Livestock** (1989): 1.75 mln. cattle; 540,000 hogs/pigs; $1.9 bln. poultry. **Timber/lumber** (1989): oak, hickory, gum, cypress, pine; 1.4 bln. bd. ft. **Nonfuel Minerals** (1990): 414.7 mln.; abrasives, bauxite, bromine. **Commercial fishing** (1986): $7.3 mln. **Chief ports:** Little Rock, Pine Bluff, Osceola, Helena, Fort Smith, Van Buren, Camden, Dardanelle, North Little Rock, West Memphis, Crosset. **Value of construction** (1990): $1.5 bln. **Employment distribution** (1990): 24.0% mfg.; 21.3% trade; 19.7% serv.; 16.4% gvt. **Per capita income** (1990): $14,218. **Unemployment** (1990): 6.9%. **Tourism** (1990): travelers spent $2.3 bln.

Finance. FDIC-insured commercial banks & trust **companies** (1990): 257. **Deposits:** $17.7 bln. **Savings institutions** (1990): 34. **Assets:** $5.3 bln.

Federal government. No. federal civilian employees (Mar. 1990): 12,344. **Avg. salary:** $27,584. **Notable federal facilities:** Nat'l. Center for Toxicological Research, Jefferson; Pine Bluff Arsenal, Little Rock AFB.

Energy. Electricity production (1990, mwh, by source): Hydroelectric: 3.7 mln.; Mineral: 22.1 mln.; Nuclear: 11.3 mln.

Education. Student-teacher ratio (1989): 17.0. **Avg. salary, public school teachers** (1990-91): $23,040.

State data. Motto: Regnat Populus (The people rule). **Flower:** Apple Blossom. **Bird:** Mockingbird. **Tree:** Pine. **Song:** Arkansas. **Entered union:** June 15, 1836; rank, 25th. **State fair at:** Little Rock; late Sept.- early Oct.

History. First European explorers were de Soto, 1541, Jolliet, 1673; La Salle, 1682. First settlement was by the French under Henri de Tonty, 1686, at Arkansas Post. In 1762 the area was ceded by France to Spain, then back again in 1800, and was part of the Louisiana Purchase by the U.S. in 1803. Arkansas seceded from the Union in 1861, only after the Civil War began, and more than 10,000 Arkansans fought on the Union side.

Tourist attractions. 5 natl. parks & 48 state parks, inc. Hot Springs National Park, water ranging from 95° to 147°F. Eureka Springs, resort since 1879; Blanchard Caverns, near Mountain View, are among the nation's largest; Crater of Diamonds, near Murfreesboro, only U.S. diamond mine; Buffalo Natl. River; Mid-America Museum, Ozark Folk Center.

Famous Arkansans include Dee Brown, Glen Campbell, Johnny Cash, Hattie Caraway, "Dizzy" Dean, Orval Faubus, James W. Fulbright, Douglas MacArthur, John L. McClellan, James S. McDonnel, Dick Powell, Winthrop Rockefeller, Mary Steenburgen, Edward Durell Stone, Archibald Yell.

Chamber of Commerce. One Spring St., Little Rock, AR 72201.

Toll-free travel information. 1-800-NATURAL.

California
Golden State

People. Population (1990): 29,760,021; **rank:** 1. **Pop. density:** 190.8 per sq. mi. **Racial distrib.:** 69.0% White; 7.4% Black; 9.6% Asian; 25.8% Hispanic. **Net change** (1980-90): 25.7%.

Geography. Total area 158,706 sq. mi.; **rank:** 3. **Land area:** 155,973 sq. mi. **Acres forested land:** 39,381,000. **Location:** on western coast of the U.S. **Climate:** moderate temperatures and rainfall along the coast; extremes in the interior. **Topography:** long mountainous coastline; central valley; Sierra Nevada on the east; desert basins of the southern interior; rugged mountains of the north. **Capital:** Sacramento.

Economy. Principal industries: agriculture, manufacturing, services, trade. **Principal manufactured goods:** foods, printed material, primary and fabricated metals, machinery, electric and electronic equipment, transportation equipment instruments. **Agriculture: Chief crops:** grapes, cotton, flowers, oranges, nursery products, hay, tomatoes, lettuce, strawberries, almonds, broccoli, walnuts, sugar beets, peaches, potatoes. **Livestock** (1990): 4.9 mln. cattle & calves; 140,000 hogs/pigs; 955,000 sheep; 281.5 mln. poultry. **Timber/lumber** (1989): fir, pine, redwood, oak; 4.7 bln. bd. ft. **Nonfuel Minerals:** (1990): $2.7 bln.; mostly asbestos, boron minerals, cement, diatomite, calcined gypsum, construction sand & gravel. **Commercial fishing** (1990): $126.9 mln. **Chief ports:** Long Beach, San Diego, Oakland, San Francisco, Sacramento, Stockton. **International airports at:** Los Angeles, San Francisco, San Jose. **Value of construction** (1990): $36.4 bln. **Employment distribution** (1990): 27.0% serv.; 23.5% trade; 16.6% mfg.; 16.1% gvt. **Per capita income** (1990): $20,795. **Unemployment** (1990): 5.6% **Tourism** (1990): $48.5 bln. **Sales tax:** 6-7%.

Finance. FDIC-insured commercial banks & trust companies (1990): 479. **Deposits:** $238.6 bln. **Savings institutions** (1990): 182. **Assets:** $370.5 bln.

Federal government. No. federal civilian employees (Mar. 1990): 210,276. **Avg. salary:** $30,677. **Notable federal facilities:** Vandenberg, Beale, Travis, McClellan AF bases, San Francisco Mint.

Energy. Electricity production (1990, mwh, by source): Hydroelectric: 23.8 mln.; Mineral: 49.6 mln.; Nuclear: 32.7 mln.

Education. Student-teacher ratio (1989): 22.4. **Avg. salary, public school teachers** (1990-91): $39,598.

State Data. Motto: Eureka (I have found it). **Flower:** Golden poppy. **Bird:** California valley quail. **Tree:** California redwood. **Song:** I Love You, California. **Entered Union** Sept. 9, 1850; **rank,** 31st. **State fair** at: Sacramento; late Aug.—early Sept.

History. First European explorers were Cabrillo, 1542, and Drake, 1579. First settlement was the Spanish Alta California mission at San Diego, 1769, first in a string founded by Franciscan Father Junipero Serra. U. S. traders and settlers arrived in the 19th century and staged the abortive Bear Flag Revolt, 1846; the Mexican War began later in 1846 and U.S. forces occupied California; Mexico ceded the province to the U.S., 1848, the same year the Gold Rush began.

Tourist attractions. Scenic regions are Yosemite Valley; Lassen and Sequoia-Kings Canyon national parks;

Lake Tahoe; the Mojave and Colorado deserts; San Francisco Bay; and Monterey Peninsula. Oldest living things on earth are believed to be a stand of Bristlecone pines in the Inyo National Forest, est. to be 4,600 years old. The world's tallest tree, the Howard Libbey redwood, 362 ft. with a girth of 44 ft., stands on Redwood Creek, Humboldt County.

Also, RMS Queen Mary, Spruce Goose, both Long Beach; Palomar Observatory; Disneyland; J. Paul Getty Museum, Malibu; Tournament of Roses and Rose Bowl.

Famous Californians include Luther Burbank, John C. Fremont, Bret Harte, Wm. R. Hearst, Jack London, Aimee Semple McPherson, John Muir, Richard M. Nixon, William Saroyan, Junipero Serra, Leland Stanford, John Steinbeck, Earl Warren.

Chamber of Commerce: 1027 10th, Sacramento, CA 95814.

Toll-free travel information. 1-800-862-2543, x T100.

Colorado
Centennial State

People. Population (1990): 3,294,394; **rank:** 26. **Pop. density:** 31.8 per sq. mi. **Racial distrib.:** 88.2% White; 4.0% Black; 12.9% Hispanic. **Net change** (1980-90): 14.0%.

Geography. Total area: 104,091 sq. mi.; **rank:** 8. **Land area:** 103,730 sq. mi. **Acres forested land:** 21,338,000. **Location:** in west central U.S. **Climate:** low relative humidity, abundant sunshine, wide daily, seasonal temperatures ranges; alpine conditions in the high mountains. **Topography:** eastern dry high plains; hilly to mountainous central plateau; western Rocky Mountains of high ranges alternating with broad valleys and deep, narrow canyons. **Capital:** Denver.

Economy. Principal industries: manufacturing, government, tourism, agriculture, aerospace, electronics equipment. **Principal manufactured goods:** computer equipment, instruments, foods, machinery, aerospace products. **Agriculture: Chief crops:** corn, wheat, hay, sugar beets, barley, potatoes, apples, peaches, pears, dry edible beans, sorghum, onions, oats. **Livestock** (1989): 2.8 mln. cattle; 220,000 hogs/pigs; 825,000 sheep; 4.0 mln. poultry. **Timber/lumber** (1989): oak, ponderosa pine, Douglas fir; 168 mln. bd. ft. **Nonfuel Minerals** (1990): $405.3 mln.; gold, construction sand & gravel, crushed stone. **International airports at:** Denver. **Value of construction** (1990): $3.3 bln. **Employment distribution** (1987 est.): 26.7% serv.; 20.8% trade; 17.0% gvt.; 10.0% mfg. **Per capita income** (1990): $18,794. **Unemployment** (1990): 4.9%. **Tourism** (1989): $5.6 bln. **Sales Tax:** 3%.

Finance. FDIC-insured commercial banks & trust companies (1990): 450. **Deposits:** $21.9 bln. **Savings Institutions** (1990): 35. **Assets:** $13.3 bln.

Federal government. No. federal civilian employees (Mar. 1990): 37,499. **Avg. salary:** $31,354. **Notable federal facilities:** U.S. Air Force Academy; U.S. Mint; Ft. Carson, Lowry AFB; Solar Energy Research Institute; U.S. Rail Transport. Test Center; N. Amer. Aerospace Defense Command; Consolidated Space Operations Center; U.S. Documents Center, Fitzsimons Army Medical Center, Federal Center.

Energy. Electricity production (1980, mwh, by source): Hydroelectric: 1.3 mln.; Mineral: 30.0 mln.

Education. Student-teacher ratio (1989): 17.6. **Avg. salary, public school teachers** (1990-91): $32,020.

State data. Motto: Nil Sine Numine (Nothing without Providence). **Flower:** Rocky Mountain columbine. **Bird:** Lark bunting. **Tree:** Colorado blue spruce. **Song:** Where the Columbines Grow. **Entered union** Aug. 1, 1876; rank 38th. **State fair** at: Pueblo; last week in Aug.

History. Early civilization centered around Mesa Verde 2,000 years ago. The U.S. acquired eastern Colorado in the Louisiana Purchase, 1803; Lt. Zebulon M. Pike explored the area, 1806, discovering the peak that bears his name. After the Mexican War, 1846-48, U.S. immigrants settled in the east, former Mexicans in the south.

Tourist attractions. 310 or more sunshine days per year; more than 1,000 peaks of 2 or more miles; Rocky Mountain National Park; Garden of the Gods; Great Sand Dunes, Dinosaur, Black Canyon of the Gunnison, and Colorado national monuments; Pikes Peak and Mt. Evans highways; Mesa Verde National Park (Ancient Anasazi Indian cliff dwellings); 35 major ski areas; the Grand Mesa tableland comprises Grand Mesa Forest, 659,584 acres, with 200 lakes stocked with trout. Mining towns of Central City, Silverton, Cripple Creek; Burlington's Old Town; Bent's Fort, outside La Junta; Georgetown Loop Historic Mining Railroad Park, Cumbres & Toltec Scenic Railroad.

Famous Coloradans include Frederick Bonfils, Molly Brown, William N. Byers, M. Scott Carpenter, Jack Dempsey, Mamie Eisenhower, Douglas Fairbanks, Scott Hamilton, "Baby Doe" Tabor, Lowell Thomas, Byron R. White, Paul Whiteman.

Toll-free travel information. 1-800-433-2656.

Connecticut

Constitution State, Nutmeg State

People. Population (1990): 3,287,116; **rank:** 27. **Pop. density:** 678.5 per sq. mi. **Racial distrib.:** 87.0% White; 8.3% Black; 6.5% Hispanic. **Net change** (1980-90): 5.8%.

Geography. Total area: 5,018 sq. mi.; **rank:** 48. **Land area:** 4,845 sq. mi. **Acres forested land:** 1,815,800. **Location:** New England state in the northeastern corner of the U.S. **Climate:** moderate; winters avg. slightly below freezing, warm, humid summers. **Topography:** western upland, the Berkshires, in the NW, highest elevations; narrow central lowland N-S; hilly eastern upland drained by rivers. **Capital:** Hartford.

Economy. Principal industries: manufacturing, retail trade, government, services, finances, insurance, real estate. **Principal manufactured goods:** aircraft engines and parts, submarines, helicopters, instruments, machinery & computer equipment, electronics & electrical equipment. **Agriculture: Chief crops:** nursery stock, vegetables, sweet corn, tobacco, apples. **Livestock** (1989): 73,000 cattle; 6,800 hogs/pigs; 8,400 sheep; 5.6 mln. poultry. **Timber/lumber** (1989): oak, birch, beech, maple; 43 mln. bd ft. **Non-fuel Minerals** (1990): $108.3 mln.; crushed stone; construction sand & gravel. **Commercial fishing** (1990): $26.9 mln. **Chief ports:** New Haven, Bridgeport, New London. **International airports at:** Windsor Locks. **Value of construction** (1990): $2.8 bln. **Employment distribution** (1989): 21.4% mfg.; 25.3% serv. **Per capita income** (1990): $25,358. **Unemployment** (1990): 5.1%. **Tourism** (1989): out-of-state visitors spent $3.2 bln. **Sales tax:** 8.0%.

Finance. FDIC-insured commercial banks & trust **companies** (1990): 70. **Deposits:** $30.7 bln. **Savings institutions** (1990): 26. **Assets:** $92.5 bln.

Federal Government. No. federal civilian employees (Mar. 1990): 9,535. **Avg. salary:** $32,285. **Notable federal facilities:** U.S. Coast Guard Academy; U.S. Navy Submarine Base.

Energy. Electricity production (1990, mwh, by source): Hydroelectric: 502,000; Mineral: 50.1 mln.; Nuclear: 19.8 mln.

Education. Student-teacher ratio (1989): 13.1. **Avg. salary, public school teachers** (1990-91): $43,847.

State data. Motto: Qui Transtulit Sustinet (He who transplanted still sustains). **Flower:** Mountain laurel. **Bird:** American robin. **Tree:** White oak. **Song:** Yankee Doodle Dandy. **Fifth** of the 13 original states to ratify the Constitution, Jan. 9, 1788.

History. Adriaen Block, Dutch explorer, was the first European visitor, 1614. By 1634, settlers from Plymouth Bay started colonies along the Connecticut River and in 1637 defeated the Pequot Indians. In the Revolution, Connecticut men fought in most major campaigns and turned back British raids on Danbury and other towns, while Connecticut privateers captured British merchant ships.

Tourist attractions. Mark Twain House, Hartford; Yale University's Art Gallery, Peabody Museum, all in New Ha-

ven; Mystic Seaport; Mystic Marine Life Aquarium; P.T. Barnum Museum, Bridgeport; Gillette Castle, Hadlyme; U.S.S. Nautilus Memorial, Groton (1st nuclear-powered submarine).

Famous "Nutmeggers" include Ethan Allen, Phineas T. Barnum, Samuel Colt, Jonathan Edwards, Nathan Hale, Katharine Hepburn, Isaac Hull, J. Pierpont Morgan, Israel Putnam, Harriet Beecher Stowe, Mark Twain, Noah Webster, Eli Whitney.

Tourist information. State Dept. of Economic Development, 865 Brook St., Rocky Hill, CT 06067.

Toll-free travel information. 1-800-CT-BOUND (282-6863).

Delaware

First State, Diamond State

People. Population (1990): 666,168; **rank:** 46. **Pop. density:** 340.8 per sq. mi. **Racial distrib.:** 80.3% White; 16.9% Black; 2.4% Hispanic. **Net change** (1980-90): 12.1%.

Geography. Total area: 2,045 sq. mi.; **rank:** 49. **Land area:** 1,955 sq. mi. **Acres forested land:** 398,000. **Location:** occupies the Delmarva Peninsula on the Atlantic coastal plain. **Climate:** moderate. **Topography:** Piedmont plateau to the N, sloping to a near sea-level plain. **Capital:** Dover.

Economy. Principal industries: chemistry, agriculture, finance, poultry, shellfish, tourism, auto assembly, food processing, transportation equipment. **Principal manufactured goods:** nylon, apparel, luggage, foods, autos, processed meats and vegetables, railroad and aircraft equipment. **Agriculture: Chief crops:** soybeans, potatoes, corn, mushrooms, lima beans, green peas, barley, cucumbers, snap beans, watermelons, apples. **Livestock** (1989): 31,000 cattle; 226.4 mln. broilers. **Nonfuel Minerals** (1990): $7.9 mln; construction sand & gravel, magnesium compounds, greensand marl. **Commercial fishing** (1990): $4.2 mln. **Chief ports:** Wilmington. **International airports at:** Philadelphia/Wilmington. **Value of construction** (1990): $805.6 mln. **Employment distribution** (1990): 79.3% non-manufacturing; 20.7% mfg. **Per capita income** (1990): $20,039. **Unemployment** (1990): 5.1%. **Tourism** (1987): out-of-state visitors spent $725 mln.

Finance. FDIC-insured commercial banks & trust **companies** (1990): 47. **Deposits:** $27.0 bln. **Savings institutions** (1990): 4. **Assets:** $5.1 bln.

Federal government. No. federal civilian employees (Mar. 1990): 2,928. **Avg. salary:** $28,706. **Notable federal facilities:** Dover Air Force Base, Federal Wildlife Refuge, Bombay Hook.

Energy. Electricity production (1989, mwh, by source): Mineral: 7.1 mln.

Education. Student-teacher ratio (1989): 16.4. **Avg. salary, public school teachers** (1990-91): $35,200.

State data. Motto: Liberty and independence. **Flower:** Peach blossom. **Bird:** Blue hen chicken. **Tree:** American holly. **Song:** Our Delaware. **First** of original 13 states to ratify the Constitution, Dec. 7, 1787. **State fair** at: Harrington; end of July.

History. The Dutch first settled in Delaware near present Lewes, 1631, but were wiped out by Indians. Swedes settled at present Wilmington, 1638; Dutch settled anew, 1651, near New Castle and seized the Swedish settlement, 1655, only to lose all Delaware and New Netherland to the British, 1664.

Tourist attractions. Ft. Christina Monument, the site of founding of New Sweden; John Dickinson "Penman of the Revolution" home, Dover; Henry Francis du Pont Winterthur Museum; Hagley Museum, Wilmington; Rehoboth Beach, "nation's summer capitol," Rehobeth; Dover Downs Intl. Speedway, Dover; Old Swedes (Trinity Parish) Church, erected 1698, is the oldest Protestant church in the U.S. still in use.

Famous Delawareans include Thomas F. Bayard, Henry Seidel Canby, E. I. du Pont, John P. Marquand, Howard Pyle, Caesar Rodney.

Chamber of Commerce. One Commerce Center, Wilmington, DE 19801.
Toll-free travel information. 1-800-441-8846.

Tourist information. Florida Division of Tourism, 126 Van Buren St., Tallahassee, FL 32399-2000, 1-904-487-1462.

Florida

Sunshine State

People. Population (1990): 12,937,926; **rank:** 4. **Pop. density:** 239.6 per sq. mi. **Racial distrib.:** 83.1% White; 13.6% Black; 12.2% Hispanic. **Net change** (1980-90): 32.7%.

Geography: Total area: 58,664 sq. mi.; **rank:** 22. **Land area:** 53,997 sq. mi. **Acres forested land:** 16,721,000. **Location:** peninsula jutting southward 500 mi. bet. the Atlantic and the Gulf of Mexico. **Climate:** subtropical N of Bradenton-Lake Okeechobee-Vero Beach line; tropical S of line. **Topography:** land is flat or rolling; highest point is 345 ft. in the NW. **Capital:** Tallahassee.

Economy. Principal industries: services, trade, gvt., manufacturing, tourism. **Principal manufactured goods:** electric & electronic equip., transp. equipment; food; printing & publishing; machinery. **Agriculture: Chief crops:** citrus fruits, vegetables, potatoes, melons, strawberries, sugar cane. **Livestock** (1987): 1.97 mln. cattle; 150,000 hogs/pigs; 7,360 sheep; 13.5 mln. poultry. **Timber/lumber** (1989): pine, cypress, cedar; 615 mln. bd. ft. **Nonfuel Minerals** (1990): $1.6 bln.; mostly cement, phosphate rock, crushed stone. **Commercial fishing** (1990): $170.5 mln. **Chief ports:** Pensacola, Tampa, Miami, Port Everglades, Jacksonville, St. Petersburg, Canaveral. **International airports at:** Miami, Tampa, Jacksonville, Orlando, Ft. Lauderdale, W. Palm Beach. **Value of construction** (1990): $16.7 bln. **Per capita income** (1990): $18,586. **Unemployment** (1990): 5.9% **Tourism** (1990): out-of-state visitors spent $26.6 bln. **Sales tax:** 6%.

Finance. FDIC-insured commercial banks & trust companies (1990): 427. **Deposits:** $112.1 bln. **Savings institutions** (1990): 141. **Assets:** $79.4 bln.

Federal government. No. federal civilian employees (Mar. 1990): 63,854. **Avg. salary:** $30,355. **Notable federal facilities:** John F. Kennedy Space Center, NASA-Kennedy Space Center's Spaceport USA; Eglin Air Force Base.

Energy. Electricity production (1990, mwh, by source): Hydroelectric: 180,000; Mineral: 101.6 mln.; Nuclear: 21.7 mln.

Education. Student-teacher ratio (1989): 17.0. **Avg. salary, public school teachers** (1990-91): $30,387.

State data. Motto: In God we trust. **Flower:** Orange blossom. **Bird:** Mockingbird. **Tree:** Sabal palmetto palm. **Song:** Old Folks at Home. **Entered union** Mar. 3, 1845; rank, 27th. **State fair** at: Tampa; early to mid-Feb.

History. First European to see Florida was Ponce de Leon, 1513. France established a colony, Fort Caroline, on the St. Johns River, 1564; Spain settled St. Augustine, 1565, and Spanish troops massacred most of the French. Britain's Francis Drake burned St. Augustine, 1586. Britain held the area briefly, 1763-83, returning it to Spain. After Andrew Jackson led a U.S. invasion, 1818, Spain ceded Florida to the U.S., 1819. The Seminole War, 1835-42, resulted in removal of most Indians to Oklahoma. Florida seceded from the Union, 1861, was readmitted, 1868.

Tourist attractions. Miami, with a variety of luxury hotels at Miami Beach; St. Augustine, oldest city in U.S.; Walt Disney World's Magic Kingdom and EPCOT; Spaceport U.S.A.

Everglades National Park preserves the beauty of the vast Everglades swamp. Castillo de San Marcos, St. Augustine, is a national monument. Also, the Ringling Museum of Art, and the Ringling Museum of the Circus, both in Sarasota; Sea World, Orlando; Cypress Gardens, Winter Haven; Busch Gardens, Tampa; Universal Studios.

Famous Floridians include Henry M. Flagler, James Weldon Johnson, MacKinlay Kantor, Henry B. Plant, Marjorie Kinnan Rawlings, Joseph W. Stilwell, Charles P. Summerall.

Georgia

Empire State of the South, Peach State

People. Population (1990): 6,478,216; **rank:** 11. **Pop. density:** 111.8 per sq. mi. **Racial distrib.:** 71.0% White; 27.0% Black; 1.7% Hispanic. **Net change** (1980-90): 18.6%.

Geography. Total area: 58,910 sq. mi.; **rank:** 21. **Land area:** 57,919 sq. mi. **Acres forested land:** 23,907,000. **Location:** South Atlantic state. **Climate:** maritime tropical air masses dominate in summer; continental polar air masses in winter; east central area drier. **Topography:** most southerly of the Blue Ridge Mtns. cover NE and N central; central Piedmont extends to the fall line of rivers; coastal plain levels to the coast flatlands. **Capital:** Atlanta.

Economy. Principal industries: manufacturing, forestry, agriculture, chemicals. **Principal manufactured goods** (1990): textiles, apparel, food, transportation equipment, printing and publishing. **Agriculture: Chief crops** (1990): soybeans, peanuts, hay, corn, cotton, wheat. **Livestock** (1990): 8.6 mln. poultry; 1.4 mln. cattle; 1.1 hogs/pigs. **Timber/lumber** (1989): pine, hardwood; 2.7 bln. bd. ft. **Nonfuel Minerals** (1990): $1.5 bln.; clays, crushed stone. **Commercial fishing** (1990): $19.8 mln. **Chief ports:** Savannah, Brunswick. **International airports at:** Atlanta. **Value of construction** (1990): $7.1 bln. **Employment distribution** (1990): 29% services; 19% mfg.; 18% retail trade; 8% gvt. **Per capita income** (1990): $16,944. **Unemployment** (1990): 5.4%. **Tourism** (1990): tourists spent $9.6 bln. **Sales tax:** 4%.

Finance. FDIC-insured commercial banks & trust companies (1990): 400. **Deposits:** $49.9 bln. **Savings institutions** (1990): 69. **Assets:** $18.9 bln.

Federal government. No. federal civilian employees (Mar. 1990): 69,473. **Avg. salary:** $29,008. **Notable federal facilities:** Dobbins AFB; Fts. Benning, Gordon, McPherson; Fed. Law Enforcement Training Ctr., Glynco, Warner Robins AFB; Centers for Disease Control, Atlanta.

Energy. Electricity production (1990, mwh, by source): Hydroelectric: 4.9 mln.; Mineral: 67.9 mln.; Nuclear: 24.8 mln.

Education. Student-teacher ratio (1989): 18.3. **Avg. salary, public school teachers** (1990-91): $28,855.

State data. Motto: Wisdom, justice and moderation. **Flower:** Cherokee rose. **Bird:** Brown thrasher. **Tree:** Live oak. **Song:** Georgia On My Mind. **Fourth** of the 13 original states to ratify the Constitution, Jan. 2, 1788.

History. Gen. James Oglethorpe established the first settlements, 1733, for poor and religiously-persecuted Englishmen. Oglethorpe defeated a Spanish army from Florida at Bloody Marsh, 1742. In the Revolution, Georgians seized the Savannah armory, 1775, and sent the munitions to the Continental Army; they fought seesaw campaigns with Cornwallis' British troops, twice liberating Augusta and forcing final evacuation by the British from Savannah, 1782.

Tourist attractions. Atlanta area: State Capitol, Stone Mt. Park, Six Flags over Georgia, Kennesaw Mt. Natl. Battlefield Park, Martin Luther King Center, Underground Atlanta, Jimmy Carter Lib. & Museum. NW: Chickamauga Battlefield Park, Chattahoochee Natl. Forest. NE: alpine village of Helen; Dahlonega, site of America's first gold rush; Brasstown Bald Mt., Lake Lanier. SW: Roosevelt's Little White House, Callaway Gardens, Andersonville Natl. Historic Site. SE: Okefenokee Swamp. Coastal: Jekyll Island, St. Simons Island, Cumberland Island Natl. Seashore, historic riverfront district in Savannah, Ft. Pulaski.

Famous Georgians include Hank Aaron, Griffin Bell, James Bowie, Erskine Caldwell, Jimmy Carter, Ray Charles, Lucius D. Clay, Ty Cobb, John C. Fremont, Joel Chandler Harris, Gladys Knight, Juliette Gordon Low, Martin Luther King Jr., Sidney Lanier, Margaret Mitchell, Flannery O'Connor, Jackie Robinson, Joseph Wheeler.

Chamber of Commerce. 235 International Blvd., Atlanta, GA 30303.

Toll-free travel information. 1-800-VISIT GA.

Hawaii

The Aloha State

People. Population (1990): 1,108,229; **rank:** 41. **Pop. density:** 172.6 per sq. mi. **Racial distrib.:** 33.4% White; 2.5% Black; 61.8% Asian or Pacific Is.; 7.3% Hispanic. **Net change** (1980-90): 14.9%.

Geography. Total area: 6,471 sq. mi.; **rank:** 47. **Land area:** 6,423 sq. mi. **Acres forested land:** 1,748,000. **Location:** Hawaiian Islands lie in the North Pacific, 2,397 mi. SW from San Francisco. **Climate:** subtropical, with wide variations in rainfall; Waialeale, on Kauai, wettest spot in U.S. (annual rainfall 444 in.) **Topography:** islands are tops of a chain of submerged volcanic mountains; active volcanoes: Mauna Loa, Kilauea. **Capital:** Honolulu.

Economy. Principal industries: tourism, defense and other government, sugar refining, pineapple and diversified agriculture, aquaculture, fishing, motion pictures. **Principal manufactured goods:** sugar, canned pineapple, clothing, foods, printing and publishing. **Agriculture: Chief crops:** sugar, pineapples, macadamia nuts, fruits, coffee, vegetables, melons, and floriculture. **Livestock** (1988): 211,045 cattle and calves; 43,000 hogs/pigs; 1.22 mln. chickens. **Nonfuel Minerals** (1990): $103.1 mln.; mostly crushed stone & cement. **Commercial fishing** (1990): $65.0 mln. **Chief ports:** Honolulu, Nawiliwili, Barbers Point, Kahului, Hilo. **International airports at:** Honolulu. **Value of construction** (1990): $2.6 bln. **Employment distribution** (1990): 24.5% trade; 26.2% serv.; 18.4% gvt. **Per capita income** (1990): $20,254. **Unemployment** (1990): 2.8%. **Tourism** (1989): visitors spent $10.9 bln. **General excise tax:** 4%; **Sales tax:** 4%.

Finance. FDIC-insured commercial banks & trust companies (1990): 21. **Deposits:** $13.8 bln. **Savings institutions** (1990): 6. **Assets:** $7.2 bln.

Federal government. No. federal civilian employees (Mar. 1990): 22,390. **Avg. salary:** $31,220. **Notable federal facilities:** Pearl Harbor Naval Shipyard; Hickam AFB; Schofield Barracks.

Energy. Electricity production (1990, mwh, by source): Hydroelectric: 23,000; Mineral: 8.0 mln.

Education. Student-teacher ratio (1989): 19.1. **Avg. Salary, public school teachers** (1990-91): $32,541.

State data. Motto: The life of the land is perpetuated in righteousness. **Flower:** Yellow Hibiscus. **Bird:** Hawaiian goose. **Tree:** Candlenut. **Song:** Hawaii Ponoi. **Entered union** Aug. 21, 1959; rank, 50th. **State fair** at: Honolulu; late May–mid-June.

History. Polynesians from islands 2,000 mi. to the south settled the Hawaiian Islands, probably between 300 A.D. and 600 A.D. First European visitor was British Capt. James Cook, 1778. Missionaries arrived, 1820, taught religion, reading and writing. King Kamehameha III and his chiefs created the first Constitution and a Legislature which set up a public school system. Sugar production began in 1835 and it became the dominant industry. In 1893, Queen Liliuokalani was deposed, followed, 1894, by a republic headed by Sanford B. Dole. Annexation by the U.S. came in 1898.

Tourist attractions. Hawaii Volcanoes, Haleakala National Parks; Polynesian Cultural Center, Waikiki Beach, Nuuanu Pali, Bishop Museum, Waimea Canyon, Wailua River State Park, Honolulu Academy of Arts.

Famous Islanders include Bernice Pauahi Bishop, John A. Burns, Father Damien de Veuster, Daniel K. Inouye, Duke Kahanamoku, King Kamehameha the Great, Queen Kaahumanu, Queen Liliuokalani, Ellison Onizuka.

Chamber of Commerce. Dillingham Bldg., 735 Bishop St., Honolulu, HI 96813.

Idaho

Gem State

People. Population (1990): 1,006,749; **rank:** 42. **Pop. density:** 12.2 per sq. mi. **Racial distrib.:** 94.4% White; 0.3% Black; 5.3% Hispanic. **Net change** (1980-90): 6.7%.

Geography. Total area: 83,564 sq. mi.; **rank:** 13. **Land area:** 82,751 sq. mi. **Acres forested land:** 21,818,000. **Location:** Pacific Northwest-Mountain state bordering on British Columbia. **Climate:** tempered by Pacific westerly winds; drier, colder, continental clime in SE; altitude an important factor. **Topography:** Snake R. plains in the S; central region of mountains, canyons, gorges (Hells Canyon, 7,900 ft., deepest in N.A.); subalpine northern region. **Capital:** Boise.

Economy. Principal industries: agriculture, manufacturing, tourism, lumber, mining, electronics. **Principal manufactured goods:** processed foods, lumber and wood products, chemical products, primary metals, fabricated metal products, machinery, electronic components. **Agriculture: Chief crops:** potatoes, peas, sugar beets, alfalfa seed, wheat, hops, barley, plums and prunes, mint, onions, corn, cherries, apples, hay. **Livestock** (1989): 1.66 mln. cattle; 296,000 sheep; 72,000 hogs; 1.1 mln. poultry. **Timber/lumber** (1989): yellow, white pine; Douglas fir; white spruce; 2.3 bln. bd. ft. **Nonfuel Minerals** (1990): $344.2 mln.; phosphate rock, silver, gold, sand & gravel. **Chief ports:** Lewiston. **Value of construction** (1990) $991 mln. **Employment distribution** (1990): 21% trade; 17% serv., 13% mfg.; 7% agric. **Per capita income** (1990): $15,160. **Unemployment** (1990): 5.8%. **Tourism** (1989): travellers spent $1.4 bln. **Sales tax:** 5%.

Finance. FDIC-insured commercial banks & trust companies (1990): 22. **Deposits:** $6.6 bln. **Savings institutions** (1990): 5. **Assets:** $904 mln.

Federal government. No. federal civilian employees (Mar. 1990): 7,261. **Avg. salary:** $30,129. **Notable federal facilities:** Ida. Nat'l. Engineering Lab, Idaho Falls; Mt. Home Air Force Base, Mt. Home.

Energy. Electricity production (1990, mwh, by source): Hydroelectric: 8.6 mln.

Education. Student-teacher ratio (1989): 20.1. **Avg. salary, public school teachers** (1990-91): $25,485.

State data. Motto: Esto Perpetua (It is perpetual). **Flower:** Syringa. **Bird:** Mountain bluebird. **Tree:** White pine. **Song:** Here We Have Idaho. **Entered union** July 3, 1890; rank, 43d. **State fair** at: Boise, late Aug.; and Blackfoot, early Sept.

History. Exploration of the Idaho area began with Lewis and Clark, 1805-06. Next came fur traders, setting up posts, 1809-34, and missionaries, establishing missions, 1830s-1850s. Mormons made their first permanent settlement at Franklin, 1860. Idaho's Gold Rush began that same year, and brought thousands of permanent settlers. Strangest of the Indian Wars was the 1,300-mi. trek in 1877 of Chief Joseph and the Nez Perce tribe, pursued by troops that caught them a few miles short of the Canadian border. In 1890, Idaho adopted a progressive Constitution and became a state.

Tourist attractions. Hells Canyon, deepest gorge in N.A.; World Center for Birds of Prey; Craters of the Moon; Sun Valley, year-round resort in the Sawtooth Mtns.; Crystal Falls Cave; Shoshone Falls; Lava Hot Springs; Lake Pend Oreille; Lake Coeur d'Alene; Sawtooth Natl. Recreation Area; River of No Return Wilderness Area.

Famous Idahoans include William E. Borah, Frank Church, Fred T. Dubois, Chief Joseph, Sacagawea.

Tourist information. Department of Commerce, 700 W. State St., Boise, ID 83720.

Toll-free travel information. 1-800-635-7820.

Illinois

The Prairie State

People. Population (1990): 11,430,602; **rank:** 6. **Pop. density:** 205.6 per sq. mi. **Racial distrib.:** 78.3% White; 14.8% Black; 7.9% Hispanic. **Net change** (1980-90): 0.0%.

Geography. Total area: 56,345 sq. mi.; **rank:** 24. **Land area:** 55,593 sq. mi. **Acres forested land:** 4,265,000. **Location:** east-north central state; western, southern, and eastern boundaries formed by Mississippi, Ohio, and Wabash Rivers, respectively. **Climate:** temperate; typically cold, snowy winters, hot summers. **Topography:** prairie and fertile plains throughout; open hills in the southern region. **Capital:** Springfield.

Economy. Principal industries: manufacturing, services, travel, wholesale and retail trade, finance, insurance, construction, gvt., health care, agriculture. **Principal manufactured goods:** machinery, electric and electronic equipment, primary and fabricated metals, chemical products, printing and publishing, food and kindred prods. **Agriculture: Chief crops:** corn, soybeans, wheat, oats, hay. **Livestock** (1990): 1.95 mln. cattle; 5.7 mln. hogs/pigs; 159,000 sheep; 3.79 mln. poultry. **Timber/lumber** (1989): oak, hickory, maple, cottonwood; 103 mln. bd. ft. **Nonfuel Minerals** (1990): $661.4 mln.; mostly crushed stone, cement, construction & industrial sand & gravel. **Commercial fishing** (1990): $444,000. **Chief ports:** Chicago. **International airports at:** Chicago. **Value of construction** (1990): $10.5 bln. **Employment distribution** (1990): 25.4% serv.; 23.9% trade; 18.7% mfg. **Per capita income** (1990): $20,303. **Unemployment** (1990): 6.2%. **Tourism** (1990): out-of-state visitors spent $14 bln. **Sales tax:** 6.25%.

Finance. FDIC-insured commercial banks & trust companies (1990): 1,102. **Deposits:** $128.9 bln. **Savings institutions** (1990): 240. **Assets:** $64.1 bln.

Federal government. No. federal civilian employees (Mar. 1990): 53,370. **Avg. salary:** $31,136. **Notable federal facilities:** Fermi Nat'l. Accelerator Lab; Argonne Nat'l. Lab; Ft. Sheridan; Rock Island; Great Lakes, Naval Training Station, Scott AFB.

Energy. Electricity production (1990, mwh, by source): Hydroelectric: 61,000; Mineral: 55.0 mln.; Nuclear: 71.9 mln.

Education. Student-teacher ratio (1989): 16.9. **Avg. salary, public school teachers** (1990-91): $34,729.

State data. Motto: State sovereignty—national union. **Flower:** Native violet. **Bird:** Cardinal. **Tree:** White oak. **Song:** Illinois. **Entered union** Dec. 3, 1818; **rank,** 21st. **State fair** at: Springfield; early Aug.; DuQuoin, late Aug.

History. Fur traders were the first Europeans in Illinois, followed shortly, 1673, by Jolliet and Marquette, and, 1680, La Salle, who built a fort near present Peoria. First settlements were French, at Fort St. Louis on the Illinois River, 1692, and Kaskaskia, 1700. France ceded the area to Britain, 1763; Amer. Gen. George Rogers Clark, 1778, took Kaskaskia from the British without a shot. Defeat of Indian tribes in Black Hawk War, 1832, and railroads in 1850s, inspired change.

Tourist attractions. Chicago museums, parks; Lincoln shrines at Springfield, New Salem, Sangamon; Cahokia Mounds, E. St. Louis; Starved Rock State Park; Crab Orchard Wildlife Refuge; Mormon settlement at Nauvoo; Fts. Kaskaskia, Chartres, Massac (parks); Shawnee Natl. Forest, Southern Illinois; Illinois State Museum, Springfield; Dickson Mounds Museum, btwn. Havana & Lewistown.

Famous Illinoisans include Jane Addams, Saul Bellow, Jack Benny, Ray Bradbury, Gwendolyn Brooks, William Jennings Bryan, St. Francis Xavier Cabrini, Clarence Darrow, John Deere, Stephen A. Douglas, James T. Farrell, George W. Ferris, Marshall Field, Betty Friedan, Benny Goodman, Ulysses S. Grant, Ernest Hemingway, Wild Bill Hickock, Abraham Lincoln, Vachel Lindsay, Edgar Lee Masters, Oscar Mayer, Cyrus McCormick, Ronald Reagan, Carl Sandburg, Adlai Stevenson, Frank Lloyd Wright, Philip Wrigley.

Tourist information. Illinois Dept. of Commerce and Community Affairs, 620 E. Adams St., Springfield, IL 62701. **Toll-free literature:** 1-800-223-0121.

Indiana

Hoosier State

People. Population (1990): 5,544,159; **rank:** 14. **Pop. density:** 154.6 per sq. mi. **Racial distrib.:** 90.6 White; 7.8% Black; 1.8% Hispanic. **Net change** (1980-90): 1.0%.

Geography. Total area: 36,185 sq. mi.; **rank:** 38. **Land area:** 35,870 sq. mi. **Acres forested land:** 4,439,900. **Location:** east north-central state; Lake Michigan on northern border. **Climate:** 4 distinct seasons with a temperate climate. **Topography:** hilly southern region; fertile rolling plains of central region; flat, heavily glaciated north; dunes along Lake Michigan shore. **Capital:** Indianapolis.

Economy. Principal industries: manufacturing, wholesale and retail trade, agriculture, government, services. **Principal manufactured goods:** primary and fabricated metals, transportation equipment, electrical and electronic equipment, non-electrical machinery, plastics, chemical products, foods. **Agriculture: Chief crops** (1987): corn, sorghum, oats, wheat, rye, soybeans, hay. **Livestock** (1987): 1.2 mln. cattle; 4.4 mln. hogs/pigs; 82,757 sheep; 28 mln. chickens. **Timber/lumber** (1989): oak, tulip, beech, sycamore; 262 mln. bd. ft. **Nonfuel Minerals** (1990): $459.3 mln.; mostly crushed stone, abrasives, cement, construction sand & gravel. **Commercial fishing** (1990): $505,000. **Chief ports:** Burns Harbor, Portage; Southwind Maritime, Mt. Vernon; Clark Maritime, Jeffersonville. **International airports at:** Indianapolis. **Value of construction** (1990): $6.1 bln. **Employment distribution** (1989): 27.9% mfg.; 24.8% trade; 19.8% serv; 12.3 gvt. **Per capita income** (1990): $16,866. **Unemployment** (1990): 5.3%. **Tourism** (1985): tourists spent $3 bln. **Sales tax:** 5%, with exemptions.

Finance. FDIC-insured commercial banks & trust companies (1990): 307. **Deposits:** $46.3 bln. **Savings institutions** (1990): 101. **Assets:** $13.5 bln.

Federal government. No. federal civilian employees (Mar. 1990): 26,322. **Avg. salary:** $28,707. **Notable federal facilities:** Naval Avionics Ctr.; Ft. Benjamin Harrison; Grissom AFB; Navy Weapons Support Ctr., Crane.

Energy. Electricity production (1990 mwh, by source): Hydroelectric: 441,000; Mineral: 97.3 mln.

Education. Student-teacher ratio (1989): 17.5. **Avg. salary, public school teachers** (1990-91): $32,178.

State data. Motto: Crossroads of America. **Flower:** Peony. **Bird:** Cardinal. **Tree:** Tulip poplar. **Song:** On the Banks of the Wabash, Far Away. **Entered union** Dec. 11, 1816; rank, 19th. **State fair** at: Indianapolis; mid-Aug.

History: Pre-historic Indian Mound Builders of 1,000 years ago were the earliest known inhabitants. A French trading post was built, 1731-32, at Vincennes and La Salle visited the present South Bend area, 1679 and 1681. France ceded the area to Britain, 1763. During the Revolution, American Gen. George Rogers Clark captured Vincennes, 1778, and defeated British forces 1779; at war's end Britain ceded the area to the U.S. Miami Indians defeated U.S. troops twice, 1790, but were beaten, 1794, at Fallen Timbers by Gen. Anthony Wayne. At Tippecanoe, 1811, Gen. William H. Harrison defeated Tecumseh's Indian confederation.

Tourist attractions. Lincoln Boyhood, George Rogers Clark memorials; Wyandotte Cave; Vincennes, Tippecanoe sites; Indiana Dunes; Hoosier Nat'l. Forest; Benjamin Harrison Home.

Famous "Hoosiers" include Larry Bird, Ambrose Burnside, Hoagy Carmichael, Jim Davis, James Dean, Eugene V. Debs, Theodore Dreiser, Paul Dresser, Gil Hodges, David Letterman, Jane Pauley, Cole Porter, Gene Stratton Porter, Ernie Pyle, James Whitcomb Riley, Oscar Robertson, Red Skelton, Booth Tarkington, Lew Wallace, Wendell L. Willkie, Wilbur Wright.

Chamber of Commerce. One North Capital, Suite 200, Indianapolis, IN 46204.

Toll-free travel information. 1-800-289-6646.

Iowa

Hawkeye State

People. Population (1990): 2,776,755; **rank:** 30. **Pop. density:** 49.7 per sq. mi. **Racial distrib.:** 96.6% White; 1.7% Black; 1.2% Hispanic. **Net change** (1980-90): −4.7%.

Geography. Total area: 56,275 sq. mi.; **rank:** 25. **Land area:** 55,875 sq. mi. **Acres forested land:** 1,562,000. **Location:** Midwest state bordered by Mississippi R. on the E and Missouri R. on the W. **Climate:** humid, continental. **Topography:** Watershed from NW to SE; soil especially rich and land level in the N central counties. **Capital:** Des Moines.

Economy. Principal industries: insurance, manufacturing, agriculture. **Principal manufactured goods:** tires, farm machinery, electronic products, appliances, office furniture, chemicals, fertilizers, auto accessories. **Agriculture: Chief crops:** silage and grain corn, soybeans, oats, hay. **Livestock** (1990): 4.5 mln. cattle; 13.5 mln. hogs; 21.9 mln. pigs; 380,000 sheep; 8.8 mln. turkeys. **Timber/lumber** (1989): red cedar; 49 mln. bd. ft. **Nonfuel Minerals** (1990): $318.7 mln.; mostly crushed stone, portland cement, construction sand & gravel. **Value of construction** (1990): 2.0 bln. **Employment distribution** (1989): 25.7% trade; 22.8% serv; 19.7% mfg.; 18.0% gvt. **Per capita income** (1990): $17,249. **Unemployment** (1990): 4.2%. **Tourism** (1989): tourists spent $2.3 bln. **Sales tax:** 4%.

Finance. FDIC-insured commercial banks & trust companies (1990): 567. **Deposits:** $27.6 bln. **Savings institutions** (1990): 45. **Assets:** $9.0 bln.

Federal government. No. federal civilian employees (Mar. 1990): 7,736. **Avg. salary:** $29,060.

Energy. Electricity production (1990, mwh, by source): Hydroelectric: 857,000; Mineral: 25.1 mln.; Nuclear: 3.0 mln.

Education. Student-teacher ratio (1989): 15.7. **Avg. salary, public school teachers** (1990-91): $27,949.

State data. Motto: Our liberties we prize and our rights we will maintain. **Flower:** Wild rose. **Bird:** Eastern goldfinch. **Tree:** Oak. **Rock:** Geode. **Entered union** Dec. 28, 1846; **rank,** 29th. **State fair** at: Des Moines; mid-Aug.

History. A thousand years ago several groups of prehistoric Indian Mound Builders dwelt on Iowa's fertile plains. Marquette and Jolliet gave France its claim to the area, 1673. It became U.S. territory through the 1803 Louisiana Purchase. Indian tribes were moved into the area from states further east, but by mid-19th century were forced to move on to Kansas. Before and during the Civil War, Iowans strongly supported Abraham Lincoln and became traditional Republicans.

Tourist attractions. Herbert Hoover birthplace and library, West Branch; Effigy Mounds Nat'l. Monument, Marquette, a pre-historic Indian burial site; Amana Colonies; Davenport Municipal Art Gallery's collection of Grant Wood's paintings and memorabilia; Living History Farms, Des Moines; Adventureland, Altoona; Boone & Scenic Valley Railroad, Boone; Greyhound Parks in Dubuque, Council Bluffs & Waterloo; Prairie Meadows horse racing, Altoona; riverboat cruises and casino gambling, Mississippi River; Iowa Great Lakes, Okoboji.

Famous Iowans include James A. Van Allen, Marquis Childs, Buffalo Bill Cody, Mamie Dowd Eisenhower, George Gallup, Susan Glaspell, James Norman Hall, Harry Hansen, Herbert Hoover, Glenn Miller, Billy Sunday, Carl Van Vechten, Henry Wallace, John Wayne, Meredith Willson, Grant Wood.

Tourist information. Division of Tourism, Iowa Dept. of Economic Development, 200 E. Grand Ave. Des Moines, IA 50309.

Toll-free travel information. 1-800-345-IOWA.

Kansas

Sunflower State

People. Population (1990): 2,477,574; **rank:** 32. **Pop. density:** 30.3 per sq. mi. **Racial distrib.:** 90.1% White; 5.8% Black; 3.8% Hispanic. **Net change** (1980-90): 4.8%.

Geography. Total area: 82,277 sq. mi.; **rank:** 14. **Land area:** 81,823 sq. mi. **Acres forested land:** 1,358,000. **Location:** West North Central state, with Missouri R. on E. **Climate:** temperate but continental, with great extremes bet. summer and winter. **Topography:** hilly Osage Plains in the E; central region level prairie and hills; high plains in the W. **Capital:** Topeka.

Economy. Principal industries: manufacturing, finance, insurance, real estate, services. **Principal manufactured goods:** transportation equip., industrial machines, food and kindred products, printing and publishing. **Agriculture: Chief crops:** wheat, sorghum, corn, hay, soybeans. **Livestock** (1990): 5.7 mln. cattle; 1.45 mln. hogs/pigs; 887,000 sheep; 1.4 mln. poultry. **Timber/lumber:** oak, walnut. **Nonfuel Minerals** (1990): $366.5 mln.; cement, salt, crushed stone. **Chief ports:** Kansas City. **International airports at:** Wichita. **Value of construction** (1990): $2.2 bln. **Employment distribution** (1989): 25.0% trade; 20.5% serv.; 19.9% gvt.; 17.1% mfg. **Per capita income** (1990): $17,986. **Unemployment** (1990): 4.4%. **Tourism** (1985): out-of-state visitors spent $1.9 bln. **Sales tax:** 6.25% maximum.

Finance. FDIC-insured commercial banks & trust companies (1990): 561. **Deposits:** $25.1 bln. **Savings institutions** (1990): 53. **Assets:** $22.0 bln.

Federal government. No. federal civilian employees (Mar. 1990): 15,794. **Avg. salary:** $28,433. **Notable federal facilities:** McConnell AFB; Fts. Riley, Leavenworth.

Energy. Electricity production (1990, mwh, by source): Hydroelectric: 12,000; Mineral: 26.0 mln; Nuclear: 7.9 mln.

Education. Student-teacher ratio (1989): 15.0. **Avg. salary, public school teachers** (1990-91): $29,923.

State data. Motto: Ad Astra per Aspera (To the stars through difficulties). **Flower:** Native sunflower. **Bird:** Western meadowlark. **Tree:** Cottonwood. **Song:** Home on the Range. **Entered union** Jan. 29, 1861; rank, 34th. **State fair** at: Hutchinson; begins Friday after Labor Day.

History. Coronado marched through the Kansas area, 1541; French explorers came next. The U.S. took over in the Louisiana Purchase, 1803. In the pre-war North-South struggle over slavery, so much violence swept the area it was called Bleeding Kansas. Railroad construction after the war made Abilene and Dodge City terminals of large cattle drives from Texas.

Tourist attractions. Eisenhower Center and "Place of Meditation," Abilene; Agricultural Hall of Fame and National Ctr., Bonner Springs, displays farm equipment; Dodge City-Boot Hill & Frontier Town; Cowtown-historic frontier town, Wichita; Ft. Scott & Ft. Larned-restored 1800s cavalry forts. Kansas Cosmosphere and Space Discovery Center, Hutchinson.

Famous Kansans include Thomas Hart Benton, John Brown, Walter P. Chrysler, John Steuart Curry, Amelia Earhart, Dwight D. Eisenhower, Ron Evans, Wild Bill Hickok, Cyrus Holliday, William Inge, Walter Johnson, Alf Landon, Carry Nation, Gordon Parks, Jim Ryun, William Allen White.

Tourist information. Kansas Dept. of Commerce, Travel and Tourism Div., 400 SW 8th St., 5th Fl., Topeka, KS 66603; 1-913-296-2009.

Toll-free travel information. 1-800-2KANSAS.

Kentucky

Bluegrass State

People. Population (1990): 3,685,296 **rank:** 23. **Pop. density:** 92.0 per sq. mi. **Racial Distrib.:** 92.0% White; 7.1% Black; Hispanic 0.6%. **Net change** (1980-90): 0.7%.

Geography. Total area: 40,410 sq. mi.; **rank:** 37. **Land area:** 39,732 sq. mi. **Acres forested land:** 12,256,000. Location: east south central state, bordered on N by Illinois, Indiana, Ohio; on E by West Virginia and Virginia; in S by Tennessee; on W by Missouri. **Climate:** moderate, with plentiful rainfall. **Topography:** mountainous in E; rounded hills of the Knobs in the N; Bluegrass, heart of state; wooded rocky hillsides of the Pennyroyal; Western Coal Field; the fertile Purchase the SW. **Capital:** Frankfort.

Economy. Principal industries: manufacturing, coal mining, construction, agriculture. **Principal manufactured goods:** nonelectrical machinery, food products, electrical & electronic products, apparel, printing and publishing. **Agriculture: Chief crops** (1990): tobacco, soybeans, corn. **Livestock** (1989): 2.5 mln. cattle; 880,000 hogs/pigs; 32,000 sheep; 1.8 mln. chickens; 1985 receipts for horse & mule sales, $450 mln. **Timber/lumber** (1989): hardwoods, pines; 426 mln. bd. ft. **Non-fuel Minerals** (1990): $334.0 mln.; mostly crushed stone. **Chief ports:** Paducah, Louisville, Covington, Owensboro, Ashland, Henderson County, Lyon County, Hickman-Fulton County. **International airports at:** Covington. **Value of construction** (1990): $3.2 bln. **Employment distribution:** 23.8% trade; 20.4% mfg.; 19.7% serv.; 18.4% gvt. **Per capita income** (1990): $14,929. **Unemployment** (1990): 5.8%. **Tourism** (1989): tourists spent $4.3 bln. **Sales tax:** 6%.

Finance. FDIC-insured commercial banks & trust companies (1990): 335. **Deposits:** $30.9 bln. **Savings institutions** (1990): 62. **Assets:** $7.8 bln.

Federal government. No. federal civilian employees (Mar. 1990): 27,962. **Avg. salary:** $26,083. **Notable federal facilities:** U.S. Gold Bullion Depository, Fort Knox; Federal Correctional Institution, Lexington.

Energy. Electricity production (1990, mwh, by source): Hydroelectric: 3.2 mln.; Mineral: 70.6 mln.

Education. Student-teacher ratio (1989): 17.7. **Avg. salary, public school teachers** (1990-91): $29,089.

State data. Motto: United we stand, divided we fall. **Flower:** Goldenrod. **Bird:** Cardinal. **Tree:** Kentucky coffee tree. **Song:** My Old Kentucky Home. **Entered union** June 1, 1792; rank, 15th. **State fair** at: Louisville.

History. Kentucky was the first area west of the Alleghenies settled by American pioneers; first permanent settlement, Harrodsburg, 1774. Daniel Boone blazed the Wilderness Trail through the Cumberland Gap and founded Fort Boonesborough, 1775. Indian attacks, spurred by the British, were unceasing until, during the Revolution, Gen. George Rogers Clark captured British forts in Indiana and Illinois, 1778. In 1792, after Virginia dropped its claims to the region, Kentucky became the 15th state.

Tourist attractions. Kentucky Derby and accompanying festivities, Louisville; Land Between the Lakes Nat'l. Recreation Area encompassing Kentucky Lake and Lake Barkley; Mammoth Cave National Park with 300 mi. of explored passageways, 200-ft. high rooms, blind fish, and Echo River, 360 ft. below ground; Shaker Village of Pleasant Hill, Harrodsburg; Lincoln birthplace, Hodgenville; My Old Kentucky Home, Bardstown; Cumberland Gap Natl. Historical Park, Middlesboro; Kentucky Horse Park, Lexington.

Famous Kentuckians include Muhammad Ali, John James Audubon, Alben Barkley, Daniel Boone, Louis D. Brandeis, John C. Breckinridge, Kit Carson, Albert B. "Happy" Chandler, Cassius Marcellus Clay, Henry Clay, Jefferson Davis, "Casey" Jones, Abraham Lincoln, Mary Todd Lincoln, Thomas Hunt Morgan, Carry Nation, Col. Harland Sanders, Diane Sawyer, Jesse Stuart, Adlai Stevenson, Zachary Taylor, Robert Penn Warren, Whitney Young, Jr.

Chamber of Commerce. 452 Versailles Rd., P.O. Box 817, Frankfort, KY 40602.

Toll-free travel information. 1-800-225-TRIP, extension 67 in U.S., Ontario & Quebec, Canada.

Louisiana

Pelican State

People. Population (1990): 4,219,973; **rank:** 21. **Pop. density:** 96.9 per sq. mi. **Racial distrib.:** 67.3% White; 30.8% Black; 2.2% Hispanic. **Net change** (1980-90): 0.3%.

Geography. Total area: 47,752 sq. mi.; **rank:** 31. **Land area:** 43,566 sq. mi. **Acres forested land:** 13,883,000. Location: south central Gulf Coast state. **Climate:** subtropical, affected by continental weather patterns. **Topography:** lowlands of marshes and Mississippi R. flood plain; Red R. Valley lowlands; upland hills in the Florida Parishes; average elevation, 100 ft. **Capital:** Baton Rouge.

Economy. Principal industries: wholesale and retail trade, government, manufacturing, construction, transportation, mining. **Principal manufactured goods** (1990): chemical products, foods, transportation equipment, electronic equipment, petroleum products, lumber, wood, and paper. **Agriculture: Chief crops** (1990): soybean, sugarcane, rice, corn, cotton, sweet potatoes, pecans, sorghum. **Livestock** (1990): 840,000 cattle; 50,000 hogs/pigs; 16,000 sheep; 2.1 mln. poultry. **Timber/lumber** (1989): pines, hardwoods, oak; 737 mln. bd. ft. **Nonfuel Minerals** (1990): $381.1 mln., mostly salt, sand & gravel, sulfur. **Commercial fishing** (1990): $263.5 mln. **Chief ports:** New Orleans, Baton Rouge, Lake Charles, S. Louisiana Port Commission at La Place, Shreveport. **International airports at:** New Orleans. **Value of construction** (1990): $2.9 bln. **Employment distribution** (1990): 23.1% trade; 23.6% serv.; 20.8% gvt.; 11.4% mfg. **Per capita income** (1990): $14,391. **Unemployment** (1990): 6.2%. **Tourism** (1989): out-of-state visitors spent $4.2 bln. **Sales tax:** 4%.

Finance. FDIC-insured commercial banks & trust companies (1990): 232. **Deposits:** $31.5 bln. **Savings institutions** (1990): 86. **Assets:** $13.3 bln.

Federal government. No. federal civilian employees (Mar. 1990): 21,755. **Avg. salary:** $28,617. **Notable federal facilities:** Barksdale, England, Ft. Polk military bases; Strategic Petroleum Reserve, New Orleans; Michoud Assembly Plant, New Orleans; U.S. Public Service Hospital, Carville.

Energy. Electricity production (1990, mwh, by source): Hydroelectric: 2.1 mln.; Mineral: 43.2 mln; Nuclear: 14.2 mln.

Education. Student-teacher ratio (1988): 18.2. **Avg. salary, public school teachers** (1990-91): $26,240.

State data. Motto: Union, justice and confidence. **Flower:** Magnolia. **Bird:** Eastern brown pelican. **Tree:** Cypress. **Song:** Give Me Louisiana. **Entered union** Apr. 30, 1812; rank, 18th. **State fair** at: Shreveport; Oct.

History. The area was first visited, 1530, by Cabeza de Vaca and Panfilo de Narvaez. The region was claimed for France by LaSalle, 1682. First permanent settlement was by French at Biloxi, now in Mississippi, 1699. France ceded the region to Spain, 1762, took it back, 1800, and sold it to the U.S., 1803, in the Louisiana Purchase. During the Revolution, Spanish Louisiana aided the Americans. Admitted to statehood, 1812, Louisiana was the scene of the Battle of New Orleans, 1815.

Louisiana Creoles are descendants of early French and/or Spanish settlers. About 4,000 Acadians, French settlers in Nova Scotia, Canada, were forcibly transported by the British to Louisiana in 1755 (an event commemorated in Longfellow's *Evangeline*) and settled near Bayou Teche; their descendants became known as Cajuns. Another group, the Islenos, were descendants of Canary Islanders brought to Louisiana by a Spanish governor in 1770. Traces of Spanish and French survive in local dialects.

Tourist attractions. Mardi Gras, French Quarter, Superdome, Dixieland jazz, Aquarium of the Americas, all New Orleans; Battle of New Orleans site; Longfellow-Evangeline Memorial Park; Kent House Museum, Alexandria; Hodges Gardens, Natchilotches.

Famous Louisianans include Louis Armstrong, Pierre Beauregard, Judah P. Benjamin, Braxton Bragg, Grace King, Huey Long, Leonidas K. Polk, Henry Miller Shreve, Edward D. White Jr.

Tourist Information. State Dept. of Culture, Recreation & Tourism, P.O. Box 94291, Baton Rouge, LA 70804-9291.

Toll-free travel information. 1-800-33-GUMBO.

Maine
Pine Tree State

People. Population (1990): 1,227,928; rank: 38. **Pop. density:** 39.8 per sq. mi. **Racial distrib.:** 98.4% White; 0.4% Black; 0.6% Hispanic. **Net change** (1980-90): 9.2%.

Geography. Total area: 33,265 sq. mi.; **rank:** 39. **Land area:** 30,865 sq. mi. **Acres forested land:** 17,713,000. **Location:** New England state at northeastern tip of U.S. **Climate:** Southern interior and coastal, influenced by air masses from the S and W; northern clime harsher, avg. +100 in. snow in winter. **Topography:** Appalachian Mtns. extend through state; western borders have rugged terrain; long sand beaches on southern coast; northern coast mainly rocky promontories, peninsulas, fjords. **Capital:** Augusta.

Economy. Principal industries: manufacturing, services, trade, government, finance, insurance, real estate, construction. **Principal manufactured goods:** paper and wood products, leather goods. **Agriculture: Chief crops:** potatoes, apples, hay, blueberries. **Livestock** (1986): 135,000 cattle; 79,000 hogs/pigs; 17,000 sheep; 4.9 mln. poultry. **Timber/lumber** (1989): pine, spruce, fir; 714 mln. bd ft. **Nonfuel Minerals** (1990): $56.0 mln.; construction sand & gravel, cement, crushed stone, dimension stone. **Commercial fishing** (1990): $129.9 mln. **Chief ports:** Searsport, Portland, Eastport. **International airports at:** Portland, Bangor. **Value of construction** (1990): $879.8 mln. **Employment distribution** (1987): 24.3% trade; 21.4% serv.; 20.1% mfg.; 18.9% gvt. **Per capita income** (1990): $17,200. **Unemployment** (1990): 5.1%. **Tourism** (1989): $2 bln. **Sales tax:** 5%.

Finance. FDIC-insured **commercial banks & trust companies** (1990): 21. **Deposits:** $6.7 bln. **Savings institutions** (1990): 14. **Assets:** $7.4 bln.

Federal government. No. federal civilian employees (Mar. 1990): 13,129. **Avg. salary:** $28,249. **Notable federal facilities:** Kittery Naval Shipyard; Brunswick Naval Air Station; Loring Air Force Base.

Energy. Electricity production (1990, mwh, by source): Hydroelectric: 2.1 mln.; Mineral: 2.1 mln.; Nuclear: 4.9 mln.

Education. Student-teacher ratio (1989): 14.1. **Avg. salary, public school teachers** (1990-91): $28,700.

State data. Motto: Dirigo (I direct). **Flower:** White pine cone and tassel. **Bird:** Chickadee. **Tree:** Eastern white pine. **Song:** State of Maine Song. **Entered union:** Mar. 15, 1820; rank, 23d.

History. Maine's rocky coast was explored by the Cabots, 1498-99. French settlers arrived, 1604, at the St. Croix River; English, 1607, on the Kennebec. In 1691, Maine was made part of Massachusetts. In the Revolution, a Maine regiment fought at Bunker Hill; a British fleet destroyed Falmouth (now Portland), 1775, but the British ship Margaretta was captured near Machiasport. In 1820, Maine broke off from Massachusetts, became a separate state.

Tourist attractions. Acadia Nat'l. Park, Bar Harbor, on Mt. Desert Is.; Funtown, Saco; Bath Iron Works and Marine Museum; Boothbay (Harbor) Railway Museum; Portland Art Museum; Sugarloaf/USA Ski Area; Ogunquit, Portland, York.

Famous "Down Easters" include James G. Blaine, Cyrus H.K. Curtis, Hannibal Hamlin, Longfellow, Sir Hiram and Hudson Maxim, Edna St. Vincent Millay, Kate Douglas Wiggin, Ben Ames Williams.

Chamber of Commerce and Industry. 126 Sewall St., Augusta, ME 04330.

Toll-free travel information. 1-800-533-9595, winter only, out of state only; 1-207-289-2423 year round.

Maryland
Old Line State, Free State

People. Population (1990): 4,781,468; rank: 19 **Pop. density:** 489.2 per sq. mi. **Racial distrib.:** 71.0% White; 24.9% Black; 2.9 Asian; 2.6% Hispanic. **Net change** (1980-90): 13.4%.

Geography. Total area: 10,460 sq. mi.; **rank:** 42. **Land area:** 9,775 sq. mi. **Acres forested land:** 2,632,000. **Location:** Middle Atlantic state stretching from the Ocean to the Allegheny Mtns. **Climate:** continental in the west; humid subtropical in the east. **Topography:** Eastern Shore of coastal plain and Maryland Main of coastal plain, piedmont plateau, and the Blue Ridge, separated by the Chesapeake Bay. **Capital:** Annapolis.

Economy. Principal industries: manufacturing, tourism. **Principal manufactured goods:** electric and electronic equipment; food and kindred products; chemicals and allied products. **Agriculture: Chief crops** (1989): corn, soybeans, greenhouse & nursery prods. **Livestock** (1989): 328,000 cattle; 180,000 hogs/pigs; 32,000 sheep; 257.8 mln. poultry. **Timber/lumber** (1990): hardwoods. **Nonfuel Minerals** (1990): $353.8 mln.; crushed stone, sand & gravel, Portland cement. **Commercial fishing** (1990): $53.9 mln. **Chief ports:** Baltimore. **International airports at:** Baltimore. **Value of construction** (1990): $5.9 bln. **Employment distribution** (1988): 27.4% serv.; 25.9% trade; 18.3% gvt. **Per capita income** (1990): $21,864. **Unemployment** (1990): 4.6%. **Tourism** (1989): tourists spent $8.3 bln. **Sales tax:** 5%.

Finance. FDIC-insured **commercial banks & trust companies** (1990): 108. **Deposits:** $41.7 bln. **Savings institutions** (1990): 102. **Assets:** $23.5 bln.

Federal government. No. federal civilian employees (Mar. 1990): 105,341. **Avg. salary:** $35,129. **Notable federal facilities:** U.S. Naval Academy, Annapolis; Natl. Agric. Research Cen.; Ft. George G. Meade, Aberdeen Proving Ground; Goddard Space Flight Center; Natl. Institutes of Health.

Energy. Electricity production (1990, mwh, by source): Hydroelectric: 2.3 mln.; Mineral: 27.9 mln.; Nuclear: 1.3 mln.

Education. Student-teacher ratio (1989): 16.8. **Avg. salary, public school teachers** (1990-91): $38,806.

State data. Motto. Fatti Maschii, Parole Femine (Manly deeds, womanly words). **Flower:** Black-eyed susan. **Bird:** Baltimore oriole. **Tree:** White oak. **Song:** Maryland, My Maryland. **Seventh** of the original 13 states to ratify Constitution, Apr. 28, 1788. **State fair** at: Timonium; late Aug.-early Sept.

History. Capt. John Smith first explored Maryland, 1608. William Claiborne set up a trading post on Kent Is. in Chesapeake Bay, 1631. Britain granted land to Cecilius Calvert, Lord Baltimore, 1632; his brother led 200 settlers to St. Marys River, 1634. The bravery of Maryland troops in the Revolution, as at the Battle of Long Island, won the state its nickname, The Old Line State. In the War of 1812, when a British fleet tried to take Fort McHenry, Marylander Francis Scott Key, 1814, wrote The Star-Spangled Banner.

Tourist Attractions. Racing events include the Preakness, at Pimlico track, Baltimore; the International at Laurel Race Course; the Maryland Million at Pimlico. Also Annapolis yacht races; Ocean City summer resort; restored Ft. McHenry, Baltimore, near which Francis Scott Key wrote The Star-Spangled Banner; Antietam Battlefield, 1862, near Hagerstown; South Mountain Battlefield, 1862; Edgar Allan Poe house, Baltimore; National Aquarium, Baltimore Harborplace; The State House, Annapolis, 1772, the oldest still in use in the U.S.; Montgomery & Prince George's County gateway to Washington, D.C.

Famous Marylanders include Benjamin Banneker, Francis Scott Key, H.L. Mencken, William Pinkney, Upton Sinclair, Roger B. Taney, Charles Willson Peale.

Chamber of Commerce. 60 West St., Suite 405, Annapolis, MD 21401.

Toll-free travel information. 1-800-543-1036.

Massachusetts

Bay State, Old Colony

People. Population (1990): 6,016,425; **rank: 13. Pop. density:** 767.6 per sq. mi. **Racial distrib.:** 89.8% White; 5.0% Black; 2.4% Asian; 4.8% Hispanic. **Net change** (1980-90): 4.9%.

Geography. Total area: 8,284 sq. mi.; **rank: 45. Land area:** 7,838 sq. mi. **Acres forested land:** 3,097,000. **Location:** New England state along Atlantic seaboard. **Climate:** temperate, with colder and drier clime in western region. **Topography:** jagged indented coast from Rhode Island around Cape Cod; flat land yields to stony upland pastures near central region and gentle hilly country in west; except in west, land is rocky, sandy, and not fertile. **Capital:** Boston.

Economy. Principal industries (1990): services, trade, manufacturing. **Principal manufactured goods** (1990): electric and electronic equipment, machinery, industrial machinery and equipment, printing and publishing, fabricated metal products. **Agriculture: Chief crops:** cranberries, greenhouse, nursery, vegetables. **Livestock** (1983): 120,000 cattle; 50,000 hogs/pigs; 8,000 sheep; 125,000 horses, ponies; 3.6 mln. poultry. **Timber/lumber** (1989): white pine, oak, other hard woods; 85 mln. bd. ft. **Nonfuel Minerals** (1990): $111.3 mln.; mostly construction sand & gravel, crushed stone. **Commercial fishing** (1990): $303.0 mln. **Chief ports:** Boston, Fall River, New Bedford, Salem, Gloucester, Plymouth. **International airport at:** Boston. **Value of construction** (1990): $5.1 bln. **Employment distribution** (1990): 30.8% trade; 23.5% serv.; 17.5% mfg. **Per capita income** (1990): $22,642. **Unemployment** (1990): 6.0%. **Tourism** (1987): out-of-state visitors spent $12.9 bln. **Sales tax:** 5%.

Finance. FDIC-insured commercial banks & trust companies (1990): 94. **Deposits:** $66.7 bln. **Savings institutions** (1990): 29. **Assets:** $98.2 bln.

Federal government. No. federal civilian employees (Mar. 1990): 31,013. **Avg. salary:** $31,176. **Notable federal facilities:** Ft. Devens; Thomas P. O'Neill Jr. Federal Bldg., J.W. McCormack Bldg., John Fitzgerald Kennedy Federal Bldg., Boston; Q.M. Laboratory, Natick.

Energy. Electricity production (1990, mwh, by source): Hydroelectric: 297,000; Mineral: 30.9 mln.; Nuclear: 5.1 mln.

Education. Student-teacher ratio (1989): 14.0. **Avg. salary, public school teachers** (1990-91): $36,090.

State data. Motto: Ense Petit Placidam Sub Libertate Quietem (By the sword we seek peace, but peace only under liberty). **Flower:** Mayflower. **Bird:** Chickadee. **Tree:** American elm. **Song:** All Hail to Massachusetts. **Sixth** of the original 13 states to ratify Constitution, Feb. 6, 1788.

History. Pilgrims settled in Plymouth, 1620; the following year they gave thanks for their survival with the first Thanksgiving Day. Indian opposition reached a high point in King Philip's War, 1675-76, won by the colonists. Demonstrations against British restrictions set off the "Boston Massacre," 1770, and Boston "tea party," 1773. First bloodshed of the Revolution was at Lexington, 1775.

Tourist attractions. Cape Cod—Plymouth Rock, Plymouth Plantation, Mayflower II, Provincetown artists colony; Boston—Freedom Trail, Museum of Fine Arts, Children's Museum, Museum of Science, New England Aquarium, JFK Library, Boston Ballet, Boston Pops, Boston Symphony Orchestra; Berkshires—Tanglewood, Jacob's Pillow Dance Festival, Hancock Shaker Village, Berkshire Scenic Railroad; Old Sturbridge Village; Walden Pond; Naismith Memorial Basketball Hall of Fame, Springfield.

Famous "Bay Staters" include John Adams, John Quincy Adams, Samuel Adams, Louisa May Alcott, Horatio Alger, Susan B. Anthony, Crispus Attucks, Clara Barton, Alexander Graham Bell, Emily Dickinson, Ralph Waldo Emerson, John Hancock, Nathaniel Hawthorne, Oliver W. Holmes, Winslow Homer, Elias Howe, John Fitzgerald Kennedy, Samuel F.B. Morse, Edgar Allan Poe, Paul Revere, Henry David Thoreau, James McNeil Whistler, John Greenleaf Whittier.

Tourist information. Massachusetts Office of Travel & Tourism, 100 Cambridge St., 13th Floor, Boston, MA 02202.

Toll-free travel information. 1-800-624-MASS.

Michigan

Great Lakes State, Wolverine State

People. Population (1990): 9,295,297; **rank: 8. Pop. density:** 165.4 per sq. mi. **Racial distrib.:** 83.4% White; 13.9% Black; 2.2% Hispanic. **Net change** (1980-90) 0.4%.

Geography. Total area: 58,527 sq. mi.; **rank: 23. Land area:** 56,809 sq. mi. **Acres forested land:** 18,220,000. **Location:** east north central state bordering on 4 of the 5 Great Lakes, divided into an Upper and Lower Peninsula by the Straits of Mackinac, which link lakes Michigan and Huron. **Climate:** well-defined seasons tempered by the Great Lakes. **Topography:** low rolling hills give way to northern tableland of hilly belts in Lower Peninsula; Upper Peninsula is level in the east, with swampy areas; western region is higher and more rugged. **Capital:** Lansing.

Economy. Principal industries: manufacturing, services, tourism, agriculture, mining. **Principal manufactured goods:** transportation equipment, machinery, fabricated metals, primary metals, food prods., rubber & plastics. **Agriculture: Chief crops:** corn, winter wheat, soybeans, dry beans, oats, hay, sugar beets, honey, asparagus, sweet corn, apples, cherries, grapes, peaches, blueberries, flowers. **Livestock** (1986): 1.4 mln. cattle; 1.2 mln. hogs/pigs; 108,000 sheep; 8.9 mln. poultry. **Timber/lumber** (1989): maple, oak, aspen; 323 mln. bd. ft. **Nonfuel Minerals** (1989): $1.37 bln.; iron ore, Portland cement, crushed stone, sand & gravel. **Commercial fishing** (1990): $10.4 mln. **Chief ports:** Detroit, Saginaw River, Escanaba, Muskegon, Saulte Ste. Marie, Port Huron, Marine City. **International airports at:** Detroit, Sault St. Marie. **Value of construction** (1990): $7.6 bln. **Employment distribution** (1990): 24% mfg.; 24% serv.; **Per capita income** (1990): $18,346. **Unemployment** (1990): 7.5%. **Tourism** (1990): travellers spent $16.5 bln. **Sales tax:** 4%.

Finance. FDIC-insured commercial banks & trust companies (1990): 255. **Deposits:** $73.2 bln. **Savings institutions** (1990): 44. **Assets:** $35.1 bln.

Federal government. No. federal civilian employees (Mar. 1990): 26,764. **Avg. salary:** $30,717. **Notable federal facilities:** Isle Royal, Sleeping Bear Dunes national parks.

Energy. Electricity production (1990, mwh, by source): Hydroelectric: 797,000 mln; Mineral: 66.6 mln.; Nuclear: 21.6 mln.

Education. Student-teacher ratio (1989): 19.7. **Avg. salary, public school teachers** (1990-91): $37,682.

State data. Motto: Si Quaeris Peninsulam Amoenam Circumspice (If you seek a pleasant peninsula, look about you). **Flower:** Apple blossom. **Bird:** Robin. **Tree:** White pine. **Song:** Michigan, My Michigan. **Entered union** Jan. 26, 1837; **rank**, 26th. **State fair** at: Detroit, late Aug.-early Sept.; Upper Peninsula (Escanaba) mid-Aug; Michigan Festival, mid.-Aug.

History. French fur traders and missionaries visited the region, 1616, set up a mission at Sault Ste. Marie, 1641, and a settlement there, 1668. The whole region went to Britain, 1763. Anthony Wayne defeated their Indian allies at Fallen Timbers, Ohio, 1794. The British returned, 1812, seized Ft. Mackinac and Detroit. Oliver H. Perry's Lake Erie victory and William H. Harrison's troops, who carried the war to the Thames River in Canada, 1813, freed Michigan once more.

Tourist attractions. Henry Ford Museum, Greenfield Village, reconstruction of a typical 19th cent. American village, both in Dearborn; Michigan Space Ctr., Jackson; Tahquamenon *(Hiawatha)* Falls; DeZwaan windmill and Tulip Festival, Holland; "Soo Locks," St. Marys Falls Ship Canal, Sault Ste. Marie.

Famous Michiganians include Ralph Bunche, Thomas A. Edison, Gerald R. Ford, Paul de Kruif, Edna Ferber, Henry Ford, Aretha Franklin, Edgar Guest, Lee Iacocca, Robert Ingersoll, Magic Johnson, Will Kellogg, Ring Lardner, Elmore Leonard, Charles Lindbergh, Joe Louis, Madonna, Pontiac, Diana Ross, Tom Selleck, Lily Tomlin, Stewart Edward White, Malcolm X.

Chamber of Commerce: 200 N. Washington Sq., Suite 400, Lansing, MI 48933.

Toll-free travel information. 1-800-543-2937.

Tourist Information. Minnesota Office of Tourism, 375 Jackson St., 250 Skyway Level, St. Paul, MN 55101.

Toll-free travel information. 1-800-328-1461.

Minnesota

North Star State, Gopher State

People. Population (1990): 4,375,099; **rank:** 20. **Pop. density:** 55.0 per sq. mi. **Racial distrib.:** 94.4% White; 2.2% Black; 1.8% Asian; 1.2% Hispanic. **Net change** (1980-90): 7.3%.

Geography. Total area: 84,402 sq. mi.; **rank:** 12. **Land area:** 79,617 sq. mi. **Acres forested land:** 16,583,000. **Location:** north central state bounded on the E by Wisconsin and Lake Superior, on the N by Canada, on the W by the Dakotas, and on the S by Iowa. **Climate:** northern part of state lies in the moist Great Lakes storm belt; the western border lies at the edge of the semi-arid Great Plains. **Topography:** central hill and lake region covering approx. half the state; to the NE, rocky ridges and deep lakes; to the NW, flat plain; to the S, rolling plains and deep river valleys. **Capital:** St. Paul.

Economy. Principal industries: agri business, forest products, mining, manufacturing, tourism. **Principal manufactured goods:** food processing, non-electrical machinery, chemicals, paper, electric and electronic equipment, printing and publishing, instruments, fabricated metal products. **Agriculture: Chief crops:** corn, soybeans, wheat, sugar beets, sunflowers, barley. **Livestock** (1990): 2.95 mln. cattle; 4.25 mln. hogs/pigs; 285,000 sheep; 12.7 mln. poultry. **Timber/lumber** (1989): needleleaves and hardwoods; 150 mln. bd. ft. **Nonfuel Minerals** (1990): 1.5 bln.; mostly iron ore. **Commercial fishing** (1990): $136,000. **Chief ports:** Duluth, St. Paul, Minneapolis. **International airports at:** Minneapolis-St. Paul. **Value of construction** (1990): $4.8 bln. **Employment distribution** (1990): 24.4% trade; 26.0% serv.; 18.3% mfg.; 15.8% gvt. **Per capita income** (1990): $18,731. **Unemployment** (1990): 4.8%. **Tourism** (1987): out-of-state visitors spent $3.6 bln. **Sales tax:** 6½%.

Finance. FDIC-insured commercial banks & trust companies (1990): 628. **Deposits:** $39.6 bln. **Savings institutions** (1990): 32. **Assets:** $13.5 bln.

Federal government. No. federal civilian employees (Mar. 1990): 14,556. **Avg. salary:** $31,108.

Energy. Electricity production (1990, mwh, by source): Hydroelectric: 658,000; Mineral: 26.3 mln.; Nuclear: 12.1 mln.

Education. Student-teacher ratio (1989): 17.2. **Avg. salary, public school teachers** (1990-91): $33,284.

State data. Motto: L'Etoile du Nord (The star of the north). **Flower:** Pink and white lady's-slipper. **Bird:** Common loon. **Tree:** Red pine. **Song:** Hail! Minnesota. **Entered union** May 11, 1858; **rank,** 32d. **State fair** at: Saint Paul; late Aug. to early Sept.

History. Fur traders and missionaries from French Canada opened the region in the 17th century. Britain took the area east of the Mississippi, 1763. The U.S. took over that portion after the Revolution and in 1803 bought the western area as part of the Louisiana Purchase. The U.S. built present Ft. Snelling, 1820, bought lands from the Indians, 1837. Sioux Indians staged a bloody uprising, 1862, and were driven from the state.

Tourist attractions. Minnehaha Falls, Minneapolis, inspiration for Longfellow's *Hiawatha*; over 15,000 lakes; 66 state parks; 25 historical sites; Minneapolis Aquatennial; Ordway Theater, St. Paul; Guthrie Theater, Minneapolis; professional baseball, football, hockey. Voyageurs Nat'l. Park, a water wilderness along the Canadian border; Mayo Clinic, Rochester; St. Paul Winter Carnival; North Shore (of Lake Superior).

Famous Minnesotans include F. Scott Fitzgerald, Cass Gilbert, Hubert Humphrey, Sister Elizabeth Kenny, Sinclair Lewis, Paul Manship, E. G. Marshall, William and Charles Mayo, Walter F. Mondale, Charles Schulz, Harold Stassen, Thorstein Veblen.

Mississippi

Magnolia State

People. Population (1990): 2,573,216; **rank:** 31. **Pop. density:** 54.8 per sq. mi. **Racial distrib.:** 63.5% White; 35.6% Black; 0.6% Hispanic. **Net change** (1980-90): 2.1%.

Geography. Total area: 47,689 sq. mi.; **rank:** 32. **Land area:** 46,914 sq. mi. **Acres forested land:** 16,693,000. **Location:** south central state bordered on the W by the Mississippi R. and on the S by the Gulf of Mexico. **Climate:** semi-tropical, with abundant rainfall, long growing season, and extreme temperatures unusual. **Topography:** low, fertile delta bet. the Yazoo and Mississippi rivers; loess bluffs stretching around delta border; sandy Gulf coastal terraces followed by piney woods and prairie; rugged, high sandy hills in extreme NE followed by black prairie belt. Pontotoc Ridge, and flatwoods into the north central highlands. **Capital:** Jackson.

Economy. Principal industries: manufacturing, food processing, seafood, government, wholesale and retail trade, agriculture. **Principal manufactured goods:** apparel, furniture, lumber and wood products, foods and kindred products, electrical machinery and equipment, transportation equip. **Agriculture: Chief crops:** cotton, soybeans, catfish, rice. **Livestock** (1989): 1.4 mln. cattle; 180,000 hogs/pigs; 387 mln. broilers. **Timber/lumber** (1989): pine, oak, hardwoods; 2.2 bln. bd. ft. **Nonfuel Minerals** (1990): $122.1 mln., mostly construction sand & gravel. **Commercial fishing** (1990): $42.3 mln. **Chief ports:** Pascagoula, Vicksburg, Gulfport, Natchez, Greenville. **Value of construction** (1990): $1.6 bln. **Employment distribution** (1990): 26.2% mfg.; 21.8% gvt.; 21.2% trade; 17.2% serv. **Per capita income** (1990): $12,735. **Unemployment** (1990): 7.5%. **Tourism** (1989): out-of-state visitors spent $1.5 bln. **Sales tax:** 6%.

Finance. FDIC-insured commercial banks & trust companies (1990): 122. **Deposits:** $18.2 bln. **Savings institutions** (1990): 40. **Assets:** $4.8 bln.

Federal government. No. federal civilian employees (Mar. 1989): 17,749. **Avg. salary:** $27,963. **Notable federal facilities:** Columbus, Keesler AF bases; Meridian Naval Air Station, John F. Stennis Space Center.

Energy. Electricity production (1990, mwh, by source): Mineral 15.6 mln.; Nuclear 7.4 mln.

Education. Student-teacher ratio (1989): 18.2. **Avg. salary, public school teachers** (1990-91): $24,443.

State data. Motto: Virtute et Armis (By valor and arms). **Flower:** Magnolia. **Bird:** Mockingbird. **Tree:** Magnolia. **Song:** Go, Mississippi! **Entered union** Dec. 10, 1817; **rank,** 20th. **State fair** at: Jackson; Fall.

History. De Soto explored the area, 1540, discovered the Mississippi River, 1541. La Salle traced the river from Illinois to its mouth and claimed the entire valley for France, 1682. First settlement was the French Ft. Maurepas, near Ocean Springs, 1699. The area was ceded to Britain, 1763; American settlers followed. During the Revolution, Spain seized part of the area and refused to leave even after the U.S. acquired title at the end of the Revolution, finally moving out, 1798. Mississippi seceded 1861. Union forces captured Corinth and Vicksburg and destroyed Jackson and much of Meridian.

Tourist attractions. Vicksburg National Military Park and Cemetery, other Civil War sites; Natchez Trace; Indian mounds; Antebellum Home; pilgrimages at Natchez, Columbus, Vicksburg; Mardi Gras and blessing of the shrimp fleet, June, both in Biloxi.

Famous Mississippians include Dana Andrews, Jimmy Buffet, Hodding Carter III, William Faulkner, Shelby Foote, Fannie Lou Hamer, Jim Henson, Robert Johnson, James Earl Jones, B.B. King, L.Q.C. Lamar, Willie Morris, Elvis Presley, Leontyne Price, Charlie Pride, Eudora Welty, Tennessee Williams, Oprah Winfrey, Richard Wright, Tammy Wynette.

Chamber of Commerce. P.O. Box 1849, Jackson, MS 39205.

Toll-free travel information. 1-800-962-2346; 1-800-647-2290 out of state.

Chamber of Commerce: 400 E. High St., P.O. Box 149, Jefferson City, MO 65101.

Toll-free travel information. 1-800-877-1234.

Missouri

Show Me State

People. Population (1990): 5,117,073; **rank:** 15. **Pop. density:** 74.3 per sq. mi. **Racial distrib.:** 87.7% White; 10.7% Black; 1.2% Hispanic. **Net change** (1980-90): 4.1%.

Geography. Total area: 69,697 sq. mi.; **rank:** 19. **Land area:** 68,898 sq. mi. **Acres forested land:** 12,523,000. **Location:** West North central state near the geographic center of the conterminous U.S.; bordered on the E by the Mississippi R., on the NW by the Missouri R. **Climate:** continental, susceptible to cold Canadian air, moist, warm Gulf air, and drier SW air. **Topography:** Rolling hills, open, fertile plains, and well-watered prairie N of the Missouri R.; south of the river land is rough and hilly with deep, narrow valleys; alluvial plain in the SE; low elevation in the west. **Capital:** Jefferson City.

Economy. Principal industries: agriculture, manufacturing, aerospace, tourism. **Principal manufactured goods:** transportation equipment, food and related products, electrical and electronic equipment, chemicals. **Agriculture: Chief crops:** soybeans, corn, wheat, hay. **Livestock** (1989): 4.5 mln. cattle; 2.7 mln. hogs/pigs; 138,000 sheep; 8.0 mln. chickens, 17.3 mln. turkeys. **Timber/lumber** (1989): oak, hickory; 385 mln. bd. ft. **Nonfuel Minerals** (1990): $1.1 bln., mostly lead, crushed stone, Portland cement. **Chief ports:** St. Louis, Kansas City. **International airports at:** St. Louis, Kansas City. **Value of construction** (1990): $3.8 bln. **Employment distribution** (1989): 25% trade; 24% serv.; 19% mfg.; 16% gvt. **Per capita income** (1990): $17,497. **Unemployment** (1990): 5.7%. **Tourism** (1990): total travelers spent $5 bln. **Sales tax:** 4.225%.

Finance. FDIC-insured commercial banks & trust companies (1990): 549. **Deposits** (1990): $49.7 bln. **Savings institutions** (1990): 80. **Assets:** $23.0 bln.

Federal government. No. federal civilian employees (Mar. 1990): 45,462. **Avg. salary:** $29,261. **Notable federal facilities:** Federal Reserve banks, St. Louis, Kansas City; Ft. Leonard Wood, Rolla; Jefferson Barracks, St. Louis; Whiteman AFB, Knob Noster.

Energy. Electricity production (1990 mwh, by source): Hydroelectric: 2.2 mln.; Mineral: 48.9 mln; Nuclear: 8.0 mln.

Education. Student-teacher ratio (1989): 15.8. **Avg. salary, public school teachers** (1990-91); $28,607.

State data. Motto: Salus Populi Suprema Lex Esto (The welfare of the people shall be the supreme law). **Flower:** Hawthorn. **Bird:** Bluebird. **Tree:** Dogwood. **Song:** Missouri Waltz. **Entered union** Aug. 10, 1821; rank, 24th. **State fair** at: Sedalia; 3d week in Aug.

History. DeSoto visited the area, 1541. French hunters and lead miners made the first settlement, c. 1735, at Ste. Genevieve. The U.S. acquired Missouri as part of the Louisiana Purchase, 1803. The fur trade and the Santa Fe Trail provided prosperity; St. Louis became the "jump-off" point for pioneers on their way West. Pro- and anti-slavery forces battled each other there during the Civil War.

Tourist attractions. Mark Twain Area, Hannibal; Pony Express Museum, St. Joseph; Harry S. Truman Library, Independence; Gateway Arch, St. Louis; Silver Dollar City, Branson Worlds of Fun, Kansas City; Lake of the Ozarks; Churchill Memorial, Fulton.

Famous Missourians include Josephine Baker, Thomas Hart Benton, George Caleb Bingham, Gen. Omar Bradley, George Washington Carver, Walter Cronkite, Dale Carnegie, Walt Disney, T.S. Eliot, Betty Grable, Jesse James, J. C. Penney, John J. Pershing, Joseph Pulitzer, Ginger Rogers, Bess Truman, Harry S. Truman, Mark Twain, Tennessee Williams.

Montana

Treasure State

People. Population (1990): 799,065; **rank:** 44. **Pop. density:** 5.49 per sq. mi. **Racial distrib.:** 92.7% White; 0.3% Black; 6.0% Amer. Indian; 1.5% Hispanic. **Net change** (1980-90): 1.6%.

Geography. Total area: 147,046 sq. mi.; **rank:** 4. **Land area:** 145,556 sq. mi. **Acres forested land:** 21,910,000. **Location:** Mountain state bounded on the E by the Dakotas, on the S by Wyoming, on the S/SW by Idaho, and on the N by Canada. **Climate:** colder, continental climate with low humidity. **Topography:** Rocky Mtns. in western third of the state; eastern two-thirds gently rolling northern Great Plains. **Capital:** Helena.

Economy. Principal industries: agriculture, timber, mining, tourism, oil & gas. **Principal manufactured goods:** food prods., wood & paper prods., primary metals, printing & publishing, petroleum & coal prods. **Agriculture: Chief crops:** wheat, barley, sugar beets, hay, oats. **Livestock** (1990): 2.35 mln. cattle; 220,000 hogs/pigs; 663,000 sheep; 890,000 poultry. **Timber/lumber** (1989): Douglas fir, pines, larch; 1.6 bln. bd. ft. **Nonfuel Minerals** (1990): $573.8 mln. mostly metallics. **International airports at:** Great Falls, Billings, Kalispell, Missoula. **Value of construction** (1990): $323.8 mln. **Employment distribution** (1989): 26.7% serv.; 22.1% trade; 18.4% govt.; 17.4% agric; 5.9% mfg. **Per capita income** (1990): $15,110. **Unemployment** (1990): 5.8%. **Tourism** (1990): non-resident visitors spent $751 mln.

Finance. FDIC-insured commercial banks & trust companies (1990): 158. **Deposits:** $6.0 bln. **Savings institutions** (1990): 10. **Assets:** $1.2 bln.

Federal government. No. federal civilian employees (Mar. 1990): 8,465. **Avg. salary:** $29,699. **Notable federal facilities:** Malmstrom AFB; Ft. Peck, Hungry Horse, Libby, Yellowtail dams, numerous missile silos.

Energy. Electricity production (1990, mwh, by source): Hydroelectric: 10.7 mln; Mineral: 15.0 mln.

Education. Student-teacher ratio (1989): 15.7. **Avg. salary, public school teachers** (1990-91): $26,210.

State data. Motto: Oro y Plata (Gold and silver). **Flower:** Bitterroot. **Bird:** Western meadowlark. **Tree:** Ponderosa pine. **Song:** Montana. **Entered union** Nov. 8, 1889; rank, 41st. **State fair** at: Great Falls; late July to early Aug.

History. French explorers visited the region, 1742. The U.S. acquired the area partly through the Louisiana Purchase, 1803, and partly through the explorations of Lewis and Clark, 1805-06. Fur traders and missionaries established posts in the early 19th century. Indian uprisings reached their peak with the Battle of the Little Big Horn, 1876. Mining activity and the coming of the Northern Pacific Railway, 1883, brought population growth.

Tourist attractions. Glacier Natl. Park, on the Continental Divide, is a scenic and recreational wonderland, with 60 glaciers, 200 lakes, and many trout streams. Yellowstone Natl. Park has 3 or 5 entrances in Montana, with 2,221,000 acres of scenic beauty, inc. geysers, mountains, canyons, streams, lakes, forests, waterfalls.

Also, Museum of the Plains Indian, Blackfeet Reservation near Browning; Custer Battlefield National Cemetery; Flathead Lake, in the NW, Lewis and Clark Caverns State Park, near Whitehall; 7 Indian reservations, covering over 5 million acres; state capitol and historical society, Helena.

Famous Montanans include Gary Cooper, Marcus Daly, Chet Huntley, Will James, Myrna Loy, Mike Mansfield, Brent Musberger, Jeannette Rankin, Charles M. Russell, Lester Thurow.

Chamber of Commerce. 2030 11th Ave., P.O. Box 1730, Helena, MT 59624.

Toll-free travel information. 1-800-541-1447.

Nebraska

Cornhusker State

People. Population (1990): 1,578,385; **rank:** 36. **Pop. density:** 20.5 per sq. mi. **Racial distrib.:** 93.8% White; 3.6% Black; 2.3% Hispanic. **Net change** (1980-90): 0.5%.

Geography. Total area: 77,355 sq. mi.; **rank:** 15. **Land area:** 76,878 sq. mi. **Acres forested land:** 722,000. **Location:** West North Central state with the Missouri R. for a NE/E border. **Climate:** continental semi-arid. **Topography:** till plains of the central lowland in the eastern third rising to the Great Plains and hill country of the north central and NW. **Capital:** Lincoln.

Economy. Principal industries: agriculture, food processing, manufacturing. **Principal manufactured goods:** foods, machinery, electric and electronic equipment, primary and fabricated metal products, transportation equipment, instruments & related prod. **Agriculture: Chief crops:** corn, sorghum, soybeans, hay, wheat, beans, oats, potatoes, sugar beets. **Livestock** (1990): 6 mln. cattle; 4.2 mln. hogs/pigs; 160,000 sheep; 6.2 mln. chickens, 2.1 mln. turkeys. **Nonfuel Minerals** (1990): $106.4 mln.; mostly Portland cement, crushed stone, construction sand & gravel. **Chief ports:** Omaha, Sioux City, Brownville, Blair, Plattsmouth, Nebraska City. **Value of construction** (1990): $1.3 bln. **Employment distribution** (1990): 25.5% trade; 24.4% serv.; 19.7% gvt.; 13.8% mfg.; 8.8% agric. **Per capita income** (1990): $17,221. **Unemployment** (1990): 2.2%. **Tourism** (1990): traveler expenditures $1.6 bln. **Sales tax:** 5%, + some local sales taxes of .5-1.5%.

Finance. FDIC-insured commercial banks & trust companies (1990): 392. **Deposits:** $16.3 bln. **Savings institutions** (1990): 23. **Assets:** $11.0 bln.

Federal government. No. federal civilian employees (Mar. 1990): 9,176. **Avg. salary:** $29,475. **Notable federal facilities:** Strategic Air Command Base, Omaha.

Energy. Electricity production (1990, mwh, by source): Hydroelectric: 1.1 mln.; Mineral: 13.0 mln.; Nuclear: 7.5 mln.

Education. Student-teacher ratio (1989): 14.7. **Avg. salary, public school teachers** (1990-91): $26,592.

State data. Motto: Equality before the law. **Flower:** Goldenrod. **Bird:** Western meadowlark. **Tree:** Cottonwood. **Song:** Beautiful Nebraska. **Entered union** Mar. 1, 1867; **rank,** 37th. **State fair** at: Lincoln; Aug. 30-Sept. 8, 1990.

History. Spanish and French explorers and fur traders visited the area prior to the Louisiana Purchase, 1803. Lewis and Clark passed through, 1804-06. First permanent settlement was Bellevue, near Omaha, 1823. Many Civil War veterans settled under free land terms of the 1862 Homestead Act; struggles followed between homesteaders and ranchers.

Tourist attractions. Architecturally unique, 400' tall state capitol, Lincoln; Stuhr Museum of the Prairie Pioneer, Grand Island; Museum of the Fur Trade, Chadron; State Museum (Elephant Hall), Lincoln; Joslyn Art Museum, Omaha; Strategic Air Command Museum, Bellevue; Boys Town, founded by Fr. Flanagan, west of Omaha; Arbor Lodge State Park, Nebraska City; Buffalo Bill Ranch State Historical Park, North Platte; Pioneer Village, Minden; Oregon Trail landmarks, Scotts Bluff National Monument, Chimney Rock Historic Site, Ft. Robinson; Hastings Museum, McDonald Planetarium, Hastings.

Famous Nebraskans include Fred Astaire, Charles W. and William Jennings Bryan, Johnny Carson, Willa Cather, William F. "Buffalo Bill" Cody, Loren Eiseley, Rev. Edward J. Flanagan, Henry Fonda, Gerald R. Ford, Rollin Kirby, Harold Lloyd, Wright Morris, J. Sterling Morton, John Neidhardt, George Norris, Gen. John J. Pershing, Chief Red Cloud, Mari Sandoz, Malcolm X, Roscoe Pound.

Chamber of Commerce. 1320 Lincoln Mall, Box 95128, Lincoln, NE 68501.

Toll-free travel information. 1-800-742-7595; 1-800-228-4307 out of state.

Nevada

Sagebrush State, Battle Born State, Silver State

People. Population (1990): 1,201,833; **rank:** 39. **Pop. density:** 10.9 per sq. mi. **Racial distrib.:** 84.3% White; 6.6% Black; 3.2% Asian; 10.4% Hispanic. **Net change** (1980-90): 50.1%.

Geography. Total area: 110,561 sq. mi.; **rank:** 7. **Land area:** 109,806 sq. mi. **Acres forested land:** 8,928,000. **Location:** Mountain state bordered on N by Oregon and Idaho, on E by Utah and Arizona, on SE by Arizona, and on SW/W by California. **Climate:** semi-arid and arid. **Topography:** rugged N-S mountain ranges; highest elevation, Boundary Peak, 13,140 ft.; southern area is within the Mojave Desert; lowest elevation, Colorado R. Canyon, 470 ft. **Capital:** Carson City.

Economy. Principal industries: gaming, tourism, mining, manufacturing, government, agriculture, warehousing, trucking. **Principal manufactured goods:** gaming devices, chemicals, aerospace prods.; lawn & garden irrigation equip.; seismic & machinery-monitoring devices. **Agriculture: Chief crops:** alfalfa seed, potatoes, hay, barley, wheat. **Livestock** (1990): 520,000 cattle; 14,000 hogs/pigs; 96,000 sheep; 14,000 poultry. **Timber/lumber:** piñon, juniper, other pines. **Nonfuel Minerals** (1990): $2.6 bln.; mostly gold, silver, barite, construction sand & gravel. **International airports** at Las Vegas, Reno. **Value of construction** (1990): $3.1 bln. **Employment distribution** (1990): 43% serv.; 20% trade; 13% gvt. **Per capita income** (1990): $19,416. **Unemployment** (1990): 4.9%. **Tourism** (1990): out-of-state travelers spent $9.1 bln. **Sales tax:** 5.75-6%.

Finance. FDIC-insured commercial banks & trust companies (1990): 19. **Deposits:** $8.3 bln. **Savings institutions** (1990): 6. **Assets:** $4.9 bln.

Federal government. No. federal civilian employees (Mar. 1990): 6,854. **Avg. salary:** $31,337. **Notable federal facilities:** Nevada Test Site; Hawthorne Army Ammunition Plant, Nellis Air Force Base & Gunnery Range; Fallon Naval Air Station; Palomino Valley Wild Horse & Burro Placement Center.

Energy. Electricity production (1990, mwh, by source): Hydroelectric: 1.7 mln.; Mineral: 17.6 mln.

Education. Student-teacher ratio (1989): 20.4. **Avg. salary, public school teachers** (1990-91): $32,209.

State data. Motto: All for our country. **Flower:** Sagebrush. **Bird:** Mountain bluebird. **Trees:** Single-leaf pinon and bristlecone pine. **Song:** Home Means Nevada. **Entered union** Oct. 31, 1864; **rank,** 36th. **State fair** at Reno; early Sept.

History. Nevada was first explored by Spaniards in 1776. Hudson's Bay Co. trappers explored the north and central region, 1825; trader Jedediah Smith crossed the state, 1826 and 1827. The area was acquired by the U.S., in 1848, at the end of the Mexican War. First settlement, Mormon Station, now Genoa, was est. 1849. In the early 20th century, Nevada adopted progressive measures such as the initiative, referendum, recall, and woman suffrage.

Tourist attractions. Legalized casino gambling provided the impetus for the development of resort facilities at Lake Tahoe, Reno, Las Vegas, and elsewhere. Ghost towns, rodeos, mountain climbing, skiing, golfing, trout fishing, water sports and hunting important. Notable are Hoover Dam, Lake Mead Natl. Recreation Area, Lake Tahoe, Great Basin Natl. Park, Valley of Fire State Park & Virginia City. Annual events inc. Helldorado Days & Rodeo, Las Vegas; Reno Rodeo; Basque Festival, Elko; Nevada Day, Carson City; Cowboy Poetry Gathering, Elko.

Famous Nevadans include Walter Van Tilburg Clark, Sarah Winnemucca Hopkins, Paul Laxalt, John William Mackay, Pat McCarran, Dat So La Lee, Key Pittman, William Morris Stewart.

Tourist Information. Commission on Tourism, Capitol Complex, Carson City, NV 89710.

Toll-free travel information. 1-800-638-2328.

New Hampshire

Granite State

People. Population (1990): 1,109,252; **rank:** 40. **Pop. density:** 123.7 per sq. mi. **Racial distrib.:** 98.0% White; 0.6% Black; 1.0% Hispanic. **Net change** (1980-90): 20.5%.

Geography. Total area: 9,279 sq. mi.; **rank:** 44. **Land area:** 8,969 sq. mi. **Acres forested land:** 5,021,000. **Location:** New England state bounded on S by Massachusetts, on W by Vermont, on N/NW by Canada, on E by Maine and the Atlantic O. **Climate:** highly varied, due to its nearness to high mountains and ocean. **Topography:** low, rolling coast followed by countless hills and mountains rising out of a central plateau. **Capital:** Concord.

Economy. Principal industries: tourism, manufacturing, agriculture, trade, mining. **Principal manufactured goods:** machinery, electrical & electronic products, plastics, fabricated metal products. **Agriculture: Chief crops:** dairy products, nursery and greenhouse products, hay, vegetables, fruit, maple syrup & sugar prods. **Livestock** (1990): 55,000 cattle; 9,000 hogs/pigs; 9,000 sheep; 365,000 poultry. **Timber/lumber** (1989): white pine, hemlock, oak, birch; 156 mln. bd. ft. **Nonfuel Minerals** (1990): $37.4 mln.; mostly construction sand & gravel, crushed & dimension stone. **Commercial fishing** (1990): $10.0 mln. **Chief ports:** Portsmouth, Hampton, Rye. **Value of construction** (1990): $997.6 mln. **Employment distribution** (1988): 22.5% mfg.; 25.7% trade; 22.4% serv; 12.9% gvt. **Per capita income** (1990): $20,789. **Unemployment** (1990): 5.6%. **Tourism** (1990): out-of-state visitors spent $3 bln.

Finance. FDIC-insured commercial banks & trust companies (1990): 43. **Deposits:** $8.1 bln. **Savings institutions** (1990): 11. **Assets:** $1.9 bln.

Federal government. No. federal civilian employees (Mar. 1990): 3,906. **Avg. salary:** $32,262.

Energy. Electricity production (1990, mwh, by source): Hydroelectric: 1.5 mln.; Mineral: 5.3 mln.; Nuclear: 4.1 mln.

Education. Student-teacher ratio (1989): 16.2. **Avg. salary, public school teachers** (1990-91): $31,329.

State data. Motto: Live free or die. **Flower:** Purple lilac. **Bird:** Purple finch. **Tree:** White birch. **Song:** Old New Hampshire. **Ninth** of the original 13 states to ratify the Constitution, June 21, 1788.

History. First explorers to visit the New Hampshire area were England's Martin Pring, 1603, and Champlain, 1605. First settlement was Odiorne's Point (now port of Rye), 1623. Indian raids were halted, 1759, by Robert Rogers' Rangers. Before the Revolution, New Hampshire men seized a British fort at Portsmouth, 1774, and drove the royal governor out, 1775. Three regiments served in the Continental Army and scores of privateers raided British shipping.

Tourist attractions. Mt. Washington, highest peak in Northeast, hub of network of trails; Lake Winnipesaukee; White Mt. Natl. Forest; Crawford, Franconia, Pinkham notches in White Mt. region—Franconia famous for the Old Man of the Mountains, described by Hawthorne as the Great Stone Face; the Flume, a spectacular gorge; the aerial tramway on Cannon Mt; Strawbery Banke, Portsmouth; Shaker Village, Canterbury; St. Gaudens, natl. historic site, Cornish; Mt. Monadnock.

Famous New Hampshirites include Salmon P. Chase, Ralph Adams Cram, Mary Baker Eddy, Daniel Chester French, Robert Frost, Horace Greeley, Sarah Buell Hale, Franklin Pierce, Augustus Saint-Gaudens, Daniel Webster.

Tourist Information. Department of Resources and Economic Development, Division of Travel & Tourism Development, P.O. Box 856, Concord, NH 03302-0856; 603-271-2666.

New Jersey

Garden State

People. Population (1990): 7,730,188; **rank:** 9. **Pop. density:** 1,041.9 per sq. mi. **Racial distrib.:** 79.3% White; 13.4% Black; 3.5% Asian; 9.6% Hispanic. **Net change** (1980-90): 5.0%.

Geography. Total area: 7,787 sq. mi.; **rank:** 46. **Land area:** 7,419 sq. mi. **Acres forested land:** 1,985,000. **Location:** Middle Atlantic state bounded on the N and E by New York and the Atlantic O., on the S and W by Delaware and Pennsylvania. **Climate:** moderate, with marked difference bet. NW and SE extremities. **Topography:** Appalachian Valley in the NW also has highest elevation, High Pt., 1,801 ft.; Appalachian Highlands, flat-topped NE-SW mountain ranges; Piedmont Plateau, low plains broken by high ridges (Palisades) rising 400-500 ft.; Coastal Plain, covering three-fifths of state in SE, gradually rises from sea level to gentle slopes. **Capital:** Trenton.

Economy. Principal industries: services, trade, manufacturing. **Principal manufactured goods:** chemicals, electronic and electrical equipment, non-electrical machinery, fabricated metals. **Agriculture: Chief crops:** hay, corn, soybeans, tomatoes, blueberries, peaches, cranberries. **Livestock** (1987): 77,500 cattle; 32,000 hogs/pigs; 12,600 sheep; 2.1 mln. poultry. **Timber/lumber** (1989): pine, cedar, mixed hardwoods; 4 mln. bd. ft. **Nonfuel Minerals** (1990): $235.3 mln.; mostly crushed stone, construction sand & gravel. **Commercial fishing** (1990): $89.3 mln. **Chief ports:** Newark, Elizabeth, Hoboken, Camden. **International airports at:** Newark. **Value of construction** (1990): $5.8 bln. **Employment distribution** (1990): 27.0% serv.; 23.9% trade; 16.4% mfg.; 15.6% gvt. **Per capita income** (1990): $24,968. **Unemployment** (1990): 5.0%. **Tourism** (1988): tourists spent $13.6 bln. **Sales tax:** 7%.

Finance. FDIC-insured commercial banks & trust companies (1990): 127. **Deposits:** $73.3. **Savings institutions** (1990): 130. **Assets:** $52.0 bln.

Federal government. No. federal civilian employees (Mar. 1990): 37,861. **Avg. salary:** $31,847. **Notable federal facilities:** McGuire AFB Fort Dix; Fort Monmouth; Picatinny Arsenal; Lakewood Naval Air Station, Lakehurst Naval Air Engineering Center.

Energy. Electricity production (1990, mwh, by source): Mineral: 12.9 mln.; Nuclear: 23.8 mln.

Education. Student-teacher ratio (1989): 13.5. **Avg. salary, public school teachers** (1990-91): $38,790.

State Data. Motto: Liberty and prosperity. **Flower:** Purple violet. **Bird:** Eastern goldfinch. **Tree:** Red oak. **Third** of the original 13 states to ratify the Constitution, Dec. 18, 1787. **State fair:** usually Aug.

History. The Lenni Lenape (Delaware) Indians had mostly peaceful relations with European colonists who arrived after the explorers Verrazano, 1524, and Hudson, 1609. The Dutch were first; when the British took New Netherland, 1664, the area between the Delaware and Hudson Rivers was given to Lord John Berkeley and Sir George Carteret. New Jersey was the scene of nearly 100 battles, large and small, during the Revolution, including Trenton, 1776, Princeton, 1777, Monmouth, 1778.

Tourist attractions. 127 miles of beaches; Miss America Pageant and hotel-casinos, Atlantic City; Grover Cleveland birthplace, Caldwell. Cape May Historic District; Edison Labs, W. Orange; Great Adventure amusement park; Liberty State Park; Meadowlands Sports Complex; Pine Barrens wilderness area; Princeton University; numerous Revolutionary War historical sites.

Famous New Jerseyans include Count Basie, Judy Blume, Aaron Burr, Grover Cleveland, James Fenimore Cooper, Stephen Crane, Thomas Edison, Albert Einstein, Alexander Hamilton, Joyce Kilmer, Gen. George McClellan, Thomas Paine, Molly Pitcher, Paul Robeson, Philip Roth, Walter Schirra, Frank Sinatra, Bruce Springsteen, Walt Whitman, William Carlos Williams, Woodrow Wilson.

Chamber of Commerce. 51 Commerce St., Newark, NJ 07102.

Toll-free travel information. 1-800-JERSEY-7.

New Mexico
Land of Enchantment

People. Population (1990): 1,515,069; **rank:** 37. **Pop. density:** 12.5 per sq. mi. **Racial distrib.:** 75.6% White; 2.0% Black; 8.9% Amer. Indian; 38.2% Hispanic. **Net change** (1980-90): 16.3%.

Geography. Total area: 121,593 sq. mi.; **rank:** 5. **Land area:** 121,364 sq. mi. **Acres forested land:** 18,526,000. **Location:** southwestern state bounded by Colorado on the N, Oklahoma, Texas, and Mexico on the E and S, and Arizona on the W. **Climate:** dry, with temperatures rising or falling 5°F with every 1,000 ft. elevation. **Topography:** eastern third, Great Plains; central third Rocky Mtns. (85% of the state is over 4,000 ft. elevation); western third high plateau. **Capital:** Santa Fe.

Economy. Principal industries: government, services, trade. **Principal manufactured goods:** foods, machinery, apparel, lumber, printing, transportation equipment. **Agriculture:** Chief crops: hay, onions, wheat, pecans, corn, cotton, sorghum. **Livestock** (1990): 1.34 mln. cattle; 27,000 hogs; 462,000 sheep; 1.43 mln. poultry. **Timber/lumber** (1989): Ponderosa pine, Douglas fir; 201 mln. bd. ft. **Nonfuel Minerals** (1990): $1.1 bln.; copper, potash, construction sand & gravel. **International airports at:** Albuquerque. **Value of construction** (1990): $1.1 bln. **Employment distribution** (1990): 26% serv.; 2% agric.; 10% mfg.; 26.2% gvt. **Per capita income** (1990): $14,228. **Unemployment** (1990): 6.3%. **Tourism** (1990): out-of-state visitors spent $2.2 bln. **Sales tax:** 5-6.75%.

Finance. FDIC-insured commercial banks & trust companies (1990): 91. **Deposits:** $9.5 bln. **Savings institutions** (1990): 24. **Assets:** $4.9 bln.

Federal government. No. federal civilian employees (Mar. 1990): 23,426. **Avg. salary:** $29,580. **Notable federal facilities:** Kirtland, Cannon, Holloman AF bases; Los Alamos Scientific Laboratory; White Sands Missile Range, National Solar Observatory, National Radio Astronomy Observatory.

Energy. Electricity production (1990, mwh, by source): Hydroelectric: 205,000; Mineral: 28.3 mln.

Education. Student-teacher ratio (1989): 18.3. **Avg. salary, public school teachers** (1990-91): $26,194.

State data. Motto: Crescit Eundo (It grows as it goes). **Flower:** Yucca. **Bird:** Roadrunner. **Tree:** Pinon. **Song:** O, Fair New Mexico, Asi Es Nuevo Mexico. **Entered union** Jan. 6, 1912; **rank,** 47th. **State fair** at: Albuquerque; mid-Sept.

History. Franciscan Marcos de Niza and a black slave Estevan explored the area, 1539, seeking gold. First settlements were at San Juan Pueblo, 1598, and Santa Fe, 1610. Settlers alternately traded and fought with the Apaches, Comanches, and Navajos. Trade on the Santa Fe Trail to Missouri started 1821. The Mexican War was declared May, 1846, Gen. Stephen Kearny took Santa Fe, August. In the 1870s, cattlemen staged the famed Lincoln County War in which Billy (the Kid) Bonney played a leading role. Pancho Villa raided Columbus, 1916.

Tourist Attractions. Carlsbad Caverns, a national park, has caverns on 3 levels and the largest natural cave "room" in the world, 1,500 by 300 ft., 300 ft. high; White Sands Natl. Monument, the largest gypsum deposit in the world.

Pueblo ruins from 100 AD, Chaco Canyon; Acoma, the "sky city," built atop a 357-ft. mesa; 19 Pueblo, 4 Navajo, and 2 Apache reservations. Also, ghost towns, dude ranches, skiing, hunting, and fishing.

Famous New Mexicans include Billy (the Kid) Bonney, Kit Carson, Peter Hurd, Archbishop Jean Baptiste Lamy, Nancy Lopez, Bill Mauldin, Georgia O'Keeffe, Kim Stanley, Al Unser, Bobby Unser, Lew Wallace.

Tourist information. New Mexico Dept. of Tourism, P.O. Box 20003, Santa Fe, N.M. 87503.

Toll-free travel information. 1-800-545-2040.

New York
Empire State

People. Population (1990): 17,990,455; **rank:** 2. **Pop. density:** 381 per sq. mi. **Racial distrib.:** 74.4% White; 15.9% Black; 3.9% Asian; 12.3% Hispanic. **Net change** (1980-90): 2.5%.

Geography. Total area: 49,108 sq. mi.; **rank:** 30. **Land area:** 47,224 sq. mi. **Acres forested land:** 18,775,000. **Location:** Middle Atlantic state, bordered by the New England states, Atlantic Ocean, New Jersey and Pennsylvania, Lakes Ontario and Erie, and Canada. **Climate:** variable; the SE region moderated by the ocean. **Topography:** highest and most rugged mountains in the NE Adirondack upland; St. Lawrence-Champlain lowlands extend from Lake Ontario NE along the Canadian border; Hudson-Mohawk lowland follows the flows of the rivers N and W, 10-30 mi. wide; Atlantic coastal plain in the SE; Appalachian Highlands, covering half the state westward from the Hudson Valley, include the Catskill Mtns., Finger Lakes; plateau of Erie-Ontario lowlands. **Capital:** Albany.

Economy. Principal industries: manufacturing, finance, communications, tourism, transportation, services. **Principal manufactured goods:** books and periodicals, clothing and apparel, pharmaceuticals, machinery, instruments, toys and sporting goods, electronic equipment, automotive and aircraft components. **Agriculture:** Chief crops: apples, cabbage, cauliflower, celery, cherries, grapes, corn, peas, snap beans, sweet corn. **Products:** milk, cheese, maple syrup, wine. **Livestock** (1989): 1.6 mln. cattle; 124,000 hogs/pigs; 63,000 sheep; 11.0 mln. poultry. **Timber/lumber** (1989): saw log production; 305 mln. bd. ft. **Nonfuel Minerals** (1990): $737 mln.; mostly crushed stone, cement, construction sand & gravel, zinc. **Commercial fishing** (1990): $56.5 mln. **Chief ports:** New York, Buffalo, Albany. **International airports at:** New York, Buffalo, Syracuse, Massena, Ogdensburg, Watertown, Niagara Falls, Newburgh, Sullivan county. **Value of construction** (1990): $13.4 bln. **Employment distribution** (1990): 29% serv.; 21% trade; 18% gvt.; 14% mfg. **Per capita income** (1990): $21,975. **Unemployment** (1990): 5.2%. **Tourism** (1988): tourists spent $20.0 bln. **Sales tax:** 4-8¼%.

Finance. FDIC-insured commercial banks & trust companies (1990): 191. **Deposits:** $263.2 bln. **Savings institutions** (1990): 86. **Assets:** $56.7 bln.

Federal government. No. federal civilian employees (Mar. 1990): 69,117. **Avg. salary:** $29,863. **Notable federal facilities:** West Point Military Academy; Merchant Marine Academy; Ft. Drum; Griffiss, Plattsburgh AF bases; Watervliet Arsenal.

Energy. Electricity production (1990, mwh, by source): Hydroelectric: 25.8 mln.; Mineral: 79.3 mln.; Nuclear: 23.7 mln.

Education. Student-teacher ratio (1989): 14.7. **Avg. salary, public school teachers** (1990-91): $41,600.

State data. Motto: Excelsior (Ever upward). **Flower:** Rose. **Bird:** Bluebird. **Tree:** Sugar maple. **Song:** I Love New York. **Eleventh** of the original 13 states to ratify the Constitution, July 26, 1788. **State fair** at: Syracuse, late Aug.-early Sept.

History. In 1609 Henry Hudson discovered the river that bears his name and Champlain explored the lake, far upstate, which was named for him. Dutch built posts near Albany 1614 and 1624; in 1626 they settled Manhattan. A British fleet seized New Netherland, 1664. Ninety-two of the 300 or more engagements of the Revolution were fought in New York, including the Battle of Bemis Heights-Saratoga, a turning point of the war.

Tourist attractions. New York City; Adirondack and Catskill mtns.; Finger Lakes, Great Lakes; Long Island beaches; Thousand Islands; Niagara Falls; Saratoga Springs racing and spas; Philipsburg Manor, Sunnyside, the restored home of Washington Irving, The Dutch Church of Sleepy Hollow, all in North Tarrytown; Corning Glass Center and Steuben factory, Corning; Fenimore House, National Baseball Hall of Fame and Museum, both in Cooperstown; Ft. Ticonderoga overlooking lakes George and Champlain; Albany's Empire State Plaza, Lake Placid Olympic Village.

The Franklin D. Roosevelt National Historic Site, Hyde Park, includes the graves of Pres. and Mrs. Roosevelt, the family home since 1867, the Roosevelt Library. Sagamore Hill, Oyster Bay, the Theodore Roosevelt estate, includes his home.

Famous New Yorkers include Susan B. Anthony, Peter Cooper, George Eastman, Millard Fillmore, Julia Ward Howe, Charles Evans Hughes, Henry and William James, Herman Melville, Franklin Delano Roosevelt, Theodore Roosevelt, Alfred E. Smith, Elizabeth Cady Stanton, Martin Van Buren, Walt Whitman.

Tourist information: N.Y. State Dept. of Economic Development, 1 Commerce Plaza, Albany, NY 12245.

Toll-free travel information. 1-800-CALLNYS, from the 48 contiguous states; 1-518-474-4116 from other areas and Canada.

North Carolina

Tar Heel State, Old North State

People. Population (1990): 6,628,637; **rank:** 10. **Pop. density:** 136.1 per sq. mi. **Racial distrib.:** 75.6% White; 22.0% Black; 1.2% Amer. Indian; 1.2% Hispanic. **Net change** (1980-90): 12.7%.

Geography. Total area: 52,669 sq. mi.; **rank:** 28. **Land area:** 48,718 sq. mi. **Acres forested land:** 18,891,000. **Location:** South Atlantic state bounded by Virginia, South Carolina, Georgia, Tennessee, and the Atlantic O. **Climate:** sub-tropical in SE, medium-continental in mountain region; tempered by the Gulf Stream and the mountains in W. **Topography:** coastal plain and tidewater, two-fifths of state, extending to the fall line of the rivers; piedmont plateau, another two-fifths, 200 mi. wide of gentle to rugged hills; southern Appalachian Mtns. contains the Blue Ridge and Great Smoky mtns. **Capital:** Raleigh.

Economy. Principal industries: manufacturing, agriculture, tobacco, tourism. **Principal manufactured goods:** textiles, tobacco products, electrical/electronic equip., chemicals, furniture, food products, non-electrical machinery. **Agriculture:** Chief crops: tobacco, soybeans, corn, peanuts, small sweet potatoes, feed grains, vegetables, fruits. **Livestock** (1990): 900,000 cattle; 2.6 mln. hogs/pigs; 19.6 mln. chickens. **Timber/lumber** (1989): yellow pine, oak, hickory, poplar, maple. 1.6 bln. bd. ft. **Nonfuel Minerals** (1990): Total $578.4 mln., mostly clay, sand & gravel, crushed stone. **Commercial fishing** (1990): $71.5 mln. **Chief ports:** Morehead City, Wilmington. **Value of construction** (1990): $6.5 bln. **Employment distribution** (1989): 29.2% mfg.; 22.9% trade; 17.6% serv.; 15.3% gvt. **Per capita income** (1990): $16,203. **Unemployment** (1990): 4.1%. **Tourism** (1990): out-of-state visitors spent $6.4 bln. **Sales tax:** 5.0%.

Finance. FDIC-insured commercial banks & trust companies (1990): 79. **Deposits:** $49.6 bln. **Savings institutions** (1990): 129. **Assets:** $21.2 bln.

Federal government. No. federal civilian employees (Mar. 1990): 29,445. **Avg. salary:** $28,059. **Notable federal facilities:** Ft. Bragg; Camp LeJeune Marine Base; U.S. EPA Research and Development Labs, Cherry Point Marine Corps Air Station; Natl. Humanities Center; Natl. Inst. of Environmental Health Science; Natl. Center for Health Statistics Lab, Research Triangle Park.

Energy. Electricity production (1990, mwh, by source): Hydroelectric: 6.9 mln.; Mineral: 47.0. mln.; Nuclear: 25.9 mln.

Education. Student-teacher ratio (1989): 17.1. **Avg. salary, public school teachers** (1990-91): $29,082.

State data. Motto: Esse Quam Videri (To be rather than to seem). **Flower:** Dogwood. **Bird:** Cardinal. **Tree:** Pine. **Song:** The Old North State. **Twelfth** of the original 13 states to ratify the Constitution, Nov. 21, 1789. **State fair** at: Raleigh; mid-Oct.

History. The first English colony in America was the first of 2 established by Sir Walter Raleigh on Roanoke Is., 1585 and 1587. The first group returned to England; the second, the "Lost Colony," disappeared without trace. Permanent settlers came from Virginia, c. 1660. Roused by British repressions, the colonists drove out the royal

governor, 1775; the province's congress was the first to vote for independence; ten regiments were furnished to the Continental Army. Cornwallis' forces were defeated at Kings Mountain, 1780, and forced out after Guilford Courthouse, 1781.

Tourist attractions. Cape Hatteras and Cape Lookout national seashores; Great Smoky Mtns. (half in Tennessee); Guilford Courthouse and Moore's Creek parks, 66 Revolutionary battle sites; Bennett Place, NW of Durham, where Gen. Joseph Johnston surrendered the last Confederate army to Gen. Wm. Sherman; Ft. Raleigh, Roanoke Is., where Virginia Dare, first child of English parents in the New World, was born Aug. 18, 1587; Wright Brothers National Memorial, Kitty Hawk; N.C. Zoo, Asheboro; N. Carolina Symphony, Raleigh.

Famous North Carolinians include Richard J. Gatling, Billy Graham, Andrew Jackson, Andrew Johnson, Wm. Rufus King, Dolley Madison, Edward R. Murrow, James K. Polk, Enos Slaughter, Moses Waddel, Thomas Wolfe.

Tourist information. Division of Travel & Tourism Development, 430 No. Salisbury St., Raleigh, NC 27603.

Toll-free travel information. 1-800-VISITNC.

North Dakota

Peace Garden State

People. Population (1990): 638,800; **rank:** 47. **Pop. density:** 9.2 per sq. mi. **Racial distrib.:** 94.6% White; 0.6% Black; 4.1% Amer. Indian; 0.7% Hispanic. **Net change** (1980-90): −2.1%.

Geography. Total area: 70,702 sq. mi.; **rank:** 17. **Land area:** 68,994 sq. mi. **Acres forested land:** 460,000. **Location:** West North Central state, situated exactly in the middle of North America, bounded on the N by Canada, on the E by Minnesota, on the S by South Dakota, on the W by Montana. **Climate:** continental, with a wide range of temperature and moderate rainfall. **Topography:** Central Lowland in the E comprises the flat Red River Valley and the Rolling Drift Prairie; Missouri Plateau of the Great Plains on the W. **Capital:** Bismarck.

Economy. Principal industries: agriculture, mining, tourism, manufacturing. **Principal manufactured goods:** farm equipment, processed foods. **Agriculture:** Chief crops: spring wheat, durum, barley, rye, flaxseed, oats, potatoes, dried edible beans, honey, soybeans, sugarbeets, sunflowers, hay. **Livestock** (1987): 2.0 mln. cattle; 285,000 hogs/pigs; 180,000 sheep; 1.4 mln. poultry. **Nonfuel Minerals** (1990): $20.4 mln. mostly lime, construction sand & gravel, crushed stone. **International airports at:** Fargo, Grand Forks, Bismarck, Minot. **Value of construction** (1990): $470.7 mln. **Employment distribution** (1990): 21.9% trade; 20.4% gvt.; 16.8% serv.; 17.2% agric. **Per capita income** (1990): $15,255. **Unemployment** (1990): 3.9%. **Tourism** (1988): $565 mln. **Sales tax:** 5%-6%.

Finance. FDIC-insured commercial banks & trust companies (1990): 152. **Deposits:** $6.2 bln. **Savings institutions** (1990): 6. **Assets:** $4.2 bln.

Federal government. No. federal civilian employees (Mar. 1990): 5,453. **Avg. salary:** $27,649. **Notable federal facilities:** Strategic Air Command bases at Minot, Grand Forks; Northern Prairie Wildlife Research Center; Garrison Dam; Theodore Roosevelt Natl. Park; Grand Forks Energy Research Center; Ft. Union Natl. Historic Site.

Energy. Electricity production (1990, mwh, by source): Hydroelectric: 1.7 mln.; Mineral: 24.9 mln.

Education. Student-teacher ratio (1989): 15.1. **Avg. salary, public school teachers** (1990-91): $23,578.

State data. Motto: Liberty and union, now and forever, one and inseparable. **Flower:** Wild prairie rose. **Bird:** Western Meadowlark. **Tree:** American elm. **Song:** North Dakota Hymn. **Entered union** Nov. 2, 1889; rank, 39th. **State fair** at: Minot; 3d week in July.

History. Pierre La Verendrye was the first French fur trader in the area, 1738, followed later by the English. The U.S. acquired half the territory in the Louisiana Purchase, 1803. Lewis and Clark built Ft. Mandan, spent the winter of 1804-05 there. In 1818, American ownership of the other half was confirmed by agreement with Britain. First permanent settlement was at Pembina, 1812. Missouri River steamboats reached the area, 1832; the first railroad, 1873, bringing many homesteaders. The state was first to hold a presidential primary, 1912.

Tourist attractions. North Dakota Heritage Center, state capitol grounds; Bonanzaville, Fargo, restored pioneer town; Ft. Union Trading Post Natl. Historic Site, built 1829; Lake Sakakawea, 180 miles of fishing, boating, 1,600 miles of shoreline. Interntl. Peace Garden, 2,200-acre tract extending across the border into Manitoba; 65,000-acre Theodore Roosevelt National Park, Badlands, contains the president's Elkhorn Ranch; Ft. Abraham Lincoln State Park and Museum, S of Mandan.

Famous North Dakotans include Maxwell Anderson, Angie Dickinson, John Bernard Flannagan; Louis L'Amour, Peggy Lee, Eric Sevareid, Vilhjalmur Stefansson, Lawrence Welk.

Chamber of Commerce. P.O. Box 2467, Fargo, ND 58108.

Toll-free travel information. 1-800-437-2077.

Ohio
Buckeye State

People. Population (1990): 10,847,115; **rank: 7. Pop. density:** 264.9 per sq. mi. **Racial distrib.:** 87.8% White; 10.6% Black; 1.3% Hispanic. **Net change** (1980-90): 0.5%.

Geography. Total area: 41,330 sq. mi.; **rank: 35. Land area:** 40,953 sq. mi. **Acres forested land:** 7,309,000. **Location:** East North Central state bounded on the N by Michigan and Lake Erie; on the E and S by Pennsylvania, West Virginia; and Kentucky; on the W by Indiana. **Climate:** temperate but variable; weather subject to much precipitation. **Topography:** generally rolling plain; Allegheny plateau in E; Lake [Erie] plains extend southward; central plains in the W. **Capital:** Columbus.

Economy. Principal industries: manufacturing, trade, services. **Principal manufactured goods:** transportation equipment, machinery, primary and fabricated metal products. **Agriculture: Chief crops:** corn, hay, winter wheat, oats, soybeans. **Livestock** (1985): 1.8 mln. cattle; 2.0 mln. hogs/pigs; 275,000 sheep; 22.0 mln. poultry. **Timber/lumber** (1989): oak, ash, maple, walnut, beech; 279 mln. bd. ft. **Nonfuel Minerals** (1990): $722.6 mln.; mostly crushed stone, construction sand & gravel, lime, Portland cement. **Commercial fishing** (1990): $3.1 mln. **Chief ports:** Toledo, Conneaut, Cleveland, Ashtabula. **International airports at:** Cleveland, Cincinnati, Columbus, Dayton. **Value of construction** (1990): $9.9 bln. **Employment distribution** (1985): 25.6% mfg.; 24.2% trade; 21.8% serv.; 15.2% gvt. **Per capita income** (1990): $17,473. **Unemployment** (1990): 5.7%. **Tourism** (1982): travelers spent nearly $5.4 bln.

Finance. FDIC-insured commercial banks & trust companies (1990): 287. **Deposits:** $85.0 bln. **Savings institutions** (1990): 217. **Assets:** $50.5.

Federal government. No. federal civilian employees (Mar. 1990): 55,519. **Avg. salary:** $31,970. **Notable federal facilities:** Wright Patterson AF base; Defense Construction Supply Center; Lewis Research Ctr.; Portsmouth Gaseous Diffusion Plant; Mound Laboratory.

Energy. Electricity production (1990, mwh, by source): Hydroelectric: 173,000; Mineral: 115.4 mln.; Nuclear: 10.7.

Education. Student-teacher ratio (1989): 17.4. **Avg. salary, public school teachers** (1990-91): $32,615.

State data. Motto: With God, all things are possible. **Flower:** Scarlet carnation. **Bird:** Cardinal. **Tree:** Buckeye. **Song:** Beautiful Ohio. **Entered union** Mar. 1, 1803; rank, 17th. **State fair** at: Columbus; mid-Aug.

History. LaSalle visited the Ohio area, 1669. American fur-traders arrived, beginning 1685; the French and Indians sought to drive them out. During the Revolution, Virginians defeated the Indians, 1774, but hostilities were renewed, 1777. The region became U.S. territory after the

Revolution. First organized settlement was at Marietta, 1788. Indian warfare ended with Anthony Wayne's victory at Fallen Timbers, 1794. In the War of 1812, Oliver H. Perry's victory on Lake Erie and William H. Harrison's invasion of Canada, 1813, ended British incursions.

Tourist attractions. Mound City Group National Monuments, a group of 24 prehistoric Indian burial mounds; Neil Armstrong Air and Space Museum, Wapakoneta; Air Force Museum, Dayton; Pro Football Hall of Fame, Canton; King's Island amusement park, King's Island; Cedar Point amusement park, Sandusky. birthplaces, homes, and memorials to Ohio's 8 U.S. presidents: Wm. Henry Harrison, Grant, Garfield, Hayes, McKinley, Harding, Taft, Benjamin Harrison; Lake Erie Islands, Sandusky; Amish Region, Tuscarawas/Holmes counties; German Village, Columbus; Sea World, Aurora; Jack Nicklaus Sports Center, Mason; Bob Evans Farm, Rio Grande.

Famous Ohioans include Sherwood Anderson, Neil Armstrong, George Bellows, Ambrose Bierce, Clarence Darrow, Paul Laurence Dunbar, Thomas Edison, Clark Gable, John Glenn, Bob Hope, Jack Nicklaus, Jesse Owens, Eddie Rickenbacker, John D. Rockefeller Sr. and Jr., Pete Rose, Gen. Wm. Sherman, Harriet Beecher Stowe, Charles Taft, Robert A. Taft, William H. Taft, James Thurber, Orville Wright.

Chamber of Commerce. 35 E. Gay St., Columbus, OH 43215.

Toll-free travel information. 1-800-BUCKEYE.

Oklahoma
Sooner State

People. Population (1990): 3,145,585; **rank: 28. Pop. density:** 45.8 per sq. mi. **Racial distrib.:** 82.1% White; 7.4% Black; 8.0% Amer. Indian; 2.7% Hispanic. **Net change** (1980-90): 4.0%.

Geography. Total area: 69,919 sq. mi.; **rank: 18. Land area:** 68,679 sq. mi. **Acres forested land:** 7,283,000. **Location:** West South Central state bounded on the N by Colorado and Kansas; on the E by Missouri and Arkansas; on the S and W by Texas and New Mexico. **Climate:** temperate; southern humid belt merging with colder northern continental; humid eastern and dry western zones. **Topography:** high plains predominate the W, hills and small mountains in the E; the east central region is dominated by the Arkansas R. Basin, and the Red R. Plains, in the S. **Capital:** Oklahoma City.

Economy. Principal industries: manufacturing, mineral and energy exploration and production, agriculture, printing & publishing. **Principal manufactured goods:** non-electrical machinery, fabricated metal products, petroleum. **Agriculture: Chief crops:** wheat, hay, peanuts, grain sorghum, soybeans, corn, pecans, oats, barley, rye. **Livestock** (1989): 5.2 mln. cattle; 240,000 hogs/pigs; 136,000 sheep; 4.65 mln. poultry. **Timber/lumber** (1989): pine, oaks, hickory; 236 mln. bd. ft. **Nonfuel Minerals** (1990): $237.2 mln.; mostly crushed stone, Portland cement, sand & gravel. **Chief ports:** Catoosa, Muskogee. **International airports at:** Oklahoma City, Tulsa. **Value of construction** (1990): $2.1 bln. **Employment distribution** (1989): 23.9% trade; 22.0% gvt.; 23.2% serv.; 14.0% mfg. **Per capita income** (1990): $15,444. **Unemployment** (1990): 5.6%. **Tourism** (1989): tourists spent $2.37 bln.

Finance. FDIC-insured commercial banks & trust companies (1990): 423. **Deposits:** $22.8 bln. **Savings institutions** (1990): 39. **Assets:** $10.2 bln.

Federal government. No. federal civilian employees (Mar. 1990): 36,697. **Avg. salary:** $28,764. **Notable federal facilities:** Federal Aviation Agency and Tinker AFB, both Oklahoma City; Ft. Sill, Lawton; Altus AFB, Altus; Vance AFB, Enid.

Energy. Electricity production (1990, mwh, by source): Hydroelectric: 2.8 mln.; Mineral: 42.3 mln.

Education. Student-teacher ratio (1989): 16.2. **Avg. salary, public school teachers** (1990-91): $24,649.

State data. Motto: Labor Omnia Vincit (Labor conquers all things). **Flower:** Mistletoe. **Bird:** Scissortailed flycatcher. **Tree:** Redbud. **Song:** Oklahoma! **Entered union** Nov. 16, 1907; rank, 46th. **State fair at:** Oklahoma City; last week of Sept.

History. Part of the Louisiana Purchase, 1803, Oklahoma was known as Indian Territory (but was not given territorial government) after it became the home of the "Five Civilized Tribes"—Cherokee, Choctaw, Chickasaw, Creek, and Seminole—1828-1846. The land was also used by Comanche, Osage, and other Plains Indians. As white settlers pressed west, land was opened for homesteading by runs and lottery, the first run taking place Apr. 22, 1889. The most famous run was to the Cherokee Outlet, 1893.

Tourist attractions. Will Rogers Memorial, Claremore; National Cowboy Hall of Fame, and Remington Park Race Track, both Oklahoma City; restored Ft. Gibson Stockade, near Muskogee, the Army's largest outpost in Indian lands; Indian pow-wows; rodeos; fishing; hunting; Ouachita National Forest; Enterprise Square, museum devoted to American economic system.

Famous Oklahomans include Carl Albert, L. Gordon Cooper, Woody Guthrie, Gen. Patrick J. Hurley, Karl Jansky, Mickey Mantle, Carry Nation, Wiley Post, Oral Roberts, Will Rogers, Maria Tallchief, Jim Thorpe.

Chamber of Commerce. 4020 N. Lincoln Blvd., Oklahoma City, OK 73105.

Tourism Dept. P.O. Box 60000, Oklahoma City, OK 73146-6000.

Toll-free travel information. 1-800-652-6552.

Oregon

Beaver State

People. Population (1990): 2,842,321; **rank:** 29. **Pop. density:** 29.6 per sq. mi. **Racial distrib.:** 92.8% White; 1.6% Black; 4.0% Hispanic. **Net change** (1980-90): 7.9%.

Geography. Total area: 97,073 sq. mi.; **rank:** 10. **Land area:** 96,003 sq. mi. **Acres forested land:** 28,057,000. **Location:** Pacific state, bounded on N by Washington; on E by Idaho; on S by Nevada and California; on W by the Pacific. **Climate:** coastal mild and humid climate; continental dryness and extreme temperatures in the interior. **Topography:** Coast Range of rugged mountains; fertile Willamette R. Valley to E and S; Cascade Mtn. Range of volcanic peaks E of the valley; plateau E of Cascades, remaining two-thirds of state. **Capital:** Salem.

Economy. Principal industries: forestry, agriculture, tourism, high technology, manufacturing. **Principal manufactured goods:** lumber & wood products, foods, machinery, fabricated metals, paper, printing & publishing, primary metals. **Agriculture: Chief crops:** hay, grass seed, farm forest prods., wheat, potatoes, onions, pears. **Livestock** (1989): 1.4 mln. cattle; 90,000 hogs/pigs; 455,000 sheep; 3.1 mln. poultry. **Timber/lumber** (1989): Douglas fir, hemlock, ponderosa pine; 8.3 bln. bd. ft. **Nonfuel Minerals** (1990): $220.6 mln.; mostly crushed stone, construction sand & gravel. **Commercial fishing** (1990): $70.5 mln. **Chief ports:** Portland, Astoria, Newport, Coos Bay. **International airports at:** Portland. **Value of construction** (1990): $3.1 bln. **Employment distribution** (1989): 25.7% trade; 23.2% serv.; 18.0% mfg.; 17.8% gvt. **Per capita income** (1990): $17,156. **Unemployment** (1990): 5.5%. **Tourism** (1989): travel expenditures, $2.1 bln.

Finance: FDIC-insured commercial banks & trust companies (1990): 49. **Deposits:** $17.9 bln. **Savings institutions** (1990): 12. **Assets:** $11.1 bln.

Federal government. No. federal civilian employees (Mar. 1990): 20,145. **Avg. salary:** $30,312. **Notable federal facilities:** Bonneville Power Administration.

Energy: Electricity production (1990, mwh, by source): Hydroelectric: 41.0 mln. Mineral: 1.9; Nuclear: 6.1 mln.

Education. Student-teacher ratio (1989): 18.4. **Avg. salary, public school teachers** (1990-91): $32,200.

State data. Motto: She flies with her own wings. **Flower:** Oregon grape. **Bird:** Western meadowlark. **Tree:** Douglas fir. **Song:** Oregon, My Oregon. **Entered union** Feb. 14, 1859; rank, 33d. **State fair at:** Salem; late Aug. to early Sept.

History. American Capt. Robert Gray discovered and sailed into the Columbia River, 1792; Lewis and Clark, traveling overland, wintered at its mouth 1805-06; fur traders followed. Settlers arrived in the Willamette Valley, 1834. In 1843 the first large wave of settlers arrived via the Oregon Trail. Early in the 20th century, the "Oregon System," reforms which included the initiative, referendum, recall, direct primary, and woman suffrage, was adopted.

Tourist attractions. John Day Fossil Beds National Monument; Columbia River Gorge; Mt. Hood & Timberline Lodge; Crater Lake National Park; Oregon Dunes National Recreation Area; Ft. Clatsop National Memorial; Oregon Caves National Monument; Shakespearean Festival, Ashland; High Desert Museum, Bend. Also, skiing, fishing; Annual Albany Timber Carnival, Pendelton Round-Up, Portland Rose Festival.

Famous Oregonians include Ernest Bloch, Ernest Haycox, Chief Joseph, Edwin Markham, Tom McCall, Dr. John McLoughlin, Joaquin Miller, Linus Pauling, John Reed, Alberto Salazar, Mary Decker Slaney, William Simon U'Ren.

Tourist Information: Economic Development Department, 775 Summer St. NE, Salem, OR 97310.

Toll-free travel information. 1-800-233-3306; 1-800-547-7842 out of state.

Pennsylvania

Keystone State

People. Population (1990): 11,881,643; **rank:** 5. **Pop. density:** 265.1 per sq. mi. **Racial distrib.:** 88.5% White; 9.2% Black; 2.0% Hispanic. **Net change** (1980-90): 0.1%.

Geography. Total area: 45,308 sq. mi.; **rank:** 33. **Land area:** 44,820 sq. mi. **Acres forested land:** 16,997,000. **Location:** Middle Atlantic state, bordered on the E by the Delaware R., on the S by the Mason-Dixon Line; on the W by West Virginia and Ohio; on the N/NE by Lake Erie and New York. **Climate:** continental with wide fluctuations in seasonal temperatures. **Topography:** Allegheny Mtns. run SW to NE, with Piedmont and Coast Plain in the SE triangle; Allegheny Front a diagonal spine across the state's center; N and W rugged plateau falls to Lake Erie Lowland. **Capital:** Harrisburg.

Economy. Principal industries: steel, travel, health, apparel, machinery, food & agriculture. **Principal manufactured goods:** primary metals, foods, fabricated metal products, non-electrical machinery, electrical machinery. **Agriculture: Chief crops:** corn, hay, mushrooms, apples, potatoes, winter wheat, oats, vegetables, tobacco, grapes. **Livestock** (1985): 1.96 mln. cattle; 800,000 hogs/pigs; 88,000 sheep; 22.5 mln. poultry. **Timber/lumber** (1989): pine, oak, maple; 617 mln. bd. ft. **Nonfuel Minerals** (1990): $1.1 bln.; mostly crushed stone, cement, lime, construction sand & gravel. **Commercial fishing** (1990): $279,000. **Chief ports:** Philadelphia, Pittsburgh, Erie. **International airports at:** Philadelphia, Pittsburgh, Erie, Harrisburg. **Value of construction** (1990): $9.7 bln. **Employment distribution** (1986): 24.4% serv.; 23.9% trade; 23.3% mfg.; 14.9% gvt. **Per capita income** (1990): $18,672 **Unemployment** (1990): 5.4%. **Tourism** (1985): out-of-state visitors spent $8.9 bln.

Finance. FDIC-insured commercial banks & trust companies (1990): 297. **Deposits:** $130.1 bln. **Savings institutions** (1990): 161. **Assets:** $42.6 bln.

Federal government. No. federal civilian employees (Mar. 1990): 87,395. **Avg. salary:** $28,387. **Notable federal facilities:** Army War College, Carlisle; Ships Control Ctr., Mechanicsburg; New Cumberland Army Depot; Philadelphia Navy Yard, Philadelphia.

Energy. Electricity production (1990, mwh, by source): Hydroelectric: 1.7 mln. Mineral: 161.9 mln. Nuclear: 57.8 mln.

Education. Student-teacher ratio (1989): 15.7. **Avg. salary, public school teachers** (1990-91): $35,471.

State data. Motto: Virtue, liberty and independence. **Flower:** Mountain laurel. **Bird:** Ruffed grouse. **Tree:** Hemlock. **Second** of the original 13 states to ratify the Constitution, Dec. 12, 1787. **State fair** at: Harrisburg; 2d week in Jan.

History. First settlers were Swedish, 1643, on Tinicum Is. In 1655 the Dutch seized the settlement but lost it to the British, 1664. The region was given by Charles II to William Penn, 1681, Philadelphia (brotherly love) was the capital of the colonies during most of the Revolution, and of the U.S., 1790-1800. Philadelphia was taken by the British, 1777; Washington's troops encamped at Valley Forge in the bitter winter of 1777-78. The Declaration of Independence, 1776, and the Constitution, 1787, were signed in Philadelphia.

Tourist attractions. Independence Hall & Natl. Historic Park, Franklin Institute Science Museum, Philadelphia Museum of Art, all in Philadelphia; Valley Forge Natl. Historic Park, Gettysburg Natl. Military Park; Pennsylvania Dutch Country; Hershey; Dusquesne Incline, Carnegie Institute, Heinz Hall, all in Pittsburgh; year 'round outdoor sports in Pocono Mtns., Pine Creek River Gorge, Alleghenies, Laurel Highlands & Presque Isle State Park.

Famous Pennsylvanians include Marian Anderson, Maxwell Anderson, James Buchanan, Andrew Carnegie, Stephen Foster, Benjamin Franklin, George C. Marshall, Andrew W. Mellon, Robert E. Peary, Mary Roberts Rinehart, Betsy Ross.

Chamber of Commerce. 222 N. 3d St., Harrisburg, PA 17101.

Toll-free travel information. 1-800-VISITPA.

Rhode Island

Little Rhody, Ocean State

People. Population (1990): 1,003,464; **rank:** 43. **Pop. density:** 960.3 per sq. mi. **Racial distrib.:** 91.4% White; 3.9% Black; 4.6% Hispanic. **Net change** (1980-90): 5.9%.

Geography. Total area: 1,212 sq. mi.; **rank:** 50. **Land area:** 1,045 sq. mi. **Acres forested land:** 399,000. **Location:** New England state. **Climate:** invigorating and changeable. **Topography:** eastern lowlands of Narragansett Basin; western uplands of flat and rolling hills. **Capital:** Providence.

Economy. Principal industries: manufacturing, services. **Principal manufactured goods:** costume jewelry, machinery, textiles, electronics. **Agriculture: Chief crops:** nursery produ., turf, potatoes, apples. **Livestock:** 7,000 cattle; 6,400 hogs/pigs; 6,500 sheep; 430,000 poultry. **Timber/lumber:** oak, chestnut. **Nonfuel Minerals** (1990): $12.4 mln.; construction sand & gravel, crushed stone. **Commercial fishing** (1990): $72.9 mln. **Chief ports:** Providence, Quonset Point, Newport. **Value of construction** (1990): $591.2 bln. **Employment distribution** (1990): 25.0% mfg.; 25.4% serv.; 22.8% trade. **Per capita income** (1990): $18,841. **Unemployment** (1990): 6.7%. **Tourism** (1987): visitors spent $1.1 bln. **Sales tax:** 7%.

Finance. FDIC-insured commercial banks & trust companies (1990): 13. **Deposits:** $11.2 bln. **Savings institutions** (1990): 4. **Assets:** $3.4 bln.

Federal government. No. federal civilian employees (Mar. 1990): 6,031. **Avg. salary:** $31,361. **Notable federal facilities:** Naval War College; Naval Underwater Systems Center.

Energy. Electricity production (1990, mwh, by source): Mineral: 592,000.

Education. Student-teacher ratio (1989): 14.5. **Avg. salary, public school teachers** (1990-91): $37,674.

State data. Motto: Hope. **Flower:** Violet. **Bird:** Rhode Island red. **Tree:** Red maple. **Song:** Rhode Island. **Thirteenth** of original 13 states to ratify the Constitution, May 29, 1790.

History. Rhode Island is distinguished for its battle for freedom of conscience and action, begun by Roger Wil-

liams, founder of Providence, who was exiled from Massachusetts Bay Colony in 1636, and Anne Hutchinson, exiled in 1638. Rhode Island gave protection to Quakers in 1657 and to Jews from Holland in 1658.

The colonists broke the power of the Narragansett Indians in the Great Swamp Fight, 1675, the decisive battle in King Philip's War. British trade restrictions angered the colonists and they burned the British revenue cutter Gaspee, 1772. The colony declared its independence May 4, 1776. Gen. John Sullivan and Lafayette won a partial victory, 1778, but failed to oust the British.

Tourist attractions. Newport mansions; summer resorts and water sports; various yachting races inc. Newport to Bermuda. Touro Synagogue, Newport, 1763; first Baptist Church in America, Providence, 1638; Gilbert Stuart birthplace, Saunderstown; Narragansett Indian Fall Festival.

Famous Rhode Islanders include Ambrose Burnside, George M. Cohan, Nelson Eddy, Jabez Gorham, Nathanael Greene, Christopher and Oliver La Farge, Matthew C. and Oliver Perry, Gilbert Stuart.

Chamber of Commerce. 30 Exchange Terr., Providence, RI 02908.

Toll-free travel information. 1-800-556-2484.

South Carolina

Palmetto State

People. Population (1990): 3,486,703. **rank:** 25. **Pop. density:** 115.8 per sq. mi. **Racial distrib.:** 69.0% White; 29.8% Black; 0.9% Hispanic. **Net change** (1980-90): 11.7%.

Geography. Total area: 31,113 sq. mi.; **rank:** 40. **Land area:** 30,111 sq. mi. **Acres forested land:** 12,257,000. **Location:** south Atlantic coast state, bordered by North Carolina on the N; Georgia on the SW and W; the Atlantic O. on the E, SE and S. **Climate:** humid sub-tropical. **Topo- graphy:** Blue Ridge province in NW has highest peaks; piedmont lies between the mountains and the fall line; coastal plain covers two-thirds of the state. **Capital:** Columbia.

Economy: Principal industries: tourism, agriculture, manufacturing. **Principal manufactured goods:** textiles, chemicals and allied products, machinery & fabricated metal products, apparel and related products. **Agriculture: Chief crops:** tobacco, soybeans, corn, cotton, peaches, hay. **Livestock** (1990): 590,000 cattle; 430,000 hogs/pigs. **Timber/lumber** (1989): pine, oak; 1.5 bln. **Nonfuel Minerals** (1990): $483.6 mln.; mostly crushed stone, Portland cement, clay. **Commercial fishing** (1990): $24.0 mln. **Chief ports:** Charleston, Georgetown, Port Royal. **International airports** at: Charleston. **Value of construction** (1990): $3.6 bln. **Employment distribution** (1988): 27.7% mfg.; 25.5% serv.; 22.8% trade; 8.2% gvt. **Per capita income** (1990): $15,099. **Unemployment** (1990): 4.7%. **Tourism** (1988): $4.6 bln. **Sales tax:** 5%.

Finance. FDIC-insured commercial banks & trust companies (1990): 84. **Deposits:** $18.0 bln. **Savings institutions** (1990): 48. **Assets:** $11.7 bln.

Federal government. No. federal civilian employees (Mar. 1990): 25,641. **Avg. Salary:** $28,017. **Notable federal facilities:** Polaris Submarine Base; Barnwell Nuclear Power Plant; Ft. Jackson; Parris Island; Savannah River Plant.

Energy. Electricity production (1990, mwh, by source): Hydroelectric: 2.7 mln.; Mineral: 23.7 mln.; Nuclear: 42.9 mln.

Education. Student-teacher ratio (1989): 17.0. **Avg. salary, public school teachers** (1990-91): $28,174.

State data. Motto: Dum Spiro Spero (While I breathe, I hope). **Flower:** Yellow jessamine. **Bird:** Carolina wren. **Tree:** Palmetto. **Song:** Carolina. **Eighth** of the original 13 states to ratify the Constitution, May 23, 1788. **State fair** at: Columbia; mid-Oct.

History. The first English colonists settled, 1670, on the Ashley River, moved to the site of Charleston, 1680. The colonists seized the government, 1775, and the royal governor fled. The British took Charleston, 1780, but were defeated at Kings Mountain that year, and at Cowpens and Eutaw Springs, 1781. In the 1830s, South Carolinians, angered by federal protective tariffs, adopted the Nullification Doctrine, holding a state can void an act of Congress. The state was the first to secede and, in 1861, Confederate troops fired on and forced the surrender of U. S. troops at Ft. Sumter, in Charleston Harbor, launching the Civil War.

Tourist attractions. Restored historic Charleston harbor area and Charleston gardens: Middleton Place, Magnolia, Cypress; other gardens at Brookgreen, Edisto, Glencairn; state parks; coastal islands; shore resorts such as Myrtle Beach and Hilton Head Island; fishing and quail hunting; Ft. Sumter National Monument, in Charleston Harbor; Charleston Museum, est. 1773, is the oldest museum in the U.S.; South Carolina State Museum, one of largest museums in South, Columbia; Riverbanks Zoo, Columbia.

Famous South Carolinians include Charles Bolden, James F. Byrnes, John C. Calhoun, DuBose Heyward, Ernest F. Hollings, Andrew Jackson, Jesse Jackson, James Longstreet, Francis Marion, Ronald McNair, Charles Pinckney, John Rutledge, Thomas Sumter, Strom Thurmond.

Tourist information: Chamber of Commerce, 930 Richland St., P.O. Box 1360, Columbia, SC 29201; and So. Carolina Dept. of Parks, Recreation, & Tourism, (803) 734-0122.

Gold was discovered, 1874, on the Sioux Reservation; miners rushed in. The U.S. first tried to stop them, then relaxed its opposition. The Sioux relinquished the land, 1877, and the "great Dakota Boom" began, 1879. A new Indian uprising came in 1890, climaxed by the massacre of Indian families at Wounded Knee.

Tourist attractions. Black Hills; Mt. Rushmore, with colossal likeness of the faces of U.S. Presidents Washington, Jefferson, Lincoln & T. Roosevelt carved by sculptor Gutzon Borglum; Needles Highway; Harney Peak, at 7,242 ft. the tallest peak between the Rockies and the Alps; Deadwood, an 1876 Gold Rush town; Custer State Park's buffalo and burro herds; Jewel Cave, the 4th largest cave in the world; Badlands Natl. Park's "moonscape"; "Great Lakes of So. Dakota"; Ft. Sisseton, restored 1864 army frontier post; Great Plains Zoo & Museum; Corn Palace in Mitchell; Wind Cave; Mammoth Site, ongoing excavation of prehistoric mammoths; Crazy Horse, mountain carving in progress.

Famous South Dakotans include Sparky Anderson, Catherine Bach, Tom Brokaw, "Calamity Jane", Mary Hart, Crazy Horse, Myron Floren, Alvin H. Hansen, Cheryl Ladd, Dr. Ernest O. Lawrence, George McGovern, Billy Mills, Allen Neuharth, Pat O'Brien, Sitting Bull.

Tourist information. South Dakota Tourism, 711 Wells Ave., Pierre, SD 57501-3335.

Toll-free travel information. 1-800-952-2217; 1-800-843-1930 out of state.

South Dakota

Coyote State, Sunshine State

People. Population (1990): 696,004; **rank:** 45. **Pop. density:** 9.17 per sq. mi. **Racial distrib.:** 91.6% White; 0.5% Black; 7.3% Amer. Indian; 0.8% Hispanic. **Net change** (1980-90): 0.8%.

Geography. Total area: 77,116 sq. mi.; **rank:** 16. **Land area:** 75,898 sq. mi. **Acres forested land:** 1,690,000. **Location:** West North Central state bounded on the N by North Dakota; on the E by Minnesota and Iowa; on the S by Nebraska; on the W by Wyoming and Montana. **Climate:** characterized by extremes of temperature, persistent winds, low precipitation and humidity. **Topography:** Prairie Plains in the E; rolling hills of the Great Plains in the W; the Black Hills, rising 3,500 ft. in the SW corner. **Capital:** Pierre.

Economy. Principal industries: agriculture, services, manufacturing. **Principal manufactured goods** (1986): food & kindred prods., machinery, electric & electronic equipment. **Agriculture: Chief crops** (1990): corn, oats, wheat, sunflowers, soybeans, sorghum. **Livestock** (1990): 3.4 mln. cattle; 1.8 mln. hogs/ pigs; 640,000 sheep. **Timber/lumber** (1989): ponderosa pine; 193 mln. bd. ft. **Nonfuel Minerals** (1990): $321.6 mln.; mostly gold, Portland cement. **Value of construction** (1990): $438 mln. **Employment distribution** (1990): 20.7% serv.; 9.8% mfg. **Per capita income** (1990): $15,872. **Unemployment** (1990): 3.7%. **Tourism** (1990): travellers' impact $860 mln. **Sales tax:** 4%.

Finance. FDIC-insured **commercial banks & trust companies** (1990): 125. **Deposits:** $9.6 bln. **Savings institutions** (1990): 12. **Assets:** $1.5 bln.

Federal government. No. federal civilian employees (Mar. 1990): 7,049. **Avg. salary:** $27,292. **Notable federal facilities:** Bureau of Indian Affairs, Ellsworth AFB, Corp of Engineers, Nat'l Park Service.

Energy. Electricity production (1990, mwh, by source): Hydroelectric: 3.9 mln.; Mineral: 2.5 mln.

Education: Student-teacher ratio (1989): 15.5. **Avg. salary, public school teachers** (1990-91): $22,363.

State data. Motto: Under God, the people rule. **Flower:** Pasque flower. **Bird:** Ringnecked pheasant. **Tree:** Black Hills spruce. **Song:** Hail, South Dakota. **Entered union** Nov. 2, 1889; rank, 40th. **State fair at:** Huron; late Aug.-early Sept.

History. Les Verendryes explored the region, 1742-43. Lewis and Clark passed through the area, 1804 and 1806. First white American settlement was at Fort Pierre, 1817.

Tennessee

Volunteer State

People. Population (1990): 4,877,185 **rank:** 17. **Pop. density:** 118.3 per sq. mi. **Racial distrib.:** 83.0% White; 16.0% Black; 0.7% Hispanic. **Net change** (1980-90): 6.2%.

Geography. Total area: 42,144 sq. mi.; **rank:** 34. **Land area:** 41,220 sq. mi. **Acres forested land:** 13,258,000. **Location:** East South Central state bounded on the N by Kentucky and Virginia; on the E by North Carolina; on the S by Georgia, Alabama, and Mississippi; on the W by Arkansas and Missouri. **Climate:** humid continental to the N; humid sub-tropical to the S. **Topography:** rugged country in the E; the Great Smoky Mtns. of the Unakas; low ridges of the Appalachian Valley; the flat Cumberland Plateau; slightly rolling terrain and knobs of the Interior Low Plateau, the largest region; Eastern Gulf Coastal Plain to the W, is laced with meandering streams; Mississippi Alluvial Plain, a narrow strip of swamp and flood plain in the extreme W. **Capital:** Nashville.

Economy. Principal industries: trade, services, construction; transp., commun., public utilities; finance, ins., real estate. **Principal manufactured goods:** chemicals & allied prods.; food & kindred prods.; nonelectrical machinery; electric/electronic equip.; apparel; fabr. metal prods.; transp. equip.; rubber/misc. plastic prods.; paper & allied prods., printing and publishing. **Agriculture: Chief crops** (1988): soybeans, greenhouse/nursery, cotton/lint. **Livestock** (1990): 2.3 mln. cattle; 0.7 mln. hogs/pigs; 12,000 sheep; 1.7 mln. poultry. **Timber/lumber** (1989): red oak, white oak, yellow poplar, hickory; 677 mln. bd. ft. **Nonfuel Minerals** (1990): $679.2 mln.; mostly clay, sand and gravel, crushed stone. **Chief ports:** Memphis, Nashville, Chattanooga, Knoxville. **International airports at:** Memphis, Nashville. **Value of construction** (1990): $4.4 bln. **Employment distribution** (1990): 23.8% mfg.; 23.6% trade; 22.2% serv.; 16.0% gvt. **Per capita income** (1990): $15,798. **Unemployment** (1990): 5.2%. **Tourism** (1989): out-of-state visitors spent $3.3 bln. **Sales tax:** 5½% state, up to 2¾% local.

Finance. FDIC-insured **commercial banks & trust companies** (1990): 260. **Deposit:** $38.4 bln. **Savings institutions** (1990): 58. **Assets:** $11.6 bln.

Federal government. No. federal civilian employees (Mar. 1990): 42,005. **Avg. salary:** $30,115. **Notable federal facilities:** Tennessee Valley Authority; Oak Ridge Nat'l. Laboratories.

Energy: Electricity production (1990, mwh, by source): Hydroelectric: 9.5 mln.; Mineral: 50.4 mln; Nuclear: 14.0 mln.

Education. Student-teacher ratio (1989): 19.1. **Avg. salary, public school teachers** (1990-91): $28,248.

State data. Motto: Agriculture and commerce. **Flower:** Iris. **Bird:** Mockingbird. **Tree:** Tulip poplar. **Song:** The Tennessee Waltz. **Entered union** June 1, 1796; rank, 16th. **State fair** at: Nashville; mid-Sept.

History. Spanish explorers first visited the area, 1541. English traders crossed the Great Smokies from the east while France's Marquette and Jolliet sailed down the Mississippi on the west, 1673. First permanent settlement was by Virginians on the Watauga River, 1769. During the Revolution, the colonists helped win the Battle of Kings Mountain, N.C., 1780, and joined other eastern campaigns. The state seceded from the Union 1861, and saw many engagements of the Civil War, but 30,000 soldiers fought for the Union.

Tourist attractions. Natural wonders include Reelfoot Lake, the reservoir basin of the Mississippi R. formed by the 1811 earthquake; Lookout Mountain, Chattanooga; Fall Creek Falls, 256 ft. high; Great Smoky Mountains National Park; Lost Sea, Sweetwater; Cherokee Natl. Forest.

Also, the Hermitage, 13 mi. E of Nashville, home of Andrew Jackson; the homes of presidents Polk and Andrew Johnson; American Museum of Science, Oak Ridge; the Parthenon, Nashville, a replica of the Parthenon of Athens; the Grand Old Opry, Nashville, Opryland, USA, theme park, Nashville; Graceland, home of Elvis Presley, Memphis; Alex Haley Home & Museum, Henning; Casey Jones Home & Museum, Jackson.

Famous Tennesseans include Davy Crockett, David Farragut, William C. Handy, Sam Houston, Cordell Hull, Grace Moore, Dinah Shore, Alvin York.

Tourist information. Dept. of Tourist Development, 5th Floor, Rachel Jackson Bldg., Nashville, TN 37219.

Texas

Lone Star State

People. Population (1990): 16,986,510; **rank: 3. Pop. density:** 64.9 per sq. mi. **Racial distrib.:** 75.2% White; 11.9% Black; 25.5% Hispanic. **Net change** (1980-90): 19.4%.

Geography. Total area: 266,807 sq. mi.; **rank: 2. Land area:** 261,914 sq. mi.; **Acres forested land:** 13,656,000. **Location:** Southwestern state, bounded on the SE by the Gulf of Mexico; on the SW by Mexico, separated by the Rio Grande; surrounding states are Louisiana, Arkansas, Oklahoma, New Mexico. **Climate:** extremely varied; driest region is the Trans-Pecos; wettest is the NE. **Topography:** Gulf Coast Plain in the S and SE; North Central Plains slope upward with some hills; the Great Plains extend over the Panhandle, are broken by low mountains; the Trans-Pecos is the southern extension of the Rockies. **Capital:** Austin.

Economy. Principal industries: trade, services, manufacturing. **Principal manufactured goods:** machinery, transportation equipment, foods, electrical and electronic equip., chemicals and allied prods., apparel. **Agriculture: Chief crops:** cotton, grain sorghum, grains, vegetables, citrus and other fruits, pecans, peanuts. **Livestock** (1985): 14.1 mln. cattle; 415,000 hogs/pigs; 1.81 mln. sheep; 17.4 mln. poultry. **Timber/ lumber** (1988): pine, cypress; 1.3 bln. bd. ft. **Nonfuel Minerals** (1990): $1.6 bln.; mostly cement, stone, sand & gravel. **Commercial fishing** (1990): $182.4 mln. **Chief ports:** Houston, Galveston, Brownsville, Beaumont, Port Arthur, Corpus Christi. **Major international airports at:** Houston, Dallas/ Ft. Worth, San Antonio. **Value of construction** (1990) $12.8 bln. **Employment distribution** (1990): 24.3% trade; 24.2% serv.; 18.1% gvt.; 14.0% mfg. **Per capita income** (1990): $16,759. **Unemployment** (1990): 6.2%. **Tourism** (1987): out-of-state visitors spent $17.6 bln. **Sales tax:** 6%, + optional 1% local, 1% transit.

Finance. FDIC-insured commercial banks & trust companies (1990): 1,236. **Deposits:** $138.8 bln. **Savings institutions** (1990): 196. **Assets:** $90.6 bln.

Federal government. No. federal civilian employees (Mar. 1990): $123,717. **Avg. salary:** $28,602. **Notable federal facilities:** Fort Hood (Killeen); Kelly AFB, and Ft. Sam Houston, both San Antonio.

Energy. Electricity production (1990, mwh, by source): Hydroelectric: 1.8 mln.; Mineral: 216.6 mln. Nuclear: 15.9 mln.

Education. Student-teacher ratio (1989): 16.7. **Avg. salary, public school teachers** (1990-91): $28,321.

State data. Motto: Friendship. **Flower:** Bluebonnet. **Bird:** Mockingbird. **Tree:** Pecan. **Song:** Texas, Our Texas. **Entered union** Dec. 29, 1845; rank, 28th. **State fair** at: Dallas; mid-Oct.

History. Pineda sailed along the Texas coast, 1519; Cabeza de Vaca and Coronado visited the interior, 1541. Spaniards made the first settlement at Ysleta, near El Paso, 1682. Americans moved into the land early in the 19th century. Mexico, of which Texas was a part, won independence from Spain, 1821; Santa Anna became dictator, 1835. Texans rebelled; Santa Anna wiped out defenders of the Alamo, 1836. Sam Houston's Texans defeated Santa Anna at San Jacinto and independence was proclaimed the same year. In 1845, Texas was admitted to the Union.

Tourist attractions. Padre Island National Seashore; Big Bend, Guadalupe Mtns. national parks; The Alamo; Ft. Davis; Six Flags Amusement Park. Named for Pres. Lyndon B. Johnson are a state park, a natl. historic site marking his birthplace, boyhood home, and ranch, all near Johnson City, and a library in Austin.

Famous Texans include Stephen F. Austin, James Bowie, Carol Burnett, J. Frank Dobie, Dwight D. Eisenhower, Sam Houston, Howard Hughes, Lyndon B. Johnson, Mary Martin, Chester Nimitz, Katharine Ann Porter, Sam Rayburn.

Chamber of Commerce. 900 Congress, Suite 501, Austin, TX 78701.

Utah

Beehive State

People. Population (1990): 1,722,850; **rank: 35. Pop. density:** 21.0 per sq. mi. **Racial distrib.:** 93.8% White; 0.7% Black; 4.9% Hispanic. **Net change** (1980-90): 17.9%.

Geography. Total area: 84,899 sq. mi.; **rank: 11. Land area:** 82,168 sq. mi. **Acres forested land:** 16,234,000. **Location:** Middle Rocky Mountain state; its southeastern corner touches Colorado, New Mexico, and Arizona, and is the only spot in the U.S. where 4 states join. **Climate:** arid; ranging from warm desert in SW to alpine in NE. **Topography:** high Colorado plateau is cut by brilliantly-colored canyons of the SE; broad, flat, desert-like Great Basin of the W; the Great Salt Lake and Bonneville Salt Flats to the NW; Middle Rockies in the NE run E-W; valleys and plateaus of the Wasatch Front. **Capital:** Salt Lake City.

Economy. Principal industries: services, trade, manufacturing, government, construction. **Principal manufactured goods:** guided missiles and parts, electronic components, food products, fabricated metals, steel, electrical equipment. **Agriculture: Chief crops:** hay, wheat, apples, barley, alfalfa seed, corn, potatoes, cherries, onions. **Livestock:** 855,000 cattle; 34,000 hogs/pigs; 600,000 sheep; 3.8 mln. poultry. **Timber/lumber:** aspen, spruce, pine. **Nonfuel Minerals** (1990): $1.2 mln.; copper, gold, magnesium. **International airports at:** Salt Lake City. **Value of construction** (1990): $1.6 bln. **Employment distribution** (1990): 25.0% serv.; 23.8% trade; 20.8% govt; 14.8% mfg. **Per capita income** (1990): $14,083. **Unemployment** (1990): 4.3%. **Tourism** (1986): travellers spent $2.0 bln. **Sales tax:** 6.25%.

Finance. FDIC-insured commercial banks & trust companies (1990): 57. **Deposits:** $9.8 bln. **Savings institutions** (1990): 13. **Assets:** $6.9 bln.

Federal government. No. federal civilian employees (Mar. 1990): 33,198. **Avg. salary:** $27,670. **Notable federal facilities:** Hill AFB; Tooele Army Depot, IRS Western Service Center.

Energy. Electricity production (1990, mwh, by source): Hydroelectric: 486,000 mln.; Mineral: 31.6 mln.

Education. Student-teacher ratio (1989): 24.8. **Avg. salary, public school teachers** (1990-91): $25,415.

State data. Motto: Industry. **Flower:** Sego lily. **Bird:** Seagull. **Tree:** Blue spruce. **Song:** Utah, We Love Thee. **Entered union** Jan. 4, 1896; rank, 45th. **State fair** at: Salt Lake City; Sept.

History. Spanish Franciscans visited the area, 1776, the first white men to do so. American fur traders followed. Permanent settlement began with the arrival of the Mormons, 1847. They made the arid land bloom and created a prosperous economy, organized the State of Deseret, 1849, and asked admission to the Union. This was not achieved until 1896, after a long period of controversy over the Mormon Church's doctrine of polygamy, which it discontinued in 1890.

Tourist attractions. Temple Square, Mormon Church hdqtrs., Salt Lake City; Great Salt Lake; fishing streams, lakes and reservoirs, numerous winter sports; campgrounds. Natural wonders may be seen at Zion, Canyonlands, Bryce Canyon, Arches, and Capitol Reef national parks; Dinosaur, Rainbow Bridge, Timpanogos Cave, and Natural Bridges national monuments. Also Lake Powell and Flaming Gorge reservoirs.

Famous Utahans include Maude Adams, Ezra Taft Benson, John Moses Browning, Mariner Eccles, Philo Farnsworth, James Fletcher, David M. Kennedy, J. Willard Marriott, Osmond Family, Merlin Olsen, Ivy Baker Priest, George Romney, Brigham Young, Loretta Young.

Tourist information. Utah Travel Council, Council Hall, Salt Lake City, UT 84114.

Vermont

Green Mountain State

People. Population (1990): 562,758; **rank:** 48. **Pop. density:** 60.8 per sq. mi. **Racial distrib.:** 98.6% White; 0.3% Black; 0.6% Asian; 0.7% Hispanic. **Net change** (1980-90): 10.0%.

Geography. Total area: 9,614 sq. mi.; **rank:** 43. **Land area:** 9,249 sq. mi. **Acres forested land:** 4,479,000. **Location:** northern New England state. **Climate:** temperate, with considerable temperature extremes; heavy snowfall in mountains. **Topography:** Green Mtns. N-S backbone 20-36 mi. wide; avg. altitude 1,000 ft. **Capital:** Montpelier.

Economy. Principal industries: manufacturing, tourism, agriculture, trade; finance, insurance, real estate, government. **Principal manufactured goods:** machine tools, furniture, scales, books, computer components, fishing rods. **Agriculture: Chief crops:** dairy products, apples, maple syrup, silage corn, hay. **Livestock** (1989): 320,000 cattle; 5,100 hogs/ pigs; 20,456 sheep; 406,000 poultry. **Timber/lumber** (1989): pine, spruce, fir, hemlock; 124 mln. bd. ft. **Nonfuel Minerals** (1990): $93.2 mln.; mostly dimension stone, crashed stone, construction sand & gravel. **International airports at:** Burlington. **Value of construction** (1990): $521.2 mln. **Employment distribution** (1990): 27% serv.; 23% trade; 18% mfg. **Per capita income** (1990): $17,436. **Unemployment** (1990): 5.0%. **Tourism** (1990): visitors spent $1.25 bln. **Sales tax.** 5%.

Finance. FDIC-insured commercial banks & trust **companies** (1990): 27. **Deposits:** $5.1 bln. **Savings institutions** (1990): 4. **Assets:** $ 565 mln.

Federal government. No. federal civilian employees (Mar. 1990): 2,557. **Avg. salary:** $29,144.

Energy. Electricity production (1990, mwh, by source): Hydroelectric: 1.2 mln.; Mineral: 68,000; Nuclear: 3.6 mln.

Education. Student-teacher ratio (1989): 13.8. **Avg. salary, public school teachers** (1990-91): $30,986.

State data. Motto: Freedom and unity. **Flower:** Red clover. **Bird:** Hermit thrush. **Tree:** Sugar maple. **Song:**

Hail, Vermont. **Entered union** Mar. 4, 1791; rank, 14th. **State fair** at: Rutland; early Sept.

History. Champlain explored the lake that bears his name, 1609. First American settlement was Ft. Dummer, 1724, near Brattleboro. Ethan Allen and the Green Mountain Boys captured Ft. Ticonderoga, 1775; John Stark defeated part of Burgoyne's forces near Bennington, 1777. In the War of 1812, Thomas MacDonough defeated a British fleet on Champlain off Plattsburgh, 1814.

Tourist attractions. Year-round outdoor sports, esp. hiking, camping and skiing; there are over 56 ski areas in the state. Popular are the Shelburne Museum; Rock of Ages Tourist Center, Graniteville; Vermont Marble Exhibit, Proctor; Bennington Battle Monument; Pres. Coolidge homestead, Plymouth; Maple Grove Maple Museum, St. Johnsbury.

Famous Vermonters include Ethan Allen, Chester A. Arthur, Calvin Coolidge, Adm. George Dewey, John Dewey, Stephen A. Douglas, Dorothy Canfield Fisher, James Fisk.

Tourist Information. Vermont Travel Division, 134 State St., Montpelier, VT 05602.

Virginia

Old Dominion

People. Population (1990): 6,187,358; **rank:** 12. **Pop. density:** 156.3 per sq. mi. **Racial distrib.:** 77.4% White; 18.8% Black; 2.6% Asian; 2.6% Hispanic. **Net change** (1980-90): 15.7%.

Geography. Total area: 40,767 sq. mi.; **rank:** 36. **Land area:** 39,598 sq. mi. **Acres forested land:** 15,968,000. **Location:** South Atlantic state bounded by the Atlantic O. on the E and surrounded by North Carolina, Tennessee, Kentucky, West Virginia, and Maryland. **Climate:** mild and equable. **Topography:** mountain and valley region in the W, including the Blue Ridge Mtns.; rolling piedmont plateau; tidewater, or coastal plain, including the eastern shore. **Capital:** Richmond.

Economy. Principal industries: services, trade, government, manufacturing, tourism, agriculture. **Principal manufactured goods:** textiles, transportation equipment, electric & electronic equipment, food processing, chemicals. **Agriculture: Chief crops:** tobacco, soybeans, peanuts, winterwheat, corn, far grain, tomatoes, apples, summer & sweet potatoes. **Livestock** (1989): 1.67 mln. cattle; 450,000 hogs/pigs; 158,000 sheep. 5.82 mln. poultry. **Timber/lumber** (1989): pine and hardwoods; 1.1 bln. bd. ft. **Nonfuel Minerals** (1990): $512.1 mln.; mostly crushed stone. **Commercial fishing** (1990): $106.6 mln. **Chief ports:** Hampton Roads, Richmond, Alexandria. **International airports at:** Norfolk, Dulles, Richmond, Newport News. **Value of construction** (1990): $7.1 bln. **Employment distribution** (1989): 24.6% serv.; 22.9% trade; 19.6% gvt.; 14.9% mfg. **Per capita income** (1990): $19,746. **Unemployment** (1990): 4.3%. **Tourism** (1989): domestic travellers spent $8 bln. **Sales tax:** 4.5%.

Finance. FDIC-insured commercial banks & trust **companies** (1990): 180. **Deposits:** $52.4 bln. **Savings institutions** (1990): 63. **Assets:** $29.9 bln.

Federal government. No. federal civilian employees (Mar. 1990): 138,712. **Avg. salary:** $33,333. **Notable federal facilities:** Pentagon; Naval Sta., Norfolk; Naval Air Sta., Norfolk, Virginia Beach; Naval Shipyard, Portsmouth; Marine Corps Base, Quantico; Langley AFB; NASA at Langley.

Energy. Electricity production (1990, mwh, by source): Hydroelectric: 428,000; Mineral: 22.9 mln.; Nuclear: 23.8 mln.

Education. Student-teacher ratio (1989): 15.9. **Avg. salary, public school teachers** (1990-91): $32,382.

State data. Motto: Sic Semper Tyrannis (Thus always to tyrants). **Flower:** Dogwood. **Bird:** Cardinal. **Tree:** Dogwood. **Song:** Carry Me Back to Old Virginia. **Tenth** of the original 13 states to ratify the Constitution, June 25, 1788. **State fair** at: Richmond; late Sept.-early Oct.

History. English settlers founded Jamestown, 1607. Virginians took over much of the government from royal Gov.

Dunmore in 1775, forcing him to flee. Virginians under George Rogers Clark freed the Ohio-Indiana-Illinois area of British forces. Benedict Arnold burned Richmond and Petersburg for the British, 1781. That same year, Britain's Cornwallis was trapped at Yorktown and surrendered.

Tourist attractions. Colonial Williamsburg; Busch Gardens; Wolf Trap Farm, near Falls Church; Arlington National Cemetery; Mt. Vernon, home of George Washington; Jamestown Festival Park; Yorktown; Jefferson's Monticello, Charlottesville; Robert E. Lee's birthplace, Stratford Hall, and grave, at Lexington; Appomattox; Shenandoah National Park; Blue Ridge Parkway; Virginia Beach; King's Dominion, near Richmond.

Famous Virginians include Richard E. Byrd, James B. Cabell, William Henry Harrison, Patrick Henry, Thomas Jefferson, Joseph E. Johnston, Robert E. Lee, Meriwether Lewis and William Clark, James Madison, George Mason, James Monroe, John Marshall, Edgar Allan Poe, Walter Reed, Zachary Taylor, John Tyler, Maggie Walker, Booker T. Washington, George Washington, Woodrow Wilson.

Chamber of Commerce: 9th South Fifth St., Richmond, VA 23219.

Toll-free travel information. 1-800-VISITVA.

Washington
Evergreen State

People. Population (1990): 4,866,692; **rank:** 18. **Pop. density:** 73.1 per sq. mi. **Racial distrib.:** 88.5% White; 3.1% Black; 4.3% Asian; 4.4% Hispanic. **Net change** (1980-90): 17.8%.

Geography. Total area: 68,139 sq. mi.; **rank:** 20. **Land area:** 66,582 sq. mi. **Acres forested land:** 21,856,000. **Location:** northwestern coastal state bordered by Canada on the N; Idaho on the E; Oregon on the S; and the Pacific O. on the W. **Climate:** mild, dominated by the Pacific O. and protected by the Rockies. **Topography:** Olympic Mtns. on NW peninsula; open land along coast to Columbia R.; flat terrain of Puget Sound Lowland; Cascade Mtns. region's high peaks to the E; Columbia Basin in central portion; highlands to the NE; mountains to the SE. **Capital:** Olympia.

Economy. Principal industries: aerospace, forest products, food products, primary metals, agriculture. **Principal manufactured goods:** aircraft, pulp and paper, lumber and plywood, aluminum, processed fruits and vegetables. **Agriculture: Chief crops:** hops, spearmint oil, raspberries, apples, asparagus, pears, cherries, peppermint oil, potatoes. **Livestock** (1986): 1.3 mln. cattle; 50,000 hogs/pigs; 59,000 sheep; 5.7 mln. poultry. **Timber/lumber** (1989): Douglas fir, hemlock, cedar, pine; 4.3 bln. bd. ft. **Nonfuel Minerals** (1990): $473.4 mln.; mostly construction sand & gravel, crushed stone, Portland cement. **Commercial fishing** (1990): $118.1 mln. **Chief ports:** Seattle, Tacoma, Vancouver, Kelso-Longview. **International airports at:** Seattle/Tacoma, Spokane, Boeing Field. **Value of construction** (1990): $6.0 bln. **Employment distribution** (1989): 24.4% trade; 20.7% serv.; 18.3% gvt.; 17.3% mfg. **Per capita income** (1990): $18,858. **Unemployment** (1990): 4.9%. **Tourism** (1988): $4.6 bln. **Sales tax:** 6.5%.

Finance. FDIC-insured commercial banks & trust companies (1990): 1,062. **Deposits:** $31.9 bln. **Savings institutions** (1990): 32. **Assets:** $17.5 bln.

Federal government. No. federal civilian employees (Mar. 1990): 49,832. **Avg. salary:** $30,985. **Notable federal facilities:** Bonneville Power Admin.; Ft. Lewis; McChord AFB; Hanford Nuclear Reservation; Bremerton Naval Shipyards.

Energy. Electricity production (1990, mwh, by source): Hydroelectric: 87.0 mln.; Mineral: 7.4 mln.; Nuclear: 5.7 mln.

Education. Student-teacher ratio (1989): 20.1. **Avg. salary, public school teachers** (1990-91): $32,975.

State data. Motto. Alki (By and by). **Flower:** Western rhododendron. **Bird:** Willow goldfinch. **Tree:** Western hemlock. **Song:** Washington, My Home. **Entered union**

Nov. 11, 1889; rank, 42d. **State fairs at:** S.E. Washington, W. Washington, N. Cent. Washington District, Cent. Washington.

History. Spain's Bruno Hezeta sailed the coast, 1775. American Capt. Robert Gray sailed up the Columbia River, 1792. Canadian fur traders set up Spokane House, 1810; Americans under John Jacob Astor established a post at Fort Okanogan, 1811. Missionary Marcus Whitman settled near Walla Walla, 1836. Final agreement on the border of Washington and Canada was made with Britain, 1846, and gold was discovered in the state's northeast, 1855, bringing new settlers.

Tourist attractions. Mt. Rainier, Olympic and North Cascades National Parks; Mt. St. Helens; Pacific beaches; Puget Sound; wineries; Indian cultures; year-round outdoor recreation: Seattle Waterfront, Seattle Center, Space Needle, San Juan Islands, Grand Coulee Dam, Spokane's Riverfront Park.

Famous Washingtonians include Bing Crosby, William O. Douglas, Henry M. Jackson, Gary Larson, Mary McCarthy, Edward R. Murrow, Theodore Roethke, Marcus Whitman, Minoru Yamasaki.

Local Chambers of Commerce. P.O. Box 658, Olympia, WA 98507.

Toll-free travel information. 1-800-544-1800.

West Virginia
Mountain State

People. Population (1990): 1,793,477. **rank:** 34. **Pop. density:** 74.5 per sq. mi. **Racial distrib.:** 96.2% White; 3.1% Black; 0.5% Hispanic. **Net change** (1980-90): −8.0%.

Geography. Total area: 24,232 sq. mi.; **rank:** 41. **Land area:** 24,087 sq. mi. **Acres forested land:** 11,942,000. **Location:** South Atlantic state bounded on the N by Ohio, Pennsylvania, Maryland; on the S and W by Virginia, Kentucky, Ohio; on the E by Maryland and Virginia. **Climate:** humid continental climate except for marine modification in the lower panhandle. **Topography:** ranging from hilly to mountainous; Allegheny Plateau in the W, covers two-thirds of the state; mountains here are the highest in the state, over 4,000 ft. **Capital:** Charleston.

Economy. Principal industries: manufacturing, services, mining, tourism. **Principal manufactured goods:** machinery, plastic and hardwood prods., fabricated metals, basic organic and inorganic chemicals, aluminum, steel. **Agriculture: Chief crops:** apples, peaches, hay, tobacco, corn, wheat, oats. **Chief products:** dairy prods., eggs. **Livestock** (1989): 500,000 cattle; 37,000 hogs/pigs; 82,000 sheep; 810,000 chickens. **Timber/ lumber** (1989): oak, yellow poplar, hickory, walnut, cherry; 411 mln. bd. ft. **Nonfuel Minerals** (1990): $132 mln.; mostly crushed stone. **Chief port:** Huntington. **Value of construction** (1990): $1.2 bln. **Employment distribution** (1989): 23% trade; 21% gvt.; 22% serv.; 14% mfg. **Per capita income** (1990): $13,747. **Unemployment** (1990): 8.3%. **Tourism** (1989): travel-related expenditures were $2.3 bln. **Sales tax:** 6%.

Finance. FDIC-insured commercial banks & trust companies (1990): 185. **Deposits:** $14.5 bln. **Savings institutions** (1990): 16. **Assets:** $2.2 bln.

Federal government. No. federal civilian employees (Mar. 1990): 10,170. **Avg. salary:** $28,680. **Notable federal facilities:** National Radio Astronomy Observatory, Green Bank; Bureau of Public Debt. Bldg., Parkersburg; Natl. Park, Harper's Ferry; Correctional Institution for Women, Alderson.

Energy. Electricity production (1990, mwh, by source): Hydroelectric: 435,000; Mineral: 76.9 mln.

Education. Student-teacher ratio (1989): 15.1. **Avg. salary, public school teachers** (1990-91): $25,958.

State Data. Motto: Montani Semper Liberi (Mountaineers are always free) **Flower:** Big rhododendron. **Bird:** Cardinal. **Tree:** Sugar maple. **Songs:** The West Virginia Hills; This Is My West Virginia; West Virginia, My Home, Sweet Home. **Entered union** June 20, 1863; rank, 35th. **State fair at:** Lewisburg (Fairlea), late Aug.

History. Early explorers included George Washington, 1753, and Daniel Boone. The area became part of Virginia and often objected to rule by the eastern part of the state. When Virginia seceded, 1861, the Wheeling Conventions repudiated the act and created a new state, Kanawha, subsequently changed to West Virginia. It was admitted to the Union as such, 1863.

Tourist attractions. Harpers Ferry National Historic Park has been restored to its condition in 1859, when John Brown seized the U.S. Armory.

Also Science and Cultural Center, Charleston; White Sulphur and Berkeley Springs mineral water spas; Monongahela Natl. Forest; state parks and forests; trout fishing; turkey, deer, and bear hunting; white water rafting, paddleboat tours, skiing; glass tours at Fenton Glass in Williamstown, Viking Glass in New Martinsville, Blenko Glass in Milton; Sternwheel Regatta, Charleston; Mountain State Forest Festival; Mountain State Arts & Crafts Fair, Ripley.

Famous West Virginians include Newton D. Baker, Pearl Buck, John W. Davis, Thomas "Stonewall" Jackson, Don Knotts, Dwight Whitney Morrow, Nick Nolte, Michael Owens, Cyrus Vance, Col. Charles "Chuck" Yeager.

Tourist information. Dept. of Commerce, State Capitol, Charleston WV 25305.

Toll-free travel information. 1-800-CALLW.VA.

State data. Motto: Forward. **Flower:** Wood violet. **Bird:** Robin. **Tree:** Sugar maple. **Song:** On, Wisconsin! **Entered union** May 29, 1848; rank, 30th. **State fair** at: West Allis; mid-Aug.

History. Jean Nicolet was the first European to see the Wisconsin area, arriving in Green Bay, 1634; French missionaries and fur traders followed. The British took over, 1763. The U.S. won the land after the Revolution but the British were not ousted until after the War of 1812. Lead miners came next, then farmers. Railroads were started in 1851, serving growing wheat harvests and iron mines.

Tourist attractions. Old Wade House and Carriage Museum, Greenbush; Villa Louis, Prairie du Chien; Circus World Museum, Baraboo; Wisconsin Dells; Old World Wisconsin, Eagle; Door County peninsula; Chequamegon and Nicolet national forests; Lake Winnebago; numerous lakes for water sports, ice boating and fishing; skiing and hunting.

Famous Wisconsinites include Edna Ferber, King Camp Gillette, Harry Houdini, Robert LaFollette, Alfred Lunt, Georgia O'Keeffe, Spencer Tracy, Thorstein Veblen, Orson Welles, Thornton Wilder, Frank Lloyd Wright.

Tourist information. Wisconsin Dept. of Development, Division of Tourism, 123 W. Washington Ave., Madison, WI 53702.

Toll-free travel information. 1-800-372-2737.

Wisconsin

Badger State

People. Population (1990): 4,891,769; **rank:** 16. **Pop. density:** 90.1 per sq. mi. **Racial distrib.:** 92.2% White; 5.0% Black; 1.9% Hispanic. **Net change** (1980-90): 4.0%.

Geography. Total area: 56,153 sq. mi.; **rank:** 26. **Land area:** 54,314 sq. mi. **Acres forested land:** 15,319,000. **Location:** North central state, bounded on the N by Lake Superior and Upper Michigan; on the E by Lake Michigan; on the S by Illinois; on the W by the St. Croix and Mississippi rivers. **Climate:** long, cold winters and short, warm summers tempered by the Great Lakes. **Topography:** narrow Lake Superior Lowland plain met by Northern Highland which slopes gently to the sandy crescent Central Plain; Western Upland in the SW; 3 broad parallel limestone ridges running N-S are separated by wide and shallow lowlands in the SE. **Capital:** Madison.

Economy. Principal industries: manufacturing, trade, services, government, transportation, communications, agriculture, tourism. **Principal manufactured goods:** machinery, foods, fabricated metals, transportation equipment, paper and wood products. **Agriculture: Chief crops:** corn, beans, beets, peas, hay, oats, cabbage, cranberries. **Chief products:** milk, butter, cheese. **Livestock** (1990): 4.2 mln. cattle, 1.3 mln. hogs/pigs; 84,000 sheep; 4.2 mln. poultry. **Timber/lumber** (1989): maple, birch, oak, evergreens; 422 mln. bd. ft. **Nonfuel Minerals** (1990): $209.6 mln.; mostly crushed stone, construction & industrial sand & gravel, lime. **Commercial fishing** (1990): $4.8 mln. **Chief ports:** Superior, Ashland, Milwaukee, Green Bay, Kewaunee, Pt. Washington, Manitowoc, Sheboygan, Marinette, Kenosha. **International airports at:** Milwaukee. **Value of construction** (1990): $4.5 bln. **Employment distribution** (1990): 24.1% trade; 25.0% mfg.; 23.1% serv.; 13.9% gvt. **Per capita income** (1990): $17,503. **Unemployment** (1990): 4.4%. **Tourism** (1989): out-of-state visitors spent $5.4 bln. **Sales tax:** 5%.

Finance. FDIC-insured commercial banks & trust companies (1990): 504. **Deposits:** $37.6 bln. **Savings institutions** (1990): 70. **Assets:** $17.1 bln.

Federal government. No. federal civilian employees (Mar. 1990): 12,222. **Avg. salary:** $26,599. **Notable federal facilities:** Ft. McCoy.

Energy. Electricity production (1990, mwh, by source): Hydroelectric: 1.8 mln.; Mineral: 32.4 mln.; Nuclear: 11.2 mln.

Education. Student-teacher ratio (1989): 15.9. **Avg. salary, public school teachers** (1990-91): $33,100.

Wyoming

Equality State

People. Population (1990): 453,588; **rank:** 50. **Pop. density:** 4.7 per sq. mi. **Racial distrib.:** 94.2% White; 0.8% Black; 2.1% Amer. Indian; 5.7% Hispanic. **Net change** (1980-90): −3.4%.

Geography. Total area: 97,809 sq. mi.; **rank:** 9. **Land area:** 97,105 sq. mi. **Acres forested land:** 9,966,000. **Location:** Mountain state lying in the high western plateaus of the Great Plains. **Climate:** semi-desert conditions throughout; true desert in the Big Horn and Great Divide basins. **Topography:** the eastern Great Plains rise to the foothills of the Rocky Mtns.; the Continental Divide crosses the state from the NW to the SE. **Capital:** Cheyenne.

Economy. Principal industries: mineral extraction, tourism and recreation, agriculture. **Principal manufactured goods:** refined petroleum products, foods, wood products, stone, clay and glass products. **Agriculture: Chief crops:** wheat, beans, barley, oats, sugar beets, hay. **Livestock** (1991): 1.2 mln. cattle; 20,000 hogs/pigs; 830,000 sheep. **Timber/lumber** (1989): aspen, yellow pine; 302 mln. bd. ft. **Nonfuel Minerals** (1990): $934.3 mln.; mostly Portland cement, crushed stone. **International airports at:** Casper. **Value of construction** (1990): $505.5 mln. **Employment distribution** (1990): 23% trade; 18% services; 9.6% mining. **Per capita income** (1990): $16,398. **Unemployment** (1990): 5.4%. **Tourism** (1989): out-of-state visitors spent $1.5 bln. **State sales tax.** 3%.

Finance. FDIC-insured commercial banks & trust companies (1990): 71. **Deposits:** $3.9 bln. **Savings institutions** (1990): 10. **Assets:** $1.2 bln.

Federal government. No. federal civilian employees (Mar. 1990): 4,824. **Avg. salary:** $29,314. **Notable federal facilities:** Warren AFB.

Energy. Electricity production (1990, mwh, by source): Hydroelectric: 645,000; Mineral: 38.7 mln.

Education. Student-teacher ratio (1989): 14.5. **Avg. salary, public school teachers** (1990-91): $28,988.

State data. Motto: Equal Rights. **Flower:** Indian paintbrush. **Bird:** Meadowlark. **Tree:** Cottonwood. **Song:** Wyoming. **Entered union** July 10, 1890; rank, 44th. **State fair** at: Douglas; late Aug.

History. Francés Francois and Louis Verendrye were the first Europeans, 1743. John Colter, American, was first to traverse Yellowstone Park, 1807-08. Trappers and fur traders followed in the 1820s. Forts Laramie and Bridger became important stops on the pioneer trail to the West Coast. Indian wars followed massacres of army detachments in 1854 and 1866. Population grew after the Union Pacific crossed the state, 1869. Women won the vote, for the first time in the U.S., from the Territorial Legislature, 1869.

Tourist attractions. Yellowstone National Park, 3,472 sq. mi. in the NW corner of Wyoming and the adjoining edges of Montana and Idaho, the oldest U.S. national park, est. 1872, has some 10,000 geysers, hot springs, mud volcanoes, fossil forests, a volcanic glass (obsidian) mountain, the 1,000-ft.-deep canyon and 308-ft.-high waterfall of the Yellowstone River, and a wide variety of animals living free in their natural habitat.

Also, Grand Teton National Park, with mountains 13,000 ft. high; National Elk Refuge, covering 25,000 acres; Devils Tower, a columnar rock of igneous origin 1,280 ft. high; Fort Laramie and surrounding areas of pioneer trails; Buffalo Bill Museum, Cody; Cheyenne Frontier Days Celebration, last full week in July, the state's largest rodeo, and world's largest purse.

Famous Wyomingites include James Bridger, Buffalo Bill Cody, Nellie Tayloe Ross.

Tourist information. Travel Commission, Etchepare Circle, Cheyenne, WY 82002.

Toll-free travel information. 1-800-CALLWYO.

District of Columbia

Area: 69 sq. mi. **Population:** (1990): 606,900. **Motto:** Justitia omnibus, Justice for all. **Flower:** American beauty rose. **Tree:** Scarlet oak. **Bird:** Wood thrush. The city of Washington is coextensive with the District of Columbia.

The District of Columbia is the seat of the federal government of the United States. It lies on the west central edge of Maryland on the Potomac River, opposite Virginia. Its area was originally 100 sq. mi. taken from the sovereignty of Maryland and Virginia. Virginia's portion south of the Potomac was given back to that state in 1846.

The 23d Amendment, ratified in 1961, granted residents the right to vote for president and vice president for the first time and gave them 3 members in the Electoral College. The first such votes were cast in Nov. 1964.

Congress, which has legislative authority over the District under the Constitution, established in 1878 a government of 3 commissioners appointed by the president. The Reorganization Plan of 1967 substituted a single commissioner (also called mayor), assistant, and 9-member City Council. Funds were still appropriated by Congress; residents had no vote in local government, except to elect school board members.

In Sept. 1970, Congress approved legislation giving the District one delegate to the House of Representatives. The delegate could vote in committee but not on the House floor. The first was elected 1971.

In May 1974 voters approved a charter giving them the right to elect their own mayor and a 13-member city council; the first took office Jan. 2, 1975. The district won the right to levy its own taxes but Congress retained power to veto council actions, and approve the city's annual budget.

Proposals for a "federal town" for the deliberations of the Continental Congress were made in 1783, 4 years before the adoption of the Constitution that gave the Confederation a national government. Rivalry between northern and southern delegates over the site appeared in the First Congress, 1789. John Adams, presiding officer of the Senate, cast the deciding vote of that body for Germantown, Pa. In 1790 Congress compromised by making Philadelphia the temporary capital for 10 years. The Virginia members of the House wanted a capital on the eastern bank of the Potomac; they were defeated by the Northerners, while the Southerners defeated the Northern attempt to have the nation assume the war debts of the 13 original states, the Assumption Bill fathered by Alexander Hamilton. Hamilton and Jefferson arranged a compromise: the Virginia men voted for the Assumption Bill, and the Northerners conceded the capital to the Potomac. President Washington chose the site in Oct. 1790 and persuaded landowners to sell their holdings to the government at £25, then about $66, an acre. The capital was named Washington.

Washington appointed Pierre Charles L'Enfant, a French engineer who had come over with Lafayette, to plan the capital on an area not over 10 mi. square. The L'Enfant plan, for streets 100 to 110 feet wide and one avenue 400 feet wide and a mile long, seemed grandiose and foolhardy. But Washington endorsed it. When L'Enfant ordered a wealthy landowner to remove his new manor house because it obstructed a vista, and demolished it when the owner refused, Washington stepped in and dismissed the architect. The official map and design of the city was completed by Benjamin Banneker, a distinguished black architect and astronomer, and Andrew Ellicott.

On Sept. 18, 1793, Pres. Washington laid the cornerstone of the north wing of the Capitol. On June 3, 1800, Pres. John Adams moved to Washington and on June 10, Philadelphia ceased to be the temporary capital. The City of Washington was incorporated in 1802; the District of Columbia was created as a municipal corporation in 1871, embracing Washington, Georgetown, and Washington County.

Outlying U.S. Areas

Commonwealth of Puerto Rico

(Estado Libre Asociado de Puerto Rico)

People. Population (1990): 3,336,000. **Pop. density:** 944.1 per sq. mi. **Urban** (1990): 66.8%. **Racial distribution** (1990): 99.9% Hispanic. **Net migration** (1985): −27,691.

Geography. Total area: 3,435 sq. mi. **Land area:** 3,421 sq. mi. **Location:** island lying between the Atlantic to the N and the Caribbean to the S; it is easternmost of the West Indies group called the Greater Antilles, of which Cuba, Hispaniola, and Jamaica are the larger islands. **Climate:** mild, with a mean temperature of 77°. **Topography:** mountainous throughout three-fourths of its rectangular area, surrounded by a broken coastal plain; highest peak is Cerro de Punta, 4,389 ft. **Capital:** San Juan.

Economy. Principal industries: manufacturing. **Principal manufactured goods:** pharmaceuticals; chemicals; machinery and metals, electric machinery and equipment, petroleum refining, food products, apparel. **Agriculture: Chief crops:** coffee; plantains; bananas; yams; taniers; pineapples; pidgeon peas; peppers; pumpkins; coriander; lettuce; tobacco. **Livestock** (1985): 579,810 cattle; 210,013 pigs; 7.4 mln. poultry. **Nonfuel Minerals** (1987): $111.6 mln., mostly cement. **Commercial fishing** (1984): $7.9 mln. **Chief ports/river shipping:** San Juan, Ponce, Mayaguez, Guayanillá, Guánica, Yabucoa, Aguirre. **Major airports at:** San Juan, Ponce, Mayaguez, Aguadilla. **Value of construction** (1987): $2.5 bln. **Employment distribution:** 24% gvt.; 18% manuf.; 19% trade; 20% serv. **Per capita income** (1985): $4,301. **Unemployment** (1988): 16%. **Tourism** (1988): Out-of-area visitors spent $1.04 bln.

Finance. No. FDIC-insured commercial banks & trust companies (1987): 14. **Deposits:** $9.7 bln. **No. savings institutions** (1987): 10. **Assets:** $6.2 bln.

Federal government. No. federal civilian employees (1985): 9,989. **Notable federal facilities:** U.S. Naval Station at Roosevelt Roads; U.S. Army Salinas Training Area and Ft. Allen; Sabana SECA Communications Center (U.S. Navy); Ft. Buchanan.

Energy Production (1985): Steam and gas: 11,938 mln. kwh; Other: 209 mln. kwh.

Education. No. schools (1985): 1,782 public, 818 private elem. and second.; 69 higher ed. **Avg. salary, public school teachers** (1985): $12,000.

Misc. Data. Motto. Joannes Est Nomen Eius (John is his name). **Flower:** Maga. **Bird:** Reinita. **Tree:** Ceiba. **National anthem:** La Borinqueña.

History: Puerto Rico (or Borinquen, after the original Arawak Indian name Boriquen), was discovered by Columbus, Nov. 19, 1493. Ponce de Leon conquered it for Spain, 1509, and established the first settlement at Caparra, across the bay from San Juan.

Sugar cane was introduced, 1515, and slaves were imported 3 years later. Gold mining petered out, 1570. Spaniards fought off a series of British and Dutch attacks; slavery was abolished, 1873. Under the treaty of Paris, Puerto Rico was ceded to the U.S. after the Spanish-American War, 1898. In 1952 the people voted in favor of Commonwealth status.

The Commonwealth of Puerto Rico is a self-governing part of the U.S. with a primary Hispanic culture. Puerto Ricans are U.S. citizens and about 2.0 million now live on the mainland, although since 1974 there has also been a reverse migration flow.

The current commonwealth political status of Puerto Rico gives the island's citizens virtually the same control over their internal affairs as the fifty states of the U.S. However, they do not vote in national elections, although they do vote in national primary elections.

Puerto Rico is represented in Congress solely by a resident commissioner who has a voice but no vote, except in committees.

No federal income tax is collected from residents on income earned from local sources in Puerto Rico.

Puerto Rico's famous "Operation Bootstrap," begun in the late 1940s, succeeded in changing the island from "The Poorhouse of the Caribbean" to an area with the highest per capita income in Latin America. This pioneering program encouraged manufacturing and the development of the tourist trade by selective tax exemption, low-interest loans, and other incentives. Despite the marked success of Puerto Rico's development efforts over an extended period of time, per capita income in Puerto Rico is low in comparison to that of the U.S. In calendar year 1985, the transfer payments from the U.S. government to individuals and governments in Puerto Rico totalled $3.2 bln., or 22% of the Gross Domestic Product of $14.8 bln.

General tourist attractions: Ponce Museum of Art; forts El Morro and San Cristobal; Old Walled City of San Juan; Arecibo Observatory; Cordillera Central and state parks; El Yunque Rain Forest; San Juan Cathedral; Porta Coeli Chapel and Museum of Religious Art, Interamerican Univ., San Germán; Condado Convention Center; Casa Blanca, Ponce de León family home, Puerto Rican Family Museum of 16th and 17 centuries and the Fine Arts Center in San Juan.

Cultural facilities, festivals, etc.: Festival Casals classical music concerts, mid-June; Puerto Rico Symphony Orchestra at Music Conservatory; Botanical Garden and Museum of Anthropology, Art, and History at the University of Puerto Rico; Institute of Puerto Rican Culture, at the Dominican Convent, and many popular festivals throughout the island.

Famous Puerto Ricans include: José Celso Barbosa, Julia de Burgos, Pablo Casals, Orlando Cepeda, Roberto Clemente, José de Diego, José Feliciano, Luis A. Ferré, José Ferrer, Doña Felisa Rincón de Gautier, Commodore Diego E. Hernández, Rafael Hernández (El Jibarito), Raúl Julia, Luis Muñoz Marín, René Marqués, Luis Palés Matos, Concha Meléndez, Rita Moreno, Adm. Horacio Rivero, Rafael Hernández Colón, Marta Casals Istomier, Miguel Hernándo Agosto.

Chamber of Commerce: 100 Tetuán P.O.Box. S-3789, San Juan, PR 00904; Ponce & South: El Señorial Bldg., Ponce, PR 00731.

Guam

Where America's Day Begins

People. Population (1990): 132,000. **Pop. density:** 631.6 per sq. mi. **Urban** (1980): 39.5%. **Major ethnic groups** (1987): Chamorro 48.8%, Filipino 25.2%, stateside immigrants 20%, remainder Micronesians. Native Guamanians, ethnically called Chamorros, are basically of Indonesian stock, with a mixture of Spanish and Filipino. In addition to the offical language, they speak the native Chamorro.

Geography. Total area: 209 sq. mi. land, 30 mi. long and 4 to 8.5 mi. wide. **Location:** largest and southernmost of the Mariana Islands in the West Pacific, 3,700 mi. W of Hawaii. **Climate:** tropical, with temperatures from 70° to 90°F; avg. annual rainfall, about 70 in. **Topography:** coral-line limestone plateau in the N; southern chain of low volcanic mountains sloping gently to the W, more steeply to coastal cliffs on the E; general elevation, 500 ft.; highest pt., Mt. Lamlam, 1,334 ft. **Capital:** Agana.

Economy. Principal industries: construction, light manufacturing, tourism, banking, defense. **Principal manufactured goods:** textiles, foods. **Agriculture: Chief crops:** cabbages, eggplants, cucumber, long beans, tomatoes, bananas, coconuts, watermelon, yams, canteloupe, papayas, maize, sweet potatoes. **Livestock** (1984): 2,000 cattle; 14,000 hogs/pigs. **Chief ports:** Apra Harbor. **International airports at:** Tamuning. **Value of construction** (1980): $80.60 mln. **Employment distribution** (1987): 61.3% private sector; 38.7% gvt. **Per capita income** (1986): $7,116. **Unemployment** (1987): 3%. **Tourism** (1980): visitors' receipts $117.9 mln.

Finance. Notable industries: insurance, real estate, finance. **No. banks:** 13; **No. savings and loan assns.:** 2.

Federal government. No. federal employees (1980): 6,600. **Notable federal facilities:** Anderson AFB; naval, air and port bases.

Education. Public elem. and second. school enrollment (1987): 25,676; **Percent of enrollment:** 91.2; **Expenditures per pupil:** $3,344.

Misc. Data. Flower: Puti Tai Nobio (Bougainvillea). **Bird:** Toto (Fruit dove). **Tree:** Ifit (Intsiabijuga). **Song:** Stand Ye Guamians.

History. Magellan arrived in the Marianas Mar. 6, 1521. They were colonized in 1668 by Spanish missionaries who named them the Mariana Islands in honor of Maria Anna, queen of Spain. When Spain ceded Guam to the U.S., it sold the other Marianas to Germany. Japan obtained a League of Nations mandate over the German islands in 1919; in Dec. 1941 it seized Guam; the island was retaken by the U.S. in July 1944.

Guam is a self-governing organized unincorporated U.S. territory. Under the jurisdiction of the Interior Department, it is administered under the Organic Act of 1950, which provides for a governor and a 21-member unicameral legislature, elected biennially by the residents who are American citizens but do not vote for president.

Beginning in Nov., 1970, Guamanians elected their own governor, previously appointed by the U.S. president. He took office in Jan. 1971. In 1972 a U.S. law gave Guam one delegate to the U.S. House of Representatives; the delegate may vote in committee but not on the House floor.

General tourist attractions. annual mid-Aug. Merizo Water Festival; Tarzan Falls; beaches; water sports, duty-free port shopping.

Virgin Islands

St. John, St. Croix, St. Thomas

People. Population (1990): 101,809 (50,139, St. Croix; 48,166, St. Thomas; 3,504, St. John). **Pop. density:** 748.60 per sq. mi. **Urban** (1980): 39%. **Racial distribution:** (1980) 15% White; 85% Black. **Major ethnic groups:** West Indian, French, Hispanic.

Geography. Total area: 133 sq. mi.; **Land area:** 136 sq. mi. **Location:** 3 larger and 50 smaller islands and cays in the S and W of the V.I. group (British V.I. colony to the N and E) which is situated 70 mi. E of Puerto Rico, located W of the Anegada Passage, a major channel connecting the Atlantic O. and the Caribbean Sea. **Climate:** subtropical; the sun tempered by gentle trade winds; humidity is low; average temperature, 78° F. **Topography:** St. Thomas is mainly a ridge of hills running E and W, and has little tillable land; St. Croix rises abruptly in the N but slopes to the S to flatlands and lagoons; St. John has steep, lofty hills and valleys with little level tillable land. **Capital:** Charlotte Amalie, St. Thomas.

Economy. Principal industries: tourism, rum, alumina prod., petroleum refining, watch industry, textiles, electronics. **Principal manufactured goods:** rum, textiles, pharmaceuticals, perfumes. **Gross Domestic Product** (1987): $1.246 bln. **Agriculture: Chief crops:** truck garden produce. **Minerals:** sand, gravel. **Chief ports:** Cruz Bay, St. John; Frederiksted and Christiansted, St. Croix; Charlotte Amalie, St. Thomas. **International airports on:** St. Thomas, St. Croix. **Value of construction** (1987): $167.0 mln. **Per capita income** (1987): $7,465. **Unemployment** (1989): 4.4%. **Tourism** (1988): $662.8. **No. banks** (1990): 8.

Education (1987): **No. public schools:** 34 elem. and second.; 1 college. **Avg. starting salary, public school teachers:** $18,001.

Misc. data. Flower: Yellow elder or yellow trumpet, local designation Ginger Thomas. **Bird:** Yellow breast. **Song:** Virgin Islands March.

History. The islands were discovered by Columbus in 1493. Spanish forces, 1555, defeated the Caribes and claimed the territory; by 1596 the native population was annihilated. First permanent settlement in the U.S. territory, 1672, by the Danes; U.S. purchased the islands, 1917, for defense purposes.

The Virgin Islands has a republican form of government, headed by a governor and lieut. governor elected, since 1970, by popular vote for 4-year terms. There is a 15-member unicameral legislature, elected by popular vote. Residents of the V.I. have been U.S. citizens since 1927. Since 1973 they have elected a delegate to the U.S. House of Representatives, who may vote in committee but not in the House.

General tourist attractions. Magens Bay, St. Thomas; duty-free shopping; Virgin Islands National Park, 14,488 acres on St. John of lush growth, beaches, Indian relics, and evidence of colonial Danes.

Tourist information. Dept. of Economic Development & Agriculture, St. Thomas, P.O. Box 6400, St. Thomas, VI 00801; St. Croix, P.O. Box 4535, Christiansted, St. Croix 00820.

American Samoa

Capital: Pago Pago, Island of Tutuila. **Area:** 77 sq. mi. **Population:** (1990) 46,773. **Motto:** Samoa Muamua le Atua (In Samoa, God Is First). **Song:** Amerika Samoa. **Flower:** Paogo (Ula-fala). **Plant:** Ava.

Blessed with spectacular scenery and delightful South Seas climate, American Samoa is the most southerly of all lands under U. S. sovereignty. It is an unincorporated territory consisting of 6 small islands of the Samoan group: **Tutuila, Aunu'u, Manu'a Group (Ta'u, Olosega and Ofu),** and **Rose.** Also administered as part of American Samoa is **Swain's Island,** 210 mi. to the NW, acquired by the U.S. in 1925. The islands are 2,300 mi. SW of Honolulu.

American Samoa became U. S. territory in Feb., 1900 by a treaty with the United Kingdom and Germany in 1899. The islands were ceded by local chiefs in April, 1900 and July, 1904, and became U.S territories. The U.S. acquired commercial rights pursuant to the convention 1899, a tripartite agreement among Great Britain, Germany, and the U.S.

Samoa (Western), comprising the larger islands of the Samoan group, was a New Zealand mandate and UN Trusteeship until it became an independent nation Jan. 1, 1962 *(see Index.)*

Tutuila and Annu'u have an area of 53 sq. mi. Ta'u has an area of 17 sq. mi., and the islets of Ofu and Olosega, 5 sq. mi. with a population of a few thousand. Swain's Island has nearly 2 sq. mi. and a population of about 100.

About 70% of the land is bush. Chief products and exports are fish products, copra, and handicrafts. Taro, bread-fruit, yams, coconuts, pineapples, oranges, and bananas are also produced.

From 1900-1951, American Samoa was under the jurisdiction of the U.S. Navy. Since 1951, it has been under the Interior Dept. On Jan. 3, 1978, the first popularly elected Samoan governor and lieutenant governor were inaugurated. Previously, the governor was appointed by the Secretary of the Interior. American Samoa has a bicameral legislature and elects its own member of Congress, who can introduce legislation and vote in committee, but not in the House.

The American Samoans are of Polynesian origin. They are nationals of the U.S.; 20,000 live in Hawaii, 65,000 in California and Washington.

Minor Caribbean Islands

Quita Sueño Bank, Roncador and Serrana, lie in the Caribbean between Nicaragua and Jamaica. They are uninhabited. U.S. claim to the islands was relinquished in a treaty with Colombia, which entered into force on Sept. 17, 1981.

Navassa lies between Jamaica and Haiti, covers about 2 sq. mi., is reserved by the U.S. for a lighthouse and is uninhabited. It is administered by the U.S. Coast Guard.

Wake, Midway, Other Islands

Wake Island, and its sister islands, **Wilkes** and **Peale,** lie in the Pacific Ocean on the direct route from Hawaii to Hong Kong, about 2,300 mi. W of Hawaii and 1,290 mi. E of Guam. The group is 4.5 mi. long, 1.5 mi. wide, and totals less than 3 sq. mi.

The U.S. flag was hoisted over Wake Island, July 4, 1898, formal possession taken Jan. 17, 1899; Wake has been administered by the U.S. Air Force since 1972. The population consists of a number of USAF personnel.

The **Midway Islands,** acquired in 1867, consist of 2, **Sand** and **Eastern,** in the North Pacific 1,150 mi. NW of Hawaii, with area of about 3 sq. mi., administered by the U.S. Navy. There is no indigenous population; it is currently populated with several U.S. military personnel.

Johnston Atoll, SW of Hawaii, area 1 sq. mi. is operated by The Defense Nuclear Agency, and **Kingman Reef,** S of Hawaii, is under Navy control.

Howland, Jarvis, and **Baker** Islands, 1,500-1,650 miles southwest of the Hawaiian group, uninhabited since World War II, are under the Interior Dept.

Palmyra is an atoll about 1,000 miles south of Hawaii, 4 sq. mi. Privately owned, it is under the Interior Dept.

Islands Under Trusteeship

The Trust Territory of the Pacific Islands was established in 1947, as the only strategic trusteeship of the 11 trusteeships established by the U.N. The territory has a heterogeneous population of about 140,000 people scattered among more than 2,100 islands and atolls in 3 major archipelagos: the Carolines, the Marshalls, and the Marianas. The entire geographic area is sometimes referred to as "Micronesia," meaning "little islands." The area of the Trust Territory covered some 3 million sq. miles of the Pacific Ocean, slightly larger than the continental U.S. However, its islands constituted a land area of only 715.8 sq. miles—half the size of Rhode Island. It formerly contained 4 political jurisdictions: The Commonwealth of the Northern Mariana Islands (CNMI), the Federated States of Micronesia (FSM), the Republic of the Marshall Islands (RMI), and the Republic of Palau (RP). As of Oct. 21, 1986, the RMI entered into free association with the U.S., as did the FSM effective Nov. 3, 1986. The CNMI became a commonwealth of the U.S., also effective Nov. 3. Only the RP remains under trusteeship.

Commonwealth of the Northern Mariana Islands

Located in the perpetually warm climes between Guam and the Tropic of Cancer, the 16 islands of the Northern Marianas form a 300-mile-long archipelago, comprising a total land area of 183.5 sq. miles. The native population, 1990, is 43,345, and is concentrated on the 3 largest of the 6 inhabited islands: **Saipan**, the seat of government and commerce (38,896), **Rota** (2,295), and **Tinian** (2,118).

The people of the Northern Marianas are predominantly of Chamorro cultural extraction, although numbers of Carolinians and immigrants from other areas of E. Asia and Micronesia have also settled in the islands. Pursuant to the Covenant of 1975, which established the Northern Marianas as a commonwealth in political union with the U.S., most natives and many domiciliaries of these islands achieved U.S. citizenship on Nov. 13, 1986, when the U.S. terminated its administration of the U.N. trusteeship as it affected the Northern Marianas. From July 18, 1947, the U.S. had administered the Northern Marianas under a trusteeship agreement with the U.N. Security Council. English is among the several languages commonly spoken.

The Northern Mariana Islands has been self-governing since 1978, when both a constitution drafted and adopted by the people became effective, and a bicameral legislature with offices of governor and lieutenant governor was inaugurated. Commercial activity has increased steadily in the last few years, with 3,537 business licenses issued in the CNM, mostly in tourism, construction, and light industry. In 1989, more than 300,000 tourists visited, an increase of 7.5% over previous years. An agreement with the U.S. for 1986-1992 entitles the Northern Marianna Islands to $228 million for capital development, government operations and special programs.

Federated States of Micronesia

The Federated States of Micronesia extends across the 1,800-mile-long Caroline Island archipelago. The 4 states of the FSM are Pohnpei, Kosrae, Truk, and Yap. Each state consists of several islands, except for Kosrae, a single island. The capital of the FSM is Pohnpei. Populations are: Pohnpei 52,000; Truk, 31,000; Kosrae, 16,500; Yap, 12,000. Pohnpei is 2,900 miles SW of Honolulu and 1,000 miles SE of Guam. The islands vary geologically from high, mountainous islands to low, coral atolls. The FSM lies between the equator and 9 degrees N and 138 degrees and 168 degrees E. Average year-round temperature is 80 degrees. Pohnpei gets the highest annual rainfall, averaging up to 250 inches.

The cultures of the FSM are very diverse. Several languages, each with dialects, are spoken throughout: Yapese, Ulithian, Woleaian, Ponapean, Nukuoran, Kapingamarangi, Trukese, and Kosraean. Each state has a constitution and government, headed by a governor. The status of free association recognizes that the FSM is a sovereign-self-governing state, with the U.S. responsible for defense and also extending agreed-upon amounts of economic and service assistance. Each of the state's constitutions recognizes a role for traditional leaders and customs.

Republic of the Marshall Islands

The Republic of the Marshall Islands consists of 2 island/atoll chains, the Ratak (sunrise) Chain, and the Ralik (sunset) Chain, totalling 31 atolls. Each atoll is a cluster of several small islands circling a lagoon. Total land area is 70 sq. miles. The capital is **Majuro**, 2,000 miles SW of Honolulu and 1,300 SE of Guam. Population is 43,000, 20,000 in Majuro. Average year-round temperature is 81 degrees.

Marshallese culture revolves around the complex clan system. Land is owned by each clan and passed down over the generations. In the late 1970's, the U.S. embarked upon an ambitious Capital Improvement Program, with a goal of building a major infrastructure (airport, dock, roads, water-power-sewer system) in Majuro. Funding was completed in 1985.

The Marshall Islands' Constitution includes both American and British concepts. The executive branch is the Nitijela (parliament) and is consulted by a Council of Iroij (local chiefs). The Nitijela elects the President from among its own members. The status of free association recognizes that the Marshall Islands is a sovereign, self-governing state, with the U.S. responsible for defense, and for extending agreed-upon amounts of economic and service assistance. A subsidiary agreement allows the U.S. continued use of Kwajalein Missile Range for 30 years. Another subsidiary agreement provides for settlement of all claims arising out of the nuclear testing programs conducted by the U.S. at Bikini and Enewetak Atolls from 1946 to 1958.

Republic of Palau

Palau consists of more than 200 islands in the Caroline chain, of which 8 are permanently inhabited. The capital of Palau, Koror, lies 3,997 miles SW of Honolulu and 813 miles S of Guam. Population of Palau is 15,122 (1990), 10,501 (1990) in Koror. Average year-round temperature is 80 degrees, average annual rainfall 150 inches.

Until 1979, a High Commissioner appointed by the U.S. president, himself appointed a district administrator for Palau to oversee programs and administration there. In support of the evolving political status, the U.S. recognized the Constitution of Palau and the establishment of the Government of Palau. The Constitution became effective in 1980. The President and Vice President are elected by popular vote. A Council of Chiefs advises the President on matters concerning traditional law and custom. Palau has a bicameral national legislature composed of a House of Delegates and a Senate.

Washington, Capital of the U.S.

Arlington National Cemetery

Arlington National Cemetery, on the former Custis estate in Virginia, is the site of the **Tomb of the Unknown Soldier** and the final resting place of John Fitzgerald Kennedy, president of the United States, who was buried there Nov. 25, 1963. A torch burns day and night over his grave. The remains of his brother Sen. Robert F. Kennedy (N.Y.) were interred on June 8, 1968, in an area adjacent. Many other famous Americans are also buried at Arlington, as well as 175,000 American soldiers from every major war.

U.S. Marine Corps War Memorial (Iwo Jima)

North of the National Cemetery, approximately 350 yards, stands the bronze statue of the raising of the United States flag on Mt. Suribachi during WWII, executed by Felix de Weldon from the photograph by Joe Rosenthal, and presented to the nation by members and friends of the U.S. Marine Corps.

Vietnam War Memorial

Dedicated on November 13, 1982, it is a symbol of the U.S.' honor and recognition of the men and women who served in the armed forces in the Vietnam War. It is inscribed with the names of the more than 58,000 who gave their lives or remain missing.

The Capitol

The United States Capitol was originally designed by Dr. William Thornton, an amateur architect, who submitted a plan in the spring of 1793 that won him $500 and a city lot.

The south, or House wing, was completed in 1807 under the direction of Benjamin H. Latrobe.

The present Senate and House wings and the iron dome were designed and constructed by Thomas U. Walter, the 4th architect of the Capitol, between 1851-1863.

The present cast iron dome at its greatest exterior measures 135 ft. 5 in., and it is topped by the bronze Statue of Freedom that stands 19½ ft. and weighs 14,985 pounds. On its base are the words "E Pluribus Unum" (Out of Many One).

The Capitol is normally open from 9 a.m. to 4:30 p.m. Tours through the Capitol, including the House and Senate galleries, are conducted from 9 a.m. to 4 p.m. without charge.

Folger Shakespeare Library

The Folger Shakespeare Library on Capitol Hill, Washington, D. C., is a research institution devoted to the advancement of learning in the background of Anglo-American civilization in the 16th and 17th centuries, and in most aspects of the continental Renaissance. It has the largest collection of Shakespeareana in the world, with 79 copies of the First Folio.

Library of Congress

Established by and for Congress in 1800, the Library of Congress has extended its services over the years to other government agencies and other libraries, to scholars, and to the general public, and it now serves as the national library. It contains over 80 million items in 470 languages.

The library's exhibit halls are open to the public. Guided tours are given every hour from 9 a.m. through 4 p.m. Monday through Friday.

Thomas Jefferson Memorial

Dedicated in 1943, The Thomas Jefferson Memorial stands on the south shore of the Tidal Basin in West Potomac park. It is a circular stone structure, with Vermont marble on the exterior and Georgia white marble inside and combines architectural elements of the dome of the Pantheon in Rome and the rotunda designed by Jefferson for the University of Virginia.

The memorial is open daily from 8 a.m. to midnight. An elevator and curb ramps for the handicapped are in service.

Lincoln Memorial

The Lincoln Memorial in West Potomac Park, on the axis of the Capitol and the Washington Monument, consists of a large marble hall enclosing a heroic statue of Abraham Lincoln in meditation sitting on a large armchair. It was dedicated on Memorial Day, May 30, 1922. The Memorial was designed by Henry Bacon. The statue was made by Daniel Chester French and sculpted by the Piccirilli family. Murals and ornamentation on the bronze ceiling beams are by Jules Guerin.

The memorial is open daily from 8 a.m. to midnight. An elevator for the handicapped is in service.

John F. Kennedy Center

John F. Kennedy Center for the Performing Arts, designated by Congress as the National Cultural Center and the official memorial in Washington to President Kennedy, opened September 8, 1971. Tours are available daily between 10:00 a.m. and 1:00 p.m.

Mount Vernon

Mount Vernon on the south bank of the Potomac R., 16 miles below Washington, D. C., is part of a large tract of land in northern Virginia.

The present house is an enlargement of one apparently built on the site of an earlier one by Augustine Washington, who lived there 1735-1738. His son Lawrence came there in 1743, when he renamed the plantation Mount Vernon in honor of Admiral Vernon under whom he had served in the West Indies. Lawrence Washington died in 1752 and was succeeded as proprietor of Mount Vernon by his half-brother, George Washington.

National Archives

The Declaration of Independence, the Constitution of the United States, and the Bill of Rights are on permanent display in the National Archives Exhibition Hall. They are sealed in glass-and-bronze cases. The National Archives also holds the permanently valuable federal records of the United States government.

National Gallery of Art

The National Gallery of Art, situated in an area bounded by Constitution Avenue and the Mall, between Third and Seventh Streets, was established by Joint Resolution of Congress Mar. 24, 1937, and opened Mar. 17, 1941.

Normally open daily from 10 a.m. to 5 p.m.; noon to 9 p.m. Sunday. Summer, 10 a.m. to 9 p.m., noon to 9 p.m. on Sunday.

The Pentagon

The Pentagon, headquarters of the Department of Defense, is one of the world's largest office buildings. Situated in Arlington, Va., it houses more than 23,000 employees in offices that occupy 3,707,745 square feet.

Tours are available Monday through Friday (excluding federal holidays), from 9 a.m. to 3:30 p.m.

Smithsonian Institution

The Smithsonian Institution, established in 1846, the world's largest museum complex, is comprised of 14 museums and the National Zoo. It holds some 100 million artifacts and specimens in its trust "for the increase and diffusion of knowledge among men." Nine museums are located on the National Mall between the Washington Monument and the Capitol; 4 other museums and the zoo are elsewhere in Washington, and the Cooper-Hewitt Museum in New York City. The National Air and Space Museum, National Museum of Natural History, and the National Portrait Gallery are some of the more popular museums. They are open daily, except Dec. 25, from 10 a.m. to 5:30 p.m. unless otherwise noted.

Washington Monument

The Washington Monument, dedicated in 1885, is a tapering shaft or obelisk of white marble, 555 ft., 5-⅛ inches in height and 55 ft., 1-½ inches square at base. Eight small windows, 2 on each side, are located at the 500-ft. level, where points of interest are indicated.

Open daily except Dec. 25, 9 a.m. to 5 p.m., 8 a.m. to 12 p.m. in summer.

The White House

The White House, the president's residence, stands on 18 acres on the south side of Pennsylvania Avenue, between the Treasury and the Executive Office Building.

The walls are of sandstone, quarried at Aquia Creek, Va. The exterior walls were painted, causing the building to be termed the "White House." On Aug. 24, 1814, during Madison's administration, the house was burned by the British. James Hoban rebuilt it by Oct. 1817.

The White House is normally open from 10 a.m. to 12 noon, Tuesday through Saturday. Only the public rooms on the ground floor and state floor may be visited.

ENVIRONMENT
Environmental Quality Index
Source: Feb.-Mar. 1991 issue of *National Wildlife* magazine

In 1991, *National Wildlife* magazine published the twenty-third in its series of annual reports on the environment. According to the report, 1990 was a year in which a lot of talk about **conservation and environmental responsibility** amounted to a disappointingly small amount of action. Important legislation was initiated on the protection of wetlands, revisions of the Clean Air Act, and on other issues, but by the time these bills were passed into law they had been significantly weakened by **concessions and lowered standards.**

Wildlife: U.S. wildlife continued to suffer from the pressures of development and deforestation in 1990. The northern spotted owl, considered by environmentalists to be a barometer of the irreplaceable old-growth woodlands of the Pacific Northwest, was officially listed as an endangered species. This status protected both the owls and their habitat, but after only four days the owl's status was rewritten to allow more logging of the old-growth forests. A new report by the World Resources Institute predicted, if trends continue, one-fourth of all plant and animal species existing in the mid-1980s would be extinct in 25 years. As if to confirm this worst case scenario, Congress granted permission for the builders of an observatory on Mount Graham in southeast Arizona to override the Endangered Species Act and begin construction, possibly signaling the end of the endangered Mount Graham red squirrel. In the coastal waters off New England, commercial fisheries stocks continued to decline to the lowest levels on record. North America's duck population also remained among the smallest ever, underlining the importance of remaining wetlands.

Air: The main cause of air pollution continued to be the automobile. Although cleaner and more efficient than in 1970, the nation's fleet of cars was now significantly larger. The American Lung Association reported that air pollution from motor vehicles was responsible for at least $40 billion in annual health care expenditure in the U.S. At the annual summit of the leaders of the seven most industrialized nations, held in Houston in 1990, the U.S. refused to take part in agreements to limit the so-called greenhouse gases, contending that the agreements ignored "growth needs." On the positive side, 1990 finally saw the passage into law of a bill that revised the Clean Air Act and contained the first regulations of emissions linked to acid rain, and the first tightening of tail-pipe emission standards in 20 years. Further, the EPA made a deal with major companies in which the firms agreed to cut emission of cancer-causing substances at 40 chemical plants in the next two years.

Water: The Environmental Protection Agency announced in 1990 that its new top priority would be the cleanup of the Great Lakes, which continued to be plagued with chemical and oil contamination, despite significant improvements in the quality of municipal and industrial sewage. The chemical contamination, including PCBs, DDT, and dioxin, had been linked to reproductive problems in bald eagles and trout of the region, and had prompted concern for its possible effects on the development of children. Despite the increased attention, funding for Great Lakes cleanup faced proposed budget cuts. The National Wildlife Federation sued the EPA for easing rules requiring states to abide by the Safe Drinking Water Act, and both a Centers for Disease Control study and a General Accounting Office report supported fears about the quality of U.S. drinking water. However, after 10 years of study, the National Acid Precipitation Assessment Program's final report for Congress was less bleak than expected: only 4 percent of U.S. lakes were acidified to the point where little could live; another 5 percent, acidic enough to threaten certain species. Concern grew in the western U.S. over diminishing underground water supplies.

Forests: Because no laws protect endangered forests, conservationists have had to focus their efforts on the endangered species that depend on these habitats. In the national forests of the Southeast, millions of acres of federal forestland were put off-limits from clear-cutting in an attempt to protect the fragile populations of red-cockaded woodpeckers. A National Research Council study accused the Forest Service of concentrating on tree production, when it should be concerned with the health of the environment. The Forest Service announced that it would do as much as possible to implement the report's recommendations, including taking "a much larger view of what a forest is ... a refuge of biological diversity and an indicator of the health of the planet." The Forest Service had already unveiled a new master plan, calling for a substantial reduction of logging in national forests from the current annual cut of 12.2 billion board feet to 10.8 billion board feet by 1995. But private sector woodlands, 80 percent of the nation's annual timber harvest, were increasingly threatened by land developers.

Energy: America's growing dependence on foreign oil, caused by declining domestic production and increased consumption, was made more obvious by the events in the oil rich Persian Gulf. Within days of Iraq's invasion of Kuwait, the price of crude oil doubled and gasoline prices rose by 20 percent. The impact of this latest oil shock was eased somewhat by the 590-million barrel U.S. strategic oil reserve. The reserve was never tapped, but its presence helped to prevent panic buying. These events also had serious implications for U.S. energy policy, but by year's end the government still had not come up with a comprehensive national energy policy. Dispute continued over possibly exploring Alaska's fragile Arctic National Refuge for oil. On the plus side, the President declared a moratorium on offshore drilling near the West Coast, Florida and in the Georges Bank area of the North Atlantic. But Administration opposition helped kill a bill calling for increased fuel efficiency in cars sold in the U.S. The nation's largest energy reserve, better conservation, remained largely untapped.

Soil: According to the World Watch Institute in Washington D.C., since 1985 America's farmers have reduced topsoil erosion by more than one-third, down to an annual loss of about 1 billion tons. The improvement was due largely to programs initiated by the 1985 federal Farm Bill, which was revised in 1990. The new bill contained no major changes in agricultural support programs, but did include some new programs for environmental protection, including forest and wetland protection and pesticide control. In 1990, the EPA found pesticide traces in the groundwater supplies of 26 states, and many insect pests were found increasingly resistant to chemical pesticides. Despite some 430 million pounds of pesticides applied yearly to U.S. crops—a ten-fold increase since WWII—crop damage seemed to have increased. But now a 40-year boom appeared to be over for the producers of chemical pesticides and fertilizers. At mid-1990, fertilizer prices were down 10 percent, as per-acre use of chemicals continued to decline. The new farm bill also included a ban on exporting farm chemicals illegal in the U.S.

Municipal Solid Waste Generation

Source: Environmental Protection Agency, 1990; figures from 1988, in millions of tons

Metals 15.3

Glass 12.5

Plastics 14.4

Rubber, Leather, Textile, Wood, Other 20.8

Yard Wastes 31.6

Food Wastes 13.2

Paper 71.8

TOTAL WEIGHT = 179.6 million tons

Municipal Solid Waste Generation 1960-2010

Source: Environmental Protection Agency

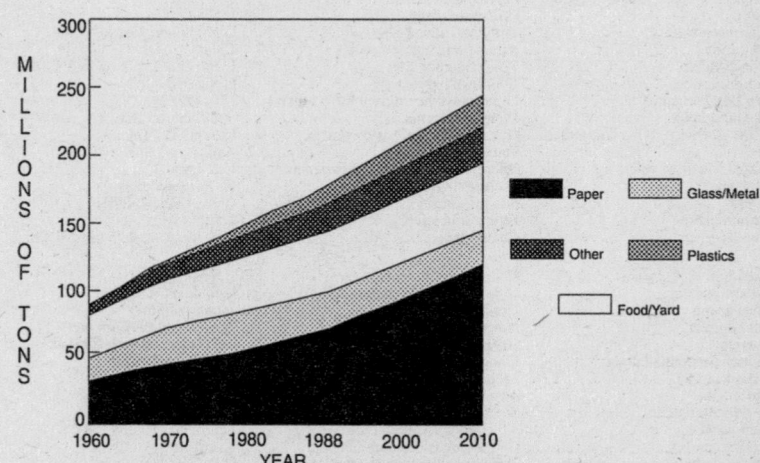

MILLIONS OF TONS

YEAR

Paper   Glass/Metal

Other   Plastics

Food/Yard

Hazardous Waste Sites

Source: Environmental Protection Agency, Natl. Priorities List Fact Book, Feb. 1991

State/Territory	Final Non-Fed.	Fed.	Total	State/Territory	Final Non-Fed.	Fed.	Total
New Jersey	103	6	109				
Pennsylvania	91	4	95	Florida	47	4	51
California	68	20	88	Washington	31	14	45
New York	79	4	83	Minnesota	40	2	42
Michigan	77	0	77	Wisconsin	39	0	39

(continued)

State/Territory	Final Non-Fed.	Fed.	Total	State/Territory	Final Non-Fed.	Fed.	Total
Illinois	32	4	36	Arizona	7	3	10
Indiana	33	0	33	Arkansas	10	0	10
Ohio	30	3	33	Maryland	8	2	10
Texas	25	3	28	New Mexico	8	2	10
Massachusetts	22	3	25	Oklahoma	9	1	10
South Carolina	22	1	23	Idaho	7	2	9
Missouri	19	3	22	Maine	7	2	9
North Carolina	21	1	22	Puerto Rico	8	1	9
Delaware	19	1	20	Montana	8	0	8
Iowa	19	1	20	Oregon	7	1	8
Virginia	19	1	20	Vermont	8	0	8
Kentucky	17	0	17	Alaska	2	4	6
Colorado	13	3	16	Nebraska	5	1	6
New Hampshire	15	1	16	West Virginia	5	0	5
Connecticut	14	1	15	South Dakota	2	1	3
Tennessee	12	2	14	Wyoming	2	1	3
Georgia	11	2	13	Mississippi	2	0	2
Alabama	10	2	12	North Dakota	2	0	2
Kansas	10	1	11	Guam	1	0	1
Louisiana	10	1	11	Hawaii	0	1	1
Rhode Island	9	2	11	Nevada	1	0	1
Utah	7	4	11	**Total**	**1073**	**116**	**1189**

Some Endangered Species

Source: Fish and Wildlife Service, U.S. Dept. of Interior; as of April 15, 1990

Common name	Scientific name	Range
Mammals		
Asian wild ass	Equus hemianus	Southwestern & Central Asia
Bobcat	Felis rufus escuinapae	Central Mexico
Ozark big-eared bat	Plecotus townsendii ingens	U.S. (Mo., Okla., Ariz.)
Brown or grizzly bear	Ursus arctos horribilis	U.S. (48 conterminous states)
Cheetah	Acinonyx jubatus	Africa to India
Eastern cougar	Felis concolor cougar	Eastern N.A.
Columbian white-tailed deer	Odocoileus virginianus leucurus	U.S. (Wash., Ore.)
Chinese river dolphin	Lipotes vexillifer	China
Asian elephant	Elephas maximas	Southcentral, Southeast Asia
San Joaquin kit fox	Vulpes macrotis mutica	U.S. (Cal.)
Gorilla	Gorilla gorilla	Central & W. Africa
Leopard	Panthera pardus	Africa, Asia
Asiatic lion	Panthera leo persica	Turkey to India
Howler monkey	Alouatta pigra	Mexico to S. America
Southeastern beach mouse	Peromyscus polionotus phasma	U.S. (Fla.)
Ocelot	Felis pardalis	U.S. (Tex., Ariz.)
Southern sea otter	Enhydra lutris hereis	U.S. (Wash., Ore., Cal.)
Giant panda	Ailuropoda melanoleuca	China
Florida panther	Felis concolor coryi	U.S. (La., Ark. east to S.C., Fla.)
Utah prairie dog	Cynomys parvidens	U.S. (Ut.)
Morro Bay kangaroo rat	Dipodomys heermanni morroensis	U.S. (Cal.)
Black rhinoceros	Diceros bicornis	Sub-Saharan Africa
Carolina northern flying squirrel	Glaucomys sabrinus coloratus	U.S. (N.C., Tenn.)
Tiger	Panthera tigris	Asia
Hualapai Mexican vole	Microtus mexicanus hualpaiensis	U.S. (Ariz.)
Gray whale	Eschrichtius robustus	N. Pacific Ocean
Wild yak	Bos grunniens	China (Tibet), India
Mountain zebra	Equus zebra zebra	South Africa
Red wolf	Canis rufus	U.S. (Southeast to central Tex.)
Birds		
Masked bobwhite (quail)	Colinus virginianus ridgwayi	U.S. (Ariz.)
California condor	Gymnogyps californianus	U.S. (Ore., Cal.)
Hooded crane	Grus monacha	Japan, USSR
Eskimo curlew	Numenius borealis	Alaska and N. Canada
Bald eagle	Haliaeetus leucocephalus	U.S. (most states), Canada
American peregrine falcon	Falco peregrinus anatum	Canada to Mexico
Hawaiian hawk	Buteo solitarius	U.S. (Hi.)
Indigo macaw	Anodorhynchus leari	Brazil
West African ostrich	Struthio camelus spatzi	Spanish Sahara
Golden parakeet	Aratinga guarouba	Brazil
Australian parrot	Geopsittacus occidentalis	Australia
Attwater's greater prairie-chicken	Tympanuchus cupido attwateri	U.S. (Tex.)
Bachman's warbler (wood)	Vermivora bachmanii	U.S. (Southeast), Cuba
Kirtland's warbler (wood)	Dendroica kirtlandii	U.S., Canada, Bahama Is.
Ivory-billed woodpecker	Campephilus principalis	U.S. (Southcentral and Southeast), Cuba
Reptiles		
American alligator	Alligator mississippiensis	U.S (Southeastern)
American crocodile	Crocodylus acutus	U.S. (Fla.)
Atlantic salt marsh snake	Nerodia fasciatia taeniata	U.S. (Fla.)
Plymouth red-bellied turtle	Pseudemys rubiventris bangsi	U.S. (Mass.)
Fishes		
Yaqui catfish	Ictalupus pricei	U.S. (Ariz.)
Bonytail chub	Gila elegans	U.S. (Ariz., Cal., Col., Nev., Ut., Wyo.)
Gila trout	Salmo gilae	U.S. (Ariz., N.M.)

Endangered and Threatened Species and Recovery Plans

Source: Fish and Wildlife Service, U.S. Dept. of Interior, July, 1991.

Group	Endangered U.S. only	Endangered U.S. & foreign	Foreign only	Threatened U.S. only	Threatened U.S. & foreign	Foreign only	Listed species total	Species with plans
Mammals	36	19	249	5	3	22	334	31
Birds	57	16	153	7	5	0	238	69
Reptiles	8	8	58	14	4	14	106	25
Amphibians	6	0	8	4	1	0	19	6
Fishes	51	2	11	27	6	0	97	49
Snails	4	0	1	6	0	0	11	7
Clams	39	0	2	2	0	0	43	30
Crustaceans	8	0	0	2	0	0	10	5
Insects	12	1	1	9	0	0	23	12
Arachnids	3	0	0	0	0	0	3	0
Subtotal	224	46	483	76	19	36	884	234
Plants	184	6	1	51	9	2	253	127
Total	408	52	484	127	28	38	1137	361

	U.S. Endangered	U.S. Threatened	Endangered & Threatened U.S.	Endangered & Threatened Foreign	Total
Animals	270	95	365	519	884
Plants	190	60	250	3	253
Totals	460	155	615	522	1137

Note: Separate populations of a species, listed both as Endangered and Threatened, are tallied twice. Those 10 species are: chimpanzee, grizzly bear (US=T & Mex.=E), leopard, gray wolf, bald eagle, piping plover, roseate tern, Nile crocodile, green sea turtle, and olive ridley sea turtle. In addition, there are 9 species of lemurs; 9 gibbons; 2 each of musk deer, sifakas, and uakaris; and 29-41 species of Oahu tree snails; these listings are each counted as one species.

Approved recovery plans	287
Species/populations in above plans	373
Listed species covered by 1 or more plans	361
Percentage of U.S. listed species covered by 1 or more plans	58.7%

Gestation, Longevity, and Incubation of Animals

Longevity figures were supplied by Ronald T. Reuther. They refer to animals in captivity; the potential life span of animals is rarely attained in nature. Maximum longevity figures are from the Biology Data Book, 1972. Figures on gestation and incubation are averages based on estimates by leading authorities.

Animal	Gestation (day)	Average longevity (years)	Maximum longevity (yrs., mos.)	Animal	Gestation (day)	Average longevity (years)	Maximum longevity (yrs., mos.)
Ass	365	12	35-10	Leopard	98	12	19-4
Baboon	187	20	35-7	Lion	100	15	25-1
Bear: Black	219	18	36-10	Monkey (rhesus)	164	15	—
Grizzly	225	25	—	Moose	240	12	—
Polar	240	20	34-8	Mouse (meadow)	21	3	—
Beaver	122	5	20-6	Mouse (dom. white)	19	3	3-6
Buffalo (American)	278	15	—	Opossum (American)	14-17	1	—
Bactrian camel	406	12	29-5	Pig (domestic)	112	10	27
Cat (domestic)	63	12	28	Puma	90	12	19
Chimpanzee	231	20	44-6	Rabbit (domestic)	31	5	13
Chipmunk	31	6	8	Rhinoceros (black)	450	15	—
Cow	284	15	30	Rhinoceros (white)	—	20	—
Deer (white-tailed)	201	8	17-6	Sea lion (California)	350	12	28
Dog (domestic)	61	12	20	Sheep (domestic)	154	12	20
Elephant (African)	—	35	60	Squirrel (gray)	44	10	—
Elephant (Asian)	645	40	70	Tiger	105	16	26-3
Elk	250	15	26-6	Wolf (maned)	63	5	—
Fox (red)	52	7	14	Zebra (Grant's)	365	15	—
Giraffe	425	10	33-7				
Goat (domestic)	151	8	18	Incubation time (days)			
Gorilla	257	20	39-4	Chicken			21
Guinea pig	68	4	7-6	Duck			30
Hippopotamus	238	25	—	Goose			30
Horse	330	20	46	Pigeon			18
Kangaroo	42	7	—	Turkey			26

Speeds of Animals

Source: Natural History magazine, March 1974. Copyright © The American Museum of Natural History, 1974.

Animal	Mph	Animal	Mph	Animal	Mph
Cheetah	70	Mongolian wild ass	40	Human	27.89
Pronghorn antelope	61	Greyhound	39.35	Elephant	25
Wildebeest	50	Whippet	35.50	Black mamba snake	20
Lion	50	Rabbit (domestic)	35	Six-lined race runner	18
Thomson's gazelle	50	Mule deer	35	Wild turkey	15
Quarterhorse	47.5	Jackal	35	Squirrel	12
Elk	45	Reindeer	32	Pig (domestic)	11
Cape hunting dog	45	Giraffe	32	Chicken	9
Coyote	43	White-tailed deer	30	Spider (Tegenaria atrica)	1.17
Gray fox	42	Wart hog	30	Giant tortoise	0.17
Hyena	40	Grizzly bear	30	Three-toed sloth	0.15
Zebra	40	Cat (domestic)	30	Garden snail	0.03

Most of these measurements are for maximum speeds over approximate quarter-mile distances. Exceptions are the lion and elephant, whose speeds were clocked in the act of charging; the whippet, which was timed over a 200-yard course; the cheetah over a 100-yard distance; man for a 15-yard segment of a 100-yard run (of 13.6 seconds); and the black mamba, six-lined race runner, spider, giant tortoise, three-toed sloth, and garden snail, which were measured over various small distances.

Giant Trees of the U.S.

Source: The American Forestry Association, Washington, D.C.

There are approximately 850 different species of trees native to the continental U.S., including a few imports that have become naturalized to the extent of reproducing themselves in the wild state.

The oldest living trees in the world are reputed to be the bristlecone pines, the majority of which are found growing on the arid crags of California's White Mts. Some of them are estimated to be more than 4,600 years old. The largest known bristlecone pine is the "Patriarch," believed to be 1,500 years old. The oldest known redwoods are about 3,500 years old.

Recognition as the National Champion of each species is determined by total mass of each tree, based on this for-

mula: the circumference in inches as measured at a point 4 1/2 feet above the ground plus the total height of the tree in feet plus 1/4 of the average crown spread in feet. Trees are compared on the basis of this formula. Trees within five points of each other are declared co-champions. The Giant Sequoia champion has the largest circumference, 83 ft. 2 in.

Anyone can nominate the candidates for the National Register of Big Trees. For information, write to National Register of Big Trees, American Forestry Assn., P.O. Box 2000, Washington, DC 20013. Following is a small selection of the trees registered.

(Figure in parentheses is year of most recent measurement; * = co-champion)

Species	Height (ft.)	Location
Ailanthus (1952)	64	Head of Harbor, L.I.
Alder, Hazel (1989)	35	Norfolk, Va.
Allthorn (1989)*	13	Midland, Tex.
Apple, Common (1986)	70	East End, Va.
Apple, Oregon Crab (1989)	79	Nisqually Natl. Wildlife Refuge, Wash.
Ash, Carolina (1988)	48	Chesapeake, Va.
Ash, Texas (1989)	66	Lost Maples State Natl. Area, Tex.
Aspen, Bigtooth (1989)*	66	Caroline Co., Md.
Avocado (1982)	40	Hallandale, Fla.
Basswood, White (1986)	75	Henderson Co., N.C.
Beech, American (1984)	130	Ashtabula Co., Oh.
Birch, Gray (1989)	77	Somers, Ct.
Birch, River (1988)*	90	Appleton Comm., Tenn.
Birch, Water (1973)	53	Wallowa Co., Ore.
Blackbead, Ebony (1986)	40	Hidalgo Co., Tex.
Bladdernut, Sierra (1986)	28	Fresno, Co., Cal.
Bluewood (1989)	30	San Juan, Tex.
Boxwood, Florida (1986)	27	Monroe Co., Fla.
Buckeye, Bottlebrush (1989)	20	Cashiers, N.C.
Buffaloberry, Silver (1975)	22	Malheur Co., Ore.
Bumelia, Tough (1987)	41	Amelia Is., Fla.
Butternut (1989)*	88	Eugene, Ore.
California Laurel (1978)	88	Siskiyou Natl. For., Ore.
Camphor-Tree (1977)	72	Hardee Co., Fla.
Catalpa, Southern (1981)	80	Henderson Co., Ill.
Catclaw, Wright (1986)	36	Uvalde Co., Tex.
Cedar, Atlantic white (1985)	88	Escambia Co., Ala.
Cherry, Bitter (1985)	104	Vashon Is., Wash.
Coconut, Palm (1979)	92	Hilo, Hi.
Cranberrybush, American (1989)*	25	Trenton, Mich.
Cypress, McNab (1981)	55	Amador Co., Cal.
Dahoon, Myrtle (1972)	46	Lawtey, Fla.
Devilwood (1989)	36	Perry, Fla.
Dogwood, Blackfruit (1986)	18	Shasta Co., Cal.
Dogwood, Swamp (1989)*	23	Chesapeake, Va.
Douglas-Fir, Coast (1989)	298	Olympic Natl. Park, Wash.
Elder, American (1987)	16	Jefferson Natl. For., Va.
Elder, Pacific Red (1989)	30	Lincoln Co., Ore.
Elm, American (1985)	125	Southampton Co., Va.
Fiddlewood, Florida (1988)	39	Dade Co., Fla.
Fig, Shortleaf (1986)	41	Monroe Co., Fla.
Fir, Grand (1987)	251	Olympic Natl. Park, Wash.
Franklinia (1968)	36	Wyndmoor, Pa.
Fringetree (1989)*	32	Fairfax Co., Va.
Gallberry, Large (1989)	27	Great Dismal Swamp Natl. Wildlife Refuge, Va.
Geiger Tree (1988)	25	Lee Co., Fla.
Guajillo (1989)	15	Starr Co., Tex.
Guiana Plum (1976)	31	Coral Gables, Fla.
Hackberry, Common (1989)	111	Rock Co., Wis.
Haw, May (1989)	12	Williamsburg, Va.
Hawthorne, Fleshy (1988)	8	Kirkwood, Mo.
Hazel, California (1984)	47	Seattle, Wash.
Hemlock, Carolina (1972)	88	Burke Co., N.C.
Hickory, Mockernut (1985)*	125	Monroe Co., Ala.
Hickory, Shellbark (1985)	105	Rixeyville, Va.
Holly, Carolina (1986)	25	Jacksonville, Fla.
Honeylocust (1972)	115	Wayne Co., Mich.
Huisache (1989)	33	Big Bend Natl. Park, Tex.

Species	Height (ft.)	Location
Jerusalem-thorn (1969)	36	Florence, Ariz.
Jujube, Common (1989)	43	Fort Worth, Tex.
Juniper, Western (1945)	86	Stanislaus Natl. Forest., Cal.
Larch, European (1989)	83	Greenwich, Ct.
Laurel, English (1985)	32	Seattle, Wash.
Loblolly Bay (1963)	94	Ocala Natl. Forest, Fla.
Locust, Black (1974)	96	Dansville, N.Y.
Magnolia, Umbrella (1969)	50	Bucks Co., Pa.
Mahogany, W. Indies (1988)	70	Lee Co., Fla.
Manzanita, Common (1989)	22	Guerneville, Cal.
Maple, Black (1976)	118	Allegan Co., Mich.
Maple, Douglas (1985)*	65	Ahsahka, Ida.
Mesquite, Honey (1984)	52	Real County, Tex.
Mountain-Laurel (1989)	25	Asheville, N.C.
Mulberry, Black (1971)	68	Westminster, Md.
Nannyberry (1989)	40	Oakland Co., Mich.
Oak, Bluejack (1985)	64	Cherokee Co., Tex.
Oak, Chestnut (1972)	75	Northport, N.Y.
Oak, Harvard (1986)	30	Yoakum Co., Tex.
Oysterwood (1986)	24	Monroe Co., Fla.
Palm, Texas Sabal (1989)	45	Hidalgo Cty., Tex.
Paloverde, Blue (1976)	53	Riverside Co., Cal.
Paper-Mulberry (1989)	34	Yorktown, Va.
Pawpaw, Common (1986)	60	Newton Co., Miss.
Peach (1986)	18	Morrisville, Va.
Pear, Common (1985)	55	Wayne Co., Mich.
Pecan (1980)	143	Cocke Co., Tenn.
Persimmon, Texas (1965)	26	Uvalde Co., Tex.
Pine, Bishop (1986)	112	Mendocino Co., Cal.
Pine, Intermountain (1951)	47	Inyo Natl. Forest, Cal.
Pine, Virginia (1989)	120	Chambers Co., Ala.
Pistache, Texas (1976)	39	Val Verde Co., Tex.
Plum, Chicasaw (1988)	32	Henderson Co., N.C.
Plum, Wildgoose (1989)	26	New Salem Village, Ill.
Poison-Sumac (1972)	16	Robins Is., N.Y.
Poplar, Balsam (1984)	138	Marquette, Mich.
Portiatree (1968)	42	Kekaha, Ha.
Privet, California (1989)*	28	Yorktown, Va.
Redbud, Eastern (1989)	36	Nashville, Tenn.
Redwood, Coast (1972)	362	Humboldt Redwoods State Park, Cal.
Ribbonbush (1977)	23	No. Warner Springs, Cal.
Russian-Olive (1982)	58	Cortez, Col.
Saffron-Plum (1987)	31	Santa Ana, Tex.
Sassafras (1954)	76	Owensboro, Ky.
Sequoia, Giant (1975)	275	Sequoia Natl. Park, Cal.
Serviceberry, Downy (1986)	60	Burkes Garden, Va.
Silktree, Mimosa (1986)*	54	Webster Parish, La.
Sophora, Mescalbean (1983)	27	Comal Co., Tex.
Spruce, Norway (1989)	94	Susquehanna City, Pa.
Stewartia, Virginia (1987)	15	Chesapeake, Va.
Sugarberry (1976)	78	Society Hills, S.C.
Sweetgum, American (1986)	136	Craven Co., N.C.
Sycamore, Arizona (1981)	114	Sierra Co., N.M.
Tamarisk (1981)	34	Columbus, N.M.
Thatchpalm, Florida (1986)	23	Monroe Co., Fla.
Walnut, Arizona (1987)	85	Mimbres Valley, N.M.
Willow, Sitka (1988)	34	Coupeville, Wash.
Willow, Weeping (1982)*	114	Asheville, N.C.
Yew, Florida (1986)	20	Torreya State Park, Fla.
Yucca, Mojave (1987)	24	Needles Res. Area, Cal.
Yucca, Torrey (1987)	23	Lincoln Natl. Forest, N.M.

Major U.S. Public Zoological Parks

Source: World Almanac questionnaire. 1991; budget and attendance in millions. (*) park has not provided up-to-date data.

Zoo	Budget	Attend- ance	Acres	Species	Major attractions
Arizona-Sonora Desert Museum (Tucson)	$12.0	0.6	186	600	"Living" museum, 90% outdoors
Audubon (New Orleans)	9.0	1.0	58	433	Asian Domain, Louisiana Swamp
Bronx (N.Y.C.)	24.6	2.1	265	674	Himalayan Highlands, African Plains, Wild Asia, MouseHouse, endangered species
Buffalo	3.0	0.5	23	215	Habicat, Gorilla Habitat, Children's Zoo
Chicago (Brookfield)	21.0	1.9	215	385	7 Seas Seascape, Tropic World
Cincinnati	10.0	1.3	65	730	Gorilla World, Insect World, white bengal tigers
Cleveland	6.0	0.9	165	470	African Plains, rhino/cheetah, Animals of China
Dallas	7.1	0.7	70	330	25-acre Wilds of Africa with monorail, nature trail, Gorilla Conservation Center
Denver	6.6	1.2	76	312	Bear Mountain, Wolf Pack Woods, Feline House
Detroit*	11.4	1.0	125	300	Penguinarium, Chimps of Harambee
Houston	3.7	1.2	43	724	Children's Zoo, white tigers, white rhinoceros
Lincoln Park (Chicago)	8.8	4.0	35	312	Great Ape House, bird house, Children's Zoo
Los Angeles	7.2	2.0	113	500	Adventure Island, World of Birds
Louisville*	2.5	0.4	73	245	African Panorama, polar bear, Siberian tiger
Memphis*	2.5	0.8	36	403	Cat Country, Primate World, The Forest
Miami Metrozoo	7.2	0.8	290	300	Koalas, Aviary, cageless exhibits, Asian River Life
Milwaukee	12.0	1.5	200	350	Sea Lion Exhibit, Predator Prey, new Aviary
Minnesota*	10.0	1.0	485	311	Tropics Trail, Minnesota Trail, koalas, dolphins
National (Wash. D.C.)*	13.0	3.0	163	509	Giant pandas, Komodo dragon lizards, gorillas
Oklahoma City	9.0	0.6	110	500	Aquaticus dolphin & sea lion shows, 300 aquariums
Philadelphia*	12.0	1.3	42	550	World of Primates, Treehouse, Rare Animal House, African Plains, Small Mammals
Phoenix*	7.0	1.0	125	300	African Veldt, Children's Zoo, Arizona Trail
Gladys Porter (Brownsville, Tex.)	2.0	0.3	31	434	Free-flight aviary, Herpetarium, Aquatic wing.
Rio Grande (Albuquerque)*	2.2	0.5	60	289	Ape Country, Free-flying Bird Show, Rainforest
Riverbanks (Columbia, S.C.)	3.2	1.0	50	439	Aquarium Reptile Complex, Riverbanks Farm
St. Louis	14.7	2.7	83	657	Living World, Bear Pits, Jungle of the Apes
San Antonio	6.8	1.0	35	700	Children's Zoo, Australian Walkabout
San Diego*	40.0	3.5	100	800	Tiger River, Southeast Asian exhibit, koalas
San Diego (Wild Animal Park)	15.0	1.3	2,150	450	Mixed-species enclosures; exotic species, mono- rail with 50-minute, narrated tour
San Francisco*	8.0	1.2	125	270	Primate Discovery Center, Koala Crossing, Go- rilla World, Penguin Island
Toledo	7.5	0.8	33	400	Hippoquarium, African Savanna, Children's Zoo
Washington Pk (Portland)	11.0	1.0	63	195	Alaska Tundra, Penguinarium, Africa exhibit
Woodland Pk (Seattle)*	5.3	0.9	90	258	African Savanna, gorillas, Asian Elephant Forest

Top 50 American Kennel Club Registrations

Breed	Rank	1990	Rank	1989	Breed	Rank	1990	Rank	1989
Cocker Spaniels	1	105,642	1	111,636	Maltese	26	15,364	27	14,420
Labrador Retrievers	2	95,768	2	91,107	Brittanys	27	14,049	26	14,557
Poodles	3	71,757	3	78,600	Pugs	28	12,833	29	11,204
Golden Retrievers	4	64,848	4	64,269	West Highland White Terriers	29	11,419	28	12,189
Rottweilers	5	60,471	6	51,291	Bichons Frises	30	10,847	30	10,639
German Shepherd Dogs	6	59,556	5	58,422	German Shorthaired Pointers	31	10,478	32	9,975
Chow Chows	7	45,271	7	50,150	Bulldogs	32	10,281	31	10,129
Dachshunds	8	44,470	8	44,305	Great Danes	33	9,118	33	9,024
Beagles	9	42,499	9	43,314	Akitas	34	8,643	37	7,531
Miniature Schnauzers	10	39,910	10	42,175	Scottish Terriers	35	8,397	35	8,759
Shetland Sheepdogs	11	39,870	11	39,665	Samoyeds	36	8,389	34	8,923
Shih Tzu	12	39,503	13	38,131	Miniature Pinschers	37	8,176	40	5,568
Yorkshire Terriers	13	36,033	12	39,268	Cairn Terriers	38	7,025	38	7,318
Pomeranians	14	34,475	14	32,109	Keeshonden	39	6,799	36	7,569
Chihuahuas	15	24,593	16	24,917	Alaskan Malamutes	40	5,647	39	5,803
Lhasa Apsos	16	24,024	15	28,810	Pembroke Welsh Corgis	41	5,041	41	4,480
Boxers	17	23,659	18	22,037	Airedale Terriers	42	4,300	43	4,412
Siberian Huskies	18	21,944	19	21,875	Chesapeake Bay Retrievers	43	4,272	42	4,427
Dalmations	19	21,603	24	17,468	St. Bernards	44	4,120	44	4,099
English Springer Spaniels	20	21,342	22	20,910	Weimaraners	45	3,731	46	3,679
Basset Hounds	21	20,945	21	21,517	Schipperkes	46	3,372	50	3,087
Doberman Pinschers	22	20,255	20	21,782	Old English Sheepdogs	47	3,352	45	3,835
Pekingese	23	18,505	17	22,986	Norwegian Elkhounds	48	3,186	47	3,520
Collies	24	17,337	23	18,227	Wire Fox Terriers	49	3,102	49	3,293
Boston Terriers	25	15,401	25	15,355	Great Pyrenees	50	2,982	53	2,645

Cat Breeds

There are 27 cat breeds recognized: abyssinian, american shorthair, balinese, birman, bombay, burmese, colorpoint shorthair, egyptian mau, exotic shorthair, havana brown, himalayan, japanese bobtail, korat, leopard cat, lilac foreign shorthair, maine coon cat, manx, ocicat, oriental shorthair, persian, rex, russian blue, scottish fold, siamese, sphynx, turkish angora, wirehair shorthair.

Major Venomous Animals

Snakes

Coral snake - 2 to 4 ft. long, in Americas south of Canada; bite is nearly painless; very slow onset of paralysis, difficulty breathing; mortality high without antivenin.

Rattlesnake - 2 to 8 ft. long, throughout W. Hemisphere. Rapid onset of symptoms of severe pain, swelling; mortality low, but amputation of affected limb is sometimes necessary; antivenin. Probably higher mortality rate for Mojave rattler.

Cottonmouth water moccasin - up to 5 ft. long, wetlands of southern U.S. from Virginia to Texas. Rapid onset of symptoms of severe pain, swelling; mortality low, but tissue destruction can be extensive; antivenin.

Copperhead - less than 4 ft. long, from New England to Texas; pain and swelling; very seldom fatal; antivenin seldom needed.

Bushmaster - up to 12 ft. long, wet tropical forests of C. and S. America; few bites occur, but mortality rate is high.

Barba Amarilla or **Fer-de-lance** - up to 7 ft. long, from tropical Mexico to Brazil; severe tissue damage common; moderate mortality; antivenin.

Asian pit vipers - from 2 to 5 ft. long throughout Asia; reactions and mortality vary but most bites cause tissue damage and mortality is generally low.

Sharp-nosed pit viper or **One Hundred Pace Snake** - up to 5 ft. long, in southern Vietnam and Taiwan, China; the most toxic of Asian pit vipers; very rapid onset of swelling and tissue damage, internal bleeding; moderate mortality; antivenin.

Boomslang - under 6 ft. long, in African savannahs; rapid onset of nausea and dizziness, often followed by slight recovery and then sudden death from internal hemorrhaging; bites rare, mortality high; antivenin.

European vipers - from 1 to 3 ft. long; bleeding and tissue damage; mortality low; antivenins.

Puff adder - up to 5 ft. long, fat; south of the Sahara and throughout the Middle East; rapid large swelling, great pain, dizziness; moderate mortality often from internal bleeding; antivenin.

Gaboon viper - over 6 ft. long, fat; 2-inch fangs; south of the Sahara; massive tissue damage, internal bleeding; few recorded bites.

Saw-scaled or carpet viper - up to 2 ft. long, in dry areas from India to Africa; severe bleeding, fever; high mortality, causes more human fatalities than any other snake; antivenin.

Desert horned viper - in dry areas of Africa and western Asia; swelling and tissue damage; low mortality; antivenin.

Russell's viper or **tic-palonga** - over 5 ft. long, throughout Asia; internal bleeding; moderate mortality rate; bite reports common; antivenin.

Black mamba - up to 14 ft. long, fast-moving; S. and C. Africa; rapid onset of dizziness, difficulty breathing, erratic heart-beat; mortality high, nears 100% without antivenin.

Kraits - in S. Asia; rapid onset of sleepiness; numbness; up to 50% mortality even with antivenin treatment.

Common or Asian cobra - 4 to 8 ft. long, throughout S. Asia; considerable tissue damage, sometimes paralysis; mortality probably not more than 10%; antivenin.

King cobra - up to 16 ft. long, throughout S. Asia; rapid swelling, dizziness, loss of consciousness, difficulty breathing, erratic heart-beat; mortality varies sharply with amount of venom involved, most bites involve non-fatal amounts; antivenin.

Yellow or Cape cobra - 7 ft. long, in southern Africa; most toxic venom of any cobra; rapid onset of swelling, breathing and cardiac difficulties; mortality high without treatment; antivenin.

Ringhals, or spitting, cobra - 5 ft. and 7 ft. long; southern Africa; squirt venom through holes in front of fangs as a defense; venom is severely irritating and can cause blindness.

Australian brown snakes - very slow onset of symptoms of cardiac or respiratory distress; moderate mortality; antivenin.

Tiger snake - 2 to 6 ft. long, S. Australia; pain, numbness, mental disturbances with rapid onset of paralysis; may be the most deadly of all land snakes though antivenin is quite effective.

Death adder - less than 3 ft. long, Australia; rapid onset of faintness, cardiac and respiratory distress; at least 50% mortality without antivenin.

Taipan - up to 11 ft. long, in Australia and New Guinea; rapid paralysis with severe breathing difficulty; mortality nears 100% without antivenin.

Sea snakes - throughout Pacific, Indian oceans except NE Pacific; almost painless bite, variety of muscle pain, paralysis; mortality rate low, many bites are not envenomed; some antivenins.

Notes: Not all snake bites by venomous snakes are actually envenomed. Any animal bite, however, carries the danger of tetanus and anyone suffering a venomous snake bite should seek medical attention. Antivenins are not certain cures; they are only an aid in the treatment of bites. Mortality rates above are for envenomed bites; low mortality, up to 2% result in death; moderate, 2–5%; high, 5–15%. Even when the victim recovers fully, prolonged hospitalization and extensive medical procedures are usually required.

Lizards

Gila monster - up to 24 inches long with heavy body and tail, in high desert in southwest U.S. and N. Mexico; immediate severe pain followed by vomiting, thirst, difficulty swallowing, weakness approaching paralysis; no recent mortality.

Mexican beaded lizard - similar to Gila monster, Mexican west-coast; reaction and mortality rate similar to Gila monster.

Insects

Ants, bees, wasps, hornets, etc. Global distribution. Usual reaction is piercing pain in area of sting. Not directly fatal, except in cases of massive multiple stings. Many people suffer allergic reactions - swelling, rashes, partial paralysis –and a few may die within minutes from severe sensitivity to the venom (anaphylactic shock).

Spiders, scorpions

Black widow - small, round-bodied with hour-glass marking; the widow and its relatives are found around the world in tropical and temperate zones; sharp pain, weakness, clammy skin, muscular rigidity, breathing difficulty and, in small children, convulsions; low mortality; antivenin.

Recluse or fiddleback and brown spiders - small, oblong body; throughout U.S.; pain with later ulceration at place of bite; in severe cases fever, nausea, and stomach cramps; ulceration may last months; very low mortality.

Atrax spiders - several varieties, often large, in Australia; slow onset of breathing, circulation difficulties; low mortality.

Tarantulas - large, hairy spiders found around the world; American tarantulas, and probably all others, are **harmless**, though their bite may cause some pain and swelling.

Scorpions - crab-like body with stinger in tail, various sizes, many varieties throughout tropical and subtropical areas; various symptoms may include severe pain spreading from the wound, numbness, severe emotional agitation, cramps; severe reactions include vomiting, diarrhea, respiratory failure; low mortality, usually in children; antivenins.

Sea Life

Sea wasps - jellyfish, with tentacles up to 30 ft. long, in the S. Pacific; very rapid onset of circulatory problems; high mortality largely because of speed of toxic reaction; antivenin.

Portuguese man-of-war - jellyfish-like, with tentacles up to 70 ft. long, in most warm water areas; immediate severe pain; not fatal, though shock may cause death in a rare case.

Octopi - global distribution, usually in warm waters; all varieties produce venom but only a few can cause death; rapid onset of paralysis with breathing difficulty.

Stingrays - several varieties of differing sizes, found in tropical and temperate seas and some fresh water; severe pain, rapid onset of nausea, vomiting, breathing difficulties; wound area may ulcerate, gangrene may appear; seldom fatal.

Stonefish - brownish fish which lies motionless as a rock on bottom in shallow water; throughout S. Pacific and Indian oceans; extraordinary pain, rapid paralysis; low mortality.

Cone-shells - molluscs in small, beautiful shells in the S. Pacific and Indian oceans; shoot barbs into victims; paralysis; low mortality.

How Much Water Is Used . . .?

Source: American Water Works Assn.

1. In the average residence during a year? **107,000 gallons**
2. By an average person daily? **168 gallons**
3. To flush a toilet? **5-7 gallons**
4. To take a shower? **25-50 gallons**
5. To brush your teeth (water running)? **2 gallons**
6. To shave (water running)? **10-15 gallons**
7. To wash dishes by hand? **20 gallons**
8. To run a dishwasher? **10 gallons**

Mammals: Orders and Major Families

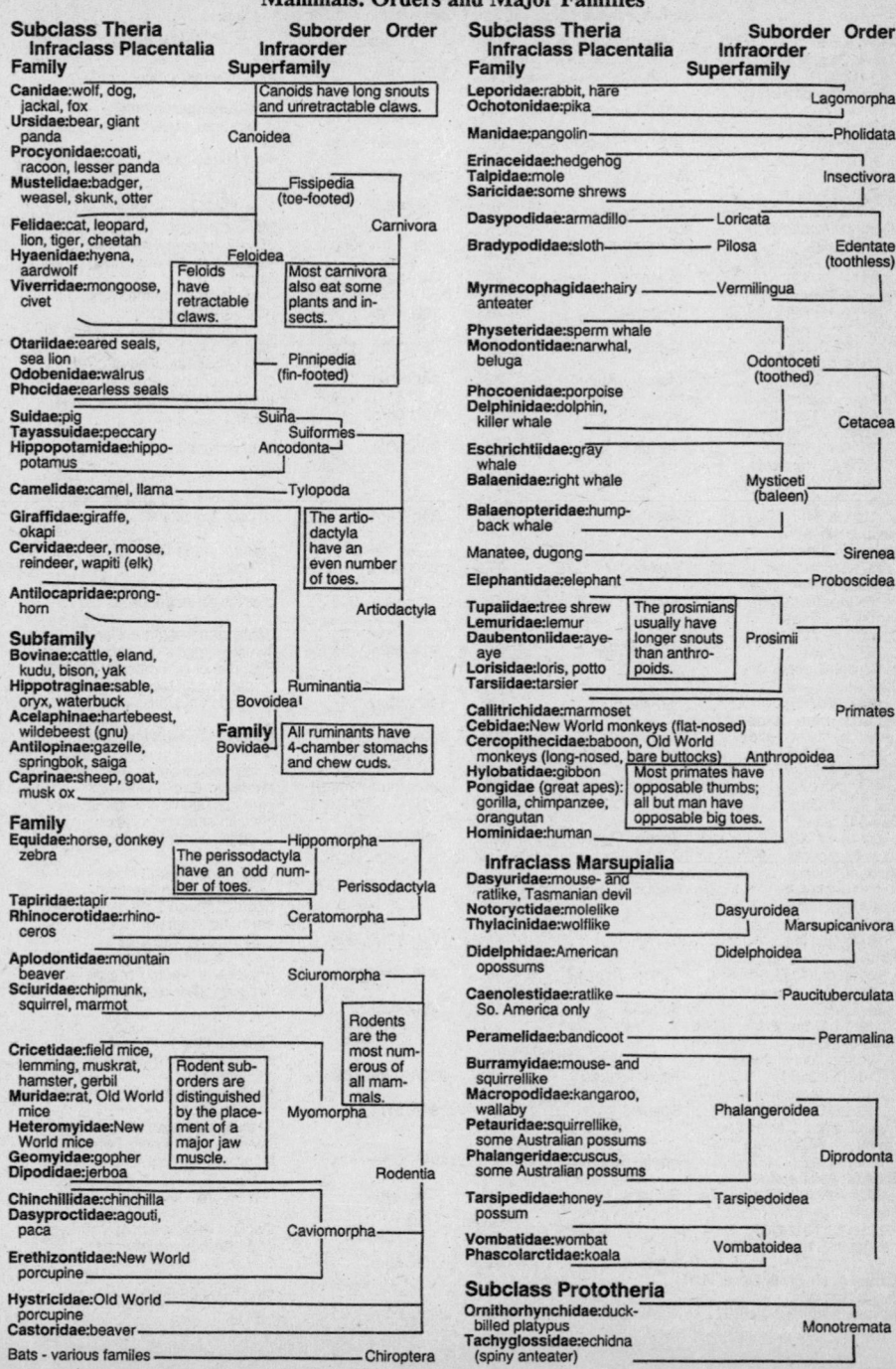

Subclass Theria
Infraclass Placentalia
Family — Suborder / Infraorder / Superfamily / Order

Canidae:wolf, dog, jackal, fox
Ursidae:bear, giant panda
Procyonidae:coati, racoon, lesser panda
Mustelidae:badger, weasel, skunk, otter

Canoidea — *Canoids have long snouts and unretractable claws.*

Felidae:cat, leopard, lion, tiger, cheetah
Hyaenidae:hyena, aardwolf
Viverridae:mongoose, civet

Feloidea — *Feloids have retractable claws.*

Fissipedia (toe-footed) — *Most carnivora also eat some plants and insects.*

Otariidae:eared seals, sea lion
Odobenidae:walrus
Phocidae:earless seals

Pinnipedia (fin-footed)

Carnivora

Suidae:pig
Tayassuidae:peccary
Hippopotamidae:hippopotamus

Suina / Suiformes / Ancodonta

Camelidae:camel, llama — Tylopoda

Giraffidae:giraffe, okapi
Cervidae:deer, moose, reindeer, wapiti (elk)

The artiodactyla have an even number of toes.

Antilocapridae:pronghorn

Artiodactyla

Subfamily
Bovinae:cattle, eland, kudu, bison, yak
Hippotraginae:sable, oryx, waterbuck
Acelaphinae:hartebeest, wildebeest (gnu)
Antilopinae:gazelle, springbok, saiga
Caprinae:sheep, goat, musk ox

Ruminantia / Bovoidea / **Family** Bovidae — *All ruminants have 4-chamber stomachs and chew cuds.*

Family
Equidae:horse, donkey, zebra

Hippomorpha — *The perissodactyla have an odd number of toes.*

Tapiridae:tapir
Rhinocerotidae:rhinoceros

Ceratomorpha

Perissodactyla

Aplodontidae:mountain beaver
Sciuridae:chipmunk, squirrel, marmot

Sciuromorpha

Cricetidae:field mice, lemming, muskrat, hamster, gerbil
Muridae:rat, Old World mice
Heteromyidae:New World mice
Geomyidae:gopher
Dipodidae:jerboa

Myomorpha — *Rodent suborders are distinguished by the placement of a major jaw muscle.*

Chinchillidae:chinchilla
Dasyproctidae:agouti, paca
Erethizontidae:New World porcupine
Hystricidae:Old World porcupine
Castoridae:beaver

Caviomorpha

Rodentia — *Rodents are the most numerous of all mammals.*

Bats - various families — Chiroptera

Subclass Theria
Infraclass Placentalia
Family — Suborder / Infraorder / Superfamily / Order

Leporidae:rabbit, hare
Ochotonidae:pika

Lagomorpha

Manidae:pangolin — Pholidata

Erinaceidae:hedgehog
Talpidae:mole
Saricidae:some shrews

Insectivora

Dasypodidae:armadillo — Loricata
Bradypodidae:sloth — Pilosa
Myrmecophagidae:hairy anteater — Vermilingua

Edentate (toothless)

Physeteridae:sperm whale
Monodontidae:narwhal, beluga
Phocoenidae:porpoise
Delphinidae:dolphin, killer whale

Odontoceti (toothed)

Eschrichtiidae:gray whale
Balaenidae:right whale
Balaenopteridae:humpback whale

Mysticeti (baleen)

Cetacea

Manatee, dugong — Sirenea

Elephantidae:elephant — Proboscidea

Tupaiidae:tree shrew
Lemuridae:lemur
Daubentoniidae:aye-aye
Lorisidae:loris, potto
Tarsiidae:tarsier

Prosimii — *The prosimians usually have longer snouts than anthropoids.*

Callitrichidae:marmoset
Cebidae:New World monkeys (flat-nosed)
Cercopithecidae:baboon, Old World monkeys (long-nosed, bare buttocks)
Hylobatidae:gibbon
Pongidae (great apes): gorilla, chimpanzee, orangutan
Hominidae:human

Anthropoidea — *Most primates have opposable thumbs; all but man have opposable big toes.*

Primates

Infraclass Marsupialia

Dasyuridae:mouse- and ratlike, Tasmanian devil
Notoryctidae:molelike
Thylacinidae:wolflike

Dasyuroidea

Didelphidae:American opossums — Didelphoidea

Marsupicanivora

Caenolestidae:ratlike So. America only — Paucituberculata

Peramelidae:bandicoot — Peramalina

Burramyidae:mouse- and squirrellike
Macropodidae:kangaroo, wallaby
Petauridae:squirrellike, some Australian possums
Phalangeridae:cuscus, some Australian possums

Phalangeroidea

Tarsipedidae:honey possum — Tarsipedoidea

Vombatidae:wombat
Phascolarctidae:koala

Vombatoidea

Diprodonta

Subclass Prototheria

Ornithorhynchidae:duck-billed platypus
Tachyglossidae:echidna (spiny anteater)

Monotremata

Memorable Manned Space Flights

Sources: National Aeronautics and Space Administration and The World Almanac.

Crew, date	Mission name	Orbits[1]	Duration	Remarks
Yuri A. Gagarin (4/12/61)	Vostok 1	1	1h 48m	First manned orbital flight.
Alan B. Shepard Jr. (5/5/61)	Mercury-Redstone 3	(2)	15m 22s	First American in space.
Virgil I. Grissom (7/21/61)	Mercury-Redstone 4	(2)	15m 37s	Spacecraft sank. Grissom rescued.
Gherman S. Titov (8/6-7/61)	Vostok 2	16	25h 18m	First space flight of more than 24 hrs.
John H. Glenn Jr. (2/20/62)	Mercury-Atlas 6	3	4h 55m 23s	First American in orbit.
M. Scott Carpenter (5/24/62)	Mercury-Atlas 7	3	4h 56m 05s	Manual retrofire error caused 250 mi. landing overshoot.
Andrian G. Nikolayev (8/11-15/62)	Vostok 3	64	94h 22m	Vostok 3 and 4 made first group flight.
Pavel R. Popovich (8/12-15/62)	Vostok 4	48	70h 57m	On first orbit it came within 3 miles of Vostok 3.
Walter M. Schirra Jr. (10/3/62)	Mercury-Atlas 8	6	9h 13m 11s	Closest splashdown to target to date (4.5 mi.).
L. Gordon Cooper (5/15-16/63)	Mercury-Atlas 9	22	34h 19m 49s	First U.S. evaluation of effects on man of one day in space.
Valery F. Bykovsky (6/14-6/19/63)	Vostok 5	81	119h 06m	Vostok 5 and 6 made 2d group flight.
Valentina V. Tereshkova (6/16-19/63)	Vostok 6	48	70h 50m	First woman in space.
Vladimir M. Komarov, Konstantin P. Feoktistov, Boris Y. Yegorov (10/12/64)	Voskhod 1	16	24h 17m	First 3-man orbital flight: first without space suits.
Pavel I. Belyayev, Aleksei A. Leonov (3/18/65)	Voskhod 2	17	26h 02m	Leonov made first "space walk" (10 min.)
Virgil I. Grissom, John W. Young (3/23/65)	Gemini-Titan 3	3	4h 53m 00s	First manned spacecraft to change its orbital path.
James A. McDivitt, Edward H. White 2d, (6/3-7/65)	Gemini-Titan 4	62	97h 56m 11s	White was first American to "walk in space" (20 min.).
L. Gordon Cooper Jr., Charles Conrad Jr. (8/21-29/65)	Gemini-Titan 5	120	190h 55m 14s	First use of fuel cells for electric power; evaluated guidance and navigation system.
Frank Borman, James A. Lovell Jr. (12/4-18/65)	Gemini-Titan 7	206	330h 35m 31s	Longest duration Gemini flight
Walter M. Schirra Jr., Thomas P. Stafford (12/15-16/65)	Gemini-Titan 6-A	16	25h 51m 24s	Completed world's first space rendezvous with Gemini 7.
Neil A. Armstrong, David R. Scott (3/16-17/66)	Gemini-Titan 8	6.5	10h 41m 26s	First docking of one space vehicle with another; mission aborted, control malfunction.
John W. Young, Michael Collins (7/18-21/66)	Gemini-Titan 10	43	70h 46m 39s	First use of Agena target vehicle's propulsion systems.
Charles Conrad Jr., Richard F. Gordon Jr. (9/12-15/66)	Gemini-Titan 11	44	71h 17m 08s	Docked, made 2 revolutions of earth tethered; set Gemini altitude record (739.2 mi.).
James A. Lovell Jr., Edwin E. Aldrin Jr. (11/11-15/66)	Gemini-Titan 12	59	94h 34m 31s	Final Gemini mission; record 5½ hrs. of extravehicular activity.
Vladimir M. Komarov (4/23/67)	Soyuz 1	17	26h 40m	Crashed after re-entry killing Komarov.
Walter M. Schirra Jr., Donn F. Eisele, R. Walter Cunningham (10/11-22/68)	Apollo-Saturn 7	163	260h 09m 03s	First manned flight of Apollo spacecraft command-service module only.
Georgi T. Beregovoi (10/26-30/68)	Soyuz 3	64	94h 51m	Made rendezvous with unmanned Soyuz 2.
Frank Borman, James A. Lovell Jr., William A. Anders (12/21-27/68)	Apollo-Saturn 8	10[3]	147h 00m 42s	First flight to moon (command-service module only); views of lunar surface televised to earth.
Vladimir A. Shatalov (1/14-17/69)	Soyuz 4	45	71h 14m	Docked with Soyuz 5.
Boris V. Volyanov, Aleksei S. Yeliseyev, Yevgeny V. Khrunov (1/15-18/69)	Soyuz 5	46	72h 46m	Docked with Soyuz 4; Yeliseyev and Khrunov transferred to Soyuz 4.
James A. McDivitt, David R. Scott, Russell L. Schweickart (3/3-13/69)	Apollo-Saturn 9	151	241h 00m 54s	First manned flight of lunar module.

Crew, date	Mission name	Orbits[1]	Duration	Remarks
Thomas P. Stafford, Eugene A. Cernan, John W. Young (5/18-26/69)....	Apollo-Saturn 10	31[4]	192h 03m 23s ..	First lunar module orbit of moon.
Neil A. Armstrong, Edwin E. Aldrin Jr., Michael Collins (7/16-24/69)......	Apollo-Saturn 11	30[3]	195h 18m 35s ..	First lunar landing made by Armstrong and Aldrin; collected 48.5 lbs. of soil, rock samples; lunar stay time 21 h, 36m, 21 s.
Georgi S. Shonin, Valery N. Kubasov (10/11-16/69)	Soyuz 6	79	118h 42m......	First welding of metals in space. Space lab construction tests made; Soyuz 6, 7 and 8 — first time 3 spacecraft 7 crew orbited earth at once.
Anatoly V. Filipchenko, Vladislav N. Volkov, Viktor V. Gorbatko (10/12-17/69).....	Soyuz 7	79	118h 41m.....	
Charles Conrad Jr., Richard F. Gordon, Alan L. Bean (11/14-24/69).....	Apollo-Saturn 12	45[3]	244h 36m 25s ..	Conrad and Bean made 2d moon landing; collected 74.7 lbs. of samples, lunar stay time 31 h, 31 m.
James A. Lovell Jr., Fred W. Haise Jr., John L. Swigart Jr. (4/11-17/70)	Apollo-Saturn 13	...	142h 54m 41s ..	Aborted after service module oxygen tank ruptured; crew returned safely using lunar module oxygen and power.
Alan B. Shepard Jr., Stuart A. Roosa, Edgar D. Mitchell (1/31-2/9/71).......	Apollo-Saturn 14	34[3]	216h 01m 57s ..	Shepard and Mitchell made 3d moon landing, collected 96 lbs. of lunar samples; lunar stay 33 h, 31 m.
Georgi T. Dobrovolsky, Vladislav N. Volkov, Viktor I. Patsayev (6/6-30/71).......	Soyuz 11	360	569h 40m......	Docked with Salyut space station; and orbited in Salyut for 23 days; crew died during re-entry from loss of pressurization.
David R. Scott, Alfred M. Worden, James B. Irwin (7/26-8/7/71).....	Apollo-Saturn 15	74[3]	295h 11m 53s ..	Scott and Irwin made 4th moon landing; first lunar rover use; first deep space walk; 170 lbs. of samples; 66 h, 55 m, stay.
Charles M. Duke Jr., Thomas K. Mattingly, John W. Young (4/16-27/72)......	Apollo-Saturn 16	64[3]	265h 51m 05s ..	Young and Duke made 5th moon landing; collected 213 lbs. of lunar samples; lunar stay line 71 h, 2 m.
Eugene A. Cernan, Ronald E. Evans, Harrison H. Schmitt (12/7-19/72)......	Apollo-Saturn 17	75[3]	301h 51m 59s ..	Cernan and Schmitt made 6th manned lunar landing; collected 243 lbs. of samples; record lunar stay of 75 h.
Charles Conrad Jr., Joseph P. Kerwin, Paul J. Weitz (5/25-6/22/73).....	Skylab 2	...	672h 49m 49s ..	First American manned orbiting space station; made long-flights tests, crew repaired damage caused during boost.
Alan L. Bean, Jack R. Lousma, Owen K. Garriott (7/28-9/25/73).....	Skylab 3	...	1,427h 09m 04s ..	Crew systems and operational tests, exceeded pre-mission plans for scientific activities; space walk total 13h, 44 m.
Gerald P. Carr, Edward G. Gibson, William Pogue (11/16/73-2/8/74)...	Skylab 4	...	2,017h 16m 30s ..	Final Skylab mission; record space walk of 7 h, 1 m., record space walks total for a mission 22 h, 21 m.
Alexi Leonov, Valeri Kubasov (7/15-7/21/75) .	Soyuz 19	96	143h 31m	U.S.-USSR joint flight. Crews linked-up in space, conducted experiments, shared meals, and held a joint news conference.
Vance Brand, Thomas P. Stafford, Donald K. Slayton (7/15-7/24/75).....	Apollo 18	136	217h 30m......	
Leonid Kizim, Vladmir Solovyov, Oleg Atkov (2/8-10/2/84).......	Salyut 7	...	237 days......	Set space endurance record. (since broken)

(1) The U.S. measures orbital flights in revolutions while the Soviets use "orbits." (2) Suborbital. (3) Moon orbits in command module. (4) Moon orbits.

Fire aboard spacecraft Apollo I on the ground at Cape Kennedy, Fla. killed Virgil I. Grissom, Edward H. White and Roger B. Chaffee on Jan. 27, 1967. They were the only U.S. astronauts killed in space tests.

U.S. Space Shuttles

Name, date	Crew	Name, date	Crew
Columbia (4/12-14/81) ...	Robert L. Crippen, John W. Young.	Challenger (4/4-9/83)	Paul Weitz, Karol Bobko, Story Musgrave, Donald Peterson.
Columbia (11/12-14/81) ..	Joe Engle, Richard Truly.		
Columbia (3/22-30/82) ...	Jack Lousma, C. Gordon Fullerton.	Challenger (6/18-24/83) ..	Robert L. Crippen, Norman Thagard, John Fabian, Frederick Hauck, Sally K. Ride (1st U.S. woman in space).
Columbia (6-27/7-4/82) ...	Thomas Mattingly 2d, Henry Hartsfield Jr.		
Columbia (11/11-16/82) ..	Vance Brand, Robert Overmyer, William Lenoir, Joseph Allen.		

(continued)

Name, date	Crew
Challenger (8/30-9/5/83).	Richard Truly, Daniel Brandenstein, William Thornton, Guion Bluford (1st U.S. black in space), Dale Gardner.
Columbia (11/28-12/8/83)	John Young, Brewster Shaw Jr., Robert Parker, Owen Garriott, Byron Lichtenberg, Ulf Merbold.
Challenger (2/3-11/84)	Vance Brand, Robert Gibson, Ronald McNair, Bruce McCandless, Robert Stewart.
Challenger (4/6-13/84)	Robert L. Crippen, Francis R. Scobee, George D. Nelson, Terry J. Hart, James D. Van Hoften.
Discovery (8/30-9/5/84)	Henry W. Hartsfield Jr., Michael L. Coats, Steven A. Hawley, Judith A. Resnik, Richard M. Mullane, Charles D. Walker.
Challenger (10/5-13/84)	Robert L. Crippen, Jon A. McBride, Kathryn D. Sullivan, Sally K. Ride, Marc Garneau (first Canadian), David C. Leestma, Paul D. Scully-Power.
Discovery (11/8-16/84)	Frederick H. Hauck, David M. Walker, Dr. Anna L. Fisher, Joseph P. Allen, Dale A. Gardner.
Discovery (1/24-27/85)	Thomas K. Mattingly, Loren J. Shriver, James F. Buchli, Ellison S. Onizuka, Gary E. Payton.
Discovery (4/12-19/85)	Karol J. Bobko, Donald E. Williams, Sen. Jake Garn, Charles D. Walker, Jeffrey A. Hoffman, S. David Griggs, M. Rhea Seddon.
Challenger (4/29-5/6/85)	Robert F. Overmyer, Frederick D. Gregory, Don L. Lind, Taylor G. Wang, Lodewijk van den Berg, Norman Thagard, William Thornton.
Discovery (6/17-6/24/85)	John O. Creighton, Shannon W. Lucid, Steven R. Nagel, Daniel C. Brandenstein, John W. Fabian, Prince Sultan Salman al-Saud (first Arab), Patrick Baudry.
Challenger (7/29-8/6/85)	Roy D. Bridges Jr., Anthony W. England, Karl G. Henize, F. Story Musgrave, C. Gordon Fullerton, Loren W. Acton, John-David F. Bartoe.
Discovery (8/27-9/3/85)	John M. Lounge, James D. van Hoften, William F. Fisher, Joe H. Engle, Richard O. Covey.
Atlantis (10/4-10/7/85)	Karol J. Bobko, Ronald J. Grabe, David C. Hilmers, William A. Pailes, Robert C. Stewart.
Challenger (10/30-11/6/85)	Henry W. Hartsfield Jr., Steven R. Nagel, Bonnie J. Dunbar, James F. Buchli, Guion S. Bluford Jr., Ernst Messerschmid, Reinhard Furrer, Wubbo J. Ockels.
Atlantis (11/26-12/3/85)	Brewster H. Shaw Jr., Bryan D. O'Connor, Charles Walker, Rodolfo Neri (first Mexican), Jerry L. Ross, Sherwood C. Spring, Mary L. Cleave.
Columbia (1/12-1/18/86)	Robert L. Gibson, Charles F. Bolden Jr., George D. Nelson, Bill Nelson (first congressman), Franklin R. Chang-Diaz, Steven A. Hawley, Robert J. Cenker.
Challenger (1/28/86- exploded after takeoff)	Francis R. Scobee, Michael J. Smith, Ronald E. McNair, Ellison S. Onizuka, Judith A. Resnik, Gregory B. Jarvis, Sharon Christa McAuliffe.
Discovery (9/29-10/3/88)	Frederick H. Hauck, Richard O. Covey, David C. Hilmers, George D. Nelson, John M. Lounge.
Atlantis (12/3-12/6/88)	Robert L. Gibson, Guy S. Gardner, Richard M. Mullane, Jerry L. Ross, William M. Shepherd.
Discovery (3/13-3/18/89)	Michael L. Coats, John E. Blaha, James F. Buchli, Robert C. Springer, James P. Bagian.
Atlantis (5/4-5/8/89)	David M. Walker, Ronald J. Grabe, Mary L. Cleave, Norman E. Thagard, Mark C. Lee.
Columbia (8/8-8/13/89)	Brewster H. Shaw Jr., Richard N. Richards, David C. Leestma, James C. Adamson, Mark N. Brown.
Atlantis (10/18-10/23/89)	Donald E. Williams, Michael J. McCulley, Shannon W. Lucid, Ellen S. Baker, Franklin R. Chang-Diaz.
Discovery (11/22-11/27/89)	Frederick D. Gregory, John E. Blaha, Manley L. Carter, F. Story Musgrave, Katherine C. Thornton.
Colombia (1/9-1/20/90)	Daniel C. Brandenstein, Bonnie J. Dunbar, James D. Wetherbee, Marsha S. Ivins, G. David Low.
Atlantis (2/28-3/4/90)	John O. Creighton, John H. Casper, David C. Hilmers, Richard M. Mullane, Pierre J. Thuot.
Discovery (4/24-4/29/90)	Bruce McCandless 2d, Kathryn D. Sullivan, Loren J. Shriver, Charles F. Bolden Jr., Steven A. Hawley.
Discovery (10/6-10/10/90)	Richard N. Richards, Robert D. Cabana, Bruce E. Melnick, William M. Shepherd, Thomas D. Akers.
Atlantis (11/15-11/20/90)	Richard O. Covey, Frank L. Culbertson, Robert C. Springer, Carl J. Meade, Charles D. Gemar.
Columbia (12/2-12/10/90)	Vance D. Brand, Guy S. Gardner, Jeffrey A. Hoffman, John M. Lounge, Robert A.R. Parker, Samuel T. Durrance, Ronald A. Parise.

(continued)

Name, date	Crew	Name, date	Crew
Atlantis (4/5-4/11/91)	Stephen R. Nagel, Kenneth D. Cameron, Linda M. Godwin, Jerry L. Ross, Jerome Apt.		Hieb, Donald R. McMonagle, Charles L. Veach.
Discovery (4/28-5/6/91) . .	Michael L. Coats, L. Blaine Hammond Jr., Guion S. Bluford Jr., Gregory J. Harbaugh, Richard J.	Atlantis (8/2-8/11/91)	John E. Blaha, Michael A. Baker, Shannon W. Lucid, G. David Low, James C. Adamson.

Notable U.S. Unmanned and Planetary Missions

Spacecraft	Launch date (GMT)	Mission	Remarks
Mariner 2	Aug. 27, 1962	Venus	Passed within 22,000 miles from Venus 12/14/62; contact lost 1/3/63 at 54 million miles
Ranger 7	July 28, 1964	Moon	Yielded over 4,000 photos
Mariner 4	Nov. 28, 1964	Mars	Passed behind Mars 7/14/65; took 22 photos from 6,000 miles
Ranger 8	Feb. 17, 1965	Moon	Yielded over 7,000 photos
Surveyor 3	Apr. 17, 1967	Moon	Scooped and tested lunar soil
Mariner 5	June 14, 1967	Venus	In solar orbit; closest Venus fly-by 10/19/67
Mariner 6	Feb. 25, 1969	Mars	Came within 2,000 miles of Mars 7/31/69; sent back data, photos
Mariner 7	Mar. 27, 1969	Mars	Came within 2,000 miles of Mars 8/5/69
Mariner 9	May 30, 1971	Mars	First craft to orbit Mars 11/13/71; sent back over 7,000 photos
Pioneer 10	Mar. 3, 1972	Jupiter	Passed Jupiter 12/3/73; exited the solar system 6/14/83
Mariner 10	Nov. 3, 1973	Venus, Mercury	Passed Venus 2/5/74; arrived Mercury 3/29/74. First time gravity of one planet (Venus) used to whip space-craft toward another (Mercury)
Viking 1	Aug. 20, 1975	Mars	Landed on Mars 7/20/76; did scientific research, sent photos; functioned 6 1/2 years
Viking 2	Sept. 9, 1975	Mars	Landed on Mars 9/3/76; functioned 3 1/2 years
Voyager 1	Sept. 5, 1977	Jupiter, Saturn	Encountered Jupiter 3/5/79; Saturn 11/13/80
Voyager 2	Aug. 20, 1977	Jupiter, Saturn, Uranus, Neptune	Encountered Jupiter 7/9/79; Saturn 8/26/81; Uranus 1/8 and 1/27/86; Neptune 8/24/89
Pioneer 12	May 20, 1978	Venus	Entered Venus orbit 12/4/78
Pioneer 13	Aug. 8, 1978	Venus	Encountered Venus 12/9/78
Titan 4	June 14, 1989	Orbit Earth	First of 41 such rockets whose primary purpose is defense

Summary of Worldwide Payloads

(A payload is something carried into space by a rocket)

Source: National Aeronautics and Space Administration

Year	Total[1]	USSR	United States	Japan	European Space Agency	India	China
1985	164	118	33	2	1	—	1
1986	132	114	9	3	0	—	3
1987	133	116	9	3	1	—	1
1988	136	107	15	2	2	2	3
1989	129	95	22	4	2	0	0
1990	160	96	31	7	1	1	5
Total	4,016	2,660	1,101	51	26	12	29

(1) Incl. launches in countries not shown.

Notable Proposed U.S. Space Missions

Source: National Aeronautics and Space Administration

Year, Month		Mission	Purpose
1992	Feb.	International Microgravity Lab (c)	Establish system for life-science studies
	May	Atmospheric Lab for Applications & Science (c)	Study variations in solar spectrum and Earth's atmosphere
	June	Small Explorer-1 (a)	First of a series to study space physics and atmospheric science
	July	TOPEX/Poseidon (a)	Study relationship of ocean systems to climate
	Sept.	Tethered Satellite System (c)	Study gas clouds and electrical fields in space
		Spacelab (c)	Low-gravity experiments
		Mars Observer (a)	Study climate and surface of Mars
		Shuttle High-energy Astrophysics Lab (c)	Study X-ray sources and spectrum in space
1993	June	Polar (a)	Study physical properties of the aurora borealis
	Oct.	Space Radar Lab (c)	Acquire radar images of Earth's surface
1994		X-ray Timing Explorer (a)	Study compact X-ray sources such as neutron stars and black holes
1995		Cassini (a)	Study Saturn
1996		Comet Rendezvous Asteroid Flyby (a)	Study origin and evolution of solar system
1998		Earth Observing System (a)	Orbit and study Earth
2000		Mars Rover Sample Return (d)	Collect Martian-soil samples and return to Earth for observation

(a) Launched by expendable rocket. (b) Launched by shuttle. (c) Carried aboard shuttle. (d) To be determined.

International Aeronautical Records

Source: The National Aeronautic Association, 1763 R St. NW, Washington, DC 20009, representative in the United States of the Federation Aeronautique Internationale, certifying agency for world aviation and space records. The International Aeronautical Federation was formed in 1905 by representatives from Belgium, France, Germany, Great Britain, Spain, Italy, Switzerland, and the United States, with headquarters in Paris. Regulations for the control of official records were signed Oct. 14, 1905. World records are defined as maximum performance, regardless of class or type of aircraft used. Records to mid-1991.

World Absolute Records—Maximum Performance in Any Class

Speed over a straight course — 2,193.16 mph — Capt. Elden W. Joersz, USAF, Lockheed SR-71; Beale AFB, Cal., July 28, 1976.

Speed over a closed circuit — 2,092.294 mph — Maj. Adolphus H. Bledsoe Jr., USAF, Lockheed SR-71; Beale AFB, Cal., July 27, 1976.

Speed around the world, non-stop, nonrefueled — 115.65 mph — Richard Rutan & Jeana Yeager, U.S., Voyager, Edwards AFB, Cal., Dec. 14-23, 1986.

Altitude — (123,523.58 feet) — Alexander Fedotov, USSR, E-266M; Podmoskovnoye, USSR, Aug. 31, 1977.

Altitude in horizontal flight — 85,068.997 ft. — Capt. Robert C. Helt, USAF, Lockheed SR-71; Beale AFB, Cal., July 28, 1976.

Class K Spacecraft

Duration — 326 days, 11 hours, 15 minutes — Col. Yuri V. Romanenko, USSR, space station *MIR*; Feb. 5 —Dec. 29, 1987.

Altitude — 234,672.5 mi. — Frank Borman, James A. Lovell Jr., William Anders, Apollo 8; Dec. 21-27, 1968.

Greatest mass lifted — 282,197 lbs. — Frank Borman, James A. Lovell Jr., William Anders, Apollo 8; Dec. 21-27, 1968.

Distance — 87,436,800 mi. — Anatoly Beresovoy & Valentin Lebedev, USSR, Salyut 7, Soyuz T5, Soyuz T7; May 13-Dec. 10, 1982.

World "Class" Records

All other records, international in scope, are termed World "Class" records and are divided into classes: airships, free balloons, airplanes, seaplanes, amphibians, gliders, and rotorplanes. Airplanes (Class C) are sub-divided into four groups: Group I — piston engine aircraft, Group II — turboprop aircraft, Group III — jet aircraft, Group IV — rocket powered aircraft. A partial listing of world records follows:

Airplanes (Class C-I, Group I—piston engine)

Distance, closed circuit — 24,986.727 mi. — Richard Rutan & Jeana Yeager, U.S., Voyager; Edwards AFB, Cal., Dec. 14-23, 1986.

Speed for 100 kilometers (62.137 miles) without payload — 469.549 mph — Jacqueline Cochran, U.S.; North American P-51; Coachella Valley, Cal., Dec. 10, 1947.

Speed for 1,000 kilometers (621.369 miles) without payload — 431.09 mph — Jacqueline Cochran, U.S.; North American P-51; Santa Rosasummit, Cal. — Flagstaff, Ariz. course, May 24, 1948.

Speed for 5,000 kilometers (3,106.849 miles) without payload — 338.39 mph — Capt. James Bauer, USAF, Boeing B-29; Dayton, Oh., June 28, 1946.

Speed around the world — 203.64 mph — D.N. Dalton, Australia; Beechcraft Duke; Brisbane, Aust., July 20-25, 1975. Time: 5 days, 2 hours, 19 min., 57 sec.

Light Airplanes—(Class C-1.d)

Great Circle distance without landing — 7,929.71 mi. — Peter Wilkins, Australia, Piper Malibu, Sydney, Aust. to Phoenix, Ariz., Mar. 30-Apr. 1, 1987.

Speed for 100 kilometers — (62,137 miles) in a closed circuit — 322.780 mph — Ms. R. M. Sharpe, Great Britain; Vickers Supermarine Spitfire 5-B; Wolverhampton, June 17, 1950.

Helicopters (Class E-1)

Great Circle distance without landing — 2,213.04 mi. — Robert G. Ferry, U.S.; Hughes YOH-6A helicopter; Culver City, Cal., to Ormond Beach, Fla., Apr. 6-7, 1966.

Speed around the world —35.40 mph — H. Ross Perot Jr.; Bell 206 L-11 Long Ranger N39112; Dallas, Tex.–Dallas, Tex.; Sept. 1-30, 1982; 29 days, 3 hrs., 8 min., 13 sec.

Gliders (Class D-I—single seater)

Distance, straight line — 907.7 mi. — Hans Werner Grosse, West Germany; ASK12 sailplane; Luebeck to Biarritz, Apr. 25, 1972.

Distance to a goal & return — 1,023.25 mi. — Thomas Knauff, U.S. Nimbus III; Williamsport, Pa., Apr. 25, 1983.

Airplanes (Class C-I, Group II—Turboprop)

Great Circle distance without landing — 8,732.09 mi. — Lt. Col. Edgar L. Allison Jr., USAF, Lockheed HC-130 Hercules aircraft; Taiwan to Scott AFB, Ill.; Feb. 20, 1972.

Altitude — (51,014 ft.) — Donald R. Wilson, U.S.; LTV L450F aircraft; Greenville, Tex., Mar. 27, 1972.

Speed for 1,000 kilometers (621.369 miles) without payload — 541.449 mph — Ivan Soukhomline, USSR; TU-114 aircraft; Sternberg, USSR; Mar. 24, 1960.

Speed for 5,000 kilometers (3,106.849 miles) without payload — 545.072 mph — Ivan Soukhomline, USSR; TU-114 aircraft, Sternberg, USSR; Apr. 9, 1960.

Speed around the world —304.80 mph — Joe Harnish, U.S., Gulfstream Commander 695A, Elkhart, Ind., Mar. 21-24, 1983.

Airplanes (Class C-1, Group III—Jet Engine)

Great Circle distance without landing — 12,532.28 mi. — Maj. Clyde P. Evely, USAF, Boeing B-52-H, Kadena, Okinawa to Madrid, Spain, Jan. 10-11, 1962.

Distance in a closed circuit — 12,521.78 mi. — Vladimir Tersky, USSR, AN-124, Podmoskovnoye, USSR, May 6-7, 1987.

Altitude — 123,523.58 ft. — Alexander Fedotov, USSR; E-226M airplane; Podmoskovnoye, USSR, Aug. 31, 1977.

Speed for 100 kilometers in a closed circuit — 1,618.7 mph — Alexander Fedotov, USSR; E-266 airplane, Apr. 8, 1973.

Speed for 500 kilometers in a closed circuit — 1,852.61 mph — Mikhail Komarov, USSR; E-266 airplane, Oct. 5, 1967.

Speed for 1,000 kilometers in a closed circuit — 2,092.294 mph — Maj. Adolphus H. Bledsoe Jr., USAF; Lockheed SR-71; Beale AFB, Cal., July 27, 1976.

Speed for 2,000 kilometers without payload — 1,250.42 mph — S. Agapov, USSR; Podmoscovnde, USSR; July 20, 1983.

Speed around the world — 637.71 mph — Allen E. Paulson, U.S., Gulfstream IV, Houston, Tex., Feb. 26-28, 1988.

Balloons-Class A

Altitude — (113,739.9 ft.) — Cmdr. Malcolm D. Ross, USNR; Lee Lewis Memorial Winzen Research Balloon; Gulf of Mexico, May 4, 1961.

Distance —(5,208.67 mi.) — Ben Abruzzo; Raven Experimental; Nagashima, Japan to Covello, Cal., Nov. 9-12, 1981.

Duration —137 hr., 5 min., 50 sec. — Ben Abruzzo, Larry Newman, and Maxie Anderson; Double Eagle II; Presque Isle, Maine to Miserey, France (3,107.61 mi.); Aug. 12-17, 1978.

FAI Course Records

Los Angeles to New York — 1,214.65 mph — Capt. Robert G. Sowers, USAF; Convair B-58 Hustler; elapsed time: 2 hrs. 58.71 sec., Mar. 5, 1962.

New York to Los Angeles — 1,081.80 mph — Capt. Robert G. Sowers, USAF; Convair B-58 Hustler; elapsed time: 2 hrs. 15 min. 50.08 sec., Mar. 5, 1962.

New York to Paris — 1,089.36 mph — Maj. W. R. Payne, U.S.; Convair B-58 Hustler; elapsed time: 3 hrs 19 min. 44 sec., May 26, 1961.

London to New York — 587.457 mph — Maj. Burl Davenport, USAF; Boeing KC-135; elapsed time: 5 hrs. 53 min. 12.77 sec.; June 27, 1958.

Baltimore to Moscow, USSR — 563.36 mph — Col. James B. Swindal, USAF; Boeing VC-137 (707); elapsed time: 8 hrs. 33 min. 45.4 sec., May 19, 1963.

New York to London — 1,806.964 mph — Maj. James V. Sullivan, USAF; Lockheed SR-71; elapsed time 1 hr. 54 min. 56.4 sec., Sept. 1, 1974.

London to Los Angeles — 1,435.587 mph — Capt. Harold B. Adams, USAF; Lockheed SR-71; elapsed time: 3 hrs. 47 min. 39 sec., Sept. 13, 1974.

Traffic at U.S. Airports in 1990

Source: Air Transport Association of America (Passenger enplanement)

Chicago O'Hare	25,607,018	New York (JFK)	9,567,157
Dallas/Ft. Worth	22,826,069	Boston	9,354,028
Atlanta	22,647,507	St. Louis	9,282,370
Los Angeles	18,107,195	Miami	9,133,761
San Francisco	13,256,191	Minneapolis/St. Paul	8,759,303
Denver	11,930,959	Honolulu	8,411,324
New York (LGA)	10,531,443	Pittsburgh	7,878,134
Phoenix	10,342,473	Orlando	7,541,636
Detroit	9,836,369	Houston	7,510,842
Newark	9,784,178	Las Vegas	7,400,107

Busiest Foreign Airports in 1990*

Source: Airport Operators Council International (passengers arriving & departing)

London, UK, Heathrow	42,964,200	Rome, Italy, Fiumicino	17,835,885
Tokyo, Japan, Haneda	40,233,031	Amsterdam, Netherlands, Schiphol	16,185,810
Frankfurt, W. Germany	28,912,145	Stockholm, Sweden, Arlanda	14,821,692
Paris, France, Orly	24,329,700	Singapore, Changi	14,403,580
Osaka, Japan	23,511,611	Bangkok	14,329,337
Paris, France, Charles De Gaulle	22,506,107	Fukuoka, Japan	13,227,659
London, UK, Gatwick	21,185,400	Zurich, Switzerland	12,694,507
Toronto, Canada, Lester B. Pearson	20,304,271	Copenhagen, Denmark	12,460,090
New Tokyo-Narita	19,264,650	Sidney, Australia	12,223,106
Hong Kong	18,687,525	Munich-Riem, W. Germany	11,218,119

*Does not include airports that did not respond to the AOCI survey.

U.S. Scheduled Airline Traffic

Source: Air Transport Association of America (thousands)

	1988	1989	1990
Passenger traffic			
Revenue passengers enplaned	454,614	453,692	465,557
Revenue passenger miles	423,301,559	432,714,309	457,915,220
Available seat miles	676,802,328	684,375,876	733,353,609
Revenue passenger load factor(%)	62.5	63.2	62.4
Cargo traffic (ton miles)	11,469,193	12,185,968	12,603,656
Freight and express	9,632,219	10,275,002	10,600,100
U.S. Mail	1,836,974	1,878,651	2,003,556
Overall traffic and service			
Total revenue ton miles—charter service	4,597,536	5,637,444	5,318,426
Total revenue ton miles—all services	58,397,186	61,095,371	63,710,362
Total available ton miles—all services	105,372,555	109,397,126	117,011,845

U.S. Airline Safety

Source: National Transportation Safety Board

	Departures (millions)	Fatal accidents	Fatalities	Fatal accidents per 100,000 departures		Departures (millions)	Fatal accidents	Fatalities	Fatal accidents per 100,000 departures
1977	4.9	3	78	0.061	1984	5.4	1	4	0.018
1978	5.0	5	160	0.100	1985	5.8	4	197	0.069
1979	5.4	4	351	0.074	1986	6.4	2	5	0.016
1980	5.4	0	0	0.000	1987	6.6	4[1]	231	0.046[1]
1981	5.2	4	4	0.077	1988	6.7	3[1]	285	0.030[1]
1982	5.0	4	233	0.060	1989	6.6	11	278	0.166
1983	5.0	4	15	0.079	1990	6.9	6	39	0.087

(1) Sabotage-caused accidents are incl. in the Accidents but not in the Accident rates.

National Aviation Hall of Fame

The National Aviation Hall of Fame at Dayton, Oh., is dedicated to honoring the outstanding pioneers of air and space.

Allen, William M.
Andrews, Frank M.
Armstrong, Neil A.
Arnold, Henry H. "Hap"
Atwood, John Leland
Balchen, Bernt
Baldwin, Thomas S.
Beachey, Lincoln
Beech, Olive A.
Beech, Walter H.
Bell, Alexander Graham
Bell, Lawrence D.
Bendix, Vincent T.
Boeing, William E.
Bong, Richard I.
Borman, Frank
Boyd, Albert
Brown, George "Scratchley"
Byrd, Richard E.
Cessna, Clyde V.
Chamberlin, Clarence D.
Chanute, Octave
Chennault, Claire L.
Cochran (Odlum), Jacqueline
Collins, Michael
Conrad Jr., Charles
Crossfield, A. Scott
Cunningham, Alfred A.
Curtiss, Glenn H.
deSeversky, Alexander P.
Doolittle, James H.
Douglas, Donald W.
Draper, Charles S.
Eaker, Ira C.

Earhart, (Putnam), Amelia
Eielson, C. Benjamin
Ellyson, Theodore G.
Ely, Eugene B.
Everest, Frank K.
Fairchild, Sherman M.
Fleet, Reuben H.
Fokker, Anthony H.G.
Ford, Henry
Foss, Joseph
Foulois, Benjamin D.
Gabreski, Francis S.
Glenn Jr., John H.
Goddard, George W.
Goddard, Robert H.
Godfrey, Arthur
Goldwater, Barry M.
Grissom, Virgil I.
Gross, Robert E.
Grumman, Leroy R.
Guggenheim, Harry F.
Haughton, Daniel J.
Hegenberger, Albert F.
Heinemann, Edward H.
Hoover, Robert A.
Hughes, Howard R.
Ingalls, David S.
Jeppesen, Elrey B.
Johnson, Clarence L.
Kenney, George C.
Kettering, Charles F.
Kindelberger, James H.
Knabenshue, A. Roy
Knight, William J.

Lahm, Frank P.
Langley, Samuel P.
Lear, William P. Sr.
LeMay, Curtis E.
LeVier, Anthony W.
Lindbergh, Anne M.
Lindbergh, Charles A.
Link, Edwin A.
Lockheed, Allan H.
Loening, Grover
Luke Jr., Frank
Macready, Carl B.
Macready, John A.
Martin, Glenn L.
McDonnell, James S.
Mitscher, Marc A.
Meyer, John C.
Mitchell, William "Billy"
Montgomery, John J.
Moorer, Thomas H.
Moss, Sanford A.
Neumann, Gerhard
Northrop, John K.
Patterson, William A.
Piper Sr., William T.
Post, Wiley H.
Read, Albert C.
Reeve, Robert C.
Rentschler, Frederick B.
Richardson, Holden C.
Rickenbacker, Edward V.
Rodgers, Calbraith P.
Rogers, Will

Rushworth, Robert A.
Ryan, T. Claude
Schirra, Walter M.
Schriever, Bernard A.
Selfridge, Thomas E.
Shepard Jr., Alan B.
Sikorsky, Igor I.
Six, Robert F.
Smith, C.R.
Spaatz, Carl A.
Sperry Sr., Elmer A.
Sperry Sr., Lawrence B.
Stanley, Robert M.
Stapp, John P.
Stearmam, Lloyd C.
Taylor, Charles E.
Towers, John H.
Trippe, Juan T.
Turner, Roscoe
Twining, Nathan F.
Vandenberg, Hoyt
von Braun, Wernher
von Karman, Theodore
von Ohain, Hans P.
Vought, Chance M.
Wade, Leigh
Walden, Henry W.
Wells, Edward
Wilson, Thornton A.
Wright, Orville
Wright, Wilbur
Yeager, Charles E.
Young, John W.

Aircraft Operating Statistics

Source: Air Transport Assn. of America

(Figures are averages for most commonly used models)

	Number of seats	Speed airborne	Flight length	Fuel (gallons per hour)	Aircraft operating cost per hour
B747-100	405	519	3,149	3,529	$6,132
L-1011-100/200	296	498	1,631	2,215	3,885
DC-10-10	288	484	1,410	2,174	4,236
A300 B4	258	460	1,221	1,482	3,526
A310-300	240	473	1,512	1,574	3,484
B767-300	230	478	1,668	1,503	3,334
B767-200	193	475	1,736	1,377	2,887
B757-200	188	449	984	985	2,301
B727-200	148	427	688	1,249	2,247
MD-80	142	416	667	882	1,861
B737-300	131	413	605	732	1,826
DC-9-50	122	378	685	848	1,830
B727-100	115	422	626	1,104	2,031
B737-100/200	112	388	440	806	1,772
F-100	103	360	384	631	1,456
DC-9-30	102	377	421	804	1,778
DC-9-10	78	376	394	764	1,588

Leading Passenger Airlines in 1990

Source: Air Transport Assn. of America

(In thousands)

Airline	Passengers	Airline	Passengers	Airline	Passengers
American	73,227	Southwest	22,064	Aloha	4,626
Delta	65,729	Eastern	21,386	West Air	2,282
USAir	60,059	Pan American	17,503	Air Wisconsin	2,248
United	57,550	America West	15,567	Horizon Air	1,816
Northwest	40,899	Midway	6,489	Trump Shuttle	1,712
Continental	35,166	Alaska	5,405	Midwest Express	754
Trans World	24,166	Hawaiian	4,735		

Notable Around the World and Intercontinental Trips

	From/To	Miles	Time	Date
Nellie Bly	New York/New York		72d 06h 11m	1889
George Francis Train	New York/New York		67d 12h 03m	1890
Charles Fitzmorris	Chicago/Chicago		60d 13h 29m	1901
J. W. Willis Sayre	Seattle/Seattle		54d 09h 42m	1903
J. Alcock-A.W. Brown (1)	Newfoundland/Ireland	1,960	16h 12m	June 14-15, 1919
Two U.S. Army airplanes	Seattle/Seattle	26,103	35d 01h 11m	1924
Richard E. Byrd (2)	Spitsbergen/N. Pole	1,545	15h 30m	May 9, 1926
Amundsen-Ellsworth-Nobile Expedition	Spitsbergen/Teller, Alaska		80h	May 11-14, 1926
E.S. Evans and L. Wells (N. Y. World) (3)	New York/New York	18,400	28d 14h 36m 05s	June 16-July 14, 1926
Charles Lindbergh (4)	New York/Paris	3,610	33h 29m 30s	May 20-21, 1927
Amelia Earhart, W. Stultz, L. Gordon	Newfoundland/Wales		20h 40m	June 17-18, 1928
Graf Zeppelin	Friedrichshafen, Ger./Lakehurst, N.J.	6,630	4d 15h 46m	Oct. 11-15, 1928
Graf Zeppelin	Friedrichshafen, Ger./Lakehurst, N.J.	21,700	20d 04h	Aug. 14-Sept. 4, 1929
Wiley Post and Harold Gatty (Monoplane Winnie Mae)	New York/New York	15,474	8d 15h 51m	July 1, 1931
C. Pangborn-H. Herndon Jr. (5)	Misawa, Japan/Wenatchee, Wash.	4,458	41h 34m	Oct. 3-5, 1931
Amelia Earhart (6)	Newfoundland/Ireland	2,026	14h 56m	May 20-21, 1932
Wiley Post (Monoplane Winnie Mae) (7)	New York/New York	15,596	115h 36m 30s	July 15-22, 1933
Hindenburg Zeppelin	Lakehurst, N.J./Frankfort, Ger.		42h 53m	Aug. 9-11, 1936
H. R. Ekins (Scripps-Howard Newspapers in race) (Zeppelin Hindenburg to Germany air planes from Frankfurt).	Lakehurst, N.J./Lakehurst, N.J.	25,654	18d 11h 14m 33s	Sept. 30-Oct. 19, 1936
Howard Hughes and 4 assistants	New York/New York	14,824	3d 19h 08m 10s	July 10-13, 1938
Douglas Corrigan	New York/Dublin		28h 13m	July 17-18, 1938
Mrs. Clara Adams (Pan American Clipper)	Port Washington, N.Y./Newark, N.J.		16d 19h 04m	June 28-July 15, 1939
Globester, U.S. Air Transport Command	Wash., D.C./Wash., D.C.	23,279	149h 44m	Oct. 4, 1945
Capt. William P. Odom (A-26 Reynolds Bombshell)	New York/New York	20,000	78h 55m 12s	Apr. 12-16, 1947
America, Pan American 4-engine Lockheed Constellation (8)	New York/New York	22,219	101h 32m	June 17-30, 1947
Col. Edward Eagan	New York/New York	20,559	147h 15m	Dec. 13, 1948
USAF B-50 Lucky Lady II (Capt. James Gallagher) (9)	Ft. Worth, Tex./Ft. Worth, Tex.	23,452	94h 01m	Feb. 26-Mar. 2, 1949
Col. D. Schilling, USAF (10)	England/Limestone, Me.	3,300	10h 01m	Sept. 22, 1950
C.F. Blair Jr.	Norway/Alaska	3,300	10h 29m	May 29, 1951
Two U.S. S-55.	Massachusetts/Scotland	3,410	42h 30m	July 15-31, 1952
Canberra Bomber (11)	N. Ireland/Newfoundland	2,073	04h 34m	Aug. 26, 1952
	Newfoundland/N. Ireland	2,073	03h 25m	Aug. 26, 1952
Three USAF B-52 Stratofortresses (12).	Merced, Cal./Cal.	24,325	45h 19m	Jan. 15-18, 1957
Max Conrad.	Chicago/Rome	5,000	34h 03m	Mar. 5-6, 1959
USSR TU-114 (13)	Moscow/New York	5,092	11h 06m	June 28, 1959
Boeing 707-320	New York/Moscow	c.5090	08h 54m	July 23, 1959
Peter Gluckmann (solo)	San Francisco/San Francisco	22,800	29d	Aug. 22-Sept. 20, 1959
Sue Snyder	Chicago/Chicago	21,219	62h 59m	June 22-24, 1960
Max Conrad (solo)	Miami/Miami	25,946	8d 18h 35m 57s	Feb. 28-Mar. 8, 1961
Sam Miller & Louis Fodor	New York/New York		46h 28m	Aug. 3-4, 1963
Robert & Joan Wallick	Manila/Manila	23,129	05d 06h 17m 10s	June 2-7, 1966
Arthur Godfrey, Richard Merrill Fred Austin, Karl Keller	New York/New York	23,333	86h 9m 01s	June 4-7, 1966
Trevor K. Brougham	Darwin, Australia/Darwin	24,800	5d 05h 57m	Aug. 5-10, 1972
Walter H. Mullikin, Albert Frink, Lyman Watt, Frank Cassaniti, Edward Shields.	New York/New York	23,137	1d 22h 50s	May 1-3, 1976
David Kunst (15).	Waseca, Minn./Waseca, Minn.	14,500	4yrs 3mos 16d	June 10, 1970-Oct. 5, 1974
Arnold Palmer	Denver/Denver	22,985	57h 25m 42s	May 17-19, 1976
Boeing 747 (14)	San Francisco/San Francisco	26,382	54h 7m 12s	Oct. 28-31, 1977
Concorde	London/Wash., D.C.	1,023 mph	03h 34m 48s	May 29, 1976
Concorde	Paris/New York	1,037.50 mph	03h 30m 11s	Aug. 22, 1978
Richard Rutan & Jeana Yeager (16).	Edwards AFB, Cal.	24,986	09d 03m 44s	Dec. 14-23, 1986

(1) Non-stop transtlantic flight. (2) Polar flight. (3) Mileage by train and auto, 4,110; by plane, 6,300; by steamship, 8,000. (4) Solo transatlantic flight in the Ryan monoplane the "Spirit of St. Louis". (5) Non-stop Pacific flight. (6) Woman's transoceanic solo flight. (7) First to fly solo around northern circumference of the world, also first to fly twice around the world. (8) Inception of regular commercial global air service. (9) First non-stop round-the-world flight, refueled 4 times in flight. (10) Non-stop jet transatlantic flight. (11) Transatlantic round trip on same day. (12) First non-stop global flight by jet planes; refueled in flight by KC-97 aerial tankers; average speed approx. 525 mph. (13) Non-stop between Moscow and New York. (14) Speed record around the world over both the earth's poles. (15) First to circle the earth on foot. (16) Circled the earth nonstop without refueling.

TRADE AND TRANSPORTATION
U.S. Foreign Trade with Leading Countries, 1990
Source: Office of Industry and Trade Information, U.S. Dept. of Commerce
(millions of dollars)

	Exports (f.a.s.)	Imports (Customs value)	Balance
Total Trade	394,044.9	495,042.0	−100,997.1
Canada	83,865.7	91,372.0	−7,506.3
20 Latin American Republics			
Other Western Hemisphere	49,424.9	61,113.1	−11,688.3
Other Western Hemisphere	4,653.2	2,820.8	1,832.2
Western Europe			
European OECD Countries			
European Economic Community			
United Kingdom	23,484.1	20,288.3	3,195.8
West Germany.	18,690.1	28,108.6	−9,418.5
Other EEC Countries			
Denmark	1,311.3	1,678.3	−366.9
Ireland.	2,539.2	1,745.5	793.7
Netherlands	13,015.9	4,971.9	8,044.0
Belgium-Luxembourg	10,448.3	4,578.4	5,869.9
France	13,652.1	13,124.0	528.1
Spain	5,208.4	3,309.7	1,898.7
Portugal.	922.3	832.6	89.7
Italy	7,987.3	12,723.5	−4,736.2
Greece	764.6	506.9	257.7
Other OECD Countries			
Iceland	231.7	163.0	68.7
Sweden	3,403.6	4,930.9	−1,527.3
Norway	1,280.6	1,847.7	−567.1
Finland	1,125.6	1,266.7	−141.1
Austria	873.4	1,315.9	−442.4
Switzerland.	4,944.4	5,451.8	−507.4
Turkey	2,253.3	1,180.2	1,073.0
Other Western Europe			
Yugoslavia	565.9	772.7	−206.8
Cyprus	129.5	18.4	111.1
Communist Areas in Europe			
German Democratic Republic	62.3	85.0	−22.7
Czechoslovakia	89.1	87.0	2.1
Hungary.	156.6	348.5	−192.0
Poland	406.4	408.6	−2.2
U.S.S.R.	3,087.6	1,065.4	2,022.2
Romania	369.0	231.1	138.0
Bulgaria.	84.3	47.3	37.0
Asia			
Communist Areas in Asia			
China	4,807.3	15,223.9	−10,416.6
Japan.	48,584.6	89,655.2	−41,070.5
Other Asia			
Near East Asia			
Syria.	150.4	52.1	98.3
Lebanon	98.1	24.3	73.9
Iraq	731.8	3,014.5	−2,282.7
Iran	166.5	7.0	159.5
Israel	3,200.3	3,312.6	−112.3
Jordan	309.1	11.5	297.6
Kuwait.	400.7	569.9	−169.2
Saudi Arabia	4,034.8	9,974.3	−5,939.5
Qatar	114.7	52.8	61.9
United Arab Emirates	998.2	888.5	109.7
Yemen (Sana)	107.1	378.1	−271.0
Oman	162.8	291.9	−129.1
Bahrain	718.4	80.7	637.7
South Asia			
India	2,486.2	3,191.2	−705.0
Pakistan.	1,142.9	609.0	534.0
Bangladesh.	181.5	538.3	−356.8
Sri Lanka (Ceylon).	137.3	538.4	−401.1
Asia, N.E.C.			
Thailand.	2,991.5	5,293.8	−2,302.3
Cambodia		0.1	−0.1
Malaysia	3,424.7	5,272.3	−1,847.6
Singapore.	8,019.1	9,839.5	−1,820.4
Indonesia	1,896.7	3,343.1	−1,446.4
Brunei.	142.7	95.7	47.0
Philippines	2,471.6	3,382.6	−911.0
South Korea	14,398.7	18,493.2	−4,094.4
Hong Kong	6,840.4	9,488.0	−2,647.6
Taiwan.	11,482.4	22,666.7	−11,184.3
Australia and Oceania			
Australia	8,534.7	4,432.7	
New Zealand.	1,133.3	1,199.4	−66.1
Africa			
Morocco	497.0	109.1	387.9
Algeria	947.7	2,645.3	−1,697.6
Tunisia	178.5	32.0	146.5
Egypt	2,248.8	396.4	1,852.4
Guinea	42.9	141.3	−98.4
Ivory Coast	78.4	199.7	−121.3
Ghana	138.4	168.6	−30.1
Nigeria	551.4	5,977.3	−5,426.0

U.S. Exports and General Imports by Principal Commodity Groupings, 1990

Source: Office of Industry and Trade Information, U.S. Commerce Department

(in millions of dollars, not seasonally adjusted)

Item	Exports	Imports
Total	**394,044.9**	**495,042.0**
Agricultural commodities. . . .	**38,715.7**	**22,378.2**
Animal feeds.	2,855.0	282.7
Bulbs, flowers, plants and		
seeds except oilseeds	457.8	379.8
Cereal flours. . . . . ──. .	684.8	568.9
Cocoa	38.2	784.3
Coffee	11.9	1,768.8
Corn	6,205.2	23.2
Cotton, raw	2,782.7	0.5
Dairy products; eggs	373.2	502.2
Furskins, undressed	144.3	78.2
Grain sorghum; rye; oats . . .	810.8	106.2
Hides and skins, undressed . .	1,613.1	94.8
Live animals	513.8	1,183.2
Meat and preparations	3,187.9	2,956.2
Oils/fats, animal.	30.6	0.5
Oils/fats, vegetable.	664.5	717.5
Rice.	801.4	71.6
Soybeans	3,595.2	15.4
Sugar.	8.2	852.7
Tobacco, unmanufactured . . .	1,441.1	696.6
Vegetables and fruit	5,011.6	5,800.8
Wheat	3,887.0	80.0
Other agricultural	3,597.4	5,414.1
Manufactured goods	**298,686.6**	**388,806.2**
ADP equipment; office mach. .	24,725.5	26,917.3
Airplanes	19,615.5	2,836.0
Airplane parts	9,554.1	3,337.8
Aluminum	2,860.3	2,844.7
Artwork/antiques	2,266.7	2,341.0
Chemicals-dyeing tanning . . .	1,588.3	1,288.5
Chemicals-fertilizers	2,574.6	955.2
Chemicals-medic./pharm. . . .	4,103.2	2,500.2
Chemicals-organic/inorganic . .	14,215.5	10,625.4
Chemicals-perfume materials .	1,962.6	1,323.2
Chemicals-plastics	9,061.6	3,747.8
Chemicals-turpentine waxes..	5,477.5	2,028.0
Clothing and footwear	2,957.5	35,108.5
Copper.	1,213.1	1,757.3
Electrical machinery	28,216.4	33,600.9
Fixtures.	678.6	1,235.8
Furniture and parts	1,596.8	5,008.0
Gem diamonds	320.1	3,977.8
General industrial machinery .	15,688.5	14,483.6
Glass	1,058.9	759.5
Gold, nonmonetary	2,983.5	1,080.8
Iron and steel mill products . .	3,243.1	8,810.6
Locomotives; railway vehicles .	495.7	635.4
Metal manufacturers, N.S.P.F..	4,722.7	6,445.7
Metalworking machinery	2,747.5	3,687.9
Motorcycles/parts		
bicycles/trailers	931.6	1,440.0
Musical inst./record media. . .	3,870.5	2,537.7
Nickel.	227.9	1,113.9
Optical goods	639.5	1,473.1
Paper paperboard and articles	4,991.8	8,510.5

Item	Exports	Imports
Photographic apparatus	2,773.4	3,359.2
Platinum	214.6	1,872.7
Pottery	71.3	1,222.1
Power generating machinery .	15,569.6	14,591.1
Printed matter.	3,158.5	1,670.2
Plastic articles, n.e.s.	1,939.4	3,142.3
Rubber articles, n.e.s.	728.4	1,020.8
Scientific instruments and parts	12,108.0	6,207.6
Silver bullion.	119.9	437.4
Spacecraft and parts	894.0	204.1
Specialized industrial mach. . .	15,254.8	12,944.6
Telecommunications apparatus	9,114.2	22,288.2
Textile yarns, fabrics	4,922.0	6,397.6
Tires and tubes—automotive . .	913.6	2,220.1
Toys/games/sporting goods .	1,820.2	9,086.6
Travel goods.	133.3	2,225.7
Umbrellas/baskets/brooms/bru-		
shes/candles, etc.	1,095.2	1,839.0
Vehicles and parts:		
Cars, new Canadian	5,833.6	13,333.3
Cars, new Japanese	581.7	19,199.2
Cars, new other countries . .	2,489.3	12,520.1
Trucks	2,997.3	8,504.0
Chassis/bodies.	206.9	590.2
Parts.	14,547.7	15,235.1
Vessels/float. structures	1,273.3	329.6
Watches/clocks/parts	209.3	1,762.2
Wood manufacturers	1,221.8	2,040.2
Zinc.	46.9	1,018.7
Other manufactured goods . .	23,859.3	31,132.2
Petroleum and petroleum		
products	**6,712.3**	**61,356.5**
Energy related.	4,418.8	60,746.9
Crude petroleum	182.9	43,870.9
Other petroleum.	4,235.9	16,876.0
Nonenergy related	2,293.5	609.6
Mineral fuels, excluding		
petroleum products.	**4,971.5**	**2,742.5**
Coal	4,464.5	86.3
Natural gas	198.7	2,149.4
Electricity.	491.1	462.5
Crude materials excluding		
agricultural and fuels	**15,468.6**	**11,118.6**
Cork, wood, lumber.	5,224.5	3,126.3
Pulp and waste paper	4,040.2	2,867.0
Metal ores; scrap	4,942.7	3,972.3
Other crude material	1,261.3	1,153.1
Fish and preparations.	**2,800.0**	**5,202.4**
Fish—fresh; chilled; frozen. . .	1,757.4	2,011.7
Beverages; tobacco excl.		
agricultural	**5,411.3**	**2,068.4**
Cigarettes	4,761.0	53.6
Distilled alcoholic beverages. .	254.0	1,727.8
Other beverages; tobacco . . .	396.3	287.0
All other	**2,178.9**	**1,124.3**

Note: Details may not equal totals due to rounding and other statistical procedures.

Value of U.S. Exports, Imports, and Merchandise Balance

Source: Office of Trade and Investment Analysis, U.S. Dept. of Commerce

(millions of dollars)

	Principal Census trade totals					Other Census totals		
Year	U.S. exports and reexports excluding military grant-aid	U.S. general imports f.a.s. transaction values[1]	U.S. merchandise balance f.a.s.[1]	U.S. general imports c.i.f.	U.S. balance exports f.a.s. imports c.i.f.	Military grant-aid shipments	Exports of domestic merchandise	Re-exports
1950	9,997	8,954	1,043	—	—	282	10,146	133
1955	14,298	11,566	2,732	—	—	1,256	15,426	128
1960	19,659	15,073	4,586	—	—	949	20,408	201
1965	26,742	21,520	5,222	—	—	779	27,178	343
1970	42,681	40,356	2,325	42,833	−152	565	42,612	634
1975	107,652	98,503	9,149	105,935	1,716	461	106,622	1,490
1980	220,626	244,871	−24,245	256,984	−36,358	156	216,668	4,115
1985	213,133	345,276[2]	−132,143	361,626	−148,493	13	206,925	6,221
1990	394,030	495,042	−101,012	516,987	−122,957	15	375,606	18,439

Note: Export values include both commercially-financed shipments and shipments under government-financed programs such as AID and PL-480. (1) Prior to 1974, imports are customs values, i.e. generally at prices in principal foreign markets. (2) In 1981 import value changes back to customs value. (3) Includes undocumented exports to Canada.

Notable Ocean Passages by Ships
Compiled by N.R.P. Bonsor

Sailing Vessels

Date	Ship	From	To	Nautical miles	Time D. H. M	Speed (knots)
1846	Yorkshire	Liverpool	New York	3150	16. 0. 0	8.46†
1853	Northern Light	San Francisco	Boston	—	76. 6. 0	—
1854	James Baines	Boston Light	Light Rock	—	12. 6. 0	—
1854	Flying Cloud	New York	San Francisco	15091	89. 0. 0	7.07†
1868-9	Thermopylae	Liverpool	Melbourne	—	63.18.15	—
—	Red Jacket	New York	Liverpool	3150	13. 1.25	10.05†
—	Starr King	50 S. Lat	Golden Gate	—	36. 0. 0	—
—	Golden Fleece	Equator	San Francisco	—	12.12. 0	—
1905	Atlantic	Sandy Hook	England	3013	12. 4. 0	10.32

Atlantic Crossing by Passenger Steamships

Date	Ship		From	To	Nautical miles	Time D. H. M	Speed (knots)
1819 (5/22 - 6/20)	Savannah (a)	US	Savannah	Liverpool	—	29. 4. 0	—
1838 (5/7 - 5/22)	Great Western	Br	New York	Avonmouth	3218	14.15.59	9.14
1840 (8/4 - 8/14)	Britannia (b)	Br	Halifax	Liverpool	2610	9.21.44	10.98†
1854 (6/28 - 7/7)	Baltic	US	Liverpool	New York	3037	9.16.52	13.04
1856 (8/6 - 8/15)	Persia	Br	Sandy Hook	Liverpool	3046	8.23.19	14.15†
1876 (12/16-12/24)	Britannic	Br	Sandy Hook	Queenstown	2882	7.12.41	15.94
1895 (5/18 - 5/24)	Lucania	Br	Sandy Hook	Queenstown	2897	5.11.40	22.00
1898 (3/30 - 4/5)	Kaiser Wilhelm der Grosse	Ger	Needles	Sandy Hook	3120	5.20. 0	22.29
1901 (7/10 - 7/17)	Deutschland	Ger	Sandy Hook	Eddystone	3082	5.11. 5	23.51
1907 (10/6 - 10/10)	Lusitania	Br	Queenstown	Sandy Hook	2780	4.19.52	23.99
1924 (8/20 - 8/25)	Mauretania	Br	Ambrose	Cherbourg	3198	5. 1.49	26.25
1929 (7/17 - 7/22)	Bremen*	Ger	Cherbourg	Ambrose	3164	4.17.42	27.83
1933 (6/27 - 7/2)	Europa	Ger	Cherbourg	Ambrose	3149	4.16.48	27.92
1933 (8/11 - 8/16)	Rex	It	Gibraltar	Ambrose	3181	4.13.58	28.92
1935 (5/30 - 6/3)	Normandie*	Fr	Bishop Rock	Ambrose	2971	4. 3. 2	29.98
1938 (8/10 - 8/14)	Queen Mary	Br	Ambrose	Bishop Rock	2938	3.20.42	31.69
1952 (7/11 - 7/15)	United States	US	Bishop Rock	Ambrose	2906	3.12.12	34.51
1952 (7/3 - 7/7)	United States* (e)	US	Ambrose	Bishop Rock	2942	3.10.40	35.59

Other Ocean Passages

Date	Ship	From	To	Nautical miles	Time D. H. M	Speed (knots)
1928 (June)	USS Lexington	San Pedro	Honolulu	2226	3. 0.36	30.66
1944 (Jul-Sep)	St. Roch (c) (Can)	Halifax	Vancouver	7295	86. 0. 0	—
1945 (7/16-7/19)	USS Indianapolis (d)	San Francisco	Oahu, Hawaii	2091	3. 2.20	28.07
1945 (11/26)	USS Lake Champlain	Gibraltar	Newport News	3360	4. 8.51	32.04
1950 (Jul-Aug)	USS Boxer	Japan	San Francisco	5000	7.18.36	26.80†
1951 (6/1-6/9)	USS Philippine Sea	Yokohama	Alameda	5000	7.13. 0	27.62†
1958 (2/25-3/4)	USS Skate (f)	Nantucket	Portland, Eng	3161	8.11. 0	15.57
1958 (3/23-3/29)	USS Skate (f)	Lizard, Eng	Nantucket	—	7. 5. 0	—
1958 (7/23-8/7)	USS Nautilus (g)	Pearl Harbor	Iceland (via N. Pole)	—	15. 0. 0	—
1960 (2/16-5/10)	USS Triton (h)	New London	Rehoboth, Del	41500	84. 0. 0	20.59†
1960 (8/15-8/20)	USS Seadragon (i)	Baffin Bay	NW Passage, Pac	850	6. 0. 0	—
1962 (10/30-11/11)	African Comet* (U.S.)	New York	Cape Town	6786	12.16.22	22.03
1973 (8/20)	Sea-Land Exchange (k) (U.S.)	Bishop Rock	Ambrose	2912	3.11.24	34.92
1973 (8/24)	Sea-Land Trade (U.S.)	Kobe	Race Rock, BC	4126	5. 6. 0	32.75

† The time taken and/or distance covered is approximate and so, therefore, is the average speed.

* Maiden voyage. (a) The Savannah, a fully rigged sailing vessel with steam auxiliary (over 300 tons, 98.5 ft. long, beam 25.8 ft., depth 12.9 ft.) was launched in the East River in 1818. It was the first ship to use steam in crossing any ocean. It was supplied with engines and detachable iron paddle wheels. On its famous voyage it used steam 105 hours. (b) First Cunard liner. (c) First ship to complete NW Passage in one season. (d) Carried Hiroshima atomic bomb in World War II. (e) Set world speed record; average speed eastbound on maiden voyage 35.59 knots (about 41 m.p.h.). (f) First atomic submarine to cross Atlantic both ways submerged. (g) World's first atomic submarine also first to make undersea voyage under polar ice cap, 1,830 mi. from Point Barrow, Alaska, to Atlantic Ocean, Aug. 1-4, 1958, reaching North Pole Aug. 3. Second undersea transit of the North Pole made by submarine USS Skate Aug. 11, 1958, during trip from New London, Conn., and return. (h) World's largest submarine. Nuclear-powered Triton was submerged during nearly all its voyage around the globe. It duplicated the route of Ferdinand Magellan's circuit (1519-1522) 30,708 mi., starting from St. Paul Rocks off the NE coast of Brazil, Feb. 24-Apr. 25, 1960, then sailed to Cadiz, Spain, before returning home. (i) First underwater transit of Northwest Passage. (k) Fastest freighter crossing of Atlantic.

Commerce at Principal U.S. Ports

Source: Corps of Engineers, Depart. of the Army (by tonnage. 1991)

	Total	Foreign		Total	Foreign
New Orleans, LA	177,522,833	69,430,222	Portland, OR	30,029,747	18,045,249
New York, N.Y.	148,590,443	54,299,365	Marcus Hook, PA	29,903,912	14,846,738
Houston, TX	125,583,156	63,523,393	St. Louis, Metro., MO	26,037,341	0
Valdez Harbor, AK.	95,436,011	10,959	Richmond, CA	25,103,335	6,311,042
Baton Rouge, LA.	82,399,896	34,266,036	Chicago, IL	23,445,821	4,241,248
Corpus Christi, TX.	60,478,858	37,706,242	Tacoma Hrbr., WA.	22,450,622	17,943,715
Long Beach, CA.	54,807,692	23,566,412	Newport News, VA	21,851,818	19,283,579
Norfolk Harbor, VA	52,055,188	41,712,428	Seattle, WA	21,763,451	14,533,929
Tampa Harbor, FL.	49,280,790	21,116,969	Paulsboro, NJ	21,445,977	12,974,771
Los Angeles, CA.	47,272,062	24,753,555	Detroit, MI	20,700,867	3,803,715
Baltimore Hrbr., MD.	44,883,667	30,351,570	Boston, MA, Port of	18,989,416	12,144,418
Texas City, TX	41,272,401	22,103,741	Huntington, WV	15,707,397	0
Lake Charles, LA	40,813,125	23,717,364	Freeport, TX	15,176,018	6,704,198
Duluth-Supr., MN	40,802,541	7,038,676	Indiana Harbor, IN	15,054,899	669,852
Mobile, AL	39,980,262	18,453,605	Jacksonville, FL	15,002,231	6,866,833
Philadelphia, PA	36,060,212	22,904,905	Toledo Harbor, OH	14,805,833	6,421,419
Pittsburgh, PA	33,416,374	0	Cleveland, OH	14,687,619	3,989,267
Beaumont, TX	31,668,257	10,618,211	Port Everglades, FL	14,684,674	4,829,738
Pascagoula, MS	31,545,792	19,257,764	Lorain Harbor, OH.	14,568,175	14,891
Port Arthur, TX.	31,127,913	19,638,929	San Juan, RQ	13,873,968	4,788,691

Commerce on U.S. Inland Waterways

Source: Corps of Engineers, Depart. of the Army, 1991

Mississippi River System and Gulf Intracoastal Waterway

Waterway	Tons
Mississippi River, Minneapolis to the Gulf	462,735,996
Mississippi River, Minneapolis to St. Louis	79,356,272
Mississippi River, St. Louis to Cairo	101,799,998
Mississippi River, Cairo to Baton Rouge	181,802,058
Mississippi River, Baton Rouge to New Orleans. .	331,655,147
Mississippi River, New Orleans to Gulf	281,225,303
Gulf Intracoastal Waterway	112,739,177
Mississippi River System.	626,384,122

Ton-Mileage of Freight Carried on Inland Waterways

System	Ton-miles
Atlantic Coast Waterways	28,204,948
Gulf Coast Waterways	42,545,820
Pacific Coast Waterways	23,999,523
Mississippi River System, including Ohio River and Tributaries.	268,089,639
Great Lakes System, U.S. Commerce only	85,847,239
Total:	**448,687,169**

Note: Tons are for calendar year 1989; all tons are in U.S. short tons (2,000 lbs per ton); ton-miles(000) have been omitted.

Important Waterways and Canals

The St. Lawrence & Great Lakes Waterway, the largest inland navigation system on the continent, extends from the Atlantic Ocean to Duluth at the western end of Lake Superior, a distance of 2,342 miles. With the deepening of channels and locks to 27 ft., ocean carriers are able to penetrate to ports in the Canadian interior and the American midwest.

The major canals are those of the St. Lawrence Great Lakes waterway — the 3 new canals of the St. Lawrence Seaway, with their 7 locks, providing navigation for vessels of 26-foot draught from Montreal to Lake Ontario; the Welland Ship Canal by-passing the Niagara River between Lake Ontario and Lake Erie with its 8 locks, and the Sault Ste. Marie Canal and lock between Lake Huron and Lake Superior. These 16 locks overcome a drop of 580 ft. from the head of the lakes to Montreal. From Montreal to Lake Ontario the former bottleneck of narrow, shallow canals and of slow passage through 22 locks has been overcome, giving faster and safer movement for larger vessels. The new locks and linking channels now accommodate all but the largest ocean-going vessels and the upper St. Lawrence and Great Lakes are open to 80% of the world's saltwater fleet.

Subsidiary Canadian canals or branches include the St. Peters Canal between Bras d'Or Lakes and the Atlantic Ocean in Nova Scotia; the St. Ours and Chambly Canals on the Richelieu River, Quebec; the Ste. Anne and Carillon Canals on the Ottawa River; the Rideau Canal between the Ottawa River and Lake Ontario, the Trent and Murrary Canals between Lake Ontario and Georgian Bay in Ontario and the St. Andrew's Canal on the Red River. The commercial value of these canals is not great but they are maintained to control water levels and permit the passage of small vessels and pleasure craft. The Canso Canal, completed 1957, permits shipping to pass through the causeway connecting Cape Breton Island with the Nova Scotia mainland.

The Welland Canal overcomes the 326-ft. drop of Niagara Falls and the rapids of the Niagara River. It has 8 locks, each 859 ft. long, 80 ft. wide and 30 ft. deep. Regulations permit ships of 730-ft. length and 75-ft. beam to transit.

Shortest Navigable Distances Between Ports

Source: Distances Between Ports. (Pub. 151 6th Edition 1991) Defense Mapping Agency Hydrographic/Topographic Center
Distances shown are in nautical miles (1,852 meters or about 6,076.115 feet). To get statute miles, multiply by 1.15.

TO	FROM New York	Montreal	Colon[1]
Algiers, Algeria	3,617	3,592	4,745
Amsterdam, Netherlands	3,418	3,162	4,825
Baltimore, Md.	410	1,820	1,901
Barcelona, Spain	3,710	3,695	4,842
Boston, Mass.	378	1,309	2,157
Buenos Aires, Argentina	5,871	6,455	5,346
Cape Town, S. Africa[2]	6,766	7,115	6,429
Cherbourg, France	3,127	2,878	4,541
Cobh, Ireland	2,879	2,603	4,308
Copenhagen, Denmark	3,720	3,241	5,129
Dakar, Senegal	3,335	3,562	3,694
Galveston, Tex.	1,895	3,165	1,492
Gibraltar[3]	3,204	3,184	4,329
Glasgow, Scotland	3,065	2,691	4,746
Halifax, N.S.	600	958	2,295
Hamburg, W. Germany	3,636	3,398	5,054
Hamilton, Bermuda	697	1,621	1,659
Havana, Cuba	1,199	2,473	998
Helsinki, Finland	4,208	3,778	5,902
Istanbul, Turkey	5,001	4,981	6,129
Kingston, Jamaica	1,474	2,690	551
Lagos, Nigeria	4,883	5,130	5,033
Lisbon, Portugal	2,980	2,941	4,155
Marseille, France	3,891	3,870	5,019
Montreal, Quebec	1,516		3,126
Naples, Italy	4,181	4,159	5,309
Nassau, Bahamas	962	2,274	1,166
New Orleans, La.	1,761	2,991	1,389
New York, N.Y.		1,516	1,974
Norfolk, Va.	287	1,697	1,779
Oslo, Norway	3,701	3,222	5,306
Piraeus, Greece	4,687	4,661	5,806
Port Said, Egypt	5,123	5,093	6,238
Rio de Janeiro, Brazil	4,770	5,342	4,367
St. John's, Nfld.	1,093	1,038	2,345
San Juan, Puerto Rico	1,399	2,445	993
Southampton, England	3,156	3,063	4,514

TO	FROM San. Fran.	Vancouver	Panama[1]
Acapulco, Mexico	1,833	2,645	1,426
Anchorage, Alas.	1,872	1,347	5,117
Bombay, India	9,791	9,519	9,248
Calcutta, India	9,006	8,728	10,929
Colon, Panama[1]	3,289	4,076	44
Jakarta, Indonesia	7,642	7,413	10,570
Haiphong, Vietnam	6,657	6,358	9,806
Hong Kong	6,044	5,756	9,195
Honolulu, Hawaii	2,091	2,423	4,685
Los Angeles, Cal.	369	1,162	2,913
Manila, Philippines	6,221	5,756	9,347
Melbourne, Australia	6,970	7,342	7,928
Pusan, S. Korea	4,914	4,623	8,074
Ho Chi Min City, Vietnam	6,878	6,606	10,017
San Francisco, Cal.		812	3,245
Seattle, Wash.	796	126	4,020
Shanghai, China	5,398	5,110	8,566
Singapore	7,353	7,078	10,505
Suva, Fiji	4,749	5,199	6,325
Valparaiso, Chile	5,140	5,915	2,616
Vancouver, B.C.	812		4,032
Vladivostok, USSR	4,563	4,262	7,739
Yokohama, Japan	4,536	4,262	7,682

TO	FROM Port Said	Cape Town[2]	Singapore
Bombay, India	3,046	4,616	2,441
Calcutta, India	4,691	5,638	1,649
Dar es Salaam, Tanzania	3,238	2,365	4,042
Jakarta, Indonesia	5,293	5,212	526
Hong Kong	6,472	7,006	1,454
Kuwait City, Kuwait	3,306	5,169	3,845
Manila, Philippines	6,348	6,777	1,330
Melbourne, Australia	7,837	6,104	3,844
Ho Chi Min City, Vietnam	5,667	6,263	649
Singapore	5,018	5,611	
Yokohama, Japan	7,907	8,503	2,889

(1) Colon on the Atlantic is 44 nautical miles from Panama (port) on the Pacific. (2) Cape Town is 35 nautical miles northwest of the Cape of Good Hope. (3) Gibraltar (port) is 24 nautical miles east of the Strait of Gibraltar.

Major Merchant Fleets of the World

Source: Maritime Administration, U.S. Commerce Department

Fleets of oceangoing steam and motor ships totalling 1 million gross tons and over as of Jan. 1, 1991. Excludes ships operating exclusively on the Great Lakes and inland waterways and special types such as channel ships, icebreakers, cable ships, etc., and merchant ships owned by any military force. Gross tonnage is a volume measurement; each cargo gross ton represents 100 cubic ft. of enclosed space. Deadweight tonnage is the carrying capacity of a ship in long tons (2,240 lbs.). Tonnage figures may not add, due to rounding.

(tonnage in thousands)

	Total			Type of Vessel — Freighters			Bulk Carriers			Tankers		
	Number	Gross Tons	Dwt. Tons	Number	Gross Tons	Dwt. Tons	Number	Gross Tons	Dwt. Tons	Number	Gross Tons	Dwt. Tons
All Countries[1]	23,596	386,736	637,493	12,441	97,296	120,037	5,446	137,154	244,253	5,361	147,815	271,749
United States[2]	636	16,103	24,342	367	6,708	7,326	26	740	1,274	233	8,501	15,650
Privately owned	408	13,306	20,771	173	4,447	4,592	25	725	1,249	207	8,056	14,900
Government owned	228	2,797	3,571	194	2,261	2,734	1	15	25	26	445	750
Argentina	131	1,681	2,722	65	547	803	17	504	880	49	630	1,039
Australia	73	2,209	3,373	23	206	239	29	1,063	1,804	21	940	1,330
Bahamas	627	14,847	25,011	251	1,807	2,378	145	4,049	6,971	188	8,080	15,442
Belgium	56	1,720	2,891	17	266	300	19	979	1,847	20	475	744
Brazil	278	5,784	9,818	95	685	918	94	2,968	5,182	87	2,129	3,716
British Dep Terr	568	13,138	22,619	276	2,109	2,700	169	5,622	10,136	118	5,366	9,769
Bulgaria	117	1,255	1,873	61	374	467	36	591	931	18	288	473
China (Communist)	1,366	13,472	20,665	897	6,339	8,878	268	5,188	8,842	183	1,800	2,868
Cyprus	1,149	18,922	34,171	572	3,506	5,273	433	9,435	17,143	140	5,954	11,748
Denmark (Dis)	241	4,562	6,915	156	1,957	2,109	13	400	722	72	2,205	4,084
France	109	3,003	4,801	52	958	1,030	8	204	336	44	1,815	3,421
Germany, Federal	484	5,000	6,331	383	3,582	4,296	33	734	1,156	59	509	826
Greece	911	21,748	40,653	238	1,747	2,548	429	10,538	19,573	214	9,263	18,431
India	304	6,022	10,079	111	1,076	1,592	127	3,164	5,429	63	1,767	3,051
Indonesia	366	1,545	2,454	250	822	1,283	18	167	246	91	549	914
Iran	127	4,621	8,616	38	405	564	50	1,066	1,771	39	3,150	6,281
Isle of Man	86	1,820	3,225	27	240	277	19	585	1,047	40	995	1,901
Italy	512	7,212	11,444	187	1,251	1,482	70	2,558	4,617	238	3,003	5,215
Japan	960	22,680	35,232	393	4,197	3,393	267	9,551	17,569	286	8,768	14,215
Korea (South)	438	7,143	11,875	221	1,637	1,943	155	4,731	8,533	62	775	1,399
Kuwait	28	1,330	2,268	5	111	148	—	—	—	23	1,219	2,120
Liberia	1,542	51,276	92,057	364	5,536	5,944	578	16,908	31,503	581	28,327	54,494
Malaysia	160	1,553	2,283	100	556	786	20	387	682	40	610	815
Malta	392	4,605	8,029	185	939	1,491	112	1,846	3,239	90	1,774	3,281
Mexico	63	1,000	1,539	14	100	134	8	173	269	41	727	1,136
Netherlands	338	2,897	3,931	267	1,746	2,257	14	362	590	53	680	1,066
Norway (Nis)	781	21,689	39,157	195	1,761	2,002	250	7,204	13,299	324	12,482	23,804
Panama	2,953	41,695	67,938	1,631	12,594	15,657	713	15,592	27,175	579	13,239	24,981
Philippines	531	8,037	13,583	230	1,261	1,692	254	6,378	11,173	38	356	695
Poland	246	3,042	4,256	144	1,269	1,404	92	1,608	2,595	7	145	247
Romania	306	3,834	6,024	219	1,258	1,665	71	1,900	3,165	16	676	1,194
Saudi Arabia	86	1,553	2,572	44	513	732	3	57	82	36	972	1,750
Singapore	427	7,987	13,084	214	2,341	2,897	81	2,312	4,183	132	3,334	6,004
Spain	287	2,911	5,511	168	421	666	45	884	1,623	72	1,588	3,216
Sweden	174	2,274	3,044	87	973	948	20	437	723	64	788	1,358
Taiwan	227	5,885	9,207	142	2,364	2,792	69	2,883	5,293	16	638	1,122
Turkey	339	3,778	6,655	200	702	1,078	85	2,253	4,082	50	803	1,488
U.A.R. (Egypt)	134	1,072	1,710	103	454	646	14	345	568	12	249	477
U.S.S.R.	2,373	18,549	24,646	1,681	9,912	11,604	239	4,105	6,529	419	4,235	6,443
United Kingdom	185	3,199	3,643	84	1,447	1,417	23	271	415	63	1,164	1,724
Vanuatu	122	2,102	3,212	62	693	692	53	1,176	2,048	7	233	472
Yugoslavia	274	3,814	6,087	166	1,432	2,002	94	2,052	3,553	11	313	527

(1) Includes Combination Passenger & Cargo Ships; (2) Excludes non-merchant type and/or Navy-owned vessels that are currently in the Nat. Reserve Fleet.

World Motor Vehicle Production, 1950-1990

Source: Motor Vehicle Manufacturers Association

(in thousands)

Year	United States	Canada	Europe	Japan	Other	World Total	U.S. Percent of World Total
1950	8,006	388	1,991	32	160	10,577	75.7%
1955	9,204	452	3,738	68	166	13,628	67.5
1960	7,905	398	6,830	482	873	16,488	47.9
1965	11,138	847	9,571	1,876	835	24,267	45.9
1970	8,284	1,160	13,243	5,289	1,427	29,403	28.2
1975	8,987	1,424	13,473	6,942	2,172	32,998	27.2
1980	8,010	1,374	15,446	11,043	2,641	38,514	20.8
1981	7,943	1,323	14,440	11,180	2,344	37,230	21.3
1982	6,986	1,276	14,808	10,732	2,311	36,113	19.3
1983	9,205	1,524	15,708	11,112	2,206	39,755	23.2
1984	10,939	1,829	15,293	11,465	2,532	42,058	26.0
1985	11,653	1,933	15,959	12,271	2,995	44,811	26.0
1986	11,335	1,854	16,701	12,260	3,147	45,297	25.0
1987	10,925	1,635	17,518	12,249	3,576	45,903	23.8
1988	11,214	1,949	18,213	12,700	4,134	48,210	23.3
1989	10,874	1,934	18,946	13,026	4,216	48,996	22.2
1990	9,780	1,896	18,614	13,487	4,336	48,113	20.3

Fastest Scheduled Passenger Train Runs in the U.S. and Canada

Source: Darrell J. Smith; 1991 timetables

Railroad	Train	From	To	Mi.	Min.	MPH
Amtrak	Eight Metroliner Service trains	Wilmington	Baltimore	68.4	42	97.7
Amtrak	16 Metroliner Service trains	Baltimore	Wilmington	68.4	43	95.0
Amtrak	Express Metroliner Service train 203	Metropark	Baltimore	160.0	103	93.0
Amtrak	Express Metroliner Service train 202	New Carrollton	New York	216.0	141	91.9
Amtrak	Express Metroliner Service train 218	Washington	Philadelphia	135.0	88	91.8
Amtrak	Express Metroliner Service train 223	New York	Baltimore	185.0	123	90.2
Amtrak	Two Metroliner Service trains	Newark	Philadelphia	80.7	55	87.7
Amtrak	Nine Metroliner Service trains	Newark	Philadelphia	80.7	56	86.8
Amtrak	Metroliner Service train 102	Philadelphia	Newark	80.7	57	84.9
VIA	Renaissance	Dorval	Kingston	165.0	117	84.6
VIA	York	Kingston	Cornwall	108.0	77	84.4
Amtrak	Two Metroliner Service trains	Philadelphia	Newark	80.7	58	83.2
VIA	York	Cornwall	Kingston	108.0	78	83.1
VIA	Renaissance	Kingston	Dorval	165.0	120	82.5

Note: The fastest schedule passenger train runs in the world are those of France's TGV Atlantique, between Paris and various cities in western France, at 186.4 mph.

Best-Selling Cars in the U.S.

Source: *Ward's Automotive Yearbooks*

1965-1969: Full-size Chevrolet Impala, Caprice, Biscayne, Bel Air
1970: Full-size Ford Custom LTD, Galaxie 500
1971-1972: Full-size Chevrolet Impala, Caprice, Biscayne, Bel Air
1973-1974: Full-size Chevrolet Impala, Caprice, Bel Air
1975: Full-size Chevrolet Impala, Caprice
1976: Oldsmobile Cutlass

1977-1979: Full-size Chevrolet Impala, Caprice
1980: Chevrolet Citation
1981: Chevrolet Chevette
1982-1983: Ford Escort
1984-1985: Chevrolet Cavalier
1986: Chevrolet Celebrity
1987-1988: Ford Escort/EXP
1989-1990: Honda Accord

Top 50 U.S. Industrial Exporters

Source: *FORTUNE* magazine; May, 1991

Rank 1990	1989	Company	Export sales $ Millions	% change 1989-90	Exports as % of Sales
1	1	Boeing	16,093.0	46.0	58.3
2	2	General Motors	10,315.9	1.3	8.2
3	4	General Electric	7,128.0	(1.9)	12.2
4	3	Ford Motor	7,098.0	14.0	7.2
5	5	Int'l Business Machines	6,195.0	13.1	9.0
6	7	Chrysler	5,004.0	(7.1)	16.2
7	6	E.I. Du Pont De Nemours	4,352.0	(10.2)	10.9
8	8	United Technologies	3,606.0	9.0	16.6
9	10	McDonnell Douglas	3,538.0	22.2	21.6
10	9	Caterpillar	3,435.0	4.4	29.8
11	11	Eastman Kodak	2,957.0	2.9	15.5
12	15	Philip Morris	2,928.0	28.0	6.6
13	12	Hewlett-Packard	2,816.0	6.9	21.3
14	14	Motorola	2,801.0	20.8	25.7
15	13	Unisys	2,203.7	(8.2)	21.8
16	17	Occidental Petroleum	2,077.0	4.1	9.5
17	16	Digital Equipment	1,920.3	(8.7)	14.7
18	18	Allied-Signal	1,838.0	8.6	14.8
19	21	General Dynamics	1,624.0	6.7	15.9
20	9	Weyerhaeuser	1,560.0	(0.9)	17.3
21	22	Raytheon	1,435.0	7.1	15.3
22	25	Dow Chemical	1,344.0	16.2	6.7
23	20	Union Carbide	1,280.0	(18.0)	16.8
24	33	Intel	1,202.3	20.5	29.1
25	31	Minnesota Mining & Mfg.	1,199.0	17.7	9.2
26	26	Westinghouse Electric	1,195.0	5.7	9.3
27	24	Archer-Daniels-Midland	1,162.7	(3.79)	14.7
28	30	Merck	1,156.3	11.3	14.8
29	35	Compaq Computer	1,121.4	25.1	30.9
30	40	Sun Microsystems	1,117.3	48.7	45.0
31	23	Textron	1,103.0	(8.8)	13.9
32	32	Exxon	1,101.0	8.0	1.0
33	27	International Paper	1,100.0	0.0	8.5
34	29	Hoechst Celanese	1,085.0	4.4	18.4
35	28	Monsanto	1,079.0	0.8	11.9
36	34	Aluminum Co. of America	926.0	(1.0)	8.5
37	37	Xerox	900.0	16.9	4.9
38	38	Bayer USA	865.0	13.9	14.7
39	48	FMC	848.0	18.4	22.6
40	36	Rockwell Int'l	835.0	4.4	6.7
41	44	Abbott Laboratories	814.5	18.9	13.1
42	41	Deere	758.0	2.2	9.6
43	42	Honeywell	750.0	4.5	10.7
44	45	Amoco	743.0	11.2	2.6
45	47	Bristol-Myers Squibb	741.0	16.1	7.1
46	46	Tenneco	711.0	10.4	4.8
47	50	Cooper Industries	662.7	16.0	10.7
48	*	Reynolds Metals	639.0	13.5	10.5
49	49	Ethyl	592.7	0.0	23.6
50	39	Lockheed	588.0	(22.0)	5.9
		Total	**$118,544.8**		

World Motor Vehicle Production, 1990

Source: Motor Vehicle Manufacturers Association

Country	Passenger Cars	Trucks and Buses	Total	Country	Passenger Cars	Trucks and Buses	Total
Argentina	81,107	18,532	99,639	Italy	1,874,672	246,178	2,120,850
Australia	360,912	23,183	384,095	Japan	9,947,972	3,538,824	13,486,796
Austria	14,741	5,265	20,006	Korea, South	986,751	334,879	1,321,630
Belgium	311,803	73,460	385,263	Mexico	598,093	222,465	820,558
Brazil	663,084	251,587	914,671	The Netherlands	121,300	29,832	151,132
Canada	1,045,498	850,608	1,896,106	Poland	295,000	70,000	365,000
China	24,202	406,840	431,042	Spain	1,679,301	374,049	2,053,350
Czechoslovakia	188,000	54,000	242,000	Sweden	335,853	74,415	410,268
France	3,294,815	474,178	3,768,993	United Kingdom	1,295,611	270,133	1,565,744
Germany, East	152,537	34,353	186,890	United States	6,077,449	3,702,787	9,780,236
Germany, West	4,660,657	315,895	4,976,552	U.S.S.R.	1,200,000	840,000	2,040,000
Hungary	—	8,525	8,525	Yugoslavia	289,362	29,754	319,116
India	176,609	187,572	364,181	**Total**	**35,675,329**	**12,437,314**	**48,112,643**

Note: As far as can be determined, production in this table refers to vehicles locally manufactured.

Selected Motor Vehicle Statistics

Source: Federal Highway Adm.; National Transportation Safety Board; Insurance Institute for Highway Safety

State	Driver's age Jan. 1, 1991 (1) Regular	(2) Juvenile	1990 Licensed drivers[3] (1,000)	1990 Registered cars, buses, trucks[3] (1,000)	State gas tax gal. cents (April 1, 1991)	1989 Vehicle-Miles of Travel (millions)	1990 Motorfuel consumption[3] Highway (millions) gallons	Non-Highway (millions) gallons	Safety belt use law[4] (Aug. 1, 1991)
Alabama	16	—	2,866	3,683	13	40,765	2,603	2,658	S
Alaska	16	—	302	368	8	3,887	261	297	S
Arizona	16	—	2,421	2,851	18	34,816	2,025	2,046	S
Arkansas	16	—	1,730	1,448	18.7	20,414	1,607	1,627	S
California	16/18	14	19,959	22,176	15	251,482	14,920	15,008	S
Colorado	18	16	2,133	3,244	22	27,577	1,667	1,709	S
Connecticut	16/18	—	2,395	2,672	22	26,183	1,590	1,555	P
Delaware	16/18	—	487	531	19	6,446	390	389	S
Dist. of Col.	18	16	397	254	18	3,414	198	194	S
Florida	16	—	9,213	11,532	11.2	108,877	6,681	6,784	S
Georgia	16	—	4,447	5,378	7.5	75,705	4,313	4,358	S
Hawaii	15	—	664	760	11	7,750	388	387	P
Idaho	16½	14	717	1,034	18	8,422	563	566	S
Illinois	16/18	—	7,277	8,123	19	81,297	5,902	6,092	S
Indiana	16/18	—	3,860	4,414	15	56,192	3,306	3,397	S
Iowa	16/18	—	1,950	2,599	20	22,571	1,667	1,633	P
Kansas	16	14	1,731	2,002	16	21,913	1,534	1,491	S
Kentucky	16	—	2,423	2,890	15.4	32,165	2,308	2,371	No
Louisiana	15/17	15	2,582	3,013	20	37,914	2,287	2,201	S
Maine	16/17	16	899	946	17	11,739	701	699	No
Maryland	16/18	16	3,163	3,580	18.5	38,922	2,419	2,323	S
Massachusetts	17/18	16 ½	4,343	3,787	21	46,214	2,676	2,618	No
Michigan	16/18	14	6,435	7,210	15	79,890	4,722	4,769	S
Minnesota	16/18	15	2,439	3,341	20	37,393	2,290	2,284	S
Mississippi	15	—	1,874	1,902	18.2	22,895	1,513	1,542	P
Missouri	16	—	3,576	3,890	11.03	48,087	3,308	3,284	S
Montana	15/16	13	599	758	20	8,250	529	534	S
Nebraska	16	14	1,081	1,387	24.2	13,781	943	949	No
Nevada	16	14	812	847	18	9,408	740	748	S
New Hampshire	16/18	16	822	955	16.6	9,819	575	566	No
New Jersey	17	16	5,688	5,593	10.5	59,898	3,848	3,885	S
New Mexico	15/16	—	1,073	1,319	17	15,839	993	1,004	P
New York	17/18	16	10,290	10,157	15.64	106,059	6,255	6,416	P
North Carolina	16/18	—	4,573	5,226	22.3	60,877	3,838	3,856	P
North Dakota	16	14	426	629	17	5,849	413	413	No
Ohio	16/18	14	7,385	9,391	20	84,418	5,811	5,781	S
Oklahoma	16	—	2,329	2,592	17	32,836	1,984	1,993	S
Oregon	16	14	2,216	2,440	20	25,820	1,634	1,669	P
Pennsylvania	17/18	16	7,844	8,027	17.8	83,855	5,481	5,555	S
Rhode Island	16/18	—	693	669	26	6,740	420	416	S
South Carolina	16	15	2,383	2,555	16	32,780	2,044	2,113	S
South Dakota	16	14	493	722	18	6,704	453	451	No
Tennessee	16	14	3,477	4,409	20	45,639	3,085	3,086	S
Texas	16/18	15	11,137	12,708	15	159,512	9,761	9,846	P
Utah	16/18	—	1,041	1,191	19	13,915	850	836	S
Vermont	18	16	414	470	16	5,765	317	318	No
Virginia	16/19	—	4,310	4,982	17.7	59,337	3,527	3,539	S
Washington	16/18	—	3,319	4,291	23	43,233	2,603	2,595	S
West Virginia	16/18	16	1,312	1,222	20.35	14,940	985	981	No
Wisconsin	16/18	14	3,314	3,567	22.2	43,086	2,470	2,479	S
Wyoming	16	14	341	493	9	5,750	468	453	S
Total[5]			**167.655**	**190.228**		**2,107,040**	**131,865**	**132,764**	

(1) Unrestricted operation of private passenger car. When 2 ages are shown, license is issued at lower age upon completion of approved driver education course. (2) Juvenile license issued with consent of parent or guardian. (3) Estimated. (4) P = an officer may stop a vehicle for a violation (primary); S = an officer may only issue a seat belt citation when the vehicle is stopped for another moving violation (secondary); (5) Figures may not add, due to rounding.

Personal Consumption Expenditures for Transportation

Source: Motor Vehicle Manufacturers Association

(in millions)

	1980	1982	1984	1986	1987	1988	1989	1990
User-Operated Transportation								
New Autos	$46,395	$53,336	$77,560	$100,329	$93,497	$101,114	$99,734	$96,089
Net Purchases of Used Autos	14,905	19,648	30,151	35,829	38,155	40,926	41,619	43,709
Other Motor Vehicles[1]	12,298	15,637	26,412	33,555	35,128	39,187	41,653	39,111
Tires, Tubes and Accessories and Parts	16,684	20,234	23,319	26,481	28,693	30,966	32,483	34,114
Repair, Greasing, Washing, Parking, Storage and Rental	32,327	35,441	42,838	51,952	55,501	63,228	69,621	76,759
Gasoline and Oil	83,721	89,090	90,006	73,457	75,162	77,254	83,804	93,754
Bridge, Tunnel, Ferry and Road Tolls	1,061	1,224	1,300	1,682	1,878	1,663	1,741	1,895
Insurance Premiums, Less Claims Paid	9,383	9,054	9,993	12,590	15,379	16,665	16,954	18,195
Total User-Operated Transportation	$216,774	$243,664	$301,579	$335,875	$343,393	$371,003	$387,609	$403,626
Purchased Local Transportation								
Transit Systems	$2,431	$3,038	$3,428	$3,855	$3,967	$4,235	$4,335	$4,503
Taxicabs	3,082	2,953	3,042	3,294	3,530	3,802	3,886	4,071
Railway Commutation	300	395	458	648	658	680	678	722
Total Purchased Local Transportation	$5,813	$6,386	$6,928	$7,797	$8,155	$8,717	$8,899	$9,296
Purchased Intercity Transportation								
Railway Excluding Commutation	$362	$445	$582	$662	$714	$825	$942	$990
Bus	1,171	1,252	1,227	1,105	1,413	1,640	1,323	1,130
Airline	13,425	14,653	17,536	18,795	21,190	22,757	24,167	25,217
Other	939	1,236	1,640	2,031	2,231	2,517	2,772	3,102
Total Purchased Intercity Transportation	$15,897	$17,586	$20,985	$22,593	$25,548	$27,739	$29,204	$30,439
Total Transportation	$238,484	$267,636	$329,492	$366,265	$377,096	$407,459	$425,712	$443,361
Total Personal Consumption Expenditures	$1,732,559	$2,050,661	$2,430,455	$2,797,437	$3,010,821	$3,238,192	$3,450,085	$3,657,304

(1) New and used trucks, recreation vehicles, etc.

Domestic and Imported Retail Car Sales in the U.S., 1978-1990

Source: Motor Vehicle Manufacturers Assn.

Calendar Year	Domestic	Imports From Japan	Imports From Germany	Imports Other Countries	Imports Total	U.S. Total	Import Percent Total	Import Percent Japan	U.S. Sponsored Imports
1978	9,311,666	1,357,337	435,952	209,124	2,002,413	11,314,079	17.7	12.0	202,738
1979	8,341,139	1,755,818	366,084	209,727	2,331,629	10,672,768	21.8	16.5	248,839
1980	6,581,307	1,905,968	305,219	186,700	2,397,887	8,979,194	26.7	21.2	223,310
1981	6,208,760	1,858,896	282,581	185,502	2,327,273	8,536,039	27.3	21.8	174,665
1982	5,758,586	1,801,969	247,080	174,508	2,223,557	7,982,143	27.9	22.6	139,767
1983	6,795,295	1,915,621	279,748	191,403	2,386,772	9,182,067	26.0	20.9	136,798
1984	7,951,543	1,906,206	344,416	188,220	2,438,842	10,390,365	23.5	18.3	116,965
1985	8,204,542	2,217,837	423,983	195,925	2,837,745	11,042,287	25.7	20.1	206,252
1986	8,214,897	2,382,614	443,721	418,286	3,244,621	11,459,518	28.3	20.8	314,358
1987	7,080,858	2,190,405	347,881	657,415	3,195,701	10,276,559	31.1	21.3	348,154
1988	7,526,038	2,022,602	280,099	700,991	3,003,692	10,529,730	28.5	19.2	393,412
1989	7,072,902	1,897,143	248,561	553,660	2,699,364	9,772,266	27.6	19.4	340,425
1990	6,896,888	1,719,839	266,775	417,802	2,404,416	9,301,304	25.8	18.5	296,778

Top 20 New Passenger Car Models Sold in the U.S., 1990

Source: Motor Vehicle Manufacturers Assn. & Ward's Automotive Reports.

Ranking and Model	Domestic*	Import	Total	Ranking and Model	Domestic*	Import	Total
1. Honda Accord	276,878	140,301	417,179	12. Cadillac DeVille/ Fleetwood	168,832	—	168,832
2. Ford Taurus	313,274	—	313,274	13. Nissan Sentra	109,575	49,479	159,054
3. Chevrolet Cavalier	295,123	—	295,123	14. Chevrolet Caprice	154,067	—	154,067
4. Ford Escort	288,727	—	288,727	15. Buick LeSabre	150,924	—	150,924
5. Toyota Camry	212,587	72,008	284,595	16. Lincoln Town Car	148,689	—	148,689
6. Chevrolet Corsica/ Beretta	277,176	—	277,176	17. Oldsmobile Ciera	133,446	—	133,446
7. Toyota Corolla	135,953	92,258	228,211	18. Ford Mustang	124,135	—	124,135
8. Honda Civic	187,240	33,612	220,852	19. Pontiac Sunbird	123,421	—	123,421
9. Chevrolet Lumina	218,288	—	218,288	20. Ford Crown Victoria	118,017	—	118,017
10. Ford Tempo	215,290	—	215,290				
11. Pontiac Grand Am	202,149	—	202,149				

* Units produced in the United States, Canada and Mexico.

Passenger Car Production, U.S. Plants

Source: Motor Vehicle Manufacturers Assn.

	1989	1990
Chrysler Corp.		
Horizon	32,937	4,327
Sundance	100,618	87,587
Acclaim	125,292	120,440
Total Plymouth	**258,847**	**212,354**
LeBaron	10	8,071
LeBaron GTS	2,946	0
LeBaron J	93,670	52,026
Fifth Avenue (Y)	26,883	41,366
Imperial	5,740	16,280
New Yorker (C)	74,375	34,876
Total Chrysler-Plymouth	**462,471**	**364,973**
Omni	34,621	4,078
Daytona	72,452	33,376
Shadow	104,145	95,681
Spirit	108,046	105,587
Lancer	1,528	0
Dynasty	132,636	123,047
Total Dodge	**453,428**	**361,769**
Total Chrysler Corp.	**915,899**	**726,742**
Ford Motor Co.		
Thunderbird	137,326	107,366
Taurus	362,144	329,852
Tempo	146,928	125,151
Escort	347,271	242,031
Mustang	172,217	129,066
Total Ford	**1,165,886**	**933,466**
Cougar	114,250	73,373
Sable	116,874	101,334
Topaz	66,554	46,729
Town Car	127,486	145,806
Mark	21,544	18,023
Continental	64,487	58,620
Total Lincoln-Mercury	**511,195**	**443,885**
Total Ford Motor Co.	**1,677,081**	**1,377,351**
General Motors Corp.		
Geo Prizm	112,111	102,296
Cavalier	355,075	360,798
Camaro	100,613	70,982
Beretta-Corsica	370,741	269,143
Celebrity	70,365	0
Chevrolet	162,792	200,006
Corvette	25,256	22,154
Total Chevrolet	**1,196,953**	**1,025,379**
Sunbird	151,177	167,405
Firebird	56,441	40,375
Grand Am	226,882	204,812
6000	78,910	51,529
Grand Prix W	125,191	112,936
Safari	2,690	0
Bonneville H	90,886	72,198
Total Pontiac	**732,177**	**649,255**
Calais	87,747	99,981
Ciera	87,908	65,339
Supreme W	115,084	93,786
Delta 88 B	7,654	3,430
Delta 88 H	140,757	99,088
Oldsmobile 98	71,497	42,346
Toronado	10,334	14,772
Total Oldsmobile	**520,981**	**418,742**
Skyhawk	6,913	0
Skylark	68,464	94,118
Century	122,766	63,780
LeSabre B	8,080	4,022
LeSabre H	156,776	154,066
Electra-Park Avenue	80,049	62,243
Reatta	6,378	5,587
Riviera	20,626	21,307
Total Buick	**470,052**	**405,123**
Cadillac C	194,264	161,609
Cadillac D	42,613	30,048
Eldorado	29,161	22,048
Seville	24,319	35,328
Allante	3,232	3,507
Total Cadillac	**293,589**	**252,540**
Total Saturn	**0**	**4,245**
Total General Motors Corp.	**3,213,752**	**2,755,284**
Diamond Star		
Mitsubishi Eclipse	40,898	58,528
Mitsubishi Mirage	0	5,340
Plymouth Laser	36,914	41,990
Eagle Talon	12,915	37,958
Eagle Summit	0	4,563
Total Diamond Star	**90,727**	**148,379**
Honda of America		
Accord	232,965	333,921
Civic	129,309	101,516
Total Honda of America	**362,274**	**435,437**
Mazda	216,501	184,428
Nissan Sentra	115,584	95,844
Subaru Legacy	0	32,461
Toyota		
Corolla	80,129	103,308
Camry	151,150	218,215
Total Toyota	**231,279**	**321,523**
Total Passenger Cars 1990	—	**6,077,449**
Total Passenger Cars 1989	**6,823,097**	—
1990/1989 Percent Change	—	**−10.93**

Countries with Safety Belt Use Laws

Source: Motor Vehicle Manufacturers Assn.

Country	Effective Date	Country	Effective Date
Australia	1/72	Hong Kong	10/83
Austria	7/76	Hungary	7/77
Belgium	6/75	Iceland	10/81
Brazil	6/72	Ireland	2/79
Bulgaria	1976	Israel	7/75
Canadian Provinces		Ivory Coast	1970
Alberta	7/87	Japan	12/71
British Columbia	10/77	Jordan	12/83
Manitoba	4/84	Luxembourg	6/75
Newfoundland	7/82	Malaysia	4/79
New Brunswick	11/83	Netherlands	6/75
Nova Scotia	1/85	New Zealand	6/72
Ontario	1/76	Norway	9/75
Prince Edward Island	1/88	Poland	1/84
Quebec	7/76	Portugal	1/78
Saskatchewan	7/77	Singapore	7/81
Czechoslovakia	1/69	South Africa	12/77
Denmark	1/76	Spain	10/74
East Germany	1/80	Sweden	1/75
Finland	7/75	Switzerland	1/76
France	10/79	Turkey	10/84
Greece	12/79		

Licensed Drivers, by Age

Source: Federal Highway Administration, U.S. Dept. of Transportation

Age	1989 Male	1989 Female	1989 Total	Percent male	Estimated 1990 Male (1,000)	Estimated 1990 Female (1,000)	Estimated 1990 Total (1,000)	Percent change total drivers 1979-1989
UNDER 16	20,623	17,076	37,699	54.70	21	17	38	−71.44
16	782,874	680,197	1,463,071	53.51	793	689	1,482	−23.24
17	1,223,631	1,068,803	2,292,434	53.38	1,239	1,082	2,321	−20.21
18	1,492,273	1,314,456	2,806,729	53.17	1,511	1,331	2,842	−16.27
19	1,632,933	1,441,420	3,074,353	53.11	1,654	1,460	3,114	−14.74
(19 AND UNDER)	5,152,334	4,521,952	9,674,286	53.26	5,218	4,579	9,797	−18.49
20	1,640,744	1,487,995	3,128,739	52.44	1,662	1,507	3,169	−14.21
21	1,675,400	1,525,991	3,201,391	52.33	1,697	1,545	3,242	−14.26
22	1,740,984	1,593,520	3,334,504	52.21	1,763	1,614	3,377	−14.04
23	1,842,013	1,694,446	3,536,459	52.09	1,865	1,716	3,581	−8.78
24	1,927,475	1,775,477	3,702,952	52.05	1,952	1,798	3,750	−3.92
(20-24)	8,826,616	8,077,429	16,904,045	52.22	8,939	8,180	17,119	−10.99
25-29	10,610,942	9,957,814	20,568,756	51.59	10,744	10,083	20,827	10.54
30-34	10,520,867	9,993,301	20,514,168	51.29	10,654	10,120	20,774	23.77
35-39	9,459,038	9,100,647	18,559,685	50.97	9,579	9,216	18,795	39.61
40-44	8,234,177	7,885,472	16,119,649	51.08	8,338	7,986	16,324	47.85
45-49	6,453,109	6,130,656	12,583,765	51.28	6,535	6,209	12,744	23.60
50-54	5,289,021	4,969,838	10,258,859	51.56	5,356	5,033	10,389	0.51
55-59	4,915,299	4,590,354	9,505,653	51.71	4,978	4,649	9,627	−2.18
60-64	4,784,316	4,529,043	9,313,359	51.37	4,845	4,587	9,432	15.95
65-69	4,236,274	4,028,846	8,265,120	51.25	4,290	4,080	8,370	28.78
70 AND OVER	6,896,429	6,391,521	13,287,950	51.90	6,984	6,473	13,457	56.51
TOTAL	85,378,422	80,176,873	165,555,295	51.57	86,460	81,195	167,655	15.54

Motor Vehicle Data by U.S. Household, 1983, 1985, and 1988

Source: Annual Energy Review, 1990, Energy Information Administration, U.S. Dept. of Energy

	Less than $25,000 1983	Less than $25,000 1985	Less than $25,000 1988	$25,000 or More 1983	$25,000 or More 1985	$25,000 or More 1988	All Income Categories 1983	All Income Categories 1985	All Income Categories 1988
Households with Vehicles (millions)	42.9	43.3	38.9	30.5	34.5	42.2	73.4	77.7	81.3
Vehicles (millions)	66.7	65.4	58.7	63.0	71.9	88.8	129.7	137.3	147.5
Vehicle Miles Traveled (billions).	589	587	550	630	766	960	1,219	1,353	1,511
Motor Fuel Consumed (billion gallons)	40.8	38.2	31.4	39.8	45.7	51.0	80.5	83.9	82.4
Motor Gasoline Consumed (billion gallons)									
Leaded	19.2	13.5	5.4	13.2	11.0	5.8	32.4	24.5	11.1
Unleaded	20.9	24.2	25.7	25.3	33.7	44.3	46.3	57.8	69.9
Motor Fuel Expenditures (billion dollars)	48.1	44.8	30.7	47.3	54.3	50.3	95.4	99.1	81.1
Averages per Household with Vehicles									
Vehicles.	1.6	1.5	1.5	2.1	2.1	2.1	1.8	1.8	1.8
Vehicle Miles Traveled	13,721	13,558	14,128	20,668	22,228	22,712	16,605	17,402	18,595
Motor Fuel Consumed (gallons)	950	883	807	1,305	1,326	1,205	1,097	1,079	1,014
Motor Fuel Expenditures (dollars)	1,121	1,035	789	1,552	1,575	1,191	1,300	1,274	998
Averages per Vehicle									
Vehicle Miles Traveled	8,837	8,972	9,383	9,996	10,658	10,816	9,400	9,855	10,246
Motor Fuel Consumed (gallons)	612	585	536	631	636	574	621	611	559
Motor Fuel Expenditures (dollars)	722	685	524	751	755	567	736	722	550
Fuel Efficiency (miles per gallon)	14.4	15.3	17.5	15.8	16.8	18.8	15.1	16.1	18.3
Price of Motor Gasoline (dollars per gallon)									
Leaded	1.14	1.11	0.90	1.14	1.11	0.90	1.14	1.11	0.90
Unleaded	1.22	1.20	0.99	1.22	1.21	1.00	1.22	1.21	1.00

Notes: Motor vehicles = automobiles, station wagons, passenger vans, cargo vans, motor homes, pickup trucks, and jeeps or similar vehicles. Excluded are motorcycles, mopeds, large trucks, and buses. Motor fuel includes motor gasoline and a small amount of other fuels such as diesel, gasohol, and propane. These data for 1983 differ from previously published 1983 data, in that the basis for estimating the number of vehicle-owning households was changed to conform with that being used for 1985. Sum of components may not equal total due to independent rounding.

Automobile Factory Sales

Source: Motor Vehicle Manufacturers Association

Year	Passenger cars Number	Motor trucks, buses Number	Total Number	Year	Passenger cars Number	Motor trucks, buses Number	Total Number
1900	4,192	—	4,190	1982	5,049,184	1,906,455	6,955,639
1910	181,000	6,000	187,000	1983	6,739,223	2,413,897	9,153,120
1920	1,905,560	321,789	2,227,349	1985	8,002,259	3,356,905	11,359,164
1930	2,787,456	575,364	3,362,820	1986	7,516,189	3,392,885	10,909,074
1940	3,717,385	754,901	4,472,286	1987	7,085,147	3,821,410	10,906,557
1950	6,665,863	1,337,193	8,003,056	1988	7,104,617	4,120,574	11,225,191
1960	6,665,863	1,194,475	7,869,271	1989	6,807,416	4,061,950	10,869,366
1970	6,546,817	1,692,440	8,239,257	1990	6,049,749	3,718,781	9,768,530

After July 1, 1964 all tactical vehicles are excluded. Federal excise taxes are excluded in all years.

Road Mileage Between Selected U.S. Cities

	Atlanta	Boston	Chicago	Cincinnati	Cleveland	Dallas	Denver	Des Moines	Detroit	Houston
Atlanta, Ga. . . .	...	1,037	674	440	672	795	1,398	870	699	789
Boston, Mass. . .	1,037	...	963	840	628	1,748	1,949	1,280	695	1,804
Chicago, Ill. . . .	674	963	...	287	335	917	996	327	266	1,067
Cincinnati, Oh. . .	440	840	287	...	244	920	1,164	571	259	1,029
Cleveland, Oh. . .	672	628	335	244	...	1,159	1,321	652	170	1,273
Dallas Tex.	795	1,748	917	920	1,159	...	781	684	1,143	243
Denver, Col. . . .	1,398	1,949	996	1,164	1,321	781	...	669	1,253	1,019
Detroit, Mich. . . .	699	695	266	259	170	1,143	1,253	584	...	1,265
Houston, Tex.. . .	789	1,804	1,067	1,029	1,273	243	1,019	905	1,265	...
Indianapolis, Ind. .	493	906	181	106	294	865	1,058	465	278	987
Kansas City, Mo. .	798	1,391	499	591	779	489	600	195	743	710
Los Angeles, Cal.	2,182	2,979	2,054	2,179	2,367	1,387	1,059	1,727	2,311	1,538
Memphis, Tenn. . .	371	1,296	530	468	712	452	1,040	599	713	561
Milwaukee, Wis. .	761	1,050	87	374	422	991	1,029	361	353	1,142
Minneapolis, Minn.	1,068	1,368	405	692	740	936	841	252	671	1,157
New Orleans, La..	479	1,507	912	786	1,030	496	1,273	978	1,045	356
New York, N.Y.. .	841	206	802	647	473	1,552	1,771	1,119	637	1,608
Omaha, Neb. . .	986	1,412	459	693	784	644	537	132	716	865
Philadelphia, Pa. .	741	296	738	567	413	1,452	1,691	1,051	573	1,508
Pittsburgh, Pa. . .	687	561	452	287	129	1,204	1,411	763	287	1,313
Portland Ore. . . .	2,601	3,046	2,083	2,333	2,418	2,009	1,238	1,786	2,349	2,205
St. Louis, Mo. . .	541	1,141	289	340	529	630	857	333	513	779
San Francisco . .	2,496	3,095	2,142	2,362	2,467	1,753	1,235	1,815	2,399	1,912
Seattle, Wash. . .	2,618	2,976	2,013	2,300	2,348	2,078	1,307	1,749	2,279	2,274
Tulsa, Okla.	772	1,537	683	736	925	257	681	443	909	478
Washington, D.C..	608	429	671	481	346	1,319	1,616	984	506	1,375

	Indianapolis	Kansas City	Los Angeles	Louisville	Memphis	Milwaukee	Minneapolis	New Orleans	New York	Omaha
Atlanta, Ga. . . .	493	798	2,182	382	371	761	1,068	479	841	986
Boston, Mass. . .	906	1,391	2,979	941	1,296	1,050	1,368	1,507	206	1,412
Chicago, Ill. . . .	181	499	2,054	292	530	87	405	912	802	459
Cincinnati, Oh. . .	106	591	2,179	101	468	374	692	786	647	693
Cleveland Oh. . .	294	779	2,367	345	712	422	740	1,030	473	784
Dallas, Tex.	865	489	1,387	819	452	991	936	496	1,552	644
Denver, Col. . . .	1,058	600	1,059	1,120	1,040	1,029	841	1,273	1,771	537
Detroit, Mich. . . .	278	743	2,311	360	713	353	671	1,045	637	716
Houston, Tex.. . .	987	710	1,538	928	561	1,142	1,157	356	1,608	865
Indianapolis, Ind. .	...	485	2,073	111	435	268	586	796	713	587
Kansas City, Mo. .	485	...	1,589	520	451	537	447	806	1,198	201
Los Angeles, Cal.	2,073	1,589	...	2,108	1,817	2,087	1,889	1,883	2,786	1,595
Memphis, Tenn. . .	435	451	1,817	367	...	612	826	390	1,100	652
Milwaukee, Wis. .	268	537	2,087	379	612	...	332	994	889	493
Minneapolis, Minn.	586	447	1,889	697	826	332	...	1,214	1,207	357
New Orleans, La..	796	806	1,883	685	390	994	1,214	...	1,311	1,007
New York, N.Y.. .	713	1,198	2,786	748	1,100	889	1,207	1,311	...	1,251
Omaha, Neb. . .	587	201	1,595	687	652	493	357	1,007	1,251	...
Philadelphia, Pa. .	633	1,118	2,706	668	1,000	825	1,143	1,211	100	1,183
Pittsburgh, Pa. . .	353	838	2,426	388	752	539	857	1,070	368	895
Portland, Ore.. . .	1,227	1,809	959	2,320	2,259	2,010	1,678	2,505	2,885	1,654
St. Louis, Mo.. .	235	257	1,845	263	285	363	552	673	948	449
San Francisco . .	2,256	1,835	379	2,349	2,125	2,175	1,940	2,249	2,934	1,683
Seattle, Wash. . .	2,194	1,839	1,131	2,305	2,290	1,940	1,608	2,574	2,815	1,638
Tulsa, Okla.	631	248	1,452	659	401	757	695	647	1,344	387
Washington, D.C..	558	1,043	2,631	582	867	758	1,076	1,078	233	1,116

	Philadelphia	Pittsburgh	Portland	St. Louis	Salt Lake City	San Francisco	Seattle	Toledo	Tulsa	Washington
Atlanta, Ga. . . .	741	687	2,601	541	1,878	2,496	2,618	640	772	608
Boston, Mass. . .	296	561	3,046	1,141	2,343	3,095	2,976	739	1,537	429
Chicago, Ill.	738	452	2,083	289	1,390	2,142	2,013	232	683	671
Cincinnati, Oh. . .	567	287	2,333	340	1,610	2,362	2,300	200	736	481
Cleveland, Oh. . .	413	129	2,418	529	1,715	2,467	2,348	111	925	346
Dallas, Tex.	1,452	1,204	2,009	630	1,242	1,753	2,078	1,084	257	1,319
Denver, Col. . . .	1,691	1,411	1,238	857	504	1,235	1,307	1,218	681	1,616
Detroit, Mich. . . .	576	287	2,349	513	1,647	2,399	2,279	59	909	506
Houston, Tex.. . .	1,508	1,313	2,205	779	1,438	1,912	2,274	1,206	478	1,375
Indianapolis, Ind. .	633	353	2,227	235	1,504	2,256	2,194	219	631	558
Kansas City, Mo. .	1,118	838	1,809	257	1,086	1,839	687	248	1,043	
Los Angeles, Cal.	2,706	2,426	959	1,845	715	379	1,131	2,276	1,452	2,631
Memphis, Tenn. . .	1,000	752	2,259	285	1,535	2,125	2,290	654	401	867
Milwaukee, Wis. .	825	539	2,010	363	1,423	2,175	1,940	319	757	758
Minneapolis, Minn.	1,143	857	1,678	552	1,186	1,940	1,608	637	695	1,076
New Orleans, La..	1,211	1,070	2,505	673	1,738	2,249	2,574	986	647	1,078
New York, N.Y.. .	100	368	2,885	948	2,182	2,934	2,815	578	1,344	233
Omaha, Neb. . . .	1,183	895	1,654	449	931	1,683	1,638	681	387	1,116
Philadelphia, Pa. .	...	288	2,821	868	2,114	2,866	2,751	514	1,264	133
Pittsburgh, Pa. . .	288	...	2,535	588	1,826	2,578	2,465	228	984	221
Portland, Ore. . .	2,821	2,535	...	2,060	767	636	172	2,315	1,913	2,754
St. Louis, Mo. . .	868	588	2,060	...	1,337	2,089	2,081	454	396	793
San Francisco . .	2,866	2,578	636	2,089	752	...	808	2,364	1,760	2,799
Seattle, Wash. . .	2,751	2,465	172	2,081	836	808	...	2,245	1,982	2,684
Tulsa, Okla.	1,264	984	1,913	396	1,172	1,760	1,982	850	...	1,189
Washington, D.C..	133	221	2,754	793	2,047	2,799	2,684	447	1,189	...

Air Distances Between Selected World Cities in Statute Miles

Point-to-point measurements are usually from City Hall.

	Bangkok	Beijing	Berlin	Cairo	Cape Town	Caracas	Chicago	Hong Kong	Hono-lulu	Lima
Bangkok......	...	2,046	5,352	4,523	6,300	10,555	8,570	1,077	6,609	12,244
Bejing	2,046	...	4,584	4,698	8,044	8,950	6,604	1,217	5,077	10,349
Berlin	5,352	4,584	...	1,797	5,961	5,238	4,414	5,443	7,320	6,896
Cairo........	4,523	4,698	1,797	...	4,480	6,342	6,141	5,066	8,848	7,726
Cape Town	6,300	8,044	5,961	4,480	...	6,366	8,491	7,376	11,535	6,072
Caracas......	10,555	8,950	5,238	6,342	6,366	...	2,495	10,165	6,021	1,707
Chicago......	8,570	6,604	4,414	6,141	8,491	2,495	...	7,797	4,256	3,775
Hong Kong	1,077	1,217	5,443	5,066	7,376	10,165	7,797	...	5,556	11,418
Honolulu......	6,609	5,077	7,320	8,848	11,535	6,021	4,256	5,556	...	5,947
London	5,944	5,074	583	2,185	5,989	4,655	3,958	5,990	7,240	6,316
Los Angeles. ..	7,637	6,250	5,782	7,520	9,969	3,632	1,745	7,240	2,557	4,171
Madrid.......	6,337	5,745	1,165	2,087	5,308	4,346	4,189	6,558	7,872	5,907
Melbourne. ...	4,568	5,643	9,918	8,675	6,425	9,717	9,673	4,595	5,505	8,059
Mexico City	9,793	7,753	6,056	7,700	8,519	2,234	1,690	8,788	3,789	2,639
Montreal......	8,338	6,519	3,740	5,427	7,922	2,438	745	7,736	4,918	3,970
Moscow	4,389	3,607	1,006	1,803	6,279	6,177	4,987	4,437	7,047	7,862
New York	8,669	6,844	3,979	5,619	7,803	2,120	714	8,060	4,969	3,639
Paris	5,877	5,120	548	1,998	5,786	4,732	4,143	5,990	7,449	6,370
Rio de Janeiro ..	9,994	10,768	6,209	6,143	3,781	2,804	5,282	11,009	8,288	2,342
Rome	5,494	5,063	737	1,326	5,231	5,195	4,824	5,774	8,040	6,750
San Francisco .	7,931	5,918	5,672	7,466	10,248	3,902	1,859	6,905	2,398	4,518
Singapore.....	883	2,771	6,164	5,137	6,008	11,402	9,372	1,605	6,726	11,689
Stockholm.	5,089	4,133	528	2,096	6,423	5,471	4,331	5,063	6,875	7,166
Tokyo	2,865	1,307	5,557	5,958	9,154	8,808	6,314	1,791	3,859	9,631
Warsaw	5,033	4,325	322	1,619	5,935	5,559	4,679	5,147	7,366	7,215
Washington, D.C..	8,807	6,942	4,181	5,822	7,895	2,047	596	8,155	4,838	3,509

	London	Los Angeles	Madrid	Mel-bourne	Mexico City	Mon-treal	Mos-cow	New Delhi	New York	Paris
Bangkok......	5,944	7,637	6,337	4,568	9,793	8,338	4,389	1,813	8,669	5,877
Bejing	5,074	6,250	5,745	5,643	7,753	6,519	3,607	2,353	6,844	5,120
Berlin	583	5,782	1,165	9,918	6,056	3,740	1,006	3,598	3,979	548
Cairo........	2,185	7,520	2,087	8,675	7,700	5,427	1,803	2,758	5,619	1,998
Cape Town	5,989	9,969	5,308	6,425	8,519	7,922	6,279	5,769	7,803	5,786
Caracas......	4,655	3,632	4,346	9,717	2,234	2,438	6,177	8,833	2,120	4,732
Chicago......	3,958	1,745	4,189	9,673	1,690	745	4,987	7,486	714	4,143
Hong Kong	5,990	7,240	6,558	4,595	8,788	7,736	4,437	2,339	8,060	5,990
Honolulu......	7,240	2,557	7,872	5,505	3,789	4,918	7,047	7,412	4,969	7,449
London	...	5,439	785	10,500	5,558	3,254	1,564	4,181	3,469	214
Los Angeles. ..	5,439	...	5,848	7,931	1,542	2,427	6,068	7,011	2,451	5,601
Madrid.......	785	5,848	...	10,758	5,643	3,448	2,147	4,530	3,593	655
Melbourne. ...	10,500	7,931	10,758	...	8,426	10,395	8,950	6,329	10,359	10,430
Mexico City	5,558	1,542	5,643	8,426	...	2,317	6,676	9,120	2,090	5,725
Montreal......	3,254	2,427	3,448	10,395	2,317	...	4,401	7,012	331	3,432
Moscow	1,564	6,068	2,147	8,950	6,676	4,401	...	2,698	4,683	1,554
New York	3,469	2,451	3,593	10,359	2,090	331	4,683	7,318	...	3,636
Paris	214	5,601	655	10,430	5,725	3,432	1,554	4,102	3,636	...
Rio de Janeiro ..	5,750	6,330	5,045	8,226	4,764	5,078	7,170	8,753	4,801	5,684
Rome	895	6,326	851	9,929	6,377	4,104	1,483	3,684	4,293	690
San Francisco .	5,367	347	5,803	7,856	1,887	2,543	5,885	7,691	2,572	5,577
Singapore.....	6,747	8,767	7,080	3,759	10,327	9,203	5,228	2,571	9,534	6,673
Stockholm.	942	5,454	1,653	9,630	6,012	3,714	716	3,414	3,986	1,003
Tokyo	5,959	5,470	6,706	5,062	7,035	6,471	4,660	3,638	6,757	6,053
Warsaw	905	5,922	1,427	9,598	6,337	4,022	721	3,277	4,270	852
Washington, D.C..	3,674	2,300	3,792	10,180	1,885	489	4,876	7,500	205	3,840

	Rio de Janeiro	Rome	San Fran-cisco	Singa-pore	Stock-holm	Teheran	Tokyo	Vienna	Warsaw	Wash., D.C.
Bangkok......	9,994	5,494	7,931	883	5,089	3,391	2,865	5,252	5,033	8,807
Bejing	10,768	5,063	5,918	2,771	4,133	3,490	1,307	4,648	4,325	6,942
Berlin	6,209	737	5,672	6,164	528	2,185	5,557	326	322	4,181
Cairo........	6,143	1,326	7,466	5,137	2,096	1,234	5,958	1,481	1,619	5,822
Cape Town	3,781	5,231	10,248	6,008	6,423	5,241	9,154	5,656	5,935	7,895
Caracas......	2,804	5,195	3,902	11,402	5,471	7,320	8,808	5,372	5,559	2,047
Chicago......	5,282	4,824	1,859	9,372	4,331	6,502	6,314	4,698	4,679	596
Hong Kong	11,009	5,774	6,905	1,605	5,063	3,843	1,791	5,431	5,147	8,155
Honolulu......	8,288	8,040	2,398	6,726	6,875	8,070	3,859	7,632	7,366	4,838
London	5,750	895	5,367	6,747	942	2,743	5,959	771	905	3,674
Los Angeles. ..	6,330	6,326	347	8,767	5,454	7,682	5,470	6,108	5,922	2,300
Madrid.......	5,045	851	5,803	7,080	1,653	2,978	6,706	1,128	1,427	3,792
Melbourne. ...	8,226	9,929	7,856	3,759	9,630	7,826	5,062	9,790	9,598	10,180
Mexico City	4,764	6,377	1,887	10,327	6,012	8,184	7,035	6,320	6,337	1,885
Montreal......	5,078	4,104	2,543	9,203	3,714	5,880	6,471	4,009	4,022	489
Moscow	7,170	1,483	5,885	5,228	716	1,532	4,660	1,043	721	4,876
New York	4,801	4,293	2,572	9,534	3,986	6,141	6,757	4,234	4,270	205
Paris	5,684	690	5,577	6,673	1,003	2,625	6,053	645	852	3,840
Rio de Janeiro ..	...	5,707	6,613	9,785	6,683	7,374	11,532	6,127	6,455	4,779
Rome	5,707	...	6,259	6,229	1,245	2,127	6,142	477	820	4,497
San Francisco .	6,613	6,259	...	8,448	5,399	7,362	5,150	5,994	5,854	2,441
Singapore.....	9,785	6,229	8,448	...	5,936	4,103	3,300	6,035	5,843	9,662
Stockholm.	6,683	1,245	5,399	5,936	...	2,173	5,053	780	494	4,183
Tokyo	11,532	6,142	5,150	3,300	5,053	4,775	...	5,689	5,347	6,791
Warsaw	6,455	820	5,854	5,843	494	1,879	5,689	347	...	4,472
Washington, D.C..	4,779	4,497	2,441	9,662	4,183	6,341	6,791	4,438	4,472	...

MANUFACTURES AND MINERALS

Industrial Production Indexes, by Industry

Source: Federal Reserve System

Major Industry Group	1970	1975	1980	1985	1988	1989	1990
Total Index.	61	66	84	94	105	108	109
Manufacturing.	56	61	79	92	106	109	110
Durable manuf.	53	57	76	92	108	111	112
Lumber and products	67	67	77	88	105	103	102
Furniture and fixtures	56	59	78	88	104	105	106
Clay, glass, and stone products. . .	71	78	92	94	106	108	106
Primary metals	115	107	111	102	110	109	108
Fabricated metal products . .	76	77	92	94	106	107	106
Nonelectrical machinery . . .	33	38	61	87	114	122	127
Electrical machinery.	40	45	73	93	106	110	111
Transportation equipment. . .	55	60	72	92	105	107	105
Instruments.	39	52	79	96	110	116	117
Nondurable manuf.	61	68	83	91	104	106	108
Food	64	71	85	95	103	105	108
Tobacco products	91	98	104	97	101	100	99
Textile mill products	74	78	92	90	100	102	101
Apparel products.	75	71	89	93	102	104	99
Paper and products	63	66	83	92	103	103	105
Printing and publishing.	53	54	70	88	104	109	112
Chemicals and products . . .	56	69	88	91	105	108	110
Petroleum products	84	91	99	93	103	106	108
Rubber and plastic products .	38	47	62	86	106	109	110
Leather and products	208	182	162	112	100	104	100
Mining	100	98	110	109	102	100	103
Utilities.	73	84	96	99	104	107	108

1987 = 100.

Manufacturing Production Worker Statistics

Source: Bureau of Labor Statistics, U.S. Dept. of Labor (p — preliminary)

Year	All employees	Production workers	Av. weekly earnings	Avg. hourly earnings	Avg. hrs. per wk.
1955	16,882,000	13,288,000	$75.30	$1.85	40.7
1960	16,796,000	12,586,000	89.72	2.26	39.7
1965	18,062,000	13,434,000	107.53	2.61	41.2
1970	19,367,000	14,044,000	133.33	3.35	39.8
1975	18,323,000	13,043,000	190.79	4.83	39.5
1980	20,285,000	14,214,000	288.62	7.27	39.7
1985	19,260,000	13,092,000	386.37	9.54	40.5
1987	19,024,000	12,970,000	406.31	9.91	41.0
1988	19,403,000	13,254,000	418.40	10.18	41.1
1989	19,612,000	13,375,000	429.27	10.47	41.0
1990	19,111,000	12,974,000	441.86	10.83	40.8
1991,P July	18,348,000	12,377,000	452.57	11.23	40.3

International Manufacturing Productivity and Labor Costs

Source: Bureau of Labor Statistics, U.S. Dept. of Labor (1982=100)

Output per hour

Country	1960	1965	1970	1975	1980	1985	1988	1989	1990
United States	58.4	72.1	77.2	89.4	96.6	114.8	132.1	133.1	136.6
Canada	51.6	66.1	76.9	90.1	99.8	119.8	117.1	118.0	121.2
Japan	18.6	28.1	52.0	69.6	92.1	112.0	126.6	133.1	138.1
France.	30.7	41.4	58.5	72.7	90.6	108.8	120.6	126.4	127.7
West Germany	38.5	51.2	67.0	84.5	98.4	112.9	115.6	120.6	124.8
Italy	28.9	40.0	54.3	67.1	95.5	122.3	130.5	134.5	138.8
Norway	47.8	58.0	74.5	88.6	96.3	116.0	119.7	124.2	127.1
Sweden	36.5	50.4	69.6	86.4	96.4	112.6	117.3	117.6	118.2
United Kingdom	49.4	58.4	70.8	83.7	89.9	117.8	137.3	143.9	145.1

Unit Labor Costs in U.S. dollars

Country	1960	1965	1970	1975	1980	1985	1988	1989	1990
United States	38.3	36.3	46.3	59.8	86.7	96.8	93.0	95.8	96.5
Canada	40.6	34.4	44.1	63.6	83.1	88.2	110.8	121.5	128.4
Japan	26.2	32.5	35.9	79.6	106.7	88.2	185.3	173.4	167.4
France.	32.2	37.4	36.2	78.8	125.2	87.8	132.4	122.1	148.0
Germany	21.7	27.2	35.8	74.1	121.2	85.0	157.8	147.7	175.8
Italy	29.6	37.6	46.2	90.2	116.3	87.5	137.9	138.9	171.0
Norway	18.7	23.2	29.8	69.2	110.2	85.7	145.2	137.7	157.6
Sweden	31.0	36.6	42.5	86.9	130.2	85.7	140.9	145.7	172.5
United Kingdom	23.4	27.0	28.7	54.9	118.1	77.4	111.8	106.4	126.2

NOTE: The data relate to all employed persons (wage & salary, the self-employed, and unpaid family workers) in the U.S. and Canada, and all employees (wage & salary earners) in the other countries.

Sales and Profits of Manufacturing Corporations by Industry Group

Source: Economic Surveys Division, Bureau of the Census, U.S. Dept. of Commerce

(millions of dollars)

Industry group	Sales 1Q 1990	Sales 4Q 1990	Sales 1Q 1991	Income after taxes 1Q 1990	Income after taxes 4Q 1990	Income after taxes 1Q 1991
All manufacturing corporations	671,404	727,932	653,662	28,064	18,779	18,343
Nondurable manufacturing corporations	345,612	387,953	348,147	16,302	14,646	16,948
Food and kindred products	95,129	104,179	97,217	3,493	2,295	5,000
Textile mill products	13,433	13,911	12,981	60	(20)	(10)
Paper and allied products	28,794	28,674	27,400	1,454	614	867
Printing and publishing	34,372	37,412	34,806	1,025	1,373	707
Chemicals and allied products	69,114	73,094	70,940	5,470	5,316	5,270
Industrial chemicals and synthetics	26,592	28,561	26,802	1,687	1,605	1,831
Drugs	14,186	15,571	16,065	2,083	2,800	2,285
Petroleum and coal products	71,777	96,961	73,242	4,116	4,843	4,889
Rubber and miscellaneous plastics products	18,813	18,653	17,823	426	30	(34)
Other nondurable manufacturing corporations	14,180	15,068	13,739	259	197	259
Durable manufacturing corporations	325,792	339,978	305,515	11,762	4,133	1,395
Stone, clay, and glass products	12,722	13,362	10,898	(6)	(474)	(542)
Primary metal industries	29,375	29,280	27,501	1,128	(351)	208
Iron and steel	13,822	13,396	12,484	322	(521)	(259)
Nonferrous metals	15,553	15,884	15,017	807	170	467
Fabricated metal products	34,131	32,629	30,184	1,343	498	515
Machinery, except electrical	61,026	66,085	59,567	2,329	3,347	(1,240)
Electrical and electronic equipment	51,998	56,620	51,901	2,044	310	1,877
Transportation equipment	84,048	86,599	74,497	2,768	(1,235)	(1,036)
Motor vehicles and equipment	49,610	48,244	40,684	1,359	(2,105)	(1,976)
Aircraft, guided missiles, and parts	31,330	34,665	30,997	1,293	447	944
Instruments and related products	24,902	26,567	24,855	1,494	1,712	1,531
Other durable manufacturing corporations	27,590	28,837	26,112	661	325	82
All mining corporations*	9,876	12,822	10,370	666	768	367
All retail trade corporations*	147,420	184,136	NA	150	4,010	NA
All wholesale trade corporations*	180,055	190,083	178,823	1,293	745	824

* With assets over $50 million.

Annual Percent Change in Productivity and Related Data, 1980-1990

Source: Bureau of Labor Statistics, U.S. Dept. of Labor

Item	1980	1981	1982	1983	1984	1985	1986	1987	1988	1989	1990
Business sector:											
Output per hour of all persons	−0.3	1.5	−0.7	2.4	2.6	2.0	2.3	1.2	1.7	0.5	−0.6
Real compensation per hour[1]	−2.6	−0.9	1.2	0.6	−0.2	0.8	3.3	0.2	0.6	−1.5	−1.7
Unit labor cost	10.9	7.7	8.3	1.4	1.5	2.3	2.8	2.6	3.0	4.8	4.3
Unit nonlabor payments[2]	5.4	13.5	1.4	7.3	7.0	2.8	0.7	2.6	2.9	4.1	2.8
Implicit price deflator[3]	9.0	9.6	5.9	3.3	3.3	2.5	2.1	2.6	2.9	3.9	3.8
Nonfarm business sector:											
Output per hour of all persons	−0.4	1.1	−0.9	3.0	2.1	1.3	2.0	1.1	2.0	0.7	−0.8
Real compensation per hour[1]	−2.6	−0.7	1.1	0.7	−0.4	0.5	3.2	−0.1	0.5	−1.5	−1.8
Unit labor cost	11.0	8.3	8.4	1.0	1.8	2.8	3.0	2.6	2.7	3.9	4.3
Unit nonlabor payments[2]	7.1	12.7	2.2	8.7	5.5	3.6	0.9	2.7	2.7	3.9	2.7
Implicit price deflator[3]	9.7	9.7	6.3	3.5	3.0	3.0	2.3	2.6	2.7	3.9	3.8
Manufacturing:											
Output per hour of all persons	0.0	2.3	2.5	5.2	5.4	4.5	3.8	3.7	2.7	3.3	3.0
Real compensation per hour	−1.6	−0.5	2.6	−0.7	−0.9	1.2	2.6	−1.0	−0.5	−0.9	−2.0
Unit labor cost[1]	11.7	7.3	6.2	−2.5	−1.9	0.3	0.7	−1.0	0.9	0.6	0.3

(1) Adjusted for changes in the CPI for all urban consumers; (2) Includes profits, capital consumption allowances, interest, rental income of persons, and indirect taxes (3) Current dollar gross product divided by constant dollar gross product.

U.S. Reliance on Foreign Supplies of Minerals

Source: Bureau of Mines, U.S. Dept. of the Interior

Mineral	Percent imported in 1990	Major sources (1986-89)	Major uses
Columbium	100%	Brazil, Canada, Thailand, Germany	Steelmaking and aerospace alloys
Graphite	100	Mexico, China, Brazil, Madagascar	Metallurgical processes
Manganese	100	Gabon, S. Africa	Steelmaking
Mica (sheet)	100	India, Belgium, France, Brazil	Electronic and electrical equipment
Strontium (Celestite)	100	Mexico, Spain, Germany	Television picture tubes, pyrotechnics
Bauxite and alumina	98	Australia, Guinea, Jamaica, Suriname	Aluminum production
Diamonds (industrial)	92	South Africa, Britain, Ireland, Zaire	Machinery for grinding and cutting
Fluorspar	90	Mexico, South Africa	Raw material for metallurgical and chemical industries
Platinum group	88	South Africa, Britain, USSR	Catalytic converters for autos, electrical and electronic equipment
Cobalt	86	Zaire, Zambia, Canada, Norway	Aerospace alloys
Tantalum	85	Thailand, Brazil, Australia, Germany	Electronic components
Nickel	83	Canada, Australia, Norway	Stainless steel and other alloys
Chromium	79	South Africa, Zimbabwe, Turkey, Yugoslavia	Stainless steel
Tin	76	Brazil, Indonesia, China	Cans, electrical construction
Tungsten	73	China, Bolivia, Germany, Peru	Lamp filaments
Barite	69	China, Morocco, India	Oil drilling fluids
Potash	68	Canada, Israel, USSR	Fertilizer
Cadmium	54	Canada, Australia, Mexico, Germany	Batteries, plating and coating of metals
Silver	NA	Canada, Mexico, Britain, Peru	Photography, electrical and electronic prods.

Minerals

Source: Bureau of Mines, U.S. Dept. of the Interior, as of mid-1991

Aluminum: the most abundant metal element in the Earth's crust. Bauxite is the main source of aluminum; convert to aluminum equivalent by multiplying by 0.211. Guinea and Australia have 46 percent of the world's reserves. Aluminum is used in the U.S. in packaging 31%, transportation 22% and building 19%.

Chromium: some 99 percent of the world's chromite is found in South Africa and Zimbabwe. The chemical and metallurgical industries use about 92% of the chromite consumed in the U.S.

Cobalt: used in superalloys for jet engines; chemicals (paint driers, catalysts, magnetic coatings); permanent magnets; and cemented carbides for cutting tools. Principal cobalt producing countries include Zaire, Zambia, and the USSR. The U.S. uses about one-third of total world consumption. Although its resources are relatively large, the U.S. has produced no cobalt since 1971; cobalt resources are low grade and production from these deposits is not economically feasible.

Columbium: used mostly as an additive in steel making and in superalloys. Brazil and Canada are the world's leading producers. There is no U.S. columbium mining industry.

Copper: main uses of copper in the U.S. are in building construction 42%, electrical and electronic products 24%, industrial machinery and equipment 13%, transportation 11%. The leading producer is Chile, followed by the U.S., USSR, Canada, Zambia, and Poland. Principal mining states are Arizona, New Mexico, and Utah.

Gold: used in the U.S. in jewelry and arts 53%, industrial (mainly electronic) 38%, dental 9%. South Africa has about half of the world's resources; significant quantities also are present in the U.S., Canada, USSR, and Brazil. Gold mining in the U.S. takes place in nearly all of the western states and Alaska.

Iron ore: the source of primary iron for the world's iron and steel industries. Major iron ore producers include the USSR, Brazil, Australia, and China.

Lead: the U.S. and Australia are the world's largest producers of lead metal. Transportation accounted for the major end use in the U.S. with 75% used in batteries, gasoline additives, and other applications. Other uses include emergency power supply batteries, construction sheeting, sporting ammunition and TV tubes. Other major mine producers include the USSR, and Canada.

Manganese: essential to iron and steel production. The U.S., Japan, and Western Europe are all nearly deficient in economically minable manganese. South Africa and the USSR have over 70% of the world's reserves.

Nickel: vital to stainless steel industry and played a key role in the development of the chemical and aerospace industries. Leading producers include the USSR, Canada, Australia, and New Caledonia.

Platinum-Group Metals: the platinum group comprises 6 closely related metals: platinum, palladium, rhodium, ruthenium, iridium, and osmium. They commonly occur together in nature and are among the scarcest of the metallic elements. They are consumed in the U.S. by the following industries: automotive 35%, electrical and electronic 32%, and dental 9%. The USSR and South Africa have nearly all the world's reserves.

Silver: used in the following U.S. industries: photography; electrical and electronic products; sterlingware, electroplated ware, and jewelry. Silver is mined in more than 56 countries. Nevada produces over 32% of the U.S. silver, Idaho 21%.

Tantalum: a refractory metal with unique electrical, chemical, and physical properties used mostly in the U.S to produce electronic components tantalum capacitors. Australia, Brazil and Canada are the leading producers. There is no U.S. tantalum mining industry.

Titanium: a metal which is mostly used in jet engines, airframes, and space and missile applications. It is produced in the USSR, Japan, and the western and central U.S., the United Kingdom, and Canada.

Vanadium: used as an alloying element in steel, as an alloying agent in aerospace titanium alloys, and as a catalyst in the production of sulfuric acid and maleic anhydride. The USSR and South Africa are the world's largest producers.

Zinc: used as protective coating on steel, as diecastings, as an alloying metal with copper to make brass, and as chemical compounds in rubber and paints. It is mined in over 50 countries with Canada the leading producer, followed by the USSR, Australia, Peru and China. In the U.S., mine production comes mostly from Tennessee, Missouri, New York and Alaska.

World Mineral Reserve Base

Source: Bureau of Mines, U.S. Dept. of the Interior, as of 1990.

Mineral	Reserve Base[1]	Mineral	Reserve Base[1]
Aluminum	25,000 mln. metric tons[2]	Nickel	121,000 thousand short tons
Chromium	6,800 mln. metric tons	Platinum—	
Cobalt	8,340 thou. metric tons.	Group Metals	66 mln. kilograms
Columbium	9,300 mln. lbs.	Silver	420,000 metric tons
Copper	574 mln. metric tons	Tantalum	76 mln. lbs.
Gold	1,510 mln. troy oz.	Titanium	330 mln. metric tons
Iron	229,000 mln. metric tons[3]	Vanadium	18,300 thousand short tons
Lead	120 mln. metric tons	Zinc	295 mln. metric tons
Manganese	3,900,000 thousand short tons		

(1) Includes demonstrated resources that are currently economic (reserves), marginally economic (marginal reserves), and some of those that are currently subeconomic. (2) Bauxite. (3) Crude ore.

U.S. Nonfuel Mineral Production—Leading States in 1989

Source: Bureau of Mines, U.S. Dept. of the Interior

State	Value (thousands)	Principal minerals
Arizona	$3,190,000	Copper, gold, sand and gravel.
California	2,839,000	Cement, boron minerals, sand and gravel (construction), stone (crushed).
Nevada	1,996,000	Gold, sand & gravel (construction), silver.
Michigan	1,586,000	Cement, sand & gravel, stone.
Florida	1,578,000	Stone (crushed), cement, phosphate rock.
Texas	1,445,000	Cement, stone (crushed), sand and gravel (construction), salt.
Minnesota	1,283,000	Iron ore, sand and gravel (construction), stone (crushed).
Utah	1,241,000	Cement, lime, sand and gravel.
Georgia	1,169,000	Clays, stone (crushed).
New Mexico	1,165,000	Potassium salts, copper.
Missouri	1,092,000	Cement, lead, stone (crushed).
Pennsylvania	1,041,000	Cement, stone (crushed), lime, sand and gravel (construction).
Wyoming	799,000	Clay, sand and gravel (construction).
Ohio	787,000	Stone (crushed), sand and gravel (construction), salt, lime.

U.S. Nonfuel Mineral Production

Source: Bureau of Mines, U.S. Dept. of the Interior

Production as measured by mine shipments, sales, or marketable production (including consumption by producers)

Metals	1987	1988	1989	1990E
Antimony (ore and concentrate)	W	W	W	W
Bauxite . . . . thousand metric tons, dried equivalent	576	588	W	W
Beryllium . . . . metric tons	220	212	184	200
Copper (recoverable content of ores, etc.) . . thousand metric tons	1,243	1,417	1,497	1,550
Gold (recoverable content of ores, etc.) . . . . metric tons	153.9	200.9	265.5	300.0
Iron ore, usable (includes byproduct material) . . million metric tons	47.6	57.5	59.0	53.9
Lead (recoverable content of ores, etc.) . . . . thousand metric tons	319	394	4.9	495
Magnesium metal (primary) . . . . thousand tons	124	142	152	150
Manganiferous ore (5% to 35% Mn)	W	W	W	W
Molybdenum (content of ore and concentrate) . thousand kilograms	34,067	43,044	65,095	60,300
Nickel (content of ore and concentrate)	NA	NA	NA	NA
Silver (recoverable content of ores, etc.) . . . . metric tons	1,241	1,661	2,007	2,000
Tungsten ore and concentrate	W	W	W	W
Zinc (recoverable content of ores, etc.) . . . . thousand metric tons	216	244	276	530
Asbestos . . . . thousand metric tons	51	18	17	20
Barite . . . . thousand metric tons	406	404	290	447
Boron minerals . . . . thousand metric tons	625	578	562	565
Bromine . . . . million kilograms	152	163	175	175
Cement: (Portland, Masonry, etc.) . . . . thousand short tons	78,198	76,867	77,189	79,700
Clays . . . . thousand metric tons	8,008	8,973	8,974	9,021
Diatomite . . . . thousand metric tons	596	629	617	619
Feldspar . . . . thousand metric tons	655	650	655	640
Fluorspar . . . . thousand metric tons	64	64	66	60
Garnet (industrial) . . . . metric tons	38,353	42,409	42,605	44,135
Gem stones	NA	NA	NA	NA
Gypsum . . . . thousand short tons	15,612	16,390	17,624	18,000
Helium (extracted from natural gas) . . . . million cubic feet	1,968	2,281	2,390	2,800
Helium (Grade A) . . . . million cubic feet	2,230	2,574	2,879	3,200
Iodine . . . . thousand kilograms	W	998	1,508	1,862
Lime . . . . thousand short tons	15,733	17,052	17,152	17,400
Mica (scrap & flake) . . . . thousand metric tons	146	130	119	113
Peat . . . . thousand short tons	955	844	755	740
Perlite . . . . thousand short tons	533	576	601	623
Phosphate rock . . . . thousand metric tons	40,954	45,389	49,817	46,000
Pumice & Pumicite . . . . thousand metric tons	356	353	424	400
Salt . . . . thousand short tons	36,943	39,170	39,278	39,400
Sand and gravel (construction) . . . . thousand short tons	895,200	923,400	897,300	924,000
Sand and gravel (industrial) . . . . thousand short tons	28,010	28,480	29,205	29,600
Sodium sulfate (natural) . . . . thousand short tons	382	398	375	380
Stone (crushed) . . . . million short tons	1,200	1,250	1,213	1,216
Stone (dimension) . . . . thousand short tons	1,179	1,189	1,207	1,186
Sulfur . . . . thousand metric tons	10,539	10,746	11,592	11,325
Talc and pyrophyllite . . . . thousand metric tons	1,163	1,234	1,253	1,261
Vermiculite . . . . thousand short tons	303	304	275	265

(E) Estimated. (W) Withheld to avoid disclosing company proprietary data. (NA) Not available.

U.S. Copper, Lead, and Zinc Production

Source: Bureau of Mines, U.S. Dept. of the Interior

Year	Copper Quantity (metric tons)	Copper Value ($1,000)	Lead Quantity (metric tons)	Lead Value ($1,000)	Zinc Quantity (metric tons)	Zinc Value ($1,000)	Year	Copper Quantity (metric tons)	Copper Value ($1,000)	Lead Quantity (metric tons)	Lead Value ($1,000)	Zinc Quantity (metric tons)	Zinc Value ($1,000)
1950	827	379,122	390,839	113,078	565,516	167,000	1984	1,103	1,625,000	322,677	181,745	252,768	270,833
1960	1,037	733,706	223,774	57,722	395,013	112,365	1985	1,105	1,631,000	413,955	174,008	226,545	201,607
1965	1,226	957,028	273,196	93,959	554,429	178,284	1986	1,144	1,666,000	339,793	165,150	202,983	170,050
1970	1,560	1,984,484	518,698	178,609	484,560	163,650	1987	1,244	2,262,000	311,381	246,720	216,281	200,529
1975	1,282	1,814,763	563,783	267,230	425,792	366,097	1988	1,417	3,764,000	384,983	315,222	244,314	324,249
1980	1,181	2,666,931	550,366	515,189	317,103	261,671	1989	1,497	4,323,000	410,915	356,476	275,883	499,103

U.S. Pig Iron and Raw Steel Output

Source: American Iron and Steel Institute (net tons)

Year	Total pig iron	Raw steel	Year	Total pig iron	Raw steel
1940	46,071,666	66,982,686	1980	68,721,000	111,835,000
1945	53,223,169	79,701,648	1984	51,904,000	92,528,000
1950	64,586,907	96,836,075	1985	50,446,000	88,259,000
1955	76,857,417	117,036,085	1986	43,952,000	81,606,000
1960	66,480,648	99,281,601	1987	48,410,000	89,151,000
1965	88,184,901	131,461,601	1988	55,745,000	99,924,000
1970	91,435,000	131,514,000	1989	55,873,000	97,943,000
1975	101,208,000	116,642,000	1990	54,750,000	98,906,000

Steel figures include only that portion of the capacity and production of steel for castings used by foundries which were operated by companies producing steel ingots.

World Gold Production

Source: Bureau of Mines, U.S. Dept. of the Interior

(Troy Ounces)

Year	World prod.	Africa South Africa	Africa Ghana	Africa Zaire	North and South America United States	North and South America Canada	North and South America Mexico	North and South America Colombia	Australia	China	Other Philippines	USSR
1972	44,843,374	29,245,273	724,051	140,724	1,449,943	2,078,567	146,061	188,137	754,866	—	606,730	—
1975	38,476,371	22,937,820	523,889	103,217	1,052,252	1,653,611	144,710	308,864	526,821	—	502,577	—
1977	38,906,145	22,501,886	480,884	80,418	1,100,347	1,733,609	212,709	257,070	624,270	—	558,554	—
1978	38,983,019	22,648,558	402,034	76,077	998,832	1,735,077	202,003	246,446	647,579	—	586,531	—
1979	38,768,978	22,617,179	362,000	69,992	964,390	1,644,265	190,364	269,369	596,910	—	535,166	—
1980	39,197,315	21,669,468	353,000	39,963	969,782	1,627,477	195,991	510,439	547,591	—	753,452	8,425,000
1982	43,082,814	21,355,111	331,000	62,233	1,465,686	2,081,230	214,349	472,674	866,815	1,800,000	834,439	8,550,000
1983	45,163,364	21,847,310	276,000	192,930	2,002,526	2,363,411	198,177	426,517	983,522	1,850,000	816,536	8,600,000
1984	46,929,444	21,860,933	287,000	117,115	2,084,615	2,682,786	270,998	730,670	1,295,963	1,900,000	827,149	8,650,000
1985	49,283,691	21,565,230	299,363	63,022	2,427,232	2,815,118	265,693	1,142,385	1,881,491	1,950,000	1,062,997	8,700,000
1986	51,534,056	20,513,665	287,127	167,827	3,739,015	3,364,700	250,615	1,285,878	2,413,842	2,100,000	1,296,400	8,850,000
1987	53,033,614	19,176,500	327,598	140,561	4,947,040	3,724,000	236,852	853,600	3,558,954	2,300,000	1,048,081	8,850,000
1988	58,453,814	19,881,126	372,979	140,000	6,459,539	4,110,000	296,689	933,000	4,887,000	2,500,000	1,134,920	9,000,000
1989	63,497,633	19,531,550	429,469	112,528	8,536,010	5,092,670	266,850	870,962	6,523,377	2,572,056	1,125,275	9,162,949
1990e	64,622,907	19,386,872	NA	NA	9,644,520	5,465,619	NA	NA	6,751,647	2,893,563	NA	9,002,196

(e) estimated. (NA) not available.

U.S. and World Silver Production

Source: Bureau of Mines, U.S. Dept. of the Interior

(metric tons)

Largest production of silver in the United States in 1915—2,332 metric tons.

Year	United States	World	Year	United States	World	Year	United States	World
1930 ..	1,578	7,736	1960 ..	1,120	7,505	1986 ..	1,074	12,970
1935 ..	1,428	6,865	1965 ..	1,238	8,007	1987 ..	1,241	13,757
1940 ..	2,164	8,565	1970 ..	1,400	9,670	1988 ..	1,661	14,167
1945 ..	904	5,039	1975 ..	1,087	9,428	1989 ..	2,007	14,452
1950 ..	1,347	6,323	1980 ..	1,006	10,556	1990 ..	2,000	14,600
1955 ..	1,134	6,967	1985 ..	1,227	13,051			

Aluminum Summary, 1980 to 1989

Source: Bureau of Mines, U.S. Dept. of the Interior

Item	Unit	1980	1984	1985	1986	1987	1988	1989
U.S. production	1,000 metric ton . .	5,914	5,859	5,262	4,810	5,329	6,066	6,084
Primary aluminum	1,000 metric ton . .	4,654	4,099	3,500	3,037	3,343	3,944	4,030
Secondary aluminum[1]	1,000 metric ton . .	1,260	1,760	1,762	1,773	1,986	2,122	2,054
Primary aluminum value	Bil. dol	7.3	7.3	6.3	5.4	5.3	9.5	7.8
Price (Primary alum.)[2]	Cents/lb	71.6	81.0	81.0	81.0	72.3	110.1	87.8
Imports for consumption[3]	1,000 metric ton . .	647	1,477	1,420	1,967	1,850	1,620	1,470
Exports[3]	1,000 metric ton . .	1,346	734	908	753	917	1,247	1,613
World production	1,000 metric ton . .	15,383	15,705	15,398	15,413	16,385	17,608	17,980

(1) Recoverable aluminum content from scrap, old and new; (2) Average prices for primary aluminum, quoted by *Metals Week;* (3) Crude and semicrude (including metal and alloys, plates, bars, etc., and scrap).

Social Security Programs

Source: Social Security Administration. U.S. Department of Health and Human Services

Old-Age, Survivors, and Disability Insurance; Medicare; Supplemental Security Income

Social Security Benefits

Social Security benefits are based on a worker's primary insurance amount (PIA), which is related by law to the average indexed monthly earnings (AIME) on which social security contributions have been paid. The full PIA is payable to a retired worker who becomes entitled to benefits at age 65 and to an entitled disabled worker at any age. Spouses and children of retired or disabled workers and survivors of deceased workers receive set proportions of the PIA subject to a family maximum amount. The PIA is calculated by applying varying percentages to succeeding parts of the AIME. The formula is adjusted annually to reflect changes in average annual wages.

Automatic increases in Social Security benefits are initiated for December of a year whenever the Consumer Price Index (CPI) of the Bureau of Labor Statistics for the third calendar quarter of a year increases relative to the CPI for the base quarter, which is either the third calendar quarter of the preceding year or the quarter in which an increase legislated by Congress becomes effective. The size of the benefit increase is determined by the actual percentage rise of the CPI between the quarters measured.

Average monthly benefits payable to all retired workers was $603.00 in December 1990. The average amount for disabled workers in that month was $587.00.

Minimum and maximum monthly retired-worker benefits payable to individuals who retired at age 65[1]

Year of attainment of age 65[2]	Minimum benefit Payable at the time of retirement	Maximum benefit Payable effective December 1990 Men[3]	Payable at the time of retirement Women	Men[3]	Payable effective December 1990 Women
1965 . . .	$44.00	$244.40	$131.70	$135.90	$653.30	$674.20
1970 . . .	64.00	244.40	189.80	196.40	1044.40	749.70
1980 . . .	133.90	244.40	572.00	. . .	1044.40	724.00
1985 . . .	(4)	(4)	717.20	. . .	895.50	. . .
1990 . . .	(4)	(4)	975.00	. . .	1027.60	. . .

(1) Assumes retirement at beginning of year. (2) The final benefit amount payable after SMI premium or any other deductions is rounded to next lower $1 (if not already a multiple of $1). (3) Benefit for both men and women are shown in men's columns except where women's benefit appears separately. (4) Minimum eliminated for workers who reach age 62 after 1981.

Amount of Work Required

To qualify for benefits, the worker must have worked in covered employment long enough to become insured. Just how long depends on when the worker reaches age 62 or, if earlier, when he or she dies or becomes disabled.

A person is fully insured if he or she has one quarter of coverage for every year after 1950 (or year age 21 is reached, if later) up to but not including the year in which the worker reaches age 62, dies, or becomes disabled. In 1991, a person earns one quarter of coverage for each $540 of annual earnings in covered employment, up to a maximum of 4 quarters per year.

The law permits special monthly payments under the Social Security program to certain very old persons who are not eligible for regular social security benefits since they had little or no opportunity to earn social security work credits during their working lifetime.

To get disability benefits, in addition to being fully insured, the worker must also have credit for 20 quarters of coverage out of the 40 calendar quarters before he or she becomes disabled. A disabled blind worker need meet only the fully insured requirement. Persons disabled before age 31 can qualify with a briefer period of coverage. Certain survivor benefits are payable if the deceased worker had 6 quarters of coverage in the 13 quarters preceding death.

Work credit for fully insured status for benefits

Born after 1929; die, become disabled, or reach age 62 in

	Years needed
1982	7¾
1983	8
1984	8¼
1985	8½
1986	8¾
1987	9
1988	9¼
1989	9½
1990	9¾
1991	10

Contribution and benefit base

Calendar year	Base
1982	$32,400
1983	35,700
1984	37,800
1985	39,600
1986	42,000
1987	43,800
1988	45,000
1989	48,000
1990	51,300
1991	53,400

Tax-rate schedule
[Percent of covered earnings]

Year	Total Employees and employers, each	OASDI	HI
1979-80	6.13	5.08	1.05
1981	6.65	5.35	1.30
1982-83	6.70	5.40	1.30
1984	7.00	5.70	1.30
1985	7.05	5.70	1.35
1986-87	7.15	5.70	1.45
1988-89	7.51	6.06	1.45
1990 and after	7.65	6.20	1.45
Self-employed			
1979-80	8.10	7.05	1.05
1981	9.30	8.00	1.30
1982-83	9.35	8.05	1.30
1984	14.00	11.40	2.60
1985	14.10	11.40	2.70
1986-87	14.30	11.40	2.90
1988-89	15.02	12.12	2.90
1990 and after	15.30	12.40	2.90

What Aged Workers Get

When a person has enough work in covered employment and reaches retirement age (currently 65 for full benefit, 62 for reduced benefit), he or she may retire and get monthly old-age benefits. The age at which unreduced benefits are payable will be increased gradually from 65 to 67 over a 21-year period beginning with workers age 62 in the year 2000; (reduced benefits will still be available as early as age 62 but with a larger reduction at age 62.) If a person aged 65 or older continues to work and has earnings of more than $9,360 in 1991, $1 in benefits will be withheld for every $3 above $9,720. The annual exempt amount for people under age 65 is $7,080 in 1991 and $1 in benefits is withheld for every $2 in earnings above the exempt amount for them. The annual exempt amount is raised automatically as the general earnings level rises. The eligible worker who is 70 receives the full benefit regardless of earnings.

For workers who reach age 65 from 1982 through 1989, the worker's benefit is raised by 3% for each year for which the worker between 65 and 70 (72 before 1984) did not receive benefits because of earnings from work or because the worker had not applied for benefits. The delayed retirement credit is 1 percent a year for workers reaching age 65 before 1982. The delayed retirement credit will gradually rise to 8% per year from 1990 through 2008. The rate for 1991 is 3½%.

Effective December 1990, the special benefit for persons aged 72 or over who do not meet the regular coverage requirements is $167.50 a month. Like the monthly benefits, these payments are subject to cost-of-living increases. The special payment is not made to persons on the public assistance or supplemental security income rolls.

Workers retiring before age 65 have their benefits permanently reduced by 5/9 of 1% for each month they receive benefits before age 65. Thus, workers entitled to benefits in the month they reach age 62 receive 80% of the PIA, while a worker retiring at age 65 receives a benefit equal to 100% of the PIA. The nearer to age 65 the worker is when he or she begins collecting a benefit, the larger the benefit will be.

Benefits for Worker's Spouse

The spouse of a worker who is getting Social Security retirement or disability payments may become entitled to a spouse's insurance benefit when he or she reaches 65 of one-half of the worker's PIA. Reduced spouse's benefits are available at age 62 (25/36 of 1% reduction for each month of entitlement before age 65). Benefits are also payable to the aged-divorced spouse of an insured worker if he or she was married to the worker for at least 10 years.

Benefits for Children of Retired or Disabled Workers

If a retired or disabled worker has a child under 18 the child will get a benefit that is half of the worker's unreduced benefit, and so will the worker's spouse, even if he or she is under 62 if he or she is caring for an entitled child of the worker who is under 16 or who became disabled before age 22. Total benefits paid on a worker's earnings record are subject to a maximum and if the total that would be paid to a family exceeds that maximum, the individual dependents' benefits are adjusted downward. (Total benefits paid to the family of a worker who retired in January 1990 at age 65 and who always had the maximum amount of earnings creditable under Social Security can be no higher than $1,799.60.)

When entitled children reach 18, their benefits will generally stop, except that a child disabled before 22 may get a benefit as long as his or her disability meets the definition in the law. Additionally, benefits will be paid to a child until age 19 if the child is in full-time attendance at an elementary or secondary school.

Benefits may also be paid to a grandchild or step-grandchild of a worker or of his or her spouse, in special circumstances.

OASDI	May 1991	May 1990	May 1989
Monthly beneficiaries, total (in thousands)	40,119	39,440	38.835
Aged 65 and over, total	29,516	28,979	28,393
Retired workers	22,432	21,960	21,455
Survivors and dependents . . .	7,078	7,010	6,926
Special age-72 beneficiaries. .	6	9	12
Under age 65, total	10,603	10,462	10,442
Retired workers	2,539	2,545	2,560
Disabled workers	3,076	2,934	2,850
Survivors and dependents . . .	4,988	4,982	5,032
Total monthly benefits (in millions).	$21,880	$20,244	$18,870

What Disabled Workers Get

If a worker becomes so severely disabled that he or she is unable to work, he or she may be eligible to receive a monthly disability benefit. Benefits continue until it is determined that the individual is no longer disabled. Each beneficiary's eligibility is reviewed periodically. When a disabled worker beneficiary reaches 65, the disability benefit becomes a retired-worker benefit.

Benefits generally like those provided for dependents of retired-worker beneficiaries may be paid to dependents of

disabled beneficiaries. However, the maximum family benefit in disability cases is generally lower than in retirement cases.

Survivor Benefits

If an insured worker should die, one or more types of benefits may be payable to survivors, again subject to a maximum family benefit as described above.

1. If claiming benefits at 65, the surviving spouse will receive a benefit that is 100% of the deceased worker's PIA. The surviving spouse may choose to get the benefit as early as age 60, but the benefit is then reduced by 19/40 of 1% for each month it is paid before age 65. However, for those whose spouses claimed their benefits before age 65, the benefit is limited to the reduced amount the worker would be getting if alive but not less than 82 1/2% of the worker's PIA. Marriage after worker's death ends the surviving spouses benefit rights. However, if he or she marries and the marriage is ended, he or she regains benefit rights (A marriage after age 60, 50 if disabled, is deemed not to have occurred for benefit purposes.). This benefit may also be paid to the divorced spouse, if the marriage lasted for at least 10 years.

Disabled widows and widowers may under certain circumstances qualify for benefits after attaining age 50 at the rate of 71.5% of the deceased worker's PIA. The widow or widower must have become totally disabled before or within 7 years after the spouse's death, the last month in which he or she received mother's or father's insurance benefits, or the last month he or she previously received surviving spouse's benefits.

2. A benefit for each child until the child reaches 18. The monthly benefit of each child of a worker who has died is three-quarters of the amount the worker would have received if he or she had lived and drawn full retirement benefits. A child with a disability begun before age 22 may receive benefits. Also, a child may receive benefits until age 19 if he or she is in full-time attendance at an elementary or secondary school.

3. A mother's or father's benefit for the widow(er), if children of the worker under 16 are in his or her care. The benefit is 75% of the PIA and he or she draws it until the youngest child reaches 16, at which time payments stop even if the child's benefit continues. They may start again when he or she is 60 (50 if disabled) unless he or she is married. If he or she has a disabled child beneficiary aged 16 or over in care, benefits also continue.

4. Dependent parents may be eligible for benefits, if they have been receiving at least half their support from the worker before his or her death, have reached age 62, and (except in certain circumstances) have not remarried since the worker's death. Each parent gets 75% of the worker's PIA; if only one parent survives the benefit is 82 1/2%.

5. A lump sum cash payment of $255. Payment is made only when there is a spouse who was living with the worker or a spouse or child eligible for immediate monthly survivor benefits.

Self-Employed

A self-employed person who has net earnings of $400 or more in a year must report such earnings for social security tax and credit purposes. The person reports net returns from the business. Income from real estate, savings, dividends, loans, pensions or insurance policies may not be included unless they are part of the business.

A self-employed person gets a quarter of coverage for each $540 (for 1991), up to a maximum of 4 quarters of coverage.

The nonfarm self-employed have the option of reporting their earnings as 2/3 of their gross income from self-employment but not more than $1,600 a year and not less than their actual net earnings. This option can be used only if actual net earnings from self-employment income is less than $1,600 and may be used only 5 times. Also, the self-employed person must have actual net earnings of $400 or more in 2 of the 3 taxable years immediately preceding the year in which he or she uses the option.

When a person has both taxable wages and earnings from self-employment, the wages are credited for Social Security purposes first; only as much of the self-employment income as will bring total earnings up to the current taxable maximum is subject to the self-employment tax.

Farm Owners and Workers

Self-employed farmers whose gross annual earnings from farming are $2,400 or less may report $2/3$ of their gross earnings instead of net earnings for social security purposes. Farmers whose gross income is over $2,400 and whose net earnings are less than $1,600 can report $1,600. Cash or crop shares received from a tenant or share farmer count if the owner participated materially in production or management. The self-employed farmer pays contributions at the same rate as other self-employed persons.

Agricultural employees. A worker's earnings from farm work count toward benefits (1) if the employer pays him $150 or more in cash during the year; or (2) if the employer spends $2,500 or more in the year for agricultural labor. Under these rules a person gets credit for one calendar quarter for each $540 in cash pay in 1991 up to four quarters.

Foreign farm workers admitted to the United States on a temporary basis are not covered.

Household Workers

Anyone working as maid, cook, laundress, nursemaid, baby-sitter, chauffeur, gardener and at other household tasks in the house of another is covered by Social Security if he or she is paid $50 or more in cash in a calendar quarter by any one employer. Room and board do not count, but carfare counts if paid in cash. The job does not have to be regular or fulltime. The employee should get a Social Security card at the social security office and show it to the employer.

The employer deducts the amount of the employee's social security tax from the worker's pay, adds an identical amount as the employer's social security tax and sends the total amount to the federal government, with the employee's social security number.

Medicare

Under Medicare, protection against the costs of hospital care is provided for Social Security and Railroad Retirement beneficiaries aged 65 and over and, for persons entitled for 24 months to receive a social security disability benefit, certain persons (and their dependents) with end-stage renal disease, and, on a voluntary basis with payment of a special premium, persons aged 65 and over not otherwise eligible for hospital benefits; all those eligible for hospital benefits may enroll for medical benefits and pay a monthly premium and so may persons aged 65 and over who are not eligible for hospital benefits.

Persons eligible for both hospital and medical insurance may choose to have their covered services provided through a Health Maintenance Organization.

Hospital insurance.—In 1988, nearly $52.7 billion was withdrawn from the hospital insurance trust fund for hospital and related benefits.

The hospital insurance program pays the cost of covered services for hospital and posthospital care as follows:

- Medicare will cover all *medically necessary* inpatient hospital care 365 days a year. The Medicare hospital patient must pay a deductible sum each year (about $560 in 1987).
- Up to 150 days' care in a skilled-nursing facility (skilled-nursing home) in each year. Hospital insurance pays for all covered services except for coinsurance for the first 8 days of SNF care each year (about $20.50 per day in 1989).
- Visits by nurses or other health workers (not doctors) from a home health agency.
- Hospice care for terminally ill individuals.

Medical insurance. Aged persons can receive benefits under this supplementary program only if they sign up for them and agree to a monthly premium ($24.80 in 1988). The Federal Government pays the rest of the cost.

In 1988, about $35 billion was paid out for medical insurance benefits. As of September 1987, about 33 million persons were enrolled — 3 million of them disabled persons under age 65.

The medical insurance program pays 80% of the reasonable charges (after the first $75 in each calendar year) for the following services:

- Physicians' and surgeons' services, whether in the doc-tor's office, a clinic, or hospital or at home (but physician's charges for X-ray or clinical laboratory services for hospital bed-patients are paid in full and without meeting the deductible).
- Other medical and health services, such as diagnostic tests, surgical dressings and splints, and rental or purchase of medical equipment. Services of a physical therapist in independent practice, furnished in his office or the patient's home. A hospital or extended-care facility may provide covered outpatient physical therapy services under the medical insurance program to its patients who have exhausted their hospital insurance coverage.
- Physical therapy services furnished under the supervision of a practicing hospital, clinic, skilled nursing facility, or agency.
- Certain services by podiatrists.
- All outpatient services of a participating hospital (including diagnostic tests).
- Outpatient speech pathology services, under the same requirements as physical therapy.
- Services of licensed chiropractors who meet uniform standards, but only for treatment by means of manual manipulation of the spine and treatment of subluxation of the spine demonstrated by X-ray.
- Supplies related to colostomies are considered prosthetic devices and payable under the program.
- Home health services even without a hospital stay are paid up to 100% *when medically necessary.*

To get medical insurance protection, persons approaching age 65 may enroll in the 7-month period that includes 3 months before the 65th birthday, the month of the birthday, and 3 months after the birthday, but if they wish coverage to begin in the month they reach 65 they must enroll in the 3 months **before** their birthday. Persons not enrolling within their first enrollment period may enroll later, during the first 3 months of each year but their premium is 10% higher for each 12-month period elapsed since they first could have enrolled.

The monthly premium is deducted from the cash benefit for persons receiving Social Security, Railroad Retirement, or Civil Service retirement benefits. Income from the medical premiums and the federal matching payments are put in a Supplementary Medical Insurance Trust Fund, from which benefits and administrative expenses are paid.

Medicare card. Persons qualifying for hospital insurance under Social Security receive a health insurance card similar to cards now used by Blue Cross and other health agencies. The card indicates whether the individual has taken out medical insurance protection. It is to be shown to the hospital, skilled-nursing facility, home health agency, doctor, or whoever provides the covered services.

Payments are made only in the 50 states, Puerto Rico, the Virgin Islands, Guam, and American Samoa, except that hospital services may be provided in border areas immediately outside the U.S. if comparable services are not accessible in the U.S. for a beneficiary who becomes ill or is injured in the U.S.

Social Security Financing

Social Security is paid for by a tax on earnings (for 1991, up to $53,400; the taxable earnings base is now subject to automatic adjustment to reflect increases in average wages). The employed worker and his or her employer share the tax equally.

Employers remit amounts withheld from employee wages for Social Security and income taxes to the Internal Revenue Service; employer Social Security taxes are also payable at the same time. (Self-employed workers pay their Social Security taxes along with their regular income tax forms). The Social Security taxes (along with revenues arising from partial taxation of the Social Security benefits of certain high-income people) are transferred to the Social Security Trust Funds (Federal Old-Age and Survivors Insurance Trust Fund, the Federal Disability Insurance Trust Fund, and the Federal Hospital Insurance Trust Fund); they can be used only to pay benefits, the cost of rehabilitation services, and administrative expenses. Money not immediately needed for these purposes is by law invested in obligations of the Federal Government, which must pay interest on the money borrowed and must repay the principal when the obligations are redeemed or mature.

Supplemental Security Income

On Jan. 1, 1974, the Supplemental Security Income (SSI) program established by the 1972 Social Security Act amendments replaced the former federal grants to states for aid to the needy aged, blind, and disabled in the 50 states and the District of Columbia. The program provides both for federal payments based on uniform national standards and eligibility requirements and for state supplementary payments varying from state to state. The Social Security Administration administers the federal payments financed from general funds of the Treasury—and the state supplements as well, if the state elects to have its supplementary program federally

administered. The states may supplement the federal payment for all recipients and must supplement it for persons otherwise adversely affected by the transition from the former public assistance programs. In May 1991, the number of persons receiving federal payments and federally administered state payments was 4,906,603 and the amount of these payments was $1.51 billion.

The maximum monthly federal SSI payment for an individual with no other countable income, living in his own household, was $407.00 in 1991. For a couple it was $610.00.

Examples of monthly cash benefit awards for selected beneficiary families with first entitlement in 1991, effective January 1991

Beneficiary Family	Low Earnings ($9,801 in 1991) (45% of average)	Career Earnings Level Average Earnings ($21,781 in 1991)[1]	Maximum Earnings ($53,400 in 1991)
Primary Insurance amount (worker retiring at 65)	$461.20	$751.10	$1,022.90
Maximum family benefit (worker retiring at 65)	692.20	1,367.90	1,790.60
Disability maximum family benefit (worker disabled at 55; in 1991)*	640.90	1,126.80	1,562.80
Disabled worker: (worker disabled at 55)			
Worker alone	461.00	751.00	1,041.00
Worker, spouse, and 1 child	639.00	1,125.00	1,561.00
Retired worker claiming benefits at age 62:			
Worker alone[2]	368.00	600.00	810.00
Worker with spouse claiming benefits at—			
Age 65 or over	598.00	975.00	1,321.00
Age 62[2]	552.00	900.00	1,219.00
Widow or widower claiming benefits at—			
Age 65 or over[3]	461.00	751.00	1,022.00
Age 60	329.00	537.00	731.00
Disabled widow or widower claiming benefits at age 50-59[4]	329.00	537.00	731.00
1 surviving child	345.00	563.00	767.00
Widow or widower age 65 or over and 1 child[5]	692.00	1,314.00	1,789.00
Widowed mother or father and 1 child[5]	690.00	1,126.00	1,534.00
Widowed mother or father and 2 children[5]	690.00	1,365.00	1,788.00

*Assumes work beginning at age 22. (1) Estimate. (2) Assumes maximum reduction. (3) A widow(er)'s benefit amount is limited to the amount the spouse would have been receiving if still living but not less than 82.5 percent of the PIA. (4) Effective January 1984, disabled widow(er)s claiming benefit at ages 50-59 will receive benefit equal to 71.5 percent of the PIA (based on 1983 Social Security Amendment provision). (5) Based on worker dying at age 65.

Social Security Trust Funds

Old-Age and Survivors Insurance Trust Fund, 1940-1990

(in millions)

Fiscal year[1]		Income				Disbursements					
	Total	Net contributions[2]	Income from taxation of benefits	Payments from the general fund of the Treasury[3]	Net interest[4]	Total	Benefit payments[5]	Administrative expenses	Transfers to Railroad Retirement program	Interfund borrowing transfers[6]	Net increase in fund	Fund at end of period
1940	$592	$550	—	—	$42	$28	$16	$12	—	—	$564	$1,745
1950	2,367	2,106	—	$4	257	784	727	57	—	—	1,583	12,893
1960	10,360	9,843	—	—	517	11,073	10,270	202	$600	—	−713	20,829
1970	31,746	29,955	—	442	1,350	27,321	26,268	474	579	—	4,425	32,616
1980	100,051	97,608	—	557	1,886	103,228	100,626	1,160	1,442	—	−3,177	24,566
1985	179,881	175,305	$3,151	105	1,321	169,210	165,310	1,589	2,310	$−4,364	6,308	33,877
1989	260,457	247,116	3,638	43	9,660	209,102	204,600	1,657	2,845	—	51,355	148,319
1990	278,607	261,506	2,924	34	14,143	223,481	218,948	1,564	2,969	—	55,126	203,445

(1) Under the Congressional Budget Act of 1974 (Public Law 93-344), fiscal years 1977 and later consist of the 12 months ending on September 30 of each year. The act further provides that the calendar quarter July-September 1976 is a period of transition from fiscal year 1976, which ended on June 30, 1976, to fiscal year 1977, which began on October 1, 1976.

(2) Beginning in 1983, includes government contributions on deemed wage credits for military service in 1957 and later.

(3) Includes payments (1) in 1947-52 and in 1967 and later, for costs of noncontributory wage credits for military service performed before 1957; (2) in 1972-83, for costs of deemed wage credits for military service performed after 1956; and (3) in 1969 and later, for costs of benefits to certain uninsured persons who attained age 72 before 1968.

(4) Net interest includes net profits or losses on marketable investments. Beginning in 1967, administrative expenses are charged currently to the trust fund on an estimated basis, with a final adjustment, including interest, made in the following fiscal year. The amounts of these interest adjustments are included in net interest. For years prior to 1967, a description of the method of accounting for administrative expenses is contained in the 1970 Annual Report of the Board of Trustees of the Fedeal Old-Age and Survivors Insurance and Disability Insurance Trust Funds. Beginning in 1983, these figures reflect payments from a borrowing trust fund to a lending trust fund for interest on amounts owed under the interfund borrowing provisions. Also, beginning in 1983, interest paid from the trust fund to the general fund on advance tax transfers is reflected. The amounts shown for 1985 and 1986 include interest adjustments of $76.5 million and $11.5 million, respectively, on unnegotiated checks issued before April 1985.

(5) Beginning in 1967, includes payments for vocational rehabilitation services furnished to disabled persons receiving benefits because of their disabilities. Beginning in 1983, figures are reduced by amount of reimbursement for unnegotiated benefit checks. The amount shown for 1983 is reduced by $288 million for all unnegotiated checks issued before 1983; reductions in subsequent years are relatively small.

(6) Positive figure represents amounts lent to the OASI Trust Fund from the DI and HI Trust Funds. Negative figures represent amounts repaid from the OASI Trust Fund to the DI and HI Trust Funds.

Disability Insurance Trust Fund, 1960-1990

(In millions)

| Fiscal year[1] | Total | Income | | | | Disbursements | | | | Interfund borrowing trans-fers[6] | Net increase in fund | Fund at end of period |
		Net contri-butions[2]	Income from taxa-tion of benefits	Payments from the general fund of the Treasury[3]	Net interest[4]	Total	Benefit pay-ments[5]	Adminis-trative expenses	Transfers to Rail-road Retire-ment program			
1960	$1,034	$987	—	—	$47	$533	$528	$32	-$27	—	$501	$2,167
1970	4,380	4,141	—	$16	223	2,954	2,795	149	10	—	1,426	5,104
1980	17,376	16,805	—	118	453	15,320	14,998	334	-12	—	2,056	7,680
1985	17,984	16,876	$217	—	891	19,294	18,648	603	43	$2,540	1,230	5,873
1989	24,479	23,694	135	—	650	23,389	22,550	751	88	—	1,090	8,363
1990	28,215	27,291	158	—	766	25,124	24,327	717	80	—	3,091	11,455

(1) Under the Congressional Budget Act of 1974 (Public Law 93-344), fiscal years 1977 and later consist of the 12 months ending on September 30 of each year. The act further provides that the calendar quarter July-September 1976 is a period of transition from fiscal year 1976, which ended on June 30, 1976, to fiscal year 1977, which began on October 1, 1976.
(2) Beginning in 1983, includes government contributions on deemed wage credits for military service in 1957 and later.
(3) Includes payments (1) in 1967 and later, for costs of noncontributory wage credits for military service performed before 1957; and (2) in 1972-83, for costs of deemed wage credits for military service performed after 1956.
(4) Net interest includes net profits or losses on marketable investments. Beginning in 1967, administrative expenses are charged currently to the trust fund on an estimated basis, with a final adjustment, including interest, made in the following fiscal year. The amounts of these interest adjustments are included in net interest. For years prior to 1967, a description of the method of accounting for administrative expenses is contained in the 1970 Annual Report of the Board of Trustees of the Federal Old-Age and Survivors Insurance and Disability Insurance Trust Funds. Beginning in 1983, these figures reflect payments from a borrowing trust fund to a lending trust fund for interest on amounts owed under the interfund borrowing provisions. Also, beginning in 1983, interest paid from the trust fund to the general fund on advance tax transfers is reflected. The amount shown for 1985 includes an interest adjustment of $14.8 million on unnegotiated checks issued before April 1985.
(5) Beginning in 1967, includes payments for vocational rehabilitation services furnished to disabled persons receiving benefits because of their disabilities. Beginning in 1983, amounts are reduced by amount of reimbursement for unnegotiated benefit checks. The amount shown for 1983 is reduced by $48 million for all unnegotiated checks issued before 1983; reductions in subsequent years are relatively small.
(6) Negative figure represents amounts lent by the DI Trust Fund to the OASI Trust Fund. Positive figures represent repayment of these amounts.

Supplementary Medical Insurance Trust Fund, 1970-1990

(In millions)

| Fiscal year[1] | Income | | | | Disbursements | | | Balance in fund at end of year[4] |
	Premium from participants	Government contribu-tions[2]	Interest and other income[3]	Total income	Benefit payments	Adminis-trative expenses	Total disburse-ments	
1970	$936	$928	$12	$1,876	$1,979	$217	$2,196	$57
1975	1,887	2,330	105	4,322	3,765	405	4,170	1,424
1980	2,928	6,932	415	10,275	10,144	593	10,737	4,532
1985	5,524	17,898	1,155	24,577	21,808	922	22,730	10,646
1989	11,548[5]	30,712	1,022[5]	43,282[5]	36,867	1,450[5]	38,317[5]	11,412[5]
1990	11,494[5]	33,210	1,434[5]	46,138[5]	41,498	1,524[5]	43,022[5]	14,527[5]

(1) For 1967 through 1976, fiscal years cover the interval from July 1 through June 30; fiscal years 1977 and later cover the interval from October 1 through September 30. (2) The payments shown as being from the general fund of the Treasury include certain interest-adjustment items. (3) Other income includes recoveries of amounts reimbursed from the trust fund which are not obligations of the trust fund and other miscellaneous income. (4) The financial status of the program depends on both the total net assets and the liabilities of the program. (5) Includes the impact of the Medicare Catastrophic Coverage Act of 1988 (Public Law 100-360).

Hospital Insurance Trust Fund, 1970-1990

(In millions)

| Fiscal Year[1] | Income | | | | | | | Disbursements | | | Trust Fund | |
	Payroll taxes	Transfers from railroad retirement account	Reimburse-ment for uninsured persons	Premiums from voluntary enrollees	Payments for military wage credits	Interest on invest-ments and other income[2]	Total income	Benefits payments[3]	Adminis-trative expense[4]	Total disburse-ments	Net increase fund	Fund at end of year
1970	$4,785	$64	617	—	$11	$137	$5,614	$4,804	$149	$4,953	$661	$2,677
1975	11,291	132	481	6	48	609	12,568	10,353	259	10,612	1,956	9,870
1980	23,244	244	697	17	141	1,072	25,415	23,790	497	24,288	1,127	14,490
1985	46,490	371	766	38	86	3,182	50,933	47,841	813	48,654	4,103[5]	21,277[5]
1989	67,527	379	515	42	86	6,567	75,116	57,433	805	58,238	16,878	82,755
1990	70,655	367	413	107	7	7,906	79,563	65,912	774	66,687	12,876	95,631

(1) Fiscal years 1976 and earlier consist of the 12 months ending on June 30 of each year; fiscal years 1977 and later consist of the 12 months ending on September 30 of each year. (2) Other income includes recoveries of amounts reimbursed from the trust fund which are not obligations of the trust fund and a small amount of miscellaneous income. (3) Includes costs of Peer Review Organizations (beginning with the implementation of the Prospective Payment System on October 1, 1983). (4) Includes costs of experiments and demonstration projects. (5) In fiscal year 1983, $12,437 million was loaned to the Old-Age and Survivors Insurance Trust Fund under the interfund borrowing provisions of the Social Security Act. Repayments of $1,824 million and $10,613 million were made in fiscal years 1985 and 1986, respectively.
NOTE: Totals do not necessarily equal the sum of rounded components.

NATIONAL DEFENSE

Data as of July, 1991

Chairman, Joint Chiefs of Staff
Gen. Colin L. Powell

The Joint Chiefs of Staff consists of the Chairman and Vice Chairman of the Joint Chiefs of Staff; the Chief of Staff, U.S. Army; the Chief of Naval Operations; the Chief of Staff, U.S. Air Force; and the Commandant of the Marine Corps.

Army

Chief of Staff—Gordon R. Sullivan
Generals

	Date of Rank
Burba, Edwin H. Jr.	Sept. 27, 1989
Foss, John W.	Aug. 2, 1989
Galvin, John R.	Feb. 25, 1985
Joulwan, George A.	Nov. 21, 1990
Powell, Colin L.	Apr. 4, 1989
RisCassi, Robert W.	Jan. 17, 1989
Saint, Crosbie E.	June 24, 1988
Schwarzkopf, H. Norman	Nov. 23, 1988
Stiner, Carl W.	July 1, 1990
Tuttle, William G.T. Jr.	Oct. 1, 1989

Navy

Chief of Naval Operations
Admiral Frank B. Kelso II (submariner)
Admirals

	Date of Rank
DeMars, Bruce (submariner)	Nov. 1, 1988
Edney, Leon A. (aviator)	Oct. 1, 1988
Howe, Johnathan T. (surface warfare)	June 1, 1989
Jeremiah, David E. (surface warfare)	Oct. 1, 1987
Johnson, Jerome L. (aviator)	July 1, 1990
Kelly, Robert J. (aviator)	Mar. 1, 1991
Larson, Charles R. (submariner)	Mar. 1, 1990
Miller, Paul D. (surface warfare)	Feb. 1, 1991
Smith, William D. (submariner)	Feb. 22, 1991

Air Force

Chief of Staff—Merrill A. McPeak.
Generals

Adams, Jimmie V.	Feb. 13, 1991
Butler, George L.	Jan. 25, 1991
Carns, Michael P.C.	May 16, 1991
Johnson, Hansford T.	Oct. 1, 1989
Kutyna, Donald J.	Apr. 1, 1990
Loh, John M.	June 1, 1990
McCarthy, James P.	Oct. 1, 1989
McDonald, Charles C.	Nov. 1, 1989
Oaks, Robert C.	July 1, 1990
Shaud, John A.	July 1, 1988
Yates, Ronald W.	Apr. 1, 1990

Marine Corps

Corps Commandant, with rank of General
Carl E. Mundy Jr. . . . . July 1, 1991

ACMC/Chief of Staff, with rank of Gen.
John R. Dailey . . . . Aug. 1, 1990

Coast Guard

Commandant, with rank of Admiral
J. William Kime. . . . . May 31, 1990

Vice Commandant, with rank of Vice Admiral
Martin H. Daniell Jr. . . . . May 31, 1990

Unified Defense Commands Commanders-in-Chief

Atlantic Command (LANTCOM) — Adm. Leon A. Edney.

U.S. European Command, Brussels — Gen. John R. Galvin (USA) (concurrently NATO Supreme Allied Commander).

U.S. Southern Command, Quarry Heights, Panama Canal Zone — Gen. George A. Joulwan (USA).

U.S. Atlantic Command, Norfolk, Virginia — Adm. Lee Baggett, Jr., (USN) (concurrently NATO Supreme Allied Commander, Atlantic).

U.S. Pacific Command, Hawaii — Adm. Huntington Hardisty (USN)

U.S. Space Command, Gen. Donald J. Kutyna (USAF)

*Strategic Air Command, Omaha — Gen. George L. Butler (USAF)

*US Forces Command — Gen. Edwin H. Burba (USA)

*U.S. Transportation Command, Gen. Hansford T. Johnson (USAF)

U.S. Special Operations Command, MacDill AFB, Fla. — Gen. Carl W. Stiner (USA)

U.S. Central Command, Gen. H. Norman Schwarzkopf (USA)

*A Specified Command.

North Atlantic Treaty Organization International Commands

Supreme Allied Commander, Europe (SACEUR) — Gen. John R. Galvin (USA)

Deputy Supreme Allied Commander Europe (DSACEUR) — Gen. Sir Brian Kenny, UK, Army (UKA)

Deputy Supreme Allied Commander Europe (DSACEUR) — Gen. Dieter Clauss (GEA)

Commander-in-Chief Allied Forces Northern Europe — Gen. Sir Patrick Palmer, UK, Army, KBE, MC (UKA)

Commander-in-Chief Allied Forces Central Europe — Gen. Hans-Henning von Sandrart (GEA)

Commander-in-Chief Allied Forces Southern Europe — Adm. J. T. Howe

Commander-in-Chief United Kingdom Air Forces — Gen. Michael Graydon (UKAF)

Chairman, NATO Military Committee — Gen. Viglik Eide (Norway)

Principal U.S. Military Training Centers
Army

Name, P.O. address	Zip	Nearest city	Name, P.O. address	Zip	Nearest city
Aberdeen Proving Ground, MD	21005	Aberdeen	Fort Knox, KY	40121	Louisville
Carlisle Barracks, PA	17013	Carlisle	Fort Leavenworth, KS	66027	Leavenworth
Fort Belvoir, VA.	22060	Alexandria	Fort Lee, VA.	23801	Petersburg
Fort Benning, GA	31905	Columbus	Fort McClellan, AL	36205	Anniston
Fort Bliss, TX	79916	El Paso	Fort Monmouth, NJ.	07703	Red Bank
Fort Bragg, NC	28307	Fayetteville	Fort Rucker, AL.	36362	Dothan
Fort Devens, MA	01433	Ayer	Fort Sill, OK.	73503	Lawton
Fort Dix, NJ	08640	Trenton	Fort Leonard Wood, MO.	65473	Rolla
Fort Eustis, VA	23604	Newport News	Joint Readiness, Ft. Chaffee, AR.	72905	Fort Smith
Fort Gordon, GA	30905	Augusta	National Training Center.	92311	Barstow, CA
Fort Benjamin Harrison, IN	46216	Indianapolis	Redstone Arsenal, AL	35809	Huntsville
Fort Sam Houston, TX.	78234	San Antonio	The Judge Advocate		Charlottes-
Fort Huachuca, AZ	85613	Sierra Vista	General School, VA.	22901	ville
Fort Jackson, SC.	29207	Columbia	U.S. Military Acad., NY.	10996	West Point

Navy

	Zip	Nearest city		Zip	Nearest city
Great Lakes, IL	60088	North Chicago	Orlando, FL	32813	Orlando
San Diego, CA	92133	San Diego			

Marine Corps

Name, P.O. address	Zip	Nearest city	Name, P.O. address	Zip	Nearest city
MCB Camp Lejeune, NC	28542	Jacksonville		Seattle	Iwakuni
MCB Camp Pendleton, CA	92055	Oceanside		98764	
MCB Camp Butler, Okinawa	FPO Seattle 98773	Futenma, Okinawa	MCAS Kaneohe Bay, Oahu, HI	San Fran- cisco 96863	Kailua
MCAGCC Twentynine Palms, CA	92278	Palm Springs			
MCCDC Quantico, VA	22134	Quantico	MCAS Futenma,		
MCRD Parris Island, SC.	29905	Beaufort	Okinawa FPO Seattle	98772	Futenma
MCRD San Diego, CA	92140	San Diego	MCAS Beaufort, SC	29904	Beaufort
MCAS Cherry Point, NC.	28533	Havelock	MCAS Yuma, AZ	85369	Yuma
MCAS El Toro (Santa Ana), CA	92709	Santa Ana	MCMWTC Bridgeport, CA.	93517	Bridgeport
MCAS Tustin, CA.	92780	Santa Ana	MCLB Albany, GA	31704	Albany
MCAS New River, NC	28545	Jacksonville	MCLB Barstow, CA.	92311	Barstow
MCAS Iwakuni, Japan	FPO				

MCB = Marine Corps Base. MCCDC = Marine Corps Combat Development Command. MCAS = Marine Corps Air Station. MCRD = Marine Corps Recruit Depot. MCAGCC = Marine Corps Air-Ground Combat Center. MCMWTC = Marine Corps Mountain Warfare Training Center. MCLB = Marine Corps Logistics Base.

Air Force

Chanute AFB, IL	61868	Rantoul	Mather AFB, CA	95655	Sacramento
Columbus AFB, MS	39701	Columbus	Maxwell AFB, AL*	36112	Montgomery
Goodfellow AFB, TX	76908	San Angelo	Randolph AFB, TX	78150	San Antonio
Gunter AFB, AL*	36114	Montgomery	Reese AFB, TX	79489	Lubbock
Keesler AFB, MS	39534	Biloxi	Sheppard AFB, TX	76311	Wichita Falls
Lackland AFB, TX	78236	San Antonio	Vance AFB, OK.	73705	Enid
Laughlin AFB, TX	78843	Del Rio	Williams AFB, AZ.	85240	Phoenix
Lowry AFB, CO.	80230	Denver	Wright-Patterson AFB, OH	45433	Dayton

*Air University Bases. All others are Air Training Command Bases.

Personal Salutes and Honors

The United States national salute, 21 guns, is also the salute to a national flag. The independence of the United States is commemorated by the salute to the union — one gun for each state — fired at noon on July 4 at all military posts provided with suitable artillery.

A 21-gun salute on arrival and departure, with 4 ruffles and flourishes, is rendered to the President of the United States, to an ex-President and to a President-elect. The national anthem or *Hail to the Chief*, as appropriate, is played for the President, and the national anthem for the others. A 21-gun salute on arrival and departure with 4 ruffles and flourishes, also is rendered to the sovereign or chief of state of a foreign country or a member of a reigning royal family; the national anthem of his or her country is played. The music is considered an inseparable part of the salute and will immediately follow the ruffles and flourishes without pause.

Rank	Salute—guns Arrive—Leave		Ruffles, flour- ishes	Music
Vice President of United States	19		4	Hail Columbia
Speaker of the House	19		4	March
American or foreign ambassador.	19		4	Nat. anthem of official
Premier or prime minister	19		4	Nat. anthem of official
Secretary of Defense, Army, Navy or Air Force	19	19	4	Honors March
Other Cabinet members, Senate President pro tempore, Governor, or Chief Justice of U.S.	19		4	Honors March
Chairman, Joint Chiefs of Staff.	19	19	4	
Army Chief of Staff, Chief of Naval Operations, Air Force Chief of Staff, Marine Commandant	19	19	4	General's or Admiral's March
General of the Army, General of the Air Force, Fleet Admiral.	19	19	4	
Generals, Admirals.	17	17	4	
Assistant secretaries of Defense, Army, Navy or Air Force	17	17	4	Honors March
Chairman of a committee of Congress.	17	17	4	Honors March

Other salutes (on arrival only) include 15 guns for U.S. envoys or ministers and foreign envoys or ministers accredited to the U.S.; 15 guns for a lieutenant general or vice admiral; 13 guns for a major general or rear admiral (upper half); 13 guns for U.S. ministers resident and ministers resident accredited to the U.S.; 11 guns for a brigadier general or rear admiral (lower half); 11 guns for U.S. charges d'affaires and like officials accredited to U.S.; and 11 guns for consuls general accredited to U.S.

Military Units, U.S. Army and Air Force

Army units. Squad. In infantry usually ten men under a staff sergeant. **Platoon.** In infantry 4 squads under a lieutenant. **Company.** Headquarters section and 4 platoons under a captain. (Company in the artillery is a battery; in the cavalry, a troop.) **Battalion.** Hdqts. and 4 or more companies under a lieutenant colonel. (Battalion size unit in the cavalry is a squadron.) **Brigade.** Hdqts. and 3 or more battalions under a colonel. **Division.** Hdqts. and 3 brigades with artillery, combat support, and combat service support units under a major general. **Army Corps.** Two or more divisions with corps troops under a lieutenant general. **Field Army.** Hdqts. and two or more corps with field Army troops under a general.

Air Force Units. Flight. Numerically designated flights are the lowest level unit in the Air Force. They are used primarily where there is a need for small mission elements to be incorporated into an organized unit. **Squadron.** A squadron is the basic unit in the Air Force. It is used to designate the mission units in operational commands. **Group.** The group is a flexible unit composed of two or more squadrons whose functions may be either tactical, support or administrative in nature. **Wing.** An operational wing normally has two or more assigned mission squadrons in an area such as combat, flying training or airlift. **Air Division.** The organization of the air division may be similar to that of the numbered air force, though on a much smaller scale. Functions are usually limited to operations and logistics. **Numbered Air Forces.** Normally an operationally oriented agency, the numbered air force is designed for the control of two or more air divisions or units of comparable strength. It is a flexible organization and may be of any size. Its wings may be assigned to air divisions or directly under the numbered air force. **Major Command.** A major subdivision of the Air Force that is assigned a major segment of the USAF mission.

U.S. Army Insignia and Chevrons

Source: Department of the Army

Grade	Insignia

General of the Armies

General John J. Pershing, the only person to have held this rank, was authorized to prescribe his own insignia, but never wore in excess of four stars. The rank originally was established by Congress for George Washington in 1799, and he was promoted to the rank by joint resolution of Congress, approved by Pres. Ford Oct. 19, 1976.

General of Army ... Five silver stars fastened together in a circle and the coat of arms of the United States in gold color metal with shield and crest enameled.

General . . . . Four silver stars
Lieutenant General . . . . . Three silver stars
Major General . . . . Two silver stars
Brigadier General . . . . . . One silver star
Colonel . . . . Silver eagle
Lieutenant Colonel . . . . Silver oak leaf
Major . . . . Gold oak leaf
Captain . . . . Two silver bars
First Lieutenant . . . . . . One silver bar
Second Lieutenant . . . . . . One gold bar

Warrant officers

Grade Four—Silver bar with 4 enamel black squares.
Grade Three—Silver bar with 3 enamel black squares.
Grade Two—Silver bar with 2 enamel black squares.
Grade One—Silver bar with 1 enamel black squares.

Non-commissioned Officers

Sergeant Major of the Army (E-9). Same as Command Sergeant Major (below) but with 2 stars. Also wears distinctive red and white shield on lapel.

Command Sergeant Major (E-9). Three chevrons above three arcs with a 5-pointed star with a wreath around the star between the chevrons and arcs.

Sergeant Major (E-9). Three chevrons above three arcs with a five-pointed star between the chevrons and arcs.

First Sergeant (E-8). Three chevrons above three arcs with a lozenge between the chevrons and arcs.

Master Sergeant (E-8). Three chevrons above three arcs.

Sergeant First Class (E-7). Three chevrons above two arcs.

Staff Sergeant (E-6). Three chevrons above one arc.
Sergeant (E-5). Three chevrons.
Corporal (E-4). Two chevrons.

Specialists

Specialist (E-4). Eagle device only.

Other enlisted

Private First Class (E-3). One chevron above one arc.
Private (E-2). One chevron.
Private (E-1). None.

U.S. Army

Source: Department of the Army

Army Military Personnel on Active Duty[1]

June 30[2]	Total strength	Commissioned officers			Warrant officers		Enlisted personnel		
		Total	Male	Female[3]	Male[4]	Female	Total	Male	Female
1940	267,767	17,563	16,624	939	763		249,441	249,441	
1942	3,074,137	203,137	190,662	12,475	3,285		2,867,762	2,867,762	
1943	6,993,102	557,657	521,435	36,222	21,919	0	6,413,526	6,358,200	55,325
1944	7,992,868	740,077	692,351	47,726	36,893	10	7,215,888	7,144,601	71,287
1945	8,266,373	835,403	772,511	62,892	56,216	44	7,374,710	7,283,930	90,780
1946	1,889,690	257,300	240,643	16,657	9,826	18	1,622,546	1,605,847	16,699
1950	591,487	67,784	63,375	4,409	4,760	22	518,921	512,370	6,551
1955	1,107,606	111,347	106,173	5,174	10,552	48	985,659	977,943	7,716
1960	871,348	91,056	86,832	4,224	10,141	39	770,112	761,833	8,279
1965	967,049	101,812	98,029	3,783	10,285	23	854,929	846,409	8,520
1969	1,509,637	148,836	143,699	5,137	23,734	20	1,327,047	1,316,326	10,721
1970	1,319,735	143,704	138,469	5,235	23,005	13	1,153,013	1,141,537	11,476
1975	781,316	89,756	85,184	4,572	13,214	22	678,324	640,621	37,703
1980 (Sept 30)	772,661	85,339	77,843	7,496	13,265	113	673,944	612,593	61,351
1984 (Sept. 30)	775,594	92,484	82,497	9,987	15,156	243	667,711	601,695	66,616
1985 (Sept. 30)	776,244	94,103	83,563	10,540	15,296	288	666,557	598,639	67,918
1988 (Mar. 30)	764,247	93,173	81,904	11,269	14,664	363	656,047	584,305	71,742
1989 (Mar. 30)	760,237	91,550	80,113	11,437	14,517	417	653,753	581,106	72,647
1990 (Mar. 30)	746,220	91,330	79,520	11,810	15,177	470	639,713	567,015	72,698
1991 (Mar. 30)	740,023	89,448	77,489	11,959	14,771	505	635,299	564,180	71,119

(1) Represents strength of the active Army, including Philippine Scouts, retired Regular Army personnel on extended active duty, and National Guard and Reserve personnel on extended active duty; excludes U.S. Military Academy cadets, contract surgeons, and National Guard and Reserve personnel not on extended active duty.
(2) Data for 1940 to 1947 include personnel in the Army Air Forces and its predecessors (Air Service and Air Corps).
(3) Includes: women doctors, dentists, and Medical Service Corps officers for 1946 and subsequent years, women in the Army Nurse Corps for all years, and the Women's Army Corps and Women's Medical Specialists Corps (dieticians, physical therapists, and occupational specialists) for 1943 and subsequent years.
(4) Act of Congress approved April 27, 1926, directed the appointment as warrant officers of field clerks still in active service. Includes flight officers as follows: 1943, 5,700; 1944, 13,615; 1945, 31,117; 1946, 2,580.

The Federal Service Academies

U.S. Military Academy, West Point, N.Y. Founded 1802. Awards B.S. degree and Army commission for a 5-year service obligation. For admissions information, write Admissions Office, USMA, West Point, NY 10996.

U.S. Naval Academy, Annapolis, Md. Founded 1845. Awards B.S. degree and Navy or Marine Corps commission for a 5-year service obligation. For admissions information, write Dean of Admissions, Naval Academy, Annapolis, MD 21402.

U.S. Air Force Academy, Colorado Springs, Col. Founded 1954. Awards B.S. degree and Air Force commission for a 5-year service obligation. For admissions information, write Registrar, U.S. Air Force Academy, CO 80840.

U.S. Coast Guard Academy, New London, Conn. Founded 1876. Awards B.S. degree and Coast Guard commission for a 5-year service obligation. For admissions information, write Director of Admissions, Coast Guard Academy, New London, CT 06320.

U.S. Merchant Marine Academy, Kings Point, N.Y. Founded 1943. Awards B.S. degree, a license as a deck, engineer, or dual officer, and a U.S. Naval Reserve commission. Service obligations vary according to options taken by the graduate. For admissions information, write Admission Office, U.S. Merchant Marine Academy, Kings Point, NY 11024.

U.S. Navy Insignia

Source: Department of the Navy

Navy
Stripes and corps device are of gold embroidery.

Stripes
Fleet Admiral . . . . . 1 two inch with 4 one-half inch.
Admiral . . . . 1 two inch with 3 one-half inch.
Vice Admiral. . . . . . 1 two inch with 2 one-half inch.
Rear Admiral (upper
  half) . . . . 1 two inch with 1 one-half inch.
Rear Admiral (lower
  half) . . . . 1 two inch.
Captain. . . . . 4 one-half inch.
Commander . . . . . . 3 one-half inch.
Lieut. Commander . . 2 one-half inch, with 1 one-quarter
  inch between.
Lieutenant . . . . . . 2 one-half inch.
Lieutenant (j.g.) . . . . 1 one-half inch with one-quarter
  inch above.
Ensign . . . . 1 one-half inch.
Warrant Officers—One 1/2" broken with 1/2" intervals of
blue as follows:

Warrant Officer W-4—1 break

Warrant Officer W-3—2 breaks, 2" apart
Warrant Officer W-2—3 breaks, 2" apart
The breaks are symmetrically centered on outer face of the
sleeve.
Enlisted personnel (non-Commissioned petty officers) . . . A
rating badge worn on the upper left arm, consisting of a
spread eagle, appropriate number of chevrons, and centered specialty mark.

Marine Corps
Marine Corps and Army officer insignia are similar. Marine Corps and Army enlisted insignia, although basically
similar, differ in color, design, and fewer Marine Corps subdivisions. The Marine Corps' distinctive cap and collar orna-
ment is a combination of the American eagle, globe, and anchor.

Coast Guard
Coast Guard insignia follow Navy custom, with certain
minor changes such as the officer cap insignia. The Coast
Guard shield is worn on both sleeves of officers and on the
right sleeve of all enlisted personnel.

U.S. Navy Personnel on Active Duty

June 30	Officers	Nurses	Enlisted	Off. Cand.	Total
1940.	13,162	442	144,824	2,569	160,997
1945.	320,293	11,086	2,988,207	61,231	3,380,817
1950.	42,687	1,964	331,860	5,037	381,538
1960.	67,456	2,103	544,040	4,385	617,984
1970.	78,488	2,273	605,899	6,000	692,660
1980.	63,100[1]	—	464,100[2]	—	527,200
1985 (Jan.)	70,291[1]	—	500,810[2]	—	571,101
1990 (Sept.)	74,429[1]	—	530,133[2]	—	604,562
1991 (June)	74,718[1]	—	524,357[2]	—	599,075

(1) Nurses are included. (2) Officer candidates are included.

Marine Corps Personnel On Active Duty

Year	Officers	Enlisted	Total	Year	Officers	Enlisted	Total	Year	Officers	Enlisted	Total
1955 . .	18,417	186,753	205,170	1970 . .	24,941	234,796	259,737	1988 . .	20,079	177,271	197,350
1960 . .	16,203	154,418	170,621	1980 . .	18,198	170,271	188,469	1989 . .	20,099	176,857	196,956
1965 . .	17,258	172,955	190,213	1985 . .	20,175	177,850	198,025	1990 . .	19,958	176,694	196,652

Veteran Population

Source: Dept. of Veterans Affairs

	March 1991
Total Veterans in civil life[a,b,c]	26,769,000
Total Wartime Veterans	20,356,700
Total Vietnam Era	8,303,000
Vietnam Era with Service in Korean Conflict	579,700
Vietnam Era with no Prior Wartime Service.	7,723,300
Total Korean Conflict	4,769,800
Korean Conflict with Service in WWII	851,600
Korean Conflict with no Prior Wartime Service	3,918,200
World War II	8,642,900
World War I	72,300
Total Peacetime Veterans	6,412,200
Total Post Vietnam Era	3,177,100
Service Between Korean Conflict and Vietnam Era Only	2,920,700
Other Peacetime	314,400

NOTE: Detail may not add to total shown due to rounding. (a) The category "War veterans" equals the sum of Vietnam
era (no service in Korean conflict), Korean conflict (no service in World War II), World War II and World War I. The data
refer only to veterans living in the U.S. and Puerto Rico since data on veterans living elsewhere are not available. (b) There is
1 living Spanish-American War veteran. There are also an indeterminate number of Mexican Border period veterans, 59 of
whom were receiving benefits in March 1991. (c) Estimates for Persian Gulf war not shown separately; data indicate that, as
of Mar. 31, 1991, there were approx. 130,000 Persian Gulf war veterans. About 80 percent are included with the Post-Viet-
nam era peacetime veteran totals; approx. 20 percent are listed as Vietnam era veterans.

Compensation and Pension Case Payments

Fiscal year	Living veteran cases no.	Deceased veteran cases no.	Total cases no.	Total disbursement dollars	Fiscal year	Living veteran cases no.	Deceased veteran cases no.	Total cases no.	Total disbursement dollars
1900. . .	752,510	241,019	993,529	138,462,130	1950. . .	2,368,238	658,123	3,026,361	2,009,462,298
1910. . .	602,622	318,461	921,083	159,974,056	1960. . .	3,008,935	950,802	3,959,737	3,314,761,383
1920. . .	419,627	349,916	769,543	316,418,029	1970. . .	3,127,338	1,487,176	4,614,514	5,113,649,490
1930. . .	542,610	298,223	840,833	418,432,808	1980. . .	3,195,395	1,450,785	4,646,180	11,045,412,000
1940. . .	610,122	239,176	849,298	429,138,465	1990 . .	2,746,329	837,596	3,583,925	15,535,069,000

USAF and Air Reserve Forces Personnel by Categories

Category	FY '87	FY '88	FY '89	FY '90	FY '91[1]	FY '92[1]
Air Force Military						
Officers	107,300	105,100	103,700	100,000	96,700	92,000
Airmen	495,200	466,900	462,800	430,800	407,500	390,500
Cadets	4,500	4,500	4,400	4,400	4,300	4,300
Total, Air Force Military	607,000	576,500	570,900	535,200	508,500	486,800
Career Reenlistments	41,400	51,500	39,400	44,600	36,300	38,800
Rate	87%	86%	87%	82%	85%	85%
First-Term Reenlistments	25,600	26,500	18,100	23,600	20,700	17,900
Rate	62%	50%	59%	51%	55%	55%
Civilian Personnel						
Direct Hire (including Technicians)	251,771	241,120	248,666	237,844	227,732	214,505
Indirect Hire—Foreign Nationals	12,559	12,041	11,909	11,031	11,397	9,653
Total, Civilian Personnel	264,330	253,161	260,575	248,875	239,129	224,158
Total, Military and Civilian[1]	871,230	829,607	831,455	784,075	747,629	710,958
Technicians (included above as Direct Hire Civilians)						
AFRES Technicians	8,772	9,111	10,061	9,596	10,316	10,343
ANG Technicians	23,221	23,409	23,644	24,119	23,521	24,639
Air Reserve Forces						
Air National Guard, Selected Reserve	114,600	115,221	114,975	117,786	116,610	118,100
Air Force Reserve, Paid	80,415	82,116	83,214	83,814	85,591	81,200
Air Force Reserve, Nonpaid[3]	43,783	51,658	49,553	68,714	65,296	65,746
Total, Ready Reserve[3]	238,798	248,995	247,742	270,314	267,497	265,046
Standby	24,479	21,772	17,299	15,369	17,075	17,075
Total, Air Reserve Forces[4]	263,277	270,767	265,041	285,683	284,572	282,121

Note: Totals may not add due to rounding. (1) President's budget request. (2) FY '87-90 are actual figures; FY '91-92 are estimates; excludes nonchargeable personnel. (3) Excludes training/pay categories J, K, and L. (4) Excludes Retired Air Force Reserve.

U.S. Air Force Personnel Strength: 1907–1992

Year[1]	Strength	Year	Strength	Year	Strength	Year	Strength
1907	3	1941	152,125	1950	411,277	1988	575,603
1918	195,023	1942	764,415	1960	814,213	1989	570,965
1920	9,050	1943	2,197,114	1970	791,078	1990	535,200
1930	13,531	1944	2,372,292	1980	557,969	1991	508,500
1940	51,165	1945	2,282,259	1986	608,200	1992	486,800

(1) Prior to 1947, data are for U.S. Army Air Corps and Air Service of the Signal Corps.

Coast Guard Personnel on Active Duty: 1970-1991

Source: U.S. Dept. of Transportation, *Annual Report of the Secretary of Transportation*.

Year	Total	Officers	Cadets	Enlisted	Year	Total	Officers	Cadets	Enlisted
1970	37,689	5,512	653	31,524	1984	38,705	6,790	759	31,156
1975	36,788	5,630	1,177	29,981	1985	38,595	6,775	733	31,087
1979	38,559	6,340	806	31,413	1986	37,284	6,577	754	29,953
1980	39,381	6,463	877	32,041	1987	38,576	6,644	859	31,073
1981	39,760	6,519	981	32,260	1988	37,723	6,530	887	30,306
1982	38,248	6,431	902	30,915	1990	37,308	6,475	820	29,860
1983	39,708	6,535	811	32,362	1991	37,390	6,783	897	29,710

Women in the Armed Forces

Women in the Army, Navy, Air Force, Marines, and Coast Guard are all fully integrated with male personnel. Expansion of military women's programs began in the Department of Defense in fiscal year 1973.

As of mid-1990, women made up 10.8 percent of the armed forces. Almost 25% of all medical and dental specialists are women; only 0.8 percent serve in the infantry, gun crews, or seamanship.

Although women are prohibited by law and directives based on law from serving in combat positions, policy changes in the Department of Defense have made possible the assignment of women to almost all other career fields. Career progression for women is now comparable to that for male personnel. Women are routinely assigned to overseas locations formerly closed to female personnel. Women are in command of activities and units that have missions other than administration of women.

Admission of women to the service academies began in the fall of 1976.

Army — Information: Chief, Office of Public Affairs, Dept. of Army, Wash., DC 20310; (as of Mar. 1990): 84,978 women, 72,698 enlisted women, 11,810 women commissioned officers, 470 women warrant officers.

Army Nurse Corps — Brig. Gen. Clara Adams-Ender, Chief Army Nurse Corps, Office of the Surgeon General, Dept. of Army, 5111 Leesburg Pike, Falls Church, VA 22041.

Navy — Information: Chief of Information, Dept. of Navy, Wash., DC 20350-1200; 8,232 women officers; 51,729 enlisted women; 674 cadets and midshipwomen, as of 6/30/91.

Navy Nurse Corps — Rear Adm. Mary F. Hall, Dir., Navy Nurse Corps, Dept. of Navy, Wash., DC 20372-2000; 2,348 women officers; 818 men. (As of 6/30/91).

Air Force — Information: Office of Public Affairs, Dept. of the Air Force, Wash., DC 20330; 14,062 women officers; 60,959 enlisted women.

Air Force Nurse Corps — Brig. Gen. Barbara A. Goodwin, Chief, Air Force Nurse Corps, Office of the Surgeon Gen., USAF, Bolling AFB, Wash., DC 20332.

Marine Corps — Information: Commandant of the Marine Corps (Code PA), Headquarters, Marine Corps, Wash., DC 20380-0001; 677 women officers; 8,679 enlisted women.

Coast Guard — Information: Commandant (G-CP), U.S. Coast Guard, 2100 Second St., SW, Wash., DC 20593-0001; 308 women commissioned officers; 15 woman warrant officer; 2,289 enlisted women.

U.S. Military Personnel Strengths—Worldwide

(As of Dec. 31, 1990)

Source: U.S. Department of Defense

U.S. Territories & Special Locations		Netherlands	1,745	Bahrain	4,128
Continental U.S.	1,046,652	Norway	219	Diego Garcia	1,310
Alaska	21,996	Portugal	1,722	Egypt	1,147
Hawaii	39,138	Spain	6,976	Saudi Arabia	51,907
Guam	6,880	Turkey	4,987	Afloat	38,396
Marshall Islands	49	United Kingdom	24,618	Total[1]	98,088
Puerto Rico	3,099	Afloat	16,155	**Other Western Hemisphere**	
Transients	57,266	Total[1]	249,565	Bermuda	1,226
Afloat	168,826	**European NATO**	233,131	Canada	537
Total[1]	1,343,996	**East Asia & Pacific**		Cuba (Guantanamo)	2,328
Western & Southern Europe		Australia	733	Honduras	1,015
		Japan	42,411	Panama	9,948
Belgium	2,245	Philippines	14,857	Afloat	1,003
Germany	171,068	Rep. of Korea	42,077	Total[1]	16,805
Greece	1,972	Thailand	155	**Total Worldwide**	2,053,328
Greenland	167	Afloat	25,873	Ashore	1,802,659
Iceland	3,197	Total[1]	126,326	Afloat	250,669
Italy	14,052	**Africa, Near East & South Asia**			

(1) Area totals include countries with less than 100 assigned U.S. military members.

Estimates of Total Dollar Costs of American Wars

(In millions of dollars, except percent)

Source: *The Military Budget and National Economic Priorities*, revised and updated by James L. Clayton, Univ. of Utah.

Item	World War II	Vietnam Conflict	Korean Conflict	World War I	Civil War: Union	Civil War: Confed-eracy	Spanish Ameri-can War	American Revolution	War of 1812	Mexi-can War
Original increment, direct costs:[1]										
Current dollars	360,000	140,600	50,000	32,700	2,300	1,000	270	100-140	89	82
Constant (1967) dollars .	816,300	148,800	69,300	100,000	8,500	3,700	1,100	400-680	170	300
Percent 1 year's GNP . .	188	14	15	43	74	123	2	104	14	4
Service-connected veterans' benefits[2]	87,629	26,175	17,024	19,273	3,290	—	2,111	28	20	26
Interest, pmts. on war loans[3]	(5)	(5)	(5)	11,000	1,200	(5)	60	20	14	10
Current cost to 1986[4] . . .	447,629	166,775	67,024	62,973	6,790	(5)	2,441	170	120	120

(1) Figures are rounded and taken from Claudia D. Goldin, *Encyclopedia of American Economic History*. (2) Total cost to Oct. 1, 1986. For World War I and later wars, benefits are actual service-connected figures from 1986 *Annual Report* of Veterans Administration. For earlier wars, service-connected veterans' benefits are estimated at 40 percent of total, the approximate ratio of service-connected to total benefits since World War I. (3) Total cost to 1986. Interest payments are a very rough approximation based on the percentage of the original costs of each war financed by money creation and debt, the difference between the level of public debt at the beginning of the war and at its end, and the approximate time required to pay off the war debts. (4) Figures are rounded estimates. (5) Unknown.

The Medal of Honor

The Medal of Honor is the highest military award for bravery that can be given to any individual in the United States. The first Army Medals were awarded on March 25, 1863, and the first Navy Medals went to sailors and Marines on April 3, 1863.

The Medal of Honor, established by Joint Resolution of Congress, 12 July 1862 (amended by Act of 9 July 1918 and Act of 25 July 1963) is awarded in the name of Congress to a person who, while a member of the Armed Forces, distinguishes himself conspicuously by gallantry and intrepidity at the risk of his life above and beyond the call of duty while engaged in an action against any enemy of the United States; while engaged in military operations involving conflict with an opposing foreign force; or while serving with friendly foreign forces engaged in an armed conflict against an opposing armed force in which the United States is not a belligerent party. The deed performed must have been one of personal bravery or self-sacrifice so conspicuous as to clearly distinguish the individual above his comrades and must have involved risk of life. Incontestable proof of the performance of service is exacted and each recommendation for award of this decoration is considered on the standard of extraordinary merit.

Prior to World War I, the 2,625 Army Medal of Honor awards up to that time were reviewed to determine which past awards met new stringent criteria. The Army removed 911 names from the list, most of them former members of a volunteer infantry group during the Civil War who had been induced to extend their enlistments when they were promised the Medal.

Since that review Medals of Honor have been awarded in the following numbers:

World War I 96   Korean War 131
World War II 432   Vietnam 238

Armed Services Senior Enlisted Adviser

The U.S. Army, Navy and Air Force in 1966-67 each created a new position of senior enlisted adviser whose primary job is to represent the point of view of his services' enlisted men and women on matters of welfare, morale, and any problems concerning enlisted personnel. The senior adviser will have direct access to the military chief of his branch of service and policy-making bodies.

The senior enlisted adviser for each Dept. is:

Army—Sgt. Major of the Army Richard A. Kidd.

Navy—Master Chief Petty Officer of the Navy Duane R. Bushey.

Air Force—Chief Master Sgt. of the AF Gary R. Pfingston.

Marines—Sgt. Major of the Marine Corps Harold G. Overstreet.

Strategic Arms Reduction Treaty

The following are highlights of the 700-page treaty signed by U.S. Pres. Bush and Soviet Pres. Gorbachev on July 31, 1991 in Moscow:

Central limits:

—1,600 Strategic Nuclear Delivery Vehicles (deployed intercontinental ballistic missiles and submarine-launched ballistic missiles and their launchers, and heavy bombers).

—6,000 "accountable" strategic warheads on these systems:

No more than 4,900 on ballistic missiles

No more than 1,100 on mobile intercontinental ballistic missiles

No more than 1,540 can be on SS-18's, the Soviet Union's 154 heavy intercontinental ballistic missiles

(To achieve these limits, the Soviet Union must eliminate 50 percent of its ballistic missile warheads, 50 percent of its SS-18 missiles, and decrease the aggregate throw-weight of its missiles by 46 percent.)

Counting rules:

—Ballistic missile warheads will count as one warhead each under the 6,000 limit.

—Warheads delivered by air will count less than one:

Heavy bombers with bombs and short-range missiles will count as carrying one warhead each, regardless of bombs or warheads carried;

U.S. heavy bombers may carry no more than 20 long-range air-launched cruise missiles each—the first 150 count as carrying 10 each;

Soviet heavy bombers may carry no more than 16 air-launched cruise missiles each—the first 180 will count as carrying 8 each.

Other provisions:

—Sea-launched cruise missiles with ranges above 373 miles will be limited to 880.

—Soviet Backfire bombers will be limited to 500.

—The treaty will run for 15 years, with the option to extend it for successive 5-year periods.

Glossary

Ballistic missile: a long-range missile that is guided by preset mechanisms in the first part of its flight, but, like an artillery shell, is a free-falling object as it approaches its target.

Cruise missile: a pilotless, warhead-equipped, miniature aircraft with its own guidance system.

Delivery vehicle: anything used to launch a warhead or cluster of warheads—such as a missile, airplane, or submarine.

Strategic nuclear weapon: nuclear weapons intended for use against a particular nation or region; tactical weapons are used on a battlefield in support of troops.

Throw-weight: a measure of how much "payload," or nuclear weaponry, can be "thrown" or carried by a missile to a distant target.

Verification: using various checks such as satellite photography and on-sight inspection to decide whether an arms control agreement has been violated.

Warhead: the part of a missile with the explosive charge.

Soviet and U.S. Nuclear Arsenals

Source: Natural Resource Defense Council; Arms Control Assn.

Estimated current number of deployed and spare nuclear warheads, and the expected levels seven years after both nations ratify START.

	Soviet Union		United States	
	Current	After treaty	Current	After Treaty
Longe-range weapons[1]: Intercontinental ballistic missiles, sea-launched ballistic missiles, long-range bombers . .	12,300	9,500	12,635	10,950
Strategic defense weapons: Air defense against ballistic missiles, aircraft, cruise missiles	2,800	2,800	0	0
Short-range weapons: missiles, aircraft, artillery	8,800	8,800	4,890	4,890
Naval weapons: bombs and depth charges for use against submarines	3,400	3,400	1,475	1,475
Totals	27,300	24,500	19,000	17,315

(1) About 11,000 Soviet and 12,000 U.S. warheads are currently (7/91) deployed. Others are not affected by START.

NATO to Reduce Forces

The North Atlantic Treaty Organization reached an agreement, May 1991, on the outline of a radical reorganization of its forces in Europe that would lead to a 50 percent reduction in American troops and a smaller reduction for the 42-year-old alliance. As of mid-year 1991, the number of active American troops in Europe was estimated at 320,000. The reductions will begin at the end of 1994 and are to be completed by the end of the decade. The reductions come as a result of the apparent end of the "cold war" marked by the dissolution of the Warsaw Pact in March 1991. The proposed military structure is based on the assumption that a direct frontal attack from the east on NATO countries, which was at the core of every NATO plan since 1949, is all but ruled out. The overall reorganization is to be formally approved late in 1991 at a meeting of heads of alliance governments.

Highlights of the agreement:

—Seven defense corps, each of 50,000 to 70,000 troops, assigned to operate in Western and Central Europe

—A rapid-reaction corps, which could respond in 5 to 7 days, including 2 British divisions and 2 multinational divisions; the U.S. could supply as much as a division, and would provide all of the planes, and helicopters and other airlift capability

—A mobile unit of about 5,000 troops that could respond within 72 hours

Nuclear Arms Treaties and Negotiations: An Historical Overview

Aug. 4, 1963—Nuclear Test Ban Treaty, signed in Moscow by the U.S., USSR, and Great Britain, prohibited testing of nuclear weapons in space, above ground, and under water.

Jan. 1967—Outer Space Treaty banned the introduction of nuclear weapons into space.

1968—Non-proliferation of Nuclear Weapons Treaty, with U.S., USSR, and Great Britain as major signers, limited the spread of military nuclear technology by agreement not to assist nonnuclear nations in getting or making nuclear weapons.

May 26, 1972—SALT I (Strategic Arms Limitations Talks) agreement, in negotiation since Nov. 17, 1969, signed in Moscow by U.S. and USSR. In the area of defensive nuclear weapons, the treaty limited antiballistic missiles to 2 sites of 100 antiballistic missile launchers in each country (amended in 1974 to one site in each country). The treaty also imposed a 5-year freeze on testing and deployment of intercontinental ballistic missiles and submarine-launched ballistic missiles. An interim short-term agreement putting a ceiling on numbers of offensive nuclear weapons was also signed. SALT I was in effect until Oct. 3, 1977.

July 3, 1974—Protocol on antiballistic missile systems and a treaty and protocol on limiting underground testing of nuclear weapons was signed by U.S. and USSR in Moscow.

Nov. 24, 1974—Vladivostok Agreement announced establishing the framework for a more comprehensive agreement on offensive nuclear arms, setting the guidelines of a second SALT treaty.

Sept. 1977—U.S. and USSR agreed to continue to abide by SALT I, despite its expiration date.

June 18, 1979—SALT II, signed in Vienna by the U.S. and USSR, constrained offensive nuclear weapons, limiting each side to 2,400 missile launchers and heavy bombers with that ceiling to apply until Jan. 1, 1985. The treaty also set a combined total of 1,320 ICBMs and SLBMs with multiple warheads on each side. Although approved by the U.S. Senate Foreign Relations Committee, the treaty never reached the Senate floor because Pres. Jimmy Carter withdrew his support for the treaty following the December 1979 invasion of Afghanistan by Soviet troops.

Nov. 18, 1981—U.S. Pres. Ronald Reagan proposed his controversial "zero option" to cancel deployment of new U.S. intermediate-range missiles in Western Europe in return for Soviet dismantling of comparable forces (600 SS-20, SS-4, and SS-5 missiles already stationed in the European part of its territory).

Nov. 30, 1981—Geneva talks on limiting intermediate nuclear forces based in and around Europe began.

May 9, 1982—U.S. Pres. Ronald Reagan proposed 2-step plan for strategic arms reductions and announced that he had proposed to the USSR that START (Strategic Arms Reduction Talks) begin in June.

May 18, 1982—Soviet Pres. Leonid Brezhnev rejected Reagan's plan as one-sided, but responded positively to the call for arms reduction talks.

June 29, 1982—START (Strategic Arms Reduction Talks) began in Geneva.

1985-1987—Disarmament talks between the U.S. and the USSR began in Geneva, Switzerland on March 12, 1985.

Dec. 8, 1987—I.N.F. (Intermediate-Range Nuclear Forces) Treaty signed in Washington, D.C. by USSR leader Mikhail Gorbachev and U.S. Pres. Ronald Reagan eliminating all medium- and shorter-range nuclear missiles; ratified with conditions by U.S Senate on May 27, 1988.

July 31, 1991—Strategic Arms Reduction Treaty (START) signed, in Moscow, by Soviet Pres. Mikhail Gorbachev and U.S. Pres. George Bush to reduce strategic offensive arms by approximately 30 percent in three phases over seven years. START is the first treaty to mandate reductions by the superpowers. (The treaty will need approval by the U.S. Senate and Soviet legislature.)

(For details and 1990-1991 developments see Index and Chronology.)

Nuclear Weapon Tests

Source: Natural Resources Defense Council

(Known nuclear tests, 1945-1988)

	United States	Soviet Union	Britain	France	China		United States	Soviet Union	Britain	France	China
1945-49	8	1	0	0	0	1970-79	190	197	5	59	16
1950-59	188	71	21	0	0	1980-90	160	188	13	94	10
1960-69	383	173	4	31	10	**Total**	**929**	**715[1]**	**43**	**186[2]**	**36**

(1) Includes 85 tests not identified by date. (2) Includes 2 tests not identified by date.

European Weapons Limits

The United States and the Soviet Union have reached an agreement that will limit or destroy many categories of nonnuclear weapons in Europe. In February 1990, the two sides agreed to reduce troops in central Europe to 195,000 men each as part of the conventional arms treaty. This treaty, which will be signed at a meeting of the 34-member Conference on Security and Cooperation in Europe, limits the number of tanks, aircraft and armored personnel carriers that the Eastern and Western alliances will be allowed to maintain in Europe from the Atlantic Ocean to the Ural Mountains. The new limits will make it extremely difficult for NATO or the Soviet Union to launch a land offensive in Europe.

Weapons	Country	1990 Level	Treaty limit[1]
Tanks	NATO	22,000	20,000
	U.S. Forces	5,700	13,300
	Soviet Forces	25,000	13,300
Armored vehicles	NATO	27,000	30,000
	U.S. Forces	5,500	20,000
	Soviet Forces	32,000	20,000
Artillery pieces	NATO	21,000	20,000
	U.S. Forces	2,650	13,700
	Soviet Forces	33,000	13,700
Helicopters	NATO	No	2,000
	U.S. Forces	figures	1,500
	Soviet Forces	available	1,500
Combat aircraft	NATO	No	6,800
	U.S. Forces	figures	5,150
	Soviet Forces	available	5,150

(1) No single country can have more than about two-thirds of the alliance's total in most categories. Alliances have worked out distribution agreements among members. Treaty limit figures are maximums allowed by 1994.

Casualties in Principal Wars of the U.S.

Data on Revolutionary War casualties is from *The Toll of Independence,* Howard H. Peckham, ed., U. of Chicago Press, 1974.

Data prior to World War I are based on incomplete records in many cases. Casualty data are confined to dead and wounded personnel and therefore exclude personnel captured or missing in action who were subsequently returned to military control. Dash (—) indicates information is not available.

Wars	Branch of service	Number serving	Casualties Battle deaths	Other deaths	Wounds not mortal[8]	Total
Revolutionary War	Total	—	6,824	18,500	8,445	33,769
1775-1783	Army	184,000	5,992	—	7,988	13,980
	Navy &	to	—	—	—	—
	Marines	250,000	832	—	457	1,289
War of 1812	Total	286,730[9]	2,260	—	4,505	6,765
1812-1815	Army	—	1,950	—	4,000	5,950
	Navy	—	265	—	439	704
	Marines	—	45	—	66	111
Mexican War	Total	78,718[9]	1,733	11,550	4,152	17,435
1846-1848	Army	—	1,721	11,500	4,102	17,373
	Navy	—	1	—	3	4
	Marines	—	11	—	47	58
Civil War	Total	2,213,363[9]	140,414	224,097	281,881	646,392
(Union forces only)	Army	2,128,948	138,154	221,374	280,040	639,568
1861-1865	Navy	—	2,112	2,411	1,710	6,233
	Marines	84,415	148	312	131	591
Confederate forces	Total	—	74,524	59,297	—	133,821
(estimate)[1]	Army	600,000	—	—	—	—
1863-1866	Navy	to	—	—	—	—
	Marines	1,500,000	—	—	—	—
Spanish-American	Total	306,760	385	2,061	1,662	4,108
War	Army[4]	280,564	369	2,061	1,594	4,024
1898	Navy	22,875	10	0	47	57
	Marines	3,321	6	0	21	27
World War I	Total	4,743,826	53,513	63,195	204,002	320,710
April 6, 1917-	Army[5]	4,057,101	50,510	55,868	193,663	300,041
Nov. 11, 1918	Navy	599,051	431	6,856	819	8,106
	Marines	78,839	2,461	390	9,520	12,371
	Coast Guard	8,835	111	81	—	192
World War II	Total	16,353,659	292,131	115,185	670,846	1,078,162
Dec. 7, 1941-	Army[6]	11,260,000	234,874	83,400	565,861	884,135
Dec. 31, 1946[2]	Navy[7]	4,183,466	36,950	25,664	37,778	100,392
	Marines	669,100	19,733	4,778	67,207	91,718
	Coast Guard	241,093	574	1,343	—	1,917
Korean War	Total	5,764,143	33,629	20,617	103,284	157,530
June 25, 1950-	Army	2,834,000	27,704	9,429	77,596	114,729
July 27, 1953[3]	Navy	1,177,000	458	4,043	1,576	6,077
	Marines	424,000	4,267	1,261	23,744	29,272
	Air Force	1,285,000	1,200	5,884	368	7,452
	Coast Guard	44,143	—	—	—	—
Vietnam (preliminary)[10]	Total	8,744,000	47,356	10,795	153,303	211,324
Aug. 4, 1964-	Army	4,368,000	30,904	7,274	96,802	134,972
Jan. 27, 1973	Navy	1,842,000	1,626	923	4,178	6,697
	Marines	794,000	13,082	1,754	51,392	66,213
	Air Force	1,740,000	1,739	842	931	3,435
	Coast Guard	—	5	2	—	7

(1) Authoritative statistics for the Confederate Forces are not available. An estimated 26,000-31,000 Confederate personnel died in Union prisons.

(2) Data are for the period Dec. 1, 1941 through Dec. 31, 1946 when hostilities were officially terminated by Presidential Proclamation, but few battle deaths or wounds not mortal were incurred after the Japanese acceptance of Allied peace terms on Aug. 14, 1945. Numbers serving from Dec. 1, 1941-Aug. 31, 1945 were: Total—14,903,213; Army—10,420,000; Navy—3,883,520; and Marine Corps—599,693.

(3) Tentative final data based upon information available as of Sept. 30, 1954, at which time 24 persons were still carried as missing in action.

(4) Number serving covers the period April 21-Aug. 13, 1898, while dead and wounded data are for the period May 1-Aug. 31, 1898. Active hostilities ceased on Aug. 13, 1898, but ratifications of the treaty of peace were not exchanged between the United States and Spain until April 11, 1899.

(5) Includes Air Service Battle deaths and wounds not mortal include casualties suffered by American forces in Northern Russia to Aug. 25, 1919 and in Siberia to April 1, 1920. Other deaths covered the period April 1, 1917-Dec. 31, 1918.

(6) Includes Army Air Forces.

(7) Battle deaths and wounds not mortal include casualties incurred in Oct. 1941 due to hostile action.

(8) Marine Corps data for World War II, the Spanish-American War and prior wars represent the number of individuals wounded, whereas all other data in this column represent the total number (incidence) of wounds.

(9) As reported by the Commissioner of Pensions in his Annual Report for Fiscal Year 1903.

(10) Number serving covers the period Aug. 4 1964-Jan. 27, 1973 (date of ceasefire). Number of casualties incurred in connection with the conflict in Vietnam from Jan. 1, 1961-Sept. 30, 1977. Includes casualties incurred in Mayaguez Incident. Wounds not mortal exclude 150,375 persons not requiring hospital care.

CONSUMER INFORMATION

Consumer Information Catalog

Source: Consumer Information Center, U.S. General Services Administration

The *Consumer Information Catalog* is a free listing of about 200 of the best federal consumer publications. They range from booklets on financial planning to planning a diet, from learning about federal benefits to getting an education, from fixing a car to dealing effectively with consumer problems, to getting a passport or a birth certificate. Many of these booklets are free.

The *Consumer Information Catalog* is published quarterly by the Consumer Information Center of the U.S. General Services Administration, so you will be able to send for the most current booklets. For your free copy of the *Consumer Information Catalog*, send your name and address to: Consumer Information Catalog, Pueblo, CO 81009. Educators, libraries, and other non-profit groups who are able to distribute 25 or more copies of the *Consumer Information Catalog* on a quarterly basis should write to the same address for an application to be placed on the mailing list. Costs prevent the Consumer Information Center from maintaining a mailing list for individuals.

The booklets listed below are available *free* from the *Consumer Information Catalog* as of Fall, 1991. Quantities of some may be limited. There is a $1 fee for handling. To order, please send your name and address, the item numbers of the booklets you want, and the $1 fee to: S. James, Consumer Information Center, Pueblo, CO 81009.

Some Free Publications

Parenting

Handbook on Child Support Enforcement. The basic steps to follow if you need child support enforcement services; tips on solving enforcement problems. 40 pp. (1989) **552X.**

Growing Up Drug Free. Shows what children should understand about drugs, including alcohol and tobacco, identifies classes and types of drugs, and resource contacts. 55 pp. (1989) **551X.**

Education

Schools Without Drugs. Guide for parents, schools, students, and communities on how to fight drug use by children. Describes extent of the problem, effects of various drugs, and signs of use. Includes legal considerations and an extensive list of resources. 94 pp. (1989) **553X.**

The Student Guide: Financial Aid. Describes federal grants, loans, and work/study programs for college, vocational and technical school students after high school. 50 pp. (1991-2) **506X.**

AIDS and the Education of Our Children. Facts about AIDS, its transmission, and how teens are at risk. Methods of protection, guidelines for selecting educational materials, and sources for more information. 34 pp. (1988) **550X.**

Federal Benefits

Request for Earnings and Benefit Estimate Statement. A form to complete and return to Social Security to get your earnings history and an estimate of future benefits. 3 pp. (1989) **510X.**

Understanding Social Security. An easy to understand overview of the Social Security system. Explains retirement, disability, and survivor's benefits; Medicare coverage; and Supplemental Security Income. 41 pp. (1991) **594X.**

Food & Nutrition

The Grazing of America: A Guide to Healthy Snacking. "Grazing" is becoming the American way of eating. Learn how to choose the best snacks for your age and lifestyle. 6 pp. (1989) **516X.**

Consumer's Guide to Food Labels. How to use food labels to make the most nutritious choices within the dates set for safe purchase and consumption. 8 pp. (1990) **512X.**

Dietary Guidelines for Americans. Seven dietary guidelines to help you stay healthy based on recent nutrition research. Charts of suggested body weights, calories used in various exercises, and a guide for selecting healthy food every day. 28 pp. (1990) **514X.**

A Word About Low Sodium Diets. Tips on how to reduce your sodium intake. Gives recipes with salt substitutes. 5 pp. (1986) **519X.**

Diet, Nutrition, and Cancer Prevention: The Good News. This booklet will help you select, prepare and serve healthier food. Includes lists of high-fiber and low-fat foods. 15 pp. (1986) **513X.**

Health

Smart Advice for Women 40 and Over: Have a Mammogram. A mammogram is an X-ray of the breast designed to find cancer in its earliest stages. Learn how often, and why, you should have one. 4 pp. (1990) **524X.**

Food and Drug Interactions. Learn how some commonly used drugs affect nutritional needs. 6 pp. (1990) **529X.**

Facing Forward: A Guide for Cancer Survivors. Advice on coping with the psychological, physical, and financial effects of this illness. Provides practical information on health care (both emotional and physical), insurance coverage, job concerns, and more. 45 pp. (1990) **577X.**

Good News for Blacks About Cancer. Blacks have a higher than average risk of getting certain cancers. Learn preventative actions to minimize your risk. 9 pp. (1987) **522X.**

Why Do You Smoke? Take this 18 question quiz to help understand what motivates your smoking, then learn practical first steps to take towards kicking the habit. 5 pp. (1990) **578X.**

Antihistamines: How to Take Your medicine. Discusses the side effects and risks, as well as when and how to take anti-histamines so they will work as effectively as possible. 8 pp. (1990) **597X.**

AIDS. How AIDS is spread, how to prevent it, and what to do if you think you've been infected. 2 pp. (1988) **533X.**

Allergies. Explains the various causes and treatments for allergic reactions from hay fever to asthma to life threatening anaphylactic shock. 7 pp. (1990) **585X.**

Breast Lumps: Questions and Answers. Straightforward discussion of benign and cancerous growths. Questions to ask your doctor, where to go for more information, and a self-examination guide. 23 pp. (1988) **534X.**

Useful Information on Alzheimer's Disease. This disease is not a normal part of aging, but a group of diseases that lead to loss of mental and physical functions. Discusses how it is diagnosed, possible causes, and current treatments. Lists references and sources of help. 25 pp. (1990) **576X.**

Getting a Second Opinion. Answers questions of the prospective patient. Includes toll-free number for locating specialists. 5 pp. (1989) **536X.**

Mental Health

A Consumer's Guide to Mental Health Services. Answers commonly asked questions about mental health and the different methods of treating mental illness. Lists resources for further help and information. 28 pp. (1987) **541X.**

Plain Talk About Depression. Nine million Americans suffer from depressive illness during any six month period. Learn about the symptoms and causes; how it's diagnosed and treated; and how to help. 4 pp. (1989) **542X.**

Plain Talk About Mutual Help Groups. Gain strength through sharing with others who have similiar problems: An overview of the many support groups available. 6 pp. (1989) **543X.**

What to Do When a Friend Is Depressed: A Guide for Students. Increases teen sensitivity to this often misunderstood condition. Identifies common myths, warning signals, and suggests ways to help. 8 pp. (1989) **600X.**

Plain Talk about Stress. What stress is and how to deal with it. 2 pp. (1987) **544X.**

Plain Talk About Wife Abuse. The causes, emotional and physical consequences, and where an abused wife can get help. 3 pp. (1983) **545X.**

Schizophrenia: Questions and Answers. Describes this chronic, debilitating illness affecting millions of Americans: its nature, causes, treatments, how others can help, and the outlook for recovery. 25 pp. (1986) **546X.**

Money Management

Investment Swindles: How They Work and How to Avoid Them. How to protect yourself against illegal telemarketing and direct mail offers. 20 pp. (1987) **548X.**

Investors' Bill of Rights. Tips to help you make an informed decision on investment risks and costs. 7 pp. (1987) **549X.**

Building your Future with Annuities: A Consumer's Guide. An annuity is a way to set aside money and have it grow on a tax deferred basis for your use some time in the future, typically at retirement. Discusses various types, features, costs, what to look for, answers common questions, and more. 10 pp. (1991) **602X.**

How to Get the Most for Your Money

Source: *Consumer's Resource Handbook.*

Before Making a Purchase:

(1) Analyze what you need and what features are important to you.

(2) Compare brands. Use word-of-mouth recommendations and formal product comparison reports. Check with your local library for magazines and other publicatons containing consumer information.

(3) Compare stores. Look for a store with a good reputation and take advantage of sales.

(4) Check for any additional charges, such as delivery and service costs.

(5) Compare warranties.

(6) Read terms of contracts carefully.

(7) Check the return or exchange policy.

After Your Purchase:

(1) Follow proper use and care instructions for products.

(2) Read and understand the warranty provisions. Keep in mind that you may have additional warranty rights in your state. Check with your state or local consumer office to find out.

(3) If trouble develops, report the problem as soon as possible. Do not try to fix the product yourself as this may void the warranty.

(4) Keep a record of efforts to have your problem remedied. This record should include names of people you speak to, times, dates, and other relevant information.

(5) Send for the *Consumer's Resource Handbook* (see *Source,* above) to find out where and how to get your problem resolved.

(6) Clearly state your problem and the solution you want.

(7) Include all relevant details, along with copies of documents (proof of purchase).

(8) Briefly describe what you have done to resolve the problem.

(9) Allow each person you contact a reasonable period of time to resolve your problem before contacting another source for assistance.

Handling Your Own Complaint:

(1) Identify your problem and what you believe would be a fair settlement. Do you want your money back? Would you like the product repaired? Will an exchange do?

(2) Gather documentation regarding your complaint. Sales receipts, repair orders, warranties, cancelled checks, or contracts will back up your complaint and help the company solve your problem.

(3) Go back to where you made the purchase. Contact the person who sold you the item or performed the service.

Calmly and accurately explain the problem and what action you would like taken. If that person is not helpful, ask for the supervisor or manager and repeat your complaint. A large percentage of consumer problems are resolved at this level. Chances are yours will be too.

(4) Don't give up if you are not satisfied with the response. If the company operates nationally or the product is a national brand, write a letter to the person responsible for consumer complaints at the company's headquarters. A listing of many of these companies can be found in the World Almanac's Business Directory on pages 781–787. If the company doesn't have a consumer office, direct your letter to the president of the company.

How to Write a Complaint Letter:

(1) If you have already contacted the person who sold you the product or service or the company is out of town, you will need to write a letter to pursue your complaint.

(2) If you need the president's name and the address of the company, first check in your phone directory to see if the company has a local office. If it does, call and ask for the name and address of the company's president. If there is no local listing, check *Standard & Poor's Register of Corporations, Directors and Executives.* It lists over 37,000 American business firms and can be found in most libraries.

(3) If you don't have the name of the manufacturer of the product, check your local library for the *Thomas Register.* It lists the manufacturers of thousands of products.

Basic Tips on Letter Writing:

(1) Include your name, address, and home and work phone numbers.

(2) Type your letter if possible. If it is handwritten, make sure it is neat and easy to read.

(3) Make your letter brief and to the point. Include all important facts about your purchase, including the date and place where you made the purchase, and any information you can give about the product or service such as serial or model numbers or specific type of service.

(4) State exactly what you want done about the problem and how long you are willing to wait to get it resolved. Be reasonable.

(5) Include all documents regarding your problems. Be sure to send COPIES, not originals.

(6) Avoid writing an angry, sarcastic, or threatening letter. The person reading your letter probably was not responsible for your problem, but may be very helpful in resolving it.

(7) Keep a copy of the letter for your records.

Business Directory

Listed below are major U.S. corporations, and major foreign corporations, whose operations—products and services—directly concern the American consumer. At the end of each listing is a representative sample of some of the company's products.

Company...Address...Phone Number...Chief executive officer...Business.

A & W Brands Inc....709 Westchester Ave., White Plains, NY 10604...(914) 397-1700...M.L. Lowenkron...soft drinks.

AMR Corp....PO Box 619616, Dallas/Ft. Worth Airport, TX 75261...(817) 355-2970...Robert Crandell...Air transportation (American Airlines).

Abbott Laboratories...One Abbott Park Rd., Abbot Park, IL 60064-3500 (708) 937-6100...D.L. Burnham...health care prods.

Aetna Life & Casualty Co....151 Farmington Ave., Hartford, CT 06156 ...(203) 273-0123 ... James T. Lynn...insurance, financial services.

H.F. Ahmanson & Co....660 S. Figueroa St., Los Angeles, CA 90017...(213) 955-4200...R.H. Deihi...operates largest S&L assn. in U.S. (Home Savings of America).

Alberto-Culver Co....2525 Armitage Ave., Melrose Park, IL 60160...(312) 450-3000...Leonard H. Lavin...hair care preparations, feminine hygiene products, household and grocery items.

Albertson's Inc....250 Parkcenter Blvd., Boise, ID 83726...(208) 385-6200...Gary Michael...supermarkets

Alcan Aluminium Ltd....1188 Sherbrooke St. W., Montreal, Que., Canada H3A 3G2...(514) 848-8050...David Morton...aluminum producer.

Alexander & Alexander Services Inc....1211 Ave. of the Amer., New York, NY 10036...(212) 840-8500...T.H. Irvin...insurance & financial services.

Allied-Signal Inc....Box 2245R, Morristown, NJ 07960...(201) 455-2000...Edward L. Hennessy Jr....aerospace, engineered materials, automotive prods.

Alltel Corp....100 Executive Pkwy., Hudson, OH 44236...(216) 650-7000...J.T. Ford...telephone service in Midwest, South, and Eastern U.S.

Aluminum Co. of America...1501 Alcoa Bldg., Pittsburgh, PA 15219...(412) 553-4545...P.H. O'Neill...mining, refining, & processing of aluminum.

Amerada Hess Corp....1185 Ave. of the Americas, N.Y., NY 10036...(212) 997-8500...L. Hess...integrated petroleum co.

American Brands, Inc....1700 E. Putnam Ave., Old Greenwich, CT 06870 (203) 698-5000...W.J. Alley...tobacco (Pall Mall, Carlton, Half and Half, Paleden pipe tobacco), whiskey (Jim Beam), snack foods, life insurance, office prods., food, financial services, toiletries.

American Cyanamid Co....One Cyanamid Plaza, Wayne, NJ 07470...(201) 831-2000...G.J. Sella Jr....medical, agricultural, chemical, and consumer products.

American Express Co....American Express Tower, N.Y., NY 10285 (212) 640-2000...J.D. Robinson 3d ... travelers checks, credit card services, insurance, investment services (Shearson Lehman).

American Greetings Corp....10500 American Rd., Cleveland, OH 44144...(216) 252-7300...M. Weiss...greeting cards, stationery, gift items.

American Home Products Corp....685 3d Ave., N.Y., NY 10017...(212) 878-5000...J.R. Stafford...prescription drugs, household prods. (Woolite, Easy-Off oven cleaner; Black Flag, Wizard air fresheners), food (Chef Boy-ar-dee), drugs (Anacin, Advil, Dristan).

American Stores Co....709 E. South Temple., Salt Lake City, UT 84102...(801) 539-0112...J.L. Scott...retail food markets, dept. & drug stores.

American Telephone & Telegraph Co....550 Madison Ave. N.Y., NY 10022...(212) 605-5500...Robert Allen...communications. (Announced merger agreement with NCR 1991).

Amoco Corp....200 E. Randolph Dr., Chicago, IL 60601...(312) 856-6111...H.L. Fuller...oil and gas exploration, production, and marketing.

Anheuser-Busch, Inc....One Busch Place, St. Louis, MO 63118...(314) 577-2000...August A. Busch 3d...brewing (Budweiser, Michelob, Bud Light, Natural Light, King Cobra, Busch), theme parks, snack foods (Eagle).

Apple Computer, Inc....10260 Bandley Dr., Cupertino, CA 95014...(408) 996-1010...John Sculley...Manuf. personal computers.

Armstrong World Industries...P.O. Box 3001, 313 W. Liberty St., Lancaster, PA 17604...(717) 397-0611...W.W. Adams...interior furnishings.

Arvin Industries, Inc....1531 13th St., Columbus, IN 47201...(812) 379-3000...J.K. Baker...auto emission & noise control systems.

Ashland Oil, Inc....P.O. Box 391, Ashland, KY 41114...(606) 329-3333...J.R. Hall...petroleum refiner, chemicals.

Atlantic Richfield Co....515 S. Flower St., Los Angeles, CA 90071 ... (213) 486-3511 ... L.M. Cook...petroleum, chemicals, other natural resources.

Avery Denison Corp....150 N. Orange Grove Blvd., Pasadena, CA 91103...(818) 304-2000...Charles D. Miller...self-adhesive labels, office prods., specialty chemicals.

Avon Products, Inc....9 West 57th St., N.Y., NY 10019...(212) 546-6015...J. E. Preston...cosmetics, fragrances, toiletries, health care.

Bally Manufacturing Corp....8700 W. Bryn Mawr Ave., Chicago, IL 60631...(312) 399-1300...A.M. Goldberg...lottery and gaming equip., hotel-casino operator, health & fitness centers.

Bausch & Lomb...One Lincoln First Square, Rochester, NY 14601...(716) 338-6000...D.E. Gill...manuf. of vision care products, accessories.

Baxter International Inc....One Baxter Pky., Deerfield, IL 60015...(708) 948-2000...Vernon R. Loucks Jr....medical care prods & services.

Bell Atlantic Corp....1600 Market St., Philadelphia, PA 19103...(215) 963-6000...R.W. Smith...telephone service in mid-Atlantic region.

BellSouth Corp....1155 Peachtree St. NE, Atlanta, GA 30367...(404) 249-2000...J.L. Clendenin...telephone service in the South.

Bethlehem Steel Corp....8th & Eaton Ave., Bethlehem, PA 18016...(215) 694-2424...W.F. Williams...steel & steel prods.

Bic Corporation...Wiley Street, Milford, CT 06401...(203) 783-2070...Bruno Bich...writing instruments, disposable lighters, and shavers.

Black & Decker Corp....701 E. Joppa Rd., Towson, MD 21204...(301) 583-3900...N.D. Archibald...manuf. power tools, household prods., small appliances.

H & R Block, Inc....4410 Main St., Kansas City, MO 64111...(816) 753-6900...Henry W. Bloch...tax preparation.

Blockbuster Entertainment Corp....901 E. Las Olas Blvd., Ft. Lauderdale, FL 33301...(305) 524-8200...H. Wayne Huizenga...video rental superstores.

Boeing Company...7755 E. Marginal Way So., Seattle, WA 98108...(206) 655-2121...F.A. Shrontz...aircraft manuf.

Boise Cascade Corp....One Jefferson Square, Boise, ID 83728...(208) 384-6161...J.B. Fery...timber, paper, wood prod.

Borden, Inc....277 Park Ave., N.Y., NY 10172...(212) 573-4000...R.J. Ventres...food, cheese and cheese products, snacks (Cracker Jack), beverages, adhesives (Elmer's, Krazy Glue), pasta (Prince, Creamette), pasta sauce (Aunt Millie's, Classico).

Bristol-Myers Squibb Co....345 Park Ave., N.Y., NY 10154...(212) 546-4000...Richard L. Gelb...toiletries (Ban anti-perspirant), hair items (Clairol), drugs (Bufferin, Nuprin, Comtrex, Excedrin), household prods.(Drano, Windex), infant formula (Enfamil).

Brown-Forman Inc....P.O. Box 1080 Louisville, KY 40210...(502) 585-1100...W.L.L. Brown Jr....distilled spirits (Jack Daniel's Early Times), wines (Bolla, Fontana Candita), champagne (Korbel), liquor (Southern Comfort), Lenox china and crystal.

Brown Group, Inc....8400 Maryland Ave., St. Louis, MO 63105...(314) 854-4000...B.A. Brightwater Jr...manuf. and wholesaler of women's and children's shoes (Buster Brown, Naturalizer); specialty retailing.

Brunswick Corp....One Brunswick Plaza, Skokie, IL 60077...(708) 470-4700...J.F. Reichert...marine, recreation prods, bowling centers & equip., fishing equip.

Burlington Coat Factory Warehouse Corp....1830 Route 130 North, Burlington, NJ 08016...(609) 387-7800...M.G. Milstein...discount apparel stores.

Burlington Northern Inc....777 Moun St., Ft. Worth, TX 76102...(817) 878-2000...G. Grinstein...rail transportation.

CBS Inc....51 W. 52d St., N.Y., NY 10019...(212) 975-4321...L.A. Tisch...broadcasting, video cassettes, leisure prods.

CPC International, Inc....International Plaza, Englewood Cliffs, NJ 07632...(201) 894-4000...Charles Shoemate...branded food items (Hellman's, Best Foods, Mazola oil,

Skippy peanut butter, Knorr Soups, Thomas English muffins), corn wet milling prods.

Caesar's World, Inc. ...1801 Century Park East, Los Angeles, CA 90067 ...(213) 552-2711 ...H. Gluck ...hotels & casinos, resort hotels.

Campbell Soup Co. ...Campbell Pl., Camden, NJ 08103 ...(609) 342-4800 ...D.W. Johnson ...canned soups, spaghetti (Franco-American), vegetable juice (V-8), pork and beans, pet foods, restaurants, confections, Le Menu frozen dinners, Prego spaghetti sauce, Mrs. Paul's frozen fish, Pepperidge Farm breads.

Capital Cities/ABC, Inc. ...77 W. 66th Street, New York, NY 10023 ...(212) 456-7777 ...T.S. Murphy ...operates television and radio stations, newspapers, cable TV (ESPN); newspapers, specialized business and consumer periodicals.

Carnival Cruise Lines Inc. ...3655 NW 87 Ave., Miami, FL 33178 ...(305) 599-2600 ...M. Arison ...Cruise Line.

Carter Hawley Hale Stores, Inc. ...444 S. Flower St., Los Angeles, CA 90071 ...(213) 620-0150 ...P.M. Hawley ...dept. stores, specialty stores.

Carter-Wallace, Inc. ...1345 Ave. of the Amer., New York, NY 10105 ...(212) 339-5000 ...H.H. Hoyt Jr. ...personal care items, anti-perspirant (Arrid), shave lathers (Rise), condoms (Trojan), laxative (Carter's Pills), pet products.

Castle & Cooke, Inc. ...10900 Wilshire Blvd., Los Angeles, CA 90024 ...(213) 824-1500 ...David Murdock ...food processing, Dole.

Caterpillar Inc. ...100 N.E. Adams St., Peoria, IL 61629 ...(309) 675-1000 ...Donald Fites ...heavy duty earthmoving equip.

Chase Manhattan Corp. ...1 Chase Manhattan Plaza, New York, NY 10081 ...(212) 552-2222 ...Thomas Rabrecque ...Bank holding co.

Chevron Corp. ...225 Bush St., San Francisco, CA 94104 ...(415) 894-7700 ...K.T. Derr ...integrated oil co.

Chrysler Corp. ...12000 Chrysler Dr., Highland Pk., MI 48288 ...(313) 956-5252 ...Lee Iacocca ...cars, trucks.

Circuit City Stores, Inc. ...9950 Maryland Dr., Richmond, VA 23233 ...(804) 527-4000 ...R.L. Sharp ...retailer of electronic equip., consumer appliances.

Circus Circus Enterprises, Inc. ...2880 Las Vegas Blvd. S., Las Vegas, NV 89109 ...(702) 734-0410 ...W.G. Bennett ...casino operator.

Citicorp ...399 Park Ave., N.Y., NY 10043 ...(212) 559-1000 ...J.S. Reed ...largest U.S. commercial bank.

Clayton Homes ...P.O. Box 15169, Knoxville, TN 37901 ...(615) 970-7200 ...J.L. Clayton ...produces & sells manufactured homes.

Clorox Co. ...1221 Broadway, Oakland, CA 94612 ...(415) 271-7000 ...C.R. Weaver ...retail consumer prods (Formula 409, Pine-Sol, Lucite paints, Kingsford charcoal briquets, Hidden Valley Ranch salad dressing, Deer Park bottled water, Soft Scrub cleanser)

Coachman Industries Inc. ...601 E. Beardsley Ave., Elkhart, IN 46514 ...(219) 262-0123 ...T.H. Corson ...manuf. recreational vehicles.

Coca-Cola Co. ...One Coca-Cola Plaza N.W., Atlanta, GA 30313 ...(404) 676-2121 ...R.C. Goizueta ...soft drink (Coca Cola, Sprite, Ramblin root beer), syrups, citrus and fruit juices (Minute Maid, Hi-C).

Colgate-Palmolive Co. ...300 Park Ave., N.Y., NY 10022 ...(212) 310-2000 ...R. Mark ...soaps (Palmolive, Irish Spring), detergents (Fab, Ajax, Fresh Start), tooth paste (Colgate, Ultra Brite), household prods. (Handy Wipes, Curad bandages).

Commodore International Ltd. ...1200 Wilson Dr., West Chester, PA 19380 ...(215) 431-9100 ...I. Gould ...microcomputer systems, semiconductors component, consumer electronics, office equipment.

Compaq Computer Corp. ...20555 SH 249, Houston, TX 77070 ...(713) 370-0670 ...J.R. Canion ...portable, desktop computers.

Control Data Corp. ...8100 34th Ave. South, Minneapolis, MN 55440 ...(612) 853-8100 ...L. Perlman ...computer systems & services.

Adolph Coors Co. ...Golden, CO 80401 ...(303) 279-6565 ...W. K. Coors ...brewery.

Corning Inc. ...Houghton Park, Corning, NY 14831 ...(607) 974-9000 ...J.R. Houghton ...glass mfg.

Crane Co. ...737 3d Ave., N.Y., NY 10017 ...(212) 415-7300 ...R.S. Evans ...fluid & pollution controls, aircraft and aerospace, building prods.

A.T. Cross Co. ...One Albion Rd., Lincoln, RI 02865 ...(401) 333-1200 ...B.R. Boss ...writing instruments.

Crystal Brands, Inc. ...Crystal Brands Rd., Southport, CT 06490 ...(203) 254-6200 ...R.F. Kral ...apparel, accessories (Evan Picone, Izod).

Culbro Corp. ...387 Park Avenue South, New York, N' 10016 ...(212) 561-8700 ...E. M. Cullman ...cigars (Corina Robert Burns, White Owl, Tiparillo's), snack foods.

Dana Corp. ...4500 Dorr St., Toledo, OH 43615 ...(419 535-4500 ...S.J. Morcott ...truck and auto parts supplies.

Data General Corp. ...4400 Computer Dr., Westboro, M' 01580 ...(508) 366-8911 ...R.L. Skates ...computer & com munications sytems manuf.

Dayton Hudson Corp. ...777 Nicollet Mall, Minneapolis, MN 55402 ...(612) 370-6948 ...K.A. Macke ...department, spe cialty, stores, Mervyn's, Target.

Deere & Co. ...John Deere Rd., Moline, IL 61265 ...(309 765-8000 ...H.W. Becherer ...farm, industrial, and outdoc power equip.

Delta Air Lines, Inc. ...Hartsfield Atlanta Intl. Airport, Atlanta GA 30320 ...(404) 765-2600 ...Ronald W. Allen ...air trans portation.

Dial Corp. ...Dial Tower, Phoenix, AZ 85077 ...(602 207-4000 ...J.W. Teets ...consumer prods (Dial, Purex), cor tract and fast food services, manuf. buses.

Diebold, Inc. ...P.O. Box 8230, Canton, OH 44711 ...(216 489-4000 ...R.W. Mahoney ...manuf. equip. for financia insts.

Digital Equipment Corp. ...146 Main St., Maynard, M/ 01754 ...(508) 493-5111 ...Kenneth H. Olsen ...compute systems manuf.

Walt Disney Co. ...500 S. Buena Vista St., Burbank, C/ 91521 ...(818) 560-1000 ...M.D. Eisner ...motion pictures CATV, amusement parks, Disneyland, Walt Disney World, Ep cot Center.

Dollar General Corp. ...427 Beach St., Scottsville, K' 42164 ...(502) 237-5444 ...Cal Turner ...self-service dis count stores.

R.R. Donnelly & Sons Co. ...2223 S. Martin Luther King Drive Chicago, IL 60616 ...(312) 326-8000 ...J.R. Walter ...larges commercial printer.

Dow Chemical Co. ...2030 Dow Center, Midland, M 48674 ...(517) 636-1000 ...F.P. Popoff ...chemicals, plas tics, metals, consumer prods. (Ziploc, Saran Wrap, Fantastik)

Dow Jones & Co. ...World Financial Center, New York, N 10281 ...(212) 416-2000 ...W. H. Phillips ...financial new service, publishing (Wall Street Journal, Barron's, Ottawa Newspapers).

Dun & Bradstreet Corp. ...299 Park Ave., New York, N 10171 ...(212) 593-6800 ...C.W. Moritz ...business informa tion and computer services, publishing; broadcasting.

E.I. du Pont de Nemours & Co. ...1007 Market St., Wilming ton, DE 19898 ...(302) 774-1000 ...Edgar Woolar Jr. ...chemicals, petroleum, consumer prods., coal.

Eastman Kodak Co. ...343 State St., Rochester, N 14650 ...(716) 724-4685 ...K.R. Whitmore ...photographi prods, chemicals, health care (Sterling Drug).

Eaton Corp. ...Eaton Center, Cleveland, OH 44114 ...(216 523-5000 ...J.R. Stover ...manuf. of electronic, electrica prods., vehicle components.

Emerson Electric Co. ...8000 W. Florissant Ave., St. Louis MO 63136 ...(314) 553-2000 ...C.F. Knight ...electrical electronics products & systems

Ethyl Corp. ...330 S. 4th St., Richmond, VA 23217 ...(804 788-5000 ...Floyd D. Gottwald Jr. ...petroleum and industria chemicals.

Exxon Corp. ...225 E. John W. Carpenter Freeway, Irving, T) 75062 ...(214) 444-1000 ...L.G. Rawl ...world's largest c co.

Family Dollar Stores, Inc. ...10401 Old Monroe Rd., Charlotte NC 28105 ...(704)847-6961 ...L. Levine ...discount varie† stores.

Fabri-Centers of America, Inc ...5555 Darrow Rd., Hudsor OH. 44236 ...(216) 656-2600 ...Alan Rosskamm ...Spe cialty fabric stores.

Fedders Corp. ...158 Highway 206, P.O. Box 265, Peapack NJ 07977 ...(201) 234-2100 ...S. Giordano ...manuf. † room air conditioners.

Federal Express Corp. ...P.O. Box 727, Memphis, Tl 38192 ...(901) 922-6443 ...F.W. Smith ...small package de livery service.

Fieldcrest Cannon, Inc. ...326 East Stadium Dr., Eden, Ne 27288 ...(919) 627-3000 ...J.B. Ely 2d ...household textil prods., rugs (Karastan, Laurelcrest).

Fleetwood Enterprises, Inc. ...P.O. Box 7638, Riverside, C, 92523 ...(714) 351-3500 ...John C. Crean ...manufacture homes, recreational vehicles.

Fluor Corp. ...3333 Michelson Dr., Irvine, CA 92730 ...(714 975-6961 ...D.S. Tappan Jr. ...engineering and constructio natural resources.

Ford Motor Co....The American Rd., Dearborn, MI 48121...(313) 845-8540...H.A. Poling...motor vehicles, Ford Tractor, Lincoln-Mercury.

Fruit of The Loom, Inc....233 S. Wacker, Chicago, IL 60606...(312) 876-1724...W. Farley...Manuf. of men's and boy's underwear.

GTE Corp....One Stamford Forum, Stamford, CT 06904...(203) 965-2789...J.L. Johnson...telecommunications system prods.

Gannett Co., Inc....1100 Wilson Blvd, Arlington, VA 22234...(703) 284-6000...J.J. Curley...newspaper publishing (USA Today), TV stations, outdoor advertising.

The GAP, Inc...1 Harrison, San Francisco, CA 94105...(415) 952-4400...D.G. Fisher...casual and activewear retailer.

Gencorp...175 Ghent Rd., Fairlawn, OH 44313...(216) 869-4200...A.W. Reynolds...aerospace, auto prods., polymer prods.

Genentech, Inc....460 Point San Bruno Blvd., S. San Francisco, CA 94080...(415) 266-1000...G.K. Raab...world's largest biotechnology corp.

General Cinema Corp....27 Boylston St., Chestnut Hill, MA 02167...(617) 232-8200...R. A. Smith...movie exhibitor, retailing.

General Dynamics Corp....Pierre Laclede Ctr., St. Louis, MO 63105...(314) 889-8200...William Anders...military and commercial aircraft, tactical missiles.

General Electric Co....3135 Easton Ave., Fairfield, CT 06431...(203) 373-2211...J. F. Welch Jr....electrical, electronic equip, finance (Kidder, Peabody & Co.), radio, television (NBC), polymer plastic prods.

General Mills, Inc....P.O. Box 1113, Minneapolis, MN 55440...(612) 540-2311...H.B. Atwater Jr....foods, toys, restaurants, fashion and specialty retailing, Total, Bisquick, Wheaties, Cheerios, Hamburger Helper, Gorton's, Betty Crocker, Red Lobster Inns.

General Motors Corp....3044 W. Grand Rapids, Detroit, MI 48202...(313) 556-5000...R. C. Stempel...world's largest auto manuf.

Genesco Inc....Genesco Park, Nashville, TN 37202...(615) 367-7000...W.S. Wire 2d...footwear and men's clothing, Jarman, Johnston & Murphy.

Genuine Parts Co....2999 Circle 75 Pkwy, Atlanta, GA 30339...(404) 953-1700...L. L. Prince...distributes auto replacement parts (NAPA).

Georgia-Pacific Corp....133 Peachtree St., NE, Atlanta, GA 30303...(404) 521-5210...T.M. Hahn Jr....building prods., pulp, paper, chemicals.

Gerber Products Co....445 State St., Fremont, MI 49412...(616) 928-2718...A.A. Piergallini...baby foods, clothing, nursery accessories.

Giant Food Inc....6300 Sheriff Rd., Landover, MD 20785...(301) 341-4100...I. Cohen...supermarkets.

Gillette Co....Prudential Tower Bldg., Boston, MA 02199...(617) 421-7000...Alfred Zeier...razors, pens (Paper Mate), toiletries (Right Guard deodorants, Foamy shaving cream, Earth Born shampoo), hair products (Toni, Adorn).

Goodyear Tire & Rubber Co....1144 E. Market St., Akron, OH 44316...(216) 796-8576...Stanley Gault...tires, rubber prods.

W.R. Grace & Co....Grace Plaza, 1114 Ave. of the Americas, N.Y., NY 10036...(212) 819-5500...J. Peter Grace...chemicals, natural resources, health care.

Great Atlantic & Pacific Tea Co....2 Paragon Dr., Montvale, NJ 07645...(201) 573-9700...James Wood...supermarket chain.

Grumman Corp....1111 Stewart Ave., Bethpage, NY 11714...(516) 575-3344...Renso Caporali...aerospace, truck bodies, electronics.

Hannaford Bros. Co....145 Pleasant Hill Rd., Scarborough, ME 04074...(207) 883-2911...J.L. Moody Jr....operates supermarkets, drug stores.

Harley-Davidson, Inc.,...3700 W. Junear Ave., Milwaukee, WI 53201...(414) 342-4680...R.F. Terrlink...manuf. of motorcycles, parts & accessories.

Hartmarx...101 N. Wacker Dr., Chicago, IL 60606...(312) 372-6300...H.A. Weinberg...apparel manufacturer and retailer (Hickey-Freeman, Hart Schaffner & Marx).

Hasbro Inc....1027 Newport Ave., Pawtucket, R.I. 02862...(401) 431-8697...A.G. Hassenfeld...toy manuf. & marketer (Milton Bradley, Playskool, G.I. Joe, Cabbage Patch Kids, Scrabble).

H.J. Heinz Co....P.O. Box 57, Pittsburgh, PA 15230...(412) 456-6014...Anthony J.F. O'Reilly...foods (Star-Kist, Ore-Ida, '57 Varieties), 9-Lives cat food, Weight Watchers.

Helene Curtis...325 N. Wells St., Chicago, IL 60610...(312) 661-0222...R.J. Gidwitz...hair care prods. (Finesse, Sauve, Salon Selectives).

Hershey Foods Corp....100 Mansion Rd., Hershey, PA 17033...(717) 534-7552...R.A. Zimmerman...chocolate & confectionery prods., (Reese's peanut butter cups, Kit Kat, Peter Paul Mounds, Almond Joy), pasta (San Giorgio, Ronzoni).

Hewlett-Packard Co....P.O. Box 10301, Palo Alto, CA 94303...(415) 857-1501...John A. Young...manuf. electronic instruments.

Hillenbrand Industries, Inc....Highway 46, Batesville, IN 47006...(812) 934-7000...D.A. Hillenbrand...manuf. burial caskets, electronically operated hospital beds, luggage.

Home Depot, Inc....2727 Paces Ferry Rd., Atlanta, GA 30339...(404) 433-8211...Bernard Marcus...retailer of building materials & home improvement prods.

Honda Motor Co., LTD...1270 Ave. of the Americas, N.Y., NY 10020...(212) 765-3804...N. Kawamoto...manuf. autos, motorcycles.

Honeywell, Inc....Honeywell Plaza, Minneapolis, MN 55408...(612) 870-5200...J.J. Renier...industrial systems & controls, aerospace guidance systems, information systems.

Geo. A. Hormel & Co....501 16th Ave. N.E., Austin, MN 55912...(507) 437-5611...R.L. Knowlton...meat packaging, pork and beef prods (Spam, Dinty Moore, Mary Kitchen).

Houghton Mifflin Co....One Beacon St., Boston, MA 02108...(617) 725-5000...Nadar F. Darehshori...book publishing.

Household International Inc....2700 Sanders Rd., Prospect Heights, IL 60070...(708) 564-5000...D.C. Clark...financial and insurance services.

Huffy Corp....7701 Byers Rd., Miamisburg, OH 45342...(513) 866-6251...H.A. Shaw 3d...bicycle manuf.

Humana, Inc....500 W. Main St., Louisville, KY 40201...(502) 580-1000...D. A. Jones...operates hospitals, provides health care plans.

ITT Corp....1330 Ave. of the Amer., N.Y., NY 10022...(212) 258-1000...R.V. Araskog...manuf., installs communication and electronic equip., auto equip., insurance, financial services, hotels, educational services.

Imperial Oil Ltd....111 St. Clair Ave. W., Toronto, Ont., Canada M5W 1K3...(416) 968-4111...A.R. Haynes...Canada's largest oil co.

International Business Machines Corp....Armonk, NY 10504...(914) 765-1900...J.F. Akers...information-handling systems, equip., and services.

International Paper Co....2 Manhattanville Rd., Purchase , NY 10577...(914) 397-1500...J.A. Georges...paper, wood prods.

Johnson & Johnson...501 George St., New Brunswick, NJ 08903...(201) 524-0400...R.S. Larsen...surgical dressings, pharmaceuticals (Tylenol), consumer prods.

Jostens, Inc....5501 Norman Center Dr., Minneapolis, MN 55437...(612) 830-3300...H. W. Lurton...school rings, yearbooks.

K mart Corp....3100 W. Big Beaver Rd., Troy, MI 48084...(313) 643-1000...J. E. Antonini...largest U.S. chain of discount stores, book stores (Walden Book), cafeterias, drug stores (Pay Less Drug Stores), home improvement retail stores.

Kellogg Co....One Kellogg Sq., Battle Creek, MI 49016...(616) 961-2765...William E. LaMothe...ready to eat cereals & other food prods., Mrs. Smith's Pie Co., Salada Foods, Eggo.

Kimberly-Clark Corp....P.O. Box 619100, DFW Airport Station, Dallas, TX 75261...(214) 830-1200...Darwin E. Smith...paper and lumber prods., consumer prods. (Kleenex, Huggies).

King World Productions, Inc....830 Morris Turnpike, Short Hills, NJ 07078...(201) 376-1313...M. King...syndicator of first-run TV programs.

Knight-Ridder, Inc....One Herold Plaza, Miami, FL 33101...(305) 376-3838...J.K. Batten...newspaper publishing, TV broadcasting, book publishing, information services.

Kroger Co....1014 Vine St., Cincinnati, OH 45201...(513) 762-4000...Joseph Pichler...grocery chain.

L.A. Gear, Inc....4221 Redwood Ave., Los Angeles, CA 90006...(213) 822-1995...Robert Greenberg...athletic & leisure footwear, casual apparel.

La-Z-Boy Chair Co....1284 N. Telegraph Rd., Monroe, MI 48161...(313) 242-1444...C. T. Knabusch...reclining chair mfg.

Land's End, Inc....One Land's End Lane, Dodgeville, WI 53595...(608) 935-9341...R.C. Anderson...direct-mail catalog co.

Eli Lilly & Company...Lilly Corp. Center, Indianapolis, IN 46285...(317) 276-2000...Richard D. Wood...mfg. human health and agricultural products.

The Limited, Inc. ...Two Limited Pkwy., Columbus, OH 43216 ...(614) 479-7000 ...L.H. Wexner ...women's apparel stores (Lane Bryant, Lerner, Victoria's Secret), Abercrombie & Fitch.

Litton Industries, Inc. ...360 N. Crescent Dr., Beverly Hills, CA 90210 ...(213) 859-5000 ...O.L. Hoch .. industrial systems & services, advanced electronic systems, electronic & electrical prods., marine engineering.

Lockheed Corp. ...4500 Park Granada Blvd., Calabasas, CA 91399 ...(818) 712-2000 ...D.M. Tellep ...commercial and military aircraft, missiles.

Loews Corp. ...667 Madison Ave., N.Y., NY 10021 ...(212) 545-2000 .. Laurence A. Tisch .. tobacco prods. (Kent, Newport, True), watches, hotels, real estate, insurance.

Long's Drug Stores Corp. ...141 North Civic Dr., Walnut Creek, CA 94596 ...(415) 937-1170 ...R.M. Long ...drug store chain.

Lowe's Cos., Inc. ...P.O. Box 1111, N. Wilkesboro, NC 28656 ...(919) 651-4000 ...L.G. Herring .. retailer of building materials & related prods.

Luby's Cafeterias, Inc. ...211 Northeast Loop 410, San Antonio, TX 78265 ...(512) 654-9000 ...R. Erben .. operates cafeterias in SW U.S.

MCI Communications Corp ...1133 19th St., NW 20036 ...(202) 887-1600 ...Bert Roberts .. long-distance telephone carrier.

Manor Care, Inc. ...10750 Columbia Pike, Silver Spring, MD 20901 ...(301) 681-9400 .. S. Bainum Jr .. operates nursing centers.

Marriott Corp. ...Marriott Dr., Wash., DC 20058 ...(301) 897-9000 ...J. Willard Marriott Jr.

Martin Marietta Corp. ...6801 Rockledge Dr., Bethesda, MD 20817 ...(301) 897-6000 ...N.R. Augustine ...electronics, aerospace.

Mattel, Inc. ...5150 Rosecrans Ave., Hawthorne, CA 90250 ...(213) 978-6300 ...J.W. Amerman ...toy & hobby prods (Barbie doll, Masters of the Universe, Hot Wheels).

May Department Stores Co. ...611 Olive Street, St. Louis, MO 63101 ...(314) 342-6300 ...D.C. Farrell ...department stores (Hecht's, Famous Barr, G. Fox, Lord & Taylor, Foley's).

Maytag Corp. ...403 W. 4th St. North, Newton, IA 50208 ...(515) 792-7000 ...Daniel J. Krumm ...manuf. home laundry equip, appliances (Magic Chef, Admiral, Norge).

McCormick & Co., Inc. ...11350 McCormick Rd., Hunt Valley, MD 21031 ...(301) 771-7301 ...C.P. McCormick Jr. ...world's leading manuf. of seasoning & flavoring prods.

McDonald's Corp. ...McDonald's Plaza, Oak Brook, IL 60521 ...(708) 575-3000 ...M.R. Quinlan .. fast service restaurants.

McDonnell Douglas Corp. ...P.O. Box 516, St. Louis, MO 63168 ...(314) 232-0232 ...J. F. McDonnell ...commercial and military aircraft, space systems & missiles.

McGraw-Hill, Inc. ...1221 Ave. of the Americas, New York, NY 10020 ...(212) 512-2000 ...J.L. Dionne .. book, magazine publishing (Business Week), information & financial services (Standard and Poor's), TV stations.

Mead Corporation ...Courthouse Plaza Northeast, Dayton, OH 45463 ...(513) 495-6323 ...B.R. Roberts .. printing and writing paper, paperboard, packaging, shipping containers, pulp and lumber.

Media General, Inc. ...333 E. Grace St., Richmond, VA 23219 ...(804) 649-6000 ...D.T. Bryan .. broadcasting, newspaper publishing.

Medtronic, Inc. ...7000 Central Ave. N.E., Minneapolis, MN 55432 ...(612) 574-4000 ...W.W. George ...manuf. prosthetic and theraputic devices.

Melville Corp. ...1 Theall Rd., Rye, NY 10580 ...(914) 925-4000 ...S.P. Goldstein .. shoe stores (Thom McAn), apparel (Marshalls, Chess King), drug stores.

Merck & Co., Inc. ...P.O. Box 2000, Rahway, NJ 07065 ...(201) 594-4000 ...P. Roy Vagelos ...human & animal health care prods.

Meredith Corp. ...1716 Locust St., Des Moines, IA 50336 ...(515) 284-3000 ...J.D. Rehm .. magazine publishing (Better Homes and Gardens, Ladies Home Journal), book publishing, broadcasting.

Merrill Lynch & Co., Inc. ...World Financial Center, N.Y., NY 10281 ...(212) 449-1000 ...W.A Schreyer ... securities broker, financial services.

Minnesota Mining & Manuf. Co. ...3M Center, St. Paul, MN 55144 ...(612) 733-1110 ...A.F. Jacobson ...abrasives, adhesives, building services & chemicals, electrical, health care, photographic, printing, recording materials, consumer prods. (Scotch Tape, Post-It).

Mobil Corp. ...322 Gallows Rd., Fairfax, VA 22037 ...(703) 846-3000 ...A.E. Murray .. international oil co., chemicals.

Monsanto Company ...800 N. Lindbergh Blvd., St. Louis, MO 63167 ...(314) 694-1000 ...R. J. Mahoney ...chemicals, agricultural prods., pharmaceutical, consumer prods. (NutraSweet).

Motorola, Inc. ...1303 E. Algonquin Rd., Schaumburg, IL 60196 ...(708) 576-5000 ...G.M.C. Fisher ...electronic equipment and components.

NCR Corp. ...1700 S. Patterson Blvd., Dayton, OH 45479 ...(513) 445-5000 ...Charles E. Exley Jr. ...business information processing systems. (Announced merger agreement with AT&T 1991).

National Medical Enterprises, Inc. ...2700 Colorado Ave., Santa Monica CA 90404 ...(213) 315-8000 ...R.K. Eamer ...operates hospitals.

National Semiconductor Corp. ...2900 Semiconductor Dr., Santa Clara, CA 95052 ...(408) 721-5000 ...P. Sprague ...manuf. of semiconductors.

Navistar Intl. Corp. ...455 N. Cityfront Plaza Dr., Chicago, IL 60611 ...(312) 836-2000 ...J.C. Cotting ...manuf. heavy duty trucks, parts.

New York Times Co. ...229 W. 43rd St., N.Y., NY 10036 ...(212) 556-3660 ...A. O. Sulzberger ...newspapers, radio, CATV stations, magazines (Family Circle, Golf Digest).

Nike, Inc. ...9000 SW Nimbus, Beaverton, OR 97005 ...(503) 644-9000 ...Philip Knight ...athletic & leisure footware.

Norfolk Southern Corp. ...One Commercial Place, Norfolk, VA 23510 ...(804) 629-2640 ...A.B. McKinnon ...operates Norfolk & Southern railways, freight carrier (North American Van Lines).

Northrop Corp. ...1840 Century Park E., Los Angeles, CA 90067 ...(213) 553-6262 ...K. Kresa ...aircraft, electronics, communications.

Nynex Corp. ...335 Madison Ave., N.Y., NY 10017 ...(212) 370-7400 ...W.C. Ferguson ...telephone co. in northeast U.S.

Occidental Petroleum Corp. ...10889 Wilshire Blvd., Los Angeles, CA 90024 ...(213) 879-1700 ...Ray Irani ...oil, gas, chemicals, coal, agriculture.

Ogden Corp. ...2 Pennsylvania Plaza, New York NY 10121 ...(212) 868-6100 ...R. Ablon ...transportation, foods, metals, financial services.

Olin Corp. ...120 Long Ridge Rd., Stamford, CT 06904 ...(203) 356-2000 ...J.W. Johnstone Jr. ...chemicals, water treatment prods., aerospace.

Olsten Corp. ...One Merrick Ave., Westbury, NY 11590 ...(516) 832-8200 ...F. N. Liguori ...provides temporary workers.

Oshkosh B', Gosh, Inc. ...112 Otter Ave, Oshkosh, WI 54901 ...(414) 231-8800 ...Charles Hyde ...manuf. of children's wear.

Outboard Marine Corp. ...100 Sea Horse Dr., Waukegan, IL 60085 ...(312) 689-6200 ...J.C. Chapman ...outboard motors (Evinrude, Johnson), boats (Four Winns, Stratos, Hydra-Sports).

Owens-Corning Fiberglas Corp. ...Fiberglas Tower, Toledo, OH 43659 ...(419) 248-8000 ...Max Weber .. glass fiber and related prods.

Oxford Industries, Inc. ...222 Piedmont Ave., N.E., Atlanta, GA 30308 ...(404) 659-2424 ...J.H. Lanier ...manuf. men's and women's apparel.

Pacific Telesis Group ...130 Kearny St., San Francisco, CA 94108 ...(415) 394-3000 ...S. L. Ginn .. telephone service.

Paramount Communications Inc. ...15 Columbus Circle, N.Y., NY 10023 ...(212) 373-8000 ...M.S. Davis ...entertainment (Paramount Pictures, Madison Square Garden), publishing (Simon & Schuster, Prentice Hall).

J.C. Penney Co. ...14841 N. Dallas Pkwy., Dallas, TX 75265 ...(214) 591-1000 ...W. R. Howell ...dept. stores, catalog sales, drug stores, insurance.

Pennzoil Co. ...P.O. Box 2967, Houston, TX 77252 ...(713) 546-4000 ...J.L. Pate .. Integrated oil and gas co.

Pep Boys—Manny, Moe & Jack ...3111 W. Allegheny Ave., Philadelphia, Pa. 19132 ...(215) 229-9000 ...M. G. Leibovitz ... automotive parts and accessories, retail stores.

PepsiCo, Inc. ...PepsiCo., Inc., Purchase, NY 10577 ...(914) 253-2000 ...D.W. Calloway .. soft drinks (Pepsi-Cola, Slice), snack foods (Ruffles, Lays, Doritos) restaurants (Pizza Hut, KFC, Taco Bell).

Perry Drug Stores, Inc. ...5400 Perry Dr., Pontiac, MI 48056 ...(313) 334-1300 ...J.A. Robinson ...drug stores, health care.

Petrie Stores Corp. ...70 Enterprise Ave., Secaucus, NJ 07094 ...(201) 866-3600 ...M.J. Petrie ...operates chain of women's specialty stores.

Pfizer Inc. ...235 E. 42d St., N.Y., NY 10017 ...(212) 573-2323 ...E.T. Pratt Jr. ...pharmaceutical, hospital, agricultural, chemical prods., consumer prods (Plax oral rinse, Ben-Gay pain relief).

Philip Morris Cos., Inc. ...120 Park Ave., N.Y., NY 10017 ...(212) 880-5000 ...H. Maxwell ...cigarettes (Marlboro, Virginia Slims), beer (Miller High Life, Lite, Lowenbrau brands), packaged foods (Jell-o, Ronzoni pasta, Entenmann baked goods, Maxwell House coffee, Kool Aid, Oscar Mayer meats, Tang, Cheez Whiz & Velveeta cheese prods.).

Phillips-Van Heusen Corp....1290 Ave. of the Americas, New York, NY 10104...(212) 541-5200...L. S. Phillips...manuf. apparel for men & women; operates retail stores.

Pitney Bowes, Inc..., Stamford, CT 06926...(203) 356-5000...G. B. Harvey...postage meters, mail handling equip., office equipment.

Playboy Enterprises, Inc....680 N. Lake Shore Dr., Chicago, IL 60611...(312) 751-8000...C. Hefner...magazine publishing, CATV, merchandising.

Polaroid Corp....549 Technology Sq., Cambridge, MA 02139...(617) 577-2000...I.M. Booth...photographic equip., supplies and optical goods.

Premark Intl., Inc...1717 Deerfield Rd. Deerfield, IL 60015...(708) 405-6000...W.L. Batts...consumer prods. (Tupperware, Hobart, West Bend).

The Price Co....2657 Arlane Dr., San Diego, CA 92117...(619) 581-4600...Robert Price...Operates "Price Club" wholesale retail warehouses.

Primerica, Corp....65 E. 55 St., N.Y., NY 10022...(212) 891-8900...S. I. Weill...insurance financial services (Smith Barney).

Procter & Gamble Co.... One Procter & Gamble Plaza, Cincinnati, OH 45202...(513) 562-1100...E. L. Artzt...soap & detergent (Ivory, Cheer, Tide, Zest), shortenings (Crisco), toiletries (Crest toothpaste, Prell, and Head and Shoulders shampoos, Noxzema, Old Spice) pharmaceuticals (Pepto-Bismol), Pampers disposable diapers, Folgers coffee, Hawaiian Punch, Charmin toilet tissues, Bounty towels, Vicks cough medicines.

Promus Cos. Inc....1023 Cherrry Rd., Memphis, TN 38117...(901) 762-8600...M.D. Rose...casinos (Harrah), lodging (Hampton Inn, Embassy Suites).

Quaker Oats Co.... Quaker Square, Chicago, IL 60604...(312) 222-7818...William D. Smithburg...foods, cereal (Quaker Oat Bran, Life, Cap'n Crunch, Puffed Wheat, Puffed Rice), foods (Aunt Jemima, Celeste pizza, Van Camp's pork and beans, Gatorade), pet foods (Ken-L-Ration, Gaines), Magic Pan restaurants.

Quaker State Corp....255 Elm St., Oil City, PA 16301...(814) 676-7676...J.W. Corn refining, marketing petroleum prods., filters, mining & marketing coal.

Ralston Purina Co.... Checkerboard Sq., St. Louis, MO 63164...(314) 982-2161...W. P. Stiritz...pet and livestock food (Purina), consumer prods. (Chex cereal, Beech-Nut baby food, Wonder bread, Hostess baked goods, Eveready batteries).

Raytheon Company...141 Spring St., Lexington, MA 02173...(617) 862-6600...Thomas L. Phillips...electronics, aviation, appliances...Amana Refrigeration, Beech Aircraft.

Reader's Digest Assn.... Pleasantville, NY 10570...(914) 238-1000...George v. Grune...magazines, books.

Reebok Intl. Ltd....100 Technology Ctr. Dr., Stoughton, MA 02072...(617) 341-5000...P.B. Fireman...athletic & casual footwear, sportswear.

Reynolds Metals Co....6601 W. Broad St., Richmond, VA 23261...(804) 281-2000...W.O. Bourke...aluminum prods.

Rite Aid Corp....P.O. Box 3165, Harrisburg, PA 17105...(717) 761-2633...A. Grass...discount drug stores, beauty aid stores, auto parts stores.

Rockwell Intl. Corp....625 Liberty Ave, Pittsburgh, PA 15222...(412) 565-2000...D. R. Beall...aerospace, electronic, automotive prods.

Rubbermaid Inc....1147 Akron Rd., Wooster, OH 44691...(216) 264-6464...Walter Williams...rubber and plastic consumer prods.

Russell Corp....P.O. Box 272, Alexander City, AL 35010...(205) 329-4000...D.L. Carlisle Jr....manuf. leisure apparel, athletic uniforms.

Ryder System, Inc....3600 NW 82d Ave., Miami, FL 33166...(305) 593-3726...M. A. Burns...truck leasing service.

Santa Fe Pacific Corp.,...224 S. Michigan Ave., Chicago, IL 60604...(708) 995-6000...Robert D. Krebs...railroad, real estate, construction, natural resources.

Sara Lee Corp....3 First National Plaza, Chicago, IL 60602...(312) 726-2600...J.H. Bryan Jr....baked goods, fresh and processed meats, fresh and frozen fruits and vegetables and other packaged foods, beverages, tobacco products, hosiery, intimate apparel and knitwear, Fuller Brush, Hanes, Kiwi, Shasta, Hillshire Farm, L' eggs, Isotoner.

Schering-Plough Corp.... One Giralda Farms, Madison, NJ 07940...(201) 822-7000...R. P. Luciano...pharmaceuticals, consumer prods.

Schlumberger Ltd....277 Park Ave., New York, NY 10172...(212) 350-9400...D.E. Baird...oilfield services, electronics, measurement and control devices.

Scott Paper Co.... Scott Plaza, Phila., PA 19113...(215) 522-5000...P. E. Lippincott...toilet tissue, paper towels, napkins.

E.W. Scripps Co....1409 Foulk Rd., Wilmington, DE 19803...(302) 478-4141...C.E. Scripps, chmn....newspapers, TV & radio stations.

Seagram Co. Ltd....1430 Peel St., Montreal, Que., Canada H3A 1S9...(514) 849-5271...E.M. Bronfman...distilled spirits & wine (Crown Royal, Chivas Regal, Calvert, Wolfschmidt Vodka, Paul Masson, Christian Brothers, Martell, Myer's Jamaica Rum); juice (Tropicana).

Sears, Roebuck & Co.... Sears Tower, Chicago, IL 60684...(312) 875-2500...E.A. Brennan...merchandising, insurance (Allstate), financial services (Dean Witter), real estate (Coldwell Banker).

Service Merchandise, Inc....P.O. Box 24600, Nashville, TN 37202...(615) 660-6000...R. Zimmerman...operates catalog showrooms.

Shaw Industries, Inc....616 E. Walnut Ave., Dalton, GA 30722...(404) 278-3812...R.E. Shaw...manuf. tufted carpeting (Magee, Philadelphia).

Sherwin-Williams Co....101 Prospect Ave. N.W., Cleveland, OH 44115...(216) 566-2000...John G. Breen...world's largest paint producer (Dutch Boy, Kem-Tone).

Skyline Corp....2520 By-Pass Rd., Elkhart, IN 46515...(219) 294-6521...Arthur J. Decio...mfg. housing and recreational vehicles.

Smucker (J.M.) Co.... Strawberry Lane, Orrville, OH 44667...(216) 682-3000...Timothy Smucker...preserves, jams, jellies, toppings.

Snap-on Tools Corp....2801 80th St., Kenosha, WI 53141...(414) 656-5449...M. F. Gregory...manuf. mechanic's tools, equip.

Sony Corp....9 W. 57th St., New York, NY 10019...(212) 371-5800...N. Ohga...manuf. televisions, radios, tape recorders, audio equip., video tape recorders, (Walkman, Betamax); entertainment (Sony Pictures).

Southwest Airlines Co....P.O. Box 36611, Love Field, Dallas, TX 75235...(214) 904-4000...H.D. Kelleher...air transportation.

Southwestern Bell Corp.... One Bell Center, St. Louis, MO 63101...(314) 235-9800...E.E. Whitacre Jr....telephone communications.

Standard Brands Paint Co....4300 W 190th St., Torrance, CA 90509...(213) 214-2411...S.D. Buchalter...retailer of home decorating prods.

Stanley Works...1000 Stanley Drive, P.O. Box 7000, New Britain CT 06050...(203) 225-5111...R.H. Ayers...hand tools, hardware, door opening equipment.

Stride Rite Corp....5 Cambridge Center, Cambridge, MA 02142...(617) 491-8800...Erwin Shames...manuf. & retailer children's footwear.

Sun Company, Inc....100 Matsonford Rd., Radnor, PA 19087...(215) 293-6000...R. McClements Jr....energy resources co.

Syms Corp.... Syms Way, Secaucus, NJ 07094...(201) 902-9600...S. Syms...operates off-price apparel stores.

Thomas), technical prods.

Tambrands Inc.... One Marcus Ave., Lake Success, NY 11042...(516) 358-8300...M.F.C. Emmett...menstrual tampons (Tampax, Maxithins).

Tandem Computers...19333 Vallco Pkwy., Cupertino, CA 95014...(408) 285-6000...T.G. Treybig...supplier of computer systems and networks.

Tandy Corp....1800 One Tandy Center, Fort Worth, TX 76102...(817) 390-3700...J.V. Roach...consumer electronics retailing & mfg, Radio Shack.

Teledyne, Inc....1901 Ave. of the Stars, Los Angeles, CA 90067...(213) 277-3311...William Rutledge...electronics, aerospace prods., industrial prods., insurance, finance.

Tenneco, Inc....P.O. Box 2511, Houston, TX 77001...(713) 757-2131...J. L. Ketelsen...oil, natural gas pipelines, shipbuilding, farm equip.

Texaco Inc....2000 Westchester Ave., White Plains, NY 10650...(914) 253-4000...J.W. Kinnear...petroleum and petroleum prods.

Texas Instruments Inc....13500 N. Central Expressway, Dallas, TX 75265...(214) 995-3773...Jerry Junkins...electrical & electronics prods.

Textron Inc....40 Westminster St., Providence, RI 02903...(401) 421-2800...B.F. Dolan...aerospace, consumer, industrial, metal prods, consumer finance, insurance, management services.

Tiffany & Co....727 5th Ave, New York, NY 10022...(212) 755-8000...W.R. Chaney...designs, manuf., and distributes jewelry & gift items.

Time Warner Inc.... Rockefeller Center, New York, NY 10020...(212) 522-1212...Steve Ross...magazine publisher (Time, Sports Illustrated, Fortune, Money, People),

CATV (HBO, Cinemax), publishing (Little, Brown, Warner Books).

Tootsie Roll Industries, Inc., ...7401 S. Cicero Ave., Chicago, IL 60629...(312) 838-3400...M.J. Gordon...candy (Tootsie Roll, Mason Dots, Mason Crows, Bonomo Turkish Taffy, Charms).

Toro Co. ...8111 Lyndale Ave. South, Bloomington, MN 55420...(612) 887-8801...K. B. Melrose...lawn and turf maintenance, (Lawn Boy); snow removal equipment.

Toys "R" Us ...461 From Rd., Paramus, NJ 07652...(201) 262-7800...Charles Lazarus...toy retailer, clothing stores (Kids "R" Us).

Transamerica Corp. ...600 Montgomery St., San Francisco, CA 94111...(415) 983-4000...J.R. Harvey...insurance, financial, business services.

Travelers Corp. ...One Tower Sq., Hartford, CT 06183...(203) 277-0111...E. H. Budd...insurance.

Tribune Co. ...435 N. Michigan Ave., Chicago, IL 60611...(312) 222-3883...C.T. Brumback...newpaper publishing, broadcasting, entertainment (Chicago Cubs baseball team).

Trinity Industries, Inc. ...2525 Stemmons Freeway, P.O. Box 10587, Dallas, TX 75207...(214) 631-4420...W.R. Wallace...manufactures variety of metal products.

TRW Inc. ...1900 Richmond Rd., Cleveland, OH 44124...(216) 291-7000...J.T. Gorman...car and truck operations, electronics, and space systems.

Turner Broadcasting System, Inc. ...1 CNN Center, Atlanta, GA 30303...(404) 827-1700...R.E. Turner...operates cable TV networks: CNN, TBS, TNT; owns MGM film library; owns Atlanta Braves, Hawks.

Tyson Foods, ...2210 W. Oaklawn, Springdale, AR 72764...(501) 756-4000...Don Tyson...produces & markets fresh & processed poultry.

USAIR Group, Inc. ...1911 Jefferson Hwy., Arlington, VA 22002...(703) 418-7000...Seth E. Schofield...air carrier of passengers, property, and mail.

UST Inc. ...100 W. Putnam Ave., Greenwich, CT 06830...(203) 661-1100...L.F. Bantle...smokeless tobacco (Copenhagen, Skoal, Happy Days), pipes, pipe tobacco.

USX-U.S. Steel Group ...600 Grant St., Pittsburgh, PA 15230...(412) 433-1121...C.A. Corry...steel manuf.

Unilever, N.V. ...390 Park Ave., New York, NY 10022...(212) 906-4694...Michael Angus, chmn....soap, detergent, margarine, frozen food, toothpaste, tea, dried soups, ice cream, cosmetics, fragrances, (Lever Brothers, Lipton, Pond's Vaseline Intensive Care, Obsession, Q-Tips, Cutex).

Union Carbide Corp. ...39 Old Ridgebury Rd., Danbury, CT 06817...(203) 794-2000...R.D. Kennedy...chemicals, industrial gases.

Union Pacific Corp. ...Martin Tower, Bethlehem, PA 18018...(215) 861-3200...D. Lewis...railroad, natural resources.

Unisys Corp. ...P.O. Box 500, Blue Bell, PA 19424...(215) 986-6999...James Unruh...business equip., data processing prods.

U.S. Shoe Corp. ...One Eastwood Dr., Cincinnati, OH 45227...(513) 527-7000...B.B. Hudson...apparel, retailer (Casual Corner), shoes (Red Cross, Joyce), eye-care stores (LensCrafters).

United Technologies Corp. ...United Technologies Bldg., Hartford, CT 06101...(203) 728-7000...R.F. Daniell...aerospace, industrial prods. & services, Carrier Corp., Otis Elevator; Pratt & Whitney, Sikorsky Aircraft.

Univar Corp. ...1600 Norton Building, Seattle, WA 98104...(206) 447-5911...J.W. Bernard...industrial and agricultural chemicals, laboratory and graphic arts products distributor, home furnishing supplies and fabrics distributors.

Universal Foods Corp. ...433 East Michigan St., Milwaukee, WI 53202...(414) 271-6755...G.A. Osborn...yeast products, cheese products, dehydrated seasonings, food colors and flavors, imported gourmet foods.

Upjohn Co. ...7000 Portage Rd., Kalamazoo, MI 49001...(616) 323-4000...T. Cooper...pharmaceuticals

(Motrin, Nuprin, Xanax, Halcion, Cleocin), chemicals, agricultural and health care prods.

VF Corp. ...1047 No. Park Rd., Wyomissing, PA 19610...(215) 378-1151...L.R. Pugh...apparel, Vanity Fair, Lee, Wrangler jeans, Bassett-Walker, Jantzen.

Wal-Mart Stores Inc. ...702 W. 8th St., Bentonville, AK 72716...(501) 273-4000...D.D. Glass...retail dept. stores.

Walgreen Co. ...200 Wilmot Rd., Deerfield, IL 60015...(708) 940-2500...Charles R. Walgreen 3d...retail drug chain, restaurants.

Wang Laboratories, Inc. ...One Industrial Ave., Lowell, MA 01851...(508) 459-5000...R.W. Miller...word processors.

Warner-Lambert Co. ...201 Tabor Rd., Morris Plains, NJ 07950...(201) 540-2000...J.D. Williams...health care prods. (Benadryl), consumer prods. (Efferdent dental cleanser, Hall cough tablets, Schick razors, Rolaids antacid, Listerine mouth wash).

Washington Post Co. ...1150 15th St., N.W., Washington, DC 20071...(202) 334-6000...Katharine Graham...newspapers, magazines (Newsweek), TV stations.

Weis Markets, Inc. ...1000 South Second Street, Sunbury, PA 17801...(717) 286-4571...S. Weis...operates supermarkets, distributes frozen foods and grocery items.

Wells Fargo & Co. ...420 Montgomery St., San Francisco, CA 94163...(415) 396-3606...C.E. Reichardt...banking.

Wendy's Intl., Inc. ...4288 W. Dublin-Granville Rd., Dublin, OH 43017...(614) 764-3100...J.W. Near...quick service restaurants.

Westinghouse Electric Corp. ...Westinghouse Bldg., Gateway Center, Pittsburgh, PA 15222...(412) 244-2000...P.E. Lego...manuf. electrical, mechanical equip.; radio and television stations.

Westvaco Corp. ...299 Park Avenue, New York, NY 10171...(212) 688-5000...J.A. Luke...manufactures paper for graphic reproduction, communications, and packaging (largest producer of envelopes in the world).

Weyerhaeuser Co. ...Tacoma, WA 98477...(206) 924-2345...George H. Weyerhaeuser...manuf., distribution of forest prods.

Whirlpool Corp. ...2000 M-63 N., Benton Harbor, MI 49022...(616) 926-5000...D.R. Whitwam...major home appliances.

Whitman Corp. ...One Illinois Ctr., 111 E. Wacker Dr., Chicago, IL 60601...(312) 565-3000...J.W. Cozad...diversified prods. and services, consumer prods., food, auto prods. (Midas).

Willamette Industries, Inc. ...3800 1st Interstate Tower, Portland, OR 97201...(503) 227-5581...William Swindells...building materials and paper prods.

Winn-Dixie Stores, Inc. ...5050 Edgewood Ct., Jacksonville, FL 32205...(904) 783-5000...A.D. Davis, chmn....supermarket chain.

Winnebago Industries, Inc. ...P.O. Box 152, Forest City, IA 50436...(515) 582-3535...J.K. Hanson, chmn....manuf. of motor homes, recreation vehicles.

Wolverine World Wide Corp. ...9341 Courtland Dr., Rockford, MI 49351...(616) 866-5500...T.D. Gleason...manuf. footwear (Hush Puppies).

Woolworth Corp. ...233 Broadway, N.Y., NY 10279...(212) 553-2000...H.E. Sells...variety stores, shoe stores (Kinney), men's clothing (Richman Brothers), children's apparel (Kid's Mart), athletic footwear (Foot Locker).

Wm. Wrigley Jr. Co. ...410 N. Michigan Ave., Chicago, IL 60611...(312) 644-2121...William Wrigley...chewing gum.

Xerox Corp. ...P.O. Box 1600, Stamford, CT 06904...(203) 329-8700...Paul Allaire...equip. for reproduction, reduction, and transmission of printed information.

Zenith Electronics Corp. ...1000 Milwaukee Ave., Glenview, IL 60025...(708) 391-8181...Jerry K. Pearlman...consumer electronic prods.

Who Owns What: Familiar Consumer Products

The following is a list of familiar consumer products and their parent companies. The address of the parent company can be found on pages 705-710.

Admiral appliances: Maytag
Ajax cleanser: Colgate-Palmolive
Allstate Insurance Co.: Sears, Roebuck
Almond Joy candy: Hershey
Anacin: American Home Products
Arrid anti-perspirant: Carter-Wallace
Aunt Millie's pasta sauce: Borden

Ban anti-perspirant: Bristol-Myers
Beech Aircraft: Raytheon
Beech Nut babyfood: Ralston Purina
Ben-Gay: Pfizer
Betty Crocker products: General Mills
Budweiser beer: Anheuser-Busch

Bufferin: Bristol-Myers Squibb
Business Week magazine: McGraw-Hill
Buster Brown shoes: Brown Group

Cap'n Crunch cereal: Quaker Oats
Carrier air conditioners: United Technologies
Celeste Pizza: Quaker Oats
Charmin toilet tissues: Procter & Gamble
Chef Boy-ar-dee products: American Home Products
Cheer detergent: Procter & Gamble
Cheerios cereal: General Mills
Clairol hair products: Bristol-Myers Squibb
Clorets mints: Warner-Lambert
Copenhagen snuff: UST

Cracker Jack: Borden
Crest toothpaste: Procter & Gamble
Crisco shortening: Procter & Gamble

Dean Witter financial services: Sears, Roebuck
Deer Park bottled water: Clorox
Doritos chips: PepsiCo
Drano: Bristol-Meyers Squibb
Dristan: American Home Products
Duncan Hines cookies: Procter & Gamble
Easy-Off oven cleaner: American Home Products
Efferdent dental cleanser: Warner-Lambert
ESPN: Capital Cities/ABC
Eveready batteries: Ralston Purina
Excedrin: Bristol-Myers

Fab detergent: Colgate-Palmolive
Family Circle magazine: New York Times
Foamy shaving cream: Gillette
Folger coffee: Procter & Gamble
Formula 409 spray cleaner: Clorox
Franco-American foods: Campbell Soup
Frito-Lay snacks: PepsiCo
Fuller Brush prods.: Sara Lee

Gatorade: Quaker Oats
Gleem toothpaste: Procter & Gamble
Hampton Inns—Promus
Handy Wipes: Colgate-Palmolive
Hanes hosiery: Sara Lee
Hawaiian Punch: Procter & Gamble
Head and Shoulders shampoo: Procter & Gamble
Hellman's mayonnaise: CPC International
Hi-C fruit drinks: Coca Cola
Hillshire Farm meats: Sara Lee
Home Box Office: Time
Hostess baked goods: Ralston Purina
Hush Puppies shoes: Wolverine World Wide

Ivory soap products: Procter & Gamble
Jack Daniel bourbon: Brown-Forman
Jell-o: Philip Morris
Jim Beam whiskey: American Brands
Ken-L-Ration pet foods: Quaker Oats
Kent cigarettes: Loews
Kinney shoe stores: Woolworth
Knorr soups: CPC International
Kool Aid: Philip Morris
La Menu frozen dinners: Campbell Soup
Ladies Home Journal magazine: Meredith
Lee jeans: VF Corp.
Lenox china: Brown-Forman
Lens Crafters: U.S. Shoe
Lerner stores: The Limited
Lipton tea: Unilever
Listerine mouth wash: Warner-Lambert
Log Cabin syrup: Philip Morris
Lord & Taylor dept. stores: May Dept. Stores
Lucite paints: Clorox
Lunch Bucket meals: Greyhound Dial

Marlboro cigarettes: Philip Morris
Mazola oil: CPC International
Maxwell House coffee: Philip Morris
Michelob beer: Anheuser-Busch
Midas automotive centers: Whitman
Miller beer: Philip Morris
Milton Bradley games: Hasbro
Minute Rice: Philip Morris

Mrs. Paul's frozen fish: Campbell Soup
NBC Broadcasting: General Electric
Newsweek magazine: Washington Post
9-Lives cat food: H.J. Heinz
North American Van Lines: Norfolk Southern
Nuprin: Bristol-Myers Squibb

Obsession fragrance: Unilever
Old Spice: Procter & Gamble
Ore-Ida frozen foods: H.J. Heinz

Pampers: Procter & Gamble
Paper Mate pens: Gillette
People magazine: Time
Pepto-Bismol: Procter & Gamble
Pepperidge Farm products: Campbell Soup
Pizza Hut restaurants: PepsiCo
Plax oral rinse: Pfizer
Playskool toys: Hasbro
Prego spaghetti sauce: Campbell Soup
Prell shampoo: Procter & Gamble
Prentice-Hall publishing: Paramount
Post-It stickers: Minn. Min. & Manuf.
Purex detergent: Dial

Q-Tips: Unilever
Radio Shack retail outlets: Tandy
Ramblin root beer: Coca Cola
Red Lobster Inns: General Mills
Reese's peanut butter cups: Hershey
Right Guard deodorant: Gillette
Rise shave lathers: Carter-Wallace
Rolaids antacid: Warner-Lambert
Ronzoni pasta: Hershey
Ruffles chips: PepsiCo

San Giorgio pasta: Hershey
Saran Wrap: Dow Chemical
Scotch tape: Minn. Min. & Manuf.
Scrabble: Hasbro
Skippy peanut butter: CPC International
Simon & Schuster publishing: Paramount
Southern Comfort liquor: Brown-Forman
Sports Illustrated magazine: Time
Sprite soda: Coca-Cola
Sugartwin: Alberto Culver
Taco Bell restaurants: PepsiCo
Thom McAn shoe stores: Melville
Thomas English muffins: CPC International
Tide detergent: Procter & Gamble
Trojan condoms: Carter-Wallace
Tropicana juices: Seagram
Tupperware: Premark
Tylenol: Johnson & Johnson
Ultra Brite toothpaste: Colgate-Palmolive
V-8 vegetable juice: Campbell Soup
Vanity Fair apparel: VF Corp.
Velveeta cheese prods.: Philip Morris
Vicks cough medicines: Procter & Gamble
Virginia Slims cigarettes: Philip Morris
Walden Book stores: K mart
Walkman: Sony
Wall Street Journal: Dow Jones
Weight Watchers: H.J. Heinz
Wheaties cereal: General Mills
White Owl cigars: Culbro
Wizard air freshener: American Home Products
Wyler's drink mixes: Borden

Shopping for Credit: Ask the Right Questions

Source: New York State Banking Department

Under federal law, all institutions that extend or arrange for the extension of consumer credit must give the borrower meaningful information about the cost of each loan. The cost must be expressed as the dollar amount of the interest or finance charge, and as the annual percentage rate computed on the amount financed.

To be sure the loan or credit agreement you are considering suits both your budget and your individual needs, shop around. Ask questions to compare and evaluate a lender's rate and services. For instance:

1. What is the annual percentage rate?
2. What is the total cost of the loan in dollars?
3. How long do you have to pay off the loan?
4. What are the number, amounts, and due dates of payments?
5. What is the cost of deferring or extending the time period of the loan?
6. What is the cost of late charges for overdue payments?
7. If you pay the loan off early, are there any prepayment penalties?
8. Does the loan have to be secured? If so, what collateral is required?
9. What is the cost of credit life or other insurance that is being offered or may be required?
10. Are there any other charges you may have to pay?

How to Check Your Credit File

Any individual can investigate the contents of his or her credit file by directly contacting one or more of the approximately 2,000 credit bureaus, or consumer credit clearinghouses, in the United States. The nearest ones can be found by calling a local Better Business Bureau or by looking in the telephone Yellow Pages under "Credit Rating or Reporting Agencies."

Although the Fair Credit Reporting Act requires that a bureau give a person no more than an oral or written credit history review, many bureaus will go beyond the technical requirements of the law and furnish the same computer-generated compilation of facts that they give the banks, retailers and other companies that subscribe to their service. An individual who has been denied credit on the basis of negative information from a credit bureau can obtain this review without charge within 30 days of the denial. Otherwise, the fee typically ranges from $8 to $12 for such a credit check.

After inspecting this record of past credit behavior, a consumer can question any item believed to be inaccurate, misleading or vague. The credit bureau must then investigate and remove any item that cannot be substantiated.

When a bureau affirms, rather than removes, a questionable item, an individual can present a 100-word explanation that must be placed in his or her file. And whenever an adverse item is deleted from the file or an explantory statement is added to one, a consumer may request that the credit bureau inform every credit grantor who received a report within the last six months.

Credit Card Rates

(As of Aug. 1, 1991)
(Prepared by Christian T. Jones, San Diego, CA)

Nearly all states have special laws dealing with rates charged for credit cards issued by state banks and other financial institutions. Although some state laws apply only to banks, under Federal parity law, the same charges can be made by other financial institutions. A national bank can charge the highest rates allowed for revolving credit extended by any other creditor in the state where the bank is located for similar types of credit, and such rates may also be charged to residents of any other state. Rates are yearly.

Ala.	No limit.	Me.	annual fees. 18%; $12 annual fee.	Oh.	25% to 1/1/92.
Alas.	17% plus fee.	Md.	24%; 2% fee.	Okla.	30-21-15% @ $840, $2,800; or 21%.
Ariz.	No limit.	Mass.	23% to $6,000; no limit over		
Ark.	5% over FRB discount rate (max. 17%).		$6,000; $20 annual fee.	Ore.	No limit.
Cal.	No limit.	Mich.	18%; no limit on annual fee.	Pa.	12% loans; 15% purchases; $15 annual fee.
Colo.	21%.	Minn.	18%; $50 annual fee.		
Conn.	15%; $10 annual fee.	Miss.	21%; or 18% plus $12 annual	P.R.	17% loans; 26% purchases.
D.C.	24%.		fee.	R.I.	18%.
Del.	No limit.	Mo.	22-10% @ $1,000.	S.C.	No limit.
Fla.	18%.	Mont.	No limit.	S.D.	No limit.
Ga.	No limit on rate or fee.	Neb.	18% plus fees.	Tenn.	24%.
Ha.	24%.	Nev.	No limit.	Tex.	18%.
Ida.	No limit.	N.H.	No limit.	Utah	No limit.
Ill.	No limit; plus fees.	N.J.	30%; $15 annual fee or $50	Vt.	18%; no limit on annual fee.
Ind.	36-21-15%, @ $810, $2,700; or 21%.		over $5,000.	Va.	No limit.
		N.M.	No limit.	Wash.	12% or 4% over U.S. T-bill rate.
Ia.	No limit.	N.Y.	25% plus annual fee to 6/30/93.	W.Va.	18%.
Kan.	18-14.45% @ $1,000.	N.C.	18%; $20 annual fee.	Wis.	No limit.
Ky.	21%; $20 annual fee.	N.D.	No limit.	Wyo.	36-21% @ $1,000; no limit over $25,000.
La.	18%; 4% cash advance and $12				

Fair Credit: What You Should Know

Source: Federal Trade Commission

Billing. The Fair Credit Billing Act permits you to dispute the accuracy of charges listed on your credit card statement and provides other important rights (such as limits on liability for unauthorized charges). To file a notice of a "billing error," send a letter to the card issuer at the address specified for "billing inquiries" within 60 days of the date that the card issuer mailed the first statement that shows the alleged error. Be sure to include your name, address, account number, the amount of the charge you dispute, and why you think an error was made. Do not send the letter in the same envelope as your payment and keep a copy.

Equal Credit. The Equal Credit Opportunity Act (ECOA) prohibits discrimination on the grounds of sex, marital status, age (provided the applicant has the capacity under state law to enter a contract), race, color, religion, or national origin. The ECOA also protects applicants whose income derives in whole or in part from any public assistance program, or those who have in good faith exercised any right under the Federal Consumer Credit Protection Act, which includes the FCBA and ECOA, among other provisions.

The creditor may inquire about your marital status, for example, if it needs to do so to determine its rights and not to discriminate in a determination of creditworthiness. Another example involves considering the age of the applicant if the inquiry is for the purpose of determining the amount and probable continuation of income levels or other elements of creditworthiness. However, a creditor may not consider race, national origin, or religion in deciding whether to extend credit.

The ECOA also requires the creditor to respond to applications within 30 days of receiving a completed application and to provide rejected applicants with a statement of specific reasons why credit was denied or a notice disclosing the consumer's rights to have the reasons if he or she requests them in writing.

Mail-Order Merchandise. By law, you have the right to have merchandise ordered through the mail shipped within 30 days, unless another shipping date has been specified in the advertisement for the merchandise. Promises such as "one week" or "4 to 6 weeks" must be met. However, if the seller is unable to ship your order when promised (or within the 30-day limit), the seller must provide you with a notice informing you that you have the right to cancel your order and get a prompt refund. If you experience a problem with late or non-delivery of merchandise ordered through the mail, contact the Federal Trade Commission.

Interest Laws and Consumer Finance Loan Rates

Source: Revised by Christian T. Jones. Editor, Consumer Finance Law Bulletin, San Diego, Ca.

All states have laws regulating interest rates. These laws fix a legal or conventional rate which applies when there is no contract for interest. They also fix a general maximum contract rate, but there are so many exceptions that the general contract maximum actually applies only to exceptional cases. Also, federal law has preempted state limits on first home mortgages, subject to each state's right to reinstate its own law, and given depository institutions parity with other state lenders.

Legal rate of interest. The legal or conventional rate of interest applies to money obligations when no interest rate is contracted for and also to judgments. The rate is usually somewhat below the general interest rate.

General maximum contract rates. General interest laws in most states set the maximum rate between 8% and 16% per year. The general maximum is fixed by the state constitution at 5% over the Federal Reserve Discount rate in Arkansas. Loans to corporations are frequently exempted or subject to a higher maximum. In recent years, it has also been common to provide special rates for home mortgage loans and variable usury rates that are indexed to market rates.

Specific enabling acts. In many states special statutes permit industrial loan companies, second mortgage lenders, and banks to charge 1.5% a month or more. Laws regulating revolving loans, charge accounts and credit cards generally limit charges between 1.5% and 2% per month plus annual fees for credit cards. Rates for installment sales contracts in most states are somewhat higher. Credit unions may generally charge 1% to 1.5% a month. Pawnbrokers' rates vary widely. Savings and loan associations, and loans insured by federal agencies, are also specially regulated. A number of states allow regulated lenders to charge any rate agreed to with the customer either for all credit or over a certain dollar amount.

Consumer finance loan statutes. Most consumer finance loan statutes are based on early models drafted by the Russell Sage Foundation (1916-42) to provide small loans to wage earners under license and other protective regulations. Since 1969 the model has frequently been the Uniform Consumer Credit Code which applies to credit sales and loans for consumer purposes. In general, licensed lenders may charge 3% a month and reduced rates for additional amounts. An add-on of 17% ($17 per $100) per year yields about 2.5% per month if paid in equal monthly installments. Discount rates produce higher yields than add-on rates of the same amount. In the table below, unless otherwise stated, monthly and annual rates are based on reducing principal balances, annual add-on rates are based on the original principal for the full term, and two or more rates apply to different portions of balance or original principal.

States with consumer finance loan laws and the rates of charge as of August 1, 1991

Maximum monthly rates computed on unpaid balances, unless otherwise stated.

Ala.. . . Annual add-on: 15% to $750, 10% to $2,000 (min. 1.5% on unpaid balances). Higher rates for loans up to $749. Over $2,000, any agreed rate. Fee: 4% (max. $25); 5% real estate.

Alas. . . 3% to $850, 2% to $10,000. Over $10,000, any agreed rate.

Ariz. . . To $1,000: 3%. Over $1,000: 3% to $500, 2% to $10,000. Over $10,000, any agreed rate.

Cal. . . 2.5% to $225, 2% to $900, 1.5% to $1,650, 1% to $2,500 (1.6% min.). Over $2,500, any agreed rate. 5% fee (max. $50) to $2,500

Colo. . 36% per year to $630, 21% to $2,100, 15% to $25,000 (21% min.).

Conn. . Annual add-on: 17% to $600, 11% to $5,000; 11% over $1,800 to $5,000 for certain secured loans. Any agreed rate for second mortgages.

Del.. . . Any agreed rate.

D.C. . . 24% per year.

Fla.. . . 30% per year to $1,000, 24% to $2,000, 18% to $25,000.

Ga.. . . 10% per year discount to 18 months, add-on to 36½months; 8% fee to $600, 4% on excess plus $2 per month. Over $3,000, any agreed rate.

Ha.. . . 3.5% to $100, 2.5% to $300; 2% on entire balance over $300 or discount rates.

Ida.. . . Any agreed rate.

Ill.. . . . Any agreed rate.

Ind.. . . 36% per year to $810, 21% to $2,700, 15% to $25,000 (21% min.).

Ia.. . . 3% to $1,000, 2% to $2,800, 1.5% to $10,000; or equivalent flat rate. Over $10,000: 21% per year.

Kan. . . 36% per year to $690, 21% to $2,300, 14.45% to $25,000 (18% min.). Fee: 2% (max. $100); 3% real estate.

Ky. . . . 3% to $1,000, 2% to $3,000. Over $3,000, 2%.

La.. . . 36% per year to $1,400, 27% to $4,000, 24% to $7,000, 21% over $7,000, plus $25 fee.

Me.. . . 30% per year to $700, 21% to $2,000, 15% to $25,000 (18% min.).

Md.. . . 2.75% to $1,000, 2% to $2,000. Over $2,000, 2%.

Mass. . 23% per year plus $20 fee to $6,000; any agreed rate over $6,000.

Mich.. . 22% per year to $8,000; 18% for second mortgages, plus 2% fee (max. $200).

Minn.. . 33% per year to $750, 19% over $750 (21.75% min.).

Miss. . 36% per year to $1,000, 33% to $1,800, 24% to $5,000, 14% over $5,000. Over $25,000, 18%. 2% fee (max. $50).

Mo.. . . 2.218% to $1,200, 1.67% over $1,200, plus 5% fee (max. $15); 1.67% plus 2% for second mortgages.

Mont.. . Any agreed rate.

Neb. . . 24% per year to $1,000. 21% over, plus fee of 7% to $2,000 and 5% over (max. $500).

Nev.. . . Any agreed rate.

N.H. . . 2% to $600, 1.5% to $1,500; Any agreed rate over $1,500 or for real estate mortgages.

N.J.. . . 30% per year to $5,000 or for second mortgages.

N.M. . . Any agreed rate.

N.Y. . . 25% per year to 6/30/93.

N.C. . . 3% to $1,000, 1.5% to $7,500; 1.5% on entire amount to $10,000. 1.5% or variable plus 2% fee for second mortgages.

N.D. . . 2.5% to $250, 2% to $500, 1.75% to $750, 1.5% to $1,000; any agreed rate over $1,000.

Ohio . . 28% per year to $1,000, 22% to $5,000; 25% on entire amount over $5,000; plus fee.

Okla.. . 30% per annum to $840, 21% to $2,800, 15% to $45,000. (21% min.). Special rates to $500.

Ore.. . . Any agreed rate.

Pa.. . . 9.5% per year discount to 48 months, 6% for remaining time plus 2% fee (max. $100); or 2% on unpaid balances; 1.85% for second mortgages over $5,000, plus 2% fee.

P.R. . . 24% per year.

R.I.. . . 3% to $300, 2.5% for loans between $300 and $800; 2% for larger loans to $5,000. 1.75% over $5,000.

S.C. . . Any agreed and posted rate.

S.D. . . Any agreed rate.

Tenn.. . Over $100, 24% per year or discount rates plus fees.

Texas . Annual add-on: 18% to $1,140, 8% to $9,500 or formula rate (18% to 24% per year on unpaid balances.)

Utah . . Any agreed rate.

Vt. . . . 2% to $1,000, 1% to $3,000 (min. 1.5%); 1.5% for second mortgages.

Va. . . . 2¾% to $800, 2% to $2,000, 1.5% to $3,500; or annual add-on of 19% to $800, 15% to $2,000, 12% to $2,800; 2% fee. Any agreed rate over $3,500 for second mortgages, plus 2% fee.

Wash. . 2.5% to $500, 1.5% to $1,000, 1% to $2,500. Over $2,500, 25% per year plus fees.

W.Va. . 36% per year to $500, 24% to $1,500, 18% to $2,000. Over $2,000, 27% per year to $2,000, 25% to $10,000, 18% on remainder, 2% fee.

Wis. . . Any agreed rate.

Wyo. . . 36% per year to $1,000, 21% to $25,000. No limit over $25,000.

Tips on Cutting Energy Costs in Your Home

Source: Con Edison Conservation Services, New York City

Heating

In many homes, in areas where temperatures drop during the winter, more energy is used for heating than anything else. Installing the right amount of insulation, storm windows and doors, caulking and weatherstripping pays off. Also consider the following advice:

- Make sure the thermostat and heating system are in good working order. An annual checkup is recommended.
- If your heating system has air filters, make sure they are clean.
- Set the thermostat no higher than 68 degrees. When no one is home, or when everyone is sleeping, the setting should be turned down to 60 degrees or lower. An automatic setback thermostat can raise and lower your home's temperature at times you specify.
- Close off and do not heat unused areas.
- Cover all air conditioner units.
- If you do not have conventional storm windows or doors, use kits to make plastic storm windows.
- Special glass fireplace doors help keep a room's heat from being drawn up the chimney when the fire is burning low. Close the damper when a fireplace is not in use.
- Use the sun's heat by opening blinds and draperies on sunny days.
- Keep radiators and warm air outlets clean. Do not block them with furniture or draperies.

Water Heater

In many homes, the water heater ranks second only to the heating system in total energy consumption.

- Put an insulation blanket on your water heater; when you go on vacation turn it to a minimum setting.
- If you have a dishwasher, set the water heater thermostat no higher than 140 degrees. If not, or if you have a separate water heater for baths, a setting as low as 110 degrees may be sufficient.
- Run the dishwasher and clothes washer only when you have a full load. Use warm or cold water cycles for laundry when you can.
- Take showers instead of tub baths. About half as much hot water is used for a shower.
- Install a water-saver shower head.
- Install aerators or restrictors on all your sink faucets.
- Do not leave the hot water running when rinsing dishes or shaving. Plug and partially fill the basin, or fill a pan with water.
- Use the right size water heater for your needs. An oversized unit wastes energy heating unneeded water. An undersized unit will not deliver all the hot water you want when you need it.
- When shopping for a water heater, look for the yellow-and-black federal EnergyGuide label to learn the estimated yearly energy cost of a unit.

Air Conditioning

- Clean or replace the filter in an air conditioner at the beginning of the cooling season. Then check it once a month and clean or change the filter if necessary. A dirty filter blocks the flow of air.
- Adjust the temperature control setting to provide a room temperature no lower than 78 degrees. Use a good wall thermometer to tell which setting will provide the desired temperature.
- Close draperies and shades to block out the sun's heat.
- When shopping for a new room air conditioner, look for the yellow-and-black federal EnergyGuide label to learn the Energy Efficiency Rating (EER) and the estimated yearly operating cost. The higher the EER, the less electricity will be used for a cooling job.
- Read the manufacturer's instructions; follow closely.
- If you have a central air conditioning system, run your hands along the ducts while it is operating to check for air leaks. Repair leaks with duct tape. Make sure the duct system is properly insulated.
- On many days, a window fan can cool an apartment as effectively as an air conditioner, and it is less costly.

Refrigerators and Freezers

The refrigerator operates 24 hours a day, every day, so it is one of the biggest users of energy in the home all year.

- Keep the condenser coils clean. The coils are on the back or at the bottom of the refrigerator. Carefully wipe, vacuum or brush the coils to remove dust and dirt at least once a year.
- Examine door gaskets and hinges regularly for air leaks. The doors should fit tightly. To check, place a piece of paper between the door and the cabinet. Close the door with normal force, then try to pull the paper straight out. There should be a slight resistance. Test all around the door, including the hinge side. If there are any places where the paper slides out easily, you need to adjust the hinges or replace the gasket, or both.
- Pause before opening your refrigerator door. Think of everything you will need before you open the door so you do not have to go back several times. When you open the door, close it quickly to keep the cool air in.
- Adjust the temperature-setting dial of the refrigerator as the manufacturer recommends. Use a thermometer to check the temperature (38 to 40 degrees is usually recommended for the refrigerator; zero degrees for the freezer). Settings that are too cold waste electricity.
- If you have a manual-defrost refrigerator, do not allow the ice to build up more than $1/4$ inch thick.
- Keep your refrigerator well-stocked but allow room for air to circulate around the food.
- The freezer, on the other hand, should be packed full. If necessary, fill empty spaces with bags of ice cubes or fill milk cartons with water and freeze.
- When you are going to be away from home for a week or more, turn off and unplug the refrigerator, empty and clean it, and prop the door open.
- If you are buying a new refrigerator, look for one with a humid-dry ("power-saver") switch. This switch is used to turn off "anti-sweat" heaters in the doors to save electricity when the heaters are not needed.
- When shopping for a new refrigerator or freezer, eliminate those too large for your needs; look for the federal EnergyGuide label to help you select an efficient unit.

Cooking

- Cook as many dishes in the oven at one time as you can instead of cooking each separately. If recipes call for slightly different temperatures, say 325, 350, and 375 degrees, pick the middle temperature of 350 to cook all 3 dishes and remove each dish as it's done.

Tips for Fuel-Efficient Driving

Source: U.S. Environmental Protection Agency

When Buying a New Vehicle

- Buy the type of vehicle that best suits your needs. Check the federal *Gas Mileage Guide*, available free at all auto dealerships, to compare the fuel economy of similar models. In general, *larger displacement engines and higher horsepower ratings will result in lower fuel economy.* The additional power and torque may be useful for mountain driving or trailer towing situations, but your fuel economy will suffer during almost all types of driving. *Avoid unnecessary optional equipment* (especially heavy options such as four-wheel drive and options such as air conditioning that tax the engine). Extra equipment adds weight and decreases the fuel economy of the vehicle. Beware of "sport" packages, which often include fuel-guzzling features such as energy robbing tires that are not reflected by *Guide* mileage values.

Conserving Fuel with your Current Vehicle:

- Drive your vehicle wisely. *Avoid idles* of more than one minute (turn off your engine in traffic jams, limit vehicle warm-ups in winter, park and go in instead of using drive-up lanes at restaurants and banks). *Go easy on the brakes and gas pedal* (anticipate stops and avoid "jack-rabbit" starts). Pay attention to speed. *You can improve your fuel economy about 15 percent by driving 55 mph rather than

65 mph.* Put your vehicle's transmission into overdrive or a "fuel economy" position when cruising on the highway. If you have manual transmission, follow recommended shift guidelines or heed your shift indicator light. *Do not carry unneeded items* that add weight. Reduce drag by placing items inside the vehicle or trunk rather than on roof racks. *Use air conditioning only when necessary.*

- Maintain your vehicle regularly. *Periodic tune-ups improve vehicle fuel economy and performance.* Dragging brakes, low transmission fluid levels, out of tune engines, and old plugged fuel or air filters all hurt fuel economy. *Inflate tires* to maximum recommended pressure and perform periodic *wheel alignments. Use energy conserving oils* which increase fuel economy by reducing internal engine friction (the best are labeled "Energy Conserving II").

- Keep track of your vehicle's fuel economy. A marked increase in the amount of fuel you use could indicate the need for a tune-up, or serve as an early signal for necessary repairs.

- Use your vehicle effectively. *Use your vehicle only when necessary.* Combine errands into one trip. If you have access to more than one vehicle, drive the one that's most fuel efficient whenever possible. Consider carpooling, bicycling, walking, or public transportation.

Fuel Economy in 1992 Cars: Comparative Miles per Gallon

Source: Environmental Protection Agency, U.S. Dept. of Energy

Highest and Lowest in Each Size

Size Class	Model	Size/No Cylinders	Trans.	City	Hwy.	Avg. Annual Fuel Cost
Highest						
2-seater	Geo Metro LSi Convertible	1.0L/3	M5	41	46	$419
Minicompact	Nissan NX	1.6L/4	M5	28	38	562
Subcompact	Geo Metro XFi	1.0L/3	M5	53	58	328
Compact	Ford Escort FS	1.9L/4	M5	32	40	515
Mid Size	Mazda 626/MX-6	2.2L/4	M5	24	31	666
Large	Saab 9000	2.3L/4	M5	20	26	819
Small Wagon	Ford Escort Wagon	1.9L/4	M5	30	37	545
	Lincoln-Mercury Tracer Wagon	1.9L/5	M5	30	37	545
Mid-Size W.	Eagle Summit Wagon	1.8L/4	M5	23	29	720
Lowest						
2-seater	Lamborghini DB 132/Diablo	5.7L/12	M5	9	14	1,841
Minicompact	Porsche 911 Turbo	3.3L/6	M5	13	21	1,266
Subcompact	Rolls-Royce Bentley Continental	6.8L/8	L4	10	14	1,687
	Rolls-Royce Corniche IV	6.8L/8	L4	10	14	1,687
Compact	BMW M5	3.5L/6	M5	12	23	1,351
Mid Size	Rolls-Royce Bentley 88/Mulsanne	6.8L/8	L4	10	14	1,687
	Silver Spirit II/Silver S	6.8L/8	L4	10	14	1,687
Large	Cadillac Fleetwood/Deville	4.9L/8	L4	16	25	1,065
	Pontiac Bonneville	3.8L/6	L4	16	25	1,065
Small Wagon	Subaru Legacy 4WD Turbo	2.2L/4	L4	18	23	1,012
Mid-Size W.	Mercedes-Benz 300TE-4Matic	3.0L/6	A4	16	20	1,126

Transmission: M=manual, A=automatic, L=lockup feature; numbers refer to speeds, W=wagon.

Other Gas Guzzlers

Size Class	Model	Size/No. Cylinders	Trans.	City	Hwy.	Avg. Annual Fuel Cost
2-Seater	Cadillac Allante	4.5L/8	L4	15	22	$1,191
	Ferrari F40	2.9L/8	M5	12	17	1,446
	Ferrari Testarossa	4.9L/12	M5	11	16	1,687
	Ferrari 348 TB/TS	3.4L/8	M5	13	18	1,351
	Jaguar XJ-S Convertible	5.3L/12	A3	13	17	1,351
	Mercedes-Benz 300SL	3.0L/6	A5	16	23	1,065
	Mercedes-Benz 500 SL	5.0L/8	A4	14	18	1,266
	Porsche 911 Carrera 4/2	3.6L/6	M5	15	23	1,126
Minicompact	Porsche 911 Carrera 4/2	3.6L/6	M5	15	23	1,126
Subcompact	Aston-Martin Virage Saloon	5.3L/8	L3	11	15	1,557
	BMW 850i	5.0L/12	L4	12	18	1,285
	Ferrari Mondial T/Cabriolet	3.4L/8	M5	13	17	1,446
	Jaguar XJ-S Coupe	5.3L/12	A3	13	18	1,351
Compact	BMW 535i	3.4L/6	L4	16	22	1,001
	Mercedes-Benz 300E-4Matic	3.0L/6	A4	16	20	1,126
Mid-Size	BMW 735i	3.4L/6	L4	15	21	1,058
	BMW 735iL	3.4L/6	L4	15	21	1,058
	BMW 750iL	5.0L/12	L4	12	18	1,285
	Infiniti Q45	4.5L/8	L4	16	22	1,126
	Infiniti Q45 Full-Active Suspension	4.5L/8	L4	14	19	1,266
	Rolls-Royce Bentley Turbo R/Turbo R(L	6.8L/8	L4	11	16	1,557
Mid-Size Wagon	Mercedes-Benz 300TE	3.0L/6	A4	17	21	1,126

U.S. Passport, Visa, and Health Requirements

Source: Bureau of Consular Affairs, U.S. Dept. of State as of Nov. 1, 1991

Passports are issued by the U.S. Department of State to citizens and nationals of the United States for the purpose of documenting them for foreign travel and identifying them as Americans.

How to Obtain a Passport

Applicants who have never been issued a passport in their own name must execute an application in person before (1) a passport agent; (2) a clerk of any federal court or state court of record or a judge or clerk of any probate court accepting applications; (3) a postal employee designated by the postmaster at a post office which has been selected to accept passport applications; or (4) a U.S. diplomatic or consular officer abroad. A DSP-11 is the correct form to use for applicants who must apply in person. All persons are required to obtain individual passports in their own name. An applicant who is 13 years of age or older is required to appear in person before the clerk or agent executing the application. A parent or legal guardian may execute the application for children under 13.

A full validity passport previously issued to the applicant, or one in which he was included, will be accepted as proof of U.S. citizenship. If the applicant has no prior passport and was born in the U.S. a certified copy of their birth certificate shall be presented to the agent accepting the passport application. To be acceptable, the certificate must show the given name and surname, the date and place of birth, and that the birth record was filed shortly after birth. A delayed birth certificate (a record filed more than one year after the date of birth) is acceptable provided that it shows acceptable secondary evidence was used for creating this record.

If such primary evidence is not obtainable, a notice from state registrar shall be submitted stating that no birth record exists. The notice shall be accompanied by the best obtainable secondary evidence such as a baptismal certificate, or a hospital birth record.

A naturalized citizen with no previous passport must present a Certificate of Naturalization. A person born abroad claiming U.S. citizenship through either a native-born or naturalized citizen parent must submit a Certificate of Citizenship issued by the Immigration and Naturalization Service; or a Consular Report of Birth or Certification of Birth Abroad issued by the Dept. of State. If one of the above documents has not been obtained, evidence of citizenship of the parent(s) through whom citizenship is claimed and evidence which would establish the parent/child relationship must be submitted. Additionally, if citizenship is derived through birth to citizen parent(s), the following documents will be required: parents' marriage certificate plus an affidavit from parent(s) showing periods and places of residence or physical presence in the U.S. and abroad, specifying periods spent abroad in the employment of the U.S. government, including the armed forces, or with certain international organizations. If citizenship is derived through naturalization of parents, evidence of admission to the U.S. for permanent residence also will be required.

Persons who possess the most recent passport in their current name issued within the last 12 years and after their 16th birthday may be eligible to apply for a new passport by mail. A form DSP-82, Application for Passport by Mail must be filled out and mailed to the nearest passport agency, together with their previous passport, 2 recent identical photographs and $35.00. The DSP-82 may not be used if the most recent passport has been altered or mutilated.

Contract Employees — Persons traveling because of a contract with the U.S. Government must submit with their application: letters from their employer stating position, destination and purpose of travel, armed forces contract number, and expiration date of contract when pertinent.

Photographs, Fees and Identity

Photographs — Submit 2 identical photographs which are sufficiently recent (normally not more than 6 months old) to be a good likeness of and satisfactorily identify the applicant. Photographs should be 2 X 2 inches in size. The image size measured from the bottom of the chin to the top of the head (including hair) should be not less than one inch nor more than 1 3/8 inches. Photographs should be portrait-type prints. They must be clear, front view, full face, with a plain, white or off-white background. Photographs which depict the applicant as relaxed and smiling are encouraged.

Fees — The passport fee is $30.00 for passports issued to persons under 18 years of age. These passports are valid for 5 years from the date of issue. The passport fee is $55.00 for passports issued to persons 18 and older. These passports are valid for 10 years from the date of issuance. An additional fee of $10.00 is charged for the execution of the application. There is no acceptance fee when using DSP-82, "Application For Passport By Mail." Applicants eligible to use this form pay only the $35.00 passport fee.

Identity—Applicants must also establish their identity to the satisfaction of the person accepting the application and to Passport Services. To establish identity, applicants may use a previous U.S. passport, a Certificate of Naturalization, a Certificate of Citizenship, a valid driver's license, or a government identification card. Applicants may not use a Social Security card, learner's or temporary driver's license, credit card, or expired identity card. Extremely old documents cannot be used by themselves. Applicants unable to establish their identity must take the identification cards they have in their own name (i.e. Social Security card) and in addition, they must be accompanied by a person who has known them for at least 2 years and who is a U.S. citizen or legal U.S. permanent resident alien. That person must sign an affidavit before the individual who executes the passport application. The witness will be required to establish his or her own identity.

The loss or theft of a valid passport is a serious matter and should be reported immediately to Passport Services, 1425 K Street, N.W., Dept. of State, Wash., D.C. 20524, tel: (202) 647-0518 or to the nearest passport agency, or the nearest U.S. embassy or consulate when abroad.

Foreign Regulations

A visa, usually rubber stamped in a passport by a representative of the country to be visited, indicates that the bearer of the passport is permitted to enter that country for a certain purpose and length of time. In most instances, you must obtain necessary visas before you leave the U.S. Apply directly to the embassy or nearest consulate of each country you plan to visit, or consult a travel agent.

The State Dept's. "Foreign Entry Requirements," contains entry requirements and application instructions for most foreign countries and is available for 50¢ from the Consumer Information Center, Dept. 438T, Pueblo, CO 81009.

The process may take several weeks, so it is important to apply well in advance and verify requirements with the embassy or nearest consulate of each country before applying.

Aliens — An alien leaving the U.S. must request a passport from the embassy of the country of their nationality, must have a permit from his local Collector of Internal Revenue, and if they wish to return, should request a re-entry permit from the Immigration and Naturalization Service if it is required.

How to Obtain Birth, Marriage, Death Records

The pamphlets, "How You May Save Time Proving Your Age and Other Birth Facts," and "Where to Write for Vital Records: Births, Deaths, Marriages, and Divorces," are available from the U.S. Dept. of Health and Human Services, National Center for Health Statistics, Rockville, MD 20852; "Guide to Geneological Research in the National Archives" is sold by the National Archives Trust Fund Board, P.O. Box 100793, Atlanta, GA 30384. "Where to Write for Birth and Death Records of U.S. Citizens Who Were Born or Died Outside the U.S. and Birth Certifications for Alien Children Adopted by U.S. Citizens" is available from Passport Services, Correspondence Branch, U.S. Dept. of State, Washington, DC 20524.

Copyright Law of The United States

Source: Copyright Office, Library of Congress

What Copyright Is

Copyright is a form of protection provided by the laws of the United States (title 17, U.S. Code) to the authors of "original works of authorship" including literary, dramatic, musical, artistic, and certain other intellectual works. This protection is available to both published and unpublished works. Section 106 of the Copyright Act generally gives the owner of copyright the exclusive right to do and to authorize others to do the following:

- *To reproduce* the copyrighted work in copies or phonorecords;
- To prepare *derivative works* based upon the copyrighted work;
- *To distribute copies or phonorecords* of the copyrighted work to the public by sale or other transfer of ownership, or by rental, lease, or lending;
- *To perform the copyrighted work publicly,* in the case of literary, musical, dramatic, and choreographic works, pantomimes, and motion pictures and other audiovisual works; and
- *To display the copyrighted work publicly,* in the case of literary, musical, dramatic, and choreographic works, pantomimes, and pictorial, graphic, or sculptural works, including the individual images of a motion picture or other audiovisual work.

It is illegal for anyone to violate any of the rights provided by the Act to the owner of copyright. These rights, however, are not unlimited in scope. Sections 107 through 118 of the Copyright Act establish limitations on these rights. In some cases, these limitations are specified exemptions from copyright liability. One major limitation is the doctrine of "fair use," which is given a statutory basis by section 107 of the Act. In other instances, the limitation takes the form of a "compulsory license" under which certain limited uses of copyrighted works are permitted upon payment of specified royalties and compliance with statutory conditions.

Copyright protection subsists from the time the work is created in fixed form; that is, it is an incident of the process of authorship. The copyright in the work of authorship *immediately* becomes the property of the author who created it. Only the author or those deriving their rights from the author can rightfully claim copyright.

In the case of works made for hire, the employer and not the employee is presumptively considered the author. Section 101 of the copyright statute defines a "work made for hire" as:

(1) a work prepared by an employee within the scope of his or her employment; or

(2) a work specially ordered or commissioned for use as a contribution to a collective work, as a part of a motion picture or other audiovisual work, as a translation, as a supplementary work, as a compilation, as an instructional text, as a test, as answer material for a test, or as an atlas, if the parties expressly agree in a written instrument signed by them that the work shall be considered a work made for hire.

The authors of a joint work are co-owners of the copyright in the work, unless there is an agreement to the contrary.

Copyright in each separate contribution to a periodical or other collective work is distinct from copyright in the collective work as a whole and vests initially with the author of the contribution.

Works published on or after January 1, 1978, are subject to protection under the copyright statute if, on the date of first publication, one or more of the authors is a national or domiciliary of the U.S., or is a national, domiciliary, or soverign authority of a foreign nation that is a party to a copyright treaty to which the U.S. is also a party, or is a stateless person, regardless of domicile, or if the work is first published either in the U.S. or in a foreign nation that on the date of first publication is a party to the Universal Copyright Convention or the Berne Union.

What Works Are Protected

Copyright protects "original works of authorship" that are fixed in a tangible form of expression. The fixation need not be directly perceptible, so long as it may be communicated with the aid of a machine or device. Copyrightable works include the following categories:

(1) literary works;

(2) musical works, including any accompanying words;

(3) dramatic works, including any accompanying music;

(4) pantomimes and choreographic works;

(5) pictorial, graphic, and sculptural works;

(6) motion pictures and other audiovisual works;

(7) sound recordings; and

(8) architectural works.

These categories should be viewed quite broadly: for example, computer programs and most "compilations" are registrable as "literary works"; maps and architectural plans are registrable as "pictorial, graphic, and sculptural works."

What Is Not Protected By Copyright

Several categories of material are generally not eligible for statutory copyright protection. These include among others:

- Works that have *not* been fixed in a tangible form of expression. For example: choreographic works that have not been notated or recorded, or improvisational speeches or performances that have not been written or recorded.
- Titles, names, short phrases, and slogans; familiar symbols or designs; mere variations of typographic ornamentation, lettering, or coloring; mere listings of ingredients or contents.
- Ideas, procedures, methods, systems, processes, concepts, principles, discoveries, or devices, as distinguished from a description, explanation, or illustration.
- Works consisting *entirely* of information that is common property and containing no original authorship. For example: standard calendars, height and weight charts, tape measures and rulers, and lists or tables taken from public documents or other common sources.

Notice of Copyright

For works first published on and after March 1, 1989, use of the copyright notice is optional, though highly recommended. Before March 1, 1989, the use of the notice was mandatory on all published works, and any work first published before that date *must* bear a notice or risk loss of copyright protection.

Use of the notice is recommended because it informs the public that the work is protected by copyright, identifies the copyright owner, and shows the year of first publication. Furthermore, in the event that a work is infringed, if the work carries a proper notice, the court will not allow a defendant to claim "innocent infringement"—that is, that he or she did not realize that the work is protected. (A successful innocent infringement claim may result in a reduction in damages that the copyright owner would otherwise receive.)

The use of the copyright notice is the responsibility of the copyright owner and does not require advance permission from, or registration with, the Copyright Office.

For visually perceptible copies, the form of the notice consists of the following: © (the letter C in a circle), the word "Copyright," or "Copr.," and the year of first publication, and the name of the owner of copyright in the work. Example: © 1991 Judy Smith. The notice must be affixed in such manner and location as to give reasonable notice of the claim of copyright.

The notice of copyright prescribed for all published phonorecords of sound recordings consists of the symbol ℗ (the letter P in a circle), the year of first publication of the sound recording, and the name of the owner of copyright in the sound recording. Example ℗ 1991 XYZ Records, Inc. The notice on phonorecords may appear on the surface of the phonorecord or on the phonorecord label or container, provided the manner of placement and location give reasonable notice of the claim.

How Long Copyright Protection Endures

Works Originally Copyrighted on or After January 1, 1978

A work that is created (fixed in tangible form for the first time) on or after January 1, 1978, is automatically protected from the moment of its creation, and is ordinarily given a term enduring for the author's life, plus an additional 50 years after the author's death. In the case of "a joint work prepared by two or more authors who did not work for hire," the term lasts for 50 years after the last surviving author's death. For works made for hire, and for anonymous and pseudonymous works (unless the author's identity is revealed in Copyright Office records), the duration of copyright will be 75 years from publication or 100 years from creation, whichever is shorter.

Works that were created but not published or registered for copyright before January 1, 1978, have been automatically brought under the statute and are now given Federal copyright protection. The duration of copyright in these works will generally be computed in the same way as for works created on or after January 1, 1978: the life-plus-50 or 75/100-year terms will apply to them as well. The law provides that in no case will the term of copyright for works in this category expire before December 31, 2002, and for works published on or before December 31, 2002, the term of copyright will not expire before December 31, 2027.

Works Copyrighted Before January 1, 1978

Under the law in effect before 1978, copyright was secured either on the date a work was published or on the date of registration if the work was registered in unpublished form. In either case, the copyright endured for a first term of 28 years from the date it was secured. During the last (28th) year of the first term, the copyright was eligible for renewal. The current copyright law has extended the renewal term from 28 to 47 years for copyrights that were subsisting on January 1, 1978, making these works eligible for a total term of protection of 75 years. However, the copyright *must* be renewed to receive the 47-year period of added protection. This is accomplished by filing a properly completed Form RE accompanied by a $12 filing fee in the Copyright Office before the end of the 28th calendar year of the original term.

International Copyright Protection

There is no such thing as an "international copyright" that will automatically protect an author's writings throughout the entire world. Protection against unauthorized use in a particular country depends, basically, on the national laws of that country. However, most countries do offer protection to foreign works under certain conditions, and these conditions have been greatly simplified by international copyright treaties and conventions. The U.S. belongs to both global, multilateral copyright treaties—the Universal Copyright Convention (UCC) and the Berne Convention for the Protection of Literary and Artistic Works.

A U.S. author may obtain copyright protection in all countries that are members of the Berne Union and the Universal Copyright Convention. A work first published in the U.S. or another Berne Union country (or first published in a non-Berne Union country, followed by publication within 30 days in a Berne Union country) is eligible for protection in all Berne member countries. There are no special requirements. In UCC member countries, where no formalities are required, the works of U.S. authors are also automatically protected. Member countries whose laws impose formalities protect U.S. works if all published copies bear a Convention notice, which consists of the symbol ©, together with the name of the copyright owner and the year of publication. Example: © JOHN DOE 1990.

For a list of countries that maintain copyright relations with the U.S., write or call the Copyright Office and ask for Circular 38a.

Copyright Registration

Copyright registration is a legal formality intended to make a public record of the basic facts of a particular copyright and is not a condition of copyright protection. Even though registration is not generally a requirement for protection, the copyright law provides several inducements or advantages to encourage copyright owners to register. Among these advantages are the following:

• Registration establishes a public record of the copyright claim;

• Before an infringement suit may be filed in court, registration is necessary for works of U.S. origin and for foreign works not originating in a Berne Union country. (For more information on when a work is of U.S. origin, contact the Copyright Office);

• If made before or within 5 years of first publication, registration will establish prima facie evidence in court of the validity of the copyright and of the facts stated in the certificate; and

• If registration is made within 3 months after first publication of the work or prior to an infringement of the work, statutory damages and attorney's fees will be available to the copyright owner in court actions. Otherwise, only an award of actual damages and profits is available to the copyright owner.

Registration may be made at any time within the life of the copyright. When a work has been registered in unpublished form, it is not necessary to make another registration when the work becomes published (although the copyright owner may register the published edition, if desired).

The process of registration is quite simple. An appropriate form is requested from the Copyright Office and completed. It is returned to the Copyright Office along with a $20 nonrefundable filing fee and the appropriate deposit(s) of the work for which registration is sought. In a common example—a published book—the deposit is two copies of the best edition of the book. A certificate of registration is sent once the paperwork is completed, a process that usually takes several months due to the large volume of registrations the Office must handle.

Although a copyright registration is not required, the Copyright Act establishes a mandatory deposit requirement for works published in the U.S. In general, the owner of copyright, or the owner of the exclusive right of publication in the work, has a legal obligation to deposit in the Copyright Office, within three months of publication in the U.S., two copies (or, in the case of sound recordings, two phonorecords) for the use of the Library of Congress. Failure to make the deposit can result in fines and other penalties, but does not affect copyright protection. Certain categories of works are *exempt entirely* from the mandatory deposit requirements, and the obligation is reduced for certain other categories.

Information on registration and application forms may be obtained free of charge by writing the Copyright Office, Information Section, LM-455, Library of Congress, Washington, DC 20559. Registration application forms and circulars may be ordered on a 24-hour basis by calling (202) 707-9100. Request Circular 1 for additional general information on copyright, including a list of which application forms to use when registering specific types of works.

Birthstones

Source: Jewelry Industry Council

Month	Ancient	Modern
January	Garnet	Garnet
February	Amethyst	Amethyst
March	Jasper	Bloodstone or Aquamarine
April	Sapphire	Diamond
May	Agate	Emerald
June	Emerald	Pearl, Moonstone, or Alexandrite

Month	Ancient	Modern
July	Onyx	Ruby
August	Carnelian	Sardonyx or Peridot
September	Chrysolite	Sapphire
October	Aquamarine	Opal or Tourmaline
November	Topaz	Topaz
December	Ruby	Turquoise or Zircon

Home Buyer's Glossary

Amortization: The gradual repayment of a mortgage over time, usually according to a predetermined schedule.

Appraisal: An opinion or estimate of the value of property, usually made by lenders before they will determine how much of a mortgage they will extend.

Assumable mortgage: The purchaser takes ownership of real estate encumbered by an existing mortgage and assumes responsibility as the guarantor for the unpaid balance of the mortgage.

Balloon payment: The final payment on a loan, usually substantially larger than previous payments, which repays the loan in full.

Binder: A preliminary and temporary agreement between the seller and the buyer, generally agreeing to the price of a house before a formal contract.

Broker: Usually, a licensed agent of, and paid by, the seller to serve as an intermediary in real estate transactions.

Closing: The day of judgment, when after writing numerous checks to cover various fees, the title passes to the buyer.

Commission: The fee paid by a seller to a broker for the sale of the house. Fee is negotiable.

Condominium: A form of ownership, not a kind of development, in which the owner gets title to a housing unit and an interest in the common areas.

Cooperative: A type of ownership in which buyers get shares in the cooperative corporation that owns the building. Those shares give the buyer a proprietary lease on an apartment in that building.

Deed: A written document that conveys title in the property.

Equity: The value of property minus the mortgage and other liens against it.

Escrow: Money paid monthly to the lender, along with the mortgage payment, for use in paying taxes and sometimes insurance. The lender keeps the funds separately and pays bills when due.

Foreclosure: Forced sale of property to meet debt obligations; usually to a lending or taxing institution.

Freddie Mac: The Federal Home Loan Mortgage Corp., a major secondary mortgage market agency that buys mortgages from lenders, allowing them to make new loans with the proceeds.

FHA: The Federal Housing Administration, a division of the Department of Housing and Urban Development that insures, but does not make, mortgages.

Fannie Mae: Federal National Mortgage Association, the largest secondary mortgage agency.

Ginnie Mae: Government National Mortgage Association, a government-owned secondary market agency that buys FHA-insured loans from lenders.

Indexing: Adjusting the interest rate on a loan in accordance with the movements of an index or economic indicator, i.e., the U.S. Treasury bill rate or the consumer price index.

Interest: Money paid for the use of money. There are two kinds of interest. Simple interest is interest that is earned and paid. Compound interest is the accumulated interest that is added to the principal amount.

Lien: A right to property obtained as collateral to a loan or debt. A mortgage is a lien.

Mortgage: A written pledge of property as collateral for a loan.

The most common type of mortgage is the *fixed rate mortgage*, in which the monthly payments remain the same over the life of the loan; and the *adjustable rate mortgage* (ARM) where the interest rate is tied to a financial index (the one-year Treasury bill rate and the savings and loan cost-of-funds index are most common). With an ARM, the monthly payments usually vary over the life of the loan. In some cases, the total number of monthly payments can be increased or decreased with the amount remaining the same. In 1989, nearly half of new mortgages were ARMs.

Another type of mortgage is the *graduated payment mortgage*, which has a fixed interest rate but lower initial payments, usually for the first 5 years of the loan. This type of mortgage is advantageous to the first-time homeowner. There is also the *shared-appreciation mortgage*, in which a borrower agrees to share the appreciation of the property with the lender in return for a lower interest rate. *Reverse mortgages* allow elderly homeowners to convert some of their accumulated housing equity into cash.

Origination Fee: A fee paid by a borrower for the cost of evaluating and documenting a loan.

Points: Additional payments made by a borrower to a lender; a point equals 1 percent of the loan.

Prepayment penalty: An extra fee charged for paying off a mortgage before it is due.

Principal: The total amount of a mortgage debt. The amount upon which the interest is computed.

Title: Evidence of a person's ownership of a piece of property.

Median Price of Existing Single-Family Homes

Source: National Association of Realtors

(Thousands of dollars)

City[1]	1988	1989	1990	City[1]	1988	1989	1990
Akron, Oh.	$59,900	$64,500	$67,700	Los Angeles, Cal.	$178,900	$214,800	$212,800
Albuquerque, N.M.	80,400	83,000	84,500	Louisville, Ky.	54,500	58,400	60,800
Anaheim/Santa Ana, Cal.	203,900	241,700	242,400	Madison, Wis.	72,000	76,500	82,300
Atlanta, Ga.	NA	84,000	86,400	Memphis, Tenn.	76,300	78,100	78,100
Baltimore, Md.	88,700	96,300	105,900	Miami/Hialeah, Fla.	82,900	86,900	89,300
Baton Rouge, La.	64,700	63,800	64,900	Milwaukee, Wis.	74,500	79,600	84,400
Birmingham, Ala.	75,700	78,500	80,800	Minneapolis/St. Paul, Minn.	85,200	87,200	88,700
Boston, Mass.	181,200	181,900	174,200	Mobile, Ala.	53,000	56,700	59,100
Bradenton, Fla.	66,100	68,100	69,600	Nashville/Davidson, Tenn.	77,600	79,900	81,800
Buffalo, N.Y.	65,500	72,500	77,200	New Haven, Conn.	169,400	163,400	153,300
Charleston, S.C.	73,100	74,500	76,200	New Orleans, La.	73,100	70,600	67,800
Chicago, Ill.	89,000	107,000	116,800	New York, N.Y.	183,800	183,200	174,900
Cincinnati, Oh.	69,700	75,800	79,800	Oklahoma City, Okla.	56,200	53,500	53,200
Cleveland, Oh.	69,200	75,200	80,600	Omaha, Neb.	59,500	60,600	63,000
Columbia, S.C.	69,700	73,900	77,100	Orlando, Fla.	79,100	79,800	62,800
Columbus, Oh.	72,600	77,900	81,600	Philadelphia, Pa.	102,400	103,900	108,700
Corpus Christi, Tex.	64,900	64,900	63,200	Phoenix, Ariz.	80,000	78,800	84,000
Dallas, Tex.	90,800	93,400	89,500	Pittsburgh, Pa.	63,200	65,800	70,100
Daytona Beach, Fla.	62,600	63,400	64,100	Portland, Ore.	64,400	70,100	79,500
Denver, Col.	81,800	85,500	86,400	Providence, R.I.	130,600	130,200	127,900
Des Moines, Ia.	55,800	57,500	60,500	Sacramento, Cal.	94,600	111,700	137,100
Detroit, Mich.	73,100	73,700	76,700	St. Louis, Mo.	78,100	76,900	75,700
El Paso, Tex.	59,600	63,100	63,600	Salt Lake City/Ogden, Ut.	67,700	69,400	69,400
Grand Rapids, Mich.	57,900	64,200	68,300	San Antonio, Tex.	65,000	64,200	63,600
Hartford, Conn.	167,600	165,900	157,300	San Diego, Cal.	153,400	181,900	183,600
Honolulu, Hi.	210,000	270,000	352,000	San Francisco, Cal.	212,900	260,600	259,300
Houston, Tex.	61,800	66,700	70,700	Seattle, Wash.	94,000	115,000	142,000
Indianapolis, Ind.	66,100	71,200	74,800	Spokane, Wash.	51,100	52,400	55,500
Jacksonville, Fla.	67,700	69,300	72,400	Syracuse, N.Y.	74,600	79,300	80,700
Kansas City, Mo.	70,500	71,600	74,100	Tampa, Fla.	65,600	71,900	71,400
Knoxville, Tenn.	67,000	71,100	75,400	Toledo, Oh.	58,400	60,800	62,800
Las Vegas, Nev.	78,800	85,700	93,000	Tulsa, Okla.	65,000	62,600	63,900
Little Rock, Ark.	63,900	63,700	64,800	Washington, D.C.	132,500	144,400	150,200

(1) All areas are metropolitan statistical areas as defined by the U.S. Office of Management and Budget. They include the named central city and surrounding suburban areas. NA=not available.

Housing Affordability

Source: National Association of Realtors

	Median-priced existing home	Average mortgage rate	Monthly principal and interest payment	Payment as percentage of median income		Median-priced existing home	Average mortgage rate	Monthly principal and interest payment	Payment as percentage of median income
1981	$66,400	15.12%	$677	36.3%	1987	$85,600	9.28	$565	21.9
1982	67,800	15.38	702	35.9	1988	90,600	9.31	591	22.0
1983	70,300	12.85	616	30.1	1989	93,100	10.11	660	23.1
1984	72,400	12.49	618	28.2	1990	97,500	10.04	673	22.7
1985	75,500	11.74	609	26.2	1991	99,700	9.51	671	22.3
1986	80,300	10.25%	563	23.0%					

Note: The average mortgage rate is based on the effective rate of loans closed on existing homes monitored by the Federal Home Loan Bank Board.

The 1991 numbers are for May.

Income Needed to Get a Mortgage

Source: National Association of Realtors

The following shows the minimum annual gross income needed for various size home loans at different rates. The figures are based on a 30-year loan and assume that the borrower's monthly payments can't exceed 28% of gross income, the ceiling most lenders use. The figures do not include property taxes and insurance as part of the monthly payment.

Interest rate (Percent)	$50,000	$75,000	Loan amount $100,000 income needed	$150,000	$200,000
8	$15,724	$23,586	$31,447	$47,171	$62,895
8½	16,477	24,715	32,954	49,430	65,907
9	17,242	25,863	34,484	51,726	68,968
9½	18,018	27,028	36,037	54,055	72,074
10	18,085	28,208	37,611	56,415	75,221
10½	19,602	29,403	39,203	58,805	78,406
11	20,407	30,611	40,814	61,221	81,628
11½	21,221	31,831	42,441	63,662	84,883
12	22,042	33,063	44,084	66,125	88,167
12½	22,870	34,305	45,740	68,610	91,479
13	23,704	35,556	47,409	71,113	94,817

Mortgage Payment Tables

Source: *The Mortgage Money Guide*, Federal Trade Commission

8% Annual Percent Rate

Monthly Payments (Principal and Interest)*

Amount Financed	10 Years	15 Years	20 Years	25 Years	30 Years
$ 25,000	303.32	238.91	209.11	192.95	183.44
30,000	363.98	286.70	250.93	231.54	220.13
35,000	424.65	334.48	292.75	270.14	256.82
40,000	485.31	382.26	334.58	308.73	293.51
45,000	545.97	430.04	376.40	347.32	330.19
50,000	606.64	477.83	418.22	385.91	366.88
60,000	727.97	573.39	501.86	463.09	440.26
70,000	849.29	668.96	585.51	540.27	513.64
80,000	970.62	764.52	669.15	617.45	587.01
90,000	1091.95	860.09	752.80	694.63	660.39
100,000	1213.28	955.65	836.44	771.82	733.76
120,000	1455.94	1146.78	1003.72	926.18	880.52
140,000	1698.58	1337.92	1171.02	1080.54	1027.28
160,000	1941.24	1529.04	1338.30	1234.90	1174.02
180,000	2183.90	1720.18	1505.60	1389.26	1320.78
200,000	2426.56	1911.30	1672.88	1543.64	1467.52

9% Annual Percent Rate

Monthly Payments (Principal and Interest)*

Amount Financed	10 Years	15 Years	20 Years	25 Years	30 Years
$ 25,000	316.69	253.57	224.93	209.80	201.16
30,000	380.03	304.28	269.92	251.76	241.39
35,000	443.36	354.99	314.90	293.72	281.62
40,000	506.70	405.71	359.89	335.68	321.85
45,000	570.04	456.42	404.88	377.64	362.08
50,000	633.38	507.13	449.86	419.60	402.31
60,000	760.05	608.56	539.84	503.52	482.77
70,000	886.73	709.99	629.81	587.44	563.24
80,000	1013.41	811.41	719.78	671.36	643.70
90,000	1140.08	912.84	809.75	755.28	724.16
100,000	1266.76	1014.27	899.73	839.20	804.62
120,000	1520.10	1217.12	1079.68	1007.04	965.54
140,000	1773.46	1419.98	1259.62	1174.88	1126.48
160,000	2026.82	1622.82	1439.56	1342.72	1287.40
180,000	2280.16	1825.68	1619.50	1510.56	1448.32
200,000	2533.52	2028.54	1799.46	1678.40	1609.24

10% Annual Percentage Rate

Monthly Payments (Principal and Interest)*

Amount Financed	10 Years	15 Years	20 Years	25 Years	30 Years
$ 25,000	330.38	268.65	241.26	227.18	219.39
30,000	396.45	322.38	289.51	272.61	263.27
35,000	462.53	376.11	337.76	318.05	307.15
40,000	528.60	429.84	386.01	363.48	351.03
45,000	594.68	483.57	434.26	408.92	394.91
50,000	660.75	537.30	482.51	454.35	438.79
60,000	792.90	644.76	579.01	545.22	526.54
70,000	925.06	752.22	675.52	636.09	614.30
80,000	1057.20	859.68	772.02	726.96	702.06
90,000	1189.36	967.14	868.52	817.83	789.81
100,000	1321.51	1074.61	965.02	908.70	877.57
120,000	1585.80	1289.52	1158.02	1090.44	1053.08
140,000	1850.12	1504.44	1351.04	1272.18	1228.60
160,000	2114.40	1719.36	1544.04	1453.92	1404.12
180,000	2378.72	1934.28	1737.04	1635.66	1579.62
200,000	2643.02	2149.22	1930.04	1817.40	1755.14

11% Annual Percentage Rate

Monthly Payments (Principal and Interest)*

Amount Financed	10 Years	15 Years	20 Years	25 Years	30 Years
$ 25,000	344.38	284.15	258.05	245.03	238.08
30,000	413.25	340.98	309.66	294.03	285.70
35,000	482.13	397.81	361.27	343.04	333.31
40,000	551.00	454.64	412.88	392.05	380.93
45,000	619.88	511.47	464.48	441.05	428.55

(Continuation — top right)

Amount Financed	10 Years	15 Years	20 Years	25 Years	30 Years
50,000	688.75	568.30	516.09	490.06	476.16
60,000	826.50	681.96	619.31	588.07	571.39
70,000	964.25	795.62	722.53	686.08	666.63
80,000	1102.00	909.28	825.75	784.09	761.86
90,000	1239.75	1022.94	928.97	882.10	857.09
100,000	1377.50	1136.60	1032.19	980.11	952.32
120,000	1653.00	1363.92	1238.62	1176.14	1142.78
140,000	1928.50	1591.24	1445.06	1372.16	1333.26
160,000	2204.00	1818.56	1651.50	1568.18	1523.72
180,000	2479.50	2045.88	1857.94	1764.20	1714.18
200,000	2755.00	2273.20	2064.38	1960.22	1904.64

12% Annual Percentage Rate

Monthly Payments (Principal and Interest)*

Amount Financed	10 Years	15 Years	20 Years	25 Years	30 Years
$ 25,000	358.68	300.05	275.28	263.31	257.16
30,000	430.42	360.06	330.33	315.97	308.59
35,000	502.15	420.06	385.39	368.63	360.02
40,000	573.89	480.07	440.44	421.29	411.45
45,000	645.62	540.08	495.49	473.96	462.88
50,000	717.36	600.09	550.55	526.62	514.31
60,000	860.83	720.11	660.66	631.93	617.17
70,000	1004.30	840.12	770.77	737.26	720.03
80,000	1147.77	960.14	880.87	842.58	822.90
90,000	1291.24	1080.15	990.98	947.90	925.75
100,000	1434.71	1200.17	1101.09	1053.23	1028.62
120,000	1721.66	1440.22	1321.32	1263.86	1234.34
140,000	2008.60	1680.24	1541.54	1474.52	1440.06
160,000	2295.54	1920.28	1761.74	1685.16	1645.80
180,000	2582.48	2160.30	1981.96	1895.80	1851.50
200,000	2869.42	2400.34	2202.18	2106.46	2057.24

13% Annual Percentage Rate

Monthly Payments (Principal and Interest)*

Amount Financed	10 Years	15 Years	20 Years	25 Years	30 Years
$ 25,000	373.28	316.32	292.90	281.96	276.55
30,000	447.94	379.58	351.48	338.36	331.86
35,000	522.59	442.84	410.06	394.75	387.17
40,000	597.25	506.10	468.64	451.14	442.48
45,000	671.90	569.36	527.21	507.53	497.79
50,000	746.56	632.63	585.79	563.92	553.10
60,000	895.87	759.15	702.95	676.71	663.72
70,000	1045.18	885.67	820.11	789.49	774.34
80,000	1194.49	1012.20	937.27	902.27	884.96
90,000	1343.80	1138.72	1054.42	1015.05	995.58
100,000	1493.11	1265.25	1171.58	1127.84	1106.20
120,000	1791.74	1518.30	1405.90	1353.42	1327.44
140,000	2090.36	1771.34	1640.22	1578.98	1548.68
160,000	2388.98	2024.40	1874.54	1804.54	1769.92
180,000	2687.60	2277.44	2108.84	2030.10	1991.16
200,000	2986.22	2530.50	2343.16	2255.68	2212.40

14% Annual Percentage Rate

Monthly Payments (Principal and Interest)*

Amount Financed	10 Years	15 Years	20 Years	25 Years	30 Years
$ 25,000	388.17	332.94	310.89	300.95	296.22
30,000	465.80	399.53	373.06	361.13	355.47
35,000	543.44	466.11	435.24	421.32	414.71
40,000	621.07	532.70	497.41	481.51	473.95
45,000	698.70	599.29	559.59	541.70	533.20
50,000	776.34	665.88	621.77	601.89	592.44
60,000	931.60	799.05	746.12	722.26	710.93
70,000	1086.87	932.22	870.47	842.64	829.42
80,000	1242.14	1065.40	994.82	963.01	947.90
90,000	1397.40	1198.57	1119.17	1083.38	1066.38
100,000	1552.67	1331.75	1243.53	1203.77	1184.88
120,000	1863.20	1598.10	1492.24	1444.52	1421.86
140,000	2173.74	1864.44	1740.94	1685.28	1658.84
160,000	2484.28	2130.80	1989.64	1926.02	1895.80
180,000	2794.80	2397.14	2238.34	2166.76	2132.76
200,000	3105.34	2663.50	2487.06	2407.54	2369.76

Marriage Laws

Source: Gary N. Skoloff, Skoloff & Wolfe, Livingston, N.J.; as of April 1, 1991

State	Age with parental consent Male	Female	Age without consent Male	Female	Physical exam & blood test for male and female Maximum period between exam and license	Scope of medical exam	Waiting period Before license	After license
Alabama*	14a	14a	18	18	—	b	—	s
Alaska	16z	16z	18	18	—	b	3 da., w	—
Arizona	16z	16z	18	18	—	—	—	—
Arkansas	17c	16c	18	18	—	—	v	—
California	aa	aa	18	18	30 da., w	bb	—	h
Colorado*	16z	16z	18	18	—	—	—	s
Connecticut	16z	16z	18	18	—	bb	4 da., w	ttt
Delaware	18c	16c	18	18	—	—	—	e, s
Florida	16a, c	16a, c	18	18	—	b	3 da.	s
Georgia*	aa	aa	16	16	—	b	3 da., g	s*
Hawaii	16d	16d	18	18	—	b	—	—
Idaho*	16z	16z	18	18	—	bb	—	—
Illinois	16	16	18	18	30 da.	b, n	—	ee
Indiana	17c	17c	18	18	—	bb	72 hrs.	t
Iowa*	18z	18z	18	18	—	—	3 da., v	tt
Kansas*y	18z	18z	18	18	—	—	3 da., w	—
Kentucky	18c, z	18c, z	18	18	—	—	—	—
Louisiana	18z	18z	18	18	10 da.	b	72 hrs., w	—
Maine	16z	16z	18	18	—	—	3 da., v, w	h
Maryland	16c, f	16c, f	18	18	—	—	48 hrs., w	ff
Massachusetts	16d	16	18	18	60 da.	bb	3 da., v	—
Michigan	16c, d	16c	18	18	30 da.	b	3 da., w	—
Minnesota	16z	16z	18	18	—	—	5 da., w	—
Mississippi	aa	aa	17gg	15gg	30 da.	b	3 da., w	—
Missouri	15d, 18z	15d, 18z	18	18	—	—	—	—
Montana*w	16	16	18	18	—	b	—	ff
Nebraskaw	17	17	18	18	—	bb	—	—
Nevada	16z	16z	18	18	—	—	—	—
New Hampshire	14j	13j	18	18	30 da.	b, l	3 da., v	h
New Jersey	16z, c	16z, c	18	18	30 da.	b	72 hrs., w	s
New Mexicoy	16d	16d	18	18	30 da.	b	—	—
New York	14j	14j	18	18	—	nn	—	24 hrs., w, t
North Carolina	16c, g	16c, g	18	18	—	m	v	—
North Dakota	16	16	18	18	—	—	—	t
Ohio*	18c, z	16c, z	18	18	30 da.	b	5 da.	t, w
Oklahoma*	16c	16c	18	18	30 da., w	b	—	s
Oregon	17	17	18	18	—	—	3 da., w	—
Pennsylvania*	16d	16d	18	18	30 da.	b	3 da., w	t
Puerto Ricoy	18c, d, z	16c, d, z	21	21	—	b	—	—
Rhode Island*	18d	16d	18	18	—	bb	—	—
South Carolina*	16c	14c	18	18	—	—	1 da.	—
South Dakota	16c	16c	18	18	—	—	—	tt
Tennessee	16d	16d	18	18	—	—	3 da., cc	s
Texas*y	14j, k	14j, k	18	18	—	—	—	s
Utah	14	14	18x	18x	30 da.	b	—	s
Vermont	16z	16z	18	18	30 da.	b	3 da., w	—
Virginia	16a, c	16a, c	18	18	—	b	—	t
Washington	17d	17d	18	18	—	bbb	3 da.	t
West Virginia	18c	18c	18	18	—	b	3 da., w	—
Wisconsin	16	16	18	18	—	—	5 da., w	s
Wyoming	16d	16d	18	18	—	bb	—	—
Dist. of Columbia*	16a	16a	18	18	30 da., w	b	3 da., w	—

*Indicates 1987 common-law marriage recognized; in many states, such marriages are only recognized if entered into many years before. (a) Parental consent not required if minor was previously married. (aa) No age limits. (b) Veneral diseases. (bb) Veneral diseases and Rubella (for female). In Colorado, Rubella for female under 45 and Rh type. (bbb) No medical exam required; however, applicants must file affidavit showing non-affliction of contagious venereal disease. (c) Younger parties may obtain license in case of pregnancy or birth of child. (cc) Unless parties are over 18 years of age. (d) Younger parties may obtain license in special circumstances. (e) Residents before expiration of 24-hour waiting period; non-residents formerly residents, before expiration of 96-hour waiting period; others 96 hours. (ee) License effective 1 day after issuance, unless court orders otherwise, valid for 60 days only. (f) If parties are under 16 years of age, proof of age and the consent of parents in person is required. If a parent is ill, an affidavit by the incapacitated parent and a physician's affidavit to that effect required. (ff) License valid for 180 days only. (g) Unless parties are 18 years of age or more, or female is pregnant, or applicants are the parents of a living child born out of wedlock. (gg) Notice to parents necessary if parties are under 21. (h) License valid for 90 days only. (j) Parental consent and/or permission of judge required. (k) Below age of consent parties need parental consent and permission of judge. (l) With each certificate issued to couples, a list of family planning agencies and services available to them is provided. (m) Mental incompetence, infectious tuberculosis, venereal diseases and Rubella (certain counties only). (n) Venereal diseases; test for sickle cell anemia given at request of examining physician. (nn) Tests for sickle cell anemia may be required for certain applicants. Marriage prohibited unless it is established that procreation is not possible. (p) If one or both parties are below the age for marriage without parental consent (3 day waiting period). (s) License valid for 30 days only. (t) License valid for 60 days only. (tt) License valid for 20 days only. (ttt) License valid for 65 days. (v) Parties must file notice of intention to marry with local clerk. (w) Waiting period may be avoided. (x) Authorizes counties to provide for premarital counseling as a requisite to issuance of license to persons under 19 and persons previously divorced. (y) Marriages by proxy are valid. (yy) Proxy marriages are valid under certain conditions. (z) Younger parties may marry with parental consent and/or permission of judge. In Connecticut, judicial approval. (zz) With consent of court.

Divorce Laws

Adapted from a revision by Gary N. Skoloff of the N.J. Bar, as of April 1, 1991. Important: almost all states also have other laws, as well as qualifications of the laws shown below and proposed divorce-reform laws pending. It would be wise to consult a lawyer in conjunction with the use of this chart.

Some grounds for absolute divorce

	Residence	Adultery	Cruelty	Desertion	Alcoholism	Impotency	Non-support	Insanity	Pregnancy at marriage	Bigamy	Separation	Felony conviction or imprisonment	Drug addiction	Fraud force, duress
PR	1 yr.	Yes	Yes	1 yr.	Yes	Yes	No	Yes	No	A	2 yrs.	Yes*	Yes	No
AL	6 mos.*	Yes	Phys. only	1 yr.	Yes	Yes*	2 yrs.	5 yrs.	Yes	A	2 yrs.*	2 yrs*	Yes	A
AK	*	Yes	Yes	1 yr.	1 yr.	Yes	No	18 mos.	No	A	No	Yes	Yes	A
AZ	90 da.	No	No	No	No	Yes	No	No	No	A	No	No	No	No
AR	60 da.	Yes	Yes	1 yr.	1 yr.	Yes	Yes	3 yrs.	No	No	3 yrs.	Yes	No	A
CA	6 mos.	No	No	No	No	A	No	Yes, A	No	A	No	No	No	A
CO	90 da.	No	No	No	No	No	No	No	No	A	No	No	No	A
CT	1 yr.*	Yes	Yes	1 yr.	Yes	A	No	5 yrs.	Yes*	A	18 mos.*	life*	No	Yes
DE	6 mos.	Yes	Yes	Yes	Yes	A	No	A	No	Yes	6 mos.	Yes	No	No
FL	6 mos.	No	No	No	No	No	No	3 yrs.	No	No	No	No	No	No
GA	6 mos.	Yes	Yes	1 yr.	Yes	Yes	No	2 yrs.	Yes	A	No	Yes*	Yes	Yes
HI	6 mos.*	No	No	No	No	No	No	A	No	A	2 yrs.*	No	No	A
ID	6 wks.	Yes	Yes	Yes	Yes	A	Yes	3 yrs.	Yes	A	5 yrs.	Yes	No	A
IL	90 da.	Yes	Yes	1 yr.	2 yrs.	Yes	No	No	No	Yes	2 yrs.*	Yes	2 yrs.	No
IN	6 mos.*	No	No	No	No	No	Yes	2 yrs.	No	A	No	Yes	No	No
IA	1 yr.*	No	No	No	No	A	No	A	No	A	No	No	No	No
KS	60 da.	No	No	No	No	No	Yes	2 yrs.	A	A	No	No	No	A
KY	180 da.	No	No	No	No	A	No	No	No	No	No	No	No	A
LA	1 yr.*	Yes	Yes	Yes	Yes	No	Yes	No	No	A	6 mos.	Yes*	No	A
ME	6 mos.*	Yes	Yes	3 yrs.	Yes	Yes	Yes	No	No	No	No	No	No	No
MD	1 yr.	Yes	No	1 yr.*	No	No	No	3 yrs.	No	A	1 yr.*	1 yr.*	No	No
MA	1 yr.*	Yes	Yes	1 yr.	Yes	Yes	Yes	No	No	A	No	5 yrs.	Yes	No
MI	180 da.	No	No	No	No	No	No	No	No	A	No	No	No	A
MN	180 da.	No	No	No	No	No	No	No	No	No	No	No	No	A
MS	6 mos.	Yes	Yes	1 yr.	Yes	Yes	No	3 yrs.	Yes	Yes	No	Yes*	Yes	A
MO	90 da.	No	No	No	No	No	No	No	No	No	No	No	No	A
MT	90 da.	No	No	No	A	No	No	No	No	No	180 da.*	No	No	A
NE	1 yr.*	No	No	No	No	A	No	No	No	A	No	No	No	A
NV	6 wks.	No	No	No	No	No	No	2 yrs.	No	A	1 yr.	No	No	A
NH	1 yr.*	Yes	Yes	2 yrs.	2 yrs.	Yes	2 yrs.	No	No	No	No	1 yr.*	No	No
NJ	1 yr.*	Yes	Yes	1 yr.	1 yr.	A	No	2 yrs.	No	A	18 mos.	18 mos	1 yr.	A
NM	6 mos.	Yes	Yes	Yes*	No	No	No	No	No	No	No	No	No	No
NY	1 yr.*	Yes	Yes	1 yr.	No	No	No	No	No	A	1 yr.	3 yrs.	No	No
NC	6 mos.	Yes	No	No	A	A	No	3 yrs.	No	A	1 yr.	No	No	No
ND	6 mos.	Yes	Yes	1 yr.	1 yr.	A	1 yr.	5 yrs.*	No	A	No	Yes	1 yr.	A
OH	6 mos.	Yes	Yes	1 yr.	Yes	Yes	Yes	No	No	Yes, A	1 yr.	Yes	No	Yes
OK	6 mos.	Yes	Yes	1 yr.	Yes	Yes	Yes	5 yrs.	Yes	Yes	No	Yes	No	Yes
OR	6 mos.*	No	No	No	No	No	No	No	No	No	No	No	No	A
PA	6 mos.	Yes	Yes	1 yr.	No	No	No	18 mos.*	No	Yes	2 yrs.*	Yes	No	A
RI	1yr.	Yes	Yes	5 yrs.*	Yes	Yes	1 yr.	No	Yes	Yes	3 yrs.	No	Yes	No
SC	1 yr.*	Yes	Phys. only	1 yr.	Yes	No	No	No	No	No	1 yr.	No	Yes	No
SD	none*	Yes	Yes	1 yr.	1 yr.	A	1 yr.	5 yrs.	No	A	No	Yes	No	A*
TN	6 mos.	Yes	Yes	2 yrs.	Yes	Yes	Yes	No	Yes	Yes	2 yrs.	Yes	Yes	A
TX	6 mos.*	Yes	Yes	1 yr.	*	A	No	3 yrs.	No	A	3 yrs.	1 yr.	No	No
UT	3 mos.	Yes	Yes	1 yr.	Yes	Yes	Yes	Yes	No	A	3 yrs.*	Yes	No	A
VT	6 mos.*	Yes	Yes	7 yrs.*	No	No	Yes	5 yrs.	No	No	6 mos.	3 yrs.	No	A
VA	6 mos.*	Yes	Yes*	1 yr.	No	A	No	No	A	A	1 yr.*	1 yr.*	No	No
WA	bona fide res.	No	No	No	No	No	No	No	No	No	No	No	No	No
WV	1 yr.	Yes	Yes	6 mos.	Yes	A	A	3 yrs.	A	A	1 yr.	Yes	Yes	No
WI	6 mos.	No	No	No	No	A	No	No	No	A	1 yr.	No	No	A
WY	60 da.*	No	No	No	No	No	No	2 yrs.	No	A	No	No	No	No
DC	6 mos.	No	No	No	No	No	No	A*	No	A	6 mos.-1 yr.	No	No	A

(*) indicates qualification-check local statutes; (A) indicates grounds for annulment.

Wedding Anniversaries

The traditional names for wedding anniversaries go back many years in social usage. As such names as wooden, crystal, silver, and golden were applied it was considered proper to present the married pair with gifts made of these products or of something related. The list of traditional gifts, with a few allowable revisions in parentheses, is presented below, followed by modern gifts in **bold** face.

1st-Paper, **clocks**
2d-Cotton, **china**
3d-Leather, **crystal & glass**
4th-Linen (silk), **electrical appliances**
5th-Wood, **silverware**
6th-Iron, **wood**
7th-Wool (copper), **desk sets**
8th-Bronze, **linens & lace**
9th-Pottery (china), **leather**

10th-Tin (aluminum), **diamond jewelry**
11th-Steel, **fashion jewelry, accessories**
12th-Silk, **pearls or colored gems**
13th-Lace, **textiles & furs**
14th-Ivory, **gold jewelry**
15th-Crystal, **watches**
20th-China, **platinum**

25th-Silver, **sterling silver jubliee**
30th-Pearl, **diamond**
35th-Coral (jade), **jade**
40th-Ruby, **ruby**
45th-Sapphire, **sapphire**
50th-Gold, **gold**
55th-Emerald, **emerald**
60th-Diamond, **diamond**

RELIGIOUS INFORMATION

Census of Religious Groups in the U.S.

Source: *1991 Yearbook of American and Canadian Churches*

The 1991 Yearbook of American and Canadian Churches reported a total of 147,607,394 members of religious groups in the U.S.—59.3 percent of the population; membership rose 1.5 percent from the previous year.

Comparisons of membership statistics from group to group are not necessarily meaningful. Membership definitions vary—e.g., Roman Catholics count members from infancy, but some Protestant groups count only "adult" members, usually 13 years or older; some groups compile data carefully, but others estimate; not all groups report annually.

The number of churches appear in parentheses. Asterisk (*) indicates church declines to publish membership figures; (**) indicates figures date from 1981 or earlier.

Group	Members
Adventist churches:	
Advent Christian Ch. (346)	25,400
Primitive Advent Christian Ch. (9)	350
Seventh-day Adventists (4,193)	701,781
American Rescue Workers (20)	2,700
Anglican Orthodox Church (40)	6,000
Baha'i Faith (1,700)	110,000
Baptist churches:	
Amer. Baptist Assn. (1,705)	250,000
Amer. Baptist Chs. in U.S.A. (5,833)	1,549,573
Baptist General Conference (792)	133,742
Baptist Missionary Assn. of America (1,339)	229,315
Conservative Baptist Assn. of America (1,126)	210,000
Duck River (and Kindred) Assn. of Baptists (85)	**8,632
Free Will Baptists (2,517)	204,489
Gen. Assn. of Regular Baptist Chs. (1,582)	216,468
Natl. Baptist Convention of America (11,398)	**2,668,799
Natl. Baptist Convention, U.S.A. (26,000)	**5,500,000
Natl. Primitive Baptist Convention (616)	**250,000
No. Amer. Baptist Conference (276)	42,629
Progressive National Baptist Convention (655)	**521,692
Seventh Day Baptist General Conference (86)	5,200
Southern Baptist Convention (37,739)	14,907,826
Brethren (German Baptists):	
Brethren Ch. (Ashland, Ohio) (126)	13,155
Church of the Brethren (1,079)	151,169
Fellowship of Grace Brethren (319)	39,481
Brethren, River:	
Brethren in Christ Ch. (189)	17,240
Buddhist Churches of America (67)	19,441
Christadelphians (850)	**15,800
The Christian and Missionary Alliance (1,829)	265,863
Christian Catholic Church (6)	2,500
Christian Church (Disciples of Christ) (4,113)	1,052,271
Christian Churches and Churches of Christ (5,579)	1,070,616
Christian Congregation (1,456)	108,881
Christian Methodist Episcopal Church (2,340)	718,922
Christian Nation Church U.S.A. (5)	200
Christian Union (114)	6,000
Churches of Christ (13,375)	1,626,000
Churches of Christ in Christian Union (250)	9,674
Churches of God:	
Chs. of God, General Conference (350)	33,909
Ch. of God (Anderson, Ind.) (2,338)	199,786
Ch. of God (Seventh Day) Denver, Col. (140)	5,000
Church of God in Christ (9,982)	3,709,661
Church of Christ, Scientist (3,000)	*
Church of God by Faith (106)	**4,500
Church of the Nazarene (5,158)	561,253
Conservative Congregational Christian Conference (180)	28,413
Eastern Orthodox churches:	
Albanian Orth. Diocese of America (2)	714
American Carpatho-Russian Orth. Greek Catholic Ch. (71)	20,000
Antiochian Orth. Christian Archdiocese of No. Amer. (160)	350,000
Diocese of the Armenian Ch. of America (66)	**450,000
Bulgarian Eastern Orth. Ch. (13)	**86,000
Coptic Orthodox Ch. (42)	165,000
Greek Orth. Archdiocese of N. and S. America (535)	**1,950,000
Orthodox Ch. in America (440)	**1,000,000
Patriarchal Parishes of the Russian Orth. Ch. in the U.S.A. (38)	9,780
Romanian Orth. Episcopate of America (37)	65,000
Serbian Eastern Orth. Ch. (68)	67,000
Syrian Orth. Ch. of Antioch (Archdiocese of the U.S.A. and Canada) (28)	30,000
Ukrainian Orth. Ch. of America (Ecumenical Patriarchate) (27)	5,000
Ukrainian Orthodox Church in the U.S.A. (107)	**87,745
The Episcopal Church in the U.S.A. (7,372)	2,433,413
Reformed Episcopal Church in America (78)	6,274
American Ethical Union (Ethical Culture Movement) (21)	3,212
Evangelical Church (185)	16,113
Evangelical Congregational Church (155)	34,779
The Evangelical Covenant Church (592)	89,014
Evangelical Free Church of America (1,040)	165,000
Evangelical associations:	
Apostolic Christian Chs. of America (80)	11,450
Apostolic Christian Ch. (Nazarean) (48)	2,799
Friends:	
Evangelical Friends Alliance (217)	24,095
Friends General Conference (505)	31,690
Friends United Meeting (543)	54,155
Grace Gospel Fellowship (50)	4,500
Independent Fundamental Churches of America (705)	73,809
Jehovah's Witnesses (9,141)	825,570
Jewish organizations:	
Union of Amer. Hebrew Congregations (Reform) (839)	1,300,000
Union of Orthodox Jewish Congregations of America (1,000)	1,000,000
United Synagogue of America (Conservative) (850)	2,000,000
Latter-day Saints:	
Ch. of Jesus Christ (Bickertonites) (63)	2,707
Ch. of Jesus Christ of Latter-day Saints (Mormon) (9,049)	4,175,400
Reorganized Ch. of Jesus Christ of Latter Day Saints (1,048)	190,183
Lutheran churches:	
Ch. of the Lutheran Brethren of America (114)	12,625
Ch. of the Lutheran Confession (69)	8,738
Evangelical Luthern Church in America (11,067)	5,238,798
Evangelical Lutheran Synod (125)	21,544
Assn. of Free Lutheran Congregations (193)	26,870
Latvian Evangelical Lutheran Church of America (56)	12,865
Lutheran Ch.-Missouri Synod (5,990)	2,609,025
Protestant Conference (Lutheran) (9)	1,065
Wisconsin Evangelical Lutheran Synod (1,198)	419,312
Mennonite churches:	
Beachy Amish Mennonite Chs. (99)	8,872
Evangelical Mennonite Ch. (26)	4,026
General Conference of Mennonite Brethren Chs. (128)	17,065
General Conference Mennonite Church (1,023)	92,682
The General Conference Mennonite Ch. (220)	33,982
Hutterian Brethren (77)	3,988
Mennonite Ch. (1,034)	92,517
Old Order Amish Ch. (785)	70,650
Old Order (Wisler) Mennonite Ch. (36)	**9,731
Methodist churches:	
African Methodist Episcopal Ch. (6,200)	**2,210,000
African Methodist Episcopal Zion Ch. (6,060)	1,220,260
Evangelical Methodist Ch. (130)	8,282
Free Methodist Ch. of North America (1,066)	75,869
Fundamental Methodist Ch. (13)	733
Primitive Methodist Ch., U.S.A. (85)	8,244
Reformed Methodist Union Episcopal Ch. (18)	3,800
Southern Methodist Ch. (137)	7,572
United Methodist Ch. (37,514)	8,979,139
Missionary Church (290)	26,332
Moravian churches:	
Moravian Ch. Northern Province (100)	31,248
Moravian Ch. in America Southern Province (55)	21,341
Unity of the Brethren (26)	4,336
Moslems	**6,000,000+
New Apostolic Church of North America (497)	37,201

Group	Members
North American Old Roman Catholic Church (133).	62,611
Old Catholic churches:	
Christ Catholic Ch. (12).	1,394
Pentecostal churches:	
Apostolic Faith (Portland, Ore.) (50)	4,100
Assemblies of God (11,192)	2,137,890
Bible Church of Christ (6)	6,500
Bible Way Church of Our Lord Jesus Christ World Wide (350).	**30,000
Church of God (Cleveland, Tenn.) (5,763)	582,203
Church of God of Prophecy (2,119).	73,430
Congregational Holiness Ch. (174)	**8,347
Gen. Council, Christian Ch. of No. Amer. (104)	13,500
Intl. Ch. of the Foursquare Gospel (1,404)	203,060
National Gay Pentecostal Alliance (2)	*
Open Bible Standard Chs. (330)	46,000
Pentecostal Assemblies of the World (550)	**4,500
Pentecostal Church of God (1,165)	90,870
Pentecostal Free-Will Baptist Ch. (141)	11,757
United Pentecostal Ch. Intl. (3,592)	500,000
Polish Natl. Catholic Church of America (162).	**282,411
Presbyterian churches:	
Associate Reformed Presbyterian Ch. (Gen. Synod) (182)	38,274
Cumberland Presbyterian Ch. (743)	90,906
Evangelical Presbyterian Ch. (160)	54,781

Group	Members
Orthodox Presbyterian Ch. (188)	19,094
Presbyterian Ch. in America (1,600)	217,374
Presbyterian Ch. (U.S.A.) (11,489)	2,886,482
Reformed Presbyterian Ch. in No. Amer. (68)	5,174
Reformed churches:	
Christian Reformed Ch. in N. America (712)	225,699
Hungarian Reformed Ch. in America (27)	9,780
Protestant Reformed Chs. in America (21).	**4,544
Reformed Ch. in America (928)	330,650
Reformed Ch. in the U.S. (34)	3,778
The Roman Catholic Church (23,500)	57,019,948
The Salvation Army (1,022)	445,566
The Schwenkfelder Church (5)	2,461
Social Brethren (40)	**1,784
Natl. Spiritualist Assn. of Churches (120).	3,406
Gen. Convention, The Swedenborgian Church (50)	2,423
Unitarian Universalist Assn. (1,010)	182,211
United Brethren:	
Ch. of the United Brethren in Christ (252)	25,462
United Christian Ch. (12)	420
United Church of Christ (6,388)	1,625,969
Universal Fellowship of Metropolitan Community Chs. (195).	22,296
Vedanta Society (13)	2,500
Volunteers of America (607)	**36,634
The Wesleyan Church (1,650).	110,027

Religious Population of the U.S.

Source: *1991 Yearbook of American and Canadian Churches*

(Membership in thousands, except as indicated)

Religious Body	1960	1965	1970	1975	1980	1989	1990
Total	114,449	124,682	131,045	131,013	134,817	145,384	147,607,394
Members as percent of population	64	64	63	61	59	58.7	59.3
Buddhists	20	92	100	60	60	100	19
Eastern Churches	2,699	3,172	3,850	3,696	3,823	4,077	4,057
Jews	5,367	5,600	5,870	6,115	5,920	5,935	5,944
Old Catholic, Polish National Catholic, Armenian Churches	590	484	848	846	924	827	980
Roman Catholics	42,105	46,246	48,125	48,882	50,450	54,919	57,020
Protestants[1]	63,669	69,088	71,173	71,043	73,479	79,329	79,387
Miscellaneous[2]	—	—	449	372	161	197	197

(1) Some bodies, e.g., Latter-Day Saints groups and Jehovahs Witnesses are strictly speaking not "Protestant" in the usual sense. (2) Officially non-Christian bodies, e.g., Spiritualists, Ethical Culture Movement, and Unitarian-Universalists.

Adherents of All Religions by Continental Areas, Mid-1990

Source: The 1990 Encyclopedia Britannica Book of the Year (in thousands)

	Africa	Asia	Europe	Latin America	Northern America	Oceania	U.S.S.R.	World	%
Christians	310,600	252,800	411,300	419,078	235,500	22,000	107,500	1,758,778	33.3
Roman Catholics	116,670	118,900	261,080	390,050	95,600	7,980	5,500	995,780	18.8
Protestants	82,900	78,380	73,500	16,600	94,900	7,310	9,700	363,290	6.9
Orthodox	27,100	3,516	35,950	1,696	5,920	560	92,200	166,942	3.2
Anglicans	25,500	680	32,760	1,250	7,230	5,560	0	72,980	1.4
Other Christians	58,430	51,324	8,010	9,482	31,850	590	100	159,786	3.0
Muslims	264,132	612,768	12,500	1,300	5,600	100	38,600	935,000	17.7
Nonreligious	1,800	686,600	52,100	16,500	22,100	3,200	83,700	866,000	16.4
Hindus	1,400	700,448	700	850	1,250	350	2	705,000	13.3
Buddhists	20	301,215	270	520	550	25	400	303,000	5.7
Atheists	300	155,280	17,500	3,100	1,300	520	55,000	233,000	4.4
Chinese folk religionists	12	179,717	60	70	120	20	1	180,000	3.4
New Religionists	20	136,009	50	510	1,400	10	1	138,000	2.6
Tribal Religionists	67,006	24,000	1	900	40	65	0	92,012	1.7
Sikhs	25	17,578	230	8	250	9	1	18,100	0.3
Jews	320	5,375	1,460	1,050	6,900	95	2,200	17,400	0.3
Shamanists	1	9,845	2	1	1	1	250	10,100	0.2
Confucians	1	5,766	2	2	26	1	2	5,800	0.1
Baha'is	1,420	2,578	90	770	360	75	7	5,300	0.1
Jains	50	3,576	15	4	4	1	1	3,650	0.1
Shintoists	2	3,097	1	1	1	1	0	3,100	0.1
Other religionists	410	11,825	1	3,433	478	4	327	17,938	0.3
Total Population	647,518	3,108,479	497,743	448,098	275,880	26,478	287,991	5,292,178	100.0

Totals not exact due to rounding.

Headquarters, Leaders of U.S. Religious Groups

Year organized in parentheses. See *Associations and Societies* section for religious organizations.

Adventist churches:

Advent Christian Church (1860) — Pres., Rev. Glennon Balser; sec., Rev. John Gallagher; P.O. Box 23152, Charlotte, NC 28212.

Primitive Advent Christian Church — Pres., Roger Hammons; sec.-treas., Hugh W. Good; 395 Frame Rd., Elkview, WV 25071.

Seventh-day Adventists (1863) — Pres., Robert S. Folkenberg; sec., G. Ralph Thompson; 12501 Old Columbia Pike, Silver Spring, MD 20904.

Baptist churches:

American Baptist Assn. (1905) — Pres., Dr. James B. Powers; sec.-treas., D.S. Madden; 4605 N. State Line, Texarkana, TX 75503.

American Baptist Churches in the U.S.A. (1907) — Pres., Beverly C. Davison; gen. sec., Daniel E. Weiss, P.O. Box 851, Valley Forge, PA 19482.

Baptist General Conference (1879) — Pres., Dr. Robert S. Ricker, 2002 S. Arlington Heights Rd., Arlington Heights, IL 60005.

Baptist Missionary Assn. of America (formerly **North American Baptist Assn.**) (1950) — Pres., Rev. Vernon R. Lee, rec. sec., Rev. Ralph Cottrell, P.O. Box 1203, Van, TX 75790.

Conservative Baptist Assn. of America (1947) — Gen. Dir., Dr. Tim Blanchard, Box 66, Wheaton, IL 60189.

Free Will Baptists (1727) — Mod., Rev. Ralph Hampton; exec. sec., Dr. Melvin Worthington, P.O. Box 1088, Nashville, TN 37202.

General Assn. of General Baptists (1823) — Mod., Rev. Ora J. Johnson; clerk, Rev. Edwin Runyon, 100 Stinson Dr., Poplar Bluff, MO 63901.

General Assn. of Regular Baptist Churches (1932) — Chpsn., Dr. John White; sec., Dr. John Greening, 1300 N. Meacham Rd., Schaumburg, IL 60173.

Natl. Baptist Convention, U.S.A. (1880) — Pres., Dr. T.J. Jemison; gen. sec., W. Franklyn Richardson, 52 S. 6th Ave., Mt. Vernon, NY 10550.

North American Baptist Conference (1865) — Mod., Rev. Harvey Mehlhaff; exec. dir., Dr. John Binder, 1 S. 210 Summit Ave., Oakbrook Terrace, IL 60181.

Progressive National Baptist Convention (1967) — Pres., Dr. Fred C. Lofton; gen. sec., Rev. Tyrone S. Pitts, 601 50th St. N.E., Washington DC 20019.

Southern Baptist Convention (1845) — Pres., Morris M. Chapman; rec. sec., David W. Atchison, 5452 Grannywhite Pike, Brentwood, TN 37027.

Brethren in Christ Church (1798) — Mod., Rev. Harvey R. Sider, gen. sec., Dr. R. Donald Shafer, P.O. Box 245, Upland, CA 91785.

Brethren (German Baptists):

Brethren Church (Ashland, Oh.) (1882) — Dir., Pastoral Min., Rev. Dave Cooksey; 524 College Ave., Ashland, OH 44805.

Church of the Brethren (1708) — Mod., Curtis Dubble; sec., Anne Myers; 1451 Dundee Ave., Elgin, IL 60120.

Buddhist Churches of America (1899) — Bishop, Rt. Rev. Seigen H. Yamaoka; exec. asst., Rev. Seikan Fukuma, 1710 Octavia St., San Francisco, CA 94109.

The Christian and Missionary Alliance (1887) — Pres., David L. Rambo; sec., R.H. Maugham, P.O. Box 35000, Colorado Springs, CO 80935.

Christian Church (Disciples of Christ) (1809) — Gen. minister and pres., John O. Humbert; v.p. for communication, Claudia E. Grant, 222 S. Downey Ave., Box 1986, Indianapolis, IN 46206.

Christian Methodist Episcopal Church (1870) — Exec. sec., Dr. W. Clyde Williams, 2805 Shoreland Dr., Atlanta, GA 30331. sec., Rev. Edgar L. Wade, P.O. Box 3403, Memphis, TN 38101.

Churches of Christ in Christian Union (1909) — Gen. supt., Dr. Daniel Tipton; gen. sec., Rev. Robert Barth, 1426 Lancaster Pike, Box 30, Circleville, OH 43113.

Grace Brethren Church, Fellowship of (1882) — Mod., Jerry Young; sec., Rev. Kenneth Koontz, 855 Turnbull St., Delona, FL 32725.

Churches of God:

Churches of God, General Conference (1825) — Pres., Pastor Stephen L. Dunn; journalizing sec., Pastor David L. Meadow, 7176 Glenmeadow Dr., Frederick, MD 21704.

Church of God (Anderson, Ind.) (1880) — Chpsn., G. David Cox; exec. sec., Edward L. Foggs; Box 2420, Anderson, IN 46018.

Church of God in Christ (1906) — Pres. Bishop, Louis Henry Ford, 272 S. Main St., Memphis, TN 38101.

Church of Christ, Scientist (1879) — Pres., Jürgen Kurt Stark; clk., Mrs. Virginia S. Harris, The First Church of Christ, Scientist, 175 Huntington Ave., Boston, MA 02115.

Church of the Nazarene (1908) — Gen. sec., Jack Stone, 6401 The Paseo, Kansas City, MO 64131.

National Association of Congregational Christian Churches (1955) — Mod., Dr. Lloyd M. Hall Jr.; exec. sec., J. Fred Rennebohm, Box 1620, Oak Creek, WI 53154.

Eastern Orthodox churches:

American Carpatho - Russian Onthodox Greek Catholic (Ecumenical Patriarchate) (1938) — Primate, Bishop Nicholas (Smisko); Chancellor, Very Rev. Protopresbyter Frank P. Milloro, 312 Garfield St., Johnstown, PA 15906.

Antiochian Orthodox Christian Archdiocese of North America (formerly **Syrian Antiochian Orthodox Archdiocese**) (1894) — Primate, Metropolitan Archbishop Philip (Saliba); aux., Archbishop Michael (Shaheen), Bishop Antoun (Khouri), 358 Mountain Rd., Englewood, NJ 07631.

Diocese of the Armenian Church of America (1889) — Primate, Eastern Diocese, Archbishop Vatche Housepian; sec., Edward Onanian; 630 Second Ave., New York, NY 10016; Western Diocese, Primate, His Eminence Archbishop Vatche Hovsepian, 1201 N. Vine St., Hollywood, CA 90038.

Coptic Orthodox Ch. — Archpriest Fr. Gabriel Abdelsayed, 427 West Side Ave., Jersey City, NJ 07304.

Greek Orthodox Archdiocese of North and South America (1864) — Pres., Archbishop Iakovos; sec., Basil C. Foussianes, 8-10 E. 79th St., N.Y., NY 10021.

Orthodox Church in America (formerly **Russian Orthodox Greek Catholic Church of North America**) (1792) — Primate, Metropolitan Theodosius; chancellor, V. Rev. Robert S. Kondratick, P.O. Box 675, Syosset, NY 11791.

Romanian Orthodox Episcopate of America (1929) — Bishop Nathaniel (Popp); sec., Rev. Fr. Laurence Lazar; 2522 Grey Tower Rd., Jackson, MI 49201.

Serbian Orthodox Church for the U.S.A. and Canada — Bishops, Rt. Rev. Georgije, Rt. Rev. Bishop Chrysostom; Bishop Christopher; St. Sava Monastery, Box 519, Libertyville, IL 60048.

Syrian Orthodox Church of Antioch, Archdiocese of the U.S.A. and Canada (1957) — Primate, Archbishop Mar- Athanasius Y. Samuel; gen. sec., Very Rev. Chorepiscopus John Meno, 45 Fairmount Ave., Hackensack, NJ 07601.

Ukrainian Orthodox Church in America (Ecumenical Patriarchate) (1928) — Primate, Rev. Bishop Vsevolod; sec., Rt. Rev. Ivan Tkaczuk, 90-34 139th St., Jamaica, NY 11435.

Ukrainian Orthodox Church of the U.S.A. (1919) — Metropolitan, Patriarch Mstyslav S. Skrypnyk, Box 495, South Bound Brook, NJ 08880.

The Episcopal Church (1789) — Presiding bishop and primate, Most Rev. Edmond L. Browning; sec., Rev. Donald A. Nickerson Jr., 815 Second Ave., New York, NY 10017.

Reformed Episcopal Church in America (1873) — Presiding bishop, Franklin Sellers; sec. Rev. Roger F. Spence; 2001 Frederick Rd., Baltimore, MD 21228.

The Evangelical Covenant Church (1885) — Pres., Dr. Paul E. Larsen; sec., John R. Hunt, 5101 N. Francisco Ave., Chicago, IL 60625.

Evangelical Friends (1965) — Mid-America YM, Roscoe Townsend, 2018 Maple, Wichita, KS 67213.

International — North Amer. Region (1990) (formerly **Evangelical Friends Alliance**)

Friends:

Friends General Conference (1900) — Gen. sec., Meredith Walton, 1520B Race St., Phila., PA 19102.

Friends United Meeting (formerly **Five Years Meeting of Friends**) (1902) — Presiding clerk, Sarah Wilson, 101 Quaker Hill Dr., Richmond, IN 47374.

Independent Fundamental Churches of America (1930) — Natl. Exec. Dir., Dr. Richard Gregory, 2684 Meadow Ridge Dr., Bryon Ctr., MI 49315.

Jehovah's Witnesses (1879) — Pres., Frederick W. Franz, 25 Columbia Heights, Brooklyn, NY 11201.

Jewish congregations:

Union of American Hebrew Congregations (Reform) — Pres., Rabbi Alexander M. Schindler, 838 5th Ave., N.Y., NY 10021.

Union of Orthodox Jewish Congregations of America — Pres., Sidney Kwestel, 45 W. 36th St., N.Y., NY 10018.

United Synagogue of America (Conservative) — Pres., Alan Tichnor, 155 5th Ave., N.Y., NY 10010.

Latter-day Saints:
The Church of Jesus Christ (Bickertonites) (1830) — Pres., Dominic R. Thomas; exec. sec., Paul Palmieri, Sixth & Lincoln Sts., Monongahela, PA 15063.
The Church of Jesus Christ of Latter-day Saints (Mormon) (1830) — Pres., Ezra Taft Benson, 50 E. North Temple St., Salt Lake City, UT 84150.
Reorganized Church of Jesus Christ of Latter Day Saints (1830) — Pres., Wallace B. Smith; sec., W. Grant McMurray, The Auditorium, P.O. Box 1059, Independence, MO 64051.

Lutheran churches:
Church of the Lutheran Brethren of America (1900) — Pres., Rev. Robert M. Overgard Sr.; sec., Rev. Richard Vettrus, 707 Crestview Dr., W. Union, IA 52175.
Church of the Lutheran Confession (1961) — Pres., Rev. Daniel Fleischer; sec., Rev. Paul F. Nolting, 620 E. 50th St., Loveland, CO 80537.
Evangelical Lutheran Church in America (1987) — Bishop, Rev. Dr. Herbert W. Chilstrom; sec., Rev. Dr. Lowell G. Almen, 8765 W. Higgins Rd., Chicago, IL 60631.
Evangelical Lutheran Synod (1853) — Pres., Rev. George Orvick; sec., Rev. Alf Merseth, 106 13th St. S., Northwood, IA 50459.
Assn. of Free Lutheran Congregations (1962) — Pres. Rev. Richard Snipstead; sec., Rev. Ronald Knutson, 402 W. 11th St., Canton, SD 57013.
Lutheran Church — Missouri Synod (1847) — Pres., Dr. Ralph A. Bohlmann; sec., Dr. Walter L. Rosin, 1333 S. Kirkwood, St. Louis, MO 63122.
Wisconsin Evangelical Lutheran Synod (1850) — Pres., Rev. Carl H. Mischke; sec., Prof. David Worgull, 1270 N. Dobson, Chandler, AZ 85224.

Mennonite churches:
The General Conference of Mennonite Brethren Churches (1860) — Mod. Edmund Janzen; sec., Roland Reimer, 8000 W. 21st St., Wichita, KS 67212.
General Conference Mennonite Church (1860) — Mod. Florence Driedger, 722 Main St., Newton, KS 67114
Mennonite Church (1690) — Mod., David W. Mann; 421 S. Second St. Ste. 600, Elkhart, IN 46516.

Methodist churches:
African Methodist Episcopal Zion Church (1796) — Sr. Bishop, John H. Adams; gen. sec., Dr. O. Urcille Infill Sr., Box 19039, E. Germantown Sta., Philadelphia, PA 19138.
Free Methodist Church of North America (1860) — Bishops R.F. Andrews, D. Bastian, G.E. Bates, D.M. Foster, B. Akulu Ilangyi, D. Ward, N. Nzeyimana, C.E. Van Valin; gen. conf. sec., Melvin J. Spencer; P.O. Box 535002, Winona Lake, IN 46590.
The United Methodist Church (1968) — Sec., Gen. Conference, Carolyn M. Marshall; 204 N. Newlin St., Veedersburg, IN 47987.
Universal Fellowship of Metropolitan Community Churches — Mod., Rev. Elder Troy D. Perry; clerk, Elder Larry Rodriguez, 5300 Santa Monica Blvd., Los Angeles, CA 90029.
Moravian Church (Unitas Fratrum) (1740) **Northern Province** — Pres., Dr. Gordon L. Sommers, 1021 Center St., P.O. Box 1245, Bethlehem, PA 18016. **Southern Province** — Pres., Rev. Graham H. Rights, 459 S. Church St., Winston-Salem, NC 27108.
Missionary Church (1883) — Pres. Dr. John Moran; sec., Rev. Paul De Merchant; 3901 S. Wayne Ave., Ft. Wayne, IN 46516.

Pentecostal churches:
Assemblies of God (1914) — Gen. supt., G. Raymond Carlson; gen. sec., Joseph R. Flower, 1445 Boonville Ave., Springfield, MO 65802.
Bible Way Church of Our Lord Jesus Christ World Wide (1927) — Interim pastor, Elder James Silver; gen. sec., Bishop Edward William, 5118 Clarendon Rd., Brooklyn, NY 11226.
Gen. Council, Christian Church of No. America (1948) — Gen. overseer; David Farina; gen. sec.-treas., Rev. R. Allen

Noyd; Rt. 18 & Rutledge Rd., Box 141-A, RD #1, Transfer, PA 16154.
The Church of God (1903) — Gen. overseer, Bishop Voy M. Bullen; gen. sec.-treas., Marie Powell, Box 13036, 1207 Willow Brook, Huntsville, AL 35802.
Church of God (Cleveland, Tenn.) (1886) — Gen. overseer, R. Lamar Vest; gen. sec.-treas., Gene D. Rice; P.O. Box 2430, Cleveland, TN 37320.
International Church of the Foursquare Gospel (1927) — Pres., Dr. John R. Holland; sec., Rev. John W. Bowers, 1100 Glendale Blvd., Los Angeles, CA 90026.
National Gay Pentecostal Alliance (1980) — Presbyter, Rev. Wm. H. Carey, P.O. Box 1391, Schenectady, NY 12301.
Open Bible Standard Churches (1919) — Gen. supt., Ray E. Smith; sec.-treas., Patrick L. Bowlin, 2020 Bell Ave., Des Moines, IA 50315.
Pentecostal Church of God (1919) — Gen. supt., Dr. James D. Gee; gen. sec.-treas., Dr. Ronald R. Minor, 4901 Pennsylvania, P.O. Box 850, Joplin, MO 64802.
Pentecostal Free Will Baptist Church (1959) — Gen. supt., Rev. Don Sauls; gen. sec., Rev. J.T. Hammond, Box 1568, Dunn, NC 28334.
United Pentecostal Church International (1945) — Gen. supt., Rev. Nathaniel A. Urshan; gen. sec.-treas., Rev. C. M. Becton, 8855 Dunn Rd., Hazelwood, MO 63042.

Presbyterian churches:
Cumberland Presbyterian Church (1810) — Mod., Rev. Thomas D. Campbell; stated clerk, Robert Prosser, 1978 Union Ave., Memphis, TN 38104.
Evangelical Presbyterian Church (1981) — Mod., James E. Rimmel; stated clerk, Rev. L. Edward Davis; 26049 Five Mile Rd., Detroit, MI 48239.
The Orthodox Presbyterian Church (1936) — Mod., Rev. Theodore J. Georgian; stated clerk, Richard A. Barker, 7401 Old York Rd., Philadelphia, Pa 19126.
Presbyterian Church in America (1973) — Mod., Dr. Cortz Cooper; stated clerk, Dr. Paul R. Gilchrist, 1852 Century Pl., Atlanta, GA 30345.
Presbyterian Church (U.S.A.) (1983) — Mod., C. Kenneth Hall; stated clerk, Rev. James E. Andrews, 100 Witherspoon St., Louisville, KY 40202.
Reformed Presbyterian Church of No. America (1871) — Mod., Robert A. Henning; clerk, J. Bruce Martin; 1328 Goodlin, Clay Center, KS 67432.

Reformed churches:
Christian Reformed Church in North America (1857) — Stated clerk, Rev. Leonard J. Hofman; gen. sec. Rev. Leonard J. Hofman; 2850 Kalamazoo Ave., SE, Grand Rapids, MI 49560.
Reformed Church in America (1628) — Pres., John E. Hiemstra; gen. sec., Edwin G. Mulder, 475 Riverside Dr., N.Y., NY 10115.
Roman Catholic Church — National Conference of Catholic Bishops. Pres., Archbishop Daniel Pilarczyk; sec., Bishop Raymond W. Lessard; 3211 Fourth St., Washington, DC 20017.
The Salvation Army (1880) — Natl. Cmdr. Commissioner James Osborne; natl. chief sec., Col. Kenneth Hood; 799 Bloomfield Ave., Verona, NJ 07044.
Sikh (1972) — Chief adm., Siri Singh Sahib, Harbhajan Singh Khalsa Yogiji; sec. gen., Mukhia Sardarni Sahiba, Sardarni Premka Kaur Khalsa, 1649 S. Robertson Blvd., Los Angeles, CA 90035.
Unitarian Universalist Assn. (1961) — Pres., Rev. William Schulz; sec., Barry Johnson-Fay, 25 Beacon St., Boston, MA 02108.
United Brethren in Christ (1789) — Chpsn., Bishop C. Ray Miller; 302 Lake St., Huntington, IN 46750.
United Church of Christ (1957) — Pres., Rev. Paul H. Sherry sec., Rev. Carol Joyce Brun; 700 Prospect Ave. E., Cleveland, OH 44115.
Volunteers of America (1896) — Pres., Raymond C. Tremont; 3813 N. Causeway Blvd., Metairie, LA 70002.
The Wesleyan Church (1968) — Gen. supt., Drs. O.D. Emery, Earle L. Wilson, Lee M. Haines, H.C. Wilson; gen. sec., Dr. Ronald R. Brannon, P.O. Box 50434; Indianapolis, IN 46250.

Religious Affiliation in the U.S., 1990

Source: 1990 Yearbook of American and Canadian Churches.

In the first Gallup audit of the 1990s, 69% of adults said they were members of a church, synagogue, or similar religious congregation. This matched the average membership of 68% during the 1980s and 70% in the 1970s, according to the Gallup organization. Membership and attendance were slightly higher during the 1930s through the 1960s, averaging 73%-74% on Gallup Poll audits. Most recently, the highest claims of church membership were found among those

who said they were "born again" (82%), and Roman Catholics (81%). Seven in ten Protestants (71%) said they had formal church affiliation. The regions with the highest proportions of their population who were church members were the Midwest (76%) and South (74%). In the East, membership was at the national average (69%), but in the West affiliation dipped to 54%. Women were somewhat more likely than men to be church members, by a margin of 72% to 66%.

Jewish Holy Days, Festivals, and Fasts

	1991 (5751-52)		1992 (5752-53)		1993 (5753-54)		1994 (5754-55)		1995 (5755-56)	
Tu B'Shvat	Jan.	30 Wed.	Jan.	20 Mon.	Feb.	6 Sat.	Jan.	27 Thu.	Jan.	16 Mon.
Ta'anis Esther (Fast of Esther)	Feb.	27 Wed.	Mar.	18 Wed.	Mar.	4 Thu.*	Feb.	24 Thu.	Mar.	15 Wed.
Purim	Feb.	28 Thu.	Mar.	19 Thu.	Mar.	7 Sun.	Feb.	25 Fri.	Mar.	16 Thu.
Passover	Mar.	30 Sat.	Apr.	18 Sat.	Apr.	6 Tue.	Mar.	27 Sun.	Apr.	15 Sat.
	Apr.	6 Sat	Apr.	25 Sat.	Apr.	13 Tue.	Apr.	3 Sun.	Apr.	22 Sat.
Lag B'Omer	May	2 Thu.	May	21 Thu.	May	9 Sun.	Apr.	29 Fri.	May	18 Thu.
Shavuot	May	19 Sun.	June	7 Sun.	May	26 Wed.	May	16 Mon.	June	4 Sun
	May	20 Mon.	June	8 Mon.	May	27 Thu.	May	17 Tue.	June	5 Mon.
Fast of the 17th Day of Tammuz	June	30 Sun.*	July	19 Sun.*	July	6 Tue.	June	26 Sun.	July	16 Sun.*
Fast of the 9th Day of Ac	July	21 Sun.*	Aug.	9 Sun.*	July	27 Tue.	July	17 Sun.	Aug.	6 Sun.
Rosh Hashanah	Sept.	9 Mon.*	Sept.	28 Mon.	Sept.	16 Thu.	Sept.	6 Tue.	Sept.	25 Mon.
	Sept.	10 Tue.	Sept.	29 Tue.	Sept.	17 Fri.	Sept.	7 Wed.	Sept.	26 Tue.
Fast of Gedalya	Sept.	11 Wed.	Sept.	30 Wed.	Sept.	19 Sun.*	Sept.	8 Thu.	Sept.	27 Wed.
Yom Kippur	Sept.	18 Wed.	Oct.	7 Wed.	Sept.	25 Sat.	Sept.	15 Thu.	Oct.	4 Wed.
Sukkot	Sept.	23 Mon.	Oct.	12 Mon.	Sept.	30 Thu.	Sept.	20 Tue.	Oct.	9 Mon.
	Sept.	29 Sun.	Oct.	18 Sun.	Oct.	6 Wed.	Sept.	26 Mon.	Oct.	15 Sun.
Shmini Atzeret	Sept.	30 Mon.	Oct.	19 Mon.	Oct.	7 Thu.	Sept.	27 Tue.	Oct.	16 Mon.
	Oct.	1 Tue.	Oct.	20 Tue.	Oct.	8 Fri.	Sept.	28 Wed.	Oct.	17 Tue.
Chanukah	Dec.	2 Mon.	Dec.	20 Sun.	Dec.	9 Thu.	Nov.	28 Mon.	Dec.	18 Mon.
	Dec.	9 Mon.	Dec.	27 Sun.	Dec.	16 Thu.	Dec.	5 Mon.	Oct.	25 Mon.
Fast of the 10th of Tevet	Dec.	17 Tue.	Jan.	3, Sun. 1993	Dec.	24 Fri.	Dec.	13 Tue.	Jan.	2 Tue. 1996

The months of the Jewish year are: 1) Tishri; 2) Cheshvan (also Marcheshvan); 3) Kislev; 4) Tebet (also Tebeth); 5) Shebat (also Shebhat); 6) Adar; 6a) Adar Sheni (II) added in leap years; 7) Nisan; 8) Iyar; 9) Sivan; 10) Tammuz; 11) Av (also Abh); 12) Elul. All Jewish holy days, etc., begin at sunset on the day previous. *Date changed to avoid Sabbath.

Greek Orthodox Movable Ecclesiastical Dates

	1992	1993	1994	1995
Triódion begins	February 16	February 7	February 20	February 12
Sat. of Souls	February 29	February 20	March 5	February 25
Meat Fare	March 1	February 21	March 6	February 26
2nd Sat. of Souls	March 7	February 27	March 12	March 4
Lent Begins	March 9	March 1	March 14	March 6
St. Theodore				
3rd Sat. of Souls	March 14	March 6	March 19	March 11
Sunday of Orthodoxy	March 15	March 7	March 20	March 12
Sat. of Lazarus	April 18	April 10	April 23	April 15
Palm Sunday	April 19	April 11	April 24	April 16
Holy (Good) Friday	April 24	April 16	April 29	April 21
Western Easter	April 19	April 11	April 3	April 16
Orthodox Easter	April 26	April 18	May 1	April 23
Ascension	June 4	May 27	June 9	June 1
Sat. of Souls	June 13	June 5	June 18	June 10
Pentecost	June 14	June 6	June 19	June 11
All Saints	June 21	June 13	June 26	June 18

Islamic (Moslem) Calendar 1991-1992 (1412-1413)

The Islamic Calendar is a lunar reckoning from the year of the *hegira*, 622 A.D., when Muhammed moved from Mecca to Medina. It runs in cycles of 30 years, of which the 2d, 5th, 7th, 10th, 13th, 16th, 18th, 21st, 24th, 26th, and 29th are leap years; 1412 is the 2nd year, 1413 the 3rd year of the cycle. Common years have 354 days, leap years 355, the extra day being added to the last month, Zu'lhijjah. Except for this case, the 12 months beginning with Muharram have alternately 30 and 29 days.

Year	Name of month	Month begins	Year	Name of month	Month begins
1412	Muharram (New Year)	July 13, 1991	1412	Shawwai	Apr. 4, 1992
1412	Safar	Aug. 12, 1991	1412	Zu'lkadah	May 3, 1992
1412	Rabia I	Sept. 10, 1991	1412	Zu'lhijjah	June 2, 1992
1412	Rabia II	Oct. 10, 1991	1413	Muharram (New Year)	July 2, 1992
1412	Jumada I	Nov. 8, 1991	1413	Safar	Aug. 1, 1992
1412	Jumada II	Dec. 8, 1991	1413	Rabia I	Aug. 30, 1992
1412	Rajab	Jan. 6, 1992	1413	Rabia II	Sept. 29, 1992
1412	Shaban	Feb. 5, 1992	1413	Jamada I	Oct. 28, 1992
1412	Ramadan	Mar. 5, 1992			

Episcopal Church Calendar and Liturgical Colors

White—from Christmas Day through the First Sunday after Epiphany; Maundy Thursday (as an alternative to crimson at the Eucharist); from the Vigil of Easter to the Day of Pentecost (Whitsunday); Trinity Sunday; Feasts of the Lord (except Holy Cross Day); the Confession of St. Peter; the Conversion of St. Paul; St. Joseph; St. Mary Magdalene; St. Mary the Virgin; St. Michael and All Angels; All Saint's Day; St. John the Evangelist; memorials of other saints who were not martyred; Independence Day and Thanksgiving Day; weddings and funerals. Red.—the Day of Pentecost; Holy Cross Day; feasts of apostles and evangelists (except those listed above); feasts and memorials of martyrs (including Holy Innocents' Day). Violet—Advent and Lent. Crimson (dark red)—Holy Week. Green—the seasons after Epiphany and after Pentecost. Black—optional alternative for funerals. Alternative colors used in some churches: Blue—Advent; Lenten White—Ash Wednesday to Palm Sunday.

(continued)

In the Episcopal Church the days of fasting are Ash Wednesday and Good Friday. Other days of special devotion (abstinence) are the 40 days of Lent and all Fridays of the year, except those in Christmas and Easter seasons and any Feasts of the Lord which occur on a Friday or during Lent. Ember Days (optional) are days of prayer for the Church's ministry. They fall on the Wednesday, Friday, and Saturday after the first Sunday in Lent, the Day of Pentecost, Holy Cross Day, and the Third Sunday of Advent. Rogation Days (also optional) are the three days before Ascension Day, and are days of prayer for God's blessing on the crops, on commerce and industry, and for the conservation of the earth's resources.

Days, etc.	1990		1991		1992		1993		1994	
Golden Number	15		16		17		18		19	
Sunday Letter	G		F		ED		C		B	
Sundays after Epiphany	8		5		8		7		6	
Ash Wednesday	Feb.	28	Feb.	13	Mar.	4	Feb.	24	Feb.	16
First Sunday in Lent	Mar.	4	Feb.	17	Mar.	8	Feb.	28	Feb.	20
Passion/Palm Sunday	Apr.	8	Mar.	24	Apr.	12	Apr.	4	Mar.	27
Good Friday	Apr.	13	Mar.	29	Apr.	17	Apr.	9	Apr.	1
Easter Day	Apr.	15	Mar.	31	Apr.	19	Apr.	11	Apr.	3
Ascension Day	May	24	May	9	May	28	May	20	May	12
The Day of Pentecost	June	3	May	19	June	7	May	30	May	22
Trinity Sunday	June	10	May	26	June	14	June	6	May	29
Numbered Proper of 2 Pentecost	#6		#4		#7		#6		#5	
First Sunday of Advent	Dec.	2	Dec.	1	Nov.	29	Nov.	28	Nov.	27

Ash Wednesday and Easter Sunday

Year	Ash Wed.		Easter Sunday		Year	Ash Wed.		Easter Sunday		Year	Ash Wed.		Easter Sunday		Year	Ash Wed.		Easter Sunday	
1901	Feb.	20	Apr.	7	1951	Feb.	7	Mar.	25	2001	Feb.	28	Apr.	15	2051	Feb.	15	Apr.	2
1902	Feb.	12	Mar.	30	1952	Feb.	27	Apr.	13	2002	Feb.	13	Mar.	31	2052	Mar.	6	Apr.	21
1903	Feb.	25	Apr.	12	1953	Feb.	18	Apr.	5	2003	Mar.	5	Apr.	20	2053	Feb.	19	Apr.	6
1904	Feb.	17	Apr.	3	1954	Mar.	3	Apr.	18	2004	Feb.	25	Apr.	11	2054	Feb.	11	Mar.	29
1905	Mar.	8	Apr.	23	1955	Feb.	23	Apr.	10	2005	Feb.	9	Mar.	27	2055	Mar.	3	Apr.	18
1906	Feb.	28	Apr.	15	1956	Feb.	15	Apr.	1	2006	Mar.	1	Apr.	16	2056	Feb.	16	Apr.	2
1907	Feb.	13	Mar.	31	1957	Mar.	6	Apr.	21	2007	Feb.	21	Apr.	8	2057	Mar.	7	Apr.	22
1908	Mar.	4	Apr.	19	1958	Feb.	19	Apr.	6	2008	Feb.	6	Mar.	23	2058	Feb.	27	Apr.	14
1909	Feb.	24	Apr.	11	1959	Feb.	11	Mar.	29	2009	Feb.	25	Apr.	12	2059	Feb.	12	Mar.	30
1910	Feb.	9	Mar.	27	1960	Mar.	2	Apr.	17	2010	Feb.	17	Apr.	4	2060	Mar.	3	Apr.	18
1911	Mar.	1	Apr.	16	1961	Feb.	15	Apr.	2	2011	Mar.	9	Apr.	24	2061	Feb.	23	Apr.	10
1912	Feb.	21	Apr.	7	1962	Mar.	7	Apr.	22	2012	Feb.	22	Apr.	8	2062	Feb.	8	Mar.	26
1913	Feb.	5	Mar.	23	1963	Feb.	27	Apr.	14	2013	Feb.	13	Mar.	31	2063	Feb.	28	Apr.	15
1914	Feb.	25	Apr.	12	1964	Feb.	12	Mar.	29	2014	Mar.	5	Apr.	20	2064	Feb.	20	Apr.	6
1915	Feb.	17	Apr.	4	1965	Mar.	3	Apr.	18	2015	Feb.	18	Apr.	5	2065	Feb.	11	Mar.	29
1916	Mar.	8	Apr.	23	1966	Feb.	23	Apr.	10	2016	Feb.	10	Mar.	27	2066	Feb.	24	Apr.	11
1917	Feb.	21	Apr.	8	1967	Feb.	8	Mar.	26	2017	Mar.	1	Apr.	16	2067	Feb.	16	Apr.	3
1918	Feb.	13	Mar.	31	1968	Feb.	28	Apr.	14	2018	Feb.	14	Apr.	1	2068	Mar.	7	Apr.	22
1919	Mar.	5	Apr.	20	1969	Feb.	19	Apr.	6	2019	Mar.	6	Apr.	21	2069	Feb.	27	Apr.	14
1920	Feb.	18	Apr.	4	1970	Feb.	11	Mar.	29	2020	Feb.	26	Apr.	12	2070	Feb.	12	Mar.	30
1921	Feb.	9	Mar.	27	1971	Feb.	24	Apr.	11	2021	Feb.	17	Apr.	4	2071	Mar.	4	Apr.	19
1922	Mar.	1	Apr.	16	1972	Feb.	16	Apr.	2	2022	Mar.	2	Apr.	17	2072	Feb.	24	Apr.	10
1923	Feb.	14	Apr.	1	1973	Mar.	7	Apr.	22	2023	Feb.	22	Apr.	9	2073	Feb.	8	Mar.	26
1924	Mar.	5	Apr.	20	1974	Feb.	27	Apr.	14	2024	Feb.	14	Mar.	31	2074	Feb.	28	Apr.	15
1925	Feb.	25	Apr.	12	1975	Feb.	12	Mar.	30	2025	Mar.	5	Apr.	20	2075	Feb.	20	Apr.	7
1926	Feb.	17	Apr.	4	1976	Mar.	3	Apr.	18	2026	Feb.	18	Apr.	5	2076	Mar.	4	Apr.	19
1927	Mar.	2	Apr.	17	1977	Feb.	23	Apr.	10	2027	Feb.	10	Mar.	28	2077	Feb.	24	Apr.	11
1928	Feb.	22	Apr.	8	1978	Feb.	8	Mar.	26	2028	Mar.	1	Apr.	16	2078	Feb.	16	Apr.	3
1929	Feb.	13	Mar.	31	1979	Feb.	28	Apr.	15	2029	Feb.	14	Apr.	1	2079	Mar.	8	Apr.	23
1930	Mar.	5	Apr.	20	1980	Feb.	20	Apr.	6	2030	Mar.	6	Apr.	21	2080	Feb.	21	Apr.	7
1931	Feb.	18	Apr.	5	1981	Mar.	4	Apr.	19	2031	Feb.	26	Apr.	13	2081	Feb.	12	Mar.	30
1932	Feb.	10	Mar.	27	1982	Feb.	24	Apr.	11	2032	Feb.	11	Mar.	28	2082	Mar.	4	Apr.	19
1933	Mar.	1	Apr.	16	1983	Feb.	16	Apr.	3	2033	Mar.	2	Apr.	17	2083	Feb.	17	Apr.	4
1934	Feb.	14	Apr.	1	1984	Mar.	7	Apr.	22	2034	Feb.	22	Apr.	9	2084	Mar.	9	Apr.	26
1935	Mar.	6	Apr.	21	1985	Feb.	20	Apr.	7	2035	Feb.	7	Mar.	25	2085	Feb.	28	Apr.	15
1936	Feb.	26	Apr.	12	1986	Feb.	12	Mar.	30	2036	Feb.	27	Apr.	13	2086	Feb.	13	Mar.	31
1937	Feb.	10	Mar.	28	1987	Mar.	4	Apr.	19	2037	Feb.	18	Apr.	5	2087	Mar.	5	Apr.	20
1938	Mar.	2	Apr.	17	1988	Feb.	17	Apr.	3	2038	Mar.	10	Apr.	25	2088	Feb.	25	Apr.	11
1939	Feb.	22	Apr.	9	1989	Feb.	8	Mar.	26	2039	Feb.	23	Apr.	10	2089	Feb.	16	Apr.	3
1940	Feb.	7	Mar.	24	1990	Feb.	28	Apr.	15	2040	Feb.	15	Apr.	1	2090	Mar.	1	Apr.	16
1941	Feb.	26	Apr.	13	1991	Feb.	13	Mar.	31	2041	Mar.	6	Apr.	21	2091	Feb.	21	Apr.	8
1942	Feb.	18	Apr.	5	1992	Mar.	4	Apr.	19	2042	Feb.	19	Apr.	6	2092	Feb.	13	Mar.	30
1943	Mar.	10	Apr.	25	1993	Feb.	24	Apr.	11	2043	Feb.	11	Mar.	29	2093	Feb.	25	Apr.	12
1944	Feb.	23	Apr.	9	1994	Feb.	16	Apr.	3	2044	Mar.	2	Apr.	17	2094	Feb.	17	Apr.	4
1945	Feb.	14	Apr.	1	1995	Mar.	1	Apr.	16	2045	Feb.	22	Apr.	9	2095	Mar.	9	Apr.	24
1946	Mar.	6	Apr.	21	1996	Feb.	21	Apr.	7	2046	Feb.	7	Mar.	25	2096	Feb.	29	Apr.	15
1947	Feb.	19	Apr.	6	1997	Feb.	12	Mar.	30	2047	Feb.	27	Apr.	14	2097	Feb.	13	Mar.	31
1948	Feb.	11	Mar.	28	1998	Feb.	25	Apr.	12	2048	Feb.	19	Apr.	5	2098	Mar.	5	Apr.	20
1949	Mar.	2	Apr.	17	1999	Feb.	17	Apr.	4	2049	Mar.	3	Apr.	18	2099	Feb.	25	Apr.	12
1950	Feb.	22	Apr.	9	2000	Mar.	8	Apr.	23	2050	Feb.	23	Apr.	10	2100	Feb.	10	Mar.	28

The Ten Commandments

According to Judeo-Christian tradition, as related in the Bible, the Ten Commandments were revealed by God to Moses, and form the basic moral component of God's covenant with Israel. The Ten Commandments appear in two different places in the Old Testament—Exodus 20:1-17 and Deuterotomy 5:6-21—the phrasing similar but not identical. Most Protestant, Anglican, and Orthodox Christians enumerate the commandments differently from Roman Catholics and Lutherans. Jewish tradition considers the introduction, "I am the Lord ..." to be the first commandment and makes the prohibition against "other gods" and idolatry the second.

Abridged Text of the Ten Commandments in Exodus 20:1-17

I. I am the Lord your God, who brought you out of the land of Egypt, out of the house of bondage. You shall have no other gods before me.
II. You shall not make for yourself a graven image. You shall not bow down to them or serve them.
III. You shall not take the name of the Lord your God in vain.
IV. Remember the sabbath day, to keep it holy.
V. Honor your father and your mother.
VI. You shall not kill.
VII. You shall not commit adultery.
VIII. You shall not steal.
IX. You shall not bear false witness against your neighbor.
X. You shall not covet.

Books of the Bible

Old Testament—Standard Protestant English Versions

Genesis	II Chronicles	Daniel
Exodus	Ezra	Hosea
Leviticus	Nehemiah	Joel
Numbers	Esther	Amos
Deuteronomy	Job	Obadiah
Joshua	Psalms	Jonah
Judges	Proverbs	Micah
Ruth	Ecclesiastes	Nahum
I Samuel	Song of Solomon	Habakkuk
II Samuel	Isaiah	Zephaniah
I Kings	Jeremiah	Haggai
II Kings	Lamentations	Zechariah
I Chronicles	Ezekiel	Malachi

New Testament—Standard Protestant English Versions

Matthew	Ephesians	Hebrews
Mark	Phillippians	James
Luke	Colossians	I Peter
John	I Thessalonians	II Peter
Acts	II Thessalonians	I John
Romans	I Timothy	II John
I Corinthians	II Timothy	III John
II Corinthians	Titus	Jude
Galatians	Philemon	Revelation

Catholic Versions

All the Catholic books of the Bible (Old Testament and New Testament) have the same names as Protestant Versions. A Catholic Version (and Pre-Reformation Bibles) simply has the books **Tobit, Judith, Wisdom, Sirach (Ecclesiasticus), Baruch, I Maccabees,** and **II Maccabees** as part of the Old Testament. The Old Testament books that a Catholic Bible includes and a Protestant Bible does not are called "Deuterocanonical Books."

Roman Catholic Hierarchy

Source: U.S. Catholic Conference; Mid-year, 1991

Supreme Pontiff

At the head of the Roman Catholic Church is the Supreme Pontiff, Pope John Paul II, Karol Wojtyla, born at Wadowice (Krakow), Poland, May 18, 1920; ordained priest Nov. 1, 1946; promoted to Archbishop of Krakow Jan. 13, 1964; proclaimed Cardinal June 26, 1967; elected pope as successor of Pope John Paul I Oct. 16, 1978; solemn commencement as pope Oct. 22, 1978.

College of Cardinals

Members of the Sacred College of Cardinals are chosen by the Pope to be his chief assistants and advisors in the administration of the church. Among their duties is the election of the Pope when the Holy See becomes vacant. The title of cardinal is a high honor, but it does not represent any increase in the powers of holy orders.

In its present form, the College of Cardinals dates from the 12th century. The first cardinals, from about the 6th century, were deacons and priests of the leading churches of Rome, and bishops of neighboring diocese. The title of cardinal was limited to members of the college in 1567. The number of cardinals was set at 70 in 1586 by Pope Sixtus V. From 1959 Pope John XXIII began to increase the number. However, the number of cardinals eligible to participate in papal elections was limited to 120. There were lay cardinals until 1918, when the Code of Canon Law specified that all cardinals must be priests. Pope John XXIII in 1962 established that all cardinals must be bishops. The first age limits were set in 1971 by Pope Paul VI, who decreed that at age 80 cardinals must retire from curial departments and offices and from participation in papal elections. They continue as members of the college, with all rights and privileges.

U.S. Cardinals

Name	Office	Born	Named Cardinal
Baum, William	Prefect of Congregation for Seminaries and Institutes of Study	1926	1976
Bevilacqua, Anthony	Archbishop of Philadelphia	1923	1991
Bernardin, Joseph	Archbishop of Chicago	1928	1983
Carberry, John*	Archbishop emeritus of St. Louis	1904	1969
Hickey, James	Archbishop of Washington	1920	1988
Krol, John*	Archbishop emeritus of Philadelphia	1910	1967
Law, Bernard F.	Archbishop of Boston	1931	1985
Mahoney, Roger	Archbishop of Los Angeles	1936	1991
O'Connor, John J	Archbishop of New York	1920	1985
Szoka, Edmund	Archbishop of Detroit	1927	1988

*Asterisk indicates cardinals ineligible to take part in papal elections.

The Major World Religions

Buddhism

Founded: About 525 BC, reportedly near Benares, India.
Founder: Gautama Siddhartha (ca. 563-480), the Buddha, who achieved enlightenment through intense meditation.
Sacred Texts: The *Tripitaka*, a collection of the Buddha's teachings, rules of monastic life, and philosophical commentaries on the teachings; also a vast body of Buddhist teachings and commentaries, many of which are called *sutras*.
Organization: The basic institution is the *sangha* or monastic order through which the traditions are passed to each generation. Monastic life tends to be democratic and anti-authoritarian. Large lay organizations have developed in some sects.
Practice: Varies widely according to the sect and ranges from austere meditation to magical chanting and elaborate temple rites. Many practices, such as exorcism of devils, reflect pre-Buddhist beliefs.
Divisions: A wide variety of sects grouped into 3 primary branches: Therevada (sole survivor of the ancient Hinayana schools) which emphasizes the importance of pure thought and deed; Mahayana, which includes Zen and Soka-gakkai, ranges from philosophical schools to belief in the saving grace of higher beings or ritual practices, and to practical meditative disciplines; and Tantrism, an unusual combination of belief in ritual magic and sophisticated philosophy.
Location: Throughout Asia, from Ceylon to Japan. Zen and Soka-gakkai have several thousand adherents in the U.S.
Beliefs: Life is misery and decay, and there is no ultimate reality in it or behind it. The cycle of endless birth and rebirth continues because of desire and attachment to the unreal "self". Right meditation and deeds will end the cycle and achieve Nirvana, the Void, nothingness.

Hinduism

Founded: Ca. 1500 BC by Aryan invaders of India where their Vedic religion intermixed with the practices and beliefs of the natives.
Sacred texts: The *Veda*, including the *Upanishads*, a collection of rituals and mythological and philosophical commentaries; a vast number of epic stories about gods, heroes and saints, including the *Bhagavadgita*, a part of the *Mahabharata*, and the *Ramayana;* and a great variety of other literature.
Organization: None, strictly speaking. Generally, rituals should be performed or assisted by Brahmins, the priestly caste, but in practice simpler rituals can be performed by anyone. Brahmins are the final judges of ritual purity, the vital element in Hindu life. Temples and religious organizations are usually presided over by Brahmins.
Practice: A variety of private rituals, primarily passage rites (eg. initiation, marriage, death, etc.) and daily devotions, and a similar variety of public rites in temples. Of the latter, the *puja*, a ceremonial dinner for a god, is the most common.
Divisions: There is no concept of orthodoxy in Hinduism, which presents a bewildering variety of sects, most of them devoted to the worship of one of the many gods. The 3 major living traditions are those devoted to the gods Vishnu and Shiva and to the goddess Shakti; each of them divided into further sub-sects. Numerous folk beliefs and practices, often in amalgamation with the above groups, exist side-by-side with sophisticated philosophical schools and exotic cults.
Location: Mainly India, Nepal, Malaysia, Guyana, Suriname, Sri Lanka.
Beliefs: There is only one divine principle; the many gods are only aspects of that unity. Life in all its forms is an aspect of the divine, but it appears as a separation from the divine, a meaningless cycle of birth and rebirth (*samsara*) determined by the purity or impurity of past deeds (*karma*). To improve one's *karma* or escape *samsara* by pure acts, thought, and/or devotion is the aim of every Hindu.

Islam

Founded: 622 AD in Medina, Arabian peninsula.
Founder: Mohammed (ca. 570-632), the Prophet.
Sacred texts: *Koran*, the words of God. *Hadith*, collections of the sayings of the Prophet.
Organization: Theoretically the state and religious community are one, administered by a caliph. In practice, Islam is a loose collection of congregations united by a very conservative tradition. Islam is basically egalitarian and non-authoritarian.
Practice: Every Moslem has 5 duties: to make the profession of faith ("There is no god but Allah ..."), pray 5 times a day, give a regular portion of his goods to charity, fast during the day in the month of Ramadan, and make at least one pilgrimage to Mecca if possible.
Divisions: The 2 major sects of Islam are the Sunni (orthodox) and the Shi'ah. The Shi'ah believe in 12 *imams*, perfect teachers, who still guide the faithful from Paradise. Shi'ah practice tends toward the ecstatic, while the Sunni is staid and simple. The Shi'ah sect affirms man's free will; the Sunni is deterministic. The mystic tradition in Islam is Sufism. A Sufi adept believes he has acquired a special inner knowledge direct from Allah.
Location: From the west coast of Africa to the Philipines across a broad band that includes Tanzania, southern USSR and western China, India, Malaysia and Indonesia. Islam claims over 2 million adherents in the U.S.
Beliefs: Strictly monotheistic. God is creator of the universe, omnipotent, just, and merciful. Man is God's highest creation, but limited and commits sins. He is misled by Satan, an evil spirit. God revealed the *Koran* to Mohammed to guide men to the truth. Those who repent and sincerely submit to God return to a state of sinlessness. In the end, the sinless go to Paradise, a place of physical and spiritual pleasure, and the wicked burn in Hell.

Judaism

Founded: About 1300 BCE.
Founder: Abrahm is regarded as the founding patriarch, but the Torah of Moses is the basic source of the teachings.
Sacred Texts: The five books of Moses constitute the written Torah. Special sanctity is also assigned other writings of the Hebrew Bible—the teachings of oral Torah are recorded in the Talmud, the Midrash, and various commentaries.
Organization: Originally theocratic, Judaism has evolved a congregational polity. The basic institution is the local synagogue, operated by the congregation and led by a rabbi of their choice. Chief Rabbis in France and Great Britain have authority only over those who accept it; in Israel, the 2 Chief Rabbis have civil authority in family law.
Practice: Among traditional practitioners, almost all areas of life are governed by strict religious discipline. Sabbath and holidays are marked by special observances, and attendance at public worship is regarded as especially important then. The chief annual observances are Passover, celebrating the liberation of the Israelites from Egypt and marked by the ritual Seder meal in the home, and the 10 days from Rosh Hashana (New Year) to Yom Kippur (Day of Atonement), a period of fasting and penitence.
Divisions: Judaism is an unbroken spectrum from ultra conservative to ultra liberal, largely reflecting different points of view regarding the binding character of the prohibitions and duties—particularly the dietary and Sabbath observations—prescribed in the daily life of the Jew.
Location: Almost worldwide, with concentrations in Israel and the U.S.
Beliefs: Strictly monotheistic. God is the creator and absolute ruler of the universe. Men are free to choose to rebel against God's rule. God established a particular relationship with the Hebrew people: by obeying a divine law God gave them they would be a special witness to God's mercy and justice. The emphasis in Judaism is on ethical behavior (and, among the traditional, careful ritual obedience) as the true worship of God.

Major Christian Denominations:
Italics indicate that area which, generally speaking, most

Denom-ination	Origins	Organization	Authority	Special rites
Baptists	In radical Reformation objections to infant baptism, demands for church-state separation; John Smyth, English Separatist in 1609; Roger Williams, 1638, Providence, R.I.	Congregational, *i.e.*, each local church is autonomous.	Scripture; some Baptists, particularly in the South, interpret the Bible literally.	Baptism, after about age 12, by total immersion; Lord's Supper.
Church of Christ (Disciples)	Among evangelical Presbyterians in Ky. (1804) and Penn. (1809), in distress over Protestant factionalism and decline of fervor. Organized 1832.	Congregational.	"*Where the Scriptures speak, we speak; where the Scriptures are silent, we are silent.*"	Adult baptism, Lord's Supper (weekly).
Episcopalians	Henry VIII separated English Catholic Church from Rome, 1534, for political reasons. Protestant Episcopal Church in U.S. founded 1789.	*Bishops, in apostolic succession, are elected by diocesan representatives; part of Anglican Communion, symbolically headed by Archbishop of Canterbury.*	Scripture as interpreted by tradition, esp. 39 Articles (1563); not dogmatic. Tri-annual convention of bishops, priests, and laymen.	Infant baptism, Holy Communion, others. Sacrament is symbolic, but has real spiritual effect.
Lutherans	Martin Luther in Wittenberg, Germany, 1517, objected to Catholic doctrine of salvation by merit and sale of indulgences; break complete by 1519.	Varies from congregational to episcopal; in U.S. a combination of regional synods and congregational polities is most common.	*Scripture, and tradition as spelled out in Augsburg Confession (1530) and other creeds. These confessions of faith are binding although interpretations vary.*	Infant baptism, Lord's Supper. Christ's true body and blood present "in, with, and under the bread and wine."
Methodists	Rev. John Wesley began movement, 1738, within Church of England. First U.S. denomination Baltimore, 1784.	Conference and superintendent system. *In United Methodist Church, general superintendents are bishops—not a priestly order, only an office—who are elected for life.*	Scripture as interpreted by tradition, reason, and experience.	Baptism of infants or adults, Lord's Supper commanded. Other rites, inc. marriage, ordination, solemnize personal commitments.
Mormons	In visions of the Angel Moroni by Joseph Smith, 1827, in New York, in which he received a new revelation on golden tablets: *The Book of Mormon.*	Theocratic; all male adults are in priesthood which culminates in Council of 12 Apostles and 1st Presidency (1st President, 2 counselors).	*The Bible, Book of Mormon and other revelations to Smith, and certain pronouncements of the 1st Presidency.*	Baptism, at age 8, laying on of hands (which confers the gift of the Holy Spirit), Lord's Supper. Temple rites: baptism for the dead, marriage for eternity, others.
Orthodox	Original Christian proselytizing in 1st century; broke with Rome, 1054, after centuries of doctrinal disputes and diverging traditions.	Synods of bishops in autonomous, usually national, churches elect a patriarch, archbishop or metropolitan. These men, as a group, are the heads of the church.	Scripture, tradition, and the first 7 church councils up to Nicaea II in 787. Bishops in council have authority in doctrine and policy.	Seven sacraments: infant baptism and anointing, Eucharist (both bread and wine), ordination, penance, anointing of the sick, marriage.
Pentecostal	In Topeka, Kansas (1901), and Los Angeles (1906) in reaction to loss of evangelical fervor among Methodists and other denominations.	Originally a movement, not a formal organization, Pentecostalism now has a variety of organized forms and continues also as a movement.	Scripture, individual charismatic leaders, the teachings of the Holy Spirit.	*Spirit baptism, esp. as shown in "speaking in tongues"; healing and sometimes exorcism; adult baptism, Lord's Supper.*
Presbyterians	In Calvinist Reformation in 1500s; differed with Lutherans over sacraments, church government. John Knox founded Scotch Presbyterian church about 1560.	*Highly structured representational system of ministers and laypersons (presbyters) in local, regional and national bodies. (synods).*	Scripture.	Infant baptism, Lord's Supper; bread and wine symbolize Christ's spiritual presence.
Roman Catholics	Traditionally, by Jesus who named St. Peter the 1st Vicar; historically, in early Christian proselytizing and the conversion of imperial Rome in the 4th century.	Hierarchy with supreme power vested in Pope elected by cardinals. Councils of Bishops advise on matters of doctrine and policy.	*The Pope, when speaking for the whole church in matters of faith and morals, and tradition, which is partly recorded in scripture and expressed in church councils.*	Seven sacraments: baptism, contrition and penance, confirmation, Eucharist, marriage, ordination, and anointing of the sick (unction).
United Church of Christ	*By ecumenical union, 1957, of Congregationalists and Evangelical & Reformed, representing both Calvinist and Lutheran traditions.*	Congregational; a General Synod, representative of all congregations, sets general policy.	Scripture.	Infant baptism, Lord's Supper.

How Do They Differ?

distinguishes that denomination from any other.

Practice	Ethics	Doctrine	Other	Denomination
Worship style varies from staid to evangelistic. Extensive missionary activity.	Usually opposed to alcohol and tobacco; sometimes tends toward a perfectionist ethical standard.	*No creed; true church is of believers only, who are all equal.*	Since no authority can stand between the believer and God, the Baptists are strong supporters of church-state separation.	Baptists
Tries to avoid any rite or doctrine not explicitly part of the 1st century church. Some congregations may reject instrumental music.	Some tendency toward perfectionism; increasing interest in social action programs.	Simple New Testament faith; avoids any elaboration not firmly based on Scripture.	Highly tolerant in doctrinal and religious matters; strongly supportive of scholarly education.	Church of Christ (Disciples)
Formal, based on *Book of Common Prayer* (1549); services range from austerely simple to highly elaborate.	Tolerant; sometimes permissive; some social action programs.	*Apostles' Creed* is basic; otherwise, considerable variation ranges from rationalist and liberal to acceptance of most Roman Catholic dogma.	Strongly ecumenical, holding talks with all other branches of Christendom.	Episcopalians
Relatively simple formal liturgy with emphasis on the sermon.	Generally, conservative in personal and social ethics; doctrine of "2 kingdoms" (worldly and holy) supports conservatism in secular affairs.	Salvation by faith alone through grace. Lutheranism has made major contributions to Protestant theology.	Though still somewhat divided along ethnic lines (German, Swede, etc.), main divisions are between fundamentalists and liberals.	Lutherans
Worship style varies widely by denomination, local church, geography.	Originally pietist and perfectionist; always strong social activist elements	No distinctive theological development; 25 Articles abriged from Church of England's 39 not binding.	In 1968, United Methodist Church joined pioneer English- and German-speaking groups. UMs leaders in ecumenical movement.	Methodists
Staid service with hymns, sermon. Secret temple ceremonies may be more elaborate. Strong missionary activity.	Temperance; strict tithing. Combine a strong work ethic with communal self-reliance.	God is a material being; he created the universe out of pre-existing matter; all persons can be saved and many will become divine. Most other beliefs are traditionally Christian.	Mormons regard mainline churches as apostate, corrupt. Reorganized Church (founded 1860) rejects most Mormon doctrine and practice except Book of Mormon.	Mormons
Elaborate liturgy, usually in the vernacular, though extremely traditional. The liturgy is the essence of Orthodoxy. Veneration of icons.	Tolerant; very little social action; divorce, remarriage permitted in some cases. Priests need not be celibate; bishops are.	Emphasis on Christ's resurrection, rather than crucifixion; the Holy Spirit proceeds from God the Father only.	Orthodox Church in America, orginally under Patriarch of Moscow, was granted autonomy in 1970. Greek Orthodox do not recognize this autonomy.	Orthodox
Loosely structured service with rousing hymns and sermons, culminating in spirit baptism.	Usually, emphasis on perfectionism with varying degrees of tolerance.	Simple traditional beliefs, usually Protestant, with emphasis on the immediate presence of God in the Holy Spirit	Once confined to lower-class "holy rollers," Pentecostalism now appears in mainline churches and has established middle-class congregations.	Pentecostal
A simple, sober service in which the sermon is central.	Traditionally, a tendency toward strictness with firm church- and self-discipline; otherwise tolerant.	Emphasizes the sovereignty and justice of God; no longer doctrinaire.	While traces of belief in predestination (that God has foreordained salvation for the "elect") remain, this idea is no longer a central element in Presbyterianism.	Presbyterians
Relatively elaborate ritual; wide variety of public and private rites, eg., mass, rosary recitation, processions, novenas.	Theoretically very strict; tolerant in practice on most issues. Divorce and remarriage not accepted. Celibate clergy, except in Eastern rite.	Highly elaborated. Salvation by merit gained through faith. Unusual development of doctrines surrounding Mary. Dogmatic.	Roman Catholicism went through a period of relatively rapid change as a result of Vatican Councils I and II.	Roman Catholics
Usually simple services with emphasis on the sermon.	Tolerant; some social action emphasis.	Standard Protestant; *Statement of Faith* (1959) is not binding.	The 2 main churches in the 1957 union represented earlier unions with small groups of almost every Protestant denomination.	United Church of Christ

NATIONS OF THE WORLD

As of mid-1991

The nations of the world are listed in alphabetical order. Initials in the following articles include UN (United Nations), OAS (Org. of American States), NATO (North Atlantic Treaty Org.), EC (European Communities or Common Market), OAU (Org. of African Unity), ILO (Intl. Labor Org.), FAO (Food & Agricultural Org.), WHO (World Health Org.), IMF (Intl. Monetary Fund), GATT (General Agreements on Tarriffs & Trade). **Sources:** U.S. Dept. of State; U.S. Census Bureau; The World Factbook; International Monetary Fund; UN Statistical Yearbook; UN Demographic Yearbook; International Iron and Steel Institute; The Statesman's Year-Book; Encyclopaedia Britannica. All embassy addresses are Wash., DC; area codes (202), unless otherwise noted. Literacy rates are usually based on the ability to read and write on a lower elementary school level. The concept of literacy is changing in the industrialized countries, where literacy is defined as the ability to read instructions necessary for a job or a license. By these standards, illiteracy may be more common than present rates suggest. Per person figures in communications and health sections are post-1986. Some nations measure national output as Gross Domestic Product. GDP is the Gross National Product less net income from current transactions with other countries.

See special color section for maps and flags.

Afghanistan

Republic of Afghanistan

De Afghanistan Jamhuriat

People: Population (1989 est.): 15,592,000. **Pop. density:** 62 per sq. mi. **Urban** (1987): 18%. **Ethnic groups:** Pushtun 50%; Tajik 25%; Uzbek 9%; Hazara 9%. **Languages:** Pushtu, Dari Persian (spoken by Tajiks, Hazaras), Uzbek (Turkic). **Religions:** Sunni Moslem 74%, Shi'a Moslem 25%.

Geography: Area: 251,773 sq. mi., about the size of Texas. **Location:** Between Soviet Central Asia and the Indian subcontinent. **Neighbors:** Pakistan on E, S, Iran on W, USSR on N; the NE tip touches China. **Topography:** The country is landlocked and mountainous, much of it over 4,000 ft. above sea level. The Hindu Kush Mts. tower 16,000 ft. above Kabul and reach a height of 25,000 ft. to the E. Trade with Pakistan flows through the 35-mile long Khyber Pass. The climate is dry, with extreme temperatures, and large desert regions, though mountain rivers produce intermittent fertile valleys. **Capital:** Kabul. **Cities** (1988 est.): Kabul 1.4 mln.

Government: Type: Communist. **Head of state, and President of the Revolutionary Council:** Pres. Mohammad Najibullah; in office: Nov. 30, 1987. **Head of Government:** Prime Min. Fazal Haq Khaliqyar; in office: May 8, 1990. **Head of Communist Party:** Secy. Gen. Mohammad Najibullah; in office: May 4, 1986. **Local divisions:** 29 provinces, each under a governor. **Defense:** 7.7% of GNP (1984).

Economy: Industries: Textiles, furniture, cement. **Chief crops:** Nuts, wheat, fruits. **Minerals:** Copper, coal, zinc, iron. **Other resources:** Wool, hides, karacul pelts. **Arable land:** 13%. **Livestock** (1988): cattle: 7.7 mln.; sheep: 19 mln. **Electricity prod.** (1988): 1.7 bln. kwh. **Labor force:** agriculture supports about 80% of the population.

Finance: Monetary unit: Afghani (Mar. 1991: 50.60 = $1 US). **Gross national product** (1988): $3.1 bln. **Per capita GNP:** $220. **Imports** (1989): $714 mln.; partners: USSR 55%, Jap. 8%. **Exports** (1989): $235 mln.; partners: USSR 72%. **International reserves less gold** (Feb. 1991): $286 mln. **Gold:** 965,000 oz t. **Consumer prices** (change in 1989): 40%.

Transport: Motor vehicles: in use (1988): 31,000 passenger cars, 30,000 comm. vehicles. **Civil aviation** (1987): 174 mln. passenger-km.

Communications: Television sets: 1 per 148 persons; **Radios:** 1 per 11 persons. **Telephones in use:** 1 per 443 persons. **Daily newspaper circ.** (1988): 10 per 1,000 pop.

Health: Life expectancy at birth (1989): 43 male; 42 female. **Births** (per 1,000 pop. 1989): 44. **Deaths** (per 1,000 pop. 1989): 21. **Natural increase:** 2.4%. **Hospital beds:** 1 per 2,054 persons. **Physicians:** 1 per 4,797 persons. **Infant mortality** (per 1,000 live births 1989): 173.

Education (1987): **Literacy:** 12%. Over 88% of adults have no formal schooling.

Major International Organizations: UN (World Bank, IMF) **Embassy:** 2341 Wyoming Ave. NW, 20008; 234-3770.

Afghanistan, occupying a favored invasion route since antiquity, has been variously known as Ariana or Bactria (in ancient times) and Khorasan (in the Middle Ages). Foreign empires alternated rule with local emirs and kings until the 18th century, when a unified kingdom was established. In 1973, a military coup ushered in a republic.

Pro-Soviet leftists took power in a bloody 1978 coup, and concluded an economic and military treaty with the USSR.

Late in Dec. 1979, the USSR began a massive military airlift into Kabul. The three-month old regime of Hafizullah Amin ended with a Soviet backed coup, Dec. 27th. He was replaced by Babrak Karmal, a more pro-Soviet leader. Soviet troops fanned out over Afghanistan fighting rebels. Fighting continued for 9 years as the Soviets found themselves engaged in a long, protracted guerrilla war.

An UN-mediated agreement was signed Apr. 14, 1988 providing for the withdrawal of Soviet troops from Afghanistan, creation of a neutral Afghan state, and repatriation of millions of Afghan refugees. The U.S. and USSR pledged to serve as guarantors of the agreement. Afghan rebels rejected the pact and vowed to continue fighting while the "Soviets and their puppets" remained in Afghanistan.

The Soviets disclosed that during the war some 15,000 soldiers were killed. They completed their troop withdrawal Feb. 15, 1989 as Afghan rebels and the government began a civil war; the rebels elected a government-in-exile Feb. 23.

There was a failed coup attempt, led by Afghan military forces, Mar. 6-8, 1990.

Albania

Peoples Socialist Republic of Albania

Republika Popullore Socialiste e Shqipërisë

People: Population (1990 est.): 3,268,000. **Pop. density:** 293 per sq. mi. **Urban** (1989): 35%. **Ethnic groups:** Albanians (Gegs in N, Tosks in S) 98%, Greeks 1.8%. **Languages:** Albanian (Tosk is official dialect), Greek. **Religions:** officially atheist; (historically) mostly Moslems. All public worship and religious institutions were outlawed in 1967. In 1990, the right to practice religion was restored.

Geography: Area: 11,100 sq. mi., slightly larger than Maryland. **Location:** On SE coast of Adriatic Sea. **Neighbors:** Greece on S, Yugoslavia on N, E. **Topography:** Apart from a narrow coastal plain, Albania consists of hills and mountains covered with scrub forest, cut by small E-W rivers. **Capital:** Tirana. **Cities** (1989 est.): Tirane 238,000; Durres 82,000; Vlore 71,000.

Government: Type: In transition. **Head of state:** Pres. Ramiz Alia, b. Oct. 18, 1925; in office: Nov. 22, 1982. **Head of government:** Premier Ylli Bufi; in office: June 5, 1991. **Local divisions:** 26 districts. **Defense:** 5.3% of GNP (1988).

Economy: Industries: Cement, textiles. **Chief crops:** Corn, wheat, cotton, potatoes, tobacco, fruits. **Minerals:** Chromium, coal, oil. **Other resources:** Forests. **Arable land:** 21%. **Livestock** (1989): 700,000 cattle; 1.6 mln. sheep. **Electricity prod.** (1988): 5.2 bln. kwh. **Labor force:** 50% agric; 50% ind. & comm.

Finance: Monetary unit: Lek (Nov. 1990: 5.41 = $1 US). **Gross national product** (1987) $4.0 bln. **Per capita GNP** (1987): $1,300. **Imports** (1986): $335 mln.; partners: Czech., Yugoslavia, Rom. **Exports** (1985): $345 mln.; partners: Czech., Yugoslavia, N. Korea, Italy.

Chief ports: Durres, Vlone, Shengjih.

Communications: Television sets: 1 per 13 persons. **Radios:** 1 per 6 persons. **Daily newspaper circ.** 48 per 1,000 pop.

Health: Life expectancy at birth (1987): 72.0 yrs. **Births** (per 1,000 pop. 1989): 25. **Deaths** (per 1,000 pop. 1989): 6.

Natural increase: 1.9%. **Hospital beds:** 1 per 176 persons. **Physicians:** 1 per 574 persons. **Infant mortality** (per 1,000 live births 1989): 59.
Major International Organizations: UN (FAO, WHO).
Education (1989): **Literacy:** 75%. Free and compulsory ages 7-15.

Ancient Illyria was conquered by Romans, Slavs, and Turks (15th century); the latter Islamized the population. Independent Albania was proclaimed in 1912, republic was formed in 1920. King Zog I ruled 1925-39, until Italy invaded.

Communist partisans took over in 1944, allied Albania with USSR, then broke with USSR in 1960 over de-Stalinization. Strong political alliance with China followed, leading to several billion dollars in aid, which was curtailed after 1974. China cut off aid in 1978 when Albania attacked its policies after the death of Chinese ruler Mao Tse-tung.

Large-scale purges of officials occurred during the 1970s. Enver Hoxha, the nation's ruler for 4 decades, died Apr. 11, 1985.

There was some liberization in 1990, including measures providing for freedom to travel abroad and restoration of the right to practice religion.

In 1991, a general strike and urban opposition forced the communist cabinet to resign; a non-communist caretaker was installed. By March, over 20,000 Albanians had left their country and sailed to Italy. James Baker became the first U.S. secy. of state to visit Albania, June 22.

Algeria

Democratic and Popular Republic of Algeria

al-Jumhuriya al-Jazāiriya ad-Dimuqratiya ash-Shabiya

People: Population (1990 est.); 25,714,000. **Age distrib.** (%): 0–14: 43.9; 15–59: 50.3; 60+: 5.8. **Pop. density:** 27 per sq. mi. **Urban** (1987): 49%. **Ethnic groups:** Arabs 75%, Berbers 25%. **Languages:** Arabic (official), Berber (indigenous language). **Religions:** Sunni Moslem (state religion).

Geography: Area: 918,497 sq. mi., more than 3 times the size of Texas. **Location:** In NW Africa, from Mediterranean Sea into Sahara Desert. **Neighbors:** Morocco on W, Mauritania, Mali, Niger on S, Libya, Tunisia on E. **Topography:** The Tell, located on the coast, comprises fertile plains 50-100 miles wide, with a moderate climate and adequate rain. Two major chains of the Atlas Mts., running roughly E-W, and reaching 7,000 ft., enclose a dry plateau region. Below lies the Sahara, mostly desert with major mineral resources. **Capital:** Algiers (El Djazair). **Cities** (1987 est.): El Djazair 1,483,000; Wahran 590,000; Qacentina 483,000.

Government: Type: Republic. **Head of state:** Pres. Chadli Benjedid; b. Apr. 14, 1929; in office: Feb. 9, 1979. **Head of government:** Prime Min Mouloud Hamroche; in office: Nov. 5, 1988. **Local divisions:** 48 wilayaat (provinces). **Defense:** 3.0% of GNP (1987).

Economy: Industries: Oil, light industry, food processing. **Chief crops:** Grains, wine-grapes, potatoes, dates, olives, oranges. **Minerals:** Mercury, iron, zinc, lead. **Crude oil reserves** (1987): 4.8 bln. bbls. **Other resources:** Cork trees. **Arable land:** 17%; **Livestock** (1988): cattle: 1.7 mln.; sheep: 14 mln. **Electricity prod.** (1988): 13.6 bln. kwh. **Crude steel prod.** (1988): 1.4 mln. metric tons **Labor force:** 30% agric.; 30% ind. and commerce; 27% government, & services.

Finance: Monetary Unit: Dinar (Mar. 1991: 17.76 = $1 US). **Gross national product** (1989): $53.1 bln. **Per capita GNP** (1989): $2,170. **Imports** (1988): $7.7 bln.; partners: EEC 64%. **Exports** (1988): $8.6 bln.; partners: EEC 74%. **National budget** (1987): $21.3 bln. **International reserves less gold** (Mar. 1991): $544 mln. **Gold:** 4.8 mln. oz t. Consumer prices (change in 1989): 7.5%

Transport: Motor vehicles: in use (1986): 712,000 passenger cars, 471,000 comm. vehicles. **Chief ports:** El Djazair.

Communications: Television sets: 1 per 15 persons. **Radios:** 1 per 4 persons. **Telephones in use:** 1 per 25 persons. **Daily newspaper circ.** (1988): 53 per 1,000 pop.

Health: Life expectancy at birth (1989): 63 male; 67 female. **Births** (per 1,000 pop. 1987): 34.6. **Deaths** (per 1,000 pop. 1987): 7.0. **Natural increase** (1987): 2.7%. **Hospital beds:** 1

per 367 persons. **Physicians:** 1 per 1,302 persons. **Infant mortality** (per 1,000 live births 1986): 82.4
Education (1989): **Literacy:** 52%. **School:** Free and compulsory to age 16; Attendance: 94% primary, 47% secondary.
Major International Organizations: UN (FAO, IMF, WHO), OAU, Arab League, OPEC.
Embassy: 2118 Kalorama Rd. NW, 20008; 328-5300.

Earliest known inhabitants were ancestors of Berbers, followed by Phoenicians, Romans, Vandals, and, finally, Arabs. Turkey ruled 1518 to 1830, when France took control.

Large-scale European immigration and French cultural inroads did not prevent an Arab nationalist movement from launching guerilla war. Peace, and French withdrawal, was negotiated with French Pres. Charles de Gaulle. One million Europeans left. Independence came July 5, 1962.

Ahmed Ben Bella was the victor of infighting, and ruled 1962-65, when an army coup installed Col. Houari Boumedienne as leader.

In 1967, Algeria declared war with Israel, broke with U.S., and moved toward eventual military and political ties with the USSR. Some 500 died in riots protesting economic hardship in 1988. In 1989, voters approved a new constitution which cleared the way for a multiparty system and guaranteed "fundamental rights and freedoms" of Algerians.

Andorra

Principality of Andorra

Principat d'Andorra

People: Population (1990 est.): 51,000. **Age distrib. (%):** 0–14: 19.0; 14–59: 68.5; 60+: 12.5. **Pop. density:** 281 per sq. mi. **Ethnic groups:** Catalan 61%, Spanish 30%, Andorran 6%, French 3%. **Languages:** Catalan (official), Spanish, French. **Religion:** Roman Catholic.

Geography: Area: 185 sq. mi., half the size of New York City. **Location:** In Pyrenees Mtns. **Neighbors:** Spain on S, France on N. **Topography:** High mountains and narrow valleys over the country. **Capital:** Andorra la Vella.

Government: Type: Co-principality. **Head of state:** Co-princes are the president of France and the Roman Catholic bishop of Urgel in Spain. **Local divisions:** 7 parishes.

Economy: Industries: Tourism, tobacco products. **Labor force:** 20% agric.; 80% ind. and commerce; services; government.

Finance: Monetary unit: French franc, Spanish peseta.

Communications: Television sets: 1 per 8 persons . **Radios:** 1 per 4 persons. **Telephones in use:** 1 per 2 persons.

Health: Births (per 1,000 pop. 1989): 10. **Deaths** (per 1,000 pop. 1989): 4. **Natural increase:** 0.7%.

Education (1989): **Literacy:** 99%. School compulsory to age 16.

The present political status, with joint sovereignty by France and the bishop of Urgel, dates from 1278.

Tourism, especially skiing, is the economic mainstay. A free port, allowing for an active trading center, draws some 10 million tourists annually. The ensuing economic prosperity accompanied by Andorra's virtual law-free status, has given rise to calls for reform.

Angola

People's Republic of Angola

República Popular de Angola

People: Population (1990 est.): 8,802,000. **Pop. density:** 18 per sq. mi. **Ethnic groups:** Ovimbundu 38%, Kimbundu 25%; Bakongo 13%. **Languages:** Portuguese (official), various Bantu languages. **Religions:** Roman Catholic 38%, Protestant 15%, indigenous beliefs 47%.

Geography: Area: 481,353 sq. mi., larger than Texas and California combined. **Location:** In SW Africa on Atlantic coast. **Neighbors:** Namibia on S, Zambia on E, Zaire on N; Cabinda, an enclave separated from rest of country by short Atlantic coast of Zaire, borders Congo Republic. **Topography:** Most of Angola consists of a plateau elevated 3,000 to 5,000 feet above sea level, rising from a narrow coastal strip. There is also a temperate highland area in the west-central region, a desert in the S, and a tropical rain forest covering Cabinda. **Capital:** Luanda (1988 est.): 1.1 mln.

Government: Type: In transition. **Head of state:** Pres. Jose Eduardo dos Santos b. Aug. 28, 1942; in office: Sept. 20, 1979. **Local divisions:** 18 provinces. **Defense:** 14.3% of GNP (1984).

Economy: Industries: Food processing, textiles, mining, tires, petroleum. **Chief crops:** Coffee, bananas. **Minerals:** Iron, diamonds (over 2 mln. carats a year), copper, phosphates, oil. **Livestock** (1989): cattle: 3.1 mln.; goats: 1 mln. **Crude oil reserves** (1987): 1.9 bln. bbls. **Arable land:** 3%. **Fish catch** (1987): 81,000 metric tons. **Electricity prod.** (1988): 737 mln.kwh. **Labor force:** 85% agric., 15% industry.

Finance: Monetary unit: Kwanza (Nov. 1990: 60 = $1 US). **Gross national product** (1989): $6.0 bln. **Per Capita GNP:** $620. **Imports** (1986): $1.1 bln.; partners: Portugal 9%, Fra. 12%; U.S. 9.2%. **Exports** (1986): $1.4 bln.; partners: U.S. 38%.

Transport: Motor vehicles: in use (1984): 56,000 passenger cars, 29,000 comm. vehicles. **Chief ports:** Cabinda, Lobito, Luanda.

Communications: Television sets: 1 per 228 persons. **Radios:** 1 per 22 persons. **Telephones in use:** 1 per 122 persons. **Daily newspaper circ.** (1984): 13 per 1,000 pop.

Health: Life expectancy at birth (1989): 42.0 male; 45.0 female. **Births** (per 1,000 pop. 1989): 47. **Deaths** (per 1,000 pop. 1989): 21. **Natural increase:** 2.6%. **Hospital beds:** 1 per 672 persons. **Physicians:** 1 per 13,489 persons. **Infant mortality** (per 1,000 live births 1989): 161.

Education (1989): **Literacy:** 30%.

Major International Organizations: UN (ILO, WHO), OAU.

From the early centuries AD to 1500, Bantu tribes penetrated most of the region. Portuguese came in 1583, allied with the Bakongo kingdom in the north, and developed the slave trade. Large-scale colonization did not begin until the 20th century, when 400,000 Portuguese immigrated.

A guerrilla war begun in 1961 lasted until 1974, when Portugal offered independence. Violence between the National Front, based in Zaire, the Soviet-backed Popular Movement, and the National Union, aided by the U.S. and S. Africa, killed thousands of blacks, drove most whites to emigrate, and completed economic ruin. Cuban troops and Soviet aid helped the Popular Movement win most of the country after independence, igniting a Civil War.

Jonas Savimbi, leader of the National Union for Total Independence of Angola (UNITA), a rebel group fighting to overthrow the government, visited the U.S. in 1986 and was favorably received by the Reagan administration.

An agreement was signed Dec. 1988 between Angola, Cuba, and S. Africa on a timetable for withdrawal of Cuban troops— Cuba completed its troop withdrawal May 25, 1991—and for the independence of Namibia. The 16-year war ended May 1, 1991, as the government and UNITA signed a peace agreement which would lead to democracy.

Antigua and Barbuda

People: Population (1990 est.) 64,000. **Urban:** (1985) 34%. **Ethnic groups:** Mostly African. **Language:** English (official). **Religion:** Predominantly Church of England.

Geography: Area: 171 sq. mi. **Location:** Eastern Caribbean. **Neighbors:** approx. 30 mi. north of Guadeloupe. **Capital:** St. John's, (1988 est.) 27,000.

Government: Type: Constitutional monarchy with British-style parliament. **Head of State:** Queen Elizabeth II; represented by Sir Wilfred E. Jacobs. **Head of Government:** Prime Min. Vere Cornwall Bird; b. Dec. 7, 1910; in office Nov. 1, 1981.

Economy: Industries: manufacturing, tourists (195,000 in 1984). **Arable Land:** 18%.

Finance: Monetary unit: East Caribbean dollar (June 1991): 2.70 = $1 U.S. **Gross national product** (1988): $215 mln.

Health: infant mortality (per 1,000 live births 1989): 11.

Education (1990): **Literacy:** 90%.

Major International Organizations: UN, Commonwealth of Nations.

Embassy: 2400 International Dr., NW 20008; 362-5122.

Antigua was discovered by Columbus in 1493. The British colonized it in 1632.

The British associated state of Antigua achieved independence as Antigua and Barbuda on Nov. 1, 1981. The government maintains close relations with the U.S., United Kingdom, and Venezuela.

Argentina
Argentine Republic
República Argentina

People: Population (1990 est.): 32,291,000. **Age distrib.** (%): 0–14: 30.3; 15–59: 56.8; 60+: 12.9. **Pop. density:** 30 per sq. mi. **Urban** (1987): 85%. **Ethnic groups:** Europeans 85% (Spanish, Italian), Indians, Mestizos, Arabs. **Languages:** Spanish (official), Italian. **Religions:** Roman Catholic 92%.

Geography: Area: 1,065,189 sq. mi., 4 times the size of Texas, second largest in S. America. **Location:** Occupies most of southern S. America. **Neighbors:** Chile on W, Bolivia, Paraguay on N, Brazil, Uruguay on NE. **Topography:** The mountains in W: the Andean, Central, Misiones, and Southern. Aconcagua is the highest peak in the Western hemisphere, alt. 22,834 ft. E of the Andes are heavily wooded plains, called the Gran Chaco in the N, and the fertile, treeless Pampas in the central region. Patagonia, in the S, is bleak and arid. Rio de la Plata, 170 by 140 mi., is mostly fresh water, from 2,485-mi. Parana and 1,000-mi. Uruguay rivers. **Capital:** Buenos Aires. (The Senate has approved the moving of the capital to the Patagonia Region). **Cities** (1990 est.): Buenos Aires 10,500,000 met.; Cordoba 969,000; Rosario 750,455; Mendoza 597,000; San Miguel de Tucuman 497,000.

Government: Type: Republic. **Head of state:** Pres. Carlos Saúl Menem; b. July 2, 1930; in office: July 8, 1989. **Local divisions:** 22 provinces, 1 natl. terr. and 1 federal dist., under military governors. **Defense:** 1.4% of GNP (1987).

Economy: Industries: Meat processing, flour milling, chemicals, textiles, machinery, autos. **Chief crops:** Grains, corn, grapes, linseed, sugar, tobacco, rice, soybeans, citrus fruits. **Minerals:** Oil, lead, zinc, iron, copper, tin, uranium. **Crude oil reserves** (1987): 2.1 bln. bbls. **Arable land:** 13%. **Livestock** (1988): cattle: 50 mln.; sheep: 29 mln. **Fish catch** (1987): 420,000 metric tons. **Electricity prod.** (1988): 48.0 bln. kwh. **Crude steel prod.** (1988): 3.6 mln. metric tons. **Labor force:** 19% agric.; 36% ind. and comm.; 20% services.

Finance: Monetary unit: Austral (June 1991: 9,420 = $1 US). **Gross national product** (1990): $70.1 bln. **Per capita GNP** (1990): $2,134. **Imports** (1989): $4.2 bln.; partners: U.S. 21%, W. Ger. 9%, Braz. 16%, Jap. 7%. **Exports** (1989): $9.3 bln.; partners: USSR 13%, Neth. 9%, U.S. 12%. **Tourists** (1988): receipts: $634 mln. **National budget** (1987): $9.5 bln. expenditures. **International reserves less gold** (Jan. 1991): $4.2 bln. **Gold:** 4.37 mln. oz t. **Consumer prices** (change in 1989): 3,079%.

Transport: Railway traffic (1987): 13.2 bln. passenger-km. **Motor vehicles:** in use (1986): 3.8 mln. passenger cars, 1.4 mln. comm. vehicles. **Civil aviation:** (1989) 8.2 mln. passenger-km. **Chief ports:** Buenos Aires, Bahia Blanca, La Plata.

Communications: Television sets: 1 per 4 persons. **Radios:** 1 per 1 person. **Telephones in use:** 1 per 9 persons. **Daily newspaper circ.** (1986): 88 per 1,000 pop.

Health: Life expectancy at birth (1989): 67 male; 74 female. **Births** (per 1,000 pop. 1989): 20. **Deaths** (per 1,000 pop. 1989): 9. **Natural increase:** 1.2%. **Hospital beds:** 1 per 186 persons. **Physicians:** 1 per 370 persons. **Infant mortality** (per 1,000 live births 1989): 32.

Education (1991): **Literacy:** 92%. School attendance: 21.5% through secondary school.

Major International Organizations: UN (WHO, IMF, FAO), OAS.

Embassy: 1600 New Hampshire Ave. NW 20009; 939-6400.

Nomadic Indians roamed the Pampas when Spaniards arrived, 1515-1516, led by Juan Diaz de Solis. Nearly all the Indians were killed by the late 19th century. The colonists won independence, 1916, and a long period of disorders ended in a strong centralized government.

Large-scale Italian, German, and Spanish immigration in the decades after 1880 spurred modernization, making Argentina the most prosperous, educated, and industrialized of the major Latin American nations. Social reforms were enacted in the

1920s, but military coups prevailed 1930-46, until the election of Gen. Juan Peron as president.

Peron, with his wife Eva Duarte effected labor reforms, but also suppressed speech and press freedoms, closed religious schools, and ran the country into debt. A 1955 coup exiled Peron, who was followed by a series of military and civilian regimes. Peron returned in 1973, and was once more elected president. He died 10 months later, succeeded by his wife, Isabel, who had been elected vice president, and who became the first woman head of state in the Western hemisphere.

A military junta ousted Mrs. Peron in 1976 amid charges of corruption. Under a continuing state of siege, the army battled guerrillas and leftists, killed 5,000 people, and jailed and tortured others. On Dec. 9, 1985, after a trial of 5 months and nearly 1,000 witnesses, 5 former junta members, including ex-presidents Jorge Videla and Gen. Roberto Eduardo Viola, were found guilty of murder and human rights abuses.

A severe worsening in economic conditions placed extreme pressure on the military government.

Argentine troops seized control of the British-held Falkland Islands on Apr. 2, 1982. Both countries had claimed sovereignty over the islands, located 250 miles off the Argentine coast, since 1833. The British dispatched a task force and declared a total air and sea blockade around the Falklands. Fighting began May 1; several hundred lost their lives as the result of the destruction of a British destroyer and the sinking of an Argentine cruiser.

British troops landed in force on East Falkland Island May 21. By June 2, the British had surrounded Stanley, the capital city and Argentine stronghold. The Argentine troops surrendered, June 14; Argentine President Leopoldo Galtieri resigned June 17.

Democratic rule returned to Argentina in 1983 as Raul Alfonsin's Radical Civic Union gained an absolute majority in the presidential electoral college and Congress. In 1989 the nation was plagued by severe financial problems as inflation reached crisis levels; over 6,000%. The hyperinflation sparked a week of looting and rioting in several cities; the government declared a 30-day state of siege May 29.

The government unveiled harsh economic measures in an effort to combat spiraling inflation and control government spending Apr. 1991.

Australia
Commonwealth of Australia

People: Population (1990 est.): 16,646,000. **Age distrib. (%):** 0–14: 21.9; 15–59; 62.6; ; 59 +: 15.5. **dop. density:** 5.4 per sq. mi. **Urban** (1984): 85%. **Ethnic groups:** European 95%, Asian 4%, aborigines (including mixed) 1.5%. **Languages:** English, aboriginal languages. **Religions:** Anglican 26%, other Protestant 25%, Roman Catholic 25%.

Geography: Area: 2,966,200 sq. mi., almost as large as the continental U.S. **Location:** SE of Asia, Indian O. is W and S, Pacific O. (Coral, Tasman seas) is E; they meet N of Australia in Timor and Arafura seas: Tasmania lies 150 mi. S of Victoria state, across Bass Strait. **Neighbors:** Nearest are Indonesia, Papua New Guinea on N, Solomons, Fiji, and New Zealand on E. **Topography:** An island continent. The Great Dividing Range along the E coast has Mt. Kosciusko, 7,310 ft. The W plateau rises to 2,000 ft., with arid areas in the Great Sandy and Great Victoria deserts. The NW part of Western Australia and Northern Terr. are arid and hot. The NE has heavy rainfall and Cape York Peninsula has jungles. The Murray R. rises in New South Wales and flows 1,600 mi. to the Indian O. **Capital:** Canberra. **Cities** (1988 est.): Sydney 3,500,000; Melbourne 3,000,000; Brisbane 1,200,000; Adelaide 1,000,000; Perth 1,100,000.

Government: Type: Democratic, federal state system. **Head of state:** Queen Elizabeth II, represented by Gov.-Gen. William Hayden; in office: Feb. 16, 1989. **Head of government:** Prime Min. Robert James Lee Hawke; b. Dec. 9, 1929; in office: Mar. 11, 1983. **Local divisions:** 6 states, 2 territories. **Defense:** 2.7% of GNP (1988).

Economy: Industries: Iron, steel, textiles, electrical equip., chemicals, autos, aircraft, ships, machinery. **Chief crops:** Wheat (a leading export), barley, oats, corn, hay, sugar, wine, fruit, vegetables. **Minerals:** Coal, copper, iron, lead, tin, uranium, zinc. **Crude oil reserves** (1987): 1.6 bln. bbls. **Other resources:** Wool (30% of world output). **Arable land:** 9%. **Livestock** (1989): cattle: 22 mln.; sheep: 162 mln.; pigs: 2.5 mln. **Fish

catch** (1988): 200,000 metric tons. **Electricity prod.** (1988): 135 bln. kwh. **Crude steel prod.** (1989): 6.6 mln. metric tons. **Labor force:** 6% agric.; 33% finance & services; 36% trade & manuf.

Finance: Monetary unit: Dollar (June 1991: 1.31 = $1.00 US). **Gross national product** (1989): $240 bln. **Per capita GNP** (1989): $14,440. **Imports** (1990): $42.0 bln; partners: U.S. 21%, Jap. 20%, UK 7%. **Exports** (1990): $39.7 bln.; partners: Jap. 27%, U.S. 11%, NZ 5%. **Tourists** (1989): $3.3 bln. receipts. **National budget** (1989): $65 bln. expenditures. **International reserves less gold** (Mar. 1991): $16.1 bln. **Gold:** 7.93 mln. oz t. **Consumer prices** (change in 1990): 6.0%.

Transport: Motor vehicles: in use (1988): 7.2 mln. passenger cars, 1.9 mln. comm. vehicles. **Civil aviation** (1989): 26.2 mln. passenger-km.; 441 airports with scheduled flights. **Chief ports:** Sydney, Melbourne, Newcastle, Port Kembla, Fremantle, Geelong.

Communications: Television sets: 1 per 2 persons. **Radios:** 1 per 2 persons. **Telephones in use:** 1 per 2 persons. **Daily newspaper circ.** (1988): 405 per 1,000 pop.

Health: Life expectancy at birth (1989): 73 male; 80 female. **Births** (per 1,000 pop. 1989): 15. **Deaths** (per 1,000 pop. 1989): 8. **Natural increase:** 8%. **Hospital beds:** 1 per 186 persons. **Physicians:** 1 per 438 persons. **Infant mortality** (per 1,000 live births 1989): 8.1.

Education (1989): **Literacy:** 99%. **School:** compulsory to age 15; attendance 94%.

Major International Organizations: UN and all its specialized agencies, OECD, Commonwealth of Nations.

Embassy: 1601 Massachusetts Ave NW 20036; 797-3000.

Capt. James Cook explored the E coast in 1770, when the continent was inhabited by a variety of different tribes. The first settlers, beginning in 1788, were mostly convicts, soldiers, and government officials. By 1830, Britain had claimed the entire continent, and the immigration of free settlers began to accelerate. The commonwealth was proclaimed Jan. 1, 1901. Northern Terr. was granted limited self-rule July 1, 1978. Their capitals and 1989 population estimates:

	Area (sq. mi.)	Population
New South Wales, Sydney	309,500	771,900
Victoria, Melbourne	87,900	321,500
Queensland, Brisbane	666,990	834,100
Western Aust., Perth	975,100	594,700
South Aust., Adelaide	379,900	424,600
Tasmania, Hobart	26,200	451,100
Aust. Capital Terr., Canberra	900	278,700
Northern Terr., Darwin	519,800	156,500

Australia's racially discriminatory immigration policies were abandoned in 1973, after 3 million Europeans (half British) had entered since 1945. The 50,000 aborigines and 150,000 part-aborigines are mostly detribalized, but there are several preserves in the Northern Territory. They remain economically disadvantaged.

On Jan. 26, 1988, some 15,000 aborigines demonstrated in Sydney to protest discrimination while the rest of the nation celebrated the 200th anniversary of the landing of the first European settlers.

Australia's agricultural success makes it among the top exporters of beef, lamb, wool, and wheat. Major mineral deposits have been developed as well, largely for exports. Industrialization has been completed.

Australia harbors many plant and animal species not found elsewhere, including the kangaroo, koalas, platypus, dingo (wild dog), Tasmanian devil (racoon-like marsupial), wombat (bearlike marsupial), and barking and frilled lizards.

Australian External Territories

Norfolk Is., area 13½ sq. mi., pop. (1985) 1,800, was taken over, 1914. The soil is very fertile, suitable for citrus fruits, bananas, and coffee. Many of the inhabitants are descendants of the Bounty mutineers, moved to Norfolk 1856 from Pitcairn Is. Australia offered the island limited home rule, 1978.

Coral Sea Is. Territory, 1 sq. mi., is administered from Norfolk Is.

Territory of Ashmore and Cartier Is., area 2 sq. mi., in the Indian O. came under Australian authority 1934 and are administered as part of Northern Territory. **Heard and McDonald Is.** are administered by the Dept. of Science.

Cocos (Keeling) Is., 27 small coral islands in the Indian O. 1,750 mi. NW of Australia. Pop. (1981) 569, area: 5½ sq. mi. The residents voted to become part of Australia, Apr. 1984.

Kiritimati (Christmas Is.) 52 sq. mi., pop. 3,000 (1983), 230 mi. S of Java, was transferred by Britain in 1958. It has phosphate deposits.

Australian Antarctic Territory was claimed by Australia in 1933, including 2,360,000 sq. mi. of territory S of 60th parallel S Lat. and between 160th-45th meridians E Long. It does not include Adelie Coast.

Austria
Republic of Austria
Republik Österreich

People: Population (1990 est.): 7,595,000. **Age distrib.** (%): 0–14: 17.4; 15–59: 62.1; 60+: 20.5. **Pop. density:** 233 per sq. mi. **Urban** (1989): 62.1%. **Ethnic groups:** German 98%, Slovene, Croatian. **Languages:** German 98%. **Religions:** Roman Catholic 85%.

Geography: Area: 32,374 sq. mi., slightly smaller than Maine. **Location:** In S Central Europe. **Neighbors:** Switzerland, Liechtenstein on W, Germany, Czechoslovakia on N, Hungary on E, Yugoslavia, Italy on S. **Topography:** Austria is primarily mountainous, with the Alps and foothills covering the western and southern provinces. The eastern provinces and Vienna are located in the Danube River Basin. **Capital:** Vienna. **Cities** (1988 cen.): Vienna 1,500,000.

Government: Type: Federal republic. **Head of state:** Pres. Kurt Waldheim; b. Dec. 21, 1918; in office: June 8, 1986. **Head of government:** Chancellor Franz Vranitzky; b. Oct. 4, 1937; in office: June 16, 1986. **Local divisions:** 9 lander (states), each with a legislature. **Defense:** 1.2% of GNP (1987).

Economy: Industries: Steel, machinery, autos, electrical and optical equip., glassware, sport goods, paper, textiles, chemicals, cement. **Chief crops:** Grains, potatoes, beets. **Minerals:** Iron ore, oil, magnesite. **Crude oil reserves** (1985): 116 mln. bbls. **Other resources:** Forests, hydro power. **Arable land:** 18.3%. **Livestock:** (1989): Cattle: 2.5 mln.; pigs: 3.8 mln. **Electricity prod.** (1989): 50.1 bln. kwh. **Crude steel prod.** (1988): 4.5 mln. metric tons. **Labor force:** 8% agric.; 35% ind. & comm.; 56% service.

Finance: Monetary unit: Schilling (June 1991: 11.91 = $1 US). **Gross national product** (1989): $131.8 bln. **Per capita GNP** (1989): $17,360. **Imports** (1990): $49.1 bln.; partners: Ger. 44%, It. 9%, Switz. 5%. **Exports** (1990): $41.2 bln.; partners: Ger. 33%, It. 9%, Switz. 7%. **Tourists** (1987): receipts: $7.6 bln. **National budget** (1987): $37.5 bln. expenditures. **International reserves less gold** (Mar. 1991): $9.0 bln. **Gold:** 20.3 mln. oz t. **Consumer prices** (change in 1990): 3.3%.

Transport: Railway traffic (1988): 6.6 bln. passenger-km. **Motor vehicles:** in use (1988): 2.7 mln. passenger cars, 234,000 comm. **Civil aviation** (1989): 2.9 bln. passenger-km; 6 airports with scheduled flights.

Communications: Television sets: 1 per 2.8 persons. **Radios:** 1 per 1.6 persons. **Telephones in use:** 1 per 1.8 persons. **Daily newspaper circ.** (1989): 389 per 1,000 pop.

Health: Life expectancy at birth (1989): 71 male; 79 female. **Births** (per 1,000 pop. 1989): 12. **Deaths** (per 1,000 pop. 1989): 12. **Natural increase:** −.0%. **Hospital beds:** 1 per 101 persons. **Physicians:** 1 per 356 persons. **Infant mortality** (per 1,000 live births 1989): 8.

Education (1989): Literacy: 99%. School years compulsory 9; attendance 95%.

Major International Organizations: UN and all of its specialized agencies, EFTA, OECD.

Embassy: 2343 Massachusetts Ave. NW 20008; 483-4474.

Rome conquered Austrian lands from Celtic tribes around 15 BC. In 788 the territory was incorporated into Charlemagne's empire. By 1300, the House of Hapsburg had gained control; they added vast territories in all parts of Europe to their realm in the next few hundred years.

Austrian dominance of Germany was undermined in the 18th century and ended by Prussia by 1866. But the Congress of Vienna, 1815, confirmed Austrian control of a large empire in southeast Europe consisting of Germans, Hungarians, Slavs, Italians, and others.

The dual Austro-Hungarian monarchy was established in 1867, giving autonomy to Hungary and almost 50 years of peace.

World War I, started after the June 28, 1914 assassination of Archduke Franz Ferdinand, the Hapsburg heir, by a Serbian nationalist, destroyed the empire. By 1918 Austria was reduced to a small republic, with the borders it has today.

Nazi Germany invaded Austria Mar. 13, 1938. The republic was reestablished in 1945, under Allied occupation. Full independence and neutrality were restored in 1955.

Austria produces most of its food, as well as an array of industrial products. A large part of Austria's economy is controlled by state enterprises. Socialists have shared or alternated power with the conservative People's Party.

An international panel of historians issued a report in 1988 which concluded that Pres. Kurt Waldheim knew of war crimes in Greece and Yugoslavia while serving in the German army during WW 2, did nothing to stop them, and later covered up his war record. The panel found no evidence that Waldheim committed war crimes.

The Bahamas
The Commonwealth of the Bahamas

People: Population (1990 est.): 251,000. **Age distrib.** (%): 0–14: 38.0; 15–59: 56.3; 60+: 5.7. **Pop. density:** 45 per sq. mi. **Urban** (1990): 60%. **Ethnic groups:** black 85%, white (British, Canadian, U.S.) 15%. **Languages:** English. **Religions:** Baptist 29%, Anglican 23%, Roman Catholic 22%.

Geography: Area: 5,380 sq. mi., about the size of Connecticut. **Location:** In Atlantic O., E of Florida. **Neighbors:** Nearest are U.S. on W, Cuba on S. **Topography:** Nearly 700 islands (30 inhabited) and over 2,000 islets in the western Atlantic extend 760 mi. NW to SE. **Capital:** Nassau. **Cities:** (1985 est.) New Providence 135,437; Freeport 16,000.

Government: Type: Independent commonwealth. **Head of state:** Queen Elizabeth II, represented by Gov.-Gen. Henry Taylor, in office: June 25, 1988. **Head of government:** Prime Min. Lynden Oscar Pindling; b. Mar. 22, 1930; in office: Jan. 16, 1967. **Local divisions:** 21 districts.

Economy: Industries: Tourism (50% of GNP), rum, banking, pharmaceuticals. **Chief crops:** Fruits, vegetables. **Minerals:** Salt. **Other resources:** Lobsters. **Arable land:** 2%. **Electricity prod.** (1988): 828 mln. kwh. **Labor force:** 5% agric.; 25% tourism, 30% government.

Finance: Monetary unit: Dollar (Apr. 1991: 1 = $1 US). **Gross national product** (1988): $1.7 bln. **Per capita income** (1988): $7,178. **Imports** (1988): $1.7 bln.; partners: U.S. 74%, EC 30%. **Exports** (1988): $1 bln. (not incl. oil); partners: U.S. 41%, U.K. 7%. **Tourists** (1988): $1.1 bln. **National budget** (1990): $557 mln. expenditures. **International reserves less gold** (Mar. 1991): $163 mln. **Consumer prices** (change in 1990): 6.4%.

Transport: Motor vehicles: in use (1986): 67,000 passenger cars, 13,200 comm. vehicles. **Chief ports:** Nassau, Freeport.

Communications: Radios: 1 per 2 persons. **Television sets:** 1 per 4.6 persons. **Telephones in use:** 1 per 2 persons. **Daily newspaper circ.** (1988): 143 per 1,000 pop.

Health: Life expectancy at birth (1989): 67 male; 74 female. **Births** (per 1,000 pop. 1989): 23. **Deaths** (per 1,000 pop. 1989): 6. **Natural increase:** 1.7%. **Infant mortality** (per 1,000 live births 1989): 17.

Education (1990): Literacy: 95%; School compulsory through age 14.

Major International Organizations: UN (World Bank, IMF, WHO), OAS.

Embassy: 600 New Hampshire Ave. NW 20037; 338-3940.

Christopher Columbus first set foot in the New World on San Salvador (Watling I.) in 1492, when Arawak Indians inhabited the islands. British settlement began in 1647; the islands became a British colony in 1783. Internal self-government was granted in 1964; full independence within the Commonwealth was attained July 10, 1973.

International banking and investment management has become a major industry alongside tourism, despite controversy over financial irregularities.

Bahrain

State of Bahrain

Dawlat al-Bahrayn

People: Population (1990 est.): 512,000. **Age distrib.** (%): 0-14: 34.7; 15-59: 61.5; 60+ 3.8. **Pop. density:** 1,872 per sq. mi. **Urban** (1986): 82%. **Ethnic groups:** Bahraini 63%, Asian 13%, other Arab 10%, Iranian 6%. **Languages:** Arabic (official), Farsi, Urdu. **Religions:** Sunni Moslem 30%, Shi'ah Moslem 70%.

Geography: Area: 258 sq. mi., smaller than New York City. **Location:** In Persian Gulf. **Neighbors:** Nearest are Saudi Arabia on W. Qatar on E. **Topography:** Bahrain Island, and several adjacent, smaller islands, are flat, hot and humid, with little rain. **Capital:** Manama. **Cities** (1988 est.): Manama 151,000.

Government: Type: Traditional monarchy. **Head of state:** Amir Isa bin Sulman al-Khalifa; b. July 3, 1933; in office: Nov. 2, 1961. **Head of government:** Prime Min. Kahlifa ibn Sulman al-Khalifa; b. 1935; in office: Jan. 19, 1970. **Local divisions:** 11 municipalities. **Defense:** 4.0% of GNP (1987).

Economy: Industries: Oil products, aluminum smelting. **Chief crops:** Fruits, vegetables. **Minerals:** Oil, gas. **Crude oil reserves** (1985): 173 mln. bbls. **Arable land:** 5%. **Electricity prod.** (1988): 5.4 bln. kwh. **Labor force:** 5% agric.; 85% ind. and commerce; 5% services; 3% gov.

Finance: Monetary unit: Dinar (Mar. 1991: 1.00 = $2.66 US). **Gross national product** (1987): $4.6 bln. **Per capita GNP** (1987): $9,994. **Imports** (1988): $2.6 bln.; partners: Sau. Ar. 60%, UK 6%, U.S. 9%. **Exports** (1988): $2.3 bln.; partners: UAE 18%, Jap. 12%, Sing. 10%, U.S. 6%. **National Budget** (1987): $2.6 bln. expenditures. **International reserves less gold** (Mar. 1991): $1.2 bln. **Gold:** 150,000 oz t. **Consumer prices** (change in 1990): 1.0%.

Transport: Motor vehicles: in use (1986): 81,000 passenger cars, 24,000 comm. vehicles. **Chief ports:** Sitra.

Communications: Television sets: 1 per 2.3 persons. **Radios:** 1 per 1.7 persons. **Telephones in use:** 1 per 3.4 persons.

Health: Life Expectancy at Birth (1989): 70 male; 75 female. **Births** (per 1,000 pop. 1989): 25. **Deaths** (per 1,000 pop. 1989): 4. **Natural Increase:** 2.1. Medical services are free. **Infant Mortality** (per 1,000 live births 1989): 22.

Education (1989): **Literacy:** 40%.

Major International Organizations: UN (GATT, IMF, WHO), Arab League.

Embassy: 3502 International Dr. NW 20008; 342-0741.

Long ruled by the Khalifa family, Bahrain was a British protectorate from 1861 to 1971, when it regained independence.

Pearls, shrimp, fruits, and vegetables were the mainstays of the economy until oil was discovered in 1932. By the 1970s, oil reserves were depleted; international banking thrived.

Bahrain took part in the 1973-74 Arab oil embargo against the U.S. and other nations. The government bought controlling interest in the oil industry in 1975.

Bangladesh

People's Republic of Bangladesh

Gama Prajātantrī Bangladesh

People: Population (1990 est.): 117,976,000. **Age distrib.** (%): 0-14: 44.3; 15-59: 50.4; 60+: 5.3. **Pop. density:** 2,028 per sq. mi. **Urban** (1988): 22%. **Ethnic groups:** Bengali 98%, Bihari, tribesmen. **Languages:** Bengali (official), Chakma, Magh. **Religions:** Moslem 85%, Hindu 14%.

Geography: Area: 55,813 sq. mi. slightly smaller than Wisconsin. **Location:** In S Asia, on N bend of Bay of Bengal. **Neighbors:** India nearly surrounds country on W, N, E; Burma on SE. **Topography:** The country is mostly a low plain cut by the Ganges and Brahmaputra rivers and their delta. The land is alluvial and marshy along the coast, with hills only in the extreme SE and NE. A tropical monsoon climate prevails, among the rainiest in the world. **Capital:** Dhaka. **Cities** (1989 est.): Dhaka (met.) 5.3 mln.; Chittagong (met.) 2.0 mln.; Khulna (met.) 940,000.

Government: Type: Presidential/parliamentary. **Head of state:** vacant. **Head of Government:** Prime Min. Khaleda Zia;

b. Nov. 1944; in office: Mar. 19, 1991. **Local divisions:** 21 districts. **Defense:** 1.8% of GNP (1987).

Economy: Industries: Cement, jute, textiles, fertilizers, petroleum products. **Chief crops:** Jute (most of world output), rice, tea. **Minerals:** Natural gas, offshore oil, coal. **Arable land:** 67%. **Livestock** (1989): cattle: 23 mln.; goats: 10.7 mln. **Fish catch** (1988): 828,000 metric tons. **Electricity prod.** (1988): 4.8 bln. kwh. **Labor force:** 59% agric; 11% ind.; 30% services.

Finance: Monetary unit: Taka (Mar. 1991: 37.79 = $1 US). **Gross national product** (1989): $20.2 bln. **Per capita GNP** (1989) $180. **Imports** (1989): $3.6 bln.; partners: Jap. 13%, U.S. 13%. **Exports** (1989): $1.3 bln.; partners: U.S. 31%, It. 9%; Pak 5%. **Tourists** (1989): $13.0 mln. receipts. **National budget** (1988): $3.3 bln. expenditures. **International reserves less gold** (Mar. 1991): $711 mln. **Gold:** 82,000 oz t. **Consumer prices** (change in 1990): 8.1%.

Transport: Railway traffic (1987): 6.0 bln. passenger-km. **Motor vehicles:** in use (1989): 39,000 passenger cars, 51,000 comm. vehicles. **Chief ports:** Chittagong, Chalna.

Communications: Radios: 1 per 24 persons. **Television sets:** 1 per 315 persons. **Telephones in use:** 1 per 572 persons. **Daily newspaper circ.** (1988) 8 per 1,000 pop.

Health: Life expectancy at birth (1989): 54 male; 53 female. **Births** (per 1,000 pop. 1989): 43. **Deaths** (per 1,000 pop. 1989): 15. **Natural increase:** 2.8%. **Hospital beds:** 1 per 3,233 persons. **Physicians:** 1 per 6,166 persons. **Infant mortality** (per 1,000 live births 1989): 138.

Education (1989): **Literacy:** 29%. **Attendance:** 24% primary school; 4% secondary school.

Major International Organizations: UN (GATT, IMF, WHO). **Embassy:** 2201 Wisconsin Ave. NW 20007; 342-8372.

Moslem invaders conquered the formerly Hindu area in the 12th century. British rule lasted from the 18th century to 1947, when East Bengal became part of Pakistan.

Charging West Pakistani domination, the Awami League, based in the East, won National Assembly control in 1971. Assembly sessions were postponed; riots broke out. Pakistani troops attacked Mar. 25; Bangladesh independence was proclaimed the next day. In the ensuing civil war, one million died and 10 million fled to India.

War between India and Pakistan broke out Dec. 3, 1971. Pakistan surrendered in the East Dec. 15. Sheik Mujibur Rahman became prime minister. The country moved into the Indian and Soviet orbits, in response to U.S. support of Pakistan, and much of the economy was nationalized.

In 1974, the government took emergency powers to curb widespread violence; Mujibur was assassinated and a series of coups followed.

Chronic destitution among the densely crowded population has been worsened by the decline of jute as a major world commodity.

On May 30, 1981, Pres. Ziaur Rahman was shot and killed in an unsuccessful coup attempt by army rivals. Vice President Abdus Sattar assumed the presidency but was ousted in a coup led by army chief of staff Gen. H.M. Ershad, Mar. 1982. Ershad declared Bangladesh an Islamic Republic in 1988. Bangladesh remains one of the world's poorest countries.

In 1988 and 1989, natural disasters and, monsoon rains brought devastation to Bangladesh: over 4,000 died, 30 million were made homeless. A cyclone struck Apr. 1991, killing over 125,000 people. Some 7,500 U.S. military aided in the relief effort.

Barbados

People: Population (1990 est.): 260,000 **Age distrib.** (%): 0-14: 24.8%; 15-59: 60.6; 60+: 14.6. **Pop. density:** 1,542 per sq. mi. **Urban** (1985): 42%. **Ethnic groups:** African 80%, mixed 16%, Caucasian 4%. **Languages:** English. **Religions:** Anglican 70%, Methodist 9%, Roman Catholic 4%.

Geography: Area: 166 sq. mi. **Location:** In Atlantic, farthest E of W. Indies. **Neighbors:** Nearest are Trinidad, Grenada on SW. **Topography:** The island lies alone in the Atlantic almost completely surrounded by coral reefs. Highest point is Mt. Hillaby, 1,115 ft. **Capital:** Bridgetown. **Cities** (1986): Bridgetown 7,400.

Government: Type: Independent sovereign state within the Commonwealth. **Head of state:** Queen Elizabeth II, represented by Gov.-Gen. Dame Nita Barrow; in office: June 6, 1990. **Head of government:** Prime Min. Erskine Sandiford; b. Mar. 24, 1937;

in office: June 1, 1987. **Local divisions:** 11 parishes and Bridgetown.

Economy: Industries: Rum, molasses, tourism. **Chief crops:** Sugar, corn. **Minerals:** Lime. **Other resources:** Fish. **Arable land:** 76%. **Electricity prod.** (1989): 484 mln. kwh. **Labor force:** 5% agric.; 17% ind. and comm.; 37% services and government.

Finance: Monetary unit: Dollar (June 1991: 2.01 = $1 US). **Gross national product** (1988): $1.5 bln. **Per capita GNP** (1987): $5,330. **Imports** (1989): $673 mln.; partners: U.S. 32%, CARACOM 12%. **Exports** (1989): $186 mln.; partners: U.S. 21%, CARACOM 27%. **Tourists** (1989): $502 mln. receipts. **National budget** (1987): $470 mln. expenditures. **International reserves less gold** (Mar. 1991): $117 mln. **Consumer prices** (change in 1990): 3.1%.

Transport: Motor vehicles: in use (1987): 34,000 passenger cars; 7,000 comm. vehicles. **Chief ports:** Bridgetown.

Communications: Television sets: 1 per 3.9 persons. **Radios:** 1 per 1.1 persons. **Telephones in use:** 1 per 2.4 persons. **Daily newspaper circ.** (1988): 161 per 1,000 pop.

Health: Life expectancy at birth (1989): male: 73 female: 77. **Births** (per 1,000 pop. 1989): 18. **Deaths** (per 1,000 pop. 1989): 8. **Natural increase:** 1.0%. **Hospital beds:** 1 per 123 persons. **Physicians:** 1 per 1,042 persons. **Infant mortality** (per 1,000 live births 1989): 17.

Education (1989): **Literacy:** 99%. **Years compulsory:** to age 16.

Major International Organizations: UN (FAO, GATT, ILO, IMF, WHO), OAS.

Embassy: 2144 Wyoming Ave. NW 20008; 939-9200.

Barbados was probably named by Portuguese sailors in reference to bearded fig trees. An English ship visited in 1605, and British settlers arrived on the uninhabited island in 1627. Slaves worked the sugar plantations, but were freed in 1834.

Self-rule came gradually, with full independence proclaimed Nov. 30, 1966. British traditions have remained.

Belgium

Kingdom of Belgium

Koninkrijk België (Dutch)
Royaume de Belgique (French)

People: Population (1990 est.): 9,895,000. **Age distrib. (%):** 0–14: 18.2; 15–59: 61.7; 60+: 20.1 **Pop. density:** 840 per sq. mi. **Urban** (1988): 76%. **Ethnic groups:** Fleming 55%, Walloon 33%. **Languages:** Flemish (Dutch) 57%, French 33%, Italian, German. **Religions:** Roman Catholic 75%.

Geography: Area: 11,799 sq. mi., slightly larger than Maryland. **Location:** In NW Europe, on N. Sea. **Neighbors:** France on W, Luxembourg on SE, Germany on E, Netherlands on N. **Topography:** Mostly flat, the country is trisected by the Scheldt and Meuse, major commercial rivers. The land becomes hilly and forested in the SE (Ardennes) region. **Capital:** Brussels. **Cities** (1988 est.): Brussels (met.) 970,000; Antwerp (met.) 479,000; Ghent 233,000; Charleroi 209,000; Liege 200,000.

Government: Type: Parliamentary democracy under a constitutional monarch. **Head of state:** King Baudouin; b. Sept. 7, 1930; in office: July 17, 1951. **Head of government:** Premier Wilfried Martens; b. Apr. 19, 1936; in office: Dec. 17, 1981. **Local divisions:** 9 provinces; 3 regions; 3 cultural communities. **Defense:** 3.1% of GNP (1988).

Economy: Industries: Steel, glassware, diamond cutting, textiles, chemicals. **Chief crops:** Wheat, potatoes, sugar beets. **Minerals:** Coal. **Other resources:** Forests. **Arable land** (incl. Lux.): 26.5%. **Livestock:** (1987): cattle: 3.0 mln; pigs: 5.7 mln. **Fish catch** (1988): 23.3 metric tons. **Electricity prod.** (1989): 60 bln. kwh. **Crude steel prod.** (1988): 11.2 mln. metric tons. **Labor force:** 2% agric.; 26% ind. & comm.; 37% services and transportation; 23% public service.

Finance: Monetary unit: Franc (June 1991: 34.85 = $1 US). **Gross national product** (1989): $162 bln. **Per capita GNP** $16,390. *Note:* the following trade and tourist data includes Luxembourg. **Imports** (1990): $119 bln.; partners: Ger. 23%, Neth. 17%, France 15%, UK 8%, U.S. 5%. **Exports** (1990): $118 bln.;

partners: Ger. 19%, France 18%, Neth. 15%, UK 6%. **Tourists** (1989): receipts: $3.5 bln. **National budget** (1989): $51 bln. expenditures. **International reserves less gold** (Mar. 1991): $12.3 bln. **Gold:** 30.2 mln. oz t. **Consumer prices** (change in 1990): 3.4%.

Transport: Railway traffic (1989): 6.3 bln. passenger-km. **Motor vehicles:** in use (1989): 3.7 mln. passenger cars, 312,000 comm. vehicles. **Civil aviation** (1989): 6.5 bln. passenger-km; 4 airports with scheduled flights. **Chief ports:** Antwerp, Zeebrugge, Ghent.

Communications: Television sets: 1 per 3.2 persons. **Radios:** 1 per 2.2 persons; **Telephones in use:** 1 per 2.1 persons. **Daily newspaper circ.** (1988): 195 per 1,000 pop.

Health: Life expectancy at birth (1989): 69.8 male; 76.6 female. **Births** (per 1,000 pop. 1989): 12. **Deaths** (per 1,000 pop. 1989): 11. **Natural increase** 0.1%. **Hospital beds:** 1 per 108 persons. **Physicians:** 1 per 317 persons. **Infant mortality** (per 1,000 live births 1989): 9.4

Education (1989): **Literacy:** 98%. School compulsory to age 18.

Major International Organizations: UN and all of its specialized agencies, NATO, EC, OECD.

Embassy: 3330 Garfield St. NW 20008; 333-6900

Belgium derives its name from the Belgae, the first recorded inhabitants, probably Celts. The land was conquered by Julius Caesar, and was ruled for 1800 years by conquerors, including Rome, the Franks, Burgundy, Spain, Austria, and France. After 1815, Belgium was made a part of the Netherlands, but it became an independent constitutional monarchy in 1830.

Belgian neutrality was violated by Germany in both world wars. King Leopold III surrendered to Germany, May 28, 1940. After the war, he was forced by political pressure to abdicate in favor of his son, King Baudouin.

The Flemings of northern Belgium speak Dutch while French is the language of the Walloons in the south. The language difference has been a perennial source of controversy and led to antagonism between the 2 groups. Parliament has passed measures aimed at transferring power from the central government to 3 regions—Wallonia, Flanders, and Brussels.

Belgium lives by its foreign trade; about 50% of its entire production is sold abroad.

Belize

People: Population (1990 est.): 180,400. **Age distrib. (%):** 0–14: 44.5; 15–59: 47.8; 60+: 7.6. **Pop. density:** 20 per sq. mi. **Ethnic groups:** African, Mestizo, Amerindian, Creole. **Languages:** English (official), Spanish, native Creole dialects. **Religions:** Roman Catholic 60%, Protestant 40%.

Geography: Area: 8,867 sq. mi. **Location:** eastern coast of Central America. **Neighbors:** Mexico on N., Guatemala on W. and S. **Capital:** Belmopan. **Cities:** (1990 est.): Belize City 60,000.

Government: Type: Parliamentary. **Head of State:** Gov. Gen. Minita Gordon. **Head of government:** Prime Min. George Cadle Price; in office: Nov. 7, 1989. **Local divisions:** 6 districts.

Economy: Sugar is the main export.

Finance: Monetary unit: Belize dollar (Mar. 1991) 2 = $1 U.S. **Gross national product** (1988): $247 mln. **Per capita GNP** (1988): $1,250. **Imports** (1989): $148 mln.; partners: U.S. 55%, UK 8%. **Exports:** (1989): $100 mln.; partners: U.S. 46%, UK 31%. **National Budget** (1990): $72 mln. expenditures.

Health: life expectancy (1989) male: 67; female: 72. **Births** (per 1,000 pop. 1989): 36. **Deaths** (per 1,000 pop. 1989): 6. **Hospital beds:** 1 per 317 persons. **Physicians:** 1 per 2,097 persons. **Infant mortality** (per 1,000 live births, 1989): 36.

Education: (1989) **Literacy:** 93%.; **Years compulsory:** 9; attendance 55%.

Major International Organizations: OAS, UN (IMF, World Bank), Commonwealth of Nations.

Embassy: 3400 International Dr., NW 20005; 363-4505.

Belize (formerly called British Honduras), was Great Britain's last colony on the American mainland, achieved independence on Sept. 21, 1981. Guatemala claims territorial sovereignty over the country and has refused to recognize Belize's independence. British troops in Belize guarantee security.

Benin

Republic of Benin

République du Benin

People: Population (1990 est.): 4,840,000. **Age distrib. (%):** 0–14: 46.5; 15–59: 49.0; 60+: 4.5. **Pop. density:** 109 per sq. mi. **Urban** (1985): 20%. **Ethnic groups:** Fon, Adja, Bariba, Yoruba. **Languages:** French (official), Fon, Yoruba, Somba. **Religions:** Mainly animist with Christian, Moslem minorities.

Geography: Area: 43,483 sq. mi., slightly smaller than Pennsylvania. **Location:** In W Africa on Gulf of Guinea. **Neighbors:** Togo on W, Burkina Faso, Niger on N, Nigeria on E. **Topography:** most of Benin is flat and covered with dense vegetation. The coast is hot, humid, and rainy. **Capital:** Porto–Novo. **Cities** (1984 est.): Cotonou 330,000.

Government: Type: Democracy. **Head of state:** Nicephore Soglo; in office: Apr. 4, 1991. **Local divisions:** 6 provinces. **Defense:** 2.1% of GNP (1988).

Economy: Chief crops: Palm products, peanuts, cotton, coffee, tobacco. **Minerals:** Oil. **Arable land:** 12%. **Livestock** (1989): sheep: 890,000; goats: 1.1 mln. **Fish catch** (1988): 41,000 metric tons. **Electricity prod.** (1988): 24 mln. kwh. **Labor force:** 60% agric; 38% serv. & comm.

Finance: Monetary unit: CFA franc (Mar. 1991: 290 = $1 US). **Gross national product** (1989): $1.7 bln. **Per capita GNP** (1989): $380. **Imports** (1986): $314 mln.; partners: Ind. 24%, Fr. 16%. **Exports** (1986): $100 mln.; partners: Port. 15%, Itl. 10% Fr. 26%. **National Budget** (1987): $159 bln. expenditures. **International reserves less gold** (Feb. 1991): $64 mln.

Transport: Railway traffic (1989): 137 mln. passenger-km. **Chief ports:** Cotonou.

Communications: Radios: 1 per 14 persons. **Televisions:** 1 per 281 persons. **Daily newspaper circ.** (1988): 3 per 1,000 pop.

Health: Life expectancy at birth (1989): 48 male; 51 female. **Births** (per 1,000 pop: 1989): 54. **Deaths** (per 1,000 pop. 1989): 17. **Natural increase:** 3.7%. **Hospital beds:** 1 per 749 persons. **Physicians:** 1 per 16,025 persons. **Infant mortality** (per 1,000 live births 1989): 124.

Education (1987): **Literacy:** 28%. Years compulsory 6; attendance 43%.

Major International Organizations: UN (GATT, IMF, WHO), OAU.

Embassy: 2737 Cathedral Ave. NW 20008; 232-6656.

The Kingdom of Abomey, rising to power in wars with neighboring kingdoms in the 17th century, came under French domination in the late 19th century, and was incorporated into French West Africa by 1904.

Under the name Dahomey, the country became independent Aug. 1, 1960. The name was changed to Benin in 1975. In the fifth coup since independence Col. Ahmed Kerekou took power in 1972; two years later he declared a socialist state with a "Marxist-Leninist" philosophy. In Dec. 1989, Kerekou announced that Marxism-Leninism would no longer be the state ideology. In 1991, Kerekou was defeated in Benin's first free presidential elections in 30 years by Nicephore Soglo.

The economy relies on the development of agriculturally-based industries.

Bhutan

Kingdom of Bhutan

Druk-Yul

People: Population (1990 est.): 1,566,000. **Age distrib. (%):** 0–14: 39.8; 15–59: 53.8; over 60: 6.4 **Pop. density:** 84 per sq. mi. **Ethnic groups:** Ngalops and Sharchops 75%. Nepalese 25%, Lepcha (indigenous), Indians. **Languages:** Dzongkha (official), Gurung, Assamese. **Religions:** Buddhist (state religion) 75%, Hindu 25%.

Geography: Area: 18,147 sq. mi., the size of Vermont and New Hampshire combined. **Location:** In eastern Himalayan Mts. **Neighbors:** India on W (Sikkim) and S, China on N. **Topography:** Bhutan is comprised of very high mountains in the N, fertile valleys in the center, and thick forests in the Duar Plain in the S.

Capital: Thimphu (Paro Dzong is administrative capital). **City** (1987 est.): Thimbu 20,000.

Government: Type: Monarchy. **Head of state:** King Jigme Singye Wangchuk; b. Nov. 11, 1955; in office: July 21, 1972. **Local divisions:** 18 districts.

Economy: Industries: Handicrafts. **Chief crops:** Rice, corn, wheat. **Other resources:** Timber. **Arable land:** 2%. **Labor force:** 90% agric.

Finance: Monetary unit: Ngultrum (Jan. 1991: 19.62 = 1 US) (Indian Rupee also used). **Gross national product** (1988): $297 mln. **Per capita GNP** (1988): $190. **Tourism** (1988): 1.9 mln. **Imports** (1988): $105.1 mln.; partners India 75%. **Exports** (1988): $60.8 mln.; partners India 99%.

Communications: Radios: 1 per 64 persons. **Telephones in use:** 1 per 675 persons.

Health: Life expectancy at birth (1987): 48.1 male; 46.8 female. **Births** (per 1,000 pop. 1989): 38. **Deaths** (per 1,000 pop. 1989): 17. **Natural increase:** 2.0%. **Hospital beds:** 1 per 1,457 persons. **Physicians:** 1 per 9,736 persons. **Infant mortality** (per 1,000 live births 1989): 139.

Education (1989): **Literacy:** 15%. School attendance: 25%. **Major International Organizations:** UN (IMF, World Bank).

The region came under Tibetan rule in the 16th century. British influence grew in the 19th century. A monarchy, set up in 1907, became a British protectorate by a 1910 treaty. The country became independent in 1949, with India guiding foreign relations and supplying aid.

Links to India have been strengthened by airline service and a road network. Most of the population engages in subsistence agriculture.

Bolivia

Republic of Bolivia

República de Bolivia

People: Population (1990 est.): 6,730,000. **Age distrib. (%):** 0–14: 41.1; 15–59: 52.4; 60+: 5.5. **Pop. density:** 17 per sq. mi. **Urban** (1988): 49%. **Ethnic groups:** Quechua 30%, Aymara 25%, mixed 30%, European 14%. **Languages:** Spanish, Quechua, Aymara (all official). **Religions:** Roman Catholic 95%.

Geography: Area: 424,165 sq. mi., the size of Texas and California combined. **Location:** In central Andes Mtns. **Neighbors:** Peru, Chile on W, Argentina, Paraguay on S, Brazil on E and N. **Topography:** The great central plateau, at an altitude of 12,000 ft., over 500 mi. long, lies between two great cordilleras having 3 of the highest peaks in S. America. Lake Titicaca, on Peruvian border, is highest lake in world on which steamboats ply (12,506 ft.). The E central region has semitropical forests; the llanos, or Amazon-Chaco lowlands are in E. **Capitals:** Sucre, (legal), La Paz (de facto). **Cities** (1988 est.): La Paz 1,000,000; Santa Cruz 615,000; Cochabamba 377,000.

Government: Type: Republic. **Head of state:** Pres. Jaime Paz Zamora, in office: Aug. 6, 1989. **Local divisions:** 9 departments. **Defence:** 3% of GNP (1987).

Economy: Industry: Textiles, food processing, mining, clothing. **Chief crops:** Potatoes, sugar, coffee, corn, coca (sold for cocaine processing). **Minerals:** Antimony, tin, tungsten, silver, zinc, oil, gas, iron. **Crude oil reserves** (1985): 157 mln. bbls. **Other resources:** rubber, cinchona bark. **Arable land:** 3%. **Livestock** (1987): cattle: 5.3 mln.; sheep: 9.5 mln.; pigs: 1.6 mln. **Electricity prod.** (1988): 1.6 bln. kwh. **Labor force:** 50% agric., 10% ind. & comm, 26% serv. & govt.

Finance: Monetary unit: Peso (Mar. 1991: 3.46 = $1 US). **Gross national product** (1989): $4.3 bln. **Per capita GNP** (1989): $600. **Imports** (1988): $604 mln.; partners: U.S. 20%, Jap. 10%, Arg. 14%, Braz. 20%. **Exports** (1988): $601 mln.; partners: Arg. 35%, U.S. 19%. **National budget** (1988): $2.8 bln. expenditures. **International reserves less gold** (Mar. 1991): $197 mln. **Gold:** 894,000 oz t. **Consumer prices** (change in 1989): 15%.

Transport: Railway traffic (1989): 368 mln. passenger-km. **Motor vehicles:** in use (1988): 83,000 passenger cars, 150,000 comm. vehicles. **Civil aviation** (1989): 1.1 bln. passenger-km.; 18 airports with scheduled flights.

Communications: Television sets: 1 per 16 persons. **Radios:** 1 per 1.8 persons. **Telephones in use:** 1 per 37 persons. **Daily newspaper circ.** (1986): 35 per 1,000 pop.

Health: Life expectancy at birth (1989): 52 male; 56 female.
Births (per 1,000 pop. 1989): 36. **Deaths** (per 1,000 pop. 1989):
13. **Natural increase:** 2.3%. **Hospital beds:** 1 per 472 persons.
Physicians: 1 per 1,595 persons. **Infant mortality** (per 1,000
live births 1989): 123.
Education (1989): **Literacy:** 63%. **Years compulsory:** ages
7-14; attendance 82%.
Major International Organizations: UN (IMF, FAO, WHO),
OAS.
Embassy: 3014 Massachusetts Ave. NW 20008; 483-4410.

The Incas conquered the region from earlier Indian inhabitants
in the 13th century. Spanish rule began in the 1530s, and lasted
until Aug. 6, 1825. The country is named after Simon Bolivar,
independence fighter.
In a series of wars, Bolivia lost its Pacific coast to Chile, the
oilbearing Chaco to Paraguay, and rubber-growing areas to Brazil, 1879-1935.
Economic unrest, especially among the militant mine workers,
has contributed to continuing political instability. A reformist government under Victor Paz Estenssoro, 1951-64, nationalized tin
mines and attempted to improve conditions for the Indian majority, but was overthrown by a military junta. A series of coups and
countercoups continued through 1981, until the military junta
elected Gen. Villa as president.
In July 1982, the military junta assumed power amid a growing
economic crisis and foreign debt difficulties. The junta resigned
in October and allowed the Congress, elected democratically in
1980, to take power.
U.S. pressure on the government to reduce the country's output of coca, the raw material for cocaine, has led to clashes between police and coca growers and increased anti-U.S. feeling
among Bolivians.

Botswana
Republic of Botswana

People: Population (1991 est.): 1,300,000. **Age distrib. (%):**
0–14: 39.6; 15–64: 48.3; 65+: 3.1. **Pop. density:** 5 per sq. mi.
Urban (1991): 25%. **Ethnic groups:** Tswana, Kalanga, others.
Languages: English (official), Tswana, Shona. **Religions:** indige-
nous beliefs 50%, Christian 50%.
Geography: Area: 231,804 sq. mi., slightly smaller than
Texas. **Location:** In southern Africa. **Neighbors:** Namibia (S.W.
Africa) on N and W, S. Africa on S, Zimbabwe on NE; Botswana
claims border with Zambia on N. **Topography:** The Kalahari
Desert, supporting nomadic Bushmen and wildlife, spreads over
SW; there are swamplands and farming areas in N, and rolling
plains in E where livestock are grazed. **Capital:** Gaborone. **Cit-
ies** (1991): Gaborone 138,000.
Government: Type: Republic, parliamentary democracy.
Head of state: Pres. Quett Masire; b. 1925; in office: July 13,
1980. **Local divisions:** 6 district councils and 6 town councils.
Defense: 3.5% of national budget (1991).
Economy: Industries: Livestock processing, mining. **Chief
crops:** Corn, sorghum, beans. **Minerals:** Copper, coal, nickel,
diamonds. **Other resources:** Big game. **Arable land:** 2%. **Electricity prod.** (1989): 845 mln. kwh. **Labor force:** 70% agric.
Finance: Monetary unit: Pula (Mar. 1991: 1.00 = $.50 US).
Gross national product (1989): $2.0 bln. **Imports** (1991): $2.2
bln.; partners: S. Africa 88%. **Exports** (1991): $2.7 bln.; part-
ners: Europe 67%, U.S. 17%, S. Africa 7%. **National budget**
(1990): $503 mln. expenditures. **International reserves less
gold** (Mar. 1991): $3.3 bln. **Consumer prices** (change in 1990):
11.4%
Transport: Railway traffic (1991): 653 mln. passenger km.
Motor vehicles: in use (1991): 26,000 passenger cars, 47,000
comm. vehicles.
Communications: Radios: 1 per 8 persons. **Daily newspaper circ.** (1989): 22 per 1,000 pop.
Health: Life expectancy at birth (1990): male: 57; female:
63. **Births** (1,000 pop. 1989): 38. **Deaths** (per 1,000 pop. 1989):
11. **Natural increase:** 2.8%. **Hospital beds** (1990): 5,022. **Physicians:** 1 per 7,185 persons. **Infant mortality** (per 1,000 live
births 1989): 63.
Education (1989): **Literacy:** 80%; 93% attend primary
school.
Major International Organizations: UN (GATT, IMF, WHO),
OAU, Commonwealth of Nations.
Embassy: 3400 International Dr. NW 20008; 244-4990.

First inhabited by bushmen, then by Bantus, the region became the British protectorate of Bechuanaland in 1886, halting
encroachment by Boers and Germans from the south and southwest. The country became fully independent Sept. 30, 1966,
changing its name to Botswana.
Cattle-raising and mining (diamonds, copper, nickel) have contributed to the country's economic growth. The economy is
closely tied to S. Africa.

Brazil
Federative Republic of Brazil
República Federativa do Brasil

People: Population (1990 est.): 153,771,000. **Age distrib.
(%):** 0–14: 35.2; 15–59: 57.7; 60+: 7.1. **Pop. density:** 47 per
sq. mi. **Urban** (1989): 76%. **Ethnic groups:** Portuguese, Africans, and mulattoes make up the vast majority; Italians, Germans, Japanese, Indians, Jews, Arabs. **Languages:** Portuguese
(official), English, German, Italian. **Religions:** Roman Catholic
89%.
Geography: Area: 3,286,470 sq. mi., larger than contiguous
48 U.S. states; largest country in S. America. **Location:** Occupies eastern half of S. America. **Neighbors:** French Guiana,
Suriname, Guyana, Venezuela on N, Colombia, Peru, Bolivia,
Paraguay, Argentina on W, Uruguay on S. **Topography:** Brazil's
Atlantic coastline stretches 4,603 miles. In N is the heavily-
wooded Amazon basin covering half the country. Its network of
rivers navigable for 15,814 mi. The Amazon itself flows 2,093
miles in Brazil, all navigable. The NE region is semiarid scrubland, heavily settled and poor. The S central region, favored by
climate and resources, has almost half of the population, produces 75% of farm goods and 80% of industrial output. The narrow coastal belt includes most of the major cities. Almost the
entire country has a tropical or semitropical climate. **Capital:**
Brasilia. **Cities** (1989 met. est.): Sao Paulo 16.8 mln.; Rio de
Janeiro 11.1 mln.; Belo Horizonte 3.4 mln.; Recife 2.9 mln.; Salvador 2.3 mln.; Porto Alegre 2.9 mln.
Government: Type: Federal republic. **Head of state:** Pres.
Fernando Collor de Mello; b. Aug. 12, 1949; in office: Mar. 15,
1990. **Local divisions:** 26 states, federal district (Brasilia). **Defense:** 0.3% of GNP (1988).
Economy: Industries: Steel, autos, ships, appliances, petrochemicals, machinery. **Chief crops:** Coffee (largest grower),
cotton, soybeans, sugar, cocoa, rice, corn, fruits. **Minerals:**
Chromium, iron, manganese, diamonds, gold, nickel, gem
stones, tin, bauxite, oil. **Crude oil reserves** (1987): 2.3 bln. bbls.
Arable land: 8%. **Livestock** (1989): cattle: 136 mln.; pigs: 33
mln.; sheep: 20 mln. **Fish catch** (1988): 830,000 metric tons.
Electricity prod. (1988): 214 bln. kwh. **Crude steel prod.**
(1988): 24.6 mln. metric tons. **Labor force:** 40% services, 35%
agric.; 25% ind.
Finance: Monetary unit: Cruzeiro (June 1991: 268 = $1
US). **Gross national product** (1989): $375 bln. **Per capita
GNP** (1988): $2,434. **Imports** (1989): $20 bln.; partners: U.S.
28%, EC 23%. **Exports** (1989): $34 bln.; partners: U.S. 26%,
EC 27%. **Tourists** (1988): receipts: $1.6 bln. **National budget**
(1986): $40.1 bln expenditures. **International reserves less
gold** (Jan. 1991): $7.3 bln. **Gold:** 3.7 mln. oz t. **Consumer
prices** (change in 1990): 2,937%.
Transport: Railway traffic (1986): 15.7 bln. passenger-km.
Motor vehicles: in use (1988): 14 mln. passenger cars, 1.6 mln.
Civil aviation (1988): 23.5 bln. passenger-km.; 126 airports with
scheduled flights. **Chief ports:** Santos, Rio de Janeiro, Vitoria,
Salvador, Rio Grande, Recife.
Communications: Television sets: 1 per 4 persons. **Radios:**
1 per 2.5 persons. **Telephones in use:** 1 per 11 persons. **Daily
newspaper circ.** (1988): 55 per 1,000 pop.
Health: Life expectancy at birth (1989): 64 male; 69 female.
Births (per 1,000 pop. 1989): 27. **Deaths** (per 1,000 pop. 1989):
7. **Natural increase:** 2.0%. **Hospital beds:** 1 per 285 persons.
Physicians: 1 per 684 persons. **Infant mortality** (per 1,000 live
births 1989): 67.
Education (1989): **Literacy:** 76%.
Major International Organizations: UN and most of its spe-
cialized agencies, OAS.
Embassy: 3006 Massachusetts Ave. NW 20008; 745-2700.

Pedro Alvares Cabral, a Portuguese navigator, is generally
credited as the first European to reach Brazil, in 1500. The coun-

try was thinly settled by various Indian tribes. Only a few have survived to the present, mostly in the Amazon basin.

In the next centuries, Portuguese colonists gradually pushed inland, bringing along large numbers of African slaves. Slavery was not abolished until 1888.

The King of Portugal, fleeing before Napoleon's army, moved the seat of government to Brazil in 1808. Brazil thereupon became a kingdom under Dom Joao VI. After his return to Portugal, his son Pedro proclaimed the independence of Brazil, Sept. 7, 1822, and was acclaimed emperor. The second emperor, Dom Pedro II, was deposed in 1889, and a republic proclaimed, called the United States of Brazil. In 1967 the country was renamed the Federative Republic of Brazil.

A military junta took control in 1930; dictatorial power was assumed by Getulio Vargas, until finally forced out by the military in 1945. A democratic regime prevailed 1945-64, during which time the capital was moved from Rio de Janeiro to Brasilia in the interior.

The next 5 presidents were all military leaders. Censorship was imposed, and much of the opposition was suppressed amid charges of torture. In 1974 elections, the official opposition party made gains in the chamber of deputies; some relaxation of censorship occurred.

Since 1930, successive governments have pursued industrial and agricultural growth and the development of interior areas. Exploiting vast mineral resources, fertile soil in several regions, and a huge labor force, Brazil became the leading industrial power of Latin America by the 1970s, while agricultural output soared. Democratic elections were held in 1985 as the nation returned to civilian rule.

However, income maldistribution and inflation have led to severe economic recession. Foreign debt is among the largest in the world.

Brazil unveiled a comprehensive environmental program for the Amazon region in 1989, amid an international outcry by environmentalists and others concerned about the ongoing destruction of the Amazon ecosystem. The Amazon rain forest was considered a global resource because of its impact on world weather patterns.

Brunei Darussalam
State of Brunei Darussalam
Negara Brunei Darussalam

People: Population (1990 est.): 372,000. **Pop. Density:** 119 per sq. mi. **Ethnic groups:** Malay 65%, Chinese 20%. **Language:** Malay, English, (both official), Chinese. **Religion:** Moslem 60%, Buddhist 14%, Christian 10%.

Geography: Area: 2,226 sq. mi.; smaller than Delaware. **Location:** on the north coast of the island of Borneo; it is surrounded on its landward side by the Malaysian state of Sarawak. **Capital:** Bandar Seri Begawan. **Cities** (1982 est.): Bandar Seri Begawan 51,000.

Government: Type: Independent sultanate. **Head of Government:** Sultan Sir Muda Hassanal Bolkiah Mu'izzadin Waddaulah; in office: Jan. 1, 1984.

Economy: Industries: petroleum (about 90% of revenue is derived from oil exports). **Chief crops:** rice, bananas, cassava. **Finance: Monetary unit:** Brunei dollar (Dec. 1990: 1.76 = $1). **Gross domestic product** (1987): $3.1 bln. **Per capita income** (1987): $20,000.

Communications: Television sets: 1 per 4.7 persons. **Radios:** 1 per 3 persons. **Telephones:** 1 per 6 persons.

Education (1987): **Literacy:** 95% among young.

Health: Life expectancy at birth: (1989): 74 male; 77 female. **Infant Mortality** (per 1,000 live births 1989): 10.

Major International Organizations: UN and some of its specialized agencies.

The Sultanate of Brunei was a powerful state in the early 16th century with authority over all of the island of Borneo as well as parts of the Sulu Islands and the Philippines. In 1888, a treaty was signed which placed the state under the protection of Great Britain.

Brunei became a fully sovereign and independent state on Jan. 1, 1984.

The Sultan of Brunei donated $10 million to the Nicaraguan *contras* in 1987; the subsequent misplacement of the funds generated much media attention in the U.S.

Bulgaria
People's Republic of Bulgaria
Narodna Republika Bulgaria

People: Population (1990 est.): 8,978,000. **Age distrib. (%):** 0–14: 20.6; 15–59: 60.5; 60+: 18.9. **Pop. density:** 203 per sq. mi. **Urban** (1990): 67%. **Ethnic groups:** Bulgarian 85%, Turk 8.5%. **Languages:** Bulgarian (official), Turkish. **Religions:** Government promotes atheism; background of people is 85% Orthodox.

Geography: Area: 44,365 sq. mi., about the size of Ohio. **Location:** In eastern Balkan Peninsula on Black Sea. **Neighbors:** Romania on N, Yugoslavia on W, Greece, Turkey on S. **Topography:** The Stara Planina (Balkan) Mts. stretch E-W across the center of the country, with the Danubian plain on N, the Rhodope Mts. on SW, and Thracian Plain on SE. **Capital:** Sofia. **Cities** (1989 est.): Sofia 1,200,000; Plovdiv 364,000; Varna 306,000.

Government: Type: In transition. **Head of state:** Pres. Zhelyu Zhelev; b. Mar. 3, 1935; in office: Aug. 1, 1990. **Head of government:** Premier Dimitar Popov; in office: Dec. 7, 1990. **Local divisions:** 9 administrative regions. **Defense:** 12.7% of GNP (1988).

Economy: Industries: Chemicals, machinery, metals, textiles, fur, leather goods, vehicles, wine, processed food. **Chief crops:** Grains, fruit, corn, potatoes, tobacco. **Minerals:** Lead, manganese, lignite, coal. **Arable land:** 38%. **Livestock** (1988): cattle: 1.8 mln.; pigs: 4.0 mln.; sheep: 8.8 mln. **Fish catch** (1989): 121,000 metric tons. **Electricity prod.** (1988): 43 bln. kwh. **Crude steel prod.** (1988): 3.0 mln. metric tons. **Labor force:** 20% agric.; 33% ind.

Finance: Monetary unit: Lev (Dec. 1990: 1.00 = $2.93 US). **Gross National Product** (1989): $50.8 bln. **Per capita GNP** (1989): $5,660. **Imports** (1987): $16.9 bln.; partners: USSR 56%. **Exports** (1987): $16.8 bln.; partners: USSR 61%. **Tourists** (1988): revenues: $359 mln. **National budget** (1987): $23.7 bln. expenditures.

Transport: Railway traffic (1989): 7.6 bln. passenger-km. **Motor vehicles:** in use (1988) 1.1 mln. passenger cars, 599,000 commercial. **Civil aviation** (1989): 3.8 bln. passenger km.; 13 airports. **Chief ports:** Burgas, Varna.

Communications: Television sets: 1 per 5.3 persons. **Radios:** 1 per 4.5 persons. **Telephones in use:** 1 per 4.3 persons. **Daily newspaper circ.** (1988): 316 per 1,000 pop.

Health: Life expectancy at birth (1989): 68 male; 74 female. **Births** (per 1,000 pop. 1989): 13. **Deaths** (per 1,000 pop. 1989): 12. **Hospital beds:** 1 per 103 persons. **Physicians:** 1 per 319 persons. **Infant mortality** (per 1,000 live births 1989): 18.

Education (1990): **Literacy:** 98%. **Years compulsory:** 8.

Major International Organizations: UN.

Embassy: 1621-22d St. NW 20008; 387-7969.

Bulgaria was settled by Slavs in the 6th century. Turkic Bulgars arrived in the 7th century, merged with the Slavs, became Christians by the 9th century, and set up powerful empires in the 10th and 12th centuries. The Ottomans prevailed in 1396 and remained for 500 years.

A revolt in 1876 led to an independent kingdom in 1908. Bulgaria expanded after the first Balkan War but lost its Aegean coastline in World War I, when it sided with Germany. Bulgaria joined the Axis in World War II, but withdrew in 1944. Communists took power with Soviet aid; the monarchy was abolished Sept. 8, 1946.

On Nov. 10, 1989, Todor Zhivkov, who had held power for 35 years, resigned. Zhivkov was imprisoned, Jan. 1990, pending the outcome of charges of corruption and abuse of power. In Jan. 1990, parliament voted to revoke the constitutionally guaranteed dominant role of the Communist Party.

Burkina Faso

People: Population (1990 est.): 8,941,000. **Pop. density:** 72 per sq. mi. **Urban** (1988): 8%. **Ethnic groups:** Voltaic groups (Mossi, Bobo), Mande. **Languages:** French (official), Sudanic tribal languages. **Religions:** animist 45%, Moslems 40%, Christian 15%.

Geography: Area: 105,869 sq. mi., the size of Colorado. **Location:** In W. Africa, S of the Sahara. **Neighbors:** Mali on NW, Niger on NE, Benin, Togo, Ghana, Côte d' Ivoire on S. **Topogra-**

phy: Landlocked Burkina Faso is in the savannah region of W. Africa. The N is arid, hot, and thinly populated. **Capital:** Ouagadougou. **Cities** (1990): Ouagadougou 500,000; Bobo-Dioulasso 250,000.

Government: Type: Military. **Head of state:** Pres. Blaise Compaore; in office: Oct. 15, 1987. **Local divisions:** 30 provinces. **Defense:** 2.7% of GNP (1988).

Economy: Chief crops: Millet, sorghum, rice, peanuts, grain. **Minerals:** Manganese, gold, limestone. **Arable land:** 10%. **Electricity prod.** (1989): 144 mln. kwh. **Labor force:** 92% agric.

Finance: Monetary unit: CFA franc (Mar. 1991: 290 = $1 US). **Gross national product** (1989): $2.7 bln. **Per capita GNP** (1989): $310. **Imports** (1988): $489 mln.; partners: EC, Côte d' Ivoire. **Exports** (1988): $142 mln.; partners: Côte d' Ivoire, EC, China. **International reserves less gold** (Jan. 1991): $300 mln. **Gold:** 11,000 oz t. **Consumer prices** (change in 1990): −.8%.

Transport: Motor vehicles: in use (1983): 21,000 passenger cars, 6,600 comm. vehicles.

Communications: Television sets: 1 per 210 persons. **Radios:** 1 per 44 persons. **Telephones in use:** 1 per 482 persons. **Daily newspaper circ.** (1989): 1 per 1,000 pop.

Health: Life expectancy at birth (1989): 45 male; 49 female. **Births** (per 1,000 pop. 1989): 47. **Deaths** (per 1,000 pop. 1989): 18. **Natural increase:** 2.9%. **Hospital beds:** 1 per 1,359 persons. **Physicians:** 1 per 29,914 persons. **Infant mortality** (per 1,000 live births 1989): 138.

Education (1989): **Literacy:** 8%. Only 8% attend school.

Major International Organizations: UN and many of its specialized agencies, OAU.

Embassy: 2340 Massachusetts Ave. NW 20008; 332-5577.

The Mossi tribe entered the area in the 11th to 13th centuries. Their kingdoms ruled until defeated by the Mali and Songhai empires.

French control came by 1896, but Upper Volta (name changed to Burkina Faso on Aug. 4, 1984), was not finally established as a separate territory until 1947. Full independence came Aug. 5, 1960, and a pro-French government was elected. A 1982 coup established the current regime.

Several hundred thousand farm workers migrate each year to Cote D'Ivoire and Ghana. Burkina Faso is heavily dependent on foreign aid.

Burma

(See Myanmar)

Burundi

Republic of Burundi

Republika y'Uburundi

People: Population (1990 est.): 5,647,000. **Age distrib. (%):** 0–14: 45.1; 15–59: 50.1; 60+: 4.8. **Pop. density:** 540 per sq. mi. **Urban** (1986): 8%. **Ethnic groups:** Hutu 85%, Tutsi 14%, Twa (pygmy) 1%. **Languages:** French, Rundi (both official). **Religions:** Christian 67%, traditional African 32%.

Geography: Area: 10,759 sq. mi., the size of Maryland. **Location:** In central Africa. **Neighbors:** Rwanda on N, Zaire on W, Tanzania on E. **Topography:** Much of the country is grassy highland, with mountains reaching 8,900 ft. The southernmost source of the White Nile is located in Burundi. Lake Tanganyika is the second deepest lake in the world. **Capital:** Bujumbura. **Cities** (1986 est.): Bujumbura 272,000.

Government: Type: Republic. **Head of state:** Pres. Maj. Pierre Buyoya; in office: Sept. 9, 1987. **Head of government:** Prime Min: Adrien Sibomana, in office: Oct. 19, 1988. **Local divisions:** 15 provinces. **Defense** (1988): 3.1% of GNP.

Economy: Chief crops: Coffee (87% of exports), cotton, tea. **Minerals:** Nickel. **Arable land:** 43%. **Electricity prod.** (1988): 54 mln. kwh. **Labor force:** 93% agric.

Finance: Monetary unit: Franc (Apr. 1991: 173 = $1 US). **Gross national product** (1989): $1.2 bln. **Per capita GNP** $220. **Imports** (1989): $187 mln.; partners: Belg.-Lux. 17%; W. Ger. 18%. **Exports** (1989): $78 mln; partners: W. Ger. 31%, Belg. 20%. **Tourism** (1988): $2 mln. receipts. **National budget** (1986): $203 mln. expenditures. **International reserves less gold** (Mar. 1991): $126 mln. **Gold:** 17,000 oz t. **Consumer prices** (change in 1990): 7.0%.

Transport: Motor vehicles: in use (1988): 10,000 passenger cars, 9,000 comm. vehicles.

Communications: Radios: 1 per 18 persons. **Telephones in use:** 1 per 622 persons.

Health: Life expectancy at birth (1989): 50 male; 53 female. **Births** (per 1,000 pop. 1989): 48. **Deaths** (per 1,000 pop. 1989): 15. **Natural increase:** 3.3%. **Hospital beds:** 1 per 724 persons. **Physicians:** 1 per 18,365 persons. **Infant mortality** (per 1,000 live births 1989): 114.

Education (1988): **Literacy:** 30%.

Major International Organizations: UN (GATT, IMF, WHO), OAU.

Embassy: 2233 Wisconsin Ave. NW 20007; 342-2574.

The pygmy Twa were the first inhabitants, followed by Bantu Hutus, who were conquered in the 16th century by the tall Tutsi (Watusi), probably from Ethiopia. Under German control in 1899, the area fell to Belgium in 1916, which exercised successively a League of Nations mandate and UN trusteeship over Ruanda-Urundi (now 2 countries).

Independence came in 1962.

An unsuccessful Hutu rebellion in 1972-73 left 10,000 Tutsi and 150,000 Hutu dead. Over 100,000 Hutu fled to Tanzania and Zaire. Burundi is pledged to ethnic reconciliation, but remains one of the poorest and most densely populated countries in Africa.

Cambodia

State of Cambodia

People: Population (1990 est.): 6,592,000. **Pop. density:** 121 per sq. mi. **Urban** (1989): 10%. **Ethnic groups:** Cambodian 90%, Vietnamese 4%, Chinese 5%. **Languages:** Khmer (official), French. **Religions:** Theravada Buddhism 95%.

Geography: Area: 70,238 sq. mi., the size of Missouri. **Location:** In Indochina Peninsula. **Neighbors:** Thailand on W, N, Laos on NE, Vietnam on E. **Topography:** The central area, formed by the Mekong R. basin and Tonle Sap lake, is level. Hills and mountains are in SE, a long escarpment separates the country from Thailand on NW. 75% of the area is forested. **Capital:** Phnom Penh. **Cities** (1990 est.): Phnom Penh 400,000.

Government: Type: No single authority controls the whole country. **Head of State:** Pres., People's Revolutionary Party Heng Samrin; in office: Jan. 7, 1979. **Head of Government:** Premier Hun Sen; in office: Jan. 14, 1985. **Local divisions:** 19 provinces and municipalities.

Economy: Industries: Rice milling, wood & rubber. **Chief crops:** Rice, corn. **Minerals:** Iron, copper, manganese. **Other resources:** Forests, rubber, kapok. **Arable land:** 16%. **Livestock** (1989): cattle: 2.0 mln. pigs: 1.5 mln. **Fish catch** (1988): 70,000 metric tons. **Electricity prod.** (1988): 142.00 mln. kwh. **Labor force:** 74% agri.

Finance: Monetary unit: Riel (Jan. 1991: 460 = $1 US). **Gross National Product** (1987): $10.4 bln. **Per capita GNP** (1987): $960. **Imports** (1988): $147 mln. **Exports** (1988): $32 mln.

Transport: Railway traffic (1986): 54 mln. passenger-miles. **Motor vehicles:** in use (1988): 4,000 passenger cars, 7,000 trucks. **Chief ports:** Kompong Som.

Communications: Television sets: 1 per 166 persons. **Radios:** 1 per 10 persons. **Telephones in use:** 1 per 129 persons.

Health: Life expectancy at birth (1989): 47 male; 50 female. **Births** (per 1,000 pop. 1989): 39. **Deaths** (per 1,000 pop. 1989): 17. **Natural increase:** 2. **Hospital beds:** 1 per 632 persons. **Physicians:** 1 per 27,000 persons. **Infant Mortality** (per 1,000 live births 1989): 131.

Education (1990): **Literacy:** 50%.

Major International Organizations: UN.

Early kingdoms dating from that of Funan in the 1st century AD culminated in the great Khmer empire which flourished from the 9th century to the 13th, encompassing present-day Thailand, Cambodia, Laos, and southern Vietnam. The peripheral areas were lost to invading Siamese and Vietnamese, and France established a protectorate in 1863. Independence came in 1953.

Prince Norodom Sihanouk, king 1941-1955 and head of state from 1960, tried to maintain neutrality. Relations with the U.S. were broken in 1965, after South Vietnam planes attacked Vietcong forces within Cambodia. Relations were restored in

1969, after Sihanouk charged Viet communists with arming Cambodian insurgents.

In 1970, pro-U.S. premier Lon Nol seized power, demanding removal of 40,000 North Viet troops; the monarchy was abolished. Sihanouk formed a government-in-exile in Peking, and open war began between the government and Khmer Rouge. The U.S. provided heavy military and economic aid.

Khmer Rouge forces captured Phnom Penh April 17, 1975. The new government evacuated all cities and towns, and shuffled the rural population, sending virtually the entire population to clear jungle, forest, and scrub, which covered half the country. Over one million people were killed in executions and enforced hardships.

Severe border fighting broke out with Vietnam in 1978; developed into a full-fledged Vietnamese invasion. The Vietnamese-backed Kampuchean National United Front for National Salvation, a Cambodian rebel movement, announced, Jan. 8, 1979, the formation of a government one day after the Vietnamese capture of Phnom Pehn. Thousands of refugees flowed into Thailand and widespread starvation was reported.

On Jan. 10, 1983, Vietnam launched an offensive against rebel forces in the west. They overran a refugee camp, Jan. 31, driving 30,000 residents into Thailand. In March, Vietnam launched a major offensive against camps on the Cambodian-Thailand border, engaged Khmer Rouge guerrillas, and crossed the border instigating clashes with Thai troops. Vietnam announced that it would withdraw all its troops by Sept. 1989.

Efforts to create a new government have been hampered by the fear both in Cambodia and internationally that the Khmer Rouge would return to power.

Cameroon
Republic of Cameroon

People: Population (1990 est.): 11,900,000. **Age distrib.** (%): 0–14: 46.1; 15–59: 48.3; 60+: 5.6. **Pop. density:** 66 per sq. mi. **Urban** (1988): 40%. **Ethnic groups:** Some 200 tribes; largest are Bamileke 30%, Fulani 7%. **Languages:** English, French (both official), numerous African groups. **Religions:** Animist 51%, Moslem 16%, Christian 33%.

Geography: Area: 179,714 sq. mi., somewhat larger than California. **Location:** Between W and central Africa. **Neighbors:** Nigeria on NW, Chad, Central African Republic on E, Congo, Gabon, Equatorial Guinea on S. **Topography:** A low coastal plain with rain forests in S; plateaus in center lead to forested mountains in W, including Mt. Cameroon, 13,000 ft.; grasslands in N lead to marshes around Lake Chad. **Capital:** Yaounde. **Cities** (1988 est.): Douala 852,000; Yaounde 700,000.

Government: Type: Republic, one party presidential regime. **Head of state:** Pres. Paul Biya; b. Feb. 13, 1933; in office: Nov. 6, 1982. **Local divisions:** 10 provinces. **Defense:** 1.9% of GNP (1987).

Economy: Industries: Aluminum processing, oil prod., palm products. **Chief crops:** Cocoa, coffee, cotton. **Crude oil reserves** (1985): 531 mln. bbls. **Other resources:** Timber. **Arable land:** 14%. **Livestock** (1989): cattle: 4.5 mln.; sheep: 3.1 mln.; pigs: 1.2 mln. **Fish catch** (1989): 83,000 metric tons. **Electricity prod.** (1988): 2.5 bln. kwh. **Labor force:** 74% agric., 11% ind. and commerce.

Finance: Monetary unit: CFA franc (Mar. 1991: 290 = $1 US). **Gross national product** (1989): $11.6 bln. **Per capita GNP** (1989): $1,010. **Imports** (1988): 1.2 bln.; partners: Fr. 42%, W. Ger. 10%. **Exports** (1988): $928 mln.; partners: Fr. 21%, U.S. 16%, Neth. 28%. **National budget** (1988): $2.2 bln. **International reserves less gold** (Jan. 1991): $55 mln. **Gold:** 30,000 oz t. **Consumer prices** (change in 1988): 8.6%.

Transport: Railway traffic (1988): 469 mln. passenger-km. **Motor vehicles:** in use (1987): 78,000 passenger cars, 43,000 comm. vehicles. **Chief ports:** Douala.

Communications: Radios: 1 per 6 persons. **Telephones in use:** 1 per 179 persons. **Daily newspaper circ.** (1988): 6 per 1,000 pop.

Health: Life expectancy at birth (1989): 48 male; 52 female. **Births** (per 1,000 pop. 1989): 42. **Deaths** (per 1,000 pop. 1989): 16. **Natural increase:** 2.6%. **Hospital beds:** 1 per 377 persons. **Physicians:** 1 per 12,540 persons. **Infant mortality** (per 1,000 live births 1989): 123.

Education (1988): **Literacy:** 65%. About 70% attend school.

Major International Organizations: UN, OAU, EC (Associate).

Embassy: 2349 Massachusetts Ave. NW 20008; 265-8790.

Portuguese sailors were the first Europeans to reach Cameroon, in the 15th century. The European and American slave trade was very active in the area. German control lasted from 1884 to 1916, when France and Britain divided the territory, later receiving League of Nations mandates and UN trusteeships. French Cameroon became independent Jan. 1, 1960; one part of British Cameroon joined Nigeria in 1961, the other part joined Cameroon. Stability has allowed for development of roads, railways, agriculture, and petroleum production. Some 3,000 died in 1986 as a result of clouds of toxic gas of volcanic origin emanating from Lake Nyos.

Canada

People: Population (1990 est.): 26,620,500. **Age distrib.** (%): 0–14: 21.4; 15–59: 63.6; 60+: 15.0. **Pop. density:** 7 per sq. mi. **Urban** (1985): 75.9%. **Ethnic groups:** British 25%; French 24%; other European 16%; mixed 28%. **Language:** English, French (both official). **Religion:** Roman Catholic 46%, Protestant 41%.

Geography: Area: 3,849,000 sq. mi., the largest country in land size in the Western Hemisphere. Canada stretches 3,223 miles from east to west and extends southward from the North Pole to the U.S. border. Its seacoast includes 36,356 miles of mainland and 115,133 miles of islands, including the Arctic islands almost from Greenland to near the Alaskan border. Climate, while generally temperate, varies from freezing winter cold to blistering summer heat. **Capitol:** Ottawa. **Cities** (met. 1986 est.): Montreal 2,921,000; Toronto 3,427,000; Vancouver 1,380,000; Ottawa-Hull 819,000; Winnipeg 625,000; Edmonton 785,000, Calgary 671,000, Quebec 603,000.

Government: Type: Confederation with parliamentary democracy. **Head of state:** Queen Elizabeth II, represented by Gov.-Gen. Ramon Hnatyshyn; in office: Jan. 29, 1990. **Head of government:** Prime Min. Brian Mulroney; born: Mar. 20, 1939; in office: Sept. 4, 1984. **Local divisions:** 10 provinces, 2 territories. **Defense:** 2% of GNP (1991).

Economy: Minerals: Nickel, zinc, copper, gold, lead, molybdenum, potash, silver. **Crude oil reserves** (1990): 6.8 bln. barrels. **Arable land:** 5%. **Livestock** (1989): cattle: 12.0 mln.; pigs: 10.8 mln.; sheep: 722,000. **Fish catch** (1988): 1.5 mln. metric tons. **Electricity prod.** (1988): 468 bln. kwh. **Crude steel prod.** (1988): 15.1 mln. metric tons. **Labor force:** 4% agric.; 52% ind. & comm., 28% services.

Finance: Monetary unit: Dollar (June 1991: 1.14 = $1 US). **Gross national product** (1989): $500 bln. **Per capita GNP** (1989) $19,020. **Imports** (1990): $124 bln.; partners: U.S. 69%, EC 8%, Jap. 5%. **Exports** (1990): $131 bln.; partners: U.S. 75%, EC 9%, Jap. 5%. **Tourists** (1989): receipts: $4.7 bln. **National budget** (1990-91): $127 bln. expenditures. **International reserves less gold** (Mar. 1991): $16.9 bln. **Gold:** 14.5 mln. oz t. **Consumer prices** (change in 1990): 4.8%.

Transport: Railway traffic (1988): 1.9 bln. passenger-km. **Motor vehicles:** in use (1987): 11.1 mln. passenger cars, 3.5 mln. comm. **Civil aviation** (1988): 52.6 bln. passenger-km: 61 airports with scheduled flights.

Communications: Television sets: 1 per 1.7 persons. **Radios:** 1 per 1.2 persons. **Telephones in use:** 1 per 1.3 persons. **Daily newspaper circ.** (1989): 221 per 1,000 pop.

Health: Life expectancy at birth (1991): 73 male; 80 female. **Births** (per 1,000 pop. 1989): 14. **Deaths** (per 1,000 pop. 1989): 7. **Natural increase:** .7%. **Hospital beds:** 1 per 148 persons. **Physicians:** 1 per 467 persons. **Infant mortality** (per 1,000 live births 1990): 7.3.

Education (1991): **Literacy:** 99%.

Major International Organizations: UN and all of its specialized agencies, NATO, OECD, Commonwealth of Nations.

Embassy: 501 Pennsylvania Ave. NW 20001; 682-1740.

French explorer Jacques Cartier, who discovered the Gulf of St. Lawrence in 1534, is generally regarded as the founder of Canada. But English seaman John Cabot sighted Newfoundland 37 years earlier, in 1497, and Vikings are believed to have reached the Atlantic coast centuries before either explorer.

Canadian settlement was pioneered by the French who established Quebec City (1608) and Montreal (1642) and declared New France a colony in 1663.

Britain, as part of its American expansion, acquired Acadia (later Nova Scotia) in 1717 and, through military victory over French forces in Canada (an extension of a European conflict between the 2 powers), captured Quebec (1759) and obtained control of the rest of New France in 1763. The French, through the Quebec Act of 1774, retained the rights to their own language, religion, and civil law.

The British presence in Canada increased during the American Revolution when many colonials, proudly calling themselves United Empire Loyalists, moved north to Canada.

Fur traders and explorers led Canadians westward across the continent. Sir Alexander Mackenzie reached the Pacific in 1793 and scrawled on a rock by the ocean, "from Canada by land."

In Upper and Lower Canada (later called Ontario and Quebec) and in the Maritimes, legislative assemblies appeared in the 18th century and reformers called for responsible government. But the War of 1812 intervened. The war, a conflict between Great Britain and the United States fought mainly in Upper Canada, ended in a stalemate in 1814.

In 1837 political agitation for more democratic government culminated in rebellions in Upper and Lower Canada. Britain sent Lord Durham to investigate and, in a famous report (1839), he recommended union of the 2 parts into one colony called Canada. The union lasted until Confederation, July 1, 1867, when proclamation of the British North America (BNA) Act launched the Dominion of Canada, consisting of Ontario, Quebec, and the former colonies of Nova Scotia and New Brunswick.

Since 1840 the Canadian colonies had held the right to internal self-government. The BNA act, which became the country's written constitution, established a federal system of government on the model of a British parliament and cabinet structure under the crown. Canada was proclaimed a self-governing Dominion within the British Empire in 1931.

In 1982 Canada severed its last formal legislative link with Britain by obtaining the right to amend its constitution (the British North America Act of 1867).

The Meech Lake Agreement was signed June 3, 1987. The historic accord, subject to ratification by Parliament and the provincial legislatures, assured constitutional protection for Quebec's efforts to preserve its French language and culture. Critics of the accord charged that it did not make any provision for other minority groups, and that it gave Quebec too much power, which might enable it to pass laws that conflicted with the nation's 1982 Charter of Rights and Freedoms. In 1988, Quebec had overridden a Canadian Supreme Court decision striking down a provincial language law that had restricted the use of any language other than French on public signs. The accord died June 22, 1990, as Newfoundland and Manitoba failed to approve it. The defeat set the stage for a possible reconsideration of Quebec separatism.

Canadian Provinces

	Sq. mi.	Population, 1990 est.
Alberta	248,800	2,472,500
British Columbia	358,971	3,138,900
Manitoba	211,723	1,090,700
New Brunswick	27,834	724,300
Newfoundland	143,510	573,000
Nova Scotia	20,402	892,000
Ontario	344,090	9,747,600
Prince Edward Island . .	2,185	130,400
Quebec	523,859	6,770,800
Saskatchewan	220,348	1,000,300
Territories		
Northwest Territories . .	1,271,442	54,000
Yukon	184,931	26,000

Prime Ministers of Canada

Canada is a constitutional monarchy with a parliamentary system of government. It is also a federal state. Canada's offical head of state is the King or Queen of England, represented by a resident Governor-General. However, in practice the nation is governed by the Prime Minister, leader of the party that commands the support of a majority of the House of Commons, dominant chamber of Canada's bicameral Parliament.

Name	Party	Term	Name	Party	Term
Sir John A. MacDonald	Conservative	1867-1873 1878-1891			1935-1948
Alexander Mackenzie	Liberal	1873-1878	R. B. Bennett	Conservative	1930-1935
Sir John J. C. Abbott	Conservative	1891-1892	Louis St. Laurent	Liberal	1948-1957
Sir John S. D. Thompson . . .	Conservative	1892-1894	John G. Diefenbaker	Prog. Cons.	1957-1963
Sir Mackenzie Bowell	Conservative	1894-1896	Lester B. Pearson	Liberal	1963-1968
Sir Charles Tupper	Conservative	1896	Pierre Elliott Trudeau	Liberal	1968-1979
Sir Wilfrid Laurier	Liberal	1896-1911	Joe Clark	Prog. Cons.	1979-1980
Sir Robert L. Borden	Cons. Union.	1911-1920	Pierre Elliott Trudeau	Liberal	1980-1984
Arthur Meighen	Cons. Union.	1920-1921	John Turner	Liberal	1984
W.L. Mackenzie King	Liberal	1921-1926[1] 1926-1930	Brian Mulroney	Prog. Cons.	1984-

(1) King's term was interrupted from June 26-Sept. 25, 1926, when Arthur Meighen again served as prime minister.

Cape Verde

Republic of Cape Verde

República de Cabo Verde

People: Population (1990 est.): 339,000. **Age distrib.** (%): 0-14: 45.6; 15-59: 47.7; 60+: 6.7. **Pop. density:** 217 per sq. mi. **Urban** (1987): 33%. **Ethnic groups:** Creole (mulatto) 71%, African 28%, European 1%. **Languages:** Portuguese (official), Crioulo. **Religions:** 80% Roman Catholic.

Geography: Area: 1,557 sq. mi., a bit larger than Rhode Island. **Location:** In Atlantic O., off western tip of Africa. **Neighbors:** Nearest are Mauritania, Senegal. **Topography:** Cape Verde Islands are 15 in number, volcanic in origin (active crater on Fogo). The landscape is eroded and stark, with vegetation mostly in interior valleys. **Capital:** Praia. **Cities** (1987 est.): Mindelo 55,000; Praia 48,000.

Government: Type: Republic. **Head of state:** Pres. Antonio Mascarenhas Monteiro; in office: Feb. 17, 1991. **Head of government:** Prime Min. Pedro Pires, b. Apr. 29, 1934; in office: July 5, 1975. **Local divisions:** 14 administrative districts.

Economy: Chief crops: Bananas, coffee, beats, corn, beans. **Minerals:** Salt. **Other resources:** Fish. **Arable land:** 10%. **Electricity prod.** (1989): 18 mln. kwh.

Finance: Monetary unit: Escudo (Dec. 1990: 68 = $1 US). **Gross national product** (1989): $281 mln. **Per capita GNP** (1989): $760. **Imports** (1986): $108 mln.; partners: Port. 33%, Neth. 12%. **Exports** (1986): $4.5 mln.; partners: Port. 32%, Ang. 21%.

Transport: Motor vehicles: in use (1988): 13,000 passenger cars, 4,000 comm. vehicles. **Chief ports:** Mindelo, Praia.

Communications: Radios: 1 per 6.8 persons. **Telephones in use:** 1 per 76 persons.

Health: Life expectancy at birth (1989): 59 male; 63 female. **Births** (per 1,000 pop. 1989): 48. **Deaths** (per 1,000 pop. 1989): 11. **Natural increase:** 3.8%. **Hospital beds:** 1 per 550 persons. **Physicians:** 1 per 4,334 persons. **Infant mortality** (per 1,000 live birth 1989): 66.

Education (1989): **Literacy:** 37%.

Major International Organizations: UN (GATT, IMF, WHO), OAU.

Embassy: 3415 Massachusetts Ave. NW 20007; 965-6820.

The uninhabited Cape Verdes were discovered by the Portuguese in 1456 or 1460. The first Portuguese colonists landed in 1462; African slaves were brought soon after, and most Cape Verdeans descend from both groups. Cape Verde independence came July 5, 1975. The islands have suffered from repeated extreme droughts and famines. Emphasis is placed on the development of agriculture and on fishing.

Antonio Mascarenhas Monteiro won the nation's first free presidential election Feb. 1991.

Central African Republic
République Centrafricaine

People: Population (1990 est.): 2,879,000. **Pop. density:** 12 per sq. mi. **Urban** (1988): 37%. **Ethnic groups:** Banda 27%, Baya 34%, Mandja 21%, Sara 10%. **Languages:** French (official), local dialects. **Religions:** Protestant 25%, Roman Catholic 25%, traditional 24%.

Geography: Area: 240,534 sq. mi., slightly smaller than Texas. **Location:** In central Africa. **Neighbors:** Chad on N, Cameroon on W, Congo, Zaire on S, Sudan on E. **Topography:** Mostly rolling plateau, average altitude 2,000 ft., with rivers draining S to the Congo and N to Lake Chad. Open, well-watered savanna covers most of the area, with an arid area in NE, and tropical rainforest in SW. **Capital:** Bangui. **Cities** (1988 est.): Bangui (met.) 596,000.

Government: Type: Republic. (under military rule). **Head of state:** Gen. Andre Kolingba; in office: Sept. 1, 1981. **Local divisions:** 16 prefectures. **Defense:** 2% of GNP (1984).

Economy: Industries: Textiles, light manuf, mining. **Chief crops:** Cotton, coffee, peanuts, tobacco. **Minerals:** Diamonds (chief export), uranium. **Other resources:** Timber. **Arable land:** 3%. **Electricity prod.** (1989): 93 mln. kwh. **Labor force:** 72% agric.

Finance: Monetary unit: CFA franc (Mar. 1991: 290 = $1 US). **Gross national product** (1989): $1.1 bln. **Per capita income** (1988): $376. **Imports** (1989): $150 mln.; partners: Fr. 44%. **Exports** (1989): $134 mln.; partners: Fr. 53%, Bel.-Lux. 23%. **National budget** (1988): $204 mln. **International reserves less gold** (Jan. 1990): $97 mln. **Gold:** 11,000 oz t.

Transport: Motor vehicles: in use (1986): 1,000 passenger cars, 20,000 comm. vehicles.

Communications: Radios: 1 per 22 persons. **Telephones:** 1 per 380 persons.

Health: Life expectancy at birth (1989): 45 male; 48 female. **Births** (per 1,000 pop. 1989): 44. **Deaths** 1 per 1,000 pop. 1989): 19. **Natural increase:** 2.5%. **Hospital beds** (1984): 3,774. **Physicians** (1984): 112. **Infant mortality** (per 1,000 live births 1989): 143.

Education (1989): Literacy: 40%. **Attendance:** primary school 79%; secondary school 18%.

Major International Organizations: UN (GATT, IMF, WHO), OAU.

Embassy: 1618 22d St. NW 20008; 483-7800.

Various Bantu tribes migrated through the region for centuries before French control was asserted in the late 19th century, when the region was named Ubangi-Shari. Complete independence was attained Aug. 13, 1960.

All political parties were dissolved in 1960, and the country became a center for Chinese political influence in Africa. Relations with China were severed after 1965. Elizabeth Domitien, premier 1975-76, was the first woman to hold that post in an African country. Pres. Jean-Bedel Bokassa, who seized power in a 1965 military coup, proclaimed himself constitutional emperor of the renamed Central African Empire Dec. 1976.

Bokassa's rule was characterized by ruthless and cruel authority, and human rights violations. Bokassa was ousted in a bloodless coup aided by the French government, Sept. 20, 1979, and replaced by his cousin David Dacko, former president from 1960 to 1965. In 1981, the political situation deteriorated amid strikes and economic crisis. Gen. Kolingba replaced Dacko as head of state in a bloodless coup.

Chad
Republic of Chad
République du Tchad

People: Population (1990 est.): 5,064,000. **Age distrib. (%):** 0–14: 42.5; 15–59: 51.7; 60+: 5.8. **Pop. density:** 11 per sq. mi. **Urban** (1986): 23%. **Ethnic groups:** 200 distinct groups. **Languages:** French, Arabic, (both official), some 100 other languages. **Religions:** Moslem 44%, animist 23%, Christian 33%.

Geography: Area: 495,755 sq. mi., four-fifths the size of Alaska. **Location:** In central N. Africa. **Neighbors:** Libya on N, Niger, Nigeria, Cameroon on W, Central African Republic on S, Sudan on E. **Topography:** Southern wooded savanna, steppe, and desert, part of the Sahara, in the N. Southern rivers flow N to Lake Chad, surrounded by marshland. **Capital:** N'Djamena. **Cities** (1988 est.): N'Djamena 500,000.

Government: Type: Republic. **Head of state:** Pres. Idriss Deby; in office: Dec. 4, 1990. **Local divisions:** 14 prefectures. **Defense:** 4.3% of GNP (1988).

Economy: Chief crops: Cotton. **Minerals:** Uranium, salt. **Arable land:** 2%. **Fish catch** (1988): 110,000 metric tons. **Electricity prod.** (1988): 69 mln. kwh. **Labor force:** 85% agric.

Finance: Monetary unit: CFA franc (Mar. 1991: 290 = $1 US). **Gross Domestic product** (1989): $1.0 bln. **Per capita GDP** (1989): $190. **Imports** (1988): $419 mln.; partners: Fr. 47%. **Exports** (1988): $141 mln.; partners Fra, EDEAC countries. **International reserves less gold** (Jan. 1990): $92 mln. **Gold:** 11,000 oz t.

Transport: Motor vehicles: in use (1985): 2,500 passenger cars, 4,000 comm. vehicles.

Communications: Radios: 1 per 4.3 persons. **Telephones in use:** 1 per 1,114 persons.

Health: Life expectancy at birth (1989): 38 male; 40 female. **Births** (per 1,000 pop. 1989): 42. **Deaths** (per 1,000 pop. 1989): 22. **Natural increase:** 2.0%. **Hospital beds** (1980): 3.500. **Physicians** (1980): 94. **Infant mortality** (per 1,000 live births 1989): 139.

Education (1989): Literacy: 17%.

Major International Organizations: UN, (GATT, IMF, WHO), OAU, EEC.

Embassy: 2002 R St. NW 20009; 462-4009.

Chad was the site of paleolithic and neolithic cultures before the Sahara Desert formed. A succession of kingdoms and Arab slave traders dominated Chad until France took control around 1900. Independence came Aug. 11, 1960.

Northern Moslem rebels, have fought animist and Christian southern government and French troops from 1966, despite numerous cease-fires and peace pacts.

Libyan troops entered the country at the request of the Chad government, December 1980. On Jan. 6, 1981 Libya and Chad announced their intention to unite. France together with several African nations condemned the agreement as a menace to African security. The Libyan troops were withdrawn from Chad in November 1981.

Rebel forces, led by Hissen Habre, captured the capital and forced Pres. Oueddei to flee the country in June 1982.

In 1983, France sent some 3,000 troops to Chad to assist Habre in opposing Libyan-backed rebels. France and Libya agreed to a simultaneous withdrawal of troops from Chad in September 1984 but Libyan forces remained in the north until Mar. 1987 when Chad forces drove them from their last major stronghold. Libyan troops abandoned almost $1 billion of military equipment during their retreat.

Chile
Republic of Chile
República de Chile

People: Population (1990 est.): 13,000,000. **Age distrib. (%):** 0–14: 30.9 15–59: 60.4; 60+: 7.7. **Pop. density:** 44 per sq. mi. **Urban** (1988): 83%. **Ethnic groups:** Mestizo 66%, Spanish 25%, Indian 5%. **Languages:** Spanish. **Religions:** Roman Catholic 89%, Protestant 11%.

Geography: Area: 292,257 sq. mi., larger than Texas. **Location:** Occupies western coast of southern S. America. **Neigh-**

bors: Peru on N, Bolivia on NE, Argentina on E. **Topography:** Andes Mtns. are on E border including some of the world's highest peaks; on W is 2,650-mile Pacific Coast. Width varies between 100 and 250 miles. In N is Atacama Desert, in center are agricultural regions, in S are forests and grazing lands. **Capital:** Santiago. **Cities** (1989 metro est.) Santiago 5,100,000.

Government: Type: Republic. **Head of state:** Pres. Patricio Aylwin; b. Nov. 26, 1918; in office: Mar. 11, 1990. **Local divisions:** 12 regions and Santiago region. **Defense:** 3.6% of GNP (1988).

Economy: Industries: Fish processing, wood products, textiles. **Chief crops:** Grain, onions, beans, potatoes, peas, fruits. **Minerals:** Copper (54% of export revenues in 1989), molybdenum, nitrates, iodine (half world output), iron, coal, oil, gas, gold, cobalt, zinc, manganese, borate, mica, mercury, salt, sulphur, marble, onyx. **Crude oil reserves** (1985): 224 mln. bbls. **Other resources:** Water, forests. **Arable land:** 7%. **Livestock** (1988): cattle: 3.3 mln.; sheep: 6.5 mln.; pigs: 1.1 mln. **Fish catch** (1989): 5.2 mln. metric tons. **Electricity prod.** (1988): 15.5 bln. kwh. **Labor force:** 19% agric., forestry, fishing; 34% ind & comm., 30% serv.

Finance: Monetary unit: Peso (June 1991: 332 = $1 US). **Gross Domestic product** (1989): $25.5 bln. **Per capita GDP** (1989): $1,979. **Imports** (1989): $6.4 bln.; partners: U.S. 19%, Braz. 9%. **Exports** (1989): $8.1 bln.; partners: Ger. 10%, Jap. 11%, U.S. 22%. **Tourists** (1988): $194 mln. receipts. **National budget** (1989): $6.9 bln. expenditures. **International reserves less gold** (Mar. 1990): $3.3 bln. **Gold:** 1.53 mln. oz. t. **Consumer prices** (change in 1990): 26.0%

Transport: Railway traffic (1988): 998 mln. passenger-km. **Motor vehicles:** in use (1987): 660,000 passenger cars, 278,000 comm. vehicles. **Civil aviation** (1989): 2.8 bln. passenger-km.; 18 airports with scheduled flights. **Chief ports:** Valparaiso, Arica, Antofagasta.

Communications: Television sets: 1 per 4.1 persons. **Radios:** 1 per 3.3 persons. **Telephones in use:** 1 per 16 persons. **Health:** Life expectancy at birth (1989): 68 male; 75 female. **Births** (per 1,000 pop. 1989): 21. **Deaths** (per 1,000 pop. 1989): 6. **Natural increase:** 1.5%. **Hospital beds:** 1 per 385 persons. **Physicians:** 1 per 922 persons. **Infant mortality** (per 1,000 live births 1989): 18.

Education (1988): Literacy: 92%. Compulsory ages 6-14.

Major International Organizations: UN and all of its specialized agencies, OAS.

Embassy: 1732 Massachusetts Ave. NW 20036; 785-1746.

Northern Chile was under Inca rule before the Spanish conquest, 1536-40. The southern Araucanian Indians resisted until the late 19th century. Independence was gained 1810-18, under Jose de San Martin and Bernardo O'Higgins; the latter, as supreme director 1817-23, sought social and economic reforms until deposed. Chile defeated Peru and Bolivia in 1836-39 and 1879-84, gaining mineral-rich northern land.

Eduardo Frei Montalva came into office in 1964, instituting social programs and gradual nationalization of foreign-owned mining companies. In 1970, Salvador Allende Gossens, a Marxist, became president with a third of the national vote.

The Allende government furthered nationalizations, and improved conditions for the poor. But illegal and violent actions by extremist supporters of the government, the regime's failure to attain majority support, and poorly planned socialist economic programs led to political and financial chaos.

A military junta seized power Sept. 11, 1973, and said Allende killed himself. The junta named a mostly military cabinet, and announced plans to "exterminate Marxism."

Repression continued during the 1980s with little sign of any political liberalization. In a plebiscite held Oct. 5, 1988, voters rejected junta-candidate Gen. Pinochet who, if victorious, would have governed Chile until 1997. Pinochet accepted the rejection and called for presidential elections. In Dec. 1989 voters removed Pinochet from office and elected Patricio Aylwin as president.

Tierra del Fuego is the largest (18,800 sq. mi.) island in the archipelago of the same name at the southern tip of South America, an area of majestic mountains, tortuous channels, and high winds. It was discovered 1520 by Magellan and named the Land of Fire because of its many Indian bonfires. Part of the island is in Chile, part in Argentina. Punta Arenas, on a mainland peninsula, is a center of sheep-raising and the world's southernmost city (pop. 67,600); Puerto Williams, pop. 949, is the southernmost settlement.

China
People's Republic of China
Zhonghua Renmin Gonghe Guo

People: Population (1990 est.): 1,130,065,000. **Pop. density:** 306 per sq. mi. **Urban** (1987): 46%. **Ethnic groups:** Han Chinese 94%, Mongol, Korean, Manchu, others. **Languages:** Mandarin (official), Yue, Wu Hakka, Xiang, Gan, Min, Zhuang, Hui, Yi. **Religions:** officially atheist; Confucianism, Buddhism, Taoism are traditional.

Geography: Area: 3,696,100 sq. mi., slightly larger than the conterminous U.S. **Location:** Occupies most of the habitable mainland of E. Asia. **Neighbors:** Mongolia on N, USSR on NE and NW, Afghanistan, Pakistan on W, India, Nepal, Bhutan, Myanmar, Laos, Vietnam on S, N. Korea on NE. **Topography:** Two-thirds of the vast territory is mountainous or desert, and only one-tenth is cultivated. Rolling topography rises to high elevations in the N in the Daxinganlingshanmai separating Manchuria and Mongolia; the Tienshan in Xinjiang; the Himalayan and Kunlunshanmai in the SW and in Tibet. Length is 1,860 mi. from N to S, width E to W is more than 2,000 mi. The eastern half of China is one of the best-watered lands in the world. Three great river systems, the Changjiang, the Huanghe, and the Xijiang provide water for vast farmlands. **Capital:** Beijing. **Cities** (1989 est.): Shanghai 7.3 mln.; Beijing 6.8 mln.; Tianjin 5.6 mln.; Canton 3.4 mln.; Shenyang 4.4 mln.; Wuhan 3.6 mln.

Government: Type: Communist Party led state. **Head of state:** Pres. Yang Shangkun; in office: Apr. 8, 1989. **Head of government:** Premier Li Peng; in office: Apr. 9, 1989. **Local divisions:** 22 provinces, 5 autonomous regions, and 3 cities. **Defense:** 3.9% of GNP (1988).

Economy: Industries: Iron and steel, textiles, agriculture implements, trucks. **Chief crops:** Grain, rice, cotton, tea. **Minerals:** tungsten, antimony, coal, iron, lead, manganese, molybdenum, tin. **Crude oil reserves** (1990): 24.0 bln. barrels. **Other resources:** Silk. **Arable land:** 11%. **Livestock** (1989): cattle: 77 mln.; pigs: 348 mln.; sheep: 102 mln. **Fish catch** (1988): 9.3 mln. metric tons. **Electricity prod.** (1988): 537 bln. kwh. **Crude steel prod.** (1988): 59.0 mln. metric tons. **Labor force:** 68% agric.; 18% ind. & comm.

Finance: Monetary unit: Yuan (Mar. 1991): 5.22 = $1 US). **Gross national product** (1989): $393 bln. **Per capita GNP** (1989): $360. **Imports** (1990): $52.2 bln.; partners: Jap. 20%, U.S. 11%, Hong Kong 20%. **Exports** (1990): $60.9 bln.; partners: Hong Kong 38%, Jap. 16%, U.S. 7%. **Tourism** (1988): $2.2 bln. receipts. **National budget** (1987): $66.1 bln. expenditures. **International reserves less gold** (Feb. 1991): $30.7 bln. **Gold:** 12.7 mln. oz t. **Consumer prices** (change in 1989): 16.3%.

Transport: Railway traffic (1989): 303 passenger-km. **Motor vehicles:** in use (1988): 1.3 mln. passenger cars, 3.1 mln. comm. vehicles. **Civil aviation** (1989): 18.7 bln. passenger km, 81 airports with scheduled flights. **Chief ports:** Shanghai, Tianjin, Luda.

Communications: Television sets: 1 per 8 persons. **Radios:** 1 per 9.1 persons. **Telephones:** 1 per 115 persons. **Daily newspaper circ.** (1986): 50 per 1,000 pop.

Health: Life expectancy at birth (1989): 68 male; 70 female. **Births** (per 1,000 pop. 1989): 23. **Deaths** (per 1,000 pop. 1989): 7. **Natural increase:** 1.6%. **Infant Mortality** (per 1,000 live births 1989): 33. **Hospital beds:** 1 per 432 persons. **Physicians:** 1 per 643 persons.

Education (1987): Literacy: 70%. Years compulsory 9; first grade enrollment 93%.

Major International Organizations: UN (IMF, FAO, WHO). **Embassy:** 2300 Conn. Ave. NW 20008; 328-2500.

History. Remains of various man-like creatures who lived as early as several hundred thousand years ago have been found in many parts of China. Neolithic agricultural settlements dotted the Huanghe basin from about 5,000 BC. Their language, religion, and art were the sources of later Chinese civilization.

Bronze metallurgy reached a peak and Chinese pictographic writing, similar to today's, was in use in the more developed culture of the Shang Dynasty (c. 1500 BC-c. 1000 BC) which ruled much of North China.

A succession of dynasties and interdynastic warring kingdoms ruled China for the next 3,000 years. They expanded Chinese political and cultural domination to the south and west, and developed a brilliant technologically and culturally advanced society. Rule by foreigners (Mongols in the Yuan Dynasty, 1271-1368, and Manchus in the Ch'ing Dynasty, 1644-1911) did not alter the underlying culture.

A period of relative stagnation left China vulnerable to internal and external pressures in the 19th century. Rebellions left tens of millions dead, and Russia, Japan, Britain, and other powers exercised political and economic control in large parts of the country. China became a republic Jan. 1, 1912, following the Wuchang Uprising inspired by Dr. Sun Yat-sen.

For a period of 50 years, 1894-1945, China was involved in conflicts with Japan. In 1895, China ceded Korea, Taiwan, and other areas. On Sept. 18, 1931, Japan seized the Northeastern Provinces (Manchuria) and set up a puppet state called Manchukuo. The border province of Jehol was cut off as a buffer state in 1933. Japan invaded China proper July 7, 1937. After its defeat in World War II, Japan gave up all seized land.

Following World War II, internal disturbances arose involving the Kuomintang, communists, and other factions. China came under domination of communist armies, 1949-1950. The Kuomintang government moved to Taiwan, 90 mi. off the mainland, Dec. 8, 1949.

The People's Republic of China was proclaimed in Peking Sept. 21, 1949, by the Chinese People's Political Consultative Conference under Mao Zedong.

China and the USSR signed a 30-year treaty of "friendship, alliance and mutual assistance," Feb. 15, 1950.

The U.S. refused recognition of the new regime. On Nov. 26, 1950, the People's Republic sent armies into Korea against U.S. troops and forced a stalemate.

By the 1960s, relations with the USSR deteriorated, with disagreements on borders, ideology and leadership of world communism. The USSR cancelled aid accords, and China, with Albania, launched anti-Soviet propaganda drives.

On Oct. 25, 1971, the UN General Assembly ousted the Taiwan government from the UN and seated the People's Republic in its place. The U.S. had supported the mainland's admission but opposed Taiwan's expulsion.

U.S. Pres. Nixon visited China Feb. 21-28, 1972, on invitation from Premier Zhou Enlai, ending years of antipathy between the 2 nations. China and the U.S. opened liaison offices in each other's capitals, May-June 1973. The U.S., Dec. 15, 1978, formally recognized the People's Republic of China as the sole legal government of China; diplomatic relations between the 2 nations were established, Jan. 1, 1979.

Internal developments. After an initial period of consolidation, 1949-52, industry, agriculture, and social and economic institutions were forcibly molded according to Maoist ideals. However, frequent drastic changes in policy and violent factionalism interfered with economic development.

In 1957, Mao Tse-tung admitted an estimated 800,000 people had been executed 1949-54; opponents claimed much higher figures.

The Great Leap Forward, 1958-60, tried to force the pace of economic development through intensive labor on huge new rural communes, and through emphasis on ideological purity and enthusiasm. The program caused resistance and was largely abandoned. Serious food shortages developed, and the government was forced to buy grain from the West.

The Great Proletarian Cultural Revolution, 1965, was an attempt to oppose pragmatism and bureaucratic power and instruct a new generation in revolutionary principles. Massive purges took place. A program of forcibly relocating millions of urban teenagers into the countryside was launched.

By 1968 the movement had run its course; many purged officials returned to office in subsequent years, and reforms in education and industry that had placed ideology above expertise were gradually weakened.

In a continuing "reassessment" of the policies of Mao Zedong, Mao's widow, Jiang Quing, and other Gang of Four members were convicted of "committing crimes during the 'Cultural Revolution,'" Jan. 25, 1981.

In the mid-1970s, factional and ideological fighting increased, and emerged into the open after the 1976 deaths of Mao and Premier Zhou Enlai. Mao's widow and 3 other leading leftists were purged and placed under arrest, after reportedly trying to seize power. The new ruling group modified Maoist policies in education, culture, and industry, and sought better ties with noncommunist countries.

Relations with Vietnam deteriorated in 1978 as China charged persecution of ethnic Chinese. In retaliation for Vietnam's invasion of Cambodia, China attacked 4 Vietnamese border provinces Feb. 17, 1979; heavy border fighting ensued.

By the mid 1980's, China had enacted far-reaching economic reforms highlighted by the departure from rigid central planning and the stressing of market-oriented socialism.

Some 100,000 students and workers staged a march in Beijing to demand democratic reforms, May 4, 1989. The demonstrations continued during a visit to Beijing by Soviet leader Mikhail Gorbachev May 15-18. It was the first Sino-Soviet summit since 1959. A million people gathered in Beijing to demand democratic reforms and the removal of Deng and other leaders. There were protests in at least 20 other Chinese cities. Martial law was imposed, May 20, but was mostly ignored by the protesters.

Chinese army troops entered Beijing, June 3-4, and crushed the pro-democracy protests. Tanks and armored personnel carriers attacked Tiananmen Square, outside the Great Hall of the People, which was the main scene of the demonstrations and hunger strikes. It was estimated that 5,000 died, 10,000 were injured, and hundreds of students and workers arrested.

China's population, the world's largest, is still increasing, but with more couples following the government's one-child policy some experts predict that the nation's population will actually decline after peaking in the early 21st century.

Manchuria. Home of the Manchus, rulers of China 1644-1911, Manchuria has accommodated millions of Chinese settlers in the 20th century. Under Japanese rule 1931-45, the area became industrialized. China no longer uses the name Manchuria for the region, which is divided into the 3 NE provinces of Heilongjiang, Jilin, and Liaoning.

Guangxi is the southernmost part of Manchuria. Russia in 1898 forced China to lease it Guandong, and built Port Arthur (Lushun) and the port of Dairen (Luda). Japan seized Port Arthur in 1905. It was turned over to the USSR by the 1945 Yalta agreement, but finally returned to China in 1950. Pop (1987 est.) 39,000.

Inner Mongolia was organized by the People's Republic in 1947. Its boundaries have undergone frequent changes, reaching its greatest extent (and restored in 1979) in 1956, with an area of 454,000 sq. mi., allegedly in order to dilute the minority Mongol population. Chinese settlers outnumber the Mongols more than 10 to 1. Pop. (1988 est.): 20.0 mln. Capital: Hohhot.

Xinjiang, in Central Asia, is 633,802 sq. mi., pop. (1988 est.): 13.8 mln. (75% Uygurs, a Turkic Moslem group, with a heavy Chinese increase in recent years). Capital: Urumqi. It is China's richest region in strategic minerals. Some Uygurs have fled to the USSR, claiming national oppression.

Tibet, 470,000 sq. mi., is a thinly populated region of high plateaus and massive mountains, the Himalayas on the S, the Kunluns on the N. High passes connect with India and Nepal; roads lead into China proper. Capital: Lhasa. Average altitude is 15,000 ft. Jiachan, 15,870 ft., is believed to be the highest inhabited town on earth. Agriculture is primitive. Pop. (1988 est.): 2 mln. (of whom 500,000 are Chinese). Another 4 million Tibetans form the majority of the population of vast adjacent areas that have long been incorporated into China.

China ruled all of Tibet from the 18th century, until independence came in 1911. China reasserted control in 1951, and a communist government was installed in 1953, revising the theocratic Lamaist Buddhist rule. Serfdom was abolished, but all land remained collectivized.

A Tibetan uprising within China in 1956 spread to Tibet in 1959. The rebellion was crushed with Chinese troops, and Buddhism was almost totally suppressed. The Dalai Lama and 100,000 Tibetans fled to India.

Colombia

Republic of Colombia

República de Colombia

People: Population (1990 est.): 32,598,000. **Age distrib.** (%): 0-14: 36.1; 15-59: 57.8; 60+: 6.1. **Pop. density:** 72 per sq. mi. **Urban** (1983): 65.4%. **Ethnic groups:** Mestizo 58%, Caucasian 20%, Mulatto 14%. **Languages:** Spanish. **Religions:** Roman Catholic 95%.

Geography: Area: 439,735 sq. mi., about the size of Texas, and New Mexico combined. **Location:** At the NW corner of S. America. **Neighbors:** Panama on NW, Ecuador, Peru on S, Brazil, Venezuela on E. **Topography:** Three ranges of Andes, the Western, Central, and Eastern Cordilleras, run through the country from N to S. The eastern range consists mostly of high table lands, densely populated. The Magdalena R. rises in Andes, flows N to Carriben, through a rich alluvial plain. Sparsely-settled plains in E are drained by Orinoco and Amazon systems. **Capital:** Bogota. **Cities** (1990 est.): Bogota 4,819,000; Medellin 1,664,000; Cali 1,637,000; Barranquilla 1,000,000.

Government: Type: Republic. **Head of state:** Pres. Cesar Gaviria Trujillo; b. Mar. 31, 1947; in office: Aug. 7, 1990. **Local divisions:** 23 departments, 8 national territories, and special district of Bogota. **Defense:** 2.1% of GNP (1985).

Economy: Industries: Textiles, processed goods, hides, steel, cement, chemicals. **Chief crops:** Coffee (50% of exports), rice, corn, cotton, sugar, bananas. **Minerals:** Oil, gas, emeralds (90% world output), gold, copper, lead, coal, iron, nickel, salt. **Crude oil reserves** (1987): 1.6 bln. bbls. **Other resources:** Rubber, balsam, dye-woods, copaiba, hydro power. **Arable land:** 5%. **Livestock** (1989): cattle: 24.6 mln.; pigs: 2.6 mln.; sheep: 2.6 mln. **Fish catch** (1988): 80,000 metric tons. **Electricity prod.** (1988): 34.7 bln. kwh. **Crude steel prod.** (1986): 500,000 metric tons. **Labor force:** 26% agric.; 21% ind.; 53% services.

Finance: Currency: Peso (June 1991: 571 = $1 US). **Gross national product** (1989): $38.6 bln. **Per capita GNP** (1989): $1,190. **Imports** (1989): $5.0 bln.; partners: U.S. 34%, EEC 14%, Jap. 11%. **Exports** (1988): $5.0 bln.; partners: U.S. 43%, EEC 38%. **Tourists** (1988): $461 mln. receipts. **National budget** (1987): $4.5 bln. expenditures. **International reserves less gold** (Mar. 1991): $4.2 bln. **Gold** 628,000 oz t. **Consumer prices** (change in 1990): 29.1.

Transport: Railway traffic (1989): 151 mln. passenger-km. **Motor vehicles** in use (1986): 840,000 passenger cars, 391,000. **Civil aviation** (1989): 4.2 bln. passenger-km; airports with scheduled flights: 67. **Chief ports:** Buena Ventura, Santa Marta, Barranquilla, Cartagena.

Communications: Television sets: 1 per 5.6 persons. **Radios:** 1 per 7.3 persons. **Telephones:** 1 per 13 persons. **Daily newspaper circ.** (1987): 61 per 1,000 pop.

Health: Life expectancy at birth (1989): 64 male; 68 female. **Births** (per 1,000 pop. 1989): 27. **Deaths** (per 1,000 pop. 1989): 7. **Natural increase:** 2.3%. **Hospital beds** (1982): 28,880. **Physicians** (1983): 21,778. **Infant mortality** (per 1,000 live births 1989): 54%.

Education (1990): **Literacy:** 80%. Only 28% finish primary school.

Major International Organizations: UN (World Bank, GATT), OAS.

Embassy: 2118 Leroy Pl. NW, 20008; 387-8338.

Spain subdued the local Indian kingdoms (Funza, Tunja) by the 1530s, and ruled Colombia and neighboring areas as New Granada for 300 years. Independence was won by 1819. Venezuela and Ecuador broke away in 1829-30, and Panama withdrew in 1903.

One of the Latin American democracies, Colombia is plagued by rural and urban violence, though scaled down from "La Violencia" of 1948-58, which claimed 200,000 lives. Attempts at land and social reform, and progress in industrialization have not succeeded in reducing massive social problems aggravated by a very high birth rate. In 1989, the government's increased activity against local drug traffickers sparked a series of retaliation killings. On Aug. 18, Luis Carlos Galán, the ruling party's presidential hopeful in the 1990 election, was assassinated. In 1990, 2 other presidential candidates were slain as the drug traffickers carried on a campaign of intimidation to stop the presidential election. Cesar Gaviria Trujillo, a strong advocate of maintaining the government's war against the nation's drug cartels, was elected president in May.

Comoros

Federal Islamic Republic of the Comoros

Jumhurīyat al-Qumur al-Itthādīyah al-Islāmīyah

People: Population (1990 est.): 459,000. **Pop. density:** 547 per sq. mi. **Ethnic groups:** Arabs, Africans, East Indians. **Languages:** Arabic, French (both official). **Religions:** Islam (official), Roman Catholic.

Geography: Area: 838 sq. mi., half the size of Delaware. **Location:** 3 islands (Grande Comore, Anjouan, and Moheli) in the Mozambique Channel between NW Madagascar and SE Africa. **Neighbors:** Nearest are Mozambique on W, Madagascar on E. **Topography:** The islands are of volcanic origin, with an active volcano on Grand Comoro. **Capital:** Moroni. **Cities** (1988 est.): Moroni (met.) 28,000.

Government: Type: Republic. **Head of state:** Pres. Said Mohammed Djohar; in office: Nov. 26, 1989. **Local divisions:** each of the 3 main islands is a prefecture.

Economy: Industries: Perfume. **Chief crops:** Vanilla, copra, perfume plants, fruits. **Arable land:** 35%. **Electricity prod.** (1988): 14 mln. kwh. **Labor force:** 80% agric.

Finance: Monetary unit: CFA franc (Mar. 1991: 290 = $1 US). **Gross national product** (1989): $209 mln. **Per capita GNP** (1989): $460. **Imports** (1986): $38 mln.; partners: Fr. 56%. **Exports** (1986): $20 mln.; partners: Fr. 35%, U.S. 18%.

Transport: Chief ports: Dzaoudzi.

Communications: Radios: 1 per 9 persons. **Telephones in use:** 1 per 740 persons.

Health: Life expectancy at birth (1989): 54 male; 58 female. **Births** (per 1,000 pop. 1989): 47. **Deaths** (per 1,000 pop. 1989): 13. **Natural increase:** 3.5%. **Infant mortality** (per 1,000 live births 1989): 91.

Education: (1989): **Literacy:** 15%; less than 20% attend secondary school.

Major International Organizations: UN (IMF, World Bank); OAU.

Embassy: 336 E. 45th St., New York, NY 10017; (212) 972-8010.

The islands were controlled by Moslem sultans until the French acquired them 1841-1909. A 1974 referendum favored independence, with only the Christian island of Mayotte preferring association with France. The French National Assembly decided to allow each of the islands to decide its own fate. The Comoro Chamber of Deputies declared independence July 6, 1975. In a referendum in 1976, Mayotte voted to remain French. A leftist regime that seized power in 1975 was deposed in a pro-French 1978 coup.

In Nov. 1989, Pres. Ahmed Abdallah was assassinated.

Congo

People's Republic of the Congo

République Populaire du Congo

People: Population (1990 est.): 2,305,000. **Pop. density:** 17 per sq. mi. **Urban** (1986): 51%. **Ethnic groups:** Bakongo 45%, Bateke 20%, others. **Languages:** French (official), Kongo, Teke. **Religions:** Christians 47% (two-thirds Roman Catholic), animists 47%, Moslem 2%.

Geography: Area: 132,046 sq. mi., slightly smaller than Montana. **Location:** In western central Africa. **Neighbors:** Gabon, Cameroon on W, Central African Republic on N, Zaire on E, Angola (Cabinda) on SW. **Topography:** Much of the Congo is covered by thick forests. A coastal plain leads to the fertile Niari Valley. The center is a plateau; the Congo R. basin consists of flood plains in the lower and savanna in the upper portion. **Capital:** Brazzaville. **Cities** (1984 est.): Brazzaville (met.) 595,000; Pointe-Noire 297,000; Loubomo 35,000.

Government: Type: People's republic. **Head of state:** Pres. Denis Sassou-Nguesso; b. 1943; in office: Feb. 8, 1979. **Head of government:** Prime Min. Pierre Moussa; in office: Dec. 3, 1990. **Local divisions:** 9 regions and capital district. **Defense:** 4.6% of GNP (1987).

Economy: Chief crops: Palm oil and kernels, cocoa, coffee, tobacco. **Minerals:** Gold, lead, copper, zinc. **Crude oil reserves** (1988): 750 mln. bbls. **Arable land:** 2%. **Fish catch** (1988): 31,000 metric tons. **Electricity prod.** (1988): 301 mln. kwh. **Labor force:** 90% agric.

Finance: Monetary unit: CFA franc (Mar. 1991: 290 = $1 US). **Gross national product** (1989): $2.0 bln. **Per capita GNP** (1989): $930. **Imports** (1989): $524 mln.; partners: Fr. 52%. **Exports** (1989): $912 mln.; partners: U.S. 45%, Fr. 15%. **Tourist receipts** (1987): $6 mln. **International reserves less gold** (Jan. 1990): $4.4 mln. **Gold:** 11,000 oz t. **Consumer prices** (change in 1989): 3.7%.

Transport: Railway traffic (1986): 456 mln. passenger-km. Motor vehicles: in use (1986): 26,000 passenger cars, 20,000 comm. vehicles. Chief ports: Pointe-Noire, Brazzaville.
Communications: Television sets: 1 per 375 persons. Radios: 1 per 9.4 persons. Telephones in use: 1 per 111 persons.
Health: Life expectancy at birth (1989): 54 male; 58 female. Births (per 1,000 pop. 1989): 46. Deaths (per 1,000 pop. 1989): 13. Natural increase: 3.4%. Hospital beds: 1 per 572 persons. Physicians: 1 per 4,334 persons. Infant mortality (per 1,000 live births 1989): 110.
Education (1989): Literacy: 80%. Years compulsory 10; attendance 80%.
Major International Organizations: UN (GATT, IMF, WHO), OAU.
Embassy: 4891 Colorado Ave. NW 20011; 726-5500.

The Loango Kingdom flourished in the 15th century, as did the Anzico Kingdom of the Batekes; by the late 17th century they had become weakened. France established control by 1885. Independence came Aug. 15, 1960.

After a 1963 coup sparked by trade unions, the country adopted a Marxist-Leninist stance, with the USSR and China vying for influence. Tribal divisions remain strong. France remains a dominant trade partner and source of technical assistance, and French-owned private enterprise retained a major economic role. However, the government of Pres. Sassou-Nguesso favored a strengthening of relations with the USSR, a socialist constitution was adopted, 1979.

In 1990, Marxism was renounced and opposition parties legalized.

Costa Rica
Republic of Costa Rica
República de Costa Rica

People: Population (1990 est.): 3,032,000. Age distrib. (%): 0–14: 36.2; 15–49: 57.4; 50+: 6.4. Pop. density: 149 per sq. mi. Urban (1989): 50%. Ethnic groups: Spanish (with Mestizo minority). Language: Spanish (official). Religions: Roman Catholic 88%.
Geography: Area: 19,575 sq. mi., smaller than W. Virginia. Location: In central America. Neighbors: Nicaragua on N, Panama on S. Topography: Lowlands by the Caribbean are tropical. The interior plateau, with an altitude of 4,000 ft., is temperate. Capital: San Jose. Cities (1988 met. est.): San Jose 890,000.
Government: Type: Democratic republic. Head of state: Pres. Rafael Angel Calderon; b. 1949; in office May 8, 1990. Local divisions: 7 provinces.
Economy: Industries: Furniture, pharmaceuticals, aluminum, textiles, fertilizers, roofing, cement. Chief crops: Coffee (chief export), bananas, sugar, cocoa, cotton, hemp. Minerals: Gold, salt, sulphur, iron. Other resources: Fish, forests. Arable land: 12%. Livestock (1989): cattle: 1.7. mln. Fish catch (1988): 20,000 metric tons. Electricity prod. (1988): 2.9 bln. kwh. Labor force: 27% agric.; 35% ind. & comm.; 33% service and government.
Finance: Monetary unit: Colone (Mar. 1991: 115 = $1 US). Gross national product (1988): $4.2 bln. Per capita income (1987): $1,584. Imports (1990): $2.0 bln.; partners: U.S. 38%, CACM 10%, Jap. 10%. Exports (1990): $1.4 bln.; partners: U.S. 45%, CACM 18%. Tourists (1988): receipts: $164 mln. National budget (1987): $791 mln. expenditures. International reserves less gold (Mar. 1991): $552 mln. Gold: 15,000 oz t. Consumer prices (change in 1990): 90.0%.
Transport: Motor vehicles: in use (1989): 143,000 passenger cars, 94,000 comm. vehicles. Civil aviation (1988): 787 mln. passenger-km; 8 airports with scheduled flights. Chief ports: Limon, Puntarenas, Golfito.
Communications: Television sets: 1 per 6.1 persons. Radios: 1 per 11 persons. Telephones: 1 per 6.9 persons. Daily newspaper circ. (1988): 110 per 1,000 pop.
Health: Life expectancy at birth (1989): 74 male; 78 female. Births (per 1,000 pop. 1989): 29. Deaths (per 1,000 pop. 1989): 4. Natural increase: 2.5%. Hospital beds: 1 per 417 persons.

Physicians: 1 per 1,045 persons. Infant mortality (per 1,000 live births 1989): 17.
Education (1989): Literacy: 93%. Years compulsory 6; attendance 99%.
Major International Organizations: UN (FAO, ILO, IMF, WHO), OAS.
Embassy: 1825 Connecticut Ave. NW, 20009; 234-2945.

Guaymi Indians inhabited the area when Spaniards arrived, 1502. Independence came in 1821. Costa Rica seceded from the Central American Federation in 1838. Since the civil war of 1948-49, there has been little violent social conflict, and free political institutions have been preserved.

Costa Rica, though still a largely agricultural country, has achieved a relatively high standard of living and social services, and land ownership is widespread.

Côte d'Ivoire
Ivory Coast
République de la Côte d'Ivoire

People: Population (1990 est.): 12,070,000. Age distrib. (%): 0–14: 45.1; 15–59: 50.2; 60+: 4.7. Pop. density: 94 per sq. mi. Urban (1986): 47%. Ethnic groups: Baule 23%, Bete 18%, Senufo 15%, Malinke 11%, over 60 tribes. Languages: French (official), Akan, Kru, Voltaic, Malinke. Religions: Moslem 20%, Christian 20%, indigenous 60%.
Geography: Area: 124,503 sq. mi., slightly larger than New Mexico. Location: On S. coast of W. Africa. Neighbors: Liberia, Guinea on W, Mali, Burkina Faso on N, Ghana on E. Topography: Forests cover the W half of the country, and range from a coastal strip to halfway to the N on the E. A sparse inland plain leads to low mountains in NW. Capital: Abidjan. Cities (1990 est.): Abidjan 2.7 mln.
Government: Type: Republic. Head of state: Pres. Felix Houphouet-Boigny; b. Oct. 18, 1905; in office: Aug. 7, 1960. Local divisions: 34 departments.
Economy: Chief crops: Coffee, cocoa. Minerals: Diamonds, manganese. Other resources: Timber, rubber, petroleum. Arable land: 9%. Livestock (1989): goats: 1.5 mln.; sheep: 1.5 mln.; cattle: 991,000. Fish catch (1988): 88,000 metric tons. Electricity prod. (1988): 2.4 bln. kwh. Labor force: 85% agric., forestry.
Finance: Monetary unit: CFA franc (Mar. 1991: 290 = $1 US). Gross national product (1989): $9.3 bln. Per capita GNP (1989): $790. Imports (1988): $2.0 bln.; partners: Fr. 31%, Jap. 5%, U.S. 5%. Exports (1988): $2.7 bln.; partners: Fr. 14%, Neth. 19%, U.S. 11%, It. 8%. Tourists (1989): $53 mln receipts; International reserves less gold (Jan. 1991): $4.0 mln. Gold: 45,000 oz t. Consumer prices (changed in 1989): 1.3%.
Transport: Railway traffic (1989): 1.0 bln. passenger-km. Motor vehicles: in use (1987): 178,000 passenger cars, 90,000 comm. vehicles. Chief ports: Abidjan, Sassandra.
Communications: Television sets: 1 per 19 persons. Radios: 1 per 8.1 persons. Telephones: 1 per 97 persons. Daily newspaper circ. (1988): 12 per 1,000 pop.
Health: Life expectancy at birth (1989): 52 male; 55 female. Births (per 1,000 pop. 1989): 46. Deaths (per 1,000 pop. 1989): 13. Natural increase: 3.3%. Hospital beds (1982): 10,062. Physicians (1982): 502. Infant mortality (per 1,000 live births 1989): 102.
Education (1990): Literacy: 45%. Years compulsory: none; attendance 75%.
Major International Organizations: UN and all of its specialized agencies, OAU.
Embassy: 2424 Massachusetts Ave. NW 20008; 483-2400.

A French protectorate from 1842, Côte D'Ivoire became independent in 1960. It is the most prosperous of tropical African nations, due to diversification of agriculture for export, close ties to France, and encouragement of foreign investment. About 20% of the population are workers from neighboring countries. Côte D'Ivoire, which officially changed its name from Ivory Coast in Oct. 1985, is a leader of the pro-Western bloc in Africa.

Students and workers staged protests, Feb. 1990, demanding the ouster of Pres. Houphouet-Boigny and multiparty democracy.

Cuba

Republic of Cuba

República de Cuba

People: Population (1990 est.): 10,582,000. **Age distrib. (%):** 0-under 15: 23.3; 15-59: 64.9; 60+: 11.8. **Pop. density:** 239 per sq. mi. **Urban** (1989): 72%. **Ethnic groups:** Spanish, African. **Languages:** Spanish. **Religions:** Roman Catholic 42%, none 49%.

Geography: Area: 44,218 sq. mi., nearly as large as Pennsylvania. **Location:** Westernmost of West Indies. **Neighbors:** Bahamas, U.S., on N, Mexico on W, Jamaica on S, Haiti on E. **Topography:** The coastline is about 2,500 miles. The N coast is steep and rocky, the S coast low and marshy. Low hills and fertile valleys cover more than half the country. Sierra Maestra, in the E is the highest of 3 mountain ranges. **Capital:** Havana. **Cities** (1989 est.): Havana 2,077,000; Santiago de Cuba 397,000; Camaguey 274,000.

Government: Type: Communist state. **Head of state:** Pres. Fidel Castro Ruz; b. Aug. 13, 1926; in office: Dec. 3, 1976 (formerly Prime Min. since Feb. 16, 1959). **Local divisions:** 14 provinces, Havana. **Defense:** 5.4% of GNP (1985).

Economy: Industries: Cement, food processing, sugar. **Chief crops:** Sugar (75% of exports), tobacco, rice, coffee, tropical fruit. **Minerals:** Cobalt, nickel, iron, copper, manganese, salt. **Other resources:** Forests. **Arable land:** 29%. **Livestock** (1986): cattle: 6.5 mln.; pigs: 2.4 mln. **Fish catch** (1989): 191,000 metric tons. **Electricity prod.** (1989): 15.2 bln. kwh. **Labor force:** 13% agric.; 29% ind. & comm.; 30% services & govt.

Finance: Monetary unit: Peso (Dec. 1990: 1 peso = $1.25 U.S.). **Gross social product:** economic measure not convertible to GNP. **Per capita income** (1990): $2,644. **Imports** (1987): $7.6 bln.; partners: USSR 72%. **Exports** (1987): $5.4 bln.; partners: USSR 72%. **Tourists** (1988): Revenues: $189 mln.

Transport: Railway traffic (1988): 2.6 bln. passenger-km. **Motor vehicles:** in use (1985): 200,000 passenger cars, 164,000 comm. vehicles. **Civil aviation** (1988): 2.7 bln. passenger-km.; 12 airports with scheduled flights. **Chief ports:** Havana, Matanzas, Cienfuegos, Santiago de Cuba.

Communications: Television sets: 1 per 5 persons. **Radios:** 1 per 3 persons. **Telephones in use** 1 per 19 persons. **Daily newspaper circ.** (1988): 155 per 1,000 pop.

Health: Life expectancy at birth (1989): 72 male; 74 female. **Births** (per 1,000 pop. 1989): 17.2. **Deaths** (per 1,000 pop. 1989): 6. **Natural increase:** 1.0%. **Hospital beds:** 1 per 174 persons. **Physicians:** 1 per 333 persons. **Infant mortality** (per 1,000 live births 1989): 16.

Education (1990): Literacy: 98%. 92% of those between ages 6-14 attend school.

Major International Organizations: UN (UNESCO, WHO).

Some 50,000 Indians lived in Cuba when it was discovered by Columbus in 1492. Its name derives from the Indian Cubanacan. Except for British occupation of Havana, 1762-63, Cuba remained Spanish until 1898. A slave-based sugar plantation economy developed from the 18th century, aided by early mechanization of milling. Sugar remains the chief product and chief export despite government attempts to diversify.

A ten-year uprising ended in 1878 with guarantees of rights by Spain, which Spain failed to carry out. A full-scale movement under Jose Marti began Feb. 24, 1895.

The U.S. declared war on Spain in April, 1898, after the sinking of the U.S.S. Maine in Havana harbor, and defeated it in the Spanish-American War. Spain gave up all claims to Cuba. U.S. troops withdrew in 1902, but under 1903 and 1934 agreements, the U.S. leases a site at Guantanamo Bay in the SE as a naval base. U.S. and other foreign investments acquired a dominant role in the economy. In 1952, former president Fulgencio Batista seized control and established a dictatorship, which grew increasingly harsh and corrupt. Fidel Castro assembled a rebel band in 1956; guerrilla fighting intensified in 1958. Batista fled Jan. 1, 1959, and in the resulting political vacuum Castro took power, becoming premier Feb. 16.

The government began a program of sweeping economic and social changes, without restoring promised liberties. Opponents were imprisoned and some were executed. Some 700,000 Cubans emigrated in the years after the Castro takeover, mostly to the U.S.

Cattle and tobacco lands were nationalized, while a system of cooperatives was instituted. By 1960 all banks and industrial companies had been nationalized, including over $1 billion worth of U.S.-owned properties, mostly without compensation.

Poor sugar crops resulted in collectivization of farms, stringent labor controls, and rationing, despite continued aid from the USSR and other communist countries.

The U.S. imposed an export embargo in 1962, severely damaging the economy. In 1961, some 1,400 Cubans, trained and backed by the U.S. Central Intelligence Agency, unsuccessfully tried to invade and overthrow the regime.

In the fall of 1962, the U.S. learned that the USSR had brought nuclear missiles to Cuba. After an Oct. 22 warning from Pres. Kennedy, the missiles were removed.

In 1977, Cuba and the U.S. signed agreements to exchange diplomats, without restoring full ties, and to regulate offshore fishing. In 1978, and again in 1980, the U.S. agreed to accept political prisoners released by Cuba some of whom, it was later discovered, were criminals and mental patients. A 1987 agreement provided for 20,000 Cubans to immigrate to the U.S. each year; Cuba agreed to take back some 2,500 jailed in the U.S. since the 1980 Mariel boat lift.

In 1975-78, Cuba sent troops to aid one faction in the Angola Civil War. All Cuban troops were withdrawn by May 1991. Cuba's involvement in Central America, Africa, and the Caribbean, has contributed to poor relations with the U.S.

In 1983, 24 Cubans died and over 700 were captured, later repatriated, as a result of the U.S.-led invasion of Grenada.

Cuba has resisted the social and economic reforms that have taken place in the USSR and other eastern bloc countries. The nation was feeling economic difficulties in the 1990s as the Soviet-bloc curtailed financial aid.

Cyprus

Republic of Cyprus

Kypriaki Dimokratia (Greek)
Kibris Cumhuriyeti (Turkish)

People: Population (1990 est.): 708,000. **Age distrib. (%):** 0-14: 25.4; 15-59: 60.4; 60+: 14.2. **Pop. density:** 194 per sq. mi. **Urban** (1982): 53%. **Ethnic groups:** Greeks 78%, Turks 18.7%, Armenians, Maronites. **Languages:** Greek, Turkish (both official), English. **Religions:** Orthodox 77%, Moslems 18%.

Geography: Area: 3,572 sq. mi., smaller than Connecticut. **Location:** In eastern Mediterranean Sea, off Turkish coast. **Neighbors:** Nearest are Turkey on N, Syria, Lebanon on E. **Topography:** Two mountain ranges run E-W, separated by a wide, fertile plain. **Capital:** Nicosia. **Cities** (1989 est.): Nicosia 166,000.

Government: Type: Republic. **Head of state:** Pres. George Vassiliou; b. May 21, 1931; in office: Feb. 28, 1988. **Local divisions:** 6 districts. **Defense:** 11% of govt. budget (1984).

Economy: Industries: Light manuf. **Chief crops:** Grains, grapes, carobs, citrus fruits, potatoes, olives. **Minerals:** Copper, pyrites, asbestos. **Arable land:** 40%. **Electricity prod.** (1988): 1.6 mln. kwh. **Labor force:** 21% agric.; 20% ind., 18% comm., 19% serv.

Finance: Monetary unit: Pound (Mar. 1991: 1.00 = $2.12 US). **GNP** (1988): $4.3 bln. **Per capita GNP** (1988): $7,812. **Imports** (1990): $2.2 bln.; partners: UK 13%, Itl. 12%. **Exports** (1990): $957 mln.; partners: UK 21%, Libya 9%. **Tourists** (1988): receipts: $782 mln. **National budget** (1987): $911 mln. expenditures. **International reserves less gold** (Mar. 1991): $1.4 bln. **Gold:** 459,000 oz. t. **Consumer prices** (change in 1990): 4.5%.

Transport: Motor vehicles: in use (1989): 159,000 passenger cars, 54,000 comm. vehicles. **Civil aviation** (1988): 1.6 bln. passenger-km; one airport. **Chief ports:** Famagusta, Limassol.

Communications: Television sets: 1 per 3.4 persons. **Radios:** 1 per 2.7 persons. **Telephones:** 1 per 2.0 persons. **Daily newspaper circ.** (1987): 157 per 1,000 pop.

Health: Life expectancy at birth (1989): 74 male; 80 female. **Births** (per 1,000 pop. 1989): 19. **Deaths** (per 1,000 pop. 1989): 7. **Natural increase:** 1.1%. **Hospital beds:** 1 per 165 persons. **Physicians:** 1 per 516 persons. **Infant mortality** (per 1,000 live births 1989): 8.

Education (1989): Literacy: 99%. **Years compulsory:** 9; attendance 99%.

Major International Organizations: UN (GATT, IMF, WHO), Commonwealth of Nations, EC (Assoc.).
Embassy: 2211 R St. NW, 20008; 462-5772.

Agitation for enosis (union) with Greece increased after World War II, with the Turkish minority opposed, and broke into violence in 1955-56. In 1959, Britain, Greece, Turkey, and Cypriot leaders approved a plan for an independent republic, with constitutional guarantees for the Turkish minority and permanent division of offices on an ethnic basis. Greek and Turkish Communal Chambers dealt with religion, education, and other matters.

Archbishop Makarios, formerly the leader of the enosis movement, was elected president, and full independence became final Aug. 16, 1960. Makarios was re-elected in 1968 and 1973.

Further communal strife led the United Nations to send a peace-keeping force in 1964; its mandate has been repeatedly renewed.

The Cypriot National Guard, led by officers from the army of Greece, seized the government July 15, 1974. Makarios fled the country. On July 20, Turkey invaded the island; Greece mobilized its forces but did not intervene. A cease-fire was arranged July 22. A peace conference collapsed Aug. 14; fighting resumed. By Aug. 16 Turkish forces had occupied the NE 40% of the island, despite the presence of UN peace forces. Makarios resumed the presidency in Dec., until his death, 1977.

Turkish Cypriots voted overwhelmingly, June 8, 1975, to form a separate Turkish Cypriot federated state. A president and assembly were elected in 1976. Some 200,000 Greeks have been expelled from the Turkish-controlled area, replaced by thousands of Turks, some from the mainland.

Turkish Republic of Northern Cyprus

A declaration of independence was announced by Turkish-Cypriot leader Rauf Denktash, Nov. 15, 1983. The new state is not internationally recognized although it does have trade relations with some countries. TRNC contains 1,295 sq mi., pop. (1990 est.): 171,000, 99% Turkish.

Czechoslovakia

Czech and Slovak Federal Republic

People: Population (1990 est.): 15,695,000. **Age distrib. (%):** 0–14: 23.5; 15–59: 59.2; 60+: 17.3. **Pop. density:** 317 per sq. mi. **Urban** (1990): 73%. **Ethnic groups:** Czechs 64%, Slovaks 31%, Hungarian, German, Ukrainian, Polish. **Languages:** Czech, Slovak (both official), Hungarian, Romany. **Religions:** Roman Catholic 77%.

Geography: Area: 49,365 sq. mi., the size of New York. **Location:** In E central Europe. **Neighbors:** Poland, E. Germany on N, W. Germany on W. Austria, Hungary on S, USSR on E. **Topography:** Bohemia, in W, is a plateau surrounded by mountains; Moravia is hilly, Slovakia, in E, has mountains (Carpathians) in N, fertile Danube plain in S. Vltava (Moldau) and Labe (Elbe) rivers flow N from Bohemia to G. **Capital:** Prague. **Cities** (1990 est.): Prague 1.2 mln.; Brno 385,000; Bratislava 413,000; Ostrava 327,000.

Government: Type: Socialist (in transition). **Head of state:** Pres. Vaclav Havel; b. Oct. 5, 1936; in office: Dec. 29, 1989. **Head of government:** Prime Min. Marian Calfa; in office: Dec. 10, 1989. **Local divisions:** Czech and Slovak republics each have an assembly. **Defense:** 6.8% of GNP (1987).

Economy: Industries: Machinery, oil products, iron and steel, glass, chemicals, motor vehicles, cement. **Chief crops:** Wheat, sugar beets, potatoes, rye, corn, barley. **Minerals:** coke, coal, iron. **Arable land:** 40%. **Livestock:** (1989): cattle: 5 mln.; pigs: 7 mln.; sheep: 1 mln. **Electricity prod.** (1989): 89.0 bln. kwh. **Crude steel prod.** (1988): 15.4 mln. metric tons. **Labor force:** 12% agric.; 37% ind.; 22% service, govt.

Finance: Monetary unit: Koruna (Apr. 1991: 30.15 = $1 US). **Gross national product** (1989): $123 bln. **Per capita GNP** (1989): $7,870. **Imports** (1990): $13.7 bln.; partners: USSR 31%, E. Ger. 10%, Pol. 6%, W. Ger. 9%. **Exports** (1990): $11.8 bln.; partners: USSR 35%, E. Ger. 7%, Pol. 7%. **Tourism** (1988): $436 mln. receipts. **International reserves less gold** (Mar. 1991): $1.2 bln. **Gold:** 2.6 mln. oz t. **Consumer prices** (change in 1990): 10.0%.

Transport: Railway traffic (1989): 20.0 bln. passenger-km. **Motor vehicles:** in use (1988): 2.9 mln. passenger cars,

460,000 comm. **Civil aviation** (1989): 2.6 bln. passenger-km.; 14 airports.

Communications: Television sets: 1 per 3.3 persons. **Radios:** 1 per 3.3 persons. **Telephones:** 1 per 3.9 persons. **Daily newspaper circ.** (1988): 327 per 1,000 pop.

Health: Life expectancy at birth (1989): 68 male; 75 female. **Births** (per 1,000 pop. 1989): 14. **Deaths** (per 1,000 pop. 1989): 12. **Natural increase:** .2%. **Hospital beds:** 1 per 99 persons; **Physicians:** 1 per 312 persons. **Infant mortality** (per 1,000 live births 1989): 13.

Education (1989): **Literacy:** 99%.
Major International Organizations: UN (GATT, WHO).
Embassy: 3900 Linnean Ave. NW 20008; 263-6315.

Bohemia, Moravia and Slovakia were part of the Great Moravian Empire in the 9th century. Later, Slovakia was overrun by Magyars, while Bohemia and Moravia became part of the Holy Roman Empire. Under the kings of Bohemia, Prague in the 14th century was the cultural center of Central Europe. Bohemia and Hungary became part of Austria-Hungary.

In 1914-1918 Thomas G. Masaryk and Eduard Benes formed a provisional government with the support of Slovak leaders including Milan Stefanik. They proclaimed the Republic of Czechoslovakia Oct. 28, 1918.

By 1938 Nazi Germany had worked up disaffection among German-speaking citizens in Sudetenland and demanded its cession. Prime Min. Neville Chamberlain of Britain, with the acquiescence of France, signed with Hitler at Munich, Sept. 30, 1938, an agreement to the cession, with a guarantee of peace by Hitler and Mussolini. Germany occupied Sudetenland Oct. 1-2.

Hitler on Mar. 15, 1939, dissolved Czechoslovakia, made protectorates of Bohemia and Moravia, and supported the autonomy of Slovakia, which was proclaimed independent Mar. 14, 1939.

Soviet troops with some Czechoslovak contingents entered eastern Czechoslovakia in 1944 and reached Prague in May 1945; Benes returned as president. In May 1946 elections, the Communist Party won 38% of the votes, and Benes accepted Klement Gottwald, a communist, as prime minister.

In February, 1948, the communists seized power in advance of scheduled elections. In May 1948 a new constitution was approved. Benes refused to sign it. On May 30 the voters were offered a one-slate ballot and the communists won full control. Benes resigned June 7 and Gottwald became president. A harsh Stalinist period followed, with complete and violent suppression of all opposition.

In Jan. 1968 a liberalization movement spread explosively through Czechoslovakia. Antonin Novotny, long the Stalinist boss of the nation, was deposed as party leader and succeeded by Alexander Dubcek, a Slovak, who declared he intended to make communism democratic. On Mar. 22 Novotny resigned as president and was succeeded by Gen. Ludvik Svoboda. On Apr. 6, Premier Joseph Lenart resigned and was succeeded by Oldrich Cernik, whose new cabinet was pledged to carry out democratization and economic reforms.

In July 1968 the USSR and 4 Warsaw Pact nations demanded an end to liberalization. On Aug. 20, the Russian, Polish, East German, Hungarian, and Bulgarian armies invaded Czechoslovakia.

Despite demonstrations and riots by students and workers, press censorship was imposed, liberal leaders were ousted from office and promises of loyalty to Soviet policies were made by some old-line Communist Party leaders.

On Apr. 17, 1969, Dubcek resigned as leader of the Communist Party and was succeeded by Gustav Husak. In Jan. 1970, Premier Cernik was ousted. Censorship was tightened and the Communist Party expelled a third of its members. In 1973, amnesty was offered to some of the 40,000 who fled the country after the 1968 invasion, but repressive policies remained in force.

More than 700 leading Czechoslovak intellectuals and former party leaders signed a human rights manifesto in 1977, called Charter 77, prompting a renewed crackdown by the regime.

The police crushed the largest anti-government protests since 1968, when tens of thousands of demonstrators took to the streets of Prague, Nov. 17, 1989. As protesters demanded free elections, the Communist Party leadership resigned Nov. 24; millions went on strike Nov. 27.

On Dec. 10, 1989 the first Cabinet in 41 years without a communist majority took power; Vaclav Havel, playwright and human rights campaigner, was chosen president, Dec. 29. The last Soviet troops left the country in May 1991.

Denmark
Kingdom of Denmark
Kongeriget Danmark

People: Population (1990 est.): 5,134,000. **Age distrib. (%):** 0–14: 17.1; 15–59: 62.5; 60+: 20.4. **Pop. density:** 308 per sq. mi. **Urban** (1990): 86%. **Ethnic groups:** Almost all Scandinavian. **Languages:** Danish. **Religions:** Evangelical Lutheran 90%.

Geography: Area: 16,633 sq. mi., the size of Massachusetts and New Hampshire combined. **Location:** In northern Europe, separating the North and Baltic seas. **Neighbors:** W. Germany on S., Norway on NW, Sweden on NE. **Topography:** Denmark consists of the Jutland Peninsula and about 500 islands, 100 inhabited. The land is flat or gently rolling, and is almost all in productive use. **Capital:** Copenhagen. **Cities** (1988, met.): Copenhagen 619,000.

Government: Type: Constitutional monarchy. **Head of state:** Queen Margrethe II; b. Apr. 16, 1940; in office: Jan. 14, 1972. **Head of government:** Prime Min. Poul Schluter; b. 1929; in office: Sept. 10, 1982. **Local divisions:** 14 counties and one city (Copenhagen). **Defense:** 2.3% of GNP (1990).

Economy: Industries: Machinery, textiles, furniture, electronics. **Chief crops:** Dairy products. **Arable land:** 62%. **Livestock** (1987): cattle: 2.3 mln.; pigs: 9.2 mln. **Fish catch** (1989): 1.9 mln. metric tons. **Electricity prod.** (1987): 27.5 bln. kwh. **Crude steel prod.** (1985): 560,000 metric tons. **Labor force:** 6% agric.; 50% ind. & comm.; 11% serv.; 27% govt.

Finance: Monetary unit: Krone (June 1991: 6.50 = $1 US). **Gross national product** (1989): $104.6 bln. **Per capita income** (1989): $20,385. **Imports** (1990): $31.6 bln.; partners: W. Ger. 24%, Swed. 12%, UK 9%, Neth. 5%. **Exports** (1990): $34.9 bln.; partners: Ger. 15%, EC 42%, U.S. 8%. **Tourists** (1989): $2.4 bln. receipts. **International reserves less gold** (Mar. 1991): $8.8 bln. **Gold:** 2.0 mln. oz t. **Consumer prices** (change in 1990): 2.6%.

Transport: Railway traffic (1989): 4.7 bln. passenger-km. **Motor vehicles:** in use (1989): 1.5 mln. passenger cars, 294,000 comm. vehicles. **Civil aviation** (1989): 4.2 bln. passenger-km; 12 airports with scheduled flights. **Chief ports:** Copenhagen, Alborg, Arhus, Odense.

Communications: Television sets: 1 per 2.7 persons. **Radios:** 1 per 2.4 persons. **Telephones:** 1 per 1.2 persons. **Daily newspaper circ.** (1986): 367 per 1,000 pop.

Health: Life expectancy at birth (1989): 72 male; 79 female. **Births** (per 1,000 pop. 1989): 11. **Deaths** (per 1,000 pop. 1989): 11. **Hospital beds:** 1 per 164 persons. **Physicians:** 1 per 375 persons. **Infant mortality** (per live births 1989): 7.8.

Education (1990): **Literacy:** 99%. Years compulsory 9; attendance 100%.

Major International Organizations: UN and all of its specialized agencies, OECD, EC, NATO.

Embassy: 3200 Whitehaven St. NW 20008; 234-4300.

The origin of Copenhagen dates back to ancient times, when the fishing and trading place named Havn (port) grew up on a cluster of islets, but Bishop Absalon (1128-1201) is regarded as the actual founder of the city.

Danes formed a large component of the Viking raiders in the early Middle Ages. The Danish kingdom was a major north European power until the 17th century, when it lost its land in southern Sweden. Norway was separated in 1815, and Schleswig-Holstein in 1864. Northern Schleswig was returned in 1920.

The **Faeroe Islands** in the N. Atlantic, about 300 mi. NE of the Shetlands, and 850 mi. from Denmark proper, 18 inhabited, have an area of 540 sq. mi. and pop. (1987) of 46,000. They are self-governing in most matters.

Greenland
(Kalaallit Nunaat)

Greenland, a huge island between the N. Atlantic and the Polar Sea, is separated from the North American continent by Davis Strait and Baffin Bay. Its total area is 840,000 sq. mi., 84% of which is ice-capped. Most of the island is a lofty plateau 9,000 to 10,000 ft. in altitude. The average thickness of the cap is 1,000 ft. The population (1989 est.) is 55,415. Under the 1953 Danish constitution the colony became an integral part of the realm with representatives in the Folketing. The Danish parliament, 1978, approved home rule for Greenland, effective May 1, 1979. Accepting home rule the islanders elected a socialist-dominated legislature, Apr. 4th. With home rule, Greenlandic place names came into official use. The technically-correct name for Greenland is now Kalaallit Nunaat; its capital is Nuuk, rather than Gothab. Fish is the principal export.

Djibouti
Republic of Djibouti
Jumhouriyya Djibouti

People: Population (1990 est.): 530,000. **Pop. density:** 59 per sq. mi. **Ethnic groups:** Issa (Somali) 47%; Afar 37%; European 8%. **Languages:** French, Arabic (both official); Afar, Issa. **Religions:** Sunni Moslem 94%.

Geography: Area: 8,950 sq. mi., about the size of New Hampshire. **Location:** On E coast of Africa, separated from Arabian Peninsula by the strategically vital strait of Bab el-Mandeb. **Neighbors:** Ethiopia on N (Eritrea) and W, Somalia on S. **Topography:** The territory, divided into a low coastal plain, mountains behind, and an interior plateau, is arid, sandy, and desolate. The climate is generally hot and dry. **Capital:** Djibouti. **Cities** (1988): Djibouti (met.) 290,000.

Government: Type: Republic. **Head of state:** Pres. Hassan Gouled Aptidon b. 1916; in office: June 24, 1977; **Head of government:** Prem. Barkat Gourad Hamadou; in office: Sept. 30, 1978. **Local divisions:** 5 cercles (districts).

Economy: Minerals: Salt. **Electricity prod.** (1988): 173 mln. kwh.

Finance: Monetary unit Franc (Mar. 1991: 177=$1 US). **Gross national product** (1986): $344 mln. **Per capita income** (1982): $400. **Imports** (1986): $197 mln.; partners: Fr. 47%, Jap. 8%, UK 8%. **Exports** (1986): $96 mln.; partners: Fr. 87%.

Transport: Motor vehicles: in use (1988): 12,000 passenger cars, 1,051 commercial vehicles. **Chief ports:** Djibouti.

Communications: Television sets: 1 per 35 persons. **Radios:** 1 per 16 persons. **Telephones:** 1 per 55 persons.

Health: Life expectancy at birth (1989): 45 male; 49 female. **Births** (per 1,000 pop. 1989): 43. **Deaths** (per 1,000 pop. 1989): 17. **Natural increase:** 2.6%. **Infant mortality** (per 1,000 live births 1989): 121.

Education (1988): **Literacy:** 20%.

Major International Organizations: UN, OAU, Arab League.

Embassy: 866 United Nations Plaza, New York, NY 10017; (212) 753-3163.

France gained control of the territory in stages between 1862 and 1900.

Ethiopia and Somalia have renounced their claims to the area, but each has accused the other of trying to gain control. There were clashes between Afars (ethnically related to Ethiopians) and Issas (related to Somalis) in 1976. Immigrants from both countries continued to enter the country up to independence, which came June 27, 1977.

Unemployment is high and there are few natural resources. French aid is the mainstay of the economy and some 5,000 French troops are present.

Dominica
Commonwealth of Dominica

People: Population (1990 est.): 85,000. **Pop. density:** 262 per sq. mi. **Ethnic groups:** nearly all African or mulatto, Caribs. **Languages:** English (official), French creole. **Religions:** mainly Roman Catholic.

Geography: Area: 290 sq. mi., about one-fourth the size of Rhode Island. **Location:** In Eastern Caribbean, most northerly Windward Is. **Neighbors:** Guadeloupe to N, Martinique to S. **Topography:** Mountainous, a central ridge running from N to S, terminating in cliffs; volcanic in origin, with numerous thermal springs; rich deep topsoil on leeward side, red tropical clay on windward coast. **Capital** (1987 est.) Roseau 22,000.

Government: Type: Parliamentary democracy; republic within Commonwealth. **Head of state:** Pres. Clarence Augustus Seignoret; in office: 1984. **Head of government:** Prime Min. Mary Eugenia Charles; b. 1919; in office: July 21, 1980. **Local divisions:** 10 parishes.

Economy: Industries: Agriculture, tourism. **Chief crops:** Bananas, citrus fruits, coconuts. **Minerals:** Pumice. **Other resources:** Forests. **Arable land:** 23%. **Electricity prod.** (1987): 16 mln. kwh. **Labor force:** 37% agric.; 20% ind & comm.; 30% services.

Finance: Monetary unit: East Caribbean dollar (May 1991: 2.70 = $1 US). **Gross national product** (1988): $91 mln. **Imports** (1988): $87 mln.; partners: UK 17%, U.S. 27%. **Exports** (1988): $55 mln.; partners: UK 50%. **Tourists** (1988): $14 mln. receipts. **Consumer prices** (change in 1988): 1.7%.

Transport: Chief ports: Roseau.

Communications: Telephones: 1 per 11 persons.

Health: Life expectancy at birth (1989): 73 male; 78 female. **Births** (per 1,000 pop. 1989): 26. **Deaths** (per 1,000 pop. 1989): 5. **Natural increase:** 2.1%. **Hospital beds:** 1 per 331 persons. **Physicians:** 1 per 2,619 persons. **Infant mortality** (per 1,000 live births 1989): 14.

Education: Literacy: 80%.

Major International Organizations: UN, OAS.

A British colony since 1805, Dominica was granted self government in 1967. Independence was achieved Nov. 3, 1978.

Hurricane David struck, Aug. 30, 1979, devastating the island and destroying the banana plantations, Dominica's economic mainstay. Coups were attempted in 1980 and 1981.

Dominica took a leading role in the instigation of the 1983 invasion of Grenada.

Dominican Republic

República Dominicana

People: Population (1990 est.): 7,253,000. **Age distrib. (%):** 0–14: 37.9; 15–59: 56.6; 60+: 5.5. **Pop. density:** 388 per sq. mi. **Urban** (1986): 55%. **Ethnic groups:** Caucasian 16%, mixed 73%, black 11%. **Languages:** Spanish. **Religions:** Roman Catholic 92%.

Geography: Area: 18,816 sq. mi., the size of Vermont and New Hampshire combined. **Location:** In West Indies, sharing I. of Hispaniola with Haiti. **Neighbors:** Haiti on W. **Topography:** The Cordillera Central range crosses the center of the country, rising to over 10,000 ft., highest in the Caribbean. The Cibao valley to the N is major agricultural area. **Capital:** Santo Domingo. **Cities** (1987 est.): Santo Domingo 1,700,000; Santiago de Los Caballeros 422,000.

Government: Type: Representative democracy. **Head of state:** Pres. Joaquin Balaguer; in office: Aug. 16, 1986. **Local divisions:** 29 provinces and Santo Domingo. **Defense:** 1.4% of GDP. (1987).

Economy: Industries: Sugar refining, cement, pharmaceuticals. **Chief crops:** sugar, cocoa, coffee, tobacco, rice. **Minerals:** Nickel, gold, silver. **Other resources:** Timber. **Arable land:** 23%. **Livestock** (1989): cattle: 2.0 mln.; pigs: 409,000. **Electricity prod.** (1988): 3.8 bln. kwh. **Labor force:** 49% agric.; 18% ind.; 34% serv. & govt.

Finance: Monetary unit: Peso (Mar. 1991: 12.83 = $1 US). **Gross national product** (1988): $4.8 bln. **Per capita GNP** (1988): $680. **Imports** (1989): $2.2 bln.; partners: U.S. 41%, Venez. 11%, Jap. 15%. **Exports** (1989): $928 mln.; partners: U.S. 50%, Neth. 18%. **Tourists** (1989): $675 mln. receipts. **National budget** (1987): $898 mln. expenditures. **International reserves less gold** (Mar. 1991): $181 mln. **Gold:** 18,000 oz t. **Consumer prices** (change in 1989): 45.4%

Transport: Motor vehicles: in use (1987): 151,000 passenger cars, 90,000 comm. vehicles. **Civil Aviation** (1988): 247 mln. passenger km.; 6 airports. **Chief ports:** Santo Domingo, San Pedro de Macoris, Puerto Plata.

Communications: Television sets: 1 per 12 persons. **Radios:** 1 per 6 persons. **Telephones:** 1 per 22 persons. **Daily newspaper circ.** (1987): 44 per 1,000 pop.

Health: Life expectancy at birth (1985): 60.7 male; 64.6 female. **Births** (per 1,000 pop. 1989): 30. **Deaths** (per 1,000 pop. 1989): 8. **Natural increase:** 2.2%. **Hospital beds:** 1 per 1,016 persons. **Physicians:** 1 per 2,147 persons. **Infant mortality** (per 1,000 live births 1989): 66.

Education (1987): **Literacy:** 68%. Years compulsory 6; attendance 60%.

Major International Organizations: UN (World Bank, IMF, GATT), OAS.

Embassy: 1712 22d St. NW 20008; 332-6280.

Carib and Arawak Indians inhabited the island of Hispaniola when Columbus landed in 1492. The city of Santo Domingo, founded 1496, is the oldest settlement by Europeans in the hemisphere and has the supposed ashes of Columbus in an elaborate tomb in its ancient cathedral.

The western third of the island was ceded to France in 1697. Santo Domingo itself was ceded to France in 1795. Haitian leader Toussaint L'Ouverture seized it, 1801. Spain returned intermittently 1803-21, as several native republics came and went. Haiti ruled again, 1822-44, and Spanish occupation occurred 1861-63.

The country was occupied by U.S. Marines from 1916 to 1924, when a constitutionally elected government was installed.

In 1930, Gen. Rafael Leonidas Trujillo Molina was elected president. Trujillo ruled brutally until his assassination in 1961. Pres. Joaquin Balaguer, appointed by Trujillo in 1960, resigned under pressure in 1962. Juan Bosch, elected president in the first free elections in 38 years, was overthrown in 1963.

On April 24, 1965, a revolt was launched by followers of Bosch and others, including a few communists. Four days later U.S. Marines intervened against the pro-Bosch forces. Token units were later sent by 5 So. American countries as a peacekeeping force.

A provisional government supervised a June 1966 election, in which Balaguer defeated Bosch by a 3-2 margin. The Inter-American Peace Force completed its departure Sept. 20, 1966. Continued depressed world prices have affected the main export commodity, sugar.

Ecuador

Republic of Ecuador

República del Ecuador

People: Population (1990 est.): 10,506,000. **Age distrib. (%):** 0–14: 41.3; 15–64: 55.0; 65+: 3.7. **Pop. density:** 95 per sq. mi. **Urban** (1988): 54% **Ethnic groups:** Indians 25%, Mestizo 55%, Spanish 10%, African 10%. **Languages:** Spanish (official), Quechuan, Jivaroan. **Religions:** Roman Catholic 95%.

Geography: Area: 109,483 sq. mi., the size of Colorado. **Location:** In NW S. America, on Pacific coast, astride Equator. **Neighbors:** Colombia to N, Peru to E and S. **Topography:** Two ranges of Andes run N and S, splitting the country into 3 zones: hot, humid lowlands on the coast; temperate highlands between the ranges, and rainy, tropical lowlands to the E. **Capital:** Quito. **Cities** (1989 est.): Guayaquil 1,600,000; Quito 1,200,000.

Government: Type: Republic. **Head of state:** Pres. Rodrigo Borja Cevallos; in office: Aug. 10, 1988. **Local divisions:** 20 provinces. **Defense:** 2.6% of GNP (1987).

Economy: Industries: Food processing, wood prods., textiles. **Chief crops:** Bananas (largest exporter), coffee, rice, sugar, corn. **Minerals:** Oil, copper, iron, lead, silver, sulphur. **Crude oil reserves** (1987): 1.2 bln. bbls. **Other resources:** Rubber, bark. **Arable land:** 6%. **Livestock** (1988): cattle: 3.8 mln.; pigs: 4.1 mln.; sheep: 2.1 mln. **Fish catch** (1987): 679,000 metric tons. **Electricity prod.** (1988): 5.7 bln. kwh. **Labor force:** 34% agric., 12% ind., 35% services.

Finance: Monetary unit: Sucre (June 1991: 966 = $1 US). **Gross national product** (1989): $10.7 bln. **Per capita GNP** (1989): $1,040. **Imports** (1990): $1.8 bln.; partners: U.S. 26%, EC 16%, Jap. 13%. **Exports** (1990): $2.7 bln.; partners: U.S. 54%. **Tourism** (1988): $173 mln. receipts. **National budget** (1987): $2.6 bln. expenditures. **International reserves less gold** (Mar. 1991): $838 mln. **Gold:** 443,000 oz t. **Consumer prices** (change in 1990): 48.5%.

Transport: Railway traffic (1987) 20 mln. passenger-km. **Motor vehicles:** in use (1987): 272,000 passenger cars, 41,000 comm. vehicles. **Civil aviation** (1989): 979 mln. passenger-km. **Chief ports:** Guayaquil, Manta, Esmeraldas, Puerto Bolivar.

Communications: Television sets: 1 per 17 persons. **Radios:** 1 per 3.4 persons. **Telephones:** 1 per 28 persons. **Daily newspaper circ.** (1987): 77 per 1,000 pop.

Health: Life expectancy at birth (1989): 64 male, 68 female. **Births** (per 1,000 pop. 1989): 31. **Deaths** (per 1,000 pop. 1989):

7. **Natural increase:** 2.4%. **Hospital beds:** 1 per 610 persons. **Physicians** (1984): 11,000. **Infant mortality** (per 1,000 live births 1989): 63.

Education (1986): Literacy: 90%. Attendance through 6th grade—76% urban, 33% rural.

Major International Organizations: UN (IMF, WHO), OAS, OPEC.

Embassy: 2535 15th St. NW 20009; 234-7200.

Spain conquered the region, which was the northern Inca empire, in 1633. Liberation forces defeated the Spanish May 24, 1822, near Quito. Ecuador became part of the Great Colombia Republic but seceded, May 13, 1830.

Ecuador had been ruled by civilian and military dictatorships since 1968. A peaceful transfer of power from the military junta to the democratic civilian government took place, 1979.

Since 1972, the economy has revolved around its petroleum exports, which have declined since 1982 causing severe economic problems. Ecuador suspended interest payments for 1987 on its estimated $8.2 billion foreign debt following a Mar. 5-6 earthquake which left 20,000 homeless, and destroyed a stretch of the country's main oil pipeline.

Ecuador and Peru have long disputed their Amazon Valley boundary.

The **Galapagos Islands,** 600 mi. to the W, are the home of huge tortoises and other unusual animals.

Egypt
Arab Republic of Egypt
Jumhūrīyah Misr al-Arabiya

People: Population (1990 est.): 54,139,000. **Age distrib (%)** 0-14: 41.8; 15-59: 52.7; 60+: 5.5. **Pop. density:** 141 per sq. mi. **Urban** (1986): 44%. **Ethnic groups:** Eastern Hamitic stock 90%, Bedouin, Nubian. **Languages:** Arabic (official), English. **Religions:** 90% Sunni Moslem.

Geography: Area: 386,650 sq. mi, about the size of Texas, Oklahoma, and Arkansas combined. **Location:** NE corner of Africa. **Neighbors:** Libya on W, Sudan on S, Israel on E. **Topography:** Almost entirely desolate and barren, with hills and mountains in E and along Nile. The Nile Valley, where most of the people live, stretches 550 miles. **Capital:** Cairo. **Cities** (1986 est.): Cairo 6,305,000; Alexandria 2,800,000; al-Jizah 1,600,000.

Government: Type: Republic. **Head of state:** Pres. Hosni Mubarak; b. 1929; in office: Oct. 14, 1981. **Head of Government:** Atef Sedki in office: Nov. 10, 1986. **Local divisions:** 26 governorates. **Defense:** 9.2% of GNP (1987).

Economy: Industries: Textiles, chemicals, petrochemicals, food processing, cement. **Chief crops:** Cotton (one of largest producers), rice, beans, fruits, grains, vegetables, sugar, corn. **Minerals:** Oil, phosphates, gypsum, iron, manganese, limestone. **Crude oil reserves** (1987): 4 bln. bbls. **Arable land:** 4%. **Livestock** (1988): cattle: 1.9 mln.; sheep: 1.1 mln. **Fish catch** (1989): 250,000 metric tons. **Electricity prod.** (1988): 42 bln. kwh. **Labor force:** 44% agric.; 22% services; 14% industry.

Finance: Monetary unit: Pound (June 1991: 3.25 = $1 US). **Gross national product** (1989): $32.5 bln. **Per capita GNP** (1989): $630. **Imports** (1989): $7.3 bln.; partners: U.S. 19%, W. Ger. 10%, It. 8%, France 8%. **Exports** (1989): $2.6 bln.; partners: It. 22%, Rom. 12%. **Tourists** (1988): $1.7 bln. receipts. **National budget** (1990): $30.3 bln. expenditures. **International reserves less gold** (Jan. 1991): $3.9 bln. **Gold:** 2.43 mln. oz t. **Consumer prices** (change in 1990): 16.8%.

Transport: Railway traffic (1986): 28.3 bln. passenger-km. **Motor vehicles:** in use (1989): 826,000 passenger cars, 550,000 comm. vehicles. **Civil aviation** (1988): 5.5 bln. passenger-km.; 11 airports. **Chief ports:** Alexandria, Port Said, Suez.

Communications: Television sets: 1 per 13 persons. **Radios:** 1 per 3.9 persons. **Telephones:** 1 per 34 persons. **Daily newspaper circ.** (1986): 88 per 1,000 pop.

Health: Life expectancy at birth (1989): 59 male; 60 female. **Births** (per 1,000 pop. 1989): 35. **Deaths** (per 1,000 pop. 1989): 10. **Natural increase:** 2.5%. **Hospital beds:** 1 per 505 persons. **Physicians:** 1 per 616 persons. **Infant mortality** (per 1,000 live births 1989): 93.

Education (1990): Literacy: 44%. Compulsory ages 6-12.

Major International Organizations: UN (IMF, World Bank, GATT), OAU.

Embassy: 2310 Decatur Pl. NW 20008; 232-5400.

Archeological records of ancient Egyptian civilization date back to 4000 BC. A unified kingdom arose around 3200 BC, and extended its way south into Nubia and north as far as Syria. A high culture of rulers and priests was built on an economic base of serfdom, fertile soil, and annual flooding of the Nile banks.

Imperial decline facilitated conquest by Asian invaders (Hyksos, Assyrians). The last native dynasty fell in 341 BC to the Persians, who were in turn replaced by Greeks (Alexander and the Ptolemies), Romans, Byzantines, and Arabs, who introduced Islam and the Arabic language. The ancient Egyptian language is preserved only in the liturgy of the Coptic Christians.

Egypt was ruled as part of larger Islamic empires for several centuries. The Mamluks, a military caste of Caucasian origin, ruled Egypt from 1250 until defeat by the Ottoman Turks in 1517. Under Turkish sultans the khedive as hereditary viceroy had wide authority. Britain intervened in 1882 and took control of administration, though nominal allegiance to the Ottoman Empire continued until 1914.

The country was a British protectorate from 1914 to 1922. A 1936 treaty strengthened Egyptian autonomy, but Britain retained bases in Egypt and a condominium over the Sudan. Britain fought German and Italian armies from Egypt, 1940-42. In 1951 Egypt abrogated the 1936 treaty. The Sudan became independent in 1956.

The uprising of July 23, 1952, led by the Society of Free Officers, named Maj. Gen. Mohammed Naguib commander in chief and forced King Farouk to abdicate. When the republic was proclaimed June 18, 1953, Naguib became its first president and premier. Lt. Col. Gamal Abdel Nasser removed Naguib and became premier in 1954. In 1956, he was voted president. Nasser died in 1970 and was replaced by Vice Pres. Anwar Sadat.

The Aswan High Dam, completed 1971, provides irrigation for more than a million acres of land. Artesian wells, drilled in the Western Desert, reclaimed 43,000 acres, 1960-66.

When the state of Israel was proclaimed in 1948, Egypt joined other Arab nations invading Israel and was defeated.

After terrorist raids across its border, Israel invaded Egypt's Sinai Peninsula, Oct. 29, 1956. Egypt rejected a cease-fire demand by Britain and France; on Oct. 31 the 2 nations dropped bombs and on Nov. 5-6 landed forces. Egypt and Israel accepted a UN cease-fire; fighting ended Nov. 7.

A UN Emergency Force guarded the 117-mile long border between Egypt and Israel until May 19, 1967, when it was withdrawn at Nasser's demand. Egyptian troops entered the Gaza Strip and the heights of Sharm el Sheikh and 3 days later closed the Strait of Tiran to all Israeli shipping. Full-scale war broke out June 5 and before it ended under a UN cease-fire June 10, Israel had captured Gaza and the Sinai Peninsula, controlled the east bank of the Suez Canal and reopened the gulf.

Sporadic fighting with Israel continued almost daily, 1968-70. Israel and Egypt agreed, Aug. 7, 1970, to a cease-fire and peace negotiations proposed by the U.S. Negotiations failed to achieve results, but the cease-fire continued.

In a surprise attack Oct. 6, 1973, Egyptian forces crossed the Suez Canal into the Sinai. (At the same time, Syrian forces attacked Israelis on the Golan Heights.) Egypt was supplied by a USSR military airlift; the U.S. responded with an airlift to Israel. Israel counter-attacked, crossed the canal, surrounded Suez City. A UN cease-fire took effect Oct. 24.

A disengagement agreement was signed Jan. 18, 1974. Under it, Israeli forces withdrew from the canal's W bank; limited numbers of Egyptian forces occupied a strip along the E bank. A second accord was signed in 1975, with Israel yielding Sinai oil fields. Pres. Sadat's surprise visit to Jerusalem, Nov. 1977, opened the prospect of peace with Israel. On Mar. 26, 1979, Egypt and Israel signed a formal peace treaty, ending 30 years of war, and establishing diplomatic relations. Israel returned control of the Sinai to Egypt in April 1982.

Tension between Moslem fundamentalists and Christians in 1981 caused street riots and culminated in a nationwide security crackdown in Sept. Pres Sadat was assassinated on Oct. 6.

Egypt was a political and military supporter of the Allied forces in their defeat of Iraq in the Persian Gulf War, 1991.

The **Suez Canal,** 103 mi. long, links the Mediterranean and Red seas. It was built by a French corporation 1859-69, but Britain obtained controlling interest in 1875. The last British troops were removed June 13, 1956. On July 26, Egypt nationalized the canal.

El Salvador

Republic of El Salvador
República de El Salvador

People: Population (1990 est.): 5,221,000. **Age distrib. (%):** 0–14: 45.3; 15–59: 51; 60+: 4.7. **Pop. density:** 642 per sq. mi. **Urban** (1987): 47%. **Ethnic groups:** Mestizo 89%, Indian 10%. **Languages:** Spanish (official). **Religions:** Roman Catholic 93%.

Geography: Area: 8,124 sq. mi., the size of Massachusetts. **Location:** In Central America. **Neighbors:** Guatemala on W, Honduras on N. **Topography:** A hot Pacific coastal plain in the south rises to a cooler plateau and valley region, densely populated. The N is mountainous, including many volcanoes. **Capital:** San Salvador. **Cities** (1987 est.): San Salvador 1.4 mln.

Government: Type: Republic. **Head of state:** Pres., Alfredo Cristiani; b. Nov, 22, 1947; in office: June 1, 1989. **Local divisions:** 14 departments. **Defense:** 3.9% of GNP (1987).

Economy: Industries: Food and beverages, textiles, petroleum products. **Chief crops:** Coffee (21% of GNP), cotton, corn, sugar. **Other resources:** Rubber, forests. **Arable land:** 27%. **Livestock** (1988): cattle: 1.1 mln.; pigs: 440,000. **Electricity prod.** (1988): 1.7 bln. kwh. **Labor force:** 40% agric.; 16% ind.; 27% services.

Finance: Monetary unit: Colon (Mar. 1991: 7.97 = $1 US). **Gross national product** (1989): $5.3 bln. **Per capita GNP** (1989): $1,040. **Imports** (1989): $1.1 bln.; partners: U.S. 39%, CACM 22%. **Exports** (1989): $497 mln.; partners: U.S. 49%, CACM 23%. **National budget** (1987): $642 mln. expenditures. **International reserves less gold** (Mar. 1991): $365 mln. **Gold:** 469,000 oz t. **Consumer prices** (change in 1990): 22.0%.

Transport: Railway traffic (1986): 4.9 mln. passenger-km. **Motor vehicles:** in use (1987): 138,000 passenger cars, 23,000 comm. vehicles. **Chief ports:** La Union, Acajutla.

Communications: Television sets: 1 per 12 persons. **Radios:** 1 per 2.6 persons. **Telephones:** 1 per 36 persons. **Daily newspaper circ.** (1988): 65 per 1,000 pop.

Health: Life expectancy at birth (1985): 62.6 male; 66.3 female. **Births** (per 1,000 pop. 1989): 33. **Deaths** (per 1,000 pop. 1989): 8. **Natural increase:** 2.5%. **Hospital beds:** 1 per 1,129 persons. **Physicians:** 1 per 2,830 persons. **Infant mortality** (per 1,000 live births 1989): 62.

Education (1987): **Literacy:** 62% (urban areas); 40% (rural areas). Years compulsory 6; attendance 82%.

Major International Organizations: UN (IMF, WHO, ILO), OAS, CACM.

Embassy: 2308 California St. NW 20008; 265-3480.

El Salvador became independent of Spain in 1821, and of the Central American Federation in 1839.

A fight with Honduras in 1969 over the presence of 300,000 Salvadorean workers left 2,000 dead. Clashes were renewed 1970 and 1974.

A military coup overthrew the Romero government, 1979, but the ruling military-civilian junta failed to quell the civil war which has resulted in some 50,000 deaths. Some 10,000 leftists insurgents, armed by Cuba and Nicaragua, control about 25% of the country, mostly in the east. Extreme right-wing death squads organized to eliminate suspected leftists were blamed for over 1,000 deaths in 1983. The Reagan administration has staunchly supported the government with military aid.

Voters turned out in large numbers in the May 1984 presidential election. Christian Democrat Jose Napoleon Duarte, a moderate, was victorious with 54% of the vote. Duarte was diagnosed as having terminal cancer in 1988.

Lefist guerrillas continued their offensive in 1990 as the civil war entered its 10th year. Nine soldiers, including 3 officers, were indicted Jan. 1990 in the Nov. 1989 slaying of 6 Jesuit priests at a university in San Salvador.

Equatorial Guinea

Republic of Equatorial Guinea
República de Guinea Ecuatorial

People: Population (1990 est.): 360,000. **Age distrib. (%):** 0–14: 38.1; 15–59: 55.2; 60+: 6.7. **Pop. density:** 35 per sq. mi.

Ethnic groups: Fangs 80%, Bubi 15%. **Languages:** Spanish (official), Fang, Bubi. **Religions:** Mostly Roman Catholic.

Geography: Area: 10,832 sq. mi., the size of Maryland. **Location:** Bioko Is. off W. Africa coast in Gulf of Guinea, and Rio Muni, mainland enclave. **Neighbors:** Gabon on S, Cameroon on E, N. **Topography:** Bioko Is. consists of 2 volcanic mountains and a connecting valley. Rio Muni, with over 90% of the area, has a coastal plain and low hills beyond. **Capital:** Malabo. **Cities** (1989 est.): Malabo 38,000.

Government: Type: Unitary Republic. **Head of state:** Pres., Supreme Military Council Teodoro Obiang Nguema Mbasogo; b. June 5, 1942; in office: Oct. 10, 1979. **Head of government:** Prime Min. Cristino Seriche Bioko. **Local divisions:** 7 provinces.

Economy: Chief crops: Cocoa, coffee, bananas, sweet potatoes. **Other resources:** Timber. **Arable land:** 8%. **Electricity prod.** (1989): 17 mln. kwh. **Labor force:** agric. 50%; public sector 40%.

Finance: Monetary unit: Bipkwele (Mar. 1991: 290 = $1 US). **Gross domestic product** (1987): $149 mln. **Per capita income** (1987): $300. **Imports** (1987): $50 mln.; partners: Spain 54%, China 17%. **Exports** (1987): $39 mln.; partners: Sp. 40%, Neth. 28%, W. Ger. 23%.

Transport: Chief ports: Malabo, Bata.

Communications: Radios: 1 per 3.5 persons.

Health: Life expectancy at birth (1989): 44.0 male; 48.0 female. **Births** (per 1,000 pop. 1989): 38. **Deaths** (per 1,000 pop. 1989): 19. **Natural increase:** 1.9% **Hospital beds** (1982): 3,200. **Infant mortality** (per 1,000 live births 1989): 125.

Education (1989): **Literacy:** 55%. About 65% attend primary school.

Major International Organizations: UN (IMF, World Bank), OAU.

Embassy: 801 2d Ave., New York, NY 10017; (212) 599-1523.

Fernando Po (now Bioko) Island was discovered by Portugal in the late 15th century and ceded to Spain in 1778. Independence came Oct. 12, 1968. Riots occurred in 1969 over disputes between the island and the more backward Rio Muni province on the mainland. Masie Nguema Biyogo, himself from the mainland, became president for life in 1972.

Masie's 11-year reign was one of the most brutal in Africa, resulting in a bankrupted nation. Most of the nation's 7,000 Europeans emigrated. In 1976, 45,000 Nigerian workers were evacuated amid charges of a reign of terror. Masie was ousted in a military coup, Aug., 1979.

The nation is heavily dependent on external aid.

Estonia

Republic of Estonia
Eesti Vabariik

People: Population (1989 cen.): 1,600,000. **Ethnic groups:** Estonian 65%, Russian 27%.

Geography: Area: 17,413 sq. mi. **Neighbors:** bounded on N., W. by the Baltic Sea, E. by Russia, S. by Latvia. **Capital:** Tallinn. **Cities** (1989 census): Tallinn 482,000.

Government: Type: Republic. **Head of state:** Arnold Ruutel. **Local divisions:** 15 districts, 33 towns, 26 urban settlements.

Economy: Industries: Agricultural machinery, electric motors. **Chief crops:** grain, vegetables. **Livestock** (1989): cattle: 823,000, sheep: 138,000.

Transport: Chief port: Tallinn.

Health: (1988): 7,600 doctors, 19,000 hospital beds.

Education: 11 year school curriculum.

Estonia was a province of imperial Russia before World War I, was independent between World Wars I and II, but was conquered by the USSR in 1940. Estonia declared itself an "occupied territory," and proclaimed itself a free nation Mar. 1990. During the Soviet coup, Estonia declared immediate full independence, Aug. 20, 1991. Several nations extended diplomatic recognition including the U.S. on Sept. 2. *(See Index & Chronology for details.)*

Ethiopia

People's Democratic Republic of Ethiopia

Ye Etiyop'iya Hezbawi Dimokrasiyawi Republek

People: Population (1990 est.): 51,375,000. **Age distrib.** (%): 0–14: 46.5; 15–59: 47.3; 60+: 6.2. **Pop. density:** 101 per sq. mi. **Urban** (1989): 11%. **Ethnic groups:** Oromo 40%, Amhara 25%, Tigre 12%, Sidama 9%. **Languages:** Amharic (official), Tigre (Semitic languages); Galla (Hamitic). **Religions:** Orthodox Christian 40%, Moslem 40%.

Geography: Area: 471,776 sq. mi., four-fifths the size of Alaska. **Location:** In E. Africa. **Neighbors:** Sudan on W, Kenya on S. Somalia, Djibouti on E. **Topography:** A high central plateau, between 6,000 and 10,000 ft. high, rises to higher mountains near the Great Rift Valley, cutting in from the SW. The Blue Nile and other rivers cross the plateau, which descends to plains on both W and SE. **Capital:** Addis Ababa. **Cities** (1984 est.): Addis Ababa 1,412,000.

Government: Type: In transition. **Head of state:** Pres. Gen. Tesfaye Gebre-Kidan; in office: May 20, 1991. **Head of Government:** Prime Min. Hailu Yimenu; in office: Nov. 8, 1989. **Local divisions:** 24 administrative zones, 5 autonomous regions. **Defense:** 8% of GNP (1987).

Economy: Industries: Food processing, cement, textiles. **Chief crops:** Coffee (61% export earnings), grains. **Minerals:** Platinum, gold, copper, potash. **Arable Land:** 13%. **Livestock** (1988): cattle: 23.4 mln.; sheep: 17.5 mln. **Electricity prod.** (1988): 815 mln. kwh. **Labor force:** 90% agric.

Finance: Monetary unit: Birr (Mar. 1991: 2.07 = $1 US). **Gross national product** (1989): $5.9 bln. **Per capita GNP** (1989): $121. **Imports** (1989): $1.2 bln.; partners: USSR 22%, U.S. 15%, Italy 10%, Jap. 6%, W.Ger. 10%. **Exports** (1989): $465 mln.; partners: U.S. 20%, W. Ger. 18%, Italy 7%. **National budget** (1987): $2.0 bln. expenditures. **International reserves less gold** (Mar. 1991): $16 mln. **Gold:** 191,000 oz t. **Consumer prices** (change in 1990): 5.2%.

Transport: Railway traffic (1986): 350 mln. passenger-km. **Motor vehicles:** in use (1988): 41,300 passenger cars, 19,000 comm. vehicles. **Civil aviation** (1988): 413 mln. passenger-km; 36 airports with scheduled flights. **Chief ports:** Masewa, Aseb.

Communications: Television sets: 1 per 815 persons. **Radios:** 1 per 5.5 persons. **Telephones:** 1 per 348 persons. **Daily newspaper circ.** (1989): 1 per 1,000 pop.

Health: Life expectancy at birth (1989): 50 male; 53 female. **Births** (per 1,000 pop. 1989): 45. **Deaths** (per 1,000 pop. 1989): 15. **Natural increase:** 3.1%. **Hospital beds:** 1 per 3,873 persons. **Physicians:** 1 per 36,660 persons. **Infant mortality** (per 1,000 live births 1989): 113.

Education (1985): **Literacy:** 18%.

Major International Organizations: UN (IMF, WHO), OAU. **Embassy:** 2134 Kalorama Rd. NW 20008; 234-2281.

Ethiopian culture was influenced by Egypt and Greece. The ancient monarchy was invaded by Italy in 1880, but maintained its independence until another Italian invasion in 1936. British forces freed the country in 1941.

The last emperor, Haile Selassie I, established a parliament and judiciary system in 1931, but barred all political parties.

A series of droughts since 1972 have killed hundreds of thousands. An army mutiny, strikes, and student demonstrations led to the dethronement of Selassie in 1974. The ruling junta pledged to form a one-party socialist state, and instituted a successful land reform; opposition was violently suppressed. The influence of the Coptic Church, embraced in 330 AD, was curbed, and the monarchy was abolished in 1975.

The regime, torn by bloody coups, faced uprisings by tribal and political groups in part aided by Sudan and Somalia. Ties with the U.S., once a major arms and aid source, deteriorated, while cooperation accords were signed with the USSR in 1977. In 1978, Soviet advisors and Cuban troops helped defeat Somalia forces. Ethiopia and Somalia signed a peace agreement in 1988.

A world-wide relief effort began in 1984, as an extended drought caused millions to face starvation and death. In 1988, victories by Eritrean guerrillas forced the government to curtail the work of foreign aid workers in drought-stricken regions. Foreign relief officials expressed the fear that suspension of their operations would lead to the starvation death of hundreds of thousands.

The Ethiopia People's Revolutionary Democractic Front (EPRDF), an umbrella group of 6 rebel armies, launched a major push against government forces, Feb. 1991. In May, Pres Mengistu resigned and left the country. The EPRDF took posession of the capital and announced plans for a coalition government.

Fiji

Republic of Fiji

People: Population (1990 est.): 772,000. **Age distrib.** (%): 0–14: 38.2; 15–59: 56.9; 60+: 4.9. **Pop. density:** 107 per sq. mi. **Urban** (1986): 39%. **Ethnic groups:** Indian 48%, Fijian (Melanesian-Polynesian) 46%, Europeans 2%. **Languages:** English (official), Fijian, Hindi. **Religions:** Christian 52%, Hindu 38%, Moslem 8%.

Geography: Area: 7,056 sq. mi., the size of Massachusetts. **Location:** In western S. Pacific O. **Neighbors:** Nearest are Solomons on NW, Tonga on E. **Topography:** 322 islands (106 inhabited), many mountainous, with tropical forests and large fertile areas. Viti Levu, the largest island, has over half the total land area. **Capital:** Suva. **Cities** (1986 est.): Suva 69,000.

Government: Type: Republic. **Head of state:** Pres. Penaia Ganilau; in office: Dec. 5, 1987. **Head of government:** Prime Min. Kamisese Mara; b. May 13, 1920; in office: Oct. 10, 1970. **Local divisions:** 4 divisions, 1 dependency.

Economy: Industries: Sugar refining, light industry, tourism. **Chief crops:** Sugar, bananas, ginger. **Minerals:** Gold. **Other resources:** Timber. **Arable land:** 8%. **Electricity prod.** (1988): 325 mln. kwh. **Labor force:** 44% agric.

Finance: Monetary unit: Dollar (Mar. 1991: 1.48 = $1.00 US). **Gross national product** (1988): $1.1 bln. **Per capita GNP** (1988): $1,540. **Imports** (1989): $615 mln.; partners: Austral. 29%, Jap. 12%, N.Z. 19%. **Exports** (1989): $370 mln.; partners; UK 32%, Aust. 25%. **Tourists** (1988): $180 mln. receipts. **National budget** (1987): $340 mln. expenditures. **International reserves less gold** (Mar. 1991): $267 mln. **Gold:** 10,000 oz t. **Consumer prices** (change in 1990): 7.9%.

Transport: Motor vehicles: in use (1989): 37,000 passenger cars, 25,000 comm. vehicles. **Civil aviation** (1989): 802 mln. passenger-km; 18 airports with scheduled flights. **Chief ports:** Suva, Lautoka.

Communications: Radios: 1 per 1.7 persons. **Telephones:** 1 per 12 persons. **Daily newspaper circ.** (1988): 56 per 1,000 pop.

Health: Life expectancy at birth (1987): 68.0 male; 72.4 female. **Births** (per 1,000 pop. 1989): 28. **Deaths** (per 1,000 pop. 1989): 5. **Natural increase:** 2.3%. **Hospital beds:** 1 per 417 persons. **Physicians:** 1 per 2,649 persons. **Infant mortality** (per 1,000 live births 1989): 19.

Education (1985): **Literacy:** 80%. 95% attend school.

Major International Organizations: UN (IMF, WHO), Commonwealth of Nations.

Embassy: 2233 Wisconsin Ave. NW 20007; 337-8320.

A British colony since 1874, Fiji became an independent parliamentary democracy Oct. 10, 1970.

Cultural differences between the majority Indian community, descendants of contract laborers brought to the islands in the 19th century, and the less modernized native Fijians, who by law own 83% of the land in communal villages, have led to political polarization.

In 1987, a military coup ousted the government; order was restored May 21 when a compromise was reached granting Lt. Col. Sitiveni Rabuka, the coup's leader, increased power. Rabuka staged a second coup Sept. 25 and in Oct. declared Fiji a republic. A civilian government was restored to power in Dec.

Finland

Republic of Finland

Suomen Tasavalta

People: Population (1990 est.): 4,977,000. **Age distrib.** (%): 0–14: 19.3; 15–59: 62.9; 60+: 17.8. **Pop. density:** 38 per sq. mi. **Urban** (1990): 61%. **Ethnic groups:** Finns 94%, Swedes, Lapps. **Languages:** Finnish, Swedish (both official). **Religions:** Lutheran 97%.

Geography: Area: 130,119 sq. mi., slightly smaller than Montana. **Location:** In northern Europe. **Neighbors:** Norway on N, Sweden on W, USSR on E. **Topography:** South and central Finland are mostly flat areas with low hills and many lakes. The N has mountainous areas, 3,000-4,000 ft. **Capital:** Helsinki. **Cities** (1990 est.): Helsinki 490,000; Tampere 170,000; Turku 160,000.

Government: Type: Constitutional republic. Head of state: Pres. Mauno Koivisto; b. Nov. 25, 1923; in office: Jan. 27, 1982. **Head of government:** Prime Min. Esko Aho; b. 1954; in office: Apr. 25, 1991. **Local divisions:** 12 laanit (provinces). **Defense:** 1.4% of GNP (1989).

Economy: Industries: Machinery, metal, shipbuilding, textiles, clothing. **Chief crops:** Grains, potatoes, dairy prods. **Minerals:** Copper, iron, zinc. **Other resources:** Forests (40% of exports). **Arable land:** 8%. **Livestock** (1988): cattle; 1.5 mln. pigs: 1.3 mln. Fish catch (1989): 160,000 metric tons. **Electricity prod.** (1988): 47.8 bln. kwh. **Crude steel prod.** (1988): 2.7 mln. metric tons. **Labor force:** 9% agric.; 54% ind., comm. & finance; 25% services.

Finance: Monetary unit: Markka (June 1991: 4.02 = $1 US). **Gross national product** (1989): $114 bln. **Per capita income** (1989): $23,153. **Imports** (1990): $24.4 bln.; partners: USSR 11%, Swed. 12%, W. Ger. 18%, UK 7%. **Exports** (1990): $26.5 bln.; partners: USSR 15%, Swed. 13%, UK 11%, W. Ger. 11%. **Tourists** (1989): $1.0 bln. receipts. **National budget** (1989): $28.9 bln. expenditures. **International reserves less gold** (Mar. 1991): $8.2 bln. **Gold** 2.0 mln. oz t. **Consumer prices** (change in 1990): 6.1%.

Transport: Railway traffic (1988): 3.1 bln. passenger-km. **Motor vehicles:** in use (1989): 1.7 mln. passenger cars, 238,000 comm. vehicles; **Civil aviation** (1989): 4.6 bln. passenger-km; 24 airports. **Chief ports:** Helsinki, Turku.

Communications: Television sets: 1 per 2.7 persons. **Radios:** 1 per person. **Telephones:** 1 per 2.1 persons. **Daily newspaper circ.** (1988): 667 per 1,000 pop.

Health: Life expectancy at birth (1989): 71 male; 79 female. **Births** (per 1,000 pop. 1989): 12. **Deaths** (per 1,000 pop. 1989): 10. **Natural increase:** .02%. **Hospital beds:** 1 per 81 persons. **Physicians:** 1 per 441 persons. **Infant mortality** (per 1,000 live births 1989): 6.

Education (1991): **Literacy:** 99%. Years compulsory 9; attendance 99%.

Major International Organizations: UN (IMF, GATT), EFTA, OECD.

Embassy: 3216 New Mexico Ave. NW 20016; 363-2430.

The early Finns probably migrated from the Ural area at about the beginning of the Christian era. Swedish settlers brought the country into Sweden, 1154 to 1809, when Finland became an autonomous grand duchy of the Russian Empire. Russian exactions created a strong national spirit; on Dec. 6, 1917, Finland declared its independence and in 1919 became a republic. On Nov. 30, 1939, the Soviet Union invaded, and the Finns were forced to cede 16,173 sq. mi., including the Karelian Isthmus, Viipuri, and an area on Lake Ladoga. After World War II, in which Finland tried to recover its lost territory, further cessions were exacted. In 1948, Finland signed a treaty of mutual assistance with the USSR. In 1956 Russia returned Porkkala, which had been ceded as a military base.

Aland, constituting an autonomous department, is a group of small islands, 572 sq. mi., in the Gulf of Bothnia, 25 mi. from Sweden, 15 mi. from Finland. Mariehamn is the principal port.

France
French Republic
République Française

People: Population (1990 est.): 56,184,000. **Age distrib.** (%): 0–14: 20.5; 15–60: 60.8; 60+: 18.7. **Pop. density:** 252 per sq. mi. **Urban** (1985): 77.2%. **Ethnic groups:** A mixture of various European and Mediterranean groups. **Languages:** French (official); minorities speak Breton, Alsatian German, Flemish, Italian, Basque, Catalan. **Religions:** Mostly Roman Catholic.

Geography: Area: 220,668 sq. mi., four-fifths the size of Texas. **Location:** In western Europe, between Atlantic O. and Mediterranean Sea. **Neighbors:** Spain on S, Italy, Switzerland, Germany on E, Luxembourg, Belgium on N. **Topography:** A wide plain covers more than half of the country, in N and W, drained to W by Seine, Loire, Garonne rivers. The Massif Central

is a mountainous plateau in center. In E are Alps (Mt. Blanc is tallest in W. Europe, 15,771 ft.), the lower Jura range, and the forested Vosges. The Rhone flows from Lake Geneva to Mediterranean. Pyrenees are in SW, on border with Spain. **Capital:** Paris. **Cities** (1990 est.): Paris 2,152,000; Marseille 801,000; Lyon 415,000; Toulouse 359,000; Nice 342,000; Nantes 245,000; Strasbourg 252,000; Bordeaux 201,000.

Government: Type: Republic. **Head of state:** Pres. François Mitterrand; b. Oct. 26, 1916; in office: May 21, 1981. **Head of government:** Prime Min. Edith Cresson; b. Jan. 27, 1934; in office: May 15, 1991. **Local divisions:** 22 administrative regions containing 95 departments. **Defense:** 4% of GNP (1987).

Economy: Industries: Steel, chemicals, textiles, wine, perfume, aircraft, electronic equipment. **Chief crops:** Grains, corn, rice, fruits, vegetables. France is largest food producer, exporter, in W. Eur. **Minerals:** Bauxite, iron, coal. **Crude oil reserves** (1985): 221 mln. bbls. **Other resources:** Forests. **Arable land:** 32%. **Livestock** (1988): cattle: 21.1 mln.; pigs: 12.5 mln.; sheep: 10.3 mln. **Fish catch** (1988): 843,000 metric tons. **Electricity prod.** (1988): 384 bln. kwh. **Crude steel prod.** (1988): 18.9 mln. metric tons. **Labor force:** 9% agric.; 45% ind. & comm.; 46% services.

Finance: Monetary unit: Franc (June 1991: 5.75 = $1 US). **Gross national product** (1989): $1 trl. **Per capita GNP** (1989): $17,830. **Imports** (1990): $234 bln.; partners: EC 51%. **Exports** (1990): $216 bln.; partners: EC 50%, U.S. 9%. **Tourists** (1989) receipts: $16.5 bln. **National budget** (1988): $208 bln. expenditures. **International reserves less gold** (Feb. 1991): $36.3 bln. **Gold:** 81.85 mln. oz t. **Consumer prices** (change in 1990): 3.5%.

Transport: Railway traffic (1989): 63.2 bln. passenger-km. **Motor vehicles:** in use (1989): 23.0 mln. passenger cars, 5.1 mln. **Civil aviation** (1989): 49.0 bln. passenger-km; 60 airports with scheduled flights. **Chief ports:** Marseille, LeHavre, Nantes, Bordeaux, Rouen.

Communications: Television sets: 1 per 2.6 persons. **Radios:** 1 per 1.1 persons. **Telephones:** 1 per 1.7 persons. **Daily newspaper circ.** (1988): 169 per 1,000 pop.

Health: Life expectancy at birth (1989): 72 male; 80 female. **Births** (per 1,000 pop. 1989): 14. **Deaths** (per 1,000 pop. 1989): 10. **Natural increase:** .3%. **Hospital beds:** 1 per 80 persons. **Physicians:** 1 per 403 persons. **Infant mortality** (per 1,000 live births 1989): 8.2.

Education (1991): **Literacy:** 99%. Years compulsory 10.

Major International Organizations: UN and most of its specialized agencies, OECD, EC, NATO.

Embassy: 4101 Reservoir Rd. NW 20007; 944-6000.

Celtic Gaul was conquered by Julius Caesar 58-51 BC; Romans ruled for 500 years. Under Charlemagne, Frankish rule extended over much of Europe. After his death France emerged as one of the successor kingdoms.

The monarchy was overthrown by the French Revolution (1789-93) and succeeded by the First Republic; followed by the First Empire under Napoleon (1804-15), a monarchy (1814-48), the Second Republic (1848-52), the Second Empire (1852-70), the Third Republic (1871-1946), the Fourth Republic (1946-58), and the Fifth Republic (1958 to present).

France suffered severe losses in manpower and wealth in the first World War, 1914-18, when it was invaded by Germany. By the Treaty of Versailles, France exacted return of Alsace and Lorraine, French provinces seized by Germany in 1871. Germany invaded France again in May, 1940, and signed an armistice with a government based in Vichy. After France was liberated by the Allies Sept. 1944, Gen. Charles de Gaulle became head of the provisional government, serving until 1946.

De Gaulle again became premier in 1958, during a crisis over Algeria, and obtained voter approval for a new constitution, ushering in the Fifth Republic. Using strong executive powers, he promoted French economic and technological advances in the context of the European Economic Community, and guarded French foreign policy independence.

France had withdrawn from Indochina in 1954, and from Morocco and Tunisia in 1956. Most of its remaining African territories were freed 1958-62.

In 1966, France withdrew all its troops from the integrated military command of NATO, though 60,000 remained stationed in Germany. France continued to attend political meetings of NATO.

In May 1968 rebellious students in Paris and other centers rioted, battled police, and were joined by workers who launched nationwide strikes. The government awarded pay increases to the strikers May 26. In elections to the Assembly in June, de Gaulle's backers won a landslide victory. Nevertheless, he resigned from office in April, 1969, after losing a nationwide referendum on constitutional reform.

On May 10, 1981, France elected François Mitterrand, a Socialist candidate, president. In September, the government nationalized 5 major industries and most private banks. In 1986, France began a privatization program in which some 80 state-owned companies would be sold. Mitterrand was elected to a 2d 7-year term in 1988.

Agents of France's external security service were responsible for the July 10, 1985 sinking of the *Rainbow Warrior*, flagship of the Greenpeace environmental movement, in the port of Auckland, New Zealand.

The island of **Corsica**, in the Mediterranean W of Italy and N of Sardinia, is an official region of France comprising 2 departments. Area: 3,369 sq. mi.; pop. (1986 est.): 248,000. The capital is Ajaccio, birthplace of Napoleon.

Overseas Departments

French Guiana is on the NE coast of South America with Suriname on the W and Brazil on the E and S. Its area is 43,740 sq. mi.; pop. (1989): 94,000. Guiana sends one senator and one deputy to the French Parliament. Guiana is administered by a prefect and has a Council General of 16 elected members; capital is Cayenne.

The famous penal colony, Devil's Island, was phased out between 1938 and 1951.

Immense forests of rich timber cover 90% of the land. Placer gold mining is the most important industry. Exports are shrimp, timber, and machinery.

Guadeloupe, in the West Indies' Leeward Islands, consists of 2 large islands, Basse-Terre and Grande-Terre, separated by the Salt River, plus Marie Galante and the Saintes group to the S and, to the N, Desirade, St. Barthelemy, and over half of St. Martin (the Netherlands portion is St. Maarten). A French possession since 1635, the department is represented in the French Parliament by 2 senators and 3 deputies; administration consists of a prefect (governor) and an elected general and regional councils.

Area of the islands is 660 sq. mi.; pop. (1989 est.) 340,000, mainly descendants of slaves; capital is Basse-Terre on Basse-Terre Is. The land is fertile; sugar, rum, and bananas are exported; tourism is an important industry.

Martinique, the northernmost of the Windward Islands, in the West Indies, has been a possession since 1635, and a department since March, 1946. It is represented in the French Parliament by 2 senators and 3 deputies. The island was the birthplace of Napoleon's Empress Josephine.

It has an area of 425 sq. mi.; pop. (1988 est.) 336,000, mostly descendants of slaves. The capital is Fort-de-France (pop. 1988: 117,000). It is a popular tourist stop. The chief exports are rum, bananas, and petroleum products.

Mayotte, formerly part of Comoros, voted in 1976 to become an overseas department of France. An island NW of Madagascar, area is 144 sq. mi., pop. (1988 est.) 77,000.

Reunion is a volcanic island in the Indian O. about 420 mi. E of Madagascar, and has belonged to France since 1665. Area, 969 sq. mi.; pop. (1988 est.) 575,000, 30% of French extraction. Capital: Saint-Denis. The chief export is sugar. It elects 3 deputies, 2 senators to the French Parliament.

St. Pierre and Miquelon, formerly an Overseas Territory, made the transition to department status in 1976. It consists of 2 groups of rocky islands near the SW coast of Newfoundland, inhabited by fishermen. The exports are chiefly fish products. The St. Pierre group has an area of 10 sq. mi.; Miquelon, 83 sq. mi. Total pop. (1988 est.), 6,300. The capital is St. Pierre. A deputy and a senator are elected to the French Parliament.

Overseas Territories

French Polynesia Overseas Territory, comprises 130 islands widely scattered among 5 archipelagos in the South Pacific; administered by a governor. Territorial Assembly and a Council with headquarters at Papeete, Tahiti, one of the **Society Islands** (which include the **Windward** and **Leeward** islands). A deputy and a senator are elected to the French Parliament.

Other groups are the **Marquesas Islands**, the **Tuamotu Archipelago**, including the **Gambier Islands**, and the **Austral Islands**.

Total area of the islands administered from Tahiti is 1,544 sq. mi.; pop. (1988 est.), 188,000, more than half on Tahiti. Tahiti is picturesque and mountainous with a productive coastline bearing coconut, banana and orange trees, sugar cane and vanilla.

Tahiti was visited by Capt. James Cook in 1769 and by Capt. Bligh in the Bounty, 1788-89. Its beauty impressed Herman Melville, Paul Gauguin, and Charles Darwin.

French Southern and Antarctic Lands Overseas Territory, comprises **Adelie Land**, on Antarctica, and 4 island groups in the Indian O. Adelie, discovered 1840, has a research station, a coastline of 185 mi. and tapers 1,240 mi. inland to the South Pole. The U.S. does not recognize national claims in Antarctica. There are 2 huge glaciers, Ninnis, 22 mi. wide, 99 mi. long, and Mentz, 11 mi. wide, 140 mi. long. The Indian O. groups are:

Kerguelen Archipelago, discovered 1772, one large and 300 small islands. The chief is 87 mi. long, 74 mi. wide, and has Mt. Ross, 6,429 ft. tall. Principal research station is Port-aux-Francais. Seals often weigh 2 tons; there are blue whales, coal, peat, semi-precious stones. **Crozet Archipelago**, discovered 1772, covers 195 sq. mi. Eastern Island rises to 6,560 ft. **Saint Paul**, in southern Indian O., has warm springs with earth at places heating to 120° to 390° F. **Amsterdam** is nearby; both produce cod and rock lobster.

New Caledonia and its dependencies, an overseas territory, are a group of islands in the Pacific O. about 1,115 mi. E of Australia and approx. the same distance NW of New Zealand. Dependencies are the **Loyalty Islands**, the **Isle of Pines**, **Huon Islands** and the **Chesterfield Islands**.

New Caledonia, the largest, has 6,530 sq. mi. Total area of the territory is 8,548 sq. mi.; population (1988 est.) 156,000. The group was acquired by France in 1853.

The territory is administered by a governor and government council. There is a popularly elected Territorial Assembly. A deputy and a senator are elected to the French Parliament. Capital: Noumea.

Mining is the chief industry. New Caledonia is one of the world's largest nickel producers. Other minerals found are chrome, iron, cobalt, manganese, silver, gold, lead, and copper. Agricultural products include coffee, copra, cotton, manioc (cassava), corn, tobacco, bananas and pineapples.

In 1987, New Caledonian voters chose by referendum to remain within the French Republic. There were clashes between French and Melanesians (Kanaks) in 1988.

Wallis and Futuna Islands, 2 archipelagos raised to status of overseas territory July 29, 1961, are in the SW Pacific S of the Equator between Fiji and Samoa. The islands have a total area of 106 sq. mi. and population (1988 est.) of 15,400. **Alofi**, attached to Futuna, is uninhabited. Capital: Mata-Utu. Chief products are copra, yams, taro roots, bananas. A senator and a deputy are elected to the French Parliament.

Gabon

Gabonese Republic

République Gabonaise

People: Population (1990 est.): 1,069,000. **Pop. density:** 11 per sq. mi. **Urban** (1985): 40%. **Ethnic groups:** Fangs 25%, Bapounon 10%, others. **Languages:** French (official), Bantu dialects. **Religions:** Tribal beliefs, Christian minority.

Geography: Area: 103,346 sq. mi., the size of Colorado. **Location:** On Atlantic coast of central Africa. **Neighbors:** Equatorial Guinea, Cameroon on N, Congo on E, S. **Topography:** Heavily forested, the country consists of coastal lowlands plateaus in N, E, and S, mountains in N, SE, and center. The Ogooue R. system covers most of Gabon. **Capital:** Libreville. **Cities** (1987 est.): Libreville 352,000.

Government: Type: Republic. **Head of state:** Pres. Omar Bongo; b. Dec. 30, 1935; in office: Dec. 2, 1967. **Head of government:** Prime Min. Casimir Oye Mba; in office: May 3, 1990. **Local divisions:** 9 provinces. **Defense:** 5.2% of GNP (1989).

Economy: Industries: Oil products. **Chief crops:** Cocoa, coffee, rice, peanuts, palm products, cassava, bananas. **Minerals:** Manganese, uranium, oil, iron, gas. **Crude oil reserves** (1985): 623 mln. bbls. **Other resources:** Timber. **Arable land:** 2%. **Electricity prod.** (1988): 877 mln. kwh. **Labor force:** 65% agric.; 30% ind. & comm.

Finance: Monetary unit: CFA franc (Mar. 1991: 290 = $1 US). **Gross national product** (1989) $3.0 bln. **Per capita GNP** (1989): $2,770. **Imports** (1988): $930 mln.; partners: Fr. 51%, U.S. 14%. **Exports** (1987): $1.7 bln.; partners: Fr. 26%, U.S.

25%. **Tourists receipts** (1987): $5 mln. **National budget** (1987): $1.2 bln. **International reserves less gold** (Jan. 1991): $1.7 mln. **Gold:** 13,000 oz t. **Consumer prices** (change in 1989): 7.0%.
Transport: Motor vehicles: in use (1985): 16,000 passenger cars, 10,000 comm. vehicles. **Civil aviation** (1986): 417 mln. passengers -km. **Chief ports** Port-Gentil, Owendo, Mayumba.
Communications: Television sets: 1 per 33 persons. **Radios:** 1 per 5 persons. **Telephones:** 1 per 98 persons.
Health: Life expectancy at birth (1990): 49.9 male; 53.2 female. **Births** (per 1,000 pop. 1989): 28. **Deaths** (per 1,000 pop. 1989): 15. **Natural increase:** 1.4%. **Hospital beds** (1985): 4,617. **Physicians** (1985): 265. **Infant mortality** (per 1,000 live births 1989): 108.
Education (1988): **Literacy:** 70%. Compulsory to age 16; attendance: 100% primary, 14% secondary.
Major International Organizations: UN (World Bank), OAU, OPEC.
Embassy: 2034 20th St NW 20009; 797-1000.

France established control over the region in the second half of the 19th century. Gabon became independent Aug. 17, 1960. It is one of the most prosperous black African countries, thanks to abundant natural resources, foreign private investment, and government development programs.

The Gambia
Republic of The Gambia

People: Population (1990 est.): 860,000. **Age distrib.** (%): 0–14: 45.9; 15–59: 54.4; 60+: 3.8. **Pop. density:** 258 per sq. mi. **Urban** (1985): 21%. **Ethnic groups:** Mandinka 42%, Fula 16%, Wolof 16%, others. **Languages:** English (official), Malinke, Wolof. **Religions:** Moslem 90%.
Geography: Area: 4,127 sq. mi., smaller than Connecticut. **Location:** On Atlantic coast near western tip of Africa. **Neighbors:** Surrounded on 3 sides by Senegal. **Topography:** A narrow strip of land on each side of the lower Gambia. **Capital:** Banjul. **Cities** (1986 est.): Banjul 40,000.
Government: Type: Republic. **Head of state:** Pres. Dawda Kairaba Jawara; b. May 16, 1924; in office: Apr. 24, 1970 (prime min. from June 12, 1962). **Local divisions:** 5 divisions and Banjul.
Economy: Industries: Tourism. **Chief crops:** Peanuts (main export), rice. **Arable land:** 16%. **Fish catch** (1988): 14,000 metric tons. **Electricity prod.** (1988): 63 mln. kwh. **Labor force:** 75% agric.; 18% ind. & comm.
Finance: Monetary unit: Dalasi (Mar. 1991: 8.64 = $1.00 US). **Gross national product** (1989): $196 mln. **Per capita GNP** (1989): $230. **Imports** (1989): $161 mln.; partners: EEC 53%. **Exports** (1988): $40 mln.; partners: EEC 45%. **Tourists** (1988): $36 mln. receipts. **National budget** (1985): $57 mln. expenditures. **International reserves less gold** (Jan. 1991): $42.1 mln. **Consumer prices** (change in 1990): 14.0%.
Transport: Motor vehicles: in use (1986): 5,200 passenger cars, 720 comm. vehicles. **Chief ports:** Banjul.
Communications: Radios: 1 per 6.1 persons. **Telephones:** 1 per 114 persons.
Health: Life expectancy at birth (1989): 39 male; 44 female. **Births** (per 1,000 pop. 1989): 48. **Deaths** (per 1,000 pop. 1989): 23. **Natural increase:** 2.5%. **Hospital beds** (1980): 635. **Physicians** (1980): 65. **Infant mortality** (per 100,000 live births 1989): 172.
Education (1989): **Literacy:** 12%.
Major International Organizations: UN (GATT, IMF, WHO), OAU.
Embassy: 19 E. 42 St., New York, NY 10017.

The tribes of Gambia were at one time associated with the West African empires of Ghana, Mali, and Songhay. The area became Britain's first African possession in 1588.

Independence came Feb. 18, 1965; republic status within the Commonwealth was achieved in 1970. Gambia is one of the only functioning democracies in Africa. The country suffered from severe famine in 1977-78.

Gambia has a treaty with Senegal to form a confederation of the 2 countries under the name of Senegambia. However, each country will retain its sovereignty.

Germany
Federal Republic of Germany
Bundesrepublik Deutschland
(Figures prior to 1990 for original 11 states)

People: Population (1991 est.): 79,070,000. **Age distrib.** (%): 0–14: 14.7; 15–59: 64.7; 60+: 20.6. **Pop. density:** 221 per sq. mi. **Urban** (1985): 86% **Ethnic groups:** German 93%. **Languages:** German. **Religions:** Protestant 44%, Roman Catholic 47%.
Geography: Area: 137,838 sq. mi. **Location:** In central Europe. **Neighbors:** Denmark on N, Netherlands, Belgium, Luxembourg, France on W, Switzerland, Austria on S, Czechoslovakia, Poland on E. **Topography:** Germany is flat in N, hilly in center and W, and mountainous in Bavaria. Chief rivers are Elbe, Weser, Ems, Rhine, and Main, all flowing toward North Sea, and Danube, flowing toward Black Sea. **Capital:** Berlin. **Cities** (1991 est.): Berlin 3.0 mln.; Hamburg 1.6 mln.; Munich 1.3 mln.; Cologne 946,000; Essen 622,000; Frankfurt 635,000; Dortmund 575,000; Dusseldorf 593,000; Stuttgart 561,000; Leipzig 549,000; Dresden 521,000.
Government: Type: Federal republic. **Head of state:** Pres. Richard von Weizsacker; b. Apr. 15, 1920; in office: May 23, 1984. **Head of government:** Chan. Helmut Kohl; b. Apr. 3, 1930; in office: Oct. 1, 1982. **Local divisions:** 16 laender (states) with substantial powers. **Defense:** 3.2% of GNP (1989).
Economy: Industries: Steel, ships, vechicles, machinery, coal, chemicals. **Chief crops:** Grains, potatoes, sugar beets. **Minerals:** Coal, potash, lignite, iron, uranium. **Arable land:** 35%. **Livestock** (1987): cattle: 14.8 mln.; pigs: 24.3 mln.; sheep: 1.2 mln. **Fish catch** (1987): 159,000 metric tons. **Electricity prod.** (1988): 439 bln. kwh. **Crude steel prod.** (1988): 41.0 mln. metric tons. **Labor force:** 5% agric.; 40% ind. & comm.; 54% services.
Finance: Monetary unit: Mark (July 1991: 1.71 = $1 US). **Gross national product** (1989): $1,208 bln. **Per capita income** (1989): $19,000. **Imports** (1990): $342 bln.; partners: EC 52%; other European 16%. **Exports** (1990): $398 bln.; partners: EC 55%; other European 19%. **Tourists** (1988): receipts $15 bln. **National budget** (1990): $245 bln. expenditures. **International reserves less gold** (Mar. 1991): $59 bln. **Gold:** 95.18 mln. oz t. **Consumer prices** (change in 1990): 2.8%.
Transport: Railway traffic (1989): 66 bln. passenger-km. **Motor vehicles:** in use (1988): 28.8 mln. passenger cars, 1.3 mln. comm. **Civil aviation** (1988): 34.0 bln. passenger-km; 27 airports with scheduled flights. **Chief ports:** Hamburg, Bremen, Lubeck.
Communications: Television sets: 1 per 2.6 persons. **Radios:** 1 per 2.3 persons. **Telephones:** 1 per 1.5 persons. **Daily newspaper circ.** (1987): 417 per 1,000 pop.
Health: Life expectancy at birth (1991): 81 male; 73 female. **Births** (per 1,000 pop. 1989): 11.4. **Deaths** (per 1,000 pop. 1989): 11.5. **Natural increase:** −.1%. **Hospital beds:** 1 per 91 persons. **Physicians:** 1 per 357 persons. **Infant mortality** (per 1,000 live births 1990): 6.0.
Education (1991): **Literacy:** 99%. **Years compulsory:** 10; attendance 100%.
Major International Organizations: UN and all of its specialized agencies, EC, OECD, NATO.
Embassy: 4645 Reservoir Rd. NW 20007; 298-4000.

Germany, prior to World War II, was a central European nation composed of numerous states which had a common language and traditions and which had been united in one country since 1871; since World War II until 1990, had been split in 2 parts.

History and government. Germanic tribes were defeated by Julius Caesar, 55 and 53 BC, but Roman expansion N of the Rhine was stopped in 9 AD. Charlemagne, ruler of the Franks, consolidated Saxon, Bavarian, Rhenish, Frankish, and other lands; after him the eastern part became the German Empire. The Thirty Years' War, 1618-1648, split Germany into small principalities and kingdoms. After Napoleon, Austria contended with Prussia for dominance, but lost the Seven Weeks' War to Prussia, 1866. Otto von Bismarck, Prussian chancellor, formed the North German Confederation, 1867.

In 1870 Bismarck maneuvered Napoleon III into declaring war. After the quick defeat of France, Bismarck formed the **German**

Empire and on Jan. 18, 1871, in Versailles, proclaimed King Wilhelm I of Prussia German emperor (Deutscher kaiser).

The German Empire reached its peak before World War I in 1914, with 208,780 sq. mi., plus a colonial empire. After that war Germany ceded Alsace-Lorraine to France; West Prussia and Posen (Poznan) province to Poland; part of Schleswig to Denmark; lost all of its colonies and the ports of Memel and Danzig.

Republic of Germany, 1919-1933, adopted the Weimar constitution; met reparation payments and elected Friedrich Ebert and Gen. Paul von Hindenburg presidents.

Third Reich, 1933-1945, Adolf Hitler led the National Socialist German Workers' (Nazi) party after World War I. In 1923 he attempted to unseat the Bavarian government and was imprisoned. Pres. von Hindenburg named Hitler chancellor Jan. 30, 1933; on Aug. 3, 1934, the day after Hindenburg's death, the cabinet joined the offices of president and chancellor and made Hitler fuehrer (leader). Hitler abolished freedom of speech and assembly, and began a long series of persecutions climaxed by the murder of millions of Jews and opponents.

Hitler repudiated the Versailles treaty and reparations agreements. He remilitarized the Rhineland 1936 and annexed Austria (Anschluss, 1938). At Munich he made an agreement with Neville Chamberlain, British prime minister, which permitted Hitler to annex part of Czechoslovakia. He signed a non-aggression treaty with the USSR, 1939. He declared war on Poland Sept. 1, 1939, precipitating World War II.

With total defeat near, Hitler committed suicide in Berlin Apr. 1945. The victorious Allies voided all acts and annexations of Hitler's Reich.

Postwar changes. The zones of occupation administered by the Allied Powers and later relinquished gave the USSR Saxony, Saxony-Anhalt, Thuringia, and Mecklenburg, and the former Prussian provinces of Saxony and Brandenburg.

The territory E of the Oder-Neisse line within 1937 boundaries comprising the provinces of Silesia, Pomerania, and the southern part of East Prussia, totaling about 41,220 sq. mi., was taken by Poland. Northern East Prussia was taken by the USSR.

The Western Allies ended the state of war with Germany in 1951. The USSR did so in 1955.

There was also created the area of Greater Berlin, within but not part of the Soviet zone, administered by the 4 occupying powers under the Allied Command. In 1948 the USSR withdrew, established its single command in East Berlin, and cut off supplies. The Allies utilized a gigantic airlift to bring food to West Berlin, 1948-1949. In Aug. 1961 the East Germans built a wall dividing Berlin, after over 3 million E. Germans had emigrated.

On Nov. 9, 1989 the E. German government announced the decision to open the border with the West signaling the end of the infamous Berlin Wall.

A New Era: As communism was being rejected in E. Germany, talks began concerning German reunification. At a meeting in Ottawa, Feb. 1990, the foreign ministers of the World War II "Big Four" Allied nations—U.S., USSR, UK, and France—as well as the foreign ministers of E. Germany and W. Germany reached agreement on a format for high-level talks on German reunification.

In May, NATO ministers adopted a package of proposals on reunification including the inclusion of the united Germany as a full member of NATO, and the barring of the new Germany from having its own nuclear, chemical, or biological weapons. In July, the USSR agreed to conditions that would allow Germany to become a member of NATO.

The 2 nations agreed to monetary unification under the W. German mark beginning in July. The merger of the 2 Germanys took place on Oct. 3, 1990, and the first all-German elections since 1937 were held Dec. 2, 1990.

(East Germany)

The German Democratic Republic was proclaimed in the Soviet sector of Berlin Oct. 7, 1949. It was proclaimed fully sovereign in 1954, but Soviet troops remained on grounds of security and the 4-power Potsdam agreement.

Coincident with the entrance of W. Germany into the European Defense community in 1952, the East German government decreed a prohibited zone 3 miles deep along its 600-mile border with W. Germany and cut Berlin's telephone system in two. Berlin was further divided by erection of a fortified wall in 1961, but the exodus of refugees to the West continued, though on a smaller scale.

E. Germany suffered severe economic problems until the mid-1960s. A "new economic system" was introduced, easing the former central planning controls and allowing factories to make profits provided they were reinvested in operations or redistributed to workers as bonuses. By the early 1970s, the economy was highly industrialized. In May 1972 the few remaining private firms were ordered sold to the government. The nation was credited with the highest standard of living among Warsaw Pact countries. But growth slowed in the late 1970s, due to shortages of natural resources and labor, and a huge debt to lenders in the West. Comparison with the lifestyle in the West caused many of the young to leave the country.

The government firmly resisted following the USSR's policy of *glasnost,* but by Oct. 1989, was faced with nationwide demonstrations demanding reform. Pres. Erich Honecker, in office since 1976, was forced to resign, Oct. 18. On Nov. 4, the border with Czechoslovakia was opened and permission granted for refugees to travel on to the West, On Nov. 9, the decision was made to open the border with the West, signaling the end of the "Berlin Wall," which separated the 2 Germanys and was the supreme emblem of the cold war.

On Aug. 23, 1990, the E. German Parliament agreed to formal unification with W. Germany; this took place on Oct. 3.

(West Germany)

The Federal Republic of Germany was proclaimed May 23, 1949, in Bonn, after a constitution had been drawn up by a consultative assembly formed by representatives of the 11 laender (states) in the French, British, and American zones. Later reorganized into 9 units, the laender numbered 10 with the addition of the Saar, 1957. Berlin also was granted land (state) status, but the 1945 occupation agreements placed restrictions on it.

The occupying powers, the U.S., Britain, and France, restored the civil status, Sept. 21, 1949. The U. S. resumed diplomatic relations July 2, 1951. The powers lifted controls and the republic became fully independent May 5, 1955.

Dr. Konrad Adenauer, Christian Democrat, was made chancellor Sept. 15, 1949, re-elected 1953, 1957, 1961. Willy Brandt, heading a coalition of Social Democrats and Free Democrats, became chancellor Oct. 21, 1969.

In 1970 Brandt signed friendship treaties with the USSR and Poland. In 1971, the U.S., Britain, France, and the USSR signed an agreement on Western access to West Berlin. In 1972 the Bundestag approved the USSR and Polish treaties and East and West Germany signed their first formal treaty, implementing the agreement easing access to West Berlin. In 1973 a West Germany-Czechoslovakia pact normalized relations and nullified the 1938 "Munich Agreement."

In May 1974 Brandt resigned, saying he took full responsibility for "negligence" for allowing an East German spy to become a member of his staff.

West Germany experienced economic growth since the 1950s. The country led Europe in provisions for worker participation in the management of industry.

The NATO decision to deploy medium-range nuclear missiles in Western Europe sparked a demonstration by some 400,000 protesters in 1983. In 1989, Chancellor Kohl's call for early negotiations with the Soviets on reducing short-range missiles caused a rift with the NATO allies, especially the U.S. and Great Britain.

In 1989, the changes in the E. German government and the opening of the Berlin Wall sparked talk of reunification of the 2 Germanys. In 1990, under the leadership of Chancellor Kohl, W. Germany moved rapidly to reunite with E. Germany.

Helgoland, an island of 130 acres in the North Sea, was taken from Denmark by a British Naval Force in 1807 and later ceded to Germany to become a part of Schleswig-Holstein province in return for rights in East Africa. The heavily fortified island was surrendered to UK, May 23, 1945, demilitarized in 1947, and returned to W. Germany, Mar 1, 1952. It is a free port.

Ghana

Republic of Ghana

People: Population (1990 est.): 15,310,000. **Age distrib.** (%): 0–14: 46.6; 15–59: 48.9; 60+: 4.5. **Pop. density:** 160 per sq. mi. **Urban** (1984): 31%. **Ethnic groups:** Akan 44%, Moshi-Dagomba 16%, Ewe 13%, Ga 8%, others. **Languages:** English (official), Akan, Mossi, Ewe, Ga-Adangme. **Religions:** Christian 52%, traditional beliefs 30%, Moslem 13%.

Geography: Area: 92,098 sq. mi., slightly smaller than Oregon. **Location:** On southern coast of W. Africa. **Neighbors:** Ivory Coast on W, Burkina Faso on N, Togo on E. **Topography:** Most of Ghana consists of low fertile plains and scrubland, cut by rivers and by the artificial Lake Volta. **Capital:** Accra. **Cities** (1988 est.): Accra 949,000.

Government: Type: Authoritarian. **Head of government:** Pres. Jerry Rawlings; b. 1947; in office: Dec. 31, 1981. **Local divisions:** 10 regions.

Economy: Industries: Aluminum, light industry. **Chief crops:** Cocoa, coffee. **Minerals:** Gold, manganese, industrial diamonds, bauxite. **Crude oil reserves:** (1980): 7 mln. bbls. **Other resources:** Timber, rubber. **Arable land:** 12%. **Livestock** (1989): Cattle: 1.1 mln.; sheep: 2.2 mln. **Fish catch** (1988): 360,000 metric tons. **Electricity prod.** (1988): 4.1 bln. kwh. **Labor force:** 55% agric.; 19% ind.

Finance: Monetary unit: Cedi (Mar. 1991: 353 = $1.00 US). **Gross national product** (1989): $5.5 bln. **Per capita GNP** (1989): $380. **Imports** (1988): $907 mln.; partners: UK 18%, W. Ger. 12%, Nigeria 12%. **Exports** (1988): $1.0 bln.; partners: UK 16%, U.S. 16%, Neth. 9%, W. Ger. 9%. **International reserves less gold** (Mar. 1991): 356 mln. **Gold:** 230,000 oz t. **Consumer prices** (change in 1990): 36.0%.

Transport: Railway traffic (1988): 389 mln. passenger-km. **Motor vehicles:** in use (1986): 26,000 passenger cars, 28,000 comm. vehicles. **Civil aviation** (1988): 286 mln. passenger-km; 3 airports with scheduled flights. **Chief ports:** Tema, Takoradi.

Communications: Television sets: 1 per 83 persons. **Radios:** 1 per 4.7 persons. **Telephones:** 1 per 191 persons.

Health: Life expectancy at birth (1989): 57 male; 62 female. **Births** (per 1,000 pop. 1989): 46. **Deaths** (per 1,000 pop. 1989): 13. **Natural increase:** 3.3%. **Physicians:** 1 per 22,127 persons. **Infant mortality** (per 1,000 live births 1989): 68.

Education (1990): **Literacy:** 30%.

Major International Organizations: UN and all of its specialized agencies, OAU.

Embassy: 3512 International Dr., 20008; 686-4500.

Named for an African empire along the Niger River, 400-1240 AD, Ghana was ruled by Britain for 113 years as the Gold Coast. The UN in 1956 approved merger with the British Togoland trust territory. Independence came March 6, 1957. Republic status within the Commonwealth was attained in 1960.

Pres. Kwame Nkrumah built hospitals and schools, promoted development projects like the Volta R. hydroelectric and aluminum plants, but ran the country into debt, jailed opponents, and was accused of corruption. A 1964 referendum gave Nkrumah dictatorial powers and set up a one-party socialist state.

Nkrumah was overthrown in 1966 by a police-army coup, which expelled Chinese and East German teachers and technicians. Elections were held in 1969, but 4 further coups occurred in 1972, 1978, 1979, and 1981. The 1979 and 1981 coups were led by Flight Lieut. Jerry Rawlings.

Greece
Hellenic Republic
Elliniki Dimokratia

People: Population (1990 est.): 10,066,000. **Age distrib.** (%): 0–14: 20.5; 15-59: 61.1; 60+: 20.4. **Pop. density:** 196 per sq. mi. **Urban** (1985): 58.0%. **Ethnic groups:** Greeks 98.5%. **Languages:** Greek. **Religions:** Greek Orthodox 97% (official).

Geography: Area: 51,146 sq. mi., the size of Alabama. **Location:** Occupies southern end of Balkan Peninsula in SE Europe. **Neighbors:** Albania, Yugoslavia, Bulgaria on N, Turkey on E. **Topography:** About 75% of Greece is non-arable, with mountains in all areas. Pindus Mts. run through the country N to S. The heavily indented coastline is 9,385 mi. long. Of over 2,000 islands, only 169 are inhabited, among them Crete, Rhodes, Milos, Kerkira (Corfu), Chios, Lesbos, Samos, Euboea, Delos, Mykonos. **Capital:** Athens. **Cities** (1981 est.): Athens (met.) 3,016,457; Thessaloniki (met.) 800,000; Patras 120,000.

Government: Type: Presidential parliamentary republic. **Head of state:** Pres. Konstantinos Karamanlis; in office: May, 1990. **Head of government:** Prime Min. Konstantinos Mitsotakis; b. Oct. 18, 1918, in office: Apr. 11, 1990. **Local divisions:** 51 prefectures. **Defense:** 6.2% of GNP (1987).

Economy: Industries: Textiles, chemicals, metals, wine, food processng, cement. **Chief crops:** Grains, corn, rice, cotton, to-

bacco, olives, citrus fruits, raisins, figs. **Minerals:** Bauxite, lignite, oil, manganese. **Crude oil reserves** (1985): 35 mln. bbls. **Arable land:** 23%. **Livestock** (1989): sheep: 11.0 mln.; goats: 5.6 mln. **Fish catch** (1989): 126,000 metric tons. **Electricity prod.** (1988): 33.1 bln. kwh. **Crude steel prod.** (1988): 970,000 metric tons. **Labor force:** 28% agric.; 29% ind., 42% service.

Finance: Monetary unit: Drachma (June 1991: 188.00 = $1 US). **Gross national product** (1989): $53.6 bln. **Per capita GNP** (1989): $5,340. **Imports** (1989): $16.1 bln.; partners: Ger. 19%, It. 12%, Fr. 7%. **Exports** (1989): $7.5 bln.; partners: Ger. 20%, It. 13%, U.S. 8%. **Tourists** (1988): $2.3 bln. receipts. **National budget** (1988): $25.3 bln. expenditures. **International reserves less gold** (Mar. 1991): $3.0 bln. **Gold:** 3.4 mln. oz t. **Consumer prices** (change in 1990): 20.4%.

Transport: Railway traffic (1988): 1.9 bln. passenger-km. **Motor vehicles:** in use (1989): 1.5 mln. passenger cars, 717,000 comm. vehicles. **Civil aviation** (1988): 7.5 bln. passenger-km; 33 airports with scheduled flights. **Chief ports:** Piraeus, Thessaloniki, Patrai.

Communications: Television sets: 1 per 5.7 persons. **Radios:** 1 per 2.4 persons. **Telephones:** 1 per 2.4 persons. **Daily newspaper circ.** (1986): 88 per 1,000 pop.

Health: Life expectancy at birth (1989): 75 male; 80 female. **Births** (per 1,000 pop. 1989): 12. **Deaths** (per 1,000 pop. 1989): 9. **Natural increase:** .2%. **Hospital beds:** 1 per 193 persons. **Physicians:** 1 per 327 persons. **Infant mortality** (per 1,000 live birth 1989): 11.

Education (1991): **Literacy:** men 96%, women 89%. **Years compulsory:** 9.

Major International Organizations: UN (GATT, IMF, WHO, ILO), EC, NATO, OECD.

Embassy: 2221 Massachusetts Ave. NW 20008; 667-3168.

The achievements of ancient Greece in art, architecture, science, mathematics, philosophy, drama, literature, and democracy became legacies for succeeding ages. Greece reached the height of its glory and power, particularly in the Athenian city-state, in the 5th century BC.

Greece fell under Roman rule in the 2d and 1st centuries BC. In the 4th century AD it became part of the Byzantine Empire and, after the fall of Constantinople to the Turks in 1453, part of the Ottoman Empire.

Greece won its war of independence from Turkey 1821-1829, and became a kingdom. A republic was established 1924; the monarchy was restored, 1935, and George II, King of the Hellenes, resumed the throne. In Oct., 1940, Greece rejected an ultimatum from Italy. Nazi support resulted in its defeat and occupation by Germans, Italians, and Bulgarians. By the end of 1944 the invaders withdrew. Communist resistance forces were defeated by Royalist and British troops. A plebiscite recalled King George II. He died Apr. 1, 1947, was succeeded by his brother, Paul I.

Communists waged guerrilla war 1947-49 against the government but were defeated with the aid of the U.S.

A period of reconstruction and rapid development followed, mainly with conservative governments under Premier Constantine Karamanlis. The Center Union led by George Papandreou won elections in 1963 and 1964. King Constantine, who acceded in 1964, forced Papandreou to resign. A period of political maneuvers ended in the military takeover of April 21, 1967, by Col. George Papadopoulos. King Constantine tried to reverse the consolidation of the harsh dictatorship Dec. 13, 1967, but failed and fled to Italy. Papadopoulos was ousted Nov. 25, 1973.

Greek army officers serving in the National Guard of Cyprus staged a coup on the island July 15, 1974. Turkey invaded Cyprus a week later, precipitating the collapse of the Greek junta, which was implicated in the Cyprus coup.

The 1981 victory of the Panhellenic Socialist Movement (Pasok) of Andreas Papandreou has brought about substantial changes in the internal and external policies that Greece has pursued for the past 5 decades. Greece has been victimized in the 1980s by incidents of international terrorism.

A scandal centered on George Kostokas, a banker and publisher, led to the arrest or investigation of about a dozen leading Socialists, implicated Papandreou, and led to the defeat of the Socialists at the polls in 1989.

Grenada

People: Population (1990 est.): 84,000. **Pop. density:** 654 per sq. mi. **Ethnic groups:** Mostly African descent. **Languages:**

English (official), French, patois. **Religions:** Roman Catholic 64%, Anglican 22%.

Geography: Area: 133 sq. mi., twice the size of Washington, D.C. **Location:** 90 mi. N. of Venezuela. **Topography:** Main island is mountainous; country includes Carriacon and Petit Martinique islands. **Capital:** St. George's. **Cities** (1990 est.): St. George's 30,000.

Government: Type: Independent state. **Head of state:** Queen Elizabeth II, represented by Gov.-Gen. Paul Scoon, b. July 4, 1935; in office: Sept. 30, 1978. **Head of government:** Prime Minister: Nicholas Braithwaite; in office: Mar. 16, 1990. **Local divisions:** 6 parishes and one dependency.

Economy: Industries: Rum. **Chief crops:** Nutmegs, bananas, cocoa, mace. **Arable land:** 41%. **Electricity prod.** (1988): 24.00 mln. kwh. **Labor force:** 33% agric.; 31% services. **Finance: Monetary unit:** East Caribbean dollar (Apr. 1991: 2.70 = $1 US). **Gross national product** (1989): $179 mln. **Per capita GNP** (1989): $1,900. **Imports** (1988): $92 mln.; partners: UK 19%, Trin./Tob. 12%, U.S. 24%. **Exports** (1988): $32 mln.; partners: UK 23%, CARICOM countries 38%. **Tourists** (1989): $30 mln. receipts. **National budget** (1989): $92.1 mln. expenditures. **International reserves less gold** (Jan. 1991): $17 mln.

Transport: Motor vehicles: in use (1981): 4,700 passenger cars, 1,000 comm. vehicles. **Chief ports:** Saint George's.

Communications: Radios: 1 per 2.4 persons. **Telephones:** 1 per 18 persons.

Health: Life expectancy at birth (1989): 69 male; 74 female. **Births** (per 1,000 pop. 1989): 37. **Deaths** (per 1,000 pop. 1989): 7. **Natural increase:** 2.9%. **Infant mortality** (per 1,000 live births 1989): 30.

Education (1991): **Literacy:** 95%; **Years compulsory:** 6. **Major International Organizations:** UN (IMF, WHO), OAS. **Embassy:** 1701 New Hampshire Ave. NW 20009; 265-2561.

Columbus sighted the island 1498. First European settlers were French, 1650. The island was held alternately by France and England until final British occupation, 1784. Grenada became fully independent Feb. 7, 1974 during a general strike. It is the smallest independent nation in the Western Hemisphere.

On Oct. 14, 1983, a military coup ousted Prime Minister Maurice Bishop, who was put under house arrest, later freed by supporters, rearrested, and, finally, on Oct. 19, executed. U.S. forces, with a token force from 6 area nations, invaded Grenada, Oct. 25. Resistance from the Grenadian army and Cuban advisors was quickly overcome as most of the population welcomed the invading forces as liberators. U.S. troops left Grenada in June 1985.

Guatemala
Republic of Guatemala
República de Guatemala

People: Population (1990 est.): 9,340,000. **Age distrib. (%):** 0–14: 45.4; 15–59: 49.5; 60+: 5.1. **Pop. density:** 233 per sq. mi. **Urban** (1986): 33%. **Ethnic groups:** Maya 55%, Mestizos 44%. **Languages:** Spanish (official), Mayan languages. **Religions:** Mostly Roman Catholic.

Geography: Area: 42,042 sq. mi., the size of Tennessee. **Location:** In Central America. **Neighbors:** Mexico N, W; El Salvador on S, Honduras, Belize on E. **Topography:** The central highland and mountain areas are bordered by the narrow Pacific coast and the lowlands and fertile river valleys on the Caribbean. There are numerous volcanoes in S, more than half a dozen over 11,000 ft. **Capital:** Guatemala City. **Cities** (1989 est.): Guatemala City 1,057,000.

Government: Type: Republic. **Head of state:** Pres. Jorge Serrano Elias; in office: Jan. 14, 1991. **Local divisions:** Guatemala City and 22 departments. **Defense:** 1.5% of GNP (1987).

Economy: Industries: Prepared foods, tires, textiles. **Chief crops:** Coffee (one third of exports), sugar, bananas, cotton, corn. **Minerals:** Oil, nickel. **Crude oil reserves** (1985): 500 mln. bbls. **Other resources:** Rare woods, fish, chicle. **Arable land:** 16%. **Electricity prod.** (1988): 2.8 bln. kwh. **Labor force:** 57% agric.; 21% ind. & comm., 12% services.

Finance: Monetary unit: Quetzal (Apr. 1991: 5.00 = $1 US). **Gross national product** (1989): $8.2 bln. **Per capita GNP** (1989): $920. **Imports** (1989): $1.6 bln.; partners: U.S. 40%, CACM 8%. **Exports** (1989): $1.1 bln.; partners: U.S. 50%, CACM 20%. **Tourism** (1988): $118 mln. **National budget**

(1987): $1.0 bln. expenditures. **International reserves less gold** (Mar. 1991): $477 mln. **Gold:** 208,000 oz t. **Consumer prices** (change in 1989): 11.4%.

Transport: Motor vehicles: in use (1986): 175,000 passenger cars, 100,000 comm. vehicles. **Civil aviation** (1988) 164 mln. passenger-km; 2 airports with scheduled flights. **Chief ports:** Puerto Barrios, San Jose.

Communications: Television sets: 1 per 18 persons. **Radios:** 1 per 22 persons. **Telephones:** 1 per 63 persons. **Daily newspaper circ.** (1983): 30 per 1,000 pop.

Health: Life expectancy at birth (1989): 59 male; 63 female. **Births** (per 1,000 pop. 1989): 36. **Deaths** (per 1,000 pop. 1989): 9. **Natural increase:** 2.7% **Health: Physicians:** 1 per 2,289 persons. **Infant mortality** (per 1,000 live births 1989): 66.

Education (1989): **Literacy:** 48%. **Years compulsory:** 6; **Attendance:** 35%.

Major International Organizations: UN (IMF, World Bank), OAS.

Embassy: 2220 R St. NW 20008; 745-4952.

The old Mayan Indian empire flourished in what is today Guatemala for over 1,000 years before the Spanish.

Guatemala was a Spanish colony 1524-1821; briefly a part of Mexico and then of the U.S. of Central America, the republic was established in 1839.

Since 1945 when a liberal government was elected to replace the long-term dictatorship of Jorge Ubico, the country has seen a swing toward socialism, an armed revolt, renewed attempts at social reform, a military coup, and in 1986, civilian rule. The Guerrilla Army of the Poor, an insurgent group founded 1975, led a military offensive by attacking army posts and succeeded in incorporating segments of the large Indian population in its struggle against the government.

Dissident army officers seized power, Mar. 23, 1982, denouncing the Mar. 7 presidential election as fraudulent and pledging to restore "authentic democracy" to the nation. Political violence has caused some 200,000 Guatemalans to seek refuge in Mexico. A second military coup occurred Oct. 8, 1983. The nation returned to civilian rule in 1986.

Guinea
Republic of Guinea
République de Guinée

People: Population (1990 est.): 7,269,000. **Pop. density:** 64 per sq. mi. **Urban** (1986): 26%. **Ethnic groups:** Foulah 40%, Malinké 25%, Soussous 10%, 15 other tribes. **Languages:** French (official), Peul, Mande. **Religions:** Moslem 85%, Christian 10%.

Geography: Area: 94,964 sq. mi., slightly smaller than Oregon. **Location:** On Atlantic coast of W. Africa. **Neighbors:** Guinea-Bissau, Senegal, Mali on N, Côte d'Ivoire on E, Liberia on S. **Topography:** A narrow coastal belt leads to the mountainous middle region, the source of the Gambia, Senegal, and Niger rivers. Upper Guinea, farther inland, is a cooler upland. The SE is forested. **Capital:** Conakry. **Cities** (1989 est.): Conakry 705,000; Labe 273,000; N'Zerekore 250,000; Kankan 278,000.

Government: Type: Republic under Military Committee For National Redressment. **Head of state:** Pres. Brig. Gen. Lansana Conte; b. 1944; in office: Apr. 5, 1984. **Local divisions:** 29 administrative regions. **Defense:** 1.2% of GNP (1988).

Economy: Chief crops: Bananas, pineapples, rice, corn, palm nuts, coffee, honey. **Minerals:** Bauxite, iron, diamonds. **Arable land:** 6%. **Electricity prod.** (1988) 243 mln. kwh. **Labor force:** 82% agric.; 9% ind. & comm.

Finance: Monetary unit: Franc (Jan. 1991: 620 = $1 US). **Gross national product** (1989): $2.4 bln. **Per capita GNP** (1989): $430. **Imports** (1988): $509 mln.; partners: Fr. 31%, U.S. 10%, It. 6%. **Exports** (1988): $553 mln.; partners: U.S. 24%, Fr. 10%. **National budget** (1988): 417 mln.

Transport: Motor vehicles: in use (1986): 12,000 passenger cars, 12,000 comm. vehicles. **Chief ports:** Conakry.

Communications: Radios: 1 per 34 persons.

Health: Life expectancy at birth (1989): 40 male; 44 female. **Births** (per 1,000 pop. 1989): 48. **Deaths** (per 1,000 pop. 1989): 22. **Natural increase:** 2.5%. **Physicians:** 1 per 9,732 persons. **Infant mortality** (per 1,000 live births 1987): 176.

Education (1989): **Literacy:** 35% (in French). **Years compulsory:** 8; **attendance:** 36% primary, 15% secondary.

Major International Organizations: UN and most specialized agencies, OAU.
Embassy: 2112 Leroy Pl. NW 20008; 483-9420.

Part of the ancient West African empires, Guinea fell under French control 1849-98. Under Sekou Toure, it opted for full independence in 1958, and France withdrew all aid.

Toure turned to communist nations for support, and set up a militant one-party state.

Thousands of opponents were jailed in the 1970s, in the aftermath of an unsuccessful Portuguese invasion. Many were tortured and killed.

The military took control of the government in a bloodless coup after the March 1984 death of Toure.

Guinea-Bissau

Republic of Guinea-Bissau

República da Guiné-Bissau

People: Population (1990 est.): 998,000. **Pop. density:** 66 per sq. mi. **Ethnic groups:** Balanta 27%, Fula 23%, Manjaca 11%, Mandinka 12%. **Languages:** Portuguese (official), Criould, tribal languages. **Religion:** Traditional 65%, Moslem 30%, Christian 4%.

Geography: Area: 13,948 sq. mi. about the size of Connecticut and New Hampshire combined. **Location:** On Atlantic coast of W. Africa. **Neighbors:** Senegal on N, Guinea on E, S. **Topography:** A swampy coastal plain covers most of the country; to the east is a low savanna region. **Capital:** Bissau. **Cities** (1979): Bissau 109,500.

Government: Type: Republic. **Head of government:** Gen. Joao Bernardo Vieira; b. 1939; in office: Nov. 14,1980. **Local divisions:** 8 regions. **Defense:** 3.3% of GNP (1987).

Economy: Chief crops: Peanuts, cotton, rice. **Minerals:** Bauxite. **Arable land:** 10%. **Electricity prod.** (1988): 15 mln. kwh. **Labor force:** 90% agric.

Finance: Monetary unit: Peso (Jan. 1991: 650 = $1 US). **Gross national product** (1989): $173 mln. **Per capita GNP** (1989): $180. **Imports** (1987): $44 mln.; partners: Port. 20%, It. 27%. **Exports** (1987): $16 mln.; partners: Port. 35%. **National Budget** (1987): $40 mln. expenditures.

Communications: Radios: 1 per 27 persons. **Daily newspaper circ.** (1988): 7 per 1,000 pop.

Health: Life expectancy at birth (1989): 44 male; 47 female. **Births** (per 1,000 pop. 1989): 43. **Deaths** (per 1,000 pop. 1989): 19. **Natural increase:** 2.4%. **Infant mortality** (per 1,000 live births 1989): 137.

Education (1989): Literacy 19%. **Years compulsory:** 4.
Major International Organizations: UN, OAU.
Embassy: 211 E 43d St., New York, NY 10017; (212) 611-3977.

Portuguese mariners explored the area in the mid-15th century; the slave trade flourished in the 17th and 18th centuries, and colonization began in the 19th.

Beginning in the 1960s, an independence movement waged a guerrilla war and formed a government in the interior that achieved international support. Full independence came Sept. 10, 1974, after the Portuguese regime was overthrown.

The November 1980 coup gave Joao Bernardo Vieira absolute power.

Guyana

Co-operative Republic of Guyana

People: Population (1990 est.): 765,000. **Age distrib. (%):** 0–14: 37.5; 5–59: 56.5; 60+: 6.0. **Pop. density:** 9.2 per sq. mi. **Urban** (1988): 39%. **Ethnic groups:** East Indians 51%, African 30%; mixed 14%. **Languages:** English (official), Amerindian dialects. **Religions:** Christian 46%, Hindu 37%; Moslem 9%.

Geography: Area: 83,000 sq. mi., the size of Idaho. **Location:** On N coast of S. America. **Neighbors:** Venezuela on W, Brazil on S, Suriname on E. **Topography:** Dense tropical forests cover much of the land, although a flat coastal area up to 40 mi. wide, where 90% of the population lives, provides rich alluvial soil for agriculture. A grassy savanna divides the 2 zones. **Capital:** Georgetown. **Cities** (1985 est.): Georgetown 170,000.

Government: Type: Republic within the Commonwealth of Nations. **Head of state:** President Hugh Desmond Hoyte; b. Mar. 9, 1929; in office: Aug. 6, 1985. **Head of Government:** Prime Min. Hamilton Green; in office: Aug. 6, 1985. **Local divisions:** 10 regions. **Defense:** 8.9% of GDP (1989).

Economy: Industries: Cigarettes, rum, clothing, furniture, drugs. **Chief crops:** Sugar, rice, citrus and other fruits. **Minerals:** Bauxite, diamonds. **Other resources:** Timber, shrimp. **Arable land:** 2%. **Electricity prod.** (1988): 530 bln. kwh. **Labor force:** 33% agric.; 45% ind. & comm.; 22% services.

Finance: Monetary unit: Dollar (Mar. 1991: 126 = $1 US). **Gross national product** (1989): $248 mln. **Per capita income** (1987): $317. **Imports** (1986): $242 mln.; partners: U.S. 21%, CARICOM 33%. **Exports** (1986): $242 mln.; partners: UK 28%, U.S. 18%, CARICOM 17%. **National budget** (1987): $229.1 mln. **International reserves less gold** (Feb. 1991): $23.2 mln. **Consumer prices** (change in 1988): 39.9%.

Transport: Motor vehicles: in use (1986): 33,000 passenger cars, 13,000 comm. vehicles. **Chief ports:** Georgetown.

Communications: Radios: 1 per 2.5 persons. **Telephones:** 1 per 25 persons. **Daily newspaper circ.** (1989): 77 per 1,000 pop.

Health: Life expectancy at birth (1989): 64 male; 69 female. **Births** (per 1,000 pop. 1989): 25. **Deaths** (per 1,000 pop. 1989): 6. **Natural increase:** 1.8% **Hospital beds:** 1 per 206 persons. **Physicians:** 1 per 5,307 persons. **Infant mortality** (per 1,000 live births 1989): 49.

Education (1989): **Literacy:** 91%. **Years compulsory:** ages 5-14.

Major International Organizations: UN (GATT, ILO, IMF, World Bank), Commonwealth of Nations, OAS.
Embassy: 2490 Tracy Pl. NW 20008; 276-6900.

Guyana became a Dutch possession in the 17th century, but sovereignty passed to Britain in 1815. Indentured servants from India soon outnumbered African slaves. Ethnic tension has affected political life.

Guyana became independent May 26, 1966. A Venezuelan claim to the western half of Guyana was suspended in 1970 but renewed in 1982. The Suriname border is also disputed. The government has nationalized most of the economy which has remained severely depressed.

The Port Kaituma ambush of U.S. Rep. Leo J. Ryan and others investigating mistreatment of American followers of the Rev. Jim Jones' People's Temple cult, triggered a mass suicide-execution of 911 cultists in the Guyana jungle, Nov. 18, 1978.

Haiti

Republic of Haiti

Républiqe d'Haiti

People: Population (1990 est.): 5,862,000. **Age distrib. (%):** 4–14: 39.2; 15–59: 52.5; 60+: 8.3. **Pop. density:** 554 per sq. mi. **Urban** (1986): 29%. **Ethnic groups:** African descent 95%. **Languages:** French, Creole (both official). **Religions:** Roman Catholics 80%, Protestants 10%; Voodoo widely practiced.

Geography: Area: 10,579 sq. mi., the size of Maryland. **Location:** In West Indies, occupies western third of I. of Hispaniola. **Neighbors:** Dominican Republic on E, Cuba on W. **Topography:** About two-thirds of Haiti is mountainous. Much of the rest is semiarid. Coastal areas are warm and moist. **Capital:** Port-au-Prince. **Cities** (1989 est.): Port-au-Prince 514,000.

Government: Type: Republic. **Head of state:** Pres. Jean-Bertrand Aristide; b. July 15, 1953; in office: Feb. 7, 1991. **Local divisions:** 9 departments. **Defense:** 1.8% of GNP (1987).

Economy: Industries: Sugar refining, textiles. **Chief crops:** Coffee, sugar, bananas, cocoa, tobacco, rice. **Minerals:** Bauxite. **Other resources:** Timber. **Arable land:** 20%. **Livestock** (1989): cattle: 1.5 mln.; goats: 1.2 mln. **Electricity prod.** (1989): 615 mln. kwh. **Labor force:** 66% agric.; 9% ind. & comm.; 25% services.

Finance: Monetary unit: Gourde (Apr. 1991: 5.00 = $1 US). **Gross national product** (1989): $2.5 bln. **Per capita GNP** (1989): $400. **Imports** (1988): $344 mln.; partners: U.S. 45%. **Exports** (1988): $183 mln.; partners: U.S. 52%. **Tourists** (1987): receipts $93 mln. **National budget** (1987): $258 mln. expenditures. **International reserves less gold** (Mar. 1991): $2.3 mln. **Gold:** 18,000 oz t. **Consumer prices** (change in 1990): 24.2%.

Transport: Motor vehicles: in use (1986): 35,000 passenger cars, 12,000 comm. vehicles. **Chief ports:** Port-au-Prince, Les Cayes.

Communications: Television sets: 1 per 221 persons. **Radios:** 1 per 41 persons. **Telephones in use:** 1 per 65 persons. **Daily newspaper circ.** (1988): 8 per 1,000 pop

Health: Life expectancy at birth (1989): 55 male; 56 female. **Births** (per 1,000 pop. 1969): 31. **Deaths** (per 1,000 pop. 1989): 12. **Natural increase:** 1.9%. **Hospital beds:** 1 per 1,258 persons. **Physicians:** 1 per 6,039 persons. **Infant mortality rate** (per 1,000 live births, 1989): 92.

Education (1987): **Literacy: 23%. Years compulsory:** 6; attendance 20%.

Major International Organizations: UN and some of its specialized agencies, OAS.

Embassy: 2311 Massachusetts Ave. NW 20008; 332-4090.

Haiti, visited by Columbus, 1492, and a French colony from 1677, attained its independence, 1804, following the rebellion led by former slave Toussaint L'Ouverture. Following a period of political violence, the U.S. occupied the country 1915-34.

Dr. Francois Duvalier was voted president in 1957; in 1964 he was named president for life. Upon his death in 1971, he was succeeded by his son, Jean-Claude. Drought in 1975-77 brought famine, and Hurricane Allen in 1980 destroyed most of the rice, bean, and coffee crops.

Following several weeks of unrest, President Jean Claude Duvalier fled Haiti aboard a U.S. Air Force jet Feb. 7, 1986, ending the 28-year dictatorship of the Duvalier family. A military-civilian council headed by Gen. Henri Namphy assumed control. In 1987, voters approved a new constitution.

The Jan. 17, 1988 elections led to Leslie Manigat being named president; opposition leaders charged widespread fraud. Gen. Namphy seized control, June 20, and named himself president of a military government. Namphy was ousted by a military coup in Sept. By mid-1990, there had been 5 governments since Duvalier fled.

A coup led by leaders of the Tonton Macoutes, the private milita of the Duvalier family, was crushed by loyalist army forces, Jan. 1991. The attempted coup sparked riots which left some 70 dead.

Honduras
Republic of Honduras
República de Honduras

People: Population (1990 est.): 5,261,000. **Age distrib. (%):** 0–14: 44.6; 15–59: 50.5; 60+: 4.9. **Pop. density:** 117 per sq. mi. **Urban** (1988): 40.0%. **Ethnic groups:** Mestizo 90%, Indian 7%. **Languages:** Spanish (official). **Religions:** Roman Catholic 95%.

Geography: Area: 43,277 sq. mi., slightly larger than Tennessee. **Location:** In Central America. **Neighbors:** Guatemala on W, El Salvador, Nicaragua on S. **Topography:** The Caribbean coast is 500 mi. long. Pacific coast, on Gulf of Fonseca, is 40 mi. long. Honduras is mountainous, with wide fertile valleys and rich forests. **Capital:** Tegucigalpa. **Cities** (1989 est.) Tegucigalpa 550,000; San Pedro Sula 399,000.

Government: Type: Democratic constitutional republic. **Head of State:** Pres. Rafael Leonardo Callejas; in office: Jan. 27, 1990. **Local divisions:** 18 departments. **Defense:** 3.8% of GNP (1987).

Economy: Industries: Textiles, wood prods, cigars. **Chief crops:** Bananas (chief export), coffee, corn, beans. **Minerals:** Gold, silver, copper, lead, zinc, iron, antimony, coal. **Other resources:** Timber. **Arable land:** 16%. **Livestock** (1989): cattle: 2.8 mln. **Electricity prod.** (1988): 1.9 bln. kwh. **Labor force:** 62% agric.; 20% services; 9% manuf.

Finance: Monetary unit: Lempira (Apr. 1991): 2.00 = $1 US). **Gross national product** (1989): $4.4 bln. **Per capita income** (1989): $1,000. **Imports** (1987): $1.7 bln.; partners: U.S. 39%, Jap. 8%. **Exports** (1987): $1.5 bln.; partners: U.S. 54%, Europe 34%. **Tourists** (1988): $28 mln. receipts. **International reserves less gold** (Mar. 1991): $62 mln. **Gold:** 16,000 oz t. **Consumer prices** (change in 1989): 9.9%.

Transport: Motor vehicles: in use (1989) 77,000 passenger cars, 24,000 comm. vehicles. **Civil aviation** (1987): 483 mln. passenger-km; 9 airports with scheduled flights. **Chief ports:** Puerto Cortes, La Ceiba.

Communications: Television sets: 1 per 31 persons. **Radios:** 1 per 2.4 persons. **Telephones:** 1 per 67 persons. **Daily newspaper circ.** (1989): 51 per 1,000 pop.

Health: Life expectancy at birth (1989): 63 male; 67 female. **Births** (per 1,000 pop. 1989): 38. **Deaths** (per 1,000 pop. 1989): 7. **Natural increase:** 3.0%. **Hospital beds:** 1 per 739 persons. **Physicians:** 1 per 1,724 persons. **Infant mortality** (per 1,000 live births 1989): 60.

Education (1989): **Literacy: 56%. Years compulsory:** 6; attendance 70%.

Major International Organizations: UN, (IMF, WHO, ILO), OAS.

Embassy: 4301 Connecticut Ave. NW 20008; 966-7700.

Mayan civilization flourished in Honduras in the 1st millenium AD. Columbus arrived in 1502. Honduras became independent after freeing itself from Spain, 1821 and from the Fed. of Central America, 1838.

Gen. Oswaldo Lopez Arellano, president for most of the period 1963-75 by virtue of one election and 2 coups, was ousted by the army in 1975 over charges of pervasive bribery by United Brands Co. of the U.S.

The government has resumed land distribution, raised minimum wages, and started a literacy campaign. An elected civilian government took power in 1982.

The U.S. has provided military aid and advisors to help withstand pressures from Nicaragua and help block arms shipments from Nicaragua to rebel forces in El Salvador. Some 3,200 U.S. troops were sent to Honduras after the Honduran border was violated by Nicaraguan forces, Mar. 1988.

Hungary
Republic of Hungary
Magyar Köztársaság

People: Population (1990 est.): 10,546,000. **Age distrib. (%):** 0–14: 20.8; 15–59: 60.5; 60+: 18.7. **Pop. density:** 293 per sq. mi. **Urban** (1990): 62%. **Ethnic groups:** Magyar 92%, German 2.5%, Gypsy 3%. **Languages:** Hungarian (Magyar). **Religions:** Roman Catholic 67%, Protestant 25%.

Geography: Area: 35,919 sq. mi., slightly smaller than Indiana. **Location:** In East Central Europe. **Neighbors:** Czechoslovakia on N, Austria on W, Yugoslavia on S, Romania, USSR on E. **Topography:** The Danube R. forms the Czech border in the NW, then swings S to bisect the country. The eastern half of Hungary is mainly a great fertile plain, the Alfold; the W and N are hilly. **Capital:** Budapest. **Cities** (1989 est.): Budapest 2,115,000; Miskolc 208,000; Debrecen 220,000.

Government: Type: Republic. **Head of state:** Pres. Arpad Goncz; in office: May 2, 1990. **Head of government:** Prime Min. Jozsef Antall; in office: May 3, 1990. **Local divisions:** 20 regions. **Defense:** 5.2% of GNP (1987).

Economy: Industries: Iron and steel, machinery, pharmaceuticals, vehicles, communications equip., milling, distilling. **Chief crops:** Grains, vegetables, fruits, grapes. **Minerals:** Bauxite, coal, natural gas. **Arable land:** 57%. **Livestock** (1989): cattle: 1.6 mln.; pigs: 7.6 mln.; sheep: 2.0 mln. **Electricity prod.** (1988): 29.2 bln. kwh. **Crude steel prod.** (1988): 3.5 mln. metric tons. **Labor force:** 19% agric.; 48% ind. & comm.; 27% services.

Finance: Monetary unit: Forint (Mar. 1991: 75 = $1 US). **Gross national product** (1989): $64.5 bln. **Per capita GNP** (1989): $6,100. **Imports** (1990): $8.6 bln.; partners: USSR 25%, W. Ger. 14%, E. Ger. 7%, Czech. 5%. **Exports** (1990): $9.5 bln.; partners: USSR 27%, E. Ger. 6%, W. Ger. 9%, Czech. 6%. **National budget** (1987): $14.9 bln. **Tourists** (1989): $825 mln. receipts. **Consumer prices** (change in 1990): 28.3%.

Transport: Railway traffic (1989): 11.8 bln. passenger-km. **Motor vehicles:** in use (1989): 1.8 mln. passenger cars, 205,000 comm. vehicles. **Civil aviation** (1989): 1.5 bln. passenger-km; 4 airports.

Communications: Television sets: 1 per 2.5 persons. **Radios:** 1 per 1.7 persons. **Telephones:** 1 per 6.3 persons. **Daily newspaper circ.** (1988): 296 per 1,000 pop.

Health: Life expectancy at birth (1989): 65.3 male; 73.2 female. **Births** (per 1,000 pop. 1989): 12. **Deaths** (per 1,000 pop. 1989): 14. **Natural increase:** −2%. **Hospital beds:** 1 per 104 persons. **Physicians:** 1 per 343 persons. **Infant mortality** (per 1,000 live births 1989): 20.2.

Education (1989): **Literacy: 98%. Years compulsory:** to age 16; attendance 96%.

Major International Organizations: UN (IMF, World Bank, GATT).

Embassy: 3910 Shoemaker St. NW 20008; 362-6737.

Earliest settlers, chiefly Slav and Germanic, were overrun by Magyars from the east. Stephen I (997-1038) was made king by Pope Sylvester II in 1000 AD. The country suffered repeated Turkish invasions in the 15th-17th centuries. After the defeats of the Turks, 1686-1697, Austria dominated, but Hungary obtained concessions until it regained internal independence in 1867, with the emperor of Austria as king of Hungary in a dual monarchy with a single diplomatic service. Defeated with the Central Powers in 1918, Hungary lost Transylvania to Romania, Croatia and Bacska to Yugoslavia, Slovakia and Carpatho-Ruthenia to Czechoslovakia, all of which had large Hungarian minorities. A republic under Michael Karolyi and a bolshevist revolt under Bela Kun were followed by a vote for a monarchy in 1920 with Admiral Nicholas Horthy as regent.

Hungary joined Germany in World War II, and was allowed to annex most of its lost territories. Russian troops captured the country, 1944-1945. By terms of an armistice with the Allied powers Hungary agreed to give up territory acquired by the 1938 dismemberment of Czechoslovakia and to return to its borders of 1937.

A republic was declared Feb. 1, 1946; Zoltan Tildy was elected president. In 1947 the communists forced Tildy out. Premier Imre Nagy, in office since mid-1953, was ousted for his moderate policy of favoring agriculture and consumer production, April 18, 1955.

In 1956, popular demands for the ousting of Erno Gero, Communist Party secretary, and for formation of a government by Nagy, resulted in the latter's appointment Oct. 23; demonstrations against communist rule developed into open revolt. Gero called in Soviet forces. On Nov. 4 Soviet forces launched a massive attack against Budapest with 200,000 troops, 2,500 tanks and armored cars.

About 200,000 persons fled the country. In the spring of 1963 the regime freed many anti-communists and captives from the revolution in a sweeping amnesty. Nagy was executed by the Russians. In Mar. 1987, some 2,000 marched in Budapest calling for democracy.

Hungarian troops participated in the 1968 Warsaw Pact invasion of Czechoslovakia. Major economic reforms were launched early in 1968, switching from a central planning system to one in which market forces and profit control much of production.

In 1989 parliament passed legislation legalizing freedom of assembly and association as Hungary shifted away from communism toward democracy. In Oct., the communist party was formally dissolved. The last Soviet troops left Hungary June 19, 1991.

Iceland

Republic of Iceland

Lýoveldio Island

People: Population (1990 est.): 251,000. **Age distrib.** (%): 0–14: 25.5; 15–59: 60.1; 60+: 14.4. **Pop. density:** 6 per sq. mi. **Urban** (1989): 90% **Ethnic groups:** Homogeneous, descendants of Norwegians, Celts. **Language:** Icelandic (Islenska). **Religion:** Evangelical Lutheran 95%.

Geography: Area: 39,769 sq. mi., the size of Virginia. **Location:** At N end of Atlantic O. **Neighbors:** Nearest is Greenland. **Topography:** Iceland is of recent volcanic origin. Three-quarters of the surface is wasteland: glaciers, lakes, a lava desert. There are geysers and hot springs, and the climate is moderated by the Gulf Stream. **Capital:** Reykjavik. **Cities** (1989 est.): Reykjavik 96,000.

Government: Type: Constitutional republic. **Head of state:** Pres. Vigdis Finnbogadottir; b. Apr. 15, 1930; in office: Aug. 1, 1980. **Head of government:** Prime Min. Steingrimur Hermannsson; in office: Sept. 28, 1988. **Local divisions:** 23 counties.

Economy: Industries: Fish products (some 80% of exports), aluminum. **Chief crops:** Potatoes, turnips, hay. **Arable land:** 0.5%. **Livestock** (1988): sheep: 586,000. **Fish catch** (1989): 1.4 mln. metric tons. **Electricity prod.** (1988): 4.9 bln. kwh. **Labor force:** 11% agric.; 55% comm. & services, 14% fisheries.

Finance: Monetary unit: Kronur (Mar. 1991: 59.66 = $1 US). **Gross national product** (1989): $5.0 bln. **Per capita GNP** (1989): $20,160. **Imports** (1989): $1.4 bln.; partners: W. Ger. 15%, UK 9%, Den. 10%. **Exports** (1989): $1.4 bln.; partners: U.S. 88%, UK 19%. **Tourists** (1988): receipts: $108 mln. **National budget** (1987): $1.2 bln. expenditures. **International reserves less gold** (Mar. 1991): $307 mln. **Gold:** 49,000 oz t. **Consumer prices** (change in 1990): 15.5%.

Transport: Motor vehicles: in use (1988): 121,000 passenger cars, 12,000 comm. vehicles. **Civil aviation** (1988): 2.3 bln. passenger-km; 31 airports with scheduled flights. **Chief ports:** Reykjavik.

Communications: Television sets: 1 per 3.3 persons. **Radios:** 1 per 1.6 persons. **Telephones:** 1 per 2.2 persons. **Daily newspaper circ.** (1988): 524 per 1,000 pop.

Health: Life expectancy at birth (1989): 75 male; 81 female. **Births** (per 1,000 pop. 1989): 15. **Deaths** (per 1,000 pop. 1989): 7. **Natural increase:** 0.8%. **Hospital beds:** 1 per 86 persons. **Physicians:** 1 per 370 persons. **Infant mortality** per (1,000 live births 1989): 6.

Education (1989): **Literacy:** 99%. **Years compulsory:** 8; **Attendance:** 99%.

Major International Organizations: UN (GATT), NATO, OECD.

Embassy: 2022 Connecticut Ave. NW 20008; 265-6653.

Iceland was an independent republic from 930 to 1262, when it joined with Norway. Its language has maintained its purity for 1,000 years. Danish rule lasted from 1380-1918; the last ties with the Danish crown were severed in 1941. The Althing, or assembly, is the world's oldest surviving parliament.

India

Republic of India

Bharat

People: Population (1990 cen.): 844,000,000. **Age distrib.** (%): 0–14: 36.8; 15–59: 56.4; 60+: 5.8. **Pop. density:** 666 per sq. mi. **Urban** (1989): 28%. **Ethnic groups:** Indo-Aryan groups 72%, Dravidians 25%, Mongoloids 3%. **Languages:** 16 languages, including Hindi (official) and English (associate official). **Religions:** Hindu 83%, Moslem 11%, Christian 3%, Sikh 2%.

Geography: Area: 1,266,595 sq. mi., one third the size of the U.S. **Location:** Occupies most of the Indian subcontinent in S. Asia. **Neighbors:** Pakistan on W, China, Nepal, Bhutan on N, Myanmar, Bangladesh on E. **Topography:** The Himalaya Mts., highest in world, stretch across India's northern borders. Below, the Ganges Plain is wide, fertile, and among the most densely populated regions of the world. The area below includes the Deccan Peninsula. Close to one quarter the area is forested. The climate varies from tropical heat in S to near-Arctic cold in N. Rajasthan Desert is in NW; NE Assam Hills get 400 in. of rain a year. **Capital:** New Delhi. **Cities** (1990 cen.): Calcutta 10.8 mln.; Bombay 12.5 mln.; New Delhi 8.3 mln.; Madras 5.3 mln.; Bangalore 4.1 mln.; Hyderabad 4.2 mln.

Government: Type: Federal republic. **Head of state:** Pres. Ramaswamy Venkataraman; b. Dec. 4, 1910; in office: July 25, 1987. **Head of government:** Prime Min. P. V. Narasimha Rao; b. June 28, 1921; in office: June 20, 1991. **Local divisions:** 24 states, 7 union territories. **Defense:** 3.8% of GNP (1987).

Economy: Industries: Textiles, steel, processed foods, cement, machinery, chemicals, fertilizers, consumer appliances, autos. **Chief crops:** Rice, grains, coffee, sugar cane, spices, tea, cashews, cotton, copra, coir, juta, linseed. **Minerals:** Chromium, coal, iron, manganese, mica salt, bauxite, gypsum, oil. **Crude oil reserves** (1987): 4.3 bln. bbls. **Other resources:** Rubber, timber. **Arable land:** 57%. **Livestock** (1989): cattle: 195 mln.; sheep: 55 mln. **Fish catch** (1988): 14.2 mln. metric tons. **Electricity prod.** (1989): 262 bln. kwh. **Crude steel prod.** (1988): 14.2 mln. metric tons. **Labor force:** 70% agric.; 19% ind. & comm.

Finance: Monetary unit: Rupee (June 1991: 20.79 = $1 US). **Gross national product** (1989): $287 bln. **Per capita GNP** (1989): $350. **Imports** (1989): $20.5 bln.; partners: Jap. 12%, U.S. 12%, W. Ger. 10%, UK 8%. **Exports** (1989): $15.8 bln.; partners: U.S. 18%, USSR 15%, UK 6%, Jap. 9%. **Tourists** (1990): receipts: $1.4 bln. **National budget** (1988): $56 bln. expenditures. **International reserves less gold** (Mar. 1991): $2.3

bln. **Gold:** 10.6 mln. oz. t. **Consumer prices** (change in 1990): 9.0%.

Transport: Railway traffic (1989): 269 bln. passenger-km. **Motor vehicles:** in use (1989): 2.2 mln. passenger cars, 1.4 mln. comm. vehicles. **Civil aviation:** (1988): 18.0 bln. passenger-km; 99 airports with scheduled flights. **Chief ports:** Calcutta, Bombay, Madras, Cochin, Vishakhapatnam.

Communications: Television sets: 1 per 42 persons. **Radios:** 1 per 15 persons. **Telephones:** 1 per 189 persons. **Daily newspaper circ.** (1988): 21 per. 1,000 pop.

Health: Life expectancy at birth (1989): 57 male; 58 female. **Births** (per 1,000 pop. 1989): 31. **Deaths** (per 1,000 pop. 1989): 11. **Natural increase:** 2.0%. **Hospital beds:** 1 per 1,130 persons. **Physicians:** 1 per 2,471 persons. **Infant mortality** (per 1,000 live births 1989): 91.

Education (1989): **Literacy:** 36%. **Years Compulsory:** to age 14.

Major International Organizations: UN (IMF, World Bank). **Embassy:** 2107 Massachusetts Ave. NW 20008; 939-7000.

India has one of the oldest civilizations in the world. Excavations trace the Indus Valley civilization back for at least 5,000 years. Paintings in the mountain caves of Ajanta, richly carved temples, the Taj Mahal in Agra, and the Kutab Minar in Delhi are among relics of the past.

Aryan tribes, speaking Sanskrit, invaded from the NW around 1500 BC, and merged with the earlier inhabitants to create classical Indian civilization.

Asoka ruled most of the Indian subcontinent in the 3d century BC, and established Buddhism. But Hinduism revived and eventually predominated. During the Gupta kingdom, 4th-6th century AD, science, literature, and the arts enjoyed a "golden age."

Arab invaders established a Moslem foothold in the W in the 8th century, and Turkish Moslems gained control of North India by 1200. The Mogul emperors ruled 1526-1857.

Vasco de Gama established Portuguese trading posts 1498-1503. The Dutch followed. The British East India Co. sent Capt. William Hawkins, 1609, to get concessions from the Mogul emperor for spices and textiles. Operating as the East India Co. the British gained control of most of India. The British parliament assumed political direction; under Lord Bentinck, 1828-35, rule by rajahs was curbed. After the Sepoy troops mutinied, 1857-58, the British supported the native rulers.

Nationalism grew rapidly after World War I. The Indian National Congress and the Moslem League demanded constitutional reform. A leader emerged in Mohandas K. Gandhi (called Mahatma, or Great Soul), born Oct. 2, 1869, assassinated Jan. 30, 1948. He advocated self-rule, non-violence, removal of untouchability. In 1930 he launched "civil disobedience," including boycott of British goods and rejection of taxes without representation.

In 1935 Britain gave India a constitution providing a bicameral federal congress. Mohammed Ali Jinnah, head of the Moslem League, sought creation of a Moslem nation, Pakistan.

The British government partitioned British India into the dominions of India and Pakistan. India became a self-governing member of the Commonwealth and a member of the UN. It became a democratic republic, Jan. 26, 1950.

More than 12 million Hindu & Moslem refugees crossed the India-Pakistan borders in a mass transferral of some of the 2 peoples during 1947; about 200,000 were killed in communal fighting.

After Pakistan troops began attacks on Bengali separatists in East Pakistan, Mar. 25, 1971, some 10 million refugees fled into India. India and Pakistan went to war Dec. 3, 1971, on both the East and West fronts. Pakistan troops in the east surrendered Dec. 16; Pakistan agreed to a cease-fire in the west Dec. 17. In Aug. 1973 India released 93,000 Pakistanis held prisoner since 1971. The 2 countries resumed full relations in 1976.

In 2 days of carnage, the Bengali population of the village of Mandai, Tripura State, 700 people, were massacred in a raid by indigenous tribal residents of the area, June 8-9, 1980. A similar year-long campaign against Bengali immigrants had been going on in Assam State.

Mrs. Indira Gandhi, was named prime minister Jan. 19, 1966. Threatened with adverse court rulings in a voting law case, and opposition protest campaign and strikes, Gandhi invoked emergency provisions of the constitution June, 1975. Thousands of opponents were arrested and press censorship imposed. Measures to control prices, protect small farmers, and improve productivity were adopted.

The emergency, especially enforcement of coercive birth control measures in some areas, and the prominent extra-constitutional role of Indira Gandhi's son Sanjay, was widely resented. Opposition parties, united in the Janata coalition, scored massive victories in federal and state parliamentary elections in 1977, turning Gandhi's New Congress Party from power.

Gandhi became prime minister for the second time, Jan. 14, 1980. She was assassinated by 2 of her Sikh bodyguards Oct. 31, 1984. Widespread rioting followed. Thousands of Sikhs were killed and some 50,000 left homeless. The assassination was in response to the government supression of a Sikh uprising in Punjab in June 1984 which included an assault on the Golden Temple, the holiest Sikh shrine. Rajiv, her son, replaced her as prime minister. He was swept from office in 1989 amid charges of incompetence and corruption. He was assassinated May 21, 1991 during an election campaign to regain the prime ministership.

Sikhs ignited several violent clashes during the 1980s. The government's May 1987 decision to bring the state of Punjab under the rule of the central government led to violence. Many died during a government siege of the Golden Temple at Amritsar, May 1988.

As India's population passed 800 mln., government officials expressed alarm that the failure to control the birth rate would lead to disaster.

Sikkim, bordered by Tibet, Bhutan and Nepal, formerly British protected, became a protectorate of India in 1950. Area, 2,740 sq. mi.; pop. 1981 cen. 315,000; capital, Gangtok. In Sept. 1974 India's parliament voted to make Sikkim an associate Indian state, absorbing it into India.

Kashmir, a predominantly Moslem region in the NW, has been in dispute between India and Pakistan since 1947. A cease-fire was negotiated by the UN Jan. 1, 1949; it gave Pakistan control of one-third of the area, in the west and northwest, and India the remaining two-thirds, the Indian state of Jammu and Kashmir, which enjoys internal autonomy.

In 1990 and 1991, there were repeated clashes between Indian army troops and pro-independence demonstrators triggered by India's decision to impose central government rule. The clashes strained relations between India and Pakistan which India charged was aiding the Moslem separatists.

France, 1952-54, peacefully yielded to India its 5 colonies, former French India, comprising Pondicherry, Karikal, Mahe, Yanaon (which became Pondicherry Union Territory, area 185 sq. mi., pop. 1981, 604,136) and Chandernagor (which was incorporated into the state of West Bengal).

Indonesia

Republic of Indonesia

Republik Indonesia

People: Population (1990 est.): 191,266,000. **Age distrib. (%):** 0–14: 39.2; 15–59: 56.5; 60+: 5.3. **Pop. density:** 255 per sq. mi. **Urban** (1985): 25%. **Ethnic groups:** Malay, Chinese, Irianese. **Languages:** Bahasa Indonesian (Malay) (official), Javanese, other Austronesian languages. **Religions:** Moslem 88%.

Geography: Area: 735,268 sq. mi. **Location:** Archipelago SE of Asia along the Equator. **Neighbors:** Malaysia on N, Papúa New Guinea on E. **Topography:** Indonesia comprises 13,500 islands, including Java (one of the most densely populated areas in the world with 1,500 persons to the sq. mi.), Sumatra, Kalimantan (most of Borneo), Sulawesi (Celebes), and West Irian (Irian Jaya, the W. half of New Guinea). Also: Bangka, Billiton, Madura, Bali, Timor. The mountains and plateaus on the major islands have a cooler climate than the tropical lowlands. **Capital:** Jakarta. **Cities** (1988 est.): Jakarta 8,800,000; Surabaya 2,500,000; Bandung 1,400,000; Medan 1,700,000.

Government: Type: Independent republic. **Head of state:** Pres. Suharto; b. June 8, 1921; in office: Mar. 6, 1967. **Local divisions:** 27 provinces, 246 districts & 55 municipalities. **Defense:** 2.5% of GNP (1985).

Economy: Industries: Food processing, textiles, light industry. **Chief crops:** Rice, coffee, sugar. **Minerals:** Nickel, tin, oil, bauxite, copper, natural gas. **Crude oil reserves** (1987): 8.4 bln. bbls. **Other resources:** Rubber. **Arable land:** 8%. **Livestock** (1989): cattle: 6.5 mln.; sheep: 5.4 mln. **Fish catch** (1987): 1.9 mln. metric tons. **Electricity prod.** (1987): 34.8 bln.

kwh. **Labor force:** 56% agric.; 23% ind. & comm.; 16% services.

Finance: Monetary unit: Rupiah (June 1991: 1,944 = $1 US). **Gross national product** (1988): $87.9 bln. **Per capita income** (1988): $435. **Imports** (1989): $16.3 bln.; partners: Jap. 23%, U.S. 12%, Sing. 6%. **Exports** (1989): $22.1 bln.; partners: Jap. 41%, U.S. 16%, Sing. 10%. **Tourists** (1988): $1.0 bln. receipts. **National budget** (1990): $21.1 bln. **International reserves less gold** (Feb. 1991): $8.0 bln. **Gold:** 3.11 mln. oz t. **Consumer prices** (change in 1989): 6.4%.

Transport: Railway traffic (1989): 7.8 bln. passenger-km. **Motor vehicles:** in use (1989): 1.1 mln. passenger cars, 1.3 mln. comm. **Civil aviation** (1989): 8.9 bln. passenger-km; 134 airports. **Chief ports:** Jakarta, Surabaya, Medan, Palembang, Semarang.

Communications: Television sets: 1 per 24 persons. **Radios:** 1 per 8 persons. **Telephones:** 1 per 193 persons.

Health: Life expectancy at birth (1989): male: 57; female 61 years. **Births** (per 1,000 pop. 1989): 28. **Deaths** (per 1,000 pop. 1989): 9. **Natural increase:** 1.9%. **Hospital beds:** 1 per 1,512 persons. **Physicians:** 1 per 7,902 persons. **Infant mortality** (per 1,000 live births 1989): 58.0.

Education (1988): **Literacy:** 85%. 84% attend primary school.

Major International Organizations: UN and all of its specialized agencies, ASEAN, OPEC.

Embassy: 2020 Massachusetts Ave. NW 20036; 775-5200.

Hindu and Buddhist civilization from India reached the peoples of Indonesia nearly 2,000 years ago, taking root especially in Java. Islam spread along the maritime trade routes in the 15th century, and became predominant by the 16th century. The Dutch replaced the Portuguese as the most important European trade power in the area in the 17th century. They secured territorial control over Java by 1750. The outer islands were not finally subdued until the early 20th century, when the full area of present-day Indonesia was united under one rule for the first time.

Following Japanese occupation, 1942-45, nationalists led by Sukarno and Hatta proclaimed a republic. The Netherlands ceded sovereignty Dec. 27, 1949, after 4 years of fighting. West Irian, on New Guinea, remained under Dutch control.

After the Dutch in 1957 rejected proposals for new negotiations over West Irian, Indonesia stepped up the seizure of Dutch property. A U.S. mediator's plan was adopted in 1962. In 1963 the UN turned the area over to Indonesia, which promised a plebiscite. In 1969, voting by tribal chiefs favored staying with Indonesia, despite an uprising and widespread opposition.

Sukarno suspended Parliament in 1960, and was named president for life in 1963. Russian-armed Indonesian troops staged raids in 1964 and 1965 into Malaysia, whose formation Sukarno had opposed.

Indonesia's Communist Party tried to seize control in 1965; the army smashed the coup. In parts of Java, communists seized several districts before being defeated; over 300,000 communists were executed.

Gen. Suharto, head of the army, was named president in 1968, reelected 1973, 1978, and 1988. A coalition his supporters won a strong majority in House elections in 1971. Moslem opposition parties made gains in 1977 elections but lost ground in the 1982 elections. The military retains a predominant political role.

In 1966 Indonesia and Malaysia signed an agreement ending hostility. After ties with Peking were cut in 1967, there were riots against the economically important ethnic Chinese minority.

Oil export earnings, and political stability have made Indonesia's economy stable.

Iran

Islamic Republic of Iran

Jomhori-e-Islami-e-Irân

People: Population (1990 est.): 55,647,000. **Age distrib. (%):** 0–14: 44.4; 15–59: 50.3; 60+: 5.2. **Pop. density:** 80 per sq. mi. **Urban** (1987): 55%. **Ethnic groups:** Persian 63%, Turkomans & Baluchis 19%, Kurds 3%, Arabs 4%. **Languages:** Farsi (official), Turk, Kurdish, Arabic. **Religions:** Shi'a Moslem 93%.

Geography: Area: 636,293 sq. mi. slightly larger than Alaska. **Location:** Between the Middle East and S. Asia. **Neighbors:** Turkey, Iraq on W, USSR of N (Armenia, Azerbaijan, Turkmenis-

tan), Afghanistan, Pakistan on E. **Topography:** Interior highlands and plains are surrounded by high mountains, up to 18,000 ft. Large salt deserts cover much of the area, but there are many oases and forest areas. Most of the population inhabits the N and NW. **Capital:** Teheran. **Cities** (1986 cen.): Teheran 6,022,000; Esfahan 1,001,000; Mashhad 1,466,000; Tabriz 994,000; Shiraz 848,000.

Government: Type: Islamic republic. **Religious head:** Ayatollah Sayyed Ali Khamenei; b. 1939; in office: June 4, 1989. **Head of state:** Pres. Hashemi Rafsanjani; in office: Aug 3, 1989. **Local divisions:** 24 provinces. **Defense:** 7.9% of GNP (1986).

Economy: Industries: Cement, sugar refining, carpets. **Chief crops:** Grains, rice, fruits, sugar beets, cotton, grapes. **Minerals:** Chromium, oil, gas. **Crude oil reserves** (1990): 92.0 bln. barrels. **Other resources:** Gums, wool, silk, caviar. **Arable land:** 9%. **Livestock** (1987): cattle: 8.3 mln.; sheep: 34.0 mln. **Electricity prod.** (1988): 43.3 bln. kwh. **Crude steel prod.** (1988) 1.2 mln. metric tons. **Labor force:** 33% agric.; 21% ind. & comm; 27% services.

Finance: Monetary unit: Rial (Mar. 1991: 65.02 = $1 US). **Gross national product** (1988): $93 bln. **Per capita GNP** (1988): $1,800. **Imports** (1989): $14.7 bln.; partners: W. Ger. 20%, Jap. 10%, UK 6%. **Exports** (1989): $13.6 bln.; partners: Jap. 13%, Neth. 12%. **National budget** (1988): $55 bln. expenditures.

Transport: Motor vehicles: in use (1983): 2.1 mln. passenger cars, 313,000 comm. vehicles. **Civil Aviation** (1989): 4.5 bln. passenger km.; 24 airports. **Chief ports:** Bandar Abbas.

Communications: Television sets: 1 per 23 persons. **Radios:** 1 per 4.7 persons. **Telephones:** 1 per 25 persons. **Daily newspaper circ.** (1988): 13 per 1,000 pop.

Health: Life expectancy at birth (1989): 57 male; 57 female. **Births** (per 1,000 pop. 1989): 44. **Deaths** (per 1,000 pop. 1989): 10. **Natural increase:** 3.4%. **Hospital beds:** 1 per 704 persons. **Physicians:** 1 per 2,992 persons. **Infant mortality** (per 1,000 live births 1989): 113.

Education (1986): **Literacy:** 48%.

Major International Organizations: UN (IMF, WHO), OPEC.

Iran was once called Persia. The Iranians, who supplanted an earlier agricultural civilization, came from the E during the 2d millenium BC; they were an Indo-European group related to the Aryans of India.

In 549 BC Cyrus the Great united the Medes and Persians in the Persian Empire, conquered Babylonia in 538 BC, restored Jerusalem to the Jews. Alexander the Great conquered Persia in 333 BC, but Persians regained their independence in the next century under the Parthians, themselves succeeded by Sassanian Persians in 226 AD. Arabs brought Islam to Persia in the 7th century, replacing the indigenous Zoroastrian faith. After Persian political and cultural autonomy was reasserted in the 9th century, the arts and sciences flourished for several centuries.

Turks and Mongols ruled Persia in turn from the 11th century to 1502, when a native dynasty reasserted full independence. The British and Russian empires vied for influence in the 19th century, and Afghanistan was severed from Iran by Britain in 1857.

Reza Khan abdicated as Shah, 1941, and was succeeded by his son, Mohammad Reza Pahlavi. Under his rule, Iran underwent economic and social change but political opposition was not tolerated.

Conservative Moslem protests led to 1978 violence. Martial law in 12 cities was declared Sept. 8. A military government was appointed Nov. 6 to deal with striking oil workers. Prime Min. Shahpur Bakhtiar was designated by the shah to head a regency council in his absence. The shah left Iran Jan. 16, 1979.

Exiled religious leader Ayatollah Ruhollah Khomeini named a provisional government council in preparation for his return to Iran, Jan. 31. Clashes between Khomeini's supporters and government troops culminated in a rout of Iran's elite Imperial Guard Feb. 11, leading to the fall of Bakhtiar's government.

The Iranian revolution was marked by revolts among the ethnic minorities and by a continuing struggle between the clerical forces and westernized intellectuals and liberals. The Islamic Constitution established final authority to be vested in a Faghi, the Ayatollah Khomeini.

Iranian militants seized the U.S. embassy, Nov. 4, 1979, and took hostages including 62 Americans. Despite international condemnations and U.S. efforts, including an abortive Apr., 1980, rescue attempt, the crisis continued. The U.S. broke diplomatic relations with Iran, Apr. 7th. The shah died in Egypt, July 27th.

The hostage drama finally ended Jan. 21, 1981 when an accord, involving the release of frozen Iranian assets, was reached.

A dispute over the Shatt al-Arab waterway that divides the two countries brought Iran and Iraq, Sept. 22, 1980, into open warfare. Iraqi planes attacked Iranian air fields including Teheran airport. Iranian planes bombed Iraqi bases. Iraqi troops occupied Iranian territory including the port city of Khorramshahr in October. Iranian troops recaptured the city and drove Iraqi troops back across the border, May 1982. Iraq, and later Iran, attacked several oil tankers in the Persian Gulf during 1984. Saudi Arabian war planes shot down 2 Iranian jets, June 5, which they felt were threatening Saudi shipping. In Aug. 1988, Iran agreed to accept a UN resolution calling for a cease fire.

In Nov. 1986, senior U.S. officials secretly visited Iran and exchanged arms for Iran's help in obtaining the release of U.S. hostages held by terrorists in Lebanon. The exchange sparked a major scandal in the Reagan administration.

A U.S. Navy warship shot down an Iranian commercial airliner, July 3, 1988, after mistaking it for an F-14 fighter jet; all 290 aboard the plane died.

In 1989, Ayatollah Khomeini offered a $1 million reward for the killing of Salman Rushdie, author of *The Satanic Verses*, a novel perceived as blasphemous to Islam. Khomeini died following a long illness, June 4, 1989.

A major earthquake struck northern Iran June 21, 1990, killing over 45,000, injuring 100,000, and leaving 400,000 homeless. A U.S. offer of assistance was accepted by the Iranian government.

Some one million Kurdish refugees crossed Iran's border to escape Iraqi forces following the Persian Gulf War.

Iraq
Republic of Iraq
al Jumhouriya al 'Iraqia

People: Population (1990 est.): 18,782,000. **Age distrib.** (%): 0–14: 45.3; 15–59: 49.6; 60+: 5.1. **Pop. density:** 104 per sq. mi. **Urban** (1988): 72%. **Ethnic groups:** Arabs, 75% Kurds, 15% Turks. **Languages:** Arabic (official), Kurdish. **Religions:** Moslem 95% (Shiites 60%, Sunnis 35%), Christian 5%.

Geography: Area: 167,924 sq. mi., larger than California. **Location:** In the Middle East, occupying most of historic Mesopotamia. **Neighbors:** Jordan, Syria on W, Turkey on N, Iran on E, Kuwait, Saudi Arabia on S. **Topography:** Mostly an alluvial plain, including the Tigris and Euphrates rivers, descending from mountains in N to desert in SW. Persian Gulf region is marshland. **Capital:** Baghdad. **Cities** (1985 est.): Baghdad (met.) 3,400,000, Basra 616,000, Mosul 570,000.

Government: Type: Republic. **Head of state:** Pres. Saddam Hussein At-Takriti, b. Apr. 29, 1937; in office: July 16, 1979. **Head of government:** Saadun Hamadi; in office: Mar. 23, 1991. **Local divisions:** 18 provinces. **Defense:** 32% of GNP (1986).

Economy: Industries: Textiles, petrochemicals, oil refining, cement. **Chief crops:** Grains, rice, dates, cotton. **Minerals:** Oil, gas. **Crude oil reserves** (1990): 100 bln. barrels. **Other resources:** Wool, hides. **Arable land:** 13%. **Livestock** (1988): cattle: 1.5 mln.; sheep 8.7 mln; goats: 1.4 mln. **Electricity prod.** (1988): 22.5 bln. kwh. **Labor force:** 33% agric.; 39% services; 28% ind.

Finance: Monetary unit: Dinar (Mar. 1991: 1.00 = $3.21 US). **Gross national product** (1988): $34 bln. **Per capita GNP** (1988): $1,950. **Imports** (1989): $10.2 bln.; partners: Tur. 10%, U.S. 11%. **Exports** (1989): $12.0 bln.; partners: U.S. 20%, Tur. 12%, Jap. 9%.

Transport: Railway traffic (1988): 1.5 bln. passenger-km. **Motor vehicles:** in use (1989): 672,000 passenger cars, 368,000 comm. vehicles. **Civil aviation** (1985): 1.2 bln. passenger-km; 3 airports. **Chief ports:** Basra.

Communications: Television sets: 1 per 18 persons. **Radios:** 1 per 5 persons. **Telephones:** 1 per 17 persons. **Daily newspaper circ.** (1989): 30 per 1,000 pop.

Health: Life expectancy at birth (1989): 65 male; 67 female. **Births** (per 1,000 pop. 1989): 45. **Deaths** (per 1,000 pop. 1989): 8. **Natural increase:** 3.8%. **Hospital beds:** 1 per 552 persons. **Physicians:** 1 per 3,324 persons. **Infant mortality** (per 1,000 live births 1989): 69.

Major International Organizations: UN (IMF, ILO), Arab League, OPEC.

Education (1987): **Literacy:** 70%. Compulsory age 6 to grade 6.
Embassy: 1801 P St. NW 20036; 483-7500.

The Tigris-Euphrates valley, formerly called Mesopotamia, was the site of some of the earliest civilizations in the world. The Sumerian city-states of 3,000 BC originated the culture later developed by the Semitic Akkadians, Babylonians, and Assyrians.

Mesopotamia ceased to be a separate entity after the conquests of the Persians, Greeks, and Arabs. The latter founded Baghdad, from where the caliph ruled a vast empire in the 8th and 9th centuries. Mongol and Turkish conquests led to a decline in population, the economy, cultural life, and the irrigation system.

Britain secured a League of Nations mandate over Iraq after World War I. Independence under a king came in 1932. A leftist, pan-Arab revolution established a republic in 1958, which oriented foreign policy toward the USSR. Most industry has been nationalized, and large land holdings broken up.

A local faction of the international Baath Arab Socialist party has ruled by decree since 1968. Russia and Iraq signed an aid pact in 1972, and arms were sent along with several thousand advisers. The 1978 execution of 21 communists and a shift of trade to the West signalled a more neutral policy, straining relations with the USSR. In the 1973 Arab-Israeli war Iraq sent forces to aid Syria. Within a month of assuming power, Saddam Hussein instituted a bloody purge in the wake of a reported coup attempt against the new regime.

Years of battling with the Kurdish minority resulted in total defeat for the Kurds in 1975, when Iran withdrew support. The fighting led to Iraqi bombing of Kurdish villages in Iran, causing relations with Iran to deteriorate.

After skirmishing intermittently for 10 months over the sovereignty of the disputed Shatt al-Arab waterway that divides the two countries, Iraq and Iran, Sept. 22, 1980, entered into open warfare when Iraqi fighter-bombers attacked 10 Iranian airfields, including Teheran airport, and Iranian planes retaliated with strikes on 2 Iraqi bases. In the following days, there was heavy ground fighting around Abadan and the adjacent port of Khorramshahr as Iraq pressed its attack on Iran's oil-rich province of Khuzistan. In May 1982, Iraqi troops were driven back across the border.

Israeli airplanes destroyed a nuclear reactor near Baghdad on June 7, 1981, claiming that it could be used to produce nuclear weapons.

Iraq and Iran expanded their war to the Persian Gulf in Apr. 1984. There were several attacks on oil tankers. An Iraqi warplane launched a missile attack on the U.S.S. *Stark*, a U.S. Navy frigate on patrol in the Persian Gulf, May 17, 1987; 37 U.S. sailors died. Iraq apologized for the attack, claiming it was inadvertent. The fierce war ended Aug. 1988, when Iraq accepted a UN resolution for a ceasefire.

Iraq attacked and overran Kuwait Aug. 2, 1990, sparking an international crisis. The United Nations, Aug. 6, imposed a ban on all trade with Iraq and called on member countries to protect the assets of the legitimate government of Kuwait. Iraq declared Kuwait its 19th province, Aug. 28. A campaign of looting, murder, and pillage was mounted against Kuwaiti civilians. Westerners caught in Iraq and Kuwait were initially held as hostages, but by the end of 1990, all were released.

A U.S.-led coalition launched air & missile attacks on Iraq, Jan. 16, 1991, after the expiration of a UN Security Council deadline for Iraq to withdraw from Kuwait. Iraq retaliated by firing scud missiles at Saudi Arabia and Israel. The coalition began a ground attack to retake Kuwait Feb. 27. Iraqi forces showed little resistance. (*See Index and Chronology for details.*)

In the aftermath of the war, there were revolts against Pres. Saddam Hussein throughout Iraq. In Feb., Iraqi troops drove Kurdish insurgents and civilians to the Iran and Turkey borders, causing a refugee crisis. The U.S. and allies established havens inside Iraq for the Kurds.

Republic of Ireland
Eire

People: Population (1990 est.): 3,557,000. **Age distrib.** (%): 0–14: 30.5; 15–59: 54.5; 60+:15.0. **Pop. density:** 137 per sq. mi. **Urban** (1985): 57%. **Ethnic groups:** Celtic, English minority. **Languages:** English predominates, Irish (Gaelic) spoken by minority. **Religions:** Roman Catholic 95%, Anglican 3%.

Geography: Area: 27,137 sq. mi. slightly larger than W. Va. **Location:** In the Atlantic O. just W of Great Britain. **Neighbors:** United Kingdom (Northern Ireland). **Topography:** Ireland consists of a central plateau surrounded by isolated groups of hills and mountains. The coastline is heavily indented by the Atlantic O. **Capital:** Dublin. **Cities** (1988 est.): Dublin 502,000; Cork (met.) 133,000.

Government: Type: Parliamentary republic. **Head of State:** Pres. Mary Robinson; in office: Dec. 3, 1990. **Head of government:** Prime Min. Charles Haughey; in office: Mar. 10, 1987. **Local divisions:** 26 counties. **Defense:** 1.3% of GNP (1988).

Economy: Industries: Food processing, metals, textiles, chemicals, brewing, electrical and non-electrical machinery, tourism. **Chief crops:** Potatoes, grain, sugar beets, fruits, vegetables. **Minerals:** Zinc, lead, silver, gas. **Arable land:** 14%. **Livestock** (1989): cattle: 5.6 mln.; pigs: 961,000; sheep: 4.9 mln. **Fish catch** (1988): 247,000 metric tons. **Electricity prod.** (1986): 12.6 bln. kwh. **Crude steel prod.** (1985): 203,000 metric tons. **Labor force:** 13% agric.; 21% ind. 47% services.

Finance: Monetary unit: Pound (June 1991: 0.64 = $1 US). **Gross national product** (1988): $28.6 bln. **Per capita income** (1988): $6,200. **Imports** (1989): $17.4 bln.; partners: UK 42%, U.S. 17%, W. Ger. 8%, Fr. 5%. **Exports** (1989): $20.6 bln.; partners: UK 33%, Fr. 9%, W. Ger. 9%. **Tourists** (1988): receipts: $1 bln. **National budget** (1990): $8.6 bln. expenditures. **International reserves less gold** (Mar. 1991): $5.3 bln. **Gold:** 360,000 oz. t. **Consumer prices** (change in 1990): 3.4%.

Transport: Railway traffic (1989): 1.2 bln. passenger-km. **Motor vehicles:** in use (1988): 748,000 passenger cars, 123,000 comm. vehicles. **Civil aviation:** (1989): 4.2 bln. passenger-km; 9 airports. **Chief ports:** Dublin, Cork.

Communications: Television sets: 1 per 3.8 persons. **Radios:** 1 per 1.7 persons. **Telephones:** 1 per 3.8 persons. **Daily newspaper circ.** (1989): 169 per 1,000 pop.

Health: Life expectancy at birth (1989): 72 male; 78 female. **Births** (per 1,000 pop. 1989): 16. **Deaths** (per 1,000 pop. 1989): 9. **Natural increase:** 8%. **Hospital beds:** 1 per 137 persons. **Physicians:** 1 per 681 persons. **Infant mortality** (per 1,000 live births 1989): 6.

Education (1988): **Literacy:** 99%. **Years compulsory:** 9; attendance 91%.

Major International Organizations: UN (GATT, IMF, World Bank), EC, OECD.

Embassy: 2234 Massachusetts Ave. NW 20008; 462-3939.

Celtic tribes invaded the islands about the 4th century BC; their Gaelic culture and literature flourished and spread to Scotland and elsewhere in the 5th century AD, the same century in which St. Patrick converted the Irish to Christianity. Invasions by Norsemen began in the 8th century, ended with defeat of the Danes by the Irish King Brian Boru in 1014. English invasions started in the 12th century; for over 700 years the Anglo-Irish struggle continued with bitter rebellions and savage repressions.

The Easter Monday Rebellion (1916) failed but was followed by guerrilla warfare and harsh reprisals by British troops, the "Black and Tans." The Dail Eireann, or Irish parliament, reaffirmed independence in Jan. 1919. The British offered dominion status to Ulster (6 counties) and southern Ireland (26 counties) Dec. 1921. The constitution of the Irish Free State, a British dominion, was adopted Dec. 11, 1922. Northern Ireland remained part of the United Kingdom.

A new constitution adopted by plebiscite came into operation Dec. 29, 1937. It declared the name of the state Eire in the Irish language (Ireland in English) and declared it a sovereign democratic state.

On Dec. 21, 1948, an Irish law declared the country a republic rather than a dominion and withdrew it from the Commonwealth. The British Parliament recognized both actions, 1949, but reasserted its claim to incorporate the 6 northeastern counties in the United Kingdom. This claim has not been recognized by Ireland. *(See United Kingdom — Northern Ireland.)*

Irish governments have favored peaceful unification of all Ireland. Ireland cooperated with England against terrorist groups.

Ireland has suffered economic hardship in the 1980's; unemployment reached 17% in 1989.

Israel
State of Israel
Medinat Israel

People: Population (1990 est.): 4,371,000. **Age distrib. (%):** 0–14: 32.4; 15–59: 55.3; 60+: 13.3. **Pop. density:** 570 per sq. mi. **Urban** (1986): 89%. **Ethnic groups:** Jewish 83%, Arab 16%. **Languages:** Hebrew and Arabic (official). **Religions:** Jewish 83%, Moslem 13%.

Geography: Area: 7,847 sq. mi. about the size of New Jersey. **Location:** On eastern end of Mediterranean Sea. **Neighbors:** Lebanon on N, Syria, Jordan on E, Egypt on W. **Topography:** The Mediterranean coastal plain is fertile and well-watered. In the center is the Judean Plateau. A triangular-shaped semi-desert region, the Negev, extends from south of Beersheba to an apex at the head of the Gulf of Aqaba. The eastern border drops sharply into the Jordan Rift Valley, including Lake Tiberias (Sea of Galilee) and the Dead Sea, which is 1,312 ft. below sea level, lowest point on the earth's surface. **Capital:** Jerusalem. Most countries maintain their embassy in Tel Aviv. **Cities** (1988 est.): Jerusalem 493,000; Tel Aviv-Yafo 317,000; Haifa 222,000.

Government: Type: Parliamentary democracy. **Head of state:** Pres. Chaim Herzog; b. Sept. 17, 1918; in office: May 5, 1983. **Head of government:** Prime Min. Yitzhak Shamir; b. 1915; in office: June 11, 1990. **Local divisions:** 6 administrative districts. **Defense:** 16.6% of GNP (1987).

Economy: Industries: Diamond cutting, textiles, electronics, machinery, food processing. **Chief crops:** Citrus fruit, vegetables. **Minerals:** Potash, copper, phosphate, manganese, sulphur. **Crude oil reserves** (1987): 700,000 mln. bbls. **Arable land:** 17%. **Livestock** (1989): cattle: 325,000; sheep: 375,000. **Fish catch** (1989): 18,000 metric tons. **Electricity prod.** (1988): 17.3 bln. kwh. **Labor force:** 6% agric.; 23% ind., 30% public services.

Finance: Monetary unit: Shekel (May 1991: 2.36 = $1 US). **GNP** (1989): $44.1 bln. **Per capita income** (1989): $9,460. **Imports** (1990): $16.5 bln.; partners: U.S. 16%, W. Ger. 13%, UK 9%. **Exports** (1990): $11.7 bln.; partners: U.S. 30%, W. Ger. 5%, UK 7%. **Tourists** (1988): receipts $1.3 bln. **National budget** (1987): $23 bln. expenditures. **International reserves less gold** (Jan. 1991): $6.5 bln. **Gold:** 823,000 oz t. **Consumer prices** (change in 1990): 17.2%.

Transport: Railway traffic (1989): 173 mln. passenger-km. **Motor vehicles:** in use (1989): 696,000 passenger cars, 140,000 comm. vehicles. **Civil aviation** (1989): 7.7 mln. passenger-km; 6 airports with scheduled flights. **Chief ports:** Haifa, Ashdod, Eilat.

Communications: Television sets: 1 per 6.9 persons. **Radios:** 1 per 2.2 persons. **Telephones:** 1 per 2.1 persons. **Daily newspaper circ.** (1989): 357 per 1,000 pop.

Health: Life expectancy at birth (1989) Jewish pop. only: 75 male; 79 female. **Births** (per 1,000 pop. 1989): 22. **Deaths** (per 1,000 pop. 1989): 7%. **Natural increase:** 1.5%. **Hospital beds:** 1 per 161 persons. **Physicians:** 1 per 345 persons. **Infant mortality** (per 1,000 live births 1989): 9.

Education (1989): **Literacy:** 88% (Jewish), 70% (Arab).

Major International Organizations: UN (GATT).

Embassy: 3541 International Dr. NW 20008; 364-5500.

Occupying the SW corner of the ancient Fertile Crescent, Israel contains some of the oldest known evidence of agriculture and of primitive town life. A more advanced civilization emerged in the 3d millenium BC. The Hebrews probably arrived early in the 2d millenium BC. Under King David and his successors (c.1000 BC-597 BC), Judaism was developed and secured. After conquest by Babylonians, Persians, and Greeks, an independent Jewish kingdom was revived, 168 BC, but Rome took effective control in the next century, suppressed Jewish revolts in 70 AD and 135 AD, and renamed Judea Palestine, after the earlier coastal inhabitants, the Philistines.

Arab invaders conquered Palestine in 636. The Arabic language and Islam prevailed within a few centuries, but a Jewish minority remained. The land was ruled from the 11th century as a part of non-Arab empires by Seljuks, Mamluks, and Ottomans (with a crusader interval, 1098-1291).

After 4 centuries of Ottoman rule, during which the population declined to a low of 350,000 (1785), the land was taken in 1917 by Britain, which in the Balfour Declaration that year pledged to support a Jewish national homeland there, as foreseen by the

Zionists. In 1920 a British Palestine Mandate was recognized; in 1922 the land east of the Jordan was detached.

Jewish immigration, begun in the late 19th century, swelled in the 1930s with refugees from the Nazis; heavy Arab immigration from Syria and Lebanon also occurred. Arab opposition to Jewish immigration turned violent in 1920, 1921, 1929, and 1936. The UN General Assembly voted in 1947 to partition Palestine into an Arab and a Jewish state. Britain withdrew in May 1948.

Israel was declared an independent state May 14, 1948; the Arabs rejected partition. Egypt, Jordan, Syria, Lebanon, Iraq, and Saudi Arabia invaded, but failed to destroy the Jewish state, which gained territory. Separate armistices with the Arab nations were signed in 1949; Jordan occupied the West Bank, Egypt occupied Gaza, but neither granted Palestinian autonomy.

After persistent terrorist raids, Israel invaded Egypt's Sinai, Oct. 29, 1956, aided briefly by British and French forces. A UN cease-fire was arranged Nov. 6.

An uneasy truce between Israel and the Arab countries, supervised by a UN Emergency Force, prevailed until May 19, 1967, when the UN force withdrew at the demand of Egypt's Pres. Nasser. Egyptian forces reoccupied the Gaza Strip and closed the Gulf of Aqaba to Israeli shipping. In a 6-day war that started June 5, the Israelis took the Gaza Strip, occupied the Sinai Peninsula to the Suez Canal, and captured Old Jerusalem, Syria's Golan Heights, and Jordan's West Bank. The fighting was halted June 10 by UN-arranged cease-fire agreements.

Egypt and Syria attacked Israel, Oct. 6, 1973 (Yom Kippur, most solemn day on the Jewish calendar). Israel counter-attacked, driving the Syrians back, and crossed the Suez Canal.

A cease fire took effect Oct. 24; a UN peace-keeping force went to the area. A disengagement agreement was signed Jan. 18, 1974. Israel withdrew from the canal's W bank. A second withdrawal was completed in 1976; Israel returned the Sinai to Egypt in 1982.

Israeli forces raided Entebbe, Uganda, July 3, 1976, and rescued 103 hostages seized by Arab and German terrorists.

In 1977, the conservative opposition, led by Menachem Begin, was voted into office for the first time. Egypt's Pres. Sadat visited Jerusalem Nov. 1977 and on Mar. 26, 1979. Egypt and Israel signed a formal peace treaty, ending 30 years of war, and establishing diplomatic relations.

Israel invaded S. Lebanon, March 1978, following a Lebanon-based terrorist attack in Israel. Israel withdrew in favor of a 6,000-man UN force, but continued to aid Christian militiamen. Violence on the Israeli-occupied West Bank rose in 1982 when Israel announced plans to build new Jewish settlements. Israel affirmed the entire city of Jerusalem as its capital, July, 1980, encompassing the annexed Arab East Jerusalem.

On June 7, 1981, Israeli jets destroyed an Iraqi atomic reactor near Baghdad that, Israel claimed, would have enabled Iraq to manufacture nuclear weapons.

Israeli jets bombed Palestine Liberation Organization (PLO) strongholds in Lebanon April, May 1982. In reaction to the wounding of the Israeli ambassador to Great Britain, Israeli forces in a coordinated land, sea, and air attack invaded Lebanon, June 6, to destroy PLO strongholds in that country. Israeli and Syrian forces engaged in the Bekka Valley, June 9, but quickly agreed to a truce. Israeli forces encircled Beirut June 14. Following massive Israeli bombing of West Beirut, the PLO agreed to evacuate the city.

Israeli troops entered West Beirut after newly-elected Lebanese president Bashir Gemayel was assassinated on Sept. 14. Israel received widespread condemnation when Lebenese Christian forces, Sept. 16, entered 2 West Beirut refugee camps and slaughtered hundreds of Palestinian refugees.

In 1989, violence continued over the Israeli military occupation of the West Bank and Gaza Strip; protesters and Israeli troops clashed frequently. Israeli police and stone-throwing Palestinians clashed, Oct. 8, 1990, around the al-Aqsa mosque on the Temple Mount in Jerusalem. Some 20 Palestinians died and 150 were injured.

The Knesset approved a new right-wing coalition government led by Prime Minister Yitzhak Shamir, June 11, 1990, following a 3-month political crisis that began with the fall of the previous "National Unity" government of Shamir and the Labor Party of Shimon Peres.

During the Persian Gulf War, Iraq fired a series of scud missiles at Israel; most were intercepted by U.S. Patriot missiles. Israel agreed in Aug. 1991 to take part in a U.S.-Soviet sponsored Middle East peace conference.

Italy

Italian Republic

Repubblica Italiana

People: Population (1990 est.): 57,657,000. **Age distrib.** (%): 0–14: 17.8; 15–59: 62.8; 60+: 19.4. **Pop. density:** 493 per sq. mi. **Urban** (1988): 67%. **Ethnic groups:** Italians, small minorities of Germans, Slovenes, Albanians. **Languages:** Italian. **Religions:** Predominantly Roman Catholic.

Geography: Area: 116,303 sq. mi., about the size of Florida and Georgia combined. **Location:** In S Europe, jutting into Mediterranean S. **Neighbors:** France on W, Switzerland, Austria on N, Yugoslavia on E. **Topography:** Occupies a long boot-shaped peninsula, extending SE from the Alps into the Mediterranean, with the islands of Sicily and Sardinia offshore. The alluvial Po Valley drains most of N. The rest of the country is rugged and mountainous, except for intermittent coastal plains, like the Campania, S of Rome. Apennine Mts. run down through center of peninsula. **Capital:** Rome. **Cities** (1989 est.): Rome 2.8 mln.; Milan 1.4 mln.; Naples 1.2 mln.; Turin 1.0 mln.

Government: Type: Republic. **Head of state:** Pres. Francesco Cossiga; b. July 26, 1929; in office: July 9, 1985; **Head of government:** Prime Min. Giulio Andreotti; in office: July 23, 1989. **Local divisions:** 20 regions with some autonomy, 94 provinces. **Defense:** 2.1% of GNP (1989).

Economy: Industries: Steel, machinery, autos, textiles, shoes, machine tools, chemicals. **Chief crops:** Grapes, olives, citrus fruits, vegetables, wheat, rice. **Minerals:** Mercury, potash, sulphur. **Crude oil reserves** (1987): 951 mln. bbls. **Arable land:** 32%. **Livestock** (1989): cattle: 8.7 mln.; pigs: 9.3 mln.; sheep: 11.6 mln. **Fish catch** (1989): 395,000 metric tons. **Electricity prod.** (1988): 197 bln. kwh. **Crude steel prod.** (1988): 23.6 mln. metric tons. **Labor force:** 10% agric.; 32% ind. and comm.; 58% services and govt.

Finance: Monetary unit: Lira (June 1991: 1,272 = $1 US). **Gross national product** (1989): $865 bln. **Per capita income** (1989): $15,052. **Imports** (1990): $181 bln.; partners: W. Ger. 20%, Fr. 15%, U.S. 7%. **Exports** (1990): $170 bln.; partners: W. Ger. 16%, Fr. 15%, U.S. 10%, UK 6%. **Tourists** (1989): receipts $11.4 bln. **National budget** (1987): $311 bln. expenditures. **International reserves less gold** (Apr. 1991): $61 bln. **Gold:** 66.67 mln. oz t. **Consumer prices** (change in 1990): 6.5%.

Transport: Railway traffic (1989): 43 bln. passenger-km. **Motor vehicles:** in use (1987): 24.3 mln. passenger cars, 1.9 mln. comm. vehicles. **Civil aviation** (1989): 21.0 bln. passenger-km; 34 airports. **Chief ports:** Genoa, Venice, Trieste, Taranto, Naples, La Spezia.

Communications: Television sets: 1 per 3.9 persons. **Radios:** 1 per 3.9 persons. **Telephones:** 1 per 2.0 persons. **Daily newspaper circ.** (1987): 121 per 1,000 pop.

Health: Life expectancy at birth (1989): 73 male; 80 female. **Births** (per 1,000 pop. 1989): 11. **Deaths** (per 1,000 pop. 1989): 10. **Natural increase:** .1%. **Hospital beds:** 1 per 127 persons. **Physicians:** 1 per 233 persons. **Infant mortality** (per 1,000 live births 1989): 8.

Education (1991): **Literacy:** 98%. **Years compulsory:** 8.

Major International Organizations: UN and all of its specialized agencies, NATO, OECD, EC.

Embassy: 1601 Fuller St. NW 20009; 328-5500.

Rome emerged as the major power in Italy after 500 BC, dominating the more civilized Etruscans to the N and Greeks to the S. Under the Empire, which lasted until the 5th century AD, Rome ruled most of Western Europe, the Balkans, the Near East, and North Africa. In 1988, archeologists unearthed evidence showing Rome as a dynamic society in the 6th and 7th centuries B.C.

After the Germanic invasions, lasting several centuries, a high civilization arose in the city-states of the N, culminating in the Renaissance. But German, French, Spanish, and Austrian intervention prevented the unification of the country. In 1859 Lombardy came under the crown of King Victor Emmanuel II of Sardinia. By plebiscite in 1860, Parma, Modena, Romagna, and Tuscany joined, followed by Sicily and Naples, and by the Marches and Umbria. The first Italian parliament declared Victor Emmanuel king of Italy Mar. 17, 1861. Mantua and Venetia were added in 1866 as an outcome of the Austro-Prussian war. The Papal States were taken by Italian troops Sept. 20, 1870, on the withdrawal of the French garrison. The states were annexed to the kingdom by plebiscite. Italy recognized the State of Vatican City as independent Feb. 11, 1929.

Fascism appeared in Italy Mar. 23, 1919, led by Benito Mussolini, who took over the government at the invitation of the king Oct. 28, 1922. Mussolini acquired dictatorial powers. He made war on Ethiopia and proclaimed Victor Emmanuel III emperor, defied the sanctions of the League of Nations, joined the Berlin-Tokyo axis, sent troops to fight for Franco against the Republic of Spain and joined Germany in World War II.

After Fascism was overthrown in 1943, Italy declared war on Germany and Japan and contributed to the Allied victory. It surrendered conquered lands and lost its colonies. Mussolini was killed by partisans Apr. 28, 1945.

Victor Emmanuel III abdicated May 9, 1946; his son Humbert II was king until June 10, when Italy became a republic after a referendum, June 2-3.

Reorganization of the Fascist party is forbidden. The cabinet normally represents a coalition of the Christian Democrats, largest of Italy's many parties, and one or 2 other parties.

Italy has enjoyed growth in industry and living standards since World War II, in part due to membership in the Common Market. Italy joined the European Monetary System, 1980. A wave of left-wing political violence began in the late 1970s with kidnappings and assassinations and continued through the 1980s. Christian Dem. leader and former Prime Min. Moro was murdered May 1978 by Red Brigade terrorists.

The Cabinet of Prime Min. Arnaldo Forlani resigned, May 26, 1981, in the wake of revelations that numerous high-ranking officials were members of an illegally secret Masonic lodge. The June 1983 elections saw Bettino Craxi chosen the nation's first Socialist premier. Craxi ended the longest tenure of an Italian leader since World War II by resigning Mar. 1987.

By mid-1991, some 20,000 Albanian refugees had entered Italy as the result of political unrest in their homeland.

Sicily, 9,926 sq. mi., pop. (1988) 5,164,000, is an island 180 by 120 mi., seat of a region that embraces the island of **Pantelleria,** 32 sq. mi., and the **Lipari** group, 44 sq. mi., 63 14,000, including 2 active volcanoes: **Vulcano,** 1,637 ft. and **Stromboli,** 3,038 ft. From prehistoric times Sicily has been settled by various peoples; a Greek state had its capital at Syracuse. Rome took Sicily from Carthage 215 BC. **Mt. Etna,** 11,053 ft. active volcano, is tallest peak.

Sardinia, 9,301 sq. mi., pop. (1988) 1,594,000, lies in the Mediterranean, 115 mi. W of Italy and 7-½ mi. S of Corsica. It is 160 mi. long, 68 mi. wide, and mountainous, with mining of coal, zinc, lead, copper. In 1720 Sardinia was added to the possessions of the Dukes of Savoy in Piedmont and Savoy to form the Kingdom of Sardinia. Giuseppe Garibaldi is buried on the nearby isle of Caprera. **Elba,** 86 sq. mi., lies 6 mi. W of Tuscany. Napoleon I lived in exile on Elba 1814-1815.

Trieste. An agreement, signed Oct. 5, 1954, by Italy and Yugoslavia, confirmed, Nov. 10, 1975, gave Italy provisional administration over the northern section and the seaport of Trieste, and Yugoslavia the part of Istrian peninsula it has occupied.

Jamaica

People: Population (1990 est.): 2,513,000. **Age distrib. (%):** 0–14: 33.7; 15–59: 56.4; 60+: 9.9. **Pop. density:** 556 per sq. mi. **Urban** (1989): 48%. **Ethnic groups:** African 76%, mixed 15%, Chinese, Caucasians, East Indians. **Languages:** English, (official), Jamaican Creole. **Religions:** Protestant 70%.

Geography: Area: 4,232 sq. mi., slightly smaller than Connecticut. **Location:** In West Indies. **Neighbors:** Nearest are Cuba on N, Haiti on E. **Topography:** The country is four-fifths covered by mountains. **Capital:** Kingston. **Cities** (1984 est.): St. Andrew 393,000, Kingston 100,000.

Government: Type: Constitutional monarchy. **Head of state:** Queen Elizabeth II, represented by Gov.-Gen. Florizel A. Glasspole; b. Sept. 25, 1909; in office: Mar. 2, 1973. **Head of government:** Prime Min. Michael N. Manley; in office: Feb. 9, 1989. **Local divisions:** 14 parishes; Kingston and St. Andrew corporate area. **Defense:** 1% of GDP (1989).

Economy: Industries: Rum, molasses, cement, paper, tourism. **Chief crops:** Sugar cane, coffee, bananas, coconuts, citrus fruits. **Minerals:** Bauxite, limestone, gypsum. **Arable land:** 19%. **Livestock** (1989): cattle: 250,000; goats: 440,000. **Electricity prod.** (1988): 2.4 bln. kwh. **Labor force:** 31% agric.; 27% services; 41% ind.

Finance: Monetary unit: Dollar (Apr. 1991: 8.44 = $1 US). **Gross national product** (1988): $2.6 bln. **Per capita GNP** (1988): $1,080. **Imports** (1989): $1.8 bln.; partners: U.S. 44%, UK 6%. **Exports** (1989): $967 mln.; partners: U.S. 40%, UK 13%, Can. 16%. **Tourists** (1988): receipts: $525 mln. **National budget** (1989): $1.0 bln. **International reserves less gold** (Feb. 1991): $178 mln. **Consumer prices** (change in 1990): 21.0%.

Transport: Railway traffic (1989): 36 mln. passenger-km. **Motor vehicles:** in use (1988): 52,000 passenger cars, 23,000 comm. vehicles. **Civil aviation** (1989): 1.9 bln. passenger km.; 6 airports with scheduled flights. **Chief ports:** Kingston, Montego Bay.

Communications: Television sets: 1 per 5.9 persons. **Radios:** 1 per 2.6 persons. **Telephones:** 1 per 13 persons. **Daily newspaper circ.** (1989): 51 per 1,000 pop.

Health: Life expectancy at birth (1989): 75 male; 78 female. **Births** (per 1,000 pop. 1989): 27. **Deaths:** (per 1,000 pop. 1989). **Natural increase:** 2.2%. **Hospital beds:** 1 per 414 persons. **Physicians:** 1 per 5,723 persons. **Infant mortality** (per 1,000 live births 1989): 17.

Education (1990): **Literacy:** 82%. Compulsory to age 14.

Major International Organizations: UN (World Bank, GATT), OAS.

Embassy: 1850 K St. NW 20008; 452-0660.

Jamaica was visited by Columbus, 1494, and ruled by Spain (under whom Arawak Indians died out) until seized by Britain, 1655. Jamaica won independence Aug. 6, 1962.

In 1974 Jamaica sought an increase in taxes paid by U.S. and Canadian companies which mine bauxite on the island. The socialist government acquired 50% ownership of the companies' Jamaican interests in 1976, and was reelected that year. Rudimentary welfare state measures were passed. Relations with the U.S. improved greatly in the 1980s following the election of Edward Seaga.

Hurricane Gilbert struck Jamaica Sept. 12, 1988, killing some 45 and causing extensive damage including half the nation's houses.

Japan

Nippon

People: Population (1990 est.): 123,778,000. **Age distrib. (%):** 0–14: 18.4; 15–59: 64.3; 60+: 17.3. **Pop. density:** 844 per sq. mi. **Urban** (1985): 76.7%. **Language:** Japanese. **Ethnic groups:** Japanese 99.4%, Korean 0.5%. **Religions:** Buddhism, Shintoism shared by large majority.

Geography: Area: 145,856 sq. mi., slightly smaller than California. **Location:** Archipelago off E. coast of Asia. **Neighbors:** USSR on N, S. Korea on W. **Topography:** Japan consists of 4 main islands: Honshu ("mainland"), 87,805 sq. mi.; Hokkaido, 30,144 sq. mi.; Kyushu, 14,114 sq. mi.; and Shikoku, 7,049 sq. mi. The coast, deeply indented, measures 16,654 mi. The northern islands are a continuation of the Sakhalin Mts. The Kunlun range of China continues into southern islands, the ranges meeting in the Japanese Alps. In a vast transverse fissure crossing Honshu E-W rises a group of volcanoes, mostly extinct or inactive, including 12,388 ft. Fuji-San (Fujiyama) near Tokyo. **Capital:** Tokyo. **Cities** (1989 est.): Tokyo 8.1 mln.; Osaka 2.5 mln.; Yokohama 3.1 mln.; Nagoya 2.1 mln.; Kyoto 1.4 mln.; Kobe 1.4 mln.; Sapporo 1.6 mln.; Kitakyushu 1 mln.; Kawasaki 1.1 mln; Fukuoka 1.2 mln.

Government: Type: Parliamentary democracy. **Head of state:** Emp. Akihito; b. Dec. 23, 1933; in office: Jan. 7, 1989. **Head of government:** Prime Min. Toshiki Kaifu; b. Jan. 2, 1931; in office: Aug. 9, 1989. **Local divisions:** 47 prefectures. **Defense:** Less than 1% of GNP (1987).

Economy: Industries: Electrical & electronic equip., autos, machinery, chemicals. **Chief crops:** Rice, grains, vegetables, fruits. **Minerals:** negligible. **Crude oil reserves** (1985): 26 mln. bbls. **Arable land:** 13%. **Livestock** (1989): cattle: 4.6 mln.; pigs: 11.7 mln. **Fish catch** (1989): 12.7 mln. metric tons. **Electricity prod.** (1988): 696 bln. kwh. **Crude steel prod.** (1987): 98.5 mln. metric tons. **Labor force:** 8% agric.; 32% manuf. & mining; 43% services & trade.

Finance: Monetary unit: Yen (June 1991: 137 = $1 US). **Gross national product** (1989): $1.8 trl. **Per capita GNP** (1989): $15,030. **Imports** (1990): $235 bln.; partners: U.S. 22%,

Middle East 26%, SE Asia 22%, EC 6%. **Exports** (1990): $287 bln.; **partners:** U.S. 33%, EC 20%, SE Asia 23%. **Tourists** (1989): $3.1 bln. receipts. **National budget** (1989): $470. bln. expenditures. **International reserves less gold** (Mar. 1991): $72 bln. **Gold:** 24.23 mln. oz. t. **Consumer prices** (change in 1990): 3.1%.

Transport: Railway traffic (1988): 361 bln. passenger-km. **Motor vehicles:** in use (1989): 30.7 mln. passenger cars, 21.4 mln. **Civil aviation** (1989): 90.3 bln. passenger-km; 65 airports with scheduled flights. **Chief ports:** Yokohama, Tokyo, Kobe, Osaka, Nagoya, Chiba, Kawasaki, Hakodate.

Communications: Television sets: 1 per 4.1 persons. **Radios:** 1 per 1.3 persons. **Telephones:** 1 per 1.8 persons. **Daily newspaper circ.** (1988): 569 per 1,000 pop.

Health: Life expectancy at birth (1989): 76 male; 82 female. **Births** (per 1,000 pop. 1989): 11. **Deaths** (per 1,000 pop. 1989): 7. **Natural increase:** 0.5%. **Hospital beds:** 1 per 77 persons. **Physicians:** 1 per 668 persons. **Infant mortality** (per 1,000 live births 1989): 5.

Education (1991): **Literacy:** 99%. Most attend school for 12 years.

Major International Organizations: UN (IMF, GATT, ILO), OECD.

Embassy: 2520 Massachusetts Ave. NW 20008; 939-6700.

According to Japanese legend, the empire was founded by Emperor Jimmu, 660 BC, but earliest records of a unified Japan date from 1,000 years later. Chinese influence was strong in the formation of Japanese civilization. Buddhism was introduced before the 6th century.

A feudal system, with locally powerful noble families and their samurai warrior retainers, dominated from 1192. Central power was held by successive families of shoguns (military dictators), 1192-1867, until recovered by the Emperor Meiji, 1868. The Portuguese and Dutch had minor trade with Japan in the 16th and 17th centuries; U.S. Commodore Matthew C. Perry opened it to U.S. trade in a treaty ratified 1854. Japan fought China, 1894-95, gaining Taiwan. After war with Russia, 1904-05, Russia ceded S half of Sakhalin and gave concessions in China. Japan annexed Korea 1910. In World War I Japan ousted Germany from Shantung, took over German Pacific islands. Japan took Manchuria 1931, started war with China 1932. Japan launched war against the U.S. by attack on Pearl Harbor Dec. 7, 1941. Japan surrendered Aug. 14, 1945.

In a new constitution adopted May 3, 1947, Japan renounced the right to wage war; the emperor gave up claims to divinity; the Diet became the sole law-making authority.

The U.S. and 48 other non-communist nations signed a peace treaty and the U.S. a bilateral defense agreement with Japan, in San Francisco Sept. 8, 1951, restoring Japan's sovereignty as of April 28, 1952.

On June 26, 1968, the U.S. returned to Japanese control the Bonin Is., the Volcano Is. (including Iwo Jima) and Marcus Is. On May 15, 1972, Okinawa, the other Ryukyu Is. and the Daito Is. were returned to Japan by the U.S.; it was agreed the U.S. would continue to maintain military bases on Okinawa.

Industrialization was begun in the late 19th century. After World War II, Japan emerged as one of the most powerful economies in the world, and as a leader in technology.

The U.S. and EC member nations have criticized Japan for its restrictive policy on imports which has given Japan a substantial trade surplus.

In Apr. 1987, the U.S. imposed 100% tariffs on Japanese electronics imports in retaliation for what the U.S. considered various unfair trade practices.

The Recruit scandal, the nation's worst political scandal since World War II, which involved illegal political donations and stock trading, led to the resignation of Premier Noboru Takeshita in May 1989.

Premier Toshiki Kaifu visited the U.S. Mar. 2-3, 1990, and met with Pres. Bush in an effort to ease the increasing economic tension between the 2 countries over the long-standing trade imbalance. A series of scandals rocked Japan's financial sector in 1991; one involved the largest bank, another the 4 largest securities firms.

Jordan

Hashemite Kingdom of Jordan

al Mamlaka al Urduniya al Hashemiyah

Population (1990 est.): 3,065,000. **Age distrib.** (%): 0-14: 48.1; 15-59: 46.9; 60+: 4.0. **Pop. density:** 80 per sq. mi. **Urban** (1986): 70%. **Ethnic groups:** Arab 98%. **Languages:** Arabic (official). **Religions:** Sunni Moslem 92%, Christian 8%.

Geography: Area: 37,737 sq. mi., slightly larger than Indiana. **Location:** In W Asia. **Neighbors:** Israel on W, Saudi Arabia on S, Iraq on E, Syria on N. **Topography:** About 88% of Jordan is arid. Fertile areas are in W. Only port is on short Aqaba Gulf coast. Country shares Dead Sea (1,296 ft. below sea level) with Israel. **Capital:** Amman. **Cities** (1989 est.): Amman 936,000; az-Zarqa 318,000; Irbid 161,000.

Government: Type: Constitutional monarchy. **Head of state:** King Hussein I; b. Nov. 14, 1935; in office: Aug. 11, 1952. **Head of government:** Prime Min. Tahir Al Masri; in office: June 17, 1991. **Local divisions:** 8 governorates. **Defense:** 13% of GNP (1987).

Economy: Industries: Textiles, cement, food processing. **Chief crops:** Grains, olives, vegetables, fruits. **Minerals:** Phosphate, potash. **Arable land:** 5%. **Electricity prod.** (1988): 3.3 bln. kwh. **Labor force:** 20% agric. 20% manuf. & mining.

Finance: Monetary unit: Dinar (Mar. 1991: 0.66 = $1 US). **Gross national product** (1989): $3.9 bln. **Imports** (1989): $2.1 bln.; **partners:** Saudi Ar. 6%, U.S. 11%, Jap. 8%. **Exports** (1989): $1.1 bln.; **partners:** Saudi Ar. 12%, Ind. 13%, Iraq. 18%. **Tourists** (1988): receipts: $621 mln. **National budget** (1989): $2.3 bln. expenditures. **International reserves less gold** (Mar. 1991): $851 mln. **Gold:** 754,000 oz t. **Consumer prices** (change in 1990): 16.2%.

Transport: Motor vehicles: in use (1989): 164,000 passenger cars, 58,000 comm. vehicles. **Civil aviation** (1989): 3.6 bln. passenger-km; 3 airports with scheduled flights. **Chief ports:** Aqaba.

Communications: Television sets: 1 per 12 persons. **Radios:** 1 per 2.7 persons. **Telephones:** 1 per 10 persons. **Daily newspaper circ.** (1989): 68 per 1,000 pop.

Health: Life expectancy at birth (1989): 67 male; 71 female. **Births** (per 1,000 pop. 1989): 42.7. **Deaths** (per 1,000 pop. 1989): 6. **Natural increase:** 3.6%. **Hospital beds:** 1 per 523 persons. **Physicians:** 1 per 881 persons. **Infant mortality** (per 1,000 live births 1989): 55.

Education (1989): **Literacy:** 71%.

Major International Organizations: UN (WHO, IMF), Arab League.

Embassy: 3504 International Dr. NW 20008; 966-2664.

From ancient times to 1922 the lands to the E of the Jordan were culturally and politically united with the lands to the W. Arabs conquered the area in the 7th century; the Ottomans took control in the 16th. Britain's 1920 Palestine Mandate covered both sides of the Jordan. In 1921, Abdullah, son of the ruler of Hejaz in Arabia, was installed by Britain as emir of an autonomous Transjordan, covering two-thirds of Palestine. An independent kingdom was proclaimed, 1946.

During the 1948 Arab-Israeli war the West Bank and old city of Jerusalem were added to the kingdom, which changed its name to Jordan. All these territories were lost to Israel in the 1967 war, which swelled the number of Arab refugees on the East Bank. A 1974 Arab summit conference designated the Palestine Liberation Organization as the sole representative of Arabs on the West Bank. Jordan accepted the move, and was granted an annual subsidy by Arab oil states.

In 1988 Jordan cut legal and administrative ties with the Israeli-occupied West Bank. In Apr. 1989, riots broke out over price increases imposed under an agreement with the International Monetary Fund.

Some 700,000 refugees entered Jordan following Iraq's invasion of Kuwait, Aug. 1990. Jordan was viewed as supporting Iraq during the Gulf crisis, which resulted in a suspension of U.S. military aid.

Kenya

Republic of Kenya

Jamhuri ya Kenya

People: Population (1990 est.): 25,393,000. **Age distrib.** (%): 0–14: 51.2; 15–59: 45.4; 60+: 3.4. **Pop. density:** 105 per sq. mi. **Urban** (1986): 20%. **Ethnic groups:** Kikuyu 21%, Luo 13%, Luhya 14%, Kelenjin 11%, Kamba 11%, others, including Asians, Arabs, Europeans. **Languages:** Swahili (official), Kikuyu, Luhya, Luo, Meru. **Religions:** Protestant 38%, Roman Catholic 26%, Moslem 6%, others.

Geography: Area: 224,960 sq. mi., slightly smaller than Texas. **Location:** On Indian O. coast of E. Africa. **Neighbors:** Uganda on W, Tanzania on S, Somalia on E, Ethopia, Sudan on N. **Topography:** The northern three-fifths of Kenya is arid. To the S, a low coastal area and a plateau varying from 3,000 to 10,000 ft. The Great Rift Valley enters the country N-S, flanked by high mountains. **Capital:** Nairobi. **Cities** (1987 est.): Nairobi 959,000; Mombasa 401,000.

Government: Type: Republic. **Head of state:** Pres. Daniel arap Moi, b. Sept., 1924; in office: Aug. 22, 1978. **Local divisions:** Nairobi and 7 provinces. **Defense:** 2.4% of GDP (1987).

Economy: Industries: Tourism, light industry, petroleum prods. **Chief crops:** Coffee, · corn, tea, cereals, cotton, sisal. **Minerals:** Gold, limestone, diatomite, salt, barytes, magnesite, felspar, sapphires, fluospar, garnets. **Other resources:** Timber, hides. **Arable land:** 4%. **Livestock** (1989): cattle: 13.4 mln. **Fish catch** (1987): 131,000 metric tons. **Electricity prod.** (1989): 2.8 bln. kwh. **Labor force:** 21% agric.; 21% ind. and commerce; 13% services; 40% public sector.

Finance: Monetary unit: Shilling (Mar. 1991: 26.59 = $1 US). **Gross national product** (1989): $8.7 bln. **Per capita GNP** (1989): $380. **Imports** (1989): $2.1 bln.; partners: UK 14%, W. Ger. 11%, Jap. 11%, Fra. 11%. **Exports** (1989): $970 mln.; partners: W. Ger. 11%, UK 18%, Ugan. 9%. **Tourists** (1988): receipts: $410 mln. **National budget** (1987): $2.6 bln expenditures. **International reserves less gold** (Mar. 1991): $119 mln. **Gold:** 80,000 oz t. **Consumer prices** (change in 1990): 11.7%.

Transport: Motor vehicles: in use (1987): 133,000 passenger cars, 110,000 comm. vehicles. **Civil Aviation** (1988): 753 mln. passenger-km; 16 airports with scheduled flights. **Chief ports:** Mombasa.

Communications: Television sets: 1 per 118 persons. **Radios:** 1 per 12 persons. **Telephones:** 1 per 70 persons. **Daily newspaper circ.** (1986): 16 per 1,000 pop.

Health: Life expectancy at birth (1989): 59 male; 63 female. **Births** (per 1,000 pop. 1989): 51. **Deaths** (per 1,000 pop. 1989): 9. **Natural increase:** 4.2%. **Hospital beds:** 1 per 703 persons. **Physicians:** 1 per 7,174 persons. **Infant mortality** (per 1,000 live births 1989): 70.

Education (1989): **Literacy:** 50%. 86% attend primary school.

Major International Organizations: UN and all of its specialized agencies, OAU, Commonwealth of Nations.

Embassy: 2249 R St. NW 20008; 387-6101.

Arab colonies exported spices and slaves from the Kenya coast as early as the 8th century. Britain obtained control in the 19th century. Kenya won independence Dec. 12, 1963, 4 years after the end of the violent Mau Mau uprising.

Kenya has shown steady growth in industry and agriculture under a modified private enterprise system, and has had a relatively free political life. But stability was shaken in 1974-5, with opposition charges of corruption and oppression.

Kenya has close ties to the West.

Kiribati

Republic of Kiribati

People: Population (1990 est.): 65,000. **Pop. density:** 244 per sq. mi. **Ethnic groups:** nearly all Micronesian, some Polynesians. **Languages:** Gilbertese and English (official). **Religions:** evenly divided between Protestant and Roman Catholic.

Geography: Area: 266 sq. mi., slightly smaller than New York City. **Location:** 33 Micronesian islands (the Gilbert, Line, and Phoenix groups) in the mid-Pacific scattered in a 2-mln. sq. mi. chain around the point where the International Date Line cuts the Equator. **Neighbors:** Nearest are Nauru to SW, Tuvalu and Tokelau Is. to S. **Topography:** except Banaba (Ocean) I., all are low-lying, with soil of coral sand and rock fragments, subject to erratic rainfall. **Capital** (1988): Tarawa 22,000.

Government: Type: Republic. **Head of state and of government:** Pres. Ieremia Tabai, b. Dec. 16, 1950; in office: July 12, 1979.

Economy: Industries: Copra. **Chief crops:** Coconuts, breadfruit, pandanus, bananas, paw paw. **Other resources:** Fish. **Electricity prod.** (1988): 8 mln. kwh.

Finance: Monetary unit: Australian dollar. **Gross national product** (1989): $48 mln.

Transport: Chief port: Tarawa.

Communications: Radios: 1 per 6.8 persons. **Telephones:** 1 per 48 persons.

Health: Hospital beds: 1 per 231 persons. **Physicians:** 1 per 4,094 persons.

Education: Literacy (1985): 90%.

A British protectorate since 1892, the Gilbert and Ellice Islands colony was completed with the inclusion of the Phoenix Islands, 1937. Self-rule was granted 1971; the Ellice Islands separated from the colony 1975 and became independent Tuvalu, 1978. Kiribati (pronounced *Kiribass*) independence was attained July 12, 1979. Under a Treaty of Friendship the U.S. relinquished its claims to several of the Line and Phoenix islands, including Christmas, Canton, and Enderbury.

Tarawa Atoll was the scene of some of the bloodiest fighting in the Pacific during WW II.

North Korea

Democratic People's Republic of Korea

Chosun Minchu-chui Inmin Konghwa-guk

People: Population (1990 est.): 23,059,000. **Pop. density:** 471 per sq. mi. **Urban** (1989): 62%. **Ethnic groups:** Korean, **Languages:** Korean. **Religions:** activities almost nonexistent; traditionally Buddhism, Confucianism, Chondokyo.

Geography: Area: 46,540 sq. mi., slightly smaller than Mississippi. **Location:** In northern E. Asia. **Neighbors:** China, USSR on N, S. Korea on S. **Topography:** Mountains and hills cover nearly all the country, with narrow valleys and small plains in between. The N and the E coast are the most rugged areas. **Capital:** Pyongyang. **Cities** (1985 est.): Pyongyang 2,639,000.

Government: Type: Communist state. **Head of state:** Pres. Kim Il-Sung; b. Apr. 15, 1912; in office: Dec. 28, 1972. **Head of government:** Premier Yong Hyong Muk; in office: Dec. 12, 1988. **Head of Communist Party:** Gen. Sec. Kim Il-Sung; in office: 1945. **Local divisions:** 9 provinces, 3 special cities. **Defense** (1988): 24% of GNP.

Economy: Industries: Textiles, petrochemicals, food processing. **Chief crops:** Corn, potatoes, fruits, vegetables, rice. **Minerals:** Coal, lead tungsten, graphite, magnesite, iron, copper, gold, phosphate, salt, fluorspar. **Arable land:** 19%. **Livestock** (1989): cattle: 1.2 mln; pigs: 3.1 mln. **Fish catch** (1988): 1.8 mln. metric tons. **Crude steel prod.** (1987) 6.1 mln. metric tons. **Electricity prod.** (1988): 41 bln. kwh. **Labor force:** 48% agric.

Finance: Monetary unit: Won (Mar. 1991): 0.97 = $1 US). **Gross national product** (1988): $20 bln. **Imports** (1988): $3.1 bln.; partners: China 17%, USSR 36%, Jap. 19%. **Exports** (1988): $2.4 bln.; partners: USSR 43% China 13%, Jap. 15%.

Communications: Television sets: 1 per 90 persons. **Radios:** 1 per 6 persons.

Transport: Chief ports: Chonglin, Hamhung, Nampo.

Health: Life expectancy at birth (1989): 67 male; 73 female. **Births** (per 1,000 pop. 1989): 29. **Deaths** (per 1,000 pop. 1989): 5. **Natural increase:** 2.4%. **Hospital beds:** 1 per 74 persons. **Physicians:** 1 per 370 persons. **Infant mortality** (per 1,000 live births, 1989): 32.

Education (1989): **Literacy:** 99%. **Years compulsory:** 11.

The Democratic People's Republic of Korea was founded May 1, 1948, in the zone occupied by Russian troops after World War II. Its armies tried to conquer the south, 1950. After 3 years of fighting with Chinese and U.S. intervention, a cease-fire was proclaimed.

Industry, begun by the Japanese during their 1910-45 occupation, and nationalized in the 1940s, had grown substantially, using N. Korea's abundant mineral and hydroelectric resources.

South Korea

Republic of Korea

Taehan Min'guk

People: Population (1990 est.): 43,919,000. **Age distrib. (%):** 0–14: 27.3; 15–59: 65.5; 60+: 7.2. **Pop. density:** 1,189 per sq. mi. **Urban** (1988): 68%. **Ethnic groups:** Korean. **Languages:** Korean. **Religions:** Christian 43%, Buddhist 18%.

Geography: Area: 38,025 sq. mi., slightly larger than Indiana. **Location:** In Northern E. Asia. **Neighbors:** N. Korea on N. **Topography:** The country is mountainous, with a rugged east coast. The western and southern coasts are deeply indented, with many islands and harbors. **Capital:** Seoul. **Cities** (1990 est.): Seoul 10.7 mln.; Pusan 3,800,000; Taegu 2,200,000; Inchon 1,600,000; Kwangju 1,200,000; Taejon 1,000,000.

Government: Type: Republic, with power centralized in a strong executive. **Head of state:** Pres. Roh Tae Woo; b. 1932; in office: Feb. 25, 1988. **Head of government:** Prime Min. Chung Won Shik; in office: May 24, 1991. **Local divisions:** 9 provinces and Seoul, Pusan, Inchon, and Taegu. **Defense:** 5.8% of GNP (1987).

Economy: Industries: Electronics, ships, textiles, clothing, motor vehicles. **Chief crops:** Rice, barley, vegetables, wheat. **Minerals:** Tungsten, coal, graphite. **Arable land:** 22%. **Livestock** (1987): cattle: 2.8 mln.; pigs: 3.3 mln. **Fish catch:** (1988): 3.2 mln. metric tons. **Electricity prod.** (1988): 85.0 bln. kwh. **Crude steel prod.** (1987): 16.7 mln. metric tons. **Labor force:** 21% agric.; 27% manuf. & mining; 52% services.

Finance: Monetary unit: Won (Mar. 1991: 724 = $1 US). **Gross national product** (1988): $171 bln. **Per capita income** (1986): $2,180. **Imports** (1990): $69 bln.; partners: Jap. 33%, U.S. 21%. **Exports** (1990): $64 bln.; partners: U.S. 40%, Jap. 15%. **Tourists** (1988): receipts: $1.3 bln. **National budget** (1988): $22.0 bln. expenditures. **International reserves less gold** (Mar. 1991): $13 bln. **Gold:** 320,000 oz t. **Consumer prices** (change in 1990): 8.6%.

Transport: Railway traffic (1988): 24 bln. passenger-km. **Motor vehicles:** in use (1988): 975,000 passenger cars, 748,000 comm. vehicles. **Civil aviation** (1989): 18.1 bln. passenger-km; 10 airlines with scheduled flights. **Chief ports:** Pusan, Inchon.

Communications: Television sets: 1 per 4.9 persons. **Radios:** 1 per 1.0 persons. **Telephones:** 1 per 4.1 persons. **Daily newspaper circ.** (1986): 24 per 1,000 pop.

Health: Life expectancy at birth (1989): 66 male; 73 female. **Births** (per 1,000 pop. 1989): 20. **Deaths** (per 1,000 pop. 1989): 6. **Natural increase:** 1.4%. **Hospital beds:** 1 per 487 persons. **Physicians:** 1 per 1,216 persons. **Infant mortality** (per 1,000 live births 1989): 25.0.

Education (1989): **Literacy:** 92%. **Attendance:** High school 90%, college 14%.

Embassy: 2320 Massachusetts Ave. NW 20008; 939-5600.

Korea, once called the Hermit Kingdom, has a recorded history since the 1st century BC. It was united in a kingdom under the Silla Dynasty, 668 AD. It was at times associated with the Chinese empire; the treaty that concluded the Sino-Japanese war of 1894-95 recognized Korea's complete independence. In 1910 Japan forcibly annexed Korea as Chosun.

At the Potsdam conference, July, 1945, the 38th parallel was designated as the line dividing the Soviet and the American occupation. Russian troops entered Korea Aug. 10, 1945, U.S. troops entered Sept. 8, 1945. The Soviet military organized socialists and communists and blocked efforts to let the Koreans unite their country. *(See Index for Korean War.)*

The South Koreans formed the Republic of Korea in May 1948 with Seoul as the capital. Dr. Syngman Rhee was chosen president but a movement spearheaded by college students forced his resignation Apr. 26, 1960.

In an army coup May 16, 1961, Gen. Park Chung Hee became chairman of the ruling junta. He was elected president, 1963; a 1972 referendum allowed him to be reelected for 6 year terms unlimited times. Park was assassinated by the chief of the Korean CIA, Oct. 26, 1979. The calm of the new government was halted by the rise of Gen. Chun Doo Hwan, head of the military intelligence, who reinstated martial law, and reverted South Korea to the police state it was under Park.

In July 1972 South and North Korea agreed on a common goal of reunifying the 2 nations by peaceful means. But there had been no sign of a thaw in relations between the two regimes until 1985 when they agreed to discuss economic issues. In 1988, radical students demanding reunification clashed with police.

On June 10, 1987, middle class office workers, shopkeepers, and business executives joined students in antigovernment protests in Seoul. They were protesting President Chun's decision to choose his successor and not allow the next president to be chosen by direct vote of the people. Following weeks of rioting and violence, Chun, July 1, agreed to permit election of the next president by direct popular vote and other constitutional reforms. In Dec., Roh Tae Woo was elected president. In 1990, the nation's 3 largest political parties merged; some 100,000 students demonstrated, charging that the merger was undemocratic.

Kuwait

State of Kuwait

Dowlat al-Kuwait

People: Population (1990 est.): 2,080,000. **Age distrib. (%):** 0–14: 40.2; 15–59: 57.6; 60+: 2.3. **Pop. density:** 285 per sq. mi. **Urban** (1986): 90%. **Ethnic groups:** Kuwaiti 39%, other Arab 39%, Iranians, Indians, Pakistanis. **Languages:** Arabic, (official). **Religions:** Moslem 85%.

Geography: Area: 6,880 sq. mi., slightly smaller than New Jersey. **Location:** In Middle East, at N end of Persian Gulf. **Neighbors:** Iraq on N, Saudi Arabia on S. **Topography:** The country is flat, very dry, and extremely hot. **Capital:** Kuwait. **Cities** (1985 est.): Hawalli 145,000; as-Salimiyah 153,000.

Government: Type: Constitutional monarchy. **Head of state:** Emir Shaikh Jabir al-Ahmad al-Jabir as-Sabah; b. 1928; in office: Jan. 1, 1978. **Head of government:** Prime Min. Shaikh Saad Abdulla as-Salim as-Sabah; in office: Feb. 8, 1978. **Local divisions:** 4 governorates. **Defense:** 5.2% of GNP (1987).

Economy: Industries: Oil products. **Minerals:** Oil, gas. **Crude oil reserves** (1990): 94 bln. barrels. **Cultivated land:** 1%. **Electricity prod.** (1988): 19.5 bln. kwh. **Labor force:** social services 45%; construction 20%.

Finance: Monetary unit: Dinar (Nov. 1990: 1.00 = $3.45 US). **Gross national product** (1989): $33.0 bln. **Per capita GNP** (1989): $16,380. **Imports** (1989): $6.1 bln.; partners: Jap. 21%, U.S. 9%. **Exports** (1989): $11.4 bln.; partners: Jap. 16%, It. 10%. **Tourists** (1988): $100 mln. receipts. **National budget** (1988): $10.5 bln. expenditures. **International reserves less gold** (Mar. 1990): $3.1 bln. **Gold:** 2.53 mln. oz t. **Consumer prices** (change in 1989): 3.3%.

Transport: Motor vehicles: in use (1989): 454,000 passenger cars, 114,000 comm. vehicles. **Civil aviation** (1989): 3.8 bln. passenger-km. 1 airport with scheduled flight. **Chief ports:** Mina al-Ahmadi.

Communications: Television sets: 1 per 2.6 persons. **Radios:** 1 per 1.8 persons. **Telephones:** 1 per 6.9 persons. **Daily newspaper circ.** (1988): 223 per 1,000 pop.

Health: Life expectancy at birth (1989): 72 male; 76 female. **Births** (per 1,000 pop. 1989): 30. **Deaths** (per 1,000 pop. 1989): 2.9. **Natural increase:** 2.7%. **Hospital beds:** 1 per 319 persons. **Physician:** 1 per 675 persons. **Infant mortality** (per 1,000 live births 1989): 14.

Education (1989): **Literacy:** 71%. **Years compulsory:** 8.

Major International Organizations: UN (World Bank, IMF, GATT), Arab League, OPEC.

Embassy: 2940 Tilden St. NW 20008; 966-0702.

Kuwait is ruled by the Al-Sabah dynasty, founded 1759. Britain ran foreign relations and defense from 1899 until independence in 1961. The majority of the population is non-Kuwaiti, with many Palestinians, and cannot vote.

Oil, first exported in 1946, is the fiscal mainstay, providing most of Kuwait's income. Oil pays for free medical care, education, and social security. There are no taxes, except customs duties.

Kuwaiti oil tankers have come under frequent attack by Iran because of Kuwait's support of Iraq in the Iran-Iraq War. In July 1987, U.S. Navy warships began escorting Kuwaiti tankers in the Persian Gulf.

In 1988, a Kuwaiti Airways jet was hijacked by pro-Iranian Shiite Moslem terrorists who demanded the release of 17 Shiite terrorists. The ordeal lasted 16 days as Kuwait refused to release the terrorists.

Kuwait was attacked and overrun by Iraqian forces Aug. 2, 1990. The Emir and senior members of the ruling family fled to Saudi Arabia to establish a government in exile. On Aug. 28, Iraq announced that Kuwait was its 19th province.

Following several weeks of aerial attacks on Iraq and Iraqi forces in Kuwait, a U.S.-led coalition began a ground attack Feb. 23, 1991. By Feb. 27, Iraqi forces were routed and Kuwait liberated. (*See Index and Chronology for details.*)

Following liberation, there were reports of abuse of Palestinians and others suspected of collaborating with Iraqi occupiers.

Laos

Lao People's Democratic Republic

Sathalanalat Paxathipatai Paxaxōn Lao

People: Population (1990 est.): 4,024,000. **Pop. density:** 42 per sq. mi. **Urban** (1987): 15%. **Ethnic groups:** Lao 48%, Mon-Khmer tribes 25%, Thai 14%, Meo and Yao 13%, others. **Languages:** Lao (official), Palaung-Wa, Tai. **Religions:** Buddhists 50%, tribal 50%.

Geography: Area: 91,428 sq. mi., slightly larger than Utah. **Location:** In Indochina Peninsula in SE Asia. **Neighbors:** Burma, China on N, Vietnam on E, Cambodia on S, Thailand on W. **Topography:** Landlocked, dominated by jungle. High mountains along the eastern border are the source of the E-W rivers slicing across the country to the Mekong R., which defines most of the western border. **Capital:** Vientiane. **Cities** (1985 cen.): Vientiane 377,000.

Government: Type: Communist. **Head of state:** Pres. Phoumi Vongvichit; in office: Oct. 31, 1986. **Head of government:** Prime Min. Kaysone Phomvihan; b. Dec. 13, 1920; in office: Dec. 2, 1975. **Local divisions:** 17 provinces. **Armed forces: Defense:** 10.5% of GNP (1984).

Economy: Industries: Wood products. **Chief crops:** Rice, corn, tobacco, cotton, opium, citrus fruits, coffee. **Minerals:** Tin. **Other resources:** Forests. **Arable land:** 4%. **Livestock** (1988): pigs: 1.5 mln. **Fish catch** (1988): 20,000 metric tons. **Electricity prod.** (1988): 900 mln. kwh. **Labor force:** 85% agric.; 6% ind.

Finance: Monetary unit: New kip (Dec. 1990): 712 = $1 US). **Gross domestic product** (1989): $693 mln. **Per capita GDP** (1989 est.): $170. **Imports** (1988): $240 mln.; partners: Thai. 45%, Jap. 20%. **Exports** (1988): $52 mln.; partners: Chi. 40%.

Transport: Motor vehicles: in use (1987): 15,800 passenger cars, 3,000 comm. vehicles. **Civil Aviation** (1987): 18 mln. passenger km; 4 airports with scheduled flights.

Communications: Radios: 1 per 7 persons.

Health: Life expectancy at birth (1989): 48 male; 51 female. **Births** (per 1,000 pop. 1989): 38. **Deaths** (per 1,000 pop. 1989): 16. **Natural increase:** 2.2%. **Hospital beds:** 1 per 369 persons. **Physicians:** 1 per 6,495 persons. **Infant mortality** (per 1,000 live births, 1989): 128.

Education: (1991): **Literacy:** 45%.

Major International Organizations: UN (FAO, IMF, WHO). **Embassy:** 2222 S St. NW 20008; 332-6416.

Laos became a French protectorate in 1893, but regained independence as a constitutional monarchy July 19, 1949.

Conflicts among neutralist, communist and conservative factions created a chaotic political situation. Armed conflict increased after 1960.

The 3 factions formed a coalition government in June 1962, with neutralist Prince Souvanna Phouma as premier. A 14-nation conference in Geneva signed agreements, 1962, guaranteeing neutrality and independence. By 1964 the Pathet Lao had withdrawn from the coalition, and, with aid from N. Vietnamese troops, renewed sporadic attacks. U.S. planes bombed the Ho Chi Minh trail, supply line from N. Vietnam to communist forces in Laos and S. Vietnam.

In 1970 the U.S. stepped up air support and military aid. After Pathet Lao military gains, Souvanna Phouma in May 1975 ordered government troops to cease fighting; the Pathet Lao took control. A Lao People's Democratic Republic was proclaimed Dec. 3, 1975.

Latvia

Republic of Latvia

Latvijas Republika

People: Population (1989 cen.): 2,700,000. **Urban** (1990): 70%. **Ethnic groups:** Latvian 54%, Russian 33%.

Geography: Area: 24,595 sq. mi. **Neighbors:** Estonia & Baltic Sea on N., Baltic Sea on W., Lithuania & Byelorussia on S., Russia on E. **Capital:** Riga.

Government: Type: Republic. **Head of state:** Anatolijs Gorbunovs. **Local divisions:** 26 districts, 56 towns, 37 urban settlements.

Economy: Industries: Electric railway passenger cars, paper. **Chief crops:** oats, barley, potatoes. **Livestock** (1989): cattle 1.5 mln.

Transport: Chief port: Riga.

Health: (1988): 13,400 doctors, 37,400 hospital beds.

From 1917, Latvia was occupied by the Soviets, and Germans. The Aug. 1939 Soviet-German agreement assigned it to the Soviet sphere of influence. It was officially accepted as part of the USSR on Aug. 5, 1940. It attempted to establish independence 1990.

During the Soviet coup, Latvia declared independence, Aug. 21, 1991. Several nations extended diplomatic recognition including the U.S. on Sept. 2. (*See Index & Chronology for details.*)

Lebanon

Republic of Lebanon

al-Jumhouriya al-Lubnaniya

People: Population (1990 est.): 3,340,000. **Age distrib. (%):** 0–14: 37.0; 15–59: 55.1; 60+: 7.9. **Pop. density:** 710 per sq. mi. **Urban** (1986): 81%. **Ethnic groups:** Lebanese 82%, Armenians 5%, Palestinian 9%. **Languages:** Arabic (official), French. **Religions:** Moslem 57%; Christian 42%.

Geography: Area: 4,015 sq. mi., smaller than Connecticut. **Location:** On Eastern end of Mediterranean Sea. **Neighbors:** Syria on E. Israel on S. **Topography:** There is a narrow coastal strip, and 2 mountain ranges running N-S enclosing the fertile Beqaa Valley. The Litani R. runs S through the valley, turning W to empty into the Mediterranean. **Capital:** Beirut. **Cities** (1991 est.): Beirut 1,100,000; Tripoli 240,000.

Government: Type: Republic. **Head of state:** Pres. Elias Hrawi; in office: Nov. 24, 1989. **Head of government:** Prime Min. Omar Karami; in office: Dec. 24, 1990. **Local divisions:** 5 governorates. **Defense:** 18% of govt. budget (1984).

Economy: Industries: Trade, food products, textiles, cement, oil products. **Chief crops:** Fruits, olives, tobacco, grapes, vegetables, grains. **Minerals:** Iron. **Arable land:** 21%. **Livestock** (1989): goats: 475,000; sheep: 145,000. **Electricity prod.** (1988): 4.8 bln. kwh. **Labor force:** 11% agric.; 79% ind., comm., services.

Finance: Monetary unit: Pound (June 1991: 921 = $1 US). **Gross national product** (1986): $1.8 bln. **Per capita GNP** (1986): $690. **Imports** (1988): $2.4 bln.; partners: It. 15%, Fr. 10%, U.S. 9%, Saudi Ar. 6%. **Exports** (1988): $709 mln.; partners: Saudi Ar. 33%, Syria 8%, Jor. 6%, Kuw. 8%. **National budget** (1989): $298 mln. expenditures. **International reserves less gold** (Mar. 1991): $550 mln. **Gold:** 9.22 mln. oz t.

Transport: Railway traffic (1982): 5.3 mln. passenger-km. **Motor vehicles:** in use (1982): 460,000 passenger cars, 21,000 comm. vehicles. **Civil aviation** (1988): 891 mln. passenger-km. **Chief ports:** Beirut, Tripoli, Sidon.

Communications: Television sets: 1 per 3.4 persons. **Radios:** 1 per 1.3 persons. **Telephones:** 1 per 18.4 persons. **Daily newspaper circ.** (1986): 211 per 1,000 pop.

Health: Life expectancy at birth (1989): 65 male; 70 female. **Births** (per 1,000 pop. 1989): 28. **Deaths** (per 1,000 pop. 1989): 7. **Natural increase:** 2.1%. **Hospital beds:** 1 per 263 persons. **Physicians:** 1 per 771 persons. **Infant mortality** (per 1,000 live births 1989): 50.

Education: (1991): **Literacy:** 75%. **Years compulsory:** 5; attendance 93%.

Major International Organizations: UN (IMF, ILO, WHO).

Embassy: 2560 28th St. NW 20008; 939-6300.

Formed from 5 former Turkish Empire districts, Lebanon became an independent state Sept. 1, 1920, administered under French mandate 1920-41. French troops withdrew in 1946.

Under the 1943 National Covenant, all public positions were divided among the various religious communities, with Christians in the majority. By the 1970s, Moslems became the majority, and demanded a larger political and economic role.

U.S. Marines intervened, May-Oct. 1958, during a Syrian-aided revolt. Continued raids against Israeli civilians, 1970-75, brought Israeli attacks against guerrilla camps and villages. Israeli troops occupied S. Lebanon, March 1978, and again in Apr. 1980.

An estimated 60,000 were killed and billions of dollars in damage inflicted in a 1975-76 civil war. Palestinian units and leftist Moslems fought against the Maronite militia, the Phalange, and other Christians. Several Arab countries provided political and arms support to the various factions, while Israel aided Christian forces. Up to 15,000 Syrian troops intervened in 1976, and fought Palestinian groups. Arab League troops from several nations tried to impose a cease-fire.

Clashes between Syrian troops and Christian forces erupted, Apr. 1, 1981, bringing to an end the ceasefire. By Apr. 22, fighting had also broken out between two Moslem factions. In July, Israeli air raids on Beirut killed or wounded some 800 persons. A cease-fire between Israel and the Palestinians was concluded July 24, but hostilities continued.

Israeli forces invaded Lebanon June 6, 1982, in a coordinated land, sea, and air attack aimed at crushing strongholds of the Palestine Liberation Organization (PLO). Israeli and Syrian forces engaged in the Bekka Valley. By June 14, Israeli troops had encircled Beirut. On Aug. 21, the PLO evacuated west Beirut following massive Israeli bombings of the city. Israeli troops withdrew from Lebanon in June 1985.

Israeli troops entered west Beirut following the Sept. 14 assassination of newly-elected Lebanese Pres. Bashir Gemayel. On Sept. 16, Lebanese Christian troops entered 2 refugee camps and massacred hundreds of Palestinian refugees.

In 1983, terrorist bombings became a way of life in Beirut as some 50 people were killed in an explosion at the U.S. Embassy, Apr. 18; 241 U.S. servicemen and 58 French soldiers died in separate Moslem suicide attacks, Oct. 23.

On Apr. 26, 1984, pro-Syrian Rashid Karami was appointed premier. The appointment failed to end virtual civil war in Beirut between Christian forces, and Druse and Shiite Moslem militias. There was heavy fighting between Shiite militiamen and Palestinian guerrillas in May 1985. In June, Beirut Airport was the scene of a hostage crisis where Shiite terrorists held U.S. citizens for 17 days. Fierce artillery duels between Christian east Beirut and Moslem west Beirut, Mar.-Apr., 1989, left some 200 dead and 700 wounded.

Kidnapping of foreign nationals by Islamic militants has become common in the 1980s. U.S., British, French, and Soviet citizens have been victims.

A treaty signed May 22, 1991, between Lebanon and Syria recognized Lebanon as a separate and independent state for the first time since the 2 countries gained independence in 1943. Critics charged that the treaty would lead to the de facto annexation of Lebanon by Syria.

Lesotho
Kingdom of Lesotho

People: Population (1990 est.): 1,757,000. **Age distrib. (%):** 0–14: 42.3; 15–59: 52.2; 60+: 5.7. **Pop. density:** 143 per sq. mi. **Ethnic groups:** Sotho 99%. **Languages:** English, Sotho (both official). **Religions:** Roman Catholic 38%, Protestant 42%.

Geography: Area: 11,716 sq. mi., slightly larger than Maryland. **Location:** In Southern Africa. **Neighbors:** Completely surrounded by Republic of South Africa. **Topography:** Landlocked and mountainous, with altitudes ranging from 5,000 to 11,000 ft. **Capital:** Maseru. **Cities** (1990 est.): Maseru 109,000.

Government: Type: Military regime & constitutional monarchy. **Head of state:** King Letsie 2d; in office: Nov. 12, 1990. **Head of government:** Col. Elias P. Ramaema; in office: Apr. 30, 1991. **Local divisions:** 10 districts. **Defense:** 2.4% of GNP (1987).

Economy: Industries: Food processing. **Chief crops:** Corn, grains, peas, beans. **Other resources:** Diamonds. **Arable land:** 13%. **Electricity prod.** (1988): 1 mln. kwh. **Labor force:** 40% agric.

Finance: Monetary unit: Maloti (Mar. 1991: 1.00 = $.37 US). **Gross national product** (1989): $816 mln. **Per capita GNP** (1989): $470. **Imports** (1988): $500 mln.; partners: Mostly So. Afr. **Exports** (1988): $60 mln.; partners: Mostly So. Afr. **National budget** (1989): $226 mln.

Transport: Motor vehicles: in use (1987): 6,000 passenger cars, 15,000 comm. vehicles.

Communications: Radios: 1 per 34 persons. **Daily newspaper circ.** (1988): 10 per 1,000 pop.

Health: Life expectancy at birth (1989): 59 male; 62 female. **Births** (per 1,000 pop. 1989): 37. **Deaths** (per 1,000 pop. 1989): 10. **Natural increase:** 2.7%. **Hospital beds:** 1 per 2,410 persons. **Physicians:** 1 per 15,728 persons. **Infant mortality** (per 1,000 live births 1989): 81.

Education (1990): **Literacy:** 59%.

Major International Organizations: UN (IMF, UNESCO, WHO), OAU.

Embassy: 2511 Massachusetts Ave. NW 20008; 797-5533.

Lesotho (once called Basutoland) became a British protectorate in 1868 when Chief Moshesh sought protection against the Boers. Independence came Oct. 4, 1966. Elections were suspended in 1970. Most of Lesotho's GNP is provided by citizens working in S. Africa. Livestock raising is the chief industry; diamonds are the chief export.

S. Africa imposed a blockade, Jan. 1, 1986, because of Lesotho's giving sanctuary to rebel groups fighting to overthrow the S. African Government. The blockade sparked a Jan. 20 military coup, and was lifted, Jan. 25, when the new leaders agreed to expel the rebels.

In 1990, King Moshoeshoe was sent into exile by the military government.

Liberia
Republic of Liberia

People: Population (1990 est.): 2,644,000. **Age distrib. (%):** 0–14: 46.8; 15–59: 48.3; 60+: 4.9. **Pop. density:** 66 per sq. mi. **Urban** (1985): 39.5%. **Ethnic groups:** Americo-Liberians 5%, indigenous tribes 95% **Languages:** English (official), tribal dialects. **Religions:** Moslem 20%, Christian 10%, traditional beliefs 70%.

Geography: Area: 38,250 sq. mi., slightly smaller than Pennsylvania. **Location:** On SW coast of W. Africa. **Neighbors:** Sierra Leone on W, Guinea on N, Côte d'Ivoire on E. **Topography:** Marshy Atlantic coastline rises to low mountains and plateaus in the forested interior; 6 major rivers flow in parallel courses to the ocean. **Capital:** Monrovia. **Cities** (1987 est.): Monrovia 400,000.

Government: Type: Civilian republic. **Head of state:** Pres. Amos Sawyer, act.; in office: Nov. 22, 1990. **Local divisions:** 13 counties. **Defense:** 3.8% of GDP (1987).

Economy: Industries: Food processing, mining. **Chief crops:** Rice, cassava, coffee, cocoa, sugar. **Minerals:** Iron, diamonds, gold. **Other resources:** Rubber, timber. **Arable land:** 1%. **Fish catch** (1988): 18,000 metric tons. **Electricity prod.** (1988): 728 mln. kwh. **Labor force:** 82% agric.

Finance: Monetary unit: Dollar (May 1991: 1.00 = $1 US). **Gross national product** (1989): $1.0 bln. **Per capita GNP** (1989): $440. **Imports** (1988): $308 mln.; partners: U.S. 32%, W. Ger. 10%, Jap. 6%, Neth. 7%. **Exports** (1987): $382 mln.; partners: W. Ger. 31%, U.S. 20%, It. 14%, Fr. 9%. **National budget** (1988): $240 mln. **International reserves less gold** (Feb. 1991): $7,000. **Consumer prices** (change in 1988): 12.2%.

Transport: Motor vehicles: in use (1987): 7,000 passenger cars, 4,000 comm. vehicles. **Chief ports:** Monrovia, Buchanan, Greenville.

Communications: Television sets: 1 per 55 persons. **Radios:** 1 per 4.4 persons. **Telephones:** 1 per 278 persons. **Daily newspaper circ.** (1987): 9 per 1,000 pop.

Health: Life expectancy at birth (1989): 53 male; 56 female. **Births** (per 1,000 pop. 1989): 45. **Deaths** (per 1,000 pop. 1989): 13. **Natural increase:** 3%. **Hospital beds** (1981): 3,000. **Physicians** (1981): 236. **Infant mortality** (per 1,000 live births 1989): 119.

Education (1989): **Literacy:** 25%; 35% attend primary school.
Major International Organizations: UN and most specialized agencies, OAU.
Embassy: 5201 16th St. NW 20011; 723-0437.

Liberia was founded in 1822 by U.S. black freedmen who settled at Monrovia with the aid of colonization societies. It became a republic July 26, 1847, with a constitution modeled on that of the U.S. Descendants of freedmen dominated politics.

Charging rampant corruption, an Army Redemption Council of enlisted men staged a bloody predawn coup, April 12, 1980, in which Pres. Tolbert was killed and replaced as head of state by Sgt. Samuel Doe. Doe was chosen president in a disputed election, and survived a subsequent coup, in 1985.

A civil war began Dec. 1989. Rebel forces seeking to depose Pres. Doe made major territorial gains and advanced on the capital, June 1990. In Sept., Doe was captured and put to death. A cease fire was declared Feb. 13, 1991. More than half of the nation's population became refugees as a result of the civil war.

Libya

Socialist People's Libyan Arab Jamahiriya

al-Jamahiriyah al-Arabiya al-Libya al-Shabiya al-Ishtirakiya

People: Population: (1990 est.): 4,280,000. **Age distrib. (%):** 0–14: 45.0; 15–59: 51.2; 60+: 3.8. **Pop. density:** 6 per sq. mi. **Urban** (1985): 64%. **Ethnic groups:** Arab-Berber 97%. **Languages:** Arabic. **Religions:** Sunni Moslem 97%.

Geography: Area: 679,359 sq. mi., larger than Alaska. **Location:** On Mediterranean coast of N. Africa. **Neighbors:** Tunisia, Algeria on W, Niger, Chad on S, Sudan, Egypt on E. **Topography:** Desert and semidesert regions cover 92% of the land, with low mountains in N, higher mountains in S, and a narrow coastal zone. **Capital:** Tripoli. **Cities** (1988 est.): Tripoli 591,000.

Government: Type: Islamic Arabic Socialist "Mass-State." **Head of state:** Col. Muammar al-Qaddafi; b. Sept. 1942; in office: Sept. 1969. **Head of government:** Premier Abu Zaid Umar Dourda; in office: Oct. 7, 1990. **Local divisions:** 46 municipalities. **Defense:** 11.1% of GNP (1987).

Economy: Industries: Carpets, textiles, petroleum. **Chief crops:** Dates, olives, citrus and other fruits, grapes, wheat. **Minerals:** Gypsum, oil, gas. **Crude oil reserves** (1987): 22 bln. bbls. **Arable land:** 2%. **Livestock** (1989): sheep: 5.8 mln.; goats: 1.0 mln. **Electricity prod.** (1988): 13.3 bln. kwh. **Labor force:** 18% agric.; 31% ind.; 27% services; 24% govt.

Finance: Monetary unit: Dinar (Feb. 1991: 1.00 = $3.57 US). **Gross national product** (1988): $20 bln. **Per capita income** (1986): $5,500. **Imports** (1988): $5.7 bln.; partners: It. 21%, W. Ger. 11%, Fr. 6%. **Exports** (1988): $5.6 bln.; partners: It. 57%, W. Ger. 27%, Sp. 13%. **International reserves less gold** (Mar. 1991): $5.8 bln. **Gold:** 3.6 mln. oz t.

Transport: Motor vehicles: in use (1986): 428,000 passenger cars, 334,000 comm. vehicles. **Chief ports:** Tripoli, Benghazi.

Communications: Television sets: 1 per 13 persons. **Radios:** 1 per 3.9 persons. **Daily newspaper circ.** (1989): 10 per 1,000 pop.

Health: Life expectancy at birth (1989): 64 male; 69 female. **Births** (per 1,000 pop. 1989): 38. **Deaths** (per 1,000 pop. 1989): 7. **Natural increase:** 3.1%. **Hospital beds** (1982): 16,051. **Physicians** (1982): 5,200. **Infant mortality** (per 1,000 live births 1989): 70.

Education (1989): Literacy: 60%. **Years compulsory:** 7; **Attendance:** 90%.

Major International Organizations: UN, Arab League, OAU, OPEC.

First settled by Berbers, Libya was ruled by Carthage, Rome, and Vandals, the Ottomans, Italy from 1912, and Britain and France after WW II. It became an independent constitutional monarchy Jan. 2, 1952. In 1969 a junta lead by Col. Muammar al-Qaddafi seized power.

In the mid-1970s, Libya helped arm violent revolutionary groups in Egypt and Sudan, and had aided terrorists of various nationalities.

Libya and Egypt fought several air and land battles along their border in July, 1977. Chad charged Libya with military occupation of its uranium-rich northern region in 1977. Libyan forces withdrew from Chad, Nov. 1981 but returned. Libyan troops were driven from their last major stronghold by Chad forces in 1987, leaving over $1 billion in military equipment behind.

The U.S. has accused Libya of masterminding numerous international terrorist actions, including the Dec. 1985 attacks on the Rome and Vienna airports.

On Jan. 7, 1986, the U.S. imposed economic sanctions against Libya, ordered all Americans to leave that country and froze all Libyan assets in the U.S. The U.S. commenced flight operations over the Gulf of Sidra, Jan. 27, and a U.S. Navy task force began conducting exercises in the Gulf, Mar. 23. When Libya fired antiaircraft missiles at American warplanes, the U.S. responded by sinking 2 Libyan ships and bombing a missile installation in Libya. The U.S. withdrew from the Gulf, Mar. 27.

The U.S. accused Libyan leader Qaddafi of having ordered the April 5 bombing of a West Berlin discotheque which killed 2, including a U.S. serviceman. After failing to get their European allies to join them in imposing economic sanctions against Libya, the U.S. sent warplanes to attack terrorist-related targets in Tripoli and Benghazi, Libya, Apr. 14.

Liechtenstein

Principality of Liechtenstein

Fürstentum Liechtenstein

People: Population (1990 est.): 28,000. **Age distrib. (%):** 0–14: 20.1; 15–59: 66.3; 60+: 11.6. **Pop. density:** 483 per sq. mi. **Ethnic groups:** Alemannic 95%, Italian 5%. **Languages:** German (official), Alemannic dialect. **Religions:** Roman Catholic 87%, Protestant 8%.

Geography: Area: 62 sq. mi., the size of Washington, D.C. **Location:** In the Alps. **Neighbors:** Switzerland on W, Austria on E. **Topography:** The Rhine Valley occupies one-third of the country, the Alps cover the rest. **Capital:** Vaduz. **Cities** (1989 cen.): Vaduz 4,920, Schaan 4,883.

Government: Type: Hereditary constitutional monarchy. **Head of state:** Prince Hans Adam; in office: Nov. 13, 1989. **Head of government:** Hans Brunhart; b. Mar. 28, 1945; in office: Apr. 26, 1978. **Local divisions:** 2 districts, 11 communities.

Economy: Industries: Machines, instruments, chemicals, furniture, ceramics. **Arable land:** 25%. **Labor force:** 54% industry, trade and building; 41% services; 4% agric., fishing, forestry.

Finance: Monetary unit: Swiss Franc. **Gross National Product** (1987): $480 mln. **Tourists** (1989): 77,000.

Communications: Radios: 1 per 2.9 persons. **Telephones:** 1 per 1.0 persons. **Daily newspaper circ.** (1987): 546 per 1,000 pop.

Health: Births (per 1,000 pop. 1989): 13. **Deaths** (per 1,000 pop. 1989): 7. **Natural increase:** .6%. **Infant mortality** (per 1,000 live births 1989): 5.

Education (1989): **Literacy:** 100%. **Years compulsory** 9; attendance 100%.

Liechtenstein became sovereign in 1866. Austria administered Liechtenstein's ports up to 1920; Switzerland has administered its postal services since 1921. Liechtenstein is united with Switzerland by a customs and monetary union. Taxes are low; many international corporations have headquarters there. Foreign workers comprise a third of the population.

The 1986 general elections were the first in which women were allowed to vote.

Lithuania

Republic of Lithuania

Lietuvos Respublika

People: Population (1989 cen.): 3,700,000. **Urban** (1988): 66%. **Ethnic groups:** Lithuanian 80%, Russian 9%, Polish 7%. **Religion:** mostly Roman Catholic.

Geography: Area: 25,170 sq. mi. **Neighbors:** Latvia on N., Byelorussia on E., S., Poland, Russia, & Baltic Sea on W. **Capital:** Vilnius.

Government: Type: Republic. **Head of state:** Pres. Vytautas Landsbergis. **Local divisions:** 44 districts, 92 towns, 22 urban settlements.

Economy: Industries: Engineering, shipbuilding. **Chief crops:** grain, potatoes, vegetables. **Arable land:** 49%. **Livestock:** cattle: 2.4 mln., pigs: 2.7 mln.
Transport: Chief Port: Klaipeda.
Communications: 147 newspapers.
Health: (1988) 16,600 doctors, 48,800 hospital beds.

Lithuania, was occupied by the German Army, 1914-18. It was annexed by the USSR but, the Soviets were overthrown, 1919. Lithuania was a democratic republic until 1926 when the regime was ousted by a coup. In 1939, the Soviet-German treaty assigned most of Lithuania to the Soviet sphere of influence. It became part of the USSR Aug. 3, 1940. Lithuania formally declared its independence from the Soviet Union Mar. 11, 1990. Soviet forces began large-scale maneuvers Mar. 18; border controls were tightened Mar. 21. Pres. Gorbachev warned Lithuania to annul its declaration of independence or face "grave consequences." The Soviets cut off oil and gas supplies Apr. 19. Lithuania agreed to suspend independence May 17, and the oil and gas supplies were renewed.

Soviet troops killed 15 protesters in Vilnius, Jan. 13, 1991, in a crackdown on pro-independence forces. During the Soviet coup in Aug., Lithuania declared full independence. Several nations extended diplomatic recognition including the U.S. on Sept. 2. *(See Index and Chronology for details.)*

Luxembourg
Grand Duchy of Luxembourg
Grand-Duché de Luxembourg

People: Population: (1990 est.): 369,000. **Age distrib. (%):** 0–14: 17.3; 15–59: 64.5; 60+: 18.2. **Pop. density:** 369 per sq. mi. **Urban** (1985): 81%. **Ethnic groups:** Mixture of French and Germans predominate. **Languages:** French, German (both official), Luxembourgish. **Religions:** Roman Catholic 97%.
Geography: Area: 998 sq. mi., smaller than Rhode Island. **Location:** In W. Europe. **Neighbors:** Belgium on W, France on S, Germany on E. **Topography:** Heavy forests (Ardennes) cover N, S is a low, open plateau. **Capital:** Luxembourg. **Cities** (1990 est.): Luxembourg 86,000.
Government: Type: Constitutional monarchy. **Head of state:** Grand Duke Jean; b. Jan. 5, 1921; in office: Nov. 12, 1964. **Head of government:** Prime Min. Jacques Santer; in office: July 21, 1984. **Local divisions:** 3 districts. **Defense:** 0.8% of GNP (1988).
Economy: Industries: Steel, chemicals, beer, tires, tobacco, metal products, cement. **Chief crops:** Corn, wine. **Minerals:** Iron. **Arable land:** 25%. **Electricity prod.** (1988): 1.0 bln. kwh. **Crude steel prod.** (1984): 3.9 min. metric tons. **Labor force:** 1% agric.; 42% ind. & comm.; 45% services.
Finance: Monetary unit: Franc (Mar. 1991: 35.29 = $1 US). **Gross national product** (1989): $7.8 bln. **Per capita GNP** (1988): $13,380. **Note:** trade and tourist data included in Belgian statistics. **Consumer prices** (change in 1990): 3.7%.
Transport: Railway traffic (1988): 276 min. passenger-km. **Motor vehicles:** in use (1988): 168,000 passenger cars, 13,000 comm. vehicles.
Communications: Television sets: 1 per 4.0 persons. **Radios:** 1 per 1.6 persons. **Telephones:** 1 per 2.3 persons. **Daily newspaper circ.** (1989): 389 per 1,000 pop.
Health: Life expectancy at birth (1989): 71 male; 78 female. **Births** (per 1,000 pop. 1989): 12. **Deaths** (per 1,000 pop. 1989): 11. **Hospital beds:** 1 per 80 persons. **Physicians:** 1 per 557 persons. **Infant mortality** (per 1,000 live births 1989): 8.
Education (1989): **Literacy:** 100%. **Years compulsory** 9; attendance 100%.
Major International Organizations: UN, OECD, EC, NATO.
Embassy: 2200 Massachusetts Ave. NW 20008; 265-4171.

Luxembourg, founded about 963, was ruled by Burgundy, Spain, Austria, and France from 1448 to 1815. It left the Germanic Confederation in 1866. Overrun by Germany in 2 world wars, Luxembourg ended its neutrality in 1948, when a customs union with Belgium and Netherlands was adopted.

Madagascar
Democratic Republic of Madagascar
Repoblika Demokratika Malagasy

People: Population (1990 est.): 11,802,000. **Pop. density:** 49 per sq. mi. **Urban** (1985): 21.8%. **Ethnic groups:** 18 Malayan-Indonesian tribes (Merina 26%), with Arab and African presence. **Languages:** Malagasy, French (both official). **Religions:** animists 52%, Christian 41%, Moslem 7%.
Geography: Area: 226,657 sq. mi., slightly smaller than Texas. **Location:** In the Indian O., off the SE coast of Africa. **Neighbors:** Comoro Is., Mozambique (across Mozambique Channel). **Topography:** Humid coastal strip in the E, fertile valleys in the mountainous center plateau region, and a wider coastal strip on the W. **Capital:** Antananarivo. **Cities** (1990 est.): Antananarivo 802,000.
Government: Type: Republic, strong presidential authority. **Head of state:** Pres. Didier Ratsiraka; b. Nov. 4, 1936; in office: June 15, 1975. **Head of government:** Prime Min. Guy Willy Razanamasy; in office: Aug. 1991. **Local divisions:** 6 provinces. **Defense:** 2.0% of GNP (1988).
Economy: Industries: Food processing, textiles. **Chief crops:** Coffee (over 50% of exports), cloves, vanilla, rice, sugar, sisal, tobacco, peanuts. **Minerals:** Chromium, graphite, coal, bauxite. **Arable land:** 5%. **Livestock** (1988): cattle: 10.4 mln.; pigs: 1.3 mln. **Fish catch** (1988): 63,000 metric tons. **Electricity prod.** (1988): 430 mln. kwh. **Labor force:** 90% agric.
Finance: Monetary unit: Franc (Mar. 1991: 1,465 = $1 US). **Gross national product** (1989): $2.5 bln. **Per capita GNP** (1989): $230. **Imports** (1988): $360 mln.; partners: Fr. 32%, U.S. 15%. **Exports** (1988): $319 mln.; partners: Fr. 34%, U.S. 14%. **Tourists** (1988): $11 mln. receipts. **National budget** (1987): $480 mln. **International reserves less gold** (Jan. 1991): $99 mln. **Consumer prices** (change in 1990): 10.8%.
Transport: Railway traffic (1987): 208 mln. passenger-km. **Motor vehicles:** in use (1987): 27,000 passenger cars, 20,000 comm. vehicles. **Civil aviation:** (1988): 422 mln. passenger-km; 40 airports with scheduled flights. **Chief ports:** Tamatave, Diego-Suarez, Majunga, Tulear.
Communications: Television sets: 1 per 89 persons. **Radios:** 1 per 5.4 persons. **Telephones in use:** 1 per 239 persons.
Health: Life expectancy at birth (1989): 50 male; 53 female. **Births** (per 1,000 pop. 1989): 47. **Deaths** (per 1,000 pop. 1989): 15. **Natural increase:** 3.2%. **Hospital beds** (1982): 20,800. **Physicians** (1982): 940. **Infant mortality** (per 1,000 live births 1989): 99.
Education (1987): **Literacy:** 53%. **Years compulsory:** 5; attendance 83%.
Major International Organizations: UN (GATT, WHO, IMF), OAU.
Embassy: 2374 Massachusetts Ave. NW 20008; 265-5525.

Madagascar was settled 2,000 years ago by Malayan-Indonesian people, whose descendants still predominate. A unified kingdom ruled the 18th and 19th centuries. The island became a French protectorate, 1885, and a colony 1896. Independence came June 26, 1960.

Discontent with inflation and French domination led to a coup in 1972. The new regime nationalized French-owned financial interests, closed French bases and a U.S. space tracking station, and obtained Chinese aid. The government conducted a program of arrests, expulsion of foreigners, and repression of strikes, 1979.

In 1990, Madagascar ended a ban on multiparty politics that had been in place since 1975.

Malawi
Republic of Malawi

People: Population (1990 est.): 9,080,000. **Age distrib. (%):** 0–14: 47.8; 15–59: 48.0; 60+: 4.2. **Pop. density:** 176 per sq. mi. **Urban** (1987): 12%. **Ethnic groups:** Chewa, 90%, Nyanja, Lomwe, other Bantu tribes. **Languages:** English, Chewa (both official), Lomwe, Yao. **Religions:** Christian 75%, Moslem 20%.
Geography: Area: 45,747 sq. mi., the size of Pennsylvania. **Location:** In SE Africa. **Neighbors:** Zambia on W, Mozambique on SE, Tanzania on N. **Topography:** Malawi stretches 560 mi.

N-S along Lake Malawi (Lake Nyasa), most of which belongs to Malawi. High plateaus and mountains line the Rift Valley the length of the nation. **Capital:** Lilongwe. **Cities** (1987 est.): Blantyre 402,000; Lilongwe 220,000.

Government: Type: One-party state. **Head of state:** Pres. Hastings Kamuzu Banda, b. May 14, 1906; in office: July 6, 1966. **Local divisions:** 24 administrative districts. **Defense:** 1.4% of GNP (1987).

Economy: Industries: Textiles, sugar, cement. **Chief crops:** Tea, tobacco, sugar, coffee. **Other resources:** Rubber. **Arable land:** 25%. **Fish catch** (1988): 88 metric tons. **Electricity prod.** (1988): 535 mln. kwh. **Labor force:** 43% agric.; 23% ind. and comm.; 17% services.

Finance: Monetary unit: Kwacha (Mar. 1991: 2.83 = $1 US). **Gross national product** (1989): $1.4 bln. **Imports** (1989): $503 mln.; partners: So. Afr. 29%, UK 24%, Jap. 6%. **Exports** (1989): $267 mln.; partners: UK 27%, S. Afr. 8%., W. Ger. 10%. **National budget** (1988): $390 mln. **International reserves less gold** (Mar. 1991): $101 mln. **Gold:** 13,000 oz t. **Consumer prices** (change in 1989): 12.5%.

Transport: Railway traffic (1987): 102 mln. passenger-km. **Motor vehicles:** in use (1987): 15,000 passenger cars, 15,000 comm. vehicles. **Civil aviation** (1988) 86 mln. passenger-km; 4 airports with scheduled flights.

Communications: Radios: 1 per 4.3 persons. **Telephones:** 1 per 172 persons. **Daily newspaper circ.** (1985): 5 per 1,000 pop.

Health: Life expectancy at birth (1989): 46 male; 50 female. **Births** (per 1,000 pop. 1989): 51. **Deaths** (per 1,000 pop. 1989): 18. **Natural increase:** 3.3%. **Hospital beds:** 1 per 627 persons. **Physicians:** 1 per 27,094 persons. **Infant mortality** (per 1,000 live births 1989): 132.

Education (1989): **Literacy:** 25%. About 45% attend school.

Major International Organizations: UN (World Bank, IMF), OAU, Commonwealth of Nations.

Embassy: 2408 Massachusetts Ave. NW 20008; 797-1007.

Bantus came in the 16th century, Arab slavers in the 19th. The area became the British protectorate Nyasaland, in 1891. It became independent July 6, 1964, and a republic in 1966.

Malaysia

People: Population (1990 est.): 17,053,000. **Age distrib.** (%): 0–14: 37.8; 15–59: 56.5; 60+: 5.7. **Pop. density:** 132 per sq. mi. **Urban** (1985): 38%. **Ethnic groups:** Malays 59%, Chinese 32%, Indian 9%. **Languages:** Malay (official), English, Chinese, Indian languages. **Religions:** Moslem, Hindu, Buddhist, Confucian, Taoist, local religions.

Geography: Area: 127,316 sq. mi., slightly larger than New Mexico. **Location:** On the SE tip of Asia, plus the N. coast of the island of Borneo. **Neighbors:** Thailand on N, Indonesia on S. **Topography:** Most of W. Malaysia is covered by tropical jungle, including the central mountain range that runs N-S through the peninsula. The western coast is marshy, the eastern, sandy. E. Malaysia has a wide, swampy coastal plain, with interior jungles and mountains. **Capital:** Kuala Lumpur. **Cities** (1986 est.): Kuala Lumpur 1 mln.

Government: Type: Federal parliamentary democracy with a constitutional monarch. **Head of state:** Paramount Ruler Sultan Azlan Shah; in office: Apr. 26, 1989. **Head of government:** Prime Min. Datuk Seri Mahathir bin Mohamad; b. Dec. 20, 1925; in office: July 16, 1981. **Local divisions:** 13 states and capital. **Defense:** 3.2% of GNP (1987).

Economy: Industries: Rubber goods, steel, electronics. **Chief crops:** Palm oil, copra, rice, pepper. **Minerals:** Tin (35% world output), iron. **Crude oil reserves** (1987): 3.2 bln. bbls. **Other resources:** Rubber (35% world output). **Arable land:** 13%. **Livestock** (1989): pigs: 2.2 mln. **Fish catch** (1989): 604,000 metric tons. **Electricity prod.** (1988): 15.8 bln. kwh. **Labor force:** 21% agric.; 22% manuf.; 11% tourism & trade.

Finance: Monetary unit: Ringgit (June 1991: 2.75 = $1 US). **Gross national product** (1989): $37.0 bln. **Per capita GNP** (1989) $2,130. **Imports** (1989): $22.4 bln.; partners: Jap. 21%, U.S. 18%, Sing. 14%. **Exports** (1989): $25.0 bln.; partners: Jap. 20%, U.S. 17% Sing. 19%, Neth. 6%. **Tourists** (1988): $766 mln. receipts. **National budget** (1988): $10.8 bln. **International**

reserves less gold (Mar. 1991): $10.0 bln. **Gold:** 2.22 mln. oz t. **Consumer prices** (change in 1990): 1.9%.

Transport: Railway traffic (incl. Singapore) (1988): 1.5 bln. passenger-km. **Motor vehicles:** in use (1987): 1.5 mln. passenger cars, 338,000 comm. vehicles. **Civil aviation:** (1989): 10.1 bln. passenger-km; 39 airports with scheduled flights. **Chief ports:** George Town, Kelang, Melaka, Kuching.

Communications: Television sets: 1 per 10 persons. **Radios:** 1 per 2.4 persons. **Telephones:** 1 per 11 persons. **Daily newspaper circ.** (1987): 109 per 1,000 pop.

Health: Life expectancy at birth (1989): 65 male; 70 female. **Births** (per 1,000 pop. 1989): 26. **Deaths** (per 1,000 pop. 1989): 6. **Natural increase:** 2.0%. **Hospital beds:** 1 per 442 persons. **Physicians:** 1 per 2,853 persons. **Infant mortality** (per 1,000 live births 1989): 31.

Education (1989): **Literacy:** 80%; 96% attend primary school, 48% attend secondary.

Major International Organizations: UN (World Bank, IMF, GATT), ASEAN.

Embassy: 2401 Massachusetts Ave. NW 20008; 328-2700.

European traders appeared in the 16th century; Britain established control in 1867. Malaysia was created Sept. 16, 1963. It included Malaya (which had become independent in 1957 after the suppression of Communist rebels), plus the formerly-British Singapore, Sabah (N Borneo), and Sarawak (NW Borneo). Singapore was separated in 1965, in order to end tensions between Chinese, the majority in Singapore, and Malays in control of the Malaysian government.

A monarch is elected by a council of hereditary rulers of the Malayan states every 5 years.

Abundant natural resources have assured prosperity, and foreign investment has aided industrialization.

Maldives
Republic of Maldives
Divehi Jumhuriya

People: Population (1990 est.): 219,000. **Age distrib.** (%): 0–14: 44.4; 15–59: 51.7; 60+: 3.9. **Pop. density:** 1,756 per sq. mi. **Urban** (1985): 26%. **Ethnic groups:** Sinhalese, Dravidian, Arab mixture. **Languages:** Divehi (Sinhalese dialect). **Religions:** Sunni Moslem.

Geography: Area: 115 sq. mi., twice the size of Washington, D.C. **Location:** In the Indian O. SW of India. **Neighbors:** Nearest is India on N. **Topography:** 19 atolls with 1,087 islands, about 200 inhabited. None of the islands are over 5 sq. mi. in area, and all are nearly flat. **Capital:** Male. **Cities** (1985 est.): Male 46,334.

Government: Type: Republic. **Head of state:** Pres. Maumoon Abdul Gayoom; b. Dec. 29, 1939; in office: Nov. 11, 1978. **Local divisions:** 19 districts.

Economy: Industries: Fish processing, tourism. **Chief crops:** Coconuts, fruit, millet. **Other resources:** Shells. **Arable land:** 10%. **Fish catch** (1988): 71,000 metric tons. **Electricity prod.** (1988): 14.0 mln. kwh. **Labor force:** 80% fishing, agriculture, & manufacturing.

Finance: Monetary unit: Rufiyaa (Mar. 1991: 9.98 = $1 US). **Gross national product** (1989): $87 mln. **Per capita GNP** (1989): $420. **Imports** (1988): $106 min.; partners: Sing., Jap., Sri Lan. **Exports** (1988): $45 mln.; partners: Jap., Europe. **Tourists** (1987): $39 mln. receipts.

Transport: Chief ports: Male Atoll.

Communications: Radios: 1 per 9.2 persons. **Telephones:** 1 per 60 persons.

Health: Life expectancy at birth (1989): 60 male; 63 female. **Births** (per 1,000 pop. 1989): 47. **Deaths** (per 1,000 pop. 1989): 10. **Natural increase:** 3.7%. **Infant morality** (per 1,000 live births 1989): 80.

Education (1989): **Literacy:** 93%. Only 6% of those aged 11-15 attend school.

Major International Organizations: UN.

The islands had been a British protectorate since 1887. The country became independent July 26, 1965. Long a sultanate, the Maldives became a republic in 1968. Natural resources and tourism are being developed; however, it remains one of the world's poorest countries.

Mali

Republic of Mali
République du Mali

People: Population (1990 est.): 9,182,000. **Age distrib. (%):** 0–14: 46.0; 15–59: 49.4; 60+: 4.6. **Pop. density:** 17 per sq. mi. **Urban** (1988): 22%. **Ethnic groups:** Mande (Bambara, Malinke, Sarakole) 50%, Peul 17%, Voltaic 12%, Songhai 6%, Tuareg and Moor, 5%. **Languages:** French (official), Bambara, Senufo. **Religions:** Moslem 90%.

Geography: Area: 478,764 sq. mi., about the size of Texas and California combined. **Location:** In the interior of W. Africa. **Neighbors:** Mauritania, Senegal on W, Guinea, Côte d'Ivoire, Burkina Faso on S, Niger on E, Algeria on N. **Topography:** A landlocked grassy plain in the upper basins of the Senegal and Niger rivers, extending N into the Sahara. **Capital:** Bamako. **Cities** (1989 est.): Bamako (met.) 800,000.

Government: Type: In transition. **Head of state:** Pres. Col. Amadou Toumani Toure; in office: Mar. 26, 1991. **Local divisions:** 7 regions and a capital district. **Defense:** 2.4% of GNP (1988).

Economy: Chief crops: Millet, rice, peanuts, cotton. **Other resources:** Bauxite, iron, gold. **Arable land:** 2%. **Livestock** (1989): sheep: 5.7 mln.; cattle: 4.8 mln. **Fish catch** (1988): 55,000 metric tons. **Electricity prod.** (1989): 204 mln. kwh. **Labor force:** 72% agric.; 12% ind. & comm.; 16% services.

Finance: Monetary unit: Franc (Mar. 1991: 290 = $1 US). **Gross national product** (1987): $1.6 bln. **Per capita income** (1987): $200. **Imports** (1988): $513 mln.; partners: Fr. 22%, Ivory Coast 25%. **Exports** (1988): $251 mln.; partners: Belg.-Lux. 25%, Fr. 15%. **Tourists** (1988): $37 mln. receipts. **National budget** (1987): $240 mln. expenditures. **International reserves less gold** (Feb. 1991): $190 mln. **Gold:** 19,000 oz t.

Transport: Railway traffic (1987): 772 mln. passenger-km. **Motor vehicles:** in use (1987): 29,000 passenger cars, 7,500 comm. vehicles.

Communications: Radios: 1 per 53 persons. **Telephones:** 1 per 580 persons.

Health: Life expectancy at birth (1989): 44 male; 47 female. **Births** (per 1,000 pop. 1989): 49. **Deaths** (per 1,000 pop. 1989): 20. **Natural increase:** 2.9%. **Hospital beds** (1983): 4,215. **Physicians** (1983): 283. **Infant mortality** (per 1,000 live births 1989): 173.

Education (1989): **Literacy:** 10%. **Attendance:** 21% attend primary school.

Major International Organizations: UN and all of its specialized agencies, OAU, EC.

Embassy: 2130 R St. NW 20008; 332-2249.

Until the 15th century the area was part of the great Mali Empire. Timbuktu was a center of Islamic study. French rule was secured, 1898. The Sudanese Rep. and Senegal became independent as the Mali Federation June 20, 1960, but Senegal withdrew, and the Sudanese Rep. was renamed Mali.

Mali signed economic agreements with France and, in 1963, with Senegal. In 1968, a coup ended the socialist regime. Famine struck in 1973-74, killing as many as 100,000 people. Drought conditions returned in the 1980s.

The military, Mar. 26, 1991, overthrew the government of Pres. Traore, who had been in power since 1968. A mutiparty democracy was promised.

Malta

Repubblika Ta' Malta

People: Population (1990 est.): 354,900. **Age distrib. (%):** 0–14: 23.6; 15–59: 61.8; 60+: 14.6. **Pop. density:** 2,900 per sq. mi. **Ethnic groups:** Italian, Arab, French. **Languages:** Maltese, English (both official). **Religions:** Mainly Roman Catholic.

Geography: Area: 122 sq. mi., twice the size of Washington, D.C. **Location:** In center of Mediterranean Sea. **Neighbors:** Nearest is Italy on N. **Topography:** Island of Malta is 95 sq. mi.; other islands in the group: Gozo, 26 sq. mi., Comino, 1 sq. mi. The coastline is heavily indented. Low hills cover the interior. **Capital:** Valletta. **Cities** (1989 est.): Birkirkara 21,000, Qormi 19,000.

Government: Type: Parliamentary democracy. **Head of state:** Pres. Censu Tabone; in office: Apr. 4, 1989. **Head of government:** Prime Min. Edward Fenech-Adami; b. Feb. 7, 1934; in office: May 12, 1987. **Local Divisions:** 13 electoral districts. **Defense:** 1.3% of GNP (1990).

Economy: Industries: Textiles, machinery, food & beverages, tourism. **Chief crops:** Potatoes, tomatoes. **Arable land:** 41%. **Electricity prod.** (1989): $1.1 bln. kwh. **Labor force:** 2% agric.; 24% manuf.; 43% services; 29% gov.

Finance: Monetary unit: Maltese Lera (Mar. 1991: 1.00 = $3.30 US). **Gross national product** (1989): $2.3 bln. **Per capita GNP** (1989): $6,564. **Imports** (1989): $1.7 bln.; partners: UK 16%, It. 30%, Ger. 14%, U.S. 4%. **Exports** (1989): $972 mln.; partners: Ger. 23%, UK 11%, It. 30%. **Tourists** (1989): receipts: $475 mln. **National budget** (1991): $1.3 bln. expenditures. **International reserves less gold** (Mar. 1991): 1.1 bln. **Gold:** 156,000 oz t. **Consumer prices** (change in 1990): 2.4% .

Transport: Motor vehicles: in use (1989): 110,000 passenger cars, 19,000 comm. vehicles. **Civil aviation** (1989): 636 mln. passenger-km; 1 airport. **Chief ports:** Valletta.

Communications: Television sets: 1 per 2.6 persons (1989). **Radios:** 1 per 3.3 persons (1989). **Telephones in use** (1989): 1 per 2.1 persons.

Health: Life expectancy at birth (1989): 74 male; 78 female. **Births** (per 1,000 pop. 1989): 14. **Deaths** (per 1,000 pop. 1989): 8. **Natural increase:** .6%. **Hospital beds:** 1 per 108 persons. **Physicians:** 1 per 489 persons. **Infant mortality** (per 1,000 live births 1989): 10.1.

Education (1988): **Literacy:** 90%. **Compulsory:** until age 16.

Major International Organizations: UN (GATT, WHO, IMF), Commonwealth of Nations.

Embassy: 2017 Connecticut Ave. NW 20008; 462-3611.

Malta was ruled by Phoenicians, Romans, Arabs, Normans, the Knights of Malta, France, and Britain (since 1814). It became independent Sept. 21, 1964. Malta became a republic in 1974. The withdrawal of the last of its sailors, Apr. 1, 1979, ended 179 years of British military presence on the island.

Malta is democratic and nonaligned.

Mauritania

Islamic Republic of Mauritania
République Islamique de Mauritanie

People: Population (1990 est.): 2,038,000. **Age distrib. (%):** 0–14: 46.4; 15–59: 49.0; 60+: 4.6. **Pop. density:** 4.5 per sq. mi. **Urban** (1987): 34%. **Ethnic groups:** Arab-Berber 80%, Negroes 20%. **Languages:** Arabic, French (both official), Hassanya Arabic (national). **Religion:** Nearly 100% Moslem.

Geography: Area: 397,954 sq. mi., the size of Texas and California combined. **Location:** In W. Africa. **Neighbors:** Morocco on N, Algeria, Mali on E, Senegal on S. **Topography:** The fertile Senegal R. valley in the S gives way to a wide central region of sandy plains and scrub trees. The N is arid and extends into the Sahara. **Capital:** Nouakchott. **Cities** (1987 est.): Nouakchott 400,000; Nouadhibou 70,000; Kaedi 22,000.

Government: Type: Military republic. **Head of Government:** President & Premier Maaouya Ould Sidi Ahmed Taya; in office: Apr. 25, 1981. **Local divisions:** 12 regions, one capital district. **Defense:** 4.2% of GNP (1987).

Economy: Chief crops: Dates, grain. **Industries:** iron mining. **Minerals:** Iron, ore, gypsum. **Livestock** (1988): sheep: 4.1 mln.; goats: 3.9 mln.; cattle: 1.2 mln. **Fish catch** (1987): 99,000 metric tons. **Electricity prod.** (1988): 97 mln. kwh. **Labor force:** 47% agric., 14% ind. & comm., 29% services.

Finance: Monetary unit: Ouguiya (Mar. 1991: 83 = $1 US). **Gross national product** (1989): $953 mln. **Per capita GNP** (1989): $490. **Imports** (1989): $222 mln.; partners: Fr. 29%, Sp. 9%. **Exports** (1989): $238 mln.; partners: Fr. 21%, It. 26%, Jap. 20%. **International reserves less gold** (Feb. 1991): $56 mln.

Transport: Motor vehicles: in use (1985): 15,000 passenger cars, 2,000 comm. vehicles. **Chief ports:** Nouakchott, Nouadhibou.

Communications: Radios: 1 per 7.8 persons.

Health: Life expectancy at birth (1989): 43 male; 48 female. **Births** (per 1,000 pop. 1989): 49. **Deaths** (per 1,000 pop. 1989): 19. **Natural increase:** 3.0%. **Hospital beds** (1984): 1,325. **Physicians** (1984): 170. **Infant mortality** (per 1,000 live births 1989): 97.

Education (1987): **Literacy:** 17%. **Attendance:** 41% in primary school, 10% in secondary school.
Major International Organizations: UN (GATT, IMF, WHO), OAU, Arab League.
Embassy: 2129 Leroy Pl. NW 20008; 232-5700.

Mauritania was a French protectorate from 1903. It became independent Nov. 28, 1960. It annexed the south of former Spanish Sahara in 1976. Saharan guerrillas stepped up attacks in 1977; 8,000 Moroccan troops and French bomber raids aided the government. Mauritania signed a peace treaty with the Polisario Front, 1980, resumed diplomatic relations with Algeria while breaking a defense treaty with Morocco, and renounced sovereignty over its share of former Spanish Sahara. Morocco annexed the territory.
Famine struck repeatedly during the 1980s.

Mauritius

People: Population (1990 est.): 1,141,900. **Age distrib. (%):** 0–14: 36.3; 15–59: 57.2; 60+: 6.4. **Pop. density:** 1,325 per sq. mi. **Urban** (1990): 41%. **Ethnic groups:** Indo-Mauritian 68%, Creole 27%, others. **Languages:** English (official), French Creole, Bhojpuri. **Religions:** Hindu 51%, Christian 30%, Moslem 16%.
Geography: Area: 790 sq. mi., about the size of Rhode Island. **Location:** In the Indian O., 500 mi. E of Madagascar. **Neighbors:** Nearest is Madagascar on W. **Topography:** A volcanic island nearly surrounded by coral reefs. A central plateau is encircled by mountain peaks. **Capital:** Port Louis. **Cities** (1990 est.): Port Louis 139,000.
Government: Type: Parliamentary democracy. **Head of state:** Queen Elizabeth II, represented by Gov.-Gen. Sir Veerasamy Ringadoo; in office: Jan. 17, 1986. **Head of government:** Prime Min. Aneerood Jugnauth; in office: June 12, 1982. **Local divisions:** 8 administrative divisions.
Economy: Industries: Tourism. **Chief crops:** Sugar cane, tea. **Arable land:** 58%. **Electricity prod.** (1988): 423 mln. kwh. **Labor force:** 20% agric. & fishing; 38% manuf.; 19% govt. services.
Finance: Monetary unit: Rupee (Mar. 1991: 15.76 = $1 US). **Gross national product** (1989): $2.0 bln. **Per capita GNP** (1989): $1,950. **Imports** (1989): $1.2 bln.; partners: UK 9%, Fr. 12%, So. Afr. 9%. **Exports** (1989): $1.0 bln.; partners: UK 50%, Fr. 22%, U.S. 8%. **Tourists** (1989): $172 mln. receipts. **National budget** (1985): $310 mln. **International reserves less gold** (Feb. 1991): $795 mln. **Gold:** 61,000 oz t. **Consumer prices** (change in 1990): 13.5%.
Transport: Motor vehicles: in use (1988): 26,000 passenger cars, 6,000 comm. vehicles. **Chief ports:** Port Louis.
Communications: Television sets: 1 per 8.2 persons. **Radios:** 1 per 4.2 persons. **Telephones:** 1 per 15 persons. **Daily newspaper circ.** (1989): 75 per 1,000 pop.
Health: Life expectancy at birth (1988): 64.4 male; 71.2 female. **Births** (per 1,000 pop. 1989): 21. **Deaths** (per 1,000 pop. 1989): 6. **Natural increase:** 1.5%. **Hospital beds:** 1 per 364 persons. **Physicians:** 1 per 784 persons. **Infant mortality** (per 1,000 live births 1989): 22.
Education (1989): **Literacy:** 94%. **Attendance:** almost all children attend school.
Major International Organizations: UN and all of its specialized agencies, OAU, Commonwealth of Nations.
Embassy: 4301 Connecticut Ave. NW 20008; 244-1491.

Mauritius was uninhabited when settled in 1638 by the Dutch, who introduced sugar cane. France took over in 1721, bringing African slaves. Britain ruled from 1810 to Mar. 12, 1968, bringing Indian workers for the sugar plantations.
The economy suffered in the 1980s because of low world sugar prices.

Mexico
United Mexican States
Estados Unidos Mexicanos

People: Population (1990 est.): 88,335,000. **Age distrib. (%):** 0–14: 36.5; 15–59: 57.8; 60+: 5.7. **Pop. density:** 115 per sq. mi. **Urban** (1990): 72%. **Ethnic groups:** Mestizo 60%,

American Indian 29%, Caucasian 9%. **Languages:** Spanish (official), Ameridian languages. **Religions:** Roman Catholic 97%.
Geography: Area: 761,604 sq. mi., three times the size of Texas. **Location:** In southern N. America. **Neighbors:** U.S. on N, Guatemala, Belize on S. **Topography:** The Sierra Madre Occidental Mts. run NW-SE near the west coast; the Sierra Madre Oriental Mts., run near the Gulf of Mexico. They join S of Mexico City. Between the 2 ranges lies the dry central plateau, 5,000 to 8,000 ft. alt., rising toward the S, with temperate vegetation. Coastal lowlands are tropical. About 45% of land is arid. **Capital:** Mexico City. **Cities** (1988 est.): Mexico City (metro) 20 mln.; Guadalajara (metro) 3 mln.; Monterrey (metro) 2.7 mln.
Government: Type: Federal republic. **Head of state:** Pres. Carlos Salinas de Gortari; b. Apr. 3, 1948; in office: Dec. 1, 1988. **Local divisions:** Federal district and 31 states. **Defense:** 0.6% of GNP (1988).
Economy: Industries: Steel, chemicals, electric goods, textiles, rubber, petroleum, tourism. **Chief crops:** Cotton, coffee, wheat, rice, sugar cane, vegetables, corn. **Minerals:** Silver, lead, zinc, gold, oil, natural gas. **Crude oil reserves** (1990): 54 bln. barrels. **Arable land:** 13%. **Livestock** (1989): cattle: 34.9 mln.; pigs: 14 mln.; sheep: 6 mln. **Fish catch** (1989): 1.3 mln. metric tons. **Electricity prod.** (1988): 91.2 bln. kwh. **Crude steel prod.** (1988): 7.7 mln. metric tons. **Labor force:** 26% agric.; 13% manuf; 31% services; 14% comm.
Finance: Monetary unit: Peso (June 1991: 3,005 = $1 US). **Gross national product** (1989): $204 bln. **Per capita GDP** (1989): $2,373. **Imports** (1989): $23.8 bln.; partners: U.S. 64%, EC 11%. **Exports** (1989): $22.8 bln.; partners: U.S. 64%, EC 10%. **Tourists** (1988): receipts: $3.9 bln. **National budget** (1985): $86.5 bln. expenditures. **International reserves less gold** (Jan. 1991): $9.8 bln. **Gold:** 919,000 oz t. **Consumer prices** (change in 1990): 30.0%.
Transport: Railway traffic (1989): 3.6 bln. passenger-km. **Motor vehicles:** in use (1988): 5.5 mln. passenger cars, 2.5 mln. comm. **Civil aviation** (1989): 12.2 bln. passenger-km; 78 airports. **Chief ports:** Veracruz, Tampico, Mazatlan, Coatzacoalcos.
Communications: Television sets: 1 in 8.7 persons. **Radios:** 1 in 5.1 persons. **Telephones:** 1 in 8.9 persons. **Daily newspaper circ.** (1986): 142 per 1,000 pop.
Health: Life expectancy at birth (1989): 67 male; 73 female. **Births** (per 1,000 pop. 1989): 30. **Deaths** (per 1,000 pop. 1989): 6. **Natural increase:** 2.5%. **Hospital beds:** 1 per 1,000 persons. **Physicians:** 1 per 1,037 persons. **Infant mortality** (per 1,000 live births 1989): 42.
Education (1989): **Literacy:** 88%. **Years compulsory:** 10.
Major International Organizations: UN (IMF, GATT), OAS.
Embassy: 1911 Pennsylvania Ave. NW 20006; 728-1600.

Mexico was the site of advanced Indian civilizations. The Mayas, an agricultural people, moved up from Yucatan, built immense stone pyramids, invented a calendar. The Toltecs were overcome by the Aztecs, who founded Tenochtitlan 1325 AD, now Mexico City. Hernando Cortes, Spanish conquistador, destroyed the Aztec empire, 1519-1521.
After 3 centuries of Spanish rule the people rose, under Fr. Miguel Hidalgo y Costilla, 1810, Fr. Morelos y Payon, 1812, and Gen. Agustin Iturbide, who made himself emperor as Agustin I, 1821. A republic was declared in 1823.
Mexican territory extended into the present American Southwest and California until Texas revolted and established a republic in 1836; the Mexican legislature refused recognition but was unable to enforce its authority there. After numerous clashes, the U.S.-Mexican War, 1846-48, resulted in the loss by Mexico of the lands north of the Rio Grande.
French arms supported an Austrian archduke on the throne of Mexico as Maximilian I, 1864-67, but pressure from the U.S. forced France to withdraw. A dictatorial rule by Porfirio Diaz, president 1877-80, 1884-1911, led to fighting by rival forces until the new constitution of Feb. 5, 1917 provided social reform. Since then Mexico has developed large-scale programs of social security, labor protection, and school improvement. A constitutional provision requires management to share profits with labor.
The Institutional Revolutionary Party has been dominant in politics since 1929. Radical opposition, including some guerrilla activity, has been contained by strong measures.
The presidency of Luis Echeverria, 1970-76, was marked by a more leftist foreign policy and domestic rhetoric. Some land redistribution begun in 1976 was reversed under the succeeding administration.

Some gains in agriculture, industry, and social services have been achieved. The land is rich, but the rugged topography and lack of sufficient rainfall are major obstacles. Crops and farm prices are controlled, as are export and import. Economic prospects brightened with the discovery of vast oil reserves, perhaps the world's greatest. But much of the work force is jobless or underemployed.

Inflation and the drop in world oil prices caused economic problems in the 1980s. The peso was devalued and private banks were nationalized to restore financial stability.

The U.S. has been critical of Mexico for its failure to combat the production of illegal drugs.

Monaco
Principality of Monaco

People: Population (1989 est.): 29,000. **Age distrib. (%):** 0–14: 12.7; 15–59: 56.3 60+: 30.7. **Pop. density:** 28,072 per sq. mi. **Ethnic groups:** French 47%, Italian 16%, Monegasque 16%. **Languages:** French (official). **Religions:** Predominantely Roman Catholic.

Geography: Area: 0.6 sq. mi. **Location:** On the NW Mediterranean coast. **Neighbors:** France to W, N, E. **Topography:** Monaco-Ville sits atop a high promontory, the rest of the principality rises from the port up the hillside. **Capital:** Monaco-Ville (1985 est.): 1,700.

Government: Type: Constitutional monarchy. **Head of state:** Prince Rainier III; b. May 31, 1923; in office: May 9, 1949. **Head of government:** Min. of State Jean Ausseil; in office: Sept. 1985.

Economy: Industries: Tourism, gambling, chemicals, precision instruments, plastics.

Finance: Monetary unit: French franc or Monégasque franc.

Transport: Chief ports: La Condamine.

Communications: Television sets: 17,000 in use (1984). **Telephones in use** (1984): 18,000.

Health: Births (per 1,000 pop. 1989): 7. **Deaths** (per 1,000 pop. 1989): 7. **Infant mortality** (per 1,000 live births 1989): 9.

Education: (1989): Literacy: 99%. **Years compulsory:** 10; attendance 99%.

An independent principality for over 300 years, Monaco has belonged to the House of Grimaldi since 1297 except during the French Revolution. It was placed under the protectorate of Sardinia in 1815, and under that of France, 1861. The Prince of Monaco was an absolute ruler until a 1911 constitution.

Monaco's fame as a tourist resort is widespread. It is noted for its mild climate and magnificent scenery. The area has been extended by land reclamation.

Mongolia
Mongolian People's Republic
Bügd Nayramdakh Mongol Ard Uls

People: Population (1990 est.): 2,185,000. **Pop. density:** 3 per sq. mi. **Urban** (1989): 52%. **Ethnic groups:** Mongol 90%. **Languages:** Mongolian (official). **Religions:** curbed by govt., traditionally Lama Buddhism.

Geography: Area: 604,247 sq. mi., more than twice the size of Texas. **Location:** In E Central Asia. **Neighbors:** USSR on N, China on S. **Topography:** Mostly a high plateau with mountains, salt lakes, and vast grasslands. Arid lands in the S are part of the Gobi Desert. **Capital:** Ulaanbaatar. **Cities** (1989 est.): Ulaanbaatar 548,000, Darhan 85,000.

Government: Type: Socialist (in transition). **Head of state:** Pres. Punsalmaagiyn Ochirbat; b. 1942; in office: Mar. 21, 1990. **Head of government:** Prime Min. Dashiyn Byambasüren; in office: Sept. 11, 1990. **Local divisions:** 18 provinces, 3 municipalities. **Defense:** 11.5% of GNP (1984).

Economy: Industries: Food processing, textiles, chemicals, cement. **Chief crops:** Grain. **Minerals:** Coal, tungsten, copper, molybdenum, gold, tin. **Arable land:** 1%. **Livestock** (1988): sheep: 13.5 mln.; cattle 2.4 mln. **Electricity prod.** (1988): 2.8 bln. kwh. **Labor force:** 52% agric.; 10% manuf.

Finance: Monetary unit: Tugrik (Jan. 1991: 3.35 = $1 US). **Gross national product** (1988): $1.3 bln. **Per capita GNP**

(1988): $660. **Imports** (1987): $1.2 bln.; partners: USSR 91%. **Exports** (1987): $768 mln.; partners: USSR 80%.

Transport: Railway traffic (1988): 531 mln. passenger-km.

Communications: Television sets: 1 per 18 persons. **Radios:** 1 per 7.5 persons. **Telephones:** 1 per 36 persons. **Daily newspaper circ.** (1988): 91 per 1,000 pop.

Health: Life expectancy at birth (1989): 63 male; 67 female. **Births** (per 1,000 pop. 1989): 35. **Deaths** (per 1,000 pop. 1989): 8. **Natural increase:** 2.8%. **Hospital beds:** 1 per 88 persons. **Physicians:** 1 per 390 persons. **Infant mortality** (per 1,000 live births 1989): 49.

Major International Organizations: UN (ILO, WHO).

Education (1985): **Literacy:** 89%. **Years compulsory:** 7 in major population centers.

One of the world's oldest countries, Mongolia reached the zenith of its power in the 13th century when Genghis Khan and his successors conquered all of China and extended their influence as far W as Hungary and Poland. In later centuries, the empire dissolved and Mongolia became a province of China.

With the advent of the 1911 Chinese revolution, Mongolia, with Russian backing, declared its independence. A Mongolian Communist regime was established July 11, 1921.

Mongolia has been changed from a nomadic culture to one of settled agriculture and growing industries with aid from the USSR and East European nations.

In 1990, the Mongolian Communist Party surrendered its monopoly on power. Free elections were held July 1990; the communists were victorious.

Morocco
Kingdom of Morocco
al-Mamlaka al-Maghrebia

People: Population (1990 est.): 26,249,000. **Age distrib. (%):** 0–14: 41.2; 15–59: 53.7; 60+: 5.1. **Pop. density:** 147 per sq. mi. **Urban** (1988): 44%. **Ethnic groups:** Arab-Berber 99%. **Languages:** Arabic (official), Berber. **Religions:** Sunni Moslems 99%.

Geography: Area: 172,413 sq. mi., larger than California. **Location:** on NW coast of Africa. **Neighbors:** W. Sahara on S, Algeria on E. **Topography:** Consists of 5 natural regions: mountain ranges (Riff in the N, Middle Atlas, Upper Atlas, and Anti-Atlas); rich plains in the W; alluvial plains in SW; well-cultivated plateaus in the center; a pre-Sahara arid zone extending from SE. **Capital:** Rabat. **Cities** (1984): Casablanca 2,600,000; Rabat 556,000, Fes 852,000.

Government: Type: Constitutional monarchy. **Head of state:** King Hassan II; b. July 9, 1929; in office: Mar. 3, 1961. **Head of government:** Prime Min. Azzedine Laraki; in office: Sept. 30, 1986. **Local divisions:** 2 prefectures, 36 provinces. **Defense:** 5.0% of GNP (1988).

Economy: Industries: Carpets, clothing, leather goods, mining, tourism. **Chief crops:** Grain, fruits, dates, grapes. **Minerals:** Copper, cobalt, manganese, phosphates, lead, oil. **Crude oil reserves** (1980): 100 mln. bbls. **Arable land:** 18%. **Livestock** (1989): cattle: 3.5 mln.; sheep; 17 mln.; goats: 5.9 mln. **Fish catch** (1989): 551,000 metric tons. **Electricity prod.** (1988): 7.7 bln. kwh. **Labor force:** 39% agric., 20% services; 17% ind.

Finance: Monetary unit: Dirham (Mar. 1991: 8.91 = $1 US). **Gross national product** (1989): $22.0 bln. **Per capita GNP** (1989): $900. **Imports** (1989): $5.4 bln.; partners: Fr. 25%, Sp. 7%, Saudi Ar. 15%. **Exports** (1989): $3.3 bln.; partners: Fr. 22%, W. Ger. 7%, Sp. 7%, It. 5%. **Tourists** (1987): $1 bln. receipts. **National budget** (1987): $5.0 bln. expenditures. **International reserves less gold** (Mar. 1991): $2.2 bln. **Gold:** 704,000 oz t. **Consumer prices** (change in 1990): 5.9%.

Transport: Railway traffic (1987): 2.0 bln. passenger-km. **Motor vehicles:** in use (1987): 554,000 passenger cars, 255,000 comm. vehicles. **Civil aviation** (1987): 2.2 bln. passenger-km; 15 airports. **Chief ports:** Tangier, Casablanca, Kenitra.

Communications: Television sets: 1 per 19.2 persons. **Radios:** 1 per 5.4 persons. **Telephones in use:** 1 per 68 persons. **Daily newspaper circ.** (1988): 12 per 1,000 pop.

Health: Life expectancy at birth (1989): 62 male; 65 female. **Births** (per 1,000 pop. 1989): 35. **Deaths** (per 1,000 pop. 1989): 9. **Natural increase:** 2.6%. **Hospital beds:** 1 per 918 persons. **Physicians:** 1 per 4,873 persons. **Infant mortality** (per 1,000 live births 1989): 79.

Education (1985): Literacy: 35%.
Major International Organizations: UN (ILO, IMF, WHO), OAU, Arab League.
Embassy: 1601 21st St. NW 20009; 462-7979.

Berbers were the original inhabitants, followed by Carthaginians and Romans. Arabs conquered in 683. In the 11th and 12th centuries, a Berber empire ruled all NW Africa and most of Spain from Morocco.

Part of Morocco came under Spanish rule in the 19th century; France controlled the rest in the early 20th. Tribal uprisings lasted from 1911 to 1933. The country became independent Mar. 2, 1956. Tangier, an internationalized seaport, was turned over to Morocco, 1956. Ifni, a Spanish enclave, was ceded in 1969.

Morocco annexed over 70,000 sq. mi. of phosphate-rich land Apr. 14, 1976, two-thirds of former Spanish Sahara, with the remainder annexed by Mauritania. Spain had withdrawn in February. Polisario, a guerrilla movement, proclaimed the region independent Feb. 27, and launched attacks with Algerian support. Morocco accepted U.S. military and economic aid. When Mauritania signed a treaty with the Polisario Front, and gave up its portion of the former Spanish Sahara, Morocco occupied the area, 1980. Morocco accused Algeria of instigating Polisario attacks.

After years of bitter fighting, Morocco controls the main urban areas, but the Polisario Front's guerrillas move freely in the vast, sparsely populated deserts. The 2 sides signed a cease-fire agreement in 1990. The UN will conduct a referendum in Western Sahara on whether the territory should become independent or remain part of Morocco.

Mozambique
Republic of Mozambique
República de Moçambique

People: Population (1990 est.): 14,718,000. **Age distrib. (%):** 0–14: 45.3; 15–59: 50.6; 60+: 4.1. **Pop. density:** 49 per sq. mi. **Ethnic groups:** Bantu tribes. **Languages:** Portuguese (official), Makua, Malawi, Shona, Tsonga. **Religions:** Traditional beliefs 60%, Christian 30%, Moslem 10%.

Geography: Area: 303,769 sq. mi., about the size of Texas. **Location:** On SE coast of Africa. **Neighbors:** Tanzania on N, Malawi, Zambia, Zimbabwe on W, South Africa, Swaziland on S. **Topography:** Coastal lowlands comprise nearly half the country with plateaus rising in steps to the mountains along the western border. **Capital:** Maputo. **Cities** (1989 est.): Maputo 1.0 mln., Beira 291,604

Government: Type: Socialist one-party state. **Head of state:** Pres. Joaquim Chissano; b. Oct. 22, 1939; in office: Oct. 19, 1986. **Head of Government:** Mario de Graca Machungo; in office: July 17, 1986. **Local divisions:** 10 provinces. **Defense:** 8.4% of GNP (1987).

Economy: Industries: Cement, alcohol, textiles. **Chief crops:** Cashews, cotton, sugar, copra, tea. **Minerals:** Coal, copper, bauxite. **Arable land:** 4%. **Livestock** (1989): cattle: 1.3 mln. **Fish catch** (1987): 37,000 metric tons. **Electricity prod.** (1988): 1.7 bln. kwh. **Labor force:** 85% agric., 9% ind. & comm., 2% services.

Finance: Monetary unit: Metical (Jan. 1991: 950 = $1 US). **Gross national product** (1988): $1.1 bln. **Per capita income** (1987): $319. **Imports** (1988): $715 mln.; partners: So. Afr. 11%, U.S. 8%, USSR 12%, It. 10%. **Exports** (1988): $103 mln.; partners: Sp. 21%, U.S. 16%, Jap. 15%. **National budget** (1987): $427 mln.

Transport: Railway traffic (1988): 75 mln. passenger-km. **Motor vehicles:** in use (1988): 87,000 passenger cars, 24,000 comm. vehicles. **Chief ports:** Maputo, Beira, Nacala, Quelimane.

Communications: Television sets: 1 per 437 persons. **Radios:** 1 per 31 persons. **Telephones:** 1 per 235 persons. **Daily newspaper circ.** (1988): 5 per 1,000 pop.

Health: Life expectancy at birth (1989): 45 male; 48 female. **Births** (per 1,000 pop. 1989): 47. **Deaths** (per 1,000 pop. 1989): 18. **Natural increase:** 2.8%. **Hospital beds:** 1 per 1,227 persons. **Physicians:** 1 per 43,536 persons. **Infant mortality** (per 1,000 live births 1989): 200.

Education (1989): **Literacy:** 14%.

Major International Organization: UN (IMF, World Bank), OAU.

The first Portuguese post on the Mozambique coast was established in 1505, on the trade route to the East. Mozambique became independent June 25, 1975, after a ten-year war against Portuguese colonial domination. The 1974 revolution in Portugal paved the way for the orderly transfer of power to Frelimo (Front for the Liberation of Mozambique). Frelimo took over local administration Sept. 20, 1974, over the opposition, in part violent, of some blacks and whites. The new government, led by Maoist Pres. Samora Machel, promised a gradual transition to a communist system. Private schools were closed, rural collective farms organized, and private homes nationalized. Economic problems included the emigration of most of the country's whites, a politically untenable economic dependence on white-ruled South Africa, and a large external debt.

In the 1980s, severe drought and civil war caused famine and heavy loss of life.

Myanmar (Formerly Burma)
Union of Myanmar
Pyeidaungzu Myanma Naingngandaw

People: Population (1990 est.): 41,279,000. **Age distrib. (%):** 0–14: 41.2; 15–59: 52.8; 60+: 6.0. **Pop. density:** 152 per sq. mi. **Urban** (1986): 24%. **Ethnic groups:** Burmans (related to Tibetans) 68%; Karen 4%, Shan 7%, Rakhine 3%. **Languages:** Burmese (official), Karen, Shan. **Religions:** Buddhist 85%; animist, Christian.

Geography: Area: 261,789 sq. mi., nearly as large as Texas. **Location:** Between S. and S.E. Asia, on Bay of Bengal. **Neighbors:** Bangladesh, India on W, China, Laos, Thailand on E. **Topography:** Mountains surround Myanmar on W, N, and E, and dense forests cover much of the nation. N-S rivers provide habitable valleys and communications, especially the Irrawaddy, navigable for 900 miles. The country has a tropical monsoon climate. **Capital:** Yangon. **Cities** (1983 est.): Yangon 2,458,712; Mandalay 458,000; Karbe ('73 cen.): 253,600; Moulmein 188,000.

Government: Type: Military. **Head of state and head of government:** Gen. Saw Maung; in office: Sept. 21, 1988. **Local divisions:** 7 states and 7 divisions. **Defense:** 3.0% of GNP (1987).

Economy: Chief crops: Rice, sugarcane, peanuts, beans. **Minerals:** Oil, lead, silver, tin, tungsten, precious stones. **Crude oil reserves** (1985): 733 mln. bbls. **Other resources:** Rubber, teakwood. **Arable land:** 15%. **Livestock.** (1988): cattle: 9.9 mln.; pigs: 3.1 mln. **Fish catch** (1988): 704,000 metric tons. **Electricity prod.** (1988): 2.9 bln. kwh. **Labor force:** 66% agric; 12% ind.

Finance: Monetary unit: Kyat (Mar. 1991: 6.40 = $1 US). **Gross national product** (1988): $9.3 bln. **Per capita income** (1989): $210. **Imports** (1989): $201 mln.; partners: Jap. 50%, EEC 20%. **Exports** (1989): $215 mln.; partners: SE Asian countries 30%; EEC 12%. **Tourism** (1987): $14 mln. receipts. **National budget** (1988): $2.2 bln. **International reserves less gold** (Mar. 1991): $312 mln. **Gold:** 251,000 oz t. **Consumer prices** (change in 1989): 27%.

Transport: Railway traffic (1987): 3.1 bln. passenger-km. **Motor vehicles:** in use (1986): 35,000 passenger cars, 45,000 comm. vehicles. **Civil aviation** (1988): 214 mln. passenger-km.; 21 airports with scheduled flights. **Chief ports:** Yangon, Sittwe, Bassein, Moulmein, Tavoy.

Communications: Television sets: 1 per 592 persons. **Radios:** 1 per 13 persons. **Telephones:** 1 per 501 persons. **Daily newspaper circ.** (1989): 14 per 1,000 pop.

Health: Life expectancy at birth (1989): 53 male; 56 female. **Births** (per 1,000 pop. 1989): 33. **Deaths** (per 1,000 pop. 1989): 13. **Natural increase:** 2.0%. **Hospital beds:** 1 per 1,498 persons. **Physicians:** 1 per 3,485 persons. **Infant mortality** (per 1,000 live births 1989): 99.

Education (1989): **Literacy:** 66%. **Years compulsory:** 4; **Attendance:** 84%.

Major International Organizations: UN (World Bank, IMF, GATT).

Embassy: 2300 S St. NW 20008; 332-9044.

The Burmese arrived from Tibet before the 9th century, displacing earlier cultures, and a Buddhist monarchy was established by the 11th. Burma was conquered by the Mongol dynasty of China in 1272, then ruled by Shans as a Chinese tributary, until the 16th century.

Britain subjugated Burma in 3 wars, 1824-84, and ruled the country as part of India until 1937, when it became self-governing. Independence outside the Commonwealth was achieved Jan. 4, 1948.

Gen. Ne Win dominated politics from 1962 to 1988, when he abdicated power, following waves of anti-government demonstrations. He led a Revolutionary Council which drove Indians from the civil service and Chinese from commerce. Socialization of the economy was advanced, isolation from foreign countries enforced.

In 1987 Burma, once the richest nation in SE Asia, was granted least developed country status by the UN. Following Ne Win's resignation, Sein Lwin and later Maung Maung, a civilian, took power but rioting and street violence continued. In Sept., Gen. Saw Maung, a close associate of Ne Win, seized power.

In 1989 the country's name was changed to Myanmar.

The first free, multiparty elections in 30 years took place May 27, 1990, with the main opposition party winning a decisive victory, but the military rulers refused to hand over power.

Namibia

Republic of Namibia

People: Population (1990 est.): 1,372,000. **Pop density:** 4 per sq. mi. **Ethnic groups:** black 86%, white 8%. **Languages:** Afrikaans, English, several indigenous languages. **Religion:** Lutheran 50%, other Christian 30%.

Geography: Area: 317,818 sq. mi., slightly more than half the size of Alaska. **Location:** In S. Africa on the coast of the Atlantic Ocean. Angola on the N., Botswana on the E., and South Africa on the S. **Capital:** Windhoek. **Cities** (1990 est.): Windhoek, 114,000.

Government: Head of state: Pres. Sam Nujoma; in office: Feb. 16, 1990. Prime Min. Hage Geingob. **Local divisions:** 26 districts.

Economy: Mining accounts for over 40% of GNP. **Minerals:** Diamonds. **Electricity prod.** (1988): 432,000 kwh.

Finance: Monetary unit: South African Rand. **Gross National Product** (1988): $1.6 bln. **Per capital GNP** (1988): $1,300. **Imports** (1987): $842 mln. **Exports** (1987): $889,000 mln.

Communications: Television sets: 1 per 42 persons. **Radios:** 1 per 5.8 persons. **Telephones:** 1 per 17 persons.

Health: Life Expectancy at Birth (1989): 57 male; 62 female. **Births** (per 1,000 pop. 1989): 45. **Deaths** (per 1,000 pop 1989): 10. **Natural increase:** 3.5. **Hospital beds:** 1 per 166 persons. **Physicians:** 1 per 4,450 persons. **Infant Mortality** (per 1,000 live births 1989): 72.

Education (1989): **Literacy:** 16% nonwhite.

Namibia was declared a protectorate by Germany in 1890 and officially called South-West Africa. South Africa seized the territory from Germany in 1915 during World War 1; the League of Nations gave South Africa a mandate over the territory in 1920. In 1966, the Marxist South-West Africa People's Organization (SWAPO) launched a guerrilla war for independence.

In 1968 the UN General Assembly gave the area the name Namibia.

In a 1977 referendum, white voters backed a plan for a multiracial interim government to lead to independence. SWAPO rejected the plan. Both S. Africa and Namibian rebels agreed to a UN plan for independence by the end of 1978. S. Africa rejected the plan, Sept. 20, 1978, and held elections, without UN supervision, for Namibia's constituent assembly, Dec., that were ignored by the major black opposition parties.

In 1982, So. African and SWAPO agreed in principle on a cease-fire and the holding of UN-supervised elections. So. Africa, however, insisted on the withdrawal of Cuban forces from Angola as a precondition to Namibian independence. On Jan. 18, 1983, South Africa dissolved the Namibian National Assembly and resumed direct control of the territory.

In 1988, a U.S. mediated plan was agreed upon by So. Africa, Angola, and Cuba, which called for withdrawal of Cuban troops from Angola and black majority rule in Namibia.

Namibia became an independent nation March 21, 1990.

Walvis Bay, the only deepwater port in the country, was turned over to South African administration in 1922. S. Africa said in 1978 it would discuss sovereignty only after Namibian independence. Discussions were held in 1991.

Nauru

Republic of Nauru

Naoero

People: Population (1990): 8,100. **Pop density:** 987 per sq. mi. **Ethnic groups:** Nauruans 57%, Pacific Islanders 26%, Chinese 8%, European 8%. **Languages:** Nauruan (official). **Religions:** Predominately Christian.

Geography: Area: 8 sq. mi. **Location:** In Western Pacific O. just S of Equator. **Neighbors:** Nearest are Solomon Is. **Topography:** Mostly a plateau bearing high grade phosphate deposits, surrounded by a coral cliff and a sandy shore in concentric rings. **Capital:** Yaren.

Government: Type: Republic. **Head of state:** Pres. Bernard Dowiyogo; in office: Dec. 12, 1989. **Local divisions:** 14 districts.

Economy: Phosphate mining. **Electricity prod.** (1988): 48 mln. kwh.

Finance: Monetary unit: Australian dollar. **Gross national product** (1986): $160 mln.

Communications: Radios: 4,000 in use (1985). **Telephones** in use (1980): 1,500.

Health: Births (per 1,000 pop. 1989): 21. **Deaths** (per 1,000 pop. 1989): 5. **Natural increase:** 1.6%. **Infant mortality** (per 1,000 live births 1989): 41.

Education (1988): Literacy 99%; compulsory ages 6-16.

The island was discovered in 1798 by the British but was formally annexed to the German Empire in 1886. After World War I, Nauru became a League of Nations mandate administered by Australia. During World War II the Japanese occupied the island.

In 1947 Nauru was made a UN trust territory, administered by Australia. Nauru became an independent republic Jan. 31, 1968.

Phosphate exports provide one of the world's highest per capita revenues for the Nauru people.

Nepal

Kingdom of Nepal

Sri Nepala Sarkar

People: Population (1990 est.): 19,158,000. **Age distrib.** (%): 0–14: 42.2; 15–59: 52.9; 60+: 4.9. **Pop. density:** 334 per sq. mi. **Urban** (1987): 8%. **Ethnic groups:** The many tribes are descendants of Indian, Tibetan, and Central Asian migrants. **Languages:** Nepali (official) (an Indic language), many others. **Religions:** Hindu (official) 90%, Buddhist 7%.

Geography: Area: 56,136 sq. mi., the size of North Carolina. **Location:** Astride the Himalaya Mts. **Neighbors:** China on N, India on S. **Topography:** The Himalayas stretch across the N, the hill country with its fertile valleys extends across the center, while the southern border region is part of the flat, subtropical Ganges Plain. **Capital:** Kathmandu. **Cities** (1987 est.): Kathmandu 422,000, Pokhara, Biratnagar, Birganj.

Government: Type: In transition to democracy. **Head of state:** King Birendra Bir Bikram Shah Deva; b. Dec. 28, 1945; in office: Jan. 31, 1972. **Head of government:** Prime Min. Giriga Prasad Koirala; in office: May 21, 1991. **Local divisions:** 14 zones; 75 districts. **Defense:** 1.2% of GNP (1987).

Economy: Industries: Sugar, jute mills, tourism. **Chief crops:** Jute, rice, grain. **Minerals:** Quartz. **Other resources:** Forests. **Arable land:** 17%. **Livestock** (1989): cattle: 6.3 mln. **Electricity prod.** (1988): 530 mln. kwh. **Labor force:** 91% agric.

Finance: Monetary unit: Rupee (Mar. 1991: 33 = $1 US). **Gross national product** (1988): $3.1 bln. **Per capita income** (1986): $160. **Imports** (1990): $686 mln.; partners: India 47%, Jap. 25%. **Exports** (1990): $210 mln.; partners: India 68%. **Tourists** (1988): receipts: $28 mln. **National budget** (1989): $733 mln. **International reserves less gold** (Mar. 1991): $331 mln. **Gold:** 152,000 oz t. **Consumer prices** (change in 1990): 8.2%.

Transport: Civil aviation (1989): 408 mln. passenger-km.

Communications: Radios: 1 per 8.5 persons. **Telephones:** 1 per 686 persons.

Health: Life expectancy at birth (1989): 50 male; 49 female. **Births** (per 1,000 pop. 1989): 40. **Deaths** (per 1,000 pop. 1989): 15. **Natural increase:** 2.4%. **Hospital beds:** 1 per 4,234 persons. **Physicians:** 1 per 20,234 persons. **Infant mortality** (per 1,000 live births 1989): 101.

Education (1989): **Literacy:** 29%. **Years compulsory:** 3; Attendance: 79% primary, 22% secondary.

Major International Organizations: UN (IMF).

Embassy: 2131 Leroy Pl. NW 20008; 667-4550.

Nepal was originally a group of petty principalities, the inhabitants of one of which, the Gurkhas, became dominant about 1769. In 1951 King Tribhubana Bir Bikram, member of the Shah family, ended the system of rule by hereditary premiers of the Ranas family, who had kept the kings virtual prisoners, and established a cabinet system of government.

Virtually closed to the outside world for centuries, Nepal is now linked to India and Pakistan by roads and air service and to Tibet by road. Polygamy, child marriage, and the caste system were officially abolished in 1963.

In response to numerous pro-democracy protests, the government, which had banned all political parties since 1960, announced the legalization of political parties in 1990. Multi-party elections were scheduled for 1991.

Netherlands

Kingdom of the Netherlands
Koninkrijk der Nederlanden

People: Population (1990 est.) 14,864,000. **Age distrib. (%):** 0–14: 18.8; 15–60: 64.2; 60+: 17.0. **Pop. density:** 931 per sq. mi. **Urban** (1990): 88.3%. **Ethnic groups:** Dutch 97%. **Languages:** Dutch. **Religions:** Roman Catholic 40%, Dutch Reformed 19.3%.

Geography: Area: 15,770 sq. mi., the size of Mass., Conn., and R.I. combined. **Location:** in NW Europe on North Sea. **Topography:** The land is flat, an average alt. of 37 ft. above sea level, with much land below sea level reclaimed and protected by some 1,500 miles of dikes. Since 1920 the government has been draining the IJsselmeer, formerly the Zuider Zee. **Capital:** Amsterdam. **Cities** (1989): Amsterdam 694,000; Rotterdam 576,100; Hague 443,500.

Government: Type: Parliamentary democracy under a constitutional monarch. **Head of state:** Queen Beatrix; b. Jan. 31, 1938; in office: Apr. 30, 1980. **Head of government:** Prime Min. Ruud Lubbers; in office: Nov. 4, 1982. **Seat of govt.:** The Hague. **Local divisions:** 12 provinces. **Defense:** 3.2% of GNP (1987).

Economy: Industries: Metals, machinery, chemicals, oil refinery, diamond cutting, electronics, tourism. **Chief crops:** Grains, potatoes, sugar beets, vegetables, fruits, flowers. **Minerals:** Natural gas, oil. **Crude oil reserves** (1987): 195 mln. bbls. **Arable land:** 26%. **Livestock** (1988): cattle: 4.7 mln.; pigs: 13.4 mln. **Fish catch** (1987): 435,000 metric tons. **Electricity prod.** (1988): 63.0 bln. kwh. **Crude steel prod.** (1988): 5.5 mln. metric tons. **Labor force:** 1% agric.; 30% ind., 44% services, 23% govt.

Finance: Monetary unit: Guilder (June 1991: 1.92 = $1 US). **Gross national product** (1989): $237 bln. **Per capita income** (1987): $13,065. **Imports** (1989): $104.2 bln.; partners: W. Ger. 26%, Belg. 14%, U.S. 9%, U.K. 9%. **Exports** (1989): $107.8 bln.; partners: W. Ger. 26%, Belg. 14%, Fr. 10%, UK 9%. **Tourists** (1989): receipts: $3.0 bln. **National budget** (1988): $91 bln. expenditures. **International reserves less gold** (Mar. 1991): $16.8 bln. **Gold:** 43.94 mln. oz t. **Consumer prices** (change in 1990): 2.5%.

Transport: Railway traffic (1988): 9.3 bln. passenger-km. **Motor vehicles:** in use (1988): 5.2 mln. passenger cars, 506,000 comm. vehicles. **Civil aviation** (1988): 23.5 bln. passenger-km; 4 airports. **Chief ports:** Rotterdam, Amsterdam, IJmuiden.

Communications: Television sets: 1 per 3.2 persons. **Radios:** 1 per 1.2 persons. **Telephones:** 1 per 1.6 persons. **Daily newspaper circ.** (1987): 312 per 1,000 pop.

Health: Life expectancy at birth (1989): 74 male; 81 female. **Births** (per 1,000 pop. 1989): 13 **Deaths** (per 1,000 pop. 1989): 9. **Natural increase:** .4%. **Hospital beds:** 1 per 157 persons. **Physicians:** 1 per 414 persons. **Infant mortality** (per 1,000 live births 1991): 6

Education (1991): **Literacy:** 99%. **Years compulsory:** 10; attendance: 100%.

Major International Organizations: UN and all of its specialized agencies, NATO, EC, OECD.

Embassy: 4200 Linnean Ave. NW 20008; 244-5300.

Julius Caesar conquered the region in 55 BC, when it was inhabited by Celtic and Germanic tribes.

After the empire of Charlemagne fell apart, the Netherlands (Holland, Belgium, Flanders) split among counts, dukes and bishops, passed to Burgundy and thence to Charles V of Spain. His son, Philip II, tried to check the Dutch drive toward political freedom and Protestantism (1568-1573). William the Silent, prince of Orange, led a confederation of the northern provinces, called Estates, in the Union of Utrecht, 1579. The Estates retained individual sovereignty, but were represented jointly in the States-General, a body that had control of foreign affairs and defense. In 1581 they repudiated allegiance to Spain. The rise of the Dutch republic to naval, economic, and artistic eminence came in the 17th century.

The United Dutch Republic ended 1795 when the French formed the Batavian Republic. Napoleon made his brother Louis king of Holland, 1806; Louis abdicated 1810 when Napoleon annexed Holland. In 1813 the French were expelled. In 1815 the Congress of Vienna formed a kingdom of the Netherlands, including Belgium, under William I. In 1830, the Belgians seceded and formed a separate kingdom.

The constitution, promulgated 1814, and subsequently revised, assures a hereditary constitutional monarchy.

The Netherlands maintained its neutrality in World War I, but was invaded and brutally occupied by Germany, 1940-45.

In 1949, after several years of fighting, the Netherlands granted independence to Indonesia, where it had ruled since the 17th century. In 1963, West New Guinea was turned over to Indonesia, after five years of controversy and seizure of Dutch property in Indonesia.

The independence of former Dutch colonies has instigated mass emigrations to the Netherlands.

Though the Netherlands has been heavily industrialized, its productive small farms export large quantities of pork and dairy foods. Rotterdam, located along the principal mouth of the Rhine, handles the most cargo of any ocean port in the world. Canals, of which there are 3,478 miles, are important in transportation.

Netherlands Antilles

The **Netherlands Antilles**, constitutionally on a level of equality with the Netherlands homeland within the kingdom, consist of 2 groups of islands in the West Indies. **Curacao, Aruba,** and **Bonaire** are near the South American coast; **St. Eustatius, Saba,** and the southern part of **St. Maarten** are SE of Puerto Rico. Northern two-thirds of St. Maarten belong to French Guadeloupe; the French call the island St. Martin. Total area of the 2 groups is 385 sq. mi., including: Aruba 75, Bonaire 111, Curacao 171, St. Eustatius 11, Saba 5, St. Maarten (Dutch part) 13.

Aruba was separated from The Netherlands Antilles on Jan. 1, 1986; it is an autonomous member of The Netherlands, the same status as the Netherland Antilles.

Total pop. (est. 1989) was 187,000. Willemstad, on Curacao, is the capital. Principal industry is the refining of crude oil from Venezuela. Tourism is an important industry, as is shipbuilding.

New Zealand

People: Population: (1990 est.): 3,397,000. **Age distrib. (%):** 0–14: 23.1, 15–59: 61.9; 60+: 15.0 **Pop. density:** 32 per sq. mi. **Urban** (1988): 84.0%. **Ethnic groups:** European (mostly British) 87%, Polynesian (mostly Maori) 9%. **Languages:** English, Maori (both official). **Religions:** Anglican 29%, Presbyterian 18%, Roman Catholic 15%, others.

Geography: Area: 103,736 sq. mi., the size of Colorado. **Location:** in SW Pacific O. **Neighbors:** Nearest are Australia on W, Fiji, Tonga on N. **Topography:** Each of the 2 main islands (North and South Is.) is mainly hilly and mountainous. The east coasts consist of fertile plains, especially the broad Canterbury Plains on South Is. A volcanic plateau is in center of North Is. South Is. has glaciers and 15 peaks over 10,000 ft. **Capital:** Wellington. **Cities** (1989 est.): Auckland 149,000; Christchurch 168,000; Wellington 137,000; Manukau 190,000.

Government: Type: Parliamentary. **Head of state:** Queen Elizabeth II, represented by Gov.-Gen. Dame Cath Tizard. **Head of government:** Prime Min. Jim Bolger; b. 1935; in office: Oct.

27, 1990. **Local divisions:** 93 counties, 12 towns & districts. **Defense:** 2.2% of GNP (1987).

Economy: Industries: Food processing, textiles, machinery, fish, forest prods. **Chief crops:** Grain. **Minerals:** Oil, gas, iron, coal **Crude oil reserves** (1987): 182 mln. bbls. **Other resources:** Wool, timber. **Arable land:** 2%. **Livestock** (1989): cattle: 7.8 mln.; sheep: 60 mln. **Fish catch** (1989): 509,000 metric tons. **Electricity prod.** (1988): 27.0 bln. kwh. **Labor force:** 11% agric. & mining; 41% ind. and commerce, 47% services and gov.

Finance: Monetary unit: Dollar (June 1991: 1.70 = $1 US). **Gross national product** (1989): $39 bln. **Per capita income** (1988): $11,040. **Imports** (1990): $9.5 bln.; partners: Austral. 22%, U.S. 16%, Jap. 20%. **Exports** (1990): $9.4 bln.; partners: UK 9%, U.S. 15%, Jap. 15%, Austral. 16%. **Tourists** (1989): receipts $1.1 bln. **National budget** (1988): $15.6 bln. **International reserves less gold** (Feb. 1991): $4.0 bln. **Gold:** 1,000 oz t. **Consumer prices** (change in 1990): 6.1%.

Transport: Railway traffic (1987): 458 mln. passenger-km. **Motor vehicles:** in use (1989): 1.4 mln. passenger cars; 297,000 comm. vehicles. **Civil aviation:** (1989): 10.5 bln. passenger-km, 36 airports. **Chief ports:** Auckland, Wellington, Lyttleton, Tauranga.

Communications: Television sets: 1 per 3.1 persons. **Radios:** 1 per 1.1 persons. **Telephones:** 1 per 1.4 persons. **Daily newspaper circ.** (1989): 306 per 1,000 pop.

Health: Life expectancy at birth (1989): 72 male; 78 female. **Births** (per 1,000 pop. 1989): 16. **Deaths** (per 1,000 pop. 1989): 8. **Natural increase:** .8%. **Hospital beds:** 1 per 111 persons. **Physicians:** 1 per 522 persons. **Infant mortality** (per 1,000 live births 1989): 10.

Education (1989): **Literacy:** 99%. Compulsory ages 6-15; attendance: 100%.

Major International Organizations: UN (GATT, World Bank, IMF), Commonwealth of Nations, OECD.

Embassy: 37 Observatory Cir. NW 20008; 328-4800.

The Maoris, a Polynesian group from the eastern Pacific, reached New Zealand before and during the 14th century. The first European to sight New Zealand was Dutch navigator Abel Janszoon Tasman, but Maoris refused to allow him to land. British Capt. James Cook explored the coasts, 1769-1770.

British sovereignty was proclaimed in 1840, with organized settlement beginning in the same year. Representative institutions were granted in 1853. Maori Wars ended in 1870 with British victory. The colony became a dominion in 1907, and is an independent member of the Commonwealth.

In July 1985, the *Rainbow Warrior*, flagship of the Greenpeace organization, was bombed and sunk in Auckland harbour by French secret service agents.

A labor tradition in politics dates back to the 19th century. Private ownership is basic to the economy, but state ownership or regulation affects many industries. Transportation, broadcasting, mining, and forestry are largely state-owned.

The native Maoris number about 250,000. Four of 92 members of the House of Representatives are elected directly by the Maori people.

New Zealand comprises **North Island**, 44,035 sq. mi.; **South Island**, 58,304 sq. mi.; **Stewart Island**, 674 sq. mi.; **Chatham Islands**, 372 sq. mi.

In 1965, the **Cook Islands** (pop. 1986 est., 17,185; area 93 sq. mi.) became self-governing although New Zealand retains responsibility for defense and foreign affairs. Niue attained the same status in 1974; it lies 400 mi. to W (pop. 1987 est., 2,500; area 100 sq. mi.). Tokelau Is., (pop. 1987 est., 1,600; area 4 sq. mi.) are 300 mi. N of Samoa.

Ross Dependency, administered by New Zealand since 1923, comprises 160,000 sq. mi. of Antarctic territory.

Nicaragua

Republic of Nicaragua

República de Nicaragua

People: Population (1990 est.): 3,606,000. **Age distrib. (%):** 0–14: 45.8; 15–59: 49.9; 60+: 4.3. **Pop. density:** 73 per sq. mi. **Urban** (1988): 60%. **Ethnic groups:** Mestizo 69%, Caucasian 17%, black 9%, Indian 5%. **Languages:** Spanish, (official). **Religion:** Roman Catholic 88%.

Geography: Area: 50,193 sq. mi., about the size of Iowa. **Location:** In Central America. **Neighbors:** Honduras on N, Costa Rica on S. **Topography:** Both Atlantic and Pacific coasts are over 200 mi. long. The Cordillera Mtns., with many volcanic peaks, runs NW-SE through the middle of the country. Between this and a volcanic range to the E lie Lakes Managua and Nicaragua. **Capital:** Managua. **Cities** (1986): Managua 1 mln.

Government: Type: Republic. **Head of Government:** Violeta Barrios de Chamorro; b. 1929; in office Apr. 25, 1990. **Local divisions:** 16 departments. **Defense:** 16.8% of GNP (1985).

Economy: Industries: Oil refining, food processing, chemicals, textiles. **Chief crops:** Bananas, cotton, fruit, yucca, coffee, sugar, corn, beans, cocoa, rice, sesame, tobacco, wheat. **Minerals:** Gold, silver, copper, tungsten. **Other resources:** Forests, shrimp. **Arable land:** 10%. **Livestock** (1989): cattle: 1.6 mln.; pigs: 680,000. **Fish catch:** (1987): 4,983 metric tons. **Electricity prod.** (1988): 1.2 bln. kwh. **Labor force:** 44% agric.; 13% Ind.; 43% services.

Finance: Monetary unit: Cordoba (May 1990: 100,000 = $1 US). **Gross national product** (1988): $2.1 bln. **Per capita GNP** (1988): $610. **Imports** (1988): $807 mln.; partners Comecon, CACM, EC. **Exports** (1988): $235 mln.; partners EC, Japan, Comecon. **National budget** (1987): $1.4 bln. expenditures. **Consumer prices** (change in 1989): 10,000%.

Transport: Railway traffic (1988): 25.5 mln. passenger-miles. **Motor vehicles:** in use (1986): 46,000 passenger cars, 30,000 comm. vehicles. **Chief ports:** Corinto, Puerto Somoza, San Juan del Sur.

Communications: Television sets: 1 per 18 persons. **Radios:** 1 per 4.3 persons. **Telephones:** 1 per 77 persons. **Daily newspaper circ.** (1989): 62 per 1,000 pop.

Health: Life expectancy at birth (1989): 61 male; 63 female. **Births** (per 1,000 pop. 1989): 39. **Deaths** (per 1,000 pop. 1989): 8. **Natural increase:** 3.1%. **Hospital beds:** 1 per 761 persons. **Physicians:** 1 per 1,678 persons. **Infant mortality** (per 1,000 live births 1989): 65.

Education (1986): **Literacy:** 66%. **Years compulsory:** 11 years or 16 years old.

Major International Organizations: UN and all of its specialized agencies, OAS.

Embassy: 1627 New Hampshire Ave. NW 20009; 939-6570.

Nicaragua, inhabited by various Indian tribes, was conquered by Spain in 1552. After gaining independence from Spain, 1821, Nicaragua was united for a short period with Mexico, then with the United Provinces of Central America, finally becoming an independent republic, 1838.

U.S. Marines occupied the country at times in the early 20th century, the last time from 1926 to 1933.

Gen. Anastasio Somoza Debayle was elected president 1967. He resigned 1972, but was elected president again in 1974. Martial law was imposed in Dec. 1974, after officials were kidnapped by the Marxist Sandinista guerrillas. Violent opposition spread to nearly all classes in 1978; nationwide strikes called against the government touched off a state of civil war. Months of simmering civil war ended when Somoza fled, July 19, 1979.

Relations with the U.S. were strained due to Nicaragua's aid to leftist guerrillas in El Salvador and the U.S. backing anti-Sandinista contra guerrilla groups.

In 1983, the contras launched their first major offensive; the Sandinistas imposed rule by decree. In 1985, the U.S. House rejected Pres. Reagan's request for military aid to the contras.

The diversion of funds to the contras from the proceeds of a secret arms sale to Iran caused a major scandal in the U.S. The plan, masterminded by the administration's national security advisor and his deputy, took place at a time when military aid to the contras was forbidden by law.

In a stunning upset, Violeta Barrios de Chamorro defeat Ortega in national elections, Feb. 25, 1990.

Niger

Republic of Niger

République du Niger

People: Population (1990 est.): 7,691,000. **Age distrib. (%):** 0–14: 46.7; 15–59: 48.5; 60+: 4.8. **Pop. density:** 15 per sq. mi. **Urban** (1988): 21%. **Ethnic groups:** Hausa 56%, Djerma 22%, Fulani 8%, Tuareg 8%. **Languages:** French (official), Hausa, Fulani. **Religions:** Sunni Moslem 80%.

Geography: Area: 489,189 sq. mi., almost 3 times the size of California. **Location:** In the interior of N. Africa. **Neighbors:** Libya, Algeria on N, Mali, Burkina Faso on W, Benin, Nigeria on S, Chad on E. **Topography:** Mostly arid desert and mountains. A narrow savanna in the S and the Niger R. basin in the SW contain most of the population. **Capital:** Niamey. **Cities** (1987 est.): Niamey 350,000.

Government: Type: Republic; military in power. **Head of government:** Pres. Ali Seibou; in office: Dec. 20, 1989. **Prime Min.** Aliou Mahamidou; in office: Mar. 2, 1990. **Local divisions:** 7 departments. **Defense:** 0.8% of GNP (1987).

Economy: Chief crops: Peanuts, cotton. **Minerals:** Uranium, coal, iron. **Arable land:** 3%. **Livestock** (1989): cattle: 3.5 mln.; sheep 3.5 mln. **Electricity prod.** (1988): 227 mln. kwh. **Labor force:** 90% agric.

Finance: Monetary unit: CFA franc (Mar. 1991: 290 = $1 US). **Gross national product** (1989): $2.1 bln. **Per capita GNP** (1989): $290. **Imports** (1988): $441 mln.; partners: Fr. 36%, Nig. 13%. **Exports** (1988): $371 mln.; partners: Fr. 36%, Nig. 17%. **National budget** (1988): $452 mln. expenditures. **International reserves less gold** (Jan. 1991): $222 mln. **Gold:** 11,000 oz t. **Consumer prices** (change in 1990): −0.8%.

Transport: Motor vehicles: in use (1988): 27,000 passenger cars, 25,000 comm. vehicles.

Communications: Television sets: 1 per 301 persons. **Radios:** 1 per 19 persons. **Telephones:** 1 per 563 persons. **Daily newspaper cir.** (1990): 1 per 1,000 pop.

Health: Life expectancy at birth (1989): 48 male; 50 female. **Births** (per 1,000 pop. 1989): 49. **Deaths** (per 1,000 pop. 1989): 17. **Natural increase:** 3.2%. **Infant mortality** (per 1,000 live births 1989): 137.

Education (1989): **Literacy:** 13%. **Years compulsory:** 6; attendance: 15%.

Major International Organizations: UN (GATT, IMF, WHO, FAO), OAU.

Embassy: 2204 R St. NW 20008; 483-4224.

Niger was part of ancient and medieval African empires. European explorers reached the area in the late 18th century. The French colony of Niger was established 1900-22, after the defeat of Tuareg fighters, who had invaded the area from the N a century before. The country became independent Aug. 3, 1960. The next year it signed a bilateral agreement with France retaining close economic and cultural ties.

Nigeria

Federal Republic of Nigeria

People: Population (1990 est.): 118,865,000. **Pop. density:** 322 per sq. mi. **Urban** (1985): 23%. **Ethnic groups:** Hausa 21%, Yoruba 20%, Ibo 17%, Fulani 9%, others. **Languages:** English (official), Hausa, Yoruba, Ibo. **Religions:** Moslem 50% (in N), Christian 40% (in S), others.

Geography: Area: 356,667 sq. mi., more than twice the size of California. **Location:** On the S coast of W. Africa. **Neighbors:** Benin on W, Niger on N, Chad, Cameroon on E. **Topography:** 4 E-W regions divide Nigeria: a coastal mangrove swamp 10-60 mi. wide, a tropical rain forest 50-100 mi. wide, a plateau of savanna and open woodland, and semidesert in the N. **Capital:** Lagos. **Cities:** (1989): Lagos 1,274,000; Ibadan 1,201,000.

Government: Type: Military. **Head of state:** Pres. Ibrahim Babangida; b. Aug. 17, 1941; in office: Aug. 30, 1985. **Local divisions:** 21 states plus federal capital territory. **Defense:** 1.0% of GNP (1987).

Economy: Industries: Crude oil (95% of export), food processing, assembly of vehicles, textiles. **Chief crops:** Cocoa (main export crop), tobacco, palm products, peanuts, cotton, soybeans. **Minerals:** Oil, gas, coal, iron, limestone, columbium, tin. **Crude oil reserves** (1987): 16.8 bln. bbls. **Other resources:** Timber, rubber, hides. **Arable land:** 31%. **Livestock** (1989): cattle: 12.1 mln.; goats: 26.3 mln.; sheep: 13.1 mln. **Fish catch** (1989): 315,000 metric tons. **Electricity prod.** (1988): 11.2 bln. kwh. **Labor force:** 54% agric., 19% ind., comm. and serv.

Finance: Monetary unit: Naira (Feb. 1991: 9.76 = $1.00 US). **Gross national product** (1989): $28 bln. **Per capita GNP** (1989): $250. **Imports** (1987): $7.8 bln.; partners: U.S., EC. **Exports** (1987): $7.3 bln.; partners: U.S., EC. **Tourist receipts** (1988): $78 mln. **National budget** (1987): $4.8 bln. expendi-

tures. **International reserves less gold** (Jan. 1991): $3.8 bln. **Gold:** 687,000 oz t. **Consumer prices** (change in 1990): 25.0%.

Transport: Motor vehicles: in use (1981): 262,000 passenger cars, 90,000 comm. vehicles. **Civil aviation** (1988): 1.1 bln. passenger-km; 13 airports. **Chief ports:** Port Harcourt, Lagos, Warri, Calabar.

Communications: Television sets: 1 per 21 persons. **Radios:** 1 per 12 persons. **Telephones:** 1 per 240 persons. **Daily newspaper circ.** (1988): 12 per 1,000 pop.

Health: Life expectancy at birth (1989): 47 male; 49 female. **Births** (per 1,000 pop. 1989): 46. **Deaths** (per 1,000 pop. 1989): 17. **Natural increase:** 2.9%. **Hospital beds:** 1 per 1,142 persons. **Physicians:** 1 per 6,900 persons. **Infant mortality** (per 1,000 live births 1989): 121.

Education (1989): **Literacy:** 42%. **Primary school attendance:** 42%.

Major International Organizations: UN (GATT, IMO, WHO), OPEC, OAU, Commonwealth of Nations.

Embassy: 2201 M St. NW 20037; 822-1500.

Early cultures in Nigeria date back to at least 700 BC. From the 12th to the 14th centuries, more advanced cultures developed in the Yoruba area, at Ife, and in the north, where Moslem influence prevailed.

Portuguese and British slavers appeared from the 15th-16th centuries. Britain seized Lagos, 1861, during an anti-slave trade campaign, and gradually extended control inland until 1900. Nigeria became independent Oct. 1, 1960, and a republic Oct. 1, 1963.

On May 30, 1967, the Eastern Region seceded, proclaiming itself the Republic of Biafra, plunging the country into civil war. Casualties in the war were est. at over 1 million, including many "Biafrans" (mostly Ibos) who died of starvation despite international efforts to provide relief. The secessionists, after steadily losing ground, capitulated Jan. 12, 1970. Within a few years, the Ibos were reintegrated into national life.

Oil revenues have made possible a massive economic development program, largely using private enterprise, but agriculture has lagged.

After 13 years of military rule, the nation experienced a peaceful return to civilian government, Oct., 1979.

Military rule returned to Nigeria, Dec. 31, 1983 as a coup ousted the democratically-elected government. The government has promised a return to civilian rule by 1992.

Norway

Kingdom of Norway

Kongeriket Norge

People: Population (1990 est.): 4,214,000. **Age distrib.** (%): 0–14: 19.0; 15–59: 59.9; 60+: 21.1. **Pop. density:** 33 per sq. mi. **Urban** (1985): 80%. **Ethnic groups:** Germanic (Nordic, Alpine, Baltic), minority Lapps. **Languages:** Norwegian (official). **Religions:** Evangelical Lutheran 94%.

Geography: Area: 125,181 sq. mi., slightly larger than New Mexico. **Location:** Occupies the W part of Scandinavian peninsula in NW Europe (extends farther north than any European land). **Neighbors:** Sweden, Finland, USSR on E. **Topography:** A highly indented coast is lined with tens of thousands of islands. Mountains and plateaus cover most of the country, which is only 25% forested. **Capital:** Oslo. **Cities** (1990): Oslo 457,000; Bergen 211,000.

Government: Type: Hereditary constitutional monarchy. **Head of state:** King Harald V; b. Feb. 21, 1937; in office: Jan. 18, 1991. **Head of government:** Prime Min. Gro Harlem Brundtland; in office: Nov. 3, 1990. **Local divisions:** Oslo, Svalbard and 18 fylker (counties). **Defense:** 3.2% of GNP (1989).

Economy: Industries: Paper, shipbuilding, engineering, metals, chemicals, food processing oil, gas. **Chief crops:** Grains, potatoes, fruits. **Minerals:** Oil, copper, pyrites, nickel, iron, zinc, lead. **Crude oil reserves** (1987): 11.1 bln. bbls. **Other resources:** Timber. **Arable land:** 3%. **Livestock** (1989): sheep: 2.3 mln.; cattle: 932,000; pigs: 750,000. **Fish catch** (1989): 1.8 mln. metric tons. **Electricity prod.** (1988): 118 bln. kwh. **Crude steel prod.** (1988): 900,000 metric tons. **Labor force:** 7% agric.; 47% ind., banking, comm.; 18% services, 26% govt.

Finance: Monetary unit: Kroner (June 1991: 6.60 = $1 US). **Gross national product** (1989): $92 bln. **Per capita GNP** (1989): $21,850. **Imports** (1990): $26.8 mln.; partners: Swed.

17%, W. Ger. 12%, UK 7%. **Exports** (1990): $34.0 bln.; partners: UK 27%, W. Ger. 11%, Swed. 12%. **Tourists** (1989): receipts: $1.4 bln. **National budget** (1988): $40.6 bln. expenditures. **International reserves less gold** (Mar. 1991): $14.1 bln. **Gold:** 1.18 mln. oz t. **Consumer prices** (change in 1990): 4.1%.
Transport: Railway traffic (1988): 2.1 bln. passenger-km. **Motor vehicles:** in use (1988): 1.6 mln. passenger cars, 313,000 comm. vehicles. **Civil aviation:** (1988): 5.6 bln. passenger-km; 48 airports. **Chief ports:** Bergen, Stavanger, Oslo, Tonsberg.
Communications: Television sets: 1 per 2.9 persons. **Radios:** 1 per 1.3 persons. **Telephones:** 1 per 1.6 persons. **Daily newspaper circ.** (1988): 540 per 1,000 pop.
Health: Life expectancy at birth (1989): 72.7 male; 79.7 female. **Births** (per 1,000 pop. 1989): 13. **Deaths** (per 1,000 pop. 1989): 11. **Natural increase:** .2%. **Hospital beds:** 1 per 171 persons. **Physicians:** 1 per 441 persons. **Infant mortality** (per 1,000 live births 1989): 7.1.
Education (1989): **Literacy:** 100%. **Years Compulsory:** 9.
Major International Organizations: UN and all of its specialized agencies, NATO, OECD.
Embassy: 2720 34th St. NW 20008; 333-6000.

The first supreme ruler of Norway was Harald the Fairhaired who came to power in 872 AD. Between 800 and 1000, Norway's Vikings raided and occupied widely dispersed parts of Europe.
The country was united with Denmark 1381-1814, and with Sweden, 1814-1905. In 1905, the country became independent with Prince Charles of Denmark as king.
Norway remained neutral during World War I. Germany attacked Norway Apr. 9, 1940, and held it until liberation May 8, 1945. The country abandoned its neutrality after the war, and joined the NATO alliance.
Abundant hydroelectric resources provided the base for Norway's industrialization, producing one of the highest living standards in the world.
Norway's merchant marine is one of the world's largest.
Petroleum output from oil and mineral deposits under the continental shelf has raised state revenues.
Svalbard is a group of mountainous islands in the Arctic O., c. 23,957 sq. mi., pop. varying seasonally from 1,500 to 3,600. The largest, Spitsbergen (formerly called West Spitsbergen), 15,060 sq. mi., seat of governor, is about 370 mi. N of Norway. By a treaty signed in Paris, 1920, major European powers recognized the sovereignty of Norway, which incorporated it in 1925. Both Norway and the USSR mine rich coal deposits.

Oman

Sultanate of Oman

Saltanat 'Uman

People: Population (1990 est.): 1,305,000. **Pop. density:** 16 per sq. mi. **Urban** (1986): 9%. **Ethnic groups:** Arab 88%, Baluchi 4%, Persian 3%, Indian 2%, African 2%. **Languages:** Arabic (official). **Religions:** Ibadhi Moslem 75%, Sunni Moslem.
Geography: Area: 82,030 sq. mi., about the size of New Mexico. **Location:** On SE coast of Arabian peninsula. **Neighbors:** United Arab Emirates, Saudi Arabia, Yemen on W. **Topography:** Oman has a narrow coastal plain up to 10 mi. wide, a range of barren mountains reaching 9,900 ft., and a wide, stony, mostly waterless plateau, avg. alt. 1,000 ft. Also the tip of the Ruus-al-Jebal peninsula controls access to the Persian Gulf. **Capital:** Muscat. **Cities** (1990 est.): Muscat 85,000.
Government: Type: Absolute monarchy. **Head of state:** Sultan Qabus bin Said; b. Nov. 18, 1942; in office: July 23, 1970. **Local divisions:** 1 province, numerous districts. **Defense:** 24% of GNP (1989).
Economy: Chief crops: Dates, fruits vegetables, wheat, bananas. **Minerals:** Oil (95% of exports). **Crude oil reserves** (1987): 4.5 bln. bbls. **Fish catch** (1988): 115,000 metric tons. **Electricity prod.** (1988): 3.5 bln. kwh. **Labor force:** 60% agric. & fishing.
Finance: Monetary unit: Rial Omani (Mar. 1991): .38 = $1 US). **Gross national product** (1989): $7.7 bln. **Imports** (1989): $2.2 bln.; partners: Jap. 21%, UAE 17%, UK 14%. **Exports** (1989): $2.6 bln.; partners: Jap. 58%, Europe 30%. **National budget** (1987): $4.2 bln. revenues; $5.4 bln. expenditures. **Inter-**

national reserves less gold (Mar. 1991): $1.6 bln. **Gold:** 289,000 oz t.
Transport: Chief ports: Matrah, Muscat.
Communications: Television sets: 1 per 1.4 persons. **Radios:** 1 per 1.6 persons. **Telephones:** 1 per 17 persons.
Health: Life expectancy at birth (1989): 55 male; 58 female. **Hospital beds:** 1 per 331 persons. **Physicians:** 1 per 1,071 persons. **Infant Mortality** (per 1,000 live births 1989): 107.
Education (1989): **Literacy:** 20%. **Attendance:** 80% primary, 30% secondary.
Major International Organizations: UN (World Bank, IMF), Arab League.
Embassy: 2342 Massachusetts Ave. NW 20008; 387-1980.

A long history of rule by other lands, including Portugal in the 16th century, ended with the ouster of the Persians in 1744. By the early 19th century, Muscat and Oman was one of the most important countries in the region, controlling much of the Persian and Pakistan coasts, and ruling far-away Zanzibar, which was separated in 1861 under British mediation.
British influence was confirmed in a 1951 treaty, and Britain helped suppress an uprising by traditionally rebellious interior tribes against control by Muscat in the 1950s.
On July 23, 1970, Sultan Said bin Taimur was overthrown by his son who changed the nation's name to Sultanate of Oman.
Oil has been the major source of income.
Oman opened its air bases to Western forces following the Iraqi invasion of Kuwait on Aug. 2, 1990.

Pakistan

Islamic Republic of Pakistan

Islam-i Jamhuriya-e Pakistan

People: Population (1990 est.): 113,163,000. **Pop. density:** 335 per sq. mi. **Urban** (1988): 32%. **Ethnic groups:** Punjabi 66%, Sindhi 13%, Pushtun (Iranian) 8.5%, Urdu 7.6%, Baluchi 2.5%, others. **Languages:** Urdu, (official), Punjabi, Sindhi, Pushtu, Baluchi, Brahvi. **Religions:** Moslem 97%.
Geography: Area: 310,403 sq. mi., about the size of Texas. **Location:** In W part of South Asia. **Neighbors:** Iran on W, Afghanistan, China on N, India on E. **Topography:** The Indus R. rises in the Hindu Kush and Himalaya mtns. in the N (highest is K2, or Godwin Austen, 28,250 ft., 2d highest in world), then flows over 1,000 mi. through fertile valley and empties into Arabian Sea. Thar Desert, Eastern Plains flank Indus Valley. **Capital:** Islamabad. **Cities** (1981 cen.): Karachi 5.1 mln.; Lahore 2.9 mln.; Faisalabad 1 mln.; Hyderabad 795,000; Rawalpindi 928,000.
Government: Type: Parliamentary democracy in a federal setting. **Head of government:** Pres. Ghulam Ishaq Khan; in office: Dec. 12, 1988. **Head of state:** Prime Min. Nawaz Sharif; in office: Nov. 6, 1990. **Local divisions:** Federal capital, 4 provinces, tribal areas. **Defense:** 6.4% of GNP (1987).
Economy: Industries: Textiles, food processing, chemicals, tobacco, **Chief crops:** Rice, wheat. **Minerals:** Natural gas, iron ore. **Crude oil reserves** (1987): 116 mln. bbls. **Other resources:** Wool. **Arable land:** 26%. **Livestock** (1989): cattle: 17.2 mln.; sheep: 28.3 mln.; goats: 34.2 mln. **Fish catch** (1989): 428,000 metric tons. **Electricity prod.** (1988): 29 bln. kwh. **Labor force:** 53% agric.; 13% ind; 33% services.
Finance: Monetary unit: Rupee (June 1991: 23.52 = $1 US). **Gross national product** (1989): $40 bln. **Per capita GNP** (1989): $370. **Imports** (1990): $7.3 bln.; partners: Jap. 16%, U.S. 11%, Kuwait 7%. **Exports** (1990): $5.5 bln.; partners: Jap. 10%, U.S. 10%. **Tourist** (1989): $133 mln. receipts. **National budget** (1987): $9.1 bln. expenditures. **International reserves less gold** (Mar. 1991): $228 mln. **Gold:** 1.94 mln. oz t. **Consumer prices** (change in 1990): 9.1%.
Transport: Railway traffic (1989): 18.7 bln. passenger-km. **Motor vehicles:** in use (1987): 540,000 passenger cars, 158,000 comm. vehicles. **Civil aviation** (1989): 8.7 bln. passenger-km; 32 airports with scheduled flights. **Chief ports:** Karachi.
Communications: Television sets: 1 per 73 persons. **Radios:** 1 per 11 persons. **Telephones:** 1 per 159 persons. **Daily newspaper circ.** (1988): 12 per 1,000 pop.
Health: Life expectancy at birth (1989): 54 male; 55 female. **Births** (per 1,000 pop. 1989): 43 **Deaths** (per 1,000 pop. 1989): 14. **Natural increase:** 2.9%. **Hospital beds:** 1 per 1,783 persons. **Physicians:** 1 per 2,081 persons. **Infant mortality** (per 1,000 live births 1989): 120.

Education (1989): Literacy: 26%.
Major International Organizations: UN (GATT, ILO, IMF, WHO).
Embassy: 2315 Massachusetts Ave. NW 20008; 939-6200.

Present-day Pakistan shares the 5,000-year history of the India-Pakistan sub-continent. At present day Harappa and Mohenjo Daro, the Indus Valley Civilization, with large cities and elaborate irrigation systems, flourished c. 4,000-2,500 BC.

Aryan invaders from the NW conquered the region around 1,500 BC, forging a Hindu civilization that dominated Pakistan as well as India for 2,000 years.

Beginning with the Persians in the 6th century BC, and continuing with Alexander the Great and with the Sassanians, successive nations to the west ruled or influenced Pakistan, eventually separating the area from the Indian cultural sphere.

The first Arab invasion, 712 AD, introduced Islam. Under the Mogul empire (1526-1857), Moslems ruled most of India, yielding to British encroachment and resurgent Hindus.

After World War I the Moslems of British India began agitation for minority rights in elections. Mohammad Ali Jinnah (1876-1948) was the principal architect of Pakistan. A leader of the Moslem League from 1916, he worked for dominion status for India; from 1940 he advocated a separate Moslem state.

When the British withdrew Aug. 14, 1947, the Islamic majority areas of India acquired self-government as Pakistan, with dominion status in the Commonwealth. Pakistan was divided into 2 sections, West Pakistan and East Pakistan. The 2 areas were nearly 1,000 mi. apart on opposite sides of India.

Pakistan became a republic in 1956. Pakistan had a National Assembly (legislature) with equal membership from East and West Pakistan, and 2 Provincial Assemblies. In Oct. 1958, Gen. Mohammad Ayub Khan took power in a coup. He was elected president in 1960, reelected in 1965.

Ayub resigned Mar. 25, 1969, after several months of violent rioting and unrest, most of it in East Pakistan, which demanded autonomy. The government was turned over to Gen. Agha Mohammad Yahya Khan and martial law was declared.

The Awami League, which sought regional autonomy for East Pakistan, won a majority in Dec. 1970 elections to a National Assembly which was to write a new constitution. In March, 1971 Yahya postponed the Assembly. Rioting and strikes broke out in the East.

On Mar. 25, 1971, government troops launched attacks in the East. The Easterners, aided by India, proclaimed the independent nation of Bangladesh. In months of widespread fighting, countless thousands were killed. Some 10 million Easterners fled into India.

Full scale war between India and Pakistan had spread to both the East and West fronts by Dec. 3. Pakistan troops in the East surrendered Dec. 16; Pakistan agreed to a cease-fire in the West Dec. 17. On July 3, 1972, Pakistan and India signed a pact agreeing to withdraw troops from their borders and seek peaceful solutions to all problems.

Zulfikar Ali Bhutto, leader of the Pakistan People's Party, which had won the most West Pakistan votes in the Dec. 1970 elections, became president Dec. 20.

Bhutto was overthrown in a military coup July, 1977. Convicted of complicity in a 1974 political murder, Bhutto was executed Apr.4, 1979. Benazir Bhutto, his daughter, returned to Pakistan from exile in Europe in 1986. Her efforts to relaunch the Pakistan People's Party sparked violence and antigovernment riots.

Pres. Mohammad Zia ul-Haq was killed when his plane exploded in Aug. 1988. Following Nov. elections, Benazir Bhutto was named Prime Minister, the first woman leader of a Moslem nation. Her party was soundly defeated in the Oct. 1990 elections; there were charges of corruption against Bhutto.

There are several million Afghan refugees now in Pakistan.

Legislation was submitted in 1991 to adopt Islamic law in place of the current secular code.

Panama

Republic of Panama

República de Panamá

People: Population (1990 est.): 2,423,000. **Age distrib. (%):** 0–14: 35.5; 15–59: 57.6; 60+: 6.9. **Pop. density:** 81 per sq. mi.

Urban (1987): 53%. **Ethnic groups:** Mestizo 70%, West Indian 14%, Caucasian 10%, Indian 6%. **Languages:** Spanish (official), English. **Religions:** Roman Catholic 93%, Protestant 6%.

Geography: Area: 29,208 sq. mi., slightly larger than West Virginia. **Location:** In Central America. **Neighbors:** Costa Rica on W., Colombia on E. **Topography:** 2 mountain ranges run the length of the isthmus. Tropical rain forests cover the Caribbean coast and eastern Panama. **Capital:** Panama. **Cities** (1990 est.): Panama City 411,000.

Government: Type: Constitutional democracy, centralized republic. **Head of state and head of government:** Pres. Guillermo Endara; in office: Dec. 20, 1989. **Local divisions:** 9 provinces, 1 territory. **Defense:** 3% of GNP (1987).

Economy: Industries: Oil refining, international banking. **Chief crops:** Bananas, pineapples, cocoa, corn, coconuts, sugar. **Minerals:** Copper. **Other resources:** Forests (mahogany), shrimp. **Arable land:** 8%. **Livestock** (1989): cattle: 1.5 mln.; pigs: 240,000. **Electricity prod.** (1988): 3.3 bln. kwh. **Labor force:** 26% agric., 28%, govt. & community services.

Finance: Monetary unit: Balboa (Apr. 1991: 1.00 = $1 US). **Gross national product** (1989): $4.2 bln. **Per capita GNP** (1989): $1,780. **Imports** (1988): $709 mln.; partners: U.S. 37%, Mexico 8%. **Exports** (1988): $280 mln.; partners: U.S. 48%, EC 16%. **Tourists** (1989): $102 mln. receipts. **National budget** (1988): $800 mln. **International reserves less gold** (Jan. 1991): $334 mln. **Consumer prices** (change in 1990): 0.6%.

Transport: Motor vehicles: in use (1989): 129,000 passenger cars, 46,000 comm. vehicles. **Civil aviation** (1986): 505 mln. passenger-km; 6 airports with scheduled flights. **Chief ports:** Balboa, Cristobal.

Communications: Television sets: 1 per 4.9 persons. **Radios:** 1 per 2.5 persons. **Telephones:** 1 per 9.3 persons. **Daily newspaper circ.** (1990): 60 per 1,000 pop.

Health: Life expectancy at birth (1989): 71 male; 75 female. **Births** (per 1,000 pop. 1989): 27. **Deaths** (per 1,000 pop. 1989): 5. **Natural increase:** 2.1%. **Hospital beds:** 1 per 299 persons. **Physicians:** 1 per 841 persons. **Infant mortality** (per 1,000 live births 1989): 23.

Education (1989): **Literacy:** 87%. **Primary school attendance:** almost 100%.

Major International Organizations: UN (IMF, IMO, World Bank), OAS.

Embassy: 2862 McGill Terrace NW 20008; 483-1407.

The coast of Panama was sighted by Rodrigo de Bastidas, sailing with Columbus for Spain in 1501, and was visited by Columbus in 1502. Vasco Nunez de Balboa crossed the isthmus and "discovered" the Pacific O. Sept. 13, 1513. Spanish colonies were ravaged by Francis Drake, 1572-95, and Henry Morgan, 1668-71. Morgan destroyed the old city of Panama which had been founded in 1519. Freed from Spain, Panama joined Colombia in 1821.

Panama declared its independence from Colombia Nov. 3, 1903, with U.S. recognition. U.S. naval forces deterred action by Colombia. On Nov. 18, 1903, Panama granted use, occupation and control of the Canal Zone to the U.S. by treaty, ratified Feb. 26, 1904.

In 1978, a new treaty provided for a gradual takeover by Panama of the canal, and withdrawal of U.S. troops, to be completed by 1999. U.S. payments were substantially increased in the interim. The permanent neutrality of the canal was also guaranteed.

President Delvalle was ousted by the National Assembly, Feb. 26, 1988, after he tried to fire the head of the Panama Defense Forces, Gen. Manuel Antonio Noriega. Noriega had been indicted by 2 U.S. federal grand juries on drug charges. A general strike followed. Despite U.S.-imposed economic sanctions Noriega remained in power. Voters went to the polls to elect a new president May 7, 1989. Noriega claimed victory but foreign observers said that the opposition had won overwhelmingly and that Noriega was trying to steal the election. The government voided the election May 10, charging foreign interference. There was an attempted coup against Noriega Oct. 3.

U.S. troops invaded Panama Dec. 20 following a series of incidents, including the killing of a U.S. Marine by Panamanian soldiers. The operation, called Operation Just Cause, had as its chief objective the capture of Noriega, who was wanted in the U.S. on drug trafficking charges.

Noriega took refuge in the Vatican diplomatic mission, but surrendered after 10 days to U.S. officials Jan. 3, 1990.

Papua New Guinea

People: Population (1989 est.): 3,613,000. **Age distrib. (%):** 0–14: 41.6; 15–59: 52.8; 60+: 5.6. **Pop. density:** 20 per sq. mi. **Urban** (1985): 14.0%. **Ethnic groups:** Papuans (in S and interior), Melanesian (N,E), pygmies; minorities of Chinese, Australians, Polynesians. **Languages:** English (official), Melanesian languages, Papuan languages. **Religions:** Protestant 63%, Roman Catholic 31%, local religions.
Geography: Area: 178,260 sq. mi., slightly larger than California. **Location:** Occupies eastern half of island of New Guinea. **Neighbors:** Indonesia (West Irian) on W, Australia on S. **Topography:** Thickly forested mtns. cover much of the center of the country, with lowlands along the coasts. Included are some of the nearby islands of Bismarck and Solomon groups, including Admiralty Is., New Ireland, New Britain, and Bougainville. **Capital:** Port Moresby. **Cities** (1987): Port Moresby 152,000; Lae 79,000.
Government: Type: Parliamentary democracy. **Head of state:** Queen Elizabeth II, represented by Gov. Gen. Sir Serei Eri; in office: Feb. 27, 1990. **Head of government:** Prime Min. Rabbie Namaliu; in office: July 4, 1988. **Local divisions:** National capital and 19 provinces with elected legislatures. **Defense:** approx. 1.5% of GNP (1989).
Economy: Chief crops: Coffee, coconuts, cocoa. **Minerals:** Gold, copper, silver. **Arable land:** 1%. **Livestock** (1989): pigs: 1.7 mln. **Electricity prod.** (1988): 1.3 bln. kwh. **Labor force:** 82% agric., 3% ind. and commerce, 8% services.
Finance: Monetary unit: Kina (Mar. 1991: 1.00 = $1.04 US). **Gross national product** (1989): $3.4 bln. **Per capita GNP** (1989): $900. **Imports** (1990): $1.1 bln.; partners: Austral. 40%, Jap. 17%; U.S. 9%. **Exports** (1990): $1.1 bln.; partners: Jap. 26%, W. Ger. 36%, Austral. 8%. **National budget** (1989): $1.4 bln. **International reserves less gold** (Mar. 1991): $333 mln. **Gold:** 63,000 oz t. **Consumer prices** (change in 1990): 6.9%.
Transport: Motor vehicles: in use (1987): 17,000 passenger cars, 26,000 comm. vehicles. **Chief ports:** Port Moresby, Lae.
Communications: Television sets: 1 per 14 persons. **Radios:** 1 per 15 persons. **Telephones:** 1 per 48 persons. **Daily newspaper circ.** (1988): 8 per 1,000 pop.
Health: Life expectancy at birth (1987): 53.0 male; 54.6 female. **Births** (per 1,000 pop. 1989): 35. **Deaths** (per 1,000 pop. 1989): 12. **Natural increase:** 2.3%. **Hospital beds:** 1 per 222 persons. **Physicians:** 1 per 11,904 persons. **Infant mortality** (per 1,000 live births 1989): 72.0.
Education (1989): **Literacy:** 32%. **Attendance:** 65% primary school; 13% secondary school.
Major International Organizations: UN (GATT), Commonwealth of Nations.
Embassy: 1330 Connecticut Ave., NW 20036.

Human remains have been found in the interior of New Guinea dating back at least 10,000 years and possibly much earlier. Successive waves of peoples probably entered the country from Asia through Indonesia. Europeans visited in the 15th century, but land claims did not begin until the 19th century, when the Dutch took control of the western half of the island.
The southern half of eastern New Guinea was first claimed by Britain in 1884, and transferred to Australia in 1905. The northern half was claimed by Germany in 1884, but captured in World War I by Australia, which was granted a League of Nations mandate and then a UN trusteeship over the area. The 2 territories were administered jointly after 1949, given self-government Dec. 1, 1973, and became independent Sept. 16, 1975.
The indigenous population consists of a huge number of tribes, many living in almost complete isolation with mutually unintelligible languages.

Paraguay

Republic of Paraguay

República del Paraguay

People: Population (1990 est.): 4,660,000. **Age distrib. (%):** 0–14: 41.0; 15–59: 52.0; 60+: 7.0. **Pop. density:** 28 per sq. mi. **Urban** (1987): 43%. **Ethnic groups:** Mestizo 95%, small Caucasian, Indian, black minorities. **Languages:** Spanish (official), Guarani. **Religions:** Roman Catholic (official) 97%.

Geography: Area: 157,047 sq. mi., the size of California. **Location:** One of the 2 landlocked countries of S. America. **Neighbors:** Bolivia on N, Argentina on S, Brazil on E. **Topography:** Paraguay R. bisects the country. To E are fertile plains, wooded slopes, grasslands. To W is the Chaco plain, with marshes and scrub trees. Extreme W is arid. **Capital:** Asunción. **Cities** (1990 est.): Asunción 607,000.
Government: Type: Republic. **Head of state:** Pres. Gen. Andres Rodriguez; in office: Feb. 3, 1989. **Local divisions:** 19 departments. **Defense:** 1.0% of GNP (1987).
Economy: Industries: Food processing, wood products, textiles, cement. **Chief crops:** Corn, cotton, beans, sugarcane. **Minerals:** Iron, manganese, limestone. **Other resources:** Forests. **Arable land:** 20%. **Livestock** (1989): cattle: 8.0 mln.; pigs: 2.3 mln. **Electricity prod.** (1988): 1.1,bln. kwh. **Labor force:** 44% agric., 34% ind. and commerce, 18% services.
Finance: Monetary unit: Guarani (Mar. 1991 1,200 = $1 US). **Gross national product** (1988): $4.7 bln. **Per capita GNP** (1988): $1,180. **Imports** (1989): $613 mln.; partners: Braz. 32%, Arg. 12%, U.S. 8%. **Exports** (1989): $970 mln.; partners: Neth. 18%, Braz. 32%. **Tourists** (1988): $113 mln. receipts. **National budget** (1987): $1 bln. expenditures. **International reserves less gold** (Mar. 1991): $718 mln. **Gold:** 35,000 oz t. **Consumer prices** (change in 1990): 39.1%.
Transport: Motor vehicles: in use (1988): 34,000 passenger cars, 5,000 comm. vehicles. **Civil aviation** (1988): 872 mln. passenger-km; 1 airport with scheduled flight. **Chief ports:** Asuncion.
Communications: Television sets: 1 per 12 persons. **Radios:** 1 per 5.4 persons. **Telephones:** 1 per 42 persons. **Daily newspaper circ.** (1987): 32 per 1,000 pop.
Health: Life expectancy at birth (1989): 67 male; 72 female. **Births** (per 1,000 pop. 1989): 36. **Deaths** (per 1,000 pop. 1989): 6. **Natural increase:** 3.0%. **Hospital beds:** 1 per 1,489 persons. **Physicians:** 1 per 1,458 persons. **Infant mortality** (per 1,000 live births 1989):49.
Education (1989): **Literacy:** 81%. **Years compulsory:** 7; **Attendance:** 83%.
Major International Organizations: UN (IMF, WHO, ILO), OAS.
Embassy: 2400 Massachusetts Ave. NW 20008; 483-6960.

The Guarani Indians were settled farmers speaking a common language before the arrival of Europeans.
Visited by Sebastian Cabot in 1527 and settled as a Spanish possession in 1535, Paraguay gained its independence from Spain in 1811. It lost much of its territory to Brazil, Uruguay, and Argentina in the War of the Triple Alliance, 1865-1870. Large areas were won from Bolivia in the Chaco War, 1932-35.
Gen. Alfredo Stroessner, who ruled since 1954, was ousted in a military coup led by Gen. Andres Rodriguez on Feb. 3, 1989. Rodriguez was elected president May 1.

Peru

Republic of Peru

República del Peru

People: Population (1990 est.): 21,904,000. **Age distrib. (%):** 0–14: 40.5; 15–59: 46.0; 60+: 5.5. **Pop. density:** 43 per sq. mi. **Urban** (1989): 70%. **Ethnic groups:** Indians 45%, Mestizos 37%, Caucasians 15%, blacks, Asians. **Languages:** Spanish, Quechua (both official), Aymara. **Religions:** Roman Catholic 90%.
Geography: Area: 496,222 sq. mi., 3 times larger than California. **Location:** On the Pacific coast of S. America. **Neighbors:** Ecuador, Colombia on N, Brazil, Bolivia on E, Chile on S. **Topography:** An arid coastal strip, 10 to 100 mi. wide, supports much of the population thanks to widespread irrigation. The Andes cover 27% of land area. The uplands are well-watered, as are the eastern slopes reaching the Amazon basin, which covers half the country with its forests and jungles. **Capital:** Lima. **Cities** (1989 est.): Lima 5,659,000; Arequipa 612,000; Callao 574,000.
Government: Type: Constitutional republic. **Head of state:** Pres. Alberto Fujimori; b. July 28, 1938; in office: July 28, 1990. **Head of government:** Prime Min. Juan Carlos Hurtado Miller; in office: July 28, 1990. **Local divisions:** 24 departments, 1 province. **Defense:** 4.9% of GNP (1987).

Economy: Industries: Fish meal, mineral processing, light industry, textiles. **Chief crops:** Cotton, sugar, coffee, corn. **Minerals:** Copper, lead, molybdenum, silver, zinc, iron, oil. **Crude oil reserves** (1987): 535 mln. bbls. **Other resources:** Wool, sardines. **Arable land:** 3%. **Livestock** (1989): cattle: 4.4 mln.; pigs: 2.3 mln.; sheep: 13.5 mln. **Fish catch** (1988): 5.8 mln. metric tons. **Electricity prod.** (1988): 14.8 bln. kwh. **Labor force:** 38% agric.; 17% ind. and mining; 45% govt. and other services.

Finance: Monetary unit: Intl (Mar. 1991: 560 = $1 US). **Gross national product** (1989): $39.3 bln. **Per capita GNP** (1988): $1,850. **Imports** (1988): $3.0 bln.; partners: U.S. 17%, EC 19%. **Exports** (1988): $2.6 bln.; partners: U.S. 66%, EC 23%, Jap. 6%. **Tourists** (1988): $447 mln. receipts. **National budget** (1987): $3.9 bln. **International reserves less gold** (Mar. 1991): $1.0 bln. **Gold:** 2.0 mln. oz t. **Consumer prices** (change in 1990): 7,650%.

Transport: Railway traffic (1987): 517 mln. passenger-km. **Motor vehicles:** in use (1987): 377,000 passenger cars, 226,000 comm. vehicles. **Civil aviation** (1989): 2.0 bln. passenger-km; 24 airports. **Chief ports:** Callao, Chimbate, Mollendo.

Communications: Television sets: 1 per 14 persons. **Radios:** 1 per 4.9 persons. **Telephones:** 1 per 32 persons. **Daily newspaper circ.** (1987): 57 per 1,000 pop.

Health: Life expectancy at birth (1989): 61 male; 66 female. **Births** (per 1,000 pop. 1989): 29. **Deaths** (per 1,000 pop. 1989): 8. **Natural increase:** 2.1%. **Hospital beds:** 1 per 625 persons. **Physicians:** 1 per 1,016 persons. **Infant mortality** (per 1,000 live births 1989): 69.

Education (1989): Literacy: 79%. Years compulsory: 10.

Major International Organizations: UN and all of its specialized agencies, OAS.

Embassy: 1700 Massachusetts Ave. NW 20036; 833-9860.

The powerful Inca empire had its seat at Cuzco in the Andes covering most of Peru, Bolivia, and Ecuador, as well as parts of Colombia, Chile, and Argentina. Building on the achievements of 800 years of Andean civilization, the Incas had a high level of skill in architecture, engineering, textiles, and social organization.

A civil war had weakened the empire when Francisco Pizarro, Spanish conquistador, began raiding Peru for its wealth, 1532. In 1533 he had the seized ruling Inca, Atahualpa, fill a room with gold as a ransom, then executed him and enslaved the natives.

Lima was the seat of Spanish viceroys until the Argentine liberator, Jose de San Martin, captured it in 1821; Spain was defeated by Simon Bolivar and Antonio J. de Sucre; recognized Peruvian independence, 1824.

On Oct. 3, 1968, a military coup ousted Pres. Fernando Belaunde Terry. In 1968-74, the military government put through sweeping agrarian changes, and nationalized oil, mining, fishmeal, and banking industries.

Food shortages, escalating foreign debt, and strikes led to another coup, Aug. 29, 1976, and to a slowdown of socialist programs.

After 12 years of military rule, Peru returned to democratic leadership under former Pres. Fernando Belaunde Terry, July 1980.

There were strikes by police, oil workers, and other labor unions in 1987 and 1988. Terrorist activity, mostly by Maoist groups, continued; the government said that guerrilla insurgency caused nearly 13,000 deaths in the 1980s.

A cholera epidemic which began in Peru in Jan. 1991, threatened to spread and could affect over 100 million people in Latin America according to the World Health Organization.

Philippines
Republic of the Philippines

People: Population (1990 est.): 66,647,000. **Age distrib.** (%): 0–14: 39.0; 15–59: 56.2; 60+: 4.8. **Pop. density:** 535 per sq. mi. **Urban** (1990): 41%. **Ethnic groups:** Malays the large majority, Chinese, Americans, Spanish are minorities. **Languages:** Pilipino (based on Tagalog), English (both official), Cebuano, Bicol, Ilocano, Pampango, many others. **Religions:** Roman Catholics 83%, Protestants 9%, Moslems 5%.

Geography: Area: 115,831 sq. mi., slightly larger than Nevada. **Location:** An archipelago off the SE coast of Asia. **Neighbors:** Nearest are Malaysia, Indonesia on S, Taiwan on N. **Topography:** The country consists of some 7,100 islands stretching 1,100 mi. N-S. About 95% of area and population are on 11 largest islands, which are mountainous, except for the heavily indented coastlines and for the central plain on Luzon. **Capital:** Quezon City (Manila is de facto capital). **Cities** (1990 est.): Manila 1.8 mln.; Quezon City 1.5 mln.; Cebu 552,000.

Government: Type: Republic. **Head of state:** Pres. Corazon C. Aquino; b. 1932; in office: Feb. 25, 1986. **Local divisions:** 12 regions, 73 provinces, 61 cities. **Defense:** 1.3% of GNP (1987).

Economy: Industries: Food processing, textiles, clothing, drugs, wood prods., appliances. **Chief crops:** Sugar, rice, corn, pineapple, coconut. **Minerals:** Cobalt, copper, gold, nickel, silver, iron, petroleum. **Other resources:** Forests (42% of area). **Arable land:** 26%. **Livestock** (1987): cattle: 1.4 mln.; pigs: 7.8 mln. **Fish catch** (1989): 2.2 mln. metric tons. **Electricity prod.** (1988): 25.0 mln. kwh. **Labor force:** 47% agric., 20% ind. and comm., 13% services.

Finance: Monetary unit: Peso (May 1991: 27.10 = $1 US). **Gross national product** (1988): $38.2 bln. **Per capita income** (1988): $667. **Imports** (1989): $11.1 bln.; partners: U.S. 25%, Jap. 16%. **Exports** (1989): $7.7 bln.; partners: U.S. 35%, Jap. 17%. **Tourists** (1987): $458 mln. receipts. **National budget** (1989): $10.7 bln. expenditures. **International reserves less gold** (Mar. 1991): $1.2 bln. **Gold:** 2.7 mln. oz t. **Consumer prices** (change in 1990): 12.7%.

Transport: Railway traffic (1988): 228 mln. passenger-km. **Motor vehicles:** in use (1988): 834,000 passenger cars, 121,000 comm. vehicles. **Civil aviation** (1989): 8.6 bln. passenger-km; 16 airports with scheduled flights. **Chief ports:** Cebu, Manila, Iloilo, Davao.

Communications: Television sets: 1 per 8.8 persons. **Radios:** 1 per 7.5 persons. **Telephones:** 1 per 6.5 persons. **Daily newspaper circ.** (1985): 44 per 1,000 pop.

Health: Life expectancy at birth (1989): 63 male; 69 female. **Births** (per 1,000 pop. 1989): 34. **Deaths** (per 1,000 pop. 1989): 7. **Natural increase:** 2.8%. **Hospital beds:** 1 per 628 persons. **Physicians:** 1 per 1,090 persons. **Infant mortality** (per 1,000 live births 1988): 52.9.

Education (1989): Literacy: 88%. Attendance: 97% in elementary, 55% secondary.

Major International Organizations: UN (World Bank, IMF, GATT), ASEAN.

Embassy: 1617 Massachusetts Ave. NW 20036; 483-1414

The Malay peoples of the Philippine islands, whose ancestors probably migrated from Southeast Asia, were mostly hunters, fishers, and unsettled cultivators when first visited by Europeans.

The archipelago was visited by Magellan, 1521. The Spanish founded Manila, 1571. The islands, named for King Philip II of Spain, were ceded by Spain to the U.S. for $20 million, 1898, following the Spanish-American War. U.S. troops suppressed a guerrilla uprising in a brutal 6-year war, 1899-1905.

Japan attacked the Philippines Dec. 8, 1941 and occupied the islands during WW II.

On July 4, 1946, independence was proclaimed in accordance with an act passed by the U.S. Congress in 1934. A republic was established.

The Philippines and the U.S. have treaties for U.S. military and naval bases and a mutual defense treaty. Riots by radical youth groups and terrorism by leftist guerrillas and outlaws, increased from 1970. On Sept. 21, 1972, President Marcos declared martial law. Ruling by decree, he ordered some land reform and stabilized prices. But opposition was suppressed, and a high population growth rate aggravated poverty and unemployment. Political corruption was widespread. On Jan. 17, 1973, Marcos proclaimed a new constitution with himself as president. His wife received wide powers in 1978 to supervise planning and development.

Government troops battled Moslem (Moro) secessionists, 1973-76, in southern Mindanao. Fighting resumed, 1977, after a Libyan-mediated agreement on autonomy was rejected by the region's mainly Christian voters.

Martial law was lifted Jan. 17, 1981. Marcos turned over legislative power to the National Assembly, released political prisoners, and said he would no longer rule by decree. He was re-elected to a new 6-year term as president.

The assassination of prominent opposition leader Benigno S. Aquino Jr, Aug. 21, 1983, sparked demonstrations calling for the resignation of Marcos.

A bitter presidential election campaign ended Feb. 7, 1986 as elections were held amid allegations of widespread fraud. On Feb. 16, Marcos was declared the victor over Corazon Aquino, widow of slain opposition leader Benigno Aquino. Aquino declared herself president and announced a nonviolent "active resistance" to overthrow the Marcos government; the 2 held separate inaugurals on Feb. 25.

On Feb. 22, 2 leading military allies of Marcos quit their posts to protest the rigged elections. Marcos, Feb. 24, declared a state of emergency as his military and religious support continued to erode. That same day U.S. President Ronald Reagan urged Marcos to resign. Marcos ended his 20-year tenure as president Feb. 26 as he fled the country. Aquino was recognized immediately as president by the U.S. and other nations.

In 1987, Aquino announced the start of land reforms. Candidates endorsed by Aquino won large majorities in legislative elections held in May, attesting to her popularity. She is plagued, however, by a weak economy, widespread poverty, communist insurgents, and lukewarm support from the military.

Rebel troops seized military bases, TV stations, and bombed the presidential palace, Dec. 1, 1989. Government forces defeated the attempted coup with the aid of air cover provided by U.S. F-4s.

The June 1991 eruption of Mt. Pinatubo led to the evacuation of 20,000 U.S. military personnel from Clark A.F.B. and their dependents at nearby bases.

The archipelago has a coastline of 10,850 mi. Manila Bay, with an area of 770 sq. mi., and a circumference of 120 mi., is the finest harbor in the Far East.

All natural resources of the Philippines belong to the state; their exploitation is limited to citizens of the Philippines or corporations of which 60% of the capital is owned by citizens.

Poland

Republic of Poland

People: Population (1990 est.): 38,363,000. **Age distrib. (%):** 0–14: 25.7; 15–59: 60.2; 60+: 14.1. **Pop. density:** 317 per sq. mi. **Urban** (1989): 60%. **Ethnic groups:** Polish 98%, Germans, Ukrainians, Byelorussians. **Language:** Polish. **Religion:** Roman Catholic 94%.

Geography: Area: 120,727 sq. mi. **Location:** On the Baltic Sea in E Central Europe. **Neighbors:** Germany on W, Czechoslovakia on S, USSR (Lithuania, Byelorussia, Ukraine) on E. **Topography:** Mostly lowlands forming part of the Northern European Plain. The Carpathian Mts. along the southern border rise to 8,200 ft. **Capital:** Warsaw. **Cities** (1987 est.): Warsaw 1.6 mln., Lodz 848,000, Kracow 740,000, Wroclaw 631,000, Poznan 570,000.

Government: Type: Socialist (in transition). **Head of state:** Pres. Lech Walesa; in office: Dec. 22, 1990. **Head of government: Prime Min.:** Tadeusz Mazowiecki; b. Apr. 17, 1927; in office: Aug. 24, 1989. **Local divisions:** 49 provinces. **Defense:** 6% of GNP (1987).

Economy: Industries: Shipbuilding, chemicals, metals, autos, food processing. **Chief crops:** Grains, potatoes, sugar beets, tobacco, flax. **Minerals:** Coal, copper, zinc, silver, zinc, sulphur, natural gas. **Arable land:** 49%. **Livestock** (1989): cattle: 10.9 mln.; pigs: 20.1 mln. **Fish catch** (1989): 636,000 metric tons. **Electricity prod.** (1987): 146 bln. kwh. **Crude steel prod.** (1988): 17.1 mln. metric tons. **Labor force:** 30% agric.; 44% ind. & comm.; 11% services.

Finance: Monetary unit: Zloty (Mar. 1991: 9,500 = $1 US). **Gross national product** (1989): $172 bln. **Per capita income** (1986): $2,000. **Imports** (1990): $8.2 bln.; partners: USSR 38%, Ger. 15%, Czech. 5%. **Exports** (1990): $13.5 bln.; partners: USSR 30%, E. Ger. 6%, Czech. 6%, W. Ger. 10%. **National budget** (1988): $24 bln. expenditures. **Tourists** (1988): $193 mln. receipts. **International Reserves Less Gold** (Mar. 1991): $4.3 bln. **Gold:** 472,000. **Consumer prices** (change in 1990): 584%.

Transport: Railway traffic (1989): 55 bln. passenger-km. **Motor vehicles:** in use (1988): 4.5 mln. passenger cars, 1.0 mln. comm. vehicles. **Civil aviation** (1989): 4.8 bln. passenger-km; 12 airports. **Chief ports:** Gdansk, Gdynia, Szczecin.

Communications: Television sets: 1 per 3.9 persons. **Radios:** 1 per 3.6 persons. **Telephones:** 1 per 8.2 persons. **Daily newspaper circ.** (1988): 217 per 1,000 pop.

Health: Life expectancy at birth (1989): 66 male; 74 female. **Births** (per 1,000 pop. 1989): 16. **Deaths** (per 1,000 pop. 1989): 10. **Natural increase:** .6%. **Hospital beds:** 1 per 174 persons. **Physicians:** 1 per 480 persons. **Infant mortality** (per 1,000 live births 1989): 21.

Education (1989): **Literacy: 98%. Years compulsory:** 8; attendance 97%.

Major International Organizations: UN (GATT, WHO).
Embassy: 2640 16th St. NW 20009; 234-3800.

Slavic tribes in the area were converted to Latin Christianity in the 10th century. Poland was a great power from the 14th to the 17th centuries. In 3 partitions (1772, 1793, 1795) it was apportioned among Prussia, Russia, and Austria. Overrun by the Austro-German armies in World War I, its independence, self-declared on Nov.11, 1918, was recognized by the Treaty of Versailles, June 28, 1919. Large territories to the east were taken in a war with Russia, 1921.

Germany and the USSR invaded Poland Sept. 1-27, 1939, and divided the country. During the war, some 6 million Polish citizens were killed by the Nazis, half of them Jews. With Germany's defeat, a Polish government-in-exile in London was recognized by the U.S., but the USSR pressed the claims of a rival group. The election of 1947 was completely dominated by the Communists.

In compensation for 69,860 sq. mi. ceded to the USSR, 1945, Poland received approx. 40,000 sq. mi. of German territory E of the Oder-Neisse line comprising Silesia, Pomerania, West Prussia, and part of East Prussia.

In 12 years of rule by Stalinists, large estates were abolished, industries nationalized, schools secularized, and Roman Catholic prelates jailed. Farm production fell off. Harsh working conditions caused a riot in Poznan June 28-29, 1956.

A new Politburo, committed to development of a more independent Polish Communism, was named Oct. 1956, with Wladyslaw Gomulka as first secretary of the Communist Party. Collectivization of farms was ended and many collectives were abolished.

In Dec. 1970 workers in port cities rioted because of price rises and new incentive wage rules. On Dec. 20 Gomulka resigned as party leader; he was succeeded by Edward Gierek; the incentive rules were dropped, price rises were revoked.

Poland was the first communist state to get most-favored nation trade terms from the U.S.

A law promulgated Feb. 13, 1953, required government consent to high Roman Catholic church appointments. In 1956 Gomulka agreed to permit religious liberty and religious publications, provided the church kept out of politics. In 1961 religious studies in public schools were halted. Government relations with the Church improved in the 1970s.

After 2 months of labor turmoil had crippled the country, the Polish government, Aug. 30, 1980, met the demands of striking workers at the Lenin Shipyard, Gdansk. Among the 21 concessions granted were the right to form independent trade unions and the right to strike — unprecedented political developments in the Soviet bloc. By 1981, 9.5 mln. workers had joined the independent trade union (Solidarity). Farmers won official recognition for their independent trade union in May. Solidarity leaders proposed, Dec. 12, a nationwide referendum on establishing a non-Communist government if the government failed to agree to a series of demands which included access to the mass media and free and democratic elections to local councils in the provinces.

Spurred by the fear of Soviet intervention, the government, Dec. 13, imposed martial law. Public gatherings, demonstrations, and strikes were banned and an internal and external blackout was imposed. Solidarity leaders called for a nationwide strike, but there were only scattered work stoppages. Lech Walesa and other Solidarity leaders were arrested. The U.S. imposed economic sanctions which were lifted when martial law was suspended December 1982.

On Apr. 5, 1989, an accord was reached between the government and opposition factions on a broad range of political and economic reforms incl. free elections. In the first free elections in over 40 years, candidates endorsed by Solidarity swept the parliamentary elections, June 4. On Aug. 19, Tadeusz Mazowiecki became the first non-Communist to head an Eastern bloc nation, when he became prime minister.

The radical economic program designed to transform the economy into a free-market system drew protests from unions, farmers, and miners. Steep price increases took effect Jan 1, 1990; wages were frozen. In 1991, the government announced the most ambitious privatization plan of any country; each adult citizen would become a shareholder in industry.

Portugal

Republic of Portugal
República Portuguesa

People: Population (1990 est.): 10,528,000. **Age distrib. (%):** 0–14: 22.7; 15–59: 59.9; 60+: 17.4. **Pop. density:** 281 per sq. mi. **Urban** (1983): 30%. **Ethnic groups:** Homogeneous Mediterranean stock with small African minority. **Languages:** Portuguese. **Religions:** Roman Catholics 97%.

Geography: Area: 36,390 sq. mi., incl. the Azores and Madeira Islands, slightly smaller than Indiana. **Location:** At SW extreme of Europe. **Neighbors:** Spain on N, E. **Topography:** Portugal N of Tajus R, which bisects the country NE-SW, is mountainous, cool and rainy. To the S there are drier, rolling plains, and a warm climate. **Capital:** Lisbon. **Cities** (1987 est.): Lisbon 2 mln. (met.), Oporto, 1.5 mln. (met.).

Government: Type: Parliamentary democracy. **Head of state:** Pres. Mario Soares; b. Dec. 7, 1924; in office: Mar. 9, 1986. **Head of government:** Prime Min. Anibal Cavaco Silva; in office: Nov. 6, 1985. **Local divisions:** 18 districts, 2 autonomous regions, one dependency. **Defense:** 2.2% of GNP (1990).

Economy: Industries: Textiles, footwear, cork, chemicals, fish canning, wine, paper. **Chief crops:** Grains, potatoes, rice, grapes, olives, fruits. **Minerals:** Tungsten, uranium, copper, iron. **Other resources:** Forests (world leader in cork production). **Arable land:** 32%. **Livestock** (1989): sheep: 5.3 mln.; pigs: 2.3 mln; cattle: 1.3 mln. **Fish catch** (1989): 346,000 metric tons. **Electricity prod.** (1988): 15.5 bln. kwh. **Crude steel prod.** (1985): 420,000 metric tons. **Labor force:** 19% agric.; 34% ind. and comm.; 46% services and govt.

Finance: Monetary unit: Escudo (June 1991: 148 = $1 US). **Gross national product** (1989): $45.0 bln. **Per capita GNP** (1989): $4,363. **Imports** (1990): $24.8 bln.; partners: W. Ger. 12%, UK 8%, Fr. 11%. **Exports** (1990): $16.3 bln.; partners: UK 15%, W. Ger. 13%, Fr. 13%. **Tourists** (1988): $2.4 bln. receipts. **National budget** (1990): $23.2 bln. expenditures. **International reserves less gold** (Mar. 1991): $14.1 bln. **Gold:** 15.7 mln. oz t. **Consumer prices** (change in 1990): 13.4%.

Transport: Railway traffic (1988): 6.0 bln. passenger-km. **Motor vehicles:** in use (1987): 2.5 mln. passenger cars, 189,000 comm. vehicles. **Civil aviation** (1988): 5.6 bln. passenger-km; 21 airports. **Chief ports:** Lisbon, Setubal, Leixoes.

Communications: Television sets: 1 per 6.2 persons. **Radios:** 1 per 4.2 persons. **Telephones:** 1 per 6.2 persons. **Daily newspaper circ.** (1987): 76 per 1,000 pop.

Health: Life expectancy at birth (1989): 71 male; 78 female. **Births** (per 1,000 pop. 1989): 15. **Deaths** (per 1,000 pop. 1989): 9. **Natural increase:** .5%. **Hospital beds:** 1 per 209 persons. **Physicians:** 1 per 388 persons. **Infant mortality** (per 1,000 live births 1989): 15.

Education (1990): **Literacy:** 83%, **Years compulsory:** 6; attendance 60%.

Major International Organizations: UN (GATT, IMF, WHO), NATO, EC, OECD.

Embassy: 2125 Kalorama Rd. NW 20008; 328-8610.

Portugal, an independent state since the 12th century, was a kingdom until a revolution in 1910 drove out King Manoel II and a republic was proclaimed.

From 1932 a strong, repressive government was headed by Premier Antonio de Oliveira Salazar. Illness forced his retirement in Sept. 1968.

On Apr. 25, 1974, the government was seized by a military junta led by Gen. Antonio de Spinola, who was named president.

The new government reached agreements providing independence for Guinea-Bissau, Mozambique, Cape Verde Islands, Angola, and Sao Tome and Principe. Despite a 64% victory for democratic parties in April 1975, the Soviet-supported Communist party increased its influence. Banks, insurance companies, and other industries were nationalized.

Parliament approved, June 1, 1989, a package of reforms that did away with the socialist economy and created a "democratic" economy and the denationalization of industries.

Azores Islands, in the Atlantic, 740 mi. W. of Portugal, have an area of 888 sq. mi. and a pop. (1987) of 252,000. A 1951 agreement gave the U.S. rights to use defense facilities in the Azores. The **Madeira Islands,** 350 mi. off the NW coast of Africa, have an area of 307 sq. mi. and a pop. (1987) of 269,000. Both groups were offered partial autonomy in 1976.

Macau, area of 6 sq. mi., is an enclave, a peninsula and 2 small islands, at the mouth of the Canton R. in China. Portugal granted broad autonomy in 1976. In 1987, Portugal and China agreed that Macau would revert to China in 1999. Macao, like Hong Kong, was guaranteed 50 years of noninterference in its way of life and capitalist system. Pop. (1989 est.): 484,000.

Qatar

State of Qatar
Dawlet al-Qatar

People: Population (1990 est.): 498,000. **Pop. density:** 80 per sq. mi. **Ethnic groups:** Arab 40%, Pakistani 18%, Indian 10%, Iranian 14%, others. **Languages:** Arabic (official), English. **Religions:** Moslem 95%.

Geography: Area: 4,247 sq. mi., smaller than Connecticut and Rhode Island combined. **Location:** Occupies peninsula on W coast of Persian Gulf. **Neighbors:** Saudi Arabia on W, United Arab Emirates on S. **Topography:** Mostly a flat desert, with some limestone ridges, vegetation of any kind is scarce. **Capital:** Doha. **Cities** (1987 est.): Doha 250,000.

Government: Type: Traditional emirate. **Head of state and head of government:** Emir & Prime Min. Khalifah ibn Hamad ath-Thani; b. 1932; in office: Feb. 22, 1972 (amir), 1970 (prime min.) **Defense:** 47% of GNP (1985).

Economy: Arable land: 2.9%. **Electricity prod.** (1988): 4.5 bln. kwh. **Labor force:** 10% agric., 70% ind., services and commerce.

Finance: Monetary unit: Riyal (Mar. 1991: 3.64 = $1.00 US). **Gross national product** (1988): $4.0 bln. **Per capita GNP** (1988): $9,920. **Imports** (1988): $1.1 bln.; partners: Jap. 20%, UK 16%, U.S. 11%. **Exports** (1987): $2.6 bln.; partners: Jap. 38%, Sing. 13%. **National budget** (1988): $3.4 bln. expenditures.

Transport: Chief ports: Doha, Musayid.

Communications: Television sets: 1 per 2.5 persons. **Radios:** 1 per 2.5 persons. **Telephones:** 1 per 3.4 persons.

Health: Life expectancy at birth (1989): 68 male; 72 female. **Hospital beds:** 1 per 399 persons. **Physicians:** 1 per 568 persons. **Infant mortality** (per 1,000 live births 1989): 29.

Education (1987): **Literacy:** 60%. **Compulsory:** ages 6-16; attendance: 98%.

Major International Organizations: UN (FAO, GATT, IMF, World Bank), Arab League, OPEC.

Embassy: 600 New Hampshire Ave. NW 20037; 338-0111.

Qatar was under Bahrain's control until the Ottoman Turks took power, 1872 to 1915. In a treaty signed 1916, Qatar gave Great Britain responsibility for its defense and foreign relations. After Britain announced it would remove its military forces from the Persian Gulf area by the end of 1971, Qatar sought a federation with other British protected states in the area; this failed and Qatar declared itself independent, Sept. 1 1971.

Oil revenues give Qatar a per capita income among the highest in the world, but lack of skilled labor hampers development plans.

Romania

People: Population (1990 est.): 23,269,000. **Age distrib. (%):** 0–14: 24.7; 15–59; 60.9; 60+: 14.4. **Pop. density:** 252 per sq. mi. **Urban** (1987): 51%. **Ethnic groups:** Romanians 89%, Hungarians 7.9%, Germans 1.6%. **Languages:** Romanian (official), Hungarian, German. **Religions:** Orthodox 80%, Roman Catholic 6%.

Geography: Area: 91,699 sq. mi., slightly smaller than New York and Pennsylvania combined. **Location:** In SE Europe on the Black Sea. **Neighbors:** USSR on E (Moldavia) and N (Ukraine), Hungary, Yugoslavia on W, Bulgaria on S. **Topography:** The Carpathian Mts. encase the north-central Transylvanian plateau. There are wide plains S and E of the mountains, through which flow the lower reaches of the rivers of the Danube system. **Capital:** Bucharest. **Cities** (1986 est.): Bucharest 1,900,000, Brasov 346,000, Timisoara 319,000, Constanta 323,000.

Government: Type: In transition. **Head of state:** Pres. Ion Iliescu; in office; Dec. 25, 1989. **Head of government:** Prime Min. Petre Roman; in office; Dec. 26, 1989. **Local divisions:** Bucharest and 40 counties. **Defense:** 4.3% of GNP (1985).

Economy: Industries: Steel, metals, machinery, oil products, chemicals, textiles, shoes, tourism. **Chief crops:** Grains, sunflower, vegetables, potatoes. **Minerals:** Oil, gas, coal. **Other resources:** Timber. **Arable land:** 45%. **Livestock** (1988): cattle: 7.2 mln.; pigs: 14.7 mln.; sheep: 18.7 mln. **Fish catch** (1988): 264,000 metric tons. **Electricity prod.** (1988): 75.3 bln. kwh. **Crude steel prod.** (1988): 15.0 mln. metric tons. **Labor force:** 28% agric.; 34% ind. & comm.

Finance: Monetary unit: Lei (Mar. 1991: 36.97 = $1 US). **Gross national product** (1989): $79.8 bln. **Per Capita GNP** (1989): $3,445. **Imports** (1989): $9.7 bln.; partners: USSR 36%, Iran 8%. **Exports** (1989): $14.2 bln.; partners: USSR 30%. **Tourists** (1988): $178 mln. receipts. **National budget** (1982): $142 mln. expenditures.

Transport: Railway traffic (1989): 33 bln. passenger-km. **Motor vehicles:** in use (1986): 105,000 passenger cars; 100,000 comm. vehicles. **Civil aviation** (1989): 1.6 bln. passenger-km; 15 airports. **Chief ports:** Constanta, Galati, Braila.

Communications: Television sets: 1 per 6.0 persons. **Radios:** 1 per 7.3 persons. **Telephones:** 1 per 11 persons. **Daily newspaper circ.** (1989): 134 per 1,000 pop.

Health: Life expectancy at birth (1989): 67 male; 73 female. **Births** (per 1,000 pop. 1989): 16. **Deaths** (per 1,000 pop. 1989): 11. **Natural increase:** 0.5%. **Hospital beds:** 1 per 107 persons. **Physicians:** 1 per 559 persons. **Infant mortality** (per 1,000 live births 1989): 25.

Education (1988): **Literacy:** 98%. **Years compulsory:** 10; attendance 98%.

Major International Organizations: UN (World Bank, IMF, GATT).

Embassy: 1607 23d St. NW 20008; 232-4748.

Romania's earliest known people merged with invading Proto-Thracians, preceding by centuries the Dacians. The Dacian kingdom was occupied by Rome, 106 AD-271 AD; people and language were Romanized. The principalities of Wallachia and Moldavia, dominated by Turkey, were united in 1859, became Romania in 1861. In 1877 Romania proclaimed independence from Turkey, became an independent state by the Treaty of Berlin, 1878, a kingdom, 1881, under Carol I. In 1886 Romania became a constitutional monarchy with a bicameral legislature.

Romania helped Russia in its war with Turkey, 1877-78. After World War I it acquired Bessarabia, Bukovina, Transylvania, and Banat. In 1940 it ceded Bessarabia and Northern Bukovina to the USSR, part of southern Dobrudja to Bulgaria, and Transylvania to Hungary.

In 1941, Romanian premier Marshal Ion Antonescu led his country in support of Germany against the USSR. In 1944 Antonescu was overthrown by King Michael and Romania joined the Allies.

With occupation by Soviet troops the communist-headed National Democratic Front displaced the National Peasant party. A People's Republic was proclaimed, Dec. 30, 1947; Michael was forced to abdicate. Land owners were dispossessed; most banks, factories and transportation units were nationalized.

On Aug. 22, 1965, a new constitution proclaimed Romania a Socialist, rather than a People's Republic.

Internal policies were oppressive. Ethnic Hungarians protested cultural and job discrimination, which has led to strained relations with Hungary.

Romania became industrialized, but lagged in consumer goods and in personal freedoms. All industry was state owned, and state farms and cooperatives owned almost all the arable land.

On Dec. 16, 1989, security forces opened fire on demonstrators in Timisoara; hundreds were buried in mass graves. President Nicolae Ceausescu declared a state of emergency as protests spread to other cities. By Dec. 21, the protests had spread to Bucharest where security forces fired on protestors. Army units joined the rebellion, Dec. 22, and a group known as the "Council of National Salvation" announced that it had overthrown the government. Fierce fighting took place between the army, which backed the new government, and forces loyal to Ceausescu.

Ceausescu was captured, Dec. 23 and, following a trial in which he and his wife were found guilty of genocide, was executed Dec. 25. The U.S. and USSR quickly recognized the new provisional government.

Following months of unrest, Bucharest was beset by violence, as anti-government protestors and pro-government coal miners clashed, June 13-15, 1990. Anti-government protests continued throughout 1991.

Rwanda

Republic of Rwanda

Republika y'u Rwanda

People: Population (1990 est.): 7,603,000. **Age distrib. (%):** 0–14: 48.7; 15–59: 47.1; 60+: 4.2. **Pop. density:** 715 per sq. mi. **Urban** (1985): 5.1%. **Ethnic groups:** Hutu 85%, Tutsi 14%, Twa (pygmies) 1%. **Languages:** French, Rwanda (both official). **Religions:** Christian 74%, traditional 25%, Moslem 1%.

Geography: Area: 10,169 sq. mi., the size of Maryland. **Location:** In E central Africa. **Neighbors:** Uganda on N, Zaire on W, Burundi on S, Tanzania on E. **Topography:** Grassy uplands and hills cover most of the country, with a chain of volcanoes in the NW. The source of the Nile R. has been located in the headwaters of the Kagera (Akagera) R., SW of Kigali. **Capital:** Kigali. **Cities** (1989 est.): Kigali 300,000.

Government: Type: In transition. **Head of state:** Pres. Juvenal Habyarimana; b. Mar. 8, 1937; in office: July 5, 1973. **Local divisions:** 10 prefectures, 143 communes. **Defense:** 2.0% of GNP (1987).

Economy: Chief crops: Coffee, tea. **Minerals:** Tin, gold, wolframite. **Arable land:** 29%. **Electricity prod.** (1988): 110 mln. kwh. **Labor force:** 91% agric.

Finance: Monetary unit: Franc (Apr. 1991: 127 = $1 US). **Gross national product** (1989): $2.1 bln. **Per capita GNP** (1989): $310. **Imports** (1987): $354 mln.; partners: Ken. 21%, Belg. 16%, Jap. 12%, W. Ger. 9%. **Exports** (1987): $113 mln.; partners: Belg.-Lux. 17%, Ugan. 12%. **National budget** (1987): $247 mln. revenues; $280 mln. expenditures. **International reserves less gold** (Mar. 1991): $38 mln. **Consumer prices** (change in 1990): 4.2%.

Transport: Motor vehicles: in use (1987): 7,000 passenger cars, 10,000 comm. vehicles.

Communications: Radios: 1 per 16 persons. **Telephones:** 1 per 652 persons.

Health: Life expectancy at birth (1989): 49 male; 53 female. **Births** (per 1,000 pop. 1989): 53. **Deaths** (per 1,000 pop. 1989): 16. **Natural increase:** 3.8%. **Hospital beds** (1984): 9,000. **Physicians** (1984): 177. **Infant mortality** (per 1,000 live births 1989): 117.

Education (1989): **Literacy:** 50%. **Years compulsory:** 8; **attendance:** 70%.

Major International Organizations: UN (GATT, IMF, WHO), OAU.

Embassy: 1714 New Hampshire Ave. NW 20009; 232-2882.

For centuries, the Tutsi (an extremely tall people) dominated the Hutus (90% of the population). A civil war broke out in 1959 and Tutsi power was ended. A referendum in 1961 abolished the monarchic system. Some 8,000 exiled Tutsi invaded Rwanda from Uganda, Sept. 1990. A new constitution was signed into effect in 1991 calling for multiparty politics, freedom of the press, and a limited presidential term.

Rwanda, which had been part of the Belgian UN trusteeship of Rwanda-Urundi, became independent July 1, 1962. The government was overthrown in a 1973 military coup. Rwanda is one of the most densely populated countries in Africa. All available arable land is being used, and is being subject to erosion. The government has carried out economic and social improvement programs, using foreign aid and volunteer labor on public works projects.

St. Kitts and Nevis

Federation of St. Kitts & Nevis

People: Population (1990 est.): 40,000. **Ethnic groups:** black African 95%. **Language:** English. **Religion:** Protestant 76%.

Geography: Area: 101 sq. mi. in the northern part of the Leeward group of the Lesser Antilles in the eastern Caribbean Sea. **Capitol:** Basseterre. (1989): 15,000.

Government: Head of State: Queen Elizabeth represented by Sir Clement Arrindell. **Head of Government:** Prime Minister Kennedy A. Simmonds; b. Apr. 12, 1936; in office: Sept. 19, 1983.

Economy: Sugar is the principal industry.

Finance: Monetary unit: E. Caribbean Dollar (Mar. 1991): 2.70 = $1 U.S. **Gross national product** (1988): $120 mln.
Tourists (1988): $54 mln. receipts.
Communications: Telephones: 1 per 6 persons.
Health: Infant mortality (per 1,000 live births, 1989): 41.
Education: Literacy (1990): 90%.

St. Kitts (known by the natives as Liamuiga) and Nevis were discovered and named by Columbus in 1493. They were settled by Britain in 1623, but ownership was disputed with France until 1713. They were part of the Leeward Islands Federation, 1871-1956, and the Federation of the W. Indies, 1958-62. The colony achieved self-government as an Associated State of the UK in 1967, and became fully independent Sept. 19, 1983. Nevis, the smaller of the islands, has the right of secession.

Saint Lucia

People: Population (1990 est.): 153,000. **Age distrib.** (%): 0–20: 44.5; 21–64: 47.5; 65+: 8.0. **Pop. density:** 537 per sq. mi. **Ethnic groups:** Predominantly African descent. **Languages:** English (official), French patois. **Religions:** Roman Catholic 90%.
Geography: Area: 238 sq. mi., about one-fifth the size of Rhode Island. **Location:** In Eastern Caribbean, 2d largest of the Windward Is. **Neighbors:** Martinique to N, St. Vincent to SW. **Topography:** Mountainous, volcanic in origin; Soufriere, a volcanic crater, in the S. Wooded mountains run N-S to Mt. Gimie, 3,145 ft., with streams through fertile valleys. **Capital:** Castries. **City:** Castries (1989 est.): 55,000.
Government: Type: Parliamentary democracy. **Head of state:** Queen Elizabeth II, represented by Gov.-Gen. S.A. James; **Head of government:** Prime Min. John Compton; in office: May 3, 1982. **Local divisions:** 11 quarters
Economy: Industries: Agriculture, tourism, manufacturing. **Chief crops:** Bananas, coconuts, cocoa, citrus fruits. **Other resources:** Forests. **Arable land:** 8%. **Electricity prod.** (1988): 80 mln. kwh. **Labor force:** 36% agric., 20% ind. & commerce, 18% services.
Finance: Monetary unit: East Caribbean dollar (Mar. 1991): 2.70 = $1 US). **Gross national product** (1989): $267 mln. **Per capita GNP** (1989): $1,810. **Imports** (1986): $155 mln.; partners: U.S. 36%, UK 12%, Trin./Tob. 11%. **Exports** (1986): $83 mln.; partners: U.S. 28%, UK 25%. **Tourists** (1989): receipts: $144 mln.
Transport: Motor vehicles: in use (1986): 7,000 passenger cars, 2,000 comm. vehicles. **Chief ports:** Castries, Vieux Fort.
Communications: Television sets: 1 per 28 persons. **Radios:** 1 per 1.5 persons. **Telephones:** 1 per 10 persons.
Health: Life expectancy at birth (1989): 68 male; 73 female. **Births** (per 1,000 pop. 1989): 34. **Deaths** (per 1,000 pop. 1989): 5. **Natural increase:** 2.8%. **Hospital beds:** 1 per 284 persons. **Physicians:** 1 per 2,636 persons. **Infant mortality** (per 1,000 live births 1989): 18.
Education: Literacy (1989) 78%; **Years compulsory:** ages 5-15; **Attendance:** 80%.
Major International Organizations: UN (IMF, ILO), CARICOM, OAS.

St. Lucia was ceded to Britain by France at the Treaty of Paris, 1814. Self government was granted with the West Indies Act, 1967. Independence was attained Feb. 22, 1979.

Saint Vincent and the Grenadines

People: Population (1990 est.): 106,000. **Pop. density:** 746 per sq. mi. **Ethnic groups:** Mainly of African descent. **Languages:** English. **Religions:** Methodists, Anglicans, Roman Catholics.
Geography: Area: 150 sq. mi., about twice the size of Washington, D.C. **Location:** In the eastern Caribbean. St. Vincent (133 sq. mi.) and the northern islets of the Grenadines form a part of the Windward chain. **Neighbors:** St. Lucia to N, Barbados to E, Grenada to S. **Topography:** St. Vincent is volcanic, with a ridge of thickly-wooded mountains running its length; Soufriere, rising in the N, erupted in Apr. 1979. **Capital:** Kingstown. **Cities** (1985 est.): Kingstown 18,378.
Government: Head of state: Queen Elizabeth II, represented by Gov.-Gen. David Jack; in office: Sept. 20 1989. **Head of government:** James Mitchell; in office: July 30, 1984.

Economy: Industries: Agriculture, tourism. **Chief crops:** Bananas (62% of exports), arrowroot, coconuts. **Arable land:** 50%. **Electricity prod.** (1988): 63 mln. kwh. **Labor force:** 30% agric.
Finance: Monetary unit: East Caribbean dollar (Mar. 1991: 2.70 = $1 US). **Gross national product** (1988): $135 mln. **Per capita GNP** (1989): $1,200. **Tourists** (1988): $45 mln. receipts. **National budget** (1984): $34 mln. expenditures.
Transport: Motor vehicles: in use (1988): 5,000 passenger cars, 2,600 comm. vehicles. **Chief port:** Kingstown.
Communications: Telephones: 1 per 13 persons.
Health: Life expectancy at birth (1989): 69 male; 74 female. **Births** (per 1,000 pop. 1989): 27. **Deaths** (per 1,000 pop. 1989): 6. **Natural increase:** 2.2%. **Infant mortality** (per 1,000 live births 1989): 26.
Education (1989): **Literacy:** 85%.

Columbus landed on St. Vincent on Jan. 22, 1498 (St. Vincent's Day). Britain and France both laid claim to the island in the 17th and 18th centuries; the Treaty of Versailles, 1783, finally ceded it to Britain. Associated State status was granted 1969; independence was attained Oct. 27, 1979.
The entire economic life of St. Vincent is dependent upon agriculture and tourism.

San Marino
Most Serene Republic of San Marino
Serenissima Repubblica di San Marino

People: Population (1990 est.): 23,000. **Age distrib.** (%): 0–14: 19.0; 15–59: 63.7; 60+: 17.3. **Pop. density:** 958 per sq. mi. **Urban** (1990): 90.5%. **Ethnic groups:** Sanmarinese 88%, Italian 11%. **Languages:** Italian. **Religion:** mostly Roman Catholic.
Geography: Area: 24 sq. mi. **Location:** In N central Italy near Adriatic coast. **Neighbors:** Completely surrounded by Italy. **Topography:** The country lies on the slopes of Mt. Titano. **Capital:** San Marino. **City** (1987 est.): San Marino 4,179.
Government: Type: Independent republic. **Head of state:** Two co-regents appt. every 6 months. **Local divisions:** 11 districts, 9 sectors.
Economy: Industries: Postage stamps, tourism, woolen goods, paper, cement, ceramics. **Arable land:** 17%.
Finance: Monetary unit: Italian lira. **Gross national product** (1987): $188 mln. **Tourists** (1989): 2.8 mln.
Communications: Television sets: 1 per 3.4 persons. **Radios:** 1 per 1.8 persons. **Telephones:** 1 per 1.6 persons.
Births (per 1,000 pop. 1989): 8. **Deaths** (per 1,000 pop. 1989): 7. **Natural increase:** 0.1%. **Infant mortality** (per 1,000 live births 1989): 9.6.
Education (1987): **Literacy:** 97%. **Years compulsory:** 8. **Attendance:** 93%.

San Marino claims to be the oldest state in Europe and to have been founded in the 4th century. A communist-led coalition ruled 1947-57; a similar coalition ruled 1978-86. It has had a treaty of friendship with Italy since 1862.

Sao Tome and Principe
Democratic Republic of Sao Tome and Principe
República Democrática de Sao Tome e Principe

People: Population (1990 est.): 125,000. **Pop. density:** 306 per sq. mi. **Ethnic groups:** Portuguese-African mixture, African minority (Angola, Mozambique immigrants). **Languages:** Portuguese. **Religions:** Christian 80%.
Geography: Area: 372 sq. mi., slightly larger than New York City. **Location:** In the Gulf of Guinea about 125 miles off W Central Africa. **Neighbors:** Gabon, Equatorial Guinea on E. **Topography:** Sao Tome and Principe islands, part of an extinct volcano chain, are both covered by lush forests and croplands. **Capital:** Sao Tome. **Cities** (1988 est.): Sao Tome 40,000.
Government: Type: Republic. **Head of state:** Pres. Miguel Trovoada; in office: Mar. 3, 1991. **Head of government:** Prime Min. Celestino Rocha da Costa; in office: Jan. 8, 1988. **Local divisions:** 7 counties.

Economy: Chief crops: Cocoa (82% of exports), coconut products. **Arable land:** 38%. **Electricity prod.** (1989): 15 mln. kwh.

Finance: Monetary unit: Dobra (Jan. 1991: 151 = $1 US). **Gross national product** (1987): $32 mln. **Per capita income** (1986): $384. **Imports** (1986): $25.6 mln.; partners: Port. 61%, Angola 13%. **Exports** (1986): $9.3 mln.; partners: Neth. 52%, Port. 33%, W. Ger. 8%.

Transport: Chief ports: Sao Tome, Santo Antonio.

Communications: Radios: 1 per 3.9 persons.

Health: Births (per 1,000 pop. 1989): 38. **Deaths** (per 1,000 pop. 1989): 7. **Natural increase:** 3.0%. **Physicians:** 1 per 2,819 persons. **Infant mortality** (per 1,000 live births 1989): 51.

Education (1988): Literacy: 50%.

Major International Organizations: UN, OAU.

Embassy: 801 2d Ave., New York, NY 10017; 212-697-4211.

The islands were uninhabited when discovered in 1471 by the Portuguese, who brought the first settlers — convicts and exiled Jews. Sugar planting was replaced by the slave trade as the chief economic activity until coffee and cocoa were introduced in the 19th century.

Portugal agreed, 1974, to turn the colony over to the Gabon-based Movement for the Liberation of Sao Tome and Principe, which proclaimed as first president its East German-trained leader Manuel Pinto da Costa. Independence came July 12, 1975. Democratic reforms were instituted in 1987. In 1991 Miguel Trovoada won the first free presidential election following the withdrawal of Pres. Manuel Pinto da Costa. da Costa had ruled the country since independence.

Agriculture and fishing are the mainstays of the economy.

Saudi Arabia

Kingdom of Saudi Arabia

al-Mamlaka al-'Arabiya as-Sa'udiya

People: Population (1990 est.): 16,758,000. **Pop. density:** 15 per sq. mi. **Urban** (1986): 73%. **Ethnic groups:** Arab tribes, immigrants from other Arab and Moslem countries. **Language:** Arabic. **Religion:** Moslem 99%.

Geography: Area: 839,996 sq. mi., one-third the size of the U.S. **Location:** Occupies most of Arabian Peninsula in Middle East. **Neighbors:** Kuwait, Iraq, Jordan on N, Yemen, South Yemen, Oman on S, United Arab Emirates, Qatar on E. **Topography:** The highlands on W, up to 9,000 ft., slope as an arid, barren desert to the Persian Gulf. **Capital:** Riyadh. **Cities** (1986 est.): Riyadh 1,380,000; Jidda 1,210,000; Mecca 463,000.

Government: Type: Monarchy with council of ministers. **Head of state and head of government:** King Fahd; b. 1922; in office: June 13, 1982. **Local divisions:** 14 provinces. **Defense:** 12.8% of GNP (1987).

Economy: Industries: Oil products. **Chief crops:** Dates, wheat, barley, fruit. **Minerals:** Oil, gas, gold, copper, iron. **Crude oil reserves** (1990): 255 bln. barrels. **Arable land:** 2%. **Livestock** (1989): sheep: 7.6 mln.; goats: 3.7 mln. **Electricity prod.** (1988): 53 bln. kwh. **Labor force:** 14% agric.; 11% ind; 53% serv., comm., & govt.; 20% construction.

Finance: Monetary unit: Riyal (June 1991: 3.74 = $1 US). **Gross national product** (1989): $89.9 bln. **Imports** (1987): $24.3 bln.; partners: US 18%, Jap. 18%, W. Ger. 7%. **Exports** (1987): $26.9 bln.; partners: U.S. 19%, Jap., 17%. **National budget** (1988): $38 bln. expenditures. **International reserves less gold** (Mar. 1991): $10.8 bln. **Gold:** 4.59 mln. oz t. **Consumer prices** (change in 1990): 1.1%.

Transport: Railway traffic (1989): 92 mln. passenger-km. **Motor vehicles:** in use (1987): 2.2 mln. passenger cars, 1.9 mln. comm. vehicles. **Civil aviation** (1989): 15.6 bln.; passenger-km.; 23 airports. **Chief ports:** Jidda, Ad-Dammam, Ras Tannurah.

Communications: Television sets: 1 per 3.5 persons. **Radios:** 1 per 3.3 persons. **Telephones:** 1 per 13 persons. **Daily newspaper circ.** (1989): 49 per 1,000 pop.

Health: Life expectancy at birth (1989): 64 male; 67 female. **Births** (per 1,000 pop. 1989): 38. **Deaths** (per 1,000 pop. 1989): 7. **Natural increase:** 3.1%. **Hospital beds:** 1 per 406 persons. **Physicians:** 1 per 852 persons. **Infant mortality** (per 1,000 live births 1989): 74.

Education (1986): Literacy: 50% (men).

Major International Organizations: UN (IMF, WHO, FAO), Arab League, OPEC.

Embassy: 601 New Hampshire Ave. NW 20037; 342-3800.

Arabia was united for the first time by Mohammed, in the early 7th century. His successors conquered the entire Near East and North Africa, bringing Islam and the Arabic language. But Arabia itself soon returned to its former status.

Nejd, long an independent state and center of the Wahhabi sect, fell under Turkish rule in the 18th century, but in 1913 Ibn Saud, founder of the Saudi dynasty, overthrew the Turks and captured the Turkish province of Hasa; took the Hejaz in 1925 and by 1926, most of Asir. The discovery of oil in the 1930s transformed the new country.

Crown Prince Khalid was proclaimed king on Mar. 25, 1975, after the assassination of King Faisal. Fahd became king on June 13, 1982 following Khalid's death. There is no constitution and no parliament. The king exercises authority together with a Council of Ministers. The Islamic religious code is the law of the land. Alcohol and public entertainments are restricted, and women have an inferior legal status.

Saudi units fought against Israel in the 1948 and 1973 Arab-Israeli wars. Many billions of dollars of advanced arms have been purchased from Britain, France, and the U.S., including jet fighters, missiles, and, in 1981, 5 airborne warning and control system (AWACS) aircraft from the U.S., despite strong opposition from Israel. Beginning with the 1967 Arab-Israeli war, Saudi Arabia provided large annual financial gifts to Egypt; aid was later extended to Syria, Jordan, and Palestinian guerrilla groups, as well as to other Moslem countries.

Faisal played a leading role in the 1973-74 Arab oil embargo against the U.S. and other nations in an attempt to force them to adopt an anti-Israel policy. Saudi Arabia joined most other Arab states, 1979, in condemning Egypt's peace treaty with Israel.

In the 1980s, Saudi Arabia's moderate position on crude oil prices often prevailed at OPEC meetings.

The Hejaz contains the holy cities of Islam — Medina where the Mosque of the Prophet enshrines the tomb of Mohammed, who died in the city June 7, 632, and Mecca, his birthplace. More than 600,000 Moslems from 60 nations pilgrimage to Mecca annually.

Two Saudi oil tankers were attacked May 1984, as Iran and Iraq began air attacks against shipping in the Persian Gulf. On May 29, the U.S., citing grave concern over the growing escalation of the Iran-Iraq war in the Persian Gulf, authorized the sale of 400 Stinger antiaircraft missiles.

In 1987, Iranians making a pilgrimage to Mecca clashed with anti-Iranian pilgrims and Saudi police; over 400 were killed. Saudi Arabia broke diplomatic relations with Iran in 1988. Some 1,426 Moslem pilgrims died July 2, 1990 when a stampede occurred in a pedestrian tunnel leading to Mecca.

Following Iraq's attack on Kuwait, Aug. 2, 1990, Saudi Arabia accepted the Kuwait royal family and over 400,000 Kuwaiti refugees. King Fahd invited Western and Arab troops to deploy on its soil in support of Saudi defense forces. During the Persian Gulf war, Iraq fired a series of Scud missiles at Saudi Arabia; most were intercepted by U.S. Patriot missiles, although 28 U.S. soldiers were killed when a scud hit their barracks in Dhahran, Feb. 25.

Senegal

Republic of Senegal

République du Sénégal

People: Population (1990 est.): 7,740,000. **Age distrib. (%):** 0–14: 47.5; 15–59: 47.5; 60+: 5.0. **Pop. density:** 101 per sq. mi. **Urban** (1986): 30%. **Ethnic groups:** Wolof 36%, Serer 17%, Peulh 17%, Diola 9%, Toucouleur 9%, Mandingo 6%. **Languages:** French (official), Wolof, Serer, Peul, Tukulor, others. **Religions:** Moslems 92%, Christians 2%.

Geography: Area: 75,750 sq. mi., the size of South Dakota. **Location:** At western extreme of Africa. **Neighbors:** Mauritania on N, Mali on E, Guinea, Guinea-Bissau on S, Gambia surrounded on three sides. **Topography:** Low rolling plains cover most of Senegal, rising somewhat in the SE. Swamp and jungles are in SW. **Capital:** Dakar. **Cities** (1986): Dakar 1.3 mln. Thies 156,000; Kaolack 132,000.

Government: Type: Republic. **Head of state: Pres.** Abdou Diouf; b. Sept. 7, 1935; in office: Jan. 1, 1981. **Local divisions:** 10 regions. **Defense:** 2.2% of GNP (1989).

Economy: Industries: Food processing, fishing. **Chief crops:** Peanuts are chief export; millet, rice. **Minerals:** Phosphates. **Arable land:** 27%. **Livestock** (1989): cattle: 2.6 mln.; sheep: 3.8 mln.; goats: 1.2 mln. **Fish catch** (1989): 255,000 metric tons. **Electricity prod.** (1988): 758 mln. kwh. **Labor force:** 77% agric.

Finance: Monetary unit: CFA franc (Mar. 1991: 290 = $1 US). **Gross national product** (1989): $4.7 bln. **Per capita GNP** (1989): $650. **Imports** (1986): $705 mln.; partners Fr. 37%, U.S. 6%. **Exports** (1986): $483 mln.; partners Fr. 25%, UK 6%. **Tourists** (1988): $123 mln. receipts. **International reserves less gold** (Jan. 1991): $11.0 mln. **Gold:** 29,000 oz t. **Consumer prices** (change in 1990): 2.0%.

Transport: Railway traffic (1988): 40 mln. passenger-km. **Motor vehicles:** in use (1985): 76,000 passenger cars, 36,000 comm. vehicles. **Chief ports:** Dakar, Saint-Louis.

Communications: Television sets: 1 per 118 persons. **Radios:** 1 per 8.7 persons. **Telephones:** 1 per 246 persons. **Daily newspaper circ.** (1988): 7 per 1,000 pop.

Health: Life expectancy at birth (1989): 51 male, 54 female. **Births** (per 1,000 pop. 1989): 46. **Deaths** (per 1,000 pop. 1989): 15. **Natural increase:** 3.1%. **Hospital beds:** 1 per 1,134 persons. **Physicians:** 1 per 17,072 persons. **Infant mortality** (per 1,000 live births 1989): 96.

Education (1988): **Literacy:** 10%. **Attendance:** 48% primary, 11% secondary.

Major International Organizations: UN and all of its specialized agencies, OAU.

Embassy: 2112 Wyoming Ave. NW 20008; 234-0540.

Portuguese settlers arrived in the 15th century, but French control grew from the 17th century. The last independent Moslem state was subdued in 1893. Dakar became the capital of French West Africa.

Independence as part, along with the Sudanese Rep., of the Mali Federation, came June 20, 1960. Senegal withdrew Aug. 20. French political and economic influence is strong.

A long drought brought famine, 1972-73, and again in 1978.

Senegal, Dec. 17, 1981, signed an agreement with The Gambia for confederation of the 2 countries under the name of Senegambia. The confederation began Feb. 1, 1982. The 2 nations retained their individual sovereignty but adopted joint defense and monetary policies.

In 1989, a border incident sparked ethnic violence against Senegalese in Mauritania and, in retaliation, against Mauritanians in Senegal.

Seychelles
Republic of Seychelles

People: Population (1990 est.): 71,000. **Age distrib.** (%): 0–14: 36.3; 15–64; 57.3; 65+: 6.4. **Pop. density:** 409 per sq. mi. **Urban** (1986): 50% **Ethnic groups:** Creoles (mixture of Asians, Africans, and French) predominate. **Languages:** English, French, (both official). **Religions:** Roman Catholic 90%.

Geography: Area: 171 sq. mi. **Location:** In the Indian O. 700 miles NE of Madagascar. **Neighbors:** Nearest are Madagascar on SW, Somalia on NW. **Topography:** A group of 86 islands, about half of them composed of coral, the other half granite, the latter predominantly mountainous. **Capital:** Victoria. **Cities** (1986): Victoria 23,000.

Government: Type: Single party republic. **Head of state: Pres.** France-Albert Rene, b. Nov. 16, 1935; in office: June 5, 1977. **Defense:** 5.6% of GNP (1984).

Economy: Industries: Food processing. **Chief crops:** Coconut products, cinnamon, vanilla, patchouli. **Electricity prod.** (1988): 67 mln. kwh. **Labor force:** 12% agric.; 19.4% tourism, comm.; 32% serv.; 40% govt.

Finance: Monetary unit: Rupee (Mar. 1991: 5.35 = $1 US). **Gross national product** (1989): $285 mln. **Per capita GNP** (1989): $4,170. **Imports** (1990): $186 mln.; partners: UK 20%, So. Afr. 13%. **Exports** (1990): $34 mln.; partners: Pak. 38%; Jap. 26%. **National Budget** (1989): $168 mln. **Tourists** (1989): $91 mln. receipts. **International reserves less gold** (Mar. 1991): $20.4 mln. **Consumer prices** (change in 1990): 4.0%.

Transport: Motor vehicles: in use (1985): 3,500 passenger cars, 1,000 comm. vehicles. **Port:** Victoria.

Communications: Radios: 1 per 3 persons. **Telephones:** 1 per 5 persons. **Daily newspaper circ.** (1990): 47 per 1,000 pop.

Health: Life expectancy at birth (1989): 65 male; 71 female. **Births** (per 1,000 pop. 1989): 28.2 **Deaths** (per 1,000 pop. 1989): 7. **Natural increase:** 2.2%. **Hospital beds:** 1 per 189 persons. **Physicians:** 1 per 980 persons. **Infant mortality** (per 1,000 live births 1989): 18.4.

Education (1989): **Literacy:** 80%. **Years compulsory** 9; attendance 98%.

Major International Organizations: UN, OAU, Commonwealth of Nations.

The islands were occupied by France in 1768, and seized by Britain in 1794. Ruled as part of Mauritius from 1814, the Seychelles became a separate colony in 1903. The ruling party had opposed independence as impractical, but pressure from the OAU and the UN became irresistible, and independence was declared June 29, 1976. The first president was ousted in a coup a year later by a socialist leader.

A new constitution, announced Mar. 1979, turned the country into a one-party state.

Sierra Leone
Republic of Sierra Leone

People: Population (1990 est.): 4,168,000. **Age distrib.** (%): 0–14: 41.4; 15–59: 53.5; 60+: 5.1. **Pop. density:** 154 per sq. mi. **Ethnic groups:** Temne 30%, Mende 29%, others. **Languages:** English (official), tribal languages. **Religions:** animist 30%, Moslem 30%; Christian 10%.

Geography: Area: 27,925 sq. mi., slightly smaller than South Carolina. **Location:** On W coast of W. Africa. **Neighbors:** Guinea on N, E, Liberia on S. **Topography:** The heavily-indented, 210-mi. coastline has mangrove swamps. Behind are wooded hills, rising to a plateau and mountains in the E. **Capital:** Freetown. **Cities** (1985 est.): Freetown 469,000; Bo, Kenema, Makeni.

Government: Type: Republic. **Head of state and head of government: Pres.** Gen. Joseph Saidu Momoh; b. Jan. 26, 1937; in office: Nov. 28, 1985. **Local divisions:** 12 districts and one region including Freetown.

Economy: Industries: Mining, tourism. **Chief crops:** Cocoa, coffee, palm kernels, rice, ginger. **Minerals:** Diamonds, bauxite. **Arable land:** 25%. **Fish catch** (1989): 52,000 metric tons. **Electricity prod.** (1988): 116 mln. kwh. **Labor force:** 75% agric.; 15% ind. & serv.

Finance: Monetary unit: Leone (Mar. 1991: 1.00 = $.04 US). **Gross national product** (1989): $813 mln. **Per capita GNP** (1989): $200. **Imports** (1990): $144 mln.; partners: UK 22%, Fr. 11%. **Exports** (1990): $138 mln.; partners: Neth. 31%; UK 15%, U.S. 9%. **National budget** (1987): $181 mln. expenditures. **International reserves less gold** (Mar. 1991): $4 mln. **Consumer prices** (change in 1990): 111.0%.

Transport: Motor Vehicles: in use (1987): 24,000 passenger cars, 9,000 comm. vehicles. **Chief ports:** Freetown, Bonthe.

Communications: Television sets: 1 per 114 persons. **Radios:** 1 per 4.2 persons. **Telephones:** 1 per 251 persons. **Daily newspaper circ.** (1987): 3 per 1,000 pop.

Health: Life expectancy at birth (1989): 41 male; 47 female. **Births** (per 1,000 pop. 1989): 46. **Deaths** (per 1,000 pop. 1989): 21. **Natural increase:** 2.5%. **Hospital beds** (1984): 4,754. **Physicians** (1984): 197. **Infant mortality** (per 1,000 live births 1989): 157.

Education (1989): **Literacy:** 15%.

Major International Organizations: UN (GATT, IMF, WHO), Commonwealth of Nations, OAU.

Embassy: 1701 19th St. NW 20009; 939-9261.

Freetown was founded in 1787 by the British government as a haven for freed slaves. Their descendants, known as Creoles, number more than 60,000.

Successive steps toward independence followed the 1951 constitution. Full independence arrived Apr. 27, 1961. Sierra Leone became a republic Apr. 19, 1971. A one-party state approved by referendum 1978, brought political stability, but the economy has been plagued by inflation, corruption, and dependence upon the International Monetary Fund and creditors.

Singapore
Republic of Singapore

People: Population (1990 est.): 2,703,000. **Age distrib.** (%): 0–14: 23.4; 15–59: 68.4; 60+: 8.2. **Pop. density:** 11,910 per sq. mi. **Ethnic groups:** Chinese 77%, Malays 15%, Indians 6%. **Languages:** Chinese, Malay, Tamil, English all official. **Religions:** Buddhism 29%, Taoism 13%, Moslem 16%, Christian 19%.

Geography: Area: 224 sq. mi., smaller than New York City. **Location:** Off tip of Malayan Peninsula in S.E. Asia. **Neighbors:** Nearest are Malaysia on N, Indonesia on S. **Topography:** Singapore is a flat, formerly swampy island. The nation includes 40 nearby islets. **Capital:** Singapore.

Government: Type: Parliamentary democracy. **Head of state:** Pres. Wee Kim Wee; in office: Sept. 3, 1985. **Head of government:** Prime Min. Goh Chok Tong; b. May 20, 1941; in office: Nov. 28, 1990. **Defense:** 5% of GNP (1988).

Economy: Industries: Shipbuilding, oil refining, electronics, banking, textiles, food, rubber, lumber processing, tourism. **Arable land:** 11%. **Livestock** (1989): pigs: 321,000. **Electricity prod.** (1988): 11.5 bln. kwh. **Crude steel prod.** (1985): 350,000 metric tons. **Labor force:** 1% agric.; 58% ind. & comm.; 35% services.

Finance: Monetary unit: Dollar (May 1991: 1.76 = $1 US). **Gross national product** (1989): $24.0 bln. **Per capita income** (1988): $8,782. **Imports** (1990): $60.8 bln.; partners: Jap. 18%, Malay. 13%, U.S. 17%, Sau. Ar. 9%. **Exports** (1990): $52.7 bln., partners: U.S. 20%, Malay. 16%, Jap. 11%, HK 6%. **Tourists** (1988): $2.3 bln. receipts. **National budget** (1988): $6.2 bln. expenditures. **Consumer prices** (change in 1990): 3.4%.

Transport: Motor vehicles: in use (1989): 271,000 passenger cars, 122,000 comm. vehicles. **Civil aviation:** (1989) 30.4 bln. passenger-km; 1 airport.

Communications: Television sets: 1 per 4.9 persons. **Radios:** 1 per 4.2 persons. **Telephones:** 1 per 2.1 persons. **Daily newspaper circ.** (1986): 270 per 1,000 pop.

Health: Life expectancy at birth (1989): 71 male; 77 female. **Births** (per 1,000 pop. 1989): 16. **Deaths** (per 1,000 pop. 1989): 5. **Natural increase:** 1.1%. **Hospital beds:** 1 per 267 persons. **Physicians:** 1 per 888 persons. **Infant mortality** (per 1,000 live births 1989): 9.

Education (1990): **Literacy:** 87%. **Years compulsory:** none; attendance 94%.

Major International Organizations: UN (GATT, IMF, WHO), ASEAN.

Embassy: 1824 R St. NW 20009; 667-7555.

Founded in 1819 by Sir Thomas Stamford Raffles, Singapore was a British colony until 1959 when it became autonomous within the Commonwealth. On Sept. 16, 1963, it joined with Malaya, Sarawak and Sabah to form the Federation of Malaysia.

Tensions between Malayans, dominant in the federation, and ethnic Chinese, dominant in Singapore, led to an agreement under which Singapore became a separate nation, Aug. 9, 1965.

Singapore is one of the world's largest ports. Standards in health, education, and housing are high. International banking has grown.

Solomon Islands

People: Population (1989 est.): 314,000. **Age distrib.** (%): 0–14: 49; 15–59: 45.5; 60+: 5.5. **Pop. density:** 29 per sq. mi. **Urban** (1986): 15%. **Ethnic groups:** Melanesian 93%, Polynesian 4%. **Languages:** English (official), Papuan, Melanesian, Polynesian languages. **Religions:** Anglican 34%, Roman Catholic 19%, Evangelical 24%, traditional religions.

Geography: Area: 10,640 sq. mi., slightly larger than Maryland. **Location:** Melanesian archipelago in the western Pacific O. **Neighbors:** Nearest is Papua New Guinea on W. **Topography:** 10 large volcanic and rugged islands and 4 groups of smaller ones. **Capital:** Honiara. **Cities** (1988): Honiara 30,000.

Government: Type: Parliamentary democracy within the Commonwealth of Nations. **Head of state:** Queen Elizabeth II, represented by Gov.-Gen. George Lepping. **Head of government:** Prime Min. Solomon Mamaloni; in office: Mar. 28, 1989. **Local divisions:** 7 provinces and Honiara.

Economy: Industries: Fish canning. **Chief crops:** Coconuts, rice, bananas, yams. **Other resources:** Forests, marine shell. **Arable land:** 2%. **Fish catch** (1984): 35,000 metric tons. **Electricity prod.** (1988): 30.0 mln. kwh. **Labor force:** 32% agric., 32% services, 18% ind. & comm.

Finance: Monetary unit: Dollar (Mar. 1991: 2.68 = $1 US). **Gross national product** (1989): $181 mln. **Per capita GNP** (1989): $570. **Imports** (1989): $117 mln.; partners: Austral. 31%, Jap. 14%, Sing. 18%. **Exports** (1989): $77 mln.; partners: Jap. 37%, UK 11%.

Communications: Radios: 1 per 4.6 persons. **Telephones:** 1 per 58 persons.

Health: Life expectancy at birth (1989): 66 male; 71 female. **Births:** (per 1,000 pop. 1989): 41. **Deaths** (per 1,000 pop. 1989): 5. **Natural increase:** 3.6%. **Infant mortality** (per 1,000 live births 1989): 41.

Education (1989): **Literacy:** 60%. **Primary school** 78%. **Secondary school:** 21%.

Major International Organizations: UN, Commonwealth of Nations.

The Solomon Islands were sighted in 1568 by an expedition from Peru. Britain established a protectorate in the 1890s over most of the group, inhabited by Melanesians. The islands saw major World War II battles. Self-government came Jan. 2, 1976, and independence was formally attained July 7, 1978.

Somalia
Somali Democratic Republic
Jamhuriyadda Dimugradiga Somaliya

People: Population (1990 est.): 8,415,000. **Pop. density:** 34 per sq. mi. **Urban** (1988): 36%. **Ethnic groups:** mainly Hamitic, others. **Languages:** Somali, Arabic (both official). **Religions:** Sunni Moslems 99%.

Geography: Area: 246,300 sq. mi., slightly smaller than Texas. **Location:** Occupies the eastern horn of Africa. **Neighbors:** Djibouti, Ethiopia, Kenya on W. **Topography:** The coastline extends for 1,700 mi. Hills cover the N; the center and S are flat. **Capital:** Mogadishu. **Cities** (1986 est.): Mogadishu 700,000.

Government: Type: Independent republic. **Head of state:** Pres. Mohammed Siad Barrah; b. 1919; in office: Oct. 21, 1969. **Head of government:** Prime Min. Muhammad Hawadle Madar; in office: Sept. 3, 1990. **Local divisions:** 16 regions. **Defense:** 6.5% of GNP (1984).

Economy: Chief crops: Incense, sugar, bananas, sorghum, corn, gum. **Minerals:** Iron, tin, gypsum, bauxite, uranium. **Arable land:** 2%. **Livestock** (1989): cattle: 5.2 mln.; goats: 20 mln.; sheep: 6 mln. **Fish catch** (1987): 17,000 metric tons. **Electricity prod.** (1988): 86 mln. kwh. **Labor force:** 82% agric.

Finance: Monetary unit: Shilling (Dec. 1990: 2,626 = $1 US). **Gross national product** (1989): $1.0 bln. **Per capita GNP** (1989): $170. **Imports** (1989): $170 mln.; partners: It. 29%, Fra. 18%. **Exports** (1987): $95 mln.; partners: It. 17%. **International reserves less gold** (Nov. 1990): $11.4 mln. **Gold:** 19,000 oz t. **Consumer prices** (change in 1990): 102%.

Transport: Motor vehicles: in use (1986): 17,000 passenger cars, 9,500 comm. vehicles. **Chief ports:** Mogadishu, Berbera.

Communications: Radios: 1 per 20 persons.

Health: Life expectancy at birth (1989): 53 male; 53 female. **Births** (per 1,000 pop. 1989): 47. **Deaths** (per 1,000 pop. 1989): 15. **Natural increase:** 3.2%. **Hospital beds:** 1 per 1,053 persons. **Physicians:** 1 per 19,071 persons. **Infant mortality** (per 1,000 live births 1989): 128.

Education (1986): **Literacy:** 40%. 50% attend primary school, 7% attend secondary school.

Major International Organizations: UN, OAU, Arab League. **Embassy:** 600 New Hampshire Ave. NW 20037; 342-1575.

The UN in 1949 approved eventual creation of Somalia as a sovereign state and in 1950 Italy took over the trusteeship held by Great Britain since World War II.

British Somaliland was formed in the 19th century in the NW. Britain gave it independence June 26, 1960; on July 1 it joined with the former Italian part to create the independent Somali Republic.

On Oct. 21, 1969, a Supreme Revolutionary Council seized power in a bloodless coup, named a Council of Secretaries of

State, and abolished the Assembly. In May, 1970, several foreign companies were nationalized.

Somalia has laid claim to Ogaden, the huge eastern region of Ethiopia, peopled mostly by Somalis. Ethiopia battled Somali rebels in 1977. Some 11,000 Cuban troops with Soviet arms defeated Somali army troops and ethnic Somali rebels in Ethiopia, 1978. As many as 1.5 mln. refugees entered Somalia. Guerrilla fighting in Ogaden continued until 1988 when a peace agreement was reached with Ethiopia.

South Africa

Republic of South Africa

Republiek van Suid-Afrika

People: Population (1990 est.): 39,550,000. **Age distrib. (%):** 0–14: 41.0; 15–59: 52.8; 60+: 6.2. **Pop. density:** 75 per sq. mi. **Urban** (1985): 55%. **Ethnic groups:** black 73%, white 18%, coloured 3%, Asian 3%. **Religions:** Mainly Christian, Hindu, Moslem minorities. **Languages:** Afrikaans, English (both official), Nguni, Sotho languages.

Geography: Area: 472,359 sq. mi., about twice the size of Texas. **Location:** At the southern extreme of Africa. **Neighbors:** Namibia (SW Africa), Botswana, Zimbabwe on N, Mozambique, Swaziland on E; surrounds Lesotho. **Topography:** The large interior plateau reaches close to the country's 2,700-mi. coastline. There are few major rivers or lakes; rainfall is sparse in W, more plentiful in E. **Capitals:** Cape Town (legislative). Pretoria (administrative), and Bloemfontein (judicial). **Cities** (1990 met.): Durban 1 mln. Cape Town 1.9 mln. Johannesburg 1.7 mln. Pretoria 850,000.

Government: Type: Tricameral parliament with one chamber each for whites, coloureds, and Asians. **Head of State:** State Pres. Frederik W. De Klerk; b. Mar. 18, 1936; in office: Sept. 20, 1989. **Local divisions:** 4 provinces, 10 "homelands" for black Africans. **Defense:** 3.7 of GNP (1986).

Economy: Industries: Steel, tires, motors, textiles, plastics. **Chief crops:** Corn, wool, dairy products, grain, tobacco, sugar, fruit, peanuts, grapes. **Minerals:** Gold (largest producer), chromium, antimony, coal, iron, manganese, nickel, phosphates, tin, uranium, gem diamonds, platinum, copper, vanadium. **Other resources:** Wool. **Arable land:** 12%. **Livestock** (1989): cattle: 11.8 mln.; sheep: 30.3 mln. **Fish catch** (1988): 1.2 mln. metric tons. **Electricity prod.** (1988): 155 bln. kwh. **Crude steel prod.** (1988): 8.7 mln. metric tons. **Labor force:** 25% agric.; 32% ind. and commerce; 34% serv.; 7% mining.

Finance: Monetary unit: Rand (June 1991: 2.78 = $1 US). **Gross national product** (1989): $85.9 bln. **Per capita GNP** (1989): $2,460. **Imports** (1990): $17.4 bln.; partners: W. Ger. 19%, U.S. 68%, UK. 12%. **Exports** (1990): $23.6 bln.; partners: U.S. 43%, Jap. 9%. **Tourism** (1988): $673 mln. receipts. **National budget** (1989): $23.3 bln. **International reserves less gold** (Mar. 1991): $1.0 bln. **Gold:** 4.7 mln. oz t. **Consumer prices** (change in 1990): 14.3%.

Transport: Railway traffic (1989): 15.1 bln. passenger-km. **Motor vehicles:** in use (1989): 3.3 mln. passenger cars, 1.2 mln. comm. vehicles. **Civil aviation:** (1988): 8.8 bln. passenger-km: 37 airports. **Chief ports:** Durban, Cape Town, East London, Port Elizabeth.

Communications: Television sets: 1 per 11 persons. **Radios:** 1 per 3.0 persons. **Telephones:** 1 per 8.5 persons. **Daily newspaper circ.** (1988): 41 per 1,000 pop.

Health: Life expectancy at birth (1987): Whites: 71 years; Asians: 67 years; Africans: 59 years. **Births** (per 1,000 pop. 1989): 35. **Deaths** (per 1,000 pop. 1989): 8. **Natural increase:** 2.7%. **Physicians:** 1 per 1,340 persons. **Infant mortality** (per 1,000 live births 1982): Africans 94, Asians 25.3, whites 14.9.

Education (1990): **Literacy:** 99% (whites), 69% (Asians), 62% (coloureds), 50% (Africans).

Major International Organizations: UN (GATT).

Embassy: 3051 Massachusetts Ave. NW 20008; 232-4400.

Bushmen and Hottentots were the original inhabitants. Bantus, including Zulu, Xhosa, Swazi, and Sotho, had occupied the area from Transvaal to south of Transkei before the 17th century.

The Cape of Good Hope area was settled by Dutch, beginning in the 17th century. Britain seized the Cape in 1806. Many Dutch trekked north and founded 2 republics, the Transvaal and the Orange Free State. Diamonds were discovered, 1867, and gold,

1886. The Dutch (Boers) resented encroachments by the British and others; the Anglo-Boer War followed, 1899-1902. Britain won and, effective May 31, 1910, created the Union of South Africa, incorporating the British colonies of the Cape and Natal, the Transvaal and the Orange Free State. After a referendum, the Union became the Republic of South Africa, May 31, 1961, and withdrew from the Commonwealth.

With the election victory of Daniel Malan's National party in 1948, the policy of separate development of the races, or apartheid, already existing unofficially, became official. This called for separate development, separate residential areas, and ultimate political independence for the whites, Bantus, Asians, and Coloreds. In 1959 the government passed acts providing the eventual creation of several Bantu nations or Bantustans on 13% of the country's land area, though most black leaders opposed the plan.

Under apartheid, blacks were severely restricted to certain occupations, and paid far lower wages than whites for similar work. Only whites could vote or run for public office. There is an advisory Indian Council, partly elected, partly appointed. In 1969, a Colored People's Representative Council was created.

At least 600 persons, mostly Bantus, were killed in 1976 riots protesting apartheid. Black protests continued through the 1980s as violence broke out in several black townships. A new constitution was approved by referendum, Nov. 1983, which extended the parliamentary franchise to the Coloured and Asian minorities. Laws banning interracial sex and marriage were repealed in 1985.

In 1963, the Transkei, an area in the SE, became the first of these partially self-governing territories or "Homelands." Transkei became independent on Oct. 26, 1976, Bophuthatswana on Dec. 6, 1977, and Venda on Sept. 13, 1979; none received international recognition.

In 1981, So. Africa launched military operations in Angola and Mozambique to combat terrorists groups; So. African troops attacked the South West African People's Organization (SWAPO) guerrillas in Angola, March, 1982. South Africa and Mozambique signed a non-agression pact in 1984.

In 1986, Nobel Peace Prize winner Bishop Desmond Tutu called for Western nations to apply sanctions against S. Africa to force an end to apartheid. President Botha announced in Apr. the end to the nation's system of racial pass laws and offered blacks an advisory role in government.

On May 19, S. Africa attacked 3 neighboring countries—Zimbabwe, Botswana, Zambia—to strike at guerrilla strongholds of the African National Congress.

A nationwide state of emergency was declared June 12, giving almost unlimited power to the security forces. On Apr. 22, 1987, a 6-week-old walkout by railway workers erupted into violence after the dismissal of 16,000 strikers. As confrontation between blacks and government increased, there was widespread support in Western nations for a complete trade embargo on S. Africa.

Some 2 million South African black workers staged a massive strike, June 6-8, 1988, to protest the government's new labor laws and the banning of political activity by trade unions and antiapartheid groups. P.W. Botha, head of the government since 1978, resigned Aug. 14, 1989 and was replaced by Frederik W. De Klerk.

In 1990, the government lifted its bar on the African National Congress, the primary black group fighting to end white minority rule. On Feb. 11, black nationalist leader Nelson Mandela was freed after more than 27 years in prison. Mandela went on a 6-week, 14-nation tour, June-July, highlighted by an 11-day, 8-city tour of the U.S. In Oct. the Separate Amenities Act was repealed, ending the legal basis of segregation in public places. In Feb. 1991 Pres De Klerk announced plans to end all apartheid racial separation laws. In June the race registration law was repealed. The government admitted, in July, making payments to the Zulu-based Inkatha Freedom Party, main rival of the African National Congress.

Bophuthatswana: Population (1990 est.): 1,959,000. **Area:** 16,988 sq. mi., 6 discontinuous geographic units. **Capital:** Mmabatho. **Head of state:** Pres. Kgosi Lucas Manyane Mangope, b. Dec. 27, 1923; in office: Dec. 6, 1977.

Ciskei: Population (1990 est.): 844,000. **Area:** 2,996 sq. mi. **Capitol:** Bisho. **Head of State:** Military council.

Transkei: Population (1990 est.): 3,301,000. **Area:** 16,855 sq. mi., 3 discontinuous geographic units. **Capital:** Umtata. **Head of government:** Gen. Bantu Holomisa; in office: Dec. 30, 1987.

Venda: Population (1990 est.): 518,000. **Area:** 2,771 sq. mi., 2 discontinuous geographic units. **Capital:** Thohoyandou. **Head of state:** Gabriel Ramushwana; in office: Apr. 5, 1990.

Spain
España

People: Population (1990 est.): 39,623,000 **Age distrib. (%):** 0–14: 24.6; 15–59: 59.5; 60+: 15.9. **Pop. density:** 204 per sq. mi. **Urban** (1987): 75%. **Ethnic groups:** Spanish (Castilian, Valencian, Andalusian, Asturian) 72.8%, Catalan 16.4%, Galician 8.2%, Basque 2.3%. **Languages:** Spanish (official), Catalan, Galician, Basque. **Religions:** Roman Catholic 90%.

Geography: Area: 194,896 sq. mi., the size of Arizona and Utah combined. **Location:** In SW Europe. **Neighbors:** Portugal on W. France on N. **Topography:** The interior is a high, arid plateau broken by mountain ranges and river valleys. The NW is heavily watered, the south has lowlands and a Mediterranean climate. **Capital:** Madrid. **Cities** (1987 est.): Madrid 3,500,000; Barcelona 2,000,000; Valencia 700,000; Seville 580,000.

Government: Type: Constitutional monarchy. **Head of state:** King Juan Carlos I de Borbon y Borbon, b. Jan. 5, 1938; in office: Nov. 22, 1975. **Head of government:** Prime Min. Felipe Gonzalez Marquez; in office: Dec. 2, 1982. **Local divisions:** 50 provinces, 2 territories, 3 islands. **Defense:** 2.2% of GNP (1988).

Economy: Industries: Machinery, steel, textiles, shoes, autos, processed foods. **Chief crops:** Grains, olives, grapes, citrus fruits, vegetables, olives. **Minerals:** Lignite, uranium, lead, iron, copper, zinc, coal. **Other resources:** Forests (cork). **Arable land:** 31%. **Livestock** (1989): cattle: 4.9 mln.; pigs: 16.9 mln.; sheep: 23.7 mln. **Fish catch** (1988): 974,000 tons. **Electricity prod.** (1988): 149 bln. kwh. **Crude steel prod.** (1988): 11.8 mln. metric tons. **Labor force:** 16% agric.; 24% ind. and comm.; 52% serv.

Finance: Monetary unit: Peseta (May 1991: 105.90 = $1 US). **Gross national product** (1989): $358 bln. **Per capita GNP** (1989): $9,150. **Imports** (1989): $71.4 bln.; partners: U.S. 11%, EC 57%. **Exports** (1989): $44.4 bln.; partners: EC 67%, U.S. 10%. **Tourists** (1989): $16.1 bln. receipts. **National budget** (1988): $77.5 bln. expenditures. **International reserves less gold** (Mar. 1991): $51.5 bln. **Gold:** 15.6 min. oz t. **Consumer prices** (change in 1990): 6.8%.

Transport: Railway traffic (1989): 15 bln. passenger-km. **Motor vehicles:** in use (1988): 10.7 mln. passenger cars, 2.0 mln. comm. **Civil aviation:** (1989): 22.8 bln. passenger-km; 31 airports with scheduled flights. **Chief ports:** Barcelona, Bilbao, Valencia, Cartagena, Gijon.

Communications: Television sets: 1 per 2.6 persons. **Radios:** 1 per 3.4 persons. **Telephones:** 1 per 2.5 persons. **Daily newspaper circ.** (1988): 76 per 1,000 pop.

Health: Life expectancy at birth (1989): 74 male; 80 female. **Births** (per 1,000 pop. 1989): 13. **Deaths** (per 1,000 pop. 1989): 8. **Natural increase:** .2%. **Hospital beds:** 1 per 198 persons. **Physicians:** 1 per 275 persons. **Infant mortality** (per 1,000 live births 1989): 11.

Education (1991): Literacy: 97%. **School compulsory:** to age 16.

Major International Organizations: UN and all of its specialized agencies, NATO, OECD, EC.

Embassy: 2700 15th St. NW 20009; 265-0190.

Spain was settled by Iberians, Basques, and Celts, partly overrun by Carthaginians, conquered by Rome c.200 BC. The Visigoths, in power by the 5th century AD, adopted Christianity but by 711 AD lost to the Islamic invasion from Africa. Christian reconquest from the N led to a Spanish nationalism. In 1469 the kingdoms of Aragon and Castile were united by the marriage of Ferdinand II and Isabella I, and the last Moorish power was broken by the fall of the kingdom of Granada, 1492. Spain became a bulwark of Roman Catholicism.

Spain obtained a colonial empire with the discovery of America by Columbus, 1492, the conquest of Mexico by Cortes, and Peru by Pizarro. It also controlled the Netherlands and parts of Italy and Germany. Spain lost its American colonies in the early 19th century. It lost Cuba, the Philippines, and Puerto Rico during the Spanish-American War, 1898.

Primo de Rivera became dictator in 1923. King Alfonso XIII revoked the dictatorship, 1930, but was forced to leave the country 1931. A republic was proclaimed which disestablished the church, curtailed its privileges, and secularized education. A conservative reaction occurred 1933 but was followed by a Popular Front (1936-1939) composed of socialists, communists, republicans, and anarchists.

Army officers under Francisco Franco revolted against the government, 1936. In a destructive 3-year war, in which some one million died, Franco received massive help and troops from Italy and Germany, while the USSR, France, and Mexico supported the republic. War ended Mar. 28, 1939. Franco was named caudillo, leader of the nation. Spain was neutral in World War II but its relations with fascist countries caused its exclusion from the UN until 1955.

In July 1969, Franco and the Cortes designated Prince Juan Carlos as the future king and chief of state. After Franco's death, Nov. 20, 1975, Juan Carlos was sworn in as king. He presided over the formal dissolution of the institutions of the Franco regime. In free elections June 1977, moderates and democratic socialists emerged as the largest parties.

Catalonia and the Basque country were granted autonomy, Jan. 1980, following overwhelming approval in home-rule referendums. Basque extremists, however, have continued their campaign for independence.

The **Balearic Islands** in the western Mediterranean, 1,935 sq. mi., are a province of Spain; they include **Majorca (Mallorca)**, with the capital, Palma; **Minorca, Cabrera, Ibiza** and **Formentera**. The **Canary Islands**, 2,807 sq. mi., in the Atlantic W of Morocco, form 2 provinces, including the islands of **Tenerife, Palma, Gomera, Hierro, Grand Canary, Fuerteventura**, and **Lanzarote** with Las Palmas and Santa Cruz thriving ports. **Ceuta** and **Melilla**, small enclaves on Morocco's Mediterranean coast, are part of Metropolitan Spain.

Spain has sought the return of Gibraltar, in British hands since 1704.

Sri Lanka
Democratic Socialist Republic of Sri Lanka
Sri Lanka Prajathanthrika Samajavadi Janarajaya

People: Population (1990 est.): 17,135,000. **Age distrib. (%):** 0–14: 35.3; 15–59: 58.1; 60+: 6.6. **Pop. density:** 692 per sq. mi. **Urban** (1985): 21.5%. **Ethnic groups:** Sinhalese 74%, Tamils 17%, Moors 7%. **Languages:** Sinhalese, and Tamil, (both official). **Religions:** Buddhist 69%, Hindu 15%, Christian 8%, Moslem 7%.

Geography: Area: 25,332 sq. mi. about the size of W. Va. **Location:** In Indian O. off SE coast of India. **Neighbors:** India on NW. **Topography:** The coastal area and the northern half are flat; the S-central area is hilly and mountainous. **Capital:** Colombo. **Cities** (1989): Colombo 1.2 mln.; Jaffna, 270,000; Galle, 168,000; Kandy, 147,000.

Government: Type: Republic. **Head of state:** Pres. Ranasinghe Premadasa; b. June 24, 1924; in office: Jan. 2, 1989. **Head of government:** Prime Minister Dingiri Banda Wijetunge, b. 1923, in office: Mar. 3, 1989. **Local divisions:** 8 provinces, 24 districts. **Defense:** 4% of GNP (1988).

Economy: Industries: Plywood, paper, milling, chemicals, textiles. **Chief crops:** Tea, coconuts, rice. **Minerals:** Graphite, limestone, gems, phosphate. **Other resources:** Forests, rubber. **Arable land:** 16%. **Livestock** (1989): cattle: 1.0 mln. **Fish catch** (1989): 197,000 metric tons. **Electricity prod.** (1988): 4.2 bln. kwh. **Labor force:** 46% agric.; 27% ind. and comm.; 26% serv.

Finance: Monetary unit: Rupee (Mar. 1991: 40 = $1 US). **Gross national product** (1989): $7.2 bln. **Per capita GNP** (1989): $430. **Imports** (1990): $2.6 bln.; partners: Jap. 15%, UK 7%. **Exports** (1990): $1.9 bln.; partners: U.S. 22%, UK 7%. **Tourists** (1988): $79 mln. receipts. **National budget** (1988): $2.7 bln. expenditures. **International reserves less gold** (Mar. 1991): $425 mln. **Gold:** 105,000 oz t. **Consumer prices** (change in 1990): 21.5%.

Transport: Railway traffic (1988): 1.9 bln. passenger-km. **Motor vehicles:** in use (1988): 155,000 passenger cars, 139,000 comm. vehicles. **Civil aviation** (1989): 2.6 bln. passenger-km; 1 airport. **Chief ports:** Colombo, Trincomalee, Galle.

Communications: Television sets: 1 per 22 persons. **Radios:** 1 per 6 persons. **Telephones:** 1 per 90 persons.

Health: Life expectancy at birth (1989): 67 male; 72 female. **Births** (per 1,000 pop. 1989): 21. **Deaths** (per 1,000 pop. 1989): 6. **Natural increase:** 1.5%. **Hospital beds:** 1 per 357 persons. **Physicians:** 1 per 6,989 persons. **Infant mortality** (per 1,000 live births 1989): 31.

Education (1988): **Literacy:** 87%. **Years compulsory:** To age 12; attendance 98%.

Major International Organizations: UN (World Bank, IMF), Commonwealth of Nations.

Embassy: 2148 Wyoming Ave. NW 20008; 483-4025.

The island was known to the ancient world as Taprobane (Greek for copper-colored) and later as Serendip (from Arabic). Colonists from northern India subdued the indigenous Veddahs about 543 BC; their descendants, the Buddhist Sinhalese, still form most of the population. Hindu descendants of Tamil immigrants from southern India account for one-fifth of the population. Parts were occupied by the Portuguese in 1505 and by the Dutch in 1658. The British seized the island in 1796. As Ceylon it became an independent member of the Commonwealth in 1948. On May 22, 1972, Ceylon became the Republic of Sri Lanka.

Prime Min. W. R. D. Bandaranaike was assassinated Sept. 25, 1959. In new elections, the Freedom Party was victorious under Mrs. Sirimavo Bandaranaike, widow of the former prime minister.

After May 1970 elections, Mrs. Bandaranaike became prime minister again. In 1971 the nation suffered economic problems and terrorist activities by ultra-leftists, thousands of whom were executed. Massive land reform and nationalization of foreign-owned plantations was undertaken in the mid-1970s. Mrs. Bandaranaike was ousted in 1977 elections. A presidential form of government was installed in 1978 to restore stability.

Tension between the Sinhalese and Tamil separatists erupted into violence repeatedly in the 1980s. In 1987, hundreds died in an attack by Tamil rebels Apr. 17. Sri Lanka forces retaliated in June with attacks on the rebel-held Jaffna peninsula. Over 17,000 have died in the civil war since 1983.

Sudan

Republic of the Sudan

Jamhuryat as-Sudan

People: Population (1990 est.): 25,164,000. **Pop. density:** 25 per sq. mi. **Urban** (1983): 35%. **Ethnic groups:** black 52%, Arab 39%, Beja 6%. **Languages:** Arabic (official), Dinka, Nubian, Nuer, Beja, others. **Religions:** Sunni Moslem 70%, animist 18%, Christians 5%.

Geography: Area: 966,757 sq. mi., the largest country in Africa, over one-fourth the size of the U.S. **Location:** At the E end of Sahara desert zone. **Neighbors:** Egypt on N, Libya, Chad, Central African Republic on W, Zaire, Uganda, Kenya on S, Ethiopia on E. **Topography:** The N consists of the Libyan Desert in the W, and the mountainous Nubia desert in E, with narrow Nile valley between. The center contains large, fertile, rainy areas with fields, pasture, and forest. The S has rich soil, heavy rain. **Capital:** Khartoum. **Cities** (1983 est.): Khartoum 476,000; Omdurman 526,000; North Khartoum 341,000; Port Sudan 206,000.

Government: Type: Military. **Head of government:** Prime Min. Gen. Omar Al-Bashir; in office: June 30, 1989. **Local divisions:** 10 regions. **Defense:** 2.4% of GNP (1988).

Economy: Industries: Textiles, food processing. **Chief crops:** Gum arabic (principal world source), durra (sorghum), cotton (main export), sesame, peanuts, rice, coffee, sugar cane, wheat, dates. **Minerals:** Chrome, copper, **Other resources:** Mahogany. **Arable land:** 5%. **Livestock** (1989): cattle: 22 mln.; sheep: 19 mln.; goats: 15 mln. **Electricity prod.** (1988): 1.2 bln. kwh. **Labor force:** 78% agric.; 9% ind., comm.

Finance: Monetary unit: Pound (Mar. 1991: 1.00 = $.22 US). **Gross national product** (1988): $8.5 bln. **Per capita GNP** (1988): $420. **Imports** (1988): $1.0 bln.; partners: UK 13%, W. Ger. 8%, Saudi Ar. 11%. **Exports** (1988): $504 mln.; partners: Eg. 13%, It. 9%, Saudi Ar. 21%. **National budget** (1990): $1.5 bln. expenditures. **International reserves less gold** (Mar. 1991): $9.4 mln. **Consumer Prices** (change in 1990): 66.3%.

Transport: Railway traffic (1988): 357 mln. passenger km. **Motor vehicles:** in use (1985): 99,000 passenger cars, 17,000 comm. vehicles. **Civil aviation:** (1988): 671 mln. passenger-km; 10 airports with scheduled flights. **Chief ports:** Port Sudan.

Communications: Television sets: 1 per 23 persons. **Radios:** 1 per 4.6 persons. **Telephones:** 1 per 338 persons. **Daily newspaper circ.** (1985): 6 per 1,000 pop.

Health: Life expectancy at birth (1989): 51 male; 55 female. **Births** (per 1,000 pop. 1989): 44. **Deaths** (per 1,000 pop. 1989): 14. **Natural increase:** 3.0%. **Hospital beds:** 1 per 1,110 persons. **Physicians** (1983): 2,169. **Infant mortality** (per 1,000 live births 1989): 98.

Education (1991): **Literacy:** 20%. **Years compulsory:** 9; attendance 50%.

Major International Organizations: UN (IMF, WHO, FAO), Arab League, OAU.

Northern Sudan, ancient Nubia, was settled by Egyptians in antiquity, and was converted to Coptic Christianity in the 6th century. Arab conquests brought Islam in the 15th century.

In the 1820s Egypt took over the Sudan, defeating the last of earlier empires, including the Fung. In the 1880s a revolution was led by Mohammed Ahmed who called himself the Mahdi (leader of the faithful) and his followers, the dervishes.

In 1898 an Anglo-Egyptian force crushed the Mahdi's successors. In 1951 the Egyptian Parliament abrogated its 1899 and 1936 treaties with Great Britain, and amended its constitution, to provide for a separate Sudanese constitution.

Sudan voted for complete independence as a parliamentary government effective Jan. 1, 1956.

In 1969, a Revolutionary Council took power, but a civilian premier and cabinet were appointed; the government announced it would create a socialist state. The northern 12 provinces are predominantly Arab-Moslem and have been dominant in the central government. The 3 southern provinces are black and predominantly pagan. A 1972 peace agreement gave the South regional autonomy. The 2 halves of the nation began a civil war in 1988.

Economic problems plagued the nation in the 1980s, aggravated by a huge influx of refugees from neighboring countries. After 16 years in power, Pres. Nimeiry was overthrown in a bloodless military coup, Apr. 6, 1985. The Sudan held its first democratic parliamentary elections in 18 years in 1986. The elected government was overthrown in a bloodless coup June 30, 1989.

Sudan agreed to allow large-scale UN relief efforts in 1991, as some 7 million people were threatened with famine.

Suriname

Republic of Suriname

People: Population (1990 est.): 408,000. **Pop. density:** 6 per sq. mi. **Ethnic groups** Hindustanis 37%, Creole 31%, Javanese 15%. **Languages:** Dutch (official), Sranantonga, English. **Religions:** Moslem 23%, Hindu 27%, Christian 25%.

Geography: Area: 63,037 sq. mi., slightly larger than Georgia. **Location:** On N shore of S. America. **Neighbors:** Guyana on W, Brazil on S, French Guiana on E. **Topography:** A flat Atlantic coast, where dikes permit agriculture. Inland is a forest belt; to the S, largely unexplored hills cover 75% of the country. **Capital:** Paramaribo. **Cities** (1989): Paramaribo 192,000.

Government: Type: Republic. **Head of State:** Pres. Johan Kraag; in office: Dec. 29, 1990. **Head of government:** Prime Min. Henck Arron; in office: Jan. 29, 1988. **Local divisions:** 9 districts.

Economy: Industries: Aluminum. **Chief crops:** Rice, sugar, fruits. **Minerals:** Bauxite. **Other resources:** Forests, shrimp. **Arable land:** 1%. **Electricity prod.** (1988): 1.9 bln. kwh. **Labor force:** 29% agric.; 15% ind. and commerce; 42% govt.

Finance: Monetary unit: Guilder (Mar. 1991: 1.78 = $1 US). **Gross national product** (1989): $1.3 bln. **Per capita GNP** (1989): $3,020. **Imports** (1986): $487 mln.; partners: U.S. 30%, Neth. 9%, Trin./Tob. 21%, Jap. 7%. **Exports** (1986): $482 mln.; partners: U.S. 13%, Neth. 26%. **Tourists** (1988): receipts: $6 mln. **National budget** (1988): $650 mln. expenditures. **International reserves less gold** (Mar. 1991): $13.8 mln. **Gold:** 54,000 oz t.

Transport: Motor vehicles: in use (1987): 33,000 passenger cars, 12,000 comm. vehicles. **Chief ports:** Paramaribo, Nieuw-Nickerie.

Communications: Television sets: 1 per 10 persons. **Radios:** 1 per 1.6 persons. **Telephones:** 1 per 10 persons. **Daily newspaper circ.** (1987): 80 per 1,000 pop.

Health: Life expectancy at birth (1989): 66 male; 71 female. **Births** (per 1,000 pop. 1989): 27. **Deaths** (per 1,000 pop. 1989): 5. **Natural increase:** 2.1%. **Infant mortality** (per 1,000 live births 1989): 40.

Education (1989): Literacy: 65%; compulsory ages 6–12.

Major International Organizations: UN (WHO, ILO, FAO, World Bank, IMF), OAS.

Embassy: 2600 Virginia Ave. NW 20037; 338-6980.

The Netherlands acquired Suriname in 1667 from Britain, in exchange for New Netherlands (New York). The 1954 Dutch constitution raised the colony to a level of equality with the Netherlands and the Netherlands Antilles. In the 1970s the Dutch government pressured for Suriname independence, which came Nov. 25, 1975, despite objections from East Indians. Some 40% of the population (mostly East Indians) emigrated to the Netherlands in the months before independence.

The National Military Council took over control of the government, Feb. 1982. The government came under democratic leadership in 1988.

Swaziland
Kingdom of Swaziland

People: Population (1990 est.): 779,000. **Age distrib. (%):** 0–14: 47.3; 15–59: 47.4; 60+: 5.3. **Pop. density:** 112 per sq. mi. **Urban** (1985): 26%. **Ethnic groups:** Swazi 90%, Zulu 2.3%, European 2.1%, other African, non-African groups. **Languages:** Swazi, English, (both official). **Religions:** Christians 57%, indigenous beliefs 43%.

Geography: Area: 6,704 sq. mi., slightly smaller than New Jersey. **Location:** In southern Africa, near Indian O. coast. **Neighbors:** South Africa on N, W, S, Mozambique on E. **Topography:** The country descends from W-E in broad belts, becoming more arid in the lowveld region, then rising to a plateau in the E. **Capital:** Mbabane. **Cities** (1990 est.): Mbabane 46,000; Manzini 53,000.

Government: Type: Monarchy. **Head of state:** King Mswati 3d; as of: Apr. 25, 1986. **Head of government:** Prime Min. Obed Dlamini; in office: July 12, 1989. **Local divisions:** 4 districts, 2 municipalities, 40 regions.

Economy: Industries: Wood pulp. **Chief crops:** Sugar, corn, cotton, rice, pineapples, sugar, citrus fruits. **Minerals:** Asbestos, iron, coal. **Other resources:** Forests. **Arable land:** 8%. **Electricity prod.** (1988): 130 mln. kwh. **Labor force:** 53% agric.; 9% ind. and commerce; 9% serv.

Finance: Monetary unit: Lilangeni (Mar. 1991: 1.00 = $.36 US). **Gross national product** (1989): $683 mln. **Per capita GNP** (1989): $900. **Imports** (1988): $404 mln.; partners: So. Afr., 96%. **Exports** (1988): $436 mln.; partners: UK 33%, So. Afr. 20%. **National budget** (1990): $181 mln. expenditures. **International reserves less gold** (Feb. 1991): $214 mln. **Consumer prices** (change in 1989): 11.7%.

Transport: Motor vehicles: in use (1986): 20,000 passenger cars, 20,000 comm. vehicles.

Communications: Radios: 1 per 6.3 persons. **Telephones:** 1 per 34 persons. **Daily newspaper circ.** (1987): 24 per 1,000 pop.

Health: Life expectancy at birth (1989): 47 male; 54 female. **Births** (per 1,000 pop. 1989): 46. **Deaths** (per 1,000 pop. 1989): 15. **Natural increase:** 3.1%. **Hospital beds** (1984): 1,608. **Physicians** (1984): 80. **Infant mortality rate** (per 1,000 live births 1989): 127.

Education (1990): **Literacy:** 65%. 82% attend primary school.

Major International Organizations: UN (IMF, WHO, FAO), OAU, Commonwealth of Nations.

Embassy: 3400 International Dr. NW 20008; 362-6683.

The royal house of Swaziland traces back 400 years, and is one of Africa's last ruling dynasties. The Swazis, a Bantu people, were driven to Swaziland from lands to the N by the Zulus in 1820. Their autonomy was later guaranteed by Britain and Transvaal, with Britain assuming control after 1903. Independence came Sept. 6, 1968. In 1973 the king repealed the constitution and assumed full powers.

Under the constitution political parties are forbidden; parliament's role in government is limited to debate and advice.

Sweden
Kingdom of Sweden
Konungariket Sverige

People: Population (1990 est.): 8,407,000. **Age distrib. (%):** 0–14: 17.9; 15–59: 59.0; 60+: 23.1. **Pop. density:** 48 per sq. mi. **Urban** (1985): 85%. **Ethnic groups:** Swedish 91%, Finnish 3%, Lapps, European immigrants. **Languages:** Swedish. **Religions:** Lutheran (official) 95%.

Geography: Area: 173,731 sq. mi., larger than California. **Location:** On Scandinavian Peninsula in N. Europe. **Neighbors:** Norway on W, Denmark on S (across Kattegat), Finland on E. **Topography:** Mountains along NW border cover 25% of Sweden, flat or rolling terrain covers the central and southern areas, which includes several large lakes. **Capital:** Stockholm. **Cities** (1990): Stockholm 672,000; Goteborg 429,000; Malmo 230,000.

Government: Type: Constitutional monarchy. **Head of state:** King Carl XVI Gustaf; b. Apr. 30, 1946; in office: Sept. 19, 1973. **Head of government:** Prime Min. vacant (as of Sept. 18, 1991). **Local divisions:** 24 lan (counties), 278 municipalities. **Defense:** 2.9% of GNP (1987).

Economy: Industries: Steel, machinery, instruments, autos, shipbuilding, shipping, paper. **Chief crops:** Grains, potatoes, sugar beets. **Minerals:** Zinc, iron, lead, copper, gold, silver. **Other resources:** Forests (half the country); yield one fourth exports. **Arable land:** 7%. **Livestock** (1989): cattle: 1.7 mln.; pigs: 2.2 mln. **Fish catch** (1989): 240,000 metric tons. **Electricity prod.** (1988): 182 bln. kwh. **Crude steel prod.** (1988): 4.6 mln. metric tons. **Labor force:** 5% agric.; 24% manuf. & mining; 37% social services.

Finance: Monetary unit: Krona (May 1991: 6.12 = $1 US). **Gross national product** (1989): $179 bln. **Per capita GNP** (1989): $19,150 **Imports** (1989): $47.8 bln.; partners: W. Ger. 21%, UK 9%, U.S. 7%. **Exports** (1989): $51.5 bln.; partners: UK 10%, W. Ger. 12%, Nor. 10%. **Tourists** (1988): $2.3 bln. receipts. **National budget** (1989): $60.5 bln. expenditures. **International reserves less gold** (Mar. 1991): $20.2 bln. **Gold:** 6.06 mln. oz t. **Consumer prices** (change in 1990): 10.5%.

Transport: Railway traffic (1988): 5.9 bln. passenger-km. **Motor vehicles:** in use (1988): 3.3 mln. passenger cars, 259,000 comm. vehicles. **Civil aviation** (1989): 7.8 bln. passenger-km; 43 airports. **Chief ports:** Goteborg, Stockholm, Malmo.

Communications: Television sets: 1 per 2.4 persons. **Radios:** 1 per 1.2 persons. **Telephones:** 1 per 1.1 persons. **Daily newspaper circ.** (1988): 572 per 1,000 pop.

Health: Life expectancy at birth (1989): 74 male; 81 female. **Births** (per 1,000 pop. 1989): 12. **Deaths** (per 1,000 pop. 1989): 12. **Natural increase:** .0%. **Hospital beds:** 1 per 148 persons. **Physicians:** 1 per 373 persons. **Infant mortality** (per 1,000 live births 1989): 6.

Education (1989): **Literacy:** 99%. **Years compulsory:** 12; attendance 100%.

Major International Organizations: UN and all of its specialized agencies, EFTA, OECD.

Embassy: 600 New Hampshire Ave. NW 20037; 944-5600.

The Swedes have lived in present-day Sweden for at least 5,000 years, longer than nearly any other European people. Gothic tribes from Sweden played a major role in the disintegration of the Roman Empire. Other Swedes helped create the first Russian state in the 9th century.

The Swedes were Christianized from the 11th century, and a strong centralized monarchy developed. A parliament, the Riksdag, was first called in 1435, the earliest parliament on the European continent, with all classes of society represented.

Swedish independence from rule by Danish kings (dating from 1397) was secured by Gustavus I in a revolt, 1521-23; he built up the government and military and established the Lutheran Church. In the 17th century Sweden was a major European power, gaining most of the Baltic seacoast, but its international position subsequently declined.

The Napoleonic wars, in which Sweden acquired Norway (it became independent 1905), were the last in which Sweden participated. Armed neutrality was maintained in both world wars.

Over 4 decades of Social Democratic rule was ended in 1976 parliamentary elections but the party was returned to power in the 1982 elections. Although 90% of the economy is in private hands, the government holds a large interest in water power production and the railroads are operated by a public agency.

Consumer cooperatives are in extensive operation and also are important in agriculture and housing.

Premier Olaf Palme was shot and killed on a Stockholm street Feb. 28, 1986. A man with a history of substance abuse and psychiatric treatment was convicted of the crime July, 1989. The conviction was overturned Oct. 12.

Switzerland
Swiss Confederation

People: Population (1990 est.): 6,628,000. **Age distrib.** (%): 0–14: 17.0; 15–59: 63.7; 60+: 19.3. **Pop. density:** 406 per sq. mi. **Urban** (1987): 60.4%. **Ethnic groups:** Mixed European stock. **Languages:** German, French, Italian (all official). **Religions:** Roman Catholic 49%, Protestant 48%.

Geography: Area: 15,941 sq. mi., as large as Mass., Conn., and R.I., combined. **Location:** In the Alps Mts. in Central Europe. **Neighbors:** France on W, Italy on S, Austria on E, Germany on N. **Topography:** The Alps cover 60% of the land area, the Jura, near France, 10%. Running between, from NE to SW, are midlands, 30%. **Capital:** Bern. **Cities** (1989): Zurich 346,000; Basel 171,200; Geneva 161,000.

Government: Type: Federal republic. **Head of government:** Pres. Arnold Koller; in office: Jan. 1, 1990. **Local divisions:** 20 full cantons, 6 half cantons. **Defense:** 2.2% of GNP (1987).

Economy: Industries: Machinery, machine tools, steel, instruments, watches, textiles, foodstuffs (cheese, chocolate), chemicals, drugs, banking, tourism. **Chief crops:** Grains, potatoes, sugar beets, vegetables, tobacco. **Minerals:** Salt. **Other resources:** Hydro power potential. **Arable land:** 10%. **Livestock** (1989): cattle: 1.8 mln.; pigs: 1.9 mln. **Electricity prod.** (1988): 58.4 bln. kwh. **Crude steel prod.** (1988): 825,000 metric tons. **Labor force:** 39% ind. and commerce, 7% agric., 50% serv.

Finance: Monetary unit: Franc (May 1991: 1.44 = $1 US). **Gross national product** (1989): $197 bln. **Per capita GNP** (1989): $30,270. **Imports** (1990): $69.6 bln.; partners: Ger. 30%, Fr. 11%, It. 10%, U.K. 5%. **Exports** (1990): $63.7 bln.; partners: W. Ger. 18%, Fr. 9%, It. 8%, U.S. 8%. **Tourists** (1989): receipts: $5.9 bln. **National budget** (1988): $17.4 bln. **International reserves less gold** (Mar. 1991): $26.5 bln. **Gold:** 83.28 mln. oz t. **Consumer prices** (change in 1990): 5.4%.

Transport: Railway traffic (1989): 10.8 bln. passenger-km. **Motor vehicles:** in use (1989): 2.7 mln. passenger cars, 239,000 comm. vehicles. **Civil aviation:** (1989): 15.8 bln. passenger-km; 5 airports with scheduled flights.

Communications: Television sets: 1 per 2.9 persons. **Radios:** 1 per 2.6 persons. **Telephones:** 1 per 1.2 persons. **Daily newspaper circ.** (1988): 429 per 1,000 pop.

Health: Life expectancy at birth (1989): 74 male; 82 female. **Births** (per 1,000 pop. 1989): 12 **Deaths** (per 1,000 pop. 1989): 10 **Natural increase:** .2%. **Physicians:** 1 per 620 persons. **Infant mortality** (per 1,000 live births 1989): 6.9.

Education (1989): **Literacy:** 99%. **Years compulsory:** 9; attendance 100%.

Major International Organizations: Many UN specialized agencies (though not a member).

Embassy: 2900 Cathedral Ave. NW 20008; 745-7900.

Switzerland, the Roman province of Helvetia, is a federation of 23 cantons (20 full cantons and 6 half cantons), 3 of which in 1291 created a defensive league and later were joined by other districts. Voters in the French-speaking part of Canton Bern voted for self-government, 1978; Canton Jura was created Jan. 1, 1979.

In 1648 the Swiss Confederation obtained its independence from the Holy Roman Empire. The cantons were joined under a federal constitution in 1848, with large powers of local control retained by each canton.

Switzerland has maintained an armed neutrality since 1815, and has not been involved in a foreign war since 1515. It is the seat of many UN and other international agencies.

Switzerland is a leading world banking center; stability of the currency brings funds from many quarters. The nation's famed secret bank accounts were due to be phased out by Sept. 1992.

Syria
Syrian Arab Republic
al-jamhouriya al Arabia as-Souriya

People: Population (1990 est.): 12,471,000. **Age distrib.** (%): 0–14: 49.3; 15–59: 44.2; 60+: 6.5. **Pop. density:** 170 per sq. mi. **Urban** (1988): 50%. **Ethnic groups:** Arab 90%, Kurd, Armenian, others. **Languages:** Arabic (official), Kurdish, Armenian. **Religions:** Sunni Moslem 74%, other Moslem 16%, Christian 10%.

Geography: Area: 71,498 sq. mi., the size of North Dakota. **Location:** At eastern end of Mediterranean Sea. **Neighbors:** Lebanon, Israel on W, Jordan on S, Iraq on E, Turkey on N. **Topography:** Syria has a short Mediterranean coastline, then stretches E and S with fertile lowlands and plains, alternating with mountains and large desert areas. **Capital:** Damascus. **Cities** (1989 est.): Damascus 1,361,000; Aleppo 1,308,000; Homs 464,000.

Government: Type: Republic (under military regime). **Head of state:** Pres. Hafez al-Assad; b. Mar. 1930; in office: Feb. 22, 1971. **Head of government:** Prime Min. Mahmoud Zuabi; in office: Nov. 1, 1987. **Local divisions:** Damascus and 13 provinces. **Defense:** 11.9% of GNP (1987).

Economy: Industries: Oil products, textiles, cement, tobacco, glassware, sugar, brassware. **Chief crops:** Cotton, grain, olives, fruits, vegetables. **Minerals:** Oil, phosphate, gypsum. **Crude oil reserves** (1987): 1.4 bln. bbls. **Other resources:** Wool. **Arable land:** 28%. **Livestock** (1989): sheep: 13 mln., goats: 1 mln. **Electricity prod.** (1988): 9.1 bln. kwh. **Labor force:** 32% agric.; 29% ind. & comm.; 39% services.

Finance: Monetary unit: Pound (Mar. 1991: 11.22 = $1 US). **Gross national product** (1989): $12.4 bln. **Per capita GNP** (1989): $1,020.1. **Imports** (1989): $2.0 bln.; partners: Iran, It., W. Ger., Fr. **Exports** (1989): $3.0 bln.; partners: It. 20%, Rom. 28%. **Tourists** (1987): receipts: $477 mln. **National budget** (1988): $4.6 bln. expenditures. **Consumer prices** (change in 1989): 11.4%.

Transport: Railway traffic (1989): 1.3 bln. passenger-km. **Motor vehicles:** in use (1988): 112,000 passenger cars, 135,000 comm. vehicles **Civil aviation** (1989): 833 mln. passenger-km; 5 airports with scheduled flights. **Chief ports:** Latakia, Tartus.

Communications: Television sets: 1 per 17 persons. **Radios:** 1 per 4.1 persons. **Telephones:** 1 per 23 persons. **Daily newspaper circ.** (1989): 21 per 1,000 pop.

Health: Life expectancy at birth (1989): 67 male; 69 female. **Births** (per 1,000 pop. 1989): 44. **Deaths** (per 1,000 1989): 6. **Natural increase:** 3.8%. **Hospital beds:** 1 per 840 persons. **Physicians:** 1 per 1,347 persons. **Infant mortality** (per 1,000 live births 1989): 40.

Education (1986): **Literacy:** 78% males. **Years compulsory:** 6; attendance: 94%.

Major International Organizations: UN (IMF, WHO, FAO), Arab League.

Embassy: 2215 Wyoming Ave. NW 20008; 232-6313.

Syria contains some of the most ancient remains of civilization. It was the center of the Seleucid empire, but later became absorbed in the Roman and Arab empires. Ottoman rule prevailed for 4 centuries, until the end of World War I.

The state of Syria was formed from former Turkish districts, made a separate entity by the Treaty of Sevres 1920 and divided into the states of Syria and Greater Lebanon. Both were administered under a French League of Nations mandate 1920-1941.

Syria was proclaimed a republic by the occupying French Sept. 16, 1941, and exercised full independence effective Apr. 17, 1946. Syria joined in the Arab invasion of Israel in 1948.

Syria joined with Egypt in Feb. 1958 in the United Arab Republic but seceded Sept. 30, 1961. The Socialist Baath party and military leaders seized power in Mar. 1963. The Baath, a pan-Arab organization, became the only legal party. The government has been dominated by members of the minority Alawite sect.

In the Arab-Israeli war of June 1967, Israel seized and occupied the Golan Heights area inside Syria, from which Israeli settlements had for years been shelled by Syria.

On Oct. 6, 1973, Syria joined Egypt in an attack on Israel. Arab oil states agreed in 1974 to give Syria $1 billion a year to aid anti-Israel moves. Some 30,000 Syrian troops entered Lebanon in 1976 to mediate in a civil war. They fought Palestinian guerrillas and, later, Christian militiamen. Syrian troops again battled Christian forces in Lebanon, Apr. 1981, ending a ceasefire that had been in place.

Following the June 6, 1982 Israeli invasion of Lebanon, Israeli planes destroyed 17 Syrian antiaircraft missile batteries in the Bekka Valley, June 9. Some 25 Syrian planes were downed during the engagement. Israel and Syria agreed to a cease fire June 11. In 1983, Syria backed the PLO rebels who ousted Yasir Arafat's forces from Tripoli.

Syria's role in promoting acts of international terrorism led to the breaking of diplomatic relations with Great Britain and the implementation of limited sanctions by the European Communities in 1986.

Syria condemned the Aug. 1990 Iraqi invasion on Kuwait and sent troops to help Allied Forces in the Gulf War.

In 1991, Syria accepted U.S. proposals for the terms of an Arab-Israeli peace conference. *(See Chronology and Index for details.)*

Taiwan

Republic of China

Chung-hua Min-kuo

People: Population (1990 est.): 20,454,000. **Age distrib.** (%): 0-14: 29.6; 15-59: 53.2; 60+: 8.1. **Pop. density:** 1,460 per sq. mi. **Urban** (1989): 72%. **Ethnic groups:** Taiwanese 85%, Chinese 14%. **Languages:** Mandarin Chinese (official), Taiwan, Hakka dialects. **Religions:** Buddhism, Taoism, Confucianism prevail.

Geography: Area: 13,885 sq. mi., about the size of Connecticut & New Hampshire combined. **Location:** Off SE coast of China, between E. and S. China Seas. **Neighbors:** Nearest is China. **Topography:** A mountain range forms the backbone of the island; the eastern half is very steep and craggy, the western slope is flat, fertile, and well-cultivated. **Capital:** Taipei. **Cities** (1990): Taipei (met.) 2,700,000; Kaohsiung 1,374,000; Taichung 747,000; Tainan 675,000.

Government: Type: One-party system. **Head of state and Nationalist Party chmn.:** Pres. Lee Teng-hui; b. Jan. 15, 1923; in office: Jan. 13, 1988. **Head of government:** Prime Min. Hau Pei-tsum; in office: May 30, 1990. **Local divisions:** 16 counties, 5 cities, Taipei & Kao-Hsiung. **Defense:** 4.6% of GNP (1987).

Economy: Industries: Textiles, clothing, electronics, processed foods, chemicals, plastics. **Chief crops:** Rice, bananas, pineapples, sugarcane, sweet potatoes, peanuts. **Minerals:** Coal, limestone, marble. **Crude oil reserves** (1987): 10 mln. bbls. **Arable land:** 25%. **Livestock** (1989): pigs: 6.9 mln. **Fish catch** (1989): 1.2 mln. metric tons. **Electricity prod.** (1988): 71.6 bln. kwh. **Crude steel prod.** (1988): 8.3 mln. metric tons. **Labor force:** 17% agric.; 41% ind. & comm.; 42% services.

Finance: Monetary unit: New Taiwan dollar (June 1991: 27.02 = $1 US). **Gross national product** (1989): $150.2 bln. **Per capita GNP** (1989): $7,510. **Imports** (1989): $52.5 bln.; partners: U.S. 27%, Jap. 30%. **Exports** (1989): $66.1 bln.; partners: U.S. 39%, Jap. 13%, Hong Kong 8%. **Tourists** (1987): $1.6 bln. receipts. **National budget** (1988): $15.6 bln.

Transport: Motor vehicles: in use (1989): 1.9 mln. passenger cars, 595,000 commercial vehicles. **Civil Aviation** (1989): 20.7 bln. passenger-km; 12 airports. **Chief ports:** Kaohsiung, Keelung, Hualien, Taichung.

Communications: Television sets: 1 per 3.2 persons. **Radios:** 1 per 1.5 persons. **Telephones:** 1 per 3.0 persons. **Daily newspaper circ.** (1989): 202 per 1,000 pop.

Health: Life expectancy at birth (1986): 70.0 male; 75.9 female. **Births** (per 1,000 pop. 1989): 16. **Deaths** (per 1,000 pop. 1989): 5. **Natural increase:** 1.1%. **Physicians:** 1 per 1,010 persons. **Hospital beds:** 1 per 227 persons. **Infant mortality** (per 1,000 live births 1987): 6.3.

Education (1988): **Literacy:** 90%. Years compulsory 9; attendance 99%.

Large-scale Chinese immigration began in the 17th century. The island came under mainland control after an interval of Dutch rule, 1620-62. Taiwan (also called Formosa) was ruled by Japan 1895-1945. Two million Kuomintang supporters fled to Taiwan in 1949. Both the Taipei and Peking governments consider Taiwan an integral part of China. Taiwan has rejected Pe-

kings efforts at reunification, but unofficial dealings with the mainland have grown more flexible in the 1980s.

The U.S. upon its recognition of the People's Republic of China, Dec. 15, 1978, severed diplomatic ties with Taiwan. It maintains the unofficial American Institute in Taiwan, while Taiwan has established the Coordination Council for North American Affairs in Washington, D.C.

Land reform, government planning, U.S. aid and investment, and free universal education have brought huge advances in industry, agriculture, and mass living standards. In 1987, martial law was lifted after 38 years and in 1991, the 43-year period of emergency rule ended.

The Penghu (Pescadores), 50 sq. mi., pop. 120,000, lie between Taiwan and the mainland. **Quemoy** and **Matsu,** pop. (1980) 61,000 lie just off the mainland.

Tanzania

United Republic of Tanzania

Jamhuri ya Mwungano wa Tanzania

People: Population (1990 est.) 26,070,000. **Pop. density:** 67 per sq. mi. **Urban** (1988): 18%. **Ethnic groups:** African. **Languages:** Swahili, English (both official), many others. **Religions:** Moslems 33%, Christians 33%, traditional beliefs 33%.

Geography: Area: 364,886 sq. mi., more than twice the size of California. **Location:** On coast of E. Africa. **Neighbors:** Kenya, Uganda on N, Rwanda, Burundi, Zaire on W, Zambia, Malawi, Mozambique on S. **Topography:** Hot, arid central plateau, surrounded by the lake region in the W, temperate highlands in N and S, the coastal plains. Mt. Kilimanjaro, 19,340 ft., is highest in Africa. **Capital:** Dar-es-Salaam. **Cities** (1989): Dar-es-Salaam 1.3 mln.

Government: Type: Republic. **Head of state:** Pres. Ali Hassan Mwinyi; b. May 8, 1925; in office: Nov. 5, 1985. **Head of government:** Prime Min. John Malecela; in office: Nov. 9, 1990. **Local divisions:** 25 regions (20 on mainland). **Defense:** 3.4% of GNP (1985).

Economy: Industries: Food processing, clothing. **Chief crops:** Sisal, cotton, coffee, tea, tobacco. **Minerals:** Diamonds, gold, nickel. **Other resources:** Hides. **Arable land:** 6%. **Livestock** (1989): cattle: 14 mln.; goats: 6.4 mln.; sheep: 5.0 mln. **Fish catch** (1989): 340,000 metric tons. **Electricity prod.** (1988): 870 mln. kwh. **Labor force:** 90% agric., 10% ind., comm. & govt.

Finance: Monetary unit: Shilling (Mar. 1991: 200 = $1 US). **Gross national product** (1988): $3.0 bln. **Per capita GNP** (1988): $120. **Imports** (1988): $800 mln.; partners: UK 14%, Jap. 12%, W. Ger. 10%. **Exports** (1988): $276 mln.; partners: W. Ger. 15%, UK 13%. **Tourists** (1988): $31 mln. receipts. **National budget** (1985): $1.0 bln. expenditures. **International reserves less gold** (Jan. 1990): $54.2 mln. **Consumer prices** (change in 1989): 24.5%.

Transport: Motor vehicles: in use (1986): 49,000 passenger cars; 33,000 comm. vehicles. **Civil aviation** (1989): $184 mln. passenger-km; 20 airports. **Chief ports:** Dar-es-Salaam, Mtwara, Tanga.

Communications: Radios: 1 per 6 persons. **Telephones:** 1 per 179 persons. **Daily newspaper circ.** (1989): 8 per 1,000 pop.

Health: Life expectancy at birth (1989): 49 male; 54 female. **Births** (per 1,000 pop. 1989): 50. **Deaths** (per 1,000 pop. 1989): 16. **Natural increase:** 3.4%. **Hospital beds** (1984): 22,800. **Physicians** (1984): 1,065. **Infant mortality** (per 1,000 live births 1989): 110.

Education (1987): **Literacy:** 85%. **Attendance:** 87% attend primary school.

Major International Organizations: UN and all of its specialized agencies, OAU, Commonwealth of Nations.

Embassy: 2139 R. St. NW 20008; 939-6125.

The Republic of Tanganyika in E. Africa and the island Republic of Zanzibar, off the coast of Tanganyika, joined into a single nation, the United Republic of Tanzania, Apr. 26, 1964. Zanzibar retains internal self-government.

Tanganyika. Arab colonization and slaving began in the 8th century AD; Portuguese sailors explored the coast by about 1500. Other Europeans followed.

In 1885 Germany established German East Africa of which Tanganyika formed the bulk. It became a League of Nations mandate and, after 1946, a UN trust territory, both under Britain. It became independent Dec. 9, 1961, and a republic within the Commonwealth a year later.

In 1967 the government set on a socialist course; it nationalized all banks and many industries. The government also ordered that Swahili, not English, be used in all official business.

Tanzanian forces drove Idi Amin from Uganda, Mar., 1979.

Zanzibar, the Isle of Cloves, lies 23 mi. off the coast of Tanganyika; its area is 621 sq. mi. The island of Pemba, 25 mi. to the NE, area 380 sq. mi., is included in the administration. The total population (1990 est.) is 375,000.

Chief industry is the production of cloves and clove oil of which Zanzibar and Pemba produce the bulk of the world's supply.

Zanzibar was for centuries the center for Arab slave-traders. Portugal ruled for 2 centuries until ousted by Arabs around 1700. Zanzibar became a British Protectorate in 1890; independence came Dec. 10, 1963. Revolutionary forces overthrew the Sultan Jan. 12, 1964. The new government ousted Western diplomats and newsmen, slaughtered thousands of Arabs, and nationalized farms. Union with Tanganyika followed, 1964. The ruling parties of Tanganyika and Zanzibar were united in 1977, as political tension eased.

Thailand

Kingdom of Thailand

Muang Thai or Prathet Thai

People: Population (1990 est.): 54,890,000. **Age distrib. (%):** 0–14: 45.0; 15–59: 49.0; 60+: 6.0. **Pop. density:** 277 per sq. mi. **Urban** (1985): 20%. **Ethnic groups:** Thais 75%, Chinese 14%, others 11%. **Languages:** Thai, (official), Chinese, Malay, regional dialects. **Religions:** Buddhist 95%, Moslem 4%.

Geography: Area: 198,456 sq. mi., about the size of Texas. **Location:** On Indochinese and Malayan Peninsulas in S.E. Asia. **Neighbors:** Myanmar on W. Laos on N, Cambodia on E, Malaysia on S. **Topography:** A plateau dominates the NE third of Thailand, dropping to the fertile alluvial valley of the Chao Phraya R. in the center. Forested mountains are in N, with narrow fertile valleys. The southern peninsula region is covered by rain forests. **Capital:** Bangkok. **Cities** (1987 est.): Bangkok (met.): 5.6 mln.

Government: Type: Military. **Head of state:** King Bhumibol Adulyadej; b. Dec. 5, 1927; in office: June 9, 1946. **Head of government:** Gen. Sunthorn Kongsompong; in office: Feb. 3, 1991. **Local divisions:** 73 provinces. **Defense:** 3.7% of GNP (1987).

Economy: Industries: Textiles, mining, wood products. **Chief crops:** Rice (a major export), corn tapioca, sugarcane. **Minerals:** Antimony, tin (among largest producers), tungsten, iron, gas. **Other resources:** Forests (teak is exported), rubber. **Arable land:** 34%. **Livestock** (1989): cattle: 4.9 mln.; pigs: 4.2 mln. **Fish catch** (1989): 2.3 mln. metric tons. **Electricity prod.** (1988): 27.0 bln. kwh. **Labor force:** 59% agric.; 26% ind. & comm.; 10% serv.; 8% govt.

Finance: Monetary unit: Baht (Mar. 1991: 25.65 = $1 US). **Gross national product** (1989): $64.4 bln. **Per capita GNP** (1989): $1,170. **Imports** (1990): $32.7 bln.; partners: Jap. 24%, U.S. 13%. **Exports** (1990): $20.0 bln.; partners: Jap. 14%, U.S. 17%, Sing. 14%. **Tourists** (1988): $3.1 mln. receipts. **National budget** (1988): $9.4 bln. **International reserves less gold** (Mar. 1991): $14.2 bln. **Gold:** 2.47 mln. oz t. **Consumer prices** (change in 1989): 5.4%.

Transport: Railway traffic (1989): 10.3 bln. passenger-km. **Motor vehicles:** in use (1988): 816,000 passenger cars, 1.1 mln. comm. vehicles. **Civil aviation** (1988): 16.6 bln. passenger-km; 24 airports with scheduled flights. **Chief ports:** Bangkok, Sattahip.

Communication: Television sets: 1 per 11 persons. **Radios:** 1 per 5.7 persons. **Telephones:** 1 per 53 persons. **Daily newspaper circ.** (1987): 50 per 1,000 pop.

Health: Life expectancy at birth (1989): 62 male; 68 female. **Births** (per 1,000 pop. 1989): 20 **Deaths** (per 1,000 pop. 1989): 7. **Natural increase:** 1.3%. **Hospital beds:** 1 per 605 persons.

Physicians: 1 per 5,564 persons. **Infant mortality** (per 1,000 live births 1989): 50.

Education (1988): **Literacy:** 89%. **Years compulsory:** 6; attendance 96%.

Major International Organizations: UN (GATT, World Bank). **Embassy:** 2300 Kalorama Rd. NW 20008; 483-7200.

Thais began migrating from southern China in the 11th century. Thailand is the only country in SE Asia never taken over by a European power, thanks to King Mongkut and his son King Chulalongkorn who ruled from 1851 to 1910, modernized the country, and signed trade treaties with both Britain and France. A bloodless revolution in 1932 limited the monarchy.

Japan occupied the country in 1941.

The military took over the government in a bloody 1976 coup. Kriangsak Chomanan, prime minister resigned, Feb. 1980, under opposition over soaring inflation, oil price increases, labor unrest and growing crime. Chatichai Choonhavan was chosen prime minister in a democratic election, Aug. 1988. In Feb. 1991, the military ousted Choonhavan in a bloodless coup.

Vietnamese troops had crossed the border and been repulsed by Thai forces in the 1980s.

Togo

Republic of Togo

République Togolaise

People: Population (1990 est.): 3,566,000. **Age distrib. (%):** 0-14: 49.8; 15-59: 44.6; 60+:5.6.**Pop. density:** 158 per sq. mi. **Urban** (1987): 23%. **Ethnic groups:** Ewe 35%, Mina 6%, Kabye 22%. **Languages:** French (official), Gur & Kwa languages. **Religions:** Traditional 50%, Christian 30%, Moslem 20%.

Geography: Area: 21,622 sq. mi., slightly smaller than West Virginia. **Location:** On S coast of W. Africa. **Neighbors:** Ghana on W, Burkina Faso on N, Benin on E. **Topography:** A range of hills running SW-NE splits Togo into 2 savanna plains regions. **Capital:** Lomé. **Cities** (1989 est.): Lomé 600,000.

Government: Type: Republic. **Head of state:** Pres. Kokou Koffigoh; in office: Aug. 28, 1991. **Local divisions:** 21 prefectures.

Economy: Industries: Textiles, shoes. **Chief crops:** Coffee, cocoa, yams, manioc, millet, rice. **Minerals:** Phosphates. **Arable land:** 26%. **Electricity prod.** (1988): 155 mln. kwh. **Labor force:** 75% agric.; 20% industry.

Finance: Monetary unit: CFA franc (Mar. 1991: 290 = $1 US). **Gross national product** (1989): $1.3 bln. **Per capita income** (1987): $390. **Imports** (1988): $335 mln.; partners: Fr., U.K., W. Ger. **Exports** (1988): $297 mln.; partners: Neth., Fr., W. Ger. **Tourists** (1988): $21 mln. receipts. **International reserves less gold** (Jan. 1991): $353 mln. **Gold:** 13,000 oz t. **Consumer prices** (change in 1990): 1.0%.

Transport: Railway traffic (1989): 109 mln. passenger-km. **Motor vehicles:** in use (1988): 47,000 passenger cars, 22,000 comm. vehicles. **Chief ports:** Lome.

Communications: Television sets: 1 per 152 persons. **Radios:** 1 per 5.0 persons. **Telephones:** 1 per 255 persons. **Daily newspaper circ.** (1989): 3 per 1,000 pop.

Health: Life expectancy at birth (1989): 53 male; 57 female. **Births** (per 1,000 pop. 1989): 47. **Deaths** (per 1,000 pop. 1989): 13. **Natural increase:** 3.3%. **Hospital beds:** 1 per 752 persons. **Physicians:** 1 per 12,992 persons. **Infant mortality** (per 1,000 live births 1989): 113.

Education (1990): **Literacy:** 45% (males).

Major International Organizations: UN (GATT, IMF), OAU. **Embassy:** 2208 Massachusetts Ave. NW 20008; 234-4212.

The Ewe arrived in southern Togo several centuries ago. The country later became a major source of slaves. Germany took control in 1884. France and Britain administered Togoland as UN trusteeships. The French sector became the republic of Togo Apr. 27, 1960.

The population is divided between Bantus in the S and Hamitic tribes in the N. Togo has actively promoted regional integration, as a means of stimulating the economy.

Tonga

Kingdom of Tonga

Pule 'anga Tonga

People: Population (1989 est.): 108,000. **Age distrib. (%):** 0–14: 44.4; 15–59; 50.5; 60+:5.1. **Pop. density:** 400 per sq. mi. **Ethnic groups:** Tongans 98%, other Polynesian, European. **Languages:** Tongan, English (both official). **Religions:** Free Wesleyan 47%, Roman Catholics 14%, Free Church of Tonga 14%, Mormons 9%, Church of Tonga 9%.

Geography: Area: 270 sq. mi., smaller than New York City. **Location:** In western S. Pacific O. **Neighbors:** Nearest is Fiji, on W, New Zealand, on S. **Topography:** Tonga comprises 169 volcanic and coral islands, 45 inhabited. **Capital:** Nuku'alofa. **Cities** (1986): Nuku'alofa (met.) 29,000.

Government: Type: Constitutional monarchy. **Head of state:** King Taufa'ahau Tupou IV; b. July 4, 1918; in office: Dec. 16, 1965. **Head of government:** Prime Min. Prince Fatafehi Tu'ipelehake; b. Jan. 7, 1922; in office: Dec. 16, 1965. **Local divisions:** 3 main island groups.

Economy: Industries: Tourism. **Chief crops:** Coconut products, bananas are exported. **Other resources:** Fish. **Arable land:** 25%. **Electricity prod.** (1988): 8 mln. kwh. **Labor force:** 45% agric, 27% services.

Finance: Monetary unit: Pa'anga (Apr. 1991: 1.29 = $1 US). **Gross national product** (1989): $89 mln. **Imports** (1985): $41 mln.; partners: N Z 45%, Fiji 7%. **Exports** (1985): $7 mln.; partners: Aust. 29%, N Z 56%. **Tourism** (1988): $8.0 mln. receipts.

Transport: Motor vehicles: in use (1987): 1,400 passenger cars, 2,400 comm. vehicles. **Chief ports:** Nuku'alofa.

Communications: Radios: 1 per 1.2 persons. **Telephones:** 1 per 24 persons.

Health: Life expectancy at birth (1989): 69 male; 74 female. **Births** (per 1,000 pop. 1989): 27. **Deaths** (per 1,000 pop. 1989): 5. **Natural increase:** 2.2%. **Infant mortality** (per 1,000 live births 1989): 25.

Education (1988): **Literacy:** 93%. **Years compulsory:** 8. **Attendance:** 77%.

The islands were first visited by the Dutch in the early 17th century. A series of civil wars ended in 1845 with establishment of the Tupou dynasty. In 1900 Tonga became a British protectorate. On June 4, 1970, Tonga became independent and a member of the Commonwealth.

Trinidad and Tobago

Republic of Trinidad and Tobago

People: Population (1990 est.): 1,270,000. **Age distrib. (%):** 0–14: 32.9; 15–59: 58.7; 60+: 8.4. **Pop. density:** 636 per sq. mi. **Ethnic groups:** Africans 43%, East Indians 40%, mixed 14%. **Languages:** English (official). **Religions:** Roman Catholic 32%, Protestant 29%, Hindu 25%, Moslem 6%.

Geography: Area: 1,980 sq. mi., the size of Delaware. **Location:** Off eastern coast of Venezuela. **Neighbors:** Nearest is Venezuela on SW. **Topography:** Three low mountain ranges cross Trinidad E-W, with a well-watered plain between N and Central Ranges. Parts of E and W coasts are swamps. Tobago, 116 sq. mi., lies 20 mi. NE. **Capital:** Port-of-Spain. **Cities** (1989 met. est.): Port-of-Spain 300,000; San Fernando 50,000.

Government: Type: Parliamentary democracy. **Head of state:** Pres. Noor Hassanali; in office: Mar. 19, 1987. **Head of government:** Prime Min. Arthur Robinson; in office: Dec. 18, 1986. **Local divisions:** 8 counties, 3 municipalities.

Economy: Industries: Oil products, rum, cement, tourism. **Chief crops:** Sugar, cocoa, coffee, citrus fruits, bananas. **Minerals:** Asphalt, oil, **Crude oil reserves** (1987): 567 mln. bbls. **Arable land:** 14%. **Electricity prod.** (1988): 3.3 bln. kwh. **Labor force:** 18% construction-utilities, 14% manuf., mining, commerce, 47% services.

Finance: Monetary unit: Dollar (Mar. 1991: 4.25 = $1 US). **Gross national product** (1989): $4.0 bln. **Per capita GNP** (1989): $3,150. **Imports** (1989): $1.2 bln.; partners: U.S. 41%, UK 11%. **Exports** (1989): $1.5 bln.; partners: U.S. 56%. **Tourists** (1988): $89 mln. receipts. **National budget** (1988): $2.1 bln. expenditures. **International reserves less gold** (Mar.

1991): $459 mln. **Gold:** 54,000 oz t. **Consumer prices** (change in 1990): 11.5%.

Transport: Motor vehicles: in use (1986): 256,000 passenger cars, 95,000 comm. vehicles. **Civil aviation:** (1987): 2.3 bln. passenger-km; 2 airports. **Chief ports:** Port-of-Spain.

Communications: Television sets: 1 per 3.6 persons. **Radios:** 1 per 3.1 persons. **Telephones:** 1 per 6.2 persons. **Daily newspaper circ.** (1988): 146 per 1,000 pop.

Health: Life expectancy at birth (1989): 68 male; 72 female. **Births** (per 1,000 pop. 1989): 27. **Deaths** (per 1,000 pop. 1989): 6. **Natural increase:** 2.1%. **Hospital beds:** 1 per 270 persons. **Physicians:** 1 per 1,025 persons. **Infant mortality** (per 1,000 pop. 1989): 15.

Education (1988): **Literacy:** 97%. **Years compulsory:** 8.

Major International Organizations: UN (GATT, IMF, WHO), Commonwealth of Nations, OAS.

Embassy: 1708 Massachusetts Ave. NW 20036; 467-6490.

Columbus sighted Trinidad in 1498. A British possession since 1802, Trinidad and Tobago won independence Aug. 31, 1962. It became a republic in 1976. The People's National Movement party has held control of the government since 1956.

The nation is one of the most prosperous in the Caribbean. Oil production has increased with offshore finds. Middle Eastern oil is refined and exported, mostly to the U.S.

In July 1990, some 120 Moslem extremists captured the parliament building and TV station and took about 50 hostages including Prime Minister Arthur Robinson, who was beaten, shot in the legs, and tied to explosives. After a 6-day siege, the rebels surrendered.

Tunisia

Republic of Tunisia

al Jumhuriyah at-Tunisiyah

People: Population (1990 est.): 8,094,000. **Age distrib. (%)** 0–14: 39.0; 15–59: 54.2; 60+: 6.8. **Pop. density:** 125 per sq. mi. **Ethnic groups:** Arab 98%. **Languages:** Arabic (official), French. **Religions:** Moslem 99%.

Geography: Area: 63,170 sq. mi., about the size of Missouri. **Location:** On N coast of Africa. **Neighbors:** Algeria on W, Libya on E. **Topography:** The N is wooded and fertile. The central coastal plains are given to grazing and orchards. The S is arid, approaching Sahara Desert. **Capital:** Tunis. **Cities** (1984 est.) Tunis 1,000,000, Sfax 475,000.

Government: Type: Republic. **Head of state:** Pres. Gen. Zine al-Abidine Ben Ami; b. Sept 3, 1936; in office: Nov. 7, 1987. **Head of government:** Prime Min. Hamed Karoui; in office: Sept. 27, 1989. **Local divisions:** 23 governorates. **Defense:** 3.1% of GNP (1987).

Economy: Industries: Food processing, textiles, oil products, construction materials. **Chief crops:** Grains, dates, olives, citrus fruits, figs, vegetables, grapes. **Minerals:** Phosphates, iron, oil, lead, zinc. **Crude oil reserves** (1987): 1.7 bln. bbls. **Arable land:** 20%. **Livestock** (1989): sheep: 5.0 mln.; goats: 1 mln. **Fish catch** (1988): 99,000 metric tons. **Electricity prod.** (1988): 4.2 bln. kwh. **Crude steel prod.** (1986): 188,000 metric tons. **Labor force:** 25% agric.; 34% industry; 40% serv.

Finance: Monetary unit: Dinar (Mar. 1991: .93 = $1 US). **Gross national product** (1990): $10.0 bln. **Per capita income** (1989) $1,253. **Imports** (1990): $5.5 bln.; partners: Fr. 26%, It. 12%. **Exports** (1990): $3.5 bln.; partners: It. 17%, Fr. 26%, Ger. 10%, U.S. 19%. **Tourists** (1988): $1.2 bln. receipts. **National budget** (1990): $3.2 bln. expenditures. **International reserves less gold** (Mar. 1991): $640 mln. **Gold:** 187,000 oz t. **Consumer prices** (change in 1990): 6.8%.

Transport: Railway traffic (1989): 1.0 bln. passenger-km. **Motor vehicles:** in use (1989): 321,000 passenger cars, 208,000 comm. vehicles; **Civil aviation:** (1989): 1.5 bln. passenger-km; 6 airports. **Chief ports:** Tunis, Sfax, Bizerte.

Communications: Television sets: 1 per 15 persons. **Radios:** 1 per 4.7 persons. **Telephones:** 1 per 24 persons. **Daily newspaper circ.** (1987): 30 per 1,000 pop.

Health: Life expectancy at birth (1989): 68 male; 71 female. **Births** (per 1,000 pop. 1989): 29. **Deaths** (per 1,000 pop. 1989): 6. **Natural increase:** 2.3%. **Hospital beds:** 1 per 482 persons. **Physicians:** 1 per 2,198 persons. **Infant mortality** (per 1,000 pop. live births 1989): 44.

Education (1990): **Literacy:** 62%. **Years compulsory:** 8; attendance 85%.
Major International Organizations: UN, Arab League, OAU.
Embassy: 1515 Massachusetts Ave. NW 20005; 862-1850.

Site of ancient Carthage, and a former Barbary state under the suzerainty of Turkey, Tunisia became a protectorate of France under a treaty signed May 12, 1881. The nation became independent Mar. 20, 1956, and ended the monarchy the following year.

Tunisia survived a Libyan-engineered raid against the southern mining center of Gafsa, Jan. 1980.

Turkey

Republic of Turkey

Turkiye Cumhuriyeti

People: Population (1990 est.): 56,549,000. **Age distrib. (%):** 0–14: 38.5; 15–59: 54.9; 60+: 6.6. **Pop. density:** 183 per sq. mi. **Urban** (1987): 55%. **Ethnic groups:** Turks 85%, Kurds 12%. **Languages:** Turkish (official), Kurdish, Arabic. **Religions:** Moslem 98%, Christian, Jewish.

Geography: Area: 301,381 sq. mi., twice the size of California. **Location:** Occupies Asia Minor, between Mediterranean and Black Seas. **Neighbors:** Bulgaria, Greece on W, USSR (Georgia, Armenia) on N, Iran on E, Iraq, Syria on S. **Topography:** Central Turkey has wide plateaus, with hot, dry summers and cold winters. High mountains ring the interior on all but W, with more than 20 peaks over 10,000 ft. Rolling plains are in W; mild, fertile coastal plains are in S, W. **Capital:** Ankara. **Cities** (1990 est.): Istanbul 6,700,000; Ankara 2,553,000; Izmir 1,700,000; Adana 931,000.

Government: Type: Republic. **Head of state:** Pres. Turgut Ozal; b. 1927; in office: Nov. 9, 1989. **Head of government:** Prime Min. Mesut Yilmaz; in office: June 24, 1991. **Local divisions:** 67 provinces. **Defense:** 3.9% of GNP (1988).

Economy: Industries: Iron, steel, machinery, metal prods., cars, processed foods. **Chief crops:** Tobacco, cereals, cotton, barley, corn, fruits, potatoes, sugar beets. **Minerals:** Chromium, mercury, boron, copper, coal. **Crude oil reserves** (1987): 139 mln. bbls. **Other resources:** Wool, silk, forests. **Arable land:** 30%. **Livestock** (1987): cattle: 12.0 mln.; sheep: 40.4 mln. **Fish catch** (1987): 562,000 metric tons. **Electricity prod.** (1988): 46.9 bln. kwh. **Crude steel prod.** (1988): 8.0 mln. metric tons. **Labor force:** 50% agric.; 21% ind. and comm.; 29% serv.

Finance: Monetary unit: Lira (Mar. 1991: 3,704 = $1 US). **Gross national product** (1989): $74.7 bln. **Per capita GNP** (1989): $1,360 **Imports** (1989): $15.7 bln.; partners: W. Ger. 16%, U.S. 13%. **Exports** (1989): $11.6 bln.; partners: W. Ger. 19%. **Tourists** (1989): $2.5 bln. receipts. **National budget** (1989): $15.5 bln. expenditures. **International reserves less gold** (Feb. 1991): $5.2 bln. **Gold:** 4.0 mln. oz t. **Consumer prices** (change in 1990): 60%.

Transport: Railway traffic (1989): 6.8 bln. passenger-km. **Motor vehicles:** in use (1988): 1.4 mln. passenger cars, 656,000 comm. vehicles. **Civil aviation** (1988): 3.8 bln. passenger-km; 14 airports with scheduled flights. **Chief ports:** Istanbul, Izmir, Mersin, Samsun.

Communications: Television sets: 1 per 6.8 persons. **Radios:** 1 per 7.8 persons. **Telephones:** 1 per 10 persons.

Health: Life expectancy at birth (1989): 63 male; 66 female. **Births** (per 1,000 pop. 1989): 30. **Deaths** (per 1,000 pop. 1989): 8. **Natural increase:** 2.2%. **Hospital beds:** 1 per 476 persons. **Physicians:** 1 per 1,275 persons. **Infant mortality** (per 1,000 live births 1989): 80.

Education (1990): **Literacy:** 90%. **Years compulsory:** 6; attendance 95%.
Major International Organizations: UN (GATT, WHO, IMF), NATO, OECD, EC.
Embassy: 1714 Massachusetts Ave. NW 20036.

Ancient inhabitants of Turkey were among the worlds first agriculturalists. Such civilizations as the Hittite, Phrygian, and Lydian flourished in Asiatic Turkey (Asia Minor), as did much of Greek civilization. After the fall of Rome in the 5th century, Constantinople was the capital of the Byzantine Empire for 1,000 years. It fell in 1453 to Ottoman Turks, who ruled a vast empire for over 400 years.

Just before World War I, Turkey, or the Ottoman Empire, ruled what is now Syria, Lebanon, Iraq, Jordan, Israel, Saudi Arabia, Yemen, and islands in the Aegean Sea.

Turkey joined Germany and Austria in World War I and its defeat resulted in loss of much territory and fall of the sultanate. A republic was declared Oct. 29, 1923. The Caliphate (spiritual leadership of Islam) was renounced 1924.

Long embroiled with Greece over Cyprus, off Turkey's south coast, Turkey invaded the island July 20, 1974, after Greek officers seized the Cypriot government as a step toward unification with Greece. Turkey sought a new government for Cyprus, with Greek Cypriot and Turkish Cypriot zones. In reaction to Turkey's moves, the U.S. cut off military aid in 1975. Turkey, in turn, suspended the use of most U.S. bases. Aid was restored in 1978. There was a military takeover, Sept. 12, 1980.

Religious and ethnic tensions and active left and right extremists have caused endemic violence. Martial law, imposed in 1978, was lifted in 1984. The military formally transferred power to an elected parliament in 1983.

Turkey was a member of the Allied forces which ousted Iraq from Kuwait, 1991. In the aftermath of the war, millions of Kurdish refugees fled to Turkey's border to escape Iraqi forces.

Tuvalu

People: Population (1990 est.): 9,000. **Pop. density:** 900 per sq. mi. **Ethnic group:** Polynesian. **Languages:** Tuvaluan, English. **Religions:** mainly Protestant.

Geography: Area: 10 sq. mi., less than one-half the size of Manhattan. **Location:** 9 islands forming a NW-SE chain 360 mi. long in the SW Pacific O. **Neighbors:** Nearest are Samoa on SE, Fiji on S. **Topography:** The islands are all low-lying atolls, nowhere rising more than 15 ft. above sea level, composed of coral reefs. **Capital:** Funafuti (pop. 1985): 2,800.

Government: Head of state: Queen Elizabeth II, represented by Gov.-Gen. Toaripi Lauti; in office: Oct. 1, 1990. **Head of government:** Prime Min. Bikenibeu Paeniu; in office: Oct. 16, 1989. **Local divisions:** 8 island councils on the permanently inhabited islands.

Economy: Industries: Copra. **Chief crops:** Coconuts. **Labor force:** Approx. 1,500 Tuvaluans work overseas in the Gilberts' phosphate industry, or as overseas seamen.
Finance: Monetary unit: Australian dollar.
Transport: Chief port: Funafuti.
Health: (including former Gilbert Is.) **Life expectancy at birth** (1989): 60 male; 63 female. **Births** (per 1,000 pop. 1989): 27. **Deaths** (per 1,000 pop. 1989): 10. **Natural increase:** 1.7%. **Infant mortality** (per 1,000 live births 1989) : 30.
Education: Literacy (1985): 96%.

The Ellice Islands separated from the British Gilbert and Ellice Islands colony, 1975, and became independent Tuvalu Oct. 1, 1978.

Uganda

Republic of Uganda

People: Population (1990 est.): 17,593,000. **Age distrib. (%):** 0–14: 48.5; 15–59: 47.3; 60+: 4.2. **Pop. density:** 180 per sq. mi. **Urban** (1984): 14%. **Ethnic groups:** Bantu, Nilotic, Nilo-Hamitic, Sudanic tribes. **Languages:** English (official), Luganda, Swahili. **Religions:** Christian 63%, Moslem 6%, traditional beliefs.

Geography: Area: 93,354 sq. mi., slightly smaller than Oregon. **Location:** In E. Central Africa. **Neighbors:** Sudan on N, Zaire on W, Rwanda, Tanzania on S, Kenya on E. **Topography:** Most of Uganda is a high plateau 3,000-6,000 ft. high, with high Ruwenzori range in W (Mt. Margherita 16,750 ft.), volcanoes in SW, NE is arid, W and SW rainy. Lakes Victoria, Edward, Albert form much of borders. **Capital:** Kampala. **Cities** (1988): Kampala 331,000.

Government: Type: Military. **Head of state:** Pres. Yoweri Kaguta Museveni; b. 1944; in office: Jan. 29, 1986. **Head of government:** Prime Min. Samson Kisekka; in office: Jan. 3, 1986. **Local divisions:** 10 provinces, 34 districts. **Defense:** 1% of GNP (1984).

Economy: Chief Crops: Coffee, cotton, tea, corn, bananas, sugar. **Minerals:** Copper, cobalt. **Arable land:** 23%. **Livestock**

(1987): cattle: 5.2 mln.; goats: 3.3 mln.; sheep: 1.3 mln. **Fish catch** (1986): 212,000 metric tons. **Electricity prod.** (1988): 312 mln. kwh. **Labor force:** 90% agric.

Finance: Monetary unit: Shilling (Mar. 1991: 620 = $1 US). **Gross national product** (1989): $4.2 bln. **Per capita GNP** (1989): $250. **Imports** (1989): $651 mln.; partners: Kenya 24%, U.K. 17%. **Exports** (1989): $251 mln.; partners: U.S. 14%, U.K. 12%, Neth. 15%. **National budget** (1988): $790 mln. expenditures. **International reserves less gold** (Nov. 1990): $19.3 mln. **Consumer prices** (change in 1990): 32%.

Transport: Motor vehicles: in use (1989): 34,000 passenger cars, 6,000 comm. vehicles.

Communications: Television sets: 1 per 183 persons. **Radios:** 1 per 46 persons. **Telephones:** 1 per 272 persons. **Daily newspaper circ.** (1989): 2 per 1,000 pop.

Health: Life expectancy at birth (1989): 49 male; 51 female. **Births** (per 1,000 pop. 1989): 49. **Deaths** (per 1,000 pop. 1989): 15. **Natural increase:** 3.4%. **Hospital beds:** 1 per 817 persons. **Physicians:** 1 per 20,000 persons. **Infant mortality** (per 1,000 live births 1989): 99.

Education (1989): **Literacy:** 52%. About 50% attend primary school.

Major International Organizations: UN (GATT, WHO, IMF), OAU, Commonwealth of Nations.

Embassy: 5909 16th St. NW 20011; 726-7100.

Britain obtained a protectorate over Uganda in 1894. The country became independent Oct. 9, 1962, and a republic within the Commonwealth a year later. In 1967, the traditional kingdoms, including the powerful Buganda state, were abolished and the central government strengthened.

Gen. Idi Amin seized power from Prime Min. Milton Obote in 1971. As many as 300,000 of his opponents were reported killed in subsequent years. Amin was named president for life in 1976.

In 1972 Amin expelled nearly all of Uganda's 45,000 Asians. In 1973 the U.S. withdrew all diplomatic personnel.

Amid worsening economic and domestic crises, Uganda's troops exchanged invasion attacks with long-standing foe Tanzania, 1978 to 1979. Tanzanian forces, coupled with Ugandan exiles and rebels, ended the dictatorial rule of Amin, Apr. 11, 1979.

Union of Soviet Socialist Republics

Soyuz Sovetskykh Sotsialisticheskikh Respublic

(As of Sept. 1, 1991)

People: Population (1990 est.): 290,939,000. **Age distrib. (%):** 0–19: 25.5; 20-59: 61.0; 60+: 13.5. **Pop. density:** 33 per sq. mi. **Urban** (1990): 66%. **Ethnic groups:** Russians 52% Ukrainians 16%, Uzbeks 5%, Byelorussians 4%, many others. **Languages:** Russian (official), Ukrainian, Byelorussian, Uzbek, Armenian, Azerbaijani, Georgian, many others. **Religions:** Russian Orthodox 18%, Moslem 9%, non-religious 70%.

Geography: Area: 8,649,496 sq. mi., the largest country in the world, nearly 2½ times the size of the U.S. **Location:** Stretches from E. Europe across N Asia to the Pacific O. **Neighbors:** Finland, Poland, Czechoslovakia, Hungary, Norway, Romania on W, Turkey, Iran, Afghanistan, China, Mongolia, N. Korea on S. **Topography:** Covering one-sixth of the earth's land area, the USSR contains every type of climate except the distinctly tropical, and has a varied topography.

The European portion is a low plain, grassy in S, wooded in N with Ural Mtns. on the E. Caucasus Mts. on the S. Urals stretch N-S for 2,500 mi. The Asiatic portion is also a vast plain, with mountains on the S and in the E; tundra covers extreme N, with forest belt below; plains, marshes are in W, desert in SW. **Capital:** Moscow. **Cities** (1989 est.): Moscow 8.5 mln.; St. Petersberg 4.8 mln.; Kiev 2.4 mln.; Tashkent 2.1 mln.; Kharkov 1.5 mln.; Baku 1.7 mln.; Nizhniy Novgorod 1.4 mln.; Novosibirsk 1.4 mln.; Minsk 1.5 mln.; Kuibyshev 1.2 mln.; Sverdlovsk 1.3 mln.

Government: Type: In transition. **Head of state:** Exec. Pres. Mikhail S. Gorbachev; b. Mar. 2, 1931; in office: Mar. 15, 1990. **Head of government:** Prime min. Valentin Pavlov; b. 1937; in office: Jan. 14, 1991. **Local divisions:** 15 union republics, 6 krays (territories), 123 oblasts (regions), 8 autonomous oblasts. **Defense:** 15-17% of GNP (1988).

Economy: Industries: Steel, machinery, machine tools, vehicles, chemicals, cement, textiles, appliances, paper. **Chief crops:** Grain, cotton, sugar beets, potatoes, vegetables, sun-

flowers. **Minerals:** Manganese, mercury, potash, bauxite, cobalt, chromium, copper, coal, gold, lead, molybdenum, nickel, phosphates, silver, tin, tungsten, zinc, oil (59%), potassium salts. **Crude oil reserves** (1990): 59 bln. barrels. **Other resources:** Forests (25% of world reserves). **Arable land:** 11%. **Livestock** (1989): cattle: 118 mln.; sheep: 142 mln.; pigs: 77 mln.; goats 142 mln. **Fish catch** (1989): 10.9 mln. metric tons. **Electricity prod.** (1988): 1,730 bln. kwh. **Crude steel prod.** (1988): 164 mln. metric tons. **Labor force:** 22% agric.; 29% industry, 26% services.

Finance: Monetary unit: Ruble (Jan. 1991: 1.00 = $1.79 US). **Gross national product** (1988): $2.5 trl. **Per capita income** (1987): $3,000. **Imports** (1988): $107.3 bln.; partners: E. Ger. 10%, Pol. 7%, Czech. 8%, Bulg. 8%. **Exports** (1988): $110.7 bln.; partners: E. Ger. 10%, Pol. 8%, Bulg. 8%, Czech. 8%. **National budget** (1989): $310 bln. expenditures. **Tourists** (1988): receipts: $216 mln.

Transport: Railway traffic (1990): 414 bln. passenger-km. **Motor vehicles:** in use (1980): 9.2 mln. passenger cars, 7.9 mln. comm. vehicles; manuf. (1982): 1.3 mln. passenger cars; 874,000 comm. vehicles. **Civil aviation** (1989): 228 bln. passenger-km; 52 airports with scheduled flights. **Chief ports:** Leningrad, Odessa, Murmansk, Tver, Archangelsk, Riga, Vladivostok.

Communications: Television sets: 1 per 3.2 persons. **Radios:** 1 per 1.5 persons. **Telephones:** 1 per 6.7 persons. **Daily newspaper circ.** (1989): 383 per 1,000 pop.

Health: Life expectancy at birth (1989): 64 male; 74 female. **Births** (per 1,000 pop. 1989): 18. **Deaths** (per 1,000 pop. 1989): 11. **Natural increase:** .8%. **Hospital beds:** 1 per 72 persons. **Physicians:** 1 per 259 persons. **Infant mortality** (per 1,000 live births 1989): 25.2.

Education (1989): **Literacy:** 99%. Most receive 11 years of schooling.

Major International Organizations: UN (ILO, UNESCO, WHO), Warsaw Pact.

Embassy: 1125 16th St. NW 20036; 628-7551.

The USSR is nominally a federation consisting of 15 republics, the largest being the Russian Republic. Many of the republics have announced their intention to withdraw from the USSR. Pres. Gorbachev warned that the unrest posed an "enormous danger" to the USSR.

Beginning in 1939 the USSR by means of military action and negotiation overran contiguous territory and independent republics, including all or part of Lithuania, Latvia, Estonia, Poland, Czechoslovakia, Romania, Germany, Finland, Tannu Tuva, and Japan. Census figures released in 1989 showed an increase in persons leaving rural areas to live in cities. The republics prior to Aug. 1991 were: *(For details after Aug. 1991 see Index & Chronology.)*

Republic	Area sq. mi.	Pop. (1989 cen.)
Russian	6,592,800	147,400,000
Ukrainian	233,100	51,700,000
Uzbek	172,700	19,900,000
Kazakh.	1,049,200	16,500,000
Byelorussian	80,200	10,200,000
Azerbaijan	33,400	7,000,000
Georgian	26,911	5,500,000
Tadzhik	54,019	5,100,000
Moldavian	13,012	4,300,000
Kirghiz	76,642	4,300,000
Lithuanian	26,173	3,700,000
Armenian	11,306	3,300,000
Turkmen	188,417	3,500,000
Latvian	24,695	2,700,000
Estonian	17,413	1,600,000

The **Russian Republic** contains over 50% of the population of the USSR and includes 76% of its territory. It extends from the old Estonian, Latvian, and Finnish borders and the Byelorussian and Ukrainian lines on the W, to the shores of the Pacific, and from the Arctic on the N to the Black and Caspian seas and the borders of Kazakh SSR, Mongolia, and Manchuria on the S. Siberia encompasses a large part of the RSFSR area. Capital: Moscow.

Boris N. Yeltsin, a critic of the slow pace of national renewal, was elected President of the SFSR in May, 1990. He called for economic and political sovereignty for the republic.

Parts of eastern and western Siberia have been transformed by steel mills, huge dams, oil and gas industries, electric railroads, and highways.

The **Ukraine**, the most densely populated of the republics, borders on the Black Sea, with Poland, Czechoslovakia, Hungary, and Romania on the W and SW. Capital: Kiev.

The Ukraine contains the arable black soil belt; the chief wheat-producing section of the Soviet Union. Sugar beets, potatoes, and livestock are important.

The Donets Basin has large deposits of coal, iron and other metals. There are chemical and machine industries and salt mines.

There is a strong independence movement in the western part of the republic.

Byelorussia (White Russia). Capital: Minsk. Chief industries include machinery, tools, appliances, bicycles, clocks, steel, cement, textiles. Main crops are grain, flax, potatoes, sugar beets.

Azerbaijan boasts near Baku, the capital, important oil fields. Its natural wealth includes deposits of iron ore, cobalt, etc. A high-yield winter wheat is grown, as are fruits. It produces iron, steel, cement, fertilizers, synthetic rubber, electrical and chemical equipment. It borders on Iran and Turkey. In 1988, clashes were reported between Moslem Azerbaijanis and the minority Christian ethnic Armenians. Soviet troops were sent to quell the ethnic civil war between the 2 factions, Jan. 1990.

Georgia, in the western part of Transcaucasia, contains the largest manganese mines in the world. There are rich timber resources and coal mines. Basic industries are food, textiles, iron, steel. Grain, tea, tobacco, fruits, grapes are grown. Capital: Tbilisi (Tiflis). Despite massive party and government purges since 1972, illegal private enterprise and Georgian nationalist feelings persist; attempts to repress them have led to violence; in Apr. 1989, soviet troops attacked nationalist demonstrators, killing some 20 persons.

Armenia is mountainous, sub-tropical, extensively irrigated. Copper, zinc, aluminum, molybdenum, and marble are mined. Instrument making is important. Armenia has sought a reunification with the Nagorno-Karabakh autonomous region of neighboring Azerbaijan. On Dec. 7, 1988, an earthquake struck in the north killing over 55,000 and leaving 500,000 homeless. An international relief effort was mounted. Soviet troops were sent to quell the ethnic civil war with Azerbaijan, Jan. 1990. Capital: Yerevan.

Uzbekistan, is the most important economically of the Central Asia republics. It is the chief cotton-growing area in the USSR. Industries include iron, steel, cars, tractors, TV and radio sets, textiles, food. Mineral wealth includes coal, sulphur, copper, and oil. Capital: Tashkent.

Turkmenistan in Central Asia, produces cotton, maize, carpets, chemicals. Minerals: oil, coal, sulphur, barite, lime, salt, gypsum. The Kara Kum desert occupies 80% of the area. Capital: Ashkhabad.

Tadzhikistan borders on China and Afghanistan. Over half the population are Tadzhiks, mostly Moslems, speaking an Iranian dialect. Chief occupations are farming and cattle breeding. Cotton, grain, rice, and a variety of fruits are grown. Heavy industry, based on rich mineral deposits, coal and hydroelectric power, has replaced handicrafts. Tadzhikistan declared sovereignty in 1990. Capital: Dushanbe.

Kazakhstan extends from the lower reaches of the Volga in Europe to the Altai Mtns. on the Chinese border. It has vast deposits of coal, oil, iron, tin, copper, lead, zinc, etc. Fish for its canning industry are caught in Lake Balkhash and the Caspian and Aral seas. The capital is Alma-Ata. About 50% of the population is Russian or Ukrainian, working in the virgin-grain lands opened up after 1954, and in the growing industries. Capital: Alma-Ata.

Kirghizia is the eastern part of Soviet Central Asia, on the frontier of Xinjiang, China. The people breed cattle and horses and grow tobacco, cotton, rice, sugar beets. Industries include machine and instrument making, chemicals. Capital: Frunze.

Moldavia, in the SW part of the USSR, is a fertile black earth plain bordering Romania and includes Bessarabia. It is an agricultural region that grows grains, fruits, vegetables, and tobacco. Textiles, wine, food and electrical equipment industries have been developed. Capital: Kishinev. The region was taken from Romania in 1940; the people speak Romanian.

Lithuania, *See Index and Chronology.*

Latvia, *See Index and Chronology.*

Estonia, *See Index and Chronology.*

Economy. The USSR is in transition to a market economy. Prior to Gorbachev's *Perestroika* policy, almost all legal economic enterprises were state-owned. A huge illegal black market played an important role in distribution.

The USSR is rich in natural resources; distant Siberian reserves are being exploited. Its heavy industry is 2d only to the U.S. It leads the world in oil and steel production. Consumer industries have lagged comparatively. Agricultural output has expanded, but in poor crop years the USSR has been forced to make huge grain purchases from the West. Shortages and rationing of basic food products periodically occur.

History. Slavic tribes began migrating into Russia from the W in the 5th century AD. The first Russian state, founded by Scandinavian chieftains, was established in the 9th century, centering in Novgorod and Kiev.

In the 13th century the Mongols overran the country. It recovered under the grand dukes and princes of Muscovy, or Moscow, and by 1480 freed itself from the Mongols. Ivan the Terrible was the first to be formally proclaimed Tsar (1547). Peter the Great (1682-1725), extended the domain and in 1721, founded the Russian Empire.

Western ideas and the beginnings of modernization spread through the huge Russian empire in the 19th and early 20th centuries. But political evolution failed to keep pace.

Military reverses in the 1905 war with Japan and in World War I led to the breakdown of the Tsarist regime. The 1917 Revolution began in March with a series of sporadic strikes for higher wages by factory workers. A provisional democratic government under Prince Georgi Lvov was established but was quickly followed in May by the second provisional government, led by Alexander Kerensky. The Kerensky government and the freely-elected Constituent Assembly were overthrown in a communist coup led by Vladimir Ilyich Lenin Nov. 7.

Lenin's death Jan. 21, 1924, resulted in an internal power struggle from which Joseph Stalin eventually emerged the absolute ruler of Russia. Stalin secured his position at first by exiling opponents, but from the 1930s to 1953, he resorted to a series of "purge" trials, mass executions, and mass exiles to work camps. These measures resulted in millions of deaths, according to most estimates.

Germany and the USSR signed a non-aggression pact Aug. 1939; Germany launched a massive invasion of the Soviet Union, June 1941. Notable heroic episode was the "900 days" siege of Leningrad, lasting to Jan. 1944, and causing a million deaths; the city was never taken. Russian winter counterthrusts, 1941 to '42 and 1942 to '43, stopped the German advance. Turning point was the failure of German troops to take and hold Stalingrad, Sept. 1942 to Feb. 1943. With British and U.S. Lend-Lease aid and sustaining great casualties, the Russians drove the German forces from eastern Europe and the Balkans in the next 2 years.

After Stalin died, Mar. 5, 1953, Nikita Khrushchev was elected first secretary of the Central Committee. In 1956 he condemned Stalin. "De-Stalinization" of the country on all levels was effected after Stalin's body was removed from the Lenin-Stalin tomb in Moscow.

Under Khrushchev the open antagonism of Poles and Hungarians toward domination by Moscow was brutally suppressed in 1956. He advocated peaceful co-existence with the capitalist countries, but continued arming the USSR with nuclear weapons. He aided the Cuban revolution under Fidel Castro but withdrew Soviet missiles from Cuba during confrontation by U.S. Pres. Kennedy, Sept.-Oct. 1962.

Khrushchev was suddenly deposed, Oct. 1964, and replaced as party first secretary by Leonid I. Brezhnev.

In Aug. 1968 Russian, Polish, East German, Hungarian, and Bulgarian military forces invaded Czechoslovakia to put a curb on liberalization policies of the Czech government.

When Egypt and Syria attacked Israel in Oct. 1973, the USSR launched huge arms airlifts to the 2 Arab nations. In 1974, the Soviet replenished the arms used or lost by the Syrians in the 1973 war, and continued some shipments to Egypt.

Massive Soviet military aid to North Vietnam in the late 1960s and early 1970s helped assure communist victories throughout Indo-China. Soviet arms aid and advisers were sent to several African countries in the 1970s, including Algeria, Angola, Somalia, and Ethiopia.

More than 130,000 Jews and over 40,000 ethnic Germans were allowed to emigrate from the USSR in the 1970s, following pressure from the West. Many leading figures in the arts also left the country.

In 1979, Soviet forces entered Afghanistan to support that government against rebels. In 1988, the Soviets announced withdrawal of their troops, ending a futile 8-year war.

There were serious food shortages reported in the early 1980s and a new agricultural program, covering 1982-90, was announced amid Soviet fears of becoming dependent on foreign, especially U.S., grain imports.

Mikhail Gorbachev was chosen Gen. Secy. of the Communist Party, Mar. 1985. He was the youngest member of the Politburo and signaled a change in Soviet leadership from those whose attitudes were shaped by Stalinism and World War II.

He held 4 summit meetings with U.S. Pres. Reagan. In 1987, in Washington, an INF treaty was signed.

In 1987, Gorbachev initiated a program of reforms, including expanded freedoms and the democratization of the political process, through openness (*glasnost*) and restructuring (*perestroika*). The reforms were opposed by some Eastern bloc countries and many old-line communists in the USSR. In 1989, the first Soviet Parliament was held since 1918.

Gorbachev faced economic problems as well as ethnic and nationalist unrest in the republics in 1990; the economy was in its worst state since WWII.

On Aug. 19, 1991, it was announced that the vice president had taken over the country due to Gorbachev's ilness. A state of emergency was imposed for 6 months with all power resting with the State Committee on the State of Emergency. The Russian republic's pres. Boris Yeltsin denounced the coup and called for a general strike. Some 50,000 demonstrated at the Russian parliament in support of Yeltsin. By Aug. 21, the coup had failed and Gorbachev was restored as pres. On Aug. 24, Gorbachev resigned as leader of the Communist Party and recommended that its central committee be disbanded. Several republics declared their independence including Russia, the Ukraine, and Kazakhstan. On Aug. 29, the Soviet parliament voted to suspend all activities of the Communist Party.

On Sept. 2, Gorbachev declared that the nation was "on the brink of catastrophe," and proposed to transfer all central authority to himself, the leaders of 10 republics, and an appointed legislative council in order to form a new kind of Soviet Union. *(See Index and Chronology for details.)*

Government. The communist party leadership dominated all areas of national life from 1917 thru 1991.

In Mar. 1990, the National Parliament repealed the party's political monopoly, revamped and strengthened the presidency, and elected Gorbachev to a 5-year term as a new-style executive president.

United Arab Emirates
Ittihād al-Imarat al-Arabiyah

People: Population (1990 est.): 2,250,000. **Pop. density:** 45 per sq. mi. **Ethnic groups:** Arab, Iranian, Pakistani, Indian. **Languages:** Arabic (official), several others. **Religions:** Moslem 94%, Christian, Hindu.

Geography: Area: 32,000 sq. mi., the size of Maine. **Location:** On the S shore of the Persian Gulf. **Neighbors:** Qatar on N, Saudi Ar. on W, S, Oman on E. **Topography:** A barren, flat coastal plain gives way to uninhabited sand dunes on the S. Hajar Mtns. are on E. **Capital:** Abu Dhabi. **Cities** (1984 est.): Abu Dhabi 537,000; Dubai 278,000.

Government: Type: Federation of emirates. **Head of state:** Pres. Zaid ibn Sultan an-Nahayan b. 1923; in office: Dec. 2, 1971. **Head of government:** Prime Min. Sheikh Maktum ibn Rashid al-Maktum; in office: Nov. 20, 1990. **Local divisions:** 7 autonomous emirates: Abu Dhabi, Ajman, Dubai, Fujaira, Ras al-Khaimah, Sharjah, Umm al-Qaiwain. **Defense:** 5.7% of GNP (1985).

Economy: Chief crops: Vegetables, dates, limes. **Minerals:** Oil. **Crude oil reserves** (1990): 98 bln. barrels. **Arable land:** 1%. **Electricity prod.** (1988): 14.5 bln. kwh. **Labor force:** 5% agric.; 85% ind. and commerce; 5% serv.; 5% gvt.

Finance: Monetary unit: Dirham (June 1991: 3.67 = $1 US). **Gross national product** (1989): $28.4 bln. **Per capita GNP** (1989) $18,430. **Imports** (1989): $10.0 bln.; partners: Jap. 18%, UK 11%, W. Ger. 6%. **Exports** (1987): $15.0 bln.; partners: Jap. 36%, U.S. 7%, Fr. 10%. **International reserves less gold** (Feb. 1991): $4.7 bln. **Gold:** 797,000 oz t.

Transport: Motor Vehicles (1985): 62,000 passenger cars; 17,000 commercial vehicles. **Chief ports:** Dubai, Abu Dhabi.

Communications: Television sets: 1 per 12 persons. **Radios:** 1 per 4.7 persons. **Telephones:** 1 per 4.3 persons.

Health: Life Expectancy at Birth (1989): 68 male, 72 female. **Hospital beds:** 1 per 267 persons. **Physicians:** 1 per 659 persons. **Infant mortality** (per 1,000 live births 1989): 29%.

Education (1989): **Literacy:** 68%. **Years Compulsory:** ages 6-12.

Major International Organizations: UN (World Bank, IMF, ILO), Arab League, OPEC.

Embassy: 600 New Hampshire Ave. NW 20037; 338-6500.

The 7 "Trucial Sheikdoms" gave Britain control of defense and foreign relations in the 19th century. They merged to become an independent state Dec. 2, 1971.

The Abu Dhabi Petroleum Co. was fully nationalized in 1975. Oil revenues have given the UAE one of the highest per capita GNPs in the world. International banking has grown in recent years.

United Kingdom of Great Britain and Northern Ireland

People: Population (1990 est.): 57,121,000. **Age distrib. (%):** 0–14: 18.9; 15–59: 60.5; 60+: 19.6. **Pop. density:** 601 per sq. mi. **Urban** (1985): 92.5%. **Ethnic groups:** English 81.5%, Scottish 9.6%, Irish 2.4%, Welsh 1.9%, Ulster 1.8%; West Indian, Indian, Pakistani over 2%; others. **Languages:** English, Welsh spoken in western Wales. **Religions:** Church of England, Roman Catholic.

Geography: Area: 94,226 sq. mi., slightly smaller than Oregon. **Location:** Off the NW coast of Europe, across English Channel, Strait of Dover, and North Sea. **Neighbors:** Ireland to W, France to SE. **Topography:** England is mostly rolling land, rising to Uplands of southern Scotland; Lowlands are in center of Scotland, granite Highlands are in N. Coast is heavily indented, especially on W. British Isles have milder climate than N Europe, due to the Gulf Stream, and ample rainfall. Severn, 220 mi., and Thames, 215 mi., are longest rivers. **Capital:** London. **Cities** (1988 est.): London 6,735,000; Birmingham 993,000; Glasgow 703,000; Leeds 710,000; Sheffield 532,000; Liverpool 469,000; Manchester 445,000; Edinburgh 433,000; Bradford 463,000; Bristol 377,000.

Government: Type: Constitutional monarchy. **Head of state:** Queen Elizabeth II; b. Apr. 21, 1926; in office: Feb. 6, 1952. **Head of government:** Prime Min. John Major; b. Mar. 29, 1943; in office: Nov. 28, 1990. **Local divisions:** England and Wales: 47 non-metro counties, 6 metro counties, Greater London; Scotland: 9 regions, 3 island areas; N. Ireland: 26 districts. **Defense:** 4.3% of GDP (1989).

Economy: Industries: Steel, metals, vehicles, shipbuilding, banking, textiles, chemicals, electronics, aircraft, machinery, distilling. **Chief crops:** Grains, sugar beets, fruits, vegetables. **Minerals:** Coal, tin, oil, gas, limestone, iron, salt, clay. **Crude oil reserves** (1987): 5.8 bln. bbls. **Arable land:** 30%. **Livestock** (1989): cattle: 12.6 mln.; pigs: 7.9 mln.; sheep: 29.0 mln. **Fish catch** (1988): 938,000 metric tons. **Electricity prod.** (1988): 344 bln. kwh. **Crude steel prod.** (1988): 19.0 mln. metric tons. **Labor force:** 1.7% agric.; 26% manuf. & eng., 64% services.

Finance: Monetary unit: Pound (June 1991: .57 = $1 US). **Gross national product** (1989): $843 bln. **Per capita GNP** (1989): $14,535. **Imports** (1990): $222 bln.; partners: W. Ger. 17%, U.S. 12%, Fr. 7%, Neth. 8%. **Exports** (1990): $185 bln.; partners: U.S. 13%, W. Ger. 10%, Fr. 8%, Neth. 8%. **Tourists** (1989): receipts: $11.2 bln.; **National budget** (1989): $283 bln. expenditures. **International reserves less gold** (Mar. 1991): $37 bln. **Gold:** 19.0 mln. oz t. **Consumer prices** (change in 1990): 9.5%.

Transport: Railway traffic (1989): 21.3 bln. passenger-km. **Motor vehicles** in use (1988): 18.4 mln. passenger cars, 2.7 mln. comm. vehicles. **Civil aviation** (1989): 68.9 bln. passenger-km: 55 airports with scheduled flights. **Chief ports:** London, Liverpool, Glasgow, Southampton, Cardiff, Belfast.

Communications: Television sets: 1 per 3 persons. **Radios:** 1 per 1 person. **Telephones:** 1 per 1.9 persons. **Daily newspaper circ.** (1989): 443 per 1,000 pop.

Health: Life expectancy at birth: (1989): 72 male; 78 female. **Births:** (per 1,000 pop. 1989): 13.2. **Deaths:** (per 1,000 pop. 1989): 12 **Natural increase:** 0.2%. **Hospital beds:** 1 per 138 persons. **Physicians:** 1 per 611 persons. **Infant mortality:** (per 1,000 live births 1989): 13.3.

Education (1991): **Literacy:** 99%. **Years compulsory:** 12; attendance 99%.

Major International Organizations: UN all of and its specialized agencies, NATO, EC, OECD.

Embassy: 3100 Massachusetts Ave. NW 20008; 462-1340.

The United Kingdom of Great Britain and Northern Ireland comprises England, Wales, Scotland, and Northern Ireland.

Queen and Royal Family. The ruling sovereign is Elizabeth II of the House of Windsor, born Apr. 21, 1926, elder daughter of King George VI. She succeeded to the throne Feb. 6, 1952, and was crowned June 2, 1953. She was married Nov. 20, 1947, to Lt. Philip Mountbatten, born June 10, 1921, former Prince of Greece. He was created Duke of Edinburgh, Earl of Merioneth, and Baron Greenwich, and given the style H.R.H., Nov. 19, 1947; he was given the title Prince of the United Kingdom and Northern Ireland Feb. 22, 1957. Prince Charles Philip Arthur George, born Nov. 14, 1948, is the Prince of Wales and heir apparent. His son, William Philip Arthur Louis, born June 21, 1982, is second in line to the throne.

Parliament is the legislative governing body for the United Kingdom, with certain powers over dependent units. It consists of 2 houses: The **House of Lords** includes 763 hereditary and 314 life peers and peeresses, certain judges, 2 archbishops and 24 bishops of the Church of England. Total membership is over 1,000. The **House of Commons** has 650 members, who are elected by direct ballot and divided as follows: England 516; Wales 36; Scotland 71; Northern Ireland 12.

Resources and Industries. Great Britain's major occupations are manufacturing and trade. Metals and metal-using industries contribute more than 50% of the exports. Of about 60 million acres of land in England, Wales and Scotland, 46 million are farmed, of which 17 million are arable, the rest pastures.

Large oil and gas fields have been found in the North Sea. Commercial oil production began in 1975. There are large deposits of coal.

Britain imports all of its cotton, rubber, sulphur, 80% of its wool, half of its food and iron ore, also certain amounts of paper, tobacco, chemicals. Manufactured goods made from these basic materials have been exported since the industrial age began. Main exports are machinery, chemicals, woolen and synthetic textiles, clothing, autos and trucks, iron and steel, locomotives, ships, jet aircraft, farm machinery, drugs, radio, TV, radar and navigation equipment, scientific instruments, arms, whisky.

Religion and Education. The Church of England is Protestant Episcopal. The queen is its temporal head, with rights of appointments to archbishoprics, bishoprics, and other offices. There are 2 provinces, Canterbury and York, each headed by an archbishop. The most famous church is Westminster Abbey (1050-1760), site of coronations, tombs of Elizabeth I, Mary of Scots, kings, poets, and of the Unknown Warrior.

The most celebrated British universities are Oxford and Cambridge, each dating to the 13th century. There are about 40 other universities.

History. Britain was part of the continent of Europe until about 6,000 BC, but migration of peoples across the English Channel continued long afterward. Celts arrived 2,500 to 3,000 years ago. Their language survives in Welsh, and Gaelic enclaves.

England was added to the Roman Empire in 43 AD. After the withdrawal of Roman legions in 410, waves of Jutes, Angles, and Saxons arrived from German lands. They contended with Danish raiders for control from the 8th through 11th centuries.

The last successful invasion was by French speaking Normans in 1066, who united the country with their dominions in France.

Opposition by nobles to royal authority forced King John to sign the Magna Carta in 1215, a guarantee of rights and the rule of law. In the ensuing decades, the foundations of the parliamentary system were laid.

English dynastic claims to large parts of France led to the Hundred Years War, 1338-1453, and the defeat of England. A long civil war, the War of the Roses, lasted 1455-85, and ended with the establishment of the powerful Tudor monarchy. A distinct English civilization flourished. The economy prospered over long periods of domestic peace unmatched in continental Europe. Religious independence was secured when the Church of England was separated from the authority of the Pope in 1534.

Under Queen Elizabeth I, England became a major naval power, leading to the founding of colonies in the new world and the expansion of trade with Europe and the Orient. Scotland was united with England when James VI of Scotland was crowned James I of England in 1603.

A struggle between Parliament and the Stuart kings led to a bloody civil war, 1642-49, and the establishment of a republic

under the Puritan Oliver Cromwell. The monarchy was restored in 1660, but the "Glorious Revolution" of 1688 confirmed the sovereignty of Parliament: a Bill of Rights was granted 1689.

In the 18th century, parliamentary rule was strengthened. Technological and entrepreneurial innovations led to the Industrial Revolution. The 13 North American colonies were lost, but replaced by growing empires in Canada and India. Britain's role in the defeat of Napoleon, 1815, strengthened its position as the leading world power.

The extension of the franchise in 1832 and 1867, the formation of trade unions, and the development of universal public education were among the drastic social changes which accompanied the spread of industrialization and urbanization in the 19th century. Large parts of Africa and Asia were added to the empire during the reign of Queen Victoria, 1837-1901.

Though victorious in World War I, Britain suffered huge casualties and economic dislocation. Ireland became independent in 1921, and independence movements became active in India and other colonies.

The country suffered major bombing damage in World War II, but held out against Germany singlehandedly for a year after the fall of France in 1940.

Industrial growth continued in the postwar period, but Britain lost its leadership position to other powers. Labor governments passed socialist programs nationalizing some basic industries and expanding social security. The Thatcher government has however, tried to increase the role of private enterprise. In 1987, Margaret Thatcher became the first British leader in 160 years to be elected to a 3d consecutive term as prime minister. She resigned as prime minister in Nov. 1990.

The UK supported the UN resolutions against Iraq and sent military forces in the Persion Gulf war.

Wales

The Principality of Wales in western Britain has an area of 8,019 sq. mi. and a population (1988 est.) of 2,857,000. Cardiff is the capital, pop. (1981 est.) 273,856.

England and Wales are administered as a unit. Less than 20% of the population of Wales speak both English and Welsh; about 32,000 speak Welsh solely. A 1979 referendum rejected, 4-1, the creation of an elected Welsh Assembly.

Early Anglo-Saxon invaders drove Celtic peoples into the mountains of Wales, terming them Waelise (Welsh, or foreign). There they developed a distinct nationality. Members of the ruling house of Gwynedd in the 13th century fought England but were crushed, 1283. Edward of Caernarvon, son of Edward I of England, was created Prince of Wales, 1301.

Scotland

Scotland, a kingdom now united with England and Wales in Great Britain, occupies the northern 37% of the main British island, and the Hebrides, Orkney, Shetland and smaller islands. Length, 275 mi., breadth approx. 150 mi., area, 30,405 sq. mi., population (1988 est.) 5,094,000.

The Lowlands, a belt of land approximately 60 mi. wide from the Firth of Clyde to the Firth of Forth, divide the farming region of the Southern Uplands from the granite Highlands of the North, contain 75% of the population and most of the industry. The Highlands, famous for hunting and fishing, have been opened to industry by many hydroelectric power stations.

Edinburgh, pop. (1986 est.) 439,000, is the capital. Glasgow, pop. (1986 est.) 733,000, is Britain's greatest industrial center. It is a shipbuilding complex on the Clyde and an ocean port. Aberdeen, pop. (1986 est.) 215,000, NE of Edinburgh, is a major port, center of granite industry, fish processing, and North Sea oil exploitation. Dundee, pop. (1986 est.) 177,000, NE of Edinburgh, is an industrial and fish processing center. About 90,000 persons speak Gaelic as well as English.

History. Scotland was called Caledonia by the Romans who battled early Celtic tribes and occupied southern areas from the 1st to the 4th centuries. Missionaries from Britain introduced Christianity in the 4th century; St. Columba, an Irish monk, converted most of Scotland in the 6th century.

The Kingdom of Scotland was founded in 1018. William Wallace and Robert Bruce both defeated English armies 1297 and 1314, respectively.

In 1603 James VI of Scotland, son of Mary, Queen of Scots, succeeded to the throne of England as James I, and effected the Union of the Crowns. In 1707 Scotland received representation in the British Parliament, resulting from the union of former separate Parliaments. Its executive in the British cabinet is the Secretary of State for Scotland. The growing Scottish National Party urges independence. A 1979 referendum on the creation of an elected Scotland Assembly was defeated.

Memorials of Robert Burns, Sir Walter Scott, John Knox, Mary, Queen of Scots draw many tourists, as do the beauties of the Trossachs, Loch Katrine, Loch Lomond and abbey ruins.

Industries. Engineering products are the most important industry, with growing emphasis on office machinery, autos, electronics and other consumer goods. Oil has been discovered offshore in the North Sea, stimulating on-shore support industries.

Scotland produces fine woolens, worsteds, tweeds, silks, fine linens and jute. It is known for its special breeds of cattle and sheep. Fisheries have large hauls of herring, cod, whiting. Whisky is the biggest export.

The Hebrides are a group of c. 500 islands, 100 inhabited, off the W coast. The Inner Hebrides include **Skye, Mull,** and **Iona,** the last famous for the arrival of St. Columba, 563 AD. The Outer Hebrides include **Lewis** and **Harris.** Industries include sheep raising and weaving. The **Orkney Islands,** c. 90, are to the NE. The capital is Kirkwall, on Pomona Is. Fish curing, sheep raising and weaving are occupations. NE of the Orkneys are the 200 **Shetland Islands,** 24 inhabited, home of Shetland pony. The Orkneys and Shetlands have become centers for the North Sea oil industry.

Northern Ireland

Six of the 9 counties of Ulster, the NE corner of Ireland, constitute Northern Ireland, with the parliamentary boroughs of Belfast and Londonderry. Area 5,463 sq. mi., 1988 est. pop. 1,578,000, capital and chief industrial center, Belfast, (1987 cen.) 303,000.

Industries. Shipbuilding, including large tankers, has long been an important industry, centered in Belfast, the largest port. Linen manufacture is also important, along with apparel, rope, and twine. Growing diversification has added engineering products, synthetic fibers, and electronics. They are large numbers of cattle, hogs, and sheep, potatoes, poultry, and dairy foods are also produced.

Government. An act of the British Parliament, 1920, divided Northern from Southern Ireland, each with a parliament and government. When Ireland became a dominion, 1921, and later a republic, Northern Ireland chose to remain a part of the United Kingdom. It elects 12 members to the British House of Commons.

During 1968-69, large demonstrations were conducted by Roman Catholics who charged they were discriminated against in voting rights, housing, and employment. The Catholics, a minority comprising about a third of the population, demanded abolition of property qualifications for voting in local elections. Violence and terrorism intensified, involving branches of the Irish Republican Army (outlawed in the Irish Republic), Protestant groups, police, and British troops.

A succession of Northern Ireland prime ministers pressed reform programs but failed to satisfy extremists on both sides. Over 2,000 were killed in over 15 years of bombings and shootings through 1990, many in England itself. Britain suspended the Northern Ireland parliament Mar. 30, 1972, and imposed direct British rule. A coalition government was formed in 1973 when moderates won election to a new one-house Assembly. But a Protestant general strike overthrew the government in 1974 and direct rule was resumed.

The turmoil and agony of Northern Ireland was dramatized in 1981 by the deaths of 10 imprisoned Irish nationalist hunger strikers in Maze Prison near Belfast. The inmates had starved themselves to death in an attempt to achieve status as political prisoners, but the British government refused to yield to their demands. In 1985, the Hillsborough agreement gave the Rep. of Ireland a voice in the governing of Northern Ireland; the accord was strongly opposed by Ulster loyalists.

Education and Religion. Northern Ireland is 2/3 Protestant, 1/3 Roman Catholic. Education is compulsory through age 15.

Channel Islands

The Channel Islands, area 75 sq. mi., est. pop. 1986 145,000, off the NW coast of France, the only parts of the one-time Dukedom of Normandy belonging to England, are **Jersey, Guernsey** and the dependencies of Guernsey — **Alderney, Brechou, Great Sark, Little Sark, Herm, Jethou** and **Lihou.** Jersey and Guernsey have separate legal existences and lieutenant governors named by the Crown. The islands were the only British soil occupied by German troops in World War II.

Isle of Man

The Isle of Man, area 227 sq. mi., 1986 est. pop. 64,000, is in the Irish Sea, 20 mi. from Scotland, 30 mi. from Cumberland. It is rich in lead and iron. The island has its own laws and a lieutenant governor appointed by the Crown. The Tynwald (legislature) consists of the Legislative Council, partly elected, and House of Keys, elected. Capital: Douglas. Farming, tourism, fishing (kippers, scallops) are chief occupations. Man is famous for the Manx tailless cat.

Gibraltar

Gibraltar, a dependency on the southern coast of Spain, guards the entrance to the Mediterranean. The Rock has been in British possession since 1704. The Rock is 2.75 mi. long, 3/4 of a mi. wide and 1,396 ft. in height; a narrow isthmus connects it with the mainland. Est. pop. 1987, 29,048.

In 1966 Spain called on Britain to give "substantial sovereignty" of Gibraltar to Spain and imposed a partial blockade. In 1967, residents voted for remaining under Britain. A new constitution, May 30, 1996, gave an elected House of Assembly more control in domestic affairs. A UN General Assembly resolution requested Britain to end Gibraltar's colonial status by Oct. 1, 1996. No settlement has been reached.

British West Indies

Swinging in a vast arc from the coast of Venezuela NE, then N and NW toward Puerto Rico are the Leeward Islands, forming a coral and volcanic barrier sheltering the Caribbean from the open Atlantic. Many of the islands are self-governing British possessions. Universal suffrage was instituted 1951-54; ministerial systems were set up 1956-1960.

The **Leeward Islands,** still associated with the UK are **Montserrat** (1987 pop. 11,600, area 32 sq. mi., capital Plymouth), the small **British Virgin Islands** (pop. 1987: 12,000), and **Anguilla** (pop. 1985: 7,000), the most northerly of the Leeward Islands.

The three **Cayman Islands,** a dependency, lie S of Cuba, NW of Jamaica. Pop. 23,000 (1987), most of it on Grand Cayman. It is a free port; in the 1970s Grand Cayman became a tax-free refuge for foreign funds and branches of many Western banks were opened there. Total area 102 sq. mi., capital Georgetown.

The **Turks and Caicos Islands,** at the SE end of the Bahama Islands, are a separate possession. There are about 30 islands, only 6 inhabited, 1987 pop. est. 9,000, area 193 sq. mi., capital Grand Turk. Salt, crayfish and conch shells are the main exports.

Bermuda

Bermuda is a British dependency governed by a royal governor and an assembly, dating from 1620, the oldest legislative body among British dependencies. Capital is Hamilton.

It is a group of 360 small islands of coral formation, 20 inhabited, comprising 20.6 sq. mi. in the western Atlantic, 580 mi. E of North Carolina. Pop., 1989 est., was 58,800 (about 61% of African descent). Density is high.

The U.S. has air and naval bases under long-term lease, and a NASA tracking facility.

Bermuda boasts many resort hotels. The government raises most revenue from import duties. Exports: petroleum products, medicine.

South Atlantic

Falkland Islands and Dependencies, a British dependency, lies 300 mi. E of the Strait of Magellan at the southern end of South America.

The Falklands or Islas Malvinas include about 200 islands, area 4,700 sq. mi., pop. (1980 est.) 1,800. Sheep-grazing is the main industry; wool is the principal export. There are indications of large oil and gas deposits. The islands are also claimed by Argentina though 97% of inhabitants are of British origin. Argentina invaded the islands Apr. 2, 1982. The British responded by sending a task force to the area, landing their main force on the Falklands, May 21, and forcing an Argentine surrender at Port Stanley, June 14. **South Georgia,** area 1,450 sq. mi., and the uninhabited **South Sandwich Is.** are dependencies of the Falklands.

British Antarctic Territory, south of 60° S lat., was made a separate colony in 1962 and comprises mainly the **South Shetland Islands,** the **South Orkneys** and **Graham's Land.** A chain of meteorological stations is maintained.

St. Helena, an island 1,200 mi. off the W coast of Africa and 1,800 E of South America, has 47 sq. mi. and est. pop., 1985 of 5,400. Flax, lace and rope making are the chief industries. After Napoleon Bonaparte was defeated at Waterloo the Allies exiled him to St. Helena, where he lived from Oct. 16, 1815, to his death, May 5, 1821. Capital is Jamestown.

Tristan da Cunha is the principal of a group of islands of volcanic origin, total area 40 sq. mi., half way between the Cape of Good Hope and South America. A volcanic peak 6,760 ft. high erupted in 1961. The 262 inhabitants were removed to England, but most returned in 1963. The islands are dependencies of St. Helena.

Ascension is an island of volcanic origin, 34 sq. mi. in area, 700 mi. NW of St. Helena, through which it is administered. It is a communications relay center for Britain, and has a U.S. satellite tracking center. Est. pop., 1985, was 1,500, half of them communications workers. The island is noted for sea turtles.

Hong Kong

A Crown Colony at the mouth of the Canton R. in China, 90 mi. S of Canton. Its nucleus is Hong Kong Is., 35½ sq. mi., acquired from China 1841, on which is located Victoria, the capital. Opposite is Kowloon Peninsula, 3 sq. mi. and Stonecutters Is., ¼ sq. mi., added, 1860. An additional 355 sq. mi. known as the New Territories, a mainland area and islands, were leased from China, 1898, for 99 years. Britain and China, Dec. 19, 1985, signed an agreement under which Hong Kong would be allowed to keep its capitalist system for 50 years after 1997, the year that the 99-year lease will expire. Total area of the colony is 409 sq. mi., with a population, 1989 est., of 5.7 million including fewer than 20,000 British. From 1949 to 1962 Hong Kong absorbed more than a million refugees from China.

Hong Kong harbor was long an important British naval station and one of the world's great trans-shipment ports.

Principal industries are textiles and apparel; also tourism, $4.2 bln. expenditures (1988), shipbuilding, iron and steel, fishing, cement, and small manufactures.

Spinning mills, among the best in the world, and low wages compete with textiles elsewhere and have resulted in the protective measures in some countries. Hong Kong also has a booming electronics industry.

British Indian Ocean Territory

Formed Nov. 1965, embracing island dependencies of Mauritius or Seychelles: the Chagos Archipelago (including Diego Garcia), Aldabra, Farquhar and Des Roches. The latter 3 were transferred to Seychelles, which became independent in 1976. Area 22 sq mi. No civilian population remains.

Pacific Ocean

Pitcairn Island is in the Pacific, halfway between South America and Australia. The island was discovered in 1767 by Carteret but was not inhabited until 23 years later when the mutineers of the Bounty landed there. The area is 1.7 sq. mi. and pop. 1983, was 61. It is a British colony and is administered by a British Representative in New Zealand and a local Council. The uninhabited islands of **Henderson, Ducie** and **Oeno** are in the Pitcairn group.

United States of America

People: Population (1990 cen.): 248,709,873. **Age distrib.(%):** 0–14: 21.7; 15–59: 61.4; 60+: 16.9. **Pop. density:** 68 per sq. mi. **Urban** (1987): 76%.

Geography: Area: 3,618,770 sq. mi. (incl. 50 states and D. of C.) about four-tenths the size of USSR. Vast central plain, mountains in west, hills and low mountains in east. **Government:** Federal republic, strong democratic tradition. **Head of state:** George Bush; b. June 12, 1924; in office: Jan. 20, 1989. **Administrative divisions:** 50 states and Dist. of Columbia. **Defense:** 5.7% of GNP (1988).

Economy: Minerals: Coal, copper, lead, molybdenum, phosphates, uranium, bauxite, gold, iron, mercury, nickel, potash, silver, tungsten, zinc. **Crude oil reserves** (1990): 25 bln. barrels. **Arable land:** 21%. **Livestock** (1988): cattle: 98 mln.; pigs: 56 mln.; sheep: 10.7 mln. **Fish catch** (1989): 3.8 mln. metric tons. **Electricity prod.** (1989): 2,781 bln. kwh. **Crude steel prod.** (1988): 90.7 mln. metric tons.

Finance: Gross national product (1989): 5.2 trl. **Per capita income** (1988): $16,444. **Imports** (1989): $492 bln.; partners: Can. 17%, Jap. 20%, Mex. 6%. **Exports** (1989): $363 bln.; partners: Can. 22%, Jap. 12%, Mex. 6%, UK 5%. **Tourists** (1989): receipts $34.3 bln. **International reserves less gold** (Mar. 1991): $66.9 bln. **Gold:** 261.0 mln. oz t. **Consumer prices** (change in 1990): 5.4%.

Transport: Railway traffic (1988): 20.2 bln. passenger-km. **Motor vehicles:** in use (1988): 141 mln. passenger cars, 40 mln. comm. vehicles. **Civil aviation** (1989): 705 bln. passenger-km; 834 airports with scheduled flights.

Communications: Television sets: 1 per 1.3 persons. **Radios:** 1 per 0.5 persons. **Telephones:** 1 per 1.9 persons. **Daily newspaper circ.** (1990): 255 per 1,000 pop.

Health: Life expectancy at birth (1989): 72 male; 79 female. **Births** (per 1,000 pop. 1989): 15. **Deaths** (per 1,000 pop. 1989): 9. **Natural increase:** .6%. **Hospital beds:** 1 per 188 persons. **Physicians:** 1 per 410 persons. **Infant mortality** (per 1,000 live births 1990): 9.1.

Major International Organizations: UN (GATT, IMF, WHO, FAO), OAS, NATO, OECD.

Education (1987): **Literacy:** 99%.

Uruguay

Republic of Uruguay

República del Uruguay

People: Population (1990 est.): 3,002,000. **Age distrib. (%):** 0–14: 26.9; 15–59: 57.7; 60+: 15.4. **Pop. density:** 43 per sq. mi. **Urban** (1985): 86.0%. **Ethnic groups:** Caucasians (Iberians, Italians) 89%, mestizos 10%, mulatto and black. **Languages:** Spanish. **Religions:** 66% Roman Catholic.

Geography: Area: 68,037 sq. mi., the size of Washington State. **Location:** In southern S. America, on the Atlantic O. **Neighbors:** Argentina on W, Brazil on N. **Topography:** Uruguay is composed of rolling, grassy plains and hills, well-watered by rivers flowing W to Uruguay R. **Capital:** Montevideo. **Cities** (1990 est.): Montevideo 1,310,000.

Government: Type: Republic. **Head of state:** Pres. Luis Alberto Lacalle; in office: Nov. 26, 1989. **Local divisions:** 19 departments. **Defense:** 1.4% of GNP (1989).

Economy: Industries: Meat-packing, textiles, wine, cement, oil products. **Chief crops:** Corn, wheat, citrus fruits, rice, oats, linseed. **Arable land:** 8%. **Livestock** (1987): cattle: 9.9 mln.; sheep: 20.6 mln. **Fish catch** (1987): 134,000 metric tons. **Electricity prod.** (1988): 4.2 bln. kwh. **Labor force** 13% agric.; 22% manuf.; 16% serv.; 20% govt.

Finance: Monetary unit: New Peso (May 1991: 1,886 = $1 US). **Gross domestic product** (1989): $8.4 bln. **Per capita GDP** (1989): $2,736. **Imports** (1989): $1.2 bln.; partners: EC 19%, Braz. 24%, Arg. 14%, U.S. 8%. **Exports** (1989): $1.6 bln.; partners: Braz. 28%, U.S. 11%, EC 23%. **Tourists** (1988): $190 mln. receipts. **National budget** (1989): $1.5 bln. expeditures. **International reserves less gold** (Jan. 1991): $512 mln. **Gold:** 2.60 mln. oz t. **Consumer prices** (change in 1990): 32%.

Transport: Railway traffic (1987): 140 mln. passenger-km. **Motor vehicles:** in use (1989): 190,000 passenger cars, 100,000 comm. vehicles. **Civil aviation** (1985): 240 mln. passenger-km; 7 airports. **Chief ports:** Montevideo.

Communications: Television sets: 1 per 6.0 persons. **Radios:** 1 per 1.0 persons. **Telephones:** 1 per 6.7 persons. **Daily newspaper circ.** (1987): 185 per 1,000 pop.

Health: Life expectancy at birth (1989): 68 male; 75 female. **Births** (per 1,000 pop. 1989): 17. **Deaths** (per 1,000 pop. 1989): 10. **Natural increase:** .7%. **Hospital beds:** 1 per 127 persons. **Physicians:** 1 per 447 persons. **Infant mortality** (per 1,000 live births 1989): 34.

Education (1990): **Literacy:** 96%.

Major International Organizations: UN (GATT, IMF, WHO), OAS.

Embassy: 1919 F St. NW 20006; 331-1313.

Spanish settlers did not begin replacing the indigenous Charrua Indians until 1624. Portuguese from Brazil arrived later, but Uruguay was attached to the Spanish Viceroyalty of Rio de la Plata in the 18th century. Rebels fought against Spain beginning in 1810. An independent republic was declared Aug. 25, 1825.

Socialist measures were adopted as far back as 1911. The state owns the power, telephone, railroad, cement, oil-refining and other industries.

Uruguay's standard of living was one of the highest in South America, and political and labor conditions among the freest. Economic stagnation, inflation, floods and drought, and a general strike in the late 1960s brought government attempts to strengthen the economy through devaluation of the peso and wage and price controls. But inflation continued in the 80's and the country asked international creditors to restructure $2.7 bln. in debt in 1983.

Terrorist activities led to Pres. Juan Maria Bordaberry agreeing to military control of his administration Feb. 1973. In June he abolished Congress and set up a Council of State in its place. Bordaberry was removed by the military in a 1976 coup. Civilian government was restored to the country in 1985.

Vanuatu

Republic of Vanuatu

Ripablik Blong Vanuatu

People: Population (1989 est.): 150,000. **Population density:** 26 per sq. mi. **Ethnic groups:** Mainly Melanesian, some European, Polynesian, Micronesian. **Languages:** Bislama, French and English all official. **Religions:** Presbyterian 40%, Anglican 14%, Roman Catholic 16%, animist 15%.

Geography: Area: 5,700 sq. mi. **Location:** SW Pacific, 1,200 mi NE of Brisbane, Australia. **Topography:** dense forest with narrow coastal strips of cultivated land. **Capital:** Vila. **Cities:** Vila (1990): 19,000.

Government: Type: Parliamentary democracy. **Head of state:** Pres. Fred Timakata; in office: Jan. 12, 1989. **Head of gov't:** Prime Min. Donald Kalpokas; in office: Aug. 7, 1991.

Economy: Industries: Fish-freezing, meat canneries, tourism. **Chief crops:** Copra (38% of export), cocoa, coffee. **Minerals:** Manganese. **Other resources:** Forests, cattle. **Fish catch** (1987): 2.9 metric tons.

Finance: Monetary unit: Australian dollar and Vanuatu franc (Mar. 1991: 111 vatu = $1 US). **Gross national product** (1989): $131 mln. **Imports** (1987): $68 mln.; partners: Aus. 36%, Fr. 8%, Japan 13%. **Exports** (1987): $17 mln.; partners: Neth. 48%, Jap. 17%, Fr. 12%, Belg.-Lux. 14%.

Health: Life expectancy at birth (1989): 67 male, 71 female. **Infant mortality** (per 1,000 live births 1989): 37.

Education: Literacy (1990): 90%. Education not compulsory, but 85-90% of children of primary school age attend primary schools.

The Anglo-French condominium of the New Hebrides, administered jointly by France and Great Britain since 1906, became the independent Republic of Vanuatu on July 30, 1980.

Vatican City

The Holy See

People: Population (1990 est.): 750. **Ethnic groups:** Italians, Swiss. **Languages:** Italian, Latin.

Geography: Area: 108.7 acres. **Location:** In Rome, Italy. **Neighbors:** Completely surrounded by Italy.

Monetary unit: Lira.

Apostolic Nunciature in U.S.: 3339 Massachusetts Ave. NW 20008; 333-7121.

The popes for many centuries, with brief interruptions, held temporal sovereignty over mid-Italy (the so-called Papal States), comprising an area of some 16,000 sq. mi., with a population in the 19th century of more than 3 million. This territory was incorporated in the new Kingdom of Italy, the sovereignty of the pope being confined to the palaces of the Vatican and the Lateran in Rome and the villa of Castel Gandolfo, by an Italian law, May 13, 1871. This law also guaranteed to the pope and his successors a yearly indemnity of over $620,000. The allowance, however, remained unclaimed.

A Treaty of Conciliation, a concordat and a financial convention were signed Feb. 11, 1929, by Cardinal Gasparri and Premier Mussolini. The documents established the independent state of Vatican City, and gave the Catholic religion special status in Italy. The treaty (Lateran Agreement) was made part of the Constitution of Italy (Article 7) in 1947. Italy and the Vatican reached preliminary agreement in 1976 on revisions of the concordat, that would eliminate Roman Catholicism as the state religion and end required religious education in Italian schools.

Vatican City includes St. Peter's, the Vatican Palace and Museum covering over 13 acres, the Vatican gardens, and neighboring buildings between Viale Vaticano and the Church. Thirteen buildings in Rome, outside the boundaries, enjoy extraterritorial rights; these buildings house congregations or officers necessary for the administration of the Holy See.

The legal system is based on the code of canon law, the apostolic constitutions and the laws especially promulgated for the Vatican City by the pope. The Secretariat of State represents the Holy See in its diplomatic relations. By the Treaty of Conciliation the pope is pledged to a perpetual neutrality unless his mediation is specifically requested. This, however, does not prevent the defense of the Church whenever it is persecuted.

The present sovereign of the State of Vatican City is the Supreme Pontiff John Paul II, Karol Wojtyla, born in Wadowice, Poland, May 18, 1920, elected Oct. 16, 1978 (the first non-Italian to be elected Pope in 456 years).

The U.S. restored formal relations in 1984 after the U.S. Congress repealed an 1867 ban on diplomatic relations with the Vatican.

Venezuela

Republic of Venezuela

Republica de Venezuela

People: Population (1990 est.): 19,753,000. **Age distrib.** (%): 0–14: 38.3; 15–59: 56.0; 60+: 5.7. **Pop. density:** 54 per sq. mi. **Urban** (1990): 83%. **Ethnic groups:** Mestizo 69%, white (Spanish, Portuguese, Italian) 20%, black 9%, Indian 2%. **Languages:** Spanish (official). **Religions:** Roman Catholic 92%.

Geography: Area: 352,143 sq. mi., more than twice the size of California. **Location:** On the Caribbean coast of S. America. **Neighbors:** Colombia on W, Brazil on S, Guyana on E. **Topography:** Flat coastal plain and Orinoco Delta are bordered by Andes Mtns. and hills. Plains, called llanos, extend between mountains and Orinoco. Guyana Highlands and plains are S of Orinoco, which stretches 1,600 mi. and drains 80% of Venezuela. **Capital:** Caracas. **Cities** (1990 est.): Caracas 1,290,000; Maracaibo 1,206,000; Barquisimeto 723,000; Valencia 955,000.

Government: Type: Federal republic. **Head of state:** Pres. Carlos Andres Perez; b. Oct. 27, 1922; in office: Feb. 2, 1989. **Local divisions:** 20 states, 2 federal territories, federal district, federal dependency. **Defense:** 3.6% of GNP (1987).

Economy: Industries: Steel, oil products, textiles, containers, paper. **Chief crops:** Coffee, rice, fruits, sugar. **Minerals:** Oil, iron (extensive reserves and production), gold. **Crude oil reserves** (1990): 58 bln. barrels. **Arable land:** 4%. **Livestock** (1989): cattle: 12.8 mln. **Fish catch** (1988): 290,000 metric tons. **Electricity prod.** (1988): 51.9 bln. kwh. **Crude steel prod.** (1988): 3.6 mln. metric tons. **Labor force:** 6% agric.; 35% ind.; 26% services.

Finance: Monetary unit: Bolivar (Apr. 1991: 55.14 = $1 US). **Gross national product** (1989): $47.1 bln. **Per capita income** (1989): $2,058. **Imports** (1990): $7.3 bln.; partners: U.S. 41%, W. Ger. 6%, Jap. 8%. **Exports** (1990): $17.5 bln.; partners: U.S. 35%, Jap. 15%. **Tourists** (1988): $425 mln. receipts. **National budget** (1987): $16.6 bln. expenditures. **International reserves less gold** (Mar. 1991): $8.8 bln. **Gold:** 11.46 mln. oz t. **Consumer prices** (change in 1990): 40.8%.

Transport: Railway traffic (1987): 22 mln. passenger-km. **Motor vehicles:** in use (1986): 2.3 mln. passenger cars, 1.2 mln. mm. vehicles. **Civil aviation** (1988): 5.1 mln. passenger-km; 26 airports with scheduled flights. **Chief ports:** Maracaibo, La Guaira, Puerto Cabello.

Communications: Television sets: 1 per 7.0 persons. **Radios:** 1 per 2.4 persons. **Telephones:** 1 per 11 persons. **Daily newspaper circ.** (1987): 111 per 1,000 pop.

Health: Life expectancy at birth (1989): 67 male; 73 female. **Births** (per 1,000 pop. 1989): 30. **Deaths** (per 1,000 pop. 1989): 6. **Natural increase:** 2.5%. **Hospital beds:** 1 per 384 persons. **Physicians:** 1 per 643 persons. **Infant mortality** (per 1,000 live births 1989): 38.

Education (1991): Literacy: 88%. **Years compulsory:** 8; attendance 82%.

Major International Organizations: UN (IMF, WHO, FAO), OAS, OPEC.

Embassy: 1099 30th St. NW 20007; 342-2214.

Columbus first set foot on the South American continent on the peninsula of Paria, Aug. 1498. Alonso de Ojeda, 1499, found Lake Maracaibo, called the land Venezuela, or Little Venice, because natives had houses on stilts. Venezuela was under Spanish domination until 1821. The republic was formed after secession from the Colombian Federation in 1830.

Military strongmen ruled Venezuela for most of the 20th century. They promoted the oil industry; some social reforms were implemented. Since 1959, the country has had democratically-elected governments.

Venezuela helped found the Organization of Petroleum Exporting States (OPEC). The government, Jan. 1, 1976, nationalized the oil industry with compensation. Oil accounts for much of total export earnings and the economy suffered a severe cash crisis in the 1980s as the result of falling oil revenues.

The government has attempted to reduce dependence on oil.

Vietnam

Socialist Republic of Vietnam

Cong Hoa Xa Hoi Chu Nghia Viet Nam

People: Population (1990 est.): 68,488,000. **Age distrib. (%):** 0-14: 40.8; 15-59: 53.6; 60+: 5.6 **Pop. density:** 519 per sq. mi. **Urban** (1989): 20%. **Ethnic groups:** Vietnamese 84%, Chinese 2%, remainder Muong, Thai, Meo, Khmer, Man, Cham. **Languages:** Vietnamese (official), Chinese. **Religions:** Buddhists, Confucians, and Taoists most numerous, Roman Catholics, animists, Muslims, Protestants.

Geography: Area: 127,330 sq. mi., the size of New Mexico. **Location:** On the E coast of the Indochinese Peninsula in SE Asia. **Neighbors:** China on N, Laos, Cambodia on W. **Topography:** Vietnam is long and narrow, with a 1,400-mi. coast. About 24% of country is readily arable, including the densely settled Red R. valley in the N, narrow coastal plains in center, and the wide, often marshy Mekong R. Delta in the S. The rest consists of semi-arid plateaus and barren mountains, with some stretches of tropical rain forest. **Capital:** Hanoi. **Cities** (1989): Ho Chi Minh City 3.9 mln.; Hanoi 3.1 mln.

Government: Type: Communist. **Head of state:** Pres. Vo Chi Cong; in office: June 18, 1987. **Head of government:** Prime Min. Vo Van Kiet; in office: Aug. 9, 1991. **Head of Communist Party:** Do Muoi; b. 1917; in office: June 27, 1991. **Local divisions:** 40 provinces, 3 municipalities, one special zone. **Defense:** 19.4% of GNP (1986).

Economy: Industries: Food processing, textiles, cement, chemical fertilizers, steel. **Chief crops:** Rice, rubber, fruits and vegetables, corn, manioc, sugarcane. **Minerals:** Phosphates, coal, iron, manganese, bauxite, apatite, chromate. **Other resources:** Forests. **Arable land:** 23%. **Livestock** (1989): cattle: 5.9 mln.; pigs: 11.7 mln. **Fish catch** (1988): 871,000 metric tons. **Electricity prod.** (1988): 5.5 bln. kwh. **Labor force:** 70% agric.; 8% ind. and commerce.

Finance: Monetary unit: Dong (Jan. 1991: 6,200 = $1 US). **Gross national product** (1988): $13.9 bln. **Per capita income** (1987): $180. **Imports** (1988): $1.9 bln.; partners: USSR 73%, Jap. 8%. **Exports** (1988): $880 mln.; partners: USSR 57%. **National budget** (1987): $4.3 bln. expenditures.

Transport: Motor vehicles: in use (1976): 100,000 passenger cars, 200,000 comm. vehicles. **Civil Aviation** (1988): 10.3 bln. passenger km; 3 airports with scheduled flights. **Chief ports:** Ho Chi Minh City, Haiphong, Da Nang.

Communications: Television sets: 1 per 29 persons. **Radios:** 1 per 10 persons. **Telephones:** 1 per 544 persons. **Daily newspaper circ.** (1989): 38 per 1,000 pop.

Health: Life expectancy at birth (1989): 62 male; 66 female. **Births** (per 1,000 pop. 1989): 33. **Deaths** (per 1,000 pop. 1989): 8. **Natural increase:** 2.5%. **Hospital beds:** 1 per 292 persons. **Physicians:** 1 per 3,040 persons. **Infant mortality** (per 1,000 live births 1989): 51.

Education (1989): Literacy: 78%.

Major International Organizations: UN (IMF, WHO).

Vietnam's recorded history began in Tonkin before the Christian era. Settled by Viets from central China, Vietnam was held by China, 111 BC-939 AD, and was a vassal state during subsequent periods. Vietnam defeated the armies of Kublai Khan, 1288. Conquest by France began in 1858 and ended in 1884 with the protectorates of Tonkin and Annam in the N. and the colony of Cochin-China in the S.

In 1940 Vietnam was occupied by Japan; nationalist aims gathered force. A number of groups formed the Vietminh (Independence) League, headed by Ho Chi Minh, communist guerrilla leader. In Aug. 1945 the Vietminh forced out Bao Dai, former emperor of Annam, head of a Japan-sponsored regime. France, seeking to reestablish colonial control, battled communist and nationalist forces, 1946-1954, and was finally defeated at Dienbienphu, May 8, 1954. Meanwhile, on July 1, 1949, Bao Dai had formed a State of Vietnam, with himself as chief of state, with French approval. China backed Ho Chi Minh.

A cease-fire accord signed in Geneva July 21, 1954, divided Vietnam along the Ben Hai R. It provided for a buffer zone, withdrawal of French troops from the North and elections to determine the country's future. Under the agreement the communists gained control of territory north of the 17th parallel, with its capital at Hanoi and Ho Chi Minh as president. South Vietnam came to comprise the 39 southern provinces. Some 900,000 North Vietnamese fled to South Vietnam.

On Oct. 26, 1955, Ngo Dinh Diem, premier of the interim government of South Vietnam, proclaimed the Republic of Vietnam and became its first president.

The North, adopted a constitution Dec. 31, 1959, based on communist principles and calling for reunification of all Vietnam. North Vietnam sought to take over South Vietnam beginning in 1954. Fighting persisted from 1956, with the communist Vietcong, aided by North Vietnam, pressing war in the South. Northern aid to Vietcong guerrillas was intensified in 1959, and large-scale troop infiltration began in 1964, with Soviet and Chinese arms assistance. Large Northern forces were stationed in border areas of Laos and Cambodia.

A serious political conflict arose in the South in 1963 when Buddhists denounced authoritarianism and brutality. This paved the way for a military coup Nov. 1-2, 1963, which overthrew Diem. Several military coups followed.

In 1964, the U.S. began air strikes against North Vietnam. Beginning in 1965, the raids were stepped up and U.S. troops became combatants. U.S. troop strength in Vietnam, which reached a high of 543,400 in Apr. 1969, was ordered reduced by President Nixon in a series of withdrawals, beginning in June 1969. U.S. bombings were resumed in 1972-73.

A ceasefire agreement was signed in Paris Jan. 27, 1973 by the U.S., North and South Vietnam, and the Vietcong. It was never implemented.

North Vietnamese forces launched attacks against remaining government outposts in the Central Highlands in the first months of 1975. Government retreats turned into a rout, and the Saigon regime surrendered April 30. North Vietnam assumed control, and began transforming society along communist lines. All businesses and farms were collectivized.

The U.S. accepted over 165,000 Vietnamese refugees, while scores of thousands more sought refuge in other countries.

The war's toll included — Combat deaths: U.S. 47,752; South Vietnam over 200,000; other allied forces 5,225. Civilian casualties were over a million. Displaced war refugees in South Vietnam totaled over 6.5 million.

The first National Assembly of both parts of the country met and the country was officially reunited July 2, 1976. The Northern capital, flag, anthem, emblem, and currency were applied to the new state. Nearly all major government posts went to officials of the former Northern government.

Heavy fighting with Cambodia took place, 1977-80, amid mutual charges of aggression and atrocities against civilians. Increasing numbers of Vietnamese civilians, ethnic Chinese, escaped the country, via the sea, or the overland route across Cambodia. Vietnam launched an offensive against Cambodian refugee strongholds along the Thai-Cambodian border in 1985; they also engaged Thai troops. Vietnam declared that it had removed all its troops from Cambodia, Sept. 1989.

Relations with China soured as 140,000 ethnic Chinese left Vietnam charging discrimination; China cut off economic aid. Reacting to Vietnam's invasion of Cambodia, China attacked 4 Vietnamese border provinces, Feb., 1979, instigating heavy fighting.

Vietnam announced a package of reforms aimed at reducing central control of the economy in 1987, as many of the old revolutionary followers of Ho Chi Minh were removed from office. By 1990, the economy was in a dire state with inflation estimated at 1,000% a year.

Progress has been made with the U.S. over the repatriating of "Amerasians," the children fathered by U.S. servicemen.

Western Samoa

Independent State of Western Samoa

Malotuto'atasi o Samoa i Sisifo

People: Population (1989 est.): 169,000. **Age distrib. (%):** 0–14: 50.4; 15–59: 45.4; 60+: 4.3. **Pop. density:** 149 per sq. mi. **Urban** (1981): 21.2%. **Ethnic groups:** Samoan (Polynesian) 88%, Euronesian (mixed) 10%, European, other Pacific Islanders. **Languages:** Samoan, English both official. **Religions:** Protestant 70%, Roman Catholic 20%.

Geography: Area: 1,133 sq. mi., the size of Rhode Island. **Location:** In the S. Pacific O. **Neighbors:** Nearest are Fiji on W, Tonga on S. **Topography:** Main islands, Savai'i (670 sq. mi.) and Upolu (429 sq. mi.), both ruggedly mountainous, and small islands Manono and Apolima. **Capital:** Apia. **Cities** (1983 est.): Apia 35,000.

Government: Type: Parliamentary democracy. **Head of state:** King Malietoa Tanumafili II; b. Jan. 4, 1913; in office: Jan. 1, 1962. **Head of government:** Prime Min. Toflau Eti Alesana; in office: Apr. 11, 1988. **Local divisions:** 11 districts.

Economy: Chief crops: Cocoa, copra, bananas. **Other resources:** Hardwoods, fish. **Arable land:** 43%. **Electricity prod.** (1988): 30 mln. kwh. **Labor force:** 67% agric.

Finance: Monetary unit: Tala (Mar. 1991: 1.00 = $.42 US). **Gross national product** (1989): $114 mln. **Per capita GNP** (1989): $720. **Imports** (1989): $67 mln.; partners: NZ 28% Austral. 10%, Jap. 13%, U.S. 30%. **Exports** (1989): $13 mln.; partners: W. Ger. 31%, NZ 26%, U.S. 12%. **International reserves less gold** (Mar. 1991): $67.4 mln. **Consumer prices** (change in 1990): 16.0%.

Transport: Motor vehicles: in use (1985): 1,700 passenger cars, 2,400 comm. vehicles. **Chief ports:** Apia, Asau.

Communications: Radios: 1 per 2.3 persons. **Telephones:** 1 per 23 persons.

Health: Life expectancy at birth (1989): 64 male; 69 female. **Births** (per 1,000 pop. 1989): 34. **Deaths** (per 1,000 pop. 1989): 7. **Natural increase:** 2.8%. **Hospital beds:** 1 per 236 persons. **Physicians:** 1 per 3,685 persons. **Infant mortality** (per 1,000 live births 1989): 48.

Education (1989): **Literacy:** 90%. 95% attend elementary school.

Major International Organizations: UN (IMF, World Bank), Commonwealth of Nations.

Western Samoa was a German colony, 1899 to 1914, when New Zealand landed troops and took over. It became a New Zealand mandate under the League of Nations and, in 1945, a New Zealand UN Trusteeship.

An elected local government took office in Oct. 1959 and the country became fully independent Jan. 1, 1962.

Yemen

Republic of Yemen

al-Jumhūrīyah al-Yamanīyah

People: Population (1990 est.): 11,500,000. **Pop. density:** 56 per sq. mi. **Ethnic groups:** Arabs, Indians, some Negroids. **Languages:** Arabic. **Religions:** Sunni Moslem 53%; Shute Moslem 46%.

Geography: Area: 205,356 sq. mi., slightly smaller than France. **Location:** On the southern coast of the Arabian Peninsula. **Neighbors:** Saudi Arabia on NE, Oman on the E. **Topography:** A sandy coastal strip leads to well-watered fertile mountains in interior. **Capital:** Sana. **Cities** (1986 est.): Sana 427,000; Aden 250,000.

Government: Type: Republic; military in power. **Head of state:** Pres. Ali Abdullah Saleh, b. 1942; in office: July 17, 1978. **Head of government:** Prime Min. Haydar Abu Bakr-al Attas; in office: May 22, 1990. **Local divisions:** 17 provinces. **Defense:** 12.4% of GNP (1988).

Economy: Industries: Food processing, mining, petroleum refining. **Chief crops:** Wheat, sorghum, fruits, coffee, cotton. **Minerals:** Salt. **Crude oil reserves** (1984): 600 mln. bbls. **Arable land:** 14%. **Livestock** (1989): goats: 3.1 mln.; sheep: 3.6 mln. **Fish catch** (1989): 73,000 metric tons. **Electricity prod.** (1988): 1 bln. kwh. **Labor force:** 64% agric.; 22% ind. and commerce; 14% serv.

Finance: Monetary unit: Rial (Apr. 1991: 12.01 = $1 US). **Gross national product** (1989): $7.2 bln. **Per capita GNP** (1989): $640. **Imports** (1987): $7.1 bln.; partners: Saudi Ar. 20%, Fr. 8%, Jap. 16%. **Exports** (1987): $3.8 mln.; partners: S. Yemen 23%, Saudi Ar. 8%, Pak. 19%. **National budget** (1986): $1.6 bln. **International reserves less gold** (Mar. 1990): $243 mln.

Transport: Motor vehicles in use (1987): 150,000 passenger cars, 220,000 commercial vehicles. **Civil Aviation** (1988): 946 mln. Passenger-km.; 13 airports with scheduled flights. **Chief ports:** Al-Hudaydah, Al-Mukha, Aden.

Communications: Television sets: 1 per 38 persons. **Radios:** 1 per 35 persons. **Telephones:** 1 per 69 persons.

Health: (N. Yemen only) Life expectancy at birth (1989): 47 male; 49 female. **Births** (per 1,000 pop. 1990): 51. **Deaths** (per 1,000 pop. 1990): 16. **Natural increase:** 3.5%. **Hospital beds:** 1 per 995 persons. **Physicians:** 1 per 5,531 persons. **Infant mortality** (per 1,000 live births 1989): 113.

Education (1989): **Literacy:** 25%. **Primary school attendance:** 59%.

Major International Organizations: UN (IMF, WHO), Arab League.

Embassy: 600 New Hampshire Ave. NW 20037; 965-4760.

Yemen's territory once was part of the ancient kindgom of Sheba, or Saba, a prosperous link in trade between Africa and India. A Biblical reference speaks of its gold, spices and precious stones as gifts borne by the Queen of Sheba to King Solomon.

Yemen became independent in 1918, after years of Ottoman Turkish rule, but remained politically and economically backward. Imam Ahmed ruled 1948-1962. Army officers headed by Brig. Gen. Abdullah al-Salal declared the country to be the Yemen Arab Republic.

The Imam Ahmed's heir, the Imam Mohamad al-Badr, fled to the mountains where tribesmen joined royalist forces; internal warfare between them and the republican forces continued. About 150,000 people died in the fighting.

There was a bloodless coup Nov. 5, 1967. In April 1970 hostilities ended with an agreement between Yemen and Saudi Arabia.

On June 13, 1974, an army group, led by Col. Ibrahim al-Hamidi, seized the government. He was assassinated in 1977.

Meanwhile, South Yemen won independence from Britain in 1967, formed out of the British colony of Aden and the British protectorate of South Arabia. It became the Arab world's only Marxist state, taking the name People's Democratic Republic of Yemen in 1970 and signing a 20-year friendship treaty with the USSR in 1979 that allowed for the stationing of Soviet troops in the south.

More than 300,000 Yemenis fled from the south to the north after independence, contributing to 2 decades of hostility between the 2 states that flared into warfare twice in the 1970's.

An Arab League-sponsored agreement between North and South Yemen on unification of the 2 countries was signed Mar. 29, 1979. An agreement providing for widespread political and economic cooperation was signed in 1988.

The 2 countries were formally united on May 22, 1990.

Yugoslavia

Socialist Federal Republic of Yugoslavia

Socijalistička Federativna Republika Jugoslavija

People: Population (1990 est.): 23,864,000. **Age distrib. (%):** 0–14: 23.5; 15-59: 63.7; 60+: 12.8. **Pop. density:** 240 per sq. mi. **Urban** (1990): 50%. **Ethnic groups:** Serbs 36%, Croats 20%, Bosnian Moslems 9%, Slovenes 8%, Macedonians 6%, Albanians 8%. **Languages:** Serbo-Croatian, Macedonian, Slovenian (all official), Albanian. **Religions:** Eastern Orthodox 41%, Roman Catholic 12%, Moslem 3%.

Geography: Area: 98,766 sq. mi., the size of Wyoming. **Location:** On the Adriatic coast of the Balkan Peninsula in SE Europe. **Neighbors:** Italy on W, Austria, Hungary on N, Romania,

Bulgaria on E, Greece, Albania on S. **Topography:** The Dinaric Alps run parallel to the Adriatic coast, which is lined by offshore islands. Plains stretch across N and E river basins. S and NW are mountainous. **Capital:** Belgrade. **Cities** (1988 est.): Belgrade 1,300,000; Zagreb 700,000; Skopje 440,000; Sarajevo 400,000; Ljubljana 300,000.

Government: Type: Communist state; Federal republic in form. **Head of state:** Pres. Stipe Mesic; in office: June 28, 1991. **Head of government:** Prime Min. Ante Markovic; in office: Mar. 16 1989. **Local divisions:** 6 republics, 2 autonomous provinces. **Defense:** 2.2% of GNP (1987).

Economy: Industries: Steel, wood products, cement, textiles, tourism. **Chief crops:** Corn, grains, tobacco, sugar beets. **Minerals:** Antimony, bauxite, lead, mercury, coal, iron, copper, chrome, zinc, salt. **Crude oil reserves** (1987): 263 mln. bbls. **Arable land:** 28%. **Livestock** (1989): cattle: 4.7 mln.; pigs: 7.3 mln.; sheep: 7.6 mln. **Fish catch** (1989): 71,000 metric tons. **Electricity prod.** (1988): 83.5 bln. kwh. **Crude steel prod.** (1988): 4.4 mln. metric tons. **Labor force:** 22% agric.; 70% ind.

Finance: Monetary unit: New Dinar (June 1991: 22.21 = $1 US). **Gross national product** (1989): $159.0 bln. **Per capita GNP** (1989): $2,490. **Imports** (1990): $19.1 bln.; partners: W. Ger. 19%, USSR 15%, It. 8%, U.S. 6%. **Exports** (1990): $14.6 bln.; partners: USSR 17%, W. Ger. 12%, It. 13%. **Tourists** (1989): $2.2 bln. receipts. **National budget** (1989): $4.5 bln. expenditures. **International reserves less gold** (Mar. 1991): $4.7 bln. **Gold:** 1.90 mln. oz t. **Consumer prices** (change in 1990): 587%.

Transport: Railway traffic (1989): 11.5 bln. passenger-km. **Motor vehicles:** in use (1989): 3.0 mln. passenger cars, 290,000 comm. vehicles. **Civil aviation** (1989): 7.9 bln. passenger-km; 20 airports. **Chief ports:** Rijeka, Split, Koper, Bar, Ploce.

Communications: Television sets: 1 per 5.7 persons. **Radios:** 1 per 6 persons. **Telephones:** 1 per 4.9 persons. **Daily newspaper circ.** (1988): 107 per 1,000 pop.

Health: Life expectancy at birth (1989): 69 male; 75 female. **Births** (per 1,000 pop. 1989): 15. **Deaths** (per 1,000 pop. 1989): 9. **Natural increase:** .6%. **Hospital beds:** 1 per 163 persons. **Physicians:** 1 per 534 persons. **Infant mortality** (per 1,000 live births 1989): 25.

Education (1989): **Literacy:** 90%. Almost all attend primary school.

Major International Organizations: UN (IMF, World Bank, GATT).

Embassy: 2410 California St. NW 20008; 462-6566.

Serbia, which had since 1389 been a vassal principality of Turkey, was established as an independent kingdom by the Treaty of Berlin, 1878. Montenegro, independent since 1389, also obtained international recognition in 1878. After the Balkan wars Serbia's boundaries were enlarged by the annexation of Old Serbia and Macedonia, 1913.

When the Austro-Hungarian empire collapsed after World War I, the Kingdom of the Serbs, Croats, and Slovenes was formed from the former provinces of Croatia, Dalmatia, Bosnia, Herzegovina, Slovenia, Voyvodina and the independent state of Montenegro. The name was later changed to Yugoslavia.

Nazi Germany invaded in 1941. Many Yugoslav partisan troops continued to operate. Among these were the Chetniks led by Draja Mikhailovich, who fought other partisans led by Josip Broz, known as Marshal Tito. Tito, backed by the USSR and Britain from 1943, was in control by the time the Germans had been driven from Yugoslavia in 1945. Mikhailovich was executed July 17, 1946, by the Tito regime.

A constituent assembly proclaimed Yugoslavia a republic Nov. 29, 1945. It became a federated republic Jan. 31, 1946, and Marshal Tito, a communist, became head of the government.

The Stalin policy of dictating to all communist nations was rejected by Tito. He accepted economic aid and military equipment from the U.S. and received aid in foreign trade also from France and Great Britain. Tito also supported the liberal government of Czechoslovakia in 1968 before the Soviet invasion.

A separatist movement among Croatians, 2d to the Serbs in numbers, brought arrests and a change of leaders in the Croatian Republic in Jan. 1972. Violence by extreme Croatian nationalists and fears of Soviet political intervention led to restrictions on political and intellectual dissent. Serbians, Montenegrins, and Macedonians use Cyrillic, Croatians and Slovenians use Latin letters.

Beginning in 1965, reforms designed to decentralize the administration of economic development and to force industries to produce more efficiently in competition with foreign producers were introduced. Yugoslavia has developed considerable trade with the West.

Pres. Tito died May 4, 1980; with his death, the post as head of the Collective Presidency and also that as head of the League of Communists became a rotating system of succession among the members representing each republic and autonomous province.

On Jan. 22, 1990, a Communist Party conference renounced its constitutionally guaranteed leading role in society and called on parliament to enact "Political Pluralism, including a multiparty system."

In Feb. 1991, the parliaments of the northern republics of Slovenia and Croatia adopted legislation that would lead to independence from the republic. The 2 republics formally declared independence June 25. In Croatia, fighting began between Croats and ethnic Serbs. In Aug., there were numerous clashes between Croatian forces and Yugoslavian army units and their Serb supporters. Serbia agreed, Aug. 31, to accept a European Community plan to send foreign observers to oversee a cease-fire in Croatia. (*See Index & Chronology for details.*)

Zaire

Republic of Zaire

République du Zaïre

People: Population (1990 est.): 35,330,000. **Pop. density:** 37 per sq. mi. **Urban** (1988): 44.2%. **Ethnic groups:** Bantu tribes 80%, over 200 other tribes. **Languages:** French (official), Kongo, Luba, Mongo, Rwanda, others. **Religions:** Christian 70%, Moslem 10%.

Geography: Area: 905,563 sq. mi., one-fourth the size of the U.S. **Location:** In central Africa. **Neighbors:** Congo on W, Central African Republic, Sudan on N, Uganda, Rwanda, Burundi, Tanzania on E, Zambia, Angola on S. **Topography:** Zaire includes the bulk of the Zaire (Congo) R. Basin. The vast central region is a low-lying plateau covered by rain forest. Mountainous terraces in the W, savannas in the S and SE, grasslands toward the N, and the high Ruwenzori Mtns. on the E surround the central region. A short strip of territory borders the Atlantic O. The Zaire R. is 2,718 mi. long. **Capital:** Kinshasa. **Cities** (1990 est.): Kinshasa 3,562,000; Lubumbashi 683,000.

Government: Type: Republic with strong presidential authority (in transition). **Head of state:** Pres. Mobutu Sese Seko; b. Oct. 14, 1930; in office: Nov. 25, 1965. **Head of Government:** Prime Min. Lunda Bululu; in office: Apr. 25, 1990. **Local divisions:** 8 regions, Kinshasa. **Defense:** 1% of GNP (1988).

Economy: Chief crops: Coffee, rice, sugar cane, bananas, plantains, manioc, mangoes, tea, cocoa, palm oil. **Minerals:** Cobalt (60% of world reserves), copper, cadmium, gold, silver, tin, germanium, zinc, iron, manganese, uranium, radium. **Crude oil reserves** (1987): 111 mln. bbls. **Other resources:** Forests, rubber, ivory. **Arable land:** 3%. **Livestock** (1989): cattle: 1.4 mln.; goats: 2.9 mln. **Fish catch** (1989): 166,000 metric tons. **Electricity prod.** (1988): 5.5 bln. kwh. **Labor force:** 75% agric..

Finance: Monetary unit: Zaire (Mar. 1991: 3,288 = $1 US). **Gross national product** (1989): $8.8 bln. **Per capita GNP** (1989): $260. **Imports** (1988): $756 mln.; partners: Chi. 38%, Belg. 16%, W. Ger. 7%, Fra. 7%. **Exports** (1988): $1.1 bln.; partners: Belg.-Lux. 36%, U.S. 19%. **International reserves less gold** (Mar. 1991): $187 mln. **Gold:** 108,000 oz t. **Consumer prices** (change in 1990): 50.1%.

Transport: Railway traffic (1989): 200 mln. passenger-km. **Motor vehicles:** in use (1985): 24,000 passenger cars, 60,000 comm. vehicles. **Civil aviation** (1988): 506 mln. passenger-km; 22 airports with scheduled flights. **Chief ports:** Matadi, Boma.

Communications: Television sets: 1 per 1,667 persons. **Radios:** 1 per 9.7 persons. **Telephones:** 1 per 1,026 persons. **Daily newspaper circ.** (1988): 1 per 1,000 pop.

Health: Life expectancy at birth (1989): 51 male; 54 female. **Births** (per 1,000 pop. 1989): 45. **Deaths** (per 1,000 pop. 1989): 14. **Natural increase:** 3.1%. **Hospital beds:** 1 per 476 persons. **Physicians:** 1 per 23,193 persons. **Infant mortality** (per 1,000 live births 1989): 107.

Education (1988): **Literacy:** 55%.

Major International Organizations: UN and all of its specialized agencies, OAU.

Embassy: 1800 New Hampshire Ave. NW 20008; 234-7690.

The earliest inhabitants of Zaire may have been the pygmies, followed by Bantus from the E and Nilotic tribes from the N. The large Bantu Bakongo kingdom ruled much of Zaire and Angola when Portuguese explorers visited in the 15th century.

Leopold II, king of the Belgians, formed an international group to exploit the Congo in 1876. In 1877 Henry M. Stanley explored the Congo and in 1878 the king's group sent him back to organize the region and win over the native chiefs. The Conference of Berlin, 1884-85, organized the Congo Free State with Leopold as king and chief owner. Exploitation of native laborers on the rubber plantations caused international criticism and led to granting of a colonial charter, 1908.

Belgian and Congolese leaders agreed Jan. 27, 1960, that the Congo would become independent June 30. In the first general elections, May 31, the National Congolese movement of Patrice Lumumba won 35 of 137 seats in the National Assembly. He was appointed premier June 21, and formed a coalition cabinet.

Widespread violence caused Europeans and others to flee. The UN Security Council Aug. 9, 1960, called on Belgium to withdraw its troops and sent a UN contingent. President Kasavubu removed Lumumba as premier; he was murdered in 1961.

The last UN troops left the Congo June 30, 1964, and Moise Tshombe became president.

On Sept. 7, 1964, leftist rebels set up a "People's Republic" in Stanleyville. Tshombe hired foreign mercenaries and sought to rebuild the Congolese Army. In Nov. and Dec. 1964 rebels slew scores of white hostages and thousands of Congolese; Belgian paratroops, dropped from U.S. transport planes, rescued hundreds. By July 1965 the rebels had lost their effectiveness.

In 1965 Gen. Joseph D. Mobutu was named president. He later changed his name to Mobutu Sese Seko. The country changed its name to Republic of Zaire on Oct. 27, 1971; in 1972 Zairians with Christian names were ordered to change them to African names.

Serious economic difficulties, amid charges of corruption by government officials, have plagued Zaire in the 1980s. In 1990, Pres. Mobutu announced an end to a 20-year ban on multiparty politics.

Zambia

Republic of Zambia

People: Population (1990 est.): 8,119,000. **Age distrib. (%):** 0–14: 48.2; 15–59: 47.8; 60+: 4.0. **Pop. density:** 26 per sq. mi. **Urban** (1985): 49%. **Ethnic groups:** Mostly Bantu tribes. **Languages:** English (official), Bantu dialects. **Religions:** Predominantly animist, Roman Catholic 21%, Protestant, Hindu, Moslem minorities.

Geography: Area: 290,586 sq. mi., larger than Texas. **Location:** In southern central Africa. **Neighbors:** Zaire on N, Tanzania, Malawi, Mozambique on E, Zimbabwe, Namibia on S, Angola on W. **Topography:** Zambia is mostly high plateau country covered with thick forests, and drained by several important rivers, including the Zambezi. **Capital:** Lusaka. **Cities** (1991): Lusaka 982,000; Kitwe 348,000; Ndola 376,000.

Government: Type: Republic. **Head of state:** Pres. Kenneth David Kaunda; b. Apr. 28, 1924; in office: Oct. 24, 1964. **Head of government:** Prime Min. Malimba Masheke; in office: Mar. 15, 1989. **Local divisions:** 9 provinces. **Defense:** 6.8% of GDP (1985).

Economy: Chief crops: Corn, tobacco, peanuts, cotton, sugar. **Minerals:** Cobalt, copper, zinc, gold, lead, vanadium, manganese, coal. **Other resources:** Rubber, ivory. **Arable land:** 7%. **Livestock** (1989): cattle: 2.8 mln. **Fish catch** (1989): 68,000 metric tons. **Electricity prod.** (1988): 8.2 bln. kwh. **Labor force:** 60% agric.; 40% ind. and commerce.

Finance: Monetary unit: Kwacha (Mar. 1991: 1.00 = $.01 US). **Gross national product** (1989): $3.0 bln. **Per capita GNP** (1989): $390. **Imports** (1989): $1 bln.; S.Af. 13%, W. Ger. 6%, U.S. 7%. **Exports** (1989): $1.3 bln.; partners: Jap. 4%, UK 3%, U.S. 10%, W. Ger. 9%. **National budget** (1987): $787 mln. expenditures. **International reserves less gold** (Jan. 1990): $135 mln. **Gold:** 12,000 oz t. **Consumer prices** (change in 1989): 154%.

Transport: Motor vehicles: in use (1982): 105,000 passenger cars, 97,000 comm. vehicles. **Civil aviation** (1989): 216 mln. passenger-km; 10 airports with scheduled flights.

Communications: Television sets: 1 per 41 persons. **Radios:** 1 per 14 persons. **Telephones:** 1 per 87 persons. **Daily newspaper circ.** (1989): 15 per 1,000 pop.

Health: Life expectancy at birth (1989): 54 male; 57 female. **Births** (per 1,000 pop. 1989): 50. **Deaths** (per 1,000 pop. 1989): 12. **Natural increase:** 3.7%. **Hospital beds:** 1 per 311 persons. **Physicians:** 1 per 8,437 persons. **Infant mortality** (per 1,000 live births 1989): 87.

Education (1991): **Literacy:** 54%. **Attendance:** less than 50% in grades 1–7.

Major International Organizations: UN (GATT, IMF, WHO), OAU, Commonwealth of Nations.

Embassy: 2419 Massachusetts Ave. NW 20008; 265-9717.

As Northern Rhodesia, the country was under the administration of the South Africa Company, 1889 until 1924, when the office of governor was established, and, subsequently, a legislature. The country became an independent republic within the Commonwealth Oct. 24, 1964.

After the white government of Rhodesia declared its independence from Britain Nov. 11, 1965, relations between Zambia and Rhodesia became strained.

As part of a program of government participation in major industries, a government corporation in 1970 took over 51% of the ownership of 2 foreign-owned copper mining companies. Privately-held land and other enterprises were nationalized in 1975, as were all newspapers. In the 1980s, decline in copper prices has hurt the economy and severe drought caused famine.

Food riots erupted in June 1990, as the nation suffered its worst violence since independence.

Zimbabwe

Republic of Zimbabwe

People: Population (1990 est.): 10,205,000. **Age distrib. (%):** 0–14: 44.9; 15–59: 51.1; 60+: 4.0. **Pop. density:** 66 per sq. mi. **Urban** (1985): 25%. **Ethnic groups:** Shona 80%, Ndebele 19%. **Languages:** English (official), Shona, Nguni. **Religions:** Predominantly traditional tribal beliefs, Christian minority.

Geography: Area: 150,803 sq. mi., slightly larger than Montana. **Location:** In southern Africa. **Neighbors:** Zambia on N, Botswana on W, S. Africa on S, Mozambique on E. **Topography:** Rhodesia is high plateau country, rising to mountains on eastern border, sloping down on the other borders. **Capital:** Harare. **Cities** (1988 est.): Harare 730,000; Bulawayo (met.) 415,000.

Government: Type: Parliamentary democracy. **Head of state:** Pres. Robert Mugabe; b. Apr. 14, 1928; in office: Jan. 1, 1988. **Local divisions:** 8 provinces. **Defense:** 5.0% of GNP (1987).

Economy: Industries: Clothing, chemicals, light industries. **Chief crops:** Tobacco, sugar, cotton, corn, wheat. **Minerals:** Chromium, gold, nickel, asbestos, copper, iron, coal. **Arable land:** 7%. **Livestock** (1989): cattle: 5.7 mln.; goats: 1.6 mln. **Electricity prod.** (1988): 7.7 bln. kwh. **Labor force:** 74% agric.; 16% serv.

Finance: Monetary unit: Dollar (Mar. 1991: 1.00 = $.33 US). **Gross national product** (1988): $5.5 bln. **Per capita income** (1986): $275. **Imports** (1987): $1.2 bln. partners: UK 14%, So. Afr. 18%, U.S. 12%, W. Ger. 7%. **Exports** (1987): $1.4 bln.; partners: UK 8%, W. Ger. 17%, Jap. 12%. **National budget** (1988): $2.8 bln. expenditures. **Total reserves less gold** (Mar. 1991): $121.7 mln. **Consumer prices** (change in 1990): 17.4%.

Transport: Motor vehicles: in use (1987): 264,000 passenger cars, 66,000 comm. vehicles. **Civil aviation** (1989): 709 mln. passenger-km. 8 airports with scheduled flights.

Communications: Television sets: 1 per 67 persons. **Radios:** 1 per 20 persons. **Telephones:** 1 per 31 persons. **Daily newspaper circ.** (1989): 23 per 1,000 pop.

Health: Life expectancy at birth (1989): 59 male; 63 female. **Births** (per 1,000 pop. 1989): 42. **Deaths** (per 1,000 pop. 1989): 9. **Natural increase:** 3.3%. **Physicians:** 1 per 6,687 persons. **Infant mortality** (per 1,000 live births 1989): 67.

Education (1988): **Literacy:** 50%. **Attendance:** 90% primary, 15% secondary for Africans; higher for whites, Asians.

Major International Organizations: UN (IMF, World Bank), OAU, Commonwealth of Nations.

Embassy: 2852 McGill Terrace NW 20008; 332-7100.

Britain took over the area as Southern Rhodesia in 1923 from the British South Africa Co. (which, under Cecil Rhodes, had conquered the area by 1897) and granted internal self-government. Under a 1961 constitution, voting was restricted to maintain whites in power. On Nov. 11, 1965, Prime Min. Ian D. Smith announced his country's unilateral declaration of independence. Britain termed the act illegal, and demanded Zimbabwe (known as Rhodesia until 1980) broaden voting rights to provide for eventual rule by the majority Africans.

Urged by Britain, the UN imposed sanctions, including embargoes on oil shipments to Zimbabwe. Some oil and gasoline reached Zimbabwe, however, from South Africa and Mozambique, before the latter became independent in 1975. In May 1968, the UN Security Council ordered a trade embargo.

A new constitution came into effect, Mar. 2, 1970. The election law effectively prevented full black representation through income tax requirements.

Intermittent negotiations between the government and various black nationalist groups failed to prevent increasing skirmishes. By mid-1978, over 6,000 soldiers and civilians had been killed. An "internal settlement" signed Mar. 1978 in which Smith and 3 popular black leaders share control until transfer of power to the black majority was rejected by guerrilla leaders.

In the country's first universal-franchise election, Apr. 21, 1979, Bishop Abel Muzorewa's United African National Council gained a bare majority control of the black-dominated parliament. Britain, 1979, began efforts to normalize its relationship with Zimbabwe. A British cease-fire was accepted by all parties, Dec. 5th. Independence was finally achieved Apr. 18, 1980.

Population of World's Largest Cities

Source: Bureau of the Census, U.S. Dept. of Commerce

The table below represents one attempt at comparing the world's largest cities. The cities are defined as population clusters of continuous built-up areas with a population density of a least 5,000 persons per square mile. The boundary of the city was determined by examining detailed maps of each city in conjunction with the most recent official population statistics. Exclaves of areas exceeding the minimum population density were added to the city if the intervening gap was less than one mile. To the extent practical, nonresidential areas such as parks, airports, industrial complexes and water were excluded from the area reported for each city, thus making the population density reflective of the concentrations in the residential portions of the city. By using a consistent definition for the city, it is possible to make comparisons of the cities on the basis of total population, area, and population density.

The population of each city was projected based on projected country populations and the proportion of each city population to the total population of the country at the time of the last 2 censuses. Figures in the table below may differ from city population figures elsewhere in The World Almanac because of different methods of determining population.

City, Country	1990 (thousands)	2000 (thousands projected)	Area (sq. mi.)	Density 1989 (pop per sq. mi.)	City, Country	1990 (thousands)	2000 (thousands projected)	Area (sq. mi.)	Density 1989 (pop per sq. mi.)
Tokyo-Yokahama, Japan	26,952	29,971	1,089	24,463	Baghdad, Iraq	3,941	5,239	97	39,304
Mexico City, Mexico	20,207	27,872	522	37,314	Belo Horizonte, Brazil	3,683	5,125	79	44,922
Sao Paulo, Brazil	18,052	25,354	451	38,528	Ho Chi Minh City, Vietnam	3,645	4,481	31	114,914
Seoul, South Korea	16,268	21,976	342	45,953	Ahmadabad, India	3,595	4,837	32	108,618
New York, U.S.	14,622	14,648	1,274	11,473	Kinshasa, Zaire	3,575	5,646	57	59,704
Osaka-Kobe-Kyoto, Japan	13,826	14,287	495	27,833	Hyderabad, India	3,563	4,765	88	39,180
Bombay, India	11,777	15,357	95	120,299	Sydney, Australia	3,515	3,708	338	10,328
Calcutta, India	11,663	14,088	209	54,607	Athens, Greece	3,468	3,866	116	29,511
Buenos Aires, Argentina	11,518	12,911	535	21,233	Miami, U.S.	3,421	3,894	448	7,498
Rio de Janeiro, Brazil	11,428	14,169	260	42,894	Guangzhou, China	3,330	3,652	79	41,942
Moscow, USSR	10,367	11,121	379	27,117	Guadalajara, Mexico	3,262	4,451	78	40,364
Los Angeles, U.S.	10,060	10,714	1,110	8,985	Surabaya, Indonesia	3,205	3,632	43	73,368
Manila, Philippines	9,880	12,846	188	50,978	Caracas, Venezuela	3,188	3,435	54	58,296
Cairo, Egypt	9,851	12,512	104	92,168	Wuhan, China	3,169	3,495	65	48,376
Jakarta, Indonesia	9,588	12,804	76	122,033	Toronto, Canada	3,108	3,296	154	20,001
London, U.K.	9,170	8,574	874	10,551	Greater Berlin, Germany	3,022	3,006	274	11,036
Teheran, Iran	9,354	14,251	112	79,594	Rome, Italy	3,021	3,129	69	43,556
Paris, France	8,709	8,803	432	20,123	Detroit, U.S.(*)	2,995	2,735	468	6,457
Delhi, India	8,475	11,849	138	59,102	Porto Alegre, Brazil	3,015	4,109	231	12,608
Karachi, Pakistan	7,711	11,299	190	39,038	Naples, Italy	2,960	3,134	62	47,424
Lagos, Nigeria	7,602	12,528	56	129,705	Melbourne, Australia	2,907	2,968	327	8,856
Essen, W. Germany	7,474	7,239	704	10,653	Alexandria, Egypt	2,899	3,304	35	81,420
Shanghai, China	6,873	7,540	78	87,659	Montreal, Canada	2,896	3,071	164	17,572
Lima, Peru	6,578	9,241	120	54,789	Casablanca, Morocco	2,891	3,795	35	80,202
Chicago, U.S.	6,526	6,568	762	8,560	Monterrey, Mexico	2,837	3,974	77	35,448
Taipei, Taiwan	6,513	8,516	138	45,710	Yangon, Myanmar	2,813	3,332	47	58,724
Istanbul, Turkey	6,461	8,875	165	37,760	Ankara, Turkey	2,782	3,777	55	48,852
Bangkok, Thailand	5,791	7,587	102	55,126	Kiev, USSR	2,751	3,237	62	43,548
Beijing, China	5,736	5,993	151	37,816	Dallas, U.S.	2,743	3,257	419	6,418
Madras, India	5,743	7,384	115	48,541	Singapore, Singapore	2,695	2,913	78	34,185
Bogota, Colombia	5,710	7,935	79	69,638	Harbin, China	2,618	2,887	30	86,591
Hong Kong	5,656	5,956	23	247,004	Washington, U.S.	2,547	2,707	357	7,082
Santiago, Chile	5,275	6,294	128	40,269	Taegu, South Korea	2,529	4,051	NA	NA
Pusan, S. Korea	4,838	6,700	54	86,284	Boston, U.S.	2,475	2,485	303	8,162
Tianjin, China	4,804	5,298	49	97,291	Poona, India	2,447	3,647	NA	NA
Milan, Italy	4,738	4,839	344	13,741	Lisbon, Portugal	2,396	2,717	NA	NA
Nagoya, Japan	4,736	5,303	307	15,236	Tashkent, USSR	2,365	2,947	NA	NA
Leningrad, USSR	4,667	4,738	139	33,474	Chengdu, China	2,349	2,591	25	93,242
Bangalore, India	4,612	6,764	50	88,191	Chongqing, China	2,339	2,961	NA	NA
Madrid, Spain	4,451	5,104	66	66,527	Vienna, Austria	2,313	2,647	NA	NA
Shenyang, China	4,248	4,684	39	108,080	Budapest, Hungary	2,301	2,335	138	16,666
Lahore, Pakistan	4,236	5,864	57	71,949	Houston, U.S.	2,298	2,651	310	7,284
Dhaka, Bangladesh	4,224	6,492	32	125,511	Salvador, Brazil	2,209	3,286	NA	NA
Barcelona, Spain	4,163	4,834	87	47,138	Birmingham, U.K.	2,170	2,078	223	9,768
Manchester, U.K.	4,050	3,827	357	11,397	Bucharest, Romania	2,150	2,271	52	41,132
Philadelphia, U.S.	4,007	3,979	471	8,515	Havana, Cuba	2,109	2,333	NA	NA
San Francisco, U.S.	3,958	4,214	428	9,167	Kanpur, India	2,076	2,673	NA	NA

(*) Includes Windsor, Canada. NA-not available.

Area and Population of the World

Source: U.S. Bureau of the Census; prior to 1950, Rand McNally & Co.

Continent	Area (1,000 sq. mi.)	% of Earth	Population (est., thousands)							% World Total, 1990
			1650	1750	1850	1900	1950	1980	1990	
North America	9,400	16.2	5,000	5,000	39,000	106,000	166,000	252,000	277,000	5.1
South America	6,900	11.9	8,000	7,000	20,000	38,000	—	—	—	
Latin America, Caribbean	—	—	—	—	—	—	166,000	364,000	450,000	8.4
Europe	3,800	6.6	100,000	140,000	265,000	400,000	392,000	484,000	499,000	9.3
Asia	17,400	30.1	335,000	476,000	754,000	932,000	1,368,000	2,494,000	2,994,000	56.1
Africa	11,700	20.2	100,000	95,000	95,000	118,000	281,000	594,000	795,000	14.9
USSR	—	—	—	—	—	—	180,000	266,000	291,000	5.4
Oceania, incl. Australia	3,300	5.7	2,000	2,000	2,000	6,000	12,000	23,000	26,000	0.4
Antarctica	5,400	9.3	Uninhabited							
World	**57,900**	**—**	**550,000**	**725,000**	**1,175,000**	**1,600,000**	**2,565,000**	**4,477,000**	**5,333,000**	**—**

Population Projections, by Region and for Selected Countries: 1995 to 2025

Source: Population Division of the United Nations

(in millions)

Region and Country	1995	2000	2025	Region and Country	1995	2000	2025
World, total . . .	**5,679.3**	**6,127.1**	**8,177.1**	Tropical South			
More developed[1] . . .	1,242.8	1,275.7	1,396.7	America[2]	276.9	304.1	436.3
Less developed[1]	4,436.4	4,851.5	6,780.4	Bolivia	8.4	9.7	18.3
Africa	**753.2**	**877.4**	**1,642.9**	Brazil	165.1	179.5	245.8
Eastern Africa[2] . . .	224.7	266.2	531.4	Colombia	34.9	38.0	51.7
Burundi	6.1	7.0	11.0	Ecuador	12.7	14.6	25.7
Ethiopia	50.1	58.4	112.0	Paraguay	4.8	5.4	8.6
Kenya	31.4	38.5	82.9	Peru	25.1	28.0	41.0
Madagascar	13.4	15.6	29.7	Venezuela.	24.2	27.2	42.8
Malawi.	9.8	11.7	23.2	**Northern America[2]. .**	**286.8**	**297.7**	**347.3**
Mozambique	18.8	21.8	39.7	Canada	28.3	29.4	34.4
Rwanda	8.8	10.6	22.2	United States . . .	258.3	268.1	312.7
Somalia	6.2	7.1	13.2	**East Asia[2]**	**1,390.4**	**1,470.0**	**1,696.1**
Uganda	22.5	26.8	52.3	China.	1,184.2	1,255.7	1,460.1
Tanzania	32.5	39.1	83.8	Hong Kong.	6.6	6.9	7.9
Zambia	9.4	11.2	23.8	Japan.	125.1	127.7	127.6
Zimbabwe	12.6	15.1	32.7	Korea, North.	24.9	27.3	37.6
Middle Africa[2] . . .	83.0	96.1	183.5	Korea, South	46.8	49.5	58.6
Angola.	11.5	13.2	24.5	**South Asia.**	**1,909.4**	**2,073.7**	**2,770.6**
Cameroon.	12.6	14.4	25.2	Eastern So. Asia[2]. .	480.8	519.7	684.7
Cen. African Rep.	3.3	3.7	6.7	Cambodia	9.2	9.9	12.5
Chad.	6.4	7.3	13.1	Indonesia	191.9	204.5	255.3
Zaire.	44.8	52.4	104.4	Laos	5.6	6.2	9.2
Northern Africa[2]. . .	164.3	185.7	295.0	Malaysia.	19.1	20.6	26.9
Algeria.	30.5	35.2	57.3	Myanmar[4].	49.8	55.2	82.2
Egypt.	58.9	65.2	97.4	Philippines.	68.3	74.8	102.3
Libya.	5.2	6.1	11.1	Singapore	2.9	3.0	3.2
Morocco.	31.9	36.3	59.9	Thailand.	61.1	66.1	86.3
Sudan	28.7	32.9	55.4	Vietnam	71.7	78.1	105.1
Tunisia.	8.9	9.7	13.6	Middle So. Asia[2] . .	1,279.9	1,385.7	1,815.9
Southern Africa[2] . .	48.1	54.5	90.7	Afghanistan	21.7	24.2	35.9
South Africa. . . .	41.6	46.9	76.3	Bangladesh	130.3	145.8	219.4
Western Africa[2]. . .	233.1	275.0	542.4	India	899.1	961.5	1,188.5
Benin	5.4	6.4	12.2	Iran.	58.7	65.5	96.2
Burkina Faso . . .	9.1	10.5	19.5	Nepal	20.7	23.0	33.9
Côte d'Ivoire[3] . . .	13.4	15.6	28.1	Pakistan	128.0	142.6	212.8
Ghana	18.7	21.9	37.7	Sri Lanka	19.5	20.8	26.2
Guinea.	7.0	7.9	13.9	Western So. Asia[2] .	148.7	168.3	270.0
Mali	10.7	12.4	21.4	Iraq.	21.6	24.9	42.7
Niger.	8.3	9.8	18.9	Israel.	5.0	5.4	7.0
Nigeria.	135.5	161.9	338.1	Jordan.	5.2	6.4	13.4
Senegal	8.7	10.0	18.9	Lebanon	3.3	3.6	5.2
Togo	3.9	4.6	9.0	Saudi Arabia . . .	16.1	18.9	33.5
Latin America.	**501.3**	**550.0**	**786.6**	Syria.	15.3	18.1	32.3
Caribbean[2]	37.7	40.8	57.7	Turkey.	62.4	68.5	99.3
Cuba.	11.2	11.7	13.6	Yemen	12.1	16.3	29.0
Dominican Rep.. .	7.7	8.4	12.2	**Europe (excl. Soviet**			
Haiti	8.6	9.9	18.3	**Union)**	**506.5**	**513.1**	**526.9**
Middle America[2] . .	134.4	149.6	222.6	Eastern Europe . . .	101.7	110.1	115.1
El Salvador	7.5	8.7	15.0	Bulgaria	9.6	9.7	10.2
Guatemala	11.1	12.7	21.7	Czechoslovakia. .	16.3	16.8	18.8
Honduras	6.0	7.0	13.3	Hungary	10.8	10.9	10.9
Mexico.	99.2	109.2	154.1	Poland.	40.2	41.4	45.9
Nicaragua	4.5	5.3	9.2	Romania.	24.8	25.6	29.2
Temperate South				Northern Europe[2]. .	83.0	83.4	83.6
America[2]	52.3	55.5	70.1	Denmark	5.1	5.1	4.8
Argentina	35.1	37.2	47.4	Finland.	5.0	5.0	4.8
Chile	14.0	14.9	18.8	Ireland.	4.0	4.2	5.2
Uruguay	3.2	3.4	3.9	Norway	4.2	4.2	4.3

Region and Country	1995	2000	2025	Region and Country	1995	2000	2025
Sweden	8.2	8.1	7.5	Belgium	9.9	9.9	9.8
United Kingdom	56.0	56.2	56.4	France	56.3	57.1	58.5
Southern Europe[2]	150.0	153.1	162.8	Germany	76.8	76.4	69.9
Albania	3.8	4.1	5.8	Netherlands	14.9	15.0	14.6
Greece	10.5	10.7	11.8	Switzerland	6.0	5.9	4.9
Italy	57.9	58.2	56.9	Soviet Union	303.1	314.8	367.1
Portugal	10.7	11.0	11.9	Oceania[2]	28.5	30.4	39.5
Spain	42.0	43.4	49.2	Australia	17.7	18.7	23.5
Yugoslavia	24.6	25.2	26.6	New Zealand	3.6	3.7	4.2
Western Europe[2]	155.3	155.6	149.3	Papua New Guinea	4.8	5.3	8.2
Austria	7.5	7.5	7.3				

(1) Regions. (2) Includes countries not shown separately. (3) Ivory Coast. (4) Formerly Burma.

Foreign Exchange Rates: 1970 to 1990

Source: International Monetary Fund

(National currency units per dollar; Data are annual averages)

Year	Australia (dollar)	Austria (schilling)	Belgium (franc)	Canada (dollar)	Denmark (krone)	France (franc)	(West) Germany (deutsche mark)	Greece (drachma)
1970	1.1136	25.880	49.680	1.0103	7.489	5.5200	3.6480	30.00
1975	1.3077	17.443	36.799	1.0175	5.748	4.2876	2.4613	32.29
1977	1.1082	16.545	35.848	1.0633	6.004	4.9160	2.3236	36.84
1978	1.1441	14.525	31.493	1.1405	5.516	4.5090	2.0096	36.75
1979	1.1177	13.387	29.342	1.1603	5.262	4.2566	1.8342	37.04
1980	1.1400	12.945	29.237	1.1693	5.634	4.2250	1.8175	42.62
1981	1.1495	15.948	37.194	1.1990	7.135	5.4396	2.2631	55.41
1982	1.0165	17.060	45.780	1.2344	8.344	6.5793	2.4280	66.87
1983	.9014	17.968	51.121	1.2325	9.148	7.6203	2.5539	87.90
1984	.8794	20.009	57.784	1.2951	10.357	8.7391	2.8454	112.73
1985	.7003	20.690	59.378	1.3655	10.596	8.9852	2.9440	138.12
1986	.6709	15.267	44.672	1.3895	8.091	6.9261	2.1715	139.98
1987	.7009	12.643	37.334	1.3260	6.840	6.0107	1.7974	135.43
1988	.7842	12.243	36.768	1.2307	6.732	5.9569	1.7562	141.89
1989	.7925	13.231	39.404	1.1840	7.310	6.3801	1.8800	162.42
1990	.7813	11.370	33.418	1.1668	6.189	5.4453	1.6157	158.51

Year	India (rupee)	Ireland (pound)	Italy (lira)	Japan (yen)	Malaysia (ringgit)	Netherlands (guilder)	Norway (kroner)	Portugal (escudo)
1970	7.576	2.3959	623	357.60	3.0900	3.5970	7.1400	28.75
1975	8.409	2.2216	653	296.78	2.4030	2.5293	5.2282	25.51
1977	8.769	1.7449	882	268.62	2.4625	2.4547	5.3239	38.34
1978	8.198	1.9184	849	210.38	2.3168	2.1642	5.2466	44.03
1979	8.156	2.0465	831	219.02	2.1721	2.0072	5.0650	48.95
1980	7.887	2.0577	856	226.63	2.1767	1.9875	4.9381	50.08
1981	8.681	1.6132	1,138	220.63	2.3048	2.4998	5.7430	61.74
1982	9.485	1.4205	1,345	249.06	2.3395	2.6719	6.4567	80.10
1983	10.104	1.2481	1,519	237.55	2.3204	2.8543	7.3012	111.61
1984	11.363	1.0871	1,756	237.52	2.3436	3.2087	8.1615	146.39
1985	12.369	1.0656	1,909	238.54	2.4830	3.3214	8.5972	170.39
1986	12.611	1.3415	1,490	168.52	2.5814	2.4500	7.3947	149.59
1987	12.962	1.4881	1,296	144.64	2.5196	2.0257	6.7375	140.88
1988	13.917	1.5261	1,301	128.15	2.6188	1.9766	6.5170	143.95
1989	16.226	1.4190	1,372	137.96	2.7088	2.1207	6.9045	157.46
1990	17.504	1.6585	1,198	144.79	2.7048	1.8209	6.2597	142.55

Year	Singapore (dollar)	South Korea (won)	Spain (peseta)	Sweden (krona)	Switzerland (franc)	Thailand (baht)	United Kingdom (pound)
1970	3.0800	310.57	69.72	5.1700	4.3160	21.000	2.3959
1975	2.3713	484.00	57.43	4.1530	2.5839	20.379	2.2216
1977	2.4394	484.00	75.99	4.4801	2.4064	20.400	1.7449
1978	2.2740	484.00	76.72	4.5206	1.7906	20.336	1.9184
1979	2.1746	484.00	67.16	4.2892	1.6643	20.419	2.1224
1980	2.1412	607.43	71.76	4.2309	1.6772	20.476	2.3243
1981	2.1053	681.03	92.40	5.0659	1.9674	21.731	2.0243
1982	2.1406	731.93	110.09	6.2838	2.0327	23.014	1.7480
1983	2.1136	776.04	143.50	7.6717	2.1006	22.991	1.5159
1984	2.1331	805.69	160.78	8.2718	2.3497	23.639	1.3366
1985	2.2002	870.02	170.04	8.6039	2.4571	27.159	1.2963
1986	2.1774	881.45	140.04	7.1236	1.7989	26.299	1.4670
1987	2.1059	822.57	123.48	6.3404	1.4912	25.723	1.6389
1988	2.0124	731.57	116.49	6.1272	1.4633	25.294	1.7813
1989	1.9508	671.46	118.38	6.4469	1.6359	25.702	1.6897
1990	1.8125	707.76	101.93	5.9188	1.3892	25.585	1.7847

The World's Refugees in 1990

Source: *World Refugee Survey 1990*, U.S. Committee for Refugees, a nonprofit corp. The refugees in this table include only those who are in need of protection and/or assistance, and do not include refugees who have resettled.

Country of Asylum	From	Number	Country of Asylum	From	Number
Total Africa		**5,443,450**	Belgium	various	13,000
Algeria	Mostly Western Sahara	189,400[1]	Canada	various	36,600
Angola	Namibia, Zaire, S. Africa.	11,900	Czechoslovakia	various	1,600
Benin	Chad.	800	Denmark	various	5,500
Botswana	S. Africa.	1,000	Finland	various	2,700
Burkina Faso	Chad.	300	France	various	56,000
Burundi	Rwanda, Zaire	90,700[1]	Germany	various	193,100
Cameroon	Chad.	6,900	Greece	various	6,200
Central African Rep.	Chad, Sudan	6,300	Hungary	various	18,300
Congo	Chad, Zaire	3,400	Italy	various	4,800
Côte d'Ivoire	Liberia.	270,500	Netherlands	various	21,200
Djibouti	Ethiopia, Somalia.	67,400	Norway	various	3,900
Egypt	Kuwait[2] Palestinians, Somalia	37,800	Portugal	various	100
			Spain	various	6,800
Ethiopia	Sudan, Somalia	783,000	Sweden	various	28,900
Gabon	various	800	Switzerland	various	37,000
Gambia	Senegal	800	Turkey	Iran, Iraq.	178,000[1]
Ghana	Liberia.	8,000	United Kingdom	various	25,000
Guinea	Liberia.	325,000	United States	Nicaragua, El Salvador, Guatemala	73,600
Guinea Bissau	Senegal	1,600	Yugoslavia	various	2,500
Kenya	Ethiopia, Rwanda, Uganda	14,400	Other European	various	7,000
Lesotho	South Africa	1,000[1]			
Malawi	Mozambique	909,000	**Total Latin America/Caribbean**		**118,950**
Mali	Mauritania.	10,600	Belize	El Salvador, Guatemala.	6,200
Mauritania	Senegal	22,000[1]	Bolivia	various	100
Morocco	various	800	Brazil	various	200
Mozambique	S. Africa.	700	Colombia	various	700
Namibia	Angola.	25,000[1]	Costa Rica	El Salvador, Nicaragua	26,900
Niger	Chad.	800	Cuba	various	3,000
Nigeria	Chad, Liberia	5,300	Ecuador	Chile, Colombia	3,750[1]
Rwanda	Burundi	21,500[1]	El Salvador	Nicaragua.	600
Senegal	Guinea Bissau, Mauritania.	55,300	French Guiana	Suriname	10,000
Sierra Leone	Liberia.	125,800	Guatemala	El Salvador, Nicaragua	6,700
Somalia	Ethiopia	358,000[1]	Honduras	El Salvador	2,700
S. Africa	Mozambique	201,000[1]	Mexico	Guatemala	53,000
Sudan	Ethiopia, Chad, Zaire	226,500[1]	Nicaragua	El Salvador	500
Swaziland	South Africa, Mozambique	47,200[1]	Panama	various	1,200
Tanzania	Burundi, Mozambique	266,200	Peru	various	600
Tunisia	various	200	Uruguay	various	100
Uganda	Rwanda, Zaire, Sudan	156,000[1]	Venezuela	Caribbean.	900
Zaire	Angola, Rwanda, Sudan.	370,900			
Zambia	Angola, Mozambique, Zaire.	133,950	**Total Middle East/South Asia**		**9,797,200**
Zimbabwe	Mozambique	186,000[1]	Bahrain	Kuwait[2]	7,500
			India	Bangladesh, Tibet, Sri Lanka	415,800[1]
Total East Asia/Pacific		**592,100**	Iran	Afghanistan, Iraq, Kuwait	2,860,000[1]
China	Myanmar	5,000	Iraq	Iran	60,000
Hong Kong	Vietnam	52,000	Nepal	Tibet.	14,000
Indonesia	Vietnam, Cambodia	20,500	Oman	Kuwait[2]	3,000
Japan	Vietnam	800	Pakistan	Afghanistan.	3,668,800
Korea	Vietnam	200	Saudi Arabia	Kuwait[2]	300,000
Macau	Vietnam	200	United Arab Emirates	Kuwait[2]	40,000
Malaysia	Vietnam	14,600	Yemen	Ethiopia	1,300
Papua New Guinea	Indonesia	8,000	Palestinians		
Philippines	Vietnam	19,600	Gaza Strip		496,300
Singapore	Vietnam	150	Jordan		921,100
Taiwan	Vietnam	150	Lebanon		306,400
Thailand	Myanmar, Laos, Cambodia	454,200	Syria		280,700
Vietnam	Cambodia	16,700	West Bank		414,300
Total Europe & No. America		**737,600+**	**Total Refugees**		**18,355,400[2]**
Austria	various	22,800			

(1) Significant variance among sources in number reported; (2) as of Apr. 1, 1991.

Principal Sources of Refugees

Afghanistan	6,027,100[1]	Kuwait	385,500*	Tibet	114,000
Palestinians	2,428,100	Cambodia	344,500	Bangladesh	75,000[1]
Mozambique	1,427,500	Sri Lanka	228,000	Laos	67,400
Ethiopia	1,066,300[1]	Iran	211,100[1]	Mauritania	60,100
Liberia	728,800	Rwanda	203,900[1]	Guatemala	57,400
Iraq	529,700	Burundi	186,200	Myanmar	50,800
Sudan	499,100	Western Sahara	165,000[1]	Zaire	50,700
Somalia	454,600[1]	Vietnam	122,200	Bangladesh	50,000[1]
Angola	435,700[1]				

(1) Significant variance among sources in number reported. *As of Apr. 1991.

Naturalization: How to Become an American Citizen

Source: The Federal Statutes

A person who desires to be naturalized as a citizen of the United States may obtain the necessary application form as well as detailed information from the nearest office of the Immigration and Naturalization Service or from the clerk of a court handling naturalization cases.

An applicant must be at least 18 years old. He must have been a lawful resident of the United States continuously for 5 years. For husbands and wives of U.S. citizens the period is 3 years in most instances. Special provisions apply to certain veterans of the Armed Forces.

An applicant must have been physically present in this country for at least half of the required 5 years' residence.

Every applicant for naturalization must:

(1) demonstrate an understanding of the English language, including an ability to read, write, and speak words in ordinary usage in the English language (persons physically unable to do so, and persons who, on the date of their examinations, are over 50 years of age and have been lawful permanent residents of the United States for 20 years or more are exempt).

(2) have been a person of good moral character, attached to the principles of the Constitution, and well disposed to the good order and happiness of the United States for five years just before filing the petition or for whatever other period of residence is required in his case and continue to be such a person until admitted to citizenship; and

(3) demonstrate a knowledge and understanding of the fundamentals of the history, and the principles and form of government, of the U.S.

When the applicant files his petition he pays the court clerk $50. At the preliminary hearing he may be represented by a lawyer or social service agency. There is a 30-day wait. If action is favorable, there is a final hearing before a judge, who administers the following oath of allegiance:

I hereby declare, on oath, that I absolutely and entirely renounce and abjure all allegiance and fidelity to any foreign prince, potentate, state or sovereignty, to whom or which I have heretofore been a subject or citizen; that I will support and defend the Constitution and laws of the United States of America against all enemies, foreign and domestic; that I will bear true faith and allegiance to the same; that I will bear arms on behalf of the United States when required by the law; that I will perform noncombatant service in the armed forces of the United States when required by the law; that I will perform work of national importance under civilian direction when required by the law; and that I take this obligation freely without any mental reservation or purpose of evasion; so help me God.

Customs Exemptions and Advice to Travelers

Source: U.S. Customs Service

U.S. residents returning after a stay abroad of at least 48 hours are usually granted customs exemptions of $400 each. The duty-free articles must accompany the traveler at the time of his return, be for personal or household use, have been acquired as an incident of his trip, and be properly declared to Customs. Not more than one liter of alcoholic beverages may be included in the $400 exemption.

If a U.S. resident arrives directly or indirectly from the U.S. Virgin Islands, or a contiguous country which maintains a free zone or a free port, the purchase may be valued up to $800 fair retail value, but not more than $400 of the exemption may be applied to the value of articles acquired elsewhere than in such insular possessions, and 5 liters of alcoholic beverages may be included in the exemption, but not more than one liter of such beverages may have been acquired elsewhere than in the designated islands.

The exemption for alcoholic beverages is accorded only when the returning resident has attained 21 years of age at the time of his arrival. One hundred cigars and 200 cigarettes may be included in either exemption. Cuban cigars may be included if obtained in Cuba and all articles acquired there do not exceed $100 in retail value.

The $400 or $800 exemption may be granted only if the exemption, or any part of it, has not been used within the preceding 30-day period and the stay abroad was for at least 48 hours. The 48-hour absence requirement does not apply if you return from Mexico or the U.S. Virgin Islands.

Gifts costing no more than $50 fair retail value or $100 from American Samoa, Guam, or the Virgin Islands, may be mailed duty-free.

Most items—including alcoholic beverages, cigars, cigarettes and perfume—made in designated Caribbean and Central American countries may enter the U.S. duty-free under the Caribbean Basin Economic Recovery Act. Countries currently designated for such duty-free treatment are: Aruba, Antigua and Barbuda, Bahamas, Barbados, Belize, British Virgin Islands, Costa Rica, Dominica, Dominican Republic, El Salvador, Grenada, Guatemala, Guyana, Haiti, Honduras, Jamaica, Montserrat, Netherlands Antilles, Nicaragua, Panama, Saint Christopher-Nevis, Saint Lucia, Saint Vincent and the Grenadines, and Trinidad and Tobago. Exceptions are: most textiles (incl. clothing), footwear, handbags, luggage, flat goods, work gloves and leather wearing apparel, and certain watches and watch parts. Alcoholic beverages and perfumes, remain subject to IRS tax.

Geneva Conventions

The Geneva Conventions are 4 international treaties designed for the protection of civilians in time of war, the treatment of prisoners of war, and the care of the wounded and sick in the armed forces. The first convention was in 1864, the second in 1906, the third in 1929, and the fourth was signed at Geneva, Switzerland on Aug. 12, 1949.

There were major revisions of the protective treaties at the conventions of 1949, sparked by outrage at the treatment of prisoners of war and civilians during World War II by some belligerents, notably Germany and Japan. The 1949 convention provided for special safeguards for the wounded, children under 15, pregnant women, and the elderly. Discrimination was forbidden on racial, religious, national, or political grounds. Torture, collective punishment, reprisals, the unwarrented destruction of property, and the forced use of civilians for an occupier's armed forces were also prohibited.

Also included in the 1949 treaty was a pledge to treat prisoners humanely, feed them adequately, and deliver relief supplies to them. They were not to be forced to disclose more than minimal information.

Most countries have formally accepted all or most of the humanitarian conventions as binding. A nation is not free to withdraw its ratification of the conventions during wartime.

Despite the war criminal trials following the second world war, which said that violation of these rules were illegal under international law, there is no machinery in place to apprehend, try, or punish violators.

U.S. Immigration Law

Source: Immigration and Naturalization Service, U.S. Dept. of Justice

The Immigration Act of 1990 became law when it was signed by President Bush on Nov. 29, 1990. Bush called the bill the "most comprehensive reform of U.S. immigration laws in 66 years." Most of its provisions amend the Immigration and Nationality Act which remains the basic law. The new law raised the total number of immigrants entering the U.S. annually in FY 1992-94 to 714,000 (excluding refugees whose admission numbers are announced annually). This figure constitutes a hard cap. The visas would be distributed as follows:

- 465,000 for family immigrants;
- 55,000 for the spouses and children of aliens legalized under IRCA;
- 140,000 for employment-based immigrants;
- 40,000 for nationals from "adversely affected" countries;
- 12,000 for Hong Kong nationals who are high-level employees of large U.S. multinationals having a subsidiary there;
- 1,000 visas for displaced Tibetans;
- 1,000 visas for aliens who were notified that they had "won" a U.S. visa under the IRCA lottery system for nationals of "adversely affected" countries (NP-5), but for whom no visas were actually available.

Beginning in FY 1995 the number drops to a minimum of 675,000. These visas would be distributed as follows:

- 480,000 for family immigrants;
- 140,000 for employment based immigrants;
- 55,000 for "diversity immigrants."

Family Immigrants

Fiscal year 1992-94: 465,000 minus the number of "immediate relatives" admitted the previous fiscal year, *plus* any numbers unused by the employment-based preference system. During this period, the number of family-sponsored visas cannot fall below 226,000 (10,000 visas higher than the current allocation). If visa availability dips below this new floor, the shortfall will be made up from the category below.

During this period, 55,000 additional visas will be made available to the spouses and children of aliens legalized under the Immigration Reform and Control Act (IRCA) of 1986.

Fiscal year 1995 and beyond: 480,000 minus the number of "immediate relatives" admitted during the previous fiscal year, plus any unused numbers under the employment-based preference system. That number may not drop below a floor of 226,000. If it does (*as it is certain to*), the "cap" simply gets pierced.

New Family Preference System

First preference—unmarried sons and daughters of U.S. citizens: 23,400 visas.

Second preference—spouses and unmarried children of Lawful Permanent Residents (LPRs): 114,200 visas, plus any visas available above the floor of 226,000 family preference visas, plus any unused visas from the previous preference.

The category is subdivided as follows: A minimum of 77 percent of the visas allocated to the category goes to the spouses and minor children of LPRs without regard to per country ceilings; these visas will be distributed in the order in which the petitions were filed; a maximum of 23 percent of the category visa allocation goes to the unmarried sons and daughters of LPRs. This group of visas will continue to be subject to per country ceilings.

Third preference—married sons and daughters of U.S. citizens; 23,400 visas plus unused visas from all earlier preferences.

Fourth preference—brothers and sisters of U.S. citizens: 65,000 plus unused visas from all earlier preferences.

Employment-Based Immigrants

A total of 140,000 plus any unused numbers under the family-sponsored system. These visas would be distributed as follows:

First preference—Priority Workers—40,000 visas plus visas unused by the fourth and fifth employment-based preferences "investors" and "special immigrants". The category is subdivided as follows: extraordinary ability, demonstrated by sustained national or international acclaim, in the sciences, arts, education, business, and athletics. No U.S. employer required;

Outstanding, internationally recognized and with at least 3 years of experience, professors and researchers seeking to enter in senior positions. U.S. employer required; executives and managers of multinationals—requires one year of prior service with the firm during the preceding 3 years. The terms are extensively defined. U.S. employer required.

Second preference—Professionals with advanced degrees and aliens of exceptional ability—40,000 visas plus any unused "priority worker" visas. A U.S. employer and labor certification are required—although the Attorney General can waive both requirements. Members of the professions with advanced degrees or exceptional ability in the sciences, arts, or business. The possession of a degree, certificate, or license is not by itself considered sufficient evidence of exceptional ability.

Third preference—Skilled workers, professionals, and "Other" Workers—40,000 visas plus any visas unused by the 2 previous categories. Requires a U.S. employer and labor certification. Skilled workers must be in an occupation that requires at least 2 years training or experience. Professionals need a Bachelor's degree. "Other" workers refers to unskilled workers. Their numbers are limited to no more than 10,000 visas per year.

Fourth preference—Special immigrants—10,000 visas. This category includes ministers of religion and persons working for religious organizations for at least 2 years, foreign medical graduates, employees of the U.S. government abroad including certain employees of the U.S. mission in Hong Kong who file for admission as special immigrants before Jan. 1, 2002, retired employees of international organizations, etc.

Fifth preference—10,000 employment creation (investor) visas—7,000 for investors of $1 million in urban areas and 3,000 for investors of no less than $500,000 in rural or high-unemployment areas. The Attorney General may increase the required investment amount up to $3 million for high employment areas. Investment must create employment for at least 10 U.S. workers.

Labor Certification

A pilot program is created for FY 1992-94 giving Dept. of Labor the authority to identify up to 10 "shortage" or "surplus" occupations and make certifications for these occupations. If the occupation is in "shortage," automatic certification would be offered; if the occupation is in "surplus," the employer may still petition for the immigrant but will be required to demonstrate that he/she has undertaken extensive recruitment.

Student Visas

A 3-year program (FY 1992-94) allows foreign students to be employed off-campus for up to 20 hours per week during the school year, and without restrictions when school is out of session. The employment can only come after their first year of school but may be unrelated to their studies.

The employer must attest that he has recruited for U.S. workers for at least 60 days and that he offers both foreign and U.S. workers the actual wage level for the occupation at the place of employment or, if greater, the prevailing wage level for the occupation in the area of employment. If the Secretary of Labor finds the attestation to be a misrepresentation, the employer can be disqualified from employing a foreign student.

Worldwide Illiteracy Shows a Decline

For the first time ever, the number of illiterate people in the world declined slightly in recent years. A report by the United Nations Educational, Scientific and Cultural Organization estimated the number of illiterate people to be 948 million in 1990, a slight drop from the 1985 estimate of 950 million.

The 948 million people represent 26.6 percent of the world's population. The report projects that the number of illiterate will decrease to 935 million, or 21.8 percent of the population by the year 2000. While the report shows a significant decrease in the proportion of illiterate people—the number in 1970 was 890 million, or 38.5 percent of the adult population—it refers to the progress of eradicating illiteracy as being "painfully slow."

Major International Organizations

As of mid-1991

Association of Southeast Asian Nations (ASEAN), was formed in 1967 to promote economic, social, and cultural cooperation and development among the non-communist states of the region. Members in 1991 are Brunei Darussalam, Indonesia, Malaysia, Philippines, Singapore, Thailand. Annual ministerial meetings set policy; a central Secretariat in Jakarta and specialized intergovernmental committees work in trade, transportation, communications, agriculture, science, finance, and culture.

Caribbean Community & Common Market, (Caricom) was established July 4, 1973. Its function is to further co-operation in economics, health, education, culture, science and technology, and tax administration, as well as the co-ordination of foreign policy. Members in 1991 are Antigua, Bahamas, Barbados, Belize, Dominica, Grenada, Guyana, Jamaica, Montserrat, St. Kitts, St. Lucia, St. Vincent, Trinidad & Tobago. Observers are Dominican Republic, Haiti, and Suriname.

Commonwealth of Nations originally called the British Commonwealth of Nations, is an association of nations and dependencies loosely joined by a common interest based on having been parts of the old British Empire. The British monarch is the symbolic head of the Commonwealth.

There are 50 self-governing independent nations in the Commonwealth, plus various colonies and protectorates. As of May 1991, the members were the United Kingdom of Great Britain and Northern Ireland and 16 other nations recognizing the British monarch, represented by a governor-general, as their head of state: Antigua and Barbuda, Australia, Bahamas, Barbados, Belize, Canada, Grenada, Jamaica, Mauritius, New Zealand, Papua New Guinea, St. Kitts-Nevis, St. Lucia, St. Vincent and the Grenadines, Solomon Islands, and Tuvalu (a special member); and 32 countries with their own heads of state: Bangladesh, Botswana, Brunei, Cyprus, Dominica, The Gambia, Ghana, Guyana, India, Kenya, Kiribati, Lesotho, Malawi, Malaysia, The Maldives, Malta, Namibia, Nauru (a special member), Nigeria, Pakistan, Samoa, Seychelles, Sierra Leone, Singapore, Sri Lanka, Swaziland, Tanzania, Tonga, Trinidad and Tobago, Uganda, Vanuatu, Zambia, and Zimbabwe. In addition various Caribbean dependencies take part in certain Commonwealth activities.

The Commonwealth facilitates consultation among member states through meetings of prime ministers and finance ministers, and through a permanent Secretariat. Members consult on economic, scientific, educational, financial, legal, and military matters, and try to coordinate policies.

European Free Trade Association (EFTA), consisting of Austria, Finland, Iceland, Norway, Sweden, and Switzerland. Created Jan. 4, 1960, to gradually reduce customs duties and quantitative restrictions between members on industrial products. By Dec. 31, 1966, all tariffs and quotas had been eliminated. The association entered into free trade agreements with the EC, Jan. 1, 1973. Trade barriers were removed July 1, 1976.

Group of Seven (G-7), organization of the major industrial democracies who meet periodically to discuss world economic issues. Members are Canada, France, Germany, Italy, Japan, UK, and U.S.

International Criminal Police Organization (Interpol), created in 1923 to ensure and promote the widest possible mutual assistance between all police authorities within the limits of the law existing in the different countries and in the spirit of the Universal Declaration of Human Rights. There are 146 members in 1991.

League of Arab States (The Arab League) was created Mar. 22, 1945. Members in 1991 are Algeria, Bahrain, Djibouti, Egypt, Iraq, Jordan, Kuwait, Lebanon, Libya, Mauritania, Morocco, Oman, Qatar, The Palestine Liberation Org., Saudi Arabia, Somalia, Sudan, Syria, Tunisia, United Arab Emirates, Yemen. The League fosters cultural, economic, and communication ties and mediates disputes among the Arab states; it represents Arab states in certain international negotiations, and coordinates a military, economic, and diplomatic offensive against Israel. As a result of Egypt signing a peace treaty with Israel, the League, Mar. 1979, suspended Egypt's membership and transferred the League's headquarters from Cairo to Tunis. Egypt was readmitted to the organization in 1989.

North Atlantic Treaty Org. (NATO) was created by treaty (signed Apr. 4, 1949; in effect Aug. 24, 1949). Members in 1991 include Belgium, Canada, Denmark, France, Germany, Greece, Iceland, Italy, Luxembourg, Netherlands, Norway, Portugal, Spain, Turkey, United Kingdom, and the U.S. The members agreed to settle disputes by peaceful means; to develop their individual and collective capacity to resist armed attack; to regard an attack on one as an attack on all, and to take necessary action to repel an attack under Article 51 of the United Nations Charter.

The NATO structure consists of a Council and a Military Committee of 3 commands (Allied Command Europe, Allied Command Atlantic, Allied Command Channel) and the Canada-U.S. Regional Planning Group.

Following announcement in 1966 of nearly total French withdrawal from the military affairs of NATO, organization hq. moved, 1967, from Paris to Brussels.

At their summit conference in July 1990, members called for a reshaping of the alliance to assure the Soviet Union of their peaceful intentions. The U.S. is planning at least a 50% reduction of its forces in Europe beginning in 1994.

Organization of African Unity (OAU), formed May 25, 1963, by 32 African countries (50 in 1991) to coordinate cultural, political, scientific and economic policies; to end colonialism in Africa; and to promote a common defense of members' independence. It holds annual conferences of heads of state. Hq. is in Addis Ababa, Ethiopia.

Organization of American States (OAS) was formed in Bogota, Colombia, in 1948. Hq. is in Washington, D.C. It has a Permanent Council, Inter-American Economic and Social Council, and Inter-American Council for Education, Science and Culture, a Juridical Committee and a Commission on Human Rights. The Permanent Council can call meetings of foreign ministers to deal with urgent security

(continued)

matters. A General Assembly meets annually. A secretary general and assistant are elected for 5-year terms. There are 35 members, each with one vote in the various organizations: Antigua, Argentina, Bahamas, Barbados, Belize, Bolivia, Brazil, Chile, Colombia, Costa Rica, Cuba, Dominica, Dominican Republic, Ecuador, El Salvador, Grenada, Guatemala, Guyana, Haiti, Honduras, Jamaica, Mexico, Nicaragua, Panama, Paraguay, Peru, St. Kitts-Nevis, St. Lucia, St. Vincent, Suriname, Trinidad & Tobago, U.S., Uruguay, Venezuela. In 1962, the OAS excluded Cuba from OAS activities but not from membership.

Organization for Economic Cooperation and Development (OECD) was established Sept. 30, 1961 to promote economic and social welfare in member countries, and to stimulate and harmonize efforts on behalf of developing nations. Nearly all the industrialized "free market" countries belong, with Yugoslavia as an associate member. OECD collects and disseminates economic and environmental information. Members in 1991 are: Australia, Austria, Belgium, Canada, Denmark, Finland, France, Germany, Greece, Iceland, Ireland, Italy, Japan, Luxembourg, Netherlands, New Zealand, Norway, Portugal, Spain, Sweden, Switzerland, Turkey, United Kingdom, United States, Yugoslavia (special member). Hq. is in Paris.

Organization of Petroleum Exporting Countries (OPEC) was created Nov. 14, 1960 at Venezuelan initiative. The group attempts to set world oil prices by controlling oil production. It is also involved in advancing members' interests in trade and development dealings with industrialized oil-consuming nations. Members in 1991 are Algeria, Ecuador, Gabon, Indonesia, Iran, Iraq, Kuwait, Libya, Nigeria, Qatar, Saudi Arabia, United Arab Emirates, Venezuela.

The European Community

The European Community (EC) is the collective designation of three organizations with common membership: the European Economic Community (Common Market), the European Coal and Steel Community, and the European Atomic Energy Community (Euratom). The 12 full members are: Belgium, Denmark, France, Germany, Greece, Ireland, Italy, Luxembourg, Netherlands, Portugal, Spain, United Kingdom. Some 60 nations in Africa, the Caribbean, and the Pacific are affiliated under the Lomé Convention.

A merger of the 3 communities executives went into effect July 1, 1967, though the component organizations date back to 1951 and 1958. The Council of Ministers, the Commission of the European Communities, the European Parliament, and the European Court of Justice comprise the permanent structure. The communities aim to integrate their economies, coordinate social developments, and bring about political union of the democratic states of Europe. There is a single passport for EC citizens and no restrictions on the movement of tourists or workers within the Community. There are also common agricultural, fisheries, and nuclear research policies.

The members have agreed that a single European market which will remove all barriers to free trade and free movement of capital and people will take effect beginning in 1993.

The legislative program will include: Mutual recognition of professional and educational degrees, so that lawyers, doctors, and engineers will be able to practice anywhere within the Community; Creation of a single customs document for truckers and first steps in deregulating ground, air, and water transportation; First steps toward liberalization of financial services, including banking, investment services, and insurance; and mutual recognition of many product standards and harmonization of others, allowing products sold in one EC country to be sold throughout the Community.

United Nations

The 46th regular session of the United Nations General Assembly opened in September, 1991.

UN headquarters are in New York, N.Y., between First Ave. and Roosevelt Drive and E. 42d St. and E. 48th St. The General Assembly Bldg., Secretariat, Conference and Library bldgs. are interconnected.

A European office at Geneva includes Secretariat and agency staff members. Other offices of UN bodies and related organizations with a staff of some 23,000 from some 150 countries are scattered throughout the world.

The UN has a post office originating its own stamps.

Proposals to establish an organization of nations for maintenance of world peace led to the United Nations Conference on International Organization at San Francisco, Apr. 25-June 26, 1945, where the charter of the United Nations was drawn up. It was signed June 26 by 50 nations, and by Poland, one of the original 51, on Oct. 15, 1945. The charter came into effect Oct. 24, 1945, upon ratification by the permanent members of the Security Council and a majority of other signatories.

Purposes: To maintain international peace and security; to develop friendly relations among nations; to achieve international cooperation in solving economic, social, cultural, and humanitarian problems and in promoting respect for human rights and fundamental freedoms; to be a center for harmonizing the actions of nations in attaining these common ends.

Roster of the United Nations

(As of Sept. 17, 1991)

The 166 members of the United Nations, with the years in which they became members.

Member	Year	Member	Year	Member	Year	Member	Year
Afghanistan	1946	Bhutan	1971	Chile	1945	Egypt[2]	1945
Albania	1955	Bolivia	1945	China[4]	1945	El Salvador	1945
Algeria	1962	Botswana	1966	Colombia	1945	Equatorial Guinea	1968
Angola	1976	Brazil	1945	Comoros	1975	Estonia	1991
Antigua and Barbuda	1981	Brunei	1984	Congo	1960	Ethiopia	1945
Argentina	1945	Bulgaria	1955	Costa Rica	1945	Fiji	1970
Australia	1945	Burkina Faso	1960	Côte d'Ivoire	1960	Finland	1955
Austria	1955	Burundi	1962	Cuba	1945	France	1945
Bahamas	1973	Byelorussia	1945	Cyprus	1960	Gabon	1960
Bahrain	1971	Cambodia	1955	Czechoslovakia	1945	Gambia	1965
Bangladesh	1974	Cameroon	1960	Denmark	1945	Germany, East	1973
Barbados	1966	Canada	1945	Djibouti	1977	Germany, West	1973
Belgium	1945	Cape Verde	1975	Dominica	1978	Ghana	1957
Belize	1981	Central Afr. Rep.	1960	Dominican Rep.	1945	Greece	1945
Benin	1960	Chad	1960	Ecuador	1945	Grenada	1974

Member	Year	Member	Year	Member	Year	Member	Year
Guatemala	1945	Libya	1955	Pakistan	1947	Sri Lanka	1955
Guinea	1958	Lithuania	1991	Panama	1945	Sudan	1956
Guinea-Bissau	1974	Luxembourg	1945	Papua New Guinea	1975	Suriname	1975
Guyana	1966	Madagascar (Malagasy)	1960	Paraguay	1945	Swaziland	1968
Haiti	1945	Malawi	1964	Peru	1945	Sweden	1946
Honduras	1945	Malaysia[1]	1957	Philippines	1945	Syria[2]	1945
Hungary	1955	Maldives	1965	Poland	1945	Tanzania[3]	1961
Iceland	1946	Mali	1960	Portugal	1955	Thailand	1946
India	1945	Malta	1964	Qatar	1971	Togo	1960
Indonesia[6]	1950	Marshall Islands	1991	Romania	1955	Trinidad & Tobago	1962
Iran	1945	Mauritania	1961	Rwanda	1962	Tunisia	1956
Iraq	1945	Mauritius	1968	Saint Christopher		Turkey	1945
Ireland	1955	Mexico	1945	& Nevis	1983	Uganda	1962
Israel	1949	Micronesia	1991	Saint Lucia	1979	Ukraine	1945
Italy	1955	Mongolia	1961	Saint Vincent and		USSR	1945
Jamaica	1962	Morocco	1956	the Grenadines	1980	United Arab Emirates	1971
Japan	1956	Mozambique	1975	Samoa (Western)	1976	United Kingdom	1945
Jordan	1955	Myanmar (Burma)	1948	Sao Tome e Principe	1975	United States	1945
Kenya	1963	Namibia	1990	Saudi Arabia	1945	Uruguay	1945
Korea, N.	1991	Nepal	1955	Senegal	1960	Vanuatu	1981
Korea, S.	1991	Netherlands	1945	Seychelles	1976	Venezuela	1945
Kuwait	1963	New Zealand	1945	Sierra Leone	1961	Vietnam	1977
Laos	1955	Nicaragua	1945	Singapore[1]	1965	Yemen	1947
Latvia	1991	Niger	1960	Solomon Islands	1978	Yugoslavia	1945
Lesotho	1966	Nigeria	1960	Somalia	1960	Zaire	1960
Liberia	1945	Norway	1945	South Africa[5]	1945	Zambia	1964
		Oman	1971	Spain	1955	Zimbabwe	1980

(1) Malaya joined the UN in 1957. In 1963, its name was changed to Malaysia following the accession of Singapore, Sabah, and Sarawak. Singapore became an independent UN member in 1965. (2) Egypt and Syria were original members of the UN. In 1958, the United Arab Republic was established by a union of Egypt and Syria and continued as a single member of the UN. In 1961, Syria resumed its separate membership. (3) Tanganyika was a member of the United Nations from 1961 and Zanzibar was a member from 1963. Following the ratification in 1964 of Articles of Union between Tanganyika and Zanzibar, the United Republic of Tanganyika and Zanzibar continued as a single member of the United Nations, later changing its name to United Republic of Tanzania. (4) The General Assembly voted in 1971 to expel the Chinese government on Taiwan and admit the Peking government in its place. (5) The General Assembly rejected the credentials of the South African delegates in 1974, and suspended the country from the Assembly. (6) Indonesia withdrew from the UN in 1965 and rejoined in 1966.

Organization of the United Nations

The text of the UN Charter, and further information, may be obtained from the Office of Public Information, United Nations, New York, NY 10017.

General Assembly. The General Assembly is composed of representatives of all the member nations. Each nation is entitled to one vote.

The General Assembly meets in regular annual sessions and in special session when necessary. Special sessions are convoked by the Secretary General at the request of the Security Council or of a majority of the members of the UN.

On important questions a two-thirds majority of members present and voting is required; on other questions a simple majority is sufficient.

The General Assembly must approve the budget and apportion expenses among members. A member in arrears will have no vote if the amount of arrears equals or exceeds the amount of the contributions due for the preceeding two full years.

Security Council. The Security Council consists of 15 members, 5 with permanent seats. The remaining 10 are elected for 2-year terms by the General Assembly; they are not eligible for immediate reelection.

Permanent members of the Council: China, France, USSR, United Kingdom, United States.

Non-permanent members are Cote D'Ivoire, Cuba, Romania, Yemen, Zaire (until Dec. 31, 1991). Austria, Belgium, Ecuador, India, and Zimbabwe (until Dec. 31, 1992).

The Security Council has the primary responsiblity within the UN for maintaining international peace and security. The Council may investigate any dispute that threatens international peace and security.

Any member of the UN at UN headquarters may participate in its discussions and a nation not a member of UN may appear if it is a party to a dispute.

Decisions on procedural questions are made by an affirmative vote of 9 members. On all other matters the affirmative vote of 9 members must include the concurring votes of all permanent members; it is this clause which gives rise to the so-called "veto." A party to a dispute must refrain from voting.

The Security Council directs the various truce supervisory forces deployed throughout the world.

Economic and Social Council. The Economic and Social Council consists of 54 members elected by the General Assembly for 3-year terms of office. The council is responsible under the General Assembly for carrying out the functions of the United Nations with regard to international economic, social, cultural, educational, health and related matters. The council meets usually twice a year.

Trusteeship Council. The administration of trust territories is under UN supervision. The only remaining trust territory is Palau, administered by the U.S.

Secretariat. The Secretary General is the chief administrative officer of the UN. He may bring to the attention of the Security Council any matter that threatens international peace. He reports to the General Assembly.

Budget: The General Assembly approved a total budget for 1992-93 of $2.36 billion.

International Court of Justice (World Court). The International Court of Justice is the principal judicial organ of the United Nations. All members are *ipso facto* parties to the statute of the Court, as are three nonmembers — Liechtenstein, San Marino, and Switzerland. Other states may become parties to the Court's statute.

The jurisdiction of the Court comprises cases which the parties submit to it and matters especially provided for in

(continued)

the charter or in treaties. The Court gives advisory opinions and renders judgments. Its decisions are only binding between the parties concerned and in respect to a particular dispute. If any party to a case fails to heed a judgment, the other party may have recourse to the Security Council.

The 15 judges are elected for 9-year terms by the General Assembly and the Security Council. Retiring judges are eligible for re-election. The Court remains permanently in session, except during vacations. All questions are decided by majority. The Court sits in The Hague, Netherlands.

Judges: 9-year term of office ending 1997: Mohamed Shahabuddeen, Guyana. Roberto Ago, Italy. Stephen Schwebel, U.S. Nikolai K. Tarasov, USSR. Mohammed Bedjaoui, Algeria. **9-year term in office ending 1994:** Ni Zhengyo, China. Jens Evensen, Norway. Manfred Lachs, Poland. Taslim Olawala Elias, Nigeria, Shigeru Oda, Japan. **9-year term in office ending 1991:** Nagendra Singh, India. Jose Maria Ruda, Argentina. Robert Y. Jennings, United Kingdom. Guy Ladreit de Lacharriere, France. Keba Mbaye, Senegal.

United Nations Secretaries General

Year	Secretary, Nation	Year	Secretary, Nation	Year	Secretary, Nation
1946	Trygve Lie, Norway	1961	U Thant, Burma	1982	Javier Perez de Cuellar, Peru
1953	Dag Hammarskjold, Sweden	1972	Kurt Waldheim, Austria		

U.S. Representatives to the United Nations

The U.S. Representative to the United Nations is the Chief of the U.S. Mission to the United Nations in New York and holds the rank and status of Ambassador Extraordinary and Plenipotentiary.

Year	Representative	Year	Representative	Year	Representative
1946	Edward R. Stettinius Jr.	1968	George W. Ball	1976	William W. Scranton
1946	Herschel V. Johnson (act.)	1968	James Russell Wiggins	1977	Andrew Young
1947	Warren R. Austin	1969	Charles W. Yost	1979	Donald McHenry
1953	Henry Cabot Lodge Jr.	1971	George Bush	1981	Jeane J. Kirkpatrick
1960	James J. Wadsworth	1973	John A. Scali	1985	Vernon A. Walters
1961	Adlai E. Stevenson	1975	Daniel P. Moynihan	1989	Thomas R. Pickering
1965	Arthur J. Goldberg				

Visitors to the United Nations

United Nations headquarters is open to the public every day of the year except Christmas and New Year's Day. The public entrance is at 46th Street and First Avenue and opens at 9 a.m.

Guided tours begin from the main lobby of the General Assembly building and are given approximately every half hour from 9:15 a.m. to 4:45 p.m. daily. The tours last about one hour. Tours in languages other than English may be arranged.

Groups of 15 or more persons should make arrangements as far in advance as possible by writing to the Group Program Unit, Visitors' Service, Room GA-56, United Nations, New York, NY 10017, or telephone (212) 963-7713. Children under 5 are not permitted on tours.

Specialized and Related Agencies

These agencies are autonomous, with their own memberships and organs which have a functional relationship or working agreement with the UN (headquarters.)

Food & Agriculture Org. (FAO) aims to increase production from farms, forests, and fisheries; improve distribution, marketing, and nutrition; better conditions for rural people. (Viale delle Terme di Caracalla, 00100 Rome, Italy.)

General Agreement on Tariffs and Trade (GATT) is the only treaty setting rules for world trade. Provides a forum for settling trade disputes and negotiating trade liberalization. (Centre William Rappard, 154 rue de Lausanne, 1211 Geneva 21, Switzerland.)

International Atomic Energy Agency (IAEA) aims to promote the safe, peaceful uses of atomic energy. (Vienna International Centre, PO Box 100, A-1400, Vienna, Austria.)

International Bank for Reconstruction and Development (IBRD) (World Bank) provides loans and technical assistance for economic development projects in developing member countries; encourages cofinancing for projects from other public and private sources. **International Development Association (IDA),** an affiliate of the Bank, provides funds for development projects on concessionary terms to the poorer developing member countries. (both 1818 H St., NW, Washington, DC 20433.) **International Finance Corporation (IFC)** an affiliate of the Bank, promotes the growth of the private sector in developing member countries; encourages the development of local capital markets; stimulates the international flow of private capital. (1818 H St., NW, Washington, DC 20433.)

International Civil Aviation Org. (ICAO) promotes international civil aviation standards and regulations. (1000 Sherbrooke St. W., Montreal, Quebec, Canada H3A 2R2.)

International Fund for Agricultural Development (IFAD) aims to mobilize funds for agricultural and rural projects in developing countries. (107 Via del Serafico, Rome, Italy.)

International Labor Org. (ILO) aims to promote employment; improve labor conditions and living standards. (4 route de Morillons, CH-1211, Geneva 22, Switzerland.)

International Maritime Org. (IMO) aims to promote cooperation on technical matters affecting international shipping. (4 Albert Embankment, London, SE1 7SR, England.)

International Monetary Fund (IMF) aims to promote international monetary co-operation and currency stabilization; expansion of international trade. (700 19th St., NW, Washington, DC, 20431.)

International Telecommunication Union (ITU) sets up international regulations of radio, telegraph, telephone and space radio-communications. Allocates radio frequencies. (Place des Nations, 1211 Geneva 20, Switzerland.)

United Nations Educational, Scientific, & Cultural Org. (UNESCO) aims to promote collaboration among nations through education, science, and culture. The U.S. withdrew from this organization in 1985 because of UNESCO's anti-Western bias. (9 Place de Fontenoy, 75700 Paris, France.)

United Nations Children's Fund (UNICEF) provides aid and development assistance to children and mothers in developing countries. (1 UN Plaza, New York, NY 10017.)

Universal Postal Union (UPU) aims to perfect postal services and promote international collaboration. (Weltpoststrasse 4, 3000 Berne, 15 Switzerland.)

World Health Org. (WHO) aims to aid the attainment of the highest possible level of health. (1211 Geneva 27, Switzerland.)

World Intellectual Property Organization (WIPO) seeks to protect, through international cooperation, literary, industrial, scientific, and artistic works. (34, Chemin des Colom Bettes, 1211 Geneva, Switzerland.)

World Meteorological Org. (WMO) aims to co-ordinate and improve world meteorological work. (Case Postale 5, CH-1211, Geneva 20, Switzerland.)

U.S. Aid to Foreign Nations in 1990

Source: Bureau of Economic Analysis, U.S. Dept. of Commerce

Figures are in millions of dollars. (*Less than $500,000.) Data include military supplies and services furnished under the Foreign Assistance Act and direct Defense Department appropriations, and include credits extended to private entities.

Net grants and credits take into account all known returns to the U.S., including reverse grants, returns of grants, and payments of principal. Also incl. are contributions received from coalition partners for Persian Gulf operations. A minus sign (−) indicates that the total of these returns is greater than the total of grants or credits. Nations with net grant or credit under $2 mln. are included with "Other and Unspecified."

Other assistance represents the transfer of U.S. farm products in exchange for foreign currencies, less the government's disbursements of such currencies as grants, credits, or for purchases.

Amounts do not include investments in the following: Asian Development Bank, $127 mln.; Inter-American Development Bank, $90 mln.; International Development Assn., $842 mln.; International Bank for Reconstruction and Development, $61 mln.; African Development Bank, $19 mln.; African Development Fund, $75 mln.; Inter-American Development Corp., $13 mln.; International Finance Corp., $75 mln.

	Total	Net grants	Net credits	Net other
Total	11,924	16,229	4,271	−34
Western Europe	−611	−222	−393	4
Austria	−10	(*)	−10	—
Belgium	−9	—	−9	—
Finland	−8	(*)	−9	(*)
France	−15	(*)	−14	—
Germany	−338	−338	—	—
Ireland	2	10	−8	—
Italy	−30	−1	−29	—
Portugal	56	94	−38	(*)
Spain	−122	1	−127	4
United Kingdom	−111	—	−111	—
Yugoslavia	−39	(*)	−39	(*)
Other & unspecified	12	12	(*)	(*)
Eastern Europe	418	311	118	−11
Poland	383	265	129	−11
Romania	64	45	19	—
USSR	−30	—	−30	—
Near East & South Asia	6,558	11,320	−4,759	−3
Afghanistan	57	60	−4	—
Bangladesh	172	228	−56	—
Cyprus	16	16	(*)	(*)
Egypt	4,977	9,907	−4,929	−1
Greece	282	4	277	(*)
India	−35	81	−115	(*)
Iraq	−17	—	−17	—
Israel	4,377	4,641	−265	—
Jordan	134	77	56	(*)
Kuwait	−2,506	−2,506	—	—
Lebanon	5	12	−7	—
Nepal	19	19	(*)	(*)
Oman	4	5	−1	—
Pakistan	522	264	258	1
Saudi Arabia	−1,614	−1,614	—	—
Sri Lanka	72	47	27	−2
Turkey	367	379	−11	−1
United Arab Emirates	−361	−361	—	—
Yemen	42	25	18	(*)
UNRWA	7	7	—	—
Other & unspecified	27	27	—	—
East Asia & Pacific	−134	−87	−49	3
Australia	−34	—	−34	—
Cambodia	5	5	(*)	—
China	71	(*)	71	—
Hong Kong	−9	(*)	−8	—
Indonesia	48	89	−41	(*)
Japan	−635	−635	—	—
Korea, South	−192	−61	−131	—
Malaysia	−1	1	−2	—
New Zealand	−2	1	−3	—
Philippines	−555	381	175	(*)
Taiwan	−7	—	−10	3
Thailand	−21	45	−66	—
Vietnam	2	1	1	—
Fed. States of Micronesia	37	37	—	—
Marshall Islands	15	15	—	—
Other & unspecified	32	33	−1	—
Africa	1,798	1,430	371	−2
Algeria	59	(*)	59	—
Angola	−16	1	−17	—
Benin	5	5	(*)	—
Botswana	17	17	(*)	—
Burkina Faso	14	14	—	(*)
Burundi	18	18	—	(*)
Cameroon	42	55	−13	(*)
Cape Verde	6	6	—	—

	Total	Net grants	Net credits	Net other
Cen. African Rep.	7	4	3	—
Chad	24	24	—	—
Congo	3	1	2	—
Cote d'Ivoire	27	8	19	—
Djibouti	8	8	—	—
Ethiopia	51	54	−3	(*)
Gabon	11	2	8	—
Gambia	13	13	—	—
Ghana	13	9	4	(*)
Guinea	15	8	7	(*)
Guinea-Bissau	8	8	—	—
Kenya	109	140	−31	(*)
Lesotho	15	15	—	—
Liberia	20	20	(*)	—
Madagascar	30	28	2	—
Malawi	31	31	(*)	—
Mali	31	31	(*)	(*)
Mauritania	11	12	−1	—
Mauritius	−4	2	−6	—
Morocco	94	93	3	−1
Mozambique	75	66	9	—
Niger	33	36	−3	—
Nigeria	156	22	134	—
Rwanda	13	13	—	—
Senegal	60	53	7	—
Seychelles	8	8	—	—
Sierra Leone	2	3	−1	—
Somalia	77	77	(*)	—
South Africa	20	20	—	—
Sudan	145	144	(*)	(*)
Swaziland	14	14	(*)	—
Tanzania	40	79	−39	—
Togo	10	10	(*)	—
Tunisia	38	56	−18	−1
Uganda	39	42	−3	(*)
Zaire	241	37	205	(*)
Zambia	58	7	51	—
Zimbabwe	10	15	−5	—
Other & unspecified	101	103	−1	—
Western Hemisphere	1,886	1,469	441	−24
Argentina	64	(*)	64	—
Belize	15	11	4	—
Bolivia	113	97	16	—
Brazil	235	2	233	—
Canada	−41	—	−41	—
Chile	−32	1	−33	(*)
Colombia	−29	46	−75	—
Costa Rica	103	94	12	3
Dominican Republic	24	18	24	−19
Ecuador	46	30	16	—
El Salvador	300	273	27	—
Guatemala	92	71	21	—
Guyana	42	1	41	(*)
Haiti	48	48	−1	(*)
Honduras	218	222	−4	—
Jamaica	107	60	48	−2
Mexico	131	32	98	—
Nicaragua	97	97	—	—
Panama	99	97	2	—
Paraguay	(*)	2	−2	(*)
Peru	78	62	16	—
St. Kitts-Nevis	2	(*)	2	—
Trinidad-Tobago	5	(*)	5	—
Uruguay	−4	3	−7	—
Venezuela	18	(*)	−18	—
Other & unspecified	190	198	−8	—
Intl. orgs. & unspecified	2,007	2,007	—	—

Ambassadors and Envoys

As of mid-1991

The address of U.S. embassies abroad is the appropriate foreign capital. The U.S. does not have diplomatic relations with the following countries: Albania,[1] Angola,[2] Cambodia,[3] Taiwan,[4] Cuba,[5] Iran,[6] Libya,[8] Vietnam,[3] N. Korea. There are informal relations with Bhutan and Vanuatu.

Countries	Envoys from United States	Envoys to United States
Afghanistan	Vacancy	Abdul Ghafoor Jawshan, Chargé
Algeria	Christopher W.S. Ross, Amb.	Adberrahmane Bensid, Amb.
Antigua & Barbuda	Vacancy	Vacancy
Argentina	Terence A. Todman, Amb.	Carlos Ortiz de Rosas, Amb.
Australia	Melvin F. Sembler, Amb.	Michael J. Cook, Amb.
Austria	Roy Michael Huffington, Amb.	Friedrich Hoess, Amb.
Bahamas	Chic Hecht, Amb.	Margaret E. McDonald, Amb.
Bahrain	Charles W. Hostler, Amb.	Ghazi M. Algosaibi, Amb.
Bangladesh	William B. Milam, Amb.	A.H.S. Ataul Karim, Amb.
Barbados	C. Philip Hughes, Amb.	William Douglas, Amb.
Belgium	Maynard W. Glitman, Amb.	Jean Cassiers, Amb.
Belize	Eugene L. Scassa, Amb.	James V. Hyde, Amb.
Benin	Harriet W. Isom, Amb.	Candide Pierre Ahouansou, Amb.
Bolivia	Robert S. Gelbard, Amb.	Jose Crespo-Velasco, Amb.
Botswana	David Passage, Amb.	Botsweletse K. Sebele, Amb.
Brazil	Richard H. Melton, Amb.	Marcilio M. Moreira, Amb.
Brunei	Christopher H. Phillips, Amb.	D.H. Mohammad Kassim, Amb.
Bulgaria	H. Kenneth Hill, Amb.	Ognian R. Pishev, Amb.
Burkina Faso	Edward P. Byrnn, Amb.	Paul-Désiré Kabore, Amb.
Burundi	Cynthia S. Perry, Amb.	Julien Kavakure, Amb.
Cameroon	Frances D. Cook, Amb.	Paul Pondi, Amb.
Canada	Edward N. Ney, Amb.	Derek H. Burney, Amb.
Cape Verde	Francis T. McNamara, Amb.	Jorge M.C. Dos Santos, Amb.
Central African Rep.	Daniel H. Simpson, Amb.	Jean-Pierre Sohahong-Kombet, Amb.
Chad	William W. Bogosian, Amb.	Mahamat Ali Adoum, Amb.
Chile	Charles A. Gillespie Jr., Amb.	Patricio Silva, Amb.
China	James R. Lilley, Amb.	Zhu Qizhen, Amb.
Colombia	Thomas E. McNamara, Amb.	Jamie Garcia-Parra, Amb.
Comoros	Kenneth N. Peltier, Amb.	Amini Ali Moumin, Amb.
Congo	James D. Phillips, Amb.	Roger Issombo, Amb.
Costa Rica	Robert O. Homme, Chargé	Gonzalo Facio, Amb.
Côte d'Ivoire	Kenneth L. Brown, Amb.	Charles Gomis, Amb.
Cyprus	Robert E. Lamb, Amb.	Michael E. Sherifis, Amb.
Czechoslovakia	Shirley Temple Black, Amb.	Rita Klimova, Amb.
Denmark	Keith L. Brown, Amb.	Peter P. Dyvig, Amb.
Djibouti	Robert S. Barrett, Amb.	Roble Olhale, Amb.
Dominica	C. Philip Hughes, Amb.	Edward I. Watty, Amb.
Dominican Republic	Paul D. Taylor, Amb.	Dario Suro, Chargé
Ecuador	Paul C. Lambert, Amb.	Jaime Moncayo, Amb.
Egypt	Frank G. Wisner, Amb.	El Sayed A. R. El Reedy, Amb.
El Salvador	William G. Walker, Amb.	Miguel A. Salaverria, Amb.
Equatorial Guinea	William Mithoefer Jr., Chargé	Damaso Obiang Ndong, Amb.
Estonia[7]		Ernst Jaakson, Consul General
Ethiopia	Robert G. Houdek, Chargé	Girma Amare, Chargé
Fiji	Evelyn I.H. Teegen, Amb.	Rutu Finau Mara, Chargé
Finland	John G. Weinmann, Amb.	Jukka Valtasaari, Amb.
France	Alan P. Larson, Amb.	Jacques Andreani, Amb.
Gabon	Keith L. Wauchope, Amb.	Alexandre Sambat, Amb.
Gambia, The	Arlene Render, Amb.	Ousman A. Sallah, Amb.
Germany	Robert M. Kimmitt, Amb.	Juergen Ruhfus, Amb.
Ghana	Raymond C Ewing, Amb.	Joseph Abbey, Amb.
Greece	Michael G. Sotirhos, Amb.	Christos Zacharakis, Amb.
Grenada	Vacancy	Denneth Modeste, Amb.
Guatemala	Thomas F. Stroock, Amb.	Norma J. Vasquez, Chargé
Guinea	Dane F. Smith, Amb.	Vacant.
Guinea-Bissau	William L. Jacobsen Jr., Amb.	Alfredo Lopes Cabral, Amb.
Guyana	Vacancy	Cedric H. Grant, Amb.
Haiti	Alvin P. Adams Jr., Amb.	Louis Harold Joseph, Chargé
Honduras	Cresencio S. Arcos, Amb.	Jorge Hernandez-Alcerro, Amb.
Hungary	Charles H. Thomas, Amb.	Eniko Bollobas, Chargé
Iceland	Charles E. Cobb Jr., Amb.	Tomas Tomasson, Amb.
India	William Clark Jr., Amb.	Abid Hussain, Amb.
Indonesia	John C. Monjo, Amb.	Abdul Rachman Ramly, Amb.
Iraq	Vacancy	Vacancy
Ireland	Richard A. Moore, Amb.	Padraic N. McKernan, Amb.
Israel	William A. Brown, Amb.	Zalman Shoval, Amb.
Italy	Peter F. Secchia, Amb.	Rinaldo Petrignani, Amb.
Jamaica	Glen A. Holden, Amb.	Richard L. Bernal, Amb.
Japan	Michael H. Armacost, Amb.	Ryohei Murata, Amb.
Jordan	Roger G. Harrison, Amb.	Hussein A. Hammami, Amb.
Kenya	Smith Hempstone Jr., Amb.	Denis D. Afande, Amb.
Kiribati	Evelyn I.H. Teegen, Amb.	Vacancy
Korea, South	Donald P. Gregg, Amb.	Hong-Choo Hyun, Amb.
Kuwait	Edward Gnehm, Amb.	Shaikh S. N. Al-Sabah, Amb.
Laos	Charles B. Salmon Jr., Chargé	Linthong Phetsavan, Chargé
Latvia[7]		Anatol Dinbergs, Chargé
Lebanon	Ryan C. Crocker, Amb.	Nassib S. Lahoud, Amb.
Lesotho	Leonard H.O. Spearman, Amb.	W. T. van Tonder, Amb.
Liberia	Peter J. de Vos, Amb.	Eugenia A. Wordsworth-Stevenson, Amb.

Lithuania[7]		Stasys Lozoraitis Jr., Chargé
Luxembourg	Edward M. Rowell, Amb.	Andre Philippe, Amb.
Madagascar	Howard K. Walker, Amb.	Pierrot J. Rajaonarivelo, Amb.
Malawi	George A. Trail 3d, Amb.	Robert Mbaya, Amb.
Malaysia	Paul M. Cleveland, Amb.	A.R. Ahmad Fuzi, Amb.
Mali	Herbert D. Gelber, Amb.	Mohamed A. Toure, Amb.
Malta	Sally J. Novetzke, Amb.	Salv Stellini, Amb.
Mauritania	William H. Twaddell, Amb.	Abdellah Ould Daddah, Amb.
Mauritius	Penne Percy Korth, Amb.	Chitmansing Jesseramsing, Amb.
Mexico	John Negroponte, Amb.	Gustavo Petricioli, Amb.
Mongolia	Joesph E. Lake, Amb.	Gendengiin Nyamdoo, Amb
Morocco	E. Michael Ussery, Amb.	Mohamed Belkhayat, Amb.
Mozambique	Townsend B. Friedman Jr., Amb.	Hipolito Patricio, Amb.
Myanmar	Vacancy	Vacancy
Namibia	Genta Hawkins Holmes, Amb.	Vacancy
Nauru	Melvin F. Sembler, Amb.	Vacancy
Nepal	Julia Chang Bloch, Amb.	Mohan Man Sainju, Amb.
Netherlands	C. Howard Wilkins Jr., Amb.	Johan H. Meesman, Amb.
New Zealand	Della M. Newman, Amb.	Denis B.G. McLean, Amb.
Nicaragua	Harry W. Shlaudeman, Amb.	Ernesto Palizio, Amb.
Niger	Carl C. Cundiff, Amb.	Moumouni A. Djermakoye, Amb.
Nigeria	Lannon Walker, Amb.	Kevin Efretei, Amb.
Norway	Loret Miller Ruppe, Amb.	Kjeld Vibe, Amb.
Oman	Richard W. Boehm, Amb.	Awadh Bader Al-Shanfari, Amb.
Pakistan	Robert B. Oakley, Amb.	Najmuddin A. Shaikh, Amb.
Panama	Deane R. Hinton, Amb.	Miguel Corro, Chargé
Papua New Guinea	Robert W. Farrand, Amb.	Margaret Taylor, Amb.
Paraguay	Timothy L. Towell, Amb.	Marcos Martinez Mendieta, Amb.
Peru	Anthony C.E. Quainton, Amb.	Ricardo Mac Lean, Amb.
Philippines	Nicholas Platt, Amb.	Emmanuel Pelaez, Amb.
Poland	Thomas W. Simons Jr., Amb.	Kazimierz Dziewanowski, Amb.
Portugal	Edward Ellis Briggs, Amb.	Joao Eduardo M. Periera Bastos, Amb.
Qatar	Mark G. Hambley, Amb.	Hamad A. Al-Kawari, Amb.
Romania	Alan Green Jr., Amb.	Virgil Constantinescu, Amb.
Rwanda	Robert A. Flaten, Amb.	Aloys Uwimana, Amb.
St. Kitts & Nevis	C. Philip Hughes, Amb.	Erstein Edwards, Chargé
St. Lucia	C. Philip Hughes, Amb.	Joseph E. Edmunds, Amb.
St. Vincent and The Grenadines	C. Philip Hughes, Amb.	Kingsley C.A. Layne, Amb.
Sao Tome and Principe	Keith L. Wauchope, Amb.	Joaquim R. Branco, Amb.
Saudi Arabia	Charles W. Freeman Jr., Amb.	Bandar Bin Sultan, Amb.
Senegal	George E. Moose, Amb.	Ibra Deguene Ka, Amb.
Seychelles	James Moran, Amb.	Marc Marengo, Chargé
Sierra Leone	Johnny Young, Amb.	George Carew, Amb.
Singapore	Robert D. Orr, Amb.	S.R. Nathan, Amb.
Solomon Islands	Robert W. Farrand, Amb.	Francis Bugotu, Amb.
Somalia	Vacancy	Abdikarim Ali Omar, Amb.
South Africa	William L. Swing, Amb.	Harry H. Schwarz, Amb.
Spain	Joseph Zappala, Amb.	Jaime de Ojeda, Amb.
Sri Lanka	Marion V. Creekmore Jr., Amb.	W. Susanta de Alwis, Amb.
Sudan	James R. Cheek, Amb.	Abdalla Ahmed Abdalla, Amb.
Suriname	John P. Leonard, Amb.	Willem A. Udenhout, Amb.
Swaziland	Stephen H. Rogers, Amb.	Absalom V. Mamba, Amb.
Sweden	Charles E. Redman, Amb.	Anders I. Thunborg, Amb.
Switzerland	Joseph B. Gildenhorn, Amb.	Edouard Brunner, Amb.
Syria	Edward P. Djerejian, Amb.	Walid Al-Moualem, Amb.
Tanzania	Edward DeJarnette Jr., Amb.	Charles M. Nyirabu, Amb.
Thailand	Daniel A. O' Donohue, Amb.	Vacancy
Togo	Harmon E. Kirby, Amb.	Ellom-Kodjo Schuppius, Amb.
Tonga	Evelyn I.H. Teegen, Amb.	Siosaia Ma'Ulupekotova, Tuita, Amb.
Trinidad and Tobago	Charles A. Gargano, Amb.	Angus A. Khan, Amb.
Tunisia	Robert H. Pelletreau, Jr., Amb.	Ismail Khelil, Amb.
Turkey	Morton I. Abramowitz, Amb.	Nuzhet Kandemir, Amb.
Tuvalu	Evelyn I.H. Teegen, Amb.	Vacancy
Uganda	John A. Burroughs Jr., Amb.	Stephen K. Katenta-Apuli, Amb.
USSR	Robert Strauss, Amb.	Viktor G. Komplektov, Amb.
United Arab Emirates	Edward S. Walker, Amb.	Abdulla Al-Nahayyan, Amb.
United Kingdom	Raymond G.H. Seitz, Amb.	Antony Acland, Amb.
Uruguay	Richard C. Brown, Amb.	Eduardo MacGillycuddy
Vatican	Thomas P. Melady, Amb.	Agostino Cacciavillan, Pro-Nuncio
Venezuela	Michael M. Skol, Amb.	Simon A. Consalvi, Amb.
Western Samoa	Della Newman, Amb.	Tuaopepe F. Wendt, Amb.
Yemen	Charles F. Dunbar, Amb.	Mohsin A. Alaini, Amb.
Yugoslavia	Warren Zimmerman, Amb.	Dzevad Mujezinovic, Amb.
Zaire	William C. Harrop, Amb.	Tatanee Manata, Amb.
Zambia	Gordon L. Streeb, Amb.	Paul J.F. Lusaka, Amb.
Zimbabwe	Vacancy	Stanislaus G. Chigwedere, Amb.

Special Missions

U.S. Mission to North Atlantic Treaty Organization, Brussels—William H. Taft 4th
U.S. Mission to the European Communities, Brussels—Thomas M.T. Niles, Amb.
U.S. Mission to the United Nations, New York—Thomas P. Pickering, Amb.
U.S. Mission to the European Office of the UN, Geneva—Morris B. Abram, Amb.
U.S. Mission to the Organization for Economic Cooperation and Development, Paris—Alan P. Larson, Amb.
U.S. Mission to the Organization of American States, Washington—Luigi R. Einaudi, Amb.

(1) Relations severed in 1939. (2) Post closed in 1975. (3) U.S. embassy closed in 1975. (4) U.S. severed relations in 1978; unofficial relations are maintained. (5) Relations severed in 1961; limited ties restored in 1977. (6) U.S. severed relations on Apr. 7, 1980. (7) U.S. does not officially recognize 1940 annexation by USSR. (8) Embassy closed, May 2, 1980. U.S. closed the Libyan mission, May 6, 1981.

SPORTS IN 1991

Olympic Games Records

The modern Olympic Games, first held in Athens, Greece in 1896, were the result of efforts by Baron Pierre de Coubertin, a French educator, to promote interest in education and culture, also to foster better international understanding through the universal medium of youth's love of athletics.

His source of inspiration for the Olympic Games was the ancient Greek Olympic Games, most notable of the four Panhellenic celebrations. The games were combined patriotic, religious, and athletic festivals held every four years. The first such recorded festival was held in 776 B.C., the date from which the Greeks began to keep their calendar by "Olympiads," or four-year spans between the games.

The first Olympiad is said to have consisted merely of a 200-yard foot race near the small city of Olympia, but the games gained in scope and became demonstrations of national pride. Only Greek citizens — amateurs — were permitted to participate. Winners received laurel, wild olive, and palm wreaths and were accorded many special privileges. Under the Roman emperors, the games deteriorated into professional carnivals and circuses. Emperor Theodosius banned them in 394 A.D.

Baron de Coubertin enlisted 9 nations to send athletes to the first modern Olympics in 1896; now more than 100 nations compete. Winter Olympic Games were started in 1924.

Sites of Olympic Games

1896 Athens	1920 Antwerp	1952 Helsinki	1976 Montreal
1900 Paris	1924 Paris	1956 Melbourne	1980 Moscow
1904 St. Louis	1928 Amsterdam	1960 Rome	1984 Los Angeles
1906 Athens*	1932 Los Angeles	1964 Tokyo	1988 Seoul
1908 London	1936 Berlin	1968 Mexico City	1992 Barcelona
1912 Stockholm	1948 London	1972 Munich	

*Games not recognized by International Olympic Committee. Games 6 (1916), 12 (1940), and 13 (1944) were not celebrated. The 1980 games were boycotted by 62 nations, including the U.S. The 1984 games were boycotted by the USSR and most eastern bloc nations. East and West Germany began competing separately in 1968.

Olympic Games Champions, 1896—1988

(*Indicates Gold Medal-Winning Record)

Track and Field — Men

100-Meter Run

1896	Thomas Burke, United States	12s
1900	Francis W. Jarvis, United States	11.0s
1904	Archie Hahn, United States	11s
1908	Reginald Walker, South Africa	10.8s
1912	Ralph Craig, United States	10.8s
1920	Charles Paddock, United States	10.8s
1924	Harold Abrahams, Great Britain	10.6s
1928	Percy Williams, Canada	10.8s
1932	Eddie Tolan, United States	10.3s
1936	Jesse Owens, United States	10.3s
1948	Harrison Dillard, United States	10.3s
1952	Lindy Remigino, United States	10.4s
1956	Bobby Morrow, United States	10.5s
1960	Armin Hary, Germany	10.2s
1964	Bob Hayes, United States	10.0s
1968	Jim Hines, United States	9.95s
1972	Valery Borzov, USSR	10.14s
1976	Hasely Crawford, Trinidad	10.06s
1980	Allan Wells, Great Britain	10.25s
1984	Carl Lewis, United States	9.99s
1988	Carl Lewis, United States	9.92s*

200-Meter Run

1900	Walter Tewksbury, United States	22.2s
1904	Archie Hahn, United States	21.6s
1908	Robert Kerr, Canada	22.6s
1912	Ralph Craig, United States	21.7s
1920	Allan Woodring, United States	22s
1924	Jackson Scholz, United States	21.6s
1928	Percy Williams, Canada	21.8s
1932	Eddie Tolan, United States	21.2s
1936	Jesse Owens, United States	20.7s
1948	Mel Patton, United States	21.1s
1952	Andrew Stanfield, United States	20.7s
1956	Bobby Morrow, United States	20.6s
1960	Livio Berruti, Italy	20.5s
1964	Henry Carr, United States	20.3s
1968	Tommie Smith, United States	19.83s
1972	Valeri Borzov, USSR	20.00s
1976	Donald Quarrie, Jamaica	20.23s
1980	Pietro Mennea, Italy	20.19s
1984	Carl Lewis, United States	19.80s
1988	Joe DeLoach, United States	19.75s*

400-Meter Run

1896	Thomas Burke, United States	54.2s
1900	Maxey Long, United States	49.4s
1904	Harry Hillman, United States	49.2s
1908	Wyndham Halswelle, Great Britain, walkover	50s
1912	Charles Reidpath, United States	48.2s
1920	Bevil Rudd, South Africa	49.6s
1924	Eric Liddell, Great Britain	47.6s
1928	Ray Barbuti, United States	47.8s
1932	William Carr, United States	46.2s
1936	Archie Williams, United States	46.5s
1948	Arthur Wint, Jamaica, B W I.	46.2s
1952	George Rhoden, Jamaica, B W I.	45.9s
1956	Charles Jenkins, United States	46.7s
1960	Otis Davis, United States	44.9s
1964	Michael Larrabee, United States	45.1s
1968	Lee Evans, United States	43.8s*
1972	Vincent Matthews, United States	44.66s
1976	Alberto Juantorena, Cuba	44.26s
1980	Viktor Markin, USSR	44.60s
1984	Alonzo Babers, United States	44.27s
1988	Steven Lewis, United States	43.87s

800-Meter Run

1896	Edwin Flack, Australia	2m. 11s
1900	Alfred Tysoe, Great Britain	2m. 1.2s
1904	James Lightbody, United States	1m. 56s
1908	Mel Sheppard, United States	1m. 52.8s
1912	James Meredith, United States	1m. 51.9s
1920	Albert Hill, Great Britain	1m. 53.4s
1924	Douglas Lowe, Great Britain	1m. 52.4s
1928	Douglas Lowe, Great Britain	1m. 51.8s
1932	Thomas Hampson, Great Britain	1m. 49.8s
1936	John Woodruff, United States	1m. 52.9s
1948	Mal Whitfield, United States	1m. 49.2s
1952	Mal Whitfield, United States	1m. 49.2s
1956	Thomas Courtney, United States	1m. 47.7s
1960	Peter Snell, New Zealand	1m. 46.3s
1964	Peter Snell, New Zealand	1m. 45.1s
1968	Ralph Doubell, Australia	1m. 44.3s
1972	Dave Wottle, United States	1m. 45.9s
1976	Alberto Juantorena, Cuba	1m. 43.50s
1980	Steve Ovett, Great Britain	1m. 45.40s
1984	Joaquim Cruz, Brazil	1m. 43.00s*
1988	Paul Ereng, Kenya	1m. 43.45s

1,500-Meter Run

1896	Edwin Flack, Australia	4m. 33.2s
1900	Charles Bennett, Great Britain	4m. 6.2s
1904	James Lightbody, United States	4m. 5.4s
1908	Mel Sheppard, United States	4m. 3.4s
1912	Arnold Jackson, Great Britain	3m. 56.8s
1920	Albert Hill, Great Britain	4m. 1.8s
1924	Paavo Nurmi, Finland	3m. 53.6s
1928	Harry Larva, Finland	3m. 53.2s
1932	Luigi Beccali, Italy	3m. 51.2s
1936	Jack Lovelock, New Zealand	3m. 47.8s
1948	Henri Eriksson, Sweden	3m. 49.8s
1952	Joseph Barthel, Luxemburg	3m. 45.2s
1956	Ron Delany, Ireland	3m. 41.2s
1960	Herb Elliott, Australia	3m. 35.6s
1964	Peter Snell, New Zealand	3m. 38.1s
1968	Kipchoge Keino, Kenya	3m. 34.9s
1972	Pekka Vasala, Finland	3m. 36.3s
1976	John Walker, New Zealand	3m. 39.17s
1980	Sebastian Coe, Great Britain	3m. 38.4s
1984	Sebastian Coe, Great Britain	3m. 32.53s*
1988	Peter Rono, Kenya	3m. 35.96s

3,000-Meter Steeplechase

1920	Percy Hodge, Great Britain	10m. 0.4s
1924	Willie Ritola, Finland	9m. 33.6s
1928	Toivo Loukola, Finland	9m. 21.8s
1932	Volmari Iso-Hollo, Finland	10m. 33.4s
	(About 3,450 mtrs. extra lap by error)	
1936	Volmari Iso-Hollo, Finland	9m. 3.8s
1948	Thore Sjoestrand, Sweden	9m. 4.6s
1952	Horace Ashenfelter, United States	8m. 45.4s
1956	Chris Brasher, Great Britain	8m. 41.2s
1960	Zdzislaw Krzyszkowiak, Poland	8m. 34.2s
1964	Gaston Roelants, Belgium	8m. 30.8s
1968	Amos Biwott, Kenya	8m. 51s
1972	Kipchoge Keino, Kenya	8m. 23.6s
1976	Anders Garderud, Sweden	8m. 08.2s
1980	Bronislaw Malinowski, Poland	8m. 09.7s
1984	Julius Korir, Kenya	8m. 11.8s
1988	Julius Kariuki, Kenya	8m. 05.51s*

5,000-Meter Run

1912	Hannes Kolehmainen, Finland	14m. 36.6s
1920	Joseph Guillemot, France	14m. 55.6s
1924	Paavo Nurmi, Finland	14m. 31.2s
1928	Willie Ritola, Finland	14m. 38s
1932	Lauri Lehtinen, Finland	14m. 30s
1936	Gunnar Hockert, Finland	14m. 22.2s
1948	Gaston Reiff, Belgium	14m. 17.6s
1952	Emil Zatopek, Czechoslovakia	14m. 6.6s
1956	Vladimir Kuts, USSR	13m. 39.6s
1960	Murray Halberg, New Zealand	13m. 43.4s
1964	Bob Schul, United States	13m. 48.8s
1968	Mohamed Gammoudi, Tunisia	14m. 05.0s
1972	Lasse Viren, Finland	13m. 26.4s
1976	Lasse Viren, Finland	13m. 24.76s
1980	Miruts Yifter, Ethiopia	13m. 21.0s
1984	Said Aouita, Morocco	13m. 05.59s*
1988	John Ngugi, Kenya	13m. 11.70s

10,000-Meter Run

1912	Hannes Kolehmainen, Finland	31m. 20.8s
1920	Paavo Nurmi, Finland	31m. 45.8s
1924	Willie Ritola, Finland	30m. 23.2s
1928	Paavo Nurmi, Finland	30m. 18.8s
1932	Janusz Kusocinski, Poland	30m. 11.4s
1936	Ilmari Salminen, Finland	30m. 15.4s
1948	Emil Zatopek, Czechoslovakia	29m. 59.6s
1952	Emil Zatopek, Czechoslovakia	29m. 17.0s
1956	Vladimir Kuts, USSR	28m. 45.6s
1960	Pyotr Bolotnikov, USSR	28m. 32.2s
1964	Billy Mills, United States	28m. 24.4s
1968	Naftali Temu, Kenya	29m. 27.4s
1972	Lasse Viren, Finland	27m. 38.4s
1976	Lasse Viren, Finland	27m. 40.38s
1980	Miruts Yifter, Ethiopia	27m. 42.7s
1984	Alberto Cova, Italy	27m. 47.54
1988	Brahim Boutaib, Morocco	27m. 21.46s*

Marathon

1896	Spiridon Loues, Greece	2h. 58m. 50s
1900	Michel Theato, France	2h. 59m. 45s
1904	Thomas Hicks, United States	3h. 28m. 63s
1908	John J. Hayes, United States	2h. 55m. 18.4s
1912	Kenneth McArthur, South Africa	2h. 36m. 54.8s
1920	Hannes Kolehmainen, Finland	2h. 32m. 35.8s
1924	Albin Stenroos, Finland	2h. 41m. 22.6s
1928	A.B. El Ouafi, France	2h. 32m. 57s
1932	Juan Zabala, Argentina	2h. 31m. 36s
1936	Kijung Son, Japan (Korean)	2h. 29m. 19.2s
1948	Delfo Cabrera, Argentina	2h. 34m. 51.6s
1952	Emil Zatopek, Czechoslovakia	2h. 23m. 03.2s
1956	Alain Mimoun, France	2h. 25m.
1960	Abebe Bikila, Ethiopia	2h. 15m. 16.2s
1964	Abebe Bikila, Ethiopia	2h. 12m. 11.2s
1968	Mamo Wolde, Ethiopia	2h. 20m. 26.4s
1972	Frank Shorter, United States	2h. 12m. 19.8s
1976	Waldemar Cierpinski, E. Germany	2h. 09m. 55s
1980	Waldemar Cierpinski, E. Germany	2h. 11m. 03s
1984	Carlos Lopes, Portugal	2h. 09m. 21 s*
1988	Gelindo Bordin, Italy	2h. 10m. 32s

20-Kilometer Walk

1956	Leonid Spirin, USSR	1h. 31m. 27.4s
1960	Vladimir Golubnichy, USSR	1h. 33m. 7.2s
1964	Kenneth Mathews, Great Britain	1h. 29m. 34.0s
1968	Vladimir Golubnichy, USSR	1h. 33m. 58.4s
1972	Peter Frenkel, E. Germany	1h. 26m. 42.4s
1976	Daniel Bautista, Mexico	1h. 24m. 40.6s
1980	Maurizio Damilano, Italy	1h. 23m. 35.5s
1984	Ernesto Canto, Mexico	1h. 23m. 13.0s
1988	Josef Pribilinec, Czech	1h. 19m. 57.0s*

50-Kilometer Walk

1932	Thomas W. Green, Great Britain	4h. 50m. 10s
1936	Harold Whitlock, Great Britain	4h. 30m. 41.4s
1948	John Ljunggren, Sweden	4h. 41m. 52s
1952	Giuseppe Dordoni, Italy	4h. 28m. 07.8s
1956	Norman Read, New Zealand	4h. 30m. 42.8s
1960	Donald Thompson, Great Britain	4h. 25m. 30s
1964	Abdon Pamich, Italy	4h. 11m. 12.4s
1968	Christoph Hohne, E. Germany	4h. 20m. 13.6s
1972	Bern Kannenberg, W. Germany	3h. 56m. 11.6s
1980	Hartwig Gauter, E. Germany	3h. 49m. 24.0s
1984	Raul Gonzalez, Mexico	3h. 47m. 26.0
1988	Vayachselav Ivanenko, USSR	3h. 38m. 29.0s*

110-Meter Hurdles

1896	Thomas Curtis, United States	17.6s
1900	Alvin Kraenzlein, United States	15.4s
1904	Frederick Schule, United States	16s
1908	Forrest Smithson, United States	15s
1912	Frederick Kelly, United States	15.1s
1920	Earl Thomson, Canada	14.8s
1924	Daniel Kinsey, United States	15s
1928	Sydney Atkinson, South Africa	14.8s
1932	George Saling, United States	14.6s
1936	Forrest Towns, United States	14.2s
1948	William Porter, United States	13.9s
1952	Harrison Dillard, United States	13.7s
1956	Lee Calhoun, United States	13.5s
1960	Lee Calhoun, United States	13.8s
1964	Hayes Jones, United States	13.6s
1968	Willie Davenport, United States	13.3s
1972	Rod Milburn, United States	13.24s
1976	Guy Drut, France	13.30s
1980	Thomas Munkelt, E. Germany	13. 39s
1984	Roger Kingdom, United States	13.20s
1988	Roger Kingdom, United States	12.98*

400-Meter Hurdles

1900	J.W.B. Tewksbury, United States	57.6s
1904	Harry Hillman, United States	53s
1908	Charles Bacon, United States	55s
1920	Frank Loomis, United States	54s
1924	F. Morgan Taylor, United States	52.6s
1928	Lord Burghley, Great Britain	53.4s
1932	Robert Tisdall, Ireland	51.7s
1936	Glenn Hardin, United States	52.4s
1948	Roy Cochran, United States	51.1s
1952	Charles Moore, United States	50.8s
1956	Glenn Davis, United States	50.1s
1960	Glenn Davis, United States	49.3s
1964	Rex Cawley, United States	49.6s
1968	Dave Hemery, Great Britain	48.12s
1972	John Akii-Bua, Uganda	47.82s
1976	Edwin Moses, United States	47.64s
1980	Volker Beck, E. Germany	48.70s
1984	Edwin Moses, United States	47.75s
1988	Andre Phillips, United States	47.19s*

High Jump

1896	Ellery Clark, United States	5ft. 11 1-4 in.
1900	Irving Baxter, United States	6ft. 2 4-5 in.
1904	Samuel Jones, United States	5ft. 11 in.
1908	Harry Porter, United States	6ft. 3 in.
1912	Alma Richards, United States	6ft. 4 in.
1920	Richmond Landon, United States	6ft. 4 in.
1924	Harold Osborn, United States	6ft. 6 in.
1928	Robert W. King, United States	6ft. 4 1-2 in.
1932	Duncan McNaughton, Canada	6ft. 5 5-8 in.
1936	Cornelius Johnson, United States	6ft. 8 in.
1948	John L. Winter, Australia	6ft. 6 in.
1952	Walter Davis, United States	6ft. 8.32 in.
1956	Charles Dumas, United States	6ft. 11 1-2 in.
1960	Robert Shavlakadze, USSR	7ft. 1 in.
1964	Valery Brumel, USSR	7ft. 1 3-4 in.
1968	Dick Fosbury, United States	7ft. 4 1-4 in.
1972	Yuri Tarmak, USSR	7ft. 3 3-4 in.
1976	Jacek Wszola, Poland	7ft. 4 1-2 in.
1980	Gerd Wessig, E. Germany	7ft. 8 3-4 in.
1984	Dietmar Mogenburg, W. Germany	7ft. 8 1-2 in.
1988	Guennadi Avdeenko, USSR	7ft 9 1-2 in.*

Long Jump

1896	Ellery Clark, United States	20ft. 10 in.
1900	Alvin Kraenzlein, United States	23ft. 6 3-4 in.
1904	Myer Prinstein, United States	24ft. 1 in.
1908	Frank Irons, United States	24ft. 6 1-2 in.
1912	Albert Gutterson, United States	24ft. 11 1-4 in.
1920	William Petterssen, Sweden	23ft. 5 1-2 in.
1924	DeHart Hubbard, United States	24ft. 5 in.
1928	Edward B. Hamm, United States	25ft. 4 1-2 in.
1932	Edward Gordon, United States	25ft. 3-4 in.
1936	Jesse Owens, United States	26ft. 5 1-2 in.
1948	William Steele, United States	25ft. 8 in.
1952	Jerome Biffle, United States	24ft. 10 in.
1956	Gregory Bell, United States	25ft. 8 1-4 in.
1960	Ralph Boston, United States	26ft. 7 3-4 in.
1964	Lynn Davies, Great Britain	26ft. 5 3-4 in.
1968	Bob Beamon, United States	29ft. 2 1-2 in.*
1972	Randy Williams, United States	27ft. 1-2 in.
1976	Arnie Robinson, United States	27ft. 4 1-2 in.
1980	Lutz Dombrowski, E. Germany	28ft. 1-4 in.
1984	Carl Lewis, United States	28ft. 1-4 in.
1988	Carl Lewis, United States	28ft. 7 1-4 in.

400-Meter Relay

1912	Great Britain	42.4s
1920	United States	42.2s
1924	United States	41s
1928	United States	41s
1932	United States	40s
1936	United States	39.8s
1948	United States	40.6s
1952	United States	40.1s
1956	United States	39.5s
1960	Germany (U.S. disqualified)	39.5s
1964	United States	39.0s
1968	United States	38.2s
1972	United States	38.19s
1976	United States	38.33s
1980	USSR	38.26s
1984	United States	37.83s*
1988	USSR (U.S. disqualified)	38.19s

1,600-Meter Relay

1908	United States	3m. 29.4s
1912	United States	3m. 16.6s
1920	Great Britain	3m. 22.2s
1924	United States	3m. 16s
1928	United States	3m. 14.2s
1932	United States	3m. 8.2s
1936	Great Britain	3m. 9s
1948	United States	3m. 10.4s
1952	Jamaica, B.W.I.	3m. 03.9s
1956	United States	3m. 04.8s
1960	United States	3m. 02.2s
1964	United States	3m. 00.7s
1968	United States	2m. 56.16s*
1972	Kenya	2m. 59.8s
1976	United States	2m. 58.65s
1980	USSR	3m. 01.1s
1984	United States	2m. 57.91 s
1988	United States	2m. 56.16s*

Pole Vault

1896	William Hoyt, United States	10ft. 10 in.
1900	Irving Baxter, United States	10ft. 10 in.
1904	Charles Dvorak, United States	11ft. 5 3-4 in.
1908	A. C. Gilbert, United States	
	Edward Cook Jr., United States	12ft. 2 in.
1912	Harry Babcock, United States	12ft. 11 1-2 in.
1920	Frank Foss, United States	13ft. 5 in.
1924	Lee Barnes, United States	12ft. 11 1-2 in.
1928	Sabin W. Carr, United States	13ft. 9 1-4 in.
1932	William Miller, United States	14ft. 1 3-4 in.
1936	Earle Meadows, United States	14ft. 3 1-4 in.
1948	Guinn Smith, United States	14ft. 1 1-4 in.
1952	Robert Richards, United States	14ft. 11 in.
1956	Robert Richards, United States	14ft. 11 1-2 in.
1960	Don Bragg, United States	15ft. 5 in.
1964	Fred Hansen, United States	16ft. 8 3-4 in.
1968	Bob Seagren, United States	17ft. 8 1-2 in.
1972	Wolfgang Nordwig, E. Germany	18ft. 1-2 in.
1976	Tadeusz Slusarski, Poland	18ft. 1-2 in.
1980	Wladyslaw Kozakiewicz, Poland	18ft. 11 1-2 in.
1984	Pierre Quinon, France	18ft. 10 1-4 in.
1988	Sergei Bubka, USSR	19ft. 9 1-4 in.*

Hammer Throw

1900	John Flanagan, United States	163ft. 1 in.
1904	John Flanagan, United States	168ft. 1 in.
1908	John Flanagan, United States	170ft. 4 1-4 in.
1912	Matt McGrath, United States	179ft. 7 1-8 in.
1920	Pat Ryan, United States	173ft. 5 5-8 in.
1924	Fred Tootell, United States	174ft. 10 1-8 in.
1928	Patrick O'Callaghan, Ireland	168ft. 7 1-2 in.
1932	Patrick O'Callaghan, Ireland	176ft. 11 1-8 in.
1936	Karl Hein, Germany	185ft. 4 in.
1948	Imre Nemeth, Hungary	183ft. 11 1-2 in.
1952	Jozsef Csermak, Hungary	197ft. 11 9-16 in.
1956	Harold Connolly, United States	207ft. 3 1-2 in.
1960	Vasily Rudenkov, USSR	220ft. 1 5-8 in.
1964	Romuald Klim, USSR	228ft. 9 1-2 in.
1968	Gyula Zsivotsky, Hungary	240ft. 8 in.
1972	Anatoli Bondarchuk, USSR	247ft. 8 in.
1976	Yuri Syedykh, USSR	254ft. 4 in.
1980	Yuri Syedykh, USSR	268ft. 4 1-2 in.
1984	Juha Tiainen, Finland	256ft. 2 in.
1988	Sergei Litinov, USSR	278ft. 2 1-2 in.*

Discus Throw

1896	Robert Garrett, United States	95ft. 7 1-2 in.
1900	Rudolf Bauer, Hungary	118ft. 3 in.
1904	Martin Sheridan, United States	128ft. 10 1-2 in.
1908	Martin Sheridan, United States	134ft. 2 in.
1912	Armas Taipale, Finland	148ft. 3 in.
	Both hands—Armas Taipale, Finland	271ft. 10 1-4 in.
1920	Elmer Niklander, Finland	146ft. 7 in.
1924	Clarence Houser, United States	151ft. 4 in.
1928	Clarence Houser, United States	155ft. 3 in.
1932	John Anderson, United States	162ft. 4 in.
1936	Ken Carpenter, United States	165ft. 7 in.
1948	Adolfo Consolini, Italy	173ft. 2 in.
1952	Sim Iness, United States	180ft. 6.85 in.
1956	Al Oerter, United States	184ft. 10 1-2 in.
1960	Al Oerter, United States	194ft. 2 in.
1964	Al Oerter, United States	200ft. 1 1-2 in.
1968	Al Oerter, United States	212ft. 6 1-2 in.
1972	Ludvik Danek, Czechoslovakia	211ft. 3 in.
1976	Mac Wilkins, United States	221ft. 5.4 in.
1980	Viktor Rashchupkin, USSR	218ft. 8 in.
1984	Rolf Dannenberg, W. Germany	218ft. 6 in.
1988	Jurgen Schult, E. Germany	225ft. 9 1-4 in.*

Triple Jump

1896	James Connolly, United States	44ft. 11 3-4 in.
1900	Myer Prinstein, United States	47ft. 5 3-4 in.
1904	Myer Prinstein, United States	47 ft.
1908	Timothy Ahearne, Great Britain, Ireland	48ft. 11 1-4 in.
1912	Gustaf Lindblom, Sweden	48ft. 5 1-4 in.
1920	Vilho Tuulos, Finland	47ft. 7 in.
1924	Anthony Winter, Australia	50ft. 11 1-4 in.
1928	Mikio Oda, Japan	49ft. 11 in.
1932	Chuhei Nambu, Japan	51ft. 7 in.
1936	Naoto Tajima, Japan	52ft. 6 in.
1948	Arne Ahman, Sweden	50ft. 6 1-4 in.
1952	Adhemar da Silva, Brazil	53ft. 2 3-4 in.
1956	Adhemar da Silva, Brazil	53ft. 7 3-4 in.
1960	Jozef Schmidt, Poland	55ft. 2 in.
1964	Jozef Schmidt, Poland	55ft. 3 1-2 in.

(continued)

1968	Viktor Saneev, USSR	57ft. 3-4 in.
1972	Viktor Saneev, USSR	56ft. 11 in.
1976	Viktor Saneev, USSR	56ft. 8 3-4 in.
1980	Jaak Uudmae, USSR	56ft. 11 1-4 in.
1984	Al Joyner, United States	56ft. 7 1-2 in.
1988	Hristo Markov, Bulgaria	57ft. 9 1-4 in.*

16-lb. Shot Put

1896	Robert Garrett, United States	36ft. 9 3-4 in.
1900	Richard Sheldon, United States	46ft. 3 1-4 in.
1904	Ralph Rose, United States	48ft. 7 in.
1908	Ralph Rose, United States	46ft. 7 1-2 in.
1912	Pat McDonald, United States	50ft. 4 in.
	Both hands—Ralph Rose, United States	90ft. 5 1-2 in.
1920	Ville Porhola, Finland	48ft. 1 1-4 in.
1924	Clarence Houser, United States	49ft. 2 1-4 in.
1928	John Kuck, United States	52ft. 3-4 in.
1932	Leo Sexton, United States	52ft. 6 in.
1936	Hans Woellke, Germany	53ft. 1 3-4 in.
1948	Wilbur Thompson, United States	56ft. 2 in.
1952	Parry O'Brien, United States	57ft. 1 1-2 in.
1956	Parry O'Brien, United States	60ft. 11 1-4 in.
1960	William Nieder, United States	64ft. 6 3-4 in.
1964	Dallas Long, United States	66ft. 8 1-2 in.
1968	Randy Matson, United States	67ft. 4 3-4 in.
1972	Wladyslaw Komar, Poland	69ft. 6 in.
1976	Udo Beyer, E. Germany	69ft. 3-4 in.
1980	Vladimir Kiselyov, USSR	70ft. 1-2 in.
1984	Alessandro Andrei, Italy	69ft. 9 in.
1988	Ulf Timmermann, E. Germany	73ft. 8 3-4 in.*

Javelin

1908	Erik Lemming, Sweden	178ft. 7 1-2 in.
	Held in middle—Erik Lemming, Sweden	179ft. 10 1-2 in.
1912	Erik Lemming, Sweden	198ft. 11 1-4 in.
	Both hands, Julius Saaristo, Finland	358ft. 11 7-8 in.
1920	Jonni Myyra, Finland	215ft. 9 3-4 in.
1924	Jonni Myyra, Finland	206ft. 6 3-4 in.
1928	Eric Lundkvist, Sweden	218ft. 6 1-8 in.

1932	Matti Jarvinen, Finland	238ft. 6 in.
1936	Gerhard Stoeck, Germany	235ft. 8 5-16 in.
1948	Tapio Rautavaara, Finland	228ft. 10 1-2 in.
1952	Cy Young, United States	242ft. 0.79 in.
1956	Egil Danielson, Norway	281ft. 2 1-4 in.
1960	Viktor Tsibulenko, USSR	277ft. 8 3-8 in.
1964	Pauli Nevala, Finland	271ft. 2 1-2 in.
1968	Janis Lusis, USSR	295ft. 7 1-4 in.
1972	Klaus Wolfermann, W. Germany	296ft. 10 in.
1976	Miklos Nemeth, Hungary	310ft. 4 in.*
1980	Dainis Kula, USSR	299ft. 2 3-8 in.
1984	Arto Haerkoenen, Finland	284ft. 8 in.
1988	Tapio Korjus, Finland	276ft. 6 in.

Decathlon

1912	Hugo Wieslander, Sweden	7,724.49 pts.(a)
1920	Helge Lovland, Norway	6,804.35 pts.
1924	Harold Osborn, United States	7,710.77 pts.
1928	Paavo Yrjola, Finland	8,053.29 pts.
1932	James Bausch, United States	8,462.23 pts.
1936	Glenn Morris, United States	7,900 pts.
1948	Robert Mathias, United States	7,139 pts.
1952	Robert Mathias, United States	7,887 pts.
1956	Milton Campbell, United States	7,937 pts.
1960	Rafer Johnson, United States	8,392 pts.
1964	Willi Holdorf, Germany	7,887 pts.(c)
1968	Bill Toomey, United States	8,193 pts.
1972	Nikolai Avilov, USSR	8,454 pts.
1976	Bruce Jenner, United States	8,617 pts.
1980	Daley Thompson, Great Britain	8,495 pts.
1984	Daley Thompson, Great Britain	8,798 pts.*(b)
1988	Christian Schenk, E. Germany	8,488 pts.

(a) Jim Thorpe of the U.S. won the 1912 Decathlon with 8,413 pts. but was disqualified and had to return his medals because he had played professional baseball prior to the Olympic games. The medals were restored posthumously in 1982. (b) Scoring change effective Apr., 1985. (c) Former point systems used prior to 1964.

Track and Field—Women

100-Meter Run

1928	Elizabeth Robinson, United States	12.2s
1932	Stella Walsh, Poland	11.9s
1936	Helen Stephens, United States	11.5s
1948	Francina Blankers-Koen, Netherlands	11.9s
1952	Marjorie Jackson, Australia	11.5s
1956	Betty Cuthbert, Australia	11.5s
1960	Wilma Rudolph, United States	11.0s
1964	Wyomia Tyus, United States	11.4s
1968	Wyomia Tyus, United States	11.0s
1972	Renate Stecher, E. Germany	11.07s
1976	Annegret Richter, W. Germany	11.08s
1980	Lyudmila Kondratyeva, USSR	11.6s
1984	Evelyn Ashford, United States	10.97s
1988	Florence Griffith-Joyner, United States	10.54s*

200-Meter Run

1948	Francina Blankers-Koen, Netherlands	24.4s
1952	Marjorie Jackson, Australia	23.7s
1956	Betty Cuthbert, Australia	23.4s
1960	Wilma Rudolph, United States	24.0s
1964	Edith McGuire, United States	23.0s
1968	Irena Szewinska, Poland	22.5s
1972	Renate Stecher, E. Germany	22.40s
1976	Barbel Eckert, E. Germany	22.37s
1980	Barbel Wockel, E. Germany	22.03
1984	Valerie Brisco-Hooks, United States	21.81s
1988	Florence Griffith-Joyner, United States	21.34s*

400-Meter Run

1964	Betty Cuthbert, Australia	52s
1968	Colette Besson, France	52s
1972	Monika Zehrt, E. Germany	51.08s
1976	Irena Szewinska, Poland	49.29s
1980	Marita Koch, E. Germany	48.88s
1984	Valerie Brisco-Hooks, United States	48.83s
1988	Olga Bryzgina, USSR	48.65s*

800-Meter Run

1928	Lina Radke, Germany	2m. 16.8s
1960	Ludmila Shevtsova, USSR	2m. 4.3s
1964	Ann Packer, Great Britain	2m. 1.1s

1968	Madeline Manning, United States	2m. 0.9s
1972	Hildegard Falck, W. Germany	1m. 58.6s
1976	Tatyana Kazankina, USSR	1m. 54.94s
1980	Nadezhda Olizaryenko, USSR	1m. 53.5s*
1984	Doina Melinte, Romania	1m. 57.6s
1988	Sigrun Wodars, E. Germany	1m. 56.10s

1,500-Meter Run

1972	Lyudmila Bragina, USSR	4m. 01.4s
1976	Tatyana Kazankina, USSR	4m. 05.48s
1980	Tatyana Kazankina, USSR	3m. 56.6s
1984	Gabriella Dorio, Italy	4m. 03.25s
1988	Paula Ivan, Romania	3m. 53.96s*

3,000-Meter Run

1984	Maricica Puica, Romania	8:35.96s
1988	Tatyana Samolenko, USSR	8:26.53s*

10,000-Meter Run

1988	Olga Boldarenko, USSR	31m. 44.69s*

400-Meter Relay

1928	Canada	48.4s
1932	United States	46.9s
1936	United States	46.9s
1948	Netherlands	47.5s
1952	United States	45.9s
1956	Australia	44.5s
1960	United States	44.5s
1964	Poland	43.6s
1968	United States	42.8s
1972	West Germany	42.81s
1976	East Germany	42.55s
1980	East Germany	41.60s*
1984	United States	41.65s
1988	United States	41.98s

1,600-Meter Relay

1972	East Germany	3m. 23s
1976	East Germany	3m. 19.23s

1980	USSR	3m. 20.02s
1984	United States	3m. 18.29s
1988	USSR	3 m. 15.18s*

80-Meter Hurdles

1932	"Babe" Didrikson, United States	11.7s
1936	Trebisonda Valla, Italy	11.7s
1948	Francina Blankers-Koen, Netherlands	11.2s
1952	Shirley Strickland de la Hunty, Australia	10.9s
1956	Shirley Strickland de la Hunty, Australia	10.7s
1960	Irina Press, USSR	10.8s
1964	Karin Balzer, Germany	10.5s
1968	Maureen Caird, Australia	10.3s*

100-Meter Hurdles

1972	Annelie Ehrhardt, E. Germany	12.59s
1976	Johanna Schaller, E. Germany	12.77s
1980	Vera Komisova, USSR	12.56s
1984	Benita Brown-Fitzgerald, United States	12.84s
1988	Jordanka Donkova, Bulgaria	12.38s*

400-Meter Hurdles

1984	Nawal el Moutawakii, Morocco	54.61s
1988	Debra Flintoff-King, Australia	53.17s*

10,000-Meter Run

1988	Olga Boldarenko, USSR	31m. 44.69s*

Heptathlon

1984	Glynis Nunn, Australia	6,390 pts.
1988	Jackie Joyner-Kersee, United States	7,215 pts.*

High Jump

1928	Ethel Catherwood, Canada	5ft. 2 1-2 in.
1932	Jean Shiley, United States	5ft. 5 1-4 in.
1936	Ibolya Csak, Hungary	5ft. 3 in.
1948	Alice Coachman, United States	5ft. 6 1-8 in.
1952	Esther Brand, South Africa	5ft. 5 3-4 in.
1956	Mildred L. McDaniel, United States	5ft. 9 1-4 in.
1960	Iolanda Balas, Romania	6ft. 3-4 in.
1964	Iolanda Balas, Romania	6ft. 2 3-4 in.
1968	Miloslava Reskova, Czechoslovakia	5ft. 11 1-2 in.
1972	Ulrike Meyfarth, W. Germany	6ft. 4 in.
1976	Rosemarie Ackermann, E. Germany	6ft. 3 3-4 in.
1980	Sara Simeoni, Italy	6ft. 5 1-2 in.
1984	Ulrike Meyfarth, W. Germany	6ft. 7 1-2 in.
1988	Louise Ritter, United States	6ft. 8 in.*

Discus Throw

1928	Helena Konopacka, Poland	129ft. 11 3-4 in.
1932	Lillian Copeland, United States	133ft. 2 in.
1936	Gisela Mauermayer, Germany	156ft. 3 in.
1948	Micheline Ostermeyer, France	137ft. 6 1-2 in.
1952	Nina Romaschkova, USSR	168ft. 8 in.
1956	Olga Fikotova, Czechoslovakia	176ft. 1 in.
1960	Nina Ponomareva, USSR	180ft. 8 1-4 in.
1964	Tamara Press, USSR	187ft. 10 in.
1968	Lia Manoliu, Romania	191ft. 2 in.
1972	Faina Melnik, USSR	218ft. 7 in.
1976	Evelin Schlaak, E. Germany	226ft. 4 in.
1980	Evelin Jahl, E. Germany	229ft. 6 in.
1984	Ria Stalman, Netherlands	214ft. 5 in.
1988	Martina Hellmann, E. Germany	237ft. 2 1-4 in.*

Javelin Throw

1932	"Babe" Didrikson, United States	143ft. 4 in.
1936	Tilly Fleischer, Germany	148ft. 2 3-4 in.
1948	Herma Bauma, Austria	149ft. 6 in.
1952	Dana Zatopkova, Czechoslovakia	165ft. 7 in.
1956	Inese Jaunzeme, USSR	176ft. 8 in.
1960	Elvira Ozolina, USSR	183ft. 8 in.
1964	Mihaela Penes, Romania	198ft. 7 1-2 in.
1968	Angela Nemeth, Hungary	198ft. 1-2 in.
1972	Ruth Fuchs, E. Germany	209ft. 7 in.
1976	Ruth Fuchs, E. Germany	216ft. 4 in.
1980	Maria Colon, Cuba	224ft. 5 in.
1984	Tessa Sanderson, Great Britain	228ft. 2 in.
1988	Petra Felke, E. Germany	245ft.*

Shot Put (8lb., 13oz.)

1948	Micheline Ostermeyer, France	45ft. 1 1-2 in.
1952	Galina Zybina, USSR	50ft. 1 3-4 in.
1956	Tamara Tishkyevich, USSR	54ft. 5 in.
1960	Tamara Press, USSR	56ft. 10 in.
1964	Tamara Press, USSR	59ft. 6 1-4 in.
1968	Margitta Gummel, E. Germany	64ft. 4 in.
1972	Nadezhda Chizova, USSR	69ft.
1976	Ivanka Hristova, Bulgaria	69ft. 5 1-4 in.
1980	Ilona Slupianek, E. Germany	73ft. 6 1-4 in.*
1984	Claudia Losch, W. Germany	67ft. 2 1-4 in.
1988	Natalya Lisovskaya, USSR	72ft. 11 1-2 in.

Long Jump

1948	Olga Gyarmati, Hungary	18ft. 8 1-4 in.
1952	Yvette Williams, New Zealand	20ft. 5 3-4 in.
1956	Elzbieta Krzesinska, Poland	20ft. 9 3-4 in.
1960	Vyera Krepkina, USSR	20ft. 10 3-4 in.
1964	Mary Rand, Great Britain	22ft. 2 1-4 in.
1968	Viorica Viscopoleanu, Romania	22ft. 4 1-2 in.
1972	Heidemarie Rosendahl, W. Germany	22ft. 3 in.
1976	Angela Voigt, E. Germany	22ft. 3-4 in.
1980	Tatyana Kolpakova, USSR	23ft. 2 in.
1984	Anisoara Stanciu, Romania	22ft. 10 in.
1988	Jackie Joyner-Kersee, United States	24ft 3 1-2 in.*

Marathon

1984	Joan Benoit, United States	2h. 24m. 52s*
1988	Rosa Mota, Portugal	2h. 25m. 40s

Swimming—Men

50-Meter Freestyle

1988	Matt Biondi, U.S.	22.14*

100-Meter Freestyle

1896	Alfred Hajos, Hungary	1:22.2
1904	Zoltan de Halmay, Hungary (100 yards)	1:02.8
1908	Charles Daniels, U.S.	1:05.6
1912	Duke P. Kahanamoku, U.S.	1:03.4
1920	Duke P. Kahanamoku, U.S.	1:01.4
1924	John Weissmuller, U.S.	59.0
1928	John Weissmuller, U.S.	58.6
1932	Yasuji Miyazaki, Japan	58.2
1936	Ferenc Csik, Hungary	57.6
1948	Wally Ris, U.S.	57.3
1952	Clark Scholes, U.S.	57.4
1956	Jon Henricks, Australia	55.4
1960	John Devitt, Australia	55.2
1964	Don Schollander, U.S.	53.4
1968	Mike Wenden, Australia	52.2
1972	Mark Spitz, U.S.	51.22
1976	Jim Montgomery, U.S.	49.99
1980	Jorg Woithe, E. Germany	50.40
1984	Rowdy Gaines, U.S.	49.80
1988	Matt Biondi, United States	48.63*

200-Meter Freestyle

1968	Mike Wenden, Australia	1:55.2
1972	Mark Spitz, U.S.	1:52.78
1976	Bruce Furniss, U.S.	1:50.29
1980	Sergei Kopliakov, USSR	1:49.81
1984	Michael Gross, W. Germany	1:47.44
1988	Duncan Armstrong, Australia	1:47.25*

400-Meter Freestyle

1904	C. M. Daniels, U.S. (440 yards)	6:16.2
1908	Henry Taylor, Great Britain	5:36.8
1912	George Hodgson, Canada	5:24.4
1920	Norman Ross, U.S.	5:26.8
1924	John Weissmuller, U.S.	5:04.2
1928	Albert Zorilla, Argentina	5:01.6
1932	Clarence Crabbe, U.S.	4:48.4
1936	Jack Medica, U.S.	4:44.5
1948	William Smith, U.S.	4:41.0
1952	Jean Boiteux, France	4:30.7
1956	Murray Rose, Australia	4:27.3
1960	Murray Rose, Australia	4:18.3
1964	Don Schollander, U.S.	4:12.2
1968	Mike Burton, U.S.	4:09.0
1972	Brad Cooper, Australia	4:00.27
1976	Brian Goodell, U.S.	3:51.93

(continued)

1980	Vladimir Salnikov, USSR	3:51.31
1984	George DiCarlo, U.S.	3:51.23
1988	Ewe Dassler, E. Germany	3:46.95*

1,500-Meter Freestyle

1908	Henry Taylor, Great Britain	22:48.4
1912	George Hodgson, Canada	22:00.0
1920	Norman Ross, U.S.	22:23.2
1924	Andrew Charlton, Australia	20:06.6
1928	Arne Borg, Sweden	19:51.8
1932	Kusuo Kitamura, Japan	19:12.4
1936	Noboru Terada, Japan	19:13.7
1948	James McLane, U.S.	19:18.5
1952	Ford Konno, U.S.	18:30.3
1956	Murray Rose, Australia	17:58.9
1960	Jon Konrads, Australia	17:19.6
1964	Robert Windle, Australia	17:01.7
1968	Mike Burton, U.S.	16:38.9
1972	Mike Burton, U.S.	15:52.58
1976	Brian Goodell, U.S.	15:02.40
1980	Vladimir Salnikov, USSR.	14:58.27*
1984	Michael O'Brien, U.S.	15:05.20
1988	Vladimir Salnikov, USSR	15:00.40

400-Meter Medley Relay

1960	United States	4:05.4
1964	United States	3:58.4
1968	United States	3:54.9
1972	United States	3:48.16
1976	United States	3:42.22
1980	Australia	3:45.70
1984	United States	3:39.30
1988	United States	3:36.93*

400-Meter Freestyle Relay

1964	United States	3:31.2
1968	United States	3:31.7
1972	United States	3:26.42
1984	United States	3:19.03
1988	United States	3:16.53*

800-Meter Freestyle Relay

1908	Great Britain	10:55.6
1912	Australia	10:11.6
1920	United States	10:04.4
1924	United States	9:53.4
1928	United States	9:36.2
1932	Japan	8:58.4
1936	Japan	8:51.5
1948	United States	8:46.0
1952	United States	8:31.1
1956	Australia	8:23.6
1960	United States	8:10.2
1964	United States	7:52.1
1968	United States	7:52.33
1972	United States	7:35.78
1976	United States	7:23.22
1980	USSR	7:23.50
1984	United States	7:15.69
1988	United States	7:12.51*

100-Meter Backstroke

1904	Walter Brack, Germany (100 yds.)	1:16.8
1908	Arno Bieberstein, Germany	1:24.6
1912	Harry Hebner, U.S.	1:21.2
1920	Warren Kealoha, U.S.	1:15.2
1924	Warren Kealoha, U.S.	1:13.2
1928	George Kojac, U.S.	1:08.2
1932	Masaji Kiyokawa, Japan	1:08.6
1936	Adolph Kiefer, U.S.	1:05.9
1948	Allen Stack, U.S.	1:06.4
1952	Yoshi Oyakawa, U.S.	1:05.4
1956	David Thiele, Australia	1:02.2
1960	David Thiele, Australia	1:01.9
1968	Roland Matthes, E. Germany	58.7
1972	Roland Matthes, E. Germany	56.58
1976	John Naber, U.S.	55.49
1980	Bengt Baron, Sweden	56.33
1984	Rick Carey, U.S.	55.79
1988	Daichi Suzuki, Japan	55.05*

200-Meter Backstroke

1964	Jed Graef, U.S.	2:10.3
1968	Roland Matthes, E. Germany	2:09.6
1972	Roland Matthes, E. Germany	2:02.82
1976	John Naber, U.S.	1:59.19*

1980	Sandor Wladar, Hungary	2:01.93
1984	Rick Carey, U.S.	2:00.23
1988	Igor Polianski, USSR	1:59.37

100-Meter Breaststroke

1968	Don McKenzie, U.S.	1:07.7
1972	Nobutaka Taguchi, Japan	1:04.94
1976	John Hencken, U.S.	1:03.11
1980	Duncan Goodhew, Great Britain	1:03.44
1984	Steve Lundquist, U.S.	1:01.65*
1988	Adrian Moorhouse, Great Britain	1:02.04

200-Meter Breaststroke

1908	Frederick Holman, Great Britain	3:09.2
1912	Walter Bathe, Germany	3:01.8
1920	Haken Malmroth, Sweden	3:04.4
1924	Robert Skelton, U.S.	2:56.6
1928	Yoshiyuki Tsuruta, Japan	2:48.8
1932	Yoshiyuki Tsuruta, Japan	2:45.4
1936	Tetsuo Hamuro, Japan	2:41.5
1948	Joseph Verdeur, U.S.	2:39.3
1952	John Davies, Australia	2:34.4
1956	Masura Furukawa, Japan	2:34.7
1960	William Mulliken, U.S.	2:37.4
1964	Ian O'Brien, Australia	2:27.8
1968	Felipe Munoz, Mexico	2:28.7
1972	John Hencken, U.S.	2:21.55
1976	David Wilkie, Great Britain	2:15.11
1980	Robertas Zhulpa, USSR	2:15.85
1984	Victor Davis, Canada	2:13.34*
1988	Jozsef Szabo, Hungary	2:13.52

100-Meter Butterfly

1968	Doug Russell, U.S.	55.9
1972	Mark Spitz, U.S.	54.27
1976	Matt Vogel, U.S.	54.35
1980	Par Arvidsson, Sweden	54.92
1984	Michael Gross, W. Germany	53.08
1988	Anthony Nesty, Suriname	53.00*

200-Meter Butterfly

1956	William Yorzyk, U.S.	2:19.3
1960	Michael Troy, U.S.	2:12.8
1964	Kevin J. Berry, Australia	2:06.6
1968	Carl Robie, U.S.	2:08.7
1972	Mark Spitz, U.S.	2:00.70
1976	Mike Bruner, U.S.	1:59.23
1980	Sergei Fesenko, USSR	1:59.76
1984	Jon Sieben, Australia	1:57.04
1988	Michael Gross, W. Germany	1:56.94*

200-Meter Individual Medley

1968	Charles Hickcox, U.S.	2:12.0
1972	Gunnar Larsson, Sweden.	2:07.17
1984	Alex Baumann, Canada.	2:01.42
1988	Tamas Darnyi, Hungary	2:00.17*

400-Meter Individual Medley

1964	Dick Roth, U.S.	4:45.4
1968	Charles Hickcox, U.S.	4:48.4
1972	Gunnar Larsson, Sweden.	4:31.98
1976	Rod Strachan, U.S.	4:23.68
1980	Aleksandr Sidorenko, USSR	4:22.89
1984	Alex Baumann, Canada.	4:17.41
1988	Tamas Darnyi, Hungary	4:14.75*

Springboard Diving — Points

1908	Albert Zurner, Germany	85.5
1912	Paul Guenther, Germany	79.23
1920	Louis Kuehn, U.S.	675.40
1924	Albert White, U.S.	97.46
1928	Pete Desjardins, U.S.	185.04
1932	Michael Galitzen, U.S.	161.38
1936	Richard Degener, U.S.	163.57
1948	Bruce Harlan, U.S.	163.64
1952	David Browning, U.S.	205.29
1956	Robert Clotworthy, U.S.	159.56
1960	Gary Tobian, U.S.	170.00
1964	Kenneth Sitzberger, U.S.	159.90
1968	Bernie Wrightson, U.S.	170.15
1972	Vladimir Vasin, USSR	594.09
1976	Phil Boggs, U.S.	619.52
1980	Aleksandr Portnov, USSR.	905.02
1984	Greg Louganis, U.S.	754.41
1988	Greg Louganis, U.S.	730.80

	Platform Diving	Points
1904	Dr. G.E. Sheldon, U.S.	12.75
1908	Hjalmar Johansson, Sweden	83.75
1912	Erik Adlerz, Sweden	73.94
1920	Clarence Pinkston, U.S.	100.67
1924	Albert White, U.S.	97.46
1928	Pete Desjardins, U.S.	98.74
1932	Harold Smith, U.S.	124.80
1936	Marshall Wayne, U.S.	113.58
1948	Sammy Lee, U.S.	130.05
1952	Sammy Lee, U.S.	156.28
1956	Joaquin Capilla, Mexico	152.44
1960	Robert Webster, U.S.	165.56
1964	Robert Webster, U.S.	148.58
1968	Klaus Dibiasi, Italy	164.18
1972	Klaus Dibiasi, Italy	504.12
1976	Klaus Dibiasi, Italy	600.51
1980	Falk Hoffmann, E. Germany	835.65
1984	Greg Louganis, U.S.	710.91
1988	Greg Louganis, U.S.	638.61

Swimming—Women

50-Meter Freestyle
1988	Kristin Otto, E. Germany	25.49*

100-Meter Freestyle
1912	Fanny Durack, Australia	1:22.2
1920	Ethelda Bleibtrey, U.S.	1:13.6
1924	Ethel Lackie, U.S.	1:12.4
1928	Albina Osipowich, U.S.	1:11.0
1932	Helene Madison, U.S.	1:06.8
1936	Hendrika Mastenbroek, Holland	1:05.9
1948	Greta Andersen, Denmark	1:06.3
1952	Katalin Szoke, Hungary	1:06.8
1956	Dawn Fraser, Australia	1:02.0
1960	Dawn Fraser, Australia	1:01.2
1964	Dawn Fraser, Australia	59.5
1968	Jan Henne, U.S.	1:00.0
1972	Sandra Neilson, U.S.	58.59
1976	Kornelia Ender, E. Germany	55.65
1980	Barbara Krause, E. Germany	54.79*
1984	(tie) Carrie Steinseifer, U.S.	55.92
	Nancy Hogshead, U.S.	55.92
1988	Kristin Otto, E. Germany	54.93

200-Meter Freestyle
1968	Debbie Meyer, U.S.	2:10.5
1972	Shane Gould, Australia	2:03.56
1976	Kornelia Ender, E. Germany	1:59.26
1980	Barbara Krause, E. Germany	1:58.33
1984	Mary Wayte, U.S.	1:59.23
1988	Heike Friedrich, E. Germany	1:57.65*

400-Meter Freestyle
1924	Martha Norelius, U.S.	6:02.2
1928	Martha Norelius, U.S.	5:42.8
1932	Helene Madison, U.S.	5:28.5
1936	Hendrika Mastenbroek, Netherlands	5:26.4
1948	Ann Curtis, U.S.	5:17.8
1952	Valerie Gyenge, Hungary	5:12.1
1956	Lorraine Crapp, Australia	4:54.6
1960	Susan Chris von Saltza, U.S.	4:50.6
1964	Virginia Duenkel, U.S.	4:43.3
1968	Debbie Meyer, U.S.	4:31.8
1972	Shane Gould, Australia	4:19.44
1976	Petra Thuemer E. Germany	4:09.89
1980	Ines Diers, E. Germany	4:08.76
1984	Tiffany Cohen, U.S.	4:07.10
1988	Janet Evans, U.S.	4:03.85*

800-Meter Freestyle
1968	Debbie Meyer, U.S.	9:24.0
1972	Keena Rothhammer, U.S.	8:53.68
1976	Petra Thuemer, E. Germany	8:37.14
1980	Michelle Ford, Australia	8:28.90
1984	Tiffany Cohen, U.S.	8:24.95
1988	Janet Evans, U.S.	8:20.20*

100-Meter Backstroke
1924	Sybil Bauer, U.S.	1:23.2
1928	Marie Braun, Netherlands	1:22.0
1932	Eleanor Holm, U.S.	1:19.4
1936	Dina Senff, Netherlands	1:18.9
1948	Karen Harup, Denmark	1:14.4
1952	Joan Harrison, South Africa	1:14.3
1956	Judy Grinham, Great Britain	1:12.9
1960	Lynn Burke, U.S.	1:09.3
1964	Cathy Ferguson, U.S.	1:07.7
1968	Kaye Hall, U.S.	1:06.2
1972	Melissa Belote, U.S.	1:05.78
1976	Ulrike Richter, E. Germany	1:01.83
1980	Rica Reinisch, E. Germany	1:00.86*
1984	Theresa Andrews, U.S.	1:02.55
1988	Kristin Otto, E. Germany	1:00.89

200-Meter Backstroke
1968	Pokey Watson, U.S.	2:24.8
1972	Melissa Belote, U.S.	2:19.19
1976	Ulrike Richter, E. Germany	2:13.43
1980	Rica Reinisch, E. Germany	2:11.77
1984	Jolanda De Rover, Netherlands	2:12.38
1988	Krisztina Egerszegi, Hungary	2:09.29*

100-Meter Breaststroke
1968	Djurdjica Bjedov, Yugoslavia	1:15.8
1972	Cathy Carr, U.S.	1:13.58
1976	Hannelore Anke, E. Germany	1:11.16
1980	Ute Geweniger, E. Germany	1:10.22
1984	Petra Van Staveren, Netherlands	1:09.88
1988	Tania Dangalakova, Bulgaria	1:07.95*

200-Meter Breaststroke
1924	Lucy Morton, Great Britain	3:33.2
1928	Hilde Schrader, Germany	3:12.6
1932	Clare Dennis, Australia	3:06.3
1936	Hideko Maehata, Japan	3:03.6
1948	Nelly Van Vliet, Netherlands	2:57.2
1952	Eva Szekely, Hungary	2:51.7
1956	Ursula Happe, Germany	2:53.1
1960	Anita Lonsbrough, Great Britain	2:49.5
1964	Galina Prozumenschikova, USSR	2:46.4
1968	Sharon Wichman, U.S.	2:44.4
1972	Beverly Whitfield, Australia	2:41.71
1976	Marina Koshevaia, USSR	2:33.35
1980	Lina Kachushite, USSR	2:29.54
1984	Anne Ottenbrite, Canada	2:30.38
1988	Silke Hoerner, E. Germany	2:26.71*

200-Meter Individual Medley
1968	Claudia Kolb, U.S.	2:24.7
1972	Shane Gould, Australia	2:23.07
1984	Tracy Caulkins, U.S.	2:12.64
1988	Daniela Hunger, E. Germany	2:12.59*

400-Meter Individual Medley
1964	Donna de Varona, U.S.	5:18.7
1968	Claudia Kolb, U.S.	5:08.5
1972	Gail Neall, Australia	5:02.97
1976	Ulrike Tauber, E. Germany	4:42.77
1980	Petra Schneider, E. Germany	4:36.29*
1984	Tracy Caulkins, U.S.	4:39.24
1988	Janet Evans, U.S.	4:37.76

100-Meter Butterfly
1956	Shelley Mann, U.S.	1:11.0
1960	Carolyn Schuler, U.S.	1:09.5
1964	Sharon Stouder, U.S.	1:04.7
1968	Lynn McClements, Australia	1:05.5
1972	Mayumi Aoki, Japan	1:03.34
1976	Kornelia Ender, E. Germany	1:00.13
1980	Caren Metschuck, E. Germany	1:00.42
1984	Mary T. Meagher, U.S.	59.26
1988	Kristin Otto, E. Germany	59.00*

200-Meter Butterfly
1968	Ada Kok, Netherlands	2:24.7
1972	Karen Moe, U.S.	2:15.57
1976	Andrea Pollack, E. Germany	2:11.41
1980	Ines Geissler, E. Germany	2:10.44
1984	Mary T. Meagher, U.S.	2:06.90*
1988	Kathleen Nord, E. Germany	2:09.51

400-Meter Medley Relay
1960	United States	4:41.1
1960	United States	4:33.9
1968	United States	4:28.3

(continued)

1972	United States	4:20.75
1976	East Germany	4:07.95
1980	East Germany	4:06.67
1984	United States	4:08.34
1988	E. Germany	4:03.74*

400-Meter Freestyle Relay

1912	Great Britain	5:52.8
1920	United States	5:11.6
1924	United States	4:58.8
1928	United States	4:47.6
1932	United States	4:38.0
1936	Netherlands	4:36.0
1948	United States	4:29.2
1952	Hungary	4:24.4
1956	Australia	4:17.1
1960	United States	4:08.9
1964	United States	4:03.8
1968	United States	4:02.5
1972	United States	3:55.19
1976	United States	3:44.82
1980	East Germany	3:42.71
1984	United States	3:43.43
1988	E. Germany	3:40.63*

Springboard Diving — Points

1920	Aileen Riggin, U.S.	539.90
1924	Elizabeth Becker, U.S.	474.50
1928	Helen Meany, U.S.	78.62
1932	Georgia Coleman U.S.	87.52
1936	Marjorie Gestring, U.S.	89.27
1948	Victoria M. Draves, U.S.	108.74
1952	Patricia McCormick, U.S.	147.30
1956	Patricia McCormick, U.S.	142.36
1960	Ingrid Kramer, Germany	155.81
1964	Ingrid Engel-Kramer, Germany	145.00
1968	Sue Gossick, U.S.	150.77
1972	Micki King, U.S.	450.03
1976	Jenni Chandler, U.S.	506.19
1980	Irina Kalinina, USSR	725.91
1984	Sylvie Bernier, Canada	530.70
1988	Gao Min, China	580.23

Platform Diving — Points

1912	Greta Johansson, Sweden	39.90
1920	Stefani Fryland-Clausen, Denmark	34.60
1924	Caroline Smith, U.S.	33.20
1928	Elizabeth B. Pinkston, U.S.	31.60
1932	Dorothy Poynton, U.S.	40.26
1936	Dorothy Poynton Hill, U.S.	33.93
1948	Victoria M. Draves, U.S.	68.87
1952	Patricia McCormick, U.S.	79.37
1956	Patricia McCormick, U.S.	84.85
1960	Ingrid Kramer, Germany	91.28
1964	Lesley Bush, U.S.	99.80
1968	Milena Duchkova, Czech	109.59
1972	Ulrika Knape, Sweden	390.00
1976	Elena Vaytsekhouskaya, USSR	406.59
1980	Martina Jaschke, E. Germany	596.25
1984	Zhou Jihong, China	435.51
1988	Xu Yanmei, China	445.20

Boxing

Light Flyweight (106 lbs)

1968	Francisco Rodriguez, Venezuela
1972	Gyorgy Gedo, Hungary
1976	Jorge Hernandez, Cuba
1980	Shamil Sabyrov, USSR
1984	Paul Gonzalez, U.S.
1988	Ivailo Hristov, Bulgaria

Flyweight (112½ lbs)

1904	George Finnegan, U.S.
1920	William Di Gennara, U.S.
1924	Fidel LaBarba, U.S.
1928	Antal Kocsis, Hungary
1932	Istvan Enekes, Hungary
1936	Willi Kaiser, Germany
1948	Pascual Perez, Argentina
1952	Nathan Brooks, U.S.
1956	Terence Spinks, Great Britain
1960	Gyula Torok, Hungary
1964	Fernando Atzori, Italy
1968	Ricardo Delgado, Mexico
1972	Georgi Kostadinov, Bulgaria
1976	Leo Randolph, U.S.
1980	Peter Lessov, Bulgaria
1984	Steve McCrory, U.S.
1988	Kim Kwang Sun, S. Korea

Bantamweight (119½ lbs)

1904	Oliver Kirk, U.S.
1908	A Henry Thomas, Great Britain
1920	Clarence Walker, South Africa
1924	William Smith, South Africa
1928	Vittorio Tamagnini, Italy
1932	Horace Gwynne, Canada
1936	Ulderico Sergo, Italy
1948	Tibor Csik, Hungary
1952	Pentti Hamalainen, Finland
1956	Wolfgang Behrendt, E. Germany
1960	Oleg Grigoryev, USSR
1964	Takao Sakurai, Japan
1968	Valery Sokolov, USSR
1972	Orlando Martinez, Cuba
1976	Yong-Jo Gu, N. Korea
1980	Juan Hernandez, Cuba
1984	Maurizio Stecca, Italy
1988	Kennedy McKinney, U.S.

Featherweight (126 lbs)

1904	Oliver Kirk, U.S.
1908	Richard Gunn, Great Britain
1920	Paul Fritsch, France
1924	John Fields, U.S.
1928	Lambertus van Klaveren, Netherlands
1932	Carmelo Robledo, Argentina
1936	Oscar Casanovas, Argentina

1948	Ernesto Formenti, Italy
1952	Jan Zachara, Czech.
1956	Vladimir Safronov, USSR
1960	Francesco Musso, Italy
1964	Stanislav Stephashkin, USSR
1968	Antonin Roldan, Mexico
1972	Boris Kousnetsov, USSR
1976	Angel Herrera, Cuba
1980	Rudi Fink, E. Germany
1984	Meldrick Taylor, U.S.
1988	Giovanni Parisi, Italy

Lightweight (132 lbs)

1904	Harry Spanger, U.S.
1908	Frederick Grace, Great Britain
1920	Samuel Mosberg, U.S.
1924	Hans Nielsen, Denmark
1928	Carlo Orlandi, Italy
1932	Lawrence Stevens, South Africa
1936	Imre Harangi, Hungary
1948	Gerald Dreyer, South Africa
1952	Aureliano Bolognesi, Italy
1956	Richard McTaggart, Great Britain
1960	Kazimierz Pazdzior, Poland
1964	Jozef Grudzien, Poland
1968	Ronald Harris, U.S.
1972	Jan Szczepanski, Poland
1976	Howard Davis, U.S.
1980	Angel Herrera, Cuba
1984	Pernell Whitaker, U.S.
1988	Andreas Zuelow, E. Germany

Light Welterweight (140 lbs)

1952	Charles Adkins, U.S.
1956	Vladimir Yengibaryan, USSR
1960	Bohumil Nemecek, Czech.
1964	Jerzy Kulej, Poland
1968	Jerzy Kulej, Poland
1972	Ray Seales, U.S.
1976	Ray Leonard, U.S.
1980	Patrizio Oliva, Italy
1984	Jerry Page, U.S.
1988	Viatcheslav Janovski, USSR

Welterweight (148 lbs)

1904	Albert Young, U.S.
1920	Albert Schneider, Canada
1924	Jean Delarge, Belgium
1928	Edward Morgan, New Zealand
1932	Edward Flynn, U.S.
1936	Sten Suvio, Finland
1948	Julius Torma, Czech.
1952	Zygmunt Chychia, Poland
1956	Nicolae Linca, Romania
1960	Giovanni Benvenuti, Italy
1964	Marian Kasprzyk, Poland

1968	Manfred Wolke, E. Germany
1972	Emilio Correa, Cuba
1976	Jochen Bachfeld, E. Germany
1980	Andres Aldama, Cuba
1984	Mark Breland, U.S.
1988	Robert Wangila, Kenya

Light Middleweight (156 lbs)

1952	Laszlo Papp, Hungary
1956	Laszio Papp, Hungary
1960	Wilbert McClure, U.S.
1964	Boris Lagutin, USSR
1968	Boris Lagutin, USSR
1972	Dieter Kottysch, W. Germany
1976	Jerzy Rybicki, Poland
1980	Armando Martinez, Cuba
1984	Frank Tate, U.S.
1988	Park Si Hun, S. Korea

Middleweight (165½ lbs)

1904	Charles Mayer, U.S.
1908	John Douglas, Great Britain
1920	Harry Mallin, Great Britain
1924	Harry Mallin, Great Britain
1928	Piero Toscani, Italy
1932	Carmen Barth, U.S.
1936	Jean Despeaux, France
1948	Laszlo Papp, Hungary
1952	Floyd Patterson, U.S.
1956	Gennady Schatkov, USSR
1960	Edward Crook, U.S.
1964	Valery Popenchenko, USSR
1968	Christopher Finnegan, Great Britain
1972	Vyacheslav Lemechev, USSR
1976	Michael Spinks, U.S.
1980	Jose Gomez, Cuba
1984	Joon-Sup Shin, S. Korea
1988	Henry Maske, E. Germany

Light Heavyweight (179 lbs)

1920	Edward Eagan, U.S.
1924	Harry Mitchell, Great Britain
1928	Victor Avendano, Argentina
1932	David Carstens, South Africa
1936	Roger Michelot, France
1948	George Hunter, South Africa
1952	Norvel Lee, U.S.
1956	James Boyd, U.S.
1960	Cassius Clay, U.S.
1964	Cosimo Pinto, Italy
1968	Dan Poznyak, USSR
1972	Mate Parlov, Yugoslavia
1976	Leon Spinks, U.S.
1980	Siobodan Kacar, Yugoslavia
1984	Anton Josipovic, Yugoslavia

1988	Andrew Maynard, U.S.	**1920**	Ronald Rawson, Great Britain	**1960**	Franco De Piccoli, Italy
	Heavyweight (200½ lbs)	**1924**	Otto von Porat, Norway	**1964**	Joe Frazier, U.S.
1984	Henry Tillman, U.S.	**1928**	Arturo Rodriguez Jurado,	**1968**	George Foreman, U.S.
1988	Ray Mercer, U.S.		Argentina	**1972**	Teofilo Stevenson, Cuba
		1932	Santiago Lovell, Argentina	**1976**	Teofilo Stevenson, Cuba
	Super Heavyweight (Unlimited)	**1936**	Herbert Runge, Germany	**1980**	Teofilo Stevenson, Cuba
	(known as heavyweight from 1904-1980)	**1948**	Rafael Inglesias, Argentina	**1984**	Tyrell Biggs, U.S.
1904	Samuel Berger, U.S.	**1952**	H. Edward Sanders, U.S.	**1988**	Lennox Lewis, Canada
1908	Albert Oldham, Great Britain	**1956**	T. Peter Rademacher, U.S.		

24th Summer Olympics

Seoul, S. Korea, Sept. 17-24, 1988

A record 13,674 athletes gathered in Seoul, South Korea in September for 16 days to compete in the Games of the XXIV Olympiad. The athletes represented 161 nations, 21 more than had participated in any previous Olympics, and competed for 237 gold medals in 26 sports at a cost of $3.1 billion to the South Korean government. The Soviet Union won the most medals, East Germany finished second, and the United States third.

The 1988 games will be remembered mostly for the long-awaited showdown in the 100-meter race between Ben Johnson, the Canadian sprinter and world record holder, and his archrival, Carl Lewis of the United States. Johnson won the race in world record time. Three days later, Johnson was stripped of his gold medal and world record because he had tested positive for the anabolic steroid stanozolol. Two weightlifters from Bulgaria were also stripped of their gold medals for taking drugs. In all, 10 of the athletes tested were disqualified by the International Olympic Committee for using banned substances.

Sports fans in the United States had much to cheer about. Swimmers Matt Biondi won 5 gold medals and Janet Evans won gold in three events. Greg Louganis repeated his 1984 performance by winning the springboard and platform diving events. Florence Griffith-Joyner won the 100 and 200-meter races while her sister-in-law, Jackie Joyner-Kersee was the Heptathlon and long jump champion. The U.S. men won the volleyball gold medal. The biggest disappointment was the defeat of the men's basketball team by the Soviet Union, only the second loss in history for a U.S. Olympic basketball team.

Final Medal Standings

	Gold	Silver	Bronze	Total		Gold	Silver	Bronze	Total
					Spain	1	1	2	4
USSR	55	31	46	132	Switzerland	0	2	2	4
East Germany	37	35	30	102	Morocco	1	0	2	3
United States	36	31	27	94	Turkey	1	1	0	2
West Germany	11	14	15	40	Jamaica	0	2	0	2
Bulgaria	10	12	13	35	Argentina	0	1	1	2
South Korea	12	10	11	33	Belgium	0	0	2	2
China	5	11	12	28	Mexico	0	0	2	2
Romania	7	11	6	24	Austria	1	0	0	1
Great Britain	5	10	9	24	Portugal	1	0	0	1
Hungary	11	6	6	23	Suriname	1	0	0	1
France	6	4	6	16	Chile	0	1	0	1
Poland	2	5	9	16	Costa Rica	0	1	0	1
Italy	6	4	4	14	Indonesia	0	1	0	1
Japan	4	3	7	14	Iran	0	1	0	1
Australia	3	6	5	14	Netherlands Antilles	0	1	0	1
New Zealand	3	2	8	13	Peru	0	1	0	1
Yugoslavia	3	4	5	12	Senegal	0	1	0	1
Sweden	0	4	7	11	Virgin Islands	0	1	0	1
Canada	3	2	5	10	Colombia	0	0	1	1
Kenya	5	2	2	9	Djibouti	0	0	1	1
Netherlands	2	2	5	9	Greece	0	0	1	1
Czechoslovakia	3	3	2	8	Mongolia	0	0	1	1
Brazil	1	2	3	6	Pakistan	0	0	1	1
Norway	2	3	0	5	Philippines	0	0	1	1
Denmark	2	1	1	4	Thailand	0	0	1	1
Finland	1	1	2	4					

Olympic Information

Symbol: Five rings or circles, linked together to represent the sporting friendship of all peoples. The rings also symbolize the 5 continents—Europe, Asia, Africa, Australia, and America. Each ring is a different color—blue, yellow, black, green, and red.

Flag: The symbol of the 5 rings on a plain white background.

Motto: "Citius, Altius, Fortius." Latin meaning "faster, higher, braver," or the modern interpretation "swifter, higher, stronger". The motto was coined by Father Didon, a French educator, in 1895.

Creed: "The most important thing in the Olympic Games is not to win but to take part, just as the most important thing in life is not the triumph but the struggle. The essential thing is not to have conquered but to have fought well."

Oath: An athlete of the host country recites the following at the opening ceremony. "In the name of all competitors I promise that we will take part in these Olympic Games, respecting and abiding by the rules which govern them, in the true spirit of sportsmanship for the glory of sport and the honor of our teams." Both the oath and the creed were composed by Pierre de Coubertin, the founder of the modern Games.

Flame: Symbolizes the continuity between the ancient and modern Games. The modern version of the flame was adopted in 1936. The torch used to kindle the flame is first lit by the sun's rays at Olympia, Greece, and then carried to the site of the Games by relays of runners. Ships and planes are used when necessary.

Other Summer Olympics Gold Medalists in 1988

Archery

Men—Jay Barrs, U.S.
Men's Team—S. Korea.
Women—Kim Soo-Nyung, S. Korea.
Women's Team—S. Korea.

Basketball

Men—1. USSR; 2. Yugoslavia; 3. U.S.
Women—1. U.S.; 2. Yugoslavia; 3. USSR.

Canoeing—Men

K1-500M—Zsolt Gyulay, Hungary.
K2-500M—Ian Ferguson, Paul MacDonald, New Zealand.
K1-1,000M—Greg Barton, U.S.
K2-1,000M—Greg Barton, N. Bellingham, U.S.
K4-1,000m—Hungary.
C1-500M—Olaf Heukrodt, E. Germany.
C2-500M—Victor Reneiski, Nikolai Jouravski, USSR.
C1-1,000M—Ivan Klementiev, USSR.
C2-1,000M—Victor Reneiski, Nikolai Jouravski, USSR.

Canoeing—Women

K1-500M—Vania Guecheva, Bulgaria.
K2-500M—Birgit Schmidt, Anke Nothnagel, E. Germany.
K4-500M—E. Germany.

Cycling

4,000 Individual Pursuit—Gintaoutas Umaras, USSR.
Sprint—Lutz Hesslich, E. Germany.
4,000 Team Pursuit—USSR.
50 Km Points Race—Dan Forst, Denmark.
1K Time Trial—Alexandr Kiritchenko, USSR.
100K Team Time Trial—E. Germany.
Road Race—Olaf Ludwig, E. Germany.
Women's Sprint—Erika Saloumiae, USSR.
Women's Road Race—Monique Knol, Netherlands.

Diving

Women's Platform—Xu Yanmei, China.
Women's Springboard—Gao Min, China.
Men's Springboard—Greg Louganis, U.S.
Men's Platform—Greg Louganis, U.S.

Equestrian

Individual 3-Day Event—Mark Todd, New Zealand.
Team 3-Day Event—W. Germany.
Individual Dressage—Nicole Uphoff, W. Germany.
Team Dressage—W. Germany.
Individual Jumping—Pierre Durand, France.
Team Jumping—W. Germany.

Fencing—Men

Foil Individual—Stefano Cerioni, Italy.
Team Foil—USSR.
Sabre Individual—Jean-Francois Lamour, France.
Team Sabre—Hungary.
Epée Individual—Arnd Schmitt, W. Germany.
Epée Team—France.

Fencing—Women

Foil Individual—Anja Fichtel, W. Germany.
Team Foil—W. Germany.

Field Hockey

Men—1. Great Britain; 2. W. Germany; 3. Netherlands.
Women—1. Australia; 2. S. Korea; 3. Netherlands.

Gymnastics—Men

Team—USSR.
All Around—Vladimir Artemov, USSR.
Floor Exercise—Sergei Kharikov, USSR.
Pommel Horse—Dimitri Bilozerchev, USSR.
Rings—Dimitri Bilozerchev, USSR.
Vault—Lou Yun, China.

Parallel Bars—Vladimir Artemov, USSR.
Horizontal Bar—Vladimir Artemov, USSR.

Gymnastics—Women

Team—USSR.
All-Around—Yelena Shoushunova, USSR.
Vault—Svetlana Boguinskaya, USSR.
Uneven Parallel Bars—Daniela Silivas, Romania.
Balance Beam—Daniela Silivas, Romania.
Floor Exercise—Daniela Silivas, Romania.

Rhythmic Gymnastics

Marina Lobatch, USSR.

Judo

133 Pounds—Kim Jae Yup, S. Korea.
143 Pounds—Lee Kyung-Keun, S. Korea.
156 Pounds—Marc Alexandre, France.
172 Pounds—Waldemar Legien, Poland.
189 Pounds—Peter Seisenbacher, Austria.
209 Pounds—Aurelio Miguel, Brazil.
Over 209 Pounds—Hitoshi Saito, Japan.

Modern Pentathlon

Individual—Janos Martinek, Hungary.
Team—Hungary.

Rowing—Men

Single Sculls—Tomas Lange, E. Germany.
Double Sculls—Netherlands.
Coxless Pairs—Great Britain.
Coxed Pairs—Italy.
Coxed Fours—E. Germany.
Coxless Fours—E. Germany.
Quadruple Sculls—Italy.
Eights—W. Germany.

Rowing—Women

Single Sculls—Jutta Behrendt, E. Germany.
Double Sculls—E. Germany.
Coxless Pairs—Romania.
Coxless Fours—E. Germany.
Quadruple Sculls—E. Germany.
Eights—E. Germany.

Shooting—Men

Smallbore Standard Rifle—Miroslav Varga, Czechoslovakia.
Smallbore Free Rifle—Malcolm Cooper, Great Britain.
Free Pistol—Sorin Babii, Romania.
Air Rifle—Goran Maksimovic, Yugoslavia.
Rapid-Fire Pistol—Afanasi Kouzmine, USSR.
Running Target—Tor Heiestad, Norway.
Air Pistol—Taniou Kiruakov, Bulgaria.

Shooting—Women

Air Rifle—Irina Cilova, USSR.
Sport Pistol—Nino Saloukvadze, USSR.
Air Pistol—Jasna Sekaric, Yugoslavia.
Smallbore Standard Rifle—Silvia Sperber, W. Germany.

Shooting—Mixed

Skeet—Axel Wegner, E. Germany.
Trap—Dmitri Monakov, USSR.

Soccer

Championship—1. USSR; 2. Brazil; 3. W. Germany.

Synchronized Swimming

Solo—Carolyn Waldo, Canada.
Duet—Michelle Cameron, Carolyn Waldo, Canada.

Table Tennis—Men

Singles—Yoo Nam Kyu, S. Korea.

Doubles—Chen Longcan, Wei Qingquang, China.

Table Tennis—Women

Singles—Chen Jing, China.
Doubles—Hyun Jung Hwa, Yang Young Ja, S. Korea.

Team Handball

Men—1. USSR. S. Korea; 3. Yugoslavia.
Women—1. S. Korea. Norway; 3. USSR.

Tennis—Men

Singles—Miloslav Mecir, Czech.
Doubles—Ken Flach, Robert Seguso, U.S.

Tennis—Women

Singles—Steffi Graf, W. Germany.
Doubles—Pam Shriver, Zina Garrison, U.S.

Volleyball

Men—1. U.S.; 2. USSR; 3. Argentina.
Women—1. USSR; 2. Peru; 3. China.

Water Polo

Championship—1. Yugoslavia; 2. U.S.; 3. USSR.

Weight Lifting

115 Pounds—Sevdalin Marinov, Bulgaria.
123 Pounds—Oxen Mirzoian, USSR.
132 Pounds—Naim Suleymanogulu, Turkey.
149 Pounds—Joachim Kunz, E. Germany.
165 Pounds—Borislav Guidikov, Bulgaria.
182 Pounds—Israil Arsamakov, USSR.
198 Pounds—Anatoli Khrapatyi, USSR.

220 Pounds—Pavel Kouzntsov, USSR.
242 Pounds—Yuri Zakharevitch, USSR.
Over 242 Pounds—Aleksandr Kourlovich, USSR.

Wrestling—Greco-Roman

106 Pounds—Vicenzo Maenza, Italy.
115 Pounds—Jon Ronningen, Norway.
126 Pounds—Andras Sike, Hungary.
137 Pounds—Kamandar Madjidov, USSR.
150 Pounds—Levon Djoulfalakian, USSR.
163 Pounds—Kim Young Nam, S. Korea.
181 Pounds—Mikhail Mamiachvili, USSR.
198 Pounds—Atanas Komchev, Bulgaria.
220 Pounds—Andrzej Wronski, Poland.
286 Pounds—Alexander Kareline, USSR.

Wrestling—Freestyle

106 Pounds—Takashi Kobayashi, Japan.
115 Pounds—Mitsuru Sato, Japan.
126 Pounds—Serguei Beloglazov, USSR.
137 Pounds—John Smith, U.S.
150 Pounds—Arsen Fadzaev, USSR.
163 Pounds—Ken Monday, U.S.
181 Pounds—Han Myang-Woo, S. Korea.
198 Pounds—Makharbek Khadartsev, USSR.
220 Pounds—Vasile Puscasu, Romania.
286 Pounds—David Gobedjichvili, USSR.

Yachting

Board Sailing—Bruce Kendall, New Zealand.
Finn—José Luis Doreste, Spain.
Flying Dutchman—Denmark.
Soling—E. Germany.
Star—Great Britain.
Tornado—France.
Men's 470—France.
Women's 470—U.S.

Winter Olympic Games Champions, 1924-1988

Sites of Games

1924 Chamonix, France	1956 Cortina d'Ampezzo, Italy	1976 Innsbruck, Austria
1928 St. Moritz, Switzerland	1960 Squaw Valley, Cal.	1980 Lake Placid, N.Y.
1932 Lake Placid, N.Y.	1964 Innsbruck, Austria	1984 Sarajevo, Yugoslavia
1936 Garmisch-Partenkirchen, Germany	1968 Grenoble, France	1988 Calgary, Alberta
1948 St. Moritz, Switzerland	1972 Sapporo, Japan	1992 Albertville, France (scheduled)
1952 Oslo, Norway		

Bobsledding

4-Man Bob

(Driver in parentheses)	Time
1924 Switzerland (Eduard Scherrer)	5:45.54
1928 United States (William Fiske) (5-man)	3:20.50
1932 United States (William Fiske)	7:53.68
1936 Switzerland (Pierre Musy)	5:19.85
1948 United States (Francis Tyler)	5:20.10
1952 Germany (Andreas Ostler)	5:07.84
1956 Switzerland (Franz Kapus)	5:10.44
1964 Canada (Victor Emery)	4:14.46
1968 Italy (Eugenio Monti) (2 races)	2:17.39
1972 Switzerland (Jean Wicki)	4:43.07
1976 E. Germany (Meinhard Nehmer)	3:40.43
1980 E. Germany (Meinhard Nehmer)	3:59.92
1984 E. Germany (Wolfgang Hoppe)	3:20.22
1988 Switzerland (Ekkehard Fasser)	3:47.51

2-Man Bob

	Time
1932 United States (Hubert Stevens)	8:14.74
1936 United States (Ivan Brown)	5:29.29
1948 Switzerland (F. Endrich)	5:29.20
1952 Germany (Andreas Ostler)	5:24.54
1956 Italy (Dalla Costa)	5:30.14
1964 Great Britain (Anthony Nash)	4:21.90
1968 Italy (Eugenio Monti)	4:41.54
1972 W. Germany (Wolfgang Zimmerer)	4:57.07
1976 E. Germany (Meinhard Nehmer)	3:44.42
1980 Switzerland (Erich Schaerer)	4:09.36
1984 E.Germany (Wolfgang Hoppe)	3:25.56
1988 USSR (Janis Kipours)	3:54.19

Luge

Men's Singles

	Time
1964 Thomas Keohler, Germany	3:26.77
1968 Manfred Schmid, Austria	2:52.48
1972 Wolfgang Scheidel, E. Germany	3:27.58
1976 Detlef Guenther, E. Germany	3:27.688
1980 Bernhard Glass, E. Germany	2:54.796
1984 Paul Hildgartner, Italy	3:04.258
1988 Jens Mueller, E. Germany	3:05.548

Men's Pairs

	Time
1964 Austria	1:41.62
1968 E. Germany	1:35.85
1972 Italy, E. Germany (tie)	1:28.35
1976 E. Germany	1:25.604
1980 E. Germany	1:19.331
1984 W. Germany	1:23.620
1988 E. Germany	1:31.940

Women's Singles

	Time
1964 Ortun Enderlein, Germany	3:24.67
1968 Erica Lechner, Italy	2:28.66
1972 Anna M. Muller, E. Germany	2:59.18
1976 Margit Schumann, E. Germany	2:50.621
1980 Vera Zozulya, USSR	2:36.537
1984 Steffi Martin, E. Germany	2:46.570
1988 Steffi Walter, E. Germany	3:03.973

Biathlon

10 Kilometers

		Time
1980	Frank Ullrich, E. Germany	32:10.69
1984	Eirik Kvalfoss, Norway	30:53.80
1988	Frank-Peter Roetsch, E. Germany	25:08.10

20 Kilometers

		Time
1960	Klas Lestander, Sweden	1:33:21.6
1964	Vladimir Melanin, USSR	1:20:26.8
1968	Magnar Solberg, Norway	1:13:45.9
1972	Magnar Solberg, Norway	1:15:55.50
1976	Nikolai Kruglov, USSR	1:14:12.26
1980	Anatoly Aljabiev, USSR	1:08:16.31
1984	Peter Angerer, W. Germany	1:11:52.7
1988	Frank-Peter Roetsch, E. Germany	0:56:33.33

30-Kilometer Relay

		Time
1968	USSR, Norway, Sweden	2:13:02.4
1972	USSR, Finland, E. Germany	1:51:44.92
1976	USSR, Finland, E. Germany	1:57:55.64
1980	USSR, E. Germany, W. Germany (30 km.)	1:34:03.27
1984	USSR, Norway, W. Germany	1:38:51.70
1988	USSR, W. Germany, Italy	1:22:30.00

Figure Skating

Men's Singles

1908	Ulrich Salchow, Sweden
1920	Gillis Grafstrom, Sweden
1924	Gillis Grafstrom, Sweden
1928	Gillis Grafstrom, Sweden
1932	Karl Schaefer, Austria
1936	Karl Schaefer, Austria
1948	Richard Button, U.S.
1952	Richard Button, U.S.
1956	Hayes Alan Jenkins, U.S.
1960	David W. Jenkins, U.S.
1964	Manfred Schnelldorfer, Germany
1968	Wolfgang Schwartz, Austria
1972	Ondrej Nepela, Czechoslovakia
1976	John Curry, Great Britain
1980	Robin Cousins, Great Britain
1984	Scott Hamilton, U.S.
1988	Brian Boitano, U.S.

Women's Singles

1908	Madge Syers, Great Britain
1920	Magda Julin-Mauroy, Sweden
1924	Herma von Szabo-Planck, Austria
1928	Sonja Henie, Norway
1932	Sonja Henie, Norway
1936	Sonja Henie, Norway
1948	Barbara Ann Scott, Canada
1952	Jeanette Altwegg, Great Britain
1956	Tenley Albright, U.S.
1960	Carol Heiss, U.S.
1964	Sjoukje Dijkstra, Netherlands
1968	Peggy Fleming, U.S.
1972	Beatrix Schuba, Austria
1976	Dorothy Hamill, U.S.
1980	Anett Poetzsch, E. Germany
1984	Katarina Witt, E. Germany
1988	Katarina Witt, E. Germany

Pairs

1908	Anna Hubler & Heinrich Burger, Germany
1920	Ludovika & Walter Jakobsson, Finland
1924	Helene Engelman & Alfred Berger, Austria
1928	Andree Joly & Pierre Brunet, France
1932	Andree Joly & Pierre Brunet, France
1936	Maxi Herber & Ernst Baier, Germany
1948	Micheline Lannoy & Pierre Baugniet, Belgium
1952	Ria and Paul Falk, Germany
1956	Elisabeth Schwartz & Kurt Oppelt, Austria
1960	Barbara Wagner & Robert Paul, Canada
1964	Ludmila Beloussova & Oleg Protopopov, USSR
1968	Ludmila Beloussova & Oleg Protopopov, USSR
1972	Irina Rodnina & Alexei Ulanov, USSR
1976	Irina Rodnina & Aleksandr Zaitzev, USSR
1980	Irina Rodnina & Aleksandr Zaitzev, USSR
1984	Elena Valova & Oleg Vassiliev, USSR
1988	Ekaterina Gordeeva & Sergei Grinkov, USSR

Ice Dancing

1976	Ludmila Pakhomova & Aleksandr Gorshkov, USSR
1980	Natalya Linichuk & Gennadi Karponosov, USSR
1984	Jayne Torvill & Christopher Dean, Great Britain
1988	Natalia Bestemianova & Andrei Bukin, USSR

Ice Hockey

1920	Canada, U.S., Czechoslovakia
1924	Canada, U.S., Great Britain
1928	Canada, Sweden, Switzerland
1932	Canada, U.S., Germany
1936	Great Britain, Canada, U.S.
1948	Canada, Czechoslovakia, Switzerland
1952	Canada, U.S., Sweden
1956	USSR, U.S., Canada
1960	U.S., Canada, USSR
1964	USSR, Sweden, Czechoslovakia
1968	USSR, Czechoslovakia, Canada
1972	USSR, U.S., Czechoslovakia
1976	USSR, Czechoslovakia, W. Germany
1980	U.S., USSR, Sweden
1984	USSR, Czechoslovakia, Sweden
1988	USSR, Finland, Sweden

Alpine Skiing

Men's Downhill

		Time
1948	Henri Oreiller, France	2:55.0
1952	Zeno Colo, Italy	2:30.8
1956	Anton Sailer, Austria	2:52.2
1960	Jean Vuarnet, France	2:06.0
1964	Egon Zimmermann, Austria	2:18.16
1968	Jean-Claude Killy, France	1:59.85
1972	Bernhard Russi, Switzerland	1:51.43
1976	Franz Klammer, Austria	1:45.73
1980	Leonhard Stock, Austria	1:45.50
1984	Bill Johnson, U.S.	1:45:59
1988	Pirmin Zurbriggen, Switzerland	1:59.63

Men's Super Giant Slalom

		Time
1988	Franck Piccard, France	1:39.66

Men's Giant Slalom

		Time
1952	Stein Eriksen, Norway	2:25.0
1956	Anton Sailer, Austria	3:00.1
1960	Roger Staub, Switzerland	1:48.3
1964	Francois Bonlieu, France	1:46.71
1968	Jean-Claude Killy, France	3:29.28
1972	Gustavo Thoeni, Italy	3:09.62
1976	Heini Hemmi, Switzerland	3:26.97
1980	Ingemar Stenmark, Sweden	2:40.74
1984	Max Julen, Switzerland	2:41.18
1988	Alberto Tomba, Italy	2:06:37

Men's Slalom

		Time
1948	Edi Reinalter, Switzerland	2:10.3
1952	Othmar Schneider, Austria	2:00.0
1956	Anton Sailer, Austria	194.7 pts.
1960	Ernst Hinterseer, Austria	2:08.9
1964	Josef Stiegler, Austria	2:11.13
1968	Jean-Claude Killy, France	1:39.73
1972	Francisco Fernandez Ochoa, Spain	1:49.27
1976	Piero Gros, Italy	2:03.29
1980	Ingemar Stenmark, Sweden	1:44.26
1984	Phil Mahre, U.S.	1:39.41
1988	Alberto Tomba	1:39.47

Men's Combined

		Points
1988	Hubert Strolz, Austria	36.55

Women's Downhill

		Time
1948	Hedi Schlunegger, Switzerland	2:28.3
1952	Trude Jochum-Beiser, Austria	1:47.1
1956	Madeleine Berthod, Switzerland	1:40.7
1960	Heidi Biebl, Germany	1:37.6
1964	Christl Haas, Austria	1:55.39
1968	Olga Pall, Austria	1:40.87
1972	Marie Therese Nadig, Switzerland	1:36.68
1976	Rosi Mittermaier, W. Germany	1:46.16
1980	Annemarie Proell Moser, Austria	1:37.52
1984	Michela Figini, Switzerland	1:13.36
1988	Marina Kiehl, W. Germany	1:25.86

Women's Super Giant Slalom

	Time
1988 Sigrid Wolf, Austria	1:19.03

Women's Giant Slalom

	Time
1952 Andrea Mead Lawrence, U.S.	2:06.8
1956 Ossi Reichert, Germany	1:56.5
1960 Yvonne Ruegg, Switzerland	1:39.9
1964 Marielle Goitschel, France	1:52.24
1968 Nancy Greene, Canada	1:51.97
1972 Marie Therese Nadig, Switzerland	1:29.90
1976 Kathy Kreiner, Canada	1:29.13
1980 Hanni Wenzel, Liechtenstein (2 runs)	2:41.66
1984 Debbie Armstrong, U.S.	2:20.98
1988 Vreni Schneider, Switzerland	2:06.49

Women's Slalom

	Time
1948 Gretchen Fraser, U.S.	1:57.2
1952 Andrea Mead Lawrence, U.S.	2:10.6
1956 Renee Colliard, Switzerland	112.3 pts.
1960 Anne Heggtveigt, Canada.	1:49.6
1964 Christine Goitschel, France	1:29.86
1968 Marielle Goitschel, France	1:25.86
1972 Barbara Cochran, U.S.	1:31.24
1976 Rosi Mittermaier, W. Germany	1:30.54
1980 Hanni Wenzel, Liechtenstein	1:25.09
1984 Paoletta Magoni, Italy	1:36.47
1988 Vreni Schneider, Switzerland	1:36.69

Women's Combined

	Points
1988 Anita Wachter, Austria	29.25

Nordic Skiing

Men's Cross-Country Events
15 kilometers (9.3 miles)

	Time
1924 Thorleif Haug, Norway.	1:14:31
1928 Johan Grottumsbraaten, Norway.	1:37:01
1932 Sven Utterstrom, Sweden.	1:23:07
1936 Erik-August Larsson, Sweden	1:14:38
1948 Martin Lundstrom, Sweden	1:13:50
1952 Hallgeir Brenden, Norway.	1:01:34
1956 Hallgeir Brenden, Norway.	49:39.0
1960 Haakon Brusveen, Norway	51:55.5
1964 Eero Maentyranta, Finland	50:54.1
1968 Harald Groenningen, Norway.	47:54.2
1972 Sven-Ake Lundback, Sweden	45:28.24
1976 Nikolai Balukov, USSR	43:58.47
1980 Thomas Wassberg, Sweden	41:57.63
1984 Gunde Svan, Sweden	41:25.6
1988 Mikhail Deviatiarov, USSR	41:18.9

(Note: approx. 18-km. course 1924-1952)

30 kilometers (18.6 miles)

	Time
1956 Veikko Hakulinen, Finland.	1:44:06.0
1960 Sixten Jernberg, Sweden.	1:51:03.9
1964 Eero Maentyranta, Finland	1:30:50.7
1968 Franco Nones, Italy	1:35:39.2
1972 Vyacheslav Vedenine, USSR.	1:36:31.15
1976 Sergei Saveliev, USSR	1:30:29.38
1980 Nikolai Zimyatov, USSR	1:27:02.80
1984 Nikolai Zimyatov, USSR	1:28:56.3
1988 Aleksei Prokourorov, USSR	1:24:26.3

50 kilometers (31.2 miles)

	Time
1924 Thorleif Haug, Norway.	3:44:32.0
1928 Per Erik Hedlund, Sweden	4:52:03.0
1932 Veli Saarinen, Finland	4:28:00.0
1936 Elis Wiklund, Sweden	3:30:11.0
1948 Nils Karlsson, Sweden	3:47:48.0
1952 Veikko Hakulinen, Finland	3:33:33.0
1956 Sixten Jernberg, Sweden	2:50:27.0
1960 Kalevi Hamalainen, Finland	2:59:06.3
1964 Sixten Jernberg, Sweden	2:43:52.6
1968 Ole Ellefsaeter, Norway.	2:28:45.8
1972 Paal Tyldum, Norway	2:43:14.75
1976 Ivar Formo, Norway	2:37:30.05
1980 Nikolai Zimyatov, USSR.	2:27:24.60
1984 Thomas Wassberg, Sweden	2:15:55.8
1988 Gunde Svan, Sweden	2:04:30.9

40-km. Relay

	Time
1936 Finland, Norway, Sweden.	2:41:33.0
1948 Sweden, Finland, Norway.	2:32:08.0
1952 Finland, Norway, Sweden.	2:20:16.0
1956 USSR, Finland, Sweden.	2:15:30.0
1960 Finland, Norway, USSR.	2:18:45.6
1964 Sweden, Finland, USSR.	2:18:34.6

1968 Norway, Sweden, Finland	2:08:33.5
1972 USSR, Norway, Switzerland	2:04:47.94
1976 Finland, Norway, USSR	2:07:59.72
1980 USSR, Norway, Finland	1:57:03.46
1984 Sweden, USSR, Finland.	1:55:06.30
1988 Sweden, USSR, Czechoslovakia.	1:43:58.60

Combined Cross-Country & Jumping

	Points
1924 Thorleif Haug, Norway.	453.800
1928 Johan Grottumsbraaten, Norway.	427.800
1932 Johan Grottumsbraaten, Norway.	446.000
1936 Oddbjorn Hagen, Norway.	430.300
1948 Heikki Hasu, Finland.	448.800
1952 Simon Slattvik, Norway	451.621
1956 Sverre Stenersen, Norway	455.000
1960 Georg Thoma, Germany	457.952
1964 Tormod Knutsen, Norway.	469.280
1968 Franz Keller, W. Germany	449.040
1972 Ulrich Wehling, E. Germany.	413.340
1976 Ulrich Wehling, E. Germany.	423.390
1980 Ulrich Wehling, E. Germany.	432.200
1984 Tom Sandberg, Norway.	422.595
1988 Hippolyt Kempf, Switzerland	235.8

Men's Team Ski Jumping (90 meters)

	Points
1988 Finland, Yugoslavia, Norway	634.400

Ski Jumping (90 meters)

	Points
1924 Jacob Thams, Norway.	227.5
1928 Alfred Andersen, Norway.	230.5
1932 Birger Ruud, Norway.	228.1
1936 Birger Ruud, Norway.	232.0
1948 Petter Hugsted, Norway.	228.1
1952 Arnfinn Bergmann, Norway.	226.0
1956 Antti Hyvarinen, Finland.	227.0
1960 Helmut Recknagel, Germany.	227.2
1964 Toralf Engan, Norway.	230.7
1968 Vladimir Beloussov, USSR	231.3
1972 Wojiech Fortuna, Poland	219.9
1976 Karl Schnabl, Austria	234.8
1980 Jouko Tormanen, Finland	271.0
1984 Matti Nykaenen, Finland.	231.2
1988 Matti Nykaenen, Finland.	224.0

Men's Team Combined

	Time
1988 W. Germany, Switzerland, Austria	1:20:46.0

Ski Jumping (70 meters)

	Points
1964 Veikko Kankkonen, Finland	229.9
1968 Jiri Raska, Czechoslovakia	216.5
1972 Yukio Kasaya, Japan	244.2
1976 Hans Aschenbach, E. Germany	252.0
1980 Anton Innauer, Austria.	266.3
1984 Jens Weissflog, E. Germany	215.2
1988 Matti Nykaenen, Finland.	229.1

Women's Events
5 kilometers (approx. 3.1 miles)

	Time
1964 Claudia Boyarskikh, USSR	17:50.5
1968 Toini Gustafsson, Sweden	16:45.2
1972 Galina Koulacova, USSR	17:00.50
1976 Helena Takalo, Finland	15:48.69
1980 Raisa Smetanina, USSR	15:06.92
1984 Marja-Liisa Haemaélainen, Finland	17:04.0
1988 Marjo Matikainen, Finland.	15:04.0

10 kilometers

	Time
1952 Lydia Wideman, Finland.	41:40.0
1956 Lyubov Kosyreva, USSR	38:11.0
1960 Maria Gusakova, USSR.	39:46.6
1964 Claudia Boyarskikh, USSR	40:24.3
1968 Toini Gustafsson, Sweden	36:46.5
1972 Galina Koulacova, USSR	34:17.82
1976 Raisa Smetanina, USSR	30:13.41
1980 Barbara Petzold, E. Germany.	30:31.54
1984 Marja-Liisa Haemaelainen, Finland	31:44.2
1988 Vida Ventsene, USSR.	30:08.3

20 kilometers

	Time
1984 Marja-Liisa Haemaelainen, Finland	1:01:45.0
1988 Tamara Tikhonova, USSR	55:53.6

20-km. Relay

	Time
1956 Finland, USSR, Sweden (15 km.)	1:09:01.0
1960 Sweden, USSR, Finland (15 km.)	1:04:21.4
1964 USSR, Sweden, Finland (15 km.)	59:20.2
1968 Norway, Sweden, USSR (15 km.)	57:30.0

(continued)

1972 USSR, Finland, Norway (15 km.)......   48:46.15
1976 USSR, Finland, E. Germany 1:07:49.75
1980 E. Germany, USSR, Norway 1:02:11.10
1984 Norway, Czechoslovakia, Finland 1:06:49.70
1988 USSR, Norway, Finland...........   59:51.1

Speed Skating

Men's 500 meters — Time

	Time
1924 Charles Jewtraw, U.S.............	0:44.0
1928 Thunberg, Finland & Evensen, Norway (tie)	0:43.4
1932 John A. Shea, U.S...............	0:43.4
1936 Ivar Ballangrud, Norway..........	0:43.4
1948 Finn Helgesen, Norway...........	0:43.1
1952 Kenneth Henry, U.S.............	0:43.2
1956 Evgeniy Grishin, USSR	0:40.2
1960 Evgeniy Grishin, USSR	0:40.2
1964 Terry McDermott, U.S...........	0:40.1
1968 Erhard Keller, W. Germany	0:40.3
1972 Erhard Keller, W. Germany	0:39.44
1976 Evgeny Kulikov, USSR	0:39.17
1980 Eric Heiden, U.S..............	0:38.03
1984 Sergei Fokichev, USSR	0:38.19
1988 Jens-Uwe Mey, E. Germany	0:36.45

Men's 1,000 meters — Time

	Time
1976 Peter Mueller, U.S.............	1:19.32
1980 Eric Heiden, U.S..............	1:15.18
1984 Gaetan Boucher, Canada	1:15.80
1988 Nikolai Guiliaev, USSR	1:13.03

Men's 1,500 meters — Time

	Time
1924 Clas Thunberg, Finland	2:20.8
1928 Clas Thunberg, Finland	2:21.1
1932 John A. Shea, U.S.............	2:57.5
1936 Charles Mathiesen, Norway	2:19.2
1948 Sverre Farstad, Norway..........	2:17.6
1952 Hjalmar Andersen, Norway........	2:20.4
1956 Grishin, & Mikhailov, both USSR (tie)	2:08.6
1960 Aas, Norway & Grishin, USSR (tie)	2:10.4
1964 Ants Anston, USSR	2:10.3
1968 Cornelis Verkerk, Netherlands	2:03.4
1972 Ard Schenk, Netherlands	2:02.96
1976 Jan Egil Storholt, Norway	1:59.38
1980 Eric Heiden, U.S..............	1:55.44
1984 Gaetan Boucher, Canada........	1:58.36
1988 Andre Hoffmann, E. Germany	1:52.06

Men's 5,000 meters — Time

	Time
1924 Clas Thunberg, Finland	8:39.0
1928 Ivar Ballangrud, Norway	8:50.5
1932 Irving Jaffee, U.S.	9:40.8
1936 Ivar Ballangrud, Norway	8:19.6
1948 Reidar Liaklev, Norway..........	8:29.4
1952 Hjalmar Andersen, Norway	8:10.6
1956 Boris Shilkov, USSR	7:48.7
1960 Viktor Kosichkin, USSR	7:51.3
1964 Knut Johannesen, Norway	7:38.4
1968 F. Anton Maier, Norway	7:22.4
1972 Ard Schenk, Netherlands	7:23.61
1976 Sten Stensen, Norway..........	7:24.48
1980 Eric Heiden, U.S.............	7:02.29
1984 Sven Tomas Gustafson, Sweden......	7:12:28
1988 Tomas Gustafson, Sweden	6:44:63

Men's 10,000 meters — Time

	Time
1924 Julius Skutnabb, Finland...........	18:04.8
1928 Event not held, thawing of ice	
1932 Irving Jaffee, U.S.	19:13.6
1936 Ivar Ballangrud, Norway...........	17:24.3
1948 Ake Seyffarth, Sweden	17:26.3
1952 Hjalmar Andersen, Norway	16:45.8
1956 Sigvard Ericsson, Sweden	16:35.9
1960 Knut Johannesen, Norway	15:46.6
1964 Jonny Nilsson, Sweden	15:50.1
1968 Jonny Hoeglin, Sweden	15:23.6
1972 Ard Schenk, Netherlands	15:01.35
1976 Piet Kleine, Netherlands..........	14:50.59
1980 Eric Heiden, U.S.............	14:28.13
1984 Igor Malkov, USSR	14:39.90
1988 Tomas Gustafson, Sweden	13:48.20

Women's 500 meters — Time

	Time
1960 Helga Haase, Germany	0:45.9
1964 Lydia Skoblikova, USSR	0:45.0
1968 Ludmila Titova, USSR	0:46.1
1972 Anne Henning, U.S.	0:43.33
1976 Sheila Young, U.S.............	0:42.76
1980 Karin Enke, E. Germany	0:41.78
1984 Christa Rothenburger, E. Germany ...	0:41.02
1988 Bonnie Blair, U.S.............	0:39.10

Women's 1,000 meters — Time

	Time
1960 Klara Guseva, USSR	1:34.1
1964 Lydia Skoblikova, USSR	1:33.2
1968 Carolina Geijssen, Netherlands.	1:32.6
1972 Monika Pflug, W. Germany	1:31.40
1976 Tatiana Averina, USSR	1:28.43
1980 Natalya Petruseva, USSR.	1:24.10
1984 Karin Enke, E. Germany	1:21.61
1988 Christa Rothenburger, E. Germany	1:17.65

Women's 1,500 meters — Time

	Time
1960 Lydia Skoblikova, USSR	2:52.2
1964 Lydia Skoblikova, USSR	2:22.6
1968 Kaija Mustonen, Finland..........	2:22.4
1972 Dianne Holum, U.S.	2:20.85
1976 Galina Stepanskaya, USSR.	2:16.58
1980 Anne Borckink, Netherlands	2:10.95
1984 Karin Enke, E. Germany	2:03.42
1988 Yvonne van Gennip, Netherlands	2:00.68

Women's 3,000 meters — Time

	Time
1960 Lydia Skoblikova, USSR	5:14.3
1964 Lydia Skoblikova, USSR	5:14.9
1968 Johanna Schut, Netherlands	4:56.2
1972 Christina Baas-Kaiser, Netherlands ...	4:52.14
1976 Tatiana Averina, USSR	4:45.19
1980 Bjoerg Eva Jensen, Norway	4:32.13
1984 Andrea Schoene, E. Germany	4:24.79
1988 Yvonne van Gennip, Netherlands	4:11.94

Women's 5,000 meters — Time

	Time
1988 Yvonne van Gennip, Netherlands	7:14:13

Winter Olympic Medal Winners in 1988

Calgary, Alberta, Canada, Feb. 13-28, 1988

	Gold	Silver	Bronze	Total		Gold	Silver	Bronze	Total
Soviet Union	11	9	9	29	United States........	2	1	3	6
East Germany	9	10	6	25	Italy	2	1	2	5
Switzerland..........	5	5	5	15	Norway	0	3	2	5
Austria	3	5	2	10	Canada	0	2	3	5
West Germany.......	2	4	2	8	Yugoslavia	0	2	1	3
Finland	4	0	3	7	Czechoslovakia	0	1	2	3
The Netherlands......	3	2	2	7	France	1	0	1	2
Sweden...........	4	0	2	6	Japan	0	0	1	1
					Liechtenstein	0	0	1	1

IGFA Freshwater & Saltwater All-Tackle World Records

Source: International Game Fish Association. Records confirmed to Jan., 1991

Saltwater Fish

Species	Weight	Where caught	Date	Angler
Albacore	88 lbs. 2 oz.	Pt. Mogan, Canary Islands	Nov. 19, 1977	Siegfried Dickemann
Amberjack, greater	155 lbs. 10 oz.	Bermuda	June 24, 1981	Joseph Dawson
Amberjack, Pacific	104 lbs.	Baja, Mexico	July 4, 1984	Richard Cresswell
Barracuda, great	83 lbs.	Lagos, Nigeria	Jan. 13, 1952	K.J.W. Hackett
Barracuda, Mexican	21 lbs.	Costa Rica	Mar. 27, 1987	E. Greg Kent
Barracuda, slender	17 lbs. 4 oz.	Sitra Channel, Bahrain	Nov. 21, 1985	Roger Cranswick
Bass, barred sand	13 lbs. 3 oz.	Huntington Beach, Cal.	Aug. 29, 1988	Robert Halal
Bass, black sea	9 lbs. 8 oz.	Virginia Beach, Va.	Jan. 9, 1987	Joe Mizelle Jr.
Bass, European	20 lbs. 11 oz.	Stes Maries de la Mer, France	May 6, 1986	Jean Baptiste Bayle
Bass, giant sea	563 lbs. 8 oz.	Anacaba Island, Cal.	Aug. 20, 1968	James D. McAdam Jr.
Bass, striped	78 lbs. 8 oz.	Atlantic City, N.J.	Sept. 21, 1982	Albert McReynolds
Bluefish	31 lbs. 12 oz.	Hatteras Inlet, N.C.	Jan. 30, 1972	James M. Hussey
Bonefish	19 lbs.	Zululand, S. Africa	May 26, 1962	Brian W. Batchelor
Bonito, Atlantic	18 lbs. 14 oz.	Fayal I., Azores	July 8, 1953	D. G. Higgs
Bonito, Pacific	23 lbs. 8 oz.	Victoria, Mahe Seychelles	Feb. 19, 1975	Anne Cochain
Cabezon	23 lbs.	Juan De Fuca Strait, Wash.	Aug. 4, 1990	Wesley Hunter
Cobia	135 lbs. 9 oz.	Shark Bay, Australia	July 9, 1985	Peter W. Goulding
Cod, Atlantic	98 lbs. 12 oz.	Isle of Shoals, N.H.	June 8, 1969	Alphonse Bielevich
Cod, Pacific	30 lbs.	Andrew Bay, Alaska	June 7, 1984	Donald Vaughn
Conger	104 lbs. 8 oz.	Brixham, England	June 5, 1988	Philip Greenway
Dolphin	87 lbs.	Papagallo Gulf, Costa Rica	Sept. 25, 1976	Manual Salazar
Drum, black	113 lbs. 1 oz.	Lewes, Del.	Sept. 15, 1975	Gerald Townsend
Drum, red	94 lbs. 2 oz.	Avon, N.C.	Nov. 7, 1984	David Deuel
Eel, African mottled	36 lbs. 1 oz.	Durban, So. Africa	June 10, 1984	Ferdie van Nooten
Eel, American	7 lb. 8 oz.	Mashpee, Mass.	May 8, 1990	Paul Peitavino
Flounder, southern	20 lb. 9 oz.	Nassau Sound, Fla.	Dec. 23, 1983	Larenza Mungin
Flounder, summer	22 lbs. 7 oz.	Montauk, N.Y.	Sept. 15, 1975	Charles Nappi
Grouper, Warsaw	436 lbs. 12 oz.	Gulf of Mexico, Destin, Fla.	Dec. 22, 1985	Steve Haeusler
Halibut, Atlantic	255 lbs. 4 oz.	Gloucester, Mass.	July 28, 1989	Sonny Manley
Halibut, California	53 lbs. 4 oz.	Santa Rosa Is., Cal.	July 7, 1988	Russell Harmon
Halibut, Pacific	356 lbs. 8 oz.	Juneau, Alaska	Nov. 8, 1986	Gregory Olsen
Jack, crevalle	54 lbs. 7oz.	Pt. Michel, Gabon	Jan. 15, 1982	Thomas Gibson Jr.
Jack, horse-eye	24 lbs. 8 oz.	Miami, Fla.	Dec. 20, 1982	Tito Schnau
Jack, Pacific crevalle	24 lbs.	Baja, Cal., Mex.	Apr. 30, 1987	Sharon Swanson
Jewfish	680 lbs.	Fernandina Beach, Fla.	May 20, 1961	Lynn Joyner
Kawakawa	29 lbs.	Clarion Is., Mexico	Dec. 17, 1986	Ronald Nakamura
Lingcod	64 lbs.	Elfin Cove, Alaska	Aug. 2, 1988	David Bauer
Mackerel, cero	17 lbs. 2 oz.	Islamorada, Fla.	Apr. 5, 1986	G. Michael Mills
Mackerel, king	90 lbs.	Key West, Fla.	Feb. 16, 1976	Norton Thomton
Mackeral, Spanish	13 lbs.	Ocracoke Inlet, N.C.	Nov. 4, 1987	Robert Cranton
Marlin, Atlantic blue	1,282 lbs.	St. Thomas, Virgin Islands	Aug. 6, 1977	Larry Martin
Marlin, black	1,560 lbs.	Cabo Blanco, Peru	Aug. 4, 1953	A. C. Glassell Jr.
Marlin, Pacific blue	1,376 lbs.	Kaaiwa Pt., Hawaii	May. 31, 1982	J.W. deBeaubien
Marlin, striped	494 lbs.	Tutukaka, New Zealand	Jan. 16, 1986	Bill Boniface
Marlin, white	181 lbs. 14 oz.	Vitoria, Brazil	Dec. 8, 1979	Evandro Luiz Caser
Permit	51 lbs. 8 oz.	Lake Worth, Fla.	Apr. 28, 1978	William M. Kenney
Pollack	26 lbs. 7 oz.	Devon, England	Dec. 30, 1984	Robert Perry
Pollock	46 lbs. 7 oz.	Brielle, N.J.	May 26, 1975	John Tomes Holton
Pompano, African	50 lbs. 8 oz.	Daytona Beach, Fla.	Apr. 21, 1990	Tom Sargent
Roosterfish	114 lbs.	La Paz, Mexico	June 1, 1960	Abe Sackheim
Runner, blue	8 lbs. 4 oz.	Bimini, Bahamas	Sept. 9, 1990	Brent Rowland
Runner, rainbow	33 lbs. 10 oz.	Clarion Is., Mexico	Mar. 14, 1976	Ralph A. Mikkelsen
Sailfish, Atlantic	128 lbs. 1 oz.	Luanda, Angola	Mar. 27, 1974	Harm Steyn
Sailfish, Pacific	221 lbs.	Santa Cruz Is., Ecuador	Feb. 12, 1947	C. W. Stewart
Seabass, white	83 lbs. 12 oz.	San Felipe, Mexico	Mar. 31, 1953	L.C. Baumgardner
Seatrout, spotted	16 lbs.	Mason's Beach, Va.	May 28, 1977	William Katko
Shark, blue	437 lbs.	Catherine Bay, N.S.W. Australia	Oct. 2, 1976	Peter Hyde
Shark, Greenland	1,708 lbs. 9 oz.	Trondheim, Norway	Oct. 18, 1987	Terje Nordtvedt
Shark, hammerhead	991 lbs.	Sarasota, Fla.	May 30, 1982	Allen Ogle
Shark, man-eater or white	2,664 lbs.	Ceduna, Australia	Apr. 21, 1959	Alfred Dean
Shark, mako	1,115 lbs.	Black R., Mauritius	Nov. 16, 1988	Patrick Guillanton
Shark, porbeagle	465 lbs.	Cornwall, England	July 23, 1976	Jorge Potier
Shark, thresher	802 lbs.	Tutukaka, New Zealand	Feb. 8, 1981	Dianne North
Shark, tiger	1,780 lbs.	Cherry Grove, S.C.	June 14, 1964	Walter Maxwell
Skipjack, black	20 lbs. 5 oz.	Baja, Mexico	Oct. 14, 1983	Roger Torriero
Snapper, cubera	121 lbs. 8 oz.	Cameron, La.	July 5, 1982	Mike Hebert
Snook	53 lbs. 10 oz.	Costa Rica	Oct. 18, 1978	Gilbert Ponzi
Spearfish	90 lbs. 13 oz.	Madeira Island, Portugal	June 2, 1980	Joseph Larkin
Swordfish	1,182 lbs.	Iquique, Chile	May 7, 1953	L. Marron
Tanguigue	99 lbs.	Natal, So. Africa	Mar. 14, 1982	Michael J. Wilkinson
Tarpon	283 lbs.	Lake Maracaibo, Venezuela	Mar. 19, 1956	M. Salazar
Tautog	24 lbs.	Wachapreagee, Va.	Aug. 25, 1987	Gregory Bell
Tope	72 lbs. 12 oz.	Parengarenga Harbor, New Zealand	Dec. 19, 1986	Melanie Feldman
Trevally, bigeye	15 lbs.	Isla Coiba, Panama	Jan. 18, 1984	Sally Timms
Trevally, giant	137 lbs. 9 oz.	McKenzie St. Park, Hawaii	July 13, 1983	Roy Gushiken
Tuna, Atlantic bigeye	375 lbs. 8 oz.	Ocean City, Md.	Aug. 26, 1977	Cecil Browne
Tuna, blackfin	42 lbs.	Bermuda	June 2, 1978	Alan J. Card
		Bermuda	July 18, 1989	Gilbert Pearman
Tuna, bluefin	1,496 lbs.	Aulds Cove, Nova Scotia	Oct. 26, 1979	Ken Fraser
Tuna, longtail	79 lbs. 2 oz.	Montague Is., N.S.W., Australia	Apr. 12, 1982	Tim Simpson

Species	Weight	Where caught	Date	Angler
Tuna, Pacific bigeye	435 lbs.	Cabo Blanco, Peru	Apr. 17, 1957	Dr. Russel Lee
Tuna, skipjack	41 lbs. 14 oz.	Mauritius	Nov. 12, 1985	Edmund Heinzen
Tuna, southern bluefin	348 lbs. 5 oz.	Whakatane, New Zealand	Jan. 16, 1981	Rex Wood
Tuna, yellowfin	388 lbs. 12 oz.	San Benedicto Island, Mexico	Apr. 1, 1977	Curt Wiesenhutter
Tunny, little	35 lbs. 2 oz.	Cap de Garde, Algeria	Dec. 14, 1988	Jean Yves Chatard
Wahoo	155 lbs. 8 oz.	Bahamas	Apr. 3, 1990	William Bourne
Weakfish	19 lbs. 2 oz.	Jones Beach Inlet, N.Y.	Oct. 11, 1984	Dennis Rooney
		Delaware Bay, Delaware	May 20, 1989	William Thomas
Yellowtail, California	78 lbs.	Alijos Rocks, Mexico	June 27, 1987	Richard Cresswell
Yellowtail, southern	114 lbs. 10 oz.	Tauranga, New Zealand	Feb. 5, 1984	Mike Godfrey

Freshwater Fish

Species	Weight	Where caught	Date	Angler
Barramundi	59 lbs. 12 oz.	Pt. Stuart, Australia	Apr. 7, 1983	Andrew Davern
Bass, largemouth	22 lbs. 4 oz.	Montgomery Lake, Ga.	June 2, 1932	George W. Perry
Bass, peacock	26 lbs. 8 oz.	Matevini R., Colombia	Jan. 26, 1982	Rod Neubert
Bass, redeye	8 lbs. 3 oz.	Flint River, Ga.	Oct. 23, 1977	David A. Hubbard
Bass rock	3 lbs.	York River, Ont.	Aug. 1, 1974	Peter Gulgin
Bass, smallmouth	11 lbs. 15 oz.	Dale Hollow Lake, Ky.	July 9, 1955	David L. Hayes
Bass, Suwannee	3 lbs. 14 oz.	Suwannee River, Fla.	Mar. 2, 1985	Ronnie Everett
Bass, white	6 lbs. 13 oz.	L. Orange, Va.	July 31, 1989	Ronald Sprouse
Bass, whiterock	24 lbs. 3 oz.	Leesville L., Va.	May 12, 1989	David Lambert
Bass, yellow	2 lbs. 4 oz.	Lake Monroe, Ind.	Mar. 27, 1977	Donald L. Stalker
Bluegill	4 lbs. 12 oz.	Ketona Lake, Ala.	Apr. 9, 1950	T.S. Hudson
Bowfin	21 lbs. 8 oz.	Florence, S.C.	Jan. 29, 1980	Robert Harmon
Buffalo, bigmouth	70 lbs. 5 oz.	Bastrop, La.	Apr. 21, 1980	Delbert Sisk
Buffalo, black	55 lbs. 8 oz.	Cherokee L., Tenn.	May 3, 1984	Edward McLain
Buffalo, smallmouth	68 lbs. 8 oz.	L. Hamilton, Ark.	May 16, 1984	Jerry Dolezal
Bullhead, brown	5 lbs. 8 oz.	Veal Pond, Ga.	May 22, 1975	Jimmy Andrews
Bullhead, yellow	4 lbs. 4 oz.	Mormon Lake, Ariz.	May 11, 1984	Emily Williams
Burbot	18 lbs. 4 oz.	Pickford, Mich.	Jan. 31, 1980	Thomas Courtemanche
Carp	75 lbs. 11 oz.	Lac de St. Cassien, France	May 21, 1987	Leo van der Gugten
Catfish, blue	97 lbs.	Missouri River, S.D.	Sept. 16, 1959	E.B. Elliott
Catfish, channel	58 lbs.	Santee-Cooper Res., S.C.	July 7, 1964	W.B. Whaley
Catfish, flathead	91 lbs. 4 oz.	L. Lewisville, Tex.	Mar. 28, 1982	Mike Rogers
Catfish, white	17 lbs. 7 oz.	Success L., Tulare, Cal.	Nov. 15, 1981	Chuck Idell
Char, Arctic	32 lbs. 9 oz.	Tree River, Canada	July 30, 1981	Jeffrey Ward
Crappie, white	5 lbs. 3 oz.	Enid Dam, Miss.	July 31, 1957	Fred L. Bright
Dolly Varden	12 lbs.	Noatak R., Alaska	July 10, 1987	Kenneth Alt
Dorado	51 lbs. 5 oz.	Corrientes, Argentina	Sept. 27, 1984	Armando Giudice
Drum, freshwater	54 lbs. 8 oz.	Nickajack Lake, Tenn.	Apr. 20, 1972	Benny E. Hull
Gar, alligator	279 lbs.	Rio Grande River, Tex.	Dec. 2, 1951	Bill Valverde
Gar, Florida	21 lbs. 3 oz.	Boca Raton, Fla.	June 3, 1981	Jeff Sabol
Gar, longnose	50 lbs. 5 oz.	Trinity River, Tex.	July 30, 1954	Townsend Miller
Gar, shortnose	5 lbs.	Sally Jones L., Oklahoma	Apr. 26, 1985	Buddy Croslin
Gar, spotted	8 lbs. 12 oz.	Tennessee R., Ala.	Aug. 26, 1987	Winston Baker
Grayling, Arctic	5 lbs. 15 oz.	Katseyedie River, N.W.T.	Aug. 16, 1967	Jeanne P. Branson
Inconnu	53 lbs.	Pah R., Alaska	Aug. 20, 1986	Lawrence Hudnall
Kokanee	9 lbs. 6 oz.	Okanagan Lake, Vernon, B.C.	June 18, 1988	Norm Kuhn
Muskellunge	69 lbs. 15 oz.	St. Lawrence River, N.Y.	Sept. 22, 1957	Arthur Lawton
Muskellunge, tiger	51 lbs. 3 oz.	Lac Vieux-Desert, Wis., Mich.	July 16, 1919	John Knobla
Perch, Nile	154 lbs. 5 oz.	Entebbe, Uganda	June 3, 1990	Frederick Dale
Perch, white	4 lbs. 12 oz.	Messalonskee Lake, Me.	June 4, 1949	Mrs. Earl Small
Perch, yellow	4 lbs. 3 oz.	Bordentown, N.J.	May, 1865	Dr. C.C. Abbot
Pickerel, chain	9 lbs. 6 oz.	Homerville, Ga.	Feb. 17, 1961	Baxley McQuaig Jr.
Pike, northern	55 lbs. 1 oz.	Lake of Grefeern, W., Germany	Oct. 16, 1986	Lothar Louis
Redhorse, greater	9 lbs. 3 oz.	Salmon R., Pulaski, N.Y.	May 11, 1985	Jason Wilson
Redhorse, silver	11 lbs. 7 oz.	Plum Creek, Wis.	May 29, 1985	Neal Long
Salmon, Atlantic	79 lbs. 2 oz.	Tana River, Norway	1928	Henrik Henriksen
Salmon, chinook	97 lbs. 4 oz.	Kenai R., Alas.	May 17, 1985	Les Anderson
Salmon, chum	32 lbs.	Behm Canal, Alas.	June 7, 1985	Fredrick Thynes
Salmon, coho	33 lbs. 4 oz.	Salmon R., Pulaski, N.Y.	Sept. 27, 1989	Jerry Lifton
Salmon, pink	12 lbs. 9 oz.	Morse, Kenai rivers, Alas.	Aug. 17, 1974	Steven A. Lee
Salmon, sockeye	15 lbs. 3 oz.	Kenai R., Alaska	Aug. 9, 1987	Stan Roach
Sauger	8 lbs. 12 oz.	Lake Sakakawea, N.D.	Oct. 6, 1971	Mike Fischer
Shad, American	11 lbs. 4 oz.	Connecticut R., Mass.	May 19, 1986	Bob Thibodo
Sturgeon, white	468 lbs.	Benicia, Cal.	July 9, 1983	Joey Pailotta 3d
Sunfish, green	2 lbs. 2 oz.	Stockton Lake, Mo.	June 18, 1971	Paul M. Dilley
Sunfish, redbreast	1 lb. 12 oz.	Suwannee R., Fla.	May 29, 1984	Alvin Buchanan
Sunfish, redear	4 lbs. 13 oz.	Marianna, Fla.	Mar. 13, 1986	Joey Floyd
Tigerfish	97 lbs.	Zaire R., Kinshasa, Zaire	July 9, 1988	Raymond Houtmans
Tilapia	6 lbs.	L. Okeechobee, Fla.	June 24, 1989	Joseph M. Tucker
Trout, Apache	2 lb. 10 oz.	Apache Res., Ariz.	June 27, 1989	Mike Shannon
Trout, brook	14 lbs. 8 oz.	Nipigon River, Ont.	July 1916	Dr. W.J. Cook
Trout, brown	35 lbs. 15 oz.	Nahuel Huapi, Argentina	Dec. 16, 1952	Eugenio Cavaglia
Trout, bull	32 lbs.	L. Pend Oreille, Ida.	Oct. 27, 1949	N.L. Higgins
Trout, cutthroat	41 lbs.	Pyramid Lake, Nev.	Dec. 1925	J. Skimmerhorn
Trout, golden	11 lbs.	Cook's Lake, Wyo.	Aug. 5, 1948	Charles S. Reed
Trout, lake	65 lbs.	Great Bear Lake, N.W.T.	Aug. 8, 1970	Larry Daunis
Trout, rainbow	42 lbs. 2 oz.	Bell Island, Alas.	June 22, 1970	David Robert White
Trout, tiger	20 lbs. 13 oz.	Lake Michigan, Wis.	Aug. 12, 1978	Pete Friedland
Walleye	25 lbs.	Old Hickory Lake, Tenn.	Aug. 1, 1960	Mabry Harper
Warmouth	2 lbs. 7 oz.	Yellow R., Holt, Fla.	Oct. 19, 1985	Tony D. Dempsey
Whitefish, lake	14 lbs. 6 oz.	Meaford, Ont.	May 21, 1984	Dennis Laycock
Whitefish, mountain	5 lbs. 6 oz.	Rioh R., Sask.	June 15, 1988	John Bell
Whitefish, river	11 lbs. 2 oz.	Nymoua, Sweden	Dec. 9, 1984	Jorgen Larsson
Whitefish, round	6 lbs.	Putahow R., Manitoba	June 14, 1984	Allen Ristori
Zander	22 lbs. 2 oz.	Trosa, Sweden	June 12, 1986	Harry Lee Tennison

National Hockey League, 1990-91

Final Standings

Wales Conference

Adams Division

	W	L	T	GF	GA	PTS
Boston	44	24	12	299	264	100
Montreal	39	30	11	273	249	89
Buffalo	31	30	19	292	278	81
Hartford	31	38	11	238	276	73
Quebec	16	50	14	236	354	46

Patrick Division

	W	L	T	GF	GA	PTS
Pittsburgh	41	33	6	342	305	88
N.Y. Rangers	36	31	13	297	265	85
Washington	37	36	7	258	258	81
New Jersey	32	33	15	272	264	79
Philadelphia	33	37	10	252	267	76
N.Y. Islanders	25	45	10	223	290	60

Campbell Conference

Norris Division

	W	L	T	GF	GA	PTS
Chicago	49	23	8	284	211	106
St. Louis	47	22	11	310	250	105
Detroit	34	38	8	273	298	76
Minnesota	27	39	14	256	266	68
Toronto	23	46	11	241	318	57

Smythe Division

	W	L	T	GF	GA	PTS
Los Angeles	46	24	10	340	254	102
Calgary	46	26	8	344	263	100
Edmonton	37	37	6	272	272	80
Vancouver	28	43	9	243	315	65
Winnipeg	26	43	11	260	288	63

Penguins Win First Stanley Cup Championship

The Pittsburgh Penguins won their first Stanley Cup championship by defeating the Minnesota North Stars 4 games to 2. Mario Lemieux of the Penguins was chosen the most valuable player in the playoffs.

Stanley Cup Playoff Results

Wales Conference

Washington defeated N.Y. Rangers 4-2
Montreal defeated Buffalo 4-2
Pittsburgh defeated New Jersey 4-3
Boston defeated Hartford 4-2
Pittsburgh defeated Washington 4-1
Boston defeated Montreal 4-3
Pittsburgh defeated Boston 4-2

Campbell Conference

Minnesota defeated Chicago 4-2
Los Angeles defeated Vancouver 4-2
St. Louis defeated Detroit 4-3
Edmonton defeated Calgary 4-3
Edmonton defeated Los Angeles 4-2
Minnesota defeated St. Louis 4-2
Minnesota defeated Edmonton 4-1

Finals

Pittsburgh defeated Minnesota 4-2

Stanley Cup Champions Since 1927

Year	Champion	Coach	Final opponent	Year	Champion	Coach	Final opponent
1927	Ottawa	Dave Gill	Boston	1960	Montreal	Toe Blake	Toronto
1928	N.Y. Rangers	Lester Patrick	Montreal	1961	Chicago	Rudy Pilous	Detroit
1929	Boston	Cy Denneny	N.Y. Rangers	1962	Toronto	Punch Imlach	Chicago
1930	Montreal	Cecil Hart	Boston	1963	Toronto	Punch Imlach	Detroit
1931	Montreal	Cecil Hart	Chicago	1964	Toronto	Punch Imlach	Detroit
1932	Toronto	Dick Irvin	N.Y. Rangers	1965	Montreal	Toe Blake	Chicago
1933	New York	Lester Patrick	Toronto	1966	Montreal	Toe Blake	Detroit
1934	Chicago	Tommy Gorman	Detroit	1967	Toronto	Punch Imlach	Montreal
1935	Montreal Maroons	Tommy Gorman	Toronto	1968	Montreal	Toe Blake	St. Louis
1936	Detroit	Jack Adams	Toronto	1969	Montreal	Claude Ruel	St. Louis
1937	Detroit	Jack Adams	N.Y. Rangers	1970	Boston	Harry Sinden	St. Louis
1938	Chicago	Bill Stewart	Toronto	1971	Montreal	Al MacNeil	Chicago
1939	Boston	Art Ross	Toronto	1972	Boston	Tom Johnson	N.Y. Rangers
1940	N.Y. Rangers	Frank Boucher	Toronto	1973	Montreal	Scotty Bowman	Chicago
1941	Boston	Cooney Weiland	Detroit	1974	Philadelphia	Fred Shero	Boston
1942	Toronto	Hap Day	Detroit	1975	Philadelphia	Fred Shero	Buffalo
1943	Detroit	Jack Adams	Boston	1976	Montreal	Scotty Bowman	Philadelphia
1944	Montreal	Dick Irvin	Chicago	1977	Montreal	Scotty Bowman	Boston
1945	Toronto	Hap Day	Detroit	1978	Montreal	Scotty Bowman	Boston
1946	Montreal	Dick Irvin	Boston	1979	Montreal	Scotty Bowman	N.Y. Rangers
1947	Toronto	Hap Day	Montreal	1980	N.Y. Islanders	Al Arbour	Philadelphia
1948	Toronto	Hap Day	Detroit	1981	N.Y. Islanders	Al Arbour	Minnesota
1949	Toronto	Hap Day	Detroit	1982	N.Y. Islanders	Al Arbour	Vancouver
1950	Detroit	Tommy Ivan	N.Y. Rangers	1983	N.Y. Islanders	Al Arbour	Edmonton
1951	Toronto	Joe Primeau	Montreal	1984	Edmonton	Glen Sather	N.Y. Islanders
1952	Detroit	Tommy Ivan	Montreal	1985	Edmonton	Glen Sather	Philadelphia
1953	Montreal	Dick Irvin	Boston	1986	Montreal	Jean Perron	Calgary
1954	Detroit	Tommy Ivan	Montreal	1987	Edmonton	Glen Sather	Philadelphia
1955	Detroit	Jimmy Skinner	Montreal	1988	Edmonton	Glen Sather	Boston
1956	Montreal	Toe Blake	Detroit	1989	Calgary	Terry Crisp	Montreal
1957	Montreal	Toe Blake	Boston	1990	Edmonton	John Muckler	Boston
1958	Montreal	Toe Blake	Boston	1991	Pittsburgh	Bob Johnson	Minnesota
1959	Montreal	Toe Blake	Toronto				

Individual Leaders

Points

Wayne Gretzky, Los Angeles, 163; Brett Hull, St. Louis, 131; Adam Oates, St. Louis, 115; Mark Recchi, Pittsburgh, 113; John Cullen, Pitts.-Hartford, 110.

Goal Scoring

Brett Hull, St. Louis, 86; Cam Neely, Boston, 51; Theo Fleury, Calgary, 51; Steve Yzerman, Detroit, 51; Mike Gartner, N.Y. Rangers, 49.

Assists

Wayne Gretzky, Los Angeles, 122; Adam Oates, St. Louis, 90; Al MacInnis, Calgary, 75; Ray Bourque, Boston, 73; Mark Recchi, Pittsburgh, 73.

Power-play goals

Brett Hull, St. Louis, 29; Mike Gartner, N.Y. Rangers, 22; Joe Nieuwendyk, Calgary, 22; Dave Gagner, Minnesota, 20; John Maclean, New Jersey, 19.

Short hand goals

Dave Reid, Toronto, 8; Theo Fleury, Calgary, 7; Dirk Graham, Chicago, 6; Craig MacTavish, Edmonton, 6; Steve Yzerman, Detroit, 6.

Shooting percentage

(minimum 80 shots)

Sergei Makarov, Calgary, 32.3; Peter Zezel, Wash.-Tor., 23.3;

Brett Hull, St. Louis, 22.1; Ken Hodge, Boston, 21.9; Mark Recchi, Pittsburgh, 21.7.

Plus/Minus

Marty McSorley, Los Angeles, 48; Theo Fleury, Calgary, 48; Al MacInnis, Calgary, 42; Jeremy Roenick, Chicago, 38; Steve Larmer, Chicago, 37.

Goaltending Leaders

(minimum 25 games)

Goals against average

Ed Belfour, Chicago, 2.47; Don Beaupre, Washington, 2.64; Patrick Roy, Montreal, 2.71; Andy Moog, Boston, 2.87; Pete Peeters, Philadelphia, 2.88.

Wins

Ed Belfour, Chicago, 43; Mike Vernon, Calgary, 31; Tim Cheveldae, Detroit, 30; Vincent Riendeau, St Louis, 29; Tom Barrasso, Pittsburgh, 27; Bill Ranford, Edmonton, 27.

Save percentage

Ed Belfour, Chicago, .910; Patrick Roy, Montreal, .906; Mike Richter, N.Y. Rangers, .903; Pete Peeters, Philadelphia, .902; Kelly Hrudey, Los Angeles, .900.

Shutouts

Don Beaupre, Washington, 5; Andy Moog, Boston, 4; Bob Essensa, Winnipeg, 4; Ed Belfour, Chicago, 4.

Individual Scoring

(42 or more games played or 40 points)

Boston Bruins

	GP	G	A	Pts	+/−	PIM
Ray Bourque	76	21	73	94	33	75
Craig Janney	77	26	66	92	15	8
Cam Neely	69	51	40	91	26	98
Ken Hodge	70	30	29	59	11	20
Dave Christian	78	32	21	53	8	41
Bob Sweeney	80	15	33	48	12	115
Glen Wesley	80	11	32	43	0	78
Randy Burridge	62	15	13	28	17	40
Petri Skriko	48	9	18	27	5−	17
Garry Galley	70	6	21	27	0	84
Jim Wiemer	61	4	19	23	3	62
Don Sweeney	77	8	13	21	2	67
Jeff Lazaro	49	5	13	18	7	67
Wes Walz	56	8	8	16	14−	32
John Carter	50	4	7	11	13−	68
Andy Brickley	40	2	9	11	4−	8
Stephane Quintal	45	2	6	8	2	89
Allen Pedersen	57	2	6	8	15	107
Andy Moog	51	0	2	2	0	20

Coach—Mike Milbury

Buffalo Sabers

	GP	G	A	Pts	+/−	PIM
Dale Hawerchuk	80	31	58	89	2	32
Pierre Turgeon	78	32	47	79	14	26
Dave Andreychuk	80	36	33	69	11	32
Alexander Mogilny	62	30	34	64	14	16
Rick Vaive	71	25	27	52	11	74
Christian Ruuttu	77	16	34	50	6−	96
Benoit Hogue	76	19	28	47	8−	74
Uwe Krupp	74	12	32	44	14	66
Grant Ledyard	60	8	23	31	13	46
Doug Bodger	58	5	23	28	8−	54
Tony Tanti	56	7	19	26	3	50
Dave Snuggerud	80	9	15	24	13−	32
Mikko Makela	60	15	7	22	2−	25
Greg Paslawski	55	11	11	22	6	14
Mike Ramsey	71	6	14	20	14	46
Rob Ray	66	8	8	16	11−	348
Dean Kennedy	64	4	8	12	5	119
Mike Hartman	60	9	2	11	10−	204
Lou Franceschetti	51	2	9	11	0	56
Jay Wells	43	1	2	3	18−	86

Coach—Rick Dudley

Calgary Flames

	GP	G	A	Pts	+/−	PIM
Theo Fleury	79	51	53	104	48	136
Al MacInnis	78	28	75	103	42	90
Joe Nieuwendyk	79	45	40	85	19	36
Doug Gilmour	78	20	61	81	27	142
Sergei Makarov	78	30	49	79	15	44
Gary Suter	79	12	58	70	26	102
Gary Roberts	80	22	31	53	15	252
Robert Reichel	66	19	22	41	17	22
Joel Otto	76	19	20	39	4−	185
Paul Fenton	78	14	21	35	5−	28
Stephane Matteau	78	15	19	34	17	93
Carey Wilson	57	11	18	29	13−	18
Brian MacLellan	57	13	14	27	15	55
Frantisek Musil	75	7	16	23	12	183
Jamie Macoun	79	7	15	22	29	84
Ric Nattress	58	5	13	18	1−	63
Tim Sweeney	42	7	9	16	1	8
Ronnie Stern	44	3	6	9	14−	230
Jim Kyte	43	0	9	9	10	155
Kevan Guy	43	1	6	7	5−	43
Mike Vernon	54	0	4	4	0	8

Coach—Doug Risebrough

Chicago Black Hawks

	GP	G	A	Pts	+/−	PIM
Steve Larmer	80	44	57	101	37	79
Jeremy Roenick	79	41	53	94	38	80
Michel Goulet	74	27	38	65	27	65
Chris Chelios	77	12	52	64	23	192
Steve Thomas	69	19	35	54	8	129
Adam Creighton	72	22	29	51	0	135
Dirk Graham	80	24	21	45	12	88
Doug Wilson	51	11	29	40	25	32
Troy Murray	75	14	23	37	13	74
Tony McKegney	59	17	17	34	27−	48
Wayne Presley	71	15	19	34	11	122
Dave Manson	75	14	15	29	20	191
Greg Gilbert	72	10	15	25	6	58
Mike Hudson	55	7	9	16	5	62
Trent Yawney	61	3	13	16	6	77
Paul Gillis	62	3	13	16	18−	144
Jocelyn Lemieux	67	6	7	13	7−	119
Keith Brown	45	1	10	11	9	55
Steve Konroyd	70	0	11	11	11	40
Bob McGill	77	4	5	9	8	153
Mike Peluso	53	6	1	7	3−	320
Ed Belfour	74	0	3	3	0	34

Coach—Mike Keenan

Detroit Red Wings

	GP	G	A	Pts	+/−	PIM
Steve Yzerman	80	51	57	108	2—	34
Sergei Fedorov	77	31	48	79	11	66
Kevin Miller	74	22	28	50	3—	67
Shawn Burr	80	20	30	50	14	112
Yves Racine	62	7	40	47	1	33
Jimmy Carson	64	21	25	46	3	28
Paul Ysebaert	62	19	21	40	7—	22
Dave Barr	70	18	22	40	19	55
Johan Garpenlov	71	18	21	39	4—	18
Bob Probert	55	16	23	39	3—	315
Doug Crossman	74	8	29	37	23—	48
Brent Fedyk	67	16	19	35	21	38
Gerard Gallant	45	10	16	26	6	111
Rick Zombo	77	4	19	23	2—	57
Steve Chiasson	42	3	17	20	0	80
Marc Habscheid	46	9	8	17	10—	22
Rick Green	65	2	14	16	10	24
Keith Primeau	58	3	12	15	12—	106
Brad McCrimmon	64	0	13	13	7	81
Bobby Dollas	56	3	5	8	6	20
Randy McKay	47	1	7	8	15—	183
Tim Cheveldae	65	0	5	5	0	2
Brad Marsh	42	1	3	4	9—	31

Coach—Bryan Murray

Edmonton Oilers

	GP	G	A	Pts	+/−	PIM
Esa Tikkanen	79	27	42	69	22	85
Petr Klima	70	40	28	68	24	113
Mark Messier	53	12	51	63	15	34
Joe Murphy	80	27	35	62	2	35
Craig Simpson	75	30	27	57	8—	66
Glenn Anderson	74	24	31	55	7—	59
Steve Smith	77	13	41	54	14	193
Martin Gelinas	73	20	20	40	7—	34
Ken Linseman	56	7	29	36	15	94
Craig MacTavish	80	17	15	32	1—	76
Anatoli Semenov	57	15	16	31	17	26
Charlie Huddy	53	5	22	27	4	32
Adam Graves	76	7	18	25	21—	127
Chris Joesph	49	5	17	22	3	59
Kevin Lowe	73	3	13	16	9—	113
Geoff Smith	59	1	12	13	13	55
Jeff Beukeboom	67	3	7	10	6	150
Craig Muni	76	1	9	10	10	77
Dave Brown	58	3	4	7	7—	160
Kelly Buchberger	64	3	1	4	6—	160
Bill Ranford	60	0	4	4	0	6

Coach—John Muckler

Hartford Whalers

	GP	G	A	Pts	+/−	PIM
John Cullen	78	39	71	110	6—	101
Pat Verbeek	80	43	39	82	0	246
Rob Brown	69	24	34	58	7—	132
Zarley Zalapski	77	15	39	54	8	65
Kevin Dineen	61	17	30	47	15—	104
Bobby Holik	78	21	22	43	3—	113
Mark Hunter	68	14	18	32	2	165
Brad Shaw	72	4	28	32	10—	29
Todd Krygier	72	13	17	30	1	95
Dean Evason	75	6	23	29	6—	170
Paul Cyr	70	12	13	25	8—	107
Sylvain Cote	73	7	12	19	17—	17
Mike Tomlak	64	8	8	16	9—	55
Mikael Andersson	41	4	7	11	0	8
Adam Burt	42	2	7	9	4—	63
Jim McKenzie	41	4	3	7	7—	108
Doug Houda	41	1	6	7	5—	82
Ed Kastelic	45	2	2	4	7—	211
Randy Ladouceur	67	1	3	4	10—	118
Peter Sidorkiewicz	52	0	4	4	0	6

Coach—Rick Ley

Los Angeles Kings

	GP	G	A	Pts	+/−	PIM
Wayne Gretzky	78	41	122	163	30	16
Luc Robitaille	76	45	46	91	28	68
Tomas Sandstrom	68	45	44	89	27	106
Tony Granato	68	30	34	64	22	156
Steve Duchesne	78	21	41	62	19	66
Todd Elik	74	21	37	58	20	58
Dave Taylor	73	23	30	53	27	148
Rob Blake	75	12	34	46	3	125
Marty McSorley	61	7	32	39	48	221
Robert Kudelski	72	23	13	36	9	46
Brian Benning	61	7	24	31	12	123
John Tonelli	71	14	16	30	3	49
Steve Kasper	67	9	19	28	3	33
Larry Robinson	62	1	22	23	22	16
Brad Jones	53	9	11	20	11	57
Jay Miller	66	8	12	20	9	259
Ilkka Sinisalo	53	5	12	17	6—	26
John McIntyre	69	8	8	16	6	140
Mike Donnelly	53	7	5	12	3	41
Rod Buskas	57	3	8	11	14	180
Tim Watters	45	0	4	4	7	92
Kelly Hrudey	47	0	0	0	0	14

Coach—Tom Webster

Minnesota North Stars

	GP	G	A	Pts	+/−	PIM
Dave Gagner	73	40	42	82	9	114
Brian Bellows	80	35	40	75	13—	43
Brian Propp	79	26	47	73	7	58
Neal Broten	79	13	56	69	3—	26
Mike Modano	79	28	36	64	2	65
Bobby Smith	73	15	31	46	9—	60
Ulf Dahlen	66	21	18	39	7	6
Mark Tinordi	69	5	27	32	1	191
Doug Smail	72	8	15	23	8—	48
Brian Glynn	66	8	11	19	5—	83
Gaetan Duchesne	68	9	9	18	4	18
Perry Berezan	52	11	6	17	2—	26
Jim Johnson	68	1	14	15	6	123
Curt Giles	70	4	10	14	3	48
Chris Dahlquist	64	3	8	11	1—	63
Neil Wilkinson	50	2	9	11	5—	117
Rob Zettler	47	1	4	5	10—	109
Jon Casey	55	0	2	2	0	22

Coach—Bob Gainey

Montreal Canadiens

	GP	G	A	Pts	+/−	PIM
Russ Courtnall	79	26	50	76	5	29
Stephane Richer	75	31	30	61	0	53
Denis Savard	70	28	31	59	1—	52
Stephan Lebeau	73	22	31	53	4	24
Shayne Corson	71	23	24	47	6	138
Guy Carbonneau	78	20	24	44	1—	63
Mike McPhee	64	22	21	43	6	50
Mike Keane	73	13	23	36	6	50
Brian Skrudland	57	15	19	34	12	85
Matt Schneider	69	10	20	30	7	63
Petr Svoboda	60	4	22	26	5	52
Eric Desjardins	62	7	18	25	7	27
Andrew Cassels	54	6	19	25	2	20
Sylvain Lefebvre	63	5	18	23	11—	20
Tom Chorske	57	9	11	20	8—	32
J.J. Daigneault	51	3	16	19	2—	31
Brent Gilchrist	51	6	9	15	3—	10
Donald Dufresne	53	2	13	15	5	55
Patrick Roy	48	0	2	2	0	6
Lyle Odelein	52	0	2	2	7	259

Coach—Pat Burns

New Jersey Devils

	GP	G	A	Pts	+/−	PIM
John MacLean	78	45	33	78	8	150
Kirk Muller	80	19	51	70	1	52
Brendan Shanahan	75	29	37	66	4	141
Peter Stastny	77	18	42	60	0	53
Claude Lemieux	78	30	17	47	8—	105
Patrik Sundstrom	71	15	31	46	7	48
Bruce Driver	73	9	36	45	11	62
Alexei Kasatonov	78	10	31	41	23	76
Eric Weinrich	76	4	34	38	10	48
Doug Brown	58	14	16	30	18	4
Jon Morris	53	9	19	28	9	27
Zdeno Ciger	45	8	17	25	3	8
David Maley	64	8	14	22	9	151
Laurie Boschman	78	11	9	20	1—	79
Ken Daneyko	80	4	16	20	10—	249
Viacheslav Fetisov	67	3	16	19	5	62
Pat Conacher	49	5	11	16	9	27
Lee Norwood	49	6	9	15	5	137
Tommy Albelin	47	2	12	14	1	44
Troy Crowder	59	6	3	9	10—	182
Chris Terreri	53	0	3	3	0	2

Coach—John Cunniff; Tom McVie

New York Islanders

	GP	G	A	Pts	+/−	PIM
Pat LaFontaine	75	41	44	85	6−	42
Dave Volek	77	22	34	56	10−	57
Brent Sutter	75	21	32	53	8−	49
Patrick Flatley	56	20	25	45	2−	74
Derek King	66	19	26	45	1	44
Randy Wood	76	24	18	42	12−	45
Ray Ferraro	76	21	21	42	12−	70
Jeff Norton	44	3	25	28	13−	16
Bill Berg	78	9	14	23	3−	67
Gary Nylund	72	2	21	23	8−	105
Wayne McBean	52	5	14	19	21−	47
Joe Reekie	66	3	16	19	17	96
Dave Chyzowski	56	5	9	14	19−	61
Hubie McDonough	52	6	6	12	14−	10
Brad Lauer	44	4	8	12	6−	45
Craig Ludwig	75	1	8	9	24−	77
Ken Baumgartner	78	1	6	7	14−	282
Mick Vukota	60	2	4	6	13−	238
Richard Pilon	60	1	4	5	12−	126
Glenn Healy	53	0	2	2	0	14
Coach—Al Arbour						

New York Rangers

	GP	G	A	Pts	+/−	PIM
Brian Leetch	80	16	72	88	2	42
Bernie Nicholls	71	25	48	73	5	96
Mike Gartner	79	49	20	69	9−	53
Darren Turcotte	74	26	41	67	5−	37
Brian Mullen	79	19	43	62	12	44
James Patrick	74	10	49	59	5−	58
John Ogrodnick	79	31	23	54	15	10
Ray Sheppard	59	24	23	47	8	21
Kelly Kisio	51	15	20	35	3	58
Kris King	72	11	14	25	1−	156
Jan Erixon	53	7	18	25	13	8
Randy Moller	61	4	19	23	13	161
Troy Mallette	71	12	10	22	8−	252
Mark Janssens	67	9	7	16	1−	172
Jody Hull	47	5	8	13	2	10
Joe Cirella	58	3	10	13	27−	111
David Shaw	77	2	10	12	8	89
Normand Rochefort	44	3	7	10	10	35
Joey Kocur	57	5	4	9	7−	289
Mark Hardy	70	1	5	6	1−	89
Mike Richter	45	0	1	1	0	4
Coach—Roger Neilson						

Philadelphia Flyers

	GP	G	A	Pts	+/−	PIM
Rick Tocchet	70	40	31	71	2	150
Per-Erik Eklund	73	19	50	69	2−	14
Murray Craven	77	19	47	66	2−	53
Ron Sutter	80	17	28	45	2	92
Gordon Murphy	80	11	31	42	7−	58
Mike Ricci	68	21	20	41	8−	64
Scott Mellanby	74	20	21	41	8	155
Keith Acton	76	14	23	37	9−	131
Terry Carkner	79	7	25	32	15−	204
Normand Lacombe	74	11	20	31	1	27
Kjell Samuelsson	78	9	19	28	4	82
Mark Pederson	59	10	16	26	5−	23
Jiri Latal	50	5	21	26	19−	14
Derrick Smith	72	11	10	21	0	37
Dale Kushner	63	7	11	18	4−	195
Craig Berube	74	8	9	17	6−	293
Murray Baron	67	8	8	16	3−	74
Martin Hostak	50	3	10	13	1	22
Dave Fenyves	40	1	4	5	1	28
Coach—Paul Holmgren						

Pittsburgh Penguins

	GP	G	A	Pts	+/−	PIM
Mark Recchi	78	40	73	113	0	48
Paul Coffey	76	24	69	93	18−	128
Ron Francis	81	23	64	87	2−	72
Kevin Stevens	80	40	46	86	1−	133
Jaromir Jagr	80	27	30	57	4−	42
Mario Lemieux	26	19	26	45	8	30
Larry Murphy	75	9	34	43	6−	68
Bob Errey	79	20	22	42	11	115

	GP	G	A	Pts	+/−	PIM
Scott Young	77	17	25	42	6−	41
Joe Mullen	47	17	22	39	9	6
Phil Bourque	78	20	14	34	7	106
Bryan Trottier	52	9	19	28	5	24
Ulf Samuelsson	76	4	22	26	17	211
Randy Gilhen	72	15	10	25	3	51
Jiri Hrdina	51	6	17	23	6−	17
Paul Stanton	75	5	18	23	11	40
Troy Loney	44	7	9	16	10	85
Gordie Roberts	64	3	13	16	17	78
Barry Pederson	46	6	8	14	2	21
Peter Taglianetti	55	3	9	12	16	107
Grant Jennings	57	2	7	9	11−	108
Tom Barrasso	48	0	5	5	0	40
Coach—Bob Johnson						

Quebec Nordiques

	GP	G	A	Pts	+/−	PIM
Joe Sakic	80	48	61	109	26−	24
Mats Sundin	80	23	36	59	24−	58
Tony Hrkac	70	16	32	48	22−	16
Stephane Morin	48	13	27	40	6	28
Mike Hough	63	13	20	33	7−	111
Bryan Fogarty	45	9	22	31	11−	24
Guy Lafleur	59	12	16	28	10−	2
Steven Finn	71	6	13	19	26−	228
Craig Wolanin	80	5	13	18	13−	89
Scott Pearson	47	11	4	15	9−	104
Owen Nolan	59	3	10	13	19−	109
Randy Velischek	79	2	10	12	19−	42
Herb Raglan	47	4	6	10	5	82
Curtis Leschyshyn	55	3	7	10	19−	49
Ron Tugnutt	56	0	0	0	0	0
Coach—Dave Chambers						

St. Louis Blues

	GP	G	A	Pts	+/−	PIM
Brett Hull	78	86	45	131	23	22
Adam Oates	61	25	90	115	15	29
Dan Quinn	78	22	38	60	33−	66
Jeff Brown	67	12	47	59	4	39
Rod Brind'Amour	78	17	32	49	2	93
Scott Stevens	78	5	44	49	23	150
Dave Lowry	79	19	21	40	19	168
Ron Wilson	73	10	27	37	1−	54
Paul Cavallini	67	10	25	35	19	89
Gino Cavallini	78	8	27	35	4	81
Bob Bassen	79	16	18	34	17	183
Rich Sutter	77	16	11	27	6	122
Garth Butcher	82	6	16	22	14−	289
Glen Featherstone	68	5	15	20	19	204
Mario Marois	64	2	14	16	17	81
Darin Kimble	61	3	6	9	3−	242
Harold Snepsts	54	1	4	5	3	50
Vincent Riendeau	44	0	2	2	0	0
Coach—Brian Sutter						

Toronto Maple Leafs

	GP	G	A	Pts	+/−	PIM
Vincent Damphousse	79	26	47	73	31−	65
Dave Ellett	77	12	37	49	8−	75
Mike Krushelnyski	74	18	27	45	1	58
Brian Bradley	70	11	31	42	9−	62
Peter Zezel	52	21	19	40	20−	14
Michel Petit	73	13	26	39	34−	179
Wendel Clark	63	18	16	34	5−	152
Dave Hannan	74	11	23	34	9−	82
Rob Ramage	80	10	24	34	2	173
Dan Marois	78	21	9	30	16−	112
Gary Leeman	52	17	12	29	25−	39
Dave Reid	69	15	13	28	10−	18
Lucien Deblois	52	12	14	26	3−	43
Bob Rouse	60	7	19	26	18−	75
Mike Foligno	68	12	12	24	1	107
Todd Gill	72	2	21	23	4−	113
Aaron Broten	47	11	8	19	9	38
Claude Loiselle	66	6	11	17	20−	88
Kevin Maguire	63	9	5	14	10−	180
Luke Richardson	78	1	9	10	28−	238
Peter Ing	56	0	0	0	0	6
Coach—Doug Carpenter; Tom Watt						

Vancouver Canucks

	GP	G	A	Pts	+/-	PIM
Trevor Linden	80	33	36	69	25-	65
Geoff Courtnall	77	33	32	65	16	64
Greg Adams	55	21	24	45	5-	10
Cliff Ronning	59	20	24	44	0	10
Dave Capuano	61	13	31	44	1	42
Doug Lidster	78	6	32	38	6-	77
Sergio Momesso	70	16	20	36	13	174
Igor Larionov	64	13	21	34	3-	14
Steve Bozek	62	15	17	32	6-	22
Robert Kron	76	12	20	32	11-	21
Jyrki Lumme	80	5	27	32	15-	59
Tom Kurvers	51	4	26	30	25-	28
Garry Valk	59	10	11	21	23-	67
Petr Nedved	61	10	6	16	21-	20
Stan Smyl	45	2	12	14	5-	87
Jim Sandlak	59	7	6	13	20-	125
Gerald Diduck	63	4	9	13	5-	105
Adrien Plavsic	48	2	10	12	23-	62
Gino Odjick	45	7	1	8	6-	296
Robert Nordmark	45	2	6	8	10-	63
Rob Murphy	42	5	1	6	11-	90
Robert Dirk	52	2	3	5	5-	120
Troy Gamble	47	0	1	1	0	14

Coach—Bob McCammon; Pat Quinn

Washington Capitals

	GP	G	A	Pts	+/-	PIM
Kevin Hatcher	79	24	50	74	10-	69
Mike Ridley	79	23	48	71	9	26
Michal Pivonka	79	20	49	69	3	34
John Druce	80	22	36	58	4	46
Calle Johansson	80	11	41	52	2-	23
Kelly Miller	80	24	26	50	10	29
Dale Hunter	76	16	30	46	22-	234
Dino Ciccarelli	54	21	18	39	17-	66
Al Iafrate	72	9	23	32	16-	237
Stephen Leach	68	11	19	30	9-	99
Peter Bondra	54	12	16	28	10-	47
Dimitri Khristich	40	13	14	27	1-	21
Mikhail Tatarinov	65	8	15	23	4-	82
Nick Kypreos	79	9	9	18	4-	196
Dave Tippett	61	6	9	15	13-	24
Tim Bergland	47	5	9	14	1-	21
Alan May	67	4	6	10	10-	264
Ken Sabourin	44	2	7	9	15	117
Rod Langway	56	1	7	8	12	24
Mike Lalor	68	1	5	6	23-	61
Don Beaupre	45	0	0	0	0	18

Coach—Terry Murray

Winnipeg Jets

	GP	G	A	Pts	+/-	PIM
Phil Housley	78	23	53	76	13-	24
Ed Olczyk	79	30	41	71	27-	82
Thomas Steen	58	19	48	67	3-	49
Pat Elynuik	80	31	34	65	13-	73
Fredrik Olausson	71	12	29	41	22-	24
Paul MacDermid	69	15	21	36	6-	128
Brent Ashton	61	12	24	36	10-	58
Doug Evans	70	7	27	34	1-	108
Teppo Numminen	80	8	25	33	15-	28
Randy Carlyle	52	9	19	28	6	46
Dave McLlwain	60	14	11	25	13-	46
Danton Cole	66	13	11	24	14-	24
Moe Mantha	57	9	15	24	20-	33
Phil Sykes	70	12	10	22	9-	59
Mark Osborne	55	11	11	22	11-	63
Scott Arniel	75	5	17	22	12-	81
Mark Kumpel	53	7	3	10	10-	10
Mike Eagles	44	0	9	9	10-	79
Gord Donnelly	57	3	4	7	13-	265
Shawn Cronin	67	1	5	6	10-	189
Bob Essensa	55	0	3	3	0	6

Coach—Bob Murdoch

Ross Trophy (Leading Scorer)

1927	Bill Cook, N.Y. Rangers	1949	Roy Conacher, Chicago	1971	Phil Esposito, Boston
1928	Howie Morenz, Montreal	1950	Ted Lindsay, Detroit	1972	Phil Esposito, Boston
1929	Ace Bailey, Toronto	1951	Gordie Howe, Detroit	1973	Phil Esposito, Boston
1930	Cooney Weiland, Boston	1952	Gordie Howe, Detroit	1974	Phil Esposito, Boston
1931	Howie Morenz, Montreal	1953	Gordie Howe, Detroit	1975	Bobby Orr, Boston
1932	Harvey Jackson, Toronto	1954	Gordie Howe, Detroit	1976	Guy Lafleur, Montreal
1933	Bill Cook, N.Y. Rangers	1955	Bernie Geoffrion, Montreal	1977	Guy Lafleur, Montreal
1934	Charlie Conacher, Toronto	1956	Jean Beliveau, Montreal	1978	Guy Lafleur, Montreal
1935	Charlie Conacher, Toronto	1957	Gordie Howe, Detroit	1979	Bryan Trottier, N.Y. Islanders
1936	Dave Schriner, N.Y. Americans	1958	Dickie Moore, Montreal	1980	Marcel Dionne, Los Angeles
1937	Dave Schriner, N.Y. Americans	1959	Dickie Moore, Montreal	1981	Wayne Gretzky, Edmonton
1938	Gordie Drillon, Toronto	1960	Bobby Hull, Chicago	1982	Wayne Gretzky, Edmonton
1939	Toe Blake, Montreal	1961	Bernie Geoffrion, Montreal	1983	Wayne Gretzky, Edmonton
1940	Milt Schmidt, Boston	1962	Bobby Hull, Chicago	1984	Wayne Gretzky, Edmonton
1941	Bill Cowley, Boston	1963	Gordie Howe, Detroit	1985	Wayne Gretzky, Edmonton
1942	Bryan Hextall, N.Y. Rangers	1964	Stan Mikita, Chicago	1986	Wayne Gretzky, Edmonton
1943	Doug Bentley, Chicago	1965	Stan Mikita, Chicago	1987	Wayne Gretzky, Edmonton
1944	Herbie Cain, Boston	1966	Bobby Hull, Chicago	1988	Mario Lemieux, Pittsburgh
1945	Elmer Lach, Montreal	1967	Stan Mikita, Chicago	1989	Mario Lemieux, Pittsburgh
1946	Max Bentley, Chicago	1968	Stan Mikita, Chicago	1990	Wayne Gretzky, Los Angeles
1947	Max Bentley, Chicago	1969	Phil Esposito, Boston	1991	Wayne Gretzky, Los Angeles
1948	Elmer Lach, Montreal	1970	Bobby Orr, Boston		

James Norris Memorial Trophy (Outstanding Defenseman)

Year	Player	Year	Player	Year	Player
1954	Red Kelly, Detroit	1967	Harry Howell, N.Y. Rangers	1980	Larry Robinson, Montreal
1955	Doug Harvey, Montreal	1968	Bobby Orr, Boston	1981	Randy Carlyle, Pittsburgh
1956	Doug Harvey, Montreal	1969	Bobby Orr, Boston	1982	Doug Wilson, Chicago
1957	Doug Harvey, Montreal	1970	Bobby Orr, Boston	1983	Rod Langway, Washington
1958	Doug Harvey, Montreal	1971	Bobby Orr, Boston	1984	Rod Langway, Washington
1959	Tom Johnson, Montreal	1972	Bobby Orr, Boston	1985	Paul Coffey, Edmonton
1960	Doug Harvey, Montreal	1973	Bobby Orr, Boston	1986	Paul Coffey, Edmonton
1961	Doug Harvey, Montreal	1974	Bobby Orr, Boston	1987	Ray Bourque, Boston
1962	Doug Harvey, N.Y. Rangers	1975	Bobby Orr, Boston	1988	Ray Bourque, Boston
1963	Pierre Pilote, Chicago	1976	Denis Potvin, N.Y. Islanders	1989	Chris Chelios, Montreal
1964	Pierre Pilote, Chicago	1977	Larry Robinson, Montreal	1990	Ray Bourque, Boston
1965	Pierre Pilote, Chicago	1978	Denis Potvin, N.Y. Islanders	1991	Ray Bourque, Boston
1966	Jacques Laperriere, Montreal	1979	Denis Potvin, N.Y. Islanders		

*Vezina Trophy (Leading Goalie)

1927	George Hainsworth, Montreal	1950	Bill Durnan, Montreal	1972	Esposito, Smith, Chicago
1928	George Hainsworth, Montreal	1951	Al Rollins, Toronto	1973	Ken Dryden, Montreal
1929	George Hainsworth, Montreal	1952	Terry Sawchuk, Detroit	1974	Bernie Parent, Philadelphia;
1930	Tiny Thompson, Boston	1953	Terry Sawchuk, Detroit		Tony Esposito, Chicago
1931	Roy Worters, N.Y. Americans	1954	Harry Lumley, Toronto	1975	Bernie Parent, Philadelphia
1932	Charlie Gardiner, Chicago	1955	Terry Sawchuk, Detroit	1976	Ken Dryden, Montreal
1933	Tiny Thompson, Boston	1956	Jacques Plante, Montreal	1977	Dryden, Larocque, Montreal
1934	Charlie Gardiner, Chicago	1957	Jacques Plante, Montreal	1978	Dryden, Larocque, Montreal
1935	Lorne Chabot, Chicago	1958	Jacques Plante, Montreal	1979	Dryden, Larocque, Montreal
1936	Tiny Thompson, Boston	1959	Jacques Plante, Montreal	1980	Sauve, Edwards, Buffalo
1937	Normie Smith, Detroit	1960	Jacques Plante, Montreal	1981	Sevigny, Larocque, Herron,
1938	Tiny Thompson, Boston	1961	John Bower, Toronto		Montreal
1939	Frank Brimsek, Boston	1962	Jacques Plante, Montreal	1982	Bill Smith, N.Y. Islanders
1940	Dave Kerr, N.Y. Rangers	1963	Glenn Hall, Chicago	1983	Pete Peeters, Boston
1941	Turk Broda, Toronto	1964	Charlie Hodge, Montreal	1984	Tom Barrasso, Buffalo
1942	Frank Brimsek, Boston	1965	Sawchuk, Bower, Toronto	1985	Pelle Lindbergh, Philadelphia
1943	Johnny Mowers, Detroit	1966	Worsley, Hodge, Montreal	1986	John Vanbiesbrouck, N.Y.
1944	Bill Durnan, Montreal	1967	Hall, DeJordy, Chicago		Rangers
1945	Bill Durnan, Montreal	1968	Worsley, Vachon, Montreal	1987	Ron Hextall, Philadelphia
1946	Bill Durnan, Montreal	1969	Hall, Plante, St. Louis	1988	Grant Fuhr, Edmonton
1947	Bill Durnan, Montreal	1970	Tony Esposito, Chicago	1989	Patrick Roy, Montreal
1948	Turk Broda, Toronto	1971	Giacomin, Villemure, N.Y.	1990	Patrick Roy, Montreal
1949	Bill Durnan, Montreal		Rangers	1991	Ed Belfour, Chicago

* Awarded to goalie who played a minimum 25 games for the team which allowed the fewest goals; since 1982, awarded to outstanding goalie.

Calder Memorial Trophy (Rookie of the Year)

1933	Carl Voss, Detroit	1952	Bernie Geoffrion, Montreal	1972	Ken Dryden, Montreal
1934	Russ Blinco, Montreal	1953	Gump Worsley, N.Y. Rangers	1973	Steve Vickers, N.Y. Rangers
	Maroons	1954	Camille Henry, N.Y. Rangers	1974	Denis Potvin, N.Y. Islanders
1935	Dave Schriner, N.Y. Americans	1955	Ed Litzenberger, Chicago	1975	Eric Vail, Atlanta
1936	Mike Karakas, Chicago	1956	Glenn Hall, Detroit	1976	Bryan Trottier, N.Y. Islanders
1937	Syl Apps, Toronto	1957	Larry Regan, Boston	1977	Willi Plett, Atlanta
1938	Cully Dahlstrom, Chicago	1958	Frank Mahovlich, Toronto	1978	Mike Bossy, N.Y. Islanders
1939	Frank Brimsek, Boston	1959	Ralph Backstrom, Montreal	1979	Bobby Smith, Minnesota
1940	Kilby Macdonald, N.Y.	1960	Bill Hay, Chicago	1980	Ray Bourque, Boston
	Rangers	1961	Dave Keon, Toronto	1981	Peter Stastny, Quebec
1941	John Quilty, Montreal	1962	Bobby Rousseau, Montreal	1982	Dale Hawerchuk, Winnipeg
1942	Grant Warwick, N.Y. Rangers	1963	Kent Douglas, Toronto	1983	Steve Larmer, Chicago
1943	Gaye Stewart, Toronto	1964	Jacques Laperriere, Montreal	1984	Tom Barrasso, Buffalo
1944	Gus Bodnar, Toronto	1965	Roger Crozier, Detroit	1985	Mario Lemieux, Pittsburgh
1945	Frank McCool, Toronto	1966	Brit Selby, Toronto	1986	Gary Suter, Calgary
1946	Edgar Laprade, N.Y. Rangers	1967	Bobby Orr, Boston	1987	Luc Robitaille, Los Angeles
1947	Howie Meeker, Toronto	1968	Derek Sanderson, Boston	1988	Joe Nieuwendyk, Calgary
1948	Jim McFadden, Detroit	1969	Danny Grant, Minnesota	1989	Brian Leetch, N.Y. Rangers
1949	Pentti Lund, N.Y. Rangers	1970	Tony Esposito, Chicago	1990	Sergei Makarov, Calgary
1950	Jack Gelineau, Boston	1971	Gilbert Perreault, Buffalo	1991	Ed Belfour, Chicago
1951	Terry Sawchuk, Detroit				

Lady Byng Memorial Trophy (Most Gentlemanly Player)

1925	Frank Nighbor, Ottawa	1948	Buddy O'Connor, N.Y.	1970	Phil Goyette, St. Louis
1926	Frank Nighbor, Ottawa		Rangers	1971	John Bucyk, Boston
1927	Billy Burch, N.Y. Americans	1949	Bill Quackenbush, Detroit	1972	Jean Ratelle, N.Y. Rangers
1928	Frank Boucher, N.Y. Rangers	1950	Edgar Laprade, N.Y. Rangers	1973	Gil Perreault, Buffalo
1929	Frank Boucher, N.Y. Rangers	1951	Red Kelly, Detroit	1974	John Bucyk, Boston
1930	Frank Boucher, N.Y. Rangers	1952	Sid Smith, Toronto	1975	Marcel Dionne, Detroit
1931	Frank Boucher, N.Y. Rangers	1953	Red Kelly, Detroit	1976	Jean Ratelle, N.Y. R.-Boston
1932	Joe Primeau, Toronto	1954	Red Kelly, Detroit	1977	Marcel Dionne, Los Angeles
1933	Frank Boucher, N.Y. Rangers	1955	Sid Smith, Toronto	1978	Butch Goring, Los Angeles
1934	Frank Boucher, N.Y. Rangers	1956	Earl Reibel, Detroit	1979	Bob MacMillan, Atlanta
1935	Frank Boucher, N.Y. Rangers	1957	Andy Hebenton, N.Y. Rangers	1980	Wayne Gretzky, Edmonton
1936	Doc Romnes, Chicago	1958	Camille Henry, N.Y. Rangers	1981	Rick Kehoe, Pittsburgh
1937	Marty Barry, Detroit	1959	Alex Delvecchio, Detroit	1982	Rick Middleton, Boston
1938	Gordie Drillon, Toronto	1960	Don McKenney, Boston	1983	Mike Bossy, N.Y. Islanders
1939	Clint Smith, N.Y. Rangers	1961	Red Kelly, Toronto	1984	Mike Bossy, N.Y. Islanders
1940	Bobby Bauer, Boston	1962	Dave Keon, Toronto	1985	Jari Kurri, Edmonton
1941	Bobby Bauer, Boston	1963	Dave Keon, Toronto	1986	Mike Bossy, N.Y. Islanders
1942	Syl Apps, Toronto	1964	Ken Wharram, Chicago	1987	Joe Mullen, Calgary
1943	Max Bentley, Chicago	1965	Bobby Hull, Chicago	1988	Mats Naslund, Montreal
1944	Clint Smith, Chicago	1966	Alex Delvecchio, Detroit	1989	Joe Mullen, Calgary
1945	Bill Mosienko, Chicago	1967	Stan Mikita, Chicago	1990	Brett Hull, St. Louis
1946	Toe Blake, Montreal	1968	Stan Mikita, Chicago	1991	Wayne Gretzky, Los Angeles
1947	Bobby Bauer, Boston	1969	Alex Delvecchio, Detroit		

Frank J. Selke Trophy (Best Defensive Forward)

1978	Bob Gainey, Montreal	1983	Bobby Clarke, Philadelphia	1988	Guy Carbonneau, Montreal
1979	Bob Gainey, Montreal	1984	Doug Jarvis, Washington	1989	Guy Carbonneau, Montreal
1980	Bob Gainey, Montreal	1985	Craig Ramsay, Buffalo	1990	Rick Meagher, St. Louis
1981	Bob Gainey, Montreal	1986	Troy Murray, Chicago	1991	Dirk Graham, Chicago
1982	Steve Kasper, Boston	1987	Dave Poulin, Philadelphia		

Hart Memorial Trophy (MVP)

1927	Herb Gardiner, Montreal	1948	Buddy O'Connor, N.Y.	1970	Bobby Orr, Boston
1928	Howie Morenz, Montreal		Rangers	1971	Bobby Orr, Boston
1929	Roy Worters, N.Y. Americans	1949	Sid Abel, Detroit	1972	Bobby Orr, Boston
1930	Nels Stewart, Montreal	1950	Chuck Rayner, N.Y. Rangers	1973	Bobby Clarke, Philadelphia
	Maroons	1951	Milt Schmidt, Boston	1974	Phil Esposito, Boston
1931	Howie Morenz, Montreal	1952	Gordie Howe, Detroit	1975	Bobby Clarke, Philadelphia
1932	Howie Morenz, Montreal	1953	Gordie Howe, Detroit	1976	Bobby Clarke, Philadelphia
1933	Eddie Shore, Boston	1954	Al Rollins, Chicago	1977	Guy Lafleur, Montreal
1934	Aurel Joliat, Montreal	1955	Ted Kennedy, Toronto	1978	Guy Lafleur, Montreal
1935	Eddie Shore, Boston	1956	Jean Beliveau, Montreal	1979	Bryan Trottier, N.Y. Islanders
1936	Eddie Shore, Boston	1957	Gordie Howe, Detroit	1980	Wayne Gretzky, Edmonton
1937	Babe Siebert, Montreal	1958	Gordie Howe, Detroit	1981	Wayne Gretzky, Edmonton
1938	Eddie Shore, Boston	1959	Andy Bathgate, N.Y. Rangers	1982	Wayne Gretzky, Edmonton
1939	Toe Blake, Montreal	1960	Gordie Howe, Detroit	1983	Wayne Gretzky, Edmonton
1940	Ebbie Goodfellow, Detroit	1961	Bernie Geoffrion, Montreal	1984	Wayne Gretzky, Edmonton
1941	Bill Cowley, Boston	1962	Jacques Plante, Montreal	1985	Wayne Gretzky, Edmonton
1942	Tom Anderson, N.Y.	1963	Gordie Howe, Detroit	1986	Wayne Gretzky, Edmonton
	Americans	1964	Jean Beliveau, Montreal	1987	Wayne Gretzky, Edmonton
1943	Bill Cowley, Boston	1965	Bobby Hull, Chicago	1988	Mario Lemieux, Pittsburgh
1944	Babe Pratt, Toronto	1966	Bobby Hull, Chicago	1989	Wayne Gretzky, Los Angeles
1945	Elmer Lach, Montreal	1967	Stan Mikita, Chicago	1990	Mark Messier, Edmonton
1946	Max Bentley, Chicago	1968	Stan Mikita, Chicago	1991	Brett Hull, St. Louis
1947	Maurice Richard, Montreal	1969	Phil Esposito, Boston		

Conn Smythe Trophy (MVP in Playoffs)

1965	Jean Beliveau, Montreal	1974	Bernie Parent, Philadelphia	1983	Billy Smith, N.Y. Islanders
1966	Roger Crozier, Detroit	1975	Bernie Parent, Philadelphia	1984	Mark Messier, Edmonton
1967	Dave Keon, Toronto	1976	Reg Leach, Philadelphia	1985	Wayne Gretzky, Edmonton
1968	Glenn Hall, St. Louis	1977	Guy Lafleur, Montreal	1986	Patrick Roy, Montreal
1969	Serge Savard, Montreal	1978	Larry Robinson, Montreal	1987	Ron Hextall, Philadelphia
1970	Bobby Orr, Boston	1979	Bob Gainey, Montreal	1988	Wayne Gretzky, Edmonton
1971	Ken Dryden, Montreal	1980	Bryan Trottier, N.Y. Islanders	1989	Al MacInnis, Calgary
1972	Bobby Orr, Boston	1981	Butch Goring, N.Y. Islanders	1990	Bill Ranford, Edmonton
1973	Yvan Cournoyer, Montreal	1982	Mike Bossy, N.Y. Islanders	1991	Mario Lemieux, Pittsburgh

NHL All Star Team, 1991

First team	Position	Second team
Ed Belfour, Chicago	Goalie	Patrick Roy, Montreal
Ray Bourque, Boston	Defense	Brian Leetch, N.Y. Rangers
Al MacInnis, Calgary	Defense	Chris Chelios, Chicago
Wayne Gretzky, Los Angeles	Center	Adam Oates, St. Louis
Brett Hull, St. Louis	Right Wing	Cam Neely, Boston
Luc Robitaille, Los Angeles	Left Wing	Kevin Stevens, Pittsburgh

Hull Scores 86 Goals

Brett Hull of the St. Louis Blues scored 86 goals during the 1990-91 regular season, the 3rd best goal total in National Hockey League history. Wayne Gretzky set the regular season goal-scoring record in 1981-82 when he scored 92 goals. The following have scored 60 or more goals in a season.

Player	Team	Season	Goals	Player	Team	Season	Goals
Wayne Gretzky	Edmonton	1981-82	92	Jari Kurri	Edmonton	1985-86	68
Wayne Gretzky	Edmonton	1983-84	87	Phil Esposito	Boston	1971-72	66
Brett Hull	St. Louis	1990-91	86	Lanny McDonald	Calgary	1982-83	66
Mario Lemieux	Pittsburgh	1988-89	85	Steve Yzerman	Detroit	1988-89	65
Phil Esposito	Boston	1970-71	76	Mike Bossy	N.Y. Islanders	1981-82	64
Wayne Gretzky	Edmonton	1984-85	73	Wayne Gretzky	Edmonton	1986-87	62
Brett Hull	St. Louis	1989-90	72	Steve Yzerman	Detroit	1989-90	62
Wayne Gretzky	Edmonton	1982-83	71	Mike Bossy	N.Y. Islanders	1985-86	61
Jari Kurri	Edmonton	1984-85	71	Phil Esposito	Boston	1974-75	61
Mario Lemieux	Pittsburgh	1987-88	70	Reggie Leach	Philadelphia	1975-76	61
Bernie Nicholls	Los Angeles	1988-89	70	Mike Bossy	N.Y. Islanders	1982-83	60
Mike Bossy	N.Y. Islanders	1978-79	69	Guy Lafleur	Montreal	1977-78	60
Phil Esposito	Boston	1973-74	68	Steve Shutt	Montreal	1976-77	60
Mike Bossy	N.Y. Islanders	1980-81	68	Dennis Maruk	Washington	1981-82	60

All-Time NHL Scoring Leaders

At end of 1990-91 season. *Active player.

	Games	G	A	Pts		Games	G	A	Pts
Wayne Gretzky*	925	718	1,424	2,142	Gil Perreault	1,191	512	814	1,326
Gordie Howe	1,767	801	1,049	1,850	Alex Delvecchio	1,549	456	825	1,281
Marcel Dionne	1,348	731	1,040	1,771	Jean Ratelle	1,281	491	776	1,267
Phil Esposito	1,282	717	873	1,590	Norm Ullman	1,410	490	739	1,229
Stan Mikita	1,394	541	926	1,467	Jean Beliveau	1,215	507	712	1,219
Bryan Trottier*	1,175	509	872	1,381	Bobby Clarke	1,144	358	852	1,210
John Bucyk	1,540	556	813	1,369	Bobby Hull	1,063	610	560	1,170
Guy Lafleur*	1,126	560	793	1,353					

NCAA Hockey Champions

1948	Michigan	1959	North Dakota	1970	Cornell
1949	Boston College	1960	Denver	1971	Boston Univ.
1950	Colorado College	1961	Denver	1972	Boston Univ
1951	Michigan	1962	Michigan Tech	1973	Wisconsin
1952	Michigan	1963	North Dakota	1974	Minnesota
1953	Michigan	1964	Michigan	1975	Michigan Tech
1954	RPI	1965	Michigan Tech	1976	Minnesota
1955	Michigan	1966	Michigan State	1977	Wisconsin
1956	Michigan	1967	Cornell	1978	Boston Univ.
1957	Colorado College	1968	Denver	1979	Minnesota
1958	Denver	1969	Denver	1980	North Dakota

1981	Wisconsin
1982	North Dakota
1983	Wisconsin
1984	Bowling Green
1985	RPI
1986	Michigan State
1987	North Dakota
1988	Lake Superior St.
1989	Harvard
1990	Wisconsin
1991	N. Michigan

Figure Skating Champions

	U.S. Champions			World Champions	
Men	**Women**	**Year**	**Men**	**Women**	
Dick Button	Tenley Albright	1952	Dick Button, U.S.	Jacqueline du Bief, France
Hayes Jenkins	Tenley Albright	1953	Hayes Jenkins, U.S.	Tenley Albright, U.S.
Hayes Jenkins	Tenley Albright	1954	Hayes Jenkins, U.S.	Gundi Busch, W. Germany
Hayes Jenkins	Tenley Albright	1955	Hayes Jenkins, U.S.	Tenley Albright, U.S.
Hayes Jenkins	Tenley Albright	1956	Hayes Jenkins, U.S.	Carol Heiss, U.S.
Dave Jenkins	Carol Heiss	1957	Dave Jenkins, U.S.	Carol Heiss, U.S.
Dave Jenkins	Carol Heiss	1958	Dave Jenkins, U.S.	Carol Heiss, U.S.
Dave Jenkins	Carol Heiss	1959	Dave Jenkins, U.S.	Carol Heiss, U.S.
Dave Jenkins	Carol Heiss	1960	Alain Giletti, France	Carol Heiss, U.S.
Bradley Lord	Laurence Owen	1961	none	none
Monty Hoyt	Barbara Roles Pursley	1962	Don Jackson, Canada	Sjoukje Dijkstra, Neth.
Tommy Litz	Lorraine Hanlon	1963	Don McPherson, Canada	Sjoukje Dijkstra, Neth.
Scott Allen	Peggy Fleming	1964	Manfred Schnelldorfer, W. Germany	Sjoukje Dijkstra, Neth.
Gary Visconti	Peggy Fleming	1965	Alain Calmat, France	Petra Burka, Canada
Scott Allen	Peggy Fleming	1966	Emmerich Danzer, Austria	Peggy Fleming, U.S.
Gary Visconti	Peggy Fleming	1967	Emmerich Danzer, Austria	Peggy Fleming, U.S.
Tim Wood	Peggy Fleming	1968	Emmerich Danzer, Austria	Peggy Fleming, U.S.
Tim Wood	Janet Lynn	1969	Tim Wood, U.S.	Gabriele Seyfert, E. Germany
Tim Wood	Janet Lynn	1970	Tim Wood, U.S.	Gabriele Seyfert, E. Germany
John Misha Petkevich	Janet Lynn	1971	Ondrej Nepela, Czech.	Beatrix Schuba, Austria
Ken Shelley	Janet Lynn	1972	Ondrej Nepela, Czech.	Beatrix Schuba, Austria
Gordon McKellen Jr.	Janet Lynn	1973	Ondrej Nepela, Czech.	Karen Magnussen, Canada
Gordon McKellen Jr.	Dorothy Hamill	1974	Jan Hoffmann, E. Germany	Christine Errath, E. Germany
Gordon McKellen Jr.	Dorothy Hamill	1975	Sergei Volkov, USSR	Dianne de Leeuw, Neth.-U.S.
Terry Kubicka	Dorothy Hamill	1976	John Curry, Gt. Britain	Dorothy Hamill, U.S.
Charles Tickner	Linda Fratianne	1977	Vladimir Kovalev, USSR	Linda Fratianne, U.S.
Charles Tickner	Linda Fratianne	1978	Charles Tickner, U.S.	Anett Potzsch, E. Germany
Charles Tickner	Linda Fratianne	1979	Vladimir Kovalev, USSR	Linda Fratianne, U.S.
Charles Tickner	Linda Fratianne	1980	Jan Hoffmann, E. Germany	Anett Potzsch, E. Germany
Scott Hamilton	Elaine Zayak	1981	Scott Hamilton, U.S.	Denise Biellmann, Switzerland
Scott Hamilton	Rosalynn Sumners	1982	Scott Hamilton, U.S.	Elaine Zayak, U.S.
Scott Hamilton	Rosalynn Sumners	1983	Scott Hamilton, U.S.	Rosalynn Sumners, U.S.
Scott Hamilton	Rosalynn Sumners	1984	Scott Hamilton, U.S.	Katarina Witt, E. Germany
Brian Boitano	Tiffany Chin	1985	Aleksandr Fadeev, USSR	Katarina Witt, E. Germany
Brian Boitano	Debi Thomas	1986	Brian Boitano, U.S.	Debi Thomas, U.S.
Brian Boitano	Jill Trenary	1987	Brian Orser, Canada	Katarina Witt, E. Germany
Brian Boitano	Debi Thomas	1988	Brian Boitano, U.S.	Katarina Witt, E. Germany
Christopher Bowman	Jill Trenary	1989	Kurt Browning, Canada	Midori Ito, Japan
Todd Eldredge	Jill Trenary	1990	Kurt Browning, Canada	Jill Trenary, U.S.
Todd Eldredge	Tonya Harding	1991	Kurt Browning, Canada	Kristi Yamaguchi, U.S.

World Pairs and Dancing Champions in 1991

Natasha Mishkutinok and Artur Dmitriev of the Soviet Union won the 1991 pairs figure skating championship in Munich, Germany. Isabelle and Paul Duchesnay of France were the ice dancing champions.

Westminster Kennel Club

Year	Best-in-show	Breed	Owner
1982	Ch. St. Aubrey Dragonora of Elsdon	Pekingese	Anne Snelling
1983	Ch. Kabik's The Challenger	Afghan	Chris & Marguerite Terrell
1984	Ch. Seaward's Blackbeard	Newfoundland	Elinor Ayers
1985	Ch. Braeburn's Close Encounter	Scottish terrier	Sonnie Novick
1986	Ch. Marjetta National Acclaim	Pointer	Mrs. Alan Robson & Michael Zollo
1987	Ch. Covy Tucker Hill's Manhattan	German shepherd	Shirley Braunstein & Jane Firestone
1988	Ch. Great Elms Prince Charming II	Pomeranian	Skip Piazza & Olga Baker
1989	Ch. Royal Tudor's Wild As The Wind	Doberman	Sue & Art Kemp, Richard & Carolyn Vida, Beth Wilhite
1990	Ch. Wendessa Crown Prince	Pekingese	Ed Jenner
1991	Ch. Whisperwind on a Carousel	Poodle	Joan & Frederick Hartsock

COLLEGE BASKETBALL

Final Regular Season Conference Standings, 1990–91

American South

	Conference W	L	Overall Record W	L
New Orleans	9	3	23	7
Arkansas State	9	3	21	8
Louisiana Tech	8	4	21	9
SW Louisiana	6	6	21	10
Lamar	4	8	15	13
Central Florida	3	9	10	17
Texas-Pan Am	3	9	7	21

Tournament Champion—Louisiana Tech.

Atlantic Coast

	Conference W	L	Overall Record W	L
Duke	11	3	25	6
North Carolina	10	4	22	5
N.C. State	8	6	18	9
Wake Forest	8	6	18	9
Virginia	6	8	20	10
Georgia Tech	6	8	16	11
Maryland	5	9	16	12
Clemson	2	12	11	16

Tournament Champion—North Carolina.

Atlantic 10

	Conference W	L	Overall Record W	L
Rutgers	14	4	19	9
Temple	13	5	21	8
George Washington	10	8	18	10
Penn State	10	8	18	10
Massachusetts	10	8	17	11
West Virginia	10	8	16	13
Duquesne	10	8	13	15
St. Joseph's	7	11	13	16
Rhode Island	6	12	11	17
St. Bonaventure	0	18	5	23

Tournament Champion—Penn St.

Big East

	Conference W	L	Overall Record W	L
Syracuse	12	4	26	4
St. John's	10	6	20	7
Seton Hall	9	7	19	8
Connecticut	9	7	18	9
Pittsburgh	9	7	20	10
Georgetown	8	8	16	11
Providence	7	9	16	11
Villanova	7	9	14	13
Boston College	1	15	11	18

Tournament Champion—Seton Hall.

Big Eight

	Conference W	L	Overall Record W	L
Oklahoma State	10	4	21	6
Kansas	10	4	21	6
Nebraska	9	5	24	6
Missouri	8	6	16	10
Iowa State	6	8	12	18
Colorado	5	9	15	12
Oklahoma	5	9	16	13
Kansas State	3	11	13	14

Tournament Champion—Missouri.

Big Ten

	Conference W	L	Overall Record W	L
Ohio State	15	3	25	3
Indiana	15	3	27	4
Illinois	11	7	21	10
Michigan State	11	7	18	10
Purdue	9	9	17	11
Iowa	9	9	20	10
Wisconsin	8	10	14	14
Michigan	7	11	14	14
Minnesota	5	13	12	16
Northwestern	0	18	5	23

Big Sky

	Conference W	L	Overall Record W	L
Montana	13	3	20	7
Nevada-Reno	12	4	17	13
Idaho	11	5	17	10
Boise State	10	6	18	9
Weber State	7	9	12	15
Idaho State	7	9	10	17
Montana State	6	10	12	16
E. Washington	5	11	11	16
N. Arizona	1	15	4	23

Tournament Champion—Montana.

Big South

	Conference W	L	Overall Record W	L
Coastal Carolina	13	1	23	7
Radford	12	2	22	7
Augusta	9	5	14	16
Davidson	6	8	10	19
Winthrop	5	9	8	20
N.C.-Asheville	5	10	8	20
Charleston Southern	4	11	9	20
Campbell	3	11	9	19

Tournament Champion—Coastal Carolina.

East Coast

	Conference W	L	Overall Record W	L
Towson State	10	2	18	10
Delaware	8	4	16	13
Hofstra	7	5	14	14
Drexel	7	5	12	16
Rider	4	8	14	15
Maryland-Balt. Co.	4	8	7	22
Cent. Conn.	2	10	4	24

Tournament Champion—Towson St.

Big West

	Conference W	L	Overall Record W	L
UNLV	18	0	27	0
New Mexico State	15	3	23	4
Pacific Univ.	9	9	13	14
UC S. Barbara	8	10	13	14
Utah State	8	10	11	16
Fullerton State	7	11	14	13
Fresno State	7	11	12	15
Long Beach State	7	11	11	16
UC Irvine	6	12	11	19
San Jose State	5	13	7	20

Tournament Champion—UNLV.

Colonial

	Conference W	L	Overall Record W	L
James Madison	12	2	19	9
Richmond	10	4	20	9
American Univ.	8	6	15	14
George Mason	6	8	13	15
William & Mary	6	8	13	15
N.C.-Wilmington	6	8	11	17
East Carolina	4	10	12	16
Navy	2	12	8	21

Tournament Champion—Richmond.

North Atlantic

	Conference W	L	Overall Record W	L
Northeastern	8	2	20	9
Maine	7	3	12	15
Vermont	5	5	15	12
Hartford	5	5	12	15
Boston Univ.	5	5	10	17
New Hampshire	0	10	3	24

Tournament Champion—Northeastern.

Northeast

	Conference W	L	Overall Record W	L
St. Francis (Pa.)	13	3	23	7
FDU	13	3	22	8
Robert Morris	12	4	17	11
Monmouth	10	6	19	10
St. Francis (N.Y.)	8	8	15	14
Mt. St. Mary's	6	10	8	19
Long Island Univ.	4	12	10	18
Marist	4	12	6	22
Wagner	2	14	4	26

Tournament Champion—St. Francis (Pa.)

Mid-Continent

	Conference W	L	Overall Record W	L
Northern Illinois	14	2	24	4
Wisconsin-Green Bay	13	3	22	6
Eastern Illinois	10	6	17	11
Cleveland State	8	8	12	16
Northern Iowa	8	8	13	18
Akron	6	10	15	13
Western Illinois	6	10	13	15
Ill.-Chicago	5	11	15	15
Valparaiso	2	14	5	22

Tournament Champion—Wisconsin-G.B.

Ivy League

	Conference W	L	Overall Record W	L
Princeton	14	0	23	2
Yale	9	5	15	11
Cornell	6	8	13	13
Brown	6	8	11	15
Harvard	6	8	9	17
Penn	6	8	9	17
Columbia	5	9	7	19
Dartmouth	4	10	8	17

Metro

	Conference W	L	Overall Record W	L
Southern Miss	10	4	21	6
Florida State	9	5	17	10
Cincinnati	8	6	17	10
Tulane	7	7	15	12
Memphis State	7	7	15	13
Virginia Tech	6	8	12	15
South Carolina	5	9	19	11
Louisville	4	10	12	15

Tournament Champion—Florida St.

Metro Atlantic

	Conference W	L	Overall Record W	L
Siena	12	4	23	9
La Salle	12	4	19	9
St. Peter's	11	5	23	6
Iona	11	5	17	12
Manhattan	8	8	13	15
Niagara	6	10	8	20
Loyola (Md.)	5	11	12	16
Fairfield	4	12	8	20
Canisius	3	13	10	19

Tournament Champion—St. Peter's.

Mid-American

	Conference W	L	Overall Record W	L
E. Michigan	13	3	21	6
Ball State	10	6	20	8
Miami (Ohio)	10	6	16	11
Bowling Green	9	7	16	11
Ohio Univ.	9	7	16	11
Cent. Michigan	8	8	14	13
Toledo	7	9	14	15
Kent State	4	12	10	17
W. Michigan	2	14	5	22

Tournament Champion—E. Michigan.

Mid-Eastern

	Conference W	L	Overall Record W	L
Coppin State	14	2	19	10
Delaware State	10	6	19	11
N. Carolina A&T	10	6	17	10
S. Carolina State	10	6	13	15
Florida A&M	9	7	17	13
Howard Univ.	7	9	8	20
Morgan State	6	10	7	22
Maryland-E. Shore	3	13	5	23
Bethune-Cookman	3	13	5	24

Tournament Champion—Florida A&M.

Midwestern

	Conference W	L	Overall Record W	L
Xavier (Ohio)	11	3	18	9
Butler	10	4	18	9
St. Louis	8	6	17	13
Dayton	7	7	14	13
Evansville	7	7	13	15
Marquette	7	7	11	17
Loyola (Ill.)	3	11	9	18
Detroit	2	12	9	18

Tournament Champion—Xavier.

Missouri Valley

	Conference W	L	Overall Record W	L
Creighton	12	4	22	7
SW Missouri	11	5	21	10
Tulsa	10	6	18	11
S. Illinois	9	7	16	13
Indiana State	9	7	14	14
Wichita State	7	9	14	17
Bradley	6	10	8	20
Drake	4	12	8	21
Illinois State	4	12	5	23

Tournament Champion—Creighton.

	Confer- ence		Over- all Record	
	W	L	W	L
Ohio Valley				
Murray State	10	2	22	8
E. Kentucky	9	3	19	9
Middle Tenn.	6	6	20	8
Austin Peay	6	6	15	14
Tenn. Tech	6	6	12	16
Morehead State . .	4	8	16	12
Tennessee State . .	1	11	5	23
Tournament Champion—Murray St.				
Pacific-10				
Arizona	14	4	26	6
UCLA	11	7	23	8
Arizona State	10	8	19	9
Southern Cal	10	8	19	9
Washington State . .	8	10	16	12
Oregon State	8	10	14	14
Oregon	8	10	13	15
Stanford	8	10	15	13
California	8	10	15	13
Washington	5	13	14	14
Patriot				
Fordham	11	1	24	6
Lehigh	10	2	19	10
Holy Cross	8	4	18	12
Bucknell	7	5	18	13
Army	3	9	6	22
Colgate	2	10	5	23
Lafayette	1	11	7	21
Tournament Champion—Fordham.				
Southern				
Furman	11	3	20	8
E. Tenn. State . . .	11	3	28	4
Tenn.-Chattanooga .	11	3	19	10
Appalachian State .	7	7	16	14
Marshall	7	7	14	14
Va. Military	5	9	10	18
W. Carolina	3	11	11	17
Citadel	1	13	6	22
Tournament Champion—E. Tenn. St.				
Southeastern				
Kentucky	14	4	22	6
Mississippi St. . . .	13	5	20	7
Louisiana St.	13	5	20	8
Alabama	12	6	18	9
Vanderbilt	11	7	17	11
Georgia	9	9	16	11
Florida	7	11	11	16
Auburn	5	13	12	15
Mississippi	3	15	9	18
Tennessee	3	15	9	21
Tournament Champion—Alabama.				

	Confer- ence		Over- all Record	
	W	L	W	L
Southland				
NE Louisiana	13	1	24	7
Texas-Arlington . . .	11	3	20	9
North Texas	11	3	17	13
S.F. Austin	6	8	11	17
Sam Houston State .	5	9	7	20
SW Texas State . .	4	10	10	16
McNeese State . . .	4	10	8	19
NW Louisiana . . .	2	12	6	22
Tournament Champion—NE La.				
Southwest				
Arkansas	15	1	28	3
Texas	13	3	20	7
Houston	10	6	18	9
Texas Christian . . .	9	7	18	9
Rice	9	7	15	12
SMU	6	10	11	16
Baylor	4	12	12	14
Texas Tech	4	12	8	22
Texas A&M	2	14	7	20
Tournament Champion—Arkansas.				
Southwestern				
Jackson State . . .	10	2	17	12
Southern Univ. . . .	8	4	19	9
Alabama State . . .	7	5	18	11
Texas Southern . . .	7	5	13	17
Miss. Valley State . .	4	8	9	19
Alcorn State	3	9	8	21
Grambling State . . .	3	9	6	22
Prairie View	0	4	21	
Tournament Champion—Jackson St.				
Sun Belt				
South Alabama . . .	11	3	21	8
Alabama-Birmingham	9	5	18	12
South Florida	8	6	19	10
W. Kentucky	8	6	14	14
Virginia Comm. . . .	7	7	14	17
N.C. Charlotte . . .	6	8	14	14
Old Dominion	5	9	14	17
Jacksonville	2	12	6	22
Tournament Champion—S. Alabama.				
Trans America				
Texas-San Antonio .	12	2	20	7
Centenary	10	4	16	11
Georgia Southern . .	9	5	13	12
Stetson	9	5	15	15
Georgia State	7	7	13	14
Arkansas-Little Rock	6	8	8	19
Samford	2	12	6	21
Mercer	1	13	2	24
Tournament Champion—Georgia St.				

	Confer- ence		Over- all Record	
	W	L	W	L
West Coast				
Pepperdine	13	1	21	8
Loyola, Marymount .	9	5	16	14
San Diego	8	6	17	12
Santa Clara	7	7	16	13
St. Mary's	7	7	13	16
Gonzaga	5	9	13	14
San Francisco . . .	4	10	12	17
Portland	3	11	5	23
Tournament Champion—Pepperdine.				
Western Athletic				
Utah	15	1	26	2
BYU	11	5	17	12
New Mexico	10	6	20	8
Wyoming	8	8	18	10
Hawaii	7	9	15	12
Texas-El Paso	7	9	15	12
Colorado State . . .	6	10	15	13
San Diego State . .	6	10	12	15
Air Force	2	14	9	19
Tournament Champion—BYU.				

Independents		
	W	L
DePaul	18	8
Wright State	17	9
Wisconsin-Milwaukee	17	10
Southern Utah	16	12
Missouri-Kansas City	14	14
Youngstown State . .	12	15
Brooklyn	11	16
Notre Dame	12	18
SE Louisiana	9	19
Miami (Fla.)	8	18
Northridge State . . .	8	19
Florida International . .	6	21
Chicago State	4	23
Liberty	4	23
Nicholls State	3	24
NE Illinois	2	24
U.S. International . . .	2	25

National Invitation Tournament Champions

Year	Champion	Year	Champion	Year	Champion	Year	Champion
1938	Temple	1952	LaSalle	1966	Brigham Young	1979	Indiana
1939	Long Island Univ.	1953	Seton Hall	1967	Southern Illinois	1980	Virginia
1940	Colorado	1954	Holy Cross	1968	Dayton	1981	Tulsa
1941	Long Island Univ.	1955	Duquesne	1969	Temple	1982	Bradley
1942	West Virginia	1956	Louisville	1970	Marquette	1983	Fresno State
1943	St. John's	1957	Bradley	1971	North Carolina	1984	Michigan
1944	St. John's	1958	Xavier (Ohio)	1972	Maryland	1985	UCLA
1945	De Paul	1959	St. John's	1973	Virginia Tech	1986	Ohio State
1946	Kentucky	1960	Bradley	1974	Purdue	1987	Southern Mississippi
1947	Utah	1961	Providence	1975	Princeton	1988	Connecticut
1948	St. Louis	1962	Dayton	1976	Kentucky	1989	St. John's
1949	San Francisco	1963	Providence	1977	St. Bonaventure	1990	Vanderbilt
1950	CCNY	1964	Bradley	1978	Texas	1991	Stanford
1951	Brigham Young	1965	St. John's				

NCAA Division I Women's Champions

Year	Champion	Coach	Final opponent	Year	Champion	Coach	Final opponent
1982	Louisiana Tech	Sonja Hogg	Cheyney	1987	Tennessee	Pat Summitt	Louisiana Tech
1983	USC	Linda Sharp	Louisiana Tech	1988	Louisiana Tech	Leon Barmore	Auburn
1984	USC	Linda Sharp	Tennessee	1989	Tennessee	Pat Summitt	Auburn
1985	Old Dominion	Marianne Stanley	Georgia	1990	Stanford	Tara VanDerveer	Auburn
1986	Texas	Jody Conradt	USC	1991	Tennessee	Pat Summitt	Virginia

1991 NCAA Basketball Tournament

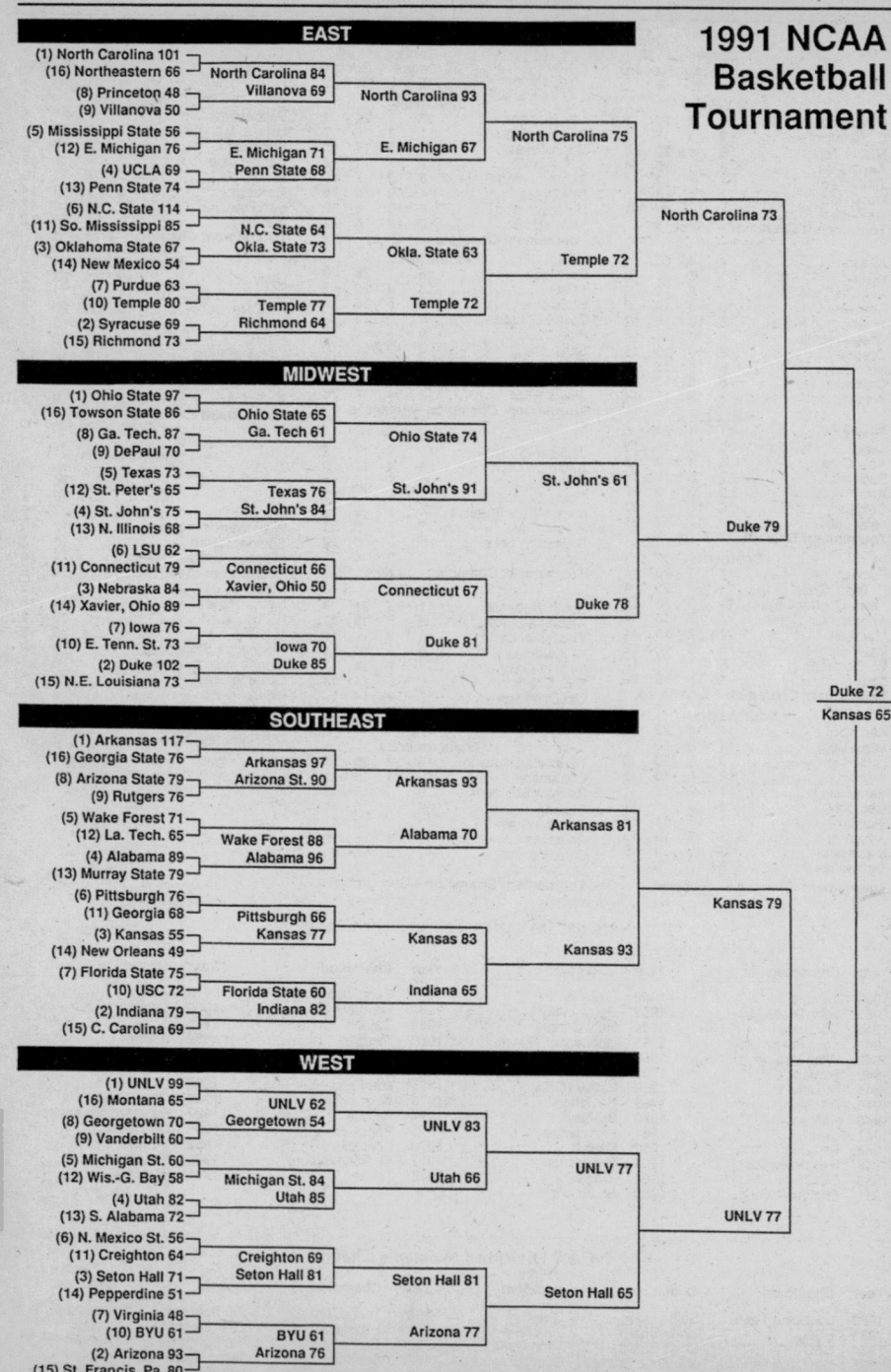

EAST

(1) North Carolina 101
(16) Northeastern 66
 — North Carolina 84
(8) Princeton 48
(9) Villanova 50
 — Villanova 69
North Carolina 93

(5) Mississippi State 56
(12) E. Michigan 76
 — E. Michigan 71
(4) UCLA 69
(13) Penn State 74
 — Penn State 68
E. Michigan 67

North Carolina 75

(6) N.C. State 114
(11) So. Mississippi 85
 — N.C. State 64
(3) Oklahoma State 67
(14) New Mexico 54
 — Okla. State 73
Okla. State 63

(7) Purdue 63
(10) Temple 80
 — Temple 77
(2) Syracuse 69
(15) Richmond 73
 — Richmond 64
Temple 72

Temple 72

North Carolina 73

MIDWEST

(1) Ohio State 97
(16) Towson State 86
 — Ohio State 65
(8) Ga. Tech. 87
(9) DePaul 70
 — Ga. Tech 61
Ohio State 74

(5) Texas 73
(12) St. Peter's 65
 — Texas 76
(4) St. John's 75
(13) N. Illinois 68
 — St. John's 84
St. John's 91

Ohio State 74 / St. John's 91 → St. John's 61

(6) LSU 62
(11) Connecticut 79
 — Connecticut 66
(3) Nebraska 84
(14) Xavier, Ohio 89
 — Xavier, Ohio 50
Connecticut 67

(7) Iowa 76
(10) E. Tenn. St. 73
 — Iowa 70
(2) Duke 102
(15) N.E. Louisiana 73
 — Duke 85
Duke 81

Duke 78

Duke 79

SOUTHEAST

(1) Arkansas 117
(16) Georgia State 76
 — Arkansas 97
(8) Arizona State 79
(9) Rutgers 76
 — Arizona St. 90
Arkansas 93

(5) Wake Forest 71
(12) La. Tech. 65
 — Wake Forest 88
(4) Alabama 89
(13) Murray State 79
 — Alabama 96
Alabama 70

Arkansas 81

(6) Pittsburgh 76
(11) Georgia 68
 — Pittsburgh 66
(3) Kansas 55
(14) New Orleans 49
 — Kansas 77
Kansas 83

(7) Florida State 75
(10) USC 72
 — Florida State 60
(2) Indiana 79
(15) C. Carolina 69
 — Indiana 82
Indiana 65

Kansas 93

Kansas 79

Duke 72
Kansas 65

WEST

(1) UNLV 99
(16) Montana 65
 — UNLV 62
(8) Georgetown 70
(9) Vanderbilt 60
 — Georgetown 54
UNLV 83

(5) Michigan St. 60
(12) Wis.-G. Bay 58
 — Michigan St. 84
(4) Utah 82
(13) S. Alabama 72
 — Utah 85
Utah 66

UNLV 77

(6) N. Mexico St. 56
(11) Creighton 64
 — Creighton 69
(3) Seton Hall 71
(14) Pepperdine 51
 — Seton Hall 81
Seton Hall 81

(7) Virginia 48
(10) BYU 61
 — BYU 61
(2) Arizona 93
(15) St. Francis, Pa. 80
 — Arizona 76
Arizona 77

Seton Hall 65

UNLV 77

NCAA Division I Champions

Year	Champion	Coach	Final opponent	Score	Outstanding player	Site
1939	Oregon	Howard Hobson	Ohio St.	46-33	None	Evanston, Ill.
1940	Indiana	Branch McCracken	Kansas	60-42	Marvin Huffman, Indiana	Kansas City, Mo.
1941	Wisconsin	Harold Foster	Washington St.	39-34	John Kotz, Wisconsin	Kansas City, Mo.
1942	Stanford	Everett Dean	Dartmouth	53-38	Howard Dallmar, Stanford	Kansas City, Mo.
1943	Wyoming	Everett Shelton	Georgetown	46-34	Ken Sailors, Wyoming	New York, N.Y.
1944	Utah	Vadal Peterson	Dartmouth	42-40(1)	Arnold Ferrin, Utah	New York, N.Y.
1945	Oklahoma St.(2)	Henry Iba	NYU	49-45	Bob Kurland, Oklahoma St.	New York, N.Y.
1946	Oklahoma St.(2)	Henry Iba	North Carolina	43-40	Bob Kurland, Oklahoma St.	New York, N.Y.
1947	Holy Cross	Alvin Julian	Oklahoma	58-47	George Kaftan, Holy Cross	New York, N.Y.
1948	Kentucky	Adolph Rupp	Baylor	58-42	Alex Groza, Kentucky	New York, N.Y.
1949	Kentucky	Adolph Rupp	Oklahoma St.	46-36	Alex Groza, Kentucky	Seattle, Wash.
1950	CCNY	Nat Holman	Bradley	71-68	Irwin Dambrot, CCNY	New York, N.Y.
1951	Kentucky	Adolph Rupp	Kansas St.	68-58	None	Minneapolis, Minn.
1952	Kansas	Forrest Allen	St. John's	80-63	Clyde Lovellette, Kansas	Seattle, Wash.
1953	Indiana	Branch McCracken	Kansas	69-68	B.H. Born, Kansas	Kansas City, Mo.
1954	La Salle	Kenneth Loeffler	Bradley	92-76	Tom Gola, La Salle	Kansas City, Mo.
1955	San Francisco	Phil Woolpert	LaSalle	77-63	Bill Russell, San Francisco	Kansas City, Mo.
1956	San Francisco	Phil Woolpert	Iowa	83-71	Hal Lear, Temple	Evanston, Ill.
1957	N. Carolina	Frank McGuire	Kansas	54-53(1)	Wilt Chamberlain, Kansas	Kansas City, Mo.
1958	Kentucky	Adolph Rupp	Seattle	84-72	Elgin Baylor, Seattle	Louisville, Ky.
1959	California	Pete Newell	W. Virginia	71-70	Jerry West, W. Virginia	Louisville, Ky.
1960	Ohio St.	Fred Taylor	California	75-55	Jerry Lucas, Ohio St.	San Francisco, Cal.
1961	Cincinnati	Edwin Jucker	Ohio St.	70-65(1)	Jerry Lucas, Ohio St.	Kansas City, Mo.
1962	Cincinnati	Edwin Jucker	Ohio St.	71-59	Paul Hogue, Cincinnati	Louisville, Ky.
1963	Loyola (Ill.)	George Ireland	Cincinnati	60-58(1)	Art Heyman, Duke	Louisville, Ky.
1964	UCLA	John Wooden	Duke	98-83	Walt Hazzard, UCLA	Kansas City, Mo.
1965	UCLA	John Wooden	Michigan	91-80	Bill Bradley, Princeton	Portland, Ore.
1966	Texas-El Paso(3)	Don Haskins	Kentucky	72-65	Jerry Chambers, Utah	College Park, Md.
1967	UCLA	John Wooden	Dayton	79-64	Lew Alcindor, UCLA	Louisville, Ky.
1968	UCLA	John Wooden	N. Carolina	78-55	Lew Alcindor, UCLA	Los Angeles, Cal.
1969	UCLA	John Wooden	Purdue	92-72	Lew Alcindor, UCLA	Louisville, Ky.
1970	UCLA	John Wooden	Jacksonville	80-69	Sidney Wicks, UCLA	College Park, Md.
1971	UCLA	John Wooden	Villanova*	68-62	Howard Porter, Villanova*	Houston, Tex.
1972	UCLA	John Wooden	Florida St.	81-76	Bill Walton, UCLA	Los Angeles, Cal.
1973	UCLA	John Wooden	Memphis St.	87-66	Bill Walton, UCLA	St. Louis, Mo.
1974	N. Carolina St.	Norm Sloan	Marquette	76-64	David Thompson, N.C. St.	Greensboro, N.C.
1975	UCLA	John Wooden	Kentucky	92-85	Richard Washington, UCLA	San Diego, Cal.
1976	Indiana	Bob Knight	Michigan	86-68	Kent Benson, Indiana	Philadelphia, Pa.
1977	Marquette	Al McGuire	N. Carolina	67-59	Butch Lee, Marquette	Atlanta, Ga.
1978	Kentucky	Joe Hall	Duke	94-88	Jack Givens, Kentucky	St. Louis, Mo.
1979	Michigan St.	Jud Heathcote	Indiana St.	75-64	Magic Johnson, Michigan St.	Salt Lake City, Ut.
1980	Louisville	Denny Crum	UCLA*	59-54	Darrell Griffith, Louisville	Indianapolis, Ind.
1981	Indiana	Bob Knight	N. Carolina	63-50	Isiah Thomas, Indiana	Philadelphia, Pa.
1982	N. Carolina	Dean Smith	Georgetown	63-62	James Worthy, No. Carolina	New Orleans, La.
1983	N. Carolina St.	Jim Valvano	Houston	54-52	Hakeem Olajuwon, Houston	Albuquerque, N.M.
1984	Georgetown	John Thompson	Houston	84-75	Patrick Ewing, Georgetown	Seattle, Wash.
1985	Villanova	Rollie Massimino	Georgetown	66-64	Ed Pinckney, Villanova	Lexington, Ky.
1986	Louisville	Denny Crum	Duke	72-69	Pervis Ellison, Louisville	Dallas, Tex.
1987	Indiana	Bob Knight	Syracuse	74-73	Keith Smart, Indiana	New Orleans, La.
1988	Kansas	Larry Brown	Oklahoma	83-79	Danny Manning, Kansas	Kansas City, Mo.
1989	Michigan	Steve Fisher	Seton Hall	80-79(1)	Glen Rice, Michigan	Seattle, Wash.
1990	UNLV	Jerry Tarkanian	Duke	103-73	Anderson Hunt, UNLV	Denver, Col.
1991	Duke	Mike Krzyzewski	Kansas	72-65	Christian Laettner, Duke	Indianapolis, Ind.

* Declared ineligible subsequent to the tournament. (1) Overtime. (2) Known as Oklahoma A&M at that time. (3) Known as Texas Western at that time.

John R. Wooden Award

Awarded annually to the nation's outstanding college basketball playing student-athlete by a poll of sports writers and broadcasters.

1977 Marques Johnson, UCLA	1982 Ralph Sampson, Virginia	1987 David Robinson, Navy
1978 Phil Ford, North Carolina	1983 Ralph Sampson, Virginia	1988 Danny Manning, Kansas
1979 Larry Bird, Indiana State	1984 Michael Jordan, North Carolina	1989 Sean Elliott, Arizona
1980 Darrell Griffith, Louisville	1985 Chris Mullin, St. John's	1990 Lionel Simmons, La Salle
1981 Danny Ainge, Brigham Young	1986 Walter Berry, St. John's	1991 Larry Johnson, UNLV

Graduation Rates for Athletes at NCAA Division I Schools

One of the most widespread surveys ever taken of graduation rates by athletes at major colleges found that the graduation rate for all Division I athletes entering school in 1984 was 56.1 percent, far ahead of the 47.9 percent graduation rate for students in general. The survey was published by the *Chronicle of Higher Education* and included responses from 262 of the 295 Division I schools. The survey took freshmen going into school in fall of 1984 and counted how many had graduated by August 1989.

Athletes in some sports were below the norm. Graduation rates for football players was 42.5 percent; graduation rates for basketball players was 39 percent. Women athletes graduated at a rate far better than men.

Late in 1992, the NCAA, for the first time, is going to release graduation information by school with each school's rates in the various sports. Racial and ethnic figures will also be provided.

Division I College Basketball Leaders in 1990-1991 Season

(through games of Tuesday, Mar. 12)

Scoring

	G	Pts	Avg
Kevin Bradshaw, U.S. International	28	1054	37.6
Alphonso Ford, Miss. Valley	28	915	32.7
Von McDade, Wis.-Milwaukee	28	830	29.6
Steve Rogers, Alabama St.	29	854	29.4
Terrell Lowery, Loyola (Cal.)	31	884	28.5
Bobby Phills, Southern-B.R.	28	795	28.4
Shaquille O'Neal, LSU	27	747	27.7
Rodney Monroe, N.C. St.	29	792	27.3
John Taft, Marshall	28	764	27.3
Terrell Brandon, Oregon	28	745	26.6

Rebounds

	G	No.	Avg
Shaquille O'Neal, LSU	27	395	14.6
Popeye Jones, Murray St.	32	461	14.4
Larry Stewart, Coppin St.	29	393	13.6
Tim Burroughs, Jacksonville	27	350	13.0
Warren Kidd, Middle Tenn. St.	30	370	12.3
Dikembe Mutombo, Georgetown	30	368	12.3
Clarence Weatherspoon, Southern Miss.	28	343	12.3
Tom Davis, Delaware St.	30	366	12.2
Ervin Johnson, New Orleans	29	353	12.2
Dale Davis, Clemson	28	340	12.1

Blocked Shots

	G	No.	Avg
Shawn Bradley, Brigham Young	32	165	5.2
Cedric Lewis, Maryland	28	143	5.1
Shaquille O'Neal, LSU	27	135	5.0
Dikembe Mutombo, Georgetown	30	145	4.8
Kevin Roberson, Vermont	28	104	3.7
Lorenzo Williams, Stetson	31	113	3.6
Jimmy Humphries, N.C. A&T	27	92	3.4

Assists

	G	No.	Avg
Chris Corchiani, N.C. St.	29	282	9.7
Danny Tirado, Jacksonville	28	259	9.3
Terrell Lowery, Loyola (Cal.)	31	283	9.1
Keith Jennings, East Tenn. St.	32	288	9.0
Greg Anthony, UNLV	30	270	9.0
Van Usher, Tennessee Tech	28	233	8.3
Orlando Smart, San Francisco	29	237	8.2
Glover Cody, Texas-Arlington	29	229	7.9

Field-Goal Percentage

	FG	FGA	Pct
Oliver Miller, Arkansas	225	320	70.3
Warren Kidd, Middle Tenn. St.	173	247	70.0
Pete Freeman, Akron	175	250	70.0
Lester James, St. Francis (N.Y.)	149	215	69.3
Marcus Kennedy, Eastern Michigan	215	312	68.9
Larry Johnson, UNLV	264	393	67.2
Chris Brooks, West Virginia	208	312	66.7
Mark Randall, Kansas	177	266	66.5
Luc Longley, New Mexico	223	336	66.4
Allen Lightfoot, Montana St.	130	196	66.3

3-Pt. FG Percentage

	FG	FGA	Pct
Keith Jennings, East Tenn. St.	81	134	60.4
Tony Bennett, Wis.-Green Bay	77	143	53.8
Mike Iuzzolino, St. Francis (Pa.)	100	187	53.5
Gary Waites, Alabama	47	89	52.8
Ross Richardson, Loyola (Cal.)	61	116	52.6
David Mitchell, Samford	41	78	52.6
Todd Leslie, Northwestern	65	127	51.2
Dave Olson, Eastern Ill.	80	160	50.0
Lance Vaughn, Boise St.	45	90	50.0
Billy Dreher, California	56	112	50.0
William Benjamin, New Mexico St.	42	84	50.0

NCAA Division I Basketball Statistical Trends

Averages and percentages are for both teams, per game.

Year	Games	FG Made	FG Att.	Pct.	FT Made	FT Att.	Pct.	PF	Pts.
1948	3945	40.6	138.7	29.3	25.3	42.2	59.8	36.9	106.5
1950	3659	43.2	136.8	31.6	28.7	46.5	61.8	39.0	115.1
1952	4009	47.5	140.6*	33.7	31.6	50.5	62.6	44.9*	126.6
1953	3754	48.0	138.1	34.7	42.1	65.8*	64.0	42.5	138.1
1955	3829	51.1	138.6	36.9	43.1*	64.7	66.5	37.9	145.3
1958	4153	51.6	134.2	38.4	33.6	50.5	66.4	36.4	136.8
1960	4295	52.6	132.3	39.8	34.7	51.5	67.4	36.7	139.9
1963	4180	53.2	127.6	41.7	32.6	47.8	68.2	36.4	139.0
1965	4520	58.3	135.4	43.1	34.7	50.3	69.0	38.5	151.4
1967	4602	57.7	131.9	43.8	34.4	49.8	69.0	38.3	149.8
1969	4883	58.2	132.8	43.8	34.8	50.8	68.4	37.9	151.2
1971	5232	60.2	135.6	44.4	35.0	51.3	68.1	38.5	155.4*
1973	5582	62.3*	139.2	44.8	26.2	38.3	68.4	38.4	150.9
1975	6147	62.9	136.7	46.0	27.4	39.7	69.0	40.3	153.1
1979	7131	59.2	124.1	47.7	29.5	42.2	69.7*	41.1	147.9
1981	7407	55.6	115.9	48.0	29.0	42.0	68.9	40.2	140.2
1983	7957	54.3	114.0	47.7	29.0	42.3	68.5	39.7	138.7
1984	8029	53.4	111.1	48.1*	29.5	42.8	68.9	39.9	136.3
1985	8269	54.5	113.9	47.9	29.3	42.5	68.9	39.3	138.3
1986	8360	54.7	114.6	47.7	29.4	42.5	69.1	39.1	138.7
1987	8580	54.4	117.3	46.6	29.7	43.0	69.1	39.3	145.5
1988	8587	54.8	116.6	47.0	30.2	43.8	68.9	39.4	147.8
1989	8677*	55.7	118.5	47.0	31.1	45.0	69.1	40.2	151.4
1990	8646	54.7	118.9	46.0	31.1	45.1	68.9	39.6	149.8

*All-time high.

World Almanac All-America Team in 1991

First team	Position	Second team
Shaquille O'Neal, LSU	Center	Christian Laettner, Duke
Larry Johnson, UNLV	Forward	Stacey Augmon, UNLV
Billy Owens, Syracuse	Forward	Calbert Cheaney, Indiana
Kenny Anderson, Georgia Tech	Guard	Eric Murdock, Providence
Jimmy Jackson, Ohio State	Guard	Rodney Monroe, N.C. State
Coach of the Year — Randy Ayers, Ohio State		Player of the Year — Larry Johnson

World Almanac All-America Women's Team in 1991

First team	Position	Second team
Daedra Charles, Tennessee	Center	Genia Miller, Cal. State-Fullerton
Andrea Stinson, N.C. State	Forward	Susan Robinson, Penn State
Kerrye Bascomb, Connecticut	Forward	Wendy Scholtens, Vanderbilt
Dana Chatman, LSU	Guard	Carolyn Jones, Auburn
Dawn Staley, Virginia	Guard	Sonja Henning, Stanford
Coach of the Year — Rene Portland, Penn State		Player of the Year — Dawn Staley, Virginia

NATIONAL BASKETBALL ASSOCIATION, 1990-91
Final Standings

Eastern Conference
Atlantic Division

	W	L	Pct	GB
Boston	56	26	.683	...
Philadelphia	44	38	.537	12
New York	39	43	.476	17
Washington	30	52	.366	26
New Jersey	26	56	.317	30
Miami	24	58	.293	32

Western Conference
Midwest Division

	W	L	Pct	GB
San Antonio	55	27	.671	...
Utah	54	28	.659	1
Houston	52	30	.634	3
Orlando	31	51	.378	24
Minnesota	29	53	.354	26
Dallas	28	54	.341	27
Denver	20	62	.244	35

Central Division

	W	L	Pct	GB
Chicago	61	21	.744	...
Detroit	50	32	.610	11
Milwaukee	48	34	.585	13
Atlanta	43	39	.524	18
Indiana	41	41	.500	20
Cleveland	33	49	.402	28
Charlotte	26	56	.317	35

Pacific Division

	W	L	Pct	GB
Portland	63	19	.768	...
Los Angeles Lakers	58	24	.707	5
Phoenix	55	27	.671	8
Golden State	44	38	.537	19
Seattle	41	41	.500	22
Los Angeles Clippers	31	51	.378	32
Sacramento	25	57	.305	38

NBA Playoff Results

Eastern Division

Chicago defeated New York 3 games to 0
Philadelphia defeated Milwaukee 3 games to 0
Boston defeated Indiana 3 games to 2
Detroit defeated Atlanta 3 games to 2
Chicago defeated Philadelphia 4 games to 1
Detroit defeated Boston 4 games to 2
Chicago defeated Detroit 4 games to 0

Western Division

L.A. Lakers defeated Houston 3 games to 0
Portland defeated Seattle 3 games to 2
Golden State defeated San Antonio 3 games to 1
Utah defeated Phoenix 3 games to 1
Portland defeated Utah 4 games to 1
L.A. Lakers defeated Golden State 4 games to 1
L.A. Lakers defeated Portland 4 games to 2

Championship

Chicago defeated L.A. Lakers 4 games to 1

Bulls Win First Championship by Defeating Lakers

The Chicago Bulls won their first National Basketball Association championship by defeating the Los Angeles Lakers 4 games to 1. Michael Jordan of the Bulls was named the most valuable player in the finals.

Los Angeles Lakers

	FG M-A	FT M-A	Reb	Ast	Avg
Worthy	35-73	6-9	12	8	19.3
Johnson	25-58	39-41	40	62	18.6
Divac	39-69	13-13	44	10	18.2
Perkins	28-69	22-29	38	5	16.6
Campbell	10-16	3-4	4	0	7.0
Green	10-32	7-12	28	1	5.8
Teagle	7-21	11-14	2	1	5.0
Smith	5-7	2-3	1	2	6.0
Scott	5-18	7-10	7	7	4.5
Drew	3-8	1-2	2	0	1.8
Thompson	0-3	0-0	0	0	0.0
Team			36		
Totals	167-374	111-137	214	96	91.6

Chicago Bulls

	FG M-A	FT M-A	Reb	Ast	Avg
Jordan	63-113	26-33	33	57	31.2
Pippen	39-86	25-29	47	33	20.8
Grant	32-51	9-12	39	8	14.6
Paxson	32-49	2-2	10	17	13.4
Cartwright	20-46	4-6	25	12	8.8
Hodges	9-23	0-0	3	1	3.8
Levingston	8-13	0-0	14	3	3.2
Armstrong	5-11	0-0	3	4	2.0
Williams	2-4	4-6	9	3	2.0
Perdue	3-5	2-2	12	1	1.6
King	0-3	2-2	1	0	1.0
Hopson	0-0	0-0	0	0	0.0
Team			30		
Totals	213-404	76-92	226	139	101.4

MVP in Playoffs

1969	Jerry West, Los Angeles	1977	Bill Walton, Portland	1985	Kareem Abdul-Jabbar, L.A. Lakers
1970	Willis Reed, New York	1978	Wes Unseld, Washington		
1971	Lew Alcindor, Milwaukee	1979	Dennis Johnson, Seattle	1986	Larry Bird, Boston
1972	Wilt Chamberlain, Los Angeles	1980	Magic Johnson, Los Angeles	1987	Magic Johnson, L.A. Lakers
1973	Willis Reed, New York	1981	Cedric Maxwell, Boston	1988	James Worthy, L.A. Lakers
1974	John Havlicek, Boston	1982	Magic Johnson, Los Angeles	1989	Joe Dumars, Detroit
1975	Rick Barry, Golden State	1983	Moses Malone, Philadelphia	1990	Isiah Thomas, Detroit
1976	Jo Jo White, Boston	1984	Larry Bird, Boston	1991	Michael Jordan, Chicago

NBA Champions 1947-1991

Year	Eastern Conference (Regular season)	Western Conference	Winner (Playoffs)	Coach	Runner-up
1947	Washington	Chicago	Philadelphia	Ed Gottlieb	Chicago
1948	Philadelphia	St. Louis	Baltimore	Buddy Jeannette	Philadelphia
1949	Washington	Rochester	Minneapolis	John Kundla	Washington
1950	Syracuse	Minneapolis	Minneapolis	John Kundla	Syracuse
1951	Philadelphia	Minneapolis	Rochester	Lester Harrison	New York
1952	Syracuse	Rochester	Minneapolis	John Kundla	New York
1953	New York	Minneapolis	Minneapolis	John Kundla	New York
1954	New York	Minneapolis	Minneapolis	John Kundla	Syracuse
1955	Syracuse	Ft. Wayne	Syracuse	Al Cervi	Ft. Wayne
1956	Philadelphia	Ft. Wayne	Philadelphia	George Senesky	Ft. Wayne
1957	Boston	St. Louis	Boston	Red Auerbach	St. Louis
1958	Boston	St. Louis	St. Louis	Alex Hannum	Boston
1959	Boston	St. Louis	Boston	Red Auerbach	Minneapolis
1960	Boston	St. Louis	Boston	Red Auerbach	St. Louis
1961	Boston	St. Louis	Boston	Red Auerbach	St. Louis
1962	Boston	Los Angeles	Boston	Red Auerbach	Los Angeles
1963	Boston	Los Angeles	Boston	Red Auerbach	Los Angeles
1964	Boston	San Francisco	Boston	Red Auerbach	San Francisco
1965	Boston	Los Angeles	Boston	Red Auerbach	Los Angeles
1966	Philadelphia	Los Angeles	Boston	Red Auerbach	Los Angeles
1967	Philadelphia	San Francisco	Philadelphia	Alex Hannum	San Francisco
1968	Philadelphia	St. Louis	Boston	Bill Russell	Los Angeles
1969	Baltimore	Los Angeles	Boston	Bill Russell	Los Angeles
1970	New York	Atlanta	New York	Red Holzman	Los Angeles

Year	Atlantic	Central	Midwest	Pacific	Winner	Coach	Runner-up
1971	New York	Baltimore	Milwaukee	Los Angeles	Milwaukee	Larry Costello	Baltimore
1972	Boston	Baltimore	Milwaukee	Los Angeles	Los Angeles	Bill Sharman	New York
1973	Boston	Baltimore	Milwaukee	Los Angeles	New York	Red Holzman	Los Angeles
1974	Boston	Capital	Milwaukee	Los Angeles	Boston	Tom Heinsohn	Milwaukee
1975	Boston	Washington	Chicago	Golden State	Golden State	Al Attles	Washington
1976	Boston	Cleveland	Milwaukee	Golden State	Boston	Tom Heinsohn	Phoenix
1977	Philadelphia	Houston	Denver	Los Angeles	Portland	Jack Ramsay	Philadelphia
1978	Philadelphia	San Antonio	Denver	Portland	Washington	Dick Motta	Seattle
1979	Washington	San Antonio	Kansas City	Seattle	Seattle	Len Wilkens	Washington
1980	Boston	Atlanta	Milwaukee	Los Angeles	Los Angeles	Paul Westhead	Philadelphia
1981	Boston	Milwaukee	San Antonio	Phoenix	Boston	Bill Fitch	Houston
1982	Boston	Milwaukee	San Antonio	Los Angeles	Los Angeles	Pat Riley	Philadelphia
1983	Philadelphia	Milwaukee	San Antonio	Los Angeles	Philadelphia	Billy Cunningham	Los Angeles
1984	Boston	Milwaukee	Utah	Los Angeles	Boston	K.C. Jones	Los Angeles
1985	Boston	Milwaukee	Denver	L.A. Lakers	L.A. Lakers	Pat Riley	Boston
1986	Boston	Milwaukee	Houston	L.A. Lakers	Boston	K.C. Jones	Houston
1987	Boston	Atlanta	Dallas	L.A. Lakers	L.A. Lakers	Pat Riley	Boston
1988	Boston	Detroit	Denver	L.A. Lakers	L.A. Lakers	Pat Riley	Detroit
1989	New York	Detroit	Utah	L.A. Lakers	Detroit	Chuck Daly	L.A. Lakers
1990	Philadelphia	Detroit	San Antonio	L.A. Lakers	Detroit	Chuck Daly	Portland
1991	Boston	Chicago	San Antonio	Portland	Chicago	Phil Jackson	L.A. Lakers

NBA Most Valuable Player

1956	Bob Pettit, St. Louis		1974	Kareem Abdul-Jabbar, Milwaukee
1957	Bob Cousy, Boston		1975	Bob McAdoo, Buffalo
1958	Bill Russell, Boston		1976	Kareem Abdul-Jabbar, Los Angeles
1959	Bob Pettit, St. Louis		1977	Kareem Abdul-Jabbar, Los Angeles
1960	Wilt Chamberlain, Philadelphia		1978	Bill Walton, Portland
1961	Bill Russell, Boston		1979	Moses Malone, Houston
1962	Bill Russell, Boston		1980	Kareem Abdul-Jabbar, Los Angeles
1963	Bill Russell, Boston		1981	Julius Erving, Philadelphia
1964	Oscar Robertson, Cincinnati		1982	Moses Malone, Houston
1965	Bill Russell, Boston		1983	Moses Malone, Philadelphia
1966	Wilt Chamberlain, Philadelphia		1984	Larry Bird, Boston
1967	Wilt Chamberlain, Philadelphia		1985	Larry Bird, Boston
1968	Wilt Chamberlain, Philadelphia		1986	Larry Bird, Boston
1969	Wes Unseld, Baltimore		1987	Magic Johnson, L.A. Lakers
1970	Willis Reed, New York		1988	Michael Jordan, Chicago
1971	Lew Alcindor, Milwaukee		1989	Magic Johnson, L.A. Lakers
1972	Kareem Abdul-Jabbar (Alcindor), Milwaukee		1990	Magic Johnson, L.A. Lakers
1973	Dave Cowens, Boston		1991	Michael Jordan, Chicago

Statistical Leaders, 1990-1991

Scoring

	G	FG	Pts	Avg
Jordan, Chicago	82	990	2580	31.5
K. Malone, Utah	82	847	2382	29.0
King, Washington	64	713	1817	28.4
Barkley, Philadelphia	67	665	1849	27.6
Ewing, New York	81	845	2154	26.6
Adams, Denver	66	560	1752	26.5
Wilkins, Atlanta	81	770	2101	25.9
Mullin, Golden State	82	777	2107	25.7
Robinson, San Antonio	82	754	2101	25.6
Richmond, Golden State	77	703	1840	23.9
Hardaway, Golden State	82	739	1881	22.9
Miller, Indiana	82	596	1855	22.6
K. Johnson, Phoenix	77	591	1710	22.2
Hawkins, Philadelphia	80	590	1767	22.1
Campbell, Minnesota	77	652	1678	21.8
Daugherty, Cleveland	76	605	1645	21.6
Drexler, Portland	82	645	1767	21.5
Worthy, L.A. Lakers	78	716	1670	21.4
Pierce, Seattle	78	561	1598	20.5
Dumars, Detroit	80	622	1629	20.4

Rebounds Per Game

	G	Def	Tot	Avg
Robinson, San Antonio	82	728	1063	13.0
Rodman, Detroit	82	665	1026	12.5
Oakley, New York	76	615	920	12.1
K. Malone, Utah	82	731	967	11.8
Ewing, New York	81	711	905	11.2
Daugherty, Cleveland	76	653	830	10.9
Parish, Boston	81	585	856	10.6
Benjamin, Seattle	70	566	723	10.3
Thorpe, Houston	82	559	846	10.3
Coleman, New Jersey	74	490	759	10.3

Field Goal Percentage

	FG	FGA	Pct
Williams, Portland	358	595	.602
Parish, Boston	485	811	.598
Gamble, Boston	548	933	.587
Barkley, Philadelphia	665	1167	.570
Divac, L.A. Lakers	360	637	.565
Polynice, L.A. Clippers	316	564	.560
Thorpe, Houston	549	988	.556
McHale, Boston	504	912	.553
Robinson, San Antonio	754	1366	.552
Paxson, Chicago	317	578	.548

Free Throw Percentage

	FT	FTA	Pct
Miller, Indiana	551	600	.918
J. Malone, Utah	231	252	.917
Pierce, Seattle	430	471	.913
Tripucka, Charlotte	152	167	.910
Johnson, L.A. Lakers	519	573	.906
Skiles, Orlando	340	377	.902
Vandeweghe, New York	259	288	.899
Hornacek, Phoenix	201	224	.897
Johnson, Seattle	229	257	.891
Bird, Boston	163	183	.891

Assists Per Game

	G	Ast	Avg
Stockton, Utah	82	1164	14.2
Johnson, L.A. Lakers	79	989	12.5
Adams, Denver	66	693	10.5
K. Johnson, Phoenix	77	781	10.1
Hardaway, Golden State	82	793	9.7
Thomas, Detroit	48	446	9.3
Richardson, Minnesota	82	734	9.0
Grant, L.A. Clippers	68	587	8.6
Douglas, Miami	73	624	8.5
Skiles, Orlando	79	660	8.4

3-Point Field Goal Percentage

	FG	FGA	Pct
Les, Sacramento	71	154	.461
Tucker, New York	64	153	.418
Hornacek, Phoenix	61	146	.418
Porter, Portland	130	313	.415
Skiles, Orlando	93	228	.408
Ainge, Portland	102	251	.406
Hawkins, Philadelphia	108	270	.400
Bird, Boston	77	198	.389
Rice, Miami	71	184	.386
Hardaway, Golden State	97	252	.385

Steals Per Game

	G	Stl	Avg
Robertson, Milwaukee	81	246	3.04
Stockton, Utah	82	234	2.85
Jordan, Chicago	82	223	2.72
Hardaway, Golden State	82	214	2.61
Pippen, Chicago	82	193	2.35
Blaylock, New Jersey	72	169	2.35
Adams, Denver	66	147	2.23
Hawkins, Philadelphia	80	178	2.23
K. Johnson, Phoenix	77	163	2.12
Mullin, Golden State	82	173	2.11

Blocked Shots Per Game

	G	Blk	Avg
Olajuwon, Houston	56	221	3.95
Robinson, San Antonio	82	320	3.90
Ewing, New York	81	258	3.19
Bol, Philadelphia	82	247	3.01
Dudley, New Jersey	61	153	2.51
Nance, Cleveland	80	200	2.50
Eaton, Utah	80	188	2.35
McHale, Boston	68	146	2.15
Benjamin, Seattle	70	145	2.07
Ellison, Washington	76	157	2.07

NBA Rookie of the Year

Year	Player
1953	Don Meineke, Ft. Wayne
1954	Ray Felix, Baltimore
1955	Bob Pettit, Milwaukee
1956	Maurice Stokes, Rochester
1957	Tom Heinsohn, Boston
1958	Woody Sauldsberry, Philadelphia
1959	Elgin Baylor, Minneapolis
1960	Wilt Chamberlain, Philadelphia
1961	Oscar Robertson, Cincinnati
1962	Walt Bellamy, Chicago
1963	Terry Dischinger, Chicago
1964	Jerry Lucas, Cincinnati
1965	Willis Reed, New York
1966	Rick Barry, San Francisco
1967	Dave Bing, Detroit
1968	Earl Monroe, Baltimore
1969	Wes Unseld, Baltimore
1970	Lew Alcindor, Milwaukee
1971	Dave Cowens, Boston; Geoff Petrie, Portland (tie)
1972	Sidney Wicks, Portland
1973	Bob McAdoo, Buffalo
1974	Ernie DiGregorio, Buffalo
1975	Keith Wilkes, Golden State
1976	Alvan Adams, Phoenix
1977	Adrian Dantley, Buffalo
1978	Walter Davis, Phoenix
1979	Phil Ford, Kansas City
1980	Larry Bird, Boston
1981	Darrell Griffith, Utah
1982	Buck Williams, New Jersey
1983	Terry Cummings, San Diego
1984	Ralph Sampson, Houston
1985	Michael Jordan, Chicago
1986	Patrick Ewing, New York
1987	Chuck Person, Indiana
1988	Mark Jackson, New York
1989	Mitch Richmond, Golden State
1990	David Robinson, San Antonio
1991	Derrick Coleman, New Jersey

Individual Statistics, 1990-1991
(Over 600 Minutes Played)

Atlanta Hawks

	Min per game	FG%	3-pt FG%	FT%	Pts avg	Reb avg	Ast avg
Wilkins.	38.0	.470	.341	.829	25.9	9.0	3.3
Rivers	32.7	.435	.336	.844	15.2	3.2	4.3
Battle	23.6	.461	.286	.854	13.6	2.0	2.7
Webb	29.3	.447	.321	.868	13.4	2.3	5.6
Willis	29.7	.504	.400	.668	13.1	8.8	1.2
Malone	23.3	.468	.000	.831	10.6	8.1	0.8
Ferrell	14.9	.489	.667	.801	6.1	2.3	0.7
Robinson	14.3	.446	.182	.588	5.6	1.5	2.8
Moncrief.	15.2	.488	.328	.781	4.7	1.8	1.4
McCormick . . .	12.3	.497	.000	.733	4.5	2.9	0.6
Koncak	25.1	.436	.125	.593	4.1	4.9	1.6

Coach—Bob Weiss

Boston Celtics

	Min per game	FG%	3-pt FG%	FT%	Pts avg	Reb avg	Ast avg
Bird	38.0	.454	.389	.891	19.4	8.5	7.2
Lewis	36.4	.491	.077	.826	18.7	5.2	2.5
McHale	30.4	.553	.405	.829	18.4	7.1	1.9
Gamble	33.0	.587	.000	.815	15.6	3.3	3.1
Parish	30.1	.598	.000	.767	14.9	10.6	0.8
Shaw	35.1	.469	.111	.819	13.8	4.7	7.6
Brown	23.7	.464	.206	.873	8.7	2.2	4.2
Pinckney	16.6	.539	.000	.897	5.2	4.9	0.6
Kleine	11.8	.468	.000	.783	3.6	3.4	0.3

Coach—Chris Ford

Charlotte Hornets

	Min per game	FG%	3-pt FG%	FT%	Pts avg	Reb avg	Ast avg
Newman	30.6	.470	.357	.809	16.9	3.1	2.3
Chapman	30.0	.445	.324	.830	15.7	2.7	3.6
Reid	30.8	.466	.000	.703	11.3	6.3	1.1
Gill	23.7	.464	.143	.835	11.0	3.2	3.7
Curry	19.9	.471	.372	.842	10.6	2.6	2.2
Gminski	27.5	.442	.143	.810	10.6	7.3	1.2
Gattison	21.6	.532	.000	.661	9.0	5.3	0.6
Tripucka.	16.7	.454	.333	.910	7.0	2.3	2.1
Bogues	28.4	.460	.000	.796	7.0	2.7	8.3
Leckner	15.6	.446	.000	.559	4.5	4.1	0.5

Coach—Gene Littles

Chicago Bulls

	Min per game	FG%	3-pt FG%	FT%	Pts avg	Reb avg	Ast avg
Jordan.	37.0	.539	.312	.851	31.5	6.0	5.5
Pippen	36.8	.520	.309	.706	17.8	7.3	6.2
Grant	33.9	.547	.167	.711	12.8	8.4	2.3
Cartwright. . . .	28.8	.490	.000	.697	9.6	6.2	1.6
Armstrong	21.1	.481	.500	.874	8.8	1.8	3.7
Paxson	24.0	.548	.438	.829	8.7	1.1	3.6
King	15.8	.467	.000	.704	5.5	2.7	0.6
Hodges	11.5	.424	.383	.963	5.0	0.6	1.3
Hopson	11.9	.426	.200	.663	4.3	1.8	1.1
Perdue	13.1	.494	.000	.670	4.1	4.5	0.6
Levingston . . .	13.2	.450	.250	.648	4.0	2.9	0.7

Coach—Phil Jackson

Cleveland Cavaliers

	Min per game	FG%	3-pt FG%	FT%	Pts avg	Reb avg	Ast avg
Daugherty.	38.8	.524	.000	.751	21.6	10.9	3.3
Nance	36.6	.524	.250	.803	19.2	8.6	3.0
Williams	30.1	.463	.000	.652	11.7	6.7	2.3
Ehlo	33.7	.445	.329	.679	10.1	4.7	4.6
Valentine	28.3	.464	.240	.831	9.4	2.6	5.4
Ferry	20.5	.428	.299	.816	8.6	3.5	1.8
Brown	20.1	.524	.000	.701	8.5	2.9	1.1
Paddio	16.9	.419	.250	.796	7.2	1.7	1.3
Morton	18.3	.438	.333	.813	5.4	1.6	3.7
Kerr	15.9	.444	.452	.849	4.8	0.6	2.3

Coach—Lenny Wilkens

Dallas Mavericks

	Min per game	FG%	3-pt FG%	FT%	Pts avg	Reb avg	Ast avg
Blackman	37.1	.482	.351	.865	19.9	3.2	3.8
Harper	37.4	.467	.362	.731	19.7	3.0	7.1
Williams	30.5	.507	.000	.638	12.5	6.0	1.6
McCray	34.6	.495	.333	.803	11.4	7.6	3.5
Donaldson	34.1	.532	.000	.721	10.0	8.9	0.8
English	22.1	.439	.000	.850	9.7	3.2	1.3
White	24.1	.398	.362	.707	8.8	6.4	0.8
Davis	17.8	.426	.259	.771	5.4	1.5	2.9

Coach—Richie Adubato

Denver Nuggets

	Min per game	FG%	3-pt FG%	FT%	Pts avg	Reb avg	Ast avg
Adams	35.5	.394	.296	.879	26.5	3.9	10.5
Woolridge.	34.4	.498	.000	.797	25.1	6.8	2.2
Jackson.	22.5	.413	.240	.857	14.1	1.8	3.1
Lichti	29.7	.439	.298	.855	14.0	3.9	2.5
Williams	26.0	.449	.363	.843	13.6	4.2	1.8
Rasmussen. . . .	33.2	.458	.400	.677	12.5	9.7	1.0
Lane	22.3	.438	.250	.411	7.5	9.3	2.0
Wolf	21.5	.451	.133	.831	7.3	5.4	1.4
Liberty	15.4	.421	.298	.630	6.7	2.9	0.8
Battle	16.9	.472	.125	.753	6.1	3.1	1.1
Cook	19.3	.417	.000	.550	5.3	5.6	0.4
Anderson	13.6	.430	.000	.522	4.3	4.7	0.2

Coach—Paul Westhead

Detroit Pistons

	Min per game	FG%	3-pt FG%	FT%	Pts avg	Reb avg	Ast avg
Dumars	38.1	.481	.311	.890	20.4	2.3	5.5
Thomas	34.5	.435	.292	.782	16.2	3.3	9.3
Aguirre	25.7	.462	.308	.757	14.2	4.8	1.8
Edwards	26.4	.484	.500	.729	13.6	3.8	0.9
Johnson.	29.1	.434	.324	.646	11.7	3.4	3.3
Laimbeer	32.5	.478	.296	.837	11.0	9.0	1.9
Rodman	33.5	.493	.200	.631	8.2	12.5	1.0
Salley	22.3	.475	.000	.727	7.4	4.4	0.9

Coach—Chuck Daly

Golden State Warriors

	Min per game	FG%	3-pt FG%	FT%	Pts avg	Reb avg	Ast avg
Mullin	40.4	.536	.301	.884	25.7	5.4	4.0
Richmond	39.3	.494	.348	.847	23.9	5.9	3.1
Hardaway.	39.2	.476	.385	.803	22.9	4.0	9.7
Marciulionis. . . .	19.7	.501	.167	.724	10.9	2.4	1.7
Higgins	24.7	.463	.332	.819	9.5	4.3	1.4
Tolbert	22.1	.423	.333	.738	8.1	4.4	1.2
Elie	19.5	.497	.400	.843	7.2	3.3	1.4
Lister	20.6	.478	.000	.569	6.4	6.3	1.2
Hill	16.1	.492	.000	.632	5.3	5.2	0.3
Petersen	13.5	.483	.250	.658	4.5	3.2	0.4
Pritchard	12.5	.384	.161	.805	3.9	1.0	1.3

Coach—Don Nelson

Houston Rockets

	Min per game	FG%	3-pt FG%	FT%	Pts avg	Reb avg	Ast avg
Olajuwon.	36.8	.508	.000	.769	21.2	13.8	2.3
K. Smith	34.6	.520	.363	.844	17.7	2.1	7.1
Thorpe	37.1	.556	.429	.696	17.5	10.3	2.4
Maxwell	35.0	.404	.337	.733	17.0	2.9	3.7
Johnson.	31.2	.477	.133	.727	13.6	4.5	1.9
Floyd	22.6	.411	.273	.752	12.3	1.9	3.9
Wood	17.3	.424	.311	.812	5.3	3.0	1.1
Winchester . . .	9.5	.400	.400	.778	3.7	1.0	0.4
L. Smith	23.7	.487	.000	.240	3.3	8.8	1.1

Coach—Don Chaney

Indiana Pacers

	Min per game	FG%	3-pt FG%	FT%	Pts avg	Reb avg	Ast avg
Miller	36.2	.512	.348	.918	22.6	3.4	4.0
Person	32.1	.504	.340	.721	18.4	5.2	3.0
Schrempf	32.1	.520	.375	.818	16.1	8.0	3.7
Fleming	28.0	.531	.220	.729	12.7	3.1	5.3
M. Williams	23.4	.499	.143	.879	11.1	2.4	4.8
Smits	22.2	.485	.000	.762	10.9	4.7	1.1
Thompson	23.7	.488	.200	.692	7.6	6.9	1.8
Sanders	17.0	.417	.200	.825	5.8	2.3	1.3
McCloud	14.5	.373	.347	.776	4.6	1.6	2.0
Dreiling	14.1	.505	.000	.600	3.5	3.5	0.7

Coach—Dick Versace; Bob Hill

Los Angeles Clippers

	Min per game	FG%	3-pt FG%	FT%	Pts avg	Reb avg	Ast avg
Smith	36.5	.469	.000	.793	20.0	8.2	1.8
Harper	35.5	.391	.324	.668	19.6	4.8	5.4
Norman	33.0	.501	.188	.629	17.4	7.1	2.3
Manning	30.0	.519	.000	.716	15.9	5.8	2.7
Polynice	26.5	.560	.000	.579	9.8	7.0	0.5
Grant	31.0	.451	.231	.689	8.7	3.1	8.6
Garland	24.7	.426	.154	.752	8.2	2.9	4.6
Martin	18.0	.422	.307	.680	7.1	1.8	0.9
Kimble	16.2	.380	.292	.773	6.9	1.9	1.2
Vaught	16.1	.487	.000	.662	5.5	4.8	0.5
Garrick	14.2	.424	.000	.759	3.9	1.9	3.3

Coach—Mike Schuler

Los Angeles Lakers

	Min per game	FG%	3-pt FG%	FT%	Pts avg	Reb avg	Ast avg
Worthy	38.6	.492	.289	.797	21.4	4.6	3.5
Johnson	37.1	.477	.320	.906	19.4	7.0	12.5
Scott	32.1	.477	.324	.797	14.5	3.0	2.2
Perkins	34.3	.495	.281	.821	13.5	7.4	1.5
Divac	28.2	.565	.357	.703	11.2	8.1	1.1
Teagle	18.3	.443	.000	.819	9.9	2.2	1.0
Green	26.4	.476	.200	.738	9.1	6.3	0.9
Thompson	15.0	.496	.000	.705	4.0	3.2	0.3
Smith	10.9	.441	.000	.702	3.7	1.1	2.1

Coach—Mike Dunleavy

Miami Heat

	Min per game	FG%	3-pt FG%	FT%	Pts avg	Reb avg	Ast avg
Douglas	35.1	.504	.129	.686	18.5	2.9	8.5
Rice	34.4	.461	.386	.818	17.4	4.9	2.5
Seikaly	33.9	.481	.333	.619	16.4	11.1	1.5
Edwards	25.3	.410	.286	.803	12.1	2.6	3.0
Burton	25.4	.441	.133	.782	12.0	3.4	1.4
Long	31.4	.492	.167	.787	9.2	7.1	2.2
Thompson	20.3	.499	.000	.718	6.8	4.3	1.5
Kessler	16.1	.425	.000	.672	6.2	4.3	0.4
Davis	18.1	.487	.500	.556	5.5	4.8	0.7
Coles	16.5	.412	.176	.747	4.9	1.9	2.8

Coach—Ron Rothstein

Milwaukee Bucks

	Min per game	FG%	3-pt FG%	FT%	Pts avg	Reb avg	Ast avg
Ellis	27.9	.474	.363	.723	16.8	3.4	1.9
Humphries	34.1	.502	.373	.799	15.2	2.8	6.7
Robertson	32.1	.485	.385	.757	13.6	5.7	5.5
Brickowski	25.5	.527	.000	.798	12.6	5.7	1.7
Roberts	25.8	.533	.160	.813	10.8	3.4	1.6
Schayes	27.2	.499	.000	.835	10.6	6.5	1.2
Sikma	25.2	.427	.341	.843	10.4	5.7	1.9
Grayer	17.3	.433	.000	.687	6.4	3.0	1.5
Lohaus	16.0	.431	.277	.685	5.3	2.7	0.9
Conner	13.6	.464	.000	.723	3.5	1.5	2.2
Henson	10.1	.418	.333	.905	3.1	0.8	1.9

Coach—Del Harris

Minnesota Timberwolves

	Min per game	FG%	3-pt FG%	FT%	Pts avg	Reb avg	Ast avg
Campbell	37.6	.434	.262	.803	21.8	4.5	2.8
Corbin	39.0	.448	.200	.798	18.0	7.2	4.2
Richardson	38.5	.470	.328	.539	17.1	3.5	9.0
Mitchell	38.1	.441	.000	.775	14.6	6.3	1.6
Spencer	25.9	.512	.000	.722	7.1	7.9	0.3
Glass	11.9	.438	.118	.684	6.9	2.0	0.8
Breuer	20.6	.453	.000	.443	5.9	4.7	1.0
Brooks	12.3	.430	.333	.847	5.3	0.9	2.6
Murphy	20.4	.396	.059	.667	4.8	4.9	1.2
West	11.0	.480	.000	.690	3.9	1.8	0.6

Coach—Bill Musselman

New Jersey Nets

	Min per game	FG%	3-pt FG%	FT%	Pts avg	Reb avg	Ast avg
Theus	36.5	.468	.361	.851	18.6	2.8	4.7
Coleman	35.2	.467	.342	.731	18.4	10.3	2.2
Baylock	35.9	.416	.154	.790	14.1	3.5	6.1
Morris	32.3	.425	.251	.734	13.2	6.6	2.8
Bowie	30.9	.434	.182	.732	12.9	7.7	2.4
Petrovic	16.6	.493	.354	.832	10.2	1.8	1.4
Gervin	13.3	.416	.250	.789	7.6	2.0	0.5
Dudley	25.6	.408	.000	.534	7.1	8.4	0.6
Mills	14.9	.465	.000	.712	5.7	4.2	0.6
Haley	15.1	.469	.000	.619	5.6	4.6	0.4
Buechler	11.6	.416	.250	.652	3.1	1.9	0.7

Coach—Bill Fitch

New York Knickerbockers

	Min per game	FG%	3-pt FG%	FT%	Pts avg	Reb avg	Ast avg
Ewing	38.3	.514	.000	.745	26.6	11.2	3.0
Vandeweghe	32.3	.494	.362	.899	16.3	2.4	1.5
G. Wilkins	31.8	.473	.209	.820	13.8	3.0	4.0
Oakley	36.0	.516	.000	.784	11.2	12.1	2.7
Jackson	22.2	.492	.255	.731	8.8	2.7	6.3
Cheeks	28.3	.499	.250	.814	7.8	2.3	5.7
Starks	19.2	.439	.290	.752	7.6	2.1	3.3
Tucker	18.4	.440	.418	.630	7.1	1.6	1.7
Quinnett	14.9	.459	.349	.722	4.7	2.1	0.8
Mustaf	13.3	.465	.000	.644	4.3	2.7	0.6
Walker	14.3	.435	.000	.780	4.3	2.9	0.2
E. Wilkins	9.8	.447	.000	.567	4.1	2.6	0.2

Coach—Stu Jackson; John McLeod

Orlando Magic

	Min per game	FG%	3-pt FG%	FT%	Pts avg	Reb avg	Ast avg
Skiles	34.4	.445	.408	.902	17.2	3.4	8.4
Scott	28.5	.425	.374	.750	15.7	2.9	1.6
Catledge	28.6	.462	.000	.624	14.6	7.0	1.1
Anderson	28.2	.467	.293	.668	14.1	5.5	1.5
Smith	25.1	.451	.196	.734	13.9	5.2	2.3
Reynolds	23.0	.434	.294	.802	12.9	3.7	2.5
Turner	23.7	.487	.400	.759	8.6	5.1	1.4
Vincent	19.9	.431	.158	.825	8.3	2.2	4.0
Ansley	13.1	.548	.000	.717	5.7	3.8	0.4
Kite	27.1	.491	.000	.512	4.8	7.2	0.7
Acres	19.3	.509	.333	.653	4.2	5.3	0.4

Coach—Matt Goukas

Philadelphia 76ers

	Min per game	FG%	3-pt FG%	FT%	Pts avg	Reb avg	Ast avg
Barkley	37.2	.570	.284	.722	27.6	10.1	4.2
Hawkins	38.9	.472	.400	.871	22.1	3.9	3.7
Gilliam	35.3	.487	.000	.815	16.6	8.0	1.4
Anderson	28.5	.485	.209	.833	14.6	4.5	1.4
Green	28.5	.463	.222	.830	10.0	1.7	5.2
Mahorn	30.5	.467	.000	.788	8.9	7.8	1.5
Turner	20.1	.439	.364	.736	5.9	2.2	4.4
Oliver	11.0	.408	.278	.732	3.8	1.1	1.2
Bol	18.6	.396	.071	.585	1.9	4.3	4.3

Coach—Jim Lynam

Phoenix Suns

	Min per game	FG%	3-pt FG%	FT%	Pts avg	Reb avg	Ast avg
K. Johnson	36.0	.516	.205	.843	22.2	3.5	10.1
Chambers	32.6	.472	.274	.826	19.9	6.4	2.6
McDaniel	32.5	.497	.000	.723	17.0	6.9	2.3
Hornacek	34.2	.518	.418	.897	16.9	4.0	5.1
Majerle	29.6	.484	.349	.762	13.6	5.4	2.8

(continued)

	Min per game	FG%	3-pt FG%	FT%	Pts avg	Reb avg	Ast avg
Ceballos	11.6	.487	.167	.663	8.2	2.4	0.6
West	23.9	.647	.000	.655	7.7	6.9	0.5
Knight	12.4	.425	.240	.602	5.3	1.1	3.0
Lang	18.3	.577	.000	.715	4.9	4.8	0.4
Rambis	14.5	.497	.000	.706	3.6	4.3	1.0

Coach—Cotton Fitzsimmons

Portland Trail Blazers

	Min per game	FG%	3-pt FG%	FT%	Pts avg	Reb avg	Ast avg
Drexler	34.8	.482	.319	.794	21.5	6.7	6.0
Porter	32.9	.515	.415	.823	17.0	3.5	8.0
Duckworth	31.0	.481	.000	.772	15.8	6.6	1.1
Kersey	32.3	.478	.308	.709	14.8	6.6	3.1
Davis	20.9	.468	.366	.915	13.0	2.5	1.8
Robinson	23.7	.463	.316	.653	11.7	4.3	1.8
Williams	32.2	.602	.000	.705	11.7	9.4	1.2
Ainge	21.4	.472	.406	.826	11.1	2.6	3.6
Bryant	14.7	.488	.000	.733	5.1	3.6	0.5
Young	12.0	.380	.346	.911	3.8	1.0	1.9
Cooper	11.1	.393	.000	.786	2.2	2.8	0.3

Coach—Rich Adelman

Sacramento Kings

	Min per game	FG%	3-pt FG%	FT%	Pts avg	Reb avg	Ast avg
Carr	32.8	.511	.000	.758	20.1	5.5	2.5
Tisdale	33.8	.483	.000	.800	20.0	7.7	2.0
Simmons	37.7	.422	.273	.736	18.0	8.8	4.0
Mays	33.5	.406	.365	.770	14.3	2.8	4.0
Sparrow	29.7	.491	.397	.699	10.4	2.3	4.5
Bonner	22.1	.448	.000	.579	7.4	4.7	1.4
Les	25.4	.444	.461	.835	7.2	2.0	5.4
Causwell	22.6	.508	.000	.636	6.9	5.1	0.9
Hansen	22.5	.375	.275	.500	6.4	2.7	2.5
Wennington	18.9	.436	.200	.787	5.7	4.4	0.9
Calloway	10.6	.391	.000	.696	3.2	1.2	1.0

Coach—Dick Motta

San Antonio Spurs

	Min per game	FG%	3-pt FG%	FT%	Pts avg	Reb avg	Ast avg
Robinson	37.7	.552	.143	.762	25.6	13.0	2.5
Cummings	32.8	.484	.212	.683	17.6	7.8	2.3
Elliott	37.1	.490	.313	.808	15.9	5.6	2.9
Anderson	34.6	.457	.200	.798	14.4	4.7	4.8
Strickland	35.8	.482	.333	.763	13.8	3.8	8.0
Pressey	24.0	.472	.281	.827	7.5	2.5	3.9
Green	16.7	.461	.000	.848	6.7	4.7	0.8

	Min per game	FG%	3-pt FG%	FT%	Pts avg	Reb avg	Ast avg
Johnson	14.1	.469	.110	.678	4.7	1.1	3.4
Greenwood	16.2	.503	.000	.734	3.8	3.5	0.8

Coach—Larry Brown

Seattle SuperSonics

	Min per game	FG%	3-pt FG%	FT%	Pts avg	Reb avg	Ast avg
Pierce	27.8	.485	.397	.913	20.5	2.4	2.2
Johnson	25.7	.484	.325	.850	16.7	3.3	1.4
McKey	34.3	.517	.211	.845	15.3	5.8	2.3
Kemp	30.1	.508	.167	.661	15.0	8.4	1.8
Benjamin	32.0	.496	.000	.712	14.0	10.3	1.7
Threatt	25.8	.519	.286	.792	12.7	1.2	3.4
Payton	27.4	.450	.077	.711	7.2	3.0	6.4
Cage	26.1	.508	.000	.625	6.4	6.8	1.3
Barros	11.4	.495	.259	.918	6.3	1.1	1.7
McMillan	18.4	.433	.355	.613	4.3	3.2	4.8

Coach—K.C. Jones

Utah Jazz

	Min per game	FG%	3-pt FG%	FT%	Pts avg	Reb avg	Ast avg
K. Malone	40.3	.527	.286	.770	29.0	11.8	3.3
J. Malone	35.7	.508	.167	.917	18.6	3.0	2.1
Stockton	37.8	.507	.345	.836	17.2	2.9	14.2
Bailey	30.3	.458	.000	.808	12.4	5.0	1.5
Edwards	26.0	.526	.250	.701	9.3	3.2	1.7
Griffith	13.4	.391	.348	.756	5.7	1.2	0.5
Eaton	32.3	.579	.000	.634	5.1	8.3	0.6
M. Brown	17.0	.454	.000	.742	4.8	4.1	0.6
Rudd	10.7	.435	.279	.831	4.0	0.8	2.6

Coach—Jerry Sloan

Washington Bullets

	Min per game	FG%	3-pt FG%	FT%	Pts avg	Reb avg	Ast avg
King	37.5	.472	.216	.790	28.4	5.0	4.6
Grant	36.9	.498	.133	.743	18.2	7.2	2.6
Eackles	24.1	.453	.237	.739	13.0	1.9	2.0
Williams	28.5	.417	.244	.753	12.5	5.4	4.0
Ellison	25.6	.513	.000	.650	10.4	7.7	1.3
English	20.6	.439	.097	.707	8.8	2.1	2.5
Workman	27.9	.454	.240	.759	8.0	3.3	4.8
Walker	32.5	.430	.000	.604	7.8	7.0	6.5
Hammonds	14.6	.461	.000	.722	5.2	2.9	0.6
Foster	11.2	.460	.000	.689	4.4	2.8	0.7
Jones	24.2	.540	.000	.580	2.6	5.8	0.8

Coach—Wes Unseld

NBA Scoring Leaders

Year	Scoring champion	Pts	Avg
1947	Joe Fulks, Philadelphia	1,389	23.2
1948	Max Zaslofsky, Chicago	1,007	21.0
1949	George Mikan, Minneapolis	1,698	28.3
1950	George Mikan, Minneapolis	1,865	27.4
1951	George Mikan, Minneapolis	1,932	28.4
1952	Paul Arizin, Philadelphia	1,674	25.4
1953	Neil Johnston, Philadelphia	1,564	22.3
1954	Neil Johnston, Philadelphia	1,759	24.4
1955	Neil Johnston, Philadelphia	1,631	22.7
1956	Bob Pettit, St. Louis	1,849	25.7
1957	Paul Arizin, Philadelphia	1,817	25.6
1958	George Yardley, Detroit	2,001	27.8
1959	Bob Pettit, St. Louis	2,105	29.2
1960	Wilt Chamberlain, Philadelphia	2,707	37.9
1961	Wilt Chamberlain, Philadelphia	3,033	38.4
1962	Wilt Chamberlain, Philadelphia	4,029	50.4
1963	Wilt Chamberlain, San Francisco	3,586	44.8
1964	Wilt Chamberlain, San Francisco	2,948	36.5
1965	Wilt Chamberlain, San Fran., Phila.	2,534	34.7
1966	Wilt Chamberlain, Philadelphia	2,649	33.5
1967	Rick Barry, San Francisco	2,775	35.6
1968	Dave Bing, Detroit	2,142	27.1
1969	Elvin Hayes, San Diego	2,327	28.4
1970	Jerry West, Los Angeles	2,309	31.2
1971	Lew Alcindor, Milwaukee	2,596	31.7
1972	Kareem Abdul-Jabbar (Alcindor), Milwaukee	2,822	34.8
1973	Nate Archibald, Kansas City-Omaha	2,719	34.0
1974	Bob McAdoo, Buffalo	2,261	30.6
1975	Bob McAdoo, Buffalo	2,831	34.5
1976	Bob McAdoo, Buffalo	2,427	31.1
1977	Pete Maravich, New Orleans	2,273	31.1
1978	George Gervin, San Antonio	2,232	27.2
1979	George Gervin, San Antonio	2,365	29.6
1980	George Gervin, San Antonio	2,585	33.1
1981	Adrian Dantley, Utah	2,452	30.7
1982	George Gervin, San Antonio	2,551	32.3
1983	Alex English, Denver	2,326	28.4
1984	Adrian Dantley, Utah	2,418	30.6
1985	Bernard King, New York	1,809	32.9
1986	Dominique Wilkins, Atlanta	2,366	30.3
1987	Michael Jordan, Chicago	3,041	37.1
1988	Michael Jordan, Chicago	2,868	35.0
1989	Michael Jordan, Chicago	2,633	32.5
1990	Michael Jordan, Chicago	2,753	33.6
1991	Michael Jordan, Chicago	2,580	31.5

All-Time NBA Statistical Leaders

(At the start of the 1990-91 season. *Includes 1990-91 season)

Scoring Average
(400 games or 10,000 Points Minimum)

	G	Pts.	Avg
*Michael Jordan	509	16,596	32.6
Wilt Chamberlain	1,045	31,419	30.1
Elgin Baylor	846	23,149	27.4
Jerry West	932	25,192	27.0
Bob Pettit	792	20,880	26.4
George Gervin	791	20,708	26.2
*Dominique Wilkins	720	18,796	26.1
Oscar Robertson	1,040	26,710	25.7
*Karl Malone	489	12,498	25.5
*Larry Bird	852	20,883	24.5

Field Goal Percentage
(2,000 FGM Minimum)

	FGA	FGM	Pct.
Artis Gilmore	9,570	5,732	.599
James Donaldson	4,494	2,617	.582
Charles Barkley	6,429	3,738	.581
Steve Johnson	4,902	2,807	.573
Darryl Dawkins	6,060	3,468	.572
Jeff Ruland	3,685	2,080	.564
Kevin McHale	10,139	5,705	.563
Kareem Abdul-Jabbar	28,307	15,837	.559
James Worthy	8,762	4,862	.555
Larry Nance	8,136	4,493	.552

Free Throw Percentage
(1,200 FTM Minimum)

	FTA	FTM	Pct.
Rick Barry	4,243	3,818	.900
Calvin Murphy	3,864	3,445	.892
Larry Bird	4,126	3,647	.884
Bill Sharman	3,357	3,143	.884
Chris Mullen	1,928	1,695	.879
Kiki Vandeweghe	2,562	3,102	.871
Mike Newlin	3,456	3,005	.870
Jeff Malone	2,231	1,939	.869
John Long	2,051	1,765	.861
Fred Brown	2,211	1,896	.858

Points

	Pts.
Kareem Abdul-Jabbar	38,387
Wilt Chamberlain	31,419
Elvin Hayes	27,313
Oscar Robertson	26,710
John Havlicek	26,395
*Moses Malone	25,737
*Alex English	25,643
Jerry West	25,192
*Adrian Dantley	23,177

Games Played

Kareem Abdul-Jabbar	1,560
Elvin Hayes	1,303
John Havlicek	1,270
Paul Silas	1,254
Alex English	1,193
Robert Parish	1,181
Moses Malone	1,164
Hal Greer	1,122
Dennis Johnson	1,100

Assists

*Magic Johnson	9,921
Oscar Robertson	9,887
*Isiah Thomas	7,431
Len Wilkens	7,211
*Maurice Cheeks	7,100
Bob Cousy	6,955
Guy Rodgers	6,917
Nate Archibald	6,476
John Lucas	6,454

Field Goals Made

Kareem Abdul-Jabbar	15,837
Wilt Chamberlain	12,681
Elvin Hayes	10,976
*Alex English	10,659
John Havlicek	10,513
Oscar Robertson	9,508
Jerry West	9,016
*Moses Malone	8,867
Elgin Baylor	8,693

Rebounds

Wilt Chamberlain	23,924
Bill Russell	21,620
Kareem Abdul-Jabbar	17,440
Elvin Hayes	16,279
*Moses Malone	15,150
Nate Thurmond	14,464
Walt Bellamy	14,241
Wes Unseld	13,769
Jerry Lucas	12,942

Individuals in The Basketball Hall of Fame

Springfield, Mass.

Players
Archibald, Nate
Arizin, Paul
Barlow, Thomas
Barry, Rick
Baylor, Elgin
Beckman, John
Bing, Dave
Borgmann, Bennie
Bradley, Bill
Brennan, Joseph
Cervi, Al
Chamberlain, Wilt
Cooper, Charles
Cousy, Bob
Cowens, Dave
Cunningham, Billy
Davies, Bob
DeBernardi, Forrest
DeBusschere, Dave
Dehnert, Dutch
Endacott, Paul
Foster, Bud
Frazier, Walt
Friedman, Max
Fulks, Joe
Gale, Lauren
Gallatin, Harry
Gates, Pop
Gola, Tom
Greer, Hal
Gruenig, Ace
Hagan, Cliff
Hanson, Victor
Havlicek, John
Hayes, Elvin
Heinsohn, Tom

Holman, Nat
Houbregs, Bob
Hyatt, Chuck
Johnson, William
Johnston, Neil
Jones, K.C.
Jones, Sam
Krause, Moose
Kurland, Bob
Lapchick, Joe
Lovellette, Clyde
Lucas, Jerry
Luisetti, Hank
Macauley, Ed
Maravich, Pete
Martin, Slater
McCracken, Branch
McCracken, Jack
McDermott, Bobby
Mikan, George
Monroe, Earl
Murphy, Stretch
Page, Pat
Pettit, Bob
Phillip, Andy
Pollard, Jim
Ramsey, Frank
Reed, Willis
Robertson, Oscar
Roosma, John S.
Russell, Honey
Russell, Bill
Schayes, Adolph
Schmidt, Ernest
Schommer, John
Sedran, Barney

Sharman, Bill
Steinmetz, Christian
Thompson, Cat
Thurmond, Nate
Twyman, Jack
Unseld, Wes
Vandivier, Fuzzy
Wachter, Edward
Wanzer, Bobby
West, Jerry
Wilkins, Lenny
Wooden, John
Coaches
Auerbach, Red
Barry, Sam
Blood, Ernest
Cann, Howard
Carlson, Dr. H. C.
Carnevale, Ben
Case, Everett
Dean, Everett
Diddle, Edgar
Drake, Bruce
Gaines, Clarence
Gardner, Jack
Gill, Slats
Hickey, Edgar
Hobson, Howard
Holzman, Red
Iba, Hank
Julian, Alvin
Keaney, Frank
Keogan, George
Knight, Bob
Lambert, Ward
Litwack, Harry

Loeffler, Kenneth
Lonborg, Dutch
McCutchan, Arad
McGuire, Frank
McLendon, John
Meyer, Ray
Meanwell, Dr. W.E.
Miller, Ralph
Newell, Pete
Rupp, Adolph
Sachs, Leonard
Shelton, Everett
Smith, Dean
Taylor, Fred
Teague, Bertha
Wade, Margaret
Watts, Stan
Wooden, John
Referees
Enright, James
Hepburn, George
Hoyt, George
Kennedy, Matthew
Leith, Lloyd
Mihalik, Red
Nucatola, John
Quigley, Ernest
Shirley, J. Dallas
Tobey, David
Walsh, David
Contributors
Abbott, Sendra B.
Allen, Phog
Bee, Clair
Brown, Walter
Bunn, John

Douglas, Bob
Duer, Al O.
Fagan, Cliff
Fisher, Harry
Fleisher, Larry
Gottlieb, Edward
Gulick, Dr. L. H.
Harrison, Lester
Hepp, Dr. Ferenc
Hickox, Edward
Hinkle, Tony
Irish, Ned
Jones, R. W.
Kennedy, Walter
Liston, Emil
Mokray, Bill
Morgan, Ralph
Morgenweck, Frank
Naismith, Dr. James
O'Brien, John
O'Brien, Larry
Olsen, Harold
Podoloff, Maurice
Porter, H. V.
Reis, William
Ripley, Elmer
St. John, Lynn
Saperstein, Abe
Schabinger, Arthur
Stagg, Amos Alonzo
Steitz, Edward
Taylor, Chuck
Tower, Oswald
Trester, Arthur
Wells, Clifford
Wilke, Lou

1991 NBA Player Draft

The following are the first round picks of the National Basketball Association.

Charlotte—Larry Johnson, UNLV
New Jersey—Kenny Anderson, Georgia Tech
Sacramento—Billy Owens, Syracuse
Denver—Dikembe Mutombo, Georgetown
Miami—Steve Smith, Michigan State
Dallas—Doug Smith, Missouri
Minnesota—Luc Longley, New Mexico
Denver—Mark Macon, Temple
Atlanta—Stacey Augmon, UNLV
Orlando—Brian Williams, Arizona
Cleveland—Terrell Brandon, Oregon
New York—Greg Anthony, UNLV
Indiana—Dale Davis, Clemson
Seattle—Rich King, Nebraska

Atlanta—Anthony Avent,[1] Seton Hall
Golden State—Chris Gatling, Old Dominion
Golden State—Victor Alexander, Iowa State
Milwaukee—Kevin Brooks,[2] SW Louisiana
Washington—LaBradford Smith, Louisville
Houston—John Turner, Phillips
Utah—Eric Murdock, Providence
L.A. Clippers—LeRon Ellis, Syracuse
Orlando—Stanley Roberts, LSU
Boston—Rick Fox, North Carolina
Golden State—Shaun Vandiver, Colorado
Chicago—Mark Randall, Kansas
Sacramento—Pete Chilcutt, North Carolina

(1) Traded to Denver, later Milwaukee. (2) Traded to Denver.

First Round NBA Draft Picks, 1966-91

Year	Team	Player, college	Year	Team	Player, college
1966	New York	Cazzie Russell, Michigan	1979	L.A. Lakers	Magic Johnson, Michigan St.
1967	Detroit	Jimmy Walker, Providence	1980	Golden State	Joe Barry Carroll, Purdue
1968	Houston	Elvin Hayes, Houston	1981	Dallas	Mark Aguirre, DePaul
1969	Milwaukee	Lew Alcindor, UCLA*	1982	L.A. Lakers	James Worthy, N. Carolina
1970	Detroit	Bob Lanier, St. Bonaventure	1983	Houston	Ralph Sampson, Virginia
1971	Cleveland	Austin Carr, Notre Dame	1984	Houston	Akeem Olajuwon, Houston
1972	Portland	LaRue Martin, Loyola-Chicago	1985	New York	Patrick Ewing, Georgetown
1973	Philadelphia	Doug Collins, Illinois St.	1986	Cleveland	Brad Daugherty, N. Carolina
1974	Portland	Bill Walton, UCLA	1987	San Antonio	David Robinson, Navy
1975	Atlanta	David Thompson,[1] N.C. State	1988	L.A. Clippers	Danny Manning, Kansas
1976	Houston	John Lucas, Maryland	1989	Sacramento	Pervis Ellison, Louisville
1977	Milwaukee	Kent Benson, Indiana	1990	New Jersey	Derrick Coleman, Syracuse
1978	Portland	Mychal Thompson, Minnesota	1991	Charlotte	Larry Johnson, UNLV

* Later Kareem Abdul-Jabbar. (1) Signed with Denver of ABA.

NBA All-League Team in 1991

First team	Position	Second team
Karl Malone, Utah	Forward	Dominique Wilkins, Atlanta
Charles Barkley, Philadelphia	Forward	Chris Mullin, Golden State
David Robinson, San Antonio	Center	Patrick Ewing, New York
Magic Johnson, L.A. Lakers	Guard	Clyde Drexler, Portland
Michael Jordan, Chicago	Guard	Kevin Johnson, Phoenix

NBA All-Defensive Team in 1991

First team	Position	Second team
Dennis Rodman, Detroit	Forward	Scottie Pippen, Chicago
Buck Williams, Portland	Forward	Dan Majerle, Phoenix
David Robinson, San Antonio	Center	Hakeem Alajuwon, Houston
Michael Jordan, Chicago	Guard	Joe Dumars, Detroit
Alvin Robertson, Milwaukee	Guard	John Stockton, Utah

Curling Champions

Source: North American Curling News

World Champions

Year	Country, skip	Year	Country, skip	Year	Country, skip
1977	Sweden, Ragnar Kamp	1982	Canada, Al Hackner	1987	Canada, Russ Howard
1978	United States, Bob Nichols	1983	Canada, Ed Werenich	1988	Norway, Eigil Ramsfjell
1979	Norway, Kristian Soerum	1984	Norway, Eigil Ramsfjell	1989	Canada, Pat Ryan
1980	Canada, Rich Folk	1985	Canada, Al Hackner	1990	Canada, Ed Werenich
1981	Switzerland, Jurg Tanner	1986	Canada, Ed Luckowich	1991	Scotland, David Smith

U.S. Men's Champions

Year	State, skip	Year	State, skip	Year	State, skip
1977	Minnesota, Bruce Roberts	1982	Wisconsin, Steve Brown	1987	Washington, Jim Vukich
1978	Wisconsin, Bob Nichols	1983	Colorado, Don Cooper	1988	Washington, Doug Jones
1979	Minnesota, Scotty Baird	1984	Minnesota, Bruce Roberts	1989	Washington, Jim Vukich
1980	Minnesota, Paul Pustover	1985	Illinois, Tim Wright	1990	Washington, Doug Jones
1981	Wisconsin, Somerville-Nichols	1986	Wisconsin, Steve Brown	1991	Wisconsin, Steve Brown

U.S. Ladies Champions

Year	State, skip	Year	State, skip	Year	State, skip
1980	Washington, Sharon Kozai	1984	Minnesota, Amy Hatten	1988	Washington, Nancy Langey
1981	Washington, Nancy Langley	1985	Alaska, Bev Birklid	1989	North Dakota, Jan Lagasse
1982	Illinois, Ruth Schwenker	1986	Minnesota, Gerri Tilden	1990	Colorado, Bev Behnke
1983	Washington, Nancy Langley	1987	Washington, Sharon Good	1991	Texas, Maymar Gemmell

Boxing Champions by Classes

As of Sept. 15, 1991 the only generally accepted title holders were in the heavyweight and lightweight division. There are numerous governing bodies in boxing including the World Boxing Council, the World Boxing Assn., the International Boxing Federation, the United States Boxing Assn., the North American Boxing Federation, and the European Boxing Union. Other organizations are recognized by TV networks and the print media. All the governing bodies have their own champions and assorted boxing divisions. The following are the recognized champions in the principal divisions of the World Boxing Association, the World Boxing Council, and the International Boxing Federation.

Class, Weight Limit	WBA	WBC	IBF
Heavyweight	Evander Holyfield, U.S.	Evander Holyfield, U.S.	Evander Holyfield, U.S.
Cruiserweight (195 lbs.)	Bobby Cruz, U.S.	Massimiliano Duran, Italy	Jeff Lampkin, U.S.
Light Heavyweight (175 lbs.)	Thomas Hearns, U.S.	Jeff Harding, Australia	Charles Williams, U.S.
Super Middleweight (168 lbs.)	Victor Cordoba, N. Ireland	Mauro Galvano, Italy	Darrin Van Horn, U.S.
Middleweight (160 lbs.)	Mike McCallum, U.S.	Julian Jackson, Virgin Islands	James Toney, U.S.
Jr. Middleweight (154 lbs.)	Vinny Pazienza, U.S.	Terry Norris, U.S.	Gianfranco Rosi, Italy
Welterweight (147 lbs.)	Meldrick Taylor, U.S.	Simon Brown, U.S.	Simon Brown, U.S.
Jr. Welterweight (140 lbs.)	Edward Rosario, Puerto Rico	Julio Cesar Chavez, Mexico	Julio Cesar Chavez, Mexico
Lightweight (135 lbs.)	Pernell Whitaker, U.S.	Pernell Whitaker, U.S.	Pernell Whitaker, U.S.
Jr. Lightweight (130 lbs.)	Joey Gamache, U.S.	Azumah Nelson, Ghana	Tony Lopez, U.S.
Featherweight (126 lbs.)	Park Yung Kyun, S. Korea	Marcos Villasana, Mexico	Troy Dorsey, U.S.
Jr. Featherweight (122 lbs.)	Luis Mendoza, Colombia	Daniel Zaragoza, Mexico	Welcome Ncita, S. Africa
Bantamweight (118 lbs.)	Luisito Espinosa, Philippines	Muangchai Kittikasem, Thailand	Orlando Canizales, U.S.
Flyweight (112 lbs.)	Yong Kang Kim, S. Korea	Muangchai Kittikasem, Thailand	Dave McAuley, Ireland

Ring Champions by Years

*Abandoned title

Heavyweights

1882-1892	John L. Sullivan (a)
1892-1897	James J. Corbett (b)
1897-1899	Robert Fitzsimmons
1899-1905	James J. Jeffries (c)
1905-1906	Marvin Hart
1906-1908	Tommy Burns
1908-1915	Jack Johnson
1915-1919	Jess Willard
1919-1926	Jack Dempsey
1926-1928	Gene Tunney*
1928-1930	vacant
1930-1932	Max Schmeling
1932-1933	Jack Sharkey
1933-1934	Primo Carnera
1934-1935	Max Baer
1935-1937	James J. Braddock
1937-1949	Joe Louis*
1949-1951	Ezzard Charles
1951-1952	Joe Walcott
1952-1956	Rocky Marciano*
1956-1959	Floyd Patterson
1959-1960	Ingemar Johansson
1960-1962	Floyd Patterson
1962-1964	Sonny Liston
1964-1967	Cassius Clay* (Muhammad Ali) (d)
1970-1973	Joe Frazier
1973-1974	George Foreman
1974-1978	Muhammad Ali
1978-1979	Leon Spinks (e), Muhammad Ali*
1978	Ken Norton (WBC), Larry Holmes (WBC) (f)
1979	John Tate (WBA)
1980	Mike Weaver (WBA)
1982	Michael Dokes (WBA)
1983	Gerrie Coetzee (WBA)
1984	Tim Witherspoon (WBC); Pinklon Thomas (WBC); Greg Page (WBA)
1985	Tony Tubbs (WBA); Michael Spinks (IBF)
1986	Tim Witherspoon (WBA); Trevor Berbick (WBC); Mike Tyson (WBC); James (Bone-crusher) Smith (WBA).
1987	Mike Tyson (WBA).
1990	James "Buster" Douglas (WBA, WBC, IBF)
1990	Evander Holyfield (WBA, WBC, IBF)

(a) London Prize Ring (bare knuckle champion).
(b) First Marquis of Queensberry champion.
(c) Jeffries abandoned the title (1905) and designated Marvin Hart and Jack Root as logical contenders and agreed to referee a fight between them, the winner to be declared champion. Hart defeated Root in 12 rounds (1905) and in turn was defeated by Tommy Burns (1906) who immediately laid claim to the title. Jack Johnson defeated Burns (1908) and was recognized as champion. He clinched the title by defeating Jeffries in an attempted comeback (1910).
(d) Title declared vacant by the WBA and other groups in 1967 after Clay's refusal to fulfill his military obligation. Joe Frazier was recognized as champion by 6 states, Mexico, and So. America. Jimmy Ellis was declared champion by the WBA. Frazier KOd Ellis, Feb. 16, 1970.
(e) After Spinks defeated Ali, the WBC recognized Ken Norton as champion. Norton subsequently lost his title to Larry Holmes.
(f) Holmes was stripped of his WBC title in 1984. He was the IBF champion when he lost to Michael Spinks.

Light Heavyweights

1903	Jack Root, George Gardner
1903-1905	Bob Fitzsimmons
1905-1912	Philadelphia Jack O'Brien*
1912-1916	Jack Dillon
1916-1920	Battling Levinsky
1920-1922	George Carpentier
1922-1923	Battling Siki
1923-1925	Mike McTigue
1925-1926	Paul Berlenbach
1926-1927	Jack Delaney*
1927-1929	Tommy Loughran*
1930-1934	Maxey Rosenbloom
1934-1935	Bob Olin
1935-1939	John Henry Lewis*
1939	Melio Bettina
1939-1941	Billy Conn*
1941	Anton Christoforidis (won NBA title)
1941-1948	Gus Lesnevich, Freddie Mills
1948-1950	Freddie Mills
1950-1952	Joey Maxim
1952-1960	Archie Moore
1961-1962	vacant
1962-1963	Harold Johnson
1963-1965	Willie Pastrano
1965-1966	Jose Torres
1966-1968	Dick Tiger
1968-1974	Bob Foster*, John Conteh (WBA)
1975-1977	John Conteh (WBC), Miguel Cuello (WBC), Victor Galindez (WBA)
1978	Mike Rossman (WBA), Mate Parlov (WBC), Marvin Johnson (WBC)
1979	Victor Galindez (WBA), Matthew Saad Muhammad (WBC)
1980	Eddie Mustava Muhammad (WBA)
1981	Michael Spinks (WBA), Dwight Braxton (WBC)
1983	Michael Spinks
1986	Marvin Johnson (WBA); Dennis Andries (WBC)
1987	Thomas Hearns (WBC); Leslie Stewart (WBA); Virgil Hill (WBA); Don Lalonde (WBC).
1988	Ray Leonard* (WBC)
1989	Jeff Harding (WBC)
1990	Dennis Andries (WBC)
1991	Thomas Hearns (WBA); Jeff Harding (WBC)

Middleweights

1884-1891	Jack "Nonpareil" Dempsey
1891-1897	Bob Fitzsimmons*
1897-1907	Tommy Ryan*
1907-1908	Stanley Ketchel, Billy Papke
1908-1910	Stanley Ketchel
1911-1913	vacant

1913	Frank Klaus, George Chip
1914-1917	Al McCoy
1917-1920	Mike O'Dowd
1920-1923	Johnny Wilson
1923-1926	Harry Greb
1926-1931	Tiger Flowers, Mickey Walker
1931-1932	Gorilla Jones (NBA)
1932-1937	Marcel Thil
1938	Al Hostak (NBA), Solly Krieger (NBA)
1939-1940	Al Hostak (NBA)
1941-1947	Tony Zale
1947-1948	Rocky Graziano
1948	Tony Zale, Marcel Cerdan
1949-1951	Jake LaMotta
1951	Ray Robinson, Randy Turpin, Ray Robinson*
1953-1955	Carl (Bobo) Olson
1955-1957	Ray Robinson
1957	Gene Fullmer, Ray Robinson, Carmen Basilio
1958	Ray Robinson
1959	Gene Fullmer (NBA); Ray Robinson (N.Y.)
1960	Gene Fullmer (NBA); Paul Pender (New York and Mass.)
1961	Gene Fullmer (NBA); Terry Downes (New York, Mass., Europe)
1962	Gene Fullmer, Dick Tiger (NBA), Paul Pender (New York and Mass.)*
1963	Dick Tiger (universal).
1963-1965	Joey Giardello
1965-1966	Dick Tiger
1966-1967	Emile Griffith
1967	Nino Benvenuti
1967-1968	Emile Griffith
1968-1970	Nino Benvenuti
1970-1977	Carlos Monzon*
1977-1978	Rodrigo Valdez
1978-1979	Hugo Corro
1979-1980	Vito Antuofermo
1980	Alan Minter, Marvin Hagler
1987	Ray Leonard* (WBC); Thomas Hearns (WBC); Sumbu Kalambay (WBA).
1988	Iran Barkley (WBC)
1989	Mike McCallum (WBA); Roberto Duran (WBC)
1991	Julian Jackson (WBC)

Welterweights

1892-1894	Mysterious Billy Smith
1894-1896	Tommy Ryan
1896	Kid McCoy*
1900	Rube Ferns, Matty Matthews
1901	Rube Ferns
1901-1904	Joe Walcott
1904-1906	Dixie Kid, Joe Walcott, Honey Mellody
1907-1911	Mike Sullivan
1911-1915	vacant
1915-1919	Ted Lewis
1919-1922	Jack Britton
1922-1926	Mickey Walker
1926	Pete Latzo
1927-1929	Joe Dundee
1929	Jackie Fields
1930	Jack Thompson, Tommy Freeman
1931	Freeman, Thompson, Lou Brouillard
1932	Jackie Fields
1933	Young Corbett, Jimmy McLarnin
1934	Barney Ross, Jimmy McLarnin
1935-1938	Barney Ross
1938-1940	Henry Armstrong
1940-1941	Fritzie Zivic
1941-1946	Fred Cochrane
1946-1946	Marty Servo*; Ray Robinson (a)
1946-1950	Ray Robinson*
1951	Johnny Bratton (NBA)
1951-1954	Kid Gavilan
1954-1955	Johnny Saxton
1955	Tony De Marco, Carmen Basilio
1956	Carmen Basilio, Johnny Saxton, Basilio
1957	Carmen Basilio*
1958-1960	Virgil Akins, Don Jordan
1960	Benny Paret
1961	Emile Griffith, Benny Paret
1962	Emile Griffith
1963	Luis Rodriguez, Emile Griffith
1964-1966	Emile Griffith*
1966-1969	Curtis Cokes
1969-1970	Jose Napoles, Billy Backus
1971-1975	Jose Napoles
1975-1976	John Stracey (WBC), Angel Espada (WBA)
1976-1979	Carlos Palomino (WBC), Jose Cuevas (WBA)
1979	Wilfredo Benitez (WBC), Sugar Ray Leonard (WBC)

1980	Roberto Duran (WBC), Thomas Hearns (WBA), Sugar Ray Leonard (WBC)
1981-1982	Sugar Ray Leonard*
1983	Donald Curry (WBA); Milton McCrory (WBC)
1985	Donald Curry
1986	Lloyd Honeyghan (WBC)
1987	Mark Breland (WBA); Marlon Starling (WBA); Jorge Vaca (WBC).
1988	Tomas Molinares (WBA); Lloyd Honeyghan (WBC).
1989	Marlon Starling (WBC); Mark Breland (WBA)
1990	Maurice Blocker (WBC); Aaron Davis (WBA)
1991	Meldrick Taylor (WBA); Simon Brown (WBC)

(a) Robinson gained the title by defeating Tommy Bell in an elimination agreed to by the NY Commission and the NBA. Both claimed Robinson waived his title when he won the middleweight crown from LaMotta in 1951.

Lightweights

1896-1899	Kid Lavigne
1899-1902	Frank Erne
1902-1908	Joe Gans
1908-1910	Battling Nelson
1910-1912	Ad Wolgast
1912-1914	Willie Ritchie
1914-1917	Freddie Welsh
1917-1925	Benny Leonard*
1925	Jimmy Goodrich, Rocky Kansas
1926-1930	Sammy Mandell
1930	Al Singer, Tony Canzoneri
1930-1933	Tony Canzoneri
1933-1935	Barney Ross*
1935-1936	Tony Canzoneri
1936-1938	Lou Ambers
1938	Henry Armstrong
1939	Lou Ambers
1940	Lew Jenkins
1941-1943	Sammy Angott
1944	S. Angott (NBA), J. Zurita (NBA)
1945-1951	Ike Williams (NBA: later universal)
1951-1952	James Carter
1952	Lauro Salas, James Carter
1953-1954	James Carter
1954	Paddy De Marco; James Carter
1955	James Carter; Bud Smith
1956	Bud Smith, Joe Brown
1956-1962	Joe Brown
1962-1965	Carlos Ortiz
1965	Ismael Laguna
1965-1968	Carlos Ortiz
1968-1969	Teo Cruz
1969-1970	Mando Ramos
1970	Ismael Laguna, Ken Buchanan (WBA)
1971	Mando Ramos (WBC), Pedro Carrasco (WBC)
1972-1979	Roberto Duran* (WBA)
1972	Pedro Carrasco, Mando Ramos, Chango Carmona, Rodolfo Gonzalez (all WBC)
1974-1976	Guts Ishimatsu (WBC)
1976-1977	Esteban De Jesus (WBC)
1979	Jim Watt (WBC), Ernesto Espana (WBA)
1980	Hilmer Kenty (WBA)
1981	Alexis Arguello (WBC), Sean O'Grady (WBA), Arturo Frias (WBA)
1982-1984	Ray Mancini (WBA)
1983	Edwin Rosario (WBC)
1984	Livingstone Bramble (WBA); Jose Luis Ramirez (WBC)
1985	Hector (Macho) Camacho (WBC)
1986	Edwin Rosario (WBA); Jose Luis Ramirez (WBC).
1987	Julio Cesar Chavez (WBA).
1989	Edwin Rosario (WBA); Pernell Whitaker (WBC).
1990	Juan Nazario (WBA); Pernell Whitaker (WBA)

Featherweights

1892-1900	George Dixon (disputed)
1900-1901	Terry McGovern, Young Corbett*
1901-1912	Abe Attell
1912-1923	Johnny Kilbane
1923	Eugene Criqui, Johnny Dundee
1923-1925	Johnny Dundee*
1925-1927	Kid Kaplan*
1927-1928	Benny Bass, Tony Canzoneri
1928-1929	Andre Routis
1929-1932	Battling Battalino*
1932-1934	Tommy Paul (NBA)
1933-1936	Freddie Miller
1936-1937	Petey Sarron

1937-1938	Henry Armstrong*
1938-1940	Joey Archibald (b)
1940-41	Harry Jeffra
1942-1948	Willie Pep
1948-1949	Sandy Saddler
1949-1950	Willie Pep
1950-1957	Sandy Saddler*
1957-1959	Hogan (Kid) Bassey
1959-1963	Davey Moore
1963-1964	Sugar Ramos
1964-1967	Vicente Saldivar*
1968-1971	Paul Rojas (WBA), Sho Saijo (WBA)
1971	Antonio Gomez (WBA), Kuniaki Shibada (WBC)
1972	Ernesto Marcel* (WBA), Clemente Sanchez* (WBC), Jose Legra (WBC)
1973	Eder Jofre (WBC)
1974	Ruben Olivares (WBA), Alexis Arguello (WBA), Bobby Chacon (WBC)
1975	Ruben Olivares (WBC), David Kotey (WBC)

1976	Danny Lopez (WBC)
1977	Rafael Ortega (WBA)
1978	Cecilio Lastra (WBA), Eusebio Pedrosa (WBA)
1980	Salvador Sanchez (WBC)
1982	Juan LaPorte (WBC)
1984	Wilfredo Gomez (WBC); Azumah Nelson (WBC)
1985	Barry McGuigan (WBA)
1986	Steve Cruz (WBA)
1987	Antonio Esparragoza (WBA)
1988	Jeff Fenech (WBC)
1990	Marcos Villasana (WBC)
1991	Park Yung Kyun (WBA)

(b) After Petey Scalzo knocked out Archibald in an overweight match and was refused a title bout, the NBA named Scalzo champion. The NBA title succession: Scalzo, 1938-1941; Richard Lemos, 1941; Jackie Wilson, 1941-1943; Jackie Callura, 1943; Phil Terranova, 1943-1944; Sal Bartolo, 1944-1946.

History of Heavyweight Championship Bouts
*Title Changed Hands

1889—July 8—John L. Sullivan def. Jake Kilrain, 75, Richburg, Miss. Last championship bare knuckles bout.
*1892—Sept. 7—James J. Corbett def. John L. Sullivan, 21, New Orleans. Big gloves used for first time.
1894—Jan. 25—James J. Corbett KOd Charley Mitchell, 3, Jacksonville, Fla.
*1897—Bob Fitzsimmons def. James J. Corbett, 14, Carson City, Nev.
*1899—June 9—James J. Jeffries def. Bob Fitzsimmons, 11, Coney Island, N.Y.
1899—Nov. 3—James J. Jeffries def. Tom Sharkey, 25, Coney Island, N.Y.
1900—May 11—James J. Jeffries KOd James J. Corbett, 23, Coney Island, N.Y.
1901—Nov. 15—James J. Jeffries KOd Gus Ruhlin, 5, San Francisco.
1902—July 25—James J. Jeffries KOd Bob Fitzsimmons, 8, San Francisco.
1903—Aug. 14—James J. Jeffries KOd James J. Corbett, 10, San Francisco.
1904—Aug. 26—James J. Jeffries KOd Jack Monroe, 2, San Francisco.
*1905—James J. Jeffries retired, July 3—Marvin Hart KOd Jack Root, 12, Reno. Jeffries refereed and presented the title to the victor. Jack O'Brien also claimed the title.
*1906—Feb. 23—Tommy Burns def. Marvin Hart, 20, Los Angeles.
1906—Nov. 28—Philadelphia Jack O'Brien and Tommy Burns, 20, draw, Los Angeles.
1907—May 8—Tommy Burns def. Jack O'Brien, 20, Los Angeles.
1907—July 4—Tommy Burns KOd Bill Squires, 1, Colma, Cal.
1907—Dec. 2—Tommy Burns KOd Gunner Moir, 10, London.
1908—Feb. 10—Tommy Burns KOd Jack Palmer, 4, London.
1908—March 17—Tommy Burns KOd Jem Roche, 1, Dublin.
1908—April 18—Tommy Burns KOd Jewey Smith, 5, Paris.
1908—June 13—Tommy Burns KOd Bill Squires, 8, Paris.
1908—Aug. 24—Tommy Burns KOd Bill Squires, 13, Sydney, New South Wales.
1908—Sept. 2—Tommy Burns KOd Bill Lang, 2, Melbourne, Australia.
*1908—Dec. 26—Jack Johnson KOd Tommy Burns, 14, Sydney, Australia. Police halted contest.
1909—May 19—Jack Johnson and Jack O'Brien, 6, draw, Philadelphia.
1909—June 30—Jack Johnson and Tony Ross, 6, draw, Pittsburgh.
1909—Sept. 9—Jack Johnson and Al Kaufman, 10, draw, San Francisco.
1909—Oct. 16—Jack Johnson KOd Stanley Ketchel, 12, Colma, Cal.
1910—July 4—Jack Johnson KOd Jim Jeffries, 15, Reno, Nev. Jeffries came back from retirement.
1912—July 4—Jack Johnson def. Jim Flynn, 9, Las Vegas, N.M. Contest stopped by police.
1913—Nov. 28—Jack Johnson KOd Andre Spaul, 2, Paris.
1913—Dec. 9—Jack Johnson and Jim Johnson, 10, draw, Paris. Bout called a draw when Jack Johnson declared he had broken his arm.
1914—June 27—Jack Johnson def. Frank Moran, 20, Paris.
*1915—April 5—Jess Willard KOd Jack Johnson, 26, Havana, Cuba.

1916—March 25—Jess Willard and Frank Moran, 10, draw, New York.
*1919—July 4—Jack Dempsey KOd Jess Willard, Toledo, Oh. Willard failed to answer bell for 4th round.
1920—Sept. 6—Jack Dempsey KOd Billy Miske, 3, Benton Harbor, Mich.
1920—Dec. 14—Jack Dempsey KOd Bill Brennan, 12, New York.
1921—July 2—Jack Dempsey KOd George Carpentier, 4, Boyle's Thirty Acres, Jersey City, N.J. Carpentier had held the so-called white heavyweight title since July 16, 1914, in a series established in 1913, after Jack Johnson's exile in Europe late in 1912.
1923—July 4—Jack Dempsey def. Tom Gibbons, 15, Shelby, Mont.
1923—Sept. 14—Jack Dempsey KOd Luis Firpo, 2, New York.
*1926—Sept. 23—Gene Tunney def. Jack Dempsey, 10, Philadelphia.
1927—Sept. 22—Gene Tunney def. Jack Dempsey, 10, Chicago.
1928—July 26—Gene Tunney KOd Tom Heeney, 11, New York; soon afterward he announced his retirement.
*1930—June 12—Max Schmeling def. Jack Sharkey, 4, New York. Sharkey fouled Schmeling in a bout which was generally considered to have resulted in the election of a successor to Gene Tunney, New York.
1931—July 3—Max Schmeling KOd Young Stribling, 15, Cleveland.
*1932—June 21—Jack Sharkey def. Max Schmeling, 15, New York.
*1933—June 29—Primo Carnera KOd Jack Sharkey, 6, New York.
1933—Oct. 22—Primo Carnera def. Paulino Uzcudun, 15, Rome.
1934—March 1—Primo Carnera def. Tommy Loughran, 15, Miami.
*1934—June 14—Max Baer KOd Primo Carnera, 11, New York.
*1935—June 13—James J. Braddock def. Max Baer, 15, New York.
*1937—June 22—Joe Louis KOd James J. Braddock, 8, Chicago.
1937—Aug. 30—Joe Louis def. Tommy Farr, 15, New York.
1938—Feb. 23—Joe Louis KOd Nathan Mann, 3, New York.
1938—April 1—Joe Louis KOd Harry Thomas, 5, New York.
1938—June 22—Joe Louis KOd Max Schmeling, 1, New York.
1939—Jan. 25—Joe Louis KOd John H. Lewis, 1, New York.
1939—April 17—Joe Louis KOd Jack Roper, 1, Los Angeles.
1939—June 28—Joe Louis KOd Tony Galento, 4, New York.
1939—Sept. 20—Joe Louis KOd Bob Pastor, 11, Detroit.
1940—February 9—Joe Louis def. Arturo Godoy, 15, New York.
1940—March 29—Joe Louis KOd Johnny Paycheck, 2, New York.
1940—June 20—Joe Louis KOd Arturo Godoy, 8, New York.
1940—Dec. 16—Joe Louis KOd Al McCoy, 6, Boston.
1941—Jan. 31—Joe Louis KOd Red Burman, 5, New York.
1941—Feb. 17—Joe Louis KOd Gus Dorzaio, 2, Philadelphia.
1941—March 21—Joe Louis KOd Abe Simon, 13, Detroit.
1941—April 8—Joe Louis KOd Tony Musto, 9, St. Louis.

1941—May 23—Joe Louis def. Buddy Baer, 7, Washington, D.C., on a disqualification.
1941—June 18—Joe Louis KOd Billy Conn, 13, New York.
1941—Sept. 29—Joe Louis KOd Lou Nova, 6, New York.
1942—Jan. 9—Joe Louis KOd Buddy Baer, 1, New York.
1942—March 27—Joe Louis KOd Abe Simon, 6, New York.
1946—June 19—Joe Louis KOd Billy Conn, 8, New York.
1946—Sept. 18—Joe Louis KOd Tami Mauriello, 1, New York.
1947—Dec. 5—Joe Louis def. Joe Walcott, 15, New York.
1948—June 25—Joe Louis KOd Joe Walcott, 11, New York.
*1949—June 22—Following Joe Louis' retirement Ezzard Charles def. Joe Walcott, 15, Chicago, NBA recognition only.
1949—Aug. 10—Ezzard Charles KOd Gus Lesnevich, 7, New York.
1949—Oct. 14—Ezzard Charles KOd Pat Valentino, 8, San Francisco; clinched American title.
1950—Aug. 15—Ezzard Charles KOd Freddy Beshore, 14, Buffalo.
1950—Sept. 27—Ezzard Charles def. Joe Louis in latter's attempted comeback, 15, New York; universal recognition.
1950—Dec. 5—Ezzard Charles KOd Nick Barone, 11, Cincinnati.
1951—Jan. 12—Ezzard Charles KOd Lee Oma, 10, New York.
1951—March 7—Ezzard Charles def. Joe Walcott, 15, Detroit.
1951—May 30—Ezzard Charles def. Joey Maxim, light heavyweight champion, 15, Chicago.
*1951—July 18—Joe Walcott KOd Ezzard Charles, 7, Pittsburgh.
1952—June 5—Joe Walcott def. Ezzard Charles, 15, Philadelphia.
*1952—Sept. 23—Rocky Marciano KOd Joe Walcott, 13, Philadelphia.
1953—May 15—Rocky Marciano KOd Joe Walcott, 1, Chicago.
1953—Sept. 24—Rocky Marciano KOd Roland LaStarza, 11, New York.
1954—June 17—Rocky Marciano def. Ezzard Charles, 15, New York.
1954—Sept. 17—Rocky Marciano KOd Ezzard Charles, 8, New York.
1955—May 16—Rocky Marciano KOd Don Cockell, 9, San Francisco.
1955—Sept. 21—Rocky Marciano KOd Archie Moore, 9, New York. Marciano retired undefeated, Apr. 27, 1956.
*1956—Nov. 30—Floyd Patterson KOd Archie Moore, 5, Chicago.
1957—July 29—Floyd Patterson KOd Hurricane Jackson, 10, New York.
1957—Aug. 22—Floyd Patterson KOd Pete Rademacher, 6, Seattle.
1958—Aug. 18—Floyd Patterson KOd Roy Harris, 12, Los Angeles.
1959—May 1—Floyd Patterson KOd Brian London, 11, Indianapolis.
*1959—June 26—Ingemar Johansson KOd Floyd Patterson, 3, New York.
*1960—June 20—Floyd Patterson KOd Ingemar Johansson, 5, New York. First heavyweight in boxing history to regain title.
1961—Mar. 13—Floyd Patterson KOd Ingemar Johansson, 6, Miami Beach.
1961—Dec. 4—Floyd Patterson KOd Tom McNeeley, 4, Toronto.
*1962—Sept. 25—Sonny Liston KOd Floyd Patterson, 1, Chicago.
1963—July 22—Sonny Liston KOd Floyd Patterson, 1, Las Vegas.
*1964—Feb. 25—Cassius Clay KOd Sonny Liston, 7, Miami Beach.
1965—May 25—Cassius Clay KOd Sonny Liston, 1, Lewiston, Maine.
1965—Nov. 11—Cassius Clay KOd Floyd Patterson, 12, Las Vegas.
1966—Mar. 29—Cassius Clay def. George Chuvalo, 15, Toronto.
1966—May 21—Cassius Clay KOd Henry Cooper, 6, London.
1966—Aug. 6—Cassius Clay KOd Brian London, 3, London.

1966—Sept. 10—Cassius Clay KOd Karl Mildenberger, 12, Frankfurt, Germany.
1966—Nov. 14—Cassius Clay KOd Cleveland Williams, 3, Houston.
1967—Feb. 6—Cassius Clay def. Ernie Terrell, 15, Houston.
1967—Mar. 22—Cassius Clay KOd Zora Folley, 7, New York. Clay was stripped of his title by the WBA and others for refusing military service.
*1970—Feb. 16—Joe Frazier KOd Jimmy Ellis, 5, New York.
1970—Nov. 18—Joe Frazier KOd Bob Foster, 2, Detroit.
1971—Mar. 8—Joe Frazier def. Cassius Clay (Muhammad Ali), 15, New York.
1972—Jan. 15—Joe Frazier KOd Terry Daniels, 4, New Orleans.
1972—May 25—Joe Frazier KOd Ron Stander, 5, Omaha.
*1973—Jan. 22—George Foreman KOd Joe Frazier, 2, Kingston, Jamaica.
1973—Sept. 1—George Foreman KOd Joe Roman, 1, Tokyo.
1974—Mar. 3—George Foreman KOd Ken Norton, 2, Caracas.
*1974—Oct. 30—Muhammad Ali KOd George Foreman, 8, Zaire.
1975—Mar. 24—Muhammad Ali KOd Chuck Wepner, 15, Cleveland.
1975—May 16—Muhammad Ali KOd Ron Lyle, 11, Las Vegas.
1975—June 30—Muhammad Ali def. Joe Bugner, 15, Malaysia.
1975—Oct. 1—Muhammad Ali KOd Joe Frazier, 14, Manila.
1976—Feb. 20—Muhammad Ali KOd Jean-Pierre Coopman, 5, San Juan.
1976—Apr. 30—Muhammad Ali def. Jimmy Young, 15, Landover, Md.
1976—May 25—Muhammad Ali KOd Richard Dunn, 5, Munich.
1976—Sept. 28—Muhammad Ali def. Ken Norton, 15, New York.
1977—May 16—Muhammad Ali def. Alfredo Evangelista, 15, Landover, Md.
1977—Sept. 29—Muhammad Ali def. Earnie Shavers, 15, New York.
*1978—Feb. 15—Leon Spinks def. Muhammad Ali, 15, Las Vegas.
*1978—Sept. 15—Muhammad Ali def. Leon Spinks, 15, New Orleans. Ali retired in 1979.

(Bouts when title changed hands only)

*1978—June 9—(WBC) Larry Holmes def. Ken Norton, 15, Las Vegas.
*1980—Mar. 31—(WBA) Mike Weaver KOd John Tate, 15, Knoxville.
*1982—Dec. 10—(WBA) Michael Dokes KOd Mike Weaver, 1, Las Vegas.
*1983—Sept. 23—(WBA) Gerrie Coetzee KOd Michael Dokes, 10, Richfield, Oh.
*1984—Mar. 10—(WBC) Tim Witherspoon def. Greg Page, 12, Las Vegas, Nev.
*1984—Aug. 31—(WBC) Pinklon Thomas def. Tim Witherspoon, 12, Las Vegas, Nev.
*1984—Dec. 2—(WBA) Greg Page KOd Gerrie Coetzee, 8, Sun City, Bophuthatswana
*1985—Apr. 29—(WBA) Tony Tubbs def. Greg Page, 15, Buffalo, N.Y.
*1985—Sept. 21—(IBF) Michael Spinks def. Larry Holmes, 15, Las Vegas, Nev.
*1986—Jan. 17—(WBA) Tim Witherspoon def. Tony Tubbs, 15, Atlanta, Ga.
*1986—Mar. 23—(WBC) Trevor Berbick def. Pinklon Thomas, 12, Miami, Fla.
*1986—Nov. 22—(WBC) Mike Tyson KOd Trevor Berbick, 2, Las Vegas.
*1986—Dec. 12—(WBA) James (Bonecrusher) Smith KOd Tim Witherspoon, 1, New York.
*(1987—Mar. 7—(WBA) Mike Tyson def. James (Bonecrusher) Smith, 12, Las Vegas.
*1990—Feb. 11—(WBA, WBC, IBF) James "Buster" Douglas KOd Mike Tyson, 10, Tokyo.
*1990—Oct. 25—(WBA, WBC, IBF) Evander Holyfield KOd James "Buster" Douglas, 3, Las Vegas.

Pan American Games in 1991

The Pan American games were contested in Havana, Cuba Aug. 4-18, 1991. Cuba won the most gold medals while the United States won the most medals overall. The U.S. had a total of 352 medals, Cuba 265, and Canada 127.

THOROUGHBRED RACING

Triple Crown Winners

Since 1920, colts have carried 126 lbs. in triple crown events; fillies 121 lbs.

(Kentucky Derby, Preakness, and Belmont Stakes)

Year	Horse	Jockey	Trainer	Year	Horse	Jockey	Trainer
1919	Sir Barton	J. Loftus	H. G. Bedwell	1946	Assault	Mehrtens	M. Hirsch
1930	Gallant Fox	E. Sande	J. Fitzsimmons	1948	Citation	E. Arcaro	H.A. Jones
1935	Omaha	W. Sanders	J. Fitzsimmons	1973	Secretariat	R. Turcotte	L. Laurin
1937	War Admiral	C. Kurtsinger	G. Conway	1977	Seattle Slew	J. Cruguet	W.H. Turner Jr.
1941	Whirlaway	E. Arcaro	B.A. Jones	1978	Affirmed	S. Cauthen	L.S. Barrera
1943	Count Fleet	J. Longden	G.D. Cameron				

Kentucky Derby

Churchill Downs, Louisville, Ky.; inaugurated 1875; distance 1-1/4 miles; 1-1/2 miles until 1896. 3-year olds.
Best time: 1:59.2, Secretariat, 1973

Year	Winner	Jockey	Year	Winner	Jockey	Year	Winner	Jockey
1875	Aristides	O. Lewis	1914	Old Rosebud	J. McCabe	1953	Dark Star	H. Moreno
1876	Vagrant	R. Swim	1915	Regret*	J. Notter	1954	Determine	R. York
1877	Baden Baden	W. Walker	1916	George Smith	J. Loftus	1955	Swaps	W. Shoemaker
1878	Day Star	J. Carter	1917	Omar Khayyam	C. Borel	1956	Needles	D. Erb
1879	Lord Murphy	C. Schauer	1918	Exterminator	W. Knapp	1957	Iron Liege	W. Hartack
1880	Fonso	G. Lewis	1919	Sir Barton	J. Loftus	1958	Tim Tam	I. Valenzuela
1881	Hindoo	J. McLaughlin	1920	Paul Jones	T. Rice	1959	Tomy Lee	W. Shoemaker
1882	Apollo	B. Hurd	1921	Behave Yourself	C. Thompson	1960	Venetian Way	W. Hartack
1883	Leonatus	W. Donohue	1922	Morvich	A. Johnson	1961	Carry Back	J. Sellers
1884	Buchanan	I. Murphy	1923	Zev	E. Sande	1962	Decidedly	W. Hartack
1885	Joe Cotton	E. Henderson	1924	Black Gold	J. D. Mooney	1963	Chateaugay	B. Baeza
1886	Ben Ali	P. Duffy	1925	Flying Ebony	E. Sande	1964	Northern Dancer	W. Hartack
1887	Montrose	I. Lewis	1926	Bubbling Over	A. Johnson	1965	Lucky Debonair	W. Shoemaker
1888	Macbeth II.	G. Covington	1927	Whiskery	L. McAtee	1966	Kauai King	D. Brumfield
1889	Spokane	T. Kiley	1928	Reigh Count	C. Lang	1967	Proud Clarion	R. Ussery
1890	Riley	I. Murphy	1929	Clyde Van Dusen	L. McAtee	1968	Dancer's Image (a)	R. Ussery
1891	Kingman	I. Murphy	1930	Gallant Fox	E. Sande	1969	Majestic Prince	W. Hartack
1892	Azra	A. Clayton	1931	Twenty Grand	C. Kurtsinger	1970	Dust Commander	M. Manganello
1893	Lookout	E. Kunze	1932	Burgoo King	E. James	1971	Canonero II	G. Avila
1894	Chant	F. Goodale	1933	Brokers Tip	D. Meade	1972	Riva Ridge	R. Turcotte
1895	Halma	J. Perkins	1934	Cavalcade	M. Garner	1973	Secretariat	R. Turcotte
1896	Ben Brush	W. Simms	1935	Omaha	W. Saunders	1974	Cannonade	A. Cordero
1897	Typhoon II.	F. Garner	1936	Bold Venture	I. Hanford	1975	Foolish Pleasure	J. Vasquez
1898	Plaudit	W. Simms	1937	War Admiral	C. Kurtsinger	1976	Bold Forbes	A. Cordero
1899	Manuel	F. Taral	1938	Lawrin	E. Arcaro	1977	Seattle Slew	J. Cruguet
1900	Lieut. Gibson	J. Boland	1939	Johnstown	J. Stout	1978	Affirmed	S. Cauthen
1901	His Eminence	J. Winkfield	1940	Gallahadion	C. Bierman	1979	Spectacular Bid	R. Franklin
1902	Alan-a-Dale	J. Winkfield	1941	Whirlaway	E. Arcaro	1980	Genuine Risk*	J. Vasquez
1903	Judge Himes	H. Booker	1942	Shut Out	W. D. Wright	1981	Pleasant Colony	J. Velasquez
1904	Elwood	F. Prior	1943	Count Fleet	J. Longden	1982	Gato del Sol	E. Delahoussaye
1905	Agile	J. Martin	1944	Pensive	C. McCreary	1983	Sunny's Halo	E. Delahoussaye
1906	Sir Huon	R. Troxler	1945	Hoop, Jr.	E. Arcaro	1984	Swale	L. Pincay
1907	Pink Star	A. Minder	1946	Assault	W. Mehrtens	1985	Spend a Buck	A. Cordero
1908	Stone Street	A. Pickens	1947	Jet Pilot	E. Guerin	1986	Ferdinand	W. Shoemaker
1909	Wintergreen	V. Powers	1948	Citation	E. Arcaro	1987	Alysheba	C. McCarron
1910	Donau	F. Herbert	1949	Ponder	S. Brooks	1988	Winning Colors*	G. Stevens
1911	Meridian	G. Archibald	1950	Middleground	W. Boland	1989	Sunday Silence	P. Valenzuela
1912	Worth	C.H. Shilling	1951	Count Turf	C. McCreary	1990	Unbridled	C. Perret
1913	Donerail	R. Goose	1952	Hill Gail	E. Arcaro	1991	Strike The Gold	C. Antley

(a) Dancer's Image was disqualified from purse money after tests disclosed that he had run with a pain-killing drug, phen-ylbutazone, in his system. All wagers were paid on Dancer's Image. Forward Pass was awarded first place money.

The Kentucky Derby has been won five times by two jockeys, Eddie Arcaro, 1938, 1941, 1945, 1948 and 1952; and Bill Hartack, 1957, 1960, 1962, 1964 and 1969; four times by Willie Shoemaker, 1955, 1959, 1965, and 1986; and three times by each of three jockeys, Isaac Murphy, 1884, 1890, and 1891; Earle Sande, 1923, 1925 and 1930, and Angel Cordero in 1974, 1976 and 1985. * Regret, Genuine Risk and Winning Colors are the only fillies to win the Derby.

Preakness

Pimlico, Baltimore, Md.; inaugurated 1873; 1 3-16 miles, 3 yr. olds. Best time: 1:53.2, Tank's Prospect, 1985

Year	Winner	Jockey	Year	Winner	Jockey	Year	Winner	Jockey
1873	Survivor	G. Barbee	1885	Tecumseh	J. McLaughlin	1900	Hindus	H. Spencer
1874	Culpepper	M. Donohue	1886	The Bard	S. H. Fisher	1901	The Parader	F. Landry
1875	Tom Ochiltree	L. Hughes	1887	Dunboyne	W. Donohue	1902	Old England	L. Jackson
1876	Shirley	G. Barbee	1888	Refund	F. Littlefield	1903	Flocarline	W. Gannon
1877	Cloverbrook	C. Holloway	1889	Buddhist	G. Anderson	1904	Bryn Mawr	E. Hildebrand
1878	Duke of Magenta	C. Holloway	1890	Montague	W. Martin	1905	Cairngorm	W. Davis
1879	Harold	L. Hughes	1894	Assignee	F. Taral	1906	Whimsical	W. Miller
1880	Grenada	L. Hughes	1895	Belmar	F. Taral	1907	Don Enrique	G. Mountain
1881	Saunterer	W. Costello	1896	Margrave	H. Griffin	1908	Royal Tourist	E. Dugan
1882	Vanguard	G. Barbee	1897	Paul Kauvar	C. Thorpe	1909	Effendi	W. Doyle
1883	Jacobus	G. Barbee	1898	Sly Fox	W. Simms	1910	Layminster	R. Estep
1884	Knight of Ellerslie	S. H. Fisher	1899	Half Time	R. Clawson	1911	Watervale	E. Dugan

(continued)

Year	Winner	Jockey	Year	Winner	Jockey	Year	Winner	Jockey
1912	Colonel Holloway	C. Turner	1938	Dauber	M. Peters	1965	Tom Rolfe	R. Turcotte
1913	Buskin	J. Butwell	1939	Challedon	G. Seabo	1966	Kauai King	D. Brumfield
1914	Holiday	A. Schuttinger	1940	Bimelech	F.A. Smith	1967	Damascus	W. Shoemaker
1915	Rhine Maiden	D. Hoffman	1941	Whirlaway	E. Arcaro	1968	Forward Pass	I. Valenzuela
1916	Damrosch	L. McAtee	1942	Alsab	B. James	1969	Majestic Prince	W. Hartack
1917	Kalitan	E. Haynes	1943	Count Fleet	J. Longden	1970	Personality	E. Belmonte
1918	War Cloud	J. Loftus	1944	Pensive	C. McCreary	1971	Canonero II	G. Avila
	Jack Hare Jr.	C. Peak	1945	Polynesian	W.D. Wright	1972	Bee Bee Bee	E. Nelson
1919	Sir Barton	J. Loftus	1946	Assault	W. Mehrtens	1973	Secretariat	R. Turcotte
1920	Man o' War	C. Kummer	1947	Faultless	D. Dodson	1974	Little Current	M. Rivera
1921	Broomspun	F. Coltiletti	1948	Citation	E. Arcaro	1975	Master Derby	D. McHargue
1922	Pillory	L. Morris	1949	Capot	T. Atkinson	1976	Elocutionist	J. Lively
1923	Vigil	B. Marinelli	1950	Hill Prince	E. Arcaro	1977	Seattle Slew	J. Cruguet
1924	Nellie Morse	J. Merimee	1951	Bold	E. Arcaro	1978	Affirmed	S. Cauthen
1925	Coventry	C. Kummer	1952	Blue Man	C. McCreary	1979	Spectacular Bid	R. Franklin
1926	Display	J. Malben	1953	Native Dancer	E. Guerin	1980	Codex	A. Cordero
1927	Bostonian	A. Abel	1954	Hasty Road	J. Adams	1981	Pleasant Colony	J. Velasquez
1928	Victorian	R. Workman	1955	Nashua	E. Arcaro	1982	Aloma's Ruler	J. Kaenel
1929	Dr. Freeland	L. Schaefer	1956	Fabius	W. Hartack	1983	Deputed Testamony	D. Miller
1930	Gallant Fox	E. Sande	1957	Bold Ruler	E. Arcaro	1984	Gate Dancer	A. Cordero
1931	Mate	G. Ellis	1958	Tim Tam	I. Valenzuela	1985	Tank's Prospect	P. Day
1932	Burgoo King	E. James	1959	Royal Orbit	W. Harmatz	1986	Snow Chief	A. Solis
1933	Head Play	C. Kurtsinger	1960	Bally Ache	R. Ussery	1987	Alysheba	C. McCarron
1934	High Quest	R. Jones	1961	Carry Back	J. Sellers	1988	Risen Star	E. Delahoussaye
1935	Omaha	W. Saunders	1962	Greek Money	J.L. Rotz	1989	Sunday Silence	P. Valenzuela
1936	Bold Venture	G. Woolf	1963	Candy Spots	W. Shoemaker	1990	Summer Squall	P. Day
1937	War Admiral	C. Kurtsinger	1964	Northern Dancer	W. Hartack	1991	Hansel	J. Bailey

Belmont Stakes

Elmont, N.Y.; inaugurated 1867; 1 ½ miles, 3 year olds. Fastest time: 2:24, Secretariat

Year	Winner	Jockey	Year	Winner	Jockey	Year	Winner	Jockey
1867	Ruthless	J. Gilpatrick	1908	Colin	J. Notter	1951	Counterpoint	D. Gorman
1868	General Duke	R. Swim	1909	Joe Madden	E. Dugan	1952	One Count	E. Arcaro
1869	Fenian	C. Miller	1910	Sweep	J. Butwell	1953	Native Dancer	E. Guerin
1870	Kingfisher	W. Dick	1913	Prince Eugene	R. Troxler	1954	High Gun	E. Guerin
1871	Harry Bassett	W. Miller	1914	Luke McLuke	M. Buxton	1955	Nashua	E. Arcaro
1872	Joe Daniels	J. Rowe	1915	The Finn	G. Byrne	1956	Needles	D. Erb
1873	Springbok	J. Rowe	1916	Friar Rock	E. Haynes	1957	Gallant Man	W. Shoemaker
1874	Saxon	G. Barbee	1917	Hourless	J. Butwell	1958	Cavan	P. Anderson
1875	Calvin	R. Swim	1918	Johren	F. Robinson	1959	Sword Dancer	W. Shoemaker
1876	Algerine	W. Donohue	1919	Sir Barton	J. Loftus	1960	Celtic Ash	W. Hartack
1877	Cloverbrook	C. Holloway	1920	Man o' War	C. Kummer	1961	Sherluck	B. Baeza
1878	Duke of Magenta	L. Hughes	1921	Grey Lag	E. Sande	1962	Jaipur	W. Shoemaker
1879	Spendthrift	S. Evans	1922	Pillory	C.H. Miller	1963	Chateaugay	B. Baeza
1880	Grenada	L. Hughes	1923	Zev	E. Sande	1964	Quadrangle	M. Ycaza
1881	Saunterer	T. Costello	1924	Mad Play	E. Sande	1965	Hail to All	J. Sellers
1882	Forester	J. McLaughlin	1925	American Flag	A. Johnson	1966	Amberoid	W. Boland
1883	George Kinney	J. McLaughlin	1926	Crusader	A. Johnson	1967	Damascus	W. Shoemaker
1884	Panique	J. McLaughlin	1927	Chance Shot	E. Sande	1968	Stage Door Johnny	H. Gustines
1885	Tyrant	P. Duffy	1928	Vito	C. Kummer	1969	Arts and Letters	B. Baeza
1886	Inspector B.	J. McLaughlin	1929	Blue Larkspur	M. Garner	1970	High Echelon	J.L. Rotz
1887	Hanover	J. McLaughlin	1930	Gallant Fox	E. Sande	1971	Pass Catcher	W. Blum
1888	Sir Dixon	J. McLaughlin	1931	Twenty Grand	C. Kurtsinger	1972	Riva Ridge	R. Turcotte
1889	Eric	W. Hayward	1932	Faireno	T. Malley	1973	Secretariat	R. Turcotte
1890	Burlington	S. Barnes	1933	Hurryoff	M. Garner	1974	Little Current	M. Rivera
1891	Foxford	E. Garrison	1934	Peace Chance	W.D. Wright	1975	Avatar	W. Shoemaker
1892	Patron	W. Hayward	1935	Omaha	W. Saunders	1976	Bold Forbes	A. Cordero
1893	Comanche	W. Simms	1936	Granville	J. Stout	1977	Seattle Slew	J. Cruguet
1894	Henry of Navarre	W. Simms	1937	War Admiral	C. Kurtsinger	1978	Affirmed	S. Cauthen
1895	Belmar	F. Taral	1938	Pasteurized	J. Stout	1979	Coastal	R. Hernandez
1896	Hastings	H. Griffin	1939	Johnstown	J. Stout	1980	Temperence Hill	E. Maple
1897	Scottish Chieftain	J. Scherrer	1940	Bimelech	F.A. Smith	1981	Summing	G. Martens
1898	Bowling Brook	F. Littlefield	1941	Whirlaway	E. Arcaro	1982	Conquistador Cielo	L. Pincay
1899	Jean Bereaud	R.R. Clawson	1942	Shut Out	E. Arcaro	1983	Caveat	L. Pincay
1900	Ildrim	N. Turner	1943	Count Fleet	J. Longden	1984	Swale	L. Pincay
1901	Commando	H. Spencer	1944	Bounding Home	G.L. Smith	1985	Creme Fraiche	E. Maple
1902	Masterman	J. Bullman	1945	Pavot	E. Arcaro	1986	Danzig Connection	C. McCarron
1903	Africander	J. Bullman	1946	Assault	W. Mehrtens	1987	Bet Twice	C. Perret
1904	Delhi	G. Odom	1947	Phalanx	R. Donoso	1988	Risen Star	E. Delahoussaye
1905	Tanya	E. Hildebrand	1948	Citation	E. Arcaro	1989	Easy Goer	P. Day
1906	Burgomaster	L. Lyne	1949	Capot	T. Atkinson	1990	Go and Go	M. Kinane
1907	Peter Pan	G. Mountain	1950	Middleground	W. Boland	1991	Hansel	J. Bailey

Eclipse Awards in 1990

Sponsored by the Thoroughbred Racing Assn., Daily Racing Form, and the National Turf Writers Assn.

Horse of the Year—Criminal Type
Best 2-year-old colt—Fly So Free
Best 2-year-old filly—Meadow Star
Best 3-year-old colt—Unbridled
Best 3-year-old filly—Go For Wand
Best colt, horse, or gelding (4-year-olds & up)—Criminal Type
Best filly or mare (4-year-olds & up)—Bayakoa
Best male turf horse—Itsallgreektome

Best turf filly or mare—Laugh and Be Merry
Best sprinter—Housebuster
Best steeplechase horse—Morley Street
Best trainer—Carl Nafzger
Best jockey—Craig Perret
Best apprentice jockey—Mark Johnston
Best owner—Frances Genter
Best breeder—Calumet Farms

Annual Leading Money-Winning Horses

Year	Horse	Amount	Year	Horse	Amount	Year	Horse	Amount
1949	Ponder	$321,825	1963	Candy Spots	$604,481	1977	Seattle Slew	$641,370
1950	Noor	346,940	1964	Gun Bow	580,100	1978	Affirmed	901,541
1951	Counterpoint	250,525	1965	Buckpasser	568,096	1979	Spectacular Bid	1,279,334
1952	Crafty Admiral	277,255	1966	Buckpasser	669,078	1980	Temperence Hill	1,130,452
1953	Native Dancer	513,425	1967	Damascus	817,941	1981	John Henry	1,148,800
1954	Determine	328,700	1968	Forward Pass	546,674	1982	Perrault	1,197,400
1955	Nashua	752,550	1969	Arts and Letters	555,604	1983	All Along	2,138,963
1956	Needles	440,850	1970	Personality	444,049	1984	Slew O'Gold	2,627,944
1957	Round Table	600,383	1971	Riva Ridge	503,263	1985	Spend a Buck	3,552,704
1958	Round Table	662,780	1972	Droll Roll	471,633	1986	Snow Chief	1,875,200
1959	Sword Dancer	537,004	1973	Secretariat	860,404	1987	Alysheba	2,511,156
1960	Bally Ache	455,045	1974	Chris Evert	551,063	1988	Alysheba	3,808,600
1961	Carry Back	565,349	1975	Foolish Pleasure	716,278	1989	Sunday Silence	4,578,454
1962	Never Bend	402,969	1976	Forego	491,701	1990	Unbridled	3,718,149

Annual Leading Jockey—Money Won

Year	Jockey	Amount	Year	Jockey	Amount	Year	Jockey	Amount
1957	Bill Hartack	$3,060,501	1969	Jorge Velasquez	$2,542,315	1980	Chris McCarron	$7,663,300
1958	Willie Shoemaker	2,961,693	1970	Laffit Pincay Jr.	2,626,526	1981	Chris McCarron	8,397,604
1959	Willie Shoemaker	2,843,133	1971	Laffit Pincay Jr.	3,784,377	1982	Angel Cordero Jr.	9,483,590
1960	Willie Shoemaker	2,123,961	1972	Laffit Pincay Jr.	3,225,827	1983	Angel Cordero Jr.	10,116,697
1961	Willie Shoemaker	2,690,819	1973	Laffit Pincay Jr.	4,093,492	1984	Chris McCarron	12,045,813
1962	Willie Shoemaker	2,916,844	1974	Laffit Pincay Jr.	4,251,060	1985	Laffit Pincay Jr.	13,353,299
1963	Willie Shoemaker	2,526,925	1975	Braulio Baeza	3,695,198	1986	Jose Santos	11,329,297
1964	Willie Shoemaker	2,649,553	1976	Angel Cordero Jr.	4,709,500	1987	Jose Santos	12,375,433
1965	Braulio Baeza	2,582,702	1977	Steve Cauthen	6,151,750	1988	Jose Santos	14,877,298
1966	Braulio Baeza	2,951,022	1978	Darrel McHargue	6,029,885	1989	Jose Santos	13,838,389
1967	Braulio Baeza	3,088,888	1979	Laffit Pincay Jr.	8,193,535	1990	Gary Stevens	13,881,198
1968	Braulio Baeza	2,835,108						

The America's Cup

The United States yacht *Stars & Stripes* defeated the New Zealand yacht *New Zealand* in 2 consecutive races to win the best-of-three series in the waters off San Diego, Cal. *Stars & Stripes* was skippered by Dennis Conner, as it had been when the Cup was recaptured from Australia in 1987.

The New Zealand syndicate, however, went to court to have the result of the races invalidated, claiming that the Americans did not live up to the America's Cup Deed of Gift which, they claim, says that the competing boats must be similar. The Americans used a catamaran, the New Zealanders a monohull ship. On Mar. 28, 1989, a New York State Supreme Court justice ruled that the San Diego Yacht Club had beaten its challenger unfairly and must forfeit the America's Cup to New Zealand. On Sept. 19, a New York appeals court overturned the ruling, and the N.Y. State Court of Appeals upheld that decision, Apr. 26, 1990. The next America's Cup competition is scheduled for May 1992 in San Diego.

Competition for the America's Cup grew out of the first contest to establish a world yachting championship, one of the carnival features of the London Exposition of 1851. The race, open to all classes of yachts from all over the world, covered a 60-mile course around the Isle of Wight; the prize was a cup worth about $500, donated by the Royal Yacht Squadron of England, known as the "America's Cup" because it was first won by the United States yacht *America*. Successive efforts of British and Australian yachtsmen had failed to win the famous trophy until 1983 when the Australian yacht *Australia II* defeated the U.S. entry *Liberty*.

Winners of the America's Cup

Year		Year	
1851	America	1930	Enterprise defeated Shamrock V, England, (4-0)
1870	Magic defeated Cambria, England, (1-0)	1934	Rainbow defeated Endeavour, England, (4-2)
1871	Columbia (first three races) and Sappho (last two races) defeated Livonia, England, (4-1)	1937	Ranger defeated Endeavour II, England, (4-0)
		1958	Columbia defeated Sceptre, England, (4-0)
1876	Madeline defeated Countess of Dufferin, Canada, (2-0)	1962	Weatherly defeated Gretel, Australia, (4-1)
1881	Mischief defeated Atalanta, Canada, (2-0)	1964	Constellation defeated Sovereign, England, (4-0)
1885	Puritan defeated Genesta, England, (2-0)	1967	Intrepid defeated Dame Pattie, Australia, (4-0)
1886	Mayflower defeated Galatea, England, (2-0)	1970	Intrepid defeated Gretel II, Australia, (4-1)
1887	Volunteer defeated Thistle, Scotland, (2-0)	1974	Courageous defeated Southern Cross, Australia, (4-0)
1893	Vigilant defeated Valkyrie II, England, (3-0)	1977	Courageous defeated Australia, Australia, (4-0)
1895	Defender defeated Valkyrie III, England, (3-0)	1980	Freedom defeated Australia, Australia, (4-1)
1899	Columbia defeated Shamrock, England, (3-0)	1983	Australia II, Australia defeated Liberty, (4-3)
1901	Columbia defeated Shamrock II, England, (3-0)	1987	Stars & Stripes defeated Kookaburra III, Australia, (4-0)
1903	Reliance defeated Shamrock III, England, (3-0)	1988	Stars & Stripes defeated New Zealand, New Zealand, (2-0)
1920	Resolute defeated Shamrock IV, England, (3-2)		

NCAA Wrestling Champions

Year	Champion	Year	Champion	Year	Champion	Year	Champion	Year	Champion
1964	Oklahoma State	1970	Iowa State	1976	Iowa	1982	Iowa	1987	Iowa State
1965	Iowa State	1971	Oklahoma State	1977	Iowa State	1983	Iowa	1988	Arizona State
1966	Oklahoma State	1972	Iowa State	1978	Iowa	1984	Iowa	1989	Oklahoma State
1967	Michigan State	1973	Iowa State	1979	Iowa	1985	Iowa	1990	Oklahoma State
1968	Oklahoma State	1974	Oklahoma	1980	Iowa	1986	Iowa	1991	Iowa
1969	Iowa State	1975	Iowa	1981	Iowa				

Notable Sports Personalities

Henry Aaron, b. 1934: Milwaukee-Atlanta outfielder hit record 755 home runs; led NL 4 times.

Kareem Abdul-Jabbar, b. 1947: Milwaukee, L.A. Lakers center; MVP 6 times; leading scorer twice; playoff MVP, 1971, 1985; all-time leading NBA scorer.

Grover Cleveland Alexander, (1887-1950): pitcher won 374 NL games; pitched 16 shutouts, 1916.

Muhammad Ali, b. 1942: 3-time heavyweight champion.

Ken Anderson, b. 1949: Cinn. Bengals quarterback led AFC in passing 4 times.

Mario Andretti, b. 1940; won Indy 500, 1969; Grand Prix champ, 1978.

Eddie Arcaro, b. 1916: jockey rode 4,779 winners including the Kentucky Derby 5 times; the Preakness and Belmont Stakes 6 times each.

Henry Armstrong, (1912-1988): boxer held feather-, welter-, light-weight titles simultaneously, 1937-38.

Arthur Ashe, b. 1943: U.S. singles champ, 1968, Wimbledon champ, 1975.

Red Auerbach, b. 1917: coached Boston Celtics to 9 NBA championships.

Ernie Banks, b. 1931: Chicago Cubs slugger hit 512 NL homers; twice MVP.

Roger Bannister, b. 1929: Briton ran first sub 4-minute mile, May 6, 1954.

Rick Barry, b. 1944: NBA scoring leader, 1967; ABA, 1969.

Sammy Baugh, b. 1914: Washington Redskins quarterback held numerous records upon retirement after 16 pro seasons.

Elgin Baylor, b. 1934: L.A. Lakers forward; 1st team all-star 10 times.

Bob Beamon, b. 1946: long jumper won 1968 Olympic gold medal with record 29 ft. 2½ ft.

Jean Beliveau, b. 1931: Montreal Canadiens center scored 507 goals; twice MVP.

Johnny Bench, b. 1947: Cincinnati Reds catcher; MVP twice; led league in home runs twice, RBIs 3 times.

Patty Berg, b. 1918: won over 80 golf tournaments; AP Woman Athlete-of-the-Year 3 times.

Yogi Berra, b. 1925: N.Y. Yankees catcher; MVP 3 times; played in 14 World Series.

Raymond Berry, b. 1933: Baltimore Colts receiver caught 631 passes.

Matt Biondi, b. 1965: swimmer won 5 gold medals at 1988 Olympics.

Larry Bird, b. 1956: Boston Celtics forward; chosen MVP 1984-86, playoff MVP, 1984, 1986.

George Blanda, b. 1927: quarterback, kicker; 26 years as active player, scoring record 2,002 points.

Wade Boggs, b. 1958: AL Batting champ, 1983, 1985-88.

Bjorn Borg, b. 1956: led Sweden to first Davis Cup, 1975; Wimbledon champion, 5 times.

Mike Bossy, b.1957: N.Y. Islanders right wing scored over 50 goals 8 times.

Ray Bourque, b. 1960: Boston Bruins defenseman won Norris Trophy 4 times.

Terry Bradshaw, b. 1948; Pittsburgh Steelers quarterback led team to 4 Super Bowl titles.

George Brett, b. 1953: Kansas City Royals 3d baseman led AL in batting, 1976, 1980, 1990; MVP, 1980.

Lou Brock, b. 1939: St. Louis Cardinals outfielder stole record 118 bases, 1974; record 938 career; led NL 8 times.

Jimmy Brown, b. 1936: Cleveland Browns fullback ran for 12,312 career yards; MVP 3 times.

Paul Brown, (1908-1991), football owner, coach; led Cleveland Browns to 3 NFL championships.

Paul "Bear" Bryant, (1913-1983), college football coach with 323 victories.

Maria Bueno, b. 1939: U.S. singles champ 4 times; Wimbledon champ 3 times.

Dick Butkus, b. 1942: Chicago Bears linebacker twice chosen best NFL defensive player.

Dick Button, b. 1929: figure skater won 1948, 1952 Olympic gold medals; world titlist, 1948-52.

Walter Camp, (1859-1925): Yale football player, coach, athletic director; established many rules; promoted All-America designations.

Roy Campanella, b. 1921: Brooklyn Dodgers catcher; MVP 3 times.

Earl Campbell, b. 1955: NFL running back; NFL MVP 1978-1980.

Jose Canseco, b. 1964: Oakland A's outfielder; AL MVP 1988.

Rod Carew, b. 1945: AL infielder won 7 batting titles; MVP, 1977.

Steve Carlton, b. 1944: NL pitcher won 20 games 5 times, Cy Young award 4 times.

Billy Casper, b. 1931: PGA Player-of-the-Year 3 times; U.S. Open champ twice.

Wilt Chamberlain, b. 1936: center was NBA leading scorer 7 times; MVP 4 times.

Bobby Clarke, b. 1949: Philadelphia Flyers center led team to 2 Stanley Cup championships; MVP 3 times.

Roger Clemens, b. 1962: Boston Red Sox pitcher; AL MVP 1986; Cy Young Award 1986, 1987.

Roberto Clemente, (1934-1972): Pittsburgh Pirates outfielder won 4 batting titles; MVP, 1966.

Ty Cobb, (1886-1961): Detroit Tigers outfielder had record .367 lifetime batting average, 12 batting titles.

Sebastian Coe, b. 1956: Briton won Olympic 1,500-meter run, 1980, 1984.

Nadia Comaneci, b. 1961: Romanian gymnast won 3 gold medals, achieved 7 perfect scores, 1976 Olympics.

Maureen Connolly, (1934-1969): won tennis "grand slam," 1953; AP Woman-Athlete-of-the-Year 3 times.

Jimmy Connors, b. 1952: U.S. singles champ 5 times; Wimbledon champ twice.

James J. Corbett, (1866-1933): heavyweight champion, 1892-97; credited with being the first "scientific" boxer.

Angel Cordero, b. 1942: jockey won over 6,000 races; leading money winner, 1976, 1982-83.

Margaret Smith Court, b. 1942: Australian won U.S. singles championship 5 times; Wimbledon champ 3 times.

Bob Cousy, b. 1928: Boston Celtics guard led team to 6 NBA championships; MVP, 1957.

Andre Dawson, b. 1954: slugger led NL in home runs, MVP, 1987.

Dizzy Dean, (1911-1974): colorful pitcher for St. Louis Cardinals "Gashouse Gang" in the 30s; MVP, 1934.

Jack Dempsey, (1895-1983): heavyweight champion, 1919-26.

Eric Dickerson, b. 1960: running back ran for NFL record 2,105 yds., 1984; led NFC 3 times, AFC twice.

Joe DiMaggio, b. 1914: N.Y. Yankees outfielder hit safely in record 56 consecutive games, 1941; MVP 3 times.

Leo Durocher, b. 1906: manager won 3 NL pennants.

Gertrude Ederle, b. 1906: first woman to swim English Channel, broke existing men's record, 1926.

Julius Erving, b. 1950: MVP and leading scorer in ABA 3 times; NBA MVP, 1981.

Phil Esposito, b. 1942: NHL scoring leader 5 times.

Chris Evert, b. 1954: U.S. singles champ 6 times, Wimbledon champ 3 times.

Patrick Ewing, b. 1962: center led Georgetown Univ. to 1984 NCAA championship.

Ray Ewry, (1873-1937): track and field star won 8 gold medals, 1900, 1904, and 1908 Olympics.

Juan Fangio, b. 1911: World Grand Prix champion 5 times.

Bob Feller, b. 1918: Cleveland Indians pitcher won 266 games; pitched 3 no-hitters, 12 one-hitters.

Peggy Fleming, b. 1948: world figure skating champion, 1966-68; gold medalist 1968 Olympics.

Whitey Ford, b. 1928: N.Y. Yankees pitcher won record 10 World Series games.

Dick Fosbury, b. 1947: high jumper won 1968 Olympic gold medal; developed the "Fosbury Flop."

Jimmie Foxx, (1907-1967): Red Sox, Athletics slugger; MVP 3 times; triple crown, 1933.

A.J. Foyt, b. 1935: won Indy 500 4 times; U.S. Auto Club champ 7 times.

Joe Frazier, b. 1944: heavyweight champion, 1970-73.

Lou Gehrig, (1903-1941): N.Y. Yankees 1st baseman played record 2,130 consecutive games; MVP, 1936.

George Gervin, b. 1952: leading NBA scorer, 1978-80, 1982.

Althea Gibson, b. 1927: twice U.S. and Wimbledon singles champ.

Bob Gibson, b. 1935: St. Louis Cardinals pitcher won Cy Young award twice; struck out 3,117 batters.

Frank Gifford, b. 1930: N.Y. Giants back; MVP, 1956.

Dwight Gooden, b. 1964: N.Y. Mets pitcher was NL Rookie of Year, 1984; Cy Young award, 1985.

Steffi Graf, b. 1969: W. German won tennis "grand slam," 1988; U.S. champ 1988, 1989.

Otto Graham, b. 1921: Cleveland Browns quarterback; all-pro 4 times.

Red Grange, b 1903: All-America at Univ. of Illinois 1923-25; played for Chicago Bears, 1925-35.

Joe Greene, b. 1946: Pittsburgh Steelers lineman; twice NFL outstanding defensive player.

Wayne Gretzky, b. 1961: Edmonton Oilers center scored record 92 goals, 212 pts., 1982; MVP, 1980-87, 1989.

Florence Griffith Joyner, b. 1959: sprinter won 3 gold medals at 1988 Olympics.

Lefty Grove, (1900-1975): pitcher won 300 AL games; 20-game winner 8 times.

Tony Gwynn, b. 1960: NL batting champ, 1984, 1987-1989.

Walter Hagen, (1892-1969): won PGA championship 5 times. British Open 4 times.

George Halas, (1895-1983); founder-coach of Chicago Bears; won 5 NFL championships.

Bill Hartack, b. 1932: jockey rode 5 Kentucky Derby winners.

John Havlicek, b. 1940: Boston Celtics forward scored over 26,000 NBA points.

Eric Heiden, b. 1958: speed skater won 5 1980 Olympic gold medals.

Rickey Henderson, b. 1958: AL outfielder stole record 130 bases, 1982; AL MVP, 1990.

Sonja Henie, (1912-1969): world champion figure skater, 1927-36; Olympic gold medalist, 1928, 1932, 1936.

Ben Hogan, b. 1912: won 4 U.S. Open championships, 2 PGA, 2 Masters.

Rogers Hornsby, (1896-1963): NL 2d baseman batted record .424 in 1924; twice won triple crown; batting leader, 1920-25.

Paul Hornung, b. 1935: Green Bay Packers runner-placekicker scored record 176 points, 1960.

Gordie Howe, b. 1928: hockey forward; NHL MVP 6 times.

Carl Hubbell, (1903-1988): N.Y. Giants pitcher; 20-game winner 5 consecutive years, 1933-37.

Bobby Hull, b. 1939: NHL all-star 10 times.

Catfish Hunter, b 1946: pitched perfect game, 1968; 20-game winner 5 times.

Don Hutson, b. 1913: Green Bay Packers receiver caught 99 NFL touchdown passes.

Reggie Jackson, b. 1946: slugger led AL in home runs 4 times; MVP, 1973; hit 5 World Series home runs, 1977.

Jack Johnson, (1878-1946): heavyweight champion, 1910-15.

Magic Johnson, b. 1959: NBA MVP 1987, 1989, 1990. Playoff MVP 1980, 1982, 1987.

Walter Johnson, (1887-1946): Washington Senators pitcher won 413 games.

Bobby Jones, (1902-1971); won "grand slam of golf" 1930; U.S. Amateur champ 5 times, U.S. Open champ 4 times.

Deacon Jones, b. 1938: L.A. Rams lineman; twice NFL outstanding defensive player.

Michael Jordan, b. 1963: NBA leading scorer, 1987-91; MVP, 1988, 1991; Playoff MVP, 1991.

Sonny Jurgensen, b. 1934: quarterback named all-pro 5 times.

Duke Kahanamoku, (1890-1968): swimmer won 1912, 1920 Olympic gold medals in 100-meter freestyle.

Harmon Killebrew, b. 1936: Minnesota Twins slugger led AL in home runs 6 times.

Jean Claude Killy, b. 1943: French skier won 3 1968 Olympic gold medals.

Ralph Kiner, b. 1922: Pittsburgh Pirates slugger led NL in home runs 7 consecutive years, 1946-52.

Billie Jean King, b. 1943: U.S. singles champ 4 times; Wimbledon champ 6 times.

Bob Knight, b. 1940: Indiana U. basketball coach lead team to NCAA championships, 1976, 1981, 1987.

Olga Korbut, b. 1955: Soviet gymnast won 3 1972 Olympic gold medals.

Sandy Koufax, b. 1935: Dodgers pitcher won Cy Young award 3 times; lowest ERA in NL, 1962-66; pitched 4 no-hitters, one a perfect game.

Guy Lafleur, b. 1951: forward led NHL in scoring 3 times; MVP, 1977, 1978.

Tom Landry, b. 1924: Dallas Cowboys head coach 1960-88.

Rod Laver, b. 1938: Australian won tennis "grand slam," 1962, 1969; Wimbledon champ 4 times.

Mario Lemieux, b. 1965: NHL leading scorer, 1988-1989; MVP, 1988; Playoff MVP, 1991.

Ivan Lendl, b. 1960: U.S. singles champ, 1985-87.

Sugar Ray Leonard, b. 1956: former world welterweight champ.

Carl Lewis, b. 1961: track and field star won 4 1984 Olympic gold medals.

Vince Lombardi, (1913-1970): Green Bay Packers coach led, team to 5 NFL championships and 2 Super Bowl victories.

Joe Louis, (1914-1981): 1914: heavyweight champion, 1937-49.

Sid Luckman, b. 1916: Chicago Bears quarterback led team to 4 NFL championships; MVP, 1943.

Connie Mack, (1862-1956): Philadelphia Athletics manager, 1901-50; won 9 pennants, 5 championships.

Bill Madlock, b. 1951: NL batting leader 4 times.

Moses Malone, b. 1955: NBA center was MVP 1979, 1982, 1983.

Mickey Mantle, b. 1931: N.Y. Yankees outfielder; triple crown, 1956; 18 World Series home runs.

Pete Maravich (1948-1988): guard scored NCAA record 44.2 ppg during collegiate career; led NBA in scoring, 1977.

Rocky Marciano, (1923-1969): heavyweight champion, 1952-56; retired undefeated.

Dan Marino, b. 1961: Miami Dolphins quarterback passed for NFL record 5,084 yds, 1984.

Roger Maris, (1934-1985): N.Y. Yankees outfielder hit record 61 home runs, 1961; MVP, 1960 and 1961.

Eddie Mathews, b. 1931: Milwaukee-Atlanta 3d baseman hit 512 career home runs.

Christy Mathewson, (1880-1925): N.Y. Giants pitcher won 373 games.

Bob Mathias, b. 1930: decathlon gold medalist, 1948, 1952.

Don Mattingly, b. 1961: N.Y. Yankees 1st baseman won 1984 AL batting title; MVP, 1985.

Willie Mays, b. 1931: N.Y.-S.F. Giants center fielder hit 660 home runs; twice MVP.

Willie McCovey, b. 1938: S.F. Giants slugger hit 521 home runs; led NL 3 times.

John McEnroe, b. 1959: U.S. singles champ, 1979-81; 1984; Wimbledon champ, 1981, 1983-84.

John McGraw, (1873-1934): N.Y. Giants manager led team to 10 pennants, 3 championships.

Mark Messier, b. 1961: Edmonton Oilers Center chosen NHL MVP, 1990; Conn Smythe Trophy, 1984.

George Mikan, b. 1924: Minn. Lakers center considered the best basketball player of the first half of the century.

Stan Mikita, b. 1940: Chicago Black Hawks center led NHL in scoring 4 times; MVP twice.

Joe Montana, b. 1956: S.F. 49ers QB was Super Bowl MVP, 1982, 1985, 1990.

Archie Moore, b. 1913: world light-heavyweight champion, 1952-62.

Howie Morenz, (1902-1937): Montreal Canadiens forward considered the best hockey player of the first half of the century.

Joe Morgan, b. 1943: National League MVP, 1975, 1976.

Thurman Munson, (1947-1979): N.Y. Yankees catcher; MVP, 1976.

Dale Murphy, b. 1956: outfielder chosen NL MVP 1982, 1983.

Stan Musial, b. 1920: St. Louis Cardinals star won 7 NL batting titles; MVP 3 times.

Bronko Nagurski, (1908-1990): Chicago Bears fullback and tackle; gained over 4,000 yds. rushing.

Joe Namath, b. 1943: quarterback led N.Y. Jets to 1969 Super Bowl title.

Martina Navratilova, b. 1956: Wimbledon champ 8 times, U.S. champ 1983-1984; 1986-87.

Byron Nelson, b. 1912: won 11 consecutive golf tournaments in 1945; twice Masters and PGA titlist.

Ernie Nevers, (1903-1976): Stanford star selected the best college fullback to play between 1919-1969.

John Newcombe, b. 1943: Australian twice U.S. singles champ; Wimbledon titlist 3 times.

Jack Nicklaus, b. 1940: PGA Player-of-the-Year, 1967, 1972; leading money winner 8 times; won Masters 6 times.

Chuck Noll, b. 1931: Pittsburgh Steelers coach led team to 4 Super Bowl titles.

Paavo Nurmi, (1897-1973): Finnish distance runner won 6 Olympic gold medals, 1920, 1924, 1928.

Al Oerter, b. 1936: discus thrower won gold medal at 4 consecutive Olympics, 1956-68.

Bobby Orr, b. 1948: Boston Bruins defenseman; Norris Trophy 8 times; led NHL in scoring twice, assists 5 times.

Mel Ott, (1909-1958): N.Y. Giants outfielder hit 511 home runs; led NL 6 times.

Jesse Owens, (1913-1980): track and field star won 4 1936 Olympic gold medals.

Satchel Paige, (1906-1982): pitcher starred in Negro leagues, 1924-48; entered major leagues at age 42.

Arnold Palmer, b. 1929: golf's first $1 million winner; won 4 Masters, 2 British Opens.

Jim Palmer, b. 1945: Baltimore Orioles pitcher; Cy Young award 3 times; 20-game winner 7 times.

Floyd Patterson, b. 1935: twice heavyweight champion.

Walter Payton, b. 1954: Chicago Bears running back has most rushing yards in NFL history; leading NFC rusher, 1976-80.

Pele, b. 1940: Brazilian soccer star scored 1,281 goals during 22-year career.

Bob Pettit, b. 1932: first NBA player to score 20,000 points; twice NBA scoring leader.

Richard Petty, b. 1937: NASCAR national champ 7 times; 7-times Daytona 500 winner.

Laffit Pincay Jr., b. 1946: leading money-winning jockey, 1970-74, 1979.

Jacques Plante, (1929-1986): goalie, 7 Vezina trophies; first goalie to wear a mask in a game.

Kirby Puckett, b. 1961: Minn. Twins outfielder won AL Batting Title, 1989; led AL in hits, 1987-89.

Willis Reed, b. 1942: N.Y. Knicks center; MVP, 1970; playoff MVP, 1970, 1973.

Jerry Rice, b. 1962: S.F. 49ers receiver chosen 1989 Super Bowl MVP.

Jim Rice, b. 1953: Boston Red Sox outfielder led AL in home runs, 1977-78, 1983; MVP 1978.

Maurice Richard, b. 1921: Montreal Canadiens forward scored 544 regular season goals, 82 playoff goals.

Branch Rickey, (1881-1965): executive instrumental in breaking baseball's color barrier, 1947; initiated farm system, 1919.

Oscar Robertson, b. 1938: guard averaged career 25.7 points per game; record 9,887 career assists; MVP, 1964.

Brooks Robinson, b. 1937: Baltimore Orioles 3d baseman played in 4 World Series; MVP, 1964.

Frank Robinson, b. 1935: slugger MVP in both NL and AL; triple crown winner, 1966; first black manager in majors.

Jackie Robinson, (1919-1972): broke baseball's color barrier with Brooklyn Dodgers, 1947; MVP, 1949.

Larry Robinson, b. 1951: NHL defenseman won Norris trophy, 1977, 1980.

Sugar Ray Robinson, (1920-1989): middleweight champion 5 times, welterweight champion.

Knute Rockne, (1888-1931): Notre Dame football coach, 1918-31; revolutionized game by stressing forward pass.

Pete Rose, b. 1941: won 3 NL batting titles; hit safely in 44 consecutive games, 1978; has most major league hits.

Wilma Rudolph, b. 1940: sprinter won 3 1960 Olympic gold medals.

Bill Russell, b. 1934: Boston Celtics center led team to 11 NBA titles; MVP 5 times; first black coach of major pro sports team.

Babe Ruth, (1895-1948): N.Y. Yankees outfielder hit 60 home runs, 1927; 714 lifetime; led AL 11 times.

Johnny Rutherford, b. 1938: auto racer won Indy 500 3 times.

Nolan Ryan, b. 1947: pitcher struck out record 383 batters, 1973; first to strike out 5,000 batters; pitched record 7 no-hitters; won 300th game, 1990.

Bret Saberhagen, b. 1964: K.C. Royals pitcher won Cy Young award, 1985, 1989; WS MVP, 1985.

Gene Sarazen, b. 1902: won PGA championship 3 times, U.S. Open twice; developer of sand wedge.

Gale Sayers, b. 1943: Chicago Bears back twice led NFC in rushing.

Mike Schmidt, b. 1949: Phillies 3d baseman led NL in home runs, 1974-76, 1980-81, 1983-84, 1986; NL MVP, 1980, 1981, 1986.

Tom Seaver, b. 1944: pitcher won NL Cy Young award 3 times, won 311 major league games.

Bill Shoemaker, b. 1931: jockey rode 3 Kentucky Derby and 5 Belmont Stakes winners; leading career money winner.

Eddie Shore, (1902-1985): Boston Bruins defenseman; MVP 4 times, first-team all-star 7 times.

Al Simmons, (1902-1956): AL outfielder had lifetime .334 batting average.

O.J. Simpson, b. 1947: running back rushed for 2,003 yds., 1973; AFC leading rusher 4 times.

George Sisler, (1893-1973): St. Louis Browns 1st baseman had record 257 hits, 1920; batted .340 lifetime.

Billy Smith, b. 1950: N.Y. Islanders goalie led team to 4 Stanley Cup championships.

Sam Snead, b. 1912: PGA and Masters champ 3 times each.

Warren Spahn, b. 1921: pitcher won 363 NL games; 20-game winner 13 times; Cy Young award, 1957.

Tris Speaker, (1885-1958): AL outfielder batted .344 over 22 seasons; hit record 793 career doubles.

Mark Spitz, b. 1950: swimmer won 7 1972 Olympic gold medals.

Amos Alonzo Stagg, (1862-1965): coached Univ. of Chicago football team for 41 years, including 5 undefeated seasons; introduced huddle, man-in-motion, and end-around play.

Willie Stargell, b. 1941: Pittsburgh Pirate slugger chosen NL, World Series MVP, 1979.

Bart Starr, b. 1934: Green Bay Packers quarterback led team to 5 NFL titles and 2 Super Bowl victories.

Roger Staubach, b. 1942: Dallas Cowboys quarterback; leading NFC passer 5 times.

Casey Stengel, (1890-1975): managed Yankees to 10 pennants, 7 championships, 1949-60.

Jackie Stewart, b. 1939: Scot auto racer retired with 27 Grand Prix victories.

John L. Sullivan, (1858-1918): last bareknuckle heavyweight champion, 1882-1892.

Fran Tarkenton, b. 1940: quarterback holds career passing records for touchdowns, completions, yardage.

Gustavo Thoeni, b. 1951: Italian 4-time world alpine ski champ.

Jim Thorpe, (1888-1953): football All-America, 1911, 1912; won pentathlon and decathlon, 1912 Olympics.

Bill Tilden, (1893-1953): U.S. singles champ 7 times; played on 11 Davis Cup teams.

Y.A. Tittle, b. 1926: N.Y. Giants quarterback; MVP, 1961, 1963.

Lee Trevino, b. 1939: won the U.S. and British Open championships twice.

Bryan Trottier, b. 1956: center led N.Y. Islanders to 4 consecutive Stanley Cup championships, 1980-83.

Mike Tyson, b. 1966: world heavyweight champion, 1987-90.

Wyomia Tyus, b. 1945: sprinter won 1964, 1968 Olympic 100-meter dash.

Johnny Unitas, b. 1933: Baltimore Colts quarterback passed for over 40,000 yds.; MVP, 1957, 1967.

Al Unser, b. 1939: Indy 500 winner, 4 times.

Bobby Unser, b. 1934: Indy 500 winner 3 times.

Norm Van Brocklin, (1926-1983): quarterback passed for game record 554 yds., 1951; MVP, 1960.

Honus Wagner, (1874-1955): Pittsburgh Pirates shortstop won 8 NL batting titles.

Tom Watson, b. 1949: golfer won British Open 5 times.

Johnny Weissmuller, (1903-1984): swimmer won 52 national championships, 5 Olympic gold medals; set 67 world records.

Jerry West, b. 1938: L.A. Lakers guard had career average 27 points per game; first team all-star 10 times.

Kathy Whitworth, b. 1939: women's golf leading money winner 8 times; first woman to earn over $300,000.

Ted Williams, b. 1918: Boston Red Sox outfielder won 6 batting titles; last major leaguer to hit over .400: .406 in 1941: .344 lifetime batting average.

John Wooden, b. 1910: coached UCLA basketball team to 10 national championships.

Mickey Wright, b. 1935: won LPGA championship 4 times, Vare Trophy 5 times; twice AP Woman-Athlete-of-the-Year.

Carl Yastrzemski, b. 1939: Boston Red Sox slugger won 3 batting titles, triple crown, 1967.

Cy Young, (1867-1955): pitcher won record 511 major league games.

Babe Didrikson Zaharias, (1914-1956): track star won 2 1932 Olympic gold medals; won numerous golf tournaments.

Pro Rodeo Championship Standings in 1990

Event	Winner	Money won
All Around	Ty Murray, Stephenville, Tex.	$213,772
Saddle Bronc	Robert Etbauer, Goodwell, Okla.	113,164
Bareback	Chuck Logue, Decatur, Tex.	112,906
Bull Riding	Jim Sharp, Kermit, Tex.	126,421
Calf Roping	Troy Pruitt, Minatare, Neb.	98,346

Event	Winner	Money won
Steer Wrestling	Scott Berry, Checotah, Okla.	$92,101
Steer Roping	Phil Lyne, Cotulla, Tex.	39,854
Women's Barrel Racing	Charmayne James Rodman, Galt, Cal.	103,323

Pro Rodeo Cowboy All Around Champions

Year	Winner	Money won	Year	Winner	Money won
1968	Larry Mahan, Salem, Ore.	$49,129	1979	Tom Ferguson, Miami, Okla.	$96,272
1969	Larry Mahan, Brooks, Ore.	57,726	1980	Paul Tierney, Rapid City, S.D.	105,568
1970	Larry Mahan, Brooks, Ore.	41,493	1981	Jimmie Cooper, Monument, N.M.	105,862
1971	Phil Lyne, George West, Tex.	49,245	1982	Chris Lybbert, Coyote, Cal.	123,709
1972	Phil Lyne, George West, Tex.	60,852	1983	Roy Cooper, Durant, Okla.	153,391
1973	Larry Mahan, Dallas, Tex.	64,447	1984	Dee Pickett, Caldwell, Ida.	122,618
1974	Tom Ferguson, Miami, Okla.	66,929	1985	Lewis Feild, Elk Ridge, Ut.	130,347
1975	Leo Camarillo, Oakdale, Cal.	50,300	1986	Lewis Feild, Elk Ridge, Ut.	166,042
	Tom Ferguson, Miami, Okla.	50,300	1988	Lewis Feild, Elk Ridge, Ut.	144,335
1976	Tom Ferguson, Miami, Okla.	87,908	1988	Dave Appleton, Arlington, Tex.	121,546
1977	Tom Ferguson, Miami, Okla.	76,730	1989	Ty Murray, Odessa, Tex.	134,806
1978	Tom Ferguson, Miami, Okla.	103,734	1990	Ty Murray, Stephenville, Tex.	213,772

NATIONAL FOOTBALL LEAGUE
Final 1990 Standings

National Conference

Eastern Division

	W	L	T	Pct	Pts	Opp
New York Giants	13	3	0	.813	335	211
Philadelphia	10	6	0	.625	396	299
Washington	10	6	0	.625	381	301
Dallas	7	9	0	.438	244	308
Phoenix	5	11	0	.313	268	396

Central Division

Chicago	11	5	0	.688	348	280
Tampa Bay	6	10	0	.375	264	367
Detroit	6	10	0	.375	373	413
Green Bay	6	10	0	.375	271	347
Minnesota	6	10	0	.375	351	326

Western Division

San Francisco	14	2	0	.875	353	239
New Orleans	8	8	0	.500	274	275
Los Angeles Rams	5	11	0	.313	345	412
Atlanta	5	11	0	.313	348	365

American Conference

Eastern Division

	W	L	T	Pct	Pts	Opp
Buffalo	13	3	0	.813	428	263
Miami	12	4	0	.750	336	242
Indianapolis	7	9	0	.438	281	353
New York Jets	6	10	0	.375	295	345
New England	1	15	0	.063	181	446

Central Division

Cincinnati	9	7	0	.563	360	352
Houston	9	7	0	.563	405	307
Pittsburgh	9	7	0	.563	292	240
Cleveland	3	13	0	.188	228	462

Western Division

Los Angeles Raiders	12	4	0	.750	337	268
Kansas City	11	5	0	.688	369	257
Seattle	9	7	0	.563	306	286
San Diego	6	10	0	.375	315	281
Denver	5	11	0	.313	331	374

NFC Playoffs—Chicago 16, New Orleans 6; Washington 20, Philadelphia 6; San Francisco 28, Washington 10; New York Giants 31, Chicago 3; New York Giants 15, San Francisco 13.

AFC Playoffs—Cincinnati 41, Houston 14; Miami 17, Kansas City 16; Buffalo 44, Miami 34; L.A. Raiders 20, Cincinnati 10; Buffalo 51, L.A. Raiders 3.

Giants Defeat Bills in Super Bowl

The New York Giants featured a strong ball-control game and defeated the Buffalo Bills, 20-19, to win Super Bowl XXV. It was the second Super Bowl victory for the Giants, who won the championship in 1987. Ottis Anderson, running back for the Giants, was chosen the game's most valuable player.

Score by Quarters

Buffalo	3	9	0	7	—19
N.Y. Giants	3	7	7	3	—20

Scoring

N.Y. Giants—Bahr 28 yd. field goal
Buffalo—Norwood 23 yd. field goal
Buffalo—D. Smith one yd. run (Norwood kick)
Buffalo—Safety (B. Smith tackled Hostetler in end zone)
N.Y. Giants—Baker 14 yd. pass from Hostetler (Bahr kick)
N.Y. Giants—Anderson one yd. run (Bahr kick)
Buffalo—Thomas 31 yd. run (Norwood kick)
N.Y. Giants—Bahr 21 yd. field goal

Individual Statistics

Rushing — Buffalo, Thomas 15-135, Kelly 6-23, K. Davis 2-4, Mueller 1-3, D. Smith 1-1. N.Y. Giants, Anderson 21-102, Meggett 9-48, Carthon 3-12, Hostetler 6-10.

Passing — Buffalo, Kelly 18-30-0-212. N.Y. Giants, Hostetler 20-32-0-222.

Receiving — Buffalo, Reed 8-62, Thomas 5-55, K. Davis 2-23, McKeller 2-11, Lofton 1-61. N.Y. Giants, Ingram 5-74, Bavaro 5-50, Cross 4-39, Baker 2-31, Meggett 2-18, Anderson 1-7, Carthon 1-3.

Team Statistics

	Buffalo	N.Y. Giants
First downs	18	24
Total net yards	371	386
Total plays	56	73
Avg gain	6.6	5.3
Rushing yards	166	172
Passing yards	205	214
Yards per pass	6.6	6.3
Punts-average	6-39	4-44
Total return yards	114	85
Penalties yards	6-35	5-31
Fumbles-lost	1-0	0-0
Time of possession	19:27	40:33

Super Bowl

Year	Winner	Loser	Winning coach	Site
1967	Green Bay Packers, 35	Kansas City Chiefs, 10	Vince Lombardi	Los Angeles Coliseum
1968	Green Bay Packers, 33	Oakland Raiders, 14	Vince Lombardi	Orange Bowl, Miami
1969	New York Jets, 16	Baltimore Colts, 7	Weeb Ewbank	Orange Bowl, Miami
1970	Kansas City Chiefs, 23	Minnesota Vikings, 7	Hank Stram	Tulane Stadium, New Orleans
1971	Baltimore Colts, 16	Dallas Cowboys, 13	Don McCafferty	Orange Bowl, Miami
1972	Dallas Cowboys, 24	Miami Dolphins, 3	Tom Landry	Tulane Stadium, New Orleans
1973	Miami Dolphins, 14	Washington Redskins, 7	Don Shula	Los Angeles Coliseum
1974	Miami Dolphins, 24	Minnesota Vikings, 7	Don Shula	Rice Stadium, Houston
1975	Pittsburgh Steelers, 16	Minnesota Vikings, 6	Chuck Noll	Tulane Stadium, New Orleans
1976	Pittsburgh Steelers, 21	Dallas Cowboys, 17	Chuck Noll	Orange Bowl, Miami
1977	Oakland Raiders, 32	Minnesota Vikings, 14	John Madden	Rose Bowl, Pasadena
1978	Dallas Cowboys, 27	Denver Broncos, 10	Tom Landry	Superdome, New Orleans
1979	Pittsburgh Steelers, 35	Dallas Cowboys, 31	Chuck Noll	Orange Bowl, Miami
1980	Pittsburgh Steelers, 31	Los Angeles Rams, 19	Chuck Noll	Rose Bowl, Pasadena
1981	Oakland Raiders, 27	Philadelphia Eagles, 10	Tom Flores	Superdome, New Orleans
1982	San Francisco 49ers, 26	Cincinnati Bengals, 21	Bill Walsh	Silverdome, Pontiac, Mich.
1983	Washington Redskins, 27	Miami Dolphins, 17	Joe Gibbs	Rose Bowl, Pasadena
1984	Los Angeles Raiders, 38	Washington Redskins, 9	Tom Flores	Tampa Stadium
1985	San Francisco 49ers, 38	Miami Dolphins, 16	Bill Walsh	Stanford Stadium, Palo Alto, Cal.
1986	Chicago Bears, 46	New England Patriots, 10	Mike Ditka	Superdome, New Orleans
1987	New York Giants, 39	Denver Broncos, 20	Bill Parcells	Rose Bowl, Pasadena
1988	Washington Redskins, 42	Denver Broncos, 10	Joe Gibbs	San Diego Stadium
1989	San Francisco 49ers, 20	Cincinnati Bengals, 16	Bill Walsh	Joe Robbie Stadium, Miami
1990	San Francisco 49ers, 55	Denver Broncos, 10	George Seifert	Superdome, New Orleans
1991	New York Giants, 20	Buffalo Bills, 19	Bill Parcells	Tampa Stadium

National Football League Champions

Year	East Winner (W-L-T)	West Winner (W-L-T)	Playoff
1933	New York Giants (11-3-0)	Chicago Bears (10-2-1)	Chicago Bears 23, New York 21
1934	New York Giants (8-5-0)	Chicago Bears (13-0-0)	New York 30, Chicago Bears 13
1935	New York Giants (9-3-0)	Detroit Lions (7-3-2)	Detroit 26, New York 7
1936	Boston Redskins (7-5-0)	Green Bay Packers (10-1-1)	Green Bay 21, Boston 6
1937	Washington Redskins (8-3-0).	Chicago Bears (9-1-1).	Washington 28, Chicago Bears 21
1938	New York Giants (8-2-1)	Green Bay Packers (8-3-0)	New York 23, Green Bay 17
1939	New York Giants (9-1-1)	Green Bay Packers (9-2-0)	Green Bay 27, New York 0
1940	Washington Redskins (9-2-0).	Chicago Bears (8-3-0)	Chicago Bears 73, Washington 0
1941	New York Giants (8-3-0)	Chicago Bears (10-1-1)(a)	Chicago Bears 37, New York 9
1942	Wash. Redskins (10-1-1)	Chicago Bears (11-0-0)	Washington 14, Chicago Bears 6
1943	Wash. Redskins (6-3-1)(a)	Chicago Bears (8-1-1)	Chicago Bears, 41, Washington 21
1944	New York Giants (8-1-1)	Green Bay Packers (8-2-0)	Green Bay 14, New York 7
1945	Wash. Redskins (8-2-0)	Cleveland Rams (9-1-0)	Cleveland 15, Washington 14
1946	New York Giants (7-3-1)	Chicago Bears (8-2-1).	Chicago Bears 24, New York 14
1947	Philadelphia Eagles (8-4-0)(a)	Chicago Cardinals (9-3-0).	Chicago Cardinals 28, Philadelphia 21
1948	Philadelphia Eagles (9-2-1).	Chicago Cardinals (11-1-0)	Philadelphia 7, Chicago Cardinals 0
1949	Philadelphia Eagles (11-1-0)	Los Angeles Rams (8-2-2)	Philadelphia 14, Los Angeles 0
1950	Cleveland Browns (10-2-0)(a)	Los Angeles Rams (9-3-0)(a)	Cleveland 30, Los Angeles 28
1951	Cleveland Browns (11-1-0).	Los Angeles Rams (8-4-0)	Los Angeles 24, Cleveland 17
1952	Cleveland Browns (8-4-0)	Detroit Lions (9-3-0)(a)	Detroit 17, Cleveland 7
1953	Cleveland Browns (11-1-0)	Detroit Lions (10-2-0)	Detroit 17, Cleveland 16
1954	Cleveland Browns (9-3-0)	Detroit Lions (9-2-1)	Cleveland 56, Detroit 10
1955	Cleveland Browns (9-2-1)	Los Angeles Rams (8-3-1)	Cleveland 38, Los Angeles 14
1956	New York Giants (8-3-1)	Chicago Bears (9-2-1).	New York 47, Chicago Bears 7
1957	Cleveland Browns (9-2-1)	Detroit Lions (8-4-0)(a)	Detroit 59, Cleveland 14
1958	New York Giants (9-3-0)(a).	Baltimore Colts (9-3-0)	Baltimore 23, New York 17(b)
1959	New York Giants (10-2-0)	Baltimore Colts (9-3-0)	Baltimore 31, New York 16
1960	Philadelphia Eagles (10-2-0)	Green Bay Packers (8-4-0)	Philadelphia 17, Green Bay 13
1961	New York Giants (10-3-1)	Green Bay Packers (11-3-0)	Green Bay 37, New York 0
1962	New York Giants (12-2-0)	Green Bay Packers (13-1-0)	Green Bay 16, New York 7
1963	New York Giants (11-3-0)	Chicago Bears (11-1-2)	Chicago 14, New York 10
1964	Cleveland Browns (10-3-1)	Baltimore Colts (12-2-0)	Cleveland 27, Baltimore 0
1965	Cleveland Browns (11-3-0)	Green Bay Packers (10-3-1)(a).	Green Bay 23, Cleveland 12
1966	Dallas Cowboys (10-3-1)	Green Bay Packers (12-2-0)	Green Bay 34, Dallas 27

(a) Won divisional playoff. (b) Won at 8:15 sudden death overtime period.

Year	Conference	Division	Winner (W-L-T)	Playoff
1967	East	Century	Cleveland (9-5-0)	Dallas 52, Cleveland 14
		Capitol	Dallas (9-5-0)	
	West.	Central	Green Bay (9-4-1).	Green Bay 28, Los Angeles 7
		Coastal	Los Angeles (11-1-2)(a)	Green Bay 21, Dallas 17
1968	East	Century	Cleveland (10-4-0)	Cleveland 31, Dallas 20
		Capitol	Dallas (12-2-0)	
	West.	Central	Minnesota (8-6-0)	Baltimore 24, Minnesota 14
		Coastal	Baltimore (13-1-0)	Baltimore 34, Cleveland 0
1969	East	Century	Cleveland (10-3-1)	Cleveland 38, Dallas 14
		Capitol	Dallas (11-2-1)	
	West.	Central	Minnesota (12-2-0)	Minnesota 23, Los Angeles 20
		Coastal	Los Angeles (11-3-0)	Minnesota 27, Cleveland 7
1970	American	Eastern	Baltimore (11-2-1).	Baltimore 17, Cincinnati 0
		Central	Cincinnati (8-6-0)	Oakland 21, Miami 14
		Western.	Oakland (8-4-2)	Baltimore 27, Oakland 17
	National.	Eastern	Dallas (10-4-0)	Dallas 5, Detroit 0
		Central	Minnesota (12-2-0)	San Francisco 17, Minnesota 14
		Western.	San Francisco (10-3-1).	Dallas 17, San Francisco 10
1971	American	Eastern	Miami (10-3-1).	Miami 27, Kansas City 24
		Central	Cleveland (9-5-0)	Baltimore 20, Cleveland 3
		Western.	Kansas City (10-3-1)	Miami 21, Baltimore 0
	National.	Eastern	Dallas (11-3-0)	Dallas 20, Minnesota 12
		Central	Minnesota (11-3-0)	San Francisco 24, Washington 20
		Western.	San Francisco (9-5-0)	Dallas 14, San Francisco 3
1972	American	Eastern	Miami (14-0-0).	Miami 20, Cleveland 14
		Central	Pittsburgh (11-3-0)	Pittsburgh 13, Oakland 7
		Western.	Oakland (10-3-1)	Miami 21, Pittsburgh 17
	National.	Eastern	Washington (11-3-0)	Washington 16, Green Bay 3
		Central	Green Bay (10-4-0)	Dallas 30, San Francisco 28
		Western.	San Francisco (8-5-1)	Washington 26, Dallas 3
1973	American	Eastern	Miami (12-2-0).	Miami 34, Cincinnati 16
		Central	Cincinnati (10-4-0)	Oakland 33, Pittsburgh 14
		Western.	Oakland (9-4-1)	Miami 27, Oakland 10
	National.	Eastern	Dallas (10-4-0)	Dallas 27, Los Angeles 16
		Central	Minnesota (12-2-0)	Minnesota 27, Washington 20
		Western.	Los Angeles (12-2-0).	Minnesota 27, Dallas 10
1974	American	Eastern	Miami (11-3-0).	Oakland 28, Miami 26
		Central	Pittsburgh (10-3-1)	Pittsburgh 32, Buffalo 14
		Western.	Oakland (12-2-0)	Pittsburgh 24, Oakland 13
	National.	Eastern	St. Louis (10-4-0)	Minnesota 30, St. Louis 14
		Central	Minnesota (10-4-0)	Los Angeles 19, Washington 10
		Western.	Los Angeles (10-4-0)	Minnesota 14, Los Angeles 10
1975	American	Eastern	Baltimore (10-4-0).	Pittsburgh 28, Baltimore 10
		Central	Pittsburgh (12-2-0)	Oakland 31, Cincinnati 28
		Western.	Oakland (11-3-0)	Pittsburgh 16, Oakland 10

Year	Conference	Division	Winner (W-L-T)	Playoff
	National	Eastern	St. Louis (11-3-0)	Dallas 17, Minnesota 14
		Central	Minnesota (12-2-0)	Los Angeles 35, St. Louis 23
		Western	Los Angeles (12-2-0)	Dallas 37, Los Angeles 7
1976	American	Eastern	Baltimore (11-3-0)	Pittsburgh 40, Baltimore 14
		Central	Pittsburgh (10-4-0)	Oakland 24, New England 21
		Western	Oakland (13-1-0)	Oakland 24, Pittsburgh 7
	National	Eastern	Dallas (11-3-0)	Minnesota 35, Washington 20
		Central	Minnesota (11-2-1)	Los Angeles 14, Dallas 12
		Western	Los Angeles (10-3-1)	Minnesota 24, Los Angeles 13
1977	American	Eastern	Baltimore (10-4-0)	Oakland 37, Baltimore 31
		Central	Pittsburgh (9-5-0)	Denver 34, Pittsburgh 21
		Western	Denver (12-2-0)	Dallas 37, Chicago 7
	National	Eastern	Dallas (12-2-0)	Minnesota 14, Los Angeles 7
		Central	Minnesota (9-5-0)	Denver 20, Oakland 17
		Western	Los Angeles (10-4-0)	Dallas 23, Minnesota 6
1978	American	Eastern	New England (11-5-0)	Pittsburgh 33, Denver 10
		Central	Pittsburgh (14-2-0)	Houston 31, New England 14
		Western	Denver (10-6-0)	Pittsburgh 34, Houston 5
	National	Eastern	Dallas (12-4-0)	Dallas 27, Atlanta 20
		Central	Minnesota (8-7-1)	Los Angeles 34, Minnesota 10
		Western	Los Angeles (12-4-0)	Dallas 28, Atlanta 0
1979	American	Eastern	Miami (10-6-0)	Houston 17, San Diego 14
		Central	Pittsburgh (12-4-0)	Pittsburgh 34, Miami 14
		Western	San Diego (12-4-0)	Pittsburgh 27, Houston 13
	National	Eastern	Dallas (11-5-0)	Tampa Bay 24, Philadelphia 17
		Central	Tampa Bay (10-6-0)	Los Angeles 21, Dallas 19
		Western	Los Angeles (9-7-0)	Los Angeles 9, Tampa Bay 0
1980	American	Eastern	Buffalo (11-5-0)	San Diego 20, Buffalo 14
		Central	Cleveland (11-5-0)	Oakland 14, Cleveland 12
		Western	San Diego (11-5-0)	Oakland 34, San Diego 27
	National	Eastern	Philadelphia (12-4-0)	Philadelphia 31, Minnesota 16
		Central	Minnesota (9-7-0)	Dallas 30, Atlanta 27
		Western	Atlanta (12-4-0)	Philadelphia 20, Dallas 7
1981	American	Eastern	Miami (11-4-1)	San Diego 41, Miami 38
		Central	Cincinnati (12-4-0)	Cincinnati 28, Buffalo 21
		Western	San Diego (10-6-0)	Cincinnati 27, San Diego 7
	National	Eastern	Dallas (12-4-0)	Dallas 38, Tampa Bay 0
		Central	Tampa Bay (9-7-0)	San Francisco 38, N.Y. Giants 24
		Western	San Francisco (13-3-0)	San Francisco 28, Dallas 27
1982	American		L.A. Raiders (8-1-0)	
	National		Washington (8-1-0)	Strike-shortened season

AFC playoffs—Miami 28, New England 13; L.A. Raiders 27, Cleveland 10; N.Y. Jets 44, Cincinnati 17; San Diego 31, Pittsburgh 28; N.Y. Jets 17, L.A. Raiders 14; Miami 34, San Diego 13; Miami 14, N.Y. Jets 0. **NFC playoffs**—Washington 31, Detroit 7; Green Bay 41, St. Louis 16; Dallas 30, Tampa Bay 17; Minnesota 30, Atlanta 24; Washington 21, Minnesota 7; Dallas 37, Green Bay 26; Washington 31, Dallas 17.

Year	Conference	Division	Winner (W-L-T)	Playoff
1983	American	Eastern	Miami (12-4-0)	Seattle 27, Miami 20
		Central	Pittsburgh (10-6-0)	L.A. Raiders 38, Pittsburgh 10
		Western	L.A. Raiders (12-4-0)	L.A. Raiders 30, Seattle 14
	National	Eastern	Washington (14-2-0)	Washington 51, L.A. Rams 7
		Central	Detroit (9-7-0)	San Francisco 24, Detroit 23
		Western	San Francisico (10-6-0)	Washington 24, San Francisco 21
1984	American	Eastern	Miami (14-2-0)	Miami 31, Seattle 10
		Central	Pittsburgh (9-7-0)	Pittsburgh 24, Denver 17
		Western	Denver (13-3-0)	Miami 45, Pittsburgh 28
	National	Eastern	Washington (11-5-0)	Chicago 23, Washington 19
		Central	Chicago (10-6-0)	San Francisco 21, N.Y. Giants 10
		Western	San Francisco (15-1-0)	San Francisco 23, Chicago 0
1985	American	Eastern	Miami (12-4-0)	New England 27, L.A. Raiders 20
		Central	Cleveland (8-8-0)	Miami 24, Cleveland 21
		Western	L.A. Raiders (12-4-0)	New England 31, Miami 14
	National	Eastern	Dallas (10-6-0)	Chicago 21, N.Y. Giants 0
		Central	Chicago (15-1-0)	L.A. Rams 20, Dallas 0
		Western	L.A. Rams (11-5-0)	Chicago 24, L.A. Rams 0
1986	American	Eastern	New England (11-5-0)	Denver 22, New England 17
		Central	Cleveland (12-4-0)	Cleveland 23, N.Y. Jets 20
		Western	Denver (11-5-0)	Denver 23, Cleveland 20
	National	Eastern	N.Y. Giants (14-2-0)	N.Y. Giants 49, San Francisco 3
		Central	Chicago (14-2-0)	Washington 27, Chicago 13
		Western	San Francisco (10-5-1)	N.Y. Giants 17, Washington 0
1987	American	Eastern	Indianapolis (9-6-0)	Cleveland 38, Indianapolis 21
		Central	Cleveland (10-5-0)	Denver 34, Houston 10
		Western	Denver (10-4-1)	Denver 38, Cleveland 33
	National	Eastern	Washington (11-4-0)	Washington 21, Chicago 7
		Central	Chicago (11-4-0)	Minnesota 36, San Francisco 24
		Western	San Francisco (13-2-0)	Washington 17, Minnesota 10
1988	American	Eastern	Buffalo (12-4-0)	Buffalo 17, Houston 10
		Central	Cincinnati (12-4-0)	Cincinnati 21, Seattle 13
		Western	Seattle (9-7-0)	Cincinnati 21, Buffalo 10
	National	Eastern	Philadelphia (10-6-0)	Chicago 20, Philadelphia 12
		Central	Chicago (12-4-0)	San Francisco 34, Minnesota 9
		Western	San Francisco (10-6-0)	San Francisco 28, Chicago 3
1989	American	Eastern	Buffalo (9-7-0)	Cleveland 34, Buffalo 30
		Central	Cleveland (9-6-1)	Denver 24, Pittsburgh 23
		Western	Denver (11-5-0)	Denver 37, Cleveland 21
	National	Eastern	N.Y. Giants (12-4-0)	San Francisco 41, Minnesota 13
		Central	Minnesota (10-6-0)	L.A. Rams 19, N.Y. Giants 13
		Western	San Francisco (14-2-0)	San Francisco 30, L.A. Rams 3

(continued)

Year	Conference	Division	Winner (W-L-T)	Playoff
1990	American	Eastern	Buffalo (13-3-0)	L.A. Raiders 20, Cincinnati 10
		Central	Cincinnati (9-7-0)	Buffalo 44, Miami 34
		Western	L.A. Raiders (12-4-0)	Buffalo 51, L.A. Raiders 3
	National	Eastern	N.Y. Giants (13-3-0)	San Francisco 28, Washington 10
		Central	Chicago (11-5-0)	N.Y. Giants 31, Chicago 3
		Western	San Francisco (14-2-0)	N.Y. Giants 15, San Francisco 13

Super Bowl MVPs

1967 Bart Starr, Green Bay	1976 Lynn Swann, Pittsburgh	1984 Marcus Allen, L.A. Raiders
1968 Bart Starr, Green Bay	1977 Fred Biletnikoff, Oakland	1985 Joe Montana, San Francisco
1969 Joe Namath, N.Y. Jets	1978 Randy White, Harvey Martin, Dallas	1986 Richard Dent, Chicago
1970 Len Dawson, Kansas City	1979 Terry Bradshaw, Pittsburgh	1987 Phil Simms, N.Y. Giants
1971 Chuck Howley, Dallas	1980 Terry Bradshaw, Pittsburgh	1988 Doug Williams, Washington
1972 Roger Staubach, Dallas	1981 Jim Plunkett, Oakland	1989 Jerry Rice, San Francisco
1973 Jake Scott, Miami	1982 Joe Montana, San Francisco	1990 Joe Montana, San Francisco
1974 Larry Csonka, Miami	1983 John Riggins, Washington	1991 Ottis Anderson, N.Y. Giants
1975 Franco Harris, Pittsburgh		

World Almanac/Bert Bell Memorial Trophy Winners

The World Almanac 's Bert Bell Memorial Trophy, named after the former NFL commissioner, is awarded annually to the outstanding NFL rookie as chosen by a panel of sports experts on behalf of The World Almanac, its co-sponsoring newspapers, and its publisher, Pharos Books.

1964 Charlie Taylor, Washington, WR	1976 AFC: Mike Haynes, New England, CB
1965 Gale Sayers, Chicago, RB	NFC: Sammy White, Minnesota, WR
1966 Tommy Nobis, Atlanta, LB	1977 Tony Dorsett, Dallas, RB
1967 Mel Farr, Detroit, RB	1978 Earl Campbell, Houston, RB
1968 Earl McCullouch, Detroit, WR	1979 Ottis Anderson, St. Louis, RB
1969 Calvin Hill, Dallas, RB	1980 Billy Sims, Detroit, RB
1970 Raymond Chester, Oakland, TE	1981 Lawrence Taylor, N.Y. Giants, LB
1971 AFC: Jim Plunkett, New England, QB	1982 Marcus Allen, L.A. Raiders, RB
NFC: John Brockington, Green Bay, RB	1983 Eric Dickerson, L.A. Rams, RB
1972 AFC: Franco Harris, Pittsburgh, RB	1984 Louis Lipps, Pittsburgh, WR
NFC: Willie Buchanon, Green Bay, DB	1985 Eddie Brown, Cincinnati, WR
1973 AFC: Boobie Clark, Cincinnati, RB	1986 Rueben Mayes, New Orleans, RB
NFC: Chuck Foreman, Minnesota, RB	1987 Bo Jackson, L.A. Raiders, RB
1974 Don Woods, San Diego, RB	1988 John Stephens, New England, RB
1975 AFC: Robert Brazile, Houston, LB	1989 Barry Sanders, Detroit, RB
NFC: Steve Bartkowski, Atlanta, QB	1990 Eric Green, Pittsburgh, TE

World Almanac/George Halas Trophy Winners

The World Almanac 's George Halas Trophy, named after football coach George Halas, is awarded annually to the outstanding defensive player in the NFL as chosen by a panel of sports experts on behalf of The World Almanac, its co-sponsoring newspapers, and its publisher, Pharos Books.

1966 Larry Wilson, St. Louis	1975 Curley Culp, Houston	1984 Mike Haynes, L.A. Raiders
1967 Deacon Jones, Los Angeles	1976 Jerry Sherk, Cleveland	1985 Howie Long, L.A. Raiders
1968 Deacon Jones, Los Angeles	1977 Harvey Martin, Dallas	Andre Tippett, New England
1969 Dick Butkus, Chicago	1978 Randy Gradishar, Denver	1986 Lawrence Taylor, N.Y. Giants
1970 Dick Butkus, Chicago	1979 Lee Roy Selmon, Tampa Bay	1987 Reggie White, Philadelphia
1971 Carl Eller, Minnesota	1980 Lester Hayes, Oakland	1988 Mike Singletary, Chicago
1972 Joe Greene, Pittsburgh	1981 Joe Klecko, N.Y. Jets	1989 Tim Harris, Green Bay
1973 Alan Page, Minnesota	1982 Mark Gastineau, N.Y. Jets	1990 Bruce Smith, Buffalo
1974 Joe Greene, Pittsburgh	1983 Jack Lambert, Pittsburgh	

World Almanac Jim Thorpe Trophy Winners

The World Almanac 's Jim Thorpe Trophy goes to the most valuable player as chosen by the NFL Players Association in 1990 on behalf of The World Almanac, its co-sponsoring newspapers, and its publisher, Pharos Books.

1955 Harlon Hill, Chicago Bears	1973 O.J. Simpson, Buffalo Bills
1956 Frank Gifford, N.Y. Giants	1974 Ken Stabler, Oakland Raiders
1957 John Unitas, Baltimore Colts	1975 Fran Tarkenton, Minnesota Vikings
1958 Jim Brown, Cleveland Browns	1976 Bert Jones, Baltimore Colts
1959 Charley Conerly, N.Y. Giants	1977 Walter Payton, Chicago Bears
1960 Norm Van Brocklin, Philadelphia Eagles	1978 Earl Campbell, Houston Oilers
1961 Y.A. Tittle, N.Y. Giants	1979 Earl Campbell, Houston Oilers
1962 Jim Taylor, Green Bay Packers	1980 Earl Campbell, Houston Oilers
1963 Jim Brown, Cleveland Browns; Y.A. Tittle, N.Y. Giants	1981 Ken Anderson, Cincinnati Bengals
1964 Lenny Moore, Baltimore Colts	1982 Dan Fouts, San Diego Chargers
1965 Jim Brown, Cleveland Browns	1983 Joe Theismann, Washington Redskins
1966 Bart Starr, Green Bay Packers	1984 Dan Marino, Miami Dolphins
1967 John Unitas, Baltimore Colts	1985 Walter Payton, Chicago Bears
1968 Earl Morrall, Baltimore Colts	1986 Phil Simms, N.Y. Giants
1969 Roman Gabriel, Los Angeles Rams	1987 Jerry Rice, San Francisco
1970 John Brodie, San Francisco 49ers	1988 Roger Craig, San Francisco
1971 Bob Griese, Miami Dolphins	1989 Joe Montana, San Francisco
1972 Larry Brown, Washington Redskins	1990 Warren Moon, Houston

Number One NFL Draft Choices, 1936-91

Year	Team	Player, Pos., College	Year	Team	Player, Pos., College
1936	Philadelphia	Jay Berwanger, HB, Chicago	1964	San Francisco	Dave Parks, E, Texas Tech
1937	Philadelphia	Sam Francis, FB, Nebraska	1965	N.Y. Giants	Tucker Frederickson, HB, Auburn
1938	Cleve.Rams	Corbett Davis, FB, Indiana	1966	Atlanta	Tommy Nobis, LB, Texas
1939	Chi.Cards	Ki Aldrich, C, TCU	1967	Baltimore	Bubba Smith, DT, Michigan St.
1940	Chi.Cards	George Cafego, HB, Tennessee	1968	Minnesota	Ron Yary, T, USC
1941	Chi.Bears	Tom Harmon, HB, Michigan	1969	Buffalo	O.J. Simpson, RB, USC
1942	Pittsburgh	Bill Dudley, HB, Virginia	1970	Pittsburgh	Terry Bradshaw, QB, La.Tech
1943	Detroit	Frank Sinkwich, HB, Georgia	1971	New England	Jim Plunkett, QB, Stanford
1944	Boston Yanks	Angelo Bertelli, QB, Notre Dame	1972	Buffalo	Walt Patulski, DE, Notre Dame
1945	Chi.Cards	Charley Trippi, HB, Georgia	1973	Houston	John Matuszak, DE, Tampa
1946	Boston Yanks	Frank Dancewicz, QB, Notre Dame	1974	Dallas	Ed "Too Tall" Jones, Tenn.St.
			1975	Atlanta	Steve Bartkowski, QB, Cal.
1947	Chi.Bears	Bob Fenimore, HB, Okla. A&M	1976	Tampa Bay	Lee Roy Selmon, DE, Oklahoma
1948	Washington	Harry Gilmer, QB, Alabama	1977	Tampa Bay	Ricky Bell, RB, USC
1949	Philadelphia	Chuck Bednarik, C, Penn	1978	Houston	Earl Campbell, RB, Texas
1950	Detroit	Leon Hart, E, Notre Dame	1979	Buffalo	Tom Cousineau, LB, Ohio St.
1951	N.Y. Giants	Kyle Rote, HB, SMU	1980	Detroit	Billy Sims, RB, Oklahoma
1952	L.A. Rams	Bill Wade, QB, Vanderbilt	1981	New Orleans	George Rogers, RB, S.Carolina
1953	San Francisco	Harry Babcock, E, Georgia	1982	New England	Kenneth Sims, DT, Texas
1954	Cleveland	Bobby Garrett, QB, Stanford	1983	Baltimore	John Elway, QB, Stanford
1955	Baltimore	George Shaw, QB, Oregon	1984	New England	Irving Fryar, WR, Nebraska
1956	Pittsburgh	Gary Glick, DB, Col. A&M	1985	Buffalo	Bruce Smith, DE, Va.Tech
1957	Green Bay	Paul Hornung, QB, Notre Dame	1986	Tampa Bay	Bo Jackson, RB, Auburn
1958	Chi.Cards	King Hill, QB, Rice	1987	Tampa Bay	Vinny Testaverde, QB, Miami (Fla.)
1959	Green Bay	Randy Duncan, QB, Iowa			
1960	L.A. Rams	Billy Cannon, HB, LSU	1988	Atlanta	Aundray Bruce, LB, Auburn
1961	Minnesota	Tommy Mason, HB, Tulane	1989	Dallas	Troy Aikman, QB, UCLA
1962	Washington	Ernie Davis, HB, Syracuse	1990	Indianapolis	Jeff George, QB, Illinois
1963	L.A. Rams	Terry Baker, QB, Oregon St.	1991	Dallas	Russell Maryland, DL, Miami

First-Round Selections in the 1991 NFL Draft

	Team	Player	Pos.	College		Team	Player	Pos.	College
1—	Dallas	Russell Maryland	DT	Miami	15—	Pittsburgh	Huey Richardson	LB	Florida
2—	Cleveland	Eric Turner	S	UCLA	16—	Seattle	Dan McGwire	QB	San Diego St.
3—	Atlanta	Bruce Pickens	CB	Nebraska	17—	Washington	Bobby Wilson	DT	Michigan St.
4—	Denver	Mike Croel	LB	Nebraska	18—	Cincinnati	Alfred Williams	LB	Colorado
5—	L.A. Rams	Todd Lyght	CB	Notre Dame	19—	Green Bay	Vincent Clark	DB	Ohio St.
6—	Phoenix	Eric Swann	DT	No college	20—	Dallas	Kelvin Pritchett	DT	Mississippi
7—	Tampa Bay	Charles McRae	OT	Tennessee	21—	Kansas City	Harvey Williams	RB	LSU
8—	Philadelphia	Antone Davis	OT	Tennessee	22—	Chicago	Stan Thomas	OT	Texas
9—	San Diego	Stanley Richard	S	Texas	23—	Miami	Randal Hill	WR	Miami
10—	Detroit	Herman Moore*	WR	Virginia	24—	L.A. Raiders	Todd Marinovich*	QB	USC
11—	New England	Pat Harlow	OT	USC	25—	San Francisco	Ted Washington	DL	Louisville
12—	Dallas	Alvin Harper	WR	Tennessee	26—	Buffalo	Henry Jones	S	Illinois
13—	Atlanta	Mike Pritchard	WR	Colorado	27—	N.Y. Giants	Jarrod Bunch	FB	Michigan
14—	New England	Leonard Russell	RB	Arizona St.			* Under classmen who chose to enter the draft.		

Pro Football Hall of Fame, Canton, Ohio

Herb Adderley	Mike Ditka	Elroy (Crazy Legs) Hirsch	George McAfee	Gale Sayers
Lance Alworth	Art Donovan	Paul Hornung	Mike McCormack	Joe Schmidt
Doug Atkins	Paddy Driscoll	Ken Houston	Hugh McElhenny	Tex Schramm
Morris (Red) Badgro	Bill Dudley	Cal Hubbard	John (Blood) McNally	Art Shell
Cliff Battles	Turk Edwards	Sam Huff	Mike Michalske	O.J. Simpson
Sammy Baugh	Weeb Ewbank	Lamar Hunt	Wayne Millner	Bart Starr
Chuck Bednarik	Tom Fears	Don Hutson	Bobby Mitchell	Roger Staubach
Bert Bell	Ray Flaherty	John Henry Johnson	Ron Mix	Ernie Stautner
Bobby Bell	Len Ford	Deacon Jones	Lenny Moore	Jan Stenerud
Raymond Berry	Dr. Daniel Fortmann	Stan Jones	Marion Motley	Ken Strong
Charles Bidwell	Frank Gatski	Sonny Jurgensen	George Musso	Joe Stydahar
Fred Biletnikoff	Bill George	Walt Kiesling	Bronko Nagurski	Fran Tarkenton
George Blanda	Frank Gifford	Frank (Bruiser) Kinard	Joe Namath	Charlie Taylor
Mel Blount	Sid Gillman	Curly Lambeau	Greasy Neale	Jim Taylor
Terry Bradshaw	Otto Graham	Jack Lambert	Ernie Nevers	Jim Thorpe
Jim Brown	Red Grange	Tom Landry	Ray Nitschke	Y.A. Tittle
Paul Brown	Joe Greene	Dick (Night Train) Lane	Leo Nomellini	George Trafton
Roosevelt Brown	Forrest Gregg	Jim Langer	Merlin Olsen	Charlie Trippi
Willie Brown	Bob Griese	Willie Lanier	Jim Otto	Emlen Tunnell
Buck Buchanan	Lou Groza	Yale Lary	Steve Owen	Clyde (Bulldog) Turner
Dick Butkus	Joe Guyon	Dante Lavelli	Alan Page	Johnny Unitas
Earl Campbell	George Halas	Bobby Layne	Clarence (Ace) Parker	Gene Upshaw
Tony Canadeo	Jack Ham	Tuffy Leemans	Jim Parker	Norm Van Brocklin
Joe Carr	John Hannah	Bob Lilly	Joe Perry	Steve Van Buren
Guy Chamberlin	Franco Harris	Vince Lombardi	Pete Pihos	Doak Walker
Jack Christiansen	Ed Healey	Sid Luckman	Hugh (Shorty) Ray	Paul Warfield
Dutch Clark	Mel Hein	Link Lyman	Dan Reeves	Bob Waterfield
George Connor	Ted Hendricks	Tim Mara	Jim Ringo	Arnie Weinmeister
Jim Conzelman	Pete Henry	Gino Marchetti	Andy Robustelli	Bill Willis
Larry Csonka	Arnold Herber	George Marshall	Art Rooney	Larry Wilson
Willie Davis	Bill Hewitt	Ollie Matson	Pete Rozelle	Alex Wojciechowicz
Len Dawson	Clarke Hinkle	Don Maynard	Bob St. Clair	Willie Wood

National Football Conference Leaders

(National Football League, 1960-69)

Passing / Pass-Receiving

Player, team	Atts	Com	YG	TD	Year	Player, team	Ct	YG	TD
Milt Plum, Cleveland	250	151	2,297	21	1960	Raymond Berry, Baltimore	74	1,298	10
Milt Plum, Cleveland	302	177	2,416	18	1961	Jim Phillips, L.A. Rams	78	1,092	5
Bart Starr, Green Bay	285	178	2,438	12	1962	Bobby Mitchell, Washington	72	1,384	11
Y.A. Tittle, N.Y. Giants	367	221	3,145	36	1963	Bobby Joe Conrad, St. Louis	73	967	10
Bart Starr, Green Bay	272	163	2,144	15	1964	Johnny Morris, Chicago	93	1,200	10
Rudy Bukich, Chicago	312	176	2,641	20	1965	Dave Parks, San Francisco	80	1,344	12
Bart Starr, Green Bay	251	156	2,257	14	1966	Charley Taylor, Washington	72	1,119	12
Sonny Jurgensen, Washington	508	288	3,747	31	1967	Charley Taylor, Washington	70	990	9
Earl Morrall, Baltimore	317	182	2,909	26	1968	Clifton McNeil, San Francisco	71	994	7
Sonny Jurgensen, Washington	442	274	3,102	22	1969	Dan Abramowicz, New Orleans	73	1,015	7
John Brodie, San Francisco	378	223	2,941	24	1970	Dick Gordon, Chicago	71	1,026	13
Roger Staubach, Dallas	211	126	1,882	15	1971	Bob Tucker, Giants	59	791	4
Norm Snead, N.Y. Giants	325	196	2,307	17	1972	Harold Jackson, Philadelphia	62	1,048	4
Roger Staubach, Dallas	286	179	2,428	23	1973	Harold Carmichael, Philadelphia	67	1,116	9
Sonny Jurgensen, Washington	167	107	1,185	11	1974	Charles Young, Philadelphia	63	696	3
Fran Tarkenton, Minnesota	425	273	2,294	25	1975	Chuck Foreman, Minnesota	73	691	9
James Harris, Los Angeles	158	91	1,460	8	1976	Drew Pearson, Dallas	58	806	6
Roger Staubach, Dallas	361	210	2,620	18	1977	Ahmad Rashad, Minnesota	51	681	2
Roger Staubach, Dallas	413	231	3,190	25	1978	Rickey Young, Minnesota	88	704	5
Roger Staubach, Dallas	461	267	3,586	27	1979	Ahmad Rashad, Minnesota	80	1,156	9
Ron Jaworski, Philadelphia	451	257	3,529	27	1980	Earl Cooper, San Francisco	83	567	4
Joe Montana, San Francisco	488	311	3,565	19	1981	Dwight Clark, San Francisco	85	1,105	4
Joe Thiesmann, San Francisco	252	161	2,033	13	1982	Dwight Clark, San Francisco	60	913	5
Steve Bartkowski, Atlanta	423	274	3,167	22	1983	Roy Green, St. Louis	78	1,227	14
						Charlie Brown, Washington	78	1,225	8
						Earnest Gray, N.Y. Giants	78	1,139	5
Joe Montana, San Francisco	432	279	3,630	28	1984	Art Monk, Washington	106	1,372	7
Joe Montana, San Francisco	494	303	3,653	27	1985	Roger Craig, San Francisco	92	1,016	6
Tommy Kramer, Minnesota	372	208	3,000	24	1986	Jerry Rice, San Francisco	86	1,570	15
Joe Montana, San Francisco	398	266	3,054	31	1987	J.T. Smith, St. Louis	91	1,117	8
Wade Wilson, Minnesota	332	204	2,746	15	1988	Henry Ellard, L.A. Rams	86	1,414	10
Joe Montana, San Francisco	386	271	3,521	26	1989	Sterling Sharpe, Green Bay	90	1,423	12
Phil Simms, N.Y. Giants	311	184	2,284	15	1990	Jerry Rice, San Francisco	100	1,502	13

Scoring / Rushing

Player, team	TD	PAT	FG	Pts	Year	Player, team	Yds	Atts	TD
Paul Hornung, Green Bay	15	41	15	176	1960	Jim Brown, Cleveland	1,257	215	9
Paul Hornung, Green Bay	10	41	15	146	1961	Jim Brown, Cleveland	1,408	305	8
Jim Taylor, Green Bay	19	0	0	114	1962	Jim Taylor, Green Bay	1,474	272	19
Don Chandler, N.Y. Giants	0	52	18	106	1963	Jim Brown, Cleveland	1,863	291	12
Lenny Moore, Baltimore	20	0	0	120	1964	Jim Brown, Cleveland	1,446	280	7
Gale Sayers, Chicago	22	0	0	132	1965	Jim Brown, Cleveland	1,544	289	17
Bruce Gossett, L.A. Rams	0	29	28	113	1966	Gale Sayers, Chicago	1,231	229	8
Jim Bakken, St. Louis	0	36	27	117	1967	Leroy Kelly, Cleveland	1,205	235	11
Leroy Kelly, Cleveland	20	0	0	120	1968	Leroy Kelly, Cleveland	1,239	248	16
Fred Cox, Minnesota	0	43	26	121	1969	Gale Sayers, Chicago	1,032	236	8
Fred Cox, Minnesota	0	35	30	125	1970	Larry Brown, Washington	1,125	237	5
Curt Knight, Washington	0	27	29	114	1971	John Brockington, Green Bay	1,105	216	4
Chester Marcol, Green Bay	0	29	33	128	1972	Larry Brown, Washington	1,216	285	8
David Ray, Los Angeles	0	40	30	130	1973	John Brockington, Green Bay	1,144	265	3
Chester Marcol, Green Bay	0	19	25	94	1974	Lawrence McCutcheon, Los Angeles	1,109	236	3
Chuck Foreman, Minnesota	22	0	0	132	1975	Jim Otis, St. Louis	1,076	269	5
Mark Moseley, Washington	0	31	22	97	1976	Walter Payton, Chicago	1,390	311	13
Walter Payton, Chicago	16	0	0	96	1977	Walter Payton, Chicago	1,852	339	14
Frank Corrall, Los Angeles	0	31	29	118	1978	Walter Payton, Chicago	1,395	333	11
Mark Moseley, Washington	0	39	25	114	1979	Walter Payton, Chicago	1,610	369	14
Ed Murray, Detroit	0	35	27	116	1980	Walter Payton, Chicago	1,460	317	15
Ed Murray, Detroit	0	46	25	121	1981	George Rogers, New Orleans	1,674	378	13
Wendell Tyler, L.A. Rams	13	0	0	78	1982	Tony Dorsett, Dallas	745	177	5
Mark Moseley, Washington	0	62	33	161	1983	Eric Dickerson, L.A. Rams	1,808	390	18
Ray Wersching, San Francisco	0	56	25	131	1984	Eric Dickerson, L.A. Rams	2,105	379	14
Kevin Butler, Chicago	0	51	31	144	1985	Gerald Riggs, Atlanta	1,719	397	10
Kevin Butler, Chicago	0	36	28	120	1986	Eric Dickerson, L.A. Rams	1,821	404	11
Jerry Rice, San Francisco	23	0	0	138	1987	Charles White, L.A. Rams	1,374	324	11
Mike Cofer, San Francisco	0	40	27	121	1988	Herschel Walker, Dallas	1,514	361	5
Mike Cofer, San Francisco	0	49	29	136	1989	Barry Sanders, Detroit	1,470	280	14
Chip Lohmiller, Washington	0	41	30	131	1990	Barry Sanders, Detroit	1,304	255	13

American Football Conference Leaders

(American Football League, 1960-1969)

Passing / Pass-Receiving

Player, team	Atts	Com	YG	TD	Year	Player, team	Ct	YG	TD
Jack Kemp, Los Angeles	406	211	3,018	20	1960	Lionel Taylor, Denver	92	1,235	12
George Blanda, Houston	362	187	3,330	36	1961	Lionel Taylor, Denver	100	1,176	4
Len Dawson, Dallas	310	189	2,759	29	1962	Lionel Taylor, Denver	77	908	4
Tobin Rote, Kansas City	286	170	2,510	20	1963	Lionel Taylor, Denver	78	1,101	10

Passing

Player, team	Atts	Com	YG	TD	Year
Len Dawson, Kansas City	354	199	2,879	30	1964
John Hadl, San Diego	348	174	2,798	20	1965
Len Dawson, Kansas City	284	159	2,527	26	1966
Daryle Lamonica, Oakland	425	220	3,228	30	1967
Len Dawson, Kansas City	224	131	2,109	17	1968
Greg Cook, Cincinnati	197	106	1,854	15	1969
Daryle Lamonica, Oakland	356	179	2,516	22	1970
Bob Griese, Miami	263	145	2,089	19	1971
Earl Morrall, Miami	150	83	1,360	11	1972
Ken Stabler, Oakland	260	163	1,997	14	1973
Ken Anderson, Cincinnati	328	213	2,667	18	1974
Ken Anderson, Cincinnati	377	228	3,169	21	1975
Ken Stabler, Oakland	291	194	2,737	27	1976
Bob Griese, Miami	307	180	2,252	22	1977
Terry Bradshaw, Pittsburgh	368	207	2,915	28	1978
Dan Fouts, San Diego	530	332	4,082	24	1979
Brian Sipe, Cleveland	554	337	4,132	30	1980
Ken Anderson, Cincinnati	479	300	3,754	29	1981
Ken Anderson, Cincinnati	309	218	2,495	12	1982
Dan Marino, Miami	296	173	2,210	20	1983
Dan Marino, Miami	564	362	5,084	48	1984
Ken O'Brien, N.Y. Jets	488	297	3,888	25	1985
Dan Marino, Miami	623	378	4,746	44	1986
Bernie Kosar, Cleveland	389	241	3,033	22	1987
Boomer Esiason, Cincinnati	388	223	3,572	28	1988
Boomer Esiason, Cincinnati	455	258	3,525	28	1989
Jim Kelly, Buffalo	346	219	2,829	24	1990

Pass-Receiving

Player, team	Ct	YG	TD
Charley Hennigan, Houston	101	1,546	8
Lionel Taylor, Denver	85	1,131	6
Lance Alworth, San Diego	73	1,383	13
George Sauer, N.Y. Jets	75	1,189	6
Lance Alworth, San Diego	68	1,312	10
Lance Alworth, San Diego	64	1,003	4
Marlin Briscoe, Buffalo	57	1,036	8
Fred Biletnikoff, Oakland	61	929	9
Fred Biletnikoff, Oakland	58	802	7
Fred Willis, Houston	57	371	1
Lydell Mitchell, Baltimore	72	544	2
Reggie Rucker, Cleveland	60	770	3
Lydell Mitchell, Baltimore	60	554	4
MacArthur Lane, Kansas City	66	686	1
Lydell Mitchell, Baltimore	71	620	4
Steve Largent, Seattle	71	1,168	8
Joe Washington, Baltimore	82	750	3
Kellen Winslow, San Diego	89	1,290	9
Kellen Winslow, San Diego	88	1,075	10
Kellen Winslow, San Diego	54	721	6
Todd Christensen, L.A. Raiders	92	1,247	12
Ozzie Newsome, Cleveland	89	1,001	5
Lionel James, San Diego	86	1,027	6
Todd Christensen, L.A. Raiders	95	1,153	8
Al Toon, N.Y. Jets	68	976	5
Al Toon, N.Y. Jets	93	1,067	5
Andre Reed, Buffalo	88	1,312	9
Haywood Jeffries, Houston	74	1,048	8
Drew Hill, Houston	74	1,019	5

Scoring

Player, team	TD	PAT	FG	Pts	Year
Gene Mingo, Denver	6	33	18	123	1960
Gino Cappelletti, Boston	8	48	17	147	1961
Gene Mingo, Denver	4	32	27	137	1962
Gino Cappelletti, Boston	2	35	22	113	1963
Gino Cappelletti, Boston	7	36	25	155	1964
Gino Cappelletti, Boston	9	27	17	132	1965
Gino Cappelletti, Boston	6	35	16	119	1966
George Blanda, Oakland	0	56	20	116	1967
Jim Turner, N.Y. Jets	0	43	34	145	1968
Jim Turner, N.Y. Jets	0	33	32	129	1969
Jan Stenerud, Kansas City	0	26	30	116	1970
Garo Yepremian, Miami	0	33	28	117	1971
Bobby Howfield, N.Y. Jets	0	40	27	121	1972
Roy Gerela, Pittsburgh	0	36	29	123	1973
Roy Gerela, Pittsburgh	0	33	20	93	1974
O.J. Simpson, Buffalo	23	0	0	138	1975
Toni Linhart, Baltimore	0	49	20	109	1976
Errol Mann, Oakland	0	39	20	99	1977
Pat Leahy, N.Y. Jets	0	41	22	107	1978
John Smith, New England	0	46	23	115	1979
John Smith, New England	0	51	26	129	1980
Jim Breech, Cincinnati	0	49	22	115	1981
Marcus Allen, L.A. Raiders	14	0	0	84	1982
Gary Anderson, Pittsburgh	0	38	27	119	1983
Gary Anderson, Pittsburgh	0	45	24	117	1984
Gary Anderson, Pittsburgh	0	40	33	139	1985
Tony Franklin, New England	0	44	32	140	1986
Jim Breech, Cincinnati	0	25	24	97	1987
Scott Norwood, Buffalo	0	33	32	129	1988
David Treadwell, Denver	0	39	27	120	1989
Nick Lowery, Kansas City	0	37	34	139	1990

* 1,011 AFC yards led conference.

Rushing

Player, team	Yds	Atts	TD
Abner Haynes, Dallas	875	156	9
Billy Cannon, Houston	948	200	6
Cookie Gilchrest, Buffalo	1,096	214	13
Clem Daniels, Oakland	1,099	215	3
Cookie Gilchrest, Buffalo	981	230	6
Paul Lowe, San Diego	1,121	222	7
Jim Nance, Boston	1,458	299	11
Jim Nance, Boston	1,216	269	7
Paul Robinson, Cincinnati	1,023	238	8
Dick Post, San Diego	873	182	6
Floyd Little, Denver	901	209	3
Floyd Little, Denver	1,133	284	6
O.J. Simpson, Buffalo	1,251	292	6
O.J. Simpson, Buffalo	2,003	332	12
Otis Armstrong, Denver	1,407	263	9
O.J. Simpson, Buffalo	1,817	329	16
O.J. Simpson, Buffalo	1,503	290	8
Mark van Eeghen, Oakland	1,273	324	7
Earl Campbell, Houston	1,450	302	13
Earl Campbell, Houston	1,697	368	19
Earl Campbell, Houston	1,934	373	13
Earl Campbell, Houston	1,376	361	10
Freeman McNeil, N.Y. Jets	786	151	6
Curt Warner, Seattle	1,446	335	13
Earnest Jackson, San Diego	1,179	296	8
Marcus Allen, L.A. Raiders	1,759	380	11
Curt Warner, Seattle	1,481	319	13
Eric Dickerson, L.A. Rams, Indianapolis	1,288*	283	6
Eric Dickerson, Indianapolis	1,659	388	14
Christian Okoye, Kansas City	1,480	370	12
Thurman Thomas, Buffalo	1,297	271	11

NFL Head Coaches in 1990

AFC

Buffalo—Marv Levy
Cincinnati—Sam Wyche
Cleveland—Bud Carson, Jim Shofner
Denver—Dan Reeves
Houston—Jack Pardee
Indianapolis—Ron Meyer
Kansas City—Marty Schottenheimer
L.A. Raiders—Art Shell
Miami—Don Shula
New England—Rod Rust

N.Y. Jets—Bruce Coslet
Pittsburgh—Chuck Noll
San Diego—Dan Henning
Seattle—Chuck Knox

NFC

Atlanta—Jerry Glanville
Chicago—Mike Ditka
Dallas—Jimmy Johnson
Detroit—Wayne Fontes

Green Bay—Lindy Infante
L.A. Rams—John Robinson
Minnesota—Jerry Burns
New Orleans—Jim Mora
N.Y. Giants—Bill Parcells
Philadelphia—Buddy Ryan
Phoenix—Joe Bugel
San Francisco—George Seifert
Tampa Bay—Ray Perkins, Richard Williamson
Washington—Joe Gibbs

World Bowl in 1991

The first World Bowl, the championship game of the World League of American Football, was won by the London Monarchs as they defeated the Barcelona Dragons 21-0. The game was played at Wembley Stadium (England) before 61,108 fans. The initial season of the WLAF saw surprising interest in Europe for their American football teams, but indifference among most U.S. fans.

1990 NFL Individual Leaders

National Football Conference

Passing

	Att	Comp	Pct comp	Yds	Avg gain	TD	Pct TD	Long	Int	Rating points
Simms, N.Y. Giants	311	184	59.2	2284	7.34	15	4.8	80	4	92.7
Cunningham, Philadelphia	465	271	58.3	3466	7.45	30	6.5	95	13	91.6
Montana, San Francisco	520	321	61.7	3944	7.58	26	5.0	78	16	89.0
Harbaugh, Chicago	312	180	57.7	2178	6.98	10	3.2	80	6	81.9
Peete, Detroit	271	142	52.4	1974	7.28	13	4.8	68	8	79.8
Everett, LA Rams	554	307	55.4	3989	7.20	23	4.2	55	17	79.3
Miller, Atlanta	388	222	57.2	2735	7.05	17	4.4	75	14	78.7
Rypien, Washington	304	166	54.6	2070	6.81	16	5.3	53	11	78.4
Testaverde, Tampa Bay	365	203	55.6	2818	7.72	17	4.7	89	18	75.6
Majkowski, Green Bay	264	150	56.8	1925	7.29	10	3.8	76	12	73.5
Rosenbach, Phoenix	437	237	54.2	3098	7.09	16	3.7	68	17	72.8
Gannon, Minnesota	349	182	52.1	2278	6.53	16	4.6	78	16	68.9
Walsh, Dall.-N.O.	336	179	53.3	2010	5.98	12	3.6	58	13	67.2
Aikman, Dallas	399	226	56.6	2579	6.46	11	2.8	61	18	66.6

Rushing

	Att	Yds	Avg	TD
B. Sanders, Detroit	255	1304	5.1	13
Byner, Washington	297	1219	4.1	6
Anderson, Chicago	260	1078	4.1	10
Cunningham, Philadelphia	118	942	8.0	5
E. Smith, Dallas	241	937	3.9	11
Johnson, Phoenix	234	926	4.0	5
Gary, L.A. Rams	204	808	4.0	14
Anderson, N.Y. Giants	225	784	3.5	11
Walker, Minnesota	184	770	4.2	5
Rozier, Hou.-Atl.	163	717	4.4	3

Interceptions

	No	Yds	Long	TD
Carrier, Chicago	10	39	14	0
Haddix, Tampa Bay	7	231	65	3
Browner, Minnesota	7	103	31	1
Waymer, San Francisco	7	64	24	0
Mayhew, Washington	7	20	15	0
Walls, N.Y. Giants	6	80	40	1
Stinson, Chicago	6	66	30	0

Pass Receiving

	No	Yds	Avg	TD
Rice, San Francisco	100	1502	15.0	13
Rison, Atlanta	82	1208	14.7	10
Byars, Philadelphia	81	819	10.1	3
Ellard, L.A. Rams	76	1294	17.0	4
Clark, Washington	75	1112	14.8	8
A. Carter, Minnesota	70	1008	14.4	8
Monk, Washington	68	770	11.3	5
Sharpe, Green Bay	67	1105	16.5	6
Martin, Dallas	64	732	11.4	0
Johnson, Detroit	64	727	11.4	6

Kickoff Returns

	No	Yds	Avg	TD
Meggett, N.Y. Giants	21	492	23.4	0
Gray, Detroit	41	939	22.9	0
Wilson, Green Bay	35	798	22.8	0
Green, L.A. Rams	25	560	22.4	1
Walker, Minnesota	44	966	22.0	0
Sanders, Atlanta	39	851	21.8	0
Dixon, Dallas	36	736	20.4	0
Fenerty, New Orleans	28	572	20.4	0
Sikahema, Phoenix	27	544	20.1	0
Delpino, L.A. Rams	20	389	19.5	0

Scoring-Touchdowns

	TD	Rush	Pass	Pts
B. Sanders, Detroit	16	13	3	96
Gary, L.A. Rams	15	14	1	90
Anderson, Chicago	13	10	3	78
Rice, San Francisco	13	0	13	78
Anderson, N.Y. Giants	11	11	0	66
E. Smith, Dallas	11	11	0	66
Rison, Atlanta	10	0	10	60
Walker, Minnesota	9	5	4	54
Williams, Philadelphia	9	0	9	54

Punt Returns

	No	Yds	Avg	TD
Bailey, Chicago	36	399	11.1	1
Meggett, N.Y. Giants	43	467	10.9	1
Gray, Detroit	34	361	10.6	0
Query, Green Bay	32	308	9.6	0
Sanders, Atlanta	29	250	8.6	1
Sikahema, Phoenix	36	306	8.5	0
V. Buck, New Orleans	37	305	8.2	0
Taylor, San Francisco	26	212	8.2	0
Drewrey, Tampa Bay	23	184	8.0	0
R. Harris, Dall.-Philadelphia	28	214	7.6	0

Scoring-Kicking

	PAT	FG	Pts
Lohmiller, Washington	41/41	30/40	131
Butler, Chicago	36/37	26/37	114
Cofer, San Francisco	39/39	24/36	111
Ruzek, Philadelphia	45/48	21/29	108
Davis, Atlanta	40/40	22/33	106
Jacke, Green Bay	28/29	23/30	97
Christie, Tampa Bay	27/27	23/27	96
Andersen, New Orleans	29/29	21/27	92
Lansford, L.A. Rams	42/43	15/24	87
Del Greco, Phoenix	31/31	17/27	82

Punters

	No	Yds	Long	Avg
Landeta, N.Y. Giants	75	3306	67	44.1
Saxon, Dallas	79	3413	62	43.2
Camarillo, Phoenix	67	2865	63	42.8
Barnhardt, New Orleans	70	2990	65	42.7
Newsome, Minnesota	78	3299	61	42.3
Feagles, Philadelphia	72	3026	60	42.0
Fulhage, Atlanta	70	2913	59	41.6
Arnold, Detroit	63	2560	59	40.6
Buford, Chicago	76	3073	59	40.4
Royals, Tampa Bay	72	2902	62	40.3

Sacks

	No		No		No
Haley, San Francisco	16.0	Doleman, Minnesota	11.0	Armstrong, Chicago	10.0
White, Philadelphia	14.0	Swilling, New Orleans	11.0	Cofer, Detroit	10.0
Greene, L.A. Rams	13.0	Taylor, N.Y. Giants	10.5	Harvey, Phoenix	10.0
Dent, Chicago	12.0				

American Football Conference

Passing

	Att	Comp	Pct comp	Yds	Avg gain	TD	Pct TD	Long	Int	Rating points
Kelly, Buffalo	346	219	63.3	2829	8.18	24	6.9	71	9	101.2
Moon, Houston	584	362	62.0	4689	8.03	33	5.7	87	13	96.8
Deberg, Kansas City	444	258	58.1	3444	7.76	23	5.2	90	4	96.3
Schroeder, L.A. Raiders	334	182	54.5	2849	8.53	19	5.7	68	9	90.8
Marino, Miami	531	306	57.6	3563	6.71	21	4.0	69	11	82.6
Brister, Pittsburgh	387	223	57.6	2725	7.04	20	5.2	90	14	81.6
Elway, Denver	502	294	58.6	3526	7.02	15	3.0	66	14	78.5
O'Brien, N.Y. Jets	411	226	55.0	2855	6.95	13	3.2	69	10	77.3
Esiason, Cincinnati	402	224	55.7	3031	7.54	24	6.0	53	22	77.0
George, Indiana	334	181	54.2	2152	6.44	16	4.8	75	13	73.8
Krieg, Seattle	448	265	59.2	3194	7.13	15	3.3	63	20	73.6
Tolliver, San Diego	410	216	52.7	2574	6.28	16	3.9	45	16	68.9
Kosar, Cleveland	423	230	54.4	2562	6.06	10	2.4	50	15	65.7
Wilson, New England	265	139	52.5	1625	6.13	6	2.3	36	11	61.6

Rushing

	Att	Yds	Avg	TD
Thomas, Buffalo	271	1297	4.8	11
Butts, San Diego	265	1225	4.6	8
Humphrey, Denver	288	1202	4.2	7
Word, Kansas City	204	1015	5.0	4
Brooks, Cincinnati	195	1004	5.1	5
Fenner, Seattle	215	859	4.0	14
Smith, Miami	226	831	3.7	8
Stephens, New England	212	808	3.8	2
Okoye, Kansas City	245	805	3.3	7
Hoge, Pittsburgh	203	772	3.8	7

Interceptions

	No	Yds	Long	TD
R. Johnson, Houston	8	100	35	1
Byrd, San Diego	7	63	24	0
Ross, Kansas City	5	97	40	0
McMillan, N.Y. Jets	5	92	25	0
Oliver, Miami	5	87	35	0
Williams, Miami	5	82	42	1
Woodson, Pittsburgh	5	67	34	0

Kickoff Returns

	No	Yds	Avg	TD
Clark, Denver	20	505	25.3	0
Elder, San Diego	24	571	23.8	0
Woodson, Pittsburgh	35	764	21.8	0
Warren, Seattle	23	478	20.8	0
Martin, New England	25	515	20.6	0
Holland, L.A. Raiders	32	655	20.5	0
McNeil, Houston	27	551	20.4	0
Metcalf, Cleveland	52	1052	20.2	2
Jennings, Cincinnati	29	584	20.1	0
D. Smith, Buffalo	32	643	20.1	0

Pass Receiving

	No	Yds	Avg	TD
Jeffires, Houston	74	1048	14.2	8
Hill, Houston	74	1019	13.8	5
Williams, Seattle	73	699	9.6	0
Givins, Houston	72	979	13.6	9
Reed, Buffalo	71	945	13.3	8
Bentley, Indiana	71	664	9.4	2
Duncan, Houston	66	785	11.9	1
Paige, Kansas City	65	1021	15.7	5
A. Miller, San Diego	63	933	14.8	7
Brooks, Indiana	62	823	13.3	5

Punt Returns

	No	Yds	Avg	TD
Verdin, Indiana	31	396	12.8	0
Woodson, Pittsburgh	38	398	10.5	1
Warren, Seattle	28	269	9.6	0
T. Brown, L.A. Raiders	34	295	8.7	0
Price, Cincinnati	29	251	8.7	1
Clark, Denver	21	159	7.6	0
Worthen, Kansas City	25	180	7.2	0
McNeil, Houston	30	172	5.7	0
Martin, Miami	26	140	5.4	0
Fryar, New England	28	133	4.8	0

Scoring-Touchdowns

	TD	Rush	Pass	Pts
Fenner, Seattle	15	14	1	90
Allen, L.A. Raiders	13	12	1	78
Thomas, Buffalo	13	11	2	78
White, Houston	12	8	4	72
Hoge, Pittsburgh	10	7	3	60
Brooks, Cincinnati	9	5	4	54
Brown, Cincinnati	9	0	9	54
Givins, Houston	9	0	9	54
Smith, Miami	9	8	1	54

Scoring-Kicking

	PAT	FG	Pts
Lowery, Kansas City	37/38	34/37	139
Norwood, Buffalo	50/52	20/29	110
Treadwell, Denver	34/36	25/34	109
Johnson, Seattle	33/34	23/32	102
Leahy, N.Y. Jets	32/32	23/26	101
Stoyanovich, Miami	37/37	21/25	100
Anderson, Pittsburgh	32/32	20/25	92
Breech, Cincinnati	41/44	17/21	92
Jaeger, L.A. Raiders	40/42	15/20	85
Carney, San Diego	27/28	19/21	84

Punters

	No	Yds	Long	Avg
Horan, Denver	58	2575	67	44.4
Stark, Indiana	71	3084	61	43.4
Johnson, Cincinnati	64	2705	70	42.3
Roby, Miami	72	3022	62	42.0
Hansen, New England	90	3752	69	41.7
Donnelly, Seattle	67	2722	54	40.6
Prokop, N.Y. Jets	59	2363	58	40.1
Kidd, San Diego	61	2442	59	40.0
Tuten, Buffalo	53	2107	55	39.8
Wagner, Cleveland	74	2879	65	38.9

Sacks

	No		No		No
D. Thomas, Kansas City	20.0	Green, Seattle	12.5	Cross, Miami	11.5
B. Smith, Buffalo	19.0	S. Jones, Houston	12.5	Perry, Cleveland	11.5
O'Neal, San Diego	13.5	Townsend, L.A. Raiders	12.5	Fletcher, Denver	11.0
Byrd, N.Y. Jets	13.0				

All-Time Professional Football Records

NFL and AFL

(at start of 1991 season)

Leading Lifetime Rushers

Player	League	Yrs	Att	Yards	Avg	Player	League	Yrs	Att	Yards	Avg
Walter Payton	NFL	13	3,838	16,726	4.4	Joe Perry	NFL	14	1,737	8,378	4.8
Tony Dorsett	NFL	12	2,936	12,739	4.3	Larry Csonka	AFL-NFL	11	1,891	8,081	4.3
Jim Brown	NFL	9	2,359	12,312	5.2	Marcus Allen	NFL	9	1,960	7,957	4.1
Franco Harris	NFL	13	2,949	12,120	4.1	Freeman McNeil	NFL	10	1,704	7,604	4.5
Eric Dickerson	NFL	8	2,616	11,903	4.6	Gerald Riggs	NFL	8	1,788	7,465	4.2
John Riggins	NFL	14	2,916	11,352	3.9	Mike Pruitt	NFL	11	1,844	7,378	4.0
O.J. Simpson	AFL-NFL	11	2,404	11,236	4.7	James Brooks	NFL	10	1,515	7,347	4.8
Ottis Anderson	NFL	12	2,499	10,101	4.0	Leroy Kelly	NFL	10	1,727	7,274	4.2
Earl Campbell	NFL	8	2,187	9,407	4.3	George Rogers	NFL	7	1,692	7,176	4.2
Jim Taylor	NFL	10	1,941	8,597	4.4	Roger Craig	NFL	8	1,686	7,064	4.2

Most Yards Gained, Season — 2,105, Eric Dickerson, Los Angeles Rams, 1984.
Most Yards Gained, Game — 275, Walter Payton, Chicago Bears vs. Minnesota Vikings, Nov. 20, 1977.
Most Games, 100 Yards or more, Season — 12, Eric Dickerson, Los Angeles Rams, 1984.
Most Games, 100 Yards or more, Career — 77, Walter Payton, Chicago Bears, 1975-87.
Most Touchdowns Rushing, Career — 110, Walter Payton, Chicago Bears, 1975-1987.
Most Touchdowns Rushing, Season — 24, John Riggins, Washington Redskins, 1983.
Most Touchdowns Rushing, Game — 6, Ernie Nevers, Chicago Cardinals vs. Chicago Bears, Nov. 8, 1929.
Most Rushing Attempts, Season — 407, James Wilder, Tampa Bay Buccaneers, 1984.
Most Rushing Attempts, Game — 45, Jamie Morris, Washington Redskins vs. Cincinnati Bengals, Dec. 17, 1988.
Longest run from Scrimmage — 99 yds., Tony Dorsett, Dallas vs. Minnesota, Jan. 3, 1983 (scored touchdown).

Leading Lifetime Passers

(Minimum 1,500 attempts)

Player	League	Yrs	Att	Comp	Yds	Pts*	Player	League	Yrs	Att	Comp	Yds	Pts*
Joe Montana	NFL	12	4,579	2,914	34,998	93.4	Jim Everett	NFL	5	2,038	1,154	15,345	82.2
Dan Marino	NFL	8	4,181	2,480	31,416	88.5	Ken Anderson	NFL	16	4,475	2,654	32,838	81.9
Boomer Esiason	NFL	7	2,687	1,520	21,381	85.8	Danny White	NFL	13	2,950	1,761	21,959	81.7
Jim Kelly	NFL	5	2,088	1,251	15,730	85.8	Bart Starr	NFL	16	3,149	1,808	24,718	80.5
Roger Staubach	NFL	11	2,958	1,685	22,700	83.4	Fran Tarkenton	NFL	18	6,467	3,686	47,003	80.4
Neil Lomax	NFL	8	3,153	1,817	22,771	82.7	Bernie Kosar	NFL	6	2,363	1,364	16,450	80.3
Sonny Jurgensen	NFL	18	4,262	2,433	32,224	82.6	Dan Fouts	NFL	15	5,604	3,294	43,040	80.2
Len Dawson	NFL-AFL	19	3,741	2,136	28,711	82.6	Warren Moon	NFL	7	3,025	1,701	22,989	79.9
Dave Krieg	NFL	11	3,291	4,909	24,052	82.3	Tony Eason	NFL	8	1,564	911	11,142	79.7
Ken O'Brien	NFL	7	2,878	1,697	20,444	82.2	Jim McMahon	NFL	9	1,840	1,056	13,398	79.3

*Rating points based on performances in the following categories: Percentage of completions, percentage of touchdown passes, percentage of interceptions, and average gain per pass attempt.

Most Yards Gained, Season — 5,084, Dan Marino, Miami Dolphins, 1984.
Most Yards Gained, Game — 554, Norm Van Brocklin, Los Angeles Rams vs. New York Yankees, Sept. 18, 1951 (27 completions in 41 attempts).
Most Touchdowns Passing, Career — 342, Fran Tarkenton, Minnesota Vikings, 1961-66; N.Y. Giants, 1967-71; Vikings, 1972-78.
Most Touchdown Passing, Season — 48, Dan Marino, Miami Dolphins, 1984.
Most Touchdown Passing, Game — 7, Sid Luckman, Chicago Bears vs. New York Giants, Nov. 14, 1943; Adrian Burk, Philadelphia Eagles vs. Washington Redskins, Oct. 17, 1954; George Blanda, Houston Oilers vs. New York Titans, Nov. 19, 1961; Y.A. Tittle, New York Giants vs. Washington Redskins, Oct. 28, 1962; Joe Kapp, Minnesota Vikings vs. Baltimore Colts, Sept. 28, 1969.
Most Passing Attempts, Season — 623, Dan Marino, Miami Dolphins, 1986.
Most Passing Attempts, Game — 68, George Blanda, Houston Oilers vs. Buffalo Bills, Nov. 1, 1964 (37 completions).
Most Passes Completed, Season — 378, Dan Marino, Miami Dolphins, 1986.
Most Passes Completed, Game — 42, Richard Todd, N.Y. Jets vs. San Francisco 49ers, Sept. 21, 1980.
Most Consecutive Passes Completed — 22, Joe Montana, S. F. vs. Cleveland, (5), Nov. 29, & Green Bay (17), Dec. 6, 1987.
Most Consecutive Games, Touchdown Passes — 47, John Unitas, Baltimore Colts, 1956-1960.

Leading Lifetime Receivers

Player	League	Yrs	No	Yds	Avg	Player	League	Yrs	No	Yds	Avg
Steve Largent	NFL	14	819	13,089	16.0	Harold Jackson	NFL	16	579	10,372	17.9
Charlie Joiner	NFL	18	750	12,146	16.2	Lionel Taylor	AFL	10	567	7,195	12.7
Art Monk	NFL	11	730	9,935	13.6	Wes Chandler	NFL	11	559	8,966	16.0
Ozzie Newsome	NFL	13	662	7,980	12.1	Stanley Morgan	NFL	14	557	10,716	19.2
Charley Taylor	NFL	13	649	9,110	14.0	J.T. Smith	NFL	13	544	6,974	12.8
James Lofton	NFL	13	633	11,834	18.7	Lance Alworth	AFL-NFL	11	542	10,266	18.9
Don Maynard	AFL-NFL	15	633	11,834	18.7	Kellen Winslow	NFL	9	541	6,741	12.5
Raymond Berry	NFL	13	631	9,275	14.7	John Stallworth	NFL	14	537	8,723	16.2
Harold Carmichael	NFL	14	590	8,985	15.2	Roy Green	NFL	12	522	8,496	16.3
Fred Biletnikoff	AFL-NFL	14	589	8,974	15.2	Bobby Mitchell	NFL	11	521	7,954	15.3

Most Yards Gained, Season — 1,746, Charley Hennigan, Houston Oilers, 1961.
Most Yards Gained, Game — 336, Willie Anderson, L.A. Rams vs. New Orleans, Nov. 26, 1989.
Most Pass Receptions, Season — 106, Art Monk, Washington Redskins, 1984.
Most Pass Receptions, Game — 18, Tom Fears, Los Angeles Rams vs. Green Bay Packers, Dec. 3, 1950 (189 yards).
Most Consecutive Games, Pass Receptions — 177, Steve Largent, Seattle Seahawks, 1976-1989.
Most Touchdown Passes, Career — 100, Steve Largent, Seattle Seahawks, 1976-1989.
Most Touchdown Passes, Season — 22, Jerry Rice, San Francisco 49ers, 1987.
Most Touchdown Passes, Game — 5, Bob Shaw, Chicago Cardinals vs. Baltimore Colts, Oct. 2, 1950; Kellen Winslow, San Diego vs. Oakland, Nov. 22, 1981; Jerry Rice, San Francisco vs. Atlanta, Oct. 14, 1990.

Leading Lifetime Scorers

Player	League	Yrs	TD	PAT	FG	Total	Player	League	Yrs	TD	PAT	FG	Total
George Blanda	NFL-AFL	26	9	943	335	2,002	Gino Cappelletti	AFL	11	42	350	176	1,130
Jan Stenerud	AFL-NFL	19	0	580	373	1,699	Ray Wersching	NFL	15	0	456	222	1,122
Jim Turner	AFL-NFL	16	1	521	304	1,439	Don Cockroft	NFL	13	0	432	216	1,080
Mark Moseley	NFL	16	0	482	300	1,382	Garo Yepremian	AFL-NFL	14	0	444	210	1,074
Jim Bakken	NFL	17	0	534	282	1,380	Jim Breech	NFL	12	0	459	201	1,062
Fred Cox	NFL	15	0	519	282	1,365	Bruce Gossett	NFL	11	0	374	219	1,031
Pat Leahy	NFL	17	0	278	528	1,362	Eddie Murray	NFL	11	0	341	225	1,016
Lou Groza	NFL	17	1	641	234	1,349	Sam Baker	NFL	15	2	428	179	977
Chris Bahr	NFL	14	0	490	241	1,213	Matt Bahr	NFL	12	0	378	199	975
Nick Lowery	NFL	12	0	375	259	1,152	Rafael Septien	NFL	10	0	420	180	960

Most Points, Season — 176, Paul Hornung, Green Bay Packers, 1960 (15 TD's, 41 PAT's, 15 FG's).
Most Points, Game — 40, Ernie Nevers, Chicago Cardinals vs. Chicago Bears, Nov. 28, 1929 (6 TD's, 4 PAT's).
Most Touchdowns, Season — 24, John Riggins, Washington Redskins, 1984 (24 rushing).
Most Touchdowns, Game — 6, Ernie Nevers, Chicago Cardinals vs. Chicago Bears, Nov. 28, 1929 (6 rushing); Dub Jones, Cleveland Browns vs. Chicago Bears, Nov. 25, 1951 (4 rushing, 2 pass receptions); Gale Sayers, Chicago Bears vs. San Francisco 49ers, Dec. 12, 1965 (4 rushing, 1 pass reception, 1 punt return).
Most Points After Touchdown, Season — 66, Uwe von Schamann, Miami Dolphins, 1984.
Most Consecutive Points After Touchdown — 234, Tommy Davis, San Francisco 49ers, 1959-1969.
Most Field Goals, Game — 7, Jim Bakken, St. Louis Cardinals vs. Pittsburgh Steelers, Sept. 24, 1967; Rich Karlis, Minn. Vikings vs. L.A. Rams, Nov. 5, 1989.
Most Field Goals, Season — 35, Ali Haji-Sheikh, N.Y. Giants, 1983.
Most Field Goals Attempted, Season — 49, Bruce Gossett, Los Angeles Rams, 1966; Curt Knight, Washington Redskins, 1971.
Most Field Goals Attempted, Game — 9, Jim Bakken, St. Louis Cardinals vs. Pittsburgh Steelers, Sept. 24, 1967 (7 successful).
Most Consecutive Field Goals — 24, Kevin Butler, Chicago Bears, 1988-1989.
Most Consecutive Games, Field Goal — 31, Fred Cox, Minnesota Vikings, 1968-1970.
Longest Field Goal — 63 yds., Tom Dempsey, New Orleans Saints vs. Detroit Lions, Nov. 8, 1970.
Highest Field Goal Completion Percentage, Season (20 attempts) — 95.24 Mark Moseley, Washington Redskins, 1982; Eddie Murray, Detroit Lions, 1988 & 1989 (20 FG's in 21 attempts).

Pass Interceptions

Most Passes Had Intercepted, Game — 8, Jim Hardy, Chicago Cardinals vs. Philadelphia Eagles, Sept. 24, 1950 (39 attempts)
Most Passes Had Intercepted, Season — 42, George Blanda, Houston Oilers, 1962 (418 attempts).
Most Passes Had Intercepted, Career — 277, George Blanda, Chicago Bears, 1949-1958; Houston Oilers, 1960-1966; Oakland Raiders, 1967-1975 (4,000 attempts).
Most Consecutive Passes Attempted Without Interception — 294, Bart Starr, Green Bay Packers, 1964-1965.
Most Interceptions By, Season — 14, Dick Lane, Los Angeles Rams, 1952.
Most Interceptions By, Career — 81, Paul Krause, Washington Redskins, 1964-67; Minnesota Vikings, 1968-79.
Most Consecutive Games, Passes Intercepted By — 8, Tom Morrow, Oakland Raiders, 1962 (4), 1963 (4).

Punting

Most Punts, Game — 15, John Teltschick, Philadelphia Eagles vs. N.Y. Giants, Dec. 6, 1987.
Most Punts, Career — 1,154, Dave Jennings, N.Y. Giants, 1974-1984; N.Y. Jets, 1985-1987.
Most Punts, Season — 114, Bob Parsons, Chicago Bears, 1981.
Highest Punting Average, Season (20 punts) — 51.40, Sam Baugh, Washington Redskins, 1940 (35 punts).
Longest Punt — 98 yds., Steve O'Neal, New York Jets vs. Denver Broncos, Sept. 21, 1969.

Kickoff Returns

Most Yardage Returning Kickoffs, Career — 6,922, Ron Smith, Chicago Bears, 1965; Atlanta Falcons, 1966-67; Los Angeles Rams, 1968-69; Chicago Bears, 1970-72; San Diego Chargers, 1973; Oakland Raiders, 1974.
Most Yardage Returning Kickoffs, Season — 1,345, Buster Rhymes, Minnesota Vikings, 1985.
Most Yardage Returning Kickoffs, Game — 294, Wally Triplett, Detroit Lions vs. Los Angeles Rams, Oct. 29, 1950 (4 returns).
Most Touchdowns Scored via Kickoff Returns, Career — 6, Ollie Matson, Chicago Cardinals, 1952 (2), 1954, 1956, 1958 (2); Gale Sayers, Chicago Bears, 1965, 1966 (2), 1967 (3); Travis Williams, Green Bay Packers, 1967 (4), 1969; Los Angeles Rams, 1971.
Most Touchdowns Scored via Kickoff Returns, Game — 2, Tim Brown, Philadelphia Eagles vs. Dallas Cowboys, Nov. 6, 1966; Travis Williams, Green Bay Packers vs. Cleveland Browns, Nov. 12, 1967; Ron Brown, Los Angeles Rams vs. Green Bay Packers, Nov. 24, 1985.
Most Kickoff Returns, Career — 275, Ron Smith, Chicago Bears, 1965; Atlanta Falcons, 1966-67; Los Angeles Rams, 1968-69; Chicago Bears, 1970-72; San Diego Chargers, 1973; Oakland Raiders, 1974.
Most Kickoff Returns, Season — 60, Drew Hill, Los Angeles Rams, 1981.
Longest Kickoff Return — 106 yds., Al Carmichael, Green Bay Packers vs. Chicago Bears, October 7, 1956; Noland Smith, Kansas City vs. Denver, Dec. 17, 1967; Roy Green, St. Louis Cardinals vs. Dallas Cowboys, Oct. 21, 1979 (all scored TD).

Punt Returns

Most Yardage Returning Punts, Career — 3,317, Billy Johnson, Houston, 1974-80, Atlanta, 1982-87, Washington, 1988.
Most Yardage Returning Punts, Season — 692, Fulton Walker, Miami-L.A. Raiders, 1985.
Most Yardage Returning Punts, Game — 207, Leroy Irvin, Los Angeles Rams vs. Atlanta Falcons, Oct. 11. 1981.
Most Touchdowns Scored via Punt Returns, Career — 8, Jack Christiansen, Detroit Lions, 1951-1958; Rick Upchurch, Denver Broncos, 1975-83.
Most Punt Returns, Career — 282, Billy Johnson, Houston Oilers, 1974-1980; Atlanta Falcons, 1982-1987, Washington, 1988.
Most Punt Returns, Season — 70, Danny Reece, Tampa Bay Buccaneers, 1979.

Miscellaneous Records

Most Fumbles, Season — 18, Dave Krieg, Seattle Seahawks, 1989; Warren Moon, Houston Oilers, 1990.
Most Fumbles, Game — 7, Len Dawson, Kansas City Chiefs vs. San Diego Chargers, Nov. 15, 1964.
Most Sacks, Career—114.5, Lawrence Taylor, N.Y. Giants, 1982-90.
Most Sacks, Season—22, Mark Gastineau, N.Y. Jets, 1984.
Most Seasons, Active Player — 26, George Blanda, Chicago Bears, 1949-1958; Houston Oilers, 1960-1966 and Oakland, 67-75.
Most Consecutive Games Played, Career — 282, Jim Marshall, Cleveland Browns, 1960; Minnesota Vikings, 1961-1979.

World Almanac All-Pro Team in 1990

Chosen by a panel of sports experts representing the World Almanac, its co-sponsoring newspapers, and its publisher, Pharos Books.

First team	Offense	Second team
Jerry Rice, San Francisco	Wide receiver	Andre Reed, Buffalo
Andre Rison, Atlanta	Wide receiver	Sterling Sharpe, Green Bay
Keith Jackson, Philadelphia	Tight end	Rodney Holman, Cincinnati
Anthony Munoz, Cincinnati	Tackle	Lomas Brown, Detroit
Jim Lachey, Washington	Tackle	Bruce Armstrong, New England
Mark Bortz, Chicago	Guard	Randall McDaniel, Minnesota
Bruce Matthews, Houston	Guard	Steve Wisniewski, L.A. Raiders
Kent Hill, Buffalo	Center	Don Mosebar, L.A. Raiders
Joe Montana, San Francisco	Quarterback	Jim Kelly, Buffalo
Barry Sanders, Detroit	Running back	Neal Anderson, Chicago
Thurman Thomas, Buffalo	Running back	Marion Butts, San Diego
Nick Lowery, Kansas City	Placekicker	John Carney, San Diego

First team	Defense	Second team
Bruce Smith, Buffalo	End	Jeff Cross, Miami
Greg Townsend, L.A. Raiders	End	Chris Doleman, Minnesota
Michael Dean Perry, Cleveland	Nose tackle	Dan Saleaumua, Kansas City
Reggie White, Philadelphia	Tackle	Ray Childress, Houston
John Offerdahl, Miami	Inside linebacker	Byron Evans, Philadelphia
Pepper Johnson, N.Y. Giants	Inside linebacker	Vaughn Johnson, New Orleans
Charles Haley, San Francisco	Outside linebacker	Mike Cofer, Detroit
Derrick Thomas, Kansas City	Outside linebacker	Leslie O'Neal, San Diego
Albert Lewis, Kansas City	Cornerback	Tim McKyer, Miami
Rod Woodson, Pittsburgh	Cornerback	Gill Byrd, San Diego
Joey Browner, Minnesota	Safety	Tim McDonald, Phoenix
Ronnie Lott, San Francisco	Safety	Steve Atwater, Denver
Sean Landeta, N.Y. Giants	Punter	Rohn Stark, Indianapolis

NFL Stadiums

Name, location	Capacity	Name, location	Capacity
Anaheim Stadium, Anaheim, Cal.	69,007	Metrodome, Minneapolis	63,000
Arrowhead Stadium, Kansas City, Mo.	78,067	Mile High Stadium, Denver, Col.	76,273
Astrodome, Houston, Tex.	60,502	Milwaukee County Stadium	56,051
Atlanta-Fulton County Stadium	59,673	Pontiac Silverdome, Mich.	80,500
Candlestick Park, San Francisco, Cal.	65,729	Rich Stadium, Buffalo, N.Y.	80,290
Cleveland Stadium	80,098	Riverfront Stadium, Cincinnati, Oh.	59,754
Foxboro Stadium, Mass.	60,794	Joe Robbie Stadium, Miami, Fla.	75,000
Giants Stadium, E. Rutherford, N.J.	76,891	San Diego Jack Murphy Stadium, San Diego	60,750
Hoosier Dome, Indianapolis, Ind.	60,127	Soldier Field, Chicago, Ill.	66,949
Robert F. Kennedy Stadium, Wash., D.C.	55,672	Sun Devil Stadium, Tempe, Ariz.	72,000
Kingdome, Seattle, Wash.	64,984	Tampa Stadium, Tampa, Fla.	74,314
Lambeau Field, Green Bay, Wis.	59,543	Texas Stadium, Irving, Tex.	65,024
Los Angeles Memorial Coliseum	92,488	Three Rivers Stadium, Pittsburgh, Pa.	59,000
Louisiana Superdome, New Orleans	69,065	Veterans Stadium, Philadelphia, Pa.	65,356

American Football League

Year	Eastern Division	Western Division	Playoff
1960	Houston Oilers (10-4-0)	L. A. Chargers (10-4-0)	Houston 24, Los Angeles 16
1961	Houston Oilers (10-3-1)	San Diego Chargers (12-2-0)	Houston 10, San Diego 3
1962	Houston Oilers (11-3-0)	Dallas Texans (11-3-0)	Dallas 20, Houston 17(b)
1963	Boston Patriots (8-6-1)(a)	San Diego Chargers (11-3-0)	San Diego 51, Boston 10
1964	Buffalo Bills (12-2-0)	San Diego Chargers (8-5-1)	Buffalo 20, San Diego 7
1965	Buffalo Bills (10-3-1)	San Diego Chargers (9-2-3)	Buffalo 23, San Diego 0
1966	Buffalo Bills (9-4-1)	Kansas City Chiefs (11-2-1)	Kansas City 31, Buffalo 7
1967	Houston Oilers (9-4-1)	Oakland Raiders (13-1-0)	Oakland 40, Houston 7
1968	New York Jets (11-3-0)	Oakland Raiders (12-2-0)(a)	New York 27, Oakland 23
1969	New York Jets (10-4-0)	Oakland Raiders (12-1-1)	Kansas City 17, Oakland 7(c)

(a) won divisional playoff (b) won at 2:45 of second overtime. (c) Kansas City defeated Jets to make playoffs.

Canadian Football League Championships (Grey Cup)

1956	Edmonton Eskimos 50, Montreal Alouettes 27	1974	Montreal Alouettes 20, Edmonton Eskimos 7
1957	Hamilton Tiger-Cats 32, Winnipeg Blue Bombers 7	1975	Edmonton Eskimos 9, Montreal Alouettes 8
1958	Winnipeg Blue Bombers 35, Hamilton Tiger-Cats 28	1976	Ottawa Rough Riders 23, Saskatchewan Roughriders 20
1959	Winnipeg Blue Bombers 21, Hamilton Tiger-Cats 7	1977	Montreal Alouettes 41, Edmonton Eskimos 6
1960	Ottawa Rough Riders 16, Edmonton Eskimos 6	1978	Edmonton Eskimos 20, Montreal Alouettes 13
1961	Winnipeg Blue Bombers 21, Hamilton Tiger-Cats 14	1979	Edmonton Eskimos 17, Montreal Alouettes 9
1962	Winnipeg Blue Bombers 28, Hamilton Tiger-Cats 27	1980	Edmonton Eskimos 48, Hamilton Tiger-Cats 10
1963	Hamilton Tiger-Cats 21, British Columbia Lions 10	1981	Edmonton Eskimos 26, Ottawa Rough Riders 23
1964	British Columbia Lions 34, Hamilton Tiger-Cats 24	1982	Edmonton Eskimos 32, Toronto Argonauts 16
1965	Hamilton Tiger-Cats 22, Winnipeg Blue Bombers 16	1983	Toronto Argonauts 18, B.C. Lions 17
1966	Saskatchewan Roughriders 29, Ottawa Rough Riders 14	1984	Winnipeg Blue Bombers 47, Hamilton Tiger-Cats 17
1967	Hamilton Tiger-Cats 24, Saskatchewan Roughriders 1	1985	B.C. Lions 37, Hamilton Tiger-Cats 24
1968	Ottawa Rough Riders 24, Calgary Stampeders 21	1986	Hamilton Tiger-Cats 39, Edmonton Eskimos 15
1969	Ottawa Rough Riders 29, Saskatchewan Roughriders 11	1987	Edmonton Eskimos 38, Toronto Argonauts 36
1970	Montreal Alouettes 23, Calgary Stampeders 10	1988	Winnipeg Blue Bombers 22, B.C. Lions 21
1971	Calgary Stampeders 14, Toronto Argonauts 11	1989	Saskatchewan Roughriders 43, Hamilton Tiger-Cats 40
1972	Hamilton Tiger-Cats 13, Saskatchewan Roughriders 10	1990	Winnipeg Blue Bombers 50, Edmonton Eskimos 11
1973	Ottawa Rough Riders 22, Edmonton Eskimos 18		

COLLEGE FOOTBALL
Annual Results of Major Bowl Games
(Note: Dates indicate the year that the game was played.)

Rose Bowl, Pasadena

1902 Michigan 49, Stanford 0	1942 Oregon St. 20, Duke 16	1967 Purdue 14, So. California 13
1916 Wash. State 14, Brown 0	(at Durham)	1968 Southern Cal. 14, Indiana 3
1917 Oregon 14, Pennsylvania 0	1943 Georgia 9, UCLA 0	1969 Ohio State 27, Southern Cal 16
1918-19 Service teams	1944 So. California 29, Washington 0	1970 Southern Cal 10, Michigan 3
1920 Harvard 7, Oregon 6	1945 So. California 25, Tennessee 0	1971 Stanford 27, Ohio State 17
1921 California 28, Ohio State 0	1946 Alabama 34, So. California 14	1972 Stanford 13, Michigan 12
1922 Wash. & Jeff. 0, California 0	1947 Illinois 45, UCLA 14	1973 So. California 42, Ohio State 17
1923 So. California 14, Penn State 3	1948 Michigan 49, So. California 0	1974 Ohio State 42, So. California 21
1924 Navy 14, Washington 14	1949 Northwestern 20, California 14	1975 So. California 18, Ohio State 17
1925 Notre Dame 27, Stanford 10	1950 Ohio State 17, California 14	1976 UCLA 23, Ohio State 10
1926 Alabama 20, Washington 19	1951 Michigan 14, California 6	1977 So. California 14, Michigan 6
1927 Alabama 7, Stanford 7	1952 Illinois 40, Stanford 7	1978 Washington 27, Michigan 20
1928 Stanford 7, Pittsburgh 6	1953 So. California 7, Wisconsin 0	1979 So. California 17, Michigan 10
1929 Georgia Tech 8, California 7	1954 Mich. State 28, UCLA 20	1980 So. California 17, Ohio State 16
1930 So. California 47, Pittsburgh 14	1955 Ohio State 20, So. California 7	1981 Michigan 23, Washington 6
1931 Alabama 24, Wash. State 0	1956 Mich. State 17, UCLA 14	1982 Washington 28, Iowa 0
1932 So. California 21, Tulane 12	1957 Iowa 35, Oregon St. 19	1983 UCLA 24, Michigan 14
1933 So. California 35, Pittsburgh 0	1958 Ohio State 10, Oregon 7	1984 UCLA 45, Illinois 9
1934 Columbia 7, Stanford 0	1959 Iowa 38, California 12	1985 So. California 20, Ohio State 17
1935 Alabama 29, Stanford 13	1960 Washington 44, Wisconsin 8	1986 UCLA 45, Iowa 28
1936 Stanford 7, So. Methodist 0	1961 Washington 17, Minnesota 7	1987 Arizona St. 22, Michigan 15
1937 Pittsburgh 21, Washington 0	1962 Minnesota 21, UCLA 3	1988 Mich. State 20, Southern Cal. 17
1938 California 13, Alabama 0	1963 So. California 42, Wisconsin 37	1989 Michigan 22, Southern Cal. 14
1939 So. California 7, Duke 3	1964 Illinois 17, Washington 7	1990 Southern Cal. 17, Michigan 10
1940 So. California 14, Tennessee 0	1965 Michigan 34, Oregon St. 7	1991 Washington 46, Iowa 34
1941 Stanford 21, Nebraska 13	1966 UCLA 14, Mich. State 12	

Orange Bowl, Miami

1935 Bucknell 26, Miami (Fla.) 0	1954 Oklahoma 7, Maryland 0	1973 Nebraska 40, Notre Dame 6
1936 Catholic U. 20, Mississippi 19	1955 Duke 34, Nebraska 7	1974 Penn State 16, Louisiana St. 9
1937 Duquesne 13, Miss. State 12	1956 Oklahoma 20, Maryland 6	1975 Notre Dame 13, Alabama 11
1938 Auburn 6, Mich. State 0	1957 Colorado 27, Clemson 21	1976 Oklahoma 14, Michigan 6
1939 Tennessee 17, Oklahoma 0	1958 Oklahoma 48, Duke 21	1977 Ohio State 27, Colorado 10
1940 Georgia Tech 21, Missouri 7	1959 Oklahoma 21, Syracuse 6	1978 Arkansas 31, Oklahoma 6
1941 Miss. State 14, Georgetown 7	1960 Georgia 14, Missouri 0	1979 Oklahoma 31, Nebraska 24
1942 Georgia 40, TCU 26	1961 Missouri 21, Navy 14	1980 Oklahoma 24, Florida St. 7
1943 Alabama 37, Boston Col. 21	1962 LSU 25, Colorado 7	1981 Oklahoma 18, Florida St. 17
1944 LSU 19, Texas A&M 14	1963 Alabama 17, Oklahoma 0	1982 Clemson 22, Nebraska 15
1945 Tulsa 26, Georgia Tech 12	1964 Nebraska 13, Auburn 7	1983 Nebraska 21, Louisiana St. 20
1946 Miami (Fla.) 13, Holy Cross 6	1965 Texas 21, Alabama 17	1984 Miami (Fla.) 31, Nebraska 30
1947 Rice 8, Tennessee 0	1966 Alabama 39, Nebraska 28	1985 Washington 28, Oklahoma 17
1948 Georgia Tech 20, Kansas 14	1967 Florida 27, Georgia Tech 12	1986 Oklahoma 25, Penn State 10
1949 Texas 41, Georgia 28	1968 Oklahoma 26, Tennessee 24	1987 Oklahoma 42, Arkansas 8
1950 Santa Clara 21, Kentucky 13	1969 Penn State 15, Kansas 14	1988 Miami (Fla.) 20, Oklahoma 14
1951 Clemson 15, Miami (Fla.) 14	1970 Penn State 10, Missouri 3	1989 Miami (Fla.) 23, Nebraska 3
1952 Georgia Tech 17, Baylor 14	1971 Nebraska 17, Louisiana St. 12	1990 Notre Dame 21, Colorado 6
1953 Alabama 61, Syracuse 6	1972 Nebraska 38, Alabama 6	1991 Colorado 10, Notre Dame 9

Sugar Bowl, New Orleans

1935 Tulane 20, Temple 14	1955 Navy 21, Mississippi 0	1973 Notre Dame 24, Alabama 23
1936 TCU 3, LSU 2	1956 Georgia Tech 7, Pittsburgh 0	1974 Nebraska 13, Florida 10
1937 Santa Clara 21, LSU 14	1957 Baylor 13, Tennessee 7	1975 Alabama 13, Penn State 6
1938 Santa Clara 6, LSU 0	1958 Mississippi 39, Texas 7	1977 (Jan.) Pittsburgh 27, Georgia 3
1939 TCU 15, Carnegie Tech 7	1959 LSU 7, Clemson 0	1978 Alabama 35, Ohio State 6
1940 Texas A&M 14, Tulane 13	1960 Mississippi 21, LSU 0	1979 Alabama 14, Penn State 7
1941 Boston Col. 19, Tennessee 13	1961 Mississippi 14, Rice 6	1980 Alabama 24, Arkansas 9
1942 Fordham 2, Missouri 0	1962 Alabama 10, Arkansas 3	1981 Georgia 17, Notre Dame 10
1943 Tennessee 14, Tulsa 7	1963 Mississippi 17, Arkansas 13	1982 Pittsburgh 24, Georgia 20
1944 Georgia Tech 20, Tulsa 18	1964 Alabama 12, Mississippi 7	1983 Penn State 27, Georgia 23
1945 Duke 29, Alabama 26	1965 LSU 13, Syracuse 10	1984 Auburn 9, Michigan 7
1946 Oklahoma A&M 33, St. Mary's 13	1966 Missouri 20, Florida 18	1985 Nebraska 28, Louisiana St. 10
1947 Georgia 20, No. Carolina 10	1967 Alabama 34, Nebraska 7	1986 Tennessee 35, Miami (Fla.) 7
1948 Texas 27, Alabama 7	1968 LSU 20, Wyoming 13	1987 Nebraska 30, Louisiana St. 15
1949 Oklahoma 14, No. Carolina 6	1969 Arkansas 16, Georgia 2	1988 Syracuse 16, Auburn 16
1950 Oklahoma 35, LSU 0	1970 Mississippi 27, Arkansas 22	1989 Florida St. 13, Auburn 7
1951 Kentucky 13, Oklahoma 7	1971 Tennessee 34, Air Force 13	1990 Miami 33, Alabama 25
1952 Maryland 28, Tennessee 13	1972 Oklahoma 40, Auburn 22	1991 Tennessee 23, Virginia 22
1953 Georgia Tech. 24, Mississippi 7	*1972 (Dec.) Okla. 14, Penn State 0	* Penn St. awarded game by forfeit
1954 Georgia Tech 42, West Virginia 19		

Fiesta Bowl, Tempe

1971 Arizona St. 45, Florida St. 38	1978 UCLA 10, Arkansas 10	1986 Michigan 27, Nebraska 23
1972 Arizona St. 49, Missouri 35	1979 Pittsburgh 16, Arizona 10	1987 Penn St. 14, Miami (Fla.) 10
1973 Arizona St. 28, Pittsburgh 7	1980 Penn St. 31, Ohio St. 19	1988 Florida St. 31, Nebraska 28
1974 Okla. St. 16, Brigham Young 6	1982 (Jan.) Penn St. 26, USC 10	1989 Notre Dame 34, W. Virginia 21
1975 Arizona St. 17, Nebraska 14	1983 Arizona St. 32, Oklahoma 21	1990 Florida St. 41, Nebraska 17
1976 Oklahoma 41, Wyoming 7	1984 Ohio State 28, Pittsburgh 23	1991 Louisville 34, Alabama 7
1977 Penn St. 42, Arizona St. 30	1985 UCLA 39, Miami 37	

Hall of Fame Bowl, Tampa

1986 (Dec.) Boston Coll. 27, Georgia 24	1989 Syracuse 23, LSU 10	1991 Clemson 30, Illinois 0
1988 (Jan.) Michigan 28, Alabama 24	1990 Auburn 31, Ohio St. 14	

Cotton Bowl, Dallas

1937 TCU 16, Marquette 6
1938 Rice 28, Colorado 14
1939 St. Mary's 20, Texas Tech 13
1940 Clemson 6, Boston Col. 3
1941 Texas A&M 13, Fordham 12
1942 Alabama 29, Texas A&M 21
1943 Texas 14, Georgia Tech 7
1944 Randolph Field 7, Texas 7
1945 Oklahoma A&M 34, TCU 0
1946 Texas 40, Missouri 27
1947 Arkansas 0, LSU 0
1948 So. Methodist 13, Penn State 13
1949 So. Methodist 21, Oregon 13
1950 Rice 27, No. Carolina 13
1951 Tennessee 20, Texas 14
1952 Kentucky 20, TCU 7
1953 Texas 16, Tennessee 0
1954 Rice 28, Alabama 6
1955 Georgia Tech 14, Arkansas 6

1956 Mississippi 14, TCU 13
1957 TCU 28, Syracuse 27
1958 Navy 20, Rice 7
1959 TCU 0, Air Force 0
1960 Syracuse 23, Texas 14
1961 Duke 7, Arkansas 6
1962 Texas 12, Mississippi 7
1963 LSU 13, Texas 0
1964 Texas 28, Navy 6
1965 Arkansas 10, Nebraska 7
1966 LSU 14, Arkansas 7
1967 Georgia 24, So. Methodist 9
1968 Texas A&M 20, Alabama 16
1969 Texas 36, Tennessee 13
1970 Texas 21, Notre Dame 17
1971 Notre Dame 24, Texas 11
1972 Penn State 30, Texas 6
1973 Texas 17, Alabama 13

1974 Nebraska 19, Texas 3
1975 Penn State 41, Baylor 20
1976 Arkansas 31, Georgia 10
1977 Houston 30, Maryland 21
1978 Notre Dame 38, Texas 10
1979 Notre Dame 35, Houston 34
1980 Houston 17, Nebraska 14
1981 Alabama 30, Baylor 2
1982 Texas 14, Alabama 12
1983 SMU 7, Pittsburgh 3
1984 Georgia 10, Texas 9
1985 Boston Coll. 45, Houston 28
1986 Texas A&M 36, Auburn 16
1987 Ohio St. 28, Texas A&M 12
1988 Texas A&M 35, Notre Dame 10
1989 UCLA 17, Arkansas 3
1990 Tennessee 31, Arkansas 27
1991 Miami (Fla.) 46, Texas 3

John Hancock Bowl, El Paso (Sun Bowl until 1989)

1936 Hardin Simmons 14, New Mex.
    St. 14
1937 Hardin-Simmons 34, Texas Mines 6
1938 West Virginia 7, Texas Tech 6
1939 Utah 26, New Mexico 0
1940 Catholic U. 0, Arizona St. 0
1941 Western Reserve 26, Arizona St. 13
1942 Tulsa 6, Texas Tech 0
1943 2d Air Force 13, Hardin-Simmons 7
1944 Southwestern (Tex.) 7,
    New Mexico 0
1945 Southwestern (Tex.) 35, U. of
    Mex. 0
1946 New Mexico 34, Denver 24
1947 Cincinnati 18, Virginia Tech 6
1948 Miami (O.) 13, Texas Tech 12
1949 West Virginia 21, Texas Mines 12
1950 Texas Western 33, Georgetown 20
1951 West Texas St. 14, Cincinnati 13
1952 Texas Tech 25, Col. Pacific 14
1953 Col. Pacific 26, Miss. Southern 7

1954 Texas Western 37, Miss.
    Southern 14
1955 Texas Western 47, Florida St. 20
1956 Wyoming 21, Texas Tech 14
1957 Geo. Washington 13, Tex.
    Western 0
1958 Louisville 34, Drake 20
1959 Wyoming 14, Hardin-Simmons 6
1960 New Mexico St. 28, No. Texas St. 8
1961 New Mexico St. 20, Utah State 13
1962 Villanova 17, Wichita 9
1963 West Texas St. 15, Ohio U. 14
1964 Oregon 21, So. Methodist 14
1965 Georgia 7, Texas Tech 0
1966 Texas Western 13, TCU 12
1967 Wyoming 28, Florida St. 20
1968 UTex El Paso 14, Mississippi 7
1969 Auburn 34, Arizona 10
1969 (Dec.) Nebraska 45, Georgia 6
1970 Georgia Tech. 17, Texas Tech. 9

1971 LSU 33, Iowa State 15
1972 North Carolina 32, Texas Tech 28
1973 Missouri 34, Auburn 17
1974 Mississippi St. 26, No. Carolina 24
1975 Pittsburgh 33, Kansas 19
1977 (Jan.) Texas A&M 37, Florida 14
1977 (Dec.) Stanford 24, Louisiana St. 14
1978 Texas 42, Maryland 0
1979 Washington 14, Texas 7
1980 Nebraska 31, Mississippi St. 17
1981 Oklahoma 40, Houston 14
1982 North Carolina 26, Texas 10
1983 Alabama 28, SMU 7
1984 Maryland 28, Tennessee 27
1985 Georgia 13, Arizona 13
1986 Alabama 28, Washington 6
1987 Oklahoma St. 35, West Virginia 33
1988 Alabama 29, Army 28
1989 Pittsburgh 31, Texas A&M 28
1990 Michigan St. 17, USC 16

Gator Bowl, Jacksonville

1946 Wake Forest 26, So. Carolina 14
1947 Oklahoma 34, N.C. State 13
1948 Maryland 20, Georgia 20
1949 Clemson 24, Missouri 23
1950 Maryland 20, Missouri 7
1951 Wyoming 20, Wash. & Lee 7
1952 Miami (Fla.) 14, Clemson 0
1953 Florida 14, Tulsa 13
1954 Texas Tech 35, Auburn 13
1955 Auburn 33, Baylor 13
1956 Vanderbilt 25, Auburn 13
1957 Georgia Tech 21, Pittsburgh 14
1958 Tennessee 3, Texas A&M 0
1959 Mississippi 7, Florida 3
1960 Arkansas 14, Georgia Tech 7
1961 Florida 13, Baylor 12

1962 Penn State 30, Georgia Tech 15
1963 Florida 17, Penn State 7
1964 No. Carolina 35, Air Force 0
1965 Florida St. 36, Oklahoma 19
1966 Georgia Tech 31, Texas Tech 21
1967 Tennessee 18, Syracuse 12
1968 Penn State 17, Florida St. 17
1969 Missouri 35, Alabama 10
1969 (Dec.) Florida 14, Tenn. 13
1971 (Jan.) Auburn 35, Mississippi 28
1972 Georgia 7, N. Carolina 3
1973 Auburn 24, Colorado 3
1973 (Dec.) Tex. Tech. 28, Tenn. 19
1974 Auburn 27, Texas 3
1975 Maryland 13, Florida 0

1976 Notre Dame 20, Penn State 9
1977 Pittsburgh 34, Clemson 3
1978 Clemson 17, Ohio State 15
1979 No. Carolina 17, Michigan 15
1980 Pittsburgh 37, So. Carolina 9
1981 No. Carolina 31, Arkansas 27
1982 Florida St. 31, West Va. 12
1983 Florida 14, Iowa 6
1984 Oklahoma St. 21, So. Carolina 14
1985 Florida St. 34, Oklahoma St. 23
1986 Clemson 27, Stanford 21
1987 LSU 30, So. Carolina 13
1989 (Jan.) Georgia 34, Michigan St. 27
1989 (Dec.) Clemson 27, W. Va. 7
1991 (Jan.) Michigan 35, Mississippi 3

Liberty Bowl, Memphis

1959 Penn State 7, Alabama 0
1960 Penn State 41, Oregon 12
1961 Syracuse 15, Miami 14
1962 Oregon State 6, Villanova 0
1963 Miss. State 16, N.C. State 12
1964 Utah 32, West Virginia 6
1965 Mississippi 13, Auburn 7
1966 Miami (Fla.) 14, Va. Tech 7
1967 N.C. State 14, Georgia 7
1968 Mississippi 34, Va. Tech 17
1969 Colorado 47, Alabama 33

1970 Tulane 17, Colorado 3
1971 Tennessee 14, Arkansas 13
1972 Georgia Tech 31, Iowa State 30
1973 No. Carolina St. 31, Kansas 18
1974 Tennessee 7, Maryland 3
1975 USC 20, Texas A&M 0
1976 Alabama 36, UCLA 6
1977 Nebraska 21, N. Carolina 17
1978 Missouri 20, Louisiana St. 15
1979 Penn St. 9, Tulane 6
1980 Purdue 28, Missouri 25

1981 Ohio State 31, Navy 28
1982 Alabama 21, Illinois 15
1983 Notre Dame 19, Boston Coll. 18
1984 Auburn 21, Arkansas 15
1985 Baylor 21, Louisiana St. 7
1986 Tennessee 21, Minnesota 14
1987 Georgia 20, Arkansas 17
1988 Indiana 34, S. Carolina 10
1989 Mississippi 42, Air Force 29
1990 Air Force 23, Ohio State 11

Freedom Bowl, Anaheim

1984 Iowa 55, Texas 17
1985 Washington 20, Colorado 17
1986 UCLA 31, Brigham Young 10

1987 Arizona St. 33, Air Force 28
1988 Brigham Young 20, Colorado 17

1989 Washington 34, Florida 7
1990 Colorado St. 32, Oregon 31

Copper Bowl, Tucson

1989 Arizona 17, N.C. St. 10

1990 California 17, Wyoming 15

Independence Bowl, Shreveport

1976 McNeese St. 20, Tulsa 16
1977 Louisiana Tech 24, Louisville 14
1978 E. Carolina 35, La. Tech 13
1979 Syracuse 31, McNeese St. 7
1980 So. Miss. 16, McNeese St. 14

1981 Texas A&M 33, Oklahoma St. 16
1982 Wisconsin 14, Kansas St. 3
1983 Air Force 9, Mississippi 3
1984 Air Force 23, Virginia Tech 7
1985 Minnesota 20, Clemson 13

1986 Mississippi 20, Texas Tech 17
1987 Washington 24, Tulane 12
1988 S. Mississippi 38, UTEP 18
1989 Oregon 27, Tulsa 24
1990 Louisiana Tech 34, Maryland 34

Citrus Bowl, Orlando

1947 Catawba 31, Maryville 6
1948 Catawba 7, Marshall 0
1949 Murray State 21, Sul Ross St. 21
1950 St. Vincent 7, Emory & Henry 6
1951 Morris Harvey 35, Emory & Henry 14
1952 Stetson 35, Arkansas St. 20
1953 East Texas St. 33, Tenn. Tech 0
1954 East Texas St. 7, Arkansas St. 7
1955 Neb.-Omaha 7, Eastern Kentucky 6
1956 Juniata 6, Missouri Valley 6
1957 West Texas St. 20, So. Miss. 13
1958 East Texas St. 10, So. Miss. 9
1958 (Dec.) East Texas St. 26, Missouri Valley 7
1960 (Jan.) Middle Tenn. 21,

Presbyterian 12
1960 (Dec.) Citadel 27, Tenn. Tech 0
1961 Lamar 21, Middle Tennessee 14
1962 Houston 49, Miami (O.) 21
1963 Western Ky. 27, Coast Guard 0
1964 E. Carolina 14, Massachusetts 13
1965 East Carolina 31, Maine 0
1966 Morgan State 14, West Chester 6
1967 Tenn.-Martin 25, West Chester 8
1968 Richmond 49, Ohio U. 42
1969 Toledo 56, Davidson 33
1970 Toledo 40, William & Mary 12
1971 Toledo 28, Richmond 3
1972 Tampa 21, Kent State 18
1973 Miami (O.) 16, Florida 7
1974 Miami (O.) 21, Georgia 10

1975 Miami (O.) 20, South Carolina 7
1976 Okla. St. 49, Brigham Young 21
1977 Florida St. 40, Texas Tech 17
1978 N.C. State 30, Pittsburgh 17
1979 LSU 34, Wake Forest 10
1980 Florida 35, Maryland 20
1981 Missouri 19, Southern Miss. 17
1982 Auburn 33, Boston College 26
1983 Tennessee 30, Maryland 23
1984 Georgia 17, Florida St. 17
1985 Ohio St. 10, Brigham Young 7
1987 (Jan.) Auburn 16, USC 7
1988 Clemson 35, Penn St. 10
1989 Clemson 13, Oklahoma 6
1990 Illinois 31, Virginia 21
1991 Georgia Tech 45, Nebraska 21

Peach Bowl, Atlanta

1968 LSU 31, Florida St. 27
1969 West Virginia 14, S. Carolina 3
1970 Arizona St. 48, N. Carolina 26
1971 Mississippi 41, Georgia Tech. 18
1972 N. Carolina St. 49, W. Va. 13
1973 Georgia 17, Maryland 16
1974 Vanderbilt 6, Texas Tech. 6
1975 W. Virginia 13, No. Carolina St. 10

1976 Kentucky 21, North Carolina 0
1977 N. Carolina St. 24, Iowa St. 14
1978 Purdue 41, Georgia Tech. 21
1979 Baylor 24, Clemson 18
1981 (Jan.) Miami 20, Virginia Tech. 10
1981 (Dec.) West Virginia 26, Florida 6
1982 Iowa 28, Tennessee2
1983 Florida St. 28, North Carolina 3

1984 Virginia 27, Purdue 22
1985 Army 31, Illinois 29
1986 Va. Tech 25, N.C. State 24
1988 (Jan.) Tennessee 28, Indiana 22
1988 (Dec.) N.C. State 28, Iowa 23
1989 Syracuse 19, Georgia 18
1990 Auburn 27, Indiana 23

All-American Bowl, Birmingham

1982 Air Force 36, Vanderbilt 28
1983 W. Virginia 20, Kentucky 16
1984 Kentucky 20, Wisconsin 19
1985 Georgia Tech 17, Michigan St. 14
1986 Florida St. 27, Indiana 13

1987 Virginia 22, Brigham Young 16
1988 Florida 14, Illinois 10
1989 Texas Tech 49, Duke 21
1990 N.C. State 31, S. Mississippi 27

Holiday Bowl, San Diego

1977 Maryland 17, Minnesota 7
1978 Texas A&M 28, Iowa St. 12
1979 Missouri 24, So. Carolina 14
1980 Arkansas 34, Tulane 15
1981 Mississippi St. 10, Kansas 0

1983 Brigham Young 21, Missouri 17
1984 Brigham Young 24, Michigan 17
1985 Arkansas 18, Arizona St. 17
1986 Iowa 39, San Diego St. 38

1987 Iowa 20, Wyoming 19
1988 Oklahoma St. 62, Wyoming 14
1989 Penn St. 50, Brigham Young 39
1990 Texas A&M 65, Brigham Young 14

1978 Navy 23, Brigham Young 16
1979 Indiana 38, Brigham Young 37
1980 Brigham Young 46, SMU 45
1981 Brigham Young 38, Wash. St. 36
1982 Ohio State 47, Brigham Young 17

Aloha Bowl, Honolulu

1982 Washington 21, Maryland 20
1983 Penn State 13, Washington 10
1984 SMU 27, Notre Dame 20

1985 Alabama 24, USC 3
1986 Arizona 30, North Carolina 21
1987 UCLA 20, Florida 16

1988 Washington St. 24, Houston 22
1989 Michigan St. 33, Hawaii 13
1990 Syracuse 28, Arizona 0

California Bowl, Fresno

1981 Toledo 27, San Jose St. 25
1982 Fresno St. 29, Bowling Green 28
1983 N. Illinois 20, Cal. State Fullerton 13
1984 Nevada-Las Vegas 30, Toledo 13

1985 Fresno St. 51, Bowling Green 7
1986 San Jose St. 37, Miami (Oh.) 7
1987 E. Michigan 30, San Jose St. 27

1988 Fresno St. 35, W. Michigan 30
1989 Fresno St. 27, Ball St. 6
1990 San Jose St. 48, Central Mich. 24

Blockbuster Bowl, Miami

1990 Florida St. 24, Penn St. 17

College Division I Football Teams

Team	Nickname	Team colors	Conference	Coach	1990 record (W-L-T)
Air Force	Falcons	Blue & silver	Western Athletic	Fisher De Berry	7-5-0
Akron	Zips	Blue & Gold	Independent	Gerry Faust	3-7-1
Alabama	Crimson Tide	Crimson & white	Southeastern	Gene Stallings	7-5-0
Alabama State	Hornets	Black & gold	Southwestern	Houston Markham	8-2-1
Alcorn State	Braves	Purple & gold	Southwestern	Cardell Jones	2-7-0
Appalachian State	Mountaineers	Black & gold	Southern	Jerry Moore	6-5-0
Arizona	Wildcats	Red & blue	Pacific Ten	Dick Tomey	7-5-0
Arizona State	Sun Devils	Maroon & gold	Pacific Ten	Larry Marmie	4-7-0
Arkansas	Razorbacks	Cardinal & white	Southwest	Jack Crowe	3-8-0
Arkansas State	Indians	Scarlet & black	Independent	Al Kincaid	3-7-1
Army	Cadets	Black, gold, gray	Independent	Bob Sutton	6-5-0
Auburn	Tigers	Orange & blue	Southeastern	Pat Dye	7-3-1
Austin Peay State	Governors	Red & white	Ohio Valley	Roy Gregory	0-11-0
Ball State	Cardinals	Cardinal & white	Mid-American	Paul Schudel	7-4-0
Baylor	Bears	Green & gold	Southwest	Grant Teaff	6-4-1
Bethune-Cookman	Wildcats	Maroon & gold	Mid-Eastern	Larry Little	4-7-0
Boise State	Broncos	Orange & Blue	Big Sky	Skip Hall	10-4-0
Boston College	Eagles	Maroon & gold	Big East	Tom Coughlin	4-7-0
Boston Univ.	Terriers	Scarlet & white	Yankee	Dan Allen	5-6-0
Bowling Green	Falcons	Orange & brown	Mid-American	Gary Blackney	3-5-2
Brigham Young	Cougars	Royal blue & white	Western Athletic	LaVell Edwards	10-3-0
Brown	Bears	Brown, cardinal, white	Ivy	Mickey Kwiatkowski	2-8-0
Bucknell	Bisons	Orange & blue	Patriot	Lou Maranzana	7-4-0
California	Golden Bears	Blue & gold	Pacific Ten	Bruce Snyder	7-4-1
Central Florida	Knights	Black & gold	Independent	Gene McDowell	10-4-0
Central Michigan	Chippewas	Maroon & gold	Mid-American	Herb Deromedi	8-3-1
Cincinnati	Bearcats	Red & black	Independent	Tim Murphy	1-10-0

Team	Nickname	Team colors	Conference	Coach	1990 record (W-L-T)
Citadel	Bulldogs	Blue & white	Southern	Charles Taaffe	7-5-0
Clemson	Tigers	Purple & orange	Atlantic Coast	Ken Hatfield	10-2-0
Colgate	Red Raiders	Maroon	Patriot	Mike Foley	7-4-0
Colorado State	Rams	Green & gold	Western Athletic	Earle Bruce	9-4-0
Colorado	Buffaloes	Silver, gold & blue	Big Eight	Bill McCartney	11-1-1
Columbia	Lions	Blue & white	Ivy	Ray Tellier	1-9-0
Connecticut	Huskies	Blue & white	Yankee	Tom Jackson	6-5-0
Cornell	Big Red	Carnelian & white	Ivy	Jim Hofher	7-3-0
Dartmouth	Big Green	Dartmouth green & white	Ivy	Buddy Teevens	7-2-1
Delaware	Fightin' Blue Hens	Blue & gold	Yankee	Harold Raymond	6-5-0
Delaware State	Hornets	Red & blue	Mid-Eastern	William Collick	7-3-0
Duke	Blue Devils	Royal blue & white	Atlantic Coast	Barry Wilson	4-7-0
East Carolina	Pirates	Purple & gold	Independent	Bill Lewis	5-6-0
East Tennessee St.	Buccaneers	Blue & gold	Southern	Don Riley	2-9-0
Eastern Illinois	Panthers	Blue & Gray	Gateway	Bob Spoo	5-6-0
Eastern Kentucky	Colonels	Maroon & white	Ohio Valley	Roy Kidd	10-2-0
Eastern Michigan	Hurons	Green & white	Mid-American	Jim Harkema	2-9-0
Eastern Washington	Eagles	Red & white	Big Sky	Dick Zornes	5-6-0
Florida	Gators	Orange & blue	Southeastern	Steve Spurrier	9-2-0
Florida A&M	Rattlers	Orange & green	Mid-Eastern	Ken Riley	7-4-0
Florida State	Seminoles	Garnet & gold	Independent	Bobby Bowden	10-2-0
Fordham	Rams	Maroon & white	Patriot	Larry Glueck	1-9-0
Fresno State	Bulldogs	Cardinal & blue	Big West	Jim Sweeney	8-2-1
Fullerton, Cal State	Titans	Blue, orange, white	Big West	Gene Murphy	1-11-0
Furman	Paladins	Purple & white	Southern	Jimmy Satterfield	9-4-0
Georgia	Bulldogs	Red & black	Southeastern	Ray Goff	4-7-0
Georgia Southern	Eagles	Blue & white	Independent	Tim Stowers	11-4-0
Georgia Tech	Yellow Jackets	Old gold & white	Atlantic Coast	Bobby Ross	11-0-1
Grambling	Tigers	Black & gold	Southwestern	Eddie Robinson	8-3-0
Harvard	Crimson	Crimson	Ivy	Joe Restic	5-5-0
Hawaii	Rainbow Warriors	Green & white	Western Athletic	Bob Wagner	7-5-0
Holy Cross	Crusaders	Royal purple	Patriot	Mike Duffner	9-1-1
Houston	Cougars	Scarlet & white	Southwest	John Jenkins	10-1-0
Howard	Bison	Blue & white	Mid-Eastern	Steve Wilson	6-5-0
Idaho	Vandals	Silver & gold	Big Sky	John L. Smith	9-4-0
Idaho State	Bengals	Orange & black	Big Sky	Garth Hall	3-8-0
Illinois	Fighting Illini	Orange & blue	Big Ten	John Mackovic	8-4-0
Illinois State	Redbirds	Red & white	Gateway	Jim Heacock	5-6-0
Indiana	Fightin' Hoosiers	Cream & crimson	Big Ten	Bill Mallory	6-5-1
Indiana State	Sycamores	Blue & white	Gateway	Dennis Raetz	4-7-0
Iowa	Hawkeyes	Old gold & black	Big Ten	Hayden Fry	8-4-0
Iowa State	Cyclones	Cardinal & gold	Big Eight	Jim Walden	4-6-1
Jackson State	Tigers	Blue & white	Southwestern	W.C. Gorden	8-4-0
James Madison	Dukes	Purple & gold	Independent	Rip Scherer	5-6-0
Kansas	Jayhawks	Crimson & blue	Big Eight	Glen Mason	3-7-1
Kansas State	Wildcats	Purple & white	Big Eight	Bill Snyder	5-6-0
Kent State	Golden Flashes	Blue & gold	Mid-American	Pete Cordelli	2-9-0
Kentucky	Wildcats	Blue & white	Southeastern	Bill Curry	4-7-0
Lafayette	Leopards	Maroon & white	Patriot	Bill Russo	4-7-0
Lehigh	Engineers	Brown & white	Patriot	Hank Small	7-4-0
Liberty	Flames	Red, White, Blue	Independent	Sam Rutigliano	7-4-0
Long Beach State	Forty-Niners	Brown & gold	Big West	Willie Brown	6-5-0
Louisiana State	Fighting Tigers	Purple & gold	Southeastern	Curley Hallman	5-6-0
Louisiana Tech	Bulldogs	Red & blue	Independent	Joe Raymond Peace	8-3-1
Louisville	Cardinals	Red, black, white	Independent	Howard Schnellenberger	10-1-1
Maine	Black Bears	Blue & white	Yankee	Kirk Ferentz	3-8-0
Marshall	Thundering Herd	Green & white	Southern	Jim Donnan	6-5-0
Maryland	Terps	Red, white, black & gold	Atlantic Coast	Joe Krivak	6-5-1
Massachusetts	Minutemen	Maroon & white	Yankee	Jim Reid	8-2-1
McNeese State	Cowboys	Blue & gold	Southland	Bobby Keasler	5-6-0
Memphis State	Tigers	Blue & gray	Independent	Chuck Stobart	4-6-1
Miami (Fla.)	Hurricanes	Orange, green, white	Big East	Dennis Erickson	10-2-0
Miami (Ohio)	Redskins	Red & white	Mid-American	Randy Walker	5-5-1
Michigan	Wolverines	Maize & blue	Big Ten	Gray Moeller	9-3-0
Michigan State	Spartans	Green & white	Big Ten	George Perles	8-3-1
Middle Tennessee St.	Blue Raiders	Blue & white	Ohio Valley	Boots Donnelly	11-2-0
Minnesota	Golden Gophers	Maroon & gold	Big Ten	John Gutekunst	6-5-0
Mississippi	Rebels	Red & blue	Southeastern	Billy Brewer	9-3-0
Mississippi State	Bulldogs	Maroon & white	Southeastern	Jackie Sherrill	5-6-0
Miss. Valley	Delta Devils	Green & white	Southwestern	Larry Dorsey	5-6-0
Missouri	Tigers	Old gold & black	Big Eight	Bob Stull	4-7-0
Montana	Grizzlies	Copper, silver, gold	Big Sky	Don Read	7-4-0
Montana State	Bobcats	Blue & gold	Big Sky	Earle Solomonson	4-7-0
Morehead State	Eagles	Blue & gold	Ohio Valley	Cole Proctor	5-6-0
Morgan State	Bears	Blue & orange	Mid-Eastern	Ricky Diggs	1-10-0
Murray State	Racers	Blue & gold	Ohio Valley	Mike Mahoney	2-9-0
Navy	Midshipmen	Navy blue & gold	Independent	George Chaump	5-6-0
Nebraska	Cornhuskers	Scarlet & cream	Big Eight	Tom Osborne	9-3-0
Nevada-Las Vegas	Rebels	Scarlet & gray	Big West	Jim Strong	4-7-0
Nevada-Reno	Wolf Pack	Silver & blue	Big Sky	Chris Ault	13-2-0
New Hampshire	Wildcats	Blue & white	Yankee	Bill Bowes	7-3-1
New Mexico	Lobos	Cherry & silver	Western Athletic	Mike Sheppard	2-10-0

Team	Nickname	Team colors	Conference	Coach	1990 record (W-L-T)
New Mexico State	Aggies	Crimson & white	Big West	Jim Hess	1-10-0
Nicholls St.	Colonels	Red & grey	Independent	Phil Greco	4-7-0
North Carolina	Tar Heels	Blue & white	Atlantic Coast	Mack Brown	6-4-1
North Carolina A & T.	Aggies	Blue & gold	Mid-Eastern	Bill Hayes	9-2-0
North Carolina State	Wolfpack	Red & white	Atlantic Coast	Dick Sheridan	7-5-0
North Texas	Mean Green, Eagles	Green & white	Southland	Dennis Parker	6-5-0
Northeast Louisiana	Indians	Maroon & gold	Southland	Dave Roberts	7-5-0
Northeastern	Huskies	Red & black	Independent	Barry Gallup	1-10-0
Northern Arizona	Lumberjacks	Blue & gold	Big Sky	Steve Axman	5-6-0
Northern Illinois	Huskies	Cardinal & black	Independent	Charlie Sadler	6-5-0
Northern Iowa	Panthers	Purple & Old Gold	Gateway	Terry Allen	8-4-0
Northwestern	Wildcats	Purple & white	Big Ten	Francis Peay	2-9-0
Northwestern State	Demons	Purple & White	Southland	Sam Goodwin	5-6-0
Notre Dame	Fighting Irish	Gold & blue	Independent	Lou Holtz	9-3-0
Ohio State	Buckeyes	Scarlet & gray	Big Ten	John Cooper	7-4-1
Ohio Univ.	Bobcats	Green & white	Mid-American	Tom Lichtenberg	1-9-1
Oklahoma	Sooners	Crimson & cream	Big Eight	Gary Gibbs	8-3-0
Oklahoma State	Cowboys	Orange & black	Big Eight	Pat Jones	4-7-0
Oregon	Ducks	Green & Yellow	Pacific Ten	Rich Brooks	8-4-0
Oregon State	Beavers	Orange & black	Pacific Ten	Jerry Pettibone	1-10-0
Pacific	Tigers	Orange & black	Big West	Walt Harris	4-7-0
Penn State	Nittany Lions	Blue & white	Independent	Joe Paterno	9-3-0
Pennsylvania	Red & Blue, Quakers	Red & blue	Ivy	Gary Steele	3-7-0
Pittsburgh	Panthers	Gold & blue	Big East	Paul Hackett	3-7-1
Princeton	Tigers	Orange & black	Ivy	Steve Tosches	3-7-0
Purdue	Boilermakers	Old gold & black	Big Ten	Jim Colletto	2-9-0
Rhode Island	Rams	Blue & white	Yankee	Bob Griffin	5-6-0
Rice	Owls	Blue & gray	Southwest	Fred Goldsmith	5-6-0
Richmond	Spiders	Red & blue	Yankee	Jim Marshall	1-10-0
Rutgers	Scarlet Knights	Scarlet	Big East	Doug Graber	3-8-0
Sam Houston State	Bear Kats	Orange & white	Southland	Ron Randleman	4-7-0
Samford	Bulldogs	Crimson & Blue	Independent	Terry Bowden	6-4-1
San Diego State	Aztecs	Scarlet & black	Western Athletic	Al Luginbill	6-5-0
San Jose State	Spartans	Gold & white	Big West	Terry Shea	9-2-1
South Carolina	Fighting Gamecocks	Garnet & black	Independent	Sparky Woods	6-5-0
South Carolina State	Bulldogs	Garnet & blue	Mid-Eastern	Willie Jeffries	4-6-0
SE Missouri St.	Indians	Red & black	Ohio Valley	John Mumford	7-3-0
Southern-Baton Rouge	Jaguars	Blue & gold	Southwestern	Gerald Kimble	4-7-0
Southern California	Trojans	Cardinal & gold	Pacific Ten	Larry Smith	8-4-1
Southern Illinois	Salukis	Maroon & white	Gateway	Bob Smith	2-9-0
Southern Methodist	Mustangs	Red & blue	Southwest	Tom Rossley	1-10-0
Southern Mississippi	Golden Eagles	Black & gold	Independent	Jeff Bower	8-4-0
SW Missouri St.	Bears	Maroon & white	Gateway	Jesse Branch	9-3-0
SW Texas St.	Bobcats	Maroon & gold	Southland	Dennis Franchione	6-5-0
Southwestern La.	Ragin' Cajuns	Vermillion & white	Independent	Nelson Stokley	5-6-0
Stanford	Cardinal	Cardinal & white	Pacific Ten	Dennis Green	5-6-0
Stephen F. Austin St.	Lumberjacks	Purple & white	Southland	Lynn Graves	2-9-0
Syracuse	Orangemen	Orange	Independent	Paul Pasqualoni	7-4-2
Temple	Owls	Cherry & white	Big East	Jerry Berndt	7-4-0
Tennessee	Volunteers	Orange & white	Southeastern	John Majors	9-2-2
Tenn.-Chattanooga	Moccasins	Navy blue & gold	Southern	Buddy Nix	6-5-0
Tennessee State	Tigers	Blue & white	Ohio Valley	Joe Gilliam Sr.	7-4-0
Tennessee Tech	Golden Eagles	Purple & gold	Ohio Valley	Jim Ragland	6-5-0
Texas	Longhorns	Orange & white	Southwest	David McWilliams	10-2-0
Texas-El Paso	Miners	Orange, white, blue	Western Athletic	David Lee	3-8-0
Texas A & M	Aggies	Maroon & white	Southwest	R.C. Slocum	9-3-1
Texas Christian	Horned Frogs	Purple & white	Southwest	Jim Wacker	5-6-0
Texas Southern	Tigers	Maroon & gray	Southwestern	Walter Highsmith	4-7-0
Texas Tech	Red Raiders	Scarlet & black	Southwest	Spike Dykes	4-7-0
Toledo	Rockets	Blue & gold	Mid-American	Gary Pinkel	9-2-0
Towson St.	Tigers	Gold & white	Independent	Phil Albert	2-9-0
Tulane	Green Wave	Olive green & sky blue	Independent	Greg Davis	4-7-0
Tulsa	Golden Hurricane	Blue & gold	Independent	Dave Rader	3-8-0
UCLA	Bruins	Navy blue & gold	Pacific Ten	Terry Donahue	5-6-0
Utah State	Aggies	Navy blue & white	Big West	Chuck Shelton	5-5-1
Utah	Utes	Crimson & white	Western Athletic	Ron McBride	4-7-0
Vanderbilt	Commodores	Black & gold	Southeastern	Gerry DiNardo	1-10-0
Villanova	Wildcats	Blue & white	Yankee	Andy Talley	6-5-0
Virginia	Cavaliers	Orange & blue	Atlantic Coast	George Welsh	8-4-0
VMI	Keydets	Red, white & yellow	Southern	Jim Shuck	4-7-0
Virginia Tech	Gobblers, Hokies	Orange & maroon	Big East	Frank Beamer	6-5-0
Wake Forest	Demon Deacons	Old gold & black	Atlantic Coast	Bill Dooley	3-8-0
Washington	Huskies	Purple & gold	Pacific Ten	Don James	10-2-0
Washington State	Cougars	Crimson & gray	Pacific Ten	Mike Price	3-8-0
Weber State	Wildcats	Purple & white	Big Sky	Dave Arsianian	5-6-0
West Virginia	Mountaineers	Old gold & blue	Big East	Don Nehlen	4-7-0
Western Carolina	Catamounts	Purple & gold	Southern	Steve Hodgin	3-8-0
Western Illinois	Leathernecks	Purple & Gold	Gateway	Randy Ball	3-8-0
Western Kentucky	Hilltoppers	Red & white	Independent	Jack Harbaugh	2-8-0
Western Michigan	Broncos	Brown & gold	Mid-American	Al Molde	7-4-0
William & Mary	Tribe	Green & gold	Independent	Jimmye Laycock	10-3-0
Wisconsin	Badgers	Cardinal & white	Big Ten	Barry Alvarez	1-10-0
Wyoming	Cowboys	Brown & yellow	Western Athletic	Joe Tiller	9-4-0
Yale	Bulldogs, Elis	Yale blue & white	Ivy	Carmen Cozza	6-4-0
Youngstown St.	Penguins	Scarlet & white	Independent	Jim Tressel	11-1-0

College Football Conference Champions

	Atlantic Coast		Ivy League		Big Eight		Big Ten
1976	Maryland	1976	Yale, Brown	1976	Oklahoma, Colorado,	1976	Michigan, Ohio State
1977	North Carolina	1977	Yale		Oklahoma State	1977	Michigan, Ohio State
1978	Clemson	1978	Dartmouth	1977	Oklahoma	1978	Michigan St., Michigan
1979	No. Carolina St.	1979	Yale	1978	Nebraska, Oklahoma	1979	Ohio State
1980	North Carolina	1980	Yale	1979	Oklahoma	1980	Michigan
1981	Clemson	1981	Yale, Dartmouth	1980	Oklahoma	1981	Iowa, Ohio State
1982	Clemson	1982	Harvard, Dartmouth, Penn	1981	Nebraska	1982	Michigan
1983	Maryland	1983	Harvard, Penn	1982	Nebraska	1983	Illinois
1984	Maryland	1984	Penn	1983	Nebraska	1984	Ohio State
1985	Maryland	1985	Penn	1984	Nebraska, Oklahoma	1985	Iowa
1986	Clemson	1986	Penn	1985	Oklahoma	1986	Michigan, Ohio State
1987	Clemson	1987	Harvard	1986	Oklahoma	1987	Michigan St.
1988	Clemson	1988	Penn, Cornell	1987	Oklahoma	1988	Michigan
1989	Virginia, Duke	1989	Yale, Princeton	1988	Nebraska	1989	Michigan
1990	Georgia Tech	1990	Dartmouth	1990	Colorado	1990	Iowa

	Mid-America		Southern		Southeastern		Southwest
1976	Ball State	1976	East Carolina	1976	Georgia	1976	Houston
1977	Miami	1977	Tenn.-Chattanooga	1977	Alabama	1977	Texas
1978	Ball State	1978	Tenn.-Chattanooga, Furman	1978	Alabama	1978	Houston
1979	Central Michigan	1979	Tenn.-Chattanooga	1979	Alabama	1979	Houston, Arkansas
1980	Central Michigan	1980	Furman	1980	Georgia	1980	Baylor
1981	Toledo	1981	Furman	1981	Georgia, Alabama	1981	SMU
1982	Bowling Green	1982	Furman	1982	Georgia	1982	SMU
1983	Northern Illinois	1983	Furman	1983	Auburn	1983	Texas
1984	Toledo	1984	Tenn.-Chattanooga	1984	Florida (title vacated)	1984	SMU, Houston
1985	Bowling Green	1985	Furman	1985	Tennessee	1985	Texas A&M
1986	Miami	1986	Appalachian St.	1986	LSU	1986	Texas A&M
1987	E. Michigan	1987	Appalachian St.	1987	Auburn	1987	Texas A&M
1988	W. Michigan	1988	Marshall, Furman	1988	Auburn, LSU	1988	Arkansas
1989	Ball State	1989	Furman	1989	Alabama, Tennessee, Auburn	1989	Arkansas
1990	Central Michigan	1990	Furman	1990	Auburn Tennessee	1990	Texas

	Pacific Ten		Western Athletic		Big West
1976	USC	1976	Wyoming, Brigham Young	1976	San Diego State
1977	Washington	1977	Brigham Young, Arizona St.	1977	Fresno State
1978	USC	1978	Brigham Young	1978	Utah St., San Jose St.
1979	USC	1979	Brigham Young	1979	San Jose St.
1980	Washington	1980	Brigham Young	1980	Long Beach State
1981	Washington	1981	Brigham Young	1981	San Jose State
1982	UCLA	1982	Brigham Young	1982	Fresno State
1983	UCLA	1983	Brigham Young	1983	Cal State-Fullerton
1984	USC	1984	Brigham Young	1984	Nevada-Las Vegas
1985	UCLA	1985	Brigham Young, Air Force	1985	Fresno State
1986	Arizona State	1986	San Diego State	1986	San Jose State
1987	UCLA, USC	1987	Wyoming	1987	San Jose State
1988	USC	1988	Wyoming	1988	Fresno State
1989	USC	1989	Brigham Young	1989	Fresno State
1990	Washington	1990	Brigham Young	1990	San Jose State

Outland Award

Honoring the outstanding interior lineman selected by the Football Writers' Association of America.

1946	George Connor, Notre Dame, T	1962	Bobby Bell, Minnesota, T	1977	Brad Shearer, Texas, DT
1947	Joe Steffy, Army, G	1963	Scott Appleton, Texas, T	1978	Greg Roberts, Oklahoma, G
1948	Bill Fischer, Notre Dame, G	1964	Steve Delong, Tennessee, T	1979	Jim Ritcher, No. Carolina St., C
1949	Ed Bagdon, Michigan St., G	1965	Tommy Nobis, Texas, G	1980	Mark May, Pittsburgh, OT
1950	Bob Gain, Kentucky, T	1966	Loyd Phillips, Arkansas, T	1981	Dave Rimington, Nebraska, C
1951	Jim Weatherall, Oklahoma, T	1967	Ron Yary, Southern Cal, T	1982	Dave Rimington, Nebraska, C
1952	Dick Modzelewski, Maryland, T	1968	Bill Stanfill, Georgia, T	1983	Dean Steinkuhler, Nebraska, G
1953	J. D. Roberts, Oklahoma, G	1969	Mike Reid, Penn State, DT	1984	Bruce Smith, Virginia Tech, DT
1954	Bill Brooks, Arkansas, G	1970	Jim Stillwagon, Ohio State, LB	1985	Mike Ruth, Boston College, DT
1955	Calvin Jones, Iowa, G	1971	Larry Jacobson, Nebraska, DT	1986	Jason Buck, BYU, DT
1956	Jim Parker, Ohio State, G	1972	Rich Glover, Nebraska, MG	1987	Chad Hennings, Air Force, DT
1957	Alex Karras, Iowa, T	1973	John Hicks, Ohio State, G	1988	Tracy Rocker, Auburn, DT
1958	Zeke Smith, Auburn, G	1974	Randy White, Maryland, DE	1989	Mohammed Elewonibi, BYU, G
1959	Mike McGee, Duke, T	1975	Lee Roy Selmon, Oklahoma, DT	1990	Russell Maryland, Miami (Fla.), DT
1960	Tom Brown, Minnesota, G	1976	Ross Browner, Notre Dame, DE		
1961	Merlin Olsen, Utah State, T				

All-Time Division I-A Coaching Victories

Paul "Bear" Bryant	323	Eddie Anderson	201	Carl Snavely	18
Amos Alonzo Stagg	314	Vince Dooley	201	Gil Dobie	18
Glenn "Pop" Warner	313	Dana Bible	198	Jerry Claiborne	17
Woody Hayes	238	Dan McGugin	197	Hayden Fry	17
Bo Schembechler	234	Fielding Yost	196	Ben Schwartzwalder	17
Joe Paterno	229	Howard Jones	194	Tom Osborne	17
Jess Neely	207	John Vaught	190	Ralph Jordan	17
Bobby Bowden	205	John Heisman	185	Frank Kush	17
Warren Woodson	203	Darrell Royal	184	LaVell Edwards	17

Eddie Robinson of Grambling State Univ. holds the record for most college football victories with 366 at the start of the 1991 season.

National College Football Champions

The NCAA recognizes as unofficial national champion the team selected each year by the AP (poll of writers) and the UPI (poll of coaches). When the polls disagree both teams are listed. The AP poll originated in 1936 and the UPI poll in 1950.

1936	Minnesota	1950	Oklahoma	1964	Alabama	1978	Alabama, So. Cal.
1937	Pittsburgh	1951	Tennessee	1965	Alabama, Mich. State	1979	Alabama
1938	Texas Christian	1952	Michigan State	1966	Notre Dame	1980	Georgia
1939	Texas A&M	1953	Maryland	1967	Southern Cal.	1981	Clemson
1940	Minnesota	1954	Ohio State, UCLA	1968	Ohio State	1982	Penn State
1941	Minnesota	1955	Oklahoma	1969	Texas	1983	Miami (Fla.)
1942	Ohio State	1956	Oklahoma	1970	Nebraska, Texas	1984	Brigham Young
1943	Notre Dame	1957	Auburn, Ohio State	1971	Nebraska,	1985	Oklahoma
1944	Army	1958	Louisiana State	1972	Southern Cal.	1986	Penn State
1945	Army	1959	Syracuse	1973	Notre Dame, Alabama	1987	Miami (Fla.)
1946	Notre Dame	1960	Minnesota	1974	Oklahoma, So. Cal.	1988	Notre Dame
1947	Notre Dame	1961	Alabama	1975	Oklahoma	1989	Miami (Fla.)
1948	Michigan	1962	Southern Cal.	1976	Pittsburgh	1990	Colorado, Georgia Tech
1949	Notre Dame	1963	Texas	1977	Notre Dame		

College Football Coach of the Year

(Selected by the American Football Coaches Assn. & the Football Writers Assn. of America)

	AFCA		FWAA		AFCA
1935	Lynn Waldorf, Northwestern	1957	Woody Hayes, Ohio St.		Woody Hayes, Ohio St.
1936	Dick Harlow, Harvard	1958	Paul Dietzel, LSU		Paul Dietzel, LSU
1937	Edward Mylin, Lafayette	1959	Ben Schwartzwalder, Syracuse		Ben Schwartzwalder, Syracuse
1938	Bill Kern, Carnegie Tech	1960	Murray Warmath, Minnesota		Murray Warmath, Minnesota
1939	Eddie Anderson, Iowa	1961	Darrell Royal, Texas		Paul "Bear" Bryant, Alabama
1940	Clark Shaughnessy, Stanford	1962	John McKay, USC		John McKay, USC
1941	Frank Leahy, Notre Dame	1963	Darrell Royal, Texas		Darrell Royal, Texas
1942	Bill Alexander, Georgia Tech	1964	Ara Parseghian, Notre Dame		Frank Broyles, Arkansas;
					Ara Parseghian, Notre Dame
1943	Amos Alonzo Stagg, Pacific	1965	Duffy Daugherty, Michigan St.		Tommy Prothro, UCLA
1944	Carroll Widdoes, Ohio St.	1966	Tom Cahill, Army		Tom Cahill, Army
1945	Bo McMillin, Indiana	1967	John Pont, Indiana		John Pont, Indiana
1946	Earl "Red" Blaik, Army	1968	Woody Hayes, Ohio St.		Joe Paterno, Penn St.
1947	Fritz Crisler, Michigan	1969	Bo Schembechler, Michigan		Bo Schembechler, Michigan
1948	Bennie Oosterbaan, Michigan	1970	Alex Agase, Northwestern		Charles McClendon, LSU;
					Darrell Royal, Texas
1949	Bud Wilkinson, Oklahoma	1971	Bob Devaney, Nebraska		Paul "Bear" Bryant, Alabama
1950	Charlie Caldwell, Princeton	1972	John McKay, USC		John McKay, USC
1951	Chuck Taylor, Stanford	1973	Johnny Majors, Pittsburgh		Paul "Bear" Bryant, Alabama
1952	Biggie Munn, Michigan St.	1974	Grant Teaff, Baylor		Grant Teaff, Baylor
1953	Jim Tatum, Maryland	1975	Woody Hayes, Ohio St.		Frank Kush, Arizona St.
1954	Henry "Red" Sanders, UCLA	1976	Johnny Majors, Pittsburgh		Johnny Majors, Pittsburgh
1955	Duffy Daugherty, Michigan St.	1977	Lou Holtz, Arkansas		Don James, Washington
1956	Bowden Wyatt, Tennessee	1978	Joe Paterno, Penn St.		Joe Paterno, Penn St.
		1979	Earle Bruce, Ohio St.		Earle Bruce, Ohio St.
		1980	Vince Dooley, Georgia		Vince Dooley, Georgia
		1981	Danny Ford, Clemson		Danny Ford, Clemson
		1982	Joe Paterno, Penn St.		Joe Paterno, Penn St.
		1983	Howard Schnellenberger, Miami (Fla.)		Ken Hatfield, Air Force
		1984	LaVell Edwards, Brigham Young		LaVell Edwards, Brigham Young
		1985	Fisher De Berry, Air Force		Fisher De Berry, Air Force
		1986	Joe Paterno, Penn St.		Joe Paterno, Penn St.
		1987	Dick MacPherson, Syracuse		Dick MacPherson, Syracuse
		1988	Lou Holtz, Notre Dame		Don Nehlen, W. Virginia
		1989	Bill McCartney, Colorado		Bill McCartney, Colorado
		1990	Bobby Ross, Georgia Tech		Bobby Ross, Georgia Tech

Longest Division I-A Winning Streaks

Wins	Team	Years	Ended by	Score
47	Oklahoma	1953-57	Notre Dame	7-0
39	Washington	1908-14	Oregon State	0-0
37	Yale	1890-93	Princeton	6-0
37	Yale	1887-89	Princeton	10-0
35	Toledo	1969-71	Tampa	21-0
34	Pennsylvania	1894-96	Lafayette	6-4
31	Oklahoma	1948-50	Kentucky	13-7
31	Pittsburgh	1914-18	Cleveland Naval Reserve	10-9
31	Pennsylvania	1896-98	Harvard	10-0
30	Texas	1968-70	Notre Dame	24-11
29	Michigan	1901-03	Minnesota	6-6
28	Alabama	1978-80	Mississippi State	6-3
28	Oklahoma	1973-75	Kansas	23-3
28	Michigan State	1950-53	Purdue	6-0
27	Nebraska	1901-04	Colorado	6-0
26	Cornell	1921-24	Williams	14-7
26	Michigan	1903-05	Chicago	2-0
25	Michigan	1946-49	Army	21-7
25	Army	1944-46	Notre Dame	0-0
25	Southern Cal	1931-33	Oregon State	0-0
25	Brigham Young	1983-85	UCLA	27-24

Heisman Trophy Winners

Awarded annually to the nation's outstanding college football player.

1935	Jay Berwanger, Chicago, HB	1954	Alan Ameche, Wisconsin, FB	1973	John Cappelletti, Penn State, RB
1936	Larry Kelley, Yale, E	1955	Howard Cassady, Ohio St., HB	1974	Archie Griffin, Ohio State, RB
1937	Clinton Frank, Yale, HB	1956	Paul Hornung, Notre Dame, QB	1975	Archie Griffin, Ohio State, RB
1938	David O'Brien, Tex. Christian, QB	1957	John Crow, Texas A & M, HB	1976	Tony Dorsett, Pittsburgh, RB
1939	Nile Kinnick, Iowa, HB	1958	Pete Dawkins, Army, HB	1977	Earl Campbell, Texas, RB
1940	Tom Harmon, Michigan, HB	1959	Billy Cannon, La. State, HB	1978	Billy Sims, Oklahoma, RB
1941	Bruce Smith, Minnesota, HB	1960	Joe Bellino, Navy, HB	1979	Charles White, USC, RB
1942	Frank Sinkwich, Georgia, HB	1961	Ernest Davis, Syracuse, HB	1980	George Rogers, So. Carolina, RB
1943	Angelo Bertelli, Notre Dame, QB	1962	Terry Baker, Oregon State, QB	1981	Marcus Allen, USC, RB
1944	Leslie Horvath, Ohio State, QB	1963	Roger Staubach, Navy, QB	1982	Herschel Walker, Georgia, RB
1945	Felix Blanchard, Army, FB	1964	John Huarte, Notre Dame, QB	1983	Mike Rozier, Nebraska, RB
1946	Glenn Davis, Army, HB	1965	Mike Garrett, USC, HB	1984	Doug Flutie, Boston College, QB
1947	John Lujack, Notre Dame, QB	1966	Steve Spurrier, Florida, QB	1985	Bo Jackson, Auburn, RB
1948	Doak Walker, SMU, HB	1967	Gary Beban, UCLA, QB	1986	Vinny Testaverde, Miami, QB
1949	Leon Hart, Notre Dame, E	1968	O. J. Simpson, USC, RB	1987	Tim Brown, Notre Dame, WR
1950	Vic Janowicz, Ohio State, HB	1969	Steve Owens, Oklahoma, RB	1988	Barry Sanders, Oklahoma St., RB
1951	Richard Kazmaier, Princeton, HB	1970	Jim Plunkett, Stanford, QB	1989	Andre Ware, Houston, QB
1952	Billy Vessels, Oklahoma, HB	1971	Pat Sullivan, Auburn, QB	1990	Ty Detmer, BYU, QB
1953	John Lattner, Notre Dame, HB	1972	Johnny Rodgers, Nebraska, RB-R		

Vince Lombardi Award

Honoring the outstanding lineman, sponsored by the Rotary Club of Houston

1970	Jim Stillwagon, Ohio State, MG	1977	Ross Browner, Notre Dame, DE	1984	Tony Degrate, Texas, DT
1971	Walt Patulski, Notre Dame, DE	1978	Bruce Clark, Penn State, DT	1985	Tony Casillas, Oklahoma, NG
1972	Rich Glover, Nebraska, MG	1979	Brad Budde, USC, G	1986	Cornelius Bennett, Alabama, DE
1973	Dave Gallagher, Michigan, DT	1980	Hugh Green, Pittsburgh, DE	1987	Chris Spielman, Ohio State, LB
1974	Randy White, Maryland, DT	1981	Kenneth Sims, Texas, DT	1988	Tracy Rocker, Auburn, DT
1975	Lee Roy Selmon, Oklahoma, DT	1982	Dave Rimington, Nebraska, C	1989	Percy Snow, Michigan St., LB
1976	Wilson Whitley, Houston, DT	1983	Dean Steinkuhler, Nebraska, G	1990	Chris Zorich, Notre Dame, DL

All-Time Division I-A Percentage Leaders

(Classified as Division I-A for the last 10 years; record includes bowl games; ties computed as half won and half lost)

	Years	Won	Lost	Tied	Pct.	Bowl Games W	L	T
Notre Dame	102	692	206	40	.759	10	6	0
Michigan	111	712	236	33	.743	10	12	0
Alabama	96	658	233	43	.728	23	17	3
Oklahoma	96	636	230	50	.722	18	10	1
Texas	98	671	257	31	.716	16	16	2
USC	98	613	236	51	.709	22	12	0
Ohio St.	101	633	257	51	.701	11	12	0
Penn St.	104	646	282	41	.688	16	9	2
Nebraska	101	644	284	39	.686	14	15	0
Tennessee	94	609	268	52	.684	17	14	0
Central Michigan	90	464	242	32	.650	3	1	0
Army	101	573	309	50	.642	2	1	0
Louisiana St.	97	561	304	46	.641	11	16	1
Miami (Ohio)	102	530	293	40	.637	5	2	0
Arizona St.	76	426	240	24	.635	9	5	1
Georgia	97	565	322	53	.630	13	13	3
Washington	101	534	303	49	.630	11	7	1
Auburn	98	537	324	45	.618	12	9	2
Florida St.	44	282	172	16	.617	11	7	2
Michigan St.	94	507	308	42	.616	5	5	0
Minnesota	107	547	334	43	.615	2	3	0
Colorado	101	532	340	33	.606	5	10	0
Arkansas	97	536	343	38	.605	9	14	3
UCLA	72	414	268	37	.602	9	7	1

World Almanac All-America Team in 1990

The following is the 1990 All-America football team as chosen by a sports panel on behalf of *The World Almanac* and its 140 co-sponsoring newspapers.

Offense

Wide receiver—Raghib Ismail, Notre Dame
Wide receiver—Herman Moore, Virginia
Tight end—Kerry Cash, Texas
Tackle—Antone Davis, Tennessee
Tackle—Mike Sullivan, Miami (Fla.)
Guard—Joe Garten, Colorado
Guard—Ed King, Auburn
Center—John Flannery, Syracuse
Quarterback—Ty Detmer, BYU
Running back—Eric Bieniemy, Colorado
Running back—Greg Lewis, Washington
Placekicker—Philip Doyle, Alabama

Defense

Lineman—Russell Maryland, Miami (Fla.)
Lineman—Chris Zorich, Notre Dame
Lineman—David Rocker, Auburn
Linebacker—Alfred Williams, Colorado
Linebacker—Maurice Crum, Miami (Fla.)
Linebacker—Mike Stonebreaker, Notre Dame
Linebacker—Mike Croel, Nebraska
Back—Todd Lyght, Notre Dame
Back—Tripp Welborne, Michigan
Back—Ken Swilling, Georgia
Back—Merton Hanks, Iowa
Punter—Jason Hanson, Washington St.

Tennis

U.S. Open Champions

Men's Singles

Year	Champion	Final opponent	Year	Champion	Final opponent
1910	William Larned	T. C. Bundy	1951	Frank Sedgman	E. Victor Seixas Jr.
1911	William Larned	Maurice McLoughlin	1952	Frank Sedgman	Gardnar Mulloy
1912	Maurice McLoughlin	Wallace Johnson	1953	Tony Trabert	E. Victor Seixas Jr.
1913	Maurice McLoughlin	Richard Williams	1954	E. Victor Seixas Jr.	Rex Hartwig
1914	Richard Williams	Maurice McLoughlin	1955	Tony Trabert	Ken Rosewall
1915	William Johnston	Maurice McLoughlin	1956	Ken Rosewall	Lewis Hoad
1916	Richard Williams	William Johnston	1957	Malcolm Anderson	Ashley Cooper
1917	Richard Murray	N. W. Niles	1958	Ashley Cooper	Malcolm Anderson
1918	Richard Murray	Bill Tilden	1959	Neale A. Fraser	Alejandro Olmedo
1919	William Johnston	Bill Tilden	1960	Neale A. Fraser	Rod Laver
1920	Bill Tilden	William Johnston	1961	Roy Emerson	Rod Laver
1921	Bill Tilden	Wallace Johnson	1962	Rod Laver	Roy Emerson
1922	Bill Tilden	William Johnston	1963	Rafael Osuna	F. A. Froehling 3d
1923	Bill Tilden	William Johnston	1964	Roy Emerson	Fred Stolle
1924	Bill Tilden	William Johnston	1965	Manuel Santana	Cliff Drysdale
1925	Bill Tilden	William Johnston	1966	Fred Stolle	John Newcombe
1926	Rene Lacoste	Jean Borotra	1967	John Newcombe	Clark Graebner
1927	Rene Lacoste	Bill Tilden	1968	Arthur Ashe	Tom Okker
1928	Henri Cochet	Francis Hunter	1969	Rod Laver	Tony Roche
1929	Bill Tilden	Francis Hunter	1970	Ken Rosewall	Tony Roche
1930	John Doeg	Francis Shields	1971	Stan Smith	Jan Kodes
1931	H. Ellsworth Vines	George Lott	1972	Ilie Nastase	Arthur Ashe
1932	H. Ellsworth Vines	Henri Cochet	1973	John Newcombe	Jan Kodes
1933	Fred Perry	John Crawford	1974	Jimmy Connors	Ken Rosewall
1934	Fred Perry	Wilmer Allison	1975	Manuel Orantes	Jimmy Connors
1935	Wilmer Allison	Sidney Wood	1976	Jimmy Connors	Bjorn Borg
1936	Fred Perry	Don Budge	1977	Guillermo Vilas	Jimmy Connors
1937	Don Budge	Baron G. von Cramm	1978	Jimmy Connors	Bjorn Borg
1938	Don Budge	C. Gene Mako	1979	John McEnroe	Vitas Gerulaitis
1939	Robert Riggs	S. Welby Van Horn	1980	John McEnroe	Bjorn Borg
1940	Don McNeill	Robert Riggs	1981	John McEnroe	Bjorn Borg
1941	Robert Riggs	F. L. Kovacs	1982	Jimmy Connors	Ivan Lendl
1942	F. R. Schroeder Jr.	Frank Parker	1983	Jimmy Connors	Ivan Lendl
1943	Joseph Hunt	Jack Kramer	1984	John McEnroe	Ivan Lendl
1944	Frank Parker	William Talbert	1985	Ivan Lendl	John McEnroe
1945	Frank Parker	William Talbert	1986	Ivan Lendl	Miloslav Mecir
1946	Jack Kramer	Thomas Brown Jr.	1987	Ivan Lendl	Mats Wilander
1947	Jack Kramer	Frank Parker	1988	Mats Wilander	Ivan Lendl
1948	Pancho Gonzales	Eric Sturgess	1989	Boris Becker	Ivan Lendl
1949	Pancho Gonzales	F. R. Schroeder Jr.	1990	Pete Sampras	Andre Agassi
1950	Arthur Larsen	Herbert Flam	1991	Stefan Edberg	Jim Courier

Women's Singles

Year	Champion	Final opponent	Year	Champion	Final opponent
1926	Molla B. Mallory	Elizabeth Ryan	1959	Maria Bueno	Christine Truman
1927	Helen Wills	Betty Nuthall	1960	Darlene Hard	Maria Bueno
1928	Helen Wills	Helen Jacobs	1961	Darlene Hard	Ann Haydon
1929	Helen Wills	M. Watson	1962	Margaret Smith	Darlene Hard
1930	Betty Nuthall	L. A. Harper	1963	Maria Bueno	Margaret Smith
1931	Helen Wills Moody	E. B. Whittingstall	1964	Maria Bueno	Carole Graebner
1932	Helen Jacobs	Carolin A. Babcock	1965	Margaret Smith	Billie Jean Moffitt
1933	Helen Jacobs	Helen Wills Moody	1966	Maria Bueno	Nancy Richey
1934	Helen Jacobs	Sarah H. Palfrey	1967	Billie Jean King	Ann Haydon Jones
1935	Helen Jacobs	Sarah P. Fabyan	1968	Virginia Wade	Billie Jean King
1936	Alice Marble	Helen Jacobs	1969	Margaret Court	Nancy Richey
1937	Anita Lizana	Jadwiga Jedrzejowska	1970	Margaret Court	Rosemary Casals
1938	Alice Marble	Nancye Wynne	1971	Billie Jean King	Rosemary Casals
1939	Alice Marble	Helen Jacobs	1972	Billie Jean King	Kerry Melville
1940	Alice Marble	Helen Jacobs	1973	Margaret Court	Evonne Goolagong
1941	Sarah Palfrey Cooke	Pauline Betz	1974	Billie Jean King	Evonne Goolagong
1942	Pauline Betz	Louise Brough	1975	Chris Evert	Evonne Goolagong
1943	Pauline Betz	Louise Brough	1976	Chris Evert	Evonne Goolagong
1944	Pauline Betz	Margaret Osborne	1977	Chris Evert	Wendy Turnbull
1945	Sarah P. Cooke	Pauline Betz	1978	Chris Evert	Pam Shriver
1946	Pauline Betz	Doris Hart	1979	Tracy Austin	Chris Evert Lloyd
1947	Louise Brough	Margaret Osborne	1980	Chris Evert Lloyd	Hana Mandlikova
1948	Margaret Osborne duPont	Louise Brough	1981	Tracy Austin	Martina Navratilova
1949	Margaret Osborne duPont	Doris Hart	1982	Chris Evert Lloyd	Hana Mandlikova
1950	Margaret Osborne duPont	Doris Hart	1983	Martina Navratilova	Chris Evert Lloyd
1951	Maureen Connolly	Shirley Fry	1984	Martina Navratilova	Chris Evert Lloyd
1952	Maureen Connolly	Doris Hart	1985	Hana Mandlikova	Martina Navratilova
1953	Maureen Connolly	Doris Hart	1986	Martina Navratilova	Helena Sukova
1954	Doris Hart	Louise Brough	1987	Martina Navratilova	Steffi Graf
1955	Doris Hart	Patricia Ward	1988	Steffi Graf	Gabriela Sabatini
1956	Shirley Fry	Althea Gibson	1989	Steffi Graf	Martina Navratilova
1957	Althea Gibson	Louise Brough	1990	Gabriela Sabatini	Steffi Graf
1958	Althea Gibson	Darlene Hard	1991	Monica Seles	Martina Navratilova

Men's Doubles

Year	Champions	Year	Champions
1947	Jack Kramer—Frederick Schroeder Jr.	1970	Pierre Barthes—Nicki Pilic
1948	Gardnar Mulloy—William Talbert	1971	John Newcombe—Roger Taylor
1949	John Bromwich—William Sidwell	1972	Cliff Drysdale—Roger Taylor
1950	John Bromwich—Frank Sedgman	1973	John Newcombe—Owen Davidson
1951	Frank Sedgman—Kenneth McGregor	1974	Bob Lutz—Stan Smith
1952	Mervyn Rose—E. Victor Seixas Jr.	1975	Jimmy Connors—Ilie Nastase
1953	Rex Hartwig—Mervyn Rose	1976	Marty Riessen—Tom Okker
1954	E. Victor Seixas Jr.—Tony Trabert	1977	Bob Hewitt—Frew McMillan
1955	Kosei Kamo—Atsushi Miyagi	1978	Stan Smith—Bob Lutz
1956	Lewis Hoad—Ken Rosewall	1979	John McEnroe—Peter Fleming
1957	Ashley Cooper—Neale Fraser	1980	Bob Lutz—Stan Smith
1958	Hamilton Richardson—Alejandro Olmedo	1981	John McEnroe—Peter Fleming
1959	Neale A. Fraser—Roy Emerson	1982	Kevin Curren—Steve Denton
1960	Neale A. Fraser—Roy Emerson	1983	John McEnroe—Peter Fleming
1961	Dennis Ralston—Chuck McKinley	1984	Tomas Smid—John Fitzgerald
1962	Rafael Osuna—Antonio Palafox	1985	Ken Flach—Robert Seguso
1963	Dennis Ralston—Chuck McKinley	1986	Andres Gomez—Slobodan Zivojinovic
1964	Dennis Ralston—Chuck McKinley	1987	Stefan Edberg—Anders Jarryd
1965	Roy Emerson—Fred Stolle	1988	Sergio Casal—Emilio Sanchez
1966	Roy Emerson—Fred Stolle	1989	John McEnroe—Mark Woodforde
1967	John Newcombe—Tony Roche	1990	Pieter Aldrich—Danie Visser
1968	Robert Lutz—Stan Smith	1991	John Fitzgerald—Anders Jarryd
1969	Fred Stolle—Ken Rosewall		

Women's Doubles

Year	Champions	Year	Champions
1947	A. Louise Brough—Margaret Osborne	1970	M. S. Court—Judy Tegart Dalton
1948	A. Louise Brough—Mrs. M. O. du Pont	1971	Rosemary Casals—Judy Tegart Dalton
1949	A. Louise Brough—Mrs. M. O. du Pont	1972	Francoise Durr—Betty Stove
1950	A. Louise Brough—Mrs. M. O. du Pont	1973	Margaret S. Court—Virginia Wade
1951	Doris Hart—Shirley Fry	1974	Billie Jean King—Rosemary Casals
1952	Doris Hart—Shirley Fry	1975	Margaret Court—Virginia Wade
1953	Doris Hart—Shirley Fry	1976	Linky Boshoff—Ilana Kloss
1954	Doris Hart—Shirley Fry	1977	Betty Stove—Martina Navratilova
1955	A. Louise Brough—Mrs. M. O. du Pont	1978	Martina Navratilova—Billie Jean King
1956	A. Louise Brough—Mrs. M. O. du Pont	1979	Betty Stove—Wendy Turnbull
1957	A. Louise Brough—Mrs. M. O. du Pont	1980	Billie Jean King—Martina Navratilova
1958	Darlene Hard—Jeanne Arth	1981	Anne Smith—Kathy Jordan
1959	Darlene Hard—Jeanne Arth	1982	Rosemary Casals—Wendy Turnbull
1960	Darlene Hard—Maria Bueno	1983	Martina Navratilova—Pam Shriver
1961	Darlene Hard—Lesley Turner	1984	Martina Navratilova—Pam Shriver
1962	Maria Bueno—Darlene Hard	1985	Claudia Kohde-Kilsch—Helena Sukova
1963	Margaret Smith—Robyn Ebbern	1986	Martina Navratilova—Pam Shriver
1964	Billie Jean Moffitt—Karen Susman	1987	Martina Navratilova—Pam Shriver
1965	Carole C. Graebner—Nancy Richey	1988	Gigi Fernandez—Robin White
1966	Maria Bueno—Nancy Richey	1989	Martina Navratilova—Hana Mandlikova
1967	Rosemary Casals—Billie Jean King	1990	Gigi Fernandez—Martina Navratilova
1968	Maria Bueno—Margaret S. Court	1991	Pam Shriver—Natilia Zvereva
1969	Francoise Durr—Darlene Hard		

Davis Cup Challenge Round

Year	Result	Year	Result	Year	Result
1900	United States 5, British Isles 0	1931	France 3, Great Britain 2	1964	Australia 3, United States 2
1901	(not played)	1932	France 3, United States 2	1965	Australia 4, Spain 1
1902	United States 3, British Isles 2	1933	Great Britain 3, France 2	1966	Australia 4, India 1
1903	British Isles 4, United States 1	1934	Great Britain 4, United States 1	1967	Australia 4, Spain 1
1904	British Isles 5, Belgium 0	1935	Great Britain 5, United States 0	1968	United States 4, Australia 1
1905	British Isles 5, United States 0	1936	Great Britain 3, Australia 2	1969	United States 5, Romania 0
1906	British Isles 5, United States 0	1937	United States 4, Great Britain 1	1970	United States 5, W. Germany 0
1907	Australia 3, British Isles 2	1938	United States 3, Australia 2	1971	United States 3, Romania 2
1908	Australasia 3, United States 2	1939	Australia 3, United States 2	1972	United States 3, Romania 2
1909	Australasia 5, United States 0	1940-45	(not played)	1973	Australia 5, United States 0
1910	(not played)	1946	United States 5, Australia 0	1974	South Africa (default by India)
1911	Australasia 5, United States 0	1947	United States 4, Australia 1	1975	Sweden 3, Czech. 2
1912	British Isles 3, Australasia 2	1948	United States 5, Australia 0	1976	Italy 4, Chile 1
1913	United States 3, British Isles 2	1949	United States 4, Australia 1	1977	Australia 3, Italy 1
1914	Australasia 3, United States 2	1950	Australia 4, United States 1	1978	United States 4, Great Britain 1
1915-18	(not played)	1951	Australia 3, United States 2	1979	United States 5, Italy 0
1919	Australasia 4, British Isles 1	1952	Australia 4, United States 1	1980	Czechoslovakia 4, Italy 1
1920	United States 5, Australasia 0	1953	Australia 3, United States 2	1981	United States 3, Argentina 1
1921	United States 5, Japan 0	1954	United States 3, Australia 2	1982	United States 3, France, 0
1922	United States 4, Australasia 1	1955	Australia 5, United States 0	1983	Australia 3, Sweden 2
1923	United States 4, Australasia 1	1956	Australia 5, United States 0	1984	Sweden 3, United States 0
1924	United States 5, Australasia 0	1957	Australia 3, United States 2	1985	Sweden 3, W. Germany 2
1925	United States 5, France 0	1958	United States 3, Australia 2	1986	Australia 3, Sweden 2
1926	United States 4, France 1	1959	Australia 3, United States 2	1987	Sweden 5, India 0
1927	France 3, United States 2	1960	Australia 4, Italy 1	1988	W. Germany 4, Sweden 1
1928	France 4, United States 1	1961	Australia 5, Italy 0	1989	W. Germany 3, Sweden 2
1929	France 3, United States 2	1962	Australia 5, Mexico 0	1990	United States 3, Australia 2
1930	France 4, United States 1	1963	United States 3, Australia 2		

All-England Champions, Wimbledon

Men's Singles

Year	Champion	Final opponent	Year	Champion	Final opponent
1933	Jack Crawford	Ellsworth Vines	1965	Roy Emerson	Fred Stolle
1934	Fred Perry	Jack Crawford	1966	Manuel Santana	Dennis Ralston
1935	Fred Perry	Gottfried von Cramm	1967	John Newcombe	Wilhelm Bungert
1936	Fred Perry	Gottfried von Cramm	1968	Rod Laver	Tony Roche
1937	Donald Budge	Gottfried von Cramm	1969	Rod Laver	John Newcombe
1938	Donald Budge	Wilfred Austin	1970	John Newcombe	Ken Rosewall
1939	Bobby Riggs	Elwood Cooke	1971	John Newcombe	Stan Smith
1940-45	not held		1972	Stan Smith	Ilie Nastase
1946	Yvon Petra	Geoff E. Brown	1973	Jan Kodes	Alex Metreveli
1947	Jack Kramer	Tom P. Brown	1974	Jimmy Connors	Ken Rosewall
1948	Bob Falkenburg	John Bromwich	1975	Arthur Ashe	Jimmy Connors
1949	Ted Schroeder	Jaroslav Drobny	1976	Bjorn Borg	Ilie Nastase
1950	Budge Patty	Frank Sedgman	1977	Bjorn Borg	Jimmy Connors
1951	Dick Savitt	Ken McGregor	1978	Bjorn Borg	Jimmy Connors
1952	Frank Sedgman	Jaroslav Drobny	1979	Bjorn Borg	Roscoe Tanner
1953	Vic Seixas	Kurt Nielsen	1980	Bjorn Borg	John McEnroe
1954	Jaroslav Drobny	Ken Rosewall	1981	John McEnroe	Bjorn Borg
1955	Tony Trabert	Kurt Nielsen	1982	Jimmy Connors	John McEnroe
1956	Lew Hoad	Ken Rosewall	1983	John McEnroe	Chris Lewis
1957	Lew Hoad	Ashley Cooper	1984	John McEnroe	Jimmy Connors
1958	Ashley Cooper	Neale Fraser	1985	Boris Becker	Kevin Curren
1959	Alex Olmedo	Rod Laver	1986	Boris Becker	Ivan Lendl
1960	Neale Fraser	Rod Laver	1987	Pat Cash	Ivan Lendl
1961	Rod Laver	Chuck McKinley	1988	Stefan Edberg	Boris Becker
1962	Rod Laver	Martin Mulligan	1989	Boris Becker	Stefan Edberg
1963	Chuck McKinley	Fred Stolle	1990	Stefan Edberg	Boris Becker
1964	Roy Emerson	Fred Stolle	1991	Michael Stich	Boris Becker

Women's Singles

Year	Champion	Year	Champion	Year	Champion	Year	Champion
1946	Pauline Betz	1958	Althea Gibson	1970	Margaret Court	1982	Martina Navratilova
1947	Margaret Osborne	1959	Maria Bueno	1971	Evonne Goolagong	1983	Martina Navratilova
1948	Louise Brough	1960	Maria Bueno	1972	Billie Jean King	1984	Martina Navratilova
1949	Louise Brough	1961	Angela Mortimer	1973	Billie Jean King	1985	Martina Navratilova
1950	Louise Brough	1962	Karen Hantze-Susman	1974	Chris Evert	1986	Martina Navratilova
1951	Doris Hart	1963	Margaret Smith	1975	Billie Jean King	1987	Martina Navratilova
1952	Maureen Connolly	1964	Maria Bueno	1976	Chris Evert	1988	Steffi Graf
1953	Maureen Connolly	1965	Margaret Smith	1977	Virginia Wade	1989	Steffi Graf
1954	Maureen Connolly	1966	Billie Jean King	1978	Martina Navratilova	1990	Martina Navratilova
1955	Louise Brough	1967	Billie Jean King	1979	Martina Navratilova	1991	Steffi Graf
1956	Shirley Fry	1968	Billie Jean King	1980	Evonne Goolagong		
1957	Althea Gibson	1969	Ann Haydon-Jones	1981	Chris Evert Lloyd		

French Open Champions

Year	Men	Women	Year	Men	Women
1969	Rod Laver	Margaret Smith Court	1981	Bjorn Borg	Hana Mandlikova
1970	Jan Kodes	Margaret Smith Court	1982	Mats Wilander	Martina Navratilova
1971	Jan Kodes	Evonne Goolagong	1983	Yannick Noah	Chris Evert Lloyd
1972	Andres Gimeno	Billie Jean King	1984	Ivan Lendl	Martina Navratilova
1973	Ilie Nastase	Margaret Court	1985	Mats Wilander	Chris Evert Lloyd
1974	Bjorn Borg	Chris Evert	1986	Ivan Lendl	Chris Evert Lloyd
1975	Bjorn Borg	Chris Evert	1987	Ivan Lendl	Steffi Graf
1976	Adriano Panatta	Sue Barker	1988	Mats Wilander	Steffi Graf
1977	Guillermo Vilas	Mima Jausovec	1989	Michael Chang	Arantxa Sanchez
1978	Bjorn Borg	Virginia Ruzici	1990	Andres Gomez	Monica Seles
1979	Bjorn Borg	Chris Evert Lloyd	1991	Jim Courier	Monica Seles
1980	Bjorn Borg	Chris Evert Lloyd			

The World Cup

The World Cup, emblematic of International soccer supremacy, was won by West Germany on July 8, 1990, with a 1-0 victory over defending champion Argentina on a penalty shot in the 84th minute. It was the lowest-scoring final in the 60 years of World Cup play. It was the 3d World Cup title for West Germany, equaling Brazil and Italy. Winners and sites of previous World Cup play follow:

Year	Winner	Final opponent	Site	Year	Winner	Final opponent	Site
1930	Uruguay	Argentina	Uruguay	1966	England	W. Germany	England
1934	Italy	Czechoslovakia	Italy	1970	Brazil	Italy	Mexico
1938	Italy	Hungary	France	1974	W. Germany	Netherlands	W. Germany
1950	Uruguay	Brazil	Brazil	1978	Argentina	Netherlands	Argentina
1954	W. Germany	Hungary	Switzerland	1982	Italy	W. Germany	Spain
1958	Brazil	Sweden	Sweden	1986	Argentina	W. Germany	Mexico
1962	Brazil	Czechoslovakia	Chile	1990	W. Germany	Argentina	Italy

Tour de France in 1991

Miguel Indurain of Spain won the 78th Tour de France, the world's most prestigious bicycle race. His margin of victory was 3 minutes 36 seconds, and he completed the 21-day, 2,445 mile race in a total time of 101 hours 1 minute 20 seconds. Gianni Bugno of Italy finished second.

Auto Racing

Indianapolis 500 Winners

Year	Winner, Car	MPH	Year	Winner, Car	MPH
1911	Ray Harroun, Marmon Wasp	74.59	1954	Bill Vukovich, Fuel Injection	130.840
1912	Joe Dawson, National	78.72	1955	Bob Sweikert, John Zink Special	128.209
1913	Jules Goux, Peugeot	75.933	1956	Pat Flaherty, John Zink Special	128.490
1914	Rene Thomas, Delage	82.47	1957	Sam Hanks, Belond Exhaust	135.601
1915	Ralph DePalma, Mercedes	89.84	1958	Jimmy Bryan, Belond A.P.	133.791
1916	Dario Resta, Peugeot	84.00	1959	Rodger Ward, Leader Card Special	135.857
1917-18	race not held		1960	Jim Rathmann, Ken Paul Special	138.767
1919	Howdy Wilcox, Peugeot	88.05	1961	A.J. Foyt, Bowes Seal Fast	139.130
1920	Gaston Chevrolet, Monroe	88.16	1962	Rodger Ward, Leader Card Special	140.293
1921	Tommy Milton, Frontenac	89.62	1963	Parnelli Jones, Agajanian Special	143.137
1922	Jimmy Murphy, Murphy Special	94.48	1964	A.J. Foyt, Sheraton-Thompson Special	147.350
1923	Tommy Milton, H.C.S.	90.95	1965	Jim Clark, Lotus-Ford	150.686
1924	L.L. Corum-Joe Boyer, Duesenberg	98.23	1966	Graham Hill, American Red Ball	144.317
1925	Pete DePaolo, Duesenberg	101.13	1967	A.J. Foyt, Sheraton-Thompson Special	151.207
1926	Frank Lockhart, Miller	95.904	1968	Bobby Unser, Rislone Special	152.882
1927	George Souders, Duesenberg	97.545	1969	Mario Andretti, STP Oil Treatment Special	
1928	Louis Meyer, Miller	99.482		cial	156.867
1929	Ray Keech, Simplex	97.585	1970	Al Unser, Johnny Lightning Special	155.749
1930	Billy Arnold, Miller-Hartz	100.448	1971	Al Unser, Johnny Lightning Special	157.735
1931	Louis Schneider, Bowes Seal Fast	96.629	1972	Mark Donohue, Sunoco McLaren	162.962
1932	Fred Frame, Miller-Hartz	104.144	1973	Gordon Johncock, STP Double Oil Filter	159.036
1933	Louis Meyer, Tydol	104.162	1974	Johnny Rutherford, McLaren	158.589
1934	Bill Cummings, Boyle Products	104.863	1975	Bobby Unser, Jorgenson Eagle	149.213
1935	Kelly Petillo, Gilmore Speedway	106.240	1976	Johnny Rutherford, Hygain McLaren	148.725
1936	Louis Meyer, Ring Free	109.069	1977	A.J. Foyt, Gilmore Coyote-Ford	161.331
1937	Wilbur Shaw, Shaw-Gilmore	113.580	1978	Al Unser, Lola Cosworth	161.363
1938	Floyd Roberts, Burd Piston Ring	117.200	1979	Rick Mears, Penske-Cosworth	158.899
1939	Wilbur Shaw, Boyle	115.035	1980	Johnny Rutherford, Chaparral-Cosworth	142.862
1940	Wilbur Shaw, Boyle	114.277	1981	Bobby Unser, Penske-Cosworth	139.085
1941	Floyd Davis-Mauri Rose, Knock-Out-Hose Clip	115.117	1982	Gordon Johncock, Wildcat-Cosworth	162.026
			1983	Tom Sneva, March-Cosworth	162.117
1942-45	race not held		1984	Rick Mears, March-Cosworth	163.621
1946	George Robson, Thorne Engineering	114.820	1985	Danny Sullivan, March-Cosworth	152.982
1947	Mauri Rose, Blue Crown Special	116.338	1986	Bobby Rahal, March-Cosworth	170.722
1948	Mauri Rose, Blue Crown Special	119.814	1987	Al Unser, March-Cosworth	162.175
1949	Bill Holland, Blue Crown Special	121.327	1988	Rick Mears, Penske-Chevy V8	144.809
1950	Johnny Parsons, Wynn Kurtis Kraft	124.002	1989	Emerson Fittipaldi, Penske PC 18-Chevy	167.581
1951	Lee Wallard, Belanger	126.224	1990	Arie Luyendyk, Lola-Chevy	185.984
1952	Troy Ruttman, Agajanian	128.922	1991	Rick Mears, Penske-Chevy	176.457
1953	Bill Vukovich, Fuel Injection	128.740			

The race was less than 500 miles in the following years: 1916 (300 mi.), 1926 (400 mi.), 1950 (345 mi.), 1973 (332.5 mi.), 1975 (435 mi.), 1976 (255 mi.). Race record—185,984 MPH, Arie Luyendyk, 1990.

Notable One-Mile Speed Records

Date	Driver	Car	MPH	Date	Driver	Car	MPH
1/26/06	Marriott	Stanley (Steam)	127.659	9/ 3/35	Campbell	Bluebird Special	301.13
3/16/10	Oldfield	Benz	131.724	11/19/37	Eyston	Thunderbolt 1	311.42
4/23/11	Burman	Benz	141.732	9/16/38	Eyston	Thunderbolt 1	357.5
2/12/19	DePalma	Packard	149.875	8/23/39	Cobb	Railton	368.9
4/27/20	Milton	Dusenberg	155.046	9/16/47	Cobb	Railton-Mobil	394.2
4/28/26	Parry-Thomas	Thomas Spl.	170.624	8/ 5/63	Breedlove	Spirit of America	407.45
3/29/27	Seagrave	Sunbeam	203.790	10/27/64	Arfons	Green Monster	536.71
4/22/28	Keech	White Triplex	207.552	11/15/65	Breedlove	Spirit of America	600.601
3/11/29	Seagrave	Irving-Napier	231.446	10/23/70	Gabelich	Blue Flame	622.407
2/ 5/31	Campbell	Napier-Campbell	246.086	10/9/79	Barrett	Budweiser Rocket	638.637*
2/24/32	Campbell	Napier-Campbell	253.96	10/4/83	Noble	Thrust 2	633.6
2/22/33	Campbell	Napier-Campbell	272.109				

*not recognized as official by sanctioning bodies.

CART Champions

(U.S. Auto Club Champions prior to 1979)

Year	Driver	Year	Driver	Year	Driver	Year	Driver
1960	A. J. Foyt	1968	Bobby Unser	1976	Gordon Johncock	1984	Mario Andretti
1961	A. J. Foyt	1969	Mario Andretti	1977	Tom Sneva	1985	Al Unser
1962	Rodger Ward	1970	Al Unser	1978	Tom Sneva	1986	Bobby Rahal
1963	A. J. Foyt	1971	Joe Leonard	1979	Rick Mears	1987	Bobby Rahal
1964	A. J. Foyt	1972	Joe Leonard	1980	Johnny Rutherford	1988	Danny Sullivan
1965	Mario Andretti	1973	Roger McCluskey	1981	Rick Mears	1989	Emerson Fittipaldi
1966	Mario Andretti	1974	Bobby Unser	1982	Rick Mears	1990	Al Unser Jr.
1967	A. J. Foyt	1975	A. J. Foyt	1983	Al Unser		

Le Mans 24-Hour Race in 1991

Johnny Herbert of the U.K., Bertrand Gachot of Belgium, and Volker Weidler of Germany, drove their Mazda to victory in the 1991 Le Mans 24-hour race. They traveled the 3,058.9 miles at an average of 127.307 mph.

NASCAR Racing in 1991

Winston Cup Races

Date	Race, site	Winner	Car
Feb. 17	Daytona 500, Daytona Beach, Fla.	Ernie Irvan	Chevrolet
Feb. 24	Pontiac Excitement 400, Richmond, Va.	Dale Earnhardt	Chevrolet
Mar. 24	Motorcraft 500, Hampton, Ga.	Ken Schrader	Chevrolet
Apr. 7	Transouth 500, Darlington, S.C.	Ricky Rudd	Chevrolet
Apr. 21	First Union 400, N. Wilkesboro, N.C.	Darrell Waltrip	Chevrolet
Apr. 28	Hanes Activewear 500, Martinsville, Va.	Dale Earnhardt	Chevrolet
May 6	Winston 500, Talladega, Ala.	Harry Gant	Oldsmobile
May 26	Coca Cola 600, Concord, N.C.	Davey Allison	Ford
June 2	Budweiser 500, Dover, Del.	Ken Schrader	Chevrolet
June 9	Banquet Frozen Foods 300, Sonoma, Cal.	Davey Allison	Ford
June 16	Champion Spark Plug 500, Pocono, Pa.	Darrell Waltrip	Chevrolet
June 23	Miller Genuine Draft 400, Brooklyn, Mich.	Davey Allison	Ford
July 6	Pepsi 400, Daytona Beach, Fla.	Bill Elliott	Ford
July 21	Miller Genuine Draft 500, Pocono, Pa.	Rusty Wallace	Pontiac
July 30	Die-Hard 500, Talladega, Ala.	Dale Earnhardt	Chevrolet
Aug. 11	Budweiser at The Glen, Watkins Glen, N.Y.	Ernie Irvan	Chevrolet
Aug. 18	Champion Spark Plug 400, Brooklyn, Mich.	Dale Jarrett	Ford
Aug. 24	Bud 500, Bristol, Tenn.	Alan Kulwicki	Ford
Sept. 1	Southern 500, Darlington, S.C.	Harry Gant	Oldsmobile
Sept. 8	Miller Genuine Draft 400, Richmond, Va.	Harry Gant	Oldsmobile
Sept. 15	Peak 500, Dover, Del.	Harry Gant	Oldsmobile
Sept. 22	Goody's 500, Martinsville, Va.	Harry Gant	Oldsmobile
Sept. 29	Tyson Holly Farms 400	Dale Earnhardt	Chevrolet

Winston Cup Champions (NASCAR)

Year	Driver	Year	Driver	Year	Driver	Year	Driver
1949	Red Byron	1960	Rex White	1971	Richard Petty	1981	Darrell Waltrip
1950	Bill Rexford	1961	Ned Jarrett	1972	Richard Petty	1982	Darrell Waltrip
1951	Herb Thomas	1962	Joe Weatherly	1973	Benny Parson	1983	Bobby Allison
1952	Tim Flock	1963	Joe Weatherly	1974	Richard Petty	1984	Terry Labonte
1953	Herb Thomas	1964	Richard Petty	1975	Richard Petty	1985	Darrell Waltrip
1954	Lee Petty	1965	Ned Jarrett	1976	Cale Yarborough	1986	Dale Earnhardt
1955	Tim Flock	1966	David Pearson	1977	Cale Yarborough	1987	Dale Earnhardt
1956	Buck Baker	1967	Richard Petty	1978	Cale Yarborough	1988	Bill Elliott
1957	Buck Baker	1968	David Pearson	1979	Richard Petty	1989	Rusty Wallace
1958	Lee Petty	1969	David Pearson	1980	Dale Earnhardt	1990	Dale Earnhardt
1959	Lee Petty	1970	Bobby Isaac				

Daytona 500 Winners

Year	Driver, car	Avg. MPH	Year	Driver, car	Avg. MPH
1959	Lee Petty, Oldsmobile	135.521	1976	David Pearson, Mercury	152.181
1960	Junior Johnson, Chevrolet	124.740	1977	Cale Yarborough, Chevrolet	153.218
1961	Marvin Panch, Pontiac	149.601	1978	Bobby Allison, Ford	159.730
1962	Fireball Roberts, Pontiac	152.529	1979	Richard Petty, Oldsmobile	143.977
1963	Tiny Lund, Ford	151.566	1980	Buddy Baker, Oldsmobile	177.602
1964	Richard Petty, Plymouth	154.334	1981	Richard Petty, Buick	169.651
1965	Fred Lorenzen, Ford (a)	141.539	1982	Bobby Allison, Buick	153.991
1966	Richard Petty, Plymouth (b)	160.627	1983	Cale Yarborough, Pontiac	155.979
1967	Mario Andretti, Ford	146.926	1984	Cale Yarborough, Chevrolet	150.994
1968	Cale Yarborough, Mercury	143.251	1985	Bill Elliott, Ford	172.265
1969	Lee Roy Yarborough, Ford	160.875	1986	Geoff Bodine, Chevrolet	148.124
1970	Pete Hamilton, Plymouth	149.601	1987	Bill Elliott, Ford	176.263
1971	Richard Petty, Plymouth	144.456	1988	Bobby Allison, Buick	137.531
1972	A. J. Foyt, Mercury	161.550	1989	Darrell Waltrip, Chevrolet	148.466
1973	Richard Petty, Dodge	157.205	1990	Derrike Cope, Chevrolet	165.761
1974	Richard Petty, Dodge (c)	140.894	1991	Ernie Irvin, Chevrolet	148.148
1975	Benny Parsons, Chevrolet	153.649			

(a) 322.5 miles. (b) 495 miles. (c) 450 miles.

World Grand Prix Champions

Year	Driver	Year	Driver	Year	Driver
1951	Jan Fangio, Argentina	1965	Jim Clark, Scotland	1978	Mario Andretti, U.S.
1952	Alberto Ascari, Italy	1966	Jack Brabham, Australia	1979	Jody Scheckter, So. Africa
1953	Alberto Ascari, Italy	1967	Denis Hulme, New Zealand	1980	Alan Jones, Australia
1954	Juan Fangio, Argentina	1968	Graham Hill, England	1981	Nelson Piquet, Brazil
1955	Juan Fangio, Argentina	1969	Jackie Stewart, Scotland	1982	Keke Rosberg, Finland
1956	Juan Fangio, Argentina	1970	Jochen Rindt, Austria	1983	Nelson Piquet, Brazil
1957	Juan Fangio, Argentina	1971	Jackie Stewart, Scotland	1984	Niki Lauda, Austria
1958	Mike Hawthorne, England	1972	Emerson Fittipaldi, Brazil	1985	Alain Prost, France
1959	Jack Brabham, Australia	1973	Jackie Stewart, Scotland	1986	Alain Prost, France
1960	Jack Brabham, Australia	1974	Emerson Fittipaldi, Brazil	1987	Nelson Piquet, Brazil
1961	Phil Hill, United States	1975	Niki Lauda, Austria	1988	Ayrton Senna, Brazil
1962	Graham Hill, England	1976	James Hunt, England	1989	Alain Prost, France
1963	Jim Clark, Scotland	1977	Niki Lauda, Austria	1990	Ayrton Senna, Brazil
1964	John Surtees, England				

Grand Prix for Formula 1 Cars in 1991

Grand Prix	Winner, car	Grand Prix	Winner, car
Belgian	Ayrton Senna, McLaren-Honda	Mexico	Riccardo Patrese, Williams-Renault
Brazilian	Ayrton Senna, McLaren-Honda	Monaco	Ayrton Senna, McLaren-Honda
British	Nigel Mansell, Williams-Renault	Portuguese	Riccardo Patrese, Williams-Renault
Canadian	Nelson Piquet, Benetton-Ford	San Marino	Ayrton Senna, McLaren-Honda
French	Nigel Mansell, Williams-Renault	Spanish	Nigel Mansell, Williams-Renault
German	Nigel Mansell, Williams-Renault	United States	Ayrton Senna, McLaren-Honda
Italian	Nigel Mansell, Williams-Renault		

Harness Racing

Harness Horse of the Year

(Chosen by the U.S. Trotting Assn. and the U.S. Harness Writers Assn.)

Year	Horse	Year	Horse	Year	Horse	Year	Horse
1951	Pronto Don	1961	Adios Butler	1971	Albatross	1981	Fan Hanover
1952	Good Time	1962	Su Mac Lad	1972	Albatross	1982	Cam Fella
1953	Hi Lo's Forbes	1963	Speedy Scot	1973	Sir Dalrae	1983	Cam Fella
1954	Stenographer	1964	Bret Hanover	1974	Delmonica Hanover	1984	Fancy Crown
1955	Scott Frost	1965	Bret Hanover	1975	Savior	1985	Nihilator
1956	Scott Frost	1966	Bret Hanover	1976	Keystone Ore	1986	Forrest Skipper
1957	Torpid	1967	Nevele Pride	1977	Green Speed	1987	Mack Lobell
1958	Emily's Pride	1968	Nevele Pride	1978	Abercrombie	1988	Mack Lobell
1959	Bye Bye Byrd	1969	Nevele Pride	1979	Niatross	1989	Matt's Scooter
1960	Adios Butler	1970	Fresh Yankee	1980	Niatross	1990	Beach Towel

The Hambletonian (3-year-old trotters)

Year	Winner	Driver	Year	Winner	Driver
1965	Egyptian Candor	Del Cameron	1979	Legend Hanover	George Sholty
1966	Kerry Way	Frank Ervin	1980	Burgomeister	Bill Haughton
1967	Speedy Streak	Del Cameron	1981	Shiaway St. Pat	Ray Remmen
1968	Nevele Pride	Stanley Dancer	1982	Speed Bowl	Tommy Haughton
1969	Lindy's Pride	Howard Beissinger	1983	Duenna	Stanley Dancer
1970	Timothy T	John Simpson Sr.	1984	Historic Freight	Ben Webster
1971	Speedy Crown	Howard Beissinger	1985	Prakas	Bill O'Donnell
1972	Super Bowl	Stanley Dancer	1986	Nuclear Kosmos	Ulf Thoresen
1973	Flirth	Ralph Baldwin	1987	Mack Lobell	John Campbell
1974	Christopher T	Bill Haughton	1988	Armbro Goal	John Campbell
1975	Bonefish	Stanley Dancer	1989	Park Avenue Joe	Ron Waples
1976	Steve Lobell	Bill Haughton	1990	Harmonious	John Campbell
1977	Green Speed	Bill Haughton	1991	Giant Victory	Jack Moiseyev
1978	Speedy Somolli	Howard Beissinger			

Leading Drivers

Races Won

Year	Driver		Year	Driver		Year	Driver		Year	Driver	
1967	Bob Farrington	277	1974	Herve Filion	637	1980	Herve Filion	474	1985	Michel Lachance	592
1968	Herve Filion	407	1975	Daryl Buse	360	1981	Eddie Davis	404	1986	Michel Lachance	770
1969	Herve Filion	394	1976	Herve Filion	445		Herve Filion	404	1987	Michel Lachance	715
1970	Herve Filion	486	1977	Herve Filion	441	1982	Herve Filion	495	1988	Herve Filion	798
1971	Herve Filion	543	1978	Herve Filion	423	1983	Eddie Davis	470	1989	Herve Filion	806
1972	Herve Filion	605	1979	Ron Waples	443	1984	Michel Lachance	466	1990	Herve Filion	660
1973	Herve Filion	445									

Money Won

Year	Driver	Dollars	Year	Driver	Dollars	Year	Driver	Dollars
1967	Bill Haughton	1,305,773	1975	Carmine Abbatiello	2,275,093	1983	John Campbell	6,104,082
1968	Bill Haughton	1,654,172	1976	Herve Filion	2,241,045	1984	Bill O'Donnell	9,059,184
1969	Del Insko	1,635,463	1977	Herve Filion	2,551,058	1985	Bill O'Donnell	10,207,372
1970	Herve Filion	1,647,837	1978	Carmine Abbatiello	3,344,457	1986	John Campbell	9,515,055
1971	Herve Filion	1,915,945	1979	John Campbell	3,308,984	1987	John Campbell	10,186,495
1972	Herve Filion	2,473,265	1980	John Campbell	3,732,306	1988	John Campbell	11,148,565
1973	Herve Filion	2,233,302	1981	Bill O'Donnell	4,065,608	1989	John Campbell	9,738,450
1974	Herve Filion	3,474,315	1982	Bill O'Donnell	5,755,067	1990	John Campbell	11,620,878

U.S. Gymnastics Championships in 1991

Cincinnati, Oh., June 6-9, 1991

Men

Floor exercise—Mike Racanelli.
Pommel horse—Chris Walker.
Still rings—Scott Keswick.
Vault—Scott Keswick.
Parallel bars—Scott Keswick.
High Bar—Lance Ringnald.
All Around—Chris Walker.

Women

Vault—Kerri Strug.
Uneven bars—Elisabeth Crandall.
Balance beam—Shannon Miller.
Floor exercise—(tie) Dominique Dawes, Kim Zmeskal
All Around—Kim Zmeskal.

World Swimming Records
As of Sept., 1991

Men's Records

Freestyle

Distance	Time	Holder	Country	Where made	Date
50 Meters	0:21.81	Tom Jager	U.S.	Nashville	Mar. 24, 1990
100 Meters	0:48.42	Matt Biondi	U.S.	Austin, Tex.	Aug. 10, 1988
200 Meters	1:46.69	Giorgio Lamberti	Italy	Bonn	Aug. 15, 1989
400 Meters	3:46.95	Ewe Dassler	E. Germany	Seoul	Sept. 23, 1988
800 Meters	7:50.64	Vladimir Salnikov	USSR	Moscow	July 4, 1986
1,500 Meters	14:50.36	Jorg Hoffmann	Germany	Perth, Australia	Jan. 13, 1991

Breaststroke

Distance	Time	Holder	Country	Where made	Date
100 Meters	1:01.49	Adrian Moorhouse	Gt. Britain	New Zealand	Jan. 25, 1990
200 Meters	2:10.60	Mike Barrowman	U.S.	Ft. Lauderdale, Fla.	Aug. 3, 1991

Butterfly

Distance	Time	Holder	Country	Where made	Date
100 Meters	0:52.84	Pablo Morales	U.S.	Orlando, Fla.	June 23, 1986
200 Meters	1:56.24	Michael Gross	W. Germany	Bonn	June 27, 1986

Backstroke

Distance	Time	Holder	Country	Where made	Date
100 Meters	0:54.51	David Berkoff	U.S.	Seoul	Sept. 24, 1988
200 Meters	1:57.30	Martin Zubero	Spain	Ft. Lauderdale, Fla.	Aug. 13, 1991

Individual Medley

Distance	Time	Holder	Country	Where made	Date
200 Meters	1:59.36	Tamas Darnyi	Hungary	Perth, Australia	Jan. 14, 1991
400 Meters	4:14.75	Tamas Darnyi	Hungary	Seoul	Sept. 21, 1988

Freestyle Relays

Distance	Time	Holder	Country	Where made	Date
400 M. (4×100)	3:16.53	Jacobs, Dalbey, Jager, Biondi	U.S.	Seoul	Sept. 23, 1988
800 M. (4×200)	7:12.51	Dalbey, Cetlinsky, Gjertsen, Biondi	U.S.	Seoul	Sept. 21, 1988

Medley Relays

Distance	Time	Holder	Country	Where made	Date
400 M. (4×100)	3:36.93	Berkoff, Schroeder, Jacobs, Biondi	U.S.	Seoul	Sept. 25, 1988

Women's Records

Freestyle

Distance	Time	Holder	Country	Where made	Date
50 Meters	0:24.98	Yang Wenyi	China	Nashville	Mar. 24, 1990
100 Meters	0:54.73	Kristin Otto	E. Germany	Madrid	Aug. 19, 1986
200 Meters	1:57.55	Heike Friedrich	E. Germany	Berlin	June 18, 1986
400 Meters	4:03.85	Janet Evans	U.S.	Seoul	Sept. 22, 1988
800 Meters	8:16.22	Janet Evans	U.S.	Tokyo	Aug. 20, 1989
1,500 Meters	15:52.10	Janet Evans	U.S.	Orlando, Fla.	Mar. 26, 1988

Breaststroke

Distance	Time	Holder	Country	Where made	Date
100 Meters	1:07.91	Silke Hoerner	E. Germany	Strasbourg, France	Aug. 21, 1987
200 Meters	2:26.71	Silke Hoerner	E. Germany	Seoul	Sept. 21, 1988

Butterfly

Distance	Time	Holder	Country	Where made	Date
100 Meters	0:57.93	Mary T. Meagher	U.S.	Brown Deer, Wis.	Aug. 16, 1981
200 Meters	2:05.96	Mary T. Meagher	U.S.	Brown Deer, Wis.	Aug. 13, 1981

Backstroke

Distance	Time	Holder	Country	Where made	Date
100 Meters	1:00.31	Krisztina Egerszegi	Hungary	Athens	Aug. 22, 1991
200 Meters	2:08.60	Betsy Mitchell	U.S.	Orlando, Fla.	June 27, 1986

Individual Medley

Distance	Time	Holder	Country	Where made	Date
200 Meters	2:11.73	Uta Geweniger	E. Germany	Berlin	July 4, 1981
400 Meters	4:36.10	Petra Schneider	E. Germany	Ecuador	Aug. 1, 1982

Freestyle Relays

Distance	Time	Holder	Country	Where made	Date
400 M. (4×100)	3:40.57	(Otto, Stellmach, Friedrich, Schulze)	E. Germany	Madrid	Aug. 19, 1986
800 M. (4×200)	7:55:47	Stellmach, Strauss, Mohring, Friedrich	E. Germany	Strasbourg, France	Aug. 18, 1987

Medley Relays

Distance	Time	Holder	Country	Where made	Date
400 M. (4×100)	4:03.69	National Team (Kleber, Gerasch, Geissler, Meineke)	E. Germany	Moscow	Aug. 24, 1984

U.S. Long Course Swimming Championships in 1991

Ft. Lauderdale, Fla., Aug. 13-17, 1991

Men

50M Freestyle—Del Cerney. **Time—0:23.09.**
100M Freestyle—Doug Gjertsen. **Time—0:50.48.**
200M Freestyle—Doug Gjertsen. **Time—1:49.69.**
800M Freestyle—Lars Jorgensen. **Time—8:02.56.**
1,500M Freestyle—Lars Jorgensen. **Time—15:22.75.**
100M Breaststroke—Seth vanNeerden. **Time—1:02.11.**
200M Breaststroke—Mike Barrowman. **Time—2:10.60.**
100M Butterfly—Trip Zedlitz. **Time—0:54.53.**
200M Butterfly—Melvin Stewart. **Time—1:56.69.**
200M Backstroke—Martin Zubero. **Time—2:58.85.**
200M Individual Medley—Trip Zedlitz. **Time—2:02.81.**
400M Individual Medley—Derek Weatherford.
Time—4:22.39.

Women

50M Freestyle—Sarah Peronni. **Time—0:26.00.**
100M Freestyle—Paige Zemina. **Time—0:56.09.**
200M Freestyle—Dara Torres. **Time—2:01.68.**
800M Freestyle—Sarah Anderson. **Time—8:48.12.**
1,500M Freestyle—Kathy Hoffman. **Time—16:40.40.**
100M Breaststroke—Emily Short. **Time—1:10.79.**
200M Breaststroke—Megan Kleine. **Time—2:33.71.**
100M Backstroke—B.J. Bedford. **Time—1:02.43.**
200M Backstroke—Paige Wilson. **Time—2:14.68.**
200M Butterfly—Jule Kole. **Time—2:11.70.**
200M Individual Medley—Mary Ellen Blanchard.
Time—2:17.91.
400M Individual Medley—Sheila Taormina. **Time—4:51.29.**

U.S. Outdoor Diving Championships in 1991

Bartlesville, Okla., Aug. 15-17, 1991

Men

One Meter—Mark Lenzi
Three Meter—Patrick Jeffrey
Platform—Scott Donie

Women

One Meter—Wendy Lucero
Three Meter—Krista Klein
Platform—Ellen McGrath

Rifle and Pistol Individual Championships in 1991

Source: National Rifle Association of America

National Outdoor Rifle and Pistol Championships

Pistol — Steve F. Reiter, Dale City, Cal., 2646-121X.
Civilian Pistol — Thomas R. Woods, Sun City, Cal., 2636-132X.
Woman Pistol — Deborah A. Storey, Pinellas Park, Fla., 2547-87X.
Smallbore Rifle Prone — Ronald O. West, Zanesville, Oh., 6390-475X.
Civilian Smallbore Rifle Prone — Ronald O. West, 6390-475X.
Woman Smallbore Rifle Prone — Carolyn Millard-Sparks, Atlanta, Ga., 6371-448X.
Smallbore Rifle NRA 3-Position — Lones W. Wigger Jr., Colorado Springs, Col., 2267-75X.
Civilian Smallbore Rifle NRA 3-Position — Lones W. Wigger Jr., 2267-75X.
Woman Smallbore Rifle NRA 3-Position — Kristin A. Peterson, Ft. Benning, Ga., 2230-78X.
Highpower Rifle — David G. Tubb, Canadian, Tex., 2373-112X.
Civilian Highpower Rifle — David G. Tubb, 2373-112X.
Woman Highpower Rifle — Nancy Tompkins-Gallagher, Prescott, Ariz., 2355-93X.

U.S. NRA International Shooting Championships

Smallbore Free Rifle Prone — Thomas A. Tamas, Columbus, Ga., 1295.1.
Smallbore Free Rifle Position — Thomas A. Tamas, Columbus, Ga., 2420.6
Air Rifle — Matthew P. Suggs, Ft. Benning, Ga., 1268.2.
Women's Standard Rifle Prone — Robin McCall, Tryon, N.C., 1182.
Women's Standard Rifle 3-Position — Launi Meili, Cheney, Wash., 1255.
Free Pistol — Ben Amonette, Radford, Va., 1121.
Rapid Fire Pistol — John T. McNally, Columbus, Ga., 1461.
Center Fire Pistol — Eduardo Suarez, Columbus, Ga., 1172.
Standard Pistol — Jimmie W. McCoy, Columbus, Ga., 1143.
Men's Air Pistol — Donald C. Nygord, La Crescenta, Cal., 1251.3.
Women's Air Pistol — Constance E. Petracek, Nashville, Tenn., 857.
Women's Sport Pistol — Constance E. Petracek, Nashville, Tenn. 1250.
International Trap — Bret E. Erickson, Buena Vista, Ga., 413.
Women's International Trap — Sharee M. Waldron, Columbus, Ga., 292.
International Skeet — Michael E. Schmidt, Jr., St. Paul, Minn., 416.
Women's International Skeet —Connie J. Fluker, Colorado Springs, Col., 309.

National Indoor Rifle & Pistol Championships

Smallbore Rifle 4-Position — Thomas A. Tamas, Columbus, Ga., 800.
Woman Smallbore Rifle 4-Position — Karen E. Monez, Colorado Springs, Col., 800.
Smallbore Rifle NRA 3-Position — James E. Meredith, Columbus, Ga., 1187.
Woman Smallbore Rifle NRA 3-Position — Karen E. Monez, 1180.
Smallbore Rifle International — Michael E. Anti, Columbus, Ga., 1179.
Woman Smallbore Rifle International — Launi Meili, Cheney, Wash., 1172.
Air Rifle — Kristin A. Peterson, St. Paul, Minn., 594.
Conventional Pistol — Ricardo Rodriguez, Stafford, Va., 885.
Woman Conventional Pistol — Kathy S. Chatterton, Millburn, N.J., 854.
International Free Pistol — Frank Woolard, Point Richmond, Cal., 554.
Woman International Free Pistol — Carol A. Baker, Brea, Cal., 486.
International Standard Pistol — Jon M. Eulette, Spring Valley, Cal., 569.
Woman International Standard Pistol — Sharon L. Allen, Scottsdale, Ariz., 543.
Air Pistol — Ronald P. Morency, Glendale, Ariz., 572.
Woman Air Pistol — Carol A. Baker, 556.

Iditarod Trail Sled Dog Race in 1991

Rick Swenson won the 1991 Iditarod Trail Sled Dog Race for a record 5th time. By winning the 1,158-mile race from Anchorage to Nome, Swenson received $50,000 in prize money. Martin Buser finished second and earned $39,500 while 4-time winner Susan Butcher finished third and earned $32,000.

Skiing

World Cup Alpine Champions

Men

1967	Jean Claude Killy, France	1976	Ingemar Stenmark, Sweden	1984	Pirmin Zurbriggen, Switzerland
1968	Jean Claude Killy, France	1977	Ingemar Stenmark, Sweden	1985	Marc Girardelli, Luxembourg
1969	Karl Schranz, Austria	1978	Ingemar Stenmark, Sweden	1986	Marc Girardelli, Luxembourg
1970	Karl Schranz, Austria	1979	Peter Luescher, Switzerland	1987	Pirmin Zurbriggen, Switzerland
1971	Gustavo Thoeni, Italy	1980	Andreas Wenzel, Liechtenstein	1988	Pirmin Zurbriggen, Switzerland
1972	Gustavo Thoeni, Italy	1981	Phil Mahre, U.S.	1989	Marc Girardelli, Luxembourg
1973	Gustavo Thoeni, Italy	1982	Phil Mahre, U.S.	1990	Pirmin Zurbriggen, Switzerland
1974	Piero Gros, Italy	1983	Phil Mahre, U.S.	1991	Marc Girardelli, Luxembourg
1975	Gustavo Thoeni, Italy				

Women

1967	Nancy Greene, Canada	1976	Rose Mittermaier, W. Germany	1984	Erika Hess, Switzerland
1968	Nancy Greene, Canada	1977	Lise-Marie Morerod, Switzerland	1985	Michela Figini, Switzerland
1969	Gertrud Gabl, Austria	1978	Hanni Wenzel, Liechtenstein	1986	Maria Walliser, Switzerland
1970	Michele Jacot, France	1979	Annemarie Proell Moser, Austria	1987	Maria Walliser, Switzerland
1971	Annemarie Proell, Austria	1980	Hanni Wenzel, Liechtenstein	1988	Michela Figini, Switzerland
1972	Annemarie Proell, Austria	1981	Marie-Theres Nadig, Switzerland	1989	Vreni Schneider, Switzerland
1973	Annemarie Proell, Austria	1982	Erika Hess, Switzerland	1990	Petra Kronberger, Austria
1974	Annemarie Proell, Austria	1983	Tamara McKinney, U.S.	1991	Petra Kronberger, Austria
1975	Annemarie Proell, Austria				

U.S. Alpine Championships in 1991

Men

Downhill—A.J. Kitt
Slalom—Joe Levins
Giant Slalom—Alain Feutrier
Super Giant Slalom—A.J. Kitt
Combined—Joe Levins

Women

Downhill—Megan Gerety
Slalom—Eva Twardokens
Giant Slalom—Eva Twardokens
Super Giant Slalom—Julie Parisien
Combined—Wendy Fisher

Chess

Source: U.S. Chess Federation

Chess dates back to antiquity, its exact origin unknown. The best players of their time, regarded by later generations as world champions, were Francois Philidor, Alexandre Deschappelles, Louis de la Bourdonnais, all France; Howard Staunton, England; Adolph Anderssen, Germany and Paul Morphy, U.S. In 1866 Wilhelm Steinitz defeated Adolph Anderssen and claimed the world champion title. Official world champions since the title was first used follow:

1866-1894 Wilhelm Steinitz, Austria	1948-1957 Mikhail Botvinnik, USSR	1969-1972 Boris Spassky, USSR
1894-1921 Emanuel Lasker, Germany	1957-1958 Vassily Smyslov, USSR	1972-1975 Bobby Fischer, U.S. (a)
1921-1927 Jose R. Capablanca, Cuba	1958-1959 Mikhail Botvinnik, USSR	1975-1985 Anatoly Karpov, USSR
1927-1935 Alexander A. Alekhine, France	1960-1961 Mikhail Tal, USSR	1985 Gary Kasparov, USSR
1935-1937 Max Euwe, Netherlands	1961-1963 Mikhail Botvinnik, USSR	
1937-1946 Alexander A. Alekhine, France	1963-1969 Tigran Petrosian, USSR	

(a) Defaulted championship after refusal to accept International Chess Federation rules for a championship match, April 1975.

United States Champions

Unofficial champions		1895-1897	Jackson Showalter	1968-1969	Larry Evans	Larry Christiansen
1857-1871	Paul Morphy	1897-1906	Harry Pillsbury	1969-1972	Samuel Reshevsky	Roman Dzindzichashvili
1871-1876	George Mackenzie	1906-1909	vacant	1972-1973	Robert Byrne	
1876-1880	James Mason	1909-1936	Frank Marshall	1973-1974	Lubomir Kavalek,	1984-1985 Lev Alburt
1880-1889	George Mackenzie	1936-1944	Samuel Reshevsky		John Grefe	1986 Yasser Seirawan
1889-1890	S. Lipschutz	1944-1946	Arnold Denker	1974-1977	Walter Browne	1987 (tie) Joel Benjamin
1890	Jackson Showalter	1946-1948	Samuel Reshevsky	1978-1980	Lubomir Kavalek	Nick DeFirmian
1890-1891	Max Judd	1948-1951	Herman Steiner	1980-1981	(tie) Larry Evans,	1988 Michael Wilder
Official champions		1951-1954	Larry Evans		Larry Christiansen,	1989 (tie) Stuart Rachels,
1891-1892	Jackson Showalter	1954-1957	Arthur Bisguier		Walter Browne	Yasser Seirawan,
1892-1894	S. Lipschutz	1957-1961	Bobby Fischer	1981-1983	(tie) Walter Browne,	Roman Dzindzichashvili
1894	Jackson Showalter	1961-1962	Larry Evans		Yasser Seirawan	1990 Lev Alburt
1894-1895	Albert Hodges	1962-1968	Bobby Fischer	1983	(tie) Walter Browne	1991 Gata Kamsky

American Power Boat Assn. Gold Cup Champions

Year	Boat	Driver	Year	Boat	Driver
1974	Pay'N Pak	George Henley	1983	Atlas Van Lines	Chip Hanauer
1975	Pay 'N Pak	George Henley	1984	Atlas Van Lines	Chip Hanauer
1976	Miss U.S.	Tom D'Eath	1985	Miller American	Chip Hanauer
1977	Atlas Van Lines	Bill Muncey	1986	Miller American	Chip Hanauer
1978	Atlas Van Lines	Bill Muncey	1987	Miller American	Chip Hanauer
1979	Atlas Van Lines	Bill Muncey	1988	Miller American	Chip Hanauer
1980	Miss Budweiser	Dean Chenoweth	1989	Miss Budweiser	Tom D'Eath
1981	Miss Budweiser	Dean Chenoweth	1990	Miss Budweiser	Tom D'Eath
1982	Atlas Van Lines	Chip Hanauer	1991	Winston Eagle	Mark Tate

GOLF

United States Open

Year	Winner	Year	Winner	Year	Winner	Year	Winner
1903	Willie Anderson	1926	Bobby Jones*	1950	Ben Hogan	1971	Lee Trevino
1904	Willie Anderson	1927	Tommy Armour	1951	Ben Hogan	1972	Jack Nicklaus
1905	Willie Anderson	1928	John Farrell	1952	Julius Boros	1973	Johnny Miller
1906	Alex Smith	1929	Bobby Jones*	1953	Ben Hogan	1974	Hale Irwin
1907	Alex Ross	1930	Bobby Jones*	1954	Ed Furgol	1975	Lou Graham
1908	Fred McLeod	1931	Wm. Burke	1955	Jack Fleck	1976	Jerry Pate
1909	George Sargent	1932	Gene Sarazen	1956	Cary Middlecoff	1977	Hubert Green
1910	Alex Smith	1933	John Goodman*	1957	Dick Mayer	1978	Andy North
1911	John McDermott	1934	Olin Dutra	1958	Tommy Bolt	1979	Hale Irwin
1912	John McDermott	1935	Sam Parks Jr.	1959	Billy Casper	1980	Jack Nicklaus
1913	Francis Ouimet*	1936	Tony Manero	1960	Arnold Palmer	1981	David Graham
1914	Walter Hagen	1937	Ralph Guldahl	1961	Gene Littler	1982	Tom Watson
1915	Jerome Travers*	1938	Ralph Guldahl	1962	Jack Nicklaus	1983	Larry Nelson
1916	Chick Evans*	1939	Byron Nelson	1963	Julius Boros	1984	Fuzzy Zoeller
1917-18	(Not played)	1940	Lawson Little	1964	Ken Venturi	1985	Andy North
1919	Walter Hagen	1941	Craig Wood	1965	Gary Player	1986	Ray Floyd
1920	Edward Ray	1942-45	(Not played)	1966	Billy Casper	1987	Scott Simpson
1921	Jim Barnes	1946	Lloyd Mangrum	1967	Jack Nicklaus	1988	Curtis Strange
1922	Gene Sarazen	1947	L. Worsham	1968	Lee Trevino	1989	Curtis Strange
1923	Bobby Jones*	1948	Ben Hogan	1969	Orville Moody	1990	Hale Irwin
1924	Cyril Walker	1949	Cary Middlecoff	1970	Tony Jacklin	1991	Payne Stewart
1925	Willie MacFarlane						

Professional Golfer's Association Championships

Year	Winner	Year	Winner	Year	Winner	Year	Winner
1922	Gene Sarazen	1940	Byron Nelson	1958	Dow Finsterwald	1975	Jack Nicklaus
1923	Gene Sarazen	1941	Victor Ghezzi	1959	Bob Rosburg	1976	Dave Stockton
1924	Walter Hagen	1942	Sam Snead	1960	Jay Hebert	1977	Lanny Wadkins
1925	Walter Hagen	1944	Bob Hamilton	1961	Jerry Barber	1978	John Mahaffey
1926	Walter Hagen	1945	Byron Nelson	1962	Gary Player	1979	David Graham
1927	Walter Hagen	1946	Ben Hogan	1963	Jack Nicklaus	1980	Jack Nicklaus
1928	Leo Diegel	1947	Jim Ferrier	1964	Bob Nichols	1981	Larry Nelson
1929	Leo Diegel	1948	Ben Hogan	1965	Dave Marr	1982	Ray Floyd
1930	Tommy Armour	1949	Sam Snead	1966	Al Geiberger	1983	Hal Sutton
1931	Tom Creavy	1950	Chandler Harper	1967	Don January	1984	Lee Trevino
1932	Olin Dutra	1951	Sam Snead	1968	Julius Boros	1985	Hubert Green
1933	Gene Sarazen	1952	James Turnesa	1969	Ray Floyd	1986	Bob Tway
1934	Paul Runyan	1953	Walter Burkemo	1970	Dave Stockton	1987	Larry Nelson
1935	Johnny Revolta	1954	Melvin Harbert	1971	Jack Nicklaus	1988	Jeff Sluman
1936	Denny Shute	1955	Doug Ford	1972	Gary Player	1989	Payne Stewart
1937	Denny Shute	1956	Jack Burke	1973	Jack Nicklaus	1990	Wayne Grady
1938	Paul Runyan	1957	Lionel Hebert	1974	Lee Trevino	1991	John Daly
1939	Henry Picard						

Masters Golf Tournament Champions

Year	Winner	Year	Winner	Year	Winner	Year	Winner
1934	Horton Smith	1950	Jimmy Demaret	1964	Arnold Palmer	1978	Gary Player
1935	Gene Sarazen	1951	Ben Hogan	1965	Jack Nicklaus	1979	Fuzzy Zoeller
1936	Horton Smith	1952	Sam Snead	1966	Jack Nicklaus	1980	Severiano Ballesteros
1937	Byron Nelson	1953	Ben Hogan	1967	Gay Brewer Jr.	1981	Tom Watson
1938	Henry Picard	1954	Sam Snead	1968	Bob Goalby	1982	Craig Stadler
1939	Ralph Guldahl	1955	Cary Middlecoff	1969	George Archer	1983	Severiano Ballesteros
1940	Jimmy Demaret	1956	Jack Burke	1970	Billy Casper	1984	Ben Crenshaw
1941	Craig Wood	1957	Doug Ford	1971	Charles Coody	1985	Bernhard Langer
1942	Byron Nelson	1958	Arnold Palmer	1972	Jack Nicklaus	1986	Jack Nicklaus
1943-1945	(Not played)	1959	Art Wall Jr.	1973	Tommy Aaron	1987	Larry Mize
1946	Herman Keiser	1960	Arnold Palmer	1974	Gary Player	1988	Sandy Lyle
1947	Jimmy Demaret	1961	Gary Player	1975	Jack Nicklaus	1989	Nick Faldo
1948	Claude Harmon	1962	Arnold Palmer	1976	Ray Floyd	1990	Nick Faldo
1949	Sam Snead	1963	Jack Nicklaus	1977	Tom Watson	1991	Ian Woosnam

British Open Golf Champions

Year	Winner	Year	Winner	Year	Winner	Year	Winner
1931	Tommy Armour	1950	Bobby Locke	1964	Tony Lema	1978	Jack Nicklaus
1932	Gene Sarazen	1951	Max Faulkner	1965	Peter Thomson	1979	Seve Ballesteros
1933	Denny Shute	1952	Bobby Locke	1966	Jack Nicklaus	1980	Tom Watson
1934	Henry Cotton	1953	Ben Hogan	1967	Roberto de Vicenzo	1981	Bill Rogers
1935	Alf Perry	1954	Peter Thomson	1968	Gary Player	1982	Tom Watson
1936	Alf Padgham	1955	Peter Thomson	1969	Tony Jacklin	1983	Tom Watson
1937	T.H. Cotton	1956	Peter Thomson	1970	Jack Nicklaus	1984	Seve Ballesteros
1938	R.A. Whitcombe	1957	Bobby Locke	1971	Lee Trevino	1985	Sandy Lyle
1939	Richard Burton	1958	Peter Thomson	1972	Lee Trevino	1986	Greg Norman
1940-45	(Not played)	1959	Gary Player	1973	Tom Weiskopf	1987	Nick Faldo
1946	Sam Snead	1960	Kel Nagle	1974	Gary Player	1988	Seve Ballesteros
1947	Fred Daly	1961	Arnold Palmer	1975	Tom Watson	1989	Mark Calcavecchia
1948	Henry Cotton	1962	Arnold Palmer	1976	Johnny Miller	1990	Nick Faldo
1949	Bobby Locke	1963	Bob Charles	1977	Tom Watson	1991	Ian Baker-Finch

Professional Golf Tournaments in 1991

Date	Event	Winner	Score	Prize
Jan. 6	Tournament of Champions, Carlsbad, Cal.	Tom Kite	272	$144,000
Jan. 13	Tucson Open, Ariz.	Phil Mickelson	*272	162,000
Jan. 20	Hawaiian Open, Honolulu	Lanny Wadkins	270	198,000
Jan. 27	Phoenix Open, Ariz.	Nolan Henke	268	180,000
Feb. 3	A.T.&T. National Pro-Am, Pebble Beach, Cal.	Paul Azinger	274	198,000
Feb. 10	Bob Hope Chrysler Classic, LaQuinta, Cal.	Corey Pyn	331	198,000
Feb. 17	Shearson Lehman Hutton Open, San Diego	Jay Don Blake	268	180,000
Feb. 24	Los Angeles Open	Ted Schulz	272	180,000
Mar. 4	Doral Ryder Open, Miami, Fla.	Rocco Mediat	*276	252,000
Mar. 11	Honda Classic, Coral Springs, Fla.	Steve Pate	279	180,000
Mar. 17	Nestle Invitational, Orlando, Fla.	Andrew Magee	203	180,000
Mar. 24	USF&G Classic, New Orleans	Ian Woosnam	*275	180,000
Mar. 31	Tournament Players Championship, Ponte Vedra, Fla.	Steve Elkington	276	288,000
Apr. 14	Masters Tournament, Augusta, Ga.	Ian Woosnam	277	225,000
Apr. 22	Heritage Classic, Hilton Head, S.C.	Davis Love 3d	271	180,000
Apr. 29	Greater Greensboro Open, N.C.	Mark Brooks	*275	225,000
May 5	Byron Nelson Classic, Irving, Tex.	Nick Price	270	198,000
May 19	Memorial Tournament, Dublin, Oh.	Kenny Perry	*273	216,000
May 26	Colonial National Tournament, Ft. Worth, Tex.	Tom Purtzer	267	216,000
June 2	Kemper Open, Potomac, Md.	Billy Andrade	*263	180,000
June 9	Buick Classic, Harrison, N.Y.	Billy Andrade	273	180,000
June 17	U.S. Open, Medinah, Ill.	Payne Stewart	*282	235,000
June 23	Anheuser-Busch Classic, Williamsburg, Va.	Mike Hulbert	*266	180,000
June 30	St. Jude Classic, Memphis, Tenn.	Fred Couples	269	180,000
July 14	New England Classic, Sutton, Mass.	Bruce Fleisher	*268	180,000
July 21	Chattanooga Classic, Tenn.	Dillard Pruitt	260	126,000
July 28	Greater Hartford Open, Cromwell, Conn.	Billy Ray Brown	*271	180,000
Aug 4	Buick Open, Grand Blanc, Mich.	Brad Faxon	271	180,000
Aug. 11	PGA Championship, Carmel, Ind.	John Daly	276	230,000
Aug. 18	The International, Castle Rock, Col.	Jose Maria Olazabal	+10 pts.	198,000
Sept. 3	Greater Milwaukee Open	Mark Brooks	270	180,000
Sept. 8	Canadian Open, Oakville, Ont.	Nick Price	273	180,000
Sept. 15	Hardee's Classic, Coal Valley, Ill.	D.A. Weibring	267	180,000
Sept. 22	B.C. Open, Endicott, N.Y.	Fred Couples	269	144,000
Sept. 29	Southern Open, Pine Mountain, Ga.	David Peoples	276	126,000
Oct. 6	Texas Open, San Antonio	Blaine McCallister	*269	162,000

Women

Date	Event	Winner	Score	Prize
Jan. 20	Jamaica Classic, Sandy Bay, Jamaica	Jane Geddes	207	$75,000
Feb. 10	Phar-Mor Classic, Lauderhill, Fla.	Beth Daniel	209	75,000
Feb. 24	Hawaiian Open, Honolulu	Patty Sheehan	207	52,000
Mar. 11	Inamori Classic, Poway, Cal.	Laura Davies	277	60,000
Mar. 17	Desert Inn International, Las Vegas	Penny Hammel	211	60,000
Mar. 24	Standard Register Classic, Phoenix, Ariz.	Danielle Ammaccapane	283	82,000
Mar. 31	Dinah Shore Invitational, Rancho Mirage, Cal.	Amy Alcott	273	90,000
May 5	Sara Lee Classic, Nashville, Tenn.	Nancy Lopez	206	63,000
May 19	Centel Classic, Tallahassee, Fla.	Pat Bradley	278	165,000
May 26	Corning Classic, Corning, N.Y.	Betsy King	273	60,000
June 2	Rochester International, N.Y.	Rosie Jones	276	60,000
June 9	Atlantic City Classic, N.J.	Jane Geddes	208	45,000
June 16	Lady Keystone Open, Hershey, Pa.	Colleen Walker	207	60,000
June 23	McDonald's Championship, Wilmington, Del.	Beth Daniel	273	112,000
June 30	Mazda Championship, Bethesda, Md.	Meg Mallon	274	150,000
July 7	Jamie Farr Toledo Classic, Oh.	Alice Miller	*205	52,000
July 15	U.S. Women's Open, Ft. Worth, Tex.	Meg Mallon	283	110,000
July 21	Big Apple Classic, New Rochelle, N.Y.	Betsy King	279	75,000
July 28	Bay State Classic, Canton, Mass.	Juli Inkster	275	60,000
Aug. 4	Phar-Mor Tournament, Vienna, Oh.	Deb Richard	*207	75,000
Aug. 11	Stratton Classic, Vt.	Melissa McNamara	278	67,000
Aug. 18	Northgate Classic, Brooklyn Park, Minn.	Cindy Rarick	211	60,000
Sept. 8	Cellular One-Ping Championship, Portland, Ore.	Michelle Estill	208	60,000
Sept. 15	DuMaurier Classic, Coquitlam, B.C.	Nancy Scranton	279	105,000
Sept. 22	Safeco Classic, Seattle, Wash.	Pat Bradley	*280	60,000
Sept. 29	MBS Classic, Buena Park, Cal.	Pat Bradley	277	52,000

*Won playoff.

U.S. Women's Open Golf Champions

Year	Winner	Year	Winner	Year	Winner	Year	Winner
1948	"Babe" Zaharias	1959	Mickey Wright	1970	Donna Caponi	1981	Pat Bradley
1949	Louise Suggs	1960	Betsy Rawls	1971	JoAnne Carner	1982	Janet Alex
1950	"Babe" Zaharias	1961	Mickey Wright	1972	Susie Maxwell Berning	1983	Jan Stephenson
1951	Betsy Rawls	1962	Murle Lindstrom	1973	Susie Maxwell Berning	1984	Hollis Stacy
1952	Louise Suggs	1963	Mary Mills	1974	Sandra Haynie	1985	Kathy Baker
1953	Betsy Rawls	1964	Mickey Wright	1975	Sandra Palmer	1986	Jane Geddes
1954	"Babe" Zaharias	1965	Carol Mann	1976	JoAnne Carner	1987	Laura Davies
1955	Fay Crocker	1966	Sandra Spuzich	1977	Hollis Stacy	1988	Liselotte Neumann
1956	Mrs. K. Cornelius	1967	Catherine Lacoste*	1978	Hollis Stacy	1989	Betsy King
1957	Betsy Rawls	1968	Susie Maxwell Berning	1979	Jerilyn Britz	1990	Betsy King
1958	Mickey Wright	1969	Donna Caponi	1980	Amy Alcott	1991	Meg Mallon

*Amateur

PGA Leading Money Winners

Year	Player	Dollars	Year	Player	Dollars	Year	Player	Dollars
1946	Ben Hogan	$42,556	1961	Gary Player	$64,540	1976	Jack Nicklaus	$266,438
1947	Jimmy Demaret	27,936	1962	Arnold Palmer	81,448	1977	Tom Watson	310,653
1948	Ben Hogan	36,812	1963	Arnold Palmer	128,230	1978	Tom Watson	362,429
1949	Sam Snead	31,593	1964	Jack Nicklaus	113,284	1979	Tom Watson	462,636
1950	Sam Snead	35,758	1965	Jack Nicklaus	140,752	1980	Tom Watson	530,808
1951	Lloyd Mangrum	26,088	1966	Billy Casper	121,944	1981	Tom Kite	375,699
1952	Julius Boros	37,032	1967	Jack Nicklaus	188,988	1982	Craig Stadler	446,462
1953	Lew Worsham	34,002	1968	Billy Casper	205,168	1983	Hal Sutton	426,668
1954	Bob Toski	65,819	1969	Frank Beard	175,223	1984	Tom Watson	476,260
1955	Julius Boros	65,121	1970	Lee Trevino	157,037	1985	Curtis Strange	542,321
1956	Ted Kroll	72,835	1971	Jack Nicklaus	244,490	1986	Greg Norman	653,296
1957	Dick Mayer	65,835	1972	Jack Nicklaus	320,542	1987	Curtis Strange	925,941
1958	Arnold Palmer	42,407	1973	Jack Nicklaus	308,362	1988	Curtis Strange	1,147,644
1959	Art Wall Jr.	53,167	1974	Johnny Miller	353,201	1989	Tom Kite	1,395,278
1960	Arnold Palmer	75,262	1975	Jack Nicklaus	323,149	1990	Greg Norman	1,165,477

LPGA Leading Money Winners

Year	Winner	Dollars	Year	Winner	Dollars	Year	Winner	Dollars
1954	Patty Berg	$16,011	1967	Kathy Whitworth	$32,937	1979	Nancy Lopez	$215,987
1955	Patty Berg	16,492	1968	Kathy Whitworth	48,379	1980	Beth Daniel	231,000
1956	Marlene Hagge	20,235	1969	Carol Mann	49,152	1981	Beth Daniel	206,977
1957	Patty Berg	16,272	1970	Kathy Whitworth	30,235	1982	JoAnne Carner	310,399
1958	Beverly Hanson	12,629	1971	Kathy Whitworth	41,181	1983	JoAnne Carner	291,404
1959	Betsy Rawls	26,774	1972	Kathy Whitworth	65,063	1984	Betsy King	266,771
1960	Louise Suggs	16,892	1973	Kathy Whitworth	82,854	1985	Nancy Lopez	416,472
1961	Mickey Wright	22,236	1974	JoAnne Carner	87,094	1986	Pat Bradley	492,021
1962	Mickey Wright	21,641	1975	Sandra Palmer	94,805	1987	Ayako Okamoto	466,034
1963	Mickey Wright	31,269	1976	Judy Rankin	150,734	1988	Sherri Turner	347,255
1964	Mickey Wright	29,800	1977	Judy Rankin	122,890	1989	Betsy King	654,132
1965	Kathy Whitworth	28,658	1978	Nancy Lopez	189,813	1990	Beth Daniel	863,578
1966	Kathy Whitworth	33,517						

TRACK AND FIELD

World Track and Field Indoor Records

As of Sept., 1991

The International Amateur Athletic Federation began recognizing world indoor track & field records as official on January 1, 1987. Prior to that, there were only unofficial world indoor bests. World indoor bests set prior to January 1, 1987 are subject to approval as world records providing they meet the prescribed IAAF world records criteria, including drug testing. To be accepted as a world indoor record, a performance must meet the same criteria as a world record outdoors except that a track performance can't be set on an indoor track larger than 200 meters. *Record pending.

Men

Event	Record	Holder	Country	Date	Where made
60 meters	*6.48	Leroy Burrell	U.S.	Feb., 1991	Madrid
200 meters	20.36	Bruno Marie-Rose	France	Feb. 22, 1987	Lievin, France
400 meters	45.04	Danny Everett	U.S.	Feb. 4, 1990	Germany
800 meters	1:44.84	Paul Ereng	Kenya	Mar. 4, 1989	Budapest
1,000 meters	2:16.62	Rob Druppers	Netherlands	Feb. 20, 1988	The Hague
1,500 meters	*3:34.16	Noureddine Morceli	Algeria	Feb. 28, 1991	Seville, Spain
1 Mile	3:49.78	Eamonn Coghlan	Ireland	Feb. 27, 1983	E. Rutherford, N.J.
3,000 meters	7:39.2	Emiel Puttemans	Belguim	Feb. 18, 1973	New York
5,000 meters	13:20.4	Suleiman Nyambui	Tanzania	Feb. 6, 1981	New York
50-meter hurdles	6.25	Mark McKoy	Canada	Jan. 27, 1985	Rosemont, Ill.
60-meter hurdles	7.36	Roger Kingdom	U.S.	Mar. 9, 1989	Athens
High Jump	7 ft. 11½ in.	Javier Sotomayor	Cuba	Mar. 4, 1989	Budapest
Pole Vault	*20 ft. 1 in.	Sergei Bubka	USSR	Mar. 23, 1991	France
Long Jump	28 ft. 10½ in.	Carl Lewis	U.S.	Feb. 27, 1984	New York
Triple Jump	58 ft. 3¼ in.	Mike Conley	U.S.	Feb. 27, 1987	New York
Shot Put	74 ft. 4¼ in.	Randy Barnes	U.S.	Jan. 20, 1989	Los Angeles

Women

Event	Record	Holder	Country	Date	Where made
60 meters	7.00	Nelli Cooman-Fiere	Holland	Feb. 23, 1986	Madrid
200 meters	*22.24	Merlene Ottey	Jamaica	Mar. 10, 1991	Seville, Spain
400 meters	49.59	Jarmila Kratochvilova	Czechoslovakia	Mar. 7, 1982	Milan
800 meters	1:56.40	Christine Wachtel	E. Germany	Feb. 13, 1988	Vienna
1,000 meters	2:34.8	Brigitte Kraus	W. Germany	Feb. 19, 1978	Dortmund, Germany
1,500 meters	4:00.27	Doina Melinte	Romania	Feb. 9, 1990	E. Rutherford, N.J.
1 Mile	4:17.13	Doina Melinte	Romania	Feb. 9, 1990	E. Rutherford, N.J.
3,000 meters	8:33.82	Elly Van Hulst	Netherlands	Mar., 1989	Budapest
5,000 meters	15:22.64	Lynn Jennings	U.S.	Jan. 7, 1990	Hanover, N.H.
50-meter hurdles	6:58	Cornelia Oschkenat	E. Germany	Feb. 20, 1988	Berlin
60-meter hurdles	7.69	Lyudmila Narozhi-Lenko	USSR	Feb. 4, 1990	USSR
High Jump	6 ft. 9 in.	Stefka Kostadinova	Bulgaria	Feb. 20, 1988	Athens, Greece
Long Jump	24 ft. 2¼ in.	Heike Dreschler	E. Germany	Feb. 13, 1988	Vienna
Shot Put	73 ft. 10 in.	Helena Fibingerova	Czechoslovakia	Feb. 19, 1977	Czech.

World Track and Field Records

As of Sept. 1991

*Indicates pending record; some new records await confirmation. The International Amateur Athletic Federation, the world body of track and field, recognizes only records in metric distances except for the mile.

Men's Records

Running

Event	Record	Holder	Country	Date	Where made
100 meters	*9.86 s.	Carl Lewis	U.S.	Aug. 25, 1991	Tokyo
200 meters	19.72 s.	Pietro Mennea	Italy	Sept. 17, 1979	Mexico City
400 meters	43.29 s.	Butch Reynolds	U.S.	Aug. 16, 1988	Zurich
800 meters	1 m., 41.73 s.	Sebastian Coe	Gr. Britain	June 10, 1981	Florence, Italy
1,000 meters	2 m., 12.18 s.	Sebastian Coe	Gr. Britain	July 11, 1981	Oslo
1,500 meters	3 m., 29.46 s.	Said Aouita	Morocco	Aug. 23, 1985	W. Berlin
1 mile	3 m., 46.32 s.	Steve Cram	Gr. Britain	July 27, 1985	Oslo
2,000 meters	4 m., 50.81 s.	Said Aouita	Morocco	July 16, 1987	Paris
3,000 meters	7 m., 29.45 s.	Said Aouita	Morocco	Aug. 20, 1989	Cologne
5,000 meters	12 m., 58.39 s.	Said Aouita	Morocco	July 22, 1987	Rome
10,000 meters	27 m., 08.23 s.	Arturo Barrios	Mexico	Aug. 18, 1989	W. Berlin
20,000 meters	57 m., 18.4 s.	Dionisio Castro	Portugal	Mar. 31, 1990	France
25,000 meters	1 hr., 13 m., 55.8 s.	Toshihiko Seko	Japan	Mar. 22, 1981	New Zealand
3,000 meter stpl	8 m., 05.35 s.	Peter Koech	Kenya	July 3, 1989	Stockholm
Marathon	2 hr., 6 m., 50 s.	Belayneh Densimo	Ethiopia	Apr. 17, 1988	Rotterdam

Hurdles

110 meters	12.92 s.	Roger Kingdom	U.S.	Aug. 16, 1989	Zurich
400 meters	47.02 s.	Edwin Moses	U.S.	Aug. 31, 1983	W. Germany

Relay Races

400 mtrs.	*37.50 s.	(Cason, Burrell, Mitchell, Lewis)	U.S.	Aug., 1991	Tokyo
800 mtrs. (4×200)	1 m., 19.38 s.	(Lewis, Everett, Burrell, Heard)	U.S.	Aug. 23, 1989	W. Germany
1,600 mtrs. (4×400)	2 m., 56.16 s.	(Matthews, Freeman, James, Evans)	U.S.	Oct. 20, 1968	Mexico City
		(Everett, Lewis, Robinzine, Reynolds)	U.S.	Oct 1, 1988	Seoul
3,200 mtrs. (4×800)	7 m., 03.89 s.	National team	Gr. Britain	Aug. 30, 1982	London

Field Events

High jump	8 ft.	Javier Sotomayor	Cuba	July 29, 1989	Puerto Rico
Long jump	*29 ft., 4½ in.	Mike Powell	U.S.	Aug., 1991	Tokyo
Triple jump	58 ft., 11½ in.	Willie Banks	U.S.	June 16, 1985	Indianapolis
Pole vault	*20 ft., ¼ in.	Sergei Bubka	USSR	Aug. 5, 1991	Malmo, Sweden
16 lb. shot put.	75 ft., 10¼ in.	Randy Barnes	U.S.	May 20, 1990	Los Angeles
Discus	243 ft.	Juergen Schult	E. Germany	June 6, 1986	E. Germany
Javelin	*318 ft. 1 in.	Seppo Raty	Finland	June 2, 1991	Finland
16 lb. hammer	284 ft., 7 in.	Yuri Sedykh	USSR	Aug. 30, 1986	Stuttgart
Decathlon	8,647 pts.	Daley Thompson	Gr. Britain	Aug. 8-9, 1984	Los Angeles

Women's Records

Running

100 meters	10.49 s.	Florence Griffith Joyner	U.S.	July 16, 1988	Indianapolis
200 meters	21.34 s.	Florence Griffith Joyner	U.S.	Sept. 29, 1988	Seoul
400 meters	47.60 s.	Marita Koch	E. Germany	Oct. 6, 1985	Canberra
800 meters	1 m., 53.28 s.	Jarmila Kratochvilova	Czech.	July 26, 1983	Munich
1,500 meters	3 m., 52.47 s.	Tatyana Kazankina	USSR	Aug. 13, 1980	Zurich
1 mile	4 m., 15.61 s.	Paula Ivan	Romania	July 10, 1989	Nice
2,000 meters	5 m., 28.69 s.	Maricica Puica	Romania	July 11, 1986	London
3,000 meters	8 m., 22.62 s.	Tatyana Kazankina	USSR	Aug. 26, 1984	Leningrad
5,000 meters	14 m., 37.33 s.	Ingrid Kristiansen	Norway	Aug. 5, 1986	Stockholm
10,000 meters	30 m., 13.74 s.	Ingrid Kristiansen	Norway	July 5, 1986	Oslo
Marathon	2 h., 21 m., 06 s.	Ingrid Kristiansen	Norway	Apr. 21, 1985	London

Hurdles

100 meters	12.21 s.	Yordanka Donkova	Bulgaria	Aug. 21, 1988	Bulgaria
400 meters	52.94 s.	Marina Stepanova	USSR	Sept. 17, 1986	USSR

Field Events

High jump	6 ft., 10¼ in.	Stefka Kostadinova	Bulgaria	Aug. 30, 1987	Rome
Shot put	74 ft., 3 in.	Natalya Lisouskaya	USSR	June 7, 1987	Moscow
Long jump	24 ft., 8¼ in.	Galina Chistyakova	USSR	June 11, 1988	Leningrad
Triple Jump	*49 ft., 4 in.	Inessa Kravets	USSR	May 10, 1991	Moscow
Discus	252 ft.	Gabriele Reinsch	E. Germany	July 9, 1988	E. Germany
Javelin	262 ft., 5 in.	Petra Felke	E. Germany	Sept. 9, 1988	Potsdam
Heptathlon	7,291 pts.	Jackie Joyner-Kersee	U.S.	Sept. 23-24, 1988	Seoul

Relay Races

400 mtrs. (4×100)	41.37 s.	National team	E. Germany	Oct. 6, 1985	Canberra
800 mtrs. (4×200)	1 m., 28.15 s.	National team	E. Germany	Aug. 9, 1980	E. Germany
1,600 mtrs. (4×400)	3 m., 15.18 s.	National team	USSR	Oct. 1, 1988	Seoul
3,200 mtrs. (4×800)	7 m., 50.17 s.	National team	USSR	Aug. 5, 1984	Moscow

Bubka Soars to New Heights

Sergei Bubka of the Soviet Union thrilled the world of track and field by setting a new record for the pole vault 8 times in 1991. He set four new world indoor records, the latest an all-time-best vault of 20 feet 1 inches at Grenoble, France on Mar. 23. He also broke the outdoor record four times. On Aug. 5, at Malmo, Sweden, he set a new official world record of 20 feet 1/4 inches (indoor records are not official world records).

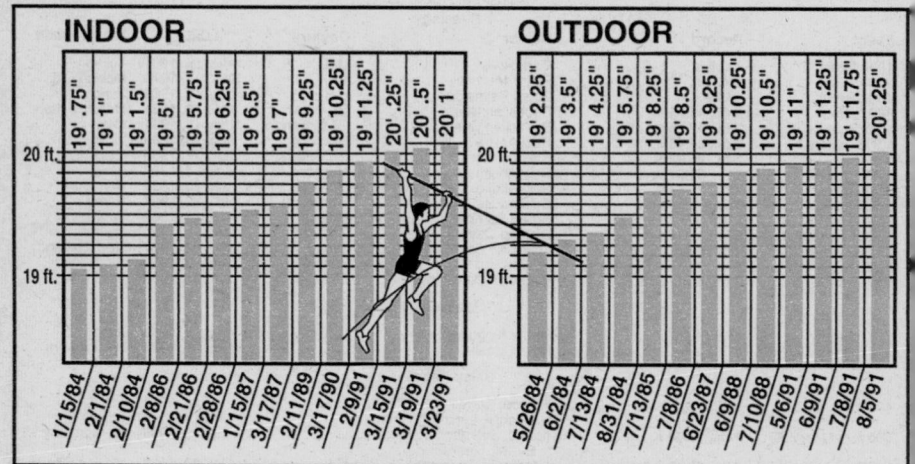

NCAA Outdoor Championships

Eugene, Ore., May 31-June 2, 1991

Men

100 Meters—Frank Fredricks, BYU. Time—0:10.03.
200 Meters—Frank Fredricks, BYU. Time—0:19.90.
400 Meters—Gabriel Luke, Rice. Time—0:45.32.
800 Meters—George Kersh, Mississippi. Time—1:45.82.
1,500 Meters—Samuel Kibiri, Washington St. Time—3:59.53.
10,000 Meters—Terry Thornton, LSU. Time—28:25.92.
110-Meter Hurdles—Greg Williams, Texas A&M. Time—0:13.55.
400-Meter Hurdles—Samuel Matete, Auburn. Time—0:49.12.
High Jump—Darrin Plab, So. Illinois. 7 ft. 6½ in.
Long Jump—George Ogbeide, Washington St. 26 ft. 8¼ in.
Triple Jump—Brian Wellman, Arkansas. 56 ft. 10¼ in.
Pole Vault—Istvan Bagyula, George Mason. 19 ft. ¼ in.
Javelin—Patrik Boden, Texas. 260 ft. 4 in.
Discus—Kamy Keshmiri, Nevada. 218 ft. 5 in.
Decathlon—Aric Long, Tennessee. 7,916 pts.
Team champion—Tennessee.

Women

100 Meters—Carlette Guidry, Texas. Time—0:10.91.
200 Meters—Carlette Guidry. Time—0:22.44.
400 Meters—Ximena Restrepo, Nebraska. Time—0:51.01.
800 Meters—Nekita Beasley, Florida. Time—2:03.29.
1,500 Meters—Darcy Arreola, Cal. State, Northridge. Time—4:11.46.
3,000 Meters—Sonia O'Sullivan, Villanova. Time—8:56.74.
5,000 Meters—Laurie Gomez, N.C. State. Time—16:07.96.
10,000 Meters—Jamie Park, Arkansas. Time—33:15.08.
100-Meter Hurdles—Dawn Bowles, LSU. Time—0:12.70.
400-Meter Hurdles—Janeene Vickers, UCLA. Time—0:55.65.
High Jump—Tanya Hughes, Arizona. 6 ft. 4½ in.
Long Jump—Diane Guthrie, George Mason. 21 ft. 10 in.
Triple Jump—Donna Crumety, St. Joseph's (Pa.). 44 ft.
Shot Put—Eileen Vanisi, Texas. 57 ft. 9 in.
Discus—Anna Mosdell, BYU. 183 ft. 10 in.
Team champion—LSU.

USA/Mobil Outdoor Championships

New York, N.Y., June 14-16, 1991

Men

100 Meters—Leroy Burrell. Time—0:09.50.
200 Meters—Michael Johnson. Time—0:20.31.
400 Meters—Antonio Pettigrew. Time—0:44.36.
800 Meters—Mark Everett. Time—1:44.28.
1,500 Meters—Terrence Herrington. Time—3:40.72.
5,000 Meters—John Trautman. Time—13:55.26.
10,000 Meters—Shannon Butler. Time—28:09.40.
110-Meter Hurdles—Greg Foster. Time—0:13.29.
400-Meter Hurdles—Danny Harris. Time—0:47.62.
3,000-Meter Steeplechase—Mark Croghan. Time—8:21.64.
High Jump—Hollis Conway. 7 ft. 7½ in.
Long Jump—Carl Lewis. 28 ft. 4¼ in.
Triple Jump—Kenny Harrison. 56 ft. 10 in.
Discus—Tony Washington. 211 ft. 11 in.
Hammer—Jud Logan. 244 ft. 10 in.
Javelin—Mike Barnett. 262 ft.
Shot Put—Ron Backes. 64 ft. 11½ in.
Decathlon—Dan O'Brien. 8,844 pts.

Women

100 Meters—Charlotte Guidry. Time—0:10.94.
200 Meters—Gwen Torrance. Time—0:22.38.
400 Meters—Lillie Leatherwood. Time—0:49.66.
800 Meters—Delisa Floyd. Time—1:59.82.
1,500 Meters—Suzy Favor Hamilton. Time—4:06.13.
3,000 Meters—Shelly Steely. Time—8:49.00.
10,000-Meters—Lynn Jennings. Time—32:45.88.
100-Meter Hurdles—Gail Devers-Roberts. Time—0:12.83.
400-Meter Hurdles—Kim Batsen. Time—0:54.18.
Long Jump—Jackie Joyner-Kersee. 22 ft. 8 in.
Shot Put—Ramona Pagel. 60 ft. 2½ in.
Javelin—Karin Smith. 197 ft. 6 in.
Discus—Lacy Barnes. 199 ft. 10 in.
High Jump—Yolanda Henry. 6 ft. 4¾ in.
Heptathlon—Jackie Joyner-Kersee. 6,878 pts.

National Track & Field Hall of Fame

Indianapolis, Ind.

Jesse Abramson	Mildred (Babe) Didrikson	Jim Hines	Bert Nelson	Helen Stephens
Dave Albritton	Harrison Dillard	Bud Houser	Cordner Nelson	James Sullivan
Roxanne Anderson	Ken Doherty	DeHart Hubbard	Parry O'Brien	Ed Temple
Horace Ashenfelter	Charles Dumas	Edward Hurt	Al Oerter	Dink Templeton
Andy Bakjian	Bill Easton	Wilbur Hutsell	Harold Osborn	John Thomas
Weems Baskin	James (Jumbo) Elliott	Nell Jackson	Jesse Owens	Earl Thomson
James Bausch	Lee Evans	Bruce Jenner	Charlie Paddock	Jim Thorpe
Bob Beamon	Barney Ewell	Rafer Johnson	Mel Patton	Eddie Tolan
Percy Beard	Ray Ewry	Hayes Jones	Eulace Peacock	Bill Toomey
Jim Beatty	Mae Faggs (Starr)	Thomas Jones	Steve Prefontaine	Forrest Towns
Greg Bell	Barbara Ferrell	Payton Jordan	Joie Ray	Wyomia Tyus
Dee Boeckman	Dan Ferris	John Kelley	Greg Rice	LeRoy Walker
Tom Botts	John Flanagan	Abel Kiviat	Bob Richards	Stella Walsh
Ralph Boston	Dick Fosbury	Alvin Kraenzlein	Betty Robinson (Schwartz)	Cornelius Warmerdam
Bill Bowerman	Bob Giegengack	Ron Laird	Ralph Rose	Martha Watson
Avery Brundage	Fortune Gordien	Clyde Littlefield	Wilma Rudolph	Willye White
Jim Bush	John Griffith	Bob Mathias	Jim Ryun	Mal Whitfield
Lee Calhoun	Archie Hahn	Randy Matson	Jackson Scholz	Fred Wilt
Milt Campbell	Evelyne Hall	Mildred McDaniel	Bob Schul	Lloyd "Bud" Winter
Ellery Clark	Brutus Hamilton	Edith McGuire (DuVall)	Bob Seagren	Rick Wohlhuter
Alice Coachman (Davis)	Glenn Hardin	Ted Meredith	Mel Sheppard	John Woodruff
Harold Connolly	Ted Haydon	Ralph Metcalfe	Martin Sheridan	Dave Wottle
Tom Courtney	Billy Hayes	Billy Mills	Frank Shorter	Frank Wykoff
Dean Cromwell	Bob Hayes	Madeline Manning-Mims	Dave Sime	Joe Yancey
Glenn Cunningham	Ward Haylett	Jack Moakley	Robert Simpson	George Young
William Curtis	Bud Held	Tom Moore	Tommie Smith	
Willie Davenport	Doris Brown Heritage	Bobby Morrow	Larry Snyder	
Glenn Davis	Ralph Higgins	Michael Murphy	Andy Stanfield	
Harold Davis	Harry Hillman	Lon Myers	Les Steers	

World Record for the One-Mile Run

The following shows how the world record for the one-mile run has been lowered since Roger Bannister broke the 4-minute barrier in 1954

3:59.4	3:58	3:57.2	3:54.5 3:54.4 3:54.1 3:53.6	3:51.3 3:51.1 3:51	3:49.4 3:49	3:48.8 3:48.53 3:48.4	3:47.33	3:46.32

| Roger Bannister (1954) | Derek Ibbotson (1957) | Peter Snell (1962) | Michel Jazy (1965) | Jim Ryun (1967) | John Walker (1975) | Steve Ovett (1980) | Steve Ovett (1981) | Steve Cram (1985) |

| John Landy (1954) | Herb Elliot (1958) | Peter Snell (1964) | Jim Ryun (1966) | Filbert Bayi (1975) | Sebastian Coe (1979) | Sebastian Coe (1981) | Sebastian Coe (1981) | |

World Track & Field Championships, 1991

The World Track & Field Championships were held in Tokyo, Japan from Aug. 23 thru Sept. 1, 1991. The star of the games was Mike Powell of the U.S. who set a long jump record of 29 feet 4½ inches, which broke the record set by Bob Beamon at Mexico City in 1968. Another highlight was Carl Lewis's record-breaking 100-meter dash at 9.86 seconds. The United States relay team of Andre Cason, Leroy Burrell, Dennis Mitchell, and Carl Lewis ran the 400-meter relay in 37.50 seconds to set a world record.

BOWLING

Firestone Tournament of Champions

Year	Winner	Year	Winner	Year	Winner	Year	Winner
1965	Billy Hardwick	1972	Mike Durbin	1979	George Pappas	1986	Marshall Holman
1966	Wayne Zahn	1973	Jim Godman	1980	Wayne Webb	1987	Pete Weber
1967	Jim Stefanich	1974	Earl Anthony	1981	Steve Cook	1988	Mark Williams
1968	Dave Davis	1975	Dave Davis	1982	Mike Durbin	1989	Del Ballard Jr.
1969	Jim Godman	1976	Marshall Holman	1983	Joe Berardi	1990	Dave Ferraro
1970	Don Johnson	1977	Mike Berlin	1984	Mike Durbin	1991	David Ozio
1971	Johnny Petraglia	1978	Earl Anthony	1985	Mark Williams		

PBA Leading Money Winners

Total winnings are from PBA, ABC Masters, and BPAA All-Star tournaments only, and do not include numerous other tournaments or earnings from special television shows and matches.

Year	Bowler	Amount	Year	Bowler	Amount	Year	Bowler	Amount
1962	Don Carter	$49,972	1972	Don Johnson	$56,648	1982	Earl Anthony	$134,760
1963	Dick Weber	46,333	1973	Don McCune	69,000	1983	Earl Anthony	135,605
1964	Bob Strampe	33,592	1974	Earl Anthony	99,585	1984	Mark Roth	158,712
1965	Dick Weber	47,674	1975	Earl Anthony	107,585	1985	Mike Aulby	201,200
1966	Wayne Zahn	54,720	1976	Earl Anthony	110,833	1986	Walter Ray Williams Jr.	145,550
1967	Dave Davis	54,165	1977	Mark Roth	105,583	1987	Pete Weber	175,491
1968	Jim Stefanich	67,377	1978	Mark Roth	134,500	1988	Brian Voss	225,485
1969	Billy Hardwick	64,160	1979	Mark Roth	124,517	1989	Mike Aulby	298,237
1970	Mike McGrath	52,049	1980	Wayne Webb	116,700	1990	Amieto Monacelli	204,775
1971	Johnny Petraglia	85,065	1981	Earl Anthony	164,735			

Leading PBA Averages by Year

Year	Bowler	Average	Year	Bowler	Average	Year	Bowler	Average
1962	Don Carter	212.844	1972	Don Johnson	215.290	1982	Marshall Holman	212.844
1963	Billy Hardwick	210.346	1973	Earl Anthony	215.799	1983	Earl Anthony	216.645
1964	Ray Bluth	210.512	1974	Earl Anthony	219.394	1984	Marshall Holman	213.911
1965	Dick Weber	211.895	1975	Earl Anthony	219.060	1985	Mark Baker	213.718
1966	Wayne Zahn	208.663	1976	Mark Roth	215.970	1986	John Gant	214.378
1967	Wayne Zahn	212.342	1977	Mark Roth	218.174	1987	Marshall Holman	216.801
1968	Jim Stefanich	211.895	1978	Mark Roth	219.834	1988	Mark Roth	218.036
1969	Bill Hardwick	212.957	1979	Mark Roth	221.662	1989	Pete Weber	215.432
1970	Nelson Burton Jr.	214.908	1980	Earl Anthony	218.535	1990	Amieto Monacelli	218.158
1971	Don Johnson	213.977	1981	Mark Roth	216.699			

PBA Hall of Fame

Performance

Bill Allen	Jim Godman	Dick Ritger
Glenn Allison	Johnny Guenther	Mark Roth
Earl Anthony	Billy Hardwick	Jim St. John
Barry Asher	Tommy Hudson	Carmen Salvino
Ray Bluth	Don Johnson	Bob Strampe
Nelson Burton Jr.	Joe Joseph	Harry Smith
Don Carter	Larry Laub	Dave Soutar
Pat Colwell	Don McCune	Jim Stefanich
Dave Davis	Mike McGrath	Dick Weber
Gary Dickinson	George Pappas	Billy Welu
Mike Durbin	Johnny Petraglia	Wayne Zahn
Buzz Fazio		

Meritorious service

John Archibald	John Jowdy
Eddie Elias	Joe Kelley
Frank Esposito	Steve Nagy
Dick Evans	Chuck Pezzano
Raymond Firestone	Joe Richards
E.A. "Bud" Fisher	Chris Schenkel
Lou Frantz	Lorraine Stilzlein
Harry Golden	Al Thompson
Ted Hoffman Jr.	

American Bowling Congress Masters Tournament Champions

Year	Winner	Year	Winner	Year	Winner
1980	Neil Burton, St. Louis, Mo.	1984	Earl Anthony, Dublin, Cal.	1988	Del Ballard Jr., Richardson, Tex.
1981	Randy Lightfoot, St. Charles, Mo.	1985	Steve Wunderlich, St. Louis, Mo.	1989	Mike Aulby, Indianapolis, Ind.
1982	Joe Berardi, Brooklyn, N.Y.	1986	Mark Fahy, Chicago, Ill.	1990	Chris Warren, Dallas, Tex.
1983	Mike Lastowski, Havre de Grace, Md.	1987	Rick Steelsmith, Wichita, Kan.	1991	Doug Kent, Canandaigua, N.Y.

Most Sanctioned 300 Games

Bob Learn Jr, Erie, Pa. 43	Mitch Jabczenski, Detroit, Mich. 21	Dave Williams, Sebastopal, Cal. 17
Jim Johnson Jr., Wilmington, Del. 34	Dave Heller, Highland Falls, N.Y. 21	Joe Vito Buenrostro, San Antonio, Tex. 17
John Wilcox Jr., Shavertown, Pa. 32	Mark Stibora, Cleveland, Oh. 20	Paul Cannon, Binghamton, N.Y. 17
Ron Woolet, Louisville, Ky. 32	Steve Carson, Oklahoma City, Okla. 20	Randy Choat, Granite City, Ill. 16
Tony Torrice, Wolcott, Conn. 29	Dave Soutar, Kansas City, Mo. 19	Don Johnson, Las Vegas, Nev. 16
Elvin Mesger, Sullivan, Mo. 27	Dick Weber, St. Louis, Mo. 18	Byron Russell, Tulsa, Okla. 16
Teata Semiz, Fairfield, N.J. 22	George Billick, Old Forge, Pa. 17	

Women's International Bowling Congress Champions in 1991

Queens Tournament—Dede Davidson, San Jose, Cal.
All Events—Debbie Kuhn, Baltimore, Md.
Doubles—Lucy Giovinco & Cindy Coburn-Carroll, Tampa, Fla. & Tonawanda, N.Y.

Team—Clear-Vu Window Cleaning, Milwaukee, Wis.

Most Sanctioned 300 Games

Jeanne Maiden, Solon, Oh. 18	Donna Adamek, Victorville, Cal. 10	Leanne Barrette, Oklahoma City, Okla. 9
Vicki Fischel, Westminster, Cal. 14	Cindy Coburn-Carroll, Tonawanda, N.Y. 10	Robin Romeo, Van Nuys, Cal. 8
Tish Johnson, Panorama City, Cal. 12	Betty Morris, Stockton, Cal. 10	Linda Kelly, Huber Hts., Oh. 8
Aleta Sill, Dearborn, Mich. 12		Cheryl Daniels, Detroit, Mich. 8

Professional Sports Directory

Baseball

Commissioner's Office
350 Park Ave.
New York, NY 10022

National League

National League Office
350 Park Ave.
New York, NY 10022

Atlanta Braves
521 Capitol Ave. SW
Atlanta, GA 30312

Chicago Cubs
Wrigley Field
Chicago, IL 60613

Cincinnati Reds
100 Riverfront Stadium
Cincinnati, OH 45202

Houston Astros
8400 Kirby Dr.
Houston, TX 77054

Los Angeles Dodgers
Dodger Stadium
Los Angeles, CA 90012

Montreal Expos
PO Box 500, Station M
Montreal, Que. H1V 3P2

New York Mets
Shea Stadium
Flushing, NY 11368

Philadelphia Phillies
PO Box 7575
Philadelphia, PA 19101

Pittsburgh Pirates
Three Rivers Stadium
Pittsburgh, PA 15212

St. Louis Cardinals
Busch Stadium
St. Louis, MO 63102

San Diego Padres
9449 Friars Rd.
San Diego, CA 92108

San Francisco Giants
Candlestick Park
San Francisco, CA 94124

American League

American League Office
350 Park Ave.
New York, NY 10022

Baltimore Orioles
Memorial Stadium
Baltimore, MD 21218

Boston Red Sox
24 Yawkey Way
Boston, MA 02215

California Angels
Anaheim Stadium
Anaheim, CA 92806

Chicago White Sox
324 W. 35th St.
Chicago, IL 60616

Cleveland Indians
Cleveland Stadium
Cleveland, OH 44114

Detroit Tigers
Tiger Stadium
Detroit, MI 48216

Kansas City Royals
P.O. Box 419969
Kansas City, MO 64141

Milwaukee Brewers
Milwaukee County Stadium
Milwaukee, WI 53214

Minnesota Twins
501 Chicago Ave. South
Minneapolis, MN 55415

New York Yankees
Yankee Stadium
Bronx, NY 10451

Oakland A's
Oakland Coliseum
Oakland, CA 94621

Seattle Mariners
P.O. Box 4100
Seattle, WA 98104

Texas Rangers
1250 E. Copeland Rd.
Arlington, TX 76011

Toronto Blue Jays
300 Bremner Blvd.
Toronto, Ont. M5V 3B3

National Basketball Association

League Office
645 5th Ave.
New York, NY 10022

Atlanta Hawks
1 CNN Center
Atlanta, GA 30303

Boston Celtics
151 Merrimac St.
Boston, MA 02114

Charlotte Hornets
Hive Drive
Charlotte, NC 28217

Chicago Bulls
980 North Michigan Ave.
Chicago, IL 60611

Cleveland Cavaliers
2923 Statesboro Rd.
Richfield, OH 44286

Dallas Mavericks
777 Sports St.
Dallas, TX 75207

Denver Nuggets
1635 Clay St.
Denver, CO 80204

Detroit Pistons
2 Championship Dr.
Auburn Hills, MI 48326

Golden State Warriors
Oakland Coliseum
Oakland, CA 94621

Houston Rockets
The Summit
Houston, TX 77046

Indiana Pacers
300 E. Market St.
Indianapolis, IN 46204

Los Angeles Clippers
3939 S. Figueroa
Los Angeles, CA 90037

Los Angeles Lakers
PO Box 10
Inglewood, CA 90306

Miami Heat
Miami Arena
Miami, FL 33136

Milwaukee Bucks
1001 N. 4th St.
Milwaukee, WI 53203

Minnesota Timberwolves
600 First Ave. N.
Minneapolis, MN 55403

New Jersey Nets
Meadowlands Arena
E. Rutherford, NJ 07073

New York Knickerbockers
4 Pennsylvania Plaza
New York, NY 10001

Orlando Magic
1 Magic Place
Orlando, FL 32801

Philadelphia 76ers
PO Box 25040
Philadelphia, PA 19147

Phoenix Suns
2910 N. Central Ave.
Phoenix, AZ 85012

Portland Trail Blazers
700 NE Multnomah St.
Portland, OR 97232

Sacramento Kings
One Sports Pkwy.
Sacramento, CA 95834

San Antonio Spurs
600 E. Market St.
San Antonio, TX 78205

Seattle SuperSonics
190 Queen Ann Ave. N.
Seattle, WA 98109

Utah Jazz
5 Triad Center
Salt Lake City, UT 84180

Washington Bullets
1 Harry S. Truman Dr.
Landover, MD 20785

National Hockey League

League Headquarters
Sun Life Bldg.
Montreal, Quebec H3B 2W2

Boston Bruins
150 Causeway St.
Boston, MA 02114

Buffalo Sabres
Memorial Auditorium
Buffalo, NY 14202

Calgary Flames
P.O. Box 1540
Calgary, Alta. T2P 3B9

Chicago Black Hawks
1800 W. Madison St.
Chicago, IL 60612

Detroit Red Wings
600 Civic Center Drive
Detroit, MI 48226

Edmonton Oilers
Northlands Coliseum
Edmonton, Alta. T5B 4M9

Hartford Whalers
One Civic Center Plaza
Hartford, CT 06103

Los Angeles Kings
3900 W. Manchester Blvd.
Inglewood, CA 90308

Minnesota North Stars
7901 Cedar Ave. S.
Bloomington, MN 55425

Montreal Canadiens
2313 St. Catherine St., West
Montreal, Quebec H3H 1N2

New Jersey Devils
Meadowlands Arena
E. Rutherford, NJ 07073

New York Islanders
Nassau Coliseum
Uniondale, NY 11553

New York Rangers
4 Pennsylvania Plaza
New York, NY 10001

Philadelphia Flyers
Pattison Place
Philadelphia, PA 19148

Pittsburgh Penguins
Civic Arena
Pittsburgh, PA 15219

Quebec Nordiques
2205 Ave. du Colisee
Quebec, Que. G1L 4W7

St. Louis Blues
5700 Oakland Ave.
St. Louis, MO 63110

San Jose Sharks
10 Almaden Blvd.
San Jose, CA 95113

Toronto Maple Leafs
60 Carlton St.
Toronto, Ont. M5B 1L1

Vancouver Canucks
100 North Renfrew St.
Vancouver, B.C. V5K 3N7

Washington Capitals
Capital Centre
Landover, MD 20785

Winnipeg Jets
15-1430 Maroons Road
Winnipeg, Man. R3G 0L5

National Football League

League Office
410 Park Avenue
New York, NY 10022

Atlanta Falcons
Suwanee Road
Suwanee, GA 30174

Buffalo Bills
1 Bills Drive
Orchard Park, NY 14127

Chicago Bears
250 N. Washington Rd.
Lake Forest, IL 60045

Cincinnati Bengals
200 Riverfront Stadium
Cincinnati, OH 45202

Cleveland Browns
Cleveland Stadium
Cleveland, OH 44114

Dallas Cowboys
One Cowboys Pkwy.
Irving, TX 75063

Denver Broncos
13655 E. Dove Valley Pkwy.
Englewood, CO 80112

Detroit Lions
1200 Featherstone Rd.
Pontiac, MI 48057

Green Bay Packers
1265 Lombardi Ave.
Green Bay, WI 54307

Houston Oilers
6910 Fannin St.
Houston, TX 77030

Indianapolis Colts
P.O. Box 53500
Indianapolis, IN 46253

Kansas City Chiefs
1 Arrowhead Drive
Kansas City, MO 64129

Los Angeles Raiders
332 Center St.
El Segundo, CA 90245

Los Angeles Rams
2327 W. Lincoln Ave.
Anaheim, CA 92801

Miami Dolphins
2269 NW 199 St.
Miami, FL 33056

Minnesota Vikings
9520 Viking Dr.
Eden Prairie, MN 55344

New England Patriots
Foxboro Stadium
Foxboro, MA 02035

New Orleans Saints
1500 Poydras St.
New Orleans, LA 70112

New York Giants
Giants Stadium
E. Rutherford, NJ 07073

New York Jets
1000 Fulton Ave.
Hempstead, NY 11550

Philadelphia Eagles
Veterans Stadium
Philadelphia, PA 19148

Phoenix Cardinals
PO Box 888
Phoenix, AZ 85001

Pittsburgh Steelers
Three Rivers Stadium
Pittsburgh, PA 15212

San Diego Chargers
P.O. Box 20666
San Diego, CA 92120

San Francisco 49ers
4949 Centennial Blvd.
Santa Clara, CA 95054

Seattle Seahawks
11220 NE 53d St.
Kirkland, WA 98033

Tampa Bay Buccaneers
1 Buccaneer Place
Tampa, FL 33607

Washington Redskins
PO Box 17247
Dulles Intl. Airport
Washington, DC 20041

Other Sports Organizations

Amateur Athletic Union
3400 W. 86th St.
Indianapolis, IN 46268

Amateur Softball Assn.
2801 NE 50th St.
Oklahoma City, OK 73111

American Horse Show Assn.
220 E. 42d St.
New York, NY 10017

American Kennel Club
51 Madison Ave.
New York, NY 10010

American Water Ski Assn.
799 Overlook Dr. SE
Winter Haven, FL 33884

Athletic Congress of the U.S.
PO Box 120
Indianapolis, IN 46206

LPGA
2570 Volusra Ave.
Daytona Beach, FL 10166

Little League Baseball
PO Box 3485
S. Williamsport, PA 17701

Major Indoor Soccer League
7101 College Blvd.
Shawnee Mission, KS 66210

National Archery Assn.
1750 E. Boulder St.
Colorado Springs, CO 80909

NASCAR
PO Box 2875
Daytona Beach, FL 32115

NCAA
6201 College Blvd.
Overland Park, KS 66211

National Rifle Assn.
1600 Rhode Island Ave. NW
Washington, DC 20036

Pro Bowlers Assn.
1720 Merriman Rd.
Akron, OH 44313

Pro Rodeo Cowboys Assn.
101 Pro Rodeo Dr.
Colorado Springs, CO 80919

Special Olympics
1350 New York Ave. NW
Washington, DC 20005

Thoroughbred Racing Assn.
3000 Marcus Ave.
Lake Success, NY 11042

U.S. Auto Club
4910 W. 16th St.
Speedway, IN 46224

U.S. Figure Skating Assn.
20 1st St.
Colorado Springs, CO 80906

U.S. Olympic Committee
1750 E. Boulder St.
Colorado Springs, CO 80909

U.S. Ski Team
1500 Kearns
Park City, UT 84060

U.S. Soccer Federation
1750 Boulder St.
Colorado Springs, CO 80909

U.S. Tennis Assn.
1212 Ave. of the Americas
New York, NY 10036

U.S. Trotting Assn.
750 Michigan Ave.
Columbus, OH 43215

Lacrosse Champions in 1991

U.S. Club Lacrosse Association Championship—Baltimore, Md., June 8: Mount Washington Club 6, New York A.C. 3.
NCAA Division I Championship—Syracuse, N.Y., May 27: North Carolina 18, Towson State (Md.) 13.
NCAA Division III Championship—Salisbury, Md., May 18: Hobart 12, Salisbury State (Md.) 11.
USILA All-Star Game-Division I—Baltimore, Md., June 7: South 15, North 12.
USILA All-Star Game-Division III—Baltimore, Md., June 8: North 14, South 7.
National Junior College Championship—Catonsville, Md., May 11: Essex (Md.) C.C. 20, Herkimer C.C. (N.Y.) 19 (O.T.).
NCAA Division I Women Championship—Ewing, N.J., May 19: Virginia 8, Maryland 6.

NCAA Division III Women Championship—Ewing, N.J., May 19: Trenton State 7, Ursinus 6.

USILA Division I All America Team

Attack: Tom Marechek, Syracuse; Dennis Goldstein, North Carolina; Mark Douglas, Maryland.
Midfield: Andy Towers, Brown; Adam Wright, Johns Hopkins; Rob Shek, Towson St.; Jay McMahon, Brown.
Defense: Pat McCabe, Syracuse; Brian Voelker, Johns Hopkins; Graham Harden, North Carolina.
Goal: Andy Piazza, North Carolina.
Coach of the Year: Dom Starsia, Brown.
Note: 4 midfielders selected for the 3 midfield positions

NCAA Division I Champions

Year	Champion	Year	Champion	Year	Champion	Year	Champion
1972	Virginia	1977	Cornell	1982	North Carolina	1987	Johns Hopkins
1973	Maryland	1978	Johns Hopkins	1983	Syracuse	1988	Syracuse
1974	Johns Hopkins	1979	Johns Hopkins	1984	Johns Hopkins	1989	Syracuse
1975	Maryland	1980	Johns Hopkins	1985	Johns Hopkins	1990	Syracuse
1976	Cornell	1981	North Carolina	1986	North Carolina	1991	North Carolina

BASEBALL

Major League Pennant Winners, 1901–1991

	National League					American League			
Year	Winner	Won	Lost	Pct	Manager	Year	Winner	Won	Lost	Pct	Manager
---	---	---	---	---	---	---	---	---	---	---	---
1901	Pittsburgh	90	49	.647	Clarke	1901	Chicago	83	53	.610	Griffith
1902	Pittsburgh	103	36	.741	Clarke	1902	Philadelphia	83	53	.610	Mack
1903	Pittsburgh	91	49	.650	Clarke	1903	Boston	91	47	.659	Collins
1904	New York	106	47	.693	McGraw	1904	Boston	95	59	.617	Collins
1905	New York	105	48	.686	McGraw	1905	Philadelphia	92	56	.622	Mack
1906	Chicago	116	36	.763	Chance	1906	Chicago	93	58	.616	Jones
1907	Chicago	107	45	.704	Chance	1907	Detroit	92	58	.613	Jennings
1908	Chicago	99	55	.643	Chance	1908	Detroit	90	63	.588	Jennings
1909	Pittsburgh	110	42	.724	Clarke	1909	Detroit	98	54	.645	Jennings
1910	Chicago	104	50	.675	Chance	1910	Philadelphia	102	48	.680	Mack
1911	New York	99	54	.647	McGraw	1911	Philadelphia	101	50	.669	Mack
1912	New York	103	48	.682	McGraw	1912	Boston	105	47	.691	Stahl
1913	New York	101	51	.664	McGraw	1913	Philadelphia	96	57	.627	Mack
1914	Boston	94	59	.614	Stallings	1914	Philadelphia	99	53	.651	Mack
1915	Philadelphia	90	62	.592	Moran	1915	Boston	101	50	.669	Carrigan
1916	Brooklyn	94	60	.610	Robinson	1916	Boston	91	63	.591	Carrigan
1917	New York	98	56	.636	McGraw	1917	Chicago	100	54	.649	Rowland
1918	Chicago	84	45	.651	Mitchell	1918	Boston	75	51	.595	Barrow
1919	Cincinnati	96	44	.686	Moran	1919	Chicago	88	52	.629	Gleason
1920	Brooklyn	93	60	.604	Robinson	1920	Cleveland	98	56	.636	Speaker
1921	New York	94	56	.614	McGraw	1921	New York	98	55	.641	Huggins
1922	New York	93	61	.604	McGraw	1922	New York	94	60	.610	Huggins
1923	New York	95	58	.621	McGraw	1923	New York	98	54	.645	Huggins
1924	New York	93	60	.608	McGraw	1924	Washington	92	62	.597	Harris
1925	Pittsburgh	95	58	.621	McKechnie	1925	Washington	96	55	.636	Harris
1926	St. Louis	89	65	.578	Hornsby	1926	New York	91	63	.591	Huggins
1927	Pittsburgh	94	60	.610	Bush	1927	New York	110	44	.714	Huggins
1928	St. Louis	95	59	.617	McKechnie	1928	New York	101	53	.656	Huggins
1929	Chicago	98	54	.645	McCarthy	1929	Philadelphia	104	46	.693	Mack
1930	St. Louis	92	62	.597	Street	1930	Philadelphia	102	52	.662	Mack
1931	St. Louis	101	53	.656	Street	1931	Philadelphia	107	45	.704	Mack
1932	Chicago	90	64	.584	Grimm	1932	New York	107	47	.695	McCarthy
1933	New York	91	61	.599	Terry	1933	Washington	99	53	.651	Cronin
1934	St. Louis	95	58	.621	Frisch	1934	Detroit	101	53	.656	Cochrane
1935	Chicago	100	54	.649	Grimm	1935	Detroit	93	58	.616	Cochrane
1936	New York	91	62	.597	Terry	1936	New York	102	51	.667	McCarthy
1937	New York	95	57	.625	Terry	1937	New York	102	52	.662	McCarthy
1938	Chicago	89	63	.586	Hartnett	1938	New York	99	53	.651	McCarthy
1939	Cincinnati	97	57	.630	McKechnie	1939	New York	106	45	.702	McCarthy
1940	Cincinnati	100	53	.654	McKechnie	1940	Detroit	90	64	.584	Baker
1941	Brooklyn	100	54	.649	Durocher	1941	New York	101	53	.656	McCarthy
1942	St. Louis	106	48	.688	Southworth	1942	New York	103	51	.669	McCarthy
1943	St. Louis	105	49	.682	Southworth	1943	New York	98	56	.636	McCarthy
1944	St. Louis	105	49	.682	Southworth	1944	St. Louis	89	65	.578	Sewell
1945	Chicago	98	56	.636	Grimm	1945	Detroit	88	65	.575	O'Neill
1946	St. Louis	98	58	.628	Dyer	1946	Boston	104	50	.675	Cronin
1947	Brooklyn	94	60	.610	Shotton	1947	New York	97	57	.630	Harris
1948	Boston	91	62	.595	Southworth	1948	Cleveland	97	58	.626	Boudreau
1949	Brooklyn	97	57	.630	Shotton	1949	New York	97	57	.630	Stengel
1950	Philadelphia	91	63	.591	Sawyer	1950	New York	98	56	.636	Stengel
1951	New York	98	59	.624	Durocher	1951	New York	98	56	.636	Stengel
1952	Brooklyn	96	57	.627	Dressen	1952	New York	95	59	.617	Stengel
1953	Brooklyn	105	49	.682	Dressen	1953	New York	99	52	.656	Stengel
1954	New York	97	57	.630	Durocher	1954	Cleveland	111	43	.721	Lopez
1955	Brooklyn	98	55	.641	Alston	1955	New York	96	58	.623	Stengel
1956	Brooklyn	93	61	.604	Alston	1956	New York	97	57	.630	Stengel
1957	Milwaukee	95	59	.617	Haney	1957	New York	98	56	.636	Stengel
1958	Milwaukee	92	62	.597	Haney	1958	New York	92	62	.597	Stengel
1959	Los Angeles	88	68	.564	Alston	1959	Chicago	94	60	.610	Lopez
1960	Pittsburgh	95	59	.617	Murtaugh	1960	New York	97	57	.630	Stengel
1961	Cincinnati	93	61	.604	Hutchinson	1961	New York	109	53	.673	Houk
1962	San Francisco	103	62	.624	Dark	1962	New York	96	66	.593	Houk
1963	Los Angeles	99	63	.611	Alston	1963	New York	104	57	.646	Houk
1964	St. Louis	93	69	.574	Keane	1964	New York	99	63	.611	Berra
1965	Los Angeles	97	65	.599	Alston	1965	Minnesota	102	60	.630	Mele
1966	Los Angeles	95	67	.586	Alston	1966	Baltimore	97	63	.606	Bauer
1967	St. Louis	101	60	.627	Schoendienst	1967	Boston	92	70	.568	Williams
1968	St. Louis	97	65	.599	Schoendienst	1968	Detroit	103	59	.636	Smith

National League

	East				West				Playoff
Year	Winner	W	L	Pct	Manager	Winner	W	L	Pct	Manager	winner
---	---	---	---	---	---	---	---	---	---	---	---
1969	N.Y. Mets	100	62	.617	Hodges	Atlanta	93	69	.574	Harris	New York
1970	Pittsburgh	89	73	.549	Murtaugh	Cincinnati	102	60	.630	Anderson	Cincinnati
1971	Pittsburgh	97	65	.599	Murtaugh	San Francisco	90	72	.556	Fox	Pittsburgh
1972	Pittsburgh	96	59	.619	Virdon	Cincinnati	95	59	.617	Anderson	Cincinnati
1973	N.Y. Mets	82	79	.509	Berra	Cincinnati	99	63	.611	Anderson	New York
1974	Pittsburgh	88	74	.543	Murtaugh	Los Angeles	102	60	.630	Alston	Los Angeles
1975	Pittsburgh	92	69	.571	Murtaugh	Cincinnati	108	54	.667	Anderson	Cincinnati
1976	Philadelphia	101	61	.623	Ozark	Cincinnati	102	60	.630	Anderson	Cincinnati

Year	Winner	East W	L	Pct	Manager	Winner	West W	L	Pct	Manager	Playoff winner
1977	Philadelphia .	101	61	.623	Ozark	Los Angeles . . .	98	64	.605	Lasorda	Los Angeles
1978	Philadelphia .	90	72	.556	Ozark	Los Angeles . . .	95	67	.586	Lasorda	Los Angeles
1979	Pittsburgh. . .	98	64	.605	Tanner	Cincinnati.	90	71	.559	McNamara	Pittsburgh
1980	Philadelphia .	91	71	.562	Green	Houston	93	70	.571	Virdon	Philadelphia
1981(a)	Philadelphia .	34	21	.618	Green	Los Angeles . . .	36	21	.632	Lasorda	(c)
1981(b)	Montreal . . .	30	23	.566	Williams, Fanning	Houston	33	20	.623	Virdon	Los Angeles
1982	St. Louis . . .	92	70	.568	Herzog	Atlanta	89	73	.549	Torre	St. Louis
1983	Philadelphia .	90	72	.556	Corrales, Owens	Los Angeles . . .	91	71	.562	Lasorda	Philadelphia
1984	Chicago. . . .	96	65	.596	Frey	San Diego	92	70	.568	Williams	San Diego
1985	St. Louis . . .	101	61	.623	Herzog	Los Angeles . . .	95	67	.586	Lasorda	St. Louis
1986	N.Y. Mets. . .	108	54	.667	Johnson	Houston	96	66	.593	Lanier	New York
1987	St. Louis . . .	95	67	.586	Herzog	San Francisco . .	90	72	.556	Craig	St. Louis
1988	N.Y. Mets. . .	100	60	.625	Johnson	Los Angeles . . .	94	67	.584	Lasorda	Los Angeles
1989	Chicago. . . .	93	69	.571	Zimmer	San Francisco . .	92	70	.568	Craig	San Francisco
1990	Pittsburgh. . .	95	67	.586	Leyland	Cincinnati.	91	71	.562	Piniella	Cincinnati
1991	Pittsburgh. . .	98	64	.605	Leyland	Atlanta	94	68	.580	Cox	Atlanta

American League

Year	Winner	East W	L	Pct	Manager	Winner	West W	L	Pct	Manager	Playoff winner
1969	Baltimore . . .	109	53	.673	Weaver	Minnesota	97	65	.599	Martin	Baltimore
1970	Baltimore . . .	108	54	.667	Weaver	Minnesota	98	64	.605	Rigney	Baltimore
1971	Baltimore . . .	101	57	.639	Weaver	Oakland	101	60	.627	Williams	Baltimore
1972	Detroit.	86	70	.551	Martin	Oakland	93	62	.600	Williams	Oakland
1973	Baltimore . . .	97	65	.599	Weaver	Oakland	94	68	.580	Williams	Oakland
1974	Baltimore . . .	91	71	.562	Weaver	Oakland	90	72	.556	Dark	Oakland
1975	Boston.	95	65	.594	Johnson	Oakland	98	64	.605	Dark	Boston
1976	New York . . .	97	62	.610	Martin	Kansas City . . .	90	72	.556	Herzog	New York
1977	New York . . .	100	62	.617	Martin	Kansas City . . .	102	60	.630	Herzog	New York
1978	New York . . .	100	63	.613	Martin, Lemon	Kansas City . . .	92	70	.568	Herzog	New York
1979	Baltimore . . .	102	57	.642	Weaver	California	88	74	.543	Fregosi	Baltimore
1980	New York . . .	103	59	.636	Howser	Kansas City . . .	97	65	.599	Frey	Kansas City
1981(a)	New York . . .	34	22	.607	Michael	Oakland	37	23	.617	Martin	(d)
1981(b)	Milwaukee . .	31	22	.585	Rodgers	Kansas City . . .	30	23	.566	Frey, Howser	New York
1982	Milwaukee . .	95	67	.586	Rodgers, Kuenn	California	93	69	.574	Mauch	Milwaukee
1983	Baltimore . . .	98	64	.605	Altobelli	Chicago	99	63	.611	LaRussa	Baltimore
1984	Detroit.	104	58	.642	Anderson	Kansas City . . .	84	78	.519	Howser	Detroit
1985	Toronto	99	62	.615	Cox	Kansas City . . .	91	71	.562	Howser	Kansas City
1986	Boston.	95	66	.590	McNamara	California	92	70	.568	Mauch	Boston
1987	Detroit.	98	64	.605	Anderson	Minnesota	85	77	.525	Kelly	Minnesota
1988	Boston.	89	73	.549	McNamara, Morgan	Oakland	104	58	.642	LaRussa	Oakland
1989	Toronto	89	73	.549	Williams, Gaston	Oakland	99	63	.611	LaRussa	Oakland
1990	Boston.	88	74	.543	Morgan	Oakland	103	59	.636	LaRussa	Oakland
1991	Toronto	91	71	.562	Gaston	Minnesota	95	67	.586	Kelly	Minnesota

(a) First half; (b) Second half; (c) Montreal and L.A. won the divisional playoffs; (d) N.Y. and Oakland won the divisional playoffs.

Baseball Stadiums

National League

Team	Stadium (built)	Surface	Home run distances (ft.) LF	Center	RF	Seating capacity
Atlanta Braves.	Atlanta-Fulton County Stadium (1966)	Natural grass	330	402	330	52,003
Chicago Cubs	Wrigley Field (1916).	Natural grass	355	400	353	38,710
Cincinnati Reds	Riverfront Stadium (1970)	Artificial	330	404	330	52,952
Houston Astros	Astrodome (1965)	Artificial	330	400	330	54,816
Los Angeles Dodgers . .	Dodger Stadium (1962)	Natural grass	330	395	330	56,000
Montreal Expos	Olympic Stadium (1977).	Artificial	325	404	325	43,739
New York Mets	Shea Stadium (1964).	Natural grass	338	410	338	55,601
Philadelphia Phillies. . .	Veterans Stadium (1971)	Artificial	330	408	330	62,382
Pittsburgh Pirates	Three Rivers Stadium (1970)	Artificial	335	400	335	58,727
St. Louis Cardinals . . .	Busch Stadium (1966)	Artificial	330	414	330	56,227
San Diego Padres	Jack Murphy Stadium (1969)	Natural grass	327	405	327	59,022
San Francisco Giants . .	Candlestick Park (1960).	Natural grass	335	400	330	58,000

American League

Team	Stadium (built)	Surface	Home run distances (ft.) LF	Center	RF	Seating capacity
Baltimore Orioles	Memorial Stadium (1954)	Natural grass	309	405	309	53,371
Boston Red Sox	Fenway Park (1912).	Natural grass	315	420	302	34,142
California Angels	Anaheim Stadium (1966)	Natural grass	333	404	333	64,593
Chicago White Sox . . .	Comiskey Park (1991)	Natural grass	347	400	347	43,500
Cleveland Indians	Cleveland Stadium (1932)	Natural grass	320	415	320	74,483
Detroit Tigers	Tiger Stadium (1912)	Natural grass	340	440	325	52,416
Kansas City Royals . . .	Royals Stadium (1973)	Artificial	330	410	330	40,625
Milwaukee Brewers . . .	Milwaukee County Stadium (1953).	Natural grass	315	402	315	53,192
Minnesota Twins	Hubert H. Humphrey Metrodome (1982) . . .	Artificial	343	408	327	55,883
New York Yankees . . .	Yankee Stadium (1923)	Natural grass	318	408	314	57,545
Oakland A's	Oakland Alameda County Coliseum (1968) . .	Natural grass	330	400	330	47,313
Seattle Mariners	Kingdome (1977)	Artificial	331	405	312	57,748
Texas Rangers	Arlington Stadium (1972)	Natural grass	330	400	330	43,521
Toronto Blue Jays	Skydome (1989)	Artificial	328	400	328	50,516

Home Run Leaders

National League

Year	Player, Club	HR
1901	Sam Crawford, Cincinnati	16
1902	Thomas Leach, Pittsburgh	6
1903	James Sheckard, Brooklyn	9
1904	Harry Lumley, Brooklyn	9
1905	Fred Odwell, Cincinnati	9
1906	Timothy Jordan, Brooklyn	12
1907	David Brain, Boston	10
1908	Timothy Jordan, Brooklyn	12
1909	Red Murray, New York	7
1910	Fred Beck, Bos., Frank Schulte, Chi.	10
1911	Frank Schulte, Chicago	21
1912	Henry Zimmerman, Chicago	14
1913	Gavvy Cravath, Philadelphia	19
1914	Gavvy Cravath, Philadelphia	19
1915	Gavvy Cravath, Philadelphia	24
1916	Dave Robertson, N.Y., Fred (Cy) Williams, Chi.	12
1917	Dave Robertson, N.Y., Gavvy Cravath, Phil.	12
1918	Gavvy Cravath, Philadelphia	8
1919	Gavvy Cravath, Philadelphia	12
1920	Cy Williams, Philadelphia	15
1921	George Kelly, New York	23
1922	Rogers Hornsby, St. Louis	42
1923	Cy Williams, Philadelphia	41
1924	Jacques Fournier, Brooklyn	27
1925	Rogers Hornsby, St. Louis	39
1926	Hack Wilson, Chicago	21
1927	Hack Wilson, Chicago; Cy Williams, Philadelphia	30
1928	Hack Wilson, Chicago; Jim Bottomley, St. Louis	31
1929	Chuck Klein, Philadelphia	43
1930	Hack Wilson, Chicago	56
1931	Chuck Klein, Philadelphia	31
1932	Chuck Klein, Philadelphia, Mel Ott, New York	38
1933	Chuck Klein, Philadelphia	28
1934	Rip Collins, St. Louis; Mel Ott, New York	35
1935	Walter Berger, Boston	34
1936	Mel Ott, New York	33
1937	Mel Ott, New York; Joe Medwick, St. Louis	31
1938	Mel Ott, New York	36
1939	John Mize, St. Louis	28
1940	John Mize, St. Louis	43
1941	Dolph Camilli, Brooklyn	34
1942	Mel Ott, New York	30
1943	Bill Nicholson, Chicago	29
1944	Bill Nicholson, Chicago	33
1945	Tommy Holmes, Boston	28
1946	Ralph Kiner, Pittsburgh	23
1947	Ralph Kiner, Pittsburgh; John Mize, New York	51
1948	Ralph Kiner, Pittsburgh; John Mize, New York	40
1949	Ralph Kiner, Pittsburgh	54
1950	Ralph Kiner, Pittsburgh	47
1951	Ralph Kiner, Pittsburgh	42
1952	Ralph Kiner, Pittsburgh; Hank Sauer, Chicago	37
1953	Ed Mathews, Milwaukee	47
1954	Ted Kluszewski, Cincinnati	49
1955	Willie Mays, New York	51
1956	Duke Snider, Brooklyn	43
1957	Hank Aaron, Milwaukee	44
1958	Ernie Banks, Chicago	47
1959	Ed Mathews, Milwaukee	46
1960	Ernie Banks, Chicago	41
1961	Orlando Cepeda, San Francisco	46
1962	Willie Mays, San Francisco	49
1963	Hank Aaron, Milwaukee, Willie McCovey, S.F.	44
1964	Willie Mays, San Francisco	47
1965	Willie Mays, San Francisco	52
1966	Hank Aaron, Atlanta	44
1967	Hank Aaron, Atlanta	39
1968	Willie McCovey, San Francisco	36
1969	Willie McCovey, San Francisco	45
1970	Johnny Bench, Cincinnati	45
1971	Willie Stargell, Pittsburgh	48
1972	Johnny Bench, Cincinnati	40
1973	Willie Stargell, Pittsburgh	44
1974	Mike Schmidt, Philadelphia	36
1975	Mike Schmidt, Philadelphia	38
1976	Mike Schmidt, Philadelphia	38
1977	George Foster, Cincinnati	52
1978	George Foster, Cincinnati	40
1979	Dave Kingman, Chicago	48
1980	Mike Schmidt, Philadelphia	48
1981	Mike Schmidt, Philadelphia	31
1982	Dave Kingman, New York	37
1983	Mike Schmidt, Philadelphia	40

American League

Year	Player, Club	HR
1901	Napoleon Lajoie, Philadelphia	14
1902	Socks Seybold, Philadelphia	16
1903	Buck Freeman, Boston	13
1904	Harry Davis, Philadelphia	10
1905	Harry Davis, Philadelphia	8
1906	Harry Davis, Philadelphia	12
1907	Harry Davis, Philadelphia	8
1908	Sam Crawford, Detroit	7
1909	Ty Cobb, Detroit	9
1910	Jake Stahl, Boston	10
1911	J. Franklin Baker, Philadelphia	11
1912	J. Franklin Baker, Philadelphia, Tris Speaker, Boston	10
1913	J. Franklin, Baker, Philadelphia	12
1914	J. Franklin, Baker, Philadelphia	9
1915	Robert Roth, Chicago-Cleveland	7
1916	Wally Pipp, New York	12
1917	Wally Pipp, New York	9
1918	Babe Ruth, Bos., Tilly Walker, Phil.	11
1919	Babe Ruth, Boston	29
1920	Babe Ruth, New York	54
1921	Babe Ruth, New York	59
1922	Ken Williams, St. Louis	39
1923	Babe Ruth, New York	41
1924	Babe Ruth, New York	46
1925	Bob Meusel, New York	33
1926	Babe Ruth, New York	47
1927	Babe Ruth, New York	60
1928	Babe Ruth, New York	54
1929	Babe Ruth, New York	46
1930	Babe Ruth, New York	49
1931	Babe Ruth, Lou Gehrig, New York	46
1932	Jimmie Foxx, Philadelphia	58
1933	Jimmie Foxx, Philadelphia	48
1934	Lou Gehrig, New York	49
1935	Jimmie Foxx, Philadelphia, Hank Greenberg, Detroit	36
1936	Lou Gehrig, New York	49
1937	Joe DiMaggio, New York	46
1938	Hank Greenberg, Detroit	58
1939	Jimmie Foxx, Boston	35
1940	Hank Greenberg, Detroit	41
1941	Ted Williams, Boston	37
1942	Ted Williams, Boston	36
1943	Rudy York, Detroit	34
1944	Nick Etten, New York	22
1945	Vern Stephens, St. Louis	24
1946	Hank Greenberg, Detroit	44
1947	Ted Williams, Boston	32
1948	Joe DiMaggio, New York	39
1949	Ted Williams, Boston	43
1950	Al Rosen, Cleveland	37
1951	Gus Zernial, Chicago-Philadelphia	33
1952	Larry Doby, Cleveland	32
1953	Al Rosen, Cleveland	43
1954	Larry Doby, Cleveland	32
1955	Mickey Mantle, New York	37
1956	Mickey Mantle, New York	52
1957	Roy Sievers, Washington	42
1958	Mickey Mantle, New York	42
1959	Rocky Colavito, Cleve., Harmon Killebrew, Wash.	42
1960	Mickey Mantle, New York	40
1961	Roger Maris, New York	61
1962	Harmon Killebrew, Minnesota	48
1963	Harmon Killebrew, Minnesota	45
1964	Harmon Killebrew, Minnesota	49
1965	Tony Conigliaro, Boston	32
1966	Frank Robinson, Baltimore	49
1967	Carl Yastrzemski, Boston, Harmon Killebrew, Minn.	44
1968	Frank Howard, Washington	44
1969	Harmon Killebrew, Minnesota	49
1970	Frank Howard, Washington	44
1971	Bill Melton, Chicago	33
1972	Dick Allen, Chicago	37
1973	Reggie Jackson, Oakland	32
1974	Dick Allen, Chicago	32
1975	George Scott, Milwaukee; Reggie Jackson, Oakland	36
1976	Graig Nettles, New York	32
1977	Jim Rice, Boston	39
1978	Jim Rice, Boston	46
1979	Gorman Thomas, Milwaukee	45
1980	Reggie Jackson, New York; Ben Oglivie, Milwaukee	41
1981	Bobby Grich, California; Tony Armas, Oakland; Dwight Evans, Boston; Eddie Murray, Baltimore	22
1982	Gorman Thomas, Milwaukee; Reggie Jackson, Cal.	39
1983	Jim Rice, Boston	39

Year	Player, Club	HR
1984	Mike Schmidt, Phil.; Dale Murphy, Atlanta	36
1985	Dale Murphy, Atlanta	37
1986	Mike Schmidt, Philadelphia	37
1987	Andre Dawson, Chicago	49
1988	Darryl Strawberry, New York	39
1989	Kevin Mitchell, San Francisco	47
1990	Ryne Sandberg, Chicago	40
1991	Howard Johnson, New York	38

Year	Player, Club	HR
1984	Tony Armas, Boston	43
1985	Darrell Evans, Detroit	40
1986	Jesse Barfield, Toronto	40
1987	Mark McGwire, Oakland	49
1988	Jose Canseco, Oakland	42
1989	Fred McGriff, Toronto	36
1990	Cecil Fielder, Detroit	51
1991	Cecil Fielder, Detroit; Jose Canseco, Oakland	44

Runs Batted In Leaders

National League

Year	Player, Club	RBI
1907	Honus Wagner, Pittsburgh	91
1908	Honus Wager, Pittsburgh	106
1909	Honus Wager, Pittsburgh	102
1910	Sherwood Magee, Philadelphia	116
1911	Frank Schulte, Chicago	121
1912	Henry Zimmerman, Chicago	98
1913	Gavvy Cravath, Philadelphia	118
1914	Sherwood Magee, Philadelphia	101
1915	Gavvy Cravath, Philadelphia	118
1916	Hal Chase, Cincinnati	94
1917	Henry Zimmerman, New York	100
1918	Frederick Merkle, Chicago	71
1919	Hi Myers, Boston	72
1920	George Kelly, N.Y., Rogers Hornsby, St. Louis	94
1921	Rogers Hornsby, St. Louis	126
1922	Rogers Hornsby, St. Louis	152
1923	Emil Meusel, New York	125
1924	George Kelly, New York	136
1925	Rogers Hornsby, St. Louis	143
1926	Jim Bottomley, St. Louis	120
1927	Paul Waner, Pittsburgh	131
1928	Jim Bottomley, St. Louis	136
1929	Hack Wilson, Chicago	159
1930	Hack Wilson, Chicago	190
1931	Chuck Klein, Philadelphia	121
1932	Don Hurst, Philadelphia	143
1933	Chuck Klein, Philadelphia	120
1934	Mel Ott, New York	135
1935	Walter Berger, Boston	130
1936	Joe Medwick, St. Louis	138
1937	Joe Medwick, St. Louis	154
1938	Joe Medwick, St. Louis	122
1939	Frank McCormick, Cincinnati	128
1940	John Mize, St. Louis	137
1941	Adolph Camilli, Brooklyn	120
1942	John Mize, New York	110
1943	Bill Nicholson, Chicago	128
1944	Bill Nicholson, Chicago	122
1945	Dixie Walker, Brooklyn	124
1946	Enos Slaughter, St. Louis	130
1947	John Mize, New York	138
1948	Stan Musial, St. Louis	131
1949	Ralph Kiner, Pittsburgh	127
1950	Del Ennis, Philadelphia	126
1951	Monte Irvin, New York	121
1952	Hank Sauer, Chicago	121
1953	Roy Campanella, Brooklyn	142
1954	Ted Kluszewski, Cincinnati	141
1955	Duke Snider, Brooklyn	136
1956	Stan Musial, St. Louis	109
1957	Hank Aaron, Milwaukee	132
1958	Ernie Banks, Chicago	129
1959	Ernie Banks, Chicago	143
1960	Hank Aaron, Milwaukee	126
1961	Orlando Cepeda, San Francisco	142
1962	Tommy Davis, Los Angeles	153
1963	Hank Aaron, Milwaukee	130
1964	Ken Boyer, St. Louis	119
1965	Deron Johnson, Cincinnati	130
1966	Hank Aaron, Atlanta	127
1967	Orlando Cepeda, St. Louis	111
1968	Willie McCovey, San Francisco	105
1969	Willie McCovey, San Francisco	126
1970	Johnny Bench, Cincinnati	148
1971	Joe Torre, St. Louis	137
1972	Johnny Bench, Cincinnati	125
1973	Willie Stargell, Pittsburgh	119
1974	Johnny Bench, Cincinnati	129
1975	Greg Luzinski, Philadelphia	120
1976	George Foster, Cincinnati	121
1977	George Foster, Cincinnati	149
1978	George Foster, Cincinnati	120
1979	Dave Winfield, San Diego	118
1980	Mike Schmidt, Philadelphia	121
1981	Mike Schmidt, Philadelphia	91

American League

Year	Player, Club	RBI
1907	Ty Cobb, Detroit	116
1908	Ty Cobb, Detroit	101
1909	Ty Cobb, Detroit	115
1910	Sam Crawford, Detroit	115
1911	Ty Cobb, Detroit	144
1912	J. Franklin Baker, Philadelphia	133
1913	J. Franklin Baker, Philadelphia	126
1914	Sam Crawford, Detroit	112
1915	Sam Crawford, Detroit	116
1916	Wally Pipp, New York	99
1917	Robert Veach, Detroit	115
1918	George Burns, Phila., Robert Veach, Detroit	74
1919	Babe Ruth, Boston	112
1920	Babe Ruth, New York	137
1921	Babe Ruth, New York	171
1922	Ken Williams, St. Louis	155
1923	Babe Ruth, New York	131
1924	Goose Goslin, Washington	129
1925	Bob Meusel, New York	138
1926	Babe Ruth, New York	145
1927	Lou Gehrig, New York	175
1928	Babe Ruth, N.Y., Lou Gehrig, N.Y.	142
1929	Al Simmons, Philadelphia	157
1930	Lou Gehrig, New York	174
1931	Lou Gehrig, New York	184
1932	Jimmie Foxx, Philadelphia	169
1933	Jimmie Foxx, Philadelphia	163
1934	Lou Gehrig, New York	165
1935	Hank Greenberg, Detroit	170
1936	Hal Trosky, Cleveland	162
1937	Hank Greenberg, Detroit	183
1938	Jimmie Foxx, Boston	175
1939	Ted Williams, Boston	145
1940	Hank Greenberg, Detroit	150
1941	Joe DiMaggio, New York	125
1942	Ted Williams, Boston	137
1943	Rudy York, Detroit	118
1944	Vern Stephens, St. Louis	109
1945	Nick Etten, New York	111
1946	Hank Greenberg, Detroit	127
1947	Ted Williams, Boston	114
1948	Joe DiMaggio, New York	155
1949	Ted Williams, Bos., Vern Stephens, Bos.	159
1950	Walt Dropo, Bos., Vern Stephens, Bos.	144
1951	Gus Zernial, Chicago-Philadelphia	129
1952	Al Rosen, Cleveland	105
1953	Al Rosen, Cleveland	145
1954	Larry Doby, Cleveland	126
1955	Ray Boone, Detroit, Jackie Jensen, Boston	116
1956	Mickey Mantle, New York	130
1957	Roy Sievers, Washington	114
1958	Jackie Jensen, Boston	122
1959	Jackie Jensen, Boston	112
1960	Roger Maris, New York	112
1961	Roger Maris, New York	142
1962	Harmon Killebrew, Minnesota	126
1963	Dick Stuart, Boston	118
1964	Brooks Robinson, Baltimore	118
1965	Rocky Colavito, Cleveland	108
1966	Frank Robinson, Baltimore	122
1967	Carl Yastrzemski, Boston	121
1968	Ken Harrelson, Boston	109
1969	Harmon Killebrew, Minnesota	140
1970	Frank Howard, Washington	126
1971	Harmon Killebrew, Minnesota	119
1972	Dick Allen, Chicago	113
1973	Reggie Jackson, Oakland	117
1974	Jeff Burroughs, Texas	118
1975	George Scott, Milwaukee	109
1976	Lee May, Baltimore	109
1977	Larry Hisle, Minnesota	119
1978	Jim Rice, Boston	139
1979	Don Baylor, California	139
1980	Cecil Cooper, Milwaukee	122
1981	Eddie Murray, Baltimore	78

Year	Player, Club	RBI	Year	Player, Club	RBI
1982	Dale Murphy, Atlanta; Al Oliver, Montreal	109	1982	Hal McRae, Kansas City	133
1983	Dale Murphy, Atlanta	121	1983	Cecil Cooper, Milwaukee; Jim Rice, Boston	126
1984	Mike Schmidt, Phil.; Gary Carter, Montreal	106	1984	Tony Armas, Boston	123
1985	Dave Parker, Cincinnati	125	1985	Don Mattingly, New York	145
1986	Mike Schmidt, Philadelphia	119	1986	Joe Carter, Cleveland	121
1987	Andre Dawson, Chicago	137	1987	George Bell, Toronto	134
1988	Will Clark, San Francisco	109	1988	Jose Canseco, Oakland	124
1989	Kevin Mitchell, San Francisco	125	1989	Ruben Sierra, Texas	119
1990	Matt Williams, San Francisco	122	1990	Cecil Fielder, Detroit	132
1991	Howard Johnson, New York	117	1991	Cecil Fielder, Detroit	133

Batting Champions

	National League				American League		
Year	Player	Club	Pct.	Year	Player	Club	Pct.
1901	Jesse C. Burkett	St. Louis	.382	1901	Napoleon Lajoie	Philadelphia	.422
1902	Clarence Beaumont	Pittsburgh	.357	1902	Ed Delahanty	Washington	.376
1903	Honus Wagner	Pittsburgh	.355	1902	Napoleon Lajoie	Cleveland	.355
1904	Honus Wagner	Pittsburgh	.349	1904	Napoleon Lajoie	Cleveland	.381
1905	James Seymour	Cincinnati	.377	1905	Elmer Flick	Cleveland	.308
1906	Honus Wagner	Pittsburgh	.339	1906	George Stone	St. Louis	.358
1907	Honus Wagner	Pittsburgh	.350	1907	Ty Cobb	Detroit	.350
1908	Honus Wagner	Pittsburgh	.354	1908	Ty Cobb	Detroit	.324
1909	Honus Wagner	Pittsburgh	.339	1909	Ty Cobb	Detroit	.377
1910	Sherwood Magee	Philadelphia	.331	1910	Ty Cobb	Detroit	.385
1911	Honus Wagner	Pittsburgh	.334	1911	Ty Cobb	Detroit	.420
1912	Henry Zimmerman	Chicago	.372	1912	Ty Cobb	Detroit	.410
1913	Jacob Daubert	Brooklyn	.350	1913	Ty Cobb	Detroit	.390
1914	Jacob Daubert	Brooklyn	.329	1914	Ty Cobb	Detroit	.368
1915	Larry Doyle	New York	.320	1915	Ty Cobb	Detroit	.369
1916	Hal Chase	Cincinnati	.339	1916	Tris Speaker	Cleveland	.386
1917	Edd Roush	Cleveland	.341	1917	Ty Cobb	Detroit	.383
1918	Zach Wheat	Brooklyn	.335	1918	Ty Cobb	Detroit	.382
1919	Edd Roush	Cincinnati	.321	1919	Ty Cobb	Detroit	.384
1920	Rogers Hornsby	St. Louis	.370	1920	George Sisler	St. Louis	.407
1921	Rogers Hornsby	St. Louis	.397	1921	Harry Heilmann	Detroit	.394
1922	Rogers Hornsby	St. Louis	.401	1922	George Sisler	St. Louis	.420
1923	Rogers Hornsby	St. Louis	.384	1923	Harry Heilmann	Detroit	.403
1924	Rogers Hornsby	St. Louis	.424	1924	Babe Ruth	New York	.378
1925	Rogers Hornsby	St. Louis	.403	1925	Harry Heilmann	Detroit	.393
1926	Eugene Hargrave	Cincinnati	.353	1926	Henry Manush	Detroit	.378
1927	Paul Waner	Pittsburgh	.380	1927	Harry Heilmann	Detroit	.398
1928	Rogers Hornsby	Boston	.387	1928	Goose Goslin	Washington	.379
1929	Lefty O'Doul	Philadelphia	.398	1929	Lew Fonseca	Cleveland	.369
1930	Bill Terry	New York	.401	1930	Al Simmons	Philadelphia	.381
1931	Chick Hafey	St. Louis	.349	1931	Al Simmons	Philadelphia	.390
1932	Lefty O'Doul	Brooklyn	.368	1932	Dale Alexander	Detroit-Boston	.367
1933	Chuck Klein	Philadelphia	.368	1933	Jimmie Foxx	Philadelphia	.356
1934	Paul Waner	Pittsburgh	.362	1934	Lou Gehrig	New York	.363
1935	Arky Vaughan	Pittsburgh	.385	1935	Buddy Myer	Washington	.349
1936	Paul Waner	Pittsburgh	.373	1936	Luke Appling	Chicago	.388
1937	Joe Medwick	St. Louis	.374	1937	Charlie Gehringer	Detroit	.371
1938	Ernie Lombardi	Cincinnati	.342	1938	Jimmie Foxx	Boston	.349
1939	John Mize	St. Louis	.349	1939	Joe DiMaggio	New York	.381
1940	Debs Garms	Pittsburgh	.355	1940	Joe DiMaggio	New York	.352
1941	Pete Reiser	Brooklyn	.343	1941	Ted Williams	Boston	.406
1942	Ernie Lombardi	Boston	.330	1942	Ted Williams	Boston	.356
1943	Stan Musial	St. Louis	.357	1943	Luke Appling	Chicago	.328
1944	Dixie Walker	Brooklyn	.357	1944	Lou Boudreau	Cleveland	.327
1945	Phil Cavarretta	Chicago	.355	1945	George Stirnweiss	New York	.309
1946	Stan Musial	St. Louis	.365	1946	Mickey Vernon	Washington	.353
1947	Harry Walker	Philadelphia	.363	1947	Ted Williams	Boston	.343
1948	Stan Musial	St. Louis	.376	1948	Ted Williams	Boston	.369
1949	Jackie Robinson	Brooklyn	.342	1949	George Kell	Detroit	.343
1950	Stan Musial	St. Louis	.346	1950	Billy Goodman	Boston	.354
1951	Stan Musial	St. Louis	.355	1951	Ferris Fain	Philadelphia	.344
1952	Stan Musial	St. Louis	.336	1952	Ferris Fain	Philadelphia	.327
1953	Carl Furillo	Brooklyn	.344	1953	Mickey Vernon	Washington	.337
1954	Willie Mays	New York	.345	1954	Roberto Avila	Cleveland	.341
1955	Richie Ashburn	Philadelphia	.338	1955	Al Kaline	Detroit	.340
1956	Hank Aaron	Milwaukee	.328	1956	Mickey Mantle	New York	.353
1957	Stan Musial	St. Louis	.351	1957	Ted Williams	Boston	.388
1958	Richie Ashburn	Philadelphia	.350	1958	Ted Williams	Boston	.328
1959	Hank Aaron	Milwaukee	.355	1959	Harvey Kuenn	Detroit	.353
1960	Dick Groat	Pittsburgh	.325	1960	Pete Runnels	Boston	.320
1961	Roberto Clemente	Pittsburgh	.351	1961	Norm Cash	Detroit	.361
1962	Tommy Davis	Los Angeles	.346	1962	Pete Runnels	Boston	.326
1963	Tommy Davis	Los Angeles	.326	1963	Carl Yastrzemski	Boston	.321
1964	Roberto Clemente	Pittsburgh	.339	1964	Tony Oliva	Minnesota	.323
1965	Roberto Clemente	Pittsburgh	.329	1965	Tony Oliva	Minnesota	.321
1966	Matty Alou	Pittsburgh	.342	1966	Frank Robinson	Baltimore	.316
1967	Roberto Clemente	Pittsburgh	.357	1967	Carl Yastrzemski	Boston	.326
1968	Pete Rose	Cincinnati	.335	1968	Carl Yastrzemski	Boston	.301
1969	Pete Rose	Cincinnati	.348	1969	Rod Carew	Minnesota	.332
1970	Rico Carty	Atlanta	.366	1970	Alex Johnson	California	.328
1971	Joe Torre	St. Louis	.363	1971	Tony Oliva	Minnesota	.337
1972	Billy Williams	Chicago	.333	1972	Rod Carew	Minnesota	.318
1973	Pete Rose	Cincinnati	.338	1973	Rod Carew	Minnesota	.350
1974	Ralph Garr	Atlanta	.353	1974	Rod Carew	Minnesota	.364

Year	Player	Club	Pct.	Year	Player	Club	Pct.
1975	Bill Madlock	Chicago	.354	1975	Rod Carew	Minnesota	.359
1976	Bill Madlock	Chicago	.339	1976	George Brett	Kansas City	.333
1977	Dave Parker	Pittsburgh	.338	1977	Rod Carew	Minnesota	.388
1978	Dave Parker	Pittsburgh	.334	1978	Rod Carew	Minnesota	.333
1979	Keith Hernandez	St. Louis	.344	1979	Fred Lynn	Boston	.333
1980	Bill Buckner	Chicago	.324	1980	George Brett	Kansas City	.390
1981	Bill Madlock	Pittsburgh	.341	1981	Carney Lansford	Boston	.336
1982	Al Oliver	Montreal	.331	1982	Willie Wilson	Kansas City	.332
1983	Bill Madlock	Pittsburgh	.323	1983	Wade Boggs	Boston	.361
1984	Tony Gwynn	San Diego	.351	1984	Don Mattingly	New York	.343
1985	Willie McGee	St. Louis	.353	1985	Wade Boggs	Boston	.368
1986	Tim Raines	Montreal	.334	1986	Wade Boggs	Boston	.357
1987	Tony Gwynn	San Diego	.369	1987	Wade Boggs	Boston	.363
1988	Tony Gwynn	San Diego	.313	1988	Wade Boggs	Boston	.366
1989	Tony Gwynn	San Diego	.336	1989	Kirby Puckett	Minnesota	.339
1990	Willie McGee	St. Louis	.335	1990	George Brett	Kansas City	.329
1991	Terry Pendleton	Atlanta	.319	1991	Julio Franco	Texas	.342

Earned-Run Average Leaders

	National League					American League			
Year	Player, club	G	IP	ERA	Year	Player, club	G	IP	ERA
1972	Steve Carlton, Philadelphia	41	346	1.98	1972	Luis Tiant, Boston	43	179	1.91
1973	Tom Seaver, New York	36	290	2.07	1973	Jim Palmer, Baltimore	38	296	2.40
1974	Buzz Capra, Atlanta	39	217	2.28	1974	Catfish Hunter, Oakland	41	318	2.49
1975	Randy Jones, San Diego	37	285	2.24	1975	Jim Palmer, Baltimore	39	323	2.09
1976	John Denny, St. Louis	30	207	2.52	1976	Mark Fidrych, Detroit	31	250	2.34
1977	John Candelaria, Pittsburgh	33	231	2.34	1977	Frank Tanana, California	31	241	2.54
1978	Craig Swan, New York	29	207	2.43	1978	Ron Guidry, New York	35	274	1.74
1979	J. R. Richard, Houston	38	292	2.71	1979	Ron Guidry, New York	33	236	2.78
1980	Don Sutton, Los Angeles	32	212	2.21	1980	Rudy May, New York	41	175	2.47
1981	Nolan Ryan, Houston	21	149	1.69	1981	Steve McCatty, Oakland	22	186	2.32
1982	Steve Rogers, Montreal	35	277	2.40	1982	Rick Sutcliffe, Cleveland	34	216	2.96
1983	Atlee Hammaker, San Fran.	23	172	2.25	1983	Rick Honeycutt, Texas	25	174	2.42
1984	Alejandro Pena, Los Angeles	28	199	2.48	1984	Mike Boddicker, Baltimore	34	261	2.79
1985	Dwight Gooden, New York	35	276	1.53	1986	Dave Stieb, Toronto	36	265	2.48
1986	Mike Scott, Houston	37	275	2.22	1986	Roger Clemens, Boston	33	254	2.48
1987	Nolan Ryan, Houston	34	211	2.76	1987	Jimmy Key, Toronto	36	261	2.76
1988	Joe Magrane, St. Louis	24	165	2.18	1988	Allan Anderson, Minnesota	30	202	2.45
1989	Scott Garrelts, San Francisco	30	193	2.28	1989	Bret Saberhagen, Kansas City	36	262	2.16
1990	Danny Darwin, Houston	48	162	2.21	1990	Roger Clemens, Boston	31	228	1.93
1991	Dennis Martinez, Montreal	31	222	2.39	1991	Roger Clemens, Boston	35	271	2.62

ERA is computed by multiplying earned runs allowed by 9, then dividing by innings pitched.

Cy Young Award Winners

Year	Player, club	Year	Player, club	Year	Player, club
1956	Don Newcombe, Dodgers	1971	(NL) Ferguson Jenkins, Cubs	1981	(NL) Fernando Valenzuela, Dodgers
1957	Warren Spahn, Braves		(AL) Vida Blue, A's		(AL) Rollie Fingers, Brewers
1958	Bob Turley, Yankees	1972	(NL) Steve Carlton, Phillies	1982	(NL) Steve Carlton, Phillies
1959	Early Wynn, White Sox		(AL) Gaylord Perry, Indians		(AL) Pete Vuckovich, Brewers
1960	Vernon Law, Pirates	1973	(NL) Tom Seaver, Mets	1983	(NL) John Denny, Phillies
1961	Whitey Ford, Yankees		(AL) Jim Palmer, Orioles		(AL) LaMarr Hoyt, White Sox
1962	Don Drysdale, Dodgers	1974	(NL) Mike Marshall, Dodgers	1984	(NL) Rick Sutcliffe, Cubs
1963	Sandy Koufax, Dodgers		(AL) Jim (Catfish) Hunter, A's		(AL) Willie Hernandez, Tigers
1964	Dean Chance, Angels	1975	(NL) Tom Seaver, Mets	1985	(NL) Dwight Gooden, Mets
1965	Sandy Koufax, Dodgers		(AL) Jim Palmer, Orioles		(AL) Bret Saberhagen, Royals
1966	Sandy Koufax, Dodgers	1976	(NL) Randy Jones, Padres	1986	(NL) Mike Scott, Astros
1967	(NL) Mike McCormick, Giants		(AL) Jim Palmer, Orioles		(AL) Roger Clemens, Red Sox
	(AL) Jim Lonborg, Red Sox	1977	(NL) Steve Carlton, Phillies	1987	(NL) Steve Bedrosian, Phillies
1968	(NL) Bob Gibson, Cardinals		(AL) Sparky Lyle, Yankees		(AL) Roger Clemens, Red Sox
	(AL) Dennis McLain, Tigers	1978	(NL) Gaylord Perry, Padres	1988	(NL) Orel Hershiser, Dodgers
1969	(NL) Tom Seaver, Mets		(AL) Ron Guidry, Yankees		(AL) Frank Viola, Twins
	(AL) (tie) Dennis McLain, Tigers	1979	(NL) Bruce Sutter, Cubs	1989	(NL) Mark Davis, Padres
	Mike Cuellar, Orioles		(AL) Mike Flanagan, Orioles		(AL) Bret Saberhagen, Royals
1970	(NL) Bob Gibson, Cardinals	1980	(NL) Steve Carlton, Phillies	1990	(NL) Doug Drabek, Pirates
	(AL) Jim Perry, Twins		(AL) Steve Stone, Orioles		(AL) Bob Welch, A's

World Almanac All-Major League Baseball Team in 1991

The team was chosen by a panel of sports experts on behalf of the World Almanac.

Position	Player, team	Position	Player, team
First base	Cecil Fielder, Detroit Tigers	Catcher	Craig Biggio, Houston Astros
Second base	Julio Franco, Texas Rangers	Right-hand pitcher	Roger Clemens, Boston Red Sox
Third base	Howard Johnson, New York Mets	Left-hand pitcher	Tom Glavine, Atlanta Braves
Shortstop	Cal Ripken Jr., Baltimore Orioles	Relief pitcher	Rick Aguilera, Minnesota Twins
Outfield	Barry Bonds, Pittsburgh Pirates	Rookie of the Year	Jeff Bagwell, Houston Astros
Outfield	Kirby Puckett, Minnesota Twins	Player of the Year	Cal Ripken Jr., Baltimore Orioles
Outfield	Joe Carter, Toronto Blue Jays	Manager of the Year	Bobby Cox, Atlanta Braves

Most Valuable Player
Baseball Writers' Association
National League

Year	Player, team	Year	Player, team	Year	Player, team
1931	Frank Frisch, St. Louis	1952	Hank Sauer, Chicago	1972	Johnny Bench, Cincinnati
1932	Charles Klein, Philadelphia	1953	Roy Campanella, Brooklyn	1973	Pete Rose, Cincinnati
1933	Carl Hubbell, New York	1954	Willie Mays, New York	1974	Steve Garvey, Los Angeles
1934	Dizzy Dean, St. Louis	1955	Roy Campanella, Brooklyn	1975	Joe Morgan, Cincinnati
1935	Gabby Hartnett, Chicago	1956	Don Newcombe, Brooklyn	1976	Joe Morgan, Cincinnati
1936	Carl Hubbell, New York	1957	Henry Aaron, Milwaukee	1977	George Foster, Cincinnati
1937	Joe Medwick, St. Louis	1958	Ernie Banks, Chicago	1978	Dave Parker, Pittsburgh
1938	Ernie Lombardi, Cincinnati	1959	Ernie Banks, Chicago	1979	(tie) Willie Stargell, Pittsburgh
1939	Bucky Walters, Cincinnati	1960	Dick Groat, Pittsburgh		Keith Hernandez, St. Louis
1940	Frank McCormick, Cincinnati	1961	Frank Robinson, Cincinnati	1980	Mike Schmidt, Philadelphia
1941	Dolph Camilli, Brooklyn	1962	Maury Wills, Los Angeles	1981	Mike Schmidt, Philadelphia
1942	Mort Cooper, St. Louis	1963	Sandy Koufax, Los Angeles	1982	Dale Murphy, Atlanta
1943	Stan Musial, St. Louis	1964	Ken Boyer, St. Louis	1983	Dale Murphy, Atlanta
1944	Martin Marion, St. Louis	1965	Willie Mays, San Francisco	1984	Ryne Sandberg, Chicago
1945	Phil Cavarretta, Chicago	1966	Roberto Clemente, Pittsburgh	1985	Willie McGee, St. Louis
1946	Stan Musial, St. Louis	1967	Orlando Cepeda, St. Louis	1986	Mike Schmidt, Philadelphia
1947	Bob Elliott, Boston	1968	Bob Gibson, St. Louis	1987	Andre Dawson, Chicago
1948	Stan Musial, St. Louis	1969	Willie McCovey, San Francisco	1988	Kirk Gibson, Los Angeles
1949	Jackie Robinson, Brooklyn	1970	Johnny Bench, Cincinnati	1989	Kevin Mitchell, San Francisco
1950	Jim Konstanty, Philadelphia	1971	Joe Torre, St. Louis	1990	Barry Bonds, Pittsburgh
1951	Roy Campanella, Brooklyn				

American League

Year	Player, team	Year	Player, team	Year	Player, team
1931	Lefty Grove, Philadelphia	1951	Yogi Berra, New York	1971	Vida Blue, Oakland
1932	Jimmie Foxx, Philadelphia	1952	Bobby Shantz, Philadelphia	1972	Dick Allen, Chicago
1933	Jimmie Foxx, Philadelphia	1953	Al Rosen, Cleveland	1973	Reggie Jackson, Oakland
1934	Mickey Cochrane, Detroit	1954	Yogi Berra, New York	1974	Jeff Burroughs, Texas
1935	Hank Greenberg, Detroit	1955	Yogi Berra, New York	1975	Fred Lynn, Boston
1936	Lou Gehrig, New York	1956	Mickey Mantle, New York	1976	Thurman Munson, New York
1937	Charley Gehringer, Detroit	1957	Mickey Mantle, New York	1977	Rod Carew, Minnesota
1938	Jimmie Foxx, Boston	1958	Jackie Jensen, Boston	1978	Jim Rice, Boston
1939	Joe DiMaggio, New York	1959	Nellie Fox, Chicago	1979	Don Baylor, California
1940	Hank Greenberg, Detroit	1960	Roger Maris, New York	1980	George Brett, Kansas City
1941	Joe DiMaggio, New York	1961	Roger Maris, New York	1981	Rollie Fingers, Milwaukee
1942	Joe Gordon, New York	1962	Mickey Mantle, New York	1982	Robin Yount, Milwaukee
1943	Spurgeon Chandler, New York	1963	Elston Howard, New York	1983	Cal Ripken Jr., Baltimore
1944	Hal Newhouser, Detroit	1964	Brooks Robinson, Baltimore	1984	Willie Hernandez, Detroit
1945	Hal Newhouser, Detroit	1965	Zoilo Versalles, Minnesota	1985	Don Mattingly, New York
1946	Ted Williams, Boston	1966	Frank Robinson, Baltimore	1986	Roger Clemens, Boston
1947	Joe DiMaggio, New York	1967	Carl Yastrzemski, Boston	1987	George Bell, Toronto
1948	Lou Boudreau, Cleveland	1968	Denny McLain, Detroit	1988	Jose Canseco, Oakland
1949	Ted Williams, Boston	1969	Harmon Killebrew, Minnesota	1989	Robin Yount, Milwaukee
1950	Phil Rizzuto, New York	1970	John (Boog) Powell, Baltimore	1990	Rickey Henderson

Rookie of the Year
Baseball Writers' Association
1947—Combined selection—Jackie Robinson, Brooklyn, 1b
1948—Combined selection—Alvin Dark, Boston, N.L. ss
National League

Year	Player, team	Year	Player, team	Year	Player, team
1949	Don Newcombe, Brooklyn, p	1964	Richie Allen, Philadelphia, 3b	1978	Bob Horner, Atlanta, 3b
1950	Sam Jethroe, Boston, of	1965	Jim Lefebvre, Los Angeles, 2b	1979	Rick Sutcliffe, Los Angeles, p
1951	Willie Mays, New York, of	1966	Tommy Helms, Cincinnati, 2b	1980	Steve Howe, Los Angeles, p
1952	Joe Black, Brooklyn, p	1967	Tom Seaver, New York, p	1981	Fernando Valenzuela, Los
1953	Jim Gilliam, Brooklyn, 2b	1968	Johnny Bench, Cincinnati c		Angeles, p
1954	Wally Moon, St. Louis, of	1969	Ted Sizemore, Los Angeles, 2b	1982	Steve Sax, Los Angeles, 2b
1955	Bill Virdon, St. Louis, of	1970	Carl Morton, Montreal, p	1983	Darryl Strawberry, New York, of
1956	Frank Robinson, Cincinnati, of	1971	Earl Williams, Atlanta, c	1984	Dwight Gooden, New York, p
1957	Jack Sanford, Philadelphia, p	1972	Jon Matlack, New York, p	1985	Vince Coleman, St. Louis, of
1958	Orlando Cepeda, S.F., 1b	1973	Gary Matthews, S.F., of	1986	Todd Worrell, St. Louis, p
1959	Willie McCovey, S.F., 1b	1974	Bake McBride, St. Louis, of	1987	Benito Santiago, San Diego, c
1960	Frank Howard, Los Angeles, of	1975	John Montefusco, S.F., p	1988	Chris Sabo, Cincinnati, 3b
1961	Billy Williams, Chicago, of	1976	(tie) Butch Metzger, San Diego, p	1989	Jerome Walton, Chicago, of
1962	Ken Hubbs, Chicago, 2b		Pat Zachry, Cincinnati, p	1990	Dave Justice, Atlanta, 1b
1963	Pete Rose, Cincinnati, 2b	1977	Andre Dawson, Montreal, of		

American League

Year	Player, team	Year	Player, team	Year	Player, team
1949	Roy Sievers, St. Louis, of	1964	Tony Oliva, Minnesota, of	1978	Lou Whitaker, Detroit, 2b
1950	Walt Dropo, Boston, 1b	1965	Curt Blefary, Baltimore, of	1979	(tie) John Castino, Minnesota, 3b
1951	Gil McDougald, New York, 3b	1966	Tommie Agee, Chicago, of		Alfredo Griffin, Toronto, ss
1952	Harry Byrd, Philadelphia, p	1967	Rod Carew, Minnesota, 2b	1980	Joe Charboneau, Cleveland, of
1953	Harvey Kuenn, Detroit, ss	1968	Stan Bahnsen, New York, p	1981	Dave Righetti, New York, p
1954	Bob Grim, New York, p	1969	Lou Piniella, Kansas City, of	1982	Cal Ripken Jr., Baltimore, ss, 3b
1955	Herb Score, Cleveland, p	1970	Thurman Munson, New York, c	1983	Ron Kittle, Chicago, of
1956	Luis Aparicio, Chicago, ss	1971	Chris Chambliss, Cleveland, 1b	1984	Alvin Davis, Seattle, 1B
1957	Tony Kubek, New York, if-of	1972	Carlton Fisk, Boston, c	1985	Ozzie Guillen, Chicago, ss
1958	Albie Pearson, Washington, of	1973	Al Bumbry, Baltimore, of	1986	Jose Canseco, Oakland, of
1959	Bob Allison, Washington, of	1974	Mike Hargrove, Texas, 1b	1987	Mark McGwire, Oakland, 1b
1960	Ron Hansen, Baltimore, ss	1975	Fred Lynn, Boston, of	1988	Walt Weiss, Oakland, ss
1961	Don Schwall, Boston, p	1976	Mark Fidrych, Detroit, p	1989	Gregg Olson, Baltimore, p
1962	Tom Tresh, New York, if-of	1977	Eddie Murray, Baltimore, dh	1990	Sandy Alomar Jr., Cleveland, c
1963	Gary Peters, Chicago, p				

National League Records in 1991
Final standings
Eastern Division

	W	L	Pct.	GB	Home	vs. RHP	Grass	Night
Pittsburgh	98	64	.605	—	52-32	64-43	20-22	73-46
St. Louis	84	78	.519	14	52-32	52-43	15-27	60-56
Philadelphia	78	84	.481	20	47-36	47-51	17-25	58-58
Chicago	77	83	.481	20	46-37	49-57	59-56	34-44
New York	77	84	.475	20½	40-42	48-52	54-61	53-55
Montreal	71	90	.441	26½	33-35	48-52	19-27	54-62

Western Division

	W	L	Pct.	GB	Home	vs. RHP	Grass	Night
Atlanta	94	68	.580	—	48-33	64-49	70-50	73-49
Los Angeles	93	69	.574	1	54-27	54-41	75-45	69-48
San Diego	84	78	.519	10	42-39	54-48	62-58	58-58
San Francisco	75	87	.463	19	43-38	51-62	58-62	41-60
Cincinnati	74	88	.457	20	39-42	47-64	22-26	54-67
Houston	65	97	.401	29	37-44	43-62	18-30	50-74

National League Championship Series

Pittsburgh 5, Atlanta 1	Pittsburgh 3, Atlanta 2	Atlanta 1, Pittsburgh 0
Atlanta 1, Pittsburgh 0	Pittsburgh 1, Atlanta 0	Atlanta 4, Pittsburgh 0
Atlanta 10, Pittsburgh 3		

Team Batting

	Avg.	AB	R	H	HR	RBI
Pittsburgh	.263	5449	768	1433	126	725
Cincinnati	.258	5501	689	1419	164	654
Atlanta	.258	5456	749	1407	141	704
St. Louis	.255	5362	651	1366	68	599
Chicago	.253	5522	695	1395	159	654
Los Angeles	.253	5408	665	1366	108	605
San Francisco	.246	5463	649	1345	141	605
Montreal	.246	5412	579	1329	95	536
Houston	.244	5504	605	1345	79	570
San Diego	.244	5408	636	1321	121	591
New York	.244	5359	640	1305	117	605
Philadelphia	.241	5521	629	1332	111	590

Team Pitching

	ERA	IP	H	BB	SO	Sv
Los Angeles	3.06	1458	1312	500	1028	40
Pittsburgh	3.44	1456	1411	401	919	51
Atlanta	3.49	1452	1304	481	969	48
New York	3.56	1437	1403	410	1028	39
San Diego	3.57	1452	1385	457	921	47
Montreal	3.64	1440	1304	584	909	39
St. Louis	3.69	1435	1367	454	822	51
Cincinnati	3.83	1440	1372	560	997	43
Philadelphia	3.86	1463	1446	670	988	35
Houston	4.00	1453	1347	651	1033	36
San Francisco	4.03	1442	1397	544	905	45
Chicago	4.03	1456	1415	542	927	40

Individual Batting (at least 150 at-bats); Individual Pitching (at least 75 innings or 10 saves)

Atlanta Braves

Batting	Avg	AB	R	H	HR	RBI
Treadway	.320	306	41	98	3	32
Pendleton	.319	586	94	187	22	86
Nixon	.297	401	81	119	0	26
Justice	.275	396	67	109	21	87
L. Smith	.275	353	58	97	7	44
Blauser	.259	352	49	91	11	54
Bream	.253	265	32	67	11	45
Gant	.251	561	101	141	32	105
Hunter	.251	271	32	68	12	50
Belliard	.249	353	36	88	0	27
Olson	.241	411	46	99	6	44
Lemke	.234	269	36	63	2	23
Berryhill	.188	160	13	30	5	14

Chicago Cubs

Batting	Avg	AB	R	H	HR	RBI
Sandberg	.291	585	104	170	26	100
Bell	.285	558	63	159	25	86
Villanueva	.276	192	23	53	13	32
Grace	.273	619	87	169	8	58
Dawson	.272	563	69	153	31	104
Dunston	.260	492	59	128	12	50
Salazar	.258	333	34	86	14	38
Walker	.257	374	51	96	6	34
Dascenzo	.255	239	40	61	1	18
D. Smith	.228	167	16	38	3	21
Wilkins	.222	203	21	45	6	22
Walton	.219	270	42	59	5	17

Atlanta Braves Pitching

Pitching	W	L	ERA	IP	BB	SO	Sv
Berenguer	0	3	2.24	64.1	20	53	17
Pena	8	1	2.40	82.1	22	62	15
Glavine	20	11	2.55	246.2	69	192	0
Stanton	5	5	2.88	78.0	21	54	7
Avery	18	8	3.38	210.1	65	137	0
Leibrandt	15	13	3.49	229.2	56	128	0
Smoltz	14	13	3.80	229.2	77	148	0
Clancy	3	5	3.91	89.2	34	50	8
Bielecki	13	11	4.46	173.2	56	75	0

Chicago Cubs Pitching

Pitching	W	L	ERA	IP	BB	SO	Sv
McElroy	6	2	1.95	101.1	57	92	3
Assenmacher	7	8	3.24	102.2	31	117	15
Maddux	15	11	3.35	263.0	66	198	0
Lancaster	9	7	3.52	156.0	49	102	3
Scanlan	7	8	3.89	111.0	40	44	1
Sutcliffe	6	5	4.10	96.2	45	52	0
Castillo	6	7	4.35	111.2	33	73	0
Boskie	4	9	5.23	129.0	52	62	0

Cincinnati Reds

Batting	Avg	AB	R	H	HR	RBI
Morris	.318	478	72	152	14	59
Larkin	.302	464	88	140	20	69
Sabo	.301	582	91	175	26	88
Doran	.280	361	51	101	6	35
Reed	.267	270	20	72	3	31
Hatcher	.262	442	45	116	4	41
Braggs	.260	250	36	65	11	39
Duncan	.258	333	46	86	12	40
O'Neill	.256	532	71	136	28	91
Davis	.235	285	39	67	11	33
Martinez	.234	154	13	36	6	19
Winningham	.225	169	17	38	1	4
Quinones	.222	212	15	47	4	20
Oliver	.216	269	21	58	11	41

Pitching	W	L	ERA	IP	BB	SO	Sv
Rijo	15	6	2.51	204.1	55	172	0
Charlton	3	5	2.91	108.1	34	77	1
Dibble	3	5	3.17	82.1	25	124	31
Gross	6	4	3.47	85.2	40	40	0
Myers	6	13	3.55	132.0	80	108	6
Power	5	3	3.62	87.0	31	51	3
Hammond	7	7	4.06	99.2	48	50	0
Browning	14	14	4.18	230.1	56	115	0
Scudder	6	9	4.35	101.1	56	51	1
Armstrong	7	13	5.48	139.2	54	93	0

Houston Astros

Batting	Avg	AB	R	H	HR	RBI
Biggio	.295	546	79	161	4	46
Bagwell	.294	554	79	163	15	82
Finley	.285	596	84	170	8	54
Candaele	.262	461	44	121	4	50
Gonzalez	.254	473	51	120	13	69
Caminiti	.253	574	65	145	13	80
Cedeno	.243	251	27	61	9	36
Yelding	.243	276	19	67	1	20
Ramirez	.236	233	17	55	1	20

Pitching	W	L	ERA	IP	BB	SO	Sv
Harnisch	12	9	2.70	216.2	83	172	0
Osuna	7	6	3.42	81.2	46	68	12
Kile	7	11	3.69	153.2	84	100	0
Corsi	0	5	3.71	77.2	23	53	0
Schilling	3	5	3.81	75.2	39	71	8
Jones	6	8	4.39	135.1	51	88	0
Portugal	10	12	4.49	168.1	59	120	1
Deshaies	5	12	4.98	161.0	72	98	0

Los Angeles Dodgers

Batting	Avg	AB	R	H	HR	RBI
Butler	.296	615	112	182	2	38
Harris	.287	429	59	123	3	38
Sharperson	.278	216	24	60	2	20
Samuel	.271	594	74	161	12	58
Strawberry	.265	505	86	134	28	99
Scioscia	.264	345	39	91	8	40
Murray	.260	576	69	150	19	96
Daniels	.249	461	54	115	17	73
Carter	.246	248	22	61	6	26
Griffin	.243	350	27	85	0	27
Webster	.222	171	21	38	2	19
Javier	.205	176	21	36	1	11

Pitching	W	L	ERA	IP	BB	SO	Sv
Belcher	10	9	2.62	209.1	75	156	0
Morgan	14	10	2.78	236.1	61	140	1
McDowell	9	9	2.93	101.1	48	50	10
Gott	4	3	2.96	76.0	32	73	2
Howell	6	5	3.18	51.0	11	40	16
Ojeda	12	9	3.18	189.1	70	120	0
Martinez	17	13	3.27	220.1	69	150	0
Crews	2	3	3.43	76.0	19	53	6
Hershiser	7	2	3.46	112.0	32	73	0
Gross	10	11	3.58	115.2	50	95	3

Montreal Expos

Batting	Avg	AB	R	H	HR	RBI
Calderon	.300	470	69	141	19	75
Da. Martinez	.295	396	47	117	7	42
Walker	.290	487	59	141	16	64
Grissom	.267	558	73	149	6	39
Owen	.255	424	39	108	3	26
DeShields	.238	563	83	134	10	51
Wallach	.225	577	60	130	13	73
Galarraga	.219	375	34	82	9	33
Reyes	.217	207	11	45	0	13
Foley	.208	168	12	35	0	15
Fitzgerald	.202	198	17	40	4	28

Pitching	W	L	ERA	IP	BB	SO	Sv
De. Martinez	14	11	2.39	222.0	62	123	0
Jones	4	9	3.35	88.2	33	46	13
Boyd	6	8	3.52	120.1	40	82	0
Nabholz	8	7	3.63	153.2	57	99	0
Gardner	9	11	3.85	168.1	75	107	0
Sampen	9	5	4.00	92.1	46	52	0
Haney	3	7	4.04	84.2	43	51	0
Barnes	5	8	4.22	160.0	84	117	0
Darling	5	8	4.37	119.1	33	69	0

New York Mets

Batting	Avg	AB	R	H	HR	RBI
Miller	.280	275	41	77	4	23
Boston	.275	255	40	70	4	21
Cerone	.273	227	18	62	2	16
Sasser	.272	228	18	62	5	35
Jefferies	.272	486	59	132	9	62
Carreon	.260	254	18	66	4	21
Johnson	.259	564	108	146	38	117
McReynolds	.259	522	65	135	16	74
Magadan	.258	418	58	108	4	51
Coleman	.255	278	45	71	1	17
Elster	.241	348	33	84	6	36
Brooks	.238	357	48	85	16	50
Templeton	.221	276	25	61	3	26
O'Brien	.185	168	16	31	2	14

Pitching	W	L	ERA	IP	BB	SO	Sv
Innis	0	2	2.66	84.2	23	47	0
Franco	5	9	2.93	55.1	18	45	30
Cone	14	14	3.29	232.2	73	241	0
Burke	6	7	3.36	101.2	26	59	6
Gooden	13	7	3.60	190.0	56	150	0
Viola	13	15	3.97	231.1	54	132	0
Whitehurst	7	12	4.19	133.1	25	87	1
Schourek	5	4	4.27	86.1	43	67	2

Philadelphia Phillies

Batting	Avg	AB	R	H	HR	RBI
Hollins	.298	151	18	45	6	21
Dykstra	.297	246	48	73	3	12
Kruk	.294	538	84	158	21	92
Jordan	.272	301	38	82	9	49
Thon	.252	539	44	136	9	44
Murphy	.252	544	66	137	18	81
Morandini	.249	325	38	81	1	20
Ready	.249	205	32	51	1	20
Backman	.243	185	20	45	0	15
Chamberlain	.240	383	51	92	13	50
C. Hayes	.230	460	34	106	12	53
Lake	.228	158	12	36	1	11
V. Hayes	.225	284	43	64	0	21
Daulton	.196	285	36	56	12	42

Pitching	W	L	ERA	IP	BB	SO	Sv
Williams	12	5	2.34	88.1	62	84	30
Greene	13	7	3.38	207.2	66	154	0
DeJesus	10	9	3.42	181.2	128	118	1
Mulholland	16	13	3.61	232.0	49	142	0
Ruffin	4	7	3.78	119.0	38	85	0
Boever	3	5	3.84	98.1	54	89	0
Hartley	4	1	4.21	83.1	47	63	2
Cox	4	6	4.57	102.1	39	46	0

Pittsburgh Pirates

Batting	Avg	AB	R	H	HR	RBI
Bonilla	.302	577	102	174	18	100
Slaught	.295	220	19	65	1	29
Bonds	.292	510	95	149	25	116
LaVilliere	.289	336	25	97	3	41
McClendon	.288	163	24	47	7	24
Merced	.275	411	83	113	10	50
Varsho	.273	187	23	51	4	23
Bell	.270	608	96	164	16	67
Lind	.265	502	53	133	3	54
Van Slyke	.265	491	87	130	17	83
Redus	.246	252	45	62	7	24
Wilkerson	.188	191	20	36	2	18

Pitching	W	L	ERA	IP	BB	SO	Sv
Tomlin	8	7	2.98	175.0	54	104	0
Drabek	15	14	3.07	234.2	62	142	0
Smiley	20	8	3.08	207.2	44	129	0
Landrum	4	4	3.18	76.1	19	45	17
Smith	16	10	3.20	228.0	29	120	0
Belinda	7	5	3.45	78.1	35	71	16
Walk	9	2	3.60	115.0	35	67	0
Palacios	6	3	3.75	81.2	38	64	3

San Diego Padres

Batting	Avg	AB	R	H	HR	RBI
Gwynn	.317	530	69	168	4	62
Roberts	.281	424	66	119	3	32
McGriff	.278	528	84	147	31	106
Fernandez	.272	558	81	152	4	38
Santiago	.267	580	60	155	17	87
Jackson	.262	359	51	94	21	49
Howard	.249	281	30	70	4	22
Clark	.228	369	26	84	10	47
Teufel	.217	341	41	74	12	44
Coolbaugh	.217	180	12	39	2	15
Howell	.206	160	24	33	6	16

Pitching	W	L	ERA	IP	BB	SO	Sv
Harris	9	5	2.23	133.0	27	95	0
Maddux	7	2	2.46	98.2	27	57	5
Benes	15	11	3.03	223.0	59	167	0
Rodriguez	3	1	3.26	80.0	44	40	0
Melendez	8	5	3.27	93.2	24	60	3
Hurst	15	8	3.29	221.2	59	141	0
Rasmussen	6	13	3.74	146.2	49	75	0
Lefferts	1	6	3.91	69.0	14	48	23
Whitson	4	6	5.03	78.2	17	40	0

St. Louis Cardinals

Batting	Avg	AB	R	H	HR	RBI
Thompson	.307	326	55	100	6	34
Jose	.305	568	69	173	8	77
O. Smith	.285	550	96	157	3	50
Zeile	.280	565	76	158	11	81
Guerrero	.272	427	41	116	8	70
Pagnozzi	.264	459	38	121	2	57
Lankford	.251	566	83	142	9	69
Pena	.243	185	38	45	5	17
Oquendo	.240	366	37	88	1	26
Perry	.240	242	29	58	6	36
Hudler	.227	207	21	47	1	15
Gilkey	.216	268	28	58	5	20

Pitching	W	L	ERA	IP	BB	SO	Sv
L. Smith	6	3	2.34	73.0	13	67	47
DeLeon	5	9	2.71	162.2	61	118	0
Terry	4	4	2.80	80.1	32	52	1
Tewksbury	11	12	3.25	191.0	38	75	0
Hill	11	10	3.57	181.1	67	121	0
Olivares	11	7	3.71	167.1	61	91	1
B. Smith	12	9	3.85	198.2	45	94	0
Agosto	5	3	4.81	86.0	39	34	2

San Francisco Giants

Batting	Avg	AB	R	H	HR	RBI
McGee	.312	497	67	155	4	43
Clark	.301	565	84	170	29	116
Williams	.268	589	72	158	34	98
Felder	.264	348	51	92	0	18
Thompson	.262	492	74	129	19	48
Mitchell	.256	371	52	95	27	69
Anderson	.248	226	24	56	2	13
Lewis	.248	222	41	55	1	15
Kennedy	.234	171	12	40	3	13
Bass	.233	361	43	84	10	40
Manwaring	.225	178	16	40	0	19
Uribe	.221	231	23	51	1	12
Herr	.209	215	23	45	1	21
Decker	.206	233	11	48	5	24

Pitching	W	L	ERA	IP	BB	SO	Sv
Brantley	5	2	2.45	95.1	52	81	15
Righetti	2	7	3.39	71.2	28	51	24
Wilson	13	11	3.56	202.0	77	139	0
Oliveras	6	6	3.86	79.1	22	48	3
Black	12	16	3.99	214.1	71	104	0
Burkett	12	11	4.18	206.2	60	131	0
Downs	10	4	4.19	111.2	53	62	0
Robinson	5	9	4.38	121.1	50	78	1

The Sporting News Gold Glove Awards in 1990

National League

Andres Galarraga, Montreal, first base.
Ryne Sandberg, Chicago, second base.
Tim Wallach, Montreal, third base.
Ozzie Smith, St. Louis, shortstop.
Tony Gwynn, San Diego, outfield.
Andy Van Slyke, Pittsburgh, outfield.
Barry Bonds, Pittsburgh, outfield.
Benito Santaigo, San Diego, catcher.
Greg Maddux, Chicago, pitcher.

American League

Mark McGwire, Oakland, first base.
Harold Reynolds, Seattle, second base.
Kelly Gruber, Toronto, third base.
Ozzie Guillen, Chicago, shortstop.
Gary Pettis, Detroit, outfield.
Ellis Burks, Boston, outfield.
Ken Griffey Jr., Seattle, outfield.
Sandy Alomar Jr., Cleveland, catcher.
Mike Boddicker, Boston, pitcher.

The following are the players at each position who have won the most Gold Gloves since the award was instituted in 1957.

First base:	Keith Hernandez	11	Shortstop:	Ozzie Smith	11	Dwight Evans 8
	George Scott	8		Luis Aparicio	9	Garry Maddox 8
Second base:	Bill Mazeroski	8	Outfield:	Roberto Clemente	12	Catcher: Johnny Bench 10
	Frank White	8		Willie Mays	12	Bob Boone 7
	Ryne Sandberg	8		Al Kaline	10	Pitcher: Jim Kaat 16
Third base:	Brooks Robinson	16		Paul Blair	8	Bob Gibson 9
	Mike Schmidt	10				

No-Hit Games in 1991

May 1— Nolan Ryan, Texas vs. Toronto, 3-0.
May 23— Tommy Greene, Philadelphia vs. Montreal, 2-0.
July 13— Bob Milacki, Mike Flanagan, Mark Williamson and Gregg Olson, Baltimore vs. Oakland, 2-0.
July 28— Dennis Martinez, Montreal vs. Los Angeles, 2-0. (Perfect Game.)

Aug. 11— Wilson Alvarez, Chicago vs. Baltimore, 7-0.
Aug. 26— Bret Saberhagen, Kansas City vs. Chicago, 7-0.
Sept. 11— Kent Mercker, Mark Wohlers and Alejandro Pena, Atlanta vs. San Diego, 1-0.

National Baseball Hall of Fame and Museum

Cooperstown, N.Y.

Aaron, Hank
Alexander, Grover Cleveland
Alston, Walt
Anson, Cap
Aparicio, Luis
Appling, Luke
Averill, Earl
Baker, Home Run
Bancroft, Dave
Banks, Ernie
Barlick, Al
Barrow, Edward G.
Beckley, Jake
Bell, Cool Papa
Bench, Johnny
Bender, Chief
Berra, Yogi
Bottomley, Jim
Boudreau, Lou
Bresnahan, Roger
Brock, Lou
Brouthers, Dan
Brown, (Three Finger), Mordecai
Bulkeley, Morgan C.
Burkett, Jesse C.
Campanella, Roy
Carew, Rod
Carey, Max
Cartwright, Alexander
Chadwick, Henry
Chance, Frank
Chandler, Happy
Charleston, Oscar
Chesbro, John
Clarke, Fred
Clarkson, John
Clemente, Roberto
Cobb, Ty
Cochrane, Mickey
Collins, Eddie
Collins, James
Combs, Earle
Comiskey, Charles A.

Conlan, Jocko
Connolly, Thomas H.
Connor, Roger
Coveleski, Stan
Crawford, Sam
Cronin, Joe
Cummings, Candy
Cuyler, Kiki
Dandridge, Ray
Dean, Dizzy
Delahanty, Ed
Dickey, Bill
DiHigo, Martin
DiMaggio, Joe
Doerr, Bobby
Drysdale, Don
Duffy, Hugh
Evans, Billy
Evers, John
Ewing, Buck
Faber, Urban
Feller, Bob
Ferrell, Rick
Flick, Elmer H.
Ford, Whitey
Foster, Andrew
Foxx, Jimmie
Frick, Ford
Frisch, Frank
Galvin, Pud
Gehrig, Lou
Gehringer, Charles
Gibson, Bob
Gibson, Josh
Giles, Warren
Gomez, Lefty
Goslin, Goose
Greenberg, Hank
Griffith, Clark
Grimes, Burleigh
Grove, Lefty
Hafey, Chick

Haines, Jesee
Hamilton, Bill
Harridge, Will
Harris, Bucky
Hartnett, Gabby
Heilmann, Harry
Herman, Billy
Hooper, Harry
Hornsby, Rogers
Hoyt, Waite
Hubbard, Cal
Hubbell, Carl
Huggins, Miller
Hunter, Catfish
Irvin, Monte
Jackson, Travis
Jenkins, Ferguson
Jennings, Hugh
Johnson, Byron
Johnson, William (Judy)
Johnson, Walter
Joss, Addie
Kaline, Al
Keefe, Timothy
Keeler, William
Kell, George
Kelley, Joe
Kelly, George
Kelly, King
Killebrew, Harmon
Kiner, Ralph
Klein, Chuck
Klem, Bill
Koufax, Sandy
Lajoie, Napoleon
Landis, Kenesaw M.
Lazzeri, Tony
Lemon, Bob
Leonard, Buck
Lindstrom, Fred
Lloyd, Pop
Lombardi, Ernie

Lopez, Al
Lyons, Ted
Mack, Connie
MacPhail, Larry
Mantle, Mickey
Manush, Henry
Maranville, Rabbit
Marichal, Juan
Marquard, Rube
Mathews, Eddie
Mathewson, Christy
Mays, Willie
McCarthy, Joe
McCarthy, Thomas
McCovey, Willie
McGinnity, Joe
McGraw, John
McKechnie, Bill
Medwick, Joe
Mize, Johnny
Morgan, Joe
Musial, Stan
Nichols, Kid
O'Rourke, James
Ott, Mel
Paige, Satchel
Palmer, Jim
Pennock, Herb
Perry, Gaylord
Plank, Ed
Radbourn, Charlie
Reese, Pee Wee
Rice, Sam
Rickey, Branch
Rixey, Eppa
Roberts, Robin
Robinson, Brooks
Robinson, Frank
Robinson, Jackie
Robinson, Wilbert
Roush, Edd
Ruffing, Red

Rusie, Amos
Ruth, Babe
Schalk, Ray
Schoendienst, Red
Sewell, Joe
Simmons, Al
Sisler, George
Slaughter, Enos
Snider, Duke
Spahn, Warren
Spalding, Albert
Speaker, Tris
Stargell, Willie
Stengel, Casey
Terry, Bill
Thompson, Sam
Tinker, Joe
Traynor, Pie
Vance, Dazzy
Vaughan, Arky
Veeck, Bill
Waddell, Rube
Wagner, Honus
Wallace, Roderick
Walsh, Ed.
Waner, Lloyd
Waner, Paul
Ward, John
Weiss, George
Welch, Mickey
Wheat, Zach
Wilhelm, Hoyt
Williams, Billy
Williams, Ted
Wilson, Hack
Wright, George
Wright, Harry
Wynn, Early
Yastrzemski, Carl
Yawkey, Tom
Young, Cy
Youngs, Ross

All-Star Baseball Games, 1933-1991

Year	Winner	Score	Location	Year	Winner	Score	Location
1933	American	4-2	Chicago	1962	National (3)	3-1	Washington
1934	American	9-7	New York	1962	American	9-4	Chicago
1935	American	4-1	Cleveland	1963	National	5-3	Cleveland
1936	National	4-3	Boston	1964	National	7-4	New York
1937	American	8-3	Washington	1965	National	6-5	Minnesota
1938	National	4-1	Cincinnati	1966	National (3)	2-1	St. Louis
1939	American	3-1	New York	1967	National (4)	2-1	Anaheim
1940	National	4-0	St. Louis	1968*	National	1-0	Houston
1941	American	7-5	Detroit	1969	National	9-3	Washington
1942	American	3-1	New York	1970*	National (2)	5-4	Cincinnati
1943*	American	5-3	Philadelphia	1971*	American	6-4	Detroit
1944*	National	7-1	Pittsburgh	1972*	National	4-3	Atlanta
1945	(not played)			1973*	National	7-1	Kansas City
1946	American	12-0	Boston	1974*	National	7-2	Pittsburgh
1947	American	2-1	Chicago	1975*	National	6-3	Milwaukee
1948	American	5-2	St. Louis	1976*	National	7-1	Philadelphia
1949	American	11-7	New York	1977*	National	7-5	New York
1950	National (1)	4-3	Chicago	1978*	National	7-3	San Diego
1951	National	8-3	Detroit	1979*	National	7-6	Seattle
1952	National	3-2	Philadelphia	1980*	National	4-2	Los Angeles
1953	National	5-1	Cincinnati	1981*	National	5-4	Cleveland
1954	American	11-9	Cleveland	1982*	National	4-1	Montreal
1955	National (2)	6-5	Milwaukee	1983*	American	13-3	Chicago
1956	National	7-3	Washington	1984*	National	3-1	San Francisco
1957	American	6-5	St. Louis	1985*	National	6-1	Minneapolis
1958	American	4-3	Baltimore	1986*	American	3-2	Houston
1959	National	5-4	Pittsburgh	1987*	National (5)	2-0	Oakland
1959	American	5-3	Los Angeles	1988*	American	2-1	Cincinnati
1960	National	5-3	Kansas City	1989*	American	5-3	Anaheim
1960	National	6-0	New York	1990*	American	2-0	Chicago
1961	National (3)	5-4	San Francisco	1991*	American	4-2	Toronto
1961	Called-rain	1-1	Boston				

(1) 14 innings, (2) 12 innings, (3) 10 innings, (4) 15 innings (5) 13 innings. * Night game.

American League Records in 1991
Final standings
Eastern Division

	W	L	Pct.	GB	Home	vs. RHP	Grass	Night
Toronto	91	71	.562	—	46-35	61-48	33-30	63-47
Boston	84	78	.519	7	43-38	63-61	70-67	59-49
Detroit	84	78	.519	7	49-32	58-56	71-63	59-52
Milwaukee	83	79	.512	8	43-37	65-54	75-62	57-60
New York	71	91	.438	20	39-42	42-59	64-74	47-64
Baltimore	67	95	.414	24	33-48	52-67	58-80	50-69
Cleveland	57	105	.352	34	30-52	45-76	53-85	38-76

Western Division

	W	L	Pct.	GB	Home	vs. RHP	Grass	Night
Minnesota	95	67	.586	—	51-30	69-49	35-27	69-47
Chicago	87	75	.537	8	46-35	62-46	74-64	65-55
Texas	85	77	.525	10	46-35	59-60	71-66	68-64
Oakland	84	78	.519	11	47-34	57-63	76-60	52-56
Seattle	83	79	.512	12	45-36	64-55	32-30	66-54
Kansas City	82	80	.506	13	40-41	62-49	31-31	60-56
California	81	81	.500	14	40-41	54-62	64-71	59-63

American League Championship Series

Minnesota 5, Toronto 4   Minnesota 3, Toronto 2   Minnesota 8, Toronto 5
Toronto 5, Minnesota 1   Minnesota 9, Toronto 3

Team Batting

	Avg.	AB	R	H	HR	RBI
Minnesota	.280	5556	776	1557	140	733
Milwaukee	.271	5611	799	1523	116	750
Texas	.270	5703	829	1539	177	774
Boston	.269	5530	731	1486	126	691
Kansas City	.264	5584	727	1475	117	689
Chicago	.262	5594	758	1464	139	722
Toronto	.257	5489	684	1412	133	649
New York	.256	5541	674	1418	147	630
California	.255	5470	653	1396	115	607
Seattle	.255	5494	702	1400	126	665
Cleveland	.254	5470	578	1390	79	546
Baltimore	.254	5604	686	1421	170	660
Oakland	.248	5410	760	1342	159	716
Detroit	.247	5547	817	1372	209	778

Team Pitching

	ERA	IP	H	BB	SO	Sv
Toronto	3.50	1462	1301	523	971	60
California	3.69	1441	1351	543	990	50
Minnesota	3.69	1449	1402	488	876	53
Seattle	3.79	1464	1387	628	1003	48
Chicago	3.79	1478	1302	601	923	40
Kansas City	3.92	1466	1473	529	1004	41
Boston	4.01	1439	1405	530	999	45
Milwaukee	4.14	1463	1498	527	859	41
Cleveland	4.23	1441	1551	441	862	33
New York	4.42	1444	1510	506	936	37
Texas	4.47	1479	1486	662	1022	41
Detroit	4.51	1450	1570	593	739	38
Oakland	4.57	1444	1425	655	892	49
Baltimore	4.59	1457	1534	504	868	42

Individual Batting (at least 150 at-bats); Individual Pitching (at least 75 innings or 10 saves)

Baltimore Orioles

Batting	Avg	AB	R	H	HR	RBI
C. Ripken	.323	650	99	210	34	114
Segui	.278	212	15	59	2	22
Orsulak	.278	486	57	135	5	43
Evans	.270	270	35	73	6	38
Martinez	.269	216	32	58	13	33
Milligan	.263	483	57	127	16	70
Devereaux	.260	608	82	158	19	59
Melvin	.250	228	11	57	1	23
Hoiles	.243	341	36	83	11	31
Horn	.233	317	45	74	23	61
Gomez	.233	391	40	91	16	45
Anderson	.230	256	40	59	2	27
Davis	.227	176	29	40	10	28
B. Ripken	.216	287	24	62	0	14
Hulett	.204	206	29	42	7	18
Bell	.172	209	26	36	1	15

Pitching	W	L	ERA	IP	BB	SO	Sv
Frohwirth	7	3	1.87	96.1	29	77	3
Flanagan	2	7	2.38	98.1	25	55	3
Mussina	4	5	2.87	87.2	21	52	0
Olson	4	6	3.18	73.2	29	72	31
Milacki	10	9	4.01	184.0	53	108	0
Williamson	5	5	4.48	80.1	35	53	4
McDonald	6	8	4.84	126.1	43	85	0
Robinson	4	9	5.18	104.1	51	65	0
Smith	5	4	5.60	80.1	24	25	0
Ballard	6	12	5.60	123.2	28	37	0
Mesa	6	11	5.97	123.2	62	64	0
Johnson	4	8	7.07	84.0	24	38	0

Boston Red Sox

Batting	Avg	AB	R	H	HR	RBI
Boggs	.332	546	93	181	8	51
Greenwell	.300	544	76	163	9	83
Quintana	.295	478	69	141	11	71
Reed	.283	618	87	175	5	60
Vaughn	.260	219	21	57	4	32
Rivera	.258	414	64	107	8	40
Burks	.251	474	56	119	14	56
Clark	.249	481	75	120	28	87
Lyons	.241	212	15	51	4	17
Pena	.231	464	45	107	5	48
Brunansky	.229	459	54	105	16	70

Pitching	W	L	ERA	IP	BB	SO	Sv
Clemens	18	10	2.62	271.1	65	241	0
Reardon	1	4	3.03	59.1	16	44	40
Hesketh	12	4	3.29	153.1	53	104	0
Harris	11	12	3.85	173.0	69	127	2
Morton	6	5	4.59	86.1	40	45	0
Lamp	6	3	4.70	92.0	31	57	0
Petry	2	3	4.79	77.0	31	30	1
Gardiner	9	10	4.85	130.0	47	91	0
Young	3	7	5.18	88.2	53	69	0
Bolton	8	9	5.24	110.0	51	64	0

California Angels

Batting

Batting	Avg	AB	R	H	HR	RBI
Joyner	.301	551	79	166	21	96
Polonia	.296	604	92	179	2	50
Gallagher	.293	270	32	79	1	30
Felix	.283	230	32	65	2	26
Winfield	.262	568	75	149	28	86
Sojo	.258	364	38	94	3	20
Venable	.246	187	24	46	3	21
Gaetti	.246	586	58	144	18	66
Hill	.239	209	36	50	1	20
Schofield	.225	427	44	96	0	31
Parrish	.216	402	38	87	19	51

Pitching

Pitching	W	L	ERA	IP	BB	SO	Sv
Harvey	2	4	1.60	78.2	17	101	46
Eichhorn	3	3	1.98	81.2	13	49	1
J. Abbott	18	11	2.89	243.0	73	158	0
Langston	19	8	3.00	246.1	96	183	0
Finley	18	9	3.80	227.1	101	171	0
McCaskill	10	19	4.26	177.2	66	71	0

Detroit Tigers

Batting

Batting	Avg	AB	R	H	HR	RBI
Barnes	.289	159	28	46	5	17
Phillips	.284	564	87	160	17	72
Whitaker	.279	470	94	131	23	78
Tettleton	.263	501	85	132	31	89
Moseby	.262	260	37	68	6	35
Fielder	.261	624	102	163	44	133
Fryman	.259	557	65	144	21	91
Cuyler	.257	475	77	122	3	33
Trammell	.248	375	57	93	9	55
Bergman	.237	194	23	46	7	29
Allanson	.232	151	10	35	1	16
Incaviglia	.214	337	38	72	11	38
Deer	.179	448	64	80	25	64

Pitching

Pitching	W	L	ERA	IP	BB	SO	Sv
Henneman	10	2	2.88	84.1	34	61	21
Tanana	13	12	3.77	217.1	78	107	0
Gullickson	20	9	3.90	226.1	44	91	0
Gleaton	3	2	4.06	75.1	39	47	2
Leiter	9	7	4.21	134.2	50	103	1
Terrell	12	14	4.24	218.2	79	80	0
Cerutti	3	6	4.57	88.2	37	29	2
Gibson	5	7	4.59	96.0	48	52	8

Chicago White Sox

Batting

Batting	Avg	AB	R	H	HR	RBI
Thomas	.318	559	104	178	32	109
Ventura	.284	606	92	172	23	100
Grebeck	.281	224	37	63	6	31
Johnson	.274	588	72	161	0	49
Guillen	.273	524	52	143	3	49
Raines	.268	609	102	163	5	50
Pasqua	.259	417	71	108	18	66
Huff	.251	243	42	61	3	25
Karkovice	.246	167	25	41	5	22
Fisk	.241	460	42	111	18	74
Cora	.241	228	37	55	0	18
Fletcher	.206	248	14	51	1	28
Sosa	.203	316	39	64	10	33

Pitching

Pitching	W	L	ERA	IP	BB	SO	Sv
Perez	8	7	3.12	135.2	52	128	1
McDowell	17	10	3.41	253.2	82	191	0
Thigpen	7	5	3.49	69.2	38	47	30
Hough	9	10	4.02	199.1	94	107	0
Hibbard	11	11	4.31	194.0	57	71	0
Fernandez	9	13	4.51	191.2	88	145	0
Garcia	4	4	5.40	78.1	31	40	0

Kansas City Royals

Batting

Batting	Avg	AB	R	H	HR	RBI
Tartabull	.316	484	78	153	31	100
Eisenreich	.301	375	47	113	2	47
Benzinger	.294	293	29	86	2	40
Pecota	.286	398	53	114	6	45
Thurman	.277	184	24	51	2	13
MacFarlane	.277	267	34	74	13	41
Seitzer	.265	234	28	62	1	25
Stillwell	.265	385	44	102	6	51
McRae	.261	629	86	164	8	64
Brett	.255	505	77	129	10	61
Mayne	.251	231	22	58	3	31
Gibson	.236	462	81	109	16	55
Shumpert	.217	369	45	80	5	34
Howard	.216	236	20	51	1	17

Pitching

Pitching	W	L	ERA	IP	BB	SO	Sv
Montgomery	4	4	2.90	90.0	28	77	33
Saberhagen	13	8	3.07	196.1	45	136	0
Appier	13	10	3.42	207.2	61	158	0
Aquino	8	4	3.44	157.0	47	80	3
Gordon	9	14	3.87	158.0	87	167	1
Boddicker	12	12	4.08	180.2	59	79	0
S. Davis	3	9	4.96	114.1	46	53	2
Gubicza	9	12	5.68	133.0	42	89	0

Cleveland Indians

Batting

Batting	Avg	AB	R	H	HR	RBI
Cole	.295	387	58	114	0	21
Baerga	.288	593	80	171	11	69
Martinez	.284	257	22	73	5	30
Belle	.282	461	60	130	28	95
Lewis	.264	314	29	83	0	30
Aldrete	.262	183	22	48	1	19
Fermin	.262	424	30	111	0	31
Hill	.258	221	29	57	8	25
Whiten	.243	407	46	99	9	45
Skinner	.243	284	23	69	1	24
James	.238	437	31	104	5	41
Browne	.228	290	28	66	1	29
Alomar	.217	184	10	40	0	7

Pitching

Pitching	W	L	ERA	IP	BB	SO	Sv
Olin	3	6	3.36	56.1	23	38	17
Swindell	9	16	3.48	238.0	31	169	0
Nichols	2	11	3.54	137.1	30	76	1
Nagy	10	15	4.13	211.1	66	109	0
Otto	2	8	4.23	100.0	27	47	0
Hillegas	3	4	4.34	83.0	46	66	7
King	6	11	4.60	150.2	44	59	0

Milwaukee Brewers

Batting

Batting	Avg	AB	R	H	HR	RBI
Randolph	.327	431	60	141	0	54
Molitor	.325	665	133	216	17	75
Hamilton	.311	405	64	126	1	57
Surhoff	.289	505	57	146	5	68
Gantner	.283	526	63	149	2	47
Spiers	.283	414	71	117	8	54
Yount	.260	503	66	131	10	77
Vaughn	.244	542	81	132	27	98
Sveum	.241	266	33	64	4	43
Bichette	.238	445	.53	106	15	59
Stubbs	.213	362	48	77	11	38
Sheffield	.194	175	25	34	2	22

Pitching

Pitching	W	L	ERA	IP	BB	SO	Sv
Henry	2	1	1.00	36.0	14	28	15
Wegman	15	7	2.84	193.1	40	89	0
Bosio	14	10	3.25	204.2	58	117	0
Machado	3	3	3.45	88.2	55	98	3
Navarro	15	12	3.92	234.0	73	114	0
Plesac	2	7	4.29	92.1	39	61	8
Crim	8	5	4.63	91.1	25	39	3
Holmes	1	4	4.72	76.1	27	59	3
August	9	8	5.47	138.1	47	62	0

Minnesota Twins

Batting	Avg	AB	R	H	HR	RBI
Puckett	.319	611	92	195	15	89
Harper	.311	441	54	137	10	69
Mack	.310	442	79	137	18	74
Bush	.303	165	21	50	6	23
Leius	.286	199	35	57	5	20
Larkin	.286	255	34	73	2	19
Hrbek	.284	462	72	131	20	89
Munoz	.283	138	15	39	7	26
Knoblauch	.281	565	78	159	1	50
Pagliarulo	.279	365	38	102	6	36
Davis	.277	534	84	148	29	93
Gagne	.265	408	52	108	8	42
Gladden	.247	461	65	114	6	52
Newman	.191	246	25	47	0	19

Pitching	W	L	ERA	IP	BB	SO	Sv
Aguilera	4	5	2.35	69.0	30	61	42
Willis	8	3	2.63	89.0	19	53	2
Tapani	16	9	2.99	244.0	40	135	0
Erickson	20	8	3.18	204.0	71	108	0
Morris	18	12	3.43	246.2	92	163	0
Guthrie	7	5	4.32	98.0	41	72	2
Bedrosian	5	3	4.42	77.1	35	44	6
Anderson	5	11	4.96	134.1	42	51	0

New York Yankees

Batting	Avg	AB	R	H	HR	RBI
Sax	.304	652	85	198	10	56
Mattingly	.288	587	64	169	9	68
Hall	.285	492	67	140	19	80
Nokes	.268	456	52	122	24	77
R. Kelly	.267	486	68	130	20	69
Espinoza	.256	480	51	123	5	33
Valarde	.245	184	19	45	1	15
P. Kelly	.242	298	35	72	3	23
Williams	.238	320	43	76	3	34
Barfield	.225	284	37	64	17	48
Meulens	.222	288	37	64	6	29
Maas	.220	500	69	110	23	63

Pitching	W	L	ERA	IP	BB	SO	Sv
Farr	5	5	2.19	70.0	20	60	23
Habyan	4	2	2.30	90.0	20	70	2
Cadaret	8	6	3.62	121.2	59	105	3
Guetterman	3	4	3.68	88.0	25	35	6
Sanderson	16	10	3.81	208.0	29	130	0
Plunk	2	5	4.76	111.2	62	103	0
Johnson	6	11	5.95	127.0	33	62	0
Taylor	7	12	6.27	116.1	53	72	0
Leary	4	10	6.49	120.2	57	83	0

Oakland A's

Batting	Avg	AB	R	H	HR	RBI
Baines	.295	488	76	144	20	90
D. Henderson	.276	572	86	158	25	85
Steinbach	.274	456	50	125	6	67
R. Henderson	.268	470	105	126	18	57
J. Canseco	.266	572	115	152	44	122
Quirk	.261	203	16	53	1	17
Blankenship	.249	185	33	46	3	21
Gallego	.247	482	67	119	12	49
Bordick	.238	235	21	56	0	21
Wilson	.238	294	38	70	0	26
Jacoby	.224	419	28	94	4	44
Riles	.214	281	30	60	5	32
McGwire	.201	483	62	97	22	75

Pitching	W	L	ERA	IP	BB	SO	Sv
Moore	17	8	2.96	210.0	105	153	0
Eckersley	5	4	2.96	76.0	9	87	43
Darling	3	7	4.08	75.0	38	60	0
Welch	12	13	4.58	220.0	91	101	0
Stewart	11	11	5.18	226.0	105	144	0
Slusarski	5	7	5.27	109.1	52	60	0
Hawkins	4	6	5.52	89.2	43	45	0

Seattle Mariners

Batting	Avg	AB	R	H	HR	RBI
Griffey Jr.	.327	548	76	179	22	100
E. Martinez	.307	544	98	167	14	52
Cotto	.305	177	35	54	6	23
Briley	.260	381	39	99	2	26
Reynolds	.254	631	95	160	3	57
T. Jones	.251	175	30	44	3	24
Schaefer	.250	164	19	41	1	11
O'Brien	.248	560	58	139	17	88
Cochrane	.247	178	16	44	2	22
Buhner	.244	406	64	99	27	77
Vizquel	.230	426	42	98	1	41
Davis	.221	462	39	102	12	69
Bradley	.203	172	10	35	0	11
Valle	.194	324	38	63	8	32

Pitching	W	L	ERA	IP	BB	SO	Sv
Swift	1	2	1.99	90.1	26	48	17
Jackson	7	7	3.25	88.2	34	74	14
Swan	6	2	3.43	78.2	28	33	2
Krueger	11	8	3.60	175.0	60	91	0
Holman	13	14	3.69	195.1	77	108	0
Hanson	8	8	3.81	174.2	56	143	0
Johnson	13	10	3.98	201.1	152	228	0
Delucia	12	13	5.09	182.0	78	98	0

Texas Rangers

Batting	Avg	AB	R	H	HR	RBI
Franco	.341	589	108	201	15	78
Palmeiro	.322	631	115	203	26	88
Sierra	.307	661	110	203	25	116
Downing	.278	407	76	113	17	49
Petralli	.271	199	21	54	2	20
Reimer	.269	394	46	106	20	69
Buechele	.267	416	58	111	18	66
Rodriguez	.264	280	24	74	3	27
Gonzalez	.264	545	78	144	27	102
Diaz	.264	182	24	48	1	22
Stanley	.249	181	25	45	3	25
Pettis	.216	282	37	61	0	19
Huson	.213	268	36	57	2	26
Palmer	.187	268	38	50	15	37

Pitching	W	L	ERA	IP	BB	SO	Sv
Ryan	12	6	2.91	173.0	72	203	0
Guzman	13	7	3.08	169.2	84	125	0
Russell	6	4	3.29	79.1	26	52	30
Brown	9	12	4.40	210.2	90	96	0
Barfield	4	4	4.54	83.1	22	27	1
Jeffcoat	5	3	4.63	79.2	25	43	1
Alexander	5	3	5.24	89.1	48	50	0
Rogers	10	10	5.42	109.2	61	73	5
Witt	3	7	6.09	88.2	74	82	0

Toronto Blue Jays

Batting	Avg	AB	R	H	HR	RBI
Alomar	.295	637	88	188	9	69
White	.282	642	110	181	17	60
Sprague	.275	160	17	44	4	20
Carter	.273	638	89	174	33	108
Myers	.262	309	25	81	8	36
Olerud	.256	454	64	116	17	68
Gruber	.252	429	58	108	20	65
Maldonado	.250	288	37	72	12	48
Mulliniks	.250	240	27	60	2	24
Borders	.244	291	22	71	5	36
Wilson	.241	241	26	58	2	28
Parker	.239	502	47	120	11	59
Lee	.234	445	41	104	0	29
Tabler	.216	185	20	40	1	21
Snyder	.175	166	14	29	3	17

Pitching	W	L	ERA	IP	BB	SO	Sv
Henke	0	2	2.32	50.1	11	53	32
Candiotti	13	13	2.65	238.0	73	167	0
D. Ward	7	6	2.77	107.1	33	132	23
Guzman	10	3	2.99	138.2	66	123	0
Key	16	12	3.05	209.1	44	125	0
Timlin	11	6	3.16	108.1	50	85	3
Wells	15	10	3.72	198.1	49	106	1
Stottlemyre	15	8	3.78	219.0	75	116	0
Acker	3	5	5.20	88.1	36	44	1

1991 World Series Composite Box Score

Braves Batting

	g	ab	r	h	2b	3b	hr	rbi	so	bb	avg	po	a	e	pct
Mark Lemke 2b	6	24	4	10	1	3	0	4	4	2	.417	14	19	1	.971
Rafael Belliard ss	7	16	0	6	1	0	0	4	2	1	.375	8	21	0	1.000
Terry Pendleton 3b	7	30	6	11	3	0	2	3	1	3	.367	2	21	2	.920
Ron Gant cf	7	30	3	8	0	1	0	4	3	2	.267	19	0	0	1.000
David Justice rf	7	27	5	7	0	0	2	6	5	5	.259	21	1	1	.957
Jeff Treadway 2b-ph	3	4	1	1	0	0	0	0	2	1	.250	1	3	1	.800
Lonnie Smith dh-lf	7	26	5	6	0	0	3	3	4	3	.231	2	0	0	1.000
Greg Olson c	7	27	3	6	2	0	0	1	4	5	.222	47	6	0	1.000
Brian Hunter lf-ph-1b	7	21	2	4	1	0	1	3	2	0	.190	6	1	1	.875
Jeff Blauser ph-ss	5	6	0	1	0	0	0	0	1	1	.167	3	3	0	1.000
Sid Bream 1b	7	24	0	3	2	0	0	0	4	3	.125	70	7	0	1.000
Francisco Cabrera ph-c	3	1	0	0	0	0	0	0	0	0	.000	0	0	0	.000
Jim Clancy p	2	1	0	0	0	0	0	0	1	0	.000	0	0	0	.000
Tom Glavine p	2	2	0	0	0	0	0	0	0	0	.000	0	3	0	1.000
Keith Mitchell lf-pr	3	2	0	0	0	0	0	0	1	0	.000	0	0	0	.000
John Smoltz p	2	2	0	0	0	0	0	0	1	0	.000	2	1	0	1.000
Steve Avery p	2	3	0	0	0	0	0	0	2	0	.000	1	0	0	1.000
Tommy Gregg ph	4	3	0	0	0	0	0	0	2	0	.000	0	0	0	.000
Charlie Leibrandt p	2	0	0	0	0	0	0	0	0	0	.000	0	1	0	1.000
Kent Mercker p	2	0	0	0	0	0	0	0	0	0	.000	0	0	0	.000
Alejandro Pena p	3	0	0	0	0	0	0	0	0	0	.000	0	0	0	.000
Randy St. Claire p	1	0	0	0	0	0	0	0	0	0	.000	0	0	0	.000
Mike Stanton p	5	0	0	0	0	0	0	0	0	0	.000	0	0	0	.000
Jerry Willard ph	1	0	0	0	0	0	0	1	0	0	.000	0	0	0	.000
Mark Wohlers p	3	0	0	0	0	0	0	0	0	0	.000	0	0	0	.000
Totals	7	249	29	63	10	4	8	29	39	26	.253	196	87	6	.979

Twins Batting

	g	ab	r	h	2b	3b	hr	rbi	so	bb	avg	po	a	e	pct
Gene Larkin ph	4	4	0	2	0	0	0	1	0	0	.500	0	0	0	.000
Al Newman ph-3b-2b-ss	3	2	0	1	0	1	0	1	0	0	.500	0	2	0	1.000
Brian Harper c-ph	7	21	2	8	2	0	0	1	2	2	.381	33	5	1	.974
Scott Leius 3b-ph-ss	7	14	2	5	0	0	1	2	2	1	.357	5	8	1	.929
Chuck Knoblauch 2b	7	26	3	8	1	0	0	2	2	4	.308	15	14	1	.967
Mike Pagliarulo ph-3b	6	11	1	3	0	0	1	2	2	1	.273	3	3	0	1.000
Kirby Puckett cf	7	24	4	6	0	2	4	7	5	2	.250	16	1	0	1.000
Randy Bush ph-rf	3	4	0	1	0	0	0	0	1	0	.250	0	0	0	.000
Dan Gladden lf	7	30	5	7	2	2	0	0	4	3	.233	25	1	1	.963
Chili Davis dh-ph-rf	6	18	4	4	0	0	2	4	3	2	.222	1	0	0	1.000
Junior Ortiz c	3	5	0	1	0	0	0	1	1	0	.200	9	0	0	1.000
Greg Gagne ss	7	24	1	4	1	0	1	3	7	0	.167	13	24	0	1.000
Shane Mack rf	6	23	0	3	1	0	0	1	7	0	.130	11	0	0	1.000
Kent Hrbek 1b	7	26	2	3	1	0	1	2	6	2	.115	66	4	0	1.000
Rick Aguilera ph-p	4	1	0	0	0	0	0	0	0	0	.000	0	0	0	.000
Scott Erickson p	2	1	0	0	0	0	0	0	1	0	.000	1	0	0	1.000
Kevin Tapani p	1	1	0	0	0	0	0	0	0	0	.000	0	2	0	1.000
Jarvis Brown rf-ph-cf-pr	4	2	0	0	0	0	0	0	0	0	.000	0	0	0	.000
Jack Morris p	3	2	0	0	0	0	0	0	1	0	.000	2	4	0	1.000
Paul Sorrento ph-1b	3	2	0	0	0	0	0	0	2	1	.000	1	1	0	1.000
Steve Bedrosian p	3	0	0	0	0	0	0	0	0	0	.000	0	0	0	.000
Mark Guthrie p	4	0	0	0	0	0	0	0	0	0	.000	0	1	0	1.000
Terry Leach p	2	0	0	0	0	0	0	0	0	0	.000	0	0	0	.000
David West p	1	0	0	0	0	0	0	0	0	0	.000	0	0	0	.000
Carl Willis p	4	0	0	0	0	0	0	0	0	0	.000	1	0	0	1.000
Totals	7	241	24	56	8	4	8	24	48	21	.232	202	75	4	.986

Braves Pitching

	g	cg	ip	h	r	bb	so	hb	wp	w	l	sv	pct	er	era
Mike Stanton	5	0	7.1	5	0	2	7	0	0	1	0	0	1.000	0	0.00
Mark Wohlers	3	0	1.2	2	0	2	1	0	0	0	0	0	.000	0	0.00
Kent Mercker	2	0	1.0	0	0	0	1	0	0	0	0	0	.000	0	0.00
John Smoltz	2	0	14.1	13	2	1	11	1	0	0	0	0	.000	2	1.26
Tom Glavine	2	1	13.1	8	6	7	8	0	0	1	1	0	.500	4	2.70
Alejandro Pena	3	0	5.1	6	2	3	7	0	0	1	0	1	.000	2	3.38
Steve Avery	2	0	13.0	10	6	1	8	0	0	0	0	0	.000	5	3.46
Jim Clancy	3	0	4.1	3	2	4	2	0	0	0	1	0	1.000	2	4.15
Randy St. Claire	1	0	1.0	1	1	0	0	0	0	0	0	0	.000	1	9.00
Charlie Leibrandt	2	0	4.0	8	5	1	3	0	0	0	0	2	.000	5	11.25
Totals	7	1	65.1	56	24	21	48	1	1	3	4	0	.429	21	2.89

Twins Pitching

	g	cg	ip	h	r	bb	so	hb	wp	w	l	sv	pct	er	era
Jack Morris	3	0	23.0	18	3	9	15	0	2	2	0	0	1.000	3	1.17
Rick Aguilera	4	0	5.0	6	1	1	3	0	0	1	1	2	.500	1	1.80
Mark Guthrie	4	0	4.0	3	1	4	3	0	1	0	1	0	.000	1	2.25
Terry Leach	2	0	2.1	2	1	0	2	0	0	0	0	0	.000	1	3.86
Kevin Tapani	2	0	12.0	13	6	2	7	0	0	1	1	0	.500	6	4.50
Scott Erickson	2	0	10.2	10	7	4	5	1	1	0	0	0	.000	6	5.06
Carl Willis	4	0	7.0	6	4	2	2	0	0	0	0	0	.000	4	5.14
Steve Bedrosian	3	0	3.1	3	2	0	2	0	0	0	1	0	.000	2	5.40
David West	2	0	0.0	4	4	4	0	0	0	0	0	0	.000	4	0.00
Totals	7	0	67.1	63	29	26	39	1	5	4	3	2	.571	28	3.74

Score By Innings

Atlanta	0	2	1	5	6	1	8	4	1	0	0	1	—	29
Minnesota	5	1	1	0	4	4	2	4	1	1	0		—	24

1991 World Series

First Game

Atlanta	ab	r	h	bi	Minnesota	ab	r	h	bi
L. Smith, dh	3	1	0	0	Gladden, lf	2	1	0	0
Treadway, 2b	3	1	1	0	Knoblauch, 2b	3	0	3	1
Pendleton, 3b	4	0	0	0	Puckett, cf	4	0	0	0
Justice, rf	2	0	1	0	Davis, dh	3	0	0	0
Gant, cf	4	0	3	2	Harper, c	4	0	2	0
Bream, 1b	4	0	0	0	Mack, rf	4	0	0	0
Hunter, lf	4	0	0	0	Hrbek, 1b	4	2	2	1
Olson, c	3	0	1	0	Leius, 3b	2	1	1	0
Belliard, ss	1	0	0	0	Pagliarulo, ph-3b	1	0	0	0
Blauser, ph-ss	2	0	0	0	Gagne, ss	3	1	1	3
Totals	30	2	6	2	Totals	30	5	9	5

Atlanta .... 0 0 0 0 0 1 0 1 0—2
Minnesota .... 0 0 1 0 3 1 0 0 x—5

Atlanta	ip	h	r	er	bb	so
Leibrandt L, 0-1	4	7	4	4	1	3
Clancy	2	1	1	1	2	0
Wohlers	1	1	0	0	1	1
Stanton	1	0	0	0	0	2
Minnesota						
Morris W, 1-0	7	5	2	2	4	3
Guthrie H, 1	2/3	1	0	0	0	0
Aguilera S, 1	1 1/3	1	0	0	0	0

E - Gladden, Treadway. LOB - Atlanta 7, Minnesota 5. 2B - Harper. HR - Hrbek, Gagne. SB - Gladden.

How runs were scored—One in Twins third: Gladden walked and stole second. Knoblauch singled scoring Gladden.

Three in Twins fifth: Hrbek doubled. Leius singled. Gagne hit a home run scoring Hrbek and Leius.

One in Braves sixth: Treadway and Justice singled. Gant singled scoring Treadway.

One in Twins sixth: Hrbek hit a home run.

One in Braves eighth: Smith and Treadway walked. Gant singled scoring Smith.

Second Game

Atlanta	ab	r	h	bi	Minnesota	ab	r	h	bi
L. Smith, dh	3	0	0	0	Gladden, lf	4	0	0	0
Pendleton, 3b	4	0	2	0	Knoblauch, 2b	3	1	0	0
Gant, cf	4	0	1	0	Puckett, cf	4	0	0	0
Justice, rf	4	1	1	0	Davis, dh	3	1	1	2
Bream, 1b	4	0	1	0	Harper, c	2	0	1	0
Hunter, lf	3	0	1	1	Mack, rf	3	0	0	0
Olson, c	4	1	1	0	Hrbek, 1b	2	0	0	0
Lemke, 2b	3	0	0	0	Leius, 3b	3	1	1	1
Gregg, ph	1	0	0	0	Gagne, ss	3	0	1	0
Belliard, ss	2	0	1	0	Totals	27	3	4	3
Totals	32	2	8	2					

Atlanta .... 0 1 0 0 1 0 0 0—2
Minnesota .... 2 0 0 0 0 0 0 1 x—3

Atlanta	ip	h	r	er	bb	so
Glavine L, 0-1	8	4	3	3	3	6
Minnesota						
Tapani W, 1-0	8	7	2	2	0	3
Aguilera S, 2	1	1	0	0	0	3

E - Justice, Leius. LOB - Atlanta 3, Minnesota 3. 2B - Bream, Olson. HR - Davis, Leius.

How runs were scored—Two in Twins first: Knoblauch walked. Davis hit a home run scoring Knoblauch.

One in Braves second: Justice singled. Bream doubled. Hunter hit a sacrifice fly scoring Justice.

One in Braves fifth: Olson doubled and went to third on a groundout. Belliard hit a sacrifice fly scoring Olson.

One in Twins eighth: Leius hit a home run.

Third Game

Minnesota	ab	r	h	bi	Atlanta	ab	r	h	bi
Gladden, lf	6	1	3	0	L. Smith, lf	4	1	1	1
Knoblauch, 2b	5	0	1	1	Mitchell, lf	2	0	0	0
Hrbek, 1b	6	0	1	0	Pendleton, 3b	4	1	0	0
Puckett, cf	4	1	1	0	Gant, cf	6	0	0	0
Mack, rf	4	0	0	0	Justice, rf	6	2	2	1
Willis, p	0	0	0	0	Bream, 1b	3	0	1	0
Sorrento, ph	1	0	0	0	Hunter, ph-1b	2	0	0	0
Guthrie, p	0	0	0	0	Olson, c	3	1	1	1
Aguilera, ph-p	1	0	0	0	Lemke, 2b	5	0	2	1
Leius, 3b	3	0	0	0	Belliard, ss	3	0	1	1
Pagliarulo, ph-3b	1	0	0	0	Blauser, ph-ss	1	0	0	0
Newman, ph-3b	1	0	0	0	Avery, p	3	0	0	0
Gagne, ss	5	0	0	0	Pena, p	0	0	0	0
Ortiz, c	2	0	1	0	Treadway, ph	0	0	0	0
Harper, ph-c	3	1	1	0	Stanton, p	0	0	0	0
Erickson, p	1	0	0	0	Cabrera, ph	1	0	0	0
West, p	0	0	0	0	Wohlers, p	0	0	0	0
Leach, p	0	0	0	0	Mercker, p	0	0	0	0
Larkin, ph	1	0	1	0	Clancy, p	0	0	0	0
Bedrosian, p	0	0	0	0	Totals	43	5	8	5
Davis, ph	1	1	1	2					
Brown, rf	0	0	0	0					
Bush, ph-rf	2	0	0	0					
Totals	47	4	10	4					

Minnesota .... 1 0 0 0 0 0 1 2 0 0—4
Atlanta .... 0 1 0 1 2 0 0 0 0 1—5

Minnesota	ip	h	r	er	bb	so
Erickson	4 2/3	5	4	3	2	3
West	0	0	0	0	2	0
Leach	1/3	0	0	0	0	0
Bedrosian	2	0	0	0	0	1
Willis	2	0	0	0	2	0
Guthrie	2	1	0	0	1	1
Aguilera L, 0-1	2/3	2	1	1	1	0
Atlanta						
Avery	7	4	3	2	0	5
Pena	2	4	1	1	0	4
Stanton	2	1	0	0	1	3
Wohlers	1/3	0	0	0	0	0
Mercker	1/3	0	0	0	0	0
Clancy W, 1-0	1/3	0	0	0	1	0

E - Knoblauch, Pendleton, Lemke. LOB - Minnesota 10, Atlanta 12. 2B - Bream, Olson. 3B - Gladden. HR - Puckett, Davis, L. Smith, Justice. SB - Knoblauch, Justice.

How runs were scored—One in Twins first: Gladden tripled. Knoblauch hit a sacrifice fly scoring Gladden.

One in Braves second: Olson walked. Lemke singled. Belliard singled scoring Olson.

One in Braves fourth: Justice hit a home run.

Two in Braves fifth: L. Smith hit a home run. Pendleton walked. Justice reached first on an error. Bream walked. Olson walked scoring Pendleton.

One in Twins seventh: Puckett hit a home run.

Two in Twins eighth: Harper reached first on an error. Davis hit a home run scoring Harper.

One in Braves twelfth: Justice singled. Olson walked. Lemke singled scoring Justice.

Fourth Game

Minnesota	ab	r	h	bi	Atlanta	ab	r	h	bi
Gladden, lf	4	0	0	0	L. Smith, lf	4	1	2	1
Knoblauch, 2b	3	0	1	0	Pendleton, 3b	4	1	2	1
Puckett, cf	4	0	1	0	Gant, cf	3	0	1	0
Hrbek, 1b	4	0	0	0	Justice, rf	3	0	0	0
Harper, c	4	1	2	0	Bream, 1b	3	0	0	0
Mack, rf	4	0	0	0	Hunter, ph-1b	1	0	0	0
Pagliarulo, 3b	3	1	3	2	Olson, c	3	0	0	0
Leius, ph-3b	1	0	0	0	Lemke, 2b	4	1	3	0
Gagne, ss	3	0	0	0	Belliard, ss	2	0	0	0
Morris, p	2	0	0	0	Treadway, ph	1	0	0	0
Larkin, ph	1	0	0	0	Blauser, ss	0	0	0	0
Willis, p	0	0	0	0	Smoltz, p	2	0	0	0
Guthrie, p	0	0	0	0	Gregg, ph	1	0	0	0
Newman, 3b	0	0	0	0	Wohlers, p	0	0	0	0
Totals	33	2	7	2	Stanton, p	0	0	0	0
					Cabrera, ph	0	0	0	1
					Willard, ph	0	0	0	0
					Totals	31	3	8	3

Minnesota .... 0 1 0 0 0 0 1 0 0—2
Atlanta .... 0 0 1 0 0 1 0 1—3

Minnesota	ip	h	r	er	bb	so
Morris	6	6	1	1	3	4
Willis	1 1/3	1	1	1	0	1
Guthrie L, 0-1	1	1	1	1	1	1
Bedrosian	1/3	0	0	0	0	0
Atlanta						
Smoltz	7	7	2	2	0	7
Wohlers	1/3	0	0	0	0	0
Stanton W, 1-0	1 2/3	0	0	0	1	0

LOB - Minnesota 5, Atlanta 7. 2B - Knoblauch, Harper, Pendleton, Lemke. 3B - Lemke. HR - Pagliarulo, L. Smith, Pendleton. SB - Knoblauch, L. Smith, Gant.

How runs were scored—One in Twins second: Harper doubled. Pagliarulo singled scoring Harper.

One in Braves third: Pendleton hit a home run.

One in Twins seventh: Pagliarulo hit a home run.

One in Braves seventh: L. Smith hit a home run.

One in Braves ninth: Lemke tripled. Willard hit a sacrifice fly scoring Lemke.

Fifth Game

Minnesota	ab	r	h	bi	Atlanta	ab	r	h	bi
Gladden, lf	5	1	1	0	L. Smith, lf	5	1	1	1
Knoblauch, 2b	3	1	1	0	Mitchell, lf	0	0	0	0
Bedrosian, p	0	0	0	0	Pendleton, 3b	4	3	2	0
Ortiz, c	1	0	0	1	Gant, cf	4	3	3	1
Puckett, cf	2	1	1	0	Justice, rf	5	2	2	5
Brown, ph-cf	2	0	0	0	Bream, 1b	2	0	0	0
Davis, rf	3	2	1	0	Hunter, ph-1b	2	2	2	2
Harper, c	2	0	0	1	Olson, c	5	1	3	0
Bush, ph-rf	1	0	0	0	St. Claire, p	0	0	0	0
Leius, 3b	2	0	1	1	Lemke, 2b	4	2	2	3
West, p	0	0	0	0	Belliard, ss	4	0	2	2
Newman, 2b	1	0	1	1	Glavine, p	2	0	0	0
Hrbek, 1b	3	0	1	0	Mercker, p	0	0	0	0
Sorrento, ph-1b	0	0	0	0	Gregg, ph	1	0	0	0
Gagne, ss	4	0	1	0	Clancy, p	1	0	0	0
Tapani, p	1	0	0	0	Cabrera, c	0	0	0	0
Larkin, ph	1	0	0	0	Totals	39	14	17	14
Leach, p	0	0	0	0					
Pagliarulo, ph-3b	2	0	0	0					
Totals	33	5	7	5					

```
Minnesota . . . . . . .   0 0 0 0 0 3 0 1 1—5
Atlanta . . . . . . . . . .  0 0 0 4 1 0 6 3 x—14
```

Minnesota	ip	h	r	er	bb	so
Tapani L,1-1	4	6	4	4	2	4
Leach	2	2	1	1	0	2
West	0	2	4	4	2	0
Bedrosian	1	3	2	2	0	1
Willis	1	4	3	3	0	0
Atlanta						
Glavine W,1-1	5⅓	4	3	3	4	2
Mercker	⅔	0	0	0	0	0
Clancy	2	2	1	1	1	2
St. Claire	1	1	1	1	0	0

E - Harper, Pendleton. LOB - Minnesota 7, Atlanta 5. 2B - Davis, Pendleton, Belliard. 3B - Gladden, Newman, Gant, Lemke (2). HR - L. Smith, Justice, Hunter. SB - Justice, Olson.

How runs were scored—Four in Braves fourth: Gant singled. Justice hit a home run scoring Gant. Olson singled. Lemke tripled scoring Olson. Belliard doubled scoring Lemke.

One in Braves fifth: Pendleton and Gant singled. Justice grounded out scoring Pendleton.

Three in Twins sixth: Knoblauch walked. Puckett singled. C. Davis walked. Harper walked scoring Knoblauch. Leius walked scoring Puckett. Hrbek grounded out C. Davis.

Six in Braves seventh: L. Smith hit a home run. Pendleton and Gant walked. Justice singled scoring Pendleton. Hunter singled scoring Gant. Lemke tripled scoring Justice and Hunter. Belliard singled scoring Lemke.

One in Twins eighth: C. Davis singled. Newman tripled scoring C. Davis.

Three in Braves eighth: Pendleton doubled. Gant tripled scoring Pendleton. Justice grounded out scoring Gant. Hunter hit a home run.

One in Twins ninth: Gladden tripled. Ortiz grounded out scoring Gladden.

Sixth Game

Atlanta	ab	r	h	bi	Minnesota	ab	r	h	bi
L. Smith, dh	3	1	0	0	Gladden, lf	4	1	0	0
Pendleton, 3b	5	1	4	2	Knoblauch, 2b	5	1	1	0
Gant, cf	5	0	1	0	Puckett, cf	4	2	3	3
Justice, rf	4	0	0	0	Davis, dh	4	0	0	0
Bream, 1b	4	0	1	0	Mack, rf	4	0	2	1
Mitchell, pr-lf	0	0	0	0	Leius, 3b	3	0	2	0
Hunter, lf-1b	5	0	0	0	Pagliarulo, ph-3b	1	0	0	0
Olson, c	5	0	0	0	Hrbek, 1b	4	0	0	0
Lemke, 2b	4	1	2	0	Ortiz, c	2	0	0	0
Belliard, ss	2	0	1	0	Harper, ph-c	2	0	0	0
Gregg, ph	0	0	0	0	Gagne, ss	4	0	1	0
Blauser, ph-ss	2	0	1	0	Totals	37	4	9	4
Totals	39	3	9	3					

```
Atlanta . . . . . . . . .  0 0 0 0 2 0 1 0 0 0 0—3
Minnesota . . . . . . . .  2 0 0 0 1 0 0 0 0 0 1—4
```

Atlanta	ip	h	r	er	bb	so
Avery	6	6	3	3	1	3
Stanton	2	0	0	0	0	1
Pena	2	0	0	0	0	2
Leibrandt L,0-2	0	1	1	1	0	0
Minnesota						
Erickson	6	5	3	3	2	2
Guthrie	⅓	1	0	0	1	1
Willis	2⅓	1	0	0	0	1
Aguilera	2	2	0	0	0	2

E - Hunter. LOB - Atlanta 7, Minnesota 5. 2B - Mack. 3B - Puckett. HR - Puckett, Pendleton. SB - Gladden, Puckett.

How runs were scored—Two in Twins first: Knoblauch singled. Puckett tripled scoring Knoblauch. Mack singled scoring Puckett.

Two in Braves fifth: Belliard singled. L. Smith grounded into fielder's choice. Pendleton hit a home run scoring Smith.

One in Twins fifth: Gladden walked, stole second, and was sacrificed to third by Knoblauch. Puckett hit sacrifice fly to score Gladden.

One in Braves seventh: Lemke singled, went to second on Guthrie's wild pitch. L. Smith walked. Pendleton singled. Gant grounded into fielder's choice scoring Lemke.

One in Twins eleventh: Puckett hit a home run.

Seventh Game

Atlanta	ab	r	h	bi	Minnesota	ab	r	h	bi
L. Smith, dh	4	0	2	0	Gladden, lf	5	1	3	0
Pendleton, 3b	5	0	1	0	Knoblauch, 2b	4	0	1	0
Gant, cf	4	0	0	0	Puckett, cf	2	0	0	0
Justice, rf	3	0	1	0	Hrbek, 1b	3	0	0	0
Bream, 1b	4	0	0	0	Davis, dh	4	0	1	0
Hunter, lf	4	0	1	0	Brown, pr-ph	0	0	0	0
Olson, c	4	0	0	0	Larkin, ph	1	0	1	1
Lemke, 2b	4	0	1	0	Harper, c	4	0	2	0
Belliard, ss	2	0	1	0	Mack, rf	4	0	1	0
Blauser, ph-ss	1	0	0	0	Pagliarulo, 3b	3	0	0	0
Totals	35	0	7	0	Gagne, ss	2	0	0	0
					Bush, ph	1	0	1	0
					Newman, pr-ss	0	0	0	0
					Sorrento, ph	1	0	0	0
					Leius, ss	0	0	0	0
					Totals	34	1	10	1

```
Atlanta . . . . . . . .   0 0 0 0 0 0 0 0 0 0—0
Minnesota . . . . . . .   0 0 0 0 0 0 0 0 0 1—1
```

Atlanta	ip	h	r	er	bb	so
Smoltz	7⅓	6	0	0	1	4
Stanton	⅔	2	0	0	1	0
Pena L,0-1	1⅓	2	1	1	3	1
Minnesota						
Morris W,2-0	10	7	0	0	2	8

LOB - Atlanta 8, Minnesota 12. 2B - Pendleton, Hunter, Gladden (2).

How runs were scored—One in Twins tenth: Gladden hit a broken-bat double, and was sacrificed to third by Knoblauch. Puckett and Hrbek were intentionally walked. Larkin, pinch hitting for Brown, singled over a drawn-in outfield scoring Gladden.

World Series Results, 1903-1991

1903 Boston AL 5, Pittsburgh NL 3	1913 Philadelphia AL 4, New York NL 1	1923 New York AL 4, New York NL 2
1904 No series	1914 Boston NL 4, Philadelphia AL 0	1924 Washington AL 4, New York NL 3
1905 New York NL 4, Philadelphia AL 1	1915 Boston AL 4, Philadelphia NL 1	1925 Pittsburgh NL 4, Washington AL 3
1906 Chicago AL 4, Chicago NL 2	1916 Boston AL 4, Brooklyn NL 1	1926 St. Louis NL 4, New York AL 3
1907 Chicago NL 4, Detroit AL 0, 1 tie	1917 Chicago AL 4, New York NL 2	1927 New York AL 4, Pittsburgh NL 0
1908 Chicago NL 4, Detroit AL 1	1918 Boston AL 4, Chicago NL 2	1928 New York AL 4, St. Louis NL 0
1909 Pittsburgh NL 4, Detroit AL 3	1919 Cincinnati NL 5, Chicago AL 3	1929 Philadelphia AL 4, Chicago NL 1
1910 Philadelphia AL 4, Chicago NL 1	1920 Cleveland AL 5, Brooklyn NL 2	1930 Philadelphia AL 4, St. Louis NL 2
1911 Philadelphia AL 4, New York NL 2	1921 New York NL 5, New York AL 3	1931 St. Louis NL 4, Philadelphia AL 3
1912 Boston AL 4, New York NL 3, 1 tie	1922 New York NL 4, New York AL 0, 1 tie	*(continued)*

1932 New York AL 4, Chicago NL 0	1953 New York AL 4, Brooklyn NL 2	1973 Oakland AL 4, New York NL 3
1933 New York NL 4, Washington AL 1	1954 New York NL 4, Cleveland AL 0	1974 Oakland AL 4, Los Angeles NL 1
1934 St. Louis NL 4, Detroit AL 3	1955 Brooklyn NL 4, New York AL 3	1975 Cincinnati NL 4, Boston AL 3
1935 Detroit AL 4, Chicago NL 2	1956 New York AL 4, Brooklyn NL 3	1976 Cincinnati NL 4, New York AL 0
1936 New York AL 4, New York NL 2	1957 Milwaukee NL 4, New York AL 3	1977 New York AL 4, Los Angeles NL 2
1937 New York AL 4, New York NL 1	1958 New York AL 4, Milwaukee NL 3	1978 New York AL 4, Los Angeles NL 2
1938 New York AL 4, Chicago NL 0	1959 Los Angeles NL 4, Chicago AL 2	1979 Pittsburgh NL 4, Baltimore AL 3
1939 New York AL 4, Cincinnati NL 0	1960 Pittsburgh NL 4, New York AL 3	1980 Philadelphia NL 4, Kansas City AL 2
1940 Cincinnati NL 4, Detroit AL 3	1961 New York AL 4, Cincinnati NL 1	
1941 New York AL 4, Brooklyn NL 1	1962 New York AL 4, San Francisco NL 3	1981 Los Angeles NL 4, New York AL 2
1942 St. Louis NL 4, New York AL 1		1982 St. Louis NL 4, Milwaukee AL 3
1943 New York AL 4, St. Louis NL 1	1963 Los Angeles NL 4, New York AL 0	1983 Baltimore AL 4, Philadelphia NL 1
1944 St. Louis NL 4, St. Louis AL 2	1964 St. Louis NL 4, New York AL 3	1984 Detroit AL 4, San Diego NL 1
1945 Detroit AL 4, Chicago NL 3	1965 Los Angeles NL 4, Minnesota AL 3	1985 Kansas City AL 4, St. Louis NL 3
1946 St. Louis NL 4, Boston AL 3	1966 Baltimore AL 4, Los Angeles NL 0	1986 New York NL 4, Boston AL 3
1947 New York AL 4, Brooklyn NL 3	1967 St. Louis NL 4, Boston AL 3	1987 Minnesota AL 4, St. Louis NL 3
1948 Cleveland AL 4, Boston NL 2	1968 Detroit AL 4, St. Louis NL 3	1988 Los Angeles NL 4, Oakland AL 1
1949 New York AL 4, Brooklyn NL 1	1969 New York NL 4, Baltimore AL 1	1989 Oakland AL 4, San Francisco NL 0
1950 New York AL 4, Philadelphia NL 0	1970 Baltimore AL 4, Cincinnati NL 1	1990 Cincinnati NL 4, Oakland AL 0
1951 New York AL 4, New York NL 2	1971 Pittsburgh NL 4, Baltimore AL 3	1991 Minnesota AL 4, Atlanta NL 3
1952 New York AL 4, Brooklyn NL 3	1972 Oakland AL 4, Cincinnati NL 3	

1991 World Series MVP

Jack Morris of the Minnesota Twins, who won the first and seventh games, was named Most Valuable Player.

Major League Leaders in 1991

National League

Batting

Pendleton, Atlanta, .319; Morris, Cincinnati, .318; Gwynn, San Diego, .317; McGee, San Francisco, .312; Jose, St. Louis, .305.

Home Runs

Johnson, New York, 38; Williams, San Francisco, 34; Gant, Atlanta, 32; McGriff, San Diego, 31; Dawson, Chicago, 31.

Runs Batted In

Johnson, New York, 117; Clark, San Francisco, 116; Bonds, Pittsburgh, 116; McGriff, San Diego, 106; Gant, Atlanta, 105.

Hits

Pendleton, Atlanta, 187; Butler, Los Angeles, 182; Sabo, Cincinnati, 175; Bonilla, Pittsburgh, 174; Jose, St. Louis, 173.

Doubles

Bonilla, Pittsburgh, 44; Jose, St. Louis, 40; Zeile, St. Louis, 36; O'Neill, Cincinnati, 36; Sabo, Cincinnati, 35; Gant, Atlanta, 35.

Triples

Lankford, St. Louis, 15; Gwynn, San Diego, 11; Finley, Houston, 10; Gonzalez, Houston, 9; Grissom, Montreal, 9.

Runs

Butler, Los Angeles, 112; Johnson, New York, 108; Sandberg, Chicago, 104; Bonilla, Pittsburgh, 102; Gant, Atlanta, 101.

Stolen Bases

Grissom, Montreal, 76; Nixon, Atlanta, 72; DeShields, Montreal, 56; Lankford, St. Louis, 44; Bonds, Pittsburgh, 43.

Pitching (16 Decisions)

Smiley, Pittsburgh, 20-8, .714; Rijo, Cincinnati, 15-6, .714; Williams, Philadelphia, 12-5, .706; Avery, Atlanta, 18-8, .692; Hurst, San Diego, 15-8, .652.

Strikeouts

Cone, New York, 241; Maddux, Chicago, 198; Glavine, Atlanta, 192; Harnisch, Houston, 172; Rijo, Cincinnati, 172.

Saves

L. Smith, St. Louis, 47; Dibble, Cincinnati, 31; Williams, Philadelphia, 30; Franco, New York, 30; Righetti, San Francisco, 24.

American League

Batting

Franco, Texas, .341; Boggs, Boston, .332; Griffey Jr., Seattle, .327; Randolph, Milwaukee, .327; Molitor, Milwaukee, .325.

Home Runs

Canseco, Oakland, 44; Fielder, Detroit, 44; C. Ripken, Baltimore, 34; Carter, Toronto, 33; Thomas, Chicago, 32.

Runs Batted In

Fielder, Detroit, 133; Canseco, Oakland, 122; Sierra, Texas, 116; C. Ripken, Baltimore, 114; Thomas, Chicago, 109.

Hits

Molitor, Milwaukee, 216; C. Ripken, Baltimore, 210; Palmeiro, Texas, 203; Sierra, Texas, 203; Franco, Texas, 201.

Doubles

Palmeiro, Texas, 49; C. Ripken, Baltimore, 46; Sierra, Texas, 44; Griffey Jr, Seattle, 42; Reed, Boston, 42; Carter, Toronto, 42; Boggs, Boston, 42.

Triples

L. Johnson, Chicago, 13; Molitor, Milwaukee, 13; R. Alomar, Toronto, 11; Devereaux, Baltimore, 10; White, Toronto, 10.

Runs

Molitor, Milwaukee, 133; Palmeiro, Texas, 115; Canseco, Oakland, 115; Sierra, Texas, 110; White, Toronto, 110.

Stolen Bases

R. Henderson, Oakland, 58; R. Alomar, Toronto, 53; Raines, Chicago, 51; Polonia, California, 48; Cuyler, Detroit, 41.

Pitching (16 Decisions)

Hesketh, Boston, 12-4, .750; Erickson, Minnesota, 20-8, .714; Langston, California, 19-8, .704; Gullickson, Detroit, 20-9, .690; Wegman, Milwaukee, 15-7, .682.

Strikeouts

Clemens, Boston, 241; R. Johnson, Seattle, 228; Ryan, Texas, 203; McDowell, Chicago, 191; Langston, California, 183.

Saves

Harvey, California, 46; Eckersley, Oakland, 43; Aguilera, Minnesota, 42; Reardon, Boston, 40; Montgomery, Kansas City, 33.

All-Time Home Run Leaders

Player	HR	Player	HR	Player	HR	Player	HR
Hank Aaron	755	Ted Williams	521	Dave Kingman	442	Johnny Bench	389
Babe Ruth	714	Willie McCovey	521	Billy Williams	426	Dwight Evans	385
Willie Mays	660	Ed Mathews	512	Darrell Evans	414	Frank Howard	382
Frank Robinson	586	Ernie Banks	512	Duke Snider	407	Jim Rice	382
Harmon Killebrew	573	Mel Ott	511	Dave Winfield	406	Orlando Cepeda	379
Reggie Jackson	563	Lou Gehrig	493	Al Kaline	399	Tony Perez	379
Mike Schmidt	548	Stan Musial	475	Eddie Murray	398		
Mickey Mantle	536	Willie Stargell	475	Dale Murphy	396		
Jimmy Foxx	534	Carl Yastrzemski	452	Graig Nettles	390		

All-Time Major League Leaders

(Includes 1991 season)

Games		At Bats		Runs Batted In		Stolen Bases	
Pete Rose	3562	Pete Rose	14,043	Hank Aaron	2297	Since 1898	
Carl Yastrzemski	3308	Hank Aaron	12,364	Babe Ruth	2204	Rickey Henderson	994
Hank Aaron	3298	Carl Yastrzemski	11,988	Lou Gehrig	1990	Lou Brock	938
Ty Cobb	3033	Ty Cobb	11,429	Ty Cobb	1961	Ty Cobb	892
Stan Musial	3026	Stan Musial	10,972	Stan Musial	1951	Eddie Collins	742
Willie Mays	2992	Willie Mays	10,881	Jimmie Foxx	1922	Max Carey	738
Rusty Staub	2951	Brooks Robinson	10,654	Willie Mays	1903	Honus Wagner	703
Brooks Robinson	2896	Honus Wagner	10,427	Mel Ott	1860	Joe Morgan	689
Al Kaline	2834	Lou Brock	10,332	Carl Yastrzemski	1844	Tim Raines	685
Eddie Collins	2826	Luis Aparicio	10,230	Ted Williams	1839	Bert Campaneris	649
						Vince Coleman	596

Runs		Hits		Strikeouts		Shutouts	
Ty Cobb	2245	Pete Rose	4256	Nolan Ryan	5461	Walter Johnson	110
Hank Aaron	2174	Ty Cobb	4191	Steve Carlton	4136	Grover C. Alexander	90
Babe Ruth	2174	Hank Aaron	3771	Tom Seaver	3640	Christy Mathewson	83
Pete Rose	2165	Stan Musial	3630	Bert Blyleven	3631	Cy Young	77
Willie Mays	2062	Tris Speaker	3515	Don Sutton	3574	Eddie Plank	69
Stan Musial	1949	Honus Wagner	3430	Gaylord Perry	3534	Warren Spahn	63
Lou Gehrig	1888	Carl Yastrzemski	3419	Walter Johnson	3508	Mordecai Brown	63
Tris Speaker	1881	Eddie Collins	3309	Phil Niekro	3340	Tom Seaver	61
Mel Ott	1859	Willie Mays	3283	Ferguson Jenkins	3192	Nolan Ryan	61
Frank Robinson	1829	Nap Lajoie	3252	Bob Gibson	3117	Bert Blyleven	60

Major League Perfect Games Since 1900

Year	Player	Clubs	Score	Year	Player	Clubs	Score
1904	Cy Young	Boston vs. Phil. (AL)	3-0	1965	Sandy Koufax	Los Angeles vs. Chic. (NL) .	1-0
1908	Addie Joss	Cleveland vs. Chicago (AL) .	1-0	1968	Jim Hunter	Oakland vs. Minn. (AL) . . .	4-0
1917	Ernie Shore (a) . . .	Boston vs. Wash. (AL) . . .	4-0	1981	Len Barker	Cleveland vs. Toronto (AL) .	3-0
1922	Charles Robertson .	Chicago vs. Detroit (AL) . .	2-0	1984	Mike Witt	California vs. Texas (AL) . .	1-0
1956	Don Larsen (b) . . .	N.Y. Yankees vs. Brooklyn .	2-0	1988	Tom Browning	Cincinnati vs. L.A. (NL). . . .	1-0
1959	Harvey Haddix (c) .	Pitts. vs. Milwaukee (NL) . .	0-1	1991	Dennis Martinez . . .	Montreal vs. L.A. (NL)	2-0
1964	Jim Bunning	Phil. vs. N.Y. Mets (NL) . . .	6-0				

(a) Babe Ruth, the starting pitcher, was ejected from the game after walking the first batter. Shore replaced him and the baserunner was out stealing. Shore retired the next 26 batters. (b) World Series. (c) Pitched 12 perfect innings, lost in 13th on an error, sacrifice bunt, walk, and double.

NCAA Baseball Champions

1960	Minnesota	1968	USC	1976	Arizona	1984	Cal. St.-Fullerton
1961	USC	1969	Arizona St.	1977	Arizona St.	1985	Miami, Fla.
1962	Michigan	1970	USC	1978	USC	1986	Arizona
1963	USC	1971	USC	1979	Cal. St.-Fullerton	1987	Stanford
1964	Minnesota	1972	USC	1980	Arizona	1988	Stanford
1965	Arizona St.	1973	USC	1981	Arizona St.	1989	Wichita St.
1966	Ohio St.	1974	USC	1982	Miami, Fla.	1990	Georgia
1967	Arizona St.	1975	Texas	1983	Texas	1991	LSU

Little League World Series in 1991

The team from Taiwan won the 1991 Little League World Series by defeating the team from San Ramon Valley, Cal. at Williamsport, Pa. It was the 15th Little League World Series title in 18 appearances for the Taiwan team.

Ten Most Dramatic Sports Events, Nov. 1990—Oct. 1991

Selected by The World Almanac Sports Staff

—Mike Powell broke Bob Beamon's 23-year-old long jump record with a leap of 29 feet 4½ inches at the world championship track & field meet in Tokyo.

—The Minnesota Twins defeated the Atlanta Braves in the World Series. The Twins became the first team to become champions after finishing last in their division the previous year.

—Duke Univ. defeated UNLV, the defending national basketball champions, who had a 45-game winning streak, 79-77 in the NCAA semi-final game. The Blue Devils went on to defeat Kansas in the championship game to win their first NCAA basketball title.

—Scott Norwood of the Buffalo Bills missed a 47-yard field goal attempt with 8 seconds remaining in Super Bowl XXV. The missed kick gave the N.Y. Giants a 20-19 victory and their second Super Bowl championship.

—Carl Lewis became the world's fastest man by setting a record for 100 meters at 9.86 seconds. He broke the record set by Leroy Burrell just 10 weeks earlier.

—Dennis Martinez of the Montreal Expos pitched a perfect game against the L.A. Dodgers. He became the 13th pitcher to hurl a perfect game in the century.

—The Chicago Bulls defeated the L.A. Lakers in 5 games to win their first NBA championship. Michael Jordan of the Bulls was chosen the playoff's most valuable player.

—Raghib (Rocket) Ismail of Notre Dame had a 91-yard punt return for a touchdown called back in the final minute of the Orange Bowl game because of a penalty. Colorado defeated the Fighting Irish 10-9.

—Rickey Henderson of the Oakland A's stole the 939th base of his career to establish a new major league record. He broke the record held by Lou Brock.

—The Pittsburgh Penguins defeated the Minnesota North Stars in 6 games to win their first Stanley Cup championship. Mario Lemieux of the Penguins was chosen the most valuable player of the playoffs.

VITAL STATISTICS

Source: National Center for Health Statistics, U.S. Department of Health and Human Services

Births

According to provisional statistics for the first quarter of 1991, there were 963,000 live births, 3 percent less than the estimated number reported for the same 3-month period in 1990 (988,000). The birth rate declined by 3 percent, from 16.0 in the first quarter of 1990 to 15.5 in the first quarter of 1991.

During the 12 months ending with March 1991, there were an estimated 4,154,000 live births, 2 percent more than reported for the comparable period ending a year earlier (4,072,000). The birth rate was 16.5, 1 percent above the rate for the 12 months ending with March 1990 (16.4).

Marriages

The total number of marriages for the first quarter of 1991 was 413,000. The marriage rate was 6.6 per 1,000 population, down 3 percent from the first quarter of 1990.

During the 12 months ending with March 1991, an estimated 2,436,000 couples married, up slightly from the same period a year before (2,427,000). However, the marriage rate for the same period was identical both years.

Divorces

A total of 285,000 couples divorced during the first quarter of 1991, fewer by 6,000 than for the first quarter of 1990. The divorce rate was 4.6 per 1,000 population, also down from the first quarter of 1990 (4.7).

During the 12 months ending with March 1991, an estimated 1,170,000 couples divorced, up slightly from the 1,168,000 during the 12 months ending March 1990. How-ever, the divorce rate for the 12-month period ending March 1991 was 4.6, 2 percent lower than during the comparable period a year before.

Deaths

According to provisional statistics, there were 560,000 deaths during the first quarter of 1991, 5 percent less than for the first quarter of 1990 (588,000). The death rate was 9.0 per 1,000 population, 5 percent lower than the Jan.-March 1990 rate. Among the deaths for the first quarter of 1991, were 9,500 deaths at ages under 1 year, yielding an infant mortality rate of 9.5 per 1,000 live births, 3 percent lower than the rate of 9.8 for the first quarter of 1990.

The death rate for the 12 months ending with March 1991 (8.5 deaths per 1,000 population) was 2 percent lower than the comparable 12-month period a year earlier. The infant mortality rate for this 12-month-period was 9.1 per 1,000 live births, 5 percent lower than the rate of 9.6 for the 12 months ending with March 1990.

Provisional Statistics
12 months ending with March

	Number		Rate*	
	1991	1990	1991	1990
Live births	4,154,000	4,072,000	16.5	16.4
Deaths	2,134,000	2,169,000	8.5	8.7
Natural increase.	2,020,000	1,903,000	8.0	7.7
Marriages	2,436,000	2,427,000	9.7	9.7
Divorces	1,170,000	1,168,000	4.6	4.7
Infant deaths. . .	37,800	38,900	9.1	9.6

*Per 1,000 population **Note:** Figures include revisions.

Annual Report for the Year 1990 (Provisional Statistics)

Highlights

The provisional number of live births in 1990 was higher than the number reported in 1989, and was the largest number reported since 1961. The birth fertility rates also increased and were the highest since the early 1970s.

In 1990 the provisional number of marriages increased 2 percent from the comparable figure for 1989. The slight rise in the marriage rate was the first increase since 1980. Despite an increase in the number of divorces in 1990, the divorce rate remained the same as in 1988 and 1989.

Births

During 1990 an estimated 4,179,000 babies were born in the United States, 4 percent more than in 1989 (4,021,000). This was the largest number reported since 1961. The birth rate was 16.7 per 1,000 total population, 3 percent above the rate for 1989 (16.2). The fertility rate was 71.1 live births per 1,000 women aged 15-44 years, 3 percent higher than 1989 (68.8) rate.

The birth and fertility rates, which increased dramatically in the 1940's and 1950's, followed by rapid declines in the 1960's and early 1970's, have been fairly steady since 1975. The birth and fertility rates have risen slightly in the last 3 years and are currently the highest since 1971 and 1972, respectively. There were increases in at least some of the age-specific birth rates.

Deaths

The provisional count of deaths in the United States during 1990 totaled 2,162,000, slightly higher than the estimated number for 1989, but below the peak number of 2,167,999 in the final count for 1988. The provisional death rate of 861.9 deaths per 1,000 population was 1 percent lower than the provisional rate for 1989 of 868.1.

The infant mortality rate for 1990 was 908.0 per 1,000 live births, compared with the rate of 9.9 for 1990. It was the lowest rate ever recorded in the U.S. Among the causes of infant death, the rate increased between 1989 and 1990 for respiratory distress syndrome.

Marriages and Divorces

The number of marriages in 1990 was 2,448,000, 2 percent more than in 1989. The marriage rate was 9.8 in 1990, a slight increase over 1989 and 1988. In the last 25 years, marriage rates have twice gone through a period of increase followed by a period of decline. In the early 1960s, marriage rates began to rise and continued through 1972, when the rate was 10.9. Beginning in 1973, the rate declined for 4 consecutive years down to 9.9 in 1977. The rate increased again in the late 1970s to a relative peak of 10.6 in 1980-82. In 1983, rates began falling again, to 9.7 in 1988-89. The increase in 1990 to 9.8 marks the first increase since 1980.

According to provisional data, 1,175,000 couples were divorced during 1990, 12,000 more than in 1989. The divorce rate, however, was the same in both years, and the same as the final rate for 1988. The divorce rate has been steady for 3 consecutive years after 2 decades of much change. In a 10-year period from 1966 to 1976, the divorce rate doubled from 2.5 to 5.0. In the remainder of the 1970s, the divorce rate climbed to its all-time peak of 5.3 in 1979. After reaching 5.3 again in 1981, the rate began a general decline until reaching its current level.

Births and Deaths in the U.S.

Refers only to events occurring within the U.S., including Alaska and Hawaii beginning in 1960. Excludes fetal deaths. Rates per 1,000 population enumerated as of April 1 for 1960, and 1970; estimated as of July 1 for all other years. Beginning 1970 excludes births and deaths occurring to nonresidents of the U.S.

	Births		Deaths	
Year	Total number	Rate	Total number	Rate
1955.	4,097,000	25.0	1,528,717	9.3
1960.	4,257,850	23.7	1,711,982	9.5
1965.	3,760,358	19.4	1,828,136	9.4
1970.	3,731,386	18.4	1,921,031	9.5
1975.	3,144,198	14.6	1,892,879	8.8
1980.	3,612,258	15.9	1,986,000	8.7
1985.	3,749,000	15.7	2,084,000	8.7
1989.	4,021,000	16.2	2,155,000	8.7
1990.	4,179,000	16.7	2,162,000	8.6

Births and Deaths by States and Regions

Source: National Center for Health Statistics.

Area	Live births 1990 Number	Rate	Deaths 1989 Number	Rate
New England	**204,145**	**15.5**	**202,027**	**15.5**
Maine	16,211	13.1	16,842	13.8
New Hampshire	16,927	15.0	17,946	16.2
Vermont	8,045	14.0	7,920	14.0
Massachusetts	95,066	16.0	96,457	16.3
Rhode Island	15,666	15.6	15,302	15.3
Connecticut	52,230	16.1	47,560	14.7
Middle Atlantic	**594,883**	**15.7**	**578,025**	**15.3**
New York	302,084	16.8	291,145	16.2
New Jersey	120,654	15.5	116,619	15.1
Pennsylvania	172,145	14.2	170,261	14.1
East North Central	**673,457**	**15.8**	**649,459**	**15.4**
Ohio	165,546	15.1	162,793	14.9
Indiana	85,202	15.1	82,764	14.8
Illinois	192,545	16.4	189,129	16.2
Michigan	157,674	16.9	142,673	15.4
Wisconsin	72,490	14.8	72,100	14.8
West North Central	**275,609**	**15.3**	**267,762**	**15.0**
Minnesota	68,353	15.5	66,593	15.3
Iowa	39,595	13.9	39,241	13.8
Missouri	83,085	16.0	80,126	15.5
North Dakota	10,483	16.0	10,862	16.5
South Dakota	10,912	15.2	10,991	15.4
Nebraska	24,317	15.0	24,317	15.1
Kansas	38,864	15.4	35,632	14.2
South Atlantic	**705,114**	**16.1**	**678,784**	**15.7**
Delaware	11,728	17.1	11,492	17.1
Maryland	75,557	15.9	67,550	14.4
District of Columbia	21,912	36.8	22,461	37.2
Virginia	96,665	15.6	93,453	15.3
West Virginia	23,202	12.6	23,079	12.4
North Carolina	105,230	15.8	102,817	15.6
South Carolina	56,521	15.9	55,214	15.7
Georgia	114,818	17.6	109,905	17.1
Florida	199,481	15.3	192,813	15.2
East South Central	**244,572**	**15.8**	**231,994**	**15.1**
Kentucky	56,753	15.2	52,591	14.1
Tennessee	77,821	15.6	76,780	15.5
Alabama	66,935	16.2	60,360	14.7
Mississippi	43,063	16.4	42,263	16.1
West South Central	**483,507**	**17.8**	**451,625**	**16.7**
Arkansas	35,499	14.7	34,997	14.5
Louisiana	71,913	16.5	68,813	15.7
Oklahoma	46,119	14.3	46,455	14.4
Texas	329,976	19.2	301,360	17.7
Mountain	**242,892**	**17.7**	**235,645**	**17.4**
Montana	11,482	14.2	11,394	14.1
Idaho	16,418	16.0	15,459	15.2
Wyoming	6,517	13.9	6,491	13.7
Colorado	53,238	16.0	52,863	15.9
New Mexico	28,252	18.3	27,324	17.9
Arizona	68,701	18.9	67,609	19.0
Utah	37,175	21.6	36,208	21.2
Nevada	21,109	18.1	18,297	16.5
Pacific	**772,564**	**19.7**	**705,189**	**18.4**
Washington	77,034	15.8	73,261	15.4
Oregon	45,851	15.9	43,835	15.5
California	617,704	20.7	557,003	19.2
Alaska	11,506	21.8	11,545	21.9
Hawaii	20,469	18.1	19,545	17.6

Notes: Data are provisional, by state of occurrence rather than state of residence, and include revisions.

Infant Mortality Rates by Race and Sex

Source: National Center for Health Statistics

	All races Both sexes	Male	Female	White Both sexes	Male	Female	Black Both sexes	Male	Female
1960	26.0	29.3	22.6	22.9	26.0	19.6	44.3	49.1	39.4
1970	20.0	22.4	17.5	17.8	20.0	15.4	32.6	36.2	29.0
1980	12.6	13.9	11.2	11.0	12.3	9.6	21.4	23.3	19.4
1981	11.9	13.1	10.7	10.5	11.7	9.2	20.0	21.7	18.3
1982	11.5	12.8	10.2	10.1	11.2	8.9	19.6	21.5	17.7
1983	11.2	12.3	10.0	9.7	10.8	8.6	19.2	21.1	17.2
1984	10.8	11.9	9.6	9.4	10.5	8.3	18.4	19.8	16.9
1985	10.6	11.9	9.3	9.3	10.6	8.0	18.2	19.9	16.5
1986	10.4	11.5	9.1	8.9	10.0	7.8	18.0	20.0	16.0
1987	10.1	1.2	8.9	8.6	9.6	7.6	17.9	19.6	16.0
1988	10.0	11.0	8.9	8.5	9.5	7.4	17.6	19.0	16.1

Estimated Death Rates for Selected Causes, 1989-90

Source: Natl. Center for Health Statistics, U.S. Depart. of Health and Human Services

Cause of death	Rate* 1989	Rate*P 1990	Cause of death	Rate* 1989	Rate*P 1990
All causes	868.1	861.9	Acute bronchitis and bronchiolitis	0.2	0.2
Viral hepatitis	0.6	0.7	Influenza and pneumonia	30.3	31.3
Tuberculosis, all forms	0.7	0.7	Influenza	0.6	0.8
Septicemia	7.7	7.9	Pneumonia	29.8	30.6
Syphilis	0.0	0.0	Chronic obstructive pulmonary diseases	34.0	35.5
All other infectious and parasitic diseases	11.5	12.8	Chronic and unspecified bronchitis	1.5	1.3
Malignant neoplasms, including neoplasms of lymphatic and hematopoietic tissues	200.3	201.7	Emphysema	6.3	6.6
			Asthma	2.1	1.8
			Ulcer of stomach and duodenum	2.7	2.5
Diabetes mellitus	18.8	19.5	Hernia and intestinal obstruction	2.2	2.2
Meningitis	0.4	0.5	Cirrhosis and chronic liver disease	10.6	10.2
Major cardiovascular diseases	376.4	366.9	Cholelithiasis, cholecystitis, and cholangitis	1.2	1.2
Diseases of heart	296.3	289.0	Nephritis, nephrosis and nephrotic syn.	8.6	8.3
Rheumatic fever and rheumatic heart disease	2.4	2.5	Infections of kidney	0.5	0.4
Hypertensive heart disease	8.5	8.7	Hyperplasia of prostate	0.2	0.1
Ischemic heart disease	200.6	195.1	Congenital anomalies	5.1	5.3
Acute myocardial infarction	96.5	99.5	Certain conditions in perinatal period	7.0	7.5
All other forms of heart disease	79.2	77.1	Symptoms, signs, ill-defined conditions	12.0	10.5
Hypertension	3.4	3.7	All other diseases	69.4	69.4
Cerebrovascular diseases	59.4	57.9	Accidents	38.2	37.3
Arteriosclerosis	7.7	6.6	Motor vehicle accidents	19.7	19.1
Other diseases of arteries, arterioles, and capillaries	9.6	9.7	Suicide	12.6	12.3
			Homicide	9.3	10.2
			All other external causes	1.0	0.9

*Per 100,000 population; based on a 10-percent sample of deaths. from Jan. through Nov. p = provisional.

Principal Types of Accidental Deaths

Source: National Safety Council

Year	Motor vehicle	Falls	Poison (solid, liquid)	Drowning	Fires, Burns	Injestion of Food, Object	Firearms	Poison (gases)
1970	54,633	16,926	3,679	7,860	6,718	2,753	2,406	1,620
1975	45,853	14,896	4,694	8,000	6,071	3,106	2,380	1,577
1980	53,172	13,294	3,089	7,257	5,822	3,249	1,955	1,242
1982	45,779	12,077	3,474	6,351	5,210	3,254	1,756	1,259
1983	44,452	12,024	3,382	6,353	5,028	3,387	1,695	1,251
1985	45,901	12,001	4,091	5,316	4,938	3,551	1,649	1,079
1986	47,865	11,444	4,731	5,700	4,835	3,692	1,452	1,009
1987	48,290	11,733	4,415	5,100	4,710	3,688	1,440	900
1988	48,900	12,200	5,100	4,600	4,700	4,000	1,500	900
1989	46,900	12,400	5,600	4,600	4,400	3,900	1,600	900
1990	46,300	12,400	5,700	5,200	4,300	3,200	1,400	800
Death rates per 100,000 population								
1970	26.8	8.3	1.8	3.9	3.3	1.4	1.2	0.8
1975	21.3	6.9	2.2	3.7	2.8	1.4	1.1	0.7
1980	23.4	5.9	1.4	3.2	2.6	1.4	0.9	0.5
1982	19.7	5.2	1.4	2.7	2.2	1.4	0.8	0.5
1983	19.0	5.1	1.4	2.7	2.1	1.4	0.7	0.5
1985	19.2	5.0	1.7	2.2	2.1	1.5	0.7	0.5
1986	19.9	4.7	2.0	2.4	2.0	1.5	0.6	0.4
1987	19.8	4.8	1.8	2.1	1.9	1.5	0.6	0.4
1988	19.9	5.0	2.1	1.9	1.9	1.6	0.6	0.4
1989	18.9	5.0	2.3	1.9	1.8	1.6	0.6	0.4
1990	8.6	5.0	2.3	2.1	1.7	1.3	0.6	0.3

U.S. Civil Aviation Accidents

Source: National Safety Council

1990	Accidents Total	Accidents Fatal	Deaths[1]	Accident Rates Per 100,000 Aircraft-Hours Total	Fatal	Per million Aircraft-Miles Total	Fatal
Large airlines	24	6	39	0.222	0.056	0.0055	0.0014
Commuter airlines	14	2	4	0.628	0.090	0.036	0.005
On-demand air taxis	104	26	40	3.28	0.82	—	—
General aviation	2,138	424	736	7.01	1.39	—	—

(1) Includes passengers, crew members and others.

Transportation Accident Passenger Death Rates, 1989

Source: National Safety Council

Kind of transportation	Passenger miles (billions)	Passenger deaths	Rate per 100 mln. pass. miles	1987-1989 avg. death rate
Passenger automobiles and taxis[1]	2,228.2	24,871	1.12	1.18
Buses	125.6	48	0.04	0.03
Intercity buses	24.0	3	0.01	0.03
Railroad passenger trains	13.1	8	0.06	0.07
Scheduled airlines	335.1	147	0.04	0.04

(1) Drivers of passenger automobiles are considered passengers.

Ownership of Life Insurance in the U.S. and Assets of U.S. Life Insurance Companies

Source: American Council of Life Insurance

Legal Reserve Life Insurance Companies (millions of dollars)

Year	Purchases of life insurance				Insurance in force					Assets
	Ordinary	Group	Industrial	Total	Ordinary	Group	Industrial	Credit	Total	
1940	6,689	691	3,350	10,730	79,346	14,938	20,866	380	115,530	30,802
1950	17,326	6,068	5,402	28,796	149,116	47,793	33,415	3,844	234,168	64,020
1960	52,883	14,645	6,880	74,408	341,881	175,903	39,563	29,101	586,448	119,576
1965	83,485	51,385*	7,296	142,166*	499,638	308,078	39,818	53,020	900,554	158,884
1970	122,820	63,690*	6,612	193,122*	734,730	551,357	38,644	77,392	1,402,123	207,254
1975	188,003	95,190*	6,729	289,922*	1,083,421	904,695	39,423	112,032	2,139,571	289,304
1980	385,575	183,418	3,609	572,602	1,760,474	1,579,355	35,994	165,215	3,541,038	479,210
1982	585,444	250,532	1,898	837,874	2,216,388	2,066,361	32,766	161,144	4,476,659	588,163
1983	753,444	271,609	1,388	1,026,441	2,544,275	2,219,573	31,354	170,659	4,965,861	654,948
1984	820,315	293,521	943	1,114,779	2,887,574	2,392,558	30,104	189,951	5,499,987	722,979
1985	910,944	319,503	722	1,231,169	3,247,289	2,561,595	28,250	215,973	6,053,107	825,901
1986	933,592	374,741*	418	1,308,751*	3,658,203	2,801,049	27,168	233,859	6,720,279	937,551
1987	986,660	365,529	324	1,352,513	4,139,071	3,043,782	26,668	242,977	7,452,498	1,044,459
1988	995,686	410,848	320	1,406,854	4,511,608	3,232,080	25,456	251,015	8,020,159	1,166,870
1989	1,020,719	420,707	252	1,441,678	4,939,964	3,469,498	24,446	260,107	8,694,015	1,299,756
1990	1,069,660	459,271	220	1,529,151	5,366,982	3,753,506	24,071	248,038	9,392,597	1,408,402

*Includes Servicemen's Group Life Insurance $27.8 billion in 1965, $17.1 billion in 1970, $1.7 billion in 1975, $45.6 billion in 1981, and $51.0 in 1986, as well as $84.4 billion of Federal Employees' Group Life Insurance in 1981 and $10.8 billion in 1986.

Accidental Deaths and Injuries by Severity of Injury

Source: National Safety Council

In 1990 accidental deaths were estimated to number 93,500, a decrease of 2 percent from the 1989 total. This was the ninth consecutive year that accidental deaths were estimated at less than 100,000. The death rate per 100,000 population was 37.5, down fom 39.8 in 1988. The rates for work, home, and motor vehicle deaths in 1990 were the lowest on record.

1990 Severity of injury	Total*	Motor vehicle	Work	Home	Public
Deaths*	93,500	46,300	10,500	21,500	19,000
Disabling injuries*	9,000,000	1,700,000	1,700,000	3,200,000	2,400,000
Permanent impairments. . . .	340,000	140,000	60,000	90,000	60,000
Temporary total disabilities. .	8,600,000	1,600,000	1,700,000	3,100,000	2,300,000

Certain Costs of Accidental Deaths or Injuries, 1990 (billions)

Total*	$173.8	$89.0	$63.8	$23.5	$13.4
Wage loss	48.2	25.2	10.2	7.9	7.2
Medical expense	28.4	6.2	8.7	10.0	4.1
Insurance administration	30.1	22.3	10.3	1.0	0.7

*Duplication between motor vehicle, work, and home are eliminated in the total column.

Home Accident Deaths

Source: National Safety Council

Year	Total home	Falls	Poison (solid, liquid)	Fires burns[2]	Suffo., ingesting object	Suffo., mechanical	Fire-arms	Poison (gases)	All Other
1950	29,000	14,800	1,300	5,000	(1)	1,600	950	1,250	4,100
1955	28,500	14,100	1,150	5,400	(1)	1,250	1,100	900	4,600
1960	28,000	12,300	1,350	6,350	1,850	1,500	1,200	900	2,550
1965	28,500	11,700	1,700	6,100	1,300*	1,200	1,300	1,100	4,100
1970	27,000	3,000	5,600	1,800	1,100	1,400	1,100	3,300	
1975	25,000	8,000	3,700	5,000	1,800	800	1,300	1,000	3,400
1980	22,800	7,100	2,500	4,800	2,000	500	1,100	700	4,100[3]
1985	21,600	6,500	3,200	4,000	2,400	600	900	700	3,300
1988	22,500	6,400	4,200	3,800	2,800	500	900	600	3,300
1989	22,500	6,600	4,700	3,300	2,700	700	900	600	3,000
1990	21,500	6,500	4,700	3,300	2,000	800	800	400	2,400

*Data for this year and subsequent years not comparable with previous years due to classification changes. (1) Included in Other. (2) Includes deaths resulting from conflagration, regardless of nature of injury. (3) Includes about 1,000 excessive deaths due to summer heat wave.

Pedalcycle Accidents

Source: National Safety Council

Year	Pedalcycles (millions)	Deaths	Death Rate[1]	Percent of Deaths by Age		
				0-14	15-24	25 & over
1940	7.8	750	9.59	48	39	13
1950	13.8	440	3.18	82	9	9
1960	28.2	460	1.63	78	9	13
1970	56.5	780	1.38	66	15	19
1980	82.3	1,200	1.46	35	36	29
1985	92.7	1,100	1.19	49	24	27
1988	100.7	1,100[2]	0.99	40[2]	24[2]	36[2]
1989	100.6	1,000	1.09	43	20	37
1990	102.4	1,000	0.98	38	17	45

(1) Deaths per 100,000 pedalcycles. (2) Data for 1988 and later are not comparable to prior years due to changes in estimating procedures. Note: A pedalcycle = a vehicle propelled by human power and operated solely by pedals; excludes mopeds.

Marriages and Divorces by States and Regions

Source: National Center for Health Statistics

Area	Marriages 1990 Number	Rate	Marriages 1989 Number	Rate	Divorces 1990 Number	Rate	Divorces 1989 Number	Rate
New England	112,240	8.5	117,905	9.0	44,006	3.4	45,218	3.5
Maine	11,773	9.5	12,420	10.2	5,275	4.3	5,708	4.7
New Hampshire	10,582	9.4	11,260	10.2	5,279	4.7	5,239	4.7
Vermont	6,144	10.7	6,016	10.6	2,616	4.5	2,473	4.4
Massachusetts	47,822	8.1	53,370	9.0	16,781	2.8	15,436	2.6
Rhode Island	8,113	8.1	8,235	8.3	3,754	3.7	3,627	3.6
Connecticut	27,806	8.6	26,604	8.2	10,301	3.2	12,735	3.9
Middle Atlantic	314,070	8.3	308,293	8.2	121,598	3.2	123,505	3.3
New York	169,264	9.4	161,834	9.0	57,863	3.2	59,520	3.3
New Jersey	58,012	7.5	60,551	7.8	23,612	3.0	25,644	3.3
Pennsylvania	86,794	7.2	85,908	7.1	40,123	3.3	38,341	3.2
East North Central	267,419[2]	8.7[2]	357,005	8.4	109,040[2]	4.3[2]	153,013[2]	4.2[2]
Ohio	95,827	8.7	98,136	9.0	50,989	4.7	49,273	4.5
Indiana	54,295	9.6	55,119	9.9	—	—	—	—
Illinois	—	—	85,720	7.4	—	—	45,892	3.9
Michigan	76,137	8.2	77,558	8.4	40,219	4.3	40,248	4.3
Wisconsin	41,160	8.4	40,472	8.3	17,832	3.6	17,570	3.6
West North Central	156,134	8.7	157,677	8.8	76,917	4.3	75,861	4.2
Minnesota	33,695	7.7	34,325	7.9	15,421	3.5	15,707	3.6
Iowa	24,813	8.7	24,266	8.5	11,060	3.9	9,975	3.5
Missouri	49,251	9.5	51,147	9.9	26,351	5.1	26,330	5.1
North Dakota	4,779	7.3	4,835	7.3	2,326	3.6	2,231	3.4
South Dakota	7,727	10.8	7,100	9.9	2,648	3.7	2,624	3.7
Nebraska	12,484	7.7	12,703	7.9	6,488	4.0	6,354	3.9
Kansas	23,385	9.2	23,301	9.3	12,623	5.0	12,640	5.0
South Atlantic	455,406	10.4	446,829	10.4	226,645	5.2	216,306	5.0
Delaware	5,628	8.2	5,940	8.8	2,985	4.4	2,987	4.4
Maryland	46,081	9.7	47,394	10.1	16,055	3.4	15,833	3.4
District of Columbia . . .	4,716	7.9	4,795	7.9	3,257	5.5	2,398	4.0
Virginia	71,257	11.5	68,868	11.3	27,266	4.4	25,799	4.2
West Virginia	13,166	7.2	13,354	7.2	9,658	5.3	9,379	5.1
North Carolina	52,070	7.8	50,590	7.7	34,017	5.1	32,384	4.9
South Carolina	55,837	15.7	54,335	15.5	16,080	4.5	14,859	4.2
Georgia	64,359	9.8	63,108	9.8	35,672	5.5	32,705	5.1
Florida	142,292	10.9	138,445	10.9	81,655	6.3	79,962	6.3
East South Central	185,473	12.0	182,821	11.9	93,809	6.1	91,791	6.0
Kentucky	51,291	13.8	50,208	13.5	21,790	5.8	20,629	5.5
Tennessee	66,597	13.4	65,005	13.2	32,295	6.5	32,278	6.5
Alabama	43,263	10.5	43,317	10.5	25,280	6.1	26,122	6.3
Mississippi	24,322	9.3	24,291	9.3	14,444	5.5	12,762	4.9
West South Central	292,857	10.8	281,746	10.4	136,823[2]	6.0[2]	133,466[2]	5.9[2]
Arkansas	35,703	14.8	34,612	14.4	16,765	6.9	16,372	6.8
Louisiana	41,161	9.4	38,990	8.9	—	—	—	—
Oklahoma	33,162	10.3	33,112	10.3	24,919	7.7	23,050	7.1
Texas	182,831	10.7	175,032	10.3	95,139	5.5	94,044	5.5
Mountain	127,551[2]	10.2[2]	241,901	17.9	87,031	6.3	83,897	6.2
Montana	7,025	8.7	6,698	8.3	4,093	5.1	4,090	5.1
Idaho	14,977	14.6	13,082	12.9	6,634	6.5	6,043	6.0
Wyoming	4,843	10.3	4,624	9.7	3,095	6.6	3,040	6.4
Colorado	31,512	9.4	32,219	9.7	18,385	5.5	18,709	5.6
New Mexico	13,175	8.5	12,746	8.3	7,652	4.9	7,598	5.0
Arizona	37,007	10.2	35,738	10.1	25,096	6.9	23,153	6.5
Utah	19,012	11.0	18,642	10.9	8,786	5.1	8,088	4.7
Nevada	—	—	118,152	106.3	13,290	11.4	13,176	11.9
Pacific	334,420	8.5	325,059	8.5	52,746[2]	5.6[2]	176,272	4.6
Washington	48,642	10.0	43,684	9.2	28,773	5.9	27,311	5.7
Oregon	25,211	8.8	23,485	8.3	15,884	5.5	15,099	5.4
California	236,693	7.9	234,120	8.1	—	—	124,889	4.3
Alaska	5,730	10.8	5,786	11.0	2,921	5.5	3,331	6.3
Hawaii	18,144	16.1	17,984	16.2	5,168	4.6	5,642	5.1

(1) Figures for marriages are marriage licenses issued for some counties; (2) Excludes figures for state shown below as not available; (3) Figures for marriages are marriage licenses issued; (4) Figures for divorces include estimates for some counties. Notes: Data are by State of occurrence, not residence. Figures reflect revisions.

Marriages, Divorces, and Rates in the U.S.

Source: National Center for Health Statistics

Data refer only to events occurring within the United States, including Alaska and Hawaii beginning with 1960. Rates per 1,000 population.

Year	Marriages[1] No.	Rate	Divorces[2] No.	Rate	Year	Marriages[1] No.	Rate	Divorces[2] No.	Rate
1895	620,000	8.9	40,387	0.6	1945	1,612,992	12.2	485,000	3.5[3]
1900	709,000	9.3	55,751	0.7	1950	1,667,231	11.1	385,144	2.6
1905	842,000	10.0	67,976	0.8	1955	1,531,000	9.3	377,000	2.3
1910	948,166	10.3	83,045	0.9	1960	1,523,000	8.5	393,000	2.2
1915	1,007,595	10.0	104,298	1.0	1965	1,800,000	9.3	479,000	2.5
1920	1,274,476	12.0	170,505	1.6	1970	2,158,802	10.6	708,000	3.5
1925	1,188,334	10.3	175,449	1.5	1975	2,152,662	10.0	1,036,000	4.8
1930	1,126,856	9.2	195,961	1.6	1980	2,413,000	10.6	1,182,000	5.2
1935	1,327,000	10.4	218,000	1.7	1985	2,425,000	10.2	1,187,000	5.0
1940	1,595,879	12.1	264,000	2.0	1990	2,448,000	9.8	1,175,000	4.7

(1) Includes estimates and marriage licenses for some states for all years. (2) Includes reported annulments. (3) Divorce rates for 1945 based on population including armed forces overseas.

Percent of Population Never Married, 1960-1990

Source: Bureau of the Census

Between 1970 and 1990 the proportion of 20- to 24-year-olds who had never married increased from 36 to 63 percent for women and from 55 to 79 percent for men. The proportion never married for 25- to 29-year-olds tripled for women (from 11 to 31 percent) and more than doubled for men (from 19 to 45 percent). Although the proportion never married declines as age increases, significant increases have occurred for persons in their thirties. Between 1970 and 1990, the proportion never married for persons 30 to 34 years old nearly tripled; among those 35 to 39 years old, the proportion never married doubled.

	Women				Men			
	1960	1970*	1980	1990	1960	1970*	1980	1990
Total, 15 years and over...	17.3	22.1	22.5	22.8	23.2	28.1	29.6	29.9
Under 40 years	28.1	38.5	38.8	40.5	39.6	47.7	48.8	50.6
40 years and over	7.5,	6.2	5.3	5.3	7.6	7.4	5.7	6.4
15-17 years	93.2	97.3	97.0	98.5	98.8	99.4	99.4	99.8
18 years	75.6	82.0	88.0	92.0	94.6	95.1	97.4	98.5
19 years	59.7	68.8	77.6	88.7	88.7	89.9	90.9	95.2
20-24 years	28.4	35.8	50.2	62.8	53.1	54.7	68.8	79.3
20 years	46.0	56.9	66.5	76.6	75.8	78.3	86.0	90.8
21 years	34.6	43.9	59.7	71.1	63.4	66.2	77.2	87.6
22 years	25.6	33.5	48.3	63.0	51.6	52.3	69.9	80.1
23 years	19.4	22.4	41.7	55.5	40.5	42.1	59.1	72.2
24 years	15.7	17.9	33.5	48.7	33.4	33.2	50.0	66.7
25-29 years	10.5	10.5	20.9	31.1	20.8	19.1	33.1	45.2
25 years	13.1	14.0	28.6	41.9	27.9	26.6	44.3	57.7
26 years	11.4	12.2	22.7	33.8	23.5	20.9	36.5	52.4
27 years	10.2	9.1	22.2	29.6	19.8	16.5	31.5	43.7
28 years	9.2	8.9	16.0	27.3	17.5	17.0	26.8	36.7
29 years	8.7	8.0	14.6	23.5	16.0	13.8	24.0	36.2
30-34 years	6.9	6.2	9.5	16.4	11.9	9.4	15.9	27.0
35-39 years	6.1	5.4	6.2	10.4	8.8	7.2	7.8	14.7
40-44 years	6.1	4.9	4.8	8.0	7.3	6.3	7.1	10.5
45-54 years	7.0	4.9	4.7	5.0	7.4	7.5	6.1	6.3
55-64 years	8.0	6.8	4.5	3.9	8.0	7.8	5.3	5.8
65 years and over	8.5	7.7	5.9	4.9	7.7	7.5	4.9	4.2

* Figures for 1970 include persons 14 years of age.

Median Age at First Marriage, 1890-1990

Source: Bureau of the Census

In 1890, the estimated median age at first marriage was 26.1 years for men and 22.0 years for women. At that time, a decline in the median age at first marriage began that did not end until 1956, when the median reached a low of 20.1 years for women and 22.5 years for men. The 66-year decline was reversed between 1956 and 1990, as the median returned to the 1890 level of 26.1 years for men and an even higher 23.6 median for women.

Year	Men	Women	Year	Men	Women
1890	26.1	22.0	1960	22.8	20.3
1900	25.9	21.9	1965	22.8	20.6
1910	25.1	21.6	1970	23.2	20.8
1920	24.6	21.2	1975	23.5	21.1
1930	24.3	21.3	1980	24.7	22.0
1940	24.3	21.5	1985	25.5	23.3
1950	22.8	20.3	1989	26.2	23.8
1955	22.6	20.2	1990	26.1	23.9

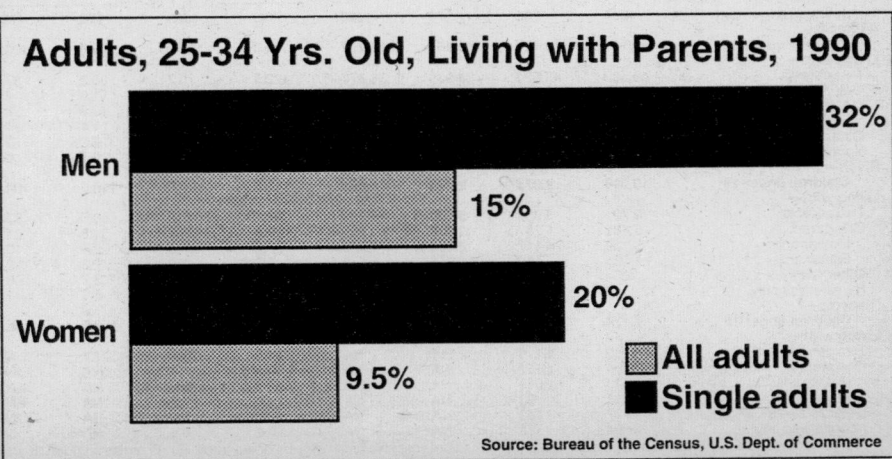

Adults, 25-34 Yrs. Old, Living with Parents, 1990

Men 32%
15%

Women 20%
9.5%

All adults
Single adults

Source: Bureau of the Census, U.S. Dept. of Commerce

Children in Families of 2 Parents, Divorced Parent, and Never-Married Parent, 1960-1990

Source: Bureau of the Census; Federal Centers for Disease Control

Only 4.2% of children lived with a never-married parent in 1960; in 1970, the percentage rose to 6.8; by 1980, to 14.6, and as of 1990, it had climbed to 30.6, according to the Bureau of the Census. Babies born to single women in 1988—the latest year for which such statistics were available—represented 26 percent of all American new-borns, the highest proportion ever; and most of the mothers were at least 20 years old, according to the Federal Centers for Disease Control. The sharpest increases in birthrates from 1980 to 1988 were among older women, with the birthrate for single women age 15 to 17 rising 29 percent and the birthrate for women age 30 to 34 rising 52 percent. The rate among single black women was 89 births per 1,000, compared with 27 for single white women. However, the rate among white women grew 51 percent from 1980 to 1988, while the rate among black women increased only by 7 percent. Children living with one divorced parent increased from 23.0% in 1960 to 30.2% in 1970, and 42.4 percent in 1980; between 1980 and 1990 there was a decline to 38.6%. Children living with 2 parents in 1960 represented 87.7 percent; in 1970, 85.2%; in 1980, 76.7%; and in 1990, 72.5%.

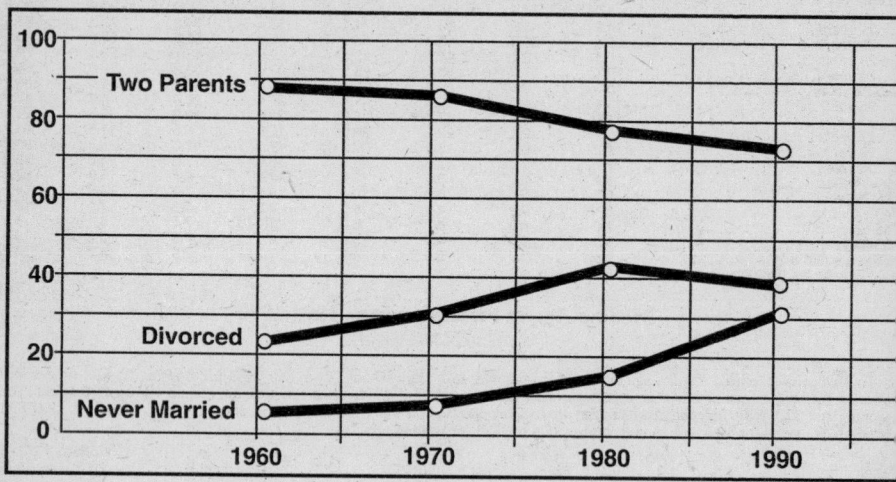

Living Arrangements of Children, 1960-1990

Source: Bureau of the Census

(Numbers in thousands. Excludes persons under age 18 who were maintaining households or family groups.)

Living arrangement	1990	1980	1970	1960	% distribution 1990	1980	1970	1960
All Races								
Children under 18 ..	64,137	63,427	69,162	63,727	100.0	100.0	100.0	100.0
Living with—								
Two parents	46,503	48,624	58,939	55,877	72.5	76.7	85.2	87.7
One parent	15,867	12,466	8,199	5,829	24.7	19.7	11.9	9.1
Mother only	13,874	11,406	7,452	5,105	21.6	18.0	10.8	8.0
Father only	1,993	1,060	748	724	3.1	1.7	1.1	1.1
Other relatives	1,422	1,949	1,547	1,601	2.2	3.1	2.2	2.5
Nonrelatives only.....	346	388	477	420	0.5	0.6	0.7	0.7
Black—[1]								
Children under 18 ..	10,018	9,375	9,422	8,650	100.0	100.0	100.0	100.0
Living with—								
Two parents	3,781	3,956	5,508	5,795	37.7	42.2	58.5	67.0
One parent	5,485	4,297	2,996	1,897	54.8	45.8	31.8	21.9
Mother only	5,132	4,117	2,783	1,723	51.2	43.9	29.5	19.9
Father only	353	180	213	173	3.5	1.9	2.3	2.0
Other relatives	654	999	820	827	6.5	10.7	8.7	9.6
Nonrelatives only.....	98	123	97	132	1.0	1.3	1.0	1.5
Hispanic—[2]								
Children under 18 ..	7,174	5,459	4,006[3]	NA	100.0	100.0	100.0	NA
Living with—								
Two parents	4,789	4,116	3,111	NA	66.8	75.4	77.7	NA
One parent	2,154	1,152	NA	NA	30.0	21.1	NA	NA
Mother only	1,943	1,069	NA	NA	27.1	19.6	NA	NA
Father only	211	83	NA	NA	2.9	1.5	NA	NA
Other relatives	177	183	NA	NA	2.5	3.4	NA	NA
Nonrelatives only....	54	8	NA	NA	0.8	0.1	NA	NA

NA = Not available. (1) Black & other races, 1960. (2) Persons of Hispanic origin may be of any race. (3) All persons under 18 yrs.

Divorced Persons Per 1,000 Married Persons With Spouse Present, 1960-1990

Source: Bureau of the Census, U.S. Dept. of Commerce

	Total	Race White	Black	Hispanic[1]		Total	Race White	Black	Hispanic[1]
Both sexes:					1970	35	32	62	40
1990	142	133	282	129	1960	28	27	45	(NA)
1980	100	92	203	98	Female:				
1970	47	44	83	61	1990	166	153	358	155
1960	35	33	62	(NA)	1980	120	110	258	132
Male:					1970	60	56	104	81
1990	118	112	208	103	1960	42	38	78	(NA)
1980	79	74	149	64					

NA-Not available. (1) Persons of Hispanic origin may be of any race.

Cohabitation and Marriage in the U.S., 1988

Source: National Center for Health Statistics, U.S. Dept. of Health and Human Services

Race, age, and Hispanic origin	Number (in thousands)	Cohabited before first marriage[1] Percent	Ever cohabited	Ever married
Total[2]				
All ages	57,900	25.4	33.5	63.6
15-19 years ...	9,179	8.2	8.4	3.7
20-24 years ...	9,413	30.3	32.4	38.6
25-29 years ...	10,796	39.1	45.1	71.0
30-34 years ...	10,930	33.3	44.9	84.4
35-39 years ...	9,583	23.9	38.4	89.5
40-44 years ...	7,999	12.3	26.3	92.5
White				
All ages	47,077	25.0	33.6	66.8
15-19 years ...	7,313	9.2	9.3	4.4
20-24 years ...	7,401	31.6	34.2	42.9
25-29 years ...	8,672	37.9	44.7	75.5
30-34 years ...	9,010	32.6	44.9	86.8
35-39 years ...	7,936	22.4	37.7	91.7
40-44 years ...	6,745	11.0	25.3	93.7
Black				
All ages	7,679	29.3	35.0	47.1
15-19 years ...	1,409	3.7	3.7	1.5
20-24 years ...	1,364	28.6	29.0	23.6
25-29 years ...	1,459	44.3	47.8	47.7
30-34 years ...	1,406	42.0	52.1	69.0
35-39 years ...	1,170	34.3	45.0	75.1
40-44 years ...	872	19.4	32.8	83.5
Hispanic origin				
Hispanic.....	5,557	25.5	32.9	62.1
Non-Hispanic ..	52,343	25.4	33.5	63.8

(1) Includes women who had cohabited but had not married. (2) Includes white, black, and other races. **Note:** Because of rounding of estimates, figures may not add to totals.

Child Care Arrangements in the U.S., 1988

Source: National Center for Health Statistics, U.S. Dept. of Health and Human Services

Characteristic	Number of children (in thousands)	Care in child's home Father	Grandparent	Other relative	Nonrelative	Care in another home Grandparent	Other relative	Nonrelative	Group care Nursery or preschool	Day care center[1]	Mother, while working
								Percent distribution[2]			
All children[3]	13,259	12.9	6.0	2.6	7.6	8.7	2.6	21.3	23.4	7.8	4.8
Age and school status											
Under 2 years	3,772	15.4	8.8	2.5	10.2	9.7	3.7	28.1	—	11.8	6.6
2-3 years	4,609	12.5	4.7	2.3	7.5	9.3	2.8	21.1	28.8	3.8	4.5
4-5 years, not in school	3,421	9.6	3.1	2.6	4.5	7.0	1.3	14.7	49.7	2.7	3.6
4-5 years, in school ..	1,323	16.4	9.5	3.8	8.7	7.6	1.5	19.1	—	25.7	3.3
Race											
White	10,854	13.2	4.7	2.1	8.2	7.6	2.3	22.9	23.6	7.6	5.4
Black	1,830	9.2	11.0	5.8	3.3	16.2	4.3	15.2	21.4	10.5	1.4
Hispanic origin											
Hispanic.........	1,352	10.1	8.0	8.1	6.7	10.2	4.9	22.7	21.1	5.1	1.9
Non-Hispanic......	11,331	12.8	5.6	2.0	7.7	8.6	2.3	21.2	23.8	8.1	5.2
Family income											
Less than $10,000...	1,119	12.6	6.7	5.5	5.5	13.0	3.4	13.1	25.1	6.5	5.5
$10,000-$24,999....	3,635	17.9	5.7	3.6	5.5	10.2	2.9	21.9	18.2	6.0	6.1
$25,000-$39,999....	3,635	13.4	4.7	1.5	6.4	9.3	2.6	23.7	22.7	9.0	4.6
$40,000 or more	3,613	8.5	4.8	1.8	10.7	6.2	1.6	22.1	28.7	8.5	3.5
Geographic region											
Northeast.........	2,242	17.0	8.3	1.8	10.5	9.8	2.0	17.5	20.0	6.9	4.5
Midwest..........	3,492	14.7	5.1	2.3	7.8	7.2	2.0	26.5	20.1	6.1	5.5
South	4,596	10.0	5.8	2.7	6.2	10.8	3.3	19.1	25.8	10.2	3.8
West	2,913	12.1	5.5	3.4	7.1	6.1	2.5	21.3	26.2	6.9	5.6
Place of residence											
MSA:											
Central city	4,035	10.9	8.9	4.2	7.5	9.9	2.3	18.9	24.1	7.3	3.4
Not central city	6,182	13.5	4.9	1.5	7.6	6.9	2.6	21.4	25.3	9.0	5.0
Not MSA	3,042	14.3	4.1	2.7	7.6	10.6	2.8	24.1	18.7	6.3	6.1
Mother's education											
Less than 12 years ..	1,488	16.5	6.8	9.4	6.6	10.3	3.6	15.3	19.7	3.7	4.2
12 years	5,308	13.3	7.7	2.5	6.5	9.8	3.5	21.5	21.4	7.2	4.1
More than 12 years ..	6,446	11.7	4.4	1.1	8.7	7.4	1.6	22.4	25.9	9.3	5.4
Mother's employment status											
Employed........	10,060	15.6	6.2	2.6	7.5	9.8	2.8	24.2	16.0	8.4	5.6
Not employed[4]	2,033	0.9	3.2	0.7	6.4	4.0	0.9	8.8	62.7	5.2	0.1

(1) Includes kindergarten extended day care and day camp. (2) Percents exclude unknown values for main source of care from numerator and denominator; numbers of children include those with missing values. (3) Includes other races and unknown origin, income, education, and employment status; also includes "other" group care. (4) Includes looking for work and not in the labor force.

Note: MSA = metropolitan statistical area.

Living Arrangements of Young Adults, 1960-1990

Source: Bureau of the Census; U.S. Dept. of Commerce

(in thousands)

Living arrangement	1960	1970	1980	1990	Percent distribution 1960	1970	1980	1990
Adults 18–24 Years, Total	14,718	22,357	29,122	25,310	100.0	100.0	100.0	100.0
Male	6,842	10,398	14,278	12,450	100.0	100.0	100.0	100.0
Child of householder[1]	3,583	5,641	7,755	7,232	52.4	54.3	54.3	58.1
Family householder or spouse	2,160	3,119	3,041	1,838	31.6	30.0	21.3	14.8
Nonfamily householder	182	563	1,581	1,228	2.7	5.4	11.1	9.9
Other	917	1,075	1,902	2,152	13.4	10.3	13.3	17.3
Female	7,876	11,959	14,844	12,860	100.0	100.0	100.0	100.0
Child of householder[1]	2,750	4,941	6,336	6,135	34.9	41.3	42.7	47.7
Family householder or spouse	4,026	5,351	5,367	3,793	51.1	44.7	36.2	29.5
Nonfamily householder	172	503	1,195	1,024	2.2	4.2	8.1	8.0
Other	928	1,164	1,946	1,908	11.8	9.7	13.1	14.8
Adults 25–34 Years, Total	22,483	24,556	36,796	43,240	100.0	100.0	100.0	100.0
Male	10,896	11,929	18,107	21,462	100.0	100.0	100.0	100.0
Child of householder	1,185	1,129	1,894	3,213	10.9	9.5	10.5	15.0
Family householder or spouse	8,557	9,455	12,024	11,998	78.5	79.3	66.4	55.9
Nonfamily householder	398	775	2,765	3,467	3.7	6.5	15.3	16.2
Other	756	570	1,424	2,784	6.9	4.8	7.9	13.0
Female	11,587	12,637	18,689	21,779	100.0	100.0	100.0	100.0
Child of householder	853	829	1,300	1,774	7.4	6.6	7.0	8.1
Family householder or spouse	9,981	10,877	14,591	15,966	86.1	86.1	78.1	73.3
Nonfamily householder	244	440	1,646	2,151	2.1	3.5	8.8	9.9
Other	509	491	1,153	1,888	4.4	3.9	6.2	8.7

(1) Child of householder includes unmarried college students living in dormitories.

Living Arrangements of the Elderly: 1980 and 1990

Source: Bureau of the Census, U.S. Dept. of Commerce

(in thousands)

Living arrangement and age	1990 Total	Men	Women	Percent distribution Men	Women	1980 Total	Men	Women	1980 Percent distribution Men	Women
65 years and over	29,566	12,334	17,232	100.0	100.0	24,157	9,889	14,268	100.0	100.0
Alone	9,176	1,942	7,233	15.7	42.0	7,067	1,447	5,620	14.6	39.4
With spouse	16,003	9,158	6,845	74.3	39.7	12,781	7,441	5,340	75.2	37.4
With other relatives	3,734	953	2,782	7.7	16.1	3,892	832	3,060	8.4	21.4
With nonrelatives only	653	281	372	2.3	2.2	417	169	248	1.7	1.7
65 to 74 years	17,979	8,013	9,966	100.0	100.0	15,302	6,621	8,681	100.0	100.0
Alone	4,350	1,042	3,309	13.0	33.2	3,750	797	2,953	12.0	34.0
With spouse	11,353	6,265	5,089	78.2	51.1	9,436	5,285	4,151	79.8	47.8
With other relatives	1,931	528	1,401	6.6	14.1	1,890	436	1,454	6.6	16.7
With nonrelatives only	345	178	167	2.2	1.7	226	103	123	1.6	1.4
75 to 84 years	9,354	3,562	5,792	100.0	100.0	7,172	2,708	4,464	100.0	100.0
Alone	3,774	688	3,086	19.3	53.3	2,664	505	2,159	18.6	48.4
With spouse	4,145	2,537	1,607	71.2	27.7	2,977	1,882	1,095	69.5	24.5
With other relatives	1,237	264	974	7.4	16.8	1,394	271	1,123	10.0	25.2
With nonrelatives only	198	73	125	2.0	2.2	137	50	87	1.8	1.9
85 years and over	2,233	758	1,475	100.0	100.0	1,683	560	1,123	100.0	100.0
Alone	1,051	213	838	28.1	56.8	653	145	508	25.9	45.2
With spouse	505	356	150	47.0	10.2	368	274	94	48.9	8.4
With other relatives	567	160	406	21.1	27.5	608	125	483	22.3	43.0
With nonrelatives only	110	29	81	3.8	5.5	54	16	38	2.9	3.4

Persons Living Alone, 1970-1990

Source: Bureau of the Census, U.S. Dept. of Commerce

(in thousands)

Between 1970 and 1990, the number of women living alone increased by 91 percent, and the number of men living along increased by 156 percent. As of 1990, more than 1 in every 9 adults age 15 and over lived alone, 61 percent of them women and the number of men fast increasing.

Age	1970[1]	1980	1990	Percent distribution 1970[1]	1980	1990
Both sexes	10,851	18,296	22,999	100.0	100.0	100.0
Men	3,532	6,966	9,049	100.0	100.0	100.0
15 to 24 years	274	947	674	7.8	13.6	7.4
25 to 34 years	535	1,975	2,395	15.1	28.4	26.5
35 to 44 years	398	945	1,836	11.3	13.6	20.3
45 to 54 years	513	804	1,167	14.5	11.5	12.9
55 to 64 years	639	809	1,036	18.1	11.6	11.4
65 to 74 years	611	775	1,042	17.3	11.1	11.5
75 years and over	563	711	901	15.9	10.2	10.0
Median age	55.7	40.9	42.5	(X)	(X)	(X)
Women	7,319	11,330	13,950	100.0	100.0	100.0
15 to 24 years	282	779	536	3.9	6.9	3.8
25 to 34 years	358	1,284	1,578	4.9	11.3	11.3
35 to 44 years	313	525	1,303	4.3	4.6	9.3
45 to 54 years	790	901	1,256	10.8	8.0	9.0
55 to 64 years	1,680	2,000	2,044	23.0	17.7	14.7
65 to 74 years	2,204	3,076	3,309	30.1	27.1	23.7
75 years and over	1,693	2,766	3,924	23.1	24.4	28.1
Median age	66.1	65.6	65.8	(X)	(X)	(X)

(X) Not applicable. (1) 1970 data are for persons 14 years and over.

Physicians by Age, Sex, and Selected Specialties

Source: American Medical Association, Jan. 1, 1989

	Total Physicians* Male	Female	Under 35 yrs. Male	Female	35–44 yrs. Male	Female	45–54 yrs. Male	Female	55–64 yrs. Male	Female
Total Physicians	502,343	98,446	100,717	37,811	143,114	33,648	99,186	13,384	75,903	6,620
Anesthesiology	20,935	4,432	5,724	1,348	6,443	1,559	4,175	949	3,288	392
Cardiovascular Disease	14,657	788	2,632	262	5,698	347	3,437	114	1,822	47
Child Psychiatry	2,805	1,418	339	267	967	576	808	316	491	169
Dermatology	5,846	1,495	836	649	1,975	554	1,542	194	860	65
Diagnostic Radiology	12,716	2,271	3,711	1,084	4,864	892	2,817	219	971	59
Emergency Medicine	11,825	1,925	2,910	800	5,869	825	1,700	210	914	74
Family Practice	38,699	7,603	10,729	3,868	14,160	2,686	5,201	647	5,513	260
Gastroenterology	6,802	414	1,297	174	3,046	185	1,586	43	590	8
General Practice	21,682	2,398	701	218	2,432	683	3,788	613	6,505	478
General Surgery	35,977	2,263	9,342	1,417	8,627	638	7,551	129	6,253	47
Internal Medicine	59,965	14,147	20,269	7,839	17,992	4,441	8,746	1,173	7,529	484
Internal Med. Subspecialities	19,331	4,043	3,126	1,289	8,407	1,923	4,799	531	2,018	200
Neurology	7,613	1,393	1,602	505	3,039	590	1,800	196	850	76
Obstetrics/Gynecology	26,052	7,043	4,354	3,354	7,625	2,341	6,437	842	4,930	326
Ophthalmology	14,487	1,473	2,701	658	4,163	538	3,867	156	2,227	76
Orthopedic Surgery	18,353	388	4,322	212	5,495	135	4,697	19	2,624	14
Otolaryngology	7,622	390	1,519	196	2,154	148	2,200	23	1,038	15
Pathology-Anat./Clin.	12,449	3,585	1,906	1,037	3,453	1,375	3,221	726	2,750	312
Pediatrics	24,603	14,854	5,866	6,249	8,117	5,268	5,136	2,115	3,494	803
Physical Med./Rehab.	2,800	1,139	821	350	858	430	477	208	401	121
Plastic surgery	4,204	288	525	77	1,563	138	1,316	47	577	18
Psychiatry	26,753	7,817	3,721	2,258	7,135	2,658	6,780	1,449	5,676	900
Pulmonary Diseases	5,508	483	1,048	173	2,635	199	1,134	60	420	25
Public Health	1,566	477	75	44	324	106	342	85	386	127
Radiation Oncology	2,264	478	535	151	720	207	583	93	305	19
Radiology	7,747	776	458	165	1,231	282	2,752	195	2,217	105
Other	6,223	949	643	162	1,350	309	1,330	182	1,488	173
Unspecified	5,303	1,660	3,090	1,135	926	318	420	117	389	54

*Includes those in 12 specialities with relatively few practitioners, those 65 years and over, those living in U.S. possessions, APO's and FPO's; and those "Inactive," "Not Classified," and with "Address Unknown."

Wanted and Unwanted Childbearing in the U.S., 1973-1988

Source: National Center for Health Statistics, U.S. Dept. of Health and Human Services

Of the nearly 16.2 million births to ever-married women that occurred from 1983 through 1988, about 5.8 million, or 35 percent, were unintended. Of those, about 30 percent were unwanted, and the other 70 percent were mistimed (wanted at a later time). The most recent statistics show an apparent increase in unwanted births for the first time since the widespread acceptance of the most effective methods of contraception. Between surveys conducted in 1973 and 1982, the proportion of recent births to ever-married women that were unwanted at the time of conception was cut almost in half, from 14.3 percent to 7.7 percent. However, the most recent data suggest that the proportion has once again risen to over 10 percent, and the pattern is consistent across subgroups of age, race, marital status, and income level.

	Births in the last 5 years 1973	1982	1988	Wanted at conception Total 1973	1982	1988	Mistimed 1973	1982	1988	Unwanted at conception 1973	1982	1988
All races[1]	Number in thousands[2]			Percent distribution								
All ages	15,901	16,300	16,466	85.6	92.1	89.5	24.0	24.0	25.0	14.3	7.7	10.3
15–24 years	5,028	4,133	2,982	91.8	94.3	91.1	39.4	43.8	42.6	8.0	5.7	8.6
25–34 years	9,105	10,176	10,794	86.3	93.1	90.8	18.3	18.5	23.3	13.5	6.7	9.0
35–44 years	1,768	1,991	2,690	64.2	82.7	82.2	9.5	11.3	12.2	35.6	17.1	17.6

(1) Includes white, black, and other races. (2) Includes births of unknown wantedness status.

Induced Terminations of Pregnancy in the U.S., 1982-1988

Source: National Center for Health Statistics, U.S. Dept. of Health and Human Services

(Ratios per 1,000 live births.)

Age of woman	1988 All races[1]	White	Black	1982-88 All races[1]	White	Black	1987-88 All races[1]	White	Black
	Ratio			Percent change			Percent change		
All ages	325.4	265.8	598.1	−12.4	−16.7	−7.8	−3.7	−3.0	−5.8
Under 14 years	1,576.1	1,786.3	1,477.7	−14.8	−21.4	−11.1	−7.6	−2.4	−11.7
14 years	1,038.5	1,305.0	876.7	−17.4	−13.5	−17.6	−9.4	4.8	−18.8
15–19 years	663.9	666.0	666.9	−7.9	−11.2	−0.3	−2.9	−2.1	−4.9
20–24 years	393.7	331.7	622.3	−1.3	−5.4	−2.2	−1.7	−1.0	−4.6
25–29 years	225.2	171.3	536.6	−7.5	−10.5	−9.6	−3.1	−2.3	−5.5
30–34 years	195.8	146.5	515.4	−19.6	−22.4	−17.5	−6.4	−6.1	−7.5
35–39 years	285.8	228.3	622.8	−30.3	−32.2	−25.2	−7.1	−5.1	−9.9
40 years and over	499.9	426.9	851.1	−35.4	−37.3	−29.6	−12.0	−11.7	−14.4

(1) Includes races other than white and black. Note: Data on induced terminations of pregnancy in 1988 come from a 14-state area and for 1982-1987, from a 13-state area. The 14-State area includes Colorado, Indiana, Kansas, Maine, Missouri, Montana, New York, Oregon, Rhode Island, South Carolina, Tennessee, Utah, Vermont, and Virginia. The 13-State area includes Colorado, Indiana, Kansas, Missouri, Montana, New York, Oregon, Rhode Island, South Carolina, Tennessee, Utah, Vermont, and Virginia.

AIDS Deaths, 1989 and 1990

Source: National Center for Health Statistics

Sex and age	All races[1] 1989 Number	Rate[2]	1990 Number	Rate[2]	White 1989 Number	Rate[2]	1990 Number	Rate[2]	Black 1989 Number	Rate[2]	1990 Number	Rate[2]
Both sexes												
All ages	21,360	8.6	24,120	9.6	14,730	7.0	16,580	7.9	6,470	21.1	7,320	23.5
Under 15 years	250	0.5	390	0.7	140	0.3	140	0.3	110	1.3	240	2.8
15-24 years	500	1.4	580	1.6	320	1.1	270	0.9	180	3.3	310	5.8
25-34 years	7,400	16.9	8,460	19.3	4,810	13.1	5,720	15.7	2,540	45.6	2,660	47.4
35-44 years	8,620	23.6	9,730	25.7	6,060	19.4	6,680	20.7	2,480	62.2	2,960	70.8
45-54 years	2,990	12.0	3,240	12.7	2,170	10.1	2,510	11.4	800	30.6	710	26.5
55 years and over	1,570	3.0	1,690	3.2	1,220	2.6	1,240	2.6	340	7.2	430	9.0
Not stated	20	—	20	—	10	—	10	—	10	—	10	—
Age-adjusted rate	—	8.3	—	9.1	—	6.7	—	7.4	—	21.7	—	23.8
Male												
All ages	19,060	15.8	21,140	17.3	13,750	13.5	15,360	14.9	5,140	35.3	5,590	37.8
Under 15 years	110	0.4	260	0.9	70	0.3	110	0.5	40	0.9	140	3.2
15-24 years	420	2.3	410	2.3	270	1.8	220	1.5	150	5.6	190	7.2
25-34 years	6,490	29.6	7,220	33.0	4,450	24.0	5,180	28.1	1,990	75.6	1,960	73.9
34-44 years	7,860	43.6	8,740	46.7	5,790	37.2	6,350	39.4	1,990	109.5	2,320	121.5
45-54 years	2,780	23.0	3,040	24.5	2,090	19.8	2,390	22.1	670	57.3	630	52.6
55 years and over	1,390	6.1	1,450	6.3	1,070	5.3	1,090	5.3	300	15.0	340	16.7
Not stated	10	—	20	—	10	—	10	—	—	—	10	—
Age adjusted rate	—	15.0	—	16.3	—	12.6	—	13.8	—	37.7	—	39.7
Female												
All ages	2,300	1.8	2,980	2.3	970	0.9	1,220	1.1	1,330	8.3	1,730	10.6
Under 15 years	140	0.5	130	0.5	70	0.3	30	0.1	70	1.7	100	2.4
15-24 years	80	0.4	170	1.0	50	0.3	50	0.3	30	1.1	120	4.4
25-34 years	910	4.2	1,240	5.7	360	2.0	540	3.0	550	18.7	690	23.3
35-44 years	760	4.1	990	5.2	270	1.7	330	2.0	490	22.6	640	28.2
45-54 years	210	1.6	200	1.5	80	0.7	120	1.1	130	9.0	80	5.4
55 years and over	180	0.6	240	0.8	140	0.5	150	0.6	40	1.5	90	3.3
Not stated	10	—	—	—	—	—	—	—	10	—	—	—
Age-adjusted rate	—	1.7	—	2.3	—	0.8	—	1.1	—	8.1	—	10.2

(1) Includes races other than white and black. (2) Figures for age not stated are included in "All ages" but are not distributed among age groups. Notes: AIDS = human immunodeficiency virus infection. Data are provisional, estimated from a 10-percent sample of deaths. Rates per 100,000 population in specified group. Figures may differ from those previously published. Due to rounding of estimates, figures may not add to totals.

Developmental, Learning, and Emotional Problems of U.S. Children, 1988

Source: National Center for Health Statistics, U.S. Dept. of Health and Human Services

Characteristic	All ages 3–17 years	3–5 years	6–11 years	12–17 years	Characteristic	All ages 3–17 years	3–5 years	6–11 years	12–17 years
	Percent								
All children[1]	19.5	9.5	19.1	25.2	Central city	18.7	8.0	19.2	24.1
Sex					Not central city	20.1	8.9	19.6	26.1
Male	22.9	10.5	22.8	29.2	Not MSA	19.4	12.3	17.9	24.6
Female	16.0	8.5	15.4	20.8	**Assessed health status**				
Race					Excellent, very good, good	19.1	8.9	18.7	24.8
White	20.7	10.0	20.3	26.7	Fair or poor	35.3	25.7	35.7	39.3
Black	14.9	5.0	14.8	19.5	**Mother's education**				
Hispanic origin					Less than 12 years	20.3	10.2	18.4	26.2
Hispanic	17.2	8.5	19.6	19.2	12 years	19.0	11.2	18.8	23.2
Non-Hispanic	19.9	9.7	19.1	25.8	More than 12 years	19.3	7.3	19.4	26.3
Family income					**Family structure**				
Less than $10,000	22.8	11.5	23.8	28.6	Biological mother and father	14.6	8.1	14.4	19.2
$10,000-$24,999	21.0	10.1	21.3	27.3	Biological mother and stepfather	29.6	14.4	27.0	34.5
$25,000-$39,999	19.5	11.3	17.6	26.0	Biological mother only[2]	24.8	11.7	24.5	31.4
$40,000 or more	18.6	6.8	18.0	24.1	All other	28.2	13.5	29.7	31.4
Place of residence									
MSA	19.6	8.5	19.5	25.4					

(1) Includes other races and unknown sociodemographic and health characteristics; "emotional problem" lasted 3 months or more or required psychological help. (2) Includes families in which the mother lived with the child's grandmother or other adult relative. Note: MSA = metropolitan statistical area.

Per Capita Spending on Mental Health Programs, By State

Source: Dept. of Health and Human Services; figures, for 1987, are rounded.

Rank	Spending	Rank	Spending	Rank	Spending	Rank	Spending
1. N.Y.	$140	14. N.H.	$51	27. Colo.	$36	40. Nev.	$28
2. D.C.	129	15. N.J.	51	28. Mont.	36	41. Ark.	27
3. Pa.	68	16. Ohio	45	29. Oregon	34	42. La.	25
4. Conn.	68	17. S.C.	44	30. Fla.	34	43. Hawaii	25
5. Mich.	67	18. Ind.	44	31. Utah	33	44. Ill.	24
6. Mass.	62	19. Kan.	44	32. Iowa	32	45. N.M.	24
7. Del.	57	20. N.D.	42	33. Mo.	31	46. Ky.	23
8. Minn.	54	21. N.C.	40	34. Wis.	31	47. W.Va.	23
9. Md.	54	22. Va.	39	35. S.D.	31	48. Miss.	22
10. Alaska	53	23. Calif.	37	36. Okla.	31	49. Tex.	21
11. Maine	53	24. Tenn.	36	37. Wyo.	30	50. Ariz.	20
12. R.I.	52	25. Wash.	36	38. Ala.	29	51. Idaho	17
13. Vt.	52	26. Ga.	36	39. Neb.	28		

U.S. Health Expenditures, 1960-1990

Source: Health Care Financing Administration. Office of the Actuary; data from Office of National Health Statistics

(in billions of dollars)

Type of expenditure	1960	1970	1980	1985	1986	1987	1988	1989	1990
National health expenditures	$27.1	$74.4	$250.1	$422.6	$454.8	$494.1	$546.0	$602.8	$666.2
Health services & supplies	25.4	69.1	238.9	407.2	438.9	476.8	526.2	582.1	643.4
Personal health care	23.9	64.9	219.4	369.7	400.8	439.3	482.8	529.9	585.3
Hospital care	9.3	27.9	102.4	168.3	179.8	194.2	212.0	232.6	256.0
Physician services	5.3	13.6	41.9	74.0	82.1	93.0	105.1	113.6	125.7
Dental services	2.0	4.7	14.4	23.3	24.7	27.1	29.4	31.6	34.0
Other professional services	0.6	1.5	8.7	16.6	18.6	21.1	23.8	27.1	31.6
Home health care	0.0	0.1	1.3	3.8	4.0	4.1	4.5	5.6	6.9
Drugs & other medical nondurables	4.2	8.8	21.6	36.2	39.7	43.2	46.3	50.6	54.6
Vision products & other medical durables	0.8	2.0	4.6	7.1	8.1	9.1	10.1	11.4	12.1
Nursing home care	1.0	4.9	20.0	34.1	36.7	39.7	42.8	47.7	53.1
Other personal health care	0.7	1.4	4.6	6.4	7.1	7.8	8.7	9.7	11.3
Program administration & net cost of private health insurance	1.2	2.8	12.2	25.2	24.6	22.9	26.8	33.9	38.7
Government public health activities	0.4	1.4	7.2	12.3	13.5	14.6	16.6	18.3	19.3
Research & construction	1.7	5.3	11.3	15.4	16.0	17.3	19.8	20.7	22.8
Research[1]	0.7	2.0	5.4	7.8	8.5	9.0	10.3	11.0	12.4
Construction	1.0	3.4	5.8	7.6	7.4	8.2	9.5	9.6	10.4

Average annual % change from previous year shown

National health expenditures	—	10.6	12.9	11.1	7.6	8.6	10.5	10.4	10.5
Health services & supplies	—	10.5	13.2	11.3	7.8	8.7	10.3	10.6	10.5
Personal health care	—	10.5	13.0	11.0	8.4	9.6	9.9	9.8	10.5
Hospital care	—	11.7	13.9	10.4	6.8	8.0	9.2	9.7	10.1
Physician services	—	9.9	11.9	12.1	10.9	13.3	13.1	8.0	10.7
Dental services	—	9.1	11.9	10.1	6.4	9.6	8.5	7.3	7.6
Other professional services	—	9.6	19.1	13.8	12.0	13.6	12.4	14.0	16.6
Home health care	—	14.5	25.2	23.3	3.6	3.6	9.6	24.9	22.5
Drugs & other medical nondurables	—	7.6	9.4	10.8	9.9	8.6	7.2	9.3	7.9
Vision products & other medical durables	—	9.6	8.5	9.4	13.0	12.3	11.8	12.9	6.1
Nursing home care	—	17.4	15.2	11.3	7.6	8.0	7.8	11.5	11.4
Other personal health care	—	7.1	12.8	6.9	11.1	10.0	12.1	11.2	16.4
Program administration & net cost of private health insurance	—	9.0	16.0	15.5	-2.5	-6.6	16.9	26.6	14.1
Government public health activities	—	13.9	18.0	11.3	9.6	8.3	13.5	10.4	5.6
Research & construction	—	12.1	7.8	6.4	3.7	8.2	14.9	4.3	10.2
Research[1]	—	10.9	10.8	7.4	9.5	5.7	14.5	6.8	11.9
Construction	—	12.8	5.6	5.4	-2.4	11.1	15.3	1.5	8.3

(1) Research and development expenditures of drug companies and other manufacturers and providers of medical equipment and supplies are excluded from "research expenditures," but included in the expenditure class in which the product falls. **Note:** Numbers may not add to totals because of rounding.

Average Length of Stay for Inpatients at Short-Stay Hospitals, 1989

Source: National Center for Health Statistics; discharges from non-Federal hospitals. excluding newborn infants

Selected characteristic	Average length of stay in days Both sexes	Male	Female	Selected characteristic	Average length of stay in days Both sexes	Male	Female
All patients. . . .	6.5	7.0	6.1	Region			
Age				Northeast	7.7	8.0	7.4
Under 15 years. .	4.9	4.9	4.9	Midwest	6.4	6.9	6.1
15-44 years. . . .	4.7	6.2	4.1	South	6.3	6.9	5.9
45-64 years. . . .	6.7	6.7	6.6	West	5.4	6.2	4.9
65 years and over	8.9	8.6	9.1				

Inpatient Surgeries

Source: National Center for Health Statistics

(Data are for non-federal short-stay hospitals and exclude newborn infants)

	Number in thousands 1988	1989	Rate per 10,000 population 1988	1989		Number in thousands 1988	1989	Rate per 10,000 population 1988	1989
All surgical procedures.	39,192	40,043	1,605.4	16,241.1	Hemic & lymphatic system	392	385	16.1	156.1
Nervous system	896	909	36.7	368.8	Digestive system	5,257	5,360	214.5	2,174.0
Endocrine system	111	113	4.5	46.0	Urinary system.	1,706	1,594	69.9	646.7
Eye	547	448	22.4	181.6	Male genital organs	633	648	25.9	262.8
Ear	198	168	8.1	68.2	Female genital organs . .	2,501	2,385	102.5	967.5
Nose, mouth, and pharynx	820	734	33.6	297.8	Obstetrical	6,042	6,383	247.5	2,588.8
Respiratory system	991	1,051	40.6	426.2	Musculoskeletal system .	3,143	3,171	128.8	1,286.1
Cardiovascular system . .	3,626	3,722	148.5	1,509.4	Integumentary system . .	1,475	1,428	60.4	579.1

Selected Chronic Conditions, 1984-88

Source: National Center for Health Statistics

Impairment	Total[1]	Limited in activity Fair or poor health	Good to excellent health	Not limited in activity Fair or poor health	Good to excellent health
		Unadjusted number per 1,000 persons			
Visual impairment	34.9	143.5	80.0	44.1	22.1
Color blindness	11.3	17.5	13.4	9.5	10.7
Cataracts	23.4	112.3	65.5	51.1	11.4
Glaucoma	7.9	33.9	23.1	16.9	4.1
Hearing impairment	89.8	280.2	210.1	155.7	61.0
Tinnitus	26.1	101.1	62.4	44.8	16.2
Speech impairment	10.6	34.8	41.5	12.7	5.8
Absence of extremities	7.0	27.9	18.4	9.1	4.3
Paralysis of extremities	5.8	45.6	29.6	2.7	0.7
Deformity or orthopedic impairment	113.1	325.5	327.2	150.4	75.3
Back	64.2	196.6	166.9	94.9	43.1
Upper extremities	13.3	48.1	48.0	15.6	7.3
Lower extremities	48.3	146.7	160.2	57.5	30.1
		Age-adjusted number per 1,000 persons			
Visual impairment	34.8	123.3	66.5	36.5	23.7
Color blindness	11.3	14.8	12.8	9.2	10.9
Cataracts	23.4	43.7	33.2	23.4	17.0
Glaucoma	7.9	17.2	13.2	9.8	5.7
Hearing impairment	89.8	200.9	166.0	115.0	73.1
Tinnitus	26.1	75.7	48.7	34.2	19.2
Speech impairment	10.6	45.0	53.1	15.8	5.6
Absence of extremities	7.0	22.6	15.7	6.2	5.0
Paralysis of extremities	5.8	42.6	29.8	2.4	0.9
Deformity or orthopedic impairment	113.1	380.2	341.8	148.6	77.5
Back	64.2	252.9	173.0	96.7	44.1
Upper extremities	13.3	49.0	51.3	12.9	7.9
Lower extremities	48.4	173.7	166.7	54.7	30.9

(1) Excludes persons whose health status was not assessed.

Persons Without Health Care Coverage, 1989

Source: National Center for Health Statistics

	All ages	Total	Under 18 years	Under 65 years 18-24 years	25-44 years	45-64 years	65 years and over
				Percent[1]			
All persons not covered[2]	13.9	15.7	14.9	27.4	15.5	10.5	1.2
Sex							
Male	15.1	16.7	15.1	31.3	17.6	9.6	1.3
Female	12.7	14.6	14.7	23.7	13.6	11.2	1.2
Race							
White	12.8	14.5	14.0	26.3	14.4	9.4	1.0
Black	20.2	21.9	18.9	34.3	22.5	17.5	2.5
Other	19.7	20.4	18.9	27.8	20.7	17.5	8.4*
Family income							
Less than $5,000	27.1	31.3	25.5	27.3	42.4	35.5	1.5*
$5,000-$9,999	27.7	36.9	31.6	43.5	43.5	32.2	1.6
$10,000-$19,999	24.3	30.1	30.2	37.5	32.0	21.3	1.1
$20,000-$34,999	10.6	11.6	10.9	22.1	11.8	6.8	1.0
$35,000-$49,999	5.8	6.0	4.0	18.4	5.8	3.9	0.8*
$50,000 or more	3.6	3.7	2.3	12.9	3.7	1.9	1.6*
Poverty status							
In poverty	32.5	36.0	32.5	35.9	42.2	35.9	2.3
Not in poverty	10.3	11.5	9.6	23.5	11.7	7.6	1.1
Employment status[3]							
Currently employed	13.9	14.3	—	26.6	13.6	9.0	1.5
Unemployed	38.3	39.2	—	44.5	40.8	26.5	
Not in labor force	10.8	18.5	—	26.0	21.2	12.8	1.2
Education[3]							
Less than 12 years	20.8	30.1	—	42.1	35.5	19.9	1.5
12 years	14.4	16.6	—	29.8	16.8	8.5	0.7
More than 12 years	8.4	9.2	—	16.0	9.0	5.8	1.3
Region							
Northeast	9.6	11.0	9.9	22.0	10.9	6.6	1.7
Midwest	9.6	10.8	8.8	22.3	10.6	7.6	0.8
South	17.5	19.7	20.5	30.9	19.2	13.4	1.1
West	17.1	18.9	16.7	32.7	19.7	13.1	1.6
Place of residence							
MSA	13.7	15.3	14.4	27.4	15.2	9.8	1.3
Central city	17.2	19.4	18.2	30.0	20.1	12.9	1.6
Not central city	11.4	12.7	12.1	25.4	12.1	8.0	1.1
Not MSA	14.7	17.1	16.5	27.6	17.0	12.6	1.1

(1) Percent calculated excluding the 9.7 million persons for whom coverage status was not determined. (2) Includes persons with unknown sociodemographic characteristics. (3) Excludes persons under 18 years of age. **Note:** MSA metropolitan statistical area.

Medicare Spending Per Beneficiary, 1975-1990

Source: U.S. Dept. of Health and Human Services; Congressional Budget Office; 1990 dollars.

	Total	Admin. costs	Inpatient hospital care	Nursing homes	Home health agencies and hospices	Outpatient hospital services	Doctors' services and laboratories
1975	$1,355	$61	$904	$25	$19	$50	$296
1976	1,481	71	970	25	26	63	326
1977	1,637	59	1,074	26	31	77	369
1978	1,744	66	1,146	24	34	87	387
1979	1,811	63	1,176	22	37	95	418
1980	1,954	61	1,266	21	40	105	460
1981	2,117	62	1,373	21	45	114	501
1982	2,300	59	1,482	21	53	135	550
1983	2,449	58	1,542	22	66	146	616
1984	2,554	63	1,588	22	76	146	659
1985	2,775	68	1,744	22	84	154	703
1986	2,817	64	1,703	21	84	185	760
1987	2,886	62	1,648	22	84	207	864
1988	2,960	67	1,636	24	80	221	931
1989	3,071	69	1,655	69	85	237	955
1990*	3,326	69	1,767	102	110	260	1,018

* 1990 subtotals are estimates.

Physician's Office Visits, 1989

Source: National Center for Health Statistics. U.S. Dept. of Health and Human Services

Physician specialty and professional identity	Number of visits in thousands	Percent distribution	Physician specialty and professional identity	Number of visits in thousands	Percent distribution
All visits	692,702	100.0	General surgery	25,379	3.7
Physician specialty			Psychiatry	16,616	2.4
General and family practice	206,301	29.8	Otolaryngology	15,956	2.3
Pediatrics	87,411	12.6	Cardiovascular disease	10,840	1.6
Internal medicine	78,816	11.4	Urological survey	10,157	1.5
Obstetrics and gynecology	58,381	8.4	Neurology	6,105	0.9
Ophthalmology	38,761	5.6	All other specialties	76,511	11.0
Orthopedic surgery	35,148	5.1	**Professional identity**		
Dermatology	26,319	3.8	Doctor of medicine	651,392	94.0
			Doctor of osteopathy	41,310	6.0

The 15 Leading Causes of Death, 1990

Source: National Center for Health Statistics

	Number	Death rate	Percent of total deaths			Number	Death rate	Percent of total deaths
All causes	2,162,000	861.9	100.0	7.	Diabetes mellitus	48,840	19.5	2.3
1. Diseases of heart	725,010	289.0	33.5	8.	Suicide	30,780	12.3	1.4
2. Malignant neoplasms, incl. neoplasms of lymphatic & hematopoietic tissues	506,000	201.7	23.4	9.	Homicide & legal intervention	25,700	10.2	1.2
3. Cerebrovascular diseases	145,340	57.9	6.7	10.	Chronic liver disease & cirrhosis	25,600	10.2	1.2
4. Accidents & adverse effects	93,550	37.3	4.3	11.	Human immunodeficiency virus infection (AIDS)	24,120	9.6	1.1
... Motor vehicle accidents	47,880	19.1	2.2	12.	Nephritis, nephrotic syndrome, & nephrosis	20,860	8.3	1.0
... Other accidents & adverse effects	45,680	18.2	2.1	13.	Septicemia	19,750	7.9	0.9
5. Chronic obstructive pulmonary diseases & allied conditions	88,980	35.5	4.1	14.	Certain conditions originating in perinatal period	17,520	7.0	0.8
6. Pneumonia & influenza	78,640	31.3	3.6	15.	Atherosclerosis	16,490	6.6	0.8
					All other causes	295,100	117.6	13.6

Note: Data are provisional, estimated from a 10-percent sample of deaths, from Jan. through Nov.; rates per 100,000 population.

Years of Potential Life Lost

While accidents are the fourth leading cause of death in the U.S., accident victims tend to be much younger than those for the three leading causes of death. Ranked by years of potential life lost before age 65, accidents are the leading cause of death, accounting for about 2.2 million such years lost in each 12-month period. The next leading causes of years of potential life lost before age 65, in order, are cancer (1.9 million), suicide/homicide (1.4 million), and heart disease (1.4 million). Motor-vehicle accidents are the leading cause of accidental deaths and also the leading cause of years of potential life lost before age 65 due to accidents. For children and youths 1 to 24 years old, accidents are not only the leading cause of death, but account for almost half of the total in the latest year for which detailed data are available, 1988. Again, motor vehicle accidents are the leading cause.

Federal Bureau of Investigation

The Federal Bureau of Investigation (FBI) is the principal investigative arm of the U.S. Department of Justice, and is located at 10th Street and Pennsylvania Avenue, Northwest, Washington, D.C. 20535. It investigates all violations of Federal law except those specifically assigned to some other agency by legislative action. The FBI's jurisdiction includes a wide range of responsibilities in the criminal, civil, and security fields. Priority has been assigned to six areas—counterterrorism, drugs, foreign counterintelligence, organized crime, white-collar crime, and violent crime. On Jan. 28, 1982, the Attorney General assigned concurrent jurisdiction for the enforcement of the Controlled Substances Act to the FBI and the Drug Enforcement Administration (DEA).

The FBI also offers cooperative services to duly authorized law enforcement agencies; these services include fingerprint identification, laboratory examination, police training, and the National Crime Information Center.

The FBI has 56 field offices in the principal cities of the country. (Consult telephone directories for locations and phone numbers.)

An applicant for the position of Special Agent of the FBI must be a citizen of the U.S., at least 23 and under 37 years old, and a graduate of an accredited law school or of an accredited college or university with a major in accounting. In addition, applicants with a four-year degree from an accredited college or university with a major in other academic areas may qualify with three additional years of full-time work experience. Specialized need areas include languages, science, and financial analysis. Those appointed to the Special Agent position must complete an initial training period of 16 weeks at the FBI Academy, Quantico, Virginia.

U.S. Fires, 1989

Source: National Fire Protection Assn., Quincy, Mass.

Fires
- Fires attended by public fire departments decreased in 1989 by a significant 13.2 percent to 2,115,000 fires.
- Fires in structures decreased by 7.7 percent to 688,000.
- Seventy-five percent, or 513,500, of all structure fires occurred in residential properties.
- Vehicle fires decreased by 8.8 percent to 435,500 fires.
- Fires in outside properties decreased by a significant 18.3 percent to 991,500 fires.
- The South had the highest fire incident rate, with 9.9 fires per thousand population.
- Every 15 seconds, a fire department responded to a fire somewhere in the nation. A fire occurred in a structure at the rate of one every 45 seconds, and a residential fire occurred every 60 seconds. There was one motor vehicle fire every 72 seconds and one fire in an outside property every 32 seconds.

Fire Deaths
- Civilian fire deaths decreased significantly in 1989 by 13.0 percent to 5,410 deaths.
- Fire deaths in the home decreased by 12.5 percent to 4,335, the lowest since 1984.
- About 80 percent of all fire deaths occurred in the home.
- The Northeast had the highest regional fire death rate in the country, with 27.4 civilian deaths per million population. This was followed closely by the South, with 26.7 deaths per million. This is the first year that the South has not had the highest civilian death rate since 1980, when tracking of overall regional statistics began.

Fire Injuries
- Civilian injuries decreased significantly in 1989, by 8.3 percent to 28,250. This estimate for civilian injuries is on the low side because civilian injuries are underreported to the fire service.

- Residential properties were the site of 20,750, or 73.5 percent, of all civilian fire injuries, while 3,275, or 11.6 percent, occurred in nonresidential structures.
- The North Central region had the highest regional injury rate, with 127.1 civilian injuries per million population. This was followed closely by the Northeast, with 124.7 civilian injuries per million.

Property Damage
- An estimated $8.655 billion in property damage occurred as a result of fire in 1989, an increase of 3.6 percent. One large industrial fire with an estimated loss of $750 million more than accounted for the increase.
- Structure fires caused $7.518 billion, or 87 percent, of all property damage.
- Residential properties incurred $3.998 billion, or 53 percent, of all structure property loss.
- The highest property loss rates occurred in the Northeast, with $40.4 per person, and the South, with $39.5 per person.

Incendiary and Suspicious Fires
- In 1989, an estimated 97,000, or 14.1 percent, of all structure fires were set deliberately or are suspected of having been set deliberately. This represents a decrease of 2.5 percent from the year before.
- Incendiary or suspicious fires in structures resulted in 615 civilian deaths, a decrease of 16.9 percent from the year before. These fires also resulted in $1.558 billion in property damage, a decrease of 2.3 percent. This represents 20.7 percent of all structure property loss.
- There were 46,000 vehicle fires of incendiary or suspicious origin, a decrease of 13.2 percent from the year before. These did $139 million in property damage, down 7.9 percent.

Fire Loss Rates Nationwide and by Region, 1989

Source: National Fire Protection Assn., Quincy, Mass.

Region	Number of Fires per Thousand Population	Civilian Deaths per Million Population	Civilian Injuries per Million Population	Property Loss per Capita
Nationwide	8.5	21.8	114.0	$34.9
Northeast	9.2	27.4	124.7	40.4
North Central	8.3	21.1	127.1	30.7
South	9.9	26.7	107.2	39.5
West	7.8	12.8	91.2	29.6

U.S. Crime Rate Up 1.4% in 1990

Source: 1990 *Uniform Crime Reports*, FBI

The crime rate rose 1.4 percent in 1990, according to the FBI's Uniform Crime Reports. From 1989 to 1990, overall violent crime increased by 10.4 percent, and property crime increased by 2 percent.

Overall, the number of crimes committed nationwide rose to 14.48 million in 1990.

The rate of murders was up 8.0 percent; rape, up 8.1 percent; robbery, 10.3 percent; aggravated assault 10.6 percent; burglary, down 3.2 percent; larceny, up 0.7 percent; and auto theft, up 4.3 percent.

The FBI urged caution in interpreting the figures.

Crime Rates by Region, Geographic Division, and State, 1990

Source: 1990 *Uniform Crime Reports*, FBI

(Per 100.000)

Area	Total	Violent crime[1]	Property crime[2]	Murder	Rape	Robbery	Aggravated assault	Burglary	Larceny-theft	Motor vehicle theft
United States Total . .	5,820.3	731.8	5,088.5	9.4	41.2	257.0	424.1	1,235.9	3,194.8	657.8
Northeast	5,193.5	756.7	4,436.7	8.6	29.0	352.8	366.4	1,020.5	2,598.5	817.8
New England	4,995.8	535.8	4,459.9	3.9	30.1	171.7	330.1	1,093.6	2,645.3	721.0
Connecticut	5,386.7	553.7	4,833.0	5.1	27.9	234.8	286.0	1,227.7	2,874.4	730.9
Maine	3,697.8	143.2	3,554.5	2.4	19.7	25.1	96.0	823.0	2,554.9	176.6
Massachusetts	5,297.9	736.3	4,561.5	4.0	33.7	217.1	481.4	1,112.7	2,525.3	923.6
New Hampshire. . . .	3,645.2	131.5	3,513.7	1.9	31.3	27.2	67.6	735.5	2,534.2	244.0
Rhode Island	5,352.7	431.9	4,920.8	4.8	24.7	122.0	280.4	1,271.1	2,695.3	954.4
Vermont	4,340.9	127.2	4,213.7	2.3	25.9	11.7	87.2	1,087.3	2,918.5	207.9
Middle Atlantic	5,262.9	834.3	4,428.6	10.2	28.6	416.4	379.2	994.8	2,582.0	851.8
New Jersey	5,447.2	647.6	4,799.7	5.6	29.8	301.0	311.1	1,017.2	2,843.0	939.5
New York	6,363.8	1,180.9	5,182.8	14.5	29.8	624.7	512.0	1,160.7	2,979.4	1,042.7
Pennsylvania	3,476.1	431.0	3,045.1	6.7	25.8	176.2	222.3	729.1	1,810.5	505.5
Midwest	5,101.9	593.9	4,507.9	7.0	42.6	198.5	345.9	983.4	3,023.8	500.7
East North Central. . .	5,321.9	662.2	4,659.7	8.1	47.4	234.2	372.6	1,007.9	3,085.9	565.9
Illinois	5,935.1	967.4	4,967.7	10.3	39.4[3]	394.0	523.6	1,063.0	3,262.0	642.8
Indiana	4,683.3	473.9	4,209.4	6.2	37.9	101.3	328.5	943.3	2,827.1	439.0
Michigan	5,994.8	790.4	5,204.4	10.4	77.6	234.0	468.4	1,143.3	3,347.4	713.7
Ohio	4,843.4	506.2	4,337.3	6.1	46.8	188.5	264.7	982.5	2,864.1	490.6
Wisconsin	4,395.1	264.7	4,130.4	4.6	20.7	112.7	126.7	751.4	2,962.6	416.5
West North Central . .	4,578.5	431.6	4,146.9	4.4	31.1	113.7	282.4	925.2	2,876.0	345.7
Iowa	4,100.9	299.7	3,801.2	1.9	18.4	39.2	240.1	808.4	2,822.9	169.9
Kansas	5,193.1	447.7	4,745.4	4.0	40.4	117.6	285.7	1,166.5	3,243.5	335.4
Minnesota	4,538.8	306.1	4,232.7	2.7	34.0	92.7	176.7	907.2	2,959.9	365.6
Missouri	5,120.6	715.3	4,405.3	8.8	32.5	216.4	457.6	1,065.8	2,800.2	539.4
Nebraska	4,213.1	330.0	3,883.1	2.7	30.0	51.1	246.2	723.8	2,981.1	178.2
North Dakota	2,922.4	73.9	2,848.5	.8	17.8	7.8	47.4	426.6	2,288.8	133.1
South Dakota	2,909.3	162.8	2,746.5	2.0	34.3	12.4	114.1	527.4	2,108.9	110.2
South.	6,333.7	766.3	5,567.4	11.8	45.4	237.1	472.0	1,498.3	3,471.1	598.0
South Atlantic	6,546.4	856.9	5,689.5	11.4	45.5	276.7	523.3	1,525.0	3,588.9	575.6
Delaware	5,360.4	655.2	4,705.1	5.0	88.1	164.8	397.3	970.5	3,290.8	443.9
District of Columbia. .	10,774.3	2,458.2	8,316.0	77.8	49.9	1,213.5	1,117.0	1,983.0	4,996.9	1,336.1
Florida	8,810.8	1,244.3	7,566.5	10.7	52.4	416.8	764.4	2,170.6	4,569.6	826.3
Georgia	6,763.6	756.3	6,007.3	11.8	53.6	263.5	427.4	1,619.4	3,714.3	673.6
Maryland	5,830.5	919.0	4,911.5	11.5	45.7	363.8	497.9	1,119.9	3,082.9	708.7
North Carolina	5,485.9	623.5	4,862.3	10.7	34.3	152.1	426.4	1,530.4	3,048.3	283.7
South Carolina	6,045.2	976.6	5,068.7	11.2	53.7	152.4	759.3	1,380.4	3,302.4	385.8
Virginia	4,440.6	350.6	4,090.0	8.8	31.0	123.3	187.6	731.1	3,031.4	327.5
West Virginia	2,503.0	169.3	2,333.7	5.7	23.6	37.9	102.1	657.1	1,522.7	153.9
East South Central. . .	4,389.1	556.6	3,832.5	10.2	39.1	131.1	376.2	1,098.4	2,374.3	359.9
Alabama.	4,915.2	708.6	4,206.7	11.6	32.6	143.7	520.7	1,103.4	2,755.4	347.8
Kentucky.	3,299.4	390.4	2,909.1	7.2	29.0	69.1	285.2	766.9	1,942.7	199.4
Mississippi.	3,869.1	340.4	3,528.8	12.2	44.1	86.2	198.0	1,251.2	2,070.0	207.6
Tennessee.	5,051.0	670.4	4,380.6	10.5	49.5	191.2	419.2	1,264.0	2,545.1	571.5
West South Central . .	7,092.0	737.7	6,354.2	13.5	48.8	232.9	442.5	1,682.2	3,902.4	769.7
Arkansas	4,866.9	532.2	4,334.7	10.3	43.3	113.2	365.4	1,210.9	2,834.4	289.4
Louisiana	6,486.7	898.4	5,588.2	17.2	42.2	269.8	569.2	1,437.9	3,548.6	601.7
Oklahoma	5,598.7	547.5	5,051.2	8.0	47.0	121.9	370.5	1,447.5	3,002.0	601.7
Texas	7,826.8	761.4	7,065.3	14.1	51.5	260.8	435.1	1,851.5	4,304.7	909.0
West	6,404.6	807.9	5,596.7	9.1	44.8	263.2	490.7	1,304.0	3,514.6	778.0
Mountain	6,268.1	516.8	3,751.3	6.0	42.3	108.8	359.7	1,286.3	3,979.2	485.8
Arizona.	7,888.7	652.4	7,236.4	7.7	40.9	160.9	442.8	1,669.9	4,703.0	863.5
Colorado.	6,053.7	526.0	5,527.8	4.2	46.2	90.6	385.0	1,208.8	3,890.6	428.4
Idaho.	4,057.1	275.7	3,781.4	2.7	27.3	15.0	230.7	813.2	2,802.7	165.5
Montana	4,502.1	159.3	4,342.8	4.9	24.4	21.7	108.4	709.1	3,391.2	242.5
Nevada	6,063.6	600.9	5,462.7	9.7	62.2	238.3	290.7	1,367.4	3,502.7	592.5
New Mexico	6,684.1	780.2	5,903.9	9.2	49.7	115.1	606.2	1,738.7	3,828.5	336.7
Utah	5,659.9	283.9	5,376.0	3.0	37.8	56.9	186.3	880.6	4,257.6	237.7
Wyoming.	4,210.6	301.4	3,909.3	4.9	29.5	15.9	251.1	631.0	3,129.3	149.0
Pacific	6,452.2	909.5	5,542.7	10.2	45.7	317.1	536.5	1,310.2	3,352.5	880.0
Alaska	5,157.7	524.5	4,628.2	7.5	72.9	76.7	367.4	894.3	3,168.5	565.4
California	6,603.6	1,045.2	5,558.4	11.9	42.6	377.0	613.6	1,345.4	3,197.5	1,015.5
Hawaii	6,106.7	280.9	5,825.8	4.0	32.5	91.4	153.0	1,228.2	4,217.1	380.5
Oregon.	5,646.0	506.8	5,139.2	3.8	46.9	141.3	311.8	1,135.4	3,545.2	458.6
Washington	6,222.9	501.6	5,721.3	4.9	64.0	130.0	302.7	1,262.9	4,011.4	447.1

Note: Populations are Bureau of the Census provisional estimates as of July 1, 1989 and decennial census counts for 1990 and are subject to change; although arson data are included in the trend and clearance tables, sufficient data are not available to estimate totals for this offense. (1) Violent crimes are offenses of murder, forcible rape, robbery, and aggravated assault. (2) Property crimes are offenses of burglary, larceny-theft, and motor vehicle theft. (3) Forcible rape figures furnished by Illinois were not in accordance with national guidelines. The totals were estimated.

Crime in the U.S., 1982-1990

Source: 1990 *Uniform Crime Reports*, FBI

Population[1]	Crime Index total[2]	Violent crime[3]	Property crime[3]	Murder and non-negligent man-slaughter	Forcible rape	Robbery	Burglary	Larceny theft
			Number of offenses					
1982-231,534,000...	12,974,400	1,322,390	11,652,000	21,010	78,770	553,130	3,447,100	7,142,500
1983-233,981,000...	12,108,600	1,258,090	10,850,500	19,310	78,920	506,570	3,129,900	6,712,800
1985-238,740,000...	12,431,400	1,328,870	11,102,600	18,980	87,670	497,870	3,073,300	6,926,400
1986-241,077,000...	13,211,900	1,489,170	11,722,700	20,610	91,460	542,780	3,241,400	7,257,200
1987-243,400,000...	13,508,700	1,484,000	12,024,700	20,100	91,110	517,700	3,236,200	7,499,900
1988-245,807,000...	13,923,100	1,566,220	12,356,900	20,680	92,490	542,970	3,218,100	7,705,900
1989-248,239,000...	14,251,400	1,646,040	12,605,400	21,500	94,500	578,330	3,168,200	7,872,400
1990-248,709,873..	14,475,600	1,820,130	12,655,500	23,440	102,560	639,270	3,073,900	7,945,700
			Percent change; number of offenses:					
1990/1989......	+1.6	+10.6	+0.4	+9.0	+8.5	+10.5	−3.0	+0.9
1990/1986......	+9.6	+22.2	+8.0	+13.7	+12.1	+17.8	−5.2	+9.5
1990/1981......	+7.8	+33.7	+4.9	+4.1	+24.3	+7.8	−11.7	+10.4
			Rate per 100,000 inhabitants:					
1982	5,603.6	571.1	5,032.5	9.1	34.0	238.9	1,488.8	3,084.8
1983	5,175.0	537.7	4,637.4	8.3	33.7	216.5	1,337.7	2,868.9
1985	5,207.1	556.6	4,650.5	7.9	37.1	208.5	1,287.3	2,901.2
1986	5,480.4	617.3	4,862.6	8.6	37.9	225.1	1,344.6	3,010.3
1987	5,550.0	609.7	4,904.3	8.3	37.4	212.7	1,329.6	3,081.3
1988	5,664.2	637.2	5,027.1	8.4	37.6	220.9	1,309.2	3,134.9
1989	5,741.0	663.1	5,077.9	8.7	38.1	233.0	1,276.3	3,171.3
1990	5,820.3	731.8	5,088.5	9.4	41.2	257.0	1,235.9	3,194.8
			Percent change; rate per 100,000 inhabitants:					
1990/1989......	+1.4	+10.4	+0.2	+8.0	+8.1	+10.3	−3.2	+0.7
1990/1986......	+6.2	+18.5	+4.6	+9.3	+8.7	+14.2	−8.1	+6.1
1990/1981......	−0.6	+23.1	−3.3	−4.1	+14.4	−0.7	−25.1	+1.8

(1) Populations are Bureau of the Census provisional estimates as of July 1, except 1990, which are preliminary census counts, and are subject to change. (2) Because of rounding, the offenses may not add to totals. (3) Violent crimes are offenses of murder, forcible rape, robbery, and aggravated assault. Property crimes are offenses of burglary, larceny-theft, and motor vehicle theft. Data are not included for the property crime of arson. **Note:** All rates were calculated on the offenses before rounding.

Law Enforcement Officers

Source: 1990 *Uniform Crime Reports*, FBI

The Nation's law enforcement community employed an average of 2.2 full-time officers for every 1,000 inhabitants as of October 31, 1990. Considering full-time civilians, the overall law enforcement employee rate was 3.1 per 1,000 inhabitants according to 12,401 city, county, and state police agencies. These agencies collectively offered law enforcement service to a population of nearly 233 million, employing 523,262 officers and 190,998 civilians.

The law enforcement employee average for all cities nationwide was 2.8 per 1,000 inhabitants. City law enforcement employee averages ranged from 2.2 per 1,000 inhabitants in those with populations from 25,000 to 49,000 to 3.7 for those with populations of 250,000 or more. Rural and suburban counties averaged full-time law enforcement employee rates of 3.8 and 3.4 per 1,000 population, respectively.

Regionally, the highest law enforcement employee rate was in the South, with 3.1. The Northeast averaged 3.0, the Midwest rate was 2.6 and the West 2.5.

Nationally, males comprised 91 percent of all sworn employees. Ninety-four percent of the officers in rural counties and 92 percent of those in cities were males, while in suburban counties they accounted for 89 percent.

Civilians made up 27 percent of the total U.S. law enforcement employee force. They represented 22 percent of the police employees in cities, 33 percent of those in rural counties, and 34 percent of the suburban law enforcement strength.

Sixty-five law enforcement officers were feloniously slain in the line of duty, the lowest since the FBI began collecting such data in the 1960s. Another 67 officers were killed due to accidents occurring while performing official duties.

Murder Weapons, 1985-1990

Source: 1990 *Uniform Crime Reports*, FBI

Weapon	1985	1986	1987	1988	1989	1990
Total	17,545	19,257	17,963	17,971	18,954	20,045
Total Firearms...............	10,296	11,381	10,612	10,895	11,832	12,847
Handguns..................	7,548	8,460	7,847	8,147	9,013	9,923
Rifles......................	810	788	776	753	865	743
Shotguns..................	1,188	1,296	1,101	1,105	1,173	1,237
Other guns	24	22	16	15	34	24
Firearms-not stated	726	815	872	875	747	920
Cutting or stabbing instruments	3,694	3,957	3,643	3,457	3,458	3,503
Blunt objects (clubs, hammers, etc.) ..	972	1,099	1,045	1,126	1,128	1,075
Personal weapons (hands, fists, feet, etc.)[1]	1,180	1,310	1,165	1,095	1,050	1,112
Poison	7	14	34	15	11	11
Explosives.................	11	16	12	34	16	14
Fire......................	243	230	200	255	234	287
Narcotics..................	31	23	24	36	17	29
Drowning..................	43	49	51	38	60	36
Strangulation...............	311	341	360	331	366	312
Asphyxiation	115	160	115	73	101	96
Other weapons or weapons not stated	642	677	702	616	681	723

(1) Pushing is included in personal weapons.

State and Federal Prison Population; Death Penalty

Source: Prison population: Bureau of Justice Statistics, U.S. Dept. of Justice, Dec. 31, 1990; Death penalty: NAACP Legal Defense and Education Fund; Bureau of Justice Statistics; "Executions" and "Death penalty" as of Dec. 31, 1990; "Under sentence of death" as of Aug., 1991.

The number of prisoners under jurisdiction of Federal or State correction authorities at year end 1990 reached a record high of 77,243. From 1980 through 1990 there was an increase of 134% in the prison population. However, the 1990 growth rate of 8.2% was less than the 1989 percentage increase of 12.8%; there were 26,271 fewer new prisoners added in 1990 than the preceding year's 80,888. In 1990 there was a nationwide need for about 1,100 new prison bedspaces per week.

	Sentenced to more than 1 yr.		% change 1989-90	Death penalty		
	Advance 1990	Final 1989		Under sentence of death	Executions	Death penalty
Total	739,763	680,955	8.6%	2,210	NA	—
Federal institutions	52,208	47,168	10.7	5	NA	Yes
State institutions	687,555	633,787	8.5	2,205	23	36
Northeast	119,062	109,394	8.8	141	0	—
Connecticut	7,771	6,309	23.2	1	0	Yes
Maine	1,480	1,432	3.4	0	0	No
Massachusetts	7,899	7,268	8.7	0	0	No
New Hampshire	1,342	1,166	15.1	0	0	Yes
New Jersey	21,128	19,439	8.7	25	0	Yes
New York	54,895	51,227	7.2	0	0	No
Pennsylvania	22,281	20,458	8.9	115	0	Yes
Rhode Island	1,585	1,469	7.9	0	0	No
Vermont	681	626	8.8	0	0	No
Midwest	145,493	136,042	6.9	348	5	—
Illinois	27,516	24,712	11.3	120	1	Yes
Indiana	12,615	12,220	3.2	50	0	Yes
Iowa	3,967	3,584	10.7	0	0	No
Kansas	5,777	5,616	2.9	0	0	No
Michigan	34,267	31,639	8.3	0	0	No
Minnesota	3,176	3,103	2.4	0	0	No
Missouri	14,919	13,921	7.2	73	4	Yes
Nebraska	2,286	2,278	.4	13	0	Yes
North Dakota	435	404	7.7	0	0	No
Ohio	31,855	30,538	4.3	92	0	Yes
South Dakota	1,345	1,252	7.4	0	0	Yes
Wisconsin	7,335	6,775	8.3	0	0	No
South	274,813	252,614	8.8	1,285	17	—
Alabama	15,365	13,575	13.2	93	1	Yes
Arkansas	6,718	6,306	6.5	31	2	Yes
Delaware	2,231	2,284	−2.3	7	0	Yes
District of Columbia	6,660	6,735	−1.1	0	0	No
Florida	44,387	39,966	11.1	294	4	Yes
Georgia	21,605	19,619	10.1	102	0	Yes
Kentucky	9,023	8,289	8.9	28	0	Yes
Louisiana	18,599	17,257	7.8	39	1	Yes
Maryland	16,684	15,378	8.5	19	0	Yes
Mississippi	8,179	7,700	6.2	45	0	Yes
North Carolina	17,713	16,628	6.5	81	0	Yes
Oklahoma	12,322	11,608	6.2	98	1	Yes
South Carolina	16,208	14,808	9.5	46	1	Yes
Tennessee	10,388	10,630	−2.3	69	0	Yes
Texas	50,042	44,022	13.7	283	4	Yes
Virginia	17,124	16,273	5.2	40	3	Yes
West Virginia	1,565	1,536	1.9	0	0	No
West	148,187	135,737	9.2	441	1	—
Alaska	1,851	1,908	−3.0	0	0	No
Arizona	13,781	12,726	8.3	86	0	Yes
California	94,122	84,338	11.6	247	0	Yes
Colorado	7,018	6,908	1.6	3	0	Yes
Hawaii	1,708	1,752	−2.5	0	0	No
Idaho	2,074	1,850	12.1	16	0	Yes
Montana	1,409	1,328	6.1	10	0	Yes
Nevada	5,322	5,112	4.1	45	1	Yes
New Mexico	2,879	2,759	4.3	2	0	Yes
Oregon	6,436	6,744	−4.6	15	0	Yes
Utah	2,482	2,368	4.8	8	0	Yes
Washington	7,995	6,928	15.4	7	0	Yes
Wyoming	1,110	1,016	9.3	2	0	Yes

Arrests for Drug Abuse Violations, 1990

Source: 1990 *Uniform Crime Reports*, FBI

(Percent distribution)

	U.S. Total	North-east	Mid-west	South	West		U.S. Total	North-east	Mid-west	South	West
Total[1]	100.0	100.0	100.0	100.0	100.0	Possession: . . .	68.4	59.0	68.3	71.6	72.1
Sale/manufacture:	31.6	41.0	31.7	28.4	27.9	Heroin or cocaine and their					
Heroin or cocaine and their						derivatives . . .	33.3	34.2	19.5	30.6	39.8
derivatives . . .	21.0	34.5	11.5	19.4	16.7	Marijuana	23.9	21.4	36.4	31.7	14.7
Marijuana	6.1	4.7	7.2	6.4	6.4	Synthetic or man-ufactured drugs	1.5	1.0	1.5	3.0	0.6
Synthetic or man-ufactured drugs	0.6	0.5	0.7	1.0	0.3	Other dangerous nonnarcotic					
Other dangerous nonnarcotic						drugs	9.7	2.4	10.8	6.3	17.0
drugs	3.9	1.4	12.4	1.6	4.5	(1) Because of rounding, percentages may not add to totals.					

Years of Life Expected at Birth

Source: National Center for Health Statistics

Year	Total	Total Male	Total Female	White Total	White Male	White Female	Black and Other Total	Black and Other Male	Black and Other Female
1920*	54.1	53.6	54.6	54.9	54.4	55.6	45.3	45.5	45.2
1930	59.7	58.1	61.6	61.4	59.7	63.5	48.1	47.3	49.2
1940	62.9	60.8	65.2	64.2	62.1	66.6	53.1	51.5	54.9
1950	68.2	65.6	71.1	69.1	66.5	72.2	60.8	59.1	62.9
1960	69.7	66.6	73.1	70.6	67.4	74.1	63.6	61.1	66.3
1965	70.2	66.8	73.7	71.0	67.6	74.7	64.1	61.1	67.4
1970	70.8	67.1	74.7	71.7	68.0	75.6	65.3	61.3	69.4
1971	71.1	67.4	75.0	72.0	68.3	75.8	65.6	61.6	69.8
1972	71.2	67.4	75.1	72.0	68.3	75.9	65.7	61.5	70.1
1973	71.4	67.6	75.3	72.2	68.5	76.1	66.1	62.0	70.3
1974	72.0	68.2	75.9	72.8	69.0	76.7	67.1	62.9	71.3
1975	72.6	68.8	76.6	73.4	69.5	77.3	68.0	63.7	72.4
1976	72.9	69.1	76.8	73.6	69.9	77.5	68.4	64.2	72.7
1977	73.3	69.5	77.2	74.0	70.2	77.9	68.9	64.7	73.2
1979	73.9	70.0	77.8	74.6	70.8	78.4	69.8	65.4	74.1
1980	73.7	70.0	77.5	74.4	70.7	78.1	69.5	65.3	73.6
1981	74.2	70.4	77.8	74.8	71.1	78.4	70.3	66.1	74.4
1982	74.5	70.9	78.1	75.1	71.5	78.7	71.0	66.8	75.0
1983	74.6	71.0	78.1	75.2	71.7	78.7	71.1	67.2	74.3
1984	74.7	71.2	78.2	75.3	71.8	78.7	71.3	67.4	75.0
1985	74.7	71.2	78.2	75.3	71.9	78.7	71.2	67.2	75.0
1986	74.8	71.3	78.3	75.4	72.0	78.8	71.2	67.2	75.1
1987	75.0	71.5	78.4	75.6	72.2	78.9	71.3	67.3	75.2
1988	74.9	71.5	78.3	75.6	72.3	78.9	71.2	67.1	75.1
1989p	75.2	71.8	78.5	75.9	72.6	79.1	71.7	67.5	75.7
1990p	75.4	72.0	78.8	76.0	72.6	79.3	72.4	68.4	76.3

p = preliminary   * Data prior to 1940 for death-registration states only.

Average Height and Weight for Children

Source: *Physicians Handbook*, 1983

Boys Age Years	ft	Height in	cm	Weight lb	kg	Girls Age Years	ft	Height in	cm	Weight lb	kg
(Birth)	1	8	50.8	7½	3.4	(Birth)	1	8	50.8	7½	3.4
½	2	2	66.0	17	7.7	½	2	2	66.0	16	7.2
1	2	5	73.6	21	9.5	1	2	5	73.6	20	9.1
2	2	9	83.8	26	11.8	2	2	9	83.8	25	11.3
3	3	0	91.4	31	14.0	3	3	0	91.4	30	13.6
4	3	3	99.0	34	15.4	4	3	3	99.0	33	15.0
5	3	6	106.6	39	17.7	5	3	5	104.1	38	17.2
6	3	9	114.2	46	20.9	6	3	8	111.7	45	20.4
7	3	11	119.3	51	23.1	7	3	11	119.3	49	22.2
8	4	2	127.0	57	25.9	8	4	2	127.0	56	25.4
9	4	4	132.0	63	28.6	9	4	4	132.0	62	28.1
10	4	6	137.1	69	31.3	10	4	6	137.1	69	31.3
11	4	8	142.2	77	34.9	11	4	8	142.2	77	34.9
12	4	10	147.3	83	37.7	12	4	10	147.3	86	39.0
13	5	0	152.4	92	41.7	13	5	0	152.4	98	45.5
14	5	2	157.5	107	48.5	14	5	2	157.5	107	48.5

This table gives a general picture of American children at specific ages. When used as a standard, the individual variation in children's growth should not be overlooked. In most cases the height-weight relationship is probably a more valid index of weight status than a weight-for-age assessment.

Average Weight of Americans by Height and Age

Source: Society of Actuaries; from the *1979 Build and Blood Pressure Study*
The figures represent weights in ordinary indoor clothing and shoes, and heights with shoes.

Men Height	20-24	25-29	30-39	40-49	50-59	60-69	Women Height	20-24	25-29	30-39	40-49	50-59	60-69
5'2"	130	134	138	140	141	140	4'10"	105	110	113	118	121	123
5'3"	136	140	143	144	145	144	4'11"	110	112	115	121	125	127
5'4"	139	143	147	149	150	149	5'0"	112	114	118	123	127	130
5'5"	143	147	151	154	155	153	5'1"	116	119	121	127	131	133
5'6"	148	152	156	158	159	158	5'2"	120	121	124	129	133	136
5'7"	153	156	160	163	164	163	5'3"	124	125	128	133	137	140
5'8"	157	161	165	167	168	167	5'4"	127	128	131	136	141	143
5'9"	163	166	170	172	173	172	5'5"	130	132	134	139	144	147
5'10"	167	171	174	176	177	176	5'6"	133	134	137	143	147	150
5'11"	171	175	179	181	182	181	5'7"	137	138	141	147	152	155
6'0"	176	181	184	186	187	186	5'8"	141	142	145	150	156	158
6'1"	182	186	190	192	193	191	5'9"	146	148	150	155	159	161
6'2"	187	191	195	197	198	196	5'10"	149	150	153	158	162	163
6'3"	193	197	201	203	204	200	5'11"	155	156	159	162	166	167
6'4"	198	202	206	208	209	207	6'0"	157	159	164	168	171	172

OBITUARIES

Deaths, Nov. 7, 1990—Oct. 15, 1991

A

Allen, George, 72; football coach who led the L.A. Rams and Washington Redskins; Rancho Palos Verdes, Cal., Dec. 31.

Appling, Luke, 83; hall of fame shortstop who twice won the American League batting title; Cummings, Ga., Jan. 3.

Arden, Eve, 83; actress who appeared in some 100 films and starred on TV in the "Our Miss Brooks" series, 1948-57; Beverly Hills, Cal., Nov. 12.

Arrau, Claudio, 88; concert pianist; Muerzzuschlag, Austria, June 9.

Arthur, Jean, 90; film actress, star of comedy, drama of the 1930s and 1940s; Carmel, Cal., June 19.

Ashcroft, Peggy, 83; actress who starred on the London stage for 50 years; London, June 14.

Ashman, Howard, 40; lyricist, playwright, and director, *Little Shop of Horrors;* New York, Mar. 14.

Atwater, Lee, 40; political tactician who guided the 1988 Bush presidential campaign; Washington, D.C., Mar. 29.

Axthelm, Pete, 47; sports author, columnist, and TV commentator; Pittsburgh, Feb. 2.

B

Barbie, Klaus, 77; Nazi Gestapo chief known as "the butcher of Lyons;" Lyons, Sept. 25.

Bardeen, Dr. John, 82; co-inventor of the transistor that led to modern electronics; won 1956, 1972 Nobel Prize in Physics; Boston, Jan. 30.

Barnet, Charlie, 77; jazz saxophonist and band leader popular during the swing era; San Diego, Sept. 4.

Barrera, Laz, 66; trainer who won the 1976 thoroughbred "Triple Crown" with Affirmed; Downey, Cal., Apr. 25.

Baruch, Andre, 83; radio and TV announcer whose career spanned some 60 years; Beverly Hills, Cal., Sept. 15.

Bell, James "Cool Papa," 87; legendary star of the Negro baseball leagues; St. Louis, Mar. 7.

Bennett, Joan, 80; actress who starred in films in the 1930s and 1940s; Scarsdale, N.Y., Dec. 7.

Bigart, Homer, 83; journalist who won Pulitzer prizes in 1946, 1951; Portsmouth, N.H., Apr. 16.

Binns, Edward, 75; character actor in numerous films and TV dramas; Brewster, N.Y., Dec. 4.

Bolling, Richard, 74; U.S. representative from Missouri, 1949-83; Washington, D.C., Apr. 21.

Brown, Paul, 82; football owner, coach, and general manager who founded the Cleveland Browns and the Cincinnati Bengals; Cincinnati, Aug. 5.

Burgess, Smokey, 64; baseball player who had 145 major league pinch hits; Asheville, N.C., Sept. 15.

Busch, Niven, 88; novelist and screenwriter; San Francisco, Aug. 25.

C

Capra, Frank, 94; film director who depicted America's common man, won 3 Oscars; La Quinta, Cal., Sept. 3.

Carter, John, 61; jazz clarinetist and composer; Los Angeles, Mar. 31.

Caulfield, Joan, 69; actress who starred in 1940s films; Los Angeles, June 18.

Chandler, A.B. "Happy", 92; Kentucky politician who served as governor, U.S. senator; commissioner of baseball, 1945-51 Versailles, Ky., June 15.

Chaplin, Oona O'Neill, 66; daughter of Eugene O'Neill; wife of Charlie Chaplin; Sorsier-sur-Vevey, Switz., Sept. 27.

Clancy, Tom, 67; Irish singer who was a founder of the Clancy Brothers folk group; Co. Tipperary, Ireland, Nov. 7.

Cleveland, Rev. James, 59; gospel singer and composer of over 400 gospel songs; Los Angeles, Feb. 9.

Collins, LeRoy, 82; governor of Florida, 1955-61; Tallahassee, Fla., Mar. 12.

Conte, Silvio, 69; U.S. representative from Massachusetts; Bethesda, Md., Feb. 8.

Convy, Bert, 57; actor and host of TV game shows; Brentwood, Cal., July 15.

Cooper, John Sherman, 89; U.S. senator from Kentucky for 17 years; Washington, D.C., Feb. 21.

Copland, Aaron, 90; best-known composer of American classical music; North Tarrytown, N.Y., Dec. 2.

Cousins, Norman, 75; editor in chief of *The Saturday Review* for over 30 years; Los Angeles, Nov. 30.

Crosby, John, 79; columnist, author of suspense novels; Esmont, Va., Sept. 7.

Cummings, Robert, 82; actor who starred in numerous films and in 4 TV series in the 1950s and 1960s; Woodland Hills, Cal., Dec. 2.

Curtis, Ken, 74; actor who was best known as Festus on the "Gunsmoke" TV series; Fresno, Cal., Apr. 28.

D

Dahl, Roald, 74; British writer of children's books and adult short stories; Oxford, England, Nov. 23.

Daly, John, 77; host of the "What's My Line?" TV game show, 1950-67; Chevy Chase, Md., Feb. 25.

Davis, Brad, 41; stage, film, and TV actor; Studio City, Cal., Sept. 8.

Davis, Miles, 65; jazz trumpeter and composer who was a major jazz innovator for 4 decades; Santa Monica, Cal., Sept. 28.

Delacorte, G.T., 97; publisher, philanthropist; New York, May 4.

Dewhurst, Colleen, 67; actress who won 2 Tony and 3 Emmy awards; South Salem, N.Y., Aug. 22.

Diaz, Bo, 37; catcher for 4 major league teams, 1977-89; Caracas, Venezuela, Nov. 24.

Dunnock, Mildred, 90; actress who appeared in the theater and in films; Oak Bluffs, Mass., July 5.

Durocher, Leo, 86; baseball player and manager who won 3 NL pennants and the 1954 world series; Palm Springs, Cal., Oct. 7.

Durrell, Lawrence, 78; British writer known for the "Alexandria Quartet" novels; Sommieres, France, Nov. 7.

E

Edmondson, Ed, 71; U.S. representative from Oklahoma, 1953-73; Muskogee, Okla., Dec. 8.

Elliott, Sumner Locke, 73; Australian novelist and playwright; New York, June 24.

F

Fedor, Eugene, 85; writer of travel guides; Torrington, Conn., Feb. 13.

Fish, Hamilton, 102; U.S. representative from New York, 1921-45; led congressional opposition to U.S. involvement in World War II; Cold Spring, N.Y., Jan. 18.

Fonteyn, Margot, 71; ballerina who redefined 20th-century dance; Panama City, Panama, Feb. 21.

Foxx, Redd, 68; comedian and actor best known for the TV series "Sanford and Son;" Los Angeles, Oct. 11.

Francescatti, Zino, 89; French violin virtuoso; La Ciotat, France, Sept. 17.

Franciscus, James, 57; actor who starred in the "Mr. Novak" TV series in the 1960s; Los Angeles, Cal., July 8.

G

Gaillard, Slim, 74; jazz pianist and composer, "Flat Foot Floogie"; London, Feb. 26.

Garry, Charles R., 82; lawyer who defended radicals in the 1960s; Berkeley, Cal., Aug. 16.

Getz, Stan, 64; jazz tenor saxophonist who won 11 Grammy awards; Malibu, Cal., June 6.

Gobel, George, 71; TV comedian, game show panelist; Encino, Cal., Feb. 24.

Goody, Sam, 87; founder of record-store chain; New York, Aug. 8.

Goren, Charles, 90; bridge player, author, and columnist; Encino, Cal., Apr. 3.

Graham, John, 82; architect; designed Space Needle for the 1962 Seattle World's Fair; Seattle, Jan. 29.

Graham, Martha, 96; dancer and choreographer; major figure in modern dance; New York, Apr. 1.

Grange, Red, 87; hall of fame running back, a legend of pro and college football; Lake Wales, Fla., Jan. 28.

Greene, Graham, 86; British author of 24 novels of suspense or moral ambiguity; Vevey, Switzerland, Apr. 3.

Guard, Dave, 56; singer and co-founder of the Kingston Trio folk group; Rollinsford, N.H., Mar. 22.

Guthrie Jr., A.B., 90; novelist who won the Pulitzer Prize in 1949 for *The Way West;* Choteau, Mont., Apr. 26.

H

Hammer, Armand, 92; industrialist who headed the Occidental Petroleum Co.; promoted U.S.-Soviet ties; Los Angeles, Dec. 10.

Heinz, John, 52; U.S. senator from Pennsylvania, since 1977; Lower Merion Township, Pa., Apr. 4.

Honda, Soichiro, 84; Japanese auto innovator who built one of the world's largest auto companies; Tokyo, Aug. 5.

Hyde-White, Wilfrid, 87; British actor in films and the theater; Woodland Hills, Cal., May 6.

I

Irwin, James B., 61; astronaut who walked on the moon in 1971; Greenwood Springs, Col., Aug. 8.

J

Jacoby, Jim, 58; bridge champion and syndicated columnist; Dallas, Feb. 8.

Jagger, Dean, 87; actor in over 100 films; Santa Monica,.Cal., Feb. 5.

Jiang Quing, 77; widow of Mao and member of the infamous "Gang of Four;" China, May 14.

K

Kahane, Rabbi Meir, 58; militant Jewish leader; New York, Nov. 5.

Kert, Larry, 60; singer who starred in the theater and cabaret; New York, June 5.

Kiker, Douglas, 61; TV journalist who was an NBC News correspondent for 25 years; Chatham, Mass., Aug. 14.

Kirk, Lisa, 62; singer who starred in Broadway musicals and cabaret; New York, Nov. 10.

Kosinski, Jerzy, 57; Polish-born author; New York, May 3.

Kulp, Nancy, 69; character actress best known as Jane Hathaway in the "Beverly Hillbillies" TV series; Palm Desert, Cal., Feb. 3.

L

Land, Edwin H., 81; inventor of the Polaroid instant camera; Cambridge, Mass., Mar. 1.

Landon, Michael, 54; actor who starred in the "Bonanza" and "Little House on the Prairie" TV series; Malibu, Cal., July 1.

Lawrence, John H., 87; scientist; a discoverer of the dangers of nuclear radiation; Berkeley, Cal., Sept. 7.

Lean, David, 83; British film director, "Lawrence of Arabia," "Bridge on the River Kwai"; London, Apr. 16.

Lefebvre, Archbishop Marcel, 85; prelate who defied the Vatican, causing a major schism; Martigny, Switzerland, Mar. 25.

Le Gallienne, Eva, 92; a major figure on the American stage as actress and director; Weston, Conn., June 3.

Luke, Keye, 86; actor who is best known as the No. 1 Son in the Charlie Chan films of the 1930s and 1940s; Whittier, Cal., Jan. 12.

M

MacMahon, Aline, 92; actress whose career spanned 50 years and 43 films; New York, Oct. 12.

Marble, Alice, 77; tennis star of the 1930s who won 4 U.S. singles titles; Palm Springs, Cal., Dec. 13.

Martin, Kiel, 46; actor who played J.D. LaRue on the "Hill Street Blues" TV series; Rancho Mirage, Cal., Dec. 28.

Martin, Mary, 76; a leading musical comedy star since the 1930s, "Peter Pan"; Rancho Mirage, Cal., Nov. 3.

Mazurki, Mike, 82; wrestler who became a character actor in many 1940s films; Glendale, Cal., Dec. 9.

McCone, John A., 89; director of the Central Intelligence Agency, 1961-65; Pebble Beach, Cal., Feb. 14.

McIntire, John, 83; character actor in over 100 films and TVs "Wagon Train"; Pasadena, Cal., Jan. 30.

McKissick, Floyd, 69; civil rights leader; Durham, N.C., Apr. 28.

McLaughlin, Emily, 61; actress who starred in the TV soap opera "General Hospital" for some 3 decades; Los Angeles, Apr. 26.

McMillan, Edwin, 83; scientist who won the Nobel Prize in Chemistry as co-discoverer of plutonium and neptunium; El Cerrito, Cal., Sept. 7.

McPartland, Jimmy, 83; cornetist, an originator of Chicago-style-jazz; Port Washington, N.Y., Mar. 13.

Mollenhoff, Clark, 69; Pulitzer prize-winning reporter, author, and syndicated columnist; Lexington, Va., Mar. 2.

Motherwell, Robert, 76; artist who was a major force in the Abstract Expressionist movement; Cape Cod, Mass., July 16.

Muggeridge, Malcolm, 87; British journalist and social critic; Sussex, England, Nov. 14.

Mullins, Chucky, 21; Univ. of Mississippi football player who had been paralyzed in a game 2 years earlier; Memphis, Tenn., May 6.

Murray, Arthur, 95; founder of dance studio franchises; Honolulu, Mar. 3.

N

Nemerov, Howard, 71; poet who won the 1978 Pulitzer prize; poet laureate of the U.S., 1988-1990; University City, Mo., July 5.

North, Alex, 81; composer who wrote the scores for over 50 films; Los Angeles, Sept. 8.

O

O'Faolain, Sean, 91; Irish short-story writer; Dublin, Apr. 20.

Olav V, 87; king of Norway since 1957; Norway, Jan. 17.

P

Pasternak, Joe, 89; producer of over 100 films during a 40-year career; Beverly Hills, Cal., Sept. 13.

Pierce, Webb, 65; singer who dominated country music in the 1950s and 1960s; Nashville, Feb. 24.

Pomus, Jerome "Doc", 65; lyricist of many rock-and-roll hits; New York, Mar. 14.

Porter, Sylvia, 77; financial columnist and author; Pound Ridge, N.Y., June 5.

R

Ray, Aldo, 64; actor who played lovable tough guys in films in the 1950s; Martinez, Cal., Mar. 27.

Reasoner, Harry, 68; newscaster who was a mainstay of network TV broadcasting for 4 decades; Norwalk, Conn., Aug. 6.

Remick, Lee, 55; actress who starred in films and TV; Los Angeles, July 2.

Revere, Anne, 87; character actress in many 1940s and 1950s films; Locust Valley, N.Y., Dec. 18.

Rice, Greg, 75; champion distance runner of the 1940s; Hackensack, N.J., May 19.

Riordon, Bill, 71; tennis promoter who managed the early career of Jimmy Connors; Naples, Fla., Jan. 20.

Ritt, Martin, 76; film and TV director, "Hud," "Norma Rae"; Santa Monica, Cal., Dec. 8.

Rizzo, Frank, 70; mayor of Philadelphia, 1971-79; Philadelphia, July 16.

Roosevelt, James, 83; 6-term U.S. representative and son of FDR; Newport Beach, Cal., Aug. 13.

Runnels, Pete, 63; baseball player who won AL batting titles in 1960 and 1962; Pasadena, Tex., May 20.

S

Schafer, Natalie, 90; actress best known as the millionaire's wife on the "Gilligan's Island" TV series; Beverly Hills, Cal., Apr. 10.

Schottzie, St. Bernard mascot of the Cincinnati Reds baseball team; Cincinnati, Aug. 7.

Schuyler, James, 67; poet who won 1980 Pulitzer Prize; New York, Apr. 12.

Serkin, Rudolf, 88; concert pianist; Guilford, Vt., May 8.

Seton, Anya, 86; author of historical and biographical novels; Old Greenwich, Conn., Nov. 8.

Seuss, Dr. (Theodor Seuss Geisel), 87; author and illustrator whose whimsical fantasies entertained millions of children; La Jolla, Cal., Sept. 24.

Shero, Fred, 65; hockey coach who led the Philadelphia Flyers to 2 Stanley Cup championships in the 1970s; Camden, N.J., Nov. 24.

Shoemaker, Vaughn, 89; editorial cartoonist who created the character "John Q. Public"; won 2 Pulitzer prizes; Carol Stream, Ill., Aug. 18.

Short, Chris, 53; pitcher who won 135 games, mostly for the Philadelphia Phillies; Wilmington, Del., Aug. 1.

Siegel, Don, 78; director of action-adventure films; Nipomo, Cal., Apr. 20.

Singer, Isaac Bashevis, 87; author who wrote about Jewish life in his native Poland and the U.S.; won 1978 Nobel Prize for literature; Miami, July 25.

Snelling, Richard A., 64; governor of Vermont; Shelburne, Vt., Aug. 14.

Staggers, Harley, 84; U.S. representative from W. Va., 1949-81; Cumberland, Md., Aug. 20.

T

Tamayo, Rufino, 91; Mexican artist; a leader of the Mexican Renaissance; Mexico City, June 24.

Thomas, Danny, 79; comedian and star of the "Make Room for Daddy" TV series, 1953-64; Los Angeles, Feb. 6.

Tower, John, 65; U.S. senator from Texas, 1961-85; nr. Brunswick, Ga., Apr. 5.

Tree, Marietta, 74; U.S. delegate to the United Nations in the 1960s; New York, Aug. 15.

Tryon, Thomas, 65; actor who became a best-selling novelist; Los Angeles, Sept. 4.

W

Wade, Leigh, 93; U.S. Air Force general and aviation pioneer; Ft. Belvoir, Va., Aug. 31.

Wagner, Robert, 80; mayor of New York City, 1954-65; New York, Feb. 12.

Walters, Bucky, 82; pitcher who won 198 games, mostly for the Cincinnati Reds; Abington, Pa., Apr. 20.

Watson, Phil, 78; hockey player and coach, mostly with the N.Y. Rangers; Vancouver, B.C., Feb. 1.

West, Dottie, 58; country singer; Nashville, Sept. 4.

Wiggins, Alan, 32; former infielder for the San Diego Padres; Los Angeles, Jan. 6.

Williams, Travis, 45; kick return specialist for the Green Bay Packers, 1967-71; Richmond, Cal., Feb. 17.

Wilson, Angus, 77; British novelist and biographer; Bury St. Edmunds, England, May 31.

Y

Yellen, Jack, 97; lyricist; Springville, N.Y., Apr. 17.

Off-Beat News Stories of 1991

Don't forget to visit our gift shop — A Soviet tour company is offering visitors a tour of the radioactive contamination zone around the Chernobyl reactor that exploded in 1986. The itinerary includes the city of Chernobyl, a radio-active waste dump at Kopachi, and the concrete "sarcophagus" built around the reactor. All trips begin and end with tests to check visitors' exposure to radiation. If medical treatment is needed, it will be provided "at no extra charge."

They ought to know — In many offices there is some sort of gambling pool based on National Football League or college football games. Few office managers protest, and most look the other way as their employees are making their weekly selections. Not so at all companies, as a memo circulated to workers at one company will attest. After reminding the employees that "gambling of any kind while working is a violation of company rules," the memo went on: "Sports betting reflects poor judgment on the part of the participants and can only inflict criticism of our organization." The memo was sent to the employees of the New York City Offtrack Betting Corporation.

Most illogical — The mystery of those giant circles and odd geometric shapes that have been showing up in recent summers in wheat fields across southern England may have been explained. There had been speculation that the circles were of such a scale and geometric precision that they must have been the work of a superior intelligence from alien spacecraft. David Chorley and Doug Bower, however, confessed that they had been skulking around the countryside under cover of darkness, trampling out patterns with wooden boards. Their joke fooled scientists from Britain and Japan who monitered the sites with scientific equipment, suspecting the circles might be the result of unusual and very sudden whirlwinds. Mystics, flying saucer fanatics, and believers in the occult also made pilgrimages to the fields trying to sense their hidden energy fields. Chorley and Bower said they followed tractor rows into the center of the fields and traced the patterns, trampling down the wheat using "two wooden boards, a piece of string and a bizarre sighting device attached to a baseball cap."

Deficit bouncing — Have you ever wondered why the United States is continually having budget deficits? One reason might be found in a General Accounting Office audit which found that the members of the House of Representatives bounced 4,325 personal checks at the House bank during the first half of 1990. Among the checks returned for insufficient funds, 581 were for at least $1,000 each, written by 134 different members. The audit found that 24 House members bounced at least one $1,000-or-more check each month. The House bank covered the overdrawn accounts and asked members to deposit funds. The average member took 7 days to do so; a few took as long as 4 weeks. A few days later, Speaker of the House Thomas Foley announced that the bank would be closed by the end of the year. Reports also showed that members owed about $300,000 in unpaid bills from the House restaurant.

Robot wrestling — The Japanese have managed to combine their love of sumo wrestling with their passion for high technology. At the All-Japan Robot Sumo Wrestling Tournament held in Tokyo, some 300 technicians with their robots, who each weighed about 6 pounds, in a ring about 5 feet in diameter. First prize was about $7,500. The contestants were divided into 2 categories. Some were controlled by radio, with their masters throwing toggle switches from controllers lifted from model race cars and airplanes, while others were autonomous, relying on their electronic wits to find their opponent and throw him out of the ring. It could be argued that there is a serious purpose in building robotic wrestlers, particularly in a country that is the biggest builder and user of industrial robots. However, one of the contestants said, "I can't think of a single useful thing I could do with this robot." Then he added, "Maybe I could teach it to attack my boss."

Pick me a winner — A study by Univ. of Wisconsin-Madison researchers will dig into rhinotillexomania, also known as nose picking. A questionnaire sent to 1,200 Madison-area residents asked questions like: "What finger do you use when picking your nose and after picking your nose how often do you find yourself looking at what you have removed?" "The habit has not been studied scientifically," said Dr. James Jefferson, a psychiatrist who specializes in compulsive behaviors. "Our assumption is that for most people, it is a harmless, private habit. But some may do it excessively in a way that causes embarrassment or social problems."

The love boat — The *Acadia*, a U.S. Navy supply vessel, was deployed to the Persian Gulf during the war with Iraq. While serving in that theater of operation, 36 of the 360 female crew members had to be transferred because they were pregnant. A Navy spokesman said that there were no indications of improper fraternization between men and women on the ship. He said 9 women became pregnant before the *Acadia* left San Diego, but were not tested until the ship was underway. Five others were transferred to the *Acadia* while it was sailing to the gulf, but their pregnancies were not discovered until after they were on board. The remaining 22 women became pregnant while the ship was deployed, perhaps on liberty calls in Hawaii, the Philippines, or other ports the ship visited. The Navy has strict rules against sexual relationships between men and women while on duty.

Call the auto club — The manager of a Olathe, Kansas fast-food restaurant found a man, wearing a George Bush mask, in his restroom after closing time. The man forced employees to open a safe and then locked them in a cooler. The bandit left the restaurant but soon returned to seek help from the manager. He couldn't start his car in the 2-degree weather. The police, who had already been called, found the manager and the robber in the restaurant parking lot trying to start the getaway car.

I'll trade you Peaches for Willie Mays — Put aside your Desert Storm and baseball cards. The newest wave in collectables are cards featuring the U.S. Customs Service drug-sniffing dogs. The 81-card set shows such canine stars as Nacho, Peaches, and Solo in action poses. The back of each card lists the dog's breed, age, weight, tattoo number, and biggest drug bust.

Hamburger helpers — Sarah Cross ordered 2 hamburgers from a Wendy's restaurant drive-in-window in Augusta, Ga. She later found that the bag the Wendy's clerk gave her did not contain the hamburgers, but it did contain $1,000 in cash. The money was returned in exchange for the hamburgers. The restaurant manager explained that he had been preparing a bank deposit and put the cash in a bag. When he turned away, the window clerk, thinking it was an order, picked it up and handed it to Cross.

Do you know me? When a third grader doubted the identity of President Bush when he visited a Virginia elementary school, the president whipped out his American Express card. He said he used his American Express card mainly for Christmas shopping and to buy dinner in restaurants. The president, who doesn't like to carry cash, used to rely on checks until store owners started collecting them.

Take me out to the crowd, revisited — The naked man and towel-clad woman who last year had an intimate interlude at the Toronto Blue Jays Sky-Dome Hotel in full view of a stadium full of fans got lots of attention (and were featured in last year's "Off-Beat News Stories). Now, guests at the hotel are required to sign a code of conduct when they check into one of the 70 rooms that overlook the playing field. Among the rules in the agreement are no activities considered inappropriate in public, and no being in a state of partial or complete undress. Violators will be evicted from their rooms.

QUICK REFERENCE INDEX

For complete Index, see pp. 3-31